THE ENCYCLOPAEDIA OF ISLAM

THE ENCYCLOPAEDIA OF ISLAM

NEW EDITION

PREPARED BY A NUMBER OF
LEADING ORIENTALISTS

EDITED BY

C. E. BOSWORTH, E. VAN DONZEL, B. LEWIS AND CH. PELLAT

ASSISTED BY F. TH. DIJKEMA AND MME S. NURIT (pp. 1-512)

C. E. BOSWORTH, E. VAN DONZEL, W. P. HEINRICHS AND CH. PELLAT

ASSISTED BY F. TH. DIJKEMA AND MME. S. NURIT (pp. 513-1044)

UNDER THE PATRONAGE OF
THE INTERNATIONAL UNION OF ACADEMIES

VOLUME VI

MAHK—MID

LEIDEN
E.J. BRILL
1991

The preparation of this volume of the Encyclopaedia of Islam was made possible in part through grants from the Research Tools Program of the National Endowment for the Humanities, an independent Federal Agency of the United States Government; the British Academy; the Oriental Institute, Leiden; Académie des Inscriptions et Belles-Lettres; and the Royal Netherlands Academy of Sciences

The articles in this volume were published in double fascicules of 128 pages, the dates of publication being:

1986: Fasc. 99-100, pp. 1-128
1987: Fascs. 101-104, pp. 129-384
1988: Fasc. 105-106, pp. 385-512
1989: Fasc. 107-112, pp. 513- 896
1990: Facs. 113-114a, pp. 897-1044

ISBN 90 04 08112 7

PRINTED IN THE NETHERLANDS

AUTHORS OF ARTICLES IN THIS VOLUME

For the benefit of readers who may wish to follow up an individual contributor's articles, the Editors have decided to place after each contributor's name the number of the pages on which his signature appears. Academic but not other addresses are given (for a retired scholar, the place of his last known academic appointment).

In this list, names in square brackets are those of authors of articles reprinted or revised from the first edition of this Encyclopaedia or from the *Shorter Encyclopaedia of Islam*. An asterisk after the name of the author in the text denotes an article reprinted from the first edition which has been brought up to date by the Editorial Committee; where an article has been revised by a second author his name appears in the text within square brackets after the name of the original author.

M. Abdesselem, University of Tunis. 911.
Z. Abrahamowicz, Cracow. 986.
Haleh Afshar, University of Bradford. 488.
I. Afshar, Tehran. 92.
Feroz Ahmad, University of Massachusetts, Boston. 74.
M. Ajami, Princeton University. 409.
Münir Aktepe, University of Istanbul. 58, 1004.
Hamid Algar, University of California, Berkeley. 225, 292.
C. H. Allen Jr., School of the Ozarks, Point Lookout, Miss. 843.
E. Allworth, Columbia University, New York. 772.
Edith G. Ambros, University of Vienna. 967, 969, 1027.
Metin And, University of Ankara. 761.
Barbara Watson Andaya, University of Auckland. 214.
L. Y. Andaya, University of Auckland. 239.
P. A. Andrews, University of Cologne. 190, 457, 700.
Ghaus Ansari, Kuwait University. 490.
A. Arioli, University of Rome. 313.
R. Arnaldez, University of Paris. 571.
the late E. Ashtor, Hebrew University, Jerusalem. 121.
R. W. J. Austin, University of Durham. 614.
A. Ayalon, Tel Aviv University, 262, 726.
D. Ayalon, Hebrew University, Jerusalem. 321.
[F. Babinger, Munich]. 1000, 1023, 1024.
J.-L. Bacqué-Grammont, French Institute of Anatolian Studies, Istanbul. 993.
M. A. Bakhit, University of Jordan, Amman. 346.
[W. Barthold, Leningrad]. 420, 433, 942.
A. F. L. Beeston, Oxford. 88.
Doris Behrens-Abouseif, Universities of Bamberg and Munich. 719.
Irène Beldiceanu-Steinherr, Centre National de la Recherche Scientifique, Paris. 278.
J. E. Bencheikh, University of Paris. 349, 626.
R. Bencheneb, Paris. 757.
N. Berkes, Hythe, Kent. 969.
[P. Berthier, Rabat]. 891.
E. Birnbaum, University of Toronto. 1020.
A. Bjørkelo, University of Bergen. 794.
W. Björkman, Uppsala. 195, 424, 1007.
J. R. Blackburn, University of Toronto. 72, 437, 912.
P. N. Boratav, Centre National de la Recherche Scientifique, Paris. 421, 827.
the late J. Bosch Vilá, Granada. 223, 577, 899, 927.
C. E. Bosworth, University of Manchester. 64, 66, 77, 87, 116, 152, 193, 270, 273, 276, 340, 419, 421, 498, 505, 539, 542, 557, 618, 621, 623, 628, 713, 726, 729, 780, 782, 783, 872, 901, 903, 912, 914, 915, 916, 918, 942, 966, 1024.
Yu. Bregel, Indiana University, Bloomington. 417, 418, 419, 420.
[C. Brockelmann, Halle]. 115, 869.
K. L. Brown, University of Manchester. 124.
J. T. P. de Bruijn, University of Leiden. 73, 86, 276, 633, 764, 835.
[Fr. Buhl, Copenhagen]. 46, 575, 918.
[M. Buret]. 137.
J. C. Bürgel, University of Bern. 340.
R. M. Burrell, University of London. 358, 730.
J. Burton-Page, Church Knowle, Dorset. 61, 87, 122, 128, 269, 343, 370, 410, 534, 536, 537, 690, 815, 839, 867, 970, 1019, 1028, 1029.
P. Cachia, Columbia University, New York. 868.
Cl. Cahen, University of Paris. 141, 144, 1017.
J. Calmard, Centre National de la Recherche Scientifique, Paris. 518, 556.
G. E. Carretto, University of Rome. 1024.
[P. de Cenival, Rabat]. 598.
the late E. Cerulli, Rome. 129, 628.
J.-Cl. Ch. Chabrier, Centre National de la Recherche Scientifique, Paris. 104.
P. Chalmeta, University of Zaragoza. 432, 521, 852.
J. Chelhod, Centre National de la Recherche Scientifique, Paris. 481, 491.
A. H. Christie, University of London. 702.
J. W. Clinton, Princeton University. 453, 783.
A. Cohen, Hebrew University, Jerusalem. 544.
[G. S. Colin, Paris]. 744, 774, 815, 1009.
[C. Collin Davies]. 87, 780.
D. C. Conrad, Stinton Beach, California. 422.
R. G. Coquin, École Pratique des Hautes Études, Paris. 144.
Chr. Correll, University of Konstanz. 309.
Nicole Cottart, Centre National de la Recherche Scientifique, Paris. 283.
[A. Cour, Constantine]. 893.
Patricia Crone, University of Oxford. 640, 848, 882.
Yolande Crowe, London. 408.
F. Dachraoui, University of Tunis. 435, 728.
H. Daiber, Free University, Amsterdam. 639.
G. Dávid, Eötvös Lorand University, Budapest. 1030.
R. H. Davison, George Washington University, Washington. 69, 1035.
G. Delanoue, French Institute of Arabic Studies, Damascus. 602.
Anne-Marie Delcambre, Paris. 870.
A. Dietrich, Göttingen. 557, 641, 727.

S. Digby, Rozel, Jersey. 784.
M. W. Dols, California State University, Hayward. 230.
F. M. Donner, University of Chicago. 917.
E. van Donzel, Netherlands Institute for the Near East, Leiden. 434, 628, 644, 910, 933.
P. Dumont, University of Strasbourg. 96.
R. M. Eaton, University of Arizona, Tucson. 269, 273.
H. Eisenstein, University of Vienna. 1003.
T. El-Achèche, University of Tunis. 438.
N. Eliséeff, University of Lyons. 383, 456, 457, 546, 548, 583, 734, 792, 871.
G. Endress, University of Bochum. 846.
J. van Ess, University of Tübingen. 458.
T. Fahd, University of Strasbourg. 247, 349, 374, 924.
Suraiya Faroqhi, University of Munich. 232, 243, 342, 510.
W. Feldman, University of Pennsylvania, Philadelphia. 1008.
C. V. Findley, Ohio State University, Columbus. 9, 11, 290, 341, 972.
Barbara Flemming, University of Leiden. 610, 837.
W. Floor, Bethesda, Maryland. 804.
J. Fontaine, Tunis. 712.
A. D. W. Forbes, University of Aberdeen. 207, 246, 703, 1022.
J. Fraenkel, Hebrew University, Jerusalem. 360.
G. S. P. Freeman-Grenville, York. 129, 203, 283, 370, 385, 704, 774, 965, 967, 1023.
Y. Friedmann, Hebrew University, Jerusalem. 440, 968.
[H. Fuchs, Mainz]. 897.
C. L. Geddes, University of Denver. 371.
G. G. Gilbar, University of Haifa. 277.
F. Müge Göçek, University of Michigan, Ann Arbor. 133, 746, 1017, 1029, 1030.
O. Grabar, Harvard University, Cambridge, Mass. 708.
W. J. Griswold, Colorado State University, Fort Collins. 613.
A. H. de Groot, University of Leiden. 532, 992, 993, 994, 995, 996, 997, 998, 999, 1000, 1001, 1002, 1003, 1025.
[M. Guidi, Rome]. 952.
Adnan Güriz, University of Ankara. 498.
U. Haarmann, University of Freiburg-im-Breisgau. 414.
[T. W. Haig, London]. 310.
H. Halm, University of Tübingen. 440, 454.
W. L. Hanaway Jr., University of Pennsylvania, Philadelphia. 609.
P. Hardy, Fulford, York. 536.
Angelika Hartmann, University of Würzburg. 430.
Mohibul Hasan, Aligarh. 47, 52, 55, 62, 63.
A. T. Hatto, London. 371.
G. R. Hawting, University of London. 625.
J. A. Haywood, Lewes, East Sussex. 272, 612, 773, 827, 953.
G. Hazai, Hungarian Academy of Sciences, Budapest. 75.
[W. Heffening, Cologne]. 200, 558.
C. J. Heywood, University of London. 129, 291, 972.
D. R. Hill, Great Bookham, Surrey. 406.
Carole Hillenbrand, University of Edinburgh. 244, 627, 932.
R. Hillenbrand, University of Edinburgh. 368, 688.
the late G. M. Hinds, University of Cambridge. 140.
H. F. Hofman, Utrecht. 131.
P. M. Holt, Oxford. 331.
[E. Honigmann, Brussels]. 231, 508, 544, 779, 792, 901.
[M. Hidayat Hosain]. 131.
R. S. Humphreys, University of Wisconsin, Madison. 782.
J. O. Hunwick, Northwestern University, Evanston, Ill. 223.
C. H. Imber, University of Manchester. 72, 228.
H. İnalcik, University of Chicago. 5, 11, 813, 961, 978, 981, 1026.
Riazul Islam, Karachi. 310.
B. S. J. Isserlin, Leeds. 298.
Fahir İz, Boğaziçi University, Istanbul. 373, 986, 989, 1003, 1016.
Penelope Johnstone, Oxford. 632.
the late T. M. Johnstone, Oxford. 85.
J. Jomier, Toulouse. 46, 361.
F. de Jong, University of Utrecht. 88, 224, 454, 627, 888, 897.
G. H. A. Juynboll, The Hague. 717.
the late A. G. Karam, American University, Beirut. 307.
Barbara Kellner-Heinkele, University of Berlin. 989, 1016.
H. Kennedy, University of St. Andrews. 206, 345, 428.
M. Khadduri, Johns Hopkins University, Washington. 740.
M. Kiel, Bonn. 1015.
D. A. King, University of Frankfort. 187, 598, 794, 840, 915.
M. J. Kister, Hebrew University, Jerusalem. 107.
J. Knappert, Barnet, Herts. 613, 828, 897.
M. Köhbach, University of Vienna. 989.
[J. H. Kramers, Leiden]. 633, 634, 983.
P. Kunitzsch, University of Munich. 376.
E. Kuran, Hacettepe University, Ankara. 1004.
Günay Alpay Kut, Boğaziçi University, Istanbul. 803.
B. Kütükoğlu, University of Istanbul. 971, 990, 991.
Ann K. S. Lambton, Kirknewton, Northumberland. 22, 485, 496, 529, 858.
[H. Lammens, Beirut]. 924.
J. M. Landau, Hebrew University, Jerusalem. 197, 400, 750, 1013.
Ella Landau-Tasseron, Hebrew University, Jerusalem. 269.
H.-P. Laqueur, Munich. 125.
J. D. Latham, University of Edinburgh. 405.
B. Lawrence, Duke University, Durham. 131.
A. Layish, Hebrew University, Jerusalem. 25, 26, 28, 29, 31, 33, 35, 36, 38, 42.
Linda Y. Leach, Richmond, Surrey. 426.
O. N. H. Leaman, Liverpool Polytechnic. 220, 347, 903.
D. S. Lev, University of Washington, Seattle. 44.
[G. Levi Della Vida, Rome]. 954.
[E. Lévi-Provençal, Paris]. 132, 188, 340, 345, 568, 923, 969.
N. Levtzion, Hebrew University, Jerusalem. 261.
A. Levy, Brandeis University, Waltham, Ma. 61.
T. Lewicki, University of Cracow. 311, 312, 453, 842, 948, 949, 1044.
B. Lewis, Princeton University. 725.
T. O. Ling, University of Manchester. 245.
O. Löfgren, Uppsala. 133.
[D. B. MacDonald, Hartford, Conn.]. 219.
D. MacEoin, Newcastle-upon-Tyne. 720, 953.
K. McPherson, Western Australian Institute of Technology, Bentley. 504.
W. Madelung, University of Oxford. 192, 219, 436, 439, 442, 847, 848, 917.

A. J. Mango, London. 984, 985.
[G. Marçais, Algiers]. 427, 441.
[D. S. Margoliouth, Oxford]. 883, 888.
J. N. Mattock, University of Glasgow. 87, 205.
[Th. Menzel]. 1027.
E. Merçil, University of Istanbul. 1018, 1019.
[E. Michaux-Bellaire]. 136.
R. E. Miller, University of Regina, Canada. 466.
[V. Minorsky, Cambridge]. 203, 385, 503, 505, 541, 542, 717, 745, 929.
A. Miquel, Collège de France, Paris. 314, 720.
S. Moreh, Hebrew University, Jerusalem. 617, 928.
M. Morony, University of California, Los Angeles. 634, 923, 952.
W. W. Müller, University of Marburg. 84, 567.
S. Munro-Hay, London. 575.
[M. Nazim]. 916.
Angelika Neuwirth, University of Munich. 189.
[R. A. Nicholson, Cambridge]. 614.
J. S. Nielsen, University of Birmingham. 935.
C. Nijland, Netherlands Institute for the Near East, Leiden. 306, 308.
Ö. Nutku, University of Izmir. 865.
G. Oman, University of Naples. 799.
R. Orazi, Rome. 720.
Solange Ory, University of Aix-Marseille. 123.
M. M. Ould Bah, Unesco, Tunis. 313.
J. D. Pearson, Cambridge. 200.
[J. Pedersen, Copenhagen]. 677.
Ch. Pellat, University of Paris. 115, 143, 188, 196, 257, 267, 344, 357, 406, 608, 628, 636, 640, 709, 710, 738, 789, 829, 843, 895, 907, 916, 933, 943, 1042.
T. Philipp, Harvard University, Cambridge, Mass. 220.
the late G. F. Pijper, Amsterdam. 701.
[M. Plessner, Jerusalem]. 205, 344, 543.
I. Poonawala, University of California, Los Angeles. 191, 1010.
Munibur Rahman, Oakland University, Rochester, Mich. 132, 271, 839.
[W. H. Rassers]. 117.
M. Rekaya, University of Paris. 339.
C. H. B. Reynolds, University of London. 247.
J. F. Richards, Duke University, Durham. 423.
J. Rikabi, Constantine. 539.
Chr. Robin, Centre National de la Recherche Scientifique, Aix-en-Provence. 832.
F. C. R. Robinson, Royal Holloway College, Egham, Surrey. 78, 874.
M. Rodinson, École Pratique des Hautes Études, Paris. 587.
W. Röllig, University of Tübingen. 1023.
[Ph. van Ronkel, Leiden]. 240.
F. Rosenthal, Yale University, New Haven. 194, 403.
[E. Rossi, Rome]. 295, 613.
G. Rotter, University of Hamburg. 740.
A. I. Sabra, Harvard University, Cambridge, Mass. 377.
J. Sadan, Tel-Aviv University. 360, 723.
A. Samb, University of Dakar. 707.
J. Samsó, University of Barcelona. 543, 602, 712.
Paula Sanders, Harvard University, Cambridge, Mass. 520, 851.
Biancamaria Scarcia Amoretti, University of Rome. 959.
[J. Schacht, New York]. 3, 25, 265, 926.
O. Schumann, University of Hamburg. 117, 733.
R. Sellheim, University of Frankfort. 635, 825, 914, 955.
Maya Shatzmiller, University of Western Ontario, London, Ontario. 441, 574.
G. W. Shaw, British Library, London. 806, 807.
S. J. Shaw, University of California, Los Angeles. 973.
H. K. Sherwani. 68.
A. Shiloah, Hebrew University, Jerusalem. 216, 262.
D. Shulman, Hebrew University, Jerusalem. 960.
I. H. Siddiqui, Muslim University, Aligarh. 1031.
J. Siegel, Cornell University, Ithaca. 239, 240.
the late Susan A. Skilliter, Cambridge. 982.
P. Sluglett, University of Durham. 902.
S. Soucek, New York Public Library. 588, 1011, 1016, 1022, 1037.
the late O. Spies, Bonn. 80.
A. J. Stockwell, University of London. 242.
[M. Streck, Jena]. 716, 923.
Abdus Subhan, Calcutta. 270, 272, 295.
M. Talbi, University of Tunis. 713.
Nada Tomiche, University of Paris. 472, 599.
G. Troupeau, Institut National des Langues et Civilisations Orientales, Paris. 130, 308.
M. Ursinus, University of Birmingham. 372.
Martine Vanhove, Paris. 303.
[R. Vasmer, Leningrad]. 942.
G. Veinstein, École des Hautes Études en Sciences Sociales, Paris. 1006.
C. H. M. Versteegh, University of Nijmegen. 346.
Ž. Vesel, Centre National de la Recherche Scientifique, Paris. 908.
Ch. Vial, University of Aix-Marseille. 77, 91, 415, 958.
F. Viré, Centre National de la Recherche Scientifique, Paris. 537, 913.
D. Waines, University of Lancaster. 809.
W. Montgomery Watt, Dalkeith, Midlothian. 147.
[A. J. Wensinck, Leiden]. 152, 632, 709, 726, 843, 874, 903.
G. M. Wickens, University of Toronto. 826.
J. C. Wilkinson, University of Oxford. 736.
the late R. B. Winder, New York University. 180.
J. J. Witkam, University of Leiden. 1031.
[A. Yu. Yakubovskii, Moscow]. 621.
F. A. K. Yasamee, University of Manchester. 90.
T. Yazici, Istanbul. 887.
H. G. Yurdaydin, University of Ankara. 844.
H. Zafrani, University of Paris. 294.
D. Zahan, University of Paris. 402.

ABBREVIATED TITLES
OF SOME OF THE MOST OFTEN QUOTED WORKS

Abu'l-Fidā', *Taḳwīm* = *Taḳwīm al-buldān*, ed. J.-T. Reinaud and M. de Slane, Paris 1840

Abu'l-Fidā', *Taḳwīm*, tr. = *Géographie d'Aboulféda, traduite de l'arabe en français*; vol. i, ii/1 by Reinaud, Paris 1848; vol. ii/2 by St. Guyard, 1883

Aghānī[1] or [2] or [3] = Abu'l-Faradj al-Iṣfahānī, *al-Aghānī*; [1] Būlāḳ 1285; [2] Cairo 1323; [3] Cairo 1345-

Aghānī, Tables = *Tables alphabétiques du Kitāb al-aghānī*, rédigées par I. Guidi, Leiden 1900

Aghānī, Brünnow = *The XXIst vol. of the Kitāb al-Aghānī*, ed. R. E. Brünnow, Leiden 1883

ʿAlī Djewād = *Memālik-i ʿOthmāniyyeniñ ta'rīkh we djughrāfiyā lughāti*, Istanbul 1313-17/1895-9.

ʿAlī Mubārak, *Khiṭaṭ* = ʿAlī Mubārak, *al-Khiṭaṭ al-tawfīḳiyya al-djadīda li-Miṣr al-Ḳāhira wa-mudunihā wa-bilādihā 'l-ḳadīma wa-'l-shahīra*, 20 vols., Būlāḳ 1304-6

Anbārī, *Nuzha* = *Nuzhat al-alibbā' fī ṭabaḳāt al-udabā'*, [1] Cairo 1294; [2] Stockholm, etc. 1963.

ʿAwfī, *Lubāb* = *Lubāb al-albāb*, ed. E. G. Browne, London-Leiden 1903-6

Babinger = F. Babinger, *Die Geschichtsschreiber der Osmanen und ihre Werke*, 1st ed., Leiden 1927

Baghdādī, *Farḳ* = *al-Farḳ bayn al-firaḳ*, ed. Muḥammad Badr, Cairo 1328/1910

Balādhurī, *Futūḥ* = *Futūḥ al-buldān*, ed. M. J. de Goeje, Leiden 1866

Balādhurī, *Ansāb* = *Ansāb al-ashrāf*, i, ed. M. Hamidullah, Cairo 1960; iv B, v. ed. M. Schlössinger and S. D. F. Goitein, Jerusalem 1936-38

Barkan, *Kanunlar* = Ömer Lûtfi Barkan, *XV ve XVI inci asırlarda Osmanlı Imparatorluğunda zirai ekonominin hukuki ve mali esasları, I. Kanunlar*, Istanbul 1943

Barthold, *Four studies* = V. V. Barthold, *Four studies on the history of Central Asia*, tr. by V. and T. Minorsky, 3 vols., Leyden 1956-63

Barthold, *Turkestan* = W. Barthold, *Turkestan down to the Mongol invasion*, London 1928 (GMS, N.S. v)

Barthold, *Turkestan*[2] = the same, 2nd edition, London 1958

Blachère, *Litt.* = R. Blachère, *Histoire de la littérature arabe*, i-ii, Paris 1952-64

Brockelmann, I, II = C. Brockelmann, *Geschichte der arabischen Literatur*, zweite den Supplementbänden angepasste Auflage, Leiden 1943-49

Brockelmann, S I, II, III = *G. d. a. L.*, Erster (zweiter, dritter) Supplementband, Leiden 1937-42

Browne, i = E. G. Browne, *A literary history of Persia, from the earliest times until Firdawsi*, London 1902

Browne, ii = *A literary history of Persia, from Firdawsi to Saʿdi*, London 1908

Browne, iii = *A history of Persian literature under Tartar Dominion*, Cambridge 1920

Browne, iv = *A history of Persian literature in modern times*, Cambridge 1924

Caetani, *Annali* = L. Caetani, *Annali dell'Islam*, Milan 1905-26

Chauvin, *Bibliographie* = V. Chauvin, *Bibliographie des ouvrages arabes et relatifs aux Arabes*, Lille 1892

Creswell, *Bibliography* = K. A. C. Creswell, *A bibliography of the architecture, arts and crafts of Islam to 1st Jan. 1960*, Cairo 1961

Ḍabbī = *Bughyat al-multamis fī ta'rīkh ridjāl ahl al-Andalus*, ed. F. Codera and J. Ribera, Madrid 1885 (BAH III)

Damīrī = *Ḥayāt al-ḥayawān* (quoted according to titles of articles)

Dawlatshāh = *Tadhkirat al-shuʿarā'*, ed. E. G. Browne, London-Leiden 1901

Dhahabī, *Ḥuffāẓ* = al-Dhahabī, *Tadhkirat al-ḥuffāẓ*, 4 vols., Hyderabad 1315 H.

Dictionnaire arabe-français-anglais = *Dictionnaire arabe-français-anglais (langue classique et moderne)*, Paris 1963-

Djuwaynī = *Ta'rīkh-i Djihān-gushā*, ed. Muḥammad Ḳazwīnī, Leiden 1906-37 (GMS XVI)

Djuwaynī-Boyle = *The history of the World-conqueror*, by ʿAṭā-Malik Djuwaynī, trans. J. A. Boyle, 2 vols., Manchester 1958

Doerfer, *Elemente* = G. Doerfer, *Türkische und mongolische Elemente im Neupersischen*, Wiesbaden 1963-

Dozy, *Notices* = R. Dozy, *Notices sur quelques manuscrits arabes*, Leiden 1847-51

Dozy, *Recherches*[3] = *Recherches sur l'histoire et la littérature de l'Espagne pendant le moyen-âge*, third edition, Paris-Leiden 1881

Dozy, *Suppl.* = R. Dozy, *Supplément aux dictionnaires arabes*, Leiden 1881 (anastatic reprint Leiden-Paris 1927)

EMA[1] = K. A. C. Creswell, *Early Muslim architecture*, 2 vols., Oxford 1932-40

EMA[2] = K. A. C. Creswell, *Early Muslim architecture*, 2nd ed., London 1969-

Fagnan, *Extraits* = E. Fagnan, *Extraits inédits relatifs au Maghreb*, Alger 1924

Farhang = Razmārā and Nawtāsh, *Farhang-i djughrāfiyā-yi Īrān*, Tehran 1949-1953

Fihrist = Ibn al-Nadīm, *K. al-Fihrist*, ed. G. Flügel, Leipzig 1871-72

Firishta = Muḥammad Ḳāsim Firishta, *Gulshan-i Ibrāhīmī*, lith. Bombay 1832

Gesch. des Qor. = Th. Nöldeke, *Geschichte des Qorāns*, new edition by F. Schwally, G. Bergsträsser and O. Pretzl, 3 vols., Leipzig 1909-38

Gibb, *Ottoman Poetry* = E. J. W. Gibb, *A history of Ottoman poetry*, London 1900-09

Gibb-Bowen = H. A. R. Gibb and Harold Bowen, *Islamic society and the West*, London 1950-1957

Goldziher, *Muh. St.* = I. Goldziher, *Muhammedanische Studien*, 2 vols., Halle 1888-90

Goldziher, *Vorlesungen* = I. Goldziher, *Vorlesungen über den Islam*, Heidelberg 1910

Goldziher, *Vorlesungen*[2] = 2nd ed., Heidelberg 1925

Goldziher, *Dogme* = *Le dogme et la loi de l'Islam*, tr. F. Arin, Paris 1920

Ḥādjdjī Khalīfa, *Djihān-nümā* = Istanbul 1145/1732

Ḥādjdjī Khalīfa = *Kashf al-ẓunūn*, ed. Ş. Yaltkaya and Kilisli Rifat Bilge, Istanbul 1941-43

Ḥādjdjī Khalīfa, ed. Flügel = *K. al-ẓ.*, Leipzig 1835-58
Ḥamd Allāh Mustawfī, *Nuzha* = *Nuzhat al-ḳulūb*, ed. G. Le Strange, Leiden 1913-19 (GMS XXIII)
Hamdānī = *Ṣifat Djazīrat al-ʿArab*, ed. D. H. Müller, Leiden 1884-91
Hammer-Purgstall, *GOR* = J. von Hammer(-Purgstall), *Geschichte des Osmanischen Reiches*, Pest 1828-35
Hammer-Purgstall, *GOR*[2] = the same, 2nd ed. Pest 1840
Hammer-Purgstall, *Histoire* = the same, trans. by J. J. Hellert, 18 vols., Bellizard [etc.], Paris [etc.], 1835-43
Hammer-Purgstall, *Staatsverfassung* = J. von Hammer, *Des Osmanischen Reichs Staatsverfassung und Staatsverwaltung*, 2 vols., Vienna 1815 (repr. 1963)
Houtsma, *Recueil* = M. Th. Houtsma, *Recueil des textes relatifs à l'histoire des Seldjoucides*, Leiden 1886-1902
Ḥudūd al-ʿālam = *The regions of the world*, translated by V. Minorsky, London 1937 (GMS, n.s. xi)
Ibn al-Abbār = *K. Takmilat al-Ṣila*, ed. F. Codera, Madrid 1887-89 (BHA V-VI)
Ibn al-Athīr = *K. al-Kāmil*, ed. C. J. Tornberg, Leiden 1851-76
Ibn al-Athīr, trad. Fagnan = *Annales du Maghreb et de l'Espagne*, tr. E. Fagnan, Algiers 1901
Ibn Bashkuwāl = *K. al-Ṣila fī akhbār aʾimmat al-Andalus*, ed. F. Codera, Madrid 1883 (BHA II)
Ibn Baṭṭūṭa = *Voyages d'Ibn Batouta.* Arabic text, ed. with Fr. tr. by C. Defrémery and B. R. Sanguinetti, 4 vols., Paris 1853-58
Ibn al-Faḳīh = *Mukhtaṣar K. al-Buldān*, ed. M. J. De Goeje, Leiden 1886 (BGA V)
Ibn Ḥawḳal = *K. Ṣūrat al-arḍ*, ed. J. H. Kramers, Leiden 1938-39 (BGA II, 2nd edition)
Ibn Ḥawḳal-Kramers-Wiet = Ibn Hauqal, *Configuration de la terre*, trans. J. H. Kramers and G. Wiet, Beirut 1964, 2 vols.
Ibn Hishām = *Sīra*, ed. F. Wüstenfeld, Göttingen 1859-60
Ibn ʿIdhārī = *K. al-Bayān al-mughrib*, ed. G. S. Colin and E. Lévi-Provençal, Leiden 1948-51; vol. iii, ed. E. Lévi-Provençal, Paris 1930
Ibn al-ʿImād, *Shadharāt* = *Shadharāt al-dhahab fī akhbār man dhahab*, Cairo 1350-51 (quoted according to years of obituaries)
Ibn Khaldūn, *ʿIbar* = *K. al-ʿIbar wa-dīwān al-mubtadaʾ wa 'l-khabar etc.*, Būlāḳ 1284
Ibn Khaldūn, *Muḳaddima* = *Prolégomènes d'Ebn Khaldoun*, ed. E. Quatremère, Paris 1858-68 (*Notices et Extraits* XVI-XVIII)
Ibn Khaldūn-Rosenthal = *The Muqaddimah*, trans. from the Arabic by Franz Rosenthal, 3 vols., London 1958
Ibn Khaldūn-de Slane = *Les prolégomènes d'Ibn Khaldoun*, traduits en français et commentés par M. de Slane, Paris 1863-68 (anastatic reprint 1934-38)
Ibn Khallikān = *Wafayāt al-aʿyān wa-anbāʾ abnāʾ al-zamān*, ed. F. Wüstenfeld, Göttingen 1835-50 (quoted after the numbers of biographies)
Ibn Khallikān, Būlāḳ = the same, ed. Būlāḳ 1275
Ibn Khallikān-de Slane = *Kitāb Wafayāt al-aʿyān*, trans. by Baron MacGuckin de Slane, 4 vols., Paris 1842-1871
Ibn Khurradādhbih = *al-Masālik wa 'l-mamālik*, ed. M. J. De Goeje, Leiden 1889 (BGA VI)
Ibn Ḳutayba, *al-Shiʿr* = Ibn Ḳutayba, *Kitāb al-Shiʿr wa'l-shuʿarā*, ed. De Goeje, Leiden 1900
Ibn Rusta = *al-Aʿlāḳ al-nafīsa*, ed. M. J. De Goeje, Leiden 1892 (BGA VII)
Ibn Rusta-Wiet = *Les Atours précieux*, traduction de G. Wiet, Cairo 1955
Ibn Saʿd = *al-Ṭabaḳāt al-kubrā*, ed. H. Sachau and others, Leiden 1905-40
Ibn Taghrībirdī = *al-Nudjūm al-zāhira fī mulūk Miṣr wa-l-Ḳāhira*, ed. W. Popper, Berkeley-Leiden 1908-1936
Ibn Taghrībirdī, Cairo = the same, ed. Cairo 1348 ff.
Idrīsī, *Maghrib* = *Description de l'Afrique et de l'Espagne*, ed. R. Dozy and M. J. De Goeje, Leiden 1866
Idrīsī-Jaubert = *Géographie d'Édrisi*, trad. de l'arabe en français par P. Amédée Jaubert, 2 vols, Paris 1836-40
Iṣṭakhrī = *al-Masālik wa 'l-mamālik*, ed. M. J. De Goeje, Leiden 1870 (BGA I) (and reprint 1927)
Juynboll, *Handbuch* = Th. W. Juynboll, *Handbuch des islāmischen Gesetzes*, Leiden 1910
Khwāndamīr = *Ḥabīb al-siyar*, Tehran 1271
Kutubī, *Fawāt* = Ibn Shākir al-Kutubī, *Fawāt al-wafayāt*, Būlāḳ 1299
LA = *Lisān al-ʿArab* (quoted according to the root)
Lane = E. W. Lane, *An Arabic-English lexicon*, London 1863-93 (reprint New York 1955-6)
Lane-Poole, *Cat.* = S. Lane-Poole, *Catalogue of oriental coins in the British Museum*, 1877-90
Lavoix, *Cat.* = H. Lavoix, *Catalogue des monnaies musulmanes de la Bibliothèque Nationale*, Paris 1887-96
Le Strange = G. Le Strange, *The lands of the Eastern Caliphate*, 2nd ed., Cambridge 1930
Le Strange, *Baghdad*, = G. Le Strange, *Baghdad during the Abbasid Caliphate*, Oxford 1924.
Le Strange, *Palestine* = G. Le Strange, *Palestine under the Moslems*, London 1890
Lévi-Provençal, *Hist. Esp. Mus.* = E. Lévi-Provençal, *Histoire de l'Espagne musulmane*, new ed., Leiden-Paris 1950-53, 3 vols.
Lévi-Provençal, *Chorfa* = E. Lévi-Provençal, *Les historiens des Chorfa*, Paris 1922
MAE = K. A. C. Creswell, *The Muslim architecture of Egypt*, 2 vols., Oxford 1952-9
Maḳḳarī, *Analectes* = *Nafḥ al-ṭīb fī ghuṣn al-Andalus al-raṭīb (Analectes sur l'histoire et la littérature des Arabes de l'Espagne)*, Leiden 1855-61
Maḳḳarī, Būlāḳ = the same, ed. Būlāḳ 1279/1862
Marquart, *Ērānšahr* = J. Marquart, *Ērānšahr nach der Geographie des Ps. Moses Xorenacʿi*, Berlin 1901
Marquart, *Streifzüge* = J. Marquart, *Osteuropäische und ostasiatische Streifzüge. Ethnologische und historisch-topographische Studien zur Geschichte des 9. und 10. Jahrhunderts* (*c. 840-940*), Leipzig 1903
Maspero-Wiet, *Matériaux* = J. Maspéro et G. Wiet, *Matériaux pour servir à la géographie de l'Egypte*, Le Caire 1914 (MIFAO XXXVI)
Masʿūdī, *Murūdj* = *Murūdj al-dhahab*, edd. C. Barbier de Meynard and Pavet de Courteille, Paris 1861-77; ed. and trans. Ch. Pellat (in press; quoted according to the paragraph)
Masʿūdī, *Tanbīh* = *K. al-Tanbīh wa 'l-ishrāf*, ed. M. J. De Goeje, Leiden 1894 (BGA VIII)
Mayer, *Architects* = L. A. Mayer, *Islamic architects and their works*, Geneva 1956
Mayer, *Astrolabists* = L. A. Mayer, *Islamic astrolabists and their works*, Geneva 1958
Mayer, *Metalworkers* = L. A. Mayer, *Islamic metalworkers and their works*, Geneva 1959

Mayer, *Woodcarvers* = L. A. Mayer, *Islamic woodcarvers and their works*, Geneva 1958

Mez, *Renaissance* = A. Mez, *Die Renaissance des Islams*, Heidelberg 1922

Mez, *Renaissance*, Eng. tr. = *The renaissance of Islam*, translated into English by Salahuddin Khuda Bukhsh and D. S. Margoliouth, London 1937

Mez, *Renaissance*, Spanish trans. = *El renacimiento del Islam*, translated into Spanish by S. Vila, Madrid-Granada 1936.

Mīrk͟hwānd = *Rawḍat al-ṣafā*, Bombay 1266/1849

Muḳaddasī = *Aḥsan al-taḳāsīm fī maʿrifat al-aḳālīm*, ed. M. J. De Goeje, Leiden 1877 (BGA III)

Munad͟jd͟jim Bas͟hī = *Ṣaḥāʾif al-ak͟hbār*, Istanbul 1285

Nallino, *Scritti* = C. A. Nallino, *Raccolta di scritti editi e inediti*, Roma 1939-48

Zubayrī, *Nasab* = Muṣʿab al-Zubayrī, *Nasab Ḳuraysh*, ed. E. Lévi-Provençal, Cairo 1953

ʿOt͟hmānlï Müʾellifleri = Bursalï Meḥmed Ṭāhir, *ʿOt͟hmānlï müʾellifleri*, Istanbul 1333

Pakalın = Mehmet Zeki Pakalın, *Osmanlı tarih deyimleri ve terimleri sözlüğü*, 3 vols., Istanbul 1946 ff.

Pauly-Wissowa = *Realenzyklopaedie des klassischen Altertums*

Pearson = J. D. Pearson, *Index Islamicus*, Cambridge 1958; S I = *Supplement, 1956-60*

Pons Boigues = *Ensayo bio-bibliográfico sobre los historiadores y geógrafos arábigo-españoles*, Madrid 1898

Samʿānī = al-Samʿānī, *al-Ansāb*, ed. in facsimile by D. S. Margoliouth, Leiden 1912 (GMS XX)

Santillana, *Istituzioni* = D. Santillana, *Istituzioni di diritto musulmano malichita*, Roma 1926-38

Sarkīs = Sarkīs, *Muʿd͟jam al-maṭbūʿāt al-ʿarabiyya*, Cairo 1346/1928

Schwarz, *Iran* = P. Schwarz, *Iran im Mittelalter nach den arabischen Geographen*, Leipzig 1896-

S͟hahrastānī = *al-Milal wa 'l-niḥal*, ed. W. Cureton, London 1846

Sid͟jill-i ʿOt͟hmānī = Meḥmed T͟hüreyyā, *Sid͟jill-i ʿOt͟hmānī*, Istanbul 1308-1316

Snouck Hurgronje, *Verspr. Geschr.* = C. Snouck Hurgronje, *Verspreide Geschriften*, Bonn-Leipzig-Leiden 1923-27

Sources inédites = Comte Henry de Castries, *Les sources inédites de l'histoire du Maroc*, Première Série, Paris [etc.] 1905 —, Deuxième Série, Paris 1922 —

Spuler, *Horde* = B. Spuler, *Die Goldene Horde*, Leipzig 1943

Spuler, *Iran* = B. Spuler, *Iran in früh-islamischer Zeit*, Wiesbaden 1952

Spuler, *Mongolen*² = B. Spuler, *Die Mongolen in Iran*, 2nd ed., Berlin 1955

Storey = C. A. Storey, *Persian literature: a bio-bibliographical survey*, London 1927-

Survey of Persian Art = ed. by A. U. Pope, Oxford 1938

Suter = H. Suter, *Die Mathematiker und Astronomen der Araber und ihre Werke*, Leipzig 1900

Suyūṭī, *Bug͟hya* = *Bug͟hyat al-wuʿāt*, Cairo 1326

TA = Muḥammad Murtaḍā b. Muḥammad al-Zabīdī, *Tād͟j al-ʿarūs* (quoted according to the root)

Ṭabarī = *Taʾrīk͟h al-rusul wa 'l-mulūk*, ed. M. J. de Goeje and others, Leiden 1879-1901

Taeschner, *Wegenetz* = Franz Taeschner, *Das anatolische Wegenetz nach osmanischen Quellen*, 2 vols., Leipzig 1924-6.

Taʾrīk͟h Bag͟hdād = al-K͟haṭīb al-Bag͟hdādī, *Taʾrīk͟h Bag͟hdād*, 14 vols., Cairo 1349/1931.

Taʾrīk͟h Dimas͟hḳ = Ibn ʿAsākir, *Taʾrīk͟h Dimas͟hḳ*, 7 vols., Damascus 1329-51/1911-31

Taʾrīk͟h-i Guzīda = Ḥamd Allāh Mustawfī al-Ḳazwīnī, *Taʾrīk͟h-i guzīda*, ed. in facsimile by E. G. Browne, Leiden-London 1910

T͟haʿālibī, *Yatīma* = *Yatīmat al-dahr fī maḥāsin ahl al-ʿaṣr*, Damascus 1304

Tomaschek = W. Tomaschek, *Zur historischen Topographie von Kleinasien im Mittelalter*, Vienna 1891.

Weil, *Chalifen* = G. Weil, *Geschichte der Chalifen*, Mannheim-Stuttgart 1846-82

Wensinck, *Handbook* = A. J. Wensinck, *A handbook of early Muhammadan Tradition*, Leiden 1927

WKAS = *Wörterbuch der klassischen arabischen Sprache*, Wiesbaden 1957-

Yaʿḳūbī = *Taʾrīk͟h*, ed. M. Th. Houtsma, Leiden 1883

Yaʿḳūbī, *Buldān* = ed. M. J. De Goeje, Leiden 1892 (BGA VII)

Yaʿḳūbī-Wiet = *Yaʿḳūbī. Les pays*, trad. par Gaston Wiet, Cairo 1937

Yāḳūt = *Muʿd͟jam al-buldān*, ed. F. Wüstenfeld, Leipzig 1866-73 (anastatic reprint 1924)

Yāḳūt, *Udabāʾ* = *Irs͟hād al-arīb ilā maʿrifat al-adīb*, ed. D. S. Margoliouth, Leiden 1907-31 (GMS VI)

Zambaur = E. de Zambaur, *Manuel de généalogie et de chronologie pour l'histoire de l'Islam*, Hanover 1927 (anastatic reprint Bad Pyrmont 1955)

Zinkeisen = J. Zinkeisen, *Geschichte des osmanischen Reiches in Europa*, Gotha 1840-83

ABBREVIATIONS FOR PERIODICALS ETC.

Abh. G. W. Gött. = *Abhandlungen der Gesellschaft der Wissenschaften zu Göttingen.*
Abh. K. M. = *Abhandlungen für die Kunde des Morgenlandes.*
Abh. Pr. Ak. W. = *Abhandlungen der preussischen Akademie der Wissenschaften.*
Afr. Fr. = *Bulletin du Comité de l'Afrique française.*
AIEO Alger = *Annales de l'Institut d'Études Orientales de l'Université d'Alger* (N.S. from 1964).
AIUON = *Annali dell' Istituto Universitario Orientale di Napoli.*
Anz. Wien = *Anzeiger der [kaiserlichen] Akademie der Wissenschaften, Wien. Philosophisch-historische Klasse.*
AO = *Acta Orientalia.*
AO Hung. = *Acta Orientalia (Academiae Scientiarum Hungaricae).*
ArO = *Archiv Orientální.*
ARW = *Archiv für Religionswissenschaft.*
ASI = *Archaeological Survey of India.*
ASI, NIS = *ditto*, New Imperial Series.
ASI, AR = *ditto*, Annual Reports.
AÜDTCFD = *Ankara Üniversitesi Dil ve Tarih-Coğrafya Fakültesi Dergisi.*
BAH = *Bibliotheca Arabico-Hispana.*
BASOR = *Bulletin of the American Schools of Oriental Research.*
Belleten = Belleten (of *Türk Tarih Kurumu*)
BFac. Ar. = *Bulletin of the Faculty of Arts of the Egyptian University.*
BÉt. Or. = *Bulletin d'Études Orientales de l'Institut Français de Damas.*
BGA = *Bibliotheca geographorum arabicorum.*
BIE = *Bulletin de l'Institut d'Égypte.*
BIFAO = *Bulletin de l'Institut Français d'Archéologie Orientale du Caire.*
BRAH = *Boletín de la Real Academia de la Historia de España.*
BSE = *Bol'shaya Sovetskaya Éntsiklopediya* (Large Soviet Encyclopaedia) 1st ed.
BSE[2] = the same, 2nd ed.
BSL[P] = *Bulletin de la Société de Linguistique de Paris.*
BSO[A]S = *Bulletin of the School of Oriental [and African] Studies.*
BTLV = *Bijdragen tot de Taal-, Land- en Volkenkunde [van Nederlandsch-Indië].*
BZ = *Byzantinische Zeitschrift.*
COC = *Cahiers de l'Orient contemporain.*
CT = *Cahiers de Tunisie.*
EI[1] = *Encyclopaedia of Islam*, 1st edition.
EIM = *Epigraphia Indo-Moslemica.*
ERE = *Encyclopaedia of Religions and Ethics.*
GGA = *Göttinger Gelehrte Anzeigen.*
GMS = *Gibb Memorial Series.*
Gr. I. Ph. = *Grundriss der Iranischen Philologie.*
IA = *Islâm Ansiklopedisi.*
IBLA = *Revue de l'Institut des Belles Lettres Arabes*, Tunis.
IC = *Islamic Culture.*
IFD = *Ilahiyat Fakültesi Dergisi.*
IHQ = *Indian Historical Quarterly.*
IQ = *The Islamic Quarterly.*
Isl. = *Der Islam.*
JA = *Journal Asiatique.*
JAfr. S = *Journal of the African Society.*
JAOS = *Journal of the American Oriental Society.*
JAnthr. I = *Journal of the Anthropological Institute.*
JBBRAS = *Journal of the Bombay Branch of the Royal Asiatic Society.*
JE = *Jewish Encyclopaedia.*
JESHO = *Journal of the Economic and Social History of the Orient.*
J[R]Num. S. = *Journal of the [Royal] Numismatic Society.*
JNES = *Journal of Near Eastern Studies.*
JPak.HS = *Journal of the Pakistan Historical Society.*
JPHS = *Journal of the Punjab Historical Society.*
JQR = *Jewish Quarterly Review.*
JRAS = *Journal of the Royal Asiatic Society.*
J[R]ASB = *Journal and Proceedings of the [Royal] Asiatic Society of Bengal.*
JRGeog. S. = *Journal of the Royal Geographical Society.*
JSFO = *Journal de la Société Finno-ougrienne.*
JSS = *Journal of Semitic Studies.*
KCA = *Körösi Csoma Archivum.*
KS = *Keleti Szemle* (Oriental Review).
KSIE = *Kratkie Soobshčeniya Instituta Étnografiy* (Short communications of the Institute of Ethnography).
LE = *Literaturnaya Éntsiklopediya* (Literary Encyclopaedia).
MDOG = *Mitteilungen der Deutschen Orient-Gesellschaft.*
MDPV = *Mitteilungen und Nachrichten des Deutschen Palästina-Vereins.*
MEA = *Middle Eastern Affairs.*
MEJ = *Middle East Journal.*
MFOB = *Mélanges de la Faculté Orientale de l'Université St. Joseph de Beyrouth.*
MGMN = *Mitteilungen zur Geschichte der Medizin und Naturwissenschaften.*
MGWJ = *Monatsschrift für die Geschichte und Wissenschaft des Judentums.*
MIDEO = *Mélanges de l'Institut Dominicain d'Études Orientales du Caire.*
MIE = *Mémoires de l'Institut d'Égypte.*
MIFAO = *Mémoires publiés par les membres de l'Institut Français d'Archéologie Orientale du Caire.*
MMAF = *Mémoires de la Mission Archéologique Française au Caire.*
MMIA = *Madjallat al-Madjmaʿ al-ʿIlmī al-ʿArabī*, Damascus.
MO = *Le Monde oriental.*
MOG = *Mitteilungen zur osmanischen Geschichte.*
MSE = *Malaya Sovetskaya Éntsiklopediya* (Small Soviet Encyclopaedia).
MSFO = *Mémoires de la Société Finno-ougrienne.*
MSL[P] = *Mémoires de la Société Linguistique de Paris.*
MSOS Afr. = *Mitteilungen des Seminars für Orientalische Sprachen, Afrikanische Studien.*
MSOS As. = *Mitteilungen des Seminars für Orientalische Sprachen, Westasiatische Studien.*
MTM = *Millî Tetebbüʿler Medjmūʿası.*
MW = *The Muslim World.*
NC = *Numismatic Chronicle.*
NGW Gött. = *Nachrichten von der Gesellschaft der Wissenschaften zu Göttingen.*
OC = *Oriens Christianus.*

OLZ = *Orientalistische Literaturzeitung.*
OM = *Oriente Moderno.*
PEFQS = *Palestine Exploration Fund. Quarterly Statement.*
Pet. Mitt. = *Petermanns Mitteilungen.*
PTF = *Philologiae Tvrcicae Fundamenta*, Wiesbaden 1959- .
QDAP = *Quarterly Statement of the Department of Antiquities of Palestine.*
RAfr. = *Revue Africaine.*
RCEA = *Répertoire chronologique d'Épigraphie arabe.*
REJ = *Revue des Études Juives.*
Rend. Lin. = *Rendiconti della Reale Accademia dei Lincei, Classe di scienze morali, storiche e filologiche.*
REI = *Revue des Études Islamiques.*
RHR = *Revue de l'Histoire des Religions.*
RIMA = *Revue de l'Institut des Manuscrits Arabes.*
RMM = *Revue du Monde Musulman.*
RO = *Rocznik Orientalistyczny.*
ROC = *Revue de l'Orient Chrétien.*
ROL = *Revue de l'Orient Latin.*
RSO = *Rivista degli studi orientali.*
RT = *Revue Tunisienne.*
SBAk. Heid. = *Sitzungsberichte der Heidelberger Akademie der Wissenschaften.*
SBAk. Wien = *Sitzungsberichte der Akademie der Wissenschaften zu Wien.*
SBBayer. Ak. = *Sitzungsberichte der Bayerischen Akademie der Wissenschaften.*
SBPMS Erlg. = *Sitzungsberichte der Physikalisch-medizinischen Sozietät in Erlangen.*
SBPr. Ak. W. = *Sitzungsberichte der preussischen Akademie der Wissenschaften zu Berlin.*
SE = *Sovetskaya Étnografiya* (Soviet Ethnography).
SO = *Sovetskoe Vostokovedenie* (Soviet Orientalism).
Stud. Isl. = *Studia Islamica.*
S.Ya. = *Sovetskoe Yazîkoznanie* (Soviet Linguistics).
TBG = *Tijdschrift van het Bataviaasch Genootschap van Kunsten en Wetenschappen.*
TD = *Tarih Dergisi.*
TIE = *Trudî instituta Étnografiy* (Works of the Institute of Ethnography).
TM = *Türkiyat Mecmuası.*
TOEM/TTEM = *Ta'rikh-i ʿOthmānī* (*Türk Ta'rikhi*) *Endjümeni medjmūʿasî.*
Verh. Ak. Amst. = *Verhandelingen der Koninklijke Akademie van Wetenschappen te Amsterdam.*
Versl. Med. Ak. Amst. = *Verslagen en Mededeelingen der Koninklijke Akademie van Wetenschappen te Amsterdam.*
VI = *Voprosî Istoriy* (Historical Problems).
WI = *Die Welt des Islams.*
WI, n.s. = the same, new series.
Wiss. Veröff. DOG = *Wissenschaftliche Veröffentlichungen der Deutschen Orient-Gesellschaft.*
WZKM = *Wiener Zeitschrift für die Kunde des Morgenlandes.*
ZA = *Zeitschrift für Assyriologie.*
ZATW = *Zeitschrift für die alttestamentliche Wissenschaft.*
ZDMG = *Zeitschrift der Deutschen Morgenländischen Gesellschaft.*
ZDPV = *Zeitschrift des Deutschen Palästinavereins.*
ZGErdk. Birl. = *Zeitschrift der Gesellschaft für Erdkunde in Berlin.*
ZS = *Zeitschrift für Semitistik.*

LIST OF TRANSLITERATIONS

SYSTEM OF TRANSLITERATION OF ARABIC CHARACTERS:

Consonants

ء	ʾ (except when initial)	ز	z	ق	ḳ
ب	b	س	s	ك	k
ت	t	ش	sh	ل	l
ث	th	ص	ṣ	م	m
ج	dj	ض	ḍ	ن	n
ح	ḥ	ط	ṭ	ه	h
خ	kh	ظ	ẓ	و	w
د	d	ع	ʿ	ي	y
ذ	dh	غ	gh		
ر	r	ف	f		

Long Vowels

ا ى	ā
و	ū
ي	ī

Short Vowels

ـَ	a
ـُ	u
ـِ	i

Diphthongs

ـَو	aw
ـَي	ay
ـيّـ	iyy (final form ī)
ـُوّ	uww (final form ū)

ة a; at (construct state)

ال (article), al- and ʾl- (even before the antero-palatals)

PERSIAN, TURKISH AND URDU ADDITIONS TO THE ARABIC ALPHABET:

پ	p	ژ	zh	ٹ	ṭ́	ڑ	ŕ
چ	č	ك or ڭ	g (sometimes ñ in Turkish)	ڈ	ḍ́	ں	ṇ

Additional vowels:

a) Turkish: e, ı, o, ö, ü. Diacritical signs proper to Arabic are, in principle, not used in words of Turkish etymology.

b) Urdu: ē, ō.

For modern Turkish, the official orthography adopted by the Turkish Republic in 1928 is used. The following letters may be noted:

c = dj	ğ = gh	j = zh	k = k and ḳ	t = t and ṭ
ç = č	h = h, ḥ and kh	ş = sh	s = s, ṣ and th	z = z, ẓ, ḍ and dh

SYSTEM OF TRANSLITERATION OF THE RUSSIAN ALPHABET:

а	a	е	e	к	k	п	p	ф	f	щ	shč	ю	yu
б	b	ж	ž	л	l	р	r	х	kh	ы	ı	я	ya
в	v	з	z	м	m	с	s	ц	ts	ь	ʾ	ѣ	ě
г	g	и	i	н	n	т	t	ч	č	ъ	ʿ		
д	d	й	y	о	o	у	u	ш	sh	э	é		

ADDENDA AND CORRIGENDA

VOLUME I

P. 56[b], **ʿABD al-ʿAZĪZ,** l. 4, *instead of* 20 June *read* 26 June.

P. 75[a], **ʿABD al-MADJĪD** I, l. 39, *instead of* 25 June *read* 26 June.

P. 106[a-b], **ABU ʾl-ʿARAB,** *add*: One of the works of Abu ʾl-ʿArab Muḥammad b. Aḥmad b. Tamīm b. Tammām b. Tamīm al-Tamīmī (thus the full *nasab*) which has been preserved (in a unique Cambridge ms.) is his *Kitāb al-Miḥan*, a work in the tradition of the *maḳātil* books. It deals with a wide range of deaths in battle, by poisoning, persecution of ʿAlids, sufferings of Aḥmad b. Ḥanbal in the *miḥna* [*q.v.*] of the early 3rd/9th century; see for an analysis of its contents, M. J. Kister, *The "Kitab al-Mihan", a book on Muslim martyrology*, in *JSS*, xx (1975), 210-18. The complete work has now been edited by Yaḥyā Wahīb al-Djabbūrī, Beirut 1403/1983.

P. 194[b], **ADHRUḤm** *add to Bibliography* A. G. Killick, *Udhruh and the early Islamic conquests*, in *Procs. of the Second Symposium on the history of Bilād al-Shām during the early Islamic period (English and French papers)*, Amman 1987, 73-8.

P. 279[a], **AḤMAD** v. **ṬŪLŪN,** end of penultimate paragraph, *instead of* March 884 *read* May 884.

P. 436[b], al-**ʿĀMILĪ,** Muḥammad b. Ḥusayn Babāʾ al-Dīn, *add* to Bibl.: A. Newman, *Towards a reconsideration of the "Isfahān school of philosophy": Shaykh Bahāʾī and the role of the Safawid ʾulamā*, in *Studia Iranica*, xv (1986), 165-98; C. E. Bosworth, *Bahāʾ al-Dīn ʿĀmilī and his literary anthologies*, Manchester 1989.

P. 847[b], **BĀBĪS,** *add* to Bibl.: Abbas Amanat, *Resurrection and renewal. The making of the Babi movement in Iran, 1844-1850*, Ithaca and London 1989.

P. 940[b], **BAHRĀM SHĀH,** al-**MALIK** al-**AMDJAD,** l. 2, *instead of* Shāhānshāh read Tūrānshāh.

P. 1007[b], **BALŪČISTĀN,** *add* to Bibl.: J. Elfenbein, *A periplus of the "Brahui problem"*, in *Stud. Iranica*, xvi (1987), 215-33.

P. 1030[b], **BARĀDŪST,** l. 37, *instead of* 395/1005 *read* 1005/1597.

P. 1300[a], **BULANDSHAHR,** l. 30, *instead of* 644/1246-665/1266 *read* 796-815/1394-1412.

P. 1345[a], **BUST,** *add* to Bibl.: T. Allen, *Notes on Bust*, in *Iran JBIPS*, xxvi (1988), 55-68, xxvii (1989), 57-66, xxviii (1990).

VOLUME II

P. 72[b], **DĀBIḲ,** paragraph three, l. 2, *instead of* 15 Radjab 922 *read* 25 Radjab 922.

P. 809[a], **FARRUKHĀN,** l. 5 from bottom, *instead of* seventy years *read* thirteen years (90-103/709-21).

VOLUME III

P. 134[a], al-**ḤAMĪDĪ,** l. 24 from bottom, *instead of* 364/974-5, *read* 564/1168-9.

P. 293[b], **ḤAWRĀN,** *add to Bibliography* M. Sartre, *Le Hawran byzantin à la veille de la conquête musulmane*, in *Procs. of the Second Symposium on the history of Bilād al-Shām during the early Islamic period (English and French papers)*, Amman 1987, 155-67.

P. 367[a], **HIDJRA,** *add to Bibliography* Z. I. Khan, *The origins and development of the concept of* Hijrah *or migration in Islam*, Ph. D. thesis, Manchester 1987, unpublished.

P. 460[b], **HINDŪ-SHĀHĪS,** *add* to Bibl.: Yogendra Mishra, *The Hindu Shahis of Afghanistan and the Punjab*, Patna 1972; Abdur Rahman, *The last two dynasties of the Śāhīs. An analysis of their history, archaeology, coinage and palaeography*, Islamabad 1979.

P. 1007[b], **ʿĪD,** l. 1, *instead of* sunset *read* sunrise.

P. 1196[a], **IN SHĀʾ ALLĀH,** l. 2 from below, *instead of* James, iv, 19 *read* James, iv, 13-15.

VOLUME IV

P. 754[b], **ḲAṬĪʿA,** *add to end*: The term *ḳaṭīʿa* is also used in the specific sense of "ransom" in the period of the Crusades; cf. al-Ṣafadī, *Wāfī*, xiii, 505.

P. 759[a], **KĀTIB,** l. 23 from below, *instead of* Amīr Khusraw *read* Amīr Ḥasan.

P. 834[a], **ḲAYS ʿAYLĀN,** *add to Bibliography* Chang-kuan Lin, *The role of internecine strife and political struggle in the downfall of the Umayyad dynasty*, M. Phil. thesis, Manchester 1987, unpublished.

P. 1100[a], **MADJMAʿ ʿILMĪ,** l. 32, *instead of* statues *read* statutes.

VOLUME V

P. 39, **KHOTAN,** *add*:

The language of ancient Khotan was a Middle Iranian language, closely related to Soghdian. It is now commonly called Khotanese, though, since it was the descendant of one of the languages of the numerous, but ill-definable, pre-historic "Saka" tribes of Central Asia, it is sometimes called "Khotan Saka" (see e.g. H. W. Bailey, *Dictionary of Khotan Saka*, Cambridge, etc. 1979). E. Leumann, one of the earliest decipherers of the language, thought that it was a separate branch of Indo-Iranian and therefore called it "Nordarisch", but this theory was shown to be untenable by scholars such as S. Konow and Bailey. See Bailey, *Indo-Scythian studies, being Khotanese texts volume IV. Saka texts from Khotan in the Hedin collection*, Cambridge 1963, introd. 1-18; R. E. Emmerick, *Saka grammatical studies*, London 1968; idem, *A guide to the literature of Khotan*, Studia Philologica Buddhica. Occasional Papers Series III, Tokyo 1979; idem, *Khotanese*, in *Compendium linguarum iranicarum*, ed. R. Schmitt, Wiesbaden 1989.

The following kings of Khotan are known from the Khotanese documents: Viśya Vikrraṃ, Viśaʾ (Viśya) Sī(m)hya, Viśaʾ Dharma, Viśaʾ Kīrtti and Viśaʾ Vāhaṃ (all probably 8th century A.D.); Viśaʾ Saṃgrāma (? 9th century); Viśaʾ Sa(ṃ)bhava/Saṃbhata (regn. 912-66), Viśaʾ Śūra (regn. 967-at least 971), Viśaʾ D(h)arma (regn. 978-at least 988). See for useful surveys, J. Hamilton, *Les règnes khotanais entre 851 et 1001*, in M. Soymié (ed.), *Contributions aux études sur Touen-Houang*, Centre de recherches d'histoire et de philologie de la IVe section de l'EPHE II, Hautes études orientales 10, Geneva and Paris 1979, 49-54; idem, *Sur la chronologie khotanaise au IXe-Xe siècle*, in Soymié (ed.), *Contributions aus études de Touen-Houang III*, Publs. de L'Ecole française d'Extrême-Orient, cxxxv, Paris 1984, 47-8; and see further, H. Kumamoto, *Some problems of the Khotanese documents*, in *Studia grammatica iranica*, ed. R. Schmitt and P. O. Skjaervø, Munich 1986, 227-44, and Skjaervø, *Kings of Khotan in the 8th-10th centuries...*, in *Acts of the colloquium on "Histoire et cultes de l'Asie Centrale préislamique: sources écrites et documents archéologiques", Paris 22-8 November 1988*, CNRS Paris (forthcoming).

The islamisation of Khotan apparently took place already around 1006, at any rate before 1008, since the Chinese annals for the year 1009 report the arrival of a *huei-hu* (= Turk) sent by the *hei-han* (= Khaghan) of Yu-t'ien (= Khotan) with tribute to the Imperial Chinese court; the envoy had been travelling for a year (see M. Abel-Rémusat, *Histoire de la ville de Khotan tirée des annales de la Chine et traduite du chinois*, Paris 1820, 86-7). The Muslim ruler at this time was the Ḳarakhānid Yūsuf Ḳadīr Khān of Kāshghar (on whom see O. Pritsak, *Die Karachaniden*, in *Isl.*, xxxi [1953-4], 30-3, repr. in *Studies in medieval Eurasian history*, London 1981, xvi, and ILEK-KHĀNS).

The conflict between Khotan and Kāshghar must have started earlier, however, for in a letter written in Khotanese by King Viśaʾ Śūra in 970, the ruler refers to "Our evil enemy the Tazhīk (Khot. Ttaśīʾkā) Tcūṃ-hyai:nä [Ts'ung hsien?], who [is] there among the Tazhīks", and in a letter in Chinese from the ruler of Sha-chou (Tun Huang) to the king of Khotan, in the Pelliot collection, from around 975 we read that "the prince of the west is leading Tadjik (Ta-shih) troops to attack [your] great kingdom" (see Bailey, *Saka documents, text vol.*, Corpus inscr. iranicarum, ii, V, London 1968, 58-61, ll. 50-1; Hamilton, *Sur la chronologie*, 48-9). Hamilton has suggested that the "evil enemy" may be Viśaʾ Śūra's brother, another son of Viśaʾ Saṃbhava (in Chinese, Li Sheng-t'ien), two of whom are known to have borne the name Tcūṃ/Ts'ung. Kumamoto, *op. cit.*, 231, suggests that this mother may have been a Ḳarakhānid. The last known king of Khotan was Viśaʾ D(h)arma (still ruling in 988), whose name shows that he was not a Muslim. The definitive struggle over Khotan must therefore have taken place during the ensuing two decades. See also M. A. Stein, *Ancient Khotan*, 2. vols., Oxford 1907, repr. New York 1975, i, 180-1; W. Samolin, *East Turkistan to the twelfth century*, The Hague, etc. 1964, 80-2.

P. 375b, AL-**KUMAYT B. ZAYD** AL-**ASADĪ**, *add* to Bibl.: W. Madelung, *The* Hāshimiyyāt *of al-Kumayt and Hāshimī Shiʿism*, in *SI*, lxx (1989), 5-26.

P. 1029b, AL-**MADJDJĀWĪ**, l. 4, *instead of* Algiers, *read* Constantine.

P. 1135b, **MADRASA,** *add. to the Bibl.*: R. Brunschvig, *Quelques remarques sur les médersas de Tunisie*, in *RT*, new ser., vi (1931), 261-85.

P. 1232a, AL-**MAHDĪ:** ll. 33-48. This passage was modified by the Editors without the author's consent. The author's original should be restored as follows:
This *ḥadīth*, whose first part is patterned upon the revolt of ʿAbd Allāh b. al-Zubayr, probably goes back to ʿAbd Allāh b. al-Ḥārith b. Nawfal b. al-Ḥārith b. ʿAbd al-Muṭṭalib, who appears in its *isnād* and claimed to have heard it from Umm Salama, widow of the Prophet. ʿAbd Allāh b. al-Ḥārith was chosen by the people of Baṣra as their governor in 64/684 after the death of the caliph Yazīd and the flight of his governor ʿUbayd Allāh b. Ziyād. He then recognised Ibn al-Zubayr as the caliph and took the pledge of allegiance of the Baṣrans for him. The *ḥadīth* was evidently proclaimed by him in this situation with the aim of stirring up support for the cause of Ibn al-Zubayr.

VOLUME VI

P. 115b, **MAḲĀMA,** *add* to Bibl.: Yūsuf Nūr ʿAwad, *Fann al-maḳāmāt bayn al-mashriḳ wa 'l-maghrib*[2], Mecca 1406/1986; Samīr Maḥmūd al-Durūbī, *Sharḥ maḳāmāt Jalāl al-Dīn al-Suyūṭī al-mutawaffā sanat 911*, 2 vols. Beirut 1409/1989.

P. 125b, **MAḲBARA,** *add to Bibliography*: J.-L. Bacqué-Grammont, H.-P. Laqueur, N. Vatin, *Stelae Turcicae*, I: *Küçük Ayasofya*, in *Istabuler Mitteilungen* xxxiv (1984), 441-539.

P. 262a, **MALIK,** *at end of Bibliography add* A. Ayalon, *'Malik' in modern Middle Eastern literature*, in *WI* xxiii-xxiv (1984), 306-19.

P. 334a, **MAʿN,** *at end of Bibliography add* Abu 'l-Wafaʾ al-Urḍī, *Maʿādin al-dhahab fī 'l-ridjāl al-musharrafa bi-him Ḥalab*, MS B.M. Or. 3618.

P. 358a, AL-**MANĀMA,** l. 3, *instead of* side *read* site.
Add to Bibliography Mahdi Abdalla al-Tajir, *Bahrain 1920-1945, Britain, the Shaikh and the administration*, London 1987.

P. 374b, AL-**MANĀZIL,** l. 8, *after* Ibn Ḳutayba *insert a comma.*
l. 27, *after* names *insert* became.
No. 5 of the list, *instead of* $\lambda\phi^{12}$. Orionis *read* $\lambda\varphi^{1,\,2}$ Orionis.
No. 9 of the list, *instead* of δ *read* $\varkappa$.

P. 375a, No. 28 of the list, instead of *al-hūt* read *al-ḥūt.*
l. 23, *instead of* 1800 *read* 180.

P. 453b, **MANŪČIHRĪ,** *add* to Bibl.: W. L. Hanaway, *Blood and wine: sacrifice in Manūchihrī's wine poetry*, in *Iran JBIPS*, xxvi (1988), 69-80.

P. 459a,, **MAPPILA,** l. 37, *instead of* 1948 *read* 1498.

P. 460a, l. 10, *instead of* ist *read* its.
l. 30, *instead of* or *read* of.

P. 461ª, l. 13 from below, *instead of* wiser *read* wider.
P. 462ᵇ, l. 17, *instead of* nor *read* not.
P. 463ᵇ, ll. 29-30 from below, *instead of* remaining *read* remains.
P. 464ª, l. 16 from below, *instead of* wisely *read* widely.
Pp. 511 and 517, **MARᶜA<u>SH</u>ĪS.** Owing to an unfortunate oversight Table A has been included twice.
P. 641ª, **MĀSAR<u>DJ</u>AWAYH,** l. 10, *instead of* πανέχτης *read* Πανδέκτης.
l. 24-25, *instead of* p. 20, 1. 341 *read* p. 20, l. 341.
l. 26, *instead of* p. 88, 11. 1860-3 *read* p. 88, ll. 1860-3.
P. 736ᵇ, **MASKAṬ,** *add* to author's signature "shortened by the Editors".
P. 764ᵇ, **MASRAḤ,** *add at the end of the Bibliography: Modern Persian drama. Anthology*, tr. G. Kapuscinski, Lanham 1987; G. Kapuscinski, *Modern Persian drama*, in *Persian literature*, ed. E. Yarshater, Albany 1988, 381-402.

SUPPLEMENT

P. 127ª, **BĀRIZ, <u>DJ</u>ABAL,** *add*: One should note the present-day settlement of Pārīz, in the northwestern part of the <u>D</u>jabal Bāriz, on the Ragsan<u>dj</u>ān-Saᶜīdābād (Sīr<u>dj</u>ān) road, which could possibly be the classical *Parikāne polis*, town of the Parikanioi. See A. D. H. Bivar, *A Persian fairyland*, in *Acta Iranica* 24: *Hommages et opera minora* X: *Papers in honour of Professor Mary Boyce*, Leiden 1985, 25-42, who here derives the legends and romances around the peris or fairies of Iran (Av. *pairikā*, MP *parīg*, NP *parī*) from indigenous Persian traditions connecting them with the Parikanioi, whose epigoni were suspect in Sāsānid times by Zoroastrian orthodoxy for their non-Zoroastrian local beliefs and customs, hence equated with demonic and supernatural beings.
P. 163ᵇ, **ČAČ—NĀMA.** The last item in the Bibliography has been published in Y. Friedmann, ed., *Islam in Asia*, i: *South Asia*, Jerusalem 1984, 23-27.
P. 395ª, **IBN NĀẒIR AL-<u>DJ</u>AY<u>SH</u>,** *add* to Bibl.: The *Ta<u>th</u>kīf* is now available in the edition of R. Veselý, IFAO, Cairo 1987; see also on the author, D. S. Richards, *The Tathqīf of Ibn Nāẓir al-Jaish: the identity of the author and the manuscripts*, in *Cahiers d'onomasticon arabe*, iv (1985-7), 97-101.

THE ENCYCLOPAEDIA OF ISLAM

NEW EDITION

PREPARED BY A NUMBER OF
LEADING ORIENTALISTS

EDITED BY

C. E. BOSWORTH, E. VAN DONZEL, B. LEWIS AND CH. PELLAT

ASSISTED BY F. TH. DIJKEMA AND MME S. NURIT

UNDER THE PATRONAGE OF
THE INTERNATIONAL UNION OF ACADEMIES

VOLUME VI

FASCICULES 99—100

MAḤKAMA — MAḲDISHŪ

LEIDEN
E. J. BRILL
1986

EXECUTIVE COMMITTEE:

All correspondence on editorial matters should be addressed to the Editorial Secretaries, whose addresses are:

For the English Edition

Dept. of Near Eastern Studies,
The University of Manchester,
Manchester,
England M13 9PL.

For the French Edition

13, rue de Santeuil
75231 Paris Cedex 05
France

AUTHORS OF ARTICLES IN THESE FASCICULES

I. Afshar, Tehran. 92.
Feroz Ahmad, University of Massachusetts, Boston. 74.
Münir Aktepe, University of Istanbul. 58.
E. Ashtor, Hebrew University, Jerusalem. 121.
A. F. L. Beeston, Oxford. 88.
J. R. Blackburn, University of Toronto. 72.
C. E. Bosworth, University of Manchester. 64, 66, 77, 87, 116.
[C. Brockelmann, Halle]. 115.
K. L. Brown, University of Manchester. 124.
J. T. P. de Bruijn, University of Leiden. 73, 86.
[Fr. Buhl, Copenhagen]. 46.
J. Burton-Page, Church Knowle, Dorset. 61, 87, 112, 128.
J.-Cl. Ch. Chabrier, Centre National de la Recherche Scientifique, Paris. 104.
[C. Collin Davies]. 87.
R. H. Davison, George Washington University, Washington. 69.
P. Dumont, Centre National de la Recherche Scientifique, Paris. 96.
C. V. Findley, Ohio State University, Columbus. 9.
Mohibbul Hasan, Aligarh. 47, 52, 55, 62, 63.
G. Hazai, Hungarian Academy of Sciences, Budapest. 75.
C. H. Imber, University of Manchester. 72.
H. İnalcik, University of Chicago. 5, 11.
T. M. Johnstone, Oxford. 85.
J. Jomier, Paris. 46.
F. de Jong, University of Utrecht. 88.
M. J. Kister, Hebrew University, Jerusalem. 107.
Ann K. S. Lambton, Kirknewton, Northumberland. 22.
H.-P. Laqueur, Institut Français d'Archéologie, Istanbul. 125.
A. Layish, Hebrew University, Jerusalem. 25, 26, 28, 29, 31, 33, 35, 36, 38, 42.
D. S. Lev, University of Washington, Seattle. 44.
A. Levy, Brandeis University, Waltham, Ma. 61.
J. N. Mattock, University of Glasgow, 87.
W. W. Müller, University of Marburg. 84.
Solange Ory, University of Aix-Marseille. 123.
Ch. Pellat, University of Paris. 115.
[W. H. Rassers]. 117.
F. Robinson, Royal Holloway College, Egham. 78.
[J. Schacht, New York]. 3, 25.
O. Schumann, University of Hamburg. 117.
H. K. Sherwani. 68.
the late O. Spies, Bonn. 80.
Ch. Vial, University of Aix-Marseille. 77, 91.
F. A. K. Yasamee, University of Manchester. 90.

Names in square brackets are those of authors of articles reprinted or revised from the first edition of this Encyclopaedia.

This fascicule was published with the financial support of the British Academy, London.

M

CONTINUATION

MAḤKAMA (A.), court. The subject-matter of this article is the administration of justice, and the organisation of its administration, in the Muslim countries, the office of the judge being dealt with in the art. ḲĀḌĪ.

The following topics are covered:

1. General
2. The Ottoman empire
   i. The earlier centuries
   ii. The reform era (*ca.* 1789-1922)
3. Iran
4. The Arab lands and Israel
   i. Egypt
   ii. Syria
   iii. Lebanon
   iv. ʿIrāḳ
   v. Palestine and Israel
   vi. Jordan
   vii. Saudi Arabia
   viii. Yemen and the People's Republic of Southern Yemen
   ix. The Gulf States
   x. Morocco
   xi. Algeria
   xii. Tunisia
   xiii. Reforms in the law applying in *Sharīʿa* courts
5. The Indo-Pakistan subcontinent
6. Indonesia

1. General

The judicial functions of the Prophet, which had been expressly attributed to him in the Ḳurʾān (IV, 65, 105; V, 42, 48-9; XXIV, 48, 51), were taken over after his death by the first caliphs, who administered the law in person in Medina. Already under ʿUmar, the expansion of the Islamic empire necessitated the appointment of judges, originally for the expeditionary forces, then, in the natural course of events, also for the conquered territories; this institution of army judges (*ḳāḍī'l-djund*) remained in being down to the Ottoman period as the *ḳāḍī-ʿaskar* [*q.v.*]. The source of jurisdiction in the *Sharīʿa* is the caliph; the judges act as delegates of the authority by which they have been appointed, and are authorised to delegate their powers in turn to other persons. The appointment of a judge is made by contract consisting of offer and acceptance in the presence of at least two witnesses. The validity of the appointment does not depend upon the legality of the appointing authority: by this open-minded disposition, the *Sharīʿa* has accommodated itself even in theory to the actual facts. On the other hand, the authorities are free to restrict the competence (*wilāya*) of the judge with regard to place, time and subject matter. In the early period, there used to be judges only in the big towns, and the judicial districts were accordingly large (the whole of Egypt, for instance); under the Ottomans this came to change, perhaps in consequence of the intense practical application of the *Sharīʿa* in their territory. The restriction with regard to subject-matter was originally intended to divide labour and alleviate the burden of the chief judge, especially by erecting into independent offices some of his functions that were not purely judicial; in modern times, the restriction with regard to time and subject-matter is used in order to modify or eliminate the application of provisions of the *Sharīʿa* without interfering directly with its material dispositions (see section 4. xiii. Reforms in the law applying in *Sharīʿa* courts, below). Under the Umayyads, the judges were as a rule appointed by the governors; the ʿAbbāsids made a point of assuming directly the exercise of this function of the sovereign; although they had to delegate it more than once to practically independent princes, they still tried to retain it, at least in form, even when their power was in full decay. The compromise between those tendencies, together with the large size, and even the accumulation in one person, of judicial districts brought about a complicated system of delegation to substitutes. The Fāṭimids, the Umayyads in Spain and the Ottoman sultans likewise appointed their judges directly; the latter continued to exercise this privilege also in ceded territories such as Egypt, of which the chief *ḳāḍī* was nominated in Istanbul until 1914. The *ḳāḍī* could be deposed at any time by the authority which had appointed him; a change of the person in charge of this function very often caused a re-filling of all the judicial posts dependent on it. According to the theory of the *fiḳh*, only a delegate, not an independent *ḳāḍī*, loses his office by the death or dismissal of the person who appointed him. Corresponding to this right of nomination is something like a right of supervision, which manifests itself in receiving complaints as well as in giving official directions. Another kind of higher instance was represented by the unanimous opinion of the learned men whom the judge ought to consult in cases of doubt; these could come to form a sort of unofficial court of appeal. A third kind of higher instance, the most important in practice, was control by the successor, which was often exercised with the utmost severity; every judgment of a *ḳāḍī* could be annulled by any of his successors, a possibility which led to an endless duration of some law-suits. All this affords certain possibilities for the revision of judgments, which in theory is not provided for at all. In theory, the *ḳāḍī* acts as a single judge; this did not prevent several judges, even if belonging to different juridical schools, from being competent for one judicial district, especially in the capitals. A judgment once pronounced cannot be changed by the same *ḳāḍī*, even if evidence to the contrary is brought in later or if the original evidence is proved to be worthless; another *ḳāḍī* can repeal it only if there was a serious fault in law, i.e. if it is contrary to the Ḳurʾān, to a recognised tradition or to unanimous opinion (*id̲j̲māʿ*). The judgment should be given according to the opinion of the law school (*mad̲h̲hab*) to which the judge belongs; if he diverges from it, the validity of the judgment is controversial. A *ḳāḍī* did not have to belong to the same juridical school als the person who appointed him, nor a substitute to the same school as the judge who delegated his powers to him; but they could always be directed to follow the opinions of a certain school. In general, the authorities preferred *ḳāḍīs* of their own juridical school; under the ʿAbbāsids this was at first the Ḥanafī and later on the S̲h̲āfiʿī one, under the Ottomans, most decidedly, the Ḥanafī, whereas under the Umayyads of Spain the Mālikī school had a jealously-guarded monopoly. The juridical school allegiance of the judge was of greater importance for the populace under his jurisdiction than for the ruler. Many judges, especially in the early period, made allowance for the people's allegiance to a school different from their own, but many difficulties arose, in particular where the people of the country were divided between several schools; to remedy this, recourse was often had (for the first time in Cairo in 525/1131) to the appointment of several *ḳāḍīs*, one of whom usually had official precedence over his colleagues, but among whom the parties could choose freely. The judge of the capital—not yet under the Umayyads but from the very beginning of the ʿAbbāsids—occupied a prominent position and was given the title of Chief Judge (*ḳāḍī 'l-ḳuḍāt*), the first being Abū Yūsuf [*q.v.*] in Bag̲h̲dād (under Hārūn al-Ras̲h̲īd); in the western lands of Islam he was called *ḳāḍī 'l-d̲j̲amāʿa*. This at first simply meant pre-eminence among his colleagues, but soon imported a right of supervision over them, which became still more pronounced when under the system of delegations the other *ḳāḍīs* were only substitutes of the Chief Judge. The most important auxiliary officials were the secretary (*kātib*) and the witnesses (*s̲h̲āhid* [*q.v.*]), who at the same time fulfilled the function of notaries; their duties were often the first steps in a judicial career. Advocacy, i.e. the representation of the interests of the parties by specialists, was rejected by the theory and discouraged by the practice of the early period; on the contrary, the task of the learned in law was supposed to be to aid the judge, as *muftīs* [see FATWĀ], in the impartial application of the sacred law. Nevertheless, the *fatwā* is often nothing more than a written pleading for one party, and advising parties and representing them in court have become a widely practised occupation of experts (*wakīl*, "representative"), who have developed in modern times into the order of advocates (*muḥāmī*) in the *S̲h̲arīʿa* courts. For the procedure, see DAʿWĀ. Besides the administration of justice by *ḳāḍīs*, the *S̲h̲arīʿa* knows the voluntary resort to arbitrators (*ḥakam*).

Along with this religious jurisdiction, we find the administrative jurisdiction of the *naẓar al-maẓālim* ("investigation of complaints") exercised by the caliphs and their political organs: viziers, governors, sultans, etc., or by judges appointed expressly for this purpose, as well as a police-like supervision by the *muḥtasib* [*q.v.*] and the *ṣāḥib al-s̲h̲urṭa* [see S̲H̲URṬA]. Whereas down to the end of the Umayyad period all jurisdiction was concentrated in the hands of the *ḳāḍī* and occasional attempts at interference by the governors were mostly frustrated, the early days of ʿAbbāsid rule saw a need for supplementing *ḳāḍī* jurisdiction, which from now on was tied to the fully-developed system of the *S̲h̲arīʿa* by the settling of complaints through the *maẓālim* procedure. A clear separation of the competences of both spheres in no way existed, notwithstanding the long lists of differences presented by theorists. Those very representatives of political authority who were anxious to assure a good administration of justice by strict supervision were apt to monopolise jurisdiction almost completely, the more so as the *ḳāḍī* possessed no executive organs of his own but had to depend on those which the authorities chose to place at his disposal. So nearly everywhere in Islam, a secular jurisdiction evolved beside the religious one [see *EI*¹, S̲H̲ARĪʿA, section 6]. It retained certain general principles of the *S̲h̲arīʿa*, but based its judgments mainly upon equity and custom and applied an elastic and often summary procedure. This state of things was to some extent sanctioned by the Ḳurʾānic injunction to obey those in authority. In the sphere of secular jurisdiction, the last and the present century brought the creation of courts on the European pattern, controlled by the government, and the introduction of modern codes. The final step was the reorganisation, again on European lines, of the *S̲h̲arīʿa* courts in a number of Muslim countries, resulting in the introduction of courts of appeal and of benches consisting of more than one judge. All this derives from the power of the authorities to restrict the competence of the *ḳāḍīs*.

In the following, we shall briefly discuss the spheres and organisation of *s̲h̲arʿī* justice in the Muslim countries, its material law and procedure, the reforms in the law applying in *S̲h̲arīʿa* courts and their application by the *ḳāḍīs*.

Bibliography: Snouck Hurgronje, *Verspr. Geschr.*, vi, index *s.v.* Kadi and Richter; Juynboll, *Handbuch*, 309 ff.; idem, *Handleiding*³, 316 ff.; López Ortiz, *Derecho musulmán*, 67 ff.; Schacht, *G. Bergsträsser's Grundzüge des islamischen Rechts*, chs. i, x, xi; Amedroz, in *JRAS* (1910), 761 ff.; (1911), 635 ff.; (1916), 287 ff.; Bergsträsser, in *ZDMG*, lxviii (1914), 395 ff.; Gabrieli, in *Rivista Coloniale*, viii/2 (1913); Pröbster, in *Islamica*, v, 545 ff. Much material is to be found in the biographical works on *ḳāḍīs*, e.g. Wakīʿ, *Kitāb Ak̲h̲bār al-ḳuḍāt*, ed. ʿAbd al-ʿAzīz Muṣṭafā al-Marāg̲h̲ī, i-iii, Cairo 1947-50; al-Kindī, *The governors and judges of Egypt*, ed. Guest; al-K̲h̲us̲h̲anī, *Historia de los jueces de Córdoba*, ed. Ribera; al-Fatḥ b. K̲h̲āḳān, *Ḳalāʾid al-ʿiḳyān*; al-Suyūṭī, *Ḥusn al-muḥāḍara*; and the works mentioned in Schacht, *Aus Kairiner Bibliotheken (II)*, 27 ff. Also the sources for political and administrative history, e.g. Ibn K̲h̲aldūn, *Muḳaddima*; al-Ḳalḳas̲h̲andī, *Ṣubḥ al-aʿs̲h̲ā*; further, the works on the history of civilisation, e.g. Mez, *Die Renaissance des Islams*, 206 ff., Span. tr. *El Renacimiento del Islam*, 267 ff. Eng. tr. Khuda Bakhsh., 216 ff.; Lévi-Provençal, *L'Espagne musulmane*, 79 ff.; R. Levy, *The social structure of Islam*, Cambridge 1957, chs, ii-iv, vi; further, the works of Schacht: *The origins of Muhammadan jurisprudence*³, Oxford 1959; *An introduction to Islamic law*², Oxford 1966, chs. 1-11, with important bibliography; and *Law and justice*, in P. M. Holt, A. K. S. Lambton and B. Lewis (eds.), *The Cambridge history of Islam*, ii, Cambridge 1970, 539-68; E. Tyan, *Histoire de l'organisation judiciaire en pays d'Islam*², Leiden 1960; M. Khadduri and H. J. Liebesny (eds.), *Law in the Middle East*, i, Washington, D.C. 1955; N. J. Coulson, *A history of*

Islamic law, Edinburgh 1964, parts i-ii; Jeanette A. Wakin, *The function of documents in Islamic law*, Albany 1972; H. J. Liebesny, *The law of the Near and Middle East*, Albany 1975, chs. 1-2; Ṣubḥī Maḥmaṣānī, *al-Awḍāʿ al-tas̲h̲rīʿiyya fi 'l-duwal al-ʿarabiyya māḍīhā wa-ḥāḍiruhā*³, Beirut 1965, with bibliography of Arabic works. (J. Schacht*)

2. The Ottoman Empire

i. The earlier centuries

As the official seat of the *ḳāḍī* [*q.v.*], the *maḥkama* was a fixed location within the bounds of a *ḳaḍāʾ* or *ḥukūma*, the jurisdiction area assigned to a *ḳāḍī*. The number of *maḥkamas* in a particular jurisdiction area was determined and fixed by the sultan, and their locations could not be changed at the will of the *ḳāḍī* (*Ḳānūn-nāme*, Turkish Hist. Soc. ms. Y4, f. 87b). When the population of a district grew or when new circumstances arose, the sultan could decide to divide the existing *ḳaḍāʾ*s in order to create new ones. The location of the *maḥkama* was usually chosen for its easy access to the commercial community, generally in the bazar or somewhere within the precincts or near to the congregational mosque of the town. For instance, one of the *maḥkamas* of Istanbul was in the courtyard of the mosque of Dāwūd Pas̲h̲a.

In the Ottoman Empire, *maḥkamas* usually had their own premises, at least in the 18th century, as appears from the court records. The exact number of the *maḥkamas* within a jurisdiction varied according to the population. In Istanbul, for example, there were five *maḥkamas* scattered in the *ḳaḍāʾ* of Istanbul, and in 993/1585 the *ḳāḍī* submitted a request for opening of new *maḥkamas* for the convenience of the population (A. Refik, *Istanbul hayatı*, i, 30). In other *ḳaḍāʾ*s of greater Istanbul, namely Eyüp (K̲h̲āṣṣlar), Galata (Pera) and Üsküdar, there were other *maḥkamas*. Bursa had seven *maḥkamas* at various parts of the city in the 11th/17th century.

The jurisdiction of a *maḥkama* and abuses of power. Within a *ḳaḍāʾ*s boundaries, an individual was free to choose which *maḥkama* to use. Some *maḥkamas* developed a speciality in a certain field; for instance, the *maḥkama* of Eyüp became the court specialising in cases of water rights (ʿO. Nūrī, *Mad̲j̲alla*, i, 1221). In the period before Süleymān's reign, important cities had judges of both the Ḥanafī and S̲h̲āfiʿī law schools. However, Süleymān ordered that all courts in the Ottoman dominions should be administered only according to the Ḥanafī rite (Abu 'l-Suʿūd, *Maʿrūḍāt*, in *MTM*, i, 340-1). Despite this rule, S̲h̲āfiʿī judges continued to function in the courts of Antakya and all the cities in the Arab provinces (see Ewliyā Čelebi, *Seyāḥat-nāme*, iii, 58). By a *ḥukm* of 928/1522 (ms. Veliyuddin 1969), the local begs were authorised to appoint *ḳāḍīs* of the S̲h̲āfiʿī school in the province of Diyārbakr. In Rad̲j̲ab 981/October-November 1573 a *firmān* confirmed that the *ḳāḍīs* in the province of Ṭarābulus al-G̲h̲arb (Libya) could follow the Mālikī school in their decisions (Mühimme defteri, xxiii, 153).

The *ḳāḍī* or *ḥākim al-s̲h̲arʿ* of a court derived his authority directly from the sultan and was responsible only to him. A *ḳāḍī* once dismissed by the sultan had no power to issue any document. In the Ottoman empire, the *ḳāḍī* administered, not only the religious law but also the secular *ḳānūn* [*q.v.*], a practice peculiar to that régime. The *ḥākim* had the power to administer *taʿzīr* [*q.v.*] punishments and to imprison debtors. Local *maḥkamas*, however, had to refer to the Porte all cases concerning the military class, state interests and public security, as well as those involving more than a certain amount of money. Some cases concerning the foreigners covered by the capitulations were also to be referred to the *dīwān-i hümāyūn* [see imtiyāzāt, ii]. The sultan could order a *ḥākim* not to hear certain kinds of cases. The *ḳāḍī*'s decision was in principle final, and there was no provision for appeal in the Ottoman judicial system. However, if the interested party complained directly to the sultan of injustice in a decision, the imperial *dīwān*, while not capable of reversing it, could order according to the circumstances either a retrial by the same *ḳāḍī*, a transfer of the case to a nearby *ḥākim*'s court, or the dispatch of the parties to the imperial *dīwān* for a new trial. Governors were strictly forbidden to interfere in the courts' activities (for the sultan's strong reaction in such a case of interference, see Tas̲h̲köprü-zāde, *S̲h̲aḳāʾiḳ al-nuʿmāniyya*, 216). In a *fatwā,* Abu 'l-Suʿūd equated such governors with infidels. If a governor-general caught a *ḳāḍī* in a flagrantly illegal action, he could put an end to his activities, but he had to notify the sultan immediately, since a *ḳāḍī* could only be tried in the imperial *dīwān* itself. The sultan could at any time decide to remove a *ḳāḍī* from office. At the beginning, the term of a *ḳāḍī*'s office was unlimited. Later, in 1001/1598-9, it was limited to three years, and afterwards to two years. From the end of the 11th/17th century onwards, the regular term of office or *muddat-i ʿurfiyya* became one year. Originally an outgrowth of the need to find appointments for the *mulāzims* or qualified candidates awaiting their turn for a post, these frequent changings of office were seen to be the prime factor in the deterioration of the Ottoman judicial system and a cause of widespread corruption (such criticisms made in the political pamphlets are summed up by K. Röhrborn, *Untersuchungen zur Osmanischen Verwaltungsgeschichte*, Berlin 1973).

Local populations had the right to complain to the sultan about their *ḥākims*' activities and behaviour, this being a fundamental right enjoyed by the *reʿāyā* against any agent of the sultan. General inspections were carried out from time to time to redress wrongs attributed to the *ḳāḍīs* (for punishments meted out after such an inspection, see Topkapı Palace Library, Revan, no. 1506; M. Cezar, *Levendler*, Istanbul 1965, document no. 1 in the appendix). In Ottoman history, popular discontent against abuses at the *maḥkama* was taken seriously by the sultans, and periodic reforms were carried out from the time of Bāyezīd I onwards. The principal subject of complaint was the collection of court fees, considered to be contrary to Islamic principles and actually denounced by the Ottoman *muftīs*. The government tried to regulate the rates at various dates, as can be seen from the following table.

These fees constituted the principal source of income of the *ḥākims*. They were prone to raise the rates or to force people to come to court unnecessarily for cases such as inheritance division or *ḳismet-i mīrāt̲h̲*. Ewliyā Čelebi gives as the normal amount the income for each *ḳaḍāʾ*, including the income from abuses. It was only in the period following the *Tanẓīmāt* [*q.v.*], when the *ḳāḍīs* were assigned fixed salaries, that such fees were finally abolished. In addition to this basic source of abuse, the *ḥākims* were inclined to increase the number of the *maḥkamas* in their jurisdiction in order to obtain extra revenues and then to farm them out to the *nāʾibs*. This practice, forbidden under Süleymān I in the regulations for Egypt of 931/1524-5, was included among the general abuses in the *ʿadālet-nāme* of 947/1540-1 (H. İnalcık, *Adâletnâmeler*, in *Belgeler*, ii, 76) and in a *firmān* of 958/1551

Table showing fees collected for certain types of cases for each of the agents officiating (in akčas)
(ND = no data)

Type of case		*884/1479*			*928/1522*			*1054/1644-5*	
	Ḳāḍī	*Nā ʾib*	*Kātib*	*Ḳāḍī*	*Nā ʾib*	*Kātib*	*Ḳāḍī*	*Nā ʾib*	*Kātib*
Manumission of slaves (*iʿtāḳ*)	30	1	1	20	6	1	50	10	6
Registration of marriage (*nikāḥ*)	20	together	5	ND	ND	ND	20	together	5
Inheritance (*mīrāt͟h*) (fees for every 1,000 *aḳčas* of the estate's value)	20	ND	ND	14	4	2	15	ND	ND
Notary service (*ḥüd͟jd͟jet*)	15	1	1	20	4	2	20	together	5
Signature (*imḍāʾ*)		ND			ND			together	12
Registration fee (*sid͟jill-i ḳayd*)		ND			together	7		together	12
Letters to authorities (*murāsala*)		ND			together	7		together	8

the due for inheritance division was dramatically reduced from 2.5% to 1.5% (see *Muns͟haʾāt mad͟jmūʿasī*, British Museum Or. 9503, f. 65b). Another widespread subject of complaint was impositions on the hospitality of the villagers during periodic tours, usually every three months, by the *ḳāḍī* or his *nā ʾib* throughout the jurisdiction.

Personnel. The *mad͟jlis al-s͟harʿ*, or council of experts on the religious law (*s͟harʿ*), used interchangeably with *maḥkamat al-s͟harʿ* in the documents, consisted of a body of learned men who assisted the judge in reaching a judgement in complete conformity with the *s͟harʿ* (for the existence of such a council from early Islamic times, see E. Tyan, *Organisation judiciaire*, 213-36). However, a *muftī* is rarely mentioned as sitting regularly in Ottoman *maḥkamas*, though local *muftīs* were often referred to for the issue of *fatwās* [*q.v.*] on particular cases. In addition, the study of *maḥkama* records reveals that the judge summoned individuals with knowledge and expertise on specific matters to act as witnesses, or *s͟huhūd al-ḥāl*, in the court, and these were registered as such at the end of the court *sid͟jills*. The use of *s͟huhūd*, an old Islamic practice [see S͟HĀHID], was designed to check the *ḳāḍī* and to ensure that a decision was reached in the presence of an unbiased and expert body. There is no evidence that in the Ottoman Empire a permanent body was appointed by the *ḳāḍī* as professional witnesses, who existed as a kind of corporation in Egypt. For everyday cases, persons in the court or court officials could be employed as witnesses. We find that the *s͟hehir ketk͟hudāsī* was regularly present at the court and was often included among the witnesses.

The personnel of a given *maḥkama* changed in number according to its importance, with a minimum of a *kātib* and a *muḥḍir*. In large *maḥkamas*, the following additional officials were to be found: a *nā ʾib* or *nā ʾibs*, *kātibs* under a *bas͟h-kātib*, chief secretary, and a *maḥkama emīni*, acting trustee. The *ḳāḍī*'s staff included in some places a *muḳayyid* or recorder and a *čuḳadār* or messenger (see Ç. Uluçay, *18. asırda Manisa*, document 27). Under a *muḥḍir-bas͟hī* (in other Islamic states, *ṣāḥib al-mad͟jlis* or *d͟jilwāz*), there were *muḥḍirs* and *yasaḳd͟jīs* (Janissaries), who acted as the court police. The *bas͟h-kātib* could also function as *nā ʾib* and the *muḥḍir-bas͟hī* as *amīn* or *emīn*. In some large *maḥkamas* were also found *dānis͟hmends*, college graduates training to become *ḳāḍīs*. *Nā ʾibs* were agents of the *ḳāḍī* appointed by him and authorised to give legal decisions on his behalf in a certain *maḥkama* or on certain specific issues. Each *maḥkama* was assigned to the control of a *nāʾib*. *Nā ʾibs*, sometimes also called simply *ḳāḍīs*, were required to have the same qualifications as *ḳāḍīs* themselves. Although in principle a *nā ʾib* was appointed by the *ḳāḍī* and exclusively responsible to him, the government imposed certain restrictions in order to prevent some common abuses. As early as Süleymān I's time (926-74/1520-66), the system of farming out the office of *nā ʾib* was officially abolished, and the practice of selecting *nā ʾibs* from the local population was also prohibited (see İnalcık, *Adâletnâmeler*, 76-7). Yet despite these measures, the farming-out of the office of *nā ʾib* became a well-established practice, since in the 12th/18th century most of the important *ḳāḍī* posts in the provinces were administered by *nā ʾibs* appointed by the great *ḳāḍīs* who remained resident in Istanbul, or by those who received their *ḳaḍāʾ* as *arpalïḳ* [*q.v.*]. Apparently the real concern in this period became how to maximise income deriving to a *ḳāḍī* from a jurisdiction area. Another category was the itinerant *nā ʾibs* who carried out inspections within the jurisdiction, handing down decisions on various offences, and determining the *niyābet resmi* or fines. Besides these, there were *nā ʾibs* appointed to deal with only a proportion of the cases or with cases involving certain expertises in a busy *maḥkama*. Among these the *ḳassām-ī baladī*, in charge of division of inheritances belonging to the non-military classes [see ḲASSĀM], may be mentioned. A separate *nā ʾib*, the *ged͟je nā ʾibi*, was appointed to hear cases at night. An *ayaḳ nā ʾibi*, or wandering *nā ʾib*, was in charge of enforcing prescriptions against religiously-forbidden things such as fraud by shop-keepers, drinking of wine, etc. In the *maḥkama* of Istanbul, the most extensive in the empire (its record books, numbering several thousands, are preserved today in a special archive attached to the *müftülük* of Istanbul), there was a *bāb nā ʾibi*, or judge for hearing ordinary cases. *Nā ʾibs* were also appointed by the *ḳāḍī* of Istanbul to oversee business at certain locations at the city's principal market places such as the flour, honey, and butter warehouses, the candle works, the vegetable market, and others. They were authorised to hear cases and to issue decisions on disputes arising in these particular locations. *Nā'ib*s were also appointed to make investigations for a *maḥkama*, the *keshif nā'ibi*, and to decide disputes in connection with payment of *ʿawāriḍ* taxes [*q.v.*], the *ʿawāriḍ nā'ibi*.

In the *ḳānūn-nāme*s of the 10th/16th century, it is repeatedly stressed that, without prior decision by a *ḥākim*, no member of the military class could impose any punishment, even a small fine, on the *reʿāyā*. The enforcement of decisions, however, was left entirely to the military. By accepting a bribe from the guilty party, they quite often omitted to enforce a *ḥākim*'s decision. This amounted in practice to a separate settlement of the case by the military. The *maḥkama* could order detention of the criminal only as a precautionary measure.

The *ḥākim* based his decisions on *sharʿī* texts, *ḳānūn-nāme*s, *daftar*s [*q.v.*], imperial *ḥukm*s and *fatwā*s. In the *ʿadālet-nāme* of 1004/1595-6 (see İnalcık, *Adâletnâmeler*, 105), it is asserted that under Süleymān I "imperial *ḳānūn-nāme*s were codified and deposited in the *maḥkama*s of *ḳāḍī*s in every city". Alongside a great many unofficial copies of the general *ḳānūn-nāme*s used by the *ḳāḍī*s in their *maḥkama*s, one official copy bearing the *tughrā* [*q.v.*] of the sultan has survived to our day (Nationalbibliothek, Vienna, Cod. mixt. 870). Because regulations were constantly being amended by imperial *ḥukm*s, the *ḥākim*s were not required to follow a universally-applied official version. As to the *sharʿī* text to be used, the *ḥākim* was free to consult any reference books, on condition that they belonged to the Ḥanafī school. In 1107/1695-6 Muṣṭafā II ordered that only *sharʿī* texts be used in the *maḥkama*s (ʿO. Nūrī, *Medjelle*, i, 568), but this seems to have lasted only a short period.

In principle, the Islamic judicial system does not recognise the institution of attorney (Tyan, *Organisation judiciaire*, 262). The system of legal representation by *wakīl*s, widely used in Islamic *maḥkama*s, including those of the Ottoman empire (R. Jennings, *The office of Vekil*, in *SI*, xlii [1975], 147-69), cannot be equated with attorneyship. Nevertheless, it appears already from 10th/16th century documents (see İnalcık, *Adâletnâmeler*, 99) that court suits of individuals were pursued by their private representatives in return for a fee, and these agents, sometimes called *daʿwā wekīli*, formed a semi-professional group in Ottoman cities, although the government tried to eliminate them from the courts, objecting to their use of false witness and other tactics to subvert the course of justice.

Cases concerning public security or injustices inflicted upon the *reʿāyā* by the local authorities, the so-called *maẓālim* [*q.v.*] cases, could be heard by the local *ḳāḍī*s' courts, by *mufattish*s or inspectors, by the *dīwān* courts set up by one of the *wezīr*s while on tour in a province, or in the final resort, by the *dīwan-i hümāyūn* [*q.v.*] itself. The *beylerbeyi*s or governor-generals held their own *dīwān*s to hear and decide on cases involving *sipāhī*s and other *tīmār*-holders in their provinces, and had the authority to inflict various disciplinary punishments, including dismissal. In their *dīwān*s, the *beylerbeyi*s also heard complaints by the *reʿāyā* of their provinces against *tīmār*-holders, but in order to be able to take action, the case and investigation had to be referred to a *toprak ḳāḍīsī*, rural *ḳāḍī*, for a legal decision. In order to save the *reʿāyā* from hardships, a sultanic decree forbade the *tīmār*-holders from taking such cases to an urban *ḳāḍī*. Any non-disciplinary case involving a *tīmār*-holder was to be referred to the *maḥkama* of the local *ḳāḍī* and to be decided according to the *sharīʿa* and the *ḳānūn*. The priority recognised to the *beylerbeyi*s for hearing cases involving people under his command was also recognised to all military regiments in the Empire whose commanding officers had the responsibility to hold *dīwān*s and to give disciplinary punishments. The heads of the community organisations, too, such as the guilds and the Dhimmī groups, were authorised to decide cases involving their internal regulations and security. Apart from these cases, the *maḥkama* was the sole place of resort for justice, and preserved this characteristic up until the 12th/18th century, when community courts began to usurp some of its authority (see Pantazopoulos, *Church and law*, 44-112).

The effects of imperial decline on the courts of the *ḳāḍī*s. *Maḥkama*s became the target of strong criticism from the writers of the late 10th/16th century, and it was from this period that the character and functions of the *maḥkama* began to change. Apart from its function as a law court, the *maḥkama* served as a town meeting-place to which the city notables, representatives of the craft guilds, as well as *imām*s representing the people of their respective districts, were invited periodically by the *ḳāḍī*. Such meetings were usually convened by the *ḳāḍī* for the purpose of explaining new orders issued by the sultan of concern to the public at large. Beginning in the 11th/17th century, however, these meetings became more frequent and assumed greater importance. The reason for this was that in that century the *ʿawāriḍ-i dīwāniyya* (extraordinary levies in the form of provisions, services or money) began to be collected on a regular basis, and distribution among the population of such impositions was decided in the town meetings held in the *maḥkama*. Also, at these meetings the city's expenses were discussed and written down in budgets. As a consequence of this development, in their capacity as representatives of the local population, town notables began to assume leadership at such meetings, supplanting the *ḳāḍī*'s authority in various fields concerning community interests. (H. İNALCIK)

ii. The reform era (*ca.* 1789-1922)

As the preceding discussion makes clear, the Ottoman Empire traditionally relied mainly on the courts of the *ḳāḍī*s for performances of judicial functions, though it also attributed some measure of judicial responsibility to other persons or organisations, such as the *dīwān*s of the sultans and senior military-administrative officials, the heads of the non-Muslim subject communities, or the guilds. Ottoman authorities recognised law based on custom (*ʿādet*) or on the sultan's decree (*ḳānūn*), as well as the *sharīʿa*, and expected those with judicial responsibilities, *ḳāḍī*s, as well as military-administrative officers (*ehl-i ʿörf*), to apply both *sharʿī* and non-*sharʿī* law. The judicial functions of the *ḳāḍī*'s courts and the *dīwān*s of the military-administrative authorities certainly differed in a variety of respects (Heyd, 252-8), but there was no formal distinction of *sharīʿa* and *maẓālim* jurisdiction. In effect, Ottoman policy was to avoid such distinction. Similarly, the remarkable development among the Ottomans of regulatory acts (*ḳānūn*, *ḳānūn-nāme* [*q.vv*]) ancillary to the *sharīʿa*—a development unmatched in other Islamic states—did not in principle signify neglect of the *sharīʿa*. Rather, the emphasis on the *ḳānūn*, an ideal means for assertion of the sultan's authority, coexisted with a larger pattern of policy aimed at legitimating the state through appeal, in law as in other matters, to Islamic values. As expressed in legal and judicial systems, this larger policy provided the basis for Schacht's opinion that the Ottoman Empire gave the *sharīʿa* "the highest degree of actual efficiency ... it had ever possessed in a society of high material civilization since early ʿAbbāsid times" (*An introduction to Islamic law*, Oxford 1964, 84).

Yet the equilibrium between *sharīʿa* and *ḳānūn*, and that between tribunals of different types, did not remain constant in every period. For example, the *ḳānūn* went into decline after the 10th/16th century. One consequence of this appears to have been an increase in emphasis on the *sharīʿa* in certain respects (Heyd, 152-57; cf. İnalcık, ḲĀNŪN, in *EI²*, iv, 560, 561). Simultaneously, the decay in the provincial military-administrative hierarchy, and the alteration in local power-relationships, seem to have enlarged and altered the functions of the *ḳāḍīs*' courts, as indicated at the end of the preceding section. Later, as the empire moved into its 19th century reform era, the balance between *sharīʿī* and non-*sharīʿī* legal systems shifted in the opposite direction. The main reason for this was that the regulatory powers of the sultans began, from the time of Selīm III (1789-1807) onward, to find a new use as the chief means for the promulgation of innovative reforms. As this occurred, a new body of law, and eventually a new system of courts, began to emerge. This time, the jurisdictions of the two types of courts did become differentiated, with the result that it now became quite exact, in a sense that had not obtained several centuries before, to refer to the *ḳāḍīs*' courts as *sharīʿa* courts. The new legal and judicial systems continued to grow in scope, however, and the end result was the closing of the *sharīʿa* courts and the creation of an exclusively secular court system under the Turkish Republic. Paradoxically, then, the same empire that had so impressed Schacht through its emphasis on the *sharīʿa* ultimately evolved in such a way as to prepare the legal and judicial foundations for the most secular Islamic state of the 20th century.

For the sake of continuity with the discussion of Ottoman tribunals of earlier periods, it will serve best, in considering the 19th century, to look first at the *sharīʿa* courts. The succeeding discussion of what became known as the *niẓāmiyye* courts will then make clear where the primary emphasis of judicial reform lay.

Reform of the *sharīʿa* courts. After earlier, episodic attempts at reform of the judiciary, a serious effort to restore standards occurred during the reign of Selīm III (Uzunçarşılı, *İlm.*, 255-60). During the 19th century, other such measures followed. Perhaps the first was a penal code applying to the *ḳāḍī-ʿaskers*, *ḳāḍīs*, and *nāʾibs*, issued at the same time as another for civil officials, in 1254/1838 (Hıfzı Veldet, *Kanunlaştırma*, 170-1). Within another three years, the first attempt to substitute salaries for compensation by fees had occurred, and seemingly also failed (İnalcık, *Tanzimat'ın uygulanması*, 626, 686). Subsequently, there were regulations defining conditions of service for *sharʿī* judicial officials, of whom all judges except those in the greatest cities came ultimately to be designated as *nāʾibs*, their judgeships being termed *niyābets* (a change presumably reflecting the increasing tendency to use the term *ḳaḍāʾ* to refer to an administrative district; Heidborn, 260 n. 177). By the 1870s, these regulations covered subjects such as appointment by examination, ranks, duration of terms of service, maintenance of systematic service records, and—once again—salaries. While some of these concepts, such as examinations and ranks, had long been known among the *ʿulemāʾ*, others were new; and all together signify the evolution, here as in other branches of government service, of essentially modern patterns of personnel administration (Aristarchi, ii, 320-4; Young, i, 290-1; Heidborn, 260-6; *Dstr.*¹, i, 315-24; ii, 721; *Dstr.*² v, 352-61). There were also efforts to upgrade *medrese* training; and in the second half of the 19th century, new schools were founded in Istanbul specifically for the training of *nāʾibs* and *ḳāḍīs* (Ergin, *Türkiye maarif tarihi*, i, 135-42; *Dstr.*², ii, 127-38; ix, 598-600). Regulations were issued to define the functions that could be performed in the various *sharīʿa* courts and the fees that were still to be collected (Aristarchi, ii, 324-38; *Dstr.*¹, 1, 301-14; *dheyl* iii, 95; v, 1). The process of legal reform and codification affected the *sharīʿa* courts, particularly through the *Medjelle* [*q.v.*], published between 1870 and 1876. Chiefly the work of Aḥmed Djewdet Pasha [*q.v.*] and based on Ḥanafī *fiḳh*, this dealt with civil law and procedure and was intended for application in both the religious and the secular (*niẓāmiyye*) courts (R. H. Davison, *Reform in the Ottoman empire*, Princeton 1962, 253-5; Heidborn, 283-6, 387-97). Under the *Medjelle*, for example, the appeal of decisions from provincial *sharīʿa* courts became a matter of system (arts. 1838-40; Young, i, 287-89; *Dstr.*¹, iv, 123; *dheyl* iii, 85-8; v, 728). Other acts regulated the division (*ḳismet*) of estates in certain circumstances (Young, i, 294-302; *Dstr.*¹, 1, 289-97; *dheyl*, iii, 88-95; vi, 394-96). As the secular courts developed, the types of cases that were to go before the *sharīʿa* courts were increasingly delimited (Young, i, 291-3; *Dstr.*¹, iii, 165-6; *EI²*, IV, 560, 561).

The Young Turk era produced more radical changes. Under the influence of Ziya Gökalp's Western-inspired concept of religion, a number of major reforms, aimed at restricting the role of the *Shaykh al-Islām* to *iftāʾ*, were carried out in 1917. One of these measure was the placing of the *sharīʿa* courts under the authority of the Minister of Justice (*Dstr.*², ix, 270-1). A new law on *sharīʿa* court procedure appeared in October 1917 (*Dstr.*², ix, 783-94), as did a new code of family law, including provisions for Christians and Jews as well as Muslims (*Dstr.*², ix, 762-81; x, 52-57; Berkes, *Secularism*, 415-19). After World War I, responsibility over the *sharīʿa* courts was briefly returned to the *Shaykh al-Islām* (Pakalın, *Kadı*, 125). But with the complete dismantling of the traditional religious establishment under the Turkish Republic, the *sharīʿa* courts were abolished in 1924 (B. Lewis, *The emergence of modern Turkey*², Oxford 1968, 265-74).

The *niẓāmiyye* courts, The best way to understand the rise of the *niẓāmiyye* courts is to begin by examining how the reassertion of the sultans' discretional legislative power stimulated a new development in the tradition of the *dīwāns*, which the Ottomans used both as consultative and as judicial bodies.

The decree-power of the sultan provided the essential legislative sanction for all the reformist initiatives, including the *Gül-khāne* Decree of 1839, the Reform Decree of 1856, and the Constitution of 1876 (İnalcık, *Pâdişah*, in *İA*, ix, 495). Concluding with the promise that new laws would be framed to elaborate its egalitarian principles, the *Gül-khāne* Decree (Hurewitz, i, 271; *Dstr.*¹, i, 6) was of particular significance. For it provided the impetus for a flood-tide of new legislation, much of it explicitly borrowed from Western models (Veldet, *Kanunlaştırma*, 175 ff.; Heidborn, 283-4, 320-54, 366-86, 416-41). The fact that the terms *niẓām* or *niẓām-nāme* now often replaced *ḳānūn* or *ḳānūn-nāme* as designations for the new laws, cannot obscure the continuity, at least as far as the underlying legislative authority is concerned, between the reformist legislation and the *ḳānūns* of earlier centuries. Rather, the two sets of terms are nearly synonymous; and the designation of major political periods of the reform era in terms of *niẓām* or its derivatives (*Niẓām-i̊ Djedīd*, *Tanẓīmāt* [*q.vv.*]) is symbolic of the new shift in the historic balance between *ḳānūn* and *sharīʿa* (Findley, *Bureaucratic reform in the Ottoman empire*, ch. v). The practice of referring to the new courts created in this period as *niẓāmiyye* courts signifies that they were responsible for trying cases under the new laws.

While some of the conciliar bodies most distinctive of the "classic" Ottoman governmental system—such as the imperial *dīwān* at the palace or the *dīwān*s of the leading military-administrative functionaries in the provinces—had long since declined, the tradition of the *dīwān*s or councils (*medjālis*), as they were more often termed during the reform era, responded to this legislative reassertion in two respects. On one hand, the Supreme Council of Judicial Ordinances (*Medjlis-i Wālā-yi̊ Aḥkām-i ʿAdliyye*), a body which Maḥmūd II created out of the *dīwān* of the Grand *Wezīr* in 1838 and which evolved into the Council of State (*Shūrā-yi̊ Dewlet*, 1868), assumed the bulk of the work of preparing the new legislation for the sultan's sanction (Shaw, *Central legislative councils*, 51-84). On the other hand, simultaneous efforts to create a new kind of local administrative apparatus led to the creation in 1840 of new local councils, referred to as *Medjlis-i Muḥaṣṣilīn*, *Müdhākere Medjlisi*, or *Memleket Medjlisi*. These were intended in part to supplant the role that the *ḳāḍī*s' courts had acquired in administrative affairs, though not of course their judicial functions in *sharʿī* cases. Both the local councils and the Supreme Council of Judicial Ordinances in Istanbul also served as judicial bodies in certain types of cases arising under the new legislation (Heidborn, 219). Including various of the local administrative officials, the *ḳāḍī* and *müftī*, the leaders of the local non-Muslim communities, and indirectly elected representatives of the local notables, the local councils were found at various administrative levels: *liwāʾ* or *sandjaḳ*, *ḳaḍāʾ* (a term used increasingly in this period to refer to the administrative subdivision of the *liwāʾ*), and sometimes on a reduced scale in lower-level subdistricts as well (Ortaylı, *Mahalli idareler*, 13 ff.; İnalcık, *Tanzimat'ın uygulanması*, 626, 633-5, 664-5; idem, *Application of the Tanzimat and its social effects*, in *Archivum Ottomanicum*, v [1973], 100-1, 107-10; Kornrumpf, *Territorialverwaltung*, 44-57 *passim*).

The assignment of judicial functions to the local councils marked the first step toward creation of the *niẓāmiyye* courts, which continued to reflect their origins in being collegial bodies. Decades were to pass before a distinct hierarchy of *niẓāmiyye* courts emerged, and—incidentally—before they were officially referred to by the term *maḥkeme* (in 1868 according to Heidborn, 226, n. 57). Even then, the local administrative councils and—except for a few years during the Young Turk period—the Supreme Council of Judicial Ordinances, later the Council of State, retained responsibility for administrative justice (Shaw, *Central legislative councils*, *passim*; Findley, *Bureaucratic reform*, 174-6, 248-9, 308-9).

Between the creation of the councils just described (1838, 1840) and the first comprehensive attempt to regulate and systematise the system of *niẓāmiyye* courts (1879), a number of steps had to be taken. The 1840s witnessed the development of a system of commercial courts, beginning with a single one in Istanbul, where cases between Ottoman subjects and non-Ottomans were tried before a panel of judges, also of mixed nationality. A special commercial code was promulgated in 1850 (Heidborn, 216-19; Young, i, 239-43). A system of penal courts to hear cases between parties of mixed nationality also came into existence, starting in 1847. The foreign consuls had the right to intervene in these courts on behalf of their nationals and, by withholding their assent, to prevent execution of judgment against such individuals. At any rate, according to Heidborn (219-20), the jurisdiction of these courts was eventually extended to cover cases to which only Ottoman subjects were parties; in addition, for the first time in Ottoman judicial procedure, the testimony of non-Muslims was accepted before these courts on a basis of equality with that of Muslims.

The reform decree of 1856 pointed toward a further generalisation and elaboration of some of these measures. It provided that commercial, correctional, and civil cases between parties of different religions be referred to mixed courts (that is, the judges were to be of different faiths) and that the parties be allowed to produce witnesses who could testify under oaths taken according to their respective religions. Laws and procedural rules for these courts were to be drafted and codified as soon as possible and published in the various languages of the empire (*Dstr.*[1], i, 11; Hurewitz, i, 317). Changes of these types did gradually occur in succeeding years.

In 1860, for example, there appeared an organic law for the commercial courts. This provided for commercial courts of specified types, which were to have one or more presidents and four or more members (*aʿḍāʾ*), part of the latter being "permanent" and part "temporary". The presidents and permanent members were to be officials, while the "temporary" members were to be merchants, chosen by assemblies including the prominent merchants of the locality, or later, once such bodies had come into existence, by the local chamber of commerce. Until 1879, the commercial courts were subordinate to the Ministry of Commerce, and there was a commercial appeals court at the ministry in Istanbul. A code of commercial procedure was adopted in 1861, and a maritime commercial code in 1863 (Heidborn, 222-3; Aristarchi, ii, 353-400; Young, i, 224-38; *Dstr.*[1], i, 375-536, 780-810).

The beginning of a distinct hierarchy of provincial *niẓāmiyye* courts occurred with the enactment of the Law on Provincial Administration of 1864 (*Dstr.*[1], i, 610-12, 615-18; Heidborn, 223-4). This established courts of first instance and appeal at the top three levels of the local administrative hierarchy: the *ḳaḍāʾ* (i.e. the administrative subdistrict headed by the *ḳāʾim-maḳām*), the *liwāʾ* or *sandjaḳ*, and the *wilāyet* or province. These were to be presided over by judges (*ḥākim*) from the *sharīʿa* courts and were also to include elected members (*mümeyyiz*). The number of these was set first at six, then raised to eight at the *ḳaḍāʾ* level (*Dstr.*[1], iii, 175). Half-Muslim and half-non-Muslim, these were to be elected by the same procedure as the elected members of the local administrative council (*medjlis-i idāre*) that became the successor, under the 1864 law, of the earlier *memleket medjlisi*. Under the provincial administration law of 1864, the provincial commercial courts, created in 1860, were also effectively integrated into the *niẓāmiyye* court system. Numerous features of the system of 1864 reflect its incipient state of development. These include reliance on *sharīʿa* court judges, as well as the fact that the hierarchy of courts thus far had only two echelons. A similar significance no doubt attaches to the fact that these provisions appeared in a law dealing with provincial administration; but this pattern proved short-lived. The new Law on Provincial Administration, promulgated in January 1871, contained virtually nothing on the courts (*Dstr.*[1], i, 625-51; Aristarchi, iii,

7-39; Young, i, 47-69); rather, they were dealt with in a separate law that appeared a year later (*Dstr.*[1], i, 352-6).

This fact reflects a new policy—separation of powers—introduced into Ottoman practice with a reform of the Supreme Council of Judical Ordinances in 1868. The Supreme Council was then separated into two bodies, one intended to perform legislative, the other judicial, functions. The new legislative body was the Council of State (*Shūrā-yi Dewlet*). This continued, aside from the short-lived parliament, to function as the main legislative body. The highest level of *niẓāmiyye* justice became the responsibility of what can probably best be envisaged as a High Court of Justice (actual title, *Dīwān-i Aḥkām-i ʿAdliyye*). The organisation and functions of this body underwent redefinition a number of times over the next several years. The various appeals courts already in existence in Istanbul for criminal and commercial cases were gradually brought together under the new agency, and it became the nucleus from which a Ministry of Justice shortly emerged (*Dstr.*[1], i, 325-42, 357-63; iii, 2-3; Aristarchi, ii, 42-55; v, 26-8; Heidborn, 225-6).

This creation of the ministry, like the promulgation of the Constitution of 1876, was essentially a response to the crises of the late 1870s and to the need which the Ottomans felt to demonstrate their ability to manage their own affairs without European interference. The constitution itself contained a few provisions on matters related to the courts, such as the independence of the judiciary, conditions of service in it, and judicial procedure. The constitution also asserted that the organisation and competence of the courts and the duties of the judges must be defined by law (*Dstr.*[1], iv, 14-16; Aristarchi, v, 19-21). A series of acts published in 1879, in the wake of the Congress of Berlin (Heidborn, 228), attempted to meet these demands.

The acts of 1879 in fact established the Ministry of Justice and the *niẓāmiyye* court system essentially as they were to remain until the Young Turk period. These acts included organic regulations for a Ministry of Justice and Religious Affairs (*ʿAdliyye ve Medhāhib Neẓāretī*), the double mission of which gave it jurisdiction over judicial and other affairs of the non-Muslim communities, as well as over the *niẓāmiyye* courts (*Dstr.*[1], iv, 125-31; Young, i, 159-66). There was also an organic law for the *niẓāmiyye* courts. This included provisions not only on the organisation and competence of the tribunals, but also on the organisation of the judiciary and on the systems of public prosecutors (*müddeʿī-yi ʿumūmī*) and judicial inspectors (*Dstr.*[1], iv, 235-50; later amendments *ibid.*, vi, 81; vii, 171-2, 1080-1; viii, 136-7, 665-6; cf. Young, i, 166-80; Heidborn, 231-48). Also among the acts of 1879 were laws on the system for execution of the judgments of the courts (*Dstr.*[1], iv, 225-35; vi, 837; viii, 752-3; Young, i, 197-210; Heidborn, 248-9), on notaries (*Dstr.*[1], iv, 338-44; 1065-8; Young, i, 193-7; Heidborn, 249-50), and on judicial fees (*Dstr.*[1], iv, 319-37; v, 582 96; vi, 156; viii, 744-7; Young, i, 210-23). There were also codes of civil and criminal procedure (*Dstr.*[1], iv, 131-224, 257-318; later modifications *ibid.*, vi, 230-1; vii, 16-17, 31-3, 89-90, 114, 151, 1081; viii, 135-6, 751-2; cf. Young, vii, 171-300; Heidborn, 397-441). About the same time, efforts were made to found a law school to train judges and lawyers competent in the new legal system (Ergin, *Maarif tarihi*, ii, 582-92; iii, 890-918; Heidborn, 280-3). Attempts to regulate the legal profession began in 1878 (*Dstr.*[1], iii, 198-209; *dheyl* iv, 35-8; v, 520-21; Young, i, 184-93; Heidborn, 250-1). Two acts of 1888 then elaborated the system for the examination and appointment of judges, who were no longer to be elected, and prescribed the keeping of systematic personnel records on all judicial officials (*Dstr.*[1], v, 1058-64; vi, 1367-8, 1476; Young, i, 182-4).

As defined in the organic regulations of 1879, the *niẓāmiyye* court system was supposed to include courts of arbitration (*ṣulḥ dāʾireleri*) in the villages and *nāḥiyes*, as well as courts of first instance (*bidāyet*), appeal (*istiʾnāf*), and cassation (*temyīz*). Heidborn (229-32) indicated that the courts of arbitration were never really set up, although various acts of the reign of ʿAbd al-Ḥamīd make clear that official interest in them did continue (*Dstr.*[1], vi, 1155-68; vii, 27-38; viii, 712-28, 747, 753). The triple-tiered system of regular courts was also not as fully developed as its nomenclature implied. The law of 1879 in fact began by stating that the courts were of two levels, first instance and appeal. There was only one court of cassation, located in Istanbul; and even the functions of the courts of first instance and appeal varied as much with the level of the administrative hierarchy at which they were found as with their ostensible placement in the judicial hierarchy.

As prescribed in 1879, however, there was to be a court of first instance in every *ḳaḍāʾ*. In a normal *ḳaḍāʾ*, the court of the first instance was empowered to hear civil cases of all types. It could decide criminal cases involving minor offences and misdemeanours (*ḳabāḥāt ve djünḥa*) and carry out preliminary investigation of major crimes (*djināyet*). It could also hear commercial cases, if there was no separate commercial court in the *ḳaḍāʾ*. The *ḳaḍāʾ* court was authorised to hear appeals from the courts of arbitration at lower levels. It was also empowered to judge in last resort in cases where the matter in question had a monetary value that fell within stated limits, as well as in minor criminal offences (*ḳabāḥāt*).

In *ḳaḍāʾ*s that coincided with the centre of a higher-level administrative circumscription, the court of first instance took on additional attributes. In the "central" *ḳaḍāʾ* of a *liwāʾ* or *sandjak*, for example, the court of first instance was to have two sections for civil and criminal cases. These functioned separately as courts of first instance for that *ḳaḍāʾ* and jointly to try major crimes (*djināyet*) or hear appeals from the other *ḳaḍāʾ*s of the *liwāʾ*.

There was also provision for a commercial court of the *liwāʾ*, which functioned similarly as a court of first instance for the central *ḳaḍāʾ* and as a court of appeal for the other *ḳaḍāʾ*s of the *liwāʾ*. The law of 1879 does not specifically mention the courts of first instance located in *ḳaḍāʾ*s that coincided with province capitals. By 1908, however, these reportedly existed, serving as courts of first instance for the *ḳaḍāʾ* in which they were located and as an appeals instance for cases coming up from the *liwāʾ* courts. There was also provision for provincial commercial courts. These are reported to have existed in most provinces, though only occasionally in lower-echelon administrative centres (Heidborn, 234).

A tribunal expressly designated as an appeals court (*istiʾnāf maḥkemesi*) was supposed to be located in every province capital. This court was to have separate civil and criminal sections. These were empowered to hear appeals from the courts of first instance located at the centres of the various *liwāʾ*s of the province, as well as from those in the *ḳaḍāʾ*s of the central *liwāʾ*. The criminal section served the central *liwāʾ* of the province as a criminal court for the trial of serious offences (*djināyet*) and as a court of appeal in cases of lesser gravity (*djünḥa*).

For Istanbul, the law of 1879 prescribed an

analogous organisation, allowing that the number of sections and staff members could be increased in case of need, as was in fact done (*Dstr.*[1], iv, 240). In addition, there was an important deviation from the provincial pattern in that the Istanbul commercial court acquired three sections, one hearing only cases between Ottoman subjects and foreigners, one only cases between Ottoman subjects, and one only maritime cases. The capital city also had an appeals court with civil, criminal, and commercial sections (Heidborn, 235-7).

At the apex of the *niẓāmiyye* court system, finally, stood the court of cassation (*maḥkeme-i temyīz*), also in Istanbul. This, too, had three sections, the functions of which were gradually defined in acts of the 1880s and 1890s (*Dstr.*[1], v, 853-4, 992; vii, 89-90; Young, i, 180-1; Heidborn, 237-8). The first section, that of petitions (*istid ʿā ʾ dā ʾiresi*), received all appeals to the court. This section had power to decide directly in certain matters, such as conflicts of jurisdiction, reassignment of cases from one court to another, or the unacceptability of petitions on grounds of technical irregularity or lapse of the period set for cassation. The petitions section referred the cases it accepted to either the civil or the criminal section, which either rejected the appeal or overtuned the lower court ruling on ground of judicial error. In major criminal cases (*d̲j̲ināyet*), judgments from the lower courts went automatically to the criminal section of the court of cassation, without need for appeal.

Under the system of 1879, all the *niẓāmiyye* courts continued to be collegial bodies, including a president, or more than one in courts with several sections, and varying numbers of members (*aʿḍā ʾ*). At least until 1908, *s̲h̲arīʿa* court judges continued to play a major role in the system, at least as far up as the province level, where the *nā ʾib* of the province normally also functioned as the president of the civil section of the court of appeal. The final article of the 1879 law on the *niẓāmiyye* courts provided, for this reason, that a representative of the Ministry of Justice should be present at the meetings of the council that selected judges for the *s̲h̲arīʿa* courts, the *Med̲j̲lis-i Intik̲h̲āb-i Ḥükkām-i S̲h̲arʿ*, when *nüwwāb* were being chosen (*Dstr.*[1], iv, 250). The commercial courts were still to include "temporary" members, chosen among the merchants of the locality.

Under the conditions of the Ḥamīdian era, the system created in 1879 cannot have functioned very effectively. The judicial inspectorate, for example, is reported to have operated only intermittently (Heidborn, 231-2; Young, i, 177 n. 4). At least at the province and *liwā ʾ* levels, for which the government yearbooks record the appropriate information, it nonetheless appears that by 1908 the system of courts had been created and staffed in essentially all parts of the empire, except the provinces of the Ḥid̲j̲āz and Yemen and perhaps also the *sand̲j̲aḳ* of Ned̲j̲d, where the *s̲h̲arīʿa* courts remained the only ones (*Sāl-nāme-i Dewlet-i ʿAliyye-i ʿOt̲h̲māniyye*, 1326/1908, 692-962 passim; Heidborn, 228 n. 70).

The Young Turk Revolution opened the way for efforts at fundamental reorganisation in the Ministry of Justice. New organic regulations for the central offices of the Ministry of Justice and Religious Affairs were issued in June 1910 (*Dstr.*[2], iii, 467-79; later modifications *ibid.*, iv, 367-8, 440-1; vi, 228-9; vii, 558-60, 634). The system for appointment of judges and other officials of the ministry underwent revision with regulations of June 1913 (*Dstr.*[2], v, 520-9; vi, 738-43, 1273-4). There were a number of amendments to the civil and penal procedure codes of 1879 (*Dstr.*[2], iii, 261-77; v, 621-23; vi, 309-10, 651-4, 1352). Other acts addressed questions such as the differentiation of the jurisdiction of *s̲h̲arʿī* and *niẓāmī* courts (*Dstr.*[2], i, 192-4; vi, 1334), the qualifications required for the practice of law (*Dstr.*[2], i, 751; Meyer, *Rechtswesen,* 148), and the reactivation of the system of judicial inspectors (*Dstr.*[2], ii, 33-7).

As concerns the *niẓāmiyye* courts proper, however, the Young Turk reforms changed the pre-existing system only at specific points. If it is correct that the courts of arbitration (*ṣulḥ dā ʾireleri*), provided for in 1879, had not been widely instituted, one of the more significant of these measures may have been the setting up, starting in April 1913, of a system of justices of the peace (*ṣulḥ ḥākimleri*). These were to be a kind of circuit judges, possessing legal qualifications, and holding court as individuals in the *ḳaḍā ʾ*s, *nāḥiye*s, and villages to hear minor cases of various types (*Dstr.*[2], v, 322-48, 619, 775-7, 827, 869-75; vi, 156-7, 294-5, 342-3, 1353; vii, 561-2; Meyer, *Rechtswesen,* 138). The patterns of organisation and staffing created in 1879 for the *niẓāmiyye* courts at the administrative levels of the *ḳaḍā ʾ*, *liwā ʾ*, province (*wilāyet*), and in Istanbul were amended at several points, starting in August 1909 (*Dstr.*[2], i, 665-6; ii, 180-1; v, 217-18, 793-5, 866). The abolition of the capitulations, effective from 1 October 1914, had important implications for the court system, inasmuch as it required the abandonment of all courts and judicial procedures specifically for the benefit of foreigners (*Dstr.*[2], vi, 1273, 1336, 1340; Meyer, *Rechtswesen*, 117-18, 135). The attack on the traditional religious institutions in 1917 was of comparable significance, since it resulted in the placement of the *s̲h̲arʿī* courts under the Ministry of Justice and the creation of a section for *s̲h̲arʿī* cases in the Cassation Court in Istanbul (Meyer, *Rechtswesen*, 139-41). Though briefly reversed during the armistice period, these changes in the status of the *s̲h̲arīʿa* courts brought Ottoman judicial systems to a point very near complete unification, which occurred with the establishment of the secular, national court system under the Ministry of Justice of the Turkish Republic.

(C. V. Findley)

Bibliography: 1. *Ḳāḍī* courts. M. Akdağ, *Türkiye'nin iktisadí ve içtimaí tarihi*, ii, Ankara 1971, 75-81; Şinasi Altundağ, *Osmanlılarda kadıların salâhiyet ve vazifeleri hakkında*, in *VI. Türk Tarih Kongresi, Kongreye sunulan bildiriler*, Ankara 1967, 342-54; Vančo Boškov, *Ein osmanischer Ketzer-Prozess im 18. Jahrhundert*, in *Südost-Forschungen*, xxiii (1974), 296-306; Amnon Cohen, *Yehudei Yerushalayim bameʾah ha-shesh-esreh/Ottoman documents on the Jewish community of Jerusalem in the sixteenth century*, Jerusalem 1976 (contains documents from the Jerusalem *s̲h̲arīʿa* court records); Panta Džambazovski and Arif Starova, tr., *Turski dokumenti za makedonskata istorija*, 5 vols., Skopje 1951-58; Yūsuf Ḍiyāʾ al-Dīn, *Ṣakk-i d̲j̲edīd*, Istanbul 1284/1867; R. Y. Ebied and M. J. L. Young, ed. and tr. *Some Arabic legal documents of the Ottoman period from the Leeds manuscript collection*, Supplement iv to the *Annual of Leeds University Oriental Society*, Leiden 1976; Osman Ersoy, *Şer'iyye sicillerinin toplu katoloğuna doğru, in AÜDTCFD*, xxi (1963), 33-65; G. D. Galabov and H. W. Duda, *Die Protokollbücher des Kadiamtes Sofia*, Munich 1960; J. Grzegorzewski, *Z sidżyllatów rumelijskich epoki wyprawy wiedeńskiej, akta tureckie*, Lwow 1912; J. von Hammer, *Des osmanischen Reichs Staatsverfassung und Staatsverwaltung*, Vienna 1815, repr. Hildesheim 1963; Hamid Hadžibergić, *Džizija ili Harač*, in *Prilozi za Orijentalnu Filologiju*, iii-iv (1952-53), 55-135, and v

(1954-55), 43-102; Mücteba İlgürel, *Şer'iyye sicillerinin toplu katoloğuna doğru*, in *İstanbul Üniversitesi Edebiyat Fakültesi Tarih Dergisi*, no. 28-9 1974-5), 123-66; H. İnalcık, *Bursa I. XV. asır sanayi ve ticaret tarihine dair vesikalar*, in *Belleten*, xxiv (1960), 45-102; idem, *Bursa şer'iyye sicillerinde Fatih Sultan Mehmed'in fermanları*, in *Belleten*, xi (1947), 693-703; idem, *Centralization and decentralization in Ottoman administration*, in *Studies in eighteenth century Islamic history*, ed. T. Naff and R. Owen, London and Amsterdam 1977, 27-52; idem, *Mahkeme*, in *İA*, vii, 149-51; idem, *Osmanlı tarihi hakkında mühim bir kaynak*, in *AÜDTCFD*, ii (1943), 89-96; idem, *Saray Bosna şer'iyye sicillerine göre Viyana bozgunundan sonraki harp yıllarında Bosna*, in *Tarih Vesikaları*, ii (1942-3), 178-87, 372-84; *Izvori za Bălgarskata istoriya*, xxi, ed. Nikolai Todorov and Mariya Kalitsin, Sofia 1977; R. C. Jennings *The development of Evḳâf in a new Ottoman province: Cyprus, 1571-1640*, paper based on Cypriot *s̲h̲arīʿa* court records, presented at the International Seminar on Social and Economic Aspects of the Muslim Waqf, Jerusalem 1979; idem, *Kadi, court, and legal procedure in 17th c. Ottoman Kayseri*, in *SI*, xlviii (1978), 133-72; idem, *Limitations of the judicial powers of the kadi in 17th c. Ottoman Kayseri*, in *SI*, 1 (1979), 151-84; idem, *Loans and credit in early 17th century Ottoman judicial records: the Sharia court of Anatolian Kayseri*, in *JESHO*, xvi (1973), 168-215; idem, *The office of Vekil (Wakil) in 17th century Ottoman Sharia courts*, in *SI*, xlii (1975), 147-69; idem, *Women in early 17th century judicial records: the Sharia court of Anatolian Kayseri*, in *JESHO*, xviii (1975), 53-114; idem, *Zimmis (non-Muslims) in early seventeenth century Ottoman judicial records*, in *JESHO*, xxi/3 (1978), 225-93; J. Kabrda, *Les anciens registres turcs des cadis de Sofia et de Vidin et leur importance pour l'histoire de la Bulgarie*, in *ArO*, xix (1951), 329-92; M. Khadduri and H. J. Liebesny, ed., *Law in the Middle East*, Washington 1955; J. E. Mandaville, *The Ottoman court records of Syria and Jordan*, in *JAOS*, lxxxvi (1966), 311-19; A. Marcus, *Men, women, and property: real estate dealers in eighteenth-Century Aleppo*, in *JESHO*, xxvi (1983), 137-63; idem, *Piety and profit: the waqf in eighteenth-century Aleppo*, paper based on Aleppo *s̲h̲arīʿa* court records, presented at the International Seminar on Social and Economic Aspects of the Muslim Waqf, Jerusalem 1979; Aleksandar Matkovski, ed., *Turski izvori za adjutstvoto i aramijstvoto vo Makedonija*, 3 vols., Skopje 1961-73; Djoko Mazalić, *Popis zaostavštine i rasulo sarajevske porodice Selaka*, in *Prilozi za Orijentalnu Filologiju*, x-xi (1960-61), 223-36; ʿO̲t̲h̲mān Nūrī, *Med̲j̲elle-yi umūr-i belediyye*, i, Istanbul 1922; I. Mouradgea d'Ohsson, *Tableau général de l'Empire othoman*, 7 vols., Paris 1788-1824; Halit Ongan, *Ankara'nın bir numaralı şer'iye sicili*, Ankara 1958; idem, *Ankara'in iki numaralı şer'iye sicili*, Ankara 1974; idem, *Ankara şer'iye mahkemesi sicillerinde kayıtlı vakfiyeler*, in *Vakıflar Dergisi*, v (1963), 213-23; Yücel Özkaya, *XVIII. yüzyılın ilk yarısında yerli ailerlerin âyânlıkları ele geçirişleri ve büyük hânedânlıkların kuruluşu*, in *Belleten*, xlii (1978), 667-723, based on court registers of various Anatolian towns; idem, *Osmanlı imparatorluğunda ayânlık*, Ankara 1977; Mehmet Zeki Pakalın, *Kadı*, in *idem, Osmanlı tarih deyimleri ve terimleri sözlüğü*, Istanbul 1946-53, ii, 119-25; N.J. Pantazopoulos, *Church and law in the Balkan peninsula during the Ottoman rule*, Thessaloniki 1967; Abdul-Karim Rafeq, *The law-court registers of Damascus, with special reference to craft-corporations during the first half of the eighteenth century*, in J. Berque and D. Chevallier, eds., *Les arabes par leurs archives (XVIe-XXe siècles)*, Paris 1976, 141-59; A. Refik, *Istanbul hayatı, 1000-1300*, 4 vols., Istanbul 1931-5; R. Repp, *Some observations on the development of the Ottoman learned hierarchy*, in Nikki Keddie, ed., *Scholars, saints and sufis: Muslim religious institutions in the Middle East since 1500*, Berkeley and Los Angeles 1972, 17-32; M. Sokoloski, A. Starova, V. Boškov, F. Ishak, eds., *Turski dokumenti za istorijata na makedonskiot narod*, Serija prva, 4 vols., Skopje 1963-72; M. Çağatay Uluçay, *Manisa şer'iye sicillerine dair bin araştırma*, in *Türkiyat Mecmuası*, x (1953), 285-98; idem, *XVII. asırda Saruhan'da eşkiyalık ve halk hareketleri*, Istanbul 1944; idem, *18. ve 19. yüzyıllarda Saruhan'da eşkiyalık ve halk hareketleri*, Istanbul 1955, documents from Manisa law court; İsmail Hakkı Üzunçarşılı, *Osmanlı devletinin ilmiye teşkilâtı*, Ankara 1965; Madeline C. Zilfi, *Elite circulation in the Ottoman Empire: great mollas in the eighteenth century*, unpublished paper 1978.

2. *Dīwāns* of Sultans, Grand *Wezīrs*, and military-administrative officials. Uriel Heyd, *Studies in old Ottoman criminal law*, ed. V. L. Ménage, Oxford 1973; Ö.L. Barkan, *XV. ve XVI. asırlarda Osmanlı imparatorluğunda ziraî ekonominin hukukî ve malî esasları, i. Kanunlar*, Istanbul 1943; Halil İnalcık, *Adâletnâmeler*, in *Belgeler*, ii (1965), 49-145; idem, *Ḳānūn*, in *EI*², iv, 556-62; idem, *Ḳānūnnāme*, in *EI*², iv, 562-6; Y. Özkaya, *XVIIIinci yüzyılda çıkarılan adâlet-nâmelere göre Türkiye'nin iç durumu*, in *Belleten*, xxxviii (1974), 445-91; Uzunçarşılı, *Osmanlı devletinin merkez ve bahriye teşkilâtı*, Ankara 1948.

3. The *Niẓāmiyye* courts. G. Aristarchi, *Législation ottomane, ou recueil des lois, règlements, ordonnances, traités, capitulations et autres documents officiels de l'Empire ottoman*, 7 vols., Constantinople, 1873-88; Niyazi Berkes, *The development of secularism in Turkey*, Montreal 1964; *Düstūr*: First Series (*Birind̲j̲i tertıb*), 4 vols., plus 4 appendices (*d̲h̲eyl*) and a later "Completion" volume (*Mütemmim*), Istanbul 1289-1335/1872-1917, as well as 4 additional vols. published as vols. v-viii, Ankara 1937-43; *Düstūr*: Second Series (*İkind̲j̲i tertıb*), 12 vols., Istanbul 1329-1297 (*sic*, i.e. 1911-27); Osman Ergin, *Istanbul mektepleri ve ilim, terbiye ve san'at müesseseleri dolayısile Türkiye maarif tarihi*, 5 vols., Istanbul 1939-43; C.V. Findley, *Bureaucratic reform in the Ottoman empire: the Sublime Porte, 1789-1922*, Princeton 1980; A. Heidborn, *Manuel de droit public et administratif de l'Empire ottoman*, i, Vienna and Leipzig 1908; J. C. Hurewitz, *The Middle East and North Africa in world politics: a documentary record*, 2 vols. to date, New Haven 1975-9: İnalcık, *Tanzimat'ın uygulanması ve sosyal tepkileri*, in *Bell.*, xxviii (1964), 623-49; idem, *Application of the Tanzimat and its social effects*, in *Archivum Ottomanicum*, v (1973), 97-127; H.-J. Kornrumpf, *Die Territorialverwaltung im östlichen Teil der europäischen Türkei vom Erlass der Vilayetsordnung (1864) bis zum Berliner Kongress (1878) nach amtlichen Veröffentlichungen*, Freiburg 1976; B. Lewis, *The emergence of modern Turkey*², London 1968; Aḥmed Luṭfī, *Mirʾāt-i ʿadālet, yāk̲h̲ūd taʾrīk̲h̲če-i ʿadliyye-i dewlet-i ʿaliyye*, Istanbul 1306/1889; F. Meyer, *Rechtswesen einschliesslich Rechtsverfolgung in der Türkei*, in J. Hellauer, ed., *Das türkische Reich: wirtschaftliche Darstellungen*, Berlin 1918, 116-52; İlber Ortaylı, *Tanzimattan sonra mahalli idareler (1840-1878)*, Ankara 1974; S. J. Shaw, *The central legislative councils in the nineteenth century Ottoman reform movement before 1876*, in *IJMES*, i (1970), 51-84; Hıfzı Veldet, *Kanunlaştırma hareketleri ve Tanzimat*, in *Tanzimat I: yüzüncü yıldönümü münasebetile*, Istanbul

1940, 139-209; G. Young, *Corps de droit ottoman: recueil des codes, lois, règlements, ordonnances et actes les plus importants du droit intérieur, et d'études sur le droit coutumier de l'Empire ottoman*, 7 vols., Oxford 1905-6.
(H. İNALCIK and C. V. FINDLEY)

3. IRAN

Under the ʿAbbāsids, as Schacht pointed out, the office of *ḳāḍī* became permanently connected with the sacred law, but, as he went on to say, the *ḳāḍīs* very soon lost control of the administration of criminal justice. Ostensibly to supplement the deficiencies of the tribunals of the *ḳāḍīs*, the *maẓālim* [*q.v.*] courts for the redress of grievances, deriving from the administrative practice of the Sāsānid kings, were set up by the political authority and received theoretical recognition (*The law*, in *Unity and variety in Muslim civilisation*, ed. G. von Grunebaum, Chicago 1955, 74-5).

Al-Māwardī [*q.v.*], recognising that the *maẓālim* court was the dominant court, attempts to bring it within the general framework of the law. In a significant statement he explains that it was charged with the enforcement of decisions made by *ḳāḍīs* not sufficiently strong to see that their judgments were carried out against defendants occupying high rank or powerful positions, and with the suppression of evil-doing and the enforcement of regulations within the jurisdiction of the *muḥtasib* but beyond his power to apply (*al-Aḥkām al-sulṭāniyya*, Cairo 1386/1966, 83). In his account of the origins of the *maẓālim* court, he attributes its emergence to the lapse into kingship after the golden age of the Medinan caliphate. It was concerned with cases against officials, suits concerning injustice in the levy of taxation, complaints by those in receipt of stipends from official sources that these had not been paid or had been reduced, and claims for the restoration of property wrongfully seized. It was also charged with the investigation of matters which concerned *awḳāf*, the care of public worship and the due performance of religious practices in general. Whereas the *ḳāḍī*'s court was bound by strict rules of evidence, the *maẓālim* court was subject to no such limits, although al-Māwardī states that in the hearing and decision of disputes in general the rules of procedure which governed cases that came before the *ḳāḍīs* and judges were to prevail (*al-Aḥkām al-sulṭāniyya*, 77 ff. See also R. Levy, *The social structure of Islam*, Cambridge 1957, 348-9). One of the most important functions of the *maẓālim* court was arbitration. In exercising this the head of the court, the *nāẓir al-maẓālim*, was, according to al-Māwardī, not to go outside the limits of what was demanded by the law and his decrees were to be in keeping with the rules expounded by the *ḳāḍīs* (*al-Aḥkām al-sulṭāniyya*, 83). Al-Māwardī further lays down that *ḳāḍīs* and jurists, to whom the *nāẓir al-maẓālim* might have recourse in case of difficulty or doubt, were to be present when the *maẓālim* court sat (*ibid.*, 80). It was thus a channel through which sanction was given to *ʿurfī* practices.

The lawbooks lay down the qualities demanded of the *ḳāḍī* and the rules of procedure for his court. They also lay down the method of his appointment; but in this Sunnī theory differs from S̲h̲īʿī. Until the Ṣafawids imposed Imāmī S̲h̲īʿism as the official religion of their empire, Persia was, apart from certain districts, predominantly Sunnī. The dominant rites were the S̲h̲āfiʿī and the Ḥanafī and it was the rules concerning *ḳaḍāʾ* laid down in the lawbooks of these schools which, for the most part, prevailed (for these see especially al-Māwardī, *al-Aḥkām al-sulṭāniyya* and idem, *Ādāb al-ḳāḍī*, ed. Muḥyī Hilāl al-Sirḥān, Bag̲h̲dād 1391/1971). According to Sunnī theory, it was essential that there should be a valid delegation of authority to the *ḳāḍī* in order that his decisions should, in turn, have validity. As long as the caliphs held political power they delegated authority to the *ḳāḍīs*. When they ceased to exercise power it was accepted that the *ḳāḍī* should be appointed by the ruler. Al-G̲h̲azālī, concerned for the legality of the life of the community, held that any *ḳāḍī* nominated by one holding power (*ṣāḥib s̲h̲awkat*) could give valid decisions (*Wad̲j̲īz*, ii, 143, quoted by E. Tyan, *Histoire d'organisation judiciaire*, i, 258). Once instituted, the *ḳāḍī* was regarded, not as the personal representative of the one who had delegated authority to him, but as the deputy or *nāʾib* of the caliph or the Prophet. With the weakening of the power of the caliph and his overthrow by the Mongols, it became the normal theory to regard the *ḳāḍīs* as the deputies of the prophet. This reinforced their independent status (see further Tyan, i, 134-5, 147-8). The death of the *imām* (or that person who had delegated authority to the *ḳāḍī*) did not result in the revocation of the *ḳāḍī*'s appointment (thus reinforcing his theoretical independence). On the other hand, the death of the *ḳāḍī* resulted in the revocation of the appointment of his deputies. If the inhabitants of a town which had no *ḳāḍī* appointed one, this designation was null and void if there was an *imām* in existence. If there was no *imām*, the appointment was valid and his judgments were to be executed (*al-Aḥkām al-sulṭāniyya*, 76). This again emphasises the independent status of the *ḳāḍī*. But his independence was relative: when a new *imām* was appointed, his agreement was required for the *ḳāḍī* to continue to exercise his functions (*ibid.*). The fact that the law administered by the *ḳāḍī* was the *s̲h̲arīʿa*, to which, in theory, the ruler was subject and which was independent of his will, also contributed to the independence of the *ḳāḍīs* (cf. Tyan, i, 149-50)—an independence which they continued to enjoy to a greater or lesser extent over the centuries. Two factors in particular, however, limited their independence. First, the ruler who had nominated them could also dismiss them, and secondly, they had to rely on the officials of the government for the enforcement of their judgments.

The competence of the *ḳāḍī* might be general or restricted. In the former case his functions were to settle disputes either by arbitration within the limits of the *s̲h̲arīʿa* between the parties to the dispute or by enforcing, after proof, liabilities by judgment in favour of those entitled to them upon persons who disputed them; to exercise control over persons who had not charge of their property by reason of madness, infancy or insolvency; to oversee *awḳāf*; to execute wills and testaments; to give widows and divorced women in marriage; to apply the legal penalties; to supervise public utilities in order to prevent encroachment upon roads and public spaces; to make the necessary investigations concerning legal witnesses; to judge between the powerful and the weak; observing equality between them; and to decide with equity cases between the *k̲h̲āṣṣ* and the *ʿāmm*. If he was invested with authority for some specific purpose, i.e. if his authority was restricted (*k̲h̲uṣūṣ*), he exercised his functions within those limits only (*al-Aḥkām al-sulṭāniyya*, 70 ff.).

Whereas the Sunnīs considered the ultimate source of the *ḳāḍī*'s authority to be the Prophet, the S̲h̲īʿa held this to be the *imāms* (see al-Kulaynī, *Uṣūl al-kāfī*, ch. on *ḳaḍāʾ*). The Imāmī S̲h̲īʿa, perhaps because their *imāms* apart from ʿAlī b. Abī Ṭālib did not hold political power, were not concerned with the valid delegation of authority by the holders of power to their subordinate officials. They regarded all government in the absence of the *imām* as unjust (*djā'ir*). In their discussions of *ḳaḍā'* they differentiate between the time when the *imām* is present and the *ghayba*, i.e. the period of occultation. However, they could not entirely escape the problem of cooperation with an unjust government, the validity of whose title to rule they did not recognise. They attempted to solve this problem by permitting a limited degree of cooperation with the adoption of *taḳiyya* [*q.v.*], dissimulation of one's belief in the event of danger.

Muḥammad b. al-Ḥasan al-Ṭūsī (d. 460/1067) sets out, in a somewhat equivocal fashion, the Imāmī Shīʿī doctrine concerning the execution of the legal penalties and the exercise of the office of *ḳāḍī* as follows: "No one has the right to execute the legal penalties except the sultan of the time, who has been appointed by God most High [i.e. the *imām*], or that person whom the *imām* has appointed to apply the legal penalties. It is not permissible for anyone except those two to apply the legal penalties on any occasion. But permission has been given for the people to apply the legal penalties to their children, their own people and their slaves in the time when the true *imāms* are not in control and tyrants have usurped power, provided that they do not fear that any harm will come to them from the tyrants and are safe from harm from them. If this is not the case, it is not permissible to apply the legal penalties. If an unjust sultan makes someone [who is an Imāmī Shīʿī] his deputy and appoints him to apply the legal penalties, it is for him to do so fully and completely, while believing that what he does he does at the command of the true sultan; and it is incumbent upon believers to cooperate with him and to strengthen him as long as he does not transgress what is right in that over which he is appointed and does not go beyond what is legal according to the *Sharīʿa* of Islam. If he does, it is not permissible to assist him or for anyone to cooperate with him in that, unless he fears for his own person, in which case it is permissible to do so while practising *taḳiyya*, as long as the killing of anyone is not involved. In no circumstance is *taḳiyya* to be practised in the case of killing anyone (*al-Nihāya fī mudjarrad al-fiḳh wa-'l-fatāwā*, Beirut 1970, 300-1, Persian text, ed. Muḥammad Bāḳir Sabzawārī, Tehran 1333/1954-6, 2 vols., i, 200-1).

Similarly, al-Ṭūsī states that it not permissible for anyone to give judgment between the people except that person to whom "the true sultan" has given permission (*ibid.*, 301, Persian text, i, 201). He continues, "The true *imāms*, upon them be peace, have cast [the mantle of] judgment (*ḥukūmat*) on the *fuḳahā'* of the Shīʿa during such time as they themselves are not in a position to exercise it in person" (*ibid.*, Persian text, i, 201; the Arabic text omits the words *a'imma-i ḥaḳḳ* and reads "They have entrusted this (the function of judging) to the *fuḳahā'* of their *shīʿa* during such time as they are not able to exercise it in person", 301). This statement, which would appear to be one of the earliest occasions when it is stated that the *fuḳahā'* are in effect the successors or deputies of the *imāms* in the giving of judgment, does not provide for any immediate source of authority for the *ḳāḍīs*. The ultimate source of their authority is the delegation by Djaʿfar al-Ṣādiḳ related in two traditions recorded by al-Kulaynī. The first, from Djaʿfar al-Ṣādiḳ, reads "Let not one of you call another to litigation before the *ahl al-djawr*. Rather look to one of your number who knows something of our judgments and set him up (to judge) between you. For I have made him a *ḳāḍī* to seek judgment from him". The second, related from ʿUmar b. Ḥanẓala, reads "I asked Abū ʿAbd Allāh (Djaʿfar al-Ṣādiḳ) concerning two of our companions who are involved in a dispute over debt or inheritance and who seek judgment before a sultan or *ḳāḍīs*. Is this lawful (*ḥalāl*)? Abū ʿAbd Allāh replied, 'He who seeks judgment from *ṭāghūt* (i.e. tyrants) and obtains judgment receives only abomination, even if his claim is valid, because he has accepted the decision of *ṭāghūt*. God has commanded that (such a one) be considered an unbeliever (*kāfir*)'. ʿUmar b. Ḥanẓala said, 'What should they do?' Djaʿfar al-Ṣādiḳ replied, 'Look to one of your number who relates our *ḥadīth*, who considers our *ḥalāl* and our *ḥarām* and who knows our *aḥkām*. Accept his judgment for I have made him a *ḥākim* over you. If he gives a decision in accord with our judgment and (the litigant) does not accept it, then it is God's judgment he has scorned and us he has rejected. One who rejects us rejects God and he is subject to the punishment due for polytheism (*ʿalā ḥadd al-shirk*)'" (*Furūʿ al-kāfī*, i, 357-9).

The qualities required for the office of *ḳāḍī* were wisdom and maturity, being learned in the Ḳur'ān and the *sunna*, and a knowledge of Arabic; it was also a condition that he who undertook this office should be devout and abstinent and much given to good works, and that he should avoid sins and refrain from lust and have an intense concern for piety. Only someone endowed with these qualities was permitted to undertake the office and to judge between the people provided that there was no fear for his life, his people, his possessions or for any believers (*al-Nihāya fī mudjarrad al-fiḳh wa'l-fatāwā*, 301, Persian text, i, 226). It was permissible to take wages and subsistence from a just sultan (i.e. the *imām*) for the exercise of the office of *ḳāḍī*, but in the case of an unjust sultan it was only permissible in the event of necessity or fear. It was, however, better, in al-Ṭūsī's opinion, to refrain in all cases from taking wages for the office of *ḳāḍī* (*ibid.*, Arabic text, 367, Persian text, i, 246).

"If," al-Ṭūsī states, "anyone is able to carry out a judgment or a settlement (*ṣulḥ*) between people or to execute a decision between two litigants, as long as he does not fear harm for himself or for anyone of the faith and is safe from harm in so doing, he will receive recompense and reward. But if he fears any of these things, in no circumstances is it permissible for him to undertake these matters. If someone calls upon one of the *fuḳahā'* of the people of the truth (i.e. the Imāmī Shīʿa) to decide something between them (the Shīʿa), and that *faḳīh* does not agree to do so, preferring that it should be referred to a person who is charged with the matter on behalf of tyrants, he will have stepped outside the truth and committed sin. It is not permissible for a person who is charged with giving a decision between two litigants, or judgment between the people, to do so except in accordance with the truth; it is not permissible to give judgment according to one of the Sunnī schools. If anyone undertakes judgment on behalf of unjust persons, let him strive to give judgments as demanded of him by the *sharīʿa* of the faith; but if he is constrained to give judgment according to the Sunnī schools because he fears for himself, his people or believers or for their property, it is permissible for him to do so [while practising *taḳiyya*], provided it does not involve the killing of anyone, because *taḳiyya* is not to be adopted in the case of killing someone" (*ibid.*, 301-2, Persian text, i, 201).

Concluding his discussion of the application of the legal penalties and the execution of judgment, al-Ṭūsī succinctly explains in what circumstances a *faḳīh* might undertake these functions under an unjust ruler and how the *faḳīh* was to believe while doing so that he was, in fact, acting on behalf of the *imām*. He states, "If a *faḳīh* exercises authority (*wilāya*) on behalf of a tyrant, let him think that in applying the penalties of the law and in giving judgment he is acting on behalf of the true *imām* and let him undertake (these duties) according to the demands of the *sharīʿa* of the faith; and whenever he is empowered to execute punishment against a transgressor, let him do so, for verily this is one of the greatest (forms) of *djihād*. If, however, someone does not know the conditions in which the penalties should be applied and cannot execute them [properly], it is not permissible, in any circumstances, for him to apply them—if he does he will be a sinner. But if he is compelled to do so, there will be nothing against him. Let him endeavour to keep himself apart from things which are illegitimate (*al-abāṭīl*). It is not permissible for anyone to choose to exercise oversight on behalf of tyrants unless he has (first) determined that he will not transgress what is obligatory and will only execute what is right and that he will allocate such things as *ṣadaḳāt* and *akhmās* and so on to their proper use. If he knows that he will not be able to control these things, it is not permissible for him voluntarily to undertake such work, but if he is compelled to do so, it is permissible. Let him strive (to act) as we have said" (*ibid.*, 302-3, Persian text, i, 201-2).

Al-Ṭūsī's theory thus made it possible for Imāmī Shīʿīs to accept the office of *ḳāḍī* from unjust rulers, whether Sunnīs or Shīʿīs, although he did not provide for any immediate source of their authority. His theory was for the most part accepted by later jurists. Ḥasan b. Yūsuf b. al-Muṭahhar al-Ḥillī (d. 726/1325), writing in the reign of Öldjeytü (703-16/1304-16), who was converted to Shīʿism, is somewhat less equivocal on the desirability of the acceptance of the office of *ḳaḍāʾ* by the *fuḳahāʾ*. When finally Imāmī Shīʿism became the official religion of Persia under the Ṣafawids, although the *fuḳahāʾ*, for the most part, continued to regard the government, in the absence of the *imām*, as unjust, the general body of *ʿulamāʾ* and *fuḳahāʾ* accepted office at their hands and from the hands of succeeding dynasties. Muḥammad b. Makkī al-ʿĀmilī al-Shāmī al-Shahīd al-Awwal (d. 786/1384-5), writing for Shams al-Dīn al-Ānī, one of the ministers of ʿAlī b. Muʿayyid, the Shīʿī Sarbadarid ruler of Sabzawār, had stated that it was the duty of the *imām* or his *nāʾib* to judge and that in the *ghayba* the *faḳīh* who was possessed of the necessary qualification to give legal decisions (*al-faḳīh al-djāmiʿ li-sharāʾiṭ al-iftāʾ*) carried out the functions of judgment. Whoever turned aside from such an individual and referred to the *ḳāḍīs* of an unjust government (*ḳuḍāt al-djawr*) was a sinner and it was incumbent upon the people to refer to him in what concerned the ordinances of the *sharīʿa*; whoever failed to do so was a sinner. Zayn al-Dīn b. ʿAlī al-ʿĀmilī al-Shahīd al-Thānī (d. 966/1559), writing in the Ottoman empire at the beginning of the Ṣafawid period, commenting on this, states "If the *muftī* is endowed with these qualities, it is incumbent upon the people to refer to him and to accept his word and to make his decision incumbent upon themselves because he is appointed by the *imām* for a general purpose (*manṣūb min al-imām ʿalā ʾl-ʿumūm*)" (*Rawḍat al-bahiyya fī sharḥ lumʿat al-dimashḳiyya*, lith. Tabrīz 1271/1854-5, 94-5). He also states with reference to the exercise of judicial functions on behalf of or under an unjust ruler that this is incumbent provided that there is safety from the commission of what is forbidden and power to enjoin the good and to forbid evil. He adds that the reason for its not being incumbent (in other circumstances) was perhaps because one who took judicial office under an unjust ruler (*ẓālim*) would in appearance (*bi-ṣūra*) be *nāʾib* to the unjust ruler (*Masālik al-ifhām fī sharḥ sharāyiʿ al-islām*, lith. 1314/1896-7, 2 vols., i, 167-8. See further N. Calder, *The structure of authority in Imāmī Shīʿī jurisprudence*, unpublished Ph. D. thesis, London University 1979, 98 ff.).

Although there were changes in the position of the *ḳāḍī* under the Ḳādjārs, his position in theory was substantially the same: the government continued to be regarded as unjust and the authority of the *ḳāḍī* derived from the *imām*, not the government from whom he received his appointment. Shaykh Djaʿfar Kāshif al-Ghiṭāʾ, the 19th century jurist, discusses the question of *ḳaḍāʾ* in his *Kashf al-ghiṭāʾ* at the end of the book on *djihād*. He follows al-Ṭūsī in the matter of the acceptance of the office of *ḳāḍī*, but he makes a distinction between the exercise of office by a *mudjtahid* and one who was not *mudjtahid*. He permits a *ḳāḍī* to carry out the *taʿzīr* punishments but states that the execution of the *ḥadd* punishments was the *mudjtahid*'s prerogative, and in carrying out a *ḥadd* punishment his inward intention (*niyyat*) must be that he was carrying it out as the deputy, not of the temporal governors (*ḥukkām*), but of the *imām*. He also states that it was not permissible for the leader of the Muslims to appoint a *ḳāḍī* or *shaykh al-islām* except with the permission of a *mudjtahid* (*Kashf al-ghiṭāʾ*, lith., pages unnumbered).

Under the Great Saldjūḳs there was a delicate balance between *sharʿī* and *ʿurfī* jurisdiction. The sultan as judge and guardian of public order sat in the *maẓālim* court. This function was delegated by him in the provinces to the provincial governor or to the *muḳtaʿ* (see further A. K. S. Lambton, *The internal situation of the Saljūq empire*, in *Cambridge history of Iran*, iv, ed. J. A. Boyle, Cambridge 1968, 247 ff.). Niẓām al-Mulk, discussing the *maẓālim* court, holds that it was indispensable for the ruler to hold such a court twice a week to hear personally, without an intermediary, what the subjects had to say (*Siyāsat-nāma*, ed. C. Schefer, Paris 1891, Persian text, 10). His main concern appears to have been to strengthen the authority of the ruler rather that to ensure that justice was done to the individual. He continues, "A few cases which are of greater importance shall be submitted [to the ruler] and he shall give an order (*mithāl*) concerning each one so that all tyrants will fear and restrain their hands from oppression. When news spreads abroad in the kingdom that the Lord of the World summons to his presence those who have grievances and those who demand redress twice a week and listens to what they have to say, no one will dare to commit tyranny or extortion for fear of punishment" (*ibid.*). Niẓām al-Mulk recommends that the plaints of those who gathered at the court should be dealt with expeditiously to avoid clamour or commotion at the court, such that strangers and envoys should be led to suppose that tyranny was rife in the kingdom (*ibid.*, 207).

A *ḳāḍī al-ḳuḍāt* was appointed in the capital and in a number of provincial cities, but there would seem to have been a decline in the importance of the office. The reasons for this—if it was indeed the case—are not clear. It may have been connected with the increased centralisation of the administration in the hands of the *wazīr* during the reign of Malik-Shāh (465-85/1072-92). The influence and prestige of the *ḳāḍīs*, however, was apparently undiminished. The immediate source of their authority was the sultan, but its ultimate source was the Prophet (cf. *Siyāsat-nāma*, 38)—in other words the sultan exercised constitutive authority with regard to the *ḳāḍī*, but the functional authority of the *ḳāḍī* derived from the *sharīʿa* (see further Lambton, *Quis custodiet custodes*, in *SI*, v [1956], 132-3).

A document issued by Sandjar's *dīwān* appointing Madjd al-Dīn Muḥammad *ḳāḍī* of Gulpāyagān states that the office of *ḳāḍī* and *ḥākim* was the greatest religious office (*shughl*) and the most delicate *sharʿī* charge (*ʿamal*) (Muntadjab al-Dīn Badīʿ al-Djuwaynī, *ʿAtabat al-kataba*, ed. ʿAbbās Iḳbāl, Tehran 1329/1950, 45). Niẓām al-Mulk also recognises that the office of *ḳāḍī* was a delicate one "because they (the *ḳāḍīs*) were empowered over the lives and properties of the Muslims" (*Siyāsat-nāma*, 38. Cf. also al-Ghazālī's letter to Fakhr al-Mulk b. Niẓām al-Mulk, *Faḍāʾil al-anām*, ed. ʿAbbās Iḳbāl, Tehran 1333/1954-5, 28). It was no doubt partly on this account that care was urged upon the *ḳāḍīs* in the drawing up of testaments, title deeds and other documents (cf. the document issued by Sandjar's *dīwān* appointing ʿImād al-Dīn Muḥammad b. Aḥmad b. Ṣāʿid *ḳāḍī* of Nīshāpūr, *ʿAtabat al-kataba*, 12). It was recognised that the office of *ḳāḍī* concerned both the people and the state (cf. the document issued by Sandjar's *dīwān* for the *ḳāḍī-yi lashkar*, *ibid.*, 58-9).

Niẓām al-Mulk states that the appointment and dismissal of the *ḳāḍī* was the responsibility of the ruler, and that the *ḳāḍīs* were to be allocated a monthly salary (*mushāhara*), sufficient to free them from the need of peculation (*khiyānat*) (*Siyāsat-nāma*, 38). They were, thus, in some measure government servants. Their function as such was probably to watch over the religious institution on behalf of the government in order to prevent the spread of unorthodox opinions (which were in the eyes of the government inevitably linked with sedition). Niẓām al-Mulk also states that the *ḳāḍīs* were to be supported by other officials and their prestige guarded. In keeping with the Sunnī principle, *kull mudjtahid muṣīb*, he states that the judgments of *ḳāḍīs*, even if wrongfully given, were to be executed by other officials. The latter were, however, to report wrong judgments to the ruler so that he might dismiss and punish a *ḳāḍī* guilty of such. Anyone who behaved presumptuously and refused to appear at the *ḳāḍī*'s court when summoned was to be forced to do so, even if he was a great man (*ibid.*). In some cases, the diploma appointing a *ḳāḍī* stipulates that he was to judge according to a particular rite. Cases are, however, recorded of *ḳāḍīs* giving *fatwās* according to more than one rite.

In Niẓām al-Mulk's theory there is a certain ambiguity in the position of the *ḳāḍī*. On the one hand he was appointed by the ruler, but on the other he enjoyed a certain independence because of his relationship to the caliph. "The *ḳāḍīs*", Niẓām al-Mulk states, "are all the deputies (*nāʾibān*) of the king. It is incumbent upon the king to support them. They must be accorded full respect and dignity because they are the deputies of the caliph, whose mantle has devolved upon them" (*ibid.*, 40-1). This statement is to be seen, perhaps, in the light of the theory that the caliph should be a *mudjtahid* and that the ruler, if he was not a *mudjtahid*, required a deputy to act on his behalf in certain matters. Niẓām al-Mulk states that "when the king is a Turk or a Persian or someone who does not know Arabic and has not studied the decrees of the *sharīʿa*, he inevitably requires a deputy to conduct affairs in his place" (*ibid.*, 40). Thus he foreshadows the theory to be put forward in the late 9th/15th century by Faḍl Allāh b. Rūzbihān Khundjī, who states that kings who were *mudjtahids* were few and far between and that if a king was not a *mudjtahid* it was incumbent upon him to appoint a *muftī* (*Sulūk al-mulūk*, B. L., ms. Or. 253, ff. unnumbered).

The documents issued by Sandjar's *dīwān* collected in the *ʿAtabat al-kataba* make clear the separation of *sharʿī* and *ʿurfī* jurisdiction and also the subordination of the provincial *ḳāḍī* to the provincial governor. In a *taḳlīd* issued in favour of Tādj al-Dīn Abu 'l-Makārim Aḥmad b. al-ʿAbbās for the office of governor (*raʾīs*) of Māzandarān, he is charged with the general supervision of the *ḳāḍīs* and is enjoined to appoint a deputy over the *ḳāḍī*'s court and the *madjlis-i-ḥakam* (? the court of arbitration) (*ʿAtabat al-kataba*, 24). He is also enjoined "to inflict upon a thief or highway robber, when caught, punishment and what is demanded by the *Sharīʿa*, with the agreement of the *ḳāḍīs*, *imāms* and notables of the province" (*ibid.*, 25. Cf. also *ibid.*, 28). A diploma in the name of Abu 'l-Fatḥ Marzbān al-Sharḳ. b. ʿAlāʾ al-Dīn Abī Bakr b. Ḳumādj for the governorship (*ayālat wa shaḥnagī*) of Balkh instructs him to give judgment and to settle cases after consultation and according to the advice of experienced and reliable persons and leaders (*muḳaddamān*). *Sharʿī* matters were to be referred to the *ḳāḍī*'s court. *Rasmiyyāt* (matters concerning salaries and allowances), *muʿāmalāt* (matters concerning *muḳāṭaʿa* contracts) and *dīwānī* affairs were to be referred to the *dīwān-i riyāsat*. Abu 'l-Fatḥ was given full powers in the preservation of order and the punishment of miscreants, but in the exercise of these powers he was to consult the *ḳāḍīs* (*ibid.*, 79). Another diploma in the name of Abu 'l-Fatḥ Yūsuf b. Khʷārazmshāh for the deputy-governorship (*niyābat-i ayālat*) of Ray enjoins him to put down the corrupt, transgressors, thieves and highway robbers and to consider the exaction of the legal penalties (*ḥudūd*), after consultation with the *ḳāḍīs*, *imāms* and reliable persons, as being among those things which are incumbent according to the *sharīʿa* and upon which the well-being and good order of religion and the world depend (*ibid.*, 43).

Among the duties of the *ḳāḍī* was the supervision of the *ḥisba*. A document issued by Sandjar's *dīwān* for the office of *ḳāḍī* and *khaṭīb* of Astarābād entrusts the grantee with the execution of the requirements of the *ḥisba*, such as the putting down of transgressors and the corrupt, the prevention of evil by them, and the adjustment of weights and measures and prices, as far as possible (*ibid.*, 52).

So far as the supervision of *awḳāf* was concerned, in the event of a *mutawallī* having been designated, the *ḳāḍī* exercised general supervision only, otherwise he administered the *waḳf*. There was in practice probably a certain conflict of jurisdiction between the *ḳāḍī* and the *wazīr* in the matter of *awḳāf*. The latter, as head of the financial administration, also exercised general supervision over *awḳāf*, though exactly what form this took is not entirely clear. In some cases the *awḳāf* of a district were placed exclusively under the *ḳāḍī* and expressly removed from the control of the *dīwān* (cf. *ibid.*, 33).

In the period between the disintegration of the Great Saldjūḳ empire and the Mongol invasion, the chief official in charge of *ʿurfī* courts appears to have been known as the *dadbeg* (see further H. Horst, *Die Staatsverwaltung der Grosselǧūqen und Ḫōrazmšāhs (1038-1231)*, Wiesbaden 1964, 92-3. See also *ibid.*, on the term *yuluk-i aʿlā*, which appears to have been some sort of *maẓālim* court). Various local officials apparently also exercised jurisdiction. A document probably belonging to the latter half of the 6th/12th century, appointing a certain Shams al-Dīn *miʿmār* of Khʷārazm and entrusting him with the agricultural development of the province, enjoins him to chastise and correct anyone who failed to further this or to exert effort in this and if such reproach and censure did not bring the culprit to see the error of his ways,

Shams al-Dīn was to refer the matter to the supreme *dīwān* so that reproof might be administered to him and he might be replaced by someone who would seek to create abundance (Bahāʾ al-Dīn b. Muʿayyad, *al-Tawassul ilā 'l-tarassul*, ed. Aḥmad Bahmanyār, Tehran 1315/1936-7, 113). That local officials had certain powers of punishment would seem to be confirmed by Nadjm al-Dīn Rāzī. He states that bailiffs, village headmen and landlords' representatives should "reprimand the corrupt and enjoin the people to do that which is recommended and to forbid them from doing that which is forbidden. If they saw presumption or corruption on the part of one of the peasants (*raʿiyyat*), they were to punish him and bring him to repentance" (*Mirṣād al-ʿibād*, ed. Ḥusayn al-Ḥusaynī al-Niʿmat Allāhī, Tehran 1312/1933-4, 296).

The distinction between *ʿurfī* and *sharʿī* jurisdiction was more sharply drawn under the Īlkhāns prior to their conversion to Islam. The Mongols brought with them their own laws and customs, though it seems improbable that the Great Yasa of Čingiz Khān existed as a written code of laws (see further D. O. Morgan, *The Great Yasa of Chingiz Khan and Mongol law in the Ilkhanate* in J. M. Rogers (ed.), *The Islamic world after the Mongol conquests* [forthcoming]; but see also D. Ayalon, *The Great Yasa of Chingiz Khan: a reexamination*, in *SI*, xxxiii â1971], 97-144, xxxiv [1971], 151-80, xxxvi [1972], 113-53, and xxxviii [1973], 107-56). There was a court of interrogation known as the *yarghu*, but we have very few details as to its terms of reference and rules of procedure. It appears to have dealt specifically with disputes between Mongols, Mongol state affairs and cases against officials, especially of alleged peculation and conspiracy (see further Morgan, *op. cit.*). With the conversion of the Īlkhāns to Islam, the *yarghu* was probably to some extent assimilated to the *maẓālim* courts and the *ḳāḍīs* associated with their proceedings. A *yarligh* for the appointment of a provincial *ḳāḍī* issued by Ghāzān Khān (694-703/1295-1304) reads as follows, "In the case of disputes which occur between two Mongols or between a Mongol and a Muslim or cases, the decision of which is difficult, we have ordered the *shaḥnas*, *maliks*, *bitikčis*, *ḳāḍīs*, ʿAlids and *ʿulamāʾ* to assemble every month for two days in the Friday mosque in the *dīwān-i maẓālim* taking the alternate reading *dīwān-i maẓālim* rather than *dīwān-i muṭālaʿa* as in the printed text to hear cases together, and after thoroughly examining a case to give judgment according to the ruling (*ḥukm*) of the *sharīʿa*.". Their decision was to be given in writing so that it might not later be abrogated (Rashīd al-Dīn, *Tārīkh-i mubārak-i ghāzānī*, ed. K. Jahn, London 1940, 219). The *Dastūr al-kātib* of Muḥammad b. Hindūshāh Nakhdjiwānī, which belongs to the late Īlkhān period, describes the functions of the *amīr yarghu*. He is instructed to act on the basis of equity (*ʿadl*, *maʿdalat*, *inṣāf*, *niṣfat* and *rāstī*) (ed. A. A. ʿAlīzādeh, Moscow, i/1 [1964], i/2 [1971], ii [1976], ii, 30, and see further Morgan, *op. cit.*).

Somewhat similar procedures appear to have prevailed in some of the succession states. Ibn Baṭṭūta, describing his arrival at the court of the *amīr* of Khwārazm, Ḳuṭlūdumūr, states "It is one of the regular practices of this *amīr* that the *qāḍī* comes daily to his audience hall and sits in a place assigned to him, accompanied by the jurists and his clerks. Opposite him sits one of the great *amīrs*, accompanied by eight of the great amirs and shaikhs of the Turks, who are called *arghujīs*. The people bring their disputes to them for decision; those that come within the jurisdiction of the religious law are decided by the *qāḍī* and all others are decided by those amirs. Their decisions are well-regulated and just, for they are free from suspicion and partiality and do not accept bribes" (*The travels of Ibn Baṭṭūta A.D. 1325-1354*, tr. H. A. R. Gibb, Cambridge 1971, iii, 545).

According to Mongol practice, the *ḳāḍīs* and *ʿulamāʾ* were granted certain tax immunities. Although they were treated with respect, prior to the conversion of the Īlkhāns to Islam, they ceased to enjoy in official circles that pre-eminence which had been theirs when religion and state were, at least in theory, one. If, as was probably the case, the *ḳāḍīs* in the main centres continued to receive their appointment from the ruler, al-Ghazālī's theory that any *ḳāḍī* nominated by anyone holding power could give a valid decision would have been of peculiar relevance. Waṣṣāf records a case in Fārs *ca.* 678/1279-80 of the joint appointment of two eminent divines to the office of *ḳāḍī al-ḳuḍāt* of Fārs. This was made by the *wazīr* of Fārs after consultation with the religious classes and the notables (*Tārīkh-i Waṣṣāf*, Bombay 1269/1853, 205-6). After the conversion of Ghāzān Khān to Islam, the influence of the *ḳāḍīs* in official circles almost certainly increased. Their tax immunities were confirmed and pensions were allocated to them on the revenue (*Tārīkh-i mubārak-i ghāzānī*, 218).

Under Ghāzān there was a *dīwān-i ḳuḍāt*, the head of which was the *ḳāḍī al-ḳuḍāt* of the empire, who once more became an important official. He was in charge of *sharʿī* officials in general and also of *awḳāf*. These appear to have increased in extent and importance in the 7th/13th century (though for what reason or reasons is not entirely clear) (see further Lambton, *Awqāf in the 7th/13th and 8th/14th centuries in Persia*, in G. Baer, ed., *Social and economic aspects of the Muslim waqf*, forthcoming). An undated document belonging to the late Īlkhān period issued by the *ḳāḍī* (who had been charged with the appointment of all *sharʿī* officials in the empire and was at the same time *mutawallī* of charitable and private *awḳāf*) for his deputy, who was also to hold the office of *ḥākim* of charitable *awḳāf*, states it was impossible for him personally to oversee *sharʿī* affairs in all regions because of his being in the retinue of the ruler. He needed a deputy. Consequently, Ḥusayn al-Asadī was appointed deputy *ḳāḍī al-ḳuḍāt* with a general designation and with a special designation over ʿIrāḳ-i ʿArab, Ādharbāydjān and various other districts. He was also appointed *mutawallī* of charitable and private *awḳāf* with power to appoint and dismiss those in charge of religious offices and the execution of Islamic decrees (*Dastūr al-kātib*, ii, 191 ff.). Another document in the same collection, delegating the office of *ḥākim* of the *awḳāf* of the empire to the *ḳāḍī al-ḳuḍāt* Shaykh ʿAlī, gives him full powers in the administration of the *awḳāf* and over the appointment and dismissal of the *mutawallīs* and *mubāshirs* and of deputies to act for him as *ḥākim-i awḳāf* in the provinces (*ibid.*, ii, 207 ff.). To ensure that the *awḳāf* were properly run and their revenues devoted to the purposes laid down by their founders was no small matter. Usurpation was common. Demands for redress came before the *ḳāḍī* and it was his duty to investigate them (cf. *ibid.*, i/1 175-6, 327-9).

Rashīd al-Dīn Faḍl Allāh, Ghāzān Khān's *wazīr*, gives an extremely unfavourable account of the administration of justice by the *ḳāḍīs* in the Īlkhān empire prior to the reign of Ghāzān Khān (as he does of other aspects of the administration). He alleges that corrupt and ignorant persons insinuated themselves into the service of the Mongols and by flattery and bribery secured the office of *ḳāḍī* and other *sharʿī* offices. Corruption was especially prevalent in transactions over landed property. Fraudulent claims based on obsolete property deeds and bonds which had remained in the hands of the original owners or their heirs after the property had changed hands were common, and there was often no means for the *ḳāḍīs* to verify the validity of such deeds. Rashīd al-Dīn states that Malik-Shāh and his *wazīr* Niẓām al-Mulk, faced by a similar situation, had issued a decree (*mithāl*), conformable to the *sharīʿa*, that claims based on title deeds which had not been preferred for thirty years should not be heard and that this decree was given to the *muftīs* of Khurāsān, ʿIrāḳ and Baghdād so that they might issue *fatwās* in accordance with the *sharīʿa*, which were then to be sent to the *dār al-khilāfa* to be signed (*tā imḍāʾ nivishta and*). Rashīd al-Dīn claims that Malik Shāh's decree was extant and that it had been shown (or reported) to Hülegü, who had issued a *yarligh* on similar lines, as had Abaḳa, Arghun and Gaykhatu (*Tārīkh-i mubārak-i ghāzānī*, 236 ff.). Rashīd al-Dīn also asserts that "before this time past sultans and Čingiz Khān in all their *farmāns* and *yarlighs* made mention that thirty-year-old claims should not be heard" (*ibid.*, 221-2). These decrees, however, had, he alleges, been inoperative, because first they had not had *sharʿī*, *ʿaḳlī* or *ʿurfī* confirmation, and secondly those charged with putting them into operation had wished to benefit themselves from the existing situation to buy property. Ghāzān Khān, on the other hand, consulted the *ḳāḍīs* and Fakhr al-Dīn Harātī, the *ḳāḍī al-ḳuḍāt* of the day, drafted a *yarligh* and wrote a decision on the back in accordance with the *sharīʿa* stating that land claims which had not been preferred for thirty years would not be heard (*ibid.*, 236 ff.). The *yarligh* is dated 3 Radjab 699/26 March 1300. Any *ḳāḍīs* who contravened it were to be dismissed and the names of any powerful persons who urged them to act in a contrary fashion were to be sent to the court so that they might be punished (*ibid.*, 221 ff.). Ghāzān also issued a *yarligh* concerning the registration and annulment of title deeds and documents (*ibid.*, 225) and another concerning appointment to the office of *ḳāḍī* and the conduct of *ḳāḍīs* in the matter of land cases (*ibid.*, 218 ff.).

ʿUrfī jurisdiction seems to have encroached upon *sharʿī* jurisdiction again under Tīmūr (d. 807/1405), but under Shāhrukh (d. 850/1446-7) there appears to have been a deliberate reassertion of *sharʿī* jurisdiction, although *ʿurfī* jurisdiction nevertheless continued to be dominant. Clavijo, who visited Tīmūr's camp in Samarḳand in 808/1405 states that all litigants and criminals were dealt with by one of three courts. The first dealt with criminal matters and bloodshed arising from quarrels, the second with money frauds such as might affect the government and the third with cases arising in the provinces. Wherever Tīmūr's camp might be, three great tents were erected, to which were brought all criminals and litigants for cases to be heard and sentences given (*Embassy to Tamerlane 1403-1405*, tr. G. le Strange, London 1928, 294-5).

When Ismāʿīl I (907-30/1502-24), the founder of the Ṣafawid dynasty, made Imāmī Shīʿism the official religion of the state, a more flexible attitude towards the acceptance of public office in general and that of *ḳāḍī* in particular developed among the Shīʿī *ʿulamāʾ* that had been the case heretofore, although there were always some who refused office out of religious scruple. The Shīʿī *ʿulamāʾ* became, like the Sunnī *ʿulamāʾ* before them, public officers and as such relied upon the machinery of the state for the execution of their judgments. Imāmī Shīʿism superseded the Sunnī schools and the Shīʿī *ʿulamāʾ* replaced the Sunnī as those in charge of *sharʿī* jurisdiction—though this did not, of course, happen overnight. Changes also took place in the religious hierarchy. The *ḳāḍī* lost some of his importance, first to the *ṣadr*, who became the chief official of the religious institution, and then to the *shaykh al-islām*, while the *mudjtahids*, who owed their pre-eminence not to any official appointment but to their own learning and sanctity, exercised a great, though undefined, influence over the religious institution and the *sharʿī* courts. The general tendency, however, was probably for *ʿurfī* jurisdiction to be strengthened, at least prior to the reign of Shāh Sulṭān Ḥusayn (1105-35/1694-1722), and for subordinate jurisdictions of a local nature to proliferate. There was a bewildering diversity at different times and in different provinces. The fact that the *shīʿa* did not accept the Sunnī principle, *kull mudjtahid muṣīb*, resulted in the decisions of the *ḳāḍī*'s courts being subject to review and reversal. It was perhaps for this reason that most Persians, according to Chardin, preferred the governments courts to the *ḳāḍī*'s courts, in which their cases were not easily brought to a decision (*Voyages*, ed. Langlès, vi, 91).

Already under Ṭahmāsp (930-84/1524-76) there was growing financial centralisation, and during the reign of Shāh ʿAbbās I (996-1038/1587-1629) centralisation spread to all aspects of the administration. The empire was divided into *khāṣṣa* and *mamālik*, i.e., regions under the central government and regions alienated from its direct control under provincial governors. The extent of the two categories varied at different times, the *khāṣṣa* reaching its greatest extent about 1071/1660-1 (see further K. Rohrborn, *Provinzen und Zentralgewalt Persiens im 16. und 17. Jahrhundert*, Berlin 1966, 113-14, 115, 118 ff.). In the *khāṣṣa*, the provincial *wazīr* had general oversight of all aspects of the administration, including the administration of justice, but probably played little part in its day to day administration (*ibid.*, 125). In some cases the provincial *wazīr* also appears to have exercised judicial functions, but this was probably exceptional (see *ibid.*, 112). Under Shāh ʿAbbās the chief *ʿurfī* judge in the capital was the *dīwānbegī*, who ranked among the great *amīrs*. Power of life and death were usually reserved to the *shāh* (*ibid*, 64-5), though in some cases he would delegate these powers to the provincial governor, especially if he was a member of the royal house.

The tradition of personal access to the ruler had remained strong and was, to some extent, a curb on the extortion and tyranny of officials, which in the absence of any clearly defined rules was widespread. On the occasion of a royal progress, the local people would bring their cases to the royal court for decision or redress. There were, however, attempts to institutionalise this. Ismāʿīl II (984-5/1576-8), shortly after his accession appointed Aḥmad Beg Ustadjlū as the officer in charge of the transmission of demands for redress (*parwānačī-i a ʿdjiza wa masākīn*) (Ḳāḍī Aḥmad, *Khulāṣat al-tawārīkh*, Berlin, Staatsbibliothek, ms. Or. 2202, f. 256 b, quoted by Rohrborn, 66; and see H. Busse, *Untersuchungen zum islamischen Kanzeleiwesen*, Cairo 1959, 71, on earlier uses of the term *parwānačī*). Shāh ʿAbbās in 1019/1610 issued an order that demands for redress should be referred to the *ṣadr-i mamālik* and the *dīwānbegī* (and not to him personally when he went out into the countryside).Chardin describes the crowds of plaintiffs who would assemble at the court (*Voyages*, v, 280).

Ismāʿīl II also set up, shortly after his accession, a *dīwān-i ʿadālat*. He appointed one of his cousins as *dīwānbegī-bāshī* and ordered him to sit twice a week with the *wazīr* of the supreme *dīwān* and two *ḳizilbāsh amīrs* to hear cases (Rohrborn, 67). There were three types of cases: *sharᶜiyyāt*, which were decided by the *ṣadr*, whose decree was sealed by the *dīwānbegī*; *ᶜurfiyyāt*, concerning *dīwān* taxation, which were referred to the *shāh*; and cases of tyranny, which were settled by the *dīwānbegī* with the cognisance of the *ṣadr* (Muḥammad-i Munadjdjim al-Yazdī, *Tārīkh-i ᶜAbbāsī*, B.L. ms., Add. 27, 241, 319a, ff. quoted by Rohrborn, *loc. cit.*). Shāh ᶜAbbās II (1052-77/1642-67), decided in 1064/1654 to hold the *dīwān-i ᶜadālat* in person three times a week. On the first day cases concerning military personnel and members of the court were heard, on the second the generality of the subjects presented their cases and on the third matters concerning *pīshkash* (obligatory "presents") were discussed (Muḥammad Ṭāhir Waḥīd-i Ḳazwīnī, *ᶜAbbās-nāma*, ed. Ibrāhīm Dihgān, 1329/1951, 175, 190, quoted by Rohrborn, *loc. cit.*).

Mīrzā Rafīᶜā describes the duties of the *dīwānbegī* in the *Dastūr al-mulūk*, a manual describing the administration of the late Ṣafawid empire (*Dastūr al-mulūk-i Mīrzā Rafīᶜā*, ed. Muḥammad Taḳī Dānishpazhūh, in *University of Tehran, Revue de la faculté des lettres et sciences humaines*, xv/5-6, 475-504, xvi/1-2, 62-93, xvi/3, 298-322, xvi/4, 416-40, xvi/5-6, 540-64. The text of this, although substantially the same as that of the *Tadhkirat al-mulūk* published by V. Minorsky, London 1943, is rather fuller. Dānishpazhūh has identified the author of the *Tadhkirat al-mulūk* as Mīrzā Rafīᶜā). He held a court four times a week in the *kashīk-khāna* of the ᶜĀlī Ḳapu in Iṣfahān to try four types of offence (*aḥdāth-i arbaᶜa*), namely murder, rape, assault (lit. breaking the teeth), and blinding; the *ṣadr-i khāṣṣa* and the *ṣadr-i ᶜāmma*, the chief officials of the religious institution (see further below) sat with him, the former on Saturdays and Sundays, the latter on Wednesdays and Thursdays. Their function would seem to have been primarily simply to give *sharᶜī* sanction to the decisions of the *dīwānbegī*. Cases of murder, in accordance with a *taᶜlīḳa* issued by the *ṣudūr* (pl. of *ṣadr*), were reported to the *shāh* by the *dīwānbegī* after the *ghassāl-bāshī* (the head of the corporation of the washers of the dead) had examined the corpse and decided the cause of death. Cases of rape, assault and blinding were investigated by the *dīwānbegī* without the *ṣudūr* (*ibid.*, xvi/1-2, 64-5, 87-8) but presumably they were associated with his verdict. The *dīwānbegī* also sat twice a week in his own house to hear *ᶜurfī* money claims (? *daᶜāwī-i ḥisābī-i ᶜurfī*). Minor claims were presumably dealt with by local officials, but anything exceeding 4-5 *tūmāns* was investigated by the *dīwānbegī*. Complaints of tyranny and extortion by *dīwānī* officials were heard by him. In the event of anyone complaining to the *dīwānbegī* of tyranny from a distance not further than 12 *farsakhs* (*ca.* 42 miles) from the capital, the two parties would be summoned to appear before him. In the case of complaints from further afield, a *muḥaṣṣil* would be sent, but Mīrzā Rafīᶜā does not give details of the procedure to be followed except to state that in a case of murder, the *dīwānbegī* would take 5 *tūmāns* caution money from the plaintiff and send one of the Adjirlū (whose particular function was to act as *muḥaṣṣils* in case of murder) to the place of the crime. Presumably they would investigate the case and if necessary bring the accused to Iṣfahān (*ibid.*, xvi/1-2, 87-8).

In financial cases there was apparently a conflict of jurisdiction between the *dīwānbegī* and the great *wazīrs*. Financial cases concerning the state and cases against the bureaucracy were sent by the *dīwānbegī* (if referred to him) to the great *wazīrs*; and cases against the *ḳurčīs*, *ghulāms*, other military personnel and employees of the royal workshops (*buyūtāt*) were referred to the elders (*rīsh-safīd*) of the relevant department. If, however, persons with a complaint against the provincial governors (the *beglarbegīs* or the *ḥukkām* and *sulṭāns*, i.e. governors of the smaller provinces) brought their case to the *dīwānbegī* instead of to the great *wazīrs*, he would investigate the matter and report to the *shāh* (*ibid.*).

In Iṣfahān, disputes between the craft guilds and the inhabitants were decided by the *kalāntar* [*q.v.*] (*ibid.*, xvi/4, 421-2), presumably on the basis of custom and equity. In the provinces there appears to have been at times a conflict of jurisdiction between the *kalāntar* and the *dārūgha* [*q.v.*]. The *mīrāb* of Iṣfahān, who was an important official, also exercised jurisdiction in disputes concerning the water of the Zāyanda-rūd. In cases affecting all the landowners and peasants, he would be ordered by the *shāh* to go, with the *wazīr* of the supreme *dīwān*. the *wazīr* of Iṣfahān, the *kalāntar* and *mustawfī* of Iṣfahān, to the districts watered by the river to decide the water rights of each district on the basis of the *dīwānī* registers and to settle disputes on the basis of common sense (*shuᶜūr*) and "according to what was customary and the practice of past years" (*ibid.*, xvi/4, 433).

In the provinces, the provincial governor was the chief *ᶜurfī* judge. Lesser cases were sometimes tried by the *dārūgha*. According to Chardin the *dārūgha* was appointed in the second half of the 11th/17th century by the *shāh*, not by the provincial governor (*Voyages*, v, 259). The provincial *wazīr*, who was appointed by the central government, or his deputies, also took part in these courts (see further, Rohrborn, 68-9).

Many districts in the provinces were alienated in the form of *tuyūls* and *suyūrghāls* from the direct control of the government and its officials. These grants frequently, though not invariably, gave the grantee immunity from the entry of government officials. In such cases the holder exercised local jurisdiction. For example, a diploma issued by Shāh Muḥammad Khudābanda, dated 989/1581, granting a *suyūrghāl* to a certain Sulṭān Ibrāhīm in Fārs, gives him immunity from a number of taxes and dues and states that "cases which occurred between the peasants (*raᶜāyā*) of the districts mentioned [i.e. those granted to him as a *suyūrghāl*] should be referred to him so that he might settle them in accordance with the law of the *sharīᶜa*" (H. Horst, *Ein Immunitätsdiplom Schah Muḥammad Ḫudābandäs vom Jahre 989/1581*, in *ZDMG*, cv/2 [1955]. 292). A powerful *tuyūldār*, even if rights of jurisdiction were not specifically granted to him, would in practice exercise such by usurpation. In cases of arbitration the local *ḳāḍī* was probably from time to time associated with the *tuyūldār* as he was with the provincial governor.

The *ṣadr* had already emerged as one of the chief officials of the religious institution under the Tīmūrids (see H. Roemer, *Staatsschreiben der Timuridenzeit*, Wiesbaden 1952, 143, and also G. Herrmann, *Zur Entstehung des ṣadr-Amtes*, in V. Harmann and P. Bachmann, eds., *Die islamische Welt zwischen Mittelalter und Neuzeit, Festschrift für H. R. Roemer*, Beirut-Wiesbaden 1979, 278-95). He acquired a new importance under the Ṣafawids and was the official through whom they controlled the religious institution. He was responsible for the appointment of *sharᶜī* officials, though the documents for the appointment of officials such as the provincial *ḳāḍī al-ḳuḍāt* continued to be issued in the name of the *shāh* (cf. the diploma issued by Ṭahmāsp for the *ḳāḍī al-ḳuḍāt* of Fārs, dated 25 Rabīᶜ II 955/3 June 1548 (H. Horst, *Zwei Erlasse Šāh*

Ṭahmāsps I in *ZDMG*, cx/2 [1961], 307-8) and the diplomas for the *aḳḍā al-ḳuḍāt* of Gīlān Biyāpīsh dated Dhu 'l-Ḥidjdja 1035/1625 and for the *ḳāḍī 'l-ḳuḍāt* of Gīlān, dated Dhu 'l-Ḥidjdja 1948/1639, issued by Shāh ᶜAbbās, in *Yak ṣad wa pandjāh sanad-i tārīkhī az Djalāʾiriyān tā Pahlawī*, ed. Djahāngīr Ḳāʾim Maḳāmī, Tehran 1348/1969-70, 26-7, 46-7). Once appointed, the *ḳāḍī al-ḳuḍāt* was empowered, in some cases at least, to appoint and dismiss *ḳāḍīs* in the region under him (cf. the diploma for the *ḳāḍī 'l-ḳuḍāt* of Gīlān quoted above). The main function of the *ṣadr* at the beginning of the Ṣafawid period was to impose doctrinal uniformity. Once this had been established, the importance of his office declined. The first holder of the office of *ṣadr* in the Ṣafawid state was the *ḳāḍī* Shams al-Dīn Lāhidjī (Gīlānī), who was appointed in 907/1501. The second holder, Muḥammad Kāshānī, appointed in 909/1503-4, was also a *ḳāḍī*. Under Shāh ᶜAbbās II, the office was left vacant for eighteen months and by the end of the Ṣafawid period the main function of the *ṣadr* was the supervision of certain classes of *awḳāf*. In the reign of Shāh Sulṭān Ḥusayn (1105-35/1694-1722), his importance further declined with the rise of the *mullā-bāshī*. Under the Afshārs, his office disappeared.

As in the case of other offices, the jurisdiction of the *ṣadr* varied at different times. Djalāl al-Dīn Astarābādī, who held the office of *ṣadr* from 920/1514 to 931/1524-5, apparently supervised *sharᶜī* affairs throughout the empire. From time to time there were joint appointments to the office, the two *ṣadrs* sometimes holding authority jointly throughout the empire and sometimes their jurisdiction being divided on a territorial basis. In 1077/1667 Shāh Sulaymān (1077-1105/1667-1694) appointed a *ṣadr-i khāṣṣa* and a *ṣadr-i ᶜāmma* (see R. M. Savory. *The principal offices of the Ṣafawid state during the reign of Ṭahmāsp I (930-84/1524-76)*, in *BSOAS*, xxiv/l [1961], 79-80 and Lambton, *Quis custodiet custodes*, in *SI*, vi, 134 ff.). Practice was far from uniform. According to Mīrzā Rafīᶜā, the office of *ṣadr-i khāṣṣa* and *ṣadr-i ᶜāmma* (also known as *ṣadr-i mamālik*) had sometimes been entrusted to one person (*op. cit.*, xvi/1-2, 66). The *ṣadr* was also in charge of *awḳāf* and the grant of *suyūrghāls* to the religious classes. *Tawfīḍī awḳāf*, i.e. *awḳāf* constituted by the Ṣafawid rulers, proliferated during the Ṣafawid period. The *ṣadr*'s supervision of these gave him potentially great influence. Mīrzā Rafīᶜā states that the *ṣadr* was not paid a salary (except in the case of the *ṣadr* Mīrzā Abū Ṭālib, who received an allowance of 1,360 *tūmāns*) but received one-tenth or one-twentieth of the value of *suyūrghāls* and something by way of *ḥaḳḳ al-tawliya* and *ḥaḳḳ al-naẓāra* from *awḳāf*, according to the conditions laid down by the *wāḳif* (xvi/1-2, 65-6). It was apparently only in the case of *tawfīḍī awḳāf* that the *ṣadr* had the right to appoint officials to the *awḳāf*. Neither the *ṣadr* nor any other *sharᶜī* official had any right of interference in the case of *sharᶜī awḳāf* (*ibid.*, xvi/1-2, 66). The precise delimitation between the *ṣadr-i khāṣṣa* and the *ṣadr-i ᶜāmma* in the matter of the supervision of *awḳāf* is not clear. Mīrzā Rafīᶜā states that "The intention in the delegation of these two great offices [that of the *ṣadr-i khāṣṣa* and that of the *ṣadr-i ᶜāmma*] was to order the affairs of all the *mawḳūfāt* of the districts of Iṣfahān, which concerned them severally, and the appointment and designation of *sharᶜī* officials (*ḥukkām-i sharᶜ*) and overseers (*mubāshirān*) of the *mawḳūfāt-i tawfīḍī* (*mawḳūfāt wa tafwīḍī* being probably a scribal error for this) and the leadership (*rīsh-safīdī*) of all the *sādāt*, *ᶜulamāʾ*, *mudarrisān*, *ḳāḍīs*, *shaykh al-islāmān*, deputy *ṣadrs*, *mutawallīs* and *nāẓirs* of the *mawḳūfāt*, prayer leaders, *khaṭībs*, *muᶜadhdhins*, *ḥuffāẓ*, *muᶜarrifān*, washers of the dead and grave-diggers (the last two on the recommendation of the *ghassāl-bāshī*), their dismissal and the payment of their pensions (*waẓīfa*) from the *mawḳūfāt*" (xvi/1-2, 64-5). *Sharᶜī* affairs in Iṣfahān and the surrounding district (which was administered by the Fayḍ Āthār department) came under the *ṣadr-i khāṣṣa* to the exclusion of the *ṣadr-i ᶜāmma* (*ibid.*, xvi/1-2, 65). The *ṣudūr*, although their importance declined in the latter part of the Ṣafawid period, nevertheless retained their pre-eminence over other officials of the religious hierarchy, as witnessed by their association with the *dīwānbegī* (see above). Mīrzā Rafīᶜā makes this point by stating that other *sharᶜī* officials had no part in the examination of the four offences known as *aḥdāth-i arbaᶜa*. The two *ṣadrs* also decided cases concerning title deeds (*ḳabāladjāt*) and *sharᶜī* deeds (*ibid.*).

In some periods, the *ṣadr-i khāṣṣa*, according to Mīrzā Rafīᶜā, also held the office of *ḳāḍī ᶜaskar* (xvi/1-2, 66). Unfortunately, he does not state which of the *ṣudūr* held this office. That the *ṣadr* should also be *ḳāḍī ᶜaskar* would seem to be a natural consequence of his succeeding the *ḳāḍī al-ḳuḍāṭ*, who also sometimes held the office of *ḳāḍī ᶜaskar*, as the most important religious official of the state. However, under Shāh Ismāᶜīl and at the beginning of the reign of Ṭahmāsp, the *ḳāḍī ᶜaskar* of Tabrīz (or Ādharbāydjān), who also had charge of the *awḳāf* of Tabrīz, was a powerful figure (see Rohrborn, 127-8). Before *ṣudūr* were appointed in Iṣfahān, the *ḳāḍī ᶜaskar* used to sit in the *kashīk-khāna* of the *dīwānbegī* and give decisions in *sharᶜī* cases for the military, but when it was laid down that the *dīwānbegī* should hear *sharᶜī* cases (unfortunately Mīrzā Rafīᶜā does not state when this was) the *ḳāḍī ᶜaskar* ceased to come to the *kashīk-khāna*; and his functions came to be confined to validating with his seal the payment orders made in favour of the army. He had no salary but received a commission of 1% from the military on their pay (*Dastūr al-mulūk*, xvi/1-2, 70).

Although the importance of the office of *ḳāḍī* was reduced by the emergence of the *ṣadr*, the *ḳāḍīs* continued to be influential and in the smaller provincial cities, where they had no rival in the person of the *ṣadr* or the *shaykh al-islām*, they probably continued to play an important part in local affairs. So far as the *shaykh al-islām* was concerned, there appears to have been some conflict of jurisdiction with the *ḳāḍī* in Iṣfahān if not elsewhere. According to Mīrzā Rafīᶜā, the *shaykh al-islām* of Iṣfahān heard the cases of the people in his house every day except Friday and enjoined the good and forbade evil. Divorce according to the *sharīᶜa* was given in his presence, and for the most part the custody of the property of orphans and those who were absent was his responsibility, though on some occasions these matters were referred to the *ḳāḍīs*. The *shaykh al-islām* also sealed documents and title deeds, which were not confined to transactions between Muslims but might also be documents exchanged between non-Muslims. Chardin mentions that the *shaykh al-islām* of Iṣfahān signed and witnessed a document concerning a financial transaction between him and some Dutch merchants in respect of a sum of money which the *shāh* owed him (*Sir John Chardin's travels in Persia*, London 1927 121-2). The *shaykh al-islām* received annually 200 Tabrīzī *tūmāns* as a pension (*waẓīfa*) from the public treasury (*Dastūr al-mulūk*, xvi/1-2, 69).

Under the early Ḳādjārs, *ᶜurfī* jurisdiction was administered by the *shāh*, the provincial governors and other local officials. There was little or no differentiation of function: matters concerning security, law and taxation were, for the most part, referred to the same officials. The lowest court was that of the village headman, who was empowered to inflict slight punishments and to impose small fines. More serious crimes were referred to the district collector (*ḍābiṭ*) and those more serious still, either because of the nature of the crime or the rank of the persons concerned, to the governor of the province. The right to pronounce the death sentence was seldom delegated by the *s̲h̲āh* except sometimes to the governors of the royal house or when the country was in rebellion.

The *ʿurfī* courts were usually held in public. This, in Sir John Malcolm's opinion, operated "as a salutary check on their proceedings". "These courts", he continues, "are sometimes very tumultuous though the judge is aided by a host of inferior officers, whose duty is to preserve order. The women who attend these courts are often the most vociferous: the servants of the magistrates are not permitted to silence them with those blows, which in the case of disturbance they liberally inflict upon the men" (*History of Persia*, London 1829, 2 vols., ii, 319). According to Malcom, *ʿurfī* officials referred to the *s̲h̲arʿī* courts all cases which for personal or political reasons they wished to be decided by their authority. In criminal cases the chief judge of the *s̲h̲arʿī* courts was associated with the *ʿurfī* officials and pronounced sentences according to the decrees of the *s̲h̲arīʿa* (*ibid.*, 320). Curzon, writing towards the end of the century aptly describes the lack of a clear dividing line between the two jurisdictions. He states, "The functions and the prerogative of the co-ordinate benches vary at different epochs, and appear to be a matter of accident or choice, rather than of necessity; and at the present time, though criminal cases of difficulty may be submitted to the ecclesiastical court, yet it is with civil matters that they are chiefly concerned. Questions of heresy or sacrilege are naturally referred to them; they also take cognisance of adultery and divorce; and intoxication as an offence, not against the common law ... but against the Koran, falls within the scope of their judgment" (*Persia and the Persian question*, London 1892, 2 vols., i, 453). Prior to the attempts at judicial reform in the reign of Nāṣir al-Dīn S̲h̲āh (1848-96), it would seem that governors and others continued to hear cases much after the fashion of the earlier *maẓālim* courts. The decisions given by them were entirely arbitrary: there were no formal rules of procedure. Torture and ill-treatment of offenders was common, and in the middle of the century became the subject of acrimonious exchanges between Nāṣir al-Ḍīn and the British and Russian missions. In 1844 a decree was issued forbidding torture. Its effect, however, was almost negligible.

The *s̲h̲ayk̲h̲ al-islām*, whose position had increased in importance since the Ṣafawid period, was the supreme judge of the *s̲h̲arʿī* courts. A *s̲h̲ayk̲h̲ al-islām* was appointed by the *s̲h̲āh* in the capital and the major provincial cities and received a salary. To this extent his position was equivocal, but in his appointment the desire and wishes of the local inhabitants, according to Malcolm, were almost invariably consulted. In the smaller towns there was only a *ḳāḍī* and in the villages seldom more than a *mullā*. The latter was competent only to perform marriage and funeral ceremonies, to draw up common deeds and to decide plain and obvious cases; anything more complicated was referred to the *ḳāḍī* in the neighbouring town and often by him to the *s̲h̲ayk̲h̲ al-islām* in the provincial capital (Malcolm, ii, 316). A *muftī* was sometimes associated with the *s̲h̲arʿī* courts. His functions, very different from those of the *muftī* in the Ottoman empire, were simply to prepare an exposition of the case before the court and to aid it with advice. To do this, however, he had to be a man of learning and his opinion often influenced the judgment (*ibid.*, 317). Although the *s̲h̲āh* nominated the *s̲h̲ayk̲h̲ al-islām*, he was no more able than preceding rulers to alter the law administered in the *s̲h̲arʿī* courts. This gave the *s̲h̲ayk̲h̲ al-islām* and the *s̲h̲arʿī* courts a certain independence, which was further strengthened by the influence of the *mud̲j̲tahids*, to whose superior knowledge cases were constantly referred by the *s̲h̲arʿī* judges. The sentence of a *mud̲j̲tahid* was irrevocable, except by that of a *mud̲j̲tahid* of greater learning and sanctity (*ibid.*, 315).

Many cases, including contracts, titles to landed property, disputed wills, intestate succession, disputed land boundaries, disputes over the ownership of landed property, the recovery of debts, and bankruptcies were decided by arbitration. A *mad̲j̲lis* or informal council of leading persons would be convoked, usually in the house of a *mullā* or notable. Both sides would state their case; the documents would be produced and inspected, and a decision, almost always in the nature of a compromise, would be given and, if reasonably fair, accepted. The verdict would then be signed and registered by the *s̲h̲ayk̲h̲ al-islām* or the *imām d̲j̲umʿa* (Curzon, *op. cit.*, i, 455-6).

The fact that there was no land registration department—title deeds and documents were not emended or abrogated and often remained in the hands of their original holders or their heirs—gave rise to much litigation, particularly over land claims (as G̲h̲āzān K̲h̲ān had found many centuries earlier, see above). In the case of disputed tenure, the general tendency was to have recourse to the local religious officials or, if one or both of the parties to the dispute were influential, to the leading religious figures in the provincial capital or Tehran for documents attesting their ownership. Land grants and *tuyūls*, which were the subject of a *farmān* or *raḳam*, were in theory registered in the royal archives and sometimes in the provincial record offices; but these records were not open to public inspection and irregularities in registration were in any case not uncommon (cf. Lambton, *The case of Ḥādjdjī Nūr al-Dīn 1823-47*, in *BSOAS*, xxx/1 [1967], 54-72). Bonds concerning financial transactions, loans to the government and its officials and transactions between individuals were commonly sealed and witnessed by religious dignitaries. Transactions with government officials were sometimes registered in the *dīwān-k̲h̲āna*, but neither practice safeguarded those by whom the documents were concluded from litigation (cf. eadem, *The case of Ḥādjdjī ʿAbd al-Karīm*, in *Iran and Islam*, ed. C. E. Bosworth, Edinburgh 1971, 331-60).

Contact with Europe had been joined in the 16th, 17th and 18th centuries, mainly in the commercial field. This had resulted in the grant of immunities to European merchants by the *s̲h̲āhs*. In the 19th century this contact took on a new form and was dominated by the strategic and political interests of the great powers. Under the commercial treaty concluded at the same time as the Treaty of Turkomānčāy (1828) extra-territorial privileges were granted to Russian subjects, which were later also claimed by other foreign states for their nationals under most favoured nation treatment [see further IMTIYĀZĀT. iii. Persia]. This treaty regulated the position of foreign merchants. Disputes to which they were a party and claims by them were removed from the control of the *s̲h̲arʿī* courts. In the provinces they were dealt with by an official known as the *kārgud̲h̲ār* and in the capital by the *dīwān-k̲h̲āna* and later by the Ministry of Foreign

Affairs. Disputes between local *dhimmīs* and Muslims were still heard in the *sharᶜī* courts, but from about the middle of the century attempts were made to transfer such cases to the *dīwān*. In 1851 when Nāṣir al-Dīn was in Iṣfahān he laid down that inheritance disputes between an Armenian, Jewish or Zoroastrian convert to Islam and an adherent of the community to which he had previously belonged were not to be referred to the *sharᶜī* or *ᶜurfī* judges in the province but that the two parties were to be sent to the capital and the matter investigated by the *dīwān-khāna* (*Rūznāma-yi waḳāyiᶜ-i ittifāḳiyya*, 3 Ṣafar 1268/1851). On the other hand, an order (*taᶜlīḳa*) was issued by the *ṣadr-i aᶜẓam* in Dhu 'l-Ḥidjdja 1270/1854 stating that any dispute between a Jew, Christian or Zoroastrian on the one hand and an *Ithnā ᶜAsharī* on the other over partnerships in trade or land should go before the Imām Djumᶜa of Iṣfahān and be settled according to the *sharīᶜa* (*ibid.*, Dhu 'l-Ḥidjdja 1270/1854). In 1863 new procedures to be followed by the *dīwān-i ᶜadliyya* in mixed cases were laid down (see *Rūznāma-i dawlat-i ᶜāliyya-i Īrān*, 17 Radjab 1279/1863).

From about the middle of the 19th century, there were various attempts by Nāṣir al-Dīn and some of his ministers to centralise the administration of justice through the *dīwān-khāna* and to extend the field of *ᶜurfī* jurisdiction, while at the same time regulating its procedure. The first was resisted by the provincial governors and the second by the *ᶜulamāʾ*. In 1854 an order was published in the official gazette stating that if anyone refused to attend the *dīwān-khāna* when summoned by the authorities, one-fifth of the claim against him, whether he was of high or low estate, a Ḳādjār prince or not, would be confiscated and he would be forced to appear (*Rūznāma-yi waḳāyiᶜ-i ittifāḳiyya*, 4 Djumādī I 1270/1854). In 1855 an attempt was made to abolish the legal force of contradictory juridical opinions. This, like the order concerning the inheritance disputes of converts to Islam, was also an encroachment on the authority of the *sharᶜī* courts.

In the same year, Mīrzā Āḳā Khān Nūrī, who had succeeded Mīrzā Taḳī Khān Amīr Kabīr as *ṣadr-i aᶜẓam* in 1851, apparently submitted a plan to the *shāh* for the promulgation of a body of laws drawn from various European codes, having as their basis the security of life, property and honour of the subject as in the Ottoman *Khaṭṭ-i sherīf-i Gülkhāna* (Great Britain. Public Record Office. F.O. 60: 201, Taylour Thomson to Clarendon, no. 23, Tehran, 18 February 1855). Nothing came of this and it was not until 1858 that further steps were taken towards legal reforms. A council of ministers was set up and regulations for the procedure of the *dīwān-khāna-yi ᶜadliyya-yi aᶜẓam*, or ministry of justice, were laid down (see further ḤUKŪMA. ii. Persia, and DUSTŪR. iv. ĪRĀN). It was further announced towards the end of the year that a department of justice (*dīwān-khāna-yi ᶜadliyya*) would be set up in each province under a *dīwānbegī*. Its decrees, if they concerned *sharᶜī* matters, were to be referred to a *mudjtahid*, and if they concerned *ᶜurfī* matters to the provincial governor. *Sharᶜı* documents were to be registered with the *dīwānbegī* (*Rūznāma-yi waḳāyiᶜ-i ittifāḳiyya*, 11 Rabīᶜ II 1275/1858). This attempt to assert the authority of the central *dīwān* over the provincial courts and of the *dīwānbegī* over *sharᶜī* as well as *ᶜurfī* courts was abortive. In the face of the opposition from both the *ᶜulamāʾ* and the provincial officials the decree was suspended. Whether it was because of the failure of these various measures designed to achieve some measure of legal reform or not, in 1860 there was a revival of the *maẓālim* court. An announcement was made on 28 Muḥarram 1277/1860 that the *shāh* would hold a *maẓālim* court every Sunday (*Rūznāma-yi waḳāyiᶜ-i ittifāḳiyya*, 28 Muḥarram 1277/1860). A rescript (*dast-khaṭṭ*) was issued for the procedure to be followed. The *īshīkāḳāsī-bāshī* and the *nasaḳčī-bāshī* and their deputies were to be on duty. The first minister and the deputy first minister were to be present and the latter was to record the answers given to the petitions. Petitioners were to be presented by the *nasaḳčī-bāshī* and the *ādjūdān-bāshī*. Petitioners were not to assemble near the guardhouse; in Tehran they were to gather in the Maydān or the Kūča-i Arg and in Shimrān, or elsewhere in summer quarters, in the open country. They were to come forward one by one or two by two. The Ḳarāwul regiment, the *farrāsh-i khalwatān* and the *pīshkhidmatān* were all to be on duty. If the petitioners made a commotion when they assembled they were to be punished. Only petitions for the redress of grievances would be received: petitions for an increase of pay, pensions or *tuyūl*s would not be heard. Petitions from the provinces could be submitted in writing through the official provincial post (*čappār*). These instructions suggest that Nāṣir al-Dīn feared both assassination and rioting by the populace; they also recall Niẓām al-Mulk's fears of commotion by petitioners at the *maẓālim* court—though apparently the Ṣafawids had no such fears (see above).

In 1863 there was an attempt to revive the measures of 1858. Mīrzā Ḥusayn Khān Mushīr al-Dawla, who had spent twelve years in Turkey as the Persian representative there, submitted draft regulations for the reorganisation of the Ministry of Justice for the *shāh*'s approval. The purpose of these regulations was to centralise the administration of justice and to limit the authority of the provincial governors. These measures brought Mīrzā Ḥusayn Khān into conflict with both the *ᶜulamāʾ* and the provincial authorities, and the proposal to set up departments of justice in the provinces under the Ministry of Justice was again shelved (*Rūznāma-yi dawlat-i ᶜāliyya-yi Īrān*, 17 Radjab 1279/1863, and Lambton, *The Persian ᶜulamā and constitutional reform*, in *Le Shiᶜisme imamite*, ed. T. Fahd, Paris 1970, 259-60. See also F. Ādamiyyat, *Fikr-i āzādī*, Tehran 1961, 72 ff.). In 1871 Mīrzā Ḥusayn Khān Mushīr al-Dawla, who had become *ṣadr-i aᶜẓam*, issued a decree in the *shāh*'s name, setting up six courts or departments of the ministry of justice and regulations for their operation. The settlement of disputes outside the court was, however, permitted, provided both parties consented to this. The decrees of the *sharᶜī* courts were to be registered and enforced by the Ministry of Justice. In the same year torture was again forbidden (see further Shaul Bakhash, *Iran: monarchy, bureaucracy and reform under the Qajars, 1858-1896*, London 1978, 83 ff.). Mīrzā Ḥusayn Khān's reforms were also abortive. On 22 May 1888, as a result of promptings by Drummond Wolff, the British minister, Nāṣir al-Dīn issued a decree giving security of life and property to all Persian subjects unless publicly condemned by a competent tribunal. The effect of this on the lives of the people was, however, negligible. One last attempt at legal reform was made after the cancellation of the Tobacco Concession in 1891, when Amīn al-Dawla urged upon the *shāh* the establishment of regular tribunals. Muḥsin Khān Mushīr al-Dawla, the minister of justice and commerce, was accordingly ordered to set up a so-called *ᶜadālat-khāna*. This plan also proved abortive (Amīn al-Dawla, *Khāṭirāt-i Mīrzā ᶜAlī Khān Amīn al-Dawla*, ed. H. Farmānfarmāniān, Tehran 1962, 164 ff.).

By the end of the century there had thus been little

change in the administration of justice. The functions of the minister were theoretically to take general note of the law throughout the country and to enforce the execution of judgments delivered by the *ʿulamāʾ*. In practice his power, like that of other ministers, was personal: at times his influence extended to the provinces, at others it barely ran even in the capital. A strong minister had his agents in the provinces, but he seldom had sufficient influence to invest them with real authority. The execution of sentences rested with officials called *farrās͟hhā* (sing. *farrās͟h*). The *farrās͟h-bās͟hī* of the capital, who was their head, was an important official and a servant of the *s͟hāh*. In the provinces the *farrās͟h-bās͟hī* was nominated by the governor or by the *farrās͟h-bās͟hī* of the capital. The religious law continued to take cognisance of many civil matters such as those concerning personal law, transfers of property, and certain criminal offences. The *ʿulamāʾ*, as formerly, depended for the execution of their decisions upon the civil authorities. All judgments, whether of the *ʿulamāʾ* or the *ʿurfī* officials, were executed by the *farrās͟hhā* (cf. F.O. 60: 566). Appendix I by Lt. Col. Picot to Sir M. Durand, in *Sir M. Durand's memo. on the situation in Persia*, Tehran, 27 September 1895 (conf. print 6704). See also *Rūznāma-yi wakāyiʿ-i ittifākiyya*, no. 46, 24 Ṣafar 1268/1851).

In the early years of the 20th century, at the suggestion of a Belgian legal adviser a codification of the law was considered, together with a reorganisation of the courts dealing with mixed cases—the need for legal reform was by this time acutely felt by foreign merchants, whose legal claims were referred in the capital to the *madjlis-i muḥākamāt*, a tribunal of the Ministry of Foreign Affairs, and in the provinces to the court of the *kārgudhār*, who frequently bought his office as a commercial speculation from the Ministry of Foreign Affairs—and the establishment of courts of first instance and appellate tribunals, which would decide mixed cases by the application of a simple commercial code based on that existing in Turkey. The plan was frustrated by the *ʿulamāʾ*, who maintained that the temporal authority was not competent to legislate in such matters and that any such legislation must be in accordance with the *s͟harīʿa*. Russia also opposed the proposal as being contrary to the Treaty of Turkomānčāy (F.O. 416: 26. no. 29, Harding to Grey, London, 23 December 1905).

After the death of Nāṣir al-Dīn S͟hāh in 1896, the movement for liberal reform, which had been gathering support during the second half of the 19th century, became more articulate. In 1903 various groups agreed to work for the establishment of a code of laws. In May 1905 an open letter was sent to the *ṣadr-i aʿẓam* demanding, *inter alia*, a code of justice and the establishment of a Ministry of Justice. In January 1906, after a large number of people had taken asylum (*bast*) in the shrine of S͟hāh ʿAbd al-ʿAẓīm outside Tehran, Muẓaffar al-Dīn, who had succeeded his father Nāṣir al-Dīn, gave orders for the establishment of a Ministry of Justice (*ʿadālat-k͟hāna-yi dawlatī*) for the purpose of executing the decrees of the *s͟harīʿa* throughout Persia so that all the subjects of the country should be equal before the law. A code (*kitābča*) in accordance with the *s͟harīʿa* was to be drawn up and put into operation throughout the country. In fact, no steps were taken to implement the promises given to the *bastī*s. A second *bast* by the religious leaders took place in Ḳumm, while merchants and members of the craft guilds of Tehran and others took refuge in the British Legation. They demanded the dismissal of the *ṣadr-i aʿẓam*, the promulgation of a code of laws and the recall of the religious leaders from Ḳumm. The *s͟hāh* yielded to their demands and on 5 August 1906 issued a rescript setting up a National Consultative Assembly. The Fundamental Law was signed on 30 December 1906 and the Supplementary Fundamental Law was ratified by Muḥammad S͟hāh on 7 October 1907 [see DUSTŪR. iv. Īrān]. Article 2 of the latter states that at no time must any legal enactment of the National Consultative Assembly (*madjlis-i s͟hawrā-yi millī*) be at variance with the sacred principles of Islam or the laws established by the prophet Muḥammad. Article 2 also provides for the setting up of a committee composed of not less than five *mudjtahid*s and pious *fukahāʾ*, who would consider all matters proposed in the *madjlis* and reject wholly or in part any proposal at variance with the sacred laws of Islam. Article 27 divides the powers of the realm into three categories, legislative, judicial and executive. It states that the judicial power belongs exclusively to the *s͟harʿī* tribunals in matters pertaining to the *s͟harīʿa* (*s͟harʿiyyāt*) and to the civil tribunals (*maḥākim-i ʿadliyya*) in matters pertaining to *ʿurf* (*ʿurfiyyāt*). Article 28 states that the three powers shall always be separate and distinct from one another, and Articles 81 and 82 affirm the irremovability and independence of the judges. (These articles were emended in the reign of Muḥammad Riḍā S͟hāh.) Article 71 states that the Supreme Ministry of Justice (*dīwān-i ʿadālat-i ʿuẓmā*) and the judicial courts are the places officially destined for the redress of public grievances, while judgment in *s͟harʿī* matters is vested in just *mudjtahid*s possessed of the necessary qualifications, thus implying that the jurisdiction of the judicial courts was general and that only those matters which were judged to pertain to the *s͟harīʿa* were to be referred to *s͟harʿī* judges. The text is, however, ambiguous, perhaps intentionally.

The committee of *mudjtahid*s laid down in Article 2 of the Supplementary Fundamental Law was set up by the second *madjlis* in 1911 but later fell into desuetude. The result of its work was the provisional law known as the *ḳānūn-i muwakkatī-yi tas͟hkīlāt wa uṣūl muḥākamāt* of 1329 (the provisional law for the regulations of judicial procedure of 1911). This law, in spite of its provisional nature, was the basis on which the judicial reforms carried out after the grant of the constitution rested. Under its authority a number of provisional laws were passed, a procedure which enabled the government to take "experimental" action and which avoided the question of whether the *madjlis* was contravening Article 2 of the Supplementary Fundamental Laws or not. Article 45 of the provisional law of 1911 defines *s͟harʿī* matters as "matters which are established in accordance with the law of the illustrious *s͟harʿ* of Islam". The lack of any more precise definition of *s͟harʿī* and *ʿurfī* matters illustrates the difficulty which the legislators experienced in making a separation between the two systems. The law further divides cases into those concerning *s͟harʿī* matters, *ʿurfī* matters and "joint" cases, i.e. cases which concerned both *s͟harʿī* and *ʿurfī* matters. The last could only be referred to the *ʿadliyya* (the Ministry of Justice) with the consent of both parties. *S͟harʿī* cases are defined *inter alia* as cases arising from ignorance of a *s͟harʿī* judgment or *s͟harʿī* matters, cases concerning marriage and divorce, debt, inheritance, *awḳāf* and the appointment of *mutawallī*s and legal guardians. The *s͟harʿī* courts (*maḥāẓir*, sing. *maḥẓar*) were presided over by a *mudjtahid* possessing the necessary qualifications (*djāmiʿ al-s͟harāʾiṭ*) and two deputies (*karīb al-idjtihād*). The effect of the provisional law, although it was perhaps intended to limit the competence of the *s͟harʿī* courts, was, in fact, to lead to the referral of most cases to the *s͟harʿī* courts. There were various reasons for this: a lack of trained personnel to administer a secular law, lack of familiarity on the part of the public with the lengthy formalities involved by the new procedures, the fact that in the provinces cases were for the most part decided by the governors on an *ad hoc* basis and the existence of a separate court in the Ministry of Foreign Affairs with branches in the provinces known as *kārgudhārīhā* for cases involving foreign subjects. For these and other reasons, reform proceeded slowly. Courts of first instance and courts of appeal, special commercial and military tribunals and a court of cassation (*dīwān-i tamyīz*) were, however, set up.

Under Riḍā Shāh (1925-42) the government embarked upon an ambitious programme of legal reform, and with the increasing power of the central government, the tendency to ride roughshod over opposition on the part of the religious classes grew. Various parts of the civil code were promulgated between 1925 and 1935, thereby increasingly limiting the competence of the *sharʿī* courts. Negotiations were begun for the abolition of the capitulations, which finally became effective from 10 May 1928, the provincial tribunals presided over by the *kārgudhārs* having already been dissolved by the law of 12 Shahrīvar 1306/3 September 1927 [see IMTIYĀZĀT, iii, Persia]. In 1305/1926-7 the Ministry of Justice was empowered to put into operation a reformed version of the provisional law of 1911, and as a result a number of new provisional laws were passed. The *ʿadliyya* was reorganised and the list of matters which were to be referred to the *sharʿī* courts was revised. By the law for the regulations of judicial procedure of 7 Day 1307/1928-9, the existence of *sharʿī* courts was reaffirmed, but their competence was limited broadly to cases referring to marriage and divorce, matters of succession and guardianship and the administration of wills and *awḳāf*. In the following year, by the law of Khurdād 1308/1929 their competence was further reduced, while the law of 10 Ādhar 1310/1930 abrogated earlier laws concerning *sharʿī* courts and recognised only those courts which were presided over by a *mudjtahid* possessing the necessary qualifications. Finally, in 1937 new Regulations for judicial procedure (*āʾīn-i dādrasī-yi madanī*) in 789 articles were presented to the *madjlis*. They were finally passed on 25 Shahrīvar 1318/1939 and replaced the earlier provisional laws.

In these various ways, which would in mediaeval terminology have been described as *ḥiyal*, an open clash between the modernists and the authorities of the religious law was avoided and a civil law was codified and brought into operation. The sections on marriage, divorce, inheritance, *awḳāf*, irrigation and dead lands were simply a codified version of *sharʿī* law already in operation with minor changes. In matters of divorce, the position was materially altered by the Family Protection Act of 1967. A penal code, based mainly on French law but also influenced by Swiss and Belgian law, was promulgated in 1928 and replaced by a new code in 1939. A provisional law for commercial courts was set up under the provisional law of 1911 and a commercial code promulgated in 1932.

Throughout the period under review down to the early 20th century *sharʿī* and *ʿurfī* jurisdictions continued side by side. The former, administered by the *ḳāḍī* and the *sharʿī* judges, covered in theory all aspects of the believer's life, was a written law, and subject to known procedures. In theory it was supreme and unchallenged, but in practice it was limited in the scope of its operation. The latter, administered by the ruler and his deputies, was unwritten, its judgments were executed by the strong hand of power and it was in practice dominant. At best it was regulated by custom and at worst wholly arbitrary and guided by the whim of the ruler. The distinction between the two jurisdictions was not, and could not be, clearly drawn since the *sharīʿa* could, in theory, have no rival. The operation of the two jurisdictions was personal: now the one, now the other, extended the field of its operation. The relationship between them was uncertain and uneasy. The power of execution in all cases rested with the *ʿurfī* officials, but so far as the *sharʿī* officials were associated with the *ʿurfī* courts, a quasi-*sharʿī* sanction was given to their proceedings.

Bibliography: Sections on *ḳaḍāʾ* are to be found in all major works on *fiḳh*, both Sunnī and Shīʿī. Material on the general principles of taking up government office is also to be found in the sections on *al-amr wa 'l-nahy* and *al-makāsib* and *al-buyūʿ*. Information on the exercise of the office of *ḳāḍī* by individuals is to be found in biographical dictionaries and histories. For the modern period, see Ahmad-Daftary, *La suppression des capitulations en Perse*, Paris 1930; idem, *Āʾīn-i dādrasī-yi madanī wa bāzargānī*, Tehran 2 vols., i, 1324/1956-7, ii, 1334/1966-7; Muṣṭafā ʿAdl Manṣūr al-Salṭana, *Ḥuḳūḳ-i madanī*[2], Tehran 1308/1929; ʿAlī Pāshā Ṣāliḥ, *Ḳuwwa-yi muḳannana wa ḳuwwa-yi ḳaḍāʾiyya*, Tehran 1343/1964-5, Muḥammad Djaʿfar Langarūdī, *Dānishnāma-yi ḥuḳūḳ*, 3 vols., Tehran 1343-52/1964-74; D. Hinchcliffe, *The Iranian family protection act*, in *The international and comparative law quarterly* (April 1968), 516-21; E. Gräf, *Der Brauch (urf/ada) nach islamischen Recht*, in K. Tauchmann, ed., *Festschrift für H. Petri*, Vienna 1973, 122-44.

(A. K. S. LAMBTON)

4. THE ARAB LANDS AND ISRAEL IN THE MODERN PERIOD

i. Egypt

In the period of direct Ottoman rule in Egypt, the *Sharīʿa* courts had a very wide jurisdiction, which comprised civil law, including personal status and *waḳf*, and also criminal and administrative matters. Their personal jurisdiction applied also to disputes between non-Muslims and Muslims, between non-Muslims of different denominations, and even between non-Muslims of the same denomination who agreed to litigate before a *Sharīʿa* court.

Muḥammad ʿAlī established many judicial authorities which took away important powers from the *Sharīʿa* courts: *madjlis aḳlām al-daʿwā* and *madjlis daʿāwā al-balad*, which dealt with claims for specific amounts and with agricultural matters; and *al-madjālis al-markaziyya*, which heard appeals against decisions of the latter courts and had original jurisdiction in claims for greater amounts. The courts of first instance (*al-madjālis al-ibtidāʾiyya*) in the provincial capitals heard criminal matters and civil claims up to substantial amounts. Their judgments were appealable to the courts of appeal (*madjālis al-istiʾnāf*). The highest appellate court was the *madjlis al-aḥkām*, which sat in Cairo. Other judicial authorities were *madjlis al-tidjāra* (a commercial court) and *madjlis mashyakhat al-balad*. Jurisdiction in criminal cases and the "investigation of complaints" in the old sense were exercised by the chief administrative office, *al-dīwān al-khidīwī*, headed by the *Kikhya* as representative of the Pasha; the chief of police (*ḍābiṭ*) and the *muḥtasib* also had considerable powers of punishment.

A major reform in the judicial system was carried

out in the days of Ismāʿīl Pas̲h̲a. The *Ḥasbiyya* Courts Law of 1873 was a first, moderate step in restricting the powers of the *S̲h̲arīʿa* courts. The *ḥasbiyya* courts (reorganised under a law of 1896 and renamed *maḥākim ḥasbiyya* rather than *mad̲j̲ālis ḥasbiyya* in 1947) were competent to look after the financial interests of local absent persons and minors, both Muslims and non-Muslims. Certain matters of personal status were also transferred to these new courts; the Public Treasury (*bayt al-māl*) was abolished. A national system of civil jurisdiction, comprising a number of *mad̲j̲ālis*, was established in 1874. In 1876, mixed tribunals were set up in which both foreign and local judges served. They heard disputes between foreigners of different nationalities and between foreigners and Egyptians. The local judges of these courts were exposed to the influence of Western legal principles and judicial norms.

The Code of Procedure of *S̲h̲arīʿa* Courts of 1880 limited the jurisdiction of the *S̲h̲arīʿa* courts to matters of personal status, succession, *waḳf* and gifts, and cases of homicide. They had concurrent jurisdiction, by the side of the provincial councils, in matters of blood-money.

The British occupation of Egypt in 1882 did not, in theory, change the juridical status of the country, which nominally continued to be part of the Ottoman Empire, though enjoying a large measure of autonomy. As a result of reorganisation, the jurisdiction of the *S̲h̲arīʿa* courts was restricted to personal status, succession and part of the law of landed property, including *waḳf* of Muslims; the *S̲h̲arīʿa* courts in the major towns had jurisdiction also in cases of homicide referred to them by the *mad̲j̲ālis niẓāmiyya.*

Until 1883, the *S̲h̲arīʿa* courts had general and residuary jurisdiction with regard to all residents of Egypt. They also had jurisdiction in matters of personal status of non-Muslims, both local and foreign, if the parties had no communal court of their own or did not signify their acceptance of *milla* (communal) jurisdiction, or if they belonged to different denominations, or if a non-Muslim husband had converted to Islam after marriage. The sphere of the *S̲h̲arīʿa* courts was restricted, either by direct limitation or by definition of the spheres of the other courts. In 1883, the judicial system was reorganised: the civil courts (*mad̲j̲ālis niẓāmiyya*) were replaced by national courts (*maḥākim ahliyya*) based on European models (the reform was only completed in 1889). Mixed and national courts took over many of the powers of the *S̲h̲arīʿa* courts. They were competent to hear criminal matters (homicide) and many matters of personal status and *waḳf*. The law of 1896 further restricted the jurisdiction of the *S̲h̲arīʿa* courts, viz. to matrimony, dower, divorce, the custody of children, maintenance (including maintenance between relatives), paternity, succession, *waḳf* and gifts; homicide was removed from their jurisdiction to that of criminal courts.

The dichotomy between the *s̲h̲arʿī* judicial system, in which the non-codified *S̲h̲arīʿa* applied, and the variegated system of the national and mixed courts, in which judges with a modern legal training applied Western-inspired codes, increasingly sharpened. In 1899, Muḥammad ʿAbduh [*q.v.*] suggested the amalgation of all judicial authorities within the framework of the *S̲h̲arīʿa* courts or, more concretely, the vesting of the *S̲h̲arīa* courts with jurisdiction in criminal matters and incidental jurisdiction in other matters (along with the hearing of matrimonial and *waḳf* cases). He also suggested integrating the *muftī*s in the higher echelons of the judicial system. His suggestions were not accepted.

Another law, of 1909-10, defined the jurisdiction of the different *S̲h̲arīʿa* courts in greater detail, but brought nothing substantively new. The law of 1931, which was in force until the abolition of the *S̲h̲arīʿa* courts, dealt more intensively with the jurisdiction of the latter. Matters relating to gifts, which had been under the jurisdiction of the *S̲h̲arīʿa* courts, were transferred to the national courts a few years before the *S̲h̲arīʿa* courts were abolished.

The establishment of the *ḥasbiyya* courts in 1947 was only the first step towards the unification of the judicial system in Egypt. In 1949, the mixed courts were abolished, and their powers were transferred to the national courts. Law no. 462 of 1955 abolished the *S̲h̲arīʿa* courts and the courts of the religious communities (*al-maḥākim al-milliyya*) with effect from 1 January 1956, and transferred their powers to the national courts, thereby closing the circle. The abolition of the religious courts was prompted by considerations of administrative efficiency—the need to prevent conflict of jurisdiction and miscarriages of justice—but above all, it was intended to demonstrate national sovereignty by removing the remnants of the judicial autonomy of foreigners. The action taken against the non-Muslim courts was more significant because in a Muslim country the *S̲h̲arīʿa* courts are identified with the state. Moreover, only the *s̲h̲arʿī ḳāḍī*s have been absorbed into the national courts, so that matters of personal status of non-Muslims can now be heard before Muslim judges, although the latter are supposed to apply the religious law of the parties.

Following the Ottoman conquest, the dominant doctrine in the Egyptian *s̲h̲arʿī* system was the Ḥanafī one, although the population was mainly S̲h̲āfiʿī (in the north) and Mālikī (in the south). The *ḳānūn* of the sultan, ostensibly designed to supplement the *S̲h̲arīʿa*, superseded it in many matters, especially criminal, in which difficulties arose in its application in the *S̲h̲arīʿa* courts. Egypt was not affected by the *Tanẓīmāt* legislation of the Ottoman Empire, and neither was the *Med̲j̲elle* introduced there.

After an endeavour had been made in 1855, under Saʿīd Pas̲h̲a, to codify the criminal law, one which only resulted in a "confused compilation" based mainly on the *S̲h̲arīʿa*, there came the greater juridical reform under Ismāʿīl Pas̲h̲a in connection with the creation of the mixed tribunals (1876). At the time of the creation of the national courts (*maḥākim aḥliyya*) (1883), new civil, criminal and commercial codes were proclaimed which were based on French models.

In the late 19th century, Muḥammad Ḳadrī Pas̲h̲a prepared codes, all based on the Ḥanafī doctrine, of several departments of law: (1) *Kitāb Murs̲h̲id al-ḥayrān ilā maʿrifat aḥwāl al-insān*, which dealt with civil law; it was not officially recognised; (2) *Kitāb Aḥwāl al-s̲h̲arʿiyya fi 'l-aḥwāl al-s̲h̲akh̲ṣiyya*, which dealt with personal status, succession, incompetence, gifts etc.; though not adopted by act of parliament, it was published by the Egyptian government in 1875 and enjoyed semi-official status; it was only intended to meet the increased need, caused by the creation of the mixed and national tribunals, for a convenient summary of the law administered by the *S̲h̲arīʿa* courts and had no authority of its own with the latter; there are official translations into French and Italian and a commentary by Muḥammad Zayd al-Ibyānī; and (3) *Ḳānūn al-ʿadl wa'l-inṣāf li'l-ḳaḍāʾ ʿalā mus̲h̲kilat al-aw-ḳāf* (Būlāḳ 1893, 1894, and later editions), which deals with pious foundations.

A law of 1880 provided that the judgments of the *S̲h̲arīʿa* courts should be based exclusively on the most approved opinion of the Ḥanafī school, except for cases of homicide, in which the *ḳāḍīs*, to avoid corruption and the spilling of innocent blood, were permitted to follow the two disciples of Abū Ḥanīfa, Abū Yūsuf and al-Shaybānī, or, in cases of deliberate homicide, the three other schools. Muḥammad ʿAbduh, within the framework of reforms in the *sharʿī* judicial system, suggested appointing a commission of *ʿulamāʾ* to prepare comprehensive codes, especially as to personal status and *waḳf*, culled from all the Sunnī doctrines according to considerations of public welfare; they were meant to be applied in the *Sharīʿa* courts by order of the ruler; but ʿAbduh's suggestion was not adopted. The *Sharīʿa* Courts Organisation Law of 1910 again required the *ḳāḍīs*, in principle, to follow the most approved opinion of the Ḥanafī school.

From 1920, Parliament engaged in extensive reformist legislation on matters of personal status, succession and *waḳf*; it deviated from the Ḥanafī doctrine and adopted elements of other Sunnī doctrines and of the Shīʿa. This legislation comprised Law no. 25 of 1920 and Law no. 25 of 1929 on maintenance, divorce and other matters; Law no. 78 of 1931 on the organisation of the *Sharīʿa* courts, introducing also reforms in family law; the Succession Law, no. 77 of 1943; the Testamentary Disposition Law, no. 71 of 1946, the *Waḳf* Laws, no. 48 of 1946 and no. 180 of 1952, and Law no. 118 of 1952 concerning the denial of guardianship over a person.

The Civil Code of 1948, prepared by ʿAbd al-Razzāḳ al-Sanhūrī, which served as model for the civil codes of several Arab countries, draws inspiration from the *Sharīʿa* as one source among many, and not the most important. It is based on the codes of 1875 and 1883, which in turn go back to the Code Napoléon. Part of the reforms were at first carried out in the Sudan, through the Grand *Ḳāḍī*, who was an Egyptian jurist.

The *Sharīʿa* Courts Abolition Law, no. 462 of 1955, provides that the national courts shall decide matters of personal status and *waḳf* in accordance with section 280 of the *Sharīʿa* Courts Organisation Law of 1931, that is to say, in accordance with the most approved opinion of the Ḥanafī school, except for matters specially provided for in that law and in statutes of the nineteen-twenties and subsequent years supplementing it. In the national courts, Islamic law applies also to non-Muslims in matters of succession and wills and where the parties do not belong to the same denomination, or one of them has converted to Islam in the course of the proceedings.

After the unification of the judiciary, there were several attempts to codify the law of personal status. There was a growing realisation that the national courts should apply a uniform material law, valid for members of all religions and for foreigners as well as for local residents. But reformist legislation was only resumed in the second half of the nineteen-seventies, and even then not to the extent planned: Law no. 26 of 1976 introduced amendment in matters of maintenance and Law no. 44 of 1979 brought important reforms in matters of maintenance, divorce, maintenance of divorced women and custody of children.

In recent years, the efforts of Islamic orthodoxy have centred on an attempt to disprove the legitimacy of statutes inconsistent with the *Sharīʿa*. The prime objective was establishing the position of the *Sharīʿa* in the constitution of the state. The provisional constitution of 1964 (i.e. of the time of ʿAbd al-Nāṣir) did not mention the *Sharīʿa* at all. The 1971 constitution (art. 2) says that Islam is the state religion and that the principles of the *Sharīʿa* are *a* chief source of legislation, i.e. one of several. On 22 May 1980, following a referendum, it was laid down that the *Sharīʿa* was the chief source of legislation. There have been several attempts by superior courts, in reliance on article 2 of the constitution, to disprove the legality of laws contrary to the *Sharīʿa* (see, e.g. *al-Daʿwa*, February 1980). The Muslim Brothers [see AL-IKHWĀN AL-MUSLIMŪN] demand that the judicature, even at its lowest levels, should be enabled to pronounce on the legality of statutes. Alternatively, they suggest including the *sharʿī* laws, especially the penal ones, among the statutes (see e.g. *al-Daʿwa*, July 1980).

Since 1972, legislation has been proposed, by both private and governmental agencies, to introduce Ḳurʾānic punishments (*ḥudūd*) for theft and embezzlement, the consumption of alcoholic beverages, armed robbery, unchastity (*zinā*), false accusation of unchastity (*ḳadhf*), and apostasy from Islam (*ridda*). In 1975, a supreme committee for the initiation of laws conforming to the *Sharīʿa* (*al-Ladjna al-ʿulyā li-taṭwīr al-ḳawānīn wafḳ al-sharīʿa*) was set up. Up till now, these efforts have had scanty results. The legislative proposals were not adopted, except for a bill concerning the consumption and sale of alcoholic beverages, which became law in 1976 (*al-Iʿtiṣām*, August 1980).

In the period prior to the occupation of Egypt by the British, procedure and the rules of evidence in *Sharīʿa* courts were based on the *Sharīʿa*. Upon the reorganisation of the courts under the law of 1880, procedure was also revised. In 1883, immediately upon the British occupation, new regulations for civil and criminal procedure, based on French models, were proclaimed (the criminal code was brought up to date in 1904); but they were only applied by civil courts. As to the *Sharīʿa* courts, in the *Règlements* since 1897, there has been an increasing tendency to do away with oral evidence of witnesses and acknowledgment (*iḳrār*) as means of proof and to prefer documentary evidence. Muḥammad ʿAbduh suggested making the use of written documents a condition of the jurisdiction of the *Sharīʿa* courts. Reformist legislation from the nineteen-twenties onwards concerning personal status and succession included also procedural provisions which served as means to circumvent substantive *sharʿī* legislation.

The *Sharīʿa* Courts Abolition Law, no. 462 of 1955, provides that the Civil Procedure Law shall apply to matters of personal status and *waḳf* in national courts, except for matters to which special provisions apply according to the *Sharīʿa* Courts Law or laws supplementing it. In addition, Law no. 57 of 1959 (amended by Law no. 106 of 1962) is to be applied to proceedings before the Court of Cassation (*maḥkamat al-naḳḍ*).

In the days of Muḥammad ʿAlī, there was in Cairo a chief *ḳāḍī*, sent every year from Istanbul, who delegated the bulk of the business to the deputy he brought with him from Istanbul. The plaintiff had, as a rule, to produce a *fatwā* from the local Ḥanafī *muftī*, who held permanent office; the *muftī*, for his part, investigated the legal dispute and the *ḳāḍī* was usually satisfied with confirming the *fatwā*. Simple cases were decided at once by the *ḳāḍī*'s deputy or by one of the official witnesses, to whom application had first of all to be made. Cases of a more complicated nature were brought before the chief *ḳāḍī*, his deputy and the *muftī* together.

In addition to this chief court of justice, there were subsidiary courts in Cairo and the suburbs at which official witnesses of the chief court administered justice as deputies and under the supervision of the chief *ḳāḍī*. In the country towns there were also *ḳāḍīs*, who were usually aided by *muftīs*. The *ḳāḍīs* were paid by the litigants and not by the state. Saᶜīd obtained the right to nominate *ḳāḍīs* (but not the chief *ḳāḍī*) and Ismāᶜīl received permission to nominate, temporarily at least, the deputy of the chief *ḳāḍī*, who himself remained in Turkey.

By a law of 1880, the benches of the *Sharīᶜa* courts in Cairo and Alexandria were made to consist of three judges, the court in Cairo became a court of appeal from the decisions of single judges, and the judgments of the two courts were made appealable to the Ḥanafī (chief) *muftī*; in cases of doubt, the courts were referred to the competent *muftīs*, but for the rest they were made independent of them.

A further step forward was marked by the *Règlement de Réorganisation des Mehkémehs* of 1897, modified in 1909-10; between the two versions came the *fatwā* of Muḥammad ᶜAbduh on the reform of *Sharīᶜa* jurisdiction of 1899. Both versions provided for an organisation of the *Sharīᶜa* courts in three stages: *sommaire* (*djuzᵓiyya*), *de première instance* (*ibtidāᵓiyya*) and *suprême* (*ᶜulyā*), according to the terminology finally adopted; single judges sat in the first stage, colleges of judges in the other stages (always three according to the earlier version, three in the intermediate instance and five in the highest court in Cairo according to the later version). The court of appeal was the next highest court; the more important cases were at once brought before the court *de première instance*. The earlier version gave the *muftīs* definite places on the bench of the collegiate courts; in the later version, the vice-president acted as *muftī*, except in Cairo. The *Règlement* of 1931 brought the number of judges in the highest court down to three.

The *Sharīᶜa* Courts Abolition Law of 1955 provides that matters of personal status shall be dealt with by national courts of three grades, to be specially established for this purpose. Those of the lowest grade, called the summary courts (*al-maḥākim al-djuzᵓiyya*), are to hear all matters of personal status, as defined in the *Sharīᶜa* Courts Law no. 78 of 1931, except paternity, repudiation and judicial dissolution on the wife's initiative, which are within the jurisdiction of the courts of first instance (*al-maḥākim al-ibtidāᵓiyya*). In addition, the courts of first instance hear matters of *waḳf* and appeals from judgments of the summary courts as far as these are appealable. Non-final judgments of the courts of first instance sitting as courts of original jurisdiction are appealable to the Personal Status Appeals Department of the Court of Cassation.

A summary court has a bench of one; a court of first instance has a bench of three and may include *sharᶜī ḳāḍīs*. The president of the court of first instance is a senior judge of the Court of Appeal. Courts of first instance exist in every provincial capital. The Personal Status Appeals Department has a bench of three, one of whom may be a *sharᶜī ḳāḍī* of the rank of *nāᵓib* or a member of the Supreme *Sharīᶜa* Court of Appeal. The president of the Supreme *Sharīᶜa* Court is made a member of the Court of Cassation, of which the Personal Status Appeals Department forms a part and which sits in Cairo.

The law of 1955 provides that the *ḳāḍīs* of the *Sharīᶜa* courts of all grades shall be integrated into the national courts system, the public prosecutor's department and the Ministry of Justice as far as matters of personal status are concerned. Actually, most *sharᶜī ḳāḍīs* have been integrated into the summary courts, in which judicial proceedings in matters of personal status are mainly conducted. At the same time, a not inconsiderable number of civil lawyers deal with matters of personal status of Muslims.

The *Sharīᶜa* Courts Law of 1931 provided that only advocates might represent parties in court, A *ḳāḍīs*' school established in 1907 trained also *sharᶜī* advocates. They set up a bar association similar to the bar association of civil advocates. Since the abolition of the *Sharīᶜa* courts, *sharᶜī* advocates have been permitted to appear, in matters that had formerly been within the jurisdiction of the *sharīᶜa* courts, before national courts of the corresponding grade.

In the mid-seventies a tendency emerged—tolerated by the authorities for reasons of domestic policy—to apply *sharᶜī* laws, even if not anchored in statutory legislation, in the jurisprudence of the national courts and to refuse to apply statutes considered inconsistent with the *Sharīᶜa* (*Rose al-Yūsuf*, 18 February 1980; *al-Daᶜwa*, February 1980, February 1981).

Bibliography: Lane, *Manners and customs of the modern Egyptians*, ch. iv; *EI*[1] art. KHEDĪW, sect. 2; Schacht, *Šarīᶜa und Qānūn im modernen Ägypten*, in *Isl.* xx (1932), 209-36; the texts of the laws and decrees in the *Journal Officiel du Gouvernement Égyptien* and separately, e.g. *Lāᵓiḥat al-maḥākim al-sharᶜiyya*, Būlāḳ 1297/1880; *Règlement de Réorganisation des Mehkémehs*, Cairo 1910; *Madjmūᶜat ḳawānīn al-maḥākim al-sharᶜiyya wa 'l-madjālis al-ḥasbiyya*, Cairo 1926; Sammarco, *Précis de l'histoire d'Égypte*, iv, 265 ff.; Muḥammad ᶜAbduh, *Taḳrīr fī iṣlāḥ al-maḥākim al-sharᶜiyya*, Cairo 1900; J. Brugman, *De betekenis van het Mohammedaanse recht in het hedendaagse Egypte* ("The place of Islamic law in contemporary Egypt"), The Hague 1960, with important bibliography; J. N. D. Anderson, *Law reform in Egypt, 1850-1950*, in P. M. Holt (ed.), *Political and social change in modern Egypt*, London 1968, 209-30; Ch. Chehata, *Droit musulman*, Paris 1970; Maḥmaṣānī, *al-Awḍāᶜ al-tashrīᶜiyya*, 220-40; F. J. Ziadeh, *Lawyers, the rule of law and liberalism in modern Egypt*, Stanford, Calif. 1968; E. Hill, *Mahkama. Studies in the Egyptian legal system*, London 1979; *Ḳawānīn al-aḥwāl al-shakhṣiyya baᶜd al-taᶜdīlāt al-djadīda, Ḳānūn Ḳabḍ al-Nafaḳa min Bank Nāṣir al-Idjtimāᶜī wa-Ḳānūn Salb al-Wilāya ᶜalā al-Nafs*, Maktab al-Maṭbūᶜāt al-Islāmiyya wa'l-Ḳānūniyya, Cario [1980]; I. Altman, *Islamic legislation in Egypt in the 1970s*, in *Asian and African Studies*, xiii/3 (1979), 199-219; further see Schacht, *Introduction*, 252, 254 f.

(J. SCHACHT - [A. LAYISH])

ii. Syria

In the Ottoman era, the *sharᶜī* judicial system of Syria was integrated in the Ottoman legal system. The powers of the *Sharīᶜa* courts were re-determined by Law no. 261 of 1926; they comprise matters of personal status, succession and *waḳf*. However, in contrast to the position in Lebanon, the *Sharīᶜa* courts are regarded as the ordinary judicial authorities in matters of personal status of non-Muslims, except for matters left to the jurisdiction of the communal courts. In matters of guardianship, succession, wills, interdiction (*ḥadjr*), legal majority (*rushd*), maintenance of relatives within the wider family, *waḳf khayrī* and the like, non-Muslims are amenable to the *Sharīᶜa* courts. Matters of personal status of foreign Muslims who in their countries of origin are subject to civil law are amenable to the civil courts. The *Sharīᶜa* court consists of a single *ḳāḍī*, whose judgment may be appealed to the *sharᶜī* department of the Court of Cassation (*maḥkamat al-tamyīz*). The judicial authority Law, no. 12 of 1961, provides for 25

Muslim courts throughout Syria, each consisting of a single *ḳāḍī*, except for those in Damascus and Aleppo, which have three *ḳāḍīs* each.

The S͟hīʿīs of Syria, unlike those of Lebanon, have no courts of their own, and are theoretically subject to the Sunnī *S͟harīʿa* courts. But it seems that they settle matters of personal status through unofficial arbitration by their leaders.

By virtue of the law of 1926, the non-Muslim communities have religious courts of their own, with jurisdiction limited to some matters not within the competence of the *S͟harīʿa* courts: betrothal, marriage, the various kinds of divorce, matrimonial maintenance and children's maintenance.

The Syrian Law of Personal Status of 1953 replaced the Ottoman Family Rights Law of 1917. It is based on the Ḥanafī doctrine and on reformist legislation anchored in other Sunnī doctrines. In the absence of an express provision in it as to a particular matter, the ruling opinion of the Ḥanafī school is to be followed. The Syrian constitutions from 1950 onwards provide that the *S͟harīʿa* shall be the principal source of legislation. The said law applies also to the S͟hīʿīs, as well as to non-Muslims (Christians and Druzes), except for those matters within the competence of the religious courts of the latter to which their religious law applies (art. 308). In other words, this law represents an attempt to frame a code of personal status applying to all citizens of Syria without distinction of school or religion.

Procedure was unified by the Law of Procedure of 1947. Under the Jurisdiction Law of 1961, *S͟harīʿa*, Christian and Druze courts apply the rules of procedure of the civil courts; the special rules of the different communities, including the Ottoman *S͟harʿī* Procedure Law, were abolished.

In the Ottoman era, the Druzes of Syria were not recognised as a religious community and were theoretically amenable to the jurisdiction of the *S͟harīʿa* courts. In practice, they settled matters of marriage, divorce, wills, *waḳf*, etc., before Druze *ḳāḍīs* lacking statutory status. Like their Lebanese brethren, the Syrian Druzes were recognised as a religious community by the Mandatory authorities in 1936 and thereby given the right to exercise communal jurisdiction in matters of personal status; but there were differences of opinion as to this with regard to the Druzes residing outside the D̲j̲abal al-Durūz and especially in Damascus.

Law no. 134 of 1945 made it possible to set up an independent judicial system for the Druzes in accordance with *mad͟hhabī* principles and customs. The powers of the courts comprise matters of marriage, divorce, maintenance and the like, as well as matters of succession and wills. Law no. 294 of 1946 and the General Judicial Powers Law, no. 56 of 1959, confirmed the powers of the Druze courts under the 1945 law.

Until 1953, the Druze courts applied Druze religious law and custom. Matters concerning Druzes heard before the *S͟harīʿa* courts were determined in accordance with the Ottoman Family Rights Law. The Syrian Personal Status Law of 1953 extends also to the Druzes, except for matters peculiar to Druze law, viz. the ban on polygamy and on the reinstatement of a divorced woman, the right of succession of an orphaned grandchild (the principle of representation) and the absolute freedom of testation (art. 307). Law no. 134 of 1945 provides that the Druze courts shall function in accordance with their own rules of procedure. Appeal proceedings before the civil Court of Cassation in Damascus, to which the Druzes resort since 1959, are conducted under the civil law of procedure.

The 1945 law established a two-grade judicial system for the Druzes: courts of first instance consisting of a single *ḳāḍī* and a court of appeal—the Principal Council (*al-hayʾa al-raʾīsiyya*)—which is the supreme *mad͟hhabī* authority and whose seat is in the province of D̲j̲abal al-Durūz. The latter's judgments were to be final. Law no. 294 of 1946 provides that the Principal Council shall consist of three *mad͟hhabi* leaders. The *ḳāḍīs* were to be appointed by the Minister of Justice upon the recommendation of the Religious Council (*al-hayʾa al-dīniyya*), on which the spiritual heads of the Druze community were represented. The judgments were to be enforced by the authorities of the state. Law no. 56 of 1959 restricted the judicial autonomy of the Druzes. It provided that a Druze *ḳāḍī* should be appointed, by order, on the recommendation of the Minister of Justice of the Syrian province of the United Arab Republic. Appeals against his judgments were to be heard before the civil Court of Cassation in Damascus (in which the Druzes were not represented) under the rules of procedure obtaining in respect of Muslim *s͟harʿī ḳāḍīs*. The Druze court of appeal was abolished and, by way of compensation, a "Druze Department of Legal Opinions" (*dāʾirat al-iftāʾ li ʾl-mad͟hhab al-durzī*) was set up, consisting of the *ḳāḍīs* of the former court of appeal. This body is unconnected with the judicial system. Law no. 56 of 1959 was amended by Law no. 98 of 1961, which provides that the election of a Druze *ḳāḍī* requires not only the recommendation of the Minister of Justice but also the consent of the High Judicial Council (*mad̲j̲lis al-ḳaḍāʾ al-aʿlā*).

The Bedouin of Syria used to settle their disputes before an arbitral board (*lad̲j̲na taḥkīmiyya*) consisting of two arbitrators and an umpire, elected by the parties, which followed tribal custom (*ʿurf*). The Tribes Law, no. 124 of 1953 (amended in 1956), forbade Bedouin, by means of penal provisions, to carry out raids (*g͟hazw*). In 1956, matters of personal status of Bedouin were assigned to the *S͟harīʿa* courts, and in 1958 the Tribes Law was repealed and the Bedouin became amenable to the ordinary legal system of the state and to the laws applying therein.

Bibliography: Maḥmaṣānī, *al-Awḍāʿ al-tas͟hrīʿiyya*, 282-97; E. T. Mogannam, *The practical application of the law in certain Arab states*, in *George Washington Law Review*, xxii (1953), 142-55; J. N. D. Anderson, *The Syrian law of personal status*, in *BSOAS*, xvii (1955), 34-49; Fuʾād S͟hubāt, *Tanẓīm al-aḥwāl al-s͟hak͟hṣiyya li-g͟hayr al-muslimīn fī Sūriyā wa-Lubnān*, [Cairo] 1966; P. Gannagé, *La compétence des juridictions confessionnelles au Liban et en Syrie*, in *Annales de l'École Française de Droit de Beyrouth*, iv/1-2 (1948), 199-247; Amīn Ṭalīʿ, *Mas͟hyak͟hat al-ʿaḳl wa ʾl-ḳaḍāʾ al-mad͟hhabī al-durzī ʿabr taʾrīk͟h*, Jerusalem 1979, 136-41, 152-3, 156. (A. Layish)

iii. Lebanon

The Lebanese legal system is mainly based on the *Règlement Organique* of 1861, which granted the Province of Mount Lebanon administrative and judicial autonomy guaranteed by the great powers. The system remained unchanged until World War I, when Turkey again ruled Lebanon directly for a short period. The *Règlement* makes no mention of the religious-legal system, but laid the foundation for the organisation of the judicial system on a communal basis. At the end of Ottoman rule, the *S͟harīʿa* courts had jurisdiction in matters of personal status, succession and *waḳf* of Muslims and some matters of Christians, such as succession, if one of the heirs requested it.

Upon the severance of Lebanon from the Ottoman Empire, the status of the Muslims was assimilated to that of the other communities. The French administration made the Muftī of Beirut a "Grand Muftī" (*al-muftī al-akbar*) heading the Sunnī Muslim community and representing it before the authorities, similar in status to the spiritual heads of the Christian communities. In 1955, he became the "Muftī of the Republic". Beside him functions the "Supreme *Sharʿī* Council" (*al-madjlis al-sharʿī al-aʿlā*), designed to assist him in running the religious affairs of the community and administering the *wakfs*. It consists of six *ḳāḍīs* and the President of the Supreme *Sharīʿa* Court.

The Lebanese Shīʿīs, unlike their brethren in Syria, were recognised as a religious community entitled to their own judicial autonomy. The powers of the Sunnī and Djaʿfarī Shīʿī *Sharīʿa* courts were defined by Law no. 241 of 1942 (amended in 1946) and by the Law Concerning the Organisation of Sunnī and Djaʿfarī *Sharʿī* Jurisdiction of 1962, which superseded the former. They comprised personal status, succession and wills and matters such as legal majority (*bulūgh*, *rushd*), interdiction (*ḥadjr*), missing persons (*mafḳūd*), control of moneys of orphans, *wakf dhurrī* and *mustathnā*. *Wakf maḍbūṭ* and *wakf mulḥaḳ* of Sunnīs are within the jurisdiction of their *wakf* administrative council, while those of Djaʿfarīs are within that of the Djaʿfarī courts.

The Ottoman Family Rights Law of 1917 is still in force in Lebanon. In the absence of an express provision in this law as to a particular matter, the Sunnī *Sharīʿa* court must follow the dominant opinion of the Ḥanafī school. The court also uses the codification of the laws of personal status of the Egyptian, Ḳadrī Pasha (see Section i above). In matters of interdiction and legal incompetence and of management of moneys of minors, the *Sharīʿa* court applies the *Medjelle* as amended by Lebanese legislation, which sometimes deviates from the Ḥanafī doctrine.

The Djaʿfarī court applies the laws of the Djaʿfarī doctrine and the provisions of the Ottoman Family Rights Law compatible with it. Where the parties do not belong to the same school (Sunnī or Djaʿfarī), the doctrine is determined by the court in accordance with the matter under consideration. In matters of succession and wills, e.g., the courts follow the school of the deceased. For reasons of convenience, a certain mobility exists among Shīʿīs and Sunnīs in matters of personal status and succession. The Ḥanafī doctrine applies to many matters of non-Muslims, such as succession (until 1959), *wakf*, interdiction and legal incompetence. The laws of 1942 and 1946 laid down also rules of court deviating in some respects from the Ottoman ones; there are certain differences in procedure between Sunnī and Djaʿfarī courts.

There are two separate systems of courts, a Sunnī one and a Djaʿfarī one. Each consists of courts of first instance, manned by a single *ḳāḍī*, in major centres and a supreme court, manned by three *ḳāḍīs*, in Beirut, which acts as a court of cassation (*maḥkamat al-tamyīz*) in some matters and as a court of appeal (*maḥkama istiʾnāfiyya*) in others. The judgments of both courts are enforced by the execution offices of the state. The state appoints and dismisses the *ḳāḍīs* and pays their salaries.

The wide autonomy of the courts of the Christian communities (*maḥākim rūḥiyya*) is another carry-over from the special status of the Province of Mount Lebanon in the second half of the 19th century. Article 156 of the Ottoman Family Rights Law of 1917 abrogated the judicial powers of the spiritual heads of the Christian communities in matters of personal status, but the French administration ignored that article; in fact, it was repealed by order of the governor of December 1921 and the Christian courts remained in existence. The powers of the courts of ten Christian communities (and of the Jewish community) were defined by laws of 1930 and 1951. These powers are wider than those courts had in the past but still narrower than those of the *Sharīʿa* courts. The widening of the powers of the Christian courts met with strong public opposition for national reasons (subjection to foreign law) and legal-professional ones. The laws of wills and succession of non-Muslims, of 1929 and 1959, respectively, freed the Christian communities from the sway of Islamic law.

The Druzes of the Province of Mount Lebanon were not recognised as a religious community under Ottoman rule. At the same time, there is evidence that they enjoyed a certain autonomy, by administrative arrangement, in matters of marriage, divorce and wills in which Druze religious law takes a special position; the Spiritual Head of the Druze community dealt with these matters "in accordance with ancient custom". That autonomy was abolished by order of the *Shaykh al-Islām* during World War I, together with the judicial autonomy of the Province of Mount Lebanon, and Druze matters of personal status were assigned to the Sunnī *Sharīʿa* courts; but the order was not implemented, and the autonomy remained in force.

In 1930, the Druze courts were granted jurisdiction in matters of personal status of the members of the community, similar to that exercised by the Sunnī and Djaʿfarī *Sharīʿa* courts. In 1936, the Mandate authorities formally recognised the Druzes as a religious community. The powers of the courts were re-defined by a law enacted in 1948 and especially by the Druze Administration of Justice Law, no. 3473 of 1960. The courts are competent to hear all matters to which Druze religious law, Druze custom and the Law of the Personal Status of the Druze Community apply.

Until 1948, the Druze courts applied non-codified religious law, Druze custom and the Ḥanafī doctrine as far as what was not inconsistent with Druze tradition and custom. The Law of the Personal Status of the Druze Community in Lebanon, of 1948—the most impressive modern family law at the time—is a synthesis of many sources of law, religious and secular, local and foreign, but its most important source of inspiration is ancient Druze religious law. In the absence of an express provision in the 1948 law as to a particular matter, the Ḥanafī doctrine is to be followed.

Order no. 3294 of 1938 requires Druze courts to apply the rules of procedure applicable in Sunnī and Djaʿfarī courts. The Druze Administration of Justice Law of 1960 provides that, in the absence of an express provision in that law as to a particular matter, the Druze courts shall apply the rules of procedure applicable in Muslim *Sharīʿa* courts, and that in the absence of an express provision also in the latter, they shall apply the general principles of civil procedure as far as they are not repugnant to Druze religious law and Druze tradition.

Before the establishment of statutory Druze courts, the two *shaykh al-ʿaḳls* served as an appellate authority acting, in a traditional manner, in accordance with customary law. The statutory status of the *shaykh al-ʿaḳls* as spiritual heads of the Druze community was regulated in 1962. In 1947, it was prescribed that the court of appeal, known as the Supreme Council (*al-*

hay'a al-ʿulyā), should consist of the two *shaykh al-ʿaḳl*s and a Druze civil judge. If it was not possible to man the Council, the Minister of Justice might appoint one or several judges of the court of first instance (other than those whose judgment was appealed against) to complete the bench. In 1958, it was ordained that if it was not possible to appoint a second *shaykh al-ʿaḳl*, the Minister of Justice should appoint a second Druze civil judge and that judgments relating to minors or legally incompetent persons, the Public Treasury (*bayt al-māl*), *waḳf*, and dissolution of a marriage on the ground of absence of the husband, might only be executed after confirmation by the appellate authority.

The Druze Administration of Justice Law of 1960 (amended in 1967) establishes a two-grade judicial system integrated in the general Lebanese legal system: courts of first instance, manned by a single *ḳāḍī madhhab*, in Beirut, ʿĀliya, Bʿaḳlīn, Rāshayyā and Ḥāṣbayyā and a court of appeal (Supreme Court), manned by a presiding judge and two assessors, in Beirut. The court of appeal performs the functions of a disciplinary committee for *ḳāḍī*s of the first instance. The status of the Druze *ḳāḍī*s is the same as that of the Muslim *sharʿī ḳāḍī*s, with certain modifications. In the absence of an express provision in that law as to a particular matter, the provisions of the Sunnī and Djaʿfarī *Sharīʿa* Justice Law are to be followed.

Bibliography: Bashīr al-Basilānī, *Ḳawānīn al-aḥwāl al-shakhṣiyya fī Lubnān*, [Cairo] 1971; Maḥmaṣānī, *al-Awḍāʿ al-tashrīʿiyya*, 246-73; P. Gannagé, *La compétence des juridictions confessionnelles au Liban et en Syrie*, in *Annales de l'École Française de Droit de Beyrouth*, iv/1-2 (1948), 199-247; E. Tyan, *Notes sommaires sur le nouveau régime successoral au Liban*, Paris 1960; R. Catala and A. Gervais (eds.), *Le droit libanais*, i-ii, Paris 1963. On Druze justice, see Ḥalīm Taḳī 'l-Dīn, *Ḳaḍā' al -muwaḥḥidīn al-durūz fī māḍīh wa-ḥāḍirih*, ʿĀliya 1979; Amīn Ṭalīʿ, *Mashyakhat al-ʿaḳl wa 'l-ḳaḍā' al-madhhabī al-durzī ʿabr al-ta'rīkh*, Jerusalem 1979; Fayṣal Nadjīb Ḳays, *Masmūʿat idjtihādāt al-maḥākim al-madhhabiyya al-durziyya 1968-1972*, Beirut 1972; J. N. D. Anderson, *The personal law of the Druze community*, in *WI*, N.S. ii (1952), 1-9, 83-94. (A. Layish)

iv. ʿIrāḳ

In the final period of Ottoman rule, a dual, *sharʿī* and civil, judicial system, integrated in the Ottoman legal system, was functioning in ʿIrāḳ. The *Sharīʿa* courts had jurisdiction in matters of personal status, succession and *waḳf*. Such courts, each consisting of a single Sunnī *ḳāḍī*, sat in towns. A judgment of the *Sharīʿa* court was appealable to the *Shaykh al-Islām* in Istanbul.

Djaʿfarī (Ithnā ʿAsharī) Shīʿī law was never officially recognised in the Ottoman Empire. Though theoretically amenable to the *Sharīʿa* courts, the Shīʿīs of ʿIrāḳ, who form over half of its population, did not in fact resort to them but settled their personal status matters, on a voluntary basis, before their *mudjtahidūn*, who had no statutory status.

Pari passu with the advance of the British forces in ʿIrāḳ in World War I, the Anglo-Indian legal system superseded the Turkish. During a short transitional period, the *Sharīʿa* courts were bereft of their status. *Ḳāḍī*s were elected *ad hoc* by the parties. They dealt with matters of personal status and succession, and their judgments were subject to confirmation by a British court. The Shīʿīs continued to resort to the *mudjtahidūn*, whose judgments were now, for the first time, recognised by the official authorities.

In July 1916, after the capture of Baghdād by the British, the *Sharīʿa* courts were reconstituted in Baghdād and other cities. Early in 1918, the *sharʿī* judicial system was reorganised with a view to adapting it to the new political situation. Personal jurisdiction was limited to Sunnīs, and matters of personal status of Shīʿīs, Christians and Jews were assigned to civil courts of first instance, which followed the personal status law of the parties or any custom applicable to them, provided it was not contrary to justice, equity or good conscience. These courts were authorised to refer such matters to the Shīʿī *mudjtahid* or to the Christian or Jewish religious authority, as the case might be. The judgments of these were subject to confirmation by the civil court. In 1921, Djaʿfarī courts were set up in Baghdād that were authorised to hear matters of personal status. Their judgments, too, were subject to confirmation by a civil court. Appeals against judgments of the Sunnī courts were heard before the *Sharīʿa* Council of Cassation (*madjlis al-tamyīz al-sharʿī*) under the *Sharīʿa* Courts Regulations of 1918.

After independence, the judicial system was reorganised. In 1923, a dual system of *Sharīʿa* courts, Sunnī and Djaʿfarī, with equal status, was set up. Their jurisdiction comprises personal status in a wide sense, succession and wills, *waḳf*, orphans' moneys, etc. A Basic Law of 1925 confirmed the dual system of courts. It provided that separate courts for the two schools should be set up in Baghdād and Baṣra, but only one court in other places, where the school of the *ḳāḍī* was to be the same as that of the majority of the inhabitants. The Establishment of Courts Law of 1945 provided that the *Sharīʿa* courts should be set up in localities where there were civil courts and that in the absence of a *ḳāḍī*, his place should be taken by a judge of the civil system.

Until 1963, appeals against judgments of *Sharīʿa* courts were heard before the *Sharīʿa* Council of Cassation, which had separate departments for Sunnīs and Djaʿfarīs. It could only confirm or set aside the judgment or direct the court to re-hear the case. The Minister of Justice had power to amend the decisions of the Council. In 1963, the Council was abolished, and appeals were henceforth heard before the State Court of Cassation (*maḥkamat tamyīz al-ʿIrāḳ*), which combined the functions of the Sunnī and Djaʿfarī Departments in the Personal Status Committee (*hay'at al-mawādd al-shakhṣiyya*).

In the Ottoman era, the *Sharīʿa* courts followed the non-codified official Ḥanafī doctrine. The two Ottoman *irāda*s of 1915 relating to personal status, and the *Medjelle*, the land law, with certain modifications, applied in ʿIrāḳ, but not the Ottoman Family Rights Law of 1917. The Ḥanafī doctrine applied also to matters of succession of Christians and Jews until special laws were enacted for them by the Civil Courts Regulations of 1918.

After World War I, the Ḥanafī *ḳāḍī*, if the parties belonged to another Sunnī school and demanded that the Ḥanafī doctrine be not applied, might either deal with the matter himself according to the school of the parties or refer it to an *ʿālim* of that school. If the parties belonged to different schools, the court, under the *Sharīʿa* Courts Law of 1923, had to follow the school of the deceased in matters of wills and intestate succession, the school of the husband in matters of marriage, divorce, dower, guardianship and the like, the school of the founder in matters of *waḳf* and the school of the defendant in matters of maintenance of relatives. In Djaʿfarī courts, the Djaʿfarī doctrine was applied. If, in a place where there were no separate courts for the two schools, a Sunnī *ḳāḍī* dealt with matters of S͟hīʿīs, he had to rely on a *fatwā* of a S͟hīʿī ʿālim, and *vice versa*.

After several abortive attempts (in the nineteen-forties) to codify the ʿIrāḳī law of personal status and succession, a Personal Status Law, applying equally to all ʿIrāḳī Muslims, both Sunnī and S͟hīʿī, was promulgated in 1959 following ʿAbd al-Karīm Ḳāsim's *coup d'état* the year before. A succession law was taken over from a European source. Other important reforms concerned marriage and divorce. The 1959 law presents a blend of Sunnī and S͟hīʿī principles in some sections, while other sections preserve separate norms for the two branches of Islam. In 1963, after ʿAbd al-Salām ʿĀrif's *coup*, under pressure from the *ʿulamāʾ*, a retreat occurred from reforms which did not seem compatible with the *S͟harīʿa*. The foreign succession law was repealed, and in its stead the system of succession of the Twelver S͟hīʿa was made applicable to all ʿIrāḳī Muslims. In 1978, further important amendments were made in the Personal Status Law of 1959 in matters of marriage, divorce, custody of children and succession. In 1922, the Ottoman *S͟harʿī* Procedure Law was adopted which, with amendments of the years 1922, 1929 and 1931, is still in force.

The courts of the non-Muslim communities (Christians and Jews) were vested, by the constitution, with jurisdiction in matters of marriage, divorce, alimony and probate. The other matters of personal status and succession are within the jurisdiction of the civil courts.

In the Ottoman era, tribal courts (*maḥākim al-ʿas͟hāʾir*) applying customary law operated among the Bedouin. These courts were reorganised by the British in 1916 on a pattern borrowed from Indian legislation. A "political officer" appointed special tribal councils (*mad͟jālis*) authorised to hear civil and criminal cases if at least one of the parties was a Bedouin. The relevant law was replaced by the Tribal Actions Regulation (*niẓām daʿāwī 'l-ʿas͟hāʾir*) of 1918, which was amended several times (in 1924, 1933 and 1951). Some of the tribal customs were abrogated by statutory legislation. The judgments of the tribal courts were made subject to scrutiny by the *mutaṣarrif*. The tribal courts were abolished in 1958, after the *coup d'état*, with a view to integrating the Bedouin into the general legal system, which included also the *S͟harīʿa* courts.

Bibliography: Maḥmaṣānī, *al-Awḍāʿ al-tas͟hrīʿiyya*, 321-40; N. el-Naqeb, *Problems of matrimonial law in contemporary Iraq*, Master of Laws thesis, University of London 1967; Muḥammad S͟hafīḳ al-ʿĀnī, *Kitāb al-Murāfaʿāt wa 'l-ṣukūk fi 'l-ḳaḍāʾ al-s͟harʿī*, Bag͟hdād 1950; idem, *Aḥkām al-aḥwāl al-s͟hakhṣiyya fi 'l-ʿIrāḳ*, [Cairo] 1970; Y. Linant de Bellefonds, *Le code du statut personnel irakien du 30 décembre 1959*, in *SI*, xiii (1960), 79-135; J. N. D. Anderson, *A law of personal status for Iraq*, in *International and Comparative Law Quarterly*, ix (1960), 542-63; idem, *Changes in the law of personal status in Iraq*, in *ICLQ*, xii (1963), 1026-31; *Taʿdīl ḳānūn al-aḥwāl al-s͟hakhṣiyya li-sanat 1959*, Law no. 21 of 11 February 1978 (Amendment no. 2 to the Law of Personal Status, no. 188 of 1959), *al-T͟hawra*, 14 February 1978; Muṣṭafā Muḥammad Ḥasanayn, *Niẓām al-masʾūliyya ʿind al-ʿas͟hāʾir al-ʿirāḳiyya al-ʿarabiyya al-muʿāṣira*, Cairo 1967. (A. Layish)

v. Palestine and Israel

Upon the severance of Palestine from the Ottoman Empire in World War I, the country ceased to be a part of a sovereign Muslim state. The status of the Muslims was assimilated in practice, though not in theory, to that of the recognised communities of the Ottoman era. In the absence of a representative Muslim body, the Mandate authorities, by order of December 1921, set up the Supreme Muslim Council (*al-mad͟jlis al-islāmī al-aʿlā*) and appointed the Muftī of Jerusalem its chairman. This body was designed to fill the vacuum which, in the absence of a Muslim sovereign, had been created in all matters relating to the Muslim religious establishment.

Article 52 of the Palestine Order in Council, 1922, which is the principal enactment determining the powers of the *S͟harīʿa* courts to this day, granted them sole jurisdiction in all matters of personal status, succession and *waḳf*, as they had had at the end of the Ottoman era, with some modifications arising out of the new political situation: their jurisdiction was limited to matters relating to the establishment and internal administration of *waḳfs* of the *mulḥaḳ* category, i.e. those administered by private *mutawallīs*. The order of 1921 gave the Muslim Council control of the *waḳfs* of the *maḍbūṭ* category, i.e. those administered by a *maʾmūr al-awḳāf* in the Ottoman era. In 1937, these powers of the Council passed to a government commission appointed under the Defence Regulations (Muslim *Waḳf*).

The personal jurisdiction of the *S͟harīʿa* courts was limited to Muslim litigants. The residuary jurisdiction they had had in respect of non-Muslims in the Ottoman era was transferred to civil courts, and their jurisdiction in matters relating to the establishment or validity of *waḳfs* of non-Muslims established before *S͟harīʿa* courts up to 1922 was changed from exclusive to concurrent.

The material law applying to matters of personal status in *S͟harīʿa* courts was mainly the Ottoman Family Rights Law of 1917, and the Ottoman Succession Law of 1913 was made applicable to property of the *mīrī* category. The *ḳāḍīs* frequently relied on Ḳadrī Pas͟ha's codification of the laws of personal status and *waḳf* (see section 4. i above), although it had no statutory status in Palestine. The doctrine dominant in the courts was the Ḥanafī—this, too, a legacy of Ottoman rule— although most of the population belongs to the S͟hāfiʿī school. The Mandatory legislator carefully maintained the *status quo* as to the material law of Muslims. The courts were regulated by the Muslim Courts Procedure Law of 1333 (1917), which is still in force with certain modifications. In the years 1918 and 1919, regulations were enacted concerning the composition and powers of the *S͟harīʿa* Court of Appeal, its procedure and the execution of its judgments.

The Supreme Muslim Council was empowered to appoint, with the approval of the government, and to dismiss *s͟harʿī ḳāḍīs*. Fifteen courts, each consisting of a single *ḳāḍī*, sat in the major towns and there was a three-man court of appeal in Jerusalem. The *muftīs*, too, were appointed by the Muslim Council. The senior status of the Muftī of Jerusalem (the "Grand Muftī" of the "Muftī of Palestine") resulted from the special status Jerusalem had had under the Ottoman administration and from the personal union between his offices and that of President of the Supreme Muslim Council. There was also a S͟hāfiʿī *muftī* in Jerusalem.

Advocates with a *s͟harʿī* training were authorised to appear before the *S͟harīʿa* courts. Also attached to the judicial system were marriage solemnisers (*maʾd͟hūn*) and "managers of orphans' money". The government paid the salaries of the *ḳāḍīs* and of the court officials.

A system of tribal courts (*maḥākim al-ʿas͟hāʾir*)

operated among the Bedouin. In the years 1919 to 1922, the government maintained a "Blood Council" (*maḏjlis al-dumūm*) which tried homicide cases, and in 1922 permanent tribal courts with specified powers were appointed; each court consisted of three representatives of the clans of the major Negev tribes, with the District Officer of Beersheba as chairman. In 1928, these courts were given power to hear criminal cases and impose light prison sentences and fines. From 1933 there was also a tribal court of appeal; it consisted of two members, with the District Officer as chairman.

The Government of Israel has reconstituted the _Sharī ʿa_ courts with the same powers as they had under the Mandate, except for a few modifications: the Age of Marriage Law, 1950, vests exclusive power to permit the marriage of a girl under seventeen in the District Court, and the Succession Law, 1965, reduces the jurisdiction of the _Sharī ʿa_ courts—like that of the other religious courts—from exclusive to concurrent in matters of succession and wills, but not in matters of personal status, in which it is still exclusive. The revocation of the Supreme Muslim Council Order of 1921 by the _Ḳāḍī_s Law, 1961, implicitly revoked the Defence (Muslim *Waḳf*) Regulations, and it seems that the powers of the _Sharī ʿa_ courts are thereby restored to their original extent, so as to include *waḳf*s of the *maḍbūṭ* category.

The Knesset intervened in many matrimonial matters with a view to equalising the legal status of women with that of men. Nevertheless, it abstained from impinging on any religious-legal prohibition or permission relating to marriage or divorce and resorted to procedural provisions and penal sanctions rather than substantive provisions as means of deterrence, and in matters for which substantive provisions were enacted, the parties were usually left an option to litigate in accordance with their religious law. It is only in matters of succession that there is—since 1965—a clear separation between religious justice, in which religious law applies, and civil justice, in which secular law is followed.

The _sharʿī_ judicial system is integrated in the general legal system. The _Sharī ʿa_ Courts (Validation of Appointments) Law, 1953, validated the appointment of courts of first instance and of a court of appeal, made by administrative action immediately after the establishment of the state. The _Ḳāḍī_s Law, 1961, regulates the appointment and tenure of the _ḳāḍī_s. They are appointed by the President of the State upon the recommendation of an appointments committee, most of the members of which are Muslims. Their salaries are paid by the Government. _Sharī ʿa_ courts of first instance, consisting of a single _ḳāḍī_, exist in Nazareth, Acre (with an extension in Haifa), Jaffa (with jurisdiction—since 1967—including also East Jerusalem (see Section 4. vi below)) and the village of Ṭayyia in the "Little Triangle".

The tribal courts have been abolished in Israel (though not their juridical basis), and the Bedouin are now amenable to the _Sharī ʿa_ courts in matters of personal status and succession. The Negev Bedouin were under the jurisdiction of the _Sharī ʿa_ Court of Jaffa till 1976. In that year, a separate court of first instance was established for them in Beersheba.

A court of appeal of two or three _ḳāḍī_s exists in Jerusalem. Until 1975, this court consisted of the _ḳāḍī_s of the courts of first instance, except the _ḳāḍī_ whose judgment was appealed against. In that year, it was administratively ordained that the court of appeal should consist of permanent members not serving in courts of first instance.

In Palestine, the Druzes were not recognised as a religious community. In the Ottoman era, the _Sharī ʿa_ court had residuary jurisdiction over them. They in fact resorted to it, especially in matters of succession. At the same time, they enjoyed a certain autonomy, within the framework of their religious and customary law, in matters of personal status and wills. The Mandatory authorities refused to recognise them as a religious community, in the interest of maintaining the *status quo* in matters of religion. They continued to recognise a certain Druze autonomy with regard to the performance of marriages, while residuary jurisdiction was transferred from the _Sharī ʿa_ courts to the civil courts, though in fact the Druzes continued to resort to the _Sharī ʿa_ courts.

In Israel, the Druzes were recognised as a religious community in 1957. Pending the establishment of their own religious courts in 1963, they continued to resort to _Sharī ʿa_ courts, although this practice has no foundation in law. But in matters in which the Druze religious-legal norm is utterly different from the Islamic, such as polygamy, divorce and wills, the Druzes turned to religious functionaries who acted by voluntary agreement of the parties; their decisions had not the effect of judgments enforceable in execution proceedings but of arbitral awards anchored in their personal authority and supported by religious and social sanctions. The arbitrators decided in accordance with custom and tradition (*ʿādāt wa-taḳālīd*); there were no strict rules of procedure.

The institutionalisation of arbitration and its transformation into a judicial proceeding began in the Ottoman era with the appointment of the first "*ḳāḍī*" in Palestine in 1909. He acted as an arbitrator, and his existence did not do away with the residuary jurisdiction, in respect of the Druzes, of the _Sharī ʿa_ court in the Ottoman era or of the District Court under the Mandate. The office of "*ḳāḍī*"-arbitrator was hereditary in the Ṭarīf family. In 1954, a "Committee of Religious-Legal Supervision" (*laḏjnat al-murāḳaba al-maḏhhabiyya*) was set up to supervise marriage solemnisers (*maʾḏhūn*) appointed under an Ordinance of 1919. In 1959, a "Committee for Druze *Waḳf* Affairs" (*al-laḏjna li-shuʾūn al-awḳāf al-durziyya*) was established. The two committees in fact also dealt with the settlement of disputes in matters of marriage and divorce. They did not act as statutory judicial authorities; their decisions were valid only with the consent of the parties and could not be enforced in execution proceedings. At the same time, they showed many characteristics of institutionalised judicial authorities. The awards of "judgments" of the committees were recognised, though with some hesitation by the various state authorities. The committees were a kind of unofficial courts of law, and most of their members later became _ḳāḍī_s of the Druze courts.

The Druze Religious Courts Law, 1962, vests the courts with exclusive jurisdiction in matters of marriage and divorce of the Druzes in Israel and with concurrent jurisdiction in all their other matters of personal status. They also have exclusive jurisdiction in matters relating to the creation or internal administration of a religious endowment established before a Druze court or in accordance with Druze custom, i.e. by will and not before any judicial authority.

In its original version, the law provides that the Court of First Instance shall consist of three _ḳāḍī madhhab_s and the Court of Appeal of not less than three. In 1967, it was laid down that if it was not possible to form such courts the court might consist of two _ḳāḍī_s, and in 1972 it was provided that the Court of First Instance might consist of one *ḳāḍī*. The *ḳāḍīs* are appointed by the President of the State on the recommendation of an appointments committee, most of the members of which are Druzes. A transitional provision prescribes that the first Court of Appeal shall consist of the members of the "Religious Council", i.e. the Spiritual Leadership of the Druze community. The Druze courts are integrated in the general legal system of the State, which enforces their judgments. Since the establishment of Druze courts, the Druzes have ceased to resort to the Muslim *Sharīʿa* courts.

The Druzes of the Golan Heights formerly settled most of their matrimonial affairs, without resort to any judicial authority, by means of religious functionaries acting as arbitrators, and in so far as they did go to a court, it was, in the Ottoman era, the Druze *madhhab* court in Djabal al-Durūz or in Ḥāṣbayyā in Lebanon, and under Syrian rule, the Muslim *Sharīʿa* court in Ḳunayṭra. In 1967, after the Six-Day War, the latter court ceased to function. In 1970, by order of the military commander of the region, a court of first instance and a court of appeal were set up with powers similar to those of the Druze courts in Israel. From 1972 onwards, the *ḳāḍīs* of the Israeli Court of First Instance and Court of Appeal acted as members of the corresponding Golan Heights courts by virtue of the above mentioned order. In 1974, a court of first instance consisting of local *ḳāḍīs* was set up in the Golan Heights.

Before being recognised as a religious community in Israel, the Druze had no codified law of personal status and succession. They dealt with these matters in accordance with their esoteric law and with custom, and in so far as they restored to a judicial authority, it was the *Sharīʿa* court, which applied the Ottoman Family Rights Law or, in the absence of an express provision in the latter, *sharʿī* law according to the Ḥanafī school. In 1961, the Spiritual Leadership of the Druze community in Israel, in its statutory capacity as the "Religious Council", adopted the Personal Status Law of the Druze Community in Lebanon of 1948 (see Section 4. iii above) with the following modifications: (a) the Ḥanafī doctrine, which served as a source of law in matters of intestate succession and in the absence of an express provision of law in a particular matter of personal status, was replaced by custom and "the law accepted by the members of the Druze community in Israel"; (b) Lebanese legislation designed to supplement the Druze Personal Status Law was replaced by Israeli legislation. The "Religious Council" sanctioned the Druze Courts Procedure Regulations of 1964, which incorporate norms of Israeli law.

The law applying to matters of personal status in the Golan Heights was until the introduction of Israeli law there on 14 December 1981 the Syrian Personal Status Law of 1953 (see Section 4. ii above). The Israeli Succession Law of 1965 was extended to the Golan Heights by the above-mentioned order of the military commander of 1970. In practice, the *ḳāḍīs*, in matters of personal status, apply the Lebanese Druze Personal Status Law, as adopted by the Religious Council. Since the introduction of Israeli law in the Golan Heights, this practice has been validated. All Israeli legislation in matters of personal status expressly referred to religious courts is likewise applicable in Druze religious courts there.

Under Egyptian military rule in the Gaza Strip, there were three *Sharīʿa* courts of first instance at Gaza, Khān Yūnis and Dayr al-Balaḥ, respectively. They had jurisdiction in matters of personal status and *waḳf* within the meaning of the Palestine Order in Council, 1922. Under Israeli military rule (since 1967), two additional courts have been set up in Djabaliyya and Rafaḥ. A *Sharīʿa* court of appeal operates in Gaza in accordance with the Egyptian Law of Procedure of Muslim Religious Courts no. 12 of 1965. The Ottoman Family Rights Law of 1917 applies in these courts. The salaries of the *ḳaḍīs* are paid by the Military Government.

Bibliography: F. M. Goadby, *Inter-religious private law in Palestine*, Jerusalem 1926; E. Vitta, *The conflict of laws in matters of personal status in Palestine*, Tel-Aviv 1947; S. D. Goitein and A. Ben Shemesh, *ha-Mishpaṭ ha-muslemi be-medinat Yisraʾel* ("Muslim law in Israel"), Jerusalem 1957; A. Layish, *Women and Islamic law in a non-Muslim state*, Jerusalem and New York 1975, and the bibl. there; idem, *The Muslim waqf in Israel*, in *Asian and African Studies*, ii (1965), 43-51; idem, *Qāḍīs and sharīʿa in Israel*, in *AAS*, vii (1971), 237-72; idem, *The family waqf and the Sharīʿa law of succession according to waqfiyyāt in the sijills of the Sharīʿa courts*, in G. Baer (ed.), *Social and economic aspects of the Muslim waqf* (forthcoming); Y. Meron, *Moslem courts, their jurisdiction in Israel and neighbouring lands*, (forthcoming); R. H. Eisenman, *Islamic law in Palestine and Israel*, Leiden 1978; Y. Meron, *The religious courts in the administered territories*, in M. Shamgar (ed.), *Military government in the territories administered by Israel 1967-1980*, Jerusalem 1982, 354, 361-2; on Druze justice, see A. Layish, *Marriage, divorce and succession in the Druze family*, Leiden 1982, and the bibl. there; idem, *The Druze testamentary waqf*, in Baer (ed.), *op. cit.* On tribal justice in Palestine see ʿĀrif al-ʿĀrif, *Kitāb al-Ḳaḍāʾ bayn al-badw*, Jerusalem 1933. (A. Layish)

vi. Jordan

The *sharʿī* legal system in Jordan is based on a medley of legal traditions. Both banks of the Jordan River were under Ottoman rule until World War I and under British Mandate thereafter. Ottoman legal tradition was preserved to a greater extent in the East Bank owing to the autonomy enjoyed by the emirate which eventually became an independent kingdom, while the influence of English law was felt more strongly in the West Bank.

After the inclusion of the West Bank in the Kingdom of Jordan, steps were taken to integrate the two legal systems, including *sharʿī* jurisdiction, which in Transjordan was regulated by *Sharīʿa* Courts Law, 1931, and to unify the organisation of the religious establishment. The law which regulated the reorganisation of the *Sharīʿa* courts in the united Hashemite Kingdom repealed the provisions of Mandated Palestine's Supreme Muslim Council Order of 1921 relating to the *sharʿī* legal system (see Section 4. v above). Closely connected therewith was the appointment of a staunch supporter of the *Amīr* ʿAbd Allāh as *Muftī* of Jerusalem in place of Amīn al-Ḥusaynī [*q.v.* in Suppl.] already in December 1948, and the transfer of the primacy from the *Muftī* of Jerusalem to the *Muftī* of the Kingdom of Jordan, whose seat is in ʿAmmān. Since unification, the Jordanian *ḳāḍī 'l-ḳuḍāt* takes the place of the President of the Supreme Muslim Council in the West Bank. He appoints the *ḳāḍīs* and *muftīs* and supervises the *waḳf* administration and the religious and educational institutions supported by it, the *ʿUlamāʾ* Council (*hayʾa*), the Council for Preaching and Guidance (*madjlis al-waʿẓ wa 'l-irshād*) and the Committee for the Rehabilitation of the al-Aḳṣā Mosque and the Dome of the Rock. He has the status of a government minister and is directly subordinate to the Prime Minister.

The jurisdiction of the *Sharīʿa* courts in the West Bank has been assimilated to that of their counterparts in the East Bank. The Jordanian constitution of 1952 and other enactments of the early nineteen-fifties vest the *Sharīʿa* courts with jurisdiction in all matters of personal status and succession as defined in Islamic law, which definition is wider than that of the Palestine Order in Council, as well as in matters of *waḳf* and blood-money (*diya*) of Muslims. Their jurisdiction in matters of personal status is limited to Muslims. Residuary jurisdiction in matters of personal status of non-Muslims has been transferred to a civil court of first instance, except where the parties agree to the jurisdiction of the *Sharīʿa* court. In matters of blood-money and of *waḳfs* established before a *Sharīʿa* court, the *Sharīʿa* courts have jurisdiction also with regard to consenting non-Muslims.

The law applying to matters of personal status on both banks of the Jordan was until 1951 the Ottoman Family Rights Law of 1917. In 1951, it was replaced by a liberal family law. Previously, in 1927, a new personal status law was adopted in Transjordan, but it was repealed in 1943 in favour of the traditional doctrine of family law. A provisional Jordanian family Rights Law, no. 26, was enacted in 1947, to be superseded by the law of 1951. The Law of Personal Status, no. 61 of 1976, replaced the law of 1951. The new law is more extensive and detailed than the earlier one and includes important amendments. The *Sharīʿa* Courts Establishment Law and the Personal Status Law of 1951 provide that the courts shall hear matters within their jurisdiction in accordance with the most approved opinion of the Ḥanafī school, save where a provision of law to the contrary exists. A similar provision exists also in the laws of personal status of 1951 and 1976. An overwhelming majority of the Kingdom's population belongs to the Shāfiʿī school. The *Sharīʿa* courts on both banks of the Jordan apply the *Sharʿī* Procedure Law, no. 31 of 1959, which replaced the Procedure Law no. 10 of 1952.

The *Sharīʿa* Courts Establishment Law of 1951 established a unitary judicial system on both banks. Twenty-four courts of first instance, each consisting of a *ḳāḍī* sitting alone, were set up at district and sub-district centres, eight thereof in the West Bank. The Court of Appeal consists of a president and two members. It passes decisions by a majority of votes and its judgments are final. The law enables the establishment of an additional court of appeal, and in fact two courts of appeal, one in ʿAmmān for the East Bank and one in Jerusalem for the West Bank, were at first set up; however, after a short time, in August 1951, it was decided that there should be only one *Sharīʿa* court of appeal, which was to have its permanent seat in ʿAmmān but might be convened in Jerusalem when necessary. The *Sharʿī* Law Council, headed by the Director of the *Sharīʿa* Office, is responsible for the appointment and dismissal of *ḳāḍīs*. Its decisions require the approval of the king.

The powers of the courts of the Christian communities in Jordan have been greatly widened compared with the Ottoman period and assimilated to those of the *Sharīʿa* courts. According to the Religious Councils Law, no. 2 of 1938, which was extended to the West Bank in 1958, and the Consitution of 1952, they have jurisdiction in all matters of personal status and succession, as well as in matters of the establishment and internal administration of *waḳfs* founded for the benefit of the community. They apply the law of the community except in matters of succession and wills, which are governed by Islamic law.

The Bedouin in Jordan are not amenable to *sharʿī* jurisdiction. They have tribal courts (*maḥākīm al-ʿashāʾir*) regulated by a law of 1966, which replaced a law of 1924. Every *mutaṣarrif* is responsible for the activities of the court in his district, and the army commander is responsible for the court in the Desert District. A law of 1949 provides that these courts shall have jurisdiction in all disputes of Bedouin, except matters of ownership and possession of immovable property and written partnership agreements concerning thoroughbred horses. The *mutaṣarrif* enforces the judgments, but the penalty for offences must not exceed one year's imprisonment and a fine of a specific amount. The *mutaṣarrif* or the army commander, as the case may be, may transfer cases from the tribal court to a civil court.

A judgment of a tribal court is appealable to a tribal court of appeal. This court may consult experts in tribal law. It may increase or reduce the penalty or return the matter to the court of first instance for a re-hearing. The tribal courts apply customary law. However, state law forbids certain customs, such as giving girls as *diya*. Procedure in tribal courts is also customary.

As a result of the Six-Day War in 1967, the West Bank was separated from the Kingdom of Jordan, but Jordanian law still applies there, except in East Jerusalem, where Israeli law has been introduced. This situation affects the functioning of the religious establishment. The *Sharīʿa* courts of first instance have been left without their court of appeal, the permanent seat of which, as stated, is in ʿAmmān.

On 24 July 1967, Muslim political leaders and religious functionaries in East Jerusalem set up a "Muslim Council" (*al-hayʾa al-islāmiyya*), which assumed authority for the conduct of Muslim affairs in East Jerusalem and the West Bank. The sole purpose of this body, which has no statutory status in either Jordanian or Israeli law, is to fill the place of the absent Muslim sovereign. The Council appointed its president to be *ḳāḍī ʾl-ḳuḍāt* of the West Bank with powers as defined by Jordanian law.

The Israeli *Sharīʿa* Court of Jaffa, the area of jurisdiction of which has been extended to include East Jerusalem (see Section 4. v above), is not recognised by most East Jerusalem Muslims, while the local *Sharīʿa* court, which is subject to the Muslim Council, is not recognised by the Israeli authorities. East Jerusalem Muslims do not resort to the Israeli court unless they are interested in the execution of a judgment or in the performance of some act in a government office on the strength of a certificate from the court. In the West Bank, the Israeli Military Government has inherited the powers of the Jordanian Government in its various spheres of activity and is consequently charged with the operation of the courts, the appointment and dismissal of the *ḳāḍīs* and the payment of their salaries, and the collection of court fees. In fact, however, it is the Jerusalem *ḳāḍī ʾl-ḳuḍāt* who appoints the *ḳāḍīs* and the Jordanian Government which pays their salaries. The Military Government recognises their appointments *ex post facto* and the executive offices subject to it enforce their judgments. As the *Sharīʿa* Court of Appeal of the West Bank is in Jerusalem, its judgments are not valid in the West Bank, but in day-to-day reality they are enforced there. The *Sharīʿa* courts of the West Bank and of East Jerusalem apply the Jordanian law of personal status and rules of procedure.

Along with their judicial tasks, several East Jerusalem *ḳāḍīs* carry out various other functions—exegetic (the *Muftī* of Jerusalem), administrative and public—connected with the religious establishment.

The Muslim Council has conferred on the *Sharī*ʿ*a* Court of Appeal the powers of the Council of Endowments and Islamic Affairs, the General Administration of Endowments and the Committee for the Rehabilitation of the al-Akṣā Mosque and the Dome of the Rock, bodies anchored in Jordanian legislation.

Bibliography: Adīb al-Halasā, *Usus al-tashrī*ʿ *wa 'l-niẓam al-ḳaḍāʾī fi 'l-Urdunn*, n.p. 1971; Maḥmaṣānī, *al-Awḍā*ʿ *al-tashrī*ʿ*iyya*, 304-13; J. N. D. Anderson, *Recent developments in Sharī*ʿ*a law. viii. The Jordanian law of family rights 1951*, in *MW*, xlii (1952), 190-206; E. T. Mogannam, *Developments in the legal system of Jordan*, in *MEJ*, vi (1952), 194-206; idem, *The practical application of the law in certain Arab states*; on the *sharī*ʿ*a* courts in the West Bank and East Jerusalem, see A. Layish, *ha-Mimsad ha-dati ha-muslemi ha-gadah ha-ma*ʿ*aravit ba-teḳufa ha-yardenit* ("Muslim religious institutions in the West Bank under Jordanian rule"), in *Medain, Mimshal vi(Y)ḥasim Beinleumiyim*, xi (1977), 97-108; D. Farhi, *ha-Mo*ʿ*atza ha-muslemit be-mizrah Yerushalayim uvi-Yehuda ve-Shomron me-az milḥemet sheshet ha-yamim* ("The Muslim Council in East Jerusalem and in Judea and Samaria since the Six-Day War"), in *Hamizrash Heḥadash*, xxviii (1979), 1-2, 3-21; Y. Meron, *The religious courts in the administered territories*, 353-68. On the position of the *Sharī*ʿ*a* and the *Sharī*ʿ*a* courts in tribal society, see J. Chelhod, *Le droit dans la société bédouine*, Paris 1971; A. Layish and A. Shmueli, *Custom and sharī*ʿ*a in the Bedouin family according to legal documents from the Judean Desert*, in *BSOAS*, xlii (1979), 1, 29-45; A. Layish, *The islamization of the Bedouin family in the Judean Desert, as reflected in the sijills of the sharī*ʿ*a court*, in E. Marx and A. Shmueli (eds.), *The changing nomad: Bedouin in and around Israel*, New Brunswick, N.J. 1983.

(A. Layish)

vii. Saudi Arabia

The Arabian Peninsula was under the nominal sovereignty of the Ottoman Empire, but the 19th century legal reforms of the Empire were not applied there except in the major urban centres of the Ḥidjāz, and even there with only limited success. At the time of his conquest of the Ḥidjāz in the early 20th century, ʿAbd al-ʿAzīz Ibn Saʿūd found there a legal system progressive by the standards of other regions of the peninsula. In the small towns of Nadjd, disputes were settled by the local *amīr* or a *ḳāḍī* appointed by him. Among the Bedouin, customary law, applied by arbitrators, reigned absolute.

The "constitution" of the Ḥidjāz of 1926 makes no express reference to the judicial system, but says that the King is limited by the *Sharī*ʿ*a* and that the legislation of the kingdom shall be based on the Ḳurʾān, the *Sunna* of the Prophet and the *idjmā*ʿ of his Companions. A *fatwā* of the ʿ*ulamā*ʾ, of 1927, demanded *inter alia* that ʿAbd al-ʿAzīz forthwith repeal the Ottoman laws in force in the Ḥidjāz and restore the position of the *Sharī*ʿ*a*.

A royal decree of 1927 established three grades of courts in the Ḥidjāz:

(1) Expeditious Courts (*maḥkama musta*ʿ*djila*), competent to try misdemeanours (*dhunaḥ*) punishable by a fine not exceeding a specific amount, offences the penalty for which was left to the discretion of the *ḳāḍī* (*ta*ʿ*zīrāt*) and felonies (*djināyāt*) entailing Ḳurʾānic punishments (*ḥudūd*), except mutilation (*ḳaṭ*ʿ) or death; they consist of a single *ḳāḍī*. Such courts were set up in Mecca and Medina and later in Riyāḍ and other major cities. Mecca had a further Expeditious Court, hearing claims by Bedouin. In small administrative units, and especially among the numerous tribes of desert Bedouin, the local *amīr* acts as *ḳāḍī*; he generally applies the *Sharī*ʿ*a* but sometimes resorts to tribal custom.

(2) Greater *Sharī*ʿ*a* Courts (*maḥkama shar*ʿ*iyya kubrā*), competent to deal with serious criminal (*djazaʾī*) matters and civil (*ḥuḳūḳī*) claims, except those under the jurisdiction of the Expeditious Courts, and with matters of personal status, probate and land. One such court exists in Mecca and one in Medina. The one in Mecca consists of three *ḳāḍīs*. Ordinary cases are heard by a single *ḳāḍī*, but the judgment is given by the full court. Cases in which the punishment may be death or mutilation are heard by the full court. The court in Medina consists of a single *ḳāḍī* (with a *nāʾib*) and so does the one in Djidda, but after the recent abolition of the Expeditious Court in Djidda the Greater *Sharī*ʿ*a* Court there hears all cases, except those under the jurisdiction of *al-madjlis al-tidjārī* (see below). In all the other towns of the Ḥidjāz and Nadjd, the court, consisting of a single *ḳāḍī*, hears all cases.

The penalties of death and mutilation in all the towns of the Ḥidjāz, all Ḳurʾānic punishments, and discretionary punishments in Mecca, require confirmation by *raʾīs al-ḳaḍā*ʾ and *hayʾat al-tamyīz* (see below) before being carried out. In Medina and other localities where the court consists of several members, a penalty for a misdemeanour, a discretionary punishment and a Ḳurʾānic punishment other than death require confirmation by the Grand *Ḳāḍī* of the town before being carried out. In towns where the court consists of a single *ḳāḍī*, judgments are only carried out if confirmed by the most senior administrative official in the town in question.

An opportunity is provided—this is an innovation which has no basis in the classical texts—to appeal from the judgment of a *Sharī*ʿ*a* court to a Greater *Sharī*ʿ*a* Court, which, as stated, is competent to try felonies as a court of first instance. In 1954, it was ordained that every judgment of a *ḳāḍī* should be carried out forthwith, except judgments against which a complaint has been lodged on the ground of injustice and judgments imposing the death penalty, mutilation or confiscation (*muṣādara*); the latter ones require confirmation by the supreme authorities, even if they are not appealed against.

By the side of every Greater *Sharī*ʿ*a* Court, there acts an official of the Public Treasury (*maʾmūr bayt al-māl*), whose task is the distribution of inheritances and the protection of the interest of minors.

(3) The Commission on Judicial Supervision (*hayʾat al-murāḳaba al-ḳaḍāʾiyya*), the seat of which is in Mecca. It comprises a Board of Judicial Review (*hayʾat al-tadḳīḳāt*) consisting of four members and headed by a *raʾīs al-ḳaḍā*ʾ. This body acts as a court of cassation (*maḥkamat al-tamyīz*). It examines judgments and confirms them or returns them to the lower court for a re-hearing in order to clarify a point or to rectify a procedural error. It may reverse judgments incompatible with the Ḳurʾān and the *Sunna* and direct the lower court to retry the case. If the *ḳāḍī* abides by his original decision, the case must be referred to another *ḳāḍī*. The Board also examines sentences of mutilation, death and confiscation. The Commission on Judicial Supervision gives legal opinions on matters not within the competence of the *Sharī*ʿ*a* courts.

The *raʾīs al-ḳaḍā*ʾ performs the functions of President of the Supreme Court and Minister of Justice. He also supervises the Public Treasury (*bayt al-māl*), the mechanism of religious-legal opinions (*iftāʾ*) and disciplinary proceedings against *ḳāḍīs*, and handles complaints about the functioning of any part of the *sharʿī* system. Moreover, he supervises all the Public Morality Committees (*hayʾat al-amr bi 'l-maʿrūf wa 'l-nahy ʿan al-munkar*) in the Ḥidjāz and Nadjd, the religious functionaries, education and *sharʿī* institutions, including the Islamic University of Medina, and religious instruction at state educational institutions.

This *sharʿī* judicial system remained in existence until the mid-seventies. Minor amendments were made by orders of the years 1931, 1936, 1938 and 1952. The name of the Commission on Judicial Supervision was changed in 1938 to Office of the Chief Justice (*riʾāsat al-ḳaḍāʾ*), but its functions remained the same. In 1967, amendments were introduced in the organisation of the judiciary and in the powers of the *ḳāḍīs*, and in 1970, a Ministry of Justice was set up. In 1974, the *sharʿī* judicial system was thoroughly reorganised. Three grades of courts were established on the Western pattern: magistrates' courts (*maḥākim djuzʾiyya*), district courts (*maḥākim ʿāmma*) and a court of cassation (*maḥkamat al-tamyīz*). Moreover, a High Judicial Council (*madjlis al-ḳaḍāʾ al-aʿlā*) was formed whose functions were to supervise the *ḳāḍīs* and to try disciplinary offences. The law ensures the independence of the *ḳāḍīs* (they cannot be removed from office); their appointment and promotion are effected by the king on the recommendation of the Judicial Council.

Sharʿī law applies to all matters within the competence of the *Sharīʿa* courts. In 1927, the *ḳāḍīs* were ordered to decide in accordance with the teachings of the Ḥanbalī school. Six books of that school, in a specific order, were recognised as authoritative sources that must be adhered to. This, in a way, introduced an element of codification and unification of the material law into the nation's judicial system. In 1927, ʿAbd al-ʿAzīz Ibn Saʿūd, inspired by Ibn Taymiyya, suggested the preparation of a code of Islamic law based not only on the Ḥanbalī doctrine but also on any other doctrine which, with regard to the matter in hand, was close to the Ḳurʾān and the *Sunna*. But he abandoned the idea under pressure from Ḥanbalī *ʿulamāʾ*. In the Ottoman era, the Ḥanbalī doctrine prevailed only in Nadjd and the Shāfiʿī doctrine in the Ḥidjāz, except for the courts in the major towns, where the Ḥanafī doctrine enjoyed official status. An order of 1930 provided that where an express provision existed in those authoritative sources as to a case being heard by a *Sharīʿa* court consisting of several *ḳāḍīs*, a decision might be given without convening the members of the court; in the absence of such a provision, they were to be convened in order to exercise their collective discretion. The *ḳāḍīs* were permitted to resort to other orthodox doctrines where the opinion of the Ḥanbalī school was likely to cause damage and was not compatible with the public interest (*maṣlaḥat al-ʿumūm*). An order of 1934 required the court, in deference to local custom, to decide matters relating to contracts of lease of agricultural land (*ʿuḳūd al-musāḳāt*) or palm plantations (*idjārāt al-nakhīl*) in accordance with the doctrine prevailing in the locality where the action was brought. In matters containing religious observances (*ʿibādāt*), the individual is free to follow the doctrine of the school to which he belongs. The *Sharīʿa* courts are subject to the *sharʿī* rules of procedure. Enactments relating to these rules were made in 1931, 1936 and 1952.

Professional lawyers have recently been authorised to appear before *Sharīʿa* courts. In 1928, a Notarial Office (*kitābat al-ʿadl*) was established for the registration of *sharʿī* documents (*ṣukūk*), powers of attorney, sales and pledges, but not of *waḳfs*, which are within the competence of the *Sharīʿa* courts. There are notaries in Mecca, Djidda and Medina. In provincial towns, the functions of the notary are performed by the *ḳāḍī*. A programmatic statement by Crown Prince Fayṣal's government in 1962 promised the creation of the post of State Public Prosecutor at the Ministry of Justice.

From time to time, the King confers quasi-judicial powers on various bodies with a view to solving problems cropping up in the economic, social or administrative sphere. Some of these bodies in fact enjoy extremely wide powers. They function concurrently with the *sharʿī* judicial system and are ostensibly designed to supplement it, but in reality restrict it.

The most important of these bodies is the Grievances Board (*dīwān al-maẓālim*), established in 1954, whose seat is in al-Riyāḍ, with an extension in Djidda. Anyone who believes that an injustice has been done to him by a decision of a judicial authority or by an administrative authority may complain to it. Its functions are to investigate the complaint and to suggest to the Royal Chancellery and to the government ministry concerned the adoption of measures against the authority in question; to investigate, together with other bodies, corruption offences, disciplinary offences in the army, and offences against economic boycott regulations (if the recommendations of the Board are rejected, the matter is to be brought before the King); to hear appeals against decisions of the Minister of Commerce in matters relating to foreign capital investments; to supervise the application of the *Sharīʿa* by the government in day-to-day life (the Board includes experts on *Sharīʿa* matters and sometimes refers complaints to the *Sharīʿa* court) and—at the special request of the King—to deal with serious matters relating to Bedouin and matters in which foreigners are involved; and to execute foreign judgments.

The chairman of the Board is appointed by the King and has the status of a government minister; since 1964, he has been responsible to the King for the work of the Board (all the decisions of the Board require the approval of the King). The Grievances Board is a permanent institution. Its simple procedure and the fact that most of its members are lawyers with a modern background ensure greater flexibility in the conduct of proceedings than prevails in *sharʿī* justice.

Other administrative-judicial bodies are the Commission on Cases of Forgery (*tazwīr*), established in 1960, headed by the Minister of Justice and including representatives of the Grievances Board; the Commission on Cases of Bribery, established in 1962 and headed by the chairman of the Grievances Board; and the Commission on the Impeachment of Ministers, competent to try various offences, ranging from interference by Ministers in the working of the judicial system to high treason (punishable with death); it is an *ad hoc* body appointed by the Prime Minister and consists of ministers and senior *ḳāḍīs*; death sentences must be passed unanimously; the judgments of the Commission are appealable to the King.

Several judicial bodies deal with commercial matters: the Central Committee on Cases of Adulteration (*ghishsh tidjārī*), which tries offences connected with food and drugs; and Chambers of Commerce (*ghurfat al-tidjāra*), established in 1963 and consisting of representatives of the economic ministries, which they act as arbitral boards in commercial disputes. The most important of these bodies was the Commercial

Tribunal (*maḥkama tidjāriyya*), first established in Djidda in 1926 for the handling of commercial disputes. Its composition and powers were laid down by a commercial regulation in 1931. It consisted of a presiding judge and seven members, one of them from the *sharʿī* legal system, who were appointed by the king. Its decisions might be appealed to the Consultative Council (*madjlis al-shūrā*). Its rules of procedure were similar to those of the *Sharīʿa* courts. Smaller commercial tribunals were established in Yanbuʿ and Dammān. Their judgments were appealable to the Commercial Tribunal in Djidda.

The commercial tribunals in Djidda, Yanbuʿ and Dammān were abolished and their functions taken over by the Ministry of Commerce in 1954. They were restored in 1965, when Commercial Disputes Arbitration Boards were set up, one in each city, each Board consisting of three officials of the Ministry of Commerce and Industry. A Commercial Disputes Appeals Board was established in 1967, consisting of three officials of the same ministry, one of them, its head, the Deputy Minister. These Boards are not bound by the *Sharīʿa*, but they can draw upon it as well as upon Western law and international law and agreements. The Saudi authorities have recently directed that agreements of commercial companies shall contain an express clause forbidding the settlement of disputes by arbitration contrary to the principles of the *Sharīʿa*.

A Supreme Board on Labour Disputes was set up in 1963; it consists of the legal advisers of the Ministry of Labour and Social Affairs and the Ministry of Petroleum and Minerals. Disciplinary Councils for Civil Servants try offenders—by virtue of regulations of 1958—only after they have been convicted by a *Sharīʿa* court. Disciplinary Councils for Military Personnel act as military tribunals by virtue of regulations of 1947. Their judgments may be set aside or commuted by the Chief of the General Staff or the Minister of Defence. Disciplinary Councils for Internal Security Personnel try police officers, members of the coast guard, frontier patrolmen, members of the fire brigade and criminal investigators. The King supervises the judicial system by virtue of his being the supreme *ḳāḍī* and sometimes sits on the bench himself, advised by *ʿulamāʾ*.

Saudi Arabia was not subject to the influence of foreign systems of law other than the Ottoman, the impact of which was limited to the Ḥidjāz. The *Sharīʿa* functioned here in a sovereign Muslim state which had grown out of the Wahhābiyya [*q.v.*], a puritanical Muslim renaissance movement which sought to apply religious law strictly and uncompromisingly in all spheres of life and in relations with the outside world. Saudi Arabia is perhaps the most theocratic state in the Sunnī Muslim world. Religion has a monopoly of the judicial system, education, public morals and the fiscal system; the *ʿulamāʾ* are integrated in the political establishment; there is no constitution and no legislative authority; and the Ḥanbalī doctrine is enforced upon the entire kingdom.

At the same time, there are significant manifestations of a decline of the status of religion and religious law in the state, although they are minimal compared with the secularisation processes in other Middle Eastern Arab countries. Important, though somewhat vague, elements of a constitution were adopted by various enactments and declarations under external pressure; an increasing number of administrative regulations made by the government and the King (*niẓām, marsūm*), which have the force of law, are ostensibly designed to supplement the *Sharīʿa* but in fact impair its substantive validity; important reforms have been made in commercial law: regulations based on the Ottoman Commercial Code of 1850, in turn based on a purely French model, have been enacted with the omission of all references to interest (that Code is applied in the tribunals of the chambers of commerce); banks have begun to operate on the basis of interest, although it is called commission; marine and other property insurance is permitted, though not, for the time being, life insurance; extensive fiscal legislation (customs duties, income and alms (*zakāt*) tax, etc.) has been enacted; contracts regulating oil concessions to foreign companies have been entered into, although the terminology is *sharʿī* as far as possible; social laws and laws regulating labour relations and transport have been enacted; slavery was abolished in 1962 in deference to international public opinion, although there are indications that reality is still stronger than the law; *sharʿī* criminal law, including the harsh Ḳurʾānic penalties (decapitation and mutilation for theft), is still mainly applied, although a tendency to replace corporal punishment by imprisonment or fines is discernible; new penalties, not strictly conforming to the provisions of the *Sharīʿa*, have been introduced (e.g. the drinking of wine (*shurb al-khamr*) entails a discretionary punishment (*taʿzīr*), not a Ḳurʾānic one (*ḥadd*); blood-money (*diya*) has been limited; penalties have been prescribed for forgery, strikes, causing death or injury in road accidents and military offences); there are deviations from the *Sharīʿa* as to the status of non-Muslims (e.g. their testimony in criminal proceedings has the same weight as that of Muslims and their oath is accepted; the same blood-money is exacted for them as for Muslims).

Bibliography: Snouck Hurgronje, *Mekka*, ii; idem, *Mekka in the latter part of the 19th century*: R. B. Winder, *Saudi Arabia in the nineteenth century*, London 1965, see index; Soliman A. Solaim, *Constitutional and judicial organization in Saudi Arabia*, Ph. D. thesis, The Johns Hopkins University, Washinton, D.C. 1970; Muḥammad Ibrāhīm Aḥmad ʿAlī, *Social responsibilities of the individual and the state in Saʿūdī Arabian law*, Ph. D. thesis, University of London 1971; Abulaziz Mohammad Zaid, *Law of bequest in traditional Islamic law and in contemporary law of Saudi Arabia*, Ph. D. thesis, University of London, 1978; Maḥmaṣānī, *al-Awḍāʿ al-tashrīʿiyya*, 354-75; Muḥammad ʿAbd al-Djawād Muḥammad, *al-Taṭawwur al-tashrīʿī fi 'l-mamlaka al-ʿarabiyya al-saʿūdiyya*, Alexandria 1977; N. Anderson, *Law reform in the Muslim world*, London 1976, see index; Liebesny, *The law of the Near and Middle East*, see index; S. von Gerd-Rüdiger Puin, *Der moderne Alltag im Spiegel ḥanbalitischer Fetwas aus ar-Riyāḍ*, in *ZDMG*, Suppl. iii, 1 (1977), 589-97; A. Layish, *ʿUlamāʾ and politics in Saudi Arabia*, in M. Heper and R. Israeli (eds.), *Islam and politics in the modern Middle East* (forthcoming). (A. LAYISH)

viii. Yemen and the People's Republic of Southern Yemen

Towards the end of their rule in Yemen, the Ottomans tried to apply their laws there and firmly to establish there the Shāfiʿī school, whose main foothold was in the Tihāma region and in the south of the country. The *Imām* resisted this attempt successfully. A sultanic *firmān* of 1913 confirmed the Treaty of Daʿʿān of 1911, by which the Ottomans agreed to the demands of the Imām, the most important of them being the reinstatement of the *Sharīʿa* as the only system of law in Yemen. The *Imām* was authorised to appoint *ḳāḍīs* to the courts in regions populated by Zaydī Shīʿis (the Ṣanʿāʾ region and the northern mountainous province). The power of the Ottoman *Wālī* was confined to the enforcement of their judgments.

After World War I, when Yemen obtained full independence, it became a theocracy. Zaydī Shīʿī law, which is nearest to Sunnī law, held unlimited sway in the imāmate. The *Imām* was the spiritual head, the head of the executive branch and the Supreme Judge (*al-ḳāḍī al-aʿlā*).

The powers of the *Sharīʿa* courts are very wide. They comprise personal status and criminal law. Severe Ḳurʾānic punishments, such as death and mutilation, are still applied, though not frequently. The *Imām* has directed that Zaydī Shīʿī law shall be applied in the courts. The *Sharīʿa* courts system consists of several grades. The court of first instance is manned by a single judge (*ḥākim*). His judgement is appealable, with the consent of the local governor (*ʿāmil*), to a higher judge and finally to the High Court of Appeal (*raʾīs al-istiʾnāf*), which has its seat in Ṣanʿāʾ. The *Imām* is the supreme appellate authority, but appeals to him are infrequent. The *Imām* appoints the judges in all the districts and sub-districts from among the graduates of al-Madrasa al-ʿIlmiyya in Ṣanʿāʾ. The *amīr al-liwāʾ* enforces their judgments, but the supervision of the *sharʿī* system is the prerogative of the *Imām*.

Concurrently with the *Sharīʿa* judicial system, a judicial system of the provincial governor (*ʿāmil*) functions which handles civil matters. Its judgments are appealable to the prince as ruler of the principality (*liwāʾ*) or, in certain cases, to the Imām. This system is governed by the *Sharīʿa* as far as commercial transactions and tax matters are concerned.

The *Sharīʿa* courts operate in the towns. Outside the towns, among the tribes, an arbitral (*manḳad*) system exists, and tribal councils adjudicate disputes concerning water, boundaries and criminal offences in accordance with tribal custom (*ʿurf*) and tradition (*taḳālīd*). Appeals against judgments of tribal courts are heard by the *ʿāmil*, whose judgments are in turn appealable to the provincial *amīr*. Here, too, the *Imām* is the supreme appellate authority. The *Imām* has sought to eliminate customary justice and to subject the Bedouin to the *Sharīʿa*. For this purpose, he has appointed persons with a religious training as judges in the customary judicial system, hoping that they will gradually substitute the *sharīʿa* for traditional customary law, but he has had only partial success. He has had to recognise *ʿurfī* justice officially by the side of *sharʿī* justice.

When Aden was a British protectorate, it had a dual judicial system, part *sharʿī* (with wide powers in matters of personal status and criminal law) and part customary. The *Imām* of Yemen accepted the situation on condition that the *Sharīʿa* was applied. Most *ḳāḍīs* were ordered to adhere to the Shāfiʿī doctrine and even more to that of Ibn Ḥadjar. There is evidence of the application of Ḳurʾānic punishments, including the death penalty. Only minor reforms were introduced during that period.

In the period preceding the British conquest of Aden in 1839, the *ḳāḍīs* of Laḥdj [*q.v.*] were appointed by the *Imām* of Yemen; their judgments were only enforced with the consent of the parties. After the British conquest, a central administration was established in the sultanate of Laḥdj and, *inter alia*, *Sharīʿa* courts equipped with wide powers, including the imposition of sanctions, were set up there by the sultan. Customary courts functioned side by side with them; their procedure and rules of evidence differed only slightly from those of the *Sharīʿa* courts. In 1950, a law establishing an Agricultural Court (*al-maḥkama al-zirāʿiyya*) was enacted in the sultanate of Laḥdj; this court applies the provisions of that law as well as custom and agricultural practice. The purpose of that law was to exclude agricultural matters from the jurisdiction of the *Sharīʿa* courts and the application of the *Sharīʿa*.

Since the achievement in 1967 of the independence of the People's Republic of Southern Yemen, of which the Aden Colony and the Western and Eastern Protectorates form part, the judicial system has, in the main, continued unchanged. On the other hand, in 1974, a family law was enacted of a radicalism unparalleled in the Muslim Middle East. Under Marxist influence, it aims at complete equality between the sexes. Some of the reforms contained in it have no basis whatsoever in Islamic law (see Section 4. x below). The courts apply a combination of customary and *sharʿī* procedure. A procedural law was under consideration at the beginning of 1972.

Bibliography: Maḥmaṣānī, *al-Awḍāʿ al-tashrīʿiyya*, 380-3; A. M. Maktari, *Water rights and irrigation practices in Laḥj*, Cambridge 1971; Anderson, *Law reform in the Muslim world*, see index; Liebesny, *The law of the Near and Middle East*, see index; M. W. Wenner, *Modern Yemen 1918-1966*, Baltimore 1967, 39, 46-8, 55, 67, 70, 155; Isam Gharem, *Social aspects of the legal systems in South-West Arabia, with special references to the application of Islamic family law in the Aden courts*, M. Phil. thesis, University of London 1972; J. Chelhod, in idem (ed.), *L'Arabie du Sud*, iii, *Culture et institutions du Yémen*, Paris 1985, 127-81. (A. Layish)

ix. The Gulf states

Under the British protectorate, most of the Persian Gulf Shaykhdoms and Trucial States had no courts of law in the accepted sense of the term. Justice was administered "under the palm tree" by the rulers themselves, who applied the *Sharīʿa* loosely and arbitrarily or were assisted by *ḳāḍīs*. Some of the Shaykhdoms had a dual judicial system: part *sharʿī*, dealing with matters of personal status, and part civil, dealing with all other, including criminal and commercial, matters and strongly influenced by English law.

After independence, the judicial system was reorganised. The Provisional Constitution of the United Arab Emirates of 1971, confirmed for another five years in 1976, provides that Islam shall be the religion of the Union and that the *Sharīʿa* shall be a principal source of the Union's legislation. But in fact, even the *sharʿī* judicial system is not, in most of the countries, based on pure *sharʿī* law. *Sharʿī* law is here attenuated or superseded by customary law or modern legislation. The civil courts apply several sources of law, of which the *Sharīʿa* is only one and not the most important. In some of the countries, a civil code modelled on the Egyptian Civil Code of 1948 has been introduced, of which the *Sharīʿa* is supposed to be one source of inspiration; but the role of the *Sharīʿa* is this context should not be exaggerated. The new graded civil system comprises many lawyers from other Arab countries.

In Kuwayt, a dual judicial system, part *sharʿī* and part civil, was functioning under the British protectorate. The jurisdiction of the *sharʿī ḳāḍīs* was confined to matters of personal status. The ruler set up two new courts, for criminal and civil matters, respectively. He had jurisdiction not only over his own subjects but also over resident nationals of some other Arab countries. Those courts applied the *Sharīʿa* and the ordinances of the ruler. The harsh Ḳurʾānic punishments were abolished. In 1959, an Organisation of Justice Law was enacted. In 1960, the *Sharīʿa* courts were abolished and their powers transferred to modern civil courts supervised by the Ministry of Justice. Domestic Courts were set up, with separate chambers for Shīʿs, Sunnīs and non-Muslims, to deal with matters of marriage, divorce, succession and wills. Criminal, civil and commercial courts were also set up. The Court of Appeal comprises departments for criminal and other matters, including personal status and succession. The legal system remained unchanged after independence (1961).

The courts apply the products of some very intensive modern law-making: codes of procedure, of criminal law and of commercial law have been enacted. Matters of personal status and blood-money (*diya*) of Muslims are still dealt with in accordance with the *Sharīʿa*, as taught by the respective schools. The Kuwaytī constitution provides that the *Sharīʿa* shall be the principal basis of legislation, but in point of fact the main source of inspiration is reformist Egyptian legislation, especially the Civil Code prepared by ʿAbd al-Razzāḳ al-Sanhūrī. In 1977, a commission was appointed "to amend and develop Kuwaytī legislation in accordance with the provisions of the *Sharīʿa*," but it is too early to assess the real significance of these terms of reference.

Under the British protectorate, a dual judicial system, part *sharʿī* and part civil, was set up in Baḥrayn. The *Sharīʿa* courts, subdivided into Sunnī and Djaʿfarī sections, dealt with matters of personal status and applied the *Sharīʿa* in accordance with the relevant doctrine. The Shaykh and members of his family acted as judges in the "civil" courts. These courts applied the ordinances of the Shaykh and customary law, which was largely based on Sudanese law; in any case, the *Sharīʿa* was not applied in these courts. The ruler also had jurisdiction over resident nationals of some other Arab states.

The dual, *sharʿī* and civil, system remained in existence after independence (1971) and so did the subdivision of the *Sharīʿa* courts (including the appeal stage) into Sunnī and Djaʿfarī sections. The powers of the *Sharīʿa* courts are confined to matters of personal status of Muslims, while the civil courts have jurisdiction in civil, commercial and criminal matters and in matters of personal status of non-Muslims. The Constitution of Baḥrayn of 1973 provides that the *Sharīʿa* shall be a principal source of legislation, and the Judicature Law of 1971 lays down that in the absence of a suitable provision in legislation, the judge shall base his decision on the principles of the *Sharīʿa* or, if the latter, too, fails to offer a solution, on custom. Local custom is to be given priority over general custom, and where no guidance is found in custom, the tenets of natural law or the principles of equity and good conscience shall be applied.

In Ḳaṭar, too, a dual, *sharʿī* and civil, judicial system was established under the British protectorate. The *Sharīʿa* courts decided matters of marriage, divorce and succession in accordance with the *Sharīʿa* as taught by the Ḥanbalī school. The ruler set up a civil court, which heard also criminal cases. It applied customary law and the decrees of the ruler. The ruler had advisers from among the religious leadership, whose task was to see that the decrees did not deviate from the *Sharīʿa*. The ban on the import, sale and consumption of alcoholic beverages was also strictly enforced. Through the activity of the ruler's British adviser, who served in the civil judiciary, English law, as applied in India and the Sudan, greatly influenced the criminal law of Ḳaṭar. The harsh Ḳurʾānic punishments, such as mutilation, had long been abolished and been replaced by imprisonment. Law no. 13 of 1971, regulating the courts of justice, left the *Sharīʿa* courts with residuary jurisdiction in matters of personal status of Muslims. It established courts with civil and criminal jurisdiction over both Muslims and non-Muslims, and a labour court.

The Amended Provisional Constitution of Ḳaṭar, of 1972, says that the *Sharīʿa* is a principal source of law. The last few years have seen a considerable output of civil and criminal legislation, which is applied in the civil courts. In 1971, a Civil and Commercial Law was enacted, based on the Egyptian Civil Code of 1948. It designates the *Sharīʿa* as a source of law only to be applied in the absence of a suitable norm in either statute or custom. There has also been legislation in specific spheres of commerce, such as the Share Companies Law, 1961, for the settlement of disputes with foreign oil companies by arbitration.

Sharʿī justice in Abū Ḏh̲abī (Ẓabī) is regulated by legislation of the years 1968 and 1970. A distinction is made between matters of personal status and succession, dealt with by *sharʿī ḳāḍīs*, and other civil matters, dealth with by civil judges. However, there is no formal distinction between a *sharʿī* and a civil judicial system. Every District Court has a *sharʿī ḳāḍī*. A civil matter other than of personal status or succession may be referred to the *sharʿī ḳāḍī* with the consent of the parties. Both the civil judges and the *sharʿī ḳāḍīs* are to act in accordance with justice or conscience or with the general principles of justice, provided that they are guided by Islamic law. The ruler appoints all the judges, including the *ḳāḍīs*.

The basic judicial system in Dubayy is still the *sharʿī* one. The entire legal system is regulated by the Courts Law of 1970. The civil courts are competent only for a few specific matters, leaving the *Sharīʿa* courts with residuary jurisdiction. Still, under the same law, the ruler may transfer any matter or action from the *Sharīʿa* court to the civil court. Most commercial matters have recently been so transferred. There are also criminal courts. The *Sharīʿa* courts are to apply the *Sharīʿa* with the modifications required by the laws of the emirate. Except for a few matters regulated by local custom and tradition, legal disputes are settled in the *Sharīʿa* court in accordance with the principles of the *Sharīʿa*. The civil courts are to apply usage and custom, the principles of natural justice, the law of equity, and the laws and legal practices of neighbouring countries, in addition to the laws of the emirate and the *Sharīʿa*. The Law of Procedure of 1971, which relates to civil and commercial matters, allows significant deviations from *sharʿī* procedure, such as written testimony. The ruler appoints the *ḳāḍīs*, including the Chief *Sharīʿa* Judge.

Until 1968, Sharjah (al-S̲h̲āriḳa) had only *Sharīʿa* courts. Sunnīs and Shīʿīs had separate courts (and *waḳf* administrations). These courts had jurisdiction in all matters. In 1968, the judicial system was reorganised: civil courts were established by the side of the *Sharīʿa* courts, whose jurisdiction was from then on confined to matters of personal status, succession and wills of Muslims, and *waḳf* and blood-money (*diya*) where at least one of the parties was a Muslim. The civil court has jurisdiction, in civil and criminal matters, also over non-Muslim foreigners. A law of 1971 reconfirmed the dual judicial system and empowered the ruler to establish *ad hoc* judicial bodies for all matters. The law applying in the *Sharīʿa* courts is

Islamic law, Sunnī or Shīʿī, as the case may be. The civil courts are to apply the statutes of the Shaykhdom, the principles of Islamic law, the decisions of Muslim jurists, common law and local custom, and the general principles of English law: right, justice and equity. There has been intensive legislative activity in the fields of criminal law, contracts, commercial law etc., as a result of which the Sharjah legal system is the most developed of any of the United Arab Emirates.

The *Sharīʿa* is the principal system of law also in ʿAdjmān, Umm al-Ḳaywayn, Raʾs al-Khayma and Fujayra. ʿAdjmān and Raʾs al-Khayma have also civil courts. In Raʾa al-Khayma, a Courts Law patterned on the corresponding law of Dubayy was enacted in 1971; it confers wide powers on the *Sharīʿa* courts, also in civil matters other than personal status and in criminal matters. A law of 1972 regulates the functioning of the *Sharīʿa* Court of Appeal. In the case of death sentences, appeal is automatic.

In the sultanate of Muscat and Oman (Masḳat and ʿUmān) (Oman since 1970), the *Sharīʿa* is about as firmly established as in Saʿūdī Arabia. There is no written constitution. The *Sharīʿa* courts have wide jurisdiction, including criminal matters involving Ḳurʾānic punishments, although there is a tendency to mitigate the latter. There are still public executions, but decapitation and mutilation are banned. The *Sharīʿa* courts apply the non-codified law of the Ibāḍī sect [see IBĀḌIYYA], to which most of the population of the sultanate belongs, with such modifications as arise out of legislation enacted by the Sultan in civil and commercial matters to meet present-day requirements, viz. legislation relating to investments by foreigners, commercial companies and baking. The judgment of the *ḳāḍī* is appealable to a bench of *ḳāḍīs* and to a Chief Court, the seat of which is in Oman. A final appeal lies to the Sultan.

There is a separate court for matters in which foreigners are involved; its seat is in Muscat. When the sultanate was a British protectorate, the Consular Court had jurisdiction in certain matters concerning British subjects, but in cases involving both British subjects and local nationals, the Sultan had jurisdiction. The Commercial Companies Law of 1974 established a Committee for the Settlement of Commercial Disputes, vested with judicial powers. In large areas of the sultanate outside the urban centres, tribal justice and custom reign almost absolute.

Bibliography: Liebesny, *The law of the Near and Middle East*, 108-11; idem, *British jurisdiction in the states of the Persian Gulf*, in *MEJ*, iii (1949), 3, 330-2; W. M. Ballantyne, *Legal development in Arabia*, London 1980; H. M. Albaharna, *The Arabian Gulf States; their legal and political status and their international problems*². Beirut 1975; N. Sinclair, in collaboration with W. Olesiuk, *Problems of commerce and law in the Arab states of the Lower Gulf*, in D. Dwyer (ed.), *The politics of law in the Middle East* (forthcoming); Anderson, *Law reform in the Muslim world*, see index.

(A. LAYISH)

x. Morocco

Before the establishment of the French and Spanish Protectorates, the peoples under the sultan's authority had recourse, more or less, for matters of personal status, property and contracts or religious endowments (*aḥbās*), to the *ḳāḍīs* who were to be found in centres of some importance. Till the middle of the 19th century, the ḳāḍī of Fās had the title of *ḳāḍī ʾl-ḳuḍāt* and filled all religious offices. Later, the Moroccan government reserved for itself the right to proceed, on the proposal of this judge, to nominate all the other *ḳāḍīs*, the staff of mosques and the professors of the University of al-Ḳarawiyyīn [*q.v.*]. The *ḳāḍīs* were aided by witnesses to deeds (*ʿadl* [*q.v.*], pl. *ʿudūl*; in French, *adel*, pl. *adoul*), who received and registered the acts of witness and drew up the judicial deeds; whilst the judges received payment on the issuing of these deeds, the *ʿudūl* had to rely on the generosity of those receiving justice. These last had the right to seek recourse to the *muftīs*, who would deliver *fatwās* to support their pleas.

On the other hand, the sultan was represented too in the towns by *pashas* and in the rural areas by *ḳāʾids* [*q.v.*] who, in the judicial field, put the *ḳāḍīs*' judgements into force and themselves gave judgement in regard to certain crimes and misdemeanours without going by any written code but basing themselves on good sense, tradition and local custom, and who held certain powers in civil and commercial cases.

Their judgements, like those of the *ḳāḍīs*, were put into practice immediately and there was no court of appeal. However, in the government itself, where the "ministerial departments" were made up of a series of little rooms (*banīḳa*, pl. *banīḳāt*) which gave out on to a courtyard and in each of which there was a "minister" (*wazīr*) seated on mats and carpets before a little desk with an inkwell, pens and paper, there was one *banīḳa* occupied by a *wazīr al-shikāyāt*, a "minister for complaints", who received all the petitions of those seeking justice and transmitted them to the sultan, who decided personally or who delegated his power here to the prime minister (*al-ṣadr al-aʿẓam*).

Out in the provinces, which were mainly peopled by Berber speakers and over which the central government had not control, local customary law was applied by the *djamāʿa* [*q.v.*] of the section or tribe, both in civil and criminal cases.

One of the first cares of the Protectorate authorities was to seek a better system of administering justice and to end abuses of power. A few days after the constituting of a commission which was aimed at combatting breaches of duty—which were common—and which was given the responsibility of revising judgements tainted by illegality, there was created, in particular by a *firmān* of 20 Dhu ʾl-Ḳaʿda 1330/31 October 1912, a Ministry of Justice (*wizārat al-ʿadliyya*), with responsibility for everything connected with the *sharīʿa*, together with the recruitment and supervision of the personnel of the *maḥkamas*, religious education in the Ḳurʾānic schools and *zāwiyas* [*q.v.*] and the higher education given at the Ḳarawiyyīn in which the *ḳāḍīs* were to be trained. This *firmān* was confirmed and amended by a dahir (*ẓahīr*) of 2 Shaʿbān 1366/21 June 1947, which added to the Ḳarawiyyīn the *madrasa* of Ibn Yūsuf founded at Marrakech by the dahir of 8 Shawwāl 1357/1 December 1938.

The *sharʿī* courts were only slightly modified under the Protectorate, but several dahirs fixed the rules of how they functioned. At the head of the *maḥkama* was a single *ḳāḍī*, who held session every day except for Thursday and Friday. He was usually accompanied by a deputy (*nāʾib*) who could act for him if the *ḳāḍī* was unable to function (dahir of 24 Rabīʿ II 1357/23 June 1938), and should need arise, by *nuwwāb* in the quarters and suburbs of the towns, as also in small places which were distant from the seat of the court. The *ḳāḍīs*, chosen from the graduates of the two colleges cited above, were recruited, after the dahir of 1 Ramaḍān 1356/5 November, from a competition organised by the Ministry of Justice, which subsequently controlled them; they were nominated, transferred on their own demand (because they were immovable) and on occasion penalised, by dahir. At the time of their nomination they received a silver seal with their own name and that of the seat of their jurisdiction. They received a fixed salary increased by 15% of the due levied by the *maḥkama*. They had jurisdiction over personal status, succession, property and contracts, and gave their judgement on the basis of the standard manuals of Mālikī *fiḳh*. Their decisions could be appealed, for a council of *ʿulamāʾ* set up by the dahir of 29 Muḥarram 1332/20 December was followed by the establishment of three appeal courts at Rabat (4 Shaʿbān 1345/7 February 1927), Tetouan and Tangiers.

In his *maḥkama*, the *ḳāḍī* is assisted by a number, fixed for each centre, of notaries which he proposes himself but who have to pass an examination unless they have certain qualifications. These *ʿudūl*, whose status was established by a decree of 24 Rabīʿ II 1357/23 June 1938, are paid, according to complicated calculations, on the issuing of the judicial deeds which they have the task of drawing up. Furthermore, the *maḥkama* has in certain cases an executive official (*ʿawn*) and a matron (*ʿarīfa*) to take care of women. After the *dahir* of 16 Shaʿbān 1342/23 March 1924, litigants could be represented by an oukil (*wakīl*, pl. *wukalāʾ*) or legal pleader whose functions were laid down in a very detailed dahir of 18 Ṣafar/7 September 1925. Advocates, for their part, could only intervene, and then only on a written basis, before an appeal court. In each *sharʿī* court, six registers had to be kept: for landed property, miscellaneous deeds, successions, lawsuits, appeals and the careers of the *ʿudūl*: after the dahir of 12 Ṣafar 1363/7 February 1944, acts of witness were entered in a separate register.

As for the *makhzan* [*q.v.*] courts (*al-maḥākim al-makhzaniyya*), that is, those of the *pashas* in the towns and of the *ḳāʾids* among the tribes, these were regulated by several dahirs, the most important of which was that of 26 Shawwāl 1336/4 August 1918. These officials had limited competence up to a certain sum of money in civil and commercial cases; they could refer complicated cases to the *ḳāḍīs* or have recourse to experts. In criminal law, they could judge misdemeanours involving theft, blows, woundings, etc., but did not have the right to inflict a prison sentence than a fixed period or a fine longer above a fixed limit. The government commissioner (who was an official of the Protectorate power) watched that the rules were kept and, in the case of any breach or shortcoming, could require an appeal to the superior Sharifian court (*al-maḥkama al-ʿulyā al-sharīfa*) set up by the above-mentioned dahir. This last jurisdiction was made up of two chambers: the first acted as an appeal court against the judgements of *pashas* and *ḳāʾids*, whilst the second was a criminal court for dealing with cases of murder, rape, procurement of abortion and other crimes falling outside the jurisdiction of the officials with judicial powers, but investigated by them, who sent along the relevant files to the criminal section of the superior court. The *pasha* had a government-paid secretariat, according to the provisions of the dahir of 29 Rabīʿ II/2 April 1946, although the *ḳāʾid* had to pay himself his secretary (*fḳīh*). In the big towns, the *pashas* had in the quarters and suburbs subordinates who had the same powers (dahir of 5 Djumādā II 1368/4 April 1949).

All these authorities made their judgements on a basis of the *sharīʿa* when it gave a solution, but more often on the *sensus communis* or unwritten custom. Among the Berber tribes, it was the *djamāʿa* which continued to decide cases between members of the group according to local customs, also unwritten. As the French forces advanced into the dissident areas, some *ḳāḍīs* were progressively installed there, but experience showed that those seeking justice continued in general to address themselves to the *djamāʿa*, which charged no fees. In any case, a dahir of 20 Shawwāl 1332/11 September 1914 already envisaged the retention of customary law (which some Berberists strove to collect and record in written form), but it was the dahir of 16 Dhu 'l-Ḥidjdja 1348/15 May 1930 (confirmed again on 23 Dhu 'l-Ḥidjdja 1352/8 April 1934) which had the greatest repercussions in the Islamic world and even in lands like the Netherlands East Indies where custom was indeed a fundamental source of law [see ʿĀDA]. France was accused of having wanted to de-Islamise Morocco, when it was simply trying to institutionalise the already existing Berber system of justice by setting up customary law courts of first instance (to which there was attached a public attorney charged with ensuring regularity in the court's functioning), and customary law appeal courts. The composition and jurisdiction of these courts were determined by a vizieral decree of 5 Djumādā II 1353/15 September 1934; another decree (7 Jafar 1357/8 April 1938) fixed there powers, procedure, structure and functioning.

For its part, the Jewish community in Morroco had, in respect of personal legal status, courts which were controlled by dahir, in 1918 in the French zone, in 1914 at Tangiers and in 1914 in the Spanish zone, as well as a rabbinical high court. Finally, foreigners and a certain number of Moroccans who had the protection, as individuals, of a foreign power benefited from the capitulations [see IMTIYĀZĀT] and thus received justice from the consular courts; these last were replaced in the French zone on 9 Ramaḍān 1331/13 August 1913 and in the Spanish one on 1 June 1914 by courts with exclusive competence in all cases where non-Moroccans were involved, whilst at Tangiers mixed courts were set up by dahir of 16 February 1924.

After independence, the Moroccan government legitimately envisaged bringing about three main objectives: first, a separation of powers by ending the intervention of the administrative authorities in the exercise of justice; second, to unify and arabise the latter by "Moroccanising" it; and third, to introduce modern codes of law based at least in part on the *sharīʿa*.

As early as 17 Muḥarram 1376/25 August 1956, the customary law courts were suppressed and replaced by *sharʿī* courts. A few months later, two dahirs promulgated simultaneously on 23 Radjab 1376/23 February 1957 created two types of Jewish courts, rabbinical and regional, together with a higher court. As for the French or Spanish courts and the international court at Tangiers, these changed their name to become the modern (*ʿaṣriyya*) courts.

Nevertheless, the authorities gave greatest attention to bringing about the objectives outlined above. By a dahir of 24 Radjab 1375/7 March 1956, there were suppressed first of all the judicial functions of the deputies (*nuwwāb*) of the *pashas*, and, on 6 Shaʿbān/19 March of the same year a dahir put an end to the interference of the executive power in the administration of justice, whose independence was asserted. The dahir of 22 Shaʿbān 1375/2 April 1956 aimed at replacing the courts of the *pashas* and *ḳāʾids* (the *maḥākim makhzaniyya*) by ordinary courts (*maḥākim ʿādiyya*) covering the kinds of courts of first instance called *sadadiyya*, regional (*iḳlīmiyya*) courts and the high Sharifian court and fixing their spheres of competence in both civil and criminal affairs. A dahir of 14 Radjab 1348/16 December 1929 had created conciliation boards with the task of settling conflicts in labour matters; these were replaced on 28 Ramaḍān 1376/29 April 1957 by labour courts (*maḥākim al-shughl*).

As for *sharʿī* justice, it had been reorganised by a dahir of 5 Djumādā I 1376/8 December 1956, which had created several new courts, apart from those which were to replace the customary law courts, and had instituted in the various regional courts boards with the task of examining appeals directed against judgements of the *ḳāḍīs*' courts. In the following year, on 23 Djumādā I 1377/16 December 1957, the procedure to be followed by the *sharʿī* courts was fixed by a law less detailed than the code of civil procedure promulgated in 1913. In the same year, on 22 Muḥarram/16 August, there was set up a commission with the task of codifying *fiḳh*. It began immediately on the law of personal status, which was naturally to remain in the sphere reserved to the *ḳāḍīs*, and it speedily brought its activities to an end. On 20 November 1962 a criminal code, in large measure based on French legislation, was promulgated.

Regarding appeal courts, the dahir of 25 Ṣafar 1377/21 September 1957 ended that of Tetouan, reorganised the one at Tangiers and created one at Rabat to replace the high Sharifian court; a third appeal court has been set up at Fās on 29 Shawwāl 1380/15 April 1961. From 2 Rabī 1377/27 September 1957 onwards, control over the Moroccan legal system was vested in the Superior Council (*al-madjlis al-aʿlā*).

The law of 23 Ramaḍān 1384/26 January 1965 made the Moroccanisation, Arabisation and unification of the administration obligatory, and this was followed by the formal unification of the judicial system and by a decree of the Minister of Justice requiring use of the Arabic language in all documents laid before the courts.

Despite the progress achieved, in particular in the sphere of criminal law, which is no longer in the hands of administrators, there still exists a certain vacillation arising from the divergent tendencies of the personnel involved, some wishing to preserve at least part of the system bequeathed by the Protectorate whilst others want to create a totally new and original system.

Bibliography: For the pre-independence period, see H. Bruno, *La justice indigène*, in *Introduction à la connaissance du Maroc*, Casablanca 1942, 413-30; A. Coudino, *Fonctionnement de la justice berbère*, in *ibid.*, 431-46; and the ch. on the legal system in the treatise of ʿAbd al-Ḥamīd Benashenhū, *al-Bayān al-muṭrib li-niẓām ḥukūmat al-Maghrib*[2], Rabat 1370/1957. For the following period, an unpublished account by Idrīs al-Ḍaḥḥāk, *al-ʿAdāla al-maghribiyya min khilāl rubuʿ ḳarn*, has been used. (Ed.)

xi. Algeria. [See Supplement]

xii. Tunisia. [See Supplement]

xiii. Reforms in the law applying in Sharīʿa courts

In the 20th century, many reforms, some of them very far-reaching, have been effected in matters of personal status, succession and *waḳf*, which are under the jurisdiction of the *Sharīʿa* courts. The most important of them are the raising of the age of competence for marriage and the imposition of restrictions on the marriage of minors; the prohibition of forced marriages; the prohibition of opposition to the marriage of persons having reached the age of competence for marriage; the prevention of great differences in age between spouses; the restriction of the institution of equality in marriage (*kafāʾa*) to the point of complete abolition and the limitation of the functions of the marriage-guardian; the limitation of the amount of the dower (Southern Yemen, 1974); the refinement of the use of stipulations in the marriage contract to improve the position of women; the performance of marriages in courts of law (ʿIrāḳ, 1978); and the prohibition of polygamy, leaving discretion to the *ḳāḍī* to permit it under special circumstances (in Southern Yemen, the consent of the District Court is required for polygamy, 1974).

The amount of maintenance of the wife is fixed in accordance with the economic position of the husband; both spouses are responsible for their own support and that of their children, each according to his or her ability (Southern Yemen, 1974); maintenance awarded by the court is paid by a government authority, which in turn recoups itself from the judgment debtor (Egypt, 1976; Israel 1972).

Wrongs resulting from the husband's right of arbitrary divorce have been redressed: repudiation pronounced under compulsion or in a state of drunkness or a fit of anger and divorce by way of an oath or a threat (provided there is no intent to divorce) are invalid; the effect of a double or triple repudiation pronounced on a single occasion has been reduced to that of one revocable divorce; divorce against the wife's will is prohibited (Israel 1951, 1959); the husband must seek judicial approval or registration of the divorce or dissolution of the marriage by the court (Southern Yemen, 1974); compensation to the amount of one or two years' maintenance, in addition to waiting-period maintenance, is due to a wife divorced without justification (Syria, 1953; Jordan, 1976; Egypt, 1979); the respective economic resources of the spouses must be equalised upon divorce (Israel, 1973). Additional grounds have been provided for dissolution on the initiative of the wife or of both spouses: a physical or mental defect of the husband, sterility of the husband; non-payment of prompt dowry (before consummation of marriage) or of maintenance to the wife; cruelty; the taking of a second wife; prolonged separation from or abandonment of the wife without legal cause (even if maintenance is provided), prevention of the wife from entering the conjugal dwelling after marriage; imprisonment of the husband for several years, together with non-supply of maintenance; and adultery of the spouse (ʿIrāḳ, 1978).

The period of the mother's custody of minors has been extended in the interest of their well-being; both parents have been declared the natural guardians of their children (Israel, 1951, 1962). The rights of heirs within the nuclear family have been strengthened, with daughters, in the absence of sons, being given preference over other Ḳurʾānic heirs; the spouse enjoys the *radd*, the residue of the estate, in the absence of Ḳurʾānic heirs and *dhawū 'l-arḥām*; germane brothers—contrary to the position of the Ḥanafī school—share the uterine brothers' portion of the estate in cases where the Ḳurʾānic portions exhaust the estate (Jordan, 1976); the Shīʿī system of succession, which is not based on the agnatic principle, has been adopted (ʿIrāḳ, 1963); the rights of heirs have been determined on the basis of equality of the sexes (ʿIrāḳ, 1959 to 1963; Palestine, 1923; Israel, 1951,

1965); bequests in favour of legal heirs have been permitted to the extent of one-third of the estate; the absence of the principle of representation has been remedied by the device of an "obligatory bequest" in favour of an orphaned grandson.

In Egypt (1946) and in Lebanon (1947), the founder of a *waḳf* has been given an option to revoke it; to stipulate whether a *khayrī waḳf* shall be perpetual or temporary (but a family *waḳf* must be temporary) and to spend the income of the *waḳf* for purposes not indicated in the *waḳf* deed; a stipulation by the founder as to the conduct of the beneficiary is no longer valid; the disinheritance of legal heirs by means of a *waḳf* exceeding one-third of the estate has been prohibited; *waḳf* property is to be administered by the beneficiaries; *waḳf* property damaged beyond repair through neglect is to be liquidated. Most of these reforms relate to *waḳf*s to be established in the future. The military régimes in Syria (1949) and Egypt (1952) abolished the family *waḳf* completely. In 1957, Egypt nationalised the property of that *waḳf* for the purposes of agrarian reform. In Israel (1965), the family and *khayrī waḳf*s as far as they comprised absentee property, were abolished; the property is to pass into the full ownership of the beneficiaries and of Muslim boards of trustees, respectively.

Important reforms have also been effected in the rules of evidence and procedure of the *Sharīʿa* courts; written evidence is now admissible and is accorded the same weight as oral testimony—in fact, with regard to some matters, documentary evidence is eligible but not oral testimony; witnesses may be cross-examined; the court is given discretion to assess the credibility of the witness and the testimony; the defendant may bring witnesses to refute the testimony of the plaintiff's witnesses; the defendant may return the oath to the plaintiff; circumstancial evidence is admissible; periods of prescription of actions have been introduced.

Rulers and parliaments have used a wide gamut of methods to introduce reforms in the law applied by the courts: (1) The procedural expedient: refusal of legal relief to parties who disregard a particular reformist norm, such as the age of competence for marriage. This method is based on the ruler's right to restrict the powers of the court (*takhṣīṣ al-ḳaḍāʾ*). (2) The *takhayyur* expedient: the selection of elements within or outside the heritage of the ruling school which suit the purpose the legislator seeks to achieve; sometimes such elements, patched together into a statute, contradict one another (*talfīḳ*). The theoretical justification of this expedient lies in the power of the ruler to direct the *ḳāḍī*, his agent, to apply a particular doctrine, and disregard others, in the public interest (*maṣlaḥa* [*q.v.*]). In the Sudan, the direction was given by means of a "judicial circular" issued by the Grand *Ḳāḍī* with the consent of the British Governor-General. (3) Administrative orders, provided that they do not conflict with the *Sharīʿa*; they rely on the duty of Muslims to obey their rulers. In Saudi Arabia, the reforms are carried out by means of royal orders based on the utility principle: *al-maṣāliḥ al-mursala* or *maṣlaḥat al-ʿumūm* or *siyāsa sharʿiyya*. (4) Criminal legislation which, while its sanctions are supposed to deter potential violators of reformist norms, such as the age of competence for marriage and the prohibition of polygamy, does not derogate from the substantive validity of the *Sharīʿa*. (5) A "modernistic" interpretation of the textual sources (Ḳurʾān and Sunna), e.g. in matters of polygamy and divorce, with a view to adapting them to the requirements of present-day society. In Saudi Arabia, the plenum of the Greater *Sharīʿa* Court may practise legal reasoning (*idjtihād*) collectively. (6) The abolition of the *Sharīʿa* courts and the application of Islamic substantive law by civil judicial authorities in accordance with civil rules of evidence and procedure. The process which took place in British India (Anglo-Muhammadan law) may now be expected to occur in Egypt and Kuwayt. It occurs to a limited extent in countries where the civil courts have incidental and other jurisdiction in matters to which Islamic law applies.

The direct approach of the reformers to the sources of religious law bears a certain, but purely technical, resemblance to the classical *idjtihād* [*q.v.*]. There are material differences as to the mode of using those sources (replacement of the deductive *ḳiyās* [*q.v.*] by the *maṣlaḥa* or utility principle) and as to the sources of inspiration and motivation of the reforms (Western ideas, and pressures arising from a disturbance of balances in Muslim society as a result of modernisation and Westernisation). The reforms rely on state-imposed, not religious, sanctions, and their somewhat forced link with Islamic sources has been severed in the process of legislation. They have an autonomous existence, independent of the sources, and should only be interpreted within the framework of the statutes in which they are embodied. In some cases, they have no basis at all in religious law. They are, first and foremost, legislative acts of secular parliaments. It is true that even in the past the secular legislation of caliphs and temporal rulers was outside the *Sharīʿa*, but there was then the pious fiction that this legislation was intended to supplement the *Sharīʿa* and that everybody, including the ruler, was subject to the latter, whereas today the parliaments are the declared sources of sovereignty and set bounds to the *Sharīʿa*. Most Arab countries are today at an advanced stage of transition from jurists' law to statute law, and the question of *idjtihād* has thus ceased to be relevant.

The purpose of resort to traditional mechanisms in legislation is a national and tactical one: the creation of the impression that the reforms are a kind of internal renovation of the *Sharīʿa*. Islamic law is conceived as part of the Arab national-cultural heritage; this prevents the creation of an ideological debt and subjection to the West. Reference to the modernists of the school of Muḥammad ʿAbduh is intended to facilitate acceptance of the reforms by the *ʿulamāʾ* and conservative circles and by the *sharʿī* judiciary.

The success of the reforms depends, to a decisive extent, on the *ḳāḍī*s charged with the application of the legislation designed for the *Sharīʿa* courts. The *ḳāḍī*s, including those integrated into the national courts in Egypt, have in their vast majority had a traditional *sharʿī* training. It seems that, contrary to the expectations of the legislator, they do not exercise the wide discretion given to them and that in many cases, out of devotion to *taḳlīd*, they ignore reformist legislation.

At the same time there have been cases (in Israel) in which that legislation impressed the *ḳāḍī*s and they explicitly relied on it in their judgments. Here the *ḳāḍī*s were not opposed to legislation in so far as it did not supersede the *Sharīʿa*. Some *ḳāḍī*s would even welcome additional legislation, procedural or penal, with a view to using the statutory sanction to buttress the *sharʿī* norm, which is sustained by a toothless ethical sanction. Druze *ḳāḍī*s still use religious and social sanctions of court. Some *ḳāḍī*s do not shrink from calling for legislation of a definitely substantive character.

The increasing ascendancy in the *Sharīʿa* courts of lawyers with a secular training and a modern social outlook will eventually, in judicial practice, lead to a kind of synthesis between the *S̲h̲arīʿa* and national law. There are *ḳāḍīs* who, in their liberal interpretation of religious law, do not hesitate to deviate from *taḳlīd* and who, by means of the techniques of *tak̲h̲ayyur* and *talfīḳ*, have scored achievements not inferior to those of parliamentary legislation. In Saudi Arabia, the *ḳāḍīs*, in the absence of an express provision as to a particular matter in authoritative Ḥanbalī literature—as designated by decree—are permitted to rely on elements from other doctrines as far as it is in the public interest to do so, and there have in fact been cases in which they applied the *maṣlaḥa* mechanism in their decisions.

The *ḳāḍīs* make use of their personal authority, sometimes with the assistance of mediators, to bring about a peaceful settlement of disputes and to give the effect of judgments to compromises that have been reached. They thereby continue a tradition of tribal arbitration. This method also prevents a confrontation with religious law. The proceedings are simple, quick and matter-of-fact. Druze *ḳāḍīs* are sometimes called upon to act as arbitrators in criminal cases heard before civil courts.

The *ḳāḍīs* react in different ways to the encounter of *S̲h̲arīʿa* and custom (*ʿurf*, *ʿāda* [*q.v.*]), according to their degree of orthodoxy, education and professional training, their social philosophy and the measure of their understanding of the Islamisation processes of a society not yet wont to regard Islam as an obligatory way of life. Some reject custom absolutely; others acquiesce in its sovereign existence by the side of the *S̲h̲arīʿa*, but there are also attempts to absorb custom, whilst compromising with it, into the *S̲h̲arīʿa*. Custom is an extremely important source of law in the jurisprudence of the Druze courts, owing to the absence of a tradition of institutionalised communal justice and the esoteric character of Druze religious law.

Following the introduction of a uniform and binding material law (secular statutes), and a hierarchy of collegial courts and appeal stages, in the *s̲h̲arʿī* judicial system, there are significant indications of the development of a case law, a phenomenon alien to the *S̲h̲arīʿa*.

For the time being, there are no significant effects of the abolition of the *S̲h̲arīʿa* courts in Egypt. The *ḳāḍīs*, who have been integrated into the national courts, continue, out of loyalty to *taḳlīd*, to apply not only Islamic substantive law but also the Islamic rules of evidence and procedure, as they used to do in the *S̲h̲arīʿa* courts. But there can be no doubt that in the long run, as their place is taken by civil judges with a secular legal training and no traditional *s̲h̲arʿī* education, the reform will make itself felt and Islamic law will be exposed to the influence of secular—national and Western—legal principles.

Bibliography: G. H. Bousquet, *Du droit musulman et de son application effective dans le monde*, Algiers 1949; idem, *et alii*, *EI*², art. ʿĀDA, with important bibliography; J. N. D. Anderson, *Recent developments in S̲h̲arīʿa law, i-ix*, in *MW*, xl-xlii (1950-2); idem, *Islamic law in the modern world*, London 1959; idem, *Law reform in the Muslim world*; Schacht, *Introduction*, 100-11, with important bibliography on 252 ff., 283; Coulson, *History*, part iii; idem, *Conflicts and tensions in Islamic jurisprudence*, Chicago and London 1969; idem, *Succession in the Muslim family*, Cambridge 1971; *Orientalisches Recht*, Leiden and Cologne 1964, 344-440; Y. Linant de Bellefonds, *Traité de droit musulman comparé*, i-iii, Paris and the Hague 1965, 1973; M. H. Kerr, *Islamic Reform*, Berkeley and Los Angeles 1966; Chehata, *Droit musulman*; Liebesny, *The law of Near and Middle East*, chs. 6-12; G. Baer, *Waqf reform*, in his *Studies in the social history of modern Egypt*, Chicago 1969, 79-92; A. Layish, *The contribution of the modernists to the secularization of Islamic law*, in *Middle Eastern Studies*, xiv (1978), 3, 263-77.

(A. LAYISH)

5. THE INDO-PAKISTAN SUBCONTINENT.
[See Supplement]

6. INDONESIA

The complex history of Islamic courts in Indonesia is evident in the many names by which they have been known over the last century in various parts of the country: among them *Pengadilan Surambi*, *Priesterraad*, *Raad Agama*, *Penghulu Gerecht*, *Rapat Kadi*, *Pengadilan Agama*, *Mahkamah Syariah*, and at the appeals level *Mahkamah Islam Tinggi*, *Kerapatan Kadi Besar*, *Mahkamah Syariah Propinsi*, and *Pengadilan Tinggi Agama*. The mixed roots of these terms reflect the subtle interplay of Islamic, pre-Islamic, and Dutch colonial influences in the evolution of the courts. When in 1980 the Ministry of Religion finally imposed a uniform religious-judicial nomenclature throughout Indonesia, *Pengadilan Agama* (*pengadilan* = court, *agama* = religion), combining Arabic and Indic roots, rather than the Arabic and Islamically derived *Mahkamah Syariah*, became the name of choice for first instance religious courts. Appellate religious courts are now called *Pengadilan Tinggi Agama* (*tinggi* = high).

Unlike many other Islamic countries, where religious courts have been progressively restricted, in Indonesia they have actually grown in number and influence. Despite continual efforts to confine or eliminate them, since the late 19th century the politics of their development has led, at every stage, to some institutional accretion. Legally, they are subordinate to civil courts, on which they depend for enforcement decrees, but socially they enjoy a measure of autonomy and authority guaranteed by Islamic commitment and political power.

The modern history of these courts began in 1882 under the colonial administration of the Netherlands East Indies. Earlier they existed in various forms throughout Java and only here and there in the other major islands, always under the control of local aristocratic authorities whose Islamic credentials were often dubious. In Java, where Islamic courts were paid most attention in the colony, they were known as *surambi* courts, from the forecourt of the mosque in which they convened, serving in part as general courts of the land and in part as Islamic courts proper. In the colony these *surambi* courts were related to the first instance colonial civil courts for Indonesians (*landraden*) in two ways: religious judges served as advisers to the *landraden*, and Islamic court decisions were required to obtain enforcement decrees (*executoire verklaring*) from the *landraden*. The first rule has long since faded, but the second still survives.

In 1882 the colonial administration reorganised the Islamic courts, which were now called *Priesterraden* (priest's courts)—though popularly *raad agama*, or *landraad agama*, after the style of the Dutch courts—on an erroneous understanding of the mosque administrators, *penghulu*, who staffed the courts. The new courts were collegial, with three judges, following from European rather than Islamic judicial traditions. The most important effect of the reform, however, was to make the courts formally more autonomous, and potentially independent of the local Javanese aristocracy that had traditionally appointed and controlled Islamic officials.

The reform of 1882 was roundly criticised by the famous Dutch Islamologist C. Snouck Hurgronje, whose arguments helped to inspire a second round of reforms, resulting in a new regulation of 1931 whose implementation, for economic and political reasons, was delayed until 1937. Applying only to Java and the nearby island of Madura, the new law responded superficially to Snouck's earlier criticism by renaming the courts *Penghulu Gerecht* (*penghulu* court) and reconstituting them, following Islamic tradition, as a single *kadi* (*ḳāḍī*) accompanied by two assessors and a clerk. Originally, the reform had called for payment of regular salaries to the religious judges and their staffs, who had acquired a reputation for venality, but this measure was put off because of budgetary shortages during the depression. Only later, during the revolution, did the Islamic courts begin to receive financial support from the state. But the heart of the 1930s reform, promoted by Dutch and Indonesian *adat* (customary) law scholars who opposed recognition of Islamic law except insofar as it was "received" by indigenous customary law, had to do with issues of substantive jurisdiction. Matters of *wakf* (*waḳf*) and, crucially, inheritance, were removed from the competence of the Islamic courts and given over to the civil *landraden*. When this provision was implemented, it caused an uproar among Islamic groups, who have tried unsuccessfully ever since to restore the inheritance jurisdiction to Islamic courts in Java. It was a major symbolic as well as practical loss for Islam, which at about the same time was able to ward off a challenge to polygamy. In compensation, the reform established a new Islamic appellate instance, the *Mahkamah Islam Tinggi* (Islamic High Court) to hear appeals from all the religious courts of Java. Although suspect at first among Islamic officials, the *Mahkamah Islam Tinggi* was eventually opened in the central Javanese city of Surakarta, where it remains today. Outside of Java, only in Kalimantan (Borneo) were similar reforms begun, also in 1937, mainly by way of reorganisation of local religious courts (*Rapat Kadi*) and the creation of appellate courts (*Kerapatan Kadi Besar*), before Japanese forces occupied the country during the second World War.

During the occupation and early in the revolution (1945-50) against the returning Dutch administration, efforts to eliminate Islamic courts failed utterly in the face of Islamic determination to preserve and develop Islamic public institutions. A political compromise led in 1946 to the establishment of a new Ministry of Religion, which soon absorbed various elements of Islamic administration, including the existing courts, and later became a driving force behind their consolidation and expansion throughout independent Indonesia. Islamic judicial affairs were organised in the Ministry under a Directorate of Religious Justice.

With the revolution, the primary issues of the Islamic judiciary shifted to the islands outside of Java, particularly Sumatra, where religious courts were few and poorly developed. In 1946, during a period of violent local conflict, Islamic groups in Aceh (northern Sumatra) established new *Mahkamah Syariah* (*S̲h̲arīʿa* councils). These courts ambitiously assumed a wide jurisdiction, which the national government later whittled away gradually by creating competitive civil courts and subjecting the *Mahkamah Syariah* to legal limits as a condition of their incorporation into the national religious bureaucracy. In response to what had happened in Aceh, however, in 1947 the republican governor of Sumatra issued an instruction to establish Islamic courts, also fashioned as *Mahkamah Syariah*, elsewhere in Sumatra. The temporary resurrection of Dutch rule prevented it from going into effect, though local Dutch administrations in Sumatra themselves set up Islamic courts here and there.

When the Dutch had finally departed, by 1950, a serious contest quickly developed within the new state over the creation of Islamic courts outside of Java. Opposition came from secular parties and the national Ministry of the Interior, which administered the provinces in close association with local élites that had long resisted the expansion of Islamic authority. On the other side, the Ministry of Religion, supported by Islamic parties, pressed the case for new religious courts assiduously. Religious Affairs Offices (*Kantor Urusan Agama*), responsible *inter alia* for registering marriages and divorces (*nikah*, *talak*, *rujuk*), established the local presence of the national Ministry and helped to generate local pressures in favor of Islamic courts. At length, in early 1957 the Achehnese courts were finally validated, and later in the same year a new regulation provided for *Mahkamah Syariah* and appellate *Mahkamah Syariah Propinsi*, modelled on the *Mahkamah Islam Tinggi* in Java, for those provinces outside of Java which did not yet have Islamic courts.

The end result was two disparate Islamic judicial régimes: one in Java and Madura based on the reforms of 1882 and 1931-7, which influenced regulations of 1937 for the Kalimantan courts, and a second, based on the regulation of 1957, for all other areas. The essential differences had to do with substantive jurisdiction. While the religious courts of Java-Madura were confined to matrimonial issues—essentially divorce—the younger courts elsewhere had also acquired jurisdiction over issues of child custody and support (*hadhanah*), *waḳf*, public religious funds (*baitulmal*), charity (*sedakah*), pre-testamentary gifts (*hibbah*), and, above all, inheritance (*waris*), which however they shared uneasily and uncertainly with civil courts. National uniformity in the competence of religious courts was very difficult to achieve because of the political sensitivity of the inheritance issue, jurisdiction over which the Islamic courts in Java wished to retrieve and those outside of Java would not relinquish.

While Islamic courts spread after 1957, problems of internal organisation and development were much harder to deal with. The courts suffered persistently from inadequate funds, poorly trained personnel, low prestige and institutional isolation. From a sociological point of view, they served their communities well enough, but beyond routine they often fell into disorder, and from a legal point of view, whether Islamic or secular, they were an easy target for critics. During the 1970s, however, some movement began on these problems, though it was inspired largely from outside the religious courts themselves.

In the 1960s, the Directorate of Religious Justice had begun to move gently towards serving as a national review instance of sorts, despite objections from local religious judges, in response to protests over procedural errors and related problems in the first instance and appellate Islamic courts. This development was cut short by a new statute of 1970 on national judicial organisation. In addition to confirming the Islamic judiciary as one line of national judicial institutions (along with civil, military, and administrative courts), the new law also provided for appeals in cassation from Islamic appellate courts to the civil Supreme Court (*Mahkamah Agung*). Although there were qualms about this among both civil and Islamic judges, for different reasons, it did finally establish a national institutional apex for the Islamic judiciary. But only a few such appeals have been heard, by late 1982, and it is too early to predict the influence of the Supreme Court on the religious courts.

The next major stage in the evolution of Islamic courts was unexpected and rather surprising in its effects. In 1973 Parliament considered a new unified marriage law for all religious groups which incensed many Muslims by its challenge to polygamy and other Ḳurʾānic legal symbols. Islamic groups protested vehemently, and after a great deal of political tension the Government revised the original drafts of the law to meet Islamic objections. One result of the new law in its final form was to place more authority and functional responsibility squarely on the Islamic courts.

Until the passage of the 1974 marriage law, the overwhelming daily fare of Islamic courts everywhere in the country was made up of divorce issues. Despite the additional jurisdiction over inheritance of the courts outside of Java, not many cases of the sort actually came to them. (Ironically, the Javanese religious courts continued informally even after 1937 to hear many inheritance cases, often deciding them in the form of *fatwa*s, advisory opinions, as people continued to bring them; sometimes because they were ignorant of the legal change, sometimes because the Islamic courts were much speedier than the civil courts, and sometimes because devout Muslims simply regarded the Islamic courts as the proper authority to take care of their inheritance problems.) The vast majority of the Islamic courts' clients were women, as only women had to go to court for a decree invoking their husband's divorce (*talak*) on prescribed grounds. Husbands bent on divorce need only pronounce the *talak* and register it at a local religious office.

The law of 1974 changed all this, however, making divorce more difficult for men by requiring them also to go to court, an equalising measure intended to promote family stability. The traffic in Islamic courts naturally increased, though less than expected because the new legal procedures themselves had the effect of discouraging divorce. In addition, all Islamic courts now have jurisdiction over a wide range of family law issues, including, among others, permission for a husband to take an additional wife, permission to marry in the absence of or disagreement among appropriate kin, dispensation from marriageable age rules, prevention of marriages, annulments, charges of neglect, determination of child custody, support of divorced wives, child support, legitimacy of children, withdrawal of parental authority, appointment of a *wali*, and review of administrative refusal to allow mixed marriages. Several of these questions require only administrative action, while others constitute litigation, but all together impress on the courts a more variegated responsibility than they have been used to. As before, decisions of the religious courts are legally enforceable only by writ of the civil courts, a requirement that the new law appears to render perfunctory, indeed mainly symbolic.

A a consequence of this burgeoning significance of the religious courts, the Ministry of Religion moved enthusiastically to demand more courts, more funds and more facilities. By ministerial regulation, two new appellate courts were provided for West and East Java, confining the old *Mahkamah Islam Tinggi* to the territorial jurisdiction of Central Java. Increasing attention has begun to be paid matters of recruitment and training of religious judges. The national standardisation of the names of the courts in 1980 implies a further commitment to uniform policies in their development.

Indonesia's Islamic courts have survived as one critical symbol of the Islamic community, but they have been progressively integrated into state administration. The law of 1974 has transformed them into rather full-blown domestic relations tribunals, responsible for profoundly important matters of social life and state policy.

Bibliography: C. Snouck Hurgronje, *Rapport ... over de Mohammedaansche Godsdienstige Rechtspraak, met name op Java, Feb. 14, 1890*, in *Adatrechtbundels*, i, 1911; Th. W. Juynboll, *Handleiding tot de Kennis van de Mohammedaansche Wet*[1], 1903; J. H. van de Velde, *De godsdienstige rechtspraak in Nederlands-Indië, staatsrechtelijk beschouwd*, 1928; Notosusanto S. H., *Peradilan Agama Islam di Djawa dan Madura* ("Islamic justice in Java and Madura"), 1953?; J. Prins, *Adat en Islamietische Plichtenleer in Indonesië*, 1954; Notususanto S. H., *Organisasi dan Jurisprudensi Peradilan Agama di Indonesia* ("Organisation and jurisprudence of Islamic justice in Indonesia"), 1963; Daniel S. Lev, *Islamic courts in Indonesia*, 1972; Dept. of Justice, Republic of Indonesia, *Sekitar Pembentukan undang-undang Perkawinan, beserta peraturan pelaksanaannya* ("On the formation of the marriage law, along with its implementing regulations"), 1974; Dept. of Justice, Republic of Indonesia, *Himpunan Undang-undang dan Peraturan-peraturan tentang Perkawinan* ("Laws and regulations concerning marriage"), 1977; S. H. M. Tahir Azhary, *Hukum Acara Perdata di Lingkungan Peradilan Agama* ("Civil procedure in the sphere of religious justice"), XII *Hukum dan Pembangunan*, no. 2 (March 1982); S. H. Ichtijanto, *Pengadilan Agama di Indonesia*, ("Religious courts in Indonesia") XII *Hukum dan Pembangunan*, no. 2 (March 1982). (D. S. Lev)

MAḤLŪL (A.), a term used in Ottoman administrative parlance to mean vacant. It is used in the registers of a grant or office which has been vacated by the previous holder, by death, dismissal, or transfer, and not yet re-allocated. The term is also used more generally for land and other assets left without heir (see also MUKHALLAFĀT). (Ed.)

MAḤMAL (modern pronunciation of the word vocalised by the lexicographers *maḥmil* or *miḥmal*), a type of richly decorated palanquin, perched on a camel and serving in the past to transport people, especially noble ladies, to Mecca (cf. al-Samʿānī, *Kitāb al-Ansāb*, under the word *al-maḥāmilī*). The famous al-Ḥadjdjādj b. Yūsuf is said to have been the first to use them.

In a more restricted and precise sense, the word designates palanquins of this same type which became political symbols and were sent from the 7th/13th century by sovereigns with their caravans of pilgrims to Mecca (or the principal caravan when it was split up) in order to bolster their prestige. In the modern period in Egypt, the head-rope of the camel which carried it was solemnly presented to the *Amīr al-Ḥadjdj*, the leader of the pilgrimage, in the course of a ceremony during which the camel, followed by some musicians, performed seven circuits on the ground in front of the officials' platform. In time, the crowds accorded these palanquins, encompassed by the glory of the Holy Places, a veneration which was excessive and at times condemned (e.g. the kissing of the head-rope, the seven circuits, the participation of the religious brotherhoods in the ceremonies, allowing the belief that it was actually a religious emblem). Forming the centre of picturesque demonstrations in Cairo, Damascus (and Istanbul) at the time of the departures and returns of the caravans of pilgrims, they were mentioned by European travellers. At the end of

1952, the Egyptian *maḥmal*, the last still in service, was suppressed by a governmental decision. The camel which carried it, a splendid and well-nourished animal, stayed resting all the year at the *dār al-kiswa*, at Khoronfish Street in Cairo, waiting for the ceremonies in default of journeys.

There exists little precise evidence, in the Middle Ages, on the form of these political *maḥmal*s. On the other hand, those of the modern period have been described, photographed and displayed in museums. In Egypt, the last ones were built of wood and approximately cubic, broader (1 m 75) than they were long (1m 35), surmounted by a four-faced pyramid, with, in the upper angles of the cube, four gilded balls and on top of the pyramid, a much larger ball surmounted by a stem, a star and a crescent: the whole was covered in an embroidered material. There existed two types of coverings: the first, for towns and the parade, was in a very rich brocade, enhanced by pompoms and fringes. The name of the sovereign and a verse of the Ḳurʾān (e.g. the "throne verse", II, 255, on that of King Fuʾād I) was embroidered respectively on the face in front of the pyramid and on a band encircling the top of the cube. The second covering of simpler material (green in recent times) was put on for the journey or minor halts. The oldest covering which has been preserved is that of the *maḥmal* of Sultan Ḳānṣawḥ al-G̲h̲ūrī (d. 922/1516) at present in Istanbul, in the Topkapı Museum (Turkish embroideries section, no. 263, Mehmel). A good photo of it is supplied in the magazine *La Turquie Kémaliste*, Istanbul, August 1941. The embroidered text expresses pious wishes but is not Ḳurʾānic. It is reproduced in J. Jomier, *Le Mahmal du sultan Qānṣūh al-Ghūrī*, in *Annales Islamologiques* (1972), 183-8. The richness of certain coverings has been mentioned by chroniclers: such as that of the *maḥmal* of the ʿIrāḳīs in 721/1321, encrusted with gold, pearls and precious stones (*Die Chroniken des Stadt Makka*, ed. Wüstenfeld, ii, Göttingen 1859, 278).

Various legends concerning these *maḥmals* are to be dismissed at the outset. The legend according to which the Egyptian *maḥmal* goes back to the reign of Queen S̲h̲ad̲j̲arat al-Durr is not found in any presently-known ancient source. Those according to which the palanquin contained Ḳurʾāns or served to transport the hangings (*kiswa*) of the Kaʿba have no firm basis. The *maḥmal* was normally empty. The word "sacred cloth" used by Westerners to designate it is pure fantasy. In Arabic it is called the noble *maḥmal*, *al-maḥmal al-s̲h̲arīf*, an adjective very often applied to that which is in contact with the Holy Places.

The (political) *maḥmal* seems to be a creation of the Mamlūk Sultan Baybars, who sent it for the first time in 664/1266. It is recorded in the context of the transfer to Cairo of the ʿAbbāsid caliphate after the capture of Bag̲h̲dād by the Mongols (656/1258). Yemen and Egypt were then rivals to offer the hangings of the Kaʿba (a gift which had always remained the caliphs' privilege of honour) until the S̲h̲arīf of Mecca promised Ḳalāwūn that only the Egyptian hangings would be hung (681/1282). The sending of the *maḥmal* coincided with the reopening of the pilgrimage route via Suez, Aqaba and the east coast of the Red Sea, closed since the Crusades (reopening in 660 A.H. plus, the manuscripts having a blank for the units' figure). Briefly, Baybars showed by his policy towards the Holy Places that he was the protector of the caliph, some of whose privileges of honour he took over. At Mecca, and then at ʿArafāt, the *maḥmal* was placed in a position where it could easily be seen, also reinforcing by its presence the symbolism of the hangings.

Very quickly other countries wanted to rival Egypt: Yemen also (from 969/1297), ʿIrāḳ, (from 718/1319) had their *maḥmals*, doubling their hangings. Hence there were conflicts of precedence, at times violent, in the course of which Egypt always insisted on the first place. Syria (from 692/1293) sent its *maḥmal*, but this was the responsibility *ipso facto* of the Mamlūk sultans of Cairo. The presence or absence of one or the other depended on the vicissitudes of politics. With the Ottoman seizure of Egypt and Syria, Istanbul took on itself this policy of prestige, and the *maḥmals* came on its behalf. In the *ḥarīm* of the Top Kapı Palace in Istanbul, the group of three *maḥmals* (Egypt, Syria and Yemen) appears three times running on the faience panels (17th century) representing the Holy Places. It is in this period that the Yemeni *maḥmal* ceased to be sent. Toward the end of the same century, M. d'Ohsson (*Tableau général de l'Empire Ottoman*, iii, Paris 1790, 263-6) mentions as customary a symbolic departure of the *maḥmal* at Istanbul, with the official delegation of the pilgrimage, this palanquin then being dismantled and returned to its store.

When the Wahhābīs seized the Holy Places in 1807, the Egyptian *maḥmal* fell into their hands and was burnt by them. Its sending was only resumed after their defeat. The war of 1914 put an end to the sending of the Syrian *maḥmal*; the Egyptian one continued to be sent until 1926, the date on which a clash between the soldiers of the escort and the Wahhābī Ik̲h̲wān caused its despatch to be definitively suppressed. The Egyptian Government and King Ḥusayn of the Ḥid̲j̲āz (1915-21) had already confronted each other on the subject of this palanquin and especially the ceremonial which was to preside over its reception. Despite exchanges of points of view, the conflict twice led to the suspension of its sending. After Ibn Saʿūd had become King of the Ḥid̲j̲āz, negotiations took place on the same subject, the Wahhābīs refusing to allow the music which accompanied the procession and various superstitious practices. Symbol of a political protection over the Holy Places, the *maḥmal* no longer had its *raison d'être* after the suppression of the caliphate and the Wahhābīs' desire for independence.

The popular festival aspect was manifest in Egypt in the course of three annual ceremonies (in the Middle Ages), in the course of which the *maḥmal* was solemnly led across the city with a large escort and parts of the caravan, accompanied by troops armed with lances and sometimes even clowns. Ladies were accustomed to go out to see the processions. The first procession announced the approach of the season of pilgrimage, the second was that of the departure and the third that of the return.

In the desert, the *maḥmal* was the centre of the principal caravan. When in 1882, and then in 1884 and after, the Egyptian caravan ceased to take the desert route and left by train (for Suez) and then by boat, the *maḥmal* was hoisted into a train (it had its own special carriage) and then embarked. From 1328 to 1331/1910-13, it went via Alexandria, the sea, Haifa and the Medina railway. In the Ḥid̲j̲āz itself, the small caravan re-formed and it was always the centre of it. The goings and comings of this caravan have been described in the valuable reports, full of realistic details, composed by the physicians who accompanied it and published *pro-manuscripto* from the beginning of the century by care of the Quarantine Service. Information and photos are also to be found in al-Batanūnī, *al-Riḥla al-ḥid̲j̲āziyya*, Cairo 1329 A.H. and Rifʿat, *Mirʾat al-ḥaramayn*, 2 vols., Cairo 1925. Two of the old processions (departure and return) lasted until 1926 in Cairo. Suppressed after the incident with the

Saʿūdī Ikhwān, they were re-established in 1937, the year in which the hangings (*kiswa*) of the Kaʿba were once again sent and accepted, although the *maḥmal* was formally refused. These processions inside Cairo lasted until 1952, the date of their definitive abolition. The custom in Egypt was for the façade of the pilgrims' houses, in the popular quarters, to be decorated around the door with naïve frescos recalling their journey. These frescos painted at the time of their return might stay in place for several years before being worn away by time. Until 1952 the *maḥmal* was almost always represented. At present it appears only rarely: the new generations no longer know what it is. See Giovanni Canova, *Nota sulle raffigurazioni popolari del pellegrinaggio in Egitto*, in *Annali della Facolta di lingue e letterature straniere di ca' Foscari*, xiv/3 (1975), 83-94, with 8 plates (University of Venice).

Finally, how can one explain the choice by Baybars of this type of symbol? Did he merely want a royal tent? Did he dream of the leather *ḳubbas*, carried on chariots in the steppes of Asia, familiar to some Mamlūks, and which had a religious meaning or at least one of honour? Or should we not look in the direction of the known symbolic palanquins of the Arabs, such as the one among the Rwāla at the beginning of this century which was the emblem of the tribe (Musil, *Die Kultur*, 1910, 8 ff., described under the name Abū Ẓhūr al-Markab), or that which bore ʿĀʾisha at the Battle of the Camel? The question remains open.

Bibliography: J. Jomier, *Le Maḥmal et la caravane égyptienne des pèlerins de la Mecque (XIIIe-XXe siècles)*, Cairo 1953; R. Tresse, *Le pèlerinage syrien aux villes saintes de l'Islam*, Paris 1937; Lane, *Manners and customs of the modern Egyptians*, London 1936, ii, 180-6, 245 ff. (with a reproduction of the Egyptian *maḥmal*); Burton, *A pilgrimage to el-Medinah and Mekka*, London 1856, iii, 12, 267; Snouck-Hurgronje, *Mekka*, i, 29, 83 ff., 152, 157 (with a photograph in the *Atlas*, Pl. v); T. Juynboll, *Handbuch des islamischen Gesetzes*, 151 ff. In Arabic, apart from the texts mentioned in Jomier, *op. cit.*, see ʿAbd al-Ḳādir al-Anṣārī al-Djazarī, *al-Durar al-farāʾid al-munaẓẓama fī akhbar al-ḥadjdj wa-ṭarīḳ Makka al-muʿaẓẓama*, especially the autograph ms. at al-Azhar (first version and the autograph ms. at Fās, Ḳarawiyyīn (completed version, printed by the Maṭbaʿa Salafiyya, Cairo 1384, sponsored by Saʿūdīs). The author was for a long time the official responsible (*kātib*) for the Pilgrimage Office (*dīwān al-ḥadjdj*) in the 10th/16th century. The work is a compendium of all the knowledge (Arab tribes, itineraries, gifts to make, functionaries, a chronicle of the pilgrimage year by year, etc.) necessary for an *Amīr al-Ḥadjdj*. (Fr. Buhl - [J. Jomier])

MAHMAND. [see mohmand]

MAḤMŪD. The following articles on a large number of personages called Maḥmūd are arranged as follows:

MAḤMUD, the name of several mediaeval rulers of Bengal.

1. Maḥmūd i, Nāṣir al-Dīn (846-64/1442-59), was a descendant of Ilyās Shāhī dynasty of Bengal. On the assassination of the tyrant, Shams al-Dīn (*ca.* 846/1442), the grandson of the usurper, Rādjā Ganesh (817-21/1414-18), a scramble for power began among the nobles, which led one of them, named Nāṣir Khān, to seize power by killing his rival, Shādī Khān. But within a week, Nāṣir Khān himself was put to death. Thereupon, the nobles chose Maḥmūd, who was a descendant of Sulṭān Ilyās Shāh and was living in obscurity, carrying on agriculture. He ascended the throne as Nāṣir al-Dīn Abu 'l-Muẓaffar Maḥmūd.

Maḥmūd was just and liberal and an able administrator. Since the Sharḳī rulers of Djawnpūr [*q.v.*], who were a constant threat to the kingdom of Bengal, were involved in conflicts with the Lodīs, Maḥmūd was able to enjoy peace, and this he utilised in promoting the prosperity of his people, in constructing mosques and *khānḳāhs*, bridges and tombs. In Gawr, his capital, he built a fort and a palace and other buildings. Unfortunately, only the five-arched bridge, the Kōtwālī Darwāza and a part of the walls of the fort have survived.

These were not the only achievements of Maḥmūd. He also strengthened his military power and extended the boundaries of his kingdom by annexing parts of the districts of Djassawr and Khulnā and a portion of the twenty-four *parganas*. He died after a successful reign of approximately seventeen years and was succeeded by his son, Rukn al-Dīn Barbek.

Bibliography: Ghulām Ḥusayn "Salīm" Zaydpūrī, *Riyāḍ al-salāṭīn*, ed. ʿAbd al-Ḥaḳḳ ʿĀbid, Bibl. Ind. Calcutta 1890-1, Eng. tr. ʿAbd al-Salām, Bibl. Ind. Calcutta 1902-4; Muḥammad Ḳāsim Hindū-Shāh, *Taʾrīkh-i Firishta*, ii, Lucknow 1281/1864; Niẓām al-Dīn, *Ṭabaḳāt-i Akbarī*, iii, ed. B. De and Hidāyat Ḥusayn, Bibl. Ind. Calcutta 1935, and Eng. tr. B. De and Baini Prashad, Bibl. Ind. Calcutta 1938; J. N. Sarkar, ed., *The history of Bengal, ii, Muslim period*, Dacca 1948; M. Ḥabīb and K. A. Niẓāmī, eds., *A comprehensive history of India (1206-1526)*, v, Dihlī 1970; W. Haig, ed., *Cambridge history of India*, iii, Cambridge 1928; Compos, *History of the Portuguese in Bengal*, 1919; F. C. Danvers, *The Portuguese in India*, London 1894; Rakhal Das Banerdjī, *The Banglar Itihās*, ii, Calcutta 1917; N. K. Bhattasalī, *Coins and chronology of the early independent Sulṭāns of Bengal*, Cambridge 1922; Aḥmad ʿAlī Khān, *Memoirs of Gaur and Pandua*, ed. H. E. Stapleton, Calcutta 1913.

2. Maḥmud II, Nāṣir al-Dīn, was the third Ḥabashī (Abyssinian) Sultan. Some modern historians consider him to be the son of Djalāl al-Dīn Fatḥ Shāh (886-92/1481-87), the last ruler of the Ilyās Shahī dynasty; but Firishta, ii, 300-1, and Niẓām al-Dīn, iii, 269, regard him as the son of Ṣayf al-Dīn Firūz (892-95/1487-90), a Ḥabashī Sulṭān of Bengal. This view seems to be correct, because it was Fīrūz who appointed a tutor for Maḥmūd's education and,

when he died, Maḥmūd succeeded him. However, since Maḥmūd was very young, the government was carried on by his tutor, Ḥabash Khān. Meanwhile, another Ḥabashī, Sīdī Badr, nicknamed Dīwāna ("the Mad"), killed Ḥabash Khān and declared himself Regent. He then put to death the young king by winning over the palace guards, and himself ascended the throne of Bengal. Maḥmūd had reigned only for about a year.

Bibliography: See that for MAḤMŪD I.

3. MAḤMŪD III, GHIYĀTH AL-DĪN (940-5/1533-8), *ruler of Bengal*. He was one of the eighteen sons of ʿAlā al-Dīn Ḥusayn Shāh (899-925/1493-1519) of Bengal, and had been nominated by his elder brother, Nuṣrat Shāh (925-39/1519-32) as his heir-apparent. But Makhdūm-i ʿĀlam, his brother-in-law and governor of North Bihār, raised to the throne Nuṣrat's son, Abu 'l-Badr, with the title of ʿĀlāʾ al-Dīn Fīrūz. He ruled only for a few months because, in 940/1533, he was put to death by his uncle, Maḥmūd, who declared himself Sulṭān and ascended the throne as Ghiyāth al-Dīn Maḥmūd III. Makhdūm, however, refused to recognise him and allied himself with Shīr Khān (later Shīr Shāh), whose power was steadily growing. Maḥmūd, on the other hand, made the mistake of entering into an alliance with the Nūhānīs of Bihār, who were weak and without an able leader. The result was that, when in 940/1533 Maḥmūd sent the Nūhānīs with Ḳuṭb Khān, governor of Monghyr, against Shīr Khān, Ḳutb was defeated and killed.

Maḥmūd next sent an army against Makhdūm, who was defeated and slain, as the Nūhānīs were able to prevent Shīr Khān from coming to his assistance. However, the victory did not benefit Maḥmūd because before setting out to fight, Makhdūm had entrusted all his treasure to Shīr Khān's envoy.

Meanwhile, Djalāl Khān, the Nūhānī ruler of Bihār, plotted the assassination of Shīr Khān, but his attempt having failed, he was affected with panic, and crossed over to Bengal with his supporters and sought the protection of Maḥmūd, which was given. Maḥmūd succeeded in occupying Bihār and, in Ramaḍān 940/March 1534, a strong force under Ibrāhīm Khān moved out of Monghyr and met Shīr Khān on the plain of Suradjgaṙh, near the town of Barh. But Ibrāhīm was defeated and killed, while Djalāl Khān again fled to Maḥmūd.

Now it was Shīr Khān's turn to retaliate and, taking advantage of Humāyūn's pre-occupation in Gudjarāt, he opened a campaign in 942/1536. Since Maḥmūd had strongly fortified the Teliyāgaṙhī Pass with Portuguese help, Shīr left behind a detachment under his son, Djalāl Khān, and having made a detour, marched through the Jharkand country and appeared before Gawr, Bengal's capital. Maḥmūd was taken by surprise. The Portuguese advised him to hold out until the outbreak of the monsoon, when Shīr's retreat could be cut off by their navy. But Maḥmūd was so demoralised that he did not follow their advice and, instead, came to a settlement with Shīr Khān, by agreeing to pay him an annual tribute of ten lacs of tankas and to cede the territory from the river Kosi to Ḥādjīpūr and from Gaṙhī to Monghyr, which was of considerable importance to the security of Bengal.

Shīr Shāh (who had by now assumed the title of Shāh) was too ambitious to remain satisfied with these gains and, on the pretext of non-payment of tribute by Maḥmūd, invaded Bengal. He entered the Teliyāgaṙhī Pass, which the Bengalis failed to defend, and laid siege to Gawr. But hearing that Humāyūn had invested Čunār, he at once set out to relieve it, leaving behind his son Djalāl to continue the siege. Maḥmūd despairing of any outside help, for the Portuguese refused immediate assistance, and being faced with dwindling supplies, sallied out of the fort to give battle. But he was wounded and fled to north Bihār. meanwhile, on 6 Dhu 'l-Ḳaʿda 944/6 April 1538, the Afghāns captured the fort by an assault. Maḥmūd, now a fugitive, appealed to Humāyūn, who immediately marched towards Gawr. But before he could reach the city, Shīr Shāh had carried away all its treasure. It was on his way to Gawr with Humāyūn that Maḥmūd heard of the murder of his two sons by the Afghāns. This effected him so much that he died soon afterwards.

Maḥmūd was a voluptuary, but the Portuguese account that he had 10,000 women in his harem is an exaggeration. He was incompetent, and inept in the art of diplomacy, lacking courage, tact and imagination. His mistake in antagonising Shīr Shāh and his failure to make an alliance with the Mughals and the Sulṭān of Gudjarāt led not only to his own overthrow but also to the loss of Bengal's independence.

Bibliography: See that for MAḤMŪD I; and for the relations of Maḥmūd III with the Afghāns, consult the following: Khwādjā Niʿmat Allāh, *Taʾrīkh-i Khān-i Djahānī*, i, ed. Imām al-Dīn, Dacca 1960; ʿAbd Allāh, *Taʾrīkh-i Dāwūdī*, ed. ʿAbd al-Rashīd, Aligarh 1954; Aḥmad Yādgār, *Taʾrīkh-i Salāṭīn-i Afāghina*, ed. Hidāyat Ḥusayn, Bibl. Ind., Calcutta 1939; K. R. Qanungo, *Sher Shah and his times*, Calcutta 1965; I. H. Siddiqi, *History of Sher Shah Sur*, Aligarh 1971. (MOHIBBUL HASAN)

MAḤMŪD, the name of two of the Dihlī sultans of mediaeval India.

1. MAḤMŪD I, NĀṢIR AL-DIN was the son of Iltutmish (Firishta, i, 70-1; Minhādj-i Sirādj Djūzdjānī, i, 471-2) and not his grandson, as some modern historians have asserted. He ascended the throne on 23 Muḥarram 644/10 June 1246 through the joint efforts of Balban [*q.v.* in Suppl.], and Maḥmūd's mother. Since Maḥmūd was weak and of a retiring disposition, devoting himself "to prayers and religious observances", and he owed his throne to Balban, the latter became very powerful. He further strengthened his position by marrying his daughter to the young Sulṭān and securing the important office of *nāʾib-i mamlakat* and the title of Ulugh Khān (Premier Khān). His younger brother, Sayf al-Dīn Aybak, was given the title of Kashlī Khān and made *amīr-i ḥādjib*, while one of his cousins, Shīr Khān, was appointed governor of Lahore and Bhatinda.

In 651/1253, however, a eunuch named ʿImād al-Dīn Rayḥān, who was jealous of Balban, organised a group of discontented Indian Muslims and some Turks and succeeded in persuading the Sulṭān to dismiss Balban and his relations. They were accordingly ordered to leave for their respective *iḳṭāʿ*s. Balban was replaced by Rayḥān, who now became *wakīl-i dar* and virtual ruler. Shīr Khān was replaced by Arslān Khān as governor of Lahore and Bhatinda.

Deprived of power and position as a result of these changes, the Turkish element became discontented and organised itself under Balban's leadership to overthrow Rayḥān and, in Ramaḍān 652/October 1254, marched towards Dihlī. Maḥmūd, under the influence of Rayḥān and his followers, moved out against the rebels and encamped near Samana. Rayḥān wanted an armed conflict, but Maḥmūd refused, because most of his nobles favoured Balban, and agreed on a compromise. Rayhān was dismissed and transferred first to Bahrāʾič and then to Badāʾūn. Balban was reappointed *nāʾib* and his kinsmen and followers were reinstated. In consequence, the Turkish nobility, and with it Balban, became even more powerful and strongly entrenched than before.

But the problems which Balban had to confront were great, because Iltutmis̲h̲ had not been able to consolidate the Sultanate; nor had his immediate successors done anything to strengthen it. In fact, it was threatened with dissolution by refractory Hindū *zamīndārs*, ambitious provincial governors and Mongol pressure.

Already in 645/1247-8, a year after Maḥmūd's accession to the throne, Balban had led a campaign against a *zamīndār* in the Dō˒āb and captured a fort called Talsindah in the Ḳannawdj̲ district. He had then attacked a Rād̲j̲pūt chief "Dulka va Mulka", who ruled over the area between the D̲j̲umnā and Kalind̲j̲ar, and defeated and expelled him. It took Balban two campaigns to secure control over the "Katahriyā infidels", who ruled Badā˒ūn and Sambhal. Balban also reduced the refractory tribes of "D̲j̲aralī and Datolī". But these successes were temporary, and he had to undertake annual campaigns in the Ganges-D̲j̲umnā area to maintain peace. In 646/1248-9 he attacked Ranthambor and Mēwāt, but the campaign was abortive. In fact, Balban's efforts to subdue the Rād̲j̲pūts during Maḥmūd's reign proved a failure; and although he led two expeditions against the Mē˒ōs [*q.v.*], who were led by the Rād̲j̲pūts, and massacred a large number of them, he failed to crush them.

Owing to the preoccupation of Maḥmūd's government with the Mongols, who had become a great threat by 635/1237, the provincial governors raised the banner of revolt. Ḳutlug̲h̲ K̲h̲ān, Maḥmūd's stepfather, who held the province of Awadh [*q.v.*] and was anti-Balban, allied himself with Rayḥān and defied royal authority. Balban therefore sent Sand̲j̲ar Sihwastānī to take over Bahrā˒ič from Rayḥān. But Ḳutlug̲h̲ came to Rayḥān's aid, intercepted and seized Sand̲j̲ar. Sand̲j̲ar managed to escape and, having collected a small force, attacked Rayḥān and killed him. Balban thereupon ordered Ḳutlug̲h̲ to leave Awadh and take over Bahrā˒ič, but the latter refused and rebelled. Balban attacked him, but he escaped to the Himalayan foothills. In 654/1256 he came out of his retreat, reoccupied Awadh and even made an attempt to occupy Karra and Mānikpūr; but Arslān K̲h̲ān, who held the province, expelled him.

In 655/1257, Yuzbek-i Tug̲h̲rïl, a Ḳïpčaḳ Turk, who was governor of Lakhnawti [*q.v.*] defied the Dihlī government. He led a successful expedition into D̲j̲ad̲j̲nagar (Orissa), occupied Awad̲h̲ and had the *k̲h̲uṭba* recited in his name. But in a campaign in Kāmrūp, he was taken prisoner by the forces of its Rād̲j̲ā and executed.

Yuzbek was succeeded by ʿIzz al-Dīn Balban-i Yuzbekī. But the latter did not rule long, for in 657-8/1259-60, Arslān K̲h̲ān, governor of Karrā, without Dihlī's permission, advanced on Lakhnawti and seized it. Yuzbekī was defeated and slain. Owing to the central government's preoccupations with other problems, it could do nothing. Fortunately however, Arslān K̲h̲ān died on 18 D̲j̲umādā I 663/27 February 1265.

The authority of Dihlī over the Pand̲j̲āb and Sind was weak partly because of the Mongol pressure and partly due to their distance from the centre. In 639/1241, Lahore had been occupied by the Mongols. About the same time Kabīr K̲h̲ān, governor of Multān had declared his independence and occupied Uččh. Shortly afterwards, Ḥasan Ḳarlig̲h̲, a lieutenant of D̲j̲alāl al-Dīn K̲h̲ʷārazm-S̲h̲āh, succeeded in occupying Multān, but on the approach of the Mongols fled to Lower Sind. Kabīr's descendants, who held Uččh, appealed to Dihlī for help. Balban at once marched with a strong army, whereupon the Mongols withdrew. Balban placed Multān under Kis̲h̲lū K̲h̲ān, while Uččh was left with Kabīr's family. Kis̲h̲lū was, however, allowed to annex Uččh as well on condition that he relinquished Nagawr. But Kis̲h̲lū refused to give up Nagawr and did so only when he was compelled. In 647/1249-50 Ḥasan Karlig̲h̲ returned from Lower Sind and seized Multān from Kis̲h̲lū. Yet he was not able to retain Multān long, for it was occupied by S̲h̲īr K̲h̲ān, governor of Lahore and Bhatinda, who not only refused to restore it to Kis̲h̲lū, but dispossessed him of Uččh as well. It is more than probable that S̲h̲īr K̲h̲ān's action was inspired by Balban.

Although Kis̲h̲lū was compensated by the governorship of Badā˒ūn, he was not reconciled to the loss of Multān and joined the anti-Balban faction led by Rayḥān. In spite of this, Kis̲h̲lū was, on Rayḥān's dismissal, given back his former possessions of Multān and Uččh according to the settlement of 652/1254. But after establishing himself firmly, Kis̲h̲lū threw off the authority of Dihlī and transferred his loyalty to Hülegü, and Maḥmūd's government was not strong enough to take any action.

Not satisfied with this, Kis̲h̲lū, early in 655/1257, joined his father-in-law, Ḳutlug̲h̲ K̲h̲ān, and together they marched on Dihlī. Balban moved out to meet them near Samana. While the two forces were preparing for a conflict, some religious leaders of Dihlī sent word to Kis̲h̲lū that they would surrender the town to them. This leaked out and the conspirators were banished. So when the rebel army reached Dihlī on 21 June 1257, after eluding Balban's forces and Kis̲h̲lū found that no support was forthcoming, he returned to Uččh. Nothing is known as to what happened to Ḳutlug̲h̲. But Kis̲h̲lū paid a visit to Hülegü in ʿIrāḳ seeking help to attack Dihlī and, at the end of 655/1257, a Mongol army under Sali Bahādur arrived in Sind; but, deterred by Balban's military preparations, it did not attack Dihlī. Balban succeeded in occupying both Multān and the Pand̲j̲āb. Twice Kis̲h̲lū tried to occupy Multān with Mongol help, but failed. Early in 656/1258, Hülegü's envoys arrived in Dihlī. Balban organised outside the city a spectacle, consisting of soldiers and common people, human heads and corpses, to express the might and invincibility of the Sultanate. It seems that Balban was able to arrive at some understanding with Hülegü, by which he was able to occupy Sind.

Maḥmūd died in 665/1266-7. No contemporary evidence exists to reveal the manner of his death. But Ibn Baṭṭūṭa and ʿIṣāmī say that he was poisoned by the ambitious Balban, and this is not improbable. On Maḥmūd's death, Balban ascended the throne as G̲h̲iyāt̲h̲ al-Dīn Balban.

Bibliography: D̲j̲ūzd̲j̲ānī, *Ṭabaḳāt-i Nāṣirī*, ed. ʿAbd al-Ḥayy Habībī, Kābul 1342/1963, also ed. Nassau Lees, K̲h̲ādim Ḥusayn and ʿAbd al-Ḥayy, Bibl. Ind. Calcutta 1864; Eng. tr. H. G. Raverty, Bibl. Ind. Calcutta 1897; ʿIṣāmi, *Futūḥ al-salāṭīn*, ed. Ag̲h̲a Mahdī Ḥusayn, Agra 1938; also ed. A. S. Usha, Madras 1948; Eng. tr. Ag̲h̲a Mahdī Ḥusayn, ii, Aligarh 1977; Ibn Baṭṭūṭa, Eng. tr. Ag̲h̲a Mahdī Ḥusayn, Baroda 1953; Ḍiyā˒ al-Dīn Baranī, *Ta˒rīk̲h̲-i Fīrūz S̲h̲āhī*, ed. Sayyid Aḥmad K̲h̲ān, Bibl. Ind. Calcutta 1862; ʿAbd al-Ḳādir Badā˒ūnī, *Muntak̲h̲ab al-tawārīk̲h̲*, i, ed. Aḥmad ʿAlī, Bibl. Ind. Calcutta 1868, Eng. tr. G. Ranking, Bibl. Ind. Calcutta 1898; Niẓām al-Dīn, *Ṭabaḳāt-i Akbarī*, i, ed. and Eng. tr. B. De, Bibl. Ind. Calcutta 1927; Muḥammad Ḳāsim Hindū-Shāh, *Taʾrīkh-i Firishta*, i, Lucknow 1281/1864-5; A. B. M. Habibullah, *The foundation of Muslim rule in India*, Allahabad 1961; M. Ḥabīb and K. A. Nizami, eds., *A comprehensive history of India (1206-1526)*, v. Dihlī 1970; W. Haig, ed., *Cambridge history of India*, iii, Cambridge 1928; R. C. Majumdar, *History and culture of the Indian people*. v, *The struggle for empire*, Bombay 1957; H. H. Howorth, *History of the Mongols*, i, London 1927; D'Ohsson, *Histoire des Mongoles*, iii, The Hague and Amsterdam 1834; P. Saran, *Politics and personalities in the reign of Naṣīr al-Dīn Maḥmūd, the Slave*, in *Studies in medieval Indian history*, Dihlī 1952; K. A. Niẓāmī, *Balban, the regicide*, in *Studies in medieval Indian history*, Aligarh 1956; G. H. Odjha, *Radjputaneka Itihas*, Adjmēr 1927.

2. Maḥmūd II, Nāṣir al-Dīn b. Sulṭān Muḥammad Shāh b. Fīrūz Shāh Tughluḳ; ascended the throne of Dihlī on 20 Djumādā 796/23 March 1394, on the death of his brother ʿAlāʾ al-Dīn Sikandar Shāh, after two weeks of discussion between the Fīrūz Shāhī slaves and the Afghān Lodī *amīrs*. Maḥmūd tried to reconcile the nobles belonging to the two groups. He appointed Malik Sarwar, a eunuch, as *wazīr* with the title of Khʷādja Djahān and Dawlat Khān Lodī as *kōtwāl* of Dihlī. ʿAbd al-Rashīd Khān Sulṭānī was given the title of Saʿādat Khān and appointed *barbek*. Sarang Khān Lodī, a cousin of Dawlat Khān was assigned Dīpalpūr, while Sārang's younger brother Mallū Iḳbāl Khan [*q.v.*] was made deputy *wazīr*.

The sultanate was in the process of disintegration. Provinces had declared their independence; even the territory around Dihlī was in a state of turmoil. In Radjab 796/May 1394, Maḥmūd sent Malik Sarwar to suppress the rebellion of a *zamīndār* in Djawnpūr and gave him the title of *Sulṭān al-Sharḳ*. Malik Sarwar suppressed the rebellion, annexed considerable territory and founded the kingdom of Djawnpūr [*q.v.*].

Meanwhile, Bīr Singh Deva, the Tomārā *zamīndār* of Danarolī, attacked Gwāliyār [*q.v.*] and occupied it. Maḥmūd marched towards Gwāliyār with Saʿādat Khān in Shaʿbān 796/June 1394, leaving behind Muḳarrab Khān, the heir-designate, in charge of Dihlī. On approaching Gwāliyār, Mallū Iḳbāl and other *amīrs*, who were jealous of Saʿādat, conspired to assassinate him. But news of this leaked out and Saʿādat put to death two of the conspirators. Mallū Iḳbāl, however, escaped to Dihlī to the protection of Muḳarrab Khān. Maḥmūd and Saʿādat therefore returned to Dihlī, but finding its gates closed to them, besieged it. In the course of the siege, which lasted for three months, Maḥmūd became dissatisfied with Saʿādat and went over to Muḳarrab. Thereupon Saʿādat withdrew to Fīrūzābād, which he seized, and, in Rabī I 797/January 1395, set up Nuṣrat Khān, another grandson of Fīrūz Shāh, as Sulṭān. But not long after, Saʿādat's fellow-slaves turned against him and he fled to Dihlī, where Muḳarrab put him to death. However, the rebel slaves remained loyal to Nuṣrat Shāh and recognised him as king. The result was that there were two rulers: Maḥmūd, who was supported by the Lodīs [*q.v.*] and held the forts of Dihlī and Sīrī and their suburbs, and Nuṣrat, who was supported by the slaves, and was in possession of Fīrūzābād, including some parts of the Dōʾāb, Sambhal, Pānīpat and Rohtak. For three years skirmishes continued between the partisans of Maḥmūd and those of Nuṣrat, until suddenly Mallū Iḳbāl, the most unscrupulous of the Dihlī nobles of the period, brought Nuṣrat to Djahānpanāh and professed loyalty to him, but then attacked him. Nuṣrat fled to Fīrūzābād and then to his *wazīr*, Tatār Khān, in Pānīpat. Mallū Iḳbāl occupied Fīrūzābād and fought against Muḳarrab for two months, and then killed him. But he did not hurt Maḥmūd, whom he now acknowledged as Sulṭān and whom he dominated.

Owing to these internecine conflicts, the Dihlī government was absolutely ineffective and, as Badāʾūnī was to observe later: "the rule of the Sulṭān of Dihlī is from Dihlī to Pālam" (*ḥukm-i khudāwand-i ʿālam az Dihlīst tā Pālam*). Gudjarāt, Rādjasthān, Bengal and Bihār no longer acknowledged the authority of Dihlī: Ḳannawdj, Dalmāw, Awadh and Bahrāʾič were annexed to the new kingdom of Djawnpūr. The Hindū *zamīndārs* to the east and west of Dihlī were in a state of rebellion. In the north-west, Khiḍr Khān held Multān; but in 798/1395-6 Sārang Khān, who had been assigned Dīpalpūr, attacked Khiḍr Khān and seized Multān with the help of his brother, Mallū Iḳbāl. He then defeated Shaykhā Khokar and appointed his younger brother, ʿĀdil Khān, as governor of Lahore. But on 15 Muḥarram 800/8 October 1397, Sārang was defeated by Tatār Khān at the battle of Kotlā.

Such was the condition of Dihlī and its provinces when the storm of Tīmūr's invasion burst on Hindustān. Already Pīr Muḥammad, Tīmūr's grandson and commander of the vanguard of his army, had occupied Uččh and Multān and killed Sārang Khān Lodī. Tīmūr crossed the Indus in the second week of Dhu 'l-Hidjdja 799/September 1399 and marched towards Dihlī, leaving behind a trail of death and destruction. On hearing of Tīmūr's approach, Maḥmūd and Iḳbāl improvised a force of 4,000 horse, 5,000 foot and 27 elephants and offered resistance near the Djahānpanāh palace, where Tīmūr had taken residence. But Mallū Iḳbāl fled after the first encounter. On 18 December, however, he and Maḥmūd confronted Tīmūr with 10,000 horse and 40,000 foot, but were completely routed, Iḳbāl fleeing to Baran and Maḥmūd to Gudjarāt and then to Mālwā. After staying in Dihlī for fifteen days, during which the city was plundered and its inhabitants ruthlessly massacred or enslaved, Tīmūr left.

Onn Tīmūr's departure, Nuṣrat occupied Dihlī, but he was driven out by Mallū Iḳbāl into Mēwāt, where he shortly after died. Iḳbāl thereupon invited Maḥmūd from Mālwā and restored him his throne on 6 Rabīʿ I 804/14 October 1401. In the same year, Maḥmūd, accompanied by Iḳbāl, marched against Ibrāhīm Sharḳī but, weary of his minister's domination, he went over to Ibrāhīm. However, as he was not treated with the respect due to him by the Djawnpūr ruler, he escaped to Ḳannawdj [see Ḳannawdj], where he established himself. Mallū Iḳbāl made an attempt on Ḳannawdj, but was unsuccessful; he then attacked Khiḍr Khān, but was defeated and slain by him on 19 Djumādā I 808/14 November 1405 on the banks of the river Dhāndā in the Adjudhan district. Maḥmūd returned to Dihlī at the invitation of Dawlat Khān Lōdī and Ikhtiyār Khān, two leading nobles. But he was faced with serious problems: in the first place, his kingdom had considerably shrunk, because the provinces had become independent; secondly, he was confronted by two formidable enemies, Sulṭān Ibrāhīm Sharḳī in the east and Khiḍr Khān in the west. In Shaʿbān 809/December 1406, Ibrāhīm Sharḳī besieged Ḳannawdj and took it after a siege of four months. Then in Djumādā I 810/October 1407 he marched towards Dihlī, but on hearing that Muẓaffar Shāh I of Gudjarāt was advancing towards Djawnpūr, withdrew to save his capital. Maḥmūd took advantage of Ibrāhīm Sharḳī's retreat to occupy Baran (Bulandshahr) and Sambhal.

It was, however, Khiḍr Khān who proved to be Maḥmūd's most dangerous enemy. He had consolidated himself in the *wilāyat* of Multān and the *shiḳḳ* of Dīpalpūr and, on the plea that Tīmūr had appointed him his viceroy, he directed his attention towards Dihlī. In Shaʿbān 809/January 1407, he occupied Ḥiṣār-Fīrūza, Samāna and Sirhind; and although the next year Maḥmūd reoccupied Ḥiṣār, it was a temporary success, for in Ramaḍān 811/January 1409, Khiḍr Khān sent Malik Ṭuḥfa, one of his lieutenants, to plunder the Dōʾāb, while he himself set out towards Dihlī and besieged Maḥmūd in Sirī and Ikhtiyār Khān in Fīrūzābād. Lack of provisions due to famine compelled Khiḍr to withdraw. But in 813/1410-11 he conquered Rohtak, and the next year he again invested Dihlī. Ikhtiyār, who held Fīrūzābād, submitted, but Maḥmūd held out in Sirī, and Khiḍr was once again compelled to withdraw on account of the lack of provisions. Maḥmūd died in Radjab 815/November 1412, and Dawlat Khān Lodī became the ruler of Dihlī. In Ramaḍān 816/November-December 1413, Khiḍr for the third time advanced on Dihlī and besieged Sirī. After holding out for four months, Dawlat Khān surrendered. He was imprisoned in Ḥiṣār-Firūza, and Khiḍr obtained possession of Dihlī on 17 Rabī I 817/6 June 1414, thus laying the foundations of the short-lived Sayyid dynasty.

Bibliography: Shams Sirādj ʿAfīf, *Taʾrīkh-i Fīrūz Shāhī*, ed. Hidāyat Ḥusayn, Bibl. Ind. Calcutta 1890; Yaḥyā b. Aḥmad b. ʿAbd Allāh Sirhindī, *Taʾrīkh-i Mubārak Shāhī*, ed. Hidāyat Ḥusayn, Bibl. Ind. Calcutta 1931, Eng. tr. K. K. Basu, Baroda 1932; Niẓām al-Din, *Ṭabaḳāt-i Akbarī*, i, ed. and tr. B. De, Bibl. Ind. Calcutta 1927; ʿAbd al-Ḳādir Badāʾūnī, *Muntakhab al-tawārīkh*, i, ed. and tr. G. A. Ranking, Bibl. Ind. Calcutta 1898; Muḥammad Ḳāsim Hindū-Shāh, *Taʾrīkh-i Firishta*, i, Lucknow 1281/1864; A. Mahdī Ḥusayn, *Tughluḳ dynasty*, Calcutta 1963; M. Ḥabīb and K. A. Niẓāmī, eds., *A comprehensive history of India (1206-1526)*, v, Dihlī 1970; W. Haig, ed., *Cambridge history of India*, iii, Cambridge 1928; R. C. Madjumdar, ed., *History and culture of the Indian people*. v. *The struggle for empire*, Bombay 1957. (MOHIBBUL HASAN)

MAḤMŪD, the name of three mediaeval rulers of Gudjarāt, [*q.v.*] in India.

1. MAḤMŪD I, SAYF AL-DĪN, BEGAṚHĀ or BEGṚĀ, a younger brother of Sulṭān Ḳuṭb al-Dīn and son of Muḥammad Shāh, ascended the throne on 1 Shaʿbān 863/3 June 1459, at the age of thirteen, with the title of Abu 'l-Fatḥ Muḥammad Shāh, after the nobles had dethroned his uncle Dāwūd. He is known as Maḥmūd Begaṛhā because of the two forts (*gaṛhs*) of Girnār and Čāmpāner which he conquered.

Four months after his accession, Maḥmūd was faced with a conspiracy of some leading nobles aimed at overthrowing his able minister, Malik Shaʿbān. They told him that the minister was plotting to depose him and thereby secured his imprisonment. But on discovering that the charges were false, Maḥmūd secured his release. Realising that the Sulṭān had come to know of their designs, the conspirators decided to attack him; however, as their followers deserted to the Sulṭān, they fled. Maḥmūd had thus crushed the plot by his courage and presence of mind. Malik Shaʿbān, though restored to his office, soon retired and Maḥmūd took the reins of government in his own hands.

In 866/1462, Maḥmūd marched to the help of Niẓām Shāh Bahmanī, whose kingdom had been invaded by Maḥmūd Khaldjī I [*q.v.*] of Mālwā. But learning that Niẓām Shāh had been defeated, he entered Khāndesh [*q.v.*] and thereby cut off the retreat of Maḥmūd Khaldjī who had to make his way back through Gondwāna after much hardship. Next year again Maḥmūd Khaldjī invaded the Dakhan, but withdrew on hearing that Maḥmūd Begaṛhā was coming to Niẓām Shāh's assistance. Henceforth, the Khaldjī ruler never again committed aggression against Niẓām Shāh.

In 867/1463, Maḥmūd invaded Dūn, situated between Gudjarāt and Konkan, because of its Rādjā's acts of piracy. The Rādjā was defeated and his fortress occupied; but it was restored to him on condition of an annual tribute.

In 871/1466, Maḥmūd attacked Girnār (Djūnāgaṛh), and compelled its chief, Rao Mandalik Čudāsama, to pay tribute. But although Maḥmūd received the tribute regularly, he decided to annex Girnār and led an invasion. The Rao retreated to his citadel of Uparkot, situated north-west of the town, but as supplies ran short, surrendered on 10 Djumādā II 875/4 December 1470. Maḥmūd had to undertake three campaigns in four years to subdue the Rao. Girnār was annexed and its chief, having entered the service of the Sulṭān, embraced Islam and was given the title of Khān-i Djahān. At the foot of the Girnār hills the Sulṭān founded the city of Muṣṭafābād, which became one of his capitals.

Maḥmūd next marched against the frontier tribes of the Sumrās, Sodhās and Kahlās who lived on the Kaččh border and who, although claiming to be Muslims, were in fact ignorant of the *Sharīʿa*. They surrendered without offering any resistance and agreed to send their leaders to Aḥmadābād to be taught the tenets of Islām.

In 877/1473, the Djāt and Balūč tribes rebelled against Maḥmūd's maternal grandfather, Djām Niẓām al-Dīn. Maḥmūd crossed the Rann of Kaččh in order to suppress the rising, but the rebels dispersed without offering any resistance. It was suggested to Maḥmūd that he should annex Sind but he refused, saying that his mother belonged to its ruling family.

On his return from Sind, Maḥmūd heard that Mawlānā Maḥmūd Samarḳandī, a poet and philosopher, who had long been in the service of the Bahmanī rulers, while sailing in a ship bound for Hormuz, had been driven to Dwārkā, situated in the north-western corner of Kathiāwār, where pirates had robbed him of all his belongings, including his womenfolk. After many hardships, the Mawlānā arrived in Muṣṭafābād. Angry at his plight, the Sulṭān marched towards Dwārkā. Its Radjput chief, Bhīm, took refuge in the island-fortress of Bet or Sankhodhar. Maḥmūd marched through dense forests, full of wild animals, and invested it. Bhīm was defeated in a sea fight and taken prisoner. The Mawlānā's goods were now restored to him.

Tired of the Sulṭān's constant wars and his plans of invading Čāmpāner, which would be a prolonged affair, the Gudjarāt nobles plotted to overthrow him and set up his son on the throne. But Ray Rayān, an important Hindū noble, revealed the plot to the *wazīr* Bahāʾ al-Dīn, who, in turn, reported it to Maḥmūd. To test the reaction of the conspirators, the Sulṭān announced that he had decided to go on a pilgrimage to Mecca. Realising that Maḥmūd had been informed of the conspiracy, and that they would not succeed in their aims, they requested him to undertake the campaign for the conquest of Čāmpāner, and then proceed to Mecca.

Accordingly, on Dhu 'l-Ḳaʿda 887/12 December 1482, he marched towards Čāmpāner on the pretext that its Rādjā, Rāwal Djay Singh, had raided his kingdom. The Rādjā was defeated and took refuge in the hill fortress of Pavagaṛh, above Čāmpāner. Maḥmūd thereupon besieged it. But learning that Maḥmūd Khaldjī I, to whom the Rādjā had appealed for aid, was marching towards Gudjarāt, Maḥmūd left his officers to continue the siege, and he himself set out to intercept the Mālwa army. But as Maḥmūd Khaldjī withdrew to Mālwa, the Sulṭān returned to prosecute the siege. Supplies in the fort ran short and, after a breach was affected by a cannonball, it was captured. Of the 700 Radjpūts, who performed the *djawhar*, all were slain except the Rādjā and his minister, who were seized and executed. But the Rādjā's son accepted Islam and was given the title of Niẓām al-Mulk and made the ruler of Idār. Čāmpāner was renamed Muḥammadabād.

Maḥmūd now turned his attention to Rādjā ʿĀdil Khān II of Khāndesh (861-907/1457-1501), who had not only not paid his annual tribute, but had asserted his independence. In 904/1498, Maḥmūd invaded Khāndesh and compelled its ruler to pay tribute and recognise his suzerainty. Later, on the death of Rādjā ʿĀdil Khān's son, Ghaznī Khān (914/1508), who left no male heir, Maḥmūd took part in the dispute over succession. Aḥmad Niẓām Shāh of Aḥmadnagar, ʿImād Shāh of Berār, and Ḥusām al-Dīn, a powerful noble, all favoured ʿĀlam Khān, who belonged to the Fārūḳī dynasty. But Maḥmūd supported his maternal grandson, also called ʿĀlam Khān, and marched with him to Thalner, the capital of the Fārūḳī rulers. Thereupon, the rulers of Aḥmadnagar and Berār, who had arrived in Burhānpūr, withdrew, and on 19 Dhu 'l-Ḥidjdja 914/10 April 1509, Maḥmūd installed ʿĀlam Khān as ʿĀdil Khān III on the throne of Khāndesh; and when, subsequently, a rebellion supported by Niẓām Shāh broke out, he sent troops to the aid of his grandson, so that the rebels fled.

The Portuguese had diverted the trade between Europe and the East from the ancient route via Egypt and the Red Sea to the new route via the Cape of Good Hope, discovered by Vasco da Gama in 1498. So, when in 913/1507 the Mamlūk Sulṭān of Egypt sent an expedition to the Gudjarāt coast to destroy the Portuguese power, Maḥmūd readily sent his naval ship under Ayāz, a Turk in his service, to his help. In a naval battle off Chaul in Ramaḍān 913/January 1508, the Portuguese were defeated and their commander, Dom Lourenço, son of the Portuguese viceroy Almeida, was killed. To avenge the defeat and the death of his son, Almeida attacked the combined Egyptian and Gudjarātī navy near Diu and scored a victory. Impressed by this victory, the Sultan sent an ambassador to the Portuguese Viceroy, Albuquerque (1505-15), and a treaty was concluded. It was agreed that the Portuguese would not hinder Gudjarāt trade and would respect the right of Gudjarātī vessels to ply in the Indian waters. In return, the Portuguese prisoners would be released and the Portuguese vessels would be permitted to visit the Gudjarāt ports. Maḥmūd released the prisoners of war and offered the Portuguese a site for a factory at Diu.

Maḥmūd died on 2 Ramaḍān 917/23 November 1511, at the age of sixty-seven, and was buried in the mausoleum which he had built for himself at Sarkhedj, about six miles south-west of Aḥmadābād. He was by far the greatest of the Sulṭāns of Gudjarāt, and his reign was the most glorious period of mediaeval Gudjarāt. Brave, just and liberal, possessing great energy and a strong will, he was not only a military genius but also an able administrator. He appointed able officers like Malik Gopī, his Hindu chief minister, to carry on the government. He advanced money to repair old houses, he dug wells, built inns, planted trees on both sides of the road, made roads safe for travellers and merchants, freed the country from internal strife and tried to exterminate piracy. Owing to these measures, trade increased, agriculture flourished and the people became prosperous.

Maḥmūd was a cultured ruler and enjoyed the society of learned men. He had the famous biographical dictionary of Ibn Khallikān translated into Persian, under the name of *Manẓar al-Islām*. He also patronised Sanskrit, and his court poet Udayarādj wrote a poem in his praise. He was also a great builder, and his contribution to Gudjarāt architecture is considerable. He laid out two beautiful gardens, Bāgh-i Firdaws and Bāgh-i Shaʿbān near Aḥmadābād. He founded the towns of Muṣṭafābād, Maḥmūdābād and Muḥammadābād-Čāmpāner and embellished them with palaces and mosques. He beautified Aḥmadābād with broad streets and a number of fine buildings. At Čāmpāner he constructed a magnificent Djāmʿ Masdjid, and at Sarkhedj he built for himself on the banks of a reservoir a grand palace. The fame of Maḥmūd's achievements spread far and wide; in Ṣafar 914/June 1508, an embassy came from Sikandar Lodī of Dihlī, and an embassy also arrived from Shāh Ismāʿīl Ṣafawī of Persia, but as the Sulṭān was lying seriously ill he could not receive the Persian envoy.

Bibliography: ʿAbd Allāh Muḥammad b. ʿUmar, *Ẓafar al-wālih bi-Muẓaffar wa-ālih*, ed. E. D. Ross, *An Arabic history of Gudjarāt*, London 1910-28; Eng. tr. of vol. i by S. Lokhandwālā, Baroda 1970; Sikandar b. Muḥammad, alias Manjhū, *Mirʾāt-i Sikandarī*, ed. S. C. Misra, Baroda 1961, Eng. tr. Faḍl Allāh Luṭf Allāh Farīdī, Bombay 1899, and by E. C. Bayley, London 1886; ʿAlī Muḥammad Khān, *Mirʾāt-i Aḥmadī*, ed. Sayyid Nawwāb ʿAlī, Baroda 1927-8, Eng. tr. M. F. Lokhandwālā, Baroda 1965; *Mirʾāt-i Aḥmadī, Supplement*, ed. Sayyid Nawwāb ʿAlī, Baroda 1930, Eng. tr. idem and C. N. Seddon, Baroda 1928; Muḥammad Ḳāsim Hindū-Shāh, *Taʾrīkh-i Firishta*, ii, Lucknow 1281/1864; Niẓām al-Dīn, *Ṭabaḳāt-i Akbarī*, iii, ed. B. De and Hidāyat Ḥusayn, Calcutta 1935, and Eng. tr. B. De and Baini Prashad, Bibl. Ind. Calcutta 1938; *The commentaries of the great Alfonso d'Alboquerque*, Eng. tr. Walter de Gray Birch, Hakluyt Society, I-IV, 1875-1905; *The book of Duarte Barbosa*, Eng.tr. M. L. Dames, Hakluyt Society 1918; M. S. Commissariat, *A history of Gudjarāt*, i, London 1938; W. Haig, ed., *Cambridge history of India*, iii, Cambridge 1928; M. Ḥabīb and K. A. Niẓāmī, eds., *A comprehensive history of India (1206-1526)*, v, Dihlī 1970; works by J. Burgess on *Muhammadan architecture of Gudjarāt*, published between 1875-1905.

2. Maḥmūd II, was the sixth son of Sulṭān Muẓaffar Shāh (917-32/1511-26), on whose death his eldest son and heir-designate, Sikandar, succeeded as Sulṭān with the support of ʿImād al-Mulk Khushḳadam and Khudāwand Khān, two powerful nobles. His third son, Laṭīf, contested the throne, but was defeated and slain. Sikandar was extremely handsome, but he surrounded himself by low favourites, gave himself up to pleasure and took no interest in affairs of state. This made him unpopular with both the nobles and Sayyids of Gudjarāt. Taking advantage of this, Khushḳadam, who was angry with Sikandar for ignoring him and not making him *wazīr*, caused him to

be assassinated on the night of 14 Sha^cbān 932/27 May 1526, and raised to the throne Muẓaffar Shāh's six-year old son Naṣīr Khān as Maḥmūd II. However, jealous of Khushḳadam, who was the *de facto* ruler, the nobles, led by Tādj Khān Narpalī, offered the throne to Muẓaffar Shāh's second son, Bahādur Khān; Khushḳadam appealed to the neighbouring princes and to Bābur, but received no help. On receiving the nobles' invitation, Bahādur, who was on his way to Djawnpūr to try his fortune there, rushed back to Aḥmadabād and ascended the throne on 26 Ramaḍān 932/July 1526. From Aḥmadabād he marched to Čāmpāner, and having occupied the fort without meeting much resistance, executed Khushḳadam and later Maḥmūd II, whose reign of about forty days thus came to an end.

Bibliography: See that for MAḤMŪD I; also Mīr Abū Turāb Wālī, *Ta'rīkh-i Gudjarāt*, ed. E. D. Ross, Bibl. Ind., Calcutta 1909.

3. MAḤMŪD III, ABU 'L-FUTŪḤĀT SA^cD AL-DĪN, was the third son of Laṭīf Khān, son of Sulṭān Muẓaffar Shāh II. On the death of Bahādur Shāh on 3 Ramaḍān 943/13 February 1537, who left no son, Muḥammad Zamān Mīrzā, the Emperor Humāyūn's brother-in-law, claimed the throne on the ground that Bahādur Shāh's mother had adopted him as his heir, and he had the *khuṭba* recited in his name in the Djāmi^c Masdjid at Diu. But the Gudjarāt nobles refused to acknowledge him as Sulṭān and offered the throne to Mīrān Muḥammad Shāh Fārūḳī, son of Bahādur Shāh's sister. Mīrān set out from Burhānpūr, but died on the way (926/1527). Thereupon, the nobles decided to set up on the throne Laṭīf's younger son Maḥmūd Khān, who, during the reign of Bahādur Shāh, had been in the custody of Mīrān Muḥammad Shāh of Khāndesh. But Mubārak Shāh, Mīrān's successor, refused to release him, he himself being a claimant to the throne of Gudjarāt. So Ikhtiyār Khān Ṣiddīḳī invaded Khāndesh and brought Maḥmūd to Aḥmadābād, where he was enthroned as Abu 'l-Futūḥāt, Sa^cd al-Dīn Maḥmūd Shāh III. But as Maḥmūd was only eleven years of age, Ikhtiyār Khān became the Regent. He was an able man, but jealous of his power, and Muḥāfiẓ Khān and Daryā Khān had him assassinated. But these two last soon fell out and fought with each other to dominate Maḥmūd. Daryā Khān emerged victorious; but not long after he was replaced by ^cĀlam Khān, another noble, who now dominated the young Sulṭān. In 856/1545 Maḥmūd, weary of being a puppet king, decided to assert himself and shifted his capital to Maḥmūdābād, which had been founded by Maḥmūd I.

On 4 September 1538, Sulaymān Pāsha, the Ottoman governor of Egypt, arrived off the coast of Diu with a large fleet in order to overthrow the Portuguese power in the Indian waters. Maḥmūd helped him when, in Djumādā I 945/October 1538, he attacked Diu abortively. In 453/1546, Maḥmūd himself made an attempt to seize Diu. The Portuguese governor, Dom João de Castro, retaliated by committing great atrocities on the Gudjarāt coast. Realising the invicibility of the Portuguese, Maḥmūd made peace with them and granted them favourable terms.

In 1551 Maḥmūd thought of invading Mālwā, but instead directed his attention to the suppression of Rādjpūt landlords, who had rebelled because of the resumption of the large land grants which they held. The rebellion was crushed with great severity and their lands were seized; but the Rādjpūt peasant was not interfered with. Maḥmūd was planning to march towards Māndū to the help of the Emperor Humāyūn when, on the night of 12 Rabī^c I 961/15 February 1554, he was assassinated by his attendant Burhān al-Dīn, in revenge for the punishment which he had once inflicted on him.

Maḥmūd was weak and incompetent, but capable of committing acts of cruelty and of displaying occasional outbursts of energy. He was nevertheless generous and distributed food and clothes to the poor, and in winter gave them firewood and even bedding. He was a cultured prince and fond of the society of the learned and the pious. In Maḥmūdābād he erected an enclosure, six miles in area, which he named the Deer Park (*Āhū-khāna)*, and in which various kinds of wild animals roamed freely. He built in it splendid buildings and laid out nice gardens and spent his time there in the company of beautiful women, with whom he hunted and played polo.

Maḥmūd left no male heir because, dreading that he would have a rival, he used to procure the abortion of any of his women who happened to become pregnant. So after Maḥmūd's death, the nobles asserted their independence in their *djāgīr*s and fought with each other for power. They first set up a boy, who was related to him as Sulṭān with the title of Aḥmad III, who ruled nominally until Sha^cbān 968/April 1561, and then Muẓaffar III who reigned until 980/1572, when the Emperor Akbar invaded Gudjarāt and put an end to the prevailing chaos by annexing it.

Bibliography: See those for MAḤMŪD I and MAḤMŪD II of Gudjarāt. (MOHIBBUL HASAN)

MAḤMŪD, the name of two mediaeval rulers of Mālwā [*q.v.*] in India.

1. MAḤMŪD KHALDJĪ I, the son of Malik Mughīth, whose mother was the sister of Dilāwar Khān, the founder of the Ghūrī dynasty of Mālwā. On the death of Sulṭān Hushang Shāh on 8 Dhu 'l-Ḥidjdja 838/5 July 1435, his son Ghaznī Shāh succeeded with the support of Maḥmūd Khān and assumed the title of Muḥammad Shāh Ghūrī. He was weak and cruel and, thinking that Maḥmūd Khān wanted to usurp the throne, tried to have him assassinated. But Maḥmūd Khān came to know of this and caused Maḥmūd Ghūrī to be poisoned. He then offered the throne to his father, but since the latter refused, he himself ascended the throne on 29 Shawwāl 839/16 May 1436. He, however, conferred on his father the title of A^cẓam Humāyūn, and permitted him the use of all the symbols of royalty. He also consulted him on all affairs of state and acted on his advice.

At the very outset of his reign, Maḥmūd was faced by the rebellion of the nobles of Muḥammad Ghūrī, who refused to recognise him as Sulṭān. This he suppressed, executing some nobles and forgiving others on the advice of his father, who suggested a policy of appeasement. However, this policy was not successful, because a rising on a much larger scale now broke out. A^cẓam Humāyūn first had Prince Aḥmad Khān, son of Hūshang Shāh, poisoned, and then eliminated the rebels one by one, so that by Radjab 841/January 1438 he had succeeded in crushing the rising.

Meanwhile, Maḥmūd was faced with a serious threat from Sulṭān Aḥmad Shāh of Gudjarāt, who championed the cause of Mas^cūd Khān, son of Muḥammad Ghūrī, and having entered Mālwā, laid siege to Māndū [*q.v.*], its capital. While the siege was in progress, Maḥmūd heard that ^cUmar Khān, youngest son of Aḥmad Shāh, had attacked Čanderī and killed its governor, Ḥādjdjī Kamāl, and that Prince Muḥammad Khān, another son of Aḥmad Shāh, was marching to ^cUmar Khān's aid. In order to intercept Prince Muḥammad, Maḥmūd marched out of Māndū towards Sārangpūr. This led to the recall of Prince Muḥammad by his father. Maḥmūd, having prevented any help reaching ʿUmar Khān, defeated and killed him and then, on hearing that Aḥmad Shāh had withdrawn to Gudjarāt because plague had broken out in his army, he returned to Māndū. But after seventeen days, he set out towards Čanderī and captured it after a siege of four months. Here he received a request of help from Bahār Khān, *muḳtaʿ* of Shahr-i Naw, which was being invested by Dungar Sen of Gwāliyār [*q.v.*]. Maḥmūd, instead of marching towards Shahr-i Naw, advanced towards Gwāliyār. This strategy was successful, because Dungar Sen, realising the danger to his capital, retired from Shahr-i Naw. Maḥmūd, having achieved his object, withdrew from Gwāliyār and proceeded to Shahr-i Naw, where Bahār Khān acknowledged his suzerainty.

After consolidating his position, Maḥmūd in 844/1440-1 turned his attention towards the border chiefs. He first advanced on Khandwa, situated between Mālwā and Khāndesh and of great strategic importance. Ray Narhar Dās, its chief, finding himself unable to resist, fled, so that Maḥmūd was able to annex it, along with Khorā and Khirkī, and secured the submission of Khērlā's chief, Narsingh Deva. From Khērlā [*q.v.*], Maḥmūd marched towards Sargūdjā. On the way, the petty *zamīndārs* sent elephants as tribute and begged him spare their territories. Rādjā Bhodjā of Sargūdjā submitted and promised to supply elephants to the Sulṭān. Similarly, the *muḳaddams* of Raypūr and Ratanpūr came forward with elephants as tribute. Maḥmūd returned from Sargūdjā to Māndū in 845/1441-2.

Maḥmūd's reputation having spread far and wide, some of the *ʿulamāʾ* of Dihlī invited him to overthrow its Sayyid ruler, Sulṭān Muḥammad Shāh (837-47/1434-43). Maḥmūd accepted the invitation and set out towards Dihlī at the end of 845/1442. But in an engagement near Dihlī he was unable to defeat Prince ʿAlāʾ al-Dīn, Sulṭān Muḥammad Shāh's son, and, finding no hope of future success, he returned to Māndū on 1 Muḥarram 846/12 May 1442.

Maḥmūd now turned his attention to Rānā Kumbha of Mēwār, against whom he nursed a grievance. The Rānā had helped Prince ʿUmar Khān of Gudjarāt to seize the throne of Mālwa, and had reduced the Rādjpūt chiefs on the borders of Mālwā, which had accepted the suzerainty of Sulṭān Hushang Shah. Maḥmūd took advantage of the rivalry between the Sisodiās and the Rāthors and of the struggle for power between Rānā Kumbha and his brother, Khem Karan. Since the latter was expelled by the Rānā, Maḥmūd used it as a pretext for its invasion. On 26 Radjab 846/30 November 1442, he advanced towards Mēwār. On reaching Kumbhalgaṙh, he attacked the Banmata temple, situated at its base, occupied it after seven days and razed it to the ground because it contained arms for the defence of the main fort and, although outwardly a temple, formed part of the defences of the main fort. Maḥmūd then marched towards Čitor, but before he could attack it, he heard the news of his father's death in Mandasor. He therefore proceeded to Mandasor and, after the period of mourning was over, returned to Čitor, but finding its capture difficult, returned to Māndū and decided to reduce Mēwār gradually. So on 13 Shawwāl 847/3 February 1444 he occupied Gagrawn and named it Muṣṭafābād. Two years later he reduced Ranthambhor. He then attempted to seize Mandalgaṙh, but failed. In 851/1447-8, he marched on Gwāliyār and defeated Dungar Sen, who was compelled to retreat into his fort. Maḥmūd proceeded to Āgra and thence to Bayana, whose chief, Muḥammad Khān, submitted to him. In 859/1455, Maḥmūd occupied Adjmer and, early in 861/January 1457, he besieged the strong fort of Mandalgaṙh. He took it on 1 Dhu 'l-Ḥidjdja 861/20 October 1457, by first breaking the dams of the fort's reservoir, which caused the water to flow out, and then affecting a breach in the fort's walls. He destroyed an old temple and built a mosque in its place, and returned to Māndū after arranging for its administration. Until the end of his life Maḥmūd made several attempts to reduce Čitor, but failed; and although he defeated Rānā Kumbha, he failed to crush him and occupy any large part of Mēwār.

In Shaʿbān 848/January 1444, Maḥmūd came into conflict with the Sharḳī ruler of Djawnpūr [*q.v.*], who had occupied Kālpī and refused to restore it to Nāṣir Khān, his vassal. This led to an armed conflict. However, through the mediation of the Shaykh al-Islām, Shaykh Djaʾilda, who enjoyed the respect of both the Sulṭāns, a settlement was arrived at and Kālpī was given back to Nāṣir Khān [see MAḤMŪD SHĀH SHARḲĪ].

Maḥmūd, taking advantage of the incompetence of Muḥammad Shāh of Gudjarāt, tried to interfere in the affairs of his kingdom. Accordingly, in 854/1450 he set out to the assistance of Gangā Dās of Čāmpāner, which had been attacked by Muḥammad Shāh. But instead of marching to Čāmpāner, he directed his attack on Aḥmadābād, capital of Gudjarāt. Alarmed for the safety of his capital, Muḥammad Shāh raised the siege of Čāmpāner and returned to Aḥmadābād. Meanwhile, having received an invitation for the invasion of Gudjarāt, Maḥmūd marched at the end of 854/January 1451 and entered Gudjarāt. But since Muḥammad Shāh had died, Maḥmūd found himself confronted by his successor, Ḳuṭb al-Dīn, at Kāparbandj. On the last night of Ṣafar 855/2 April 1451, he made a night attack on the Gudjarāt army, but it proved abortive. In an engagement the next day, Maḥmūd suffered a defeat and had to retreat with the loss of eighty elephants and his baggage. On his return to Māndū, Maḥmūd, to avenge his defeat, sent Prince Ghiyāth to raid the Gudjarāt ports of Surat and Rainder. Accordingly, the prince plundered the suburbs and countryside of Surat and returned to Māndū with the booty. However, realising that his chances of success against the Gudjarāt army were remote, Maḥmūd decided to compel Ḳuṭb al-Dīn to make peace by a show of his military power. This device worked, for when, on 6 Dhu 'l-Ḥidjdja 855/30 December 1451, he sent an army to invade Gudjarāt, Ḳuṭb al-Dīn agreed upon a treaty by which they were to respect each other's territories and Mēwār was to be divided into two parts for the military activities of the two rulers.

In Muḥarram 857/January-February 1453, Maḥmūd invaded the Deccan under the impression that the Bahmanī Sulṭān ʿAlāʾ al-Dīn Aḥmad II, had died. But on reaching the borders of Māhur, he discovered that the Bahmanī ruler was not only alive, but had personally come to attack him; hence he returned to Mālwā.

In 866/1461 Maḥmūd again invaded the Deccan, defeated the Bahmanī forces at Maheskar on the Mandjar river and invested Bīdar. The Dowager Queen, mother of the boy-king, Niẓām Shāh, sent an army under Maḥmūd Gāwān and at the same time appealed to Maḥmūd I of Gudjarāt [*q.v.*] for aid. Realising that he was not strong enough to fight the two armies simultaneously, Maḥmūd withdrew to

Mālwā. He for the third time invaded the Deccan on 26 Rabīʿ I 867/19 December 1462, and occupied Dawlatābād, but on hearing of the approach of Maḥmūd Begaṙhā [*q.v.*], he again withdrew. But since the route via Khāndesh was blocked by the Gudjarātī forces, Maḥmūd had to make his way back through the forests of Gondwāna and suffer great hardship. Convinced that he would not be able to conquer the Deccan, Maḥmūd came to a settlement with the Bahmanids. It was agreed that Eličpur [*q.v.* in Suppl.] would be the boundary between the kingdoms of Mālwā and the Bahmanids, and that Maḥmūd would not in future invade the Deccan.

Maḥmūd died on 19 Dhu 'l-Ḳaʿda 873/31 May 1469 at the age of sixty-eight and was succeeded by his eldest son, Ghiyāth al-Dīn Shah. He had been a precocious child and, impressed by his intelligence, Sulṭān Hushang Shāh used to keep him by his side, and gave him the title of Khān when he was only sixteen. So it was no surprise that Maḥmūd proved to be the greatest ruler of mediaeval Mālwā, which reached the height of glory under him. He was wise, brave and benevolent, and a man of great energy and determination. Although religious, he was tolerant towards Hindus and associated them in his government; Sangrāma Singh was his treasurer and Rāy Rayān Siva was one of his most important and respected nobles. It is true he destroyed some temples, but this was done in the territory of his enemies in the course of his campaigns; in his own kingdom he respected the sanctity of Hindu places of worship.

Maḥmūd tried to promote the welfare of his subjects. When the crops were damaged by the marches and counter-marches of his troops, he compensated the peasants for their losses. He encouraged trade by patronising the Jains and encouraging them to settle in Mālwā, and he made the roads safe for the movements of goods. He established a big hospital in Māndū which he richly endowed. He also opened a college with a hostel, where board and lodging was provided for both teachers and students.

The fame of Maḥmūd's achievements reached as far as distant Egypt and Transoxiana. In 867/1462 al-Mustandjid bi'llāh, the puppet ʿAbbāsid caliph of Egypt, sent an envoy to Māndū with a *khilʿa* [*q.v.*] and a diploma of investiture, conferring on Maḥmūd sovereign powers. Some years later, in 867/1462, an envoy came from Tīmūr's great-grandson, Abū Saʿīd of Transoxiana and Khurāsān, with presents for Maḥmūd. In return, when the envoy left, he was accompanied by Prince ʿAlāʾ al-Dīn and his father's envoy and carried rich presents for Abū Saʿīd. Unfortunately, no details of Maḥmūd's mission to Harāt are available.

Maḥmūd was an enthusiastic builder. He completed the mosque and tomb of Hūshang Shāh, whose foundations had been laid by the latter. He also erected a number of buildings to commemorate his victory over Rānā Kunbha of Mēwār.

Bibliography: ʿAbd Allāh Muḥammad b. ʿUmar, *Ẓafar al-wālih bi-Muẓaffar wa-ālih*, ed. E. D. Ross, *An Arabic history of Gudjarāt*, London 1910-28; ʿAlī b. Muḥammad al-Kirmānī, *Maʾāthir-i Maḥmūd Shāhī*, ed. Nūr al-Ḥasan, Dihlī 1968; Yaḥyā b. Aḥmad b. ʿAbd Allāh al-Sirhindī, *Taʾrīkh-i Mubārak Shāhī*, ed. Hidāyat Ḥusayn, Bibl. Ind., Calcutta 1931, Eng. tr. K. K. Basu, Baroda 1932; Niẓām al-Dīn, *Ṭabaḳāt-i Akbarī*, iii, ed. B. De and Hidāyat Ḥusayn, Bibl. Ind., Calcutta 1935 and Eng. tr. B. De and Baini Prashad, Bibl. Ind., Calcutta 1938; Muḥammad Ḳāsim Hindū Shāh, *Taʾrīkh-i Firishta*, Lucknow 1281/1864; U. N. Day, *Medieval Mālwa (1401-1561)*, Dihlī 1965; M. Ḥabīb and K. A. Niẓāmī, eds., *A comprehensive history of India (1206-1526)*, Delhi 1965; W. Haig, ed., *Cambridge history of India*, iii, Cambridge 1928; G. Yazdānī, *Māndū: the city of joy*, Oxford 1929.

2. Maḥmūd Khaldjī I, whose real name was Aʿẓam Humāyūn, the third son of Sulṭān Naṣīr al-Dīn Shāh (906-16/1501-10). The latter had designated his eldest son, Shihāb al-Dīn, as his successor, but as Shihāb al-Dīn had rebelled, he nominated Aʿẓam Humāyūn to succeed him, and gave him the title of Maḥmūd Shāh. Accordingly, on the death of his father, Maḥmūd declared himself Sulṭān. But his two elder brothers, Shihāb al-Dīn and Ṣāḥib Khān, refused to recognise him. The former set out towards Māndū, but his advance was checked by Muḥāfiẓ Khān and Khawāṣṣ Khān, who were in favour of Maḥmūd. In consequence, he retired to Khāndesh [*q.v.*]. Maḥmūd, who had been following him, succeeded in entering Māndū and ascended the throne on 6 Rabīʿ I 917/3 June 1511.

Maḥmūd was weak, incompetent, fickle-minded and a puppet in the hands of his nobles, who struggled with each other to dominate him. He first came under the influence of Iḳbāl Khān and Mukhtaṣṣ Khān, who were so powerful as to assassinate the *wazīr*, Basant Rāy, in the audience hall, and secure the banishment of Sangrān Sonī, the treasurer. But Maḥmūd soon turned against them and allowed himself to be dominated by Muḥāfiẓ Khān. Iḳbāl and Mukhtaṣṣ thereupon recalled Shihāb al-Dīn, and finding their life in danger, left Māndū to join the pretender. Shihāb al-Dīn advanced from Khāndesh by quick marches, but died on the way due to heat and exhaustion. Meanwhile, Maḥmūd, weary of Muḥāfiẓ Khān's domination, tried to overthrow him. But before he could take any action, the minister himself struck and raised to the throne his elder brother, Ṣāḥib Khān, as Muḥammad Shāh II. Maḥmūd, finding himself helpless, escaped from Māndū and went first to Udjdjayn and then to Čanderī, where its governor refused to help him. However, he secured the help of Ray Čand Pūrbiya, upon whom he conferred the title of Mednī Rāy, and attacked Ṣāḥib Khān. He defeated him and then besieged him in Māndū. Ṣāḥib Khān, unable to hold out, fled to Gudjarāt with Muḥāfiẓ Khān and was given protection by its ruler. Muẓaffar II.

Maḥmūd, in recognition of Mednī Rāy's services, made him his *wazīr.* But this aroused the hostility of the nobles like Sikandar Khān of Satwas and Bahdjat Khān of Čanderī, who rebelled and took up the cause of Ṣāḥib Khān, who had returned to Mālwā. Mednī Rāy succeeded in reducing Sikandar Khān to obedience, but operations against the other rebels had to be postponed because Muẓaffar II invaded Mālwā and besieged Māndū. Fortunately, however, finding Māndū too strong to be reduced, Muẓaffar withdrew and Maḥmūd, with Mednī Rāy's help, was able to occupy Čanderī and expel Ṣāḥib Khān in Djumādā I 920/July 1514.

The victories achieved by Mednī Rāy made him very powerful, and he began to fill all the important posts by his own Rādjpūt followers, dismissing old Muslim officers. Maḥmūd resented these changes, and chafing under Mednī Rāy's domination, demanded that the dismissed Muslim officers be reinstated, and that the Rādjpūts should not keep Muslim women as mistresses. Mednī Rāy accepted these conditions, but his assistant Salivahan refused. Maḥmūd therefore decided to get rid of both of them by assassination. Mednī Rāy escaped with minor injuries, but Salivahan was killed. This led to the revolt of the Rād̲j̲pūts. Mednī Rāy, however, pacified them and continued as *wazīr*. But Maḥmūd, having failed to overthrow him, escaped from Māndū at the end of 923/1517 to Gud̲j̲arāt and sought the aid of Muẓaffar II. The latter, thereupon, invaded Mālwā in order to restore Maḥmūd's authority. On hearing of the invasion, Mednī Rāy proceeded to Čitor to seek the aid of Rānā Sàngarāmā Sengh, leaving his son, Rāy Pithora, in charge of Mandū. Meanwhile, Muẓaffar II invested Māndū and having taken it by an escalade on 4 Ṣafar 924/15 February 1518, ordered the massacre of the Rād̲j̲pūts who had defended the fort. He reinstated Maḥmūd and returned to Gud̲j̲arāt, leaving behind 10,000 troops for his protection.

These events completely alienated Mednī Rāy and his Rād̲j̲pūt followers from Maḥmūd. Mednī Rāy occupied Gagrawn and, when Maḥmūd besieged him, he appealed to Rānā Sāngarāmā for help. The Rānā marched to his relief. Maḥmūd raised the siege and set out to intercept the Rānā, but was defeated, wounded and taken prisoner. He was taken to Čitor, and allowed to return to Mālwā after his wounds were healed, but had to surrender his crown and leave behind his son as a hostage.

On his return to Māndū, he found his position extremely weak; and it was further weakened by the withdrawal of the Gud̲j̲aratī forces by Muẓaffar II at his request. The result was that Rānā Sanga occupied Mandasor; Mednī Rāy seized Čanderi; Silhadi occupied Bhilsa and Raisin; and Sikandar K̲h̲ān declared his independence in Satwāʾ. The disintegration of Maḥmūd's power was almost complete, and he was left with only a small territory around Māndū. But instead of consolidating his position and trying to recover his territories, Maḥmūd committed the mistake of giving asylum and support to Čānd K̲h̲ān against his brother, Bahādur K̲h̲ān, who had ascended the throne of Gud̲j̲arāt. Bahādur K̲h̲ān was greatly offended and invaded Mālwa. He besieged Māndū, captured it by assault on 9 S̲h̲aʿbān 937/2 April 1531, and caused the *k̲h̲uṭba* to be recited in his name. Mālwā thus passed into his possession. Maḥmūd and his sons were sent as prisoners to Čampāner. On the way, he made an attempt to escape, but was seized and killed along with his sons on the night of 14 S̲h̲aʿbān 837/2 April 1531; with his death the K̲h̲ald̲j̲ī dynasty of Mālwā came to an end.

Bibliography: See that for MAḤMŪD K̲H̲ALD̲J̲Ī I.

(MOHIBBUL HASAN)

MAḤMŪD, the name of two Ottoman sultans.

1. MAḤMŪD I (1143-68/1730-54), (with the title of G̲h̲āzī and the literary nom-de-plume of Sabḳatī). The eldest son of Sultan Muṣṭafā II, he was born on the night of 3 Muḥarram 1108/2 August 1696 in the Palace at Edirne. His mother was Wālide Ṣāliḥa Sulṭān. He undertook his first studies on Wednesday, 20 D̲h̲u 'l-Ḥid̲j̲d̲j̲a 1113/18 May 1702 with a grand ceremony at the Edirne Palace which his father Muṣṭafā II attended in person, and was given his first lesson by the *S̲h̲ayk̲h̲ al-Islām* Sayyid Fayḍ Allāh Efendi. In due course, the latter's son Rūmeli Pāyeli Ibrāhīm Efendi was appointed to act as his tutor. Following the deposition of his father Muṣṭafā II as a result of the "Edirne Incident" and the accession of his uncle Aḥmad III on 10 Rabīʿ II 1115/23 August 1703, Prince Maḥmūd, together with his mother and her other children, was taken into custody by the insurgents at the Palace in Edirne and was subsequently taken to Istanbul along with the Ottoman palace staff and shut up in a private apartment in the Imperial Palace (the Sarāy-i d̲j̲edīd). His circumcision was effected with a simple ceremony on Thursday, 22 D̲h̲u 'l-Ḥid̲j̲d̲j̲a 1116/17 April 1705.

Prince Maḥmūd's life of seclusion in the Palace continued for 27 years up to 1730. It was only when Aḥmad III was forced to abdicate the Ottoman throne as a result of the Patrona K̲h̲alīl revolt that he was set free, becoming sultan on Monday, 19 Rabīʿ I 1143/2 October 1730. Having ordered his release from the apartment in the Palace where he had been shut up, his uncle invited Maḥmūd to spend the night of 1-2 October with him so that he could advise him on the administration of the Empire. He then joined his two sons in swearing allegiance to Maḥmūd and was thus the first ro recognise him officially as sultan. The formalities necessary for his accession were completed at Eyyūb on Friday, 23 Rabīʿ I 1143/6 October 1730, when he girded on the sword and the *k̲h̲uṭba* was read in his name for the first time.

During the first days of Maḥmūd's reign, the rebels had complete control over the affairs of the state. In particular, their leader Patrona K̲h̲alīl forced the sultan to carry out his wishes with regard to new appointments, while Maḥmūd I also complied with the rebels' demands by agreeing to the abolition of one category of taxes and to changes in the way some others were collected, and he had to sit idly by as the buildings at pleasure-grounds such as Kāg̲h̲ıtk̲h̲āne and Fenerbāg̲h̲česi were demolished by the insurgents. However, disorderly conduct of this kind was not permitted for much longer. Under the leadership of Maḥmūd's mother Ṣāliḥa Sulṭān, some of the Empire's most experienced statesmen—the *Ḳızlar ag̲h̲ası* Bes̲h̲īr Ag̲h̲a, Ḳaplan Girāy, a former *K̲h̲ān* of the Crimea, and the *Ḳapudan-i deryā* D̲j̲ānım-K̲h̲ōd̲j̲a Meḥmed Pas̲h̲a—cooperated with Ḳabakulaḳ Ibrāhīm Ag̲h̲a and others in arranging for the leading rebels to be put to death in the Imperial Palace—inside the Rewān Ḳaṣrıand the Sünnet Odası—on 25 November 1730, and Maḥmūd was thus assured of the freedom to rule without such interventions.

Despite the outbreak of a second uprising on 25 March 1731, which seems to have been a continuation of the first revolt and may even have been organised by Fāṭima Sulṭān, the daughter of Aḥmad III and widow of the executed Grand Vizier News̲h̲ehirli Ibrāhīm Pas̲h̲a, in order to revenge herself on the new Sultan, the people's manifest support for Maḥmūd and the strong measures taken by the Grand Vizier Ḳabakulaḳ Ibrāhīm Pas̲h̲a and the *Ḳapudan-i deryā* D̲j̲ānım K̲h̲ōd̲j̲a Meḥmed Pas̲h̲a meant that this disturbance was confined to the neighbourhoods of Bāyezīd and Aḳsaray and was suppressed before it could gain strength.

After achieving a strong position in the internal affairs of the Empire, Maḥmūd I turned his attention to the problems facing it abroad. His first moves were against Nādir S̲h̲āh, who was causing the Ottoman Empire difficulties in the East. The forces which he sent against Iran under the command of the governor of Bag̲h̲dād, Eyyūbī Aḥmad Pas̲h̲a, won the first success of his reign at the battle of Korıd̲j̲an on 13 Rabīʿ I 1144/15 September 1731, and by the treaty signed on 10 January 1732 the Ṣafawid ruler S̲h̲āh Ṭahmāsp II agreed to cede the districts of Gand̲j̲a, Tiflīs, Rewān, S̲h̲īrwān and Dāg̲h̲istān to Maḥmūd. Nevertheless, the war between the Ottomans and Iran could not be concluded because of Maḥmūd's objections over the question of Tabrīz, and it continued to rage with full force through the districts of al-Mawṣil, Kirkūk, Bag̲h̲dād, Tabrīz, Gand̲j̲a, Tiflīs and Ḳars until the end of 1735, during the period when Nādir

S͟hāh was acting as guardian to ʿAbbās Mīrzā (III). It was on account of the successes of the Ottoman forces during the early years of this war that Maḥmūd I adopted the title of G͟hāzī. Later on, however, the Ottoman army suffered defeat after defeat and eventually, as a result of negotiations which were initially conducted by the representatives of Nādir S͟hāh and a Turkish delegation under the commander of Gand͟ja, Genč ʿAlī Pas͟ha, in the Mūg͟hān steppe in Ād͟harbāyd͟jān and later by an Iranian delegation led by ʿAbd al-Bāḳī K͟hān and Maḥmūd I himself in Istanbul, an agreement was reached between the two powers in 1736 which dealt with the border question but left the *mad͟hhab* dispute unsettled.

At this point, Nādir S͟hāh wished to turn his attention to Iran's eastern borders, while Maḥmūd I was intent on dealing with the Russian threat from the north. Relations between Maḥmūd I and the Russian Empress Anna Ivanovna had been soured by the Polish question and a number of other border disputes, and because, in the course of the struggle with Nādir for control of Ḳars and the surrounding area in 1735, a contingent of Crimean troops had crossed Kabartay territory on their way to reinforce the Ottoman army in northeastern Anatolia. Finally, after the Russian attack on the fortress of Azak on 31 March 1736, Maḥmūd I held a great *dīwān* in Istanbul on 2 May and personally took the decision to declare war on Russia. However, as Talman, the Habsburg Emperor's representative in Istanbul, who later joined the Ottoman army in the field, followed a policy of distracting the Ottoman government with plans for peace, this campaign was not given the necessary degree of importance and the Ottoman commanders were therefore unable to gain any success during the first year. Furthermore, from June 1737 onwards, when the Habsburg Emperor Charles VI took Russia's side in this war, Maḥmūd was forced to defend the borders of the Empire along a very broad front. There were engagements on the banks of the Sava in northern Bosnia, in the Nis͟h and Vidin areas south of Belgrade as well as in Little Wallachia, along the Aksu (Bug) and Turla (Dnestr) rivers near Özü and Bender, in the Crimea, and around Azak. In his attempts to gain the upper hand against both these states, Maḥmūd I frequently changed his Grand Vizier. Eventually, the victories which the Ottoman forces won against the Austrians on the western front, which was considered the more important, forced both states to come to terms with Maḥmūd through the good offices of the French ambassador, the Marquis de Villeneuve, and led to the signing of the treaty of Belgrade on 18 September 1737.

Maḥmūd I thereby regained from the Habsburg Empire a number of towns, Belgrade being the most important, which had been lost by the treaty of Passarowitz in 1718. For their part, the Russians had to evacuate several areas they had occupied in northern Moldavia. In return for the Marquis de Villeneuve's services, France's commercial advantages were increased by the capitulation dated 30 May 1740. At the same time, in order to improve his political relations with Russia, Maḥmūd I sent the *Defteremīni* Meḥmed Emnī Beyefendi on an embassy to St Petersburg, while the *Birind͟ji rūznāmčed͟ji* D͟jānib ʿAlī Efendi was dispatched as ambassador to the Habsburg Empire. Meanwhile, a commercial treaty had been signed with the kingdom of Sweden in 1737 and a defence pact in 1740, in which same year a purely commercial agreement was reached between the Empire and the kingdom of the Two Sicilies.

However, while Maḥmūd I was still putting his political relations with the European states in good order, his relations with Nādir S͟hāh reached another crisis point. Nādir S͟hāh, who had returned from his campaign in India, again marched to Iran's western borders and laid siege to the Ottoman cities of Bag͟hdād and Kirkūk in the spring of 1743 under the pretext that, during the truce, Maḥmūd I had not accepted the D͟jaʿfarī school as the fifth *mad͟hhab*, as Nādir had proposed. Because the Turkish mission which Maḥmūd I had previously sent to Iran under Münīf Muṣṭafā Efendi in July 1741 had been unable to prolong the good relations with Nādir S͟hāh, the second phase of the war between the Ottomans and Iran had begun before the gates of Bag͟hdād, Kirkūk and al-Mawṣil. However, Maḥmūd I, with the assistance of Aḥmad Pas͟ha, the *Ser ʿasker* of Ḳars, had Ṣafī Mīrzā, a member of the Ṣafawī dynasty who was living in the Ottoman Empire, sent to the Iranian frontier and turned a number of *k͟hān*s in the Dāg͟histān and S͟hīrwān areas south of the Caucasus against Nādir S͟hāh by granting them their independence. Nādir S͟hāh was therefore unable to remain in the Bag͟hdād and al-Mawṣil areas and had to lift the sieges of these two cities and abandon Kirkūk, which he had already taken, in order to move to the area around Ḳars. The fighting in this area and around Rewān continued until the end of 1745. In the end, in the face of the determination and perseverance shown by Maḥmūd I and despite the fact that he had gained a number of victories, Nādir S͟hāh, who was also influenced by events at home, abandoned the struggle for the Ḳars region and made a serious peace proposal to Maḥmūd. The peace negotiations between the Ottomans and Iran began at a great *dīwān* on 1 February 1746, after the delegation which Nādir had sent under the leadership of Fatḥ ʿAlī K͟hān had arrived in Istanbul.

Maḥmūd I reacted favourably to the proposals put forward by Nādir S͟hāh on this occasion and, having decided upon a new border settlement which was based on the Ḳaṣr-i S͟hīrīn treaty of 1639, but leaving aside the problem of the D͟jaʿfarī school, he dispatched a Turkish delegation to Iran under the leadership of Muṣṭafā Naẓīf Efendi on 9 March 1746 with authority to negotiate with Nādir S͟hāh. This delegation met Nādir S͟hāh in the Kardan steppe between Ḳazwīn and Tehran and, as a result of their negotiations, peace was declared between the two states on 17 S͟haʿbān 1159/4 September 1746. Maḥmūd I, who signed the instruments of this settlement in December 1746, sent the text of the treaty back to Nādir S͟hāh in the care of the ambassador Kesriyeli Aḥmed Pas͟ha.

After Nādir's death, Maḥmūd I followed a conciliatory policy towards his neighbours such as Iran, Russia and Austria up until his own death. Meanwhile, however, the internal problems of the Empire, such as the agitation among the Palace Ag͟has after the death of the *Ḳîzlar ag͟hasî* Bes͟hīr Ag͟ha, the suppression of the Lewend bandits [*q.v.*]. who were bringing destruction to Anatolia, the murder of Sayyid Fatḥī in Syria, the revolt of the Janissary garrison at Nis͟h, the Wahhābī movement in Nad͟jd, the uprising in Istanbul on 2 July 1748, and many other similar incidents, occupied his attention. Maḥmūd died at the Demirḳapî in the Imperial Palace while on his way back from the Friday prayers on 27 Ṣafar 1168/13 December 1754. He was not interred in the mausoleum which he had built beside the Nūr-i ʿOt͟hmāniyye mosque, but was buried beside his grandfather Meḥemmed IV and his father Muṣṭafā II in the mausoleum of Wālide Turk͟han K͟hadīd͟je Sulṭān in the Yeñi D͟jāmiʿ complex by order of his brother and successor ʿOt͟hmān III.

He was a thin, short, well-tempered man, who gave priority to the maintenance of public order inside Istanbul and would go to meetings of the *dīwān* in order to hear the people's complaints. He was keen on the sports of *dj̲erīd* [*q.v.*], horse-racing and swimming and was knowledgeable about poetry and music. We know that he used the *mak̲h̲laṣ* Sabḳatī and that he wrote poetry in Arabic (S̲h̲ehrīzāde Saʿīd Efendi, *Mak̲h̲zan al-ṣafāʾ*, Belediye Kütüphanesi, ms. Muallim Cevdet 0.74, f. 53b; Tayyār-zāde Aḥmad ʿAṭāʾ, *Ta'rīk̲h̲-i ʿAṭāʾ*, iv, Istanbul 1293, 67; ʿAlī Emīrī, *Dj̲awāhir al-mulūk*, Istanbul 1319, 30). He knew enough about music to be a composer in his own right, but he is more often spoken of as an instrumentalist and as a patron of other musicians (Yılmez Öztuna, *Türk mûsikîsi lûgatı*, 120, 407; Subhi Ezgi, *Nazarî, amelî Türk mûsikîsi*, Istanbul 1940, iv, 93). This Sultan, who was interested in chess and had a passion for flowers, is also known to have lavished a good deal of attention on the cultivation of tulips. In his free time and when the weather permitted, he would make trips to the pleasure-grounds along the Bosphorus, at Kāg̲h̲ītk̲h̲āne and at Fenerbāg̲h̲česi, and would spend his time in the summer houses there. Although the Nūr-i ʿO̲t̲h̲māniyye complex, with its mosque, *madrasa*, *maktab*, library, mausoleum, *ʿimāret* and *sebīl*, was built at his orders, it was given its present name because it was completed in the reign of his brother ʿO̲t̲h̲mān III. Similarly, the Yīldīz-Dede and Defterdār Ḳapīsī mosques and the mosque of the Ṭulumbadj̲īlar Odasī near the Yalī Kös̲h̲kü, the landing-stage at Rumeli Ḥiṣārī, the ʿArab Iskelesi at Bes̲h̲iktas̲h̲, the Friday mosques at Üsküdar which were named after him and at Kandilli on the Bosphorus were also built by this Sultan. In addition, he had the Opuzlu reservoir built to collect the water from the streams passing between Bāg̲h̲čeköy and Balabanköy near Kāg̲h̲ītk̲h̲āne in order to supply the famous Meydān Čes̲h̲mesi fountain which he had had constructed in Ṭopk̲h̲āne via the cistern at Taḳsīm, while water from the same cistern was used to supply water for around 40 fountains in Ḳāsīmpas̲h̲a, Tepebas̲h̲ī, G̲h̲alaṭa and in the Bes̲h̲iktas̲h̲ area. He also had three libraries built, one in the Ayasofya Mosque in 1740, the second beside the Fātiḥ Mosque, in 1742 and the third in the G̲h̲alaṭa Sarāyī in 1754. The Bes̲h̲iktas̲h̲ Sāḥil Sarāyī, the Bayīldīm Ḳaṣrī at Dolmabāg̲h̲če, and the Toḳat Kös̲h̲kü near Yūs̲h̲ā were all repaired in his reign. Furthermore, in his time the Kandilli quarter on the Bosphorus was also called Newābād, as he had had it built up from scratch and had had the Mihrābād summer palace constructed there.

As Ottoman sultan, his political and social activities were numerous. Because neither he nor his brother ʿO̲t̲h̲mān had any children, the Ottoman dynasty was continued by the children of his uncle Aḥmad III.

Bibliography: Silaḥdār Fīndīklīlī Meḥmed Ag̲h̲a, *Nuṣret-nāme*, ed. İsmet Parmaksızoğlu, i/2, Istanbul 1963, 169-70, ii/l, 1966, 90-2, ii/2, 1969, 220; Rās̲h̲id, *Waḳāyiʿ-nāme*, Istanbul 1282/1865-6, ii, 557, iii, 79; Destārī Ṣāliḥ Efendi, *Taʾrīk̲h̲*, ed. Bekir Sıdkı Baykal, Ankara 1962, text, 26, 30 ff., 36-41; ʿAbdī, *Taʾrīk̲h̲*, ed. Faik Reşid Unat, Ankara 1943, 41-5, 45-8, 62 ff.; *Relation des deux rebellions arrivées à Constantinople en 1730 et 1731*, The Hague 1737, 41 ff., 130-52; Crouzenac, *Histoire de la dernière revolution arrivée dans l'Empire Ottoman*, Paris 1740, 26-9; Dispatches of the Marquis de Villeneuve dated November 1730 in the French Foreign Ministry Archives: Turquie, V, 82; Ṣalāḥī (Sīrr-kātibi), *Ḍabṭ-i waḳāyiʿ-i yewmiyye-i ḥaḍret-i s̲h̲ehriyārī*, Istanbul University Library, ms. TY 2518, ff. 7-11, 65b (another copy: Topkapı Sarayı Müzesi, ms. Revan 1315/2); ʿÖmer Efendi, *Rūz-nāme* (for the years 1153-63/1740-50), Millet Kütüphanesi, ms. Ali Emiri, Tarih 423; Sāmī-S̲h̲ākir-Ṣubḥī, *Waḳāyiʿ-nāme*, Istanbul 1198/1784, ff. 9, 17, 25 ff., 55 ff., 89, 93-95, 113, 119 ff.; ʿIzzī Süleymān, *Waḳāyiʿ-nāme*, Istanbul 1199/1785, ff. 8-11, 15, 86-107; Meḥmed Hāḳim, *Waḳāyiʿ-nāme*, Topkapı Sarayı Müzesi, ms. Bagdat 231; Mahdī K̲h̲ān, *Nādir S̲h̲āh Taʾrīk̲h̲i* (tr. of Ḳarslī Ḥidj̲ābī), Süleymaniye Library, ms. Esʿad Efendi 2179; *Taʾrīk̲h̲-i Nādir S̲h̲āh* (tr.), Topkapı Sarayı Müzesi, ms. Bagdat 285, f. 31; Muṣaffā Muṣṭafā, *Taʾrīk̲h̲-i Sulṭān Maḥmūd-i ewwel*, Topkapı Sarayı Müzesi, ms. Revan 1324/1 and 1325/2; Ismāʿīl Ḍiyāʾ al-Dīn, *Maṭāliʿ al-ʿaliyya fī g̲h̲urrat al-g̲h̲aliyya*, Istanbul University Library, ms. TY 2486, ff. 42b ff., 56 ff.; ʿAbd al-G̲h̲affār Ḳīrīmī, *ʿUmdat al-ak̲h̲bār*, Süleymaniye Library, ms. 2331, fl. 239; Newres, *Taʾrīk̲h̲če*, Süleymaniye Library, ms. Esʿad Efendi 2252; ʿÖmer Efendi, *Aḥwāl-i ḳaḍawāt dar diyār-i Bosna*, Istanbul 1154/1741-2, ff. 3-4, 10-56; Münir Aktepe, *Mehmed Eminî Beyefendi'nin Rusya sefâret-nâmesi*, Ankara 1974, *passim*; Muṣṭafā Raḥmī, *Sefāret-nāme-yi Īrān*, Istanbul University Library, ms. TY 3782; Rāg̲h̲ib Pas̲h̲a, *Fetḥiyye-yi Belg̲h̲rad*, Süleymaniye Library, ms. Esʿad Efendi 3655/2, ff. 11-25; Muṣṭafā Münīf, *Fetḥ-nāme-yi Belg̲h̲rad*, Süleymaniye Library, ms. Esʿad Efendi 3655/3, ff. 26-48 (another copy: Topkapı Sarayı Müzesi, ms. Revan 1324/2); Muṣṭafā Naẓīf, *Sefāret-nāme-yi Īrān*, Topkapı Sarayı Müzesi, ms. Hazine 1635 (another copy: Millet Kütüphanesi, ms. Ali Emiri, Tarih 824); Ḳāḍī Nuʿmān Efendi, *Tadbīrāt-i pasandīde*, part II, Süleymaniye Library, ms. Reşid Efendi, Tarih 667; Sīrrī (*Dīwān-i humāyūn kātibi*), *Maḳāle-yi wāḳiʿa-yi muḥṣara-yi Ḳars*, Süleymaniye Library, ms. Esʿad Efendi 2417 (another copy: Topkapı Sarayı Müzesi, ms. Revan 1427); *Sulṭān Maḥmūd-i ewwel zamānīnda Fransīz muʿāhedesi*, Istanbul University Library, ms. TY 2270; *Ḍiyāfet-nāme* (describing the banquet given at the opening of the Taḳsīm cistern), Topkapı Sarayı Müzesi, ms. Hazine 1441; ʿO̲t̲h̲mān, *I Maḥmūd devrinde Haremeyne gönderilen eşya defteri* Topkapı Sarayı Muzesi, ms. Hazine 1636; Niʿmet Efendi, *I Maḥmūd'un 1749 yılında Hicaz'a gönderdiği eşya defteri*, Istanbul University Library, ms. TY 2505; S̲h̲emʿdānī-zāde Fīndīḳlīlī Süleymān Efendi, *Murʿī 'l-tawārīk̲h̲*, ed. Münir Aktepe, i, Istanbul 1976, ii, 1978, *passim*; Aḥmad Wāṣif, *Taʾrīk̲h̲*, Istanbul 1219/1804-5, i, 40 ff.; Ḥalīm Giray, *Gülbün-i k̲h̲ānān*, Istanbul 1287/1870-1, 86; A. Vandal, *Une ambassade française en Orient sous Louis XV*, Paris 1887, 249 ff., 348 ff.; J. von Hammer, *Histoire de l'Empire Ottoman*, Paris 1839, xiv, xv; Hüseyin Ayvansarāyī, *Ḥadīḳat al-dj̲awāmiʿ*, Istanbul 1281/1864-5, i, 12, 204, ii, 33, 61, 152, 166; Jouannin, *Turquie*, Paris 1840, 344; ʿAbd al-Raḥmān S̲h̲eref, *Taʾrīk̲h̲-i dewlet-i ʿO̲t̲h̲māniyye*, Istanbul 1312/1894-5, ii, 162; Gabriel Efendi Noradounghian, *Recueil d'actes internationaux de l'Empire Ottoman*, Paris 1897, i, 65-73, 239-314; Meḥmed T̲h̲üreyyā, *Sidj̲ill-i ʿO̲t̲h̲mānī*, Istanbul 1308/1890-l, i, 72; V. Minorsky, *Esquisse d'une histoire de Nāder-chāh*, Paris 1934; Lockhart, *Nādir S̲h̲āh*, London 1938; Mary Lucille Shay, *The Ottoman Empire from 1720 to 1734 as revealed in despatches of the Venetian Baili*, Urbana 1944; İ. Hakkı Uzunçarşılı, *Osmanlı tarihi*, iv/1 and 2 Ankara 1956; Münir Aktepe, *Patrona isyanı (1730)*, Istanbul 1958; A. D. Alderson, *The structure of the Ottoman dynasty*,

Oxford 1956, 36, 45, 67, 80, 105, 107, 110, 129, 130, Table XLII; Ibrahim Hilmi Tanışık, *İstanbul çeşmeleri*, i, Istanbul 1943, ii, 1945; M. de la Croix, *Abrégé chronologique de l'Histoire Ottomane*, Paris 1748, ii, 725-6; M. Mignot, *Histoire de l'Empire Ottoman depuis son origine jusqu'à la paix de Belgrade en 1740*, Paris 1773, iv, 340-446; Jouannin and Jules van Gaver, *Turquie*, Paris 1840, 334-44; Rāg͟hib Pas͟ha, *Taḥḳīḳ ve tewfīḳ*, Istanbul University Library, ms. TY 3371; R. W. Olson, *The Siege of Mosul and Ottoman-Persian relations, 1718-1743*, Indiana 1975, 83-90, 131, 148-50, 155, 191; Mustafa Ali Mehmed, *Istoria Turcilor*, Bucharest 1970; G. R. Bosscha Erdbrink, *At the Threshold of Felicity: Ottoman-Dutch relations during the embassy of Cornelis Calkoen at the Sublime Porte, 1726-1744*, Ankara 1975.

(Münír Aktepe)

2. Maḥmūd II (reigned 1223-55/1808-39). Born at Topkapı palace on 13 Ramaḍān 1199/20 July 1785, he was the youngest of twelve sons of sultan ʿAbd al-Ḥamīd I. He succeeded to Muṣṭafā IV on 28 July 1808. An armed coup led by the provincial governor Muṣṭafā Bayraḳdār [*q.v.*] aimed at restoring to the throne the formerly deposed sultan Selīm III. In the course of the action, however, Selīm was assassinated, the reigning Muṣṭafā deposed, and Maḥmūd, as the only remaining legitimate candidate, was declared sultan. Until his ascendance to the throne, Maḥmūd had spent his entire life in seclusion, according to Ottoman practice.

At this point the Ottoman empire appeared to be on the verge of final disintegration. The central government wielded minimal authority over the provinces, administered largely by self appointed local rulers [see aʿyān, derebey]. A temporarily inactive state of war with Russia and Britain imposed further strains on the political fabric. In Istanbul itself political power was exercised by extra-legitimate forces, composed mainly of *ʿulamāʾ* and soldiers. The sultan's office was reduced to political impotency (D̲jewdet, ix, 16).

During the first months of Maḥmūd's reign real power was wielded by Bayraḳdār, who had himself appointed grand vizier. He convened an assembly of provincial rulers in Istanbul which adopted the Deed of Agreement [see dustūr. ii. turkey]. This document sought to change the constitutional framework of the empire by limiting the sultan's sovereignty and establishing a quasi-feudal political system. In addition, it aimed at reviving Selīm III's military reforms. In mid-November 1808, Bayraḳdār's government was brought down by a popular uprising led by the Janissaries of Istanbul. It was the culmination of a movement opposed to reform as well as to the seizure of the central government by provincial elements.

Following their victory, the Janissaries set up in Istanbul a reign of terror and once again began to interfere in state affairs. The anarchy which prevailed at the capital since the fall of Selīm III in May 1807 left the political élite hopelessly divided and demoralised. Meanwhile, Maḥmūd exhibited characteristics of strong leadership and dedication to traditional values. The religious and bureaucratic élites desiring the re-establishment of orderly government began to turn to the court for guidance (D̲jewdet, ix, 59-61). Thus were laid the foundations for the restoration of the court as an active centre of government. Maḥmūd seized this opportunity to curb the Janissaries. Throughout his reign he consistently endeavoured to strengthen the court's position by subordinating all other political forces. Gradually, he formed a network of advisers and assistants who helped him carry out his policies. Some of these at various times attained positions of great influence [see ḥālet efendi], but throughout, Maḥmūd remained the supreme autocrat.

In January 1809 a peace treaty was concluded with Britain, in spite of strong protests by Napoleonic France. But negotiations with the Russians, who had in 1806 occupied Bessarabia, Moldavia and Wallachia, failed. In April 1809 the war was resumed with the Russians attacking south of the Danube. The Ottomans suffered defeat in several battles, but succeeded in foiling a Russian attempt to take Shumla and to storm across the Balkan mountains. Faced with the mounting threat of war with France, the Russians were prepared to compromise. The war was terminated with the Treaty of Bucharest (May 28, 1812) which ceded Bessarabia to Russia, while the Ottomans regained Moldavia and Wallachia.

Meanwhile, Maḥmūd initiated a policy designed to restore central authority over the provinces, and when the war ended this became his primary concern. By 1820 Istanbul succeeded in re-asserting its power over most of the provincial centres in Anatolia, as well as over Thrace, Macedonia and the Danube districts. The local ruling notables were replaced by governors appointed from Istanbul. In the view of the government, all local notables were usurpers of legitimate authority (*müteg͟hallibe*). Consequently, their suppression was often ruthless and indiscriminate. This tended to destroy the local administrative infrastructure, weakening thereby the very bases of Ottoman power (cf. S͟hānīzāde, ii, 230-1, 246-7; D̲jewdet[2], x, 146-8, 181-7, 217-19). This was a factor which facilitated the emergence of the national movements of the Serbs and Greeks.

During the same period, the sultan intervened occasionally in the affairs of his Syrian and Mesopotamian provinces, but achieved ephemeral results only. In Arabia the power of the Wahhābīs was curbed by enlisting the military services of Muḥammad ʿAlī, the governor of Egypt. While still maintaining his allegiance to the sultan, Muḥammad ʿAlī gradually transformed Egypt into a formidable state. The sultan had no means with which to reassert his authority over the distant African provinces of Tripoli, Tunis and Algiers, but he still claimed suzerainty over them.

The Serbs had taken advantage of the weakening of Ottoman provincial administration to rise in 1804-13 and again in 1815. Under Russian pressure the sultan agreed to grant the Serbs complete autonomy. The process was gradual, and was completed in 1829. The drawn-out conflict between the sultan and Tepedelenli ʿAlī Pas͟ha [see ʿalī pas͟ha tepedelenli], the most powerful notable in Albania and Greece, aided the Greek cause. The sultan initiated the conflict with ʿAlī in July 1820 and the Peloponnesus was up in arms in March 1821. Although Maḥmūd was profoundly shaken by the outbreak of the Greek uprising, for almost another year he continued to direct the main military efforts against ʿAlī, whom he considered the greater threat to the realm (A. Levy, *Ottoman attitudes to... Balkan nationalism*). ʿAlī was finally defeated and executed in February 1822. Meanwhile, a series of border skirmishes with Iran in 1820 escalated into a full-scale war. After several years of desultory fighting, peace was restored in July 1823. The sultan now concentrated all his efforts to subdue Greece. Uprisings in Macedonia and Thessaly were suppressed, but the Ottoman forces proved incapable of advancing into the Peloponnesus and a stalemate ensued. The sultan once again appealed to Muḥammad ʿAlī for assistance, promising to cede to him the governorship of Crete and the Peloponnesus in return for his services. In February 1825 the modernised Egyptian army landed in Greece, drastically altering the military balance. The Ottomans renewed their attacks and by April 1826, with the fall of the key fortress of Missolonghi, the Greek position became desperate.

The Greek uprising made a great impact not only on the Ottoman political élite but also on wide segments of the Muslim population at the centre of the empire. The proximity of the fighting and the destruction of long-established Turkish communities in Greece and the islands were among the main reasons which caused Muslim society to view this conflict as a threat to its very survival. In addition, the poor performance of the largely untrained Ottoman troops could be compared with the effectiveness of the modernised Egyptian army. This created a perceptible change in the mood of Ottoman society favouring military reform (Djewdet, xii, 139-46, 159). Since early in his reign Maḥmūd had been cautiously introducing significant improvements in several military branches, especially in the artillery and navy. But in the spring of 1826, with his authority restored at the capital and in many provinces, and with the Greek rising appearing close to extinction, it seemed to Maḥmūd that the time had come to carry out more comprehensive reforms. But he adopted a gradual approach. The first project called for reorganising part of the Janissary corps as an élite unit of active soldiers called *Eshkindjiyān*. The sultan took precautions to enlist the support of the religious and bureaucratic élites as well as the Janissary officers themselves. Nevertheless, on the night of 14 June the Janissaries rose up in arms. The sultan reacted with speed and determination. He mustered loyal troops and on 15 June, within hours, the rebellion was crushed with considerable bloodshed. Two days later an imperial order declared the Janissary corps abolished.

It is difficult to exaggerate the impact which the suppression of the Janissaries made on contemporary Ottoman society as well as on Europe. It was considered the end of one era and the beginning of another. In an effort to gain for it universal approval, the régime termed the incident the "Beneficial Affair" (*waḳʿa-yi khayriyye*) and the court historian Esʿad Efendi was charged with recording the official version for future generations. Esʿad's detailed account entitled *The foundation of victory* (*Üss-i ẓafer*) was printed in 1828. Indeed, the ease with which the suppression of the Janissaries was carried out and its general acceptance by the public were indications of the changing times.

Now the *Eshkindjiyān* project was abandoned in favour of a more ambitious plan calling for the formation of an entirely new army organised and trained on western models. The new force was named the "Trained Victorious Troops of Muḥammad" (*Muʿallem ʿasākir-i manṣūre-yi muḥammadiyye*), or *Manṣūre*, for short. But the project encountered great difficulties from its very inception and its progress was much slower than had been expected. By spring 1828 the new army had some 30,000 men only, poorly organised, trained and equipped.

Meanwhile, the plight of the Greeks elicited European intervention. Britain, Russia and France offered mediation. The Ottomans rejected the proposals, arguing that the conflict was an internal matter. The European powers countered by sending their fleets to Greece where on 20 October 1827, inside the harbour of Navarino, they destroyed an Ottoman-Egyptian fleet. Ottoman losses alone amounted to 37 ships with over 3,000 sailors, comprising more than two-thirds of the entire seaworthy navy. In May 1828 the Russians launched an offensive against the Ottoman dominions in Europe and Asia. In 1829 they achieved complete victory. A Russian army under the leadership of General Diebitsch bypassed Shumla, stormed through the passes of the Balkan Mountains, captured Edirne (August 20) and threatened to march on Istanbul. The sultan was forced to sue for peace. By the Treaty of Edirne/Adrianople (14 September 1829) the Ottomans ceded to Russia the Danube delta in Europa and the province of Akhaltsikhe (Akhi̊skha) in Asia. In addition, they were required to pay to Russia a heavy war indemnity as well as to recognise the autonomy of Serbia, Moldavia, Wallachia and Greece under Russian protection. Later, in negotiations between the European powers, it was determined that Greece should become an independent monarchy. In July 1832 the sultan accepted these terms.

Military defeat and the apparent failure of the government's reform policies rekindled unrest and rebellion in widely flung provinces, especially in Bosnia, Albania, eastern Anatolia and Baghdād. These movements, sometimes led by former Janissaries and their sympathisers, were partly a delayed conservative reaction against the government's reforms. More commonly, they represented protest against increased taxes, forced conscription and, in general, the sultan's heavy-handed centralising policies. The government was generally successful in putting down these movements by employing the new disciplined troops, which proved sufficiently effective as an instrument of suppression and centralisation. Nevertheless, throughout the remaining years of Maḥmūd's reign, unrest and rebellion continued to flare up in various districts.

In 1830 the sultan tried unsuccessfully to prevent the French occupation of Algiers. Meanwhile, Muḥammad ʿAlī became determined to seek compensation for his losses in Greece. His perception of the sultan's military weakness encouraged him to demand the governorship of Syria. When this was refused, in October 1831 the Egyptian army invaded Syria, defeated two Ottoman armies and completed the conquest by July 1832. When the sultan countered by preparing yet another army, the Egyptians marched into Anatolia, defeated the Ottomans again at Ḳonya (21 December), occupied Kütahya (2 February 1833) and were in a position to march on Istanbul. The sultan sought help from the great powers, but only the Russians dispatched a naval force to defend Istanbul (February 1833). This induced Britain and France to offer mediation, resulting in the Convention of Kütahya (April 8). It conferred on Muḥammad ʿAlī the government of Syria and the province of Adana. Meanwhile, Russian paramountcy in Istanbul was underscored by the Treaty of Hünkâr (Khūnkār) Iskelesi (8 July), a Russian-Ottoman defensive alliance. But the treaty alarmed other European powers, especially Britain, who became determined to help the Ottomans liberate themselves of Russian dependence. The Ottoman empire now came under the protection of the European Concert, and its foreign relations with Britain, Austria and Prussia were increasingly improving.

In spite of military disasters and political setbacks, during the 1830s Sultan Maḥmūd relentlessly proceeded with his reformatory measures. His main objectives continued to focus on centralisation of government and the attainment of greater efficiency in its work. In 1835 the entire administration was reconstituted into three independent branches: the civil bureaucracy (*ḳalemiyye*), the religious-judicial hierarchy (*ᶜilmiyye*) and the military (*seyfiyye*). Their respective heads—the grand vizier, the *sheykh ül-Islām* and the *ser-ᶜasker*—were now considered equals, and therefore, responsible directly to the sultan (*BBA*, *HH* 24031; Luṭfī, v, 25-6). Throughout most of Maḥmūd's reign the court had been the most important centre of power. Now it was officially recognised as such. The aggrandisement of the court was mainly at the expense of the grand vizier's office. Traditionally, the grand vizier was considered the sultan's absolute deputy (*wekīl-i muṭlaḳ*) and as such the head of the entire government, civilian and military. To underscore the reduction of his authority, in March 1838 the grand vizier's title was officially changed to that of chief deputy, or prime minister (*bash wekīl*). At the same time, the grand vizier's chief assistants were given the title of minister (*nāẓir* and later *wekīl*). These changes were combined with attempts to attain a better definition of administrative responsibilities. Consequently, from 1836 government departments were being regrouped into ministries (*neẓāret*) for internal, foreign and financial affairs. A further distinction was made between the executive and the legislative. Consultative councils were established to supervise military and civil matters and to propose new legislation. The highest of these, the Supreme Council for Judicial Ordinances (*Medjlis-i wālā-yi aḥkām-i ᶜadliyye*), established in 1838, acted as an advisory council to the sultan. New regulations granted the civil servants increased security, but also required higher standards of performance. But all these were mere beginnings. The difficulties were due mainly to the lack of trained personnel. In most cases the staffs of new departments were drawn from old ones, and the administrative reforms often amounted to a mere reshuffle of offices. Nevertheless, the groundwork was prepared for the emergence of a new generation of administrators with a more modern outlook.

The military, which during Maḥmūd's last years was allocated about 70% of the state's revenues, continued to be the focal point of reform. Most significant was the gradual extension of the authority of the commander-in-chief (*ser-ᶜasker*) of the *Manṣūre* over other services and branches. Thus the headquarters of the *ser-ᶜasker* (*Bāb-i Ser-ᶜAsker* [*q.v.*]) gradually came to combine the roles of a ministry of war and a general staff and was in charge of all land forces. The navy continued to operate as a separate organisation under the grand admiral, whose administration comprised a separate ministry. In the different branches of the army, larger permanent units were formed with their regular commanding officers and staffs. Segments of the old feudal (*tīmārlu*) cavalry were reformed. In 1834 a provincial militia (*redīf*) was established. The last two measures were intended to provide the regular army with reserve forces as well as to co-opt the provincial notability into the new system by conferring on them commissions and honours. After 1833 the strength of the regular armed forces was considerably increased, and by the end of Maḥmūd's reign there were some 90,000 men in all the services, exclusive of the militia and other semi-regular organisations. Several European governments began extending modest military assistance. The Russians and British each sent a few military instructors. The British also helped establish the beginnings of a modern arms industry and sent teams of engineers and workmen. Most useful services were rendered by the Prussian military mission which increased from one officer (Helmuth von Moltke) in 1835 to twelve by 1837. This was the beginning of a continuing pattern of military cooperation which was to last until the 20th century. At the same time, the sultan rejuvenated the military engineering schools which had been founded in the 18th century and had subsequently fallen into decay. He also established a military medical school (1827) and an officer school (1834). The sultan enlisted the support and cooperation of the *ᶜulamāʾ* in many of his military reforms (A. Levy, *Ulema*). But the paucity of adequately trained personnel and limited financial resources made progress difficult. The commissary system could not support the rapid increase of the military establishment as demanded by the sultan. Epidemics were rife and over a quarter of all recruits succumbed to disease. Desertion was also very high, and it was necessary to replenish the ranks continuously with new, untrained conscripts (*BBA*, *Kepeci* 6799; Moltke, *Briefe*, 349-50).

In May 1835 the international community was taken by surprise when an Ottoman expeditionary force occupied Tripoli in Africa, claiming it back to the sultan. In the following years Ottoman fleets appeared several times before Tunis, but were turned back by the French navy (*BBA*, *MMD*, ix, 99-110). The continued occupation of Syria by Muḥammad ᶜAlī could not be tolerated by an autocratic ruler like Maḥmūd. In the spring of 1839, believing that his army had sufficiently recovered and that a general uprising in Syria against Egyptian rule was imminent, Maḥmūd precipitated another crisis. On June 24 the Egyptians, once again, decisively routed the Ottoman army at Nizīb. On July 1 Maḥmūd died, probably without learning of his army's last defeat.

During Maḥmūd's reign, due to the inertia effects of long historical processes, the Ottoman empire continued to decline in relation to the West. Its dependence on Europe increased and it continued to suffer military humiliation and territorial losses. Yet, within the reduced confines of his realm Maḥmūd's achievements were considerable. He resurrected the sultan's office, and with that he reformed and rejuvenated the central government. He arrested the disintegration of the state and even initiated a process of consolidation. In spite of his intensive reformatory activity, Maḥmūd was inherently dedicated to traditional values. He did not attempt to alter the basic fabric of Ottoman society, but rather to strengthen it through modern means. He generally succeeded in integrating the old élites into the new institutions. This was in keeping with his strong attachment to the ideal of justice in the traditional Ottoman sense. The sobriquet he selected for himself, *ᶜAdlī*, "the Just," is an indication of the cast of his mind. It may be said, therefore, that the principles which guided him throughout his reign were Islam, autocracy and justice. Nevertheless, though he may not have intended it, the reforms which Maḥmūd introduced were to produce basic change and to launch Ottoman society on the course of modernisation in a final and irrevocable manner.

Bibliography: The Ottoman archives contain a vast number of relevant documents dispersed in numerous collections. All the documents cited above are from Başbakanlık Arşivi (abbreviated as *BBA*). For a description of the holdings of this archive see M. Sertoğlu, *Muhteva bakımından Başvekâlet Arşivi*, Ankara 1955. Especially valuable concentration of documents are located in the following collections: *Kanunnâme-i askerî defterleri* (abbreviated as *KAD*), vols. i, ii, vi (military legislation, organisation, history); *Mühimme-i mektum defterleri* (abbreviated as *MMD*), vols. v-ix (mainly internal political matters); *Maliyeden müdevver defterleri*, vol. 9002 (financial and administrative matters); *Tev-*

cihat ve redif ve mevad ve mühimme-i asâkir defterleri (abbreviated as *TRD*), vol. xxvi (military reform and financial administration); *Tevziat, zehayir, esnaf ve ihitisab defterleri*, vols. xxiv - xxxii (taxation, provisions and various matters); *Kamil Kepeci tasnifi* (numerous documents dealing with the financial administration of the government and armed forces). The *Cevdet tasnifi* and *Hatt-ı hümâyuñlar* (abbreviated as *HH*) collections are very useful, but more disparate.

European archives contain extensive information in the correspondence and reports of envoys stationed in the Ottoman empire. At the Archives de la Guerre, Paris, carton no. MR1619 contains an especially valuable collection of detailed and informed reports on political and military conditions.

The Ottoman chronicles for this period are: Aḥmed ʿĀṣim, *Taʾrīkh*, 2 vols., Istanbul n.d. (vol. ii discusses the events of 1808); S̲h̲ānīzāde Meḥmed ʿAṭāʾullāh, *Taʾrīkh*, 4 vols., Istanbul 1290-1/1873-4 (events of 1808-21); Meḥmed Esʿad, *Taʾrīkh*, 2 vols., unpublished ms. (events of 1821-6); Aḥmed Djewdet, *Taʾrīkh*, 12 vols., Istanbul 1270-1301/ 1854-83; 2nd rev. ed. 1302-9/1884-91 (vols. ix-xii discuss events of 1808-26; Aḥmed Luṭfī, *Taʾrīkh*, 8 vols., Istanbul 1290-1328/1873-1910 (vols. i-vi discuss the period 1825-39).

Other important Ottoman historical works are: Aḥmed Djewād, *Taʾrīkh-i ʿaskerī-yi ʿOthmānī* (5 books in 3 vols.), vol. i— *Yeñičeriler*, Istanbul 1297/1880 (tr. G. Macridès, *État militaire...*; tome i, livre I—*Le corps des janissaires*, Constantinople 1882); vols. ii, iii, unpublished ms. (vol. ii, book IV discusses Maḥmūd's military reforms). Ḥāfiẓ Khiḍr (Khizîr) Ilyās, *Weḳāʾiʿ-i leṭāʾif-i enderūn*, Istanbul 1276/1859 (life and politics at Maḥmūd's court); Meḥmed Esʿad, *Üss-i ẓafer*, Istanbul 1243/1828 (the destruction of the Janissaries; tr. Caussin de Perceval, *Précis historique de la destruction du corps des janissaires...*, Paris 1833); Muṣṭafā Nūrī, *Netāʾidj al-wuḳūʿāt*, 4 vols., Istanbul 1294-1327/ 1877-1909 (vol. iv discusses political, military and economic developments).

Of the extensive western travel accounts, memoirs and other contemporary works, the following have special value: A. F. Andreossy, *Constantinople et le Bosphore de Thrace³*, Paris 1841; A. Boué, *La Turquie d'Europe...*, Paris 1840; J. E. Dekay, *Sketches of Turkey in 1831 and 1832*, New York 1833; V. Fontanier, *Voyages en Orient...*, Paris 1829; A. Juchereau de St. Denys, *Les révolutions de Constantinople en 1807-1808*, Paris 1819; idem, *Histoire de l'empire Ottoman depuis 1792 jusqu'en 1844*, Paris 1844; C. MacFarlane, *Constantinople in 1828*, London 1829; idem, *Turkey and its destiny...*, London 1850; Helmuth von Moltke, *Briefe...*, Berlin 1841; R. Wagner, *Moltke und Mühlbach zusammen unter den Halbmonde*, Berlin 1893 (very useful; based on private and public documents).

In addition to numerous articles in *EI* and *İA*, modern studies discussing this reign include: N. Berkes, *The development of secularism in Turkey*, Montreal 1964, 89-135; C. V. Findley, *The legacy of tradition to reform: origins of the Ottoman foreign ministry*, in *IJMES*, i (1970), 334-57; idem, *The foundation of the Ottoman foreign ministry: the beginnings of bureaucratic reform under Selîm III and Maḥmūd II*, in *IJMES*, iii (1972), 388-416; H. İnalcık, *Sened-i Ittifak ve Gülhane Hatt-ı Hümâyunu*, in *Belleten*, xxviii (1964), 603-22; A. Levy, *The officer corps in Sultan Mahmud II's new Ottoman army, 1826-1839*, in *IJMES*, ii (1971), 21-39; idem, *The Ottoman ulema and the military*

reforms of Sultan Mahmud II, in *Asian and African Studies*, vii (1971), 13-39; idem, *The eshkenji-project—an Ottoman attempt at gradual reform (1826)*, in *Abr-Nahrain*, xiv (1973-4), 32-9; idem, *Ottoman attitudes to the rise of Balkan nationalism*, in B. K. Király and G. E. Ruthenberg, eds., *War and Society in east central Europe during the 18th and 19th centuries*, i, New York 1979, 325-45; B. Lewis, *The emergence of modern Turkey*, London 1961, 75-104; S. J. Shaw and E. Kural Shaw, *History of the Ottoman empire and modern Turkey*, ii, Cambridge 1977, 1-54; F. R. Unat, *Başhoca İshak efendi*, in *Belleten*, xxviii (1964), 89-116.   (A. LEVY)

MAḤMŪD KHAN, NAṢĪR AL-DĪN, the founder of a short-lived dynasty ruling in Kālpī [*q.v.*] in the first half of the 9th/15th century. He was the son of Malikzāda Fīrūz b. Tādj al-Dīn Turk, the *wazīr* of G̲h̲iyāth al-Dīn Tug̲h̲luḳ II, who was killed with his sovereign in Dihlī in 791/1389; after that event he fled to Kālpī, his *iḳṭāʿ*, gave it the honorific name of Muḥammadābād, and "aspired to independence" (*dam az istiḳlāl mīzad*). This was not difficult to attain in the disrupted conditions of the Dihlī sultanate after Tīmūr's sack and withdrawal, and Maḥmūd consolidated his position at the expense of his Hindū neighbours. His status was never really secure against the growing power of the neighbouring sultanates of Mālwā and D̲j̲awnpur [*q.vv.*], and the historians of those regions indicate that the arrogated titles of *shāh* and *sulṭān* were resented by the rulers of the larger and more powerful regions. Maḥmūd died in 813/1410-11 and was succeeded by his son (Ikhtiyār al-Dīn Abu 'l-Mudjāhid) Ḳādir Khān, referred to by Firis̲h̲ta as ʿAbd al-Ḳādir *al-mawsūm ba*-Ḳādir S̲h̲āh (Lucknow lith., ii, 306, 307), d. *ca.* 835/1432; in a war of succession between his three sons, Mālwā and D̲j̲awnpur again intervened, resulting in a son called Djalāl Khān being installed under the suzerainty of Mālwā; he managed to assert his independence more firmly than his father or grandfather, for he issued coins as Fatḥ al-Dunyā wa 'l-Dīn Djalāl S̲h̲āh Sulṭānī in 841/1437-8. The length of his reign is not known, but his brother Naṣīr Khān, ruling in 847/1443, was chastised by the D̲j̲awnpur forces and temporarily deprived of Kālpī after being suspected of apostasising from Islam; thereafter, this semi-independent dynasty does not appear in the historians.

Bibliography: The prime text is Muḥammad Bihāmad Khānī, *Taʾrīkh-i Muḥammadī*, B.M. ms. Or. 137 (Rieu, *Cat. Pers. mss.*, i, 84 ff.), completed in 842/1438-9; the author was brought up in the house of Maḥmūd Khān's father, and later served under Maḥmūd's brother and *wazīr* Djunayd Khān, receiving the *iḳṭāʿ* of Irič for military services. His information is corroborated by Yaḥyā b. Aḥmad Sirhindī, *Taʾrīkh-i Mubārak Shāhī*, and Firis̲h̲ta, and he is cited as an authority by Niẓām al-Dīn Aḥmad, *Ṭabakāt-i Akbarī* (whence also the later information on Naṣīr Khān); S. H. Hodivālā, *The unassigned coins of Jalāl Shāh Sulṭānī*, in *JASB*, NS xxv (1929), Numismatic Supplement N. 41-6.
                                           (J. BURTON-PAGE)

MAḤMŪD SHĀH SHARḲĪ, ruler in Djawnpūr [*q.v.*], the eldest son of Ibrāhīm S̲h̲āh Sharḳī, ascended the throne in 844/1440. In 846/1442, he decided to invade Bengal, but owing to reasons not clear he refrained from carrying out his plans. The account in the *Maṭlaʿ al-saʿdayn* that he did so because of a warning from the Tīmūrīd S̲h̲āh Rukh, seems to be apocryphal.

In 847/1443, hearing that Nāṣir S̲h̲āh, ruler of Kālpī (Maḥmūdābād), had plundered the town of

Shāhpūr and harassed its Muslim population, Maḥmūd decided to punish him, and with the permission of Maḥmūd Khaldjī [*q.v.*] of Mālwā, whose feudatory Nāṣir Shāh's father, Ḳādir Khān, had been, Maḥmūd Sharḳī marched on Kālpī. Nāṣir fled to Čanderi and appealed to Maḥmūd Khaldjī for help. The latter wrote to the Sharḳī Sulṭān to restore Kālpī to Nāṣir, but since the Sharḳī ruler ignored this, Maḥmūd Khaldjī advanced towards Eračh on 2 Shaʿbān 848/14 November 1444 and attacked him. Although both sides suffered losses, the result of the conflict was indecisive, and hostilities ended through the mediation of the Shaykh al-Islām, Shaykh Djaʾilda, a holy man much respected by both the rulers; Maḥmūd Sharḳī agreed to restore Kālpī to Nāṣir Shāh.

Soon afterwards, Maḥmūd crushed a rebellion in Čunār and annexed a greater portion of it. He then invaded Orissa which he plundered and, after laying the foundations of two mosques at Pahārpūr, returned to Djawnpūr.

Maḥmūd now put forward a claim to the throne of Dihlī on the ground that its ruler Sulṭān ʿAlāʾ al-Dīn ʿĀlam Shāh (847-83/1443-76) was his wife's brother. The Sulṭān was a puppet in the hands of his *wazīr*, Ḥamīd Khān, who was the *de facto* ruler. But weary of his minister's domination, he had gone away to Badāʾūn. Ḥamīd Khān, finding his position insecure on account of the machinations of the Sulṭān and the hostility of some Dihlī nobles, invited Bahlūl from Sirhind. Bahlūl immediately set out towards Dihlī and occupied it on 17 Rabīʿ I 855/19 April 1451. He then imprisoned Ḥamīd Khān and declared himself king.

At the beginning of 856/1452, Maḥmūd Shāh, instigated by his queen, Bībī Rādjī, and invited by the nobles who detested the uncouth Afghāns, advanced towards Dihlī with 170,000 cavalry and 1,400 war elephants and invested it. Meanwhile, Bahlūl Lodī hastened from Dīpalpūr to the help of his son, Khʷādja Bāyazīd, whom he had left in charge of Dihlī. On hearing of Bahlūl's approach, Maḥmūd Shāh despatched an army of 30,000 cavalry and 30 elephants under Daryā Khān Lodī and Fatḥ Khān Harāwi, who met Bahlūl at Narela, 17 miles north of Dihlī. Before the battle Sayyid Shams al-Dīn, a loyal follower of Bahlūl, won over Daryā Khān by appealing to his racial feelings. The result of Daryā Khān's defection was that the Sharḳī army became demoralised and, although numerically superior, it was defeated by Bahlūl's 7,000 troops. Fatḥ Khān was taken prisoner and beheaded. Maḥmūd Sharḳī had no alternative except to return to Djawnpūr.

In 858/1454 Maḥmūd sent a force to occupy Udjdjayn, whose chief, Īshwar Singh, Djawnpūr's feudatory, had declared his independence. Īshwar Singh fled, but was pursued and captured and then put to death (859/1455). Udjdjayn was then annexed.

Emboldened by his victory at Narela, Bahlūl Lodī decided to extend his territories. He occupied Raprī and expelled the Sharḳī governor of Etāwah. Maḥmūd marched against the Afghan army, which he met at Etāwah (856/1452-3). The battle was indecisive, and peace was brought about through the mediation of Ḳuṭb Khān, cousin and brother-in-law of Bahlūl, and Ray Pratāp, ruler of Bhongāon and Kampil. It was agreed that Bahlūl would return the seven elephants he had captured at Narela; that each would retain possession of the territories which had belonged to Ibrāhīm Sharḳī and Mubārak Shāh Sayyid of Dihlī; and lastly, that Shamsābād would be ceded to Bahlūl.

But hostilities again broke out in 861/1456-7 because Djawna Khān, the Sharḳī governor of Shamsābād, refused to surrender it. Bahlūl therefore attacked him and after expelling him, handed over Shamsābad to Ray Karan. Maḥmūd hastened to the aid of Djawna Khan. Ḳuṭb Khān and Daryā Khān made a night attack on him, but this proved abortive and Ḳuṭb Khān was taken prisoner. Greatly distressed on hearing of Ḳuṭb Khān's imprisonment, Bahlūl set out to attack Maḥmūd. But the latter fell ill and died in 862/1458. He was succeeded by his eldest son, Bhīkam Khān, who ascended the throne of Djawnpūr as Sulṭān Muḥammad Sharḳī.

Maḥmūd was an able ruler and his subjects were happy and prosperous during his reign. He is said to have spent his time in the society of the *ʿulamāʾ* and Ṣūfīs. He was interested in architecture and built the famous Lāl Darwāza Mosque in Djawnpūr, and adjacent to it a magnificent palace for his queen, Bībī Rādjī. He also built a bridge and *madrasas*, and laid the foundations of another palace outside Djawnpūr.

Bibliography: Niẓām al-Dīn, *Ṭabaḳāt-i Akbarī*, iii, ed. B. De, Bibl. Ind., Calcutta 1935 and Eng. tr. B. De and Baini Prashad, Bibl. Ind., Calcutta 1938; Muḥammad Ḳāsim Hindū-Shāh, *Taʾrīkh-i Firishta*, ii, Lucknow 1281/1864; ʿAbd al-Bāḳī Nihāwandī, *Maʾāthir-i raḥīmī*; Mawlāwī Khayr al-Dīn Muḥammad Allāhābādī, *Djawnpūr-nāma*, Djawnpūr 1875, 1895, abridged Eng. tr. Faḳīr Khayr al-Dīn Muḥammad, Calcutta 1814, Urdu tr. Nadhīr al-Dīn Aḥmad, Djawnpūr 1921; Miyān Muḥammad Saʿīd, *The Sharḳī Sulṭāns of Djawnpūr*, Karāčī 1972; M. Ḥabīb and K. A. Niẓāmī, eds., *A comprehensive history of India (1206-1526)*, v, Dihlī 1970; Sir W. Haig, ed., *Cambridge history of India*, iii, Cambridge 1928; M. A. Raḥīm, *A history of the Afghāns in India*, Karāčī 1961; S. Ḥasan ʿAskarī, *Discursive notes on the Sharḳī monarchy of Djawnpūr*, in the *Procs. of the Ind. Hist. Congress, 1960*, Part i; R. R. Diwarkar, ed., *Bihār through the ages*, Calcutta 1959; Percy Brown, *Indian architecture. The Islamic period*, Bombay 1956. (Mohibbul Hasan)

MAḤMŪD SHIHĀB AL-DĪN, the fourteenth ruler of the Bahmanī dynasty [*q.v.*] in the Dakhan (Deccan). He ascended the throne at Muḥammadābād-Bīdar at the age of twelve on the death of his father, Shams al-Dīn Muḥammad III, on 5 Ṣafar 887/26 March 1482. During Maḥmūd's long reign of twenty-six years, the kingdom continued on its downward course on account of his own incompetence and the greed and intrigues of his nobles. The bitter rivalry between the Dakhanīs, consisting of the natives and old settlers, and the Newcomers called Āfāḳīs or Gharībīs, comprising Turks, Persians and Arabs, continued in all its intensity. Malik Ḥasan Niẓām al-Mulk, a Hindū convert to Islām and governor (*ṭarafdār*) of Telingānā, became the leader of the Dakhanīs and planned to destroy the Āfāḳīs, already weakened since the death of Maḥmūd Gāwān [*q.v.*] on 5 Ṣafar 886/5 April 1481. He succeeded in persuading the boy-king to order the massacre of the Turkish population of the town. Accordingly, the gates of the town were shut and about 4,000 Turks were massacred in cold blood. Fortunately, Yūsuf ʿĀdil, *ṭarafdār* of Bīdjāpūr and leader of the Āfāḳīs, who had come to attend the king's coronation ceremony, was saved because he had encamped outside the town wall, and after the massacre left for Bidjapūr.

The government was carried on by a Regency with the Queen-Mother as President of the Council of Regency; Malik Ḥasan Niẓām al-Mulk as Mīr Nāʾib; Fatḥ Allāh ʿImād al-Mulk, also a Hindū convert to

Islām, as *wazīr* and Mīr Djumla as finance minister. Ḳāsim Barīd, a Turk who had watched the massacre of the people of his own race with indifference, was appointed *kōtwāl* [*q.v.*].

In 891/1486, four years after his accession, Maḥmūd, anxious to assert his power, conspired with Ḳāsim Barīd and Dastūr Dīnār, the leader of the Abyssinians (Ḥabashīs), to get rid of both Niẓām al-Mulk and ʿImād al-Mulk. But the plot leaked out and the Sulṭān apologised to them. However, ʿImād al-Mulk, realising his life to be in danger, left for his own province of Berār, never to return again. Niẓām al-Mulk, who took no precaution, was strangled to death by his friend, Dilpasand Khān, at the instigation of Maḥmūd.

Niẓām al-Mulk's removal from the scene led to the victory of the Āfāḳīs. But the Dakhanīs, alarmed and angry by the murder of their leader, plotted to assassinate the king with the support of the Ḥabashīs; and on 21 Dhu 'l-Ḳaʿda 892/8 November 1487, they entered the palace, locking the gate behind them so that no one else could enter. They killed the Turkish guards, but Ḳāsim Barīd, with a detachment of 12,000 men, scaled the walls of the palace and rescued the king. The next morning, Maḥmūd ordered the massacre of the Dakhanīs, and for three days this continued until it was stopped by the intercession of Shāh Muḥibb Allāh, son of the saint Khalīl Allāh.

Taking advantage of these events, Ḳāsim Barīd raised the banner of revolt, and compelled Maḥmūd to make him *wakīl* or prime minister (897/1492). Meanwhile, Malik Aḥmad, Niẓām al-Mulk's son, who was at his *djāgīr* [*q.v.*] of Djunayr, on hearing of his father's death, adopted the title of Niẓām al-Mulk and without seeking the permission of the king, conquered all the forts in Mahārāshtra, including the whole of Konkon and the territory up to the river Godāvarī. He then came to Bīdar, where he was received by Maḥmūd and confirmed in his new possessions; but at the same time Maḥmūd sent troops against Malik Aḥmad and also ordered Yūsuf ʿĀdil to march against him. The royal troops were defeated, while Yūsuf ʿĀdil, in defiance of the king's order, congratulated Malik Aḥmad on his success. It was in 895/1490 that Malik Aḥmad, on achieving his victory over the king's army, had founded the town of Aḥmadnagar [*q.v.*], which became the capital of the Niẓām Shāhī dynasty [*q.v.*].

Encouraged by the incompetence of the ruler, the governors in the provinces began to assert their independence. Bahādur Khān Gīlānī, *kōtwāl* of Goa, took possession of the whole west coast from Goa up to Dābul as well as the greater portion of southern Mahārāshtra. But on 5 Ṣafar 900/5 November 1494, he was defeated and killed by Sulṭān Ḳulī Ḳuṭb al-Mulk, *ṭarafdār* of Telingāna. Dastūr Dīnār, the Ḥabashī, who held the *djāgīrs* of Culbarga, Aland and Gangāwatī, also declared his independence in 901/1496. But although he was defeated by Yūsuf ʿĀdil, he was forgiven by Maḥmūd and his *djāgīrs* restored to him.

Yūsuf ʿĀdil's position became strong due to the betrothal of his daughter to the crown prince, Aḥmad, early in 903/1497, which enabled him to secure the *djāgīrs* of Gulbarga, Aland and Gangāwatī which had been assigned to Dastūr Dinār. Previously to this, Ḳāsim Barīd, being jealous of Yūsuf ʿĀdil, had contrived his overthrow. He had suggested to Narasa Nāyak, the prime minister of Vidjayānagar, to occupy Rayčūr and Mudgal which were in Yūsuf ʿĀdil's possession, and had also tried to win over Malik Aḥmad against Yūsuf by offering him Panhāla, Konkon and Goa, which were at the time in Bahādur Gīlānī's possession. But Yūsuf ʿĀdil had succeeded in foiling Malik Aḥmad's plans. He had first marched towards Bīdar and defeated Ḳāsim Barīd, who was accompanied by Maḥmūd, near the capital. He had then directed his attention towards the Vijayānagar army, which he had defeated on 1 Radjab 899/18 April 1493 and had reoccupied Rayčūr and Mudgal, thus upsetting Ḳāsim Barīd's plans.

Disenchanted with Ḳāsim Barid, Maḥmūd now invited Yūsuf ʿĀdil and Ḳuṭb al-Mulk to his rescue at the end of Dhu 'l-Ḥidjdja 903/August 1497. They came and besieged Ḳāsim in his *djāgīr* of Ausa, but gained no success, for the minister was soon reconciled to the king. However, in 909/1503-4, Ḳāsim Barīd was replaced by Khān-i Djahān, also a Turk, until Ḳāsim Barid contrived his death. Thereupon, Yūsuf ʿĀdil, Ḳuṭb al-Mulk and Dastūr Dīnār marched on Bīdar to wrest power from Ḳāsim. The latter was defeated and fled, but this did not improve things, because he once again won over Maḥmūd. Frustrated in their attempts to rescue the king, the *ṭarafdārs* in disgust returned to their respective *djāgīrs*, leaving Ḳāsim Barīd as powerful as before. When he died in 910/1504-5 he was succeeded by his son Amīr ʿAlī Barīd, whose domination was even more effective than that of his father.

Taking advantage of these internecine conflicts, Krishnādevarāya compelled Yūsuf ʿĀdil to evacuate the Dōʾāb. The Gandjpatīs of Orissa, on the other hand, occupied the whole east coast which had belonged to the Bahmanids. In 923/1517, Maḥmūd tried to recover the Dōʾāb from the Rādja of Vidjayānagar, but he was defeated and wounded and compelled to retreat.

Maḥmūd's last days were unhappy. In addition to these territorial losses, there were risings of his *ṭarafdārs*, who were engaged in carving out independent kingdoms for themselves, which he was helpless to prevent; soon his writ did not run beyond the walls of Bīdār, and even there he was subject to the will of Amīr ʿAlī Barīd.

Maḥmūd died on 4 Dhu 'l-Ḥidjdja 924/7 December 1518. He was succeeded by four kings, one after another, set up or set aside according to ʿAlī Barīd's pleasure. Kalīm Allāh, Maḥmūd's son, was the last king. He wrote to Bābur for help against ʿAlī Barīd, but as the latter found this out, Kalīm Allāh fled to Bīdjāpūr and thence to Aḥmadnagar, where he is supposed to have died in 945/1538.

Bibliography: Sayyid ʿAlī Ṭabāṭabā, *Taʾrīkh-i Burhān-i maʾāthir*, ed. Sayyid Hāshim, Dihlī 1355/1936; Muḥammad Ḳāsim Hindū-Shāh, *Taʾrīkh-i Firishta*, i, Lucknow 1281/1864; Niẓām al-Dīn, *Ṭabaḳāt-i Akbarī*, iii, ed. B. De and Hidāyat Ḥusayn, Bibl. Ind. Calcutta 1935, Eng. tr. B. De and Baini Prashad, Bibl. Ind. Calcutta 1938; H. K. Sherwānī, *The Bahmanis of the Deccan*, Hyderabad 1953: H. K. Sherwānī and P. M. Djoshi, eds., *History of medieval Deccan (1295-1724)*, 2 vols., Hyderabad 1973-4; M. Ḥabīb and K. A. Niẓāmī, eds., *A comprehensive history of India (1206-1526)*, v, Dihlī 1970; G. Yazdānī, *Bīdar and its history and its monuments*, Oxford 1947. (MOHIBBUL HASAN)

MAḤMŪD B. ISMĀʿĪL. [See LUʾLUʾ, BADR AL-DĪN].

MAḤMŪD B. MUḤAMMAD B. MALIK-SHĀH, MUGHĪTH AL-DUNYĀ WA 'L-DĪN ABU 'L-ḲĀSIM, Great Saldjūḳ sultan in western Persia and ʿIrāḳ 511-25/1118-31.

The weakening of the Great Saldjūḳ central power in the west, begun after Malik-Shāh's death in the period of the disputed succession between Berk-yaruḳ and Muḥammad [*q.vv.*], but arrested somewhat once Muḥammad had established his undisputed authority, proceeded apace during Maḥmūd's fourteen-year reign. This arose in part from the latter's initial youthfulness (he came to the throne, at the age of 13 and as the eldest of his father's five sons, on 24 Dhu 'l-Ḥidjdja 511/18 April 1118, through the support of Kamāl al-Mulk Simīrumī, subsequently his vizier), but stemmed mainly from the continued vitality among the Saldjūḳs of a patrimonial concept of rule which made clear-cut father-eldest son succession difficult to enforce. Maḥmūd's uncle Sandjar [*q.v.*] remained as undisputed ruler of the eastern Persian lands, and from his seniority and experience became regarded as head of the Saldjūḳ family, even though since the time of Ṭoghrīl Beg the holder of the seat of power in the western half of the sultanate had normally been regarded as supreme sultan. But what made Maḥmūd's reign so full of strife were the pretensions of his four brothers, Masʿūd, Ṭoghrīl, Sulaymān Shāh and Saldjūḳ Shāh. All of them held some degree of power in various parts of the western sultanate at different times, and the first three of them eventually achieved the title of sultan itself, though their reigns followed after the brief one of Maḥmūd's son Dāwūd (525-6/1131-2) and were interspersed with those of two other sons, Malik-Shāh III (547-8/1152-3) and Muḥammad II (548-55/1153-60).

The claims of these fraternal rivals for power during Maḥmūd's reign could not have been sustained without military support from their own Atabegs or guardians [see ATABAK] and other Turkish commanders, through whose control large sections of the sultanate were frequently abstracted from Maḥmūd's direct rule, with deleterious effects on his finances, his ability to pay his troops and therefore his enforcing his authority. As lamented by Anūshīrwān b. Khālid [*q.v.*], who acted as Maḥmūd's vizier 521-2/1127-8, "they [sc. Maḥmūd's rivals] split up the kingdom's unity and destroyed its cohesion; they claimed a share with him in the power, and left him with only a bare subsistence" (Bundārī, 134). Maḥmūd's sultanate also witnessed further steps in the process of the revival of the ʿAbbāsid caliphs in Baghdād's temporal power, and the growing confidence of Maḥmūd's contemporary al-Mustarshid (512-29/1118-35) was only held in check by the caliph's enemies in central ʿIrāḳ, the Shīʿī Arab dynasty of the Mazyadids [*q.v.*] under Dubays b. Ṣadaḳa.

The ascendancy over the young sultan Maḥmūd immediately established by the Chief *Ḥādjib* ʿAlī Bār soon led to an invasion by Sandjar, who came westwards with a powerful army, defeated Maḥmūd at Sāwa and dictated peace to him, but on a fairly amicable basis (513/1119); Sandjar secured control of the Caspian provinces and Ray, but gave Maḥmūd one of his daughters in marriage and made him his heir. Meanwhile, Maḥmūd was losing control of the northern parts of his dominions, for his brother Ṭoghrīl's cause was espoused in northern Djibāl by the Atabeg Küntoghdī, and from a base at Ḳazwīn, Ṭoghrīl defied Maḥmūd for the whole of his reign. Also, Ādharbāydjān and al-Djazīra had been granted to Masʿūd b. Muḥammad, with Ay-Aba Djuyūsh Beg as his Atabeg. The separatist tendencies of local Turkish and Kurdish chiefs, including ʿImād al-Dīn Zangī, encouraged Masʿūd, and in 514/1120 he and Ay-Aba rebelled openly, but were defeated by Maḥmūd's general Aḳ Sunḳur Bursuḳī at Asadābād near Hamadhān, and Masʿūd's vizier al-Ḥasan b. ʿAlī al-Ṭughrāʾī [*q.v.*], the famous poet and stylist, was executed. Ay-Aba had hoped to incite Dubays b. Ṣadaḳa against Maḥmūd, and over the next few years the *amīr* of Ḥilla's hopes of reducing Saldjūḳ influence in ʿIrāḳ were raised. Fortunately for Maḥmūd, fear of the Shīʿī threat had the effect of forcing the caliph al-Mustarshid into close co-operation with Maḥmūd's own vizier Shams al-Mulk ʿUthmān b. Niẓām al-Mulk, and in 520/1126 Maḥmūd came with an army to Baghdād to enforce his rights and reinforce the authority of his *shiḥna* or military governor there.

On the extreme northern fringes of the sultanate, a threat had arisen from the resurgent Georgians [see AL-KURDJ] under David IV the Restorer (1089-1125), who had stopped paying tribute to the Saldjūḳs (see W. E. D. Allen, *A history of the Georgian people*, London 1932, 96-100). An army sent by Maḥmūd in 515/1121, and including Ṭoghrīl, Dubays and the Artuḳid Il-Ghāzī, failed to halt the Georgians, who captured Tiflis and Ānī and dislodged the latter's Shaddādid prince, and a further expedition to Shīrwān led personally by the sultan (517/1123) achieved nothing either. Ṭoghrīl and Dubays tried soon after this to stir up ʿIrāḳ against Maḥmūd and al-Mustarshid, but failed and had to flee to Khurāsān. They persuaded Sandjar to move westwards to Ray in 522/1128, but Maḥmūd became reconciled to his uncle; Dubays had eventually to move to Syria, and in 524/1130 Maḥmūd and Masʿūd made peace, the latter being confirmed in his appanage centred on Gandja in Ādharbāydjān.

Maḥmūd died in Djibāl on 15 Shawwāl 525/10 September 1131 at the age of only 27, and his death was to plunge the western sultanate into sharp succession disputes. Despite an alleged love of luxury, Maḥmūd achieved a favourable mention from historians for his justice and reasonableness and for his Arabic scholarship, rare among the Saldjūḳ rulers. He patronised many of the leading poets of his time, and both he and the caliph al-Mustarshid were the *mamdūḥs* of Ḥayṣa Bayṣa [*q.v.*] (see ʿAlī Djawād al-Ṭāhir, *al-Shiʿr al-ʿarabī fi 'l-ʿIrāḳ wa-bilād al-ʿAdjam fi 'l-ʿaṣr al-Saldjūḳī*, Baghdād 1958-61, index s.v. *Maḥmūd*). The ten grave accusations levelled against Maḥmūd by Anūshīrwān b. Khālid (listed in Bundārī, 120-4), including those of breaking up the unity of the Saldjūḳ house and of causing disharmony in ʿIrāḳ, of squandering his father's treasury, of splitting up the royal *ghulāms*, of raising the siege of Alamūt because of Ismāʿīlī sympathies, of encouraging an atmosphere of immorality at court, etc., and the further accusations laid at the door of the vizier Ḳiwām al-Dīn Darguzīnī or Ansabādhī (Anūshīrwān's predecessor and then successor in office), contain palpable exaggerations, and do not take sufficient account of the parlous financial state of the sultanate, because of which Maḥmūd was compelled to grant out to his commanders more and more land as *iḳṭāʿs* and thus reduce his own income.

Bibliography: 1. Sources. See the general chronicles, Ibn al-Athīr, Ibn al-Djawzī and Sibṭ al-Djawzī; and of the Saldjūḳ, sources, Bundārī, *Zubdat al-nuṣra*, 119-56; Rāwandī, *Rāḥat al-ṣudūr*, 203-6; Ṣadr al-Dīn Ḥusaynī, *Akhbār al-dawla al-Saldjūḳiyya*, 88-9, 96-9; Ibn al-Ḳalānisī, *Dhayl Taʾrīkh Dimashḳ*, 198 ff. There is a biography in Ibn Khallikān, ed. Iḥsān ʿAbbās, v, 182-3, no. 174, tr. de Slane, iii, 337-8.

2. Studies. See M. A. Köymen, *Büyük Selçuklu imparatorluğu tarihi. ii. İkinci imparatorluk devri*, Ankara 1954, 5-148, 164-73; C. E. Bosworth, in *Cambridge hist. of Iran*, v, 119-24.

(C. E. BOSWORTH)

MAḤMŪD B. SEBÜKTIGIN, sultan of the G̲h̲aznawid dynasty [*q.v.*], reigned 388-421/998-1030 in the eastern Islamic lands.

Abu 'l-Ḳāsim Maḥmūd was the eldest son of the Turkish commander Sebüktigin, who had risen from being one of the slave personal guards of the *Ḥād̲j̲ib-i buzurg* or commander-in-chief Alptigin [see ALP TAKĪN] under the Sāmānids to becoming the virtually independent *amīr* of a principality centred on G̲h̲azna [*q.v.*], at that time on the far eastern fringe of the Sāmānid empire. Maḥmūd was born in 361/971, his mother being from the local Iranian (?) gentry stock of Zābulistān [*q.v.*], the district around G̲h̲azna in what is now eastern Afg̲h̲ānistān; hence in the eulogies of his court poets, Maḥmūd is sometimes called "Maḥmūd-i Zābulī".

Maḥmūd was involved at his father's side in the confused, internecine warfare which marked the last years of the Sāmānid amīrate. In 384/994 the two of them fought on behalf of the *amīr* Nūḥ II b. Manṣūr against the rebels Abū ʿAlī Sīmd̲j̲ūrī and Fāʾiḳ K̲h̲āṣṣa, and Maḥmūd was rewarded with the honorific title Sayf al-Dawla and command of the army of K̲h̲urāsān in place of Abū ʿAlī. Control of this powerful military force was of prime value to Maḥmūd when, in S̲h̲aʿbān 387/August 997, Sebüktigin died and Maḥmūd had to establish by force of arms his own claim to the amīrate in G̲h̲azna against that of Ismāʿīl, his younger brother, whom Sebüktigin had by a somewhat puzzling decision appointed his successor (388/998) but who had no military experience or reputation comparable to that of Maḥmūd.

Once securely in power, the latter's first step was to re-establish the position in K̲h̲urāsān by ejecting the general Begtuzun, who had taken over the province whilst Maḥmūd was involved in civil war with Ismāʿīl. By securing a decisive victory over all his opponents in K̲h̲urāsān, Maḥmūd was able to turn against his old masters the Sāmānids on pretext of seeking vengeance for the deposed *amīr* Manṣūr b. Nūḥ II; he then secured from the ʿAbbāsid caliph al-Ḳādir [*q.v.*] direct investiture of the governorships of K̲h̲urāsān and G̲h̲azna and the *laḳab*s of Yamīn al-Dawla and Amīn al-Milla (the former honorific being that by which Maḥmūd became most widely-known, to the point that the whole G̲h̲aznawid dynasty was often referred to later as the Yamīniyān). With the final disintegration of the Sāmānid state in the face of a fresh invasion from the north by the Ḳarak̲h̲ānids or Ilek K̲h̲āns [*q.v.*], it was a question for Maḥmūd of moving quickly to consolidate his hold over his own share of the former Sāmānid dominions, those south of the Oxus, for the Ilig K̲h̲ān Naṣr b. ʿAlī coveted K̲h̲urāsān also. Whilst Maḥmūd was pre-occupied in India in 396/1005-6, a Ḳarak̲h̲ānid army invaded K̲h̲urāsān, and the united forces of the Ilig and his kinsman Yūsuf Ḳadïr K̲h̲ān of Kās̲h̲g̲h̲ar were not finally driven out till 398/1008, after which Maḥmūd's grip on K̲h̲urāsān was never again threatened from that quarter.

Maḥmūd's 32 years of rule were filled with almost ceaseless campaigning over a vast expanse of southern Asia, so that by his death he had assembled an empire greater than any known in eastern Islam since the decline of the ʿAbbāsid caliphs. Continuance of his father's policy of raids into the Indian subcontinent enabled Maḥmūd to build up a great contemporary reputation as hammer of the heretical Ismāʿīlī S̲h̲īʿīs in Multān and other centres of Sind, but above all, of the pagan Hindus. In retrospect, it appears to us that the prime motivation for Maḥmūd's raids was financial greed rather than religious zeal. The temple treasures of India were thereby tapped, and the proceeds used to beautify mosques and palaces in G̲h̲azna and at places like Lashkar-i Bāzār [*q.v.*], but above all, to maintain the central bureaucracy and the highly expensive, multi-national professional army which could not be stood down between campaigns. For the army, indeed, the manpower of India, in the form of infantrymen and elephant-drivers, was pressed into service, and it does not seem that Maḥmūd baulked at employing these men whilst they were still pagan. The details of Maḥmūd's Indian campaigns, usually enumerated at 17 in all, can conveniently be read in Nāẓim's *Sulṭān Maḥmūd* (see *Bibl.*), 86-122. Briefly, the Hindūs̲h̲āhī [*q.v.*] dynasty of Wayhind, which had stood as a bulwark in northwestern India against Muslim expansion down the Indus valley and across to the Gangetic plains, was assaulted in several campaigns, and successive Rād̲j̲ās, D̲j̲aypāl (d. 393/1002-3), Anandpāl, Triločanpāl (d. 412/1021-2) and Bhimpāl (d. 417/1026, the last of his line) humbled, despite their attempts at alliance with other threatened potentates such as the Rād̲j̲ās of Kālind̲j̲ār, Ḳanawd̲j̲, Gwāliyōr, Dihlī and Ud̲j̲d̲j̲ayn. Expeditions against these latter rulers led Maḥmūd well into the Dōʾāb and into Central India, whilst a spectacular march across the Thar Desert in 416/1026 gained him fabulous plunder from the idol-temple at Sōmnāth in Kāṭhīāwāṛ, ancient Sawrās̲h̲ṭra, an enhanced reputation throughout the Muslim world, and the fresh *laḳab* of Kahf al-Dawla wa 'l-Islām. Nor were Muslim dissidents spared, and the Ismāʿīlī ruler of Multān, Abu 'l-Fatḥ Dāwūd b. Naṣr, one of the local Arab rulers in Sind who had acknowledged the distant suzerainty of the Fāṭimids, was subdued and finally deposed in two campaigns (396/1006 and 401/1010).

The raiding of India was thus a financial necessity for maintaining the momentum of the G̲h̲aznawid military machine. A political annexation and the mass conversion of the Hindus were probably never envisaged, and could not have been maintained in face of the strenous opposition offered by the Hindu princes except by an enormous army of occupation and the settlement of myriads of Muslim colonists. By the end of Maḥmūd's reign, Islam must have had a good hold in the lower and middle Indus valley regions, but Lahore remained for nearly two centuries essentially a frontier bastion for Muslim *g̲h̲āzī* activity against Hindu-held territory which lay not far to the east; it was to be the task of Muʿizz al-Dīn Muḥammad G̲h̲ūrī and his commanders really to establish Islamic political control over northern India in the 7th/13th century [see G̲H̲ŪRIDS and DIHLĪ SULTANATE].

The other aspect of Maḥmūd's imperialist policies concerned the Iranian world, where, as successor-state to the Sāmānids, the sultan employed a mixture of direct conquest and the extension of tributary states over outlying regions. Thus the local Ṣaffārid rulers of Sīstān were reduced to vassalage (393/1003), as had been already at Maḥmūd's accession the Farīg̲h̲ūnids [*q.v.* in Suppl.] in Gūzgān [*q.v.*] and the S̲h̲ērs or princes of G̲h̲arčistān [*q.v.*]; whilst the rulers of Ḳuṣdār and Makrān [*q.vv.*] in modern Balūčistān had to acknowledge Maḥmūd in 402/1011 and at the sultan's accession respectively. His forcible annexation of the ancient kingdom of K̲h̲ʷārazm [*q.v.*] on the lower Oxus and the extinguishing of the native Maʾmūnid dynasty of K̲h̲ʷārazm-S̲h̲āhs [*q.v.*] in Gurgānd̲j̲ in 408/1017, an isolated outpost of conquest which Maḥmūd's son Masʿūd had to relinquish only five or six years after his father's death, nevertheless enabled the G̲h̲aznawids to turn the flank of the western branch of the Karakhānids, who under ʿAlītigin had never ceased to show hostility to the sultan, and to achieve a position of dominant influence in Central Asia.

Maḥmūd inherited from the Sāmānids a tradition of rivalry with the Daylamī Būyids [see BUWAYHIDS] concerning possession of Ray and northern Persia and concerning the exercise of suzerainty over the petty rulers of the Caspian region. The death of Faḵẖr al-Dawla [q.v.] of Ray and Djibāl in 387/997 inaugurated a period of weaker rule for the northern Būyid amīrate under his youthful son Madjd al-Dawla Rustam [q.v.] and his imperious mother and regent Sayyida. Maḥmūd made the Ziyārid ruler of Gurgān and Ṭabaristān Manūčihr b. Kābūs [see ZIYĀRIDS] his vassal, but only towards the end of his life did he feel freed from his many other commitments to lead a full-scale expedition against the Būyids (an expedition into the Būyid province of Kirmān in 407/1016-17 in support of a Būyid claimant to the governorship there had achieved no lasting result). Madjd al-Dawla was dethroned and his amīrate annexed, and the Ghaznawid troops pushed into northwestern Persia, temporarily subduing local Daylamī and Kurdish princes like the Kākuyids and Musāfirids [q.vv.] (420/1029). The whole campaign was retrospectively justified by propaganda denouncing the Būyids for their Shīʿism, their encouragement of heretics and their tutelage of the caliphs in Baghdād, and grandiose plans for advancing on ʿIrāḳ and confronting the Fāṭimids on the Syrian Desert fringes envisaged. All these plans were cut short by the sultan's death at the age of 59 on 23 Rabīʿ II 421/30 April 1030 and rendered impossible of execution for his son Masʿūd because of the growing menace from the Turkmen incursions, which were to lead eventually to the triumph of the Saldjūḳs at Dandānḳān [q.v. in Suppl.] and the Ghaznawids' loss of Ḵẖurāsān.

The contemporary image of Maḥmūd was that of a Sunnī hero, sedulous in sending presents to the caliph in return for honorifics and investiture patents, and zealous to maintain orthodoxy within his dominions against all religious dissent and against odd pockets of paganism in regions of Afghānistān like Ghūr and Kāfiristān [q.vv.]. The centralised, despotic machinery of state with the sultan at its head, as created by Maḥmūd and his Persian officials, typifies the Perso-Islamic "power-state" in which the ruling institution of officials and soldiers was clearly set apart from the masses of tax-paying subjects, the raʿāyā. It was not for nothing that within half-a-century of Maḥmūd's death, the great vizier Niẓām al-Mulk [q.v.] could hold the sultan up in his Siyāsat-nāma as an exemplar for his own Saldjūḳ, masters, and the military state typified by that of the Ghaznawids became the model for many later Islamic powers, a large proportion of them likewise directed by Turkish military castes. However, the figure of Maḥmūd also exemplifies how speedily and successfully the Islamic cultural milieu could attract and mould in its own image an outsider whose father had been a barbarian from the pagan Turkish steppes; for amongst other things, the literary and intellectual circles at Maḥmūd's court, which nurtured several leading poets like ʿUnṣurī, Farruḵẖī and, for a short time, Firdawsī [q.vv.] and provided a congenial centre of work for the scientist al-Bīrūnī [q.v.], show that the sultan conceived of himself as a full member of the comity of Islamic prince-patrons.

Bibliography: 1. Primary sources. The main contemporary source is ʿUtbī's al-Taʾrīkh al-Yamīnī, together with that of a generation or so later, Gardīzī's Zayn al-aḵẖbār; this last plus Ibn al-Athīr contain valuable material from the lost Taʾrīkh Wulāt Ḵẖurāsān of Sallāmī. Although the relevant volumes of Bayhaḳī's Mudjallāt for Maḥmūd's reign have not survived, those subsequent ones forming the Taʾrīkh-i Masʿūdī give important retrospective information, e.g. for the conquest of Ḵẖwārazm. The later biographies of viziers, such as Nāṣir al-Dīn Munshī Kirmānī's Nasāʾim al-ashār and Sayf al-Dīn ʿUḳaylī's Āthār al-wuzarāʾ, are important, as are adab works and collections of anecdotes, including ʿAwfī's Djawāmiʿ al-ḥikāyāt and Faḵẖr-i Mudabbir's Adab al-ḥarb wa 'l-shadjāʿa.

2. Secondary sources. M. Nāẓim's The life and times of Sulṭān Maḥmūd of Ghazna, Cambridge 1931, is a detailed, somewhat eulogistic, full-scale study; briefer, but more critical, is M. Habib's Sultan Mahmud of Ghaznin², Dihli 1951. Other studies containing important information include Barthold, Turkestan down to the Mongol invasion², London 1928; C. E. Bosworth, The Ghaznavids, their empire in Afghanistan and eastern Iran 994-1040, Edinburgh 1963; idem, in Camb. hist. of Iran, iv, ch. 5, v, ch. 1; and idem, The medieval history of Iran, Afghanistan and Central Asia, London 1977 (contains several reprinted relevant articles). For a survey of later historiography about Maḥmūd, see P. Hardy, Mahmud of Ghazna and the historians, in Jnal. of the Panjab Univ. Historical Soc., xiv (Dec. 1962), 1-36.

(C. E. BOSWORTH)

MAḤMŪD EKREM BEY. [See EKREM BEY].

MAḤMŪD GĀWĀN, Ḵẖwādjā ʿImād al-Dīn, Bahmanī minister in South India during the years 862-87/1458-82.

He was born in 813/1411 (al-Sakhāwī, al-Ḍawʾ al-lāmiʿ, x), and arrived at Bīdar [q.v.] the capital of the Bahmanī kingdom [q.v.] at the age of 43. His family had held high office in Gīlān in the Caspian coastlands, but it had fallen into disgrace and Maḥmūd had been compelled to leave the land of his birth. After wandering from place to place, he at last reached the Bahmanī port of Dābul with the intention of entering the profession of merchant. From Dābul he wended his way to the metropolis of the Deccan in order to sit at the feet of Shāh Muḥibb. Allāh, son of the famous saint Shāh Niʿmat Allāh of Kirmān, who had made the Deccan his home. It was not long after this that he caught the attention of the sulṭān, Aḥmad II (839-62/1435-58), who appointed him manṣabdār of 1,000 and ordered him to go and suppress the rebellion of the royal kinsman Djalāl Ḵẖān at Nalgunda. After desultory fighting, the rebels soon surrendered to Maḥmūd on his promise to intercede with the sultan for their lives and safety, and this was the beginning of the policy of conciliation and compromise which Maḥmūd tried to pursue during the whole of his life.

Aḥmad II was succeeded by Humāyūn Shāh (862-5/1458-61). Maḥmūd had already secured a considerable position in the kingdom, and the new king appointed him as his prime minister, later bestowing on him the highly-esteemed title of Malik al-Tudjdjār, "Prince of Merchants". On Humāyūn's death his eldest son, who was barely eight years old, succeeded him as Niẓām al-Dīn Aḥmad III (865-7/1461-3). The late king had willed that the country should be governed during the minority of the new sulṭān by a council of regency consisting of Maḥmūd Gāwān, Ḵẖwādja Djahān Turk and the dowager queen, Maḵẖdūma Djahān Nargis Bēgam, who was to act as the president of the council with a casting vote on all matters of policy. The regency lasted throughout the reign of Aḥmad III and during the minority of the next sultan, Muḥammad III (867-87/1463-82). The short reign of Aḥmad III saw two major military operations, namely, a war with Kapilēs̲h̲war of Uṛisā (Orissa), who took advantage of the sultan's youth to invade the Deccan from the north-east, and the struggle with Maḥmūd K̲h̲ald̲j̲ī of Mālwā, who invaded it from the north; in both of these, Maḥmūd Gāwān's policy and strategy were successful. While Kapilēs̲h̲war had to retreat and pay a large indemnity, Maḥmūd K̲h̲ald̲j̲ī, who menaced the very existence of the Deccan as an independent state, was defeated with the help of the sulṭān of Gud̲j̲arāt [*q.v.*]. This alliance of Gud̲j̲arāt with the Deccan was initiated at the instance of Maḥmūd Gāwān and became the corner-stone of the foreign policy of the Bahmanī kingdom for many years to come.

Three years after the accession of Muḥammad III in 867/1463, a palace intrigue caused the murder of one of the members of the council of regency, K̲h̲ʷād̲j̲a D̲j̲ahān Turk, followed later by the retirement of the dowager queen from the day-to-day affairs of state. Maḥmūd Gāwān was now invested with the insignia of premiership and the title of K̲h̲ʷād̲j̲ā D̲j̲ahān [*q.v.*] conferred on him. Maḥmūd K̲h̲ald̲j̲ī was again repulsed with the help of Gud̲j̲arāt, and following the policy of conciliation already exercised effectively, the Deccan now entered into a treaty of friendship with Mālwā. Soon an opportunity arose for interference in the affairs of Uṛisā when in 875/1470-1 two factions came to grips at D̲j̲ād̲j̲nagar, the capital of the Gad̲j̲apatis, and one of them sought the help of the Bahmanī sultan (*JASB* [1893], and *Burhān-i maʾāt̲h̲ir*). Maḥmūd Gāwān thereupon sent Malik Ḥasan Baḥrī (later Niẓām al-Mulk and ancestor of the Niẓām-S̲h̲āhī dynasty of Aḥmadnagar [*q.v.*]) to Uṛisā. Malik Ḥasan not only succeeded in putting the rightful claimant on the Uṛisā throne, but also in annexing Rād̲j̲āmanḍrī and Konḍavidu to the Bahmanī Kingdom.

It was now the turn of the lands beyond the Western Ghāṭs to be pacified. Goa had already been reduced by the founder of the dynasty, ʿAlāʾ al-Dīn Bahman S̲h̲āh (748-59/1347-58), but it seems that it had subsequently passed into Vid̲j̲ayanagar's orbit. Moreover, certain local chieftains were in the habit of waylaying Bahmanī ships plying in the Arabian Sea. By a series of brilliant campaigns which lasted three years from 873/1469 to 876/1472, Maḥmūd Gāwān successfully negotiated the difficult terrain, captured the great fort of Sangamēs̲h̲war and boldly marched to Goa, which he entered on 20 S̲h̲aʿbān 876/1 February 1472.

The frontiers of the kingdom had now reached the Bay of Bengal in the east and the Arabian Sea in the west, and Maḥmūd Gāwān rightly felt that it was time to reform the administration which had remained more or less static since the reign of Muḥammad I (759-76/1358-75). He ordered that the whole land should be measured and a record of rights kept, thus forestalling the reforms of Akbar the Great and Rād̲j̲ā Tōḍar Mal by about a century. He re-divided the kingdom into eight instead of four *aṭrāf* (sing. *ṭaraf*) or provinces, brought certain tracts in each province under the direct rule of the sultan as royal domain, made *k̲ilʿadārs* or commanders of fortresses in each province directly responsible to the centre, and demanded accounts from military *d̲j̲āgīrdārs* or fiefholders. He thus curbed the power of the fiefholders and provincial magnates, who had exercised absolute power for several decades. Although himself an *Āfāk̲ī* or "Newcomer", he tried to keep the balance between the native *Dakhnīs* and the *Āfāk̲īs* in the matter of the distribution of high posts, and thus strove to solve a problem which had adversely affected the body-politic. Two significant events vastly increased the prestige of the kingdom, and with it that of the K̲h̲ʷād̲j̲ā. One was the complete rout of Purus̲h̲ottam of Uṛisā, who had advanced to the banks of the Godāvarī to make common cause with the rebels of Konḍavidu, and the other was the state visit of ʿĀdil K̲h̲ān Fārūk̲ī of K̲h̲āndēs̲h̲ to Bīdar. ʿĀdil K̲h̲ān's visit is remarkable in that it resulted in the circulation of Bahmanī coins in K̲h̲āndēs̲h̲ as well as the mention of the Bahmanī sultan's name in the *k̲h̲uṭba* at Burhānpur, the capital of the principality. Thus K̲h̲āndēs̲h̲, which was once at daggers drawn with the Deccan, became virtually a protectorate of the Bahmanīs at this time.

It was when Muḥammad III was away on an expedition to Nellur and Kānčī (Conjiverum) in S̲h̲awwāl 885/December 1481 that a conspiracy was formed in the royal camp at Konḍāpallī (Muṣṭafānagar, now in the Kris̲h̲na district of Āndhra Prades̲h̲) against Maḥmūd Gāwān. The old feudal lords resented the loss of their power at the hands of the K̲h̲ʷād̲j̲ā, while the *Dakhnīs* had never reconciled themselves to the rise of a mere "Newcomer" to such heights. Niẓām al-Mulk Baḥrī, who was the leader of the conspirators, persuaded Maḥmūd Gāwān's Ḥabs̲h̲ī private secretary, under the influence of strong drink, to affix the K̲h̲ʷād̲j̲ā's seal to a piece of paper. The conspirators then forged a letter purporting to be from the K̲h̲ʷād̲j̲ā to the Rād̲j̲ā of Uṛisā and suggesting that the time was opportune for an invasion of the Deccan. This letter was shown to the sultan on his return from the south. He at once summoned the K̲h̲ʷād̲j̲ā to his presence, and as his ears had been poisoned against him from time to time ever since he had been leading the western campaigns, he did not even enquire how the letter had come in the possession of Niẓām al-Mulk. The old man was decapitated forthwith as a traitor, on the sultan's orders, on 5 Ṣafar 886/5 April 1481 when he was 73 lunar years old.

The K̲h̲ʷād̲j̲ā was not merely the political and military leader of the Deccan, but was its cultural leader as well. He no doubt re-built a number of forts such as the one at Parenḍā, but it is the noble edifice of the great *madrasa* at Bīdar which was to remain a permanent symbol of his concern for the public welfare. The college is a three-storeyed building, covering a site of 205 ft by 180 ft., and is surrounded by a large courtyard which was once fringed by a thousand cubicles where students lived and were provided not only with free education but with food and clothes as well. The library was the central feature of the institution, and it is related that no one could give the K̲h̲ʷād̲j̲ā a more acceptable present than a rare manuscript. This and other works of utility such as water-works and numerous public buildings must have made Bīdar known far and wide. The Russian traveller, Afanasy Nikitin, who was in the Deccan from 1469 to 1474, says that this city was "the chief town of Hindustan" and was the centre of trade in horses, cloth, silk, pepper and many other species of merchandise.

Maḥmūd Gāwān continued the policy of making the kingdom the resort of the learned which had been initiated by Fīrūz S̲h̲āh (800-25/1397-1422). He was himself a scholar of renown and was recognised as one of the most learned exponents of the Persian language. He has left us two important works, namely the *Manāẓir al-inshā*ʾ and the *Riyāḍ al-inshā*ʾ. The former, which was compiled in 880/1475, is a handbook of Persian diction of the ornate type in fashion in those days, treating of the subject in a prolegomenon, two discourses and an epilogue. The *Riyāḍ al-inshā*ʾ is a collection of his letters written to kings, ministers, princes and divines in practically all the states in India and the Middle East. It contains historical material of almost unsurpassed value, as it is the only contemporary record of many important events in which the Kh^w^ādjā was the chief actor.

Maḥmūd Gāwān's real character may be gleaned from the contrast between the image of the public minister and the real, private man. Nikitin says that 500 men belonging to all walks of life sat down to dine with the minister every day and that his stables contained 2,000 horses of the best breed, while his mansion was guarded by a hundred armed men night and day. But as transpired after his death, he was personally a man of extremely simple habits. His treasurer swore to the sultan that the late minister's personal expenses did not exceed twelve silver pieces per day, and even this amount came out of the forty thousand *lārīs* which he had brought from Gīlān. The sultan realised too late the worth of the servant who had been so summarily done to death by his orders, and his remorse was so great that he himself died just one lunar year after the deed (5 Ṣafar 887/26 March 1482). Maḥmūd Gāwān's death was one of the causes of the downfall of the dynasty which he had served so well, and hastened the day when the provincial governors (sc. the ʿĀdilshāhīs at Bīdjāpur, the Barīdshāhīs at Bīdar, the ʿImādshāhīs in Berār and the Ḳuṭbshāhīs in Tilangāna [*q.vv.*]) became virtually autonomous and ultimately independent of the central authority.

Bibliography: Maḥmūd Gāwān, *Riyāḍ al-inshā*ʾ, Haydarābād Dn., 1948; al-Sakhāwī, *al-Ḍawʾ al-lāmiʿ*, x; Firishta, *Gulshan-i Ibrāhīmī*; V. Major, *India in the fifteenth century*; J. S. King, *History of the Bahmanī dynasty*; H. K. Sherwani, *Maḥmūd Gāwān, the great Bahmanī Wazīr*, Bombay 1942; idem, *The Bahmanīs of the Deccan, an objective study*, Hyderabad 1953; G. Yazdani, *Bidar, its history and monuments*, Oxford 1947; *The history and culture of the Indian people*. vi. *The Delhi sultanate*, Bombay 1960, 266-9, and bibl. at 768-9. (H. K. Sherwani)

MAḤMŪD KEMĀL. [See Inal].

MAḤMŪD NEDĪM PASHA, Ottoman bureaucrat and twice Grand Vizier under Sultan ʿAbd al-ʿAziz, was born in Istanbul in 1233/1817-18. He was the younger son of Gürdjü Meḥmed Nedjib Pasha (d. 1267/1850-1), who had a distinguished governmental career and became *wālī* of Syria and of Baghdād. After the traditional elementary education, Maḥmūd Nedīm at age 14 entered the scribal bureaucracy, in the *ṣadāret mektūbi*. He rose fairly rapidly, perhaps in part owing to his father's position, but also because he was intelligent and attracted the favourable notice of Muṣṭafā Reshīd Pasha [*q.v.*] and, later, of Meḥmed Emīn ʿĀlī Pasha [*q.v.*].

In 1256/1840-1 he entered the *āmedī ḳalemleri*. In Rabīʿ I 1263/February-March 1847 he was promoted to the first rank, second class, in the correspondence office of the grand vizier Reshīd Pasha. In Radjab 1265/May-June 1849, again under Reshīd's auspices, he became the deputy *āmeddji* [*q.v.*] of the *dīwān-i hümāyūn* [*q.v.*], and by Muḥarram 1266/November-December 1849 attained the full position. In 1270/1853 he became *beylikdji* of the *dīwān-i hümāyūn*.

Maḥmūd Nedīm's career then shifted into near-ministerial levels. Under Muṣṭafā Nāʾilī Pasha he was *ṣadāret müsteshārī* for three months from 23 Djumāda II 1270/24 March 1854, and then *müsteshār* of the Foreign Ministry from 29 Ramaḍān 1270/25 June 1854. For 16 days he was detached to carry orders to the commander-in-chief Ekrem ʿÖmer Pasha, in Bulgaria, during the war with Russia. On 7 Djumāda II 1271/25 February 1855 Maḥmūd Nedīm attained the rank of *wezīr* with appointment as *wālī* of Sidon. He was transferred as *wālī* to Damascus in Rabīʿ II 1272/December 1855 and to Izmir in Muḥarram 1274/August-September 1857. He managed to return to the capital in Radjab 1274/February-March 1858 as a member of the *Tanẓīmāt* Council. Two months later he was acting Foreign Minister for a time while the minister, Fuʾād Pasha [*q.v.*], was at the Paris conference on the Danubian Principalities. He became a minister, finally, on 20 Muḥarram 1275/30 August 1858 with the portfolio of commerce, from which he was dismissed in Djumādā I 1276/November-December 1859. For half a year he was unemployed.

Till this point, Maḥmūd Nedīm had a mixed reputation. He was thought to be able, but some considered him a sycophant and untrustworthy. Reshīd Pasha once compared him to mushy soap, suitable neither for washing hands nor for doing laundry. He knew the bureaucratic forms and language, but no foreign tongue save Arabic.

On 19 Dhu 'l-Ḥidjdja 1276/8 July 1860 Maḥmūd Nedīm was named *wālī* of Ṭarābulus-i Gharb, a post not much sought-after, at his own request, and remained there for seven years. Toward the end of this period occurred the original conspiracy of the small group of New Ottomans [see Yeñi ʿOthmānlîlar], of which Maḥmūd Nedīm's nephew Saghîr Aḥmed-zāde Meḥmed Bey was a member. Meḥmed Bey proposed that the grand vizier ʿĀlī Pasha, whom the conspirators detested, be replaced by his uncle Maḥmūd Nedīm. The plan was leaked to the authorities and known to ʿĀlī Pasha. Therefore in Dhu 'l-Ḥidjdja 1283/April-May 1867 Maḥmūd Nedīm returned to Istanbul to clear his name with the Grand Vizier. Although ʿĀlī at first refused to see him, Maḥmūd Nedīm eventually talked his way back into ʿĀlī's good graces. By 15 Ṣafar 1284/18 June 1867 Maḥmūd Nedīm was a member of the *Medjlis-i wālā-i aḥkām-i ʿadliyye*, on 23 Rabīʿ II 1284/24 August 1867 he was *daʿāwī nāẓirî*, and on 11 Dhu 'l-Ḳaʿda 1284/5 March 1868 was briefly *ṣadāret müsteshārî* for the second time. Eight days later he became Minister of Marine, a post which he held for more than three years, during ʿĀlī Pasha's last grand vizierate. Maḥmūd Nedīm cultivated relations with the Palace, catered to Sultan ʿAbd al-ʿAzīz's interests, and emerged as the sultan's choice to succeed ʿĀlī Pasha after ʿĀlī's death.

On 22 Djumāda II 1288/8 September 1871 Maḥmūd Nedīm entered on his first grand vizierate, which lasted eleven months. His administration was chaotic, marked by a constant shifting of officials both in provincial posts and in the capital (in 11 months: five *serʿaskers*, four navy ministers, four justice ministers, five finance ministers, six arsenal commanders, etc.). He cut salaries in the name of economy, exiled important rivals, among them Ḥusayn ʿAwnī [*q.v.*], to the provinces, hobbled the *wilāyet* system and in general created new enemies for himself. He evidently took bribes from the Khedive Ismāʿīl of Egypt. Although the New Ottomans at first welcomed his appointment as an improvement over the "tyrant" ʿĀlī, they were soon disenchanted. Nāmîḳ Kemāl [*q.v.*] in his newspaper *ʿIbret* began to criticise Maḥmūd Nedīm, who then suspended the paper and ordered Nāmiḳ Kemāl out of Istanbul to the post of *mutaṣarrif* of Gelibolu. The Russian ambassador, Ignatyev, however, thought well of Maḥmūd Nedīm's anti-*Tanẓīmāt* activities. The public began to use the nickname "Nedimoff" for the grand vizier. Eventually Sultan ʿAbd al-ʿAzīz seems to have become disillusioned, too; he later called Maḥmūd Nedīm duplicitous and corrupt, and spoke of him to the British ambassador. "in terms so disparaging that I have some hesitation in recording them in a despatch" (PRO. FO 78/2220, Elliot, 2 Nov. 1872). Maḥmūd Nedīm was dismissed suddenly on 25 Djumādā I 1289/31 July 1872 as the result of Midḥat Pasha's [*q.v.*] energetic representations to the sultan about the harm the Grand Vizier was causing. Midḥat, already and for ever after an opponent of Maḥmūd Nedīm, replaced him. Public rejoicing ensued.

For nearly three years Maḥmūd Nedīm was under a cloud. He was investigated and condemned for irregular financial dealings, but pardoned by ʿAbd al-ʿAzīz. In Rabīʿ II 1290/June 1873 he was sent into provincial exile as *wālī* of Kastamonu, after a month or two was transferred to forced residence in Trabzon, then on 22 Shaʿbān 1290/15 October 1873 was sent on to be *wālī* of Adana, from which post he was finally allowed to return to Istanbul on 23 Ṣafar 1292/31 March 1875. Somehow he had retained or regained the sultan's favour. He apparently persuaded ʿAbd al-ʿAzīz that he could deal with the revolt that broke out in July in Herzegovina, and spread to Bosnia. On 19 Radjab 1292/21 August 1875 Maḥmūd Nedīm was made president of the *Shūrā-yi dewlet* [*q.v.*], and four days later replaced Esʿad Pasha as Grand Vizier.

Maḥmūd Nedīm's second grand vizierate was, if anything, less successful than his first. He was confronted with a treasury crisis. Without funds for payment of the October coupons of Ottoman bonds, his ministry defaulted on half the amount on 6 October 1875, arousing much enmity from domestic and foreign bondholders. The revolt in Bosnia and Herzegovina grew, attracting support from Montenegro. Bulgarian revolutionaries rose in revolt early in May 1876; they were put down with much bloodshed. The French and German consuls in Salonika were killed by a mob as a by-product of a religious controversy. These events brought ineffectual reform palliatives from Maḥmūd Nedīm's government and provoked pressures and diplomatic intervention by the great powers. Russian backing for "a Grand Vizier devoted to Russia" (Nelidow, "Souvenirs...," *Revue des deux mondes*, 6th per., 27 [1915], 308) brought no solutions. Public sentiment rose against Maḥmūd Nedīm. On 8 May 1876, theological students in Istanbul began to strike; on 10 May, encouraged by Midḥat Pasha, they demonstrated to demand dismissal of Maḥmūd Nedīm. The sultan bowed and let him go on 11 May. The next day Müterdjim Meḥmed Rüshdī was appointed Grand Vizier, and allowed Maḥmūd Nedīm to go to Česhme rather than suffer more distant exile; actually, he took up residence on Sakïz Ada.

In 1879, when Tunuslu Khayr al-Dīn Pasha [*q.v.*] was Grand Vizier, Maḥmūd Nedīm was offered and declined the governorship of Mawṣil *wilayet*. He then lived on Midilli until 3 Dhu 'l-Ḳaʿda 1296/19 October 1879, in Meḥmed Saʿīad Pasha's grand vizierate, when he was appointed Minister of the Interior. On 20 Rabīʿ II 1300/26 February 1883, owing to a lengthy illness, he was dismissed and put on unemployment pay. He died on 7 Radjab 1300/14 May 1883 and was buried in Djaghaloghlu in Istanbul.

Maḥmūd Nedīm's reputation has generally been unsavoury. His opponents have stressed his Russophile views, his alleged venality, a character that included fickleness and deceitfulness, and his chaotic administrations. Yūsuf Kemāl Pasha thought him qualified only to be a chief secretary to a vizier. In each session of the Ottoman Chamber of Deputies, 1877 and 1878, there were votes to try him for crimes and incompetence. This was not done. Among Maḥmūd Nedīm's writings are some unpublished poems, a published one (*Ḥasb-i ḥāl*) on his career, and an unpublished *apologia pro vita sua*, *Mudāfaʿa-nāme* or *Reddiyye*, much quoted in Pakalın and İnal.

Bibliography: Ibnülemin Mahmud Kemal İnal, *Osmanlı devrinde son sadrıazamlar*, Istanbul 1940-53, 264-321 and picture at 258; Mehmed Zeki Pakalın, *Mahmud Nedim Paşa*, Istanbul 1940. These two quote extensively from the standard Ottoman histories and memoirs, and are the most informative. Meḥmed Thüreyyā, *Sidjill-i ʿOthmānī*, Istanbul 1308-15, iv, 336-7; İ. A. Gövsa, *Türk meşhurları ansiklopedisi*, Istanbul 1946, 235; *La Turquie*, 9 September 1871; Ahmed Cevdet, *Tezâkir*, 4 vols., Ankara 1953-67, indices; R. H. Davison, *Reform in the Ottoman Empire, 1856-1876*, Princeton 1963, index; Maḥmūd Djalāl al-Dīn, *Mirʾāt-i ḥaḳīḳat*, Istanbul 1326-7, i, 35-6, 91-4; ʿAbd al-Raḥmān Sheref, *Taʾrīkh muṣāḥabeleri*, Istanbul 1339, 187-8; Mithat Cemal Kuntay, *Namık Kemal*, Istanbul 1944-56, i, 152, 231, ii, 116-9; ʿAlī Ḥaydar Midḥat, *Midḥat Pasha, ḥayāt-i siyāsiyyesi*. i. *Tabṣira-yi ʿibret*, Istanbul 1325, 125-34; Meḥmed Memdūḥ, *Mirʾāt-i shuʾūnāt*, Izmir 1328, 45-66; Aḥmed Ṣāʾib, *Waḳʿa-yi Sulṭān ʿAbd al-ʿAzīz*, Cairo 1320, 190-91; R. Devereux, *The First Ottoman Constitutional period*, Baltimore 1963, 193, 240.

(R. H. Davison)

MAḤMŪD PASHA (? - 879/1474), Ottoman Grand Vizier. Contemporary Ottoman historians tell us nothing of his origins. Authors of *tadhkiras* from the 10th/16th century down to ʿOthmānzāde Tāʾib (*Ḥadīḳat al-wuzarāʾ*, Istanbul 1271/1854-5, 9; facs. repr., Freiburg 1969) state that he was a native of Aladja Ḥiṣār (Kruševac) in Serbia, but this seems unlikely. According to Phrantzes, he was born of a Serbian mother and a Greek father. Chalcocondylas makes his mother Bulgarian, while Kritovoulos (Turkish tr., *Taʾrīkh-i Meḥemmed Khān-i thānī*, in *TOEM*, Suppl. 1328/1910, 192) makes him the descendant of a noble Greek family, whose father, Michael, was a descendant of Alexios III Philathropenos. According to Martinus Crusius (*Turcograecia*, Basel 1584, 21), Maḥmūd Pasha was, on his mother's side, the Serbian-born grandson of the Byzantine nobleman Marko Yagari. He also tells us that Maḥmūd Pasha's cousin, George Amirutzes, the *protovestiarius* of the Comnene Emperor of Trebizond, David, was a grandson of the same Yagari. According to F. Babinger (*Mehmed the Conqueror and his time*, Eng. tr. R. Manheim, ed. W. Hickman, Princeton 1978, 115), based on Chalcocondylas (*L'Histoire de la décadence de l'Empire Grec*, Paris 1620, i, 229, 246), he was the son of Michael Angelus of Novo Brdo. He was in all probability a scion of the Angeli, i.e. the Thessalian branch of the Serbian despotate.

It is uncertain when the Ottomans captured Maḥmūd Pasha. The accounts in Chalcocondylas (*op. cit.*, i, 246), Tashköprüzāde (*al-Shaḳāʾiḳ al-nuʿmāniyya*, tr. Medjdī, Istanbul 1269/1852-3, 176) and ʿĀshïḳ Čelebi (*Tadhkira*, University Library, Istanbul, Turkish ms. 2406, f. 215a) are identical in all but a few minor details. They each relate how the commander Meḥmed Agha took Maḥmūd Pasha and his mother prisoner on the road between Novo Brdo and Smederovo and, since Ta<u>sh</u>köprüzāde (*loc. cit.*) tells us of Meḥmed A<u>gh</u>a's taking Maḥmūd from the "lands of infidelity" to Edirne, together with Mawlānā ʿAbd al-Karīm and Mawlānā Ayās (cf. ʿĀ<u>sh</u>ıḳ Čelebi, *loc. cit.*), it seems likely that Meḥmed A<u>gh</u>a patronised all three, and it is undoubtedly through him that he was presented to Murād II. Ta<u>sh</u>köprüzāde's claim that Murād II attached him to the suite of Prince Meḥemmed, later Meḥemmed II, is probably false (cf. ʿĀ<u>sh</u>ıḳ Čelebi, *op. cit.*, f. 214a).

He underwent a period of education in the Palace at Edirne and, after the accession of Meḥemmed II in 855/1451, began to receive royal favours. He attained the rank of *od<u>j</u>aḳ a<u>gh</u>asî*, and was in the sultan's company at the siege of Constantinople. According to some accounts, the sultan sent him to Constantinople at the beginning of the siege at the end of Rabīʿ I 857/beginning of April 1543 to demand the surrender of the city. During the siege, Maḥmūd Pa<u>sh</u>a and the *beglerbegi* of Anadolu, Isḥāḳ Pa<u>sh</u>a, received the command to attack the city wall between modern Edirne Kapı and Yedi Kule, and a section of the sea-walls in this area (Kritovoulos, *op. cit.*, 48, 76). Those *ta<u>dh</u>kiras* which include a biography of Maḥmūd Pa<u>sh</u>a and certain histories claim that Maḥmūd Pa<u>sh</u>a participated in the siege as a vizier and *beglerbegi*, but this information is almost certainly false. The most reliable sources agree that his promotion to the vizierate followed not the fall of <u>Kh</u>alīl Pa<u>sh</u>a <u>D</u>jandarlî [*q.v.*], but the dismissal of Zaganos Pa<u>sh</u>a in 858/1454 (Ibn Kemāl, *Tevârih-i âl-i Osmân, VII. defter*, ed. Şerafeddin Turan, Ankara 1954, 147; Ne<u>sh</u>rī, *Kitâb-i cihân-nümâ*, ed. F. R. Unat and M. A. Köymen, Ankara 1957, ii, 717; Enwerī, *Dustūr-nāme*, ed. Mükrimin Halil Yınanç, Istanbul 1928, 103; Idrīs-i Bitlīsī, *He<u>sh</u>t behi<u>sh</u>t*, Ali Emiri Library, Istanbul, Persian ms. 806, f. 83a). Since his uncle Ḳara<u>dj</u>a Beg was *beglerbegi* until his death at the siege of Belgrade in 860/1456 (Tewḳīʿī Meḥmed Pa<u>sh</u>a, *Tewārī<u>kh</u> al-salāṭīn al-ʿO<u>th</u>māniyya*, ed. Mükrimin Halil Yınanç, in *Türk taʾrī<u>kh</u>i en<u>dj</u>ümeni me<u>dj</u>mūʿasi* [1340/1921-2], 147), Maḥmūd Pa<u>sh</u>a must have become *beglerbegi* after his siege, as Oru<u>dj</u> Beg (*Tewārī<u>kh</u>-i āl-i ʿO<u>th</u>mān*, ed. F. Babinger, Hanover 1925, 72) and Chalcocondylas (*op. cit.*, i, 252) confirm (cf. also Ibn Kemāl, *op. cit.*, 147; ʿĀ<u>sh</u>ıḳ Čelebi, *op. cit.*, f. 214b). The statement by Küčük Ni<u>sh</u>ān<u>dj</u>î Ramaḍānzāde Meḥmed (*Taʾrī<u>kh</u>*, Istanbul 1279/1862-3, 162), that he was at the same time *ḳāḍī ʿasker*, is probably based on a reference in the *Menāḳib-nāme (Menāḳib-i Maḥmūd Pa<u>sh</u>a-yi Welī*, Ali Emiri Library, Istanbul, Turkish ms. 43, f. 50a), which makes it clear that he received his appointment temporarily while the *ḳāḍī ʿasker* ʿAlī Efendi performed the pilgrimage.

Maḥmūd Pa<u>sh</u>a accompanied Meḥemmed II on a number of campaigns, in all of which he achieved outstanding successes. The Sultan promoted him to the vizierate in recognition of his courageous exploits at the siege of Belgrade (Ibn Kemāl, *op. cit.*, 122), after which he served as vizier and *beglerbegi* of Rumelia. When, on 24 <u>D</u>jumādā I 863/31 March 1458, the Serbian Queen removed Maḥmūd Pa<u>sh</u>a's brother Michael Anglović and appointed a Catholic Bosnian in his stead, the Serbian boyars contacted Meḥemmed II and offered him suzerainty over Serbia (J. W. Zinkeisen, *Geschichte des Osmanischen Reiches in Europa*, Gotha 1845, ii, 116). The Sultan ordered Maḥmūd Pa<u>sh</u>a to settle the Serbian question. To the Rumelian troops which he had equipped at his own expense, Maḥmūd Pa<u>sh</u>a added the troops of Anadolu and 1,000 Janissaries which the Sultan had allotted to him (Dursun Beg, *Taʾrī<u>kh</u>-i Ebu 'l-Feth*, in *TOEM*, Suppl. 1330/1912, 82; Saʿd al-Dīn, *Tā<u>dj</u> al-tewārī<u>kh</u>*, Istanbul 1279/1862-3, i, 465) and marched to Sofia. He succeeded, with numerous promises, in overcoming the objections of the troops, who refused to advance when the Serbs announced that they would observe the terms of the agreement only if the Sultan came in person, and that otherwise they would refuse to surrender the fortresses and join with the Hungarians. Continuing the advance, the Ottoman forces seized several fortified places, the most important being Resava and Kuruca (for the other fortresses, see ʿĀ<u>sh</u>ıḳ-Pa<u>sh</u>a-zāde, *Tewārī<u>kh</u>-i āl-i ʿO<u>th</u>mān*, ed. ʿĀlī, Istanbul 1332/1913-14, 150; Dursun Beg, *op. cit.*, 86). Maḥmūd Pa<u>sh</u>a then unsuccessfully laid siege to Smederovo, before withdrawing to the fortress which the Sultan had built nearby. Shortly afterwards, he improved the fortifications, and captured the castles of Ostrovica and Rudnik (Dursun Beg, *op. cit.*, 89; Enwerī, *op. cit.*, 103; Ibn Kemāl, *op. cit.*, 154; Bihi<u>sh</u>tī, *Tewārī<u>kh</u>-i āl-i ʿO<u>th</u>mān*, BL ms., Add. or. 7869, f. 168a).

After celebrating *bayram* at Yellü Yurt near Ni<u>sh</u>, Maḥmūd Pa<u>sh</u>a appeared before Golubac. He seized and repaired the fort before despatching Minnet Beg-O<u>gh</u>lu Meḥmed Beg with *aḳın<u>dj</u>î* troops to raid into Hungary. He then joined the Sultan in Skoplje. It was he who dissuaded the Sultan from demobilising the army when the Hungarians crossed the Danube. A number of sources state wrongly that Maḥmūd Pa<u>sh</u>a commanded the Serbian expedition which resulted in the fall of Smederovo in 864/1459 (cf. J. von Hammer, *GOR*, i, 447), whereas Dursun Beg (*op. cit.*, 90) and Idrīs-i Bitlīsī (*op. cit.*) make the Sultan himself the commander (cf. also Zinkeisen, *op. cit.*, ii, 116).

In 864/1460, Maḥmūd Pa<u>sh</u>a took part in Meḥemmed II's Morean campaign (see D. Zakythinos, *Le despotat grec de Morée*, Paris 1932, i, 285 ff.) On the Sultan's command he laid siege to the fortress of Mistra which the Despot Demetrios held and, with the Sultan's Greek secretary, Thomas Katavolenos, acting as intermediary, he persuaded the Despot to surrender and sent him, on 9 <u>Sh</u>aʿbān/30 May, to the Sultan in Istanbul. Since the Despot had voluntarily surrendered the fortress, the Sultan treated him well (Ducas, *Historia Byzantina*, Bonn 1834, 521; Kritovoulos, *op. cit.*, 128; Dursun Beg, *op. cit.*, 94; Ibn Kemāl, *op. cit.*, 168).

In the following year, Maḥmūd Pa<u>sh</u>a served with great distinction under the sultan on the campaign against Sinop, Amasra and Trebizond. Meḥemmed II apparently attached great importance to the conquest of the Genoese-held Amasra, which earlier sultans had neglected to capture (ʿA<u>sh</u>ıḳ Pa<u>sh</u>a-zāde, *op. cit.*, 153; Ne<u>sh</u>rī, *op. cit.*, ii, 739), and despatched Maḥmūd Pa<u>sh</u>a to blockade the city with a force of 150 ships, while he himself came overland. In 865/1461, the city surrendered to the Ottomans (Ne<u>sh</u>rī, *loc. cit.*; Ibn Kemāl, *op. cit.*, 185; Ḥadīdī, *Tewārī<u>kh</u>-i āl-i ʿO<u>th</u>mān*, University Library, Istanbul, Turkish ms. 1268, f. 126b). Maḥmūd Pa<u>sh</u>a also mounted the operations which resulted in the fall of Sinop. Sending a fleet of 100 galleys from Istanbul, with a letter written by Dursun Beg, he himself went first to Edirne and then to Bursa with the assembled troops. In describing the campaign Ne<u>sh</u>rī (*op. cit.*, ii, 743) wrote: "Maḥmūd Pa<u>sh</u>a was now at the height of his glory. It was as though the sultan had renounced the sultanate and bestowed it on Maḥmūd". In describing the council held at Bursa in the Sultan's presence, the Ottoman writers tell how Maḥmūd Pa<u>sh</u>a influenced the other members by speaking against the enemy of the Ottomans, Isfendiyār-Og͟hlu Ismāʿīl Beg of Sinop, and attribute the preparations for the expedition to Maḥmūd Pas͟ha. According to an anonymous *Taʾrīk͟h-i āl-i ʿOt͟hmān* (Library of the Topkapı Sarayı, ms. Revan 1099, 91), he spread the rumour that the expedition was aimed against Trebizond. At Ankara, the sultan announced the true goal of the campaign, and sent Maḥmūd Pas͟ha ahead to Sinop. Despatching a letter composed by Dursun Beg, Maḥmūd Pas͟ha secured Ismāʿīl Beg's submission to the Sultan (Dursun Beg, *op. cit.*, 98; ʿĀs͟hiḳ-Pas͟ha-zāde, *op. cit.*, 156; Chalcocondylas, *op. cit.*, i, 274. See also Yaşar Yücel, *Candar oğulları beyliği*, in *Belleten*, xxxiv/135 (1970), 373-407).

Before the Trebizond campaign, Maḥmūd Pas͟ha accompanied the sultan on his way to confront Uzun Ḥasan Aḳ Ḳoyunlu, as far as Yassī Čimen, where, according to one account, a joint deputation from Uzun Ḥasan's mother Sara and Kürd S͟heyk͟h Ḥasan, the *beg* of Čemis͟hgezek, secretly presented him with a petition for peace (Saʿd al-Dīn, *op. cit.*, i, 479). Afterwards, he took part in the Trebizond campaign as commander of the troops of Rumelia. At the head of the left wing in the vanguard of the army, Maḥmūd Pas͟ha appeared before Trebizond, and persuaded first the townspeople, and then the Emperor David and his family to surrender (Chalcocondylas, *op. cit.*, i, 278; Crusius, *op. cit.*, 21, 121). As David's *protovestiarius*, Maḥmūd Pas͟ha's cousin, the philosopher George Amirutzes played an important role as intermediary, which had led a number of Greek writers to accuse him of treachery (Ducas, *op. cit.*, 343; on the fall of Trebizond, see J. P. Fallmerayer, *Geschichte des Kaisertums Trapezunt*, Munich 1827; Heath Lowry, *The Ottoman tahrir defters as a source for urban demographic history: the case study of Trabzon*, Ph. D. thesis, UCLA 1977, unpublished, ch. i [in course of revision by the author]).

In 866-7/1462, Maḥmūd Pas͟ha participated in the Wallachian campaign, where he successfully prevented Vlad Drakul from routing Ewrenos Beg's *aḳind͟jī* troops and repulsed Vlad's night attack (Enwerī, *op. cit.*, 104; Dursun Beg, *op. cit.*, 106). Vlad sought refuge in Hungary, where he was imprisoned by Matthias Corvinus. According to S. Ferencs (*Magyaroszág a török hoditas korban*, Budapest 1886, 41), Matthias' motive in imprisoning him was a letter which he had sent in the same year to Meḥemmed II and Maḥmūd Pas͟ha, offering Transylvania to the Ottomans (cf. Zinkeisen, *op. cit.*, ii, 176). In 862/458, the Duke of Lesbos, Niccolò II Gattilusio, had strangled his brother Domenico, whom he accused of collaboration with the Ottomans. This provided Meḥemmed II with a pretext to attack the island in 866/1462. Placed in command of the expedition, Maḥmūd Pas͟ha besieged Lesbos with a fleet of about 60 galleys and 7 transport vessels (sources differ as to the exact number of ships) and a portion of the army. He bombarded the city with 27 guns and captured it on 24 D͟hu 'l-Ḥid͟jd͟ja 866/19 September 1462. According to some sources, the city was stormed (Dursun Beg, *op. cit.*, 112); according to others, it surrendered voluntarily (Ducas, *op. cit.*, 346, 511; Kritovoulos, *op. cit.*, 163; ʿĀs͟hiḳ-Pas͟ha-zāde, *op. cit.*, 163). Maḥmūd Pas͟ha imprisoned the Duke and made a register of the booty (Nes͟hrī, *op. cit.*, ii, 759) and gave the government of the island to ʿAlī al-Bisṭāmī (F. Babinger, *op. cit.*, 211).

When the Bosnian king Stjepan Tomašević laid claim to Smederovo and failed to send tribute, the Sultan determined on the conquest of Bosnia. On 3 Ramaḍān 867/22 May 1463, the Sultan seized Bobovac and, resolving to capture the king at Jajce, sent Maḥmūd Pas͟ha to lay siege to this fortress. Maḥmūd Pas͟ha sent Ṭurak͟hān-Og͟hlu ʿÖmer Beg ahead on a raid. The king surrendered when he heard that the Sultan had besieged Jajce. Maḥmūd Pas͟ha then received orders to prevent the attacks of the Venetians who were inciting the Greek towns in the Morea to rebellion (H. Kretschmayr, *Geschichte von Venedig*, Gotha 1920, ii, 372). He marched to the Morea, routed the Venetians and captured Argos. His victories frightened the Greek rebels into submission. He then sent ʿÖmer Beg to raid the Venetian territories in the Morea, while he himself was despatched to relieve Lesbos which the Venetians were besieging. Within 12 days, he raised a fleet of 110 ships and pursued the Venetians, who had abandoned Lesbos and retreated to Euboea.

In 868/early 1464, when the Hungarians had passed to the attack, the Sultan, himself occupied with the siege of Jajce, ordered Maḥmūd Pas͟ha on a winter campaign against Hungary. Maḥmūd Pas͟ha sent words of encouragement to Zvornik to resist the Hungarians and, shortly afterwards, sent Mīk͟hāl-og͟hlu ʿAlī Beg to this fortress with *aḳind͟jī* troops, forcing the Hungarians to withdraw (Enwerī, *op. cit.*, 105; Ibn Kemāl, *op. cit.*, 273; Kritovoulos, *op. cit.*, 178). In 869-70/1465, Maḥmūd Pas͟ha conducted negotiations with Venice and, in the following year, took part in campaigns in Albania under the command of the Sultan (*Müns͟heʾāt*, ms. Selim Ağa Library, Istanbul 862; Kritovoulos, *op. cit.*, 189; Ibn Kemāl, *op. cit.*, 300).

In 872/1468, Meḥemmed II intervened in the troubles in Ḳaramān following the death of Ḳaramān-og͟hlu Ibrāhīm Beg. Accompanying the Sultan to Konya and Gevele, Maḥmūd Pas͟ha received orders to pursue the *beg* of Ḳaramān, Pīr Aḥmed, whom he was, however, unable to capture. Maḥmūd Pas͟ha's rival, Rūm Meḥmed Pas͟ha, used this opportunity to win the Sultan and the army to his cause, by ascribing Maḥmūd Pas͟ha's failure to negligence. Although the event angered the sultan (Saʿd al-Dīn, *op. cit.*, i, 511), he concealed his wrath and sent Maḥmūd Pas͟ha firstly in pursuit of the Ṭurg͟hudlu Turcomans and then, shortly afterwards, commanded him to deport all the master-craftsmen from Konya and Lārenda to Istanbul. Maḥmūd Pas͟ha could not, however, restrain himself from absolving some of these from deportation, and offering his consolation to the rest (Ibn Kemāl, *op. cit.*, 291). To discredit him further, his rivals claimed that he had deported only the poor, and spared the rich in return for bribes (Ḥadīdī, *op. cit.*, f. 139b; ʿĀs͟hiḳ-Pas͟ha-zāde, *op. cit.*, 170). It was not long before these accusations influenced the Sultan. Maḥmūd Pas͟ha's post went to Rūm Meḥmed Pas͟ha and, according to an unsubstantiated report (F. Babinger, *op. cit.*, 272) the former Grand Vizier's tent was collapsed over his head when his army arrived at Afyon Karaḥiṣār. Through the misrepresentations of Rūm Meḥmed Pas͟ha, he had been dismissed from both the vizierate and the *beglerbegilik* of Rumelia.

Ibn Kemāl (*op. cit.*, 293) and Ḥadīdī (*op. cit.*, f. 140a) state that, shortly after his dismissal, Maḥmūd Pas͟ha retired to his *k͟hāṣṣ* but, before long, he was appointed Admiral (*ḳapudan*) with the rank of *sand͟jaḳ begi* of Gelibolu, with the task of restoring and equipping the Ottoman fleet (spring 873/1469 or 874/1470).

On 5 D͟hu 'l-Ḥid͟jd͟ja 874/5 June 1470, he left Gelibolu at the head of a large fleet to attack the Venetian island of Euboea (Negroponte, Eğriboz). Maḥmūd Pas͟ha arrived off Euboea after capturing the island of Skiros and warding off the Venetian Admiral Niccolò da Canale. Approaching the island from the mainland with a large army (Maʿnawī, *Feth-nāme-yi Eğriboz*, in *Fatih ve Istanbul*, Istanbul 1954, i, 305), he persuaded the Sultan, who was hesitant, despite having had a bridge built on which he had crossed over from the mainland, to press on with the conquest of the island (Maʿālī, *Khünkār-nāme*, ms. Library of the Topkapı Sarayı, 1417, f. 9a; Dursun Beg, *op. cit.*, 140; Chalcocondylas, *op. cit.*, ii, 113; Orudj Beg, *op. cit.*, 127). The island capitulated on 13 Muḥarram 875/12 July 1470.

When Uzun Ḥasan's troops began to advance into Anatolia, Maḥmūd Pasha, in recognition of his part in the conquest of Euboea, replaced Rūm Meḥmed Pasha as Grand Vizier (Dursun Beg, *op. cit.*, 148; Ibn Kemāl, *op. cit.*, 350). In Istanbul, he attended the council which the Sultan had convened to consider what measures to take against Uzun Ḥasan. At Maḥmūd Pasha's suggestion, the *beglerbegi* of Anadolu, Dāwūd Pasha, serving nominally under Prince Muṣṭafā, was sent against Uzun Ḥasan. According to contemporary sources, Maḥmūd Pasha's refusal of the leadership led to a breach between himself and the sultan.

On 13 Dhu 'l-Ḳaʿda 877/11 April 1473, Maḥmūd Pasha left Istanbul with the sultan and marched to Sivas, where he encouraged Meḥemmed to attack Ḳaraḥiṣār-i Sharḳī (Shebīnḳaraḥiṣār) [see ḲARA ḤIṢĀR]. The Sultan rejected his advice and, at the battle of Otluḳ Beli, cast him in a secondary role by positioning him with the *beglerbegi* of Rumelia, Khāṣṣ Murād Pasha. Maḥmūd Pasha acted with great perspicacity and, perceiving Uzun Ḥasan's strategy, warned Khāṣṣ Murād not to cross the Euphrates. Khāṣṣ Murād ignored him and, after his death, Maḥmūd Pasha fought with Uzun Ḥasan's son, Ughurlu Muḥammad (Maʿālī, *op. cit.*, f. 29a). At the battle of Bashkent on 19 Rabīʿ I 878/11 August 1473, he fought among Dāwūd Pasha's forces (R. R. Arat, *Fatih Sultan Mehmed'in yarlığı*, in *Turkiyat mecmuası*, vi [1936-9], 285-322). Popular opinion attributed the victory to Maḥmūd Pasha (Maʿālī, *op. cit.*, 154); but Maḥmūd Pasha's enemies disgraced him in the sultan's eyes and caused his downfall (Bihishtī, *op. cit.*, f. 202b).

He retired to his estates at Khāṣṣköy, but returned to Istanbul on the death of Prince Muṣṭafā and, against the advice of his *khʷādja*, Kürt Ḥāfiẓ, appeared before the sultan. The sultan received him coldly. Suspecting him of taking pleasure in the death of Prince Muṣṭafā, he imprisoned him in Yedi Ḳule. He was executed shortly afterwards on 3 Rabīʿ I 879/18 July 1474 (Ibn Kemāl, *op. cit.*, 376-7; Saʿd al-Dīn, *op. cit.*, i, 553 gives the month as Rabīʿ II) and buried in the *türbe* near the mosque in Istanbul which he had endowed (built 867/1462).

Bibliography: for further references see *İA* art. *Mahmûd Paşa* (M. Şehabeddin Tekindağ) of which this article is an abridged and slightly emended translation. See also Konstantin Mihailović, *Memoirs of a Janissary*, tr. B. Stolz, with historical commentary by S. Soucek, Michigan 1975; Selahettin Tansel, *Osmanlı kaynaklarına göre Fatih Sultan Mehmed'in siyasi ve askeri faaliyeti*, Ankara 1953. (C. H. IMBER)

MAḤMŪD PASHA, an Ottoman governor or *beylerbeyi* of Yemen and of Egypt in the 10th/16th century, whose avarice and devotion to self-promotion led to the near-expulsion of the Ottomans from southwestern Arabia. A Bosnian by birth, Maḥmūd was selected at Damascus in 944/1538 by Dāwūd Pasha, the new governor of Egypt (945-56/1538-49), as his *ketkhudā*. He subsequently held various positions in Egypt, including those of *amīr al-ḥadjdj* for 957/1550 and 958/1551 and of *sandjaḳ beyi*, making both enemies and friends in his pursuit and distribution of wealth. In 967/1560, he gained the governorship of Yemen through the influence of Khādim ʿAlī Pasha, the governor of Egypt (966-7/1559-60), and probably by purchase. His appointment proved the first in a series of unfortunate appointments to the governorship of Yemen, where Ottoman authority had recently been much expanded and consolidated. Arriving deeply in debt, Maḥmūd's only apparent goal in Yemen was to exploit its riches for his own gain. Towards this, he demoralised the Ottoman soldiery by grossly further debasing the silver coinage to retain the surplus precious metal for himself; and he alienated Ottoman allies among the non-Zaydī population by seizing their wealth without pretext and levying taxes on previously tax-exempt communities.

When recalled in 972/1565, Maḥmūd lavished much of his accumulated fortune among the influential persons of Istanbul in order to gain the governorship of Egypt. To enhance his reputation and chances of success, he persuaded the Grand Vizier Ṣoḳollu Meḥmed Pasha, a fellow-Bosnian, to divide Yemen into two *beylerbeyiliks* (5 Djumādā II 973/28 December 1565). This arrangement proved destructive to Ottoman interests for the three years during which it remained in effect, and contributed to the collapse of Ottoman rule in Yemen by 976/1568-9. In 973/1566, Maḥmūd secured his long-coveted posting to Cairo, where, according to Egyptian chronicles, he ruthlessly extorted private wealth, and from where he was able to manipulate official dispatches from Yemen reflecting adversely on his reputation and warning of the degenerating situation there. The steady erosion of Ottoman authority in Yemen was thus concealed from Istanbul until after his assassination at Cairo in Djumādā I 975/November 1567.

Bibliography: The only comprehensive contemporary source is the Arabic chronicle by Ḳuṭb al-Dīn al-Nahrawālī, *al-Barḳ al-yamānī*, published as *Ghazawāt al-djarākisa wa 'l-atrāk fī djunūb al-djazīra*, ed. Ḥamad al-Djāsir, al-Riyāḍ 1967. Its author, who met with Maḥmūd Pasha on at least three occasions, incorporated all of the relevant material provided by the Egyptian chronicles, including *al-Minaḥ al-raḥmāniyya* by Ibn Abi 'l-Surūr al-Bakrī. Two modern studies dealing in part with this individual are M. Sālim, *al-Fatḥ al-ʿUthmānī al-awwal li-'l-Yaman*, Cairo 1969, and J. R. Blackburn, *The collapse of Ottoman authority in Yemen*, in *WI*, xix (1980), 119-76. (J. R. BLACKBURN)

MAḤMŪD B. ʿABD AL-KARĪM B. YAḤYĀ **SHABISTARĪ**, (or SHABUSTARĪ, according to modern Azeri writers) Shaykh Saʿd al-Dīn, Persian mystic and writer.

He was born at Shabistar, a small town near the north-eastern shore of Lake Urmiya. The date of his birth is unknown, but would have to be fixed about 686/1287-8 if the report that he died at the age of 33 (mentioned in an inscription on a tombstone erected on his grave in the 19th century) is accepted. He is said to have led the life of a prominent religious scholar at Tabrīz. Travels to Egypt, Syria and the Ḥidjāz are mentioned in the introduction to the *Saʿādat-nāma.* He may also have lived for some time at Kirmān where, in later times, a group of mystics, known as the Khʷādjagān, claimed to descend from a marriage of his contracted in that city (cf. Zayn al-ʿĀbidīn Shīrwānī, *Riyāḍ al-siyāḥa*, Tehran

1334/1955, 89-90). In the Persian *tadhkiras*, dates varying between 718/1318 and 720/1320-1 are given for his death. The tomb at Shabistar, where he was buried next to his teacher Bahāʾ al-Dīn Yaʿḳūb Tabrīzī, has become a place of pilgrimage. It has been restored several times during the last century.

The fame of Maḥmūd rests entirely on a short *mathnawī* (1,008 *bayats* in the most recent edition), the *Gulshan-i rāz* ("The rose garden of the secret"). According to the poet's introduction, it was written in the month of Shawwāl 717/December 1317-January 1318 in reply to a versified letter (*nāma*) sent by a "well-known notable" (*buzurgī mashhūr*) from Khurāsān. A generally accepted tradition, appearing for the first time at the end of the 9th/15th century in Djāmī's *Nafaḥāt al-uns* (ed. Tehran 1337/1958, 605), specifies that the letter contained questions on difficult points of mystical doctrine and was composed by Ḥusaynī Sādāt Amīr [*q.v.*], who was an expert writer on the subject in his own right. These details are not confirmed by the text of the poem. The text of the letter, which is extant in some manuscripts of the *Gulshan-i rāz*, was probably only put together afterwards with lines taken from the lines of the poem itself, which precede each of the fifteen main divisions under the heading *suʾāl* ("question"). The answers given by the poet are subdivided into theoretical parts (*ḳāʾida*) and illustrative parts (*tamthīl*). The subject-matter of the poem is the doctrine of man's perfection through gnosis. This involves a number of cosmological, psychological and metaphysical themes as well as topics proper to the Ṣūfī traditions, such as the problem posed by expressions of identification with the Divine Being. The influence of Ibn al-ʿArabī, acknowledged by Maḥmūd in his *Saʿādāt-nāma*, is quite obvious. He also continues, however, the older tradition of Persian religious poetry as it appears from his treatment of poetical images as mystical symbols in the last sections of the *Gulshan-i rāz*, and from a reference to ʿAṭṭār [*q.v.*] as his example.

The great value attached to the poem is reflected, especially, in the many commentaries which were written on it throughout the centuries. The diversity of its contents, in spite of its concision, made the *Gulshan-i rāz* into a convenient starting-point to elaborate expositions of mystical doctrine, like the celebrated *Mafātīḥ al-iʿdjāz* by Shams al-Dīn Muḥammad b. Yaḥyā al-Lāhidjī al-Nūrbakhshī, dated 877/1472-3 (several editions, the latest by Ghulām-Riḍā Kaywān-Samīʿī, Tehran 1337/1958). Other notable commentators were Ḍiyāʾ al-Dīn ʿAlī Turka Khudjandī (d. 835/1431-2), Niẓām al-Dīn Maḥmūd al-Ḥusaynī "al-Dāʿī ilā 'llāh" (d. *ca.* 869/1464-5) and Shudjāʿ al-Dīn Kurbālī, who wrote his work between 856/1452-3 and 867/1462-3. As early as 829/1425-6, a Turkish translation in *mathnawī* verses was dedicated to the Ottoman sultan Murād II by Elwān Shīrāzī (cf. E. Rossi, *Elenco di manoscritti turchi della Bibl. Vaticana*, Vatican City 1953, 236; B. Flemming, *Türkische Handschriften*, i, Wiesbaden 1968, no. 366). Imitations were composed until the present century, e.g. the *Gulshan-i rāz-i djadīd*, an appendix to the *Zabūr-i ʿadjam* (1927) by Muḥammad Iḳbāl. (See further on the commentaries, translations and imitations of the *Gulshan-i rāz*: A. Gulčīn-i maʿānī, in *Nuskhahā-yi khaṭṭī*, iv, Tehran 1344/1965, 53-124; Munzawī, ii/1, 1248-53 and *passim.*) A manuscript with glosses by an anonymous Ismāʿīlī author was brought to notice by W. Ivanow (*JBBRAS*, viii [1932], 69-78) and published by H. Corbin.

The 17th-century traveller Jean Chardin was the first Western writer to note the importance of this poem to the Persian Ṣūfīs as a "somme théologique" (*Voyages*, ed. Langlès, Paris 1811, iv, 453). It was then used by F. A. D. Tholuck as a source of his study on Persian mysticism (*Sufismus*, Berlin 1821; wrongly ascribed to "Asisi") and his anthology of mystical poetry in German translation (*Blüthensammlung aus der morgenländischen Mystik*, Berlin 1825). The text, with a full translation, was published by J. von Hammer-Purgstall (*Rosenflor des Geheimnisses*, Pesth-Leipzig 1838) and by E. H. Whinfield (*The mystic rose garden*, London 1880; repr. 1978). Several other editions were published in Iran and on the Indian subcontinent. A critical edition was prepared by Gurban-eli Memmedzade (Baku 1973).

Of the other works ascribed to Maḥmūd Shabistarī, the most likely to be authentic are the *mathnawī* called the *Saʿadat-nāma*, on mystical theology, containing also valuable data for the biography of the author (cf. Rieu, ii, 871; Ateş, no. 351/1; Munzawī, iv, 2909-10) and *Ḥaḳḳ al-yaḳīn fī maʿrifat rabb al-ʿālamīn*, a prose work which was repeatedly printed (cf. Browne iii, 149-50; Munzawī, ii/1, 1129-30). The *Mirʾāt al-muḥaḳḳiḳīn*, also in prose, is in some manuscripts ascribed to Ibn Sīnā or others (cf. Munzawī, ii/1, 842-4 and 1374-5). No longer extant are the *Shāhid-nāma*, mentioned in *Ḥaḳḳ al-yaḳīn* as well as in Gāzurgāhī's *Madjālis al-ʿushshāḳ*, and a translation of Muḥammad al-Ghazālī's *Mishkāt al-anwār*. The *mathnawī* called *Kanz al-ḥaḳāʾiḳ*, published under Maḥmūd Shabistari's name (Tehran 1344/1965), seems to be identical with a poem wrongly attributed to ʿAṭṭār (cf. H. Ritter, in *Isl.*, xxv [1939], 158 f.; idem, in *Oriens*, xi (1958), 21 f.; Ateş, no. 122/13). The real author is probably Pahlawān Maḥmūd Pūryār Khʷārazmī (cf. Ateş, under nos. 351/2 and 382; Munzawī, iv, 3059-60). Some of his *ghazals* and quatrains are extant in anthologies (cf. e.g. Ethé, *India Office*, no. 1747; Ismailov, 165).

Bibliography: Ch. Rieu, *Cat. of the Pers. mss. in the Brit. Museum*, ii, London 1881; H. Ethé, in *Gr.I.Ph.*, ii; idem, *Cat. of the Pers. mss. in the Library of the India Office*, Oxford 1903; Browne, iii, 146-50; H. H. Schaeder, in *ZDMG*, lxxix (1925), 253 ff.; M. A. Tarbiyat, in *Armaghān*, xii (1310/1931), 601-10; idem, *Dānishmandān-i ʿĀdharbāydjān*, Tehran 1314/1935, 334-8; Kaywān-Samīʿī, introd., to the ed. of *Mafātīḥ al-iʿdjāz*, Tehran 1337/1958, pp. lxxvii ff.; Tahsin Yazıcı, in *İA*, s.v. *Şebisteri*; H. Corbin, *Trilogie ismaélienne*, Tehran-Paris 1961; E. E. Bertel's, *Izbraniye trudi. Sufizm i sufiyskaya literatura*, Moscow 1965, 109-25; A. Ateş, *İstanbul kütüphanelerinde farsça manzum eserler*, i, Istanbul 1968; A. Munzawī, *Fihrist-i nuskhahā-yi fārsī*, ii/1, Tehran 1349/1970 and iv, Tehran 1351/1972; Shaig Ismailov, *Filosofiya Makhmuda Shabustari*, Baku 1976.

(J. T. P. de Bruijn)

MAḤMŪD SHEWḲAT PASHA (1856-1913), Ottoman general, war minister and Grand-Vizier (1913), was born in Baghdād. He came from a Georgian family long settled in ʿIrāḳ and thoroughly Arabised, so much so that he was known as ʿArab Maḥmūd at the War Academy. His father Ketkhudāzāde Süleymān was a former *mutaṣarrif* of Baṣra, and his mother an Arab lady of the ancient house of al-Farūkhī. After completing his early education in Baghdād he entered the War Academy in Istanbul, graduating in 1882 at the head of his class. He was appointed to the General Staff with the rank of captain and thereafter promotions came with regularity. He rose to the rank of major in 1886, colonel (1891), brigadier-general (1894), and divisional general or *ferīḳ* (1901). In 1905 he became army commander or *birindji ferīḳ* and was appointed governor of Ḳosova, one of the most troublesome provinces in Ottoman Macedonia. He soon established a reputation as a tough, efficient, and fair-minded administrator who did not kow-tow to the Ḥamīdian clique in Istanbul. As a result, immediately after the constitution was proclaimed in July 1908, Shewḳat Pasha was appointed commander of the Third Army at Salonica and in November, acting Inspector-General of Rumelia, succeeding Ḥüseyn Ḥilmī [*q.v.*].

In April 1909 when military insurrection and counter-revolution broke out in Istanbul, Shewḳat Pasha marched with his Third Army from Salonica and crushed it with ruthless determination. He soon emerged as the most powerful political-military figure in the Empire. Though he permitted the creation of a civilian government, Shewḳat Pasha, as martial law commander and Inspector-General of the first three army corps, refused to accept its authority, especially its attempts to control the military budget. For a time there was even tension between the Pasha and the Committee of Union and Progress (*Ittiḥād we Teraḳḳī Djemʿiyyeti* [*q.v.*]), whose fortune he had saved in April 1909, but which resented the Pasha's independence of cabinet control. When Ibrāhīm Ḥaḳḳī Pasha [*q.v.*] became Grand Vizier in 1910, he tried to bring Maḥmud Shewkat under cabinet control by appointing him Minister of War. But this scheme did not work either and the Pasha even resigned (October 1910) when the Finance Minister attempted to inspect military spending. The ministerial crisis that followed was resolved on the Pasha's terms: the audit law was not to be applied to the War Ministry.

By the beginning of 1911, as the government faced rebellion in the Yemen, Albania and Macedonia, as well as political dissension at home, there were rumours in the press that Shewḳat Pasha intended to seize power and set up a military dictatorship. Despite his independence of and contempt for the civilians, Shewḳat Pasha had no such intentions. He denied these charges in the Assembly, claiming that he had not availed of such an opportunity when it had presented itself in April 1909. His position—and that of the CUP—declined following the outbreak of an unsuccessful war with Italy in September 1911. By the spring of 1912 an anti-CUP opposition had emerged in the army, reminiscent of the movement of 1908. Shewḳat Pasha introduced legislation to curb this movement, but with no effect. The rebellion continued unabated, and he was forced to resign as War Minister on 9 July 1912 though he retained his military command.

Shewḳat Pasha remained in political eclipse until 23 January 1913 when the CUP seized power. Again, the Unionists turned to the Pasha because of his popularity with the army and the people, and had him appointed Grand Vizier and War Minister. But now the Unionists were in control, and used Shewḳat Pasha's talents to reorganise the Ottoman army after the disasters of the Balkan Wars. It was under Maḥmud Shewḳat's influence that the decision to invite a German military mission under Liman von Sanders was taken. Meanwhile, in the turmoil following the fall of Edirne (26 March 1913), the Liberal opposition began to conspire to overthrow the CUP. As a part of that conspiracy, Shewḳat Pasha was assassinated on 11 June as he drove to the Sublime Porte.

Maḥmūd Shewḳat Pasha was one of the most important military-political figures of the Young Turk period. Despite the role he played, he lacked political ambition and his principal concern was always the interest of the amy and the state. He created neither a clique in the army nor a political faction in the CUP. He therefore found himself totally isolated in the political crisis of 1912 and was forced to resign. While he collaborated with the Unionists, he did not trust them nor they him: any co-operation between them was based on the shared goal of an independent and strong Ottoman state. While Turkish sources do not deal adequately with his alleged financial corruption, German sources, quoted by George Hallgarten, find him "hardly less corrupt than other Turks" (*Imperialismus vor 1914*, ii, Munich 1951, 139). Yet it is worth noting that he did prevent the Unionists from investigating the pilfering of the Yīldīz Palace treasure by martial law authorities after April 1909. He was always considered pro-German, and there can be little doubt that his ten years in Germany and the influence that Field Marshal von der Goltz had upon him inclined him in that direction. But there was no question of his seizing power in order to set up a military régime devoted to German interests, as a Unionist paper claimed, even in 1909. Maḥmud Shewḳat Pasha was primarily a professional soldier and a cautious statesman devoted entirely to the Ottoman state, and unwilling to involve it in any rash adventure. While he was alive there was little danger that he would take any risks that would threaten the Empire's very existence. Had he lived, he might have provided the stable leadership to prevent the war party in the CUP from taking Turkey into the World War at a time not of its choosing.

Bibliography: Mahmud Kemal İnal, *Osmanlı devrinde son sadri-âzamlar*, 14 pts., Istanbul 1940-53, 1869-92; Glen Swanson, *Mahmud Şevket Paşa and the defense of the Ottoman empire: a study of war and revolution during the Young Turk period*, unpublished Ph. D. thesis, Indiana University 1970; Generalfeldmarschall Freiherr von der Goltz, *Erinnerungen an Mahmud Schewket Pascha*, in *Deutsche Rundschau*, xl/1-2, October and November 1913, 32-46, 184-209; Sina Akşin, *31 Mart olayı*, Ankara 1970; idem, *Jön Türkler ve İttihat ve Terakki*, Istanbul 1980; Feroz Ahmad, *The Young Turks: the Committee of Union and Progress in Turkish politics 1908-1914*, Oxford 1969; Mehmed Cavit, *Meşrutiyet devrine ait Cavit Beyin hatıraları*, in *Tanin* (Istanbul), 3 August 1943 ff.; Halid Ziya Uşakliğil, *Saray ve ötesi*, i, Istanbul 1940; F. McCullagh, *The fall of Abd-ul-Hamid*, London 1910; Halil Menteşe, *Eski meclisi mebusan reisi Halil Menteşe'nin hatırları*, in *Cumhuriyet*, 18 October 1946; Ali Fuad Türkgeldi, *Görüp isittiklerim*², Ankara 1951; İ. H. Danişmend, *İzahlı Osmanlı tarihi kronolojisi*², iv, Istanbul 1961; *31 Mart vak'ası*, Istanbul 1961; General Pertev Demirhan, *Generalfeldmarschall Colmar Freiherr von der Goltz*, Göttingen 1960. (FEROZ AHMAD)

MAḤMŪD TARDJUMĀN, interpreter and diplomat for the Ottomans. Born in Bavaria of a noble family, he was taken captive (probably at the age of 16) by the Turks at the battle of Mohács (1526) while serving as page to Louis II. Sent to the Palace School in Istanbul, he became famous for his extraordinary knowledge of languages. From 1550 at the latest, he served as interpreter to the Porte, with the title *agha*, and in 1573 he was promoted to chief interpreter, with the title *beg*. As Turkish ambassador he played an important role in the diplomatic relations of the Porte with the Hungarian king John Sigismund and the latter's widow Isabella (1553-4). In 1569 a diplomatic mission brought him to France, and in 1570 he was sent as ambassador to Venice in order to summon the Republic to withdraw from Cyprus. The negotiations remained inconclusive, war broke out and Maḥmūd was kept back in Verona. Only in 1573 did he return to Istanbul. In 1574 he was sent to Vienna and in 1575 to Prague, where he died. His body was brought to Gran (Esztergom), then on the boundary of the Hungarian region which had been conquered by the Turks. Maḥmūd was described by his contemporaries as a learned and capable diplomat. Although it cannot be proved unequivocally, it is assumed that Maḥmūd can be identified with the author of the same name who wrote the *Taʾrīkh-i Ungurus*, chronicle of the history of Hungary in Turkish, the unique manuscript of which is in the collection of the Library of the Hungarian Academy of Science (Török. F. 57).

Bibliography: J. Matuz, *Die Pfortendolmetscher zur Herrschaftszeit Süleymans des Prächtigen*, in *Südostforschungen*, xxiv (1975), 26-60. (G. Hazai)

MAḤMŪD TAYMŪR (born in Cairo 16 June) 1894, died in Lausanne 25 April 1973), Egyptian writer whose prolific output includes novels and short stories, theatrical pieces, accounts of journeys, articles and various studies, in particular relating to Arabic language and literature. He is beyond doubt the best known of the Taymūr family, although his brother Muhammad (1892-1921) was a talented short-story writer and dramatist.

Hagiography has claimed the most remote origins for this family. Henceforward, the most reliable source for information on these origins is "the story of the Taymūrs", from the pen of the learned *adīb* Aḥmad Taymūr, father of Muḥammad and of Maḥmūd, which figures as supplement to his work *Luʿab al-ʿArab* "The games of the Arabs", 1st ed., Ladjnat al-muʾallafāt al-Taymūriyya, Cairo 1367/1948.

The first known ancestor of the Taymūrs, Muḥammad b. ʿAlī Kurd Taymūr, was a Kurd from the region of Mawṣil who arrived in Egypt with the troops sent by the Porte after the departure of the French forces of Bonaparte (1801). Rising through the military echelons he became a general, then a senior official—the title of *kāshif* is also attached to his name. Having been the confidant of Muḥammad ʿAlī, he was to become that of his son Ibrāhīm.

The Taymūrs were thus installed in Egypt from the beginning of the 19th century. The devotion of these foreigners to the Arabic language and the people of Egypt intrigued and delighted the Egyptians, whether historians of literature or literary critics. Their ascendancy otherwise poses no problems since the Kurds, it is said, are pure Arabs, descended from Ḳaḥṭān. But what is astonishing is to see this dignitary of the Ottoman state and his descendants showing a clear predilection for the Arabic language and not keeping themselves aloof from the Egyptians, not displaying towards them that arrogance which is so typical of a foreign aristocracy.

Furthermore, Ismāʿīl, the son of the *kāshif*, marks the transition between official and man of letters. His mastery of Turkish and of Persian earned him the post of private secretary of Muḥammad ʿAlī, and he subsequently exercised important functions in the Khedival *Dīwān* under Ibrāhīm, ʿAbbās I, Saʿīd and Ismāʿīl. But it was no secret that he preferred the company of books to dealings with people. It was he who laid the foundations of a library which was to become famous.

The son and one of the two daughters of Ismāʿīl are the two first renowed members of the family in the modern era. The daughter, ʿĀʾisha (1840-1902), received, at home, a very substantial education, both religious and poetic, in Arabic, Turkish and Persian, and produced a corpus which is all the more remarkable in view of the fact that Arab poetesses were at that time scarcely numerous. The son, Aḥmad Taymūr (1871-1930), who became a Pasha in 1919, devoted his entire life to Arabic language and literature; at his death, he bequeathed to the National Library of Cairo 4,134 volumes, including many manuscripts, wich constitute the Taymūr collection.

Maḥmūd, the third son of Aḥmad, was born on 16 June 1894 in Cairo, in the Darb al-Saʿāda quarter, between the street of the Mūskī and Bāb al-Khalḳ. Subsequently, the family was to dwell in another quarter of Cairo, al-Ḥilmiyya, and, between these two stages, took up residence in ʿAyn Shams, a suburb still barely urbanised. Many cultured visitors frequented the home of Aḥmad Pasha Taymūr, some of them famous: the Imām Muḥammad ʿAbduh, the erudite Maghribī al-Shanḳīṭī and the orientalist Kratchkovski.

In this propitious milieu, Maḥmūd and his brother Muḥammad, two years his senior, were able to satisfy their precocious appetite for literature. Their father definitely possessed too strong a classical background not to make them learn by heart the *Muʿallaḳa* of Imruʾ al-Ḳays, but he was sufficiently imaginative to encourage them to read the *Thousand and one nights*. While still adolescents, the two brothers developed a passion for the theatre and, in emulation of Salāma al-Ḥidjāzī whom they saw at every opportunity, they composed plays which they performed before their family and their friends; they were also enthusiasts for journalism and, with the means at their disposal (the *bālūẓa* was the stencil of that time), they circulated on a very small scale the family newspaper which they edited.

Maḥmūd was to find himself the beneficiary of another advantage. Shortly before the outbreak of the First World War, his brother Muḥammad, returning from France where he had studied law for four years, revealed to him the existence of a realist trend in literature and acquainted him with the work of Maupassant. He accepted these discoveries with admiration but also with circumspection, because the change of direction to which he saw himself called was considerable. He had believed that he had realised his cultural *aggiornamento* in applauding the attempts made by Syro-Lebanese emigrants to America to liberate Arabic language and thought from ponderous classical clichés; his sensibility had been aroused by reading the *al-Adjniḥa al-mutakassira*, the poetic "novel" of Djabrān (1883-1931), the greatest of the "Americans", just as he appreciated the heart-rending stories, original or adapted, which the Egyptian al-Manfalūṭī (1876-1924) [*q.v.*] related in such exquisite Arabic. Now, his brother assured him, literature worthy of the name did not need to flee from reality to take refuge in romantic exaltation, but should cling as close as possible to life such as it is, to everyday Egyptian life. Of all contemporary Arabic writing, he said, two works alone deserved to find favour: the *Ḥadīth ʿĪsā Ibn Hishām* of Muḥammad al-Muwayliḥī (1858-1939) and *Zaynab* of Muḥammad Ḥusayn Haykal (1888-1956) [*q.vv.*].

He therefore took some time assimilating this doctrine, though he did not dispute its worth. Appearing after some poems which he had composed in free verse, the first story which he published in the review *al-Sufūr* in September 1916 was sentimental and, in his own estimation, mediocre. On the other hand, in the same period his brother Muḥammad was for his part attempting to apply the new principles; he worked with other enthusiastic amateurs for the creation of a popular Egyptian theatre, and published, in different reviews, short stories which count among the first realist Egyptian publications to mark an epoch. His untimely death persuaded Maḥmūd to engage resolutely in the path which his brother had traced out, and as a first step he published, one year after his death, an edition of his collected works in three volumes (1922).

However, the stories indicating that Maḥmūd had really taken up the mantle of Muḥammad seem to have been slow in coming. The first narrative to reflect his move towards realism, *al-Shaykh Djumʿa*, dates from 1921, but it was in 1925 that his *Ūsṭā Shaḥḥāta yuṭālibu bi-adjrihi* "The coachman Shaḥḥata claims his due", drew attention to him. The *al-Fadjr* review of avant-garde literature in which the text was published, saw its author as "the Egyptian Maupassant", and the critics stressed, not necessarily as a compliment, the audacious nature of this little tableau of manners. One of them reckoned that Oriental society was still too hypocritical to allow itself to be stripped bare by a Zola.

This was the real departure. Henceforth, his production became more prolific and he began publishing compilations: two for the one year 1925, each containing a dozen short stories, and another appearing in the following year. These first three compilations had particular importance for him because about ten years later (1937) he published a selection from them under the title *al-Wathba al-ūlā* "The first leap". It could in fact be said that here is a collection of the first truly meritorious works, on account of which he is considered the creator of the Arabic short story, an opinion held not only in Egypt and the Arab world but also in Europe, where the orientalists Kratchkovski, Schaade and Wiet presented and translated his writing. Until 1939, he published on average one collection of short stories every year. After a certain slowing down due to the war, the rhythm was subsequently sustained. It may be noted that from the decade of the 1940s onward, the storyteller also began writing novels and theatrical pieces which have added little to his reputation. Suffice it to say that as novelist or dramatist, Maḥmūd Taymūr followed the same preoccupations as in his short stories. Always painstaking in his clarity and accuracy, here too he drew upon various sources of inspiration: the most immediate present (the war in *al-Makhbaʾ raḳm 13* "Shelter no. 13", play, 1942); social questions (the condition of woman is the basis of *Ḥawwāʾ al-khālida* "Eternal Eve", play, 1945, and of *Ilā al-liḳāʾ ayyuhā al-ḥubb* "Farewell, love", novel, 1959); and historico-legendary evocations tending towards fantasy and humour (*Kliyūbātra fī Khān al-Khalīlī* "Cleopatra in Khān al-Khalīlī", novel, 1946, and *Ibn Djalaʾ* (= al-Ḥadjdjādj, play, 1951). There are, however, particular features: only full-length fiction gave him the opportunity to develop the kind of psychological analysis to which he had always aspired (*Salwā fī mahabb al-rīḥ* "Salwā to the four winds", novel, 1944).

The fact remains that Maḥmūd Taymūr was before all else a short story writer—in the course of his life he published a total of some thirty compilations. From the start, he aimed to produce an Egyptian œuvre. Much attention is therefore given to the local colour in his writing, and it is taken as evidence of his patriotism. In fact, if he locates the majority of his tales in a context familiar to the Egyptians, he does so out of concern for authenticity and writes with such sobriety, with such mastery of ellipsis, that the predominant impression gained from his work is one of technical virtuosity. In addition, nothing could be less banal than the plots and the characters that he presents. The *futuwwa*, that is the bad boy, leader of a gang of ruffians, is indeed a familiar type among the common folk of Egypt; making him a *ḥādjdj* is not consistent with natural logic, but bestowing upon him this title and the dignity which accompanies it by having him serve as a hairdresser to a group of pilgrims travelling by train to Mecca, is something which departs totally from traditional norms and reveals the mischievous attitude of the author (*al-Ḥādjdj Shalabī*, in the collection bearing this title, 1930). Realism requires thus! In the quest for the desired effect, the writer leaves nothing to chance. He begins with an existing situation, a character who may be of any kind but is easily recognisable and, without any unnecessary delay, he brings out the weakness of the character, the incident which, breaking the daily routine, will prepare the way for catastrophe. In other cases, pathology plays a part from the outset; inspired and possessed persons abound in his work, as well as beings beset by obsessive beliefs and those whom misery, frustration or sickness have unbalanced. But all of this would be incapable of holding the attention of the reader were it not for the interplay of artistic qualities: narration which is clear yet precise, judicious choice of eloquent detail or of striking formula, sense of suspense and, essential to all the preceding, firmness of writing.

The question of language was central, in fact, in the art and in the life of Maḥmūd Taymūr. Out of concern for realism, he opted first for the spoken language which he employed in his early stories and theatrical pieces. Taking part in a Congress of Orientalists held in 1932 in Leiden, he expressed the opinion that classical Arabic language should be simplified and relieved of certain cumbersome grammatical forms in order to meet the needs of hitherto unknown literary genres, sc. the novel and drama. This being the case, his recourse to dialect, the natural language of conversation, is clearly explicable. But subsequently he was to take a different view. No doubt he felt himself obliged to employ a more polished, more "academic" language when official recognition was accorded to him: in 1947 the Fuʾād I Academy awarded him the short story prize for the corpus of his works written in the classical language; in 1950 he was elected a member of this Academy; and in 1952 he received the State Prize, which he shared with Tawfīḳ al-Ḥakīm.

It would, however, be a mistake to overstress this aspect and to forget that on his own account, for reasons of taste and also out of concern for efficacy and appeal, he had taken the side of the *fuṣḥā*. That which he lost in Egyptian parochialism, he gained in universality, but above all he was capable of expressing himself in a language simultaneously pure and adapted to the objectives that he imposed upon himself: a narrative, living language, freed from the traditional rhetorical tinsel which would in fact be totally out of place. On the other hand, those expressive classical idioms which had been unjustly abandoned are restored and rehabilitated in his work. This style which is both functional and mildly anachronistic gives to Taymūr's stories their distinguishing mark, their peculiar flavour. Most often the phrase is brief, but the syntax and vocabulary recall and embellish the technique of the prose masters of antiquity.

It may be that he attached too much importance to these questions of language. Not only did he eschew dialect completely in his later works but he systematically set about rewriting the earlier ones, or at least those of them closest to his heart. Dramatic pieces and stories received their definitive version, revised and corrected to an extent that would satisfy the most rigorous academic standards. A lengthy text dating from 1934 (*Abū ʿAlī ʿāmil artist*) was thus revised twenty years later, becoming *Abū ʿAlī al-fannān* (1954). Of course, the removal of dialect was not always the only reason for the revision, which could be influenced equally by considerations of composition (lengthy passages are abbreviated, the profound sense of history is modified, etc.). However, it is impossible not to regret this perfectionism which drove a great writer to the rewriting of works which had been published many years before. To a certain extent, these scruples are a credit to a craftsman anxious to produce fine work, but they also have the effect of preventing the artist from developing truly original creations. In the end, it is certainly true that the art of Taymūr, too cultivated, too polished, could no longer, at a given moment, respond to the curiosities and dissatisfactions of new generations, in Egypt and in other Arab countries. It has come about that his successors, many of them his disciples, denounce his romantic or theatrical style of writing but furthermore, question the realism and the rationalism of which he was a resolute partisan.

Bibliography: Brockelmann, S III, 218-26; H. Pérès, *Le roman dans la littérature arabe moderne*, in *AIEO Alger*, v (1939-41), 167-86; ʿAbd al-Muḥsin Ṭāhā Badr, *Taṭawwur al-riwāya al-ʿarabiyya al-ḥadīt͟ha fī Miṣr* (1870-1938), Cairo 1963; Yaḥyā Ḥaḳḳī, *Fad͟jr al-ḳiṣṣa al-miṣriyya*, Cairo; J. Landau, *Studies in the Arab theater and cinema*, Philadelphia 1962, Fr. tr. Paris 1965; ʿAbbās K͟hiḍr, *al-Ḳiṣṣa al-ḳaṣīra fī Miṣr mund͟hu nas͟hʾatihā ḥattā 1930*, Cairo 1966; Ch. Vial, *Contribution à l'étude du roman et de la nouvelle en Egypte des origines à 1960*, in, *ROMM*, iv/2, 1967; E. Gálvez Vázquez, *El Cairo de Maḥmūd Taymūr—Personajes literarios*, Séville 1974; eadem, *Cuentos egipcios de Maḥmūd Taymūr*, Madrid n.d. [1976]; N. K. Kotsarov, *Pisateli Egipta*, Moscow 1975, 212-17; Fatḥī al-Ibyārī, *ʿĀlam Taymūr al-ḳaṣaṣī*, Cairo 1976; *La littérature égyptienne*, in *L'Egypte d'aujourd'hui*, ouvrage collectif du GREPO d'Aix-en-Provence, CNRS, Paris 1977; K.A.S. El Beheiry, *L'influence de la littérature française sur le roman arabe*, Sherbrooke, Québec 1980, index. (CH. VIAL)

MAḤMŪD YALAWAČ, minister in Central Asia and China of the Mongol K͟hāns in the 13th century A.D.

Barthold surmised (*Turkestan*³, 396 n. 3) that Maḥmūd Yalawač was identical with Maḥmūd the K͟hʷārazmian mentioned by Nasawī as one of the leaders of Čingiz's embassy of 1218 to the K͟hʷārazm-S͟hāh ʿAlāʾ al-Dīn Muḥammad [see K͟HʷĀRAZM-S͟HĀHS]. It is true that the *Secret history of the Mongols* (tr. E. Haenisch, *Die Geheime Geschichte der Mongolen*², Leipzig 1948, 132) refers to Maḥmūd Yalawač and his son Masʿūd Beg [*q.v.*] as K͟hʷārazmians (Ḳurums͟hi) and that *yalawač/yalawar* means "envoy" in Turkish (Clauson, *Etymological dictionary*, 921: perhaps of Iranian origin?). He was clearly from the merchant class, and must have rendered services to the Mongols, for under the Great K͟hān Ögedey (1227-41) he achieved high office, being appointed over all the sedentary population of Transoxania and Mog͟holistan [*q.v.*] (i.e. the steppelands to the north of Transoxania) and ruling these from K͟hud͟jand [*q.v.*]. During his governorship, a serious popular revolt aimed against the Mongol overlords and the local notables broke out in Buk͟hārā under the leadership of the sieve-maker Maḥmūd Tārābī (1238), and it was only Maḥmūd Yalawač's intercession which saved the city from savage Mongol reprisals. Soon after this, he fell into dispute with Čag͟hatay, to whom part of Transoxania and Mog͟holistan had been granted as an *ind͟jü* or appanage [see ČAG͟HATAY K͟HĀN and MĀ WARĀʾ AL-NAHR. 2. History], and was dismissed by Čag͟hatay. Ögedey expressed disapproval, but accepted his brother's excuses and then appointed Maḥmūd Yalawač as governor of Peking in northern China, an office later confirmed by Güyük and Möngke K͟hāns, where he died in 1254; his son Masʿūd Beg succeeded him as minister for the Mongols in Central Asia. Maḥmūd Yalawač is accordingly mentioned in Chinese sources as Ya-lao-wa-čʾi (E. Bretschneider, *Mediaeval researches from eastern Asiatic sources*, London 1888, i, 11-12).

D͟juwaynī praises the beneficent rule in Transoxania of Maḥmūd Yalawač and his son: they restored a city like Buk͟hārā to something of its old splendour, after the Mongol devastations, and Maḥmūd abolished compulsory labour and military services and extraordinary imposts (*ʿawāriḍ* [*q.v.*]).

Bibliography: (in additions to references already given); D͟juwaynī-Boyle, index, s.v.; Ras͟hīd al-Dīn, tr. Boyle, *The successors of Genghis Khan*, New York and London 1971, index, s.v.; W. Barthold, *Turkestan down to the Mongol invasion*³, London 1968, 465, 469 ff.; idem, *Histoire des Turcs d'Asie Centrale*, Paris 1945, 142-3; V. Minorsky, *Four studies on the history of Central Asia*, i, Leiden 1962, 45-6. (C. E. BOSWORTH)

MAḤMŪDĀBĀD FAMILY, a leading landed family of north India prominent in public life under the Mug͟hals, the Kings of Awadh [*q.v.*] and the British. These Ṣiddīḳī S͟hayk͟hs trace their descent from Abū Bakr through one Naṣr Allāh, a *ḳāḍī* of Bag͟hdād who is said to have come in the 7th/13th century to India, where his descendants were *ḳāḍīs* of Dihlī. In the 8th/14th century, *ḳāḍī* Naṣr Allāh's great-grandson, *ḳāḍī* Nuṣrat Allāh, acquired land in Awadh, and under the Mug͟hals his descendants, Nawwāb Dāwūd K͟hān, Nawwāb Maḥmūd K͟hān and Bāyazīd K͟hān, rose high in the imperial service. Nawwāb Maḥmūd K͟hān founded the town of Maḥmūdābād in the Sītapur district of Awadh, which gave its name to the junior branch of the family, dominant over the last 150 years, and whose palace lay on its outskirts.

In recent times, the family's fortunes were founded by Nawwāb ʿAlī K͟hān (d. 1858) a S͟hīʿī poet, scholar and able estate manager. Between 1838 and 1858 he took advantage of the disturbed conditions of Awadh to add to the few lands he inherited, using all means at his disposal, until he possessed what Sleeman described as a "magnificent estate"; see P. D. Reeves, ed., *Sleeman in Oudh*, Cambridge 1971, 269-73. Although he took a prominent part in the uprising against the British of 1857-8, the Maḥmūdābād estate which was his great achievement did pass in large part to his son, Amīr Ḥasan K͟hān. The British policy of clemency, and their aim to create an Indian aristocracy in Awadh, thus enabled the family to consolidate the gains made under the Awadh régime and to emerge in the late 19th century as one of the largest Muslim landlords in India.

The wealth of the Maḥmūdābād estate provided the basis on which the descendants of Nawwāb ʿAlī K͟hān were able to play leading roles in Indian and Muslim affairs under the British. Rād͟jā Amīr Ḥasan K͟hān's (d. 1903) activities were those of a cultivated landed gentleman. He followed literary pursuits, in particular, writing elegies on the Imām al-Ḥusayn, whilst he was a great public benefactor in Awadh, supporting schools and a public library. In 1871 he became vice-president, and from 1882 to 1892 President, of the British Indian Association, the organisation of the Awadh *taʿallukdārs*. He also served on the Viceroy's council and was prominent in opposing the Indian National Congress.

The Rādjā's son, Muḥammad ʿAlī Muḥammad Khān, played a more varied and yet more distinguished role in public life. He maintained the traditions established by his father. He gave generously to educational projects like the Lucknow University and Lucknow Medical College and founded the Lucknow Madrasat al-Wāʿiẓīn. Moreover, he not only gave to the Muslim University at ʿAlīgaṛh [*q.v.*] but also played a very active part in the movement to raise the funds to transform ʿAlīgaṛh College into the University of which he was the first Vice-Chancellor from 1920 till 1923. He was President of the British Indian Association 1917-21 and 1930-1, and served on the United Provinces' Legislative Council 1904-9 and the Governor-General's Council 1907-20. From 1920 to 1925 he was the first Home Member of the United Provinces' government, and consequently had the embarassing task of putting many personal friends, Congressmen and Khilāfatists, in prison. In 1925 he was given the personal title of Mahārādjā.

More important were Muḥammad ʿAlī Muḥammad's activities as a leading Muslim politician, and as patron of other politicians. He became involved in the politics of protest for the first time in 1909, demanding joint electorates in the negotiations leading to the Morley-Minto Legislative Council reforms, when the majority of North Indian Muslims were asking for separate ones. From 1909 to 1917 he was closely associated with the radical wing of Muslim politics. He took the part of the radicals in the Muslim University movement, he protested most vigorously to government over the Kānpur mosque incident of 1913 [see KĀNPUR] and helped bring about the pact between the All-India Muslim League and the Indian National Congress at Lucknow in 1916, by which time his political stance had annoyed the government so much that it threatened to confiscate his estates. From 1915 to 1919 he was President of the All-India Muslim League and presided over its sessions in 1917, 1918 and 1928. Throughout much of his life he helped to support, both financially and in other ways, young men who were just entering politics, for instance, Sayyid Wazīr Ḥasan, the secretary of the All-India Muslim League 1912-19, Rādjā Ghulām Ḥusayn, the editor of *New era*, Čawdharī Khāliḳ al-Zamān, who for a while he made his education secretary, and the leading Pan-Islamist politicians Muḥammad and Shawkat ʿAlī. However, his political support was not restricted to Muslim causes alone; he was also a nationalist and counted leading Congressmen like Motilal and Jawaharlal Nehru amongst his friends. In the last years of his life he strove, in the teeth of much Muslim opposition, to draw his community behind the Nehru Report of 1928, the Congress response to the communal problem which supported the creation of Muslim provinces but rejected separate representation, and then threw his weight behind the Muslim Nationalist Party founded in 1929. He died in May 1931.

The Mahārādjā was succeeded by his eldest son, Rādjā Muḥammad Amīr Aḥmad Khān (1914-73), who, though he began as an Indian nationalist in politics, soon became absorbed in Muslim separatism. In 1936, as a young man, he was drawn into the All-India Muslim League by Djinnah, a close family friend for over two decades and a trustee of the Maḥmūdābād estate. From 1937 to 1947 he played a leading role in the League, as treasurer, chairman of the Working Committee and a major benefactor. In particular, he operated as the link between the League and Muslim youth; he was president of the All-India Muslim Students Federation and devoted himself especially to organising the student forces which played such a considerable role in the League's campaigns for support. But Amīr Aḥmad Khān did not follow League policy in all things. A deeply religious man, in the early 1940s he became involved in the Islāmī Djamāʿat and advocated, against Djinnah, that Pakistan should be an Islamic state.

After the partition of India, Amīr Aḥmad Khān lived for a time in ʿIrāḳ and in Pakistan. He played little part in Pakistani politics, and rejected Ayyūb Khān's demand that he refound the Muslim League on the grounds that Pakistan needed a "party with socialist aims wedded to Islamic justice"; see *Dawn* (Karachi) for 15 October 1973. From 1968 until his death he was Director of the Islamic Cultural Centre in London, where his principal achievements were to bring to fruition plans to complete the London Mosque and to establish an Islamic Science Foundation. His life was distinguished by his faith, his simplicity, his generosity and a high level of cultivation in Urdu, Arabic, Persian and English, a level of scholarship which had been the hall-mark of his ancestors in the previous three generations.

Bibliography: There is a family history by Shaykh ʿAlī Ḥasan, the *Taʾrīkh-i Maḥmūdābād*, ms., Lucknow n.d.; short histories of the family can be found in Nurul Hasan Siddiqui, *Landlords of Agra and Avadh*, Lucknow 1950 and H. R. Nevill, *Sitapur: a gazetteer, being Volume XL of the District Gazetteers of Agra and Oudh*, Allahabad 1905; T. R. Metcalf, *Land, landlords and the British Raj: Northern India in the nineteenth century*, Berkeley and Los Angeles 1979, P. D. Reeves, *The landlords' reponse to political change in the United Provinces of Agra and Oudh, India, 1921-1937*, Ph. D. thesis, Australian National University, 1963, unpublished, and idem, ed., *Sleeman in Oudh*, Cambridge 1971, throw light on the family as *taʿallukdārs*; while F. Robinson, *Separatism among Indian Muslims: the politics of the United Provinces' Muslims 1860-1923*, Cambridge 1974, Choudhuri Khaliquzzaman, *Pathway to Pakistan*, Lahore 1961, and the Rāja of Mahmudabad, *Some memories*, in C. H. Philips and M. D. Wainwright, eds. *The partition of India: policies and perspectives 1935-1947*, London 1970, offer information on the political careers of Amīr Ḥasan Khān, Muḥammad ʿAlī Muḥammad Khān, and Amīr Aḥmad Khān.

(F. ROBINSON)

MĀHPAYKAR. [see KÖSEM].

MAHR (A.), Hebrew *mohar*, Syriac *mahrā*, "bridal gift", originally "purchase-money", synonymous with *ṣadāḳ* which properly means "friendship", then "present", a gift given voluntarily and not as a result of a contract, is in Muslim law the gift which the bridegroom has to give the bride when the contract of marriage is made and which becomes the property of the wife.

1. Among the pagan Arabs, the *mahr* was an essential condition for a legal marriage, and only when a *mahr* had been given did a proper legal relationship arise. A marriage without a *mahr* was regarded as shameful and looked upon as concubinage. In the romance of ʿAntar, the Arab women, who are being forced to marry without a *mahr*, indignantly reject such a marriage as a disgrace. Victors alone married the daughters of the conquered without giving them a *mahr*.

In the pre-Islamic period, the *mahr* was handed over

to the *walī*, i.e. the father, or brother or relative in whose guardianship (*walāʾ*) the girl was. Here the original character of the marriage by purchase is more apparent. In earlier times the bride received none of the *mahr*. What was usually given to the woman at the betrothal was the *ṣadāḳ*; the *mahr*, being the purchase price of the bride, was given to the *walī*.

But in the period shortly before Muḥammad, the *mahr*, or at least a part of it, seems already to be given to the woman. According to the Ḳurʾān, this is already the prevailing custom. By this amalgamation of *mahr* and *ṣadāḳ*, the original significance of the *mahr* as the purchase price was weakened and became quite lost in the natural course of events. There can be no doubt that the *mahr* was originally the purchase price. But the transaction of purchasing, in course of long development, had become a mere form. The remains, however, as they survived in the law of marriage in Islam, still bear clear traces of a former marriage by purchase.

2. Muḥammad took over the old Arab patriarchal ceremony of marriage as it stood and developed it in several points. The Ḳurʾān no longer contains the conception of the purchase of the wife and the *mahr* as the price, but the *mahr* is in a way a reward, a legitimate compensation which the woman has to claim in all cases. The Ḳurʾān thus demands a bridal gift for a legal marriage: "And give them whom ye have enjoyed their reward as a wedding-gift" (lit. *farīḍa* "allotment of property", IV, 24) and again: "And give the women their dowries voluntarily" (IV, 3); cf. also IV, 25, 34; V, 5; IX, 10.

The bridal gift is the property of the wife; it therefore remains her own if the marriage is dissolved. "And if ye wish to exchange one wife for another and have given one a talent, take nothing of it back" (IV, 20). Even if the man divorces the wife before he has cohabited with her, he must leave half the *mahr* with her (II, 236-7).

Up to the Muslim period, the wife was considered after the death of the husband as part of his estate; the heir simply continued the marriage of the deceased. Such levirate marriages are found in the Old Testament also. Muḥammad abolished this custom, which still remained in his time, by sūra IV, 19; "O ye who are believers, it is not permitted to you to inherit women against their will". In his social reforms, Muḥammad made the *mahr* into a settlement in the wife's favour.

3. There was an ample store of traditions about the *mahr*, and these pave the way for the theories laid down by the jurists in the *fiḳh* books. From all the traditions, it is clear that the *mahr* was an essential part of the contract of marriage. According to a tradition in Bukhārī, the *mahr* is an essential condition for the legality of the marriage: "every marriage without *mahr* is null and void". Even if this tradition, so brief and to the point, is not genuine, a number of traditions point to the fact that the *mahr* was necessary for the marriage, even if it only consisted of some trifling thing. Thus in Ibn Mādja and al-Bukhārī, traditions are given according to which the Prophet permitted a marriage with only a pair of shoes as *mahr* and approved of a poor man, who did not even possess an iron ring, giving his wife instruction in the Ḳurʾān as *mahr*.

A few *ḥadīths* endeavour to show that the *mahr* must be neither too high nor too low. From the traditions we also learn what *mahr* was given in particular cases in the Prophet's time: for example, the bridal gift of ʿAbd al-Raḥmān b. ʿAwf was an ounce of gold, that of Abū Hurayra 10 *ūḳiyas* and a dish, that of Sahl b. Saʿd an iron ring.

In the *ḥadīths* we again frequently find the Ḳurʾānic regulation that in a divorce after cohabitation the woman has the right to the whole *mahr*.

4. According to Muslim *fiḳh*-books, marriage is a contract (*ʿaḳd*) made between the bridegroom and the *walī* of the bride. An essential element in it is the *mahr* or *ṣadāḳ*, which the bridegroom binds himself to give to the bride. The marriage is null without a *mahr*. The jurists themselves are not quite agreed as to the nature of the *mahr*. Some regard it practically as purchase-money (e.g. Khalīl: "the *mahr* is like the purchase-money") or as equivalent (*ʿiwaḍ*) for the possession of the woman and the right over her, so that it is like the price paid in a contract of sale; while other jurists see in the *mahr* a symbol, a mark of honour or a proper legal security of property for the woman.

All things can be given as *mahr* that are things (*māl*) in the legal sense and therefore are possible to deal in, that is, can be the object of an agreement. The *mahr* may also—but opinions differ on the point—consist in a pledge to do something or in doing something, e.g. instructing the woman in the Ḳurʾān or allowing her to make the pilgrimage. The whole of the *mahr* can either be given at or shortly after the marriage or it may be paid in instalments. When the latter is the case, it is recommended to give the woman a half or two-thirds before cohabitation and the rest afterwards. The woman may refuse to allow consummation of the marriage before a part is given.

Two kinds of *mahr* are distinguished:

a. *Mahr musammā*, "specified *mahr*", the amount of which is exactly laid down in the wedding contract.

b. *Mahr al-mithl* "*mahr* of the like", i.e. unspecified dower, in which the amount is not exactly laid down, but the bridegroom gives a bridal gift befitting the wealth, family and qualities of the bride. This *mahr al-mithl* is also applied in all cases in which nothing definite about the *mahr* was agreed upon in the contract.

The *mahr* becomes the property of the wife and she has full right to dispose of it as she likes. In the case of any dispute afterwards as to whether certain things belong to the *mahr* or not, the man is put upon oath.

The *Sharīʿa* lays down no maximum. There is also no upper limit to the *mahr*: whatever is agreed upon in the contract must be paid. The *mahr* generally is adjusted to what other women of equal status (sister, daughter, aunt) have received. As regards the minimum for the amount of the *mahr*, limitations were introduced by the various law-schools; the Ḥanafīs and Shāfiʿīs insist upon 10 *dirhams* as a minimum and the Mālikīs three *dirhams*. The difference in the amount fixed depends on the economic conditions in the different countries where the *madhhabs* in question prevail.

If the man pronounces a divorce, the *mahr* must be paid in every case if cohabitation has taken place; but the bridegroom may withdraw from the marriage before it is consummated; in this case he is bound to give the woman half the *mahr*.

Bibliography: W. Robertson Smith, *Kinship and marriage in early Arabia*, Cambridge 1885 (cf. thereon Th. Nöldeke, in *ZDMG*, xl [1886], 148-9); Wellhausen, *Die Ehe bei den Arabern*, in *Nachrichten der G. W. zu Gött.* (1893), 431 ff.; G. Jacob, *Altarabisches Beduinenleben*, Berlin 1897; R. Roberts, *The social laws of the Qorân*, London 1925, 29, 124; Gertrude H. Stern, *Marriage in early Islam*, London 1939; W. Montgomery Watt, *Muhammad at Medina*, Oxford 1956, 283, 393.—For the *ḥadīths*, cf. Wensinck, *Handbook*, 145; the chapters *Nikāḥ* and *Ṣadāḳ* or *Mahr* in the *Fiḳh*-books. Further:

Mahomed Yusoof, *Mohamedan law relating to marriage, dower, divorce, legitimacy and guardianship of minors according to the Soonees*, i-iii, Calcutta 1895-8; Ameer Ali, *Mahommadan law*, i[4], Calcutta 1912, ii[5], Calcutta 1929; T. Juynboll, *Handbuch des islam. Gesetzes*, 181 ff.; E. Sachau, *Muhammadanisches Recht*, 34 ff.; D. Santillana, *Istituzioni di diritto Musulmano Malichita*, Rome 1926, p. 168 sqq.; van den Berg, *Principes du droit musulman* (tr. France de Tersant), Algiers 1896, 75; Khalīl, *Mukhtaṣar*, Italian tr. Santillana, Milan 1919, ii, 39 ff., French tr. G.-H. Bousquet, *Abrégé*, Algiers 1956-62; Tornauw, *Moslem. Recht*, Leipzig 1855, 74 ff.; G. Bergsträsser, *Grundzüge*, index; J. Schacht, *The origins of Muhammadan jurisprudence*, Oxford 1959; idem, *An introduction to Islamic law*, Oxford 1964, 167-8; Asaf A. A. Fyzee, *Outlines of Muhammadan law*[3], Oxford 1964, 126-38,[4] Delhi 1974, 132-45; N. J. Coulson, *A history of Islamic law*, Edinburgh 1964, 40, 137-8, 207-8; see also the works of Milliot, Bousquet, Linant de Bellefonds and Brunschvig.

(O. Spies)

MAHRA, a tribe living in the south-eastern part of the Arabian peninsula, in a stretch of land along the coast of the Indian Ocean between Ḥaḍramawt and ʿUmān, and in the hinterland belonging to that region.

More accurately, the boundaries of Mahra-land run in the west from the coast along Wādī Masīla, a continuation of Wādī Ḥaḍramawt, in the north-west along Wādī Ramāʾ as far as Ṣanāw, from there east-north-east, and reach via Anḍawr the north-eastern coast at Rās Ḥāsik, to the north of Ḥāsik, the ancient Mahra settlement. These boundaries enclose also the territories of other tribes, namely of the Shaḥāra, the Ḳarā and the Baṭāḥira in Ẓufār. At the present time, Mahra-land comes within the People's Democratic Republic of Yemen in the west and in the Sultanate of ʿUmān in the east. Until very recently, the Mahra of the Ẓufār province in the Sultanate of ʿUmān, living mainly on the highlands between the desert and the mountains, led a Bedouin life; but those living on the coast have always been sedentary. The present-day sixth governorate (*muḥāfaẓa*) of South Yemen, with its chief town Ḳishn [*q.v.*], corresponds more or less with the former Mahra sultanate, with the same centre.

The Mahra can be considered not only as a tribe but as a separate people, since they speak a language of their own, Mahrī [*q.v.*], and have until very recently retained a high degree of autonomy. That the Mahra are mentioned by classical Arabic authors is mainly due to this fact that they have their own language, not understood by anybody else (Ibn al-Mudjāwir, 271, l. 17).

A member of the Mahra tribe is indicated in their own language as *mahrī* or *mehrī*, pl. *mahrē* or *mehrē* (A. Jahn, *Mehri-Sprache*, 130, l. 14); the corresponding feminine forms are *mehriūt* (Hein, *Mehri-Texte*, 137, l. 2), plural *mehreyten* (Jahn, 210). They indicate Mahra-land as *raḥbēt dha-mahrē* (cf. Jahn's map, *op cit.*, 211).

According to Yāḳūt (*Muʿdjam*, iv, 700, l. 8), the correct form is Mahara, not Mahra, but he stands alone in this opinion, which is moreover uncorroborated by any proof. Mahara is perhaps an incorrect reconstruction of an alleged plural Maharāt, a place name in the Nadjd of Mahra land (*Muʿdjam*, iv, 697, l. 2). Ibn Durayd (*Kitāb al-Ishtiḳāḳ*, ed. ʿA. M. Hārūn, 2nd ed. Baghdād 1979, 552, ll. 3 f.) derives the name Mahra from Arabic *māhir* "skilful, experienced". Ibn al-Mudjāwir (271, ll. 8-14) relates an aetiological story, according to which the Mahra are descendants of three hundred virgins who, having escaped a massacre in a place called al-Dabādib, were given a dowry (*mahr*) by the people of the surrounding mountains and then married by them.

The most important of the still-existing sub-tribes of the Mahra (their orthography not being always consistent in the sources) are: Bayt Kalshāt, Bayt Ṣamūdat, Bayt Thuwār, Bayt Zaʿbanāt, Bayt Ḥarāwīz, Bayt Ziyād, Bayt Bāraʿfīt, Bayt Ḳamṣīt and Bayt Balḥāf (see the charts and lists of the Mahra tribes in Dostal, *Beduinen*, 77 ff.; H. ʿA. Luḳmān, *Taʾrīkh al-djuzur al-yamaniyya*, Beirut 1972, 47-50: *Ḳaʾil al-mahrī fī Ḥaḍramawt*; Carter, *Tribal structures*, 46-8). W. Dostal (*Beduinen*, 34) estimates the number of their able-bodied, weapon-carrying men as 8,000. J. Carter (*Tribal structures*, 37) supposes that there are 5,000 members of this tribe in ʿUmān, and T. M. Johnstone (*The Modern South Arabian languages*, Malibu 1975, 2) is of the opinion that the individuals of all Mahra groups taken together amount to some 15,000. According to the *Gazetteer of Arabia. A geographical and tribal history of the Arabian peninsula*, ed. Sh. A. Scoville, i, Graz 1979, 80, the number of the Mahra on the mainland, the Bedouin included, amounted to 50,000 in the then Aden Protectorate at the time of the First World War. A census carried out in 1983 numbers the population of the sixth governorate of the People's Democratic Republic of Yemen at 60,000. If one takes into account that on the one side people from Ḥaḍramawt and elsewhere have immigrated into the country of the Mahra and that on the other hand members of the Mahra tribes have emigrated to other provinces and to the Gulf Emirates the total number of the Mahra, i.e. the people speaking Mahrī, can be estimated at about 60,000 (A. Lonnet, *The Modern South Arabian Languages in the P.D.R. of Yemen*, in *Proceedings of the Seminar for Arabian Studies*, xv [1985], 51).

It cannot be maintained any longer that Mahra-land was already known to the ancient Greek writers, nor that Mamali, with the variant Mali, named by Theophrastus (*Historia plantarum*, ix, 4,2) as the fourth South Arabian land next to Sabaʾ, Ḥaḍramawt and Ḳatabān [*q.vv.*], is probably a corruption of Mahra and should be identified with it (F. Hommel, *Ethnologie und Geographie des Alten Orients*, Munich 1926, 137). E. Glaser's endeavour (*Skizze der Geschichte und Geographie Arabiens*, ii, Berlin 1890, 26) to identify Minaia, mentioned by Strabo (*Geographia*, xvi, 4,4 = 768), who refers to Eratosthenes, with Mahra-land, has also been proved to be incorrect. The earliest attestation of the Mahra is apparently found in the Ḥaḍramite inscription RES 4877 from al-ʿUḳla, a pre-Islamic stronghold to the west of the capital Shabwa. The text, presumably dating from the beginning of the 3rd century A.D., runs as follows: (1) *shhrm/bn* (2) *w ʾlm/kb* (3) *r/ʾmhrn*, "Shāhirum (or Shahrum), son of Wāʾilum, chief of the Mahrites". It is true that A. F. L. Beeston (*The Philby collection of old South-Arabian inscriptions*, in *Le Muséon*, li [1938], 324) translates *kbr/ʾmhrn* as "chief of the artificers", and A. Jamme (*The Al-ʿUqlah texts*, Washington 1963, 50) as "leader of the specialised workers". But in the inscriptions, *kabīr* almost always indicates the leader or the chief of a tribe, and is followed by the name of the tribe or by the *nisba* plural in the form *ʾfʿln*, *afʿūlān*, usual in ancient South Arabian, e.g. *kbr/fyshn* (RES 3913,1) "*kabīr* (of the tribe) of Fayshān", *kbr/ṣrwḥ* (RES 3951, 1 f.) "*kabīr* (of the city-tribe) of Ṣirwāḥ", *kbr/kl/shʿbn/ʾrymn* (RES 4085,1) "*kabīr* of the entire tribe of the Raymānites", *kbr/ḥśrn* (Ja 816,2) "*kabīr* (of the tribe) of the Ḥaśirān", etc.; the "leader of the Bedouin of the king of Sabaʾ" (*kbr/ʾʿrb/mlk/sbʾ*: Ja

665, 1 f.) is indicated in the same way. Thus *ʾmhrn* is the *nisba* of an unattested * *mhryn* "Mahrite", i.e. Amhūrān, or perhaps Amhārān, since the place-name Burḳat al-Amhār, mentioned as lying next to al-Ghayḍa (Mahrī: Ghayḍat) (Hamdānī, *Ṣifa*, 147, l. 17), certainly does not mean anything else but "Burḳa of the Mahrites". W. Dostal's conjecture (*Beduinen*, 134) that the Mahra, being neighbours of the highly-developed culture of ancient South Arabia, served as mercenaries already in the armies of the pre-Islamic kings in the same way as they went into service occasionally later, is confirmed by inscription RES 4877. A further evidence for the country and the tribe of Mahra has been found in the Sabaean rock-inscription from Wādī ʿAbadān from the middle of the fourth century A.D., in which military campaigns "towards the country of Mahra" (line 7: *qbl/ʾrḍ/mhrt*) and "against the Mahra" (line 21: *ʿly/mhrt*) are mentioned (cf. the reproduction of the text in J. Pirenne, *Deux prospections historiques au Sud-Yémen*, in *Raydān. Journal of Ancient Yemeni Antiquities and Epigraphy*, iv [1981], 235). F. Hommel's assumption (*Süd-arabische Chrestomathie*, Munich 1893, 45) that the form Amhār is still alive in the name of Amhara people, who allegedly have migrated from Mahra land to Ethiopia, is wrong. Already A. Sprenger (*Alte Geographie*, 268) had wrongly maintained that the Semites of Ethiopia were of Mahra origin. An alleged form *mhrt*, found in the late Sabaean inscription RES 4069,5 from Niṣāb, has nothing to do with the Mahra; the passage should rather be read as *wmhrg/wkbwr/sh ʿbn/sybn*, and translated as "and the administrators and the leaders of the Saybān tribe".

The Yemenite authors al-Hamdānī and Ibn al-Mudjāwir excepted, the classical Arabic geographers who localised Mahra-land in the region between Ḥaḍramawt and ʿUmān (al-Iṣṭakhrī, 12, l. 20; al-Muḳaddasī, 53, ll. 9-11), had only a superficial knowledge of it; the interior in particular was almost completely unknown to them. Al-Hamdānī (*Ṣifa*, 45, ll. 18 f.; see also *Iklīl*, i, 72, l. 19) names al-Asʿāʾ as the centre of the Mahra. C. de Landberg (*Ḥaḍramoût*, Leiden 1901, 158) wanted to correct this name into al-Ashghā, but there is no necessity for this, for the place-name al-Asʿāʾ, apparently not mentioned any more since the early Islamic period, is now verified as *ʾsʿyn* (Asʿāyān; Yanbuḳ 47, l. 7) in a late Sabaean inscription from Yanbuḳ in Ḥaḍramawt (M. A. Bafaqih, *New light on the Yazanite dynasty*, in *Proceedings of the Seminar for Arabian Studies*, ix [1979], 7; M. Bāfaqīh et Chr. Robin, *Inscriptions inédites de Yanbug*, in *Raydān. Journal of Ancient Yemeni Antiquities and Epigraphy* ii [1979] 49 f.). According to E. Glaser (*Die Abessinier in Arabien und Afrika*, Munich 1895, 87), the co-ordinates given by al-Hamdānī for the position of al-Asʿāʾ point to the region of Damḳōt and Rās Ḍarbat ʿAlī, thus rather precisely to the middle of the coastal strand which was, moreover, at a later time still inhabited by the Mahra. This conclusion corresponds with al-Hamdānī's indication, given in another passage (*Ṣifa*, 87, 11, 21 f.), that al-Asʿāʾ is a port. Elsewhere (*Ṣifa*, 127, l. 4), al-Hamdānī counts Mahra among the coastal lands of the Arabian Sea. According to him, the Wādī al-Aḥḳāf (for the term al-Aḥḳāf [*q.v.*], see also L. Forrer, *Südarabien nach al-Hamdānī's "Beschreibung der Arabischen Halbinsel"*, Leipzig 1942, 220, n. 4) flows for several days' journeys from the land of Ḥaḍramawt into Mahra-land (*Ṣifa*, 87, l. 10), and likewise to the left of the great wādī, the Wādī Thawba where the tomb of the Prophet Hūd is to be found (*Ṣifa*, 87, l. 8). Mahra-land is considered to belong to the farthest part of Yemen (Yāḳūt, *Muʿdjam*, i, 280, ll. 1 f.; ii, 510, l. 13; etc.) and is named as one of its *mikhlāf*s (Yāḳūt, *Muʿdjam*, iv, 700, ll. 11 f.). The steppe region between the slope down to the coast in the south and the desert in the north is called Nadjd, as was already done by al-Ṭabarī (*Taʾrīkh*, i, 1980, l. 12), Yāḳūt (*Muʿdjam*, iii, 681, l. 11; iv, 697, l. 2.; etc.) and others; from that region originates also the *nadjdī*, a highly-appreciated kind of frankincense (A. Grohmann, *Südarabien als Wirtschaftsgebiet*, i, Vienna 1922, 137 f.). Al-Shiḥr is also mentioned as a main centre of Mahra-land (al-Iṣṭakhrī, 25, ll. 10 f.; Ibn Khaldūn, *Mukhtaṣar*, 132, l. 2). Muḥammad b. Ḥabīb (*Kitāb al-Muḥabbar*, ed. I. Lichtenstaedter, Ḥaydarābād 1942, 266, ll. 4-6) counts al-Shiḥr in Mahra as one of the markets of the Arabs in pre-Islamic times; it is said to lie at the foot of the mountains in which the tomb of the Prophet Hūd is found, and said further that no tithe is levied on that market because the town does not belong to any kingdom. Al-Shiḥr is occasionally even identified with Mahra-land (Ibn Khaldūn, *Muktaṣar*, 132, ll. 1, 4 f.), as can also be concluded from Nashwān b. Saʿīd al-Ḥimyarī, *Shams al-ʿulūm*, when he (under the root *s-ʿ-y*) defines al-Asʿā (*sic*) as a place in al-Shiḥr, i.e. in Mahra-land. This is also the case when, for the year 694/1294-5, during the zenith of the power of the Rasūlids [*q.v.*] under al-Ashraf, it is said that the latter's domination was firmly established in the Yemen, in al-Shiḥr (i.e. in Mahra-land) and in Ḥaḍramawt (Yaḥyā b. al-Ḥusayn, *Ghāyat al-amānī fī akhbār al-ḳuṭr al-yamānī*, Cairo 1968, 477, ll. 6 f.). Thereafter, for long al-Shiḥr, once the residence of a Mahra sultan, did not belong any more to Mahra-land; it passed into the possession of the Ḳuʿayṭī sultans of al-Shiḥr and Mukallā. Only families like the Āl Ḳiraynūn, living there in isolation, testify to the former presence of the Mahra in al-Shiḥr.

The Mahra trace their genealogy back to their ancestor Mahra b. Ḥaydān b. ʿAmr b. al-Ḥāf. Already A. Sprenger (*Alte Geographie*, 266) recognized in these names some geographical and ethnographical names of places on the South Arabian coast, e.g. in Ibn al-Ḥāf the port of Bal-Ḥāf, lying to the west of Bīr ʿAlī. Early Arabic authors traced these geneaological connections further back to Ḳaḥṭān: al-Ḥāf b. Ḳuḍāʿa b. Mālik b. Ḥimyar b. Ḳaḥṭān (see the genealogy of the descent of the Mahra in Carter, *Tribal structures*, 38). On the descendants of Mahra b. Ḥaydān and the sub-divisions of the Mahra according to Arabic sources, see al-Hamdānī, *al-Iklīl*, i, 72, l. 19-74, l. 8, and the remarks by W. W. Müller on some of the names mentioned there in *OLZ*, lxiv (1969), 265-6. Less reliable than this South Arabian source is the rendering of the often specifically Mahra names by North Arabian authors like Ibn al-Kalbī, *Djamharat al-nasab*, ed. W. Caskel, i, Leiden 1966, Table 328. The Mahra genealogy as given by the Arabic authors shows in any case a tendentious endeavour to reconstruct a pattern of origins for the tribes which often does not coincide with the genealogy handed down by the Mahra themselves. Their genealogy distinguishes clearly between the authentic Mahra (cf. the groups indicated in al-Hamdānī, *Iklīl*, i, 73, l. 12 as *afṣaḥ Mahra* and the "mahricised" Arabs (cf. the groups which are said newly to have come to join them: *dakhala fī Mahra*, al-Hamdānī, *Iklīl*, i, 73, ll. 20 f.), and thus reflects the fusion of Arab groups with the Mahra and their assimilation to the latter's genealogy. Rivalry between these Arab groups and those who claim descent from Mahra exists until today. Of these two groups which differ genealogically, the one, whose members are considered to be "pure" Mahra, claim descent from the Banū Sharāwiḥ; the others who are said to be of Arabic origin, are brought together in the Banū Sār. Each of these two great confederacies is sub-divided again into several patrilineal groups (see the tables of the classification of the Mahra tribes and their attribution to these two groups in Dostal, *Beduinen*, 77). The greater part of the Mahra coastal area is in the hands of the Banū Sār, while the inland zone belongs to the Banū Sharāwiḥ, who have access to the coast only between Ḳishn and Ḍabōt and possess a small enclave further north (for a general outline of the region where both of the Mahra confederacies are at present dwelling and roaming, see the map in Dostal, *Beduinen*, 125). This spread of the Mahra over two areas is perhaps reflected already in al-Ṭabarī (*Taʾrīkh*, i, 1980, l. 9-1981, l. 3), who mentions two groups of the Mahra under two different leaders, one dwelling in the plain around Djayrūt (this form is also found in Ibn al-Mudjāwir 260, l. 9), the other in Nadjd, i.e. in the highland zone.

According to Ibn al-Mudjāwir (271, ll. 15 f.), the origin of the Mahra is to be sought in the remains of the people of ʿĀd; when God destroyed the greater part of them, this group of people was saved and went to live in the mountains of Ẓufār and the islands of Suḳuṭrā (Socotra) and al-Maṣīra. Ibn Khaldūn (*Mukhtaṣar*, 132, ll. 11 f.) also says that the land, afterwards inhabited by the Mahra, in prehistoric times belonged to the ʿĀd mentioned in the Ḳurʾān.

The first Ḳaḥṭānid to settle in this area is said to have been Mālik b. Ḥimyar, who was succeeded by his son Ḳuḍāʿa. The latter's possessions, however, became restricted to the land which later was named after his great-grandson (Yāḳūt, *Muʿdjam*, iv, 700, l. 10; Ibn Khaldūn, *Mukhtaṣar*, 132, ll. 13-17). Ibn Khaldūn goes on to say that the Mahra have come to their later dwelling-places from Ḥaḍramawt or from the Ḳuḍāʿa, but this certainly does not correspond with reality. The derivation of the Mahra from the Ḳaḥṭān through Ḳuḍāʿa and Ḥimyar is a mere construction of Arabic genealogists which does not withstand examination. Immigration from further west is also out of the question. Although the Mahra do not have written historical traditions, yet in their oral transmission the memory survives of large parts of ʿUmān having belonged in earlier times to the regions where they were living and roaming and of their being expelled from there by the Arabs. The pressure of their eastern neighbours must have caused the Mahra to withdraw to the west and brought about their great loss of fertile regions. W. Dostal (*Beduinen*, 184-8) supports this tradition of the Mahra by collating non-Arabic place-names in south-east Arabia ending in *-ūt*, *-ōt* and *-īt*. He also illustrates this tradition with the aid of a map showing the spread of Mahrī place-names (*Beduinen*, 133, Pl. 19). Further criteria for Mahrī place-names in this region are: the ending *-ēt* occuring as a variant of *-īt*, the feminine plural endings *-ōten* and *-ūten*, the relative frequency of place-names with the prefixes *ya-* and *yi-*, and finally the etymology which in many cases indicates a place-name as being clearly Mahrī. The majority of these place-names, mostly names of wādīs, lies in the interior. On the coast they are only found in the area which is traditionally Mahrī. Their greatest density occurs between long. 51° and 55° and lat. 16° and 18°. Since more than half of these non-Arabic place-names lie in regions now inhabited by Arabic-speaking tribes, this finding shows at the same time the present limitations of the Mahrī living space. Al-Hamdānī (*Ṣifa*, 52, ll. 5 ff.; *Iklīl*, i, 73, l. 15) still attests that the Banū Riyām, a group of the Mahra tribe of the Ḳamar, were settled in ʿUmān; other tribes, too, he remarks, have their dwelling places in the region of ʿUmān (*Iklīl*, i, 73, l. 5) or on the sea-coast of ʿUmān (*Iklīl*, i, 73, l. 4). Other groups, like the Banū Khanzirīt (*Ṣifa*, 51, ll. 25 ff.) and the Thugharā (*Ṣifa*, 52, ll. 2 ff.) were entangled in warlike altercations with Arabs who pressed forward along the coast into Mahra-land. Al-Hamdānī (*Ṣifa*, 51, ll. 16 ff.) still includes in his description of the "Green Yemen" the territory of the Mahra tribes of the Ghayth, Ḳamar and ʿUḳār. On the island of Suḳuṭrā [*q.v.*] (Socotra), Mahra are also to be found living (al-Hamdānī, *Ṣifa*, 53, l. 1), i.e. members of all Mahra tribes (*Iklīl*, i, 74, l. 9). Ibn Ruzayḳ attests that even in the year 884/1479-80, part of ʿUmān was in the possession of the Mahra, since in that year the Ibāḍī *Imām* compelled the departure of the Mahra from ʿUmān.

After 608/1211-12, the Mahra tribe of the Banū Ẓanna pushed forward into the eastern part of Ḥaḍramawt, where they exercised control over the town of Tarīm for some time after 673/1274-5. In 945/1538-9 serious danger was brought to the Mahra by the Banū Kathīr under sultan Badr Bū Ṭuwayriḳ. The latter occupied great parts of the Mahra territory, and in 952/1545-6 conquered even the Mahra port of Ḳishn, where they murdered almost all the members of the family of the sultan of the Banū ʿAfrār, the *mashāyikh* of the Mahra. But in 955/1548-9 sultan Saʿīd b. ʿAbd Allāh of the Banū ʿAfrār succeeded in reconquering the town of Ḳishn from the Banū Kathīr. He started from the island of Suḳuṭrā, where the Mahra had constructed a fortress after the retreat of the Portuguese in 917/1511-2. Since the Kathīr had joined the Ottomans, the Mahra were supported by the Portuguese. In 1876 the Mahra sultan of Suḳuṭrā and Ḳishn guaranteed not to surrender any of his possessions except to the British Government and in 1886 he agreed to a Treaty of Protectorate with Great Britain.

The Mahra also participated in the Islamic campaigns of conquest. Together with other South Arabians, they settled in ʿIrāḳ and in even greater numbers in Egypt. In Kūfa and in Old Cairo they lived in their own quarters (cf. the *khiṭṭat Mahra* of al-Fusṭāṭ in al-Ḳalḳashandī, *Ṣubḥ al-aʿshā*, iii, 327, l. 12). There were also communications between the coast of Mahra-land and the island of Suḳuṭrā on the one hand, and with East Africa on the other, where the Mahra may have had settlements. Thus on Vasco da Gama's first journey, the Mahrī Ibn Mādjid [*q.v.*] guided the Portuguese as a pilot from Malindi to India. As well as Sulaymān Mahrī [*q.v.*], he left behind nautical texts. In 923/1517 the Mamlūk sultan Barsbāy enlisted Mahra as soldiers for his undertaking in the Yemen (see L. O. Schuman, *Political history of the Yemen at the beginning of the 16th century. Abū Makhrama's account of the years 906-927 h. (1500-1522 A.D.) with annotations*, Groningen 1960, 27 ff.). Mahra are attested in Zaylaʿ during the years 944-5/1537-9, and a group of about seventy Mahra with their chiefs (*muḳaddams*) are repeatedly mentioned in the *Futūḥ al-Ḥabasha* (see Serjeant, *Portuguese*, 81, n. 5). The Comoro Islands [see KUMR] allegedly owe their name to the Ḳamar or Moon mountains of Mahra-land (see H. Ingrams, *Arabia and the Isles*³, New York 1966, 64). For Mahra immigrants to Somalia, see E. Cerulli, *Un gruppo Mahri nella Somalia Italiana*, in *RSO*, xi (1926-8), 25-6.

The Mahra are "tall handsome people" (Ibn al-

Mudjāwir, 271, 1. 17) of brown complexion with black, often curly, hair. Because of these physical characteristics they have been considered as not belonging to the Mediterranean race but as related rather to the Veddas in South India. Until circumcision, boys have their hair shaven at both sides, so that only a tuft remains in the middle of the head. Circumcision of boys takes place at the age of twelve or also, as was usual in earlier days, only immediately before the wedding. After circumcision the hair grows long, either tied into a knot or falling down loosely and only kept together with a long braid, either plaited or made of leather; growing a beard is forbidden. Sedentary Mahra wear an indigo-coloured loin cloth and a skirt, the Bedouin generally only a loin cloth, an extremity of which can be thrown over the shoulder. Boys' ornaments consist of amulets and occasionally also necklaces; men adorn themselves with a leather belt equipped with characteristic ornamentation and sometimes stitched with pearls. Many Bedouin also wear an earring in the right ear and an armlet above the right elbow. Tattooing scars are also found, and all men carry the curved dagger (*djanbiyya*), more as an ornament than as a weapon. Nowadays, rifle and cartridge-belt are carried as weapons; formerly there were used the spear and the throwing stick terminating almost in a point, together with a sword without a sheath and a round shield. The Mahra have their own war-cry. They greet each other with a threefold kiss on the cheek, starting with the right cheek, then the left and the right again. Girls are circumcised immediately after birth. Mahra women wear the hair braided and go unveiled. Women's dress is preferably also indigo-coloured and has an open square or round neck. Women like to wear many silver ornaments like chains at the forehead, rings at nose, ears, fingers and ankles, and armlets (Ibn al-Mudjāwir, 271, 1. 12, describes Mahra virgins as *mukhalkhalāt mudamladjāt* "provided with armlets and ankle rings"), and occasionally wearing head or neck ornament hanging down to the belt, single parts of which are adorned with geometrical embellishments and cornelians (*aķīķ*). At the neck, an amulet of leather, silver or gold is also worn, and one side of the nose is usually perforated in order to wear a precious stone as ornament. The breast ornament is an indication of the social status of the wearer. Women also use face-painting.

The nomads among the Mahra make do with modest shelters. They live mainly in caves, seek refuge under protruding rocks or make a roof against the sun amongst trees and shrubs. Remarks that the Mahra in these dwelling-places resemble animals (Ibn al-Mudjāwir, 272, 11. 2 ff.) and are like wild animals (*wuḥūsh*) in those sands (Ibn Khaldūn, *Mukhtaṣar*, 132, 1. 12), may allude to their modest way of life and their familiarity with the surrounding nature. In their land, the Mahra do not know the cultivation of date-palms or agriculture (al-Iṣṭakhrī, 25, l. 12); this information refers of course to the Bedouin and not to the sedentary Mahra who, in the western part of their land, at the edge of Wādī Masīla, practice a well-developped farming and lay out palm plantations. The riches of the Mahra consist of camels and goats, while they live on meat, milk and a kind of small fish on which they also feed the animals (Ibn Khaldūn, *Muktaṣar*, 132, 11. 3 ff.). This fish is the sardine-like *ᶜayd*, found in great numbers along the coast and which, after having been dried, is given to the animals, especially when other food is lacking. Goats are still predominant among the Mahra and more appreciated than sheep. Camels bred by the Mahra (sing. *mahriyyat*^{un}, pl. *mahārā*, *mahār*^{in} *and mahāriyy*^{u}) were considered from ancient times as a particularly good breed (al-Hamdānī, *Ṣifa* 100, 11. 1 ff.). Among these were valued as noble the ᶜĪdite camels, named after ᶜĪdī (vocalisation according to al-Hamdānī, *Iklīl*, i, 73, 1. 11), a Mahra tribe (*Ṣifa*, 201, 1. 14). Already in the biography of the Prophet (Ibn Hishām, *Sīra*, ed. F. Wüstenfeld, 963, 1. 9) Mahra camels are mentioned; they were valued by the caliphs (al-Ķazwīnī, *ᶜAdjāʾib*, i, 41, 11. 3 ff.) and repeatedly celebrated by the ancient poets (e.g. Abū Tammām, *Dīwān*, ed. M. ᶜA. ᶜAzzām, ii, 132, 1. 4 = *Aghānī*^{1}, xv, 106, 1. 16). They spread as far as North Africa, where the form *mahrī* (pl. *mahārā*) made its way into French as *méhari* "riding camel" (pl. *méhara*) from which term was derived *méhariste* to indicate a member of the camel riders. Besides making use of their herds, the Mahra provide the transport of merchandise by procuring caravan service, convey pilgrims to the places of pilgrimage and supply local markets with camels. If they do not possess their own incense trees, a supplementary source of livelihood consists in employment as seasonal workers in Ẓufār at the time of the incense harvest in order to scrape the gum off the trees; The Ķarā leave their incense trees to the Bedouin to take half of the harvest. The Mahra living on the coast are mostly fishermen; a few are also merchants and seafarers. With the rise of the oil industry in the Arab countries of the Gulf, many Mahras have departed thither as labourers.

Among the Mahra exists a patrilinear system of kinship; however, still-remaining traces of matriliny point to an earlier matrilineal social structure. Monogamy is the prevailing form of marriage; if polygamy occurs, it is in fact mainly a multi-local polygamy based on uxorilocal marriage.

The Mahra settle their social and political affairs almost exclusively inside their tribe. The sultanate of the Banū ᶜAfrār exercised authority only in name, and thus had only a limited influence on the political situation of the mainland, the more so because the sultan used to reside on Suķuṭrā, with another member of the ᶜAfrār family acting as his representative in Ķishn. The real power over the individual tribes is in the hands of their chiefs, the *muķaddams*, who have always enjoyed great esteem. Feuds exist between the Mahra and almost all of their neighbouring tribes (see the charts on inter-tribal relations in Dostal, *Beduinen*, 109); lasting hostility exists especially with the Manāhil. Friendly relations exist only with the Banū Kathīr and the Banū Rāshid, bringing about also marriages between members of these tribes and the Mahra.

Al-Hamdānī (*Ṣifa*, 87, 1. 11) relates that the Mahra visit at all times the tomb of the Prophet Hūd. Besides this pilgrimage place, the Mahra also venerate other holy places like the tomb of Bin ᶜAlī in Mirbāṭ, of *shaykh* ᶜAfīf in Ṭāķa or of Bin ᶜArībat in Raysūt. Oath-taking and vows play an important rôle among them (see T. M. Johnstone, *Oath-taking and vows in Oman*, in *Arabian Studies*, ii [1975], 7-18). In order to prove their innocence, they swear on the tombs of the saints and invoke divine judgement by way of ordeal by fire. They practise all kinds of charms, especially against malevolent *djinn* or against the evil eye. Ibn al-Mudjāwir (271, 11. 17-272, 1. 1) even wanted to derive from *siḥr* "witchcraft" the term Saḥara, another name for the Mahra which has not as yet been satisfactorily explained. He attributes (272, 1. 1) to the Mahra ignorance (*djahl*) and reason (*ᶜaķl*) and some demoniac possession (*djunūn*), moreover, and continues (272, 1. 2) by saying that they benefit from God's blessings without giving praise and thanks, and that they worship not Him but someone else. The first statement probably refers to the indifference in religious matters and to the non-performance of the prescribed worship, which can be observed especially among the nomadic Mahra. The last statement, on the other hand, may be attributed to the fact that the Mahrī language does not know either the word *Allāh* or the word *rabb*, but speaks of God as *bālī* (literally "my Lord"), so that an Arab, not understanding this word might infer that they serve another deity. Ibn Khaldūn (*Mukhtaṣar*, 132, 11. 12 ff.), however, rightly remarks that, so far as religious confession is concerned, the Mahra are Khāridjīs, in fact Ibāḍīs [*q.vv.*]. Information about the Mahra's conversion to Islam is given by Ibn Saʿd, *Ṭabaḳāt*, i/2, Leiden 1917, 83, 11. 13-26. After the Prophet's death, Mahra-land also formed part of the areas joining the *ridda* movement; but ʿIkrima, one of Abū Bakr's commanders, succeeded in reconquering Mahra-land for Islam (al-Ṭabarī, *Taʾrīkh*, i, 1980, 1. 5 - 1982, 1. 2).

Bibliography: Apart from the works quoted in the text, only the more frequently quoted and most important sources are mentioned here: Ṭabarī, *Taʾrīkh*; Hamdānī, *Ṣifat djazīrat al-ʿArab*, i, ed. D. H. Müller, 1884; Hamdānī, *al-Iklīl*, i/2, ed. O. Löfgren, Uppsala 1965; Iṣṭakhrī; Muḳaddasī; Yāḳūt, *Muʿdjam al-buldān*; Ibn al-Mudjāwir, *Taʾrīkh al-mustabṣir*, ii, ed. O. Löfgren, Leiden 1954; Ibn Khaldūn, *Mukhtaṣar al-taʾrīkh*, with H. C. Kay, *Yaman, its early mediaeval history*, London 1892, 103-38 of the Arabic text; A. Sprenger, *Die alte Geographie Arabiens*, Bern 1875; A. Jahn, *Die Mehri-Sprache in Südarabien*, Vienna 1902; W. Hein, *Mehri- und Ḥaḍrami-Texte*, Vienna 1909; J. Tkatsch, art. *Mahra*, in *EI*[1] (contains numerous further details on the history of the exploration of Mahra-land and the Mahrī language); R. B. Serjeant, *The Portuguese off the South Arabian coast*, Oxford 1963; W. Dostal, *Die Beduinen in Südarabien*, Vienna 1967 (this is the most important work on the Mahra, based on field-studies; it has been much utilised for the present article), cf. the review of W. W. Müller, in *ZDMG*, cxviii (1968), 399-402; T. M. Johnstone, *Folklore and folk literature in Oman and Socotra*, in *Arabian Studies*, i (1974), 7-23; J. Carter, *Tribal Structures in Oman*, in *Proceedings of the Seminar for Arabian Studies*, vii (1977), 11-68, esp. 37-49. (W. W. MÜLLER)

MAḤRAM BILḲĪS. [see MĀRIB].

MAHRATTAS. [see MARĀTHĀ].

MAHRĪ. The Mahrī language, called by its speakers Məhrayyət, is spoken by many thousands, both Bedouin and settled people, over a large area of South Arabia extending in a great half-circle from Mukallā in South Yemen to the small coastal towns of Ẓufār or Dhofar. In South Yemen, the speakers are Bedouin, merchants, fishermen and seamen, but many Mahra of the more prosperous classes are now monolingual in Arabic. In Ẓufār, the Mahrī speakers are, or were, mainly concentrated in Nadjd, the high desert area of Ẓufār behind the fertile part of the long mountain range (Mahrī *śaḥayr*) which is largely populated by speakers of Djibbālī. For a long time, however, there have been large settlements of Mahra in the eastern coastal towns and their hinterlands, and in some of these coastal towns (like Sidḥ, for example), the Mahra speak only Arabic and Djibbālī.

The Mahra also continuously penetrate the *śaḥayr*, the fertile part of the Ẓufār mountain which gets the monsoon rains, not without some resistance from the Ḳarā, the dominant Djibbālī-speaking group. Many of these immigrants lose their Mahrī language also, and come to speak only Djibbālī and Arabic. The western dialect is not confined entirely to South Yemen, and is spoken in the coastal area of Ẓufār nearest to South Yemen (where there is also a definably western dialect of Djibbālī).

A number of non-Mahrī groups within this area speak what may be defined as dialects of Mahrī, or as languages closely related to Mahrī. Within Ẓufār, a small group of people, the Baṭāḥira, speak a language or dialect closely related to Mahrī. Now fishermen, formerly of humble status, they were apparently driven from their homes in the fertile hinterland of the coastal towns of Shuwaymiyya and Sharbithāt, at or near where they are now mainly settled. It seems likely that they learnt their language from the invaders, unlike the Ḳarā who would seem to have learnt their language from the original inhabitants of the fertile area they conquered. In the desert between the Ẓufār province and the Sharḳiyya province of ʿUmān, in the area between Haymā and the Wādī Ḥalfayn, is the small tribe of the Ḥarāsīs, apparently of Arab origin. Ḥarsūsī, which is fairly easily understood by Mahra, shows signs of having been acquired by them on the borders of Ẓufār and South Yemen. In the same border area is the last of the groups speaking a Mahrī-related language, namely Hobyot. Hobyot is spoken by a small number of people in little settlements on both sides of the border. It shares a few features with Ḥarsūsī: thus, "I want" is *xōm* in Ḥarsūsī and *xom* in Hobyot, as against Mahrī *ḥōm* and Baṭḥarī *ḥām*.

Nadjdī Mahrī (NM) appears to be a more conservative dialect than the South Yemen dialect (SM). Thus NM retains the interdentals *ṯ*, *ḏ* and *ḏ̣*, which in (most dialects of) SM are replaced by *t*, *d̄*, and *ṭ*. The Austrian expedition (SAE) publications give no indication that SM has a definite article, a passive voice, or conditional verb forms. This does not conclusively prove that they do not occur in SM, however, since the SAE publications also give no indication that glottalised consonants occur in SM, though they do occur in SM texts recorded by the present writer.

The principal features of interest in the phonology of Mahrī (M) are, firstly, the occurence of the glottalised consonants *ḏ̣* (mainly NM), *ḳ*, *ṣ*, *ṣ́*, and *ṭ* (as against the series of emphatic/velarised consonants in Arabic), the occurrence of the laterals *ś* and *ź* (which probably occurred in early pre-literary Arabic) and finally the (virtual) non-occurrence of the voiced pharyngal (Ar. *ʿayn*).

The syllabication of M is also of considerable historical and comparative interest. In M all forms with a final Cv (C) syllable (other than -CəC) have final stress. This stress results in a lengthening of the vowel of the final syllable where it was not already long, and the reduction to *ə* of the short (or lengthened) vowels of the non-final syllables.

Thus consider *katūb* ("he wrote", from earlier **katab(a)*), *kətəbūt* ("she wrote" from **katabat*), and *kətəbīs* ("he wrote it", f., from **katab-a-s*). Non-final stress occurs in many earlier monosyllables. Thus *baḏr*, "seed" has become *bēḏər*, but in affixed forms it remains *-baḏr-*, as, e.g., *abaḏrəh*, "his seed", where the *a*-element is a definite article. It is a puzzling feature of phonology that the vowel of the stressed syllable of nominal forms is not always of the same quality as that of the comparable verbal forms. Thus contrast *səyūr*, "he went", with *səbēb*, "cause"; and *bēḏər*, "seed" with *ṯībər*, "it got broken". Even if it is likely that the nouns lost their final vowels before the verbs (though some plural nouns like *ḥādūtən*, "hands", still have a final nunation which is elided on affixation), this does not throw much light on the problem. Fem.

nouns, for example, may be characterised by an *-ēt*, *-īt*, *-ōt*, or *-ūt* ending.

The noun in M is not inflected for case but has two genders, masc. and fem., and three numbers, sing., dual and pl. Some common nouns, such as *bayt*, "house" and *nəhōr*, "day", are fem. in M (and indeed, in all the Modern South Arabian languages). The dual in M ends in *-i*, thus *gawgi*, "two men" and *fakhi*, "[two] halves". It rarely occurs without a following numeral *ṯərō* (masc.) or *ṯərayt* (fem.), "two", and, unlike dual verb forms, can be considered to be obsolescent. Thus speakers clearly believe when they say "two boys" that they are saying *gəggēn iṯrō*, and not *gəggēni ṯrō*.

Nouns have sound or broken plurals. Masc. nouns for the most part have broken plurals, while fem. nouns mostly have sound pls. in *-ōtən*, *ūtən*, *-áttən*, etc. The noun in NM can be defined by the prefixation of *a*. This can, however, be affixed only to words with an initial voiced or glottalised consonant. Thus *kətōb*, "a/the book", *abēḏər*, "the seed", and *aṣayd*, "the fish".

The verb in M has two main simple themes and six derived themes, namely:

Simple	CəCūC (a) and CīCəC (b)
Intensive-conative	(a)CōCəC
Causative	həCCūC
Reflexive	CatCəC (a) and əCtəCūc (b)
Causative-reflexive	šəCCūc (a) and šəCēCəC (b)

The reflexive types (a) and (b) often overlap in their conjugation.

The verb has a perfective and an imperfective aspect. The imperf. indic. and subj. patterns are markedly different from Arabic. Thus consider *kətūb* (perf.)/*yəkūtəb* (indic.)/*yəktēb* (subj.)/*yəktēbən* (cond.). Conditional forms occur relatively rarely, mainly in sentences involving hypothetical conditions. All dependent verbs are subj., and the subj. also functions as a jussive and occasionally as a kind of future. Imperative forms are subj. in syllable structure but lack the personal prefixes, so, e.g. *k(ə)tēb!*, "write'.". The verb has the following persons: 3 m.s., 3 f.s., 2 m.s., 2 f.s., 1 c.s.; 3 m.du., 3 f.du., 2 c.du., 1 c.du; 3 m.pl., 3 f.pl., 2 m.pl., 2 f.pl., 1 c.pl. The verb has also verbal nouns, and active and passive participles. The active participle (as, e.g., m.s. *kətbōna*, f.s. *kətbīta*, etc.) functions as a future.

Mahrī (or at least NM) has a large vocabulary relatively little affected by Arabic, and there is a good deal of resistance to borrowings from Arabic. Lexical items may be considered to be for comparative purposes in a number of categories: words which have no cognates in literary or colloquial Arabic (as, e.g., *śxəwəlūl*, "he sat"); words which have Ar. cognates but cannot, for phonological or morphological reasons, be borrowings (as, e.g., *źáfōr*, Dhofar/Ẓafār); words which have the same radicals as the equivalent Ar. words (as, e.g., *səd*, "it sufficed"); words which have been borrowed and modified to become completely Mahrī in terms of phonology and morphology (such as, perhaps, *əbtōdi*, "he began"); and borrowings from Ar. which have been left virtually unchanged (as, e.g., *məftāḥ*, "key"). There is a large area of the vocabulary, which is not possible to categorise with any degree of certainty. Since M and Ar. have lived side by side for many centuries, it is difficult to say in many cases which language has borrowed from the other. Thus *səyūr*, "he went", is paralleled by *sār* in most Ar. dialects of the South. It is just as likely, however, that such Ar. dialects are influenced by Mahrī as that Mahrī has been influenced by Arabic.

Bibliography: All references up to his date of publication are collected in W. Leslau, *Modern South Arabian languages—a bibliography*, New York 1946; for later references, see E. Wagner, *Syntax der Mehri-Sprache...*, Berlin 1953. The most important of these earlier sources are the following (all published in Vienna) by the Austrian South Arabian Expedition (*SAE*) associates: (grammar) A. Jahn, *Grammatik der Mehri-Sprache in Südarabien*, in *SB Ak. Wien*, Phil.-Hist. Kl., Bd. 150, Abh. 6, 1905; M. Bittner, *Studien zur Laut- und Formenlehre der Mehri-Sprache in Südarabien*, in *SB Ak. Wien*, Phil.-Hist. Kl., Bd. 162, Abh. 5; Bd. 168, Abh. 2; Bd. 172, Abh. 5; Bd. 174, Abh. 4; Bd. 178, Abh. 2, 3, 1909-15; (texts) A. Jahn, *SAE* 3, 1902 (with vocabulary); W. Hein, *SAE* 9, 1909 (ed. D. H. Müller); D. H. Müller, *SAE* 7, 1907. For more recent work, see the following publications of T. M. Johnstone: *Ḥarsūsi lexicon*, Oxford 1977; *A definite article in the Modern South Arabian languages*, in *BSOAS*, xxxiii/2 (1970); *Dual forms in Mehri and Ḥarsūsi*, in *BSOAS*, xxxiii/3 (1970); *Diminutive patterns in the Modern South Arabian languages*, in *JSS*, xviii (1973); *Folklore and folk-literature in Oman and Socotra*, in *Arabian Studies*, i (1973); *Contrasting articulations in the Modern South Arabian languages*, in *Hamito-Semitica*, Leiden 1975; *Oath-taking and vows in Oman*, in *Ar. St.*, ii (1975); *Knots and curses*, in *Ar. St.*, iii (1976); *A St. George of Dhofar*, in *Ar. St.*, iv (1977); *Jibbāli lexicon*, 1981; *Mehri lexicon*, 1984.

(T. M. Johnstone)

MAHSATĪ (the most probable interpretation of the consonants *mhsty*, for which other forms, like Mahistī, Mahsitī or Mihistī, have been proposed as well; cf. Meier, 43 ff.) a Persian female poet whose historical personality is difficult to ascertain.

She must have lived at some time between the early 5th/11th and the middle of the 6th/12th century. The earliest sources situate her alternatively in the environment of Maḥmūd of Ghazna, of the Saldjūḳ Sultan Sandjar, or of a legendary king of Gandja in Ādharbāydjān. The qualification *dabīr* or *dabīra* is often attached to her name, but it is uncertain whether she actually worked as a professional scribe, the function designated by this term. Usually, she is represented as a singer and a musician as well as a poet of the court, though not as a panegyrist. The poems attributed to her name are almost without exception quatrains. Their dominating theme is the lover's complaint about the absence, the lack of attention or the cruelty of his or her beloved. Several poems belong to the genre of *shahrāshūb* poetry in which the beloved is presented as a young craftsman. Mahsatī has acquired a reputation as a writer of bawdy verse. Mystical and fatalistic thoughts, often expressed in Persian quatrains, are absent and the antinomism of the *ḳalandariyyāt* can only seldom be found. The authenticity of these poems remains in each case questionable. An original collection is not known to exist. The current *dīwāns* of Mahsatī are modern compilations from many different sources.

Mahsatī became already at an early date the heroine of romantic tales. The oldest specimen is contained in ʿAṭṭār's *Ilāhī-nāma* (Meier, 53-6; tr. J. A. Boyle, Manchester 1976, 218-20). A similar story, embellished by inserted quatrains, was used by ʿAbd Allāh Djawharī in a commentary on the *ḳaṣīda-yi ḥawliyya*, a poem about alchemy, towards the end of the 7th/13th century. It is, however, not derived from ʿAṭṭār's story (Meier, 63-7). The *Dāstān-i Amīr Aḥmad-u Mahsatī* is a popular romance, built upon an extensive cycle of quatrains, dealing with the love between two poets, of whom the former is sometimes referred to as "the son of the preacher of Gandja" (*pūr-i khaṭīb-i Gandja*). It is extant in two versions of different lengths (Meier, 123 and *passim*; E. E. Bertel's, *Nizami i Fuzuli*, 78, n. 12).

Bibliography: The fundamental study by F. Meier, *Die schöne Mahsati. Ein Beitrag zur Geschichte des persischen Vierzeilers. Band I*, Wiesbaden 1963, gives full references to the preceding literature. It also contains a critical edition of 279 poems with translation and commentary; the quatrains which only occur in the *Dāstān*, have been excluded. See further: E. E. Bertel's, *Istoriya persidsko-tadžikskoy literaturî*, Moscow 1960, 425, 489 f.; idem, *Nizami-i Fuzuli*, Moscow 1962, 77-81; Īradj Afshār, *Fihrist-i maḳālāt-i fārsī*, i, Tehran 1340/1961, 693-6 and ii, Tehran 1348/1969, 495; A. Gulčīn-i maʿānī, *Shahr-āshūb dar shiʿr-i fārsī*, Tehran 1346/1967, 15-7; J. Rypka *et alii*, *History of Iranian literature*, Dordrecht 1968, 199.

(J. T. P. de Bruijn)

MAHSŪD, the name of a Paṭhān tribe on the north-west frontier of Pakistan, in British Indian times the fiercest opponents there of British rule. The Mahsūds inhabit the heart of Wazīristān around Kāniguram and are shut off from Pakistan territory by the Bhittanni country. On all other sides they are flanked by Darwīsh Khēl Wazīrīs. It is now generally accepted that they left their original home in the Birmal hills of modern Afghānistān sometime towards the close of the 8th/14th century and gradually extending eastwards occupied the country in which they now reside. The tribe has three main branches: the Bahlōlzay, Shaman Khēl, and the ʿAlīzay.

The Mahsūds have always been the scourge of the Bannū and Dēradjāt borders. This was the case in the days of Sikh rule and, after the annexation of the Pandjāb in 1849, they still continued to plunder and devastate the borders of British India. This and the fact that their rocky mountain fastnesses command the Gōmal and Toči, two of the five main passes connecting India with Afghānistān, compelled the British to resort to reprisals. On three occasions, in 1860, 1881 and 1894, the Mahsūds became so troublesome that punitive expeditions had to be undertaken against them. On the conclusion of the 1860 expedition, a temporary peace was patched up by which each of the three main sections of the tribe agreed to hold themselves responsible for outrages committed by their respective clansmen. From 1862 to 1874 various sections of the tribe were at one time or another placed under a blockade until, in 1873 and 1874 respectively, the Shaman Khēl and Bahlōlzay, finding their continued exclusion from British territory irksome, made full submission. The burning of Tank by a band of Mahsūds in 1879 and other outrages brought about the expedition of 1881, when a British force penetrated Wazīristān as far as Kāniguram and Makīn. For the next ten years, British subjects were left practically unmolested and the whole of the Wazīrī border enjoyed a period of comparative peace. So peacefully disposed were the Mahsūds that, in 1883, they even rendered assistance in the survey of the country around Khadjuri Kač, and, in 1890, were granted allowances for the watch and ward of the Gōmal pass.

In 1894, under the influence of Mullā Powinda, a Shābī Khel *mullā* belonging to the ʿAlīzay section of the tribe, the Mahsūds attacked the British boundary demarcation camp in defiance of the subsidised *maliks*. From this time the Mullā's influence steadily increased, and all efforts to uphold the authority of the *maliks* against his faction failed. Continued depredations along the British borders after 1897 called for reprisals. From December 1900 to March 1902, the Mahsūds were subjected to a stringent blockade, but it was only after the blockade had been varied by sudden punitive sallies into the Mahsūd hills that they were forced to come to terms. During this period, there were two factions in the country, the one headed by the *maliks*, the other by their enemy, the Mullā Powinda (to whom also, in an effort at conciliation, a monthly allowance had been granted in 1900); and from 1902 onwards the Mullā's influence was paramount. After 1908 the Mahsūd question became acute again, and a series of raids into British territory were traced to him. On his death in 1913, his place was taken by Mullā ʿAbd al-Ḥākim, who continued the policy of attempting to preserve the independence of the Mahsūd country between British India and Afghānistān by exploiting the marauding proclivities of the tribesmen. From 1914 to 1917 the history of the Dēra Ismāʿīl Khān district was one long tale of rapine and outrage. Eventually, in 1917, troops marched into the Mahsūd country, but were able to effect only a temporary settlement. British preoccupations elsewhere delayed the day of retribution, and during 1919 and 1920, the wind-swept *raghzas* of Wazīristān witnessed the severest fighting in the annals of the Indian frontier.

During the disturbances in Afghānistān following on the abdication of Amān Allāh [*q.v.* in Suppl.] and the brief assumption of power by the adventurer Bačča-yi Saḳāō (1928), Mahsūds and Wazīrs joined the returning Nādir Khān in his march on Kābul, and were the spearhead of his successful bid for the throne. But they were disappointed at not receiving a licence to loot indiscriminately, and were subsequently stirred up by the partisans of Amān Allāh, so that in 1933 a Mahsūd and Wazīr *lashkar* crossed the Durand Line and besieged Matun in the Khōst district till repulsed by Nādir's brother Hāshim Khān.

From 1936 onwards, the Mahsūds were further inflamed by the presence amongst them of the virulently anti-British "Faḳīr of Ipi" [*q.v.* in Suppl.], Ḥādjdjī Mīrzā ʿAlī Khān, and in 1938 they and the Wazīrs were stirred up by the "Shāmī Pīr", Saʿīd al-Djīlānī from Syria, who established himself at Kāniguram with the aim of working for a restoration in Afghānistān of Amān Allāh, until the Pīr was bought off by a large subsidy from the Government of India.

Mahsūds and Wazīrs took part enthusiastically in the Kashmiri *djihād* against India in 1948; since Partition, considerable numbers of Mahsūds have migrated down to the Indus valley and other parts of Pakistan in search of work.

Bibliography: C. U. Aitchison, *Treaties, engagements and sanads*, xi, Bombay 1909; R. I. Bruce, *The Forward Policy and its results*, London 1900; C. C. Davies, *The problem of the North-West Frontier*, Cambridge 1932; idem, *Coercive measures on the Indian borderland*, in *Army Quarterly Review*, April 1928; R. H. Davies, *Report showing relations of British Government with tribes on N.W.F. of the Punjab, 1855-1864*, 1864; *Frontier and overseas expeditions from India (confidential)*, ii, 1908; *North-West Frontier Province administration reports* (published annually in British Indian times); *Operations in Waziristan, 1919-1920*, 1921; W. H. Paget and A. H. Mason, *Record of expeditions against the N.W.F. Tribes since the annexation of the Punjab*, London 1884; *Panjab administration reports*, 1850-1900; *Parliamentary papers*, lxxi, Cd. 1177, 1902; H. Priestley, *Ḥayāt-i Afghānī*, 1874; H. A. Rose, *Glossary of tribes and castes of the Punjab and North-West Frontier Province*, iii, s.v. Wazīr; H. C. Wylly, *From the Black Mountain to Waziristan*, 1912;

Sir Olaf Caroe, *The Pathans 550 B.C.-A.D. 1957*, London 1958, 392-4, 397, 406-9; J. W. Spain, *The Pathan borderland*, The Hague 1963, 52-3.

(C. Collin Davies*)

MAḤSŪSĀT (A.), "sensibilia". For the theories of sense-perception held by the principal *falāsifa* of Islam, see ḤISS. In addition to these, it should be mentioned that Ibn Bād̲j̲dja is perhaps the philosopher who most closely follows Aristotle's views on this subject, and that his *Kitāb al-Nafs* (ed. M. S. Ḥasan Maʿṣūmī, Damascus 1960; tr. as *Ibn Bajja's ʿIlm al-nafs*, Karachi n.d.), while undoubtedly an original work, may be regarded as almost a paraphrase of Aristotle's *De anima*. In particular, he differs from other Islamic philosophers in not referring to to "internal" and "external" senses or to *al-ḳuwwa al-mus̲h̲tarika*.

In *falsafa*, *maḥsūsāt* are frequently contrasted with *maʿḳūlāt*, "intelligibilia'. In *taṣawwuf*, however, both are regarded as equally unreliable as means of arriving at the truth and are contrasted with *d̲h̲awḳ*. For a clear statement of this position, see al-G̲h̲azālī, *al-Munḳid̲h̲ min al-ḍalāl* (where *ʿaḳliyyāt* is used rather than *maʿḳūlāt*). In spite of the Ṣūfīs' avowed rejection of *falsafa*, such views as these may, to some degree, be considered to represent less a complete abandonment of it than a turning away from Aristotelianism towards Platonism (in neo-Platonic guise). That *falsafa* continued to exercise an influence may be seen from D̲j̲alāl al-Dīn Rūmī's references in the *Mat̲h̲nawī* to the "internal" and "external" senses and to the "common sense".

Bibliography: Given in the article and in ḤISS.

(J. N. Mattock)

MĀHŪR, a small town of mediaeval India in the extreme north of the former Hyderabad State of British India. It is situated in lat. 19° 49′ N. and long. 77° 58′ E. just to the south of the Pengangā river, a left-bank affluent of the Godavari, where it forms the boundary between the former regions of northern Hyderabad [see ḤAYDARĀBĀD] and Berār [*q.v.*] in Central India.

In pre-Muslim times, Māhūr had the shrine of Śrī-Dattātreya. In the middle years of the 8th/14th century, the territory up to Māhūr was conquered by the Deccani power of the Bahmanīs [*q.v.*]. In 857/1453 Maḥmūd I K̲h̲ald̲j̲ī [*q.v.*] of Mālwa besieged the fortress of Māhūr, but was unable to conquer it from the Bahmanīs, and in 872/1468 it was again a bone of contention between the two powers. In later times, however, it relapsed into insignificance. In British Indian times, it fell after 1905 within the ʿĀdilābād District and *taʿalluḳ*, the district being described in the 1901 census as sparsely-populated forest land, with 76% of the people being Hindus, 11% animistic Gonds and 5% Muslims, whilst, from the linguistic point of view, 44% were Telugu-speaking and 28% Marāṭhī-speaking. In the Indian Union, after the 1956 administrative reorganisation, the Māhūr region was placed within Maharashtra State, and is now in Nanded District and Kinvat *taʿalluḳ*. Māhūr village had in 1971 a population of 380.

Māhūr has an important fortress, which may have been in existence in pre-Bahmanid times. It stands on a steep hill 380 feet/120 m. above the valley of the Pengangā, and is irregularly shaped since it occupies the edges of two adjacent spurs (the intermediate valley is converted into a large tank through the construction of a massive connecting wall); the hill is precipitous on the east, south and west, its northern access being defended by multiple gateways. The main northern gateway (known as Čīnī Darwāza, from the panels of Bahmanid tilework on its façade) encloses a defended entry with guard rooms along each side, and the *Ḳilʿadār*'s residence is set in an upper storey.

Bibliography: *Gazeteer of India. Provincial series. Hyderabad State*, Calcutta 1909; G. Yazdani, *Report on ʿĀdilābād District*, in *Annual Report, Archaeol. Dept. Hyderabad*, 1327 F./1917-18, 6-8; *Maharashtra State District gazeteers. Nanded*, Bombay 1971; Description of some of the antiquities in *Jnal. Hyderabad Archaeol. Soc.* (1918), 48-59.

(C. E. Bosworth-J. Burton Page)

MAḤYĀ, a communal nightly liturgical ritual in which the recital of supplications for divine grace for the Prophet [see ṢALAWĀT] is central.

Such sessions were originally introduced as a mystical method [see ṬARĪḲA] by Nūr al-Dīn al-S̲h̲ūnī (d. 944/1537; cf. Brockelmann, II, 438, for the titles and additional details about the *ṣalawāt* composed by him), a *s̲h̲ayk̲h̲* of ʿAbd al-Wahhāb al-S̲h̲aʿrānī [*q.v.*] at the mosque of Aḥmad al-Badawī in Ṭanṭā and at al-Azhar mosque in Cairo in the year 897/1491-2 (ʿAbd al-Wahhāb al-S̲h̲aʿrānī, *al-Ṭabaḳāt al-kubrā*, Cairo 1954, ii, 172-3; cf. Nad̲j̲m al-Dīn b. Muḥammad al-G̲h̲azzī, *al-Kawākib al-sāʾira fī aʿyān al-miʿa al-ʿas̲h̲ira*, Beirut 1945-59, ii, 216-19). The meetings were held after the *mag̲h̲rib* prayer on Thursday night until the *ad̲h̲ān* for the Friday prayer the following noon. Later, *maḥyā* sessions were held on Monday night as well (*al-Ṭabaḳāt*, ii, 171). In these sessions many candles were burnt. This aspect brought about criticism from the side of the students at the mosque. They condemned it as an act of Mazdaism. It elicited a *fatwā* from al-Burhān b. Abī S̲h̲arīf who denounced the lightning of more candles than were necessary for sufficient illumination (al-G̲h̲azzī, ii, 216), while Abu 'l-ʿAbbās Aḥmad b. Muḥammad al-Ḳasṭallānī [*q.v.*] wrote a treatise in its defence (see al-G̲h̲azzī, *ibid.*).

The spread of this new institution in Egypt and from there to Syria, North Africa, Takrūr and the Hid̲j̲āz during al-S̲h̲ūnī's life-time (see *al-Ṭabaḳāt*, ii, 172) may be viewed as one of the manifestations of the growing reverence for the Prophet, particularly from the 7th/13th century onwards (cf. T. Andrae, *Die Person Muhammeds in Lehre und Glauben seiner Gemeinde*, Stockholm 1918, 379, 388, and I. Goldziher, *Ueber den Brauch der Maḥjâ Versammlungen im Islam*, in *WZKM* xv [1901], 38 f.).

At al-Azhar, supervision and organisation of these meetings became institutionalised in an office. The incumbent to this office was known as *s̲h̲ayk̲h̲ al-maḥyā*. The names of the *mas̲h̲āyik̲h̲ al-maḥyā* from al-S̲h̲ūnī until the year 1057/1647-8 are mentioned by Muḥammad al-Muḥibbī, *K̲h̲ulāṣat al-at̲h̲ar fī aʿyān al-ḳarn al-ḥādī ʿas̲h̲ar*, Cairo 1284, i, 266, iii, 382 f. (see also ʿAbd al-Wahhāb al-S̲h̲aʿrānī, *al-Ṭabaḳāt al-ṣug̲h̲rā*, Cairo 1970, 88 f. for data concerning al-S̲h̲ūnī's *k̲h̲alīfa*, S̲h̲ihāb al-Dīn al-Bulḳīnī, d. 960/1553). After this year, no incumbents are known and no information concerning the exact nature of the office has become available. It seems likely, however, that the office of *s̲h̲ayk̲h̲ al-maḥyā* has been similar to the offices of *s̲h̲ayk̲h̲ ḳurrāʾ al-Ḥizb* and *s̲h̲ayk̲h̲ ḳirāʾat Dalāʾil al-K̲h̲ayrāt* existing in 19th century Egypt (cf. F. De Jong, *Ṭuruq and ṭuruq-linked institutions in nineteenth century Egypt. A historical study in organizational dimensions of Islamic mysticism*, Leiden 1978, 112). The office of *s̲h̲ayk̲h̲ al-maḥyā* must have become redundant or greatly insignificant during the 18th century, since no mention of an incumbent is made in ʿAbd al-Raḥmān al-D̲j̲abartī, *ʿAd̲j̲āʾib al-āt̲h̲ār fi 'l-tarād̲j̲im wa 'l-ak̲h̲bār*, while the term *maḥyā* itself lost its specific meaning and became synonymous with *dhikr* [*q.v.*]; cf. Abu 'l-Fayḍ Muḥammad Murtaḍā al-Zabīdī, *Tādj al-ʿarūs min sharḥ djawāhir al-Ḳāmūs*, Cairo 1306-7, x, 110.

In this sense, and more particularly in the sense of weekly *ḥaḍra* [*q.v.*], the term is used in a treatise by the well-known Rifāʿiyya *shaykh* Muḥammad Abu 'l-Hudā al-Ṣayyādī (1859-1909), *al-Ṭarīḳa al-Rifāʿiyya*, Baghdād 1969, 131. In the 7th/13th century another Rifāʿiyya author uses the term *maḥyā* (ʿIzz al-Dīn Aḥmad al-Ṣayyād al-Rifāʿī, *al-Maʿārif al-Muḥammadiyya fi 'l-waẓāʾif al-Aḥmadiyya*, Cairo 1305, 41, 89; the context, however, defies identification of its meaning). The term is equally employed to denote the *ḥaḍra* of the Demirdāshiyya order [*q.v.*] in Cairo, which is not a *maḥyā* of the type introduced by al-Shūnī, as is erroneously supposed by Goldziher (*ibid.*, 49 f.; cf. E. Bannerth, *La Khalwatiyya en Egypte. Quelques aspects de la vie d'une confrérie*, in *MIDEO*, viii [1964-6], 47; and idem, *Über den Stifter und Sonderbrauch der Demirdāšiyya Sufis in Kairo*, in *WZKM*, lxii [1969], 130, for a description of the ritual. For the texts recited during the *ḥaḍra*, see also Ḥusayn Amīn al-Ṣayyād, *al-Fuyūḍāt al-nūrāniyya fī maḥyā al-ṭarīḳa al-Demirdāshiyya*, Cairo n.d., 12 ff.). In Egypt, the increasing institutionalisation of Islamic mysticism, in particular in the 9th/15th century, in *ṭarīḳas*, some of which, like the Shādhiliyya [*q.v.*], held the recital of *ṣalawāt* as part of the *ḥaḍra*, and the rise of al-Shaʿrāniyya [*q.v.*] as an independent *ṭarīḳa* after the death of ʿAbd al-Wahhāb al-Shaʿrānī (d. 973/1565), who had been *shaykh al-maḥyā* in al-Ghamurī mosque (cf. al-Ghazzī, ii, 217), may have contributed to the decline of the *maḥyā* as an institution independent from the main stream of Islamic mysticism.

Before the middle of the 10th/16th century, the *maḥyā* had also become institutionalised in Mecca, as is testified by a *fatwā* given by Ibn Ḥadjar al-Haytamī [*q.v.*], *al-Fatāwī al-ḥadīthiyya*, Cairo 1307, 137-40, relative to the *ṣalawāt* formulae recited on these occasions. No other data on the *maḥyā* in this part of the Islamic world have come down to us.

In Damascus, the *maḥyā* was introduced by ʿAbd al-Ḳādir b. Muḥammad b. Suwār (921-1014/1515-1605). The first *maḥyā* in this city was held in al-Buzūrī mosque in Radjab 970/March 1563. Shortly afterwards, a weekly *maḥyā* was started in the Umayyad mosque (cf. al-Muḥibbī, ii, 454; iii, 276; Muḥammad Khalīl al-Murādī, *Silk al-Durar fī aʿyān al-ḳarn al-thānīʿashar*, Būlāḳ, 1301, i, 112 f.; ii, 160; iii, 179; and al-Ghazzī, ii, 218). In Damascus, as in Cairo, organisation and supervision of the *maḥyā* sessions became an office which is referred to in the sources as *shaykh al-maḥyā* (Aḥmad al-Budayrī, *Ḥawādīth Dimashḳ al-yawmiyya (1154-75/1741-62)*, ed. Aḥmad ʿIzzat ʿAbd al-Karīm, Cairo 1359, 180, 230; al-Muḥibbī, i, 281, 336; ii, 454; iv, 375) and *shaykh sadjdjādat al-maḥyā al-sharīf* (al-Murādī, iii, 142). This office, about which little is known, was hereditary within the Ibn Suwār family. Members of this family conducted *maḥyā* sessions twice weekly at the mosques mentioned, until the end of the 19th century at least (cf. Goldziher, 49).

In addition, the term *laylat al-maḥyā* (night of the *maḥyā*, i.e. the night made alive by devotional activity; cf. Goldziher, 42; and al-Ghazzī, ii, 217, for etymological details and references) was used to denote the night of 27 Radjab, when religious gatherings were held at the shrine of ʿAlī, in early 8th/14th century al-Nadjaf (Ibn Baṭṭūṭa, i, 417-8); the night of 27 Ramaḍān, when the Ḥarīriyya order commemorated the death of the order's founder, in 8th/14th century Damascus (Kutubī, *Fawāt*, Cairo 1951, ii, 91); and the night of mid-Shaʿbān in, as would seem, several parts of the Islamic world in that period (see Muḥammad b. Muḥammad al-ʿAbdarī (= Ibn al-Ḥādjdj), *al-Mudkhal*, Cairo 1320, i, 260; and also ʿAlī b. al-Ḥasan b. Aḥmad al-Wāsiṭī, *Khulāṣat al-iksīr fī nasab sayyidinā al-Ghawth al-Rifāʿī al-Kabīr*, Cairo 1306, 92).

Bibliography: Given in the article.

(F. de Jong)

MAIMONIDES. [see ibn maymūn].

MAʿIN, name of an ancient people of Southwest Arabia, mentioned by the 3rd century B. C. Greek geographer Eratosthenes as one of the four principal peoples (*ethnē*) of the area, under the form Minaioi.

In Strabo and Pliny they figure as largely engaged in the aromatics trade between South Arabia and the Mediterranean; according to Pliny, they were the initiators of the frankincense trade. Apart from sparse notices in Greek and Latin sources, our knowledge of them is based on their own inscriptions, in a distinctive language which has however some afinities with the language of Saba [*q.v.*]. The widespread nature of their trade is evidenced by Minaean inscriptions from the island of Delos and from the Egyptian Fayyūm, but apart from such scattered examples, all the texts in this language come from in and around their main centre Ḳarnaw (Khirbet Maʿin) at the eastern end of the South Arabian Djawf, from the oasis of Yathill (Barāḳish) a little south of there (both these places still show impressive town walls), and from their trading settlement at Dedan (al-ʿUlā in the northern Ḥidjāz). But they certainly had other similar trading posts elsewhere, and a Ḳatabanian language text from Timnaʿ in the Wādī Bayhān [see ḳatabān] mentions a "magistrate of the Minaeans in Timnaʿ".

In effect, the term Minaeans seems to have had a double application. There must have been an original Minaean folk who, to judge from Pliny's remark that "they possessed palmgroves, but their main wealth lay in cattle", may perhaps most plausibly be sited in the steppe country north of Ḳarnaw. But considered as a trading organisation, they were subdivided in a number of *ahālī* or "folks", of whom the most significant in the texts are the *ahl GBʾN*. Earlier scholars did not hesitate to identify these with Pliny's Gebbanitae, and although in recent years there has been a tendency to equate them with the Ḳatabanians, the earlier view still seems more probable, since Pliny's Gebbanitae (and also Strabo's Gabaioi) figure as principally concerned with the frankincense trade up the west coast of Arabia. The Minaean language texts all belong within the Ptolemaic period, and after Pliny (whose information may well be already a little out-of-date when he wrote), they disappear from the records. Evidently, therefore, their trading monopoly had broken up by about the turn of he Christian era, the west coast trade having been taken over by Nabataeans and other north Arabian peoples, while the Minaeans seem to have sunk back into obscurity.

Bibliography: Strabo, *Geogr.*, xvi. 4 4; Pliny, *Nat. hist.*, xii. 54, 63-4, 68-9, 88; *Les monuments de Maʿīn*, i by M. Tawfik, ii by K. Y. Nami (Publs. Inst. Fr. d'Arch. Or. du Caire, Etudes sudarabiques, 1-2), Cairo 1951-2; J. Pirenne, *Paléographie des inscriptions sud-arabiques*, i, Brussels 1956; A. F. L. Beeston, *Pliny's Gebbanitae*, in *Procs. Fifth Seminar for Arabian Studies*, London 1972, 5-8; idem, *Some observations on Greek and Latin data relative to South Arabia*, in *BSOAS*, xlii (1979), 7-12).

(A. F. L. Beeston)

MĀḲADŪNYĀ, the Ottoman Turkish name for

Macedonia, a region which occupies the centre of the Balkan Peninsula. Despite its historically mixed population of Slavs, Ottoman Turks, Greeks, Albanians, Vlachs, Sephardic Jews and others, Macedonia forms a geographical unit. Its boundaries are sometimes disputed, but may be said to follow the line of peaks which stretches from the Šar Planina in the north to the Rhodope range and the river Mesta in the east, and to the Albanian mountains and the Pindus in the west. On the southern side it is naturally limited by the Gulf of Salonica. Macedonia was visited by the early Arab traveller Hārūn b. Yaḥyā, and is mentioned in the form *Maḳadūniyā* by the ʿAbbāsid geographer Ibn Khurradādhbih (257/870) and by the anonymous *Ḥudūd al-ʿālam* (372/982).

1. Ottoman Macedonia. Immediately before the Ottoman conquest, Macedonia was loosely divided between the Byzantine and various local potentates. In 784/1383, during the reign of Murād I, Ottoman forces penetrated as far as Seres, and in 787/1385 captured Ishtīp (Štip), Manāstir, (Monastir, Bitola) and Pirlepe (Prilep). Üsküb (Skopje) fell in 794/1391. Selānīk (Salonica) was briefly held from 789/1387, but not finally secured until 834/1430. Thereafter Ottoman rule was consolidated. The frontier marches were replaced by *sandjaḳ*s dependent on the *beglerbeglik* of Rūmelī, and the *tīmār* system was introduced. Turkish settlements began at an early date. Anatolian *yürük*s were established in the neighbourhood of Selānīk, Ishtīp and Üsküb. The *dewshirme* [*q.v.*] was levied, and during the 9th-10th/15th-16th centuries, conversion to Islam proceeded at a significant rate. Institutions of Islamic culture and learning were established in the major towns. Popular Islam was in the hands of the dervish orders, amongst whom the Bektāshīs were prominent. The 11th/17th century saw the emergence of an intractable *ḥaydūd* or brigandage problem. Economically, the region was a traditional exporter of grain; the development of *čiftlik*s [*q.v.*] in the 12th/18th century led to an expansion of rice and tobacco cultivation. The Ottoman Empire did not recognise Macedonia as an administrative unit, and the *sandjaḳ*s, into which the *beglerbeglik*, subsequently *eyālet*, of Rūmelī was divided, bore little relation to Macedonia's geographical borders. In 1864 the *Law of the Wilāyets* divided the region between the *wilāyet*s of Ḳoṣowa, Manāstir and Selānīk, and apart from a brief period when the *wilāyet* of Manāstir was suppressed, this administrative partition survived to the end of Ottoman rule.

2. "The Macedonian question". Macedonia acquired a political significance during the 19th century as a result of the revival of the Christian nationalities and the rival aspirations of Greeks, Serbs and Bulgarians to establish themselves in Macedonia as the Ottoman Empire's prospective successor. The Greeks were the first to mount an effective national propaganda designed to secure the allegiance of the Macedonian Christians, but they were rapidly challenged by the Bulgarians, who won ecclesiastical independence with the establishment of the Bulgarian Exarchate in 1870. Russia obliged Sultan ʿAbd al-Ḥamīd II to agree to the inclusion of most of Macedonia in an autonomous Bulgarian principality at the Treaty of San Stefano (3 March 1878), but the subsequent Treaty of Berlin (13 July 1878) restored Macedonia to Ottoman control. Greek, Serbian and Bulgarian propaganda continued, and began to assume a violent form. In 1893 local Slavs formed the Internal Macedonia-Adrianople Revolutionary Organisation to fight for the establishment of an autonomous Macedonia. It was soon rivalled by the overtly pro-Bulgarian Supreme Macedonian Committee. There was an upsurge of guerilla and terrorist activity in which Greeks, Vlachs and Albanians soon joined. The Internal Organisation's abortive Ilinden Rising in August 1903 led the Powers to impose a programme of administrative reforms upon Sultan ʿAbd al-Ḥamīd, but their intervention fanned existing discontent among Ottoman troops stationed in Macedonia, where the *Ittiḥād we Teraḳḳī Djemʿiyyeti* [*q.v.*] was increasingly active. As a result, it was from Macedonia that the sucessful Young Turk Revolution was launched in July 1908. The Young Turk régime attempted to alter the confessional balance in Macedonia by encouraging the immigration of Muslims from Bosnia, but lost all of Macedonia in the Balkan Wars of 1912-13. Macedonia was partitioned between Greece, Bulgaria and Serbia (subsequently Yugoslavia). Bulgaria's share was reduced somewhat after World War I. The partition has had far-reaching ethnic consequences. Thanks to immigration from Asia Minor, the population of Greek Macedonia now consists overwhelmingly of Hellenes. Before World War II, attempts were made to Serbianise Yugoslav Macedonia; however, the subsequent Communist régime has recognised the Macedonian Slavs as a separate historic Macedonian nation. The Turkish population has been drastically reduced by emigration to Asia Minor. In 1913 Turks accounted for 29.5% of the population of Greek Macedonia, and numbered some 300,000: all were deported during the Greco-Turkish population exchanges of the 1920s. Bulgarian Macedonia, where Turks accounted for 16.3% of the population in 1913, has been similarly cleared. The Turkish population of Yugoslav Macedonia has been reduced by voluntary emigration from a total of 209,000 in 1913 to 129,000 in 1971, falling as a proportion of the total population from 19.3% to 6.6%. Against this, the Albanian population of Yugoslav Macedonia rose from 13% of the total in 1961 to 17% in 1971. The surviving Turkish community in Yugoslav Macedonia enjoys full minority rights.

Bibliography: The geography and ethnography of Ottoman Macedonia is outlined in S. Gopčevič, *Makedonien und Alt-Serbien*, Vienna 1889; Benderev, *Voennaya geografiya i statistika Makedonii i sosyednikh s neyu oblastey Balkanskogo poluostrova*, St. Petersburg 1890; and J. Cvijić, *Mazedoien und Altserbien*, Gotha 1908. For mediaeval Islamic geographers, see V. Minorsky, tr., *Ḥudūd al-ʿālam*, London 1937, 156, 420. There exists no comprehensive account of Macedonia under Ottoman rule. *Istorija na Makedonskiot narod*, 3 vols., Skopje 1969, is sketchy. Local Ottoman administrative materials have been translated into Macedonian and published in the two series, *Turski dokumenti za istorija na Makedonskiot narod*, i-iv, Skopje 1963-72, and *Turski dokumenti za Makedonskata istorija*, i-v, Skopje 1952-8. Documents from Istanbul are published as *Makedonija vo XVI i XVII vek: dokumenti od carigradskite arhivi (1557-1645)*, Skopje 1955. A. Birken, *Die Provinzen des Osmanischen Reiches*, Wiesbaden 1976, describes provincial organisation, as does B. Cvetkova, *Les institutions ottomanes en Europe*, Wiesbaden 1978, which also deals with economic and social questions. The *sālnāme*s of the *wilāyet*s of Ḳoṣowa, Manāstir and Selānīk give basic information for the later Ottoman period, as does Maḥmūd, *Manāstir wilāyetiniñ taʾrīkhčesi*, Manāstir n.d. Popular religion is dealt with in F. M. Hasluck, *Christianity and Islam under the sultanate*, 2 vols., Oxford 1929. The question of Islamisation is broached in B. Cvetkova, *op. cit.* Settlement of *yürüks* is dealt with in M. Tayyib Gökbilgin, *Rumeli'de Yürükler, Tatarlar ve Evlâd-ı Fâtihân*, Istanbul 1957. The *ḥaydūd* problem is documented in J. Vasdravellis, *Klephts, Armatoles and pirates in Macedonia during the rule of the Turks 1627-1821*, Thessaloniki 1975, and in two volumes of documents published as *Turski izvori za ajdutstvoto i aramistvoto vo Makedonija*, Skopje 1961. See also A. Stojanovski, *Dervendžistvoto vo Makedonija*, Skopje 1974. Aspects of economic history are covered in N. Todorov (ed.), *La ville balkanique, XVe-XIXe siècles*, Sofia 1970; Khr. Khristov, *Agrarnite otnosheniya v Makedoniya prez XIX v. i načalato na XX v.*, Sofia 1964; Zografski, *Razvitokot na kapitalističkite elementi vo Makedonija*, Skopje 1967, contains much data. See also M. Lascaris, *Salonique à la fin du XVIII siècle d'après les rapports consulaires français*, Athens 1939; N. Svoronos, *Le commerce de Salonique au XVIII siècle*, Paris 1956; F. Bianconi, *Carte commerciale de la province de Macedoine*, Paris 1888; Khr. Gandev. *Tărgovskata obmena na Evropa s bălgarskite zemi prez XVIII i nachaloto na XIX vek*, in *Godishnik na sofiiskiya univerzitet*, xl, Sofia 1944; A. Matkovski, *G'určin Kokaleski*, Skopje 1959. The literature of the Macedonian question is extensive and highly controversial. F. Adanır, *Die macedonische Frage*, Wiesbaden 1979, uses Turkish materials; E. Barker, *Macedonia*, London 1950, concentrates on the post-Ottoman period. The issue is approached from varying national standpoints by E. Kofos, *Nationalism and Communism in Macedonia*, Thessaloniki 1964; I. Katardžiev, *Serskiot okrug od kresnenskoto vostanie do mladoturskata revolucija*, Skopje 1968; G. Kyosev, *Istoriya na makedonskoto natsionalno revolyutsionno dvizhenie*, Sofia 1954. Useful information is found in D. Dakin, *The Greek struggle in Macedonia 1897-1912*, Thessaloniki 1966; Khr. Silyanov, *Osvoboditelnite borbi na Makedoniya*, 2 vols., Sofia 1933-43. Some light is shed on the attitudes of ʿAbd al-Ḥamīd II and his advisers by M. Hocaoğlu, *Abdülhamit Han'ın muhtırları*, Istanbul n.d.; H. K. Bayur, *Sadrazam Kâmil Paşa*, Ankara 1954; Saʿīd Pasha, *Saʿīd Pasha'niñ khāṭirāti*, ii, Istanbul 1328. The Macedonian background to the Young Turk Revolution is traced in Aḥmed Niyāzī, *Khāṭirāt-i Niyāzī*, Istanbul 1326; Kâzim Nami Duru, *Arnavutluk ve Makedonya hatıralarım*, Istanbul 1959; *Şevket Süreyya Aydemir, Enver Paşa*, i, Istanbul 1970. Albanian aspects are covered by J. Bartl, *Die albanischen Muslime zur Zeit der nationalen Unabhängigkeitsbewegung (1878-1912)*, Wiesbaden 1968; Stavro Skendi, *The Albanian national awakening 1878-1912*, Princeton 1967. Tahsin Uzer, *Makedonya eşkıyalık tarihi ve son osmanlı yönetimi*, Ankara 1979, is a personal memoir of the *Ittiḥād we Teraḳḳi Djemʿiyyeti* in Macedonia. For a brief account of the fate of the Turkish population of Macedonia since 1913, R. Grulich, *Die türkische Volksgruppe in Jugoslawien*, in *Materiala Turcica*, i, Bochum 1975, the Yugoslav Turkish periodicals *Sesler*, *Çevren*, and *Birlik* may also be consulted. (F. A. K. Yasamee)

MAḲĀLA (a.), article.

1. In Arabic

This *maṣdar mīmī* from the root *ḳ-w-l* "to say", has etymologically the sense of "statement", "utterance", etc. It will be noted, however, that in a typical hundred pages of text from the classical period, it is found only once with this "oral" sense (Ch. Vial, *Al-Ǧāḥiẓ, quatre essais*, ii, Cairo 1979, 132). On the other hand, its usage in contemporary Arabic is remarkably frequent, all the more so in that its sense is henceforward almost exclusively related to the written rather than the spoken text. The modern user designates by the word *maḳāl* or *maḳāla* that which we call "article", and doubtless there would be nothing further to add in this context were it not that the history of the word impinges upon the recent history of Arabic literature.

It being unnecessary to dwell in detail on an evolution which is now well-known, it will simply be recalled that modern Arabic prose has been forged through the intermediary of the press. It was a a result of the creation and development of Arab journals and reviews at the end of the 19th century that the affected and inflated language which had hitherto prevailed rapidly gave way to a convenient and direct means of expression. In avoiding the conventional attractions of hackneyed rhythm and rhyme (*sadjʿ*), the writer simultaneously freed himself from the mould of entrenched ideas which had hitherto been imposed on a variety of subjects. The liberation of the language was accompanied to a certain extent by a liberation of thought. This fundamental change was effected by departure from the domain of the classical Arabic humanities and by contact with European languages. There were genuine grounds for fearing that a movement of such magnitude might compromise the very nature of the Arabic language. There was much concern that, by dint of inspiration from foreign press agencies and the desire to imitate the style of European periodicals, the grammatical correctness of articles appearing in the Arabic press would be severely impaired. Authoritative voices—linguists, professors and writers—were raised to engage in often impassioned debate on the most common defects and on the means of preventing the corruption of the Arabic language. The development of education, the visceral attachment of the Arabs to their language, the frequent criticism brought to bear on the linguistic correctness of texts of all kinds, the painstaking work of academies of the Arabic language [see madjmaʿ ʿilmī. 1.], all these elements have enabled "the language of the press" to maintain a thoroughly respectable standard, even though—in Arabic as elsewhere—a number of eminent individuals protest at the liberties taken by the press, and more recently by radio and television, with the rules of the language (cf. in particular the arguments between linguists at the end of the last and the beginning of the present century; among them, the Lebanese Ibrāhīm al-Yāzidjī and his *Lughat al-djarāʾid*, Cairo 1901).

But the *maḳāla* does not represent only the testing bench or laboratory of that which, more elaborated and better adapted, has become the contemporary literary prose. It represents a mode of expression regarded as special, and some would go as far as to see it as a whole literary genre in its own right. In the same way that there is talk of oratorical literature (*adab al-khaṭāba*) it has come about that there is talk of literature of the article (*adab al-maḳāla*). There is an impression that, *mutatis mutandis*, the treatment of this term today is similar to the treatment undergone in the Middle Ages and until more recent times by the word *risāla* [*q.v.*]. In the latter case, the notion of "epistle" was abandoned in favour of that of a literary text of variable length and sometimes very long, retaining nothing in common with the idea of epistolary form other than the more or less fictitious existence of a recipient (sc. the one to whom the text is dedicated). Henceforward, the original sense of "letter", "missive", "epistle", was no longer appropriate and, as works of undisputed literary quality dealing in principle with a relatively circumscribed subject which is considered in an original manner, it became appropriate to regard them as "essays" (cf. Vial, *op. cit.*, i, 2-3). Also, it will be noted that the definition of this *risāla* genre is so vague that it becomes impossible to lay down the guidelines according to which literature is to be conceived either as a manifestation of thought or as an artistic effect, in other words, closer to the original expression of a consistent thought or more akin to gratuitous rhetorical cliché. Precisely the same considerations apply to the *maḳāla* (cf. Anouar Abdel-Malek, *Anthologie de la littérature arabe contemporaine.* ii. *Les essais*, Paris 1965).

On the one hand, Arab intellectuals who have acquired a western culture are inspired both by the ideas and the style of the French and English writers whom they have taken as models and masters. Djabrān, ʿArīḍa and Nuʿayma in America, al-ʿAḳḳād, Ṭāhā Ḥusayn and al-Māzinī in Egypt, have attempted to present and adapt to the Arab public a new conception of literature and of reflection, and the framework in which they have expressed themselves is precisely that of the *maḳāla*, where the temperament and style of each of these authors is revealed: the concise phrase of Nuʿayma, the causticness of al-ʿAḳḳād, the fulsome sentence-structure of Ṭāhā Ḥusayn, etc. Moreover, it is by no means absurd to consider an article of *Ḥaṣād al-Hashīm* by al-Māzinī as being just as revealing of his literary personality as one of his stories of *Bayt al-ṭāʿa*.

This close connection between essay and the narrative text enables a further step to be taken in the assessment of the role of the *maḳāla*. It is a known fact that the contemporary period has seen the development of a novelistic genre among the Arabs. As has been indicated above, the modernisation of the language, achieved as a direct result of the development of the press, gives to novelists an appropriate tool which they can perfect still further. But, on the other hand, there is a danger that the *maḳāla* may impose itself as a screen or as a substitute for narrative fiction as such. The first Arabic novels, those which attempt to evoke the problems of oriental society in the framework of an imported genre, often have the appearance of political or sociological articles. The first narrative essays of the ʿIrāḳī Dhu 'l-Nūn Ayyūb represent the transition between the article and the story and it is the author himself who calls them *al-maḳāṣṣa* (= *maḳāla ḳiṣṣa*). But even in the case of confirmed novelists, it is not unusual for the writer to indulge in an art which is located on the fringe of fiction. Examples are very numerous, but worthy of mention are the collections of articles by Yaḥyā Ḥaḳḳī and in particular one of his mixed collections (*ʿAntara wa-Djuliyat*) in which "tableaux" (*lawḥāt*) are found alongside "stories" in the true sense of the term. It is easy to demonstrate that, in this case as in other similar ones, the literary article which becomes the outline of a narrative corresponds to particular conditions of composition and readership; a journal is assured of the weekly collaboration of a writer of repute (in this case, for his humanity and his humour). The result of this is a special tone midway between the free expression of opinion or dilettante story-telling, and literary narration proper. The interest of the reader whose sympathy must be rapidly gained is attracted by the use of language that is apparently amiable and relaxed, but where the use of a carefully chosen dialectal term responds to strategic considerations. This having been said, it appears quite superfluous to consider *maḳāla* as a separate genre in itself, since if it were so, it would risk confusion with the "diverse" category, those *varia* which defy classification by any reputable catalogue.

Bibliography: Mainly given in the text, but see also ʿAbd al-Djabbār Dāwūd al-Baṣrī, *Ruwwād al-maḳāla al-adabiyya fi 'l-adab al-ʿirāḳī al-ḥadīth*, Baghdād n.d.; Muhammad Yūsuf Nadjm, *Fann al-maḳāla*, Beirut 1957; ʿAbd al-Laṭīf Ḥamza, *Adab al-maḳāla al-ṣuḥufiyya*, 8 vols., Cairo 1965, 1966 ff.

(Ch. Vial)

2. In Persian.

Maḳāla has been used in Persian to denote a collection of discourses, spoken or written, on a given subject (e.g. *Čahār maḳāla* by Niẓāmi-yi ʿArūḍī, ed. M. Muʿīn, 135; Khāḳānī's *Munshaʾāt*, ed. M. Rawshan, 174; Ḥamdīdī's *Maḳāmāt*, ed. Gh. Āhanī, 5, 17, 38; Bābā Afḍal's *Writings*, ed. Y. Mahdawī and M. Minōwī, ii, 393; *Djuwaynī's Tārīkh-i Djahāngushā*, ed. M. Ḳazwīnī, i, 32; and also the poems of Nāṣir-i Khusraw and Saʿdī). *Maḳāla* was used in reference to spoken discourses and sermons up to the late 19th century (see Muḥammad-Ḥasan Iʿtimād al-Salṭana, *al-Maʾāthir wa 'l-āthār*, under the biography of Burhān al-Wāʿiẓīn of Gīlān, 1306 A.H., 201 col. 1).

Maḳāla has also been used to designate a book's inner divisions, synonymously with such other terms as *faṣl*, *bāb*, *bakhsh* or *guftār*. Niẓāmī-yi ʿArūḍī, *op. cit.*, 19, writes: "The book, therefore, comprises four *maḳālat* ..., in each *maḳālat* whatever was found befitting in the domain of philosophy was included." The title of his work, *Čahār maḳāla*, was not bestowed upon it by its author. The book was found to contain four discourses, and so it became popularly known as *Čahār maḳāla*, and Ḥādjdjī Khalīfa appears to be the first person to have recorded down its title as such (see *Kashf al-ẓunūn*, under *Čahār maḳāla*).

The term *maḳālāt* has been also used for the utterances, statements and dictations of Ṣūfī *shaykhs*, the best-known of these being the *Maḳālāt-i Shams*; to the same category also belongs the *Maḳālāt-i ʿAlāʾ al-Dawla Simnānī*.

Maḳāla in contemporary Persian is synonymous with *article* in English and *article* or *essai* in French. It started with the practice of modern journalism in 19th century Iran, and was applied to almost any kind of writing produced for the printed page (even a news story, short story or play was often referred to as *maḳāla* in place of *nivishta* or *maṭlab*), and the person who engaged in such writing would be called *maḳāla-nivīs* or equally *maṭlab-nivīs* (see Afḍal al-Mulk Zandī, *Afḍal al-tawārīkh*, ed. M. Ittiḥādiyya and S. Saʿdwandiyān, Tehran 1361 A.H.S.).

The leading article of a newspaper, or its editorial, would be called *sar-maḳāla* in Persian, and a series that would be carried over several issues would be *maḳālāt-i musalsal* or *silsila maḳālāt*.

Scholarly papers, which usually get published in academic journals, are also referred to as *maḳāla* (see Zarrīnkūb's *Naḳd-i adabī*, ii, 640), and a volume containing a collection of such papers would be called *maḳālāt* or *madjmūʿa maḳālāt*, e.g. the *Maḳālāt-i Taḳīzāda* or *Maḳālāt-i Kasrawī*. Sometimes the number of papers contained in such a volume will provide an appropriate title for it, e.g. *Bīst* [20] *maḳāla-yi Ḳazwīnī*, *Bīst maḳāla-yi Taḳīzāda*, *Čihil* [40] *maḳāla-yi Ḥusayn Nakhdjawānī* and *Čand* [several] *maḳāla-yi Naṣr Allāh Falsafī*.

The practice of indexing published articles and papers does not go back a long time. For a listing of selected writings in the field of Iranian studies, Īradj Afshār's *Fihrist-i maḳālāt-i Fārsī* is available. Three volumes have been published so far, containing references to some 16,000 maḳālāt that have appeared between 1915 and 1971 in Iran. The fourth volume, unpublished as yet, deals with the writings of the past decade. Some other fields for which indexes are already available are geography, social sciences, economics, and law.

Bibliography: Given in the article.

(I. AFSHAR)

3. In Turkey

In the majority of Turkish dictionaries of the 19th century, the term maḳāla figures with the primary sense of "discourse", of "monograph" or of "thing said or written regarding any given subject" (Shams al-Dīn Sāmī, Ḳāmūs-i Türkī). In this period it is usually encountered, often in the plural (maḳālāt), in the titles of collected editions of the "sayings" or "writings" of a certain writer or eminent person. However, since the middle of the 19th century, with the development of the Turkish language press, it has appeared more and more frequently as a designation of an article published in a periodical, progressively displacing from current usage other words such as bend or baḥth.

Although a noun of Arabic origin, maḳāla has resisted quite well the various trends towards turkification of vocabulary which have characterised the history of the Turkish language in the 20th century. At the present time, this term is still in current use in the sense of an article in a journal or review (its primary sense of "thing said" having been forgotten), even though the word yazı "writing") which some would seek to substitute for it is gradually gaining ground, in spite of its inaccuracy.

Specialists in Turkish literature readily present maḳāla as a specific literary genre, distinct from the essay (deneme) or the anecdotal account (fıkra). It is thus, for example, that Cevdet Kudret defines it as a "writing composed with the object of exposing, defending or supporting a point of view on a certain subject" and states specifically that this type of work should not be confused with the essay (C. Kudret, Örneklerle edebiyat bilgileri, Istanbul 1980, ii, 372). In practice, however, it seems very difficult to assign precise limits to the maḳāla genre, this term being applied in fact, in customary usage, to every kind of article, ranging from the editorial of a daily newspaper to a learned study published in a specialist review, and including the article of literary criticism (generally classed in the category of "essays"), the "paper" of the historian or the political pamphlet.

While not constituting a major genre, the maḳāla is clearly a means of expression particularly valued by Turkish writers. The majority have written them while some, among the most eminent, have published nothing other than journalistic articles, promoting this type of production to the status of genuine artistic creation.

If the maḳāla has thus become the literary genre probably most widely practised in Turkey, this fact is to be explained in terms of the spectacular rise enjoyed by the periodical press in this country, beginning in the second half of the 19th century (see DJARĪDA. iii). The first Turkish language journals—the Taḳwīm-i waḳāʾiʿ, founded in 1832, and the Djerīde-yi ḥawādith launched by the Englishman William Churchill in 1840—accorded only limited space for "articles", and essentially offered their readers short stories and official bulletins. However, with the appearance in 1860 of Terdjumān-i aḥwāl, published by Agāh Efendi in collaboration with Shināsī [q.v.], one of the most talented

literary figures of the period, matters were to change in a radical manner. In fact, under the influence of Shināsī and of all those writers who were soon to become active in the same field, the nascent Turkish press rapidly acquired the objective not only of informing the public but also of working for the reform of society, and the journalistic article, in particular the editorial (soon to be designated by the term bash maḳāla), henceforward became a licensed instrument of education.

In the Turkish periodicals of the 1860s and 1870s, the majority of the leading contemporary literary figures are encountered. Besides Shināsī, who launched in 1861 his own journal, the Taṣwīr-i efkār, writers of renown including Ziyā (Ḍiyāʾ) Pasha, ʿAlī Suʿāwī, Nāmiḳ Kemāl, Shams al-Dīn Sāmī and Ebü l-Ziyā (Abū l-Ḍiyāʾ) Tewfīḳ, contributed to making the maḳāla one of the most flourishing genres. It was to a great extent through their articles, published in increasingly numerous intellectual journals, that ideas of reform began to spread at an accelerated pace. Neither political institutions, nor social structures, nor traditional culture escaped the criticism of these intellectuals of liberal tendency, most of whom belonged to the "Society of Young Ottomans" (Yeñi ʿOthmānlĭlar Djemʿiyyeti), which sought to transform Turkey into a modern country based on the model of the West, a state endowed with a constitutional régime and directed towards new manners of thought, life and action.

During this period of genesis, the newspaper article did not constitute only a means for the propagation of ideas received from elsewhere. It also played the role of a spear-head in the elaboration of a new literary language, closer to spoken Turkish. Shināsī and Ḍiyāʾ Pasha were among the first advocates of this simplification of the written language. They were soon followed by Nāmiḳ Kemāl—who was not always capable of putting into practice his own precepts on the matter—Shams al-Dīn Sāmī and numerous others.

While the maḳāla genre thus flourished in the context of the intellectual press, there also came into being in Turkey in the same period of time, a specialised periodical press—scientific reviews, women's magazines, professional organs, literary journals, etc.—in which there were to be found, alongside numerous translations, scholarly studies, articles of literary criticism and historical pieces comparable, in their professionalism, to writings of the same type promulgated by the Western press. Among these periodicals, one of the most notable was the Medjmūʿa-yi fünūn, founded in 1861 by Munīf Pasha. This monthly, which was presented as the organ of the "Ottoman Society of Sciences" (Djemʿiyyet-i ʿIlmiyye-yi ʿOthmāniyye [q.v.]) and which included articles dealing with such diverse disciplines as geography, history, geology, philosophy or natural sciences, was distinguished, during the few years of its existence, by the quality of its presentation and it played in Turkey of the mid-19th century a role similar to that of the Grande Encyclopédie in France of the Enlightenment.

Conscious of the danger which could be posed by these periodicals, which were continually growing in number, the Ottoman government had, since 1864, enacted various measures aimed at limiting the freedom of the press. With the accession to power of ʿAbd al-Ḥamīd II in 1876, the weight of bureaucratic interference was to become even more oppressive. But censorship, while preventing for several decades the publication of articles judged subversive, did not halt the development of Turkish journalistic production.

Indeed, on the contrary, as has been noted by Niyazi Berkes (*The development of secularism in Turkey*, Montreal 1964, 277), the prohibition, beginning at the end of the 1870s, of subjects of political nature, was largely balanced by the proliferation of writings on scientific or cultural themes, which led to the accelerated diffusion of new ideas and knowledge.

Aḥmed Midḥat Efendi is definitely the most representative publicist of the Ḥamīdian period. Becoming a fervent supporter of ʿAbd al-Ḥamīd II, after having flirted for some time with the adversaries of absolutism, he was very careful to write nothing which could have been interpreted as a criticism of the régime. This did not prevent him publishing an incalculable number of articles on the most diverse subjects, using the press, and in particular his own journal, the *Terdjümān-i ḥaḳīḳat*, founded in 1878, as a veritable instrument of popular instruction.

The same encyclopaedic, somewhat disorderly curiosity is encountered in the case of Abu 'l-Ḍiyā' Tewfīḳ who, for almost thirty years, was practically the sole contributor to the *Medjmūʿa-yi Abu 'l-Ḍiyā'*, one of the best cultural periodicals of the reign of ʿAbd al-Ḥamīd.

Among other great names of the Turkish press in this period, it is appropriate to mention also Aḥmed Iḥsān Bey, founder of the *Therwet-i fünūn*, a scientific and literary magazine which brought together, until *ca.* 1900, the best writers of the time, notably the poet Tewfīḳ Fikret and the essayist Djanāb Shihāb al-Dīn, thus opening the way to the development of a whole literary school, subject to diverse influences but especially interested in symbolism and realism as then practised in France.

This having been said, although *maḳāla*s on scientific or cultural themes represented, in these last years of the 19th century, the essence of Turkish journalistic production, political literature was also being developed. In fact, while within Turkey the periodical press employed its best efforts to avoid the attention of the Ḥamīdian censorship, abroad there was a proliferation of opposition journals, entirely devoted to anti-government diatribe. The Young Turk leader Aḥmed Riḍā Bey, who in 1895 had founded *Meshweret* in Paris, was one of the foremost exponents of the political *maḳāla* and an expert at transcribing into Turkish the effects of French eloquence. His rivals were the founder of *Mīzān*, Murād Bey, and various other revolutionaries, among whom particular mention is due to ʿAbd Allāh Djewdet, whose *ʿOthmānlî*, set in motion in Geneva in 1897, was for several years the most widely read organ of the Committee for Union and Progress.

After the Young Turk Revolution, which finally broke out in July 1908, the *maḳāla* genre was to enter a new stage in its development. The period of instability which ensued was marked not so much by liberalisation of control of the press as by the spectacular rise of a resolutely nationalist literature. In the daily press, it was the *Ṭanīn*, headed by Ḥüseyn Djāhid and Tewfīḳ Fikret, which played the role of the leading mouth-piece of this effervescent nationalism. But the Turkish intellectuals had at their disposal a large number of literary and scientific reviews in which they were able to publish considerably more "considered" articles than those destined for the daily consumption of the readers of newspapers.

According to a survey undertaken by Aḥmed Emīn in 1913 (*The development of modern Turkey as measured by its press*, New York 1914, 113-16), there were at this time in Istanbul, besides the official newspaper and 8 ministerial weekly bulletins, 60 periodicals, classified as follows: 6 dailies, 3 humorous magazines, 5 illustrated magazines, 6 "nationalist" reviews, 11 reviews intended for children, 2 women's journals, 6 religious reviews, 4 professional organs, 5 agricultural reviews, 6 military reviews and 7 scientific reviews. A large number of these periodicals had appeared after 1910, on the full crest of the nationalist wave, and they expressed, with different nuances and according to various approaches, the same aspiration towards a national rebirth. While the illustrated magazines accorded an ever increasing amount of space to photographs, the majority of the other reviews were composed almost entirely of *maḳāla*s, often quite long. It was not unusual, for example, for *Türk Yurdu*, one of the leading nationalist organs of the period, to publish articles ten or more pages in length, in the form of serials continued over several issues. *Maḳāla*s also occupied a relatively significant place in the daily press. According to the survey made by Aḥmed Emīn, *maḳāla*s of all kinds (editorials, points of view) covered between 30 and 52% of the space of the six journals in circulation when the survey was conducted in 1913. The editorial alone occupied 11.74% of the space in *Ṣabāḥ*, an independent pro-government journal, 11.20% in *Tanẓīmāt*, an organ of the extreme left, 1017% in *Yeñi Gazete*, favourable to the opposition and between 6 and 10% in *Ṭanīn*, official organ of the government, *ʿAlemdār* (opposition) and *Iḳdām* (moderate). These by no means negligible percentages testify in fact to the fidelity of the Turkish publicists to the tradition of the preceding decades where the *bash maḳāla*, the "leading article", constituted the essential and indispensable element of the newspaper, sometimes occupying as much as a quarter of the space available.

When this prolific production of articles is considered in total, the constant recurrence of certain themes cannot be other than striking. Among the questions of greatest interest to Turkish intellectuals in these years, the most prominent was the long-standing debate over the simplification and modernisation of the written language. The publication, in the review *Genč Ḳalemler* of Salonica, of a series of articles by ʿÖmer Seyf al-Dīn and ʿAlī Djānib proposing the adoption of the spoken Turkish of Istanbul as a means of literary expression was to open the way, in 1911, to the movement of the "new language". The impassioned discussions which took place around this theme mobilised a large number of writers, some favourable to the theses defended in *Genč Ḳalemler*—prominent among those belonging to this category was Ḍiyā' Gökalp, one of the leading advocates of the nationalist trend—others opposed to them, among whom it is appropriate to mention Köprülüzāde Meḥmed Fu'ād and Djanāb Shihāb al-Dīn, resolutely hostile to what they considered a debilitating debasement of the language. Another vigorous debate, in a quite different scheme of ideas, revolved around economic questions. Since the end of the 19th century, certain Turkish publicists, including Aḥmed Midḥat, had begun to express concern at Western control over the Ottoman economy and had advanced propositions aimed at putting an end to this state of affairs. Immediately after the Young Turk Revolution, controversies on this theme resumed in earnest, pitting the advocates of a liberal policy, favourable to foreign investments and freedom of commercial exchanges, against the supports of a strategy of tight government control, capable of opening the way to the establishment of a "national economy." Practically all the major periodicals of the period took part in these discussions, giving column space either to "enlightened amateurs" such as Ḍiyā' Gökalp and Muṣṭafā Ṣubḥī, or to genuine specialists such as Alexander Israël Helphand, alias Parvus (one of the leading figures of German Social Democracy who lived in Turkey from 1910 to 1915) or Tekin Alp (penname of Moïse Cohen), editor-in-chief of *Iktiṣādiyyat Medjmū ͨasi*, the leading economic review of the period.

In some publications, a very important place was also accorded to the literature and history of the Turks. In the review *Türk Yurdu* especially, writers whose origins lay in the Russian Empire, including Yūsuf Akčura, ͨAlī Hüseynzāde and Aḥmed Aghaoghlu, supported by Ottoman intellectuals including the novelist Khālid Edīb, the poet Djelāl Sāhir, the historian Köprülüzāde Meḥmed Fu'ād and the literary critic ͨAlī Djānib, skilfully exalted the prestigious past of the "Turkish race" and pleaded unceasingly for a reunification, if only cultural, of the peoples derived from the primal Central Asian stem. Among the periodicals contributing to this exploration of the literary and historical foundations of Turkish nationalism, also worthy of mention are the monthly *Bilgi* and the weekly *Khalḳa Doghru*, both published by Djelāl Sāhir, and, in particular, the *Ta'rīkh-i ͨOthmānī Endjümeni Medjmū ͨasi*, organ of the Ottoman Historical Society which, through the medium of the works of scholars such as Aḥmed Refīḳ and ͨAbd al-Raḥmān Sheref, the last official chronicler of the Imperial Court, was to give decisive encouragement to the development of a "national" Turkish historiography.

To the range of themes which caused the greatest amount of ink to flow in the Young Turk decade, it is appropriate to add, finally, the religious question. In this domain, the controversies were particularly impassioned. While Muslim periodicals such as *Volkan*, *Beyān al-ḥaḳḳ* or *Sebīl ül-reshād* pressed for various forms of Islamic revival, advocating the teaching of the Ḳur'ān as the effective response to the evils of the age, certain nationalists and the "westernists" who had as their principal mouth-piece the review *Idjtihād* of the doctor ͨAbd Allāh Djewdet, published numerous articles which, if not overtly anti-religious, at least favoured a "rationalisation" of Islam and went so far as to demand a strict secularisation of Ottoman institutions which would free civil society from all religious domination.

The entry of the Ottoman Empire into war in 1914 did not bring about a fundamental change in the subject-matter of the *maḳālas* published by Turkish men of letters. In fact, a large proportion of the work produced in the preceding years had already constituted a literature of propaganda, intended principally to equip public opinion with ideological weapons in readiness for the approaching conflict, signalled in advance by a succession of regular crises. However, with the outbreak of hostilities there was witnessed a sharp radicalisation of the points of view expressed in the periodical press. Learned controversies were replaced by slogans, the exaltation of the national identity was transformed into belligerence and the eulogy of "Turkish" cultural values became racism. This nationalism exacerbated by war did, however, allow numerous Turkish individuals to clarify their positions. It was during the war years that Tekin Alp and some others put the finishing touches to theories of "national economy". It was also during the war years that Ḍiyā' Gökalp, who had become the foremost ideologue of the régime, promoted in the most excessive terms the cause of "Turkism".

Naturally, the circumstances were hardly favourable to freedom of expression. Literary men were obliged to take into account not only the imperatives of the war but also the increasingly marked authoritarianism of the Committee for Union and Progress, the holders of absolute power since 1912. It was not until the end of the global conflict that a genuine plurality of opinions was once more established in the Turkish periodical press. To be sure, occupied by the forces of the Entente, Istanbul, the intellectual capital of the country, was obliged for many years to bow to the censorship of the Allied High Commissions. But that which could not be said and written in the Ottoman capital could be blazoned forth in Anatolia, where Muṣṭafā Kemāl was leading the struggle for Turkish independence, and conversely, writings which would not be tolerated by the Anatolian government could be published without difficulty in the regions controlled by the Entente.

In Istanbul, a large number of journalists and writers took advantage of this situation to oppose systematically the ideas propounded by the nationalists, and to campaign with equally vigorous propaganda against those who still supported the Committee of Union and Progress in opposition to Muṣṭafā Kemāl and his partisans. The most virulent among them was ͨAlī Kemāl Bey, editor-in-chief of *Peyām-i Ṣabāḥ*, whose editorials bore witness to a particularly incisive polemical talent. For their part, literary men who supported the nationalist movement undertook as their primary task to put a stop to defeatism, using their writings to stimulate Turkish patriotism. But some also pondered over the future of Turkey and indulged in speculation as to the form which would be taken by the future Turkish state. No reader of the journalism dating from the beginning of the War of Independence can fail to notice, in particular, to what an extent the nationalists were fascinated by the Soviet experience. In *Yeñi Gün*, editorials favourable to the Soviets—most of them owed to Yūnus Nādī, the proprietor of the newspaper, or to Maḥmūd Esͨad—could be counted by the score. Articles of similar type, though fewer in number, were also published by *Ḥākimiyyet-i milliyye*, the official organ of the Kemālist government. It is, however, appropriate to state that this love affair with revolutionary Russia was short-lived. At a very early stage, the ideologues of the national movement—prominent among whom was Muṣṭafā Kemāl himself, who did not hesitate to take to the pen to express his point of view—were putting forward concepts very similar to those championed some years previously by the theorists of the Young Turk régime, leaving the defence of the Soviets to genuine Communists such as Shefīḳ Ḥüsnü and Ṣadr al-Dīn Djelāl, the two leading contributors to the review *Aydīnlīḳ*.

Undoubtedly the most remarkable phenomenon in these years was the emergence of a genre closely related to that of the *maḳāla*, the *fiḳra*, a kind of short news item generally of entertaining nature, combining anecdote with comment on some matter of contemporary importance. The first major practitioner of this literary genre, Aḥmed Rāsim, had begun to publish his articles towards the end of the 19th century. Subsequently, numerous other writers, in particular the poet Aḥmed Hāshim and the journalist Ḥuseyn Djāhid Yalčīn, made names for themselves as eminent authors of *fiḳras*. But it was especially after the First World War, with the appearance of new specialists such as Refīḳ Khālid Karay and Fāliḥ Rīfḳī Atay, that this type of news-item came to occupy a position of major importance in newspapers and reviews, possibly because the anecdotal tone which was its distinguishing feature enabled it to discuss political questions in a manner unlikely to alarm the censors, possibly also because the public expressed an ever-increasing interest in this form of expression.

Extremely sensitive to the fluctuations of political circumstance, the Turkish periodical press was obliged once again to change its complexion in the mid-1920s, with the establishment in Turkey, shortly after the proclamation of the Republic, of a single-party régime. In fact, although this did not lead to the total disappearance of opposition newspapers and reviews, the monopoly exercised by Muṣṭafā Kemāl's creation, the Republican People's Party, over the conduct of public affairs was accompanied by a spectacular inflation—especially noticeable after 1930—in the press entrusted with the defence of the official line. This development of a republican press was made possible only by means of a vast mobilisation of intellectuals. Journalists, writers, historians, economists, sociologists, all were called upon to make their contribution to the building of the new Turkey. Those who responded to this appeal—and there were many of them—did so by producing for the Kemālist periodicals *makala*s remarkable, whatever the subject tackled, for the eagerness of their commitment.

It is probably in the monthly *Kadro*, published between 1932 and 1934, that there appeared the most remarkable and significant articles of the period. Motivated by a relatively limited team of writers including in particular Yakup Kadri Karaosmanoğlu, Vedat Nedim Tör, Şevket Süreyya Aydemir, Ismail Husrev and Burhan Asaf, this review was especially concerned with economic and social questions, and it contributed in a significant manner to the refinement of Kemalist theses in these domains. Writers involved with this magazine were responsible for the most convincing arguments in favour of the state control policy adopted by the régime in economic matters, from the beginning of the 1930s.

The articles published in *Kadro*, often relatively long and technical, were addressed to an educated public of bureaucrats and intellectuals. *Makala*s of a more accessible type were to be found for example in the numerous organs of the "People's Houses" [see KHALKEVI], kinds of public forums established by the Republican People's Party to propagate Kemalist values throughout the country. The reviews, of which the best was *Ülkü*, the monthly magazine of the People's House of Ankara, provided an impressive collection of works, generally modest in scale but sometimes of very high quality, concerning the folklore, the history, the arts and the social life of Turkey all of which had the aim, often in explicit manner, to stimulate the national pride of the population and to lay the foundations of a new culture compatible with republican ideas.

With the spread of universities, high schools and research institutions, Kemalist Turkey was also soon to be endowed with various specialised reviews, among which it is appropriate to mention in particular *Türkiyat Mecmuasi*, organ of the Institute of Turcology of the University of Istanbul, and *Belleten*, review of the Foundation for Turkish History. The scientific *makala*s published in these periodicals were generally of a quality comparable to that of articles of similar type produced in countries with a long university tradition. However, some writers willingly took account of the directives and principles of the régime, eager to construct from all their work hypotheses and theories capable of supporting them.

This said, even though writings inspired by official doctrines constituted until the end of the Second World War the major portion of the material appearing in the Turkish periodical press, dissidents were not deprived of the opportunity for self-expression, provided that they did not overstep certain limits. It was thus for example that one of the most talented journalists of the period, Peyami Safa, was responsible for a large number of subtly reactionary *makala*s and *fikra*s of which some were even published in government journals such as Yunus Nadi's *Cümhuriyet* and *Ulus*, the official organ of the Republican Party. Similarly, persons suspected of Communist sympathies such as Zekeriya Sertel, Sabahattin Ali, Aziz Nesin, Sadrettin Celal and numerous others, were able for many years to write in periodicals known for their progressive ideas—in particular the daily *Tan* and the monthly *Yurt ve Dünya*—without being unduly molested. It was only in 1945, in the wake of violent polemical struggle with Pan-Turkist organs, that they were obliged to put an end to their activities, some of them even being forced into exile.

After the Second World War, with the establishment of a pluralist régime and the emergence of new political parties, the various constituents of Turkish opinion were able to make their points of view known with greater ease than in the past, on condition however of exercising a degree of self-censorship. Only extremist factions, in particular all those considered to be Communists, as well as certain religious or ultra-nationalist groups, found themselves deprived for rather more than a decade of freedom of expression. This was however gradually restored to them in the wake of the *coup d'état* of 1960 which inaugurated in Turkey a period characterised by a growing liberalisation of political life and ideological debate.

This was a climate eminently favourable to the development of the press, as the statistics demonstrate. In 1951, there was a total of 551 periodicals in Turkey; by the end of the 1970s, the number had risen to more than 1,400. In such circumstances, the *makala* genre could not but prosper.

The political *makala* in particular flourished remarkably, especially in the period beginning in the mid-1960s. Among the outstanding specialists in the genre, mention should be made, on the left, of Doğan Avcioğlu, who in 1961 launched the weekly *Yön*, the first of a whole series of increasingly subversive periodicals which were to come into existence in succeeding years, as well as journalists of great talent including Çetin Altan, Abdi Ipekçi and İlhami Soysal. As for the conservative camp, besides Peyami Safa, who continued to produce extremely corrosive *makala*s until his death in 1961, worthy of mention, among many other polemicists of great virulence, are the poet Necip Fazil Kısakürek, founder of the Islamic and nationalist review *Büyük Doğu*, Ahmet Kabaklı, author of a large number of news-items of fundamentalist tone published in various journals, and Nazli Ilıcak, editor-in-chief of the daily *Tercüman*.

During the same period, literary criticism and the related genre of the essay (*deneme*) also developed in a remarkable manner. Nurullah Ataç, who died in 1957, had dominated the preceding decades with his refined sensibility and literary talent, leaving to posterity thousands of articles dispersed among scores of periodicals. Slightly younger than him, Suut Kemal Yetkin, Sabahattin Eyuboğlu, Azra Erhat and Tahir Alangu had also contributed to the enrichment of modern Turkish letters in these two domains. In their wake, with the proliferation of literary reviews from 1950 onwards, there appeared a host of new talents, of whom there is space here to mention only a few such as Asım Bezirci and Fethi Naci, very productive literary critics; Mahmut Makal, the pioneer in Turkey of the essay on rural themes; Salah Birsel, who was responsible in particular for numerous theoretical writings on poetry; and most of all Atilla İlhan, author of news-items of a very personal tone on problems of contemporary Turkish society.

Finally, it is appropriate to note the remarkable proliferation of works of academic type published in reviews intended for a limited audience. Until recently, only establishments of higher education had at their disposal organs capable of accommodating such production. Several reviews of wider circulation, designed with the aim of laying the results of scientific research before an educated public, have begun to appear since the mid-1970s, at the initiative of private individuals or associations. The most characteristic example which may be cited in this context is the quarterly *Toplum ve Bilim*, founded by Sencer Divitçioğlu which, since its inception, has given a new impetus to works in the domain of economic and social history.

If the *makala* appears as a whole to be an ever-expanding genre, it should nevertheless be noted that, in the daily press, the tradition of the *bas̲h̲ maḳāla* has tended, for its part, to disappear. An essential element of the newspaper in the 19th century and during the Young Turk period, from the end of the 1930s the editorial occupied no more than approximately 1 to 2% of available space in organs such as *Cümhuriyet* or *Ulus*. Today, it has disappeared from the majority of dailies—including *Cümhuriyet*, in spite of its long-lived traditional role as a journal of opinion—or survives only in the form of articles of variable regularity relegated to the interior of the newspaper. This abandonment of the *bas̲h̲ maḳāla* is perhaps a result of the proliferation, in newspapers, of particular rubrics—*fıkra*, news of foreign politics, economic news, etc.—enabling different members of the staff to express their point of view on matters of the moment. It is explained, above all, by the radical transformation experienced by the Turkish daily press after 1960. The appearance of non-political newspapers of mass circulation—in 1982 *Günaydin* had a readership of more than 800,000 and *Hürriyet* approximately 600,000—and the competition posed by television have had a drastic effect on the ideological press which, to survive, has found itself in many cases obliged to adopt the formulae operated by the mass-circulation dailies: development of photographic reportage, expansion of space reserved for sport, for humorous cartoons, for entertainments, multiplication of short stories at the expense of serious articles. The most successful example of this adaptation to the new circumstances of journalism is provided by the conservative daily *Tercüman* which in 1982 drew a readership of almost 400,000. However, as has been seen, these structural changes have not prevented the *makala* on political themes from prospering. The traditional *bas̲h̲ maḳāla* has been replaced not only by the news-items and diverse "points of view" published on the inside pages of daily newspapers, but also by the widespread production of weekly or bi-monthly periodicals of all shades of opinion, whose proliferation has only been temporarily halted by the measures taken to restrict the freedom of the press in the aftermath of the military intervention of 1980.

Bibliography: Ṇermin Abadan, *Cumhuriyet ve Ulus gazeteleri hakkında muhteva tahlili*, in *Ank. Univ. Siyasal Bilgiler Fakültesi Dergisi*, xvi/2 (June 1961), 93-118; Korkmaz Alemdar, *Basında Kadro dergisi ve Kadro hareketi ile ilgili bazı görüşler*, in *Kadro* (new facs. edn. by Cem Alpar), Ankara 1978, i, 21-42; Niyazi Berkes, *The development of secularism in Turkey*, Montreal 1964; Ömer Sami Coşar, *Milli mücadele basını*, n.p., n.d.; Server Iskit, *Türkiye' de neşriyat hareketleri tarihine bir bakış*, Istanbul 1939; A. D. Želtyakov, *Türkiye'nin sosyo-politik ve kultûrel hayatında basin (1729-1908 yılları)*, n.p., n.d. (tr. from Russian); Alpay Kabacalı, *Türkiye'de yazarın kazancı*, Istanbul 1981; Kemal Karpat (ed.), *Political and social thought in the contemporary Middle East*, New York 1968; Cevdet Kudret, *Örneklerle edebiyat bilgileri*, 2 vols., Istanbul 1980; J. Landau, *Radical politics in modern Turkey*, Leiden 1974; idem, *Pan-Turkism in Turkey. A study in irredentism*, London 1981; B. Lewis, *The emergence of modern Turkey*², Oxford 1968; Şerif Mardin, *The genesis of Young Ottoman thought*, Princeton 1962; Rauf Mutluay, *50 yılın türk edebiyatı*³, Istanbul 1976; idem, *Çagdaş türk edebiyatı (1908-1972)*, Istanbul 1973; Fuat Süreyya Oral, *Türk basın tarihi*, 2 vols., n.p., n.d.; Ragıp Özdem, *Tanzimattan beri yazı dilimiz*, in *Tanzimat*, i, Istanbul 1940, 859-931; Ahmet Hamdi Tanpınar, *19uncu asır türk edebiyatı tarihi*², Istanbul 1956; Zafer Toprak, *Türkiye'de "Milli İktisat" (1908-1918)*, Ankara 1982; Tarık Zafer Tunaya, *Islamcılık cereyanı*, Istanbul 1962; Hilmi Ziya Ülken, *Türkiye'de çağdaş düşünce tarihi*², Istanbul 1979; M. Bülent Varlık, *Türkiye basın-yayın tarihi kaynakçası*, Ankara 1981; idem, *Türkiye'de basın-yayın tarihi kaynakçasına ek-I* in *İletişim*, 1982/4, 351-84; Ahmed Emin [Yalman], *The development of modern Turkey as measured by its press*, New York 1941. (P. Dumont)

MAKALLA. [see al-mukallā].

MAḲĀM (a., pl. *maḳāmāt*), literally "place, position, rank", began to appear in Islamic musical treatises at the end of the ʿAbbāsid period, to designate Arabo-Irano-Turkish and assimilated musical modes and, in this musical sense, it is still predominantly used today. It is thought that this usage comes from the place assigned to the musician with a view to the interpretation of a given musical mode; but it will be seen later that each mode also has a defined place and a position on the fingerboard and fingering of the ʿ*ūd* [*q.v.*].

Maḳām has a broader meaning than its translation "mode". *Maḳām* defines both the "formulary mode" (J. Chailley), the Greek concept of the systemic mode, the "scale-system" (J.-Cl. Ch. Chabrier) with the heptatonic octave (*sullam, dīwān asāsī*) or, going beyond the octave, the analysed modal structure, standardised or conceived on the ʿ*ūd* through a joining-together of tri-, tetra-, or pentachordal genres (*d̲j̲ins*, pl. *ad̲j̲nās*), the plan, process or "operational protocol" of improvisation or interpretation of the mode according to the models, forms, formulas or musical cadences, and finally "the ethos" or "modal sentiment" (*rūḥ al-d̲j̲ins*), linked to the conception or perception of the given musical mode.

Such a fairly broad meaning of the word, comprising the system, structure, form and aura of the mode, entails a relative synonymity of the term *maḳām* with other generic names of modes, used concurrently by the musicologists of mediaeval Islam, such as *laḥn, d̲j̲amʿ, ṭarīḳa, dastān, mad̲j̲rā, tarkīb, d̲j̲ins, dawr, s̲h̲add, murakkab, s̲h̲uʿba, barda, āwāz, gūs̲h̲a, baḥr*, etc. In the 20th century, even if the term *maḳām* remains the most classical and widespread, other generic names designate the musical mode in various regions: *nag̲h̲ma, nag̲h̲am* (Arab East); *ṭab, ṣanʿa* (Mag̲h̲rib); *āwāz, dastgāh, nag̲h̲ma* (Iran). The term *maḳām* becomes *makam* in Turkey, *mugām* in Ād̲h̲arbāyd̲j̲ān and Turkmenistan and *makom* in Central Asia.

A musicological controversy places in opposition to

one another at present the partisans of the *maḳām-system* and the partisans of the *maḳām-form*. The ambiguity arises from the fact that a *maḳām*-system being made musically concrete entails the illustration of its structures in the form of a solo melodic modal improvisation entrusted to an instrumentalist (this is the *taḳsīm*), to the human voice without written music (this is the *layālī*), or in the form of a memorised or written elaboration entrusted to an instrumental group (*takht* or *djawḳ*) or to an orchestra with soloists, singers and choral voices. In the latter case, the listener retains the written music or poetry and the form more than the system. In some countries, e.g. those of the Maghrib or Central Asia, as in Iran, Ādharbāydjān or ʿIrāḳ, the *maḳām* is understood precisely through the agency of its forms or models transmitted on the instrument from master to pupil or entrusted to solo artists acquainted with the traditional répertoire (*nawba* in the Maghrib, *makom* in Central Asia, *radīf* in Iran, *mugām* in Ādharbāydjān or *maḳām* in ʿIrāḳ, for example).

Whatever may be the ascendancy of human voices and the impact of words and poems on the Islamic populations, even if it remains at the central core of Islamic culture, the Arabo-Irano-Turkish *maḳām* appears in the history of musical language to be a relation which has evolved from the ancient musical mode, rethought, conceived and standardised on the fingerboard of the *ʿūd* through an association of genres (*adjnās*). The understanding of the *maḳām* is thus inseparable, on the level of the analysis of modal structures, from a study of the language of the *ʿūd*, an instrument which has defined the scale of sounds and tested the types constituting the modes. The modal languages of Islam were developed under the finger (*iṣbaʿ*, pl. *aṣābiʿ*), on the finger-board (*dastān*) and along the scale-range of the *ʿūd*. This process of elaboration allowed each *maḳām*, from the time of its creation, to go beyond its own technical and intellectual conception and each system to be transmuted into a process and a form which would put into a concrete shape the "idea-material", the "*maḳām-ʿūd*" relationship. Hence the risk constituted by the representation of a *maḳām* or its modal structures on a musical stave in the 20th century.

Formation and evolution of the theoretical scale of sounds.—The first technical and modal problem of music within Islam seems to have been the combination of the autochtonous or empirical systems inherited from the *Djāhiliyya* with the scholarly systems borrowed from the Byzantines, Lakhmids and Sāsānids. The artists and theoreticians, therefore, until the end of the ʿAbbāsid period, had to find on the finger-board of the lute theoretical scales whose intervals and "finger-degrees" or "scaling-fingerings" might be compatible with the local practices and Greek theories which were regarded as ideal [cf. MŪSĪḲĪ].

As the Greek modes had been conceived on the lyre and the local modes on long-necked lutes, it was necessary to multiply the number of fingering-degrees and positions on the finger-board of the *ʿūd*, a short-necked lute adopted with the rise of Islam, so as to ratify the juxtaposition of various scales with different intervals and to open up the possibility of producing sound-degrees to suit various systems and temperaments.

The technical genesis of the *maḳām*, heir of the ancient mode, passed according to mediaeval treatises through the following stages:

1. Calculation of a theoretical scale, defining sounds and intervals;
2. Study of tetrachordal genres on the finger-board of the *ʿūd*; and
3. Elaboration of heptatonic octave scale system.

In fact, the theoreticians proceeded rather in the opposite way; starting with musical modes in use, they analysed their genres and attempted to conceive a rational theoretical scale.

What must be intended here by a theoretical scale is a series (*ṭabaḳa*) or a framework of available consecutive sounds disposed from low to high within an octave and over several octaves, to depart from which knowledgeable musicians could select the intervals or standardise the fingering-degrees, then the genres, and finally the modes of a piece of music in a given temperament. Throughout the evolution of the musical sciences within Islam, various theoretical scales were conceived and used, either successively or concurrently.

The first theoretical scale of tones, which existed before Islam and was known to the ancient Greeks, was based on the division of the string into forty aliquot parts, and, following from this, the division of the first octave into twenty musically unequal intervals. Al-Fārābī, writing in the 4th/10th century, describes the *ṭunbur* of Baghdād in these terms, distinguishing five first fingerings in use since the *Djāhiliyya* and five others which are his own invention. Theoretically, this acoustic system defines numerous intervals which are to be found in earlier or later systems. Worthy of mention are a sub-quarter-tone diesis (40/39) of Eratosthenes, a sub-limma (40/38 = 20/19; 89 cents), a sub-neutral-second, prefiguring that of Ibn Sīnā, (40/37), a minor harmonic tone (40/36 = 10/9; 182 cents), a maximal tone (40/35 = 8/7; 231 cents). Furthermore, al-Fārābī proposes a subminor-third (40/34 = 20/17; 281 cents), a sub-neutral-third (40/33), a major harmonic third (40/32 = 5/4; 386 cents), an implicit diminished fourth (40/31) and a perfect fourth (40/30 = 4/3; 498 cents). If this system is pursued, the logical outcome will be a sub-diminished fifth (40/29), a harmonic tritone (40/28 = 10/7; 617 cents), a short fifth (40/27) and a super-"wolf's-fifth" (40/26). But al-Fārābī restricts his description to the fourth, and no evidence is available concerning the details of the diffusion of this system in proto-Islamic or early Islamic music.

In Baghdād, in the 2nd-3rd/8th-9th centuries, the eminent and skilled classical soloists of the *ʿūd*, like Isḥāḳ al-Mawṣilī, seemed more inclined to employ the Pythagorean Hellenistic system. The latter was characterised by a limma (256/243; 90 cents), an implicit apotome (2187/2048; 114 cents), a major tone (9/8; 204 cents), a minor third (32/27; 294 cents), a major (third) or ditone (81/64; 408 cents), a perfect fourth (4/3; 498 cents), an implicit tritone subsequently described by al-Fārābī with reference to the harp (729/512; 612 cents) and a perfect fifth (3/2; 702 cents).

The two systems were thus only compatible on the level of the limma and of the fourth. At the same time, Manṣūr Zalzal, a virtuoso lutist, apparently reconciled the popular and learned traditions by giving official status to a para-Pythagorean system based on empirical and equidistant longitudinal divisions of the string of the *ʿūd*, following the Pythagorean fingering-degrees.

Zalzal thus recommended the use of the following complementary degrees: a "Persian" neutral second (162/149; 145 cents; 6,4 holders), a "Zalzalian" neutral second (54/49; 168 cents; 7,4 holders), a "Persian" minor third (81/68; 303 cents; 13,4 holders) and a "Zalzalian" neutral third (27/22; 355

RĒVERIES SUR LE MAQĀM FARAḤFAZĀ
SUITE MODALE (19'30").
P 1979, réédition 1984 arabesques-récitalbum.

album 6 arabesques
LUTH AU YEMEN classique
ᶜUD JAMIL GHANIM
rêveries récital à Aden
récitalbum ARÂ — RA 333 106

arabesques-récitalbum. anthologie phonographique du récital oriental éditée avec la participation de l'Institut du Monde Arabe, du Ministère de la Culture (Diréction de la Musique), et sous le patronage du Centre National de la Recherche Scientifique.

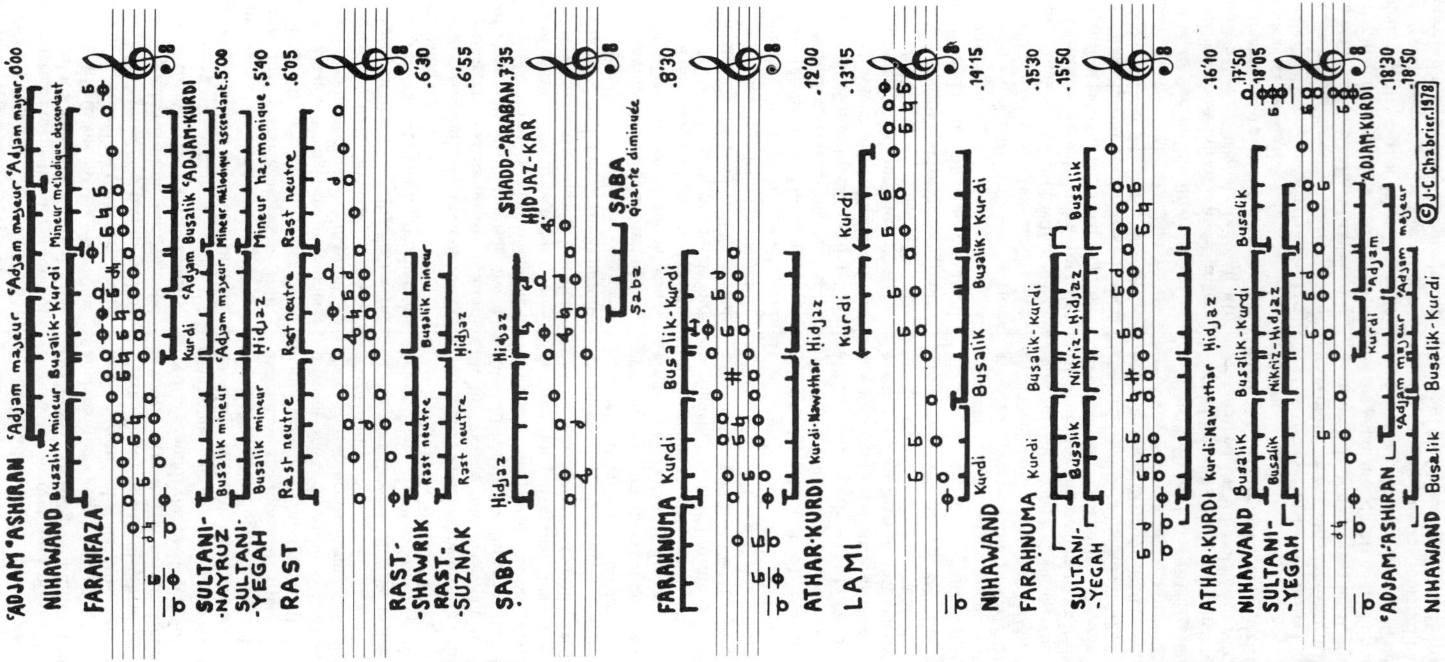

L'accordature du ᶜūd de Jamil Ghânim implique une échelle à *râst* en *fa*2. Le doigté *râst* (ton-clef) donne un *fa*, le degré *yegâh* (1° corde vide) un *do*2. Les modes et genres (commatiques) s'insèrent logiquement dans ce système : *Farahfazâ (yegâh-nawâ-do*, 6° corde en *sol*1), *Nihâwand (râst-fa*, 6° corde en *fa*1).

Les analyses et schémas consignent les modes, genres, degrés, intervalles constitutifs ou de modulation identifiés à l'oreille et sont transcrits à la hauteur réelle jouée. Les altérations précisent les quarts-de-tons ou commas conformément au style du musicien et à notre code *"arabesques"*.

Le code d'altérations *arabesques* confronte les codes arabes, iraniens, turcs, les quarts-de-tons et commas. Assimilant 1 quart à 2 commas, il reprend de nombreux signes déjà utilisés sur portées orientales et en crée quelques nouveaux pour situer des altérations touchant les 9 commas du ton majeur.

Code d'altérations *arabesques* avec division du ton en 4 quarts - 9 commas
© J.C. Chabrier, 1978.

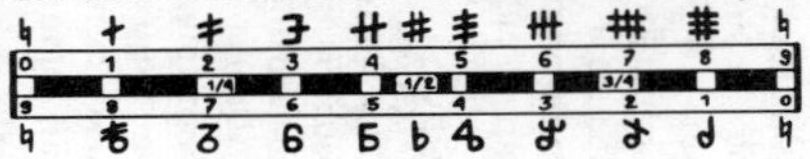

cents; 15,7 holders.) Thus there came about, in regard to the fingerboard of the ʿ*ūd*, the confrontation between the Hellenistic or universal acoustic systems and the specific or empirical Arabo-Irano-Turanian musical systems.

The treatises of al-Kindī, al-Munadjdjim (3rd/9th century), al-Fārābī, al-Iṣfahānī, the Ikhwān al-Ṣafāʾ (4th/10th century), Ibn Sīnā (5th/11th century) and many other scholars thus had as their object or desired aim to position on the finger-board of the ʿ*ūd* a theoretical scale capable of standardising the intervals of these different systems.

The ideal solution seems to have been found in the 7th/13th century by the Systematists with Ṣafī al-Dīn al-Urmawī and Ḳuṭb al-Dīn al-Shīrāzī, thanks to a commatic scale supporting the Pythagorean system and assimilating, by justifying them by longitudinal measures and mathematical calculations, the intervals of the *Djāhiliyya* and the neutral intervals. It all led in practice to the (theoretical) comma, the limma (4 commas), the apotome (5 commas), the minor tone (8 commas), the major tone (9 commas) divided into two limmas and a comma, and their combinations, amongst these being a minor third (13 commas), a neutral third which became "natural" (17 commas), a major third (18 commas) and a perfect fourth (22 commas).

Subsequently, Iran, Central Asia and the outer regions moved away from reference to the ʿ*ūd* and returned to empirical systems. The Arab world was to experience the recession before adopting from the 18th century, and more precisely with Mikhāʾīl Mushāka (19th century), under the influence of Europe, a theoretical scale dividing the octave into twenty-four quarter-tones (*rub*ʿ). Only the Ottomans and the heirs of ʿAbbāsid élitism were able to perpetuate the commatic system of the Systematists.

In the 20th century, a comparative Arabo-Irano-Turkish study entails the reconstitution of a theoretical scale of sounds confronting the three systems of contemporary Arab, Iranian and Turkish temperaments. In spite of divergences, the octave can be divided into twenty-four intervals defining twenty-five fingering-degrees or scaling-fingerings (*daradja*, *barda*, *perde*), supposing there to be four per major tone. The traditional names of these fingering-degrees are somewhat variable from one language to another (e.g. *segāh-sīkāh*, *čahārgāh-djahārkāh*).

The preliminary division of the octave into fifty-three Holderian commas among the Turks and twenty-four quarter-tones among the Arabs and Iranians only presents minor problems of temperament, illustrated by the controversies as to the height of the "neutral" fingering-degrees, as, for example, the *segāh* higher in the Zarlinian third (17 commas, Turkey, Aleppo, Baghdad than in the Zalzalian third (16 commas or 7 quarters, Cairo, Damascus). Of the twenty-five theoretical fingering-degrees, modern Iranian treatises mention only eighteen fingering-degrees to the octave, dividing the octave into seventeen intervals which are unequal, having a semi-tone and two quarter-tones in a major tone. So it is not a case of seventeen third-tones.

This theoretical scale is transposable in its entirety in terms of the pitch (*ṭabaḳa*) then of the height of reference chosen. Also the guide mark and key tone of the scale, *yegāh* and *rāst*, can be aligned on a frequency, a pitch and then an equivalent Latin note which varies according to the countries, schools or, obviously, voices to be accompanied. The *rāst*, key tone, can be a *si*^{b}, a *do* (Mediterranean), a *ré* (Turkey), a *fa* or a *sol* (ʿIrāḳ, Iran) or even a *la*, and the whole scale is led by it like a mobile keyboard or a set of *nāys* (oblique flutes) of various pitches.

This theoretical scale can be deduced from the historical ʿ*ūd* which conceived it and is reducible to the modern ʿ*ūd* which is its ideal standard. For this reason, it is influenced by "units" of fourths, and presents in the 20th century preferential degrees corresponding to the open strings of the ʿ*ūd* with classical tuning, supposing that, from low to high, is a bass string: *karār-rāst* or *karār-dūgāh*, 1st string *yegāh*, 2nd string ʿ*ashīrān*, 3rd. string *dūgāh*, 4th string *nawā*, 5th string *gardān*. So it is not equalised like a piano scale.

This theoretical scale is only a range without an immediate melodic outcome. The twenty-five sounds disposable on the octave are not played in conjunction or simultaneously. A given modal structure uses normally only four degrees to the fourth or eight degrees to the octave in the rules of heptatonic diatonism.

Value of the intervals and formation of the genres. Historically in the treatises and logically in analysis, the approach to the *maḳāmāt* entails, the unit of measure and theoretical scale of sounds being known, a study of the intervals and fingering-degrees which, in dividing the fourth or the fifth, seek to define the tri-, tetra- or pentachordal genres constituting the *maḳāmāt*. The genre (*djins*, *baḥr*, ʿ*iḳd*, in Arabic, *dörtlü-beşli* in Turkish) is thus the elementary unit of the modal structures in contemporary Arabic and Turkish treatises. In Iranian treatises it is not explicitly identified, but a modal analysis should reveal its presence.

The selection of a given genre brings a choice of fingering-degrees on the theoretical scale of sounds and also ordains a specific series of juxtaposed intervals. The value of these intervals is determined by the systems or temperaments adopted.

In the Arab countries and Iran, the intervals are measured in quarter-tones at the rate of twenty-four quarters per octave. The chromatic quarter-tone is exceptional. The current melodic intervals are the semitone (2 qs.), the three-quarter-tone (3 qs.), the major tone (4 qs.), the maxim tone (5 qs.), the trihemitone (an augmented second of (6 qs.). The thirds are minor (6 qs.), neutral (7 qs.) or major (8 qs.). The fourths are perfect (10 qs.), but the shortened fourth (6 qs.) of the *ṣabā* genre should be noted as well as the augmented fourth (tritone of 12 qs.) of the *nikrīz*, *nawathar* and *kurdī-athar* genres. The perfect fifths are 14 qs. The intervals are more flexible in Iran.

In Turkey and the academic schools (Aleppo, Mosul, Baghdad) the intervals are measured in Holderian commas at the rate of fifty-three commas per octave. The current intervals are the limma (4 commas), the apotome (5 cs.), the minor tone (8 cs.), the major tone (9 cs.), the "trilimma" or trihemitone (augmented seconds of 12 or 13 cs.). The thirds are minims (12 cs.), minors (13-14 cs.), rarely neutrals (15-16 cs.), Zarlinian naturals (17 cs) or Pythagorician majors (18 cs.). The fourths are perfect (22 cs.), shortened (18) or augmented (26 cs.), in the genres mentioned above. The perfect fifths are of 31 commas.

The Arab, Iranian and Turkish treatises give the specific intervals historical names, of which the variants will not be mentioned here. The fingering-degrees or scaling-fingerings are not always designated by their Eastern names, and, under the influence of European notation, Latin names of the notes are frequently used by giving them adapted inflections. Also, more precisely since the Congrès de musique du Caire (1932), a note lowered a quarter-tone (made semi-flat) can be called *nuṣṣ-bémol*, *kar-*

bémol or *koron.* Raised a quarter-tone (made semi-sharp), it becomes *nuṣṣ-dièze, kar-dièze* or *sorī.* The Turkish codes of inflection are clearly more rigid due to the commatic system. There are regular new initiatives, amongst which is a code of the Colloque de Beyrouth (1972). One of the most recent (code arabesque, 1978) normalises the signs and transcribes all the commatic inflections.

Just as the theoretical scale of sounds is only a range, the quarter-tone and the comma are only units of measure and not melodic or chromatic intervals. Heptatonic diatonism theoretically escapes the proliferation of fingering-degrees or scaling-fingerings beyond eight to the octave, when there is a given modulation. Further, the conception of the genres on the finger-board of the *ʿūd* can only use the open string and four fingers, which reinforces the link between the fifth and the playing of a pentachord and does not stir the musician to imagine micro-intervals smaller than the limma which do not exist in the traditional genres. Here, moreover, the *maḳām* owes more to the *ʿūd* than to the laboratory.

Nevertheless, some "micro-intervals" are smaller than the semi-tone or the limma. In diatonism, they may be detected below the fingering-degree *segāh* of the rare genres *awdj-ārā* and *sāz-kār* described by Erlanger (quarter-tone between *ré dièze* and mi semi-bémol). There is also a leading note at the same level in the *segāh* genre, which is superimposed on diatonism. However, it would appear to be a matter of Turkish limmas, which, transposed in the Arabic quarter-tone system, are devalued. In chromatism, there are micro-intervals in the execution of the rare *mukhālif* genre of ʿIrāḳ; but it is, in this case, an alternated overlapping of the *ṣabā* and *segāh* genres on the same part of the scale. In this case, it is even possible to analyse a *maḳām Mukhālif* formed from the overlapping of the three *Ṣabā, Segāh* and *Huzam maḳāmāt* mobilising twelve degrees per octave (cf. *Arabesques* record 5, *Luth en Iraq traditionnel, ʿUd Jamîl Bachîr).*

As the selection of a genre brings a choice of fingering-degrees and ordains a specific series of juxtaposed intervals, the genre is an elementary and invariable modal structure which should be identified on analysis in terms of the value of its intervals and independently of the temperament adopted. The ear itself is probably aided by characteristic melodic formulae of the genre and by an intuitive perception. However, apart from the variations of temperament from one country to another, the universal laws of music "temper" the rigidity of the specific intervals.

Some fingering-degrees of the genre, in particular the two poles or extremities often inserted in an open string of the *ʿūd*, are rigorously fixed, except, for instance, in the Iranian-ʿIrāḳıān *Dashtī-Dasht* mode. Others, the intermediaries, can be mobile. This mobility is frequently linked to phenomena of ascending or descending gradient or enharmonic change, quite natural on instruments with a non-fretted finger-board such as the *ʿūd* or the violin, and more artificial on instruments such as the *ḳānūn.* It also responds to phenomena of attraction or repulsion valid in other kinds of music.

Also, such a fingering-degree or scaling-fingering will be raised more in ascending than in descending. In spite of the fairly rigid commatic precision of the system applied in Turkey, the third fingering-degree *segāh* of the *rāst* genre occurs at 17 commas of the finale in ascending and 16 in descending, also inflecting a Zarlinian third and a Zalzalian third. By contrast, if this *segāh* fingering-degree becomes the finale of the *segāh* genre it becomes a modal pole and it is fixed more especially as it is doubled with a leading note given the space of several commas.

It may be remarked that the mobile degrees are frequently linked, as historical treatises or musical practice confirm, with the index or medius finger on the finger-board of the historical or modern *ʿūd.* In the modes of Iran, these mobile fingering-degrees, which the analysts do not associate with the role of the *ʿūd,* are called *mutaghayyir.*

The establishment of a nomenclature of Arabo-Irano-Turkish musical genres can only lead to a didactic compromise due to the complexity of the criteria allowing the specificity of a genre to be confirmed. However, the same term can designate different genres, or the same genre may be designated variously according to the countries. An Arabo-Turkish terminology will be normalised here.

Erlanger presents an Arabo-Turkish system marked by the academic tradition of Aleppo with a quarter-tone scale and enumerates seventeen genres. An Arabo-Turkish system will be presented here marked by the *ʿūd* school of Baghdād with a commatic scale. A progression of structures will follow from the "Hellenic" scale (tones and semi-tones) to the "Islamic" scale (which includes also neutral seconds and thirds). The reverse approach would also be plausible.

Attention will be given to eight structures of the main genres by giving precise information on their characteristic interval: *čahārgāh* or *ʿadjam-ʿashīrān* (major); *būsalīk* (minor); *kurdī* (minor second and third); *ḥidjāz* (with trihemitone-augmented second); *bayātī* and *nawā* tetrachords or *ḥusaynī* and *ʿushshāḳ* pentachords (neutral second and minor third); *ṣabā* (neutral second, minor third and diminished fourth); *segāh* and *ʿirāḳ* (finale on a neutral fingering-degree with apotome and short neutral third), *rāst*, an academic and classical genre (major second and neutral third).

Six structures will also be cited derived from the main genres by correlation, overlapping, combination, inflection: *kurdī-athar* (*kurdī/ḥidjāz* correlation); *nikrīz* and *nawathar* (*būsalīk/ḥidjāz* correlation); *mukhālif* (*ṣabā-segāh* overlapping); *huzam* (*segāh/ḥidjāz* combination); *mustaʿār* inflection of the *segāh*); and *zawīl* (*ḥidjāz/rāst* interaction).

All these genres are compatible with the fifth and can be represented in the form of pentachords on a diagram illustrating the real value of the intervals and the preferred insertion on the scale of sounds, itself transposable. However, so as to facilitate reading, a scale of sounds is often chosen with a *rāst* key tone in *do* (Mediterranean) and one may also remark the equivalence in Latin notes of the height of the fingering-degrees or scaling-fingerings by giving their inflections precisely.

Formation of the musical modes from the genres.—The mode (*maḳām* in Arabic; *dastgāh, āwāz, naghma* in Persian; *makam* in Turkish) is formed by the combination of genres. However, musicologists who do not play the *ʿūd*, Iranian authors and numerous Western musicologists study the mode as a whole like a Greek mode or an Indian *raga.*

In popular traditions and archaic practices, a single tri-, tetra- or pentachordal genre can constitute a *maḳām* of limited ambitus. In general, it is a genre more autochthonous than Hellenic such as the *ḥidjāz*, the *bayātī*, the *ṣabā* or the *rāst.* A Bedouin's improvisation on his *rabāba* is often limited to a tetrachord. But an educated artist can decide to play deliberately in the popular style and produce an astonishing result (e.g. Djamīl Bashīr interpreting the *swīḥlī-nāʿil* on the

ʿ*ūd*; cf. *Arabesques* record 5, *Luth en Iraq traditionnel*, *ʿUd Jamîl Bachîr*).

Two genres joined from low to high can form the "scale system" (*dīwān asāsī*, *sullam* in Arabic; *dizi* in Turkish) of a classical heptatonic *maḳām* bearing a tonic finale (*asās*, *mayé*, *durak*), a witness-pivot (*ghammāz*, *shāhid*, *güçlü*), normally placed at the juncture of the two genres and corresponding most often to an open string of the ʿ*ūd*, which, in fact, by structural and acoustic definition, is a preferential degree. Other degrees can be preferential or mobile according to the genres and modes played and in terms of what the ethnomusicologists call the hierarchy of degrees.

Musical treatises class *maḳāmāt* in terms of the degree on which they are inserted and progress from low to high. Here it will be limited to a small number of heptatonic "scale systems", simple or compound according to the identical (or theoretically identical) or different genres from which they are formed. All the *maḳāmāt* cited point to Arabo-Turkish academic traditions and a certain number of these *maḳāms* seem to be of relatively recent creation from the time of the Ottoman Empire (18th-19th centuries).

The constituent genres will be mentioned from low to high with and by their arbitrary limitation to the main octave (*dīwān asāsī*).

1. The principal *maḳāmāt* formed by the combination of two identical genres are called simple, and often bear the same name as their constituent genre or the fingering-degree of insertion on the theoretical scale of sounds:

Čahārgāh or *ʿAdjam-ʿAshīrān* (or *Māhūr*): major; major pentachord + major tetrachord.

Nihāwand or *Būsalīk*: minor; *būsalīk* tetrachord + *būsalīk* pentchord

Faraḥnumā, *Ḥidjāz-kār-kurdī*, *Kurdī*: two disjointed kurdī tetrachords (or *Kurdī tetrachord* + *būsalīk* pentachord

Lāmī: two descending, joined *kurdī* tetrachords (minor without finale)

Shadd-ʿArabān, *Sūzidil*, *Ḥidjāz-kār*, *Shāhnāz*: *ḥidjāz* pentachord + *ḥidjāz* tetrachord (or the latter + *nikrīz-nawathar* pentachord)

Ḥusaynī: *bayātī-ʿushshāḳ* pentachord + *bayātī* tetrachord (pivot on 5th degree)

Rāst: *rāst* pentachord + *rāst* tetrachord (two neutral thirds) (3rd and 7th degrees are neutral)

2. Some compound *maḳāmāt* are formed by joining two different genres constituting a heptatonic blend (*tarkīb*, *mürekkep*):

Sulṭānī-yegāh, *Nihāwand-kabīr*: harmonic minor; *būsalīk* pentachord + *ḥidjāz* tetrachord (or *būsalīk* tetrachord + *nikrīz* pentachord)

Athar-kurdī: *kurdī-athar* pentachord + *ḥidjaz* tetrachord

Nikrīz: *nikrīz* pentachord + modulating *rāst* tetrachord

Nawathar: *nikrīz nawathar* pentachord + *ḥidjāz* tetrachord

Ḥidjāz: *ḥidjāz* tetrachord + modulating *rāst* pentachord

Bayātī, *Nawā*: *bayātī* tetrachord + modulating *rāst* pentachord (*būsalīk* pentachord in the Turkish *Bayātī*)

Kardjighār: *bayātī* tetrachord + modulating *ḥidjāz* pentachord

Shūr: *bayātī* tetrachord + modulating *bayātī*, *būsalīk*, *rāst* or *ḥidjaz* pentachord (mobile 5th and 6th degrees)

Dasht: *bayātī-ʿushshāḳ* pentachord (mobile 5th degree witness-pivot) + modulating *Kurdī* tetrachord).

Sūznāk: *rāst* pentachord + *ḥidjāz* tetrachord

3. Some complex *maḳāmāt* are reducible to three different genres by their octave system (a theory not found in Turkey):

Huzam: *segāh* trichord + *ḥidjāz* tetrachord + *rāst* trichord

Segāh: *segāh* trichord + modulating *rāst* or *bayātī* tetrachord + *rāst* trichord

ʿIrāḳ: *segāh* trichord + *bayātī tetrachord* + *rāst* trichord

Sabā: *ṣabā* tetrachord + *ḥidjāz* overlapping (no octave)

4. Some *maḳāmāt* are reducible to an overlapping of genres or modes: *Faraḥfazā*: minor-major modal relativity with several leading notes

Mukhālif: overlapping of *ṣabā*, *segāh* and *huzam* (chromatism)

The definition of the *maḳām* limited to the octave is only a didactic diagram, for only archaic improvisations are limited to the octave. The extension of the system beyond the octave can be made in various ways. In the most common case, the heptatonic structure is recommenced in the adjacent low and high octaves. In scholastic practice, the theory or science of the musician adds new structures to the high and low in the form of connected genres or modes. It also leads to the formation of *maḳāmāt* of a broad ambitus, of which many are described in treatises. Going beyond the register of the human voice, they apply to instruments covering three octaves such as the ʿ*ūd* with six courses of strings, the *ḳānūn*, the *sanṭūr* or the *nāy*. In this way, the *maḳām* is freed from its antiquity.

On the occasion of an improvisation (*taḳsīm*), Arabic and Turkish traditions define for each *maḳām* a point of departure (*mabdaʾ*, *zemin*), a process of melodic movement (*tawr*, *seyr*), stopping points (*marākiz*, *asma kararlar*), specific melodic formulas such as the *ḳafla* before returning to the finale (*karār*). Iranian traditions entail the unrolling of a certain number of melodic models (*gūshas*) according to a fixed protocol in the official répertoire (*radīf*), with the periodic return of a conclusive formula-coda (*forūd*) such as *bāl-i kabutar*.

Apart from the vertical association of genres and modes from low to high, horizontal associations in time allow for improvisation by modulating from a *maḳām* of reference. Genres and modes constituting the initial modal system are renewed in terms of the laws of Arabo-Turkish modulation (*talwīn*, *geçki*) by the substitution or evolution of structures engendering a succession of genres and modes at intermediate stages (*miyāna*, *meyan*) and illustrating a rich procession of ten or twenty *maḳāmāt* before returning to the initial *maḳām* (e.g. "Reveries sur le maqām Faraḥfazā", *Arabesques* record 6, *Luth au Yemen classique*, *ʿUd Jamîl Ghânim*)

Al-makām al-ʿirāḳī, based on the same process, is a typically ʿIrāḳī genre whose poem is entrusted to a solo singer (*maḳāmčī*) and the accompaniment to an instrumental quartet (*čalghī*) from the beginning (*taḥrīr*) to the finale (*taslīm*) (e.g. "Meditations sur des naghams traditionnels d'Iraq", in *maḳām Pandjgāh*, *Arabesques* record 1, *Luth en Iraq classique*, *ʿUd Munîr Bachîr*).

Insertion, height in frequency, transposition, gradient, ethos.—*Maḳāmāt* are not of a fixed height in frequency with reference to universal physical principles. But they have for preferential insertion that of their main genre, which is done more readily on certain fingering-degrees of the scale of sounds. Also the *Shadd ʿArabān*, the *Yegāh* are inserted on *yegāh*; the *Sūzidil* on *ʿashīrān*; the *ʿAdjam-ʿAshīrān* on *nim-ʿadjam*; the *ʿIrāḳ* on *ʿirāḳ*; the *Nihāwand*, *Nikrīz*, *Nawathar*, *Ḥidjāz-kār*, *Rāst* on *rāst*; the *Kurdī*, *Ḥidjāz*, *Bayātī*, *Nawā*, *Ḥusaynī*, *ʿUshshāḳ*, *Ṣabā*, *Shāhnāz* on *dūgāh*; *Segāh*, *Huzam*, *Mustaʿār* on *segāh*; etc.

As the height in frequency of the fingering-degrees or scaling-fingerings is in terms of the height in frequency of the theoretical scale of sounds and the latter varies from one country to another and one school to another, it would be difficult to speak of absolute height, more especially as the European pitches, which are often cited in reference, have continued to rise since the 18th century. Recourse to the *nāy*, sometimes evoked as a pitch, presents the same risk since, with the fixed fingering-degrees, the *nāy* transposes the scale in terms of its size.

In the Mediterranean Arab countries, the *rāst* is generally assimilated to a *do2* and played as such by trained musicians. In Turkey the scale has been deliberately fixed and the *rāst* key tone, called *sol* and written *sol* by convention is a *ré2* in official institutions. In ʿIrāḳ and Iran, the *rāst* is more readily a *fa2* or a *sol2*. These heights suit baritone singers quite well. At all times, in practice, the instrumentalists choose their scale and the soloist singers impose theirs in terms of their vocal aptitudes.

The *maḳāmāt* can be transposed in various ways, in addition to transposition by total displacement of the tuning-pitch of the instrument or the theoretical scale of sounds. Transposition can be obtained on the *nāy* by preserving the fingerings and changing the *nāy*. On the *ḳānūn* and the *sanṭūr*, the playing is displaced after the tuning-pitch has been refined. On the *ʿūd* all the fingering-degrees of a course of strings can be transferred to the next course, corresponding to a translation of a fourth without modification of the internal acoustic equilibrium of the *maḳām*. Also a *bayātī* on a *dūgāh* (3rd open string) can be transposed on a *nawā* (4th open string) or on an *ʿas̲h̲īrān* (2nd open string) without breaking its structure, since the finale and the pivot (4th degree) remain inserted on the open strings. In some cases, the *maḳām* transposed in this way takes on a new name.

In other cases, a musician displaces the finale in a longitudinal fashion on the string, which leads to a transposition with translation of all the fingering-degrees and a modification of the acoustic structure of the *maḳām*. Such would be the case of a *maḳām Rāst* played on a *segāh* finale, a particularly arduous performance which alters the acoustic role of the pivot (5th degree), usually on an open string (*nawā*), and plays it on a fingering in the middle of a string.

Some *maḳāms* have, observed on a stave, octave scale systems absolutely identical with those of other *maḳāmāt*, whose height of insertion on the theoretical scale is different. Such is the case of *maḳāmāt S̲h̲add-ʿArabān* (on *yegāh*), *Sūzidil* (on *ʿas̲h̲īrān*), *Ḥid̲j̲āz-kār* (on *rāst*), Turkish *Zengüle* and *S̲h̲āhnāz* (on *dūgāh*). Played on a *ḳānūn* in the absence of a criterion of height, they could only be differentiated from one another by formulas, details of modulation or cadence. By contrast, on an *ʿūd*, they have their own acoustic equilibrium. The *yegāh* finale (1st open string) of the *S̲h̲add-ʿArabān* is on the *ʿūd* a preferential and fundamental degree. On the other hand, the *rāst* finale (on a fingering of minor third on *ʿas̲h̲īrān* 2nd string) of the *Ḥid̲j̲āz-kār*, which is a very important key tone, is not an acoustically preferential degree. Consequently, a *maḳām Ḥid̲j̲āz-kār* is not a transposed *S̲h̲add-ʿArabān*.

The question of the gradient of the *maḳāmāt* has given rise to several controversies. Some *maḳāmāt*, at the time of their improvised melodic evolution, deliberately display ascending melody, others no less deliberately descending melody. The musicologists of Turkey give precise information in their works as to the nature of the pitch to be given its value. At times, two *maḳāmāt* of identical modal structure and identical insertion have different gradients. Also, the Turkish *Bayātī* is descending and the Turkish *ʿUs̲h̲s̲h̲āḳ* ascending; the Turkish *Ḥid̲j̲āz* ambivalent and the *ʿUzzāl* ascending; the Turkish *Nevā* ascending and the Turkish *Tahīr* descending. In ʿIrāḳ, two popular *maḳāmāt* based on the modal structure of the *Ṣabā* are respectively the *Manṣūrī*, usually ascending, and the *Nāʿil*, usually descending.

Historically, each genre and mode is supposed to correspond to a certain ethos (*rūḥ*) or a "modal sentiment", which conditions the inspiration of the artist, and the perception or sensation of his accompanists and audience, when he improvises. Each mode or genre even had in former times its preferred hour, at dawn (*maḳām Rāhawī*), at the end of the evening (*maḳām Zirāfkand*), if reference is made to the *Anonymous treatise dedicated to the Ottoman sultan Mehemmed II* (9th/15th century). But in the 20th century, the holding of musical sessions in the evening and the influence of the media have upset the nyctemeral *rūḥ* as they have the sentimental *rūḥ*.

Nevertheless, the *Rāst* is classical and academic, the *Bayātī* has a rural and collective tendency and is well-suited to popular songs, the *Segāh* expresses lofty sentiments and is claimed by the mystics, the *Ṣabā*, linked to the fresh wind of dawn, expresses the weariness of the end of the night with a clear tendency to sadness and depression. It is all together strange, on the other hand, to the idea of waking up and is not an arousing *maḳām*. The *Ḥid̲j̲āz* is a *maḳām* able to evoke sadness without depression and it is remarkable to Western ears. In a certain measure, the calls to prayer maintain a kind of nyctemeral ethos of the *maḳāmāt*, since they are supposed to change the *maḳām* at each call.

Nomenclature and comparative approaches.—The number of real or fictitious *maḳāmāt* is difficult to determine in the absence of a preconceived idea and due to the plurality of musical traditions perpetuated in the heart of Arabo-Irano-Turkish Islam.

A Persian theoretician of the Sāsānid period, Bārbad̲h̲, had elaborated a mystical and cosmogonous musical system describing seven *k̲h̲usrawānīs* (modes), thirty *laḥns* (genres?) and three hundred and sixty *dastgāhs* (modulations?). This type of nomenclature as the basis of fatidical numbers has not disappeared and some contemporary musicologists retain seven notes and forty intervals to the octave so as to reach three hundred and sixty *maḳāmāt*. In the 7th/13th century, Ṣafī al-Dīn described twelve *s̲h̲udūd*, six *āwāzāt*, one *murakkab* and two undetermined modes.

Apart from large mediaeval treatises which studied the scales, intervals, genres and modes conceived on the *ʿūd*, and which established the nomenclatures for the classification of the modes used, we should take account of the delicate art and patronage which encouraged musicians to create a new mode and present it to the prince amidst a circle of initiates or on the occasion of a collective feast. Also, throughout thirteen centuries, hundreds of *maḳāmāt* have been described and it has been possible to elaborate thousands. However, the present current practice is limited to a few tens of simple or compound *maḳāmāt* and a hundred transposed *maḳāmāt*.

In the 20th century, Erlanger describes one hundred and nineteen Eastern *maḳāmāt* and twenty-nine Tunisian *maḳāmāt* belonging to the Hispano-Arabic tradition. S. al-Mahdī describes forty *maḳāmāt*. Alexis Chottin notes the existence of twenty-four *nawbāt* of North Africa, corresponding to twenty-four modes. Hüseyin Sadeddin Arel describes a hundred Turkish *makamlar*. Nelly Caron and Dariouche Safvate describe twelve Iranian modes, seven being *dastgāh* and five *āwāz*. Jürgen Elsner notes the existence of the system of six *makomot* in Central Asia, usually characterised by their forms. Habib Hassan Touma evaluates the *mugām* of Ādharbāydjān as more than seventy. Among all these structures there exist similarities and divergences.

Aesthetic, natural musical and universal laws, the limited character of the theoretical scale of sounds and a large number of historical interferences explain how numerous Arabo-Irano-Turkish *maḳāmāt* or those of Central Asia may be identical with Indian modes (*ragas*), Greek modes or modes perpetuated in the Eastern churches or among the minorities.

As for the similarities with India, we can recognise the identity of structure between the Indian *Bhairavi* and the *Kurdī*. As for the Greek heritage, it must be remarked that classical musicians of the end of the 2nd/8th century such as Isḥāk al-Mawṣilī [*q.v.*] used exclusively the Pythagorean Hellenic scale. The rehabilitation of autochthonous structures in academic music seems to be undertaken with Manṣūr Zalzal and his neutral fingering-degrees. Since then, "Greek" and "local" structures coexist. Some musicologists of Islam do not fail to underscore the homology between "Islamic" and Greek genres: Ionian, Aeolian, Dorian and Phrygian. The process, nevertheless, suffers from the multiplicity of classifications of the Greek genres. Thus we have to remark the presence of a major and a minor and the similarities with the modes of Greek churches, namely *Rāst*-natural diatonic, *Bayātī*-minor chromatic, and *Ḥidjāz-kār*-major chromatic.

The similarities with the Greek modes arise equally from the European influences of the 19th century which provoked a paradoxical re-Hellenisation. After the ʿAbbāsid period, which marked the flight of Arabo-Irano-Turanian musical syncretism, academic musical forms regressed among the Arabs and Iranians and were to discover a new brilliance at the court of the Ottomans. But from the 19th century onwards, imperial patronage and the taste of Istanbul were more and more influenced by Europe. A recrudescence of the *Nihāwand* (minor) took place and the "creation" of *maḳāmāt* for grand occasions, with a very broad ambitus, and a "tempered" tendency such as the *Nawathar* (*neveser*), *Sulṭānī-yegāh* (harmonic minor), *Ḥidjāz-kār-kurdī* (*Kürdilī-Ḥidjāz-kār*), *Faraḥfazā* and *Faraḥnumā*. It is these *maḳāmāt*, along with so many others perpetuated at the Ottoman court, which were to be introduced in Egypt by ʿAbdū al-Ḥammūlī so as to regenerate music which was at that time in a parlous condition, if the descriptions of Villoteau are to be believed.

The similarity between the modes of Islam and the modes of the Eastern churches is at times striking, despite divergences of form and style. It might as well be attributed to relics of the common ancient heritage claimed by both traditions, to a period of modal syncretism, or to the fruits of a coexistence which lasted more than ten centuries. The same question can be posed as regards the commatic chant of the churches whose territory was administered by the Ottomans, when the latter perpetuated the Byzantine artistic heritage and commatic system.

The problem of the musical modes perpetuated by the minorities reveals the same ambiguous similarities. As regards the Kurds, for example, it is well-known in Turkey, ʿIrāḳ and Iran that the Kurdish singers and instrumentalists interpret more readily the *Ḥusaynī* or *Dasht* modes according to their own forms and styles. The form and style can also be ascribed to the mountainous environment as well as to precise ethnic criteria. But, if it is a matter of reconciling a citizenship or a race to the modes, it is noteworthy that the same *Ḥusaynī* or *Dasht* modes were perpetuated with the same structures and more classical forms or styles in Istanbul, Baghdād or Tehran.

Some modes, endowed with structures that can be found throughout the Arabo-Irano-Turkish world, have taken a form, style and name which makes them characteristic of a region. But they are not linked especially strictly to a nation. Also, the *Shūr* and *Dashtī* modes (*bayātī* structure) or *Afshārī* (*segāh* structure) of Iran, perpetuated equally in Ādharbāydjān, correspond respectively, as far as structure is concerned, to the *Shūrī*, *Dasht* and *Awshār maḳāmāt* of ʿIrāḳ, and it may be supposed that they derive from a common regional ancestral patrimony in these three countries.

A classical mode can present local variants. Also the *Segāh*, remarkable for its finale on a neutral fingering-degree, is articulated according to various patterns: in the 3rd degree, on a modulating *rāst/būsalīk* tetrachord (in the Arab countries) or on the equivalent of a *bayātī* genre (in Iran), or, in the fifth degree, on a *ḥidjāz* tetrachord (in Turkey). Another mode called *maḳām Nawā/dastgāh-i Nawā/Nevā maḳāmi* is also constituted:
— a *Bayātī* tetrachord (hardly variable) inserted on the *dūgāh* fingering-degree (3rd open string on the ʿ*ūd*)
— a modulating variable pentachord inserted on the *nawā* fingering-degree (4th open string on the ʿ*ūd*) which may be

(a) a *rāst* pentachord in Turkey (5th degree hardly mobile);

(b) a *rāst* or *būsalīk* pentachord in the Arab countries (5th degree mobile); or

(c) a *rāst*, *būsalīk*, *Bayātī* or *ḥidjāz* pentachord in Iran (5th and 6th degrees mobile)

A comparative approach to the Arab, Iranian and Turkish modes would allow, by making an abstraction of nationalisms, separatisms or claims of paternity, the discovery of a large number of divergent structures under a common name or common structures under different names. However, ambiguities of terminology are involved. What is called a *maḳām/Čahārgāh* among the Arabs and Turks is a major, while the *Čahārgāh* of Iran corresponds to an Arabo-Turkish *Ḥidjāzkār*. The major is called *Māhūr* or *Rāst-pandjgāh* in Iran, while the Arab *Māhūr* is not a major. The *maḳāmāt* called *Pandjgāh* and *Shūrī* in ʿIrāḳ would be called *Sūznāk* and *Ḳardjighār* in Turkey and Syria.

The fruitless efforts since the Congress of Arabic Music in Cairo in 1932 show that it is too late to establish normalised Arabo-Irano-Turkish nomenclature and that it is illusory to want to fix the height of the neutral degrees, very high in Istanbul and very low in Cairo. Finally, the two recent Baghdād Congresses of Music in 1975 and 1978 have allowed us to ascertain that it is just as impossible to agree to a definition of the term *maḳām* in its musical sense.

Moreover, every amateur and every musicologist will persist in perceiving the *maḳām* in terms of his sensibility or formation: familiar melodic formulas, recollection of a cultural identity, expression of an ethnic music, modal system, heptatone on a stave, modal protocol, form of improvisation, aesthetic vestige of the Golden Ages, obstacle to progress by harmonisation, communication of a state of soul, linguistic system of the ʿ*ūd* and specific language, etc.

Bibliography: There is a very full bibliography on the *maḳām* as understood by orientalist musicologists or ethnomusicologists, on *mūsīḳī* and the ʿ*ūd* in J. Elsner, *Zum Problem des Maquam*, in *Acta musicologica*, xlvii/2 (1975), 208-30; H. G. Farmer, arts. MŪSĪḲĪ and ʿŪD in

EI[1]—Interpretation of mediaeval treatises. Evolution of music and of the *ᶜūd* in Islam. Translations: Th. Antar, *Šams al-Dīn Muḥammad al-Ṣaydawī al-Dimašqī. Livre de la connaissance des tons et leur explication*, Sorbonne typed thesis, Paris 1979; J. E. Bencheikh, *Les musiciens et la poésie. Les écoles d'Isḥāq al-Mawṣilī (m. 225 H.) et d'Ibrāhīm al-Mahdī (m. 224 H.)*, in *Arabica*, xxii (1975), 114-152; J.-C. Chabrier, *Un mouvement de rehabilitation de la musique arabe et du luth oriental. L'école de Bagdad de Cherif Muhieddin à Munîr Bachîr*, Sorbonne typed thesis, Paris 1976; A. Chottin, *La musique arabe*, in Roland-Manuel (ed.), *Histoire de la musique*, Paris 1960, 526-43; R. d'Erlanger, *La musique arabe*, i-iv, Paris 1930-8; H. G. Farmer, *The lute scale of Avicenna*, in *JRAS* (1937), 245-57; L. Ronzevalle, *Un traité de musique arabe moderne*, in *MFOB*, iv (1913), 1-120; J. Rouanet, *La musique arabe* and *La musique arabe dans le Maghreb*, in A. Lavignac (ed.), *Histoire de la musique*, Paris 1922, 2676-2939; A. Shiloah, *L'epître sur la musique des Ikhwān aṣ-Ṣafā*, annotated translation, in *REI* (1964), 125-62, (1966), 159-93; idem, *Al-Ḥasan ibn Aḥmad ibn ᶜAlī al-Kātib. La perfection des connaissances musicales*, Paris 1972; idem, *Un ancient traité sur le ᶜūd d'Abū Yūsuf al-Kindī*, in *Israel Or. Studies*, iv (1974), 179-205; idem, *The theory of music in Arabic writings c. 900-1900*, in *R.I.S.M.*, Bx, Munich 1979; O. Wright, *The modal system of Arab and Persian music. A.D. 1250-1300*, Oxford 1978; Z. Yusuf, *Ibn al-Munadjdjim, Risāla fi 'l-mūsīḳā*, critical ed., Cairo 1964; Chabrier, *Évolution du luth-ᶜud et periodisation des structures musicales arabo-islamiques*, in R. Petcos (ed.), *Proceedings of the ninth congress of the U.E.A.I.*, Leiden 1981, 31-47; G. Villoteau, *De l'état actuel de l'art musical en Egypte ou Relation historique et descriptive des recherches et observations faites sur la musique en ce pays par M. Villoteau*, in *Description de l'Égypte*, 2nd ed., xiv, Paris 1826.—Modes and scales in general: J. Chailley, *Formation et transformations du langage musical*, Sorbonne duplicated handbook, Paris 1955, 1-24, 69-143, 191-200; idem, *Essai sur les structures melodiques*, in *Revue de Musicologie*, xliv (1959), 139-75; idem, *L'Imbroglio des modes*, Paris 1960, 5-9, 35-41, 10-28; Chailley, and H. Challan, *Théorie complète de la musique*, Paris 1951; E. Weber (ed.), *La resonance dans les échelles musicales* (C.N.R.S. Colloquium 1960), Paris 1963.—*Maḳām* and *taḳsīm* in the Arab countries: D̲j̲amīl Bas̲h̲īr, *al-ᶜUd wa-ṭarīḳat tadrīsih*/*ᶜUd, ways and methods of teaching*, Bag̲h̲dād 1962; d'Erlanger, *La musique arabe*, v, Paris 1949; Elsner, *Zum Problem des Maquam*; idem, *Der Begriff des maqâm in Ägypten*, in *Beiträge zur musikwissenschaftlichen Forschung in DDR*, v (1973); E. Gerson-Kiwi, *On the technique of Arab Taqsim composition*, in *Festschrift W. Graf*, Vienna-Cologne-Graz 1970, 66-73; M. Guettat, *La musique classique du Maghreb*, Paris 1980; M. Khemakhem, *La musique tunisienne traditionnelle. Structures et formes*, Sorbonne typed thesis, Paris 1974; S. Mahdī, *La musique arabe*, Paris 1972; idem (Ṣāliḥ al-Mahdī), *Maḳāmāt al-mūsīḳā al-ᶜArabiyya*, Tunis (1982); R. Riddle, *Taqsim Nahawand, a study of sixteen performances by Jihad Racy*, in *Yearbook of the International Folk Music Council* (1973); B. Nettl, *Thoughts on improvisation. A comparative approach*, in *The Musical Quarterly*, 1x/1 (1974), 1-19; Aly Jihad Racy, *Musical change and commercial recording in Egypt, 1904-1932*, thesis Univ. of Illinois, Urbana 1977; A. Shiloah, *The Arabic concept of mode*, in *JAMS* xxxiv/1, 1981; H. H. Touma, *Maqam, une forme d'improvisation*, in *The World of Music*, xii/3 (1970), 22-31; idem, *The Maqam phenomenon: an improvisation technique in the music of the Middle East*, in *Ethnomusicology* (1971); idem, *Der Maqam Bayati im arabischen Taqsim*, Hamburg 1976; H. A. Mahfuz, *Muᶜd̲j̲am al-mūsīḳā al-ᶜarabiyya*, Baghdad 1964.—*Maḳām ᶜirāḳī* and *maḳāmāt* in ᶜIrāḳ: Chabrier, thesis, cited above; B. Fāʾiq, *The Iraqī maqam*, in *Baghdad*, x (May 1975), 25-8; ᶜA. Bilāl, *al-Nag̲h̲am al-mubtakar fi 'l-mūsīḳa al-ᶜirākiyya wa 'l-ᶜarabiyya*, Baghdad 1969; al-Ḥād̲j̲d̲j̲ M. Hās̲h̲im-Rad̲j̲ab, *al-Maḳām al-ᶜirāḳī*, Bag̲h̲dād 1961; M.S. D̲j̲alālī, *al-Maḳāmāt al-mūsīḳiyya fi 'l-Mawṣil*, Mawṣil 1941.—Modal structures in Iran: M. Barkechli and M. Maᶜrufī, *La musique traditionnelle de l'Iran et les systèmes de la musique traditionnelle (Radīf)*, Tehran 1963; M. Barkechli, *La musique iranienne,* in Roland-Manuel (ed.), *Histoire de la musique*, 453-525; N. Caron and D. Safvate, *Iran. Les traditions musicales*, Paris 1966; H. Farhat, *Form and style in Persian music*, in *The World of Music*, ii (1978), 108-14; Gerson-Kiwi, *The Persian doctrine of Dastga composition*, Tel Aviv 1963; Khatschi-Khatschi, *Der Dastgah, Studien zur neuen persischen Musik*, in *Kölner Beiträge zur Musikforschung*, xix (1962); M. F. Massoudieh, *Āwāz-e Šūr, Zur Melodiebildung in der persischen Kunstmusik*, in *ibid.*, xlix (1968); B. Nettl and B. Foltin, *Darâmad of Chahârgâh: a study in the performance practice of Persian music*, in *Detroit monographs in musicology*, ii (1972); G. Tsuge, *Notation in Persian music*, in *The World of Music*, ii (1978), 119-20; E. Zonis, *Classical Persian music, an introduction*, Harvard-Cambridge 1973.—Modal structures in Turkey: H. S. Arel, *Türk musikisi nazariyati dersleri*, Istanbul 1968; S. Ezgi, *Nazari ve ameli türk musikisi*, 5 vols., Istanbul 1933-53; B. Mauguin, *Utilisation des échelles dans la tradition musicale turque contemporaine*, typed thesis, Paris 1969; G. Oransay, *Die melodische Linie und der Begriff Makam der traditionellen türkischen Kunstmusik vom 15. bis zum 19. Jahrhundert*, Ankara 1966; Y. Öztuna, *Türk musikisi ansiklopedisi*, Istanbul 1969, 3 vols.; A. Saygun, *La musique turque*, in Roland-Manuel (ed.), *Histoire de la musique*, 573-617; K. L. Signell, *Makam: modal practice in Turkish art music*, thesis, Seattle 1977; R. Yekta-Bey, *La musique turque*, in A. Lavignac (ed.), *Histoire de la musique*, Paris 1922, 1845-3064.—Modal structures in C. Asia, *makom* and the *s̲h̲as̲h̲-makom* system: J. Elsner, see above; V. M. Belyaev, *Očerki po istorii musiki narodov S.S.S.R.*, I, Mosow 1962.

Specific discography: There are analyses of the Arabo-Irano-Turkish modal structures with tables of transposition, finger-boards of the *ᶜūd* and transcription of all the perceived modulations in J.-C. C. Chabrier (ed.), *Arabesques—récitalbum. Anthologie phonographique du récital oriental*, ten albums, Paris 1974-9 (with the cooperation and patronage of the C.N.R.S. and the Institut du Monde Arabe, to be reissued): 1. *Luth en Iraq classique, Méditations. ᶜUd Munîr Bachîr* 2. *Cithare au Liban classique. Qânûn. Muhammad Sabsabi* 3. *Flûte en Syrie classique. Nây. Selim Kosur* 4. *Luth en Syrie. Thèmes damascènes. ᶜUd. ᶜOmar Naqichbendî* 5. *Luth en Iraq traditionnel. Évocations. ᶜUd Jamîl Bachîr* 6. *Luth au Yemen classique. Rêveries. ᶜUd Jamîl Ghânim* 7. *Cithare en Égypte. Le Caire. Qânûn. Muhammad ᶜAtiya ᶜOmar* 8. *Luth au Liban traditionnel. Buzuq. Nasser Makhoul* 9. *Flute en Turquie mystique. Nay. Soufi Hayrî Tümer* 10. *Cithare en Iran classique. Sanṭûr. Farâmarz Payvar.*

(J.-Cl. Ch. Chabrier)

MAḲĀM IBRĀHĪM denotes, according to Ḳurʾān, II, 125 (... *wa-ttak̲h̲id̲h̲ū min maḳāmi Ibrāhīmi* *muṣallan ...)* a place of prayer. Some commentators interpreted, however, the word *muṣallan* as "a place of invocations and supplications", a definition which would considerably modify the status of the place. The reading of the verb in the phrase became the subject of discussion. Several scholars read it in the perfect tense "... *wa-ttak͟had͟hū* ...", and they rendered it" ... and they took to themselves Abraham's station for a place of prayer", linking it with the preceding clause" ... and when We appointed the House to be a place of visitation for the people and shelter and they took to themselves ..." (see e.g. Mud͟jāhid, *Tafsīr*, ed. ʿAbd al-Raḥmān al-Sūratī, Islāmābād n.d., i, 88, 89 n. 1; al-S͟hawkānī, *Fatḥ al-ḳadīr*, Beirut n.d., i, 138; Ibn Mud͟jāhid, *Kitāb al-Sabʿa fī 'l-ḳirāʾāt*, ed. S͟hawḳī Ḍayf, Cairo 1972, 169, no. 45; al-ʿAynī, *ʿUmdat al-ḳārī*, Cairo 1348, repr. Beirut, ix, 212). In the other version, the verb is read as an imperative "... *wa-ttak͟hid͟hū* ..." and rendered "... and take to yourselves ..."; this is the reading preferred by the majority of Muslim scholars. The verse was connected with the person of ʿUmar, who according to tradition approached the Prophet asking him to establish the spot on which the stone known as *maḳām Ibrāhīm* was located as a place of prayer. After a short interval, God revealed to the Prophet the verse of sūra II, 125 "... and take to yourselves ...". This is one of the miraculous cases in which ʿUmar's advice proved to be congruent with the will of God, the Ḳurʾānic verses lending confirmation to his suggestion (see Abū Nuʿaym, *Ḥilyat al-awliyāʾ*, Cairo 1351/1932, iii, 302, 377, iv, 145; al-Ṭabarānī, *al-Muʿd͟jam al-ṣag͟hīr*, ed. ʿAbd al-Raḥmān Muḥammad ʿUt͟hmān, Cairo 1388/1968; al-Muttaḳī al-Hindī, *Kanz al-ʿummāl*, Hyderabad 1390/1970, xvii, 99, nos. 283-5; al-Fak͟hr al-Rāzī, *al-Tafsīr al-Kabīr*, Cairo n.d., xxiii, 86; Amīn Maḥmūd K͟haṭṭāb, *Fatḥ al-malik al-maʿbūd, takmilat al-manhal al-ʿad͟hb al-mawrūd, s͟harḥ sunan al-Imām Abī Dāwūd*, Cairo 1394/1974, ii, 11; al-ʿAynī, *op. cit.*, ix, 212; al-Ḳurṭubī, *Tafsīr* [*al-D͟jāmiʿ li-aḥkām al-Ḳurʾān*], Cairo 1387/1967, ii, 112; al-S͟hawkānī, *op. cit.*, i, 140 inf.; Anonymous, *Manāḳib al-ṣaḥāba*, ms. Br. Mus., Or. 8273, fol. 3a). Ibn al-D͟jawzī is reported to have wondered why ʿUmar had asked for a practice from the faith of Abraham (*millat Ibrāhīm*) to be introduced into the ritual of Islam despite the fact that the Prophet had forbidden him to quote passages from the Torah. Ibn al-D͟jawzī tries to explain this, saying that Abraham is revered in Islam as an *imām*, the Ḳurʾān urges people to follow in his steps, the Kaʿba is linked with his name and the prints of his feet are like the marks of the mason; that is the reason why ʿUmar asked to turn the *maḳām* into a place of worship (see al-ʿAynī, *op. cit.*, iv, 145; Ibn Ḥad͟jar, *Fatḥ al-bārī*, Cairo 1300 [repr. Beirut], viii, 128). One of the commentators states that the injunction is linked with sūra II, 122 ("... Children of Israel, remember my blessing...") and that the Children of Israel are those who were addressed by it (al-Fak͟hr al-Rāzī, *op. cit.*, i, 472); another one says that the injunction is incumbent upon the Jews at the time of the Prophet (al-Ṭabarī, *Tafsīr*, ed. Maḥmūd and Muḥammad S͟hākir, Cairo n.d., iii, 31); a third commentary connects the injunction with II, 124: "... and when his Lord tested Abraham ...". According to this last interpretation, the *maḳām Ibrāhīm* is one of the words of the Lord by which Abraham was tested (al-S͟hawkānī, *op. cit.*, i, 139; Ibn Kat͟hīr, *Tafsīr*, Beirut 1385/1966, i, 291).

There was disagreement among Muslim scholars as to the significance of the expression *maḳām Ibrāhīm*. Some of them claimed that the expression denotes the whole place of the pilgrimage, others said that ʿArafa, Muzdalifa [*q.vv.*] and the D͟jimār are meant; a third group maintained that *maḳām Ibrāhīm* refers to ʿArafa only, while the fourth view identifies it with the *Ḥaram* of Mecca (see e.g. al-ʿAynī, *op. cit.*, iv, 130, ix, 212; Abu 'l-Baḳāʾ Muḥammad b. al-Ḍiyāʾ al-ʿAdawī, *Aḥwāl Makka wa 'l-Madīna*, ms. Br. Mus., Or. 11865, fol. 84b; Amīn Maḥmūd K͟haṭṭāb, *op. cit.*, ii, 11). The great majority of the scholars identified *maḳām Ibrāhīm* with the stone in the sanctuary of Mecca which commonly bears this name (see e.g. al-ʿAynī, *op. cit.*, ix, 212; A. Spitaler, *Ein Kapitel aus den* Faḍāʾil al-Qurʾān *von Abū ʿUbaid al-Qāsim b. Salām*, in *Documenta islamica*, Berlin 1952, 6, nos. 29-30) and behind which the Prophet prayed when he performed the circumambulation of the Kaʿba (see e.g. al-Wāḳidī, *al-Mag͟hāzī*, ed. M. Jones, London 1966, 1098; al-Ḥarbī, *al-Manāsik*, ed. Ḥamad al-D͟jāsir, al-Riyāḍ 1389/1969, 433, 500; al-Ṭabarānī, *op. cit.*, i, 22; Muḥibb al-Dīn al-Ṭabarī, *al-Ḳirā li-ḳāṣid umm al-ḳurā*, ed. Muṣṭafā al-Saḳḳā, Cairo 1390/1970, 342 sup.).

The sanctity of the stone was enhanced by the fact that it bears the footprints of Abraham (see e.g. al-Isfarāʾīnī, *Zubdat al-aʿmāl wa-k͟hulāṣat al-afʿāl*, ms. Br. Mus., Or. 3034, fol. 6b). The footprints of the Prophet had exactly the same size as the footprints in the *maḳām* (see e.g. al-Ṭabarsī, *Iʿlām al-warā*, ed. ʿAlī Akbar al-G͟haffārī, Tehran 1379, 73; al-Kāzarūnī, *Sīrat al-nabī*, ms. Br. Mus. Add. 18499, fols. 70b, 88a, 89a). Some traditions say that the miracle of Abraham's footprints in the stone appeared when Abraham built the Kaʿba; when the walls became too high he mounted the *maḳām* which miraculously rose and went down in order to let Ismāʿīl hand him the stones for the building (see e.g. al-Sind͟jārī, *Manāʾiḥ al-karam bi-ak͟hbār Makka wa 'l-Ḥaram*, ms. Leiden, Or. 7018, fol. 22b; al-Sayyid al-Bakrī, *Iʿānat al-ṭālibīn ʿalā ḥall alfāẓ fatḥ al-muʿīn*, Cairo 1319, repr. Beirut, ii, 295 inf.-296 sup.; al-Isfarāʾīnī, *op. cit.*, fol. 83b; al-K͟hargūs͟hī, *Lawāmiʿ*, ms. Vatican, Arab. 1642, fol. 67b; al-Suyūṭī, *al-Ḥāwī li 'l-fatāwī*, ed. Muḥammad Muḥyī al-Dīn ʿAbd al-Ḥamīd, Cairo 1378/1959, ii, 201; al-Ṣāliḥī, *Subul al-hudā wa 'l-ras͟hād fī sīrat k͟hayr al-ʿibād*, ed. Muṣṭafā ʿAbd al-Wāḥid, Cairo 1392/1972, i, 181; Muḥibb al-Dīn al-Ṭabarī, *op. cit.*, 343); other traditions claim that the miracle occurred when the wife of Ismāʿīl washed the head of Abraham (see e.g. al-Masʿūdī, *It͟hbāt al-waṣiyya*, Nad͟jaf 1374/1955, 39 inf.-40 sup.; Abu 'l-Baḳāʾ al-ʿAdawī, *op. cit.*, fol. 85a; al-ʿAynī, *op. cit.*, ix, 212); a third tradition says that it happened when Abraham mounted the *maḳām* in order to summon the people to perform the pilgrimage to Mecca (see e.g. Abu 'l-Baḳāʾ al-ʿAdawī, *loc. cit.*; al-Ṣāliḥī, *op. cit.*, i, 184-5; anon., *ʿArf al-ṭīb*, ms. Leiden, Or. 493, fol. 70a; Muḥibb al-Dīn al-Ṭabarī, *op. cit.*, 342; al-Sind͟jārī, *op. cit.*, fol. 28b; al-Mad͟jlisī, *Biḥār al-anwār*, Tehran 1388, xcix, 182, 188). Certain traditions affirm that Abraham took the stone as a *ḳibla* [*q.v.*]; he prayed at the stone turning his face to the Kaʿba (see e.g. al-Isfarāʾīnī, *op. cit.*, fol. 83b; Muḥibb al-Dīn al-Ṭabarī, *loc. cit.*; Abu 'l-Baḳāʾ al-ʿAdawī, *loc. cit.*). Some scholars, however, defined the stone merely as a means to mark the *ḳibla*, bidding the believer to have the stone placed in front of himself while facing the Kaʿba (al-ʿAynī, *op. cit.*, iv, 130: *fa-inna 'l-maḳāma innamā yakūnu ḳiblatan id͟hā d͟jaʿalahu al-muṣallī baynahu wa-bayn al-ḳibla*). Certain scholars pointed out that the prayer at the *maḳām* is not obligatory (al-ʿAynī, *op. cit.*, ix, 212: *wa-hiya ʿalā wad͟jh al-ik͟htiyār wa 'l-istiḥbāb dūn al-wud͟jūb* ...).

Numerous traditions about the qualities and virtues

of the *maḳām* report that the stone was sent down from Heaven, that supplications at the *maḳām* will be answered and sins will be forgiven (see e.g. al-Ṣāliḥī, *op. cit.*, i, 204; al-Sindjārī, *op. cit.*, fol. 23b; anon., *ʿArf al-ṭīb*, fol. 73b; al-Madjlisī, *op. cit.*, xcix, 219, 230, 231; al-Fāsī, *Tuḥfat al-kirām*, ms. Leiden Or. 2654, fol. 66b; Muḥibb al-Dīn al-Ṭabarī, *op. cit.*, 324; al-Shiblī, *Maḥāsin al-wasāʾil fī maʿrifat al-awāʾil*, ms. Br. Mus., Or. 1530, fol. 38b; al-Isfarāʾīnī, *Zubdat al-aʿmāl*, fols. 76b-77a; al-Khwarazmī, *Mukhtaṣar ithārat al-targhīb wa 'l-tashwīḳ*, ms. Br. Mus., Or. 4584, fols. 11a-13a; al-Ḳazwīnī, *Āthār al-bilād*, Beirut 1382/1962, 118; Ibn Abī Shayba, *al-Muṣannaf*, Hyderabad 1390/1970, iv, 108-9; ʿAbd al-Razzāḳ, *al-Muṣannaf*, ed. Ḥabīb al-Raḥmān al-Aʿẓamī, Beirut 1392/1972, v, 32, no. 8890; al-Sayyid al-Bakrī, *op. cit.*, ii, 295). The sanctity of the *maḳām* was associated with that of the *rukn* and with *zamzam*; 99 prophets are buried at this spot, among them Hūd, Ṣāliḥ, Nūḥ and Ismāʿīl (see e.g. al-Sindjārī, *op. cit.*, fol. 26a; al-Suyūṭī, *al-Durr al-manthūr*, Cairo 1314, i, 136). Prayer at the graves was permitted on the ground that this was a cemetery of prophets; as prophets are alive in their graves, prayer is not only permitted but even meritorious (cf. al-Sayyid al-Bakrī, *op. cit.*, ii, 277). Scholars criticised the practice of kissing the stone, stroking it, and even performing a kind of circumambulation round it (see Ibn Abī Shayba, *op. cit.*, iv, 61, 116; Muḥibb al-Dīn al-Ṭabarī, *op. cit.*, 357, no. 109; anon., *ʿArf al-ṭīb*, *loc. cit.*; but see Ibn Djubayr, *al-Riḥla*, Beirut 1388/1968, 55, ... *tabarraknā bi-lamsihi wa-taḳbīlihi* ...).

The *maḳām* is a stone of small dimensions: 60 cm. wide by 90 cm. high (see the data recorded by al-Fāsī, *Tuḥfat al-kirām*, fol. 67a; measured by al-Fāsī *anno* 753 AH; and see al-Sindjārī, *op. cit.*, fol. 23a). It is now "closely surrounded by glass and bars set into a polygonal base, the whole structure, capped by a much narrower kind of 'helmet', being about three yards above ground level" (A. J. Wensinck-J. Jomier, art. KAʿBA). In the early periods of Islam, the stone, encased in a wooden box, was placed on a high platform so as to prevent its being swept by a torrent. During the prayer led by the ruler or his deputy, the box used to be lifted and the *maḳām* shown to the people attending the prayer; after the prayer, the box was again locked and placed in the Kaʿba (cf. al-Muḳaddasī, 72). It was sad to see how al-Ḥadjdjādj tried with his leg to set up the *maḳām Ibrāhīm* back to its place after it had moved (see ʿAbd al-Razzāḳ, *op. cit.*, v, 49, no. 8959).

In 160/777 the *maḳām* was brought to the abode of al-Mahdī in Mecca when he performed the pilgrimage. In the next year, when the *maḳām* was raised carelessly by one of its keepers, it fell down and cracked; it was repaired at the order of al-Mahdī and its upper and lower parts were braced with gold. Al-Mutawakkil in 241/855-6 improved the pedestal of the *maḳām*, embellished the *maḳām* itself with gold and ordered the building of a cupola over the *maḳām* (cf. al-Sindjārī, *op. cit.*, fol. 120b). In 252/866 the *maḳām* was stripped of its gold by the governor of Mecca Djaʿfar b. al-Faḍl; the gold was then melted down for minting *dīnārs*, which he spent in his struggle against the rebel Ismāʿīl b. Yūsuf b. Ibrāhīm (see al-Sindjārī, *op. cit.*, fols. 120a ult. - 120b, 121a; on Ismāʿīl b. Yūsuf, see al-Fāsī, *al-ʿIḳd al-thamīn*, ed. Fuʾād Sayyid, Cairo 1383/1963, iii, 311, no. 783). A thorough restoration of the *maḳām* was carried out in 256/870 by the governor ʿAlī b. al-Ḥasan al-Hāshimī (see on him al-Fāsī, *op. cit.*, vi, 151, no. 2050). Al-Fākihī gives a detailed description of the stone in its place (cf. *Le Muséon*, lxxxiv [1971], 477-91). When the stone was brought to the *dār al-imāra*, al-Fākihī noticed the inscription on it and tried to copy parts of it. R. Dozy reproduced the inscription and tried to decipher it (R. Dozy, *Die Israeliten zu Mekka*, Leipzig 1864, 155-61). His reading and interpretation are implausible (Prof. J. Naveh's opinion, communicated verbally).

Lengthy and heated discussions took place among the scholars about the place of the *maḳām*. The traditions about whether the stone was established in its place are divergent and even contradictory (see e.g. Ibn Abi 'l-Ḥadīd, *Sharḥ Nahdj al-balāgha*, ed. Muḥammad Abu 'l-Faḍl Ibrāhīm, Cairo 1964, xii, 160; al-Ḳuḍāʿī, *Taʾrīkh*, Bodleian ms. Pococke 270, fol. 58a; al-Ḥarbī, *al-Manāsik*, ed. Ḥamad al-Djāsir, 500; al-Shiblī, *op. cit.*, fol. 38a-b; al-Muttaḳī al-Hindī, *op. cit.*, xvii, 97-9, nos, 278-81; Ibn Ḥibbān al-Bustī, *al-Thiḳāt*, Hyderabad 1395/1975, ii, 218; ʿAbd al-Raḥmān b. Abī Ḥātim al-Rāzī, *ʿIlal al-ḥadīth*, ed. Muḥibb al-Dīn al-Khaṭīb, Cairo 1343, i, 298). These traditions were divided by al-Sindjārī into five groups. According to some reports, ʿUmar was the first who removed the stone. Others say that in the time of Abraham the stone was in the same place as it is now, but in the time of the Djāhiliyya it had been attached to the Kaʿba and so it remained during the periods of the Prophet and of Abū Bakr and for some time during the caliphate of ʿUmar, who returned it to its proper place. A third series of traditions claims that the Prophet removed the stone from its original place (next to the Kaʿba) and put it in its present location. A fourth tradition maintains that ʿUmar moved the stone to its present place and returned it to the same spot after it had been swept away by a torrent. Finally, some scholars say that the *maḳām* has always been in the place where it is nowadays; ʿUmar re-installed it to this place after it was swept away by a torrent (see al-Sindjārī, *op. cit.*, fols. 23a-b, 76b-78a). A tradition which contains new aspects of the location of the *maḳām* is recorded by Ibn Kathīr. The stone was in the Kaʿba; the Prophet took it out of the Kaʿba and attached it to its wall (i.e. of the Kaʿba). Then he said, "O people, this is the *ḳibla*" (Ibn Kathīr, *Tafsīr*, ii, 322). It is noteworthy that in this tradition there is no mention of ʿUmar, of his advice or of the changes carried out by him. It is quite plausible that ʿUmar's change had to be legitimised and duly justified. Muḥibb al-Dīn al-Ṭabarī tries to explain this discrepancy by reporting that ʿUmar inquired after the death of the Prophet about the place in which Abraham put the stone. In the time of the Prophet, the stone was indeed attached to the wall of the Kaʿba; but ʿUmar was aware of the Prophet's will to follow the *sunna* of Abraham, and returned the *maḳām* to its original place, the place in which it had been put by Abraham (*al-Ḳirā*, 347; quoted by Abu 'l-Baḳāʾ al-ʿAdawī, *Aḥwāl Makka wa 'l-Madīna*, fols. 86b-87a). A divergent report is recorded by al-Sindjārī on the authority of Ibn Surāḳa. Between the door of the Kaʿba and the place of Adam's prayer (where God accepted his repentance) there were nine cubits; it was the place of *maḳām Ibrāhīm* and there the Prophet performed two *rakʿas* after finishing the *ṭawāf* and after receiving the relevation of the verse "... and take the *maḳām Ibrāhīm* as a place of prayer...". It was the Prophet himself who later removed the stone to the place where it is nowadays, sc. at a distance of 20 cubits from the Kaʿba (al-Sindjārī, *op. cit.*, fol. 77a). Instructive is the report of Ibn Djubayr. The ditch (*ḥufra*) at the door of the Kaʿba (in which the water gathers when the Kaʿba is washed) is the place of the *maḳām* in the time of Abraham; the place is crowded by believers who pray there; the stone was moved by the Prophet to the present place (see *al-Riḥla*, 55 inf. - 56; al-Sindjārī, *op. cit.*, fol. 78a). The change of the place of the *maḳām* and the possibility that the stone should be moved to another place of the *ḥaram* led to a disturbing question: would it be incumbent upon the believer to pray, in such a case, in the new place (since the injunction clearly makes it necessary to take the *maḳām* as a place of prayer), or to stick to the original place? (See al-Sindjārī, *op. cit.*, 77b and also fol. 78a: the former *maḳām* occupied half of the ditch (*ḥufra*) at the *ḥidjr*).

Shīʿī scholars were aware of the change carried out by ʿUmar. Shīʿī *imāms* are said to have recommended prayer at the former place of the *maḳām Ibrāhīm*. This "former place" is described as being between the *rukn al-ʿirāḳī* and the door of the Kaʿba. Second in merit is the prayer behind the present *maḳām* (cf. al-Madjlisī, *op. cit.*, xcix, 230, no. 4, 231 nos. 6-7). Ibn Bābawayh sketches the history of the changes as follows. Abraham attached the stone to the Kaʿba, stood on it and summoned the people to perform the pilgrimage to Mecca; on that occasion his footprints were moulded in the stone. The people of the Djāhiliyya then removed the stone and put it in its present place in order to make the circumambulation of the Kaʿba easier. When the Prophet was sent, he reinstalled the *maḳām* in the place where it had been put by Abraham. ʿUmar asked where its location had been during the period of the Djāhiliyya, and returned it to that place; hence the present place of the *maḳām Ibrāhīm* is the same as it was in the time of the Djāhiliyya (see Ibn Bābawayh, *ʿIlal al-sharāʾiʿ*, ed. Muḥammad Ṣādiḳ Baḥr al-ʿulūm, Nadjaf 1385/1966, 423, *bāb* 160; quoted by al-Madjlisī, *op. cit.*, xcix, 232, no. 1; cf. anon., untitled ms. Vatican Arab. 1750, fol. 32b).

Some traditions related by al-Fākihī add certain peculiar details about the change carried out by ʿUmar. A report traced back to Saʿīd b. Djubayr says that Abraham placed the stone in front of the Kaʿba. ʿUmar removed the stone and placed it in its present spot, as he was afraid that people performing the *ṭawāf* might tread on it; it is now facing the former *maḳām*. Another report given on the authority of Hishām b. ʿUrwa and transmitted to him by his father ʿUrwa says that the Prophet prayed facing the Kaʿba; afterwards, both Abū Bakr and ʿUmar in the early part of his caliphate prayed in the same direction. But later, ʿUmar announced that God, blessed He is and lofty, says "... and take to yourselves the *maḳām Ibrāhīm* as a place of prayer ..."; thereafter, he moved the stone to the (present) place of the *maḳām* (al-Fākihī, *Taʾrīkh Makka*, fol. 331a). Both these reports recorded by al-Fākihī are sober, concise and devoid of miraculous features or of obligatory divine injunctions, and deserve a fair degree of confidence. The conclusion must be that it was ʿUmar who relocated the place of the *maḳām*, probably out of pragmatic considerations.

The latest change in the place of the *maḳām* has been carried out by the Saʿūdī government: the *maḳām* was moved to the rear in order to widen the path for the circumambulation of the Kaʿba (see in al-Ḥarbī, *op. cit.*, 500, n. 2 of Ḥamad al-Djāsir).

Bibliography: In addition to references given in the text, see the bibl. in *Le Muséon*, lxxxiv (1971), 477-91. (M. J. KISTER)

MAḲĀMA, a purely and typically Arabic literary genre. The word is generally translated as "assembly" or "session" (Fr. "séance"), but this is an approximation which does not convey exactly the complex nature of the term.

Semantic evolution of the term. The semantic study of this vocable for the period previous to the creation of the genre is complicated by the fact that the plural *maḳāmāt*, which is frequently used, is common to two nouns, *maḳāma* and *maḳām* [*q.v.*]. Both are derived from the radical *ḳ-w-m*, which implies the idea of "to rise, to stand in order to perform an action", but which is often weakened in that it simply marks the beginning of an action, whether the agent rises or not, and even loses its dynamic sense altogether, taking on the static sense of "to stay in a place". *Maḳām* occurs fourteen times in the Ḳurʾān with the general sense of "abode, a place where one stays", more specifically in the beyond, but in one verse (XIX, 74/73), where it is used in conjunction with *nadī*, "tribal council", it must refer to a meeting of important people; the same applies to a verse of Zuhayr b. Abī Sulmā (Cheikho, *Shuʿarāʾ al-Naṣrāniyya*, 573, v. 6: *maḳāmāt ... andiya*). Otherwise, from the archaic period onward, *maḳām* naturally conveyed the sense of "situation, state", and, in a verse of Kaʿb b. Zuhayr (*Bānat Suʿād*, ed. and tr. R. Basset, Algiers 1910, v. 41), the *maḳām* of the poet, which is certainly dramatic, is judged terrifying (*hāʾil*) by the commentator. It is probable that an analysis of ancient poetry would supply more precise and illuminating examples, but it seems likely that by means of a transference of meaning, starting with "a tragic situation", *maḳām* came to designate a battle, a combat, a mêlée, and that, as a result of a confusion of the two terms or the simple exigencies of metre, *maḳāma* also took on this sense. In a verse of Djarīr in *-sī* (*Sharḥ Dīwān Djarīr*, ed. Ṣāwī, Cairo n. d., 326, v. 1 of the 2nd poem), *maḳāma* seems to signify, not *madjlis* "assembly" (as it is glossed by the editor, who confines himself to reproducing the dictionary definition), but "battle"; similarly, in a verse of Abū Tammām in *-dā* (*Badr al-tamām fī sharḥ Dīwān Abī Tammām*, ed. M.I. al-Aswad, Beirut 1347/1928, i, 222, v. 5), *maḳāma* (read as *muḳāma* by the editor, but glossed as "scene of warlike actions") is used in conjunction with *muʿtarak* and doubtless has the sense of "theatre of warlike valour". In other examples of this type it is the plural which is attested, and it is not known to which singular it corresponds. In any case, it is certainly in the sense of "battles, military actions" that this plural is to be best understood in a passage of the *Kitāb al-Bukhalāʾ* of *al-Djāḥiẓ* (ed. Ḥādjirī, 184, 1. 2; rectify accordingly the translation by Pellat, 289), where there is a case of Bedouins talking of battles of the pre-Islamic period (*ayyām* [*q.v.*]) and of *maḳāmāt*, acts of heroism.

In assemblies of important people, eloquence was a natural feature, and it is not surprising that, by means of another transference of meaning, *maḳām* should also refer to the topics discussed in the course of these meetings, then, by extension, to more or less edifying addresses delivered before a distinguished audience. This evolution is attested, in the 3rd/9th century by Ibn Ḳutayba [*q.v.*] who, in his *ʿUyūn al-akhbār* (ii, 333-43), gives the title *Maḳāmāt al-zuhhād ʿind al-khulafāʾ wa ʾl-mulūk* to a chapter in which he reproduces pious homilies designated, in the singular, by the term *maḳām*. Before him, the Muʿtazilī al-Iskāfī (d. 240/854 [*q.v.*]) had written a *Kitāb al-Maḳāmāt fī tafḍīl ʿAlī*, and in the following century, al-Masʿūdī [*q.v.*] (*Murūdj*, iv, 441 = § 1744) speaks of homilies by ʿAlī b. Abī Ṭālib and (v, 421 = § 2175) of a sermon by ʿUmar b. ʿAbd al-ʿAzīz, delivered on the occasion of their *maḳāmāt*, where it is impossible to tell whether the corresponding singular is *maḳām* or *maḳāma*. Whatever the case may be, al-Hamadhānī was perhaps thinking primarily of the latter interpretation, while retaining in the background the memory of the concept of feats of arms when he adopted the term *maḳāma* to designate the speeches, which he considered instructive, if not edifying, of Abu 'l-Fatḥ al-Iskandarī and the "sketches", the "sessions", in the course of which they are reported by ʿĪsā b. Hishām; then, this word came to be applied to a whole genre, and was ultimately confused often, as will be seen in due course, with *risāla* [*q.v.*]. W. J. Prendergast (*The Maqámát of Badíʿ al-Zamán al-Hamadhání*, London-Madras 1915, repr. with introd. by C. E. Bosworth, London-Dublin 1973, 11-14) has collected a number of occurrences of *maḳāma* and *maḳāmāt* in poetry and prose predating Badīʿ al-Zamān, but the most exhaustive research has been that of R. Blachère, *Étude sémantique sur le nom* maqāma, in *Machriq* (1953), 646-52 (repr. in *Analecta*, Damascus 1975, 61-7).

Birth of the genre. In the *maḳāmāt* described by Ibn Ḳutayba, it is often a Bedouin or a person of rather shabby appearance, although extremely eloquent, who addresses an aristocratic audience. Before an audience of common people, an analogous role was performed by the *ḳāṣṣ* [*q.v.*], who originally delivered edifying speeches but, as is well-known, in the course of time soon took on the dual function of storyteller and mountebank, whose activity was to a certain extent comparable to that of the *mukaddī* [*q.v.*], the wandering beggar or vagrant who went from town to town and easily gathered around him an audience who rewarded him financially for the fascinating stories that he told. It seems probable that the first to introduce these colourful characters into Arabic literature was al-Djāḥiẓ [*q.v.*], who devoted a long treatment to them in the *Kitāb al-Bukhalāʾ* and wrote at least two other pieces on the stratagems of thieves (*Ḥiyal al-luṣūṣ*) and of beggars (*Ḥiyal al-mukaddīn*), of which al-Bayhaḳī (*Maḥāsin*, ed. Schwally, i, 521-3, 622-4) has preserved extracts which are unfortunately very short (see Pellat, *Arabische Geisteswelt*, Zürich-Stuttgart 1967 = *The life and works of Jāḥiẓ*, London-Berkeley-Los Angeles 1969, texts xlii and xliii). The interest taken by the aristocracy and men of letters, not only in the popular classes, but also in members of the "milieu" is remarkably illustrated by the *Ḳaṣīda sāsāniyya* of Abū Dulaf al-Khazradjī (4th/10th century) [*q.v.*] which has given C. E. Bosworth occasion to write a masterly work (*The medieval underworld, the Banū Sāsān in Arabic society and literature*, Leiden 1976, 2 vols.) to which the reader must be referred; he will find there, in particular, a very well-documented first chapter on vagabonds and beggars, as well as a discussion (97-9) of opinions regarding the birth of the *maḳāma*. In the formation of the latter it is in fact possible to discern a certain influence from earlier literature relating to the adventures of some marginal elements of society, and in particular from the *ḳaṣīda* of Abū Dulaf (cf. al-Thaʿālibī, *Yatīma*, Damascus 1885, iii, 176). To this influence there should no doubt be added that of mimes [see ḤIKĀYA], since the *maḳāma* contains an undeniable theatrical element, at least in the make-up of the hero and the posture of the narrator. Recently, A. F. L. Beeston (*The genesis of the* maqāmāt *genre*, in *Journal of Arabic literature*, ii [1972], 1-12) has endeavoured to show that the reputation of al-Hamadhānī has been to some extent exaggerated and that the anecdotal literature represented especially by the *Faradj baʿd al-shidda* of his contemporary al-Tanūkhī (329-84/939-94 [*q.v.*]) also presented persons of pitiable appearance who prove to be endowed with an exceptional talent for oratory. The contrast between the external appearance and eloquence or wisdom is a commonplace of *adab*, and while the anecdotal literature discussed by Beeston has certainly exercised an influence, it has not been the only one to do so.

As early as 1915, Prendergast (*op. laud.*, 6) had drawn attention to and translated a subsequently well-known passage of the *Zahr al-ādāb* (ed. Z. Mubārak, Cairo 1344, i, 235; ed. Budjāwī, Cairo 1972/1953, i, 261) of al-Ḥuṣrī (d. 413/1022 [*q.v.*]), who states that al-Hamadhānī imitated (*ʿāraḍa*) the forty *ḥadīth*s of Ibn Durayd [*q.v.*] and composed four hundred "sessions" on the theme of the *kudya*, the activity of the *mukaddūn*. After Margoliouth had, in the first edition of the *EI* (s.v. AL-HAMADHĀNĪ), given credit to this passage, Z. Mubārak, in 1930, adopted the same point of view in *al-Muḳtaṭaf* (lxxvi, 412-20, 561-4) and reproduced it in his thesis on *La prose arabe au IVe siècle* (Paris 1931), while, in the same volume of the *Muḳtaṭaf* (588-90), Ṣādiḳ al-Rāfiʿī refuted his arguments by emphasising the weakness of the source on which he relied. R. Blachère and P. Masnou (*al-Hamadānī, choix de Maqāmāt*, Paris 1957, 15) criticise the exploitation of the information supplied by al-Ḥuṣrī and write that the only conclusion to be drawn from it "is that at the end of the 10th century or at the beginning of the 11th, a Muslim scholar discovered a link between the 'sessions' of Hamadānī and the stories attributed to a philologist-poet of Iraq, Ibn Duraid"; as Prendergast had done, these authors observe that no work of this genre features in the list of Ibn Durayd's writings, and C. E. Bosworth, in his introduction to the reprinted edition of Prendergast, concludes that al-Ḥuṣrī's information is suspect. Powerful evidence in support of this conclusion is supplied by the silence of a compatriot of the latter, Ibn Sharaf (d. 460/1067, *q.v.*), who at the beginning of his *Masāʾil al-intiḳād* (ed.-tr. Pellat, Algiers 1953, 5) declares that he himself has been inspired by the *Kalīla wa-Dimna*, by Sahl b. Hārūn [*q.v.*], who also wrote about animals, and by Badīʿ al-Zamān, but makes no mention of Ibn Durayd.

In another context, in his account of the great rival of al-Hamadhānī, al-Khwārazmī [*q.v.*], Abū Bakr (323-83/934-93), Brockelmann (S I, 150) adds, having listed the mss. of the *Rasāʾil* of this author, "nebst *Maqāmen*, in denen wie bei al-Hamadānī ʿĪsā b. Hišām auftritt"; moreover, al-Ḳalḳashandī (*Ṣubḥ*, xiv, 128-38) reproduces, from the *Tadhkira* of Ibn Ḥamdūn (495-562/1102-66 [*q.v.*]), a *maḳāma* of Abu 'l-Ḳāsim al-Khwārazmī in which the author recounts his victory over a learned opponent encountered in the course of a journey. Even allowing for the fact that al-Ḳalḳashandī made a mistake over the *kunya* of this Khwārazmī, this *maḳāma* is certainly of a later period than the first *Séances* of Badīʿ al-Zamān. The same can probably be said of the *Ḥikāya* of Abu 'l-Muṭahhar al-Azdī [*q.v.* in Suppl.] (A. Mez, *Abulkâsim, ein bagdâder Sittenbild*, Heidelberg 1902) of which the connections with *maḳāma* are not clear [see ḤIKĀYA].

Whatever the case may be, it may be asserted that the idea of the "session" as we know it was in the air and that, in the absence of information to the contrary, the first to have adopted it for the creation of a new literary genre was, as all the critics agree, al-Hamadhānī (358-98/968-1008 [*q.v.*]). It does not seem obligatory, in fact, to search desperately for a model whenever an innovation appears, since the most elementary justice demands that allowance be made for personal invention. Prendergast (*op. laud.*, 20-1) poses the question as to whether Badīʿ al-Zamān owes anything to Greek or Byzantine models, but considers such influence totally improbable and concludes that "the same demons of difficulty, obscurity and pedantry entered the orators and poets of both nations in different periods". This assessment, the accuracy of which will become apparent in the course of the study of the evolution of the *maḳāma*, cannot, however, be fully applied to al-Hamadhānī. It is undeniable that this author was, in the framework of Arabic literature and Arab-Islamic society in general, subject to various influences, but he should be given credit for having succeeded, through a commendable work of synthesis, in setting in motion two principal characters charged with precise roles, in particular a hero who symbolises a whole social category.

Structure of the original *maḳāma*. From the point of view of form, this genre is characterised, in the work of its initiator, by the almost invariable use of *sadj*ᶜ [*q.v.*], of rhymed and rhythmic prose (sometimes blended with verse) which, in the 4th/10th century, tended to become the almost universal mode of literary expression, especially in the class of administrative secretaries to which al-Hamadhānī belonged, and was to remain so until the end of the 19th century. As regards the structure of an individual *maḳāma*, the fundamental characteristic is the existence of a hero (in this case Abu 'l-Fatḥ al-Iskandarī) whose adventures and eloquent speeches are related by a narrator (in this case ᶜĪsā b. Hishām) to the author who, in turn, conveys them to his readers. As Abd El-Fattah Kilito has quite correctly observed in a suggestive article (*Le genre "séance"*, in *St. Isl.*, xliii [1976], 25-51), in the *maḳāma*, a text is obtained through the research of a *rāwī* and transmitted through a second *rāwī* (the author), in such a way that the mode of transmission recalls that of ancient poetry and, still more precisely, that of *ḥadīth*, with the difference that the text, the person who speaks it and the first *rāwī* are fictitious. In a typical *maḳāma*, Kilito adds (48), the order of events is as follows: arrival of the *rāwī* in a town, encounter with the disguised *balīgh* (the eloquent man = the hero), speech, reward, recognition, reproach, justification, parting. It need hardly be said that this general scheme does not apply invariably to all the *maḳāmat* of al-Hamadhānī, still less to those of his successors. From the start, this literary form was employed to cover a great variety of subjects: criticism of ancient and modern poets, of prose-writers like Ibn al-Muḳaffaᶜ and al-Djāḥiẓ, of the Muᶜtazilīs, exposure of the sexual slang and jargon of vagabonds, display of lexicographical knowledge, etc.; six *maḳāmat* of Badīᶜ al-Zamān celebrate the author's benefactor, Khalaf b. Aḥmad, the ruler of Sidjistān, to whom Margoliouth (*art. cit.*) believes that the whole work may have been dedicated. It is not, however, certain that all these compositions were put together in a compilation constituted *ne varietur*. In fact, Ibn Sharaf (*op. laud.*, 5) counts no more than twenty of them and adds that they were not all available to him, while al-Hamadhānī (*Rasāʾil*, Beirut 1890, 390, 516), quoted by al-Thaᶜālibi (*Yatīma*, Damascus 1885, iv, 168) and al-Ḥuṣrī (see above), claims to have written four hundred of them, which is highly improbable; current editions contain fifty-one each (fifty-two in all), so that fifty may be reckoned the average number of *maḳāmāt* of Badīᶜ al-Zamān in circulation in the Middle Ages; the figure of fifty was subsequently considered artificially to be a traditional characteristic and was respected by numerous imitators of al-Ḥarīrī (see below), who had himself adopted it.

In summary, the original *maḳāma* appears to be characterised fundamentally by the almost exclusive use of rhymed prose (with the insertion of verse) and the presence of two imaginary persons, the hero and the narrator. As for its content, this appears to be a complex amalgam having recourse to numerous genres such as the sermon, description, poetry in various forms, the letter, the travelogue, the dialogue, the debate, etc., which allowed the successors of al-Hamadhānī the greatest of latitude in the choice of their subjects.

Development of the genre. These authors had no difficulty in obeying the exigencies of the form, namely rhymed prose, but it was not long before they indulged in verbal acrobatics, the first manifestations of which are encountered in the works of the most eminent successor of Badīᶜ al-Zamān, al-Ḥarīrī (446-516/1054-1122 [*q.v.*]). The latter retains the structure created by his predecessor and presents a hero and a narrator, but many of his imitators were to dispense with the former character, if not with both. The diversity of themes dealt with in primitive *maḳāmāt* set the scene for the exploitation of the genre for the most varied of purposes and we shall see that if the objective of the genre is that of the authentic *adab*, seeking to instruct through entertainment, by means of a harmonious blending of the serious and the joking (*al-djidd wa 'l-hazl* [*q.v.*]), many *maḳāmāt* deviate from this purpose and in this respect follow the evolution of the *adab* which has a tendency either to neglect the *djidd* or to forget the *hazl*.

Furthermore, some compositions corresponding approximately to the exigencies of this genre are known by other names, such as *risāla* or *ḥadīth*, while some so-called *maḳāmāt* show none of the fundamental features of "sessions". What has happened is an evolution similar to that of the word *ṭabaḳāt*, which after usually designating biographical works arranged according to generation (*ṭabaḳa*), is ultimately applied to those which follow alphabetical order. A confusion between *risāla* and *maḳāma* is already visible in the *Risālat al-Tawābiᶜ wa 'l-zawābiᶜ* of Ibn Shuhayd (382-426/992-1035 [*q.v.*]), who was well-acquainted with Badīᶜ al-Zamān since he makes use of his *ṣāḥib*, his inspiring spirit (ed. B. al-Bustānī, Beirut 1951, 172-4); J. Vernet goes so far as to assert (*Literatura árabe*, Barcelona n.d., 114) that he was inspired by the *maḳāma iblīsiyya* in the writing of his *Risāla*, which in effect contains two features of the "sessions", rhymed prose and the presence of a companion of the author, in this case a genie who questions the *tawābiᶜ* of various representatives of Arabic literature. Other evidence is supplied at an early date by Ibn Sharaf (see above) who gives the title *ḥadīth* to his compositions, while one manuscript of the surviving fragment bears the title *Masāʾil al-intiḳād* and another, *Rasāʾil al-intiḳād*; the subject-matter comprises questions of literary criticism articulated by a scholar expressing his opinions of ancient and modern poets, somewhat in the style of al-Hamadhānī, but without an intermediary *rāwī* (see Iḥsān ᶜAbbās, *Taʾrīkh al-naḳd al-adabī ᶜind al-ᶜArab*, Beirut 1391/1971, 460-9).

These two authors were writing in al-Andalus where, on the other hand, the word *maḳāma* was to be used "to designate any rhetorical exercise in rhymed verse, with or without an ingredient of poetry, whatever the theme inspiring it: congratulating a recently-appointed provincial judge, accompanying a basket of first-fruits sent as a gift, describing a landscape, recounting an incident of minimal importance or the perils of a journey, giving praise or blame or simply indulging in caprice, as an antidote to boredom. Any theme is considered valid, and this type of composition, laden to the point of asphyxia with all the devices of language, erudition and pedantry and well-nigh indecipherable, is indiscriminately called *risāla* or *maḳāma*, without any account being taken of the theme (if indeed it has one...)" (F. de la Granja, *Maqāmas y risālas andaluzas*, Madrid 1976, p. xiv). The above remarks could equally well be applied to many of the oriental *maḳāmāt*.

History of the genre. Independently of the al-Kh ʷārazmī mentioned above, whose dates cannot be precisely established, a contemporary of al-Hamadhānī, Ibn Nubāta al-Saʿdī (d. 405/1014) wrote a "session" which is preserved in Berlin (see Brockelmann, I, 95; Blachère and Masnou, *op. laud.*, 39 and n. 1), but it cannot be said whether it is an imitation or an original work. Again in the 4th/10th century, ʿAbd al-ʿAzīz al-ʿIrāḳī was the author of a *maḳāma* on the resurrection (Brockelmann, I, 524). Chronologically, it is here that one should place Ibn Shuhayd (see above) and Ibn Sharaf (see above) who confines himself to presenting his *ḥadīth* in the form of the beginning of a dialogue followed by a long monologue of the scholar who takes the place of the hero and the *rāwī*; one gains the impression that, for this learned Tunisian who made his home in Spain, the essential features of *maḳāma* are rhymed prose and the intervention of a fictional character who is an eloquent speaker (*balīgh*). It is thus that many later authors interpret the scheme of Badīʿ al-Zamān, when they do not eliminate the hero. In any case, the works of Ibn Shuhayd and of Ibn Sharaf, not to mention the *Zahr al-ādāb* of al-Ḥuṣrī, testify to the rapid diffusion of the *Maḳāmāt* of al-Hamadhānī in Ifrīḳiya and al-Andalus where, in the same century, a poet, Ibn Fattūḥ, was the author of a *maḳāma* on the poets of his time which was also presented in the form of a dialogue (Ibn Bassām *Dhakhīra*, i/2, 273-88; F. de la Granja, *op. laud.*, 63-77), and where Ibn al-Shahīd [*q.v.*] made the account of a journey by a member of a group of travellers in a *maḳāma* (*Dhakhīra*, i/2, 104-95; F. de la Granja, 81-118) which exercised a certain influence on the genre as developed in Hebrew (see below). Ibn Bassām (*Dhakhīra*, i/2, 246-57) mentions another *maḳāma* by Abū Muḥammad al-Ḳurṭubī (443-83/1051-92; see R. Arié, *Notes sur la* maqāma *andalouse*, in *Hespéris-Tamuda*, ix/2 [1968], 204-5).

In the east, a close successor of Badīʿ al-Zamān, the physician Ibn Buṭlān (d. after 460/1068 [*q.v.*]) was the author of a *Maḳāma fī tadbīr al-amrāḍ* (Brockelmann, S I, 885) which might well deserve examination. However, one of his most eminent imitators was Ibn Nāḳiya (410-85/1020-92 [*q.v.*]), nine of whose *maḳāmāt* are available to us; this author renounces the oneness of the hero and introduces several narrators, but this plurality would amount to nothing more, according to Blachère and Masnou (39-40), "than a mark of respect paid to the model", Badīʿ al-Zamān, to the extent that the possibility of varying the methods of narration has been understood (ed. Istanbul 1331; O. Rescher, *Beiträge zur Maqāmen-Literatur*, iv, 123-52; tr. Cl. Huart, in *JA*, 10th series, xii [1908], 435-54). Nevertheless, the most eminent successor of al-Hamadhānī is incontestably al-Ḥarīrī (446-516/1054-1122 [*q.v.*]) who gave the genre its classic form, freezing it, so to speak, and diverting it from its actual function; according only a secondary interest to the content and placing his entire emphasis on the style which often takes on the nature of ponderous obscurity, al-Ḥarīrī's ultimate aim is the preserving and teaching of the rarest vocabulary, to such an extent that some twenty philologists have commented on his *maḳāmāt* and many of his imitators accompany their own compositions with lexicographical commentaries. (In the same way, a Maghribī author was to write 12 *maḳāmāt* in dialectical Arabic in order to improve the language spoken in southern Algeria; see G. Faure-Biguet and G. Delphin, *Les séances d'El-Aouali, textes arabes en dialecte maghrébin de Mohammed Qabîh al-Fa'l (M. le Mauvais sujet)*, in *JA*, 11th ser., ii [1913], 285-310, iii [1914], 303-74, iv [1914], 307-78.) The success of al-Ḥarīrī's *Maḳāmāt*, which appealed to the taste of readers to such an extent that, after the Ḳurʾān, children were made to memorise them, overshadowed those of al-Hamadhānī, which were too easily intelligible, and prompted many later writers to imitate the rhetorical artifices invented by al-Ḥarīrī (see Prendergast, 22-5; Crussard. *Études sur les Séances de Ḥarīrī*, Paris 1923; Blachère and Masnou, 42-6) and to take such little interest in the substance that verbal richness remained in fact the principal, if not the only specific characteristic of this original and fertile literary genre in its principle.

In spite of the specialisation of the term which designates it, we still see al-Ghazālī (d. 505/1111 [*q.v.*]) in his *Maḳāmāt al-ʿulamāʾ bayna yaday al-khulafāʾ wa 'l-umarāʾ* (ms. Berlin 8537/1) and al-Samʿānī (d. 562/1167 [*q.v.*]) in his *Maḳāmāt al-ʿulamāʾ bayna yaday al-umarāʾ* (Ḥādjdjī Khalīfa, no. 12702), of which the titles and content recall the chapter of Ibn Ḳutayba mentioned above, returning to the previous notion of *maḳām*/*maḳāma* = "pious discourse"; the same applies to al-Zamakhsharī (467-538/1074-1143 [*q.v.*]), who, while appearing to take his inspiration from al-Hamadhānī and al-Ḥarīrī, composed fifty *maḳāmāt* in which he addresses to himself a number of moral exhortations, also entitled *Naṣāʾih al-kibār*; they would appear to testify to the repentance of the author who has decided, after an illness, to renounce profane literature (see Brockelmann, S I, 511; Blachère and Masnou, 40-1; ed. Cairo 1312, 1325; tr. Rescher, *Beiträge*, vi, 1913), but, unable to forget that he is also a philologist, he produces a commentary on his own compositions (Yāḳūt, *Udabāʾ*, xix, 133).

Two authors of the 6th/12th century are also credited with *maḳāmāt* composed in imitation of al-Ḥarīrī: al-Ḥasan b. Ṣafī, nicknamed Malik al-Nuḥāt (489-568/1095-1173; see Yāḳūt, *Udabāʾ*, viii, 123-4; al-Suyūṭī, *Bughya*, 220) and Aḥmad b. Djamīl (d. 577/1182) of Baghdād, whose only work cited by Yāḳūt (*Udabāʾ*, ii, 282) is a *Kitāb Maḳāmāt*.

The work of al-Ḥarīrī soon became known in Spain, where the most celebrated commentary on it, that of al-Sharīshī (d. 619/1222 [*q.v.*]), was written. These *maḳāmāt* were already being imitated there, apparently, by a slightly younger contemporary of their author, Ibn al-Ashtarkūwī (d. 538/1143) in *al-Maḳāmāt al-Saraḳusṭiyya*, which numbering the henceforward traditional fifty, may perhaps be, according to F. de la Granja (*op. laud.*, p. xiii) the only Spanish ones which conform to the classical norms; in addition, the other title by which they are known, *Kitāb al-Khamsīn maḳāma al-luzūmiyya*, could be an indication of the influence of al-Maʿarrī and of his *Luzūmiyyāt* (cf. LUZŪM MĀ LĀ YALZAM; A. M. al-ʿAbbādī, in *RIEEIM*, ii/1-2 [1954], 161); two of them, which deal with literary criticism, have been the object of a study on the part of Iḥsān ʿAbbās (*op. laud.*, 500-1), but the others would doubtless merit closer examination (on the mss., see Brockelmann, S I, 543). It was also at the beginning of the 6th/12th century that the *wazīr* Abū ʿĀmir Ibn Arḳam composed a *maḳāma* in praise of the Almoravid *amīr* of Granada Tamīm b. Yūsuf b. Tashfīn (see R. Arié, *art. cit.*, 206); judging by the fragment which has been preserved by al-Fatḥ b. Khāḳān (*Ḳalāʾid al-ʿiḳyān*, ed.

Paris, repr. Tunis 1966, 153-4), this composition in rhymed prose is related to the *raḥīl* of the *ḳaṣīda*, but there appears in it a fictitious person who engages the author in a discussion on the *mamdūḥ*. Al-Fatḥ b. Khāḳān himself (d. ca. 529/1134 [*q.v.*]) composed a *maḳāma* on his master al-Baṭalyawsī (H. Derenbourg, *Mss. de l'Escurial*, 538), and Ibn Khayr al-Ishbīlī (502-75/1108-79 [*q.v.*]) mentions in his *Fahrasa* (328, 450) a further seven *maḳāmāt* written by the *wazīr* Abu 'l-Ḥasan Sallām al-Bāhilī (see al-ʿAbbādī, art. cit., 162; R. Arié, *art. cit.*, 205). For his part, al-Maḳḳarī (*Azhār al-riyāḍ*, ed. Cairo 1361/1942, iii, 15) attributes a number of them to a *faḳīh* of Granada named ʿAbd al-Raḥmān b. Aḥmad b. al-Ḳaṣīr (d. 576/1180; see Arié, 206). In Spain in the 6th/12th century, we may note (Ibn al-Abbār, *Takmila*, 407) a further two *maḳāmās* by al-Wādī Āshī (d. 553/1158), one of which is written in praise of the *ḳāḍī* ʿIyāḍ (476-544/1083-1149 [*q.v.*]), but, contrary to a widespread opinion, this eminent person is neither the author nor the dedicatee of *al-Maḳāma al-dawḥiyya* or *al-ʿIyāḍiyya al-ghazaliyya* which is the work of Muḥammad b. ʿIyāḍ al-Sabtī and of which Ibn Saʿīd has preserved a few lines (see F. de la Granja, *op. laud.*, 121-8). Ibn Ghālib al-Ruṣāfī (d. 572/1177) composed a *Maḳāma fī waṣf al-ḳalam* of which a brief surviving fragment has been edited and translated by F. de la Granja (131-7). It was very probably in Syria that Ibn Muḥriz al-Wahrānī (d. 575/1179) wrote *al-Maḳāma al-fāsiyya*, in which the hero is questioned about a number of real actual people who are characterised in a few sometimes incisive lines (ed. S. Aʿrāb, in *al-Baḥth al-ʿilmī*, Rabat, no. 5 [1965], 195-204).

Too much attention should not be given to the *Maḳāmāt ṣūfiyya* of al-Suhrawardī al-Maḳtūl (d. 587/1191 [*q.v.*]) which deal with Ṣūfī terminology (Brockelmann, S I, 783), even less to the *Maḳāmāt* or Stages on the Mystic Way, of another Suhrawardī, Abū Ḥafṣ ʿUmar (d. 632/1234 [*q.v.*]). Neither shall we enlarge on the various collections of *Maḳāmāt* dealing with mystical ethics rightly or wrongly ascribed (see O. Yahia, *Histoire et classification de l'œuvre d'Ibn ʿArabī*, Damascus 1964, nos 415, 416, 417) to Ibn ʿArabī (560-638/1165-1240 [*q.v.*]).

Abu 'l-ʿAlāʾ Aḥmad b. Abī Bakr al-Rāzī al-Ḥanafī, who dedicated thirty "sessions" to the grand *ḳāḍī* Muḥyī 'l-Dīn al-Shahrazūrī, seems to belong to the end of the 6th/12th century. He strives to imitate al-Hamadhānī and al-Ḥarīrī, like them presenting a hero and a narrator, but he uses simpler language; he is fond of rich descriptions of a high-spirited nature which are not always free of obscenity and he composes *maḳāmāt* which go together in pairs and are mutually explanatory (ed. Rescher, *Beiträge*, iv, 1-115).

At the beginning of the 7th/13th century, attention may be drawn to *al-Maḳāma al-mawlawiyya al-ṣāḥibiyya* of al-Wazīr al-Ṣāḥib Ṣafāʾ al-Dīn, which deals with judicial questions (Brockelmann, S I, 490; ed. Rescher, *Beiträge*, iv, 153-99), then to an imitation of al-Ḥarīrī's work, *al-Maḳāmāt al-zayniyya*, fifty in number, composed in 672/1273 by al-Djazarī (d. 701/1301 [*q.v.* in Suppl.]). In the course of the same century, the names of Ibn Ḳarnas (*ca.* 672/1273), of al-Barāʿī (*ca.* 674/1275) and of al-Ḳāḍī Ḥāshid (*ca.* 690/1291) are mentioned by Brockelmann (I, 278), as well as those of the young poet al-Shābb al-Ẓarīf (661-88/1263-89 [*q.v.*]), author of the amorously-inspired *Maḳāmāt al-ʿushshāḳ* (S I, 458), and Ibn al-Aʿmā (d. 692/1293) who wrote a *Maḳāma baḥriyya* (S I, 445). His contemporary Ẓahīr al-Kāzarūnī (d. 697/1298) presents a narrator and a hero who visits Baghdād with him and describes some early customs in a *Maḳāma fī ḳawāʿid Baghdād fi 'l-dawla al-ʿAbbāsiyya*, published by K. and M. ʿAwwād, in *al-Mawrid*, viii/4 (1979), 427-40. Ibn al-Ṣā'igh (645-722/1247-1322) is credited with a *Maḳāma shihābiyya* which did not survive.

In the 8th/14th century, imitations seem to proliferate, often applying to religious or parenetic subjects. In 730/1229, Ibn al-Muʿaẓẓam al-Rāzī is still using the term *maḳām* which we have encountered in the work of Ibn Ḳutayba in the title of his twelve compositions, *al-Maḳāmāt al-ithnāʿashar* (ed. Ḥarāʾirī, Paris 1282/1865, Tunis 1303; Brockelmann, II, 192, S II, 255); the Tunisian-born Ibn Sayyid al-Nās (d. 734/1334 [*q.v.*]) celebrates the Prophet and his Companions in *al-Maḳāmāt al-ʿaliyya fi 'l-karāmāt al-djaliyya*. Shams al-Dīn al-Dimashḳī (d. 727/1327) puts the form of the *maḳāma* to a mystical purpose in *al-Maḳāmāt al-falsafiyya wa-tardjamat al-Ṣūfiyya* which are fifty in number (Brockelmann, S II, 161). The *Dīwān* of Ibn al-Wardī (689-749/1290-1349 [*q.v.*]), published by Fāris al-Shidyāḳ in Constantinople in 1300, contains some *maḳāmāt* and a *risāla/maḳāma*, *al-Nabāʾ ʿan al-wabāʾ*, concerning an epidemic in which he died shortly afterwards (Brockelmann, II, 140, S II, 174, 175). An author of Maghribī origin, Aḥmad b. Yaḥyā al-Tilimsānī, also known as Ibn Abī Ḥadjala (725-776 or 777/1325 to 1374-5 or 1375-6), who spent most of his literary career in Cairo, was renowned in his day as a writer of *maḳāmāt*, and one curiosity of his is a *maḳāma* on chess which he dedicated to the Artuḳid ruler of Mārdīn, al-Malik al-Ṣāliḥ Shams al-Dīn Ṣāliḥ, presumably himself a chess enthusiast (see Brockelmann, II², 5-6, S II, 5, and J. Robson, *A chess maqāma in the Rylands Library*, in *Bull. John Rylands Library*, xxxvi [1953], 111-27).

An Andalusian, Ibn al-Murābiʿ (d. 750/1350 [*q.v.*]) drew attention to himself with his *Maḳāmāt al-ʿīd*, published by A. M. al-ʿAbbādī (in *RIEEIM*, ii/1-2 [1954], 168-73) and translated by F. de la Granja (*op. laud.*, 173-99); the hero is a beggar, one of the Banū Sāsān, searching for a victim to sacrifice on the occasion of the Great Feast, and the text also supplies information concerning the history of Granada, the home of an eminent contemporary of the author, Ibn al-Khaṭīb (713-76/1313-75 [*q.v.*]). In the extensive and varied literary output of the latter there are a number of compositions which borrow certain features of the "session"; of the four texts analysed by R. Arié (*Notes*, 207-14): *Khaṭrat al-ṭayf fī riḥlat al-shitāʾ wa 'l-ṣayf* (account of a journey), *Mufākharat Mālaḳa wa-Salā* (a eulogy of Malaga), *Miʿyār al-ikhtiyar fī dhikr al-maʿāhid wa 'l-diyār* and *Maḳāmat al-siyāsa*, it is the two last which are most closely related to the *maḳāma*. In the *Miʿyār* (ed. A. M. al-ʿAbbādī, *Mushāhadāt Lisān al-Dīn Ibn al-Khaṭīb fī bilād al-Maghrib wa 'l-Andalus*, Alexandria 1958, 69-115), the author presents a traveller who describes thirty-four towns and villages of al-Andalus, and a doctor who eulogises sixteen localities in the Maghrib; as in the second text mentioned above, the reader is faced with a *mufākhara* or a *munāẓara*, a debate, of which a large number of examples is found in the "sessions" which ultimately absorbed this particular genre (see below). The similarity with the classical *maḳāma* is more marked in the *Maḳāmat al-siyāsa* (*apud* al-Maḳḳarī, *Nafḥ al-ṭīb*, ed. Cairo, ix, 134-49), in which the author brings into the presence of Hārūn al-Rashīd an old man of unprepossessing appearance who gives him advice on good administration and the duties of the ruler (see D. M. Dunlop, *A little-known work on politics by Lisān al-Dīn b. al-Ḫaṭīb*, in *Miscelanea de estudios árabes y hebraicos*, viii/1 [1959], 47-54).

While still dealing with al-Andalus, we may further

recall that the *kāḍī 'l-djamāʿa* of Granada, al-Nubāhī [*q.v.*], inserted in his *Nuzhat al-Baṣāʾir wa 'l-abṣār*, in 781/1379, a commentary on his own *Maḳāma nakhliyya* presented in the form of an erudite, obscure and pedantic dialogue between a palm-tree and a fig-tree (see R. Arié, *art. cit.*, 212-12). In Spain in the following century, in 844/1440, a similar calamity to that described by Ibn al-Wardī (see above) inspired ʿUmar al-Mālaḳī al-Zadjdjal to write his *Maḳāma fī amr al-wabāʾ* which is preserved by al-Maḳḳarī in his *Azhār al-riyāḍ* (ed. Saḳḳāʾ *et alii*, Cairo 1939-42, i, 125-32) and translated by F. de la Granja (*op. laud.*, 201-30); this jurist-poet is also the author of the *Tasrīḥ al-niṣāl ilā maḳātil al-faṣṣāl* which according to the same Maḳḳarī, who twice reproduced the text of it (*Azhār*, i, 117-24 and *Nafḥ al-ṭīb*, ed. Cairo, vi, 345-50), was appreciated by the populace but rejected by the *khāṣṣa* on account of the *mudjūn* [*q.v.*] which characterised it.

In the East, the names of some writers of the 8th/14th century have been mentioned by Brockelmann: al-Shādhilī (702-60/1302-58; S II, 148); al-Ṣafadī (696-764/1296-1363 [*q.v.*]), the author of the *Wāfī*, who wrote a *maḳāma* on wine, *Rashf al-raḥīḳ fī waṣf al-ḥarīḳ* (S II, 29); and al-Bukhārī (d. 791/1389; S II, 289).

Al-Ḳalḳashandī (d. 821/1418 [*q.v.*]) reproduces in a chapter of the *Ṣubḥ* (xiv, 110-38) a text of al-Khwārazmī (see above) and a *maḳāma* of his own invention regarding the function of the secretary to a chancellery (see C. E. Bosworth, *A maqāma on secretaryship: al-Qalqashandī's al-Kawākib al-duriyya fi 'l-manāqib al-badriyya*, in *BSOAS*, xxvii/2 [1964], 291-8). Naturally, the prolific writer al-Suyūṭī (849-911/1445-1505 [*q.v.*]) could not avoid cultivating the *maḳāma* genre, which he uses in the form of dialogues, abandoning the traditional structure and dispensing with hero and narrator, to deal with religious and secular questions, such as the fate of the family of Muḥammad in Heaven, the qualities of perfumes, flowers and fruits, and obscene subjects are not excluded (see Rescher, *Zu Sojūṭī's Maqāmen*, in *ZDMG*, lxiii [1919], 220-3; Brockelmann, S II, 183, 187, 197, 198; L. Nemoy, *Arabic MSS in the Yale University Library*, New Haven 1956, ms. L. 754, fols. 47-50). His contemporary, the South Arabian Zaydī Ibrāhīm b. Muḥammad al-Ḥādawī Ibn al-Wazīr (d. 914/1508) applies this form to theological questions in *al-Maḳāma al-naẓariyya/al-manẓariyya wa 'l-fākiha al-khabariyya* (Brockelmann, II, 188, S II, 248; Nemoy, *op. laud.*, ms. L-366, fols. 140-7), and al-Suyūṭī's rival, Aḥmad b. Muḥammad al-Ḳasṭallanī (d. 923/1517) did likewise in his *Maḳāmāt al-ʿārifīn* (Brockelmann, II, 72). Brockelmann also mentions al-Birkawī (929-81/1523-73; S II, 658), al-Ghazāfī (*ca.* 997/1589; S II, 383), al-Mārdīnī (*ca.* 1000/1591; S II, 383), al-Ḳawwās (*ca.* 1000/1591), author of nine "sessions" (II, 272, S II, 383) and al-Fayyūmī (d. 1022/1614; S II, 486). Not mentioned by Brockelmann is the Indian author from Multān, Abū Bakr al-Ḥusaynī al-Ḥaḍramī (*floruit* late 10th/16th century) who wrote a set of fifty *maḳāmāt* inspired by al-Ḥarīrī; cf. L. Cheikho, *Madjānī 'l-adab*, Beirut 1957, vi, 76-8, and R. Y. Ebied and M. J. L. Young, *Arabic literature in India: two maqāmāt of Abū Bakr al-Ḥaḍramī*, in *Studies in Islam* (1978), 14-20.

In the period of literary decadence which marked the 11th and 12th/17th and 18th centuries, the "session" was still used to deal with a wide range of subjects. In 1078/1697, Djamāl al-Dīn Abū ʿAlī Fatḥ Allāh b. ʿAlawān al-Kaʿbī al-Ḳabbānī composed one describing the war conducted by Ḥusayn Pasha and ʿAlī Pasha Afrāsiyāb of Baṣra against a Turkish army commanded by Ibrāhīm Pasha, and added a commentary, the *Zād al-musāfir* (printed in Baghdād in 1924; Brockelmann II, 373; S II, 501). Also encountered are the names of al-Kāshī/al-Kāshānī (1007-90/1598-1679; S II, 585), ʿArīf (d. 1125/1713; S II, 630), Baʿbūd al-ʿAlawī who produced in 1128/1715 (S II, 601) an imitation of al-Ḥarīrī in which al-Nāṣir al-Fattāh (the victorious conqueror) recounts the fifty adventures, in India, of Abu 'l-Ẓafar al-Hindī al-Sayyāḥ ("the triumphant Indian vagabond") under the title *al-Maḳāmāt al-hindiyya* (lith. 1264), and al-Djazāʾirī (1050-1130/1640-1718; S II, 586).

In Morocco, the genre is represented by Muḥammad b. ʿĪsā (d. 990/1582) and Muḥammad al-Maklātī (d. 1041/1631-2), whose *Maḳāma bakriyya* is a eulogy of Maḥammad b. Abī Bakr al-Dilāʾī (d. 1021/1612 [see DILĀʾ in Suppl.]), the son of the founder of *al-Zāwiya al-dilāʾiyya* (see M. Lakhdar, *La vie littéraire au Maroc sous la dynastie ʿalawide (1075-1311/1664-1894)*, Rabat 1971, 42). Muḥammad al-Masnāwī al-Dilāʾī (1072-1136/1661-1724) describes this *zāwiya* and laments its destruction in *al-Maḳāma al-fikriyya fī maḥāsin al-zāwiya al-bakriyya*, which is of classical structure, with hero and narrator (see Lakhdar, 156-8).

Nemoy (*op. laud.*) records a ms. (Yale L-182) of *al-Maḳāma al-rūmiyya* of al-Bakrī (1099-1162/1688-1749 [*q.v.*]), which is part of his *Tafrīḳ al-humūm wa-taghrīḳ al-ghumūm fi 'l-riḥla ilā bilād al-Rūm*. ʿAbd Allāh b. al-Ḥusayn al-Baghdādī al-Suwaydī (d. 1174/1760) and his son Abu 'l-Khayr ʿAbd al-Raḥmān (d. 1200/1786) use this form (Brockelmann, II, 374, 377, S II, 508) as a means of bringing together, in an entertaining fashion, a whole series of ancient and modern proverbs, the father, in *Maḳāmāt al-amthāl al-sāʾira* (Cairo 1324), and the son, in *al-Maḳāma djāmiʿat al-amthāl ʿazīzat al-imthāl* (ms. Berlin 8582/3).

In the same way that al-Ḥarīrī, in the two *risāla*s called *al-sīniyya* and *al-shīniyya*, employed only words containing respectively a *sīn* and a *shīn*, ʿAbd Allāh al-Idkawī (d. 1184/1770) wrote *al-Maḳāma al-iskandariyya wa 'l-taṣḥīfiyya* in which pairs of words which differ only in diacritical points are placed beside each other (Brockelmann, II, 283). A display of erudition is the main characteristic of *al-Maḳāma al-Dudjayliyya wa 'l-maḳāla al-ʿUmariyya* of Uthmān b. ʿAlī al-ʿUmarī al-Mawṣilī (d. 1184/1770) which contains essentially a list and a brief definition of Islamic sects (Brockelmann, S II, 500; Rescher, *Beiträge*, iv, 191-285, where other products in this style are to be found). Nemoy (*op. laud.*) further mentions (Yale L-302) *Maḳāmāt* in mixed prose and verse by Aḥmad al-Armanāzī (18th century?).

The popular theme of competitive debate (see Steinschneider, *Rangstreitliteratur*, in *SB Ak. Wien*, clv/4 [1908]; Brockelmann, in *Mél. Derenbourg*, 231; Blachère and Masnou, 48 and n. 2; H. Massé, *Du genre littéraire "Débat" en arabe et en persan*, in *Cahiers de civilisation médiévale*, iv, 1961), is developed in the *Maḳāmat al-muḥākama bayn al-mudām wa 'l-zuhūr* (ms. Berlin, 8580) of Yūsuf b. Sālim al-Ḥifnī (d. 1178/1764), also the author of *al-Maḳāma al-ḥifniyya* (B. M. 1052/1; Brockelmann, II, 283; S II, 392). The Cretan Aḥmad b. Ibrāhīm al-Rasmī (1106-79/1694-1783) also experimented with this genre and wrote *al-Maḳāma al-zulāliyya al-bishāriyya* (Brockelmann, II, 430). Of the work of al-Badrī (d. 1215/1800) there survives a brief *maḳāma* (Yale L-30a) composed in *sadjʿ* and verse (Nemoy, *op. laud.*). In a similar way, by inserting numerous verses of his own composition, the Tunisian poet al-Warghī (d. 1190/1776) put together three *maḳāmāt* edited by ʿAbd al-ʿAzīz al-Gīzānī at Tunis in 1972 and called *al-Bāhiyya* (on the founder of the *zāwiya bāhiyya* in 1160/1747), *al-Khitāniyya* (on the occasion of the circumcision of the Bey ʿAlī b. al-Ḥusayn's sons in 1178/1764) and *al-Khamriyya* (in praise of this same Bey in 1183/1769). His compatriot and contemporary al-Ghurāb (d. 1185/1771) likewise left three *maḳāmāt* behind, of which two, *al-Hindiyya* and *al-Bāhiyya*, have a hero and a narrator, without however conforming to all the genre's exigencies, whilst the third, *al-ʿAbāʾiyya* or *al-Ṣābāniyya*, is merely a *risāla* (see Ḥ. Ḥ. al-Ghazzī, *al-Adab al-tūnisī fi 'l-ʿahd al-ḥusaynī*, Tunis 1972, 95-7; see also 154-60, on al-Warghī). Another Tunisian, Ismāʿīl al-Tamīmī (d. 15 Djumādā I 1248/10 October 1832) wrote a *Maḳāma fī ḥaḳḳ al-shaykh sayyidī Ismāʿīl ḳāḍī al-ḥadra al-ʿaliyya bi-Tūnis*, which has been published by Ḥ.Ḥ. al-Ghuzzī, in *al-Fikr*, xxv/2 (April 1980), 25-9 (see also the latter's study on *al-Maḳāma al-tūnisiyya bayn al-taḳlīd wa 'l-taṭawwur al-marḥalī naḥw al-ḳiṣṣa*, in *ibid.*, xxvii/5-6 (1982), 33-9, 96-103).

Other names which could be mentioned are those of ʿAbd al-Raḥmān b. ʿAbd Allāh al-Suwaydī (1134-1200/1721-86; II, 374), al-Barbīr (1160-1226/1748-1811; S II, 750), Ḥamdūn Ibn al-Ḥādjdj al-Fāsī (1174-1232/1760-1817; S II, 875) whose *Maḳāma ḥamdūniyya* is said to be found in ms. in Cairo (M. Lakhdar, *op. laud.*, 282). Again in Morocco, Abū Muḥammad ʿAbd Allāh al-Azārīfī (d. 1214/1799-1800) addressed to the sultan's *khalīfa* in Sūs a *maḳāma* comprising a hero and a narrator and describing the conditions prevailing in Saharan areas in the 12th/18th century (text in *al-Baḥth al-ʿilmī*, xiii/2 [1396/1971], 166-72). Another Moroccan writer al-Zayyānī (1147-1249/1734-1833) is the author of a *maḳāma fī dhamm al-ridjāl* directed against the conspirators who deposed Mawlāy Sulaymān (Lakhdar, 323). Another well-known Moroccan, Akansūs (1211-94/1796-1877 [*q.v.*]) left a *maḳāma* of mystical appeal (ms. Rabat D 1270) designed to show the vanity of the things of this world; it contains a hero and a *rāwī* and comprises poems, dialogues and descriptions (Lakhdar, 343-5).

Thus we arrive at the 19th century, where the first name to be noted is that of al-ʿAṭṭār (d. 1250/1824; Brockelmann, S II, 720), then that of Abu 'l-Thanā al-Ālūsī (1217-70/1802-53), author of five *maḳāmāt* without hero or narrator which contain advice to the writer's children, autobiographical information, descriptions and reflections on death (see Brockelmann, II, 498, S II, 786; *EI*², s.v. AL-ĀLŪSĪ); they were lithographed in 1273 at Karbalāʾ, but do not seem to have enjoyed great success (see M. M. al-Baṣīr, *Nahḍat al-ʿIrāḳ al-adabiyya*, Baghdad 1365/1946, 230-4).

It was precisely in the period of the *Nahḍa*, the renaissance, that a number of writers set themselves the task of reviving this genre in accordance with the classical norms, believing that, as a genre exclusive to Arabic literature, it was the best means of stimulating the interest of readers and of putting back into circulation a rich vocabulary that had fallen into disuse over the course of the preceding centuries. In this respect, the most eminent writer of the 19th century is the Lebanese Christian Nāṣīf al-Yāzidjī (1800-71 [see AL-YĀZIDJĪ]), who, with his *Madjmaʿ al-baḥrayn*, offered the public, for didactic purposes, a successful imitation of al-Ḥarīrī; in his work, which nevertheless contains sixty *maḳāmāt* (instead of the fateful number of fifty) accompanied by his own commentary, the hero and the narrator meet sometimes in the town, but often in the desert, a traditional setting for eloquent speech (see also Blachère and Masnou, 49-50).

Brockelmann also mentions al-Djazāʾirī (S II, 758, III, 379), al-Hamsh (S III, 338) and ʿAbd Allāh Pasha Fikrī (d. 1307/1890 [*q.v.*]), whose works (*al-Āthār al-fikriyya*, Būlāḳ 1315) contain a number of *maḳāmāt* including *al-Maḳāma al-fikriyya fi 'l-mamlaka al-bāṭiniyya* which has been published separately in Cairo in 1289 (Brockelmann, II, 475, S II, 722). Some *Maḳāmāt* by Maḥmūd Rashīd Efendi were edited in Cairo in 1913 (S III, 85). In ʿIrāḳ, Dāwūd Čelebi (*Makhṭūṭāt al-Mawṣil*, 299) has found a *maḳāma* on Baghdād by ʿAbd Allāh b. Muṣṭafā al-Fayḍī al-Mawṣilī (late 19th century). In the Lebanon, Ibrāhīm al-Aḥdab (1242-1308/1826-91 [*q.v.*]) left eighty-eight "sessions" of traditional structure, with hero and *rāwī*, which are as yet unedited (see Dj. ʿAbd al-Nūr, in *Dāʾirat al-maʿārif*, vii, 172).

In 1907, in Cairo, Muḥammad Tawfīḳ al-Bakrī published a collection of *maḳāmāt*, *Sahārīdj al-luʾluʾ*, a number of which were chosen by ʿUthmān Shākir and included, in 1927, in his work entitled *al-Luʾluʾ fi 'l-adab*.

It is not our intention to dwell here on the *Ḥadīth ʿĪsā b. Hishām* of al-Muwayliḥī (1868-1930 [*q.v.*]) of which the first edition in book form dates from 1907; this "novel", which is both the first major achievement of 20th century Arabic literature and the swan-song of classical literature, has been the object of a number of studies, the list of which is to be found in G. Widmer, *Beiträge zur neuarabischen Literatur*, iv, in *WI*, n.s. iii/2 (1954), 57-126; H. Pérès, in *Mélanges Massignon*, iii, Damascus 1957, 233; N. K. Kotsarev, *Pisateli Egipta xx vek*, Moscow 1975, 157-9. It will however be recalled that while still being published in instalments, this satire on contemporary mores had inspired an imitation, *Layālī Saṭīḥ*, on the part of Ḥāfiẓ Ibrāhīm (1872-1932 [*q.v.*]), who also aspired, although with less success, to present a satirical portrait of society in the form of a long *maḳāma* (see H. Pérès, in *B. Ét. Or.*, x [1943-4], 13 ff.; Kotsarev, *op. laud.*, 104-7). The *Wadjdiyyāt* of Muḥammad Farīd Wadjdī, published in Cairo in 1910, contain eighteen "sessions" which have not attracted much interest (but see the Tunisian review *al-Mabāḥith*, xxxi ff.). Finally, it is possible that other writers of the first half of the 20th century have composed, as rhetorical exercises or for a specific purpose, *maḳāmāt* which have not come to the attention of literary critics and historians. This applies notably to Amīn al-Rīḥānī (1876-1940 [*q.v.*]), whose *Rīḥāniyyāt* contain (ed. 1956, ii, 83-6) *al-Maḳāma al-kabkadjiyya*, where the narrator is a moth-grub (*ʿuththa*) searching for an attractive book in a library.

The above list cannot be regarded as exhaustive; it is based essentially on the article *Maḳāma* by Brockelmann in *EI*¹ and his *Geschichte der arabischen Litteratur*, the material of which has already been exploited by Blachère and Masnou (*op. laud.*, 123-9); our intention has been to complete this inventory by means of less ancient works but, in order to achieve a more satisfactory result, it would be necessary to go through recently published or still unedited biographical works, as well as catalogues of manuscript collections, and to carry out research in certain libraries whose riches have not been explored. As our list has been compiled in approximately chronological order, no mention has been made of a dozen or so fairly late authors whose dates have not been precisely located. Blachère and Masnou mention the following: al-Sukkarī (Brockelmann, S II, 906), al-Khanīnī (S II, 908), al-Ḥāʾirī (Rescher, *Beiträge*, iv, 328), al-Ṣāghānī (*ibid.*, iv, 335), al-Shāfiʿī (S II, 908), Ibn Rayyān (S II, 909), Ibrāhīm b. ʿAlī b.

Aḥmad b. al-Hādī (S II, 909), al-Anṭākī (Rescher, iv, 116), al-Munayyir (S II, 1010), al-Ḥusaynī (Rescher, iv, 311), al-Rasʿanī (Rescher, iv, 339), al-ʿUmarī al-Mawṣilī (Rescher, iv, 199).

In general, however, it seems certain that the most significant representatives of the genre have not escaped scrutiny, giving rise to the works enumerated in the bibliographies of the notices devoted to them by the present *Encyclopaedia*. But alongside those authors whose *maḳāmāt* are known only by a sometimes misleading title or by a brief mention in one or other of the bibliographical works, there are a number whose surviving works deserve, if not an edition, at least a fairly thorough examination, in order to allow for a more confident judgment. The general observations which follow are therefore still fragmentary.

Of the characteristics of primitive *maḳāma*, all the authors have essentially retained the use of rhymed prose, more or less rhythmic and mingled with verse, and, taking the example of al-Hamadhānī and especially of al-Ḥarīrī, a vocabulary obscure to the point of being sometimes impenetrable; furthermore, *sadj*ʿ, which sometimes goes to acrobatic extremes, is all the less likely to make use of simple language since the object of many of the authors is to make a display of their verbal dexterity. Quite apart from this common feature, the presence of two characters is not always felt to be necessary, so that the hero and the narrator are the same person in a large number of *maḳāmāt*, where this device is still retained.

From a theoretical point of view, the "séance", which belongs to *adab* is, by this definition, certainly designed to entertain, but also to instruct, since it is inconceivable that, originally, prose literature could have lacked any purpose. While the didactic function was to be served by means of the educational or edifying content, it was soon the form which fulfilled this role to the detriment of the essence, through the accumulation, scarcely bearable today for the average reader, of rare and unnecessary words, through a disagreeable pedantry and an impenetrable obscurity. The first objective, for its part, was to be realised, as in the case of *adab*, by a mixture of the serious and the joking, by the interesting quality of the adventures related and the theatrical element introduced by the two imaginary characters. Now, just as the *risāla*, being a convenient means of display on the part of authors full of false modesty, tended to be nothing more than a rhetorical exercise, in the same way the *maḳāma*, while supplying authors with an opportunity safely to express personal opinions in fictitious guise, enabled many others simply to make a show of their lexicographical expertise, at the same time, however, aiming at a certain aestheticism, one is tempted to say, at art for art's sake. This tendency is an expression of the love of Arabic-speakers for fine verbal style, and one gains the impression that an exquisite form sometimes conceals nothing more than a total vacuum. It is, however, not impossible that at least some of the compositions which appear most hollow lend themselves to different interpretations at a level which has yet to be ascertained.

The authors of manuals on the history of Arabic literature, when tackling the subject of *maḳāma*, rightly cite al-Hamadhānī and al-Ḥarīrī as those whose works are considered the first milestone on the path followed by this original genre; subsequently, they maintain their silence and, for the next seven centuries are unaware of one author worthy of mention as an eminent representative of the "session", which is evidently the sign of an unfortunate decline; more detailed studies will perhaps enable one to correct this severe judgment, but the fact remains that, in the absence of evidence to the contrary, it is necessary to wait until the 19th century to find, in the *Madjmaʿ al-baḥrayn* of al-Yāzidjī, a third significant milestone, although the new lease of life given to the *maḳāma* by this author did not inspire any notable works, perhaps because his object was far too didactic. In any case, the fourth and final milestone was planted by al-Muwayliḥī, whose *Ḥadīth ʿĪsā b. Hishām* is sometimes described as a novel. But at this time rhymed prose had already begun to lose its appeal, and the educated public turned for entertainment, either in the original, or in translation, to foreign works which inspired modern Arabic literature to the detriment of a henceforward discredited genre.

The theatrical element contained in classical *maḳāmāt* has not been satisfactorily exploited, for we do not see many playwrights drawing from them their inspiration and staging some of them. ʿAlī al-Rāʿī (*Some aspects of modern Arabic drama*, in R.C. Ostle (ed.), *Studies in modern Arabic literature*, Warminster 1975, 172 ff.) thinks that the shadow-plays of Ibn Dāniyāl [*q.v.*] are linked to Arabic literature through the *maḳāma* and points out that the Moroccan al-Ṭayyib al-Ṣiddīḳī has based himself on the famous *Maḍīra* [*q.v.*] and other sections of al-Hamadhānī to write plays which have met a great success; but this is an isolated attempt.

Imitation in other literatures. The success of the genre created by al-Hamadhānī and consolidated by al-Ḥarīrī was so remarkable in Arabic-speaking circles that some authors, who normally expressed themselves in other languages but had direct access to the Arabic texts, conceived the idea of composing *maḳāmāt* of their own.

In Persia, particularly highly esteemed were the twenty-four "sessions" which Ḥamīd al-Dīn Balkhī (d. 559/1156) composed in 551/1156 in imitation of the two great Arabic authors (Ḥādjdjī Khalīfa, no. 12716; lith. Tehran and Cawnpore); some of them consist of debates between a young man and an old, a Sunnī and a Shīʿī, a doctor and an astronomer; others contain descriptions of summer and autumn, love and folly, judicial and mystical discussions, but the sense is always sacrificed to the form (see H. Massé, *Du genre "Débat"*, 143-4). The example of Ḥamīd al-Dīn does not seem to have been much followed; nevertheless, the journalist Adīb al-Mamālik (d. 1917) composed a series of *maḳāmāt* (Browne, iv, 349).

In Spain, Yehūdā ben Shlōmō Ḥarīzī (1165-1225 A.D.) first translated al-Ḥarīrī into Hebrew (in 502/1205), then composed fifty *maḳāmāt* which he entitled *Sefer Taḥkemōni*; in these "sessions" the style of the model is imitated by means of a very skilful use of Biblical quotations; as for the content, it has been noted that Ḥarīzī was inspired by a *maḳāma* of Ibn al-Shahīd which we have mentioned above (see S. M. Stern, in *Tarbiz*, xvii [1946], 87-100; J. Schirmann, *ibid.*, xxiii [1952], 198-202; J. Razahbi, *ibid.*, xxvi [1957], 424-39); the work had been the object of partial translations into German, by Krafft (in *Literaturblatt des Orients*, xiii [1840], 196-8, xiv, 213-5) and L. Dukes (*Ehrensäulern*, etc., Vienna 1873, 92-4), before being published by P. de Lagarde, under the title *Iudae Harizii Macamae* (Göttingen 1881, 2nd ed. Hanover 1924).

A contemporary of Ḥarīzī, Jacob ben Eleazar of Toledo (beginning of the 13th century A.D.) for his part composed ten *maḳāmāt* which he intitled *Meshālīm*, with a narrator, but no hero; this work has been studied by J. Schirmann, *Les contes rimés de Jacob ben*

Eleazar de Tolede (in *Etudes d'orientalisme ... Lévi-Provençal*, ii, 285-97). In addition, J. M. Millás Vallicrosa mentions, in *La poesía sagrada hebraico-española* (Barcelona 1948, 133-4, 136-7, 144) other Jewish writers of Spain whose works could be compared to *makāmāt*.

The archbishop of Nisibin, ʿEbedyeshū ʿ/ʿAbdīshū ʿ (d. 1318 A.D.) composed in 1290-1, in imitation of al-Ḥarīrī, fifty "sessions" in Syriac verse of religious and edifying content, divided into two parts designated under the names Enoch and Elias; he himself explained, in a commentary written in 1316, the extremely artificial language abounding with acrostics and verses which can be read indifferently from right to left or from left to right (see Chabot, *Littérature syriaque*, Paris 1934, 141); the first half of these "sessions" was published by Gabriel Cardahi in Beirut, in 1899, under the title *Paradaisa dha Edhen seu Paradisus Eden carmina auctore Mar Ebediso Sobensis.*

Apparently there is no *makāma* composed or translated into Latin or Romance during the Middle Ages, but it is quite clear that the hero of the picaresque novel, the *pícaro*, closely resembles in many ways the characters of Abu 'l-Fatḥ al-Iskandarī or Abū Zayd al-Sarūdjī, and the diffusion in Spain of the work of al-Hamadhānī, and later and more significantly that of al-Ḥarīrī, suggests a direct or indirect influence of the *makāma*. The works which have been undertaken in this area (in particular by Menéndez Pelayo, *Orígenes de la novela*, 1943, i, 65 ff.; A. Gonzáles Palencia, *Del Lazarillo a Quevedo*, Madrid 1946, 3-9) appear as so far inconclusive. On the other hand, A. Rumeau (*Notes au Lazarillo*, in *Langue néo-latines*, no. 172 (May 1965), 3-12) has shown that the central episode, *La casa lóbrega y oscura*, of the *Lazarillo de Tormes* is closely related to an anecdote mentioned by al-Ibshīhī (*Mustaṭraf*, tr. Rat, ii, 670), but already figuring in the work of al-Bayhaḳī, who probably borrowed it from al-Djāḥiẓ; thus it is likely that the long road travelled from the *fatā* and the *mukaddī* of the latter to the *pícaro* passes through the *makāma*. This question, linked to that of the influence of the *1001 Nights*, has been recently discussed in an extensive thesis by M. Tarchouna, *Les margitans dans les récits picaresques arabes et espagnols*, Tunis 1982, which contains a profound comparison between the two sources mentioned above and the picaresque literature (and extensive bibl.)

Bibliography: To the references in the text, the following may be added: V. Chauvin, *Bibliographie des ouvrages arabes ou relatifs aux Arabes*, ix, Liège 1904; the studies published in the Tunisian review *al-Mabāḥith*, xxiii-xxv, xxvii-xxviii; A. Mez, *Renaissance*, index; G. E. von Grunebaum, *The spirit of Islam as shown in its literature*, in *SI*, i (1953), 114-19; Dj. Sulṭān, *Fann al-ḳiṣṣa wa 'l-makāma*, Damascus 1362/1943; Shawḳī Ḍayf, *al-Makāma*, Caire 1954; ʿAbd al-Raḥmān Yāghī, *Raʾy fi 'l-makāma*, Beirut 1969; Jareer Abu-Haydar, *Maqāmāt literature and the picaresque novel*, in *JAL*, iii (1974), 1-10; M. R. Ḥasan, *Athar al-makāma fī nashʾat al-ḳiṣṣa al-miṣriyya al-ḥadītha*, Cairo 1974; H. Nemah, *Andalusian maqāmāt*, in *JAL*, iii (1974), 83-92; R. Marzūḳī, *Taṭawur al-makāma shaklan wa-maḍūman*, in CERES, *Ḳaḍāyā 'l-adab al-ʿarabī*, Tunis 1978, 299-335; R. Droury, *Ḥawl ḳawāʿid tabaddul al-ḳāfiya fī l-makāma*, in S. Somekh (ed.), *Abḥāth fī 'l-lugha wa 'l-uslūb*, Tel Aviv 1980, 7-13; and A. Kilito, *Les séances*, Paris 1983. Several "maîtrise" theses dealing with the *makāma* have been presented in recent years to the University of Tunis; see also the general studies in manuals of the history of Arabic literature, in particular H. A. R. Gibb, *Arabic Literature*[2], 1963, index, s.v. *maqāma*; F. Gabrieli, *Storia della letteratura araba*, Milan 1951, 202-7; G. Wiet, *Introduction à la littérature arabe*, Paris 1966, 174-9; and J. Vernet, *Literatura árabe*, Barcelona n.d., 125-9. (C. BROCKELMANN - [CH. PELLAT])

MAḲĀN B. KĀKĪ, ABŪ MANṢŪR, Daylamī soldier of fortune who played an important part in the tortuous politics and military operations in northern Persia, involving local Daylamī chiefs, the ʿAlids of Ṭabaristān and the Sāmānids, during the first half of the 4th/10th century.

The house of Kākī were local rulers of Ashkawar in Rānikūh, the eastern part of Gīlān in the Caspian coastlands. Mākān rose to prominence in Ṭabaristān in the service of the ʿAlid princes there, and as the ʿAlids themselves dissolved into internecine rivalries, he became the contender with a fellow-commander, Asfār b. Shīrūya [see ASFĀR B. SHĪRAWAYHĪ] for control over the Caspian lands. Mākān allied with the Ḥasanid *al-Dāʿī al-Ṣaghīr* al-Ḥasan b. al-Ḳāsim [q.v. in Suppl.] against the latter's rival Djaʿfar b. al-Ḥasan b. al-Uṭrūsh and his supporter Asfār, but was worsted in battle in 316/928 by the rule of the ʿAlids in Ṭabaristān, and Mākān had temporarily to flee into Daylam. His fortunes nevertheless revived, and by 318/930 he was master of Ṭabaristān, Gurgān and even of Nīshāpūr in Khurāsān, and had repelled an attack by Asfār's supplanter Mardāwīdj b. Ziyār [q.v.], master of Ray (319/931).

Mardāwīdj's élan could not be stemmed by Mākān, who lost Ṭabaristān and had to retire to Sāmānid territory in Khurāsān, receiving from the *amīr* Naṣr b. Aḥmad [q.v.] the governorship of Kirmān. However, when Mardāwīdj was assassinated in 323/935 by his slave troops (according to Gardīzī, at Mākān's instigation), Mākān returned from the east to the Caspian region, established himself as governor of Gurgān for the Sāmānids, and allied with another local leader, Mardāwīdj's brother Wushmagīr, founder of the subsequent Ziyārid dynasty [q.v.]. With Wushmagīr's support, he threw off the control of Bukhārā, but the *amīr* sent against him an army under Abū ʿAlī Aḥmad b. Muḥtādj Čaghānī. Mākān was dislodged from the town of Gurgān and compelled to fall back on Ray; and outside the town, at a village called Ishāḳābād on the Dāmghān road, the forces of Wushmagīr and Mākān were defeated on 21 Rabīʿ I 329/25 December 940. Mākān was killed and his head sent first to Bukhārā and then to the caliph in Baghdād.

Mākān's career is typical of several Daylamī condottieri in the early stages of the "Daylamī intermezzo" of Persian history, when the decline of caliphal power in northern Persia allowed various local interests to vie for power there; but in the long run, it was the Būyids who were able to establish the most enduring domination (ʿAlī b. Būya, the later ʿImād al-Dawla [q.v.], seems to have taken an important step forward in his career by joining Mākān's army as a commander, perhaps in ca. 316/928, but left Mākān when the latter was temporarily eclipsed by Mardāwīdj, see above). Collateral relatives of Mākān, the family of his cousin al-Ḥasan b. Fīrūzān, continued to rule locally in Daylam till the end of the century.

Bibliography: 1. Sources: Masʿūdī, *Murūdj*, ix, 6-8 = §§ 3578-9; ʿArīb, 137-8; Miskawayh, in *Eclipse of the ʿAbbasid caliphate*, i, 275 ff., ii, 3-6; Gardīzī, ed. Nāzim, 30-1, ed. Ḥabībī, 83-5, 153; Hamadhānī, *Takmila*, ed. Kanʿān, i, index; Ibn Isfandiyār, tr. Browne, 208-li; Niẓāmī ʿArūḍī Samarḳandī, *Čahār maḳāla*, ed. Ḳazwīnī and

Muʿīn, 24-7, Browne's revised tr. 16-18 (chronologically confused anecdote): Ibn al-Athīr, viii, 140-292, *passim*; Ẓahīr al-Dīn, ed. Dorn, 171-6; 2. Studies. H. L. Rabino, *Mázandarán and Astarábád*, 140; V. Minorsky, *La domination des Daïlamites*, in *Iranica, twenty articles*, Tehran 1964, 17, 27; Spuler, *Iran*, 89-94; W. Madelung, in *Cambridge hist. of Iran*, iv, 141-2, 211-12, 253-4; *EI*¹ s.v. (M. Nāẓim). (C.E. Bosworth)

MAKARI. [see KOTOKO]

MAKASSAR, since 1972 renamed "Ujung Pandang" with reference to one of its oldest quarters around the harbour, is the capital of the Indonesian Province of Sulawesi Selatan (South Celebes). It has 434,168 inhabitants, among them 332,618 Muslims. After World War II, Makassar was the capital of the Dutch-sponsored East Indonesian State (until 1950). It still remains the dominant cultural, administrative, economic and traffic centre in East Indonesia, its population comprising notable minorities of Torajas, Menadonese, Ambonese, Timorese, etc.

Its name "Makassar" originates from the people living in its hinterland, stretching over the most southern part of the south-western peninsula of Sulawesi. The population of the island of Selayar, to the south, is usually also counted among the Makassars, although their dialect shows a number of differences from genuine Makassarese. Their neighbours to the north are the Buginese, who are closely related to the Makassars in their customs, manners, and language. At the present, there are about 1,250,000 people living in the predominently Makassarese-speaking *kabupatens* (regencies) of Gowa, Takalar, Jene Ponto, Bantaeng, Maros, and Pangkajene (here mixed with Buginese).

Originally, as H. J. Friedericy had pointed out by examining the old Bugis-Makassarese epic *La Galigo*, Makassarese society was divided into three main groups: the *ana' karaëng*, or family of the king, the *to deceng*, or free people, and the *ata*, or slaves, who were either captives, those who could not repay their debts, or who had acted against the *adat* (customary law). Since the beginning of the 20th century, slavery has been abolished. An outstanding feature of the character of the Makassars (and Buginese) is called *siri'*, a feeling of humiliation and shame if the rules of *adat* are broken; it usually leads to revenge.

Little is known about the history of Makassar in pre-Islamic times. In the middle of the 14th century, the area was under the rule of the Javanese kingdom of Majapahit. According to the chronicles of Gowa and Tallo', which are the names of the two ancient Makassarese kingdoms, Gowa originally consisted of an alliance of nine small districts, each under a noble; after the government had passed into the hands of one man and the kingdom had expanded, to include for example the lands of what was later Tallo', Gowa is said, after the death of the sixth king (the first one described as an ordinary mortal), to have been divided between his two sons; the one became ruler of Gowa and the other of Tallo'. Both kingdoms usually had close relations and were known to the Europeans as the "kingdom of the Makassars". About the year 1512, one year after the conquest of Malacca by the Portuguese, "Malays" were given permission to settle in Makassar and to build a mosque in their quarter. Also, in other ports on the west coast of South Sulawesi, Muslim traders began to settle. Those in Pangkajene were resisting tendencies among the family of the local ruler to adopt the Christian belief. But on the whole, during the 16th century, the Makassars and their rulers were still adhering to their traditional religion, and an even-handed policy was pursued towards the Muslim traders, most of whom originated from Johore, Malacca, Pahang, Blambangan, Patani, Banjarmasin, and the Minangkabau in West Sumatra on one hand, and the Portuguese on the other.

When the Makassarese kings started to become interested in trade affairs, they usually asked the Portuguese for their good services. The *karaëng* of Tallo', Tu Nipasuru' (first half of the 16th century) is said to have travelled to Malacca and Johore for trade reasons. During the reign of Tu Nijallo as *karaëng* of Gowa (1565-1590), the *sulṭān* of Ternate, Bāb Allāh, visited Makassar about 1580. Besides trying to solve their political disputes, Bāb Allāh, a fervent enemy of the Portuguese who had murdered his father, urged the *karaëng* to adopt Islam. It seems doubtful that he had any success, and it was not until 9 Djumādā I 1014/22 September 1605 that the young *karaëng* of Tallo', I Mallingkaang Daeng Nyonri, who at the same time acted as *patih* (prime minister) of Gowa, publicly confessed the Islamic *shahāda*. Later he was known as Sultan ʿAbd Allāh Awwal al-Islām. The *karaëng* of Gowa, I Mangu' rangi Daeng Nanra'bia, soon followed his example and adopted the name Sulṭān ʿAlāʾ al-Dīn. On 18 Radjab 1016/16 November 1607, the islamisation of the two Makassarese kingdoms was officially declared to be completed. This was followed by successful wars against the Buginese neighbours, who thus were forced to convert to Islam too. One of the most celebrated teachers of Islam at that time was the miraculous Dato' riBandang, a mystic from Kota Tengah in the Minangkabau, who is said to have been a pupil of Sunan Giri in Java. Other outstanding teachers were Dato' riTiro and Dato' Patimang. Their tombs became centres of worship.

In the first half of the 17th century, the kingdom of Makassar extended very much, so that it brought under its suzerainty almost the whole of Sulawesi, Buton, Flores, Sumbawa, Lombok and the east coast of Kalimantan. In 1609, the Dutch East India Company was granted permission to establish a factory, but disputes about the trade with the Moluccas gave cause to repeated warfare and treaties which reduced the sovereignty of the Makassarese kings, and led to the expulsion of the Portuguese and later, in 1667, of the British as well. A treaty dictated by Admiral C. Speelman in 1667, which was reconfirmed in 1669, gave the right to the Dutch to settle there permanently. These wars are the topic of the *Sjaʿir Perang Mangkasara'*.

Although the main port in South Sulawesi was (and is) Makassar, the most skilled sailors and shipmakers, however, were not the Makassars but the Buginese, especially those from Wajo, who formed in Makassar—like in some other major ports, e.g. in East Kalimantan—their own community supervised by the *matoa*. The third *matoa*, Amanna Gappa, assisted by two of his colleagues from other ports, compiled in about 1676 a code of trade and navigation law which reflects at the same time their understanding of the cosmic order, together with Islamic and traditional elements.

Both the Makassars and likewise the Buginese are usually considered as strong, and sometimes fanatical confessors of Islam. Generally speaking, most of the legal duties of Islam are conscientiously observed. But this does not prevent them from maintaining, at the same time, pre-Islamic religious convictions, and a number of "mystical movements" are still in existence or are even gaining in strength, especially among the villagers, but also among intellectuals. Since the beginning of this century, modernist Muslim ideas have been spread by Zaini Dahlan, a former pupil of the *Sumatra Thawalib*, and the journal *al-Islâm* which was published since 1906 for some years by a Sumatran living in Malaya, and which resembled *al-Manār* in its orientation. A branch of the modernist *Muhammadiyah* movement was established in 1929.

In 1950, Makassar became the starting point of the "Darul-Islam" rebellion led by Kahar Muzakkar. In 1963 came the establishment of the *Ikatan Masjid dan Mushalla Indonesia Mutahhidin*, or Association of United Indonesian Mosques and Prayer Houses (abbrev. *IMMIM*), which tries to propagate the principles of unity in the *ʿaḳīda*, but tolerance in matters of the *khilāfiyyāt*. Thus among its members are mosques which are owned by the *Muhammadiyah*, or by the traditionalist *Nahdlatul Ulama* party, or by other groups. They are urged by the leaders of the *IMMIM* to keep their special convictions among themselves in order to avoid public turmoil. It has branches now in Central and Southeast Sulawesi, in the Moluccas and in Irian Jaya.

Bibliography: see article MACASSAR in *EI*[1]; T. Leigh and D. Midwinter, *An historical description of the Kingdom of Macasar in the East Indies*, London 1701, republ. 1971; H. J. Friedericy, *De Standen bij de Boegineezen en Makassaren*, in *BKI*, xc (1933), 447-602; J. Tideman, *Een Makassaarsch Adat huwelijk*, in *Koloniaal Tijdschrift*, xxiii (1934), 66-77; H. T. Chabot, *Verwantschap, Stand en Sexe in Zuid-*Celebes, Groningen-Jakarta 1950; G. J. Resink, *Volkenrecht in vroeger Makassar*, in *Indonesië*, v (1952-3), 393-410; J. Noorduyn, *De Islamisering van Makasar*, in *BKI*, cxii (1956), 247-66; M. Sjarif Saleh Daeng Paesa, *Analisa Perjuangan Muhammadijah di Sulawesi Selatan*, in *Almanak Muhammadijah Tahun Hijra 1380*, Jakarta 1960, 132-49; Ph. O. L. Tobing, *Hukum Pelayaran dan Perdagangan Amanna Gappa* (*The Navigation and Commercial Law of Amanna Gappa*), Makassar 1961, repr. Jakarta-Ujung Pandang 1977 (with an abbreviated English version); Mattulada, *Siri' dalam Hubungannya dengan Perkawinan Masjarakat Mangkasara'*, Makassar 1962; C. Skinner, *Sjaʿir Perang Mengkasar (The Rhymed Chronicle of the Macassar War) by Entji' Amin*, 's-Gravenhage 1963 (= VKI 40); G. J. Wolhoff and Abdurrahim, *Bingkisan Sedjarah Gowa*. Makassar 1964; Bahar Mattalioe, *Kahar Muzakkar dengan Petualangannja*. Jakarta 1965; Abdurrazak Daeng Patunru', *Sedjarah Gowa, Makassar* 1967; Mattulada, *Kebudajaan Bugis-Makassar*, in Koentjaraningrat (ed.), *Manusia dan Kebudajaan di Indonesia*, Jakarta 1971, 264-83; *Bingkisan Budaya Sulawesi Selatan*, new series since 1976 (ed. by South Sulawesi Cultural Foundation, Ujung Pandang); Hamka, *Pandangan Islam terhadap Siri'*, in *Panji Masyarakat* No. 227, 15 July 1977; Chr. Pelras, *Les premières données occidentales concernant Celebes-Sud*, in *BKI*, cxxxiii (1977), 227-60 (with useful bibliography); *IMMIM menuju persatuan ummat dengan kerja*, in *Panji Masyarakat* No. 263, 15 January 1979.
(W. H. RASSERS - [O. SCHUMANN])

MAKĀYIL (A.), "measures of capacity" (sing. *mikyal(a)*; var. *makāyīl*, sing. *mikyāl*), and **MAWĀZĪN** (A.) "weights" (sing. *mīzān*). On the measures of length and surface area, see MISĀḤA.

1. In the Arabic, Persian and Turkish lands.

In the history of Oriental metrology, the spread of Islam meant no abrupt break. Whereas Charlemagne imposed in his empire a uniform system of weights and measures and introduced a much heavier pound than the Roman libra of 327.45 g, neither Muḥammad nor ʿUmar made such a reform; and as later rulers could not claim canonical character for their systems of weights and measures, their bewildering diversity was in the Muslim countries even greater than in mediaeval Europe, where Charlemagne's system remained as a firm basis. The weights and measures which were used in the countries conquered by the Muslims were however not altogether different, as preceding oriental conquerors had introduced their metrological systems in other countries and, secondly, a mutual influence shaped them to a certain extent. For the needs of the fiscal administration [see BAYT AL-MĀL and DĪWĀN] and the market supervision [see ḤISBA], every governor and finance director of the provinces of the caliphal empire had to enforce what the caliph decreed concerning weights and measures. But rulers who had in mind to establish a truly new régime fixed new weights and measures, just as they built up an administration different from that of their predecessors. The Būyid prince ʿAḍud al-Dawla, the Fāṭimids, the Il-Khān Ghāzān and the Turcoman Uzun Ḥasan introduced new metrological systems.

For the study of Muslim weights one has recourse to the accounts in literary sources, the analysis of glass weights which served as standards and, thirdly, to data in European sources, such as Merchants' Guides. But despite the relatively rich information, research in Muslim metrology has not resulted in generally-accepted conclusions. From the accounts of the Muslim authors and the archaeological findings, different values have been calculated. The data in the European sources mostly point to smaller ones, which cannot be considered as mistaken.

The names of the weights and measures of capacity point to their origins: the *raṭl*, the most common weight, is an Aramaic form of the Greek λίτρον; the *ḳinṭār* (100 *raṭls*) is obviously the Latin *centenarius*; and the *ḳafīz* is the Persian name of a measure of capacity. When the Arabs conquered the lands of the Near East, all these names were already used for different weights and measures. The *mudd*, a measure of capacity, was in ʿIrāḳ of (about) 1.05 litres, in Syria of 3.673 litres, and in Egypt of 2.5 litres. The diversity of the weights and measures called by the same name was a phenomenon common to all Muslim countries. Almost every district had its own weights and measures, and in some countries those used in the capitals were different from those of the countryside. This is what the Arabic geographers tell about Djibāl and its capital Rayy, about Khūzistān and its capital al-Ahwāz and about Aleppo (Ḥalab) and its province. Further different weights were used for various commodities: in many provinces meat was weighed by a *raṭl* different from that of other articles. In all provinces of Upper Egypt there was a *raṭl* for meat and bread and another for other commodities. In many countries there were particular *raṭls* for pepper, silk, etc. For grain, one used in all Arabic countries measures of capacity; for liquids one had other measures of this kind. One learns, however, from the sources that in course of time there was a trend in several countries to use for liquids (e.g. olive oil) weights, and secondly, there was a tendency to replace weights (and measures of capacity) by bigger ones. Despite the mutual influence between the metrological systems of the Near Eastern countries, there remained through the Middle Ages (and also later) a marked difference between the Persian and

Arab countries (although there was some overlapping). The mutual influence and the age-old Roman-Byzantine rule over the Near East resulted, however, in a two-sided structure of the metrological systems of all the Muslim countries: they were both sexagesimal and decimal. This was indeed also a characteristic feature of the metrological system of the Greco-Roman world. The survival of the metrological systems of antiquity overshadows the almost insignificant influence of the weights and measures of Arabia upon the newly-conquered countries. The measures of capacity which were used in the Ḥidjāz in the days of Muḥammad, the *ṣāᶜ* equal to 4 *mudds* and the *wasḳ* equal to 60 *mudds*, did not spread to other countries (except perhaps in Algeria and Tunisia where the *ṣāᶜ* is still used, with varying equivalences). But the basic weight used at Baghdād became widely accepted as a standard weight. This was clearly the influence of ᶜAbbāsid rule. On the other hand, the Muslim rulers did not introduce "Royal measures" for collecting taxes or making payments; some of them established special measures for these purposes, but these latter ones did not become new standards. The striking feature of the metrological systems of the mediaeval Arab countries was their diversity. Nevertheless, the Muslims tried to give the obviously different systems a common theoretical basis, adapted to the monetary system of the caliphs which was considered as canonical. Thus a metrological theory was elaborated.

Every weight was supposed to consist of a certain number of weight *dirhams* (to be distinguished from the weight of the coin called by the same name). The French scholars who came with Bonaparte to Egypt found that this *dirham* was equal to 3.0884 g, whereas a commission appointed by the Egyptian government in 1845 concluded that it was of 3.0989 g, and this latter value was taken by Sauvaire as basis for his calculations. Decourdemanche concluded that it was 3.148 g, and Hinz 3.125 g. But the Egyptian government established in 1924 that it is 3.12 g, and both the glass weights of the caliphal period and the data in the late mediaeval Merchants' Guides point to a smaller value. In addition, mediaeval Muslim writers say that this unity was not equal everywhere. For in Central Syria it was, according to them, lighter than in other Near Eastern countries. Another standard weight unity was the *mithḳāl*. Just as 10 silver *dirhams* should have the same weight as 7 gold *dīnārs*, so 10 weight *dirhams* should be equal to the weight of 7 *mithḳāls*. The authorities of the caliphal empire had the *dirham* weight stamped on the standard weights, and Arab writers usually give the value of a (real) weight in these theoretical units. They also established further relationships: a weight *dirham* consists of 60 barley grains (*ḥabba*), each equal to 70 grains of mustard; a *mithḳāl* too is equal to 60 barley grains, but of 100 mustard grains each. The *mithḳāl* was also divided into 24 *ḳīrāṭs* (from the Greek κεράτιον), and consequently the weight *dirham* was reckoned at 164/5 *ḳīrāṭs*. But the *mithḳāl* was not everywhere the same; thus that of Damascus was lighter than the Egyptian one.

In the time of Muḥammad and his first successors, the weight system of Mesopotamia had apparently already been introduced into Arabia. Both in Mecca and in ᶜUmān there was used a *raṭl* which was the double of what was later called "the *raṭl* of Baghdād", so that it weighed 402.348 g. The *raṭl* of Yemen was equal to the Baghdād *raṭl*. The *raṭl* of Medina weighed 617.96 g. The basic unity of the measures of capacity was the *mudd*, which contained a Meccan *raṭl* of wheat, and this was considered as the canonical *mudd* of Islam.

The data which we have about the weights and the measures of capacity which were used in the Middle Ages in Syria and in Egypt are much more numerous than data about those in other Islamic countries, and both archaeological findings and the information provided by Westerners enable us to draw a comprehensive sketch of the metrological development of these two countries.

For weighing small quantities one used in these countries everywhere the *raṭl*. Under Umayyad rule, one had in Syria a *raṭl* of 337.5 g or 340 g, obviously equal to the Roman pound. In the 4th/10th century, one used in most provinces of Syria and Palestine a heavy *raṭl*, numbering 600 *dirhams*, i.e. 1.853 kg. The *raṭl* of Damascus was, however, according to al-Muḳaddasī, slightly lighter. In this town it remained unchanged throughout the Middle Ages. In northern Syria, however, other *raṭls* were used. In the 5th/11th century, the Aleppo *raṭl* was equal to 1.483 kg. In the 6th/12th century one had in Aleppo a *raṭl* of 2.335 kg, in Ḥamāt one of 2.039 kg and in Shayzar one of 2.114 kg. According to the Arabic sources, the Damascus *raṭl* was in the Mamlūk period still equal to 1.85 kg, but the Italian Merchants' Guides make it 600 light Venetian pounds, i.e. 1.8072 kg. The *raṭl* of the northern provinces of Syria was in the 7th/13th and 8th/14th centuries, according to the Arabic sources, equal to 2.22 kg, and according to the Italian sources it was of 2.1688 kg. In the 11th-13th/17th-19th centuries the *raṭl* of Aleppo was slightly heavier and weighed 2.28 kg. Even in Palestine every district had its own *raṭl*; that of Jerusalem (also used in Nābulus) was in the Middle Ages of 2.47 kg and in the 19th century of 2.78 kg.

Grain was measured in southern Syria and in Palestine by the *ghirāra*, a measure of capacity which was however of different size in every province. The *ghirāra* of Damascus was equal to 731/2 *mudds*, containing 2.84 kg of wheat each, or to 3 Egyptian *irdabbs*. So it contained 208.74 kg of wheat. But in Jerusalem, the *ghirāra* contained, at least at the end of the Middle Ages, three times as much, sc. 626.22 kg of wheat, and in Ghazza 313.1 kg. In northern Syria one used for weighing grains the *makkūk*. Even this was a name given to different measures. The *makkūk* of Aleppo and Tripoli contained 83.5 kg of wheat and that of Ḥamāt 92.77 kg, according to Ibn Faḍl Allāh al-ᶜUmarī and al-Ḳalḳashandī. But in the period of the Crusades, the *makkūk* was smaller. Ibn al-ᶜAdīm recounts that the *makkūk* of Aleppo was in the 6th/12th century half of the *makkūk* of his own day, so that it must then have been of about 40 kg of wheat. Once more one becomes aware of a characteristic trend of the development of weights and measures in the mediaeval Near East: that there was a tendency to use heavier and bigger ones. In the 19th century one used in Syria the *kayl* of 28.18 kg of wheat.

Judging from the glass weights found in Egypt, the standard *raṭl* in Umayyad times was in that country equal to 440 g, whereas the ᶜAbbāsids introduced a lighter *raṭl*, weighing 390-400 g. But in ᶜAbbāsid Egypt also a "big *raṭl*" (*raṭl kabīr*) of 493 g was used. Under the Fāṭimids, several *raṭls* were used. According to the Arabic writers of that period and shortly afterwards, such as Eliya of Nisibin, writing in the firts half of the 5th/11th century, al-Makhzūmī of the late 6th/12th century and Ibn Mammātī, at the beginning of the 7th/13th century, and a later text referring to a happening in the early 5th/11th century, they were the following: the *raṭl* called *miṣrī* of 144 *dirhams*, i.e. 444.9 g, used for weighing bread, meat and other articles; that of 150 *dirhams*, i.e. 463 g, used for spices (and therefore called *fulfulī*, pepper *raṭl*) and also for cotton; the *raṭl laythī* of 200 *dirhams*, i.e. 617.96 g, used for flax; and the *raṭl djarwī* of 312 *dirhams*; i.e. 964 g, used for honey, sugar, cheese and metals. However, according to the Italian Merchants' Guides the *raṭl fulfulī* was equal to 1.4 - 1.46 light Venetian pounds, i.e. 420 - 440 g, the *raṭl laythī* (called after the governor al-Layth b. Faḍl, year 802), equalled 602.46 - 617.52 g, and the *raṭl djarwī* 939.8376 - 951.8868 g or, as other Italian sources have it, 300 light Venetian pounds, i.e. 903.69 g. Although one can quote other data from these European sources, the comparison of the data in the Arabic and European sources shows clearly that the European merchants who carried on trade in the Near East were accustomed to lighter standards. Several authors of the European Merchants' Guides, such as Pegolotti, emphasise that these *raṭls* were used in Cairo, Alexandria and Damietta alike, and others point to minimal differences, but from the Arabic sources one learns that different *raṭls* were used in almost all provinces of Egypt. The Fayyūm, Asyūṭ, Manfalūṭ, Ikhmīm and Ḳūṣ in Upper Egypt, Ḳalyūb, Fuwwa, al-Maḥalla and Samannūd in Lower Egypt, all had their own *raṭls*. The variety of the Egyptian weights was even much greater than that of the weights used in Syria, as in the major towns of this latter country many more commodities were weighed by the same weights. In Damascus, for instance, all the spices and the metals were weighed by the Damascene *raṭl* (and *ḳinṭār*). In Egypt, on the other hand, some spices were weighed by the *mann*, which was equal, according to the Arabic sources, to 260 *dirhams*, i.e. 803.348 g, according to Pegolotti to 840 g, and according to other Merchants' Guides to $2^1/_2$ light Venetian pounds, i.e. 753 g. Spices weighed by the *mann* comprised cinnamon, nutmeg, mace, cloves, cubeb and borax.

The measures of capacity which were used in Egypt in the caliphal period for grain were the *ṭillīs* and different *irdabbs*, but from the middle of the 5th/11th century the first of these measures dropped out of use. Al-Muḳaddasī says that it was of 96.4 kg of wheat and that it was no more used in his days. But in various accounts of the third decade and of the middle of the 5th/11th century, the *tillīs* is still mentioned; perhaps this was another *ṭillīs*. The *irdabb* (from ἀρτάβη) was originally a Persian measure of capacity which had been used in Egypt for a long time under the Ptolemies and the Byzantines. According to al-Muḳaddasī, it contained 72.3 kg of wheat. This was the *irdabb* of the Egyptian capital; it consisted of 6 *waybas* of 12.05 kg of wheat each. In the various provinces there were other *irdabbs*, such as that of Fayyūm comprising 9 *waybas* or 103.22 kg of wheat. In the Mamlūk period, the *irdabb* of Cairo corresponded to 68.8 kg. of wheat, whereas, judging from the equations made by Pegolotti and in two anonymous Merchants' Guides, the *irdabb* of Alexandria was already in that period twice as much. In the 18th and 19th centuries the *irdabb* was apparently everywhere doubled, and nowadays it is in the Buḥayra of 140.8 kg of wheat and in the Ṣaʿīd of 148.3 kg. Flour was weighed by the *buṭṭa*, equal to 50 Egyptian *raṭls*, i.e. 22.245 kg. A *ṭillīs* of flour weighed, according to Ibn Mammātī, 150 of these *raṭls*, i.e. 66.735 kg.

For olive oil, one used in the period of the Umayyad and the ʿAbbāsid caliphs measures of capacity. There were three measures called *ḳisṭ* (ξέστης, *sextarius*), one containing 476 g olive oil, another 1.07 kg and yet another 2.14 kg. But according to al-Maḳrīzī, a *ḳisṭ* contained 2.106 1 (or .1.93 kg) of olive oil. Other measures of capacity for liquids were the *maṭar* (derived from the Greek μετρήτης) which, according to a Venetian source, contained, in the later Middle Ages, about 17 kg of olive oil. But under the rule of the Ayyūbids, one began to weigh olive oil by the *ḳinṭār (raṭl) djarwī*, as is borne out by an account of Ibn Mammātī.

For great quantities of various commodities, one used some kinds of "loads". The *ḥiml* was reckoned at 600 "Egyptian *raṭls*", i.e. 266 kg, but as far as spices were concerned it consisted of 500 *raṭls* only, i.e. 222.45 kg. This latter unity is that which the Italian traders called *sporta* and reckoned at 720 (later 700) light Venetian pounds, i.e. 216.885 kg.

Weights in ʿIrāḳ, where the old Persian tradition prevailed, were altogether different from those used in Syria and in Egypt, although some had the same name. The *raṭl* of Baghdād which was equal to 401.674 g (according to others, to 397.26 g) (130 or 128 4/7 *dirhams* respectively) was considered as the "canonical" *raṭl* of the Muslims, because it was used from the days of the first caliphs. Al-Muḳaddasī recounts that this *raṭl* was also used in Upper Mesopotamia. But a short time later, Eliya of Nisibin says that in his native town one had a *raṭl* of 926.49 g (210 *mithḳāls*) and he mentions also a *raṭl* of Balad as being twice as much, i.e. 1.8529 kg. His contemporary Nāṣir-i Khusraw mentions the *raṭl* of Mayyāfāriḳīn which was equal to 1.483 kg. The measures of capacity which were used in ʿIrāḳ fitted into a sexagesimal system. Small quantities of grain were sold by *ḳafīz*. In the 4th/10th century one used various *ḳafīzs*. One of them contained 10 kg of wheat (25 Baghdādī *raṭls*); Baghdād and Kūfa had a *ḳafīz* containing 120 *raṭls* or 48.2 kg wheat, whereas the *ḳafīz* of Wāsiṭ and Baṣra was only half of it, i.e. equal to 24.1 kg. The measure of capacity used for greater quantities of grains was the *kurr*. There were, however, different *kurrs*. The so-called "reformed *kurr*" (*kurr muʿaddal*) contained, according to al-Būzadjānī, an author of the Būyid period, 2829 kg of wheat, since it was equal to 60 *ḳafīzs*; the "full *kurr*" (*kurr kāmil*) was half of it. In Upper Mesopotamia, one used the "Sulaymānī" *kurr* which contained 771.2 kg of wheat (1920 *raṭls* of Baghdād). In the period of the caliphs, one measured in this latter region small quantities of grain by a *makkūk* containing 6.025 kg of wheat, but in the period of the Crusades the *makkūk* of this region was bigger. It contained, according to Ibn al-Athīr, $^1/_{14}$ of a Damascene *ghirāra*, that is, 14.91 kg of wheat. The data which one finds in the Arabic sources about the measures of capacity which were used in ʿIrāḳ for liquids are rather scanty. According to Eliya of Nisibin, one used for olive oil a *ḳisṭ* containing 3 Baghdādī *raṭls* and another which was twice as much.

The weights and measures of capacity of Persia had almost nothing in common with the metrological system which had been established by the Arabs in Syria, in Egypt and in other countries on the basis of the Roman-Byzantine tradition. The ancient Persian tradition on the whole withstood the Muslim-Arab influence, but was nevertheless not wholly untouched by it.

In the provinces of Persia adjacent to ʿIrāḳ, many towns had the *raṭl* as the basic weight unit for small quantities of various commodities, but most of them shared with the *raṭls* used in the lands of the Fertile Crescent only the name. One exception to this rule was the town of al-Ahwāz, where one used the Baghdādī *raṭl*. Al-Iṣṭakhrī recounts that one used almost everywhere a *mann* which weighed twice as much as the *raṭl* of Baghdād. This is undoubtedly an exaggeration. In Rayy, the capital of Djibāl, one had a *raṭl* of 300 *dirhams*, i.e. 926.94 g. This *raṭl* was also used in some provinces of Ādharbāydjān, as in those of Khūy and Urmiya. But outside Rayy, one used in Djibāl a *raṭl* which was the double of the Rayy one, and in other provinces of Ādharbāydjān one used the *raṭl* of Baghdād. The *raṭl* of Ardabīl weighed, according to al-Iṣṭakhrī, 1,040 *dirhams*, i.e. 3.213 kg, and according to al-Muḳaddasī 1,200 *dirhams*, i.e. 3.7 kg. In Shīrāz one weighed bread and meat by the *raṭl* of Baghdād, whereas other commodities were weighed by the same *raṭl* as that used in Ardabīl (eight times as much as that of Baghdād). The standard weight for small quantities of dry (and even liquid commodities) was in most provinces of Persia the *mann* (also called *manā*), which had spread widely in western Persia. But even *mann* was a name given to different weights. In the province of Khūzistān, outside the town of al-Ahwaz, it was equal to 4 *raṭls* of Baghdād, so that it weighed 1.6 kg. In the neighbouring province of Fārs, one used in some towns, like Arradjān, a *mann* of 1.2 kg (equal to 3 Baghdādī *raṭls*) and in others one of 926.94 g. In Iṣṭakhr one used a *mann* of 400 *dirhams*, i.e. 1.235 kg, and in Fasā one of 300 *dirhams*, i.e. 926.94 g. The *mann* of Rayy was of 1.853 kg, and that of other towns of Djibāl 1.2359 kg (600 and 400 *dirham* respectively). The *mann* of Rayy was widely used. It was also the standard weight of the provinces of Daylam and Ṭabaristān, whereas Ḳūmis had a *mann* of 926.94 g. Despite the bewildering variety of all these weights, they point to a striking difference between the metrological system of the Persian provinces of the caliphate and those formerly belonging to the Byzantine empire: the basic unit was much heavier than that used in the latter countries. The *mann* remained also in the later Middle Ages, and even in subsequent periods, the basic weight of the provinces of Persia. Ghāzān imposed the *mann* of Tabrīz, which was equal to 260 *dirhams*, i.e. 803.348 g, as the standard weight in the whole kingdom of the Il-Khāns, and even grain was weight by this *mann*. However, according to Pegolotti, spices were weighed by a *mann* equal to 903.69 g. After the downfall of the Il-Khāns, in the middle of the 8th/14th century, it fell out of use. Uzun Ḥasan introduced another weight, the so-called *batman*, equal to 5.76 kg, and this was apparently the standard weight in most Persian provinces under the rule of the Ṣafawids. Then in the 11th/17th and 12th/18th centuries a *mann* of 2.88 - 2.9 kg spread everywhere. Obviously, this was a variation of half the pound of Uzun Ḥasan. From the beginning of the 19th century, it was mostly equal to 3 kg, and later it was indeed fixed at exactly 3 kg. In 1926 the equivalence of Persian and metric weights was fixed by law, and in 1935 the metric system was introduced, although in practice the ancient weights are still used.

The use of measures of capacity was in Persia much less common than in the Arab-speaking countries, although in the days of the caliphs, the *ḳafīz* was widely used. According to the reports of the Arabic authors of the 4th/10th century, one used in Nīshāpūr a *ḳafīz* which was equal to 70 *manns*, i.e. 56.23 kg of wheat. In Fārs one had various *ḳafīzs*, containing 3.2 - 6.4 kg wheat. For greater quantities, one used there the *djarīb*, equal to 10 *ḳafīzs* of 16 *raṭls*, i.e. 64.26 kg, but the inference of al-Iṣṭakhrī is that this only is an indication of its average weight, since he adds to this equation with the *raṭl* (of Baghdād) the statement that the weight of the *ḳafīz* depended upon the commodity measured (and this was probably true for other equivalents of measures of capacity and weights). In his native town of Iṣṭakhr, one called *ḳafīz* a measure which was half of the *ḳafīz* of Shīrāz. In Khūzistān one used a *kurr* containing 1004 kg of wheat (but for government crops, only 963.5 kg). Another unit of weight which was in all periods widespread in the Persian lands was the *kharwār*, a donkey's load. The Būyid ruler ʿAḍud ad-Dawla fixed it at 96.35 kg, and Ghāzān Khān at 80.29 kg; but in the later Middle Ages a heavier *kharwār* was introduced, weighing 288 kg, and at present a *kharwār* of 297 kg is widespread (although others are used).

In the Muslim regions of Asia Minor one used, according to Eliya of Nisibin, in the 5th/11th century a *raṭl* which was equal to 317.89 g, but later authors say that the *raṭl rūmī* weighed 120 *dirhams*, i.e. 370.776 g. Ibn Faḍl Allāh al-ʿUmarī, who wrote in the first half of the 8th/14th century, mentions the different *raṭls* of several provinces of Asia Minor. According to him, one used in some (as in those of Anṭālya, Aḳsarāy and Ḳarā Ḥiṣār) a *raṭl* of 1.779 kg; in Bursa a *raṭl* of 9.64 kg; and in Ḳasṭamūnī a *raṭl* of 7.118 kg. As to the *raṭl* of Sīwās, the contemporary Pegolotti says that it was of 4.8 kg, whereas one learns from an Arabic source that it was of 4.618 kg. In the 18th century Istanbul had a *raṭl* of 2.8 kg, and Konya had in the 19th century a *raṭl* of 481 g. Beside these different *raṭls*, one used everywhere in the Ottoman empire another weight, the *okka*, which was equal to 1.283 kg. For grain, one used in the Middle Ages in the Turkish provinces of Asia Minor measures of capacity, which in some places equalled the Egyptian *irdabb*. Ibn Faḍl Allāh al-ʿUmarī lists them and says also that in Bursa one used a *mudd* which was bigger by a quarter. In the Ottoman period the *mudd* contained 513 kg of wheat (being of 666.4 l).

In North Africa the *raṭl* of Baghdād, being considered as the canonical, was the most common as long as the ʿAbbāsids exercised suzerainty there. The Fāṭimids, however, introduced a heavier *raṭl*, which had been previously used for weighing pepper. It was reckoned at 140 *dirhams*, i.e. it was equal to 432.572 g, according to the detailed account of al-Muḳaddasī. Ibn Ḥawḳal, who probably describes conditions prevailing at the beginning of their rule, says that meat was weighed in al-Ḳayrawān by a *raṭl* of 128 *dirhams*, i.e. 395.49 g, whereas other commodities were weighed by a *raṭl* of 4.94 kg. Eliya of Nisibin gives for the common Maghribī *raṭl* $137^1/_7$ *dirhams*, thereby confirming the account of al-Muḳaddasī. Ibn Ḥawḳal's report about a heavy *raṭl* of al-Ḳayrawān refers certainly to that used in this town, according to the later al-Bakrī, for figs, nuts and other victuals, and this was 10 times heavier than the pepper *raṭl*. The latter author gives also some data about the weights used in various other provinces of the Maghrib, in the post-Fāṭimid period there. According to him, one used in Tenes, Melīla and Nakūr, a *raṭl* of 330 *dirhams*, i.e. 1.019 kg, whereas meat was both in Tenes and in other towns weighed by much heavier *raṭls*. Ibn Baṭṭūṭa makes two statements about the common Maghribī *raṭl*: in one he says that it was equal to a quarter of a Damascene *raṭl*, that is 463.47 g, and in another that it was $^5/_4$ of an Egyptian *raṭl*, i.e. 556.164 g. From Pegolotti, one learns that one used in the first half of the 8th/14th century in Tunis a *raṭl* of 490.7 g. For grains, one had in the Maghrib various *mudds*. According to al-Bakrī, there was used in Fās a small *mudd* of 4.31 l, but in most places bigger units were used. Al-Muḳaddasī says that in al-Ḳayrawān a *mudd* was used which equalled 201 l, and al-Bakrī reports that the people of Tāhart had a *mudd* of 243 l. For liquids, such as olive oil, there was used in Tunis in the 19th century the *ḳulla* of 10.08 l and the *maṭar*, twice its weight.

In Muslim Spain, a *raṭl* of 503.68 g was commonly used. But for weighing meat, one had a *raṭl* four times as heavy. For grain, one used a *ḳafīz* containing 60 *raṭls* of wheat, i.e. 30.22 kg. Olive oil was weighed by a *thumn* containing $2^1/_4$ *raṭls*, i.e. 1.12 kg; the *ḳulla* was equal to 12 *thumns*.

Bibliography: Iṣṭakhrī, 156, 191, 203, 213; Muḳaddasī, 99, 129, 145 f., 181 f., 204, 240, 381, 397, 417 f., 452; Bakrī, ed. de Slane, 26 f., 62, 69, 89, 91117, 145; Ibn Mammātī, *Ḳawānīn al-dawāwīn*, Cairo 1943, 360 ff.; Ibn al-Ukhuwwa, *Maᶜālim al-ḳurba*, London 1938, ch. ix; Ibn al-ᶜAdīm, *Zubdat al-ṭalab min taʾrīkh Ḥalab*, Damascus 1954, ii, 182; al-Ḳalḳashandī, *Ṣubḥ al-aᶜshā*, iii, 445, iv, 181, 198, 216, 233, 237, 422 f.; Maḳrīzī, *Khiṭaṭ*, Būlāḳ 1270, ii, 274, 1. 27; al-Saḳaṭī, *Un manuel hispanique de ḥisba*, ed. Lévi-Provençal, 11, 13, 39; Ibn Baṭṭūṭa, iii, 382, iv, 317; Pegolotti, *La practica della mercatura*, ed. Evans, 30 f., 69 ff., 89 ff., 135, 166; Zibaldone da Canal, ed. A. Stussi, Venice 1967, 56, 65 ff.; *Tarifa zoè noticia dy pexi e mexure di luogi e tere che s'adovra mar-cadantia per el mondo*, Venice 1925, 26 ff., 63; *Il manuale di mercatura di Saminiato de' Ricci*, ed. A. Borlandi, Genoa 1963, 120; *Il libro di mercatantie et usanze de' paesi*, ed. Fr. Borlandi, Turin 1936, 70 f., 72 ff., 75 ff., 99 ff.; Sauvaire, *Matériaux pour servir à l'histoire de la numismatique et de la métrologie musulmane*, in *JA* (1884-6); idem, *On a treatise on weights and measures by Eliya, archbishop of Nisibin*, in *JRAS* (1877), 291 ff.; R. Brunschvig, *Mesures de capacité de la Tunisie médiévale*, in *RAfr.*, 1935/3-4, 86-90; idem; in *AIEO Alger* (1937), 74-87; W. Hinz, *Islamische Masse und Gewichte*, Leiden 1955, Russian tr. with corrections, together with a treatise about weights in Central Asia, *Musul'man-skie meri is vesa s perevodom w metričeskuyu sistemu*, tr. Y. Bregel, (with) E. A. Davidovič, *Materialī po metrologii srednevekovoy sredney Asii*, Moscow 1970; P. Balog, *Umayyad, Abbasid and Tulunid glass weights and vessel stamps*, New York 1976; A. Grohmann, *Einführung und Chrestomathie zur arabischen Papyruskunde*, Prague 1955, 139 ff.; F. Vivé, *Dénéraux, estampilles et poids musulmans en verre en Tunisie*, in *CT*, iv (1956), 17-90; A. S. Ehrenkreutz, *The kurr system in medieval Iraq*, in *JESHO*, v (1962), 309 ff.; Cl. Cahen, *Douanes et commerce dans les ports méditerranéens de l'Égypte médiévale d'après le Minhadj d'al-Makhzumi*, in *JESHO*, vii (1964), 275 ff.; B. Lewis, *Studies in the Ottoman archives*, in *BSOAS*, xvi (1954), 489; E. Ashtor, *Histoire des prix et des salaires dans l'Orient médiéval*, Paris 1969, 103, 125; A. K. S. Lambton, *Landlord and peasant in Persia*², London 1969, 405 ff.; C. E. Bosworth, *Abū ᶜAbdallāh al-Khwārazmī on the technical terms of the secretary's art*, in *JESHO*, xii (1969). (E. Ashtor)

2. In Muslim India

It appears that the earliest Muslims in India of whose fiscal regulations we have any records had assimilated the indigenous system of weights of northern India for everyday trade; for the more precise requirements of the coinage, there is excellent numismatic evidence that indigenous standards had been adopted from the beginning and maintained thenceforth, except for a few anomalous periods. The interconnexion between precise and general weights, however, varies enormously from time to time and from region to region, so that there can be considerable difficulties in interpreting references before the 19th century.

An attempt was made by the East India Company in 1833 to standardise the weights system in *Regulation VII*, "A regulation for altering the weight of the Fur-ruckabad [i.e. Farrukhābād] rupee and for assimilating it to the legal currency of the Madras and Bombay Presidencies; for adjusting the weight of the Company's sicca rupee, and for fixing a standard unit of weight for India". This provided for the following scale:

8 *rattī*	= 1 *māshā*
12 *māshā*	= 1 *tōlā*
80 *tōlā*	= 1 *sēr*
40 *sēr*	= 1 *man*

The *sēr* was further divisible into 16 *čhaṭānk* (just as the rupee was divisible into 16 *ānā* "annas", the *ānā* being originally not a coin but merely a money of account, "sixteenth share". The central unit here, the *tōlā*, was fixed at 180 grains, i.e. 11.6638 gm.; thus the "official seer", *sēr*, was fixed at 2.057 lbs.av. = 0.933 kg., and the "official maund", *man*, at 82.286 lbs.av = 37.32 kg. *The Indian weights and measures act*, Act. XI of 1870, provided for the extension of this system, throughout British India, and provided for a future redefinition of the *sēr* as precisely equal to the standard kilogram, although with the death of Lord Mayo, the proposer of the Act, this scheme did not materialise at the time, and the above system of weights remained in force until the official introduction of the metric system after Indian independence (persisting unofficially in country districts up to the present day). The *anglicé* form "maund" derives from *man* through Port. *mão*, possibly influenced by an old Eng. "maund", a hamper of eight bales, etc.; see *OED*, s.v. *Maund*.

This relative scale was general throughout north and central India and Bengal, although the values of *sēr* and *man* were very variable; the situation is further complicated by the presence side by side of a *kaččā* and a *pakkā sēr* and *man* almost everywhere (cf. mediaeval Europe: "almost every city in Italy had its *libra grossa* and *libra sottile*"; and the former distinction in England between lb.av. and lb.troy. See Hobson-Jobson, s.v. PUCKA, *Pucka*, and cf. variations in the Eng. pound for different commodities in *OED*, s.v. *Pound*. Thus Tavernier (*Les six voyages...*, Paris 1676, ed. and Eng. tr. V. A. Ball, London 1889) and Grose (*Voyage to the East Indies...*, London 1757) agree that the ordinary *man* is 69 livres/pounds, but that used for weighing indigo is only 53. Grose further mentions the *man* of Bombay as 28 lb., that of Goa 14 lb., that of Surat 37 lb., of Coromandel 25 lb., but of Bengal 75 lb. Some, but not all, of these estimates correspond with those of Prinsep (E. Thomas, ed., *Essays on Indian antiquities of the late James Prinsep ... to which are added his Useful Tables*, London 1858), whose list is the most complete; his largest *man* is of Aḥmadnagar, of 64 *sēr* and = 163.25 lbs, the smallest that of "Colachy" (Kolačel) in Travancore, of 18.80 lbs.

Absolute values have been cited first from European travellers, since they describe transactions of their own times and offer some standards for comparison. The question becomes more difficult when interpreting the Muslim historians: e.g. Ḍiyāʾ al-Dīn Baranī, discussing (*Taʾrīkh-i Fīrūz Shāhī*, 316 ff.) the first *ḍabīṭa* of ᶜAlāʾ al-Dīn Khaldjī on the regulations of grain prices some sixty years after the events, details the prices for various commodities in terms of *djītals* or *tankas* per *man* or *sēr*; only Firishta's explanation—some three hundred years after ᶜAlāʾ al-Dīn's time—that the *sēr* was at that time of 24 *tōlās* allows the rough calculation that the *man* referred to must have been about 11.2 kg., provided that one can depend on the accuracy of both Baranī and Firishta [*q.vv.*]. Ibn Baṭṭūṭa (iii, 290, tr. Gibb, iii, 695), describing the famine of 734/1334, refers to the Dihlī *man*, and to its half, the *raṭl*, and elsewhere equates the Dihlī *raṭl* as 20 Maghribī *raṭl* (Hinz, *Islamische Masse*, 32, makes the Morocco *raṭl* 468.75 gm). Some writers confuse the issue further (e.g. ʿAbd al-Razzāḳ Shīrāzī, *Maṭlaʿ al-saʿdayn*; Djahāngīr, in *Tūzuk*), by referring to a foreign *man*, although Djahāngīr does explain that 500 Hindūstānī *man* = 4000 Wilāyatī; the "Hindūstānī" must be the recently established *man-i Akbarī*, equivalent to *man-i tabrīzī*.

The smaller weights present fewer problems, since they are relatable to the coinage and one possesses the ponderal evidence of the coins themselves. Here the standard is the *tōlā*, the weight of the *ṭanka*, calculated as equal to 96 *rattī*. The *rattī* ("red one", Skt. *raktikā*; Abu 'l-Faḍl in *Āʾīn-i Akbarī* calls it *surkh*) is the seed of a small red-flowered leguminous creeper, *Abrus precatorius*; the actual weight of such a seed varies from 80 to 130 mg, its notional weight, at least up to the end of the 8th/14th century, being 116.6 mg. (for fuller discussion of the metrological problem see SIKKA. India). The *rattī* is in Hindu theory a high multiple of the smallest particle, the "mote in a sunbeam"; there are several factitious tables of increments in the ancient authors, some of which are related by al-Bīrūnī (ed. Sachau, text i, 76 ff.; Eng. tr. i, 160 ff.), who complains of weights being "different for different wares and in different provinces". He relates some of these weights to his *mithḳāl*, but not consistently, giving the *mithḳāl* a weight of about 5.5 gm. But the weight of the *mithḳāl* has similarly varied; the term is used occasionally by Indian authors, especially in the *Bābur-nāma* and *Humāyūn-nāma*, where it is expressly stated to be the weight of a *shāhrukhī*, the especial currency of Kābul, two-fifths the value of an Akbarī rupee, and weighing only about 4.67 gm (S.H. Hodivala, *Historical studies in Mughal numismatics*, Calcutta 1923, s.v. "Shāhrukhīs", 1-10).

The *rattī* and, less frequently, the *māshā* are also used as the common jewellers' weights; in some cases the jewellers' *rattī* is known to have been a "double *rattī*"; this brings it to nearly the weight of another seed notionally used in South India, including Golkoṇḍā and Bīdjāpur, the *mandjāḷī* (Telugu) or *mandjāḍī* (Tamil), of about 260 mg. (Hobson-Jobson, s.v. *Mangelin*).

There were no measures of capacity in regular Indian use, liquids and grain being regularly accounted by weight only. When precision was of small importance, water might be accounted by the skinful, *dahī* (curds) by the jarful, small quantities of grain by the handful, etc. Al-Bīrūnī, *loc. cit.*, does mention some Indian measures of capacity, of which only the *bīsī* seems to have survived but not now to be identifiable. Factory records (e.g. those at Ḍhākā, see Abdul Karim, *Dacca: the Mughal capital*, Dacca 1964) show cloth as being accounted simply by the "piece", or (tantalisingly) for smaller or fractional lengths, by the *rēza*.

Bibliography: In addition to references in the article, see for the metrology especially, H. N. Wright, *The coinage and metrology of the sultans of Delhi*, Oxford (for the Manager of Publications, Delhi) 1936, App. A. (J. BURTON-PAGE)

MAḲBARA (or *maḳbura*, *maḳbira*, *miḳbara*, *maḳbar* and *maḳbur*) (A.), "cemetery". The word occurs only in the Ḳurʾān in the plural form *maḳābir*: "Rivalry distracts you, until you visit the cemeteries" (CII,2). Its synonyms *djabbāna*, *madfan* and *turba* do not figure in the Holy Book.

1. In the central Arab lands

The Arab authors supply little information of use in tracing the history of Muslim cemeteries. Works of *fiḳh* refer only to prohibitions concerning tombs (*ḳabr*, pl. *ḳubūr* [*q.v.*]) and the visiting of burial-places (*ziyāra* [*q.v.*]). At the most, a few occasional references may be gleaned from these sources: Ibn Baṭṭa and Ibn Ḳudāma recall, for example, the dictum of the Prophet forbidding prayer in cemeteries (cf. H. Laoust, *La profession de foi d'Ibn Baṭṭa*, Damascus 1958, 80, 149, and idem, *Le précis de droit d'Ibn Qudāma*, Beirut 1950, 21). Ibn Taymiyya notes that the cemeteries of Christians and Jews must not be located in proximity to those of the faithful (cf. idem, *Essai sur les doctrines sociales et politiques d'Ibn Taimiyya*, Cairo 1939, 372). For more substantial information, it is necessary to consult works of topography, guides to pilgrimage and the accounts of travellers. Even here, it very often happens that such information is dispersed and responds only partially to the requirements of the historian. Thus in his topography of the city of Damascus, Ibn ʿAsākir devotes a whole chapter to the cemeteries, but he is primarily concerned with locating the tombs of the revered individuals who are buried there. While he identifies the site of the first cemetery of Damascus, that of Bāb Tūmā (currently Shaykh Raslān) where the Muslims killed at the time of the conquest of the city were buried, it is only by chance that he mentions those of al-Bāb al-Ṣaghīr and al-Farādīs, in referring to the tombs of the Companions of the Prophet (cf. Ibn ʿAsākir, *Taʾrīkh madīnat Dimashḳ*, ii, ed. Ṣ. Munadjdjid, Damascus 1954, 188-200, tr. N. Elisséeff, *La Description de Damas*, Damascus 1959, 303-16). His aim is not to describe the history of the cemeteries, their creation, development and abandonment, but to give a topography of the tombs.

It is in the same manner that the authors of topographies of the two holy cities—Mecca and Medina—describe the cemeteries. They recount the traditions relating to their origin, but are concerned above all with the topographical landmarks of tombs of the members of the family of the Prophet whose names are listed. They accord the same treatment to the Ṣaḥāba and the Tābiʿūn (cf. al-Azraḳī, *Akhbār Makka wa-mā djāʾa fī-hā min al-āthār*, Mecca 1965, 209-13; al-ʿAbbāsī, *Kitāb ʿUmdat al-akhbār fī madīnat al-mukhtār*, Cairo n.d., 147-62).

Somewhat different is the account given by al-Maḳrīzī in the chapter of the *Khiṭaṭ* devoted to the cemeteries of Cairo. He locates them, tells the story of the acquisition of the site of the Ḳarāfa at the time of the conquest, and gives a brief account of its development and extension. But the greater part of the chapter deals with the localisation of the monuments—mosques, palaces, *ribāṭs*, *muṣallās*—dispersed throughout that massive expanse at the feet of the hill of al-Muḳaṭṭam known as the "city of the dead" (cf. al-Maḳrīzī, *al-Mawāʿiẓ wa 'l-iʿtibār bi-dhikr al-khiṭaṭ wa 'l-āthār*, Beirut n.d., ii, 442-3, 451-3).

By adding to the information supplied by topographical works that which may be gleaned from the accounts of travellers, it is possible to identify the privileged sites where Muslim cemeteries were established: in general, according to a comprehensible urban logic, they are laid out on the exterior of the ramparts, close to the gates of the town: for example, in the case of Damascus, the cemeteries of Shaykh Raslān near Bāb Tūmā, of al-Bāb al-Ṣaghīr, of Bāb Kaysān, of Daḥdaḥ near Bāb al-Farādīs, of al-Ṣūfiyya near Bāb al-Djābiya, etc. (cf. Kh. Moaz and S. Ory, *Inscriptions arabes de Damas, les stèles funéraires. I. Le cimetière d'al-Bāb al-Ṣaghīr*, Damascus 1977, 9-13); in the case of Mecca, the cemetery of al-Ḥadjūn, close to Bāb Maʿlā (cf. al-Azraḳī, *op. cit.*, ii, 3, 81; Ibn Baṭṭūṭa, *Riḥla*, i, 330, Eng. tr. Gibb, i, 206-8; Ibn Djubayr, *Riḥla*, Fr. tr. Gaudefroy-Demombynes, Paris 1951, ii, 129); in the case of Medina, al-Baḳīᶜ, near the gate of the same name (Ibn Djubayr, *op. cit.*, ii, 227; Ibn Baṭṭūṭa, i, 286, tr. i, 179; in the case of Baghdād, the cemeteries of Bāb Dimashḳ, of Bāb al-Tibn, of Bāb al-Ḥarb, of Bāb al-Kunās, of Bāb al-Baradān, of Bāb Abraz (cf. al-Khaṭīb al-Baghdādī, *Taʾrīkh Baghdād*, i, Cairo 1931, 120-7; J. Lassner, *The topography of Baghdad in the early Middle Ages*, Detroit 1970, ch. *The cemeteries of Baghdād*, 111-18; G. Maḳdīsī, *Ibn ᶜAḳīl et la resurgence de l'Islam traditionel* Damascus 1963, index s.v. *cimetières*; etc.).

The slopes or foot of mountains imbued with an atmosphere of sanctity are also propitious sites for cemeteries. The cemeteries of the Ḳarāfa in Cairo, at the feet of the Djabal al-Muḳaṭṭam, are the best examples of this. Also worthy of mention in this context are the cemeteries of al-Ḥadjūn in Mecca, on the hill of the same name (cf. above), and that of Ṣāliḥiyya in Damascus, at the foot of Mount Ḳāsiyūn [*q.v.*].

While the perspective in which cemeteries are described in the works of Arabic topography does not fully respond to all the requirements of the historian, it does, on the other hand, identify well the relations existing between the cemetery and the town, ambivalent relations which reflect the difficulties of reconciling legal prescriptions with living reality, difficulties similar to those already mentioned in the context of tombs (cf. Y. Raghib, *Les premiers monuments funéraires de l'Islam*, in *Annales Islamologiques*, ix [1970], 21-2). In fact, in the view of some of the *fuḳahāʾ*, the cemetery is an impure case. It will be recalled that Ibn Ḳudāma and Ibn Baṭṭa (*op. cit.*, 80, 149) include it in the list of places unsuited to prayer, in the same manner as public baths, enclosures where camels shed excrement, abattoirs and rubbish dumps. However, for the majority of authors and the consensus of believers, the cemetery is a holy place, seeing that it contains the tombs of individuals venerated in Islam: members of the Prophet's family, the Ṣaḥāba or Companions, the Tābiᶜūn or successors, *awliyāʾ* and *ṣāliḥūn*. Ibn Baṭṭūṭa and al-Maḳrīzī, referring to the mosque of the cemetery of the Ḳarāfa, call it the *Djāmiᶜ al-awliyāʾ*, and when al-Harawī (*Ziyārāt*, ed. and tr. J. Sourdel-Thomine, Damascus 1953-7, 33/76, 37/86, 74/166, 76/172) mentions a cemetery, it is always in terms of the saints and righteous men buried there. Special blessings are attached to these tombs. Every major city of Islam claims the honour of possessing the tombs of such venerated persons, irrespective of the fact that several cities may boast of the burial-place of the same individual (cf. Moaz-Ory, *op. cit.*, tomb of Bilāl al-Ḥabashī, 79).

A whole literature has developed around this theme. These are the books of *faḍāʾil* [*q.v.*], listing the holy persons still present, in a certain sense, in the town, and conferring upon it merit, glory and blessing (cf. for example al-Rubaᶜī, *Faḍāʾil al-Shām wa-Dimashḳ*, ed. Ṣ. Munadjdjid, Damascus 1950; Ibn al-Zayyāt, *al-Kawākib al-sayyāra fī tartīb al-ziyāra fi 'l-Ḳarāfatayn al-kubrā wa'l-ṣughrā*, Baghdād n.d., chs. 1-3, pp. 5-12). Very similar to these works, and sometimes overlapping with them, are the books of *ziyārāt* [*q.v.*] for the use of pilgrims who come to visit these tombs in order to benefit from the privileges associated with them (cf. Y. Rāghib, *Essai d'inventaire chronologique des guides à l'usage des pèlerins du Caire*, in *REI* xli/2 [1973], 259-80; al-Harawī, *op. cit.*; J. Sourdel-Thomine, *Les anciens lieux de pèlerinage damascains*, in *BEO*, xiv [1954], 65-85). For these pilgrims to cemeteries, itineraries of visits are established (cf. L. Massignon, *La cité des morts au Caire*, Cairo 1958, 45-6) and rituals composed. Today still, Shīᶜī pilgrims who visit the tombs of Fāṭima and Sukayna, in the cemetery of Bāb Ṣaghīr, recite, wailing, the litanies specially written for these visits.

In conjunction with these rituals, a veritable funeral liturgy was developed in certain cemeteries, in particular in that of the Ḳarāfa. Readings of the Ḳurʾān were performed over the tombs visited by members of the company of *ḳurrāʾ* [see ḲĀRIʾ] and, on feast-days, ceremonies took place with *dhikr* [*q.v.*], dances and chanting, organised by the disciples of the brotherhoods (cf. L. Massignon, *op. cit.*, 46-8). These gatherings in the cemeteries sometimes led to abuses which the jurists were obliged to remedy. Thus in Baghdād, the caliphate authorities were obliged to place a guard on the cemetery, so intense were the demonstrations of devotion on the part of the pilgrims over the tomb of Ibn Ḥanbal (on the legality of these visits, see ḲABR).

The tombs of these holy persons were often the basis for the creation of new necropolises or "quarters" in pre-existing cemeteries. Their topography thus led to the appearance of nuclei, grouping together in small enclosures within the cemetery, the tombs of members of the Prophet's family, the Ṣaḥāba and the Tābiᶜūn. In Baghdād, in the cemetery of Bāb al-Ḥarb, a number of Ḥanbalīs are buried in the shadow of the tomb of Ibn Ḥanbal, and Ḥanafīs around that of Abū Ḥanīfa (cf. Makdisi, *op. cit.*, 258, 259, n. 1, 446, n. 2, 447, 448, 453, n. 1, 388). At Karbalā, Shīᶜīs were buried in the cemetery which developed around the tomb of the *imām* al-Ḥusayn and, in the small Syrian town of Buṣrā [*q.v.*], they established their own cemetery around the *masdjid* of al-Khiḍr [*q.v.*].

At the present day, Muslim cemeteries display an extremely varied typology. A vast extent of stones, with barely perceptible tombs, where the dead lie in anonymity conforming to the most rigorous injunctions of the *fuḳahāʾ*, or a city where the visitor becomes lost in the labyrinth of streets fringed with the façades of false buildings, behind which shelter tombs and funeral monuments, a veritable "city of the dead", desert necropolises gathered together in the hollows of dunes and fields of flowers from which funeral steles emerge, cemeteries built into the walls of cities or dispersed in palm-groves or forests of cork-oak—all of these constitute the cemeteries of Islam.

Bibliography: Given in the article, to which should be added, M. Galal, *Essai d'observations sur les rites funéraires en Égypte actuelle...*, in *REI*, xi (1937), 131-299. (S. ORY)

2. In North Africa

The most common terms used to designate a cemetery in the languages and dialects of the Maghrib are the plural forms *mḳābeṛ* and *ḳbōṛ l-maᶜmōra* and *rōḍa* (in Moroccan and Algerian Arabic); and *djebbāna* (Tunisian and Algerian Arabic); the Berber form include *timəḳbəṛt* or *ləmḳabəṛ* (Kabyle); *aᶜammar*, *issəndal*, *timədlin* (Middle, High and Anti-Atlas Mts.), *imdṛan* (Rif), etc.

The cemeteries of North African towns and villages may be both *extra* and *intra muros*. Thus Fās, for example, has at least ten important graveyard sites. These include the Bāb Futūḥ, which is separated by a small valley and stream into two halves: the so-called al-Ḳbāb "the cupolas" (because of its numerous mausoleums of holy men) to the west, and Sīdī Ḥarāzəm to the east. The whole of the cemetery overlooks the *madīna* of Fās from the south. At the same time, there are within the city walls immense graveyards, such as Bāb al-Ḥamra and Sīdī ʿAlī al-Mzālī (cf. R. Le Tourneau, *Fès avant le protectorat*, Casablanca 1949, 114, 135 and index, 638). The various sites may differ in social composition and rank, and within any given cemetery there may exist a diversity of types of graves and elaborations of these. In some tribal localities, there is a tendency for particular lineage groups to have their graves within a particular plot (cf. D. M. Hart, *The Aith Waryaghar of the Moroccan Rif*, Tucson 1976, 144). It may be the case, in regard to some towns of the region, that urban growth "is hindered particularly by the stiff collar of cemeteries which modern Islamic towns have had the greatest difficulty in breaking through" (X. de Planhol, *The world of Islam*, Ithaca, N.Y. 1959 (original French ed. Paris 1957), 11), but this is not everywhere so; there are examples, at least in Tunisia, of cemeteries having been moved in order to facilitate urban expansion; elsewhere, formerly external sites have now become, because of expansion, part of city centres.

Some writers have noted a striking contrast between the cemeteries of Europe and those of the Islamic shores of the Mediterranean: that the former are enclosed, sad places, whilst the latter are open spaces, favoured especially by women and children, and used for visiting, for strolling about and for picnics. It seems that in the Muslim towns of the Mediterranean lands, attitudes towards death and the dead imply certain specific rights and duties that are absent in Christian Europe; cf. J.-P. Charay, *La vie musulmane en Algérie d'après la jurisprudence de la première motié du XXᵉ siècle*, Paris 1965, 237; Hart, *op. cit.*, 147.

In the far west of Islam, during mediaeval times, judging on the basis of 6th/12th century Seville, the *ʿulamāʾ* were concerned about the maintenance of cemeteries both from the physical and the moral points of view. The *ḳāḍī* Ibn ʿAbdūn remarks upon the tendency to construct buildings within cemeteries and to use these buildings and the space around them for purposes considered illicit or indecent (E. Lévi-Provençal, *Séville musulmane au début du XIIᵉs.*, Paris 1947, 57-8). Some dynasties constructed elaborate necropolises for their dead, e.g. Chella (Shāla [*q.v.*]), built by the Marīnid sultans Abu Saʿīd and Abu 'l-Ḥasan between 710/1310 and 739/1339 on the site of the ancient Roman city of Sala (see H. Basset and Lévi-Provençal, *Chella, une nécropole mérinide*, in *Hespéris*, ii [1922], 1-92, 255-316, 385-425), and the Saʿdian tombs of Marrakesh, mostly built during the reign of Aḥmad al-Manṣūr (986-1012/1578-1603) (see G. Deverdun, *Marrakech des origines à 1912*, Rabat 1959, 381 ff.).

A number of customs and rituals are associated with cemeteries in the Maghrib. Most of these include ceremonial visits and meals, usually accompanied by prayers at gravesides. Thus in Fās, at least until World War II, the family of a deceased person on the day after the death sent a meal to the grave to be distributed to the poor assembled there (*ʿashat l-ḳbaṛ* "the supper of the grave"). Generally, various individuals or groups (family, men, women) visit graves on specific occasions, such as *ʿĀshūrāʾ* day, on 26 Ramaḍān, and on ʿArafa, the day before the Greater Festival. In most urban centres, the obligatory outdoor place of prayer, *muṣallā*, is in the major cemetery. There the chief religious rite of the Greater and Lesser Festivals, the morning worship of the first day, takes place; and on the Greater Festival, the initial sacrifice of the local community is carried out by the *ḳāḍī* (see E. Westermarck, *Ritual and belief in Morocco*, London 1926, ii, 105, 254, 457, 478-9, 511, 547). Another rite often carried out at the *muṣallā* is the "prayer for rain" (*ṣalāt al-istisḳāʾ* [see ISTISḲĀʾ]); see K. L. Brown, *The impact of the Dahir Berbère in Salé*, in E. Gellner and C. Micauld (eds.), *Arabs and Berbers*, London 1973, 209.

The general attitude towards the space within cemeteries has been mentioned above. It appears to be marked by a mixture of dread and security. Thus according to Westermarck, Moroccans fear to pass near or through cemeteries at night, because in them dwell the *mwālīn l-aṛd*, i.e. the *žnūn*; but as Hart remarks, these *žnūn* are considered harmless. Moreover, travellers are said to have stayed the night in cemeteries because of the security and protection provided by the *mwālīn l-ḳbōṛ* "the masters of the graves", i.e. the dead, amongst whom there was likely to be some holy man (see Westermarck, ii, 374, and Hart, *loc. cit.*).

The sanctuaries of holy men (*awliyāʾ*) are often alongside or within cemeteries, and this in part explains why these latter places may be considered and filled with mystery. In tales, it is said that the prophets whilst crossing through them heard the voices of the dead; and mystics, especially those considered divinely-possessed (*madjdhūb* [*q.v.*]), are supposed to have gone into retreat within them. Yet the fact of being sacred does not result from the simple agglomeration of graves, but depends on the presence and veneration of the tomb (*ḳubba*) of a holy man; cf. E. Dermenghem, *Le culte des saints dans l'Islam maghrébin*, Paris 1957, 135-6. Private sepulchres which become sanctuaries (*rawḍa*) may or may not be considered as cemeteries in the broader sense. Thus Mawlāy Idrīs, the main sanctuary in the heart of Fās, is not properly speaking a cemetery. But in other places, the tomb of a holy man will be at the centre of a town's graveyard.

Finally, it should be noted that the cemeteries of North Africa offer precious sources for historical and demographic research. The use of such data has hardly begun, but see J. Bourrilly and E. Laoust, *Stèles funéraires marocaines*, Paris 1927, and P. Pascon and D. Schroeter, *Le cimetière juif d'Iligh (1751-1955), étude des épitaphes comme documents d'histoire sociale (Tazerwalt, Sud-Ouest Marocain)*, in *ROMM*, xxiv (1982), 39-62.

Bibliography: Given in the article.

(K. L. BROWN)

3. In Turkey

Funerary monuments in both the pre-Ottoman and Ottoman periods are characterised by the use of durable material as well as sometimes by rich decoration, neither of which accord with orthodox Sunnī tradition. Pre-Islamic Turkish traditions, as well as manners and customs of other peoples with whom the Turks came into contact during their migration towards the West, are here at variance with the stringent regulations of Sunnī Islam, according to which a tomb should be simple and made of transient material. Particularly in eastern Anatolia and in Ādharbāydjān, these traditions and contacts are at the origin of gravestones in the form of animals, connected with animistic religious belief, as well as of types based on the tradition of local industrial art (e.g. at Akhlāṭ).

Not much is known about early Ottoman tombs before about the 10th/17th century. Since only a small number of authentic gravestones have been preserved, no further conclusions can be made. It cannot be ascertained whether their disappearance is to be attributed to the influence of time alone: European travellers of the 16th and 17th centuries mention bricks as material for tombs (Geuffroy, *Erste Theil der Hoffhaltung Des Türckischen Keysers* ... ed. Hoeniger, Basel 1596, i, p. clii). The use of this transient material, if in fact not limited to isolated cases, could explain the small number of tombs which have survived from this period. This might then support the hypothesis according to which the funerary art of the later Ottoman period began to develop in the 10th-11th/16th-17th centuries only.

One of the characteristics of the Ottoman gravestone—unparalleled in this form—is its anthropomorphic shape, with a reproduction on top of some kind of headgear. Such a representation is reserved for tombs of men, but it is not the only form used. (Only further investigation can confirm the assertion, repeatedly put forward, that the form of the upper part of tombs for women, widespread since the 11th/18th century, can indeed be traced to an old Turkish, nomadic headgear.) The headgear on tombs of men—in a comparable form and frequency not to be found in any other region of the Islamic world—can be proved to have been in existence since *ca.* 900/1494-5. The oldest example in Istanbul is the tomb of a Dervīs̲h̲ Meḥmed in Eyüp (918/1512-3). In the next 200 years, hardly any social differentiation can be detected in the form of the headgear, since only a small number of turban forms appear which cannot be clearly ascribed to any particular social group. Since the 11th/18th century, it became customary in Istanbul to represent, on gravestones of men, a headgear which was specific for a certain social class, or to express the social affiliation in another way (representations in relief of headgear and other distinctive marks). In the same way in which the graves of dervishes began to show the turbans of the various *ṭarīḳas*, and not the headgear in general use, the form of the turban started to indicate the differentiation between the various professional and social groups in other areas of society. Besides, one finds other representations in relief which indicate to which group the deceased belonged: insignia of *bölük* and *d̲j̲emāʿat* for Janissaries, rosettes (*gül*) of the various *ṭarīḳas*, especially for women from *ca.* 1250/1834-5, and, rather infrequently, images of utensils and instruments.

For about a century, this strong differentiation marks the image of Ottoman gravestones. The introduction of the fez from 1829 onwards leads, again, to a general levelling and standardisation. (In other parts of the empire this development appears with some delay; e.g. in Bosnia, turban forms, which in the capital had fallen into disuse at the beginning of the 18th century, were still used towards the end of the 19th century.) Besides the fez, turbans remained in use, but in Istanbul they were, since about 1850, almost exclusively reserved for *ʿulamāʾ* and dervishes. Finally, the Atatürk reforms, especially the reform of the script and the legislation on headgear, mark the end of the tradition of Ottoman graves.

As in other fields of Ottoman art, an ever-increasing degree of European influence upon grave ornamentation can be detected from the second half of the 18th century onwards. Before that period, gravestones had hardly been decorated, but now vegetational motifs, both of traditionally oriental (cypresses, etc.) and of western origin (flower-baskets, cornucopias, etc.) were spreading more and more. By the roundabout way of Europe, older Islamic motifs, like the arabesque, were rediscovered for tombstone art towards the end of the 19th century. In general, the development of ornamentation of tombstones went parallel to that of representative and architectural art.

Whereas tomb inscriptions in Arabic can be found for the early period, Ottoman became the dominant language in the 10th/16th century. With regard to their contents, these inscriptions underwent but very few alterations: they follow a formula which corresponds largely to that of Ottoman documents (see Kraelitz, *Osmanische Urkunden in türkischer Sprache*, Vienna 1921, 12 ff., adapted to gravestones by Prokosch, *Osmanische Inschriften auf Gräbern bei der Moschee des Karabaş-Klosters in Tophane-Istanbul*, Istanbul 1976, 3-4):

1. *invocatio*: mostly *hüve 'l-bāḳī*, or another of the 99 names of God [see AL-ASMĀʾ AL-ḤUSNĀ].
2. *benedictio*: *merḥūm ve mag̲h̲fūr*, occasionally more elaborate.
3. *inscriptio*: statements about the deceased. Apart from the name, details on his origin, relationship and profession, may be given here.
4. request for prayer: mostly *rūḥīyčün* or *rūḥuna fātiḥa.*
5. date.

Such concise and rather uniform inscriptions were standard during a long period, even if particular components occasionally are expressed more elaborately. From the 18th century onwards, poetical expressions on the transitoriness of temporal existence are often inserted between the *invocatio* and the *benedictio*, in which reference is almost always made to the same limited and reiterated répertoire of verses of this kind. In the same period, chronograms are more and more used, especially for dervishes. In later times, there is a clear tendency towards more elaborate inscriptions. Instead of the original 5-6 lines of concise text, there often appear 15-20 lines which, however, do not provide more factual information.

Traditional Ottoman Islamic society did not allow the digging out of tombs, or their re-use; burial-places had to remain for ever. Yet the loss of many tombstones, and above all of most of the (uninscribed) foot-end stones might be attributed to their being used again by Ottoman masons. Since the middle of the 19th century, the construction of roads for traffic and new buildings has become another source for destruction of cemeteries, and consequently of tombstones, a problem which has still not been solved. However, at present most of the permanent losses cannot be imputed to such interferences (in which, as a rule, at least part of the tombstones are erected again at some other places), but to the hardly supervised re-use of historical cemeteries.

Bibliography: H.-P. Laqueur, *Osmanische Grabsteine, bibliographische Übersicht*, in *Travaux et Recherches en Turquie, 1982, Collection Turcica* ii, Louvain 1983, 90-6. A survey of the most important historical descriptions of Ottoman cemeteries can be found in idem, *Grabsteine als Quellen zur osmanischen Geschichte-Möglichkeiten und Probleme*, in *Osmanlı Araştırmaları/Journal of Ottoman Studies*, iii (1982), 21-44 (esp. 21-8). (H.-P. LAQUEUR)

4. In Iran [see Suppl.]

5. India

The word *maḳbara* is used in India for both graveyard and mausoleum, although *ḳabristān* is also heard for the former; *ḳabr* may, besides the grave itself, signify a monumental tomb, especially of the simpler variety; *dargāh* is used especially for the tomb or shrine of a *pīr*, where there may be also such associated buildings as mosque(s), *mihmān-k̲h̲āna*, etc.; in Kas̲h̲mīr a *pīr*'s tomb is usually called *ziyārat*, and the related *mazār* may also be used, especially for the smaller wayside shrine; *rawḍa* is commonly used for a monumental tomb within an enclosure, not necessarily of a *pīr*.

The solitary grave is rare; the individual may select an appropriate site in his lifetime, usually on his own ground (but sometimes by a roadside, since it is believed that the dead like to be within sound of human activity). But because this action then precludes the use of the ground for other purposes, the individual grave becomes a focus for other sepultures. In this way many family graveyards especially have come into being—"family" in the case of a *pīr* being held to include *murīds*. There is a tendency in some regions for graveyards of the Muslim community to be situated to the south of habitations, possibly an extension of the Hindū association of the south as the "quarter of Yama", the god of death: in the Lodī period the entire region of Dihlī south of Fīrūzābād and Purānā Ḳilʿa down to the Ḳuṭb complex was used mostly as a vast necropolis. Khuldābād, near Dawlatābād, was originally called simply Rawḍa and was a necropolis village. Community graveyards may be enclosed by a low boundary wall, but protection is generally careless and graves and walls may fall into early ruin. Some enclosures are known to be family graveyards, where the standard of upkeep is higher; there may be an imposing entrance to the east and a tall and substantial wall to the west, with arched openings or depressions which serve to indicate the *ḳibla*; some of the Dihlī examples (Yamamoto *et al.* list and illustrate some 72 graveyards) stand on high arcaded plinths and may have such features as substantial corner towers and the position of the central *miḥrāb* indicated on the exterior wall, precisely as in mosques. In the Ḳadam Sharīf [*q.v.*] at Dihlī the enclosure wall is fortified, as a measure of protection for the special relic; but the fortified rocky outcrop on which stands the tomb of Tughluḳ Shāh is primarily an extreme outpost of the fortifications of Tughluḳābād (plan at Vol. ii, p. 257 above). In Aḥmadābād the tombs of the queens of the Aḥmad Shāhī dynasty are enclosed in a large screened chamber (Rānī kā ḥudjra) which forms part of a royal precinct; a fine enclosed graveyard known as "Niẓām al-Dīn's" in Čānderī [*q.v.*] contains tombs and many individual *miḥrābs* from the early 9th/15th century with a rich design repertory. Some graveyards may contain one or more substantial mausoleums in addition to simple graves. An indication of the *ḳibla* may be provided, even in unenclosed graveyards, by one or more "*ḳibla* walls", with an odd number of arched necesses; individual mausoleums may also be provided with such a separate structure on the *ḳibla* side, or the enclosure wall may be modified in such a way as to incorporate one: e.g. the tomb of Sikandar Lodī in Dihlī has three arches and a raised platform in the west enclosure wall which presumably formed a *ḳanātī* mosque. A mausoleum very often has openings on three sides with the west wall solid to incorporate an internal *miḥrāb* (the tombs of the Barīd Shāhīs [*q.v.*], however, are regularly open on all four sides). The larger mausoleums may be provided with a full-scale mosque (without *minbar*), either replacing or in addition to an internal *miḥrāb*; Bīdjāpur [*q.v.*] provides many excellent examples, of which the Ibrāhīm Rawḍa is the finest example with tomb and mosque of similar proportions and sumptuous decoration standing on a common platform in an elaborate enclosure; the Tādj Maḥall [see MAḤALL] has not only a superb mosque on the *ḳibla* side but an identical building on the east essentially for the symmetry of the plan but incidentally to serve as a *mihmān-khāna*. (The converse arrangement, wherein a single tomb is subsidiary to a mosque, is common, especially when both have the same founder.) Some major mausolea, however, are without any indication of the *ḳibla* at all: e.g. Humāyūn's tomb at Dihlī (plan at Vol. ii, p. 265 above) has neither internal *miḥrāb* nor external mosque or other structure (the building on the west, where a mosque might be expected, is in fact the main gateway); although the enclosure wall on the south-east has a range of *exterior* arches which formed the *ḳibla* wall of the earlier "Nīlā gunbad". At some graveyards there is a special mortuary provided for the *ghassāls* to work in: outstanding examples at the graveyard of Afḍal Khān's wives at Bīdjāpur, and the tombs of the Ḳuṭb Shāhī kings at Golkonḍā. Some form of well is of course a common adjunct; a *bāʾolī* [*q.v.*] is commonly found included in a Čishtī dargāh complex, and occasionally elsewhere (e.g. within the fortified enclosure of the tomb of the "Sayyid" sultan Mubārak Shāh at Koflā Mubārakpur, Dihlī).

There has been no study of the typology of gravestones (i.e. the stone or brick structures above ground level, the *taʿwīdh*) in India as a whole, although many types with regional variation can be recognised. Djaʿfar Sharīf [*q.v.*], referring primarily to the Deccan, says that on a man's tomb, above the (commonly) three diminishing rectangular slabs, a top member is placed "resembling the hump on a camel's back, or the back of a fish", and adds that in north India tombs of men are distinguished by a small stone pencase (*ḳalamdān*) raised on the *flat* upper surface; but in fact both types can be seen side by side in Dihlī graveyards. The tombs of women are generally flat above the diminishing rectangular slabs, and more frequently in north India than in the Deccan may display a flat *takhtī*, in form like a child's slate, where those of men have the *ḳalamdān* (the explanation commonly given is that only males are literate and so can carry a pencase, whereas women have to have everything written for them!); in south India in particular a woman's tomb may have instead a basin-like hollow on the upper surface. The woman's tomb, given the same date and provenance, is lower than the man's. In the case of the larger mausoleums, this applies to the cenotaph *taʿwīdh* as much as to the *taʿwīdh* of the actual grave. There may be, in both men's and women's tombs, a mere stepped surround with the internal rectangular space filled with earth (e.g. grave of Awrangzēb at Khuldābād) or grass (e.g. grave of Djahānāra Bēgam, daughter of Shāhdjahān, within the *dargāh* of Niẓām al-Dīn Awliyāʾ at Dihlī, where however the surround and the enclosure are of white marble and there is an inscribed marble headstone; plan at Vol. ii, p. 263 above). This is much approved by the pious, but leads to quick decay of the structure if the grave is not attended. In parts of western India in particular a cylindrical boss may be found at the head of the tomb of a man, sometimes in addition to an inscribed headstone. In Gudjarāt the "casket" style of tomb is favoured, at least for the more exalted personages, in which a rectangular chamber with vertical sides, about a cubit high, rises from the base and is capped by the shallow diminishing rectangular slabs, finished flat in the case of women, arched or triangular in cross-section for men; they may have in addition cylindrical corner stones with vertical ribbing and two or three cross-mouldings. Dr Zajadacz-Hastenrath, describing similar forms in the Čawkhanḍī tombs, sees here a representation of the *čārpāʾī* (string bed) with rope lashings which would have been used as the bier. A *čirāghdān*, to carry lamps or on which fragrant substances may be burnt, may be placed at the head of or alongside any tomb; the actual grave may, in the case of the illustrious, be covered with a pall kept in place by ornamental weights (*mīr-i farsh*). The tomb of a *pīr* may be marked also by a white (or green in the case of a sayyid) triangular flag carried on a tall bamboo, especially in country districts.

It is only in the case of the remarkable Čawkhandī tombs that anything like a systematic study has been made (Salome Zajadacz-Hastenrath, *Chaukhandigräber: Studien zur Grabkunst in Sind und Baluchistan*, Wiesbaden 1978). In the most characteristic (but not the only) style one, two or three diminishing rectangular hollow "caskets" are superimposed, and are capped by a final slab set vertically on edge. The cylindrical boss at the head may be added in the case of males. They are richly carved, either with geometrical patterns (the author gives ten plates of "Steinmetzmuster" alone), flowers, whorls, *miḥrāb*-like blind arches, swords, bows, and even the figure of a horseman carrying a spear, sometimes led by an attendant. Similar carvings (or paintings on wood) are reported in Crooke's ed. of Dja'far Sharīf (ref. below) from Afghānistān, Kurdistān, and the Orakzay Paṭhāns; this ethnological aspect stands in need of further investigation.

A curious class of tomb, sparsely but widely distributed, is that of the "nine-yard saints", *naw gaz pīr*, usually ascribed to warrior saints of the earliest days of Islam in India. Many of these have the reputation of miraculously extending their length over the ages. (Miracles are reported at other tombs: lumps of silver in the pavement of the *dargāh* of Muntadjib al-Dīn "Zar Bakhsh" at Khuldābād are said to be the remains of silver trees which grew after the saint's death, which were broken off for the upkeep of the shrine; hairs from the Prophet's beard at the same place are said to increase in number yearly.) Many tombs have the reputation of curing various ailments through the thaumaturgic power of a *pīr* persisting; e.g. women still tie ribbons on the lattice screens on the tomb of Salīm Čishtī at Fatḥpur Sikrī as a cure for barrenness. (The virtue is not confined to Muslims: I have seen an obviously Hindū woman making oblations at the tomb of the Ḳādirī brothers at Bīdjāpur.)

Tombs may bear inscriptions (and inscribed tombs, from reverence for the written word, stand a better chance of being looked after in later years): on the *ta'wīdh* itself sometimes simply a name and date of decease, more often the *kalima* or Ḳur'ānic verses such as the *Āyat al-kursī*, II.256, the conclusion of II.157, or the very end of Sūra II; there may be, especially with the tombs of men in Gudjarāt, a sizeable headstone with a more elaborate epitaph; but so many tombstones are devoid of any information on the deceased that many obviously major mausolea cannot be now identified. The cenotaph of Akbar, of white marble, is inscribed on the sides with the ninety-nine Names of God, and on the ends the Dīn-i Ilāhī formulae *Allāh^{u} Akbar* and *Djalla djalālah^{u}*. On the *ta'wīdh* of Djahāngīr the Names are inscribed in *pietra dura*. Often in the case of mausolea an inscription is placed within the entrance or on a wall, and copious Ḳur'ānic texts may be inscribed on the façade, e.g. at the Tādj Maḥall.

The graves above belong to the mainstream tradition of Islamic art, which may be described as the "Greater Tradition"; graves of a "Lesser Tradition", belonging to a stream of folk-art, have been observed in Gilgit, Punial, the Swāt valley and the Yūsufzay country, and may have a more extensive area. These, which do not always distinguish between the graves of males and females, have a crude indication of the north-south axis marked by slabs of stone, or by wooden planks which may be carved into various shapes, or by turned wooden posts; they may also be surrounded by an open wooden framework which, it is suggested, represents the bier inverted over the sepulture, and may be analogous to the *čārpā'ī* representations in the Čawkhandī tombs. A fuller description, with map and drawings, in J. Burton-Page, *Muslim graves of the "Lesser Tradition": Gilgit, Punial, Swat, Yusufzai*, in *JRAS* (1986).

The typology of the mausoleum is too complicated for any but the simplest treatment here; further information is provided in the articles HIND. vii. Architecture, MUGHALS: Architecture, and on the various regional dynasties. The simplest type, in that it provides a covered place over the *ta'wīdh*, is the *čhatrī* [see MIẒALLA], a single dome supported on pillars; those covering a square or octagonal area are the commonest, although the hexagonal plan is known. From the use of the umbrella in both Buddhist and Hindū funerary practices, there is possibly here a persistence of an eschatological idea (but the Hindū use of the *čhatrī* to mark the site of a cremation, so common with the Rādjpūt rulers at e.g. Udaypur and Djaypur, is a borrowing back from Muslim forms). Even with this simplest type there is the possibility of the common principle that a funeral building (or its site; cf. the tomb of Tughluḳ Shāh mentioned above) might be intended for a different purpose during its owner's lifetime. An elaboration is to support a square roof on twelve pillars, thereby furnishing three openings on each side as well as making possible a larger area (this type of building, *bāradarī*, is also of wide secular use for pleasaunces). Filling in the openings with stone screens (*djālī*), leaving an entrance on each side, is frequently practised, although as noticed above the western side is often completely closed to provide an indication of *ḳibla*; Tomb 2 at Thālnēr [*q.v.*; see plan of tombs] is a *bāradarī* whose sides have been filled in with purpose-cut masonry. An extension of this type is characteristic of Gudjarāt, whereby both an inner chamber and a surrounding veranda are provided with screened walls; after the Mughal conquest of Gudjarāt tombs of this type are found in north India, e.g. those of Muḥammad Ghawth at Gwālyār, Salīm Čishtī at Fatḥpur Sikrī. When a tomb is given greater prominence by being raised on a plinth, the sepulchral chamber may be placed at earth level in a *tahkhāna*, with a cenotaph *ta'wīdh* immediately above it on an upper floor; but where this applies to the principal inhumation at a large mausoleum, it is not practised for later and subsidiary burials, and is not held to be required for burials within a raised mosque *ṣaḥn*. The preponderant form of the masonry mausoleum is a square chamber surmounted by a dome; an idiosyncratic type occurs in the royal Bahmanī tombs (Haft Gunbad) at Gulbargā [*q.v.*], where two square domed chambers are conjoined on a single plinth (the sultan in one chamber, his immediate family adjoining); but the octagonal form [see MUTHAMMAN] is also known from the 8th/14th century (popular for royal tombs of the "Sayyid" and Lodī dynasties, tombs of *pīrs* at Multān and Uččh [*qq.v.*], nobles of the Sūr dynasty [see especially SHĒR SHĀH SŪRĪ], and not infrequently in Mughal times); in the earliest monumental tomb, that of Nāṣir al-Dīn Maḥmūd ("Sulṭān Ghārī") at Dihlī, the plinth of the structure accommodates a vaulted octagonal sepulchral chamber. In two of the Sūrī tombs at Sasarām [*q.v.*] the mausoleum stands in the middle of an artificial lake, approached by a gateway and causeway; the idea recurs in the Mughal period with fine but anonymous examples at

Iʿtimādpur, near Āgrā, and Nārnawl [*q.v.*], where the idea of a pleasaunce for use in the lifetime of the subject seems patent. Mughal mausolea introduce new plans: the oblong, the square or oblong with chamfered corners to produce a "Baghdādī octagon" (e.g. the Tādj Maḥall), a square chamber with engaged corner rooms (e.g. Humāyūn's tomb, tomb of ʿAbd al-Raḥīm Khānkhānān) or engaged corner turrets (e.g. tomb of Ṣafdar Djang). They may also incorporate independent symmetricaly disposed minarets (see MANĀRA, 2. India), and may stand within a formal garden (see BŪSTĀN, and further references in MĀʾ, 12). The wooden tombs of Kashmīr do not fall into any of the above categories, and are described under ZIYĀRA.

Bibliography: In addition to references in the article and the Bibliographies to other articles cited: for graveside requirements and practices see DJANĀZA; Djaʿfar Sharīf, *Ḳānūn-i Islām*, Eng. tr. as *Herklots' Islam in India*, ed. W. Crooke, Oxford 1921, esp. ch. ix, "Death"; W. Crooke, *Popular religion and folklore of northern India*, Allahabad 1894, Chap. iv, "The worship of the sainted dead", which has illuminating references to Hindū-Muslim syncretisms. F. Wetzel, *Islamische Grabbauten in Indien in der Zeit der Soldatenkaiser*, Leipzig 1918, provides a typological framework for the study of monumental tombs of the Dihlī sultanate, rich in plans and sections. T. Yamamoto, M. Ara and T. Tsukinowa, *Delhi: architectural remains of the Delhi sultanate period*, i, Tokyo 1967, describe (in Japanese) and illustrate 142 monumental tombs and 72 graveyards of Dihlī, excellent photographs; idem, ii, Tokyo 1968, analyse in depth several of the same monumental tombs. Some good illustrations of "Niẓām al-Dīn's graveyard" at Čāndērī in R. Nath, *The art of Chanderi*, Delhi 1979. Much of the information above is based on a personal photographic collection, which will eventually be housed in Victoria and Albert Museum, London.

(J. BURTON-PAGE)

MAḲBŪL IBRĀHĪM PASHA, [see IBRĀHĪM PASHA].

MAḲDISHŪ, the capital of the Somali Republic, independent since 1960, comprising the former Italian Somalia and British Somaliland, lies in lat. 2° N. on the East African shore of the Indian Ocean.

Although it is not specifically mentioned in the *Periplus of the Erythraean Sea* (*ca.* A.D. 106), this Alexandrine report attests the presence of Arab and Egyptian traders on the coast. The principal exports were cinnamon, frankincense, tortoise-shell and "slaves of the better sort, which are brought to Egypt in increasing numbers." Recent excavations at Rās Ḥāfūn by H. N. Chittick, as yet unpublished, disclosed Egyptian pottery of Roman Imperial date, probably 2nd to 3rd century A.D. Apart from some ruins of uncertain date that are possibly South Arabian, Maḳdishū is stated by a 16th century *Chrónica dos Reyes de Quiloa*, preserved in a summary form by João de Barros, to have been founded by "the first people of the coast who came to the land of Sofala [*q.v.*] in quest of gold." This date is uncertain, but it was at some time between the 10th and 12th centuries A.D., when the Sofala gold trade became the monopoly of Kilwa (Port. Quiloa) [see KILWA]. It is not to be thought that there was any single immigration of Arabs; rather, they came in trickles, and from different regions of the Arabian peninsula; the most remarkable one came from al-Aḥsā on the Gulf, probably during the struggles of the caliphate with the Ḳarmaṭians. Probably at the same time, Persian groups emigrated to Maḳdishū, for inscriptions found in the town refer to Persians from Shīrāz and Naysābūr dwelling there during the Middle Ages. The foreign merchants, however, found themselves obliged to unite politically against the nomadic, Somali, tribes that surrounded Maḳdishū, and against invaders from the sea. In the 10th century A.D. a federation was formed of 39 clans: 12 from the Muḳrī tribe; 12 from the Djidʿatī tribe; 6 from the ʿAḳabi, 6 from the Ismāʿīlī and 3 from the ʿAfīfī. Under conditions of internal peace, trade developed; and the Muḳrī clans, after acquiring a religious supremacy and adopting the *nisba* of al-Ḳaḥṭānī, formed a kind of dynasty of *ʿulamāʾ* and obtained from the other tribes the privilege that the *ḳāḍī* of the federation should be elected only from among themselves. It is not known at what period Islam became established, but the earliest known dated inscription in Arabic in Somalia is an epitaph at Barāwa of 498/1105.

In the second half of the 7th/12th century, Abū Bakr b. Fakhr al-Dīn established in Maḳdishū an hereditary sultanate with the aid of the Muḳrī clans, to whom the new ruler recognised again the privilege of giving the *ḳāḍī* to the town. In 722/1322-3 the ruler was Abū Bakr b. Muḥammad: in that year he struck dated billon coins in his name, but without title. During the reign of Abū Bakr b. ʿUmar, Maḳdishū was visited by Ibn Baṭṭūṭa, who describes the town in his *Riḥla*. The relationship of this sultan with his predecessors is not known, but he was probably from the family of Abū Bakr b. Fakhr al-Dīn; and under this dynasty Maḳdishū reached, in the 8th/14th and 9th/15th centuries, the highest degree of prosperity. Its name is quoted in the *Maṣḥafa Milād*, a work by the Ethiopian ruler Zareʾa Yāʿḳob, who refers to a battle fought against him at Gomut, or Gomit, in Dawaro by the Muslims on 25 December 1445. To these centuries are to be ascribed, in addition to the billon coins issued by Abū Bakr b. Muḥammad, the undated copper issues of ten rulers whose names are commemorated on their coins, but whose sequence even is not known. They are linked by a simularity of script, weight, type and appearance, and certain of the issues share with contemporary Kilwa issues a reverse legend contrived to rhyme with the obverse. To this period belongs also the foundation of the three principal mosques in Maḳdishū, all dated by inscriptions, the Friday Mosque in 636/1238, that of Arbaʿ Rukūn in 667/1268, and that of Fakhr al-Dīn in Shaʿbān 667/April-May 1269. Their handsome proportions witness to the prosperity of the times there.

In the 10th/16th century, the Fakhr al-Dīn dynasty was succeeded by that of Muẓaffar. It is possible that one copper issue refers to a ruler of this dynasty. In the region of the Wēbi Shabēllä, the true commercial hinterland of Maḳdishū, the Adjurān (Sōmālī), who had constituted there another sultanate which was friendly with and allied to Maḳdishū, were defeated by the nomadic Hawiya (Sōmālī), who thus conquered the territory. In this way, Maḳdishū was separated by the nomads from the interior, and began to decline from its prosperity, a process which was hastened by Portuguese colonial enterprise in the Indian Ocean and later by the Italians and the British. When Vasco da Gama returned from his first voyage to India in 1499, he attacked Maḳdishū, but without success; and similarly in 1507 Da Cunha failed to occupy it. In 1532 Estavão da Gama, son of Vasco, came there to buy a ship. In 1585 Maḳdishū surrendered to the Ottoman *amīr* ʿAlī Bey, who came down the coast in that year with two galleys as far as

ADDENDA AND CORRIGENDA

VOLUME I

P. 56^{b}, **ʿABD al-ʿAZĪZ**, l. 4, *instead of* 20 June *read* 26 June.
P. 75^{a}, **ʿABD al-MADJĪD** I, l. 39, *instead of* 25 June *read* 26 June.
P. 106^{a-b}, **ABU ʾl-ʿARAB**, *add*: One of the works of Abu ʾl-ʿArab Muḥammad b. Aḥmad b. Tamīm b. Tammām b. Tamīm al-Tamīmī (thus the full *nasab*) which has been preserved (in a unique Cambridge ms.) is his *Kitāb al-Miḥan*, a work in the tradition of the *maḳātil* books. It deals with a wide range of deaths in battle, by poisoning, persecution of ʿAlids, sufferings of Aḥmad b. Ḥanbal in the *miḥna* [*q.v.*] of the early 3rd/9th century; see for an analysis of its contents, M. J. Kister, *The "Kitab al-Mihan", a book on Muslim martyrology*, in *JSS*, xx (1975), 210-18. The complete work has now been edited by Yaḥyā Wahīb al-Djabbūrī, Beirut 1403/1983.
P. 279^{a}, **AḤMAD b. ṬŪLŪN**, end of penultimate paragraph, *instead of* March 884 *read* May 884.
P. 940^{b}, **BAHRĀM SHĀH, al-MALIK al-AMDJAD**, l. 2, *instead of* Shāhānshāh read Tūrānshāh.
P. 1030^{b}, **BARĀDŪST**, l. 37, *instead of* 395/1005 *read* 1005/1597.
P. 1300^{a}, **BULANDSHAHR**, l. 30, *instead of* 644/1246-665/1266 *read* 796-815/1394-1412.

VOLUME II

P. 72^{b}, **DĀBIḲ**, paragraph three, l. 2, *instead of* 15 Radjab 922 *read* 25 Radjab 922.
P. 809^{a}, **FARRUKHĀN**, l. 5 from bottom, *instead of* seventy years *read* thirteen years (90-103/709-21).

VOLUME III

P. 134^{a}, al-**ḤAMĪDĪ**, l. 24 from bottom, *instead of* 364/974-5, *read* 564/1168-9.
P. 1196^{a}, **IN SHĀʾ ALLĀH**, l. 2 from below, *instead of* James, iv, 19 *read* James, iv, 13-15.

VOLUME IV

P. 754^{b}, **ḲAṬĪʿA**, *add to end*: The term *ḳaṭīʿa* is also used in the specific sense of "ransom" in the period of the Crusades; cf. al-Ṣafadī, *Wāfī*, xiii, 505.

VOLUME V

P. 1029^{b}, al-**MADJDJĀWĪ**, l. 4, *instead of* Algiers, *read* Constantine.
P. 1135^{b}, **MADRASA**, *add. to the Bibl.*: R. Brunschvig, *Quelques remarques sur les médersas de Tunisie*, in *RT*, new ser., vi (1931), 261-85.
P. 1232^{a}, al-**MAHDĪ**: ll. 33-48. This passage was modified by the Editors without the author's consent. The author's original should be restored as follows:
This *ḥadīth*, whose first part is patterned upon the revolt of ʿAbd Allāh b. al-Zubayr, probably goes back to ʿAbd Allāh b. al-Ḥārith b. Nawfal b. al-Ḥārith b. ʿAbd al-Muṭṭalib, who appears in its *isnād* and claimed to have heard it from Umm Salama, widow of the Prophet. ʿAbd Allāh b. al-Ḥārith was chosen by the people of Baṣra as their governor in 64/684 after the death of the caliph Yazīd and the flight of his governor ʿUbayd Allāh b. Ziyād. He then recognised Ibn al-Zubayr as the caliph and took the pledge of allegiance of the Baṣrans for him. The *ḥadīth* was evidently proclaimed by him in this situation with the aim of stirring up support for the cause of Ibn al-Zubayr.

VOLUME VI

P. 125^{b}, **MAḲBARA**, *add to Bibliography*: J.-L. Bacqué-Grammont, H.-P. Laqueur, N. Vatin, *Stelae Turcicae*, I: *Küçük Ayasofya*, in *Istanbuler Mitteilungen* xxxiv (1984), 441-539.

SUPPLEMENT

P. 127^{a}, **BĀRIZ, DJABAL**, *add*: One should note the present-day settlement of Pārīz, in the northwestern part of the Djabal Bāriz, on the Rafsandjān-Saʿīdābād (Sīrdjān) road, which could possibly be the classical *Parikānē polis*, town of the Parikanioi. See A. D. H. Bivar, *A Persian fairyland*, in *Acta Iranica* 24: *Hommages et opera minora* X: *Papers in honour of Professor Mary Boyce*, Leiden 1985, 25-42, who here derives the legends and romances around the peris or fairies of Iran (Av. *pairikā*, MP *parīg*, NP *parī*) from indigenous Persian traditions connecting them with the Parikanioi, whose epigoni were suspect in Sāsānid times by Zoroastrian orthodoxy for their non-Zoroastrian local beliefs and customs, hence equated with demonic and supernatural beings.

ISBN 90 04 08311 1

PRINTED IN THE NETHERLANDS

Early Mahdism

Politics and Religion in the Formative Period of Islam

by

JAN-OLAF BLICHFELDT

(Studia Orientalia Lundensia, 21)

1985. (xi, 137 p.) **Gld. 48.—**
ISBN 90 04 07643 3

The belief in a restorer of religion and justice who will rule in the period preceding the end of the world forms an integral part both of Sunnī and Shīʿī Islam to this day. The notion of this restorer, or Mahdī, emerged shortly after Mohammed's death. Much attention has so far been paid to Islamic theological literature on this subject, but there have been few attempts at understanding the birth and early development of Mahdism in its historical context.

On the basis of a detailed examination of the early religio-political history of Islam the author demonstrates the importance of contemporary political and social conditions as determinants of the birth hour and the characteristic features of Mahdism.

The book throws much new light on Mahdism and its origins. It will be of interest both to students of Islam and early Islamic history and of religion in general.

Der Islam im Spiegel zeitgenössischer Literatur der islamischen Welt

Vorträge eines Internationalen Symposiums an der Universität Bern 11.-14. Juli 1983

Herausgegeben von

J. C. BÜRGEL

in Verbindung mit

MARIANNE CHENOU — MICHAEL GLÜNZ — MARGUERITE REUT

1985. (xi, 305 p.) (T) **Gld. 90.—**
ISBN 90 04 07707 3

Inhalt

J. C. Bürgel, Größe und Grenzen gewaltlosen Handelns. Aktualisierung islamischer Mystik in einem modernen türkischen Drama; *P. Cachia*, In a glass darkly. The faintness of Islamic inspiration in modern Arabic literature; *P. Chelkowski*, Islam in modern drama and theatre; *W. Ende*, Wer ist ein Glaubensheld, wer ist ein Ketzer? Konkurrierende Geschichtsbilder in der modernen Literatur islamischer Länder; *H. Fähndrich*, Andere Prioritäten? Weniges Islamisches in einigen palästinensischen Prosawerken; *G. Kraft*, Zum Gottesbegriff in der türkischen Lyrik der kemalistischen Ära; *J. Marek*, The impact of Islamic culture on Urdu drama; *N. Naderpour*, Une contradiction: l'âme iranienne et l'esprit islamique; *C. Nijland*, Naguib Mahfouz and Islam. An analysis of some novels; *J. Oliverius*, Der traditionelle Islam in der Konfrontation mit den sozialen Umwandlungen auf dem algerischen Lande. ʿAbdalḥamīd Benhadūqas Roman *Rīḥ al-ǧanūb*; *A. Schimmel*, Das Ḥallāj-Motiv in der modernen islamischen Literatur; *K. Skarżyńska-Bocheńska*, Le reflet de l'islam dans la poésie tunisienne contemporaine; *F. Steppat*, Konfessionalismus im libanesischen Roman: Taufīq Yūsuf ʿAwwāds *Ṭawāhīn Bairūt*; *N. Tomiche*, Procédés d'ironie dans le traitement des valeurs traditionnelles et modernes dans la littérature arabe actuelle; *W. Walther*, Von Sozialkritik bis Mystik. Der Islam im Spiegel irakischer Erzählliteratur; *R. Wielandt*, Die Bewertung islamischen Volksglaubens in ägyptischer Erzählliteratur des 20. Jahrhunderts; *S. Wild*, Judentum, Christentum und Islam in der palästinensischen Poesie; *F. Baykurt*, Die neue Moschee. Erzählung.

Sonderdruck aus der Zeitschrift „Die Welt des Islams", N.S. Bd. XXIII und XXIV.

THE ENCYCLOPAEDIA OF ISLAM

NEW EDITION

PREPARED BY A NUMBER OF
LEADING ORIENTALISTS

EDITED BY

C. E. BOSWORTH, E. VAN DONZEL, B. LEWIS AND CH. PELLAT
ASSISTED BY F. TH. DIJKEMA AND MME S. NURIT

UNDER THE PATRONAGE OF
THE INTERNATIONAL UNION OF ACADEMIES

VOLUME VI

FASCICULES 101—102

MAḲDISHŪ — MALḤŪN

LEIDEN
E. J. BRILL
1987

All correspondence on editorial matters should be addressed to the Editorial Secretaries, whose addresses are:

For the English Edition

Dept. of Near Eastern Studies,
The University of Manchester,
Manchester,
England M13 9PL.

For the French Edition

13, rue de Santeuil
75231 Paris Cedex 05
France

AUTHORS OF ARTICLES IN THESE FASCICULES

Names in square brackets are those of authors of articles reprinted or revised from the first edition of this Encyclopaedia.

This fascicule was published with financial support of the British Academy, London.

Mombasa; all along the coast, the suzerainty of the Ottoman Sultan was recognised. In 1587, however, the Portuguese re-asserted their authority with a strong fleet, but no attempt was made to attack Maḳdishū. The vials of their wrath fell on Faza, where large numbers of people were slaughtered and 10,000 palm trees destroyed. ʿAlī Bey returned with five ships in 1589, but, although the coast again declared for the Ottomans, he was himself defeated and captured in Mombasa harbour, from which he was deported to Lisbon. Although this was the end of Ottoman attacks on the eastern African coast, at Maḳdishū new copper coins were issued by no less than eleven rulers. All these bear a *ṭughrā* in imitation of Ottoman coinage, and are probably to be ascribed to the 10th/16th to 11th/17th centuries.

In 1700 a British squadron of men-of-war halted before Maḳdishū for several days, but without landing. After the ʿUmānī Arabs had taken Mombasa from the Portuguese in 1698 Maḳdishū and other towns on the Sōmālī coast were occupied at uncertain dates, but after a while their troops were ordered back to ʿUmān. The sultanate of Maḳdishū continued to decline, and the town was divided into two quarters, Ḥamar-Wēn and Shangānī, by civil wars. Little by little the Sōmālī penetrated into the ancient Arabian town, and the clans of Maḳdishū changed their Arabic names for Sōmālī appellatives: the ʿAḳabī became the rēr Shēkh, the Djidʿatī the Shanshiya, the ʿAfīfī the Gudmanä, and even the Muḳrī (Ḳaḥṭanī) changed their name to rēr Faḳīh. In the 12th/18th century the Darandollä nomads, excited by exaggerated traditions of urban wealth, attacked and conquered the town. The Darandollä chief, who had the title of *imām*, set himself up in the Shangānī quarter, and once again the Ḳaḥṭānī privilege of electing the *ḳāḍī* was recognised. In 1823 Sayyid Saʿīd of ʿUmān attempted to assert his authority over Maḳdishū, and arrested two of the notables. It was not until 1843 that he was able to appoint a governor. He chose a Sōmālī, but the new governor shortly retired inland to his own people. When Charles Guillain visited Maḳdishū in 1848, he found only "an old Arab" who presided over the customs house. Guillain's fourth volume, an *Album*, contains some admirable engravings of Maḳdishū at this period which have been reproduced in Cerulli's work. It was only at the end of the century, during the reign of Saʿīd's son Barghash (1870-88), that Zanzibari authority was finally established over Maḳdishū, only to be ceded to Italy, along with Barāwa, Merca and Warsheikh, for an annual rent of 160,000 rupees, in 1892.

Bibliography: Yāḳūt, i, 502; Ibn Baṭṭūṭa, *Riḥla*, ii, 183, ed. Cairo 1322, i, 190; J. de Barros, *Da Ásia*, Decade i, iv, xi, and 1.viii, iv, 1552; F. S. Caroselli, *Museo della Garesa: Catalogo: Mogadiscio* 1934; De Castanhoso, *Dos feitos de Dom Christovam da Gama*, ed. Esteves Pereira, Lisbon 1898, p. xi; E. Cerulli, *Somalia, scritti vari editi ed inediti*, i, Rome 1957 (reprinting earlier articles on Somalia); H. N. Chittick and R. I. Rotberg, *East Africa and the Orient*, New York 1975; Gaspar Correa, *Lendas da India*, Lisbon 1858-66, t.i, vol. ii, 678; t. iii, vol. ii, 458, 540; Diogo do Couto, *Decadas da Asia*, Lisbon 1778, dec. iv., 1.viii, cap. ii; G.S.P. Freeman-Grenville, *Coins from Mogadishu, c. 1300 to c. 1700*, in *Numismatic Chronicle* (1963); idem and B. G. Martin, *A preliminary handlist of the Arabic inscriptions of the Eastern African coast*, in *JRAS* (1973); C. Guillain, *Documents sur l'histoire, la géographie et le commerce de l'Afrique orientale*, Paris 1856, i; I. M. Lewis, *The modern history of Somaliland*, London 1965; C. Conti Rossini, *Vasco da Gama, Pedralvarez Cabral e Giovanni da Nova nella Cronica di Kilwah*, in *Atti del 3° Congresso geografico Italiano*, ii, Florence 1899; idem, *Studi su populazioni dell'Etiopa*, in *RSC*, vi, 367, n. 2; S. A. Strong, *History of Kilwa*, in *JRAS* (1895); A. Nègre, *A propos de Mogadiscio au moyen âge*, in *Annales de l'Univ. du Benin*, ii (Nov.-Dec. 1975), 175-200, repr. in *Annales de l'Univ. d'Abidjan*, Série 1, vol. v (1977), 5-38.

(E. Cerulli - [G. S. P. Freeman-Grenville])

AL-**MAḲDISI** [see AL-MUḲADDASĪ; AL-MUṬAHHAR B. ṬĀHIR]

MAKHAČ-ḲALʿE (Russ. Makhačkala), a town on the western coast of the Caspian Sea at the point where the narrow coastal plain running north from Bākū and Derbend [*q.v.*], at the eastern extremity of the Caucasus range, debouches into the Nogay Steppe. The present name of what is now (since 1921) the chef-lieu of the Dagestan A.S.S.R. is neither Islamic nor of any great antiquity, reflecting the eponym of a local revolutionary leader Muḥammad ʿAlī Dakhadayev (d. 1918), but Makhač-ḳalʿe stands on or near the site of a number of places significant in the mediaeval history of the Caucasus: Balanghar (= Arm. Varačʿan), the capital of the Hun tributaries of the Khazar kingdom (J. Marquart, *Osteuropäische und ostasiatische Streifzüge*, Leipzig 1903, 16: Samandar, "four (eight) days march from Derbend"); and Ṭarkhū/Ṭarḳī, briefly occupied by the Ottomans in the late 10th/16th century. The present town may be traced back to the Russian foundation of Petrovsk, known subsequently as Temīr-Khān-Shūrā and (in the years 1917-20) as Shāmil-ḳalʿe.

Bibliography: O. Pritsak, in *Harvard Jnl. of Ukrainian Studies*, ii (1978), 263; A. Bennigsen and H. Carrère d'Encausse, in *REI* (1955), 7-56 (with details of the ethnic composition of Makhač-kalʿe); *İA*, art. *Dâğistân* (Mirza Bala); *EI²*, art. *Dāghistān* (W. Barthold-[A. Bennigsen]); *BSE²*, s.vv. *Makhač*, *Makhačkala*. (C. J. Heywood)

MAKHĀRIDJ AL-ḤURŪF (A.), "the places of emission of the letters", i.e. the points of articulation of the phonemes of Arabic. The singular may be either *makhradj*, noun of place from form I of the verb *kharadja* "go forth, be emitted", or else *mukhradj*, passive participle of form IV *akhradja* "emit, send forth" serving as the noun of place. The word *ḥurūf* (sing. *ḥarf*) denotes both the graphic elements of the language (= letters) and the phonetic ones (= consonants and vowels) which they represent.

The first description which we possess of the points of articulation of the 29 Arabic phonemes is that of al-Khalīl (d. 175/791 [*q.v.*]) in his *K. al-ʿAyn* (ed. Anastase al-Karmalī, Baghdād 1914, 4, 11. 8-9). This description is given according to two classifications, which present certain differences. In the first, al-Khalīl enumerates, going from the throat towards the lips, 10 zones (*ḥayyiz*) of articulation, each of these comprising several degrees (*madradja*):

1. The pectoral cavity (*djawf*) and air (*hawāʾ*); the sounds made in the cavity or made with the air *wāw*, *yāʾ*, *alif* and *hamza*.
2. The back (*aḳṣā*) part of the throat (*ḥalḳ*): the gutturals *ʿayn*, *ḥāʾ* and *hāʾ*.
3. The fore (*adnā*) part of the throat: the gutturals *khāʾ* and *ghayn*.
4. The uvula (*lahāt*): the uvular sounds *ḳāf* and *kāf*.
5. The side (*shadjr*) of the mouth: the laterals *djīm*, *shīn* and *ḍād*.
6. The apex (*asala*) of the tongue: the apical sounds *ṣād*, *sīn* and *zāy*.
7. The alveoles (*niṭʿ*) of the palate: the alveolars *ṭāʾ*, *dāl* and *tāʾ*.
8. The gum (*litha*): the gingivals *ẓāʾ*, *dhāl* and *thāʾ*.

9. The tip (*dhawlaḳ*) of the tongue: the sounds pronounced at the tip of the tongue *rā*ʾ, *lām* and *nūn*.
10. The lips (*shifā*): the labials *fā*ʾ, *bā*ʾ and *mīm*.

In the second classification, less detailed than the first, al-Khalīl enumerates them in the opposite way, i.e. from the lips to the throat, but with only six articulatory zones:

1. The lips: *fā*ʾ, *bā*ʾ and *mīm*.
2. The tip of the tongue and the extremity (*ṭaraf*) of the palate (*ghār*): *rā*ʾ, *lām* and *nūn*.
3. The back (*ẓahr*) of the tongue and the zone going from the interior (*bāṭin*) of the middle incisors (*thanāyā*) to the palate: *thā*ʾ to *shīn*.
4. The back part of the mouth, between the root (ʿ*akada*) of the tongue and the uvula: *djīm*, *ḳāf* and *kāf*.
5. The throat: ʿ*ayn*, *ḥā*ʾ, *khā*ʾ and *ghayn*.
6. The back part of the throat: *hamza*.

It will be noted that, in this scheme of classification, the place of emission of the *djīm* is placed with that of *kāf* (which might suppose a realisation as *gīm*), and that that of *wāw*, *yā*ʾ and *alif* is not given with precision, whilst that of the *hamza* is placed in the throat.

The second description of the points of articulation of the phonemes of Arabic is provided for us by Sībawayhi (d. *ca.* 180/796 [*q.v.*] in his *Kitāb* (ed. H. Dérenbourg, Paris 1889, ii, 452-3). In this, Sībawayhi enumerates, going from the throat towards the lips, 16 places of emission of the sounds:

1. The back part of the throat: *hamza*, *hā*ʾ and *alif*.
2. Its middle part (*awsaṭ*): ʿ*ayn* and *ḥā*ʾ.
3. Its fore part: *ghayn* and *khā*ʾ.
4. The back part of the tongue and palate (*ḥanak*): *ḳāf*.
5. A little lower (*asfal*) than the place (*mawḍi*ʿ) of the *ḳāf*: *kāf*.
6. The middle part of the tongue and the middle part of the palate: *djīm*, *shīn* and *yā*ʾ.
7. The beginning of the edge (*ḥāffa*) of the tongue and its molars (*aḍrās*): *ḍād*.
8. The edge of the tongue, from its forward part to its extremity, and the palate, a little bit below the pre-molar (*ḍāḥik*), the caninc tooth (*nāb*) and the incisors (*rabā*ʿ*iyya* and *thaniyya*): *lām*.
9. The tip of the tongue and a little bit below the middle incisors: *nūn*.
10. The same position, but a little further towards the inner part of the back of the tongue: *rā*ʾ.
11. The tip of the tongue and the bases (*uṣūl*) of the middle incisors: *ṭā*ʾ, *dāl* and *tā*ʾ.
12. The tip of the tongue and a little bit above the middle incisors: *zāy*, *sīn* and *ṣād*.
13. The tip of the tongue and the tips of the middle incisors: *ẓā*ʾ, *dhāl* and *thā*ʾ.
14. The inside of the lower lip and the tips of the upper middle incisors: *fā*ʾ.
15. The two lips: *bā*ʾ, *nūn* and *wāw*.
16. The nasal cavities (*khayāshīm*): nun realised lightly (*khafīfa*).

The most important difference between the description of al-Khalīl and that of Sībawayhi lies in the fact that al-Khalīl indicates the place of emission of *wāw* and *yā*ʾ realised as long vowels (*ū* and *ī*), whereas Sībawayhi indicates these places of emission realised as consonants (*w* and *y*).

It was Sībawayhi's description which was to prevail for all the later grammarians, in whose works it is found cited en bloc, sometimes with a few variations. Thus al-Mubarrad (*K. al-Muḳtaḍab*, Cairo 1963, i, 192-3) separates the place of emission of *shīn* from that of *djīm*, and names the place of emission of *ḍād* by a word which denotes the corner of the mouth (*shidḳ*).

One should finally note that the *makhāridj al-ḥurūf* have been the subject of a very interesting study by a Moroccan scholar, Muḥammad b. ʿAbd al-Salām al-Fāsī (1717-99), in his commentary on the *Lāmiyya* of Abu 'l-Ḳāsim al-Shāṭibī.

Bibliography: J. Cantineau, *Cours de phonétique arabe*, in *Études de linguistique arabe*, Paris 1960, 1-125; H. Fleisch, *Études de phonétique arabe*, in *MUSJ*, xxviii (1949), 225-85; idem, *La conception phonétique des Arabes*, in *ZDMG*, cviii (1958), 74-105; idem, *Traité de philologie arabe*, i, Beirut 1969, 51-70; G. Troupeau, *Le commentaire d'al-Sīrāfī sur le chap. 265 du Kitāb*, in *Arabica*, v (1958), 168-82; A. Roman, *Le système consonantique de la koinè arabe d'après le Kitāb de Sībawayhi*, in *CLOS*, ix (1977), 63-98; idem, *Les zones d'articulation de la koinè arabe d'après l'enseignement d'al-Ḫalīl*, in *Arabica*, xxiv (1977), 58-65. (G. Troupeau)

MAKHDŪM-I DJAHĀNIYĀN. [see DJALĀL BUKHĀRĪ].

MAKHDŪM ḲULĪ "Firāḳī", perhaps rather Makhtūm Ḳulī (local forms Magtïmkulï and Fragï), a prominent 18th century Turkmen poet (1733?-1782?).Much of the information about this poet is obscure, and sources are unreliable. Among the 10,000 lines ascribed to him, a substantial amount must certainly be considered spurious, invalidating their informative value. Moreover, it is unclear whether the events alluded to have a real historical significance or are merely literary devices. Hence it is uncertain whether he was really born in the Gürgen River region, studied at the Shīrghāzī and Kökildāsh *madrasas* in Khīwa and Bukhārā respectively, worked for a time as a silversmith and a cobbler, bewailed a brother, who had disappeared into captivity in Persia (where he himself had suffered too), lost an infant son and was separated from his love. However, there is a personal flavour in the relevant descriptions. Such uncertainties are often met with when discussing major Turkmen poets.

It does however seem that he was a son of Dawlat Muḥammad "Āzādī", that he travelled widely, and that he was well versed in classical Persian and Turkish letters as well as in the folk literature of Central Asia, Iran and Ādharbāydjān. A master of the elevated style and technique, he nevertheless introduced popular forms, such as syllabic quatrains, into Turkmen poetry. He wrote fiery patriotic verses during the warfare between the Turkmens, Iran and Khīwa. His lyrical and didactic (not epic, and—though Yasawī-like elements spring to the eye—not strictly religious) poetry remained widely appreciated, not only among his compatriots but in the whole of Central Asia.

Bibliography: 1. Editions: A. Chodzko, *Specimens of the popular poetry of Persia*, London 1842, 389-94; N. Berezin, *Turetskaya khrestomatiya*, ii, Kazan 1857-76; H. Vambéry, *Die Sprache der Turkomanen und der Diwan Machdumkulis*, in *ZDMG*, xxxiii (1879), 388-444, (31 poems and 10 fragments, with German tr.; not too reliable); Shaykh Muḥsin Fānī, *Makhtūm-ḳulī dīwānï we yedi* ʿ*aṣïrlïḳ bir manẓūme*, Istanbul 1340/ 1924 (a bad repr. of Vambéry); B. M. Kerbabaev, *Sbornik izbrannïkh proizvedeniy turkmenskoyo poëta Makhtum-Kuli (II. pol. XVIII. veka)*, Ashkhābād 1926 (289 poems, Arabic script, useful). A. Gyurgenli (?), *Magtïmgulï, saylanan goshgïlar*, Ashkhābād 1940 (uncritical); Kurban, *Maktïmkulï*, Berlin 1944; *Magtïmgulï, saylanan èserler*, Ashkhābād 1957, 2 vols. (375 poems). 2. Studies and translations: A. Samoylovič, *Ukazetal' pesnyam Makhtūm-kuli*, in

ZVOIRAO, xix (1909), 0125-0147, additions in *ibid.*, 0216-0218 and xxii (1914), 127-39; Russian tr. *Izbranniya stikhotvoreniya*, Moscow 1941; *Makhtum-Kuli fragi, izbrannye stikhi*, Moscow 1945; *Makhtum-kuli, Stikhotvoreniya*, Leningrad 1949; *Izbrannoe* (*sic*), Moscow 1960. 3. General surveys: Zeki Velidi, in *TM*, ii (1928), 465-74; Köprülü-zāde Fuʾād, *EI*[1], art. *Turkomans. Literature*; J. Benzing, in *PTF*, ii, Wiesbaden 1954, 726-7; 739-40; B. A. Karryev, in *BSE*[3], xv, 526.

(H. F. Hofman)

MAKHDŪM AL-MULK, a Mughal religious leader, whose real name was Mawlānā ʿAbd Allāh. He was the son of Shaykh Shams al-Dīn of Sulṭānpūr. His ancestors had emigrated from Multān and settled at Sulṭānpūr near Lahore. The pupil of Mawlānā ʿAbd al-Ḳādir Sirhindī, he became one of the foremost religious scholars and functionaries of his day. A committed Sunnī, he never trusted Abu 'l-Faḍl ʿAllāmī (d. 1011/1602 [*q.v.*]) and looked upon him from the beginning as a dangerous man. Contemporary monarchs had great respect for Makhdūm al-Mulk. The Emperor Humāyūn (937-63/1530-56) conferred on him the title of *Shaykh al-Islām*. When the empire of Hindūstān came into the possession of Shēr Shāh (946-52/1539-45), the latter further honored him with the title of *Ṣadr al-Islām*. He was a man of especially great importance during the reign of Akbar (963-1014/1556-1605). Bayram Khān Khānān (d. 968/1560) exalted his position very much by giving him the sub-divison of Thānkawāla which yielded an annual income of one *lakh* of rupees, while Akbar gave him the title of *Makhdūm al-Mulk*, by which designation he has become known to posterity. When the Emperor introduced his religious innovations and tried to convert people to his "Divine Faith" [see dīn-i ilāhī], however, Makhdum al-Mulk opposed him. Akbar became very angry. He ordered Makhdum al-Mulk to go on a pilgrimage to Mecca and Medina. Setting out in 987/1579, he completed the enforced canonical journey within two years' time. On his return from the Hidjāz, Makhdūm al-Mulk died or was poisoned in 990/1582 in Aḥmadābād.

He was the author of the following books, none of which are now extant: (1) *ʿIṣmat al-anbiyāʾ*, a work on the sinlessness of prophets (cf. Badāʾūnī, iii, 70); (2) *Minhādj al-dīn*, a life of the Prophet (cf. *Maʾāthir al-umarāʾ*, iii, 252); (3) *Ḥāshiya Sharḥ Mullāh*, a gloss on Djāmī's commentary on Ibn al-Ḥādjib's *Kāfiya* (cf. *Maʾāthir al-umarāʾ*, iii, 252); (4) *Sharḥ Shamāʾil al-Tirmidhī*, a commentary on Tirmidhī's *Shamāʾil al-nabī* (cf. Badāʾūnī, iii, 70).

Bibliography: ʿAbd al-Ḳādir Badāʾūnī, *Muntakhab al-tawārīkh*, iii, 70; Shāhnawāz Khān Awrangābādī, *Maʾāthir al-umarāʾ*, iii, 252; *Khazīnat al-aṣfiyāʾ*, 443, 464; *Āʾīn-i Akbarī*, tr. Blochman, 172, 544.

(M. Hidayet Hosain - [B. Lawrence])

MAKHDŪM AL-MULK Sharaf al-Dīn Aḥmad b. Yaḥyā **MANĪRĪ** or **MANĒRĪ,** celebrated saint of mediaeval Bihār. Born in Shawwāl 661/August 1263 at Manīr or Manēr, a village in the north Bihārī district of Patna, Sharaf al-Dīn was educated at Sunargaon, Bengal by the Ḥanbalī traditionist Abū Tawwāma. On completing his studies, he travelled to Dihlī, where he met the premier Čishtī *shaykh* of the Sultanate period, Niẓām al-Dīn Awliyāʾ (d. 725/1325). He subsequently enrolled as the disciple of Nadjīb al-Dīn Firdawsī (d. 691/1291) and spent several years in the forests of Bihīya and Rādjgīr secluded from human company and engaged in meditation on God. When he re-emerged at Bihār Sharīf (*ca.* 60 miles from Patna city) in the 1320s, he was acknowledged as a spiritual preceptor and guide of extraordinary power. From the *khānaḳāh* built for him by friends and later enlarged by Sultan Muḥammad b. Tughluḳ (reigned 1325-1351), Sharaf al-Dīn established the Firdawsī *silsila* throughout northern Bihār and western Bengal. He died at Bihār Sharīf on 6 Shawwāl 782/3 January 1381.

The several writings of Sharaf al-Dīn reveal him to be a knowledgeable traditionist as well as a skilled dialectician of Ṣūfī categories and concepts. He is best known for one of his collections of letters, *Maktūbāt-i ṣadī*. He has also been credited with three other epistolary volumes: *Rukn-i fawāʾid*, *Maktūbāt-i dū ṣadī*, and *Maktūbāt-i bīst-u hasht*. Numerous are the compilations of *awrād* (invocatory prayers) and *ishārāt* (practical directives) attributed to Sharaf al-Dīn, but his most comprehensive work was a *sharḥ* (commentary) on the Ṣūfī catechism, the *Ādāb al-murīdīn* of Abū Nadjīb Suhrawardī (d. 561/1168).

The literary and spiritual tradition of Sharaf al-Dīn was continued by the several notable Firdawsī saints who were his successors, beginning with Muẓaffar Shams Balkhī (d. 803/1401). The attainments of this regionally delimited *silsila* were lauded throughout Hindustan; its major *shaykhs* found recognition in the most popular pan-Indian *tadhkiras*, e.g., ʿAbd al-Ḥaḳḳ Dihlawī's *Akhbār al-akhyār* and Ghulām Sarwar Lāhōrī's *Khazīnat al-aṣfiyāʾ*.

Bibliography: Shuʿayb b. Djalāl al-Dīn Manīrī, *Manāḳib al-aṣfiyāʾ*, Calcutta 1895; Zayn al-Dīn Badr-i ʿArabī, *Maʿdin al-maʿānī*, Bihār 1884; ʿAbd al-Ḥaḳḳ Dihlawī, *Akhbār al-akhyār*, Dihlī 1309/1891, 113-118; Ghulām Sarwar Lāhōrī, *Khazīnat al-aṣfiyāʾ*, Lucknow 1290/1873, ii, 290-92; M. Muʿīn al-Dīn Dardāʾi, *Taʾrīkh-i silsila-yi Firdawsiyya* [Urdū], Gaya 1962, 137-244; M. Ishaq, *India's contribution to the study of hadith literature*, Dacca 1955, 66-71; S. H. Askari, *Sufism in medieval Bihar*, in *Current Studies* (Patna College), vii (1957), 3-37, viii (1958), 107-29; B. Lawrence, *Notes from a distant flute: the extant literature of pre-Mughal Indian Sufism*, Tehran 1978, 72-77; S. A. A. Rizvi, *A history of Sufism in India*, i, Dihlī 1978, 228-40

(B. Lawrence)

MAKHFĪ, the much-disputed pen-name of Zīb al-Nisāʾ Begum, eldest child of the Mughal emperor Awrangzīb (1068-1118/1658-1707).

She was born in 1638 at Dawlatābād in the Deccan. Her mother, Dilras Bānū Begum (d. 1657), was the daughter of Shāhnawāz Khān (d. 1659), a dignitary of Shāhdjahān's reign. For her early education she was assigned to Ḥāfiẓa Maryam, a learned lady who was the mother of one of Awrangzīb's trusted nobles, ʿInāyat Allāh Khān (d. 1139/1726-7). Under Ḥāfiẓa Maryam's guidance, Zīb al-Nisāʾ memorised the Ḳurʾān, for which Awrangzīb rewarded her with a purse of 10,000 gold pieces. Later, she studied under some of the best scholars of the time, foremost among them being Muḥammad Saʿīd Ashraf (d. 1116/1708-9), a poet and man of learning who came to India from Persia during the early part of Awrangzīb's reign. Her accomplishments included mastery of Arabic and Persian languages as well as skill in calligraphic writing. She was a great lover of books, and is said to have collected a library which was unrivalled in its time. Many writers and scholars benefited from her generous patronage, and some of them composed books bearing her name. Significant among such writing was Ṣafī al-Dīn Ardabīlī's *Zīb al-tafāsīr*, which was a Persian translation of Fakhr al-

Dīn Rāzī's exegesis of the Ḳurʾān. Zīb al-Nisā remained unmarried throughout her life. It is reported that she was involved in a love intrigue with ʿĀḳil K͟hān, a nobleman of Awrangzīb's court, but this is pure fiction invented by some 19th-century Urdu writers. She incurred Awrangzīb's wrath for complicity with her brother, Akbar, in his unsuccessful rebellion against the emperor. In 1681 she was imprisoned in the Salīmgaṙh fort at Dihlī, where she spent the remaining years of her life until her death in 1702.

Whether or not Zīb al-Nisāʾ left behind a *dīwān* of her poems is a disputed question. A collection of verse published in her name under the title of *Dīwān-i Mak͟hfī* has been subjected to critical scrutiny, and is regarded as the work of someone other than Zīb al-Nisāʾ. Sporadic verses attributed to her indicate that she was a promising poet, favouring a lyrical style.

Bibliography: Mustaʿīd K͟hān Sāḳī, *Maʾāt͟hir-i ʿĀlamgīrī*, tr. Jadunath Sarkar, Calcutta 1947; Aḥmad K͟hān Hās͟himī Sandīlawī, *Tad͟hkira-yi mak͟hzan al-g͟haraʾib*, ii, ed. Muḥammad Bāḳir, Lahore 1970; Muḥammad Ḳudrat Allāh Gopāmawī, *Tad͟hkira-yi natāʾid͟j al-afkār*, Bombay 1336/1957-8; *Dīwān-i Mak͟hfī*, Cawnpore 1283/1866-7; Muḥammad b. Muḥammad Rafīʿ "Malik al-Kuttāb" S͟hīrāzī, *Tad͟hkirat al-k͟hawātīn*, Bombay 1306/1888; S͟hams al-Dīn Sāmī, *Ḳāmūs al-aʿlām*, iv, Istanbul 1889; T. W. Beale, *An oriental biographical dictionary*, London 1894; Magan Lal and Jessie Duncan Westbrook, *The diwan of Zeb-un-Nissa*, New York 1913; P. Whalley, *The tears of Zebunnisa*, London 1913; *Journal of the Bihar and Orissa Research Society*, xiii (March 1927); S͟hiblī Nuʿmānī, *Sawāniḥ-i Zīb al-Nisāʾ Begum*, Lucknow n.d.; Jadunath Sarkar, *History of Aurangzib*, iii, repr. Dihlī 1972; idem, *Studies in Aurangzib's reign*, Calcutta 1933; Muḥammad ʿAlī Tarbiyat, *Dānis͟hmandān-i Ād͟harbāyd͟jān*, Tehran 1314/1935-6; M. Ishaque, *Four eminent poetesses of Iran*, Calcutta 1950; J. Rypka, *History of Iranian literature*, Dordrecht 1956; ʿAlī Akbar Mus͟hīr Salīmī, *Zanān-i suk͟hanwar*, ii, Tehran 1335/1956-7; Nūr al-Ḥasan Anṣārī, *Fārsī adab bi-ʿahd-i Awrangzīb*, Dihlī 1969; Punjab University, *Urdū dāʾira-yi maʿārif-i Islāmiyya*, x, Lahore 1973; P. N. Chopra, *Life and letters under the Mughals*, Dihlī 1976.

(Munibur Rahman)

MAK͟HLAD, Banū, a family of famous Cordovan jurists who, from father to son, during ten generations, distinguished themselves in the study of *fiḳh*. The eponymous ancestor of the family was Mak͟hlad b. Yazīd, who was *ḳāḍī* of the province of Reyyoh (the *kūra* in the south-west of Spain, the capital of which was Malaga), in the reign of the *amīr* ʿAbd al-Raḥmān II, in the first half of the 3rd/9th century. His son, Abū ʿAbd al-Raḥmān Baḳī b. Mak͟hlad [*q.v.*], was by far the most famous member of the family, and his direct descendants devoted their intellectual activity mainly to commenting on the masterpieces of their celebrated ancestor. A list of these scholars, with bibliographical references, is supplied in a little monograph devoted to the family of the Banū Mak͟hlad by Rafael de Ureña y Smenjaud, *Familias de jurisconsultos: Los Benimajlad de Córdoba*, in *Homenaje a D. Francisco Cordera*, Saragossa 1904, 251-8.

Bibliography: Add to the *Bibl. of* Baḳī b. Mak͟hlad: Manuela Marín, *Baqī ibn Majlad y la introducción del estudio del ḥadīt en al-Andalus*, in *al-Qanṭara*, i (1980), 165-208; W. Werkmeister, *Quellenuntersuchungen zum Kitāb al-ʿIqd al-farīd*, Berlin 1983, 267-70 and index. (E. Lévi-Provençal)

MAK͟HLAṢ [see takhalluṣ].

MAK͟HRAMA, Bā or Abū, a South Arabian Ḥimyarite clan of S͟hāfiʿī jurists and Ṣūfīs who lived in Ḥaḍramawt and Aden in the 9th/15th and 10th/16th centuries. Prominent members of it were the following:

1. ʿAfīf al-Dīn Abu 'l-Ṭayyib ʿAbd Allāh b. Aḥmad b. ʿAlī b. Ibrāhīm Bā Mak͟hrama al-Ḥimyarī al-S͟haybānī (or al-Saybānī?) al-Had͟jarānī al-Ḥaḍramī al-ʿAdanī, b. 833/1430 in Had͟jarayn [*q.v.*], d. 903/1497 in Aden, where he was appointed *ḳāḍī* by the sultan ʿAlī b. Ṭāhir but resigned after four months, without losing his popularity (in Brockelmann, S II, 239 f.; these biographical dates are by mistake attributed to his son al-Ṭayyib, below, 2.). His writings include remarks (*nukat*) on *D͟jāmiʿ al-muk͟htaṣarāt* by al-Nasāʾī (Brockelmann, II, 199/254) and the *Alfiyya* of Ibn Mālik, a commentary on the *Mulḥa* of al-Ḥarīrī, an abstract of Ibn al-Hāʾim's commentary on the *Urd͟jūza al-Yāsamīniyya* (Brockelmann, S I, 858:7.I.1), *rasāʾil* and *fatāwī*.

2. Abū Muḥammad al-Ṭayyib b. ʿAbd Allāh b. Aḥmad ... al-ʿAdanī (son of 1.), b. 870/1465, d. 947/1540, jurist and scholar of wide learning, teaching *fiḳh*, *tafsīr*, *ḥadīt͟h*, *naḥw* and *lug͟ha*. He had studied under his father, Muḥammad Bā Faḍl and Muḥammad al-Ḳammāṭ (both d. 903/1497) and shared his reputation as a *faḳīh* with Muḥammad b. ʿUmar Bā Ḳaḍḍām (d. 951/1544) belonging to another branch of the Mak͟hrama family. Sickness evidently prevented him from finishing his two main works: the "Chronicle of Aden" *Taʾrīk͟h T͟hag͟hr ʿAdan* (ed. Löfgren 1936-50) and *Ḳilādat al-naḥr fī wafayāt aʿyān al-dahr* (*ṭabaḳāt* work, with historical supplement ed. Schuman 1960). He also wrote *Mus͟htabih al-nisba ilā 'l-buldān* (Serjeant, *Materials*, no. 11) and *Asmāʾ rid͟jāl Muslim*. In the *Ḳilāda* are biographies of the brothers Aḥmad (d. 911/1505-6), ʿAbd Allāh al-ʿAmūdī and Muḥammad, who at his death in S͟hiḥr in 906/1500-1 bequeathed his library to students of theology in Aden, under the supervision of his brothers Aḥmad and al-Ṭayyib (see *MO*, xxv, 131-8).

3. ʿUmar b. ʿAbd Allāh b. Aḥmad (son of 1.), b. 884/1479 in Had͟jarān, d. 952/1545 in Saywūn (a residential town in Wādī Ḥaḍramawt between Tarīm and S͟hibām), famous Ṣūfī scholar and poet. Having completed his juridico-theological training in Aden under his father, the local saint Abū Bakr al-ʿAydarūs [*q.v.*] and Muḥammad b. ʿAlī D͟jirfīl al-Dawʿanī (d. 903/1497-8), he met with the Ṣūfī ʿAbd al-Raḥmān b. ʿUmar Bā Hurmuz [see hurmuz, bā], was converted to mysticism, and became a local spiritual leader residing in Saywūn, where he collected numerous disciples and was buried in a mausoleum close to that of the Kat͟hīrī sultans. He was a productive poet in classical as well as indigenous (*ḥumaynī*) metre; his *Dīwān* was collected in several volumes by al-Ḥudaylī Ṣāḥib al-Ḳāra (d. 1037/1627-8, al-Muḥibbī, ii, 366, cf. Serjeant, *Materials*, no. 28). Specimens of it are given in *al-Nūr al-sāfir*, 33-7, and *Taʾrīk͟h al-S͟huʿarāʾ al-Ḥaḍramiyyīn*, i, 134 ff. Two verses on *maʿiyya* written shortly before his death were treated by ʿAbd al-Raḥmān al-ʿAydarūs under three titles, *Irs͟hād d͟hawī 'l-lawd͟haʿiyya ʿalā baytay al-maʿiyya*, *Itḥāf d͟hawī 'l-almaʿiyya fī taḥḳīḳ maʿnā 'l-maʿiyya*, and *al-Nafḥa al-ilāhiyya fī taḥḳīḳ maʿnā 'l-maʿiyya* (cf. Ismāʿīl Pas͟ha, *Īḍāḥ al-maknūn*, i, 18, ii, 668). Other writings by him include *al-Wārid al-ḳudsī fī s͟harḥ āyat al-kursī*, *S͟harḥ Asmāʾ Allāh al-ḥusnā*, *al-Maṭlab al-yasīr min al-sālik al-faḳīr*.

4. ʿAfīf al-Dīn ʿAbd Allāh b. ʿUmar b. ʿAbd Allāh (son of 3.), b. 907/1501 in S͟hiḥr, d. 972/1565 in Aden, where he finished his legal career as *muftī*

and was buried at the side of his father and his uncle al-Ṭayyib close to the mausoleum of the Ṣūfī Djawhar al-ʿAdanī (6th/12th century, cf. *Taʾrīkh Thaghr ʿAdan*, ii, 39 ff.). Having studied under his father, his uncle and ʿAbd Allāh b. Aḥmad Bā Surūmī al-Shiḥrī (d. 943/1536-7) he was *ḳāḍī* in Shiḥr twice, became a great authority (*ʿumda*) on *fiḳh*, and was consulted from all parts of the Yaman and Ḥaḍramawt. As will be seen from the list of his writings, he was not only a *faḳih* and theologian, but pursued a special interest of astronomy and chronology. He also wrote some poetry (*arādjīz*).

His writings include *Dhayl Ṭabaḳat al-Shāfiʿiyya* by al-Asnawī (Brockelmann, II, 91/111) *Nukat* on Ibn Ḥadjar al-Haythamī's commentary on al-Nawawī's *Minhādj*, 2 vols., *Fatāwī*, *al-Durra al-zahiyya fī sharḥ [al-Urdjūza] al-Raḥbiyya* (16 vv. in Ambr. NF D 256), *Ḥaḳīḳat al-tawḥīd (radd ʿalā ṭāʾifat Ibn ʿArabī)*, *al-Miṣbāḥ fī sharḥ al-ʿUdda wa ʾl-silāḥ (li-mutawallī ʿuḳūd al-nikāḥ*, by Muḥammad b. Aḥmad Bā Faḍl, d. 903/1497-8), (cf. Brockelmann, S II, 972:5 *Mishkāt al-miṣbāḥ*, identical); astronomy-chronology: *al-Djadāwil al-muḥaḳḳaḳa al-muḥarrara fī ʿilm al-hayʾa*, *al-Lumʿa fī ʿilm al-falak* (Rabat 2023), *al-Shāmil fī dalāʾil al-ḳibla*, etc., *rasāʾil* on *ikhtilāf al-maṭāliʿ wa-ttifāḳihā*, *al-rubʿ al-mudjayyab*, *samt al-ḳibla*, *ẓill al-istiwāʾ* (several details from the work of King, see *Bibl. below*).

Bibliography: O. Löfgren, *Arabische Texte zur Kenntnis der Stadt Aden im Mittelalter*, i-ii, Leiden 1936-50: edition of *Taʾrīkh Thaghr ʿAdan*; idem, *Über Abū Maḥrama's Ḳilādat al-naḥr*, in *MO*, xxv, 120-39; R. B. Sergeant, *Materials for South Arabian history*, in *BSOS*, xiii, 281-307, 581-601; L. O. Schuman, *Political history of the Yemen at the beginning of the 16th century*, 1960; D. A. King, *Mathematical astronomy in medieval Yemen* (unpublished study); al-ʿAydarūs(ī), *al-Nūr al-sāfir ʿan akhbār al-ḳarn al-ʿashir*, *passim*; al-Saḳḳāf, *Taʾrīkh al-Shuʿarāʾ al-Ḥaḍramiyyīn*, i; Sakhāwī, *al-Ḍawʾ al-lāmiʿ*, v, 8; Ibn al-ʿImād, *Shadharāt al-dhahab*, viii, 268, 367; Kaḥḥāla, *Muʿdjam al-muʾallifīn*, vii, 293; Ziriklī, *al-Aʿlām*, iv, 193, 227, 249, v. 213. (O. Löfgren)

MAKHREDJ (A.), "outlet, going out", an Ottoman term used in education and law. In education, the term was used in reference to two schools in the 19th century, of which one prepared students for employment in Ottoman administrative offices, the other for the military schools.

Makhredj-i aḳlām designated the post-secondary school were secondary school students were prepared to "go out" to work at Ottoman administrative offices, *aḳlām* (pl. of *ḳalam* [*q.v.*]). The *Makhredj-i aḳlām* was founded in 1862 when Ottoman administrators decided that the quality of secondary school training was insufficient. The first graduates of the school were examined in 1864 by the Educational Council, *medjlis-i maʿārif*, and were appointed to the aḳlām. The school was superseded in 1876 by a school of higher education for civil servants, *mekteb-i fünūn-u mülkiyye*.

Makhredj-i mekātib-i ʿaskeriyye was the secondary school which prepared students "going out" to military schools. The foundation for the school was laid in 1862 when the Naval and Civil Engineering, Warfare, and Medical Schools established introductory classes to train their students. The students were admitted to these classes only after completing classes called *makhredj*. In 1864, all introductory classes were combined into a preparatory school, *iʿdādi-i ʿumūmī*. The *makhredj* classes were collected into a secondary school, *makhredj-i mekātib-i ʿaskeriyye*. This school was replaced in 1875 by a newly formed military secondary-school, *ʿaskerī rüshdiyye*.

In law, the term makhredj had two meanings. Certain judicial districts in the Ottoman Empire were referred to as *makhredj mewlewiyyeti* [see MEWLEWIYYET]. The name derived from a common attribute of the judges appointed to these districts. All were judges "going out" to their first appointment after teaching in schools, *madrasa* [*q.v.*]. The judges who had completed this appointment and were awaiting assignment to a higher ranking judicial district were called *makhredj mewālīsi*.

In inheritance law, makhredj was the term for the denominator which was used to divide an inheritance among heirs. In the case of the inheritance of a deceased woman, for example, where her husband and daughter each received one-fourth of the inheritance and her son received two-fourths, the *makhredj* of the inheritance would be four.

Bibliography: O. Ergin, *İstanbul mektepleri ve ilim, terbiye ve san'at müesseseleri dolayısile Türkiye maarif tarihi*, ii, İstanbul 1940, 397-400, 413, 418-21; M.Z. Pakalın, *Osmanlı tarih deyimleri ve terimleri sözlüğü*, İstanbul 1951, 385-7; İ.A. Gövsa, *Resimli yeni lugat ve ansiklopedi*, iii, 1708; İ.H. Uzunçarşılı, *Osmanlı devletinin ilmiye teşkilatı*, Ankara 1965, 90, 101, 120, 265; M. Sertoğlu, *Resimli Osmanlı tarihi ansiklopedisi*, İstanbul 1958, 194; Gibb-Bowen, i/2, 89, 126, 151. (F. Müge Göçek)

MAKHZAN (A.), from *khazana*, "to shut up, to preserve, to hoard". The word is believed to have been first used in North Africa as an official term in the 2nd/8th century applied to an iron chest in which Ibrāhīm b. al-Aghlab, *amīr* of Ifrīḳiya, kept the sums of money raised by taxation and intended for the ʿAbbāsid caliph of Baghdād. At first this term, which in Morocco is synonymous with the government, was applied more particularly to the financial department, the Treasury.

It may be said that the term *makhzan* (pronounced *makhzen*) meaning the Moroccan government, and everything more or less connected with it, at first meant simply the place where the sums raised by taxation were kept, intended to be paid into the treasury of the Muslim community, the *bayt al-māl* [*q.v.*]. Later, when the sums thus raised were kept for use in the countries in which they were collected, and they became, as it were, the private treasuries of the communities in which they were collected, the word *makhzan* was used to mean the separate local treasuries and a certain amount of confusion arose between the *makhzan* and the *bayt al-māl*.

We do find in Spain the expression *ʿabīd al-makhzan*, but it still means slaves of the treasury rather than slaves of the government, and in al-Andalus, later it seems than in Morocco, in proportion as the state became separated from the rest of the Muslim community after being successively under the Umayyads of Damascus, the ʿAbbāsids of Baghdād, the Umayyads of Spain and the Fāṭimids of Egypt, that *makhzan* came to be used for the government itself.

To sum up, the word *makhzan*, after being used for the place where the sums intended for the *bayt al-māl* of the Islamic empire were kept, was used for the local treasury of the Muslim community of Morocco, when it took shape under the great Berber dynasties; later, with the Sharīfī dynasties, the word was applied not only to the treasury but to the whole organisation more or less administrative in nature which lives on the treasury, that is to say the whole government of Morocco. In tracing through history the changes of meaning of the word *makhzan*, one comes to the conclusion that not only is the institution to which it is applied not religious in character but, on the contrary, it represents the combined usurpations of powers, originally religious, by laymen, at the expense of which it has grown up through several centuries. The result of these successive usurpations is that the makhzan ended up by representing to the Moroccans the sole principle of authority.

In rapidly surveying the history of the makhzan, we can see how it became gradually established, while using the prescriptions of Islam, and how it succeeded in forming, in face of the native Berber element which surrounded it, a kind of Arab façade, behind which the Berbers, in spite of the slowness of their gradual islamisation, have preserved their institutions and their independence.

No organisation was made at the first conquest by ʿUḳba b. Nāfiʿ in 63/682. All the Arab conquerors had to do was to levy heavy tributes in money and slaves to satisfy their own greed and to enable them to send valuable gifts to the caliph of Damascus.

It was the same in 90/708 with Mūsā b. Nuṣayr, but the conquest of Spain brought over to Islam a large number of Berber tribes by promising them a share in plundering the wealth of the Visigoths. On the other hand, the spread of Khāridjī doctrines made any unity of power impossible and on the contrary increased decentralisation.

The Idrīsid dynasty, which its Sharīfī origin gives a claim to be the first Muslim dynasty of Morocco and which completed the conversion of the country to Islam, only exercised its power over a small part of Morocco. Alongside of it, the Barghawāṭa [q.v.] heretics and numerous Khāridjī amīrs continued to exist. It was not till the 5th/11th century, under the Almoravids, that in the reign of Yaʿḳūb b. Tāshfīn we can see the beginnings of a makhzan which only becomes clearly recognisable under the Almohads.

It was under the latter that religious unity was first attained in Morocco. The heresy of the Barghawāṭa and all other schisms were destroyed, and a single Muslim community, that of the Almohads, replaced the numerous more or less heterodox sects which had been sharing the country and its revenues. It may be said that the organisation of the makhzan as it existed in Morocco at the opening of the 20th century is fundamentally based on this unification and the measures which resulted from it. The Almohads were able to apply to all the territory of their empire the ideal Muslim principle for dealing with land, i.e. that all the lands conquered by them from non-Almohads, and even from Almohads whose faith was regarded as suspect, were classed as lands taken from infidels and became ḥubus (pl. aḥbās) of the Muslim, i.e. Almohad community. These landed properties are those whose occupants have to pay the kharādj tax. In order to levy this, the sultan ʿAbd al-Muʾmin had all his African empire surveyed from Gabès to the Wādī Nūn.

A few years later, Yaʿḳūb al-Manṣūr brought to Morocco the Djusham and Banū Hilāl Arabs and settled them on lands which had been uninhabited since the destruction of the Barghawāṭa, the wars of the Almohads with the last Almoravids and the extensive despatches of troops to Spain.

These Arab tribes who formed the gīsh [see DJAYSH] of the Almohads did not pay the kharādj for the lands of the Muslim community which they occupied. They were makhzan tribes who rendered military service in place of kharādj. We shall find later the remains of this organisation with the gīsh tribes and the tribes of nāʾiba. The efforts of the Marīnids to reconstitute a gīsh with their own tribes did not succeed, and they had to return to the makhzan of Arab tribes brought to Morocco by Yaʿḳūb al-Manṣūr and even added to it contingents of the Maʿḳil [q.v.] Arabs of the Sūs.

Under the Banū Waṭṭās, this movement became more marked, and Spanish influences became more and more felt in the more complicated organisation of the central makhzan and by the creation of new offices at the court and in the palace.

The conquests by the Christians, by causing the development of the zāwiyas and the fall of the Banū Waṭṭās, brought about the rise of the Saʿdids [q.v.] of Wādī Darʿa. The latter, with their customs as Saharan tribes and under the religious influence of the shaykhs of the brotherhoods, began to try to bring back the exercise of power to the patriarchal simplicity with which it was wielded in the early days of Islam. The necessities of the government, the intrigues of the tribes and the wars of members of the ruling family against one another soon made necessary the constitution of a proper makhzan with its military tribes; ministers, its crown officials of high and low degree, its governors to whom were soon added the innumerable groups of palace officials which will be mentioned below.

The frequent intercourse between the Saʿdids and the Turks, who had come to settle in Algeria at the beginning of the 10th/16th century, brought to the court of Morocco a certain amount of eastern ceremonial, a certain amount of luxury and even a certain degree of pomp in the life of the sovereign and in that of his entourage and of all the individuals employed in the makhzan.

The increasing official relations of Morocco with European powers, the exchange of ambassadors, the commercial agreements and the ransoming of Christian slaves, largely contributed to give this Makhzan more and more the appearance of a regular government. The jealousies of the powers, their desire to maintain the status quo in Morocco and the need to have a regular government to deal with them further strengthened the makhzan both at home and abroad and enabled the sultan Mawlāy al-Ḥasan to conduct for nearly twenty years this policy of equilibrium between the powers on one side, and the tribes on the other, who kept till his death the empire of Morocco in existence, built up of very diverse elements, of which the makhzan formed the façade.

The very humble, almost humiliating, attitude imposed on the European ambassadors at official receptions increased the prestige of the sultan and the makhzan in the eyes of the tribes. The envoy of the Christian power, surrounded by the presents which he brought, appeared on foot in a court of the palace and seemed to have come to pay tribute to the commander of the Muslims, who was on horseback. All the theatrical side was developed to strike the imagination of the makhzan with much care, and it succeeded in creating an illusion of the real efficiency of this organisation in the eyes of both tribes and powers.

Under the Berber dynasties, the Almohads, the Marīnids and the Banū Waṭṭās, the military tribes, the djaysh (gīsh) were almost all Arab; under the Saʿdids they were entirely Arab; to the Djusham and Banū Hilāl Arabs were added the Maʿḳil Arabs of the Sūs. On the other hand the Saʿdids had removed from the registers of the djaysh a certain number of the Arab tribes who then paid in money the kharādj for the aḥbās lands of the Muslim community which they occupied. These tribes, in contrast to the djaysh, were called tribes of the nāʾiba, that is to say, according to the etymology proposed for the word, they were under the tutelage of the makhzan (from nāʾib "tutor" or "substitute" for a father), or rather, they paid the tribes of the djaysh a sum for replacing them (from nāba "to act as a substitute").

From this time onwards, Morocco assumed the appearance which it had when France established her protectorate there. The frontier, settled with the Turks in the east, had hardly been altered by the occupation of Algeria by France and the territory of Morocco was divided into two parts: 1. *bilād al-makhzan* or conquered territory; 2. *bilād al-sība* [*q.v.*] or land of schism; the latter was almost exclusively occupied by Berbers.

The *bilād al-makhzan*, which represented official Morocco, was formed of territories belonging to the *aḥbās* of the Muslim community, liable to the *kharādj* and occupied by Arab tribes, some *gīsh*, other *nāʾiba*.

The Berber tribes of the *bilād al-sība* not only refused to allow the authority of the *makhzan* to penetrate among them, but even had a tendency to go back to the plains from which they had gradually been pushed into the mountains. One of the main endeavours of the present dynasty, the ʿAlawīs of Tafilalt, which succeeded the Saʿdids in the 11th/17th century, has been to oppose this movement of expansion of the Berber tribes. This is why Mawlāy Ismāʿīl, the most illustrious sultan of this dynasty, built 70 *ḳaṣbas* on the frontier of the *bilād al-makhzan* to keep down the Berbers. Hence we have this policy of equilibrium and intrigues which has just been mentioned and which up till the 20th century was the work of the *makhzan*.

As has already been said, it was not a question of organising the country nor even of governing it, but simply of holding their own by keeping rebellion within bounds with the help of the *gīsh* tribes by extracting from the ports and from the *nāʾiba* tribes all that could be extorted by every means. From time to time, expeditions led by the sultan himself against the unsubjected tribes asserted his power and increased his prestige.

The *makhzan*, gradually formed in course of centuries by the possibilities and exigencies of domestic policy as well as by the demands of foreign policy, seems to have attained its most complete development in the reign of Mawlāy al-Ḥasan, the last great independent sultan of Morocco (1873-94). The government of Mawlāy al-Ḥasan consisted in the first place of the sultan himself, at once hereditary and also, if not exactly elected, at least nominated by the *ʿulamāʾ* and notables of each town and tribes from among the sons, brothers, nephews and even the cousins of the late ruler. This proclamation is called *bayʿa*. It is, in general, he who takes control of the treasury and of the troops when the moment comes to assume the right of succession. It sometimes happens that the late sovereign has nominated his successors, but this does not constitute an obligation on the electors to obey it. There is then no rule of succession to the throne.

Formerly there was only one vizier, the grand vizier (*al-ṣadr al-aʿẓam*); the grand vizierate, a kind of Ministry of the Interior was divided into three sections, each managed by a secretary (*kātib*):

1. From the Strait of Gibraltar to the Wād Bū Regreg.
2. From Bū Regreg to the Sahara.
3. The Tafilalt.

In the reign of Sīdī Muḥammad (1859-73), the more frequent and intimate relations with Europe and more particularly the working of the protectorate, made it necessary to found a special office for foreign relations, and a *wazīr al-baḥr*, literally Minister of the Sea, was appointed. This did not mean minister for the navy, but for all that came by sea, i.e. Europeans. This minister had a representative in Tangier, the *nāʾib al-sulṭān*, who was the intermediary between European representatives and the central *makhzan*. His task was to deal with European complaints and claims from perpetual settlements and to play off against one another the protégés of the European powers, who were certainly increasing in numbers and frequently formed an obstacle to the traditional arbitrary rule of the *makhzan*. The régime of the consular protectorate, settled and regulated in 1880 by the Convention of Madrid, had also resulted in discouraging the *makhzan* from extending its authority over new territory.

The exercise of this authority was in fact automatically followed by the exercise of the right of protection and, from the point of view of resistance to European penetration, the *makhzan* had everything to gain by keeping in an apparent political independence the greater part of the territory in order to escape the influence which threatened in time to turn Morocco into a regular international protectorate.

By a conciliatory policy and cautious dealing with the local chiefs, the *shaykhs* of the *zāwiyas* and the Sharīfī families, the *makhzan* was able to exert even in the remotest districts a real influence and never ceased to carry on perpetual intrigues in order to divide the tribes against one another. It maintained its religious prestige by the hope of preparation for the holy war which was one day to drive out the infidels, and sought to penetrate by spreading the Arabic language and the teaching of the Ḳurʾān and gradually substituting the principles of Islamic law of the *sharʿ* for Berber customs. In a word, it continued the conquest of the country by trying to complete its islamisation and making Islam permeate its customs.

In the reign of Mawlāy al-Ḥasan, the *makhzan* consisted of the grand vizier, the *wazīr al-baḥr*, minister of foreign affairs, the *ʿallāf*—afterwards called minister of war—, the *amīn al-umanāʾ*.—afterwards minister of finance—, the *kātib al-shikāyāt*, secretary for complaints, who became minister of justice by combining his duties with that of the *ḳāḍī ʾl-ḳuḍāt*, Ḳāḍī of Ḳāḍīs. These high officials had the offices (*banīḳa*, pl. *banāʾiḳ*) in the *mashwar* at the Palace.

The offices were under the galleries which were built round a large courtyard. At the top of the *mashwar* was the office of the grand vizier, beside which was that of the *ḳāʾid al-mashwar*, a kind of captain of the guard, who also made presentations to the sultan. The *ḳaʾid al-mashwar* was in command of the police of the *mashwar* and he had under his command the troops of the *gīsh*, *mashwariyya*, *masakhriyya* as well as all the bodies of servants outside the palace (*ḥanāṭī*, sing. *ḥanṭa*); the *mawlā* (*mūl*) *al-ruwā*, grand-master of the stables, and the *frāʾigiyya*, who had charge of the sultan's encampments (*āfrāg* [*q.v.*]).

In addition to these *banīḳas* of the *mashwar*, mention must be made of an individual who could play a more considerable part in the government than his actual office would lead one to expect. This is the *ḥādjib* [*q.v.*], whose *banīḳa* was situated between the *mashwar* and the palace proper; he had charge of the interior arrangements of the sultan's household. Under his orders were the various groups of domestic servants (*ḥanāṭī al-dākhliyyīn*), *mwālīn al-uḍūʾ*, who looked after the washing arrangements, *mwālīn al-frash*, who attended to the beds, etc.; he also commanded the eunuchs and even was responsible for the discipline of the sultan's women, through the *ʿarīfas* or mistresses of the palace. The *ḥādjib* is often called grand chamberlain, although he does not exactly correspond to this office.

Around these officers gravitated a world of secretaries of different ranks, of officers of the *gīsh*, then the *ḳāʾid al-raḥā*, who was in theory in command of 500 horsemen, the *ḳāʾid al-mīʾa*, who commanded

100, down to a simple *muḳaddam*. All this horde of officials, badly paid when paid at all, lived on the country as it could, trafficking shamelessly in the influence which it had or was thought to have and in the prestige it gained from belonging to the court, whether closely or remotely.

In this organisation it may be noticed that the authority of the *makhzan* properly so-called, i.e. of a lay power, continually increased at the expense of the religious power by a series of changes. No doubt the basis continued to be religious, but the application of power became less and less so and the civil jurisdiction of the *ḳāʾid*s and of the *makhzan* more and more took the place of the administration of the sharʿ by the *ḳāḍī*s, which finally became restricted to questions of personal law and landed property [see MAḤKAMA. 4. x].

The sultan's authority was represented in the towns and in the tribes by the *ḳāʾid*s, appointed by the grand vizier and by the *muḥtasib*s, who supervised and controlled the gilds, fixed the price of articles of food and inspected weights and measures and coins [see ḤISBA].

The tax of the *nāʾiba*, which represented the old *kharādj*, was levied on the non-*gīsh* tribes by the *ḳāʾid*s of these tribes. It was one of the principal causes of abuses; the amount of this tax was never fixed and the sums which came from it were in reality divided among the *ḳāʾid*s, the secretaries of the *makhzan* and the vizier without the sultan or the public treasury getting any benefit from it.

The grand vizier also appointed the *nāḍir* (< *nāẓir*) officials who, from the reign of Mawlāy ʿAbd al-Raḥmān, had been attached to the local *nāẓir*s of the *aḥbās* of the mosques and sanctuaries. The financial staff, *umanāʾ*, who controlled the customs, the possessions of the *makhzan* (*al-amlāk*), the *mustafādāt* (market-dues and tolls, etc., called *mukūs*, pl. of *maks*), the controller of the *bayt al-māl* (popularly *abu 'l-mawārīth*), i.e. the official who intervened to collect the share of the Muslim community from estates of deceased persons and who also acted as curator of intestate estates (*wakīl al-ghuyyāb*). All these officers were appointed by the *amīn al-umanāʾ*, who was later known as the minister of finance.

This organisation was completely centralised, i.e. its only object was to bring all the resources of the country into the coffers of the state and of its agents; but no provision was made for utilising these resources in the public interest. No budget was drawn up, no public works, no railways, no navy, no commerce and no post was provided for. Military expenses were confined to the maintenance of a regiment commanded by an English officer, of a French mission of military instruction, of a factory of arms at Fās directed by Italian officers and of the building at Rabāṭ of a fort by a German engineer. These were really rather diplomatic concessions to the powers interested than a regular military organisation. In the spirit of the *makhzan*, the defence of the territory was to be the task of the Berber tribes, carefully maintained out of all contact with Europeans behind the elaborate display maintained by the court.

In the event of war, the *makhzan*, faithful to its system of equal favour, purchased arms and munitions from the different powers and kept them in the Makīna of Fās in order to be able, when necessity arose, to distribute them to the tribes when proclaiming a holy war.

The expenses of the education service were limited to the very modest allowances granted to the *ʿulamāʾ* of al-Ḳarawiyyīn [*q.v.*]. These allowances were levied from the *aḥbās* and augmented by the gifts made by the sultan on the occasion of feasts (*ṣila*).

Nothing was done for public health, and one could not give the name of hospitals to the few *māristān*s to be found in certain towns, where a few miserable creatures lived in filth, receiving from the *aḥbās* and the charity of the public barely enough to prevent them dying of hunger and without, of course, receiving any medical assistance.

On the repeated representation of the Powers, the sultan had ultimately delegated his powers to the members of the diplomatic corps in Tangier, which had been able to form a public health committee in order to be able to refuse admission if necessary to infected vessels. In spite of its defects, the *makhzan* constituted a real force; it formed a solid bloc in the centre of surrounding anarchy which it was interested in maintaining, in order to be able to exploit it more easily on the one hand and on the other to prevent the preservation in the country of any united order which might become a danger to it.

In brief, we may say that the *makhzan* in Morocco was an instrument of arbitrary government, which worked quite well in the social disorder of the country, and thanks to this disorder, we may add, it worked for its own profit and was in a way like a foreign element in a conquered country. It was a regular caste with its own traditions, way of living, of dressing, of furnishing, of feeding, with its own language, *al-lugha al-makhzaniyya*, which is a correct Arabic intermediate between the literary and the spoken Arabic, composed of official formulae, regular clichés, courteous, concise and binding to nothing.

This *makhzan*, which was sufficient in the old order of things which it had itself contributed to create and maintain, was forced, if it was not to disappear at once, to undergo fundamental modifications from the moment this state of things had rendered necessary the establishment of a protectorate. The vizierate of foreign affairs and that of war were then handed over to the Resident-General, and that of finance to the Director-General of Finance, who administered the revenue of the empire like those of a regularly-organised state. The director-generalships of agriculture and education, which were regular ministries, were held by French officials, as were the management of the postal service, telegraph and telephone, and the board of health.

Two new vizierates had been created, that of the regal domains (*al-amlāk*) and that of the *aḥbās*. The vizierate of the *amlāk* was soon suppressed and the domains were henceforward administered by a branch of the finance department. The vizierate of the *aḥbās* was under that of the Sharīfian affairs. This organisation represented the principle of protectorate in the Moroccan government itself, in order to realise "the organisation of a reformed Sharīfian *makhzan*" in keeping with the treaty. (E. MICHAUX-BELLAIRE*)

Bibliography: 1. On the evolution of the meaning of the word *makhzan*: E. Lévi-Provençal, *Documents inédits d'histoire almohade*, Paris 1928, Arabic text, 71 and glossary, and esp. Dozy, *Supplément*, s.v. *kh.z.n*, and the *bibl.* cited there. For the sense of the term in Algeria, see F. Pharaon, *Notes sur les tribus de la Subdivision de Médéa*, in *RA* (1856-7), 393; in *ibid.* (1873), 196 ff.; N. Robin, *Note sur l'organisation militaire et administrative des Turcs dans la Grande Kabylie*, in *ibid.* (1873), 196 ff.; E. Mangin, *Notes sur l'histoire de Laghouat*, in *ibid.* (1895), 5 ff., 109 ff.

2. On the history of this institution: (a) Arabic works: *Kitāb al-Baydaḳ*, in Lévi-Provençal, *op. cit.*; Ibn Abī Zarʿ, *Ḳirṭās*, lith. Fās 1305; Ibn Baṭṭūṭa, *Riḥla*; Ibn Khaldūn, *Muḳaddima*; Ifrānī, *Nuzhat al-ḥādī*, Arabic text, lith. Fās 1307, tr. O.

Houdas, Paris 1889; Zayyānī, *al-Turdjumān al-mu'rib*, extract published and tr. Houdas, *Le Maroc de 1631 à 1812*, Paris 1886; Nāṣīrī, *Kitāb al-Istiḳṣā*, Cairo 1312/1894, 4 vols. (tr. of vol. i. by A. Graulle, G. S. Colin and Ismael Hamet, in *AM*, xxx, xxxi, xxxii, tr. of vol. iv. by Fumey, in *AM*, ix and x); Akansūs, *al-Djaysh al-'aramram*, lith. Fās 1336/1918; *al-Ḥulal al-bahiyya fi mulūk al-dawla al-'alawiyya*, anonymous ms. of the beginning of the 20th century; E. Fumey, *Choix de correspondances marocaines*, Paris 1903; M. Nehlil, *Lettres chérifiennes*, Paris 1915.

(b) European works: Diego de Torrès, *Relation de l'origine et Succez des Cherifs*, Paris 1637, 315-20; Sieur Mouëtte, *Relation de captivité* and *Histoire des conquêtes de Mouley Archy*, both Paris 1682, *passim*; Marmol, *L'Afrique*, tr. Paris 1667, *passim*; Pidou de St. Olon, *Estat présent de l'empire de Maroc*, Paris 1694, 58 ff. and 153 ff.; P. Dominique Busnot, *Histoire du règne de Mouley Ismael*, Rouen 1714, 35-62; P. P. Jean de la Faye, Denis Mackar, etc., *Relations du voyage pour la redemption des captifs aux rouames de Maroc et d'Alger*, Paris 1726, 146 ff.; Braithwaite, *Histoire des révolutions de l'Empire de Maroc*, French tr., Amsterdam 1731, 214; Georg Höst, *Efter retninger om Marókos*, Copenhagen 1779, 158-71; I. S. de Chénier, *Recherches historiques sur les Maures et histoire de l'empire de Maroc*, Paris 1787, iii, 161-70, 226-44, 391-4, 480-1; *Voyages d'Ali Bey et Abbassi*, Paris 1814, i, *passim*; Jacopo Gråberg di Hemsö, *Specchio geografico e statistico dell' Empero di Marocco*, Genoa 1834, 194-217; Garcin de Tassy, *Mémoire sur les noms propres et les titres musulmans*, Paris 1878, 38-41; Dr. Oskar Lenz, *Die Machaznyah in Marokko*, in *Deutsche Rundschau für Geogr.* (1882); J. Erckmann, *Le Maroc moderne*, Paris 1885; H. de la Martinière, *Le Sultan du Maroc et son Gouvernement*, in *Rev. fr. de l'Et. et des Col.* (1885), ii, 282-5; L. de Campou, *Un empire qui croule*, Paris 1886; Ch. de Foucauld, *Reconnaissance au Maroc*, Paris 1888, *passim*; de Campou, *Le Sultan Mouley, Haçen et le Makhzen Marocain*, Paris 1888; E. Reclus, *Géographie universelle*, xi, Paris 1890; Leo Africanus, *Description de l'Afrique*, *passim*; Rouard de Card, *Les traités entre la France et le Maroc*, Paris 1898; Budgett Meakin, *The Moorish empire*, New York 1899, 197-236; E. Aubin, *Le Maroc d'aujourd'hui*, Paris 1904, 172-256; Dr. Fr. Weisgerber, *Trois mois de campagne au Maroc*, Paris 1904; G. Veyre, *Au Maroc, Dans l'intimité du Sultan*, Paris *ca.* 1905; H. de Castries, *Sources inédites de l'histoire du Maroc*, Paris 1905 ff., *passim*; G. Wolfrom, *Le Maroc, ce qu'il faut en connaître*, Paris 1906; L. Massignon, *Le Maroc dans les premières années du 16ème siècle. Tableau géographique d'après Léon Africain*, Algiers 1906, 172-84; Chevrillon, *Un crépuscule d'Islam*, Paris 1906, 190-2; Cte. Conrad de Buisseret, *A la Cour de Fez*, Brussels 1907, 40-8; G. Jeannot, *Étude sociale, politique et économique sur le Maroc*, Dijon 1907, 185-268; H. Gaillard and Ed. Michaux-Bellaire, *L'administration au Maroc—Le Makhzen—Étendue et limites de son pouvoir*, Tangier 1909; Michaux-Bellaire, *L'administration au Maroc*, in *Bull. de la Société de Géographie d'Alger et de l'Afrique du Nord*, Algiers 1909; J. Becker, *Historia de Marruecos*, Madrid 1915, *passim*; A. Bernard, *Le Maroc*[3], Paris 1915.

Articles in journals: Salmon, *L'administration marocaine à Tanger*, in *AM*, i, 1 ff.; Michaux-Bellaire, *Les impôts marocains*, in *ibid.*, i, 56 ff.; idem, *Essai sur l'histoire politique du Nord marocain*, in *ibid.*, ii, 1-99; X. Lécureuil, *Historique des douanes au Maroc*, in *ibid.*, xv, 33 ff.; A. Péretié, *Le Raïs El Khadir Ghaïlan*, in *ibid.*, xviii, 1-187; Michaux-Bellaire, *Un rouage du gouvernement marocain, la Beniqat ech-chikayat de Moulay Abd el-Hafid*, in *RMM*, v, 242-74; idem, *Au palais du Sultan Marocain*, in *ibid.*, v, 646-62; *L'Islam et l'état marocain*, in *ibid.*, viii; idem, *L'organisme marocain*, in *ibid.*, ix, 1-43; A. le Châtelier, *Lettre à un Conseiller d'État*, in *ibid.*, xii, 87-91; idem, *Enquête sur les corporations musulmanes, l'influence du Makhzen*, in *ibid.*, lviii, 104-7; *Le voyage du Sultan*, in *Bulletin du Comité de l'Afrique française* (1902), 420; René Manduit, *Le Makhzen marocain*, in *ibid.* (1903), Suppl. 293-304; Général Derrécagaix, *La crise marocaine*, in *ibid.* (1904), 4; idem, *L'évolution du Makhzen*, in *ibid.*, 50; Commandant Ferry, *La réorganisation marocaine*, in *ibid.* (1905), 517-28; *Le Sultan et la Cour*, in *ibid.* (1906), 335; *Le Gouvernement marocain*, in *ibid.* (1907), 102; *Le Sultan du Sud*, in *ibid.*, 367; *Le déplacement de la Cour de Fez*, in *ibid.*, 368; E. Doutté, *Les causes de la chute d'un Sultan, la Royauté marocaine*, in *ibid.* (1909), 185 ff.

(M. BURET)

MAKHZŪM, BANŪ, a clan of Ḳurays̲h̲ [*q.v.*] which achieved a prominent position in pre-Islamic Mecca. Although in the course of the 7th century A.D. the clans of 'Abd S̲h̲ams and Hās̲h̲im [*q.v.*] went on to achieve greater prominence, a role of some importance was played in early Islamic history by Makhzūmīs. They were for the most part descendants of al-Mughīra b. 'Abd Allāh b. 'Umar b. Makhzūm, in whom the *bayt* of Makhzūm reposed (al-Muṣ'ab al-Zubayrī, *Nasab Ḳuraysh*, ed. Lévi-Provençal, 300; al-Balādhurī, *Ansāb al-ashrāf*, Süleymaniye ms. ii, 523; Ibn Ḥazm, *Djamhara*, ed. Hārūn, 144), rather than members of the cadet branches of the clan associated with his nineteen (according to Ibn al-Kalbī, *Djamhara*, ed. Caskel, table 23) or more brothers and cousins.

The extent of the power and influence of Makhzūm in Mecca during the 6th century A.D. cannot be established with any certainty; all we know is that Muslim accounts of the two major Ḳuras̲h̲ī alignments there at that time—the Muṭayyabūn and the Aḥlāf—place Makhzūm in the latter grouping, along with the clans of 'Abd al-Dār, Sahm, Djumaḥ and 'Adī (Watt, *Mecca*, 5). Near the end of the century, however, at about the time of the formation of the Ḥilf al-Fuḍūl [*q.v.*] as a third grouping at Mecca (which took 'Adī away from the Aḥlāf), the Makhzūmī leader His̲h̲ām b. al-Mug̲h̲īra came to occupy a prominent position in Meccan political life. He was "the *sayyid* of Ḳuraysh in his time"; (Ibn Durayd, *al-Ishtiḳāḳ*, ed. Hārūn (following Wüstenfeld's pagination, 92); Mug̲h̲īra had inherited the *siyāda*, and the Banū His̲h̲ām were the foremost of the Banu 'l-Mug̲h̲īra (Ibn Durayd, 87); "in the *djāhiliyya* the genealogy of Ḳuraysh was linked with that of His̲h̲ām" (*nusibat Ḳuraysh ilā His̲h̲ām fi 'l-Djahiliyya*: Ibn Durayd, 94); when His̲h̲ām died, the Meccans were called on to witness the funeral of their lord (*rabb*: Ibn Durayd, 63); and it is reported that Ḳuraysh used a dating system in which His̲h̲ām's death was taken as the starting point (al-Muṣ'ab, 301; Ibn Ḥabīb, *al-Munammaḳ*, ed. Fāriḳ, 412; al-Balādhurī, *Ansāb*, ms., ii, 524; al-Mubarrad, *al-Kāmil*, ed. Wright, 313; *Aghānī*[1], xv, 11 (where a second report says, less credibly, that the death of [his brother] al-Walīd b. al-Mug̲h̲īra was taken as the starting point). The economic interests of Makhzūm at this time appear to have been focussed on trade in the Yemen and Ethiopia, where they constituted the predominating Meccan presence; in that connection, the sources name His̲h̲ām, his brother al-Walīd, and

Descendants of al-Mug͟hīra b. ʿAbd Allāh b. ʿUmar b. Mak͟hzūm

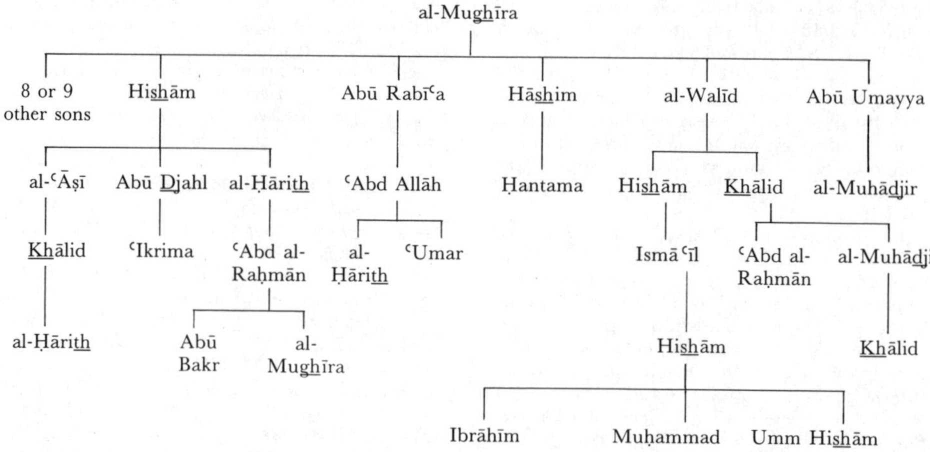

two more of the sons of al-Mug͟hīra, together with four of their sons (P. Crone, *Meccan trade* (forthcoming), ch. v).

The emergence of Muḥammad as Prophet in the second decade of the 7th century A.D. met with strenuous opposition on the part of the Mak͟hzūmī leader of the time, Abū D̲jahl b. His͟hām b. al-Mug͟hīra [*q.v.*]; he it was who in particular brought into effect the boycott of the Banū Hās͟him in *ca.* 616-18 (Watt, *Mecca*, 117 ff.). In addition, his uncle, the *ḥakam* [*q.v.*] (Ibn Ḥabīb, 460; al-Fāsī, ed. Wüstenfeld, in *Die Chroniken der Stadt Mekka*, ii, 143) al-Walīd b. al-Mug͟hīra, was one of the "deriders" (*al-mustahziʾūn*) against whom verses in the Meccan sūras of the Ḳurʾān are said to have been directed (Muʾarrid̲j al-Sadūsī, *Ḥad͟hf min nasab Ḳurays͟h*, ed. al-Munad̲jd̲jid, 68; Ibn His͟hām, 272; Ibn Ḥabīb, 485-6; Ibn Durayd, 60-1, 94). But the tables were turned on Mak͟hzūm by the Prophet shortly after the *hid̲jra* at the battle of Badr [*q.v.*], where the Meccan force which went to the assistance of the threatened caravan was led by Abū D̲jahl. The Mak͟hzūmī losses were heavy: seven or eight of al-Mug͟hīra's twenty-five or so grandsons were killed on the Meccan side at Badr (among them Abū D̲jahl himself), together with a similar number and proportion of the same generation of the cadet branches of Mak͟hzūm, and others were taken captive (for details, see Ibn al-Kalbī, tables 22-3 and Register; al-Muṣʿab, 299-346; Watt, *Mecca*, 176-7); the three Mak͟hzūmīs who fought on the Prophet's side at Badr, viz. al-Arḳam b. ʿAbd Manāf, Abū Salama b. ʿAbd al-Asad, and S͟hammās b. ʿUt͟hmān, were all from the cadet branches of Mak͟hzūm, not from the Banu 'l-Mug͟hīra (Muʾarrid̲j, 73-4; Watt, *Mecca*, 176, and cf. 93). Losses of an order such as this inevitably weakened the position of Mak͟hzūm at Mecca, and in particular vis-à-vis Abū Sufyān [*q.v.*] and ʿAbd S͟hams. It was not until shortly before the Prophet's conquest of Mecca in late 8/January 630 that ʿIkrima b. Abī D̲jahl began to exert influence there as the new Mak͟hzūmī leader—one who was strongly opposed to entering into negotiations with the Prophet (Watt, *Medina*, 58, 62, 64); but by that stage more Mak͟hzūmīs were among those who had gone over to the Prophet, including K͟hālid b. al-Walīd b. al-Mug͟hīra [*q.v.*], who had earlier played a vigorous part in the Meccan military opposition to him. K͟hālid participated in the conquest of Mecca; and ʿIkrima fled to the Yemen.

Following the conquest of Mecca, Mak͟hzūm were incorporated into the new order. Two of their number, al-Ḥārit͟h b. His͟hām b. al-Mug͟hīra and Saʿīd b. Yarbūʿ, were among "those whose hearts were reconciled" (*al-muʾallafa ḳulūbuhum*: Watt, *Medina*, 74), presumably in their capacity as leaders of the Banu 'l-Mug͟hīra and the cadet branches respectively (Muʾarrid̲j, 74, also names a second person from the cadet branches in this connection). ʿIkrima received a pardon, returned from the Yemen, played a conspicuous part in the suppression of the *ridda* [*q.v.*] in 11/632-3 (see al-Ṭabarī, index; the Yemen was among the places to which this activity took him, but Muʾarrid̲j seems to be alone in holding the view (69) that Abū Bakr appointed him over the Yemen), and was subsequently mortally wounded in battle against the Byzantines in Syria (at either al-Ad̲jnādayn [*q.v.*] or al-Yarmūk [*q.v.*]: al-Muṣʿab, 303, 310; Ibn Saʿd, v, 329; Ibn Durayd, 93; al-Balād͟hurī, *Ansāb*, ms., ii, 526; al-Ṭabarī, i, 2100-1, iii, 2307). The continuing Mak͟hzūmī link with the Yemen also becomes apparent with the appointments there of al-Muhād̲jir b. Abī Umayya b. al-Mug͟hīra and ʿAbd Allāh b. Abī Rabīʿa b. al-Mug͟hīra; there is disagreement in the sources about points of detail, but it would seem that al-Muhād̲jir was appointed as governor of Ṣanʿāʾ by the Prophet in 10/631 but did not go there, was reappointed by Abū Bakr, went there, and was still there at the time of Abū Bakr's death in 13/634 (Muʿarrid̲j, 71; Ibn Durayd, 62, who incorrectly calls him al-Muhād̲jir b. ʿAbd Allāh b. Abī Umayya; al-Ṭabarī, i, 1750, 2013, 2135, iii, 2357). Even more confused are the reports relating to ʿAbd Allāh b. Abī Rabīʿa, who is one of those named in the earlier context of Mak͟hzūmī trade in the Yemen. He was appointed over al-D̲janad and its *mik͟hlāfs* by the Prophet (*Ag͟hānī*[1], i, 32), over all or part of the Yemen by Abū Bakr (al-Balād͟hurī, *Ansāb*, ms., ii, 531), and over the Yemen by ʿUmar (al-Muṣʿab, 317; Ibn Saʿd, v, 328, K͟halīfa b. K͟hayyāṭ, *Taʾrīk͟h*, ed. Zakkār, 154; Ibn Ḥazm, 146); he was governor of al-D̲janad at the time of ʿUmar's death (al-Ṭabarī, i, 2798; *Ag͟hānī*[1], i, 32) in 23/644 and at the time of the death of ʿUt͟hmān (al-Ṭabarī, i, 3057 Add.) in 35/656.

Two other Mak͟hzūmīs who were particularly active in this period were K͟hālid b. al-Walīd [*q.v.*] and al-Ḥārit͟h b. His͟hām. K͟hālid overcame the resistance of al-Musaylima [*q.v.*] in the Yamāma and subsequently played a leading role in the conquest of Syria. Al-

Ḥāri<u>th</u> also took part in the conquest of Syria and later migrated there with 70 of his *ahl bayt*, apparently because of his displeasure at being allocated by ʿUmar a stipend which reflected the tardiness of his conversion; he and all but four (or two) of those with him perished, variously in battle and of plague (al-Muṣʿab, 302; al-Ṭabarī, i, 2411-12, 2516, 2524). His surviving son ʿAbd al-Raḥmān was brought to Medina by ʿUmar, who awarded him an allocation of land (*<u>kh</u>iṭṭa* [*q.v.*]) there (al-Muṣʿab, 303). In this connection, it can be noted not only that ʿUmar's mother was from the Banu 'l-Mu<u>gh</u>īra (Ḥantama bint Hā<u>sh</u>im b. al-Mu<u>gh</u>īra: al-Muṣʿab, 301, 347; al-Balā<u>dh</u>urī, *Ansāb*, ms., ii, 531; al-Ṭabarī, i, 2728; al-Masʿūdī, *Murū<u>dj</u>*, iv, 192 = § 1525; Ibn Ḥazm, 144. Al-Masʿūdi says that she was black, from which Lammens (*Études*, 8 n.) inferred that she was "esclave des Maḫzoûmites"), but also that one of his wives, Umm Ḥakīm, was a daughter of al-Ḥāri<u>th</u> b. Hi<u>sh</u>ām (al-Muṣʿab, 349-50, cf. 302).

The line of ʿAbd al-Raḥmān b. al-Ḥāri<u>th</u> b. Hi<u>sh</u>ām was to be of particular importance within the large and influential Hi<u>sh</u>ām branch of the Banu 'l-Mu<u>gh</u>īra. ʿAbd al-Raḥmān fathered thirteen or fourteen sons (five or six of them by Fā<u>kh</u>ita bint ʿUtba of ʿĀmir b. Luʾayy) and eighteen daughters; al-Muṣʿab al-Zubayrī, writing in the first half of the 9th century A.D. remarks (419) on the large numbers of descendants of ʿAbd al-Raḥmān and Fā<u>kh</u>ita in his own time. Some idea of 7th century Ma<u>kh</u>zūmī connections can be gained not only from the information that ʿAbd al-Raḥmān's own wives included a daughter of al-Zubayr (who was herself a granddaughter of Abū Bakr) and a daughter of ʿU<u>th</u>mān (al-Muṣʿab, 111, 307-8; al-Balā<u>dh</u>urī, *Ansāb*, ms., ii, 526), but also from data relating to twenty-five marriages (all of them within Ḳuray<u>sh</u>) of his daughters: ten of these were with Ma<u>kh</u>zūmīs (all of them from the Banu 'l-Mu<u>gh</u>īra), eight of them were with Umayyads (including Muʿāwiya, although that was a childless union terminated by divorce), and five were with Zubayrids (ʿAbd Allāh b. al-Zubayr in two instances); the marriage settlement of 40,000 *dīnār*s paid by ʿAbd al-Malik's uncle, Yaḥyā b. al-Ḥakam in respect of one of these ladies, while it may not have been typical, does at least give us an indication of how large such a settlement could be (al-Muṣʿab, 306-8). In the following generation, the ten recorded marriages involving the six daughters of al-Mu<u>gh</u>īra b. ʿAbd al-Raḥmān are also instructive: one with a Ma<u>kh</u>zūmī (an *ibn ʿamm*), three with Marwānids (including one of ʿAbd al-Malik's sons) and five with other Ḳura<u>sh</u>is (descendants of Abū Bakr, ʿUmar, ʿU<u>th</u>mān, al-ʿAbbās and Ṭalḥa respectively); the tenth of these marriages, that of Umm al-Banīn bint al-Mu<u>gh</u>īra b. ʿAbd al-Raḥmān to al-Ḥa<u>djdj</u>ā<u>dj</u> b. Yūsuf [*q.v.*] (al-Muṣʿab, 310), represents the earliest indication of a Ma<u>kh</u>zūmiyya being given in marriage to a non-Ḳura<u>sh</u>ī (the two other examples of this phenomenon given by al-Muṣʿab (309, 310) involve sons of al-Ḥa<u>djdj</u>ā<u>dj</u>).

A second branch of the Banu 'l-Mu<u>gh</u>īra to which attention should be paid is that of al-Walīd b. al-Mu<u>gh</u>īra, particularly in the lines of his sons <u>Kh</u>ālid, Hi<u>sh</u>ām and al-Walīd. The distinction of <u>Kh</u>ālid's line lies above all in his own accomplishments and those of his son ʿAbd al-Raḥmān [*q.v.*], who was governor of Ḥimṣ and the <u>D</u>jazīra for Muʿāwiya and achieved renown as the leader of campaigns against the Byzantines. Al-Muṣʿab states quite categorically that the line came to an end in the time of (their agnate relative) Ayyūb b. Salama (328), i.e. by the end of the Umayyad period or conceivably just after; all forty or so of <u>Kh</u>ālid's male descendants died in a plague in Syria (Ibn Ḥazm, 148). The line of Hi<u>sh</u>ām b. al-Walīd is of interest because his grandson, Hi<u>sh</u>ām b. Ismāʿīl, in addition to being ʿAbd al-Malik's governor of Medina, was also the father of ʿAbd al-Malik's wife Umm Hi<u>sh</u>ām (Muʾarri<u>dj</u>, 71; al-Muṣʿab, 328; al-Balā<u>dh</u>urī, *Ansāb*, ms., ii, 541; Ibn Ḥazm, 148 (Umm Hā<u>sh</u>im); Ibn Ḥazm, *Ummahāt al-<u>kh</u>ulafāʾ*, ed. al-Muna<u>djdj</u>id, 17: her name was either ʿĀʾi<u>sh</u>a or Fāṭima). When her son Hi<u>sh</u>ām became caliph, he appointed his maternal uncles Ibrāhīm and Muḥammad, the sons of Hi<u>sh</u>ām b. Ismāʿīl, to terms of office as governors of Medina; they later ran foul of his successor, al-Walīd b. Yazīd, and were tortured to death on his instructions by the governor of ʿIrāḳ, Yūsuf b. ʿUmar [*q.v.*] (al-Muṣʿab, 329; al-Balā<u>dh</u>urī, *Ansāb*, ms., ii, 541 (Muḥammad was governor of Mecca and then of Medina)). As far as the line of al-Walīd b. al-Walīd is concerned, its interest lies primarily in the fact that it produced Umm Salama bint Yaʿḳūb b. Salama, who married the future first ʿAbbāsid caliph, Abu 'l-ʿAbbās; their daughter Rayṭa married the caliph al-Mahdī and bore him two sons (Muʾarri<u>dj</u>, 72; al-Muṣʿab, 330; al-Balā<u>dh</u>urī, *Ansāb*, iii, ed. al-Dūrī, 161, 180; Ibn Ḥazm, 148).

Although there were some Ma<u>kh</u>zūmīs in Syria (at least until <u>Kh</u>ālid's line became extinct) and some in ʿIrāḳ (mainly Baṣra) in the course of the Umayyad period, the main concentration of Ma<u>kh</u>zūm was in the Ḥi<u>dj</u>āz, at Mecca and Medina. The Ma<u>kh</u>zūm of Medina appear to have come into conflict with ʿU<u>th</u>mān on account of his maltreatment of the Companion ʿAmmār b. Yāsir [*q.v.*] (al-Masʿūdī, *Murū<u>dj</u>*, iv, 266, 299 = §§ 1591, 1602), who was a *mawlā* of theirs as a result of Abū Ḥu<u>dh</u>ayfa b. al-Mu<u>gh</u>īra's manumission of him (Ibn Ḥabīb, 312; Ibn Saʿd, iii/1, 176; al-Ṭabarī, iii, 2388). In the events following the murder of ʿU<u>th</u>mān, some Ma<u>kh</u>zūmī support for Ṭalḥa [*q.v.*] and al-Zubayr [*q.v.*] is indicated by the Ma<u>kh</u>zūmī casualities (<u>Kh</u>ālifa, 209) at the battle of the Camel (al-<u>D</u>jamal [*q.v.*]). In the ensuing confrontation between ʿAlī and Muʿāwiya, Muʿāwiya had the support of ʿAbd al-Raḥmān b. <u>Kh</u>ālid, who distinguished himself at the battle of Ṣiffīn [*q.v.*], where he bore the standard of the Syrian army (Lammens, *Études*, 5); and the Ma<u>kh</u>zūm of the Ḥi<u>dj</u>āz may be presumed to have preferred Muʿāwiya to ʿAlī. The presence on ʿAlī's side of <u>D</u>jaʿda b. Hubayra, who was from one of the cadet branches of Ma<u>kh</u>zūm, is explained by the identities of his mother and his wife: his mother was a daughter of Abū Ṭālib and his wife was a daughter of ʿAlī (Muʾarri<u>dj</u>, 75; al-Muṣʿab, 39, 45, 344, 345; Ibn Ḥazm, 141). Less easy to explain is the pro-Hā<u>sh</u>imite stance of <u>Kh</u>ālid's son al-Muhā<u>dj</u>ir, who was killed on ʿAlī's side at Ṣiffīn (Ibn Ḥabīb, 450; al-Balā<u>dh</u>urī, *Ansāb*, ms., ii, 543; *A<u>gh</u>ānī*[1], xv, 13).

If we are to judge by the pattern emerging from the marriages reported by al-Muṣʿab al-Zubayrī, however, it would seem that Muʿāwiya's ultimate victory was not particularly to the advantage of Ma<u>kh</u>zūm. Their links by marriage were stronger with the Zubayrids and the descendants of ʿU<u>th</u>mān and al-Ḥakam than with the Sufyānids. Moreover, relations between Muʿāwiya and Ma<u>kh</u>zūm deteriorated when ʿAbd al-Raḥmān b. <u>Kh</u>ālid was (at least allegedly) poisoned in 46/666 by Muʿāwiya's physician Ibn U<u>th</u>āl (reportedly on account of his growing popularity as potential successor to Muʿāwiya) and Ibn U<u>th</u>āl himself was killed in vengeance by ʿAbd al-Raḥmān's nephew <u>Kh</u>ālid b.

al-Muhād̲j̲ir (al-Muṣᶜab, 327; Ibn Ḥabīb, 449 ff.; al-Balād̲h̲urī, *Ansāb*, ms., ii, 542; *Ag̲h̲ānī*[1], xv, 13; al-Ṭabarī (ii, 82-3) seems to be alone in attributing the murder of Ibn Uthāl to K̲h̲ālid b. ᶜAbd al-Rahmān—the other sources know of no son of ᶜAbd al-Raḥmān's by that name. Cf. Lammens, *Études* 7-10). It is noticeable that there were no Mak̲h̲zūmī governors of Mecca from 48/668 until the end of Muᶜāwiya's caliphate in 60/680, although K̲h̲ālid b. al-ᶜĀṣī b. His̲h̲ām had hitherto held that post on several occasions (Ibn Saᶜd, v, 330; al-Fāsī, 161-6). Yazīd b. Muᶜāwiya did appoint K̲h̲ālid's son, the poet al-Ḥārit̲h̲ b. K̲h̲ālid, to the post (al-Muṣᶜab, 313, 390; al-Balād̲h̲urī, *Ansāb*, ms., ii, 531; Ibn Ḥazm, 146; al-Fāsī, 166), but it was also a Mak̲h̲zūmī (ᶜAbd Allāh b. Abī ᶜAmr b. Ḥafṣ b. al-Mug̲h̲īra) who was the first to forswear allegiance to Yazīd (al-Muṣᶜab, 332; al-Balād̲h̲urī, *Ansāb*, ms., ii, 539; Ibn Ḥazm, 149). In the ensuing second civil war, Mak̲h̲zūm were pro-Zubayrid with the single exception of al-Ḥārit̲h̲ b. K̲h̲ālid, who was pro-Marwānid (*Ag̲h̲ānī*[1], iii, 102); and they were accordingly represented among the governors appointed by Ibn al-Zubayr (al-Ḥārit̲h̲ al-Ḳubāᶜ b. ᶜAbd Allāh b. Abī Rabīᶜa b. al-Mug̲h̲īra at Baṣra; and ᶜAbd Allāh al-Azraḳ b. ᶜAbd al-Raḥmān b. al-Walīd b. ᶜAbd S̲h̲ams b. al-Mug̲h̲īra at al-D̲j̲anad (al-Muṣᶜab, 332)).

The defeat of the Zubayrids obviously affected the interests of Mak̲h̲zūm adversely, and ᶜAbd al-Malik saw the wisdom of being magnanimous in victory by drawing them closer to him. In addition to reinstating al-Ḥārit̲h̲ b. K̲h̲ālid as governor of Mecca, he appointed the Mak̲h̲zūmī His̲h̲ām b. Ismāᶜīl (from Banu 'l-Walīd b. al-Mug̲h̲īra) as governor of Medina and married his daughter; a second Mak̲h̲zūmiyya (Umm al-Mug̲h̲īra bint al-Mug̲h̲īra b. K̲h̲ālid b. al-ᶜĀṣī b. His̲h̲ām) is also identified as having been one of ᶜAbd al-Malik's wives (al-Muṣᶜab, 165; al-Mug̲h̲īra b. K̲h̲ālid is not otherwise known; al-Ḥārit̲h̲ b. K̲h̲ālid would make perfect sense); and the blind religious scholar, Abū Bakr b. ᶜAbd al-Raḥmān b. al-Ḥārit̲h̲ b. His̲h̲ām b. al-Mug̲h̲īra (d. in or *ca.* 93/711-12), whose predilection for ritual prayer, fasting and asceticism earned him the sobriquet "the monk" (*rāhib*) of Ḳuraysh", enjoyed the caliph's special favour (*kāna d̲h̲ā manzila min ᶜAbd al-Malik*: al-Muṣᶜab, 304; Ibn Saᶜd, v, 151; al-Balād̲h̲uri, *Ansāb*, ms., ii, 527-8; Ibn Ḥad̲j̲ar, *Tahd̲h̲ib*, xii, 31). There is not, however, any evidence of similar caliphal attention having been paid to Mak̲h̲zūm by ᶜAbd al-Malik's immediate successors. Al-Walīd dismissed His̲h̲ām b. Ismāᶜīl from his post at Medina, and the sources tell us little of Mak̲h̲zūm thereafter until the caliph His̲h̲ām appointed his maternal uncles as governors of Medina in the 720s to 740s; their demise at the hands of Yūsuf b. ᶜUmar shortly preceded the end of the Umayyad caliphate.

It is apparent that, as the Ḥid̲j̲āz became more and more a political backwater after the defeat of the Zubayrids, the role of Mak̲h̲zūm became increasingly restricted to one of being merely local gentry. Individual Mak̲h̲zūmīs crop up in the sources mainly in the context of religious learning and the application of Islamic law: In addition to Abū Bakr b. ᶜAbd al-Raḥmān (see above), special mention should be made of the *faḳīh* Saᶜīd b. al-Musayyab [*q.v.*], who was from one of the cadet branches of Mak̲h̲zūm; a list of Mak̲h̲zūmīs who transmitted *ḥadīth* is given by al-Ṭabarī (iii, 2383-8); ᶜAbd al-ᶜAzīz b. ᶜAbd al-Muṭṭalib (from one of the cadet branches) served as *ḳāḍī* of Medina in the time of the caliphs al-Manṣūr and al-Mahdī (al-Muṣᶜab, 341. Ibn Ḥazm, 142, says Mecca and Medina in the time of al-Manṣūr and al-Hādī), Muḥammad al-Awḳaṣ b. ᶜAbd al-Raḥmān (from the Banū His̲h̲ām b. al-Mug̲h̲īra) served as *ḳāḍī* of Mecca in the time of al-Mahdī (al-Muṣᶜab, 315; Ibn Ḥazm, 146; al-Balād̲h̲urī, *Ansāb*, ms., ii, 531 says in the time of Abū D̲j̲aᶜfar), and His̲h̲ām b. ᶜAbd al-Malik al-Aṣg̲h̲ar (from the Banū His̲h̲ām b. al-Mug̲h̲īra) served as *ḳāḍī* of Medina in the time of the caliph Hārūn al-Ras̲h̲īd (al-Muṣᶜab, 309; Ibn Ḥazm, 145). There are in addition indications that in the early ᶜAbbāsid period Mak̲h̲zūmī links with ᶜAlids, notably Ḥasanids, became closer (al-Muṣᶜab, 52-3, 56, 63); in particular, the mother of Idrīs b. ᶜAbd Allāh [*q.v.*], who founded the Idrisid dynasty in the Mag̲h̲rib at the end of the 8th century A.D., was ᶜĀtika bint ᶜAbd al-Malik b. al-Ḥārit̲h̲ b. K̲h̲ālid b. al-ᶜĀṣī (from the Banū His̲h̲ām b. al-Mug̲h̲īra: al-Muṣᶜab, 54, 315).

The bulk of the wealth and assets of Mak̲h̲zūm may be presumed to have been in the Ḥid̲j̲āz: they owned much land and property in and around Mecca (al-Azraḳī, ed. Wüstenfeld, in *Die Chroniken der Stadt Mekka*, i, 468-72 for details), as well as the *k̲h̲iṭṭa* at Medina awarded by ᶜUmar to ᶜAbd al-Raḥmān b. al-Ḥārit̲h̲ b. His̲h̲ām; and the report that ᶜAbd al-Raḥmān's son al-Mug̲h̲īra endowed an estate as a *waḳf* [*q.v.*] for the provision of food to pilgrims at Minā [*q.v.*] (al-Muṣᶜab, 305-6) does prompt the question of whether Mak̲h̲zūmīs may have had a stake in the business of provisioning more generally. There is not a great deal of evidence of Mak̲h̲zūmī economic involvement elsewhere: ᶜAmr b. Ḥurayt̲h̲, who was from one of the cadet branches, prospered greatly in al-Kūfa from early on (al-Muṣᶜab, 333; Ibn Durayd, 61); and Muḥammad b. ᶜUmar b. ᶜAbd al-Raḥmān b. al-Ḥārit̲h̲, who took the head of the rebel Yazīd b. al-Muhallab [*q.v.*] to the caliph Yazīd b. ᶜAbd al-Malik, was rewarded for his pains with the rebel's *dār* (sc. at al-Baṣra) and some of his estates (al-Balād̲h̲urī, *Ansāb*, ms., ii, 528). Insufficient evidence also prevents much being said about the nature of Mak̲h̲zūmī links with the Yemen after ᶜAbd Allāh b. Abī Rabīᶜa: the sole subsequent Mak̲h̲zūmī appointee there was Ibn al-Zubayr's governor of al-D̲j̲anad (see above); the land in the Yemen owned by ᶜAbd Allāh b. Abī Rabīᶜa (al-Ṭabarī, i, 2757) may have stayed in the family; and his son, the poet ᶜUmar (b. ᶜAbd Allāh) b. Abī Rabīᶜa [*q.v.*], had maternal relatives (*ak̲h̲wāl*) there (*Ag̲h̲ānī*[1], i, 49). As for Ethiopia, it remains to be ascertained whether there was any continuum between pre-Islamic Mak̲h̲zūmī activities there and the Mak̲h̲zūmī sultanate of Shoa, which ruled from the last decade for the ninth century A.D. until 1285 (*Cambridge History of Africa*, iii, 106, 140).

Bibliography: In addition to the items given in the article, see Ibn Abi 'l-Ḥadīd, *S̲h̲arḥ Nahd̲j̲ al-balāg̲h̲a*, ed. Ibrāhīm, xviii, 285-309; Schwarz, *Der Diwan des ᶜUmar ibn Abi Rebiᶜa*, 4 (Schluss-) Heft, Leipzig 1909, 1-33, esp. 9-12 (M. Hinds)

AL-**MAK̲H̲ZŪMĪ**, Abu 'l-Ḥasan ᶜAlī b. ᶜUt̲h̲mān al-Ḳuras̲h̲ī, author of an important, long-forgotten fiscal treatise, *al-Minhād̲j̲ fī ᶜilm k̲h̲arād̲j̲ Miṣr*, a large part of which was recently discovered in the acephalous ms. Add. 23,483 in the British Museum. Al-Mak̲h̲zūmī belonged to a great family dating back to the origins of Islam. He was a *ḳāḍī* and it was owing to this title, although he was a S̲h̲āfiᶜī as were nearly all the Egyptians, that the Fāṭimids, as was their custom, entrusted him with the duties of controlling the employees of the tax office, nearly all Copts. He performed these duties for a long time in Alexandria, and it is plain that he had acquired a concrete experience of the work, which his illustrious contemporary, Ibn Mammātī [*q.v.*] did not possess. Although the two works have similar documentary sources for some points and present almost the same form of administration (that of the later Fāṭimids prolonged under Saladin), they differ profoundly: the *Ḳawānīn al-dawāwīn* presents a clear, methodical account, without technical details which would be difficult for the senior civil servant to understand, of the fiscal régime of Egypt; the *Minhādj* is concerned, with the concrete activities performed by the employees of the tax office. For us, its remarkable originality lies in the minute description it gives of the customs and commercial administration of the Mediterranean ports frequented by Italian merchants; it provides despite the lacunas of the manuscript and the mediocrity of the style, something which no other work gives us in any corresponding measure. There is also an important chapter on the army, a very short one on the currency, the *ṭirāz*, etc. The author of the present article has devoted to the contents of the *Minhādj*, especially in *JESHO* for 1962, 1963, 1965 and 1972, a series of articles now gathered together in his *Makhzūmiyyāt* (Leiden 1978) and hopes to produce in the near future the complete Arabic text. The manuscript, however, comprises in its first part some historical developments and traditions which will be left aside, owing to the very poor state of these pages, of which al-Maḳrīzī reproduces all the main points. The *Minhādj* has been used to advantage by some young contemporary scholars, such as H. Rabie, in his *Financial system of Egypt*; R. Cooper, most recently in *JAOS* (1976); Gladys Frantz-Murphy (unpublished thesis); etc. (CL. CAHEN)

AL-**MAʿḲIL,** Arab tribe, probably of Yemeni origin, who, having come from Arabia at the same time as the Banū Hilāl [*q.v.*], crossed Egypt and Libya, entered the Maghrib towards the middle of the 5th/11th century, led a nomadic life for a short time to the west of Gabès (Ibn Khaldūn, *Berbères*, i, 36), but left only a small number of their members in the south of Ifrīḳiya (*Berbères*, i, 116; cf. R. Brunschvig, *Ḥafṣides*, ii, 170); in fact, they proceeded towards the west (*taghriba*), following the northern border of the Sahara (cf. al-Zayyānī, *Turdjumāna*, Fr. tr. Confourier, in *AM*, vi [1906], 448, who notes their route). However, it happened that they strayed from their route on occasion and also that, in 496/1103, the Ḥammādid al-Manṣūr (481-98/1088-1104 [*q.v.*]) was able to march on Tlemcen after having gathered together some Arab contingents including some Maʿḳil (*Berbères*, i, 54-5, 295). Similarly, at the beginning of the 6th/12th century, a clan of the tribe, the Thaʿāliba, occupied the region stretching from Titteri to Médéa and supplied the local rulers with auxiliary troops (*Berbères*, i, 92, 123, 253); Leo Africanus (ii, 349) mentions that in 915/1510 a member of this clan had become ruler of Algiers and held on to power for several years before being strangled in a *ḥammām* and replaced by Barbarossa [see KHAYR AL-DĪN], who dealt harshly, moreover, with the Thaʿāliba.

But it is principally in the oasis of Touat and Gourara (southern Algeria), and then in Morocco (where they began to infiltrate in the first decades of the 7th/13th century, so as to constitute an important collection of groups who were authentically Arab, at least in origin), that the majority of the Maʿḳil settled. They approached this land from the south-east and expanded rapidly in the eastern and southern regions of what constituted at that time al-Maghrib al-Aḳṣā, on the one hand between the west of the Oran region and the valley of the Moulouya (Malwiyya) as far as the Mediterranean coast and, on the other hand, in the south-east of present-day Morocco, in Tafilalt, Darʿa and Sous, as far as the Atlantic coast to the south of the High Atlas. The clans known as Dhawī Ḥassān and Shabbānāt, established further to the north, were to be summoned to Sous by ʿAlī b. Yedder (Idder = Yaḥyā or Yaʿīsh), who had rebelled against the Almohad al-Murtaḍā (646-65/1248-66) in 652/1254-5 (*Berbères*, i, 131, ii, 276-7), but it is quite possible that these clans may already have been in the area. Whatever may be the case, the Maʿḳil were not slow to impose their domination on the sedentary Berbers of the *ḳṣūr* and the oases, to levy tolls on the caravans that they were supposed to protect and to sow disorder in these lands which were already fairly turbulent; in fact, even if, according to Ibn Khaldūn (*Berbères*, i, 117), they did not always devote themselves to brigandage, they upset the economic situation and political structures quite considerably. Some of them remained nomads (camel breeders), especially in the steppes of eastern Morocco, but the majority settled, not without allying themselves at times with the local Berber groups in order to resist more effectively the sultan and his agents, should the occasion arise.

Even though on their arrival in Ifrīḳiya the Maʿḳil were, we are told, fewer than 200 (*Berbères*, i, 116), they increased considerably and added to their number allogenous elements, after having attained the goal of their principal migration. They formed, according to Ibn Khaldūn (*Berbères*, i, 115-34), three large groups called Dhawī (Dwi) ʿUbayd Allāh (between Tlemcen, Taourirt and the mouth of the Moulouya, in the plain of the Angād), Dhawī Manṣūr (who constituted the majority and occupied the region stretching from Taourirt to Darʿa, as well as the countryside around Taza, Fez, Meknès, and even Tadla) and Dhawī Ḥassān (between Darʿa and the Atlantic Ocean). The author of the *Kitāb al-ʿIbar* enumerates in great detail the families grouped within these three branches. He rejects the claim of the Maʿḳil to be descended from Djaʿfar b. Abī Ṭālib [*q.v.*] and, while being quite convinced that their origin is unknown, he is compelled by his intellectual honesty to consult Ibn al-Kalbī's *Djamhara*, retains two possible genealogies, and finally inclines in favour of that which links them with the Banū Madhhidj [*q.v.*]: in fact, the eponymous ancestor of the tribe is sometimes called Rabīʿa, and the Maʿḳil of the Madhhidj in fact bears the personal name of Rabīʿa b. Kaʿb (= al-Aratt) b. Rabīʿa (see Ibn al-Kalbī-Caskel, *Ǧamharat an-nasab*, Tab. 258). Moreover, G. Kampffmeyer (in *MSOS* [1899], 176) considers that the use of Dhawī pleads in favour of the Yemeni origin of the Maʿḳil. For his part, Leo Africanus does not indulge in the same speculations as Ibn Khaldūn, but he also divides the Maʿḳil into three branches (i, 27, 30-2) called Mukhtār, ʿUthmān and Ḥassān (cf. *Berbères*, i, 119, where the two first names only designate subdivisions). In both authors, the large groups contain an important number of families whose territory is mentioned with relative precision; however, they are far too numerous, and the nomenclature is much too variable, to be able to contemplate enumerating them here with any degree of reliability. It is even impossible, within the restricted limits of the present article, to relate the history of the most notable clans, even supposing that it were known sufficiently. We will therefore confine ourselves to the facts which appear the most remarkable.

It is probably in the last years of the Almohad dynasty (515-668/1121-1269) [see AL-MUWAḤḤIDŪN] that the Maʿkil settled in the pre-Saharan areas of Morocco, where they began to dominate the local populations without, however, playing a political role wide enough to be termed national. But on the accession of the Marīnids (668-823/1269-1420 [*q.v.*]), the situation was modified. Shortly after the unsuccessful siege (660/1261-2) of Sidjilmāsa [*q.v.*] by a Marīnid prince, the inhabitants of the town, which had fallen into the hands of the Maʿḳilī clan of the Munabbāt, appealed to the ʿAbd al-Wādids (7th-10th/13-16th centuries [*q.v.*]) of Tlemcen (*Berbères*, ii, 278-9), which led the Marīnid Yaʿḳūb b. ʿAbd al-Ḥaḳḳ (656-85/1258-86) to come to seize it in 672/1274 (*Berbères*, iv, 68-9) and to massacre the population. Various clans of the Maʿḳil, such as the Shabbānāt and the Dhawī Ḥassān, also tried to oppose the interference of the new sultans in the territories of the south where they were solidly established (*Berbères*, ii, 132). Profiting from this troubled situation, a relative of the sultan Abū Yaʿḳūb (685-706/1286-1307) passed over in 686/1287 to the Dhawī Ḥassān and "raised the standard of revolt"; the sovereign sent against the rebels, to the east of Darʿa, his nephew Manṣūr b. Abī Mālik who slaughtered them in large numbers and seized their herds and womenfolk. Several months later, the sultan himself went to Darʿa to punish some Maʿḳil who were practising brigandage (*Berbères*, iv, 123). Generally, eastern Morocco suffered from the opposition of these tribes to the Marīnid sovereigns, until the time when Abū ʿInān (749-59/1349-58 [*q.v.*]) appointed to Darʿa a governor who won their friendship and succeeded in imposing his authority, but he had to grant them *iḳṭāʿ*s and entrust them with collecting taxes (*Berbères*, i, 117, 132); these privileges, from which some clans benefited, did not prevent several others from continuing to plunder the whole region; at the end of the 8th/14th century, the Maʿḳil brought anarchy to Sous and seized revenues which should have been paid to the Marīnids (*Berbères*, i, 133).

It is probably towards the end of this dynasty that, not content with controlling the oases and Saharan borders, some Maʿḳil proceeded as far as the Ḥawz of Marrakech, devastating on their way cultivated lands and forests (see J. Berque, *Antiquités Seksawa*, in *Hespéris* [1953], 379, 401-2). In the following century, the plain of Shīshāwa and the town of Amizmiz on the northern slopes of the High Atlas were suffering from the presence of "Arabs" who overtaxed the people (Leo, i, 98).

At almost the same period, i.e. in the 8th-9th/14th-15th centuries, some Dhawī Ḥassān, who were accustomed to spending the winter in the area called al-Sāḳiya al-ḥamrāʾ [*q.v.*], spread into the western Sahara. It is not known under exactly what conditions this partial migration took place towards a region which today forms part of the Republic of Mauritania, but as the groups in question had received the title of *makhzan* tribes [see DJAYSH, iii], it could be considered a conquest on behalf of the sultans of Morocco (on this problem of territorial distribution, see MŪRĪTĀNIYA). In any case, the dialect of the Arabic speakers of the land, *Ḥassāniyya*, is related to those who are known as the clan of the Dhawī Ḥassān, without, from an ethnic point of view, necessarily being associated with the confederation of the Maʿḳil (see D. Cohen, *Le dialecte arabe* ḥassānīya *de Mauritanie*, Paris 1963).

The decadence of the Marīnids also encouraged other Maʿḳil to speed up their movement northwards and to enter the Middle Atlas in search of summer pastures; they appeared in the region of Khunayḳ al-Ghirbān, on the direct route from Tafilalt to Fez, before spreading, at the beginning of the 11th/17th century, in the region of Sefrou, bringing in their wake migrations of Berber tribes (see G. S. Colin, *Origine arabe des grands mouvements de populations berbères dans le Moyen-Atlas*, in *Hespéris*, 1938/2-3, 265-8). And it is probably at the end of the 9th/15th century that the Zaër (Zaʿīr), who are authentic Maʿḳil (al-Ifrānī, *Nuzha*, Fr. tr. Houdas, 329), moved northwards across the mountainous massifs of the High and Middle Atlas. Leo Africanus (i, 249-50) mentions them near Khenifra, and they then descended the valleys of the Bou Regreg and its tributaries to come to settle to the south of Rabat, where they are still to be found (see V. Loubignac, *Textes arabes des Zaër*, PIHEM, xlvi, Paris 1953).

Leo Africanus also recalls (ii, 426-7) that in the same period the Maʿḳil were the masters of Sidjilmāsa and that they controlled the traffic, levying a toll; but, even if they did not attack caravans, their presence made the traditional routes from the Maghrib to the Sudan impracticable, so that travellers had to make detours.

At the end of the 9th/15th century, they were powerful enough in the south-west of Morocco to participate in the agreements reached in 904/1499 between the Berbers and Castile (D. Jacques-Meunié, *Maroc Saharien*, i, 317), Subsequently, their attitude towards the Portuguese regarding the position of Santa Cruz of the Cap de Gué [see AGADIR-IGHIR] seems to have been conditioned by their relations with the Saʿdids (961-1064/1544-1654 [*q.v.*]). In fact, in the period which witnessed the birth of the movement which was to result in the foundation of this dynasty, the Berbers of Sous, exhausted by the oppression that the Arabs had inflicted upon them, supported the action of these more or less genuine *sharīfs* whom they continued to uphold, whereas the clan of the Shabbānāt of the plain of Sous and the western High Atlas were, it seems, the only one to rally to the Saʿdids, whose famous sultan Aḥmad al-Manṣūr (986-1012/1578-1603 [*q.v.*]) married a wife from this family.

The Maʿḳil who remained in the region of Guercif towards the end of the Saʿdid dynasty gathered in 1051/1641-2 around the ʿAlawid Mawlāy Muḥammad b. al-Sharīf (1050-75/1640-64), who seized Oujda and pressed his advantage as far as the south of Algeria, but his followers abandoned him in 1074/1664 and recognised his brother Mawlāy al-Rashīd (1075-82/1664-72 [*q.v.*]) whom they proclaimed in Oujda. These events were not able to limit the activity of other Maʿḳil, who continued for their part to trouble public order. It was also in 1069/1659 that Karrūm al-Ḥādjdj occupied Marrakech and, ten years later, Mawlāy al-Rashīd found the Shabbānāt masters of the capital of the South (see G. Deverdun, *Marrakech des origines à 1912*, Rabat 1959-66, i, 460). The brother and successor of this latter sultan, Mawlāy Ismāʿīl (1082-1139/1672-1727 [*q.v.*]) added to his army some Maʿḳil from the oases to form the *gīsh* (*djaysh*) of Ūdāya, but he treated other members of the tribe harshly (see al-Zayyānī, *Turdjumān*, Fr. tr. Houdas, 35), the Aḥlāf (= ʿAmārna and Munabbāt of the Dhawī Manṣūr from the region of Sidjilmāsa); after his death, these clans recovered their old power.

It would be difficult today to trace the descendants of the various groups of Maʿḳil, more especially as the names which designated them changed frequently in the course of centuries. Furthermore, it is probable that some members of this confederation were distinguished in the religious or literary sphere, but the adjective Maʿḳilī does not appear to be used, and it would be necessary to search in the lists—without any assurance of success—for those members of the tribe corresponding to the numerous families cited by Ibn Khaldūn. We will restrict ourselves to remarking that the Thaʿālibīs of Algeria, who produced a renowned theologian (788-873/1386-1468 [*q.v.*]) and probably belonged to the Maʿḳil, occupy a prominent position till our own day. Ibn ʿAskar (*Dawḥat al-nāshir*, ed. Ḥadjdjī, Rabat 1396/1976, 101) notes that the *faḳīh* and saint by the name of ʿUmar al-Ḥusaynī who died in the years 940s/1530s, was *min ḳabīlat Ḥuṣayn min ʿArab al-Maʿḳil* (more precisely, from the Dhawī Manṣūr); such a note is however isolated. It is also not impossible that the Maʿḳil may be have taken part in the spread of the popular poetry known in Morocco by the name of *məlḥūn* [see MALḤŪN].

It is evident from the brief account that precedes that different groups of this tribe were scattered over a territory which, within the present Moroccan frontiers, forms a crescent going from the Mediterranean to the Atlantic Ocean, crossing the High and Middle Atlas and turning its convex side towards the desert. But the vast territory occupied by these Arabs is not continuous, to such an extent that, being intimately mixed with Berber populations, they scarcely have the feeling of belonging to a homogeneous ethnic group. This situation explains how the various clans would often rally to opposite camps, favouring moreover the weakest dynasty (cf. *Berbères*, i, 120-1). If some of them, still partially nomadic, rebelled spontaneously, those who were settled in Tafilalt and Sous provided a refuge rather for princes who were in more or less open rebellion and who found on the spot combatants ready to help them, at least provisionally. So the almost constant policy of the authorities established in the capital was to suppress energetically any sign of insubordination and to prevent these Arabs—although employed at times as auxiliaries—from moving northwards to settle in more fertile regions, which they nevertheless succeeded at times in doing, when the central power showed signs of weakness.

Bibliography: Among the Arabic sources, the richest is the *Kitāb al-ʿIbar* of Ibn Khaldūn, of which only the French translation of de Slane is cited, entitled *Histoire des Berbères*, 2nd ed., Paris 1925-34, 1956). From Ibn ʿIdhārī (7th-8th/13th-14th centuries), whose *Bayān* (vol. iii) published by A. Huici Miranda in Tetuan in 1963 had been used by the latter in the preparation of his *Historia política del imperio almohade*, Tetuan 1956, the Arab historians of the Maghrib and especially of Morocco (notably al-Ifrānī/Ufrānī, *Nuzhat al-ḥādī*, Fr. tr. O. Houdas, Paris 1888-9, Ibn Abī Zarʿ, *Rawḍ al-ḳirṭās*, Rabat 1972, and al-Nāṣirī, *Istiḳṣāʾ*, Casablanca 1954-6) were led by force of circumstances to cite the Maʿḳil. The same applies to even the authors of general histories such as Ch.-A. Julien, *Histoire de l'Afrique du Nord*[2], Paris 1952, H. Terrasse, *Histoire du Maroc*, Casablanca 1949-50, and A. Laroui, *Histoire du Maghreb*, Paris 1970.

Apart from Ibn Khaldūn, another important source is Leo Africanus, whose *Description de l'Afrique*, Fr. tr. Épaulard, Paris 1956, gives an idea of the situation at the beginning of the 16th century. Independently of the partial studies, of which some have been cited in the art., two works are of particular interest: those of G. Marçais, *Les Arabes en Berbérie du XIe au XIVe siècle*, Constantine-Paris 1913, 364-404, 548-81 and index (with a map of the distribution of tribes at the end of the work) and Mme D. Jacques-Meunié, *Le Maroc saharien des origines à 1670*, Paris 1982, index, *s.vv.* Arabes Maâqil and Maâqil (with an extensive bibliography); the other works of the latter author, notably *Cités anciennes de Mauritanie*, Paris 1961, also contain useful information. See also F. de La Chapelle, *Esquisse d'une histoire du Sahara occidental*, in *Hespéris* xi/1-2 (1930), 35-95, esp. 65-70. Finally, one should cite an unpublished thesis submitted in Paris in 1984 by M. Kably and entitled *Société, pouvoir et religion au Maroc, des Mérinides aux Waṭṭāsides (XIVe-XVe siècles)*, index. (CH. PELLAT)

AL-**MAKĪN** B. AL-ʿ**AMĪD**, DJIRDJIS, (602-72/1205-73) Arabic-speaking Coptic historian whose *History*, covering the period from the creation of the world to the year 658/1260, was one of the very first mediaeval oriental chronicles to become known in Europe and consequently played a significant role in the early researches of modern Islamic scholars.

The encyclopaedists, who since the 18th century have provided a biography of al-Makīn which is still reproduced by Brockelmann (I, 348) and Graf (*GCAL*, i, 348), have omitted to indicate their sources; all that is known is that the history of the family of al-Makīn was related in his own appendix to a manuscript with which these scholars were evidently familiar. However, this account, an enlargement from his biography, is certainly the basis of the version supplied by the Christian Arab al-Suḳāʿī, *Tālī kitāb Wafayāt al-aʿyān* (ed. J. Sublet, no. 167) and subsequently reproduced by al-Ṣafadī and al-Maḳrīzī in the *Muḳaffā*. Al-Makīn was descended from a merchant of Takrīt who settled in Egypt under the caliphate of al-ʿĀmir; the younger son of this merchant (if our biographers are not missing out a generation) held high offices in the *dīwān al-djaysh* from Ṣalāḥ al-Dīn to al-Ṣāliḥ Ayyūb, offices in which he was succeeded by his son al-Makīn, first in Egypt and later in Damascus. Implicated in the unrest which broke out in Syria at the time of the Mongol invasion and the beginning of the reign of Baybars, al-Makīn spent several years in prison; he ended his life in Damascus, but remained in close contact with Egyptian Coptic scholars, like al-ʿAssāl, who possessed a manuscript of the history of al-Makīn (Graf, *loc. cit.*).

This history, *al-Madjmūʿ al-mubārak*, generally known by the simple title of *History*, is a universal chronicle covering the period from the origins of the world to the accession of Baybars (658/1260). It is divided into two major sections: the first concerning pre-Islamic history as far as the eleventh year of Heraclius; the second, Islamic history to the year 658. (i) *Pre-Islamic section*. It is today difficult, if not impossible, to determine the originality of the *History* of al-Makīn, for two reasons: on the one hand, the manuscripts have not been classified; on the other, the similar work of his contemporary Ibn al-Rāhib [*q.v.* in Suppl.], which al-Makīn frequently quotes, has not yet been edited. G. Wiet, who undertook an edition of the history, has given some indications as to the manuscript transmission of the earlier section, in J. Maspero, *Histoire des Patriarches d'Alexandrie*, Paris 1923, 219-22, n. 2. He identified two distinct groups of manuscripts, one transmitting the original text of al-Makīn, the other, which he calls the vulgate, being an edition adapted according to the model of Eutychius/Ṣāʿid b. al-Biṭrīk (it was a manuscript of this vulgate which was utilised by al-Maḳrīzī, e.g. B.N. ar. 4729).

In addition, al-Makīn makes frequent textual quotations from Ibn al-Rāhib. Before the researches of A. Sidarus, *Ibn al-Rāhibs Leben und Werk*, Freiburg-i.-Br. 1972, the latter's *Universal history* was known only in the form of an abbreviated edition which has misled more than one historian (L. Cheikho, *Petrus ibn Rahib chronicon orientale*, in *CSCO*, xlv, Louvain 1903). But there is now available a complete manuscript of the *K. al-Tawārīkh*, a work dating from 1257, and the forthcoming publication of this text will no doubt make it possible to assess how much of al-Makīn's work is to be considered original.

Whatever may prove to be the case, al-Makīn presents universal history in the form of biographies: to the year 586 B.C., it is naturally enough the biblical account which provides the format, the biographical series beginning with Adam; after the destruction of the Temple of Solomon he traces the ancient dynasties of Asia, then those of Alexander, the Romans, the Byzantines.

(ii) *Islamic section.* The second part of al-Makīn's history is quite unconnected with the first and appears to be an abridged version of al-Ṭabarī, supplemented with material from more recent sources dealing with the history of Syria and Egypt. But in fact it seems that al-Makīn was not directly responsible for this work; a comparison between his text and the *Taʾrīkh Ṣāliḥī* of Ibn Wāṣil (unedited) leads to the conclusion that al-Makīn virtually copied either this work, or a hitherto unidentified common source; the only doubt arises from the fact that the correspondence between the texts ceases with the death of Ṣalāḥ al-Dīn, although Ibn Wāṣil's history extends to the year 635/1238; for the early stages of this final period al-Makīn clearly lacks source-material.

Whatever the case may be, the abbreviated nature of the greater part of this history makes it less useful to us than to our predecessors. Only the last part, contemporary with the life of the author, is more detailed and of vastly superior originality and interest. By an unfortunate chance, Erpenius, who edited the work in the 17th century, stopped short at the year 525/1130, with the result that the final section has remained virtually unknown until the present day and its publication by Cl. Cahen (in *BEO*, xv [1955]; cf. *Arabica*, vi, 198-9, and *al-Makīn et Ibn Wāṣil*, in *Hispano-Arabica... Fr. Pareja*, i, Madrid 1974, 158-67).

A characteristic apparently common to all Arabic historiography, Christian or Muslim, is that authors of both persuasions write in almost the same manner and indulge in mutual plagiarism. As has been observed, al-Makīn follows a Muslim predecessor and is utilised in his turn by Shāfiʿ b. ʿAlī. The only difference is that the Christian supplements the Hegirian chronology with a Christian chronology (in this case the Era of the Martyrs) and includes in his account episodes of ecclesiastical history (which were to be borrowed by al-Maḳrīzī). Certain copyists continue his list of patriarchs as far as the year 720/1320. It is not known whether al-Makīn utilised the history of the patriarchs compiled by Severus b. al-Muḳaffaʿ and his successors.

The final section of the work of al-Makīn, the part contemporary with his own life, is totally undeserving of the pejorative judgment of it expressed on the author by Renaudot (*Hist. Patriarch. Alex.*, Paris 1713, 10); it is intellectually comparable with the works of the major historians of the period, with a particularly sensitive interest in military administration, reflecting the professional career of the author. Most important of all, the principal historians of this time, even though they deal with Egypt, are of Syrian nationality; together with the Muslim Ibn Muyassar, whose treatment of the Ayyūbids is accessible to us only through al-Nuwayrī's version, al-Makīn is the only Egyptian historian of his generation. His work was continued by al-Mufaḍḍal b. Abi 'l-Faḍāʾil, who was of the same family but who makes no mention of him.

Also published, but erroneously, under the name of al-Makīn was a doctrinal study, *al-Ḥāwī*, ed. Taridus Basili, Cairo, Maison Copte (cf. *Abstracta Isl.*, 1966 no. 831).

Bibliography: Given in the article; supplementary details concerning the early section are given by M. Plessner in *EI*[1], *s.v.*

(CL. CAHEN and R. G. COQUIN)

MAKKA (in English normally "Mecca", in French "La Mecque"), the most sacred city of Islam, where the Prophet Muḥammad was born and lived for about 50 years, and where the Kaʿba [*q.v.*] is situated.

1. THE PRE-ISLAMIC AND EARLY ISLAMIC PERIODS

Geographical description.—Mecca is located in the Ḥidjāz about 72 km. inland from the Red Sea port of Jedda (Djudda [*q.v.*]), in lat. 21° 27′ N. and long. 39° 49′ E. It is now the capital of the province (*manāṭiḳ idāriyya*) of Makka in Suʿūdī Arabia, and has a normal population of between 200,000 and 300,000, which may be increased by one-and-a-half or two millions at the time of the Ḥadjdj or annual pilgrimage.

Mecca lies in a kind of corridor between two ranges of bare steep hills, with an area in the centre rather lower than the rest. The whole corridor is the *wādī* or the *baṭn Makka*, "the hollow of Mecca", and the lower part is al-Baṭḥāʾ, which was doubtless the original settlement and where the Kaʿba stands. Originally some of the houses were close to the Kaʿba, but apparently there was always a free space round it, and in the course of centuries this has been enlarged to constitute the present mosque. Into the Baṭḥāʾ converged a number of side-valleys, each known as a *shiʿb*, and often occupied by a single clan. The outer and higher area of settlement was known as the *ẓawāhir.* The situation of Mecca was advantageous for trade. Important routes led northwards to Syria (Gaza and Damascus); north-eastwards through a gap in the mountain chain of the Sarāt to ʿIrāḳ; southwards to the Yemen; and westwards to the Red Sea, where there were sailings from Shuʿayba (and later from Djudda) to Abyssinia and other places. Rainfall is scant and irregular. There may be none for four years. When it does come, it may be violent and a *sayl* or torrent may pour down each *shiʿb* towards the *Ḥaram* or sacred area round the Kaʿba. There are accounts of the flooding of the *Ḥaram* from time to time. The supply of water depended on wells, of which that at Zamzam beside the Kaʿba was the most famous. One of the leading men of Mecca was always charged with the *siḳāya*, that is, with the duty of seeing there was sufficient water for the pilgrims taking part in the *Ḥadjdj*. Needless to say, there was no agriculture in the neighbourhood of Mecca. The climate of Mecca was described by the geographer al-Muḳaddisī as "suffocating heat, deadly winds, clouds of flies". The summer was noted for *ramḍāʾ Makka*, "the burning of Mecca", and the wealthier families sent their children to be brought up in the desert for a time.

Pre-Islamic Mecca.—Mecca had been a sacred site from very ancient times. It was apparently known to Ptolemy as Macoraba. The Ḳurʾān has the name Makka in XLVIII, 24, and the alternative name Bakka in III, 96/90. It also (II, 125-7/119-21) speaks of the building of the Kaʿba by Abraham and Ishmael, but this is generally not accepted by occidental scholars, since it cannot be connected with what is otherwise known of Abraham. According to Arabian legend, it was for long controlled by the tribe of Djurhum [*q.v.*], and then passed to Khuzāʿa [*q.v.*], though certain privileges remained in the hands of older families. After a time, presumably in the 5th century A.D., Khuzāʿa were replaced by Ḳuraysh [*q.v.*]. This came about through the activity of Ḳuṣayy [*q.v.*], a descendant of Ḳuraysh (or Fihr), who became powerful through bringing together hitherto disunited groups of the tribe of Ḳuraysh and gaining the help of allies from Kināna and Ḳuḍāʿa. It is probable that Ḳuṣayy was the first to make a permanent settlement here as distinct from temporary encampments. In later times a distinction was made between Ḳuraysh al-Biṭāḥ (those of the Baṭḥāʾ or centre) and Ḳuraysh al-Ẓawāhir (those of the outer area); and it is significant that all the descendants, not only of Ḳuṣayy but of his great-grandfather Kaʿb, are included in the former. These are the clans of ʿAbd al-Dār, ʿAbd Shams, Nawfal, Hāshim, al-Muṭṭalib, Asad (all descended from Ḳuṣayy), and Zuhra, Makhzūm, Taym, Sahm, Djumaḥ and ʿAdī. The most important clans of Ḳuraysh al-Ẓawāhir were Muḥārib, ʿĀmir b. Luʾayy and al-Ḥārith b. Fihr. There are no grounds, however, for thinking this distinction was equivalent to one between patricians and plebeians.

In the 6th century A.D. divisions appear within Ḳuraysh al-Biṭāḥ. ʿAbd al-Dār had succeeded to some of the privileges of his father Ḳuṣayy, but in course of time his family was challenged by the descendants of another son of Ḳuṣayy, ʿAbd Manāf, represented by the clan of ʿAbd Shams. ʿAbd Manāf had the support of Asad, Zuhra, Taym and al-Ḥārith b. Fihr; and this group was known as the Muṭayyabūn ("perfumed ones" [see LAʿAḲAT AL-DAM]). ʿAbd al-Dār's group, known as the Aḥlāf or Confederates, included Makhzūm, Sahm, Djumaḥ and ʿAdī. A compromise agreement was reached without actual fighting. About the year 605 (Ibn Habīb, *Munammaḳ*, 46) a league is mentioned called the Ḥilf al-Fuḍūl [*q.v.*] which seems to be a continuation of the Muṭayyabūn. It comprised the same clans as the latter, except that of the four sons of ʿAbd Manāf only Hāshim and al-Muṭṭalib were in the Ḥilf al-Fuḍūl, while Nawfal and ʿAbd Shams remained aloof. The ostensible reason for this league was to help a Yamanī merchant to recover a debt from a man of Sahm (al-Masʿūdī, *Murūdj*, iv, 123 f. = §§ 1451-3; cf. Ibn Ḥabīb, *Muḥabbar*, 167; idem, *Munammaḳ*, 45-54; Ibn Hishām, 85-7; al-Ṭabarī, i, 1084 f.). This suggests that the Ḥilf al-Fuḍūl was not a general league against injustice (as maintained by Caetani, *Annali*, i, 164-6) but was an association of commercially weaker clans attempting to curb unfair monopolistic practices by stronger and wealthier clans—the repudiation of debts would discourage non-Meccans from sending caravans to Mecca and increase the profits of the caravans of the great merchants of Mecca (sc. those not in the Ḥilf al-Fuḍūl).

From many other pieces of evidence it is clear that by this time Mecca had become an important commercial centre. Because of the sanctuary at Mecca and the institutions of the sacred months, when blood feuds were in abeyance, there had doubtless been some commerce for many centuries. It would appear, however, that during the second half of the 6th century A.D. the trade of Mecca had increased enormously. It might be conjectured that the wars between the Byzantines and Persians had made the route through western Arabia more attractive than that from the Persian Gulf to Aleppo. Even if this is not so, the leading merchants of Mecca had gained control of a great volume of trade passing between Syria and the Mediterranean on the one hand and South Arabia and the Indian Ocean on the other. Despite the Ḥilf al-Fuḍūl, it would appear that most of the merchandise was carried in caravans organised by wealthy Meccans. The Ḳurʾān (XVI, 2) speaks of "the winter and summer caravans", and it is usually stated that the former went to the Yemen and the latter to Syria [see ĪLĀF]. Normally, a caravan carried goods belonging to many groups and individuals, who presumably gave a proportion of their profits to the organisers. The organisers had to enter into agreements with the political authorities in Syria and South Arabia, and possibly also with the ruler of al-Ḥīra and the Negus of Abyssinia, in order to be allowed to buy and sell; and they had to ensure the safety of the caravans by agreements with the nomadic chiefs through whose areas they passed.

It is possible that the expedition of the "men of the elephant" (Ḳurʾān, CV, 1) was occasioned by the growing prosperity of Mecca, and that Abraha [*q.v.*], the Abyssinian ruler of the Yemen, wanted to reduce its commerce by attacking the sanctuary which facilitated it.

The war of the Fidjār [*q.v.*] certainly marks a stage in the growth of Meccan commercial strength, since it appears to have resulted in the elimination of al-Ṭāʾif as a rival centre of trade and its incorporation into the Meccan system in a subordinate position. The term "system" is appropriate since Mecca was a financial centre, and not a mere focus of trade. By about 600 A.D., the leading men were skilled in the manipulation of credit and interested in possibilities of investment along the routes they travelled, such as the mines in the territory of the tribe of Sulaym. It may be noted that one or two women were merchants, trading on their own account and employing men as their agents; such were Khadīdja [*q.v.*], Asmāʾ bint Mukharriba, mother of Abū Djahl, and Hind, wife of Abū Sufyān. Among the goods carried were leather, ingots of gold and silver, gold dust (*tibr*), perfumes and spices, the two latter from South Arabia or India. From Syria they conveyed the products of Mediterranean industry, such as cotton, linen and silk fabrics, and also arms, cereals and oil. Some of these goods would be sold to nomadic tribesmen, others would be sold in markets at the further end of the trade route.

Henri Lammens spoke of Mecca as a "merchant republic", and this description fits up to a point, but the underlying political concepts were those of Arabia, not of Greece or Italy. Almost the only organ of government, apart from clan assemblies, was the *malaʾ* or "senate". This was in fact a meeting of the chiefs and leading men of various clans, but had no executive powers. Any punitive measures could be taken only by the chief of the offender's clan, since otherwise the *lex talionis* [see ḲIṢĀṢ] would be invoked. There was no president or doge, but sometimes a man's personal talents gave him a degree of primacy (as Abū Sufyān had for three years after the defeat at Badr in 624). The Ḳuraysh, however, were renowned for their *ḥilm* [*q.v.*] or "steadiness", and this in practice meant putting their commercial interests before all other considerations. Because of this, the *malaʾ* was often able to compose differences between its members and come to a common mind. Thus most of the leading men were agreed on a policy of neutrality in the struggle of the two giant empires of the day, the Byzantine Greek one and the Sāsānid Persian one. Both were trying to extend their spheres of influence in Arabia. When, in about 570 or 575, the Persians conquered the Yemen from the Abyssinians, it became all the more necessary for the Meccans to remain neutral. Some years after the war of the Fidjār, a man of the clan of Asad called ʿUthmān b. al-Ḥuwayrith entered into negotiations with the Byzantines and told his fellow-Meccans that he could get favourable trade terms for them if they accepted him as their leader; though he was denounced by a men of his clan as aiming at kingship, the rejection of his proposition was doubtless also due to the need of avoid too close an association with the Byzantines.

In addition to the *malaʾ*, there were certain traditional offices or functions, usually attached to specific families. The *siḳāya* or superintendence of the water-supply, especially for pilgrims, has already been mentioned. The *rifāda* was the provisioning of pilgrims; the *liwāʾ* was the carrying of the standard in war; the *nasī* was the privilege of deciding when an intercalary month should be inserted to keep the lunar calendar in line with the solar year; and there were several others.

The culture and religion of the Meccans were essentially the same as those of their nomadic neighbours. They applied the *lex talionis* in much the same way, and had similar ideas about the relations of a chief or *sayyid* to the full members of his clan or tribe, namely, that he was only *primus inter pares*. They likewise gave a central place to the conception of honour [see ʿIRḌ], though in detail Meccan ideas of honour may have been modified by the ideas of wealth and power. Like most nomadic Arabs, the majority of Meccans were pagans, acknowledging many gods, but probably having little faith in these and being mainly materialistic in outlook. The Ḳurʾān, however, in a number of passages, describes pagans who, besides the minor deities, acknowledging Allāh as a "high god" or supreme god, and especially his function of creating. This form of belief is known to have been predominant among the Semitic peoples of a whole wide region (cf. J. Teixidor, *The pagan god*, Princeton 1977). In addition, besides Byzantine visitors or temporary residents, one or two Meccans seem to have become Christians, such as ʿUthmān b. al-Ḥuwayrith, and others are said to have been attracted to monotheism [see ḤANĪF]. One or two, whose business contacts were with ʿIrāḳ, had some interest in Persian culture.

Mecca and the beginnings of Islam.— Although the Ḳurʾānic message had from the first a universal potential, it was originally addressed to Meccans. The attraction of the message for many Meccans was due to its relevance to the moral, social and spiritual malaise which had developed in Mecca as a result of the great increase in wealth. It is thus not accidental that Mecca still remains the focus of the religion of Islam. The career of Muḥammad and the early history of the religion which he proclaimed will be found in the article MUḤAMMAD. Here the relation of these events to the town of Mecca will be briefly noted.

Muḥammad was born in Mecca into the clan of Hāshim about 570 A.D. This clan may have been more important earlier, but was not now among the very wealthy clans, and played a prominent part in the Ḥilf al-Fuḍūl, which was directed against monopolistic practices. Because Muḥammad was a posthumous child and his grandfather died when he was about eight, he was excluded by Arabian custom from inheriting anything from either. Most of his near kinsmen were engaged in trade, and Muḥammad accompanied his uncle Abū Ṭālib on trading journeys to Syria. Then he was employed as a steward by the woman merchant Khadīdja and subsequently married her. This was about 595, and thereafter he seems to have continued to trade with her capital and in partnership with one of her relatives. It was no doubt his personal experience of these consequences of being an orphan which made Muḥammad specially aware of the problems facing Meccan society; and it was about 610, after he had long meditated on these matters, that the Ḳurʾānic revelation began to come to him.

The Ḳurʾān may be said to see the source of the troubles of Mecca as the materialism of many Meccans and their failure to believe in God and the Last Day. In particular, it attacked the great merchants for their undue reliance on wealth and their misuse of it by neglecting the traditional duties of the leading men to care for the poor and unfortunate. At the same time, the Ḳurʾān summoned all men to believe in God's power and goodness, including his position as final Judge, and to worship him. In the years up to 614 or 615 many people responded to this summons, including sons and younger brothers of the great merchants. By 614 some of these great merchants, especially younger ones like Abū Djahl, had come to feel their position threatened by Muḥammad, since his claim to receive messages from God and the number of people attracted by his preaching might eventually give him great political authority. A movement of opposition to the new religion then appeared. The great merchants applied pressures of various kinds to Muḥammad and his followers to get them to abandon their beliefs, or at least to compromise. Some of his followers, persecuted by their own families, went to Abyssinia for a time. Muḥammad himself was able to continue preaching so long as he had the protection of his clan. About 619, however, his uncle Abū Ṭālib died and was succeeded as head of the clan by another uncle, Abū Lahab, who was in partnership with some of the great merchants and found a pretext for denying clan protection to Muḥammad. In 622, therefore, Muḥammad accepted an invitation to go to Medina where a great many people were ready to accept him as a prophet. His move from Mecca to Medina was the *Hidjra* or emigration.

The greater part of the period between the *Hidjra* and Muḥammad's death was dominated by the struggle between Muḥammad's supporters and the great merchants of Mecca. After some fruitless Muslim razzias against Meccan caravans, the Meccans were provoked by the capture of a small caravan under their noses, as it were, at Nakhla early in 624. Because of this they sent a relatively large force to protect a very wealthy caravan returning from Syria in March 624; and this expedition ended disastrously for them in the battle of Badr, where they lost many of their leading men by death or capture, including the leader of the expedition, Abū Djahl. Meccan affairs were guided by Abū Sufyān for the next three years. His attempt in 625 to avenge the defeat of Badr led to his having the better of the fighting at Uḥud in the oasis of Medina, but he failed to disturb Muḥammad's position there. His next attempt in 627, with numerous allies, was a more ignominious failure through Muḥammad's adoption of the *khandaḳ* or trench and the break-up of the alliance. Abū Sufyān then seems to have worked for peace and reconciliation with the Muslims, while other men still hoped to retrieve the fortunes of Mecca, and, for example, forcibly prevented Muḥammad and 1,600 Muslims from making the pilgrimage in 628. Nevertheless, they made the treaty of al-Ḥudaybiyya [*q.v.*] with him as with an equal. A breach of the terms of this treaty by Meccan allies led to a great Muslim expedition against Mecca with some 10,000 men. The town was surrendered almost without a blow, and all the Meccans, except a handful who were guilty of specific offences against Muḥammad or some Muslim, were assured their lives and property would be safe if they behaved honourably. For some time, Muḥammad had been aiming at reconciling the Meccans rather than crushing them by force. When, a week or two after the capture or *fatḥ*, it was learnt that there was a large concentration of nomads to the east of Mecca, some 2,000 Meccans took to the field with Muḥammad and helped him to gain the victory of Ḥunayn [*q.v.*]. Some of the pagan Meccans became Muslims almost at once, others only after a longer period.

A young Muslim of a Meccan family was left as governor of Mecca and it was made clear that Medina would remain the capital. The Kaʿba had for many years been the *ḳibla* [*q.v.*] or direction towards which all Muslims turned in prayer. At the *fatḥ* it was purged of idols and became a centre of Islamic worship, while the Black Stone was retained as an object to be reverenced. The annual *Ḥadjdj* [*q.v.*] was retained as an Islamic ceremony, and this also gave special importance to Mecca in Islamic eyes. Its commercial activity appears to have dwindled away, perhaps largely because many of the leading men moved to Medina and subsequently found their administrative abilities fully employed in organising an empire. After the capture of ʿIrāḳ, the trade between the Indian Ocean and the Mediterranean seems to have resumed the old route by the Euphrates valley.

Mecca from 632 to 750.—Not much is heard about Mecca under the first four caliphs. ʿUmar and ʿUthmān were concerned with the danger of flooding and brought Christian engineers to build barrages in the high-lying quarters. They also constructed dykes and embankments to protect the area round the Kaʿba. The first Umayyad caliph, Muʿāwiya, the son of Abū Sufyān, though mostly living in Damascus, took an interest in his native town. He had new buildings erected, developed agriculture in the surrounding district, and improved the water-supply by digging wells and building storage dams. The work of flood prevention continued under the Umayyads. In an attempt to control the *sayl*, a new channel was dug for it and barriers were erected at different levels. Despite these improvements, the problem was not fully solved, since the Baṭḥāʾ was a basin with no outlet. In the course of operations, buildings on the bank of the *sayl* and adjoining the Kaʿba were taken down, and the appearance of Mecca was thus considerably altered.

For a brief period after the death of Muʿāwiya, Mecca had again some political importance as the seat of the rival caliph ʿAbd Allāh b. al-Zubayr [*q.v.*]. The succession to Muʿāwiya of his son Yazīd in 611/680 was disliked by many members of Ḳuraysh, and Ibn al-Zubayr took advantage of such feelings to build up a party of supporters in Mecca, and eventually had himself proclaimed caliph there. For a time he controlled most of Arabia and ʿIrāḳ, but the Umayyad ʿAbd al-Malik gradually consolidated his power, and in 73/692 his general al-Ḥadjdjādj defeated and killed Ibn al-Zubayr, thus ending his bid for power and restoring to Umayyad rule Mecca and the other regions acknowledging the Zubayrids. In 63/682, when Ibn al-Zubayr was deep in intrigue but had not yet openly claimed the caliphate, an Umayyad army was sent to Mecca, and during its presence there the Kaʿba was partly destroyed by fire, probably through the carelessness of a supporter of Ibn al-Zubayr. Subsequently, the latter had the Kaʿba rebuilt, including the Ḥidjr within it; but this change was reversed by al-Ḥadjdjādj. The caliph al-Walīd I is credited with the construction of galleries circling the vast courtyard round the Kaʿba, thus giving the mosque (*al-masdjid al-ḥaram*) its distinctive form. In the period of the decline of the Umayyads, in 130/747 Mecca was briefly occupied by Abū Ḥamza, a Khāridjī rebel from the Yemen, but he was soon surprised and killed by an army sent by the caliph Marwān II. For most of the Umayyad period, Mecca had a sub-governor responsible to the governor of the Ḥidjāz who resided at Medina. It attracted wealthy people who did not want to be involved in politics and became a place of pleasure and ease with many poets and musicians. There were also some religious scholars, but fewer than at Medina.

Bibliography: 1. - Sources. Ibn Hishām, *Sīra*; Wāḳidī, *Maghāzī*, ed. Marsden Jones; Ibn Saʿd, *Ṭabaḳat*; Yaʿḳūbī, *Historiae*, ed. Houtsma, ii; Ṭabarī, *Annales*, series I, ii; Wüstenfeld, *Chroniken der Stadt Mekka*, esp. those of Azraḳī and Fārisī, i, ii; Bakrī, *Muʿdjam*; Yāḳūt, *Muʿdjam*; Muḳaddasī, *Aḥsan al-taḳāsīm*, 71-9; Masʿūdī, *Murūdj al-dhahab*, iii.

2. Studies. H. Lammens, *La Mecque à la veille de l'hégire*, in *MFOB*, ix (1924); idem, *La république marchande de la Mecque vers l'an 600 de notre ère*, in *BIE* (1910); idem, *Les chrétiens à la Mecque à la veille de l'hégire*, in *BIFAO*, xiv; idem, *Les juifs à la Mecque à la veille de l'hégire*, in *RSR*, xiv; C. Snouck Hurgronje, *Mekka*, i; M. Gaudefroy-Demombynes, *Le pélerinage à la Mekka*, Paris 1923; L. Caetani, *Annali*, i, ii; F. Buhl, *Das Leben Muhammeds*, Leipzig 1930; W. M. Watt, *Muhammad at Mecca*, Oxford 1953; P. Crone, *Meccan trade and the rise of Islam*, Princeton, forthcoming. (W. Montgomery Watt)

2. From the ʿAbbāsid to the modern period

i. Mecca under the ʿAbbāsids down to the foundation of the Sharīfate (132-350/750-961).

Although the political centre of gravity in Islam now lay in Baghdād, this period at first presents the same picture as under Umayyad rule. The *Ḥaramayn* are as a rule governed by ʿAbbāsid princes or individuals closely connected with them (*Die Chroniken der Stadt Mekka*, ed. Wüstenfeld, ii, 181 ff.). Sometimes Mecca and Ṭāʾif were under one ruler, who was at the same time leader of the *Ḥadjdj*, while Medina had a separate governor of its own.

Arabia had, however, from the 1st century A.H. contained a number of ʿAlid groups, who, as was their wont, fished in troubled waters, lay in wait as brigands to plunder the *Ḥadjdj* caravans, and from time to time hoisted their flags when they were not restrained either by the superior strength or by the bribes of the caliphs. We find al-Manṣūr (136-56/754-74) already having trouble in Western Arabia. Towards the end of the reign of al-Mahdī (156-69/774-85) a Ḥasanid, Ḥusayn b. ʿAlī, led a raid on Medina, which he ravaged; at Fakhkh [*q.v.*] near Mecca, he was cut down with many of his followers by the ʿAbbāsid leader of the *Ḥadjdj*. The place where he was buried is now called al-Shuhadāʾ. It is significant that he is regarded as the "martyr of Fakhkh" (al-Ṭabarī, iii, 551 ff.; *Chron. Mekka*, i, 435, 501).

Hārūn al-Rashīd on his nine pilgrimages expended vast sums in Mecca. He was not the only ʿAbbāsid to scatter wealth in the holy land. This had a bad effect on the character of the Meccans. There were hardly any descendants left of the old distinguished families, and the population grew accustomed to living at the expense of others and were ready to give vent to any dissatisfaction in rioting. This attitude was all too frequently stimulated by political conditions.

In the reign of al-Maʾmūn (198-218/817-33) it was again ʿAlids, Ḥusayn al-Afṭas and Ibrāhīm b. Mūsā, who extended their rule over Medina, Mecca and the Yemen (al-Ṭabarī, iii, 981 ff.; *Chron. Mecca*, ii, 238), ravaged Western Arabia and plundered the treasures of the Kaʿba. How strong ʿAlid influence already was at this time is evident from the fact that al-Maʾmūn appointed two ʿAlids as governors of Mecca (al-Ṭabarī, iii, 1039; *Chron. Mecca*, ii, 191 ff.).

With the decline of the ʿAbbāsid caliphate after the death of al-Maʾmūn, a period of anarchy began in the holy land of Islam, which was frequently accompanied by scarcity or famine. It became the regular custom for a number of rulers to be represented at the *Ḥadjdj* in the plain of ʿArafāt and to have their flags unfurled; the holy city was rarely spared fighting on these occasions. The safety of the pilgrim caravans was considerably affected; it was very often ʿAlids who distinguished themselves in plundering the pilgrims.

The ʿAlid cause received an important reinforcement at this time by the foundation of a Ḥasanid dynasty in Ṭabaristān (al-Ṭabarī, iii, 1523-33, 1583 ff., 1682-5, 1693 ff., 1840, 1880, 1884 ff, 1940). In Mecca the repercussion of this event was felt in the appearance of two Ḥasanids (*Chron. Mekka*, i, 343; ii, 10, 195, 239 ff.), Ismāʿīl b. Yūsuf and his brother Muḥammad, who also ravaged Medina and Djudda in the way that had now become usual (251/865-6).

The appearance of the Ḳarmaṭians [see ḲARMAṬĪ] brought still further misery to the country in the last fifty years before the foundation of the sharīfate (al-Ṭabarī, iii, 2124-30). Hard pressed themselves at the heart of the empire, the caliphs were hardly able even to think of giving active support to the holy land, and, besides, their representatives had not the necessary forces at their disposal. From 304/916 onwards the Ḳarmatians barred the way of the pilgrim caravans. In 318/930, 1,500 Ḳarmaṭian warriors raided Mecca, massacred the inhabitants by the thousand and carried off the Black Stone to Baḥrayn. It was only when they realised that such deeds were bringing them no nearer their goal—the destruction of official Islām—that their zeal began to relax and in 339/950 they even brought the Stone back again. Mecca was relieved of serious danger from the Ḳarmaṭians. The following years bear witness to the increasing influence of the ʿAlids in western Arabia in connection with the advance of Fāṭimid rule to the east and with Būyid rule in Baghdād. From this time, the Meccan ʿAlids are called by the title of Sharīf, which they have retained ever since.

ii. From the foundation of the Sharīfate to Ḳatāda (*ca.* 350-598/960-1200).

a. The Mūsāwīs. The sources do not agree as to the year in which Djaʿfar took Mecca; 966, 967, 968 and the period between 951 and 961 are mentioned (*Chron. Mekka*, ii, 205 ff.). ʿAlids had already ruled before him in the holy land. It is with him, however, that the reign in Mecca begins of the Ḥasanids, who are known collectively as Sharīfs, while in Medina this title is given to the reigning Ḥusaynids.

The rise and continuance of the Sharīfate indicates the relative independence of Western Arabia in face of the rest of the Islamic world from a political and religious point of view. Since the foundation of the Sharīfate, Mecca takes the precedence possessed by Medina hitherto.

How strongly the Meccan Sharīfate endeavoured to assert its independence, is evident in this period from two facts. In 365/976 Mecca refused homage to the Fāṭimid caliph. Soon afterwards, the caliph began to besiege the town and cut off all imports from Egypt. The Meccans were soon forced to give in, for the Ḥidjāz was dependent on Egypt for its food supplies (Ibn al-Athīr, *Kāmil*, viii, 491; *Chron. Mekka*, ii, 246).

The second sign of the Sharīfs' feeling of independence is Abu 'l-Futūḥ's (384-432/994-1039) setting himself up as caliph in 402/1011 (*Chron. Mekka*, ii, 207; Ibn al-Athīr, ix, 233, 317). He was probably induced to do this by al-Ḥākim's heretical innovations in Egypt. The latter, however, was soon able to reduce the new caliph's sphere of influence so much that he had hurriedly to return to Mecca where in the meanwhile one of his relatives had usurped the power. He was forced to make terms with al-Ḥākim in order to be able to expel his relative.

With his son Shukr (432-53/1039-61) the dynasty of the Mūsāwīs, i.e. the descendants of Mūsā b. ʿAbd Allāh b. Mūsā b. ʿAbd Allāh b. Ḥasan b. Ḥasan b. ʿAlī b. Abī Ṭālib, came to an end. He died without leaving male heirs, which caused a struggle within the family of the Ḥasanids with the usual evil results for Mecca. When the family of the Banū Shayba (the Shaybīs) went so far as to confiscate for their private use all precious metals in the house of Allāh, the ruler of Yemen, al-Ṣulayḥī (*Chron. Mekka*, ii, 208, 210 ff.; Ibn al-Athīr, ix, 422; x, 19, 38 [see ṢULAYḤIDS], intervened and restored order and security in the town. This intervention by an outsider appeared more intolerable to the Ḥasanids than fighting among themselves. They therefore proposed to al-Ṣulayḥī that he should instal one of their number as ruler and leave the town.

He therefore appointed Abū Hāshim Muḥammad (455-87/1063-94) as Grand Sharīf. With him begins the dynasty of the:

b. Hawāshim (455-598/1063-1200), which takes its name from Abū Hāshim Muḥammad, a brother of the first Sharīf Djaʿfar; the two brothers were descendants in the fourth generation from Mūsā II, the ancestor of the Mūsāwīs.

During the early years of his reign, Abū Hāshim had to wage a continual struggle with the Sulaymānī branch, who thought themselves humiliated by his appointment. These Sulaymānīs were descended from Sulaymān, a brother of the above-mentioned Mūsā II.

The reign of Abū Hāshim is further noteworthy for the shameless way in which he offered the suzerainty, i.e. the mention in the *khuṭba* as well as the change of official rite which is indicated by the wording of the *adhān*, to the highest bidder i.e. the Fāṭimid caliph or the Saldjūḳ sultan (*Chron. Mekka*, ii, 253; Ibn al-Athīr, x, 67). It was very unwelcome to the Meccans that imports from Egypt stopped as soon as the official mention of the Fāṭimid in the *khuṭba* gave way to that of the caliph. The change was repeated several times with the result that the Saldjūk, tired of this comedy, sent several bodies of Turkomans to Mecca.

The ill-feeling between sultan and Sharīf also inflicted great misery on pilgrims coming from ʿIrāḳ. As the leadership of the pilgrim caravans from this country had gradually been transferred from the ʿAlids to Turkish officials and soldiers, Abū Hāshim did not hesitate occasionally to fall upon the pilgrims and plunder them (*Chron. Mekka*, ii, 254; Ibn al-Athīr, x, 153).

The reign of his successors is also marked by covetousness and plundering. The Spanish pilgrim Ibn Djubayr, who visited Mecca in 578/1183 and 580/1185, gives hair-raising examples of this. Even then, however, the Hawā<u>sh</u>im were no longer absolutely their own masters, as over ten years before, the Ayyūbid dynasty had not only succeeded to the Fāṭimids in Egypt but was trying to get the whole of nearer Asia into their power.

The Ayyūbid ruler Ṣalāḥ al-Dīn (Saladin)'s brother, who passed through Mecca on his way to South Arabia, abandoned his intention of abolishing the <u>Sh</u>arīfs, but the place of honour on the Ḥa<u>dj</u>dj belonged to the Ayyūbids and their names were mentioned in the *<u>kh</u>uṭba* after those of the ʿAbbāsid caliph and the <u>Sh</u>arīf (Ibn <u>D</u>jubayr, 75, 95). The same Ayyūbid in 582/1186 also did away with the <u>Sh</u>īʿī (here Zaydī, for the <u>Sh</u>arīfs had hitherto been Zaydīs) form of the *a<u>dh</u>ān* (*Chron. Mekka*, ii, 214), had coins struck in Ṣalāḥ al-Dīn's name and put the fear of the law into the hearts of the <u>Sh</u>arīf's bodyguard, who had not shrunk from crimes of robbery and murder, by severely punishing their misdeeds. A further result of Ayyūbid suzerainty was that the <u>Sh</u>āfiʿī rite became the predominant one.

But even the mighty Ṣalāḥ al-Dīn could only make improvements in Mecca. He could abolish or check the worst abuses, but the general state of affairs remained as before.

iii. The rule of Ḳatāda and his descendants down to the Wahhābī period (*ca.* 596-1202/1200-1788).

Meanwhile, a revolution was being prepared which was destined to have more far-reaching consequences than any of its predecessors. Ḳatāda, a descendant of the same Mūsā (see above) from whom the Mūsāwīs and the Hawā<u>sh</u>im were descended, had gradually extended his estates as well as his influence from Yanbuʿ to Mecca and had gathered a considerable following in the town. According to some sources, his son Ḥanẓala made all preparations for the decisive blow on the holy city; according to others, Ḳatāda seized the town on 27 Ra<u>dj</u>ab when the whole population was away performing a lesser *ʿumra* in memory of the completion of the building of the Kaʿba by ʿAbd Allāh b. al-Zubayr, which was celebrated on this day along with the festival of Muḥammad's ascension to heaven. However it came about, Ḳatāda's seizure of the town meant the coming of an able and strong-willed ruler, the ancestor of all later <u>Sh</u>arīfs. He steadfastly followed his one ambition to make his territory an independent principality. Everything was in his favour; that he did not achieve his aim was a result of the fact that the Ḥi<u>dj</u>āz was once again at the intersection of many rival lines of political interest.

Ḳatāda began by ruining his chances with the great powers; he ill-treated the son of the Ayyūbid al-Malik al-ʿĀdil (540-615/1145-1218 [see AL-ʿĀDIL]) in brutal fashion (*Chron. Mekka*, ii, 263). He roused the ire of the caliph by his attitude to pilgrims from ʿIrāḳ. He was able, however, to appease the latter and the embassy he sent to Bag<u>h</u>dād returned with gifts from the caliph. The caliph also invited him to visit Bag<u>h</u>dād. According to some historians, however, the <u>Sh</u>arīf turned home again before he actually reached Bag<u>h</u>dād. On this occasion, he is said to have expressed his policy of the "splendid isolation" of the Ḥi<u>dj</u>āz in verse, as he did in his will in prose (see Snouck Hurgronje, *Qatâdah's policy of splendid isolation*, cited in *Bibl.*).

On the other hand, Ḳatāda is said to have vigorously supported an *Imām* of Ḥasanid descent in founding a kingdom in the Yemen. After the reconquest of this region by a grandson of al-ʿĀdil, the Ayyūbids of Egypt, Syria, and South Arabia were mentioned in the *<u>kh</u>uṭba* in Mecca along with the caliph and <u>Sh</u>arīf.

Ḳatāda's life ended in a massacre which his son Ḥasan carried out in his family to rid himself of possible rivals (*Chron. Mekka*, ii, 215, 263 ff.; Ibn al-A<u>th</u>īr, xii, 262 ff.). The Ayyūbid prince Masʿūd, however, soon put a limit to his ambition and had Mecca governed by his generals. On his death, however, power again passed into the hands of the <u>Sh</u>arīfs, whose territory was allowed a certain degree of independence by the rulers of the Yemen as a bulwark against Egypt.

About the middle of the 7th/13th century, the world of Islam assumes a new aspect as the result of the advent of persons and happenings of great importance. In 656/1258 the taking of Bag<u>h</u>dād by the Mongol <u>Kh</u>ān Hülegü put an end to the caliphate. The pilgrim caravan from ʿIrāḳ was no longer of any political significance. In Egypt, power passed from the Ayyūbids to the Mamlūks; Sultan Baybars [*q.v.*] (658-76/1260-77) was soon the most powerful ruler in the lands of Islam. He was able to leave the government of Mecca in the hands of the <u>Sh</u>arīf, because the latter, Abū Numayy, was an energetic individual who ruled with firmness during the second half of the 7th/13th century (652-700/1254-1301). His long reign firmly established the power of the descendants of Ḳatāda.

Nevertheless, the first half century after his death was almost entirely filled with fighting between different claimants to the throne. ʿA<u>dj</u>lān's reign also (747-76/1346-75) was filled with political unrest, so much so that the Mamlūk Sultan is said on one occasion to have sworn to exterminate all the <u>Sh</u>arīfs. ʿA<u>dj</u>lān introduced a political innovation by appointing his son and future successor Aḥmad co-regent in 762/1361, by which step he hoped to avoid a fraticidal struggle before or after his death.

A second measure of ʿĀ<u>dj</u>lān's also deserves mention, namely the harsh treatment of the *muʾa<u>dh</u>dhin* and *imām* of the Zaydīs; this shows that the reigning <u>Sh</u>arīfs had gone over to the predominant rite of al-<u>Sh</u>āfiʿī and forsaken the Zaydī creed of their forefathers.

Among the sons and successors of ʿA<u>dj</u>lān, special mention may be made of Ḥasan (798-829/1396-1426) because he endeavoured to extend his sway over the whole of the Ḥi<u>dj</u>āz and to guard his own financial interests carefully, at the same time being able to avoid giving his Egyptian suzerain cause to interfere.

But from 828/1425 onwards, he and his successors had to submit to a regular system of control as regards the allotment of the customs.

From the time of Ḥasan, in addition to the bodyguard of personal servants and freedmen, we find a regular army of mercenaries mentioned which was passed from one ruler to another. But the mode of life of the <u>Sh</u>arīfs, unlike that of other Oriental rulers, remained simple and in harmony with their Arabian surroundings. As a vassal of the Egyptian sultan, the <u>Sh</u>arīf received from him every year his *tawḳīʿ* [*q.v.*] and a robe of honour. On the ceremonies associated with the accession of the <u>Sh</u>arīfs, see Snouck Hurgronje, *Mekka*, i, 97-8.

Of the three sons of Ḥasan who disputed the position in their father's lifetime, Barakāt (I) was chosen by the sultan as co-regent; twenty years later, he succeeded his father and was able with slight interruptions to hold sway till his death in 859/1455. He had to submit to the sultan, sending a permanent garrison of 50 Turkish horsemen under an *amīr* to Mecca. This *amīr* may be regarded as the precursor of the later governors, who sometimes attained positions of considerable influence under Turkish suzerainty.

Mecca enjoyed a period of prosperity under

Barakāt's son Muhammad (*Chron. Mekka*, ii, 341 ff.; iii, 230 ff.), whose reign (859-902/1455-97) coincided with that of Ḳāʾitbay [*q.v.*] in Egypt. The latter has left a fine memorial in the many buildings he erected in Mecca.

Under Muḥammad's son Barakāt II (902-31/1497-1525), who displayed great ability and bravery in the usual struggle with his relatives, without getting the support he desired from Egypt (*Chron. Mekka*, ii, 342 ff.; iii, 244 ff.), the political situation in Islam was fundamentally altered by the Ottoman Sultan Selīm's conquest of Egypt in 923/1517.

Although henceforth Constantinople had the importance for Mecca that Baghdād once had, there was little real understanding between Turks and Arabs, Mecca at first experienced a period of peace under the Sharīfs Muḥammad Abū Numayy 931-73/1525-66) and Ḥasan (973-1009/1566-1601). Under Ottoman protection, the territory of the Sharīfs was extended as far as Khaybar in the north, to Ḥalī in the south and in the east into Nadjd. Dependence on Egypt still existed at the same time; when the government in Constantinople was a strong one, it was less perceptible, and vice-versa. This dependence was not only political but had also a material and religious side. The Ḥidjāz was dependent for its food supply on corn from Egypt. The foundations of a religious and educational nature now found powerful patrons in the Sultans of Turkey.

A darker side of the Ottoman suzerainty was its intervention in the administration of justice. Since the Sharīfs had adopted the Shāfiʿī *madhhab*, the Shāfiʿī *ḳāḍī* was the chief judge; this office had also remained for centuries in one family. Now the highest bidder for the office was sent every year from Istanbul to Mecca; the Meccans of course had to pay the price with interest.

With Ḥasan's death, a new period of confusion and civil war began for Mecca. In the language of the historians, this circumstance makes itself apparent in the increasing use of the term *Dhawī*... for different groups of the descendants of Abū Numayy who dispute the supremacy, often having their own territory, sometimes asserting a certain degree of independence from the Grand Sharīf, while preserving a system of reciprocal protection which saved the whole family from disaster (Snouck Hurgronje, *Mekka*, i, 112 ff.).

The struggle for supremacy, interspersed with disputes with the officials of the suzerain, centred in the 11th/17th century mainly around the ʿAbādila, the Dhawī Zayd and the Dhawī Barakāt.

Zayd (1040-76/1631-66) was an energetic individual who would not tolerate everything the Turkish officials did. But he was unable to oppose successfully a measure which deserves mention on account of its general importance. The ill-feeling between the Sunnī Turks and the Shīʿī Persians had been extended to Mecca as a result of an order by Sultan Murād IV to expel all Persians from the holy city and not to permit them to make the pilgrimage in future. Neither the Sharīfs nor the upper classes in Mecca had any reason to be pleased with this measure; it only served the mob as a pretext to plunder well-to-do Persians. As soon as the Turkish governor had ordered them to go, the Sharīfs however gave permission as before to the Shīʿīs to take part in the pilgrimage and to remain in the town. The Sharīfs likewise favoured the Zaydīs, who had also been frequently forbidden Mecca by the Turks.

The further history of Mecca down to the coming of the Wahhābīs is a rather monotonous struggle of the Sharīfian families among themselves (Dhawī Zayd, Dhawī Barakāt, Dhawī Masʿūd) and with the Ottoman officials in the town itself or in Djudda.

iv. The Sharīfate from the Wahhābī period to its end. The Kingdom.

Although the Wahhābīs [*q.v.*] had already made their influence perceptible under his predecessors, it was Ghālib (1788-1813) who was the first to see the movement sweeping towards his territory like a flood; but he left no stone unturned to avert the danger. He sent his armies north, east and south; his brothers and brothers-in-law all took the field; the leaders of the Syrian and Egyptian pilgrim caravans were appealed to at every pilgrimage for help, but without success. During the period of the French occupation of Egypt (1798-1801), he made a rapprochement with the French there, hoping to ensure the continuance of the corn imports from Egypt upon which the Ḥidjāz relied and to reduce Turkish influence there (see M. Abir, *Relations between the government of India and the Sharif of Mecca during the French invasion of Egypt, 1798-1801*, in *JRAS* [1965], 33-42). In 1799 Ghālib made a treaty with the *amīr* of Darʿiyya, by which the boundaries of their territories were laid down, with the stipulation that the Wahhābīs should be allowed access to the holy territory. Misunderstandings proved inevitable, however, and in 1803 the army of the *amīr* Suʿūd b. ʿAbd al-ʿAzīz approached the holy city. After Ghālib had withdrawn to Djudda, in April Suʿūd entered Mecca, the inhabitants of which had announced their conversion. All *ḳubba*s were destroyed, all tobacco pipes and musical instruments burned, and the *adhān* purged of praises of the Prophet.

In July, Ghālib returned to Mecca but gradually he became shut in there by enemies as with a wall. In August, the actual siege began and with it a period of famine and plague. In February of the following year, Ghālib had to submit to acknowledging Wahhābī suzerainty while retaining his own position.

The Sublime Porte had during all these happenings displayed no sign of life. It was only after the Wahhābīs had in 1807 sent back the pilgrim caravans from Syria and Egypt with their *maḥmals* [*q.v.*], that Muḥammad ʿAlī [*q.v.*] was given instructions to deal with the Ḥidjāz as soon as he was finished with Egypt. It was not till 1813 that he took Mecca and there met Ghālib who made cautious advances to him. Ghālib, however, soon fell into the trap set for him by Muḥammad ʿAlī and his son Tusun. He was exiled to Salonika, where he lived till his death in 1816.

In the meanwhile, Muḥammad ʿAlī had installed Ghālib's nephew Yaḥyā b. Sarūr (1813-27) as Sharīf. Thus ended the first period of Wahhābī rule over Mecca, and the Ḥidjāz once more became dependent on Egypt. In Mecca, Muḥammad ʿAlī was honourably remembered because he restored the pious foundations which had fallen into ruins, revived the consignments of corn, and allotted stipends to those who had distinguished themselves in sacred lore or in other ways.

In 1827, Muḥammad ʿAlī had again to interfere in the domestic affairs of the Sharīfs. When Yaḥyā had made his position untenable by the vengeance he took on one of his relatives, the viceroy deposed the Dhawī Zayd and installed one of the ʿAbādila, Muḥammad, usually called Muḥammad b. ʿAwn (1827-51). He had first of all to go through the traditional struggle with his relatives. Trouble between him and Muḥammad ʿAlī's deputy resulted in both being removed to Cairo in 1836.

Here the Sharīf remained till 1840 when by the treaty between Muḥammad ʿAlī and the Porte the Ḥidjāz was again placed directly under the Porte. Muḥammad b. ʿAwn returned to his home and rank. Ottoman suzerainty was now incorporated in the person of the *wālī* of Djudda. Friction was inevitable between him and Muḥammad b. ʿAwn; the latter's friendship with Muḥammad ʿAlī now proved of use to him. He earned the gratitude of the Turks for his expeditions against the Wahhābī chief Fayṣal in al-Riyāḍ and against the ʿAṣīr tribes. His raids on the territory of Yemen also prepared the way for Ottoman rule over it.

In the meanwhile, the head of the Dhawī Zayd, ʿAbd al-Muṭṭalib (1851-56), had made good use of his friendship with the grand vizier and brought about the deposition of the ʿAbādila in favour of the Dhawī Zayd. ʿAbd al-Muṭṭalib, however, did not succeed in keeping on good terms with one of the two pashas with whom he had successively to deal. In 1855 it was decided in Istanbul to cancel his appointment and to recall Muḥammad b. ʿAwn. ʿAbd al-Muṭṭalib at first refused to recognise the genuineness of the order; and he was supported by the Turkophobe feeling just provoked by the prohibition of slavery. Finally, however, he had to give way to Muḥammad b. ʿAwn, who in 1856 entered upon the Sharīfate for the second time; this reign lasted barely two years. Between his death in March 1858 and the arrival of his successor ʿAbd Allāh in October of the same year, there took place the murder of the Christians in Djidda (15 June) and the atonement for it (cf. DJUDDA, and Snouck Hurgronje, *Een rector der mekkaansche universiteit*, in *Bijdragen t. d. Taal-, Land- en Volkenkunde van Ned.-Indië*, 5e volgr., deel ii, 381 ff., 399 ff.).

The rule of ʿAbd Allāh (1858-77), who was much liked by his subjects, was marked by peace at home and events of far-reaching importance abroad. The opening of the Suez Canal (1869) meant on the one hand the liberation of the Ḥidjāz from Egypt, on the other, however, more direct connection with Istanbul. The installation of telegraphic connections between the Ḥidjāz and the rest of the world had a similar importance. The reconquest of Yemen by the Turks was calculated to strengthen the impression that Arabia was now Turkish territory for ever.

The brief reign of his popular elder brother Ḥusayn (1877-80) ended with the assassination of the Sharīf by an Afghān. The fact that the aged ʿAbd al-Muṭṭalib (see above) was sent by the Dhawī Zayd from Istanbul as his successor (1880-82) gave rise to an obvious suspicion.

Although the plebs saw something of a saint in this old man, his rule was soon felt to be so oppressive that the notables petitioned for his deposition (Snouck Hurgronje, *Mekka*, i, 204 ff.). As a result in 1881, the energetic ʿOthmān Nūrī Pasha was sent with troops to the Ḥidjāz as commander of the garrison with the task of preparing for the restoration of the ʿAbādila. ʿAbd al-Muṭṭalib was outwitted and taken prisoner; he was kept under guard is one of his own houses in Mecca till his death in 1886.

ʿOthmān Pasha, who was appointed *wālī* in July 1882, hoped to see his friend ʿAbd Ilāh, one of the ʿAbādila, installed as Grand Sharīf alongside of him. ʿAwn al-Rafīḳ (1882-1905) was, however, appointed (portrait in Snouck Hurgronje, *Bilder aus Mekka*). As the *wālī* was an individual of great energy, who had ever done much for the public good and ʿAwn, although very retiring, was by no means insignificant, but was indeed somewhat tyrannical, trouble between them was inevitable, especially as they had the same powers on many points, e.g. the administration of justice and supervision of the safety of the pilgrim routes. After a good deal of friction, ʿOthmān was dismissed in 1886. His successor was Djemāl Pasha, who only held office for a short period and was succeeded by Ṣafwat Pasha. Only Aḥmad Rātib could keep his place alongside of ʿAwn, and that by shutting his eyes to many things and being satisfied with certain material advantages. After ʿAwn's death, ʿAbd Ilāh was chosen as his successor. He died, however, before he could start on the journey from Istanbul to Mecca. ʿAwn's actual successor was therefore his nephew ʿAlī (1905-8). In 1908 he and Aḥmad Rātib both lost their positions with the Turkish Revolution.

With Ḥusayn (1908-1916-1924 [see ḤUSAYN B. ʿALĪ]), also a nephew of ʿAwn's, the last Sharīf came to power as the nominee of the young Turks in Istanbul. But for the Great War, his Sharīfate would probably have run the usual course. The fact that Turkey was now completely involved in the war induced him to declare himself independent in 1916. He endeavoured to extend his power as far as possible, first as liberator (*munḳidh*) of the Arabs, then (22 June 1916) as king of the Ḥidjāz or king of Arabia and finally as caliph. Very soon however, it became apparent that the ruler of Nadjd, ʿAbd al-ʿAzīz Āl Suʿūd, like his Wahhābī forefathers, was destined to have a powerful say in the affairs of Arabia. In September 1924 his troops took al-Ṭāʾif, and in October, Mecca. King Ḥusayn fled first to ʿAḳaba and from there in May 1925 to Cyprus. His son ʿAlī retired to Djudda. Ibn Suʿūd besieged this town and Medina for a year, avoiding bloodshed and complications with European powers. Both towns surrendered in December 1925.

We owe descriptions of social life in Mecca during the last decades of the pre-modern period to two Europeans, the Briton Sir Richard Burton, who as the dervish-physician Mīrzā ʿAbd Allāh visited Mecca in 1853 at the time of the pilgrimage, and the Dutchman Snouck Hurgronje, who lived in Mecca for some months during 1884-5 with the express aim of acquiring a knowledge of the daily life of the Meccans, but also with a special interest, as a Dutchman, in the Djāwa or Indonesians who went as pilgrims to Mecca and who often stayed there as *mudjāwirūn*.

The institution of the pilgrimage and the ceremonies connected with the various holy sites in or near the city dominated Meccan life, many of its citizens having specific roles concerning the religious rites and being organised in special gilds, such as the *zamzamiyyūn* who distributed water from the well of Zamzam in the courtyard of the Kaʿba; the Bedouin *mukharridjūn* or camel brokers, who arranged transport between Djudda, Mecca, al-Ṭāʾif and Medina; and above all, the *muṭawwifūn* or guides for the intending pilgrims and their conductors through the various rites (*manāsik*) of the *Ḥadjdj* [*q.v.*]. These *muṭawwifūn* had their connections with particular ethnic groups or geographical regions of the Islamic world (there were, in Snouck Hurgronje's time, 180 guides plus hangers-on who were concerned with the Djāwa pilgrims alone), and their agents (*wukalāʾ*) in Djudda would take charge of the pilgrims as soon as they disembarked. Such groups as these, together with the townspeople in general who would let out their houses or rooms, were geared to the exploitation of the pilgrims, and it was only in the rest of the year that tradesmen, scholars, lawyers, etc., could really pursue their other vocations.

At this time also, the slave trade was still of considerable importance. There were a few white Circassians (Čerkes [*q.v.*]), but much more important for hard manual labour like building and quarrying were the black negro slaves (*sūdān*), and, for domestic service, the somewhat lighter-skinned so-called Abyssinians (*ḥubūsh*). Despite the prohibitions of slave-trading imposed in their own colonial territories and on the high seas, Snouck Hurgronje further observed some slaves from British India and the Dutch East Indies, and the Mecca slave market was a flourishing one.

Bibliography: Azraḳī, *Akhbār Makka*, in *Die Chroniken der Stadt Mekka*, ed. Wüstenfeld; Ṭabarī; Ibn al-Athīr, *Kāmil*; Aḥmad b. Zaynī Daḥlān, *Khulāṣat al-kalām fī bayān umarāʾ al-balad al-ḥarām*, Cairo 1305; Wüstenfeld, *Die Scherife von Mekka im XI. (XVII.) Jahrhundert*, in *Abh. G. W. Gött.*, xxxii (1885); C. Snouck Hurgronje, *Mekka*, The Hague 1888-9 (on this work is based the above sketch down to the beginning of ᶜAwn's reign); idem, *Een rector der Mekkaansche Universiteit*, in *BTLV*, 5e reeks, ii, 344 ff. = *Verspr. geschr.*, iii, 65 ff.; idem, *Qatâdah's policy of splendid isolation of the Ḥijâz*, in *A volume of oriental studies presented to E. G. Browne*, Cambridge 1922, 439-44 = *Verspr. geschr.*, iii, 355-62); idem, *The revolt in Arabia* (New York 1917 = *Verspr. geschr.*, iii, 311 ff.); idem, *Prins Faisal Bin Abdal-Aziz al-Saoed*, in *Verspr. geschr.*, vi, 465 ff.; J. L. Burckhardt, *Travels in Arabia*, London 1829, i, 170 ff.; Ali Bey, *Travels*, London 1816, chs. vi-x, R. Burton, *Personal narrative of a pilgrimage to El Medinah and Meccah* London 1855-6, iii; T. F. Keane, *Six months in Mecca*, London 1881; H. St. J. B. Philby, *The heart of Arabia*, London 1922; idem, *The recent history of the Hijaz*, London 1925; Ibrāhīm Rifᶜat Pasha, *Mirʾāt al-Ḥaramayn*, Cairo 1343/1925; Zambaur, *Manuel*, 19-23 (for list of the governors and Sharīfs); Snouck Hurgronje, *Mekka in the latter part of the 19th century*, Leiden-London 1931; Naval Intelligence Division, *Western Arabia and the Red Sea*, London 1946, 243-99; ᶜAbd al-Ḥamīd al-Baṭrīq, *Turkish and Egyptian rule in Arabia 1810-1940*, London Univ. Ph. D. thesis, 1947, unpublished; G. de Gaury, *Rulers of Mecca*, London 1951; Aḥmad al-Sibāᶜī, *Taʾrīkh Makka*, Mecca 1372/1952-3; Sāṭiᶜ al-Ḥuṣrī, *al-Bilād al-ᶜArabiyya wa 'l-dawla al-ᶜUthmāniyya*, Cairo 1376/1957; Emel Esin, *Mecca the blessed, Madinah the radiant*, London 1963; R. Bayly Winder, *Saudi Arabia in the nineteenth century*, London and New York 1965; Muḥammad ᶜAbd al-Raḥmān al-Shāmikh, *A survey of Ḥijāzī prose literature in the period 1908-41, with some reference to the history of the press*, London Univ. Ph. D. thesis, 1967, unpublished; ᶜAlī b. Ḥusayn al-Sulaymān, *al-ᶜIlāqāt al-Ḥidjāziyya al-Miṣriyya*, Cairo 1393/1973; D. G. Hogarth, *Hejaz before World War I*, repr. Cambridge 1978; Ṣāliḥ al-ᶜAmr, *al-Ḥidjāz taḥt al-ḥukm al-ᶜUthmānī 1869-1914 m.*, al-Riyāḍ 1978; Nāṣir ᶜAbd Allāh Sulṭān al-Barakātī, *Itḥāf fuḍalāʾ al-zaman bi-taʾrīkh wilāyat Banī 'l-Ḥasan by Muḥammad b. ᶜAlī al-Ṭabarī, critical edition ...*, Manchester Univ. Ph. D. thesis, 3 vols. 1983, unpublished.

(A. J. Wensinck - [C. E. Bosworth])

3. The Modern City

Politics and administration. ᶜAlī b. al-Ḥusayn b. ᶜAlī, was declared king of al-Ḥidjāz on 5 Rabīᶜ I 1346/4 October 1924 following the abdication of his father the previous day, but the odds against his stabilising a collapsing situation were insurmountable. Wahhābī forces under Khālid b. Luʾayy and Sulṭān b. Bidjād had already occupied al-Ṭāʾif, where excesses had taken place, and a significant number of Makkans, in fear for their lives, had fled to al-Madīna and Djudda. Since, unlike other Ḥidjazī cities, Makka had no walls, and since King ᶜAlī's "army" probably did not exceed 400 men, the monarch ordered his troops out of the capital on 14 Rabīᶜ I 13 October 1924 to take up new positions in Baḥra about half-way between Makka and Djudda. The next morning, the city was looted, not by the Ikhwān (Wahhābīs) but by local Bedouin who found it unguarded. ᶜAbd al-ᶜAzīz b. ᶜAbd al-Raḥmān Āl Suᶜūd, the sultan of Nadjd and its Dependencies, was in al-Riyāḍ and had ordered Khālid b. Lu'ayy and Ibn Bidjād not to enter Makka by force before his own arrival, for fear of further savagery in Islam's holiest city. However, when Khālid and Ibn Bidjād found that the enemy had fled, they decided to move. On 17 Rabīᶜ I/16 October, by which time the Bedouin had left, Ibn Bidjād ordered four Ikhwān from Ghaṭghaṭ to enter the shuttered city without weapons and wearing *iḥrām* clothing. As they traversed the deserted streets, they read a proclamation annexing the city and guaranteeing the safety of its inhabitants. Slowly the citizenry began to re-emerge. On the following day, Khālid and Sulṭān led their forces, all *muḥrimūn*, into the holy city to the *Ḥaram*, where the *ᶜumra* was performed. There was some sporadic destruction of water pipes, tobacco supplies, Sharīfian property and domed tombs, and the Ikhwān delivered sermons. Among the revered antiquities destroyed was the reputed birthplace of the Prophet and two houses revered as those of Khadīdja and of Abū Bakr. But on the whole, good order was kept. As a Suᶜūdī official observed, the Ikhwān entered Makka saying "Lā ilāha illā Allāh" and "Allāhu Akbar", not fighting and killing. Khālid b. Lu'ayy was "elected" *amīr* and promptly installed himself in the Sharīfian reception room to receive the submission of the civil and religious notables.

The *amīr* of Makka served unaided for a month-and-a-half, and had to confront both domestic and international problems almost at once. On 6 Rabīᶜ II 1343/4 November 1924, the consuls resident in Djudda (British, Dutch, French, Iranian and Italian), who no doubt anticipated an immediate Suᶜūdī advance on Djudda, sent Ibn Luʾayy a letter addressed to Sultan ᶜAbd al-ᶜAzīz holding the Nadjdīs responsible for the safety of the subjects and citizens of their several countries but also indicating their neutrality in the ongoing conflict with the reduced Sharīfian kingdom. Ibn Luʾayy forwarded it on to the sultan. Ibn Luʾayy also received a rather treasonable communication of 7 Rabīᶜ II/5 November from the Ḥidjāz National Party in Djudda. This group, which was nominally led by Shaykh ᶜAbd Allāh Sarrādj, the *muftī* of Makka, who reputedly had been the only official of al-Ḥusayn's government who had been willing to stand up to him in debate, had been transformed into King ᶜAlī's cabinet. Following Baker's account, we learn that they nevertheless, secretly, wrote to Ibn Luʾayy seeking some accommodation. Ibn Luʾayy responded on 20 Rabīᶜ II/18 November curtly, "We, the Muslims, have no aim but to subject ourselves to God's orders and to love those who carry out those orders even if he be an Abyssinian negro, to fight the *kuffār* ... or the *mushrikīn* ... As God said (LVIII, 22) in his Holy Book... 'Thou wilt not find those who believe in God and the last day loving those who resist God and His Prophet even though they be their fathers, sons, brothers or kin' ... if you look at our own situation and consider our actions you will see that this is our way of defending Islam." He enclosed a copy of ᶜAbd al-ᶜAzīz's pro-

Fig. 1. Aerial view of ᶜArafāt during the *ḥadjdj*. (Photograph by courtesy of the Embassy of the Kingdom of Saoudi Arabia, The Hague).

Fig. 2. Pilgrims at Minā. (Photograph by courtesy of the Embassy of the Kingdom of Saoudi Arabia, The Hague)

Fig. 3. Aerial view of Minā during the *ḥadjdj*. (Photograph by courtesy of the Embassy of the Kingdom of Saoudi Arabia, The Hague).

Fig. 4. Interior of the *Mas*^{c}*ā*. (Photograph by courtesy of the Embassy of the Kingdom of Saoudi Arabia, The Hagu

clamation to the people of Djudda and Makka suggesting an international conference on the future of al-Ḥidjāz and meanwhile assuring security for all. The Ḥidjāz committee responded to the effect that, since al-Ḥusayn had gone and since King ʿAlī and the Party accepted the same kind of Islam that Sultan ʿAbd al-ʿAzīz believed in, there was no reason to continue fighting. They asked to send delegates to Makka so that a truce could be signed pending the decision of the international conference. Khālid gave them no encouragement; he wrote on 22 Rabiʿ II/20 November, "God has already purified the Holy *Ḥaram* by ridding it of Ḥusayn... We shall oppose all those who continue to support ʿAlī." Muḥammad al-Ṭawīl, who was the real power in the Ḥidjāz National Party, nevertheless, requested permission to send a delegation; Khālid agreed, and the delegation went to Makka the next day. Any lingering doubt as to Wahhābī intentions was removed by the ultimatum which Khālid gave his visitors. They could arrest ʿAlī, get him out of the country, or join the Wahhābīs in seizing Djudda.

Sultan ʿAbd al-ʿAzīz had left al-Riyāḍ with an army of 5,000 sedentaries on 13 Rabiʿ II 1343/11 November 1924 for Makka and arrived there in remarkably fast time on 8 Jumādā I/5 December. Upon his departure from al-Riyāḍ he had issued a proclamation (text in Wahba, *Djazīra*, 253) on his purposes in going to Makka. He also sent an advance party of three close advisors, Dr. ʿAbd Allāh al-Damlūdjī (from al-Mawṣil), Shaykh ʿAbd Allāh Āl Sulaymān (from ʿUnayza in al-Ḳaṣīm, Nadjd), and Shaykh Ḥāfiẓ Wahba (of Egyptian origin) to study out the situation in Makka and to assist in reassuring the population. Shaykh Ḥāfiẓ reports (*Khamsūn*, 63 ff.) that he delivered a number of speeches to ulema, merchants and government employees in various meetings. He stressed that ʿAbd al-ʿAzīz would reform corruption, end the isolation of al-Ḥidjāz from the mainstream of the Muslim world and put the administration of the country, and especially of the Ḥaramayn, on a sound basis. These speeches probably helped; in any case, just before ʿAbd al-ʿAzīz's arrival, Shaykh Ḥāfiẓ received a letter from the director of the Egyptian *takiyya*, Aḥmad Ṣābir, congratulating him on one of them.

Sultan ʿAbd al-ʿAzīz himself reached al-Ṭāʾif on 6 Djumāda I/3 December, changed into *iḥrām*, entered the city and then, by the Bāb al-Salām, entered the sacred mosque. No member of his house had prayed there since 1227-8/1812. Ibn Suʿūd eschewed the Sharīfian palaces and instead set up his camp outside the city in al-Shuhadāʾ, where for two weeks he received all and sundry. Universal report is that his humility, his unpretentiousness, his sincere apologies for what had happened at al-Ṭāʾif and his rejection of sycophancy (to those who tried to kiss his hand he said that his custom was only to shake hands) combined to win local hearts. The proclamation that he had issued on 12 Djumādā I 1343/9 December when he entered the city had already made a favourable impression (text in Wahba, *Djazīra*, 254-5). Article 4 was as follows: "Every member of the ulema in these regions and each employee of al-Ḥaram al-Sharīf or *muṭawwif* with a clear title shall be entitled to his previous entitlement. We will neither add to it nor subtract anything from it, with the exception of a man against whom people bring proof of unsuitability for a post, for unlike the past situation, such practices will be forbidden. To whomever has a firm previous claim on the *bayt al-māl* of the Muslims, we will give his right and take nothing from him."

Having established some rapport with the citizens of Makka, Sultan ʿAbd al-ʿAzīz now took command of his forward troops located at al-Raghāma about 4 km. east of Baḥra. The governance of the city rested still with Ibn Luʾayy, but ʿAbd al-ʿAzīz now turned the civil administration of the city over to ʿAbd Allāh al-Damlūdjī and to Ḥāfiẓ Wahba on a kind of rotating basis. He then decided he would rather have al-Damlūdjī close at hand and left the administration of Makka divided so that Khālid b. Luʾayy handled Ikhwān and military affairs and Shaykh Ḥāfiẓ civil matters. Soon thereafter the administration was further elaborated. The municipality was turned over to a Makkan, Shaykh Aḥmad al-Subaḥī, and an embryonic consultative council was established under the chairmanship of Shaykh ʿAbd al-Ḳādir al-Shaybī, the keeper of the key of the Kaʿba. This simple council was the kernel of the later *Madjlis al-Shūrā*. This administrative set-up continued until the capture of Djudda a year later.

The dual amīrate was not harmonious. Shaykh Ḥāfiẓ reports perpetual conflicts between himself and Khālid. It was, he says, a conflict between Bedouin and sedentary mentalities. "He wanted to confiscate all the houses and seize their contents because their owners had fled. Since they had only fled out of fright, I tried and in many cases succeeded in preserving them; in other cases I failed." Smoking was a perpetual source of trouble. Ibn Luʾayy wanted to use force on offenders; Ḥāfiẓ, kindness. One of the ironies was that although smoking had been banned, cigarettes were taxed.

There were other problems. King ʿAlī, attempts at reconciliation having failed, stopped all supplies going from Djudda to Makka. Since 300-400 camel loads a day were needed, the situation became very strained. ʿAbd al-Ḳādir al-Shaybī wrote to King ʿAlī as follows: "How far do your deeds differ from the statement of God. What is the reason for stopping our food? We are not responsible for the Nejdi Army entering Mecca; you are, for the following reasons (i) you did not settle differences with the Sultan of Nejd, (ii) when the Nejd army entered Taif we asked you to evacuate our families and belongings, but you refused. You promised to protect us but you ran away. When you came to Mecca we asked you and your father to protect us... and again you ran away... we would like to ask your Highness if the neighbours of the House of God are animals. We beg your Highness to leave us and Jeddah." (quotation from Baker, 214-15). ʿAlī sent one of his dilapidated aircraft to drop a leaflet in reply saying that he had left in order to prevent a repetition of the *émeutes* in al-Ṭāʾif. ʿAbd al-ʿAzīz's response to him was more concrete. He sent the Ikhwān to capture Rābigh and al-Līth thus (a) giving them something to do; (b) breaking the blockade; and (c) cutting the communications between Djudda and al-Madīna.

In fact, the situation in Makka improved while that in Djudda slowly deteriorated. Not only did Makkans begin to return home, but native Djuddāwīs themselves began to arrive in Makka. The superior administration in Makka was a noticeable factor. In April an interesting visitor arrived, Comrade Karīm Khān Ḥakīmoff, the Soviet consul in Djudda. He had been granted permission by King ʿAlī to mediate and arrived with his Iranian colleague. They were of course received by ʿAbd al-ʿAzīz. Reportedly, Ḥakīmoff characterised the hostilities as resulting from imperialist plots, but he did get permission for Fuʾād al-Khaṭīb, King ʿAlī's foreign minister, to come and negotiate. On 2 May, ʿAbd al-ʿAzīz met with al-Khaṭīb at a coffee shop midway between the warring lines. The sultan never wavered: the former King al-Ḥusayn now in al-ʿAḳaba was still really running affairs; even if he were not, King ʿAlī was indistinguishable from him; both had to go.

The sieges of al-Madīna and D̲j̲udda dragged on, but the approaching *Ḥad̲j̲d̲j̲* season of 1344/June-July 1925 began to occupy ʿAbd al-ʿAzīz's attention. Despite the difficulty that the siege of D̲j̲udda imposed, he was anxious for the *Ḥad̲j̲d̲j̲* to go well. He announced that Rābig̲h̲, al-Līth and al-Ḳunfud̲h̲a were official pilgrim ports and sent out a general invitation (*nidāʾ ʿāmm*) to all Muslims (text in Wahba, *K̲h̲amsūn*, 67) which incidentally indicated that charitable contributions and economic development projects would be welcome.

This was the year that Eldon Rutter, an English Muslim, made the pilgrimage and left a first-hand account thereof. Of course, the number who came was very small. His *muṭawwif* claimed normally to have had some 1,000 plus clients, but this year he had only Eldon Rutter. The Englishman estimated that the total number who came was approximately 70,000, of whom he thought some 25-30,000 were Nad̲j̲dīs. They camped apart, and Rutter notes that they took no notice of the tobacco that was on sale everywhere. "It is the smoking ... which is unlawful, not the selling of it!" At ʿArafāt, while returning toward his tent from a visit to Masd̲j̲id Namira (also known as Masd̲j̲id Ibrāhīm and Masd̲j̲id ʿArafa), Rutter and his companions "passed the burly figure of Ibn Saʿûd, dressed in a couple of towels and bestriding a beautiful Nejd horse which looked rather like a little animated rocking horse under his long form. He was attended by four mounted guards carrying rifles." Another of Rutter's vivid descriptions is that of the break-up of the pilgrim throng at ʿArafāt: "Far out on the northern side of the plain rode the scattered hosts of the Nejd Ikhwân—dim masses of hosting camelry, obscurely seen in the falling dusk. Here and there in the midst of the spreading multitude, a green standard, born aloft, suddenly flashed out from the dust-cloud, only to disappear the next moment behind the obscuring screen, which rose in spreading billows from beneath the feet of the thousands of trotting deluls." There were also Wahhābīs riding as police against the returning crowd on the look-out for thieving, which was much less that year because potential thieves knew that the Wahhābīs would apply Islamic law literally and promptly. The Nad̲j̲dī flag was flying over the hospital at Munā, where ʿAbd al-ʿAzīz had pitched his tent on the "cope-stoned earthen platform where the tents of the Sharîf of Mekka were formerly pitched at this season." All guests, including Rutter, were received by the sultan, and he rose to greet each and every one. By this time, the sultan had apparently settled for more comfortable quarters when in the city. Rutter mentions passing his residence in al-Abṭaḥ (al-Muʿābada), a spacious well-built mansion which belonged to ʿUmar al-Saḳḳāf and over which the green flag flew. Rutter met with ʿAbd al-ʿAzīz a number of times, learned that he personally approved the editorials in the new official journal, *Umm al-Ḳurā*, and on one occasion heard the king say that his three concerns were Allāh, "my beloved" Muḥammad and the Arab nation.

In short, despite occasional harassment of foreign pilgrims by the Ik̲h̲wān, the pilgrimage was a brilliant success for the new régime. The numbers who came were obviously small but the organisation was excellent. Glowing reports filtered back to home countries, and the bogey man image of the Wahhābī leader began to recede.

Meanwhile, the sieges were dragging down to their end. Rutter describes one aerial attack in which the S̲h̲arīfian bombs were dropped on the hills bordering al-Muʿābada. He opines that they were probably aimed at the house in al-Abṭaḥ. The result was not impressive; the straw hut of a Takrūnī (African) was destroyed, and an old woman was slightly wounded in the leg. Autumn brought visitors. Philby on a personal mission was received by the sultan at al-S̲h̲umaysī on the edge of the sacred territory. Sir Gilbert Clayton, who was negotiating with ʿAbd al-ʿAzīz at his camp in Baḥra, noted in his diary for 22 Rabīʿ I/21 October the arrival of an Iranian delegation. Led by Mīrzā ʿAlī Akbar K̲h̲ān Bahmān, the Iranian minister in Egypt, and Mīrzā Ḥabīb K̲h̲ān Huwayda, the consul-general of Iran in Palestine, its function was to investigate alleged Wahhābī desecration and destruction of shrines in Makka and al-Madīna. ʿAbd al-ʿAzīz received them most cordially and sent them on to Makka by car. The sultan said he welcomed the investigation because the charges were false. Incidentally, Clayton indicated in his diary (19 October 1925) his belief that Ibn Suʿūd could have captured D̲j̲udda whenever he wanted, but that he was going slowly because, *inter alia*, he wanted "to gauge more fully the effect which his attack on the Holy Places and his capture of Mecca has had on the Moslem world in general and especially in India and Egypt." In any case, by the middle of November 1925, large numbers of Wahhābīs began to arrive in groups ranging from half-a-dozen to several hundred. The wadi from D̲j̲abal al-Nūr to the city was crowded with them and many were sent on to the front. Clearly, the sultan was preparing to storm D̲j̲udda, but it turned out not to be necessary. Al-Madīna surrendered on 19 D̲j̲umādā I 1344/5 December 1925, followed two weeks later by D̲j̲udda. On 20 D̲j̲umāda II 1344/5 January 1926, certain notables in D̲j̲udda formally approached the sultan of Nad̲j̲d to ask him if he would also become king of al-Ḥid̲j̲āz, hoping by this device to maintain the integrity of al-Ḥid̲j̲āz. When they had left. ʿAbd al-ʿAzīz convened the ulema and other notables. They approved. On 22 D̲j̲umādā II/7 January in Makka, Ibn Suʿūd released a formal statement of his intentions pointing out that there had been almost no response to his appeal for a conference to discuss the problem of al-Ḥid̲j̲āz. "So, as I find that the Islamic World is not concerned about this important matter, I have granted them [the people of the Ḥid̲j̲āz] the freedom to decide what they will.' The wishes of the "people" manifested themselves the same evening in the form of a petition confirming their support for ʿAbd al-ʿAzīz: "We acknowledge you, Sultan Abdulaziz, as king of Hejaz in accordance with the Holy Book and the *Sunna* of the Prophet and that Hejaz will be for the Hejazeen ... Mecca will be the capital and we shall be under your protection" (Baker, 230). Rutter was present in the Great Mosque for the *mubāyaʿa*: "Upon a Friday [23 D̲j̲umādā II/8 January] after the midday prayer, I mounted the crumbling stone steps of the school el Madrassat el Fakhrîya, which stands beside the Bâb Ibrâhîm, in order to visit an acquaintance who was employed as a schoolmaster there. As we sat sipping tea beside a window looking into the Haram, we were surprised to observe a sudden rush of people toward Bâb es-Safâ. They were evidently attracted by something which was happening near that gate.

Rising, we descended the steps and passed into the Haram. Making our way toward Bâb es-Safâ, we came upon a great press of Mekkans and Bedouins. In the midst of them was one of the Haram preachers [probably ʿAbd al-Malik Murād] perched upon a little wooden platform or pulpit, apparently addressing the multitude. Elbowing our way into the crowd, we were able to see Ibn Saʿûd sitting in a prepared place near the gate. The preacher was addressing to the Sultân a speech of adulation. Presently, he made an end, and then several of the Ashrâf, the Shaybi, and other prominent Mekkans in turn, took the Sultan's hand and acknowledged him King of the Hijâz. Ibn Saʿûd received these advances with his usual cordial smile, and upon the conclusion of the ceremony he rose, and accompanied by his armed guards, made his way slowly through the crowd towards the Kaaba and proceeded to perform the towâf. Having completed this, and prayed two prostrations in the Makâm Ibrâhîm, he left the Mosque and went to the Hamîdîya where he held a general reception... Suddenly one of the old guns in the Fort of Jiyâd [Adjyād], boomed and was immediately followed by another on Jebel Hindi. The troops of the garrison were saluting the new king. A hundred and one times the peace of the city was broken." Rutter reports some hostile reactions to the elevation of al-Suʿūdī, as some Makkans dubbed their king, but contrasts most favourably the honest treatment received by pilgrims under the new dispensation.

The hostilities over, the new king of the Ḥidjāz remained in his new capital, Makka, and addressed himself to these major issues: the *Ḥadjdj* of 1344/1926, the Islamic conference which he had previously announced and which was scheduled in conjunction with it, and the administration of the kingdom. The *Ḥadjdj* that summer attracted 191,000, approximately an eight-fold increase over the previous year, but the Holy City was also the scene of the rather serious *maḥmal* [*q.v.*] affair. The Egyptian *maḥmal* arrived in the usual way with the *kiswa* [*q.v.*], with the retinue of civilians and soldiers including their flags and bugles, and with contributions of cash and kind much of which represented *wakf* [*q.v.*] income dedicated to the *Ḥaram* from Egypt. The Egyptian *amīr al-Ḥadjdj* was Maḥmūd ʿAẓmī Pasha. The whole procedure was almost programmed for trouble, given the cultural differences of the groups involved and especially the religious sensitivities of the Ikhwān. As Lacey (202) observed: "The glorious shoulder-borne litter smacked to them of idolatry [and] its retinue of armed guards piqued their pride...". In the event, the Kaʿba was dressed in its new Egyptian *kiswa* without incident, and the ceremonies were proceeding normally, but on the eve of 9 Dhū 'l-Ḥidjdja (some report the day of 10 Dhū 'l-Ḥidjdja) the situation exploded. One report is that the spark was some music (= probably bugling) played by the Egyptian soldiers. Other reports indicate that the Nadjdī Bedouin simply saw the *maḥmal* and began to shout out that it was an idol. Whatever the precise trigger event was, in the crowded mass of pilgrims between Munā and ʿArafāt some Ikhwān tried to interfere with the Egyptians and began to throw stones at them. The Egyptians responded with gunfire reportedly at the order of Maḥmūd ʿAẓmī. In all, some 25 men and women pilgrims were killed and 100 wounded; 40 camels were also killed; but the carnage could easily have been much worse. Just as the Ikhwān were preparing a massive assault on the Egyptians, King ʿAbd al-ʿAzīz rode up and at considerable personal risk managed to separate the two groups and to cool the hot blood. Once order was restored, the king ordered his son Fayṣal to guard the Egyptians with a detachment of Suʿūdī troops until the end of the ceremonies. When the *Ḥadjdj* had ended, he ordered Mushārī b. Suʿūd b. Djalwī to escort the Egyptians to Djudda with a detachment of Suʿūdī troops, and as a cable (text in Wahba, *Khamsūn*, 257) of 16 Dhu 'l-Ḥidjdja 1344/from ʿAbd Allāh Āl Sulaymān in Makka to Ḥāfiẓ Wahba, then serving as the king's envoy in Cairo, makes clear, the departure of the Egyptians from Makka was scarcely willing, but the king was going to have them out, willing or not. As Lacey had summarised it (*loc. cit.*), "the Mahmal never trooped again in glory through the streets of Mecca", but the incident further soured Egypto-Suʿūdī relations to the degree that diplomatic relations were not established between the two countries as long as King Fuʾād reigned in Cairo.

Since the fall of the city to his arms, King ʿAbd al-ʿAzīz had repeatedly proclaimed his intention to convene an Islamic conference in Makka to which delegates from all Muslim countries and communities would be invited. The stated idea was to discuss the governance of Islam's holiest sites and ceremonies, but the basic motivation was to put to rest the fears of Muslims beyond Arabia over the capability of a Suʿūdī-Nadjdī-Wahhābī régime to care for the Ḥaramayn responsibly. In the event, the conference probably attained its goal, but the results were passive not active. Egypt had declined to attend, and the *maḥmal* incident was most distracting. The delegates who did attend debated with great freedom a wide variety of religious subjects but to no very particular point. On the underlying political issue, it was crystal-clear that ʿAbd al-ʿAzīz was going to run the country and there was no indication of any incapacity on his part. That issue was settled without being raised.

The series of *ad hoc* administrative arrangements made by the king during and after the conquest now gave way to more permanent arrangements. It should be remembered that until the unification of the "dual kingdom" (on 25 Radjab 1345/29 January 1927 ʿAbd al-ʿAzīz had been proclaimed king of Nadjd and its Dependencies) as the Kingdom of Suʿūdī Arabia in 1932, and even beyond that time, al-Ḥidjāz and especially its capital Makka received most of the government's attention. It is not always easy to separate what applied: (a) to Makka as a city, (b) to al-Ḥidjāz as a separate entity including Makka, and (c) to both the Kingdom of al-Ḥidjaz and the Kingdom of Nadjd, equally including Makka. The evolution of advisory or quasi-legislative councils was as follows. Immediately after the Suʿūdī occupation of Makka (7 Djumādā I 1343/19 December 1924), ʿAbd al-ʿAzīz convened a partly elected, partly appointed body of notables called *al-Madjlis al-Ahlī* (the national council). It was elected and then it was re-elected on 11 Muḥarram 1344/1 August 1925. Representation was on the basis of town quarters, and included prominent merchants and ulema, but in addition, the king appointed a number equal to the elected members and also appointed the presiding officer; indeed, no elected member could take his seat without ʿAbd al-ʿAzīz's approval. After the second election, this group came to be known as *Madjlis al-Shūrā* (consultative council). After the Islamic conference ended, this arrangement was significantly changed. A national (Ḥidjāzī) council—a kind of constituent assembly—with 30 Makkan members was convened to study an organic statute (*al-Taʿlīmāt al-Asāsiyya li 'l-Mamlaka 'l-Ḥidjāziyya*). Known as *al-Djamʿiyya al-ʿUmūmiyya* (the general assembly), it accepted on 21 Ṣafar 1345/31 August 1926 Ibn Suʿūd's draft of the organic statute which specified that Makka was the capital of the kingdom, that administration of the kingdom was "in the hand of King ʿAbd al-ʿAzīz," and that a *nā'ib ʿāmm* (deputy general, viceroy) would be appointed on behalf of the king. Fayṣal b. ʿAbd al-ʿAzīz, the king's second living son, was appointed *nā'ib ʿāmm*. Under his chairmanship and in accordance with the statute, a new *Madjlis al-Shūrā* of 13 members (five from Makka), this time all appointed, was convened. Various administrative and budgetary matters were routinely discussed by it. (For the rapid evolution of the *Madjlis al-Shūrā*, see Nallino, 33-5, 235-6 and M.T. Ṣādiķ, 21-47.) The *Madjlis al-Shūrā*, no matter how limited its real powers were, did play a major role as a sounding board in al-Ḥidjāz for various government policies. It has never been dissolved and even under the very much changed situation caused by oil price increases in 1973, it apparently still meets ceremonially from time to time.

One should also note that the *Madjlis al-Shūrā*, meeting in Makka on 16 Muḥarram 1352/11 May 1933, recognised the king's oldest living son, Suʿūd b. ʿAbd al-ʿAzīz, as heir designate (*walī al-ʿahd*). The prince himself was not present, and Fayṣal b. ʿAbd al-ʿAzīz received the *bayʿa* on his behalf. The decree was read aloud in the *Ḥaram* and the ministers, notables and ordinary people filed by to present their congratulations. The organic statute also established arrangements for local government and national departments; all of the latter were in Makka. Nor did this situation change radically with the proclamation of the unified Kingdom of Saudi Arabia in 1351/1932. As late as 1952, the Minister of Health and Interior (H.R.H. Prince ʿAbd Allāh b. Fayṣal b. ʿAbd al-ʿAzīz) and the ministry officials were in Makka as was the Ministry of Finance under ʿAbd Allāh Āl Sulaymān Āl Ḥamdān and the Directorates General of Education, P.T.T., Public Security, *awķāf*, and other central government agencies. It may be noted here that Fayṣal was named Minister of Foreign Affairs in 1349/1930, but also that his father continued to make all important decisions in all matters as long as he was vigorous.

Initial branches (originally called *aķsām*, sing. *ķism*) of the new government, each under a director (*mudīr*) were: *sharīʿa* affairs, internal affairs, foreign affairs, financial affairs, public education affairs and military affairs. Courts, *waķfs* and mosques, including the Makkan *Ḥaram*, were under the *sharīʿa* branch; municipal matters were under internal affairs. It should also be noted that a *Ḥadjdj* committee composed of the heads of all departments concerned with pilgrimage matters plus members nominated by the king was formed under the chairmanship of the viceroy. Finally, one may note that the titles of departments, their heads and the loci of responsibility all evolved over time. For example, in 1350/1932 a Council of Agents (*Madjlis al-Wukalā'*) was announced, and for the first time the germ of the idea of ministerial responsibility was introduced.

Makka was one of only five cities in the Ḥidjāz that had had a municipality in Ottoman and Hāshimite times. The municipality was re-established by the Suʿūdī regime in 1345/1926 with its own organisational structure. Three years later, its powers and responsibilities were increased and its name was changed to *Amānat al-ʿĀṣima*. According to Hamza, the underlying idea of the king was to turn purely local matters over to local people. Further organisational adjustments were made in 1357/1938. The budget was in reality under the control of the king and his deputy general, but formaly it was under the purview of the *Madjlis-al-Shūrā*. Once the budget was approved, the municipality apparently enjoyed a certain independence in administering it. It was able to levy local fees (*rusūm*). Figures are very incomplete, but in 1345/1926-7 the municipal budget totaled SR 158,800 and in 1369/1949-50 SR 4,034,000. Municipality responsibilities included city administration, cleaning, lighting, supervision of establishments, roads, installation of awnings, condemnation and destruction of properties, land registration, price regulation (for necessities), cleanliness of food preparers, slaughter houses, weights and measures, supervision of elections of guilds of industries and trades and of their activities, supervision of burial procedures, kindness to animals and fines. No other municipality in the land had such broad responsibilities.

The one area where Nadjdīs played an important role in the Makkan scene after the conquest was in organised religion. As early as Djumādā II 1343/January 1925, conferences between the Wahhābī ulema of Nadjd and the local ulema of Makka were going forward with minimal difficulty. Shortly after the conquest, ʿAbd al-ʿAzīz had transferred ʿAbd Allāh b. Bulayhid (1284-1359/1867 to 1940-1) from the *ķaḍā'* of Ḥā'il to that of Makka, where he remained for about two years. He was succeeded by ʿAbd Allāh b. Ḥasan b. Ḥusayn b. ʿAlī b. Ḥusayn b. Muḥammad b. ʿAbd al-Wahhāb. Philby, writing around 1369-70/1950, referred to him as the "archbishop of Mecca" and Aramco, *Royal Family*... still reported him to be chief *ķāḍī* in Dhu 'l-Ķaʿda 1371/July 1952. Yet care was taken not to alienate the local ulema. For example, when the Ḥidjāzī *Hay'at al-Amr bi'l Maʿrūf wa'l-Nahy ʿan al-Munkar* was established in 1345/1926, ʿAbd Allāh al-Shaybī was made chairman of the committee. The function of the *Hay'a* was in general to supervise morals, encourage prayer, control muezzins and *imāms* of mosques, and report infractions of the *sharīʿa* (details in Nallino, 100-2.) In general, the influence of the ulema was high and they were deferred to. The king could not dispose of *sharīʿa* questions on his own and regularly referred them to either a *ķāḍī* or to the full "bench" of the Makkan or Riyāḍī ulema. The king's direct influence over this largely autonomous group was through the power of appointment, but he was of course influential indirectly.

Makka was one of only three cities in al-Ḥidjāz that had had police at the time of the Suʿūdī takeover; however, since King ʿAlī had taken them all to Djudda as part of his military forces, none were immediately available. According to Rutter, a squad of powerful black slaves belonging to ʿAbd al-ʿAzīz kept order. Makka was also the seat of police administration. A police academy was started in 1353/1933-4 and, at that time at least, the police supervised the orphanage and an old persons' home which had 44 residents. In 1953-5, a new government building was constructed in Djarwal as the main headquarters for the police, and in 1385/1965-6 a police emergency squad was established which responded to the emergency telephone number of 99. In the first decades after the conquest, police were almost all recruited from ʿAsīr [*q.v.*] and Nadjd. By the mid-1930s, they wore European-style uniforms and numbered 33 officers and 896 other ranks. As long as it was necessary, the police force also included a special squad called *Ķalam Taftīsh al-Raķīķ* (section for the inspection of slaves). Executions were usually carried out on Fridays after the noon prayer between the Ḥamīdiyya (government house) and the southern corner of the *Ḥaram*. Philby (*Jubilee*, 118-20) details a triple execution in 1931 over which Fayṣal presided from a window in the *madjlis* of al-Ḥamīdiyya, where a group of notables had also gathered. There was a large crowd of commoners in the street. When the beheadings were over, the police tied the corpses "each with its head by its side" to the railings of the building until sundown.

There were three levels of judicial jurisdiction established by the court regulations (*niẓām tas̲h̲kīlāt al-maḥākim al-s̲h̲arʿiyya*) issued in Ṣafar 1346/August 1927, at least up until the post-World War II period. The lowest was the summary court (*maḥkamat al-umūr al-mustaʿd̲j̲ila*) presided over by a single *ḳāḍī* with jurisdiction over petty civil cases and criminal cases not involving execution or loss of limb. The higher court (*maḥkamat al-s̲h̲arīʿa al-kubrā*) had a *ḳāḍī* as president plus two of his colleagues. In cases involving loss of limb or execution, the sentence had to be pronounced by the full court. The appeals court sat only in Makka and was presided over by a president and four other ulema. It functioned as a court of appeals (criminal cases) and of cassation (civil cases). Appeals have to be filed within 20 days and if the court refuses to take the case, the verdict of the lower court stands. The president, who was S̲h̲ayk̲h̲ ʿAbd Allāh b. Ḥasan Āl al-S̲h̲ayk̲h̲, also administers the whole system and supervises all courts and *ḳāḍīs*. There has also been, since 1350-1/1932, an inspector of courts. Notaries (sing. *kātib al-ʿadl*) were instituted in 1347/1928-9, and Hamza reports that in Makka at the time he was writing the incumbent was ʿUrābī Sid̲j̲īnī.

A few other administrative notes are in order. Immediately after the conquest, the government overprinted "Sultanate of Nad̲j̲d and al-Ḥid̲j̲āz" on the Hās̲h̲imite stamps, but Suʿūdī ones were soon in use and the Suʿūdī government joined the International Postal Union of Berne in 1345-6/1927. In 1357-8/1939 Makka's post office was one of only four (the others being at D̲j̲udda, al-Madīna and Yanbuʿ) in the country that could handle all operations specified by the international conventions including the telegraph. There was a daily service to D̲j̲udda and al-Ṭāʾif and a twice-weekly service to al-Madīna. In 1384/1964-5, Makka's post office, which was handling in that year's *ḥad̲j̲d̲j̲* 350,000 letters daily, became a postal centre independent of D̲j̲udda. Rent control was imposed at the time of the conquest and was still in force as late as 1374/1955-6. There was a customs office in the city which, like its counterpart in al-Madīna, was presumably a branch of the main office in D̲j̲udda. *Waḳf* administration in Makka reported directly to the viceroy. Early directors of the Directorate of *Awḳāf* were Muhammad Saʿīd Abu 'l-K̲h̲ayr (1343/1924-8) and Mad̲j̲id al-Kurdī (1347-50/1928-31). By a royal decree of 27 D̲h̲u 'l-Ḥid̲j̲d̲j̲a 1354/21 March 1936 the Makkan Directorate of *Awḳāf* was changed into a directorate general to which the other *awḳāf* directorates of al-Ḥid̲j̲āz would report. Sayyid ʿAbd al-Wahhāb Nāʾib al-Ḥaram was appointed director general.

As far as fire fighting is concerned, Rutter (228) describes a reasonably effective volunteer system in use before modern systems were adopted. He comments that in case of fire "the neighbours regard it as a point of honour to render all the assistance in their power, and official notice of the occurrence is taken by the police, some of whom also turn out and help." The first student mission sent abroad to train in fire fighting and life-saving methods was some time before 1367/1947-8.

One may at this point reasonably inquire as to general Makkan acceptance of Suʿūdī hegemony in the pre-oil period. Leaving aside Ik̲h̲wān discontent at the régime's alleged softness toward religious laxity in Makka and discounting near-by tribal unhappiness ("taxing" pilgrims was no longer possible), there was general acceptance of the régime and great pleasure at the total security and basic fairness. There was also some unhappiness which doubtless increased with the very straitened circumstances concomitant with the general world-wide depression. In 1345-6/1927 Ḥusayn Ṭāhir al-Dabbāg̲h̲, whose father had been Minister of Finance both under King al-Ḥusayn and under King ʿAlī and who himself headed a business house, established in Makka an anti-Suʿūdī "Ḥid̲j̲āz liberation organisation" called *And̲j̲umānī Ḥizb al-Aḥrār*. Its basic platform opposed any monarch in al-Ḥid̲j̲āz. Ḥusayn was exiled in 1346-7/1928, but he probably left behind a clandestine cell of his party which also maintained an open operation in Egypt. We get another glimpse of anti-Suʿūdī feeling in Makka in 1354-5/1936 from the report of a Muslim Indian employee of the British legation in D̲j̲udda named Iḥsān Allāh. According to him, dissatisfaction was widespread; older conservative merchants and ulema wished for an Egyptian takeover with British support, whereas middle-aged merchants and government officials simply viewed the government as backward, a "set of old fools"; younger businessmen, army officers, and pilots longed for an Atatürk [*q.v.*] or a Mussolini. Iḥsān notes, however, that there was no action and that the preferred way to seek relief was by working for Ḥid̲j̲āzī interests through the *Mad̲j̲lis al-Shūrā*. Intelligence reports are notoriously unreliable, but it would have been surprising had there not been some level of discontent. With the coming of oil, separatist feelings doubtlessly disappeared, and Makka participated to the full in the extraordinary development that the Kingdom enjoyed as a whole. The extraordinary events of 1400/1979 were the only dramatic break in the standard rhythms of the city's life.

Seizure of the *Ḥaram*. Not since the followers of Ḥamdān Ḳarmat [*q.v.*] seized Makka and carried the Black Stone back to their headquarters in al-Ahsāʾ [*q.v.*] had there been such an astonishing event as that which unfolded in the *Ḥaram* at dawn on Tuesday, 1 Muḥarram 1400/20 November 1979. It was of worldwide interest not only because of its intrinsic importance for one of the world's major religions, but also against the background of the Soviet-American global rivalry, of the recent revolution in Iran, and of the general religious fervour surging through the Muslim world.

The events can be quickly told. The Ḥaram may have had 50,000 people in it, which is not many for a structure designed to accommodate 300,000. It had more than usual at that hour because the day was the first of the new Islamic century and thus deserved some special observance. The *imām*, S̲h̲ayk̲h̲ Muḥammad b. Subayyil, had gone to the microphone to lead the prayer, but he was then pushed aside. Several dozens of men produced rifles from their robes; firing broke out, the worshippers ran, and the armed men moved quickly to seal the 29 gates. Many people were wounded in these first exchanges, and a number were killed. Meanwhile two men, subsequently identified as D̲j̲uhaymān ("little glowerer") b. Muḥammad al-ʿUtaybī and Muḥammad b. ʿAbd Allāh al-Ḳaḥṭānī, were at the microphone proclaiming that the latter was the *Mahdī*. The rebels, a number of whose grandfathers had been killed while fighting as Ik̲h̲wān against ʿAbd al-ʿAzīz in 1347-8/1929, who considered themselves neo-Ik̲h̲wān, and who numbered in all some 250 including women and children, let the worshippers out aside from 30-odd who were kept as hostages. With apparent presence of mind, S̲h̲ayk̲h̲ Muḥammad had removed his clerical garb and made his way to a telephone in his office according to some reports—a public phone according to others—and notified the authorities of the seriousness of what was happening. He managed to slip out with the other worshippers. At the beginning of the ensuing siege, the rebels used the powerful public address system, which had speakers in the 90 m. high minarets and which was designed to be heard in the streets and plazas outside the mosque, to proclaim their message that the *Mahdī* was going to usher in justice throughout earth and that the *Mahdī* and his men had to seek shelter and protection in al-Ḥaram al-S̲h̲arīf because they were everywhere persecuted. They had no recourse except the *Ḥaram*. Attacks on the House of Suʿūd and its alleged policies and practices were virulent; the rebels opposed working women, television, football, consumption of alcohol, royal trips to European and other pleasure spots, royal involvement in business, and the encouragement of foreigners who came to Arabia and corrupted Islamic morality. Details of names and business contracts were specified. The *amīr* of Makka came in for particular attack. Meanwhile, Suʿūdī Arabia was alive with rumours, some officially encouraged, to the effect that the D̲j̲uhaymān was a homosexual, that he was a drug addict, a drunkard, etc.

The reaction of the Suʿūdī government was hesitant at first but never in doubt. Prince Fahd b. ʿAbd al-ʿAzīz, the heir designate, was out of the country attending an international conference in Tunis. Prince ʿAbd Allāh b. ʿAbd al-ʿAzīz second in line to the throne was on vacation in Morocco. The king, K̲h̲ālid b. ʿAbd al-ʿAzīz, was awakened at seven in the morning and informed of what had happened. He immediately ordered that all communication with the outside world to be cut. The ensuing communications blackout was so total that it was reported that even Prince Fahd had been unable to find out what was going on. In Makka a police car, which may have been the first concrete reaction, drove toward the mosque to investigate. It was promptly fired on and left. Later the *amīr* drove up to try to assess the situation, only to have his driver shot in the head. The men inside were evidently well armed, trained and ruthless. By mid-afternoon, the 600-man special security force was in Makka and national guard, police, and army units were being airlifted in from Tabūk [*q.v.*] in the north and K̲h̲amīs Mus̲h̲ayt [*q.v.*] in the south. Prince Sulṭān b. ʿAbd al-ʿAzīz, the Minister of Defence; Prince Nāʾif b. ʿAbd al-ʿAzīz, the Minister of Interior; and Prince Turkī b. Fayṣal b. ʿAbd al-ʿAzīz, the Chief of Exernal Intelligence, all arrived in Makka. In al-Riyāḍ, the king had simultaneously called together the senior ulema in order to get a *fatwā* authorising the use of force in the *Ḥaram*, since force there is by definition forbidden. The *fatwā* approving the action was apparently issued immediately but not published for several days. Authority was found in the *āya* of the Ḳurʾān: "Do not fight them near the Holy Mosque until they fight you inside it, and if they fight you, you must kill them, for that is the punishment of the unbelievers" (II, 149).

By Tuesday evening the siege was on, and the rebels had no way to escape, despite the fact that they had secretly and ingeniously cached large supplies of weapons, ammunition and food in the mosque. Electricity and all other services to the mosque were cut, but D̲j̲uhaymān's snipers covered the open ground around the mosque. Horrified by what was going on, some national guardsmen (*mud̲j̲āhidūn*) wanted to storm the mosque, but the king had ordered that casualties be minimised. The situation was extremely delicate, for Prince Sulṭān could hardly order heavy weaponry to destroy the mosque and Bayt Allāh. Ultimately, Prince Sulṭān ordered an attack on the *masʿā* which juts out from the mosque enclosure like an open thumb from a closed fist (see plan). According to some, an "artillery barrage" was laid down, but when the troops advanced, they suffered heavy losses and accomplished little. There was considerable confusion on the government side and some lack of coordination among the various services. At one point, two soldiers reportedly ran firing into the courtyard in order to be shot down and die as martyrs. Others were reported to have been unhappy at being called on to fight in the mosque. Since the national guardsmen were tribal, and it had become known that the leaders of the insurrection were tribal, suspicion of the national guardsmen arose. Sulṭān tried another approach involving a disastrous helicopter attack into the courtyard. It failed; the soldiers were winched down in daylight, and most died. When government soldiers died, the rebels are said to have exclaimed *amr Allāh* ("at the order of God"), when one of their own died, they either shot or burned off his face—a job the women mostly performed—to conceal his identity. In a very difficult situation, friendly governments including the American, French and Pakistani "were prodigal with advice, much of it conflicting" (Holder and Johns, 524). By Friday, 4 Muḥarram/23 November, however, the superiority of the government forces began to tell. Using tear gas, they forced an entrance into the mosque including the second storey, and they drove the rebel marksmen from two of the minarets. Once inside, government forces were able to rake D̲j̲uhaymān's people, and despite a desperate pillar-to-pillar defence backed by barricades of mattresses, carpets and anything else that could be found, the rebels were gradually pushed down toward the maze-like complex of basement rooms. By Monday, 7 Muḥarram/26 November the government had gained control of everything above ground. But the fighting continued in nightmarish conditions below ground even though the number of the rebels was by then much reduced. By Wednesday the courtyard had been sufficiently cleared and cleaned to broadcast prayers live on TV and to begin to calm down the city and the country.

Below ground, difficult fighting continued. The rebels were few and their supplies now scant, but accompanied in some cases by their women and children they fought desperately. Gas, flooding, and burning tires were all tried in an effort to flush them out—without success. The fate of Muḥammad b. ʿAbd Allāh al-Ḳaḥṭānī is not clear. Some reports indicate that he was killed early in the fighting; others that, in the depths of despair, D̲j̲uhaymān had shot him. With many wounded, the hour of the rebels had come. At an hour-and-a-half after midnight on Wednesday 16 Muḥarram/5 December D̲j̲uhaymān led his people out. "It is said that as they emerged, many weeping and too tired to stand, muttering constantly, spat on and reviled, one of the band turned to a National Guardsman and asked: 'What of the army of the north?'" (Holder and Johns, 526.) But many had to be individually overpowered. D̲j̲uhaymān is reported to have been kicking and struggling even as his arms were pinned. Suʿūdī TV covered this scene, and D̲j̲uhaymān "stared defiantly at the cameras, thrusting forward his matted beard, his eyes fierce and piercing like a cornered beast of prey" (Lacey, 487).

The investigation and trial of the rebels did not take long. On Wednesday a.m., 21 Ṣafar 1400/9 January

1980 (not following the Friday noon prayer as was customary) in eight different Saudi cities amongst which they had been divided, 63 of the rebels were beheaded. Their citizenship was as follows: Suᶜūdīs 41, Egyptians 10, South Yamanīs 6, Kuwaytīs 3, North Yamanīs 1, Sudanese 1 and ᶜIrāḳīs 1. Twenty-three women and thirteen children had surrendered along with their men. The women were given two years in prison and the children were turned over to welfare centres. The authorites found no evidence of foreign involvement. In addition, 19 who had supplied arms were jailed, while another 38 so accused were freed. The government casualty count listed 127 troops killed and 461 wounded, rebel dead as 117, and dead worshippers as 12 or more (all killed the first morning). Popular reaction to these extraordinary events was uniformly hostile to the rebels as defilers of God and his house. The only reported approval is by other members of the ᶜUtayba tribe, who reportedly admired the fact that D̲j̲uhaymān had in no way buckled under during interrogation.

Population and Society. Consistent population figures for Makka are not easy to find. Those that follow are perhaps suggestive:

Date	Estimated population	Source
Before Suᶜūdī-S̲h̲arīfian war	125,000	Rutter
1923	60,000	Rutter
1932	100,000*	Wahba, *D̲j̲azīra*
1940	80,000	*Western Arabia & the Red Sea*
1953	150,000	Philby, *Saᶜudi Arabia*
1962	71,998	ᶜAbd al-Raḥmān Ṣādiḳ al-S̲h̲arīf
1970	112,000	ᶜAbd al-Raḥmān Ṣādiḳ al-S̲h̲arīf
1974	198,186	ᶜAbd al-Raḥmān Ṣādiḳ al-S̲h̲arīf
1976	200,000 plus	Nyrop

* Excluding women

Incidentally, the population density for Makka district (not the city) has been estimated as 12 per km². The age distribution in the city for 1974 was estimated to be as follows (in percentage):

Age	Makka	Kingdom of Suᶜūdī Arabia
Under 10	35	37
10 - 29	36	30.8
30 - 49	22	21.4
Over 50	7	10

Given the fact that Makka has for centuries been the centre for a pilgrimage that was often slow and tortuous, and given the desire of the pious to live and die near Bayt Allāh, it is natural and has been observed by many that the population is a highly mixed one. Faces from Java, the Indian sub-continent and sub-Saharan Africa are noticeable everywhere. Almost every cast of feature on the face of the earth can be found. And the process continues; Nyrop (140) estimated that 20% of the population consisted of foreign nationals in the early 1960s—a figure which is particularly remarkable when one reflects that the non-Muslim foreigners who flocked to other Arabian cities in that era were absent from Makka. In a way, this has constituted an important benefit for Makka because the city is the continual recipient of new blood.

Outsiders have frequently complained about the people of Makka. Nor were the early Wahhābīs least in their low opinion of Makkans. ᶜAbd al-ᶜAzīz is reported to have said that he "would not take the daughters of the Sharif or of the people of Mecca or other Moslems whom we reckon as *mushrikīn*" (Helms, 98 quoting W. Smalley, *The Wahhabis and Ibn Saᶜud*, in *MW*, xxii [1932], 243). Philby (*Jubilee*, 126) quotes the king in 1930 as having dismissed them with, *Ahl Makka dabas̲h̲* ("the people of Makka are trash"). Nor was Philby's own opinion of them high: "In truth, the citizen of God's city, by and large, is not an attractive character: his whole life being concentrated on the making of money out of gullible people, especially pilgrims, by a studied mixture of fawning and affability." H. R. P. Dickson reports the Bedouin view that "every foul vice prevails there." But of course, not all reports are bad. Wahba (*D̲j̲azīra*, 31) opines that Makkans (along with Medinese) care more about the cleanliness of their houses and their bodies than do other Arabians. One might finally note the establishment in Makka of the *Sundūḳ al-Birr* (the piety fund), which was started by one family and joined in by others, including the royal family. The organisation distributes welfare support to some hundreds of needy families and also helps victims of accidents and calamities. It proved to be a model for similar funds in other cities in Suᶜūdī Arabia. Actual Makkan manners and customs seem unexceptionable (as the comments above about cooperative neighbourly firefighting suggest), and Rutter, who gives many interesting details of life in Makka just after the Wahhābī conquest, specifically states that the city is not as immoral as it is pictured and that for example, Makkans use foul language much less than do Egyptians.

Marriages were arranged by the prospective bridegrooms's mother or other female relative, who negotiated with the prospective bride's parents. Both normally give their consent. Once the dowry and other details have been agreed, the bride's parents prepare a feast to which the groom and his friends are invited. Two witnesses are required, but there is usually a crowd. After instruction by the *s̲h̲ayk̲h̲*, the girl's father takes the groom's hand and states that he is giving him his daughter in marriage for a dowry of the agreed amount. The groom accepts this contract and the parties are at that point married. No women are present. Neither party has seen the other unless accidentally or as children. Consummation, if the individuals are old enough, is usually about a month later at the bride's house. The same night, she is escorted quietly by her family to the groom's house, and the whole procedure ends the evening after that with a party at the groom's house to which relatives of both families male and female are invited. The sexes are, however, still segregated on this occasion. In Rutter's day there was some polygyny and many slave concubines, but little divorce. He thought Makkan women, for whom silver was the commonest jewelry, were generally fairer than the men and notes that many women could play the lute and drum. They also smoked a great deal. Prostitution was never seen by him. A week after the birth of a child, the father invites his and his wife's relatives for the ceremony naming the infant. Again, the women are upstairs and the men down. When all have assembled, the father goes up and brings the child down on a cushion and places it on the floor while saying things like *ma shā᾽ Allāh* [*q.v.*]—but not too vigorously lest devils be attracted. The father arranges the child so that his head is toward the Kaᶜba and his feet away from it. The father kneels, says *aᶜūdhu bi-Allāh min al-Shayṭān al-radjīm*, then bends over the child's head with his mouth close to the right ear of the infant and repeats the *adhān* [*q.v.*] three times. He then says: "I name thee so-and-so. "The child is now a Muslim. The guests repeat the name, invoke God's blessing, and each puts a coin under the pillow. Another person then rings an iron pestle against a brass mortar. This is the signal to the women upstairs that the child has been named. They respond with *zaghradāt* (trilling ululations) of joy. With that, the father picks the infant up, the guests kiss it on the cheek, and the father takes it back upstairs to the women. He redescends with a tray full of sweets. On the 40th day after birth, every child is taken to the *Ḥaram* and placed for a moment on the threshhold of the Kaᶜba. Other aspects of child rearing, at least up to Rutter's time, included the use of foster mothers by the wealthy and the *ashrāf*'s turning their male children over to Bedouin foster mothers for the three-fold purpose of developing their independent spirit, learning the "pure" language of the desert and creating an indissoluble alliance with the tribe. Up to the age of four, clothes worn are scanty and sketchy. Starting at five, boys go to *kuttāb*s [*q.v.*] and girls are veiled. Boys are circumcised at six or seven, and female circumcision is also practised. Rutter characterises children as generally submissive and respectful. Rutter thought that life expectancy was not great because of the lack of movement of air during the heat of the long summer and because of the high humidity during the wet season (November-February). Death is marked by brief keening, after which the women friends of the family come to comfort the bereaved women. The body is washed, then carried on a bier without a coffin and placed on the pavement of the *maṭāf* in front of the door of the Kaᶜba. The mourners stand, and one repeats the burial prayers. The bier is then lifted, taken out the appropriately named Djamā᾽iz Gate to the Maᶜlā Cemetery north of the *Ḥaram.* Mourners and even passers-by rapidly rotate in carrying the bier. Burial is in shallow graves, and the shrouds have commonly been soaked in Zamzam water. After the burial, male friends pay a brief visit of condolence to the males of the deceased's family. There are often Ḳur᾽ān readings on the 7th and 40th days after death.

As to recreation, there was little sport, but impromptu wrestling and foot races sometimes occurred. Singing, the lute, the reed pipe and drums were popular both in homes and in the open air coffee houses just outside of town, but all music was discouraged by the Nadjdī puritans. "The club of the Mekkans," wrote Rutter (375), "is the great quadrangle of the Haram. Here friends meet by accident or appointment, sit and talk of religious or secular matters, read, sleep, perform the towâf in company, have their letters written (those of them who are illiterate) by the public writers who sit near Bâb es-Salâm, or feed the sacred pigeons." There are, incidentally, many pigeons and they enjoyed a beneficial *wakf* for the supply of the grain. They had drinking troughs and two officials to serve them, one to dispense their grain and the other to fill the water troughs. Popular belief is that no bird ever perches on the roof of the Kaᶜba. Rutter himself says that in months of sleeping on a roof overlooking the Kaᶜba, even when the courtyard and the *maḳāms* of the *imāms* were covered with birds, the roof of the Kaᶜba was bare. Another popular belief concerns those who fall asleep in the *Ḥaram.* Should their feet point toward the Kaᶜba, they are sharply turned around to conform with custom. There were other pleasures. One of the greatest was repairing to the outdoor, half-picnic, half-tea or coffee house sites out of town. Rutter describes one in a ravine at the southeast end of Adjyād where a small stream of clear water often flows. Many groups would go there with samovars and waterpipes (*shīshas*). At sunset, after performing ablutions in the stream, all would pray. There was a singer, some of whose lays were religious, others, amorous. Along with these latter went clapping and dancing. In pre-Wahhābī times, alcohol may have been served and pederasty practiced. Incidentally, he comments that King al-Ḥusayn had already stopped the open drinking and prostitution of Ottoman times. Rutter also provides (291-4) an interesting account of a visit to the oasis and farms of al-Ḥusayniyya about 20 km southeast of the city (and see Nallino's reference (202) to similar visits to al-Sanūsiyya, 20 km northeast of the capital). He also paints a picture of how Makkans spend a week or two on the upland (2,000 m) plain of al-Hada overlooking the escarpment to the west of al-Ṭā᾽if. The largest house there belonged to the Kaᶜba key-keeper, al-Shaybī. Religious occasions also formed part of the rhythm of participation in the life of the city. Twice yearly in Radjab and Dhu'l-Ḳaᶜda there occurs the ritual of washing the inside of the Kaᶜba. These occasions constitute major festivals. All the important people and important visiting pilgrims attend and a big crowd gathers. Al-Shaybī provides the water in a large bottle and brooms which the dignitaries use for the purpose. There are some distinctly un-Islamic folk practices, such as people washing themselves in the used washing water and actually also drinking it. During Ramaḍān, there is much recitation of the Ḳur᾽ān. One hears it as one walks down the street. Purely secular "clubs" also existed in the form of coffee houses which provided tea, light food and *shīshas*. One of their characteristics is the high (about 1 m.) wood-framed platforms about two m. long with rush-work surface. Characteristically, the mat work is done by Sudanese. These high mats are used as chairs, on which three or four can sit, or used as beds. The cafés have linen available if the latter use is required. These establishments are open day and night. Al-Kurdī indicates that there were two Ottoman-era *ḥammāms* [*q.v.*], but that the first, which had been near Bāb al-ᶜUmra, was torn down to make way for the mosque expansion and the second, in al-Ḳashāshiyya quarter, was closed—a victim no doubt of private residential baths and showers.

Finally, some mention must be made of slaves. King ᶜAbd al-ᶜAzīz had agreed as early as 1345/1927 to cooperate with the British government in suppressing the international slave trade, but slavery as such was not outlawed in Su^c ūdī Arabia until 1382/1962. In 1365/1946 Ḥāfiẓ Wahba described it (*Djazīra*, 32-3) as a reasonably flourishing institution. Makka was the largest slave market in Arabia—possibly because it was secure from prying non-Muslim eyes. Meccans trained male slaves (sing. *ʿabd*) and female slaves (sing. *djāriya*) well for household duties, and Wahba quotes prices as being £60 for a male and £120 for a female. Ethiopians were considered the best because they were more loyal and more sincere in their work. He indicates that they worked mostly in domestic chores or in gardens, but that Bedouin chiefs also acquired them as bodyguards. *Djāriyas* he notes were also used for other things. Manumission is an act of piety, and Shaykh Ḥāfiẓ says that hardly a master died who did not free some of his slaves and leave them a legacy. Apparently non-slave servants were very difficult to find, and Shaykh Ḥāfiẓ opined that a sudden prohibition of slavery would cause a revolution. He also notes that the trade was declining.

The coming of the Suʿūdī régime also had an important impact on the top of the social structure in that the privileged position formerly held by the *sharīfs* was eliminated. Merchants, ulema and *muṭawwifūn* stood high on the local social scale, with pride of place perhaps going to the Shayba family.

Because of the cosmopolitan nature of the population, city quarters seem not to have had quite the same degree of near water-tight ethnic or religious compactness that is found in some other cities, but quarters did and do exist. Some generalised comments applying mostly to the pre-oil period follow. Djarwal, an extensive mixed area northwest of the *Ḥaram*, was the site of many offices and the garages of motor transport companies. It is also the quarter in which Philby lived, the quarter where ʿAbd Allah Āl Sulaymān, the Minister of Finance under King ʿAbd al-ʿAzīz, had his palace, and the quarter in which immigrants from west and central Africa used to live—mostly in hovels. Writing in the early 1960s, al-Kurdī indicates (ii, 264) that the Djarwal and al-Misfala quarters had heavy concentrations of *bidonvilles* inhabited by poor Sudanese and Pakistanis. Their shanty dwellings were, however, being replaced by modern buildings. Al-Shubayka, to the west and a little south of the *Ḥaram*, was, pre-World War II, mainly populated by Central Asian, Indian and East Indian *muṭawwifūn*. Adjyād, southeast of the *Ḥaram*, was the old Ottoman quarter sometimes called "government quarter." It continued in Suʿūdī times to contain a number of important institutions, including the first modern hospital, the Egyptian *takiyya*, the Ministry of Foreign Affairs, the Ministry of Finance, the public security office, *al-Maʿhad al-ʿIlmī al-Suʿūdī*, the *Kiswat al-Kaʿba* factory), the Egyptian Bank and the Directorate of Education. Adjyād is dominated by an imposing looking Ottoman fort, Ḳalʿat Adjyād, which is perched on the heights to the south of it. The quarter is said to have the best climate and the best views in the city. It was also the location of most of the better older houses and hotels. Pre-oil city quarters numbered 15 in all, as follows: Sūḳ al-Layl, Shiʿb ʿAlī, Shiʿb ʿĀmir, al-Sulaymāniyya, al-Muʿābada, Djarwal, al-Naḳā, al-Falḳ, al-Ḳarāra, al-Shāmiyya, Adjyād, al-Ḳashāshiyya, al-Shubayka, Hārat al-Bāb and al-Misfala. There are also eleven modern outlying quarters: al-ʿUtaybiyya, al-Hindawiyya, al-ʿAzīziyya (earlier known as Ḥawḍ al-Baḳar), al-Shishsha, al-Rawḍa, al-Khānisa, al-Zāhir, al-Tanbudāwī, al-Raṣīfa, al-Mishʿaliyya and al-Nuzha. Some of these are dubbed *ḥayy*; others, *ḥāra*; and the last three *maḥalla*. Each quarter has an *ʿumda* as its administrative head.

The importance and centrality of the *Ḥaram* dictated that areas immediately adjacent to it were of high importance and prestige, at least as long as the pilgrim business was the main source of revenue. Thus before the extension of the mosque, there were a number of *sūḳs* which surrounded it or nearly so. These included al-Suwayḳa just north of the northern corner which was the drapery and perfume bazaar; Sūḳ al-ʿAbīd the slave market; al-Sūḳ al-Ṣaghīr *ca.* 100 m southeast of Bāb Ibrāhīm, which was in the main water course and often washed out in floods; Sūḳ al-Ḥabb the grain market some 700 m north of the mosque; and finally the fruit market, also to the north, which was simply called al-Ḥalaḳa, the market. Al-Masʿā formerly was paved and covered during the early days of ʿAbd al-ʿAzīz' reign, but it was still a public street with book and stationery stores at the southern (al-Ṣafā) end and stalls selling items for pilgrims along the rest of it. Another transient demographic feature that may be noticed is that in pre-oil days, the camps used by pilgrims were on the outskirts of the city nearest the direction from which they came, *i.e.*, those coming from Syria camped north of the city, etc.

With the broader economic and transportation possibilities available since World War II (and especially after the oil price increases of 1973 and beyond) and with the number of pilgrims swelling to almost two million (with attendant traffic and other problems), centre city has probably become less desirable.

The physical City. Constrained as it is by the wadi courses and low mountains of its location, the size and physical appearance of Makka has changed dramatically in the six decades since the Wahhābīs most recently captured it. It should be borne in mind that the *Ḥaram* is in the widest part of the central, south-flowing wadi and that main streets follow wadi valleys. Before the most recent enormous enlargement of the mosque structure, a noticeable feature was what Philby called "oratory houses." These surrounded the entire periphery and abutted on the mosque itself. They had first floor balconies on the roof of the mosque's surrounding colonnade and were more or less considered an integral part of the mosque. Since the inhabitants of these houses could pray at home while observing the Prophet's injuction that whoever lives near the mosque should pray in it, they were in high demand at high rentals. On the other hand, the residents were said to have run up rather large hospitality bills! In the pre-oil era, Makkan buildings were mostly built of local dark grey granite, but by and large they gave no great impression of grandeur. The larger ran to about four storeys. Even before modernisation, major streets in Makka were fairly wide. King al-Ḥusayn had electrified the *Ḥaram* during his brief reign, but probably it was not until after the second World War that streets were lighted electrically. Previously they were lighted, on special occasions only, by oil lamps attached to the corners of houses. Al-Ḥusayn's palace had been located northeast of the *Ḥaram* in al-Ghazza, but when King ʿAbd al-ʿAzīz built his own palace, he chose a site well to the north in al-Muʿābada, where incidentally, the pre-oil wireless station was also built in the immediate vicinity of the king's palace. At the present time (1405/1985) this tradition continues, for the amīrate, the municipality secretariat, its technical units and the main courthouse are all located at that site. Expansion of the city in the period before there were adequate roads tended to be along the Djudda road.

Modernisation in the oil era has brought completely different architectural approaches and materials, and

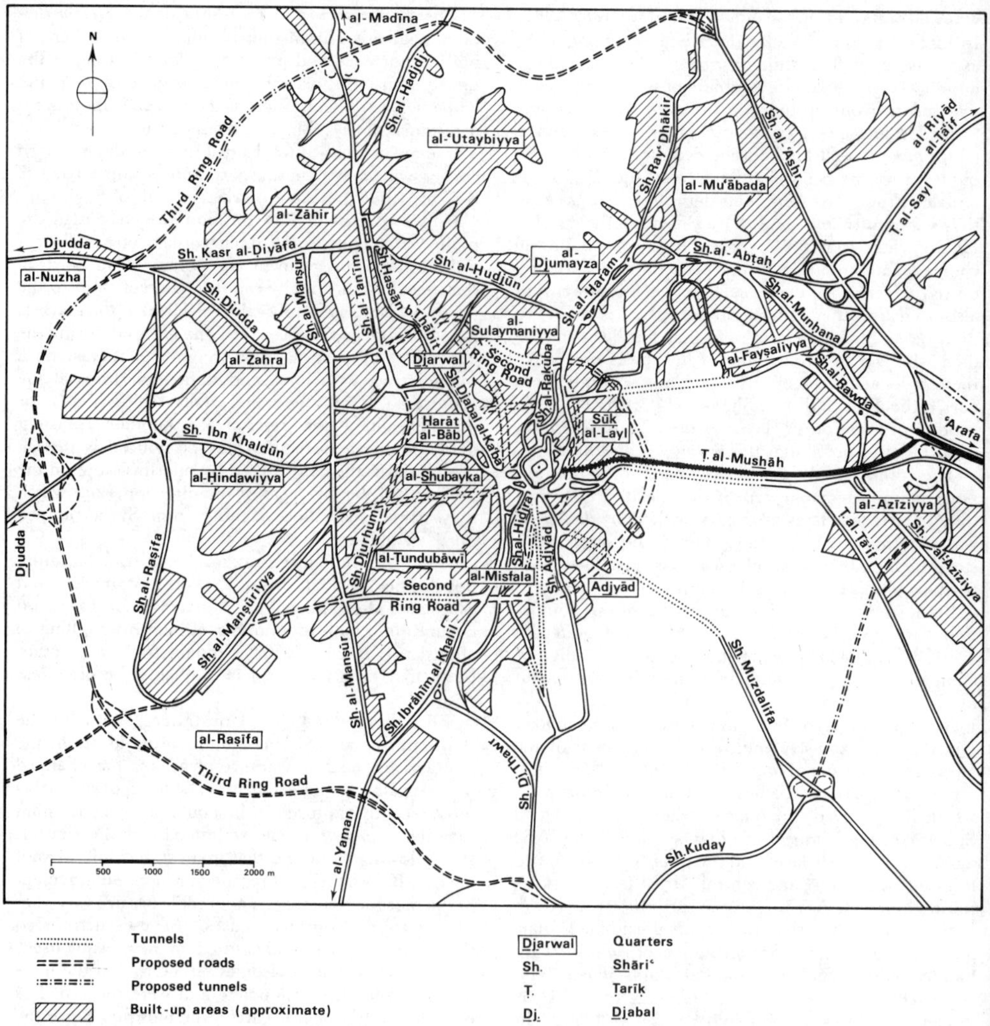

Fig. 1. Makka in the 1980s: built-up areas. After Fārisī.

much of the old has been swept away. Air conditioners are everywhere, cement and reinforced concrete reign, and buildings of up to 13 or more storeys high are everywhere visible. City planning in Suʿūdī Arabia has become pervasive, and the master plan studies and designs for Makka were projected to be ready for implementation in 1976. Given the pilgrimage, traffic circulation had to be a major part of the plan. Key features of the traffic plan were: a series of broad open plazas around the *Ḥaram*, a major north-south road which essentially followed the main wadi bottom, a set of four concentric ring roads (none of which had been completed by 1402-3/1982-3), and a remarkable complex of roads leading to Munā, Muzdalifa, and ʿArafāt. Especially to be noted is the extensive tunnelling under Makka's rocky crags for a number of these roads, not excluding a major "pedestrian way" for pilgrims which goes due east from al-Ṣafā before bending southwest toward ʿArafāt. About one kilometer of the "pedestrian way" is a tunnel (Nafaḳ al-Sadd) under Djabal Abī Ḳubays, the north-south running mountain east of the *Ḥaram*. In addition to the roads themselves—all built to international standards with clover-leaf intersections, overpasses and the like—there are vast systematic parking areas, helicopter pads and other facilities. Makka may have some areas left without modern amenities such as running water and electricity, but essentially it is a modern city with all the assets and problems that modern implies. The growth in the area of the built-up section of Makka can only be roughly estimated, but according to Rutter's map (facing p. 117), the maximum length of the built-up section on the north-south axis was about 3 km; on the east-west axis it was about $2^1/_2$ km. Fārisī's map (1402-3/1982-3) indicates a north-south axis of about 8 km and an east-west of just under $5^1/_2$ km. This massive growth does not include very extensive new built up areas such as al-Fayṣaliyya and al-ʿAzīziyya—the latter reaching all the way to Muzdalifa.

E c o n o m y. The economy of Makka consists of only two basic factors, commerce and industry concerned with the local market, and the pilgrimage. Agriculture is essentially non-existent in Makka. Food was imported: fruit from al-Ṭāʾif, vegetables largely from the Wādī Fāṭima and a few other oases

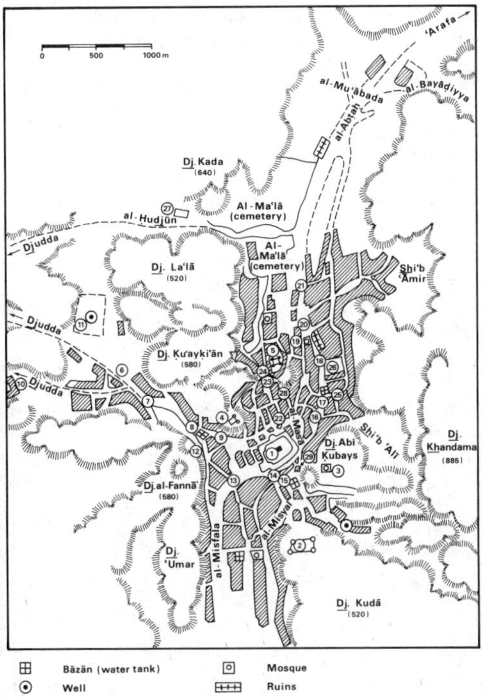

Fig. 2. Makka in late Ottoman, Hāshimite and early Suʿūdī times. After Rutter and *Western Arabia and the Red Sea.* The numbers indicate approximate heights in metres above the central valley.
Key: 1. al-Masdjid al-Ḥarām—2. Ḳalʿat Adjyād—3. Masdjid Bilāl—4. Ḳalʿat Djabal Hindī—5. Ḳalʿat Fulful—6. Shaykh Maḥmūd—7. Djarwal—8. Ḥārat al-Bāb—9. al-Shubayka—10. Ottoman barracks—11. Walled garden—12. Graveyard—13. al-Sūḳ al-Ṣaghīr—14. al-Ḥamīdiyya—15. Dār al-Takiyya al-Miṣriyya—16. al-Ḳashāshiyya—17. Sūḳ al-Layl—18. al-Ghazza—19. al-Djawdhariyya—20. Sūḳ al-Ḥabb—21. al-Maʿlā—22. al-Suwayḳa—23. al-Ḳarāra—24. al-Falḳ—25. Prophet's birthplace—26. Sharīfian palace—27. Slaughterhouse— 28. al-Ṣafā.

such as al-Ḥusayniyya. They included egg plant, radishes, tomatoes, vegetable marrows, spinach, Egyptian clover (*birsīm*) for fodder and hibiscus. Makka itself had to content itself with a few date trees in the gardens of the wealthy (see al-Kurdī, ii, 208-15). Industry in 1390/1970-1 counted 35 establishments employing 800 people with an estimate of SR (= Suʿūdī riyals) 22 million in use. By way of contrast, neighbouring Djudda had 95 establishments with 4,563 employees and SR 329 million in use. Among the Makkan enterprises were corrugated iron manufacturing, carpentry shops, upholstering establishments, sweets manufacturies, vegetable oil extraction plants, flour mills, bakeries, copper smithies, photography processing, secretarial establishments, ice factories, bottling plants for soft drinks, poultry farms, frozen food importing, barber shops, book shops, travel agencies and banks. The first bank in Makka was the National Commercical Bank (*al-Bank al-Ahlī al-Tidjārī*) which opened in 1374/1954. Hotels and hostels are another major activity. According to al-Kurdī (ii, 173), there were no hotels before the Suʿūdī régime began. Important pilgrims were housed in a government rest house, others stayed in private homes as actual or paying guests. The first hotel project was undertaken and managed by Banque Misr for the account of the Ministry of Finance in 1355/1936-7. A decade later it was bought by Ṣidḳa Kaʿkī, a member of Makka's most successful business family. Banque Misr also managed a second hotel that belonged to Shaykh ʿAbd Allāh Āl Sulaymān and which opened in 1356/1937-8. This had its own electric power, an elevator, running water and some private baths. Construction activity, long important in Makka, has obviously grown with the oil-fired building boom. The traditional building trades with their interesting organisation and special skills in stone masonry (details in al-Kurdī, ii, 261-6) are fading away. It is also interesting to note that in 1936 a *Djamʿiyyat al-Ḳirsh* was founded with its seat in Makka with the goal of encouraging economic development in order to make the country economically independent by stimulating new and existing industrial and agricultural projects. Goods available in the markets in the 1930s were almost all imported. Cotton textiles came from Japan, silk from China and India, and carpets, rosaries (*subḥa, misbaḥa*), and copper and silver items—the kinds of items that pilgrims wanted—came variously from Syria, India and al-ʿIrāḳ. Many of the merchants catering to the pilgrim trade were foreigners or of foreign extraction and employed native Makkans as hawkers. Visitors felt that prices were high, profits large and local employees inadequately paid.

The importance of the *Ḥadjdj* for the economy of Makka through most of the city's history is simple. As Rutter has put it, "[Makkans] have no means of earning a living but by serving the hâjjis." Fifty years later, D. Long confirms that "the Hajj constitutes the largest single period of commercial activity during the year," and that no one in the country is unaffected thereby. Indeed, once al-Ḥidjāz had been conquered, *ḥadjdj* income was supposed to finance Nadjd in addition to the Holy Land. The money came in different ways. A direct tax, instituted by ʿAbd al-ʿAzīz in 1345-6/1927, was seven gold rupees ($16.80). In addition there was a kind of service charge, dubbed "landing and service fee," which amounted to £1.5 ($7.20) in the early thirties. As late as 1972, this charge, now called "fee for general services" was SR 63 ($11.88). There were also taxes on internal motor transport, for example £7.5 (36.00) on the round trip car hire fare between Makka and al-Madīna in the 1920s, reduced to £6.00 (28.00) in 1931. In addition to direct levies, the government received indirect income from licence fees charged those who served the pilgrims, from customs duties on goods imported for re-sale to pilgrims and from other indirect levies. As D. Long (much followed in this section) has noted, when the world-wide depression struck, King ʿAbd al-ʿAzīz, despite his successful efforts to eliminate gross exploitation of the pilgrims, was forced to impose fees on the pilgrims in order to maintain the solvency of the government. Later, oil income essentially eliminated government dependence on pilgrim fees, and in 1371/1952 the king abolished the head tax altogether. That the government continued to be sensitive to the public relation aspects of any fees at all, is made clear by the official *Ḥadjdj* instructions for 1972 (quoted by Long) to the effect that such charges only cover the actual costs of necessary services. For Makka, the *Ḥadjdj* has of course continued to be a major source of cash income. On the other hand, from a national Suʿūdī viewpoint, servicing the pilgrims became a major expenditure category far exceeding the income generated, though one should note that in recent years the national airline, Saudia, derived some 12% of its revenue from *Ḥadjdj*-generated customers. D. Long has also made detailed estimates (101-5) of the effect of the *Ḥadjdj* on the private sector in Djudda, al-Madīna and especially Makka. Roughly, he estimates that in 1972 pilgrims paid the guilds (*muṭawwifūn*, *wukalāʾ* and *zamāzima*) a total of $7.9 million in fees, a figure which excludes gratuities. Lodging during the late 1960s cost each pilgrim an average of $60, for a total housing income of $40 million. The transportation syndicate's income based on fares paid by land and air pilgrims for internal transportation is estimated at $11 million. All these estimates are for gross income. Net income is difficult to calculate, especially because fixed costs of capital items, such as accommodation at Munā and ʿArafāt which is only filled for a few days a year, are normally not counted. Makkan merchants continue to see the two months of pilgrim business as more or less their whole year's business, and as in the case of holiday expenditures in other countries the merchants raise their prices, despite government attempts to protect the pilgrims. Animals for ritual slaughter approximately double in value. The foreign provenance of pilgrim-specific goods continued in later years. Cheap ($1 to $10 each), European-manufactured prayer rugs sell a million or more each year, but it may be noted that in the 1970s prayer beads were manufactured by a local Makkan plastics factory. In more general categories, Swiss and Japanese watches move briskly; most textiles still come from Asia, though expensive ones may be from Europe; United States products predominate among cosmetics, better quality canned foods and drugs; wheat is almost exclusively American; whilst China has predominated in cheap fountain pens, parasols and cheaper canned goods. One final point is that many non-Suʿūdī pilgrims who can afford them purchase luxury consumer items which are either heavily taxed or unavailable in their own countries. Foreign exchange trading also constitutes a brisk business for the Makkan banks—all nationalised by about 1400/1979-80. Long notices another economic factor, that more and more foreign pilgrims have come in the sixties, seventies and early eighties, but the shift in mode of travel has been equally dramatic as the chart below shows:

Mode of travel of non-Suʿūdī pilgrims
(Selected years)

Year	Mode of Travel			Total Number
	Land	Sea	Air	
1381/1961	32%	43%	25%	216,455
1391/1971	30	20	50	479,339
1403/1982	22	6	72	1,003,911

The dramatic increase in numbers and equally dramatic shift to air travel have meant that the average length of stay has decreased from two to three, or even more, months to an average stay of only a few weeks. Purchases of food and rentals for lodging have declined proportionately with the decrease in time, and in addition, because of baggage limitations on air travel, gift items have trended toward the watch and away from bulky items. Sales to pilgrims as a proportion of total sales by Meccan merchants have also declined. Long (based on Djudda information) estimated that they had declined from 33-50% of the total in 1381/1961 to about 25% in 1391/1971—still highly significant. Based on an estimate of per capita expenditures of *ca.* $230, Long estimates that gross sales by Suʿūdī merchants to foreign pilgrims aggregated $53 million from the *Ḥadjdj*. If one adds Suʿūdī pilgrims, the figure rises to $90 million. His estimate of *Ḥadjdj* income from all sources for the 1391/1971 *Ḥadjdj* was *ca.* $213 million. It is not easy to know the proportion of this total which went to Makka and Makkans, but the number has to be quite significant locally when one considers the size of the city and the concentrated nature of the business.

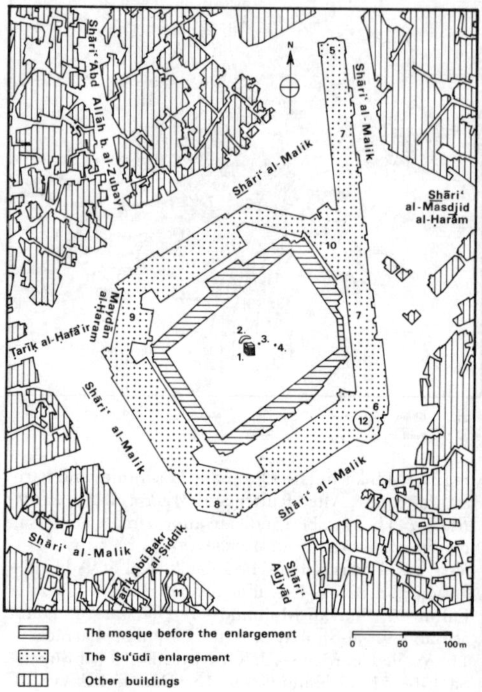

Fig. 3. al-Masdjid al-Ḥarām after the Suʿūdī enlargement. After Bundūḳdjī.
Key: 1. al-Kaʿba—2. al-Ḥuṭaym—3. Maḳām Ibrāhīm—4. Zamzam—5. al-Marwa—6. al-Ṣafā—7. al-Masʿā—8. Bāb al-Malik—9. Bāb al-ʿUmra—10. Bāb al-Salām—11. al-Ḥaram Library—12. Dome.

Al-Masdjid al-Ḥarām and other religious buildings. From the moment ʿAbd al-ʿAzīz entered Makka, he and his successors have expended time, money and effort on the Great Mosque of Makka. (For description of the mosque at the beginning of the Suʿūdī régime, see Rutter, 252-63.) In the spring of 1344/1925, the king was anxious to make the best impression possible for the first *Ḥadjdj* under his auspices. He ordered a general tidying-up, and when the pilgrims arrived, they found everything freshly painted and clean. An innovation of 1345/1926 was the erection of tents inside the cloister to give relief from the sun; but unfortunately they could not withstand the wind. In 1346/1927 the king ordered a thorough restoration to be undertaken "at his personal expense." The work was entrusted to Shaykh ʿAbd Allāh al-Dihlawī on the basis of his successful work over a number of years at ʿAyn Zubayda. This programme lasted about a year and cost 2,000 gold pounds. The accomplishments included replacing tiles and marble, cleaning the domes of the cloister, repairing doors and pillars, repairing and painting (green)

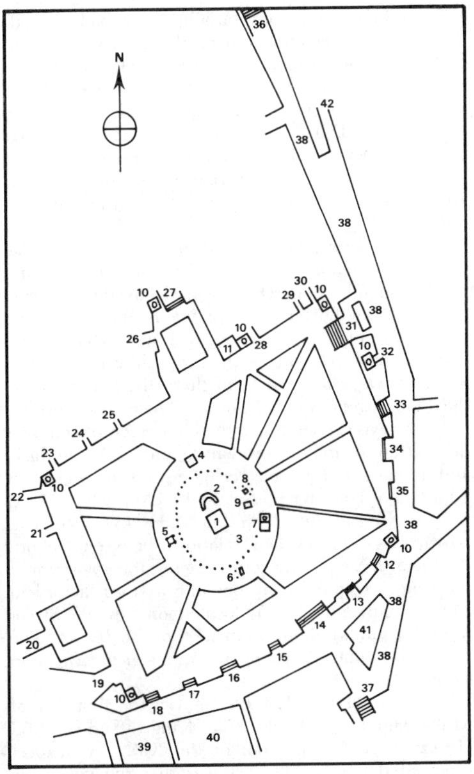

Fig. 4. Plan of the Ḥaram in late Ottoman, Hāshimite and early Suᶜūdī times. After Snouck Hurgronje, Rutter and *Western Arabia and the Red Sea*.
Key: 1. al-Kaᶜba—2. al-Ḥuṭaym—3. al-Maṭāf—4. al-Maḳām al-Ḥanafī—5. al-Maḳām al-Mālikī—6. al-Maḳām al-Ḥanbalī—7. Zamzam—8. Banī Shayba portal—9. Maḳām Ibrāhim—10. Minarets (7)—11. Ḳāḍī's office—12. Bāb Bāzān—13. Bāb al-Baghla—14. Bāb al-Ṣafā—15. Bāb al-Raḥma—16. Bāb Djiyād—17. Bāb Adjlān—18. Bāb Umm Hāniʾ—19. Bāb al-Widāᶜ—20. Bāb Ibrāhīm—21. Bāb al-Dāʾūdiyya—22. Bāb al-ᶜUmra—23. Bāb ᶜAmr b. al-ᶜĀṣ—24. Bāb al-Zamāzima—25. Bāb al-Bāsiṭa—26. Bāb al-Ḳuṭbī—27. Bāb al-Ziyāda—28. Bāb al-Maḥkama—29. Bāb al-Madrasa—30. Bāb al-Durayba—31. Bāb al-Salām—32. Bāb Ḳāʾit Bāy—33. Bāb al-Nabī—34. Bāb al-ᶜAbbās—35. Bāb ᶜAlī—36. al-Marwa—37. al-Ṣafā—38. al-Masᶜā—39. al-Ḥamīdiyya—40. Dār al-Takiyya al-Miṣriyya—41. Guardhouse—42. Sūḳ al-Layl.

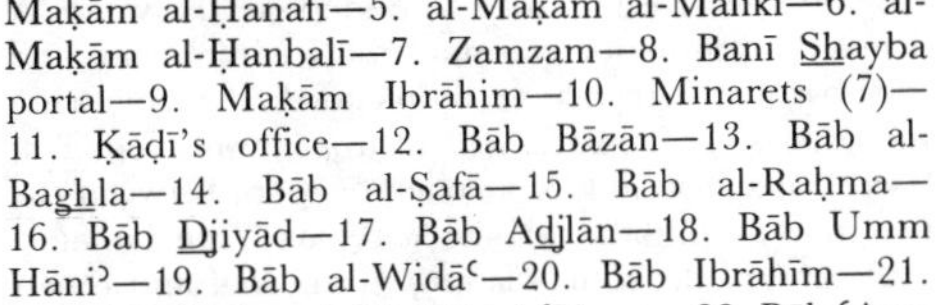

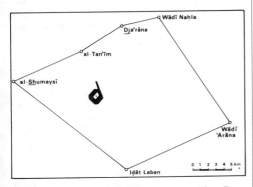

Fig. 5. Boundary of the Ḥaram area. After Bundūḳdjī, *Maps of hajj*.

the roofs of the Maḳām Ibrāhīm and of al-Maḳām al-Ḥanafī. The Zamzam building was much beautified, the stones of the Kaᶜba were pointed, and Bāb Ibrāhīm was widened and beautified. Moreover, determined to do something to protect worshippers from the fierce sun, ᶜAbd al-ᶜAzīz, for the 1346 *Ḥadjdj*, ordered ᶜAbd Allāh Āl Sulaymān to erect all around the inside of the cloister a massive wooden frame to which heavy canvas was fixed as an awning. Once the pilgrims had left, this canopy was removed. But apparently there were some serious structural problems, for in 1354/1935-6 a more general study was undertaken. The order for this created a special four-man committee (ᶜAbd Allāh b. ᶜAbd al-Ḳādir al-Shaybī of the *Madjlis al-Shūrā*, chairman, Sulaymān Azhar, Assistant Director of *awḳāf*; Hāshim b. Sulaymān, Administrator of the Ḥaram (*nāʾib al-Ḥaram*); and ᶜAlī Muftī of the Makka municipality). Its mission was to carry out a general survey and then make recommendations for repairs and restoration. The committee recommendations (details in Bāsalāma, 285) included such things as disassembling walls and rebuilding them, using cement for mortar. Costs for this work, which began in Ramaḍān, were split between the Directorate of *Awḳāf* and King ᶜAbd al-ᶜAzīz.

The electrification of the mosque had been instituted under the Hāshimite al-Ḥusayn, but was steadily improved under ᶜAbd al-ᶜAzīz with generous outside support. In 1346/1927-8 Ḥādjdj Dāwūd Atba (?) of Rangoon donated a 300 kilowatt generator, and as a result the king was able to increase the number of bulbs from al-Ḥusayn's 300 to 1,000. In 1349/1930-1 new generating equipment was acquired so that "a reader could read his book by electric lights anywhere in the mosque" (Bāsalāma, 257). In addition, large free-standing, brass electric candelabra mounted on reinforced concrete columns 3 m high were placed in the mosque and six other brass candelabra were mounted on al-Ḥuṭaym, the semicircular wall enclosing the Ḥadjar Ismāᶜīl. An even larger contribution was made in 1353/1934-5 by Djanāb Nawwāb Bahādur Dr. al-Ḥādjdj Sir Muḥammad Muzammil Allāh Khān (1865-1938) of Bhikhampur, India, who presented much more elaborate equipment to the mosque. It consisted of a 52 h.p. engine, a 220 volt, 34 kilowatt generator and required that the mosque engineer (Ismāᶜīl al-Dhabīḥ) go to India in order to familiarise himself with it. He stayed there several months and, interestingly, returned with additional contributions in kind (elaborate candelabra put on the gates, on the *maḳāms*, and on the Zamzam dome) from Muslim philanthropists in Cawnpore, Lucknow and Karachi. Toward the end of 1354/1935-6, all was in working order and "the *Maṭāf* was as though in sunlight." Microphones and loudspeakers were first used in the mosque in 1368/1948-9.

Attention should now be turned to several specific features of the mosque area.

Al-Masᶜā. — Firstly, it may be noted that the Hāshimite al-Ḥusayn was the first person in Islamic history to improve physically the running place, in effect a street at that time, between al-Ṣafā and al-Marwa when in 1339/1920-1 he ordered ᶜAbd al-Wahhāb al-Ḳazzāz to erect a cover over it. A steel structure with wooden roof was built to the general benefit of all. This continued in use for many years, with some later improvements made by the municipality (then directed by ᶜAbbās Ḳaṭṭān) at the order of King ᶜAbd al-ᶜAzīz. The king also undertook another major improvement early in his reign (1345/1926-7) when he ordered al-Masᶜā, which was rough ground, to be paved. To oversee the work, a high-level unit was constituted within the administration framework of the *Amānat al-ʿĀṣima*, that is, the municipality. It was presided over by ʿAbd al-Wahhāb b. Aḥmad, the *Naʾib al-Ḥaram*, and included his former assistant Muḥammad Surūr al-Ṣabbān, later Director (Minister) of Finance, along with the ubiquitous ʿAbd Allāh Āl Sulaymān (as the king's representative), several members of the *Madjlis al-Shūrā* and some technical people. The decision was reached to use square granite stones mortared with lime. Initial expenses were to be covered by the *Amānat al-ʿĀṣima* and subsequent ones from the national treasury (*bayt al-māl*). Once protruding living rock had been levelled, the work began ceremonially with a large gathering that saw H. R. H. Prince Fayṣal b. ʿAbd al-ʿAzīz lay the "corner stone" and heard invocations from the *khaṭīb* of the mosque. This enterprise, completed before the *Ḥadjdj* of 1345, resulted in the first paved street in the history of the city.

Zamzam. — In the early repairs carried out under al-Dihlawī's direction, the king paid special attention to the well of Zamzam and the two-chambered building above it. Two new *sabīl*s [*q.v.*] were constructed, one of six taps near Bāb Ḳubbat Zamzam, the other of three near the Ḥudjrat al-Aghawāt; in addition, the older Ottoman *sabīl* was renovated. All this was beautifully done in local marble with fine calligraphic inscriptions including the phrase "Imām [*sic*] ʿAbd al-ʿAzīz b. ʿAbd al-Raḥmān al-Suʿūd [*sic*] built this *sabīl*."

Kiswa. — With the outbreak of World War I, the *kiswa* came as it had for many years previously from Egypt. When the Ottoman Empire entered the war on the side of Germany, the authorities in Makka assumed that British-controlled Egypt would no longer send the *kiswa* and so they ordered one to be made in Istanbul. It was a particularly fine one and was dispatched by train to al-Madīna, thence to be taken to Makka. In the event, the Egyptian government did send the *kiswa*, bearing the embroidered name of Ḥusayn Kāmil, sultan of Egypt as well as that of Sultan Muḥammad Rashād. The Istanbul-manufactured *kiswa* remained in al-Madīna, and the Cairo one (with Ḥusayn Kāmil's name removed) was hung on the Kaʿba. After the Sharīf al-Ḥusayn revolted against the Ottomans, the Egyptians continued to send *kiswa*s until 1340/1922. In that year, at the end of Dhu 'l-Ḳaʿda, as a result of a dispute between the Sharīf al-Ḥusayn and the Egyptian government, al-Ḥusayn sent the *maḥmal*, the Egyptian guard, the wheat ration, medical mission, *ṣurra* (traditional funds forwarded from Egypt), alms, oblation and *kiswa* back from Makka to Djudda. With only a very short time left before the *ḥadjdj*, al-Ḥusayn cabled to the *amīr* of al-Madīna immediately to forward the Ottoman *kiswa* stored there to Rābigh [*q.v.*]. Simultaneously, he dispatched the steamship *Rushdī* to proceed from Djudda to Rābigh. All worked well, and the Ottoman *kiswa* reached Makka in time to be "dressed" on the Kaʿba by the deadline date of 10 Dhu 'l-Ḥidjdja. Subsequently, al-Ḥusayn ordered a *kiswa* woven in al-ʿIrāḳ, lest the dispute with Egypt not be settled by the 1342/1923 *ḥadjdj*; however, in that year the Egyptian *kiswa* arrived and was used as usual. When the *ḥadjdj* of 1343/1924 approached, ʿAbd al-ʿAzīz ruled Makka, and relations with Egypt had become so bad that Egypt did not send the *kiswa*. Luckily, the king had a fall-back position, namely, the *kiswa* that King al-Ḥusayn had had made in al-ʿIrāḳ. In the next year, the Egyptians did send the *kiswa*, but that was the year of the famous *maḥmal* incident as a result of which Egypto-Suʿūdī relations became very bad indeed. The Suʿūdī expectation apparently was that the Egyptians would again send the *kiswa* in 1345, but in fact they forbade it along with the other customary items. The Suʿūdī government learned of this only at the beginning of Dju 'l-Ḳaʿda, and once again the king called on ʿAbd Allāh Āl Sulaymān, this time to have a *kiswa* made locally on a rush basis. Shaykh ʿAbd Allāh and the Makkan business community fell to, and by 10 Dhu 'l Ḥidjdja—the due date—a black broadcloth *kiswa*, brocaded with silver and gold as usual, had been produced. For the first time the name of the Suʿūdī monarch appeared—as the donor—brocaded on the band above the Kaʿba door. The *kiswa* continued to be made in a special factory in Makka until relations with Egypt improved, after which it was reordered from there. In 1377/1957-8, the donor legend was as follows: "The manufacture of the *kiswa* was carried out in the United Arab Republic during the régime of President Djamāl ʿAbd al-Nāṣir and donated to the noble Kaʿba during the régime of Khādim al-Ḥaramayn, Suʿūd b. ʿAbd al-ʿAzīz Āl Suʿūd, King of Suʿūdī Arabia, A.H. 1377" (text in Kurdi, iv, 220). When relations between Suʿūdī Arabia and Egypt later soured again, the government once more responded by opening a *kiswa* factory in Makka (currently [1985] located on Djudda Street [Shāriʿ Djudda] about 8 km west of the *Ḥaram*. The factory is managed by a deputy minister of *ḥadjdj* and *awḳāf*.

Repair of the Kaʿba. — On the first day of Muḥarram 1377/29 July 1957, King Suʿūd b. ʿAbd al-ʿAzīz went to the roof of the Kaʿba to inspect reported damage. The fact was that the venerable building had an outer roof which needed repair, an inner wooden roof which was rotting and walls that were beginning to crumble. Repairs were needed immediately. Two commissions, one technical, the other religious, were established to undertake the work. A detailed examination was made on 7 Muḥarram, and a subsequent report recommended the following remedial steps: replacement of upper roof, repair of lower roof, insertion of a concrete beam between the two roofs around the perimeter, repair of the damaged walls and of the stairs leading to the roof and repair of the marble lining the inner walls. A royal decree (text in al-Kurdī, iv, 68) was issued instructing Muḥammad b. ʿAwaḍ b. Lādin al-Ḥaḍramī, the Director of Public Works (*inshāʾāt ʿumūmiyya*) to carry out the work. All workers were Makkan; the architects and engineers were mostly Egyptian. Specifications were that all materials should be local, the wood of the roof should be of the highest quality, the roof not be painted or decorated in any way and the concrete beam be exactly the same thickness as the original space between the two roofs. On 18 Radjab 1377/1957, Fayṣal b. ʿAbd al-ʿAzīz presided over the start of these repairs, and on 11 Shaʿbān, H. M. King Suʿūd b. ʿAbd al-ʿAzīz placed the last piece of marble facingstone in the walls inside the Kaʿba. This was followed by two large dinners on successive nights.

Even before the repair of the Kaʿba, the mosque had begun to undergo the most stupendous expansion in its history. This development in Makka had no doubt been informally decided upon by the king and other senior officials, even as the expansion of *al-Ḥaram al-Nabawī* in al-Madīna was getting under way in 1370/1951. In any case, the increase in the number of pilgrims after World War II had brought facilities of all sorts to acute levels of congestion and inadequacy to the degree that pilgrims in Makka were praying in roads and lanes far outside the confines of the mosque. The first public indication of what was to happen came on 5 Muḥarram 1375/24 August 1955 when it was announced that all the equipment and machinery which had been used on the now completed enlargement in al-Madīna would be moved to Makka. A month later (6 Ṣafar/24 September) a royal decree established: (1) a Higher Committee chaired by Fayṣal b. ʿAbd al-ʿAzīz, the heir designate, to supervise the planning; (2) an executive committee to supervise implementation; and (3) a committee to assess values of expropriated property. Later, the first two were merged into a higher executive committee with King Suʿūd b. ʿAbd al-ʿAzīz as chairman and the minister of finance as vice chairman. The basic concept of the final design was little short of inspired, and may be considered an extension of the design concept developed for the enlargement of the mosque in al-Madīna. It consisted of two ideas: (1) to maintain the old mosque intact and surround it by the new construction; and (2) to incorporate al-Masʿā fully into the mosque complex.

Work began in Rabīʿ II 1375/November 1955 with road diversions, cutting of cables and pipes, land clearing and other diversionary work, and was concentrated in the Adjyād and al-Masʿā areas. A foundation-stone ceremony was held five-and-a-half months later in front of Bāb Umm Hāniʾ with the king and other dignitaries in attendance, and this marked the beginning of construction. Incidentally, by *ḥadjdj* time, pilgrims were able to perform the *saʿy* undisturbed by hawkers and traffic for the very first time. Work concentrated in Stage I on the southeastern side of the mosque and also on the al-Masʿā "thumb." This latter, completed, is 394.5 m long. The ground floor is 12 m high and the second storey 9 m. It is noteworthy that there is a low partitioning in the middle of the Masʿā which provides for a special lane for the handicapped and ensures one-way traffic in each direction. There is no basement under al-Masʿā, but a full one under the rest of the new construction. A particular problem was the floods which sweep south down the wadi systems, around both sides of the mosque (but especially on the east). To deal with this problem an underground conduit 5 m wide and 4-6 m deep was run under the road now known as Shāriʿ al-Masdjid al-Ḥarām (formerly Shāriʿ al-Maʿlā) starting in al-Ḳashāshiyya quarter then under the area of al-Ṣafā, and under Shāriʿ al-Hidjra where, well south of the mosque, it resurfaces in the Misfala quarter. Among the buildings removed in this phase of the work were those of the old general post, the Ministry of Education and the Egyptian *takiyya*; in addition, there was some other non-mosque construction carried out as a part of the whole project, including a three-story building near al-Ṣafā to house government offices and the mosque-project offices and just northwest of al-Marwa a group of buildings with office and apartments on the upper floors. In Stage II, work continued in a counter-clockwise direction. Special note may be made of the demolition of the cells along the Bāb al-Salām and Bāb Adjyād façades, where the *zamāzima* used to store water for pilgrims, and the construction of replacement cells under the old ones. Not as lucky were the *madrasa*s adjoining the mosque on the Adjyād façade; they were simply demolished. Public fountains were also built on the new exterior façades as the work progressed. In Stage III, the southwest and northwest arcades and façades were built. The work was completed in 1398/1978.

All walls of the new construction are covered with local marble. The marble came from quarries in Wādī Fāṭima, Madraka and Farsān. The quarries were developed by Muḥammad b. Lādin, who had also started the companion marble processing factory in 1950 in preparation for the enlargement of the mosque in al-Madīna. He identified the quarries by asking local Bedouin to bring him samples and then by purchasing the most promising land from the government. The equipment in the factory was all Italian, and a force of nine Italian marble specialists directed and trained a total work force of 294 Suʿūdīs and others on a three-shift, round-the-clock basis. According to the Italian technicians, the marble is much harder than the famous Italian Carrara marble. Another feature of the marble operations was the production of "artificial marble." Remnant pieces and chips of marble from the main operation were sent to a crushing plant in Djudda, where they were ground into carefully graded pellets. To these were added waste from the cutting operations. This material was then mixed with a binding agent and poured into a variety of moulds of decorative panels. There were 800 different moulds "the patterns for which were created by a master of the art from Carrara." The mosque project as a whole called for processing 250,000 m² of marble.

Some over-all statistics and other information on the new structure follow:

1. Areas of old building	29,127 m²
Area of new building, including al-Masʿa	131,041 m²
Total	160,168 m²

2. The building can accommodate an estimated 300,000 worshippers with a clear view of the Kaʿba.
3. The old gate names were retained for the new gates except for the new Bāb al-Malik Suʿūd (probably subsequently renamed Bāb al-Malik).
4. There are six main stairways and seven subsidary ones. Stairs leading directly form the street have gentle slopes in order to make it easier for elderly pilgrims.
5. There are seven minarets, 90 m high each. (The old minarets are one feature that did not survive; they also numbered seven.)
6. By Radjab 182/December 1962, demolition of 768 houses and 928 stores and shops had been carried out against indemnities of SR 239,615,300.
7. The work force in 1382/1962 was:

architect-engineers	6
administrative employees	208
skilled workers	150
unskilled workers (maximum)	3,000

8. The total cost of the mosque expansion is estimated at $155 million.
9. The width of the streets around the new mosque is 30 m, with large plazas in front of the main gates.

There is one final aspect of the mosque enlargement and renovation that deserves mention, sc. Zamzam. In 1383/1963-4, the building that had long covered it was torn down and the space was levelled. Access to the well is now below ground down an ample sloping marble staircase; there is no above-ground structure whatsoever.

Like other shrines, *al-Masdjid al-Ḥarām* has its servants and its administration. In late Ottoman days the administration was headed by the *wālī* of Makka who was, therefore, the nominal *shaykh al-Ḥaram*, and it depended financially on the *ewḳāf* (*awḳāf*) in Istanbul. The operational head was the *nāʾib al-Ḥaram* (deputy of the *Ḥaram*) who was appointed by the sultan. The Hāshimite contribution was to institute a special security force whose assignment was to watch out for thieves and corruption and also to provide needed services such as "lost and found." Once he assumed power, King ʿAbd al-ʿAzīz appointed the nāʾib al-Ḥaram, and he also established a three-man administrative council (Madjlis Idārat al-Ḥaram al-Sharīf) over which the nāʾib presided. Financially, since income ceased coming from many waḳfs after the Suʿūdī takeover, King ʿAbd al-ʿAzīz ordered the financing of all services to come from the public treasury. He also initially doubled the salaries of those who served. His own waḳf department had support of the Ḥaram building as one of its main charges. According to Rutter, below the nāʾib came the "opener of God's House" (sādin), who since pre-Islamic times had always been from the Shayba (nisba: Shaybī) family. Not the least of the perquisites of the sādin was the right to cut the kiswa up after the Ḥadjdj and to sell the small pieces to pilgrims as religious tokens. Incidentally, a member of the Banū Shayba could not become nāʾib al-Ḥaram. Below the "opener" were two or three lieutenants who supervised the numerous lesser personages and the actual workers. All, according to Rutter, took special pride in this work. Rutter's estimate is that the total work force declined to 400 during the Wahhābī invasion but that in better times it rose to as many as 800. This latter figure would have included 100 imāms and preachers, 100 teachers, 50 muezzins, plus hundreds of sweepers, lamp cleaners, door keepers and Zamzam water drawers (zamzamī, pl. zamāzima). The Maṭāf, the circular inner area around the Kaʿba, was in the care of 50 black eunuchs who also doubled as mosque police. They were either Africans or of African origin and are called aghās or, colloquially, ṭawāshī (pl. ṭawāshiya, sc. eunuchs). Their chief ranked directly below the Shaybī. They wore distinctive clothes and were diligent in instantly removing any litter. The rationale for having eunuchs was that, if women became involved in any incident in the mosque or had to be ejected, the aghās could deal with them without impropriety. They apparently had large incomes (especially from awḳāf in al-Baṣra) and maintained expensive establishments including "wives" and slave girls as well as slave boys. They all lived in al-Hadjla at the northern end of al-Misfala quarter. The young boys destined for this service, who normally had been castrated in Africa, lived together in a large house, there to receive instruction both in their faith and in their duties. Literally slaves of the mosque and not of any individual, the aghās were nevertheless greatly venerated both by pilgrims and Makkans. "The middle-class Makkans also invariably rise when addressed by an Agha, and treat him in every way as a superior" (Rutter, 251). Others give a lower estimate for the numbers of mosque employees. Hamza (Bilad, 217) writing in 1355/1936-7 numbers as follows: muezzins 14, eunuchs 41, supervisors 80, water drawers 10, sweepers 20 and doormen 30. His list does not include teachers or preachers. Al-Kurdī (iv, 249), writing in the 1960s, notes that there are 26 eunuchs including their shaykh and their naḳīb. He also notes that the aghās have their own internal organisation (niẓām) and that amongst themselves they use special nicknames.

There are, naturally enough, numerous religious sites in Makka other than al-Masdjid al-Ḥarām. Brief remarks: 1. Mawlid al-Nabī (the Prophet's birthplace), located in the Shiʿb ʿAlī ravine near Sūḳ al-Layl. First the dome and minaret and later the whole structure was torn down by the Wahhābīs. The place is still pointed out. 2. Mawlid Sayyidatnā Fāṭima (the birthplace of our Lady Fāṭima). Same remarks. 3. Masdjid al-Arḳam b. al-Arḳam. The home of a Companion of the Prophet and reputed site of ʿUmar's ac-

ceptance of Islam. Destroyed during the recent expansion of al-Ḥaram, its location is now a parking lot east of al-Masʿā. 4. In Rutter's time the small mosques marking the houses of other Companions had mostly already been destroyed. 5. Cemetery of al-Maʿlā. It is located about 1 km due north of al-Ḥaram. In it are buried Āmina, the Prophet's mother; Khadīdja, his first wife; ʿAbd Manāf, his great-great grandfather; ʿAbd al-Muṭṭalib, his grandfather and guardian; and hosts of Muslims, famous and unknown, from the earliest days until the present. In the first flush of the occupation, Wahhābī zealots destroyed the small domes which covered some of the most famous sites, and those guardians who had sought alms from pious visitors were faced with other work. As in the case of al-Baḳīʿ cemetery in al-Madīna, bodies decompose quickly (six months) in al-Maʿlā, and there is "continuous" burial in the same place. 6. Masdjid al-Djinn (also called Masdjid al-Bayʿa and Masdjid al-Ḥaras). It is on Shāriʿ al-Ḥaram next to al-Maʿlā cemetery and marks the reputed place (see Ḳurʾān, XLVI, 29) where a party of djinn, having heard the Prophet chanting the Ḳurʾān were converted to Islam. An older Ottoman building was replaced by a modern mosque in 1399/1978-9. 7. Ghār Ḥirāʾ. Site of the first revelation (XCIV, 1-5), the cave of Ḥirāʾ is near the top of the mountain from which it takes it name (the mountain is more commonly called Djabal al-Nūr today). It lies about 5.2 km northeast of al-Ḥaram al-Sharīf—a steep climb to the top. The Wahhābīs pulled down the dome which earlier had ornamented it. 8. Ghār Thawr. Seven km south-southeast of al-Masdjid al-Ḥarām lies the cave on the top of Djabal Thawr in which the Prophet took refuge with Abū Bakr at the beginning of the hidjra; a difficult ascent. 9. al-Tanʿīm. Seven km north of al-Masdjid al-Ḥarām on Shāriʿ al-Tanʿīm which turns into Ṭarīḳ al-Madīna. This is the limit of the sacred area in this direction, and it is the place where Makkans often go to don the iḥrām when they want to perform the ʿumra. They go there not because it is necessary for them but because it is the place where the Prophet, returning from al-Madīna, announced his intention of performing the ʿumra. Formerly also a pleasant picnic spot, al-Tanʿīm in the 1980s has become a suburban quarter. There is a small mosque called Masdjid al-ʿUmra. 11. Masdjid al-Khayf. A mosque in Munā in which (at least formerly) were several large vaults which were opened for the receipt of bodies in plague years. It is especially meritorious for prayer on the ʿĪd al-Aḍḥā and has been rebuilt and enlarged by the Suʿūdīs. The new mosque has many columns, splendid carpets and a permanent imām. 12. Masdjid Ibrāhīm or, more commonly today, Masdjid Bilāl. Formerly outside the city on the slope of Djabal Abī Ḳubays 250 m due east of the Kaʿba; now a built-up area. 13. Masdjid al-Namira. Also known as Masdjid Ibrāhīm al-Khalīl and as Masdjid ʿArafa. It is located almost 2 km west of Djabal al-Raḥma in the plain of ʿArafāt and takes its name from a low mountain about 2 km further west. 14. Al-Kurdī estimates (ii, 269) that in all there are 150 mosques in Makka, but he adds that Friday prayers are only allowed to be performed in 15 of them (not counting al-Ḥaram) in 1375/1955-6. This relaxation of the traditional restriction on performing the Friday noon prayers only in al-Ḥaram was in response to the growth of the city and the disruption of al-Masdjid al-Ḥarām by the new construction there. The 15 mosques (with their locations) are as follows: Masdjid (thereafter, M.) al-Djinn (al-Sulaymāniyya), M. al-Djumazya (al-Muʿābada), M. al-Amīra Ḥassa (al-Ḥudjūn), M. Ḥamdān al-Faraḥ (al-ʿUtaybiyya),

M. Ibn Rushd al-Hamzānī (?) (al-Muᶜābada), M. al-Malik ᶜAbd al-ᶜAzīz (al-Muᶜābada), M. Ḥayy al-Tawfīḳ (Djarwal), M. al-Malik ᶜAbd al-ᶜAzīz (al-Zāhir), M. Biʾr al-Ham (?m)am (Shiᶜb ᶜĀmir), M. al-Amīr Bandar (al-Muᶜābada), M. Ḥasan Āl al-Shaykh (Shāriᶜ al-Manṣūr), M. al-Kuwaytī (Shariᶜ al-Manṣūr), M. al-Ṭabīshī) (Djarwal), M. al-Kaᶜkī (Djarwal), and M. al-Badawī (or M. al-Rāya or M. al-Djawdariyya) (al-Djawdariyya). From their names, it is clear that most of these are modern mosques. (For more detail on all the above and other mosques, see al-Bilādī, esp. *s.v. masdjid.*).

Pilgrimage. From time immemorial, the life of Makka has been punctuated by the inflow of pilgrims, and even mighty oil has not interfered with this annual surge. Indeed, it has rather confirmed it. D. Long's admirable study of the modern *Ḥadjdj* begins, "Over 1,500,000 people [by 1403/1982 the total figure was probably a little under 2,000,000] annually attend the Hajj, or Great Pilgrimage to Makkah, making it one of the largest exercises in public administration in the world. Nearly every agency of the Saudi government becomes involved, either in regulating the privately operated Hajj service industry, or in providing direct administrative services. Such a task would tax the most sophisticated government bureaucracy; and yet Saudi Arabia, where public administration is still in a developing stage, manages to get the job done each year. Moreover, since non-Muslims are not allowed in Makka, it is done with almost no administrative assistance from more developed countries." The brief tent city annually erected on the plain of ᶜArafat and the vast multitude that inhabits it creates as moving a picture of religious faith as any that human society affords.

Ḥadjdj arrival figures (or estimates) for the period under review from various sources:

Foreign *Ḥadjdj* arrivals (in 000s)

Year	No.	Year	No.
1324/1907	120	1373/1954	164
1343/1925	25	1374/1955	233
1344/1926	—	1375/1956	221
1345/1927	191	1376/1957	216
1346/1928	96	1377/1958	209
1347/1929	91	1378/1959	207
1348/1930	82	1379/1960	253
1349/1931	39	1380/1961	286
1350/1932	29	1381/1962	216
1351/1933	20	1382/1963	197
1352/1934	25	1383/1964	267
1353/1935	34	1384/1965	283
1354/1936	34	1385/1966	294
1355/1937	50	1386/1967	316
1356/1938	67	1387/1968	319
1357/1939	60	1388/1969	375
1358/1940	32	1389/1970	406
1359/1941	9	1390/1971	431
1360/1942	24	1391/1972	479
1361/1942-3	25	1392/1973	645
1362/1943	63	1393/1973-4	608
1363/1944	38	1394/1974-5	919
1364/1945	38	1395/1975	895
1365/1946	61	1396/1976	719
1366/1947	55	1397/1977	739
1367/1948	76	1398/1978	830
1368/1949	90	1399/1979	863
1369/1950	108	1400/1980	813
1370/1951	101	1401/1981	879
1371/1952	149	1402/1982	854
1372/1953	150	1403/1983	1,004

In the period under review, three aspects of the *Ḥadjdj* must be considered: the transitional period running from the Suᶜūdī conquest to the end of World War II, during which the camel gave way to the motor vehicle; the increasing Suᶜūdī regulation of what D. Long has called the *Ḥadjdj* service industry; and the *Ḥadjdj* in the era of mass air transport.

1. *The* Ḥadjdj *in the era of camel and car.* In general, what must be emphasised is that the security which the *pax Suᶜūdiana* brought to the Ḥidjāz transformed the pilgrimage. No longer were pilgrims subjected to capricious "taxes" or thinly veiled threats of much worse as they passed through tribal areas. No longer were the exploitative tendencies of merchants, transporters, *muṭawwifs* and officials allowed to run unchecked and unheeded. The policy was to make the pilgrimage as dignified and comfortable a spiritual experience as possible. King ᶜAbd al-ᶜAzīz turned his attention to the improvement of the lot of the pilgrims as he first entered Makka. It has already been noted that, when the king entered the city, his initial decree confirmed all *muṭawwifūn* "with a clear title" in their positions. The organic statute of 1345/1926 established a committee, *Ladjnat Idārat al-Ḥadjdj* (committee on administering the *Ḥadjdj*), to assist the viceroy, Fayṣal b. ᶜAbd al-ᶜAzīz, in supervising the pilgrimage. The committee was to include the heads of all government departments involved in the *Ḥadjdj* and a number of qualified notables, which latter category was probably intended to include senior members of the *muṭawwif* organisation. The committee was vested with investigatory powers, and all aspects of the pilgrimage were within its purview. But the king remained the final authority, as Article 16 makes clear: "'All regulations made by the Pilgrimage Committee should be enforced by the Agent-General [viceroy] after they have been sanctioned by His Majesty the King'" (quoted in Long, 55).

Philby reports (*Pilgrim*, 20 ff.) in some detail on the 1349/1931 pilgrimage. The king personally supervised matters like an officer in his command post. The royal party itself travelled in 300 automobiles, but it was not until 1352/1934 that ordinary citizens were allowed to use vehicles to go to ᶜArafāt. Houses in Minā were being rented for £40 for the four or five days of the *Ḥadjdj*, but again note that they were used for only some of the 350 days of the lunar year. The government discouraged various extravagant practices and did not allow access to the summit of Djabal al-Raḥma; guards were posted about half-way up. Exactly at sunset on 9 Dhu 'l-Ḥidjdja, the return to Makka begins, and on arrival at Muzdalifa the worshippers find a city which had not been there when the pilgrims passed through on the previous day. The pilgrimage is attended by various kinds of difficulties, for the régime which is responsible, not excluding political difficulties. Philby notes (*Jubilee*, 160) that during the 1349/1931 *Ḥadjdj*, the king felt it necessary discreetly to stop Amān Allāh Khān [*q.v.* in Suppl.], the former king of Afghanistan, from making political propaganda for his cause with Afghan pilgrims. ᶜAbd al-ᶜAzīz's policy was that any Muslim was welcome, but that the occasion was for religious not political purposes. A different, attempted political use of the pilgrimage occurred during the 1353/1935. As the king and his eldest son Suᶜūd were performing the *ṭawāf al-ifāḍa* (circumambulation of the Kaᶜba on 10 Dhu 'l-Ḳaᶜda), three Yamanīs, probably hoping to revenge some loss incurred in the Suᶜūdī-Yamanī war the previous year, fell on King ᶜAbd al-ᶜAzīz and on Suᶜūd b. ᶜAbd al-ᶜAzīz with daggers. Both received light wounds, but the assailants were shot dead.

The pilgrimage is also a socio-political affair, and

King ᶜAbd al-ᶜAziz and his successors have extended their hospitality generously and advantageously. ᶜAbbās Ḥamāda, who was a delegate from al-Azhar and whose account of his pilgrimage in 1354/1936 contains many interesting observations, vividly retells his reception by the king. He and others were invited to a royal dinner on the night of 6 Dhu 'l-Hidjdja. They gathered in front of the Ministry of Foreign Affairs to wait for cars to take them to al-Muᶜābada palace. A little before sunset, the group left. Paraphrasing and skipping, his account reads (70-3): "We were let off in front of a great palace built like a strong military fort outside Makka to the northeast in al-Muᶜābada. Opposite the palace lies Djabal Durūd, on the summit of which was a fort. When I entered the outside door, I found the royal guard on both sides armed to the teeth wearing splendid Arab dress. Most of them were slaves of the king. I walked until I entered a large reception hall furnished with splendid oriental carpets. When all the visitors had assembled, excellent Arabian coffee was passed around several time. During this stage, the chief of the *dīwān* was going around and greeting people warmly. When the muezzin called out sunset prayer time, we hastened to the mosque inside the palace. After praying, we climbed to the upper floor where superb Arab food was spread out for the guests. It combined the best oriental practice with the most modern European. H. R. H. Prince Suᶜūd b. ᶜAbd al-ᶜAzīz, the heir designate, sat at one table; Prince Fayṣal b. ᶜAbd al-ᶜAzīz, at another; and the chief of the royal *dīwān* at a third. After the meal, we went into an area reserved for receptions and then to the main royal reception hall where King ᶜAbd al-ᶜAzīz ibn al-Suᶜūd was surrounded by ulema, princes, ministers and Eastern leaders who had come to Makka for the pilgrimage. When all had gathered, ᶜAbd al-ᶜAzīz delivered an Islamic sermon. His talk reminded me of the Orthodox caliphs. When he finished, various speakers and poets rose to praise him. I got up and gave my speech [text, which is not without interest, at pp. 71-3]. We all left full of thanks, praise, and loyalty." Nor was that dinner the only time Ḥamāda was entertained by the royal family. He was later received by the king in Minā, and on another occasion Suᶜūd b. ᶜAbd al-ᶜAzīz sent for him to attend his *madjlis*.

Ḥamāda makes other observations. He speaks of the general lack of consideration for the old and weak in the surge of people performing the *ṭawaf.* Some would die, he opines, were it not for the police. A custom that he reports (61) is that some men take their wives' heads and shove them hard against the Black Stone. If blood flows, he calls out: "*Ḥadjdjī*" because the flowing blood means that the pilgrimage is acceptable. There is also shouting for forgiveness as people run around the Kaᶜba. These folk practices and ideas, including the belief of some ignorant pilgrims that it is a blessing if they are hit by droppings from the *Ḥaram* pigeons, or the practice by others of kissing the stone of the *Maḳam Ibrāhīm*, are the kind that the Suᶜūdī régime discouraged; Ḥamāda condemns them vigorously in his turn. He also discusses (67) begging. At *Ḥadjdj* time, thousands of poor Bedouin flocked to Makka and, along with the Makkan poor, became an army of beggars who constituted a considerable nuisance for the pilgrims. It was more or less a profession, in his view. Since his pilgrimage was made just when the conversion from camel to automobile transport was taking place, Ḥamāda makes a number of remarks (*passim*) on the subject. Most importantly, cars are much more comfortable than camels and much quicker. He contrasts the 12 days it took by camel from Makka to al-Madīna with the 18 hours that it took by car, although he notes that the conversion might deprive many Bedouin of their livelihood. He himself went to ᶜArafāt with a group that had 400 camels, and he paid 60 Egyptian piasters for the round trip. The outgoing trip encountered a severe thunderstorm, and it took six hours to reach the destination. On the problem of conversion from camel transport to motor vehicles, Philby notes (*Forty years*, 173) that the chaos initially engendered by cut-throat and dishonest competition among motor transport companies had by 1348-9/1930 been ended through the government's forcing all the motor companies to combine into a single monopoly company backed and regulated by the government.

2. *The* Ḥadjdj *service industry.* This service has long been a key element in the year-to-year functioning of the pilgrimage. It has grown up over centuries, is highly specialised, is divided among families and is organised into guilds. Two guilds are specifically Makkan, the *muṭawwifūn* (sing. *muṭawwif* "one who causes [others] to make the *ṭawāf* or circumambulation of the Kaᶜba"; an alternate term sometimes encountered is *shaykh al-ḥadjdj*); and the *zamāzima* (sing. *zamzamī*, a "Zamzamer"). A third guild which is related to Makka, but which is largely based in Djudda, is that of the *wukalā'* (sing. *wakīl*, "agent") whose task, as agents for the *muṭawwifūn*, is to meet pilgrims arriving in Djudda, help them choose a *muṭawwif* if by chance they do not have one, be responsible for them in Djudda until they depart for Makka and again when they return to Djudda. (For the guild of *adillā'*, sing. *dalīl*, "guide" of al-Madīna, see art. AL-MADĪNA; for the now defunct guild of camel brokers, *mukharridjūn*, sing. *mukharridj*, "dispatcher", see Long, 46.) The task of the *muṭawwifūn* is to assist the pilgrim while in Makka, by supplying his material needs and in performing the rites of the pilgrimage. In the years immediately following the Suᶜūdī conquest, the *muṭawwifūn* functioned much as they had in previous times. They delegated many of their responsibilities to assistants, who were called *ṣabī* (boy) if apprentices and *dalīl* (guide; unrelated to the *adillā'* of al-Madīna) if experienced. *Muṭawwifūn* commonly owned property which they either rented out directly to their clients or to another *muṭawwif* for his clients. Rutter notes (149) that particular national groups have their own attitudes. Malaysians, for example, like to be housed near the *Masdjid al-Ḥarām* and are willing to pay handsomely for the privilege. Thus a *muṭawwif* with a house there will rent it to a *muṭawwif* of Malaysians and put his own group in cheaper quarters. Rutter's own *muṭawwif* was the model for this generalisation. Aside from his own living quarters, he had rented his house to a *muṭawwif* of Malaysians for a three-month period for £30 per year. Incidentally, Rutter reports that in the previous year 1342/1924 his *muṭawwif* had had 1,000 clients whereas in the starving year of 1343/1925 he had only Rutter. One of the obligations of a *muṭawwif* even in Rutter's time was to keep a register of each pilgrim who died, along with a list of his or her effects. Twenty-seven of this *muṭawwif*'s 1,000 clients had died during the 1342/1924 pilgrimage. Most had been destitute or had possessed only a pound or two. The *muṭawwifūn* were organised according to the areas from which their clients came, and frequently the *muṭawwif* was originally from the same area. Thus he spoke the language and knew the characteristics of his customers who in turn would, if warranted, report favourably on him when they returned home.

Muṭawwifūn specialising in a particular country

formed sub-guilds (Long's term, 30) which rigidly excluded other *muṭawwifūn*. These sub-guilds were called *ṭawāʾif (sing. ṭāʾifa)*, and each was headed by a *shaykh al-mashāʾikh*. The title of the over-all guild leader was *shaykh al-muṭawwifīn*. He both represented the guild to the authorities and also had the responsibility of seeing that government regulations were applied. The normal pool for admitting new members was those proven assistants who were members of the family of a *muṭawwif*. "In cases of an interloper, however, the muṭawwifīn would rise to a man to prevent him from becoming established. The few outsiders who persisted were called *jarrārs* (those who drag [someone] along) and dealt primarily with Hajjis too poor to hire the services of a bona fide muṭawwif" (Long, 30). The final decision on admissibility lay with the *shaykh al-muṭawwifīn*. Some *muṭawwifūn* were large operators, with recruiters who travelled annually to the country or countries of specialisation; others were much smaller. Long (31) estimates that in the mid-1930s, there may have been 500 *muṭawwifūn* who, with helpers and apprentices, would have totalled "several thousand." The *muṭawwifūn* were compensated for their work in a variety of ways, although it should be noted that in theory there was no charge for guiding the pilgrim in the actual performance of his duties. In fact, there were no set fees and the pilgrims were expected to pay a gratuity according to their means. Should a pilgrim be too poor to pay, a *muṭawwif* would help him with the rites without pay; however, according to Rutter (446), "such an act is rarely done out of kindness. It is done in order to sustain the delusion that rites performed without the guidance of a mutawwif are valueless in the sight of Allah—for such is the impious connection advanced by the fraternity of guides for their own financial advantage." Yet such a flexible system doubtless cut both ways, especially for the apprentices and guides, and some at least worked hard for little. Additional sources of income were rentals, commissions for referring clients to various associated merchants, *zamāzima*, coffee shops, etc. It should also be realised that the government got a "cut" of *muṭawwif* income by issuing licenses (sing. *taḳrīr*) to the *muṭawwifūn*. In theory, these licenses once issued had been good for life, but prior to the Suʿūdī take-over, revalidation fees of various sorts had caused the system to break down. The *zamāzima* are basically organised in the same way as the *muṭawwifūn*. Membership is hereditary, members employ young helpers, they have their own *shaykh*, and they also specialise by the country or area of their clients' origin. As indicated above, they normally have client-sharing relationships with the *ṭāʾifa* of *muṭawwifūn*, specialising in the same linguistic or national group as themselves. Many are bi- or multilingual. The basic function of the *zamāzima* is to distribute the sacred water of Zamzam to those who desire it, whether in the mosque precincts or at home, where it was delivered twice a day to those who ordered it. Naturally, business was much greater during the *Ḥadjdj*. Selling water in containers to be taken home by a pilgrim was also a most important part of their business. Although in principle anyone could draw his own water, the practice was hardly encouraged by the *zamāzima*, and in addition, they performed a considerable service during the long hot periods by cooling the otherwise warm water in porous earthenware jars. The members of the guild of *wukalāʾ* of Djudda have formal relationships with the Makkan *muṭawwifūn* for whom they do it in fact work as agents.

Regulation of the guilds began shortly after the occupation of al-Ḥidjāz. In Rabīʿ II 1345/-October-November 1926, Fayṣal issued comprehensive regulations for the guilds, in the first article of which it was made clear that the king nominated *muṭawwifūn*. However, the fact that these guilds were powerful is indicated by the fact that they made King ʿAbd al-ʿAzīz back down on two separate occasions. The first was very shortly after he took Makka, when he tried to break the monopoly that had grown up whereby a pilgrim was compelled to accept as *muṭawwif* a *muṭawwif* who had acquired rights to all pilgrims from the given pilgrim's home area, but the affected interests were too powerful, and the king had to accept the old system. The second time was in the late 1920s, when the king wanted to pump water from Zamzam and lead it by pipe to taps in locations where it would be more readily available to pilgrims and also more sanitary. The *zamāzima* and the *sāḳīs* (water haulers) saw their interests threatened, and they aroused the local Nadjdīs against the king's plan. With the Ikhwān trouble brewing, ʿAbd al-ʿAzīz decided it was more politic to retreat, and the pumps and pipes that had been ordered sat uselessly. Nevertheless, government control over the guilds gradually increased. In 1348/1930, the king devoted much effort to the reorganisation of the *Ḥadjdj*, and the committee's name became *Ladjnat al-Hadjdj wa 'l-Muṭawwifīn* (Committee on the *Ḥadjdj* and the *muṭawwifūn*). During the 1351/1932-3 sessions of the *Madjlis al-Shūrā*, its policy mandate was enlarged to include "caring for pilgrimage and pilgrims ... because efforts expended in serving the interests of pilgrims in this holy land constitutes one of the ways of approaching God.... It is a duty in the interest of this country to care for them and their interests with vigilance" (text in Hamza, 101). Bureaucratically, *Ḥadjdj* affairs were under the Ministry of Finance. The committee was composed of ten members, as follows: chairman (appointed by the government), four members elected by the trustees (*hayʾat umanāʾ*) of the *muṭawwif* guild (two to represent Turkish *muṭawwifūn*; two, other nationalities), two members from the trustees of the Djāwā ("Java" = Southeast Asia) *ṭāʾifa*, two members from the trustees of the "Indian" (= South Asia) *ṭāʾifa*, and one member from the trustees of the *zamāzima*. Licensing of guildsmen was spelled out by the Suʿūdī régime in some detail. The bases for possession of a valid licence were: 1. inheritance of a licence; 2. service under a licenced *muṭawwif* for a period of 15 years conditional on the applicant's receiving a certification of competence and good character from a licensed *muṭawwif*, plus nomination by the relevant *ṭāʾifa* and approval by the *shaykh al-muṭawwifīn*; 3. a grant (*inʿām*) from the ruler (*walī al-amr*); and 4. holding a license from a previous ruler. Two types of these licenses had been issued, a first type that gave the head of a given geographical area's *ṭāʾifa* the right to assign pilgrims to individual *muṭawwifūn* within the *ṭāʾifa*, and a second type introduced by the Hāshimite régime, in which the process of assigning pilgrims was opened up. At the time Fuʾād Ḥamza was writing, these guilds were divided into three divisions (his term is *ḳism*) each led by a head (his term is *raʾīs*): 1. the "Javan" *shaykhs* ((headed by Shaykh Ḥāmid ʿAbd al-Mannān), whose ten trustees were elected by the 500 members. 2. The "Indian" *muṭawwifūn* (headed by Shaykh ʿAbd al-Raḥmān Maẓhar), who also have trustees and who number in all 350. 3. The *muṭawwifūn* of other races (headed by Shaykh Muḥammad Harsānī), who also have ten trustees and a membership of 350. Ḥamza notes that there were 200 *zamāzima* (headed by Sulaymān Abū Ghaliyya), with a similar organisation. Ḥamza's estimate then is for a total of 1,400 Makkan guildsmen, not counting the *mukharridjūn*. For the 1386/1967 *Ḥadjdj*, regulations on the assignment of clients to *muṭawwifūn* were liberalised so that a pilgrim arriving without a pre-selected *muṭawwif* could be assigned to any *muṭawwif* by the *Su*ʾ*āl* (Interrogation [committee]). A *Su*ʾ*āl*, composed of *wukalā*ʾ and Ministry of Ḥadjdj officials, sits at every port of entry. The purpose of the change was to prevent *muṭawwifūn* who specialised in areas whence many pilgrims came, from getting too large a share, relatively, of the market. To the same end, the fees collected were set on a sliding scale which reduced the fee as the number of a *muṭawwif*'s clients increased. Nevertheless, nothing prevented *muṭawwifūn* from employing doubtful tactics to lure pilgrims before their arrival in Suʿūdī Arabia and after the 1386/1967 pilgrimage, controls in this regard were tightened to force each *muṭawwif* formally to declare his area of specialisation. Simultaneously, the three *ṭā*ʾ*ifa*s were also formalised as follows: Arab *ṭā*ʾ*ifa* (Arab countries plus Turkey, Iran and Europe [?plus the Americas], Indian *ṭā*ʾ*ifa* (Afghanistan, Ceylon, India and Pakistan), Djāwā *ṭā*ʾ*ifa* (Indonesia, Philippines, Burma, China, Malaysia, Thailand and Japan). As a double check, each *ṭā*ʾ*ifa* board had to approve the *muṭawwif*'s declaration. The net result was that no *muṭawwif* was allowed to solicit clients outside the area of his approved declaration. Balancing this limitation was the rule that thereafter, pilgrims arriving with no pre-selected *muṭawwif* would automatically be assigned to a *muṭawwif* specialising in the area from which he came.

Gradually, the government was also able to establish set fees. In 1948 the total fee for a pilgrim was SR 401.50/£35.50 (see *Madjallat al-Ḥadjdj*, n. 10, p. 47; cited by Long, 38). This fee included all charges. The part of it dedicated to Makkans was as follows: *muṭawwif*, SR 51; *shaykh al-muṭawwifīn* and his board, SR 4.5; *naḳīb* (? later term for a *dalīl*), SR .5; poor *muṭawwifūn*, SR .5; *zamzamī*, SR 3.5. Thus the total cost for guild services in Makka was SR 60/£5.31.

Various new decrees and amendments continued to increase the regulatory control until on 9 Djumādā I 1385/5 September 1965 a comprehensive royal decree (*marsūm*) was issued which detailed the responsibilities of all guilds, including those in Djudda and in al-Madīna, reset fees and established travel instructions. The fee for the services of a *muṭawwif*, *zamzamī* and a *wakīl* was SR 74/$16.44. This fee was paid in Djudda to the *wakīl*, who deposited it in the central bank, the Saudi Arabian Monetary Agency. The government then paid the guildsmen. Under new streamlined procedures, the pilgrim was to go to a reception centre run by the Ministry of *Ḥadjdj* and *Awḳāf* where he or she was processed and introduced to the *muṭawwif* or his staff. Duties to the client were specified as follows: 1. to receive the arriving pilgrim, take his passport, and issue him a special travel document giving his name, nationality, address in Makka, name of his *muṭawwif*, departure date and means of transport; 2. to assist the pilgrim to find lodging at a rate he can afford, according to a rent-control schedule of SR 100 for a house in Makka and SR 30 for a tent in ʿArafāt and Minā. There is an Accommodation Control Committee charged with oversight of housing and investigation of abuses. The *muṭawwif* must also assist the pilgrim in obtaining reasonable prices for food and other goods in stores; 3. to guide the pilgrim through all the prescribed rites in Makka, ʿArafat, and Minā; 4. to supervise the transportation and the stay at ʿArafāt and Minā. For this purpose a second card is issued showing the site of his tent in ʿArafāt and Minā. According to the regulation, "cards shall include the number of the plot, square, and street." In addition, the *muṭawwif* must erect signs giving the same information "so that the Hajjis may see clearly their places in ʿArafāt and Mina" (Long, 41-2); and 5. to assist the pilgrim in arranging his ongoing travel. Three days before departing from Makka, the pilgrim's name "is submitted to the Hajj Ministry for inclusion on a departure list and for checking reservations and tickets... Passports, tickets, and reservations are then returned to the Hajji" (Long, 42). The *zamzamī* had under the 1965 regulations two responsibilities: 1. to supply pilgrims with Zamzam water within *al-Masdjid al-Ḥarām* and twice a day in their rooms; and 2. to help them during prayers, i.e., to supply water for ablutions. All guildsmen are responsible for carrying out set procedures to help lost pilgrims, to report suspected disease to health officials and to deal with death. Finally, the government has also tried to regulate the quality of the guildsmen's helpers. Long indicates (45-6) that the royal decree of 1965 "states that every employee must be of good conduct, physically fit, of suitable age to perform his required services, and competent and licensed for that service. It further stipulates that: 'The muṭawwif... and zamzami, for their part must take the necessary steps to supervise the said persons during their work and guarantee good performance. Each is to be supplied with a card containing all the [required] information including the name of his employer.'"

3. *The* Ḥadjdj *in the era of air travel.* The pilgrimage entered its latest phase in the wake of World War II with the simultaneous appearance of air travel and of greatly increased income from oil. The first pilgrim flights were in chartered ex-military transports; in the 1980s, almost all pilgrims came by "wide-bodied" jets, and the number have increased dramatically as noted above. One might start this section on the post-war period by reporting that the direct tax imposed by the king in 1345-6/1927 was lifted in 1371/1952, by which year oil income had exceeded *Ḥadjdj* income. The circumstances were as follows. ʿAbd al-ʿAzīz, just a year before his death, was heard to say: "The goal of my life is to lift the *Ḥadjdj* fees from the Muslims." One of his oldest advisors, Shaykh Yūsuf Yāsīn, who was present, said: "The king almost immediately turned to me and said, 'Telegraph Ibn Sulaymān [ʿAbd Allāh Āl Sulaymān, Minister of Finance] to abolish the pilgrims' fees.' So I wired him in the king's name as directed. He replied to the king, 'O Long of Life: Thirty million *riyāl*s—from what shall I compensate them in the budget?" ʿAbd al-ʿAzīz replied to him: '*Dabbir nafsaka*' ("solve your own problems")!" The fees were abolished forthwith. (See al-Ziriklī, 1416.) Other positive moves followed. By 1376/1956-7, the Ministry of Health had built a large modern hospital in Minā, including specialised sunstroke facilities, even though the town really existed only a few days a year. Al-Kurdī describes (ii, 194) the government's provision of shaded rest areas and ice water taps along the way between Minā and ʿArafāt (in addition to the numerous coffee houses which serve fruit and other food as well as drinks). There were also important administrative changes. In 1383-4/1964 following Fayṣal's accession to the throne, direct supervision of the *Ḥadjdj* was relinquished by the new king and devolved upon the *amīr* of Makka. For the pilgrimage of 1385/1966, the old committee was superseded by a new Supreme Ḥadjdj Committee (*Ladjnat al-Ḥadjdj al-ʿUlyā*). "Chaired by

the amir, its members include the mayors of Jiddah and Makkah; the senior representatives in the Hijaz for the Ministries of Health, Interior, Hajj and Waqfs, and other interested ministries; and representatives from the local police, customs, quarantine, and other offices'' (Long, p. 56). All policy on the ever-more complicated *Ḥadjdj* operation was set, under the over-all supervision of the king, by this committee. Another new aspect of the *Ḥadjdj* is the growth of hotels. The city now boasts not less than 25 hotels, and several of them belong to major international chains; many meet international standards. To give a small insight into the way things have changed in the latest phase, it is enough to mention that at ʿArafāt there are lost children's tents stocked with toys to divert them until their parents claim them. It is also pertinent to note that in 1974, the *kiswa* factory employed 80 craftsmen who wove 2,500 feet of material on hand looms. The finished cloth weighs about 5,000 lbs.

The annual traffic problem may be the most challenging in the world. An excellent picture is provided by the following extended quotation:

''In order to get some idea of the magnitude of the traffic problem at ʿArafat during the nafrah, one might picture about twelve [major] football games all getting out at the same time, with all the fans heading for the same place; only, in the case of the Hajj, there is a multitude of different languages, types of vehicles, and many foreign drivers not familiar with the road system. In order to cope with this situation, special cadres of traffic police are trained for the Hajj and are given extra assistance by the Saudi army. In recent years such modern devices as closed circuit television have also been installed to help guide the traffic flow. Moreover Hajjis traveling overland are required to use designated routes on entering al-Madīnah, Makkah, Muzdalifah, and Minā; the vehicles must be parked in designated places until the Hajjis are scheduled to depart. While in these cities and at ʿArafat the Hajjis must utilize Saudi transportation (for which they have paid anyway).

Despite all these measures the traffic situation can still get out of hand. In 1968 a mammoth traffic jam developed during the nafrah, and some Hajjis were delayed as much as twenty hours trying to get from ʿArafāt to Muzdalifah. Making matters worse, an exceptionally large number of Saudis attended the Hajj because of the special religious significance of Standing Day falling on Friday and because of the extension of the highway system throughout the kingdom. Not subject to the parking regulations for non-Saudi Hajjis, many took their private autos to ʿArafāt. In addition many Turkish buses, which had been allowed to drive to ʿArafāt because they contained sleeping and eating facilities, broke down during the long tie-ups, further contributing to the traffic jam. Sixteen new, black-and-white-checkered police cars especially marked for the purpose, were wrecked as they sought to cross lanes of moving or stalled traffic. In the post-Hajj evaluation by the Supreme Hajj Committee, traffic control was a major topic, and since then no such major tie-ups have been reported'' (Long, 64).

It is clear that, in totally changed circumstances, pilgrimage to the *Bayt Allāh* in Makka is a continuing, vital process not only for Muslims around the world but most especially for Makka al-Mukarrama.

Education and cultural life. Formal education, traditional or modern, was little developed in Makka in late Ottoman and Hās͟himite times. The first major attempt to improve the situation had been made by the distinguished public-spirited D̲j̲udda merchant, Muḥammad ʿAlī Zaynal Riḍā, who founded the Madrasat al-Falāḥ in Makka in 1330/1911-12 as he had founded a school of the same name in D̲j̲udda in 1326/1908-9. He is reported to have spent £400,000 of his own money on these two schools before the world depression of 1929 forced him to curtail his support, at which point ʿAbd al-ʿAzīz assigned a share of the D̲j̲udda customs' duties to support the institutions. These two schools, the best in the land, had enormous influence through their graduates, even though they followed the old principles of excessive reliance on memorisation with little emphasis on independent thought. There were also in pre-Has͟himite days some Indian religious institutes, and of course, Islamic sciences were taught in *al-Masd̲j̲id al-Ḥarām*. During the Hās͟himite period, what Wahba calls (125) schools-in-name appeared, including an academic school (al-Madrasa al-Rāḳiya) as well as agricultural and military schools. By the time of the Suʿūdī occupation, the city counted one public elementary (*ibtidāʾī*) and 5 public preparatory (*taḥḍīrī*) schools. Private schools in addition to al-Falāḥ included 20 Ḳurʾān schools (*kuttāb*) and perhaps 5 other private schools. Rutter noted that a good deal of study went on among the pilgrims and opined that the Makkans were better educated than the contemporary Egyptians. Ḥamāda, writing a decade later, agrees about the first point, for he says that during his pilgrimage hundreds of pilgrims gathered nightly to hear the lesson given by the *imām*, S͟hayk͟h Muḥammad Abū Samḥ ʿAbd al-Ẓāhir. He taught *tafsīr [q.v.]* according to Ibn Kat͟hīr [*q.v.*], but Ḥamāda complains that his lecture wandered, often to the question of intercession with God—a sensitive point for the Wahhābīs—and wishes that he would concentrate on subjects of more interest to his listeners. He also comments that the majority of the population were illiterate and opines that the highest diploma awarded by the Falāḥ school, the *ʿālimiyya*, was equivalent to the *ibtidāʾiyya* of al-Azhar in Cairo.

In any case, King ʿAbd al-ʿAzīz moved rapidly in the field of education as in other areas. In 1344-5/1926 he established al-Maʿhad al-ʿIlmī al-Suʿūdī (Science Institute) for instruction in *s͟harīʿa* and Arabic language and linguistics, but also for social, natural and physical sciences as well as physical education. In 1356-7/1938, the Maʿhad was divided into four departments, *s͟harīʿa*, calligraphy, teacher training, and secondary instruction. The faculty was largely Egyptian, and by 1935 was also giving instruction in the English language. In addition, by that time the government had established other schools, the K͟hayriyya, ʿAzīziyya, Suʿūdiyya and Fayṣaliyya, in addition to starting student missions abroad. These developments were praised by Ḥamāda. Another development in the growth of education in Makka was the establishment in 1352/1932 of the Dār al-Ḥadīth (the *ḥadīth* academy) by Imām Muḥammad Abū Samḥ ʿAbd al-Ẓāhir. *Ḥadīth* was the only subject taught, and that at a relatively low level. Based on Ḥamza's summary (220-2), Makkan schools in about 1354/1935 were as shown in the table overleaf.

Thus, based on a population of perhaps 80,000, there were some 5,000 students enrolled in schools. Many of the teachers were ''foreigners,'' Egyptians, Southeast Asians, Muslims from British India and Central Asians, but then many in the population as a whole were people of non-Arabian origin. Students in many of these schools received stipends based on the financial capability of the several schools.

Educational facilities continued to expand, especially after oil income began to flow on a significant scale

Name	Level	No. of teachers	No. of students
Public schools			
al-Maʿhad al-ʿIlmī al--Suʿūdī		7	57
al-ʿAzīziyya	elementary & preparatory	15	452
al-Raḥmāniyya	,,	10	300
al-Suʿūdiyya	,,	10	300
al-Fayṣaliyya	,,	10	250
al-Muḥammadiyya	elementary	5	100
al-Khālidiyya	,,	5	90
Night Schools		6	100
Police Department supervised orphanage		?	49
Sub-total		68	1,698
Private schools			
al-Falāḥ			796
al-Fakhriyya			371
al-Ṣawlatiyya			575
al-Fāʾizīn			120
al-Māḥī			138
al-Taraḳḳī al-ʿIlmī			79
al-ʿUlūmiyya al-Djāwiyya			500
al-Indūnisiyyā			30
Dār al-Ḥadīth			30
20 *kuttāb*s			685
Sub-total			3,324
Total			5,022

after World War II. Secondary school education developed as follows. The first school to become a regular secondary school was the ʿAzīziyya, which had been upgraded to that status in 1355-6/1937. By 1363-4/1944, the number had grown to four with total enrollments of 368. Nine years later, there were 12 secondary schools with 1,617 students, and by 1381-2/1962 there were 18 with 2,770 pupils. The first institution of higher learning was established in 1370/1949-50, namely, the Kulliyyat al-Sharīʿa (*sharīʿa* college), which subsequently became the Faculty of Sharīʿa of King ʿAbd al-ʿAzīz University, most faculties of which are in Djudda. According to Thomas's survey (published 1968) the Faculty of Sharīʿa was comprised of departments of *sharīʿa*; Arabic language and literature; and history and Islamic civilisation. The undergraduate programme lasts four years and grants a bachelor's degree. Master's degrees and doctorates are also granted. (For curricular details, see Thomas, 68-70.) A College of Education followed in 1370-1/1951. Its departments in the mid-60s were: education and psychology; geography; English; mathematics; and physics. It only granted the bachelor's degree in the 1960s, but planned to develop masters' and doctoral programs. (For curricular details, see Thomas, 74-7.) In 1981 the university faculties in Makka were constituted into a separate university called Djāmiʿat Umm al-Ḳurā, which included four faculties; *sharīʿa* and Islamic studies; science; Arabic language; and education, to which last there was also attached a centre for the English language. In 1379-80/1960 another higher institution was created, the police academy, which required a secondary school certificate for admission. By 1386/1966-7 there was also in existence Maʿhad al-Nūr (the Institute of Light), a school for the blind and deaf, which counted 87 students. It may also be noted that an intermediate vocational school teaching auto mechanics, shop, electronics, printing and book binding had opened.

An official survey of the academic year 1386-7/1966-7 (from Kingdom of Suʿūdī Arabia, Ministry of Finance, *passim*) reveals the picture for institutions which are part of the Ministry of Education shown on the facing page.

There is little information available on female education. According to Ḥamāda, girls in the 1930s only attended *kuttāb*s taught by *faḳīh*s and after the first few years had to continue study at home. He also comments on the generally low level of women's knowledge and deprecates the use of female diviners or fortune-tellers (sing. *ʿarrāfa*) for medical purposes. But Ḥamāda also notes that even in his day, young men were seeking more educated wives, and he calls on the government to support female education and in particular to replace the *faḳīh*s with "enlightened" teachers. The chart above indicates that, although female education has expanded a great deal, it has continued to lag behind male.

In the 1970s and the 1980s, educational expansion has continued on a large scale. One estimate—possibly high—is that in 1402/1982 there were 15 secondary schools in Makka.

Educational administration of Makkan institutions followed general trends in the country. The Department of Education was established in 1344/1926 under the direction of Ṣāliḥ Shaṭṭa, and regulations for it were issued by the government of al-Ḥidjāz in Muḥarram 1346/July 1927. *Inter alia*, these gave the department its own policy board (*madjlis*). The budget was £5,665. In Muḥarram 1357/March 1938 a vice-regal decree (*amr sāmⁱⁿ*) was issued which thoroughly reorganised the department now called *Mudīriyyat al-Maʿārif al-ʿĀmma.* All education except military fell under its aegis. Four departments were established: policy board, secretariat, inspectorate, and instruc-

Type	No. of institutions	No. of Suᶜūdi teachers	No. of non-Suᶜūdī teachers	Total teachers	No. of students
Elementary	56	527	213	740	18,654
Intermediate	7	94	95	189	2,768
Intermediate/secondary	1	7	15	22	387
Secondary	1	9	27	36	767
Teacher training institutes of elementary schools	2	—	—	—	343
Teacher training institutes for secondary schools	1	2	7	9	65
Commercial intermediate school	1	2	6	8	57
Adult education	19				2,226
Institute for blind	1	8	8	16	87
Private schools	13	25	72	97	1,563
Public girls schools	21	—	—	318	9,882
Private girls schools	6	—	—	74	1,984
Faculty of Sh̲arīᶜa	1	12	11	23	737
Total	130				39,520

tional office (details in Nallino, 44-7). These new regulations brought private education under full government control. They specified that the principal had to be a Suᶜūdī citizen and that preference in hiring teachers should also go to citizens. Foreign nationals had to be approved by the Department of Education. In curricular terms, those private schools which received government support were required to teach *sh̲arīᶜa* according to any one of the four recognised *mad̲h̲habs*. In the religious institutions, *kalām* [*q.v.*] was forbidden and *fiḳh* was limited to the Ḥanbalī *mad̲h̲hab*. Little budgetary information on the schools of Makka is available. Directors of the department were as follows: Ṣāliḥ Sh̲aṭṭa, Muḥammad Kāmil al-Ḳaṣṣāb (of Damascus, who served only briefly), Mād̲j̲id al-Kurdī, Ḥāfiẓ Wahba (in addition to his other duties; his deputy, who ran the department, was Ibrāhīm al-Sh̲ūrī, a graduate of Dar al-ᶜUlūm in Cairo), Muḥammad Amīn Fūda (1347-1352/1928-9 to 1933-4), Ṭāhir al-Dabbāg̲h̲ (until 1378/1959), Muḥammad b. ᶜAbd al-ᶜAzīz al-Māniᶜ (of Nad̲j̲dī origin). It may be mentioned that when independent, fully-formed ministries were established at the end of ᶜAbd al-ᶜAzīz's reign, Prince (later King) Fahd b. ᶜAbd al-ᶜAzīz became the first Minister of Education. Subsequently, the ministry was divided into a Ministry of Education (*Wizārat al-Maᶜārif*, under Dr. ᶜAbd al-ᶜAziz al-K̲h̲uwayṭir from approximately 1395/1975 to the present, 1405/1985) and a Ministry of Higher Education (*Wizārat al-Taᶜlīm al-ᶜĀlī*, under Sh̲ayk̲h̲ Ḥasan b. ᶜAbd Allāh b. Ḥasan Āl al-Sh̲ayk̲h̲ from approximately 1975 to the present).

The most important library in Makka is the *Ḥaram* Library (*Maktabat al-Ḥaram*) as it became known in 1357/1938. The basis of the collection was 3,653 volumes donated by Sultan ᶜAbd al-Med̲j̲īd. These were placed under a dome behind the Zamzam building, but were badly damaged during the flood of 1278/1861-2. The sultan then ordered the construction of a *madrasa*/library next to the Egyptian *takiyya* (by the southern corner of the *Ḥaram*), but died before its completion. In 1299/1881-2 the dome above Bāb al-Durayba was used to house the remains of the damaged library. New accretions began; Sh̲arīf ᶜAbd al-Muṭṭalib b. G̲h̲ālib (d. 1303/1886) donated *wakf* books, to which were added those of Sh̲ayk̲h̲ Ṣāliḥ ᶜIṭird̲j̲ī, and still other volumes brought from different mosques and *ribāṭs*. In 1336/1917-8 another addition was made by *wakf* from Sh̲ayk̲h̲ ᶜAbd al-Haḳḳ al-Hindī. A more important accretion occurred in 1346/1927-8 under the new Suᶜūdī régime when the 1,362-volume library of Muḥammad Rush̲dī Pash̲a al-Sh̲irwānī (d. 1292/1875-6), a former Ottoman *wālī* of al-Ḥid̲j̲āz, was added to the growing collection. By 1386/1965 the collection was officially estimated as 200,000 volumes used in the course of the year by 100,000 readers. The main public library, founded in 1350/1931-2, contained 500,000 volumes and was used by 400,000 people per year. Other libraries include: 1. The Dihlawī library results from a combination of the library of Sh̲ayk̲h̲ ᶜAbd al-Sattār al-Dihlawī (1286-1355/1869-70 to 1936-7) composed of 1714 volumes with that of Sh̲ayk̲h̲ ᶜAbd al-Wahhāb al-Dihlawī which in fact had been collected by Sh̲ayk̲h̲ ᶜAbd al-D̲j̲abbār (? al-Dihlawi). It is said to have many choice items. 2. The Mād̲j̲idiyya library was assembled by Sh̲ayk̲h̲ Muḥammad Mād̲j̲id al-Kurdī, sometime director of the Department of Education, and consists of 7,000 volumes of rare printed works and manuscripts. Sh̲ayk̲h̲ Mād̲j̲id not only acquired the books but systematically organised and indexed them. After al-Kurdī's death, ᶜAbbās al-Ḳaṭṭān purchased the library from al-Kurdī's children and set it up in a building that he had built. Although al-Ḳaṭṭān died in 1370/1950, the library was moved to the building and was attached to the *wakf* libraries of the Ministry of Ḥad̲j̲d̲j̲ and Awḳāf. 3. Another library reputed to contain manuscripts and rare printed works is that of Sh̲ayk̲h̲ Ḥasan ᶜAbd al-Sh̲ukūr, a "Javan" *sh̲ayk̲h̲*. 4. Other libraries are those of ᶜAbd Allāh b. Muḥammad G̲h̲āzī, al-Madrasa al-Ṣawlatiyya, Madrasat al-Falāḥ, Sulaymān b. ᶜAbd al-Raḥmān al-Ṣanīᶜ (d. 1389/1969), Muḥammad Ibrāhīm al-G̲h̲azzāwī (brother of the poet laureate), Muḥammad Surūr al-Ṣabbān, al-ᶜAmūdī, Ibrāhīm Fūda, Aḥmad ᶜAbd al-G̲h̲afūr ᶜAṭṭār, and the late distinguished writer ᶜAbd al-Ḳuddūs al-Anṣārī. (Section on libraries basically from al-Ziriklī, iii, 1035-7.)

Presses and publishing in Makka have been rather restricted. The first press was brought to the city *ca.*

1303/1885-6 by ᶜOthmān Nūrī Pasha, who had arrived as Ottoman *wālī* in November 1881. Probably it was briefly directed by the historian Aḥmad b. Zaynī Daḥlān (d. 1304/1886-7). During the Hāshimite period, it was used to print the official gazette, *al-Ḳibla*. It was of course taken over by the Suᶜūdī régime, new equipment was purchased, and other small local presses were bought by the government and added to it. The new enlarged operation was called Maṭbaᶜat Umm al-Ḳurā after the new Suᶜūdī official gazette *Umm al-Ḳurā*, which was published thereon. Subsequently, a separate administration was set up for it and its name was changed to Maṭbaᶜat al-Ḥukūma (the government press). A Syrian expert at the same time was brought in to teach Suᶜūdīs zinc etching and stamping (*ᶜamal al-ṭawābiᶜ*). A special plant was set up for this purpose in 1346/1927. The next press to arrive was brought in by Muḥammad Mādjid al-Kurdī in 1327/1909. Called al-Maṭbaᶜa al-Mādjidiyya, it was installed in his house and printed many books. His sons continued it after his death. The third press was that introduced by the famous Djudda scholar, Shaykh Muḥammad Ṣāliḥ Naṣīf, which he called al-Maṭbaᶜa al-Salafiyya, but which he soon sold. Other presses include: al-Maṭbaᶜa al-ᶜArabiyya (or al-Sharika al-ᶜArabiyya li-Ṭabāᶜ wa'l-Nashr) used to print *Ṣawt al-Ḥidjāz* newspaper (subsequently called *al-Bilād al-Suᶜūdiyya*, subsequently *al-Bilad*); the press of Aḥmad al-Fayḍ Ābādī established in 1357/1938 on German equipment; Maṭābiᶜ al-Nadwa, established in 1373/1953-4; the beautifully-equipped press of Ṣāliḥ Muḥammad Djamāl (for printing books); Maṭbaᶜat Ḳuraysh, established by Aḥmad al-Sibāᶜī, the author of the well-known history of Makka; and Maṭbaᶜat Maṣḥaf Makka al-Mukarrama established in 1367/1948 with American equipment. Most of these were hand presses up until the 1960s, but many have doubtless been highly automated since then. (For other lesser presses, see al-Kurdī, ii, 156, who along with al-Ziriklī, 1023-4, is much followed in this section, and also Kingdom of Saudi Arabia, Mudīriyya, 235.)

Newspapers and magazines published in Makka in modern times include in chronological order the following: 1. The first periodical in Makka (and in the Ḥidjāz) was an official gazette called *al-Ḥidjāz* which began publication in both Arabic and Turkish in 1326/1908 (not, apparently, in 1301/1884 as reported by Philippe Ṭarrāzī). It appeared in four small pages and ceased publication a year later with the Young Turk Revolution. It reappeared under a new name, *Shams al-Haḳīḳa* ("The Sun of Truth") that same year again in Arabic and Turkish as the organ of the Committee on Union and Progress in Istanbul. Its editor was Muḥammad Tawfīḳ Makkī and his assistant was Ibrāhīm Adham. Under the Hāshimites, *al-Ḳibla*, their official gazette, appeared starting in 1334/1916 on a weekly basis. Those who participated in the editorial work were Fuʾād al-Khaṭīb, Muḥyī al-Dīn Khaṭīb, and Aḥmad Shākir al-Kar(?a)mī. When ᶜAbd al-ᶜAzīz Āl Suᶜūd captured Makka, the official gazette re-emerged once again on a weekly basis as *Umm al-Ḳurā*. The speed with which it began once again illustrates the energy of the new régime, for it started on 15 Djumādā I 1343/12 December 1924, exactly one week after the sultan of Nadjd had entered the newly-conquered city. According to Ḥamāda, circulation was 3,000 during the *Ḥadjdj*. The paper has remained the unrivalled documentary source for Suᶜūdī affairs, but also has included much non-official material, especially literary. Successive editors of *Umm al-Ḳurā* starting with vol. i, no. 1 were Yūsuf Yāsīn, Rushdī Malḥaṣ, Muḥammad Saᶜīd ᶜAbd al-Maḳṣūd, ᶜAbd al-Ḳuddūs al-Anṣārī, and in 1952, al-Ṭayyib al-Sāsī. 2. *Ṣawt al-Ḥidjāz*, ("The Voice of the Ḥidjāz"), appeared in 1350/1932 as a weekly paper and lasted with that title for seven years. Like *Umm al-Ḳurā*, it had four, small-format pages. Its publisher was the well-known Muḥammad Ṣāliḥ Naṣīf and its initial editor was ᶜAbd al-Wahhāb Āshī. His successors were a kind of *Who's Who*, including Aḥmad Ibrāhīm al-Ghazzāwī, Ḥasan al-Faḳī, Muḥammad Saᶜīd al-ᶜAmūdī, Muḥammad Ḥasan ᶜAwwād, Aḥmad al-Sibāᶜī, Muḥammad ᶜAlī Riḍā and Muḥammad ᶜAlī Maghribī. 3. *al-Manhal* ("The Spring or Pool"), a magazine which was first published in al-Madīna in 1355/1936, but transferred to Makka a year later. It ceased publication for a while during World War II along with other periodicals (see below), and then resumed in Makka. It is essentially a literary magazine and was published and edited by the well-known ᶜAbd al-Ḳuddūs al-Anṣārī. In the 1960s, *al-Manhal*'s operations were moved to Djudda. 4. *al-Ḥadjdj* magazine started publication in 1366/1947 under the initial editorship of Hāshim al-Zawāwī, who was succeeded therein in 1370/1951 by Muḥammad Ṭāhir al-Kurdī. It is religiously oriented and includes literary and historical materials. It is published under the auspices of the Ministry of Ḥadjdj and Awḳāf. 5. *al-Iṣlāḥ* ("Reform") ran for two years as a monthly magazine starting in 1347/1928. It was published by the Department of Education and edited by Muḥammad Ḥāmid al-Faḳī. It is not to be confused with its late Ottoman predecessor of the same title. 6. *al-Nidāʾ al-Islāmi* was a bilingual monthly magazine (Arabic and Indonesian) which began publication in 1357/1938. It is to be noted that on 27 Djumādā II/1360/21 July 1941, the government issued an official communiqué which ordered the cessation of all newspapers and magazines except *Umm al-Ḳurā* because of the war-time shortage of newsprint. When the wartime emergency was over, *al-Manhal* and *al-Ḥadjdj* reappeared and have continued publication. 7. *Ṣawt al-Ḥidjāz* also reappeared but with a different name, *al-Bilād al-Suᶜūdiyya* ("The Suᶜūdi Land")—first as a weekly again, then as a half-weekly. Starting in 1373/1953, it became the first daily in all of Suᶜūdī Arabia. Its name was subsequently shortened simply to *al-Bilād* and, according to al-Ziriklī, (ii, 1024-8), much followed here, it was by far the best paper in the country from almost all points of view. Its editor was ᶜAbd Allāh ᶜUrayf for a long period after the Second World War, and it is worth noting that, as with several other periodicals, Makka lost *al-Bilād* to Djudda in the 1960s. 8. A newer Makkan daily is *al-Nadwa*. It was founded in 1378/1958-9 and in 1387/1967 boasted a circulation of 9,000. 9. Finally, note should be taken of *Madjallat al-Tidjāra wa'l-Ṣināᶜa* ("The Journal of Commerce and Industry"), a monthly founded in 1385/1965 with a circulation of 2,000. (For additional journals, see al-Kurdī, ii, 156-60.) Both Nallino and Ḥamāda, writing about the same time, note that censorship existed. The former indicates that the *Hayʾat al-Amr bi'l-Maᶜrūf* had responsibility for censorship and states that among books which had been disallowed were polemics against Ibn Taymiyya [*q.v.*], the forerunner of Wahhābism, books by Aḥmad b. Zaynī Daḥlān, and Muḥammad Ḥusayn Haykal's *Fī manzil al-waḥy*, the latter for its criticism of Wahhābī extremism. Ḥamāda says only that "a committee" oversees writers and journalists and passes on imported books. He wonders if his book will be approved.

Before turning to Makkan writers, we may notice

one or two incidental aspects of cultural life in the city. Bookstores were formerly clustered around the *Ḥaram* near its gates. When the enlargement of the mosque took place, they were forced to move and relocate in scattered directions. Of 12 listed by al-Kurdī (ii, 138, 148), four belonged to the Āl Bāz and three to the Āl Faddāᶜ families, but al-Kurdī reports that only two were sought by scholars and students. The first was Maktabat al-Ḥaram al-Makkī, which was, he opines, founded "a number of centuries ago" by an Ottoman sultan. Originally, it was located facing Zamzam "in a room above a small dome," but when the Ottoman mosque renovation (? by Sultan ᶜAbd al-Medjīd) took place, it was relocated inside the mosque at Bāb al-Durayba. When the Suᶜūdī expansion took place, the store was once again moved to a special place near Bāb al-Salām. The second, Maktabat Makka al-Mukarrama, he describes as newly-established. Information on the time spent in penning careful calligraphy is not commonly given. Muḥammad Ṭāhir al-Kurdī, whose history has often been cited in this article, started the calligraphy for a Ḳurᵓān in 1362/1943-4. He published it, as *Maṣḥaf Makka al-Mukarrama* in 1369/1949-50. Some mention should also be made of the *waḳf*-established *ribāṭs* of Makka, best defined perhaps as hospices. Some were for students; others for the poor and the wayfarer. They were, according to al-Kurdī (ii, 149), "numerous" and not a few were for women. Established for the most part by *waḳfs*, they usually provided students with single rooms. They were generally located adjacent to or in the immediate vicinity of the *Ḥaram*. When the Suᶜūdī régimes pulled everything down around the mosque to make way for the enlargement, the *ribāṭs* of course went. Some were paid compensation and hence rebuilt elsewhere; others were not, and hence have disappeared forever. Al-Kurdī remembers six of the latter, and claims that none was less than 400 years old. (For details of the Italo-Muslim hospice in Makka, *al-Ribāṭ al-Īṭālī al-Islāmī*, see Nallino, 109-10.)

Makka has not failed to produce its share of modern writers, some of whom were primarily poets, others prose authors. Many had other work, often in publishing, journalism and printing. Many of the names that follow (based on Nallino, 132-7, who based his work in turn on ᶜAbd al-Maḳṣūd and Balkhayr's *Waḥy al-ṣaḥrāᵓ*), have appeared earlier in this article: 1. Aḥmad Ibrāhīm al-Ghazzāwī (b. Makka 1318/1900-1). A poet, he studied at the al-Ṣawlatiyya and al-Falāḥ schools and held public positions both under the Hāshimites and the Suᶜūds. A member of the *Madjlis al-Shūrā* in 1936. Was designated "poet of the king" (*shāᶜir al-malik*; poet laureate, in Philby's words) in 1932. (For a sample of his verse see al-Zirikli, ii, 675-6). 2. Aḥmad Sibāᶜī (b. Makka 1323/1905/6). Travelled abroad and studied two years at the Coptic High School in Alexandria. On his return, he taught in schools and then became the director of *Ṣawt al-Ḥidjāz* in 1354/1935-6. His *Taᵓrīkh Makka* ("History of Makka"), the most judicious, comprehensive history of the city, was first published in 1372/1953. The sixth edition appeared in 1404/1984, a year after he was judged first in the state prize of honour (*djāᵓizat al-dawla al-taḳdīriyya*). 3. Amīn b. ᶜAḳīl (b. Makka 1329/1911). Amīn studied at al-Falāḥ and then moved with his family to Mukalla in South Yemen, where he continued to study. He also was in Laḥidj for a year-and-a-half and then returned to Makka and completed his studies at al-Falāḥ. In 1351/1932, along with a group of Ḥidjāzīs, he was briefly exiled in al-Riyāḍ on political grounds. His medium was prose. 4. Ḥusayn Khaznadār (b. Makka 1336/1917-18). He studied at al-Khayriyya school and finished his studies at al-Falāḥ: a poet. 5. Ḥusayn Sarḥān (b. Makka 1334/1915-16). A member of the al-Rūsān section of the ᶜUtayba tribe, he also studied at al-Falāḥ and was a poet. 6. Ḥusayn Sarrādj (b. 1330-1/1912). Primary studies at al-Falāḥ, secondary in Jordan, he received his B.A. from the American University of Beirut in 1936; a poet. 7. ᶜAbd al-Wahhāb Āshī (b. Makka 1323/1905). He studied at al-Falāḥ, taught at al-Fakhriyya school and at al-Falāḥ. A member of the Automobile Association, he became editor-in-chief of *Ṣawt al-Ḥidjāz*. In 1932 he was imprisoned for political reasons and exiled in Nadjd for two months. On his return, he joined the Ministry of Finance and in time became head of the correspondence section. 8. ᶜAbd Allāh ᶜUmar Balkhayr (b. al-Ḥaḍramawt 1333/1914-15). He soon moved with his father to Makka, studied at al-Falāḥ and then at the American University of Beirut. Co-author of *Waḥy al-ṣaḥrāᵓ* (with Muḥammad Saᶜīd [b.] ᶜAbd al-Maḳṣūd; Cairo, 1355[/1936-7]), an anthology of prose and poetry by then living Ḥidjāzī authors, this talented young man was diverted from writing into government service. He became the translator from English of world-wide radio reporting for King ᶜAbd al-ᶜAzīz during World War II and rose to be Minister of Information under King Suᶜūd b. ᶜAbd al-ᶜAzīz. When the latter was deposed, Shaykh ᶜAbd Allāh retired and in the 1980s has begun to write again. 9. ᶜUmar Ṣayrafī (b. Makka 1319/1901-2). Upon completing his studies, Ṣayrafī taught in South Yaman and subsequently at al-Maᶜhad al-Suᶜūdī al-ᶜIlmī. Prose was his forte. 10. ᶜAbd al-Salām ᶜUmar (b. Makka 1327/1909-10 studied at al-Falāḥ and also taught there until he took a post with the Ministry of Finance in the correspondence department, to which a number of writers—given the very high levels of illiteracy in the country—gravitated. ᶜAbd al-Salām wrote prose. 11. ᶜUmar ᶜArab (b. Makka 1318/1900). Having studied in a *kuttāb* and then at al-Falāḥ, he taught at al-Falāḥ school in Djudda, became secretary of the municipal council of Makka and then was transferred to the correspondence section of the viceroy's secretariat. 12. Muḥammad b. Surūr al-Ṣabbān (b. al-Ḳunfudha 1316/1899) moved with his family first to Djudda then to Makka, where he enrolled in al-Khayyāṭ school. At first he became a merchant and then, under the Hāshimites, accountant of the Makkan municipal government. He retained this post under the Suᶜūdī régime. He was imprisoned on political grounds but released after the fall of Djudda to ᶜAbd al-ᶜAzīz. Thereafter, he became assistant to the head (*amīn*) of the municipality of Makka, but in 1346/1927 he was incarcerated in al-Riyāḍ for more than a year. After his release, he became head of the correspondence department in the Ministry of Finance, of which he ultimately became the minister. He was the author of *Adab al-Ḥidjāz* (Cairo 1344/1925-6), an anthology of Ḥidjāzī authors. 13. Muḥammad Saᶜīd al-ᶜAmūdī (b. Makka 1323/1905-6), attended a *kuttāb* and al-Falāḥ school. After a stint in commerce, he was employed by the ᶜAyn Zubayda authority. After several other posts, he became head of the correspondence department of the Department of Posts and Telegrams. He was also editor of *Ṣawt al-Ḥidjāz*. Al-ᶜAmūdī wrote both prose and poetry. 14. Muḥammad Ḥasan Faḳī (b. Makka 1330/1911-12) attended both al-Falāḥ of Djudda and that of Makka. He taught at the latter for three years, and he also became editor of *Ṣawt al-Ḥidjāz*. This poet and prose author was also chief of the contracts' department in the Ministry of Finance. 15. Muḥammad Ḥasan Kutubī (b. Makka 1329/1911) studied at al-Falāḥ and was a member of the mission that Muḥammad ʿAlī Zaynal Riḍā sent at his own expense to Bombay, India, for the study of religious science. After receiving his diploma there, Kutubī returned and he also became editor of *Ṣawt al-Ḥidjāz*. In addition, he taught courses for prospective *kāḍīs* at al-Maʿhad al-ʿIlmī al-Suʿūdī and later became director of public schools in al-Ṭāʾif. 16. Muḥammad Ṭāhir b. ʿAbd al-Ḳādir b. Maḥmūd al-Kurdī (b. Makka *ca.* 1323/1904-5. Al-Kurdī attended al-Falāḥ school, and after graduation entered al-Azhar in 1340/1921-2. That trip was the first of many to Egypt. He was a member of the executive committee on replacing the roof of the Kaʿba and on enlarging the Great Mosque. His works number more than 40, not all of which have been published. Among the published works are *Maḳām Ibrāhīm ʿalayhi 'l-Salām* (Cairo 1367/1947-8), *Maṣḥaf Makka al-Mukarrama* (1369/1949-50), *Taʾrīkh al-Ḳurʾān wa-gharāʾib rasmihi wa-ḥukmihi, al-Tafsīr al-Makkī*, a book (title unknown) on calligraphy, and *al-Taʾrīkh al-Ḳawīm li-Makka wa-Bayt Allāh al-Karīm*, 4 vols. (Makka 1385/[1965]; a fifth volume is promised. His work is traditional in conception, but scrupulous and comprehensive.

Health care. Because of the *Ḥadjdj* and its attendent health problems and because of the world-wide reach of returning pilgrims, health facilities in Makka are of more than passing importance. In the late Ottoman and Hāshimite periods, there were two "hospitals" one in Adjyād and the other in al-Madʿā. They had about five doctors between them, and al-Kurdī reports (ii, 225) that the equipment was satisfactory. These doctors were all foreign—Indians, Indonesians, Algerians, etc. There was one proper pharmacy near al-Marwa and other shops which sold drugs on a casual basis. In a general way, observers noted that the combination of primitive sanitary facilities, low standards of personal hygiene and an oppressively hot climate were unhealthy, although Rutter said that vermin were almost non-existent as a result of the heat and summer dryness. Mosquitoes were apparently common enough but non-malaria bearing. Shortly after ʿAbd al-ʿAzīz reached Makka, he deputed his personal physician, Dr. Maḥmūd Ḥamdī Ḥamūda, to re-establish the medical services, and among his first acts was the appointment of doctors to the Department of Health and the reopening of the Adjyād hospital. The hospital reportedly (Hamza, 200) had 275 beds and its facilities included an operating room, X-ray department, microscope room, pharmacy, obstetrics department and an outpatient clinic. It may be pointed out that it had become normal over the years for countries with large Muslim populations, and hence many pilgrims, to dispatch medical teams to Makka at *Ḥadjdj* time. In 1345/1927 the regulations for the health department (*Maṣlaḥat al-Ṣiḥḥa al-ʿĀmma*) were established, and by the mid-1930s the spectrum of medical facilities in addition to the Adjyād hospital included the following: 1. a mental hospital. 2. a contagious disease hospital. 3. a brand new hospital in al-Shuhadāʾ section with completely up-to-date equipment. 4. the Egyptian hospital in Dār al-Takiyya al-Miṣriyya—the official Egyptian presence in Makka. 5. an emergency aid society (*Djamʿiyyat al-Isʿāf*) founded 1355/1936, which held a conference on hygiene and first aid and which owned its own ambulances and motor cycles. In its first year it treated 922 victims of misfortunes, almost all of them in its own facilities. The king, heir designate, and viceroy all contributed to this society, and it was authorised to levy a special 1/4 piastre stamp on top of the regular postage for the support of its activities. This society probably came into existence because of needs arising from the 1934 Suʿūdī war against the Yaman. It grew into the Red Crescent society of the whole country (Philby, *Pilgrim*, 39); 6. a school for midwives. Philby estimated that during the pilgrimage of 1349/1931, there were 40 deaths out of total pilgrims numbering 100,000 and in 1352/1934, 15 deaths out of 80,000 pilgrims. In the post-World War II period, there was predictably a great increase in facilities, and to the above list must be added: 7. The Dr. Aḥmad Zāhir hospital with 400 beds and 16 doctors. 8. an obstetrical hospital. 9. an eye hospital. 10. a bilharzia (schistosomniasis) control station (1975). 11. a venereal disease control demonstration centre.

As noted earlier, various governments send medical missions to Makka during the *ḥadjdj* season. Ḥamāda reported (69) that in the 1930s, the Egyptian mission consisted of two units, one in Ḥārat al-Bāb near Djarwal, the other in the permanent Egyptian mission building (al-Takiyya al-Miṣriyya), which used to face *al-Masdjid al-Ḥarām* before it was torn down to make way for the mosque enlargement. The latter unit was in addition to the permanent Egyptian medical service in the same building. In 1355-6/1937, the countries sending medical missions were Egypt, India, the Dutch East Indies, Algeria, Afghanistan and the USSR. They contributed a total of ten doctors plus pharmacists, assistants and supplies to the available medical services. During the same period, Hamza noted (200) that at *Ḥadjdj* time there were a total of 13 government hospitals and clinics spread between Makka and ʿArafāt. Physicians, nurses and orderlies were hired on a temporary basis to man them. Reading from Fārisi's map, one finds that the latest indications are as follows: there were six hospitals, seven clinics (*mustawṣaf*) and three medical centres (*markaz ṭibbī*) in Makka proper and ten dispensaries in Minā, one hospital in Muzdalifa, and one medical centre in ʿArafāt. These latter doubtlessly function only during the *Ḥadjdj*.

Communications. By 1985 Makka, like other Suʿūdī cities, was possessed of the most modern telephone, telex, radio and TV communications. Its roads were of the most modern design, and it was linked to the rest of the country by first-class highways, many of them divided and of limited access. Since Djudda, which has one of the world's largest and most modern airports, is only some 60 km away and since a major airport at Makka would be difficult, both because of the terrain and because of the problem of non-Muslims being in proximity to the *ḥaram* area, there is no important airport in Makka. It may, however, be noted that a Djudda-Makka service had been authorised in 1936 to Misr Air (now Egypt Air). It was cancelled following an accident in 1938. In a similar vein, a railroad project from Djudda to Makka was authorised by a royal decree in 1351/1933 with a concession granted to ʿAbd al-Ḳādir al-Djīlānī. It was revoked 18 months later because of his failure to carry it out.

The modernisation of communications has been dramatically rapid. Rutter describes (455) how in 1925 camel caravans for al-Madīna assembled in an open space called Shaykh Maḥmūd on the western edge of Djarwal; a camel in Djarwal in 1985 would be about as common as a horse in Paris. The use of cars spread very rapidly after the Suʿūds' conquest and the development of the Djudda-Makka road was a natural early priority because of the pilgrim traffic. It was first asphalted in the period just before the outbreak of World War II.

Telecommunications were early emphasised by King ᶜAbd al-ᶜAzīz because they represented a means of control as well as a convenience. In King al-Ḥusayn's time, there had been about 20 telephones in the city—all reserved for high officials and probably only functional within the city. By 1936, subscribers in Makka had grown to 450 (slightly over half of all those in Suᶜūdī Arabia), and lines had been extended to Djudda and al-Ṭāʾif (but not al-Riyāḍ or al-Madīna). Ḥamza also reports (230-1) that, in addition to the regular telephones, there were "automatic" (?) telephones which were used by officials. Of this type, 50 were in Makka. After World War II, the first telephone training mission (10 persons) was sent abroad in 1367/1947-8. By 1385/1965-6, Makka had 5,000 telephones but service was still through operators. Dial phones were introduced soon after this, and within a dozen years there was fully automatic direct-dial service anywhere in the world. There had been limited radio communication within the Ḥidjāz under the Hāshimites. In 1348/1929, using Philby as an intermediary (for details see *Jubilee*, 173-4; *Days*, 286-9; *Saᶜudi Arabia*, 316-17), the king contracted with the Marconi company for wireless stations in various towns. That of Makka was of 25 kw power (as was al-Riyāḍ), and by the spring of 1932 the network was fully functional. Soon after World War II, by contract with the German Siemens company, this network was greatly expanded and improved. Radio communication has been used at various key points in directing the pilgrimage since about 1370/1950. Public radio broadcasts were initiated on *yawm al-wuḳūf* ("standing day") during the pilgrimage of 1368/1949 with *Hunā Makka* ("This is Makka") as the opening words. Initial power was only 3 kw, but with the creation of the Directorate General of Broadcasting, Press and Publications (by a decree of 1374/1955) under ᶜAbd Allāh ᶜUmar Balkhayr, there was rapid improvement. Within less than a year, power had increased to 10 kw, and it was boosted in 1377/1957 to 50 kw, making Radio Makka one of the most powerful in the Near East at that time. Later, power was increased still more to 450 kw. In keeping with Wahhābī tradition, music was initially kept off the air, but it was gradually introduced. TV in Makka began service in 1386/1966-7 and has since become a pervasive part of life there as everywhere else in the world.

Water supply. Before oil-induced modernisation, the water supply of Makka came from two basic sources. The first was local wells. The water of these, of which Zamzam is one, was generally brackish, and they were located in houses. The second was fresh or sweet water most of which came from ᶜAyn Zubayda by man-made underground channels of the *ḳanawāt* [see ḲANĀT] type. Locally, the system is called *kharaz*. A very sporadic third source was rainfall which, although it brought the threat of destructive floods, was eagerly collected in every way possible. Water distribution was by hand. A man carried two 20 litre petrol tins (*tanaka*) attached to the ends of a stout board or pole on his shoulders to the individual houses of those who could afford such service. Philby noted (*Forty years*, 172) that in the 1930s, 8 gallons cost one penny. His monthly bill seldom exceeded five shillings. The mass of the people went individually to get their own water at one of the small reservoirs or cisterns (*bāzān*). Of these in Rutter's time, there were seven in the city and one each in Minā, Muzdalifa, and ᶜArafa. The water for all of these came from ᶜAyn Zubayda.

The immediate source of the ᶜAyn Zubayda water is the mountains (Djabal Saᶜd and Djabal Kabkāb) which lie a few kilometers east of Djabal ᶜArafa or about 20 km east southeast of Makka. The main source is a spring in the mountains, ᶜAyn Ḥunayn, which according to Rutter is a two-hour walk from the Wādī Naᶜmān plain. Several other small springs are led to the beginning of the subterranean aqueduct which starts at the foot of the mountain. The aqueduct is attributed to Zubayda [*q.v.*], the wife of Hārūn al-Rashīd, but in all probability it far predates her, and she should be credited with improvement of the system rather than creation of it. Like other *ḳanawāt*, the ᶜAyn Zubayda system is characterised by access wells (*fataḥāt*) at intervals of about one km which are marked by circular erections around them. King ᶜAbd al-ᶜAzīz did not lack interest in the water supply system, and made personal financial contributions from time to time. Philby reports (*Jubilee*, 116-17) an expedition of autumn 1930 when the king and his party drove out to inspect work in progress at one of the access wells which was being cleaned. A thorough cleaning of the whole system had been ordered because flow had been declining as a result of inadequate maintenance in the prior, disturbed years. A pit some 30 m deep had been dug "at the bottom of which the *top* [Philby's italics] of one of the original manholes could be seen." Philby theorised that the valley silt had built up at a rate of about 3 m a century. In any case, the new pit was surfaced with masonry and the channel between it and the next pit thoroughly cleaned. When the whole process was completed, the flow of water in Makka increased greatly, although Philby notes that the growth of private gardens in the suburbs was putting pressure on supplies. The ᶜAyn Zubayda system (as well as other lesser ones) was so important to the city that a separate ᶜAyn Zubayda administrative authority had been created. Its budget came from the government and fell under the purview of the *Madjlis al-Shūrā*. In addition, pilgrims often made pious contributions to the upkeep of the system. Ḥamāda notes (77) that supervision of it had to be increased during pilgrimage season because of the danger of defilement. He also, writing for an Egyptian audience, assures his readers that Zubayda water is little inferior to Nile water! In the early 1950s, a modern pipline was run from al-Djadīda, 35 km northwest of Makka at the head of the Wādī Fāṭima, to the city. It doubled the water supply. One may assume that by the 1980s, water was piped into most Makkan houses, offices and apartments and that indoor plumbing and metered water, desalinated from sea water, were the norm. Detailed information is not, however, readily available.

Floods in Makka have been a danger since earliest times. Al-Kurdī counts a total of 89 historic ones, including several in the Suᶜūdī period. The most severe one was in 1360/1942 when it rained for several hours. Water reached the sill of the Kaᶜba's door, and prayers and *ṭawāf* were cancelled. The streets of the city filled with mud, and there was severe damage to stocks in stores. Tombs in al-Maᶜlā were washed out and houses were destroyed (al-Kurdī, ii, 200). Philby also reports (*Saᶜudi Arabia*, 320) a flood in 1950 which reached a depth of seven feet in the mosque. Soon thereafter the improved modern technologies and easier financial situation led to the construction of dams, one on the Wādī Ibrāhīm, which is the main source of floods, the other across the Wādī al-Zāhir, which threatens the northern and western sections. These dams were helpful, and the great underground conduit built in connection with the mosque enlargement may have permanently ameliorated the problem of floods.

Bibliography: Fundamental works on Suᶜūdī Arabia including Makka in the 1920s, 30s, and 40s are those of F. Ḥamza, C. Nallino, H. St. J. B. Philby, and Ḥ. Wahba. Muḥammad Surūr al-Ṣabbān, *Adab al-Ḥidjāz*, Cairo 1344/1926 (not consulted; unavailable); E. Rutter, *The holy cities of Arabia*, London and New York 1930 (most important source on Makka in immediate wake of Suᶜūdi take-over); Muḥammad Saᶜīd ᶜAbd al-Maḳṣūd and ᶜAbd Allāh ᶜUmar Balkhayr, *Waḥy al-ṣaḥrā*ʾ, Cairo 1354/1936 (important for literature, unconsulted); ᶜAbbās Mutawallī Ḥamāda, *Mushāhadātī fi 'l-Ḥidjāz sanata 1354/1936*, Cairo 1355/1936 (interesting photos and other material by a semi-official Egyptian pilgrim); Fuʾād Ḥamza, *al-Bilād al-ᶜArabiyya al-Suᶜūdiyya*, Makka 1355/1936-7; C. Nallino, *Raccolta di scritti editi e inediti*. v. 1. *L'Arabia Saᶜūdiana (1938)*, Rome 1939; Great Britain, Admiralty, Naval Intelligence Division, Geographical Section, *Western Arabia and the Red Sea*, [London] 1946; Ḥāfiẓ Wahba, *Djazīrat al-ᶜArab fi 'l-ḳarn al-ᶜishrīn*, Cairo 1365/1946; H. St. J. B. Philby, *A pilgrim in Arabia*, London 1946; idem, *Arabian days*, London 1948; Arabian American Oil Co., Government Relations, Research and Translation Division, *The Royal Family, officials of the Saudi Arab government and other prominent Arabs*, (typescript), Dhahran 1952; Philby, *Arabian jubilee*, London 1952; Abdul Ghafur Sheikh, *From America to Mecca on air borne pilgrimage*, in *The National Geographic magazine*, civ, (July 1953), 1-60; Ḥusayn Muḥammad Naṣīf, *Māḍī al-Ḥidjāz wa-ḥāḍiruha* (probably important, unavailable); Kingdom of Saudi Arabia, Ministry of Commerce, *al-Mamlaka al-ᶜArabiyya al-Suᶜūdiyya: tasdjīl wa-taᶜrīf*, Damascus [?1955]; Philby *Saᶜudi Arabia*, London 1955; Kingdom of Saudi Arabia, al-Mudīriyya al-ᶜĀmma li-Idhāᶜa wa'l-Ṣiḥāfa wa'l-Nashr, *al-Mamlaka al-ᶜArabiyya al-Suᶜūdiyya fi ᶜahdihā 'l-ḥāḍir* [Djudda] 1376/1956-7; Philby, *Forty years in the wilderness*, London 1957; ᶜUmar ᶜAbd al-Djabbār, *Durūs min māḍī al-taᶜlīm wa-ḥāḍirihi bi'l-Masdjid al-Ḥarām*, Cairo 1379/1959-60; Ṣāliḥ Muḥammad Djamāl, *Sundūḳ al-birr*, in *Ḳāfilat al-zayt*, vii/6, 10; Ḥāfiẓ Wahba, *Khamsūn ᶜāman fī Djazīrat al-ᶜArab*, Cairo 1380/1960; *Marble for Mecca*, in *Aramco world*, xi (Nov. 1962), 3-7; Muḥammad Tawfīḳ Ṣādiḳ, *Taṭawwur al-ḥukm fi 'l-mamlaka al-ᶜArabiyya al-Suᶜūdiyya*, al-Riyāḍ 1385/1965; Muḥammad Ṭāhir b. ᶜAbd al-Ḳādir b. Maḥmūd al-Kurdī, *al-Taʾrīkh al-ḳawīm li-Makka wa-Bayt Allāh al-Karīm*, 4 vols. Makka 1385/1965-6; Kingdom of Saudi Arabia, Ministry of Information, *Enlargement of the Prophet's mosque at Medina and the Great Mosque in Mecca*, [?al-Riyāḍ n.d.]; A. Thomas, *Saudi Arabia: a study of the educational system of the kingdom of Saudi Arabia*, Washington 1968; Kingdom of Saudi Arabia, Ministry of Finance and National Economy, Central Department of Statistics, *Statistical Yearbook, 1387 A. H., 1967 A. D.*, [al-Riyāḍ ?1388/1968]; Sir Gilbert Clayton, *An Arabian diary*, ed. R. O. Collins, Berkeley 1969; Khayr al-Dīn al-Ziriklī, *Shibh al-djazīra fī ᶜahd al-Malik ᶜAbd al-ᶜAzīz*, 3 vols., Beirut 1390/1970; *The Hajj: a special issue*, in *Aramco world* xxv (Nov.-Dec. 1974), 1-45 (excellent photographs); ᶜAbd al-Raḥmān b. ᶜAbd al-Laṭīf b. ᶜAbd Allāh Āl al-Shaykh, *Mashāhir ᶜulamāʾ Nadjd wa-ghayrihim*, [al-Riyāḍ] 1394/1974-5; Kingdom of Saudi Arabia, Saudi Arabian Monetary Agency, *Annual report*, al-Riyāḍ 1396/1976; ᶜAbd al-Raḥmān Ṣādiḳ al-Sharīf, *Djughrāfiyat al-mamlaka al-ᶜArabiyya al-Suᶜūdiyya*, i, al-Riyāḍ 1397/1977; Ḥusayn Ḥamza Bunduḳdjī, *Maps of hajj to the holyland: Mecca-Medina*, Cairo 1397/1977; idem, *Djughrāfiyat al-mamlaka al-ᶜArabiyya al-Suᶜūdiyya*, 2nd printing, Cairo 1397/1977; R. F. Nyrop *et alii*, *Area handbook for Saudi Arabia*³, Washington 1977; idem, *Atlas of Saudi Arabia*, Oxford 1398/1978; R. Baker, *King Husain and the Kingdom of Hejaz*, Cambridge 1979; D. Long, *The hajj today: a survey of the contemporary pilgrimage to Makkah*, Albany 1979 (a fundamentally important piece of research); ᶜAbd al-Madjīd Bakr, *Ashhar al-masādjid fi 'l-Islām*, i. *al-Biḳāᶜ al-Muḳaddasiyya*, Djudda [1400]/1979-80 (has major treatment of Suᶜūdī enlargement of *al-Masdjid al-Ḥarām*); Anon. (Abū Dharr, pseudonym), *Thawra fī riḥāb Makka*: *haḳīkat al-niẓām al-Suᶜūdī* [n.p. ? Kuwayt], Dār Ṣawt al-Ṭalīᶜa 1980 (an anti-Suᶜūdī, pro-neo-Ikhwān defence of the seizure of the Great Mosque in 1979); ᶜĀtiḳ b. Ghayth al-Bilādī, *Maᶜālim Makka al-taʾrīkhiyya wa'l-athariyya*, Makka 1400/1980; Ḥusayn ᶜAbd Allāh Bāsalāma, *Taʾrīkh ᶜimārat al-Masdjid al-Ḥarām* (series: al-Kitāb al-ᶜArabī al-Suᶜūdī, no. 16), Djudda 1400/1980 (originally published in 1354/1935-6); D. Stewart, *Mecca*, New York 1980; C. M. Helms, *The cohesion of Saudi Arabia*, London 1981; D. Holden and R. Johns, *The house of Saud*, London 1981; Ḥusayn Ḥamza Bunduḳdjī, *City map of Makkah Al Mukkaramah*, Jidda 1401/1981 (a useful map); Hamza Kaïdi, *La Mecque et Médine aujourd'hui*, Paris [1981]; R. Lacey, *The kingdom*, New York and London 1981; Zakī Muḥammad ᶜAlī Fārisī, *City map and Hajj guide of Makka Al Mukkaramah*, Jidda 1402-3/1982-3 (the best map available); J. Kostiner, *The making of Saudi Arabia 1917-1936* (unpubl. PhD diss., London School of Economics and Political Science), n.d.; ᶜAbd al-Laṭīf Ṣāliḥ, *Al-Mutawwif – The pilgrim's guide*, in *Ahlan wasahlan*, vii, (Dhu 'l-Ḥidjdja 1403/September 1983), 8-11; Aḥmad al-Sibāᶜī, *Taʾrīkh Makka*: *dirāsāt fi 'l-siyāsa wa'l-ᶜilm wa'l-idjtimāᶜ wa'l-ᶜumrān*,⁶ 2 vols. in 1, Makka 1404/1984; Kingdom of Saudi Arabia, Saudi Arabian Monetary Agency, Research and Statistics Department, *Statistical summary*, al-Riyāḍ 1404/1984. Important works unfortunately not consulted in the compilation of this article are: G. A. W. Makky, *Mecca: The pilgrimage city. A study of pilgrim accommodation*, London 1978; Z. Sardar and M. A. Z. Badawi, eds., *Hajj studies*, i, London [1977].

(R. B. Winder)

4. As the centre of the world

Introduction.

In Ḳurʾān, II, 144, Muslims are enjoined to face the sacred precincts in Mecca during their prayers. The Kaᶜba was adopted by Muḥammad as a physical focus of the new Muslim community, and the direction of prayer, *ḳibla*, was to serve as the sacred direction in Islam until the present day.

Since Muslims over the centuries have faced the Kaᶜba during prayer, mosques are oriented so that the prayer wall faces the Kaᶜba. The *miḥrāb* [*q.v.*] or prayer-niche in the mosque indicates the *ḳibla*, or local direction of Mecca. Islamic tradition further prescribes that certain acts such as burial of the dead, recitation of the Ḳurʾān, announcing the call to prayer, and the ritual slaughter of animals for food, be performed in the *ḳibla*, whereas expectoration and bodily functions should be performed in the perpendicular direction. Thus for close to fourteen centuries,

Muslims have been spiritually and physically oriented towards the Kaʿba and the holy city of Mecca in their daily lives, and the *ḳibla* or sacred direction is of fundamental importance in Islam [see KAʿBA and ḲIBLA, i. Ritual and legal aspects].

A statement attributed to the Prophet asserts that the Kaʿba is the *ḳibla* for people in the sacred mosque which surrounds the Kaʿba, the Mosque is the *ḳibla* for the people in the sacred precincts (*ḥaram*) of the city of Mecca and its environs, and the sacred precincts are the *ḳibla* for people in the whole world. To ʿĀʾisha and ʿAlī b. Abī Ṭālib, as well as to other early authorities, is attributed the assertion that Mecca is the centre of the world. The early Islamic traditions with Mecca as the centre and navel of the world constitute an integral part of Islamic cosmography over the centuries (see Wensinck, *Navel of the earth*, 36), although they do not feature in the most popular treatise on the subject from the late mediaeval period, namely, that of al-Suyūṭī [*q.v.*]; see Heinen, *Islamic cosmology*.

From the 3rd/9th century onwards, schemes were devised in which the world was divided into sectors (*d̲j̲iha* or *ḥadd*) about the Kaʿba. This sacred geography had several manifestations, but the different schemes proposed shared a common feature, described by al-Maḳrīzī, "The Kaʿba with respect to the inhabited parts of the world is like the centre of a circle with respect to the circle itself. All regions face the Kaʿba, surrounding it as a circle surrounds its centre, and each region faces a particular part of the Kaʿba" (*K̲h̲iṭaṭ*, i, 257-8).

Islamic sacred geography was quite separate and distinct from the mainstream Islamic tradition of mathematical geography and cartography, which owed its inspiration to the *Geography* of Ptolemy [see D̲J̲UG̲H̲RĀFIYA and K̲H̲ARĪṬA]. Indeed, it flourished mainly outside the domain of the scientists, so that a scholar such as al-Bīrūnī [*q.v.*] was apparently unaware of this tradition: see his introduction to astronomy and astrology, the *Tafhīm*, tr. R. R. Wright, London 1934, 141-2, where he discusses the Greek, Indian and Persian schemes for the division of the world, but makes no reference to any system centred on Mecca or the Kaʿba.

The orientation of the Kaʿba.

In the article KAʿBA, it is asserted that the corners of the Kaʿba face the cardinal directions. In fact, the Kaʿba has a rectangular base with sides in the ratio *ca.* 8:7 with its main axis at about 30° counter-clockwise from the meridian. When one is standing in front of any of the four walls of the Kaʿba, one is facing a significant astronomical direction; this fact was known to the first generations who had lived in or visited Mecca. In two traditions attributed to Ibn ʿAbbās and al-Ḥasan al-Baṣrī [*q.vv.*], and in several later sources on folk astronomy, it is implied that the major axis of the rectangular base of the Kaʿba points towards the rising of Canopus, the brightest star in the southern celestial hemisphere, and that the minor axis points towards summer sunrise in one direction and winter sunset in the other (Heinen, *Islamic cosmology*, 157-8).

For the latitude of Mecca, the two directions are indeed roughly perpendicular. (A modern plan of the Kaʿba and its environs, based upon aerial photography, essentially confirms the information given in the texts, but reveals more: for epoch 0 AD, the major axis is aligned with the rising of Canopus over the mountains on the southern horizon to within 2°, and the minor axis is aligned with the southernmost setting point of the moon over the south-western horizon to within 1°. This last feature of the Kaʿba is not known to be specifically mentioned in any mediaeval text, and its significance, if any, has not yet been established.) In early Islamic meteorological folklore, which appears to date back to pre-Islamic times, the Kaʿba is also associated with the winds. In one of several traditions concerning the winds in pre-Islamic Arabia, the four cardinal winds were thought of as blowing from the directions defined by the axes of the Kaʿba. This tradition is in some sources associated with Ibn ʿAbbās (see MAṬLAʿ and also Heinen, 157).

The term *ḳibla*, and the associated verb *istaḳbala* for standing in the *ḳibla*, appear to derive from the name of the east wind, the *ḳabūl*. These terms correspond to the situation where one is standing with the north wind (*al-s̲h̲amāl*) on one's left (*s̲h̲amāl*) and the Yemen on one's right (*yamīn*); see Chelhod, *Pre-eminence of the right*, 248-53; King, *Astronomical alignments*, 307-9. In other such traditions recorded in the Islamic sources, the limits of the directions from which the winds blow were defined in terms of the rising and setting of such stars and star-groups as Canopus, the Pleiades, and the stars of the handle of the Plough (which in tropical latitudes *do* rise and set), or in terms of cardinal directions or solstitial directions [see MAṬLAʿ].

It appears that in the time of the Prophet, the four corners of the Kaʿba were already named according to the geographical regions which they faced and which the Meccans knew from their trading ventures: namely, Syria, ʿIrāḳ, Yemen, and "the West". As we shall see, a division of the world into four regions about the Kaʿba is attested in one of the earliest sources for sacred geography. Since the Kaʿba has four sides as well as four corners, a division of the world into eight sectors around it would also be natural, and, as we shall see, eight-sector schemes were indeed proposed. However, in some schemes, the sectors were associated with segments of the perimeter of the Kaʿba, the walls being divided by such features as the waterspout (*mīzāb*) on the north-western wall and the door on the north-eastern wall (see Fig. 1).

The directions of sunrise and sunset at midsummer, midwinter and the equinoxes, together with the north and south points, define eight (unequal) sectors of the horizon, and, together with the directions perpendicular to the solstitial directions, define 12 (roughly equal) sectors. Each of these eight- and 12-sector schemes was used in the sacred geography of Islam.

The determination of the sacred direction

The article ḲIBLA, ii. Astronomical aspects, ignores the means which were used in popular practice for determining the sacred direction, since at the time when it was written, these had not yet been investigated. It is appropriate to consider them before turning to the topic of sacred geography *per se*.

From the 3rd/9th century onwards, Muslim astronomers working in the tradition of classical astronomy devised methods to compute the *ḳibla* for any locality from the available geographical data. For them, the *ḳibla* was the direction of the great circle joining the locality to Mecca, measured as an angle to the local meridian. The determination of the *ḳibla* according to this definition is a non-trivial problem of mathematical geography, whose solution involves the application of complicated trigonometric formulae or geometrical constructions. Lists of *ḳibla* values for different localities and tables displaying the *ḳibla* for each

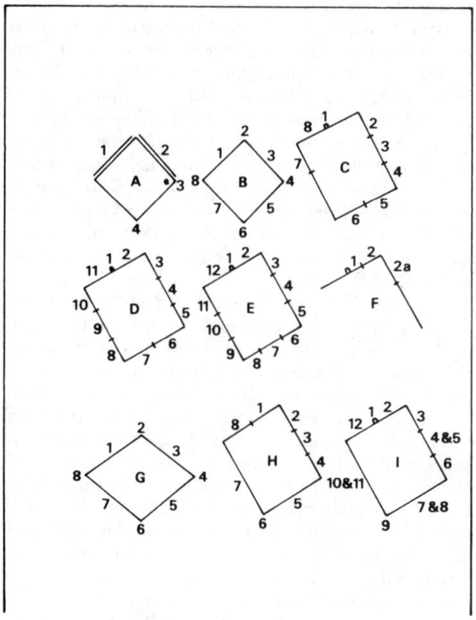

Fig. 1. Different schemes for dividing the perimeter of the Kaᶜba to correspond to different localities in the surrounding world. The Black Stone is in the south-eastern corner; the door is on the north-eastern wall; the blocked door is on the south-western wall; and the waterspout is on the north-western wall.

degree of longitude and latitude difference from Mecca were available. Details of this activity are given in ḲIBLA. ii. Astronomical aspects. However, mathematical methods were not available to the Muslims before the late 2nd/8th and early 3rd/9th centuries. And what is more important, even in later centuries, the *ḳibla* was not generally found by computation anyway.

In some circles, the practice of the Prophet in Medina was imitated: he had prayed southwards towards Mecca, and there were those who were content to follow his example and pray towards the south wherever they were, be it in Andalusia or Central Asia. Others followed the practice of the first generations of Muslims who laid out the first mosques in different parts of the new Islamic commonwealth. Some of these mosques were converted from earlier religious edifices, the orientation of which was considered acceptable for the *ḳibla*; such was the case, for example, in Jerusalem and Damascus, where the *ḳibla* adopted was roughly due south.

Other early mosques were laid out in directions defined by astronomical horizon phenomena, such as the risings and settings of the sun at the equinoxes or solstices and of various prominent stars or star-groups; such was the case, for example, in Egypt and Central Asia, where the earliest mosques were aligned towards winter sunrise and winter sunset, respectively. The directions known as *ḳiblat al-ṣaḥāba*, the "*ḳibla* of the Companions", remained popular over the centuries, their acceptability ensured by the Prophetic dictum: "My Companions are like stars to be guided by: whenever you follow their example you will be rightly guided".

Astronomical alignments were used for the *ḳibla* because the first generations of Muslims who were familiar with the Kaᶜba knew that when they stood in front of the edifice, they were facing a particular astronomical direction. In order to face the appropriate part of the Kaᶜba which was associated with their ultimate geographical location, they used the same astronomically-defined direction for the *ḳibla* as they would have been standing directly in front of that particular segment of the perimeter of the Kaᶜba. This notion of the *ḳibla* is, of course, quite different from that used by the astronomers. Such simple methods for finding the *ḳibla* by astronomical horizon phenomena (called *dalāʾil*) are outlined both in legal texts and in treatises dealing with folk astronomy. In the mediaeval sources, we also find *ḳibla* directions expressed in terms of wind directions: as noted above, several wind schemes, defined in terms of solar or stellar risings and settings, were part of the folk astronomy and meteorology of pre-Islamic Arabia.

The non-mathematical tradition of folk astronomy practiced by Muslims in the mediaeval period was based solely on observable phenomena, such as the risings and settings of celestial bodies and their passages across the sky, and also involved the association of meteorological phenomena, such as the winds, with phenomena in the sky [see ANWĀʾ, MANĀZIL, MAṬLAᶜ and RĪḤ]. Adapted primarily from pre-Islamic Arabia, folk astronomy flourished alongside mathematical astronomy over the centuries, but was far more widely known and practised. Even the legal scholars accepted it because of Ḳurʾān, XVI, 16, "... and by the star[s] [men] shall be guided". There were four main applications of this traditional astronomical folklore: (1) the regulation of the Muslim lunar calendar; (2) the determination of the times of the five daily prayers, which are astronomically defined; (3) finding the *ḳibla* by non-mathematical procedures; and (4) the organisation of agricultural activities in the solar calendar (see King, *Ethnoastronomy*, and Varisco, *Agricultural almanac*).

Historical evidence of clashes between the two traditions is rare. Al-Bīrūnī made some disparaging remarks about those who sought to find the *ḳibla* by means of the winds and the lunar mansions (*Kitāb Taḥdīd nihāyāt al-amākin*, tr. J. Ali as *The determination of the coordinates of cities*, Beirut 1967, 12 (slightly modified): "When [some people] were asked to determine the direction of the *ḳibla*, they became perplexed because the solution of the problem was beyond their scientific powers. You see that they have been discussing completely irrelevant phenomena such as the directions from which the winds blow and the risings of the lunar mansions".

But the legal scholars made equally disparaging and far more historically significant remarks about the scientists. According to the 7th/13th century Yemeni legal scholar al-Aṣbaḥī (ms. Cairo Dār al-Kutub, *mīḳāt* 984, 1, fol. 6a-b): "The astronomers have taken their knowledge from Euclid, [the authors of] the *Sindhind*, Aristotle and other philosophers, and all of them were infidels".

It is quite apparent from the orientations of mediaeval mosques that astronomers were seldom consulted in their construction. Indeed, from the available architectural and also textual evidence, it is clear that in mediaeval times several different and often widely-divergent *ḳibla*s were accepted in specific cities and regions. Among the legal scholars there were those who favoured facing the Kaᶜba directly (*ᶜayn al-Kaᶜba*), usually with some traditionally acceptable astronomical alignment such as winter sunrise, and others who said that facing the general direction of the Kaᶜba (*djihat al-Kaᶜba*) was sufficient (see Pl. 1).

Thus, for example, there were legal scholars in mediaeval Cordova who maintained that the entire south-eastern quadrant could serve as the *ḳibla* (see King, *Qibla in Cordova,* 372, 374).

Islamic sacred geography

The earliest known Kaʿba-centred geographical scheme is recorded in the *Kitāb al-Masālik wa 'l-mamālik,* ed. de Goeje, 5, of the 3rd/9th century scholar Ibn Khurradādhbih [*q.v.*]. Even if the scheme is not original to him, there is no reason to suppose that it is any later than his time. In this scheme, represented in Fig. 2, the region between North-West Africa and Northern Syria is associated with the north-west wall of the Kaʿba and has a *ḳibla* which varies from east to south. The region between Armenia and Kashmir is associated with the north-east wall of the Kaʿba and has a *ḳibla* which varies from south to west. A third region, India, Tibet and China, is associated with the Black Stone in the eastern corner of the Kaʿba, and, for this reason, is stated to have a *ḳibla* a little north of west. A fourth region, the Yemen, is associated with the southern corner of the Kaʿba and has a *ḳibla* of due north.

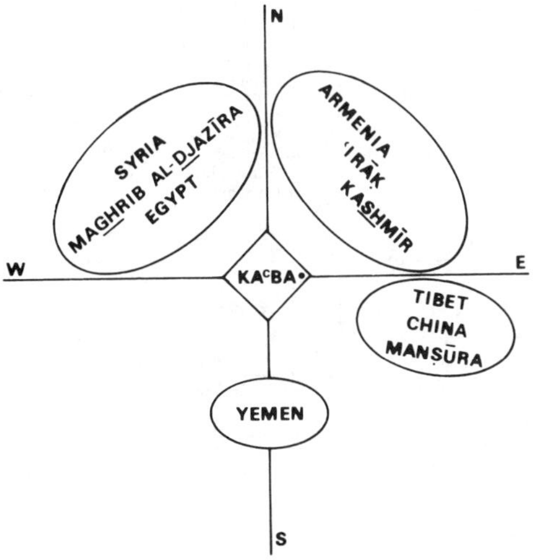

Fig. 2. A simple scheme of sacred geography in the published text of the *Kitāb al-Masālik* of Ibn Khurradādhbih.

The 4th/10th century legal scholar Ibn al-Ḳāṣṣ wrote a treatise entitled *Dalāʾil al-ḳibla* which is unfortunately not extant in its entirety. The Beirut ms. is lost, and the Istanbul and Cairo mss. (Veliyuddin 2453,2 and Dār al-Kutub, *mīḳāt* 1201) are quite different in content. In the Istanbul copy, Ibn al-Ḳāṣṣ states that the world is centred on the Kaʿba and then presents a traditional Ptolemaic survey of the seven climates [see IḲLĪM]. In the Cairo copy, he surveys the different stars and star-groups used for finding the *ḳibla.*

The principal scholar involved in the development of sacred geography was Muḥammad b. Surāḳa al-ʿĀmirī, a Yemeni *faḳīh* who studied in Basra and died in the Yemen in 410/1019. Little is known about this individual, and none of his works are known to survive in their original form. However, from quotations in later works, it appears that he devised a total of three distinct schemes, with eight, 11 and 12 sectors around the Kaʿba. In each scheme, several prescriptions for finding the *ḳibla* in each region are outlined. Ibn Surāḳa explains in words and without recourse to any diagrams how one should stand with respect to the risings or settings of some four stars and the four winds; the actual direction which these prescriptions are intended to help one face is not specifically stated. Thus, for example, people in ʿIrāḳ and Iran should face the north-east wall of the Kaʿba, and to achieve this one should stand so that the stars of the Plough rise behind one's right ear, the lunar mansion al-Hanʿa rises directly behind one's back, the Pole Star is at one's right shoulder, the East wind blows at one's left shoulder, and the West wind blows at one's right cheek, and so on (see Table 1). Ibn Surāḳa did not actually point out that the *ḳibla* in ʿIrāḳ was toward winter sunset.

Ibn Surāḳa's eight-sector scheme is known from the writings of one Ibn Raḥīḳ, a legal scholar of Mecca in the 5th/11th century, who wrote a treatise on folk astronomy (extant in the unique Berlin ms. Ahlwardt 5664; see especially fols. 23a-25b). Several significant regions of the Muslim world were omitted from this scheme. A similar but more refined eight-sector scheme is proposed by the 7th/13th century Libyan philologist Ibn al-Adjdābī [*q.v.*] (*Kitāb al-Azmina...*, ed. I. Hassan, 120-35). Here eight sectors are neatly associated with the four walls and the four corners of the Kaʿba, and the *ḳibla*s in each region are defined in terms of the cardinal directions and sunrise and sunset at the solstices. A cruder scheme based on the same notion is proposed by the 6th/12th century Egyptian legal scholar al-Dimyāṭī (ms. Damascus, Ẓāhiriyya 5579, fol. 14a). He represents the Kaʿba by a circle and associates each of the eight regions around the Kaʿba with a wind (see Pl. 2).

Yet another eight-sector scheme is presented in an anonymous treatise preserved in a 12th/18th century Ottoman Egyptian manuscript (Cairo, Ṭalʿat, *madjāmīʿ* 811,6, fols. 59a-61a (see Pl. 3). From internal evidence, it is clear that this scheme, in which the *ḳibla*s are actually defined in terms of the stars which rise or set behind one's back when one is standing in the *ḳibla* and in terms of the Pole Star, was already at least five centuries old when it was copied in this manuscript. For example, various 7th/13th century Yemeni astronomical sources contain 12-sector schemes based on precisely the same eight *ḳibla* directions. In the eight-sector scheme, Palestine had been omitted and two regions were associated with two entire walls of the Kaʿba. The individual who first devised this particular 12-sector scheme added a sector for Palestine and three more for segments of those two walls.

Ibn Surāḳa's 11-sector scheme is known from an 8th/14th (?) century Egyptian treatise (ms. Milan Ambrosiana, II.75 (A75), 20, fols. 174a-177b), and in it he has simply added three sectors to his eight-sector scheme and modified the prescriptions for finding the *ḳibla.* His 12-sector scheme is yet more refined. It was used by al-Dimyāṭī in his *Kitāb al-Tahdhīb fī maʿrifat dalāʾil al-ḳibla* (ms. Oxford, Bodleian Marsh 592, fols. 97b-101b, and 126a-28a), who complained that Ibn Surāḳa had placed Damascus and Medina in the same sector, and so he himself presented a 13-sector scheme, subdividing the sector for Syria and the Ḥidjāz. Ibn Surāḳa's 12-sector scheme was also used by the 7th/13th century Yemeni astronomer al-Fārisī in his treatise on folk astronomy. The unique copy of this work (ms. Milan Ambrosiana X73 sup.) includes diagrams of Ibn Surāḳa's 12-sector scheme and the different 12-sector scheme discussed above (see Pl. 4).

Table 1: *Ḳibla* indicators in the eight- and eleven-sector schemes of Ibn Surāḳa

Ms. Berlin Ahlwardt 5664, fols. 23a-25b		Ms. Milan Ambrosiana A75,20, fols. 174a-177b	
BN = Banāt Naʿsh; EW = east wind; NW = north wind; PS = Pole Star; SW = south wind; WW = west wind			
1. Medina, Palestine (Waterspout)	BN setting behind Canopus rising in front (al-Dimyāṭī (ms. Oxford Marsh 592. fol. 100b) attributes: NW intermediate wind behind BN setting behind PS behind left shoulder)	1. As in 8-sector scheme ,,	BN setting behind Canopus rising in front Vega rising at left ear Vega setting behind right ear EW at left eye NW behind left ear WW behind right ear SW at right eyebrow
		2. Syria (Waterspout to Syrian Corner)	BN rising behind left ear PS at left shoulder, al-Haḳʿa rising at left EW at left cheek NW at joint of right shoulder WW at right ear towards nape SW in front
2. Djazīra, Armenia (Syrian Corner to *Muṣallā* of Adam)	Winter sunrise at bone behind left ear EW at left shoulder NW at right cheek WW in front SW at left eye	3. As in 8-sector scheme ,,	Capella rising between behind left ear and nape Capella setting at right side PS between right ear and behind nape Winter sunrise at bone behind left ear EW at left shoulder NW at right cheek WW at right side of neck SW at left eye
3. C. ʿIrāḳ, N. Iran, Transoxania (*Muṣallā* of Adam to Door)	BN rising behind right ear al-Hanʿa rising behind PS at right shoulder EW at left shoulder NW between right side of neck and nape WW at right cheek SW at left cheek	4. ,, ,,	BN rising at right ear al-Hanʿa rising between directly behind and behind left ear PS at right shoulder EW at left shoulder NW between right side of neck and nape WW at right cheek SW at left cheek
4. S. ʿIraḳ, S. Iran, China (Door to ʿIrāḳī Corner)	PS at right ear Vega rising behind al-Shawla setting in front Summer sunrise behind right shoulder EW at left shoulder NW at right ear WW in front SW at left side of neck	5. ,, ,,	PS at right ear Vega [rising] behind al-Shawla setting in front Summer sunrise behind right shoulder EW at left shoulder NW at right ear WW at right cheek SW at left eye
5. Sind, India, Afghanistan (ʿIrāḳī Corner to *Muṣallā* of the Prophet)	BN rising at left cheek (*sic*) PS behind (*sic*) EW behind left ear NW at right cheek SW at left shoulder	6. ,, ,,	BN rising at righ cheek PS at right eye EW behind right ear NW at right cheek WW at left cheek SW at left shoulder
6. Yemen, Hadramawt (*Muṣallā* of the Prophet to Yemeni Corner)	PS in front Canopus rising at right ear (*sic*) Canopus setting behind left ear Winter sunrise at right ear EW at right shoulder NW in front SW at right shoulder (*sic*)	7. ,, ,,	PS in front Canopus rising at right ear (*sic*) Canopus setting behind left ear Winter sunrise at right ear EW at right shoulder NW in front WW at left side SW at left shoulder
		8. Ethiopia (Yemeni Corner to Blocked Door)	Pleiades rising in front Sirius and Capella rising at right eye PS at left ear EW at right ear NW in front WW on left SW behind
		9. Sudan (Blocked Corner to 7 cubis short of Western Corner)	Capella rising in front Pleiades rising at right eye al-Shawla setting behind PS at left cheek Summer sunrise in front Winter sunset behind EW at right eye NW at left eyebrow WW at left ear SW at left shoulder
7. Andalusia, Maghrib, Ifrīḳiya, Ethiopia (7 cubits from Western Corner to Corner itself)	Pleiades rising in front Sirius rising at right eye EW in front WW behind NW at left shoulder SW at right shoulder	10. Andalusia, Maghrib, Ifrīḳiya As in 8-sector scheme	Pleiades rising in front Sirius rising at righ eye Capella setting behind nape EW in front WW behind NW at left shoulder SW at right shoulder
8. Egypt, coast of Maghrib and Ifrīḳiya	BN setting at right shoulder BN rising at left shoulder PS behind WW at right	11. ,, ,,	*al-Zubānā* (*al-Aḥmira*) rising in front BN setting at left shoulder BN rising at left ear NW behind left ear EW at left side

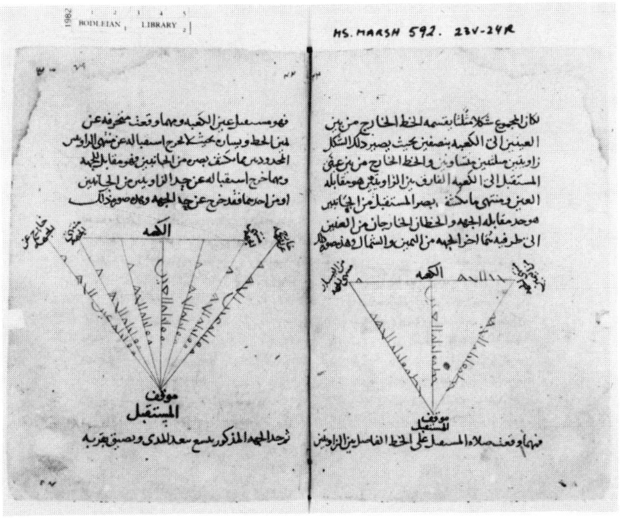

1. Diagrams in the unique manuscript of the *Tahdhīb* of al-Dimyāṭī displaying the notions of *ʿayn al-Kaʿba*, facing the Kaʿba head on, and *djihat al-Kaʿba*, facing the general direction of the Kaʿba, that is, anywhere within the field of vision (*ca.* 90°) of a person facing the Kaʿba head on. Taken from ms. Oxford Bodleian Marsh 592, fols. 23b-24a.

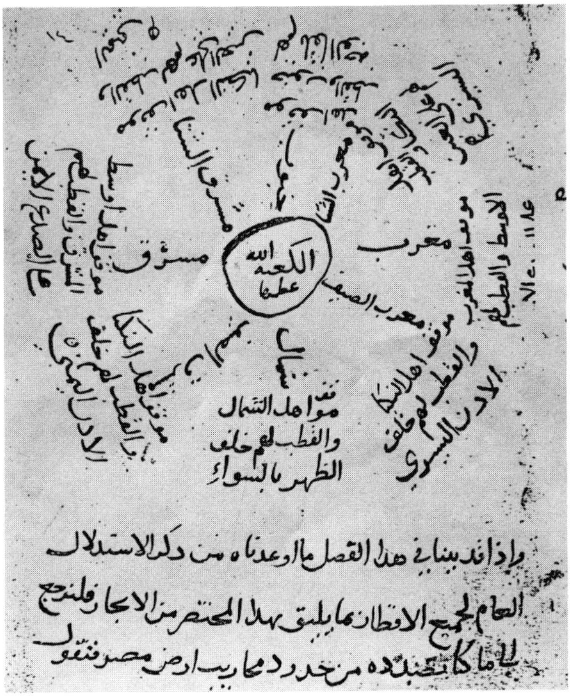

2. An illustration of al-Dimyāṭī's eight-sector *ḳibla* scheme in the unique copy of his shorter treatise on the *ḳibla*. The directions of the *ḳibla* are defined in each sector in terms of the Pole Star. Taken from ms. Damascus Ẓāhiriyya 5579, fol. 14a.

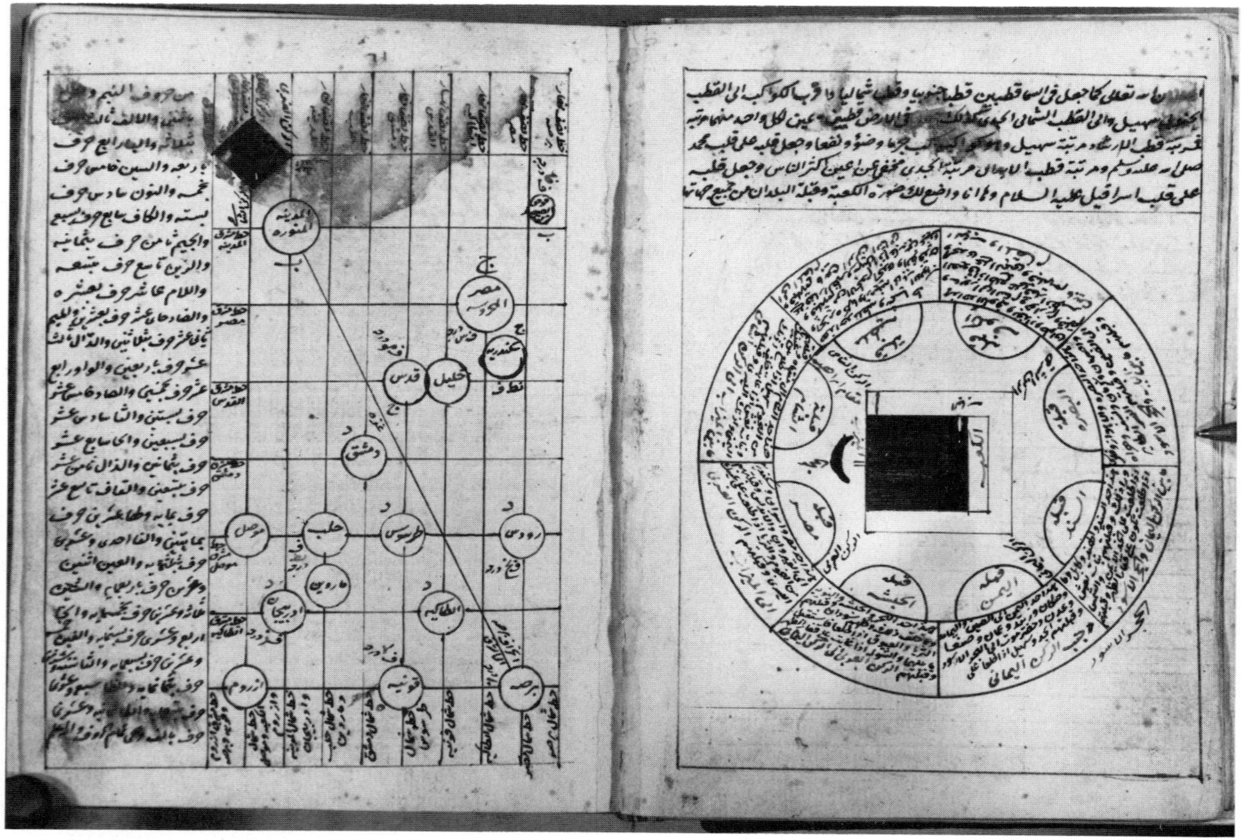

3. Two illustrations from an anonymous treatise on the *ḳibla* and the Kaʿba of uncertain provenance. On the left is a latitude and longitude grid with various localities marked, as well as the Kaʿba, shown in the upper left corner, inclined to the meridian. (No such diagram is contained in any scientific treatise from the mediaeval Islamic period.) On the right is an eight-sector *ḳibla* scheme not attested in any other known source. The main *ḳibla* indicators used in each sector are the risings or settings of prominent stars which should be *directly behind* the person facing the *ḳibla*: this suggests that they were determined by someone standing with his back to the appropriate part of the Kaʿba looking towards those regions. Taken from ms. Cairo Talʿat *madjāmīʿ* 811, fols. 59b-60a.

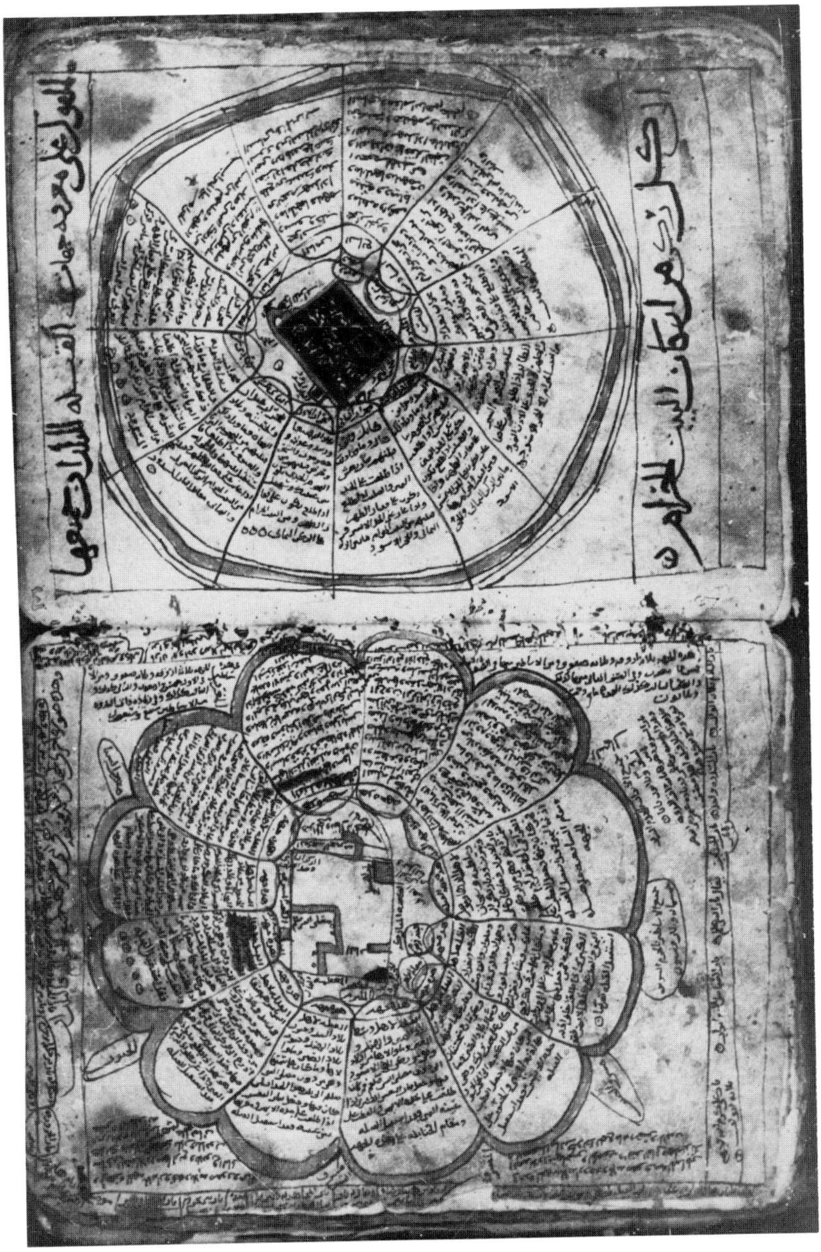

4. Two 12-sector diagrams occuring at the end of the unique complete copy of a treatise on folk astronomy by the 7th/13th century Yemeni scholar Muḥammad b. Abī Bakr al-Fārisī. The one on the left corresponds roughly to the scheme described in the text of al-Fārisī's treatise. Notice that the scheme is surrounded by a schematic representation of the Sacred Mosque. The one on the right is developed from the eight-sector scheme of Ibn Surāḳa. Taken from ms. Milan Ambrosiana Griffini 37, unfoliated.

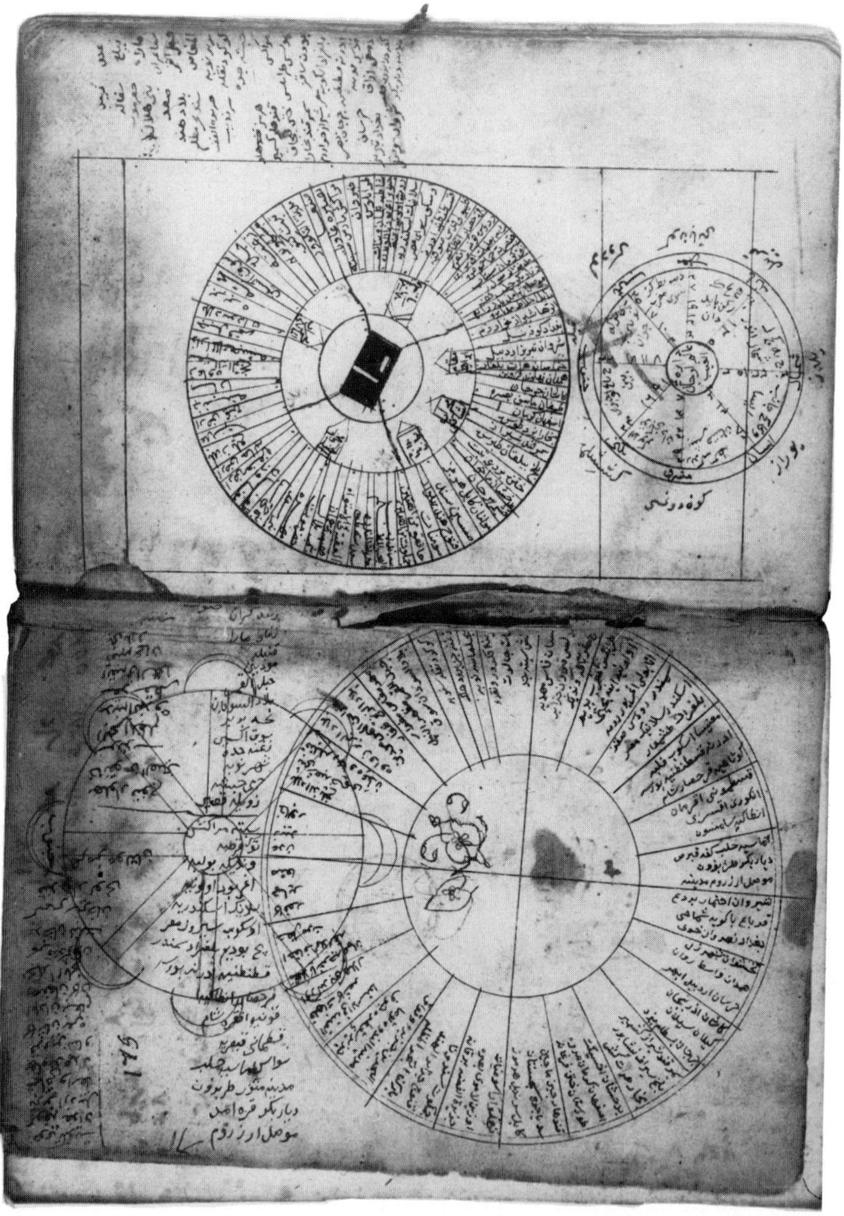

5. On these flyleaves of an Ottoman Turkish copy of a 10th/16th century Syrian *zīdj* are preserved four different schemes of sacred geography. Two are represented graphically, and two others by ordered lists of localities (upper left and upper right). In addition, there is (lower right) a diagram for locating the so-called *ridjāl al-ghayb*, intermediaries between God and man, belief in whom was widespread amongst Ṣūfīs in Ottoman times. Taken from ms. Paris B.N. ar. 2520.

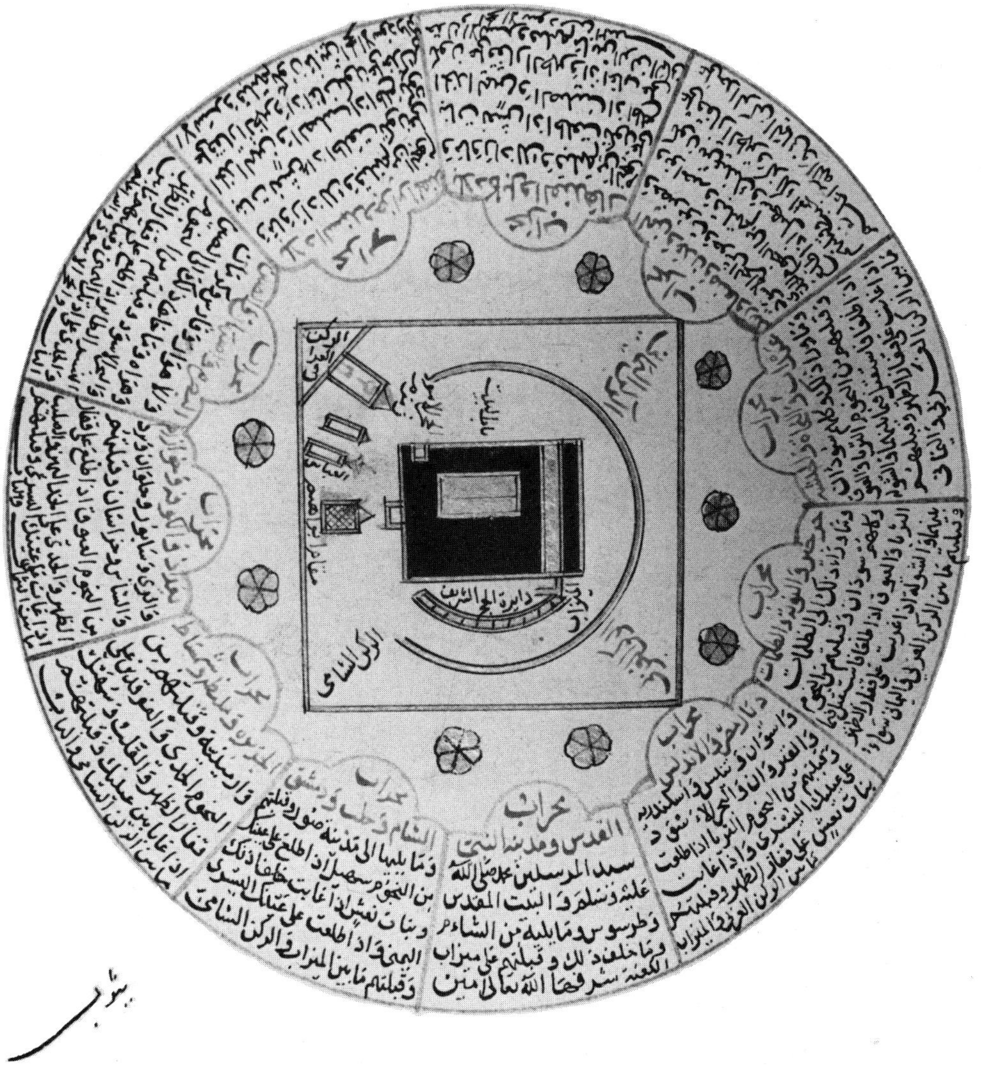

6. A defective diagram of a 12-sector scheme (simplified from that of Ibn Surāḳa) in an elegantly copied manuscript of Ibn al-Wardī's *Cosmography*. As in some diagrams of this kind in various copies of al-Ḳazwīnī's *Āthār al-bilād*, there are only 11 sectors: presumably at some stage in the transmission someone noticed that, because of copyists' errors in some copies of the text, Medina occurred in two sectors. The one omitted here is the one in which Medina had been entered by mistake. Taken from ms. Istanbul Topkapi Ahmet III 3020, fol. 52b.

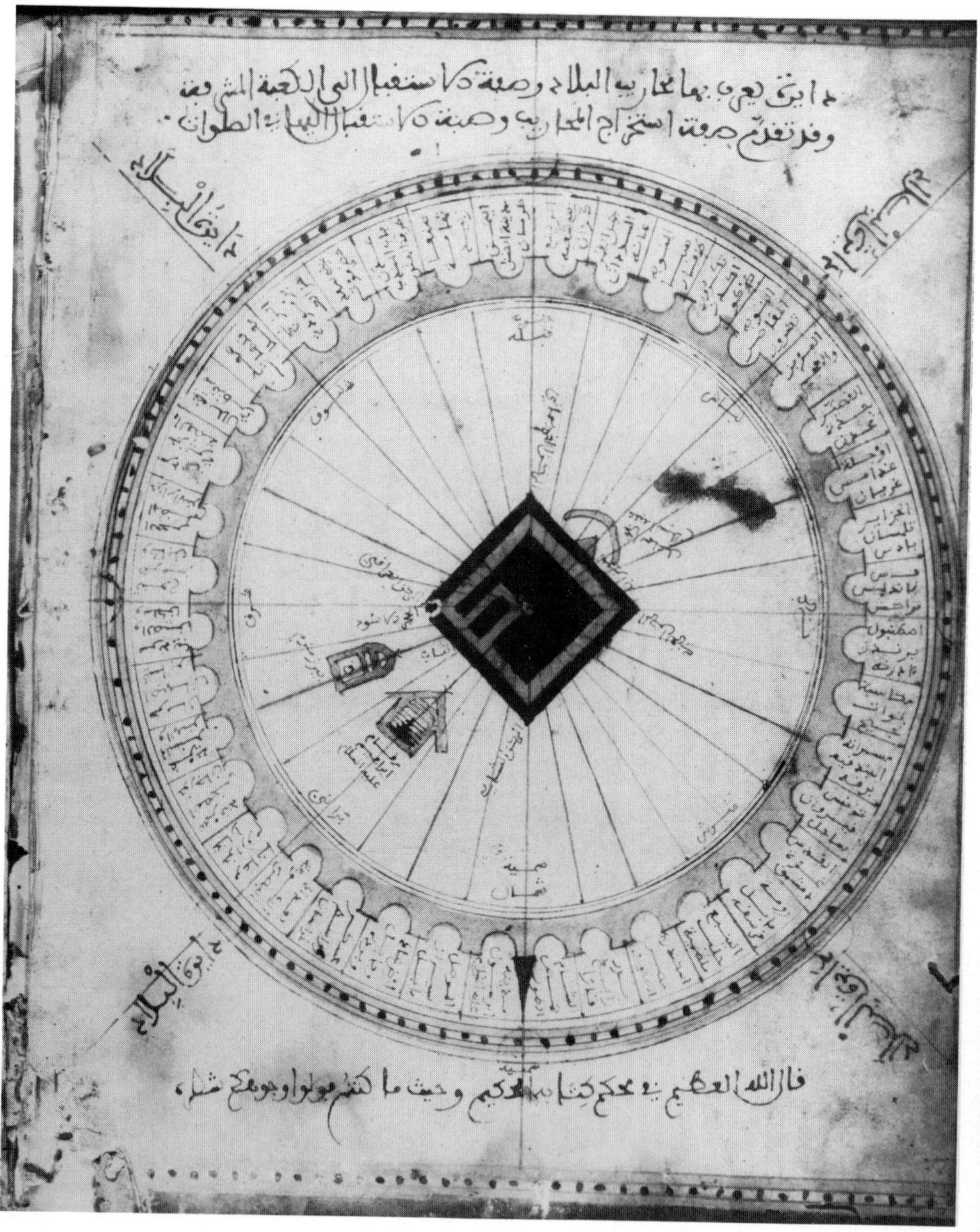

7. The 40-sector scheme of al-Ṣafāḳusī, superimposed on a 32-division windrose. The order of the localities around the Kaᶜba differs somewhat in the two extant copies of this chart. Taken from ms. Paris B.N. ar. 2278, fol. 2b.

Several sources contain schemes in which the prescriptions for finding the *ḳibla* in each region of the world are based only on the Pole Star (*al-Djudayy* or *al-Ḳuṭb*). Although the earliest known scheme of this kind dates from the 6th/12th century, others must have been in circulation prior to this time, since al-Bīrūnī (*Taḥdīd*, tr. Ali, 13, modified) wrote: "Of the majority of people [who write about the *ḳibla* in non-mathematical terms], none are closer to the truth than those who use (*iʿtabarahu bi-*) the Pole Star known as *al-Djudayy*. By means of its fixed position, the direction of a person travelling can be specified approximately".

The most detailed scheme of this kind is recorded by the 7th/13th century Egyptian legal scholar Shihāb al-Dīn al-Ḳarāfī [*q.v.*] in his *Dhakhīra*, ed. Cairo, i, 489-508; in this, some nine regions of the world are identified and instructions for finding the *ḳibla* are given as follows: "[The inhabitants of] Sind and India stand with [the Pole star] at their [right] cheeks and they face due west, etc." See Fig. 3 for a simplified version of this kind of scheme.

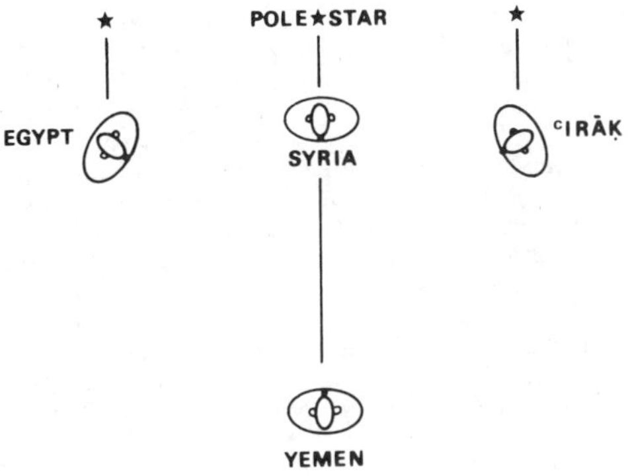

Fig. 3. A simple scheme for using the Pole Star to face Mecca recorded in a late Ottoman Egyptian text, typical of much earlier prescription for finding the *ḳibla*.

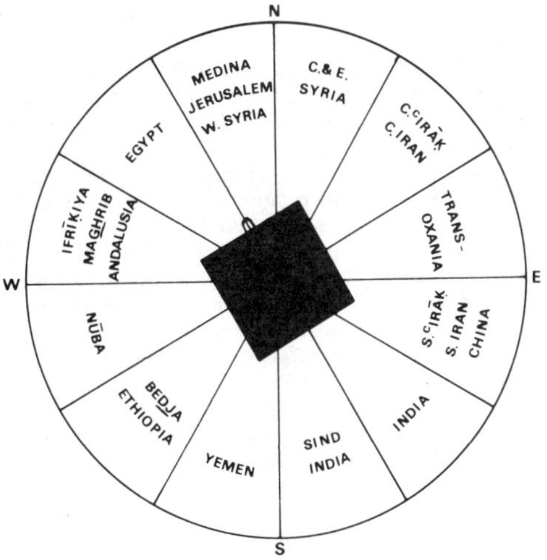

Fig. 4. A simplified version of the 12-sector scheme of sacred geography found in some manuscripts of the *Āthār al-bilād* of al-Ḳazwīnī.

At least one of the 12-sector schemes mentioned above must have been in circulation outside the Yemen before the 7th/13th century, because it was copied by the geographer Yāḳūt (*Buldān*, Eng. tr. Jwaideh, 51), who worked in Syria in *ca.* 600/1200. The instructions for finding the *ḳibla* are omitted from his diagram. A similar diagram is presented in al-Ḳazwīnī's *Āthār al-bilād*, 76, (see Fig. 4), and the same scheme is described in words in al-Ḳalḳashandī, *Ṣubḥ*, iv, 251-5. Another such simple 12-sector scheme occurs in the cosmography *Kharīdat al-ʿadjāʾib* of the 9th/15th century Syrian writer Ibn al-Wardī [*q.v.*], a work which was exceedingly popular in later centuries. In some copies of this, a diagram of an eight-sector scheme is presented. In others, diagrams of 18-, 34-, 35-, or 36-sectors schemes occur. In one manuscript of a Turkish translation of his treatise (ms. Istanbul Topkapı, Turkish 1340 = Bağdat 179), there is a diagram of a scheme with 72 sectors. In the published edition of the Arabic text (Cairo 1863, 70-1), extremely corrupt versions of both the 12- and the eight-sector schemes are included.

These simple diagrams were often much abused by ignorant copyists, and even in elegantly copied manuscripts we find the corners of the Kaʿba mislabelled and the localities around the Kaʿba confused. In some copies of the works of al-Ḳazwīnī and Ibn al-Wardī containing the 12-sector scheme, Medına occurs in more than one sector. In other copies, one of these two sectors has been suppressed and only 11 sectors appear around the Kaʿba (see Pl. 5).

Yet another scheme occurs in the navigational atlas of the 10th/16th century Tunisian scholar ʿAlī al-Sharafī al-Ṣafāḳusī (see Pl. 6). There are 40 *miḥrāb*s around the Kaʿba, represented by a square with its corners facing in the cardinal directions, and also by the fact that the scheme is superimposed upon a 32-division wind-rose, a device used by Arab sailors to find directions at sea by the risings and settings of the stars. Even though al-Ṣafāḳusī had compiled maps of the Mediterranean coast, the order and arrangement of localities about the Kaʿba in his diagram in each of the available copies (mss. Paris, B.N. ar. 2273 and Oxford, Bodleian Marsh 294) are rather inaccurate. Again, no *ḳibla* indications are presented.

Mainly through the writings of al-Ḳazwīnī and Ibn al-Wardī, these simplified 12-sector schemes were copied right up to the 19th century. By then, their original compiler had long been forgotten, and Muslim scholars interested in the sciences were starting to use Western geographical concepts and coordinates anyway. In most regions of the Islamic world, traditional *ḳibla* directions which had been used over the centuries were abandoned for a new direction computed for the locality in question using modern geographical coordinates.

The orientation of Islamic religious architecture

A variety of different *ḳibla* values was used in each of the major centres of Islamic civilisation (see King, *Sacred direction*). In any one locality, there were *ḳibla*s advocated by religious tradition, including both cardinal directions and astronomical alignments advocated in texts on folk astronomy or legal texts, as well as the directions computed by the astronomers (by both accurate and approximate mathematical procedures). This situation explains the diversity of mosque orientations in any given region of the Islamic world. However, since very few mediaeval mosques have been surveyed properly for their orientations, it is not yet possible to classify them, and for the present we are forced to rely mainly on the information contained in the mediaeval written sources.

In Cordova, for example, as we know from a 6th/12th century treatise on the astrolabe, some mosques were laid out towards winter sunrise (roughly 30° S. of E.), because it was thought that this would make their *ḳibla* walls parallel to the north-west wall of the Kaᶜba. The Grand Mosque there faces a direction perpendicular to summer sunrise (roughly 30° E. of S.), for the very same reason: this explains why it faces the deserts of Algeria rather than the deserts of Arabia. In fact, the axis of the Mosque is "parallel" to the main axis of the Kaᶜba.

In Samarḳand, as we know from a 5th/11th century legal treatise, the main mosque was oriented towards winter sunset, in order that it should face the north-east wall of the Kaᶜba. Other mosques in Samarḳand were built facing due west because the road to Mecca left Samarḳand towards the west, and yet others were built facing due south because the Prophet, when he was in Medina, had said that the *ḳibla* was due south, and some religious authorities interpreted this as being universally valid.

Similar situations could be cited for other mediaeval cities. In some of these, the *ḳibla*, or rather, the various different directions accepted for the *ḳibla*, have played an important role in the development of the entire city in mediaeval times. Investigations of the orientations of Islamic cities are still in an early phase. However, the city of Cairo represents a particularly interesting case of a city oriented towards the Kaᶜba.

The first mosque in Egypt was built in Fusṭāṭ in the 1st/7th century facing due east, and then a few years later was altered to face winter sunrise (about 27° S. of E.). The first direction was probably chosen to ensure that the Mosque faced the Western Corner of the Kaᶜba, the second to ensure that it faced the north-western wall, but these reasons are not mentioned in the historical sources. When the new city of al-Ḳāhira was founded in the 4th/10th century, it was built with a roughly orthogonal street plan alongside the Pharaonic canal linking the Nile with the Red Sea. Now, quite fortuitously, it happened that the canal was perpendicular to the direction of winter sunrise. Thus the entire city was oriented in the "*ḳibla* of the Companions". The Fāṭimids who built al-Ḳāhira erected the first mosques in the new city (the Mosque of al-Ḥākim and the Azhar Mosque) in the *ḳibla* of the astronomers, which at 37° S. of E. was 10° south of the *ḳibla* of the Companions. Thus their mosques were skew to the street plan.

The Mamlūks built their mosques and *madrasas* in such a way that the exteriors were in line with the street plan and the interiors skew to the exteriors and in line with the *ḳibla* of the astronomers. When they laid out the "City of the Dead" outside Cairo, they aligned the street and the mausolea with the *ḳibla* of the astronomers. In the other main area of greater Cairo known as al-Ḳarāfa, both the streets and the mosques follow a southerly *ḳibla* orientation. Al-Maḳrīzī discussed the problem of the different orientations of mosques in Egypt, but without reference to the street plan of Cairo. Now that the methods used in mediaeval times for finding the *ḳibla* are understood, the orientation of mediaeval Islamic religious architecture in particular and cities in general is a subject which calls out for further investigation.

Concluding remarks

This purely Islamic development of a sacred geography featuring the world centred on the Kaᶜba, provided a simple practical means for Muslims to face the Kaᶜba in prayer. For the pious, to whom the "science of the ancients" was anathema, this tradition constituted an acceptable alternative to the mathematical *ḳibla* determinations of the astronomers. As noted above, it was actually approved of by the legal scholars, not least because of Ḳurʾān XVI, 16. The number and variety of the texts in which this sacred geography is attested indicate that it was widely known from the 4th/10th century onwards, if not among the scientific community. The broad spectra of *ḳibla* values accepted at different times in different places attest to the multiplicity of ways used by Muslims to face the Kaᶜba over the centuries, and all of this activity was inspired by the belief that the Kaᶜba, as the centre of the world and the focus of Muslim worship, was a physical pointer to the presence of God.

Bibliography: On the early Islamic traditions about Mecca as the centre of the world, see A. J. Wensinck, *The ideas of the Western Semites concerning the Navel of the Earth,* Amsterdam 1915, repr. in *Studies of A. J. Wensinck,* New York 1978. On early Islamic traditions about cosmology in general, see A. Heinen, *Islamic cosmology: a study of al-Suyūṭī's al-Hayʾa al-saniyya fī al-hayʾa al-sunniyya,* Beirut 1982.

On the Kaᶜba, see in addition to the bibliography cited in KAᶜBA, J. Chelhod, *A Contribution to the problem of the pre-eminence of the right, based upon Arabic evidence* (tr. from the French), in R. Needham, *Right and left,* Chicago 1973, 239-62; B. Finster, *Zu der Neuauflage von K. A. C. Creswell's Early Muslim Architecture,* in *Kunst des Orients,* ix (1972), 89-98, esp. 94; G. S. Hawkins and D. A. King, *On the orientation of the Kaᶜba,* in *Jnal. for the Hist. of Astronomy,* xiii (1982), 102-9; King, *Astronomical alignments in medieval Islamic religious architecture,* in *Annals of the New York Academy of Sciences,* ccclxxxv (1982), 303-12; G. Lüling, *Der christliche Kult an der vorislamischen Kaaba ...,* Erlangen 1977, and other works by the same author; G. R. Hawting, *Aspects of Muslim political and religious history in the 1st/7th century, with especial reference to the development of the Muslim sanctuary,* University of London Ph. D. thesis, 1978 unpublished.

On Islamic folk astronomy, see in addition to the articles ANWĀʾ, MANĀZIL and MAṬLAᶜ, King, *Ethnoastronomy and mathematical astronomy in the Medieval Near East,* and D. M. Varisco, *An agricultural almanac by the Yemeni Sultan al-Ashraf,* in *Procs. of the First International Symposium on Ethnoastronomy, Washington, D.C. 1983* (forthcoming).

All available sources on Islamic sacred geography (some 30 in number) are surveyed in King, *The sacred geography of Islam,* in *Islamic Art,* iii (1983) (forthcoming). For an overview of the *ḳibla* problem, see idem, *The world about the Kaᶜba: a study of the sacred direction in Islam* (forthcoming), and its summary, *The sacred direction in Islam: a study of the interaction of science and religion in the Middle Ages,* in *Interdisciplinary Science Reviews,* x (1984), 315-28.

On the possibility of a *ḳibla* towards the east before the adoption of the *ḳibla* towards the Kaᶜba, see W. Barthold, *Die Orientierung der ersten muhammadanischen Moscheen,* in *Isl.,* xviii (1929), 245-50, and King, *Astronomical alignments,* 309.

On the orientation of Islamic religious architecture, see King, *op. cit.,* and on the situations in Cordova, Cairo and Samarḳand, see *Three sundials from Islamic Andalusia, Appx. A: Some medieval values of the Qibla at Cordova,* in *Jnal. for the Hist. of Arabic Science,* ii (1978), 370-87; *Architecture and astronomy:*

the ventilators of medieval Cairo and their secrets, in *JAOS,* civ (1984), 97-133; *Al-Bazdawī on the Qibla in Transoxania,* in *JHAS,* vii (1983), 3-38. In 1983, a treatise on the problems associated with the *ḳibla* in early Islamic Iran by the 5th/11th century legal scholar and mathematician ʿAbd al-Ḳāhir al-Baghdādī was identified in ms. Tashkent, Oriental Institute 177; this awaits investigation. No doubt other treatises on the problems of the *ḳibla* in West and East Africa and in India were prepared, but these have not been located yet in the manuscript sources. (D. A. KING)

AL-**MAḲḲARĪ**, SHIHĀB AL-DĪN ABU 'L-ʿABBĀS AḤMAD B. MUḤAMMAD B. AḤMAD B. YAḤYĀ AL-TILIMSĀNĪ AL-FĀSĪ AL-MĀLIKĪ, man of letters and biographer, born at Tilimsān (Tlemcen) in *ca.* 986/1577, d. at Cairo in Djumādā II 1041/ Jan. 1632. He belonged to a family of scholars, natives of Maḳḳara (about 12 miles from Msīla [see MASĪLA]). One of his paternal ancestors, Muḥammad b. Muḥammad al-Maḳḳarī, had been chief *ḳāḍī* of Fās and one of the teachers of the famous Lisān al-Dīn Ibn al-Khaṭīb [*q.v.*] of Granada. He himself received a wide education from his early youth; one of his principal teachers was his paternal uncle Abū ʿUthmān Saʿīd (d. at Tlemcen in 1030/1620-1; on him, see Ben Cheneb, *Idjâza,* § 103).

In 1009/1600, al-Maḳḳarī went to Morocco. At Marrākush, he met numerous scholars and followed the teaching of Aḥmad Bābā [*q.v.*], who on 15 Rabīʿ 1010/13 October 1601 gave him an *idjāza* (text in al-Maḳḳarī's *Rawḍa,* 305-12) authorising him to teach the *Muwaṭṭaʾ,* the two *Ṣaḥīḥ*s of al-Bukhārī and Muslim, the *Shifāʾ* of the *Ḳāḍī* ʿIyāḍ and his own works, to the spreading of which he must have contributed greatly (see M. A. Zouber, *Aḥmad Bābā de Tombouctou,* Paris 1977, 57-8 and index). It was probably round about this time that he began to frequent the *zāwiya dilāʾiyya,* where his special master for *ḥadīth* was Maḥammad b. Abī Bakr (967-1046/1559-1636) [see AL-DILĀʾ in Suppl.]. He kept up cordial relations with the latter until his last days, judging by a letter written at Cairo early in 1041/1631 and entrusted to Maḥammad's son Muḥammad al-Ḥādjdj, on his return from the Pilgrimage; this letter, in which he gives some details about his latest works and journeyings, is preserved in the Rabat ms. 471 K (it has been published by M. Ḥadjdjī, *al-Zāwiya al-dilāʾiyya,* Rabat 1384/1964, 282-4).

Al-Maḳḳarī remained then in Fās, where he became *imām* and *muftī* at the al-Ḳarawiyyīn mosque [*q.v.*] from 1022/1613 to 1027/1617. It was during the stay there that he composed his *Azhār al-riyāḍ* (see below). But he was accused of favouring a turbulent tribe, and decided to leave for the East in order to make the Pilgrimage. In 1027 or 1028/1617-18 he accordingly left Fās, leaving there, besides his books, a daughter and a wife (to whom he gave, in the above-cited letter, the power to obtain a divorce), and after having accomplished the Pilgrimage (1028/1618), he went to Cairo, where he remained for some months and got married. In the next year, he undertook a trip to Jerusalem, and then returned to Cairo. From there, he went back on several occasions to the Holy Places and, both at Mecca and at Medina, gave a course in *ḥadīth* which excited great attention. He made fresh trips to Jerusalem and Damascus, where he was welcomed at the Čaḳmaḳiyya *madrasa* by the scholar Aḥmad b. Shāhīn; in this last city too, his courses on the Islamic traditions were much frequented by students. He went back to Cairo, and just as he was preparing to return to Damascus and stay there permanently, he fell ill and died.

In spite of his long stay in the East, it was in Morocco that al-Maḳḳarī collected the essential materials for his work as the historian and biographer of Muslim Spain, especially at Marrākush in the library of Saʿdian Sultans (now preserved in part in the Escorial; see Lévi-Provençal, *Les manuscrits arabes de l'Escurial,* iii, Paris 1928, pp. viii-ix). Indeed, his masterpiece, written at Cairo in 1038/1629 at the suggestion of Ibn Shāhīn, is a long monograph on Muslim Spain and on the famous encyclopaedist of Granada, Lisān al-Dīn Ibn al-Khaṭīb, *Nafḥ al-ṭīb min ghuṣn al-Andalus al-raṭīb wa-dhikr wazīrihā Lisān al-Dīn Ibn al-Khaṭīb,* an immense compilation of historical and literary information, poems, letters and quotations very often taken from works now lost. It is this that gives the *Nafḥ al-ṭīb* an inestimable value and puts it in the first rank for our sources of Muslim Spain from the conquest to the last days of the Reconquista.

The *Nafḥ al-ṭīb* consists of two quite distinct parts, a monograph on the history and literature of Muslim Spain and the monograph on Ibn al-Khaṭīb. The first part is divided as follows: 1. Physical geography of al-Andalus. 2. Conquest of al-Andalus by the Arabs, period of the governors. 3. History of the Umayyad caliphs and of the petty dynasts (*Mulūk al-ṭawāʾif*). 4. Description of Cordova, its history and its monuments. 5. Spanish Arabs who made the journey to the East. 6. Orientals who made the journey to Spain. 7. Sketches of literary history, the intellectual and moral qualities of the Spanish Arabs. 8. The Reconquista of Spain and the expulsion of the Muslims. The second part contains: 1. Origin and biography of the ancestors of Ibn al-Khaṭīb. 2. Biography of Ibn al-Khaṭīb. 3. Biographies of his teachers. 4. Letters in rhymed prose of the chanceries of Granada and of Fās, sent or received by Ibn al-Khaṭīb (*mukhāṭabāt*). 5. Selection of his work in prose and verse. 5. Analytical list of his works.

The first part was published at Leiden from 1855 to 1861 under the title of *Analectes sur l'histoire et la littérature des Arabes d'Espagne,* by R. Dozy, G. Dugat, I. Krehl and W. Wright. In 1840, D. Pascual de Gayangos had published in English, at London, under the title *The history of the Muhammadan dynasties in Spain,* a version adapted from the part of the first half which deals with the history of Muslim Spain. The complete Arabic text of the *Nafḥ al-ṭīb* was first printed at Būlāḳ in 1279, at Cairo in 1302 and 1304 in 4 volumes, then at Cairo in 1367/1949 in 10 volumes and finally, by Iḥsān ʿAbbās at Beirut in 1968 (8 volumes). Although various texts given by al-Maḳḳarī have been translated, in addition to the work of Pascual de Gayangos mentioned above, a complete version of this monumental work still remains to be done.

Another important work of this author is the *Azhār al-riyāḍ fī akhbār ʿIyāḍ,* a long monograph on the *Ḳāḍī* ʿIyāḍ (476-544/1083-1149 [*q.v.*]), which is enriched by numerous pieces of information on scholars of Morocco and al-Andalus and by citations from otherwise lost works. Of this work, the autograph ms. (incomplete) is in the Royal Library in Rabat (no. 784), and there is a good ms. in the General Library of Rabat (no. 229 K); this has been the object of an edition begun in Tunis (1322/1904), and then 3 volumes have been published in Cairo in 1359-61/1939-42; the vols. iv and v at al-Muḥammadiyya in 1978-80.

A third work by al-Maḳḳarī, the *Rawḍat al-ās al-ʿaṭirat al-anfās fī dhikr man laḳītuhu min aʿlām al-ḥaḍratayn Marrākush wa-Fās,* contains biographies of scholars and other Moroccan personalities, together, like the preceding two works, various others texts, in

particular, *idjāza*s received by or conferred by the
author (ed. Rabat 1383/1964).

As well as these historical and biographical compilations, al-Maḳḳarī is said to have left behind a commentary on the *Muḳaddima* of Ibn Khaldūn (Ḥādjdjī
Khalīfa, ii, 106) which has not yet been found, but
there are extant several others of his works which are
of varying interest. From the lists given of his works
(see Ben Cheneb, *Idjāza*, § 102; Brockelmann, II²,
381-3, S II, 407-8; M. Ḥadjdjī, *op. cit.*, 110-13), there
will be mentioned here those which are extant and
which deal with: — (1) the Prophet: *Fatḥ al-mutaᶜāl
fī madḥ al-niᶜāl* (*ḥadīth*s, verses and citations from the
texts of Moroccan poets and writers, in particular, on
the Prophet's sandals). This is a lengthy rewriting (ed.
Hyderabad 1334/1916) of a compilation made in
Cairo under the title of *al-Nafaḥāt al-ᶜanbariyya fī niᶜāl
khayr al-bariyya.* The ms. 565 Dj. of Rabat contains the
Fatḥ and an *urdjūza* on the same topic addressed to
Maḥammad b. Abī Bakr. Another text, *Azhār/Zahr al-
kimāma fī sharaf al-ᶜimāma*, is an *urdjūza* of 305 verses on
the Prophet's turban, written at Medina and sent to
this same Dilāᶜī, which contains lexicographical
details on Muḥammad's clothing (cf. ms. Rabat 984
D, ff. 96b-103a). — (2) theology: *Iḍāᵓat al-dudjunna
bi-ᶜaḳāᵓid ahl al-sunna*, a profession of faith in 500
radjaz verses, which al-Maḳḳarī asserts (in the letter
cited above) he taught and commented upon at Mecca, Jerusalem, Damascus, Cairo, Alexandria, Rosetta
and Ghazza. More than 2,000 copies, most of them
with his signature, are said to have been made
(numerous ms., including Rabat 1227 D, 2742 K; ed.
Cairo 1304). *Itḥāf al-mughram al-mughrā fī sharḥ al-
Ṣughrā*, a commentary on the *ᶜaḳīda ṣughrā* of al-Sanūsī
[*q.v.*] (mss. Royal Library at Rabat nos. 3544 and
5928). — (3) fiḳh: *Iᶜmāl al-dhihn wa 'l-fikr fi 'l-masāᵓil
al-mutanawwiᶜat al-adjnās al-wārida min al-Shaykh Sayyidī
Maḥammad b. Abī Bakr*, barakat al-zamān wa-baḳiyyat al-
nās (in al-Ḥawwāt, *al-Budūr al-ḍāwiya*, ms. Rabat 261
D, ff. 64a-71b). — (4) magical formulae and
devices: *Nayl al-marām al-mughtabiṭ li-ṭālib al-
mukhammas al-khālī al-wasaṭ* (ms. Rabat 2878 K).

Al-Maḳḳarī was essentially a compiler who
felicitously preserved a host of texts otherwise lost
which he had copied out before leaving for the East,
and one hopes that he did not rely too much on his
own memory, which was remarkble. His master
Maḥammad b. Abī Bakr, despite their friendly relations, did not have a very high opinion of his reliability in regard to *ḥadīth*, and al-Ifrānī (*Safwa*, 74), repeats
a judgement of al-ᶜAyyāshī according to which he
always refused to give a legal opinion twice on the
same question, for fear of contradicting himself.
Nevertheless, he was a skilful versifier, and in the
passages composed by himself, his rhymed prose remains relatively smooth-flowing and readable.

Bibliography (in addition to works cited in the
article): Mayyāra, *al-Durr al-thamīn*, Cairo
1305/1887, i, 41; Yūsī, *Muḥāḍarāt*, lith. Fās
1317/1899, 59; Khafādjī, *Rayḥanat al-alibbāᵓ*, Cairo
1283, 293; Ibn Maᶜṣūm, *Sulāfat al-ᶜaṣr*, Cairo 1324,
589; Muḥibbī, *Khulāṣat al-athar*, Cairo 1284, i,
302 ff.; Ifrānī, *Safwat man intashar*, lith. Fās n.d.,
22 ff.; Ḳādirī, *Nashr al-mathānī*, lith. Fās 1310/1892,
i, 157-60; Dugat, in introd. to the *Analectes*; E.
Lévi-Provençal, *Chorfa*, 93, n. 3; Kattānī, *Fihris al-
fahāris*, Fās 1346/1927, i, 337-8; M. Hajji, *L'activité
intellectuelle au Maroc à l'époque saᶜdide*, Rabat 1977,
423-4 and index.

                    (E. Lévi-Provençal - [Ch. Pellat])

AL-**MAKKĪ.** [See ABŪ ṬĀLIB].

MAKKĪ, ABŪ MUḤAMMAD MAKKĪ B. ABĪ ṬĀLIB B.
(?) ḤAMMŪSH B. MUḤAMMAD B. MUKHTĀR AL-ḲAYSĪ

AL-ḲAYRAWĀNĪ AL-ANDALUSĪ AL-ḲURṬUBĪ, Mālikī
lawyer and Ḳurᵓān reader, born at al-
Ḳayrawān on 23 Shaᶜbān 354/25 August 965, died at
Cordova in 437/1045, one of the earliest and most distinguished scholars in the science of Ḳurᵓān reading
(*kirāᵓa* [*q.v.*]) and especially the theory and art of
recitation (*tadjwīd* [*q.v.*]) in the Muslim West.

It is largely due to him that the new development
in Ḳurᵓān reading scholarship which is connected
with the Baghdādī *Imām al-ḳurrāᵓ*, Ibn Mudjāhid (d.
324/936 [*q.v.*]) spread so soon via Aleppo and Cairo
to Spain. Makkī started his studies in Cairo at the age
of thirteen, and accomplished most of his learning
there during the years 368-74/978-84, 377-9/987-9
and 382-3/992-3, concentrating on philology, *ḳirāᵓāt*
and *tadjwīd*, and frequenting at an advanced stage
such illustrious authorities as the commentator Abū
Bakr al-Udfuwī (304-88/916-98, *GAS*, i, 46) and Abu
'l-Ṭayyib ᶜAbd al-Munᶜim b. Ghalbūn al-Ḥalabī (d.
389/999). The latter had studied with Ibn Mudjāhid's
pupil Ibn Khālawayh [*q.v.*] during Sayf al-Dawla's
reign in Aleppo [see ḤALAB, III, 86a] and become
famous for his works on *ḳirāᵓa* (*GAS*, i, 15). Makkī also
studied with Abu 'l-Ṭayyib's son Ṭāhir b. Ghalbūn
(d. 399/1008), the same scholar, who was to become
the teacher of Makki's 17 years' younger Maghribī
colleague, Abū ᶜAmr al-Dānī [*q.v.*], who came to
Cairo some 20 years later. It is Ṭāhir b. Ghalbūn's
teaching and his *K. al-Tadhkira fī 'l-ḳirāᵓāt* (*GAS*, i, 16)
that were to become the foundations of two influential
ḳirāᵓāt-works by each of Makkī (*K. al-Tabṣira, K. al-
Kashf*) and al-Dānī (*K. al-Taysīr, K. Djāmiᶜ al-bayān*).
During Makki's short residence at home in
374-77/984-7, he studied with two outstanding Ḳayrawānī scholars: the legal scholar and traditionist al-
Ḳābisī (d. 403/1011 [*q.v.*]) and the lawyer Ibn Abī
Zayd (d. 386/996 [*q.v.*]). In 387/998 he set off for his
last journey to the east. Staying three years in Mecca,
frequenting Meccan scholars and performing the
ḥadjdj several times, he wrote in 389/999 his *K.
Mushkil gharīb al-Ḳurᵓān*, a summary of which is probably extant in a unique ms. (ed. Yūsuf ᶜAbd ar-
Raḥmān al-Marᶜashlī, Beirut 1981; its authenticity is,
however, doubted by Aḥmad Farḥāt, see preliminary
note to Marᶜashlī's edition). On his way back to al-
Ḳayrawān via Cairo, two other works were completed: (1) *K. Mushkil iᶜrāb al-Ḳurᵓān*, written in
390/1001 in Jerusalem (16 mss. extant, Brockelmann,
I, 515, S I, 719, and cf. introd. to the critical edition
by Yāsīn M. al-Sawwās, Damascus n.d., 2 vols.; further edition by Ḥātim S. al-Ḍāmin, Baghdād *ca.*
1970); and (2) *K. al-Tabṣira*, originally meant as a
mere introduction to be memorised by beginners,
which was later elaborated by Makkī and published in
424/1038 as *K. al-Kashf ᶜan wudjūh al-ḳirāᵓāt al-sabᶜ* (4
mss., ed. Muḥyī al-Dīn Ramaḍān, Damascus, 2
vols.; Ḥātim S. al-Ḍāmin, Baghdād *ca.* 1970). This
longer version not only gives the fuller *isnād*s for the
readings but also grammatical justifications (*taᶜlīl*) for
them, following closely the method first adopted by
Abū ᶜAlī al-Fārisī (d. 377/987 [*q.v.*]), whose *K. al-
Ḥudjdja*, which was well known to Makkī, constitutes
a complete Ḳurᵓān commentary discussing the
readings presented by Ibn Mudjāhid in his *K. al-
Sabᶜa*, see *GdQ*, iii, 116-43.

Makkī did not remain long in his home town, but
— for reasons unknown to us — left al-Ḳayrawān for
al-Andalus in 393/1003 and established himself as a
teacher of Ḳurᵓān reading (*muḳri*ᵓ) at Cordova at the
Masdjid al-Nukhayla in the ᶜAṭṭārīn quarter. He soon
won a wide reputation for his learning, and was appointed between 397/1007 and 399/1009 by al-
Muẓaffar ᶜAbd al-Malik b. Abī ᶜĀmir [see ᶜĀMIRIDS]

as *muḳri*ʾ to the Mosque of the Zāhira quarter, newly established by the ʿĀmirids. After the fall of the ʿĀmirid rule in 399/1009, he was called by the caliph Muḥammad b. Hishām al-Mahdī (399/1009) to teach at the Friday Mosque of Cordova. There he continued to teach until the end of the civil war, when the vizier Abu 'l-Ḥazm b. Djahwar [see DJAHWARIDS] appointed him *imām* and preacher to the same mosque (after 425/1031), which office he held until his death on 2 Muḥarram 437/21 July 1045).

At Cordova, most of his works (numbering over 80, on various topics such as *fiḳh, ḥadīth*, but mostly on *ḳirāʾa*) were written. Two of the extant *tadjwīd* works have played a major role in the development of the *ḳirāʾa* disciplines, *al-Riʿāya li-tadjwīd al-ḳirāʾa wa-lafẓ al-tilāwa* (preserved in 9 mss, ed. Aḥmad Farḥāt, Damascus 1973) is considered as one of the earliest systematic treatises on *tadjwīd*. His *Sharḥ kallā wa-balā wa-naʿam wa 'l-waḳf ʿalā kulli wāḥidatin minhunna wa-dhikr maʿānīhā wa-ʿilalihā* (4 mss., ed. Aḥmad Farḥāt, Damascus 1978) treats the rhetorical qualities of the three particles monographically and is a useful source for the study of Ḳurʾān rhetorics. A work unique of its kind is his *K. al-Ibāna fī maʿāni 'l-ḳirāʾāt* (4 mss., ed. Muḥyī al-Dīn Ramaḍān, Damascus 1979, previous edition by ʿAbd al-Fattāḥ Shalabī, Cairo 1960) discussing problems arising from the existence of several different and equally canonical readings. Whereas his comprehensive Ḳurʾān commentary *al-Hidāya* seems to be lost, his monograph on the special *tafsīr* problem of the abrogated verses is extant: *al-Īḍāḥ li-nāsikh al-Ḳurʾān wa-mansūkhih* (4 mss., ed. Aḥmad Farḥāt, Riyadh 1976). Makkī's work has in later generations been overshadowed by that of his younger colleague al-Dānī and the later scholastic commentaries resting upon al-Dānī's writings. Yet some of Makkī's treatises have exercised even a direct influence on later scholars, see Pretzl, in *GdQ*, iii, 214. Some of his work has come to light again only in recent years, and has still to be studied as to its intrinsic value and its impact on later developments.

Bibliography: Basic studies: G. Bergstraesser and O. Pretzl, *Geschichte des Qorans*, iii. *Die Geschichte des Korantexts*, Leipzig 1938, repr. Hildesheim 1961, see Index, s.v. Makkī b. Abī Ṭālib; O. Pretzl, *Die Wissenschaft der Koranlesung* (*ʿilm al-qirāʾa*). *Ihre literarischen Quellen und ihre Aussprachegrundlagen (uṣūl)*, in *Islamica*, vi (1933-4), 1-47, 230-46, 290-331.

Biographical sources: Ibn Bashkuwāl, *K. al-Ṣila fī taʾrīkh aʾimmat al-Andalus*, Cairo 1966, ii, 631-3; Abū Barakāt al-Anbārī, *Nuzhat al-alibbāʾ fī ṭabaḳāt al-udabāʾ*, ed. I. al-Samarrāʾi, Baghdād 1970, 238; al-Ḍabbī, *Bughyat al-multamis fī taʾrīkh ridjāl ahl al-Andalus*, Cairo 1967, 469; Yāḳūt al-Rūmī, *Muʿdjam al-udabāʾ*, ed. Margoliouth, London 1925, vi, 7, 173-5; al-Ḳifṭī, *Inbāh al-ruwāt ʿalā anbāh al-nuḥāt*, ed. Abu 'l-Faḍl Ibrāhīm, Cairo 1955, iii, 313-15; Ibn Khallikān, *Wafayāt al-aʿyān*, ed. I. ʿAbbās, Beirut 1968, v, 274-7; al-Dabbāgh, *Maʿālim al-īmām fī maʿrifat ahl al-Ḳayrawān*, ed. M. Māḍūr *et alii*, Tunis 1968-78, iii, 171-2; al-Dhahabī, *al-ʿIbar fī khabar man ghabar*, ed. F. Sayyid, Kuwayt 1961, iii, 187; Ibn al-Djazarī, *Ṭabaḳāt al-ḳurrāʾ*, ed. Bergstraesser, Cairo 1932, ii, 309-10; al-Suyūṭī, *Bughyat al-wuʿāt*, ed. Abu 'l-Faḍl Ibrāhīm, Cairo 1964, 396-7; al-Maḳḳarī, *Nafḥ al-ṭīb min ghuṣn al-Andalus al-raṭīb*, ed. I. ʿAbbās, Beirut 1968, iii, 179. See also H. A. Idris, *Deux juristes Ḳairouanais*, in *AIEO Alger*, xii (1954), 152; Ch. Bouyahia, *La vie littéraire sous les Zirides*, Tunis 1972, 129-30.

(ANGELIKA NEUWIRTH)

MAKLĪ, the elongated, flat hilltop, running north and south some 2 miles/3 km. to the northwest of the city of Thaṭṭhā (Tatta or Thatta) [*q.v.*] in lower Sind [*q.v.*] on the road to Karāčī and now in Pakistan, which served as a necropolis for the local Sammā, Arghūn, and Tarkhān dynasties, besides being the burial ground for countless thousands of ordinary Muslims. The etymology is obscure, though possibly derived from *mukallaʾ* "a river bank", as it lies along the old bed of the Indus. Within its irregularly curving width, the mausolea are arranged in roughly chronological order, with the oldest at the northern end. Their architecture, strongly local and somewhat provincial in character, though influenced by buildings in Iran, is executed in two distinct techniques; the brick characteristic of the country is either clad in tilework, both polychrome and mosaic, or built in courses alternating with glazed bricks whose edges are recessed and glazed white to simulate a mortar joint about 1.5 cm wide on two or more sides (though some real mortar joints in white plaster can also be found) to create a vertical emphasis, a horizontal one, or both. Other monuments, however, are in carved ashlar of yellow, grey or red sandstone slabs on a rubble core, which in many cases has crumbled with disastrous effects; some of this stone is local, from Djangshāhī, and the rest imported from Rādjpūtāna and Gudjarāt. The brick buildings are set on stone bases to withstand the rise of moisture charged with destructive saltpetre. The glazes are generally white, cobalt, and turquoise; though the tile designs may be stereotyped, the technical standard of the dense red brickwork is very high, and the true joints can hardly be seen. Glazed brick in chevron patterns is also used to face some domes internally, as may be seen in one of the earliest buildings on the hill, the tomb of Fatḥ Khān's sister (898/1492).

The mausoleum of Djām Niẓām al-Dīn Nindō (915/1509) at the northernmost end of the site illustrates the recently Hindu origin of the Rādjpūt Sammās; square in plan, its four stone walls are decorated entirely with Hindu carving, except for a frieze of Ḳurʾānic inscriptions in beautiful *thulth*. The almost cubical mass is articulated by twelve other horizontal bands of motifs, including one of geese, alternating with plain stone. This is set off by the heavily-worked carving on the rear of the *miḥrāb*, surmounted by a corbelled balcony with arched openings. The incomplete nature of this work shows that it has been borrowed from a Hindu temple, complete with a miniature *śikhara*, though some panels are Islamic. The interior is dominated by the use of squinch arches, in tiers of first eight, then sixteen, to carry the missing dome. Both their scale and the corbelled technique are reminiscent of Iltutmish's tomb at Dihlī (*ca.* 632/1235), though the ornament is again limited to flat bands, friezes and rosettes like tilework. Two *čhatrī* pavilions nearby, each on eight columns, also incorporate Hindu work, with corbelled domes, monolithic banded pillars, and *kalsā* finials (late 15th century).

The tomb of Sulṭān Ibrāhīm (966/1558), son of ʿĪsā Khān Tarkhān I, is an octagonal brick structure surrounding a square cell inside with a carefully-proportioned Persian dome on a cylindrical drum above. Each of the faces houses a recess within a pointed arch outside, those at the cardinal sides being taller, and containing a door with a window above in the flat *īwān* wall, while those at the angles form five-faceted niches. It may have been derived from the tomb of Mullā Ḥasan at Sulṭāniyya [*q.v.*] (*ca.* 936/1530), though it lacks double storeys at the angles, and its proportions are more compact. Traces of turquoise tiling can be seen on the dome, though little remains elsewhere except for three small panels of Ḳurʾānic phrases, one of them signed. Another cenotaph within is dated 952/1545, and that of Amīr Sulṭān Muḥammad stands outside. The structure anticipates the monument to Dj̲ānī Bēg (1009/1601), and ultimately that to Āṣaf Kh̲ān at Lāhawr [*q.v.*].

The tomb of ʿĪsā Kh̲ān Tarkh̲ān I (973/1565) with five others of his family lies in the centre of a court whose stone walls still stand. Outside, recessed panels house blank arches with rosettes in relief, and arched *dj̲ālī* screens alternately, under bold string courses which rise around the *pīsh̲ṭāḳ* of the entrance. It is Iranian in its restraint. The mausoleum of the apparently paranoid Mīrzā Muḥammad Bāḳī Tarkh̲ān (d. 993/1585), which follows the same pattern, still has merlons over the *pīsh̲ṭāḳ*, diaper-work on the lintel, and bolder entrance steps; the inscription shows it to have been built for his son Sh̲āh-zāda Sh̲āhrukh̲ in 992/1584. Like other enclosures of this type, the court has been used for subsequent family burials in separate compartments over a generation. Just to the south again, the similar mausoleum of Āhinsa Bāʾī (995/1587) has finely-carved relief between the string-courses, in a frieze of palmettes carried over a tall *miḥrāb* to the west, and the *dj̲ālī* frets are geometrically more intricate.

Although Mīrzā Dj̲ānī Bēg, the last independent Tarkh̲ān ruler, died while in submission to Akbar's court, he too was buried at Maklī, in the southernmost great tomb, in 1009/1601. Set in a once similar stone enclosure, with fine Ḳurʾānic epigraphs around the gate, which has four rosettes set boldly in the tympanum, and over the *miḥrāb* elaborated with a faceted recess, flanked by miniature lotus posts and superimposed aedicules, the mausoleum itself is a domed octagon, whose alternating courses of venetian red and turquoise brick, with both joints picked out in white glaze, reflect the alternately broad and narrow coursing of the yellow sandstone. The plan differs from Sulṭān Ibrāhīm's tomb only in that the panels housing the angle arches are recessed. The outer dome has fallen, though its septal reinforcements remain. The inner one still carries sections of tilework, and on the walls below is a tiled dado, which once had a counterpart outside. The three *īwāns* and the tympanum of the doorway to the south house geometric *dj̲ālīs*, surmounted by panels of Ḳurʾānic inscription in white on cobalt.

The building housing the tomb of Dj̲ān Bābā (d. 1017/1608), with others from 964/1557 onwards, is by contrast a rectangular pavilion originally covered by three domes, of which the central one remains. The brown stone enclosure wall is heavily carved with both relief and incised work, with blank arcading carrying fully developed pole medallions and rosettes. The rich *miḥrāb*, with *muḳarnas* vaulting, is housed in a carefully-conceived two storied backing.

The mausoleum of ʿĪsā Kh̲ān Tarkh̲ān II (d. 1054/1644) combines a square domed central cell with surrounding verandahs in two stories, two rows of ten square columns being on each face. The middle two columns in the outer row rise free of the gallery behind, like those of the Dj̲āmiʿ Masdj̲id at Aḥmadābād, to support triple arches with lotus-buds on the intrados, below a remarkable rising parapet which is effectively a *pīsh̲ṭāḳ* for each face. The main dome, surmounted by a *mahāpadma* finial, is surrounded by low hemispherical ones over each bay; it has, unusually, eight facets. The buff Kāṭhiāwāṛ sandstone surfaces of walls, pillars and lintels are wrought with carving of both types which in its swarming intricacy recalls that of Fatḥpūr Sikri (1568-85) [*q.v.*]. The monolithic pillars of the upper level have scrolled bracket capitals of an Indian type, but those below have tapering honeycombs of a western Islamic kind. The building is at the centre of a large court with high stone walls, arcaded within, and with a massive *īwān* in the middle of each side once crowned by a smooth squinched vault. Hindu influence is evident in the *dj̲arōkhā* balconies projecting either side of these, and in the rows of niches forming the plinth. The work is reported to have been built in the Nawwāb's life-time.

Best preserved is the tomb of the Dīwān Sh̲urfā Kh̲ān (1048/1638), again a square cell rising into a dome, with an *īwān* on each cardinal face outside, but here the corners are built as heavy cylindrical towers containing spiral stairs, and the dome, slightly bulbous above a recessed springing, is apparently the first of its kind in Northern India: it is close to that of the Masdj̲id-i Sh̲āh at Mash̲had (855/1451) in shape, and was once sheathed in light blue tile. The walls, outside and in, are of unglazed red brick with blue strips in the joints. Glazed bricks make a chevron pattern inside the dome, with bands of tiles below. The cenotaph and headstone carry especially fine carving. Another bulbous dome, with more pronounced shoulders, roofs the open tomb of Ṭugh̲rul Beg (1090/1679), surrounded by merlons and *čhadj̲dj̲ās*, above twelve carved square pillars. Honeycomb capitals support a trabeated octagon below the arches of an Islamic zone of transition, and chevron vaulting.

Bibliography: The available material is uneven. For tilework, see H. Cousens, *Portfolio of illustrations of Sind tiles*, London 1906. His descriptions of Maklī in his *Antiquities of Sind*, Calcutta 1929, repr. Oxford and Karachi 1975, contains some mistakes in identification and dating, particularly of Bāḳī Bēg with Muḥammad Bāḳī Tarkh̲ān (p. 119). Shamsuddin Ahmad, *A guide to Tattah and the Makli Hill*, Karachi 1952, is still a useful pocket guide, but dates need revision; M. Idris Siddiqi, *Thatta*, Karachi 1958 and Islamabad 1970; M. A. Ghafur, *Muslim architecture in Sind area*, Karachi 1964; idem, *The calligraphers of Thatta*, Karachi 1978 (useful history and dating, with transcriptions of epigraphy); Shaukat Mahmood, *Islamic inscriptions in Pakistani architecture to 1707*, unpublished Ph.D. thesis, Edinburgh 1981, 3 vols., 254-320 (new analyses of inscriptions and chronograms). See also HIND. vii. Architecture. xii. Sind.

(P. A. ANDREWS)

AL-**MAKRAMĪ**, ṢAFĪ AL-DĪN MUḤAMMAD B. FAHD, the progenitor of the Makramī (pl. al-Makārima, so called after their supposed ancestor Ibn Makram b. Sabaʾ b. Ḥimyar al-Aṣgh̲ar) family which headed the Sulaymānī branch of the Ismāʿīlī-Mustaʿlī-Ṭayyibī *daʿwa* [see ISMĀʿĪLIYYA] in Yaman and also wielded political power in Nadj̲rān [*q.v.*] during the past two centuries.

He was appointed by Sulaymān b. Ḥasan (d. 1005/1597) [*q.v.*] as the acting *dāʿī* to manage the affairs of the *daʿwa* during the minority of his son Dj̲aʿfar b. Sulaymān. He lived first in Ṭayba, a town northwest of Ṣanʿāʾ, then migrated to Nadj̲rān where he preached and succeeded in winning the confidence of the most influential Yām [*q.v.*] tribe settled in that region (Fuad Hamza, *Najran*, in *JRCAS*, xxii [1935], 631-40; the author, an official of the Saudi Arabian government, visited Nadj̲rān probably in 1934 and derived his information from the then deputy of the *dāʿī*, Ḥusayn b. Aḥmad al-Makramī). Here in the

Yām territory he took Badr, situated at an altitude of 6,600 feet in *wādī* Badr, which later became the Makramī capital, as his new residence and died there on 1 Sha^c^bān 1042/11 February 1633. Through his farsightedness the groundwork laid by him among the Yām came to fruition in the succeeding generations by providing the Yāmī support for the *da^c^wa* and thereby raising its religious prestige in the Nadjrān province. He was also a prolific author. Most of his works deal with the succession dispute after the death of Dāwūd b. ^c^Adjab in *ca.* 999/1591 which split the Musta^c^lī-Ṭayyibī *da^c^wa* into the Dāwūdī and Sulaymānī branches (for a comprehensive list see I.K. Poonawala, *Biobibliography of Ismā^c^īlī literature,* Malibu 1977, 244-6).

Bibliography: in addition to the works cited in the article: ^c^Abd Allāh al-Djarāfī, *al-Muktaṭaf min ta^ɔ^rīkh al-Yaman,* Cairo 1951, 233; Muṣṭafā al-Dabbāgh, *Djazīrat al-^c^Arab,* Beirut 1963, i, 234-5, 270; M. Wenner, *Modern Yemen,* 1918-66, Baltimore 1967, 34, 76-7. (I. POONAWALA)

MAKRAMIDS, a family which has held the spiritual and political leadership of the Banū Yām [*q.v.*] and the Sulaymānī Ismā^c^īlī community [see ISMĀ^c^ĪLIYYA] in Nadjrān and Yaman since the 11th/17th century. The name evidently refers to the Banū Makram of Hamdān who are settled in Ṭayba in the Wādī Ḍahr and in some other villages to the west of Ṣan^c^ā^ɔ^. There is evidence that the family came from Ṭayba, an old Ismā^c^īlī stronghold. A pedigree linking them rather to a Makram b. Saba^ɔ^ b. Ḥimyar al-Aṣghar is fictitious. The term Makārima is often also extended to their followers.

The earliest known member of the family, Ṣafī al-Dīn Muḥammad b. al-Fahd al-Makramī [*q.v.*], is said to have been the first of them to settle in the town of Badr in the Wādī Ḥibawnā in northern Nadjrān, which later remained the usual residence of the Makramī *dā^c^īs*. When Sulaymān b. Ḥasan, founder of the Sulaymānī *da^c^wa* and its 27th *dā^c^ī muṭlak* since the disappearance of the *Imām* al-Ṭayyib, died in 1005/1597, he became acting (*mustawda^c^*) *dā^c^ī* during the minority of Sulaymān's son Dja^c^far, the 28th *dā^c^ī muṭlak*. He wrote numerous treatises, mostly polemics against the Dāwūdī *da^c^wa,* and died in 1042/1633. A Djābir b. al-Fahd al-Makramī, also known as the author of a religious treatise, was probably his brother. Ṣafī al-Dīn's son Ibrāhīm succeeded to the leadership of the Sulaymānī community as the 30th *dā^c^ī muṭlak* in 1088/1677, and died in 1094/1683 in Nadjrān (according to H. St. J. Philby, *Arabian Highlands,* Ithaca 1952, 358, in Ṭayba). Since then, the position has remained in various branches of the family except in the time of the 46th *dā^c^ī,* the Indian Ḥusām al-Dīn Ghulām Ḥusayn (1355-7/1936-8). A list of the Sulaymānī chief *dā^c^īs* and their death dates has been given by A. A. A. Fyzee (*JBBRAS,* N.S. x [1934], 13-14, xvi [1940], 101-4), followed and continued by I. Poonawala (*Biobibliography of Ismā^c^īlī literature,* Malibu 1977, 368-9), and a geneaological chart of the family is provided by Philby (*op. cit.*, 719). The 43rd *dā^c^ī,* whose name is given there as ^c^Abd Allāh b. ^c^Alī, was, according to E. Glaser, ^c^Abd Allāh b. Aḥmad b. Ismā^c^īl, son of the 42nd *dā^c^ī* (see D. H. Müller and N. Rhodokanakis, eds., *Eduard Glasers Reise nach Mârib,* Vienna 1913, 128). Nos. 48 and 49 in Poonawala's list are evidently identical.

The Makramī *dā^c^īs* remained politically independent as rulers of Yām until the inclusion of Nadjrān in the Sa^c^ūdī kingdom in 1934. Their history is only fragmentarily known from occasional reports, mostly in Yamanī and Wahhābī chronicles. The Zaydī *Imām* al-Manṣūr al-Ḥusayn b. al-Mutawakkil after his accession in 1131/1719 sought the support of the tribes of Yām and the Makramīs under the 32nd *dā^c^ī* Hibat Allāh b. Ibrāhīm (1109-60/1697-1747) against rebels in his family and, in recognition of their services, granted him control of the Ismā^c^īlī territories of Ḥarāz in Yaman. When his rule was solidly established, al-Manṣūr tried to recover Ḥarāz, provoking raids of the Yām into his territories in Tihāma. At this time, Muḥammad b. Aḥmad b. Khayrāt, *amīr* of Abū ^c^Arīsh and the Mikhlāf al-Sulaymānī, sought an alliance with them against hostile tribes. Overthrown by his uncle Ḥawdhān in 1157/1744, he found refuge in Nadjrān and was restored to power by an army of Yām. The Makramīs thereafter continued to interfere, by force and diplomacy, in the affairs of the Āl Khayrāt dynasty until its fall *ca.* 1285/1868. They were aided by the fact that the Āl Khayrāt were usually forced to employ Yām mercenaries as the backbone of their army.

The power of the Makramī *dā^c^īs* reached a peak under Hibat Allāh's son and successor Ḍiyā^ɔ^ al-Dīn Ismā^c^īl (1160-84/1747-70). Ismā^c^īl asserted his authority over the Ismā^c^īlī community in Yaman by conquering a mountain fortress in Ṣa^c^fān (before 1164/1751) and holding it against all attacks of the Zaydī *imām* and of the adventurer Abū ^c^Ulāma al-Mashdja^c^ī. He forced the *amīr* Muḥammad al-Khayrātī into an alliance. According to modern Haḍramī authors, he invaded Ḥaḍramawt, for the first time in 1170/1756-7, and pretended to uphold the *sharī^c^a* there and to abolish tribal law and customs. The Makramī sway over Ḥaḍramawt appears to have lasted for some time, perhaps still during the reign of his brother Ḥasan (see R. B. Serjeant, *Hūd and other pre-Islamic prophets of Ḥaḍramawt,* in *Le Muséon,* lvii [1954], 132, repr. in idem, *Studies in Arabian history and civilization,* London 1981, with addendum, p. 1). In 1178/1764 he invaded Nadjd and inflicted a crushing defeat on the Wahhābīs at al-Ḥā^ɔ^ir. He pushed on further, approaching al-Riyāḍ, but then agreed to a settlement and withdrew, spurning the offer of an alliance and joint anti-Wahhābī action by ^c^Uray^c^ir, the ruler of al-Aḥsā^ɔ^. The Wahhābī chronicles seem to be mistaken in identifying the leader of the campaign as Ḥasan b. Hibat Allāh. They, as well as Niebuhr, describe the leader as the lord of Nadjrān. Yet it is certain that Ḥasan did not succeed his brother Ismā^c^īl before the latter's death six years later. Ismā^c^īl is also the author of an esoteric Ismā^c^īlī commentary on the Ḳur^ɔ^ān, *Mizādj al-tasnīm* (ed. R. Strothmann, Göttingen 1944-55), of answers to questions by Ḥasan b. Sahnā^ɔ^ and of other works (listed by Strothmann, *op. cit.*, introd. 39). His brother and successor Ḥasan b. Hibat Allāh (1184-9/1770-5) after his accession reaffirmed the Makramī domination in the territories of Muḥammad al-Khayrātī, who had tried to assert his independence, by defeating him and occupying the town of Ḥaraḍ for two months. In 1189/1775 he led a second campaign against the Wahhābīs to al-Ḥā^ɔ^ir and Ḍurmā. The Wahhābī defence proved more effective this time, and Ḥasan, struck by illness, decided to retreat and died on the way back. In 1202/1788 "the lord of Nadjrān", presumably the 36th *dā^c^ī* ^c^Abd Allāh b. ^c^Alī (1195-1225/1781-1810), joined forces with some of the tribes of al-Dawāsir in order to prevent the Wahhābīs from taking possession of this region neighbouring Nadjrān, but was forced to retreat unsuccessfully. In 1220/1805 Sa^c^ūd b. ^c^Abd al-^c^Azīz sent a numerous Wahhābī army to conquer Nadjrān. After an unsuccessful assault on Badr, the Wahhābīs built a fortress near the town and left a garrison there.

The Makramīs now became more active in Yaman.

In 1237/1822 they seized Zabīd for six months, and in 1241/1825-6 they sacked al-Ḥudayda. In 1256/1840 they took possession of al-Manākha, the capital of Ḥarāz. The 41st *dāʿī*, Ḥasan b. Ismāʿīl b. Muḥsin Āl Shibām al-Makramī (1262-89/1846-72), who belonged to a collateral line of unknown relationship to the main branch of the family, established himself there and pursued expansionist designs. In 1277/1860 he seized al-Ḥayma and held it against all Zaydī efforts to expel him. Other conquests were of less duration. According to Manzoni (*El Yèmen*, Rome 1884, 177-8), he entered into an anti-Ottoman alliance with the Khedive Ismāʿīl of Egypt, cut the Ottoman trade between al-Ḥudayda and Ṣanʿāʾ, and raided the Ottoman provinces of al-Ḥudayda and al-Luḥayya. In 1289/1872 the Ottoman Aḥmad Mukhtār Pasha set out from al-Ḥudayda to conquer Ḥarāz. The *dāʿī* surrendered in the mountain fortress of ʿAttāra after having received a promise of safety. When the Pasha was informed of the heretical doctrines contained in the captured Ismāʿīlī books, he ordered the *dāʿī*, his sons and other leading Makramīs to be sent to the Porte. The *dāʿī* died on the way in al-Ḥudayda, perhaps murdered, and his son Aḥmad perished at sea. Thereafter, the Makramī *daʿīs* again resided in Badr. They reached a *modus vivendi* with the Ottomans in Yaman and declined an invitation of the Sayyid Muḥammad b. ʿAlī al-Idrīsī, ruler of ʿAsīr, to join an anti-Ottoman alliance, fearing Ottoman reprisals against their possessions in Ḥarāz.

In 1352/1933, after the failure of prolonged Saʿūdī-Yamanī negotiations concerning the status of Nadjrān, the army of *Imām* Yaḥyā Ḥamīd al-Dīn seized Badr. The 45th *dāʿī*, ʿAlī b. Muḥsin Āl Shibām (1331-55/1913-36), probably a descendant of Ḥasan b. Ismāʿīl, fled to Abhā in Saʿūdī territory. The Yamanī army destroyed the houses of the Makramī *dāʿīs* and desecrated the tombs of their ancestors. Strong local reaction forced it to withdraw and paved the way for the Saʿūdī takeover of Nadjrān, which was sealed by the Saʿūdī-Yamanī treaty of May 1934. ʿAlī b. Muḥsin was allowed to return to Badr, and all members of the family in Nadjrān, said to have numbered 145, were given a small pension by the Saʿūdī government in lieu of the contributions which they used to receive from their followers.

Bibliography (In addition to the works mentioned in the article): anon., *Tuḥfat al-zaman fīmā djarā min al-nukat bi-ḳiyām Abī ʿUlāma fi 'l-Yaman*, ms. Brit. Mus. Or. 3790, fols. 14a, 16a; C. Niebuhr, *Beschreibung von Arabien*, Copenhagen 1772, 250, 267, 172-4, 347; Ibn Ghannām, *Rawḍat al-afkār*, Bombay n.d., ii, 76-8, 101-2, 103-5, 150-1; Ibn Bishr, *ʿUnwān al-madjd*, Mecca 1349, i, 47-8, 63-4, 136; al-Nuʿamī, *Taʾrīkh al-Yaman*, ms. Brit. Mus. Or. 3265, fols. 170-1, 182b, 185b, 219b; al-Ḥarāzī, *Riyāḍ al-rayāḥīn*, ms. Brit. Mus. Or. 3912, fols. 52b, 59, 60b, 61a, 65a, 66a, 70b, 74a-75a; Aḥmad Rāshid, *Taʾrīkh Yaman wa-Ṣanʿāʾ*, Istanbul 1291, i, 265, 301, 311-2, ii, 86-90, 206; al-Wāsiʿī, *Taʾrīkh al-Yaman*, Cairo 1346/1927-8, 83, 85, 102-3, 106, 108, al-Djarāfī, *al-Muḳtaṭaf min taʾrīkh al-Yaman*, Cairo 1951, 205, 207, 243-4; al-Sayyid Muṣṭafā Sālim, *Takwīn al-Yaman al-ḥadīth*², Cairo 1971, 367-70; Muḥammad b. Aḥmad al-ʿAḳīlī, *Taʾrīkh al-Mikhlāf al-Sulaymānī*², al-Riyāḍ 1982, esp. i, 393-424, ii, 1111-14. The anonymous Yemenite chronicle published by ʿAbd Allāh Muḥammad al-Ḥibshī under the title *Ḥawliyyāt Yamaniyya min sanat 1224 h. ilā sanat 1316 h.*, n.p., n.d. [1980?], gives some variant dates for the Makramī campaigns in the first half of the 19th century (pp. 17-18, 28, 36). (W. MADELUNG)

MAKRĀN, the coastal region of southern Balūčistān, extending roughly from the Somniani Bay in the East to the eastern fringes of the region of Bashkardia [see BASHKARD in Suppl.] in the west. The modern political boundary between Pakistan and Iran thus bisects the mediaeval Makrān. The east-to-west running Siyāhān range of mountains, just to the north of the Mashkēl and Rakhshān valleys, may be regarded as Makrān's northern boundary. In British Indian times, this range formed the boundary between the southwestern part of the Kalāt native state [see KILĀT] and the Khārān one [*q.v.*]; the easternmost part of Makrān fell within the other native state of Las Bēla [*q.v.*]. At this time, the part of Makrān within British India was often called Kēč Makrān to distinguish it from Persian Makrān.

The topography of Makrān comprises essentially east-west running parallel ranges of mountains; the coastal range, going up to 5,180 feet; the central Makrān range, going up to 7,500 feet; and the Siyāhān range, going up to 6,760 feet. Between these lie the narrow Kēč valley and the rather wider Rakhshān-Mashkēl one, where some agricultural activity, chiefly dates, cereals and rice, can be practised by irrigation. Considerable fishing is possible from the coastland itself, otherwise arid, but this region possesses few major harbours, except for Pasni and Gwādar [*q.v.* in Suppl.] in what is now Pakistani Makrān, and Čāhbahār (now an important base of the Iranian Navy, with free access to the Indian Ocean) and Djāsk in what is now Persian Makrān. The only inland town of significance in Pakistani Makrān is Turbat, in the Kēč valley; the main towns of inland Persian Makrān are Nīkshahr, Bampūr [*q.v.*] and the modern administrative centre of Persian Balūčistān, Īrānshahr (the mediaeval Fahradj). Climatically, the coasts are in part affected by the southwestern monsoon, but the inland parts are extremely hot and arid. Makrān as a whole can never have supported more than an exiguous population.

The etymology of the name Makrān has been much discussed, but the popular Persian etymology from *māhī-khūrān* "fish eaters", echoing the Greek description of the inhabitants of the coastlands as *ichthyophagoi*, cannot of course be credited. More likely is a connection with the name Magan, which is known in texts of the Sumerian and old Akkadian period as a territory somewhere in or beyond the lower Persian Gulf region having trade connections with Mesopotamia. Recently, J. Hansman has propounded the identification of the ancient Magan with modern western, substantially Persian, Makrān, and the other region of Melukhkha, described as being beyond Magan according to the ancient Mesopotamian texts, with modern Pakistani Makran (*A Periplus of Magan and Meluḫḫa*, in *BSOAS*, xxxvi [1973], 554-87). Magan would therefore be the Maka of the Old Persian inscriptions (described as a satrapy of Darius, and here apparently covering the whole of Makran or Balūčistān), and the Makarēnē, seemingly so-called in the Seleucid period and certainly called thus in Byzantine Greek sources; but a derivation from Magan does not explain the intrusive *r* of Makrān. By the time of Alexander the Great, eastern Makrān was known to the Greeks as Gedrosia and its people as Gedrosii (a name possibly Iranian in origin, hence younger than the ancient one Melukhkha); the conqueror travelled through here on his way back from the Indus valley in 325 B.C., turning northwestwards and inland, probably from near modern Gwādar, to the Bampūr valley and the Djāz Muryān depression, whilst his general Nearchus sailed along the Makrān coast to Charax at the head of the Gulf. In Parthian usage we have the

form Makuran (*Mkwrn* in the S̲h̲āpūr inscription of
the Ka'ba-yi Zaradus̲h̲t) and in Pahlavi the form
Makulān (*Mkwl'n*) in the Kārtīr inscription of Naḳs̲h-
i Rustam) (P. Gignoux, *Glossaire des inscriptions
pehlevies et parthes*, Corpus inscriptionum iranicarum,
Suppl. Series, i, London 1972, 28, 57), echoed in early Islamic times in the Makurrān/Mukurrān of Arabic
poetry (e.g. al-Ḥakam b. 'Amr al-Tag̲h̲libī, in al-
Ṭabarī, i, 2708, and A'<u>s̲h̲</u>ā Hamdān, *Dīwān*, ed.
Geyer, 328). In general, however, eastern Makrān
must have remained until the Muslim invasions within the cultural and political sphere of India, and latterly under the influence of the Brahman kings of Sind.

Arab raiders reputedly entered Makrān from Kirmān during 'Umar's caliphate, but were deterred by
the appalling desolation and inhospitableness of the
terrain (sentiments subsequently further expressed by
A'<u>s̲h̲</u>ā Hamdān in his verses, see *loc. cit.*). In
Mu'āwiya's caliphate, Ziyād b. Abīhi, governor of
the east, sent thither Sinān b. Salama b. al-Muḥabbiḳ
al-Hud̲h̲alī, who planted a garrison there; according
to another tradition, Makrān was invaded by Ḥakīm
b. D̲j̲abala al-'Abdī (al-Balād̲h̲urī, *Futūḥ*, 433-4;
Yāḳūt, *Buldān*, ed. Beirut, v, 179-80). From here,
raids were directed northwards into Ḳīḳān in the
region known to the Arabs at the time as Ṭūrān [*q.v.*
in *EI*[1]], which came to contain the mediaeval Islamic
town of Ḳuṣdār [*q.v.*], and Makrān also formed the
springboard for Muḥammad b. Ḳāsim al-T̲h̲aḳafī's
invasion of Sind [*q.v.*] in 92/711.

The mediaeval Islamic geographers describe
Makrān as a region of scant population and few
amenities, its main product being sugar-cane syrup
(*fānīd̲h̲*, see *EI*[1] art. SUKKAR). The *Ḥudūd al-'ālam* (*ca.*
372/982), tr. 123, § 27, comm. 373, reckons Makrān
as part of Sind. It names Tīz, in the Čāhbahār bay,
as Makrān's chief port, together with inland towns
which were centres of trading like Kīz or Kīd̲j̲
(modern Kēč), the seat of the king of Makrān, and
Rāsk, Pand̲j̲būr. etc.; Tīz is described by al-
Muḳaddasī, 478, as a flourishing port with fine *ribāṭ*s,
and Pand̲j̲būr as the *ḳaṣaba* or chef-lieu of the region.
The local ruler of Makrān whose seat was at Kīz must
have been from the family mentioned in connection
with early G̲h̲aznavid history. According to
Miskawayh, in *Tad̲j̲ārib al-umam*, ii, 298-9, tr. v,
320-1, 'Aḍud al-Dawla's general 'Ābid b. 'Alī had
penetrated to Tīz and western Makrān in 360/970 as
part of the operations to subdue the disturbed province of Kirmān, and had brought all these regions
under Būyid allegiance (cf. Bosworth, *The Banū Ilyās
of Kirmān (320-57/932-68)*, in *Iran and Islam, in memory
of the late Vladimir Minorsky*, ed. idem, Edinburgh 1971,
117-18). With the subsequent rise of the G̲h̲aznawids
[*q.v.*], the local ruler of Makrān, named by Bayhaḳī
as Ma'dān, submitted to Sebüktigin and Maḥmūd.
After 417/1026, his son 'Īsā likewise acknowledged
G̲h̲aznawid suzerainty, but Sultan Maḥmūd's son
Mas'ūd during 421-2/1030-1 sent an army into
Makrān which placed 'Īsā's brother Abu 'l-'Askar on
the throne there; clearly, Makrān was at this time a
loosely-tributary state of the G̲h̲aznawid empire on
the same sort of footing as the Ziyārids of Gurgān and
Ṭabaristān or the Ṣaffārids of Sīstān before the imposition of G̲h̲aznawid direct rule in 393/1003 (M.
Nāzim, *The life and times of Sulṭān Maḥmūd of Ghazna*,
Cambridge 1931, 79-80; R. Gelpke, *Sulṭān Mas'ūd I.
von Gazna. Die drei ersten Jahre seiner Herrschaft
(421/1030-424/1033)*, Munich 1957, 87-9).

During the succeeding centuries, Makrān appears
little on the general scene of eastern Islamic history.
At times, outside empires, like those of the G̲h̲ūrids
and K̲h̲ʷārazm-S̲h̲āhs [*q.vv.*] and the *amīr*s of the Il-

K̲h̲ānids after the death of Abū Sa'īd (Ibn Baṭṭūṭa, ii,
124; *amīr* Malik Dīnār), exercised some measure of
suzerainty there, but local potentates must have held
all internal power. Marco Polo sailed along the
Makrān coast on his way home in 1290, describing it
as Kesmacoran (= Kīd̲j̲ Makrān) and as the last of
the provinces of India, under a separate ruler of its
own (Sir Henry Yule, *The book of Ser Marco Polo the
Venetian*, London 1871, ii, 334-5; cf. P. Pelliot, *Notes
on Marco Polo*, ii, 759-60). It was during these centuries that Makrān was largely colonised by Balūč
tribes, Makrān being predominantly Balūčī-speaking
today. The region's history may now be followed in
the *EI*[1] art. BALŌČISTĀN and the *EI*[2] arts. KILĀT and
LAS BĒLA.

Bibliography: (in addition to references given
in the article): W. Tomaschek, *Zur historische
Topographie von Persiens*, in *SB Ak. Wien*, cii (1883),
44 ff.; Pauly-Wissowa, vii/1, cols. 895-903, art.
Gedrosia (Kiessling); Sir Thomas Holdich, *Notes on
ancient and mediaeval Makran*, in *Geogr. Jnal.*, vii
(1896), 387-405; Le Strange, *The lands of the Eastern
Caliphate*, 329-30; Marquart, *Ērānšahr*, 31-4,
179 ff.; R. Hughes-Buller, *Baluchistan District
gazeteers series. vii. Makrán*, Bombay 1906.

(C. E. BOSWORTH)

MAḲRĪN B. MUḤAMMAD AL-BUG̲H̲TŪRĪ [see
AL-BUG̲H̲TŪRĪ].

AL-MAḲRĪZĪ, TAḲĪ AL-DĪN ABŪ 'l-'ABBĀS AḤMAD
B. 'ALĪ B. 'ABD AL-ḲĀDIR (766-845/1364-1442),
Egyptian historian.

His father (d. 779/1378 at the age of fifty), married
a daughter of the wealthy philologist and jurist Ibn al-
Ṣā'ig̲h̲ (d. 776/1375). He was born in Cairo, apparently in 765/1363-4. The *nisba* Maḳrīzī refers to a
quarter in Ba'labakk where his paternal family came
from. His paternal grandfather, 'Abd al-Ḳādir b.
Muḥammad (*ca.* 677-733/1278-1332, see Ibn Ḥad̲j̲ar,
Durar, ii, 391 f.) was a Ḥanbalī, his maternal grandfather, who influenced his early upbringing, a Hanafī.
His father was a S̲h̲āfi'ī, and he himself opted for
S̲h̲āfi'ism in early manhood; he also developed (non-
juridical) Ẓāhirī tendencies (cf. I. Goldziher, *Die
Ẓāhiriten*, Leipzig 1884, 196-202). He received the
thorough education of a youth born into a well-to-do
scholarly family, studying with famous scholars and
eventually being able to boast of "600 *s̲h̲aykh*s." Like
his father, but with greater success initially, he exercised a variety of administrative and scholarly functions, such as those of writer of *tawḳī'*s, deputy judge,
muḥtasib (for terms lasting only a few months each in
801, 802, and 807), preacher in the Mosque of 'Amr
and the Madrasa of al-Ḥasan, *imām* and chief administrator of the Mosque of al-Ḥākim, and professor
of *ḥadīt̲h̲* in the Mu'ayyadiyya. In Damascus, where
he spent about ten years beginning in 810/1408, he
held teaching positions at the As̲h̲rafiyya and
Iḳbāliyya, and was chief financial administrator of the
Ḳalānisiyya and the great Nūrī Hospital, although
this last position was reserved by law for the S̲h̲āfi'ī
judge of Damascus. He had actually been offered that
judgeship by al-Nāṣir b. Barḳūḳ, but had refused.
While in Syria, he appears to have decided to give up
an unsatisfactory public career and devote himself
full-time to historical scholarship (instead of part-time
as he had done before). He did so after his return to
Egypt. He spent a number of years in Mecca and died
in Cairo in early February 1442. The last of his
children had died already in 826/1423 (*Sulūk*, iv, 2,
651). A nephew, Nāṣir al-Dīn Muḥammad b.
Muḥammad (801-67/1399-1462), survived him (al-
Sak̲h̲āwī, *Ḍaw'*, ix, 150).

The germs of his determination to become an

historian were perhaps planted by Ibn Khaldūn, with whom he appears to have been on familiar terms; according to *Ḍaw'*, ii, 24, he once predicted on the basis of Ibn Khaldūn's horoscope when the latter would again be appointed to office. With his fellow historians, such as al-ʿAynī [*q.v.*] and Ibn Ḥadjar, he seems to have had professional, and perhaps also personal, difficulties, although relations remained outwardly proper. Ibn Ḥadjar's devoted student al-Sakhāwī displays an outspokenly negative attitude toward him. His contemporaries were sometimes critical of his scholarship, cf., e.g., Ibn Taghrībirdī, *Nudjūm,* ed. Popper, vi, 756, tr., part iv, 143, *anno* 841. Yet his works were not only numerous and often planned on the grand scale, but they also proved to be of lasting importance.

For older editions, translations, and studies, most of them still useful for scholarship, see Brockelmann (below, *Bibliography*), whose bibliographical references are not repeated here. Best known is *al-Mawāʿiẓ wa 'l-iʿtibār fī dhikr al-khiṭaṭ wa 'l-āthār,* commonly referred to as *Khiṭaṭ* (the incomplete ed. of G. Wiet covers about one-half of the ed. Būlāḳ 1270, repr. Beirut, *ca.* 1970; English translation by K. Stowasser in progress). It deals with the topography of Fusṭāṭ and Cairo as well as with Alexandria and Egyptian history in general. According to the critical Ibn Ḥadjar (al-Sakhawī), al-Maḳrīzī used much of the material assembled earlier by al-Awḥadī (761-811/1359-1408). He made no mention of that in the *Khiṭaṭ* (in the way in which, for instance, Ibn Ḳuṭlūbughā acknowledged that he had used al-Maḳrīzī's notes for his *Tādj al-tarādjim*), but elsewhere he spoke of his indebtedness to al-Awḥadī (see *Ḍaw'*, i, 358 f.). The accusation of plagiarism seems much too harsh. The preservation of older sources now apparently lost is one of the *Khiṭaṭ*'s greatest merits.

Among his many other works are a history of the Fāṭimids (*Ittiʿāẓ al-ḥunafā'*, ed. Djamāl al-Dīn al-Shayyāl, Cairo 1367/1948, 1387/1967; ed. A. Hilmy, Cairo, 1971-3, see C. Cahen and M. Adda, in *Arabica,* xxii [1975], 302-20) and a history of the Ayyūbids and Mamlūks (*al-Sulūk li-maʿrifat al-mulūk,* ed. M. M. Ziyāda and S. ʿA. ʿĀshūr, Cairo 1934-73; English translation of the history of the Ayyūbids by R. J. C. Broadhurst [Boston 1980]; for source studies, see e.g. D. P. Little, in *JSS,* xix [1974], 252-68), also extensive biographical works, which remained uncompleted, on prominent Egyptians, entitled *al-Muḳaffā* and *Durar al-ʿuḳūd*, as well as a world history, *al-Khabar ʿan al-bashar,* which he also did not live to complete; it contains his last eloquent statement on the value of history. His short monographs are remarkable for the interesting subjects they deal with, such as the differences between Umayyads and ʿAbbāsids (*al-Nizaʿ wa 'l-takhāṣum,* ed. G. Vos, Leiden 1888, Cairo 1937; Eng. tr. C. E. Bosworth *Al-Magrīzī's "Book of contention and strife...",* Manchester 1981, see idem in *Islam: past influence and present challenge = W. M. Watt Festschrift,* Edinburgh 1979, 93-104), the Arab tribes which came to Egypt (*al-Bayān wa 'l-iʿrāb,* ed. ʿAbd al-Madjīd ʿĀbidīn, Cairo 1961), the Muslim rulers of Ethiopia (*al-Ilmān bi-akhbār man bi-arḍ al-Ḥabasha min mulūk al-Islām*), or the geography of the Ḥaḍramawt (*al-Ṭurfa al-gharība*). His interest in the economic factors in history is evident in the *Sulūk* and in treatises on measures and on coins (al-Nadjaf 1387/1967, Turkish translation by İ. Artuk, in *Belleten,* xvii [1953], 367-92) as well as on famines and inflation in Egypt (*Ighāthat al-umma,* Cairo 1940; ed. al-Shayyāl, Cairo 1957; French translation by G. Wiet, in *JESHO,* v [1962], 1-90). A work on certain aspects of the biography of the Prophet (*Imtāʿ al-asmāʿ*, ed. Maḥmūd Shākir, Cairo 1941), a biography of Tamīm al-Dārī (*Ḍaw' al-sārī,* ed. M. A. ʿĀshūr, Cairo 1392/1972), a treatise on caliphs and rulers who performed the pilgrimage (*al-Dhahab al-masbūk,* ed. al-Shayyāl, Cairo 1955), a discussion of the preferred position of the Prophet's family (*Maʿrifat mā yadjibu li-āl al-bayt al-sharīf min al-ḥaḳḳ ʿalā man ʿadāhum,* ed. M. A. ʿĀshūr, Cairo 1973), attest to his religious interests, as does a work on dogmatics not yet studied (*Tadjrīd al-tawḥīd,* cf. also *al-Bayān al-mufīd fī 'l-farḳ bayn al-tawḥīd wa 'l-talḥīd,* of somewhat doubtful attribution, ed. and tr. by G. C. Anawati, see *MIDEO,* xii [1974], 150). He also published brief treatises on minerals (*al-Maḳāṣid al-saniyya*) and bees (*ʿIbar,* or *Dhikr al-naḥl,* ed. al-Shayyāl, Cairo 1946). A general work on geography, entitled *Djāmiʿ al-azhār min al-Rawḍ al-miʿṭār,* has not yet been sufficiently studied, see IBN ʿABD AL-MUNʿIM AL-ḤIMYARĪ, at the end.

Bibliography: Ibn Ḥadjar, *Inbā'*, ix, Hyderabad 1396/1976, 170-2; Sakhāwī, *Ḍaw'*, ii, 21-25; Ibn Taghrībirdī, *Manhal,* ed. A. Y. Nadjātī, Cairo 1375/1956, i, 394-9, and *Nudjūm,* ed. W. Popper, vi, 277-9, tr., part v, 182. Still later biographical notes, such as the one in Ibn Iyās, ed. M. Mostafa, ii, 231 f. (*Bibl. Isl.* 5b), contain no new information. Further, Brockelmann, II, 47-50, 675, S II, 36-8, also *EI*¹, art. *al-Maḳrīzī; Dirāsāt ʿan al-Maḳrīzī,* Cairo 1391/1971 (lectures given in 1966 by six scholars). (F. ROSENTHAL)

MAKRŪH (A.) "reprehensible action, action disapproved of", one of the five juridical qualifications (*aḥkām* [*q.v.*]) of human actions according to the *Sharīʿa* [*q.v.*].

MAKS, toll, customs duty, is a loanword in Arabic and goes back to the Aramaic *maksā,* cf. Hebrew *mekes* and Assyr. *miksu;* from it is formed a verb *m-k-s* I, II, III and *makkās,* the collector of customs. According to the Arabic tradition preserved in Ibn Sīda, even in the Djāhiliyya there were market-dues called *maks,* so that the word must have entered Arabic very early. It is found in Arabic papyri towards the end of the 1st century A.H.

C. H. Becker dealt with the history of the *maks,* especially in Egypt, and we follow him here. The old law books use *maks* in the sense of *ʿushr,* the tenth levied by the merchants, more properly the equivalent of an excise duty than of a custom. They still show some opposition to the *maks,* then give it due legal force, but the word continued to have unpleasant association, cf. the *ḥadīth*: *inna ṣāḥib al-maks fī 'l-nār* "the tax-collector will go to hell": Goldziher has suggested that the Jewish view of the publican may have had some influence here. There are six traditions about *maks* in the *Kitāb al-Amwāl* by Abū ʿUbayd al-Ḳāsim b. Sallām (Cairo 1353, nos. 1624-9, Brockelmann, S I, 166), and al-Suyūṭī wrote a *Risāla fī dhamm al-maks* (Brockelmann, II, 152, no. 174).

The institution of the customs duty was adopted by Islam about the beginning of the Umayyad period or shortly before it. While theological theory demanded a single customs area in Islam, the old frontiers remained in existence by land and water, and Egypt, Syria and Mesopotamia were separate customs areas. The amount of the duty in the canon law was settled not so much by the value of the goods as by the person, i.e. the religion of the individual paying it; but in practice, attention was paid to the article and there were preferential duties, and no attention was paid to the position of the owner in regard to Islam. The laws of taxation were very complicated and graduated; the duties rose in course of time from the tenth (*ᶜus̲h̲r*) to the fifth (*k̲h̲ums*).

The Egyptian *maks* was levied on the frontier at al-ᶜArīs̲h̲ and in the ports (*sawāḥil*) ᶜAyd̲h̲āb, al-Ḳusayr, al-Ṭūr and al-Suways, but there was also an octroi to be paid in al-Fusṭāṭ, at a place called Maks. This name is said to have replaced an old Umm Dunayn and then became identified with the Maks = custom-house of Cairo. At Alexandria there was a *maks al-munāk̲h̲* for caravans, and today Maks is the name of a quarter there, cf. K̲h̲alīl Muṭrān, *Waṣf al-Maks* (Nak̲h̲la, *Muk̲h̲tārāt*, ii, 139-41). All grain had to pass through here before it could be sold, and two *dirhams* per *artaba* and a few minor charges had to be paid on it. Further details of the administration of the *maks* in the earliest period are not known; but there are references towards the end of the 1st century A.H. to a *ṣāḥib maks Miṣr* in papyri and in literature also.

The conception of the *maks* was extended in the Fāṭimid period, when all kinds of small dues and taxes became known as *mukūs*, especially—emphasising the already mentioned unpleasant associations of the word—the unpopular ones which the people regarded as unjust. Such occasional taxes had been levied from time to time in the early centuries of Islam. The first to make them systematic was the dreaded financial secretary and noted opponent of Aḥmad b. Ṭūlūn, Aḥmad b. al-Mudabbir [see IBN AL-MUDABBIR]. The latter introduced not only an increase in the ground-tax and the three great monopolies of pasture fisheries and soda (in connection with which it is interesting to note a reversion was made to old Roman taxes), but also a large number of smaller taxes which were called *maᶜāwin* and *marāfiḳ* and included among the *hilālī*, the taxes to be paid according to lunar years. Such artifices (known as *mukūs* from the Fāṭimid period and later as *maẓālim, ḥimāyāt, rimāyāt* or *mustaʾd̲j̲arāt*) were destined to develop in time into the main form of oppressing the people and to become one of the principal causes of the economic decline in Egypt, until under the Mamlūks a limit was reached where hardly anything was left untaxed and *mukūs* were even granted as fiefs and "misfortune became general" (*wa-ᶜammat al-balwā*). These small taxes, however, (but not the monopolies) were repeatedly abolished by reforming rulers, indeed *ibṭāl al-mukūs* (other terms are *radd, musāmaḥat, isḳāṭ, waḍᶜ, rafᶜ al-mukūs*) even formed part of the style and title of such rulers. Thus it is recorded of Aḥmad b. Ṭūlūn that he abolished some duties, and later of Ṣalāḥ al-Dīn, Baybars, Ḳalāwūn and his sons K̲h̲alīl and Nāṣir Muḥammad, of al-As̲h̲raf S̲h̲aᶜbān, Barḳūḳ and D̲j̲aḳmaḳ. Al-Maḳrīzī gives a long list of *mukūs* abolished by Ṣalāḥ al-Dīn, and al-Ḳalḳas̲h̲andī gives copies of the texts of *musāmaḥāt*, which are decrees of the Mamlūk sultans abolishing taxes or granting exemption from dues which were sent to the governors and read from the *minbars* and sometimes contain very full details, while shorter decrees were probably carved on stone and are given among the fragments published by van Berchem. It would of course be wrong to deduce from such abolitions of taxes that the government was a particularly good one, while on the other hand, the continually-recurring extortion of the same taxes shows that the abuses had been restored in the interval. Al-Maḳrīzī, *K̲h̲iṭaṭ*, i, 111, concludes with the well-known jibe at the Copts: "even now there are *mukūs*, which are in the control of the vizier, but bring nothing to the state but only to the Copts, who do exactly as they like with them to their great advantage". A group which particularly suffered from the *mukūs* were the pilgrims to Mecca from the Mag̲h̲rib. The Spanish traveller Ibn D̲j̲ubayr [*q.v.*], who as a pilgrim passed by Egypt in 1183, saw at Alexandria, ᶜAyd̲h̲āb and D̲j̲udda many proofs of *mukūs* and *waẓāʾif mukūsiyya*. He wrote a poem about them and sent it to Ṣalāḥ al-Dīn, whom he admired. But he noted *tamkīs* and *ḍarība maksiyya* even in Syria and Sicily. About that time, al-Mak̲h̲zūmī wrote his *Minhād̲j̲*, with lists of *mukūs* and other duties (*k̲h̲ums, wād̲j̲ib, ḳāf, matd̲j̲ar*).

Among the great variety of dues, which were of course not all levied at the same place and at the same time, were the following: *hilālī* taxes on houses, baths, ovens, mills and gardens; harbour dues in al-D̲j̲īza, in Cairo at "the corn-quay" (*sāḥil al-g̲h̲alla*) and at the arsenal (*ṣināᶜa*), also levied separately on each passenger; market-dues for goods and caravans (*baḍāʾiᶜ wa-ḳawāfil*) especially for horses, camels, mules, cattle, sheep, poultry and slaves; meat, fish, salt, sugar, pepper, oil, vinegar, turnips, wool, silk, linen and cotton; wood, earthenware, coal, halfa grass, straw and henna; wine and oil-presses, tanned goods; brokerage (*samsara*) charges on the sale of sheep, dates and linen. There were taxes on markets, drinking-houses and brothels, which were euphemistically called *rusūm al-wilāya*. Warders deprive prisoners of everything they have; indeed, this right is sold to the highest bidder; officers consume the fiefs of their soldiers; peasants pay their lords forced labour and give them presents (*barāṭil, hadāyā*) and many officials (*s̲h̲ādd, muḥtasib, mubās̲h̲irūn* and *wulāt*) also accept them; when a campaign is begun, the merchants pay a special war-tax and a third of inheritances falls to the state; when news of victories is received and when the Nile rises, levies are made; the *d̲h̲immīs*, in addition to paying the poll-tax, have to contribute to the maintenance of the army; pilgrims to the Holy Sepulchre pay a tax in Jerusalem; separate special taxes are levied to maintain the embankments, the Nilometer etc.

Outside of Egypt we occasionally hear of the *maks* as toll or market-due, e.g. in D̲j̲udda and in North Africa (cf. Dozy, *Suppl.*, ii, 606). Ibn al-Ḥād̲j̲d̲j̲, *Madk̲h̲al*, iii, 67, mentions a *musāmaḥat maẓālim*, but does not use the word *mukūs* in this sense.

Bibliography: Ibn Mammātī, *Ḳawānīn al-dawāwīn*, 10-26; Maḳrīzī, *K̲h̲iṭaṭ*, i, 88 ff., 104-11; ii, 267; Ḳalḳas̲h̲andī, iii, 468 ff. (= Wüstenfeld, 169 ff.); xiii, 30 ff., 117; C. H. Becker, *Papyri Schott-Reinhardt*, 51 ff.; idem, *Beiträge zur Geschichte Ägyptens*, 140-8; idem, *EI*[1], ii, 15; idem, *Islamstudien*, i, 177, 267, 273 ff.; M. van Berchem, *Matériaux pour un Corpus Inscriptionum Arabicarum*, i, 59, 560; ii, 297, 332 ff., 374, 377, 384; A. Mez, *Renaissance*, 111 ff., 117; W. Heffening, *Fremdenrecht*, 53 ff.; H. Bowen, *The life and times of ᶜAlī b. ᶜĪsā, the "Good Vizier"*, Cambridge 1928, 124; Wensinck, *Handbook*, 228; Fagnan, *Additions*, 165; Yāḳūt, iv, 606, on *Maks*; Ibn D̲j̲ubayr, *Travels*, ed. Wright[2], 14, 55, 62, 69, 77, 301, 331; Cl. Cahen, *Douanes et commerce dans les ports méditerranéens de l'Égypte médiévale d'après le Minhādj d'al-Makhzoumi*, in *JESHO*, vii (1964), 217-314 (= *Mak̲h̲zūmiyyāt* [57]-[154]). (W. BJÖRKMAN)

MAḲṢŪRA (A.), a name given to a poem whose rhyme is constituted by an *alif maḳṣūra* (ى). According to al-Masᶜūdī (*Murūd̲j̲*, viii, 307 = § 3462), the first author of a piece of this type was the S̲h̲īᶜī Naṣr b. Nuṣayr al-Ḥulwānī [*q.v.*], who preceded the most famous versifier in this field, Ibn Durayd (died 321/933 [*q.v.*]. The author of the *Murūd̲j̲* also cites someone called Ibn Warḳāʾ (unidentified) who had composed a *maḳṣūra* on that of Ibn Durayd, and declares that the latter had often been imitated

(*ʿāraḍahā ... d̲j̲amāʿa min al-s̲h̲uʿarāʾ*; viii, 305 3461), but he only names in this connection a certain ʿAlī b. Muḥammad al-Tanūk̲h̲ī, whose *Maḳṣūra* was dedicated to the praise of the Tanūk̲h̲. As the *Murūd̲j̲* dates from 332/943, some imitations must have been made in the first third of the 4th century, testifying also to the immediate vogue of the masterpiece of Ibn Durayd; this success, due in large part to the didactic value of the piece of verse, was not contradicted in the course of the following centuries, to judge by the exceptional number of manuscripts of the *Maḳṣūra* which survive and by the *tak̲h̲mīs*s, *tasmīṭ*s and commentaries which it inspired (see Brockelmann, S I, 172-3; Ben Salem, cited in the *Bibl.*). Among the *s̲h̲urūḥ* which were devoted to it, al-Ṣafadī (*Wāfī*, ii, 1301) and al-Bag̲h̲dadī, himself author of a brief commentary (*K̲h̲izāna*, ed. Būlāḳ, i, 490 = ed. Cairo, iii, 105) appreciate in particular that of Ibn His̲h̲ām al-Lak̲h̲mī [*q.v.* in Suppl.] which was partially edited, with a Latin translation of the *Maḳṣūra*, by Boysen, in 1828. The Dutch were interested from an early date in this famous *Maḳṣūra*; by 1773, Haitsma had translated it into Latin and published it at Franeker, following it with the commentary of Ibn K̲h̲ālawayh; this work had served as the basis of the edition-translation, also in Latin, of Sceidus (1786), and there exists in ms., in Leiden, a Latin version of N. G. Schroeder (1721-98), as well as a commentary of the same author and another anonymous Latin translation accompanied by a commentary (see P. Voorhoeve, *Handlist of Arabic manuscripts*, Leiden 1957, 192). In 1808, Bilderdijk brought out in the Hague a new edition and Dutch translation of the same *Maḳṣūra* which, since then, has been made the subject of several oriental editions: Tehran 1859 and 1910, Istanbul 1300/1883 with the commentary of al-Zamak̲h̲s̲h̲arī, Cairo 1328/1910, 1358/1939.

The text of the poem calls for some remarks. In its present state, it numbers 249 and even 25 verses of *rad̲j̲az* in Ibn Sālim's ed. of the *Dīwān* of Ibn Durayd (Tunis 1973, 115-37), while al-Bag̲h̲dadī (*loc. cit.*) counts only 239, so that it must be considered that several verses have been interpolated. In fact, al-Suyūṭī (*Bug̲h̲ya*, 32) asserted that the original *maṭlaʿ* opened with a conditional particle, then a protasis without an apodosis, followed by a feminine, of which it was not known to what it related; it is Kamāl al-Dīn Ibn al-Anbārī (died 577/1181) [see AL-ANBĀRĪ]) who allegedly composed a prologue of ten verses, of which the last may have been retained as a true *maṭlaʿ*. Independently of probable additions, the plan of this poem composed in praise of the Mīkālīs [*q.v.*] appeared barely coherent: at the beginning, there is the topic of the beloved, the separation, the cruel destiny of the poet, then comes the relation of a pilgrimage containing a certain number of toponyms in *-ā*; the personal glorification, followed by the panegyric of the Mīkālīs (vv. 96-110), but the beloved appears again later on, possibly justifying the nostalgia experienced by the poet for the city of Baṣra, and one can scarcely see why he glorifies himself anew, before delivering moral reflections, recounting a journey to the Mīkālis, returning to the *nasīb*, inserting some verses on wine and finally expressing his satisfaction. In spite of all these faults, the *Maḳṣūra* aroused the admiration of the litterati, philologists and *fuḳahāʾ*. The former, and particularly the poets, see in it a kind of tour-de-force because of the difficulty of the rhyme and the diversity of the themes treated; for the philologists, it contains a third of the nouns in *alif maḳṣūra* and may consequently serve for the teaching of vocabulary; the *fuḳahāʾ*, for their part, were seduced by the moral reflections which incline towards resignation.

Another important *Maḳṣūra* is that of Ḥāzim al-Ḳarṭad̲j̲annī (died 684/1285 [*q.v.*]) which contains no less than 1,006 verses of *rad̲j̲az* and was composed in imitation of Ibn Durayd and in praise of the Ḥafṣid al-Mustanṣir. As it has already been discussed in the article on Ḥāzim, we shall confine ourselves here to a few pieces of information. The plan of the poem is hardly more homogeneous than that of its model: *nasīb* (vv. 1-52), praise of al-Mustanṣir's ancestors and services rendered by the latter (vv. 53-172), recollection of the poet's youth in various towns in Spain (vv. 173-84), glorification of love and description of the sky (vv. 185-97), recollection of past pleasures (vv. 198-502), return to the beloved (vv. 503-66), laments (vv. 567-788), panegyric of al-Mustanṣir (vv. 789-974), and finally, eulogy of the poet's masterpiece (vv. 975-1006).

The text of this *Maḳṣūra* was published in Cairo in 1344, then by Mahdī ʿAllām, in *Ḥawliyyat Kulliyyat al-Ādāb* of ʿAyn S̲h̲ams University 1953-4, 1-110. Apart from the commentary of al-G̲h̲arnāṭī (*Rafʿ al-ḥud̲j̲ub al-mastūra ʿan maḥāsin al-Maḳṣūra*, Cairo 1344/1925), M. Lakhdar (*Vie littéraire*, 37) mentions another of Abu 'l-Ḳāsim al-Sabtī (died 760/1358).

Among the other pieces of verse which bear the title of *Maḳṣūra*, that of Abū Madyan (died 594/1197 [*q.v.*]) met with a great success, and there exist several mss. of it (see for example, G. Vajda, *Catalogue*, 460; Brockelmann, S II, 785). The BN in Paris also possesses one of Ḥasan b. Ḥabīb (Vajda, 459) and another of Muḥammad b. Aḥmad al-Hawwārī (*ibid.*; Brockelmann, II², 15). Ḥamdūn b. al-Ḥād̲j̲d̲j̲ (1174-1232/1760-1817) has also left us a *Maḳṣūra* on prosody and rhymes (E. Lévi-Provençal, *Manuscrits arabes de Rabat*, 292 (5), 497 (11); Lakhdar, *Vie littéraire*, 282).

Bibliography: Apart from the works cited in the article, see: on Ibn Durayd, A. Ben Salem, *Ibn Durayd, vie, oeuvre et influence*, thesis Paris 1968, 100-9, 313-7, 324-30 (published in Arabic, Tunis 1972); on Ḥāzim, E. Garcia Gómez, *Quelques remarques sur la "qaṣīda maqṣūra" d'Abū 'l-Ḥasan Ḥāzim al-Qarṭājannī*, in *Actes du XVIIIᵉ Congrès des Orientalistes*, 1931, 242-3; idem, *Observaciones sobre la "Qaṣīda maqṣūra" de Abū 'l-Ḥāzim al-Qarṭāŷannī*, in *And.*, i (1933), 80-103; M. ʿAllām, *Abu 'l-Ḥasan al-Ḳarṭād̲j̲annī wa-fann al-maḳṣūra fi 'l-adab al-ʿarabī*, in *Ḥawliyyat Kulliyyat al-Ādāb*, ʿAyn S̲h̲ams University, 1951, 1-31; M. H. Belkhodja, ed. of *Manhad̲j̲ al-bulag̲h̲āʾ* of Ḥāzim, Tunis 1966, introd. 81-6.

(CH. PELLAT)

MAḲṢŪRA [see MASD̲J̲ID].

MAKTAB (A.), pl. *makātib*, was an appellation for the Islamic traditional school frequently known also as *kuttāb* [*q.v.*; a brief discussion of the uses of *maktab* will be found there]. The same applies to its equivalents in Persian, *maktab*, and in Turkish, *mekteb*. In Egypt, the Copts too used *maktáb* to denote their own traditional schools. Later, however, the term came also to mean "school", more generally, as in the Ottoman Turkish *mekteb-i ṣanāʾiʿ* ("vocational school") or even *mekteb gemisi* ("training ship"). In both Ottoman Turkish and Arabic the term was borrowed, mainly during the 19th century, to denote—in various word-combinations—some of the more modernised educational institutions which were then being established. Thus during the reign of Maḥmūd II, the *Mekteb-i ṭibbiyye s̲h̲āhāne*, the *Mekteb-i maʿārif-i ʿadliyye* and the *Mekteb-i ʿulūm-i ḥarbiyye* were set up to teach, respectively, medicine, general knowledge for government service and military studies. Later, in 1859, the *Mekteb-i mülkiyye* was founded as a civil service school. In a parallel manner, in Muḥammad ʿAlī's Egypt, *al-Maktab al-ʿālī,* which the French called "École des Princes", was inaugurated in the 1820s as a military college for the male members of Muḥammad ʿAlī's family and of some others. In 1833, a *Maktab al-muhimmāt al-ḥarbiyya* was set up in Cairo and closed down after three years, probably purveying for munitions or serving as military workshops. In 1836, a *Maktab raʾīs al-muḥāsaba* was set up to train the accountants which were so badly needed. In the Khedive Ismāʿīl's days, the general sense of "school" for *maktab* seems to have become so prevalent in Egypt that the term *makātib ahliyya,* i.e. "national schools" or "local schools", as were called the primary schools founded between 1868 and 1879 in Cairo, its suburbs and the provincial centres, was accepted unquestioningly. From there, the usage seems to have spread into other Arab lands, although *maktab* continued too to be widely used as synonymous with *kuttāb.* In our days, in Turkey, a primary school is called *ilk mektep* and the next stage, the "middle school", *orta mektep.* In Malaysia, it has recently been used for "Institute", as in *Maktab Perguruan Ilm Khas* ("Specialised Teachers' Training Institute") in Kuala Lumpur. *Mekteb* was also the title of a journal, published since 1307 A.H., in Istanbul, in Turkish, first as a weekly, then twice a month, for the benefit of educators. In modern Persian usage, in addition to its basic meaning of "school", *maktab* has acquired also the connotation of an "instructing manual", as in *Maktab-i Islām* ("A manual of instruction into Islam", 2 vols., Tehran 1375-8/1334-7), Mihrdād Mihrīn's *Maktab-i falsafa-yi igzīstansiyālīzm* ("A manual—or study—of existentialism", Tehran 1343), *Maktab-i tas̲h̲ayyuʿ* ("A manual of instruction in S̲h̲iʿism", annual, i, 1378-/1338-), or even *Maktab-i ʿis̲h̲k* ("A manual of love", title of a play by ʿAlī Aṣg̲h̲ar S̲h̲arīf, Tehran 1313). Otherwise, during the 20th century, *maktab* has increasingly come to mean, in Arabic, "bureau" or "department", generally in the official sense, such as *Maktab al-buḥūt̲h̲* ("Bureau of research") and *Maktab dāʾim* ("Permanent bureau") or *Maktab al-ṣiḥḥa* ("Department of Health"); or else "office" as in *Maktab al-barīd* ("Post office"); or even "agency", as in *Maktab al-anbāʾ* ("News agency"). This applies to both administrative and military terms, sometimes with slight differences of usage, in various countries.

Bibliography: See the bibl. for KUTTĀB and also the arts. in *EI*[1], *İA* and *Türk Ansikl.*, s.v. Further, *Mekteb-i ṣanāʾiʿ niẓām-nāmesī,* n.p. [Istanbul] 1285; Meḥmed Nüzhet, *Mekātib-i rus̲h̲diyye oḳunmaḳ üzere muk̲h̲taṣar mens̲h̲eʾet dir,* Istanbul 1289; H. Vámbery, *Der Islam im neunzehnten Jahrhundert,* Leipzig 1875, 171 ff.; Fāḍīl, *Mekātib-i ʿaskariyye-yi s̲h̲ākirdanine mak̲h̲ṣūṣ müswedde numūneleri,* Istanbul 1314; Maʿārif-i ʿUmūmiye Neẓāretī, *Mekātib-i iʿdādīyede tedrīs ōlunān ʿulūm ve-funūn müfredāt prog̲h̲rāmī,* fasc. 1-7, Istanbul 1327; idem, *Mekātib-i ibtidāʾiyye ders müfredātī,* Istanbul 1329; idem, *Mekātib-i Sulṭāniyyenin̄ ṣunūf-ī ibtidāʾiyye ve-tāliye ders prog̲h̲rāmlarī,* Istanbul 1329; Ibrāhīm ʿAs̲h̲ḳī, *Mekteb terbiyesı,* Istanbul 1330; Fāʾiḳ Ṣabrī, *Mekteblerde d̲j̲og̲h̲rāfiyā tedrīsātī,* Istanbul 1331; *Mekteb-i Sulṭānīnin̄ ellind̲j̲ sene-yi dewriyye-yi teʾsīsī münāsebetile nes̲h̲rolunmus̲h̲tur,* Istanbul 1334/1918; Maʿārif-i ʿUmūmiyye Neẓāretī, *Mekātib-i Sulṭāniyye ʿArabī ve-Ed̲j̲nebī lisānlarī müfredāt prog̲h̲rāmlarinin̄ muʿaddal ṣūretleri,* Istanbul 1335; *Mekteb-i mülkiyye-yi s̲h̲āhāne taʾrīk̲h̲česī,* n.p. 1337 (lith.); D̲j̲elāl ʿAbdī, *Muk̲h̲taṣar-i mekteb ḥifẓ-i ṣiḥḥasī,* Istanbul 1340; Mekteb-i Ḥarbiyye—Birind̲j̲ī dewre, *Ḍābiṭān kürsü 1340 senesi ʿumūmī imtiḥān prog̲h̲rāmlarī,* Istanbul 1340; Kāẓīm Nāmī, *Mekteblerde ak̲h̲lāḳī nāṣil telḳīn eytmeli?* Istanbul 1343/1925; T. Kāllīktyeyev, *Mektepte ōḳūtūd̲j̲ūlar üčun metōdīkte yōldās̲h̲ī,* Kazan 1927; Ḥifẓ al-Raḥmān Rās̲h̲id, *Mektebčiliğin kaʿbesinde,* Istanbul 1928; Safattin Rıza, *Eski tarihte mektep,* in *Atsız Mecmua* (Istanbul), 6 (15 October 1931), 130-1; Şevket Süreyya, *Mektep kooperatifçiliği ve tasarruf terbiyesi,* Ankara 1932; Naci Kasım, *Mektep kitaplari ve Türk irfan hayatı,* Istanbul 1933; *Tek kitap kanuna dair: mektep kitapları tâbilerinin bazi dilekleri,* Istanbul 1933; H. A. Malik, *Köyde mektep,* in *Ülkü* (Ankara), i/6 (July 1933), 481-4; F. Uzun, *Mektepçiliğe dair,* Istanbul 1935; J. Heyworth-Dunne, *An introduction to the history of education in modern Egypt,* London n.d. [1938], 139-42, 207-8, 371-2; İhsan Sungu, *Mekteb-i Maarif-i Adliyyenin tesisi,* in *Tarih Vesikaları,* i/3 (1941), 1-14; *Statuto della communità musulmana in Jugoslavia (25 ottobre 1936),* in *OM,* xxii (1942), 105-9; K. K. Pahlen, *Mission to Turkestan,* London, N.Y. and Toronto 1964, esp. 37-49, 58, 61, 63, 74 (for 1908-9); S.Z. Shaw and E. K. Shaw, *History of the Ottoman Empire and modern Turkey,* ii, Cambridge 1977, index s.v. *Mekteb-i;* İlhan Tekeli, *Toplumsal dönüşüm ve eğitim tarihi üzerine konuşmalar,* Ankara 1980; ʿAbd al-ʿAzīz al-Sayyid al-Miṣrī, *Ḳiṣṣat awwal madrasa islāmiyya fī g̲h̲ābāt Siera Leone,* in *al-Dawḥa* (Ḳaṭar), lxxiii (Jan. 1982), 35-9; P. X. Jacob, *L'enseignement religieux dans la Turquie moderne,* Berlin 1982, 12-38; Avraham Cohen, *Maktab: ha-Ḥeder bĕ-Faras* (Hebr., "Maktab: the Ḥeder in Persia"), in *Peʿamim,* Jerusalem, xiv (1982), 57-76.

(J. M. LANDAU)

MAKTABA, library, is the word now normally used in the Arab world for this institution. In Iran *kitāb-khāna* is used (the entry-word for the article in *EI*[1]), and in modern Turkey *kütüphane.* Other equivalents are *k̲h̲izānat al-kutub* and *dār al-kutub.*

With the zeal for literary pursuits and the ever increasing composition of books, after the period of conquests, men of literary tastes accumulated handsome private collections of books and from the example of the Kūfan philologist Abū ʿAmr al-S̲h̲aybānī we can reasonably assume that it was a custom for authors to deposit copies of their works for reference in the mosque of their town or quarter.

The libraries of the Umayyads contained books on all the principal branches of knowledge cultivated at that time. Librarians were appointed to take charge of them, and translators may have worked in them or, at least, have deposited their works in them.

Youssef Eche, by dint of reading most of the relevant Arabic literature, manuscript or printed, on history and geography, belles-lettres in prose or poetry, *fiḳh* and *waḳf,* has assembled all available information on public and semi-public libraries in ʿIrāḳ, Syria and Egypt during the mediaeval period (up to the death of Hülegü). Hence there is no need to look further than this valuable compendium for the history of libraries in the Arab world during these centuries.

The first public libraries formed a fundamental part of the first academies known as *bayt al-ḥikma* [*q.v.*]. That established by Muʿāwiya contained collections of *ḥadīt̲h̲* and works such as that of ʿAbīd b. S̲h̲ariyya, composed at the order of the caliph. This was inherited by his grandson, K̲h̲ālid b. Yazīd [*q.v.*], who devoted his life to the study of Greek sciences, particularly alchemy and medicine. We are told that he caused such books to be translated, and when an epidemic occurred at the beginning of the reign of ʿUmar b.

ᶜAbd al-ᶜAzīz, he commanded the books to be fetched out of the library (*khizāna*) to be made available for the people.

The *bayt al-ḥikma* underwent its greatest development in the time of the ᶜAbbāsid caliph al-Maʾmūn in Baghdād. To make this library as comprehensive as possible he had valuable Greek manuscripts purchased in the Byzantine empire and translated by a number of competent scholars into Arabic. This library contained books in all the sciences cultivated by the Arabs. After the transfer of the caliphate from Baghdād to Sāmarrā under al-Muᶜtaṣim, successor of al-Maʾmūn, the *bayt al-ḥikma* lost its academic character and was known solely as *khizānat al-Maʾmūn*. Visited by scholars up to the end of the 4th/10th century, it is not mentioned by writers after that time, and is thought either to have been incorporated into the library of one of the caliphs or to have been dispersed by the Saldjūḳs. It is known, however, that some of its books carrying the emblem of al-Maʾmūn were presented to Ibn Abī Uṣaybiᶜa [*q.v.*] at the time of his compiling the *Ṭabaḳāt al-aṭibbāʾ*.

The period of the *bayt al-ḥikma* was followed by that of the *dār al-ᶜilm* [*q.v.*], an institution of semi-official character, established in the style of a public library with its own building for the purposes of disseminating sectarian propaganda and teaching the natural sciences. These were set up in Baghdād, Mawṣil, Baṣra, Rām-Hurmuz and elsewhere; that in Baṣra, founded by Ibn Sawwār, being said to be the first ever established by *waḳf*. All of these are described in detail by Eche, and some by Mackensen (see *Bibl.*). The *dār al-ᶜilm* engendered the *madrasa* [*q.v.*], and so the library is the father of the Arab university. Other celebrated libraries were those attached to the Niẓāmiyya and the Mustanṣiriyya *madrasas* in Baghdād, where there existed also many others attached to *madrasas*, mosques, *ribāṭs* and mausoleums. Eche describes more than twenty of these, most of which were destroyed by Hülegü in 656/1258, as were those of other cities in ᶜIrāḳ. Similar libraries were founded in Damascus, Aleppo and other cities in Syria, and in Egypt.

The library collected by the Fāṭimid caliph al-Ḥākim [*q.v.*] in Cairo contained untold literary treasures and we learn that in the year 435/1043-4 the *wazīr* Abu 'l-Ḳāsim ᶜAlī b. Aḥmad al-Djardjarāʾī gave instructions for a catalogue of the books to be made and the bindings to be renewed, and he appointed Abū Khalaf al-Ḳuḍāᶜī and Ibn Khalaf al-Warrāḳ to superintend the work. This library remained intact till the death of the last Fāṭimid caliph al-ᶜĀḍid, when Ṣalāḥ al-Dīn ordered it to be dissolved and the Ḳāḍī 'l-Fāḍil [*q.v.*] acquired most of the books and deposited them in the library of the Fāḍiliyya *madrasa* which he founded, where they were soon neglected, and by the time of al-Ḳalḳashandī most of them had disappeared. This library is stated to have contained 6,500 volumes on the exact sciences alone, such as mathematics, astronomy, etc., and among its treasures was a globe of copper stated to have been constructed by Ptolemy and bearing an inscription stating that it had been acquired by Khālid b. Yazīd b. Muᶜāwiya.

The Spanish Umayyad caliphs at Cordova possessed a library which achieved great renown. Al-Ḥakam II [*q.v.*] devoted his life to it, employing agents to collect books from all Islamic lands. It is said to have contained some 400,000 volumes, described in a catalogue of 44 volumes, each containing 40 leaves. Disastrously, it was plundered and largely destroyed in the time of his successors. After the conquest of Granada by the Catholic kings, in order to facilitate the conversion of the Moriscos, the order was given that all books in their possession should be handed over to the authorities for examination by experts, so that all useful works of philosophy, medicine and history might be retained and all others destroyed. Cardinal Cisneros, however, decreed that all books in Arabic should be burnt in a public square in Granada. We are frequently told of valuable private libraries which were placed at the disposal of learned men, as e.g. in the biographies of al-Ṣūlī [*q.v.*] we read of his large collection of books which were tastefully bound in red and yellow leather. Al-Ṣafadī [*q.v.*] records in the biography of Ghars al-Niᶜmat al-Ṣābī that he founded in Baghdād a library of about 300 volumes for the use of students and that this library was shamelessly robbed by the librarian who had been placed in charge.

In Persia, libraries allegedly existed at the time of the Achaemenids, as we hear from Ibn Nadīm, but these were destroyed by Alexander the Great. In the ᶜAbbāsid period libraries are recorded at Rām-Hurmuz (founded by Ibn Sawwār), Rayy and Iṣfahān (plundered by the Ghaznawid troops in 420/1029 and removed to Ghazna, but later destroyed there by the Ghūrid Sulṭān ᶜAlāʾ al-Dīn Ḥusayn). In Shīrāz, the celebrated library founded by ᶜAḍud al-Dawla contained a copy of all books written up to that time in all branches of learning (al-Maḳrīzī, 449, tr. in Pinto [see *Bibl.*], 228).

When early in the 7th/13th century the Mongols swept over Persia we read that in addition to the loss of human life and the destruction of other valuable property untold quantities of priceless books were wantonly destroyed. Although some of the sultans of Dihlī patronised scholars and were keen friends of learning, no mention of a library from that period has as yet been found. The earliest of which we hear is, however, that of the saint Niẓām al-Dīn Awliyāʾ, a contemporary of the Khaldjī and Tughluḳid sultans. Many of the Mughal emperors and their courtiers were dedicated bibliophiles and possessed private collections of great value, and fostered the development of the imperial library. This was dispersed after the traumatic events of the 1857-8 Indian Mutiny, and some of its valuable manuscripts came to the India Office Library and the Royal Asiatic Society; but many remain in various libraries of India and Pakistan. Sezgin records 46 libraries in India and 8 in Pakistan which have published catalogues of their Islamic manuscripts, among them the Bānkīpur [*q.v.*] Library at Patna (6,000 manuscripts), the Buhār collection in the National Library at Calcutta (485 Persian and 465 Arabic manuscripts), and the Rāmpur State Library (10,500 manuscripts in Arabic, Persian and various Indian languages).

After the conquest of Constantinople, Meḥemmed II Fātiḥ [*q.v.*] assembled the manuscripts in Greek, Latin and other languages which had survived the holocaust into the library which he founded in the Eski Sarāy, which now forms part of his palace, the Ṭopḳapï Sarāy. Aḥmed III [*q.v.*] established no fewer than five libraries in Istanbul, including his Enderūn-i Hümāyūn Kütübkhānesi, of which the poet Nedīm [*q.v.*] was appointed curator. He also prohibited the export of rare manuscripts. Most of the libraries formerly attached to mosques in the capital have now been transferred to the Süleymaniye Public Library. In Istanbul alone there were said to be in 1959 over 135,000 manuscripts, many of them known only to scholars through the very inadequate *defters* published in the late Ottoman period.

Most countries in the Middle East now possess a national library performing the functions of such libraries everywhere, including, it may be, the publication of the national bibliography (see Auchterlonie, *Libraries* [see *Bibl.*], 245-9). Public, university, special and school libraries have been set up, schools of librarianship inaugurated, and library associations founded.

Arrangements, administration and use of libraries. In the 4th/10th century there were already buildings devoted solely to libraries and erected specially for this purpose. For example, Sābūr b. Ardas͟hīr, the vizier of Bahā᾽ al-Dawla [*q.v.* in Suppl.], built in 381/991 in Bag͟hdād in the Kark͟h quarter a *Dār al-kutub,* which contained over 10,000 volumes (Ibn al-At͟hīr, ix, 246; Yāḳūt, i, 799). The geographer al-Muḳaddasī (449) found in S͟hīrāz a huge library which had been built by the Būyid ᶜAḍud al-Dawla (338-72/949-82). This library was a separate building and consisted of a great hall, a long vaulted building along the three sides of which were a series of rooms (*k͟hazā᾽in*). Along the walls of the central vaulted room and along the side-rooms were cases of carved wood three ells high and three broad, with doors which were let down from the top. The books lay on shelves one above the other. The cases used in the Fāṭimid library in Cairo were somewhat different (al-Maḳrīzī, *K͟hiṭaṭ*, Cairo 1270, i, 409); the bookcases (*rufūf*) were divided by partitions into separate compartments (*ḥād͟jiz*) each of which was closed by a door with hinges and locks. Open cases, which also were divided into small compartments, are illustrated in a miniature by Yaḥyā b. Maḥmūd of the year 634/1237 in the Paris manuscript of al-Ḥarīrī, ms. arabe, 5847), which shows a library in Baṣra (Blochet, *Les enlumineurs des manuscrits orientaux,* Paris 1926, Pl. 10). Unlike our custom, we find the books lying one above the other in the small compartments, as is still usual in the East. This explains the oriental custom (which is only occasionally found in the West) of writing a short title of the works on the upper and lower edge.

The books were systematically arranged, classified according to the various branches of knowledge. Copies of the Ḳur᾽ān had usually a special place; in the Fāṭimid library, for example, they were kept on a higher level than the others. The various books were often present in several copies; this made it possible not only to lend the same work to several readers, but the scholar was also enabled to read corrupt passages at once in a manuscript by referring to another copy. The Fāṭimid library of Cairo, for example, had thirty copies of the *Kitāb al-ᶜAyn* of al-K͟halīl, twenty copies of the *Ta᾽rīk͟h* of al-Ṭabarī and, if the figure is not wrong, actually a hundred copies of the *D͟jamhara* of Ibn Durayd.

The *wakfiyya* drafted when the books were deposited normally served as the catalogue. Occasionally we hear of a special catalogue (*fihrist* [*q.v.*]) being compiled by the librarian. These catalogues sometimes ran into several volumes, that of al-Ḥakam II in Cordova filling 44 of 20 leaves each (Ibn K͟haldūn, *ᶜIbar,* iv, 146). In the Fāṭimid library, to the door of each bookcase was affixed a list of the books contained therein.

Libraries usually had a director (*ṣāḥib*) and one or more librarians (*k͟hāzin*) according to the size of the institution, also copyists (*nāsik͟h*) and attendants (*farrās͟h*). We find that some of the most celebrated scholars were librarians: thus the historian Ibn Miskawayh was librarian to the vizier Abu 'l-Faḍl b. al-ᶜAmīd in Rayy (Ibn Miskawayh, *Tad͟jārib al-umam*, ed. Amedroz and Margoliouth, Oxford 1921, text, ii, 224, tr. v, 237); al-S͟hābus͟hī (d. 390/1000), the author of the *Kitāb al-Diyārāt,* was librarian of the Fāṭimid library in Cairo under al-ᶜAzīz (Ibn K͟hallikān, *Wafayāt,* i, 338).

The books were acquired partly by purchase and partly by the copyists attached to the libraries copying manuscripts. Al-Maḳrīzī has preserved for us the budget of a library (i, 459); according to this, the caliph al-Ḥākim (386-411/996-1020) spent 207 *dīnār*s a year on the *Dār al-ᶜIlm* founded by him. This was allotted as follows:

	*dīnār*s
Mats from ᶜAbbādān, etc.	10
Paper for copyist	90
Salary of the librarian	48
Drinking water	10
Wages of the attendant	15
Wages of the keeper of paper, ink, and reed pens	12
Repairing the door-curtains	1
Repairing books	12
Felt carpets for the winter	5
Blanket for the winter	4

Libraries were open to everyone free of charge. Paper, ink and reed-pens were supplied by the authorities. Some private libraries even provided for the maintenance of scholars who had come from a long distance. A deposit had usually to be made if books were taken outside the library buildings; at least Yāḳūt (iv, 509-10) praises the liberality of the libraries in Marw, where he always had two hundred and more volumes to the value of two hundred *dīnār*s in his house without a deposit. Instructive in this connection also is the *wakf* document of 21 Ṣafar 799/24 November 1396) by which Ibn K͟haldūn bestowed his *Kitāb al-ᶜIbar* on the library of the D͟jāmiᶜ al-Ḳarawiyyīn in Fās; according to it, this manuscript was only to be lent out to trustworthy, reliable men for two months at the most in return for a substantial deposit, for this period was long enough to copy or study the borrowed work. The director of the library was to take care that this rule was observed (Lévi-Provençal, in *JA*, cciii [1923], 164).

But at the same time we find in Muslim lands purely reading libraries. One of these was the library of the Madrasa al-Maḥmūdiyya founded in Cairo in 797/1395. By the will of the founder, the Ustādār D͟jamāl al-Dīn Maḥmūd b. ᶜAlī (d. 799/1397), no book was to leave the rooms of the *madrasa.* The manuscript of the *Tad͟jārib al-umam* of Ibn Miskawayh (Gibb Mem. Ser., vii/6) published in facsimile by Caetani belonged to this library; in the *wakf* document on the first page of this manuscript, dated 15 S͟haᶜbān 797/5 June 1395) it is written: "The above-named donor makes the condition that neither the whole work nor a single volume of it shall be lent from the library, either against a deposit or without one".

Nevertheless by the year 826/1423 when the books were checked, it was found that 400 volumes (exactly a tenth of the total) were missing, whereupon the then director of the mosque was dismissed (cf. Ibn Ḥad͟jar al-ᶜAsḳalānī, in Quatremère, *Mémoire* [see *Bibl.*], 64, 70; al-Maḳrīzī, *K͟hiṭaṭ*, ii, 395).

If we think of the above statements, which are true even of the 4th/10th century, it can safely be asserted that Muslim libraries were in every respect centuries in advance of those of the west; there was a general need for public libraries felt in Muslim lands much earlier than in the west.

Bibliography: 1. General. Quatremère, *Mémoire sur le goût des livres chez les Orientaux,* in *JA*, Ser. 3, vi (1838), 35-78; and the supplementary notes by Hammer-Purgstall in *JA,* Ser. 4, xi (1848), 187-98; Mez, *Renaissance des Islâms,* Heidelberg 1922, 164 ff.; A. Grohmann, *Bibliotheken und Bibliophilen im islamischen Orient,* in *Festschrift der Nationalbibliothek in Wien,* Vienna 1926, 431-42; M. Hartmann, *Das Bibliothekwesen in den islamischen Ländern,* in *Centralblatt f. Bibliothekwesen,* xvi (1899), 186 ff.; idem, *Zur litterarischen Bewegung und zum Buch- u. Bibliothekwesen in den islamischen Ländern,* in Catalogue No. 4 of the Buchhandlung Rudolf Haupt, Halle 1905. 2. The Arab world. J. Ribera y Tarrago, *Bibliófilos y bibliotecas en la España musulmana,* in his *Disertaciones y opúsculos,* Madrid 1928, 181-228; S. M. Imamuddin, *Hispano-Arab libraries, books, and manuscripts,* in *J. Pak. Hist. Soc.*, vii (1959), 101-19; G. Gozalbes Busto, *El libro y las bibliotecas en la España musulmana,* in *Cuad. Bibl. Esp. Tetuán,* v (1972), 17-46; Eva Thurmann, *Bibliophilie im islamischen Spanien,* in *Philobiblon,* xviii (1974), 195-203; O. Pinto, *Le biblioteche degli Arabi nell' età degli Abbasidi,* in *Bibliofilia,* xxx (1928), 139-65, tr. F. Krenkow as *The libraries of the Arabs in the time of the Abbasids,* in *IC,* iii (1929), 210-43; Ruth Mackensen, *Moslem libraries and sectarian propaganda,* in *Amer. J. Sem. langs. lit.*, li (1934-5), 83-113; *eadem, Arabic books and libraries,* in *ibid.*, lii (1935-6), 245-53; liii (1936-7), 239-50; liv (1937), 41-61; lvi (1939), 149-57; *eadem, Background of the history of Moslem libraries,* in *ibid.*, li (1934-5), 114-25; lii (1935-6), 22-33, 104-10; *eadem, Four great libraries of medieval Baghdad,* in *Library Qtly,* ii (1932), 279-99; Youssef Eche, *Les bibliothèques arabes publiques et semi-publiques en Mésopotamie, en Syrie et en Egypte au Moyen Age,* Damascus 1967; J. P. C. Auchterlonie, *Libraries,* in *Arab Islamic bibliography,* ed. D. Grimwood-Jones, Hassocks 1977, 235-65; J. A. Dagher, *Répertoire des bibliothèques du Proche et Moyen-Orient,* Paris 1951; Aḥmad Badr, *Dalīl dūr al-makhṭūṭāt wa 'l-maktabāt wa-marākiz al-tawthīḳ wa-maʿāhid al-biblūdjrāfiyya fi 'l-duwal al-ʿarabiyya,* Cairo 1965; Arab League, *Dalīl al-maktabāt fi 'l-waṭan al-ʿarabī,* Cairo 1973. 3. Persia. Rukn al-Dīn Humāyūn Farrūkh, *History of books and the imperial libraries,* tr. Abū Ṭālib Sārimī, Tehran 1968; idem, *Tāʾrīkhča-yi kitāb-khānahā-yi Īrān az ṣadr-i Islām tā ʿaṣr-i kunūnī,* Tehran 1347 sh., esp. 199-216; Īrādj Afshār, *Kitāb-khānahā-yi Īrān wa muḳaddama-ī dar bāra-yi kitāb-khānahā-yi ḳadīm,* in *Yaghmā,* xiv (1964), 331-6, 418-22 and suppl., 1-16; M. Weisweiler, *Avicenna und die iranischen Fürstenbibliotheken seiner Zeit,* in *Avicenna commem. vol.*, Calcutta 1956; Abazar Sipihrī, *Rāhnamā-yi kitāb-khānahā-yi Īrān (A directory of Iranian libraries.* i. *West Azarbayjan, East Azarbayjan, Kordestan, Kermanshahan, Gilan, Hamadan),* Tehran 1970; Firishta Raḍawī, *Rāhnamā-yi kitāb-khanahā-yi shimāl-sharḳ-i Īrān,* Tehran 1349 sh. (Khurāsān, Māzandarān, Simnān); Hooshang Ebrami, *Iran, libraries in,* in *Enc. of library and information science,* xiii, 15-53. 4. Muslim India. Sh. Abdul Aziz, *The imperial library of the Mughals,* Lahore 1967; S. A. Zafar Nadvi, *Libraries during the Muslim rule in India,* in *IC,* xix (1945), 329-47; xx (1946), 3-20; Dharma Bhanu, *Libraries and their management in Mughul India,* in *J. Ind. Hist.*, xxxi (1953), 157-73; idem, *The Mughul libraries,* in *J. Pak. Hist. Soc.*, ii (1954), 287-301; V.C.S. O'Connor, in *An Eastern library,* Glasgow 1920 (Bankipore); Hidayat Hosain, *The founders of the Buhar Library,* in *IC,* vii (1933), 125-46; S. M. Imamuddin, *A visit to the Rampur State Library,* in *IC,* xxi (1947), 360-78; Hidayat Hosain, *The Library of Tipu Sultan,* in *IC,* xiv (1940), 139-67; C. Stewart, *A descriptive catalogue of the oriental library of the late Tippoo Sultan of Mysore,* Cambridge 1809; S. C. Sutton, *Guide to the India Office Library*², London 1967, 34 n.; A. Sprenger, *A catalogue of the Arabic, Persian and Hindustany manuscripts of the libraries of the King of Oudh,* Calcutta 1854. 5. Turkey. *Türkologischer Anzeiger,* section AC, *passim;* A. Deissmann, *Forschungen und Funde im Serai,* Berlin 1933; Abdullah Savaşçı Nurten Eke, *Türk kütüphanecilik bibliyografyası,* Ankara 1976; *Türk kütüphaneleri rehberi (Répertoire des bibliothèques de Turquie),* Ankara 1957; Muzaffer Gökman, *Istanbul kütüphaneleri ve yazma tıp kitapları (Libraries of Istanbul and their medical manuscripts),* Istanbul 1959; Halit Dener, *Süleymaniye Umumî Kütüphanesi,* Istanbul 1957. 6. Outside the Islamic world. For libraries outside the Middle East with collection of Islamic manuscripts and printed books see, in addition to the works listed by Auchterlonie, *op. cit.*, and Sezgin, *Levinus Warner and his legacy,* Leiden 1970; F. Taylor, *The Oriental manuscript collections in the John Rylands Library,* in *BJRL,* liv (1972), 449-78; H. J. Goodacre and A. P. Pritchard, *Guide to the Department of Oriental Manuscripts and Printed Books,* London 1977; T. J. Martin, *North American collections of Islamic Manuscripts,* Boston 1977; H. Halén, *Handbook of Oriental collections in Finland,* London and Malmo 1978; E. Apor, ed., *Jubilee volume of the Oriental Collection,* Budapest 1978.

(W. Heffening - [J. D. Pearson])

al-**MAKTŪL** [see al-suhrawardī].

MĀKŪ, a former khānate in the Persian province of Adharbāydjān, and now the name of a town and of modern administrative units around it (see below).

Mākū occupies the north-western extremity of Persia and forms a salient between Turkey (the old *sandjaḳ* of Bāyazīd, modern *vilayet* of Ağri) and Soviet Transcaucasia. In the west the frontier with Turkey follows the heights which continue the line of the Zagros in the direction of Ararat. The frontier then crosses a plain stretching to the south of this mountain (valley of the Ṣarī-ṣu) and runs over the saddle between Great and Little Ararat. Down to 1920 Great Ararat formed the frontier between Russia and Turkey, while Little Ararat was divided between Russia and Persia. Since 1920 Great Ararat has been completely surrounded by Turkish territory, while Little Ararat is divided between Turkey and Persia. The Turco-Persian frontier at the present day comes down to the Araxes. The Lower Ḳara-ṣu and the Araxes (to its confluence with its right bank tributary Ḳotur-čay) form the frontier between Mākū and the autonomous territory of Nakhčuwān which forms part of the Armenian SSR. The third side of the triangle i.e. the inner boundary between the khānate and the Persian province of Khōī [*q.v.*] is somewhat vague. When the prestige of its khāns was as its greatest, their lands stretched to the districts of Čay-pāra, Čāldīrān (Ḳara-ʿAynī) and Äländ. The little khānate of Awadjīḳ (30 villages belonging to the Ayrumlu Khāns) on the Bāyazīd-Čāldīrān-Khōī road formed a little enclave close to the Turco-Persian frontier.

The region of Mākū consists of a series of heights and fertile valleys. In the centre between the valley of the Zängimār and that of the Akh-čay rises the isolated mass of Soḳkar. At the foot of the Little Ararat along the frontier chain and on the slopes of Soḳkar there are excellent pastures.

The lands of Mākū are very well-watered. The streams that flow into the Araxes on the right bank are as follows: 1. in the northwest the lower Ḳara-ṣu, which runs almost parallel to the Araxes and receives on the right bank the waters from Dambat (a high plateau to the south-east of Little Ararat where in 1905 Minorsky discovered the ruins of the ancient town which local Armenian tradition identifies with Arshakawan, cf. Moses of Chorene, iii, 27, and *ibid.,* i, 30); 2. the mountain-torrents Yïlandäräsi and Ṣarï-čay; 3. the river Zängimār (Zängibār, Mākū-čay) which consists of three main branches, one coming from the khānate of Awadjïḳ; the other, the Tïghnït, from the south-east corner of the plain of Čāldïrān from the vicinity of the village of Tïghnït (Armenian *tlmut* = "muddy"); and the third from the central canton of Bābādjik. The combined waters run through the defile in which lies the town of Mākū and water the rich district of Zangibasar ("watered by the Zängimār"). Here the Zängimār receives on its right bank the waters from the central massif of Soḳḳar (this tributary seems to have been once known as the Ḳaban), and on the left bank the Ṣarï-ṣu (different from the above mentioned Ṣarï-sū) which rises in Turkish territory in the north of Bāyazīd and flows a considerable distance parallel to the central course of the Zängimār. 4. The Akh-čay, the sources of which are on the eastern face of the chain which separates Turkey from Persia and on the southern face of the transverse chain (Älägän) which separates Akh-čay from Tïghnït. The waters of the Akh-čay and its tributary irrigate the canton of Sögmän-āwā, flow into the fertile plain of Čaypāra and flow into the Ḳotur-čay which waters the plain of Khōī. Below this confluence, the Akh-čay receives on its right bank the waters of the district of Äländ which rise near the Turco-Persian frontier to the south of the sources of the Akh-čay and the north of those of the Ḳotur-čay.

The town. Mākū is situated in long. 44° 30′ and lat. 39° 18′ at an altitude of 1,294 m./4,245 feet. Its site, 170 miles from Tabrīz and on the main Tabrīz-Erzerum road, is very striking. It lies in the short gorge through which the Zängimār here runs. The cliffs rise perpendicularly on the right bank. The cliffs on the left bank rise to a height of 600 feet above the river. The little town lies in an amphitheatre on the slope. Above the town at the foot of the rocks, are the ruins of ancient fortifications and a spring. Then the mountain wall rises almost perpendicularly, and at a height of 180 to 200 feet leans forward. There is therefore an incredible mass of rock suspended over the town. (According to Monteith's estimate, the dimensions of the cavern thus formed are: height 600 feet, depth of the cavern 800 feet (?), breadth 1,200 feet, thickness at the top of the arch 200 feet.) It is only for a brief period daily that the sun penetrates into this gigantic cave. Just above is a cave which used to be entered by a perilous scaffolding. At a later date, when the cave was used as a prison, the prisoners were hoisted up by a rope. (The only European who has been inside it is A. Ivanovski.)

The population. The population of the town of Mākū in *ca.* 1950 was 6,670, comprising Turkish-speaking Shīʿīs. The population of Mākū consists of Turks and Kurds. The former, who are in the majority, occupy villages along the rivers of the khānate. They are the remains of the Turkoman tribes of Bayat, Pornäk etc. The canton at the foot of the Soḳḳar is called Ḳaraḳoyunlu. The people (about 900 houses in the earlier decades of this century, grouped into 26 villages) belong to the Ahl-i Ḥaḳḳ [*q.v.*] faith (*RMM,* xl, 66) which is indirect but interesting evidence of the character of the heresy of which the Turkoman dynasty of the Ḳara-Ḳoyunlu was accused (Münedjdjim-bashï, iii, 153). The old enmity between the Turkoman tribes survives in the general name applied by the Ḳara-Ḳoyunlu to their Shīʿa "Twelver" neighbours: they call them Aḳ-Ḳoyunlu (Gordlevsky, 9).

The Kurds of the khānate are semi-nomads. The Djalālī (cf. on their supposed ancestors, *ʿĀlam-ārā,* 539, under the years 1017-18) occupy the slopes of Ararat, and in summer betake themselves to the pasturages along the Turco-Persian frontier. Many sections of them lead a troglodyte life in the caves of the Dambat region.

The Milān live between the Araxes and the massif of Soḳḳar, where they pass the summer. At Ḳara-ʿaynī (in Kurdish Ḳaleni) there are Ḥaydarānlu.

Before the First World War there were only 1,200 Armenians left in Mākū. It was remarkable that the confidential servants in the houses of the khāns were of this nationality. The celebrated and imposing monastery of St. Thaddeus (Thadevos-Arakel = Ḳara-Kilisa among the Muslims), rebuilt in 1247 (St. Martin, *Mémoires sur l'Arménie,* ii, 463), is in the central canton of Bābādjik. It is regarded with a certain respect even by Muslims, who kiss the Gospels on entering it. A long inscription recording the *firmān* of protection given it by Shāh ʿAbbās adorns the doorway. At one time the villages at Mākū and at Khōī belonged to the monastery and paid their rents to it. Another Armenian monastery (Surp-Stephanos; Dāniyāl-Payghambar among the Muslims) lies below the mouth of the Ḳotur-čay on the borders of Mākū. The little village of Djabbārlu is inhabited by Yazīdīs [*q.v.*].

Ancient history. The oldest monuments of Mākū go back to the period of the Urartian (Vannic) kingdom. The chamber carved in the rock near Sangar (on the Mākū-Bāzirgān-Bāyazīd road) is one of a number of similar constructions in Bāyazīd and in the country west of Urmia (Minorsky, *Kela-shīn,* in *ZVOIRAO,* xxiv, 171; S. Matheson, *Persia, an archaeological guide,* London 1972, 81-5). A Vannic inscription known as that of "Mākū" seems to come from Bastām on the Akh-čay (district of Čay-pāra). It is of king Rusa II, son of Argishti (*ca.* 680-645 B.C.; cf. Sayce, *A new Vannic Inscription,* in *JRAS* [1912], 107-13; N. Y. Marr, *Nadpis Rusï II iz Mākū,* in *ZVOIRAO,* xxv [1921], 1-54). The inscription is important as showing that the power of the kings of Vān extended to the region of Khōī.

Mākū later formed part of Armenia. It corresponds to the canton of Artaz of the province of Vaspurakan (Armenian 7th century *Geography*). According to Moses of Chorene, the district was at first known as Shawarshan, but was given the name of Artaz in memory of the old home of the Alān whom Artashēs transplanted hither (cf. Ardoz in Ossetia). The name Shawarshakan may be explained from the rule of the Artsruni kings among whom the name Shawarsh (Xšayāršan = Ξέρξης = Mod. Pers. Siyāwush) was frequent (cf. Marquart, *Ērānšahr,* 4, 177). The suggestion of this scholar that Artaz is connected with the older Ἄζαρα etc., Strabo, xi, 14, 3, is untenable because Azara is above Artaxata, which again is above the land of Artaz = Mākū. The Amatuni kings who later established themselves north of the Araxes must also have ruled in Artaz, for the diocese of Mākū is called Amantuneacʿtan (Adontz).

The names Mākū and Hacʿium (= Hasun) north of Mākū are mentioned in the *History* of Thomas Artsruni written in the 10th century, in the passage (ii, § 3) describing the frontier of the lands ceded by the Sāsānid Khusraw to the emperor Maurice in 591

(Brosset, *Coll. d'hist. arm.*, St. Petersburg 1874, i, 78). On the many Armenian monuments in the land of Mākū, cf. the work of Minorsky on the antiquities of the k͟hānate; cf. also Hübschmann, *Die altarm. Ortsnamen,* 1904, 344, and Adontz, *Armenia v epokhu Justiniana,* St. Petersburg 1908, index.

According to a legend recorded by Moses of Chorene (i, 30; ii, 49), Tigranes, having defeated the Mede (in Arm. *Mar*) Aždahak, settled his descendants all around Masis (Ararat). Neither the Arab historians (al-Ṭabarī, Ibn al-At͟hīr) nor geographers know this corner of Armenia, although the name looks very old. It would be tempting to explain Mākū as Māh + kūh = "Mountain of the Medes" (Pers. *māh* and Arm. *mār* go back to the old Iranian Māda). The form Mākūya (*Mākōya) which is found in Ḥamd Allāh Mustawfī, however, presupposes a different final element.

History under Islam. Ḥamd Allāh Mustawfī (*Nuzhat al-ḳulūb,* ed. Le Strange, 89) is the first writer (740/1340) to mention Mākū among the cantons of the *tūmān* of Nak͟hčuwān: it is a castle in the cleft of a rock and at the foot lies a village which stands in the shade till midday. In this place lives the Christian chief priest (*ḳas͟hīs͟h*) whom they call Mar-Ḥasiyā (this reading is preferable to *Mardjanitha* of Le Strange; cf. Aram. *Mar-K͟hasīā* "the Lord Bishop".)

The Spanish Ambassador Clavijo who visited Mākū on 1 June 1404 still found it inhabited by Armenian Catholics ruled by their prince Noradin, who enjoyed practical independence. Tīmūr did not succeed in taking Mākū, but by a treaty Noradin agreed to supply him with 20 horsemen when required. The eldest son of Noradin was taken to the court of ʿUmar Mīrzā and converted to Islam, when he was given the name of Sorgatmix (Suyurg͟hatmīs͟h); as to another son, Noradin intended to send him to Europe to be consecrated a bishop. Clavijo mentions a monastery of Dominicans at Mākū, "en el dicho lugar" (Frayles de Sancto Domingo, *Vida y hazañas,* ed. Sreznevski, St. Petersburg 1881, 158-62, 376; tr. Le Strange, London 1928, 144-5). Clavijo gives an accurate description of the town (a castle in the valley; on the slope, the town surrounded by walls; higher, a second wall, which was reached by steps cut in the rock).

On the death of Tīmūr, Ḳara Yūsuf the Ḳara-Ḳoyunlu reappeared on the scene and Mākū was one of the first places he conquered in 809/1406 (*S͟haraf-nāma,* i, 376). Henceforth the country must have become rapidly Turkicised. According to the *S͟haraf-nāma* (i, 295, 308), in 982/1574 the Ottoman government ordered the Kurd ʿIwaḍ Beg of the Maḥmūdī tribe [see KURDS] to take Mākū (one of the cantons of Nak͟hčuwān) from the Persians and to restore the fortress. ʿIwaḍ was given Mākū as *odjaklïk*. After his death in 1002/1593-4, Sultan Meḥemmed II gave the fortress to Muṣṭafā Beg, son of ʿIwaḍ.

When in the summer of 1014/1605 S͟hāh ʿAbbās was in the vicinity of K͟hōī, the Maḥmūdī Kurds of the district of Mākū and Pasak (a village on the Äländ-čay to the west of K͟hōī) did not come to pay homage to the S͟hāh. ʿAbbās I transferred the clan of Manṣūr-beg to Persian ʿIrāḳ and took the field in person against Muṣṭafā, *beg* of Mākū. The historian Iskandar Muns͟hī mentions two forts at Mākū, one at the foot of the mountain (*pāy-i kūh*) and the other on its side (*miyān-kūh*). The former was soon taken by the S͟hāh's troops, but the capture of the other was "not so easy". Orders were given to plunder the Maḥmūdī tribe, which was done. The women and children were carried off and the Maḥmūdī men executed. The booty was so great that cows were sold at 2 *dirhams* = 200 (Persian) *dīnārs* a head. The royal camp remained for 10 days at Mākū, but the upper fortress "in spite of the constrictedness of the place and the lack of water" held out and the S͟hāh left for Nak͟hčuwān without having obtained its surrender (*ʿĀlam-āra,* 479).

The Turks and Persians attached great importance to the position of Mākū. Murād IV in the campaign of 1045/1635-6 himself realised the importance of Ḳotur and Mākū, and in the instructions given in 1048/1638-9 to Ḳara Muṣṭafā Pas͟ha ordered him to demand that the Persians should destroy the two fortresses. Indeed, by the treaty of 1049/1639 the Persians decided to raze Ḳotur Mākūr (read Mākū) and Mag͟hazberd (*Taʾrīkh-i Naʿīmā,* i, 686). However, Murād IV died and in the reign of Sultan Ibrāhīm, the Persians reoccupied Ḳotur and Mākū (Ewliyā Čelebi, iv, 279).

The next stage is recorded in the Persian inscription engraved on the rock above the fortress. (Minorsky, *Drevnosti,* 23). It tells us that S͟hāh ʿAbbās II ordered the destruction of the fortress because it sheltered the unsubdued (*mufsidān*). The fortress is compared to a Ḳalʿa-yi Ḳābān; the executor of the S͟hāh's order was a certain Akbar and the date is 1052/1642-3 (chronogram *g͟h-n-b*). The history of ʿAbbās II (*Ḳiṣaṣ al-K͟hāḳānī,* Bib. Nat. Paris, Suppl. Pers. no. 227) throws no light on the incident, but as (f. 74b) an Ottoman embassy to the court of the young S͟hāh in 1052/1642-3 is mentioned, it is probable that it was not without influence on the destruction of the fortress, on the preservation of which Persia had formerly laid stress.

Contrary to the tenor of the inscription, Ewliyā Čelebi, ii, 337-9, claims that it was the Ottomans who, after the peace of 1049/1639, destroyed Mākū and at the same time recalled the Maḥmūdī Beg who was their representative there. In 1057/1647 the Kurd *beg* of S͟hūs͟hīk (a stronghold on the borders of Persia) rebelled against the Turks. The Persians, while protesting against his raids, seized the occasion to introduce to Mākū 2,000 musketeers from Māzandarān. The Ottomans sent an army of 72,000 men against S͟hūs͟hīk. Muṣṭafā Beg of S͟hūs͟hīk was defeated and sought refuge in Mākū. Ewliyā accompanied the Pas͟ha and the detachment that went to Mākū to demand the extradition of the rebel. Satisfaction was given them, and the *wālī* of Erzerūm, Meḥmed Pas͟ha, treated the Persian envoys in a very friendly fashion. He told them, however, that if the Persians did not withdraw their troops from Mākū and destroy the fortress, he would attack Eriwān and Nak͟hčuwān. The result is not known, but Persia's possession of Mākū recognised in 1049/1639 does not seem to have again been seriously disputed by Turkey.

The family which ruled Mākū from 1747 to 1923 belonged to the Bayat tribe, the clan settled around the Soḳḳar (on the Bayat, cf. Köprülü-zāde Meḥmed Fuʾād, *Og͟huz etnolozhisine dāyir taʾrīk͟hī notalar,* in *Türkiyyāt Medjmūʿasī* [Istanbul 1925], 16-23). According to oral tradition, Aḥmad Sulṭān Bayat was in K͟hurāsān in the service of Nādir S͟hāh. After the latter's assassination, he seized one of his wives and a part of his treasure and returned to Mākū. Very little is known about him or his son Ḥusayn K͟hān (Monteith's host?) who died in 1835. It is possible that under the Zand dynasty and at the beginning of the Ḳādjārs, the real authority in the region north-west of Ād͟harbāydjān belonged to the family of Dumbulī K͟hāns [cf. KURDS], whose headquarters was at K͟hōī (cf. TABRĪZ; the special history of the Dumbulī is not accessible in Europe). The disappearance of the Dumbulī must have opened the way to the Bayat. ʿAlī Khān (1775-1865), son of Ḥusayn Khān, is often mentioned by travellers (Fraser, Abich, Flandin, Čirikov, Likhutin) as an influential chief jealous of his prerogatives. We know that the Bāb was entrusted to the guardianship of ʿAlī Khān from June to December 1847 and that the latter treated him very kindly. The Bāb in his esoteric language calls Mākū *djabal-i bāsiṭ* in contrast to *djabal-i shahīd* (= Čahrīk, see SALMĀS), where his imprisonment was more rigorous (cf. Browne, *A traveller's narrative,* 1891, ii, 16, 271-7; Djānī-Kāshānī, *Nuḳṭat al-ḳāf*, GMS, xv, Leiden 1910, 131-2). During the war of 1853-6, ʿAlī Khān derived great material advantage from the neutrality of his territory, which lay between Russia and Turkey. His son Tīmūr Pasha Khān (1820-95?) profited by a similar situation during the Russo-Turkish war of 1877-8. In 1881, his appearance at the head of the Mākū horsemen in the district of Salmās accelerated the collapse of the invasion of Kurds under Shaykh ʿUbayd Allāh. Tīmūr Pasha Khān was hailed as the saviour of Ādharbāydjān and the people even called him *Mākū Pādshāhī.*

His son and successor Murtaḍā Ḳulī Khān Iḳbāl al-Salṭana (1863-1923) at first continued the policy of isolation and aggrandisement of the khānate, but his activity aroused suspicion on all sides. At the beginning of the First World War in 1914, Russian distrust earned him a forced stay in Tiflis. In time, Mākū became part of the theatre of war. The Russian troops built a light railway from Shāh-takhtī (on the Araxes) to Bāyazīd, and the station of Mākū became a busy centre. In 1917 the Sardār returned home and held his position till the coming of Riḍā Shāh Pahlawī, when, accused of intrigues, he was arrested on 25 Mihr 1302/17 October 1923) and transported to the prison of Tabrīz where he died suddenly. A Persian officer was appointed governor of Mākū (Nawbakht, *Shāhinshāh-i Pahlawī,* Tehran 1332, 112).

In modern Iran, Mākū town is described as having a population of 6,670, all Turkish-speaking and Shīʿī in faith. It is also the centre of a *bakhsh* (population 22,420), together with two others, making up the *shahrastān*(population 100,854) of the same name in the province or *ustān* of Western Ādharbāydjān, which is based on Riḍāʾiyya (Rezaiyyeh) (since the Iranian Revolution of 1978-9, re-named Urumiyya (Urmia)).

Bibliography: Monteith, *Journal of a tour through Azerbidjan,* in *JRGS,* iii (1933), 40-9 (ʿArablar-Bilga-Mākū-Surp Thadewos-Zāwiya-Malhamlu); E. Smith and Dwight, *Missionary researches,* London 1834, 313 (Khōī-Zorawa-Awadjiḳ); J. B. Fraser, *Travels in Koordistan,* London 1840, ii, 314-21 (Khōī-Ḳara-Ziyaddīn-Sūfiyān-Mākū-Bāzirgān); Ritter, *Erdkunde,* ix, 916-24; E. Flandin, *Voyage en Perse,* Paris 1851, i; Likhutin, *Russkiye v Aziat. Turtsii,* St. Petersburg 1863, 244-50; Čirikov, *Putevoi zhurnal,* 1875, 506-8 (visit in September 1852: Bāyazīd-Mākū); M. Schachtachtinski, *Aus dem Leben eines orientalischen Kleinstaates an der Grenze Russlands,* in *Das Ausland,* Stuttgart 1887, ix, 23-6; H. Abich, *Aus kaukasischen Ländern,* Vienna 1896, i, 97-11, 121-5 (visit to Mākū in 1844), ii, 121; S. Wilson, *Persian life and customs,* London 1896, 85-9; A. Ivanovski, *V Makinskom khanstve,* in *Russk. Vedomosti* (1897), nos. 314, 323, 325; A. Ivanovski, *Po Zakavkazyu v 1893-4,* in *Mater. po arkheol. Kavkaza,* vi (1911), 68; Frangean, *Atrpatakan,* Tiflis 1905, 10-27: Mākū; 27-43: Surp Thadewos; Minorsky, *Otčet o poyezdke v Makinskoye khanstvo v 1905,* in *Mater. po izuč. Vostoka,* St. Petersburg 1909, 1-62; idem, *Drevnosti Mākū,* 1-29 (repr. from *Vostoč. Sbornik,* Petrograd 1916, ii); M. Philips Price, *A journey through Azerbaijan,* The Persian Society, 1913, 13-17; *Makinskoye khanstvo,* in *Novīi Vostok,* Moscow 1922, i, 334-44; V. A. Gordlevsky, *Ḳara-Ḳoyunlu* [canton of Mākū], in *Izv. Obshč. obsledov. Azerbaidjanī,* Bākū 1927, 5-33; *Farhang-i djughrāfiyāʾi-yi Īrān,* iv, 481-3; L. Adamec, ed., *Historical gazeteer of Iran. i. Tehran and northwest Iran,* Graz 1976, 428-9.

(V. MINORSKY*)

MĀKŪLA, BANŪ [see IBN MĀKŪLĀ].

MAKUA, the largest tribal group in Mozambique [*q.v.*], where they occupy the greatest part of the area north of the Zambezi River. A few also are found in Masasi, Kilosa and Tunduru districts in Tanzania. In 1980 they were approximately 30% of the total Mozambique population of some 12m. Almost all of them are Muslims. Their traditions assert that they reached Mozambique from the north during the 16th century, among other Bantu-speaking peoples then entering southern Africa. The Dominican missionary Fr Joâo dos Santos OP recorded a brief description of their customs during his travels in the country at the end of the 16th century, when they were still pagan. A few words of their language, Kimakua, were recorded in 1607 by the French sea captain Jean Moquet, some of which are akin to Swahili. Their conversion to Islam, which is almost total, most probably did not take place until after 1870, when members of the Ḳādiriyya and Shādhiliyya fraternities from the nearby Comoro Islands [see ḲUMR] penetrated the area as missionaries and traders. It seems that the Arabs, who had had contacts on the coast already for a millenium, had made no religious headway among them. The Makua who inhabit the areas nearest to the coast speak a form of Swahili. Other than the Yao [*q.v.*], their immediate neighbours have, however, apparently been impervious to Islam, and have been considerably Christianised. Although the question has not been explored in detail, this is probably due, as in neighbouring Tanzania, to the local limits of the activity of the Comorian missionaries. In spite of Islam, the Makua preserve matrilineal reckoning of descent, and are ruled by village chiefs without any central organisation of their own.

Bibliography: E. Jardim da Vilhena, *A influencia islamica na costa oriental d'Africa,* in *Boletim da Sociedade da Geografica de Lisboa,* xxiv/a (1906); B. G. Martin, *Muslim Brotherhoods in nineteenth century Africa,* Cambridge 1976; Jean Moquet, *Voyages en Afrique, Asie, Indes Orientales,* Paris 1617, recording a visit of 1607; Joâo dos Santos OP, *Ethiopia Oriental,* Evora 1609, ed. Mello d'Azevedo, 2 vols., Lisbon 1891, recording visits in the 1590s; Mary Tew, *Peoples of the Lake Nyasa region,* Ethnographical Survey of Africa, Oxford 1950; G. S. P. Freeman-Grenville, *The Sidi and Swahili,* in *Bull. of the British Assoc. of Orientalists,* vi (1971).

(G. S. P. FREEMAN-GRENVILLE)

AL-**MAḲŪLĀT** (A.), "Categories", the translation of the title of the work of Aristotle [see ARISṬŪṬĀLĪS] on that subject, which is also referred to, by the transliteration of the Greek title as *Ḳāṭīghūriyā* or *Ḳāṭīghūriyās.* The singular is usually *maḳūla,* but *maḳūl* is also found. *Al-Maḳūlāt* is used also in the titles of works by Muslim authors on the same subject.

The ten Aristotelian categories are commonly rendered as follows (but for a detailed analysis of renderings by various Arab authors, see the table at the end of the article):

1. οὐσία (Substance, "what?") *djawhar*
2. ποσόν (Quantity, "how large?") *kam*

3. ποιόν	(Quality, "of what kind?")	*kayfa*
4. πρὸς τί	(Relation, "in what relationship to anything?")	*iḍāfa* or *muḍ*
5. ποῦ	(Place, "where?")	*ayna*
6. πότε	(Time, "when?")	*matā*
7. χεῖσθαι	(Posture, "in what attitude?")	*mawḍūᶜ* or *waḍᶜ*
8. ἔχειν	(Possession, "having/ containing what?")	*(an yakūn) lahu* or *djida* or *milk*
9. ποιεῖν	(Action, "doing what?")	*(an) yafᶜal* or *fiᶜl*
10. πάσχειν	(Affection, "suffering what?")	*(an) yanfaᶜil* or *infiᶜāl*

The earliest appearance known to us of the *Categories* in Arabic is in a version of a Greek compendium of part of the *Organon* attributed to Ibn al-Muḳaffaᶜ [*q.v.*] (said to be preserved in Beirut ms. Univ. St.-Joseph 338). This compendium is said also to have been translated by Abū Nūḥ (*flor. ca.* 184/800).

The full translation that we possess, however, which was that used by later philosophers, is attributed to Isḥāḳ b. Ḥunayn [*q.v.*]. Ḥunayn is himself credited with a translation, but this seems to have been into Syriac. Isḥāḳ may have referred to his father's version in preparing his own, but this appears to have been made directly from the Greek. It certainly has no connexion with the Syriac version of James of Edessa (ed., with Isḥāḳ's Arabic version, K. Georr, *Les Catégories d'Aristote dans leurs versions syro-arabes,* Beirut 1948). Isḥāḳ's version is stylish and, on the whole, clear and accurate. It survives in a recension by al-Ḥasan b. Suwār (d. *ca.* 408/1017), based on Yaḥyā b. ᶜAdī's copy and furnished with an introduction and critical notes. In these, Ibn Suwār makes use of a large amount of earlier material, including a commentary by Ibn ᶜAdī.

The controversy in the classical world concerning the authenticity of the work appears not to have suvived its transmission to the Islamic world. Ibn Suwār mentions it, no doubt drawing on his Greek sources, but he accepts the work as genuine, as do the other commentators.

Many commentaries on the work were made. Among those mentioned by the bibliographers but not, as far as we know, extant are works by Abū Bishr Mattā, Thābit b. Ḳurra, Djābir b. Ḥayyān (attrib.), Abu 'l-Ḳāsim b. al-ᶜAbbād, and ᶜAbd al-Laṭīf al-Baghdādī. Epitomes are also attributed to Ibn Bahrīz (a bishop of Mawṣil and a patron of Ḥunayn), al-Kindī, Aḥmad b. al-Ṭayyib (d. 286/899), and Muḥammad b. Zakariyyāʾ al-Rāzī. Surviving works based on the *Categories* include a paraphrase by al-Fārābī (ed. D. M. Dunlop, *Al-Farabi's paraphrase of the* Categories *of Aristotle,* in *IQ,* iv [1958], 168-87, v [1959], 21-54), a large section of Ibn Sīnā's *al-Shifāʾ* (*al-Manṭiḳ 2 - al-Maḳūlāt*), ed. G. Anawati *et alii,* Cairo 1959), a commentary by Abu 'l-Faradj b. al-Ṭayyib [see IBN AL-ṬAYYIB] (d. 434/1043) (preserved in Cairo ms. Bibl. Eg. 7772; anon. paraph. India Office ms. Or. 3832), notes by Ibn Bādjdja [*q.v.*] on al-Fārābī's paraphase (preserved in Escurial ms. 612), and Ibn Rushd's *Compendium* (in Hebrew tr.) and *Middle Commentary* (ed. M. Bouyges, *Averroès: Talkhiç kitab al-maqoulat,* Beirut 1932). The work or, at any rate, the subject with which it deals is also, of course, referred to, if at no great length, in other Islamic philosophical works, e.g. the *Rasāʾil Ikhwān al-Ṣafāʾ* and al-Ghazālī's *Miᶜyār al-ᶜilm.*

It might well be thought that the *Categories* received more attention from the earlier Islamic philosophers than it merited, particularly in view of the difficulty of determining precisely what it is about. This question is still disputed; I. Madkour (introd. to ed. of *al-Shifāʾ* cited above) characterises it as "... à la fois une recherche sur la substance et les accidents et un essai de déterminer exhaustivement le nombre des genres suprêmes; par là, elle se rattache à la fois à la métaphysique et à la logique." Others maintain, more simply and perhaps more plausibly, that it is merely an early attempt by Aristotle to list all the predicates that can be attached to a given man, and that it is therefore indisputably an adjunct, if a minor one, to the study of logic. The choice of *al-maḳūlāt* as the translation of the title may perhaps indicate that Isḥāḳ himself inclined to the latter view (*ḳāla* ... *ᶜalā* ... "to predicate ... of ..."). It may be that the digressions in the work itself, the mass of commentary, in Greek, Syriac and Arabic, that it attracted, and the inclusion of a similar treatment of the categories in *Metaphysics* △ (where, according to Ross, it is clearly out of place) combined to obscure the significance of the title. Whether most of the Islamic commentators really considered it to be an integral part of the *Organon,* or their respect for Aristotle forced them to retain it as such, is not clear. Ibn Sīnā is the only philosopher to give an independent opinion on the nature

Early Arabic nomenclature of the categories

(compiled by F. Zimmermann)

Aristotle	Muḥammad b. ᶜAbd Allāh	al-Kindī	al-Yaᶜḳūbī	Abu 'l-Ḥusayn al-Kātib	Isḥāk b. Ḥunayn	al-Fārābī	Ikhwān al-Ṣafāʾ	al-Khʷārazmī	Avicenna
οὐσία	*ᶜayn (djawhar)*	*djawhar*	*djawhar*	*djawhar*	*djawhar*	*djawhar*	*djawhar*	*djawhar*	*djawhar*
ποσόν	*ᶜadad*	*kammiyya*	*kammiyya*	*ᶜadad*	*kam*	*kammiyya*	*kam*	*kam*	*kammiyya*
ποιόν	*ṣifa*	*kayfiyya*	*kayfiyya*	*ḥāl*	*kayfa*	*kayfiyya*	*kayfa*	*kayfa*	*kayfiyya*
πρός τι	*muḍāf*	*muḍāf*	*muḍāf*	*iḍāfa*	*iḍāfa*	*iḍāfa*	*muḍāf*	*iḍāfa*	*iḍāfa*
πού	*makān (ayna)*	*ayna*	*ayna*	*makān*	*ayna*	*ayna*	*ayna*	*ayna*	*ayna*
ποτέ	*waḳt (matā)*	*matā*	*matā*	*zamān*	*matā*	*matā*	*matā*	*matā*	*matā*
κεῖσθαι	*nuṣba*	*waḍᶜ (nuṣba)*	*waḍᶜ*	*nuṣba*	*mawḍūᶜ*	*waḍᶜ*	*nuṣba (waḍᶜ)*	*waḍᶜ (nuṣba)*	*waḍᶜ*
ἔχειν	*djida*	*lahu*	*djida*	*ḳunya*	*(an yakūna) lahu*	*lahu*	*malaka*	*dhū (djida)*	*djida, milk*
ποιεῖν	*fiᶜl*	*fāᶜil (fiᶜl)*	*fāᶜil*	*fāᶜil*	*yafᶜal*	*yafᶜal*	*yafᶜal*	*yafᶜal*	*yafᶜal (fiᶜl)*
πάσχειν	*mafᶜūl*	*munfaᶜil*	*mafᶜūl*	*munfaᶜil*	*yanfaᶜil*	*yanfaᶜil*	*yanfaᶜil*	*yanfaᶜil*	*yanfaᶜil (infiᶜāl)*

and the value of the work. He takes its object to be to assert—not to prove—that ten things are *summa genera* (*adjnās ʿāliya*), which comprehend all that exists (*taḥwī 'l-mawdjūdat*), and to which alone single terms (*al-alfāẓ al-mufrada*) can be applied. One of these is substance and the nine others are accidents. Consequently, he considers it to be metaphysical rather than logical and, although he grudgingly accords it a certain value for the theory of definition, wishes to remove it completely from the syllabus of the study of logic. He is, he claims, merely following tradition in including in his logical works a treatise (a most substantial, detailed and critical one, it must be said) on a subject that is of little use and may indeed confuse and harm the reader. In *al-Nadjāt,* he refers to the categories only in connection with the theory of definition, and in *al-Ishhārāt* he omits all mention of them.

Ibn Rushd does not tell us his opinion of the work or indicate whether he made his commentary on it for its own sake or out of loyalty to Aristotle. After him, at all events, it would seem that Ibn Sīnā's assessment of its worth commanded general assent, for it makes few further appearances.

Bibliography (in addition to references in the text): I. Madkour, *L'Organon d'Aristote dans le monde arabe*², Paris 1969; F. E. Peters, *Aristoteles Arabus,* Leiden 1968; idem, *Aristotle and the Arabs,* New York 1968; R. Walzer, *New light on the Arabic translations of Aristotle,* in *Greek into Arabic,* Oxford 1962 (repr. from *Oriens,* vi [1953]); I. Alon and F. Zimmermann, ed. and tr., *An account of elementary logic attributed to Muḥammad b. ʿAbdallāh b. al-Muqaffaʿ* (forthcoming).

(J. N. MATTOCK)

MAKURRA [see NŪBA].

MĀL (A.), means in the old language possession, property, referring among the Bedouins particularly to camels, but also to estates and money, and in any case to concrete things. The word is formed from *mā* and *li* and means properly anything that belongs to any one. As a noun it is of course treated as a med. *w* stem from which a verb is then formed. In the meaning "money", the word is used in the expression *māl ṣāmit* "dumb property" in contrast to *māl nāṭiḳ* "speaking property", applied to slaves and cattle. There is a full definition of the conception in the introduction to the *Ishāra ilā maḥāsin al-tidjāra* of Abu 'l-Faḍl Djaʿfar b. ʿAlī al-Dimashḳī (Cairo 1318/1900-1, 2 ff.), studied and for the most part translated by H. Ritter, in *Isl.*, vii (1916), 1-91. There and in the *Mafātīḥ al-ʿulūm* (see *Bibl.*), 59, the different classes of property are enumerated. As *māl* includes property in its different aspects, the word can also mean "taxes".

The attitude of the Muslim religion to money and property and its acquisition was of course a subject of discussion from the beginning of the literature. The authoritative religious and ethical point of view is that of al-Ghazālī in the second ten of the books of the *Iḥyāʾ,* especially book 13 (Ritter, *op. cit.*, gives an analysis) and 14 (tr. H. Bauer, *Erlaubtes und verbotenes Gut = Islamische Ethik,* iii, 1922; cf. R. Hartmann in *Isl.*, xiv; analysis of the two books in G.-H. Bousquet, *Ihʾyâ ʿouloûm eddîn,* Paris 1955, 121-53).

The acquisition, conservation and disposal of property is one of the four main sections of domestic economy (*tadbīr al-manzil*), the second part of practical philosophy, which is divided into ethics, economics and politics, just as it entered Islam with the rest of Hellenistic sciences. As the *Politics* of Aristotle, the first book of which deals with economics, was not translated into Arabic, the Muslims had to be content with the only translated work on economics, composed by the Neo-Pythagorean Ps.-Bryson, which has had a deciding influence on the whole economic literature of Islam. The text, the Greek original of which is lost, was first edited by L. Cheikho in *Machriq*, xix (1921) and has been recently published with the Hebrew and Latin versions and a German translation by M. Plessner. The interesting chapter on *māl* in it was further expanded by Muslim authors of the school of the Ps.-Bryson, particularly from religious literature. A standard work is the *Akhlāḳ-i nāṣirī* of al-Ṭūsī [*q.v.*], of which the economic section has been analysed and translated by Plessner. The view of the origin of money which Aristotle holds in the *Nicomachaean ethics* reached Islam direct, besides coming through the Ps.-Bryson; it is first found in the *Tahdhīb al-akhlāḳ* of Miskawayh, e.g. Cairo 1322, 1904-5, 38 [cf. also NĀMŪS and DHAHAB].

The word *māl* very early became a technical term in arithmetic. It is first found in exercises in dividing inheritances applied to the property of the testator which is to be divided. We later find the word used regularly for the unknown quantity in an equation; in this meaning it was afterwards replaced by *shayʾ* [*q.v.*]. Used for the unknown in quadratic equations, it became the word for the square of a number. The fourth power is called *māl al-māl*, the fifth *mālᵘ kaʿbⁱⁿ*, the square of the cube. The history of this change of meaning has been elucidated by J. Ruska, *Zur ältesten arabischen Algebra und Rechenkunst*, in *S.B.Ak. Heid.*, Phil.-hist. Kl. (1917), no. 2, esp. ch. vi, cf. also index s.v. *Māl.*

Bibliography: Brockelmann, *Grundriss,* i; H. Ritter, *Ein arabisches Handbuch der Handelswissenschaft,* in *Isl.,* vii (1916), 1-91 (cf. esp. the passages quoted on p. 45, n. 3, from the Arab lexicographers, the *LA* and Dozy, *s.v.*); M. Plessner, *Der οἰκονομικός des Neupythagoreers "Bryson" und sein Einfluss auf die islamische Wissenschaft,* 1928; Merx, *Die Einführung der aristotelischen Ethik in die arabische Philosophie,* in *Verhandlungen des XIII. Intern. Orientalistenkongresses,* 290 ff.; on the meaning in algebra, cf. the references given in Ruska, *op. cit.*; al-Khʷārazmī, *Mafātīḥ al-ʿulūm,* ed. van Vloten, 1895, 59, 198-9 (the latter passage tr. by Wiedemann, *Beiträge zur Geschichte der Naturwissenschaften,* xiv = *SBPMS Erl.*, xl [1908].

(M. PLESSNER)

MĀL AL-BAYʿA (A.), also *ḥaḳḳ al-bayʿa, rasm al-bayʿa* and *ṣilat al-bayʿa*, a term used for the payments made to the *djund* at the time of the swearing of the oath of allegiance (*bayʿa* [*q.v.*]) to a new ruler.

The practice was unknown among the Umayyads and early ʿAbbāsids, and the first example seems to be the payments made to the *djund* in Baghdād following the death of al-Mahdī in 169/785, when each man was given eighteen months' or two years' salary (*rizḳ*) after they had caused disturbances. It is not clear, however, that this was directly related to the *bayʿa,* and it may have been settlement of arrears of pay. Nonetheless, this seems to have become a precedent, and extra *ʿaṭāʾ* [*q.v.*] was paid at the time of Hārūn's accession the next year. After the death of Hārūn in 193/809, al-Amīn's supporters in Baghdād paid two years' *rizḳ* to the army, while in Marw his brother al-Maʾmūn paid one year's salary at the time of the *bayʿa.* By this time, such payments seem to have been regarded as standard practice, and the harmful effects were soon apparent; when Ibrāhīm b. al-Mahdī was proclaimed caliph in Baghdād in 201/817 in opposition to al-Maʾmūn, he promised six months *ʿaṭāʾ,* but was unable to pay the full amount, hence drafts were given to the troops so that they could collect payment in kind from the surrounding country. There is no mention of payment at the accessions of al-Muʿtaṣim (218/833) or al-Wāthiḳ (227/842), but whether this meant that the practice was in abeyance or that it had become routine is impossible to tell. On the accession of al-Mutawwakil (232/847), eight months' salary was paid, and some, but by no means all, of his successors followed the practice. Under al-Muḳtadir, the abuse of the system became glaringly obvious. The troops in Baghdād received *māl li 'l-bayʿa* at the time of his accession, while those escorting the *ḥadjdj* rioted when they did not receive *djāʾizat al-bayʿa* which they clearly felt was their due. After the abortive revolt of Ibn al-Muʿtazz in the next year, the *djund* were given a second payment for renewing the oath. In 317/929 a revolt was launched with the object of deposing al-Muḳtadir and making al-Ḳāhir caliph, but the attempt collapsed when the leaders were unable to supply the year's *rizḳ* demanded by the army as a reward. The re-establishment of al-Muḳtadir meant that *māl al-bayʿa* was required for the third time in his caliphate, and this led to the selling off of state lands at very low prices in an effort to satisfy the troops. The accession of al-Ḳāhir in 320/932 meant a further payment.

Thereafter, the practice seems to have become less regular; at the accession of al-Muttaḳī in 329/940, the Turkish *amīr al-umarāʾ* Badjkam [*q.v.*] reduced payments and restricted them to his own followers. Payments were sometimes made under the Būyids, as at the accession of Bahāʾ al-Dawla [*q.v.* in Suppl.] in 379/989, when *rasm al-bayʿa* was paid, and the army also extorted it on the accession, in suspicious circumstances, of the ʿAbbāsid caliph al-Ḳādir in 381/991. Under the later Būyids, extra payments continued to be demanded, and sometimes made, at accessions and other times of crisis, but the decline of the system of regular salaries, and the bankruptcy of the state, meant that the practice was irregular.

Bibliography: See descriptions of accessions in Ṭabarī, iii; Miskawayh, *Tadjārib*, ed. Amedroz; Rūdhrāwarī, *Dhayl Tadjārib*, ed. Amedroz; Ibn al-Athīr; and also INʿĀM. (H. KENNEDY)

MĀL-I AMĪR (See ĪDHADJ].

MĀL-I IRSĀLIYYE [See IRSĀLIYYE].

MALABAR, the name first given by Arab and Persian mariners in mediaeval times to a pepper-producing coastal region of the south-western Indian Deccan approximately conterminous with the modern state of Kerala. The name "Malabar" is probably derived from a combination of the Dravidian term *malai* = "mountain" and the Persian *bār* = "country" (Logan, i, 1), though the affix *bar* may alternatively be derived from the Arabic *barr* = "a continent", or the Sanskrit *vāra* = "a slope" (*Hobson-Jobson*, 539; cf. *Madras glossary*, 460). The name Malabar is not generally employed by the indigenous inhabitants of the region, who have traditionally preferred the Dravidian *Malayaḷam* = "the hill country", or the more classical *Keraḷam*, a name thought to be derived from the former Chēra kingdom of the Indian Deccan (Logan, i, 224; see also Menon, *op. cit., passim*).

According to *Hobson-Jobson*, the substantive part of the name Malabar, variously appearing as *Malai, Male, Maliāh*, etc., is to be found "in the earlier post-classical notices of India, whilst in the great Temple-Inscription at Tanjore we find the region in question called *Malai-naḍu*". The affix *bār* would seem to appear for the first time (in the form *Manībar*) in al-Idrīsī's mid-6th/12th century geographical study *Nuzhat al-mushtāḳ fī 'khtirāḳ al-āfāḳ* (Nainar, 19), whilst Yāḳūt includes the name Malībār in his 7th/13th century geographical dictionary, the *Muʿdjam al-buldān* (Nainar, 19; cf. Miller, 18). In its original usage, the name Malabar was applied by the Arabs and Persians to the whole coast of the south-western Deccan from Mt. D'eli in the north to Cape Comorin in the south. Although originally an exclusively Arabo-Persian designation, the name Malabar soon attained widespread international currency, being employed by John of Montecorvino in 693/1293 (Yule, *Cathay*, i, 215) and by Marco Polo in 698/1298 (Bk. iii, ch. 25). The name Malabar also occurs in Ming Chinese sources, both in the rather obscure form *Ma-li-mo* employed in Chau Ju-kua's 7th/13th century *Chu-fan-chi* (Hirth and Rockhill, 88, 90) and in the immediately recognisable form *Ma-lo-pa* listed in Feng Ch'eng-chün's *Hsi-yü ti-ming*.

Although the name Malabar was adopted by the Portuguese and applied by them to the whole region of modern Kerala, from the beginning of the British period the name was applied to an increasingly restricted area, being employed to designate that part of the south-western Deccan which came under direct British rule. This area, which covered the northern third of present-day Kerala, became the administrative district of Malabar, a part of the Madras Presidency situated between 10° and 12°30′ north which included the important ports of Kannanūr (Cannanore) [*q.v.*] and Kozhikode (Calicut), as well as the important Māppila [*q.v.*] Muslim centre of Ponnani. After the incorporation of Malabar within the modern Indian state of Kerala in 1956, the old Malabar district was divided into three smaller districts: Kozhikode, Kannanūr and Palghat. In 1969 a fourth district, Malappuram, was carved out of these three (Miller, 18). Under the British, Minicoy Island and the Laccadives [*q.v.*] were attached to Malabar for administrative purposes, though when Malabar was incorporated within Kerala in 1956, the Laccadive, Minicoy and Amindivi Islands were reorganised in the separate Indian Union Territory of Lakshadweep.

Arab contacts with the Malabar region pre-date the Islamic era by many centuries, and the foundations of the present Māppila Muslim community of South India were laid within a few years of the *hidjra*, certainly well before Muḥammad b. Ḳāsim's conquest of Sind in 93-5/711-13 (Miller, 39-43; Ahmad, 77; Logan, i, 231-45; Cherian, *op. cit., passim*); Malabar is therefore the site of the earliest Muslim community to have been established on the South Asian subcontinent.

Today South India's Māppila community numbers some five millions and extends beyond the frontiers of Kerala into Tamil Nadu and Karnataka. Māppila communities are also to be found in Bangalore, Madras and Bombay as well as overseas in Arabia, Sri Lanka, Malaysia and Burma. The former district of Malabar remains, however, the Māppila homeland *par excellence;* thus according to *Census of India* figures for 1921, out of a total population of 2,039,333 there were 1,004,327 Muslims living in the Malabar district, 93.60% of whom were Sunnīs. Nearly all the Malabari Muslims are Māppilas, but there is also a sizeable Labbai [*q.v.*] community, and there are lesser numbers of Pathans and Arabs. According to the 1971 *Census of India,* there were 4,162,718 Māppilas in Kerala state, of whom 2,765,747 lived in the four administrative districts (Kozhikode, Kannanūr, Palghat and Malappuram) which correspond approximately to the former Malabar District. (In 1971 the total population of this same region was 8,012,759, of whom 4,789,198 were Hindus; Miller, 315.) Today the administrative region of Malabar no longer exists, but the name is still widely applied to coastal Kerala, and may almost be said to have reverted to its original Arabo-Persian meaning, that is, the whole littoral of the south-western Indian Deccan between Mt. D'eli in the north and Cape Comorin in the south.

Bibliography: W. Logan, *Malabar,* 3 vols., Madras 1887; *Madras glossary,* vol. iii of *Manual of the administration of the Madras Presidency,* Madras 1893; K. P. Menon, *Discursive notes on Malabar and its place names,* in *Indian Antiquary,* xxxi (1902), 349-50; Sir H. Yule, *The Book of Ser Marco Polo,* 2 vols., London 1903; idem and A. C. Burnell, *Hobson-Jobson*², London 1903 (repr. 1968); W. W. Hunter, *The Imperial Gazetteer of India*², Oxford 1908, s.v.; C. A. Innes, *Madras District Gazetteer: Malabar and Anjengo,* Madras 1908; F. Hirth and W. W. Rockhill, *Chau Ju-kua: his work on the Chinese and Arab trade in the twelfth and thirteenth centuries,* St. Petersburg 1911 (repr. Taipei 1970); Sir H. Yule, *Cathay and the way thither*², 4 vols., London 1915-16; S. Muhammad Nainar, *Arab geographers' knowledge of Southern India,* Madras 1942; Feng Ch'eng-chün. *Hsi-yü ti-ming* ("Names of places in western regions")², Peking 1957; Aziz Ahmad, *Studies in Islamic culture in the Indian environment,* Oxford 1964; A. Cherian, *The genesis of Islam in Malabar,* in *Indica* (1969), 1-13; G. Bouchon, *Les Musulmans du Kerala à l'époque de la découverte portugaise,* Centre des Recherches d'Histoire et de Philologie de la IVᵉ Section de l'École Pratique des Hautes Études (IV, Hautes Études Islamiques et Orientales d'Histoire Comparée), 5; *Mare Luso-Indicum,* Geneva-Paris, ii, 1-59; R. E. Miller, *Mappila Muslims of Kerala,* Madras 1976; F. S. Dale, *Islamic society on the South Asian frontier: the Māppiḷas of Malabar 1498-1922,* Oxford 1980.

(A. D. W. FORBES)

MALACCA, a town situated on the west coast of the Malay peninsula, in lat. 2° 12′ N and long. 102° 15′ E. The common anglicised form is Malacca, but the official spelling now used in Malaysia is Melaka. Giving its name to the Malacca Straits separating the Malay peninsula from Indonesian Sumatra, Malacca is the administrative centre of Malacca State and is 152 km. from the Malaysian capital of Kuala Lumpur. The town is distinguished from other Malaysian cities by its 19th century Chinese Malay shop houses and old Portuguese and Dutch buildings. Together with Central Malacca district, it currently numbers about 250,630 inhabitants. Relatively quiet today, Malacca was in the 9th/15th century the bustling heart of the most powerful kingdom in Malay history, the Malacca sultanate, which played a key role in the expansion of Islam through the Archipelago.

Origins. Malacca's origins are obscure. Although a plausible date for its founding is *ca.* 802-3/1400, Malacca is not mentioned in any pre-9th/15th century sources. The first verifiable reference is Rabīʿ II 806/October 1403, which comes from the imperial records of the Ming dynasty. At that time the new Yung Lo Emperor (804-28/1402-24) first heard of Malacca's existence, possibly from some Muslim Indian envoys then in Peking. It was already important enough to warrant the despatch thither of a Chinese mission, and its growth must thus have been extremely rapid. According to Albuquerque's commentaries (983-4/1576), one purported derivation of "Malacca" was a word (as yet unidentified) meaning "to meet", because so many people settled there in such a short time. In an effort to explain why Malacca was able to develop so quickly, scholars have been drawn by Malay traditions which attribute its founding to a prince from a mighty kingdom situated in Palembang in southeast Sumatra.

Malay accounts of Palembang's former greatness have been supported by archaeological evidence as well as by references in Chinese sources. It is believed that a prosperous trading kingdom, which the Chinese called San-fo-chi (reconstructed as Śrīvijaya) rose in southeastern Sumatra in the 1st/7th century. Acting as an entrepot to serve the trade between India and China, Śrīvijaya flourished and became a noted centre for Buddhist studies. At the height of its power, it claimed overlordship over the interior and east coast of Sumatra, the Malay peninsula, and the islands of the Riau-Lingga archipelago and the South China Sea. By the 6th/13th century, Śrīvijaya appears to have been weakening as neighbouring kingdoms challenged its commercial hegemony and sought to take advantage of new opportunities for trade with China. Attacks by Chola India in 415-16/1025 and recurring hostilities with Java further undermined its position. From 772-3/1371, Java claimed suzerainty in southeastern Sumatra, but around 792-3/1390 a Palembang prince apparently attemped to assert his independence. Shortly afterwards, he was ousted by an invading Javanese army. When a Chinese fleet visited Palembang early in the 9th/15th century, it was still an important port, but was under the control of a Chinese pirate chief.

Two major sources contain the Malay legend of a Palembang prince who left Sumatra, founding a dynasty which ultimately ruled in Malacca. The first is the *Sejarah Melayu,* a Malacca court text, of which the oldest extant version dates from the 11th/17th century but which was probably based on earlier recensions since lost. The second is the *Suma oriental,* a work by a Portuguese apothecary, Tomé Pires, sent to Malacca in 914-15/1509 by the Portuguese to investigate trading conditions there. Though the two sources differ in detail, the core of the legend is similar. According to the *Sejarah Melayu,* a descendant of Alexander the Great (in Malay, Iskandar Zul-karnain) appeared miraculously on a hill in Palembang named Bukit Si Guntang. A covenant was concluded between him and the local chief in which he promised that he and his descendants would govern the people justly in return for their loyalty. With the title Sri Tri Buana, he was then made ruler. Subsequently, seeking a suitable site for a city, Sri Tri Buana came to an island which he renamed Singapore after glimpsing a strange beast which he took to be a lion (*singa*) there. During the succeeding four reigns, Singapore developed into a great trading city, but the fourth and fifth rulers flouted Sri Tri Buana's earlier covenant, unjustly punishing their subjects. In retribution, Singapore was attacked not only by giant swordfish but by Javanese armies. The ruler, Iskandar S͟hāh, fled up the coast to Muar, but was twice forced to relocate his settlement. Finally, he came to a place called Bertam which he deemed auspicious after he saw one of his hounds kicked by a courageous mouse deer. Because he was standing under a *melaka* tree (*phyllanthus emblica; tetramerista glabra*) he decided to call the place Melaka.

The broad outlines of Pires' version are similar. According to the *Suma oriental,* a Palembang prince entitled Parameśvara would not acknowledge his subservience to Java and proclaimed his independence. The Javanese attacked and Parameśvara fled to Singapore with a following which included thirty *orang laut,* proto-Malay sea people whose habitat was the coasts and offshore islands of Sumatra and the peninsula. In Singapore, Parameśvara killed the local chief, a vassal of the Thai kingdom of Ayudhya, and established himself instead. When the Thais attacked five years later, Parameśvara fled to Muar where he settled, while the *orang laut* moved about 8 km. further north to the mouth of the Malacca River. Discovering an attractive area up-river (Bertam), they persuaded Parameśvara to establish his residence there. Parameśvara gave the port at the estuary the name Malacca, which according to Pires' version means "hidden fugitive", although no satisfactory derivation is known. Another suggested derivation given in the *Sejarah Melayu* is the Arabic *malakat* (written ملاكة in Malay and ملاقة or ملعقة in early Arab trading manuals) = "possession", which the text interprets to mean "a place where merchants gather".

The Malacca dynasty. The precise chronology of the first five rulers varies according to the source, and gravestones have established the reign dates of only some of the later rulers. The following is the currently accepted dynastic list of the Malacca dynasty:

mented, "There is no doubt that Malacca is of such importance and profit that it seems to me it has no equal in the world."

If the Sumatran origins of Malacca are accepted, it can be argued that a primary reason for its rapid rise was the fact that its founders brought with them the prestige, administrative traditions and commercial experience of the formerly great port of Śrīvijaya.

However, there were more tangible factors in Malacca's success as an entrepôt. It was strategically placed on the narrow Straits through which shipping between China and India passed and where the dominant monsoonal wind systems met. Ports in the Straits region had a guaranteed clientèle because seaborne trading patterns followed the cycle of the monsoon winds. Ships from India and the western lands arrived at various periods between March and January, while traders from China and the east came between November and March and those from the western archipelago between May and September. For some shipping, there was an enforced wait before they could return home as the monsoon changed direction or gained force; other traders, taking advantage of dif-

Parameśvara (died 816/1413-14)
|
Megat Iskandar Shah (817/1414 - 826/1423-4)
|
Sri Maharaja Sultan Muhammad Shah (827/1424 - 847/1444?)

- Raja Ibrahim, Sri Parameśvara Dewa Shah (848-9/1445? - 850/1446?)
- Raja Kasim, Sultan Muzafar Shah (850/1446 - 863-4/1459?)
  |
  Raja Abdullah, Sultan Mansur Shah (863-4/1459? - 882/1477)
  |
  Sultan Alauddin Riyat Shah (882/1477 - 893/1488)
  |
  Sultan Mahmud Shah (893/1488-934-5/1528)

After 917/1511, when Malacca was captured by the Portuguese, the dynasty ruled from capitals in the Riau archipelago and peninsular Johor. The last direct descendant was murdered in 1111/1699.

Malacca as an international entrepôt. In order to appreciate the reasons for Malacca's place in the expansion of Islam, it is necessary to understand its emergence as an entrepôt. It has been said that Malacca was founded, rather than grew into, a trading city. Its life blood was always commerce, for the soil around was unsuitable for large-scale rice growing, and rice imports became vital for feeding its population. Some sago was grown, together with fruits such as sugar cane, jackfruit, lichi and bananas. The ordinary people subsisted by fishing from simple dugout canoes, by collecting forest and marine products, by panning tin and by weaving mats for barter in Malacca's market. These local activities, however, were economically of minor importance beside Malacca's role as an exchange centre in the international trading network which by the 10th/16th century reached from China through India and the Middle East to Europe.

By 805-6/1403, presumably within a few years of its founding, Malacca was sufficiently important to receive a mission from the Chinese Emperor. During the course of the 9th/15th century, it eclipsed its rivals, notably the ports of Pasai and Aru on Sumatra's northeast coast, which had long since participated in international trade. Tomé Pires com-

ferent wind systems, needed to wait only a short period before they left. Malacca proved ideally suited as a stapling port where goods could be stored, ships reprovisioned and cargoes sold and purchased quickly. It had an attractive harbour with approaches free from shoals and mangrove swamps and, because it lay in the lee of Sumatra, was more sheltered from storms than Pasai. By tropical standards, the climate was pleasant; there were good stands of timber for masts in the jungles nearby; and to the northeast of the settlement was a supply of potable water. Malacca was also well-placed as a collecting point for local jungle and marine products which were valued in India and China. A portage route linked the upper Malacca River with the gold mines of inland Pahang, and numerous rivers that disembogue on both sides of the Straits facilitated the transport of goods between the coast and interior. Finally, the hill to the east of the settlement (Malacca or St. Paul's Hill) was a natural vantage point where lookouts could be posted to warn against any impending attack.

Diplomatic initiatives by the first rulers further contributed to Malacca's commercial success. The patronage of China, the greatest Asian power at the time, was assiduously cultivated. When a large Chinese mission arrived in 806/1404, Malacca responded by sending envoys back to the imperial court. As a sign of the emperor's favour, Parameśvara was granted an elevated title and Malacca became the first foreign nation to receive the Yung Lo Emperor's personal inscription. Between 806-7/1404 and 838-8/1435, twenty missions were sent from Malacca to China, several of which were headed by the ruler himself. By offering the apropriate tribute and fulfilling its obligations to its Chinese overlord, the new settlement retained China's favour and protection in the initial stages of its development. For their part, the Ming Emperors obtained as a vassal an important commercial centre which could act as a base for the Chinese naval fleets that periodically sailed to the Indian Ocean. Although the Imperial court withdrew from active involvement in overseas affairs after 837-8/1434, junk trade with Malacca continued. Nor were the close ties of the past forgotten. Sultan Muzafar, Sultan Mansur and Sultan Mahmud requested investiture by China and it was to China that the last Malacca ruler looked for assistance when the Portuguese attacked in 916-17/1511.

The new settlement also reached if not friendship then at least a *modus vivendi* with its two powerful neighbours, the Thai kingdom of Ayudhya and Majapahit in Java. Founded in 751-2/1351, Ayudhya continued to claim suzerainty over the entire peninsula, and Majapahit too exercised a vague overlordship in the southern peninsula. Accordingly, until the latter part of the 9th/15th century, Malacca rulers acknowledged themselves to be Ayudhya's vassals. In return, Malacca received supplies of food and people as well as valued trading privileges. When Ayudhya attempted to impose its control there in 809-10/1406, 822/1419 and 834-5/1431, Malacca was able to appeal to its patron China, who ordered the Thais to desist. The relationship with Majapahit, on the other hand, was more harmonious. Malacca continued to accept vassal status till the end of the century, and ties with Majapahit were fostered through regular missions and royal marriages. This ensured a mutually advantageous trade and guaranteed Malacca access to Javanese rice.

From Malacca's inception, its rulers sought to attract inhabitants. Not only was manpower a vital economic resource, but a kingdom's prestige was always measured in terms of the people it controlled. According to Portuguese accounts, within four months of his arrival Parameśvara's new settlement had a population of a hundred people, which soon increased to 2,000. By the second reign, the population had swelled to 6,000 and it continued to grow as Malacca's trade expanded. Peoples from the archipelago itself, especially Sumatra and the peninsula, were the most numerous, but there were also large groups of foreigners, especially Indians, who took up semi-permanent residence in Malacca and frequently became prominent officials. At the beginning of the 10th/16th century the inhabitants of Malacca were estimated at 100,000, though this is probably an exaggeration. According to Pires, no less than 84 languages could be heard in the streets and 4,000 foreign merchants resided there. The town itself spread out for three leagues (about 15 km.) on both sides of the Malacca river, encompassing a large commercial quarter on the northern shore, a Javanese settlement on the southern side, impressive buildings on Malacca Hill, and fishing villages at the estuary and along the river marshes.

Militarily, Malacca was able to assert its superiority in the region and thus ensure that its commercial hegemony was maintained. Portuguese figures for Malacca's fighting men vary from 4,000 in the city proper to 100,000, including the neighbouring areas. In the Portuguese attack on Malacca in 917/1511, 3,000 guns were taken, but this was believed to be less than half the town's artillery. The prime component in Malacca's forces were the *orang laut,* the sea people of the coasts and river reaches, who manned its fleets. In the early stages of Malacca's development *orang laut* patrols were sent out to compel passing vessels to patronise Malacca rather than rival ports, and they were crucial in guarding Malacca's sea lanes from pirate raids by other kingdoms. Their prestige in Malacca was considerable. Several of their leaders were related to the Malacca dynasty through marriage, and some of the highest ministers traced their descent from *orang laut.*

A prime factor in Malacca's success was the quality of its administration. High priority was given to security within the town and to the protection of foreign merchants and their goods. One very practical measure was the construction of underground warehouses so that stored goods would be less vulnerable to theft and fire. An early Chinese account mentions men patrolling the streets ringing bells, and both Malay and Portuguese sources describe the active part taken by rulers themselves in supervising the enforcement of law. By the middle of the 9th/15th century, a body of laws had been codified regulating punishments and attempting to control abuses such as bribery, especially of judges. A separate maritime code set out the powers of a ship's captain when at sea and his relationship with the merchants whose goods he was carrying. The fact that foreigners in Malacca had ready access to a legal authority in cases of dispute must have been a great attraction to traders.

Commercial transactions were aided by an efficient administrative system shaped to the needs of the mercantile community. Four Shahbandars or harbour masters were appointed, each representing a group of trading nations. One was for the Gujeratis alone, since they were the most numerous (estimated at 1,000 by Pires); another was for other Indians and for traders from Pegu and Pasai; another for those from Java, the Moluccas, Banda, Palembang, Borneo and the Philippines; the fourth was for traders from Champa, China and the Ryukyu Islands (probably including Japan). Each Shahbandar had the responsibility of welcoming individual traders, assigning warehouses, overseeing the affairs of his particular group, maintaining a check on weights, measures and coinage, adjudicating disputes between ships' captains and merchants, and generally supervising the market place.

Customs duties were also carefully regulated. In general, these were paid in accordance with the value of the cargo, with additional gifts presented to the ruler and leading ministers. Though the bulk of Malacca's revenue came from these duties, they were somewhat lower than those of its chief rivals. The Chinese, furthermore, were exempt from any gift-offering. For large ships, a flat rate of 6% of the total value was levied, eliminating the need for further gifts. To minimise the possibility of extortion or corruption, a consortium of Malacca merchants under the supervision of the Temenggung often bought up the entire cargo of these larger vessels. Each merchant then received a proportion of the cargo equivalent to the amount he had contributed. This proved a speedy and efficient method of clearing cargoes, enabling captains to buy up new supplies and prepare for their homeward journey with the appropriate monsoon. The smaller Malay traders of Malacca acted as middlemen, by selling or bartering the goods in front of their homes, in licensed stalls erected on the bridge over the Malacca River, or in the market place itself. They also carried cargoes by boat to other areas in the archipelago. Because of the middleman role of Malays, and because their language was easily learnt when compared with most regional languages, Malay became the *lingua franca* in ports throughout the archipelago.

Thanks to its attractive mercantile environment, Malacca emerged as the collecting centre for spices from the eastern archipelago as well as a distribution point for Indian textiles. This dual role was vital in its commercial success, giving it a great advantage over nearby ports and ensuring its dominance in the Straits region. By the beginning of the 10th/16th century, Pires valued Malacca's trade at 2.4 million cruzados annually, well over half that of Seville, one of Europe's major commerical cities.

Statecraft in Malacca. The prestige which came to Malacca was linked not only to its wealth but to the development of a court culture. A fundamental part of this culture was the formulation of a concept of statecraft that reinforced the status of the dynasty and of Malacca itself. At the apex of the kingdom was the ruler, whose exalted lineage was traced to Sri Tri Buana, the prince who had miraculously appeared on Bukit Si Guntang in Palembang. The legend of the contract made by Sri Tri Buana with the Palembang chief stressed that a terrible retribution would be meted out to any subject guilty of *derhaka* or disloyalty to the ruler. Although the latter was enjoined to treat all his subjects with respect, the punishment of a wicked king must be left to Allah Almighty. But when a ruler governed justly and wisely, the kingdom would flourish, for the prosperity of the state found its ultimate source in the king. Divine powers were inherent in him, in pre-Islamic times perhaps subsumed in the Sanskrit word *śakti* or old Malay *andeka* but later denoted by the Arabic term *daulat*.

Despite the king's theoretical sanctity and total authority, there were checks against arbitrary rule. It was customary for all state decisions to be based on *muafakat* or consultation between the ruler and his ministers. The interaction between the two is well expressed by the *Sejarah Melayu,* which compares the ruler to the fire and the ministers to the firewood "and fire needs wood to produce a flame". Since the ministers were responsible for the daily functioning of the kingdom, they wielded great power. The most important was the Bendahara, originally of commoner and perhaps *orang laut* birth, but whose line in time became intimately linked with the royal house through intermarriage. Following him came the Penghulu Bendahari, the head of all Shahbandars, who controlled state revenues as well as royal servants and scribes. The Temenggung, originally third in line but later regarded as Bendahara designate, was chief of police and chief magistrate. Finally, the Laksamana headed the military administration and was commander of the ruler's bodyguard and the fleets of *orang laut.*

Below them were many other nobles, although the numbers are unknown. Some noble positions were created as royal favours, but many others were inherited. The nobles shared in the process of government through collective decision-making in a large assembly where consensus was highly valued. Because of their commercial interests, these men were often extremely wealthy and could call on a large following. Indeed, the greatest challenge a ruler could face was a coterie of hostile ministers and nobles. It is not surprising, therefore, that by the mid-9th/15th century Malaccan theories of statecraft had been translated into laws which spelt out special royal prerogatives in dress and ceremonial and the severe penalties for any who flouted this rigid sumptuary code. In extreme cases, such as the use of words forbidden to any but the king, the offender would be put to death.

While these notions of kingship did not originate in Malacca, it was there that they were fully developed and most clearly articulated. Malacca's great achievement was to refine a court culture which was then consciously imitated throughout other parts of the Malay-speaking world. Despite local variations, the style of dress, literature and dance, social norms and courtly language were similar throughout the peninsula and east-coast Sumatra, with considerable influence in Borneo and parts of the eastern archipelago. The fact that this highly-respected dynasty also adopted Islam was not only an important ingredient in its own prestige, but was also fundamental to the spread of Islam in the Malay-Indonesian archipelago.

Islam in Malacca. Arab and Indian Muslim traders had been in the archipelago for several centuries, but Islam did not begin to attract converts in significant numbers until after the 7th/13th century (for the coming of Islam, see MALAY PENINSULA and INDONESIA). By 692-3/1292 the town of Perlak and by 696/1297 Samudra-Pasai on the north-eastern coast of Sumatra had Muslim rulers, but on the peninsula the earliest evidence of an Islamic king is the Trengganu Stone from the east coast. It has a partly illegible *hidjra* date which could read between 702/1303 and 789/1387. Various dates for the conversion of the Malacca ruler, ranging from 811-12/1409 to 839-40/1436, have been suggested, but the precise year is still speculative. While the Islamic name of Iskandar is attributed to Malacca's founder by the *Sejarah Melayu,* it is unlikely that the first ruler was himself Muslim. Pires attributes the conversion to the second ruler, whom he calls Iskandar. Since his dynastic list omits one king, it is more probable that the conversion he describes can be identified with the third ruler, Sultan Muhammad Shah, whom the *Sejarah Melayu* depicts as the first royal convert. The second, and conceivably the first ruler, may have assumed the name Iskandar and the Persian title of Shāh to enhance their status, but Muhammad is a more appropriate name for a newly-converted king.

The *Sejarah Melayu* presents the conversion of the third ruler as an act of divine revelation. The Prophet, appearing to him in a dream, instructs him to recite the confession of faith, gives him the new name Muhammad, and tells him of the imminent arrival of a teacher from Jeddah. When the king awakes, he finds that he has been miraculously circumcised and that he is able to recite the creed. That afternoon a religious teacher arrives as his dream had foretold and, convinced by this event, both the ruler and his court embrace Islam.

The precise reasons for the ruler's conversion are still debated. According to Pires' account, the (second) Malacca ruler was aware that the commercial vitality of Malacca's rival, Muslim Pasai, was largely due to its patronage by Indian Muslim cloth merchants. He therefore took active steps to emulate Pasai's success and himself attract Muslims to Malacca. Muslim traders were granted commercial privileges; residences and mosques were built for them and they were welcomed at court. Pasai, assuming the prestigious role of proselytiser, encouraged this development by sending teachers to Malacca. Pires goes on to say that under the influence of both Pasai and prominent Muslim merchants, the (second) ruler at the age of 72 adopted Islam and married the King of Pasai's daughter.

Pasai's example and Malacca's desire to attract

merchants must have been persuasive in Malaccan court circles. Arguments in favour of taking definitive measures to secure Muslim trade would have been strengthened after the third ruler returned from a mission to China in 838-9/1435, presumably aware that the Emperor intended to abolish imperial trade, which had previously brought Malacca valued revenue, and revert to the tribute system.

But the decision to embrace Islam would not have been purely the result of commercial considerations. The new faith would have heightened the dynasty's already considerable prestige, since it linked the ruler with the wider Muslim world. The impressive ceremonial accompanying the reception of foreign envoys at the Malacca court must have been even more significant when the missions came from the Muslim princes of such places as Aden, Hormuz, Cambay and Bengal. Scholars have also suggested that the changing doctrinal mood of Islam may have been another inducement. By the 8th/13th century, the mystical Ṣūfī orders had become more influential within Islam and had become closely associated with trade guilds. The tolerance of Ṣūfism when confronted with non-Islamic practices as well as the Ṣūfīs' syncretistic theosophy, moderating the more stringent demands of orthodox Islam, may have helped to make the new faith acceptable to the Malacca court [see MALAY PENINSULA].

Little is known of the nature of Islam in Malacca. The main source for information about its theological content has been the *Sejarah Melayu*, but although the text contains scattered references to Islam, these cannot be considered as particularly revealing. The reshaping of the royal genealogy to incorporate Alexander the Great (Iskandar Zul-karnain), regarded as a great Muslim warrior who converted the ruler of India, conveys more about Malay attitudes to ancestry than to religion. The Islamic invocation at the conclusion of each chapter and the death-bed testimonies of various rulers are purely formulaic phrases. Stories similar to that describing the miraculous conversion of the third ruler can be found in other parts of the Indonesian world and are hardly unique.

Scholars have been attracted by apparent references to mysticism, but the *Sejarah Melayu* itself does not demonstrate any deep knowledge of Ṣūfī thought. The great Persian theologian and mystic, al-G͟hazālī (d. 505/1111 [*q.v.*]) is mentioned simply as an example of a very learned man; similarly, the episodes which describe the exchange of missions between Malacca and Pasai, apparently over questions of doctrinal interest, may be equally related to the Malay love of riddles and the rivalry between the two courts. In one of these episodes, a teacher from Mecca is sent from Malacca by Sultan Mansur to Pasai to have his book on mysticism, *Durr manzum,* either authenticated or explained. In another, Sultan Mansur poses to the Pasai court the question of whether those in heaven or hell abide there forever, from which it has been inferred that the work of the late 8th/14th century and early 9th/15th century mystic ʿAbd al-Karīm al-D͟jīlī (d. 820/1417 [*q.v.*]) was known in Malacca. Sultan Mahmud later sent a further mission to Pasai to resolve an apparent contradiction between two statements concerning the nature of unbelief. But while the deliberately undisclosed answer may possibly imply a mystic response, the debate over what distinguished an infidel from an unbeliever was of general concern to Muslims in these early stages of Islamicisation.

Available sources do no more than suggest that Islamic teaching in Malacca was tinged with mysticism. Historical evidence is more revealing about Malacca's prestige as a thriving Muslim centre in the 9th/15th century and about the contribution of Islam to the shaping of Malay culture.

Within Malacca, Islam helped to strengthen the dominance of the court. By the time Islam was formally adopted in Malacca, the influence of Persian notions of kingship, stressing the monarch's sacral nature and elevating him to a place high above ordinary mortals, had spread through much of the Islamic world. The Malacca ruler became part of this tradition. Already regarded as semi-divine, he was now able to assume other new and imposing titles. Coins from Malacca proclaim the ruler as Sultan and Shah, raising him above all other princes in the region who, with the exception of Pasai, bore the simpler title *raja.* He was also "Helper of the World and of the Religion" (*Nāṣir al-dunyā wa 'l-dīn*), "Allah's Shadow Upon the Earth" (*Ẓill Allāh fī 'l-ʿālam*), to whom obedience was due as a religious obligation. In the words of the *Sejarah Melayu,* "When you do your duty to the Prophet and Allah, with whom a good king is joined, then it is as though you are doing your duty to Allah himself".

There have been suggestions that the Hinduised titles of Sultan Muḥammad's successor imply a short-lived rejection of Islam. In general, however, the promotion of Islam in Malacca was very much a royal undertaking, with the rulers themselves actively encouraging proselytisation. In the reign of Sultan Mansur, marriages between Muslims and infidels were arranged to attract new converts, and apostasy was forbidden. The daily prayers were made obligatory for Muslims, and to a considerable extent the legal system began to favour Muslims, especially as witnesses and in property disputes. The adoption of Islam became increasingly necessary in order to maintain high positions in the court; while able non-Muslims could still rise, they usually eventually converted to the new faith. Nothing is known of the Islamic religious hierarchy, although there are passing references to *imām*, *ḳāḍī*, and *k͟haṭīb*. It seems that the major religious official, who also played a prominent role in court affairs, was termed *Kadi.* He had far greater authority than did the *ḳāḍī* or judge in the Islamic heartlands, and in at least one case the position passed from father to son. Other religious officials, especially the ruler's own teacher, similarly gained influence in court circles and Malacca's administration because of their assumed piety and superior knowledge.

The high point of royal encouragement of Islam came during the reign of Sultan Mansur, who built a great new mosque for Malacca and made preparations to make the pilgrimage. He died before this could be accomplished, but his son, Sultan Alauddin, said to be devoted to mosque affairs, also announced his intention of going to Mecca. Though he too abandoned his goal, the projects assume greater significance when it is realised that until the late 19th century no Malay kings had made the *haj.*

In the development of Malacca's court culture, Islam's great strength was its willingness, within certain limits, to tolerate many non-Islamic beliefs and traditions. An examination of Malacca's laws (*Undang-Undang Melaka*) shows that Islam made continuing compromises with existing practices, particularly in regard to criminal punishments and sexual offences. These laws, though drawn up by Islamic jurisconsults and modified over several reigns, often include two penalties for the same crime, one following custom (*ʿadat*) and the other said to be that of "the law of Allah". In fact, the so-called "law of Allah" was often adapted from *sharīʿa* law to conform with local conditions. This fusion of Islam and Malaccan custom was encouraged as local religious scholars and scribes took over the task of rewriting and amending the existing law code. While some sections of the Malacca laws seem to have been copied verbatim from Islamic law books, the language was not uncommonly corrupt because *sharīʿa* law was not always fully understood.

To some Muslims, especially non-Malays, this accomodation was not always acceptable. An Arab sailor-author whose account is dated 866/1462 considered that, in Islamic terms, Malacca had no culture; he was critical of the marriage between Muslims and infidels, and the fact that divorce was not regarded as a religious act; he also condemned the failure to observe Islamic restrictions against certain foods, especially the eating of dogs and drinking of wine. The *Sejarah Melayu* hints at the continuing tension between Malays and foreign Muslims who looked down on a society they might well consider morally and spiritually lax. One incident describes how a Malacca noble, coming to his religious class intoxicated, accuses his teacher of being in Malacca purely for financial gain; another noble defends the subtlety of Malay pronunciation in comparison with that of Arabic.

From an orthodox point of view, Malacca Malays might not have been deeply versed in Islamic theology or punctilious observers of strict *sharīʿa* law. On the other hand, even when the faith was only newly-established in Malacca, the sources contain no hint that Muslims from eastern Asia questioned its orthodoxy. Ma Huan, a Chinese Muslim interpreter whose account may relate to any period between 812-13/1409 and 855/1451, notes simply that "the king of the country and all the people follow the Muslim faith, fasting, doing penance and chanting liturgies". By the second half of the 9th/15th century, Malacca was regarded as a focal point for Islamic scholarship, with religious teachers attracted by the patronage of the court and the possibility of supporting themselves by taking on pupils. Malacca became a dissemination point for Islam as much as for trading goods, and all over the archipelago, in the southern Philippines, Borneo and Java, legends link royal conversions to teachers arriving from Malacca or to local figures who received instruction there. The explication and dispersal of Islamic beliefs was facilitated because Malay was already established as a regional *lingua franca.* Furthermore, the process of Islamicisation was fostered by the later Malacca rulers, who regarded themselves and were perceived as the champions of Islam in the region. Sultan Muzafar was said to have actively encouraged princes in the northern coastal ports of Java to adopt Islam, and one Javanese non-Muslim ruler was driven to complain to the Portuguese about Malacca's Muslim fervour. While Malacca laid down the basis for much of Malay culture, Islam itself became so associated with Malays that, in places such as Borneo, to embrace Islam was to *masuk Melayu,* to enter Malayness.

The spread of Islam in neighbouring courts owed much to the example of the prosperous and prestigious Malacca, but its acceptance was not only a result of peaceful persuasion. As Malacca expanded territorially, gaining control over greater economic resources, food-producing areas and manpower, it brought its religion as well as overlordship. In the second reign, Malacca's borders extended to include all land between Kuala Linggi and Kuala Kesang (respectively the northern and southern borders of the modern Malacca state) and from the mid-9th/15th century, territorial expansion proceeded apace. Confronted by an aggressive Ayudhya, Sultan Muzafar waged several campaigns against the Thais, the victory, according to the *Sejarah Melayu,* being finally assured by the magical power of a Malacca *sayid.* Following the conclusion of peace with Ayudhya and emboldened by his friendship with Pasai, China and Majapahit, Sultan Muzafar extended his control north to Selangor, south to Singapore and west to Pahang, where the ruler adopted Islam at Muzafar's request. Although he never succeeded in defeating Aru, Malacca traditions successfully propagated the notion that the people of Aru, though converted before Malacca, practised a form of Islam inferior to that found in Malacca. Sultan Muzafar did, however, defeat the rulers of Kampar and Indragiri on the east coast of Sumatra, forcing them to become Muslim and gaining access to the pepper and gold of the Sumatran interior. His son Sultan Mansur extended suzerainty over Perak, gained after wars with Kedah, Ayudhya's vassal. His control was strengthened along the east coast of Sumatra, where Siak was defeated and Mansur's daughter married to its ruler. Mansur's sister, who married the ruler of Minangkabau, also induced her husband to accept Islam. The next ruler, Sultan Alauddin, incorporated the entire Riau-Lingga archipelago in his territory, and to ensure his hold over key areas of his empire, retained the kings of Pahang, Kampar and Indragiri at the Malacca court, where he was said to have instructed them on Islamic matters.

Islam must have provided the last ruler of Malacca, Mahmud, with a rallying point around which to mobilise his subjects in campaigns against the Buddhist Thais. During his reign Malacca attacked Kelantan, a Thai vassal in the northern Peninsula, and in 902-3/1497 moved as far north as Ligor. A Thai prince of Patani agreed to accept Melaka's suzerainty and adopt Islam, while the ruler of Kedah also revoked Thai overlordship. When Mahmud formally renounced any Thai claims to suzerainty in the region, relations with Ayudhya were broken off. In 905-6/1500 the Thais attacked Malacca again and possibly made another unsuccessful Siamese assault prior to the first arrival of the Portuguese in 941-5/1509. But by this stage, Malacca's hold over the central and southern peninsula was so strong that Ayudhya was only able to impose overlordship over the most northerly Malay states.

During the 9th/15th century, the nexus between flourishing international trade and a thriving religious environment, characteristic of major maritime ports in the archipelago, is well-exemplified in Malacca. Islam became an integral part of the court culture of Malacca which, admired and emulated throughout the Malay world, also laid the basis for the evolution of modern Malay society. While Malacca played a vital role in the Islamicisation process, Islam was equally important in contributing to Malacca's special place in Malay history. Perhaps the measure of Malacca's prestige is expressed most vividly by the last ruler, Sultan Mahmud, who claimed that Malacca was so great that it could be made into Mecca itself. Although implications of Ṣūfī teaching on the unimportance of the *haj* have been read into this, it is as easy to see it simply as the boast of a proud, wealthy and successful dynasty. But the statement clearly created a dilemma for orthodox Muslims, and according to later Malay arguments it was Sultan Mahmud's unacceptable hubris which brought down divine retribution from far-off Portugal.

In Rabīʿ II-Djumādā I 917/July 1511, Malacca was

attacked by a Portuguese fleet under the command of Afonso de Albuquerque. The Portuguese aim was to establish a post for their expanding Asian trade, to gain access to and command of eastern spices, and to strike a major blow at Christianity's great rival, Islam. Internal dissensions in Malacca, and Portuguese military superiority, led to the flight of Sultan Mahmud with 3,000 men and the fall of the city itself on 21 Djumādā I 917/10 August 1511. There can be little doubt that at the time both Malays and Portuguese felt the religious nature of the conflict to be as compelling as the commercial one. Several Portuguese taken hostage in Malacca in 914-15/1509 were circumcised and forcibly converted by Sultan Mahmud's orders. His refusal to negotiate with Albuquerque two years later was attributed to the influence of Muslim merchants, especially those from India who had already experienced conflict with the Portuguese. Albuquerque for his part saw "Moors" as Portugal's implacable enemies, both on commercial and spiritual grounds, and gave orders that any Malay captured should be put to death. The Hindu merchants of Malacca regarded the Christian Portuguese as a natural ally against their Muslim rivals and gave Albuquerque valued assistance both before and after Malacca's fall.

In the aftermath of the attack, Malacca was sacked and mosques and royal graves destroyed to provide stone for the great fortress, La Formosa, built on the site of Sultan Mansur's great mosque. A Portuguese governor and administration was appointed, Hindus were placed in high positions and relations with neighbouring non-Muslim rulers were cultivated. In time, a *modus vivendi* was reached with other Muslim states whose economy had come to be closely linked with Malacca's. But despite sustained efforts, the Portuguese were never successful in reviving Malacca's former commercial supremacy. While it remained an important entrepôt, foreign merchants complained of high duties and official corruption, and Muslim traders preferred to patronise Islamic Atjeh [*q.v.*] because of the unsympathetic Portuguese attitude towards those of the Muslim faith. The Portuguese were thus unable to command the exchange trade in spices and cloth which, largely in Muslim hands, had been so fundamental in Malacca's former success.

Furthermore, Portuguese Malacca faced the continuing hostility of the Malacca dynasty's heirs. Setting up a new capital in the Riau-Lingga archipelago, they made repeated attacks on Malacca in an effort to recapture the city. When the Dutch appeared in the area in the early 11th/17th century, the Malacca dynasty, now based in peninsular Johor, were more than ready to assist the Dutch East India Company (VOC) in a siege of Malacca, perhaps hoping that they might thereby return. However, after Malacca's fall to Dutch forces in Shawwāl 1050/January 1641, it became simply one more post in the vast VOC trading network. Unlike the Portuguese, the Dutch never saw Malacca as an important commercial centre. Its major function was to act as a strategic guard post on the Malacca Straits, with commercial traffic focussed on Batavia, the VOC capital.

Under the Dutch administration, the Malay population (including Malay speakers from elsewhere in the archipelago) slowly increased to more than 5,000. Indian Muslim traders did frequent Malacca, but not in great numbers, being always the object of Dutch suspicion. But Islam fared better under the Protestant VOC than under the Roman Catholic Portuguese. The VOC did not encourage missionary activities among Muslims, and in many ways was more concerned about Catholicism. However, without a Malay court to act as a religious sponsor, and without the links to the Muslim world provided by a cosmopolitan trading port, Malacca made no further significant contribution to the development of Malay Islam. In 1795, during the Napoleonic Wars, it was taken over by the British to prevent its capture by the French. Under the British, the famous fort was destroyed to forestall its use by hostile forces in the future. Malacca reverted briefly to the Dutch in 1818 but in 1824, by the terms of the Anglo-Dutch Treaty, was returned to the British in exchange for Benkulen (west Sumatra). In 1826 it was incorporated into the Straits Settlements, but was always subservient commercially to Penang and Singapore, which became renowned centres for Islamic study. In 1867 the Straits Settlements were transferred from the Government of India and brought directly under the Colonial Office. During the colonial period (1874 until 1957), Malacca was under the control of a British Resident responsible to the Governor in Singapore. It became part of the independent Federation of Malaysia in 1957.

Bibliography: A collection of essays surveying Malacca's history from early times to the present day is found in two volumes edited by Kernial Singh Sandhu and P. Wheatley, entitled *Melaka: the transformation of a Malay capital, c. 1400-1980,* Kuala Lumpur 1983. R.O. Winstedt, *A history of Malaya,* revised ed. Singapore 1968, is dated but still useful. The background to Malacca's founding is given in O.W. Wolters, *The fall of Śrivijaya in Malay history,* Ithaca and London 1970, and P. Wheatley, *The Golden Khersonese,* Kuala Lumpur 1961. Early relations with China are discussed in J.V.G. Mills (tr. and ed.), Ma Huan, *Ying-Yai Sheng-Lan. The overall survey of the Ocean's shores (1433),* Cambridge 1970; see especially Wang Gungwu, *The opening of relations between China and Malacca,* 1403-5, in J. Bastin and R. Roolvink, eds., *Malayan and Indonesian studies,* London 1964, 34-62, and *The first three rulers of Malacca,* in *JMBRAS,* xli/1 (1968), 11-22. The Arabic navigational texts are discussed by G. R. Tibbetts, *A study of the Arabic texts containing material on South-East Asia,* Leiden and London 1979. The standard Malay account is C. C. Brown, *Sejarah Melayu or Malay Annals,* in *JMBRAS,* xxv/2-3 (1953), which is discussed by R. J. Wilkinson, *The Malacca Sultanate,* in *JMBRAS,* xxi/2 (1935), 22-67. Legal codes are Liaw Yock Fong, *Undang-Undang Melaka,* The Hague 1976, and R. O. Winstedt and P. E. Josseling de Jong, *The maritime laws of Malacca,* in *JMBRAS,* xxix/3 (1956), 22-59. A. Cortesão, ed., *The Suma oriental of Tomé Pires,* ii, London 1944, remains the most valuable source on most aspects of Malacca's history, providing the basis for M.A.P. Meilink-Roelofsz's standard work, *Asian trade and European influence in the Indonesian Archipelago between 1500 and about 1630,* The Hague 1962. Information on Islam is limited, but see C. H. Wake, *Malacca's early kings and the reception of Islam,* in *Jnal. of Southeast Asian History,* v/2 (1964), 104-28; A. H. Johns, *Islam in Southeast Asia: reflections and new directions,* in *Indonesia,* xix (1975), 33-55; A. C. Milner, *Islam and Malay kingship,* in *JRAS* (1981), 46-70. For the Portuguese conquest, see W. de Gray Birch, ed. and tr. *The Commentaries of the Great Afonso Dalboquerque,* iii, London 1884; A. Bausani, ed. and tr. *Lettera di Giovanni da Empoli,* Rome 1970; M. L. Dames, tr. *The Book of Duarte Barbosa. An account of the countries bordering on the Indian Ocean and their inhabitants, A.D. 1518,* London 1918. Malacca's dealings with Malay states under the Portuguese and Dutch are covered in L. Y. Andaya, *The Kingdom of Johor, 1641-1728,* Kuala Lumpur 1975, and Dianne Lewis, *The Dutch East India Company and the Straits of Malacca, 1700-84,* unpubl. Ph. D. thesis, A.N.U. Canberra 1970. The period of British rule is discussed in C. M. Turnbull, *The Straits Settlements 1826-7,* Kuala Lumpur 1972.

(Barbara Watson Andaya)

MALAGA [see mālaḳa].

MALĀHĪ (a., pl. of *malhā*), appears in a number of sources, in a figurative sense, as the equivalent of musical instruments; it is sometimes replaced by *ālat al-lahw* or linked with the word *lahw* which means "game, pastime, amusement", as e.g. in certain works called *kitāb al-lahw wa 'l-malāhī.* According to the *LA,* the verb *lahā* denotes an action aimed at amusing and at securing *ṭarab,* the emotion of joy or sadness; this further term, closely associated with music and its power, gives birth to another appellation of musical instruments, *ālāt al-ṭarab.* Dozy, in his *Supplement,* ii, 554, lists several terms which come from the same root and are connected with the same idea: *mulhī* "musician, instrumental player, minstrel, balladeer whose profession is to amuse the masses"; the feminine *mulhiya* would mean "dancer", according to Quatremère, but Dozy remarks "I believe rather that it means a female musician"; finally, we have *arbāb al-malāhī* "musicians" and *ālāt al-malāhī* "musical instruments". We have thus already three equivalent terms denoting the same idea.

These few explanations of the usage of the term *malāhī* underline very clearly the association of the designated object with the idea of game, pastime, diversion and amusement, a point which leads us to examine certain questions of principle. Does this obvious connection with games and diversion indicate a certain ideological and conceptual attitude which could be at the very origin of the term in its relationship with music? Is it therefore possible that the term was adopted at a given moment and in particular circumstances? Was it, together with its variants, the sole term used to designate the musical facts to which it corresponds? Are the various meanings given by Dozy exceptional ones, or do they rather indicate that the term *malāhī* is a wider one and extends beyond the idea of musical instruments to denote, e.g., music in general, and above all, the art-forms of music? Is there perhaps a more restricted sense denoting e.g., a particular category of instruments? As we shall see, it seems that *malāhī* is a term with manifold usages.

A study of the sources on music reveals to us a very significant state of affairs. On one side, the term *malāhī*, either alone or linked with *lahw,* appears in the title of 7 or 8 works which, accordingly, set forth systematically the facts concerning it. On the other, *malāhī* appears in the chapters and passages devoted to music which form part of works belonging to certain categories of writings, but is almost absent from treatises with a speculative character. These last, which examine closely the mathematical, theoretical and philosophical aspects of music, like those of al-Kindī, al-Fārābī, Ibn Sīnā, etc., use other terms to denote the musical instruments or the other concepts covered by *malāhī*, such as *ālāt* pure and simple, or *ālāt al-mūsīḳī, ālāt al-ṭarab* and *ālāt al-g̲h̲inā*ʾ. The Epistle of the Ik̲h̲wān al-Ṣafāʾ, which is on the borderline between the opposing categories, uses on one occasion at the beginning of the treatise the term in the combination *ṣināʿat al-malāhī* (instrumental art or *musica instrumentalis*), but in the definition of music and its aims twice repeated we read "*mūsīḳī* is *g̲h̲inā*ʾ, the *mūsīḳār* is the musician and the *mūsīḳāt* are musical instruments, *ālāt al-g̲h̲inā*ʾ". Amongst the rare exceptions in the speculative treatises, one may cite the case of a late, anonymous treatise called *Maʿrifat al-ang̲h̲ām wa 'l-hunūk wa 'l-ṭarab fi 'l-ith̲nay ʿas̲h̲ar wa 'l-sitta* "Knowledge about the melodies and modes and the happy emotions caused by the 12 and 6 modes" (ms. Top Kapu Sarayı A. 2130, pp. 2-47), where it says "The search for *ṭarab* has led to the invention of *malāhī* (musical instruments) by the philosophers".

It is interesting to note that seven out of the eight treatises completely dedicated to *malāhī* saw the light in the 3rd/9th century; the eighth one, the *D̲h̲amm al-malāʿib wa 'l-malāhī* by Ibn al-Kayyāl (d. 938/1532), is conceived in the same spirit and bears almost the same title as one of the seven others, Ibn Abi 'l-Dunyā's *D̲h̲amm al-malāhī* (author d. 281/894). Like this last, Ibn al-Kayyāl brings together games and music in his treatise (ms. Chester Beatty 3419, fols. 1-77a), of which the first two-thirds are devoted to games and the last third to music, dancing and musical instruments, whose origin is attributed to Satan. Given that the theologian and jurist Ibn Abi 'l-Dunyā's *D̲h̲amm al-malāhī* is the oldest extant work of this kind, it is plausible to suggest that it was indeed he who established the model of the systematic and expanded connection of "music and musical instruments" with "games, pastimes and amusements".

Ibn Abi 'l-Dunyā in fact attacks violently music, which he regards as a diversion from the life of devotion and piety; his attack covers all kinds of musical activity, including the instruments linked up with games and other types of pleasure. This treatise accordingly became a source of inspiration for later generations of theologians and jurists who opposed music. Discussion concerning *malāhī* in either a wide or a more restrained sense crops up again whenever it is a question of *samāʿ* [*q.v.*]. In the numerous passages about the problem of *malāhī,* we find attitudes varying from total prohibition to total admissibility of music, dancing and all instruments. Hence in certain cases, the term *malāhī* acquires a very wide sense, embracing the art-forms of music and the dance; in others, it is restricted to a limited number of forbidden instruments. Al-Adfuwī, e.g. in his treatise *al-Imtāʿ bi-aḥkām al-samāʿ* (which exists in various mss., see Shiloah, *The theory of music in Arabic writings,* 50-2), discusses the case of several instruments, such as the *duff* (tambourine) and the *s̲h̲abbāba* and *yarāʿ* (flutes), then he deals separately with the *malāhī,* which are identified with *maʿāzif* (a generic term for stringed instruments). In this case, one must understand that *malāhī* denoting the forbidden instruments for amusement correspond essentially with stringed instruments, those par excellence of art-form music. The Mālikī jurist Ibn al-Ḥad̲j̲d̲j̲ (d. 737/1336) confirms in some measure this remark in his *Madk̲h̲al al-s̲h̲arʿ al-s̲h̲arīf,* where he states that *g̲h̲inā*ʾ, listening to slave musicians, to the *ʿūd,* the *ṭunbūr* and other instruments of amusement (*malāhī*) is to be condemned. An attitude similar to al-Adfuwī's turns up again in the treatise of Ibn al-Ḳaysarānī, *Fī d̲j̲awāz al-samāʿ,* in which the author begins also by putting forward the idea that certain instruments are allowable, but then devotes a passage to *mazāmīr* and *malāhī,* which are absolutely forbidden. The jurist al-S̲h̲āmī (d. 993/1585) in his *Niṣāb al-iḥtisāb* writes that if the *ʿūd,* the *ṭunbūr* and the *zamr* are publicly on view, it is the *muḥtasib*'s duty to destroy them. Finally, in this type of writings, the term *malāhī* or *ālāt al-lahw* is taken, according to the attitude of the various authors, at times as the equivalent of all the concepts concerning art-form music and the dance and at times as designating certain instruments which are universally condemned.

In the general schema of the literature on *samā*ʿ, there are other points of view about the term and concept of *malāhī*. Al-Nābulusī (d. 1143/1731) in his *Īḍāḥ al-dalālāt fī samā*ʿ *al-ālāt* (ed. Damascus 1302/1884) puts forward the idea that the word *lahw*, by which one describes the instruments (*malāhī* or *ālāt al-lahw*), does not necessarily indicate that musical instruments are invariably used with the aim of amusement. This qualification and the prohibition which follows from it are justifiable when the end sought is mere amusement. But when they contribute to the spiritual elevation of the Ṣūfī, this idea of distraction and amusement is no longer valid, since an instrument as such is not to be condemned because of its shape or the harmonious sounds which it makes; thus listening to the beautiful sounds made by birds is not forbidden. We find exactly the same attitude again, set forth in more or less the same terms, in the work of al-Nābulusī's pupil al-Dikdikidjī (d. 1189/1775), *Raf*ʿ *al-mushkilāt fī ḥukm ibāḥat samā*ʿ *al-ālāt bi 'l-naghamāt al-ṭayyibāt* (ms. Berlin, We 1811, fols. 1-29).

With this refutation, which reduces to some extent the pejorative sense of *malāhī* and which rejects the ideological attitude which associates them wholly with maleficient effects, we can pass on to the class of writings which presents the point of view of literary exponents and is seen in the other works of the 3rd/9th century devoted to *malāhī*. Amongst these, some are unfortunately lost, and we only have the titles in bibliographical works. Ibn al-Ḳifṭī, in his *T. al-Ḥukamā*ʾ, mentions a treatise by al-Sarakhsī (d. 286/899), whose complete title is *Kitāb al-Lahw wa 'l-malāhī fi 'l-ghināʾ wa 'l-mughannīn wa 'l-munādama wa 'l-mudjālasa*. Ibn Abī Uṣaybiʿa, in his ʿ*Uyūn al-anbā*ʾ, gives an abridged title for the same work, *K. al-Lahw wa 'l-malāhī*, and Ḥādjdjī Khalīfa refers merely to a *K. al-Lahw*; in the light of the practices of al-Sarakhsī's time, it may be that we have here more than one work. Amongst the lost treatises on music of Thābit b. Ḳurra (d. 288/901), a *Kitāb al-Lahw wa 'l-malāhī* is mentioned in the previously-cited work of Ibn al-Ḳifṭī. Finally, in the *Fihrist*, Ibn al-Nadīm cites a lost work of Muḥammad b. Yaḥyā b. Abī Manṣūr al-Mawṣilī (3rd/9th century) which had the title *Kitāb al-*ʿ*Ūd wa 'l-malāhī*.

We come now to two final works of the 3rd/9th century which dealt with *malāhī* and which are, at the same time, the oldest treatises on music which have come down to us. The first, the *Kitāb al-Malāhī*, is that of the famous grammarian of the Kūfan school al-Mufaḍḍal b. Salama (d. *ca.* 292/905 [*q.v.*]). The work is essentially apologetic, and takes up the defence of two causes set forth in the introduction in the following order:

(1) Refutation of the opinion, probably that of the Shuʿūbiyya [*q.v.*], according to which the Arabs did not know the ʿ*ūd* and the other *malāhī* and the Arabic language did not possess the technical terms for the different parts of the instrument and for other musical features; and (2) demonstration of the fact that music and musical instruments were not illicit. The author begins with the second proof, to which he devotes a few lines only, adducing some pieces of evidence in favour of music and musical instruments. The greater part of the treatise is thus devoted to the first proof, in which the attitude of the grammarian becomes clear. He comments upon a large number of Arabic terms relating to instruments and to music which he has gleaned from classical Arabic poetry. The method of presentation starts off from the origin of each instrument considered, most frequently, in the style of the *awāʾil* [*q.v.*] literature. The ʿ*ūd*, regarded as the king of instruments, comes first; in this connection, the author quotes Hishām Ibn al-Kalbī for the legend of its invention by Lamech [see LAMAK]. After having mentioned other Biblical inventors of instruments (Tzila, daughter of Lot, etc.), he moves on to details of terminology, supporting each piece of commentary by references to poetry. Thus he passes under review the different names for the ʿ*ūd*, sc. *kirān, mizhar, barbaṭ* and *muwattar*; the term for "string", sc. *watar, maḥbaḍ* and *sharʿa*; the special name for the ʿ*ūd*'s four strings, sc. *zīr, mathnā, mathlath* and *bamm*; its frets (*dasātīn*), called in Arabic ʿ*iḳāb*, the Arabic equivalents of the *ṭunbūr*, a lute with a long neck and plucked strings, sc. *dirrīdj* and *alwān*; and the names of the ten different kinds of wind instruments, sc. *mizmār, mizmar, zammāra, nāy, ḳuṣṣab, mushtaḳ, yarā*ʿ, *zanbaḳ* and *hanbuḳa*. Still on the lexicographical level, at the end of the treatise the author adds the first forms of singing developed in the pre-Islamic period, sc. *ḥidā*ʾ, *naṣb, sinād* and *hazadj*. In addition to its lexicographic importance, the work has a special interest for musicology in its aspect of organology (i.e. the science dealing with musical instruments). This interest extends in fact to all the categories of the literature on *malāhī*, and provides information to the scholar about a large number of instruments since fallen into disuse. Thus al-Shalaḥī (8th/14th century) mentions in his *Kitāb al-Imtā*ʿ *wa 'l-intifā*ʿ *fī masʾalat samā*ʿ *al-samā*ʿ 28 different instruments, and the total number to be gleaned from this literature amounts to several dozen.

To the same period as al-Mufaḍḍal b. Salama's work belongs that of the geographer Ibn Khurradādhbih (3rd/9th century [*q.v.*]), his *Kitāb al-Lahw wa 'l-malāhī*. Despite certain similarities to the preceding work, this latter one is much more complex and sophisticated. In the same fashion as the *Kitāb al-Malāhī*, it opens with a section refuting the opinions of those who prohibit music and gives the story of the invention of the ʿ*ūd* by Lamech as well as the stories of other inventors of musical instruments in Biblical times, but Ibn Khurradādhbih slants his work towards wider and more universal horizons. His interest is indeed more centred on cultural and historical than lexicographical questions. In furtherance of these, he touches on the music of other peoples, in particular, on that of the Persians and Greeks; and he pictures the musical world on a wide scale, dealing with the power of music and its different effects. From his glimpse at world music, he passes to its development among the Arabs, and then devotes the greater part of the work to a series of biographies of all the famous musicians from the beginnings of Islam to his own time. As a result, the term *malāhī* has here a wider sense and becomes the equivalent of "music". Hence it is not by chance that al-Masʿūdī (d. 345/956 [*q.v.*]) has cited, in the form of a dialogue in his *Murūdj al-dhahab* (see *Bibl.*) the essential part of Ibn Khurradādhbih's work. Al-Masʿūdī related indeed that the caliph al-Muʿtamid, who was a fervid lover of music, asked Ibn Khurradādhbih to compose for him a treatise on the origins and evolution of music; the discourse which Ibn Khurradādhbih sets forth in response to the caliph's request follows amost word-for-word the first part of the *K. al-Lahw wa 'l-malāhī* as far as the point where the long series of biographies begins.

These two works are the beginning and the end of this category of writings on the *malāhī*. They are also the opening of a genre of writings on music which borrows from that *adab* literature which has anecdotal and edifying works which do not however use the word *malāhī* any longer in their title. Nevertheless, the term was to remain for a long while in use sporadically. It is often to be found in the *Kitāb al-Aghānī,* as e.g. in the passage concerning the caliph al-Muʿtamid cited above, in which it is said that he had a passion for *malāhī.* Moreover, in regard to the caliph Yazīd (60-4/680-3), the same source states that "he was the first to introduce *malāhī* (musical instruments) and singers at court".

In conclusion, we are inclined to admit that the term *malāhī* came into current usage of the 3rd/9th century above all with the sense of musical instruments. Within the circles of those religious authorities opposed to music, their association with amusement is seized upon and stress laid on this pejorative connotation, which at times enables these authorities to attack what they regard as the negative side of music and its emotive power. It is accordingly in this sense that the term *malāhī* is perpetuated in the corresponding literature. In the circles of literary adepts, the sense of amusement is taken up as the equivalent of *ṭarab,* the dominating and much sought-after effect of music in that period. Its substitution takes place at the moment when the theoretical writings on music become formed, without the influence of Greek treatises translated into Arabic, i.e. towards the beginning of the 4th/10th century. The term disappears fairly rapidly from this literature, because the philosophers and theorists inveighed against the identification of music with playing, pastimes and amusement; hence they had no interest in utilising a term which denoted the very thing which they wished to avoid.

Bibliography: ʿA. al-ʿAzzāwī, *al-Mūsīḳā al-ʿirāḳiyya fī ʿahd al-Mughūl wa 'l-Turkumān,* Baghdād 1370/1951, 73-89, 94-101; H. G. Farmer, *Studies in Oriental musical instruments,* London 1931; idem, *Ibn Khurdadhbih on musical instruments,* in *JRAS* (1928), 509-18; idem, *A Maghribi work on musical instruments,* in *ibid.* (1935) 339-53; I. A. Khalifé, *Mukhtaṣar Kitāb al-Lahw wa 'l-malāhī li'bn Khurradādhbih,* in *Machriq* (1960), 129-67 (2nd ed. *Mukhtār min K. al-Lahw wa'l-malāhī li'bn Khurradādhbih,* Beirut 1969); Masʿūdī, *Murūdj,* viii, 88-99 = §§ 3213-26; J. Robson, *The* Kitāb al-malāhī *of Abū Ṭālib al-Mufaḍḍal ibn Salama,* in *JRAS* (1938), 231-49; idem, *A Maghribi MS. on listening to music,* in *IC, xxvi*/1 (1952), 113-31; idem (ed. and tr.), *Tracts on listening to music: being* Dhamm al-malāhī *by Ibn Abi 'l-Dunyā and* Bawāriq al-ilmāʿ *by Majd al-Dīn al-Ṭūsī al-Ghazālī,* London 1938; A. Shiloah, *L'épître sur la musique des Ikhwān al-Ṣafā,* in *REI* (1964), 125-62, 1966, 159-93; idem, *The ʿūd and the origin of Music,* in *Studia orientalia memoriae D. H. Baneth,* Jerusalem 1979, 395-407; idem *The theory of music in Arabic writings (c. 900-1900),* in *Répertoire international des sources musicales,* Bx, Munich 1979.

(A. Shiloah)

MALĀḤIM (A.), pl. of *malḥama* [*q.v.*], which is the subject of the article below mainly devoted to the *Malḥamat Dāniyāl* and its several versions culminating in an apocalyptic current, at first in connection with the announcing of the approach of the Mahdī [*q.v.*], and then oriented towards the predictions concerning the fate of different dynasties. These oracles gave birth to the elaborating of so-called *malāḥim* (or *ḥidthān*) works, which have been already spoken of in the article DJAFR, and the subject is only raised again here in order to note the use of the term in the sense of predictions of a historical character (see e.g. al-Masʿūdī, *Murūdj,* i, 8, ii, 335 = §§ 6, 756) and to highlight the fact that Ibn Khaldūn enumerates several of these writings in a section about the beginnings of states and of nations which he places in the last pages of ch. 3 of Book i of the *Muḳaddima* (Ar. text, ii, 193 ff., tr. de Slane, ii, 226 ff., tr. Rosenthal, ii, 200 ff.). There follows here a list of the texts of which he acquired knowledge, mainly in the Maghrib, but some also in the Orient:

— A *ḳaṣīda* of Ibn Murrāna on the Lamtūna, i.e. the Almoravids, who seized Ceuta [see SABTA] in 476/1083-4;

— A *ḳaṣīda* of 500 verses or 1,000 verses called *al-Tubbaʿiyya* and concerning the Almohads;

— A *malʿaba* "amusing piece" or "plaything" of about 500 verses given in *zadjal* [*q.v.*] form, attributed to a Jew and also concerning the Almohads;

— A *ḳaṣīda* on the Ḥafṣids of Tunis attributed to Ibn al-Abbār [*q.v.*], but belonging to a person of the same name who was a tailor;

— Another *malḥama* on the Hafsids;

— A *malʿaba* attributed to a certain Hawshanī and written in dialect Arabic in such an hermetical style that it would need an allegorical commentary.

In the Orient, Ibn Khaldūn acquired knowledge of a *malḥama* attributed to Ibn al-ʿArabī [*q.v.*], the *Ṣayḥat al-būm* (see O. Yahia, *Histoire et classification de l'oeuvre d'Ibn ʿArabī,* Damascus 1964, no. 708; T. Fahd, in AL-DJAFR, above), as well as several others attributed to Ibn Sīnā, to Ibn Abi 'l-ʿAḳb (see Goldziher, in *ZDMG,* lxxv [1921]) or, on the Turks, to the Ṣūfī al-Bādjurbaḳī.

One should note that the works consulted by Ibn Khaldūn in the Maghrib are all in verse (classical or dialectical), that they were widespread in his own time and that he himself attached no credence to any of them.

Bibliography: In addition to references given in the article, see A. Kovalenko, *Magie et Islam,* Geneva 1981, index, and the *Bibls.* to AL-DJAFR and MALḤAMA.

(Ed.)

MALĀʾIKA (A.) angels (Persian "angel" = *firishta*).

1. In the Ḳurʾān and in Sunnī Islam.

The form *malāʾika* is the broken plural in Arabic of a word going back to early North-West Semitic (there is no cognate in Akkadian), Ugar. *mlʾk* "messenger", Aram. *malʾak* and O.T. Hebr. *malʾāk* "messenger, angel", the root in Arabic being referred by the lexicographers and commentators to a root *m-l-k, ʾ-l-k* or even *l-ʾ-k* (see *LA,* xii, 272-4, 370-1; al-Ṭabarī, *Tafsīr,* i, 150; Lane, *Lexicon,* i, 81c), which they consider original to Arabic. A. Jeffery, *The foreign vocabulary of the Qur'ān,* 269-70, following e.g. K. Ahrens, *Christliches im Qoran,* in *ZDMG,* lxxxiv (1930), 24, thought it fairly certain that the proximate source of the word in Arabic was nevertheless the Ethiopic *malʾāk,* pl. *malāʾeket,* the usual equivalent in that language for Grk. *angelos* "messenger > angel"; the word was presumably a loanword into Ethiopic from Aramaic or Hebrew. Since it is so frequently used in the Ḳurʾān, Muḥammad's audience was obviously familiar with it, and it must have been a pre-Islamic borrowing. The singular in Arabic is normally *malak* without *hamza,* and so always in the Ḳurʾān; although *LA* in two places (xii, 274,8; 371,5) quotes the same verse as a proof that *mal'ak* does occur, but as an exceptional form (*shādhdh*). Both singular and plural in Arabic are used only in the sense "angel". In the Ḳurʾān it occurs twice in the dual (*malakayn,* II, 96; VII, 19); of the two angels Hārūt and Mārūt [*q.v.*, and SIḤR], and of Adam and Eve being tempted in the

Garden to believe that they may become angels. The plural occurs very often in the Ḳurʾān (in Flügel's *Concordance* under *l-ʾ-k,* 171) but the singular only 12 times (Flügel, under *m-l-k,* 183). These are of the people demanding revelation by an angel rather than a human being (*ba<u>sh</u>ar,* VI, 8, 9, 50? XI, 15, 33; XVII, 97; XXV, 8); women think Joseph an angel for his beauty rather than a human being (*ba<u>sh</u>ar,* XII, 31); an angel's intercession (*<u>sh</u>afāʿa,* LIII, 26) does not avail; twice as collective for angels, beside the *ʿar<u>sh</u>* (LXIX, 17), and in rows and rows (LXXXIX, 23).

In XXXII, 11 "the angel of death" (*malak al-mawt*) occurs but not by name; see ʿIZRĀʾĪL, and references in tradition in Wensinck, *Handbook of early Muhammadan tradition,* 22b. <u>Dj</u>ibrīl, the angel of revelation, is named three times (II, 91, 92; LXVI, 4); cf. traditions on him in Muslim, Constantinople 1333, i, 109-11 and other references in Wensinck, 59. In Ḳurʾān XXVI, 193-5, <u>Dj</u>ibrīl unnamed, is called "the Faithful Spirit" (*al-rūḥ al-amīn*); he brings down the revelation to the *ḳalb* of Muḥammad in a clear Arabic tongue. There are other descriptions of him, still unnamed, in LIII, 5-18 and LXXXI, 19-25, as appearing plainly to Muhammad in revelation. He, as "our Spirit" (*rūḥanā*), was sent to Maryam (XIX, 17). He is called "the Holy Spirit" (*rūḥ al-ḳudus*) in XVI, 104 and Allāh aided ʿĪsā with the name (II, 84, 254; V, 109). Mīkāʾīl (variant Mīkāl) is named (II, 92) as an angel of the same rank as <u>Dj</u>ibrīl; see a long and apparently true story of how his naming came about in al-Bayḍāwī (ed. Fleischer, i, 74, 18 ff.); in traditions he, with <u>Dj</u>ibrīl, appears to Muḥammad and instructs him; he does not laugh (Wensinck, 152b); Muḥammad called the two his *wazīrs* of the angels. To Isrāfīl [*q.v.*], the angel with the trumpet of resurrection, there is no reference either in the Ḳurʾān or in canonical traditions, but very much in eschatological legend. In Ḳurʾān, XLIII, 47, the tortured in hell call to the keeper of hell, "O Mālik!" and in XCVI, 18, the guards of hell are called al-Zabāniyya, an otherwise unused word, meaning apparently, "violent thrusters" (*LA,* xvii, 55); the number of these, LXXIV, 30, is nineteen, and they are asserted specifically to be angels, apparently to guard against the idea that they are devils; they are called "rough, violent" (*<u>gh</u>ilāẓ <u>sh</u>idād*). Another class of angels are those "Brought Near" [to Allāh], *al-muḳarrabūn* (IV, 170); these praise Allāh day and night without ceasing (XXI, 20); al-Bayḍāwī calls them also *al-ʿalawiyyūn* (on Ḳurʾān, II, 28; ed. Fleischer, i, 47, 23); and *al-karrūbiyyūn* (כרובים) on Ḳurʾān, IV, 170 (ed. Fleischer, i, 243, 25) as those that are around the *ʿar<u>sh</u>*. The same term, *muḳarrab,* is used of ʿĪsā (III, 40) as he is in the company of the angels nearest Allāh; cf. ʿĪSĀ for his semi-angelic character. At the beginning of the Sūra of the Angels (XXXV) there is a significant description: "making the angels messengers (*rusul^an^*), with wings two and three and four; He increases in the creation what He wills"; this has had much effect on later descriptions and pictures. They are guardians (*ḥāfiẓīn*) over mankind, cognisant of what man does and writing it down (*kātibīn*; LXXXII, 10-12), in XXI, 94 the writing down is ascribed to Allah himself. In LXX, 4; LXXVIII, 38; XCVII, 4, there occurs the very puzzling phrase "the angels and *al-rūḥ*". Al-Bayḍāwī on the first two passages shows how perplexing the distinction was found (ed. Fleischer, ii, 356,5, 383,4): "the *rūḥ* is an angel set over the spirits (*al-arwāḥ*); or he is the whole genus of spirits; or <u>Dj</u>ibrīl; or a creation (*<u>kh</u>alḳ*) mightier than the angels"; cf. too, al-Ḳazwīnī's *ʿA<u>dj</u>āʾib,* ed. Wüstenfeld, 56. For spirits and the conception "spirit" in Islam, see RŪḤ. In the Ḳurʾān there is no reference to the two angels, Munkar and Nakīr, who visit the dead man in his grave, on the night after his burial, and catechise him as to his Faith. Thereafter, if he is an unbeliever, his grave becomes a preliminary hell, and if he is a believer, it becomes a preliminary purgatory from which he may pass at the Last Day into paradise; it may even, if he is a saint, be a preliminary paradise. This is called technically the Questioning (*suʾāl*) of Munkar and Nakīr and, also, the Punishment of the grave (*ʿa<u>dh</u>āb al-ḳabr* [*q.v.*]). This doctrine, similar to the Lesser Judgement of Christian theology, is one of the *samʿiyyāt* (to be believed on oral testimony) and is based on the implicit meaning of Ḳurʾānic passages (XIV, 32; XL, ii, 49; LXXI, 25) and upon explicit traditions (al-Taftazānī's commentary on al-Nasafī's *ʿAḳāʾid,* Cairo 1321, 109; the *Mawāḳif* of al-Ī<u>dj</u>ī with commentary of al-<u>Dj</u>ur<u>dj</u>ānī, Būlāḳ 1266, 590 ff.). There is a still fuller account and discussion by the Ḥanbalī theologian Ibn Ḳayyim al-<u>Dj</u>awziyya (Brockelmann, II, 106, no. 23) in his *Kitāb al-Rūḥ,* Ḥaydarābād 1324, 62-144, §§ vi-xiv.

The angels are also called the heavenly host, or multitude (*al-malaʾ al-aʿlā,* XXXVII, 8; XXXVIII, 69) and guard the walls of heaven against the "listening" of the *<u>dj</u>inn* and *<u>sh</u>ayṭān.* See further on this under SIḤR.

The Ḳurʾān lays stress on the absolute submission and obedience of the angels to Allah "To Him belong those who are in the heavens and in the earth and those who are with Him (*indahu*) are not too proud for His service (*ʿibāda*) and they do not become tired. They praise, night and day, without intermission" (XXI, 19, 20). "They do not anticipate Him in speech and they labour on His command (XXI, 27). At the creation of Adam they are distinguished in this respect from him and his future race: "while we praise Thee and sanctify Thee" (II, 28). Over the Fire there are set certain terrible and powerful angels, "they do not rebel against Allāh as to what He commands them and they do what they are commanded" (LVI, 6). But does this absolute obedience extend to impeccability (*ʿiṣma* [*q.v.*])? The Ḳurʾān is emphatic as to their obedience, but is in contradiction as to their created nature and as to their relationship in that respect to the *<u>dj</u>inn* and to the *<u>sh</u>ayṭāns*. Thus in several passages in the Ḳurʾān, the story is told of the creation of man out of clay and that the angels were bidden by Allāh to prostrate themselves to him. This they all did "except *Iblīs*" (*illā Iblīs*; II, 32, VII, 10; XV, 31; XVIII, 48; XXXVIII, 74). Iblīs, therefore, must have been an angel; as al-Bayḍāwī says, "If not, the command to them did not apply to him and his being excepted from them was illegitimate" (ed. Fleischer, i, 51, 21). This would mean that the angels were not impeccable. But, again, in XVIII, 48, the statement is expanded, "except Iblīs; he was of the *<u>dj</u>inn*; so he departed from the command of his Lord" (*fasaḳa ʿan amr^i^ rabbihi*). Further, in VII, 11; XXXVIII, 77, Iblīs pleads in justification that man was created of clay (*ṭīn*) but he of fire (*nār*); and the *<u>dj</u>inn* are acceptedly created of fire; "fire of the *samūm*" in VI, 27, "of a *māri<u>dj</u>* of fire" in LV, 14. The meaning of *māri<u>dj</u>* is unknown; *LA*, iii, 189, 13-19, gives a number of contradictory explanations, but it is probably an unidentified loan-word. Iblīs and the *<u>dj</u>inn,* then, were created of fire; but there is no statement in the Ḳurʾān as to the material out of which the angels were formed. A tradition traced back to ʿĀʾi<u>sh</u>a is the foundation of the accepted position that the angels were formed of light: "The Prophet said, 'The angels were formed of light (*<u>kh</u>uliḳat min nūr*) and the *<u>dj</u>ānn* were formed of a *māridj* of fire and Adam of that which was described to you'' (Muslim, Constantinople 1333, vii, 226; al-Bayḍāwī, i, 52,4). Another difficulty in the doctrine of the impeccability of the angels is the Ḳurʾānic statement as to Hārūt and Mārūt referred to above. These two angels are supposed to have yielded to sexual temptation, to be confined in a pit near Bābil and there to teach magic to men. But, it is answered, (a) the Ḳurʾān says nothing of their fall; (b) teaching magic is not practising magic; (c) they always first warn those who come to them, ''We are only a temptation (*fitna*); so do not disbelieve'' (Ḳurʾān, II, 96); cf. further, al-Taftāzānī on the *ʿAḳāʾid* of al-Nasafī, Cairo 1321, 133.

In al-Bayḍāwī on Ḳurʾān, II, 32, there is a long discussion of the angelic nature (ed. Fleischer, i, 51, 20 to 52,8) which, however, runs out in the despairing statement that knowledge on the point is with Allāh alone (*al-ʿilm ʿinda-'llāh*ⁱ). Perhaps Iblīs was of the *djinn* as to his actions (*fiʿlan*) but of the angels as to species (*nawʿ*). Also, Ibn ʿAbbās has a tradition that there was a variety (*ḍarb*) of the angels who propagated their kind (this has always been regarded as an essential characteristic of the *djinn* and of the *shayṭāns* as opposed to the angels) and who were called *al-djinn*; and Iblīs was one of these. Or, that he was a *djinnī* brought up among the angels and identified with them. Or, that the *djinn* were among those commanded to prostrate themselves to Adam. Or, that some of the angels were not impeccable, although that was their characteristic in general, just as some men, e.g. the prophets, are guarded against sin but most are not. Further, perhaps a variety of the angels are not essentially different from the *shayṭāns* but differ only in accidents and qualities as men are virtuous or evil, while the *djinn* unite both, and Iblīs was of this variety. The tradition from ʿĀʾisha is no answer to this explanation, for light and fire in it are not to be taken too precisely; they are used as in a proverb, and light is of the nature of fire and fire of light, they pass into another; fire can be purified into light and light obscured to fire. So al-Bayḍāwī.

With this should be compared the scholastic discussion in the *Mawāḳif* of al-Īdjī, with the commentary of al-Djurdjānī, Būlāḳ 1266, 576. In it the objector to the *ʿiṣma* of the angels has two grounds'': (a) their urging upon Allāh that he should not create Adam showed defects (slander, pride, malice, finding fault with Allāh) in their moral character; (b) that Iblīs was rebellious, as above. These grounds are then answered scholastically. Then various Ḳurʾānic texts, as above, on the submission and obedience of the angels are quoted. But it is pointed out that these texts cannot prove that all of them, at all times, are kept free from all sins. The point, therefore, cannot be absolutely decided. Individual exceptions under varying circumstances may have occurred, just as, while the *shayṭāns* as a class were created for evil (*khuliḳū li 'l-sharr*), there is a definite tradition (*Sharḥ* by al-Māturīdī on *al-Fiḳh al-akbar* ascribed to Abū Ḥanīfa, Ḥaydarābād 1321, 25) of one Muslim *shayṭān*, a great-grandson of Iblīs, who appeared to Muḥammad and was taught by him certain sūras of the Ḳurʾān.

The story of Hārūt and Mārūt suggests that the angels possess sex, although they may not propagate their kind. But ''they are not to be described with either masculinity or femininity'' (*ʿAḳāʾid* of al-Nasafī, Cairo 1321, 133). Al-Taftāzānī and the other commentators in this edition explain that there is no authority (*naḳl*) on this point and no proof by reason (*ʿaḳl*); it should, therefore, be left unconsidered and that, apparently, was the course followed by al-Īdjī and al-Djurdjānī. They may have sex and not use it. In that respect, man, who has in himself the possibility of sin and must himself rule his appetites of lust (*shahwa*) and of anger (*ghaḍab*), has a higher potentiality of excellency than the angels (al-Bayḍāwī on II, 28, ed. Fleischer, i, 48, 28).

This leads to the second question as to the angels which scholastic theology has considered, the relative excellency of angels and men, and especially, of angels and prophets. This is stated shortly by al-Nasafī, 147: (a) ''The Messengers (*rusul*) of mankind (*al-bashar*) are more excellent than the Messengers of the angels; and (b) the Messengers of the angels are more excellent than the generality of mankind; and (c) the generality of mankind are more excellent than the generality of the angels''. Al-Taftāzānī develops the theme that there is general and indeed necessary agreement on the excellency of the messengers of the angels over mankind in general, but that the other two statements (a and c) will bear argument. He urges (a) the prostrating of the angels to Adam; (b) that Adam was taught all the names of things (Ḳurʾān, 29); (c) that Allāh ''chose'' (*iṣṭafā*) Adam and Nūḥ and the family of Ibrāhīm and the family of ʿImrān over all created things (*ʿalā 'l-ʿālamīn*, III, 30); and (d) that mankind achieves excellencies and perfections of knowledge and action in spite of the hindrances of lust and anger. But the Muʿtazilīs and the ''philosophers'' (*al-falāsifa*) and some Ashʿarīs held the superior excellence of the angels. They urged (a) that they were spirits, stripped of materiality (*arwāḥ mudjarrada*), complete actually, free of even the beginnings of evils and defects, like lust and anger, and from the obscurities of form and matter (*ẓulumāt al-hāyūlā wa 'l-ṣūra*), capable of doing wonderful things, knowing events (*kawāʾin*), past and to come, without error. The answer is that this description is based on philosophical and not Muslim principles. (b) That the prophets learn from the angels, as in Ḳurʾān, XXVI, 193; LIII, 5. The answer is that the prophets learn from Allāh and that the angels are only intermediaries. (c). That there are multiplied cases both in Ḳurʾān and in tradition where mention of the angels precedes that of the prophets. The answer is that precedence is because of their precedence in existence or because their existence is more concealed (*akhfā*) and, therefore, faith in them must be emphasised. (d) In Ḳurʾān, IV, 170, ''*al-masīḥ* does not disdain to be an *ʿabd* to Allāh nor do the angels'' must mean, because of linguistic usage, that the angels are more excellent than ʿĪsā. The answer is that the point is not simple excellency but to combat the Christian position that ʿĪsā is not an *ʿabd* but a son to Allāh. In the *Mawāḳif*, 572-8, there is a similar but much fuller discussion which involves a philosophical consideration of the endowment—mental, physical, spiritual—of all living creatures from immaterial spirits to the lower animals (*al-bahīma*).

In the *ʿAdjāʾib al-makhlūḳat* of al-Ḳazwīnī, ed. Wüstenfeld, 55-63, there is an objective description of the angels in all their classes, in which the statements of Ḳurʾān and Sunna are adjusted to the Aristotelian-Neoplatonic universe with its spheres (*al-aflāk*), in accordance with al-Ḳazwīnī's general aim to give a picture of the created universe in its details and wonders. Yet apparently, while the angels possess the quality of ''life'' (*ḥayāt*) and are the inhabitants of the heavens and of the heavenly spheres (*sukkān al-samawāt*), they are not to be reckoned among the animals (*al-ḥayawān*). Al-Damīrī includes mankind and the *djinn*, even the diabolic (*mutashayṭana*) *djinn*, such as the *ghūl*, in his *Ḥayāt al-ḥayawān* but not the angels. Equally acute and scholastic with the discussion in the *Mawāḳif,* and more spiritual than that by al-Ḳazwīnī, is al-Ghazālī's treatment of the mystery of the angelic nature in some of his specialist smaller treatises. For him, it is part of the general question of the nature of spirit to which his smaller *Maḍnūn* is devoted. See, too, the larger *Maḍnūn,* Cairo 1303, in *Rukn,* ii, 23 and the translation by W. H. T. Gairdner of his *Mishkāt al-anwār*, London, Royal Asiatic Society, 1924 *passim.* Muslim literature also takes account of non-Muslim ideas on the angels, such as those of "philosophers", Christians, dualists, idolaters. These will be found given briefly by al-Bayḍāwī on Ḳurʾān, II, 28, ed. Fleischer, i, 47, 18, and in more detail in al-Tahānāwī, *Dict. of techn. terms,* 1337 ff.

Bibliography: In addition to references given in the article, see W. Eickmann, *Angelologie und Dämonologie des Korans,* New York and Leipzig 1908; T. P. Hughes, *A dictionary of Islam,* 15-16; D. B. Macdonald, *The religious attitude and life in Islam,* Chicago 1912, index; J. Horovitz, *Muhammeds Himmelfahrt,* in *Isl.*, ix (1919), 159-83; idem, *Jewish proper names in the Koran,* in *HUCA,* ii (1925), 144-227; idem, *Koranische Untersuchungen,* Berlin 1926; L. Jung, *Fallen angels in Jewish, Christian and Mohammadan literature,* in *JQR,* N.S., xv (1924-5), 267-502, vii (1925-6), 287-336; P. A. Eichler, *Die Dschinn, Teufel und Engel im Koran,* Leipzig 1928; *ERE,* art. *Charms and amulets (Muhammadan)* (Carra de Vaux), *Demons and spirits (Muslim)* (M. Gaudefroy-Demombynes); S. Zwemer, *The worship of Adam by angels,* in *MW,* xxvii (1937), 115-27; R. Guénon, *Notes sur l'angélologie de l'alphabet arabe,* in *Etudes traditionnelles,* xliii (1938), 324-7; J. Macdonald, *The creation of man and angels in the eschatological literature,* in *Isl. Studies,* iii (1964), 285-308; W. M. Watt, *Bell's Introduction to the Qur'ān,* Edinburgh 1970, indices at 216, 242; L. Gardet, *Les anges en Islam,* in *Studia missionalia,* xxi (1972), 207-27; F. Jaadane, *La place des anges dans la théologie cosmique musulmane,* in *SI,* xli (1975), 23-61; A. T. Welch, *Allah and other supernational beings: the emergence of the Qur'anic doctrine of Tawḥīd,* in *Jnal of the American Acad. of Religion, Thematic Issue,* xlvii/4 (Dec. 1979), 739 ff., 749 ff.; Fazlur Rahman, *Major themes of the Qur'ān,* Minneapolis-Chicago 1980, index; arts. DJABRĀʾĪL/DJIBRĪL, HĀRŪT WA-MĀRŪT, ISRĀFĪL, ʿIZRĀʾĪL, MĪKĀL.

(D. B. MACDONALD*)

2. In Shīʿism.

In Imāmī Shīʿism, angels are closely associated with the *Imāms*. Imāmī doctrine consistently upheld the dogma that the *Imāms*, just like the prophets, were more excellent before God than the angels with whom they shared in divine protection from sin and error (*ʿiṣma*), and leading theologians, like the Shaykh al-Mufīd, wrote treatises in support of it. The *Imāms* are, however, guided and aided by angels. According to a well-known Imāmī tradition, the *Imāms* could only hear the voices of the angels but could not see them, in contrast to the messenger prophets (*rusul*), who could see angels while awake and would converse with them, and to ordinary prophets who could hear and see them in their sleep. This was countered, however, by other traditions which affirmed that the *Imāms* also see the angels, and the restriction was held to apply only at the time of their receiving divine instruction through the angel. According to a tradition attributed to the *Imām* Djaʿfar, the angels regularly come to the *Imāms*, tread on their beds, attend their tables, come forth to them from every plant in its season, shake their wings above the children of the *Imāms*, prevent beasts from reaching them and join them in every prayer. Angels will, according to Imāmī belief, appear in the sky at the advent of the Twelfth *Imām* and will call out his name; Gabriel and Michael will rally the faithful to swear allegance to him. Imāmī doctrine adds to the Islamic angels of death, Munkar and Nakīr, who question and torment the dead in their tomb, a positive counterpart, Mubashshir and Bashīr, who are sent to the saintly dead to comfort them. According to some, they are the same pair as Munkar and Nakīr and merely change their function, while according to others they are a different pair.

In Ismāʿīlism, the hierarchy of ranks (*ḥudūd*) of the spiritual world are sometimes described as angels. In particular, the triad of Djadd, Fatḥ and Khayāl, which mediates between the Universal Intellect and Soul and the prophets and *Imāms* in the physical world, are commonly identified with the archangels Djibrāʾīl, Mīkāʾīl and Isrāfīl. In an early Ismāʿīlī cosmogony, seven Cherubim (*karūbiyya*) are named and described as having been created out of the light between the first two principles of the spiritual world. After them a group of twelve "spiritual beings (*rūḥāniyya*)" was created to form their counterpart. In later Ṭayyibī Ismāʿīlism, the third to ninth Intellects of the spiritual world are called the seven Cherubim. Ismāʿīlī doctrine, however, also recognises angels of a more conventional character. They are described as being all of a single substance, with only their names varying in accordance with their functions. Some inhabit the spiritual world, others the heavenly spheres, and still others the physical world in order to preserve all its regions. They are seen only by prophets and those who rise spiritually to become like prophets.

Bibliography: The Imāmiyya: al-Madjlisī, *Biḥār al-anwār*; for references to angels throughout this encyclopaedia, see ʿAbbās al-Ḳummī, *Safīnat al-biḥār,* Nadjaf 1355, ii, 546-9; the main section on angels in the new edition of *Biḥār al-anwār* is in vol. lix, Tehran 1386, 144-326. M. J. McDermott, *The theology of al-Shaikh al-Mufīd,* Beirut 1978, index s.v. Angels. The Ismāʿīliyya: ʿAlī b. Muḥammad [b.] al-Walīd, *Tādj al-ʿaḳāʾid,* ed. ʿA. Tāmir, Beirut 1967, 45-6; R. Strothmann, *Gnosistexte der Ismailiten,* Göttingen 1943, 29, 44, 46; H. Corbin, *Histoire de la philosophie islamique,* i, Paris 1964, 118-36; H. Halm, *Kosmologie und Heilslehre der frühen Ismāʿīlīya,* Wiesbaden 1978, index s.v. *Karūbīya*; S. M. Stern, *Studies in early Ismāʿīlism,* Jerusalem 1983, 20-9.

(W. MADELUNG)

MALAK, MALʾAK [SEE MALĀʾIKA]

MALAK ḤIFNĪ NĀṢIF (1886-1918), pen-name of Bāḥithat al-Bādiya, daughter of Ḥifnī Nāṣif, a follower of Muḥammad ʿAbduh [*q.v.*], and pioneer protagonist of women's rights in Egypt. She was in 1903 one of the first Egyptian women to receive a teacher's primary certificate and became a teacher in the government girls' school. Her marriage to ʿAbd al-Sattār al-Bāsil took her to the Fayyūm, where she observed the life of women in nomadic and rural society. She was herself faced with the problem of polygamy, since her husband had married a second wife.

The intellectual influence of her father, her professional training and experience, and the experience of her marriage caused her to become the first Egyptian woman to speak out publicly for the emancipation of women. She wrote articles on the topic in *al-Djarīda* and such women's magazines as *al-Djins al-laṭīf* and founded her own women's organisation, the *Ittiḥād al-Nisāʾ al-Tahdhībī.* In 1911 she gave a speech before the Egyptian Congress in Helipolis, in which she developed a ten-point programme for the improvement of the conditions of women.

In her ideas on emancipation, she was certainly influenced by the writings of Ḳāsim Amīn [*q.v.*], though her goals usually remained more moderate and her concern with proper Islamic norms was strong. She defended the veil, but was bitterly opposed to polygamy. She attributed great importance to the proper education of women in such subjects as hygiene, household economics, child-rearing, first aid, etc., i.e., to the provision of an education which would prepare the woman for her role as mother and household manager. In this she addressed herself especially to upper-class women, whose idleness in seclusion and ignorance she perceived as the major cause for the weakness of their social position, and whose style of life she contrasted with a somewhat romanticised view of the active life of rural and nomadic woman. Although she propagated the possibility of higher education for women, she did not envisage an independent professional life for women, and opposed any suggestion of their participation in public life and politics. Concurring with the general trend of the emancipation movement for women at the time, she did not postulate the legal and social equality of women with men.

Bibliography: For a collection of her essays, addresses, and lectures, see Madjd al-Dīn Nāṣif (ed.), *Āthār Bāḥithat al-Bādiya,* Cairo 1962, and Bāḥithat al-Bādiya, *al-Nisāʾiyyāt,* Cairo 1328/1910, which includes all her articles published in *al-Djarīda.* ʿUmar Riḍā Kaḥḥāla, *Aʿlām al-nisāʾ fī ʿālamay al-ʿarab wa 'l-islām,* Damascus 1959, v, 74-101, and Rawḥiyya al-Ḳallīnī, *Shāʿirāt ʿarabiyyāt,* Cairo 1964, 37-57, have comprehensive biographies on her, the latter work discussing especially her poetic works. For a general analysis of her role, see T. Philipp, *Feminism and nationalist politics in Egypt,* in N. Keddie and L. Beck (eds.), *Women in the Muslim world,* Cambridge, Mass. 1978. (T. Philipp)

MALAKA (a.), a philosophical term used to translate the Greek *hexis,* "a being in a certain state or habit". It is contrasted with privation (*ʿadam - steresis*) in translations and commentaries on Aristotle: whatever the possession (*malaka*) naturally occurs in, anything capable of receving a possession is deprived of it when it is completely absent from that which naturally has it. It is also used in the expression *al-ʿaḳl bi 'l-malaka* (the *nous kath-hexin* of Alexander of Aphrodisias) to represent the intellect *in habitu,* a stage in the development of the human intellect where basic primary truths are cognised on the route to the intellect *in actu* where a complete set of primary and secondary (imaginative) truths are cognised and applied in the philosophy of mind of al-Fārābī, Ibn Sīnā and Ibn Rushd. According to Ibn Sīnā, all forms of thought exist in the intellect, which is in a state (*malaka*) in which it can by itself perform the act of thinking. Ibn Rushd uses the contrast between *malaka* or habit and *ʿāda* (the Greek *ethos*) or custom to criticise al-Ghazālī's reduction of causal language to language about God's customs. Talking about God having habits is to suggest impiously that there is change in God "from which a repetition of his act often follows" (*Tahāfut al-Tahāfut,* 425.6). There is also a significant use of *malaka* by Ibn Khaldūn to explain the survival of civilisation despite serious political upheavals. The acquisition of habits embodying civilisation is a matter of education and involves the learning through continuous repetition of skills or science, which then persist in very different circumstances.

Bibliography: P. H. Hannes, *Des Averroes Abhandlung: über die Möglichkeit der Conjunction,* Halle a.S. 1892, 10, 53; Ibn Sīnā, *K. al-Ishārāt wa 'l-tanbīhāt,* ed. J. Forget, Leiden 1892, 126-7; Ibn Rushd, *Tahāfut al-Tahāfut,* ed. M. Bouyges, Beirut 1930; Ibn Sīnā, *K. al-Nadjāt,* ed. G. Anawati and S. Zayed, Cairo 1938, 160-1; Kh. Georr (ed.), *Les Catégories d'Aristote dans leurs versions syro-arabes,* Beirut 1948, 347 f.: Ibn Rushd, *Talkhīṣ K. al-Nafs,* ed. A. Ahwānī, Cairo 1950; F. Rahman, *Avicenna's psychology,* London 1952, 117-20; Ibn Khaldūn, *The Muqaddimah,* tr. F. Rosenthal, London 1958, i, p. lxxxiv; Ibn Sīnā, *Shifāʾ: De anima,* ed. F. Rahman, London 1959, 48-50; H. Wolfson, *The philosophy of the Kalam,* London 1976, 545, 556; F. Zimmermann, *Al-Farabi's commentary and short treatise on Aristotle's De interpretatione,* London 1981, 29 n. 2; I. M. Lapidus, in Barbara D. Metcalf (ed.), *Moral conduct and authority, the place of Adab in South Asian Islam,* Berkeley and Los Angeles 1984, 53-6 (on *malaka* in Ibn Khaldūn). (O. N. H. Leaman)

MĀLAḲA, Arabic form of the name of Málaga (in ancient times Malaca), which is today a major city of southern Spain, on the Mediterranean coast between Algéciras and Alméria, and regional centre of the province of the same name. It is situated in the centre of a bay and lies at the foot of a hill known as Gibralfaro (Djabal Fāruh). The town is divided from north to south by a ravine which, at times of heavy rainfall, carries the waters of the Guadelmedina (Wādī 'l-Madīna). To the west stretches the Hoya of Málaga, a fertile plain formerly covered with various crops and especially tropical fruits, but today severely damaged by the enormous tourist development of the region.

The geographers of al-Andalus, of the Maghrib and even of the Orient, provide lavish descriptions of Málaga in which they stress the outstanding qualities of the town just as much as the products of its soil. Its port, always a centre of intense traffic, was visited by numerous traders from all countries and especially from the mercantile republics of Italy, the Genoese in particular. The arsenal (*dār al-ṣināʿa,* the name of which is preserved in that of *atarazana*) drew the admiration of the German traveller J. Münzer in October 1494. The town, in the Islamic period and particularly from the 5th/11th century onward, was magnificent and possessed remarkable buildings; there were two densely-populated quarters, that of Fuentecilla or Fantanella (Funtanalla) in the upper city and that of the fig merchants (al-Tayyānīn) in the lower city, attractive public baths (*ḥammāmāt*) and well-stocked markets. According to al-Ḥimyarī (*Rawḍ,* text 178, tr. 214), five gates were let into the wall, of which two, to the south, overlook the sea; to the east, or rather to the west, was the Bāb al-Wādī; the north gate, according to the same author, was called Bāb al-Khawḳa; the *ḳāḍī* of Málaga Ibn ʿAskar (d. 636/1239) mentions the fifth, the Bāb al-Riyāḥ or "gate of the winds". The fortifications of the town in the time of Ibn al-Khaṭīb, comprising a fortress, double walls, a ditch, bastions, towers set out at short intervals and well-defended gates, rendered Málaga an impregnable stronghold. The same Ibn al-Khaṭīb (*Mufākharat Mālaḳa wa-Salā,* in *Mushāhadāt fī bilād al-Maghrib wa 'l-Andalus,* ed. A. M. al-ʿAbbādī, Alexandria 1968, 57-66; tr. E. García Gómez, *El parangon entre Málaga y Salé,* in *al-And.*, ii [1934], 190-1) stresses the attractive appearance and the elegance of its population, the liveliness of its streets, markets and suburbs, as well as the beauty of its buildings and palaces and the size of its country houses.

The Vega, now known as the Hoya of Málaga, was cultivated in its entirety. The texts stress the abundance of fruits, especially delicious figs, almonds and raisins. The figs of Málaga (*tīn rayyī*) were much in demand on the markets and, when dried, were exported to Egypt, Syria, ʿIrāḳ and even India. The Málaga region was densely planted with fig-trees, vineyards, groves of almonds, olives and pomegranates, without counting other crops and the timber plantations. The wine was excellent with the result that, rightly or wrongly, it became proverbial, as is described by al-S͟haḳundī in his *Risāla* (tr. E. García Gómez, *Elogio del Islam español,* Madrid 1934, 111). Ibn al-K͟haṭīb draws attention to the fact that Málaga enjoyed the benefits of the sea, which offers abundance and variety of fish, and of the land, so fertile that it produces lavish crops which not only allow it to be self-sufficient but also provide, through surpluses and the harvests from the common lands, considerable revenues. It is also appropriate to take into account the development, from the 5th/11th century onward, of the textile industry, in particular the manufacture of silk of different colours with a fringe of gold (*was͟hy*) known in Europe by the names, among others, of *algüexi, albeci, alveici* and *oxi,* and the making of muslin for bonnets and turbans. The industry of leather and precious stones, used in the manufacture of sword scabbards, belts, straps and cushions, was no less important; the iron industry, producing especially knives and chisels is also to be noted; there was also the manufacture of glazed and gilded ceramics which, of unique type, were an exported product. In the markets of the town, baskets were woven from both osiers and esparto-grass. The curing of fish, anchovies in particular, was characteristic of Málaga. The tending of bees and silk-worms were also well developed industries; silk had become one of the most highly-prized export products.

Málaga possessed a considerable number of mosques. One of the first must have been that which, situated inside the fortress, was constructed at the initiative of the traditionist from Ḥimṣ, Muʿāwiya b. Ṣāliḥ (d. 158/775). The Great Mosque, which occupied the present site of the cathedral, in the centre of the former *madīna*, had five naves according to the author of *al-Rawḍ al-miʿṭār.* The courtyard of this mosque was planted with orange and palm trees. The fortress was built or rebuilt by the Zīrid Bādīs after he captured Málaga in 449/1057; it was reinforced in the 8th/14th centuries by the Naṣrids, because for them the town constituted a vital strategic point. There were, it is known, at least five cemeteries; the largest was situated to the north-east, outside the gate of the Fontanella; there were also those of the Muṣallā and of the Rawḍa of the Banū Yaḥyā, according to L. Torres Balbás (*Ciudades hispano-musulmanas,* i, 277). On the banks of the Gibralfaro, in the 9th/14th century, there lay, not far from the Jewish quarter, to the east of the town, the cemetery of the Jewish community; this then numbered just over 1,500 persons.

Concerning the social and economic life of Málaga, especially in the 7th/13th century, information is available from an exceptional document, sc. the treatise on *ḥisba* by al-Saḳaṭī, which offers a vivid and expressive account of customs, weights and measures, corporations, the price of foodstuffs, etc. The description of Málaga, like that of other towns in the region, offered by Ibn al-K͟haṭīb in his *Miʿyār al-ik͟htiyār* (ed. M. Kamal S͟habāna, Rabat 1396/1976, 87-92, and ed. A. M. al-ʿAbbādi, in *Mus͟hāhadāt Lisān al-Dīn Ibn al-K͟haṭīb*, 76-8) permits the formation of a close impression of the reality of life in Málaga in the later centuries of its Islamic history.

In the politico-administrative division of al-Andalus, Málaga, perhaps on the fall of the caliphate, came to be the regional centre of the *kūra* of Rayya (some read Rayyu) in place of Archidona (Ars͟hid͟hūna or Arḏjid͟hūna). The limits of the *kūra* are, exceptionally, indicated for the beginning of the 5th/11th century by the 8th/14th century author who was a native of Málaga, al-Nubāhī, in his *K. al-Marḳaba al-ʿulyā,* Cairo 1948, 82: the region included Alhama (al-Ḥamma) of Granada: to the west, the limit was formed by the Montemayor (Munt Mayūr, previously Ḥiṣn al-Wād) near Marbella; to the north by the Rio Genil (Wādī S͟hanīl) alongside the Benameji (Ḥiṣn Banī Bas͟hīr) and the Castillo of Anzur (al-Ranisūl); the limit subsequently passed through the territory of Aljonós (al-K͟hunūs), of Gilena (Ḳaryat Ḏjilyāna), near Estapa (Istabba) as far as the limit (*ḥawz*) of Morón (*Mawrūr*). Among the strongholds and towns of the *kūra* were Marbella, Fuengirola (Suhayl), Cártama, Iznájar, Comares, Vélez Málaga, Coín, Alhama and Antequera and, for some time, probably also Estepa (cf. J. Vallvé, *De nuevo sobre Bobastro,* in *al-And.*, xxx [1965], 139-74).

The perimeter of Málaga enclosed an area of some 34 hectares at the end of the 5th/11th century, which allows a calculation of the population, in these years, at 20,000 inhabitants, mostly residing in homes of 50 to 100 m² (although some exceeded 150 m² or were smaller than 40). During the same century, according to Ibn Ḥazm in his *Ḏjamharat ansāb al-ʿArab* (cf. Elías Terés, *Linajes árabes en al-Andalus,* in *al-And.*, xxii [1957], index) a number of Arab tribes settled in the region of Málaga, among them As͟hʿarīs, Lak͟hmīs, Nahdīs and Ḳaysīs descended from Ḥimyar, (Ḥabībī) Umayyads, and Berbers of diverse origin (Lamāya, Mag͟hīla, Nafza, among others of the race of the Ṣanhāḏja and the Zanāta), all of these on a broad base mostly Hispano-Christian and Hispano-Muslim, with a considerably smaller Hispano-Jewish element.

Málaga and its *kūra* knew almost eight centuries of Islamic history from the moment when, according to certain sources, an army sent from Ecija by Ṭāriḳ, in 92/711, took the town, then an episcopal see and one of the most important ports of the peninsula in the Roman period. However, Ibn ʿAskar, who seems to take his information from Ibn Ḥayyān (cf. J. Vallvé, *Una fuente importante de la historia de al-Andalus. La "Historia" de Ibn ʿAskar,* in *al-And.*, xxxi [1966], 244-5) presents in some detail a version according to which it was ʿAbd al-ʿAlāʾ, son of Mūsā b. Nuṣayr, who besieged the town and took it by storm, without thereby discounting the obliging *wa-yuḳāl* which indicates that it was Ṭāriḳ who sent the army to the conquest of Málaga. In the time of the *wālī* Abu 'l-K͟haṭṭār, in 125/742, the Syrian *ḏjund* of Jordan (al-Urdunn) became established in the *kūra.* In the last decade of the period of the *wālīs*, the territory of Málaga experienced the effects of rivalries between Kalbīs and Ḳaysīs who were seeking power, and the Syrians. One of these pretenders was Yaḥyā b. Ḥurayt͟h, an Arab of the Ḏjud͟hām, who had to be content to govern the province of Rayya, but for only a short time, since he was soon to be stripped of power by Yūsuf al-Fihrī, appointed in 131/747 *wālī* of al-Andalus.

Málaga gave a warm welcome to ʿAbd al-Raḥmān I al-Dāk͟hil and supported him after his landing at Almuñécar and his journey across the *kūra* of Ilbīra. Until the second half of the 3rd/9th century, the chronicles record no event of importance, apart from the fact that, for an expedition against Ḏjillīḳiya, the *kūra* of Málaga supplied 2,600 horsemen to the imposing army which was formed with contributions from other provinces. In the period of al-Mun͟dhir, and at the outbreak of the civil wars which marked the major crisis of the amīrate, Málaga and other regions of southern al-Andalus found themselves involved in the series of rebellions which ensued and of which the leading protagonist was the *muwallad* ʿUmar b. Ḥafṣūn, who established his operational base and the centre of his revolt in the territory of Málaga, where he could rely on the decisive aid of the city chieftains and of strong fortresses. This action obliged the authorities in Cordova to send troops in order to defeat and punish the rebels. One of the most important of these expeditions dispatched in the time of the *amīr* ʿAbd Allāh was that of 291/904 which, commanded by Abān, brother of the *amīr*, routed the forces of Ibn Ḥafṣūn near Antequera. Some years later, the same Abān marched against Málaga, laid siege to the city, set fire to the suburbs and overran part of the neighbouring littoral. A fresh expedition was sent against the rebels of Málaga in 297/910 and achieved a result favourable to the troops of the *amīr*. In the first years of the reign of ʿAbd al-Raḥmān III, various campaigns were undertaken in the region with the object of putting an end to the rebellion of ʿUmar b. Ḥafṣūn, who had found support there especially from the population of Spanish origin, both Christians and Muslims. One of these was the campaign of Belda, directed by ʿAbd al-Raḥmān III himself in 306/919, and crowned with success. Once Málaga had been subdued, all the strongholds of the *kūra* met the same fate, as a result of repeated expeditions, and once the territory had been pacified, the *kūra* of Rayya experienced a long period of prosperity which was to last throughout the caliphate, until the turbulent years of the *fitna*.

In the first third of the 5th/11th century, at the beginning of the period of the *Mulūk al-ṭawāʾif* (in fact as early as the time of the *fitna*), Málaga declared itself independent under the government of the Ḥammūdids [*q.v.*], recognised as caliphs by the majority of Berbers of southern al-Andalus. Under the caliphate of ʿAlī b. Ḥammūd, proclaimed in Cordova in 407/1016, who, arriving from Ceuta had disembarked at Málaga, the town began to play a national role in the affairs of al-Andalus. It was in fact the refuge of al-Ḳāsim b. Ḥammūd when he was forced to leave Cordova in 412/1021 and, in 413/1023, of his nephew Yaḥyā b. ʿAlī, who sustained his rebellion in Málaga and was recognised as caliph by the people of Seville and by the neighbouring Berber chieftains. Some time later, al-Ḳāsim, besieged in Xérès and taken prisoner by his nephew, was incarcerated in Málaga, where he was strangled on the orders of Idrīs b. ʿAlī b. Ḥammūd in 427/1036. In fact, Málaga was transformed into another *taifa* kingdom and was the rival of Seville, where the *ḳāḍī* al-Ḳāsim b. ʿAbbād employed a fraud consisting of displaying and having recognised a double of Hi͟shām II al-Muʾayyad. Yaḥyā, son of Idrīs, was proclaimed in Málaga on the death of his father in 431/1039 and was recognised by the people of the town, but at the price of estrangement from another Ḥammūdid prince, Ḥasan, based in Ceuta. Confronted by action undertaken by troops loyal to the latter, Yaḥyā surrendered and abdicated in favour of Ḥasan, who was proclaimed four months later, having taken power (432/1040), and was recognised as rightful caliph by the Zīrid *amīr* of Granada and by other provincial chieftains. In 434/1043 the Ḥammūdid Idrīs II was in charge of the political affairs of Málaga, but the inhabitants turned against him and he was forced to seek refuge in Bobastro, where he appealed to Bādīs for assistance in regaining his throne. When his enterprise failed, in spite of the support that he received, he withdrew to Ceuta. Power then fell to Muḥammad b. Idrīs b. ʿAlī b. Ḥammūd who adopted, like his predecessors, the title of caliph. He reorganised public administration but, proving cruel and bloodthirsty, he was deposed, and Muḥammad b. al-Ḳāsim, governor of Algéciras, was appointed in his place.

The history of Málaga under the later Ḥammūdids remains fairly obscure, and there is evidence that the situation was fairly precarious and showing symptoms of weakness and instability, since Bādīs of Granada took steps to annex Málaga and its entire region to his own possessions and achieved this in 448/1056, according to al-Nubāhī, who follows the account of ʿIbn ʿAskar, or in 449/1057-8, according to al-Maḳḳarī and other sources. Bādīs, as has been said previously, then built or reconstructed the old fortress and entrusted the government of Málaga to his son Buluggin. The successor to the latter, Tamīm, showed hostility to his brother ʿAbd Allāh, the Zīrid of Granada, and, around 474/1082, he appealed unsuccesfully to Yūsuf b. Ta͟shfīn for aid against the latter. In 483/1090, Tamīm was deposed by Yūsuf, and Málaga was henceforward ruled by Almoravid *ḳuwwād*, but no significant information is available until the time that Ibn Ḥassūn, *ḳāḍī* of the town, rebelled against the Almoravids (538/July 1143-July 1144) and subsequently repelled the Almohads in Rabīʿ I 547/June 1182. Málaga had been besieged by the *s͟hayk͟h* Abū Ḥafṣ ʿUmar al-Īntī who had not succeeded in breaching its defences, but when the inhabitants rebelled and Ibn Ḥassūn was deposed and imprisoned, the people invited the Almohads to enter the town. In years marked by the overall insurrection of al-Andalus against the Almohads, ʿAbd Allāh b. ʿAlī b. Zannūn began a revolt in Málaga and recognised the authority of Ibn Hūd in 621/1229. Ibn ʿAskar supplies a quite detailed account of the political activities of Ibn Zannūn and of his tragic end.

Finally, in Ramaḍān 635/April 1238, Málaga was incorporated into the Naṣrid kingdom of Granada. The Banū As͟hkilūla, the kinsmen of Muḥammad I b. Naṣr, who governed the town, consolidated themselves there, rebelled against the latter and offered allegiance to Alfonso X of Castile who was at war with Granada. In 665/1267, Málaga was besieged without success for three months by the Granadan; in D͟hu 'l-Ḥid͟dj͟a 674/June 1275, Muḥammad II also attacked the town without success, and subsequently the Banū As͟hkilūla, who had obtained the favour of the Marīnids and recognised them as sovereigns, handed over the town to them on 6 S͟hawwal 676/2 March 1278. Six years later, the Marīnid sultan renounced his claim to Málaga and other places in favour of Muḥammad II al-Faḳīh of Granada. Henceforward, a Naṣrid governor was appointed over the town. The plague of 1348 claimed some hundred victims each day, with the result that the inhabitants panicked and abandoned the town. In the later years of the crisis of the Naṣrid kingdom, from 1455 onwards and in the time of the sultans Saʿd and of Muḥammad XI, Málaga found itself embroiled in dynastic quarrels and civil war, while its plain was subjected to reprisals on the part of the Castilians. In the course of the campaign between 1485 and 1488 and, more especially in that which began in the spring of 1487 against Vélez-Málaga, the old capital of the Ḥammūdids, after three-and-a-half months of siege, its chieftain then being Aḥmad al-T͟hag͟hrī, fell on 27 Shaʿbān 892/18 August 1487 to the might of the armies of the Catholic Kings.

Bibliography (in addition to references given in the article): see especially (on Rayya as well as Málaga), *Crónica del Moro Rasis,* ed. D. Catalán and M. S. de Andrés, Madrid 1975, 105-8; Idrīsī, *Opus geographicum,* Naples-Rome 1975, v, 570-1; Zuhrī, *K. al-Dja*ʿ*rafiyya,* ed. M. Hadj-Sadok, in *B. Et. Or.*, xxi (1968), 179; Ibn Saʿīd, *K. Basṭ al-arḍ,* ed. J. Vernet, Tetouan 1958, 74 and idem, *España en la geografía de Ibn Sa*ʿ*īd al-Magribī,* in *Tamuda,* vi (1958), 313; *al-Mughrib,* ed. Shawḳī Ḍayf, Cairo n.d., i, index; E. Fagnan, *Extraits inédits,* Algiers 1924, index; Yāḳūt, s.v.; Abu 'l-Fidāʾ, *Taḳwīm al-buldān,* ed. Reinaud and de Slane, 174-5; Ibn Ghālib, ed. Luṭfī ʿAbd al-Badīʿ, in *RIMA,* i/2 (1955), 294; Ibn Baṭṭūṭa, *Riḥla,* ed. Beirut 1388/1968, 254-5 (various trs., including the latest, the Spanish one by S. Fanjul and F. Arbós, *A través del Islam,* Madrid 1981, 761-3). To the descriptions of the geographers and historians, add Ibn al-Khaṭīb, *Iḥāṭa,* ed. ʿAbd Allāh ʿInān, Cairo 1393-7/1973-7, index; *Lamḥa,* ed. Cairo 1347, index; Maḳḳarī, *Nafḥ al-ṭīb,* ed. Iḥsān ʿAbbās, Beirut 1388/1968, index; For political history, as well as the sources cited in ISHBĪLIYA, see *Akhbār madjmūʿa,* 10, 12, 58, 80, 119 Arabic text, and 23, 25, 64, 79, 108 tr.; Ibn Ḥayyān, *Muḳtabas,* v, ed. P. Chalmeta, Madrid 1979, index; Ibn ʿIdhārī, *Bayān*; ʿAbd Allāh b. Buluggīn, *K. al-Tibyān,* ed. E. Lévi-Provençal, *Mudhakkarāt al-amīr* ʿ*Abd Allāh,* Cairo 1955, index, tr. E. García Gómez, *El siglo XI en la persona. Les "Memorias" de* ʿ*Abd Allāh, último Rey Zirí de Granada destronado por los almorávides (1090),* Madrid 1980, index. As well as the works of R. Dozy, E. Lévi-Provençal, A. Prieto Vives, J. Bosch Vilá and A. Huici Miranda, cited in ISHBĪLIYA, see L. Seco de Lucena, *Los Ḥammūdíes, señores de Málaga y Algeciras,* Malaga 1955; H. R. Idris, *Les Zīrīdes d'Espagne,* in *al-And.*, xxix (1964), 39-144, index; R. Arié, *L'Espagne musulmane au temps des Naṣrides (1232-1492),* Paris 1973; F. Guillén Robles, *Málaga musulmana. Sucesos, antigüedades, ciencias y letras malagueñas durante la edad media,* Malaga 1957; of special interest for the last years of the Islamic history of Málaga is the work of José E. López de Coce Castañer, *La tierra de Málaga a fines del siglo XV,* University of Granada 1977.

(J. BOSCH VILÁ)

MALAM (pl. *malamai*), a Hausa term derived from the Arabic *mu*ʿ*allim* with the meaning "teacher", formerly used to designate a man versed in the Arabic language and Islamic sciences to whatever extent. The tasks of a *malam* were many and various and included any or all of the following: preparing talismans (Hausa: *hatimi* from the Arabic *khātam*), dispensing medical cures both herbal and Ḳurʾānic, advising on propitious days, slaughtering animals at circumcision, naming and other ceremonies, officiating at marriages, offering prayers on behalf of patrons, teaching the Ḳurʾān, copying and selling books, etc. A *malam* of higher scholastic attainments, often known as *babban malam* "a great *malam*", would devote himself mainly to teaching the Islamic sciences or to such offices as *ḳāḍī* (Hausa, *alkali*) or *imām* (Hausa, *limam*).

Nowadays, although the traditional *malam* described above remains a familiar feature of Hausa society, the term itself has been debased to the point where (like the Arabic term *al-sayyid*) it merely serves the function of the English "Mr.". Similarly, *Shehu* (from Arabic *al-shaykh*), once the coveted title of a great teacher and scholar, is now commonly used as a personal name. Combined with the word *malam,* however, in the phrase *shehu malami,* it is used as an epithet for a distinguished exponent of the Islamic sciences.

Among the black communities of Algiers where the Hausa *bori* (possession) cult has been influential, the term *malam* is used as a title in the *diyār* of Sīdī Bilāl. The *malam* is in charge of musical arrangements during ceremonies at the *dār* and officiates at minor sacrifices outside it.

Bibliography: For the autobiography of a *malam*, see *Alhaji Koki, Kano malam,* ed. and tr. N. Skinner, Zaria 1979. On the usage of the term in Algiers, J.-B. Andrews, *Les Fontaines des génies (Sebâ Aioun), croyances soudanaises à Alger,* Algiers 1903.

(J. O. HUNWICK)

MALĀMATIYYA, an Islamic mystical tradition which probably originated in 3rd/9th century Nīshāpūr.

1. IN THE CENTRAL ISLAMIC LANDS

The foundation of this tradition has been attributed to Ḥamdūn al-Ḳaṣṣār (d. 271/884-5 [*q.v.* and see further on him below, section 2]). One of the main sources for the study of its doctrine is the *Risālat al-Malāmatiyya* by ʿAbd al-Raḥmān Muḥammad b. al-Ḥusayn al-Sulamī (330-412/941-1021). This treatise (see *Bibl.*) contains a number of sayings by early authorities concerning the Malāmatiyya and an enumeration of the principles (*uṣūl*) of Malāmatī teaching. This teaching is not a closely reasoned internally consistent system, but rather a number of tenets which centre around the basic Malāmatī doctrine that all outward appearance of piety or religiosity, including good deeds, is ostentation. The most important of these tenets are: 1. the display of ʿ*ibāda* [*q.v.*] is *shirk* [*q.v.*]; 2. the display of a *ḥāl* [*q.v.*] is *irtidād* [*q.v.*]; 3. in all *aḥwāl*, suspicion of one's *nafs* [*q.v.*] is obligatory (and in conjunction, man is an opponent of his *nafs*, therefore he must not find pleasure in any *ḥāl*); and 4. a man must struggle against finding satisfaction in doing good, since every action and every pious deed which he looks upon with appreciation is worthless. In accordance with these tenets, the Malāmatī has to struggle continuously against his desire for divine reward and for approval by man. This explains the requirements: 1. not to say prayers (*du*ʿ*ā*ʾ) except (under special conditions) for those in distress; 2. not to dress differently from others and/or isolate oneself from the world, but to dress like everybody else and to live a normal life in conformity with the requirements of society; 3. to take up a despised profession and to refuse a prestigious one; and 4. to conceal one's poverty (if revealed, one enters the state of neediness and will attract attention). The required struggle against the desire for the approval of men in conjunction with the concern to hide his *ḥāl* may bring the Malāmatī to show only his bad qualities. In doing so, he may make himself an object of blame (Ar. *malām, malāma,* from the root *lāma* "to blame").

The Malāmatī attitude is older than Islam. R. Reitzenstein, *Hellenistische Wundererzählungen,* Leipzig 1906, 65 ff., was drawn upon by I. Goldziher, *Vorlesungen über den Islam,* Heidelberg 1925, 167-8, Eng. tr. *Introduction to Islamic theology and law,* Princeton 1981, 149-50, who traced back the essence of Malāmatī thought to the ancient Greek philosophical school of the Cynics, while M. Molé, *Les mystiques musulmans,* Paris 1965, 72-7, has shown that the Malāmatī trend to hide one's virtuous actions, in order not to divulge one's saintly state, was to be found among the early Syrian Christians. Most contemporary Muslim authors (see *Bibl.*) on al-Malāmatiyya are in unanimous agreement that this tradition is not Islamic, neither in its spirit nor in its theory.

In the 4th/10th century, the Malāmatiyya tradition reached Baghdād and Mecca in the persons of Abu ʿUmar al-Zadjdjādjī, Abu 'l-Ḥasan b. Bandār, Abu 'l-Ḥasan b. Sahl al-Būshandjī, Abū Yaʿḳūb al-Nahradjūrī and Muḥammad b. Aḥmad al-Farrāʾ (cf. ʿAbd al-Ḳādir Maḥmūd, *al-Falsafa al-Ṣūfiyya fi 'l-Islām,* Cairo 1967, 415). In later centuries, the Malāmatī orientation frequently took the form of an explicit invitation of reproach and rejection by intentional repulsive behaviour. Sometimes, such behaviour became the hall-mark and proof of sanctity.

Intentional and systematic transgression of the norms and values of society is particularly practised by the Ḳalandariyya [*q.v.*], which have been looked upon (e.g. by A. Le Chatelier, *Les confréries musulmanes du Hedjaz,* Paris 1887, 253 ff.) as the continuation of the Malāmatī tradition within the framework of a more or less regular *ṭarīḳa.* This idea of continuity must be discarded, however. Fundamental differences exist between Malāmatī and Ḳalandarī thinking and practice, as has already been pointed out by Shihāb al-Dīn Abū Ḥafṣ ʿUmar b. Muḥammad al-Suhrawardī (539-632/1144-1235) and lately by J. S. Trimingham, *The Sufi orders in Islam,* Oxford 1971, 264-9. In al-Suhrawardī's life-time, the Malāmatī tradition still had its adepts in Khurāsān and in ʿIrāḳ, where, however, the epithet Malāmatī was not applied to them (al-Suhrawardī, *ʿAwārif al-maʿārif,* Cairo 1971, i, 228).

Elements of the Malāmatī tradition, notably silent *dhikr,* abstinence of ritual activity in public and the requirement of "mental isolation" in the world while actively engaged in it, seem to have been absorbed into the teaching of the Naḳshbandiyya [*q.v.*] order and filtered into the mystical traditions in the Arab lands; for this process, see section 2 below.

The origins of the version of the Malāmatiyya order which had active adherents in the Hidjāz in the 19th century were in a Syrian congregation of the Ḥamzawiyya (see below). These adherents were most numerous in the town of al-Ṭāʾif, where this Malāmatiyya order had been introduced by the *ḳāḍī* of the town, Ḥasan Fatḥ al-Karkhī. Leadership of the order in the Ḥidjāz used to be held by his descendants. A *zāwiya* [*q.v.*] existed in Mecca at the end of the 19th century (Le Chatelier, 256).

Bibliography: Basic texts on the Malāmatī mystical tradition are Abū ʿAbd al-Raḥmān al-Sulamī, *Risālat al-Malāmatiyya,* ed. Abu 'l-ʿAlāʾ ʿAfīfī in his *al-Malāmatiyya wa 'l-taṣawwuf wa-ahl al-futuwwa,* Cairo 1945, 71-120 (for an analysis of this text, see R. Hartmann, *As-Sulamī's Risālat al-Malāmatīja,* in *Isl.,* viii [1918], 157-203); Abu 'l-Ḥasan ʿAlī b. ʿUthmān al-Hudjwīrī, *Kashf al-maḥdjūb,* ed. V. A. Zhukovskii, Leningrad 1926, repr. Tehran 1399/1979, 68-78, tr. R. A. Nicholson, *The "Kashf al-Maḥjūb", the oldest Persian treatise on Sufism by al-Hujwīrī,* GMS, London 1911, see 19-74 for the Malāmatiyya; Shihāb al-Dīn Abū Ḥafṣ ʿUmar b. Muḥammad al-Suhrawardī, *ʿAwārif al-maʿārif,* Cairo 1971 (several editions exist), ch. 8 (*fī dhikr al-Malāmatiyya wa-sharḥ ḥālihā*). Dispersed and fragmentary information may be found in a number of classical texts, which are all mentioned in ʿAbd al-Ḳādir Maḥmūd, 407. See also Muḥyī 'l-Dīn b. ʿArabī, *al-Futūḥāt al-Makkiyya,* Būlāḳ 1293/1876, iii, 44-6.

For short discussions by contemporary Muslim authors based mainly upon these texts, see Abu 'l-ʿAlāʾ al-ʿAfīfī, *al-Taṣawwuf, al-thawra al-rūḥiyya fi 'l-Islām,* Beirut n.d., 268-70; ʿAbd al-Ḳādir Maḥmūd, *op. cit.*, 406-20; Ibrāhīm Hilāl, *al-Taṣawwuf al-Islāmī bayn al-dīn wa 'l-falsafa,* Cairo 1979, 11-14. In addition to these works and the works mentioned in the article, see A. J. Arberry, *Sufism, an account of the mystics of Islam,* London 1956, 70, 74; H. Ritter, *Philologika XV. Farīduddīn ʿAṭṭār. III.*, in *Oriens,* xii (1959), 14 ff.; M.S. Seale, *The ethics of Malāmātīya Sufism and the Sermon on the Mount,* in *MW,* lviii (1968), 12-23 (contains an abridged translation of al-Sulamī's enumeration of Malāmatī tenets); P. Nwyia, *Ibn ʿAṭāʾ Allāh et la naissance de la confrérie šādilite,* Beirut 1972, 243-4; M. G. S. Hodgson, *The venture of Islam,* ii, Chicago 1974, 457; A. Schimmel, *Mystical dimensions of Islam,* Chapel Hill 1975, 86-8; R. Gramlich, *Die Schiitischen Derwischorden Persiens. Zweiter Teil: Glaube und Lehre,* Wiesbaden 1976, 346-7; Taḳī 'l-Dīn Ibn Taymiyya, *al-Tuḥfa al-ʿIrāḳiyya fi 'l-aʿmāl al-kalbiyya,* Cairo n.d., 45 (for a condemnation of the Malāmatiyya in its antinomianist form); Aḥmad Muḥammad Riḍwān, *al-Nafaḥāt al-rabbāniyya,* Cairo 1970, 113 (a short characterisation of the Malāmatiyya and the observation that al-Khiḍr [SEE AL-KHAḌIR] is one of them). (F. DE JONG)

2. IN IRAN AND THE EASTERN LANDS

The concept of blame that underlies the designation Malāmatiyya (both in the sense of self-reproach and of exposing oneself to reproach by others) derives from Ḳurʾān, V, 54 ("they struggle in the path of God and fear not the blame of any blamer"), a verse referring to the Prophet and his Companions, whom the Mālamatīs indeed claimed as the first of their number (Hudjwīrī, *Kashf al-maḥdjūb,* Leningrad, 1926, repr. Tehran 1399/1979, 78). But as a historically identifiable group, the Mālāmatiyya first appeared in Iran in the 3rd/9th century, and since they remained confined to Iran, at least in their original form, it is permissible to define the Malāmatiyya as an Iranian or, more narrowly, as a Khurāsānian form of spirituality.

As noted in the preceding section, the major figure of the Malāmatiyya was Abū Ṣāliḥ Ḥamdūn al-Ḳaṣṣār, after whom the early Malāmatīs were sometimes known as al-Ḥamdūniyya or al-Ḳaṣṣāriyya. Born in Nīshāpūr where he spent most of his life and gathered his following, he was himself a student of Abu 'l-Ḥasan Sālim al-Bārūsī (for whose putative spiritual descent see Cavit Sunar, *Melamilik ve Bektaşilik,* Ankara 1975, 9). Al-Bārūsī was a critic of the effusive and public devotions of the Karrāmiyya sect [*q.v.*] in Nīshāpūr, and insofar as the emergence of the Malāmatiyya may be taken as a reaction against contemporaneous trends, it is in the Karrāmiyya rather than the Ṣūfīs that the counterpoint to the Malāmatīs should be sought. Shunning fame for piety and the concomitant danger of hypocrisy, Ḥamdūn al-Ḳaṣṣār and his associates believed it necessary to conceal all acts of superrogatory worship and declared public appearances to be a matter of indifference; the pleasure of God and the pleasure of men were irreconcilably opposed goals. The appetitive self was their exclusive object of blame (cf. the expression "reproachful soul"—*al-nafs al-lawwāma*—in Ḳurʾān, LXXV, 2), to such a degree that they allowed the duty of publicly "forbidding the evil" (*al-nahy ʿan al-munkar*) to fall into abeyance. The emphasis on inward, secretive devotion also led the Malāmatīs to a deliberate shunning of distinctive forms of dress, of the writing of treatises setting forth their principles, of the musical sessions of the Ṣūfīs known as *samāʿ* [*q.v.*] and even of vocal—and hence audible—*dhikr* [*q.v.*].

Abū Ḥafṣ al-Ḥaddād and ʿAbd Allāh Munāzil, the latter a pupil of al-Ḳaṣṣār, are clearly identifiable with the Malāmatiyya, but other figures sometimes designated as Malāmatīs have been claimed by the Ṣūfīs as their own; this is the case notably with Abū ʿUthmān al-Ḥīrī. In addition, Malāmatī features are to be found in persons who have no direct relation with the Malāmatī circle of Nīshāpūr, especially in Bāyazīd Bisṭāmī [see ABŪ YAZĪD AL-BISṬĀMĪ], who on several occasions changed popular acclaim into blame by apparent violations of the *Sharīʿa*. It is evident, then, that the demarcation between Malāmatīs and Ṣūfīs was not always sharp. Ḥamdūn al-Ḳaṣṣār himself met with Sahl al-Tustarī and al-Djunayd [*q.vv.*] while on a visit to Baghdād and earned their approval, surely an indication of compatibility between the Malāmatiyya and the "sober" school of ʿIrāḳī Ṣūfism.

Nonetheless, the shunning of all outward indications of one's inward state was a clear point of difference from the Ṣūfīs, one implying criticism of them. In return, the Ṣūfīs politely condemned the unceasing Malāmatī preoccupation with the wretchedness of the *nafs*, which seemed to them a form of implicit ontological dualism, setting the soul up as a reality confronting God. Echoing earlier writers, Djāmī said of the Malāmatīs: "Although this group is precious and their state is noble, the veil of creaturely existence has not been fully lifted from them" (ʿAbd al-Raḥmān Djāmī, *Nafaḥāt al-uns*, ed. Mahdī Tawḥīdīpūr, Tehran 1336 *sh*./1957, 9). Likewise, the preoccupation with reproach of the *nafs* seemed to some Ṣūfīs to bar the Malāmatīs from all progress beyond the station (*maḳām*) of sincerity of devotion (*ikhlāṣ*); al-Suhrawardī said that while the Ṣūfī has "lost awareness of *ikhlāṣ* because of *ikhlāṣ* ... the Malāmatī is fixed at the station of *ikhlāṣ*" (*ʿAwārif al-maʿārif*, in supplementary volume to al-Ghazālī, *Iḥyāʾ ʿulūm al-dīn*, Beirut n.d., 71).

A close relationship appears to have existed between the first Malāmatīs and the practitioners of *futuwwa* [*q.v.*] the members of the craft guilds. Like them, the Malāmatīs wore the common dress of the bazaar and followed various callings, rejecting the work-denying interpretation of *tawakkul* made by certain Ṣūfīs. Both Ḥamdūn al-Ḳaṣṣār and Abū Ḥafṣ al-Ḥaddād are on record as offering definitions of *futuwwa*, and it is significant that al-Sulamī—whose maternal grandfather was Abū ʿUthmān al-Ḥīrī—treated *malāma* and *futuwwa* as twin concepts in his writing. Aḥmad Khiḍrawayh was identified by al-Ḳushayrī as a *fatā* and by Hudjwīrī as a *malāmatī*; this, too, must indicate an overlapping between the two affiliations. After the disappearance of the Malāmatiyya in their original form, the craft guilds and organs of *futuwwa* seem to have become one of the chief repositories of Malāmatī influence, with their emphasis on self-effacing probity and practical devotion.

Although no prominent individuals are identified as Malāmatī after the 4th/10th century, the original Malāmatiyya may have survived in Khurāsān for considerably longer. In the 6th/12th century, al-Suhrawardī wrote in his *ʿAwārif al-maʿārif*, 71, "There is still a group of them (sc. of Malāmatīs) in Khurāsān; they have their elders who expound their fundamental principles and make known to them the conditions of their states. I have seen people that follow the same path in ʿIrāḳ but they are not known by this name". Early on, however, the name Malāmatī had been usurped by antinomians who actively sought the blame of others, instead of simply being ready to accept it; instead of hidden piety, libertinism was their hallmark. Although both Hudjwīrī (*Kashf al-maḥdjūb*, 72) and al-Suhrawardī (*op. cit.*, 72) sought to clarify the difference between the true and the false Malāmatī, it seems that the false gradually came to prevail, at least numerically. *Ḳalandar* [*q.v.*] a term designating a vagabond of scandalously offensive behaviour, became interchangeable with Malāmatī in popular usage.

The true heirs of the early Malāmatiyya of Khurāsān were, it appears, the Naḳshbandīs, although they did not claim initiatic descent from them (the notion of a *silsila*, like many other appurtenances of Ṣūfism, was in any event alien to the Malāmatīs). The Naḳshbandīs followed the Malāmatis in their avoidance of a distinctive garb, their shunning of vocal *dhikr* and *samʿ*, their prohibition of ceaseless voyaging, and their closeness to the people of the bazaar. The most prolific of early Naḳshbandī authors, Khʷādja Muḥammad Pārsā (d. 823/1420) quoted approvingly and at length from Hudjwīrī's discussion of the Malāmátiyya; he said of Abū Bakr al-Ṣiddīḳ, Salmān al-Fārisī and Bāyazīd Bisṭāmī—all key figures in the spiritual ancestry of the Naḳshbandī order—that they were to be regarded as Malāmatis; and concluded that "whatever holds true of the Malāmatīs holds true of our masters (*khʷādjagān*) also" (extract from Pārsā's *Faṣl al-khiṭāb*, quoted in Saʿīd Nafīsī, *Sarčishma-yi taṣawwuf dar Īrān*, Tehran 1343 *sh*./1964, 172-80). More generally, the original concept of the Malāmatiyya continued to be celebrated as a spiritual virtue or station in Ṣūfī literature, while in later Persian poetry—suffused with the terminology and concepts of Ṣūfism—*malāmat* became ubiquitous as a usefully rhyming antonym to *salāmat* ("safety"): the lover had to be ready, it was held, to accept the former and renounce the latter, for the sake of his beloved.

The original concept of the Malāmatiyya does not seem to have entered India and Central Asia, except as mediated by the Naḳshbandiyya. The term Malāmatī was, however, sometimes applied to antinomian (*bīsharʿ*) groups such as the Djalāliyya, a derivative of the Suhrawardiyya that was addicted to narcotics and ate scorpions.

Bibliography: Aziz Ahmad, *An intellectual history of Islam in India*, Edinburgh 1969, 44-5; Farīd al-Dīn ʿAṭṭār, *Tadhkirat al-awliyāʾ*, ed. R. A. Nicholson, London and Leiden 1905, i, 322-35; Jacqueline Chabbi, *Remarques sur le développement historique des mouvements ascétiques et mystiques au Khurasan*, in *SI*, xlvi (1977), 32-4, 53-7; Khʷādja ʿAbd Allāh Anṣārī Harawī, *Ṭabaḳāt al-Ṣūfiyya*, ed. Muḥammad Sarwar Mawlāʾī, Tehran 1362 *sh*./1983, 113-17, 121-2; Djāmī, *Nafaḥāt al-uns*, 9-10; Saʿīd Nafīsī, *Sarčishma-yi taṣawwuf dar Īrān*, 160-81; Abu 'l-Ḳāsim al-Ḳushayrī, *al-Risāla al-Ḳushayriyya*, ed. ʿAbd al-Ḥalīm Maḥmūd, Cairo 1974, i, 118-19, 129-31; Suhrawardī, *ʿAwārif al-maʿārif*, in supplementary vol. to Ghazālī, *Iḥyāʾ ʿulum al-dīn*, 70-2; Sunar, *Melamilik ve Bektaşilik*, 8-12; F. Taeschner, *Zünfte und Bruderschaften im Islam*, Zürich and Munich 1979, 27; ʿAbd al-Ḥusayn Zarrīnkūb, *Ahl-i malāmat va rāh-i ḳalandar*, in *Yādnāma-yi Marḥūm Ustād Badīʿ al-Zamān Furūzānfar (Madjalla-yi Dānishkada-yi Adabiyyāt wa ʿUlūm-i Insānī, Dānishgāh-i Ṭihrān*, no. 89 [Spring 1354 *sh*./1975]), 61-100.

(HAMID ALGAR)

3. IN OTTOMAN TURKEY.

In the Ottoman Empire, the name Malāmatiyya attached itself to a heretical offshoot of the Bayrāmiyya [*q.v.*]. An account of the original split between the orthodox and the heretical branches of the Bayrāmiyya survives only as a legend recorded first in the 10th/16th century. According to this, ʿÖmer the Cutler (d. 880/1475-6), a dervish who had followed first Shaykh Ḥāmid (d. 815/1412-13) and then Ḥāmid's disciple, Ḥādjdjī Bayrām [*q.v.*], refused to join the disciples of Ḥādjdjī Bayrām's appointed successor, Aḳ Shams al-Dīn [*q.v.*] in performing *dhikr* [*q.v.*], or to kiss Aḳ Shams al-Dīn's hand. Thereupon, Aḳ Shams al-Dīn threatened to divest ʿÖmer of the distinguishing cloak (*khirḳa*) and headgear (*tādj*) of the new order. ʿÖmer's retort was to invite Aḳ Shams al-Dīn and his followers to his house, where he lit a fire in the courtyard. He then walked through the fire, which burned off his headgear and cloak but left his body unscathed. After this ʿÖmer's followers—the Malāmatiyya-yi Bayrāmiyya—wore no distinguishing garments (Maḥmūd of Caffa, *Katāʾib,* quoted in A. Gölpınarlı, *Melâmîlik ve melâmîler,* Istanbul 1931, 41; ʿAṭāʾī [*q.v.*], *Dhayl-i shaḳāʾiḳ*, Istanbul 1268/1851-2, 65). The real reason why the Malāmatiyya wore no distinguishing clothing must, in fact, have been because their heretical beliefs led to occasional persecutions, and their survival could depend on concealing their identities from the authorities. To wear identifiable clothing would invite investigation. However, the sect continued to abjure special garments right down to the 13th/19th century, by which time it had long since become an orthodox Ṣūfī group, accepting the authority of the *Sharīʿa* [*q.v.*] (J. P. Brown, *The dervishes,* London 1868, repr. 1968, 61. On the orthodoxy of the later Malāmatiyya, see Brown's translation of a *risāla* by Laʿlīzāde ʿAbd al-Bāḳī, in *op. cit.,* 232 ff.). The legend of ʿÖmer's dispute with Aḳ Shams al-Dīn suggests that their rivalry was personal. This seems probable since, although Ḥādjdjī Bayrām had nominated him as his successor or *khalīfa* [*q.v.*], Aḳ Shams al-Dīn had been one of the last to join the group, so displacing candidates of "forty years'" standing. His nomination no doubt aroused jealousy. However, the essential split was doctrinal, and it was doctrinal differences that caused it to be permanent.

There are no surviving 9th/15th century Malāmī writings to give an account of the original doctrines and affiliations of the sect. Links with Badr al-Dīn of Simawne [*q.v.*] and the early Ṣafawiyya [*q.v.*], through ʿÖmer's and Ḥādjdjī Bayrām's connection with Shaykh Ḥāmid have been suggested (H. J. Kissling, *Zur Geschichte des Derwischordens der Bajramijje,* in *Süd-Ost Forschungen,* xv [1956], 237-68). The writings of 10th/16th and 11th/17th-century Malāmī *shaykhs,* however, clearly reveal the sect's doctrines and permit speculation as to its 9th/15th century origins. These show that the sect espoused Ṣūfism of a Ḥallādjian type, striving not, as orthodox Ṣūfīs, for *fanāʾ fi'llāh*—the total loss of individual identity in God—but believing in the manifestation of God in the individual member of the sect: "Know that the Mirror of Man is the outward form of the Merciful God", in the words of Aḥmed the Cameleer (d. 952/1545-6), or "The *ḳibla* is Man", in the words of "The Hidden" Idrīs (d. 1024/1615) (quoted by A. Gölpınarlı, *op. cit.,* 59, 127). The orthodox *ʿulamāʾ,* with some justification, regarded this form of Ṣūfism as leading to a disavowal of the *Sharīʿa,* the true source of divine authority, since its adepts believed the divine authority to be within themselves. This disavowal, the *ʿulamāʾ* believed, expressed itself in a denial of the distinction between what is canonically legitimate (*ḥalāl* [*q.v.*]) and what is canonically forbidden (*ḥarām*). The surviving verses attributed to the Malāmī martyr Ismāʿīl Oghlan Shaykh (d. 935/1529) (quoted by A. Gölpınarlı, *op. cit.,* 51-4) do, in fact, strongly suggest that he flouted the concepts of *ḥalāl* and *ḥarām* by, for example, linking "the mosque and the wineshop" or "the mosque of the Muslim worshipper (*maʿbed-i ʿābid*) and the idol-house of the priest" in a way which went far beyond accepted Ṣūfī convention. In his guidelines for the trial of the Malāmī suspect Ghaḍanfer Dede (d. 974/1566-7), Abu 'l-Suʿūd [*q.v.*] instructed the examiners to pay particular attention to his statements on *ḥalāl* and *ḥarām* (ʿAṭāʾī, *op. cit.,* 87-8).

Although Ḥallādjian beliefs were not peculiar to any one sect, there is evidence that they came to the Malāmatiyya specifically from the original Ḥurūfiyya [*q.v.*]. Ḥurūfī doctrines appear not only in the Ḥallādjism of Malāmī writings, but also in certain specific details. In the verses attributed to Oghlan Shaykh, there are references to God's appearing in the human face: "Today, O heart, look at the beauty of the Beloved's face", and in a *ghazal* [*q.v.*] of "The Hidden" Idrīs, there is a reference to the indisputably Ḥurūfī concept of "The Seven Lines" of the face as a visible form of the *fātiḥa* [*q.v.*], which in turn represents the Sum of the Universe (i.e. God plus what is beside God): "The Seven Lines are the 'Mother of the Book' (i.e. the *fātiḥa*). They are the visible testimony from God". Oghlan Shaykh also makes the Ḥurūfī equation between the "Name" (*ism*) and the "Named" (*musammā*): "You whose name is Man gives news of the Named". Furthermore, one of his *ghazals* is a *naẓīra* of one by the Ḥurūfī martyr Nesīmī [*q.v.*] (d. 820/1417). These Ḥurūfī echoes occur in poems of the 10th/16th and early 11th/17th centuries, but it is possible that the doctrines themselves date from the earliest days of the sect in the first half of the 9th/15th century, since this was the period when the disciples of Faḍl Allāh [*q.v.*] were actively preaching Ḥurūfī doctrines in Anatolia and Syria (see H. Ritter, *Die Anfänge der Hurūfī-sekte,* in *Oriens,* vii [1954], 1-54; Ibn Ḥadjar al-ʿAskalānī [*q.v.*], *Inbāʾ al-ghumr,* Cairo 1973, 136; for the Ḥurūfī preacher in Edirne in 848/1444, see F. Babinger, *Von Amurath zu Amurath,* in *Oriens,* iii [1950], 229-65). ʿÖmer the Cutler and his followers may well have absorbed their doctrines.

A distinguishing feature of *malāmī* writings is their exhortation to believers to conceal their beliefs from the "ignorant", meaning non-members of the sect. In this they resemble the original Malāmatiyya; but concealment of belief had the immediate practical purpose of preventing persecution by the Ottoman authorities. They also maintained that "although there can be no place like Man for the manifestation of God's essence" (Oghlan Shaykh, quoted by A. Gölpınarlı, *op. cit.,* 52), God can be manifest only in a "believer" that is, a member of the sect. Non-believers are mere "animals".

The Malāmatiyya began as a sect in central Anatolia and appear not to have spread beyond this region until the first quarter of the 10th/16th century. ʿÖmer's *khalīfa,* Benyāmīn or Ibn Yāmīn (d. 926/1520) came from Ayash near Ankara [*q.v.*]. His successor, Pīr ʿAlī Dede (d. 935/1528-9) was a native of Aḳsaray [*q.v.*], where he is also buried. The Malāmī *shaykh* Ḥusām al-Dīn, a *khalīfa* of Aḥmed the Cameleer, came from the region of Ankara (ʿAṭāʾī, *op. cit.,* 70). In 960/1553 he was imprisoned and executed in the citadel of that town. He still had followers in the nearby region of Haymana, whom the Ottoman government investigated in 975/1568 (*Mühimme defteri,* text in

A. Refik, *On altıncı asırda Rafizîlik ve Bektaşîlik,* Istanbul 1932, 24-5). By the time of Ḥusām al-Dīn's end, however, the sect had spread far beyond the region of its origin.

The expansion began in 934/1528 when Ismāʿīl, the son of Pīr ʿAlī Dede, known as Og̲h̲lan S̲h̲ayk̲h̲, began to preach in Istanbul. For a year he preached and performed ceremonies, apparently in mosques, attracting many followers, including soldiers (ʿAṭāʾī, *op. cit.,* 79). These were probably *ḳapïḳulï* troops stationed in the capital. In 935/1529, after numerous warnings and condemnatory *fatwās* [*q.v.*], the authorities executed him on the At Meydānï, with the sanction of a *fatwā* from Kemāl Pas̲h̲a-zāde [*q.v.*].

The underlying question in the trial of Og̲h̲lan S̲h̲ayk̲h̲ was whether or not he accepted the authority of the *S̲h̲arīʿa,* and therefore of its officially appointed interpreters, the Ottoman *ʿulamāʾ*. However, the examination centred specifically around the question of whether he and his followers regarded the gyrating dance which constituted their *d̲h̲ikr* as *ʿibāda* [*q.v.*], obligatory worship, or simply as a permissible (*mubāḥ*) religious ceremony. To regard it as *mubāḥ* did not occur the death-penalty: it merely branded its practitioners as "dissolutes", to be corrected by flogging (*taʿzīr*). However, to regard it as *ʿibāda* made the death-penalty inevitable. Since the term *ʿibāda* refers specifically to the forms of obligatory worship laid down by the *S̲h̲arīʿa,* to claim any other form of worship as *ʿibāda* is to arrogate to oneself the authority which properly belongs to the *S̲h̲arīʿa,* the revealed command of God. This Og̲h̲lan S̲h̲ayk̲h̲ did, and, furthermore, defended his position with quotations from the Ḳurʾān and *Ḥadīth* [*q.vv.*] (John Rylands Library, Manchester, Turkish ms. no. 39 [the *fatwās* of Kemāl Pas̲h̲a-zāde], fols. 377a-b. This section, entitled *Maṭlab-i Zeyd-i Ṣūfī,* appears to refer to the case of Og̲h̲lan S̲h̲ayk̲h̲). In doing so, he conformed precisely to the definition of a heretic (*zindīḳ* [*q.v.*]) which Kemāl Pas̲h̲a-zāde had propounded, following the case of Mollā Ḳābiḍ [*q.v.*] in the previous year. A *zindīḳ* was someone who, while "concealing his unbelief, also propagates it" by "extracting his seditious propaganda from the Truth" (Kemāl Pas̲h̲a-zāde, *Risāla fī taḥḳīḳ lafẓ al-zindīḳ,* printed in *Rasāʾil Ibn Kemāl,* Istanbul 1316/1898-9, 240-9). A heretic was, in fact, someone who, like Og̲h̲lan S̲h̲ayk̲h̲, supported "erroneous" opinions by arguments from the Ḳurʾān, *Ḥadīth* or other "true sources" of Islam (for a summary—how accurate a one we can only surmise—of the *s̲h̲erʿiyye sid̲j̲illi* entry on the trial of Og̲h̲lan S̲h̲ayk̲h̲, see M. Akdağ, *Türkiye'nin iktisadî ve içtimaî tarihi,* ii, Ankara 1971, 48-9).

The trial of Og̲h̲lan S̲h̲ayk̲h̲ may have assisted the Ottoman authorities in formulating a definition of heresy, but was otherwise counterproductive. In executing him, they created the first Malāmī martyr. A body of legend, relating essentially to the injustice of his execution collected around him (ʿAṭāʾī, *op. cit.,* 70) and continued to circulate for at least a century and a half after his death (Evliya Čelebi [*q.v.*], *Seyāḥatnāme,* i, Istanbul 1314/1896-7, 456). Years after his execution, Abu 'l-Suʿūd ruled that if a person claimed that Og̲h̲lan S̲h̲ayk̲h̲'s execution was unjust and also belonged to the "sect of Og̲h̲lan S̲h̲ayk̲h̲", he incurred the death-penalty (M. E. Düzdağ, *Şeyhülislâm Ebussuûd Efendi fetvaları,* Istanbul 1972, 196). In the case of G̲h̲aḍanfer Dede, Abu 'l-Suʿūd also wrote that "no good" could come of him if the reports were true that he was "from the *silsila* [*q.v.*] of Og̲h̲lan S̲h̲ayk̲h̲" (ʿAṭāʾī, *op. cit.,* 88). An Imperial Decree of 967/1559 concerns the arrest of a *s̲h̲ayk̲h̲* who preached around Üsküdar [*q.v.*] and was a "disciple of Og̲h̲lan S̲h̲ayk̲h̲'s father" (*Mühimme defteri,* text in A. Refik, *op. cit.,* 17). This frequent re-occurrence of Og̲h̲lan S̲h̲ayk̲h̲'s name suggests that his martyrdom advanced the fortunes of the Malāmatiyya.

Og̲h̲lan S̲h̲ayk̲h̲ brought Malāmī doctrines to the capital. It is possible that Aḥmed the Cameleer, a native of Hayrabolu in Thrace, where he is also buried (ʿAṭāʾī, *op. cit.,* 65), carried them into Europe. In 980-1/1572-3, the Imperial *Dīwān* ordered the *ḳāḍī* of Hayrabolu and the *ḳāḍīs* of the neighbouring districts of Rodosčuḳ (Tekirdağı) and Burgos (Lüle Burgaz) to examine suspects in certain villages who were adherents of the martyred Malāmī Ḥamza (d. 968/1561) (*Mühimme defteri,* text in A. Refik, *op. cit.,* 33-4; *Mühimme defteri,* xxii, 228). It may have been Aḥmed the Cameleer who established the sect in his native region. His itinerant profession would also have given him the opportunity to proselytise in different areas. A later *s̲h̲ayk̲h̲,* "The Hidden" Idrīs, also travelled a great deal, making frequent trips as a merchant to "Belgrade (Belgrad), Plovdiv (Filibe), Sofia, Edirne and Gallipoli (Gelibolı)" (ʿAṭāʾī, *op. cit.,* 602). It is likely that travelling *s̲h̲ayk̲h̲s* such as these both spread the sect and maintained contact between members in different regions. By whatever means it spread, it is clear that by about 1560 Malāmī doctrines had reached and had become deep-rooted in Bosnia. There is no obvious reason why this should have been so, but it is worth noting that pre-Ottoman Bosnia had been a centre of dualist Christianity, with remnants of the Bogomil sect surviving into the Ottoman period, showing that Bosnia had long been receptive to heterodox forms of religion.

The Malāmī *s̲h̲ayk̲h̲* Ḥamza, a *k̲h̲alīfa* of Ḥusām al-Dīn, was a Bosnian by birth. His public preaching in Istanbul led to his execution there in 968/1561 and to an investigation of his followers in Bosnia, of whom "many were arrested and executed" (ʿAṭāʾī, *op. cit.,* 70-1). ʿAṭāʾī's report (*loc. cit.*) that a *baltad̲j̲ï* [*q.v.*] committed suicide in grief at his execution suggests that he, like Og̲h̲lan S̲h̲ayk̲h̲, had a following among the *ḳapïḳulï* troops.

The execution of Ḥamza, like the execution of Og̲h̲lan S̲h̲ayk̲h̲, had the effect of creating a new martyr, and one so revered that the Malāmatiyya came to be known as the Ḥamzawīs until the last days of the sect (Brown, *loc. cit.*). Nor did the persecutions in Bosnia after his death eliminate his followers in the area. In 981/1573, the year of similar investigations in Thrace, the Imperial *Dīwān* received reports about "disciples of the heretic Ḥamza, who was previously arrested and executed" and ordered the *sand̲j̲aḳ beyis* of Hercegovina (Hersek [*q.v.*]), Bosnia and Požega, and the *beylerbeyi* of Buda (Budin [*q.v.*]), to arrest and imprison them while awaiting further instructions (*Mühimme defteri,* xxii, 194). The authorities' efforts seem again to have been ineffective, since in 990/1582, the *ḳāḍīs* of Zvornik, Gracanica and Tuzla in Bosnia again investigated a group belonging to the "sect of Ḥamza, who was executed when his heresy was proven" (*Mühimme defteri,* xlvii, 185; xlviii, 151). At the same time, the government clearly continued to treat with suspicion adherents of the sect in the capital. At an unspecified date, it issued a *fermān* for the arrest of "The Hidden" Idrīs, after the "great *s̲h̲ayk̲h̲s* of the city", Sīwāsī Efendi and ʿÖmer Efendi, had publicly denounced him for heresy. Idrīs, however, avoided arrest by using his name Ḥād̲j̲d̲j̲ī ʿAlī Beg in public, rather than his *laḳab* [*q.v.*] of Idrīs, and by spending most of his time in the seclusion of his own house (ʿAṭāʾī, *op. cit.,* 602; Kātib Čelebi [*q.v.*],

Fedhleke, Istanbul 1286/1869-70, i, 373-4, after ʿAṭāʾī). The sect's last martyr was a certain Beshīr Agha who, together with "forty" disciples, was executed in Istanbul in 1073/1662-3. He apparently had a number of Ḥurūfīs in his following (A. Gölpınarlı, *op. cit.,* 128, 158-60, after Laʿlīzāde ʿAbd al-Bāḳī, *Sergüzesht*).

There are, however, indications that, by the time of Beshīr Agha, the Malāmatiyya had largely changed, or were changing their character to become an orthodox *ṭarīḳa* [*q.v.*]. The Bosnian Malāmī *shaykh* Ḥüseyn-i Lāmekānī (d. 1035/1625) (Kātib Čelebi, *op. cit.,* ii, 71), for example, while still defending the sect's gyrating dance with the same *ḥadīth* as Oghlan Shaykh had used, apparently upheld the primacy of the *Sharīʿa*: "[The believer] should be a Ḥanafī, a Sunnī and pious ..." (quoted by A. Gölpınarlı, *op. cit.,* 82). By the time of Laʿlīzāde (d. 1165/1751-2), the sect appears to have accepted without question the authority of the *Sharīʿa*. The report that the vizier Ferhād Pasha [*q.v.*] (d. 1004/1595) became a disciple or *murīd* of Ḥüseyn-i Lāmekānī is perhaps significant; as members of the Ottoman ruling establishment began to join the sect, it would, by definition, become orthodox.

The organisation and membership of the sect remains as obscure as the Malāmīs themselves obviously intended it to be. It is not clear, for example, whether one *ḳuṭb* [*q.v.*] could ever claim the allegiance of the entire sect. This was probably the case until the death of Benyāmīn (926/1520), when the order was confined to central Anatolia. ʿAṭāʾī (*op. cit.,* 65), however, gives him three *khalīfas*: his son Shaykh Ibrāhīm, Abū Leylī Shaykh Süleymān and the influential Pīr ʿAlī of Aḳsaray. He then lists three *khalīfas* of Pīr ʿAlī: Aḥmed the Cameleer, Pīr Aḥmed of Edirne (d. 1000/1591-2) and Shaykh Yaʿḳūb the *ḥelvā*-maker (d. 989/1581-2). The last two appear to have been too young to have been Pīr ʿAlī's personal disciples, but the number of apparently very long-lived Malāmī *shaykh*s whom he lists, and other peculiarities, cast doubt upon ʿAṭāʾī's chronology. Among Pīr ʿAlī's successors, one should also mention his son Ismāʿīl Oghlan Shaykh. Aḥmed the Cameleer's *khalīfa* Ḥusām al-Dīn, in turn claimed three *khalīfas*: the martyred Ḥamza, Ḥasan the Tailor, from Bursa (d. 1010/1601-2) and "The Hidden" Idrīs. Ḥüseyn-i Lāmekānī was a *khalīfa* of Ḥasan. The most influential *ḳuṭbs* down to 1024/1615 seem to have been ʿÖmer—Benyāmīn—Pīr ʿAlī and his son—Aḥmed—Ḥusām al-Dīn—Ḥamza—Ḥasan—Idrīs. However, another branch descended from Aḥmed the Cameleer: ʿAlāʾ al-Dīn of Vize (d. 970/1562-3) (for verses attributed to this *shaykh*, see A. Gölpınarlı, *Türk tasavvuf şiiri antolojisi,* Istanbul 1972, 119-31) and his *khalīfa* Ghaḍanfer Dede, who won acquittal in his trial for heresy. His successors were, in turn, Bālī Efendi of Vize, his son Ḥasan and Emir Efendi of Ḳāsim Pasha.

The number of *khalīfas* whom ʿAṭāʾī records after the death of Benyāmīn points to the success and spread of the sect from the time of Pīr ʿAlī. However, it is by no means certain that his list represents any kind of recognised succession or hierarchy within the order itself. The apparent confusion within the line of succession suggests that, as the sect spread over a wide area after 926/1520, it became less cohesive, with various *ḳuṭbs* acquiring fame and a personal following not universally recognised by all members. It is possible, for example, that the following of ʿAlāʾ al-Dīn, Ghaḍanfer Dede and Bālī Efendi did not extend beyond the region of Vize. The difficulty of communication within a widely-dispersed and underground order must have caused fragmentation, and the order probably had no recognised and formal hierarchy.

If information on the Malāmī leaders is inadequate, that on their followers is even more so. The recorded professions of the *shaykh*s suggests that it was largely a movement of artisans, although the verses and other writings of some of them suggest that they had received an education wider than a simple craft-training. The founder, ʿÖmer was a cutler, Shaykh Yaʿḳūb a *ḥelvā*-maker, Aḥmed a cameleer, and Ḥasan was a tailor who was "both director of a workshop, and intent upon guiding the people of the *ṭarīḳat*" (ʿAṭāʾī, *op. cit.,* 169). Ghaḍanfer Dede was a tanner, and "The Hidden" Idrīs made a fortune as a merchant, but had begun his career as an apprentice to his uncle, who was a tailor to the Grand Vizier Rüstem Pasha [*q.v.*] (ʿAṭāʾī, *op. cit.,* 602). The list of Bosnian suspects in 990/1582 (*Mühimme defteri, loc. cit.*) refers to two of them as knife-grinders (*čarkčí*), and to one of them as *khalīfa*, a title which, in this context, probably refers to that position in a craft-gild (*kalfa*). However, Oghlan Shaykh and Ḥamza seem also to have numbered *ḳapiḳulí* troops among their followers, and the 981/1573 investigations in Thrace suggest that it had spread beyond the towns to the villages of the area.

The doctrines of the sect, which could lead its members to claim a source of divine authority outside the *Sharīʿa*, imply that they also disavowed the authority of the Ottoman dynasty which claimed, as a source for its legitimacy, to "prepare the path for the precepts of the Manifest *Sharīʿa*". The clearest statement of opposition to the dynasty occurs in a poem by Aḥmed the Cameleer, which he almost certainly composed during the reign of Süleymān I [*q.v.*]: "If I could find the most minute message from your ruby lips / I would not buy the Kingdom of Solomon (Turkish: *Süleymān*) for the smallest coin" (quoted by A. Gölpınarlı, in *op. cit.,* 59). There is further evidence from the 990/1582 investigations in Bosnia. Part of the accusation against the group was simply that they had "declared lawful that which is *ḥarām*" and "associated with women outside the permitted degrees" (*Mühimme defteri, loc. cit.*). These accusations, while quite possibly true, are simply stereotyped phrases found in most indictments of heretics. However, the additional accusation that one of them claimed to be "the Sulṭān who had succeeded Sulṭān Ḥamza", while others claimed to be "viziers", a "*ḳāḍī*" and a "*defterdār*" [*q.v.*], does suggest that this group, at least, did regard itself as self-governing and beyond the authority of the Ottoman state, whose titles and organisation it mimicked. While any evidence produced in a heresy hunt is suspect, this piece does seem credible in that it does not fit into the stereotyped pattern of orthodox accusations.

Bibliography: Given in article.

(C. H. Imber)

MALANG (etymology uncertain: not Pandjābī, possibly Persian; in Urdu, *malangi,* masc. = "salt worker", fem. = "loose, wanton woman"), a term used in Muslim India, including in the Pandjāb but also in the Deccan, to denote wandering dervishes of the Ḳalandarī, *bī-sharʿ* or antinomian type [see ḲALANDAR, ḲALANDARIYYA]. Djaʿfar Sharīf [*q.v.*] at one place of his *Ḳānūn-i Islām* puzzlingly names their founder as Djalāl al-Dīn Bukhārī, Makhdūm-i Djahāniyān-i Djahāngasht [*q.v.*], and at another, as Djamandjatī, a disciple of Zinda Shāh Madār (*Islam in India,* ed. W. Crooke, London 1921, 141-2, 172-3,

290), but describes the term Malang as a general one for unattached religious mendicants.

Malangs aim at total distinctiveness from the external world, in which are included the prescriptions of the _Sh_arīʿa as followed by the more orthodox, *bā-_sh_arʿ* Ṣūfīs, in order to enter the inner spiritual world. Hence the use of hashish and other narcotics is common amongst them, as is the wearing of a particular style of dress and type of long hair arrangement, together with the use of bangles, rings and other feminine ornaments to symbolise the Malang's role as the bride of God, hence subservient to Him; cf. the descriptions of Dj̲aʿfar _Sh_arīf, *loc. cit.*

Bibliography: Dj̲aʿfar _Sh_arīf, see above; H. A. Rose, *A glossary of the tribes and castes of the Punjab and North West Frontier Province,* Lahore 1911-19, i, 579, iii, 57; M. T. Titus, *Indian Islam,* London 1930, 127, 130; Katherine Ewing, Malangs *of the Punjab, intoxication or* adab *as the path to God?*, in Barbara D. Metcalf (ed.), *Moral conduct and authority, the place of* adab *in South Asian Islam,* Berkeley, Los Angeles and London 1984, 357-71 (Ed.)

MALĀRYĀ, a neologism in Arabic for malaria, an infection of the blood by a minute plasmodium parasite. The disease is characterised clinically by fever, which is often periodic; varying degrees of anaemia; splenic enlargement; and various syndromes resulting from the physiological and pathological involvement of certain organs, including the brain, liver and kidneys. The severity of the disease is dependent on the age, health, and degree of immunity of the victim and the particular species of the plasmodium parasite. Under suitable environmental conditions, malaria is transmitted by the mosquito genus *Anopheles*; out of about 375 species of anopheline mosquitoes, more than 70 are vectors of the four species of human malaria, i.e. *P. falciparum, P. vivax, P. malariae,* and *P. ovale.* Although the geographical distributions of plasmodial and anopheline species are not uniform, malaria is today a serious endemic disease in most Islamic countries from North Africa to South-East Asia, evoking widespread eradiction programs.

Malaria seems to have originated in tropical Africa in prehistoric times. With the Neolithic revolution, the infection appears to have spread and established itself in the great centres of riverine civilisation in Mesopotamia, India, South China and the Nile valley, from which it invaded the Mediterranean littoral. From these five foci, malaria extended its hold over most of the tropical world and much of the land in the temperate climates. Moreover, it appears that high gene frequencies of abnormal haemoglobins were created that protected human population against malaria and allowed for the exploitation of malarious areas.

Considerable attention has been devoted to the history of malaria and its deleterious effects on Graeco-Roman civilisation. It would appear, that malaria became endemic in Greece and Italy at least by the 5th century B.C. Because of the prevalence of the disease, malarial symptoms were recorded in the Hippocratic corpus and later medical works (see W. H.S. Jones, *Malaria and Greek history,* Manchester 1909, ch. 3). Aside from simplistic cultural notions of degeneration, the major effects of malaria on a population are a high infant mortality rate and a reduction in its work efficiency.

A priori, malaria seems to have existed from late antiquity until modern times in most of the regions where Islam was established as the predominant religion. The spread of rice cultivation in the mediaeval period, especially, may have significantly augmented the disease. The history of malaria in Islamic society, however, has not been the subject of any systematic investigation. The medical literature, particularly, has not been studied with regard to malaria; in one instance, al-Rāzī gives a case that had been misdiagnosed as malarial (E. G. Browne, *Arabian medicine,* Cambridge 1921, 51 ff.; M. Meyerhof, *Thirty-three clinical observations by Rhazes (circa 900 A.D.),* in *Isis,* xxiii [1934], 332 f.). Generally, the descriptions of fevers (*ḥummayāt*) in Arabic medicine appear to be greatly dependent on the Greek medical tradition (see M. Meyerhof, *ʿAlī at-Ṭabarī's "Paradise of wisdom", one of the oldest Arabic compendiums of* medicine, in *Isis,* xvi [1931], 29 f.; idem, *The "Book of treasure", an early Arabic treatise on medicine,* in *Isis,* xiv [1930], 71 f.; M. Ullmann, *Die Medizin im Islam,* Leiden 1970, 42, 137 f., 214).

Bibliography: The literature on malaria—its epidemiology, treatment, and eradication—is quite extensive. Useful accounts include: G. Harrison, *Mosquitoes, malaria and man: a history of the hostilities since 1880,* New York 1978; L. W. Hackett, *Malaria in Europe. An ecological study,* London 1937; P. F. Russell, *Man's mastery of malaria,* London 1955. For a valuable description of the disease, see. B. Maegraith, "Malaria", in Adams and Maegraith, *Clinical tropical diseases*[6], Oxford 1976, ch. 6. The following works discuss malaria with special reference to Islamic countries: E. H. Ackerkneckt, *The history of malaria,* in *Ciba Symposia,* vii (1945), 38-68; J. L. Angel, *Porotic hyperostosis, anemias, malarias, and marshes in the prehistoric Eastern Mediterranean,* in *Science,* ser. 2, vol. cliii (1966), 760-3; E. N. Borza, *Some observations on malaria and the ecology of Central Macedonia in Antiquity,* in *American Journal of Ancient History,* iv (1979), 102-24; L. C. Bruce-Chwatt, *Paleogenesis and paleo-epidemiology of primate malaria,* in *Bulletin, WHO,* xxxii (1965), 363-87; P. A. Buxton, *Rough notes: anopheles mosquitoes and malaria in Arabia,* in *Transactions of the Royal Society of Tropical Medicine and Hygiene,* xxxviii (1944), 205-14; S. R. Christophers and H. E. Short, *Malaria in Mesopotamia,* in *Indian Journal of Medical Research,* viii (1921), 508-52; Ch. Comte, *Note sur l'historique de la lutte contre le paludisme en Tunisie (1903-1929),* in *Compte-Rendu du Deuxième Congrès International du Paludisme (Alger 1930),* ii, Algiers 1931, 117-25; W. Fisher, *Quelques facteurs géographiques de la répartition de la malaria en moyen-orient,* in *Annales de Géographie,* lxi (1952), 263-74; Hackett, *Conspectus of malaria incidence in Northern Europe, the Mediterranean region and the Near East,* in *Malariology,* ed. M. F. Boyd, Philadelphia and London 1948, ii, 788-99; A. Halawani and A. A. Shawarby, *Malaria in Egypt,* in *Journal of the Egyptian Medical Association,* xl (1957), 753-92; Hussameddin, *La lutte contre le paludisme en Turquie,* in *Compte-Rendu du Deuxième Congrès International du Paludisme (Alger 1930),* ii, 359-401; *International symposium on malaria in Rabat,* in *Wiadomosci parazytologiczne,* xx (1974), 900-3; S. Jarcho, *A cartographic and literary study of the word malaria,* in *Journal of the History of Medicine,* xxv (1970), 31-9; I. J. Kligler, *The epidemiology and control of malaria in Palestine,* Chicago 1930; Carol Laderman, *Malaria and progress: some historical and ecological considerations,* in *Social Science and Medicine,* ix (1975), 587-94; H. S. Leeson, *Anopheline surveys in Syria and Lebanon,* in *Anopheles and malaria in the Near East,* London School of Hygiene and Tropical Medicine Memoir no. 7, London 1950, 1-46; K. Lindberg, *Le paludisme dans l'Iran,* in *Acta Medica*

Scandinavica, cvii (1941), 547-78; W. H. R.
Lumsden and J. Yofe, *Anophelism and malaria in
Transjordan and in the neighbouring parts of Palestine and
Syria,* in *Anopheles and malaria in the Near East,*
47-108; T. T. Macan, *The anopheline mosquitoes of
Iraq and North Persia,* in *ibid.,* 109-220; M. Motabar,
I. Tabibzadeh and A. V. Manouchehri, *Malaria
and its control in Iran,* in *Tropical and Geographical
Medicine,* xxvii (1975), 71-8; A. A. Shawarby *et alii,
The response of malaria and its vectors to environmental
changes in the southern oases of U.A.R.,* in *Journal of the
Egyptian Public Health Association,* xlii (1967), 19-33;
H. Soulié, *Histoire du paludisme en Algérie,* in *Compte-
Rendu du Deuxième Congrès International du Paludisme
(Alger, 1930),* ii 420 ff.; S. Tomaszunas, *Human
milieu and malaria eradication in Afghanistan,* in *Przegl.
epidemiol.,* xxviii (1974), 139-48; A. R. Zahar,
*Review of the ecology of malaria vectors in the WHO
Eastern Mediterranean Region,* in *Bulletin, WHO,* 1
(1974), 427-40; J. de Zulueta, *Malaria and Mediterranean history,* in *Parasitologia,* xv (1973), 1-15; idem
and D. A. Muir, *Malaria eradication in the Near East,*
in *Transactions of the Royal Society of Tropical Medicine
and Hygiene,* lxvi (1972), 679-96. (M. W. DOLS)

AL-**MALAṬĪ**, ABU 'L-ḤUSAYN MUḤAMMAD B.
AḤMAD B. ʿABD AL-RAḤMĀN, S̲h̲āfiʿī *faḳīh* and
specialist in the Ḳurʾānic readings, born at
Malaṭya [*q.v.*] and died at ʿAsḳalān in 377/987,
whence the *nisba* of al-ʿAsḳalānī which he also bears.
He was the author of a *ḳaṣīda* of 59 verses on the
readings and the readers, in imitation of a poem by
Mūsā b. ʿUbayd Allāh al-K̲h̲āḳānī, but he deserves
the notice of Islamicists through his having left behind
one of the oldest treatises on heresiography, the *Kitāb
al-Tanbīh wa 'l-radd ʿalā ahl al-ahwāʾ wa 'l-bidaʿ,* which
has been edited and published on various occasions,
in particular, by S. Dedering, Bibl. Islamica, ix,
Istanbul-Leipzig 1936, and by Muḥammad Zāhid al-
Kawt̲h̲arī, Bag̲h̲dād 1388/1968.

Bibliography: Subkī, *Ṭabaḳāt al-S̲h̲āfiʿiyya,* ii,
112 (ed. Cairo 1384/1965, no. 111, iii, 77-8); Ibn
K̲h̲ayr al-Is̲h̲bīlī, *Fahrasa,* 73; Ibn al-Dj̲azarī,
Ṭabaḳāt al-ḳurrāʾ, ii, 67; Massignon, *Passion d'al-
Halladj,* 510; Ritter, in *Isl.,* xviii, 41; Ziriklī, *Aʿlām,*
vi, 202; Brockelmann, S I, 332, 348; H. Laoust,
L'hérésiographie musulmane sous les Abbasides, in *Cahiers
de Civilisation médiévale,* 1967, 157-78.   (ED.)

MALAṬYA, an old-established town of
eastern Anatolia, not far from the upper
Euphrates. It lies at the junction of important roads
(in antiquity: the Persian royal road and the
Euphrates route; in modern times Samsūn-Siwās-
Malaṭya-Diyārbakr and Ḳayṣariyya-Albistān-
Malaṭya-K̲h̲arpūt) in a plain (the fertility and richness
of which in all kinds of vegetables and fruits was
celebrated by the Arab geographers, as in modern
times by von Moltke and others) at the northern foot
of the Taurus, not very far south of Tok̲h̲ma-sū
(Arabic Nahr al-Ḳubāḳib), which is there crossed by
the old bridge of Ḳīrkgöz. The town was supplied with
drinking-water by the springs of ʿUyūn Dāwūdiyya
and by the Euphrates. Weaving used to be a
flourishing industry there; according to Ibn al-
S̲h̲iḥna, there were once 12,000 looms for spinning
wool in Malaṭya, but they no longer existed in his
time. Its attitude is 2,900 ft./884 m.

1. Pre-Ottoman history.

The town appears as Melidda in Assyrian cuneiform
inscriptions and two "Hittite" stelae have been found
there (to be more accurate: at Arslān Tepe, a little
south of Malaṭya: Messerschmidt, *Corpus Inscr. Het-*

titic., in *MVAG* [1900], part iv, 13; [1906], part v, 7).
It is probably also to be identified with the district
called *M-l-z* (last letter uncertain) in the inscription of
king *Z-k-r* of Hamāt (*ca.* 800 B.C.) which Pognon
found in ʿAfis near Aleppo. Pliny (*Nat. hist.,* vi, 8)
calls the town *Melita a Samiramide condita;* the name of
the legendary foundress has perhaps survived in that
of the fortress of S̲h̲amrīn which Michael the Syrian
(*Chronicle,* tr. Chabot, iii, 272) mentions in the 12th
century in the land of Sawād in the region of Malaṭya.
To its position on the Oriental *limes* Malaṭya owed its
great prosperity in the Roman period. From the time
of Titus it was the headquarters of the *Legio XII
Fulminata;* it was much extended by Trajan, and
under Justinian raised to be the capital of the province
of Armenia III. Anastasius and Justinian refortified
and beautified it. After his severe defeat at Malaṭya in
the autumn of 575, K̲h̲usraw I Anūs̲h̲irwān burned
the town (John of Ephesus, vi, 9; E. Stein, *Studien zur
Gesch. d. Byzant. Reiches,* Stuttgart 1919, 66-8, 83 n. 9).

In the period of the early Arab conquests, Ḥabīb b.
Maslama al-Fihrī first took Malaṭya, but when
Muʿāwiya became governor of Syria, he had to send
Ḥabīb again to Malaṭya in 36/656-7, and he then captured it by storm. It subsequently became one of the
frontier fortresses [see ʿAWĀṢIM, T̲H̲UG̲H̲ŪR] and was
used as a base for the summer campaigns into Byzantium. In the time of ʿAbd al-Malik, it reverted to the
Greeks, and was resettled by Armenian and Nabaṭī
(i.e. Aramaic-speaking) peasants. In the course of the
2nd/8th century, Malaṭya was once more occupied by
the Muslims, rebuilt by His̲h̲ām, razed to the ground
by Constantine VI Copronymos in 133/750 and then
again rebuilt by al-Manṣūr's governor of al-Dj̲azīra
and the marches, ʿAbd al-Wahhāb b. Ibrāhīm b.
Muḥammad, the caliph's nephew. The same pattern
of struggles for possession of the town continued
throughout the subsequent ʿAbbāsid period, with control of it oscillating between the Arabs and the Greeks,
with an intermediate element in the 3rd/9th century
in the shape of the Paulician heretics (Arabic, *al-
Bayālika*), who lived to the north and west of Malaṭya
and who were often aided by the Muslims against the
Byzantines, e.g. by the *amīr* of Malaṭya ʿUmar b.
ʿAbd Allāh al-Aḳṭaʿ. Then in the 4th/10th century,
the Domestikos Joannes Kurkuas (in Ibn al-At̲h̲īr,
viii, 221, al-Dumistiḳ Ḳurḳās̲h̲), himself of Armenian
origin, seems to have granted Malaṭya and Samosata
(Sumaysāṭ [*q.v.*]) to the Armenian prince Mleh
(Arabic, Malīḥ; Greek, Melías), who was however
driven out of the two towns in 320/932 by the Ḥamdānid Saʿīd al-Dawla of Mawṣil. When Nicephorus
Phocas reconquered Syria, he wished to rebuild and
to repopulate Malaṭya with Greek settlers, but they
refused to live there because of the town's exposure to
Arab raids; hence Syrian Jacobites were in 969 invited
to settle there, with the result that by the year 1100
there were said to be 53 churches in Malaṭya and its
district and 60,000 Jacobite and Melkite Christians
capable of bearing arms (Michael of Tinnīs and
Barhebraeus).

During the years of Byzantine re-occupation,
Malaṭya was held for a time by the rebel and claimant
to the imperial throne Bardas Scleros (366/976-7), but
in the following century began the attacks of the
Turkmens. The first raid is recorded in the Syriac and
Armenian sources as taking place in 1058, or slightly
earlier in the reign of Constantine IX, and soon the
Greeks were being by-passed by Turkmens raiding as
far as Kayseri and beyond, making their tenure of
Malaṭya impossible. Hence it was held for a while by
the Armenian Philaretos as the centre of his

ephemeral principality on the *thughūr,* under caliphal protection. Despite help from the Frankish Crusaders, recently established in Edessa, Malaṭya was captured by the Turkmen *amīr* of Sīwās Gümüshtigin b. Dānishmend [see DĀNISHMENDIDS] in Dhu 'l-Ḳaʿda 494/September 1101. There were now several contenders for control of the area, including the Dānishmendids, the Saldjūḳs of Rūm, the Mengüdjekids of Kemākh [*q.v.*], the Franks of Edessa and the Greek Comnenoi emperors. By the end of the 6th/12th century, the Saldjūḳs were generally the holders of power there, in alliance with the Ayyūbids. In 628/1231 the Mongols penetrated to Ḥiṣn Ziyād and the neighbourhood of Malaṭya, and after their victory at Köse Dagh [*q.v.*] near Sīwās in 641/1243, Malaṭya was on two occasions besieged by the Mongols and its vicinity laid waste; then in the time of the Il-Khān Abaḳa (663-80/1265-82), Malaṭya fell within the share of the Saldjūḳ sultanate of Rūm allotted, under Mongol suzerainty, to Ghiyāth al-Dīn Masʿūd b. ʿIzz al-Dīn Kay Kāwūs. It is from the Saldjūḳ period that the oldest monument in Malaṭya, the Ulu Djāmiʿ, stems.

In the 12th and 13th centuries lived the two great Syriac historians, both born in Malaṭya, to whose chronicles we mainly owe our knowledge of the history of the town: the patriach Michael I (1126-99), son of the priest Eliyā, who belonged to the family of Kindasī in Malaṭya and the Mafrʿyān Gregor Abu 'l-Faradj called Barhebraeus (1226-86 [see IBN AL-ʿIBRI]), whose father, the baptised Jewish physician Ahrōn, had restrained his fellow citizens in Malaṭya from stupidly flying before the Tatars (Baumstark, *Gesch. d. syr. Lit.,* 298-300, 312-20). Michael's principal authority, Ignatius (d. 1104), was also metropolitan of Malaṭya (Baumstark, *op cit.,* 291).

The increasing weakness of the Saldjūḳs about 1300 favoured the formation of local Turkmen and Armenian petty states, especially in the east of Asia Minor. According to Abu 'l-Fidāʾ, Christians and Muslims in Malaṭya in those days lived on the best of terms with one another; the town took the side of the Tatars and informed them of everything that went on in the country. During his war against the Tatars, Sulṭān al-Malik al-Nāṣir Muḥammad b. Ḳalāwūn in 715/1315 decided to send a large army under the *nāʾib* of Damascus, Sayf al-Dīn Dengiz, who was joined by his vassal Abu 'l-Fidāʾ of Ḥamāt, against Malaṭya. The army went by Ḥalab, ʿAynṭāb, Ḥiṣn Manṣūr and Zibaṭra to Malaṭya and encamped before the town on 28 April. The inhabitants sent their *ḥākim* Djamāl al-Dīn al-Khiḍr, whose father and grandfather had filled the same office in their time, through the south gate, Bāb al-Ḳāḍī, to Dengiz, who was willing to afford them protection and security, if they surrendered the town. But he was unable to fulfil his pledge, for the soldiers could not be restrained from plundering and ravaging in the town. Among the prisoners was the Tatar Ibn Kerboghāʾ and the *ṣāḥib* of Ḥiṣn Arkanāʾ, Shaykh Mindū. The greater part of the town was finally burned down (Abu 'l-Fidāʾ, *Annales Moslemici,* ed. Reiske, v, 286-92; ed. Istanbul 1286, iv, 77-8; tr. also in *Rec. hist. or. Crois.,* i, 180; Weil, *Gesch. d. Chalif.,* iv, 310-11). The sultan made the territory of Malaṭya a separate frontier province, which included seven districts (Khalīl al-Ẓāhirī, *Zubda,* ed. Ravaisse, 52). There were seven citadels around the town; Mūshār or Minshār, Kūmī, Ḳaraḥiṣār, Kadarbirt, Ḳalʿat Akdja, Ḳalʿat Nawḥamām (?) and Ḳalʿat al-Akrād (Khalīl, *op. cit.*; Gaudefroy-Demombynes, *La Syrie à l'époque des Mamelouks,* 97, 105).

Malaṭya for the next few decades belonged to the Mamlūk sultans. As their remotest province, it was with Ḥalab in 791/1389 the scene of a great rebellion led by the governors Minṭāsh and Yilboghā against Barḳūk [*q.v.*]. About this time, the Turkish family of the Dulghadir or Dhu 'l-Ḳadr-oghlu [see DHU 'L-ḲADR] began to rise to power in the region of Malaṭya and Albistān, where they ruled till 921/1515 under Mamlūk suzerainty. About 794/1391-2, Bāyezīd I conquered the town, and in 903/1400 Tīmūr. By the battle of Ḳōč Ḥiṣār (922/1516) it fell into the hands of Selīm I [*q.v.*] who destroyed the Dhu 'l-Ḳadr-oghlu. This was the cause of his war against Egypt, which was rapidly decided on the field of Mardj Dābiḳ [*q.v.*]. At a later date under the Ottomans, the *eyālet* to which the *sandjaḳ* of Malaṭya belonged was still called Dhu 'l-Ḳadrıyya.

Bibliography: Geography: Khʷārazmī, *Kitāb Ṣūrat al-arḍ,* ed. H. von Mžik in *Bibl. arab. Histor. u. Geogr.,* iii, Leipzig 1926, 25 (no. 366); Battānī, *Opus astronom.,* ed. Nallino, ii, 40, iii, 238 (no. 143); Iṣṭakhrī, 62; Ibn Ḥawḳal, ii, 120, Ibn al-Faḳīh, 114; Ibn Khurradādhbih, 97, 108, 173-4; Ḳudāma, 233, 254; Ibn Rusta, 97, 107; Yaʿḳūbī, *Buldān,* 238, 362; Masʿūdī, *Tanbīh,* 52, 58, 169, 183, 189; Idrīsī, ed. Gildemeister, in *ZDPV,* viii, 26; Yāḳūt, *Muʿdjam,* iv, 633; Ṣafī al-Dīn, *Marāṣid al-iṭṭilāʿ,* ed. Juynboll, iii, 144; Abu 'l-Fidāʾ, ed. Reinaud, 235; Ḥamd Allāh Mustawfī, tr. Le Strange, 98-9; Ḳalḳashandī, *Ṣubḥ al-aʿshāʾ,* iv, 131-2, 228; tr. in Gaudefroy-Demombynes, *La Syrie à l'époque des Mamelouks,* Paris 1923, 97, 217; Ibn al-Shiḥna, *al-Durr al-muntakhab fī taʾrīkh Ḥalab,* tr. A. v. Kremer, in *Denkschr. Akad. Wien,* iii (1850), 42-3; W. M. Ramsay, *The historical geography of Asia Minor,* London 1890, index; Le Strange, *Palestine under the Moslems,* 499-500 and index; idem, *The lands of the eastern caliphate,* Cambridge 1905, 120; E. Reitemeyer, *Die Städtegründungen der Araber im Islam,* Munich 1912, 79-80; E. Honigmann, *Die Ostgrenze des Byzantinischen Reiches,* Brussels 1935, index.

History: Pauly-Wissowa, xxix, 549-50; Balādhurī, *Futūḥ,* 184-8, 190, 199; Abu 'l-Fidāʾ, *Annales Moslemici,* ed. Reiske, ii, 4, 10, v, 286; Michael the Syrian, *Chronicle,* ed. and tr. J.-B. Chabot, index, 50; Barhebraeus, *Chronicon syriacum,* ed. Bedjan, Paris 1890, *passim*; Ibn al-Athīr, *al-Kāmil,* index, ii, 813; Yaḥyā b. Saʿīd al-Anṭākī, ed. Rosen, 1-3, 20, 49 (= 1-3, 22, 51 of the Russian tr.), in *Zapiski Imper. Akad. Nauk.,* xliv (1883); Ibn Bībī, in Houtsma, *Recueil de textes rel. à l'histoire des Seldjoucides,* iv, index, 358; Cl. Cahen, *Pre-Ottoman Turkey,* London 1968, index.

(E. HONIGMANN)

2. The Ottoman and modern periods.

Reliable information on the size of Malaṭya begins with the 10th/16th century. A first list of taxable inhabitants was prepared in 924/1518, shortly after the end of Mamlūk rule. In 929/1522-3, the town possessed 1,540 taxpayers, who probably represented a total population of 6,900-7,000 inhabitants. Almost forty years later, in 967/1559-60, the number of taxpayers had risen to 1,946. By this time, the total population should have amounted to about 8,700 inhabitants.

Malaṭya's commercial importance during the 10th/16th century was great enough to warrant the construction of a covered market (*bedestān*). In addition, the existence of a bridge toll collected at the Ḳırkgöz bridge, a Saldjūḳ structure over which the road to Sīwās crossed the Tokhma Ṣuyu, equally shows that 10th/16th century Malaṭya played a certain role in local and interregional trade. Moreover, it seems also during this period to have possessed at least one major *khān* [*q.v.*]. Of the constructions which existed in the middle of the 10th/16th century and produced appreciable revenues for the Sultan's treasury, nothing at present remains. But in 1046/1636-7, Sultan Murād IV's *ḳapudan-i deryā*, Silāḥdār Muṣṭafā Pasha, had a new *khān* constructed, which survives today and about whose original shape ample information can be found in contemporary documents. This *khān*, in which several hundreds of camels could be stabled, probably possessed military as well as commercial functions.

For the 11th/17th and 12th/18th centuries, only indirect information concerning the population of Malaṭya is available. In *ca.* 1068/1657-8, the town consisted of 293 taxable units (*ʿawāriḍ-khāne*). At the beginning of the 12th/18th century, the town consisted of almost 100 taxable units (*ʿawāriḍ-khāne*), while the number of houses inhabited by tax-paying families amounted to about 370. Even if a large number of people lived in one house, the town must have declined appreciably between 967/1559-60 and the early 12th/18th century.

Throughout the 11th/17th century, Malaṭya, as described by travellers such as Ewliyā Čelebi and Kātib Čelebi, appears to have functioned primarily as a marketing centre for the fruit and other agricultural produce grown on the rich irrigated land surrounding the town. In summer, most of the inhabitants moved out of Malaṭya proper to live among their gardens and vineyards. This custom gave rise to the development of summer settlements, among which Aspuzu gradually took on the characteristics of a separate town.

Both the gradual decline of Malaṭya, and the rise of Aspuzu were accelerated by eternal factors. In 1838-9 the Ottoman army under Ḥāfiẓ Pasha, on campaign against the Egyptian forces of Muḥammad ʿAlī and his son Ibrāhīm, established winter quarters in Malaṭya. The townsmen were therefore obliged to spend the winter in their summer settlement, and after their return found that the town had been too badly destroyed to make reconstruction worthwhile. As a result, the name as well as the old foundations of Malaṭya were gradually transferred to Aspuzu. The old settlement, first known as Eskishehir and later as Eski Malaṭya, continued to exist as a good-sized village and *nāḥiya* centre.

Similar to other Anatolian towns, Malaṭya toward the end of the 19th and the beginning of the 20th century went through a period of growth. Before the beginning of World War I, population had increased to 40,000. But the economic difficulties of the war years caused a sharp decline, and the first population count of the Turkish Republic in 1927 recorded only about 20,000 inhabitants. However, in the subsequent years, the town soon recovered and then surpassed its previous level, to become one of the most rapidly growing cities of Turkey. According to the census of 1975, Malaṭya possessed a population of 154,505, thereby ranking as a major provincial centre.

Bibliography: Among unpublished documents, see particularly the Ottoman tax registers Tapu Tahrir nos. 387, 408, 257 (Başbakanlık Arşivi, Istanbul) and Tapu Kadastro Genel Müdürlüğü, Kuyudu Kadime no. 146 (Ankara). Compare also the *ḳāḍī* registers of 1068/1657-8, p. 198, and 1129-33/1716-21, pp. 121-30 (photostat copies in Orta Doğu Teknik Üniversitesi Library, Ankara). The Ottoman period, with particular emphasis on geographical factors, has been treated by Besim Darkot in his *İA* article s.v. (fundamental; excellent bibliography). Further references include: Ewliyā Čelebi, *Seyāḥat-nāmesi*, ed. Aḥmed Djevdet *et alii*, 10 vols., 1313/1895-6 to 1935, iv, 7-20; Kātib Čelebi, *Djihān-numā*, Istanbul 1145/1732-3), 600, *Malatya il yıllığı*, 1967, Ankara; W. F. Ainsworth, *Travels and researches in Asia Minor, Mesopotamia, Chaldea, and Armenia*, 2 vols. London 1842, i, 252-6; Ch. Texier, *Description géographique, historique et archéologique des provinces et des villes de la Chersonnèse d'Asie*, Paris 1862, 586-9; Helmuth von Moltke, *Briefe über Zustände und Begebenheiten in der Türkei*, Berlin 1877, 297 ff.; V. Cuinet, *La Turquie d'Asie. Géographie administrative. Statistique descriptive et raisonnée de chaque province de l'Asie Mineure*, 4 vols. Paris 1891-4, ii, 369-75; *Murray's handbook, Asia Minor, Transcaucasia, Persia, etc.*, London 1895, 256-7; G. L. Bell, *Amurath to Amurath*, London 1911, 336-8; E. Banse, *Die Türkei. Eine moderne Geographie*, Brunswick 1916, 223-4; E. Chaput, *Voyages d'études géologiques et géomorphogéniques en Turquie*, Istanbul 1936, 134 ff.; A. Gabriel, *Voyages archéologiques dans la Turquie orientale*, 2 vols. Paris 1940, i, 263-75, 352-4; ii, 94-7; Zeki Oral, *Malatya kitabeleri ve tarihi*, in *III Türk Tarih Kongresi, Kongreye sunulan tebliğler*, Ankara 1948, 434-40; Celal Yalvaç, *Eski Malatya Ulu Camii*, in *Türk Yurdu*, v (1966), 22-9; M. Oluş Arık, *Malatya Ulu Camiinin asli planı ve tarihi hakkında*, in *Vakıflar Dergisi*, viii (1969), 141-5; Erol Özbilgen, *Eski Malatya'da Silahdar Mustafa Paşa Hanı'nin restitüsyonu hakkında*, in *Tarih Enstitüsü Dergisi*, i (1970), 93-102; Nejat Göyünç, *Eski Malatya'da silahdar Mustafa Paşa Hanı*, in *Tarih Enstitüsü Dergisi*, i (1970), 63-92; idem, *Silahdar Mustafa Paşa Hanına ait bir vesika*, in *Tarih Dergisi*, xxv (1971), 73-8; idem, *Kanuni devrinde Malatya şehri*, in *VII Türk Tarih Kongresi, Kongreye sunulan bildiriler*, 2 vols. Ankara 1973, ii, 654-9; Cevet Çulpan, *Türk taşköprüleri, Ortacağdan Osmanlı devri sonuna kadar*, Ankara 1975, 119-20.

(S. Faroqhi)

MALAY PENINSULA. 1. Geographical considerations. The Malay peninsula, together with the Borneo states of Sabah (formerly North Borneo) [see BORNEO in Suppl.] and Sarawak, became the Federation of Malaysia in 1963. The population of the Federation in 1977 was estimated at 12.74 million, of whom 10.5 million lived on the peninsula, and the ethnic composition (according to 1970 census figures) was approximately: Malay 46.8%, Chinese 34.1%, Indians 9%, Dayaks (including Ibans) 3.7%, Kadazan 1.8%, other native groups 3.2%, and others (Eurasians, Arabs, Siamese, Filipinos, Indonesians, etc.) 1.4%. While almost all Malays, Indonesians, and some of the native groups are Sunnī Muslims of the Shāfiʿī school, the other ethnic communities are mainly Christian, Buddhist and Hindu. "Peninsular Malaysia", as the Malay peninsula is officially known to distinguish it from the Borneo half, covers some 131,794 square kilometres and comprises the eleven states of Perlis, Kedah, Penang, Perak, Selangor (in which is located the separate Federal Capital Territory of Kuala Lumpur), Malacca, Johor, Negri Sembilan, Pahang, Trengganu and Kelantan.

Peninsular Malaysia's unique location explains much about its prominent role in the history of Islam in Southeast Asia. Lying athwart the Straits of Malacca, the Malay peninsula is the southernmost extension of mainland Southeast Asia and forms, with the islands of the Indonesian archipelago, a large breakwater between the Pacific and Indian Oceans. Until the advent of air travel, seaborne traffic moving between the major civilisations of the East and the West was forced to sail through either the Sunda Straits, separating the Indonesian islands of Java and Sumatra, or the Malacca Straits. The latter was indeed almost the only passageway used until the Sunda Straits became better known in the 10th/16th century, with the invention of ships capable of open sea sailing and with the discovery of the winds known as the "Roaring Forties", enabling ships to sail quickly and easily from east coast Africa to Indonesia.

The Malay peninsula is also strategically located in terms of the seasonal monsoon winds circulating over the Indian Ocean and the China Sea. With the onset of the southwest monsoon in April, the winds blow from the Indian Ocean on to the Sumatra coast then in May across the Malay peninsula. While this monsoon gradually decreases, the northeast monsoon develops in the northern part of the South China Sea in October. It reaches a peak in January, when it covers all equatorial Southeast Asia except for Java and southern Sumatra, and then slowly lessens in intensity until the cycle begins again in April. Sailing ships in earlier centuries were dependent upon these winds to move quickly between east and west, and experienced mariners soon realised that the Straits of Malacca were ideal as a harbouring place because they were sheltered from the winds and were the beginning and end points of the monsoons.

Another important geographical consideration is the Malay peninsula's virtually inaccessible interior and its long coastlines. Along the whole length of the peninsula for about 483 km is a north-south mountain range varying between 914 and 2,134 m. above sea level. This main range and inhospitable interior jungles have been the main barriers to trans-peninsular contact by land. On the opposite shore of the Straits, in Sumatra, fairly similar conditions are found. From very early on, therefore, inhabitants living on the Malay peninsula and east-coast Sumatra have regarded the rivers and seas around them as the primary means of contact with one another. The Straits of Malacca between the west coast of the peninsula and the east coast of Sumatra became an internal lake linking the people living in lands adjoining it and helping to create a basically common culture. Communication between these peoples was often even closer than that between those living on the west and east coasts of the peninsula itself.

2. Early contact with the outside world. It is generally accepted that by the 2nd century A.D. there were Indian traders in the area of the Straits. The search for gold may have provided the initial impetus, but soon a profitable exchange of local products with Indian goods sustained the trade. The participation of the Chinese and other traders from the East and the Indonesian archipelago, all using the Straits as a convenient harbouring place and later exchange site, was an added attraction to Indian traders. Enterprising native chieftains quickly seized the opportunity to make their particular settlement the centre of trade. The few places which developed into major entrepôts had responded successfully to the demands of foreign merchants and provided the physical facilities and the legal and governmental apparatus to assure the rapidity, fairness and security of trade.

Through contact with Indians, the Malays were introduced to religio-political and cultural ideas which struck a familiar chord, since both societies shared a basic Monsoon Asian belief system. What was different and hence attractive to the locals was the elaboration and refinement of these ideas from India which had been a result of the incorporation of the Indo-European Aryan culture to local Monsoon Asian belief. Although little is known of how this "Indianisation" process occurred in the Malay areas, its success can be gauged by the survival of Indian terms, themes, and practices in present-day Malay language, literature and court ceremonies. India, then, was regarded from early times by Malays as the homeland of a rich culture worthy of consideration and emulation.

China's contact with the Malay peninsula was much more limited since it only began using a sea route to the West from about the 5th century A.D. Even then, China's political philosophy regarding the self-sufficiency of the kingdom discouraged official involvement in international trade. Nevertheless, some trade under various guises and rationalisations did occur and was carried on principally by Persians and Arabs in the first millenium A.D. Only later in the period of the famous Ming voyages of the late 8th/14th and early 9th/15th centuries did the Malay areas begin to appreciate the splendour and the might of the culture from China. Like India, China now became regarded by Malays as a respectable source of goods and ideas.

A third group to have visited the Malay areas in earlier centuries was the Arabs. By the 3rd/9th century, Arab traders knew a large part of Southeast Asia, but appeared to have neglected this area in favour of the lucrative China trade. Although Arab sources mention the northwestern and eastern coasts of Sumatra, the Malacca Straits down to Palembang, Johor, part of the Riau-Lingga archipelago and Pulau Tioman, there is no hint of organised Arab trade with these areas until the mid-4th/mid-10th century. By the 7th/13th century, Arab trade to Southeast Asia was all but superseded by that of their Muslim brethren from India, and it is to them that the spread of Islam through the archipelago is generally attributed.

3. The coming of Islam to the Malay lands. The Malay areas were accustomed to regard India as a source of respectable and exciting ideas, and they welcomed Indians bearing tidings of Islam in the same way that they had greeted their predecessors with their Hindu-Buddhist ideas. Although the question as to which Indian group was responsible for the conversion of Southeast Asia may never be answered conclusively, the direct relationship between trade and the spread of Islam is rarely denied. After the fall of Bag͟hdād and the destruction of the ʿAbbāsid caliphate by the Mongols in 657/1258, the spice route from the east through the Persian Gulf, up to the Levantine coast, and thence to northern Europe, was effectively closed. A new route now went from the east to India, then to Aden in southern Arabia, through the Red Sea up to Alexandria, and thence northward. Since the authorities in Egypt refused any but Muslim trading as far as Alexandria, the Muslim ports of Cambay, Surat and Diu in Gud͟jarāt province of India acquired great importance as trans-shipment centres for spices. Growing demand for Eastern spices by a prosperous Renaissance Europe and the cessation from the 8th/14th century of direct Chinese trade to India brought the Gud͟jarātī merchants into great prominence as intermediaries in the spice trade. Their great numbers in Malacca [*q.v.*], the major emporium in the Malay-Indonesian archipelago in the 9th/15th and early 10th/16th centuries, facilitated the work of Muslim missionaries in spreading the ideas of Islam in the region. By the beginning of the 10th/16th cen-

tury, in addition to the thousand or so Gudjarātī merchants resident in the city of Malacca, there were about three to four thousand others always en route between this port and those in Gudjarāt. But the Gudjarātīs did not have the exclusive control of trade to Southeast Asia. There were substantial numbers of other Indian traders from the Malabar [*q.v.*] and Coromandel Coasts in South India, as well as from Bengal. In fact, some of the strongest arguments, based on local traditions and survival of certain religious terms, have been made for a Southern Indian origin of the Islamic ideas which came to Southeast Asia.

A theory has recently been advanced which does not attempt to single out any particular group for the honour of bringing Islam to Malay shores. Instead, it suggests that there was a general Islamic "fall-out" around the shores of the Indian Ocean which "showered" the Malay areas. When the Portuguese fleet rounded the Cape of Good Hope in 904/1498, they entered what has been described as an "Arabic-speaking Mediterranean". The extensive trading network which stretched from east-coast Africa to India was dominated by Muslims, and Arabic was the *lingua franca.* Malays had already long been a part of this trading world in which the Muslim network was simply the latest development. A 6th/12th century Arab account mentions Malays from Zābag (identified with Srīvijaya, a kingdom which flourished in the Straits of Malacca area between the 1st/7th and 8th/14th centuries) participating in the trade to east coast Africa, while an 8th/14th century Arabic source describes a trip from China to Sumatra on a junk manned by Malays. The latter had moved from being simply engaged in facilitating the trade of others to active traders themselves. They, therefore, according to this theory of "fall-out", were already subject to Islamic ideas prevalent in the Indian Ocean area.

Another theory concerning the coming of Islam to the Malay lands points to an easterly route, from China to Champa in central Vietnam and then to the western half of the Malay-Indonesian archipelago. The participation of Muslim Arabs and Persians as shippers for the Chinese traders in earlier centuries, and the later direct involvement of Malays in the trade to China, would have provided the vehicle for movement of ideas from Muslims in China to these trading intermediaries. Early Chinese contacts with the Malay areas, especially with the 9-10th/15-16th century kingdom of Malacca, had already made such an avenue for ideas both acceptable and respectable.

4. The adoption of Islam by Malay society. A foreign Muslim trading colony is said to have existed at some time in the 4th/10th century in Kalah [*q.v.*] a place tentatively located in the northern part of the Malay peninsula. Other evidence of early Muslim activity on the peninsula itself is scattered and difficult to corroborate. In 1965 a Muslim tombstone was found in Kedah bearing the Arabic date 291 A.H. (903 A.D.). Another find was a gold coin in Kelantan in 1914, which local Islamic scholars claim dates from a 6th/12th century Muslim kingdom in that state. But the most interesting and reliable discovery of early Muslim activity in the peninsula is the Trengganu Stone, dated between 703/1303 and 788-9/1386-7. The stone, which was intended as a pillar, contains the oldest Malay text in the Perso-Arabic script. It refers to certain Islamic laws in a way which indicated that the population, if converted, was not yet deeply Muslim. However, the first evidence accepted by historians as indicating sustained local Muslim activity in the Straits of Malacca is not on the peninsula but on Sumatra, where Marco Polo in 692/1292 mentioned a Muslim town in Perlak on the northeastern coast.

The manner in which Islam, once brought to the Straits area through the trading connection, took root is still a matter of speculation. If the Indianisation process, though imperfectly known, can be used as a guide, there had to be certain perceived benefits which the new religion or religio-political ideas could confer on the receiving society. There are some who have argued that the rulers of the Malay areas were attracted by the resplendent titulary and traditions of the Perso-Islamic kingship which had arrived via India. An epithet borrowed from the Babylonian rulers, "God's Shadow on Earth", became incorporated into the titles of the Muslim rulers, as did the Persian title of Shāh. From Baghdād to Morocco and from the north of India in Dihlī to the south in Madura, Muslim rulers assumed grandiloquent titles or *laḳabs* [*q.v.*] to mark their uniqueness. To belong to such a distinguished company and to acquire the appellations and ceremonies associated with this new religion would have appealed to a Malay ruler, always awake to the possibilities of enhancing his position.

Another perceived benefit of Islam among the local ruling classes would have been the prospects of closer economic links with the powerful and prosperous Muslim kingdoms, whence came most of the traders to the Malay areas. After Malacca's foundation some time in the beginning of the 9th/15th century, it vied with a number of centres to become the dominant entrepôt in the region. One of its competitors was Pasai on the northeastern coast of Sumatra which had accepted Islam toward the end of the 8th/14th century. Malacca's rulers may have justifiably attributed Pasai's prosperity to the presence of large numbers of Muslim Indian cloth merchants in that city. Since Indian cloth was an essential component of the complex exchange system which operated in the Southeast Asian region, any ruler able to attract Indian cloth merchants was assured of a lucrative trade in his port. As an Islamic city, Pasai offered to Muslim traders mosques and the protection of an Islamic ruler, advantages which neighbouring non-Muslim kingdoms were unable to match. For Malacca's rulers, therefore, there seemed much to gain and little to lose by embracing this new faith.

While the paraphernalia of Perso-Islamic kingship and hopes of increased trade with powerful Muslim kingdoms may have been appreciated by the ruling classes, such arguments would have probably been insufficient to convince many of the common folk. In some areas in the Malay-Indonesian archipelago, local sources indicate that, despite the conversion of the rulers, some resistance to Islam was encountered among the common people. But initial distrust gave way to cautious acceptance as the people began to view Islam as yet another source of ideas and spiritual power to strengthen the community.

One reason for the success of the proselytisation effort among the people may be attributed to Ṣūfism. The impressive flourishing in 10-11th/16-17th century Atjèh in north Sumatra of Ṣūfī ideas has given rise to the suggestion that Ṣūfism may have been the vehicle by which Islam became the religion of the archipelago. Ṣūfism's moderate religious demands, incorporation of local pre-Islamic beliefs, and similarity to certain existing spiritual practices are seen as positive factors in its general acceptance. In the Malay areas the Ṣūfī recitation of prescribed prayer formulae (*awrād,* sing. *wird*) resembled local incantations to the spirits; the trance-inducing Ṣūfī sessions of the *dhikr* [*q.v.*] were similar to the seances of the local shaman (*pawang*); and the healing powers attributed to the Ṣūfī were a trait also associated with the traditional village doctor (*bomoh*). The successful co-existence of Islamic and local spirit practices is clearly demonstrated in a 12th/18th century Malay text from Perak, the *Misa Melayu*. It describes how, when the sultan was ill, prayers were offered to the Prophet, the saints, as well as the ancestors. *Pawang*s commonly ascribed their incantations to the Hindu deities Śiva and Brahma, as well as to Luḳmān al-Ḥakīm, father of Arabian magic [see LUḲMĀN]. Among Malay farmers today there are various *Kitab Tib,* Islamic works on magic, saint worship, and other practices considered to be only vaguely Muslim. One of the most well-known of these works is the *Taj ul-Muluk* (*Tādj al-mulūk*) respected among Malay farmers as the standard source on Islamic magic.

Another factor which may have facilitated conversion to Islam was the introduction of Muslim tales into the already vast international repertory of stories found among the Malays. Tales of Islamic heroes appealed to the people as much as the heroes of the well-known episodes from the Indian epics, the *Mahābhārata* and the *Rāmāyaṇa*. Stories of the lives of Muslim saints were a source of entertainment and religious edification, and treatises on magic and divination helped confirm Islam as another important, if not the most superior, source of spiritual power for the Malay community.

One other reason should be cited for the adoption of Islam as a religion among Malays. In all levels of society, there would have been people who would have understood the basic teachings of the religion and seen their value for this life and for that in the hereafter. For such people, the act of embracing Islam was a spiritual commitment to the basic tenets preached by the Prophet Muḥammad.

5. The role of Malays and the Malay language in the propagation of Islam. The conversion of Malacca to Islam [see MALACCA] was an important factor in that kingdom's rise to become one of the greatest commercial emporiums in the 9th/15th century world and the centre for the propagation of Islam to other areas of Southeast Asia. With Malacca as the hub of a vast international trading network, which included even the easternmost islands of the Indonesian archipelago, Malay and other traders prepared the way for more formal conversion by Muslim missionaries. Malacca's predominance on the Malay peninsula meant that Islam quickly became established as a religion in all the vassal courts and riverine settlements.

The incorporation of the Malay peninsula and other areas in the archipelago into the Muslim *ummat* provided a basis for united action against the Christian Europeans who began appearing in the area from the beginning of the 10th/16th century. But unity was more a hope than a reality, and in 917/1511 the famous entrepôt kingdom of Malacca fell to the Portuguese, to be replaced by new centres of power in the Muslim kingdoms of Atjèh [*q.v.*] in northern Sumatra and Banten in West Java [see INDONESIA]. Malacca's royal family roamed the wide reaches of their kingdom before finally settling at a site on the Johor River in the southern tip of the Malay peninsula. As the ruling house of the new kingdom of Johor, the Malacca dynasty continued to conduct itself in the manner of the former days of glory, but the direction in the Islamic world in the archipelago was shifting to the rising power of Atjèh.

At the court of Atjèh in the 11th/17th century, important religious tracts on Ṣūfī mysticism were being translated into Malay by such writers as Ḥamza Fanṣūrī, Shams al-Dīn, Nūr al-Dīn al-Rānīrī, and ʿAbd al-Raʾūf of Singkel [SEE INDONESIA. iv. History. (a) Islamic period]. Although Malay was not the mother tongue of any of these writers, it was the *lingua franca* in the archipelago as a result of Malacca's long dominance in the trading world. In order to reach the largest number of readers, these mystic scholars were forced to use Malay to explain Islamic concepts in a way which was comprehensible to those with only a limited understanding of Islam. Toward the end of the 12th/18th century, Malay theologians followed the trends in the Middle East and turned to the mysticism of al-Ghazālī. The latter's famous work, the *Iḥyāʾ ʿulūm al-dīn,* was translated into Malay over a ten-year period by ʿAbd al-Ṣamad of Palembang, while Dāwūd b. ʿAbd Allāh b. Idrīs of Patani also translated this work and al-Ghazālī's *Kitāb al-Asrār* and *Kitāb al-Ḳurba ilā Allāh* into Malay. For more serious debate within the Islamic world itself, these writers read, wrote, and discussed in Arabic.

For anyone wishing to go beyond the few rudiments of Islamic law and doctrine, a knowledge of Malay was essential. Even in those few manuals written in other regional languages there were numerous Malay words. But the more important information was contained in *kitab*s, which are works written in Malay but derived and compiled from Arabic sources. In general, only the introduction, the conclusion, and a few comments are the original work of the local "author", while the remainder is simply a translation. These *kitab*s were the principal tools of Islamic learning for many who were unable to read Arabic. One inhabitant in early 19th century Malacca describes how a poor Arab *sayyid* (Malay, *sayid*) from the Ḥaḍramawt with a knowledge of both Arab and Malay gave lessons on Islam for five dollars per year per pupil. The first text used was the *Ummu 'l-barahin* (*Umm al-barāhīn*), and then he went on to other manuscripts, all in Malay, to teach canon law, matters concerning prayers and similar devotional practices, various branches of Islamic knowledge and didactic stories. Malay, then, had become a language of Islam and an essential vehicle for the spread of religious ideas throughout the Southeast Asian Islamic world.

6. Impressions of Islamic institutions before the mid-19th century. There is very little material about Islam in the Malay peninsula before the early period of British rule in the mid-19th century. What one knows about Islamic institutions before this must perforce remain as impressions from scattered and often disparate evidence in Malay sources and contemporary European reports. It appears that one of the most important Islamic officials in the Malay states was the *kadi* (*ḳāḍī*). In early 12th/18th century Johor, the *kadi* was ranked next to the principal ministers as the most powerful individual in the kingdom. His respected status may have been a result of his Muslim learning, which would have still been considered to be a rare achievement in the Malay world at this time. Even in the early 19th century, an episode is related in the *Hikayat Abdullah* of how the rare appearance in Malacca of a learned *sayid* from Atjèh resulted in a virtual self-imposed seclusion of those who previously had claimed to be local religious scholars. The *kadi* appeared to have had close ties with the royal family and may even have married into local royalty. His knowledge of Islam would have made him in the eyes of the local people a superior individual with access to strong spiritual powers. But as the number of Muslim

teachers and scholars increased, especially in the second half of the 18th and 19th centuries, the *kadi* gradually lost his unique standing. Nevertheless, in the 19th century he was still described as "presiding over a number of mosques".

The only indication that one has of a religious hierarchy, although not necessarily an official one, is from the *Misa Melayu.* At the occasion of the opening of a new palace (*mahaligai*), which coincided with the Prophet Muḥammad's birthday, special celebrations were arranged with the secular and religious guests seated according to rank. On the first level was the sultan and his religious counterpart, the *sharif*; on the second level the nobles and the *ulama*; on the third level the court attendants and the *imam*; on the fourth level the district official (*hulubalang*) and the *khatib*; on the fifth level the official in charge of a settlement around a mosque (*penghulu mukim*) and the *bilal* (i.e. the muezzin); on the sixth level the ordinary people and the experts on religious matters (*lebai* and *alim*); and on the lowest level, the foreign traders, itinerant travellers and the religious mendicants (*fakir*).

The *sharif* family was especially honoured in Perak, but everywhere else in the Malay peninsula, descendants of the Prophet, whether *sayid* or *sharif* (Malays rarely distinguished between the two), generally were accorded a high place in society and even regarded as suitable marriage partners for the royal children. But pre-19th century sources rarely speak of them until the arrival of Ḥaḍramawt *sayid*s and *sharif*s in the archipelago from the mid-12th/18th century. Once again, as the *kadi* in Johor in the early 12th/18th century, the prominent position of the *sayid* or *sharif* was most likely due to his religious knowledge, which would have been substantially greater than most other Muslims in the kingdom. But more important, the *sharif* or *sayid* had an even greater claim to respect and honour among the Malays because of his direct descent from the Prophet.

While there does not appear to have been any official hierarchy extending from the chief religious figures at the court to the other Muslim officials in the kingdom, there was a definite ranking at the village level. The *imam*, usually a member of a prominent village family, was the head of the village prayer house (*surau*), which functioned as the gathering place for Friday prayers, village Islamic rituals, village education, and certain community-wide religious celebrations. Mosques were usually found only in the larger settlements and in the towns. Below the *imam* was the *khatib* who delivered the Friday sermons and performed the wedding ceremonies. Next in line was the *bilal*, who called the faithful to prayer and officiated at funerals; and finally there was the *penghulu mukim*, combining both secular and religious administrative duties, who kept the mosque in good order, assisted in ceremonies, reminded the faithful of the Friday services, reported absences to the *imam* and beat the wooden gong outside the mosque to summon the people to prayer. The *kadi* and the village elders screened individuals before selecting them for these posts. Funds for the partial remuneration of these religious functionaries and for the upkeep of the *surau* or mosque were obtained through a collection of the annual *zakat* and *fitrah* (*zakāt al-fitr*), the taxes or alms, from the villagers.

Other than the small village Islamic officialdom, with the *kadi* at the apex in charge of a number of village *suraus* or mosques, there is no mention in the sources of any formal kingdom-wide religious hierarchy. A study of the state of Kelantan suggests that above this village hierarchy may have functioned a nominally state-wide authority of a *mufti* and *kadi* with the various other officials associated with the religious courts. But in other states the picture is less clear, and the only reference one has of any united Islamic effort is when holy war is declared against the Europeans. But such calls for Muslim unity were mainly unsuccessful since personal, ethnic, and state rivalries and antagonisms often proved stronger than the appeal to a common religious bond.

7. Islam in British Malaya. Only in the 19th century with the establishment of British rule in Singapore (1819) and the Malay peninsula (1874-1919) did a more formal organisation of Islam occur. The British long maintained the pretence that they were merely advisers to the Malay sultans, while effectively exercising control over all aspects of government except "religion and custom". This latter sphere was regarded as being under the jurisdiction of the sultans. Unable to exercise much authority in matters of government, the sultans in the last two decades of the 19th century created a religious administration modelled after the centralised bureaucratic system imposed by the British to govern the Malay states. In Kelantan, which together with Trengganu, Perlis and Kedah were under Siam until 1909, religious administrative change occurred toward the end of the 19th century more as a result of a reaction to Siamese provincial reform efforts than to any British example.

By the second decade of the 20th century, most states had a form of centralised Islamic bureaucracy which was co-ordinated by bodies such as Perak's Council of Chiefs and Ulamas, Kelantan's Council of Religion and Malay Custom, Selangor's various committees under the State Council, and Johor's Council of Ministers. These bodies, which included the State *Mufti* (*Shaikh ul-Islam*) and the Chief *Kadi* as ex-officio members, were appointed by the sultan and served as his religious advisers. What differed significantly from the past was the presence in these organisations of a majority of non-Islamic officials from the royal household and senior chiefs, a development which reflected the limited opportunities now open to the traditional ruling classes in the new British colonial government. Their participation in the newly-formalised religious hierarchy further strengthened the long-standing mutually supportive relationship between religious and secular authorities. This alliance guaranteed that any Islamic reform movement which threatened to weaken the established religion would find little favour among the ruling classes. It is noteworthy that the reformist Wahhābī movement which made such a great impression in Indonesia, especially in Sumatra at the end of the 18th and 19th centuries, created barely a ripple in the Malay peninsula.

In the new Islamic bureaucracy, the previously-independent village Muslim officals became incorporated into a system which bound them closer to the secular authorities than ever before. Although implementation of policies from the centre was often difficult because of the relative inaccessibility of some of the villages, the new religious structure did reinforce, at least in the eyes of the people, Islam's traditional support for the ruler.

Islamic scholarship, too, became much more organised and extensive in the peninsula in the 19th century. One major factor in this development was the new Islamic intellectual activity being fostered in such centres as Atjèh, Palembang and Riau. Malay translations from the Arabic of authoritative Muslim treatises on doctrine, law, exegesis, commentary,

Ṣūfism, prayer and catechism were produced, together with popular religious works in Malay which arose independent of the Middle East. Riau's reputation as the guardian of the Malay heritage, which now also included the purity of Islam, made it an exemplar of Islamic thought and attitudes for the rest of the Malay world. From the beginning of the 19th century, reformist Islamic ideas were encouraged on Riau, as were the Ṣūfī mystical brotherhoods divested of their "accretions". In the congenial atmosphere of the Riau court, particularly that of the Raja Muda on the island of Penyengat, religious writings and theological debates flourished, attracting Muslim scholars from all parts of the archipelago.

One of the members of the Raja Muda family and a prominent Malay scholar was Raja Ali Haji ibni Raja Ahmad (*ca.* 1809-*ca.* 1870). He encouraged the recruitment of Islamic teachers and was sufficiently regarded as an Islamic scholar himself to have been consulted on religious doctrine by the royal family and even appointed as the religious adviser to the Raja Muda. He was greatly influenced by al-G͟hazālī's *Iḥyāʾ ʿulūm al-dīn* and *Naṣīḥat al-mulūk*, as can be seen by Raja Ali Haji's application of theological and ethical argument in viewing the Malay past in his monumental work, the *Tuḥfat al-nafīs*. Raja Ali Haji also had sisters and sons who promoted the study of Islam in such groups as the *Persekutuan Rusydiah*. But Raja Ali Haji remained the dominant intellectual figure in Riau, and his religious ideas became the basis for many of the views expounded later by the *Kaum Muda* group in Singapore.

The Straits Settlements of Malacca, Penang and Singapore, geographically and culturally on the edge of Malay society, contributed further to the development of Islamic thought in the region. Created as an administrative unit by the British in 1867, the Straits Settlements were cosmopolitan centres serving as a gateway for the flow of labour, capital and ideas to the Malay peninsula. The wealth and dynamism of Penang and Singapore, enjoying the protection of British rule, fostered religious and political ideas which were less acceptable in the Malay states. A heterogeneous Muslim community became resident in these cities, especially in Singapore, since it was an important port of call for Southeast Asian Muslims going on the pilgrimage to Mecca.

From the last two decades of the 19th century until about 1920, when Penang challenged its position, Singapore had a reputation as a principal centre of Islamic learning. Muslims from Southeast Asia, India, and the Middle East gathered in the city to debate the latest religious ideas, and Islamic tracts in Arabic were translated and simplified into Malay for consumption throughout the archipelago, a practice which had already begun in the 9th/15th century in the heyday of the Malacca kingdom. No stronger comment can be made concerning the vitality of Islam in Singapore than to mention that those in the archipelago wishing to study Islamic law or theology went either to Mecca or to Singapore. The establishment of a number of hand lithograph presses in Singapore in the late 19th century operated principally by *Jawi Peranakan* (those of mixed Malay-Indian origin) enabled the publication of a growing body of Islamic literature in Arabic, Malay and even in some regional languages. The generally liberal attitude of the British authorities toward religious activities in the Straits Settlements facilitated the publication of works and journals not in favour with the religious establishment in the peninsula.

In July 1906 a periodical *Al-Imam*, modelled intellectually after the Egyptian periodical *al-Manār*, began publication in Singapore, promoting the modernist Islamic ideas of the Egyptian thinker, Muḥammad ʿAbduh. Although *Al-Imam's* readership was small, limited mainly to the intellectuals in urban areas, its ideas did percolate to the countryside in the peninsula. The presence of *Al-Imam's* representatives in most Malay states and the interest which it generated among religious teachers in the modernist Islamic schools, the *madrasahs*, assured the transmission of its viewpoints to an audience outside the cities. This, and other similar publications, advocated a return to the original strength of early Islam and the rejection of accretions to Islam which had prevented the revival of the Malay nation. A number of *madrasahs* began to be established introducing a more modern curriculum than that offered by the *pondok* ("hut") schools, which employed the method of recitation and exegesis by a teacher as the principal means of imparting religious knowledge to the pupils. The *madrasahs* were intended to put into practice the ideas advanced in the modernist Islamic publications. Instruction was by no means confined to Islam, and such commercial subjects as mathematics, history, English, business, techniques for wet-rice agriculture, and soap- and soy sauce-making were also introduced to instruct a good Muslim how to survive and flourish in a modern society.

Because of the traditionally supportive role between the religious and secular authorities in the Malay states, the modernist Islamic press attacks on established religious officialdom became viewed as an attack on the ruling classes. Attempts were made to prevent entry of these publications into the peninsula from the Straits Settlements. In 1934 there was a public burning of a tract on free will written by a Malay modernist who had studied at al-Azhar university in Cairo. But the debate could not be stifled. Opponents of the movement referred to the modernists as *Kaum Muda*, the "Younger Faction", while reserving for themselves the more respectable appellation of *Kaum Tua*, or "Older Faction". The modernists objected to their label, since they regarded themselves as the true "Older Faction" who advocated a return to the original pure teachings of the Prophet. Despite the forcefulness of the rhetoric in the modernist Islamic literature and the progress made in the establishment of *madrasahs*, the impact of modernist ideas was much less in the countryside than in urban areas. With the British creation of Malay vernacular schools throughout the countryside, and the introduction of Ḳurʾān lessons within these schools, the village Muslim officials were able to strengthen their influence among the people. Their new formal positions provided them with security and respectability, and reinforced their traditional ties with the existing secular authorities. The opposition of these village Muslim officials to the modernist Islamic ideas being propagated via the Straits Settlements seriously weakened the impact of such ideas in the Malay countryside. During the Japanese Occupation in Malaya (1942-5), the links between the ruler and the Islamic hierarchy were further reinforced, since more of the secular functions of the ruler were removed, leaving him basically only with religion as an area of responsibility.

8. Islam since independence. Since the independence of Malaya in 1957, there has been constitutionally a separation between Church and State. The various sultans are regarded as the head of religion in their respective states, and in Malacca and Penang, which have no sultans, the quinquennially-

elected Paramount Ruler (*Yang Dipertuan Agung*) is regarded as the religious head. Since 1948 every state has had a religious affairs department, a type of council of religion, the *Sharīʿa* court, the Treasury or *Bayt al-Māl*, and a department of *zakāt*. While Islam is the proclaimed official religion of Malaysia today, freedom to worship any other religion is guaranteed by the Constitution. The protection of the non-Muslim citizen is evident in the controlled application of *hukum syaraʿ* or *Sharīʿa* law. The religious courts (*mahkamah syariah*) deal mainly with Muslim personal law, especially with marriage, divorce and property matters, but have no jurisdiction over non-Muslims. In any conflict between the religious courts and the civil courts, the latter prevail.

The most significant religious development in the peninsula since independence has been the *dakwah* movement. *Dakwah* is described in Malaysia today as a call inviting those who are not yet Muslim to embrace the faith, and those who are Muslims to practice it in their lives. The movement stresses Islam as *deen*, a total system, which provides an effective alternative to Western materialism and secularisation. The movement seems strongest among government officials, teachers, and young urban Malays from English or Malay schools, rather than from Islamic educational institutions as one would have expected. Even among Muslim students studying abroad, there has been a noticeable increase in *dakwah* participation.

The origins of the movement can be traced directly to the government's policy after 1969 to increase Malay enrolments in the universities. Many of these graduates, who became teachers or bureaucrats in the education system, were the *dakwah* activists of the 1970s. The movement gained popularity, particularly after 1974, when government restrictions on student political activity on the campuses led many to re-channel their discontent via the *dakwah* movement, with its stress on Islam as a total system. So pervasive is the movement that the term *dakwah* has been used to categorise behaviour (returning to the simple, less materialistic life style), dress (wearing short praying veils for women, and the turban and long white, green, or black robes for men) and organisation (any group viewing itself as advancing the cause of the movement). Such dedication is encouraged by a steady supply of Islamic literature, both in Indonesian and English, now filling the bookstores in the urban areas.

The basic *dakwah* ideas are in the tradition of earlier Islamic reform movements, such as Wahhābism and the modernism of Muḥammad ʿAbduh. They all preach the rejection of "corrupt" Islamic accretions and the return to the purity of Islam as practised by the Prophet. And as in earlier reformist waves, the *dakwah* movement is seen as a threat to the existing religious and secular authorities and has been resisted by both. In the villages, many of the Muslim officials reject the movement and have managed to retain the loyalty of the villagers. In the urban areas, where the movement is strongest, traditional religious officials have to a large extent been sheltered by the government's cautious attitude toward the movement. The government has sought to contain or domesticate the movement by creating its own *dakwah* organisations within the various departments. While fears have been expressed concerning the possibility of an Islamic revolution along the lines which have transformed Iran into a theocratic state, the more realistic concern is the movement's threat to disrupt the fragile unity painfully created by the nation's leaders between the Malays and the large non-Muslim Chinese and Indian minorities in the country. The movement is viewed suspiciously by some of the latter as yet another instrument by which the Malays would justify their dominance over the other ethnic communities.

The strength of the traditional relationship between the religious and secular authorities has thus far succeeded in diverting *dakwah* energies along the least disruptive channels. Unlike earlier reformist movements, however, *dakwah* activities have become much more forceful and prominent because of the resurgence of Islamic pride and power throughout the world. Yet one can still detect in the movement, and the attempts by established authority to contain and guide it, the process by which new ideas have always filtered into the Malay peninsula. The Malays are now undergoing a re-examination of their religion and society and will no doubt, as in the past, select only those ideas which will best strengthen and make more meaningful their chosen way of life.

Bibliography: For a general history of the Malay peninsula and of Malaysia in general, see B. W. Andaya and L. Y. Andaya, *A history of Malaysia*. London 1982. An enlightening work on Malay society is R. W. Winstedt, *The Malays, a cultural history*, 6th ed., London 1961.

The importance of early trade as a source of goods and ideas to the Malay areas is the subject of O. W. Wolters, *Early Indonesian commerce*, Ithaca 1967; see also idem, *The fall of Srivijaya in Malay history*, Ithaca 1970; P. Wheatley, *The Golden Khersonese*, Kuala Lumpur 1961; G. R. Tibbetts, *Early Muslim traders in South-East Asia*, in *JMBRAS*, xxx/1 (1957), 1-45; J. A. E. Morley, *The Arabs and the eastern trade*, in *JMBRAS*, xxii/1 (1949), 143-76. Theories of how Islam was introduced to the Malay world are discussed in A. H. Johns, *Islam in Southeast Asia: reflections and new directions*, in *Indonesia*, xix (April 1975), 33-55; idem, *Sufism as a category in Indonesian literature and history*, in *Jnal. of Southeast Asian History*, ii/2 (1961), 10-23; idem, *From coastal settlement to Islamic school and city: Islamization in Sumatra, the Malay peninsula and Java*, in *Hamdard Islamicus*, iv/4 (1981), 3-28; G. W. J. Drewes, *New light on the coming of Islam to Indonesia*, in *Bijdragen tot de Taal-, Land- en Volkenkunde*, cxxiv/4 (1968), 433-59; S.Q. Fatimi, *Islam comes to Malaysia*, Singapore 1963.

Impressions of Islamic institutions prior to the 19th century in the Malay peninsula can be gleaned from such works as A. H. Hill, ed. and tr., *The Hikayat Abdullah*, Kuala Lumpur 1970; J. M. Gullick, *Indigenous political systems of Western Malaya*, London 1958; W. R. Roff, ed., *Kelantan: religion, society and politics in a Malay State*, Kuala Lumpur 1974; B. W. Andaya, *Perak: the Abode of Grace*, Kuala Lumpur 1979; L. Y. Andaya, *History of Johor, 1641-1728*, Kuala Lumpur 1975.

For a discussion of the Islamic intellectual climate and writings in the Malay areas in the 19th and early 20th centuries, see B. W. Andaya and V. Matheson, *Islamic thought and Malay tradition: the writings of Raja Ali Haji of Riau (ca. 1809-ca. 1870)*, in A. Reid and D. Marr, *Perceptions of the past in Southeast Asia*, Singapore 1979; Roff, *The origins of Malay nationalism*, Kuala Lumpur 1967; R. W. Winstedt, *A history of classical Malay literature*, Kuala Lumpur 1969. An interesting account of the blend of Islamic, Hindu and spirit beliefs among Malay villagers in idem, *The Malay magician, being Shaman, Saiva and Sufi*, rev. ed. London 1951. A more general account of the role of Islam in Malay society in the 19th and 20th centuries can be found in D. Noer, *Islam in Indonesia and Malaysia: a preliminary study,* in *Review of Indonesian and Malayan Affairs,* ix/2 (July-Dec. 1975), 51-70; M. A. Rauf, *A brief history of Islam, with special reference to Malaya,* Kuala Lumpur 1964; Syed Naguib al-Attas, *Some aspects of Sufism as understood and practised among the Malays,* Singapore 1963; Roff, *Kelantan: religion, society and politics in a Malay State*; idem, *The origins of Malay nationalism*; M. L. Lyon, *The Dakwah movement in Malaysia,* in *Review of Indonesian and Malayan Affairs,* xiii/2 (1979), 34-45; Khoo Kay Kim, ed., *Tamadun di Malaysia,* Kuala Lumpur 1980 (a collection of articles, many written by members of the Islamic Studies departments in the various universities in Malaysia); V. S. Naipaul, *Among the believers. An Islamic journey,* London 1981. (L. Y. ANDAYA)

MALAYS, a people of South-East Asia. The Malays speak Malay, one of the languages of the Austronesian language family. Inscriptions from the area of Palembang in Sumatra dating from the 7th century are the oldest evidence of Malay. They show that Malay functioned as an official language in an Indianised kingdom. It is sometimes assumed, on somewhat tenuous ground, that this region of Sumatra and the islands off its east coast are the homeland of the Malays.

The Malay language takes three forms. It is a series of local dialects; it is a *lingua franca,* and it is the official language of Indonesia, of Malaysia, of Brunei and one of the national languages of Singapore. Its speakers rank sixth in number amongst those of other world languages. Most of these, however, do not have Malay as their first language. Malay is spoken also in Southern Thailand, in Sri Lanka by descendants of slaves brought there, and in the Netherlands by 40,000 Moluccan Malays. What is sometimes called Cape Malay is actually not Malay at all, but Afrikaans with unimportant Malay influence. As the official language of Indonesia [SEE INDONESIA, iii. Languages] it is one of approximately 800 languages. It is spoken as a local dialect in the southern part of Sumatra, around the city of Medan on that island and in the islands of Bangka, Billiton, and in Riau; in Kalimantan it is spoken around the rim of the island; in Java it is spoken as a local dialect in pockets along the north coast. "Moluccan Malay" is one name given to several varieties of the local dialects in Eastern Indonesia. From a linguistic point of view, the situation of dialects has not yet been properly studied. Teeuw notes that the varieties of types of influence—via traders, religious figures, wanderers and others—has left "an intricate complex of Malay, Malay-like and Malay-influenced languages and dialects". In Malaysia, the language of Johor and Riau is considered the correct language. There is much divergence from this form of Malay. However, linguistic study does not yet allow us to specify how many dialects can be isolated.

Malay already existed as a *lingua franca* during the period of Portugese activity in Eastern Indonesia. Its status as a national language was furthered by its use by both Dutch and British in dealing with their colonial subjects. The Japanese replaced Dutch and English with Malay during World War II and thus helped development of Malay as a language of administration and learning. This marked the beginning of efforts to expand the use of the language that continue to the present. Malay is more of a success as a national language in Indonesia than in Malaysia. It has often become the language of domestic life in major Indonesian cities, as well as the language of youth.

The complicated Malay linguistic situation makes it difficult to decide which groups are Malay and which are not. In Malaysia the term *bumiputera,* meaning "son of the soil" is used to distinguish Malays from Chinese and Indians. When it is so used it refers to native speakers of Malay who are Muslim and born in Malaysia. The same term in Borneo, however, refers to tribes who may or may not speak a form of Malay. Though the term *bumiputera* is recent, the notion, as Gullick notes, goes back to British rule. Before colonial times, it is doubtful that an equivalent term was used by anyone to designate themselves, Malay speakers rather referring to themselves as inhabitants of certain places or followers of certain rulers.

Before the colonial period, Malay states were typically situated at the mouths of rivers. Revenues collected from the control of trade were the source of the ruler's power. With these revenues, the ruler maintained a band of retainers. Before the coming of the British, peasants fled from one area to the next as they felt pressure from rulers to pay taxes or perform labour services. The limitation of aristocratic power and the bringing of peace to the Malay Peninsula allowed for the building of permanent Malay setlements. It resulted also in immigration from Sumatra to the central areas of the peninsula. Rubber became a major smallholder crop between 1910 and 1920 and thus a mainstay of the Malay economy on the West Coast. In other states, rice became the chief crop. The growing of those crops along with fishing, the cultivation of copra and palm oil, work on estates and in the civil service comprise the chief occupations of Malaysians today.

It is more difficult to isolate a notion of "Malay" in Indonesia with its more complicated linguistic and ethnic composition and different colonial history. What have been termed "Coastal Malays" have been little studied. Pigeaud has used the Malay word meaning "coastal" to term the culture that includes coastal Malays as well as other groups, "Pasissir culture". Hildred Geertz has elaborated this notion. She sees Pasissir culture as developing around the spice trade of the 14th to the 18th centuries and associated with the spread of Islam. In this process, Malay culture was mixed with other influences—Javanese and Makassarese as well as Arabic and south Indian, with different mixtures evolving in different localities. In addition to Islam, Geertz stresses an orientation to the market and the development of literary forms as features of Pasissir culture. As was the case in the Malay states, a system of status was tied to actual political power so that office was not a sure sign of authority, rulers having to validate their power through the maintenance of retainers.

Malays are Sunni Muslims. Their religious institutions vary from place to place. There is usually a village religious official, often termed a *lebai.* In the traditional states, there were religious officials, including *kadi*s, associated with the courts as well as religious functionaries independent of the states and connected often with mosques or with religious boarding schools in the countryside. Peripatetic teachers from the Middle East as well as the pilgrimage have long been important vehicles of influence. The oldest Malay texts which show Muslim influences come from Trengganu in Malaysia and Atjèh in Indonesia. Both date from the 14th century. Tomb inscriptions showing adherence to Islam date from the 15th century. (J. SIEGEL)

Of pre-Islamic Malay literature, nothing is known. As far as may be concluded from a few old inscriptions in Hindu script, it seems that Malay was written in Kawi-like characters, but literature, in its earliest known form, is written in Arabic letters only. The oldest manuscripts are preserved in the Cambridge and Oxford libraries; they date from the last years of the 16th and the first decade of the 17th century. The only literary-historical evidence of the existence of written literature in the 16th century is the mention, in a 17th century chronicle, of the use made of a royal library at Malacca at the time when the Portuguese endeavoured to capture that town (1511). Malay literature, as it presents itself now, is only for a very small part original. Hardly any of the chronicles, tales and poems are derived from Arabic sources directly, most of the religious and semi-historical romances having been translated from Persian; but all these literary products are imbued with the Muslim atmosphere, being full of Arabic words and phrases and laden with Islamic theory. There are, it is true, some indigenous farcical tales, and some fables, especially the sometime highly appreciated mouse-deer tales, moreover some original romances with Hinduistic influences, and several adapted old Javanese tales, that do not betray real Islamic influence; but the very fact that all these books are written in Arabic characters makes them overflow with Arabic words in a way that shows that they belong to Islamic mentality. In this short account, there will be no mention of literary products going back to the great Sanskrit epic poems, nor of the tales that do not show traces of Muslim influence; only in so far as Malay literature has Islamic features will it be treated here. The originally genuine Indonesian deer-fable has undergone an Islamic correction. The historical writings, more or less mythical and semi-romantic, are almost absolutely Islamised. To that class of works the chronicle *Sejarah Melayu,* and other ones, as the chronicles of Kutawaringin, Kutai, Atjèh and Pasai, are to be reckoned. A partly historical but for the greater part fictitious, romance is the *Hikayat Hang Tuah.* A host of romances, dealing with foreign princes and princesses and their endless adventures, has been spread over a great part of the Malay-reading East-Indian World; the titles of all those popular, but for European readers less attractive, books, may be found in the catalogues of Malay manuscripts at Leiden, Batavia and London. Some books of fiction have been translated from Persian, Arabic or Hindustani. A group of them is to be traced to the *Hitopadeṣa*-collection, another one to the *Tūtī-nāma*-series, a third one to the *Bak͟hitar* cycle. Only exceptionally have foreign authors written in Malay; e.g. the Rād͟jput Nūr al-Dīn al-Rānīrī, who wrote a great encyclopaedic chronicle at the instigation of an Atjèhnese queen. A very great number of texts deals with the former prophets, the Prophet Muḥammad, his family and friends. Those works, like e.g. the romances of Amīr Ḥamza and Muḥammad b. al-Ḥanafiyya, have Persian originals. The purely religious books cannot be regarded as Malay literature.

Poetical literature has a different character. The real Malay kind of poetry, though not devoid of Persian influences, is the *pantun*, i.e., popular quatrains, whose first two kinds deal with a natural fact, or a well known event, and are intended to prelude, phonetically, the third and fourth lines, that contain the real meaning of the usually erotic poem. The other "genre" is the *shaʾir.* Its form is the stanza of four rhyming lines. Some of these very extensive overloaded poems are from the Javanese, some others are versified versions of prose romances, moreover historical events, love-scenes, religious matters, mystical speculations etc. are dealt with in innumerable *shaʾir.* (Ph. van Ronkel)

The development of Malay as a modern literary language is generally said to begin with the writings of Abdullah bin Abdul Kadir Munshi, 1796-1854 (known as Munshi Abdullah), who introduced a colloquial style and who relied on his own observations for the content of his writing. The Islamic features of the literature that developed after Munshi Abdullah are difficult to specify. The progress of modern literature meant a decisive break with older forms, such as the *shaʾir,* with their strong Muslim overtones. At the same time, the development of contemporary forms such as the novel and short story can be seen as a means of continuing the expression of traditional social tensions which often centred around Islam. Writers from the 1920s and 1930s who were responsible for the acceptance of modern styles were most often from the Minangkabau region of Sumatra. Taufik Abdullah has shown that a continuous tension and resolution between Minangkabau tradition which featured matrilineal descent and Islam resulted in the perpetual generation of new social forms. The modern novel and short story as exemplified in the works of writers such as Marah Rusli, born 1889, Nur Sutan Iskandar, born 1893, and Sutan Takdir Alisjahbana, born 1908, can be seen as continuing the expression of this tension. At the same time, one cannot point to a specifically Islamic literature, though writers such as Hadji Abdul Malik Karim Amrullah, born 1908 (known as Hamka) continue to deal with Islamic themes.

Bibliography: The standard history of the earliest Malay kingdom is O. W. Wolters, *Early Indonesian commerce: a study of the origins of Srivijaya,* Ithaca 1967. On the Malay language, see A. Teeuw, *A critical survey of studies on Malay and Bahasa Indonesia,* The Hague 1961; P. Voorhoeve, *Critical survey of studies on the languages of Sumatra,* The Hague 1955; A. A. Cense and E. M. Uhlenbeck, *Critical survey of studies on the languages of Borneo,* The Hague 1985. On Malay literature, the standard works are Sir Richard Winstedt, *A history of Classical Malay literature,* in *JMBRAS,* xxxi (1958), 1-261; C. Hooykaas, *Over Maleise Literatuur,* Leiden 1947; A. Teeuw, *Modern Indonesian literature,* The Hague 1967.

On Pasissir culture, see Th. Pigeaud, *Javanese Volksvertoningen,* Batavia 1938, and H. Geertz, *Indonesian cultures and communities,* in R. McVey (ed.), *Indonesia,* New Haven 1963. Important studies of Malay society include R. Firth, *Malay fishermen: their peasant economy,* London 1946; J. Djamour, *Malay kinship and marriage in Singapore,* London 1959; J. M. Gullick, *Indigenous political systems of Western Malay,* London 1958; idem, *Malaysia,* London 1985; C. Kessler, *Islam and politics in a Malay state: Kelantan 1838-1969,* Ithaca 1978; W. Roff, *The origins of Malay nationalism,* New Haven 1967; Taufik Abdullah, *Schools and politics in the Kaum Muda movement in West Sumatra (1927-1933),* Ithaca 1971; idem, *Modernization in the Minangkabau world. West Sumatra in the early decades of the twentieth century,* in Claire Holt (ed.), *Culture and politics in Indonesia,* Ithaca 1972. (J. Siegel)

MALAYSIA. Political developments since 1957. The Federation of Malaya (consisting of nine peninsular Malay states plus Penang and Melaka) achieved sovereign independence within the Commonwealth on 31 August 1957. The written constitution (amended at various times since) provided a strong central authority comprising the Yang di-Pertuan Agong (the constitutional monarch who is elected at five-yearly intervals by and from the nine hereditary Malay Rulers), a partially nominated Senate and a wholly elected House of Representatives. The Malay Rulers remained heads of their respective states (though Governors occupied this position in Penang and Melaka), each of which was provided with an executive council responsible to the state assembly. The Rulers were also confirmed as heads of the Islamic religion in their states. For a society where differences between Malays, Chinese and Indians are marked, a single nationality was created with provisions enabling all persons to qualify for citizenship either by birth or according to requirements of residence, language and allegiance. Though this would allow the proportion of non-Malay citizens to rise steadily, it was made acceptable to the Malays by constitutional safeguards for their religion, language and "special position" in public service, education, land reservations, etc. Lawyers and politicians have had some difficulty reconciling the historic principles of "the special position of the Malays" with the more modern concept of "common nationality".

Tunku Abdul Rahman's Alliance coalition of the United Malays National Organization (UMNO), Malayan Chinese Association (MCA) and Malayan Indian Congress (MIC) was intended to make compatible the interests of the three major communities. The arrangement allowed Malay political hegemony and non-Malay domination of the economy in the short term while holding out the prospect of a gradual breakdown of these respective preserves. The Alliance majority was confirmed at the 1959 elections and on 1 August 1960 it was confident enough to end the Emergency which has been declared on the outbreak of the communist insurrection (June 1948). Controversial educational and rural developmental policies were launched to improve the economic lot of the Malays.

On 27 May 1961 the Tunku proposed the formation of "Malaysia" from Malaya and the British dependencies of Singapore, Brunei, North Borneo (Sabah) and Sarawak. Neither the Tunku nor Lee Kuan Yew (Chief Minister of Singapore) believed that an independent Singapore could survive on its own, while the former was confident that the peoples of Borneo would counter-balance the Chinese of Singapore. Reassured about their military base in Singapore, the British were prepared to decolonise the rest of their Southeast Asian empire via the Malaysia plan. Despite protests in Borneo (e.g. the Sarawak United People's Party; Azahari's revolt in Brunei, December 1962), the Cobbold Commission and a UN Mission separately concluded that the majorities in Sabah and Sarawak favoured Malaysia which was inaugurated, but without Brunei's membership, on 16 September 1963.

The new federation faced problems within and without. Sukarno condemned it as a "neo-colonial" conspiracy and "confrontation" between Indonesian and Malaysian-Commonwealth forces lasted until May 1966, while the Philippines laid claim to Sabah. Relations between Kuala Lumpur and some state governments were also strained. The Pan-Malayan Islamic Party (PMIP) controlled Kelantan, and the federal government had to intervene in the affairs of Sabah and Sarawak to ensure state governments to its liking. Lee Kuan Yew's commitment to a "Malaysian Malaysia" challenged the Alliance formula for the harmonisation of communal differences and roused UMNO "ultras". In August 1965, Singapore was forced to secede from Malaysia. Nevertheless, the Alliance had increased its majority in the 1964 federal elections.

The elections five years later, however, were bitterly contested. The PMIP and some Malays within UMNO criticised Tunku Abdul Rahman for "giving in" to the Chinese, while the Democratic Action Party (DAP), Gerakan and People's Progressive Party complained about the disadvantages suffered by non-Malays. Reduction of the Alliance majority, particularly the MCA's poor performance, provoked demonstration and counter-demonstration which spilled into communal violence in Kuala Lumpur on 13 May 1969. Probably many hundreds were killed. Parliamentary government was suspended until February 1971.

1969 is a turning-point in the modern history of Malaysia. Tun Abdul Razak, for years the Tunku's deputy, assumed the leadership of government, first as Director of the National Operations Council and later as Prime Minister (September 1970 to January 1976). Razak evolved a strategy for stability which was continued by Hussein Onn (1976-81) and Mahathir (since 1981). The *Rukunegara* (national creed) was proclaimed, but public and parliamentary debate of "sensitive issues", notably the paramountcy of the Malay Rulers, the special position of *bumiputras* ("princes of the soil", i.e. Malays and other indigenous peoples) and the citizenship rights of non-Malays, was outlawed. Authoritarianism has been a characteristic of Malaysian government; in 1960 when the Emergency ended, the executive equipped itself with even wider emergency powers by amending the Internal Security Act, and detention without trial and news censorship have been features of the period since the return to parliamentary government in 1971. The coalition has been enlarged to incorporate former opposition parties, including the Parti Islam Sa-Malaysia (PAS, previously PMIP), between 1973 and 1977, but not the DAP. This National Front (NF or *Barisan National*), like the old Alliance, has been dominated by UMNO. In the 1974 elections, the NF won well over two-thirds of the federal seats (the amount needed to amend the constitution) and control of all 13 states.

Perhaps the most significant result of the 1969 riots lay in economic planning. One of the most prosperous countries in Asia and enjoying an enviable growth rate, Malaysia has nonetheless suffered from rural poverty and an uneven distribution of income. To break down the communal compartmentalisation of society, in which *bumiputras* were identified with traditional activities while Chinese and Indians were obviously associated with the modern sector, the New Economic Policy (NEP) was devised. Through a series of Five Years Plans (1971-5, 1976-80, 1981-5), the NEP has aimed to eradicate poverty and to increase the *bumiputras*' share of corporate wealth to 30% by 1990. There is tension between these objectives, and irritation arising from their immediate pursuit or failure to attain long-term goals could exacerbate communal relations and popular grievances. Since independence, the economy has diversified considerably and the manufacturing sector has been developed, but Malaysia still relies on the export of commodities (petroleum, rubber, tin, palm oil, timber and more recently cocoa) and is thus vulnerable to world-market fluctuations. Since the mid-70s, government has been aware that world recession might upset the timetable of the NEP. So, too, might the rapid growth of population (currently at 2.7% p.a.) which, according to the 1983 estimate, totalled 14,744,000 and is ethnically divided in the approximate proportions of Malays 47%, Chinese 33%, Indians 9% and Borneo peoples 9% (plus 2% others), and is distributed geographically between Peninsular Malaysians 83% and East Malaysians 17%.

In foreign affairs, too, the early 1970s saw a shift in emphasis. The Anglophile Tunku had stayed firmly in the Western camp; though Malaysia had not joined SEATO, the Anglo-Malayan (Malaysian) Defence Agreement (AMDA) had underwritten the country's security, and Malaysia had supported the US in Vietnam. In 1971 AMDA was replaced by the Five Power Defence Arrangement (Australia, Britain, Malaysia, New Zealand, Singapore) in which Britain played a less prominent role. At the same time, Malaysia became interested in the neutralisation of the region through the Association of Southeast Asian Nations (ASEAN, 1967). Without compromising its anti-communism, it established diplomatic relations with China (1974). Communist expansion and Sino-Soviet rivalry in Indo-China since 1975 has been tackled by Malaysia as an ASEAN matter rather than through the Commonwealth, in which the present Prime Minister shows little interest.

In 1975-6, world recession, resurgent terrorism, political crisis in Sabah, corruption involving the Selangor Chief Minister and the death of Tun Razak (January 1976) might have shaken the régime, but the calm control asserted by Datuk (later Tun) Hussein Onn was endorsed by the 1978 elections. In July 1981 he was succeeded by the more abrasive Datuk Seri Dr Mahathir Mohamad, a vigorous champion of Malays within a "Greater Malaysia". "Leadership by example", "Malaysia incorporated" and "Look East" are some of the slogans illustrating his drive for administrative efficiency, entrepreneurial zeal and international repute. Since the NF's landslide victory in the elections of April 1982, however, he has been embarrassed by a constitutional wrangle with the Rulers, a financial scandal arising from the Bank Bumiputra's involvement in property development in Hong Kong, the Islamic revivalism of PAS and the defeat of the NF party (Berjaya) in the Sabah state election (April 1985). Though Mahathir's command of UMNO, the NF and the country is unassailable at the moment (June 1985), he has to counter the blandishments of PAS and guard against splits between NF partners and within parties such as the MCA and MIC, which are notoriously disunited. Apart from the politics of the moment, some are exercised by the fear of a slump in Malaysia's economy whose continuing buoyancy is essential to the integration of this new state.

Bibliography: Barbara Watson Andaya and L. Y. Andaya, *A history of Malaysia,* London 1982; J. Gullick, *Malaysia: economic expansion and national unity,* London 1981; D. Lim, *Economic growth and development in West Malaysia, 1947-1970,* Kuala Lumpur 1973; Mahathir b. Mohamad, *The Malay dilemma,* Singapore 1970, republ. 1981; D. K. Mauzy and R. S. Milne, *Politics and government in Malaysia,* Vancouver 1978; G. P. Means, *Malaysian politics,* London, 2nd ed. 1976; R. S. Milne and K. J. Ratnam, *Malaysia—new states in a new nation: political development of Sarawak and Sabah in Malaysia,* London 1974; Mohamed Noordin Sopiee, *From Malayan union to Singapore separation: political unification in the Malaysia region, 1945-65,* Kuala Lumpur 1974; Tun Mohamed Suffian, H. P. Lee, F. A. Trindade, eds., *The constitution of Malaysia, its development 1957-1977,* Kuala Lumpur 1978; K. von Vorys, *Democracy without consensus: communalism and political stability in Malaysia,* Princeton 1975; see also the *Far Eastern Economic Review* and its *Year Book (Asia Year Book,* 1973—), Hong Kong; *The Far East and Australasia,* London, 1969—; Institute of Southeast Asian Studies, *Southeast Asian Affairs,* Singapore 1975-

(A. J. Stockwell)

MALĀZGIRD. 1. The town. The modern Turkish Malazgird constitutes a district (*ilçe*) centre in the province (*il*) of Muş in eastern Anatolia. The area surrounding the town is rich in cuneiform inscriptions, and it is possible that the battle between Tiglathpileser I and the Naīri kings took place in the area. The name of the town itself, which probably goes back no further than the Parthian period, in Old Armenian is recorded as Manavazakert, Manavazkert and Manazkert, while the oldest Arabic form is Manāzdjird. It has been supposed that this name preserves the memory of the Urartu king Menuas of Van, whose name is mentioned in many inscriptions which have been found in the Malāzgird area.

Very little is known about the town's pre-Islamic history. Constantine Porphyrogenitus remarks that the local dynasty who held Malāzgird in the 4th/10th century paid tribute to the Byzantine Empire. However, the members of this dynasty, which originally had been subordinate to the Bagratids, bore Arabic names, the *nisba* derived from Malāzgird being recorded as al-Manāzī. Thus during the campaign of the Ḥamdānid Sayf al-Dawla into eastern Anatolia (328/940), we hear of a prince of Malāzgird named ʿAbd al-Ḥamīd. In 353/964 a *ghulām* of Sayf al-Dawla's conquered the town, and in 359/969-70 it was taken by the Byzantines. The Byzantine occupation of Malāzgird must have been very brief, for in 382/992-3 another Byzantine army tried to take possession of the town, this time without success. On the other hand, by 446/1054-5 Malāzgird must have once again fallen into Byzantine hands, because Ibn al-Athīr records that in 446/1054-5 Malāzgird resisted a siege by the Saldjūḳ Ṭoghrīl Beg.

However, the main event in the history of the town was the battle of Malāzgird between the Saldjūḳ sultan Alp Arslan and the Byzantine ruler Romanus Diogenes (463/1071) [for details, see 2. below]. The outcome of this battle led to the gradual settlement of Anatolia by Turkish nomads and then townsmen, and to the establishment of the Rūm Saldjūḳ sultanate in central and eastern Anatolia.

On the other hand, the town of Malāzgird itself never played a prominent role, neither in the Saldjūḳ nor during the Ottoman period. During the 7th/13th century, the name of Malāzgird is occasionally mentioned in chronicles (particularly Ibn al-Athīr), but no references can be found concerning the economic life of the town. Equally sparse is the material for the Ottoman period. Thus it has not been possible to locate an enumeration of Malāzgird tax-payers in the *taḥrīrs* of the 10th/16th century, although an Ottoman document from the year 1001/1592-3 refers to a *sandjaḳ* of Malāzgird, in the *wilāyet* of Diyārbekir, which was inhabited by the Ḳara Ulus nomads (Başbakanlık Arşivi, Divan-ı hümayun Ruus Kalemi, 253/46a, p. 63). However, Kātib Čelebi (*Djihān-numā*, 426) makes a brief reference to the existence of the town, which in the 11th/17th century could be reached in two days' travel from Erzurum. Moreover, the town lay on a road connecting Adilcevaz and Bitlis, which was used by the Ottoman army on one of its campaigns in ʿIrāḳ.

In the 1890s, Malāzgird appears as the centre of a *ḳaḍā*ʾ (*sandjaḳ* of Mush, *wilāyet* of Bitlis) comprising 50 villages, the main settlement containing 213 houses and 19 shops. The *ḳaḍāʾ*, then as now, depended mainly upon agriculture and animal husbandry. According to the *İl yıllığı* of Muş (1967), Malāzgird appears as an *ilçe* (formerly *nahiye*) centre of 7,826 inhabitants, mostly engaged in field agriculture, such as the cultivation of wheat, barley, beans, and maize. Vegetables and industrial cultures (sunflowers, sugarbeet) were being encouraged by government projects. The number of craftsmen was low, and the *ilçe* possessed no industry.

According to the *İl yıllığı* of Muş published in 1973, the town had by 1970 grown to 10,711 inhabitants (1975: 13,094). A hydroelectrical power plant had been established, so that Malāzgird is now supplied with electricity. As an administrative centre, the town also provides educational services for its district: a high school (*lise*) was opened in 1971, and the construction of a cultural and sports centre began about 1970. An irrigation project had equally been undertaken by 1970, and the first producers' cooperatives were making their appearance. However industry continues to be practically absent from the *ilçe* of Malāzgird.

Bibliography: Apart from V. F. Büchner's *EI*[1] art., revised and augmented by Besim Darkot in *İA*, see: Kātib Čelebi, *Djihān-nümā*, Istanbul 1145/1732; Naṣūḥ al-Silāḥī (Maṭrakčī), *Beyān-i menāzil-i sefer-i ʿIrāḳayn*, ed. H. G. Yurdaydın, Ankara 1976, 105; Samy-Bey Fraschery, *Ḳāmūs al-aʿlām*, 6 vols., Istanbul 1316/1898, vi, 4388; V. Cuinet, *La Turquie d'Asie*, Paris 1894, iii, 589-91; Le Strange, *The lands of the eastern caliphate*, 115-16, 139; E. Banse, *Die Türkei, eine moderne Geographie*, Berlin, Hamburg, Brunswick 1916, 210, 214; M. Canard, *Histoire de la dynastie des H'amdânides*, Algiers 1951, 187 and n. 279, 473-5, 481-3, 629-32, 668; *Muş il yıllığı 1967*, Elaziğ 1967; *Cumhuriyetin 50. yılında Muş*, Elaziğ 1973; *Genel nüfus sayımı, idari bölümü*, 26.10.1975, Ankara 1977, § 49, p. 6.

(S. Faroqhi)

2. The battle. As noted above, the most important event with which the name of the town is connected is the battle of Mantzikert fought in Ḏhu 'l-Ḳaʿda 463/August 1071 between Alp Arslan [*q.v.*] and Romanus IV Diogenes. This event is treated by a variety of sources, Byzantine Greek, Armenian, Syriac and Arabic. The most valuable account is surely that of Attaliates, who was present at the battle itself as well as being an adviser of the Emperor, whereas that of Psellus, tutor of Michael VII Ducas who was to replace Romanus on the imperial throne after the battle (see below), is hostile. Although Cahen (1934, see *Bibl.*) was critical of Attaliates' detailed testimony, more recently Vryonis and Cheynet (see *Bibl.*) have reinstated him as the prime source for the battle. A relevant Western source is the Gesta Roberti Wiscardi of William of Apulia (see *Bibl.*); other later Christian writers such as Michael the Syrian and Matthew of Edessa are strongly anti-Byzantine, viewing the Saldjūḳ invasions of Anatolia as divine retribution for the Emperors' treatment of non-Melkite religious minorities of the empire. There is no contemporary Muslim account, the earliest extant one being that of Ibn al-Ḳalānisī (d. 555/1160), but the long description by Sibṭ b. al-Ḏjawzī (probably deriving from Ghars al-Niʿma Muḥammad b. Hilāl al-Ṣābiʾ's lost *ʿUyūn al-tawārīkh*) is, among other Muslim sources, detailed and valuable.

The policy adopted by Romanus when he became Emperor in January 1068 was to take the offensive against the Muslim enemy beyond the Byzantine frontiers rather than to wait for raids to take place, and the campaign which culminated at Malāzgird was the last of three conducted by the Emperor himself, for which he left Constantinople in spring 463/1071, aiming to securing against the Saldjūḳs the Armenian fortresses of Akhlāṭ [*q.v.*] and Malāzgird. Alp Arslan was for his part besieging Edessa in the spring, but on hearing of the arrival of the Byzantine army in the east, decided to move in that direction, probably via Mawṣil and Khūy, to assemble reinforcements. Romanus detached a contingent of his army under the Norman Roussel of Bailleul to take Akhlāṭ, whilst he took and garrisoned Malāzgird itself. Preliminary skirmishes took place, during which time some of the Uze (sc. Ghuzz) mercenaries in the Byzantine army deserted to the enemy, whilst Roussel and the Georgian Joseph Trachaniotes fled westwards from Akhlāṭ, deserting the Emperor, at the approach of Alp Arslan. The Muslim side offered peace, but Romanus refused any terms, feeling that he had numerical superiority and being unwilling to throw away the immense effort put behind his campaign. The Muslim sources emphasise Alp Arslan's pessimism before the battle, but the fact that the battle took place on a Friday meant that the force of universal Muslim prayer was felt as an advantage (cf. al-Ḥusaynī, *Akhbār al-dawla al-saldjūḳiyya*, 47-9, which purports to give the text of special prayers offered up throughout the Sunnī world at the caliph al-Ḳāʾim's orders).

Although the figures in the Muslim sources for Romanus's army (from 200,000 to 400,000) must be exaggerated, the Emperor must, despite defections, have had superiority in numbers; Cheynet estimates his army at probably 60,000, with much baggage and impediment. Its morale however was not high, and its composition very heterogeneous; amongst foreign mercenaries are mentioned Franks, Arabs, Rūs, Pechenegs, Georgians, Abkhazians, Khazars, Ghuzz, Ḳıpčaḳ, Scyths, Alans and Armenians. Alp Arslan is generally credited in the Muslim sources with having 15,000 troops at the battle. The exact date of the battle has not hitherto been established with certainty, but the fact that it was a Friday in Ḏhu 'l-Ḳaʿda seems to limit the possibilities to 20 Ḏhu 'l-Ḳaʿda/19 August or the next week; in fact, astronomical indications, confirming Attaliates' information that the night before the battle was moonless, point to 27 Ḏhu 'l-Ḳaʿda 463/26 August 1071, as is shown in a recent popular book on the battle, A. Friendly, *The dreadful day*, London 1981, 178. The exact location of the field of battle is likewise uncertain, though it was along the road between Malāzgird and Akhlāṭ; the al-Rahwa (cf. Yāḳūt, ii, 880) of Sibṭ b. al-Ḏjawzī, Ibn al-Ḏjawzī and Ibn al-ʿAdīm seems most probable.

The course of the battle is described in most detail by Attaliates and by the anti-Romanus, later writer Nicephorus Bryennius. A Byzantine return to camp at nightfall seems to have been interpreted as a retreat; the rearguard under Andronicus Ducas left the field, leaving the army's rear unprotected; and in the later stages, the Saldjūḳ forces lured the Greeks into ambushes. The Emperor was captured and was honourably treated by Alp Arslan; several sources record the famous conversation in which the sultan asked Romanus what treatment should be meted out to him. A peace agreement was drawn up, the precise terms of which are not known, but which probably included a ransom, the cession of various frontier fortresses, and the provision of troops and annual tribute to the sultan; but since during Romanus's brief captivity, Michael VII Ducas had been proclaimed Emperor and Romanus was eventually blinded and killed by his supplanter (August 1072), it is likely that these terms were never put into force anyway.

Romanus's defeat seems to have sprung in part from inadequate intelligence about the movements of the A<u>kh</u>lāṭ force, which was to rejoin him, and a poor choice of terrain, one favourable to the Sal<u>dj</u>ūḳs' mounted archers; but internal dissensions within the Byzantine empire, moreover, had been reflected in the army itself, for Andronicus Ducas, cousin of the future Emperor Michael VII, had been ill-disposed towards Romanus. A Fāṭimid involvement in the campaign has recently been suggested by Hamdani (see *Bibl.*), but this remains speculative.

Was the battle indeed "the greatest disaster of Byzantine history" (Grousset)? In many ways, it was the decade of internecine strife within the Empire after the battle which harmed the Empire more and allowed Turks to infiltrate Byzantine territory. Byzantine prestige abroad was certainly harmed by the ignominy of Romanus's capture, and some Crusader chroniclers (e.g. William of Tyre) see Western European involvement in the Levant as dating from this time, with the Franks replacing the Greeks as upholders of Christianity against Islam there. The Muslim historians, for their part, tend to overdramatise the event, probably because it was the only major military confrontation during the infiltration process.

Bibliography: 1. Primary sources: (i) Arabic: Ibn al-Ḳalānsī, *<u>Dh</u>ayl taʾrī<u>kh</u> Dima<u>sh</u>ḳ*, ed. Amedroz, 99; Ibn al-Azraḳ al-Fāriḳī, *Taʾrī<u>kh</u> al-Fāriḳī*, ed. B.A.L. ʿAwaḍ, Cairo 1959, 186-90; Ḥusaynī, *A<u>kh</u>bār al-dawla al-sal<u>dj</u>ūḳiyya*, ed. Iḳbāl, 46-53; al-Makīn b. al-ʿAmīd, *Historia saracenica*, ed. T. Erpenius, Leiden 1625, 555-6; Ibn al-ʿAdīm, *Zubdat al-ḥalab min taʾrī<u>kh</u> Ḥalab*, ed. S. Dahhān, Damascus 1954, ii, 23-30; Ibn al-<u>Dj</u>awzī, *al-Muntaẓam*, viii, 260-5; Sibṭ al-<u>Dj</u>awzī, *Mirʾāt al-zamān, apud* Ibn al-Ḳalānisī, in *op. cit.*, 100-5; Bundārī, *Zubdat al-nuṣra wa-nu<u>kh</u>bat al-ʿuṣra*, ed. Houtsma, ii, 36-44; Ibn al-A<u>th</u>īr, x, 43-6. (ii) Persian: Ẓahīr al-Dīn Nī<u>sh</u>āpurī, *Sal<u>dj</u>ūḳ-nāma*, Tehran 1332, 24-7; Mīr<u>kh</u>ʷānd, *Rawḍat al-ṣafā*, Tehran 1853-4. (iii) Eastern Christian: Aristakes of Lastiverd, *Récit des malheurs de la nation arménienne*, ed. M. Canard et H. Berberian, Brussels 1973, 124-8; Michael the Syrian, facs. ed. and tr. J.-B. Chabot, *Chronique de Michel le Syrien*, Paris 1899-1914, 168-70; Matthew of Edessa, *Patmut'iwn*, tr. E. Dulaurier, *Chronique de Matthieu d'Edesse (962-1136)* ..., Paris 1858, 163-70; Bar Hebraeus, *The chronography of Gregory Abu 'l-Faraj* ..., ed. and tr. E. A. W. Budge, London 1932, 220-2. (iv) Byzantine: Attaliates, *Historia*, ed. I. Bekker, in *CSHB*, Bonn 1853, 144-69; Nicephorus Bryennius, *Historia*, tr. P. Gautier, *Nicephore Bryennios Histoire*, Brussels 1975, 104-20; Skylitzes, *Ioannes Skylitzes continuatus*, ed. E. T. Tsolakes, Thessalonika 1968; Michael Psellus, *Chronographia*, tr. E. R. A. Sewter, *The Chronographia of Michael Psellus*, London 1953, 271-4; Zonaras, *Ioannis Zonarae epitomae historiarum*, ed. T. Büttner-Wobst, in *CSHB*, Bonn 1897, 696-703. (v) Western Christian: William of Apulia, *Gesta Roberti Wiscardi*, in *MGH Scriptorum*, 1851, ix, 239-98.

2. Secondary sources: C. Oman, *A history of the art of war*, London 1898, 216-21; J. Laurent, *Byzance et les Turcs Seldjoucides dans l'Asie occidentale jusqu'en 1081*, Nancy 1913, 43-4; C. Cahen, *La campagne de Mantzikert d'après les sources musulmanes*, in *Byzantion*, ix (1934), 613-42; E. Honigmann, *Die Ostgrenze des Byzantinischen Reiches*, Brussels 1935, 189-90 and index; R. Grousset, *Histoire de l'Arménie*, Paris 1947, 624-30; M. Mathieu, *Une source négligée de la bataille de Mantzikert. Les "Gesta Roberti Wiscardi" de Guillaume d'Apulie*, in *Byzantion*, xx (1950), 89-103; S. Runciman, *A history of the Crusades*, Cambridge 1954, i, 62-5; İ. Kafesoğlu, *İA*, art. *Malazgirt*; A. Hamdani, *A possible Fatimid background to the battle of Manzikert*, in *AÜDTCFD*, vi (1968), 1-39; Cahen, *Pre-Ottoman Turkey*, London 1968, 26-30; J. C. Cheynet, *Mantzikert: un désastre militaire?*, in *Byzantion*, 1 (1980), 410-38; S. Vryonis, Jr., *The decline of medieval Hellenism in Asia Minor and the process of Islamization from the eleventh through the fifteenth century*, Berkeley, etc. 1971, 96-104; N. Kaymaz, *Malazgirt savaşı ile Anadolu'nun fethi ve türkleşmesine dair*, in *Malazgirt armağanı*, Ankara 1972, 259-68; A. Sevim, *Malazgirt meydan savaşı ve sonuçları*, in *ibid.*, 219-30; A. Hamdani, *Byzantine - Fatimid relations before the battle of Manzikert*, in *Byzantine Studies*, ii/2 (1974), 169-79; F. Sümer, *Malazgird savaşına katılan Türk beyleri*, in *Selçuklu Araştırmaları Dergisi*, iv (1975), 197-207.

(Carole Hillenbrand)

MĀLDA (properly Māldah or Māldaha) a district of India, in the Jalpaiguri Division of the State of West Bengal, area 3,713 sq. km. (1971), population 1,612,657 (1971), of whom 827, 706 were males and 784,951 were females. Of the total population, 53.64% were Hindus and 46.18% were Muslims.

It is possible that the name of the district town, Mālda, is derived from the element *māl* and refers to the wealth of the place as a centre of trade in the mediaeval period. In more ancient times, the area was known as Gaur (Gauḍa) from the city of that name, capital of the Senas (a Hindu dynasty). Between 1201 and 1203 the whole area was conquered by Muḥammad Ba<u>kh</u>tiyār <u>Kh</u>al<u>dj</u>ī, who was until that time a *<u>dj</u>āgīrdār* under the Muslim governor of Oudh. Muḥammad Ba<u>kh</u>tiyār <u>Kh</u>al<u>dj</u>ī was murdered in 1206 by ʿAlī Mardān <u>Kh</u>al<u>dj</u>ī; the latter was subsequently appointed by the Sultan of Dihlī as governor in Lakhnawtī [*q.v.*] which had become the Muslim capital in western Bengal. Islamic institutions were established throughout the area; numerous mosques, *maktabs* and *madrasas* were constructed. In 1345, Sultan <u>Sh</u>ams al-Dīn Ilyās <u>Sh</u>āh became ruler of the area independently of Dihlī. The <u>Sh</u>āhī dynasty he founded was noted for its liberal patronage of Bengali culture, and the <u>Sh</u>āhīs are generally acknowledged to have been tolerant and enlightned rulers. The beginning of Mu<u>gh</u>al rule in Bengal at the end of the 10th/16th century was a period of disorder and upheaval, followed by eventual peace, but not by the same identification with Bengali culture as under the <u>Sh</u>āhīs. In the 11th/17th century, under the Mu<u>gh</u>al rulers, trade with various European merchants flourished, notably with the English, whose assumption of the *Dīwānī* in 1765 led to the eventual economic decline of the area. The ruins of magnificent mosques at Mālda, Lakhnawtī and Pandu remain as evidence of the district's Islamic history; of the ten *<u>th</u>ānas* into which the district is divided, four (on the western side of the district) have Muslim population majorities.

Bibliography: <u>Gh</u>ulām Ḥusayn Salīm, *Riyāḍ al-salāṭīn*, tr. Abdus Salam, Calcutta 1902-4, repr. Dihlī 1975; Sir Jadunath Sarkar (ed.), *The history of Bengal: Muslim period, 1200-1757*, Patna 1973; Montazur Rahman Tarafdar, *Husain Shahi Bengal, 1494-1538: a socio-political study*, Dacca 1965; Jatindra Chandra Sengupta, *West Bengal District Gazetteers. Māldā*, Calcutta 1969; Bhaskar Ghose, *Census of India 1971. Series 22. West Bengal,* Part II A, *General population tables,* Dihlī 1973; G. Michell (ed.), *The Islamic heritage of Bengal,* UNESCO Protection of the cultural heritage, Research papers 1, Paris 1984, 106-7, 154, 196-7 (on the monuments).

(T. O. LING)

MALDIVES, a group of islands in the Indian Ocean.

1. History and social organisation.

The Republic of Maldives, formerly a Sultanate, forms an independent Asian state located in the north-central Indian Ocean some 650 km. south-west of Ceylon [*q.v.*]. The name "Maldives" is a foreign designation, probably derived from the Sanskrit *māladvīpa,* "garland of islands"; the indigenous name Divehi Rājjē "island realm" is gradually attaining some international currency.

The Maldive Archipelago consists of a narrow, 750 km. long chain of coral islands, lying scattered on a north-south axis between lat. 7°6′ N. and 0°42′ S and long. 72° and 74° E. The country is divided into nineteen administrative atolls, comprising an estimated 1,196 islands, of which 211 are presently (1980) inhabited. According to the 1977 Maldivian Government Census, the total population was 143,469, of whom 29,555 lived in Malé, the capital and only town of the archipelago.

The Maldives are believed to have been settled by the first of several waves of Sinhalese in the 5th or 4th century B.C., though both legend and scientific evidence point to the presence of an earlier Veddoid or Tamil population (Bell, 1940, 16; Maloney, 1980, 28-71). The islands seem never to have passed under Ceylonese political control, however, and with the exception of a brief period of Portuguese domination (965-81/1558-73) have remained effectively independent throughout recorded history.

Little is known of the history or culture of the Maldive Islanders in the pre-Islamic period. There are indications both of an indigenous primal religious pantheon (in which Rannamārī, a powerful deity of sea and storm, may have played a leading role), and of Hindu influence, both etymologically (Maloney, 1980, 51) and archaeologically (a Shivalingam, possibly indicating the site of a former Hindu temple, was excavated in Ari Atoll, Ariyaddu Island, in 1959). It is clear, however, that from *ca.* 300 A.D. onwards, Theravada Buddhism emanating from neighbouring Ceylon came to dominate the archipelago (Bell, 1940, *passim*; Reynolds, 1974, 1978; Maloney, 1980, 72-98). Thus by the 4th/10th century, Buddhist monasteries and stupas existed throughout the country, but especially in the southern and central atolls.

The initial advent of Islam to the islands remains shrouded in mystery. However, it is clear that the existence of the Maldives must have been known to Arab (and Persian) mariners even in pre-Islamic times, and it is therefore reasonable to assume that Muslim merchants and sailors first visited the remote archipelago as early as the 1st/7th century (Forbes, 1981, 62-77). For the next four centuries, Buddhism remained established as the dominant religious creed of the islands, though it is possible that, during the 4th-5th/10th-11th centuries, some of the northern atolls fell under the political and cultural influence of the (Hindu) Chola monarchs Rājarāja I and Rājendra I (Sastri, 1953, 220; Forbes, 1979, 138). During this period a mixed Arabo-Maldivian population, albeit of small size, must have developed at Malé, in some respects paralleling the development of the neighbouring Mappila [*q.v.*] community of Malabar [*q.v.*] and elsewhere on the Indian Ocean littoral. As with the Mappilas, this nascent Maldivian Muslim community is likely to have wielded economic, political and cultural influence out of all proportion to its numbers.

According to the Maldivian *Taʾrīkh* (a historical chronicle dating from the early 12th/18th century—see Bell, 1940, 18-43), the last Buddhist monarch of the Maldives, who bore the Sinhalese-style *biruda* (epithet) "Sirī Bavanādītta", was converted to Islam by a Muslim visitor to the islands on the 12th day of Rabīʿ II 548 (1153 A.D.), upon which he adopted the Muslim name and title "Sulṭān Muḥammad al-ʿĀdil". Certain controversies surround this arcane event. Thus, according to Ibn Baṭṭūṭa (who visited the islands between 1343-4 and again in 1346), the *shaykh* responsible for the conversion was a Maghribī styled Abu 'l-Barakāt al-Barbarī, a Sunnī Muslim of the Mālikī *madhhab* (text, iv, 127; English tr. Gray, 1882, 14). In contrast, the Maldivian *Taʾrīkh* ascribes the conversion to one Shaykh Yūsuf Shams al-Dīn Tabrīzī, by *nisba* almost certainly a Persian or perhaps a Turk, of uncertain rite (Bell, 1940, 18-19). Today, Abu 'l-Barakāt is officially recognised as the *shaykh* responsible for the conversion, and his tomb stands in Malé's Henveru district, the most venerated *ziyāra* in the country. Other early epigraphic evidence ascribing the conversion to Shams al-Dīn is extant, however (Bell, 1940, 190; Forbes, 1982), and the exact role played by "Tabrīzugefānu" (who is still widely revered throughout the country) remains uncertain.

Following the conversion of Muḥammad al-ʿĀdil to Islam, both the *Taʾrīkh* and Ibn Baṭṭūṭa's *Riḥla* are agreed that the new faith was rapidly embraced by all Maldivians. Recently-translated epigraphic evidence casts doubt on this claim, however. Thus according to a copper-plate grant (*lōmāfānu*) preserved at the Boḍugalu Mosque in Malé, more than half-a-century after the initial conversion, it was necessary for the Malé authorites to send a military expedition to crush an "infidel" (presumably Buddhist) king in the south of the country (a transcript of this *lōmāfānu* is currently in press at Malé). It may be safely assumed, however, that by the late 7th/13th century the country was universally Muslim, a situation which remains unchanged today.

Following the initial Portuguese assault upon the traditional trade network of the Indian Ocean, much of the indigenous, Muslim-dominated trade of the Malabar region was re-routed via the Maldives, thus exposing the islanders to more direct and regular contact both with Arabia and with Islamic South-East Asia. This development led in turn to an increased (and unfriendly) Portuguese interest in the islands, culminating in the brief but destructive Portuguese occupation when, between 965-81/1558-73, Malé passed under the control of the hated "Adiri Adiri" and "the sea grew red with Muslim blood" (*Taʾrīkh*: Bell, 1940, 26). In response to this Portuguese aggression, the Maldivians, under the inspired leadership of Muḥammad Boḍu Takurufānu, a son of the *khaṭīb* of Utīm in the north of the country, waged an unremitting guerilla struggle. By 981/1573 the Portuguese were forced to withdraw, and Muḥammad Takurufānu became sultan. One lasting result of the Portuguese occupation was a change in the *madhhab* followed by the Maldivians. Thus according to the *Taʾrīkh* (Bell, 1940, 27), following the expulsion of the Portuguese it was discovered that the Maldivian *ʿulamāʾ* had been decimated, and that no *shaykh* of the Mālikī *madhhab* remained alive. At this time there chanced to return to Malé from southern Arabia one Muḥammad Djamāl al-Dīn Huvadu (a native of Huvadu/Suvadiva Atoll in the south of the country), a Maldivian ʿālim who had spent many years studying at the Shāfiʿī centres of the Wādī Ḥaḍramawt and at Zabīd in the Yemen. He was subsequently appointed ḳāḍī by Muḥammad Takurufānu, and from this time the Mālikī *madhhab* was replaced by the Shāfiʿī one as the formal rite of the Maldives.

From 981/1573 to the present day, the Maldives have remained effectively independent, though in 1887 an agreement was signed between Sultan Ibrāhīm Nūr al-Dīn and the British Crown by which the islands assumed British protectorate status in matters of foreign policy, but retained internal self-government. In 1932 a constitution was introduced for the first time, though the Sultanate was retained for a further 21 years, when the First Republic was established under the Presidency of Muḥammad Amīn Dīdī. In 1954, following the overthrow and death of the latter, the Sultanate was briefly re-established. However in 1968, three years after the attainment of full independence from Britain, the Sultanate was finally abolished and a Second Republic proclaimed under the Presidency of Ibrahim Nasir. Today, the President of the Republic of Maldives is Maumoon Abdul Gayoom, a graduate of al-Azhar who is fluent in both Arabic and English.

The people of the Maldive Islands are predominantly of Indo-European origin, being linked ethnically and culturally with the Sinhalese people of Ceylon and the inhabitants of Minicoy Island, now grouped with the neighbouring Laccadive Islands [*q.v.*] to the north. Other important constituent elements in Maldivian culture are the Dravidian and the Arabo-Muslim ones. Maldivians are 100% Sunnī Muslims of the Shāfiʿī *madhhab*. The only non-Muslims to be found in the country are foreign experts or businessmen, all of whom are resident on a strictly temporary basis, and none of whom may acquire property or Maldivian nationality without first becoming Shāfiʿī Sunnīs. The Ismāʿīlī Bohra community (originating from Gudjarāt [SEE BOHORĀS]) which dominated Maldivian trade from the late 19th century to the early 1950s has been expelled, and their solitary mosque (in Malé) has passed under Shāfiʿī control. Unlike the neighbouring Laccadive Islands, the Maldives are patrilineal; nor is "caste" a factor, though class distinctions were—and in some cases remain—strong. Maldivian Islam is therefore distinguished by considerable orthodoxy at the official level. At a popular level, however, it is characterised by an unusually widespread belief in spirits and in all manner of *djinn*, as well as by the extensive practice of *fańḍita* (cf. Sanskrit *paṅḍit*, "a learned person"), a religio-magical science widely accepted throughout the archipelago and described by Maloney (1980, 242-73) as "a parallel religious system". Today the Maldivian religious establishment—which draws much of its inspiration from the reformist ideologies with their roots in Arabia and elsewhere in the Middle East—is anxious to limit the role played by *fanḍita* in Maldivian society, and actively discourages *sīhuru* (cf. Ar. *siḥr* "magic"), *fańḍita*'s black magic counterpart. Despite these pressures, however, widespread belief in *fańḍita* and in a plethora of *djinn* persists, providing intriguing evidence of parallels between popular Islam in the Maldives and in its counterpart in the Malay-Indonesian archipelago.

Bibliography: Ibn Baṭṭuṭa, iv, 110-67; cf. A. Gray, *Ibn Batuta in the Maldives and Ceylon*, in *JRAS (Ceylon Branch)*, extra no. (1882), 60 pp.; F. Pyrard, *The voyage of François Pyrard of Laval*, ed. and tr. A. Gray and H. C. P. Bell, Hakluyt Society, Cambridge 1888, 3 vols. in 2, i, 60-320; H. C. P. Bell, *The Maldive Islands: an account of the physical features, climate, history, inhabitants, productions and trade*, Ceylon Government Sessional Paper xliii (1881), Colombo 1883; *idem, The Maldive Islands: report on a visit to Malé*, Ceylon Government Sessional Paper xv (1921), Colombo 1921); *idem, The Maldive Islands: monograph on the history, archaeology and epigraphy*, Colombo 1940; K. A. Nilakanta Sastri, *The Colas*, Madras 1953; C. H. B. Reynolds, *Buddhism and the Maldivian Language*, in L. Cousins (ed.), *Buddhist studies in honour of I. B. Horner*, Dordrecht 1974, 193-8; J. Carswell, *Mosques and tombs in the Maldive Islands*, in *Art and Archaeology Research Papers*, ix (July 1976), 26-30; Reynolds, *Linguistic strands in the Maldives*, in *Contributions to Asian Studies*, xi (1978), 155-66; C. Maloney, *Divehi*, in R. V. Weekes (ed.), *Muslim peoples: a world ethnographic survey*, London and Connecticut 1978, 128-33; A. D. W. Forbes, *Sources towards a history of the Laccadive Islands*, in *South Asia*, ii/1-2 (1979), 130-50; *idem, Archives and resources for Maldivian history*, in *ibid.*, iii/l (1980), 70-82; C. Maloney, *People of the Maldive Islands*, Madras 1980; Forbes, *Southern Arabia and the Islamicisation of the Central Indian Ocean Archipelagoes*, in *Archipel*, xxi (1981), 55-92; *idem, The mosque in the Maldive Islands: a preliminary historical survey*, in *ibid.*, xxiv (1982); N. F. Munch-Petersen, *The Maldives, history, daily life and art-handicraft*, in *Bull. du Centre d'Etudes du Moyen-Orient et de la communauté Islamique*, Brussels, i/1-2 (1982), 74-103. See also LACCADIVES, *Bibl.*

(A. D. W. FORBES)

2. Language and literature. The Maldivian language, called Divehi, is an Indo-Aryan tongue closely related to Sinhalese, with which it shares such distinctive features as the half-nasals before voiced stops and the "umlaut" of *a* to *e* in certain positions. It maintains the distinction, now lost in Sinhalese, between dental *l* and retroflex *ĺ*. It was formerly written in a script derived ultimately from Brāhmī and closely resembling earlier forms of Sinhalese script. This script, known as *Dives akuru* ("Maldivian letters"), survives on tombstones and inscriptions and in some manuscripts, but was gradually replaced during the 18th century by a script called *tāna*, written from right to left (which facilitated the use of Urdu or Persian loanwords written in Arabic script). This script contains 24 letters (one of which is known as *alifu*, though it has more than one function). It was a local invention; the first nine letters are forms of the Arabic numerals. In 1977, an official romanisation scheme was introduced by the government.

No ancient literature has survived. Surviving writings on palmleaf are mostly magical or medical treatises. A few historical works exist, though not generally available for inspection. Learned works were sometimes written in Arabic; thus an Arabic *taʾrīkh* of the Maldivian Kingdom (*Divehi rājje*) exists, compiled in 1725 and brought up to date in 1821, as well as some 18th-century histories in Maldivian called *Rādavali* ("line of Kings"); these histories all begin from the time of adoption of Islam in 548/1153. Surviving poems include *Diyōge raivaru* ("The song of Diyō"), an obscure romance of travels in the Indian Ocean dating from about 1810.

It is only with the 20th century that books became common and duplication of texts was practised. Grammatical formulation of the Maldivian language may be dated from the publication of *Sullam al-arīb* by Shaykh Ibrāhīm Rushdī in A.H. 1355. Amīn Dīdī, Chief Minister and later first President of the Maldives (1909-54), was a prolific writer and encouraged and promoted literary compositions by others. Literary magazines feature among the early newspapers which date from the 1930s, and poetry competitions became fashionable at the time. Amīn Dīdī also wrote historical and biographical works, including a history of the Maldives during the 1939-45 war.

There was also a tradition of religious writing, usually of a commentarial character. Literary figures of the recent past who wrote on both secular and religious subjects are Shaykh Ṣalāḥ al-Dīn (d. 1950) and Bodufenvaluge Sīdī (also known as ʿAfīf al-Dīn) (d. 1969). Most of their works remain in manuscript.

Bibliography: H. C. P. Bell, *The Máldive Islands: monograph on the history, archaeology and epigraphy*, Colombo 1940. (C. H. B. Reynolds)

MALḤAMA (a) in modern times designates an epic [see ḥamāsa] and also corresponds to a usage already in evidence in the Old Testament, where *milḥamōt* is applied to the wars of Yahweh (I Sam. xviii, 17, xxv, 28), but in the Islamic Middle Ages this word meant a writing of a divinatory character, the *Malḥamat Dāniyāl* [cf. dāniyāl]. It is a question of a collection of meteorological signs with their divinatory meanings, derived from the day of the week on which 1 January falls (from the Saturday to the Friday), eclipses of the moon, following the same order, lightning, thunder, the appearance of halos around the sun and the moon, a rainbow, the appearance of a sign in the sky and earthquakes. This first series of signs is followed by another, referring to the effects of the winds on events, those of days of the week and those of days of the week on which 1 Thôt of the Coptic year falls, and the first day of the Arab year (cf. Istanbul ms. Bayezit, Veliüddin Ef. 2294,3, fols. 58-65).

Another recension of this *malḥama* (Istanbul, Bağdatlı Vehbi 2234, fols. 1-6a) enlarges the range of these predictions based on the lunar mansions, thunder according to months, eclipses of the moon, earthquakes, new moons, a rainbow, parhelions (*al-ghubār ʿalā wadjh al-shams*), the moon's disc, snow, hail, clouds, comets, the blowing of winds, rains, etc.

A third recension (Istanbul, Reisülküttab Mustafa Ef. 1164,2, fols. 15a-93a) enumerates the signs and information supplied by "celestial and terrestrial phenomena in deserts and at sea, earthquakes, eclipses, new moons, according to the signs of the zodiac, tempests, black winds, clouds seen as silhouettes of people; what will happen in the lands of the Persians, Arabs and other peoples and in the islands and mountains".

These popular astrological portents trace their origin to the Akkadian divinatory tablets and the Syriac writings which preserve echos of them. The most complete Syriac witness to this is the *K. al-Dalāʾil* (= *Ktōbō d-shūdōʿē*) "Book of Prognostications" of al-Ḥasan b. Bahlūl (cf. Istanbul, Hekimoğlu 572, fols. 1-300a, fine large *naskhī*, dating from 556/1160-1). The prognostications which it incorporates are derived from the seasons, months, weeks and festivals, according to the calendar of the Christians, Muslims, Jews, Armenians and Copts. This compilation contains, in addition, various calculations, information on the festivals of the Ḥarrānians, where Ibn al-Bahlūl refers to the *Fihrist* (of Ibn al-Nadīm), whose author he gives as Yaḥyā b. Ḥātim Ipnā (?) (ايني), and an account of the Mandaeans of Wāsiṭ. One table brings together prognostications derived from atmospheric phenomena; a chapter on physiognomy (based on the *Kunnāsh al-Manṣūrī* of Abū Bakr al-Rāzī and other writings); symptoms of poisons and their antidotes; signs of the humours which predominate in the body; rules for the purchase of slaves; the diagnosis of illness; the recognition of horses' illnesses; a compendium of dream interpretation.

There follows (fols. 302-356a) a *malḥama* of Daniel in which the meteorological and astrological *malḥama* develops into the apocalyptical *malḥama*. Indeed, in the introduction we read the following definition: "This is *Malḥamat al-bayān fī maʿrifat al-sinīn wa 'l-duhūr wa 'l-azmān* on the celestial bodies, the movements of the stars, the phenomena of the universe, order and corruption, how to see the shifts of fortune, the oppression that kings exercise over one another, the succession of their states and what will befall them" (fol. 2a). The work is presented as a reply by Kaʿb al-Aḥbār [*q.v.*] to a question asked by Muʿāwiya concerning the Mahdī.

This apocalyptical current reaches its peak in *al-Shadjara al-nuʿmāniyya fī 'l-dawla al-ʿuthmāniyya*, a work attributed to Muḥyī 'l-Dīn Ibn al-ʿArabī (d. 638/1240) and commented on, in particular, by his disciple Ṣadr al-Dīn al-Ḳūnawī (d. 672/1263), Ṣalāḥ al-Dīn al-Ṣafadī (d. 764/1363). Aḥmad b. Muḥammad al-Maḳḳarī (d. 1041/1632), Muṣṭafā Ef. b. Sahrab and al-Shahrāfī. The earliest form of this work, recast and adapted at a later date in Egypt (cf. Istanbul, Nuruosmaniye 2819, 82 fols., dating from 1111/1699-1700; Saray, Revan 1742, fols. 65b-180b; Üniv. Kütüphanesi A 6257, fols. 26b-34a), then in the Ottoman Empire, on the authority of Ibn al-ʿArabī, is thought to go back to the Fāṭimid period and to have dealt with the Mahdī. It is to be found in *madjmūʿāt* of an apocalyptical character, such as ms. A 542 of Istanbul University, containing: (1) *al-Shadjara al-nuʿmāniyya wa-hiya 'l-kubrā min thalāth dawāʾir* (fol. 2b); (2) *al-Dāʾira fī bayān ẓuhūr al-ḳāʾim min ʿilm al-djafr* (fols. 1b-2b) and (3) *al-Risāla al-sharīfa al-ḥarfiyya fī bayān rumūz al-djafriyya* (fols. 3a-20a). Similarly, Bursa ms. Ulucami 3544, *naskhī* from 1096/1684-5, contains an anonymous commentary on *al-Shadjara al-nuʿmāniyya* (fols. 94a-140a) preceded by the *Risālat al-burhān fī ʿalāmat mahdī ākhir al-zamān* (fols. 1-92b) of ʿAlī b. Ḥusām al-Dīn known by the name of al-Muttaḳī (d. between 975 and 977/1567-9).

With this current of apocalyptical *malḥama, malāḥim* [*q.v.*] literature is associated.

Bibliography: T. Fahd, *La divination arabe*, Leiden 1966, 224-8, 408-12; F. Sezgin, *GAS*, vii, Leiden 1979, 312-17, 282-3, 328; A. Abel, *Changements politiques et littérature apocalyptique dans le monde musulman*, in *SI*, ii (1954), 23-43; Sophia Grotzfeld, *Dāniyāl in der arabischen Legende*, in *Festgabe H. Wehr*, Wiesbaden 1969, 72-85; G. Furlani, *Di una raccolta di tratti astrologici*, in *RSO*, vii (1916-18), 885-9; *idem*, *Eine Sammlung astrologischer Abhandlungen in arabischer Sprache*, in *ZA*, xxxiii (1921), 157-64; G. Bergsträsser (ed.), *Neue meteorologische Fragmente des Theophrast*, in *SBAk. Heidelberg*, Phil.-hist. Kl. (1918), Abh. 9, 6-7; G. Vajda, *Quelques observations sur Malḥamat Dāniyāl*, in *Arabica*, xxiii (1976), 84-7; A. Fodor, *Malḥamat Dāniyāl*, ed. and tr. in *The Muslim East. Studies in honour of Julius Germanus*, ed. G. Káldy-Nagy, Budapest 1974, 85-133. (T. Fahd)

MALḤŪN (*məlḥūn*) designates the state of the language which served for the expression of certain forms of dialectal poetry in the Maghrib, as well as this poetry itself. Although the verse composed may be generally intended to be intoned and chanted by amateurs or professionals with a momentary musical accompaniment, this term does not come from *laḥn* "melody", as Muḥammad al-Fāsī would have it (*Adab sha ʿbī,* 43-4), but from *laḥana* (cf. Djirārī, *Ḳaṣīda,* 55-7) understood in the sense of "to stray from the linguistic norm" i.e. from literary Arabic [see LAḤN AL-ʿĀMMA]. In the Maghrib there are various forms of popular poetry in dialect which grew up there or were imported [see in particular BUḲĀLA, ḤAWFĪ and ZADJAL], but, although the distinction may not always be perceived or even perceptible, *məlḥūn* properly so-called, which also has various names such as *ḳaṣīda zadjaliyya* or *ʿilm mawhūb/mūhūb* because this art was innate (see Djirārī, 54-64) or simply *klām,* comprises more specifically strophic poems or ones derived from the classical *ḳaṣīda* [*q.v.*], whose fundamental characteristic appears to be (apart from liberties taken by poets) the tendency to use an internal rhyme, the first hemistichs of all the lines rhyming throughout the poem or in each of the strophes.

In the present article, we will not neglect Tripolitania, and we will concern ourselves with Tunisia, where popular poetry is still very much alive, but more particularly with Morocco and Algeria, for it is concerning these two countries that there is the most information, due to the significant number of bards (*gawwāl,* pl. *gawwālīn*) and poets (*shā ʿir, nāẓim, shaykh*) who were famous there from an earlier period, and due also to the abundance of works which have been devoted to them. However, we will limit ourselves to citing those of them who are the most renowned and, as it is impossible to reserve a notice for each of them in this *Encyclopaedia,* we will indicate in brief the principal references which concern them, asking the reader to refer to the general bibliography, where the titles will be given in their complete form.

The origin of *məlḥūn.* *Məlḥūn* does not appear to have arisen from any of the categories of poetic production in dialectal Arabic with which Spain [see ZADJAL] and the Near East (see Ṣafī al-Dīn al-Ḥillī, *al-ʿĀṭil al-ḥālī,* ed. W. Hoenerbach, *Die vulgärarabische Poetik,* Wiesbaden 1956) were already acquainted in the Middle Ages. Ibn Khaldūn, to whom the merit, among other things, must be acknowledged of taking popular poetry into account, does not use the word *məlḥūn,* but he cites at the end of the *Muḳaddima* (iii, 417 ff.; French tr. de Slane, iii, 445 ff. Eng. tr. Rosenthal, iii, 466 ff.) some examples of townspeople's poetry which he calls *ʿarūḍ al-balad* and whose creation he attributes to an Andalusian by the name of Ibn ʿUmayr who had emigrated to Fās. It is a strophic poetry with a double rhyme which Ibn Khaldūn regards as deriving from the *muwashshaḥ* [*q.v.*] and whose structure is similar to certain pieces of urban *məlḥūn* (see A. Tahar, *Poésie populaire,* 363 ff.). The author of the *Muḳaddima* adds that Ibn ʿUmayr respected *i ʿrāb,* but that the Fāsīs abandoned it because it did not interest them. Despite its undeniable value, this evidence does not allow us to ascertain the period in which the first manifestations of the genre which concerns us arose; that of Leo Africanus [*q.v.*] (10th/16th century) is not of much more help; he says in fact (*Description de l'Afrique,* 214-15) that there were in Fās many poets composing love poems in the "vernacular" and, each year, on the occasion of the festival of the Prophet's birthday (*mawlid/mūlūd*) [*q.v.*], a piece of verse in his praise [see MAWLIDIYYĀT], but it is quite likely that the "vernacular" in question was Hispanic Arabic, as this must also have been the language of the *ʿarūḍ al-balad.* According to G.S. Colin (in *Initiation au Maroc,* 224-7; *EI*[1], art. MOROCCO, vii. 2), two periods are to be distinguished in the evolution of popular poetry; during the first, which stretches until the beginning of the Saʿdids (middle of the 10th/16th century), Moroccan poetry in dialectal Arabic was a direct heritage from al-Andalus and was expressed in Hispanic Arabic, having become the "classical" language of the *zadjal;* the second begins in the 10th/16th century, and it is under the "Bedouinising dynasties" of the Saʿdids and ʿAlawids (from 1076/1666) that *məlḥūn* properly so-called, a special language influenced by Bedouin dialects made its appearance and developed. The word designating, in Algeria, the popular poet (*gawwāl* and not *ḳawwāl*), the significant number of bards belonging to nomad or at least rural tribes, and the fact that the oldest specimens of the genre which have been preserved date from the 10th/16th century, seem to lend credence to G.S. Colin. However, this *məlḥūn* was not born overnight, and it is probable that the Arab tribes who had emigrated into North Africa in the 5th/11th century had preserved their traditions and that they composed some verse in their own dialect; only a study of the language of the most ancient remnants of dialectal poetry could shed some light on this problem. It is actually dangerous to contest G.S. Colin's theory by citing, as Djirārī had done (549-60), poets earlier than the 10th/16th century, without taking account of the language—which is really hard to define—that they used in their compositions.

Whatever may be the case, the first who is known was one called Ibn ʿAbbūd who lived in Fās at the end of the Waṭṭāsid dynasty (first half of the 10th/16th century); he is famous in Morocco for a "war poem" (*ḥarbī*) inspired by the battle of 942/1536 between Waṭṭāsids and Saʿdids, at which he was present (Rabat ms. G594; see E. Dermenghem and M. El Fasi, *Poèmes marocains,* 96; M. El Fasi, in *La Pensée,* no. 1 (November 1962), 68; M. al-Fāsī, *Adab sha ʿbī,* 46). Two poets of the same period, the Moroccan al-Madjdjūb [*q.v.*], author of well-known quatrains which constitute a category on their own, and the Algerian Sīdī Lakhḍar Bəkhkhlūf (al-Akhḍar, *alias* al-Akhḍal b. ʿAbd Allāh b. Makhlūf), of the Mostaganem region, are counted among the earliest; in a poem on the Battle of Mazagran delivered against the Spaniards in 965/1558, the latter asserts that he participated in this combat in person, so that if this detail is authentic, he supplies a valuable chronological reference; the works of this bard are still appreciated, so that it has been possible to collect them in a *Dīwān* published by M. Bekhoucha in Rabat in 1951 (31 poems, among which figure several panegyrics of the Prophet, which are still sung by the *ṭolba,* in funerary vigils, to the tune of the *Burda* [*q.v.*]; see also J. Desparmet, *Blida,* 146-66; idem, *Chansons de geste,* 195, 216-19; Sonneck, no. 112; M. al-Ḳāḍī, *Kanz,* 7-15; A. Tahar, index).

The principal poets from the 10th/16th century to the present. In the second half of the century there lived another Moroccan originally from the Tāfīlālt called Abū Fāris ʿAbd al-ʿAzīz al-Maghrāwī (d. 1014/1605) who has also remained famous, to the point that there is a proverb *kull ṭwīl khāwi, ghēr ən-nəkhla w-əl-Məghrāwi* "Everything tall is empty, except the palm-tree and al-Maghrāwī", because he was very tall and expressed such wisdom in his verses that sanctity was attributed to him (see Rabat ms. Bibl. Royale 860), although he also left erotic poems which we do not know whether to interpret symbolically; in his finely-executed work figure *ghazawāt* (see below) and, in particular, a *marthiya* [*q.v.*] in dialectal Arabic composed on the death of Sultan al-Manṣūr al-Dhahabī (985-1012/1578/1603), whose favourite he was (see Rabat ms. 594; Aubin, *Le*

Maroc, 343; Colin, *op. laud.,* 225; al-G͟hawt͟hī, *Kas͟hf,* 87-9; Ḳāḍī, *Kanz,* 205-10; Bekhoucha, *Poèmes erotiques,* 156-78; idem and Sekkal, *Printanières,* 61-5; M. al-Fāsī, *Adab s͟haᶜbī,* 57, who estimates at about 50 the number of the poems preserved; Belhalfaoui, 120-37, hymn to the Prophet; D̲j̲irārī, 587-91; Tahar, index).

In the course of the 11th/17th century, when Tlemcen had already become a flourishing centre of this genre of popular poetry, Moroccan *məlḥūn* received a fresh impetus from Tlemceni poets in exile (see below). Towards the end of the century, another *s͟hāᶜir* originally from the Tāfīlālt (see M. al-Fāsī, *Adab s͟haᶜbī,* 57; D̲j̲irārī, 592-6), al-Maṣmūdī, "noted the principal tunes, that the people had gradually adapted for their songs, and he also became the creator of the" *grīḥa* (< *ḳarīḥa,* which designates a light music and some easy tunes for popular poems, with a vague instrumentation"; Aubin, *op. laud.,* 342-3); with regard to this, it is said that al-Maṣmūdī is one of the branches of poetry, while al-Mag͟hrāwī is its trunk.

Məlḥūn did not cease to find favour with all classes of Moroccan society, but after these two poets, it experienced a certain stagnation until the end of the 12th/18th century. In this period, one of those who revived it was Sultan Sīdī Muḥammad b. ᶜAbd Allāh (1171-1204/1759-89) who had no scruples about cultivating it himself (see M. al-Fāsī, *Adab s͟haᶜbī,* 58). Among his successors one can mention Sīdī Muḥammad b. ᶜAbd al-Raḥmān (1276-90/1859-73), with whom Tuhāmī al-Madg͟harī (Mdəg͟hri) of the Tāfīlālt (see below) lived on intimate terms, and it is said that many *ḳaṣīdas* issued in the latter's name were really the work of the prince (Aubin, *op. laud.,* 343-4; M. al-Fāsī, *Adab s͟haᶜbī,* 62-3). The last sultan who was particularly interested in dialectal poetry was Mawlāy ᶜAbd al-Ḥafīẓ (1909-13), who is said to have composed the 39 pieces of verse collected in his *Dīwān* lithographed in Fās (n.d.); it is, however, doubtful whether they were all of his creation (see M. al-Fāsī, *op. laud.,* 64), and the names of three poets are cited who may have participated in the fraud (see D̲j̲irārī, 663-9).

In an erotico-mystical poem on Mecca, the Moroccan al-Ḥād̲j̲d̲j̲ Muk͟htār al-Baḳḳālī (d. 1255/1839; see Ibn Zaydān, *Itḥāf,* v, 339, 341, 443) wants to confide his anxieties to 21 of his predecessors and contemporaries and asks them for their intercession (text and French tr. in Belhalfaoui, 56-61); although he may not be one of the most remarkable, this poet gives an idea of the unity which existed in the field of dialectal poetry between Morocco and Algeria and, without compiling an honours list properly speaking, or testifying to the tastes of all his contemporaries, he nevertheless supplies precious information on the names to bear in mind by recording in the first lines, alongside more obscure personages and ones who are harder to identify, the greatest representatives of *məlḥūn* from the 10th/16th century to the first decades of the 13th/19th. Apart from al-Mag͟hrāwī, Sīdī Lak͟hḍar and al-Maṣmūdī already cited, there appear notably:

al-Ḥād̲j̲d̲j̲ ᶜĪsā of Lag͟hwāṭ (d. *ca.* 1150/1737-8), author, in particular, of hunting poems (see Sonneck, no. 63; M. Sidoun, *Chasse au faucon,* 272-94; Ḳāḍī, *Kanz,* 179-81; C. Trumelet, *Les Français dans le désert,* 499).

Muḥammad b. Āmsāyb (Ben Msayeb *et var.*) of Tlemcen (d. 1182/1768), who had to go into exile in Morocco after having sung of love and wine, and composed on his return several panegyrics of the Prophet and saints; he is still held in public favour and his "poems of love and religious inspiration always move men and women at weddings" (S. Bencheneb, in *Initiation à l'Algérie,* 302; see Sonneck, no. 32; M. Ben Cheneb, *Itinéraire*; Desparmet, *Blida,* 8; Ḳāḍī, *Kanz,* 134-42, 147-9; A. Hamidou, *Poésie vulgaire,* 1007-30; Bekhoucha, *Poèmes érotiques,* 6-33; idem and Sekkal, *Printanières,* 124-7; Belhalfaoui, 72-91; Tahar, index; *al-D̲j̲awāhir al-ḥisān* 285-316; his *Dīwān* (31 poems) was collected and published in Tlemcen in 1370/1951 by M. Bekhoucha.

ᶜAlī Kūra (end of the 12th/18th century), of the Relizane region, who celebrated Platonic and mystical love (see Belhalfaoui, 148-53; Tahar, 208, 210).

Ibn Swīkāt (Bessouiket), an Oranian of the same period, who achieved fame through his opposition to the Turkish occupation, although al-Baḳḳālī claims that he was a Turk (see A. Cour, *Poésie politique,* 486; Belhalfaoui, 144-7, on his dying horse; Tahar, index).

ᶜAlī al-Bag͟hdādī, a Moroccan poet of the same period, whose fame rests on a *ḳaṣīda* entitled *al-Ḥarrāz* (watchman = *raḳīb* of the Andalusians = *gardador* of the troubadours), which is a little satirical comedy (French tr. E. Dermenghem and M. El Fasi, *Poèmes marocains,* reproduced in H. Duquaire, 213-22 and E. Dermenghem, *Les plus beaux textes arabes,* Paris 1951, 522-31; see also M. al-Fāsī, *Adab s͟haᶜbī,* 61-2).

Ibn Ḥammādī of Relizane (early 13th/19th century) who exalted love and the Prophet (see Belhalfaoui, 138-43; Tahar, index).

Ibn ᶜAlī: this poet who is cited by al-Baḳḳālī must be Muḥammad b. ᶜAlī wuld/u Rzīn of Tāfīlālt (d. 1237/1822), whose best known work today in Morocco is a love poem in which the *ṭars͟hūn* ("young hawk") symbolises the loved one (text and French tr. by M. El Fasi, *Le* tarchoun (*le petit faucon*) *de Ben ᶜAli Chérif,* in *Hespéris-Tamuda,* vi [1965], 39-52; see also Sonneck, no. 59; Aubin, 343; Bekhoucha, *Poèmes érotiques,* 115-54; idem and Sekkal, *Printanières,* 75-89; M. al-Fāsī, *Adab s͟haᶜbī,* 60-1); he is notable for his composition of a poem (preserved, but inaccessible) on Bonaparte's expedition to Egypt (see D̲j̲irārī, 625-7).

al-ᶜAmīrī of Meknès (middle of the 13th/19th century), who attracted attention on account of his poems called *d̲j̲afriyya* full of reflections of a political character which led him to make predictions about future events (see M. al-Fāsī, *Adab s͟haᶜbī,* 62; D̲j̲irārī, 627-8).

al-Ḥād̲j̲d̲j̲ Muḥammad al-Nad̲j̲d̲j̲ār of Marrakesh, son-in-law and copyist of Mt͟hīrəd (see below), who left many panegyrics of the Prophet, a poem in which he alluded to an eclipse and a *mart͟hiya* of Ḥamdūn b. al-Ḥād̲j̲d̲j̲ [see IBN AL-ḤADJ̲DJ̲ in Suppl.] which is preserved in Rabat ms. 396D (see Aubin, 343; Bekhoucha and Sekkal, *Printanières*; M. al-Fāsī, *Adab s͟haᶜbī,* 58; D̲j̲irārī, 616-19).

His contemporary Ḳaddūr al-ᶜAlamī of Meknès (d. 1266/1850), who is one of the most popular; that al-Baḳḳālī, who was his master, cites him among his authorities is an indication of the prestige which he already enjoyed. This illiterate poet, who claimed descent from ᶜAbd al-Salām b. Mas͟hīs͟h [*q.v.*] and led a pious life, is a kind of saint regarded as possessing thaumaturgical gifts; moreover, he recounts several miracles in his poems which he composed with extreme facility. There appears to have been no attempt to collect his works, but a certain number of them, preserved by his disciples and *rāwīs* (also called in Morocco *həffāḍ* < *ḥaffāẓ*), still enjoy great popularity, even in the humblest circles. Sīdī Ḳaddūr, who belongs to the urban school, is the author of *zad̲j̲als* dealing with mystical and profane subjects and of *ḳṣāyd* (*ḳaṣāᵓid*) to which a religious character is attributed, even when they have an entirely erotic appearance. One of his most famous compositions is that in which he tells the story of his house, sold, miraculously recovered and transformed into a much-frequented *zāwiya,* where he was later buried. His biography, which figures in Ibn Zaydān (*Itḥāf,* v, 336-52) has been discussed by M. T. Buret, in *Hespéris,* xxv/1 (1938), 85-92 (see also Lakhdar, *Vie littéraire,* 337-8; on his verses, see the *Itḥāf, loc. cit.*; Sonneck, no. 12; A. Fischer, *Liederbuch,* nos. 17, 26, 29, 34; Lévi-Provençal, in *Arch. Berb.,* iv [1919-20], 67-75; Ḳādī, *Kanz,* 143; Bekhoucha, *Poèmes érotiques*; J. Jouin, in *Hespéris,* 1959/1-2, 87-103; M. al-Fāsī, *Adab sha*ᶜ*bī,* 62-3; Djirārī, 629-39; Tahar, index; Belhalfaoui, 47, for whom a line of Ḳaddūr rightly recalls the beginning of a famous poem of Rutebeuf).

Abu 'l-Aṭbāḳ, who is doubtless Mubārak Abu 'l-Aṭbāḳ (Mbārk Bū Leṭbāḳ), an Oranian poet, author of *ghazawāt* (see Desparmet, *Chansons de geste,* 195; M. al-Fāsī, *Adab sha*ᶜ*bī,* 56, 58).

Al-Baḳḳālī further cites an Ibn ᶜArūs, who is perhaps identical with al-ᶜArūsī al-Tilimsānī (see Desparmet, *Chansons de geste,* 195, 205 ff.), and four other unidentified poets.

On the other hand, several great names have been omitted and, although the limits of this article do not allow mention of all the *gawwālīn* whose work is not totally forgotten, we will go back in time a little to add to the preceding list those who appear the best known: Abū ᶜUthmān Saᶜīd b. ᶜAbd Allāh al-Tilimsānī al-Mandasī, who lived in the entourage of three sultans of Morocco: Mawlāy Maḥammad b. al-Sharīf (1045-74/1635-64), Mawlāy al-Rashīd (1075-82/1664-72) and Mawlāy Ismāᶜīl (1082-1139/1672-1729). This poet originally from Tlemcen enjoyed great prestige among his colleagues due to his profound knowledge of literary Arabic in which he also composed, as well as to his taste for rare rhymes and for the transposition in dialect of classical poems. He is known particularly as the author of the *ᶜAḳīḳa,* a famous poem of 303 lines composed in 1088/1677 in praise of the Prophet, with a commentary in literary Arabic by Muḥammad Abū Raʾs al-Nāṣirī (1164-1237/1751-1822) entitled *al-Durra al-anīḳa fī sharḥ al-ᶜAḳīḳa,* later edited and translated by G. Faure-Biguet, *L'Aqîqa* (*la Cornaline*), Algiers 1901 (see also al-Ghawthī, *Kashf,* 51-75; Ḳādī, *Kanz,* 21-43, 190-6; M. al-Fāsī, *Adab sha*ᶜ*bī,* 58; Djirārī, 604-8; Tahar, index).

Al-Mandasī had as his pupil his fellow-citizen Aḥmad b. al-Trīkī (Ben Triki or Ben Zengli) who died at the beginning of the 18th century. A singer of love, he was exiled by the Turks in 1083/1672 and, like his master, had to seek refuge for some time in Morocco. On his return, he composed mainly panegyrics of the Prophet (see Sonneck, no. 33; al-Ghawthī, *Kashf,* 75-84; Desparmet, *Blida,* 130-1; Bekhoucha, *Poèmes érotiques*; idem and Sekkal, *Printanières,* 50-4; A. Hamidou, *Poésie vulgaire,* 1030-6; Djirārī, 608; Belhalfaoui, 100-15; Tahar, index; *al-Djawāhir al-ḥisān,* 85-106, 317-70).

After the stagnation which has been alluded to above, the Moroccan *məlḥūn* experienced a new flowering at the end of the 18th century and the beginning of the 19th, less probably due to the panegyrist of the Prophet ᶜAbd al-Madjīd al-Zabādī (d. 1163/1750; see Lakhdar, *Vie littéraire,* 94) than to

Djilālī Mthīrəd, who lived in the reign of Sīdī Muḥammad b. ᶜAbd Allāh, has already been cited as a poet in dialect. Mthīrəd, a Filālī born in Marrakesh where he worked as a vegetable seller, composed principally *khamriyyāt* [*q.v.*] and some love poems; he is regarded as the best of his time and perhaps in Morocco, and it is quite astonishing that al-Baḳḳālī, who cites his son-in-law al-Nadjdjār, passes over him in silence, unless he knew him under another name (see M. al-Fāsī, *Adab sha*ᶜ*bī,* 58-60; idem, *Jilali Mthired,* in *La Pensée,* no. 5 [March 1963], 42-54; Djirārī, 611-16).

In the reign of Mawlāy Sulaymān (1206-38/1792-1823), Muḥammad b. Sulaymān al-Fāsī, a pupil of the Ibn ᶜAlī mentioned by al-Baḳḳālī, found himself in disagreement with his master, and his verses carry an echo of this misunderstanding; a *ḳaṣīda* undoubtedly composed on his death-bed is one of his most remarkable works (see Aubin, 343; Sonneck, no. 5; Bekhoucha and Sekkal, *Printanières,* 65-71; M. al-Fāsī, *Adab sha*ᶜ*bī,* 61; Djirārī, 625-7).

For his part, the Darḳāwī Muḥammad al-Ḥarrāḳ of Tetwan (d. 1261/1845) is the author of mystical *ḳaṣīdas* which have been preserved and published at the end of his *Dīwān* (lith. Tunis and Fās n.d.; ed. Meknès, n.d.); he was himself made the subject of a monograph, *al-Nūr al-lāmi*ᶜ *al-barrāḳ fī tardjamat Muḥammad al-Ḥarrāḳ* (Rabat ms. 960; see Lévi-Provençal, *Chorfa,* 343, n. 8).

Tuhāmī al-Madghārī (d. 1273/1856) whom we have already encountered, composed also in classical Arabic; his works consist of some occasional poems, *khamriyyāt* and *ghazal,* as well as the panegyric of the prince Muḥammad b. ᶜAbd al-Raḥmān (see Sonneck, no. 14; Ḳādī, *Kanz,* 162-4; Desparmet, in *Bull. Soc. Géog. Alger,* xxii [1917], 40-51; M. al-Fāsī, *Adab sha*ᶜ*bī,* 63-4; *Un poème marocain inédit: «les Buveurs» de si Thami al-Oldaghi,* recueilli et traduit par M. El Fasi et E. Dermerghem, in *L'Islam et l'Occident, Cahiers du Sud,* 1947, 343-8; Djirārī, 643-9).

Aḥmad al-Ganduz, who lived in the reign of Mawlāy ᶜAbd al-Raḥmān (1238-76/1823-59) and his son Muḥammad (1276-90/1859-73), is the author of an elegy on the first and poems in honour of the Ḥamādsha [*q.v.* in Suppl.] (see Djirārī, 650-2).

al-Madanī al-Turkumānī (d. 1303/1886) is regarded as a specialist in humorous *ḳaṣīdas* (see Sonneck, no. 11; M. al-Fāsī, *Adab sha*ᶜ*bī,* 64).

Idrīs b. ᶜAlī, surnamed al-Ḥansh (d. 1319/1901), left a classical *dīwān* and a *maḳāma* [*q.v.*] in addition to his poems in *məlḥūn* (see Djirārī, 656-7).

Several more or less renowned Moroccan poets might also be cited in the three principal centres of composition; Fās, Meknès and Marrakesh (see al-Fāsī, *Adab sha*ᶜ*bī,* 64; Djirārī, 534-704, *passim*).

In Algeria, we should not pass over in silence the Tlemceni singer of love, Muḥammad b. Sahla (end of the 12th/18th century), whose works enjoy a lasting success (see Sonneck, nos. 29, 30; Desparmet, *Blida,* 8; J. Joly, *Répertoire algérois,* 58-66; Bekhoucha, *Poèmes érotiques,* 70-111 (on Muḥammad b. Sahla and his son); idem and Sekkal, *Printanières,* 122-4; Hamidou, *Poésie vulgaire,* 1025, 1037; Belhalfaoui, 170-9; *al-Djawāhir al-ḥisān,* 371-88). His son Abū Madyan (Boumediène) followed his father's example and also sang of love (see Sonneck, no. 31; El Boudali Safir, in *Hunā 'l-Djazāʾir,* no. 61 [1958], 35-7; Tahar, index; *al-Djawāhir al-ḥisān,* 389-97).

In the 19th century, Ibn al-ᶜAbbās (Belabbès) of Mascara, combined with love poetry philosophical and political themes (see Belhalfaoui, 116-19), while his fellow citizen Ḥabīb b. Gannūn (Benguennoun) composed principally during his long life (1761?-1864) erotic poems (see Bresnier, *Cours,* Algiers 1846, 636-7; A. Tahar, in *Bull. des Ét. Ar.,* no. 12 [1943], 42-3; Belhalfaoui, 92-9; Tahar, index).

The most famous *gawwāl* is, however, Muṣṭafā b.

Ibrāhīm (Məṣṭfa bən Bṛāhīm, 1800?-67), whose rich *Dīwān* was collected by ᶜAbd al-Ḳādir ᶜAzza (see below); having had much success with women and celebrated love at length, this Oranian bard, following a gallant adventure, had to seek exile in Fez, where he expressed his nostalgia in a highly-esteemed poem, *əl-Gomri* "the dove" (*Dīwān*, no. 34, 242-84). He then returned to his country and, like all his compatriots on returning from exile, ceased to sing of women in order to turn to religious poetry. Some of his poems are still sung at weddings and circumcision feasts.

At the beginning of the 20th century, the most popular of the *gawwālīn* appears to have been ᶜAbd Allāh b. Kerrīw of Lag̲h̲wāṭ (d. 1921), whose romances are still appreciated (see J. Joly, in *R Afr.*, liii [1909], 285-303; *Hunā 'l-Dj̲azāʾir,* no. 13 [1953], 22, no. 27 [1954], 27-8; S. Bencheneb, in *Initiation à l'Algérie,* 302; Tahar, 87-9).

The poems of Tripolitanian origin gathered by Sonneck (nos. 16, 17, 45, 101, 102) are generally anonymous and come from the Maḥāmīd tribe. As for Stumme (*Beduinenlieder*), it was an informant from the Maṭmāṭa, illiterate but provided with a collection, who supplied him with his documentation on Tripolitania and South Tunisia. The specimens collected by P. Marty (*Chants lyriques*) at the beginning of the century in this latter region are all anonymous; those which Stumme reproduced in *Märchen und Gedichte,* relying on an informant from Tunis, are also unnamed, whereas the authors of some of the 23 Tunisian poems which figure in Sonneck's collection are known, but are not very old and barely go back to the 19th century. Among them can be cited ᶜAbd Allāh b. Bū G̲h̲āba of al-Kāf (no. 107) who, like Məṣṭfa b. Bṛāhīm, entrusted a message to a pigeon in a strophic *ḳaṣīda*; Sāsī b. Muḥammad (19th-20th century) of the Dj̲ibāliyyīn (nos. 46, 65, 67, 75) who describes at length the horse and its rider (no. 65) as well as a hunting party (no. 67); ᶜUt̲h̲mān Ulīdī of Bizerta, who celebrates (no. 106) the construction of a bridge; Aḥmad b. K̲h̲ūdj̲a who exalts the merits of the saint ᶜĀʾis̲h̲a al-Mannūbiyya [*q.v.*]; finally Aḥmad b. Mūsā (d. 1893; see Briquez) to whom is attributed, probably wrongly (see Marzūḳī, *Mallāk,* 10) the authorship of a poem of 29 strophes of 5 lines of which each one, packed with proverbs and maxims, is introduced by a letter of the alphabet followed by a word beginning with the same letter; however, this poem (*Alīf al-adab*) is more likely to be the work of Aḥmad Mallāk of Sfax, who was his contemporary and lived in a period when popular poetry had developed, in part due to the impetus given it by Aḥmad Bey (1253-71/1837-55). The *Dīwān* of this latter poet, who deals with all kinds of subjects (social, wise, religious, but also amorous, satirical and rural) was published in the form of extracts by Muḥammad al-Marzūḳī, *Aḥmad Mallāk, s̲h̲āᶜir al-ḥikma wa 'l-malḥama,* Tunis 1980. Mallāk is described here as an epic poet, but we do not know exactly whether it is him or Ḥamdūn S̲h̲albī who is the author of a kind of narrative poem inspired by the legend of Ḥassūna al-Laylī; the latter was made the subject of another poem of Sālim al-ᶜAydūdī that M. Marzūḳī published and studied, with the preceding poem, in *Ḥassūna al-Laylī, malḥama s̲h̲aᶜbiyya,* Tunis 1976.

In our own time, *məlḥūn* is always very much in favour in the whole of North Africa. Dj̲irārī further cites (671-87) several contemporary Moroccan poets who bear witness to the vitality of dialectal poetry. In Algeria, Muḥammad ᶜAbābsa (d. 1953), surnamed the "Bard of the tribes" (*s̲h̲āᶜir al-aᶜrās̲h̲*), expresses "philosophical" ideas, e.g. on peace and fraternity (in *Hunā 'l-Dj̲azāʾir,* no. 10 [1953], 16-17). Al-Ṭāhir Raḥāb greets the spring, the month of Ramaḍān, the feast of the sacrifices, tells of a journey to Sicily and eulogises his mother in some poems of 26-43 lines (see *Hunā 'l-Dj̲azāʾir,* nos. 11, 14 [1953], 43, 44 [1956], 56 [1957], 61 [1958]).

In Tunisia, the government encourages not only the study of popular poetry of the past, but also the composition of poems on the occasion of anniversaries of national events which have marked the recent fortunes of the country: festivals of the Revolution (18 January), Independence (20 March), Victory (1 June), the Republic (25 July), the Departure of the occupiers (15 October), as well as that of the birth of President Bourguiba (3 August); the Minister of Cultural Affairs publishes, under the suggestive title *ᶜUkāẓiyya* [see ᶜUKĀẒ], a selection of these occasional poems. The authors will not be cited, as they are still alive, but by way of information we will note that the *ᶜUkāẓiyyāt* of the years 1977-80 and of 18 January 1981 contain a total of 73 poems by 24 poets, among whom several provided 4 to 10 compositions.

Subjects treated in *məlḥūn.* As suggested by the preceding, poetry in dialectal Arabic covers the same fields as that which is expressed in literary Arabic, and the classical genres are present in it, sc. *madīḥ, hidj̲āʾ, rit̲h̲āʾ, g̲h̲azal,* etc., but certainly in different proportions. As S. Bencheneb rightly remarks (in *Initiation à l'Algérie,* 302), the *gawwālīn* "derive their inspiration from all sources, chivalrous adventures as well as love stories, miracles as well as everyday life"; for his part, G. S. Colin (in *Initiation au Maroc,* 226) makes out poems which are amorous, mystico-erotic, satirical, political (against the French presence), didactic (or on wisdom themes), burlesque, to which must be added those which celebrate wine (mystical or not), sing the beauties of nature, glorify the Prophet and the saints or eulogise a person living or dead. M. al-Fāsī presents (*Adab s̲h̲aᶜbī,* 51-6) a comprehensive list of the subjects treated, and Dj̲irārī devotes a very long discussion (198-529) to the themes of the Moroccan *məlḥūn* which he analyses with great care. Although no statistics are available, we cannot help but remark on the important place occupied by love in spontaneous dialectal poetry, very often in a symbolic form behind the erotic (or erotico-Bacchic) appearance, in which it is sometimes very hard for the profane, but not for the initiated, to detect a mystical meaning, as is the case with al-Baḳḳālī's poem cited above. Moreover, what is particularly striking is the abundance of religious songs, hymns to the Prophet, to the patron saints of the different towns and local saints, *klām al-dj̲əadd* as opposed to *klām al-həzl*; one can even read (Belhalfaoui, 66-71) a mystical poem dedicated to ᶜAbd al-Ḳādir al-Dj̲īlānī [*q.v.*] by ᶜAbd al-Ḳādir al-Ṭubdj̲ī (beginning of the 19th century).

Among the Bedouins, beside love, nature and animals, both wild and domesticated (horse, camel, pigeon), are very often celebrated in accordance with archaic tradition, and hunting with the falcon is a traditional theme (see above, al-Ḥādj̲dj̲ ᶜĪsā and Gen. A. Margueritte, *Chansons de l'Algérie*), while wars between tribes gave further inspiration to the bards of the south at the times when these wars were still endemic (see P. Marty, *Chants lyriques*).

As the poets enjoy much freedom, some acts of daily life and family events are a source of inspiration which is not negligible (we will mention notably a poem on the death of his wife, a relatively rare theme in Arabic literature [see MART̲H̲IYA], by Ibn Giṭūn Wulā al-Ṣag̲h̲īr of the Biskra region; Sonneck, no. 41 and *Hunā 'l-Dj̲azāʾir,* no. 19 (1953), 14-15).

Some dramatic events which made a deep impression also find an echo in popular poetry. Venture de Paradis had collected *Un chant algérien du XVIIIe siècle* of 114 lines (published in *RAfr.*, xxxviii [1894], 325-45) on a bombardment of Algiers, in 1770, by the Danes (?). An accident which occurred in 1885 provides the material for a *Complainte sur la rupture du barrage de Saint-Denis-du-Sig,* edited by G. Delphin and L. Guin, Paris-Oran 1886. S. Bencheneb (*Initiation à l'Algérie,* 307) mentions that the first Orléansville (al-Aṣnām) earthquake, in 1954, inspired melodies full of sadness and hope, and it is probable that the one in 1980 will also be lamented in *məlḥūn.* It has been seen earlier that Bonaparte's expedition to Egypt was made the subject of a Moroccan poem, just as the construction of a bridge at Bizerta had been celebrated in its time.

The events which have so far been alluded to until now have a lesser weight, in the eyes of the Maghribīs, than the conquest and colonisation of North Africa. In Algeria, they have, since 1830, given rise to a whole series of compositions (see e.g. Gen. E. Daumas, *Mœurs et coutumes de l'Algérie*[3], 1858, 160-74, on the capture of Algiers; J. Desparmet, *La conquête racontée par les indigènes*, in *Bull. Soc. Géogr. Alger.*, cxxxii [1932], 437-56). The resistance of the *amīr* ʿAbd al-Ḳādir [*q.v.*] was bound to find an echo among *məlḥūn* poets, such as Ḳaddūr wuld Muḥammad al-Burdjī, called Bū Ngāb (d. 1850), of the Mascara region (see A. Cour, *Poésie politique,* 463-76; Ḳādī, *Kanz,* 92, 94, 96, 100, 104-6; Moh. Abderrahman, *Enseignement de l'arabe parlé*[2], 1923, 44 ff.) or Ṭāhir al-Ḥawwa who fought him, was taken prisoner, then eulogised him after having been freed (see A. Cour, *Poésie politique,* 478-83; Ḳāḍī, *Kanz,* 75-8; Desparmet, *Elégies et satires,* 48-9).

In a general way, the poets who tackle political themes deplore what they consider as the ruin of Maghribī civilisation, and pour out their sarcasm on that which their conquerors bring them (see Desparmet, *Elégies et satires*). Opposition to the French penetration is manifested indirectly in some poems which the *məddāḥ*s declaim in public: some accounts relating the warlike exploits of the Prophet's contemporaries and some Muslim heroes which, in classical Arabic, constitute the pseudo-*Maghāzī,* are in part adapted in dialectal Arabic and form a kind of little epics; very much in vogue from the time of ʿAbd al-Ḳādir in order to stimulate the ardour of the combatants, then at the end of the 19th century and in the 20th century to recall the glories of the past and give consolation for the present humiliation, these *ghazawāt* are an evident manifestation of Maghribī nationalism (see J. Desparmet, *Chansons de geste*).

Different events which took place after the conquest also inspired the *gawwālīn.* By way of example, we will cite Mḥammad b. al-Khayr (Belkheïr) who was deported to Corsica after taking part in the insurrection of the Awlād Sīdī Shaykh of 1864-6; he addresses a prayer to God and expresses in touching terms his nostalgia, in a poem which deserves to be cited among the works composed by prisoners (see Sonneck, no. 44; Ḳāḍī, *Kanz,* 177-9; Tahar, 74-83).

The 38 poems gathered by P. Marty in southern Tunisia, between 1902 and 1907, are classified into 4 categories (see *Chants lyriques*) according to the subject which inspires them: love, war between tribes, nature, and finally the situation created in Tunisia by the installation of the French protectorate; in this "modern cycle" (for the other poems are older) some poets express their surprise and their anxieties or glorify the epic action for independence of some rebels, whilst others discover in the new themes material for irony or for reflection (see e.g. Sonneck, nos. 70 and 71, against the French in 1881).

The two World Wars have also found an echo in *məlḥūn* (see Desparmet, *Chanson d'Alger*), and it is probable that the events which took place in Algeria from 1954 to 1962 have given rise to a certain form of heroic poetry, but the author of the present article only possesses in this connection some works of poets writing in French. In southern Tunisia, al-Fītūrī Tlīsh (d. after 1943) derives his inspiration from the political and military situation during the Second World War, and uses symbols to express his hostility with regard to the French authorities who had thrown him into prison; but horses and camels are not absent from his work, which has been collected in a *Dīwān* and published by M. Marzūḳī (Tunis 1976). Today, the *ʿUkāẓiyyāt* are eloquent, and the patriotic themes are greatly developed in them.

Transmission and preservation of *məlḥūn.* As was said at the beginning of this article, the compositions in *məlḥūn* of the poets earlier than the 10th/16th century, if they existed, have not been preserved. It can be still ascertained that, among the Bedouins, the *gawwālīn* used to go, in the manner of troubadours, from encampment to encampment, from the house of a notable to the tent of a tribal chief in order to provide a spectacle on the occasion of festivals: wedding, circumcision, anniversary, etc., being accompanied by a rudimentary orchestra playing the oboe, flute and tambourine, while, sometimes, dancers complete the troupe. Several authors who have described these festivals (e.g. C. Trumelet, *Les Français dans le désert,* 249-61; P. Marty, *Chants lyriques,* in *RT*, 1936/1, 96) stress the transmission of the traditions of song in families. "It is rare", adds Marty, "for them to make them publicly known or for a stranger to be allowed to record them ... But the refrains are known by everyone or at least learnt and remembered at once, and the whole audience, especially the women who are always very excited, repeat in chorus this refrain, which is ordinarily indicated by the two last rhymes of the couplet." In southern Algeria, a distinction is established between the *gawwāl* proper, the *məddāḥ* who sings the works of others, and the *fəṣṣāḥ* who improvises and modifies from his own inspiration a theme which is learnt and known, without always distinguishing exactly what he has remembered from what is of his own creation. In Morocco, Aubin (343) says with regard to the *ḳaṣīda* that "it is the work of a poet who, himself, is not a musician and who is content to provide professionals with his compositions and entrust them with retailing them from house to house. The latter learn by heart the new song and apply to it a known tune which appears to suit it." M. el-Fasi confirms this information (in *Hespéris-Tamuda,* vi [1965], 39) and states that the town poets who compose *ḳaṣīdas* without ever writing them "entrust them to the memory of a *ḥaffāḍ* or *rāwī* who teaches them to the *šiāḫ* [*shyākh*, pl. of *shaykh*/*shēkh*] musicians. They sing them to the accompaniment of the violin and the *taʿrīja* (tambourine), while the *āliyīn* who sing to classical 'Andalusian' music, have an orchestra formed by the lute, the *rbāb* (rebeck) with two strings, the tambourine (*ṭarr*) and the violin."

Thus, as among the ancient Arabs, the popular poets do not make a point of writing their compositions, more especially as they are often illiterate, and the executants, who trust to their extraordinary memory, only rarely transcribe them in notebooks (*kunnāsh*) or on loose leaves, so as more surely to retain the monopoly. Dialectologists and ethnologists have sometimes succeeded in procuring some of these documents, and in 1898 A. Fischer could have at his disposal, in Tangier, a rich songbook (*Liederbuch*, pp. vii-viii) containing poems in dialectal Arabic, all anonymous, and some poems of well-known classical authors, such as al-ʿAbbās b. al-Aḥnaf, Ibn al-Rūmī, Abu 'l-Atāhiya, Abū Nuwās and al-Mutanabbī. Not all investigators have been as fortunate, and H. Stumme states (*Beduinenlieder*, 2-3) that he was refused the possibility of examining a collection whose existence he knew of. The jealous care with which the written documents are preserved by their owners is a constant trait of which researchers do not cease to complain (see e.g. the complaints of Djirārī, 5, whose entreaties often met with no response, or of Marzūḳī, *Mallāk*, 6). In a general way, in a period in which the tape recorder did not exist, the investigators had to be content with collecting from the mouth of more complaisant informants, some texts which they transcribed and, in many cases, translated. Jeanne Jouin relates (in *Hespéris*, 1959/1-2, 78) that she was able to have a Moroccan girl or woman, whose father owned a collection of the works of Ḳaddūr al-ʿAlamī (see above), recite a *ḳaṣīda* "which he was often pleased to chant aloud for the joy and edification of his family who appreciated it very much" and had ended by learning it by heart. Fortunately, Djirārī (700-3) supplies a long list of manuscript sources, and ʿAzza (see below) states that he had procured a collection of al-Madgharī's poems. Without waiting to have at their disposal technical means of recording them, some scholars and ardent amateurs succeeded, after minute and difficult inquiries, in putting together some important anthologies (see al-Ghawthī, Ḳāḍī, Bekhoucha, Marzūḳī, etc.), and even, in assembling patiently some scattered remnants, to reconstitute at least partially some *dīwāns* and publish them in Arabic script, in spite of the inconvenience that this procedure presents (see below). Fraudulent attributions are doubtless more numerous than those which have been laid bare, but, after all, this poetry is a common patrimony, and it is not of great importance that the authorship of each poem be exactly defined. As P. Marty writes (*Chansons lyriques,* 97), whose collection is all anonymous: "The singers do not, however, have the glory of the author" (even if they assert that such a passage is *mən klāmi* "of my creation").

The reader has been able to remark a revival of interest in productions in dialectal Arabic, and particularly in Tunisia where, until recently, they encountered a "hostile prejudice" (L. Bercher, in *Initiation à la Tunisie,* Paris 1950, 194). Although several Muslims did not have scruples about showing, by publishing specimens and translating them, their taste for popular poetry, it should be recognised that the opposition had two principal causes: on the one hand, many scholars, even if they took pleasure in listening to *məlḥūn*, could not admit that they were seriously concerned with dialectal Arabic and the literature expressed in it (and Djirārī states that there was an attempt to dissuade him from submitting in Cairo a thesis on the *ḳaṣīda* in *məlḥūn*); on the other hand, in the eyes of many, to bring these works to light, was to play the game of "colonialism" which a certain propaganda presented as determined to transform dialectal Arabic into a national and official language. Still today, when this unfounded worry has been dissipated, M. al-Fāsī begins his article on *Adab shaʿbī* with a profession of faith in the future of literary Arabic and A. Tahar feels constrained (p. v) "to reaffirm his position which is entirely favourable to classical Arabic as a means of communication both written and oral". There is no doubt, he adds, "that the liberation of the Arab lands has ruined the hopes of those who speculated on linguistic partition in order to divide them so as to perpetuate their rule over them", and then he justifies (p. vi) "his assistance in the work of a salvaging enterprise to rescue from oblivion the little which remains of popular poetry". No-one ever really believed in the propaganda which aroused this speculation on "linguistic partition", and especially not A. Tahar who, an ardent admirer of *məlḥūn*, had begun to study it well before the independence of Algeria; in 1933, in fact, he had presented an (unpublished) mémoire on Ben Guennoun and, some years later, promised his collaboration to Henri Pérès. The latter, after having given in the *BEA,* no. 1 (1940), 17-19, a general bibliography of Algerian popular poetry, published (*ibid.,* no. 4, 111-15) under an engaging title (*Pour un corpus des poésies populaires de l'Algérie*), a list of 85 *gawwālīn* whose works had to be collected and edited according to a necessarily subjective order of urgency. In the period, five *dīwāns* were in the course of preparation, but to our knowledge, only three of them have been published: those of Sīdī Lakhdar (who came quite low in the order of urgency), Ibn Amsāyb (see above) and Mṣṭfa bən Bṛāhīm (see below). Actually, the project of H. Pérès was quite ambitious and difficult to achieve integrally, but it is regrettable that it was not more largely carried out. Aware of the interest that popular poetry presents as an authentic element of the national patrimony, an eloquent representative of the personality of a country and evidence of a sensibility which cannot always be expressed in classical Arabic, the author of the present article accepted the supervision of three theses on this subject: those of Abdelkader Azza (*Məṣṭfa bən Bṛāhīm, barde de l'Oranais et chantre des Beni ʿAmer*), M. Belhalfaoui (*La poésie arabe maghrébine d'expression populaire*) and A. Tahar (*La poésie populaire algérienne (melhûn). Rythmes, mètres et formes).* All three have been printed, but only the latter *in extenso* (Algiers 1975); to elaborate on the first, which was treated in H. Pérès' list, the candidate had collected the works of Məṣṭfa bən Bṛāhīm and had transcribed them in Arabic and Latin script and commented on them; his work was published after his death, but exclusively in Arabic (D. (= *Duktūr*) ʿAbd al-Ḳādir ʿAzza, *Muṣṭafā b. Ibrāhīm, shāʿir Banī ʿĀmir wa-maddāḥ al-ḳabāʾil al-wahrāniyya,* Algiers 1977). The case of the second is entirely different, for M. Belhalfaoui, in order to publish it in Paris in 1973, had to remove the apparatus criticus and transcriptions into Latin script, so as to present a literary study only—of high quality and very suggestive—as well as a selection of poems reproduced in Arabic script and translated. Actually, a fourth thesis ought to be added, that of Mohamd El Moktar Ould Bah, which was submitted in 1969, but has remained unpublished; it is a collection of Mauritanian poems in literary as well as dialectal Arabic, which the author presented in a *Introduction à la poésie mauritanienne (1650-1900),* published in *Arabica* (xviii [1971], 1-48); a paragraph in it was devoted to the popular poetry which is expressed in the dialect of the country, *Ḥassāniyya,* and is called *ghnāʾ* (*ghināʾ*), although, in an unspecified work of Muḥammad al-Yadalī, it also bears the name *malḥūn*; the reader will find several examples of it in this *Introduction* (which he will be able to supplement with Aḥmad al-Shinkīṭī, *al-Wasīṭ fī tarādjim udabāʾ Shinkīṭ,* Cairo 1960, studied by A. B. Miské, in *BIFAN,* B, xxx/1 [1968]; A. Leriche, *Poésie et musique maures,* in *BIFAN,* xiii [1951], 1227-56; D. Cohen, *Ḥassānīya,* 236-43; H. T. Norris, *Shingīṭī folk literature and song,* Oxford 1968).

It is essential to insist on the necessity of not restricting oneself to publishing in Arabic script the texts gathered, if one wants to write a useful work and present a study which can be used beyond the limits of one land or indeed region. The efforts of M. El-Fas to explain how he arranges the Arabic writing so as to allow the correct reading of a text (*Hespéris-Tamuda,* vi [1965], 45) would certainly have been more conclusive if he had added to the good translation of the poem studied a transcription in Latin script, especially as his article is in French and is addressed to a public who may well be ignorant of Arabic. For his part, Djirārī doubtless devised an analogous system, but could not prevent the printer from omitting the vowels and reading signs, conscious though he was of the difficulty that is encountered in reading a dialectal poem. The vowels which figure in the *ʿUkāẓiyyāt* and in certain publications of M. Marzūḳī are useful, without being totally satisfactory. The thesis of A. Tahar proves that it is possible to produce works which combine a care to preserve the poems in their Arabic script with a concern to make them appreciated and studied by Arabists and, thanks to translations, to procure proper evidence to nourish fruitful studies in comparative literature.

The language of *məlḥūn*. If we have insisted on the importance of presenting transcriptions and translations (accompanied by suitable annotation), it is also because this poetry is not always perfectly clear; the differences of interpretation which can be brought forward among qualified experts are an irrefutable proof. With regard to Morocco, E. Aubin (343) writes: "The song—qaçida—is composed in the common language and permits, consequently, the dialect of each province", which would appear evident. On the other hand, A. Fischer (*Liederbuch,* p. ix) distinguishes, midway between the dialectal (*Vulgärsprache*) and the classical (*Schriftsprache*), some poems in a mixed language (*Mischsprache*), and G. S. Colin (*op. laud.,* 225) describes, for his part, the language of popular poetry as a "kind of literarised poetic *koiné,* based on common Moroccan Arabic, but influenced above all by Bedouin dialects. "It seems furthermore", he adds, "that this poetry may be of Bedouin origin". This last suggestion seems very plausible, and one cannot help thinking of the poetic *koiné* of the pre-Islamic period which transcended the speech of the tribes and tended to a certain unity. *Mutatis mutandis*, a similar phenomenon has been able to take place with *məlḥūn* which serves so to speak as a common language for poets of different regions, without extending, however, to the whole of North Africa. On the other hand, the literary genre also represented was not limited to the Bedouins and countryfolk, and it must be recognised that a more or less independent *məlḥūn* developed in certain towns and adopted, besides, some rather different structures (see below).

Given that the language of popular poetry has still not been studied in depth, in spite of the efforts of M. al-Fāsī (*Lughat al-malḥūn*), it is best to be very prudent and beware of any peremptory assertion. M. Belhalfaoui (53-4) describes *məlḥūn* as "a language whose expression, while remaining popular and current, possesses a vocabulary which is sometimes entirely that of classical Arabic, with some minor modifications; some forms which are often actually the same as those of classical Arabic, without our losing sight of the notable differences in morphology and above all the semantic evolutions which confer here and there on the dialectal expression a stamp *sui generis* far removed from the classical source ... We believe that we can assert that the dialectal language—that of the people and that of the bards—is today remarkably similar to that which was already attested in the works of El-Maghraoui or Lakhdar Ben Khlouf and Abderrahmane El-Mejdoub, all three of the 16th century" and, he could have added, of different origin. Here we have a highly optimistic assertion, and certainly an imprudent one in the present state of our knowledge. Even if the language of the bards appears palpably that of the people, one cannot fail to remark some differences, which thorough comparisons and exhaustive inventories would reveal more clearly. Proofs of these particulars are not lacking: A. Joly (*Poésie moderne*) and Abdelkader Azza (at the end of his original thesis) gave a list of words which do not figure in Beaussier's dictionary; M. al-Fāsī (*Lughat al-malḥūn,* 199) recognises that the language of *məlḥūn* is not easily intelligible, and Djirārī writes (6): "It has not been easy for us to understand these texts, especially those which were recorded in writing, because of the evolution of the language and our ignorance of the meaning of many words and their pronunciation." M. Marzūḳī takes care to explain, at the end of each of the poems that he publishes, the difficult terms, and often claims that only the context enlightens them. Fortunately these exist a number of texts in *məlḥūn* transcribed in Hebrew characters, so that further studies in this respect will probably yield useful information.

When the poets are educated (like al-Mandasī in the *ʿAḳīḳa*), it is understandable and inevitable that they use classical words and forms (omitting the *iʿrāb* and certain short internal vowels), but the illiterate poets themselves, formed by the tradition and example of their masters or predecessors, are acquainted with some of them and use them in their compositions. Some at the very least provide food for thought; thus the word *rāḥ* (wine), already poetic in classical, is quite frequent in *məlḥūn*; is it a case of a borrowing or a survival from the poetic tradition brought by the conquerors and consequently a pre-classical word? As Djirārī has rightly perceived, it is the whole problem of the Arabisation of North Africa which is hereby posed (see W. Marçais, *Comment l'Afrique du Nord a été arabisée*).

Apart from classical words, certain poets go as far as inserting in their verses, as a pleasantry (*li 'l-ḍaḥik*; Sonneck, no. 117, of ʿAlī b. al-Ṭāhir of Djelfa), some French words (or Berber, notably in Mauritania) possessing the required syllabic quantity, and this remark must lead us directly to another problem which appears to be a very difficult one, that of metre.

The metrics of *məlḥūn*. The first researchers who concerned themselves with popular poetry were Arabists, naturally inclined to look for connections with classical metrics, but they stumbled against the problem of identifying the rhythm and proposed various solutions. H. Stumme (*Tunisische Märchen und Gedichte,* 87-103) detects in the verses studied a metre based on accent, then discovers in the Bedouin *məlḥūn* of Tunisia and Tripolitania (*Beduinenlieder,* 24, 38, 39, 40, 44, 45) some iambic lines of classical poetry. W. Marçais (*Tlemcen,* 208-9) discerns in his turn in the *ḥawfī* [*q.v.*] a classical *basīṭ*. R. Basset finds a *radjaz madjzūʾ* in *Une complainte arabe,* 4. However, J. Desparment (*Blida,* 445) considers that the rhythm of the *məlḥūn* is based on the "numeration of syllabes which are accented in conformity with dialectal pronunciation". For G. S. Colin (in *Initiation au Maroc,* 225 and *EI*[1], art. MOROCCO, vii/2), the metre is "based exclusively on the number of syllables of each line (as in French)". S. Bencheneb (*Chansons satiriques,* 90) emphasises the number of syllables and the rhyme. A.

Chottin (*Musique marocaine,* 154) is of the opinion that the rhythm rests on the number of syllables and on an accentuation which he can hardly define. E. Dermenghem and M. El Fasi (*Poèmes marocains,* 99) imply that the *məlḥūn* is characterised by the number of syllables and the rhyme. For Azza, it is the number of syllables which characterises the verse of Bən Bṛāhīm. Dj̲irārī (131-46) recognises that the metre of al-K̲h̲alīl [*q.v.*] cannot be applied to *məlḥūn,* and says that the Moroccan *zad̲j̲d̲j̲al*s have particular *tafʿīlāt* which they call *ṣurūf* and which are of two kinds: the *dandana* (*dāndānī*) and *mālī mālī,* owed respectively to al-Mag̲h̲rāwī and al-Maṣmūdī (592-6). M. al-Fāsī, who undertook a study in depth of the structure of *məlḥūn,* also considers (*ʿArūḍ al-malḥūn,* 8-9) that the rhythm is syllabic, but remarks that certain poems pose quite complicated problems.

A. Tahar, after having been won over to the view of S. Bencheneb, not without taking into account the accentuation (*Métrique,* in *BÉA,* no. 11 [1943], 1-7), endeavoured to deepen his study of the question and finally discovered and explained, in his thesis cited above, a new theory which appears attractive. Given that Mag̲h̲ribī Arabic possesses only end short open syllables (Cv̆), while such syllables are preserved in literary Arabic in the body of the word, a line in *məlḥūn* cannot be scanned according to the classical metres [see ʿARŪḌ]; all the syllables are thus long (Cv̆C, Cv̄) or overlong, and the latter (Cv̄C, Cv̆CC, CCv̄C, CCC, Cv̄CC, CCv̄CC) present a particular importance. So, after having examined a considerable number of lines and separated the syllables which they contain, this scholar has come to the conclusion that the rhythm of the *məlḥūn* is essentially characterised by the identity of the number and the place of the over-long syllables in the lines of a poem. Here is an example taken from the work of the Moroccan Ḳaddūr al-ʿAlamī:

līn yərkən mən bārət lū žmīʿ l-əḥyāl
ʿād mənzəl dīwānū b-əl-kdār mālī

"Where will he go to take refuge whose stratagems have all been in vain
And whose cares fill up the place of his assemblies?"

scanned (61) as follows (the over-long syllables in roman type):

līn / *yər*/*kən*/*mən*/*bā*/*rət*/lūž/mīʿ/*ləḥ*/yāl
ʿād/*mən*/*zəl*/*dī*/*wā*/*nū*/bəlk/dār/*mā*/*lī*

In spite of the impressive number of examples cited, this theory does not seem to be applicable to all poetry in *məlḥūn,* at least when one attempts to put it into practice on written texts; however, it is worthy of being taken into consideration.

Pursuing his researches, A. Tahar has tried to determine the different "metres" according to the number of syllables and the place of the over-long ones and, in imitation of al-K̲h̲alīl, has even given them names. For example, the line above belongs to metre no. 1, called *əl-ʿtīḳ* "the old", formed by two decasyllabic hemistichs with four over-long syllables in the first and three in the second. In all, seven metres have been distinguished, but some of them contain a considerable series of variants, so that the question, in so far as it is of interest, would have to be reconsidered. In any case, pp. 176-349, which are devoted to the analysis of the metres, have the additional advantage of containing a mass of verse reproduced in Arabic script, transcribed and translated.

The structure and forms of *məlḥūn.* In an *urd̲j̲ūza* of some 5,000 lines, *al-Uḳnūm fī mabādiʾ al-ʿulūm,* which is a veritable encyclopaedia (see M. Lakhdar, *Vie littéraire,* 93-5), ʿAbd al-Raḥmān al-Fāsī (d. 1096/1685 [see AL-FĀSĪ in Suppl.]) approaches the *ʿilm mīzān al-malḥūn* (see Dj̲irārī, 62) and counts 15 *awzān,* of which the last is *al-ḳaṣīd al-d̲j̲ārī*; one might as well say that one can hardly make use of this document where *wazn* appears to designate at once the form and the rhythm. Anyway, analysis is complicated by a confusion in the terminology and the extension of the word *məlḥūn* to everything which is composed in dialectal Arabic, and notably to *zad̲j̲al,* in which is included the *ḳaṣīda,* also known as *grīḥa.* In fact, although the forms of *məlḥūn* may be extremely varied, it is permissible to distinguish, for the sake of simplication, two principal categories: the Bedouin type and the urban type.

Among the Bedouins and the townsfolks who follow the Bedouin tradition, we meet with isometric poems generally described as *ḳaṣīda* or *ḳaṣīd* (*gṣēda*/*gṣēd*) and recalling the old *ḳaṣīda,* with, however, some essential differences: the bi- or tripartite frame is not compulsory; the rhythm (see above) has nothing in common with classical metres and especially the *ḳāfiya,* the final rhyme, is doubled by an internal rhyme, i.e. all the first hemistichs rhyme also within themselves. For example, the line of Ḳaddūr al-ʿAlamī cited above belongs to a poem in which the odd hemistichs end in *-āl,* and the even, in *-lī*; in al-Baḳḳālī's poem used at the beginning of the present article, the hemistichs rhyme respectively in *-dī* and *-rā*; G. Boris (*Documents,* 166-7) reproduces a satire of seven lines rhyming in *-rā* and *-ān.* The examples could be multiplied, and it suffices to go over the great collections in order to take account of the importance of internal rhyme, which appears so fundamental that it is respected even in the case where the bard takes the liberty of changing the rhyme of the second hemistich in each line.

The word *ḳaṣīda* (*et var.*) naturally applied to poems of the preceding type, is extended, among the Bedouins themselves to a strophic structure which, far from being uniform, presents very numerous varieties which it is impossible to reduce to only a few forms. A. Tahar has undertaken a work analogous to that of Ibn Sanāʾ al-Mulk [*q.v.*] on the *muwas̲h̲s̲h̲aḥ* [*q.v.*], and one can only refer to his analysis (363-404). The simplest form to be recognised is constituted, in Bedouin *məlḥūn,* by a succession of strophes with a double rhyme whose designation is variable from one region to another. We are not able to enter here into all these details, and will limit ourselves to recalling that in Algeria these strophes, which alternate with one another, are called *hədda* and *frās̲h̲,* the poem beginning and ending with a *hədda*; such an arrangement is particularly regular in the *Dīwān* of Məṣṭfa bən Bṛāhīm. In Morocco, the *ḳaṣīda* with a double rhyme contains several divisions called *ḳsām* (pl. of *ḳsəm*), themselves having subdivisions whose terminology does not seem clearly fixed. It is the same in Tunisia, and this question will merit being made the subject of an analysis in depth. Finally, the quatrain is also to be met with in Bedouin *məlḥūn.*

As for the urban type, which may be compared with the *ʿarūḍ al-balad* cited by Ibn K̲h̲aldūn, it also presents some variable forms, for the strophic arrangement which is prevalent leaves the field open to all the improvisations, and the terminology, here again, is quite confused. For example, in Algeria, a prelude (*maṭlaʿ* or *məd̲h̲həb*) is followed by strophes of two or three parts: *bīt* or *ʿarūbī,* then *ḳufl* or *bīt, dawr* and *ḳufl.* The structure and terminology of Moroccan *məlḥūn* have been made the subject of a thorough study by M. al-Fāsī (*ʿArūḍ al-malḥūn*). Dj̲irārī (147-73) analyses a *ḳaṣīda* containing a prelude (*sarrāba*) intended to set the rhythm and comprising an introduction (*dkhūl*) followed by two or three lines forming a *nāᶜūra,* of one strophe and one linking hemistich (*rədma*); then comes the *ḳsām* which follow a refrain (*ḥarba*); the latter *ḳsām* often contain the name of the author and the date of the composition clearly announced or in a cryptic form and, for the latter, by means of the Maghribī *abdjad* [*q.v.*] (an example in Belhalfaoui, 168).

In his edition of the *Ṭarshūn* (*Hespéris-Tamuda* [1965], 39 ff.), M. El-Fasi divides the poem into: *ḳsəm* of introduction followed by a *ḥarba* (refrain), then four other *ḳsām* constituted by a strophe (*nāᶜūra*), a *ḥarība* (small refrain), a *ḳsəm* and a *ḥarba.* So we see that the structure of *məlḥūn* and the terms which designate the different parts of a *ḳaṣīda* are extremely variable. The common point remains, nevertheless, the principle of the double rhyme, which tends to be quite widely respected in each of the constituent elements.

It is clear from all that precedes that the Maghribī *məlḥūn* which we have attempted to present concisely by abstaining from approaching the difficult question of melody (on the different modes, see M. al-Fāsī, *ᶜArūḍ al-malḥūn*), is a question which, from a scientific point of view, merits being studied more deeply, now that the obstacles, real or imagined, have in large part been raised, for this "poetry of popular expression", as M. Belhalfaoui wishes to describe it, not only remains very much cultivated and even to a certain point competitive with poetry in classical Arabic, as the Tunisian *ᶜUkāẓiyyāt* notably prove, but still offers to the Arabist and comparativist an extremely extensive field of research. Although the corpus already available, thanks to dialectologists and enlightened amateurs, may as a whole be considerable, it will be desirable in the first place to collect the greatest possible number of poems preserved in the memory of the *rāwī*s or in notebooks still too jealously guarded, to transcribe them in Arabic and Latin script and translate them or at least elucidate the obscure passages. The national radios today give a large place to popular poetry, and the singers hardly have reasons to refuse to communicate their répertoire; so it will be necessary to record it in such a way as to be in a position to resolve definitively the problem of rhythm and see to what extent the theory of A. Tahar can be generally applied. One would then have to attempt to set to rights a terminology which seems anarchic, and finally to make an inventory of the vocabulary so as to determine the origin of the different elements which constitute it.

Bibliography: Although some references have appeared in full in the main article, they are repeated here also.

I.—There is a general bibl. on the Algerian *məlḥūn*, by H. Pérès, in *Bull. des études arabes* (*BEA*), no. 1 (1941), 17-19; the same author completed it up to 1958 in *L'arabe dialectal algérien et saharien: Bibliographie analytique avec un index méthodique* (see "poésie"), Algiers 1958; a summary bibl. comes after the names of the poets listed by idem, *Pour un corpus des poésies populaires de l'Algérie,* in *BEA,* no. 4 (1941), 111-15.

II.—Collections and anthologies (in chronological order): H. Stumme, *Tunisische Märchen und Gedichte,* Leipzig 1893; idem, *Tripolitanisch-tunisische Beduinenlieder,* Leipzig 1894 (partial Fr. tr. A. Vagnon, *Chants des Bédouins de Tripoli et de la Tunisie,* Paris 1894); idem, *Märchen und Gedichte aus der Stadt Tripolis,* Leipzig 1898; M. Hartmann, *Lieder der libyschen Wüste,* in *Abh. für d. Kunde des Morgenland,* xi/3 (1899); Sonneck = M. C. Sonneck, *Chants arabes du Maghreb. Étude sur le dialecte et la poésie populaire de l'Afrique du Nord,* 2 tomes in 3 vols. Paris 1902-4 (i. Arabic text of 117 pieces. ii/1. Transcription of 6 songs and Fr. tr. of the whole collection, apart from nos. 113-17. ii/2. Phonological and morphological study, glossary). There are reproduced in this collection, as nos. 2, 29, 41, 59, 101 and 108, by the same author, the *Six chansons arabes en dialecte maghrébin*, published in *JA,* 3ᵉ série, xiii (1899), 471-520, xiv (1899), 121-56, 223-58); A. Joly, *Remarques sur la poésie moderne chez les nomades algériens,* in *RAfr.*, xliv (1900), 283-311, xlv (1901), 208-36, xlvii (1903), 171-94, xlviii (1904), 5-55, 211-63 (numerous texts); Abū ᶜAlī al-Ghawthī, *Kashf al-ḳināᶜ ᶜan ālāt al-samāᶜ,* Algiers 1322/1904 (*muwashshaḥāt, azdjāl* and a selection of the works of six poets); J. Desparmet, *Blida = La poésie actuelle à Blida et sa métrique,* in *Actes du XIVᵉ Congrès Intern. des Orient.*, iii, Paris 1907, 437-602 (various songs, and list of poets from the end of the 19th century); J. C. E. Falls, *Beduinenlieder des libyschen Wüste,* Cairo 1908; M. Sidoun, *Chants sur la chasse au faucon attribués à Sid El Hadj Aïssa, Chérif de Laghouat,* in *RAfr.*, lii (1908), 272-94 (5 songs, text and tr.); J. Joly, *Chansons du répertoire algérois,* in *RAfr.,* liii (1909), 46-66; idem, *Poésies du Sud,* in *RAfr.*, liii (1909), 285-307; A. Fischer, *Das Liederbuch eines marokkanischen Sängers,* Leipzig 1918 (125 pieces, tr. and notes); A. Cour, *La poésie populaire politique au temps de l'Émir Abdelqader,* in *RAfr.*, lix (1918), 458-93; J. Desparmet, *La conquête racontée par les indigènes,* in *Bull. Soc. Géog. Alger,* cxxxii (1932), 437-56; idem, *Elégies et satires politiques de 1830 à 1914,* in *ibid.*, cxxxiii (1933), 35-54 (translated extracts from 8 poets); idem, *La chanson d'Alger pendant la Grande Guerre,* in *RAfr.*, lxxiii (1932), 54-83 (tr. and Arabic text); idem, *Les chansons de geste de 1830 à 1914 dans la Mitidja,* in *ibid.*, lxxxiii (1939), 192-226; Muḥammad al-Ḳāḍī, *al-Kanz al-maknūn fi 'l-shiᶜr al-malḥūn,* Algiers 1928 (selected works from 30 poets); S. Bencheneb, *Chansons satiriques d'Alger, 1ʳᵉ moitié du XIVᵉ siècle de l'hégire,* in *RAfr.*, lxxiv (1933), 75-117, 296-352 (Arabic text, tr. and notes); M. Bekhoucha and A. Sekkal, *Anthologie d'auteurs arabes. Les printanières ou romantisme arabe: Kitāb Nafḥ al-azhār wa-waṣf al-anwār wa-aṣwāt al-aṭyār wa-nighām al-awtār,* Tlemcen 1934 (works of 14 Algerian and Moroccan poets); E. Chimenti, *Èves marocaines,* Tangier 1935; A. Hamidou, *Le Bonheur éternel,* Tlemcen 1935; idem, *Aperçu sur la poésie vulgaire de Tlemcen. Les deux poètes populaires de Tlemcen: Ibn Amsaïb et Ibn Triki* (Deuxième Congrès de la Fédération des Soc. savantes de l'Afrique du Nord), in *RAfr.*, lxxix (1936), 1007-46; P. Marty, *Les chants lyriques populaires du Sud Tunisien,* in *RT,* nos. xxv (1936/1), 83-135, xxvi (1936/2), 256-95, xxix (1937/1), 138-77, xxxi (1937/3-4), 433-69 (38 pieces, text in Arabic characters and tr.); M. Bekhoucha, *Anthologie arabe. Deuxième livre. Poèmes érotiques: Kitāb al-ḥubb wa-l-maḥbūb,* Tlemcen 1939 (notices and poems by 7 authors); E. Dermenghem and M. El Fasi, *Poèmes marocains du genre melhûn,* in *Cahiers du Sud,* Feb. 1940; E. Chimenti, *Chants de femmes arabes,* Paris 1942; H. Duquaire, *Anthologie de la littérature marocaine,* Paris 1943, 213-31; the journal *al-Amal* (Algiers), Nov.-Dec. 1969 (some 20 poems); M. Belhalfaoui, *La poésie arabe maghrébine d'expression populaire,* Paris 1973 (17 poems in Arabic characters and tr.); *ᶜUkāẓiyyāt min al-shiᶜr al-shaᶜbī,* years 1977-80, Tunis 1981 (69 poems from 24 poets, including one woman), year 1981 (4 pieces from 4 poets, including one woman); anon., *Kitāb al-*

CORRIGENDA

VOLUME VI

Fasc. 99-100, p. 2 of cover, list of contributors:
Instead of T. M. JOHNSTONE, Oxford. 85. *read: the late* T. M. JOHNSTONE, University of London. 85.
Instead of H.-P. LAQUEUR, Institut Français d'Archéologie, Istanbul. 125. *read* H.-P. LAQUEUR, German Archaeological Institute, Istanbul. 125.

SUPPLEMENT

P. 163[b], **ČĀČ—NĀMA.** The last item in the Bibliography has been published in Y. Friedmann, ed., *Islam in Asia*, i: *South Asia*, Jerusalem 1984, 23-27.

ISBN 90 04 08521 1

PRINTED IN THE NETHERLANDS

Humanism in the Renaissance of Islam

The Cultural Revival during the Buyid Age

by

JOEL L. KRAEMER

1986. (ix, 329 p.)
ISBN 90 04 07259 4 *cloth* **Gld. 128.—**

Under the enlightened rule of the Buyid dynasty (945-1055 A.D.) the Islamic world witnessed an unequalled cultural renaissance. The main expression of this renaissance was a philosophical humanism that embraced the scientific and philosophical heritage of Classical Antiquity as a cultural and educational ideal. Along with this philosophical humanism, a literary humanism was cultivated by litterateurs, poets, and government secretaries. This renaissance was marked by a powerful assertion of individualism in the domains of literary creativity and political action. It thrived in a remarkably cosmopolitan atmosphere. Baghdad, the center of the ʿAbbāsid empire and of Buyid rule, was the rendezvous for scholars from far and wide, of diverse cultural and religious backgrounds. Philosophers belonged to a class of their own, transcending particular loyalties, united by the pursuit of the truth and the love of reason.

This book is an investigation into the nature of the environment in which the cultural transformation took place and into the cultural elite who were its bearers. After an extensive introductory section setting the stage the book deals with the main schools and circles and with the outstanding individual representatives of this renaissance.

Philosophy in the Renaissance of Islam

Abū Sulaymān al-Sijistānī and his Circle

by

JOEL L. KRAEMER

1986. (xvi, 354 p.)
ISBN 90 04 07258 6 *cloth* **Gld. 140.—**

During the renaissance of Islamic civilization under the Buyid dynasty philosophy flourished as never before or after. This can be conveniently illustrated by the life and deeds of Abū Sulaymān al-Sijistānī (ca. 912-ca. 985 A.D.), a Socratic figure at the center of a ramified circle of scholars in Baghdad who contributed significantly to the assimilation and dissemination of the Classical legacy in the Islamic culture sphere.

This book deals with Sijistānī's life and his philosophical doctrine and intellectual contribution. It shows the extent to which Sijistānī and his colleagues were conversant with technical discussions of philosophical issues of Greek and late Antiquity. The author takes issue with the view that the bearers of Islamic civilization failed to understand the cultural legacy of Antiquity in general and its educational and cultural ideas in particular.

The book contributes to our understanding of the humanist tradition in Islam.

E. J. Brill — P.O.B. 9000 — 2300 PA Leiden — The Netherlands

THE ENCYCLOPAEDIA OF ISLAM

NEW EDITION

PREPARED BY A NUMBER OF
LEADING ORIENTALISTS

EDITED BY

C. E. BOSWORTH, E. van DONZEL, B. LEWIS and Ch. PELLAT

ASSISTED BY F. Th. DIJKEMA AND Mme S. NURIT

UNDER THE PATRONAGE OF
THE INTERNATIONAL UNION OF ACADEMIES

VOLUME VI

FASCICULES 103-104

MALḤŪN — MĀND

LEIDEN
E. J. BRILL
1987

All correspondence on editorial matters should be addressed to the Editorial Secretaries, whose addresses are:

For the English Edition

Dept. of Near Eastern Studies,
The University of Manchester,
Manchester,
England M13 9PL.

For the French Edition

13, rue de Santeuil
75231 Paris Cedex 05
France

AUTHORS OF ARTICLES IN THESE FASCICULES

HAMID ALGAR, University of California, Berkeley. 292.
A. ARIOLI, University of Rome. 313.
A. AYALON, Tel Aviv University. 262.
D. AYALON, Hebrew University, Jerusalem. 321.
M. A. BAKHIT, University of Jordan, Amman. 346.
IRÈNE BELDICEANU-STEINHERR, Centre national de la recherche scientifique. 278.
J. E. BENCHEIKH, University of Paris. 349.
C. E. BOSWORTH, University of Manchester. 270, 273, 276, 340.
J. T. P. DE BRUIJN, University of Leiden. 276.
J. C. BÜRGEL, University of Bern. 340.
R. M. BURRELL, University of London. 358.
J. BURTON-PAGE, Church Knowle, Dorset. 269, 343, 370.
CHR. CORRELL, University of Konstanz. 309.
NICOLE COTTART, Centre national de la recherche scientifique, Paris. 283.
R. M. EATON, University of Arizona, Tucson. 269, 273.
N. ELISSÉEFF, University of Lyons. 383.
T. FAHD, University of Strasbourg. 349, 374.
SURAIYA FAROQHI, Middle East Technical University, Ankara. 342.
C. V. FINDLEY, Ohio State University, Columbus. 290, 341.
J. FRAENKEL, Hebrew University, Jerusalem. 360.
G. S. P. FREEMAN-GRENVILLE, Sheriff Hutton, York. 283, 370.
C. L. GEDDES, University of Denver. 371.
G. G. GILBAR, University of Haifa. 277.
[T. W. HAIG, London]. 310.
A. T. HATTO, London. 371.
J. A. HAYWOOD, Lewes, Sussex. 272.
C. J. HEYWOOD, University of London. 291.
R. HILLENBRAND, University of Edinburgh. 368.
P. M. HOLT, Oxford. 331.
RIAZUL ISLAM, Karachi. 310.
B. S. J. ISSERLIN, Leeds. 298.
FAHİR İZ, Boğaziçi University, Istanbul. 373.
J. JOMIER, Toulouse. 361.
the late A. G. KARAM, American University, Beirut. 307.
H. KENNEDY, University of St. Andrews. 345.
P. KUNITZSCH, University of Munich. 376.
[H. LAMMENS, Beirut]. 266.
ELLA LANDAU-TASSERON, Hebrew University, Jerusalem. 269.
O. N. H. LEAMAN, Liverpool Polytechnic. 347.
[E. LÉVI-PROVENÇAL, Paris]. 340, 345.
N. LEVTZION, Hebrew University, Jerusalem. 261.
T. LEWICKI, University of Cracow. 311, 312.
A. MIQUEL, Collège de France, Paris. 314.
C. NIJLAND, Netherlands Institute for the Near East, Leiden. 306, 308.
M. M. OULD BAH, Unesco, Tunis. 313.
CH. PELLAT, University of Paris. 257, 267, 344, 357.
[M. PLESSNER, Jerusalem]. 344.
MUNIBUR RAHMAN, Oakland University, Rochester. 271.
M. REKAYA, University of Paris. 339.
[E. ROSSI, Rome]. 295.
A. I. SABRA, Harvard University, Cambridge, Mass. 377.
J. SADAN, Hebrew University, Jerusalem. 360.
K. S. SALIBI, American University, Beirut. 344.
[J. SCHACHT, New York]. 265.
A. SHILOAH, Hebrew University, Jerusalem. 262.
ABDUS SUBHAN, Calcutta. 270, 272, 295.
G. TROUPEAU, Institut national des langues et civilisations orientales, Paris. 308.
M. URSINUS, University of Birmingham. 372.
MARTINE VANHOVE, Paris. 303.
C. H. M. VERSTEEGH, University of Nijmegen. 346.
H. ZAFRANI, University of Paris. 294.

Names in square brackets are those of authors of articles reprinted or revised from the first edition of this Encyclopaedia.

This fascicule was published with financial support of the British Academy, London.

Djawāhir al-ḥisān fī-naẓm awliyāʾ Tilimsān, ed. ʿAbd al-Ḥamīd Ḥādjiyāt, Algiers 1982 (Arabic characters).

III.—*Dīwāns*: ʿAbd al-Ḥafīẓ, lith. Fās n.d.; *Dīwān de Ben Msaïb,* by M. Bekhoucha, Tlemcen 1370/1951; al-Ḥarrāḳ, lith. Tunis 1331, Fās n.d., printed Meknès n.d.; *Dîwân de Sidî Lakhdar Ben Khloûf,* by M. Bekhoucha, Rabat 1958; Aḥmad Mallāk, by M. Marzūḳī, Tunis 1980; al-Fītūrī Tlīsh, by idem, Tunis 1976; Muṣṭafā b. Ibrāhīm, by A. ʿAzza, see below, V).

IV.—Isolated texts: original or tr. (alphabetical order): Achour Abdelaziz, *Un chant maghribin: la qasida de la «Tête de mort»,* in *RMM,* xxxix (1920), 134-50; R. Basset, *Une complainte arabe sur Mohammed et le chameau,* in *Giornale della società asiatica italiana,* xv (1902), 1-26; A. Bel, *La Djazya. Chanson arabe précédée d'observations sur quelques légendes arabes et sur la geste de Banū Hilāl,* in *JA,* 9e série, xix (1902), 289-347, xx (1902), 169-236, 10e série, i (1903), 311-66; M. Ben Cheneb, *Itinéraire de Tlemcen à La Mekke par Ben Messaïb (XVIIIe siècle),* in *RAfr.,* xliv (1900), 261-82 (text and tr.); G. Boris, *Documents linguistiques et ethnographiques sur une région du Sud Tunisien (Nefzaoua),* Paris 1951, 160-2/175, 166/179; L. J. Bresnier, *Cours pratique et théorique de langue arabe,* Algiers 1846; H. Briquez, *Un poète populaire tunisien: chansons du Cheikh Ben Moussa El Fathaïri,* in *RT* (1917), 286-304; D. Cohen, *Le dialecte arabe* ḥassānīya *de Mauritanie,* Paris 1963; A. Cour, *Constantine en 1902 d'après une chanson populaire de Cheïkh Belqâsem Er-Rehmouni El-Haddad,* in *RAfr.,* lx (1919), 224-40 (text, tr. and comm.); G. Delphin and L. Guin, *Complainte arabe sur la rupture du barrage de Saint-Denis-du-Sig,* Paris-Oran 1886; M. El Fasi, *Le tarchoun (le petit faucon) de Ben ʿAlī Chérif,* in *Hespéris-Tamuda,* vi (1965), 39-52; Gen. G. Faure-Biguet, *L'Aqîqa (La cornaline) par Abou-Otman Saïd ben Abdallah Et-Tlemsani el-Mendasi,* Algiers 1901 (text and tr.); J. Jouin, *Un poème de Si Qaddour-el-ʿalami,* in *Hespéris,* xlvi/1-2 (1959), 87-103 (transcription and tr.); E. Lévi-Provençal, *Un chant populaire religieux du Djebel marocain,* in *RAfr.,* lix (1918), 215-48 (text and tr.); idem, *La chanson dite Sīdī 'l-ʿAlwi,* in *Arch. Berb.,* iv (1919-20), 67-75; M. al-Marzūḳī, *Ḥassūna al-Laylī, malḥama shaʿbiyya,* Tunis 1976 (2 poems); A. Tahar, *Le cheval de Ben Guennûn,* in *BEA,* no. 12 (1943), 42-3; Venture de Paradis, *Un chant algérien du XVIIIe siècle,* published by E. Fagnan, in *RAfr.,* xxxviii (1894), 325-45 (text and tr.).

V.—Studies, commentaries, translations, etc. (alphabetical order): Abū Raʾs al-Nāṣirī, *al-Durra al-anīḳa fī sharḥ al-ʿAḳīḳa* (see Faure-Biguet, who partially reproduced this comm.); ʿAbd al-Ḳādir ʿAzza, *Muṣṭafā b. Ibrāhīm shāʿir Banī ʿĀmir wa-maddāḥ al-ḳabāʾil al-wahrāniyya,* Algiers [1977]; ʿAbd al-Raḥmān al-Fāsī, *al-Uḳnūm fī mabādiʾ al-ʿulūm* (mss. in Rabat); E. Aubin, *Le Maroc d'aujourd'hui,* Paris 1912, 343-4; M. Bekhoucha, *Énigmes, contes et chansons tlemcéniennes,* Tlemcen 1942; A. Bel, *La Djazya,* see above, IV; M. Belhalfaoui, see above, II; S. Bencheneb, *La littérature populaire,* in *Initiation à l'Algérie,* Paris 1957, 301-9; M. T. Buret, *Sīdī Qaddūr el-ʿAlamī,* in *Hespéris,* xxv/1 (1938), 85-92; C. Cerbella, *Poesie e conti popolari arabi,* in *Libia,* iv (1956), 27-39; A. Chottin, *Tableau de la musqiue marocaine,* Paris 1938; G. S. Colin, *Littérature arabe dialectale,* in *Initiation au Maroc,* Paris 1937, 224-7; idem, in *EI*[1], s.v. MOROCCO = *EI*[2] AL-MAGHRIB, AL-MAMLAKA AL-MAGHRIBIYYA; Gen. A. Daumas, *Mœurs et coutumes de l'Algérie,* Paris[3] 1858; ʿAbbās Djirārī, *al-Zadjal fī l-Maghrib: al-ḳaṣīda,* Rabat 1390/1970 (715 pp.); idem, *Dalīl ḳaṣāʾid al-zadjal fi 'l-Maghrib* (unpubl.); M. El Fasi, *La littérature populaire,* in *La Pensée* (Rabat), no. 1 (Nov. 1862); idem, *Jilali Mthried,* in *ibid.,* no. 5 (March 1963), 42-54; idem (Muḥammad al-Fāsī), *al-Adab al-shaʿbī al-maghribī al-malḥūn,* in *al-Baḥth al-ʿilmī,* i (1964), 41-64 (see also *Tiṭwān,* ix (1964), 7-30; idem, *Lughat al-malḥūn,* in *al-Baḥth al-ʿilmī,* iv-v (1965), 199-203; idem, *ʿArūḍ al-malḥūn wa-muṣṭalaḥātuh,* in *al-Thaḳāfa al-maghribiyya,* i (1970), 7-29, ii-iii (1970), 5-23, iv (1971), 1-2, v (1971), 1-19 (study of the structure and, from I, 17, onwards of the terminology of the *məlḥūn*); idem, *Chants anciens de femmes de Fès,* Paris 1968 (tr. of 168 pieces); Ibn al-Sāʾiḥ (B. Bessaïh), *Funūn al-taṣwīr fi 'l shiʿr al-shaʿbī al-malḥūn,* in *Hunā 'l-Djazāʾir = Ici-Alger,* no. 33 (1955), 4-5; idem, *Naẓra khāṭifa ʿalā l-shiʿr al-djazāʾirī al-malḥūn,* in *ibid.,* no. 44 (1956), 12; Ibn Zaydān, *Itḥāf aʿlām al-nās,* Rabat 1347-52/1929-33; Idrīs al-Idrīsī, *Kashf al-ghiṭāʾ ʿan sirr al-mūsīḳī wa-natāʾidj al-ghināʾ,* Rabat 1935; M. Lacheraf, *Poésie du Sud,* in *Cahiers du Sud* (1947), 323-33; M. Lakhdar, *La vie littéraire au Maroc sous la dynastie ʿalawide,* Rabat 1971; J. Lecerf, *La place de la «culture populaire» dans la civilisation musulmane,* in *Classicisme et déclin culturel dans l'histoire de l'Islam,* Paris 1957, 351-67; Leo Africanus, *Description de l'Afrique, tr.* Épaulard, Paris 1956; A. Leriche, *Poésie et musique maures,* in *BIFAN,* xiii (1951), 1227-56; E. Lévi-Provençal, *Les historiens des Chorfa,* Paris 1922; A. Maïza, *Sidi Guessouma, patron des «hechaïchis» de Constantine,* in *Recueil de notices et mémoires de la Soc. archéol. de Constantine,* 5e série, xv (1927), 83-166; W. Marçais, *Le dialecte arabe parlé à Tlemcen,* Paris 1902; idem, *Comment l'Afrique du Nord a été arabisée,* in *AIEO Alger,* iv (1938) and xiv (1956); Gen. A. Margueritte, *Chasses de l'Algérie et notes sur les Arabes du Sud,* Paris[3] 1884; M. al-Marzūḳī, *al-Shiʿr al-shaʿbī fī Tūnis,* in *Madjallat al-Funūn al-shaʿbiyya,*. i (Cairo 1965); M. M. Ould Bah, *Introduction à la poésie mauritanienne (1650-1900),* in *Arabica,* xviii/1 (1971), 1-48; Aḥmad al-Shinḳīṭī, *al-Wasīṭ fī tarādjim ʿulamāʾ Shinḳīṭ,* Cairo 1960; P. M. de Styx, *Chants de Grenade et du Maghreb,* Paris 1953; A. Tahar, *La métrique de la poésie populaire,* in *BEA,* no. 11 (1943), 1-7; idem, *La poésie populaire algérienne (melḥûn). Rythmes, mètres et formes,* Algiers 1975 (fundamental); Col. C. Trumelet, *Les Français dans le désert,* Paris[2] 1885, 249-61. (CH. PELLAT)

MALI, a kingdom of mediaeval West Africa. The West African Republic of Mali is named after the ancient kingdom of Mali. In the 13th and 14th centuries, ancient Mali expanded over the whole territory of the modern Republic of Mali and beyond into the present Republics of Senegal, Gambia and Niger.

The dominant ethnic group in ancient Mali were the Malinke (i.e. "the people of Mali"), also known as Mandinka, of the large group of Mande-speaking peoples.

The history of ancient Mali is known to us from oral traditions and from Arabic written sources. The two categories represent different, but complementary, viewpoints, Whereas in the oral traditions the African traditional themes are prominent, the Arabic sources emphasise Islamic aspects.

In 460/1067-8 al-Bakrī (ed. Algiers 1911, 178) describes the small chiefdom of Malal amidst stateless, loosely-organised peoples. Its ruler embraced Islam after a Muslim visitor had prayed for rain and had saved the country from severe drought. The Malal of al-Bakrī must have been one of several chiefdoms which, according to oral traditions, emerged among the Malinke during the 11th and 12th centuries. Muslims reached that area of the Upper Niger river on their way to the goldfields of Burne, the exploitation of which began about that time.

Mali was Ghana's successor as the hegemonic power in the Western Sudan. But in between (towards the end of the 12th century), after the decline of Ghāna [*q.v.*] and before the rise of Mali, the Susu, a southern Soninke group, conquered territories to the north (Ghāna) and south (the Malinke chiefdoms).

The Susu represented a traditional reaction to Islam, which by then had become a significant factor in quite a few chiefly courts. The Malinke war of liberation from the rule of the Susu was led by Sundjata, who became recognised as head of all the Malinke, with the title of *mansā*.

In the first half of the 13th century, following the victory over the Susu, the new kingdom of Mali expanded northwards to the Sahel. The termini of the trans-Saharan trade, where Muslim communities flourished, became part of Mali, and served as a link with the Muslim world north of the Sahara. As the small Malinke chiefdom turned into a multi-ethnic kingdom, with influential Muslim elements inside and extensive Islamic relations with the outside, the rulers of Mali adopted an Islamic-oriented policy.

Mansā Ulī (or Walī), son of the founder of Mali, extended the conquests of his father. He secured the northern frontiers of Mali in the Sahara, which permitted him to perform the pilgrimage to Mecca. He passed through Cairo during the reign of Baybars (658-76/1260-77). There was a long tradition of royal pilgrims in West Africa, especially among the more powerful rulers. Ibn Khaldūn, to whom we are in debt for an excellent chronicle of the kings of Mali in the 13th and 14th centuries (ed. Paris 1847, i, 264-8), recorded also the pilgrimage of Sakūra during the second reign of al-Malik al-Nāṣir b. Ḳalāwūn (698-708/1299-1309). But the most famous of all royal pilgrims was Mansā Mūsā [*q.v.*], who visited Cairo in 724/1324.

Visits of kings of Mali to North Africa, Egypt and Mecca established the fame of Mali (often referred to as Takrūr in Egyptian chronicles) as a Muslim kingdom rich in gold. Religious, cultural and commercial relations between Egypt and Mali became more intensive. At home, the blessing (*baraka*) ascribed to pilgrims was respected by Muslims and non-Muslims alike and added to the authority of the king. The performance of the pilgrimage, and the encounter with the central lands of Islam, called the rulers' attention to the laxity of Islam in their own lands. Mansā Mūsā pursued a more vigorous Islamic policy after his return from the *ḥadjdj*; he built new mosques and sent local *ʿulamāʾ* to study abroad in Fās. In 737/1337, Mansā Mūsā initiated the exchange of ambassadors and gifts with the Moroccan Sultan Abu 'l-Ḥasan ʿAlī of the Marīnid dynasty, which were continued under their successors until 762/1360-1.

The Moroccan traveller Ibn Baṭṭūṭa visited Mali in 753-4/1352-3, during the reign of Mansā Sulaymān, the brother of Mansā Mūsā. In many Malian towns, Ibn Baṭṭūṭa met residents from Morocco.

Ibn Baṭṭūṭa's account reveals strong traditional survivals in Mali beneath a veneer of Islam. Royal presence at the public prayer of the two Islamic festivals turned them into official ceremonies to which non-Muslims were also attracted. In return, the prestige of Islam was used to exhort loyalty to the king during the *khuṭba*. As national feasts, the Islamic festivals had to accommodate pre-Islamic rites, which were among the sources of the king's legitimacy. Ibn Baṭṭūṭa condemned this and other pre-Islamic customs at the court of Mali. But he also had words of praise for the devotion to the prayer of Malian Muslims, in particular the Friday prayer, and their concern with the study of the Ḳurʾān by heart. The ritual rather than the legal aspects of Islam were of greater significance. The precepts of the *Sharīʿa* were observed only by foreign residents and by a small but committed group of local traders and clerics.

Islam penetrated into African societies through the rulers' courts. But it was in the purely Muslim towns, mostly commercial centres, that Islam was more vigorous and the *ʿulamāʾ* were in authority. The kings of Mali respected the autonomy of these towns, the most important of which was Timbuktu [*q.v.*].

Timbuktu, which had begun as a summer camp and a trading entrepôt for the Tuaregs, developed into an important commercial town and a cultural centre of Islam since the 14th century. The Andalusian poet and architect Abū Isḥāḳ al-Sāḥilī, who accompanied Mansā Mūsā back to Mali from the *ḥadjdj*, died in Timbuktu in 1346. Timbuktu must have been by then an intellectual centre of some importance for al-Sāḥilī to have settled there.

By the beginning of the 15th century, Timbuktu was "full of Sudanese *fuḳahāʾ*" (al-Saʿdī, *Taʾrīkh al-Sūdān*, 51). One of the leading scholars of Timbuktu was Modibo Muḥammad, who had come from the town of Kābora on the Niger south of Timbuktu. This town was mentioned by Ibn Baṭṭūṭa (iv, 395) together with Diāgha, the people of which "were Muslims of old, and are distinguished by their piety and their quest for knowledge".

Towards the end of the 14th century, Mali was weakened by rivalries over the royal succession and lost its hold over the Sahelian provinces. In 837/1433-4 Timbuktu passed into the hands of the Tuaregs. The political vacuum caused by the decline of Mali invited the expansion of the rising kingdom of Songhay [*q.v.*] into the area west of the Niger bend. The hegemony of Songhay over the northern section of the present republic of Mali in the second half of the 15th and through the 16th centuries coincided with the most illustrious period in the economic and intellectual history of Timbuktu. The history of Songhay and Timbuktu may be reconstructed from the biographical treatises of Aḥmad Bābā (d. 1036/1627) and from the mid-17th century chronicles of Timbuktu, the *Taʾrīkh al-Sūdān* by al-Saʿdī and the *Taʾrīkh al-Fattāsh* by Ibn al-Mukhtār. Djenne, which was linked by the Niger waterway with Timbuktu, was the commercial and Islamic metropolis of the Sudanic hinterland. About the level of Islamic learning in Djenne, one may learn from the career of two of its sons, the brothers Muḥammad and Aḥmad Baghyughu, who moved to Timbuktu and were among the leading scholars there. From Djenne and its region, the Dyula and Marka, Muslim traders who spoke Malinke and Bambara dialects extended their commercial network southwards as far as the fringes of the forest. These traders were known also as Wangara. Their impact on Hausaland is recorded by the Kano chronicle (*J. of the Anthropological Institute* [1908], 70): "The Wangarawa came from Mali bringing with them the Mohammedan religion."

The Songhay empire expanded mainly along the Niger river as far as Djenne in the south. Mali contracted to its Malinke nucleus, but survived repeated attacks until the beginning of the 17th century. Niani, the capital of Mali, was on the Sankarani, one of the tributaries of the Upper Niger (today in Guinea). Because its ethnic and political base was deep in the Savannah, Mali survived longer than the two other powers of the Western Sudan, Ghāna and Songhay. Both had their centres in the northern Sahel, exposed to external intervention: the Almoravids [see AL-MURĀBIṬŪN] in the 11th century and the Moroccans at the end of the 16th century.

In 1591 a Moroccan expeditionary force sent by the Sultan Aḥmad al-Manṣūr [*q.v.*] defeated the Songhay army by its superior fire-arms and conquered Gao, Timbuktu and Djenne. Timbuktu became the capital of a *pashalik*, which soon became virtually independent of Morocco, and ruled by a hereditary military caste, the descendants of the Moroccan conquerors, known as *al-rumāt* or *arma*. The *pashalik* survived until the beginning of the 19th century.

As seen from the north, through Muslim records, Mali was reduced to a kingdom of local importance during the 15th and 16th centuries. But the Portuguese, who about that time reached the Gambia, became aware of the powerful inland ruler of Mali, whose authority extended to the Atlantic coast. Mali's westward expansion was consolidated by the migration of Malinke warriors, peasants and traders to the Gambia. In 1621, sailing up the Gambia river, the British voyager Jobson met many hundred of Muslims traders and clerics who "have free recourse through all places" even in times of war (Jobson, in E. W. Bovill, *The golden trade of the Moors,* London 1932, 17-8, 84, 106).

In Mali and Songhay, Islam had become integrated into the imperial texture ideologically and institutionally. Yet even the great *mansās* and *askiyas*, who had been exposed to external Islamic influences and ruled over centres of Islamic learning, remained attached to the pre-Islamic heritage of their people. Islam was confined to urban traders and *ʿulamāʾ*. Similar patterns persisted into the 17th and 18th centuries, except that the rulers of smaller states, which had emerged as a result of the fragmentation of the great empires, had no contacts with Islamic centres north of the Sahara and had fewer and smaller towns. Consequently, Islamic influences were mitigated by traditional particularisms.

The Bambara, one of the major ethnic groups in present day Mali, are closely related to the Malinke and speak a similar dialect. They call themselves Banmana, and the term Bambara has the connotation of "infidels". Under ancient Mali they were among the subject peoples, the common peasantry, who had no share in the imperial culture of which Islam was an important component. Following the disintegration of Mali, the Bambara entered upon a process of state-building, which culminated with the establishment of the powerful Bambara states of Segu and Kaarta in the 18th century. With Bambara clans in political authority, their chiefs came under Islamic influences. Muslim elements penetrated the culture of the Bambara, but the latter remained traditionally-oriented. They were treated as infidels by most of the militant Islamic leaders of the 19th century.

The northern frontiers of the modern Republic of Mali cut deep into the Sahara to incorporate important Arabo-Berber groups. Thus Mali, like Niger and Chad, accommodates both the pastoralists of the southern Sahara and the peasants of the Sahel and the savannah. Tension between these two elements is an important feature in the political life of these states. Though the present frontiers were determined by colonial France, the interaction between desert and Sahel has a longer tradition. The southern Sahara was of strategic importance for the Sudanic states as the outlet of the desert trade routes. On the other hand, the pastoralists of the southern Sahara were attracted, mainly during years of drought, to the more promising pastures of the Sahel.

Whenever a strong state dominated the Sahel (Ghāna of the 11th century, Mali of the 14th century and Songhay of the 16th century), its authority extended over the Tuareg of the southern Sahara. But in between these periods, the pastoralists pressed south. The most decisive and lasting invasion of the Tuareg into the Niger bend began in the second half of the 17th century with the decline of the power of the *pashalik* of Timbuktu.

The southern Sahara was not, however, only a threat to the Sahel, but also a source for religious and spiritual leadership. The most prominent scholars of Timbuktu, such as the famous Aḳīt family, were of Ṣanhādja origin. The harshness of the desert pastoralists was mitigated by the marabouts, from holy families, whose religious prestige carried political influence. In the 18th century the Kunta [*q.v.*], a clan of Arab and Berber descent, established one of its centres in Azawad, north of Timbuktu. Their leader Sīdī al-Mukhtār al-Kuntī (1728-1811) was venerated by the Tuareg warriors, and through them he extended his influence over the Niger bend and the city of Timbuktu. His religious authority expanded even farther as the head (*muḳaddam*) of the Ḳādiriyya Ṣūfī brotherhood [*q.v.*], which was for the first time spread effectively among Islamic communities of the Savannah by Sīdī al-Mukhtār's numerous disciples.

The introduction of Ṣūfism into the western Sudan contributed to Islamic revivalism and militancy, which bred the *djihād* movements. In 1818 Shekhu Aḥmadu (Shaykh Aḥmad), a scholar of Fulbe origin and a follower of the Kuntī Ḳādiriyya, initiated a *djihād* against the Fulbe clan leaders in Massina who practiced mixed Islam. He also challenged the religious authority of the established *ʿulamāʾ* of Djenne, who sanctioned the existing socio-political order and reconciled it with the marginal role of Islam. The military success of Shekhu Aḥmadu resulted in the creation of a theocratic state (known as *dina*) with its capital in the new town of Ḥamdallāhi. The state existed for over forty years under the successive rule of Shekhu Aḥmadu, his son and grandson.

In 1862 Ḥamdallāhi was conquered and destroyed by a rival *mudjāhid*, al-Ḥādjdj ʿUmar b. Saʿīd. Al-Ḥādjdj ʿUmar, whose way to his own land of Futa Toro, on the lower Senegal, had been blocked by the French, turned east against the infidel Bambara state of Segu. He then attacked the theocratic state of Ḥamdallāhi, which he anathemised as an ally of the infidel Bambara. Behind this pretext was the fierce conflict between two Ṣūfī brotherhoods; the Ḳādiriyya of Ḥamdallāhi and the Tidjāniyya of al-Ḥādjdj ʿUmar. The Tidjāniyya represented a more vigorous, radical and populist way (*ṭarīḳa*) which challenged the aristocratic, established way of the Ḳādiriyya. The leader of the Ḳādiriyya Aḥmad al-Bakkāʾī (grandson of the great Sīdī al-Mukhtār al-Kuntī), who had first resented the militant aggression of Ḥamdallāhi, now rose to oppose the Tidjānī threat of al-Ḥādjdj ʿUmar. The forces which he mobilised fought al-Ḥādjdj ʿUmar, who was killed in battle in 1864.

The latter's son Aḥmad ruled for almost thirty years in Segu, the former Bambara capital. His authority had to be enforced by his army, composed of Tokolor followers and local conscripts (*sofa*), against continuous resistance of local ethnic groups.

The French military commanders in their advance towards the Niger exploited the internal dissensions in the Tid̲j̲ānī empire of Segu, until its final defeat in 1893. The non-Muslim ethnic groups, like the Bambara, greeted their liberation from Tid̲j̲ānī rule. Many of those who had been forcibly converted to Islam by the Tid̲j̲ānīs now returned to their ancestral ways.

During the colonial period (when the present Republic of Mali was known as the French Sudan), Islam progressed among most ethnic groups, winning over those who moved to the growing towns and those who joined the seasonal labour migration to the more prosperous colonies. With better roads and greater security, more clerics (*marabouts*) visited villages, converted non-Muslims and invigorated religion among long-established Muslim communities.

These marabouts helped the spread of Ṣūfī brotherhoods. The younger and more vigorous Tid̲j̲āniyya expanded faster and further than the old Ḳādiriyya. But the Tid̲j̲āniyya in its turn was challenged by a new brotherhood, a splinter group, the Ḥamāliyya, named after its founder Ḥamāhullāh (1883-4 to 1943). The French colonial authorities, seeking to avoid instability, intervened in defence of the old Tid̲j̲āniyya brotherhood. They deported Ḥamāhullāh, harassed his followers and as in other cases of self-fulfilling prophecies, provoked the Ḥamāllists to violence.

In the 1930s, some young Muslim scholars who returned from studies at al-Azhar resented the growing influence of the Ṣūfī brotherhoods and deplored the exploitation of the believers by the marabouts. The reformists, sometimes referred to as neo-Wahhābīs, considered ignorance as the source of all evils and devoted themselves to the promotion of Islamic education, with emphasis on the teaching of Arabic. Bamako, the capital of the French Sudan, was an important centre for their activities. Religious reformism and fundamentalism soon had political implications; at home they challenged the authority of the old marabouts, and abroad they subscribed to pan-Islamic ideologies. Both trends were considered a threat to the public security, and the reformists were closely watched by the French colonial authorities and their activities were severely curtailed. The reformists were among the first supporters of the radical, anti-colonial party, the Union Soudanaise (US - RDA).

The post-war political struggle in the French Sudan was between the US and the PPS (Parti Progressiste Soudanaise). The latter was the party supported by the traditional chiefs and favoured by the French colonial authorities. It was stronger in the villages among non-Muslims and away from the main commercial routes. It survived longer among the Bambara and the Fulbe, the two ethnic groups most hostile to the Tid̲j̲ānī empire and those who had most to gain from its destruction by the French. The US was stronger in the towns, along commercial routes, among traders, and the more committed and politically-articulate Muslims. The political leaders of the US soon discovered the effectiveness of an Islamic vocabulary for mass mobilisation. Radical Muslim ideas were incorporated into the political ideology of the US. It won the elections of 1956 and formed the first autonomous African government of the French Sudan. After independence, the radical government of the US pursued a "scientific" though not an atheistic socialism. In its economic policies, it soon alienated the Dyula Muslim traders, who had been among the supporters of US during the period of decolonisation. The government also curtailed the activities of the *ʿulamāʾ*. Islam was integrated into the national ethos of Mali, but only at the symbolic level. The coup d'état in November 1968 brought to power young officers, mostly of Bambara origin, who were little concerned with Islam. In 1971 by a government decree, the modern Islamic schools established by Muslim reformists (l'Union Culturelle Musulmane) were closed.

Modern Malians have strong historical sentiments and consider themselves heirs to the traditions of ancient Mali, to the intellectual achievements of Timbuktu and to the religious experience which was enriched through the interplay of Islam and ethnic religions.

Bibliography: Arabic sources: Bakrī, *K. al-Masālik wa 'l-mamālik*, ed. M. G. de Slane, Algiers 1911; ʿUmarī, *Masālik al-abṣār fī mamālik al-amṣār*, ms. B.N. 5868; Ibn Baṭṭūṭa, *Tuḥfat al-nuẓẓār fī g̲h̲arāʾib al-amṣār*, ed. and tr. Defrémery and Sanguinetti, repr. Paris 1922; Ibn K̲h̲aldūn, *K. Taʾrīk̲h̲ al-duwal al-islāmiyya bi 'l-mag̲h̲rib min Kitāb al-ʿIbar*, ed. de Slane, Paris 1847; Aḥmad Bābā, *Nayl al-ibtihād̲j̲ fī taṭrīz al-dībād̲j̲*, Cairo 1956; Saʿdī, *Taʾrīk̲h̲ al-Sūdān*, ed. O. Houdas, Paris 1900; [Ibn al-Muktār], *Taʾrīk̲h̲ al-Fattās̲h̲*, ed. Houdas and M. Delafosse, Paris 1913; anon., *Tad̲h̲kirat al-nisyān*, Paris 1901; M. Eisenstein, *Die Herrscher von Mali nach al-Qalqašandī*, in *Orientalia Lovaniensia periodica* xvi (1985), 197-204.

Ancient Mali: Ch. Monteil, *Les empires du Mali*, Paris 1927; R. Mauny, *Tableau géographique de l'Ouest Africain au moyen âge*, Dakar 1961; D. T. Niane, *Soundiata ou l'épopée mandingue*, Paris 1960; N. Levtzion, *Ancient Ghana and Mali*, London 1973; J. M. Cuoq, *Recueil des sources arabes concernant l'Afrique Occidentale du 8e au 16e siècle (Bilād al-Sūdān)*, Paris 1975; M. Ly Tall, *L'empire du Mali*, Dakar 1977; W. Filipowiak, *Études archéologiques sur la capitale médiévale du Mali*, Warsaw 1979; J. F. P. Hopkins and N. Levtzion (annot. tr.), *Corpus of early Arabic sources for West African history*, Cambridge 1980.

Songhay, Timbuktu, the *Pas̲h̲alīḳ* and the Bambara states (15th-18th centuries): Ch. Monteil, *Les Bambara du Ségou et du Kaarta*, Paris 1924; idem, *Une cité soudanaise: Djenné*, Paris 1932; J. Rouch, *Contribution à l'histoire des Songhai*, Dakar 1953; J. O. Hunwick, *Religion and state in the Songhay empire, 1464-1591*, in *Islam in Tropical Africa*, ed. I. M. Lewis, London 1966; S. M. Cissoko, *Tombouctou et l'empire Songhay*, Dakar 1975; M. A. Zouber, *Aḥmad Bābā de Tombouctou*, Paris 1977; M. Abitbol, *Tombouctou et les arma*, Paris 1977.

The 19th-century d̲j̲ihād movements: A.H. Ba et J. Daget, *L'empire peul du Macina*, Paris 1962; Y. Person, *Samori: une révolution dyula*, Dakar 1968; A. S. Kanya-Forstner, *The conquest of the Western Sudan*, Cambridge 1969; W. A. Brown, *The caliphate of Ḥamdallāhi: ca. 1818-1864*, unpubl. Ph.D. diss., U. of Wisconsin 1969; Y. J. Saint-Martin, *L'empire toucouleur, 1848-1897*, Paris 1970; B. O. Oloruntimehin, *The Segu Tukulor empire, 1848-1893*, London 1972; A. A. Batran, *Sīdī al-Mukhtār al-Kuntī and the recrudescence of Islam in the Western Sudan and the middle Niger, c. 1750-1811*, unpubl. Ph.D. diss., U. of Birmingham 1972; A. Zebadia, *The career and correspondence of Aḥmad al-Bakkāʾī of Timbuktu, 1847-1865*, unpubl. Ph.D. diss., U. of London (SOAS) 1974.

The French Sudan and modern Mali: A. Le Chatelier, *L'Islam dans l'Afrique Occidentale*, Paris 1899; M. Delafosse, *Haut-Sénégal-Niger*, Paris 1912; P. Marty, *Études sur l'Islam et les tribus du Soudan*,

Paris 1920-1; M. Chailley, *Aspects de l'Islam au Mali,* in *Notes et études sur l'Islam en Afrique noire,* Paris 1962; R. Schachter-Morgenthau, *Political parties in French-speaking West Africa,* Oxford 1964; W. J. Foltz, *From French West Africa to the Mali Federation,* New Haven 1965; P. Alexandre, *The Hammalism,* in *Protest and power in Black Africa,* ed. Rotberg and Mazrui, New York 1970; L. Kaba, *The Wahhabiyya: Islamic reform and politics in French West Africa,* Evanston 1974; J. M. Cuoq, *Les Musulmans en Afrique,* Paris 1975, 175-89. (N. Levtzion)

MALIK, the Arabic word for king (pl. *mulūk*), stemming from the old Semitic root *m-l-k* (the Hebrew equivalent is *melekh*; Aramaic *malkā*; Akkadian *malku*; Assyrian *malku, maliku*), which signifies "possession" and, by extension, "rule" or "government". As a kingly title, the term appears repeatedly in pre-Islamic inscriptions from southern Arabia and the Syrian desert fringes (e.g. the Namāra epitaph of Imruʾ al-Ḳays, "King of the Arabs", from 328 A.D. [see LAKHMIDS]). The Ḳurʾān mentions several historical and legendary kings (*mulūk*), among them Pharaoh and Saul (II, 246-7; XII, 42 f.); and the *ḥadīth* discusses numerous others.

Islam, however, presented a new order in which God alone was "the King, the Truth", "the Possessor of Heavens and Earth" as the Ḳurʾān says, "Say, O God, Possessor of sovereignty (*mālik al-mulk*), You give sovereignty to whomever You choose and take it from whomever You choose" (III, 26). In this view, heads of the community of believers, the caliphs, were vested with the exercise of God's sovereignty so that they could administer His divinely-created polity; yet its ultimate possession, as well as the kingly title, remained exclusively His. Accordingly, a man's claim to such a title was regarded as a contemptible feature of the prior, unholy order that Islam sought to replace (an analogous approach may be seen in the Old Testament, where the idea of human kingship is discredited as unfit for the pious community of the People of Israel; cf. Judges, viii, 22-3; I Samuel, viii, 4-20). *Malik* thus came to connote the temporal, mundane facet of government—the antithesis of *khalīfa* and *imām* [*q.vv.*] which signified piety and righteousness. The Umayyads were termed *mulūk* and their rule *mulk* by their opponents, who thus expressed disdain for an irreligious and worldly-minded government. Considered to be a term of abuse, *malik* was not officially assumed by Muslim rulers in the early centuries of Islam; on the other hand, it was commonly applied, sometimes with unconcealed scorn, to non-Muslim monarchs.

The spread of the Islamic empire brought it under the impact of non-Arab traditions, which played a major role in shaping the Muslim concept of government in the early centuries of Islam. Under Sāsānid influence, authors of "Mirrors for princes", from the beginning of the ʿAbbāsid period, introduced theories on the divine right of kings. God, it was stated, "bestowed upon kings His special grace (*karāmatihi*) and endowed them with His authority (*sulṭānihi*)" (*Kitāb al-Tādj fī akhlāḳ al-mulūk*, attributed to al-Djāḥiẓ, ed. Aḥmad Zakī, Cairo 1914, 2). Discussing in great detail the privileges, duties and recommended conduct of kings, this literature emphasised the elevated status of a *malik* within his community. The principles underlying these writings, distant from the initial Islamic theory of rulership, represented the revival of pre-Arab concepts in the formerly Persian regions of the empire.

The use of the royal title in such a manner gradually led to a modification in its import, and consequently to its adoption by Muslim rulers. Towards the middle of the 4th/10th century the Būyids, new rulers of the empire, were reviving the Sāsānid tradition of regnal epithets: in the year 325/936 ʿAlī b. Būya, one of the three founders of the dynasty, assumed the persian title *shāhānshāh* (i.e. "king of kings" [*q.v.*]); and his nephew and heir, ʿAḍud al-Dawla (338-72/944-83 [*q.v.*]) added *malik* to his list of epithets (al-Maḳrīzī, *Sulūk*, 28). Meanwhile, in the north-eastern provinces, Sāmānid rulers likewise assumed kingship as a measure of asserting their independence from ʿAbbāsid and Būyid dominion: on coins dating from the years 339/950-1, i.e. from the reign of Nūḥ b. Naṣr (331-43/943-54), the latter is designated *al-malik al-muʾayyad.* Later members of his dynasty employed the title in a similar way (S. Lane Poole, *Catalogue of coins in the British Museum,* ii, 100, 103, 105-6, 109-10, 115-16). Other non-Arab dynasties followed suit: Khwārazmī, Ghaznawid and Saldjūḳ rulers called themselves *malik,* usually in combination with honorific adjectives, e.g. *al-kāmil, al-ṣāliḥ, al-ʿādil,* which accordingly became a highly common feature of mediaeval Islamic titulature. On the western flank of the Islamic empire, Fāṭimid rulers in the late 5th/11th century similarly adopted *malik* as their royal epithet. The Ayyūbids inherited it from them (one of Ṣalāḥ al-Dīn's titles was *al-malik al-nāṣir*), and in turn passed it on to the Mamlūks. In the Būyid, Saldjūḳ, Fāṭimid, Ayyūbid, and Mamlūk states the title was not reserved for the heads of the monarchy alone, but was rather freely applied to princes, *wuzarāʾ* and provincial governors as well (see examples in Ḥasan al-Bāshā, *al-Alḳāb al-Islāmiyya,* Cairo 1957, 496-500).

The increasing number of potentates identifying themselves as *malik* gradually rendered the name less majestic, for it came to imply limited sway over one realm among many, and subjection to a supreme suzerain. Its devaluation, once again, was reflected in the fact that many a ruler assumed, in addition to *malik,* other and more pretentious designations. Several Būyid heads of state (e.g. Djalāl al-Dawla, Bahāʾ al-Dawla) and Ayyūbid ones (e.g. al-ʿĀdil) adopted the epithet *malik al-mulūk,* modelled on the Persian *shāhānshāh*; while others called themselves *sulṭān* [*q.v.*], a title superior to *malik* as it conveyed a sense of independent sovereignty. The Mamlūks, in a similar manner, combined these last two names, identifying themselves as *al-malik al-sulṭān,* while calling high-ranking governors in the Egyptian and Syrian provinces *malik al-umarāʾ* i.e. chief *amīr.* In one instance in the Mamlūk state the term was employed in the feminine, as the regnal designation of Shadjar al-Durr [*q.v.*] (d. 655/1257), who entitled herself *malikat al-muslimīn.* Another occurrence of the name in the feminine was in India, where *malik* was not otherwise in use; the queen Raḍiyya [*q.v.*] of Dihlī (634-7/1236-40), the only female ruler in Muslim India, adopted it in lieu of the title *sulṭān* carried by the male members of the dynasty.

The depreciation of the title was apparently the main reason for its disappearance in later times. The Ottoman Sultans did not commonly use it. By the time when they were in power, the name retained but little of its former glory.

In the 20th century, *malik* has appeared again in the Muslim countries, carrying a new sense of grandeur. Following more than a century of contacts with European monarchies, the idea of kingship acquired new respect in the Islamic countries, and *malik* lost whatever was left of its uncomplimentary associations. Its reappearance was, thus, not a revitalisation of the old title but rather a calque of "king" or "roi" in the modern European sense. The first to use *malik* in this novel sense was the Hāshimite Ḥusayn, the *sharīf* of Mecca, who in 1916 declared himself "King of the Arab countries"; after some international discussion, he was recognised by Britain and France as "King (*malik*) of the Ḥidjāz". The Hāshimite kingdom of the Ḥidjāz existed until 1925, when it was conquered by the Saᶜūdī ᶜAbd al-ᶜAzīz Ibn Saᶜūd, the Sultan of Nadjd. In 1926 the latter declared himself "Sultan of Nadjd and King of the Ḥidjāz and its Dependencies", and in 1932 he merged the different units, thereby becoming *malik* of the "Kingdom of Saudi Arabia".

The style of royal titles reached the peak of its prestige in the Islamic countries in the 1920s, when several kingdoms were established. In 1920 the Hāshimite King Ḥusayn's son, Fayṣal, was declared King of Syria; his monarchy lasted for four short months, at the end of which he left for ᶜIrāḳ, where he became king in 1921. In the following year, the Sultan of Egypt, Fuʾād I [see FUʾĀD AL-AWWAL], followed the latter's footsteps and assumed the title *malik*. In 1926 Amān Allāh [*q.v.* in Suppl.], the *amīr* of Afghānistān, abandoned his former title and declared himself king; and in the same year the *Imām* Yaḥyā of Yemen was first recognised as *malik* in a treaty with Italy. Yemenī rulers, more commonly known by the title *Imām*, were thereafter formally acknowledged as kings in international documents. Muslim rulers continued to adopt the royal epithet in later years: in Trans-Jordan in 1946 the Hāshimite *amīr* ᶜAbd Allāh took the title "King of Trans-Jordan" (since 1948: of "the Hāshimite Kingdom of Jordan"); in 1951 the *amīr* Idrīs al-Sanūsī of Cyrenaica was declared *malik* of the nascent state of Libya; and in Morocco in 1957, the Sultan Muḥammad V changed his title to *malik*, thus marking his intention to introduce a modern type of government.

By that time, however, *malik* was no longer the venerated and popular title it used to be in the earlier part of the century. Anti-monarchical revolutions and revolts swept away most kings reigning in the Islamic countries—in Egypt in 1952; in ᶜIrāḳ in 1958; in Yemen in 1962; in Libya in 1969; and in Afghānistān in 1973. Thus the last third of the 20th century has witnessed, once again, a decline in the standing of the kingly title, which has lost ground to more attractive alternatives inspired by leftist, revolutionary trends.

Bibliography: *LA*, s.v.; Ibn al-Athīr, *Taʾrīkh al-dawla al-atābakiyya*, in *Recueil des historiens des croisades*, x, Paris 1876, s.v., in index; Ḳalḳashandī, *Ṣubḥ al-aᶜshā*, v, 486-8; Goldziher, *Muh. Stud.*, ii, 31 ff., Eng. tr. ii, 40 ff.; A. K. S. Lambton, *The theory of kingship in Naṣīḥat ul-mulūk of Ghazālī*, in *IQ*, i (1954), 47-55; W. Madelung, *The assumption of the title shāhānshāh by the Būyids and 'the reign of the Daylam (dawlat al-Daylam)'*, in *JNES*, xxviii (April 1969), 84-108, (July 1969), 168-83; C. E. Bosworth, *The titulature of the early Ghaznavids*, in *Oriens*, xv (1962), 210-33; Ḥasan al-Bāshā, *al-Alḳāb al-islāmiyya*, Cairo 1957, 496-507 and *passim* (a fundamental work); cf. also LAḲAB, PĀDISHĀH, SHĀH, SULṬĀN.

(A. AYALON)

MĀLIK b. ABI 'L-SAMḤ AL-ṬĀʾĪ (d. *ca.* 136/754), one of the great musicians of the 1st/7th century. According to a tradition given in the *Aghānī*, the famous Isḥāḳ al-Mawṣilī classed him among the four finest singers, of whom two were Meccans, Ibn Muḥriz and Ibn Suraydj, and two Medinans, Maᶜbad and Mālik.

His father, who came from a branch of the tribe of Ṭayy, died when Mālik was still very young; his mother, who came from the Ḳurayshite tribe of Makhzūm [*q.v.*], had to leave the mountains of the Ṭayy because of famine and settled with her children in Medina. According to the *Aghānī* again, Mālik became fascinated by singing, and spent his days at the door of ᶜAbd Allāh b. al-Zubayr's son Ḥamza, listening to the latter's protégé, the famous singer Maᶜbad, and in whose company he spent the greater part of his time. One day, the *amīr* invited in the strange young Bedouin who had stationed himself at the door, and after a brief audition, instructed Maᶜbad to teach him music. The relations between master and pupil were not always unequivocal.

Subsequently, Mālik attached himself to Sulaymān b. ᶜAlī al-Hāshimī, who became his patron. When al-Saffāḥ came to power, he nominated his uncle Sulaymān as governor of the lower Tigris region. The latter installed himself at Baṣra and summoned thither his protégé Mālik. After a short stay, Mālik decided to return to Medina, where, after some time, he died at over 80 years old.

Mālik learnt very easily the songs which he heard; but although he could easily remember the tunes, with all their nuances, he found it hard to remember the poetic texts. Ever since his first meeting with Ḥamza, he showed a remarkable mastery in the exact and tasteful reproduction of the melodies of Maᶜbad, whom he captivated when listening at the door. In regard to the words, he confessed frankly that he could not remember them. In accordance with the norms of the period, Mālik was not considered as a creative artist and he himself did not consider himself as such. His practice was to declare that he was happy to embellish and enrich the works of others. Accordingly, he was in some way a musical aesthete whose whole imagination and energy were concentrated on the refinement and embellishment of the melody and on the beauty of its execution, rather than on the creation of new songs. Being careful to discover an exact expression of the facts just mentioned, he questioned his confrère Ibn Suraydj about the qualities of the perfect musician, and heard this reply: "The musician who enriches the melody, has good wind, gives the correct proportion to the phrases, underlines the pronunciation, respects the grammatical endings of words, gives long notes their proper value, separates clearly the short notes and, finally, uses correctly the various rhythmical modes, can be considered as perfect". It is very likely that Mālik embodied these qualities of the perfect musician.

Finally, Mālik remained faithful to his origins among the people, for we read on several occasions that he took as the basis of this compositions folkloristic melodies which a mourning woman, a weaver, an ass-driver, etc., sang.

Bibliography: *Aghānī*, Cairo 1932, i, 251, 315, v, 101-21; Ibn ᶜAbd Rabbihi ᶜ*Iḳd*, Cairo 1949, vi, 29-30; *JA* (Nov.-Dec. 1873), 497-500.

(A. SHILOAH)

MĀLIK b. ANAS, a Muslim jurist, the *Imām* of the *madhhab* of the Mālikīs, which is named after him [see MĀLIKIYYA], and frequently called briefly the *Imām* of Medina.

1. The sources for Mālik's biography.

The oldest authority of any length for Mālik, Ibn Saᶜd's account (d. 230/845 [*q.v.*]), which is based on al-Wāḳidī (d. 207/822 [*q.v.*]) and which places him in the sixth class of the Medinan "successors", is lost, as there is a hiatus in the manuscript of the work; but it is possible to reconstruct the bulk of it from the quotations preserved, mainly in al-Ṭabarī (iii, 2519 ff), in the *Kitāb al-ᶜUyūn* (*Fragm. hist. arab.*, i, 297 ff.), in Ibn Khallikān and in al-Suyūṭī (7, 6 ff., 12 ff., 41, 46).

From this, it is evident that the brief biographical notes in Ibn Ḳutayba (d. 276/889 [*q.v.*]) and the somewhat more full ones in the *Fihrist* (compiled in 377/987) are based on Ibn Saᶜd. The article on Mālik in al-Ṭabarī's (d. 310/922 [*q.v.*]) *Dhayl al-Mudhayyal* is essentially dependent on the same source, while a few other short references there and in his history are based on other authorities. Al-Samᶜānī (wrote *ca.* 550/1156 [*q.v.*]) with the minimum of bare facts gives only the legendary version of an otherwise quite well established incident, while in Ibn Khallikān (d. 681/1282 [*q.v.*]), and particularly in al-Nawawī (d. 676/1277 [*q.v.*]), the legendary features are more pronounced, although isolated facts of importance are also preserved by them. Al-Suyūṭī (d. 911/1505 [*q.v.*]) gives a detailed compilation drawn from Ibn Saᶜd and other works, most of which are now no longer accessible but are for the most part of later date and unreliable, like the *Musnad Ḥadīth al-Muwaṭṭa*ʾ of al-Ghāfiḳī, the *Ḥilya* of Abū Nuᶜaym, the *Kitāb al-Muttafaḳ wa 'l-mukhtalaf* of al-Khaṭīb al-Baghdādī, the *Kitāb Tārtīb al-madārik* of al-Ḳāḍī ᶜIyāḍ and the *Faḍāʾil Mālik* of Abu 'l-Ḥasan Fihr. The bulk of the later *Manāḳib* [*q.v.*], for example that of al-Zawāwī, are of no independent value.

2. Mālik's life.

Mālik's full name was Abū ᶜAbd Allāh Mālik b. Anas b. Mālik b. Abī ᶜĀmir b. ᶜAmr b.-al-Ḥārith b. Ghaymān b. Khuthayn b. ᶜAmr b. al-Ḥārith al-Aṣbaḥī; he belonged to the Ḥumayr, who are included in the Banū Taym b. Murra (Taym Ḳuraysh).

The date of his birth is not known; the dates given, varying between 90 and 97/708-16, are hypotheses, which are presumably approximately correct. As early as Ibn Saᶜd we find the statement that he spent three years in his mother's womb (over two, according to Ibn Ḳutayba, 290), a legend, the origin of which in a wrong interpretation of an alleged statement by Mālik on the possible duration of pregnancy, is still evident in the text of Ibn Saᶜd. According to a tradition preserved by al-Tirmidhī, Muḥammad himself is said to have foretold his coming as well as that of Abū Ḥanīfa and al-Shāfiᶜī. His grandfather and his uncle on the father's side are mentioned by al-Samᶜānī as traditionists, so that there is nothing remarkable in his also being a student. According to the *Kitāb al-Aghānī*, he is said to have first wanted to become a singer, and only exchanged his career for the study of *fiḳh* on his mother's advice on account of his ugliness (cf. Goldziher, *Muh. Studien,* ii, 79, n. 2); but such anecdotes are little more than evidence that someone did not particularly admire him. Very little reliable information is known about his studies, but the story that he studied *fiḳh* with the celebrated Rabīᶜa b. Farrukh (d. 132 or 133 or 143/749-60), who cultivated *raʾy* in Medina, whence he is called Rabīᶜat al-Raʾy, can hardly be an invention, although it is only found in somewhat late sources (cf. Goldziher, *op. cit.,* ii, 80). Later legends increase the number of his teachers to incredible figures: 900, including 300 *tābiᶜūn* are mentioned. He is said to have learned *ḳirāʾa* from Nāfiᶜ b. Abī Nuᶜaym. He transmitted traditions from al-Zuhrī, Nāfiᶜ, the *mawlā* of Ibn ᶜUmar, Abu 'l-Zinād, Hāshim b. ᶜUrwa, Yaḥyā b. Saᶜīd, ᶜAbd Allāh b. Dīnār, Muḥammad b. al-Munkadir, Abu 'l-Zubayr and others, but the *isnād*s of course are not sufficient evidence that he studied with the authorities in question; a list of 95 *shuyūkh* is given by al-Suyūṭī, 48 ff.

A fixed chronological point in his life, most of which he spent in Medina, is his being involved in the rising of the ᶜAlid pretender Muḥammad b. ᶜAbd Allāh in 145/762 (on the other hand, the story of Mālik's alleged dealings with Ibn Hurmuz in the same year gives the impression of being quite apocryphal). As early as 144/761, the caliph al-Manṣūr sent to the Ḥasanids of Mecca through him a demand that the two brothers Muḥammad and Ibrāhīm b. ᶜAbd Allāh, suspected of being pretenders to the supreme power, should be handed over to him; this shows that he must have already attained a position of general esteem and one at least not openly hostile to the government; he was even rewarded out of the proceeds of the confiscated property of the captured ᶜAbd Allāh, father of the two brothers above named. This mission met with no success. When Muḥammad in 145/762 by a coup made himself master of Medina, Mālik declared in a *fatwā* that the homage paid to al-Manṣūr was not binding because it was given under compulsion, whereupon many who would otherwise have held back joined Muḥammad. Mālik took no active part in the rising but stayed at home. On the failure of the rebellion (147/763), he was punished by flogging by Djaᶜfar b. Sulaymān, the governor of Medina, when he suffered a dislocation of the shoulder, but this is said to have still further increased his prestige and there is no reason to doubt that the stories of Abū Ḥanīfa's ill-treatment in prison are based on this episode in the life of Mālik. He must have later made his peace with the government; in 160/777 the caliph al-Mahdī consulted him on structural alterations in the Meccan sanctuary, and in the year of his death (179/796) the caliph al-Rashīd visited him on the occasion of his pilgrimage. While this fact may be considered certain, the details in the *Kitāb al-ᶜUyūn* are already somewhat legendary and in al-Suyūṭī, following Abū Nuᶜaym, quite fantastic. The story of al-Manṣūr found as early as Ibn Saᶜd, in a parallel *riwāya* in al-Ṭabarī from al-Mahdī, is quite fictitious, and is given again with fantastic detail in al-Suyūṭī (from Abū Nuᶜaym) from al-Rashīd, that the caliph wanted to make the *Muwaṭṭa*ʾ canonical and only abandoned his intention at the representations of Mālik.

Mālik died, at the age of about 85 after a short illness, in the year 179/796 in Medina and was buried in al-Baḳīᶜ. ᶜAbd Allah b. Zaynab, the governor there, conducted his funeral service. An elegy on him by Djaᶜfar b. Aḥmad al-Sarrādj is given in Ibn Khallikān. Pictures of the *ḳubba* over his grave are given in al-Batanūni, *al-Riḥla al-Ḥidjāziyya*², opposite p. 256, and in Ibrāhim Rifᶜat Pasha, *Mirʾāt al-Ḥaramayn,* i, opposite p. 426.

As early as Ibn Saᶜd (certainly going back to al-Wāḳidī), we have fairly full description of Mālik's personal appearance, his habits and manner of life, which cannot however claim to be authentic, nor can the sayings attributed to him, which became more and more numerous as time went on. The few certain facts about him have been buried under a mass of legends; the most important facts have already been noted and the others will be found in al-Suyūṭī and al-Zawāwī.

On the transmitters of his *Muwaṭṭa*ʾ and the earliest members of his *madhhab,* see MĀLIKIYYA. Here we will only mention the most important scholars who handed down traditions from him. These were ᶜAbd Allāh b. al-Mubārak, al-Awzāᶜi, Ibn Djuraydj, Ḥammād b. Zayd, al-Layth b. Saᶜd, Ibn Salama, al-Shāfiᶜī, Shuᶜba, al-Thawrī, Ibn ᶜUlayya, Ibn ᶜUyayma, Yazīd b. ᶜAbd Allāh and his *shaykhs* al-Zuhrī and Yaḥyā b. Saᶜīd; al-Suyūṭī, (18 ff.) gives a long list of transmitters, but most of them are not corroborated. We may just mention the apocryphal story of Mālik's meeting with the young al-Shāfiᶜī (*Fragm. hist. ar.,* i, 359; Wüstenfeld, in *Abh. Gött. AW* [1890], 34, and [1891], 1 ff.), which is simply an expression of the view that was held of the relation between the two *Imāms*.

3. Mālik's writings. Further sources for his teachings.

A. Mālik's great work is the *Kitāb al-Muwaṭṭaʾ* which, if we except the *Corpus juris* of Zayd b. ʿAlī, is the earliest surviving Muslim law-book. Its object is to give a survey of law and justice; ritual and practice of religion according to the *idjmāʿ* of Islam in Medina, according to the *sunna* usual in Medina; and to create a theoretical standard for matters which were not settled from the point of view of *idjmāʿ* and *sunna*. In a period of recognition and appreciation of the canon law under the early ʿAbbāsids, there was a practical interest in pointing out a "smoothed path" (this is practically what *al-muwaṭṭaʾ* means) through the far-reaching differences of opinion even on the most elementary questions. Mālik wished to help this interest on the basis of the practice in the Ḥidjāz, and to codify and systematise the customary law of Medina. Tradition, which he interprets from the point of view of practice, is with him not an end but a means; the older jurists are therefore hardly ever quoted except as authorities for Mālik himself. As he was only concerned with the documentation of the *sunna* and not with criticism of its form, he is exceedingly careless as far as order is concerned in his treatment of traditions. The *Muwaṭṭaʾ* thus represents the transition from the simple *fiḳh* of the earliest period to the pure science of *ḥadīth* of the later period.

Mālik was not alone among his contemporaries in the composition of the *Muwaṭṭaʾ*; al-Mādjashūn (d. 164/781) is said to have dealt with the consensus of the scholars of Medina without quoting the pertinent traditions, and works quite in the style of the *Muwaṭṭaʾ* are recorded by several Medinan scholars of the same time (cf. Goldziher, *op. cit.*, ii, 219 ff.) but nothing of them has survived for us. The success of the *Muwaṭṭaʾ* is due to the fact that it always takes an average view on disputed points (see below, section 4).

In transmitting the *Muwaṭṭaʾ*, Mālik did not make a definitive text, either oral or by *munāwala*, to be disseminated; on the contrary, the different *riwāyas* (recensions) of his work differ in places very much (cf. Goldziher, *op. cit.*, ii, 222). The reason for this, besides the fact that in those days every little stress was laid on accurate literal repetition of such texts and great liberty was taken by the transmitters (cf. Goldziher, *op. cit.*, ii, 221), lies probably in the fact that Mālik did not always give exactly the same form to his orally-delivered teachings. But the name *Muwaṭṭaʾ*, which certainly goes back to Mālik himself, and is found in all recensions, is a guarantee that Mālik wanted to create a "work" in the later sense of the term, although of course the stories which make Mālik talk of his writings reflect the conditions of a later period. In later times, the *Muwaṭṭaʾ* was regarded by many as canonical (cf. Goldziher, *op. cit.*, ii, 213, 265 ff.; al-Suyūṭī, 47) and numerous legends deal with its origin (al-Suyūṭī, 42 ff.).

Fifteen recensions in all of the *Muwaṭṭaʾ* are known, only two of which were to survive in their entirety, while some five were studied in the 3rd-4th/9th-10th centuries in Spain (Goldziher, *op. cit.*, ii, 222, nn. 2 and 4) and twelve were still available to al-Rudānī (d. 1094/1693) (Heffening, *Fremdenrecht*, 144, n. 1):

a. the vulgate of the work transmitted by Yaḥyā b. Yaḥyā al-Maṣmūdī (d. 234/848-9), often printed e.g. Delhi 1216, 1296 (without *isnāds* and with Hindustānī translation and commentary), 1307, 1308, Cairo 1279-80 (with the commentary of Muḥammad b. ʿAbd al-Bāḳī al-Zurḳānī, d. 1122/1710), Lahore 1889, Tunis 1280; numerous commentaries, editions and synopses; cf. Brockelmann, I, 176, S I, 297-9; Ahlwardt, *Katalog Berlin,* 1145; Muḥammad ʿAbd al-Ḥayy al-Lakhnawī (Introduction to the edition of the recension *b*), Lucknow 1297, 21 ff.; al-Suyūṭī, 3 *passim* (work of al-Ghāfiḳī), 57 (on Ibn ʿAbd al-Barr) and 58 (chief passage); Goldziher, *op. cit.*, ii, 230, n. 2; Schacht, in *Abh. Preuss. Ak.* (1928), no. 2 *c*; and al-Suyūṭī, *Isʿāf al-mubaṭṭaʾ bi-ridjāl al-Muwaṭṭaʾ*, Delhi 1320, and Muḥammad b. Ṭāhir al-Patnī, *Madjmaʿ biḥār al-anwār,* Lucknow 1283.

b. the recension of Muḥammad b. al-Ḥasan al-Shaybānī (d. 189/805) which is also an edition and critical development of Mālik's work, as al-Shaybānī at the end of most chapters gives his own views and that of Abū Ḥanīfa on the questions discussed, sometimes with very full reasonings; often printed, e.g. Lahore 1211-13 (with Hindustānī translation and notes), Ludhiana 1291, 1292, 1293, Lucknow 1297 (with introduction and commentary by Muḥammad ʿAbd al-Ḥayy al-Lakhnawī), Kazan 1910 (with the same); several commentaries; cf. Brockelmann, *op. cit.*; Schacht, *op. cit.*, nos. 2, 2*a*, 2*b*; and the works quoted under *a*.

On the relation of these *riwāyas* to one another, cf. Goldziher, *op. cit.*, ii, 223 ff.

c. The quotations from the recension of ʿAbd Allāh b. Wahb (d. 197/813) which are preserved in the two fragments of al-Ṭabarī's *Kitāb Ikhtilāf al-fuḳahāʾ* (ed. Kern, Cairo 1902, and Schacht, *op. cit.*, no. 22) are fairly comprehensive; this *riwāya* follows that of Yaḥyā b. Yaḥyā quite closely.

The other recensions of the *Muwaṭṭaʾ* are given by al-Lakhnawī, *op. cit.*, 18 ff.; further lists of transmitters of the *Muwaṭṭaʾ* are given in al-Suyūṭī, 48, 51, and in al-Nawawī.

B. Whether Mālik composed other works besides the *Muwaṭṭaʾ* is doubtful (the statements in the *Fihrist,* 199,$_9$, which speak of a number of works by Mālik are quite vague and uncertain). The books ascribed to him fall into two groups: legal and otherwise. Among the legal ones we read of a *Kitāb al-Sunan* or *al-Sunna* (*Fihrist,* 199, ll. 9, 16) transmitted by Ibn Wahb or by ʿAbd Allāh b. ʿAbd al-Ḥakam al-Miṣrī, a *Kitāb al-Manāsik* (al-Suyūṭī, 40), a *Kitāb al-Mudjālasāt,* transmitted by Ibn Wahb (*ibid.*), a *Risāla fi 'l-aḳḍiya,* transmitted by ʿAbd Allāh b. ʿAbd al-Djalīl (*ibid.*, 41) and a *Risāla fi 'l-fatwā,* transmitted by Khalīd b. Nazzār and Muḥammad b. Muṭarrif (*ibid.*). The genuineness of all these is, however, uncertain, and even if they go back to Mālik's immediate pupils (sometimes they are actually attributed to the latter; cf. al-Lakhnawī, *op. cit.*, 19), Mālik's own share in them would be still uncertain. A work (Gotha 1143) said to have been transmitted by ʿAbd Allāh b. ʿAbd al-Ḥakam al-Miṣrī and heard by him along with Ibn Wahb and Ibn al-Ḳāsim is certainly apocryphal and does not pretend moreover to give any utterances of Mālik himself.

Of other titles, there are mentioned a *Tafsīr*, a *Risāla fi 'l-ḳadar wa 'l-radd ʿalā 'l-ḳadariyya*, a *Kitāb al-Nudjūm* and a *Kitāb al-Sirr* (al-Suyūṭī, 40 ff.), which are in the usual style of the apocryphal literature. The suspicion of falsity is also strong in the case of the *Risāla* containing advice to the caliph al-Rashīd, mentioned as early as the *Fihrist* alongside of the *Muwaṭṭaʾ* (printed *Būlāḳ* 1311; cf. Brockelmann, *op. cit.*) which looks like a Mālikī counterpart of the *Kitāb al-Kharādj* of Abū Yūsuf: even al-Suyūṭī (41) doubted its genuineness, although for reasons which are not convincing to us.

C. There are two other main sources for Mālik's

teaching (setting aside the later accounts of the doctrine of the Mālikī *madhhab*):

The more important is the *al-Mudawwana al-kubrā* of Saḥnūn (d. 240/854 [*q.v.*]) which contains replies by Ibn Ḳāsim (d. 191/807) according to the school of Mālik, or according to his own *raʾy,* to questions of Saḥnūn as well as traditions and opinions of Ibn Wahb (d. 197/813) (cf. Brockelmann, *op. cit.,* 177; Heffening, *op. cit.,* 144; Krenkow, in *EI*¹ art. SAḤNŪN).

Al-Ṭabarī, who in his *Kitāb Ikhtilāf al-fuḳahāʾ* has preserved fragments of the *Muwaṭṭaʾ* recension of Ibn Wahb (cf. above), also quotes frequently traditions and opinions of Mālik in his commentary on the Ḳurʾān on the "legal" verses.

4. Mālik's position in the history of *fiḳh*. Mālik represents, in time, a stage in the development of *fiḳh* in which the reasoning is not yet thorough and fundamental but only occasional and for a special purpose, in which the legal thought of Islam has not yet become jurisprudence; and, in place, the custom of the town of Medina where the decisive foundations of Muslim law were laid down. One of the main objects in the juristic thought that appears in the *Muwaṭṭaʾ* is the permeation of the whole legal life by religious and moral ideas. This characteristic of the formation of legal ideas in early Islam is very clear, not only in the method of putting questions but in the structure of the legal material itself. The legal material, having in itself no connection with religion, that has to be permeated by religious and moral points of view, is the customary law of Medina, by no means primitive but adapted to the demands of a highly developed trading community, which for us is the principal representative of old Arabian customary law: it appears in Mālik sometimes as *sunna* "use and wont"; sometimes it is concealed under the Medina *idjmāʿ,* which he ascertains with great care. Broadly speaking, this only means that objections on religious grounds have not been raised by anyone against a principle, etc., of customary law. The older jurisprudence had another main object: the formation of a system which sets out from principles of a more general character, which aims at the formation of legal conceptions in contrast to the prevailing casuistry and is to some extent rounded off in a codification, if still a loose one, of the whole legal material.

While the Islamisation of the law had been already concluded in its essential principles before Mālik, many generations had still to work at its systematisation; therefore, Mālik's own legal achievement can only have consisted in the development of the formation of a system. How great his share in it was cannot be ascertained with certainty from the lack of material for comparison. The surprising success achieved by the *Muwaṭṭaʾ,* out of a number of similar works, would in any case be completely explained by the fact that it recorded the usual consensus of opinion in Medina without any considerable work of the author's own and came to be regarded as authoritative as the expression of compromise (just as the works on Tradition came to be regarded as canonical). The *Muwaṭṭaʾ* would in this case have to be regarded less as evidence of Mālik's individual activity than as evidence of the stage reached in the general development of law in his time. It may be said that this average character was just what Mālik aimed at (cf. above, section 3, A).

The high estimation in which Mālik is held in the older sources is justified by his strict criticism of *ḥadīth*s and not by his activity in the interests of *fiḳh* (al-Ṭabarī, iii, 2484, 2492; al-Samʿānī; al-Nawawī; Goldziher, *op. cit.,* ii, 147, 168; idem, *Ẓâhiriten,* 230); even this only means that with his *ḥadīth*s he kept within the later consensus. That al-Shāfiʿī devoted special attention to him out of all the Medinan scholars (cf. his *Kitāb Ikhtilāf Mālik wa 'l-Shāfiʿī*) is explained by the fact that he was a disciple of his.

As to the style of legal reasoning found in the *Muwaṭṭaʾ, ḥadīth* is not by any means the highest or the only court of appeal for Mālik; on the one hand, he gives the *ʿamal,* the actual undoubted practice in Medina, the preference over traditions, when these differ (cf. al-Ṭabarī, iii, 2505 ff), and on the other hand, in cases where neither Medinan tradition nor Medinan *idjmāʿ* existed, he laid down the law independently. In other words, he exercises *raʾy,* and to such an extent that he is occasionally reproached with *taʿarruḳ,* agreement with the ʿIrāḳīs (cf. Goldziher, *Muh. Studien,* ii, 217; idem, *Ẓâhiriten,* 4 ff., 20, n. 1). According to a later anti-*raʾy* legend, he is said to have repented of it on his deathbed (Ibn Khallikān). It is scarcely to be supposed that he had diverged seriously from his Medinan contemporaries in the results of his *raʾy*.

5. Mālik's pupils.

In the strict sense, Mālik no more formed a school than did Abū Ḥanīfa; evidence of this is found in the oldest names *Ahl al-Ḥidjāz* and *Ahl al-ʿIrāk*, etc. compared for example with *Aṣḥāb al-Shāfiʿī.* These names at once indicate the probable origin of the Mālikī *madhhab*; after a regular Shāfiʿī school had been formed, which in view of al-Shāfiʿī's personal achievement, is quite intelligible in the development of *fiḳh* (cf. Bergsträsser, *op. cit.,* 76, 80 ff.), it became necessary for the two older schools of *fiḳh,* whose difference was probably originally the result of geographical conditions in the main, also to combine to form a regular school, when a typical representative of the average views like Mālik or Abū Ḥanīfa was regarded as head. In the case of Mālik, the high personal esteem, which he must have enjoyed even in his lifetime (see above, section 2) no doubt contributed to this also. But it is to his pupils that his elevation to the head of a school is mainly due. Traces of this process are still to be found in the varying classification of old jurists as of the Ḥidjāz school or as independent *mudjtahid*s (cf. also *Fihrist,* 199, 1.22).

On the Mālikī law school, see MĀLIKIYYA.

Bibliography: On Mālik's life: Ibn Ḳutayba, *Kitāb al-Maʿārif,* ed. Wüstenfeld, 250, 290; Ṭabarī, *Annales,* index; *Kitāb al-Fihrist,* ed. Flügel, 198; Samʿāni, *Kitāb al-Ansāb,* GMS, xx, fol. 41a; Ibn Khallikān, ed. Wüstenfeld, no. 500; Nawawī, ed. Wüstenfeld, 530; De Goeje, *Fragmenta historicorum arabicorum,* index; al-Suyūṭī, *Tazyīn al-mamālik,* in Ibn al-Ḳāsim, *al-Mudawwana,* i, Cairo 1324; ʿĪsā b. Masʿūd al-Zawāwī, *Manāḳib sayyidnā al-Imām Mālik,* Cairo 1324; the further *manāḳib* and Mālikī *ṭabaḳāt* literature; a modern list by Muḥammad ʿAbd al-Ḥayy al-Lakhnawī in the introduction to his edition of the *Muwaṭṭaʾ* of al-Shaybānī [*q.v.*].

On Mālik's writings: Brockelmann, I, 175, S I, 297-9; Sezgin, *GAS,* i, 457-84; Goldziher, *Muhammedanische Studien,* ii, 213 ff. (Fr. tr. L. Bercher, 269 ff.; Eng. tr. S. M. Stern and C. M. Barber, ii, 198 ff.); al-Lakhnawī, *op. cit.*

On Mālik's position in the history of *fiḳh*: Bergsträsser, in *Isl.,* xiv, 76 ff.; Goldziher, *op. cit.*

(J. SCHACHT)

MĀLIK B. ʿ**AWF** B. SAʿD B. RABĪʿA AL-NAṢRĪ, Bedouin chief and contemporary of Muḥammad, who belonged to the clan of the Banū Naṣr b. Muʿāwiya of the powerful Ḳaysī tribe of the

Hawāzin, whom he commanded at the battle of Ḥunayn [*q.v.*] against the Muslims; it is mainly through this rôle that he has achieved a place in history.

We know little about his early history, but one may assume that he early found opportunities to display his personal bravery. He was still *amrad,* beardless, that is, barely out of his first years of adolescence (*Aghānī*[1], xix, 81) when he commanded a detachment of the Hawāzin in the Fidjār [*q.v.*] war.

This distinction he perhaps also owed to the consideration which his clan, the Banū Naṣr b. Muʿāwiya, enjoyed among the Banū Hawāzin. Allies of the tribe of Thaķīf (Aghānī, xii, 46), the Banū Naṣr found themselves in the same position with regard to the latter and the town of Ṭāʾif as the Aḥābīsh with respect to the Ķuraysh and Mecca. They supplied mercenaries to Ṭāʾif and were given the task of defending the town and protecting against the depredations of marauders the fine gardens that covered the Thaķafī territory. Their relations were, as a rule, peaceful and friendly, but occasionally it happened that the anarchical instincts of the Bedouins, gaining the upper hand, drove them to encroach on the domain of their allies, the citizens of Ṭāʾif. This situation enables us to understand how in the struggle that was about to develop against Islam, the Thaķīf were ready to march under the banner of a Bedouin commander.

In 8/629, Muḥammad, at the head of a strong force, was preparing to attack Mecca. This news disturbed the people who lived on the hills of the Sarāt. They asked themselves, if, once master of Mecca, the Prophet would not be tempted to invade their country. It was then that Mālik b. ʿAwf succeeded in combining for their joint defence the majority of the Ķaysī tribes settled on the frontiers of Nadjd and of the Ḥidjāz. The Thaķafīs joined their forces to those of their Hawāzin allies. The only result was the defeat at Ḥunayn [*q.v.*]. The commander-in-chief Mālik had had the unfortunate idea of bringing the women, children and flocks along with the actual combatants. The whole of this enormous booty fell into the hands of the Muslims.

The defeated side did not distinguish themselves by bravery on the battlefield; the tradition of the Banū Hawāzin attempts the impossible when it endeavours to hide this failure and save Mālik's reputation. After the débâcle, he is said to have bravely sacrificed himself to cover the retreat of his comrades-in-arms. This same tradition attributes to him a series of poetical improvisations on this occasion, in which, after the fashion of the old Bedouin paladins, he explains and excuses his flight.

Mālik tried to make a stand at Liyya, a few hours south of Ṭāʾif where he had a *ḥuṣn*. What was a *ḥuṣn*? In Medina at the time of the *hidjra,* the name was given to an enclosure commanded by an *uṭum* or tower. Mālik's had probably only brick walls like the little stronghold in Yemen described by al-Muķaddasī (*Aḥsan al-taķāsīm,* 84). A century ago, the traveller Maurice Tamisier (*Voyage en Arabie,* Paris 1840, ii, 6) passing through Liyya saw there "une forteresse flanquée de tours" intended as in earlier times, to guard the road. Muḥammad easily destroyed Mālik's fort, and when the latter learned of the approach of the Muslims, he tought it prudent to seek refuge behind the ramparts of Ṭāʾif.

In the interval, all the booty taken by the Muslims at Ḥunayn had been collected in the camp at Djiʿrāna, including Mālik's family and flocks. To the Hawāzin deputies sent to negotiate the ransom of the prisoners, Muḥammad said: "If Mālik comes to embrace Islam, I shall return him his family and property with the addition of a gift of a hundred camels". Whatever the decision adopted by Mālik, this declaration could not fail to compromise him with the Thaķafīs. He rightly recognised that his position in Ṭāʾif had become untenable. He succeeded in escaping from the town and presented his submission to Muḥammad, who fulfilled his promise to the letter. Mālik then pronounced the Muslim confession of faith and, to use the traditional formula, "his Islam was of good quality".

The new proselyte had extensive connections and was remarkably well acquainted with the Thaķafī region. The Prophet was glad to use him against Ṭāʾif, which he had been unable to take by force. He put Mālik at the head of the Ķaysī tribes who had adopted Islam. Mālik therefore organised a guerilla war against his old allies in Thaķīf. No caravan could leave Ṭāʾif without being intercepted by Mālik's men. Exhausted by this unceasing struggle, the Thaķafīs decided to sue for terms. Mālik then became the representative of the Prophet among the Banū Hawāzin, and the caliph Abū Bakr later confirmed him in the office. He took part in the wars of conquest, and was at the taking of Damascus and the victory of al-Ķādisiyya in ʿIrak.

Bibliography: Ibn Hishām, *Sīra,* ed. Wüstenfeld, 840, 852, 854, 867, 872, 879; Ibn Ķutayba, *Maʿārif,* 315; Ibn al-Kalbī-Caskel, *Djamhara,* Tab. 115; *Naķāʾiḍ Djarīr wa 'l-Farazdaķ,* ed. Bevan 495; Yāķūt, s.v. *Liyya*; Ibn Saʿd. *Ṭabaķāt,* ed. Sachau, vi, 17; Nawāwī, *Tahdhīb al-asmāʾ,* ed. Wüstenfeld, 539; *Aghānī*[1], viii, 160, xvi, 141, xix, 81; Ibn al-Athīr, *Usd al-ghāba,* iv, 289-90; Caetani, *Annali,* ii, 119, 152, 162 ff., 189, 359, 559; H. Lammens, *La cité arabe de Ṭāʾif à la veille de l'hégire,* in *MFOB,* viii/4 (1922), 61, 63, 65, 74-5.

(H. Lammens)

MĀLIK b. **DĪNĀR** al-Sāmī, Abū Yaḥyā, preacher and moralist of Baṣra, who copied the Holy Book for a living and who was interested, it seems, in the question of the Ķurʾānic readings (Ibn al-Djazarī, *Ṭabaķāt al-ķurrāʾ,* ii, 36).

He was the *mawlā* of a woman of the Banū Sāma b. Luʾayy, to whom he owed his *nisba,* and had the occasion to follow more or less regularly the teaching of Baṣran traditionists and mystics as famous as Anas b. Mālik, Ibn Sīrīn, al-Ḥasan al-Baṣrī and Rabīʿa al-ʿAdawiyya [*q.vv.*]. He was considered to have led an ascetic life himself, and posterity went so far as to attribute to him thaumaturgic gifts. In reality, he seems to have been above all a most eloquent *ķāṣṣ* [*q.v.*], who nevertheless admired the eloquence of al-Ḥadjdjādj [*q.v.*] whom he naturally could see at Baṣra. According to Ibn al-Faķīh, *Buldān,* 190, tr. Massé, 231, he brought honour to his native town because he was accounted one of the six Baṣrans who were without equals at Kūfa. Abū Nuʿaym, *Ḥilyat al-awliyāʾ,* ii, 357-89, and Ibn al-Djawzī, *Ṣifat al-ṣafwa,* Ḥaydarābād 1356, iii, 197-209, reproduce a host of sayings attributed to Mālik b. Dīnār whose authenticity is nevertheless very doubtful; the idea of *djihād* within oneself is even traced back to him (*djāhidū ahwāʾakum kamā tudjāhidūn aʿdāʾakum* "fight against your desires just as you fight against your enemies"; al-Mubarrad, *Kāmil,* ed. Zakī Mubārak, Cairo 1355/1936, i, 180, ii, 520; Abū Nuʿaym, *op. cit.,* ii, 363). It is not impossible, as Abū Nuʿaym suggests (ii, 358, 359, 369, 370, 382, 386), that he was strongly influenced by the Christian scriptures. His moralistic tendency is seen in a fairly numerous collection of pieces of advice for behaviour, as well as in the reproaches which he launched at Ba<u>shsh</u>ār b. Burd [*q.v.*], who was accused of bringing dishonour on the Baṣrans and inciting the population to debauchery (*A<u>gh</u>ānī*[1], iii, 41, vi, 49).

He died just before the epidemic of plague which caused considerable ravages in Baṣra in 131/748-9; the *Fihrist,* ed. Cairo 10, places his death in 130/747-8, and Ibn al-ʿImād, *<u>Sh</u>a<u>dh</u>arāt,* i, 173, places it in 127/744-5.

Bibliography: In addition to sources given in the article, see <u>Dj</u>āḥiẓ, *Bayān,* index; Ibn Ḳutayba, *Maʿārif,* 470, 577; Ibn Saʿd, *Ṭabaḳāt,* vii/2, 11; Ṭabarī, iii, 281; Abu 'l-ʿArab, *Ṭabaḳāt ʿulamāʾ Ifrīḳiya,* ed. and tr. M. Ben Cheneb, Algiers 1915-20, 17; Makkī, *Ḳūt al-ḳulūb,* iv, 187; Nawawī, *Tah<u>dh</u>īb,* 537; Pellat, *Milieu,* 99-100, 257.

(CH. PELLAT)

MĀLIK B. **MISMAʿ** [see MASĀMIʿA].

MĀLIK B. **NUWAYRA** B. <u>DJ</u>AMRA B. <u>SH</u>ADDĀD B. ʿUBAYD B. <u>TH</u>AʿLABA B. YARBŪʿ, ABU 'L-MI<u>GH</u>WĀR, brother of the poet Mutammim [*q.v.*] and a poet in his own right, considered as the chief of the B. Yarbūʿ during Muḥammad's lifetime. The B. Yarbūʿ was one of the most powerful tribes of the Tamīm confederacy, and was involved in many of the battles (*ayyām al-ʿarab* [*q.v.*] in the <u>Dj</u>āhiliyya. The office of *ridāfa*—a kind of viceroyship in the court of al-Ḥīra—was traditionally held by members of Yarbūʿ, among whom was Mālik b. Nuwayra (there is, however, an account according to which he was offered the *ridāfa,* but rejected it. See <u>Dj</u>arīr, *Dīwān,* 261-2). Mālik's clan, the B. <u>Th</u>aʿlaba b. Yarbūʿ, was incorporated into the body-politic of Mecca in the <u>Dj</u>āhiliyya, through the organisation of the *ḥums* (see M. J. Kister, *Mecca and Tamīm,* in *JESHO,* iii/2 [1965], 139, 146).

Mālik is usually portrayed as a noble, ambitious and brave warrior, a hero of whom the Yarbūʿī poet <u>Dj</u>arīr boasts, referring to him as "the knight (*fāris*) of <u>Dh</u>u 'l-<u>Kh</u>imār" (heroes often being called after their horses). The saying "a man but not like Mālik" (*fatā wa-lā ka-Mālik*) is taken to reflect his bravery. Notwithstanding all these descriptions, concrete details of his heroic exploits are sparse if not altogether lacking, and in the abundant and detailed material concerning the *ayyām* of Yarbūʿ he is hardly mentioned at all. The few verses attributed to him concerning certain battles do not necessarily indicate that he participated in them (see e.g. Yāḳūt, *Buldān,* s.v. *Mu<u>kh</u>aṭṭaṭ*). There is, however, an incident in which it is implied that Mālik held a senior position in his clan: during a conflict between groups of Tamīm, peace was proposed to the B. Ḥanẓala (the larger tribal group which includes the B. Yarbūʿ), and all its leaders accepted except for Mālik. Nevertheless, he had to comply with the decision of the others (*Naḳāʾiḍ,* ed. Bevan, i, 258-9, al-Maydāni, *Ma<u>dj</u>maʿ al-am<u>th</u>āl,* Beirut 1962, ii, 525, al-Alūsī, *Bulū<u>gh</u> al-arab,* ii, 75). It seems, then, that Mālik's fame as a chief and warrior in the <u>Dj</u>āhiliyya has no solid basis in actual accounts of his glorious exploits. Indeed, even the saying "a man but not like Mālik" seems originally to refer to his reliability rather than his valour (see Abū Ḥātim al-Si<u>dj</u>istānī, *al-Muʿammarūn wa 'l-waṣāyā,* ed. ʿAbd al-Munʿim ʿĀmir, 1961, 15). It is rather his brother's descriptions of him which have earned him his fame. Mutammim, who lamented bitterly Mālik's death, glorified him in elegies which have come to be counted among the most famous of their kind in Arabic literature.

Not much is known about Mālik's attitude towards Islam during the lifetime of the Prophet. There is a dubious tradition which records that when the sage Ak<u>th</u>am b. Ṣayfī [*q.v.*] recommended to Tamīm that they should adopt Islam, Mālik objected. However, he is said to have been appointed by Muḥammad as tax-collector (in the year 9 or 11 A.H.). His responsibilities are said to have included the tribe of Yarbūʿ or the larger group of Ḥanẓala. Both versions seem to be exaggerations caused by the careless way in which tradition uses tribal names. It is safer to accept Abū Rayyā<u>sh</u>'s statement, that Mālik was appointed over his own clan only, namely, the B. <u>Th</u>aʿlaba b. Yarbūʾ (see Abū Tammām, *Ḥamāsa,* ed. Freytag, i, 370, al-Ba<u>gh</u>dādī, *<u>Kh</u>izāna,* ed. ʿAbd al-Salām Hārūn, ii, 24).

In contrast to the sparsity of information about Mālik's life, there is an abundance of details concerning the circumstances of his death. This is due to the fact that his execution during the *ridda* wars, apparently by order of <u>Kh</u>ālid b. al-Walīd, aroused a fierce dispute among the Muslims. Some claimed that Mālik was an apostate (*murtadd*) and therefore deserved his fate, while others maintained that he was a Muslim, and that <u>Kh</u>ālid had him murdered because he coveted his wife. The affair was used in political conflicts, as <u>Kh</u>ālid's enemies, both from among the Ḳuray<u>sh</u> and the Anṣār, used it against him, while the <u>Sh</u>īʿa accused Abū Bakr of having ordered Mālik's execution for his alleged support of ʿAlī (see al-Ma<u>dj</u>lisi, *Biḥār al-anwār,* [Tehran 1301-15], viii, 267; Ibn Abi 'l-Ḥadīd, *<u>Sh</u>arḥ Nah<u>dj</u> al-balā<u>gh</u>a,* Cairo 1963, xvii, 202). Also reflected in this affair is the juridical and theological debate concerning the conditions required from a man in order to be considered a Muslim (see e.g. al-Hay<u>th</u>amī, *Ma<u>dj</u>maʿ al-zawāʾid wa-manbaʿ al-fawāʾid,* Cairo 1352-3, vii, 293-4). All details of the traditions about Mālik's execution should be examined in the light of these debates.

The sources are in agreement that Mālik was killed by the Muslims in the year 11 A.H. There are, generally speaking, three different accounts of the events.

Account (a), the most prevalent of the three, runs as follows: Mālik was the tax-collector of his people. Upon Muḥammad's death he did not hand over to Medina the camels which he had collected as *ṣadaḳa,* but instead gave them back to his fellow-tribesmen; hence his nickname al-<u>Dj</u>afūl (it should however be noted that *<u>dj</u>afūl* also means "one who has abundant hair", a trait for which Mālik was known. See e.g. Ibn Nubāta, *Sarḥ al-ʿuyūn,* Cairo 1321, 54). When Abū Bakr learned of Mālik's deed he was furious, and had <u>Kh</u>ālid b. al-Walīd promise before God that he would kill Mālik if he could lay hands on him. As <u>Kh</u>ālid was advancing through Na<u>dj</u>d, having conquered some rebellious tribes, one of his detachments came upon a group of twelve Yarbūʿīs, among whom was Mālik b. Nuwayra. The Yarbūʿīs offered no resistance, declared that they were Muslims, and were taken to <u>Kh</u>ālid's camp at al-Buṭāḥ (or Baʿūḍa) where they were executed as rebels. Some of the captors, chiefly the Anṣārī Abū Ḳatāda, tried to prevent the execution by arguing that the captives were inviolable, since they had declared themselves to be Muslims and performed the ritual prayer. <u>Kh</u>ālid, however, disregarded these arguments, ordered the execution, and married Mālik's widow. When ʿUmar learned of <u>Kh</u>ālid's conduct, he pressed Abū Bakr in vain to punish him, or at least to dismiss him. Eventually, Abū Bakr openly forgave <u>Kh</u>ālid, after having heard his version of the story.

Account (b), the unique tradition of Sayf b. ʿUmar (preserved in the annals of al-Ṭabarī, Ibn al-A<u>th</u>īr and Ibn Ka<u>th</u>īr, and in the *A<u>gh</u>ānī*). This tradition connects Mālik with the so-called false prophetess Sa<u>dj</u>āḥ [*q.v.*]. It relates that Muḥammad's death found the confederacy of Tamīm in a state of internal conflict, with groups of it preparing for war against one another. At this point, Sadjāḥ and her army reached Tamīmī territory. Mālik persuaded her to abandon her original plan, which was to attack Medina, and to join him against his (Tamīmī) enemies. A battle took place, in which the combined forces of Sadjāḥ, Mālik and another chief of Ḥanẓala were defeated. Sadjāḥ's army was defeated in yet another battle, whereupon she headed for al-Yamāma, while Mālik stayed behind, realising that his policy had failed. He ordered his men to disperse and cautioned them not to offer any resistance to the Muslims who would reach their territory, but to submit and adopt Islam. He himself retreated to his dwelling-place, where he was captured by the Muslims. The details of his capture and execution closely resemble those given above in account (a). Into these two accounts are sometimes woven traditions justifying the conduct of Khālid b. al-Walīd. For instance, it is recorded that in a conversation held between Khālid and Mālik, the latter referred to Muḥammad as "your man" (or "your master") instead of "our man" (or "our master"), thus excluding himself from the Muslim community. In a variant of this tradition, Mālik further insisted on withholding the *ṣadaḳa* payment, and therefore Khālid put him to death (needless to say, this additional detail spoils the original argument, because if Mālik withheld the *ṣadaḳa*, which was the *casus belli* of the *ridda,* it was immaterial how he referred to Muḥammad in a conversation). Another tradition claims that the captives were killed by mistake, as Khālid's soldiers misinterpreted his orders, due to dialectal differences (cf. the same motif in quite another story, in *LA,* s.v. *ḥ-m-r*). Strangely enough, though, traditions which openly accuse Mālik of rebellion against Islam do not mention his co-operation with Sadjāḥ, but only his refusal to pay *ṣadaḳa.* Moreover, it is stated that this co-operation was not tantamount to *ridda* (e.g. Ibn al-Athīr, *Usd al-ghāba,* s.v. *Mālik b. Nuwayra*).

Account (c), the unique tradition quoted from Abū Rayyāsh (Aḥmad b. Abī Hāshim) (preserved in al-Baghdādī's *Khizāna* and al-Tabrīzi's commentary to the *Ḥamāsa*). This tradition records that upon Muḥammad's death, Mālik raided the place called Raḥraḥān and drove off 300 camels which had been collected from various tribes as their *ṣadaḳa* payment. When Abū Bakr learned about this, he ordered Khālid b. al-Walīd to kill Mālik, should he capture him. While advancing through Nadjd, Khālid arrived at the plain where the clans of Yarbūʿ were encamped. He encamped there as well, and they showed no fear of him. Then he attacked the clans of Ghudāna and Thaʿlaba (Mālik's clan), because he did not hear the call to prayer (*adhān*) among them. He disregarded their protestations that they were Muslims, and not rebels, so Mālik took to arms. Only a part of his clan followed suit, but they fought vigorously till they had to surrender. Khālid offered Mālik security (*dhimma*) in return for his acceptance of Islam, to which Mālik consented. Later, Khālid broke the agreement on the ground that he had promised Abū Bakr to kill Mālik, and so he ordered his execution.

Obviously, the three accounts are very different from one another, and can hardly be harmonised so as to make one coherent story. Two additional details should be mentioned here. Firstly, the actual executioner of Mālik, whether or not by order of Khālid b. al-Walīd, was Ḍirār b. al-Azwar al-Asadī, whose clan had been in a state of war with Mālik's clan. Secondly, the affair of Mālik's execution closely resembles another affair, where Khālid, on a mission on behalf of Muḥammad to invite people to embrace Islam, wrongfully executed members of the B. Djadhīma. Indeed, some of the accounts of the two affairs are practically identical. It thus seem that the truth behind Mālik's career and death will remain buried under a heap of conflicting traditions.

Bibliography: Sources: Diyārbakrī, *Taʾrīkh al-khamīs,* 1302/1885, ii, 225, 232-3; Sulaymān b. Mūsā al-Kalaʿī al-Balansī, *Taʾrīkh al-Ridda,* ed. Kh. A. Fāriq, New Delhi 1970, 10, 50-5; Ibn Ḥubaysh, *Kitāb Dhikr al-ghazawāt wa 'l-futūḥ,* ms. Leiden, Or. 343, pp. 13, 28-30; Ibn Aʿtham, *Futūḥ,* Hyderabad 1388/1968, 21-3; Ps.-Wāḳidi, *al-Ridda,* ms. Bankipore, Cat. xv, 1042, fols. 16b-17b; Makkī, *Simṭ al-nudjūm,* Cairo 1380, ii, 351-3; Ṭabarī, *Taʾrīkh,* ed. Muḥammad Abu 'l-Faḍl Ibrāhīm, iii, 147, 268-70, 276-8, 304-5; Ibn al-Athīr, *Kāmil,* Beirut 1385/1965, i, 598-600, 650, ii, 357-60; Ibn Kathīr, *Bidāya,* Cairo 1351/1932, vi, 320-3; Iṣfahānī, ed. al-Shanḳīṭī, Cairo n.d., xiv, 63-9; Djumaḥi, *Ṭabaḳāt al-shuʿarāʾ,* ed. Hell, 48-50; Marzubānī, *Muʿdjam al-shuʿarāʾ,* ed. Krenkow, 360-1; Ibn Ḳutayba, *Shiʿr,* Cairo 1350/1932, 119-122; Bakrī, *Muʿdjam mā 'staʿdjam,* s.vv. *Baʿūḍa, al-Buṭāḥ, al-Mala, al-Dakādik,* and index; Yāḳūt, s.vv. *Baʿūḍa, al-Buṭāḥ,* and index; Ibn Khallikān, *Wafayāt al-aʿyān,* tr. De Slane, iii, 648-56; Ibn Abi 'l-Ḥadīd, *Sharḥ Nahdj al-balāgha,* Cairo 1963, xvii, 202-7, 212-14; Madjlisi, *Biḥār al-anwār,* viii, 264-7; Ibn Ḥadjar, *Iṣāba,* s.vv. *Mālik b. Nuwayra, Mutammim b. Nuwayra, Ḍirār b. al-Azwar, Fātik b. Zayd, Khālid b. al-Walīd, Aktham b. Ṣayfi*; Ibn al-Athīr, *Usd al-ghāba,* s.vv. *Mālik b. Nuwayra, Ḍirār b. al-Azwar*; Ibn ʿAbd al-Barr, *Istīʿāb,* s.vv. *Mutammim b. Nuwayra, Khālid b. al-Walīd*; Mughlṭay b. Ḳilidj al-Bakdjarī, *al-Zahr al-bāsim fī siyar Abi 'l-Ḳāsim,* ms. Leiden Or. 370, fol. 279b; Tibrīzī, *Sharḥ al-Ḥamāsa,* ed. Freytag, 370-2; Marzūḳī, *Sharḥ al-Ḥamāsa,* 1371/1951, 797-9; Baghdādī, *Khizāna,* ed. ʿAbd al-Salām Hārūn, Cairo 1387/1967, ii, 24-8; Muḥammad b. Ḥabīb, *Asmāʾ al-mughtālīn min al-ashrāf fī al-djāhiliyya wa 'l-Islām,* in *Nawādir al-makhṭūṭāt,* ed. ʿAbd al-Salām Hārūn, Cairo 1374/1954, ii, 244-5; idem, *Kunā 'l-shuʿarā,* in *ibid.*, ii, 295; Mubarrad, *al-Kāmil,* ed. Wright, 7, 317, 612, 692, 761-3; Dhahabī, *Siyar aʿlām al-nubalāʾ,* i, Cairo 1956, 271; idem, *Taʾrīkh al-Islām,* Cairo 1367, i, 353-8; Thaʿālibi, *Thimār al-ḳulūb,* Cairo 1384/1965, 24; Maḳdisī, *Badʾ,* ed. Huart v, 159-60; al-Khālidiyyān, *al-Ashbāh wa 'l-naẓāʾir min ashʿār al-mutaḳaddimīn wa 'l-djāhiliyya wa 'l-mukhaḍramīn,* ed. Muḥammad Yūsuf, Cairo 1965, ii, 345-7; Ibn ʿAsākir, *Taʾrīkh,* Damascus 1332, iii, 105-6, 112; Kutubī, *Fawāt,* Būlāḳ 1299, ii, 143-4; al-Muttaḳī 'l-Hindī, *Kanz al-ʿummāl,* Hyderabad 1374/1954, v, 360-1 (no. 2309); Khalīfa b. Khayyāṭ, *Taʾrīkh,* Nadjaf 1386/1967, 63, 69-70; Balādhurī, *Futūḥ,* Cairo 1377/1957, 137; Yaʿḳūbī, *Taʾrīkh,* Beirut 1379/1960, ii, 76, 79, 122, 131-2; Ibn Nubāta, *Sarḥ al-ʿuyūn,* Cairo 1321, 14-5, 54-7; Ḥimyarī, *al-Ḥūr al-ʿīn,* Cairo-Baghdād 1948, 130-2; Yazīdī, *Amālī,* Hyderabad 1367/1948, 18-26.

For modern studies and résumés of Mālik's career, see Nöldeke, *Beiträge zur Kenntniss der Poesie der alten Araber,* Hanover 1864, 87-95, 134; Caussin de Perceval, *Essai,* iii, 366-70; Ahlwardt, in *Sammlungen alter Arabischer Dichter,* i (*Elaçmaʿijjat*), 7-8, and Ar. text, 25-6; Lyall, *Translations of ancient Arabian poetry,* London 1930, 35-6; idem, tr. and notes to *Mufaḍḍaliyyāt,* ii, 20, 205-6; E. Shoufani, *al-Ridda and the Muslim conquest of Arabia,* Toronto 1972, index; Wellhausen, *Skizzen,* vi, 12-15; Caetani, *An-*

nali, ii, 650-8 (*anno* 11, §§ 175-84); W. M. Watt, *Muhammad at Medina,* 138-9; Ibtisām Marhūn al-Ṣaffār, *Mālik wa-Mutammim ibnā Nuwayra,* Baghdād 1968. A study by Aḥmad Muḥammad Shākir is mentioned by Aḥmad Amīn and Hārūn in their edition of the *Ḥamāsa* (797, n.). This study was published in *al-Muḳtaṭaf,* August 1945, and *al-Hady al-nabawī,* Shaʿbān 1364.

Verses attributed to Mālik have been collected by Nöldeke, *op. cit.,* and al-Ṣaffār, *op. cit.* To these may be added the following references: *Mufaḍḍaliyyāt,* 25, 77, 565, 720; *ʿIḳd,* v, 234-5; *Naḳāʾiḍ,* 258, 412; Ibn Hishām, iii, 260; Zamakhsharī, *al-Mustaḳṣā fī amthāl al-ʿarab,* Hyderabad 1381/1962, ii, 387, Djarīr, *Dīwān,* 262; Abū Hilal al-ʿAskari, *Dīwān al-maʿānī,* Cairo 1352, ii, 55.

(Ella Landau-Tasseron)

AL-MALIK AL-ʿĀDIL, AL-MALIK AL-KĀMIL, AL-MALIK AL-MANṢŪR, etc.; see for those Ayyūbid monarchs with names of this type, the second element of the name, i.e. AL-ʿĀDIL, AL-KĀMIL, AL-MANṢŪR, etc.

AL-MALIK AL-NĀṢIR. [see ṢALĀḤ AL-DĪN].

MĀLIK AL-ṬĀʾĪ. [see MĀLIK B. ABI 'L-SAMḤ].

MALIK AḤMAD BAḤRĪ, later styled Aḥmad Niẓām Shāh Baḥrī and regarded as the first independent ruler of the Niẓām Shāhī [*q.v.*] sultanate, was the son of Malik Ḥasan Niẓām al-Mulk Baḥrī, the converted Hindū who eventually became a *wazīr* of thc Bahmanī sultanate after the murder of Maḥmūd Gāwān [*q.v.*] in 886/1481.

There is no reliable evidence concerning his date of birth or his early years, but he is known to have accompanied his father when the latter was appointed governor of Telingānā in 875/1471. Here his ability and promise were so conspicuous that Maḥmūd Gāwān separated father and son, sending Aḥmad to Māhūr [*q.v.*] as a commander of 300, where he spent five years before becoming his father's deputy governor at Rādjamundarī. After Malik Ḥasan came to power in Bīdar, when the boy king Maḥmūd had succeeded to the Bahmanī throne, he strengthened his following by conferring assignments on his own men, his son Malik Aḥmad receiving Bīr and Dhārūr and other districts around Dawlatābād and Djunnār, residing in the latter place and successfully suppressing Marāthā oppression; later, at his father's bidding, he attacked the Marāthā hill-forts whose chieftains had been withholding the annual tribute, and extended his control over the entire Konkan coast. In 891/1486 Malik Ḥasan was murdered and Aḥmad assumed his title of Niẓām al-Mulk; he continued his campaign of conquest against Marāthā-held forts, and soon held the entire north up to the river Godāvarī, where his good administration commanded much local respect and support. The court party, mostly of Āfāḳīs, at Bīdar was against him and his successes; but an army sent against him was defeated near Nikāpur, later named Bāgh, from the garden which Aḥmad laid out to commemorate his victory in 895/1490; a palace he built there (Bāgh-i Niẓām) became his residence, and the city which grew around it was named Aḥmadnagar. He then styled himself Aḥmad Niẓām Shāh Baḥrī, and omitted the name of the Bahmanī sultan from the *khuṭba*; this, and his use of the white umbrella, were resented by some Bahmanī loyalists, but he had become too strong and his independence dates from this time.

For his future history, and for Bibliography, see further under Niẓām Shāhī. (J. Burton-Page)

MALIK ʿAMBAR, a Ḥabashī *wazīr* and military commander who served the Niẓām Shāhī dynasty of Aḥmadnagar in the Deccan.

Born around 955/1548 in Abyssinia, Malik ʿAmbar was sold into slavery in Baghdād and subsequently brought to India, where he was sold to the *wazīr* of the Niẓām Shāhī court. After his patron died, he sought, but was refused, the patronage of other local powers in the Deccan. He then returned to Aḥmadnagar, where in 1006/1596 he commanded a cavalry of 150 horse. The fall of Aḥmadnagar fort to Mughal arms in 1009/1600 created turmoil in the kingdom, during which Malik ʿAmbar rose to particular prominence. Supported by Deccanis and other Ḥabashīs, he managed to rescue the dynasty from extinction by raising a member of the royal family, Murtaḍā Niẓām Shāh II, to the throne. The monarch's power was only *de jure,* however, as the *wazīr* wielded effective power from this point until his death in 1035/1626. Malik ʿAmbar fended off not only his rival for military supremacy within the kingdom, Miyān Rādjū, who was finally suppressed in 1016/1607, but also the armies of the ʿĀdil Shāhī dynasty of Bīdjāpur to his south, European naval powers on the Konkan coast and above all, the armies of the Mughal Empire to his north. Throughout the period 1009-35/1600-26, the emperors Akbar and Djihāngīr [*q.vv.*] mounted large-scale invasions of the Deccan in repeated attempts to subdue the Ḥabashī *wazīr.*

Malik ʿAmbar's name has endured for several reasons. First, he represents perhaps the most striking example of Ḥabashī slave mobility in Indo-Muslim history. Second, despite his preoccupation with military matters, he placed the land revenue system of the kingdom on a firm and rational basis, probably imitating the reforms of Rādjā Todar Mal in this respect. Third, it was he who pioneered the recruiting and training of Marāthā [*q.v.*] light cavalry and also the organised use of guerrilla tactics in Indian warfare. Even his arch-opponent, the Mughal Emperor Djahāngīr, acknowledged that as a commander, Malik ʿAmbar was without equal. Finally, he promoted the social and political fortunes of several Marāthā families—most notably that of Shāhdjī Bhonsle, father of the Marāthā chieftain Shīvādjī—which contributed to the subsequent rise of Marāthā power in western India.

Bibliography: Original authorities include the *Akbar-nāma,* completed in 1010/1602 by Abu 'l-Faḍl b. Mubārak, Calcutta 1873-87, tr. H. Beveridge, Calcutta 1897-1921; *Futūḥāt-i ʿĀdil Shāhī,* completed *ca.* 1054/1644 by Hāshim Bēg Astarābādī, ms. London, British Library; Firishta, abridged tr. J. Briggs, *History of the Rise of the Mahomedan Power in India,* Calcutta 1910; *Iḳbāl-nāma-yi Djahāngīrī,* completed 1028-9/1619-20 by Muḥammad Sharīf Muʿtamad Khān, Lucknow 1870; *Maʾāthir-i Raḥīmī,* completed 1047/1637 by ʿAbd al-Bāḳī Nihāwandī, Calcutta 1910-31. Secondary authorities include J. G. Duff, *A history of the Mahrattas,* ed. J. P. Guha, New Delhi 1971; W. H. Moreland, *Pieter van den Broeke at Surat (1620-29),* in *Journal of Indian History,* x (1931), 235-50; xi (1932), 1-16, 203-18; idem, *From Gujarat to Golconda in the reign of Jahangir,* in *ibid.,* xvii (1938), 135-50; D. R. Seth, *The Life and times of Malik Ambar,* in *IC,* xxxi (1957), 142-55; Radhey Shyam, *Life and times of Malik Ambar,* New Delhi 1968. (R. M. Eaton)

MALIK AYĀZ, Indian Muslim admiral, administrator and statesman, one of the most distinguished personalities of the reigns of the Gudjarāt Sultans Maḥmūd I (863-917/1458-1511) and Muẓaffar II (917-32/1511-26).

Ayāz, according to the Portuguese historian João de Barros, was originally a Russian slave, born in Georgia, who fell into the hands of the Turks and thus found his way to Istanbul, where he was sold to a trader having business connections with India. Endowed by nature with valour and wisdom, he proved to be the "jewel of a great price" in the estimate of his master who later, in one of his business trips to Gudjarāt, made a gift of him to the reigning Sultan Maḥmūd I, popularly known in history as Sultan Begādā. A legend has it that he attained instant fame when he brought down, with a well-aimed arrow, a hawk which defecated on the head of the Sultan during an expedition against Mālwā; the delighted Sultan granted him freedom on the spot and conferred on him the title of *Malik*. By showing gallantry on the battle-field and prudence in council, Ayāz rose steadily in the confidence of the king, who ultimately made him governor of Dīv [see DIU], an island situated off the coast of Una in the extreme south of the Kathiawar peninsula.

In 1484, Malik Ayāz played a vital part in securing form Maḥmūd I the great and impregnable Rādjput hill-fortress of Pavagaṙh in Čāmpanēr, following its investment over a period of 20 months. Its fall signalled the end of the centuries-old sovereignty of the Rādjput dynasty of Patai Paval over Čāmpanēr, which for the next 50 years remained the political capital of Gudjarāt under the Muslims. In 1511, Malik Ayāz was called upon by Sultan Muẓaffar II to salvage the prestige of Gudjarāt, severely mauled by the inroads of Rana Sangha of Čitōr. Placed in supreme command of what is described as 100,000 cavalry and assisted by generals like Malik Sārang and Mubāriz al-Mulk, Ayāz proved his mettle in capturing enemy strongholds like Dungarpur and Mandasor, and also through his diplomatic skill concluded peace with Rana Sangha.

But it is round the administration of the historic island city of Dīv that the career of Malik Ayāz is mainly centred. In view of its strategic situation and commercial importance, the island during the late 15th century had become a bone of contention between the maritime powers of Europe and the Gudjarāt Sultans. The most determined challenge came from the Portuguese, who had already made their appearance on the western shores of India. They made persistent demands from the Muslim rulers for permission to build a fortress in Dīv, whose possession was in fact the cornerstone of the very survival of Malik Ayāz. Ever since he was given charge of Dīv, Malik Ayāz set about fortifying the island. He built a tower there on a submarine rock and drew from it a massive iron chain across the mouth of the harbour so as to block the entry of enemy ships into the island waters. He also built a bridge over the creek lying between the island and the mainland. The resulting naval base was meant for his fleet of at least 100 *fustas*, large war vessels and many armed merchant ships, which ultimately made Dīv invulnerable to Portuguese attacks. Both the contemporary native historians and Portuguese chroniclers testify to Malik Ayāz's complete authority over the Gudjarāt sea-coast as long as he lived, and his invincible armada did not allow any intruding vessel to enter Dīv except for the purpose of trade.

The Portuguese now tried diplomacy, and won supporters among courtiers such as Malik Gopi in order to secure approval for building a fortress in Dīv, but were frustrated by the intelligence and influence of Malik Ayāz. Afonso de Albuquerque, conqueror and Governor of Goa, whom the Malik met and entertained at Dīv in 1513, records that "he had never known a more suave courtier; nor a person more skilful in deception while at the same time leaving one feeling very satisfied". The last Portuguese attempt during Malik Ayāz's life was in 1520 under Diogo Lopes de Sequeira, the next Governor of Goa, who nevertheless found the island's defences too strong for his ambitions.

Malik Ayāz died at Una in 928/1522, and lies buried there near the tomb of Shāh Shams al-Dīn. In his death, the Gudjarāt Sultān lost a brave soldier and astute statesman and the Portuguese an inveterate adversary. The disastrous consequences suffered by the kingdom soon after the Portuguese were granted the much-sought-after concessions by Sultan Bahādur in 1535 provide the highest justification of the unbending policy of exclusion which Malik Ayāz had followed in respect of the Portuguese.

The *Mirʾāt-i Sikandarī* contains many anecdotes about Malik Ayāz and his mode of life; his dinner table used to be stocked with the delicacies of India, Persia and Turkey. The *Ẓafar al-wālih* speaks of his generosity, charity and hospitality, and his conciliation of his subjects with presents and bounties. He amassed immense wealth and affluence, and attained a position second in power only to the Sultan himself.

Bibliography: Sikandar b. Muḥammad, *alias* Mandjhū b. Akbar, *Mirʾāt-i Sikandarī,* ed. S. C. Misra and M. L. Rahman, Baroda 1961, Eng. tr. Sir E. Clive Bayley in his *Local Muhammadan dynasties: Gudjarat,* London 1886, and by Faḍl Allāh Luṭf Allāh Farīdī, Dharampur n.d.; ʿAlī Muḥammad Khān, *Mirʾāt-i Aḥmadī,* ed. Syed Nawāb ʿAlī, Baroda 1927-30; Eng. tr. C. N. Seddon, S. N. Ali and M. F. Lokhandwala, Baroda 1928, 1965; ʿAbd Allāh Muḥammad al-Makkī al-Āṣafī Ulughkhānī Ḥādjdjī al-Dabīr, *Ẓafar al-wālih bi-Muẓaffar wa-ālih,* ed. E. Denison Ross, London 1910-28, Eng. tr. M. F. Lokhandwala, i, Baroda 1970; Afonso de Albuquerque, *Commentaries,* Eng. tr. London 1875-84; Duarte Barbosa, *The Book of Duarte Barbosa,* London 1918-21; João de Barros, *Decadas da Asia,* Lisbon 1945-6; M. S. Commisariat, *History of Gujarat,* Bombay 1938-57; M. N. Pearson, *Merchants and rulers of Gujarat,* London 1976. (ABDUS SUBHAN)

AL-**MALIK** AL-ʿ**AZĪZ,** ABŪ MANṢŪR KHUSRAW-FĪRŪZ, eldest son of Djalāl al-Dawla Shīrzīl, Būyid prince (407-41/1016 or 1017-1049). In the lifetime of his father Djalal al-Dawla [*q.v.*], ruler of Baghdād, he was governor of Baṣra and Wāsiṭ and latterly heir to the throne, but when his father died in Shaʿbān 435/March 1044, Khusraw-Fīrūz was away from the capital in Wāsiṭ, and superior financial resources enabled his more forceful cousin ʿImād al-Dīn Abū Kālīdjār Marzubān [*q.v.*] to secure the loyalty of the Būyid troops in Baghdād and to establish himself firmly in ʿIrāḳ. Khusraw-Fīrūz was forced to wander between local courts such as those of the Mazyadids at Ḥilla and the ʿUḳaylids at Mawṣil [*q.vv.*], making abortive military attempts to secure his father's throne, and died at Mayyāfāriḳīn in Rabīʿ I 441/August 1049 whilst staying with the Marwānids of Diyārbakr [*q.v.*].

Bibliography: The main primary source is Ibn al-Athīr. See also H. Bowen, *The last Buwayhids,* in *JRAS* (1929), 230-3; Mafizullah Kabir, *The Buwayhid dynasty of Baghdad,* Calcutta 1964, 109-10; C. E. Bosworth, in *Camb. hist. of Iran,* v, 39-40; H. Busse, *Chalif und Grosskönig, die Buyiden im Iraq (945-1055),* Beirut-Wiesbaden 1969, 110-13.

(C. E. BOSWORTH)

MALIK DĀNISHMAND [see DĀNISHMANDIDS].

MALIK KĀFŪR, military commander of the Dihlī sultans.

Originally a Hindu eunuch, nicknamed *Hazār-*

dīnārī, "a thousand *dīnār* slave", from his purchase price, was included in the large booty captured from the port city of Kambayāt (modern Cambay) following the Khaldjī conquest of Gudjarāt [*q.v.*] in 698/1299, and brought to Sultan ʿAlāʾ al-Dīn Khaldjī, whose fascination he attracted by dint of his personal ability. He gradually attained the title of *nāʾib malik* "Regent of the King", a position which was next only to the Sultan. Malik Kāfūr reached the zenith of his meteoric career when he showed his martial prowess conclusively as the commander of the first Muslim army to cross the Vindyachal into South India. In 706/1307, he opened his Deccan adventure by leading an army of 30,000 horsemen to Devagiri (modern Dawlatābād in Maharashtra State), whose king Ramachandra Deva surrendered without offering any resistance. By subjugating in 709/1310 Warangal, the capital of the Kakatiya kingdom of Telingana, Kāfūr secured for his master the vassalage of its ruler Rai Prataprudra, along with a vast quantity of treasures, which were carried to Delhi by a thousand camels. In 710/1311, the Hoysala dynasty of Dwarasamudra, the ruins of which can still be seen at Halebid in the Hassan district of modern Karnataka State, was the third Deccan kingdom to fall to the invading hordes of Kāfūr, and its ruler Vir Ballala III became bound by a peace treaty to pay a substantial war indemnity to the Dihlī Sultan, apart from acknowledging his suzerainty. Malik Kāfūr continued his spectacular march towards the extreme south of the peninsula and after a few days' march arrived at Madura, the seat of Pandya kingdom (known to Muslim writers as Maʿbar [*q.v.*]), only to find it abandoned by its fleeing king Vir Pandya. The Khaldjī general stopped only when confronted by the sea at the coastal town of Rameswaram, where he built a mosque named after ʿAlāʾ al-Dīn Khaldjī. He returned to Dihlī with an enormous spoils which included 312 elephants; 20,000 horses; 2,750 pounds of gold, whose value equalled nearly ten crores of *tankas*; and chests of jewels. The capital had never before seen such a large booty.

Kāfūr's brilliance on the battlefield was overshadowed by the civil strife which marked the rest of his life. The Sultan's infatuation with him proved anathema to the influential Khaldjī nobles, so much so that within only 35 days of the Sultan's death he fell a victim to the assassin's sword on 12 Dhu 'l-Kaʿda 715/11 February 1316.

Bibliography: Ḍiyāʾ al-Dīn Baranī, *Taʾrīkh-i-Fīrūz Shāhī,* Calcutta 1860-6; ʿIṣamī, *Futūḥ al-salāṭīn,* Agra 1938; Amīr Khusraw, *Khazāʾin al-futūḥ,* Calcutta 1953, Eng. tr. Muḥammad Ḥabīb, Bombay 1931; K. S. Lal, *History of the Khaljis (1290-1320),* Dihlī 1967; S. K. Aiyangar, *South India and her Muhammadan invaders,* Madras 1921.

(ABDUS SUBHAN)

AL-**MALIK** AL-**KĀMIL** II [see SHAʿBĀN]

MALIK ḲUMMI, Indo-Muslim poet, was born at Ḳum in about 934/1528. The author of the *Maykhāna* states that his full name was Malik Muḥammad.

He went at an early age to Kāshān, where he stayed nearly twenty years, and then spent approximately four years in Ḳazwīn, frequenting the company of writers and scholars in both places. Already during his youth he seems to have won distinction for himself in poetical competitions with his contemporaries, and was regarded highly by such literary figures as Muḥtasham of Kāshān (d. 996/1587-8) and Ḍamīrī of Iṣfahān (d. *ca.* 1578) for his innovative tendencies. He was respected in important circles, and was sought after by Ṣafawī nobles and other Persian dignitaries. He left Ḳazwīn, according to Āzād Bilgrāmī, in 987/1579 and, reaching India, took up residence at Aḥmadnagar, enjoying the favours of Murtaḍā Niẓām Shāh I (1565-88) and, upon the latter's death, of Burhān Niẓām Shāh II (1590-5) [see NIẒĀM-SHĀHS]. It is mentioned in the *Maʾāthir-i Raḥīmī* that after the fall of Aḥmadnagar to Akbar's forces, he served temporarily under ʿAbd al-Raḥīm Khān-i Khānān, whom he praises in several of his *ḳaṣīdas*. Finally, he settled down in Bīdjāpūr, attaching himself to the ruler of that state, Ibrāhīm ʿĀdil Shāh II (1580-1627) [see ʿĀDIL-SHĀHS]. There he reached the highest point of his career, with his appointment as poet laureate in the Bīdjāpūr court. In Aḥmadnagar, and later in Bīdjāpūr, he developed close relations with Ẓuhūrī (*ca.* 1537-1616), to whom he gave his daughter in marriage. The two poets collaborated in several literary ventures which they undertook for Ibrāhīm ʿĀdil Shāh. The report that they also worked jointly in producing *Naw ras,* a book of songs attributed to the above-mentioned ruler, and received 9,000 gold pieces as a reward for their efforts, is disputed by modern writers. Towards the end, Malik Ḳummī seems to have led a life of retirement dedicated to austerity and devotion. He died, most probably, in 1025/1616, a date confirmed by the chronogram composed on his death by Abū Ṭālib Kalīm.

Apart from Ẓuhūrī, Malik Ḳummī was the only other significant poet in the Deccan during his time. According to Badāʾūnī, he was known by the title of Malik al-Kalām. Most writers speak highly of his literary talents. He was the author of many works, written either independently or in collaboration with Ẓuhūrī. In his personal life he was inclined towards mysticism, and has been praised for his pious habits and purity of character.

Bibliography: *Kulliyyāt,* ms. I.O. 1499; ʿAbd al-Bāḳī Nihāwandī, *Maʾāthir-i Raḥīmī,* iii, ed. Muḥammad Hidāyat Ḥusayn, Calcutta 1931; ʿAbd al-Ḳādir Badāʾūnī, *Muntakhab al-tawārikh,* iii, tr. T. W. Haig, Calcutta 1925; Amīn Aḥmad Rāzī, *Haft iḳlīm,* ii, ed. Djawād Fāḍil, Tehran n.d.; Iskandar Munshī, *Taʾrīkh-i ʿālam ārā-yi ʿAbbāsī,* i, ed. Naṣr Allāh Falsafī, Tehran 1334/1955-6; ʿAbd al-Nabī Fakhr al-Zamānī Ḳazwīnī, *Maykhāna,* ed. Aḥmad Gulčīn Maʿānī, Tehran 1340/1961-2; Luṭf ʿAlī Beg Ādhar, *Ātash-kada,* ed. Sayyid Djaʿfar Shahīdī, Tehran 1337/1958; Ghulām ʿAlī Khān Āzād Bilgrāmī, *Sarw-i āzād,* Hyderabad 1913; idem, *Khizāna-yi ʿāmira,* Cawnpore 1871; Aḥmad ʿAlī Khān Hāshimī Sandīlawī, *Tadhkira-yi makhzan al-gharāʾib,* ms. Bodleian 395; Lačhmī Narāyan Shafīḳ, *Shām-i gharībān,* ed. Akbar al-Dīn Ṣiddīḳī, Karachi 1977; Muḥammad Ḳudrat Allāh Gopāmawī, *Tadhkira-yi natāʾidj al-afkār,* Bombay 1336/1957-8; Shiblī Nuʿmānī, *Shiʿr al-ʿAdjam,* iii, repr. Aʿẓamgaṙh 1945; E. G. Browne, *LHP,* iv, repr. Cambridge 1953; Muhammad ʿAbdu'l Ghani, *A history of Persian language and literature at the Mughal court,* iii, Allahabad 1930; Muḥammad ʿAlī Mudarris Tabrīzī, *Rayḥānat al-adab,* iv, Tabrīz 1371/1952; J. Rypka, *History of Iranian literature,* Dordrecht 1956; Nazir Ahmad (ed.), *Kitāb-i nawras,* Delhi 1956; T. N. Devare, *A short history of Persian literature at the Bahmani, the Adilshahi, and the Qutbshahi courts, Deccan,* Poona 1961; H. K. Sherwani (ed.), *History of medieval Deccan,* ii, Hyderabad 1974; P. N. Chopra, *Life and letters under the Mughals,* Delhī 1976.

(MUNIBUR RAHMAN)

AL-**MALIK** AL-**MANṢŪR** [see ḲALĀWŪN].

MALIK MUGHĪTH, military commander under the rulers of Mālwā [*q.v.*].

The son of a Turkish noble named ʿAlī S̲h̲īr K̲h̲urd, he played a conspicuously important role in the history of mediaeval Mālwā. He came into prominence during the reign of Sultan Hus̲h̲ang S̲h̲āh G̲h̲ūrī (809-38/1406-35), who appointed him minister in recognition of his meritorious service and conferred on him the titles of As̲h̲raf al-Mulk and K̲h̲ān-i-D̲j̲ahān. He was instrumental in bringing about the accession of his son Maḥmūd K̲h̲ald̲j̲ī I (839-73/1436-69), whom he helped to achieve signal victories against rival chieftains of central India, to extend the limit of frontiers to its widest extent and to bring unprecedented glory to Mālwā. The galaxy of honorific denominations which Malik Mug̲h̲īth received, such as Amīr al-Umarāʾ, Zubdat al-Mulk, K̲h̲ulāṣat al-Mālwa, Aʿzam-i Humāyūn and Masnad-i ʿĀlī, amply reflect the influence and prestige which he enjoyed throughout his life. His death in 846/1443, following a brief illness while laying a siege to the fort of Mandasor, left the Sultan so distracted with grief that he "tore his hair and raved like one bereft of his senses" (Firis̲h̲ta, ii, 488). He lies buried in the K̲h̲ald̲j̲ī family mausoleum at Māndū [q.v.] where he has also left an architectural legacy in the shape of an elegant mosque called the Masd̲j̲id-i Malik Mug̲h̲īth, which he built in 835/1432.

Bibliography: Ghulam Yazdani, Mandu, City of Joy, Oxford 1929; Upendra Nath Dey, Medieval Malwa (1401-1562), Dihlī 1965.(ABDUS SUBHAN)

MALIK MUḤAMMAD D̲J̲ĀYASĪ (D̲J̲ĀYSĪ/D̲J̲AYSĪ) (?900/1493 to ?949/1542), Indian Ṣūfī and poet, was born at D̲j̲āyas (D̲j̲ays) in Awadh [q.v.] and died at nearby Amēt̲h̲ī. Educated locally, he became a disciple of the Čis̲h̲tī S̲h̲ayk̲h̲ Muḥyī 'l-Dīn. He had Hindu as well as Muslim teachers, and showed a religious tolerance which some ascribe to the influence of Kabīr. He wrote poetry in Awadhī, a form of Eastern Hindī, including two fairly short religious poems, one of which, Āk̲h̲irī kalām, is on the Day of Judgement. But he is famed chiefly for his Padumāvat, a narrative and descriptive poem of over 5,000 verses probably, but not conclusively, written in Persian script, although it is best preserved in Nāgarī, and moreover probably the earliest major work in any Indian vernacular extant in authentic form, apart from its intrinsic literary merits. It combines some elements of the earlier Hindī bardic epic, elements of the traditional mahākāvya and some metrical resemblances to the Persian mat̲h̲nawī, being a story of war and love, the heroine of the title being a paragon among women. It ends with the death of Padumāvatī's husband, who is ruler of Čitōr, and her satī, followed by the capture of Čitōr by ʿAlāʾ al-Dīn, Sulṭān of Dihlī.

Despite the apparent secular nature of the poem, K. B. Jindal (History, 45, see Bibl.) regards it as a Ṣūfī love poem. The poet, in his envoi (if this is authentic and not a later addition), states that it is an allegory, briefly explaining the symbolism: but A.G. Shirreff (Padmavatī, p. viii, see Bibl.) describes it as "half fairy-tale and half historical romance". The first canto (again, if this is authentic) is of interest to Islamologists. The poet praises God, Muḥammad the Prophet, the first four caliphs, S̲h̲ēr S̲h̲āh, the Sulṭān of Dihlī, the poet's Čis̲h̲tī teachers and predecessors and the city of D̲j̲āyas. Hindu and Islamic terminology is intermingled, the Ḳurʾān being so named and also called purāna, for example. All the essentials of Islam are referred to in Hindu terms, with a deliberately propagandist intent in accordance with Čis̲h̲tī ideals, e.g. ʿUthmān is called paṇdit, Allāh vidhi, "the book" giranth = Granth, the Companions mīt (Skr. mitra "friend"), as well as the Ḳurʾān called purān.

Malik Muḥammad D̲j̲āyasī has been revered on religious grounds by both Hindus and Muslims of the sub-continent, while his poetry gives him importance in the history of both Hindī and, to a lesser extent, Urdu literature.

Bibliography: Brief critical accounts of the poet will be found in F.E. Keay, A history of Hindi literature, London, etc. 1920, 31-3; K. B. Jindal, A history of Hindi literature, Allahabad 1955, 44-7; G. A. Grierson and N. A. Dvivedi, The Padumāvatī of Malik Muḥammad Jaisi, Calcutta 1911, i, Introd. 1-5; A. G. Shirreff, Padmāvatī, Calcutta 1944, containing an annotated English translation of the whole poem; the text of the collected poetry is found in Rāmčandra S̲h̲ukla, D̲j̲āyasī granthāvalī, 1st ed. Benares 1924, 5th ed., Allahabad 1951, and Mātāprasād Gupta, D̲j̲āyasī granthāvalī, Allahabad 1952 (both in the Dēvanāgarī script). Grierson and Dvivedi's work contains the text of about half of the Padumāvatī in the same script, with a translation in vol. ii. Lakshmi Dhar, Padumāvatī - a linguistic study of 16th century Hindi (Avadhi), London 1949, gives the text of cantos 26-31 (out of 57) in Roman transliteration, with an indifferent or worse English translation and lexical analyses. There are five mss. of the text in Persian script, three dating from around the end of the 11th/17th century, in the India Office Library, London. Unfortunately, there is no authoritative printed edition in the Persian script, scholars having largely concentrated on producing a reliable Dēvanāgarī version, since the Persian script, even when fully vowelled, is not entirely satisfactory for Hindī. They have compared Persian-script mss. with earlier ones in Dēvanāgarī, but the process of establishing a definitive version is not yet complete. For further bibliography, including historical and religious background, see Shirreff, op. cit., pp. xi-xiii, to which should be added, as the best modern study, Vāsudev Śaran Agravāl, Padmārat, Jhansī 2012 V.S./1955, with a critical introd., analysis, edited text based largely on Gupta's but also taking into account recently-discovered mss., translation and commentary. See also HINDĪ and HINDŪ.   (J. A. HAYWOOD)

AL-MALIK AL-RAḤĪM, ABŪ NAṢR K̲H̲USRAW-FĪRŪZ, Būyid amīr, d. 450/1058. When Abū Kālīd̲j̲ār, ruler in K̲h̲ūzistān, Fārs, Kirmān, ʿUmān and Baṣra in parallel with his uncle D̲j̲alāl al-Dawla [q.v.] of Bag̲h̲dād, died in 440/1048, the eldest of his ten or so sons, K̲h̲usraw-Fīrūz, succeeded as amīr with the title, unwillingly extracted from the caliph, of al-Malik al-Raḥīm. However, his succession was challenged by various of his brothers, and especially by Fūlād-Sutūn, and during his seven years' reign, K̲h̲usraw-Fīrūz reigned undisputedly only in ʿIrāḳ, with Fūlād-Sutūn established in S̲h̲īrāz and generally controlling southern Persia, fighting off K̲h̲usraw-Fīrūz's attempts to secure Fārs and K̲h̲ūzistān.

These squabbles were ominous for the future of the Būyid dynasty, whose position in northern Persia had already been destroyed by the G̲h̲aznawids [see MAD̲J̲D AL-DAWLA], in that it allowed the Sald̲j̲ūḳ leader Ṭog̲h̲rïl Beg to intervene in the remaining Būyid lands. Already in 444/1052-3 marauding Og̲h̲uz reached S̲h̲īrāz; in the next year Fūlād-Sutūn placed Ṭog̲h̲rïl's name in the k̲h̲uṭba before those of K̲h̲usraw-Fīrūz and his own; and in 446/1054-5 Ṭog̲h̲rïl was in control of K̲h̲ūzistān. K̲h̲usraw-Fīrūz's seven-year reign in Bag̲h̲dād was marked by continuous civil strife there, with the caliph al-Ḳāʾim's vizier, the raʾīs al-ruʾasāʾ Ibn al-Muslima [q.v.] upholding the Sunnī, Ḥanbalī cause, and the Turkish commander Arslan Basāsīrī [q.v.] inclining towards the S̲h̲īʿīs, being uspected of furthering the designs of the Fāṭimids on Irāḳ. Ṭog̲h̲rïl marched on Bag̲h̲dād and entered it in Ramaḍān 447/December 1055, with his name pronounced in the *k̲h̲uṭba* there. K̲h̲usraw-Fīrūz was soon afterwards arrested and deposed, and spent the last four years of his life in captivity, dying at Ray in 450/1058. The rule of the Būyids in ʿIrāḳ accordingly ended, though it continued for a few years more in Fārs under Fūlād-Sutūn.

Bibliography: The main primary sources are Ibn al-At̲h̲īr, al-Bundārī and Ibn al-D̲j̲awzī. See also H. Bowen, *The last Buwayhids,* in *JRAS* (1929), 234-8; Mafizullah Kabir, *The Buwaihid dynasty of Baghdad,* Calcutta 1964, 112-15; C. E. Bosworth, in *Camb. hist. of Iran,* v, 45-7; H. Busse, *Chalif und Grosskönig, die Buyiden im Iraq (945-1055),* Beirut-Wiesbaden 1969, 119-24. (C. E. BOSWORTH)

MALIK SARWAR, or K̲H̲ʷĀD̲J̲A D̲J̲AHĀN, the founder of the sultanate of D̲j̲awnpūr [*q.v.*] in northern India. A eunuch of common birth, Malik Sarwar rose in the service of Sultan Fīrūz Tug̲h̲luḳ to become the governor of the city of Dihlī. In the political confusion that followed the death of Sultan Fīrūz in 790/1388, Malik Sarwar lent powerful support to Prince Muḥammad, his chief patron and a younger son of Fīrūz, in Muḥammad's bid for the throne. Several years later the prince eventually ascended the Dihlī throne as Sultan Muḥammad S̲h̲āh, and in 795/1392 he elevated Malik Sarwar from governor of Dihlī to *wazīr* of the sultanate, conferring upon him the title K̲h̲ʷād̲j̲a D̲j̲ahān. But the sultan died the next year, and the state of political affairs in Dihlī plunged still deeper in chaos, with provincial governors and Hindu chieftains openly defying the authority of the court.

In these circumstances, Sultan Naṣīr al-Dīn Maḥmūd S̲h̲āh, shortly after becoming sultan in 796/1394, made Malik Sarwar governor of all the Dihlī's sultanate's possessions from Kanawd̲j̲ to Bihār, and conferred upon him the title Malik al-S̲h̲arḳ or "Lord of the East". The new governor promptly repaired to these domains with twenty elephants and a large army. After a victorious campaign, in which he succeeded in subduing rebellious princes throughout the lower D̲j̲umna-Ganges Dōāb and Bihār, Malik Sarwar established himself in the provincial capital of D̲j̲awnpūr as a virtually independent monarch, a circumstance enhanced by Dihlī's own preoccupation with Tīmūr's invasion of India in 801/1398. During his brief rule, Malik Sarwar's power increased and his administration flourished, with even the kings of Bengal paying to him the tribute formerly sent up to Dihlī. Upon his death in 802/1399, he bequeathed to his adopted son Ḳaranfūl a vast kingdom stretching from just east of Dihlī through the heart of the Gangetic plain to Bengal. Through the patronage of Malik Sarwar's successors, the S̲h̲arḳi kings of D̲j̲awnpūr, the city of D̲j̲awnpūr emerged as an important regional centre of Indo-Muslim culture in the 9th/15th century.

Bibliography: *Taʾrīk̲h̲-i Mubārak S̲h̲āhī,* completed *ca.* 837/1434 by Yaḥyā b. Aḥmad Sirhindī, Calcutta 1931, tr. K. K. Basu, Baroda 1932; *Ṭabaḳāt-i Akbarī,* compiled in 1001/1593 by Niẓām al-Dīn Aḥmad, Calcutta 1913, tr. B. De, Calcutta 1927-31; Mīyān Muḥammad Saeed, *The Sharqi sultanate of Jaunpur,* Karachi 1972.

(R. M. EATON)

MALIK-SHĀH, the name of various Sald̲j̲ūḳ rulers.

1. MALIK-S̲H̲ĀH I B. ALP ARSLAN, D̲J̲ALĀL AL-DAWLA MUʿIZZ AL-DIN ABU 'L-FATḤ, Great Sald̲j̲ūḳ sultan, born in 447/1055, reigned 465-85/1072-92. During his reign, the Great Sald̲j̲ūḳ empire reached its zenith of territorial extent—from Syria in the west to K̲h̲urāsān in the east—and military might.

Alp Arslan [*q.v.*] had made Malik-S̲h̲āh his *walī 'l-ʿahd* or heir to the throne in 458/1066, when various governorships on the eastern fringes were at this same time distributed to several members of the ruling family. Although Alp Arslan was fatally wounded during his Transoxanian campaign against the Ḳarak̲h̲ānids [see ILEK-K̲H̲ĀNS], he lingered long enough to make clear his intended arrangements for the future of the empire, leaving his son Ayāz in the upper Oxus provinces and his brother Ḳāwurd [*q.v.*] to continue in the largely autonomous principality of Kirmān which he had carved out. Through the prompt action of the experienced vizier Niẓām al-Mulk [*q.v.*], Malik-S̲h̲āh's succession to the sultanate was officially notified to the caliph in Bag̲h̲dād, and the key city in K̲h̲urāsān of Nīs̲h̲āpūr and its treasury secured for the young prince. The revolt of the disgruntled Ḳāwurd, who regarded his position as senior member of the Sald̲j̲ūḳ family as giving him a superior claim, was quelled at Hamadān in 466/1074 and Ḳāwurd strangled, though the sultan subsequently (467/1074) restored his sons Sulṭān-S̲h̲āh and Tūrān-S̲h̲āh to Kirmān (see E. Merçil, *Kirman Selçukları,* Istanbul 1980, 45 ff.).

Malik-S̲h̲āh's preoccupation with Ḳāwurd at this time in western Persia had emboldened the Ḳarak̲h̲ānid S̲h̲ams al-Mulk Naṣr b. Tamg̲h̲ač K̲h̲ān Ibrāhīm (460-72/1068-80) to invade Balk̲h̲ and Ṭuk̲h̲āristān, necessitating Malik-S̲h̲āh's hurried return to the east. He drove the Ḳarak̲h̲ānids out of Tirmid̲h̲ and dictated terms to the K̲h̲ān in his own capital of Samarḳand (466/1074); the subsequent disputes of S̲h̲ams al-Mulk Naṣr with the eastern branch of his dynasty in Kās̲h̲g̲h̲ar kept the K̲h̲ān generally submissive to Sald̲j̲ūḳ suzerainty over the ensuing years (see W. Barthold, *Turkestan down to the Mongol invasion,* London 1928, 314-15). Ayāz b. Alp Arslan died just before the Transoxanian campaign of his elder brother, and Malik-S̲h̲āh now gave Balk̲h̲ and Ṭuk̲h̲āristān to his other brother Tekis̲h̲. For some years, Tekis̲h̲ governed his territories peacefully, but in 473/1080-1 took into his service 7,000 mercenary troops discharged by Malik-S̲h̲āh as an economy measure, even though Niẓām al-Mulk had warned him of the dangers of throwing such a large group of desperadoes out of employment (cf. *Siyāsat-nāma,* ch. xli, ed. H. Darke, Tehran 1340/1962, 209-10, tr. idem, London 1960, 170-1). With these soldiers, Tekis̲h̲ rebelled, but failed to capture Nīs̲h̲āpūr and had to submit. The sultan pardoned him, but four years later, in 477/1084, Tekis̲h̲ again renounced his allegiance whilst Malik-S̲h̲āh was in the D̲j̲azīra at the other end of the empire; this time, Malik-S̲h̲āh showed no mercy, and after quelling the outbreak, blinded and jailed Tekis̲h̲. These draconian measures kept further potential trouble-makers within the Sald̲j̲ūḳ family quiet for the rest of the reign.

Peace was also established on the eastern fringes by the achievement of a *modus vivendi* with the G̲h̲aznawids [*q.v.*] of eastern Afg̲h̲ānistān and India. The succession quarrels at the outset of Malik-S̲h̲āh's reign tempted the G̲h̲aznawid sultan Ibrāhīm b. Masʿūd (451-92/1059-99) to make a bid for the recovery of the G̲h̲aznawid territories in K̲h̲urāsān lost to the Sald̲j̲ūḳs 30 years before. Ibrāhīm attacked the Sald̲j̲ūḳ prince ʿUt̲h̲mān b. Čag̲h̲rï Beg Dāwūd in northern Afg̲h̲ānistān and captured him, but Malik-

Shāh sent an army and restored the situation there (465/1073). Thereafter, Ibrāhīm seems to have been reconciled to the permanent loss of the Ghaznawid former western provinces, and peaceful relations between the two empires became the norm; there were marriage links between the two royal houses, and Saldjūḳ cultural influence, e.g. in regard to titulature and coinage patterns, was increasingly felt within the Ghaznawid dominions (see C. E. Bosworth, *The later Ghaznavids, splendour and decay: the dynasty in Afghanistan and northern India 1040-1186,* Edinburgh 1977, 50-8). Within the buffer zone between the two empires, the principality of Sīstān, governed by scions of the once-mighty Ṣaffārid dynasty [*q.v.*] as vassals of the Saldjūḳs, Malik-Shāh's authority was reasserted, and joint operations conducted by the Saldjūḳ and Ṣaffārid forces against the Ismāʿīlīs of Ḳūhistān [*q.v.*].

Saldjūḳ-Ḳarakhānid relations also remained pacific, as noted above, for the rest of Shams al-Mulk Naṣr's reign and during the short reign of Khiḍr Khān b. Ibrāhīm and then of the latter's son Aḥmad, nephew of Malik-Shāh's Ḳarakhānid wife Terken Khātūn, whom the sultan had married when a child in 456/1064. But the discontent of the orthodox *ʿulamāʾ* in Transoxania led Malik-Shāh to invade Transoxania once more in 482/1089, to depose Aḥmad Khān (though he was later restored before his final deposition and execution, ostensibly because of his Ismāʿīlī sympathies, in 488/1095) and to penetrate as far as Semirečye, overawing the eastern Ḳarakhānid ruler of Kāshghar and Khotan, Hārūn Khān b. Sulaymān, who now acknowledged Malik-Shāh in the *khuṭba* of his dominions. Recognition of the Saldjūḳs here represented the culmination of Saldjūḳ prestige in the east (see Barthold, *Turkestan,* 316-18).

Timely displays of military force were sufficient to subdue ambitious Saldjūḳ rivals, to bring into line Ḳarakhānid princes torn by family dissensions and to persuade the Ghaznawids that their fortunes now lay in the exploitation of India rather than in futile irredentist dreams in the west. The situation on the western borders of the Great Saldjūḳ empire was more complex and the frontier, towards which Türkmen adventures and *ghāzī*s had for some time been deflected by government policy, more fluid and shifting. There was a zone of local Arab and Kurdish amīrates, jealous of their independence, mingled with ambitious Turkish slave commanders and Türkmen *begs*; beyond them, in western Transcaucasia and western Anatolia, lay the hostile Christian powers of Georgia and Byzantium. Hence the special importance to the Saldjūḳs of defending the northwestern provinces of Ādharbāydjān, Arrān and Armenia against Georgian attacks and of preserving these regions as areas of concentration for Türkmen forces. Soon after he came to the throne, Malik-Shāh took steps to strengthen his frontier by deposing the Kurdish Shaddādid [*q.v.*] prince of Gandja and Dvin Faḍl(ūn) III b. Faḍl II (466-8/1073-5) and installing there the veteran Turkish slave commander of Alp Arslan's, Sawtigin, who was already well-familiar with the situation in the Caucasus region. Malik-Shāh campaigned here personally in 471/1078-9, after the Georgian king had temporarily captured Kars from the Muslims, and again in 478/1085 after the restored Shaddādid Faḍl III had rebelled (see V. Minorsky, *Studies in Caucasian history,* London 1953, *I. New light on the Shaddādids of Ganja,* 67-8). This time, the main line of the Shaddādids in Gandja was extinguished, although a collateral branch continued in Ānī till the end of the 6th/12th century (see *ibid.*, *II. The Shaddādids of Ani,* 79-106). The submission of the Shīrwān-Shāh Farīburz [see SHĪRWĀN] was also received. Much of the Araxes-Kur basin, i.e. eastern Transcaucasia, was now parcelled out as *iḳṭāʿs* [*q.v.*] for the sultan's Turkish commanders, with Malik-Shāh's cousin Ḳuṭb al-Dīn Ismāʿīl b. Yāḳūtī as overlord.

The overrunning of Anatolia and the gradual pushing-back of the Greeks continued essentially as an enterprise of individual Türkmen leaders, prominent among whom were the sons of the Saldjūḳ Ḳutlumush b. Arslan Isrāʾīl, Sulaymān and Manṣūr. Although the later historiography of the Rūm Saldjūḳs makes Malik-Shāh officially invest these princes with the governorship of Anatolia, the assumption of the title of sultan by these last seems to have been a unilateral act which Malik-Shāh probably could only regard as one of *lèse-majesté*; and two others of Ḳutlumush's sons actually fought at the side of the Fāṭimids in Palestine against the Saldjūḳ cause (see Cl. Cahen, *Qutlumush et ses fils avant l'Asie Mineure,* in *Isl.*, xxxix [1964], 26-7; idem, *Pre-Ottoman Turkey,* London 1968, 73 ff.).

In the Arab lands of ʿIrāḳ, the Djazīra and Syria, Saldjūḳ policy aimed at containing the Ismāʿīlī Fāṭimids [*q.v.*] in Palestine, at curbing their influence among the Shīʿī Arab amīrates of the desert fringes and within the Arabian peninsula, at assuring Sunnī control of major cities like Aleppo and Damascus, and at establishing some measure of control over the Türkmen bands ranging across these lands of Syria and the Djazīra and competing with the existing Arab population for pasture-grounds. The caliphal vizier Fakhr al-Dawla Ibn Djahīr [see DJAHĪR, BANŪ] secured Saldjūḳ military help in order to reduce the Kurdish principality of the Marwānids [*q.v.*] of Diyārbakr in 478/1085, eventually incorporating it into the Saldjūḳ empire. Malik-Shāh's authority in Syria was imposed in the face of opposition from the Armenian former general of the Byzantines. Philaretos, in the middle Taurus Mountains region, from the ʿUḳaylids [*q.v.*] under their *amīr* Muslim b. Ḳuraysh in the lands between Mawsil and Aleppo, and from Sulaymān b. Ḳutlumush, firstly through the agency of Malik-Shāh's brother Tutush and then in 477-8/1084-5 by an army from the capital Iṣfahān under the caliph's personal command (see Cahen, *La Syrie du Nord à l'époque des Croisades,* Paris 1940, 177 ff.; idem, *Pre-Ottoman Turkey,* 30-2). Triumphing over his rivals, Malik-Shāh's authority was now extended as far as the Mediterranean shores, and Turkish slave commanders installed as governors in Antioch, Aleppo and Edessa. Saldjūḳ influence was even carried southwards into the Arabian peninsula, for in 469/1076-7 Malik-Shāh's commander Artuḳ b. Ekseb (later, the founder of a dynasty of Türkmen *begs* in Diyārbakr [see ARTUḲIDS]) marched into al-Aḥsā in eastern Arabia against the Carmathians [see ḲARĀMIṬA]; the *Sharīf*s of Mecca were suborned from their Fāṭimid allegiance; and Yemen and Aden were temporarily occupied.

Relations with the ʿAbbāsid caliphs were necessarily important for a power like the Saldjūḳs which claimed to be the spearhead of Sunnī orthodoxy and protector of the Commander of the Faithful against Shīʿī threats. Malik-Shāh did not manage personally to visit Baghdād until 479-80/1086-7, when al-Muḳtadī [*q.v.*] formally granted him the *salṭana* or secular authority. As Cahen has pointed out (*op. cit.*, 42), Malik-Shāh and Niẓām al-Mulk regarded the sultanate, whose protectorate over the caliph had been established by Malik-Shāh's great-uncle Ṭoghrïl Beg [*q.v.*], as an institution deriving its legitimacy from its very self and having a full entitlement to intervene even in religious matters. The caliphs could not of course concede the validity of this constitutional interpretation of the ordering of affairs in Islam, hence the inevitability of a state of tension, in greater or lesser degree, between the two focuses of authority (see G. Makdisi, *Les rapports entre calife et sulṭān à l'époque Saljûqide*, in *IJMES*, vi [1975], 228-36).

The sultans had installed in Bag̲h̲dād a *s̲h̲ihna* [*q.v.*] or military commander, who had to keep order in the city and often in ʿIrāḳ in general, and an *ʿamīd* [*q.v.*] or official in charge of civil and financial matters, including the allocation to the caliph of his *iḳṭāʿ*s and allowances. These personages could, and at times did, exert considerable pressure on the caliphs. Central policy in the Sald̲j̲ūḳ state was directed from the *dīwān* of the great vizier Niẓām al-Mulk, who had been first appointed under Alp Arslan; for a detailed survey of his policy, see NIẒĀM AL-MULK. Part of this policy lay in facilitating the revival of Sunnī Islam, as the authority of S̲h̲īʿī powers like the Būyids or Buwayhids [*q.v.*] and Fāṭimids disappeared or waned, by financial and other support to the orthodox religious institution, including the encouragement of the founding of *madrasas* [*q.v.*], and this in theory meant harmonious co-operation with the ʿAbbāsid caliphs, the moral heads of Sunnī Islam. In practice, strains arose between Niẓām al-Mulk and the Banū D̲j̲ahīr, viziers to the caliphs from al-Ḳāʾim to al-Muḳtafī, with a nadir of bad relations in 471/1079 when Niẓām al-Mulk secured Fak̲h̲r al-Dawla Ibn D̲j̲ahīr's dismissal. The arranging of the betrothal of one of Malik-S̲h̲āh's daughters to al-Muḳtadī in 474/1081-2 (another daughter was later to marry the next caliph al-Mustaẓhir) only brought about détente when the sultan came personally to Bag̲h̲dād and the marriage was celebrated in 480/1087. Even then, relations speedily deteriorated, and on his second visit to Bag̲h̲dād, shortly before his death, the caliph was largely ignored by Malik-S̲h̲āh, who set in motion extensive building operations, including a great mosque, the D̲j̲āmiʿ al-Sulṭān, and palaces for the great men of state, intending to make Bag̲h̲dād his winter capital (see Makdisi, *The topography of eleventh-century Baġdād, materials and notes*, in *Arabica*, vi [1959], 292, 298-9). It seems that the sultan planned to set up his infant grandson D̲j̲aʿfar, the "Little Commander of the Faithful" and fruit of the alliance between the caliph and the Sald̲j̲ūḳ princess, as caliph; but in the middle of S̲h̲awwāl 485/November 1092, not very long after Niẓām al-Mulk's assassination, of complicity in which some people thought him guilty, Malik-S̲h̲āh died of fever at the age of 58, suspectedly poisoned (see M. T. Houtsma, *The death of Nizam al-Mulk and its consequences*, in *Jnal. of Indian history*, iii [1924], 147 ff.). The caliph was thereby assured of a reprieve. Terken K̲h̲ātūn and her protégé the *mustawfī* Tād̲j̲ al-Mulk Abu 'l-G̲h̲anāʾim endeavoured to place Terken K̲h̲ātūn's four-year old son Maḥmūd on the throne, but the Niẓāmiyya, the relatives and partisans of the dead vizier, succeeded in killing Tād̲j̲ al-Mulk and eventually securing the succession of the thirteen-year old Berk-yaruḳ, Malik-S̲h̲āh's eldest son by another wife, Zubayda K̲h̲ātūn. The Great Sald̲j̲ūḳ sultanate now entered a period of internal dissension under Malik-S̲h̲āh's sons [see BARK-YĀRUḲ; MUḤAMMAD B. MALIK-S̲H̲ĀH; SAND̲J̲AR], so that the political authority of the caliphate could revive in the 6th/12th century as that of the sultans declined. Malik-S̲h̲āh's body was carried back to Iṣfahān and buried in a *madrasa* there.

Malik-S̲h̲āh is praised in the sources, Christian as well as Muslim, for his noble and generous character. Although probably no more cultured than the rest of the early Sald̲j̲ūḳ sultans, he acquired, in the conventional pattern of Islamic rulers, the reputation of being a patron of learning and literature. The great Arabic poet and stylist al-Ṭug̲h̲rāʾī [*q.v.*] served in his chancery, and amongst Persian poets, Muʿizzī [*q.v.*] in fact derived his *tak̲h̲alluṣ* from Malik-S̲h̲āh's honorific of Muʿizz al-Dīn. ʿUmar K̲h̲ayyām [*q.v.*] seems to have been attracted into the Sald̲j̲ūḳ service at the time of Malik-S̲h̲āh's Transoxanian campaign against S̲h̲ams al-Mulk Naṣr, and to have played a leading role in the reform of the calendar, involving the introduction of the new Malikī or D̲j̲alālī era (after the sultan's *laḳab* of D̲j̲alāl al-Dawla [see D̲J̲ALĀLĪ]), and in the construction of an observatory at Iṣfahān. A collection of legal *responsa*, the *Masāʾil al-Maliks̲h̲āhiyya fi 'l-ḳawāʿid al-s̲h̲arʿiyya*, perhaps composed for the sultan, is mentioned in certain sources, e.g. in Muḥammad b. Muḥammad al-Ḥusaynī's abridgement of Rāwandī, *al-ʿUrāḍa fi 'l-ḥikāya al-sald̲j̲ūḳiyya*, ed. K. Süssheim, Leiden 1909, 69-71.

Bibliography: (in addition to works mentioned in the article): Of primary sources, see the standard Arabic and Persian ones for the period, such as Ẓahīr al-Dīn Nīs̲h̲āpūrī, Rāwandī, Bundārī, Ṣadr al-Dīn al-Ḥusaynī, Ibn al-At̲h̲īr, Ibn al-D̲j̲awzī, Sibṭ b. al-D̲j̲awzī, and the Syriac one of Barhebraeus. Ibn K̲h̲allikān, ed. Iḥsān ʿAbbās, v, 283-9, tr. de Slane, iii, 440-6, has a biography of Malik S̲h̲āh, deriving material for it from the continuation of Miskawayh by Muḥammad b. ʿAbd al-Malik al-Hamad̲h̲ānī (d. 521/1127).

Of secondary sources, see İ. Kafesoğlu, *Sultan Melikşah devrinde Büyük Selçuklu imparatorluğu*, Istanbul 1953; C. E. Bosworth, in *Cambridge history of Iran*, v, 66-102, for political and dynastic history, and A. K. S. Lambton in *ibid.*, 203 ff. for administrative history; O. Turan, *Selçuklar tarihi ve Türk-Islam medeniyeti*, Istanbul 1969, 152-75.

2. MALIK-S̲H̲ĀH II B. BERK-YARUḲ, infant son of sultan Berk-yaruḳ, who, after the latter's death in 498/1105, was briefly proclaimed sultan in Bag̲h̲dād, with Ayāz as his Atabeg and Saʿd al-Mulk Abu 'l-Maḥāsin as vizier, but who soon had to yield to Muḥammad b. Malik-S̲h̲āh I [*q.v.*].

Bibliography: Bosworth, in *Camb. hist. of Iran*, v, 111.

3. MALIK-S̲H̲ĀH III B. MAḤMŪD B. MUḤAMMAD MUʿĪN AL-DĪN (547-8/1152-3), son of sultan Maḥmūd [*q.v.*], who, with the support of the *amīr* K̲h̲āṣṣ Beg Arslan and of Ildegiz [*q.v.*], Atabeg of Arrān and most of Ād̲h̲arbāyd̲j̲ān, briefly became sultan in western Persia after the death of his uncle Masʿūd b. Muḥammad [*q.v.*] without direct heir. His incapability as a ruler—the caliph al-Muḳtafī was now able to get rid of all Sald̲j̲ūḳ authority from Bag̲h̲dād and ʿIrāḳ—speedily led to his deposition in favour of his brother Muḥammad. He was imprisoned, escaped and then was granted the governorship of Fārs by Muḥammad, but died at Iṣfahān in 555/1160.

Bibliography: Bosworth, in *Camb. hist. of Iran*, vi, 169, 175-7.

4. MALIK-S̲H̲ĀH was also the name of two members of the Sald̲j̲ūḳs of Rūm in the 6th/12th century: (a) MALIK-S̲H̲ĀH B. ḲÏLÏD̲J̲ ARSLAN I B. SULAYMĀN B. ḲUTLUMUS̲H̲ (for a brief spell after his father's death in 500/1107); and (b) MALIK-S̲H̲ĀH B. ḲÏLÏD̲J̲ ARSLAN II B. MASʿŪD, ḲUṬB AL-DĪN, who during the division of territories during the latter part of his father's reign (i.e. 551-88/1156-92), received Sīwās and Aḳsaray, and who then kept his father in semi-captivity in Konya [see ḲÏLÏD̲J̲ ARSLAN II].

Bibliography: Zambaur, *Manuel,* 143; O. Turan, *Selçuklu zamanında Türkiye,* Istanbul 1971, 149 n. 2, 154, n. 17; S. Vryonis, *The decline of medieval Hellenism in Asia Minor,* Berkeley and Los Angeles 1971, 147, 150 n. 48.(C. E. BOSWORTH)

MALIK AL-SHUᶜARĀᵓ (A.), "King of the Poets", honorific title of a Persian poet laureate, which is also known in other forms. It was the highest distinction which could be given to a poet by a royal patron. Like other honorifics [see LAKAB], it confirmed the status of its holder within his profession and was regarded as a permanent addition to his name which sometimes even became a hereditary title. Corresponding to this on a lower level was the privilege, given occasionally to court poets, of choosing a pen name [see TAKHALLUṢ] based on the name or one of the *laḳabs* of their patron.

Certain responsibilities went with the title, at least during the Middle Ages. The poet laureate was a supervisor of the poets assembled at the court and passed judgment on poems before they were presented to the patron. He also decided about the admission of applicants to the position of a court poet, but it is evident from some of the anecdotes related by Niẓāmī-yi ᶜArūḍī that such introductions could equally be sought through the intermediacy of other dignitaries. Being the guardian of the ruler's reputation as a benefactor of letters, he occupied a position of trust; it is frequently mentioned that the poet laureate was a prominent boon companion (*nadīm* [*q.v.*]) of his patron. E. E. Bertels ascribed an important role in the development of Persian poetry before the Mongol period to the institution; the influences exerted by a poet laureate on the poets under his control fostered the rise of local traditions marked by common stylistic features.

The scarce information about literary life at the Sāsānid court available to us suggests that the rank of favourite artist was known in Iran prior to Islam. The story about the rivalry between Sarkash and Bārbad over the first place among the minstrels of Khusraw Parvīz can be taken as an indication (cf. A. Christensen, *L'Iran sous les Sassanides,* Copenhagen 1944, 484). The founding of a *dīwān al-shiᶜr* for the distribution of rewards to poets by the Barāmika [*q.v.*] and the appointment of Abān al-Lāḥiḳī (died about 200/815-16 [*q.v.*]) as an official critic of the poems presented to these Iranian viziers of the ᶜAbbāsids, point into the same direction (see also D. Sourdel, *Le vizirat ᶜAbbāside de 749 à 936,* Damascus 1959-60, i, 143 f.).

Dawlatshāh (*flor.* at the end of the 9th/15th century) recorded the formal appointment of ᶜUnṣurī as a poet laureate by Maḥmūd of Ghazna through a *mithāl-i malik al-shuᶜarāᵓī* in the early 5th/11th century. The duties of this office were similar to those incumbent on the holder of the office instituted by the Barmakids (*Tadhkirat al-shuᶜarāᵓ,* London-Leiden 1901, 44 f.). Although the actual title is not mentioned in sources from his own time, there is little reason to doubt that ᶜUnṣurī did occupy the leading position at the Ghaznawid court ascribed to him. This need not mean, however, that he was the first Persian poet who was honoured in this manner. The chapter on the poets in the *Čahār maḳāla,* the anecdotes of which illustrate the most important aspects of early court poetry, refers to the special position held by Rūdakī under the Sāmānids in the 4th/10th century. Particularly informative is the story on Niẓāmī-yi ᶜArūḍī's visit to Amīr Muᶜizzī [*q.v.*] in 510/1116-17 in order to get a reward for a *ḳaṣīda* presented to this poet-laureate of the Saldjūḳ sultan. It contains a detailed account of Muᶜizzī's succession to the post of *amīr al-shuᶜarāᵓ* which was held already by his father Burhānī. The remunerations attached to this function consisted of a *djāmagī* and an *idjrāᵓ*, the kinds of salary regularly assigned to officials [see DJĀMAKIYYA]. Another anecdote tells about a conflict at the court of the Khāḳānīyān (i.e. the Ilek-Khāns [*q.v.*]) of Transoxania between rival poets. Rashīdī defies successfully the authority of the *amīr al-shuᶜarāᵓ* ᶜAmᶜaḳ and wins for himself the title of *sayyid al-shuᶜarāᵓ*. It should be noted that the title of *malik al-shuᶜarāᵓ*, which later appears to be in general use, does not occur in the *Čahār maḳāla.*

The institution remained a part of the organisation of courts wherever poetry was practised according to the Persian tradition. We find it under the Saldjūḳs of Anatolia as well as under the Muslim rulers of the Indian subcontinent. For the later periods, it is difficult to decide to what extent its significance exceeded that of a merely honorary office. A remarkable revival of mediaeval customs came about in 19th-century Iran under the Ḳādjār dynasty. Fatḥ ᶜAlī Shāh tried to imitate the literary splendour of the ancient court of Ghazna by attracting a great number of court poets who were united in a society called *andjuman-i Khāḳān.* He gave the title of *malik al-shuᶜarāᵓ* to Ṣabā, the author of the *Shāhinshāh-nāma,* which in the style of the *Shāh-nāma* glorified the exploits of Fatḥ ᶜAlī Shāh. Many honorifics of this kind were handed out by Shāhs, viziers and provincial governors to their favourite poets throughout this period. Among the last who received the title of *malik al-shuᶜarāᵓ* was Muḥammad Taḳī Bahār [*q.v.*]. In 1904, when he was only eighteen, Muẓaffar al-Dīn Shāh allowed him to adopt this title which was previously held by his father Ṣabūrī. In spite of his subsequent renouncing of feudal poetry, the title remained attached to Bahār's name till the end of his days.

Bibliography: Niẓāmī-yi ᶜArūḍī, *Čahār maḳāla,* ed. M. Ḳazwīnī and M. Muᶜīn, Tehran 1955-7, 49 ff.; E. E. Bertels, *Izbrannïe trudï. Istoriya persidskotadzikskoy literaturï,* Moscow 1960, 125 f., 332, 355; F. Machalski, *Persian court poetry of the Kaǵar period,* in *Folia Orientalia,* vi (1964), 1-40; J. Rypka, *History of Iranian Literature,* Dordrecht 1968, 173, 203, 326, 328 f., 345; J. W. Clinton, *The Divan of Manūchihrī Dāmghānī,* Minneapolis 1972, 29 ff.
(J. T. P. DE BRUIJN)

MALIK AL-TUDJDJĀR (A. "king of the big merchants"), an office and a title which existed in Iran from Ṣafawid times (J. Chardin, *Journal de voyages du Chevalier Chardin, en Perse, et autres lieux de l'Orient* ..., ed. L. Langlès, v, Paris 1811, 262), and probably earlier, until the end of the Ḳādjār period.

It is not clear precisely what the functions of the *malik al-tudjdjār* were during the Ṣafawid and early Ḳādjār periods, or to what extent the office existed in the various commercial centres of the country. It is, however, obvious, that not all major towns had a *malik al-tudjdjār* in the first half of the 19th century. In Djumādā I 1260/May-June 1844 Muḥammad Shāh (1834-48) issued a *farmān* which ordered that a *malik al-tudjdjār* be appointed "in every place in Persia where extended commerce is carried on ..." ("Firman relating to bankruptcies ...", in L. Hertslet [ed.], *A complete collection of the treaties and conventions ... between Great Britain and foreign powers,* ix, London 1856, 614). By the second half of the 19th century, big merchants (*tudjdjār*) acting as *malik al-tudjdjār* were to be found in most major commercial centres of Iran (Mīrzā Muḥammad Ḥasan Khān Iᶜtimād al-Salṭana [Ṣaniᶜ al-Dawla], *Mirᵓāt al-buldān-i Nāṣirī,* Tehran

1297-1300/1880-83, ii, 270; iii, 2, 4-5, 25, 33, 120; Ḥādjdjī Mīrzā Ḥasan Fasāʾī, *Fārs-nāma-yi Nāṣirī*, Tehran 1313/1895-6, i, 308-9; ii, 205; *Rūznāma-yi Dawlat-i ʿAliyya-yi Īrān* [Tehran], 486, 2 Ramaḍān 1277; 26 Dhu 'l-Ḥidjdja 1280; Aḥmad ʿAlī Khān Wazīrī, *Djughrāfiyā-yi Kirmān*, ed. M. Bāstānī Pārīzī, Tehran 1346/1967, 67, 159; J. E. Polak, *Persien: Das Land und seine Bewohner, ethnographische Schilderungen*, Leipzig 1865, ii, 188; E. G. Browne, *A year amongst the Persians,* London 1893, 372, 407; W. M. Floor, *The merchants (tujjār) in Qājār Iran,* in *ZDMG,* cxxvi (1976), 107-9). In Nāṣir al-Dīn Shāh's reign (1848-96), the *malik al-tudjdjār* of Tehran was officially recognised as the superior *malik al-tudjdjār* of the country, and received the title *malik al-tudjdjār al-mamālik* (Mīrzā Muḥammad Ḥasan Khān Iʿtimād al-Salṭana [Ṣāniʿ al-Dawla], *Taʾrīkh-i muntaẓam-i Nāṣirī,* Tehran 1300/1883, iii, 231; *Rūznāma-yi Dawlat-i ʿAliyya-yi Īrān,* 642, 16 Rabīʿ I 1287). It seems that the prominent big merchants of each main town chose one from out of their ranks and recommended his name to the authorities, which would then nominate him to that office (*Rūznāma-yi Dawlat-i ʿAliyya-yi Īrān,* 486, 2 Ramaḍān 1277; 26 Dhu 'l-Ḥidjdja 1280; Polak, *Persien,* ii, 188; J. Greenfield, *Die Verfassung des persischen Staates,* Berlin 1904, 145). It appears that the office almost always fell into the hands of one of the most prominent and wealthy big merchants of any given commercial centre (Dr. J.-B. Feuvrier, *Trois ans à la Cour de Perse,* new ed., Paris 1906, 284; J. G. Lorimer, *Gazetteer of the Persian Gulf, ʾOmān, and Central Arabia,* i/2, Calcutta 1915, 2618; "Maʾdan" and "Shīrāz" in Government of India, *Gazetteer of Persia,* Simla 1910, i, 497-8, 502-3; iii, 852; J. Greenfield, *Verfassung,* 143), and that a strong hereditary tendency developed in the holders of the office (*Rūznāma-yi Dawlat-i ʿAliyya-yi Īrān,* 642, 16 Rabīʿ I 1287; Iʿtimād al-Salṭana, *Mirʾāt,* iii, 120; Fasāʾī, *Fārs-nāma,* ii, 205).

The *malik al-tudjdjār* was not a government official. He did not receive any payment for holding the office, nor was he officially a member of any government department. He had two main functions: (1) he was the merchants' representative, or better, the link between the trading community of a given town or province and the authorities, and (2) he was entrusted with authority to settle disputes between the Iranian merchants and their customers, among the merchants themselves, and between local and foreign merchants and trading-firms (Polak, *Persien,* ii, 188-9; J. M. de Rochechouart, *Souvenir d'un voyage en Perse,* Paris 1867, 176; C. J. Wills, *Persia as it is,* London 1886, 45; G. N. Curzon, *Persia and the Persian question,* London 1892, i, 450; A. Houtum-Schindler, art. *Persia. I. Geography and statistics,* in *Encyclopaedia Britannica,* 10th ed., London 1902, xxxi, 619; Greenfield, *Verfassung,* 143; idem, *Das Handelsrecht ... von Persien,* Berlin 1906, 22, 27). It was the latter function, especially so far as it concerned the claims of foreign merchants in cases of the bankruptcies of Iranian merchants, that provoked the issue of Muḥammad Shāh's abovementioned *farmān.* Nāṣir al-Dīn Shāh extended the functions of the *malik al-tudjdjār* to include, in collaboration with the provincial official in charge of trade and commerce (*raʾīs tudjdjārat*), the encouragement of commercial activity in particular and of the economy of the country in general (Greenfield, *Verfassung,* 143). In Tehran, the *malik al-tudjdjār* was consulted by the government on commercial and various other economic issues. He was asked by Nāṣir al-Dīn to form a council of the prominent big merchants of the capital which would hold regular meetings, in which the question of developing and encouraging trade and commerce, should be discussed, and the results of its deliberations communicated to the government (Iʿtimād al-Salṭana, *Taʾrīkh,* iii, 231. Cf. Houtum-Schindler, in *EB*[10], xxxi, 619).

The economic developments of the 1870s and 1880s were bound to bring to an end the co-operation which had existed between the government and the big merchants. While the central government found itself faced by growing fiscal difficulties, the big merchants became wealthier. Against this background, the government initiated new economic measures. The tobacco concession (1890) and the new customs administration and regulations (1898-1904) in particular aroused the opposition of the big merchants to the government. Big merchants holding the office of *malik al-tudjdjār* in several major towns played a central role in the protest movements which brought about the cancellation of the tobacco concession in 1892, and the granting of a constitution (*ḳānūn-i asāsī*) and the establishment of a national consultative assembly (*madjlis-i shūrā-yi millī*) in 1906 (see further Mihdī Malikzāda, *Taʾrīkh-i inḳilāb-i mashrūṭiyyāt-i Īrān,* Tehran 1328/1949, i, 128-30, 278-9; ii, 28, 168-72; Ibrāhīm Taymūrī, *Taḥrīm-i tanbākū yā awwalīn muḳāwamat-i manfī dar Īrān,* Tehran 1328/1949, 78-9, 112; Nāẓim al-Islām Kirmānī, *Taʾrīkh-i bīdārī-yi Īrāniyān,* Tehran 1332/1952, 12; Mīrzā ʿAlī Khān Amīn al-Dawla, *Khāṭirāt-i siyāsī-yi Mīrzā ʿAlī Khān Amīn al-Dawla,* ed. Ḥāfiẓ Farmānfarmāyān, Tehran 1341/1962, 155; Yaḥyā Dawlatābādī, *Taʾrīkh-i muʿāṣir yā ḥayāt-i Yaḥyā,* Tehran n.d., i, 108; A. K. S. Lambton, *The tobacco regie: prelude to revolution,* in *SI,* xxii [1965], 124-42; eadem, *Persia: The breakdown of society,* in *The Cambridge history of Islam*, i, Cambridge 1970, 459-67; eadem, *The Persian constitutional revolution of 1905-6,* in P. J. Vatikiotis (ed.), *Revolution in the Middle East,* London 1972, 175-82; N. R. Keddie, *Religion and rebellion in Iran, the tobacco protest of 1891-1892*, London 1966, 49-53, 85, 90-1; eadem, *Iranian politics 1900-1905: background to revolution,* in *Middle Eastern Studies*, v [1969], 7, 12, 155-6, 163, 236, 240, 243; G. G. Gilbar, *The big merchants (tujjār) and the Persian constitutional revolution of 1906,* in *Asian and African Studies*, [The Hebrew University, Jerusalem], xi [1976], 288-303; idem, *Persian agriculture in the late Qājār period, 1860-1906: some economic and social aspects,* in *ibid.*, xii [1978], 334-46).

With the fall of the Ḳādjārs and the adoption of modern forms of government and Western institutions, the office of *malik al-tudjdjār* lapsed, its functions being taken over by the Chambers of Commerce of the major towns and by several government departments.

Bibliography: Given in the article.

(G. G. GILBAR)

MĀLIKĀNE, a technical term made up of Arabic *mālik* "owner" and the Persian suffix *-āne* which gives the meaning of "in the manner of, way of" to the word to which it is added. It is used to describe intangible property, i.e. fiscal revenues, whenever the enjoyment of them is connected with full ownership. The term's content has nevertheless changed over the centuries. The oldest attestation of it known to us appears in a grant of Ghiyāth al-Dīn Pīrshāh, ruler of Khwārazm, d. 627/1230 (see H. Horst, *Die Staatsverwaltung der Grosselǧūqen und Ḫōrazmšāhs (1038-1231)*, Wiesbaden 1964, 142). Under the Saldjūḳs of Asia Minor and their subsequent successor states, including the Ottomans, the term *mālikāne* was applied to the tithe (i.e. the tax levied according to the religious law) or to a proportion of it ceded by the state either subject to various liabilities or freely to a certain person, who could sell it, make it into a pious foundation or bequeath it to his descendants. It is thus contrasted with those fiscal revenues called *dīwānī* which were composed of customary rights. Under this form, the *mālikāne* system was able to maintain itself only in certain long-established pious foundations, since the Ottoman state would not tolerate any fiscal revenue slipping from its control.

In 1695, the *defterdār* [see DAFTARDĀR] of the time elaborated the bases of a new form of *mālikāne,* i.e. a grant of the enjoyment of revenues for life, with care to protect the properties of the state from the dilapidation allowed by uncaring lessees, heedless of the ultimate fate of properties granted to them. The fiscal revenues were, as in ordinary leases, put up for auction and sold to the highest bidder. This last paid over to the state the "price" of the lease called *muʿad͟jd͟jele* and contracted to hand over each year a fixed sum corresponding to the fiscal revenues taken on lease. In the case of a new sovereign coming to the throne, he paid additionally 25% of the cost of the lease, and in times of war, 10%. Given the fact that the holders of these leases for life came from the class of high officials and persons (such as civilian and military dignitaries and scholars) who usually lived in the capital, they in turn sub-let the properties they had leased. In 1715 a *firman* decreed the abolition of the system, but it continued in existence till *ca.* 1839.

Bibliography: Ö. L. Barkan, *Türk-islam toprak hukuku tatbikatının osmanlı imparatorluğunda aldığı şekiller. Mâlikâne-divânî sistemi,* in *Türk hukuk ve iktisat tarihi mecmuası,* ii (1932-9), Istanbul 1939, 119-84; M. Z. Pakalın, *Osmanlı tarih deyimleri ve terimleri sözlüğü,* ii, Istanbul 1951, 3, 395-7; M. Genç, *Osmanlı maliyesinde malikane sistemi,* in *Türkiye iktisat tarihi semineri,* ed. O. Okyar, Publ. of Hacettepe Univ. no. C 13, Ankara 1975, 231-96; I. Beldiceanu-Steinherr, *Fiscalité et formes de possession de la terre arable dans l'Anatolie préottomane,* in *JESHO,* xix/3 (1976), index x.v. *mālikāne.*

(I. BELDICEANU-STEINHERR)

MĀLIKIYYA, a juridical-religious group of orthodox Islam which formed itself into a school (*al-mad͟hhab al-mālikī*) after the adoption of the doctrine of Imām Mālik b. Anas [*q.v.*] who died at Medina in 179/795.

In the 2nd/8th century, when the islamisation of law had been partially accomplished but different systems coexisted, the need for a uniform judicial code became imperative. The second ʿAbbāsid caliph, Abū D͟jaʿfar al-Manṣūr (d. 159/775), approached the Medinan jurist with a proposal to establish a judicial system which would unify the different methods then in force in the different Islamic countries. This project was in accordance with the spirit of ʿAbbāsid policy, and Mālik b. Anas was chosen because he represented Medina, where the principles of Islamic law had been determined, and because it is almost certain that, at the time that this proposal was put to him, his doctrine had already been diffused and circulated by his pupils in the Mag͟hrib and in Spain.

1. DOCTRINE

The sources. The originality of the teaching of Mālik consists in the fact that he introduced in the *Kitāb al-Muwaṭṭaʾ* the recognition of *ʿamal,* i.e. the effective and unanimous practice of Medina, which he established as an organised judicial system. The *Muwaṭṭaʾ* is the earliest Islamic judicial work which has survived to the present day; a treatise of *fiḳh* based on *ḥadīt͟h* which plays the role of judicial argument, it has two objects in view: religious worship (*ʿibādāt*) and general law (*muʿāmalāt*). In its final edition, the *Muwaṭṭaʾ* contains approximately a hundred *ḥadīt͟hs*, 222 *mursals*, 613 *mawḳūfs* [see ḤADĪTH] and 285 opinions of *Tābiʿūn.* All the individuals mentioned are Medinans or scholars who had frequented Mecca or Medina. The bulk of the traditions are traced back to ʿAbd Allāh b. ʿUmar. The success enjoyed by the *Muwaṭṭaʾ* is owed to the fact that it represented the moderate view then holding sway in Medina and that, without being a particularly original work, it bore witness to the judicial level attained by the consensus of opinion in Medina (for an analysis of the *Muwaṭṭaʾ*, see A. Békir, *Histoire de l'école mālikite.*) The *Muwaṭṭaʾ* is thus a code of legislation according to a description of law, statute and dogma as practised according to the consensus and the tradition (*sunna*) of Medina, augmented by personal remarks of Mālik. On the recensions of the *Muwaṭṭaʾ*, see MĀLIK B. ANAS, and al-Suyūṭī, *Tazyīn al-mamālik bi-manāḳib sayyidinā al-Imām Mālik,* where there is a list of authors who have passed on a *riwāya* of the work.

The other principal source for the study of the doctrine of Mālik is intitled *al-Mudawwana al-kubrā.* It is the work of the Ḳayrawānī Saḥnūn (160-240/776-854 [*q.v.*]), and is a collection of Mālikī *fiḳh* which contains the corrections and responses made to Saḥnūn by Ibn al-Ḳāsim al-ʿUtāḳī (d. 191/806), a disciple of Mālik, according to the opinions of Mālik himself, of his contemporaries and his masters in tradition including al-Zuhrī (d. 124/740), Nāfiʿ (d. 116/734) and Rabīʿat al-Raʾy. The *Mudawwana* was also called the *Muk͟htaliṭa*, since it completed and improved upon, through the diversity of subjects considered, the *Asadiyya* of Ibn al-Furāt (d. 213/828), a work based on the teaching of Mālik and of the Ḥanafīs of ʿIrāḳ. The practical interest of the *Mudawwana* consists in the fact that it illustrates the connections between religion and trade and that it describes mercantile practices (documentation, bills of exchange and all kinds of commercial transactions). See G. H. Bousquet, *La Mudawwana. Index* (*avec la table générale des matières*), in *Arabica,* xvii/2 (1970), 113-50.

This work gave rise to a whole literature of commentaries of which the principal examples will be indicated here, and some of which have been translated. The first to be mentioned are the works of Ibn Abī Zayd al-Ḳayrawānī (d. 386/996): the *Ik͟htiṣār al-Mudawwana* and the *Kitāb al-Nawādir wa 'l-ziyādāt ʿalā 'l-Mudawwana,* a summary of the precepts of the school, supplemented by a study of cases not foreseen by Saḥnūn. Ibn Abī Zayd al-Ḳayrawānī is also the author of a famous *Risāla,* a précis of Mālikī law, translated by L. Bercher, Algiers 1952 (see H. R. Idris, *Note sur l'identification du dédicataire de la Risâla d'Ibn Abî Zaid al-Qairâwânî,* in *CT,* i [1953], 63-8). Another work which enjoyed great success in North Africa is the *Tahd͟hīb al-Mudawwana,* Tunis ms. Zaytūna, of Abū Saʿīd al-Bard͟haʿī (d. 400/1009). In imitation of Saḥnūn, the Andalusian Ibn Ḥabīb (d. 238/845) composed *al-Wāḍiḥa* after a visit to Egypt as the guest of Ibn al-Ḳāsim. One of his pupils, al-ʿUtbī (d. 255/869), made an abridged version of it entitled *al-ʿUtbiyya.* The Mudawwana also inspired Ibn Ḥād͟jib (d. 646/1248) who restated the precepts of the Mālikī school in his *Muk͟htaṣar fi 'l-furūʿ.* K͟halīl b. Isḥāḳ (d. 776/1374 [*q.v.*]) is the author of a *Muk͟htaṣar* of this work. It has been translated into French by Perron (*Précis de jurisprudence musulmane,* 2nd éd., Paris 1877); into Italian by Guidi and Santillana in 1919, and again into French by G. H. Bousquet (*Abrégé de la loi musulmane selon le rite de l'Imâm Mâlik,* Algiers-Paris 1956-63), to say nothing of partial translations.

This *Mukhtaṣar* of Khalīl, a basic text of Mālikī law, is in its turn barely usable without the aid of commentaries, of which the best known are:
—*al-Sharḥ ʿalā Mukhtaṣar Khalīl* of al-Zurḳānī (d. 1099/1687, published in Cairo in 1307 with a commentary by al-Bannānī (a version highly valued in the Orient);
—*al-Sharḥ al-ṣaghīr* of Dardīr (d. 1201/1786), Būlāḳ 1289, and, of the same author;
—*al-Sharḥ al-kabīr,* Būlāḳ 1295, with glosses by al-Dasūḳī;
—*Mukhtaṣar Khalīl* of al-Khirshī, with glosses by al-ʿAdawī, Būlāḳ 1316, vols, iv and v;
—*al-Djuzʾ al-awwāl min Kitāb Mawāhib al-Djalīl li-sharḥ Mukhtaṣar Sīdī Khalīl* of al-Mawwāḳ, vols. iii and iv; Abu 'l-Walīd al-Bādjī (d. 474/1081), a celebrated polemicist who composed a *Mukhtaṣar fī masāʾil al-Mudawwana* is also the author of the *Muntaḳā sharḥ al-Muwaṭṭaʾ,* published in Cairo in 1312.

Transmission of the doctrine. According to Ibn Khaldūn (*Muḳaddima,* Cairo n.d.), until the 5th/11th century the Mālikī school was divided into three tendencies (*ṭuruḳ*): Kayrawānī, Andalusian and eastern, the last-named including the ʿIrāḳī, Egyptian and Alexandrian transmissions. The following are the lines of transmission from Mālik onwards:

Ḳayrawānī *sanad:* Ibn al-Ḳāsim (d. 191/806), Saḥnūn (d. 240/854), who also inherited from Asad b. al-Furāt (d. 213/828) and, by this indirect means, from the disciples of Abū Ḥanīfa. After Saḥnūn, there are the commentaries of Abū Zayd al-Ḳayrāwānī (d. 386/996), of al-Bardhaʿī (d. 400/1009), of Ibn Yūnus (d. 451/1059), of Ibn Muḥriz (d. 450/1058), of al-Tūnisī (d. 443/1051) and of al-Lakhmī (d. 478/1085). This line of transmission established the reputation of the *Mudawwana* and of its commentaries for the Maghrib.

Andalusian *sanad*: Yaḥyā b. Yaḥyā al-Laythī (d. 234/848), al-Aṣbagh (d. 224/838), Ibn al-Mādjishūn (d. 214/829), al-Muṭarrif (d. 220/835), Ibn al-Ḳāsim (d. 191/806) who transmitted to Ibn al-Ḥabīb (d. 238/845) and in his turn to al-ʿUtbī (d. 255/869). The Andalusian transmission for its part accords the greatest respect to the *ʿUtbiyya,* of which the best known commentary is the *Bayān* of Ibn Rushd (d. 520/1126 [*q.v.*]).

ʿIrāḳi *sanad*: Ḳāḍī Ismāʿīl (d. 246/860), Ibn Khuwayzmindād, Ibn al-Labbān and al-Abḥarī (d. 375/985) who transmitted to ʿAbd al-Wahhāb (d. 421/1030). The last-named, who settled in Egypt, was to influence directly and profoundly the Egyptian *sanad.*

Egyptian *sanad*: Ibn ʿAbd al-Hakam (d. 214/829), Ibn al-Ḳāsim (d. 191/806) and Ashhab (d. 204/819); al-Ḥārith b. Miskīn (d. 250/864) inherited from both these last two. The following may be regarded as the most significant links in this chain of transmission: Ibn al-Rashīḳ (d. 632/1234) and Ibn al-Ḥādjib (d. 646/1248), the latter inheriting via the Alexandrian *sanad* from Ibn ʿInān (d. 541/1146), Ibn ʿAṭāʾ Allāh (d. 612/1215) and Ibn ʿAwf (d. 581/1185), and transmitting to al-Ḳarāfī (d. 684/1285). The connection between eastern and Andalusian transmission was established in the 6th/12th century with Abū Bakr al-Ṭurṭushī (d. 520/1126), who travelled to Egypt and secured employment as a teacher in Alexandria (see V. Lagardère, *L'unificateur du malikisme oriental et occidental à Alexandrie: Abū Bakr al-Ṭurṭushī,* in *ROMM,* i [1981]). This connection with the Egyptian school, already much influence by the ʿIrāḳi transmission in the person of the *ḳāḍī* ʿAbd al-Wahhāb, was to have as its consequence the abandonment, in the 7th/13th century, of the *Mudawwana* and of the *ʿUtbiyya* in favour of the *Mukhtaṣar fī 'l-furūʿ* of Ibn al-Ḥādjib (d. 646/1248). These two basic works of Mālikī doctrine, which had led to the production of a significant corpus of judicial writing, continued to be influential for some time after the disappearance of Cordova and Ḳayrawān as centres of learning, but lost their effective role at the end of the 8th/14th century.

Principles and judicial theory. Like other schools of Sunnī Islam, Mālikism bases its doctrine on the Ḳurʾān, the *Sunna* and *idjmāʿ* [*q.v.*]; nevertheless, divergencies of greater or lesser significance exist in regard to the other rites. While there is unanimity surrounding the Holy Book, a primary difference appears concerning the *Sunna.* The tradition of the Prophet Muḥammad and that of the Companions constitute the *Sunna* according to Mālik, who excludes from it the tradition of ʿAlī, which other schools incorporate (in fact, in refusing to choose between ʿAlī and ʿUthmān, Mālik would have recognised the legitimacy of their caliphate, but, according to another trend of opinion, he would have agreed as to the superiority of ʿUthmān, which would seem more likely in view of the fact that his school also flourished at Baṣra in an ʿUthmānī milieu).

To *idjmāʿ,* universal consensus of the Muslims, there is added the Medinan *idjmāʿ* which proceeds from the *ʿamal,* the effective practice of Medina. It can even result that this consensus prevails over *ḥadīth,* Medinan opinion being considered to testify to the acts of the Prophet. For Mālik, *ḥadīth* is thus not the most important source, and personal judgment, *raʾy,* is to be used in parallel, when *idjmāʿ* cannot provide the answer to a question and only if this procedure does not injure the public good (*maṣlaḥa*). Mālik is sometimes reproached for making too much use of this method. *Ḳiyās* [*q.v.*], reasoning by analogy, which had many opponents among the Sunnīs, is applied by the Mālikīs in cases of *idjmāʿ al-umma.*

Mālikism and schismatics. It was the intolerance of Mālik towards schismatics which made his school so successful. The hostility of his teaching towards the Ḳadariyya [*q.v.*] and the Khāridjīs is based on the fact that they are considered to be disturbers of public order and agents of corruption (*fasād*). Khāridjīs must make an act of repentance (*tawba*); if they refuse, they are condemned to capital punishment. For the *zindīḳ* [*q.v.*], even repentance is not allowed; he is immediately condemned to death for the crime of apostasy. The temporal authorities, notably the ʿAbbāsid caliphate, often had recourse to a Mālikī *ḳāḍī* to judge heretics, public agitators or those considered as such. Thus it was the Mālikī Grand *Ḳāḍī* of Baghdād, Abu ʿUmar Ibn Yūsuf, who tried and condemned to death al-Ḥallādj [*q.v.*] in 319/922. Two Shīʿī extremists of the Middle Ages are known to have perished in similar circumstances: Ḥasan b. Muḥammad al-Sakākīnī, executed at Damascus in 744/1342, and ʿAlī b. al-Ḥasan al-Ḥalabī, executed in 755/1354.

Mālikism and mysticism. There is *a priori* no place for mysticism in the school of Mālik. A *ḥadīth* of the Prophet forbids monasticism, which is even regarded as *bidʿa.* Nevertheless, under the impulse of piety an ascetic movement was established, and until the 2nd/8th century it attracted little attention. But, stimulated by the intense intellectual activity which developed in the Orient from the end of this century, mysticism spread widely and attained proportions which were disturbing for the prevailing orthodoxy. In the Maghrib, in spite of *fatwās* promulgated to condemn and ban the works of al-Ghazālī (d. 505/1111), Ṣūfism gained ground with the Almoravids and even flourished under the Almohads. In al-Andalus, where the milieu was particularly intolerant, the mystical movement enjoyed a brief period of ascendancy with Ibn Masarra (d. 319/931) [*q.v.*] and his disciples (see V. Lagardère, *La Ṭarīqa et la révolte des Murīdūn en 539H/1144 en Andalus*, in *ROMM*, i [1983]).

The following may be named among the Mālikī mystics: Abu 'l-Ḳāsim al-Shiblī (d. Baghdād, 334/945), the Ifrīḳiyan Abū ʿUthmān Ibn Sallāmī al-Maghribī (d. Nīsābūr, 373/983). After al-Ghazālī, mysticism triumphed with the Ḥanbalī ʿAbd al-Ḳādir al-Djīlī (d. 561/1166), whose school spread widely both in the East and the West. Abū Madyān al-Andalusī diffused his doctrine in the Maghrib, and one of his pupils was ʿAbd al-Salām b. Mashīsh (d. 624/1227), the teacher of al-Shādhilī (d. 656/1258), who was educated in Ifrīḳiya and in Egypt and had numerous disciples in Syria and the Ḥidjāz. From this time onwards, there were many Ṣūfis among the Mālikīs. In Syria, around Ibn al-ʿArabī (d. 638/1240), the greatest mystic of Muslim Spain, a complete organisation was established and *zāwiya*s were built for his followers. Among known Mālikī Ṣūfis, also worthy of mention are Muhammad b. Aḥmad al-Bisāṭī (d. 842/1438), Mālikī *ḳāḍī* and *shaykh* of the Ṣūfīs of Cairo, and ʿAlī b. Muḥammad al-Ḳurashī (d. Alexandria, 808/1405). Another who should be mentioned is a famous Egyptian Ṣūfi who introduced gnosis (*maʿrifa*) into his doctrine, Dhu 'l-Nun al-Miṣrī; a Mālikī, he is the author of a version of the *Muwaṭṭaʾ*.

Works of Ṭabaḳāt, *other sources for the knowledge of Mālikism and of its disciples.* Although the first text of Mālikī *ṭabaḳāt* is owed to the pen of Ibn Abī Dalīm (d. 351/962), under the title of *Kitāb al-Ṭabaḳāt fī man yarwī ʿan Mālik wa-atbāʿihim min ahl al-amṣār,* it is not this that is regarded by posterity as a fundamental work, both of *ṭabaḳāt* and of history of the doctrine, but the second of the genre in chronological order, that of the *ḳāḍī* ʿIyāḍ (d. 544/1149 [*q.v.*]), which bore the title *Tartīb al-madārik wa-taḳrīb al-masālik.* This source is particularly important for the reason that, in addition to the biographies of Eastern and Western Mālikīs, it contains a lengthy study of the life of Mālik, his work, the eminence of his doctrine and the causes of its expansion before dealing with the expansion itself. The next text, which contains the biographies of Mālikīs who lived after the time of ʿIyāḍ until the end of the 8th/14th century, is the work of the Andalusian Ibn Farḥūn (d. 799/1396) and is intitled *al-Dībādj al-mudhhab fī maʿrifat aʿyān ʿulamāʾ al-madhhab.*

The Shāfiʿi al-Sakhāwī (d. 780/1378) is the author of *Ṭabaḳāt mālikiyya* which is composed on the basis of some twenty sources mentioned in the conclusion. Two further works of *ṭabaḳāt* directly inspired by the *Dībādj* of Ibn Farḥūn should be noted: *Nayl al-ibtihādj bi-taṭrīz al-Dībādj* of Aḥmad Bābā (d. 1032/1622 [*q.v.*]), printed in the margins of the *Dībādj,* and the *Tawshīḥ al-Dībādj* of al-Ḳarāfī (d. 1008/1600). The last text of Mālikī *ṭabaḳāt* is that of the Tunisian Muḥammad Makhlūf who lived at the beginning of the 20th century; it is intitled *Shadjarat al-nūr al-zākiyya fī ṭabaḳāt al-Mālikiyya* and was published in Cairo in 1931. This is the most complete source, since it relates the biographies of the Prophet, of the Companions, of the *tābiʿūn,* then those of the eminent *fuḳahāʾ* of the Ḥidjāz, of ʿIrāḳ, of Egypt, of the Maghrib and of Andalusia, concluding with those of the masters who instructed the author in 1922.

2. The expansion of Mālikism

The Orient. In general, in the East as in the West, it was the disciples of Mālik who took upon themselves the task of spreading his doctrine in his lifetime. In the *Tartīb al-madārik,* the *ḳāḍī* ʿIyāḍ informs us that it was in Egypt, at Alexandria, that the second centre of Mālikism after Medina was established, through the efforts of ʿUthmān b. ʿAbd al-Ḥakam al-Djudhāmī (d. 163/779), Saʿīd b. ʿAbd Allāh al-Maʿāfirī who introduced Mālikism to Alexandria, and Ibn al-Ḳāsim al-ʿUtāḳī who lived for a long time at Medina as an intimate of Mālik and was the intermediary through whom the doctrine gained sway in the Maghrib and Muslim Spain. On his death in 191/806, ʿAbd Allāh b. Wahb (d. 197/812) succeeded him as leader of the Mālikīs of Egypt. These eminent *fuḳahāʾ* were successful in definitively implanting Mālikism in this country in spite of the difficulties caused by living in proximity with Shāfiʿism which was ultimately to supplant it; today, this school is dominant in Egypt, but Mālikism remains active in the Ṣaʿīd.

In his *Rafʿ al-iṣr ʿan ḳuḍāt Miṣr*, Cairo 1957, Ibn Ḥadjar al-ʿAsḳalānī (d. 852/1449) provides a list of the Mālikī *ḳāḍīs* of Egypt from the origin of the post until the middle of the 9th/15th century. Al-Ḳalḳashandī, in the *Ṣubḥ al-aʿshā*, xii, explains how the Mālikīs were addressed under the Mamlūks. For the modern period, see also G. Delanoue, *Moralistes et politiques musulmans dans l'Egypte du XIX siècle (1798-1882),* Cairo 1982.

In ʿIrāḳ, it was ʿAbd al-Raḥmān al-Kaʿnabī (d. 221/835), of Medinan origin, who spread the doctrine of Mālik in the region of Baṣra. One of the most eminent figures of the ʿIrāḳī school is the *ḳāḍī* Ismāʿīl b. Isḥāḳ who, by his judical and political activities, represents the Mālikī authority *par excellence* of his period. Other figures, no less renowned, including Abū Bakr al-Bāḳillānī or al-Abharī, continued the enterprise and spread the doctrine in Khurāsān and Syria. But the crises provoked by the Shāfiʿī movement at the beginning of the 5th/11th century led to the eviction of Mālikism from ʿIrāḳ. In Khurāsān, the doctrine did not long resist the competition of the new ideologies, and in Syria, after promising beginnings, Mālikism could not succeed in supplanting the doctrine of al-Awzāʿī and did not survive in that country.

In the Yemen, it stood firm for more than a century, but was ultimately ousted by Shāfiʿism.

At Medina, after the demise of the first disciples of the *Imām* Mālik, all trace of the school is lost. Nevertheless, some Mālikī scholars are attested before the time of the arrival of the Fāṭimids, notably ʿAbd al-ʿAzīz b. Abī Ḥāzim, Muḥammad b. Dīnār al-Djuhaynī (d. 182/798) and ʿAbd al-Malik al-Mādjishūn (d. 213/828). It was not until the triumph of Sunnism in the 8th/14th century that Mālikism returned to Medina (see A. Békir, *op. cit.*).

In the present day, the Shāfiʿī rite holds sway in the Ḥidjāz, but Mālikī nuclei exist in the cities. In the contemporary United Arab Emirates, there exists a small Mālikī community represented by a section of the Ḥinawī clan.

The Muslim West. North Africa. It was Asad Ibn al-Furāt who introduced Mālikism into North Africa and Saḥnūn who established it as a formal sect. A Mālikism of extreme severity then dominated the Maghrib, in particular Ifrīḳiya under the Aghlabid dynasty, and this continued until the arrival of the Fāṭimids (298/910), which marked the triumph of Shīʿism. A vigorous resistance was directed against the latter by the Mālikī scholars of Ḳayrawān, but it was not until 440/1048 that Mālikism was definitively adopted in the Maghrib following the expulsion of the Fāṭimids from Ifrīḳiya.

However, the intransigent doctrine which became the norm in the Maghrib had the effect of suppressing intellectual effort and religious feeling. In fact, the study of the Ḳurʾān and of *ḥadīth*, as well as *idjtihād* (personal effort at interpretation) were abandoned in favour of the manuals of applied *fiḳh* (*furūʿ*). The Almoravid sovereigns gave their support to these methods and encouraged the *fuḳahāʾ* to accord supreme importance to the study of manuals of *furūʿ*. This abandonment of recourse to the Ḳurʾān and the *Sunna* is denounced by al-Ghazālī in the *Iḥyāʾ ʿulūm al-dīn,* which shows that Mālikism as practised by its disciples no longer had any connection with the religion as it had developed. He also condemns the important role played by the *fuḳahāʾ* in political life. Ibn Tūmart [*q.v.*] went even further than al-Ghazālī. Inspired by his principles, he declared war on the Almoravids, appointed himself judge of morals, appropriated the title of *Mahdī* and, by violent means, restored true orthodoxy. He banned the works of *furūʿ*, and established as the basis of his doctrine elements of the purest orthodoxy, sc. Ḳurʾān, *Sunna* and consensus of the *umma.* The doctrine of Ibn Tūmart was to be the impulse for an important mystical movement throughout the whole of the Maghrib, and in spite of the collapse of the Almohad empire, and thus of its political support, it was to imprint upon victorious Mālikism an indelible mark of austerity (segregation of the sexes, fasting, dietary prohibitions, among other elements characteristic of Maghribi austerity).

It is, on the one hand, with the Ḥafṣid civilisation in Ifrīḳiya, under the influence of the judicial schools of Tunis, Bougie and Ḳayrawān, and of scholars of the calibre of Ibn ʿArafa (d. 804/1401), and on the other, with the Marīnid civilisation in the Western Maghrib, and the famous *madrasas* of Fās and Tlemcen, that the renaissance of Mālikism in North Africa is observed. If, today, Maghribī Islam seems particularly rigorous, this is due to Mālikism. In fact, practice and doctrine have remained totally unchanged since the middle of the 7th/13th century, immediately after the fall of the Almohads. The success of Mālikism in North Africa may be explained by reference to the theory of Ibn Khaldūn (d. 808/1406) according to whom Bedouin culture accounts for the predominance of this school in the Muslim West. Effectively, Mālikism is loyal to the Tradition and hostile to rational explanations; it is perfectly suited to the Berber mentality of the Maghribīs who refuse to accept any idea unless it can be traced back to a tradition. It is for this reason that Maghribī Mālikism seems rigid in comparison to that of the East, which does not reject effort at interpretation (*idjtihād*). In contemporary North Africa, Mālikism is predominant in Morocco, Algeria, Tunisia and Libya; it coexists with some Ibāḍī and Ḥanafī centres in the three last-named countries. It is exclusive in Mauritania where it has been the object, over the centuries, of an interesting adaptation (see Ould Bah, *Littérature juridique*).

Muslim Spain. It was at the end of the 2nd/8th century that Mālikism was introduced into Muslim Spain where it superseded the Syrian doctrine of al-Awzāʿī. Those who brought to the country the principles of the *Imām* of Medina were Andalusian scholars, initiated by Mālik himself or by his pupils. The best known among them are Ziyād b. ʿAbd al-Ḥakam, Yaḥyā b. Yaḥyā al-Laythi, Yaḥyā b. Muḍar and ʿĪsā b. Dīnār. This class of scholars was the nucleus of a clerical aristocracy which, throughout the duration of the Umayyad dynasty, exercised real power in the state and made Mālikism the sole official rite of al-Andalus. This state of affairs, which lasted for nearly two centuries, coincided with the period of the transmitters of Mālik and of the Medinan tradition, of the commentaries on the *Muwaṭṭaʾ* and compilations of *responsa.* Andalusian Mālikism was characterised then by an intransigent austerity, exclusively attached to the study of manuals of jurisprudence (*furūʿ*), forsaking, in the manner of its Maghribī neighbour, the study of *ḥadīth*s and proscribing all effort at personal reflection (*idjtihād*).

The fall of the Umayyad caliphate, then the emergence of regional principalities (*mulūk al-ṭawāʾif*) in the 5th/11th century, and later, the domination of the Almohads, put an end to the supremacy of jurisprudence. Political decentralisation, stimulated, at an early stage, a socio-cultural renewal with individuals including Ibn ʿAbd al-Barr (d. 463/1070), al-Bādjī (d. 474/1081) and Ibn Ḥazm (d. 456/1063); with the last-named, a Ẓāhirī jurist who opposed the Mālikī doctrine, *ḥadīth,* the *uṣūl al-fiḳh* and polemics of judicial methodology (*djadal*) became the order of the day (see in this context, the edition of *al-Minhādj fī tartīb al-ḥidjadj* of Bādjī, edited by A. M. Turki, Paris 1978, and Turki, *Polémique entre Ibn Ḥazm et Bāǧī sur les principes de la loi musulmane,* Algiers 1976).

This opening towards the exterior, towards other systems of thought, is given formal expression in the work of Ibn Rushd (d. 595/1198), especially with the *Bidāyat al-mudjtahid wa-nihāyat al-muḳtaṣid* (ed. Cairo 1329). Nevertheless, the class of the *fuḳahāʾ* retained a dominant position until the last days of the Andalusian principalities and in particular that of Granada, by means of individuals like Ibn Lubb and Muḥammad al-Saraḳusṭī in the 8th/14th and 9th/15th centuries, and through them, Mālikism, as the compilations of biographies testify.

Africa, Bilād al-Sūdān. Islam was propagated at an early stage in the Sudan, among the Nūba of the Nile Valley. But it was not until the 10th/16th century that it was introduced to Dār Fūr by Arab tribes. The progress of Islam became most definitive towards the end of the 13th/19th century under the influence of the *Mahdī* Muḥammad Aḥmad. At the present time, the majority of the Muslims of the Sudan are of the Mālikī rite and use the *Mukhtaṣar* of Khalīl. Islam spread to Kanem in the 5th/11th century and was firmly established around Lake Chad from the 9th/15th century onwards.

In West Africa, Mālikism was introduced by the Almoravid conquest of the Takrūr (Fūta Tōro) among tribes which were to a greater or lesser extent vassals of Ghāna. At the end of the 5th/11th century, Islamisation gained sway in the Gold Coast. Timbuktu became the Islamic metropolis of the western Sudan in the 8th/14th century, and its influence lasted until the conquest of Songhay by Morocco in 1000/1591. It was especially among political functionaries and senior officials that the Muslim faith was spread. It was not until the 12th/18th and 13th/19th centuries that theocratic monarchies were established in Fūta Djallon and Fūta Tōro, following the victories of the Toucouleur Muslims over the Peuls who were forcibly converted. The Touçouleur Usmānu Fōdjo preached *djihād* and founded the empire of Sokoto in 1207/1802. Muslim law was introduced to Masīna by the Peul Sēku Ḥamadu Bari in 1225/1810 and, in 1236/1820, the Toucouleur al-Ḥādjdj ʿUmar had himself appointed *khalīfa tidjānī* for the Sudan. A vast empire was established in which the Muslim faith was the state religion. At the present time, there are Mālikī Muslims in the Black African states of Senegal, Mali, Niger, Togo, Chad and Nigeria.

Bibliography: I. For the general study of

Mālikī doctrine, law and juridical applications: Mālik b. Anas, *Kitāb al-Muwaṭṭaʾ*, Cairo 1951; Saḥnūn, *al-Mudawwana al-kubrā*, Cairo 1905; Ḳarāfī, *Tanḳīḥ al-fuṣūl fī l-uṣūl*, Tunis 1921; idem, *Kitāb al-Furūḳ*, Cairo 1925; ʿAbd al-Wahhāb al-Bag̲h̲dādī, *Kitāb al-Is̲h̲rāf ʿalā masāʾil al-k̲h̲ilāf*, Tunis n.d.; ʿIyāḍ, *Tartīb al-Madārik wa-takrīb al-masālik li-maʿrifat aʿlām mad̲h̲hab Mālik*, ed. A. Békir, Beirut 1965; idem, *al-Ilmāʿ ilā maʿrifat usūl al-riwāya wa-takyīd al-samāʿ*, ed. A. Saḳḳar, Cairo 1978; Ibn D̲j̲uzay, *al-Ḳawānīn al-fiḳhiyya*, Tunis 1925; S̲h̲āʿibī, *al-Muwāfaḳāt fī uṣūl al-s̲h̲arīʿa*, Cairo n.d.; Wans̲h̲arīsī, *al-Miʿyār al-mug̲h̲rib*, ed. E. Amar, Paris 1908; al-Kurdī al-Irbilī, *Hidāyat al-ṭālibīn li-aḥkām al-dīn*, Cairo 1913; Ibn ʿĀsim, *al-ʿĀṣimiyya*, or *Tuḥfat al-ḥukkām fī nukat al-ʿuḳūd wa-aḥkām*, tr. Houdas and Martel, Algiers 1893; Nubāhī, *Kitāb al-Marḳaba al-ʿulyā*, Cairo 1948; E. Fagnan, *Le D̲j̲ihād ou guerre sainte selon l'école mālikite*, Algiers 1908; F. Peltier, *Le livre des ventes du Muwaṭṭaʾ de Mālik Ibn Anas*, Algiers 1911; R. Brunschvig, *Le livre de l'Ordre et de la Défense d'al-Muzānī*, Damascus 1945-6; idem, *De la filiation maternelle en droit musulman*, in *SI*, ix (1958), 49-59; idem, *Corps certain et chose de genre dans l'obligation en droit musulman*, in *ibid.*, xxix (1969), 83-102; idem, *Variations sur le thème du doute dans le fiqh*, in *Stud. Orient.... G. Levi Della Vida*, i, Rome 1956, 61-82 (repr. in *Etudes d'Islamologie*, Paris 1976, ii, 133-54); idem, *Polémiques médiévales autour du rite de Mālik*, in *al-And.*, xv/2 (1950), 377-435 (repr. in *Et. d'Isl.*, ii, 65-101); idem, *Averroès juriste*, in *Et. d'Or. ... Lévi-Provençal*, Paris 1962, i, 35-68; G. H. Bousquet, *Précis élémentaire de droit musulman*, Algiers 1935; idem, *Une petite erreur de Juynboll et de Perron à propos d'une institution peu connue*, in *Mélanges William Marçais*, Paris 1950, 48-53; Y. Linant de Bellefonds, *Un problème de sociologie juridique: les terres «communes» en pays d'Islam*, in *SI*, x (1959), 111-36; idem, *Traité de droit musulman comparé*, Paris 1973; E. Tyan, *La procédure du «défaut» en droit musulman*, in *SI*, vii (1957), 115-33; idem, *Méthodologie et source du droit en Islam*, in *SI*, x (1959), 79-109; idem, *L'organisation judiciaire en pays d'Islam*, Beirut 1960; idem, *L'autorité de la chose jugée en droit musulman*, in *SI*, xvii (1962), 81-90; J. Schacht, *Problems of modern Islamic legislation*, in *SI*, xii (1960), 99-129; idem, *On Abū Muṣʿab and his «Mujtaṣar»*, in *al-And.*, xxx/1 (1965), 1-14, and *Further on Abū Muṣʿab and his «Mujtaṣar»*, in *ibid.*, xxx/2; idem, *Origins of Muhammadan jurisprudence*, Oxford 1950 (Fr. tr. J. and F. Arin, *Esquisse d'une histoire du droit musulman*, Paris 1953); idem, *Sur la transmission de la doctrine dans les écoles juridiques de l'Islam*, in *AIEO Alger*, x (1952), 399-419; idem, *An introduction to Islamic law*, Oxford 1964 (Fr. tr. P. Kempf et A. M. Turki, Paris 1983); A. Békir, *Histoire de l'école mālikite en Orient jusqu'à la fin du Moyen Age*, Tunis 1962; A. Demeerseman, *Recherches tunisiennes sur le mālikisme*, in *IBLA* (1963); M. Abu Zahra, *Mālik. sa vie, son époque, sa théologie*, Cairo 1952; J. Lapanne-Joinville, *La filiation maternelle naturelle en droit musulman mālikite*, in *Revue marocaine de droit*, 1952; J. Chelhod, *Le sacrifice chez les Arabes*, Paris 1955; J. Sublet, *Deux commentaires homonymes des deux Muhtaṣar-s d'Ibn al-Ḥāğib*, in *Bull. de l'IRHT*, xiii (1964-5), 95-9; Ch. Chehata, *Logique juridique en droit musulman*, in *SI*, xxiii (1965), 5-25; A. Ben Abdallah, *Lexique juridique du rite mālikite, arabe-français*, Rabat 1965; H. Laoust, *Les schismes dans l'Islam*, Paris 1965; V. Berger-Vachon, *Le ribā*, in *Normes et valeurs de l'Islam contemporain*, Paris 1966; M. Bernand-Baladi, *L'id̲j̲māʿ, critère de validité juridique*, in *ibid.*; A. Turki, *Situation du «tributaire» qui insulte l'Islam*, in *SI*, xxx, (1969), 39-72; idem, *Ibn Khaldūn, historien des sciences religieuses*, in *Théologiens et juristes de l'Espagne musulmane*, Paris 1980; L. Gardet and M. H. Anawati, *Introduction à la théologie musulmane*, Paris 1970; J.-P. Charnay, *Pluralisme normatif et ambiguïté dans le fiqh*, in *SI*, xix (1973), 65-82; W. M. Watt, *The closing of the door of iğtihād*, in *Orientalia Hispanica*, Leiden 1974, 675-8; I. Fierro, *El principo mālikī "Sadd al-d̲h̲arāʾiʿ"*, in *al-Qantara*, ii, Madrid 1981; M. Arcas Campoy, *al-Kitāb Muntajab al-Aḥkām de Ibn Abī Zamānīn*, (ed., tr. and study of the summary of Book 1, doctoral thesis, Madrid 1982); *Uṣūl al-fiqh*, Procs. of Colloquium at Princeton March 1983), to appear in *SI* (1984); J. S. Trimingham, *The Ṣūfī orders in Islām*, Oxford 1971. — II. For the expansion of the Mālikī doctrine and its application: Aḥmad Pas̲h̲a Taymūr, *Naẓra taʾrīk̲h̲iyya fī ḥudūt̲h̲ al-mad̲h̲āhib al-arbaʿa*, Cairo 1844; Bergsträsser, in *ZDMG* (1914), 410 ff.; I. Massignon, *Annuaire du monde musulman*^{4}, Paris 1955, index. Expansion in the Mag̲h̲rib: K̲h̲ushanī, *Kitāb Ṭabaḳāt ʿulamāʾ Ifrīḳiyā*, Cairo 1966; Mālikī, *Riyāḍ al-nufūs fī ṭabaḳāt ʿulamāʾ al-Ḳayrāwān wa-Ifrīkiya*, ed. Ḥ. Muʾnis, Cairo 1951; Dabbāg̲h̲ Ibn Nād̲j̲ī, *Maʿālim al-īmān fī maʿrifat ahl al-Ḳayrāwān*, Cairo 1968-72; ʿIyāḍ, *Biographies aghlabides extraites des Madārik*, ed. Talbi, Tunis 1968; I. Goldziher, *Introduction au Livre de Mohammed Ibn Toumert*, Algiers 1903; O. Pesle, *Le marriage chez les Mālikites d'Afrique du Nord*, in *Hespéris*, xxiv (1937); Snoussi, *Code du status personnel tunisien*, Tunis 1958; J. Roussier, *Dispositions nouvelles dans le statut successoral en droit tunisien*, in *SI*, xii (1969), 121-44; H. Monès, *Le Malékisme et l'échec des Fatimides en Ifriqya*, in *Et. d'Or. ... Lévi-Provençal*, Paris 1962, i, 197-220; M. Talbi, *Kairouan et le mālikisme espagnol*, in *ibid.*, i, 317-37; idem, *L'émirat aghlabide 184-286/800-909*, Paris 1966; idem, *Opérations bancaires en Ifrīqiya à l'époque d'al-Māzarī (453-536/1061-1141)*, in *Recherches d'Islamologie*, Louvain 1977; A. al-Fāsī, *Difāʿ ʿan al-s̲h̲arīʿa*, Rabat 1966; R. Brunschvig, *La Berbérie orientale sous les Ḥafṣides*, Paris 1940-7; idem, *Fiqh fâtimide et histoire de l'Ifrîqiya*, in *Mélanges d'histoire et d'archéologie de l'Occident musulman. Hommage à G. Marçais*, Algiers 1957, ii, 13-20; idem, *Justice religieuse et justice laïque dans la Tunisie des Deys et des Beys jusqu'au milieu du XIXe siècle*, in *SI*, xxiii (1965), 27-70; H. R. Idris, *Deux juristes kairouanais de l'époque zîrîde: Ibn Abî Zaid et al-Qâbisî*, in *AIEO Alger*, xii (1954), 122-98; idem, *Deux maîtres de l'école juridique kairouanaise sous les Zîrîdes (XI^{e}s.): Abû Bakr b. ʿAbd al-Raḥmân et Abû ʿImrân al-Fâsî*, in *ibid.*, xiii (1955), 30-60; idem, *Le crépuscule de l'école mâlikite kairouanaise (fin du XIe s.)*, in *CT*, iv, 1956; idem, *Une des phases de la lutte du mâlikisme contre le šīʿisme sous les Zîrîdes (XIe s.)*, in *ibid.*; idem, *Quelques juristes ifrîqiyens de la fin du Xe siècle*, in *RAfr.*, c/446-9 (1956), 349-73; idem, *L'école malikite de Mahdia: l'imām al-Māzarī (m. 536 H./1141)*, in *Et. ... Lévi-Provençal*, 153-63; idem, *Contribution à l'histoire de la vie religieuse en Ifrīqiya zīrīde (Xème-XIème siècles)*, in *Mélanges Louis Massignon*, Damascus 1957, ii, 327-59; idem, *La Berbérie orientale sous les Zîrîdes*, Paris 1962; idem, *L'aube du mālikisme ifrīqiyen*, in *SI*, xxxiii (1971); M. Bormans, *Status personnel et famille au Mag̲h̲reb de 1940 à nos jours*, Paris 1977. — Expansion en Espagne musulmane: J. López-Ortiz, *La recepción de la escuela malaquí en España*, in *Anuario de historia del derecho español*. Madrid 1931; E. Lévi-

Provençal, *Le malikisme andalou et les apports doctrinaux de l'Orient*, in *RIEEI*, i (1953), 159-71; idem, *Histoire de l'Espagne musulmane*, Paris 1953; P. Nwyia, *Ibn ʿAbbād de Ronda*, Beirut 1961; H. Menèz, *Le rôle des hommes de religion dans l'histoire de l'Espagne musulmane jusqu'à la fin du califat*, in *SI*, xx (1964), 47-88; H. R. Idris, *Réflexions sur le mālikisme sous les Umayyades d'Espagne*, in *Atti del III congresso di Studi Arabi i Islamici*, Ravello 1966; A. M. Turki, *La vénération pour Mālik et la physique du malikisme andalou*, in *Théologiens et juristes de l'Espagne musulmane*, Paris 1982; idem, *La place d'Averroès juriste dans l'histoire du malikisme et de l'Espagne musulmane, ibid.*; R. Arié, *L'Espagne musulmane au temps des Naṣrides* (1232-1492), Paris 1973; D. Urvoy, *Le monde des ulémas andalous du Vᵉ/XIᵉ s. au VIIᵉ/XIIIᵉ s.*, Geneva 1978. — Expansion en Afrique: J. Schacht, *Islam in northern Nigeria*, in *SI*, viii (1957), 123-46; J. S. Trimingham, *Islam in West Africa*, Oxford 1959; idem, *A history of Islām in West Africa*, Oxford 1962; M. Zouber, *Aḥmad Bābā de Tombouctou*, Paris 1977; J. Cuoq, *Recueil des sources arabes concernant l'Afrique occidentale du VIIIᵉ au XVIᵉ s.*, Paris 1975; idem, *Les musulmans en Afrique*, Paris 1975; V. Monteil, *L'Islam noir*, Paris 1980; Sidi Mohamed Mahibou et J. L. Triaud, *Voilà ce qui est arrivé, Bayān mā waqaʿa d'al-Ḥādjdj ʿUmar al-Fūtī*, Paris 1983; Mohamed El Mokhtar Ould Bah, *La littérature juridique et l'évolution du Mālikisme en Mauritanie*, Tunis 1981.

(N. Cottart)

MALINDI, a town on the Kenya coast in lat 4°N. It is first mentioned in literature by al-Idrīsi (*ca.* 1150); the Ma-in mentioned by Ou-yang Hsiu, *Hsin T'ang-shu, ca.* 1060, is more likely to have been situated in Somalia. Al-Idrīsi says that it was a town of hunters and fishermen, whose inhabitants owned and exploited iron mines. Iron was their greatest source of profit. The iron, however, as A. O. Thompson has shown, was not mined, but recoverable from seashore deposits. Al-Idrīsi also mentions Malindi as a centre of witchcraft, a view also confirmed by Abu 'l-Fidāʾ (1273-1331), who adds that it was the capital of the King of the Zandj; he is likewise aware of the exploitation of iron. Malindi was visited by the Chinese admiral Cheng Hô in the course of his fifth diplomatic and commercial voyage in the Indian Ocean. Otherwise, little is known of the town in the Middle Ages.

It was from Malindi that Vasco da Gama set off for India in 1498 under the guidance of the pilot Aḥmad b. Mādjid al-Nadjdjī [see IBN MĀDJID]. Da Gama had been cold-shouldered at Mombasa, but was well-received at Malindi, where the ruler had an ancient enmity against Mombasa. The town of Malindi, which in Swahili means "deep-water anchorages", lay in a bay and extended along the shore. A more detailed description is given by Duarte Barbosa in *ca.* 1517-18. The place was well laid out, with many storeyed houses with flat roofs. The people traded gold, ivory and wax, importing rice, millet and wheat from Cambay. It was visited briefly by St. Francis Xavier in 1542, when he had a conversation with a *ḳāḍī*, who would seem to have been a Shīʿī. He reported that the practice of Islam had greatly declined in recent years, and that, out of seventeen mosques, only three were in use. A later missionary, Fr. João dos Santos O.P., reported in 1609 that the whole coast from Mozambique to Lamu was Shīʿī.

The royal family of Malindi was of Shīrāzī descent, and possibly related to that of Kilwa [*q.v.*]. When the royal line of Mombasa failed in *ca.* 1590, the Portuguese donated Mombasa to the Malindi dynasty, which then reigned from Mombasa until 1632 [see MOMBASA]. In the 18th century the Malindi traders at Kilwa had as their chief an officer known as the Malindāni, who had virtually sovereign powers over them which even the Sultan of Kilwa could not overrule. After the move of the royal house to Mombasa, the town lost its importance. Captain Owen found it deserted in 1827. The modern seaside resort contains few Islamic antiquities: two ruined mosques, a cemetery, and a pillar tomb which is possibly near the site of the former royal palace.

Ten miles from Malindi to the south, and two miles inland, is the very remarkable Islamic site of Gedi, which was occupied from the 11th until the 17th century, when it was abandoned to nature. The outer wall encloses an area of about 45 acres, and may have contained a population of some 10,000. Within the inner wall are a palace, a Friday mosque and several other small mosques, numerous houses and what may have been a commercial centre. The place is not mentioned either in Arabic or Portuguese literature. Its proximity to Malindi, and the fact that it lies some two miles from the sea, suggests that, unlike other eastern African coastal sites, which were primarily trading centres, Gedi was, as it were, a country residence of the *sulṭāns* of Malindi, around which a small town had grown up. Three architectural features of the houses are of especial interest: the houscs are divided into two distinct compartments, presumably for a wife each; of these compartments one has a store especially designed for cowrie shells, the local currency; and the palace and houses have elaborately constructed water conduits, leading to internal ablutions and latrines.

Bibliography: J. Brodrick, S. J., *Saint Francis Xavier (1506-52)*, London 1952; J. J. L. Duyvendak, *China's discovery of Africa*, London 1949; G. S. P. Freeman-Grenville, *The French at Kilwa Island*, Oxford 1965; idem, *The East African coast: select documents* (contains relevant Arabic and Portuguese sources), 2nd edn., Oxford 1975; idem, *Shīʿī rulers at Kilwa*, in *Num. Chron.* (1978); P. S. Garlake, *The early Islamic architecture of the East African coast*, Nairobi 1966; J. S. Kirkman, *The Arab city of Gedi: excavations at the Great Mosque*, London 1954; idem, *Gedi: the palace*, The Hague 1963; João dos Santos, *Ethiopia oriental* (1609), Mello de Azevedo, Lisbon 1891; J. Strandes, *The Portuguese period in East Africa* (1899), tr. J. F. Wallwork, ed. J. S. Kirkman, 2nd edn., Nairobi 1968; S. A. Strong, *History of Kilwa*, in *JRAS* (1895); A. O. Thompson, *Geological survey of Kenya*, report no. 36, 1956; St. Francisci Xavieri, *Epistolae*, t.i. 20 Sept. 1542, ed. G. Schurhammer and J. Wicki, *Monumenta Historica Societatis Iesu*, lxvii, Rome 1944.

(G. S. P. Freeman-Grenville)

MĀLIYYE. In the Ottoman Empire and successor states. In the 19th and 20th centuries, this term has been used in Arabic and Turkish to refer to financial affairs and financial administration. In the Ottoman Empire, and in various of its successor states, the term has also acquired a more specific reference to the Ministry of Finance (*Māliyye Neẓāreti* under the empire; *Māliyye Wekāleti* or *bakanlığı* under the Turkish Republic; *Wizārat al-Māliyya* in the Arab states). The history of financial institutions in the Ottoman Empire and its successor states still awaits thorough research. In part, this fact is attributable to problems of the original sources, which remain largely inaccessible even for the empire (e.g., Çetin, 28-35, 42, 83, 128, 133-4, 135, 158-60; Sertoğlu, 62-7, 72,

74, 78-9, 85). In part, the challenge of studying the history of the financial institutions, or financial problems more generally, derives from the fact that the economic and fiscal problems of the Middle East cannot be fully understood as unique, local occurrences. Increasingly, as time passes, they have been manifestations of world-encompassing patterns of economic relationships that only become clear when seen in a comparative perspective, preferably one of global scope.

While it is essential to acknowledge this fact, a brief article can only be selective in coverage. Since much of the scholarship on economic and financial topics has concentrated on problems of particular interest to people outside the Islamic world, this discussion will concentrate on *māliyye* in the sense of institutions for financial administration. Even within that limit, it will focus on the Ministry of Finance of the Ottoman Empire and the Republic of Turkey. A concluding section will offer comments aimed at setting Ottoman and republican Turkish developments in a comparative perspective that encompasses other Islamic states.

1. The late Ottoman Empire. During the last quarter of the 18th century, the Ottoman financial agencies were still concentrated in a large building situated between Ṭop Ḳapï Palace and the Sublime Porte and referred to by terms such as *Bāb-ï Defterī*. These agencies were presided over by three officials known respectively as the *defterdār*s [*q.v.*] of the first, second, and third "divisions" (*defterdār-ï s͟hïḳḳ-ï ewwel, t͟hānī, t͟hālit͟h*). In the 18th century, the first *defterdār* functioned as the real head of the financial departments, and the other two as assistants to him. Different sources from the period show the *Bāb-ï Defterī* as including a slightly varying list of bureaux, numbering close to 30. In addition to records on the revenues and disbursements of the empire, these bureaux kept the muster rolls and pay records of various categories of military personnel and palace functionaries, as well as the records on the provisioning of the capital city and major fortresses. Other responsibilities of the offices of the *Bāb-ï Defterī* included processing the papers for appointments of Muslim religious functionaries, maintaining records on relations between the imperial government and the non-Muslim religious authorities of the empire, and disposing of the estates (*muk͟hallefāt*) of important officials, when these estates reverted to the sultan by death or expropriation. As was characteristic of Ottoman government agencies of the period, these responsibilities were parcelled out among the various bureaux in a way that reflected the effects of accretion over time, more than any effort at systematisation. At the head of each bureaux stood an official holding the rank of the scribal élite (*k͟hʷād͟jegān*). The potential for gradual change among the financial agencies, even before the beginning of serious efforts at innovative reform, was illustrated by the introduction, at the beginning of the reign of Selīm III, of a type of internal debt securities (*eshām*) and the creation of a new bureau to maintain the records on them (*Eshām Muḳāṭaʿasï Ḳalemi*). According to a source of *ca.* 1770-90 (Top Kapu Sarayı Arşivi D3208), the number of officals employed in the offices discussed here was about 650. This fact made the *Bāb-ï Defterī* the largest, though not the most influential, of the scribal agencies.

Eighteenth-century Ottoman financial practice displayed several traits of particular significance for later periods. One was the custom of assigning specific revenues to specific expenses and limiting the extent to which transfers could be made. This practice goes back to the beginnings of Islamic fiscal practice and is still found in many parts of the world, but is in contrast to the preferred modern practice, at least in the West, of pooling revenues in a unified budget (Heidborn, ii, 12-14). A second characteristic was particularly prominent among the Ottomans in the era of imperial decline: revenue collection by means of tax farms, either on an annual basis (*iltizām*) or for life (*mālikāne* [*q.v.*]; Issawi, *Turkey*, 343-7). A third practice, which helps to explain the reliance on tax farming, was that some of the most important revenues continued to be collected in kind.

The chief business of the offices of the *Bāb-ï Defterī* was to keep records of transactions organised on these bases. In furtherance of this, the staff included, in addition to the bureaux discussed above, an auctioneer (*mīrī dellāl bas͟hïsï*) to conduct auctions of tax farms, an *ʿālim* appointed with the title *mīrī kātibi* to hear cases arising between the financial department and revenue farmers or other individuals; and staffs of quasi-police officers (*bas͟h bāḳī ḳulï, k͟harād͟j bas͟h bāḳī ḳulï*) whose responsibility was to collect overdue revenues (d'Ohsson, iii, 375-9; Hammer, *Staats.*, ii, 145-69; Uzunçarşılı, 319-73).

In the late 18th century, the treasury was still located in Ṭop Ḳapï Palace. In fact, there were two treasuries. One was known as the outer treasury (*k͟hazīne-yi bīrūn, tas͟hra k͟hazīnesi*) or state treasury (*k͟hazīne-yi ʿāmire*). The other was known as the inner treasury (*k͟hazīne-yi enderūn, ič k͟hazīnesi*). The latter was supposed to be a reserve treasury, filled at least in part out of the surplus of the former and bound to aid the former in event of shortage. In addition, there were a number of so-called *k͟hazīne*s, including a "privy purse" (*d͟jeyb-i hümāyūn*) at the palace and a number of others located in specific government agencies [see K͟HAZĪNE]. These were little more than special funds or cashiers' offices for specific needs or departments (Deny, 119-20).

Substantial efforts at reform of Ottoman financial institutions began under Selīm III (1789-1807 [*q.v.*]) in conjunction with his programme of military reform. To finance his new military force, he created a "new receipts treasury" (*īrād-ï d͟jedīd k͟hazīnesi*), under the direction of the former *defterdār* of the "second division" (*s͟hïḳḳ-i t͟hānī*), and assigned a number of revenues to him. The new treasury survived until the end of Selīm's reign, when, like other reforms of his "new order" (*niẓām-ï d͟jedīd* [*q.v.*]), it was eliminated. Those of its revenue sources that were still productive were reassigned to the "treasury" of the Mint (*ḍarbk͟hāne-i ʿāmire k͟hazīnesi*), which was a branch of the inner or private treasury (Muṣṭafā Nūrī, iv, 113-4; Pakalın, *OTD*, ii, 79-80; Shaw, *Old and new*, 128-34). Selīm's reforms also included some efforts to limit fiscal exactions and to reorganise the state treasury (*ibid.*, 170, 174).

Under Maḥmūd II (1808-39 [*q.v.*]), financial reform resumed in the 1820s, at first, it appears, as a concomitant of efforts in other fields. For example, Maḥmūd assigned a number of Anatolian *sand͟jaḳs* to a kind of collection agents (*mütesellim*), rather than the normal type of provincial administrators (*wālī, mutaṣarrïf*). Such assignment of *mütesellims* was not new, but this time the revenues that would otherwise have gone to the *wālī* or *mutaṣarrïf* were diverted to Istanbul [see K͟HAZĪNE, IV, 1185]. Another of Maḥmūd's policies affected the *tïmar* [*q.v.*] system and the provincial cavalry (*sipāhīs* [*q.v.*]) who had traditionally benefited from it. In 1241/1825-6, Maḥmūd began re-assigning *tïmars* and *sipāhīs* to other types of military forces (D͟jewdet, *Taʾrīk͟h* xii, 143-4). In 1831, he attempted to abolish what remained of the *tīmar*-system and to carry out a land survey and census (Lewis, 90-2).

While the exact course of events is still not entirely clear, Maḥmūd's reforms had clearly extended by then into a direct reorganisation of financial offices. With the abolition of the Janissaries in 1826, the one of the offices of the *Bāb-i̊ Defterī* that had been responsible for maintaining records of that corps, that of the *yeñi-čeri kātibi*, went through a series of changes of name and function, emerging as a "military supervisorship" (*ʿaskerī neẓāreti*; Luṭfī, i, 132, 143; Pakalın, *Maliye*, iii, 22-3). By 1831, further change had produced at least two financial "supervisorships", a *maṣārīfāt neẓāreti*, responsible for military expenditures, and a *muḳāṭaʿāt neẓāreti*, responsible for other aspects of government finance. This nomenclature is somewhat confusing, since presumably the revenues assigned to both agencies were farmed out, although the term *muḳāṭāʿa* might be taken to indicate that this was true only of the second (Heidborn, ii, 37; Pakalın, *Maliye*, i, 10; idem, *OTD*, ii, 578). Over the next several years, there were a number of further reorganisations, a persistent feature, at least until 1838, being maintenance of one agency for military finance and another for government finance more generally (Hammer, *Histoire*, xvii, 182; Luṭfī, iv, 111). In 1250/1834-5, for example, we find a state treasury (*khazīne-yi ʿāmire*) and a financial agency for the army, referred to as the *manṣūre defterdārlighi* (Heidborn, ii, 37; Pakalın, *OTD*, ii, 406-7). In 1251/1835-6, the state treasury (*khazīne-yi ʿāmire*) was combined with that of the mint (*ḍarb-khāne*), the new agency being placed under the headship of a *ḍarb-khāne defterdārī* (Luṭfī, v, 17). Then on 3 Dhu 'l-Ḥidjdja 1253/28 February 1838, the *manṣūre defterdārlighī* was added to the organisation, the mint was again separated out, and the result became known as the Ministry of Financial Affairs (*Umūr-i̊ Māliyye Neẓāreti*).

The second half of the 1830s was when Maḥmūd organised the larger departments of the Ottoman government into European-style ministries, for which he adopted the generic term *neẓāret*. From that point onwards, that term continued, as in the past, to refer both to small-scale agencies, where it is more appropriately translated as "supervisorship", and to the new ministries. The financial agency created in 1838 was clearly of the latter type (Luṭfī, v, 104-5; Pakalın, *Maliye*, i, 25-6).

Following the death of Maḥmūd II, the development of the Ottoman system of financial administration reflected both the goals of reformers like Muṣṭafā Reshīd [*q.v.*] and the intensity of the political struggle that surrounded them. At the death of Maḥmūd, Khosrew Pasha [*q.v.*] seized the grand vizierate and set to work undoing many of the reforms of the late sultan and his civilian bureaucratic advisers, who were Khosrew's enemies. Among other things, Khosrew abolished the Ministry of Financial Affairs (Djumādā 'l-Ūlā 1255/July-August 1839), replacing it with a dual system of a state treasury (*khazīne-yi ʿāmire*) and a *defterdārlīḳ* for farmed revenues (*muḳāṭaʿāt*; Pakalın, *Maliye*, iii, 96). When Muṣṭafā Reshīd and his friends managed to topple Khosrew in 1840, they also launched an ambitious attempt to replace tax-farming with direct collection of revenues, at least in selected localities. About the same time, it appears that they converted the *defterdārlīḳ* for farmed revenues into a Ministry of Finance (*Māliyye Neẓāreti*) responsible for supervision of the system of direct collection, relegating responsibility for revenues that continued to be administered in the "old way" to the state treasury (*khazīne-yi ʿāmire*; Luṭfī, vi, 68-9, 106). At the beginning of 1257/1841, the treasury was again combined with the ministry to form a single Ministry of Financial Affairs (*Umūr-i̊ Māliyye Neẓāreti*; Pakalın, *Maliye*, i, 26). Muṣṭafā Reshīd and his friends did not consolidate their hold on high office until *ca.* 1845; however, the history of the Ministry of Finance was continuous from 1841 onwards. By the early 1840s, the bureaux formerly attached to the *Bāb-i̊ Defterī* had also undergone considerable modification; and the ministry had acquired a number of new functionaries and agencies. The resulting organisation remained essentially unchanged from that point until 1297/1880 (Luṭfī, v, 105, 116; vi, 125-6; Pakalın, *Maliye*, i, 26-7; iii, 29-31, 34).

Had Muṣṭafā Reshīd and his colleagues succeeded in realising the policy goals that lay behind these changes of organisation, the results might have done a lot to provide the *Tanẓīmāt* [*q.v.*] reforms with the sound economic foundation that they never acquired. What the reformers intended was a fundamental reorganisation of the system of taxation: eliminating many of the old taxes, especially the arbitrary exactions (*tekālīf-i ʿörfiyye*), substituting direct collection for revenue farming, centralising receipts and disbursements in the state treasury, and assigning salaries to all officials to replace the prebendal forms of compensation and the revenue forms on which most of them had previously depended. In 1838, the tax reforms were inaugurated on an experimental basis in selected provinces, and the salary system was supposed to go into effect. The Gülkhāne Decree of 1839 proclaimed the general principles underlying the changes. Subsequent acts generalised the fiscal reforms to a larger number of provinces. The chief agents of the new system of revenue-collection were to be collectors (*muḥaṣṣils*) appointed to assess and collect revenues in collaboration with locally appointed administrative councils (*medjlis-i idāre*), which were to include both ex officio members and representatives of the local populace (ʿAbd al-Raḥmān Wefīḳ, i, 346-7; ii, 6-50; İnalcık, *Tanzimat'in uygulanması*, 623 ff.; idem, *Application of the Tanzimat*, 97 ff.; Shaw, *Tax reform*, 422). These reforms failed, and the Ottomans never succeeded in overcoming the consequences. In part, the failure resulted from the fact that the Ottoman system of financial administration was not ready for the demands that fiscal centralisation made on it. In part, the problem resulted from the opposition of former tax farmers or *ṣarrāfs* [*q.v.*], who had vested interests in the old system (Pakalın, *Maliye*, iii, 52-4; Shaw, *Tax reform*, 422). In any case, revenue receipts fell off. In 1258/1842, tax farming (*iltizām*, but not the life farms, *mālikāne*) had to be restored (Pakalın, *OTD*, ii, 397). Direct collection was later revived for some taxes. But for the tithe on agricultural produce (*aʿshār*), the most important single revenue, tax farming continued at least into the Young Turk period (Heidborn, ii, 117-30; Lewis, 385-6, 458; Shaw, *Tax reform*, 428-9; Issawi, *Turkey*, 351-60). The failure of the effort at centralisation of revenue collection crippled the new system of official salaries from the start. And that was not all.

The extent to which the Ottoman Empire had been integrated, prior to the 19th century, into the worldwide system of European economic dominance is clear from the evolution of the capitulations (*imtiyāzāt* [*q.v.*]) and the abuses that developed out of them. One of the saddest ironies of the *Tanẓīmāt* is that the economic subordination of the empire underwent a critical tightening in 1838, just as the new period was about to open. This occurred with the adoption of the Anglo-Ottoman Commercial Convention of Balta Liman. This, and comparable treaties concluded later with other states, marked the substitution of negotiated bilateral treaties for the capitulations. More important, it forced Ottoman statesmen, who were desperate at that point for European help against the Egyptian challenge, to accept what amounted to free trade (Bailey, Kütükoğlu). The effects on an unindustrialised economy, in which customs revenues had traditionally been one of the most important cash revenues, were very serious. Not only were Ottoman markets now opened wide to European industrial goods, but the ability of the Ottoman government to raise new revenue, either by taxation or by setting up monopolies or other government enterprises, was limited by the terms of the treaties (du Velay, 338). The deteriorating economic situation, and the political and military crisis with Egypt, led to the issue in 1840 of the first Ottoman paper money (*ḳāʾime* [*q.v.*]). This remained in circulation until 1862, and gave rise to serious problems of counterfeiting and depreciation. Paper money was again issued in the wake of the Russo-Turkish War and during World War I (Toprak, 205 ff.). The coinage, too, was in disarray (Schaefer, 25 ff.; Issawi, *Turkey*, 326-31). The monetary problems were aggravated by the lack, prior to the second half of the century, of modern banking facilities; when created, these were essentially foreign enterprises (du Velay, 132 ff.; Biliotti; Issawi, *Turkey*, 339-42).

To make matters worse, the Ottoman government began during the Crimean War to contract foreign loans (D̲j̲ewdet, *Ted̲h̲ākir, 1-12*, 20-3; du Velay, 134 ff.). In a little over twenty years, the empire acquired a foreign debt of 200 million pounds sterling (Blaisdell, 74) and experienced a complete collapse of its credit. The crisis over the public debt resulted in Muḥarram 1299/1881 in the creation of an international Council of the Public Debt (*duyūn-i ʿumūmiyye* [*q.v.*]), to which the Ottoman government was forced to cede control of a number of revenues (du Velay, 463 ff.; Young, v, 55 ff.; Blaisdell, 90 ff.; Issawi, *Turkey*, 361-5). The Russo-Turkish War also left the empire saddled with an indemnity of 35 million Turkish pounds to pay to Russia (Blaisdell, 85; Heidborn, ii, 294-5; Milgrim, 519 ff.). The liabilities that the Ottomans incurred under concessions for various economic development projects—example, the kilometric guarantees granted to assure a profit to foreign railway builders—were another drain (du Velay, 550 ff.). Over the course of time, the government ceded more of its revenues to the Public Debt Administration in order to cover further commitments, until that agency controlled almost one-quarter of Ottoman revenue (Blaisdell, 150-1).

Considering the swift failure of its most important attempts at fiscal reform and the continuing decline in the economic independence of the Empire, it is not surprising that Ottoman financial institutions of the reform era made little progress in achieving increased efficiency. The Public Debt is only the most conspicuous example of the extent to which control of public revenues remained dispersed among a number of different agencies. By the last years of the reign of ʿAbd al-Ḥamīd II (1876-1909), there were twenty or more official or semi-official bodies in Istanbul with power to collect and disburse revenues directly. The most important were the Public Debt Administration and the privy treasury (*k̲h̲azīne-yi k̲h̲āṣṣa*). As successor to the old privy purse (*d̲j̲eyb-i hümāyūn*), this became a very large and powerful organisation, thanks to the growth of ʿAbd al-Ḥamīd's enormous personal fortune. The Minister of Finance really had control only over fiscal resources not otherwise accounted for. Even there, the control was not effective. Partly because the economy was overwhelmingly agricultural, with important revenues still collected in kind, tax collection was always in arrears (Heidborn, ii, 162 ff.). The weakness of central control over provincial finance is clear from the use, as a favourite mode of payment, of the *ḥawāle*. This was an order to pay, drawn against a provincial "treasury", which might or might not have funds to honour the order. Ottoman bankers and *ṣarrāf*s made a business of discounting these orders. The Ministry of Finance seldom had enough money on hand to pay more than a few of its creditors in cash. Procedures were so complicated that even this favoured few had to "jump through many fiery hoops" before getting their money (Pakalın, *Maliye*, i, 38). Favouritism and irregularity in salary payments were but a variation on this theme. By inflating the numbers of officials in all departments, ʿAbd al-Ḥamīd's policy of using the bureaucracy as a vast patronage machine made the financial situation much worse.

Under these circumstances, it was out of the question for Ottoman officials to use budget preparation as an effective instrument of fiscal policy. What look like modern budgets began to be prepared in 1863; there had been somewhat similar documents earlier in the *Tanẓīmāt* (Shaw, *Tax reform,* 449-50; idem, *Ottoman expenditures,* 373-8; Findley, 349-52, 384 n. 123, 396 n. 178, 404 n. 124; Issawi, *Turkey,* 348-9). Contemporary experts were united in the opinion that the budgets bore little correspondence to reality, especially before 1908 (Heidborn, ii, 45-9; du Velay, 174-88, 317-24).

The late 19th century nonetheless witnessed some efforts to improve the organisation and efficiency of financial institutions. There was an attempt in 1277/1861 to organise a hierarchy of fiscal officials to serve in the local administrative system then being created (*Düstūr*[1], ii, 4-25). Under ʿAbd al-Ḥamīd, there were further acts on this subject and on the related issue of tax collection (Young, v, 18-21). The Constitution of 1876 contained a special section on financial affairs, including articles on taxation, budgeting, and the creation of an independent Board of Audit (*Dīwān-i Muḥāsebāt*; *Düstūr*[1], iv, 16-17, arts. 96-107). The law of 1877 on provincial municipalities authorised them to have their own budgets (Young, i, 69-84; *Düstūr*[1], iv, 538-53). After the Russo-Turkish War, there was a flurry of effort at reorganisation on a number of fronts, the purpose being to convince the major powers of the empire's capacity for reform. Among the measures then enacted were one of 1296/1879 setting up the Board of Audit (*Dīwān-i Muḥāsebāt*; *Düstūr*[1], iv, 602-13) and another of 1297/1880 reorganising the Ministry of Finance (*ibid.*, iv, 674-84; Pakalın, *Maliye*, i, 28-30, 32-7). The latter measure reorganised the ministry and its personnel into two components, the central organisation (*heyʾet-i merkeziyye*) and the attached agencies (*heyʾet-i mülḥaḳa*), located either in the provinces or in other ministries at the centre. The central organisation was to include a corps of inspectors (*heyʾet-i teftīs̲h̲iyye*) empowered to investigate the accounts of all central and provincial departments. Under the Ḥamīdian régime, control measures such as the inspectorate and the Board of Audit produced little real effect. The practice of filling the post of undersecretary of finance (*māliyye müstes̲h̲ārī*) with a foreign expert did at least provide a continuing source of critical perspective on fiscal affairs (Young, v, 16).

There was also another extensive reorganisation of the ministry in *ca.* 1305/1888. The ministry in this form appears to have been distinguished by the complexity of its internal organisation and records-keeping procedures (Pakalın, *Maliye,* i, 37-52). Like most governmental agencies under ʿAbd al-Ḥamīd, it also became grossly overstaffed. The number of officials in its central offices stood at 650 in 1879, 750 in 1888, and perhaps 1,400 at the time of the Young Turk Revolution (*ibid.*, i, 36, 52).

The 1908 Revolution opened the way for efforts at fundamental reform in finance, as in other fields. The most important reforms of the period appear to have been three in number. First, as part of a program affecting the bureaucracy in general, there was a purge (*tensīḳāt*) of superfluous and unreliable officials and a reduction of salaries for all others (Findley, 296-8). The purge was carried out in several waves and reduced the number of officals in the central offices of the ministry for a time to about 500. Second, as a natural extension of the purge, there was a reorganisation of the ministry. Thenceforth, its central agencies consisted of the minister, his undersecretary, a directorate general for accounts, eight specialised departments, and two consultative bodies. One of these, the Financial Reform Commission (*Iṣlāḥāt-ï Māliyye Komisyonï*), included foreign as well as Ottoman members and served to study reform proposals and draft legislation on them; the other, the Consultative Committee (*Endjümen-i Müs̲h̲āwere*), was to advise on implementation of a new accounting system. Even more important, the inspectorate of finance and the Board of Audit (*Dīwān-ï Muḥāsebāt*) were at last made into active institutions. The ongoing practice of training financial inspectors by a period of apprenticeship abroad dates from this period (Ayni, 25). The third major reform of the Young Turk years was a new system of accountability, embodied in a law (*uṣūl-ï muḥāsebe-yi ʿumūmiyye ḳānūnï*) that went into effect in 1911. The new system centralised control of revenue and expenditure in the Ministry of Finance, established in principle the universality of the state budget, defined the system for budget preparation, and provided for a directorate of accounts, controlled by the minister of finance, in every ministry. These major reforms of the Young Turk period were the most important innovations attempted in government finance since the beginning of the *Tanẓīmāt* (Heidborn, ii, 42-65; Pakalın, *Maliye*, i, 30-1, 50-5).

In addition, the Young Turk years also included many other financial innovations. Publication of budgets and other acts of fiscal relevance began for the first time on a prompt and regular basis, and the budgets were much more realistic than any published before (see *Bibl.*). Some taxes were abolished, and the assessment and collection of many others revised. The law of 1913 on provincial administration allowed each province to have a budget consisting of revenue and expenditure items controlled at the provincial level (*Düstūr*², v, 144, 186-216, arts. 79-83; vi, 505-8). The Land Registry Office (*Defter-i K̲h̲āḳānī* [*q.v.*]), was attached to the Ministry of Finance. A special school for financial officials (*Māliyye Mektebi*) was founded in 1910. The privileges that foreigners enjoyed under the capitulations were unilaterally repudiated in 1914. In response to wartime needs, a Ministry of Supply (*I-ʿās̲h̲e Neẓāreti*) was eventually created. Many of these reforms occurred during the four periods between 1909 and 1918 when D̲j̲āwīd Bey [*q.v.*] was minister of finance (Pakalın, *Maliye*, iv, 238-9, 243, 246-7). He exemplifies the energy and determination characteristic of the period.

2. The Turkish Republic. Following the collapse of the empire, the Turkish Republic managed to extricate itself from the problems that had done most to breach Ottoman economic sovereignty. The position of the Public Debt Administration had previously been undermined by the wartime loss of co-operation among its European members, the collapse of the Ottoman monetary system, and the shrinkage during the armistice period of the territory under control of the Ottoman government (Blaisdell, 179 ff.). The Treaty of Lausanne (1923) recognised the end of the capitulatory régime in Turkey and apportioned the Ottoman debt among the various successor states, setting the share of the Turkish Republic at 67%. The Turkish government accepted the debt obligations assigned to it, but later unilaterally suspended payment, and in 1943 made a final offer to redeem outstanding bonds at a reduced rate (Robinson, 98-9).

Meanwhile, the development of the Ministry of Finance, as of other agencies of the new government, was "evolutionary, rather than revolutionary" (Dodd, 47). Although the matter appears not to have been studied, there must have been substantial initial carry-over of personnel and organisation from the imperial government. Serious efforts at financial reorganisation came only with the abolition of the tithes (*aʿs̲h̲ār*) in 1925 and subsequent tax reforms (Ayni, 29), then in 1929 with a reorganisation of the Ministry of Finance under a law on unification and equalisation of government payrolls (*devlet memurlarının maaşlarının tevhid ve taadül hakkındaki kanun*; Ülker, 91). These provisions were superseded by a law of 1936 on the organisation and duties of the Ministry of Finance (*maliye bakanlığı teşkilât ve vazifeleri hakkındaki kanun*; Gorvine and Barber, 78-89). With numerous amendments, this remained in effect in the mid-1970s (Ülker, 91-2; *Teşkilât rehberi 1976*, 332).

Under the Republic, the mission of the Ministry of Finance has been defined as "to carry out the financial administration of the State in harmony with the efforts directed toward the economic development of the country" (*Organization and functions*, 164). In keeping with this extension of the old concept of financial administration into the newer one of economic development, the internal organisation and the size of the ministry have become considerably greater than in the Ottoman period, while a number of other organisations with related missions have also come into existence.

In contrast to the bipartite organisation of central and attached officials prescribed for the ministry in 1880, the Republican Ministry of Finance comprises four categories of agencies: central, provincial, international, and attached (*bağlı*) or related (*ilgili*). During the mid-1970s, the central organisation had at its top the minister, with his undersecretary, assistant undersecretaries, and private secretariat. There were five advisory and staff units, including the Financial Inspectorate (*teftiş kurulu*), the Board of Accounting Experts, and the Board of Certified Bank Examiners (*bankalar yeminli murakıpları kurulu*). The ministry had six principal organisational units, including a department for legal counsel and general directorates for budget and financial control, accounts (*muhasebat*), revenues (*gelirler*), and the treasury, the last also serving as a general secretariat for international economic co-operation. There were also support agencies in charge of personnel (*özlük işleri*), the mint and printing plant, the accounts of the ministry itself, etc. The provincial agencies of the Ministry of Finance were found at the two highest jurisdictional levels of the local administrative hierarchy, the *il* (province) and the *ilçe.*

At the province level, the chief financial officer continued to bear the old title *defterdar*. There were a number of agencies attached to him with functions parallel to various of the central agencies. The most important of these provincial agencies were those responsible for assessment and collection of taxes. At the next lower administrative level, the *ilçe*, the senior official was the *mal müdürü*, whose functions and staff were a reduced-scale replica of those of the provincial *defterdar*. The international agencies included financial representatives serving with the Turkish missions to organisations like the North Atlantic Treaty Organisation (Brussels) or the United Nations (New York), as well as financial counsellors attached to embassies and consulates. The category of agencies attached or related to the Ministry of Finance included the Central Bank, the State Investment Bank, the government retirement fund, and the national lottery (*Turkish government organization manual*, 138 ff.; Ülker, 92 ff.; *Teşkilât rehberi 1976*, 333 ff.).

During the mid-1960s, the staff of the ministry reportedly stood on average at 2,000 in the central offices and 15,000 in all (Ülker, 92). A decade later, it was reported at 5,600 in the central offices and over 40,000 in total (*Teşkilât rehberi 1976*, 342). The comparison between these two sets of figures is startling, suggesting that political forces have again been at work, as in the days of ʿAbd al-Ḥamīd, to bloat the bureaucracy. Whatever the explanation of the short-term contrast, that between either of these sets of figures and those dating from the empire is probably more significant. Whatever other factors may be at work, the presence of many times more financial officials in a state much smaller than the empire surely reflects the greater demands made on the ministry in a society committed not just to financial administration, but to economic development.

Indeed, the growth of the Ministry of Finance is only a partial illustration of this point. To appreciate it fully, one must also note the proliferation of governmental agencies with financial and economic responsibilities. The empire in its day had ministries, which appear not to have been very effective, for trade, agriculture, public works, forests and mines, as well as certain state enterprises. Atatürk committed the Republic to eliminating the hold of foreign interests over the economy and to étatism, and the first state plan for economic development went into effect in 1934 (Robinson, 103 ff.; Hershlag, 31 ff.; Issawi, *Turkey*, 367-8). By then, the development of a new series of official and semi-official agencies had begun. By the mid-1960s, this series included the State Planning Organisation (*Devlet Plânlama Teşkilâti,* created 1960), Board of Audit (now known as *Sayıştay* instead of *Dīwān-ī Muḥāsebāt*), the ministries of customs and monopolies, commerce, industry, public works, communications, agriculture, health and social assistance, reconstruction and settlement, tourism and information, plus other agencies or enterprises concerned with banking, energy, natural resources, land tenure, and various forms of industrial production (*Organization and functions*, 62-6, 163-4, 198-317). The obvious need for coordination among so many agencies has given rise to several interministerial bodies intended to perform this function in support of the development plans (*Teşkilât rehberi 1976,* 139-43, 156-8). Where the Ministry of Finance is concerned, probably the most critical need for co-ordination arises between it and the State Planning Organisation, which not only prepares the economic development plans for the state but also plays a central role, together with the Ministry of Finance, in budget preparation (Dodd, 245-6; *Organization and functions,* 175-76).

The Ministry of Finance of the Turkish Republic, though vastly larger in size and wider-ranging in functions than its imperial prototype, has thus been surrounded with a galaxy of agencies with financial and economic responsibilities. According to recent sources, some major developmental needs of the ministry are still unmet. These include improved coordination with other agencies, especially the planning organisation; the full acceptance of "programme budgeting", as opposed to dispersion of sums needed for a given project under different headings; and an end to the age-old practice of assigning specific revenues to specific needs (Dodd, 246; *Organization and functions,* 170-1, 179-80). The last point, in particular, shows that the Ottoman tradition dies hard. To these problems must, of course, be added others of general economic significance, such as the monetary instability and mounting public debt that have again come to plague the republic.

3. Comparative note. In the 19th century, the financial and economic history of autonomous regions within the Empire passed through stages parallel to those observable in Istanbul. The similarities derive from a common institutional heritage, similar economic and environmental constraints, and confrontation with the same set of problems in dealing with the outside world. At many points, there is not only parallelism, but also contemporaneity, in the major economic events occurring in different locales. In the 20th century, parallelisms are equally noticeable, the main difference being the proliferation of sovereign states and the growth of emphasis on economic development. In both periods, similar traits can be found in Islamic states beyond the frontiers or former frontiers of the empire, as well as farther afield.

In the 19th century, there were two regions in the Islamic parts of the empire that the Ottomans acknowledged as autonomous. These were the "privileged provinces" (*eyālāt-ī mümtāze*) of Egypt and Tunisia. As early as the time of Muḥammad ʿAlī (1805-49), Egypt, at least, began to develop financial agencies that resembled, and for a time anticipated, those of Istanbul in their development. Both Tunisia and Egypt professedly adopted a European-style system of ministries in the 1850s; the Istanbul government had done so in the late 1830s. Tunisia and Egypt resembled their suzerain in the form and weakness of procedures for budgeting and revenue control. They shared the same problems where the privileges of foreigners were concerned. Tunis, Cairo, and Istanbul all began to accumulate a foreign debt between 1854 and 1862. Bankruptcy occurred for Tunis as early as 1866; for Cairo and Istanbul, it came a decade later, although Egypt had been in deep trouble ever since the collapse of the cotton boom enjoyed during the American Civil War (1861-5). Fiscal control agencies, dominated by Europeans, were established in all three places between 1870 and 1881. In Egypt, there was not only a *Caisse de la dette,* but also an Anglo-French dual controllership over the remainder of government finance. Even the personal fortune of the Khedive was taken under European control (Deny, 104-20, 131-43, 398-414, 519-48; Rivlin, 75-136; Landes, 278 ff.; Issawi, *Egypt: an economic and social analysis,* 23-5; idem, *Economic history of the Middle East and North Africa,* 62-70; Owen, 122-52, 216-43; Brown, 134-7, 245-50, 335-49; Ganiage, 99-112, 186-216, 298-334, 348-402). It is true that Tunisia came under direct European domination in 1881, and Egypt did in 1882, while the territories remaining under control of the Istanbul government did not. Yet for the Istanbul government, as for the few other

Asian and African states that retained nominal independence in this period, sovereignty became almost a fiction. With its fiscal system a weaker version of the Ottoman one, and its economy even more dominated by foreign interests, Ḳādjār Īrān is one of the clearest examples (Bakhash, *Evolution,* 139 ff.; idem, *Iran,* 102-4, 110-14, 142-4, 166-7, 263-6, 270-81).

Following World War I, the dismantling of the Ottoman Empire meant that all its Islamic territories outside what became the Republic of Turkey fell under European control, if they had not been before. The only exceptions—to the extent that it can be spoken of as former Ottoman territory—were in the Arabian peninsula. The fact that the Turkish Republic managed, through the Treaty of Lausanne, to escape the peace terms inflicted on the empire following World War I, while others of the successor states did not, meant that some aspects of the old régime survived elsewhere, after being abolished in Turkey. For example, the capitulatory privileges of foreigners were not abolished in Egypt until 1937 (Issawi, *Egypt: an economic and social analysis,* 172). In Egypt, the development of financial institutions continued in this period under the British-dominated monarchy. In the Fertile Crescent, the development of such institutions, beyond what had existed as part of the Ottoman provincial administration, began in the 1920s under the mandatory régimes controlled by the French and British. Whether for the mandate period or for that of independence, detailed examination would disclose important parallelisms between economic and fiscal developments in the Arab successor states and Republican Turkey. Major traits in common include demands that economic and financial institutions provide an increasing range and quality of services, a growing number of government agencies with responsibilities of such types, and an increasing emphasis on social welfare. Government control of important sectors of the economy, efforts to restrict foreign enterprises, reliance on centralised planning for economic development are now also generally characteristic. In recent years, the chief factor in differentiating the economic fortune of the various successor states has been the presence or absence of significant petroleum resources (see e.g. Issawi, *Economic history of the Middle East and North Africa,* 170 ff.; on Egypt, idem, *Egypt in Revolution,* 46-75, 169-80, 246-315; Hansen and Marzouk, 1-21, 246-316; Mabro, 107-63; Ikram, *passim;* on ʿIrāḳ, Penrose and Penrose, 148-81, 240-73, 381-530, 538-44; on Saudi Arabia, El Mallakh, *Saudi Arabia,* passim).

Bibliography: 1. Ottoman Empire and Turkish Republic. H. T. Ayni, *Maliye sistemimiz ve vergi usullerimiz,* in *Ankara Üniversite'si Siyasal Bilgiler Fakültesi yüzüncü yıl armağan'i,* Ankara 1959, 9-35; F. E. Bailey, *British policy and the Turkish reform movement: a study in Anglo-Turkish relations, 1826-1853,* Cambridge, Mass. 1942; A. Biliotti, *La Banque impériale ottomane,* Paris 1909; D. C. Blaisdell, *European financial control in the Ottoman Empire: a study of the establishment, activities, and significance of the Ottoman public debt,* New York 1929; A. Çetin, *Başbakanlık Arşivi kılavuzu,* Istanbul 1979; S. Dilik, *Die Geldverfassung und die Währungspolitik der Türkei bis 1958, mit einem statistischen Anhang für die Zeit nach 1958,* Ankara 1969; Aḥmed Djewdet, *Taʾrīkh-i Djewdet,* 2nd ed. (*tertīb-i djedīd*), 12 vols., Istanbul 1309/1891-92; idem, *Tedhākir, 1-12, 13-20, 21-39, 40-tetimme,* 4 vols., ed. Cavid Baysun, Ankara 1953-67; C. H. Dodd, *Politics and government in Turkey,* Berkeley and Los Angeles 1969; C. V. Findley, *Bureaucratic reform in the Ottoman Empire: the Sublime Porte, 1789-1922,* Princeton 1980; A. Gorvine and L. Barber, *Organization and functions of Turkish ministries,* Ankara 1957; W. Hale, *The political and economic development of modern Turkey,* London and New York 1981; J. von Hammer, *Des osmanischen Reichs Staatsverfassung und Staatsverwaltung,* 2 vols., Vienna 1815 (repr. Hildesheim 1963); idem, *Histoire de l'Empire ottoman, depuis son origine jusqu'à nos jours,* xvii, tr. J.-J. Hellert, Paris 1841; A. Heidborn, *Manuel de droit public et administratif de l'Empire ottoman,* 2 vols., Vienna-Leipzig 1908-12; Z. Y. Hershlag, *Turkey: the challenge of growth*², Leiden 1968; H. İnalcık, *Application of the Tanzimat and its social effects,* in *Archivum Ottomanicum,* v (1973), 97-127; idem, *Tanzimat'ın uygulanmasi ve sosyal tepkileri,* in *Belleten,* xxvii (1964), 623-49; A. Karamursal, *Osmanlı malî tarihi hakkında tetkikler,* Ankara 1940; Ç. Keyder, *Ottoman economy and finances (1881-1918),* in *Social and economic history of Turkey (1071-1920),* ed. O. Okyar and H. İnalcık, Ankara 1977, 323-8; H. Kızılyallı, *Türk vergi sisteminin ekonomik analizi,* Ankara 1969; E. Kurnow, *The Turkish budgetary process,* Ankara 1956, published in Turkish as *Türkiye'de bütçenin hazırlanışı,* tr. S. Aren, Ankara 1956; M. S. Kütükoğlu, *Osmanlı-İngiliz iktisadî münâsebetleri. II (1830-1850),* Istanbul 1976; B. Lewis, *The emergence of modern Turkey*², Oxford 1968; Aḥmed Luṭfī, *Taʾrīkh-i Luṭfī,* 8 published vols., the 8th ed. ʿAbd al-Raḥmān Sheref, Istanbul 1290-1328/1873-1910 (many quotations from later, unpublished volumes in Pakalın, *Maliye*); J. W. Martin and F. C. E. Cush, *Final report on the administration of the Turkish ministry of finance,* Ankara 1951; M. Milgrim, *An overlooked problem in Turkish-Russian relations: the 1878 war indemnity,* in *IJMES,* ix (1978), 519-37; C. Morawitz, *Les finances de la Turquie,* Paris 1902; Muṣṭafā Nūrī, *Netāʾidj al-wuḳūʿāt,* 4 vols., Istanbul 1327/1909; I. Mouradgea d'Ohsson, *Tableau général de l'Empire othoman,* 3 vols., Paris 1787-1820; Pakalın, *Maliye teşkilâtı tarihi,* 4 vols., Ankara 1977; idem, *Osmanlı tarih deyimleri ve terimleri sözlüğü,* 3 vols., Istanbul 1971-2, 2d printing; idem, *Tanzimat maliye nazırları,* Istanbul 1939; D. H. Quataert, *Ottoman reform and agriculture in Anatolia, 1876-1908,* unpubl. diss., UCLA, 1973; idem, *Social disintegration and popular resistance in the Ottoman empire 1881-1908: reactions to European economic penetration,* New York 1983; R. D. Robinson, *The first Turkish republic: a case study in national development,* Cambridge, Mass. 1963; A. Schaefer, *Geldwesen und Staatsbankfrage in der Türkei,* in *Das Türkische Reich: Wirtschaftliche Darstellungen,* ed. J. Hellauer, Berlin 1918, 25-48; M. Sertoğlu, *Muhteva bakımından Başvekâlet Arşivi,* Ankara 1955; S. J. Shaw, *Between old and new: the Ottoman empire under Sultan Selim III, 1789-1807,* Cambridge, Mass 1971; idem, *The nineteenth century Ottoman tax reforms and revenue system,* in *IJMES,* vi (1975), 421-59; idem, *Ottoman expenditures and budgets in the late nineteenth and early twentieth centuries,* in *IJMES,* ix (1978), 373-8; A. L. Sturm and C. Mıhçıoğlu, *Bibliography on public administration in Turkey,* Ankara 1959; Süleymān Sūdī, *Defter-i muḳteṣid,* 3 vols., Istanbul *1307-8/1890;* İ. Tekeli and S. İlkin, *Para ve kredi sisteminin oluşumunda bir aşama: Türkiye cumhuriyeti merkez bankası,* Ankara 1981; J. Thobie, *Finance et politique extérieure: L'administration de la dette publique ottomane 1881-1914,* in *Social and economic history of Turkey (1071-1920),* ed. O. Okyar and H. İnalcık, Ankara 1977, 311-22; V. Tönük, *Türkiyede idare teşkilâtı'nın tarihî gelişimi* *bügünkü durumu*, Ankara 1945; Z. Toprak, *Osmanlı devleti'nin birinci dünya savaşı finansmanı ve para politikası*, in *Orta Doğu Teknik Üniversitesi Gelişme Dergisi—Middle East Technical University Studies in Development*, 1979-80, special issue, 205-38; M. Ülker, *Malî idare: kuruluşu, görev, yetki ve sorumlulukları, merkez ve taşra örgütleri, bunlar arasında bağlantı ve işbirliği*, in *Maliye enstitüsü konferansları*, Ankara 1966, 87-115; İ. H. Uzunçarşılı, *Osmanlı devletinin merkez ve bahriye teşkilâtı*, Ankara 1948; ʿAbd al-Raḥmān Wefīḳ, *Tekālīf ḳawāʿidi*, 2 vols., Istanbul 1328-1330/1910-12; A. du Velay, *Essai sur l'histoire financière de la Turquie, depuis le règne du Sultan Mahmoud II jusqu'à nos jours*, Paris 1903; E. Yavuz, O. Kurmuş and Ş. Pamuk, *19. y.y. Türkiye iktisat tarihi kaynakları: bir bibliyografya denemesi*, in *ODTÜ Gelişme Dergisi-METU Studies in Development*, 1979-80, special number, 329-71; F. Yavuz, *A survey on the financial administration of Turkish municipalities*, Ankara 1962; G. Young, *Corps de droit ottoman*, 7 vols., Oxford 1905-6; H. Yücelen, *Türk malî tarihine toplu bir bakış ve maliyeci şairler antolojisi*, Istanbul 1973.

2. Official publications. *Düstur:* first series (*birindji tertīb*), 4 vols. plus 4 appendices (*dheyl*) and a "completion" volume (*Mütemmim*), Istanbul 1289-1335/1872-1917, as well as 4 more vols., published as vols. v-viii, Ankara 1937-42; second series (*ikindji tertīb*), 12 vols., Istanbul 1329-1927 [*sic*]/1911-27; third to fifth series (*üçüncü, dördüncü, beşinci tertib*), published under Turkish Republic, Ankara; fifth series continues. Publications of the Institute of Public Administration for Turkey and the Middle East Türkiye ve Orta Doğu Amme İdaresi Enstitüsü: *Merkezî hükûmet teşkilâtı kuruluş ve görevleri*, Ankara 1963, published in English as *Organization and functions of the central government of Turkey: report of the managing board of the central government organization research project*, Ankara 1965; *T.[ürkiye] C.[umhuriyeti] teşkilâtı rehberi*, Ankara 1963, published in English as *Turkish government organization manual*, Ankara 1966; *T.[ürkiye] C.[umhuriyeti] devlet teşkilâtı rehberi 1976*, Ankara 1977. Publications of the Ottoman Ministry of Finance (*Māliyye Neẓāreti*): *Dewlet-i ʿothmāniyyeniñ 1325 senesine makhṣūṣ büddjesidir* (series continues annually till at least 1334), Istanbul 1325-34 *mālī*/1909-18 (on earlier budgets, see Shaw, *Tax reforms*, 449-50); *Iḥṣāʾiyyāt-i māliyye: wāridāt ve maṣārif-i ʿumūmiyyeyi muḥtewīdir*, 3 (?) vols., Istanbul 1325-7 *mālī*/1909-11; *Ḳawānīn-i māliyye*, 4 (?) vols. for 1333-6 *mālī*, Istanbul 1336-7 *mālī*/1920-1; *Ḳawānīn ve niẓāmāt ve muḳarrerāt-i māliyye medjmūʿasi*, 6 vols., Istanbul 1327-9 *mālī*/1911-13; *1325 senesi eylūlünden shubāṭi ghāyesine ḳadar khazīne-i djelīleden meʾmūrīn-i māliyyeye yazilan muḥarrerāt-i ʿumūmiyye ṣūretlerini muḥtewī medjmūʿadir* (title varies by year: e.g. *1333 senesi muḥarrerāt-i ʿumūmiyye medjmūʿasidir*), Istanbul 1326-36 *mālī*/ 1910-20. Publications of the Republican Ministry of Finance at first take the form of continuations of some of the series just named: e.g. *1341 sene-i māliyyesine makhṣūṣ büdjedir*, Istanbul 1341 *mālī*/1925; *Ḳawānīn ve niẓāmāt ve muḳarrerāt-i māliyye medjmūʿasi*, vol. vii, Istanbul 1339-41 *mālī* (?)/1923-5; for names of later series, see *Teşkilât rehberi 1976*, 971 ff.

3. Sources cited in Comparative Section. S. Bakhash, *The evolution of Qajar bureaucracy: 1779-1879*, in *Middle Eastern Studies*, vii (1971), 139-68; idem, *Iran: monarchy, bureaucracy and reform under the Qajars, 1858-1896*, London 1978; L. C. Brown, *The Tunisia of Ahmad Bey, 1837-1855*, Princeton 1974; J. Deny, *Sommaire des archives turques du Caire*, Cairo 1930; R. El Mallakh, *Saudi Arabia: rush to development*, Baltimore 1982; J. Ganiage, *Les origines du protectorat français en Tunisie (1861-1881)*, Paris 1959; B. Hansen and G. A. Marzouk, *Development and economic policy in the UAR (Egypt)*, Amsterdam 1965; K. Ikram, *Egypt: economic management in a period of transition*, Baltimore 1981; C. Issawi, *Economic history of the Middle East and North Africa*, New York 1982; idem, *The economic history of the Middle East, 1800-1914*, Chicago 1966; idem, *The economic history of Iran, 1800-1914*, Chicago 1971; idem, *The economic history of Turkey, 1800-1914*, Chicago 1981; idem, *Egypt: an economic and social analysis*, London 1947; idem, *Egypt at mid-century*, London 1954; idem, *Egypt in revolution; an economic analysis*, London 1963; D. S. Landes, *Bankers and pashas: international finance and economic imperialism in Egypt*, Cambridge, Mass. 1958; R. Mabro, *The Egyptian economy, 1952-1972*, Oxford 1974; R. Owen, *The Middle East in the world economy*, London 1981; Edith and E. F. Penrose, *Iraq: international relations and national development*, London 1978; Helen Anne B. Rivlin, *The agricultural policy of Muḥammad ʿAlī in Egypt*, Cambridge, Mass. 1961; A. Schölch, *Ägypten den Ägyptern. Die politische und gesellschaftliche Krise der Jahre 1878-1882 in Ägypten*, Zürich and Freiburg im Breisgau n.d.

(C. V. Findley)

MALḲARA (modern Turkish Malkara; Ottoman Maʿlghara < Mīghalghara/Mīghalḳara; oldest forms: Mīghal Ḳarā (in a *waḳfiyya* of Murād I of 767/1366—but cf. Wittek, in *WZKM*, lviii [1962], 180); Mīghalḳarā (temp. Meḥemmed II, cf. Gökbilgin, *Edirne*, 167, 193) < ? *Μεγάλη ἀγορά/*Μεγάλη χαρύα cf. Jacopo de Promontorio, *ca.* 1475: "Magalicarea"), a township in European Turkey (pop. 1973, 12,204), approximately 95 km to the south-south-east of Edirne [*q.v.*] and lying 57 km. to the west of Tekirdağ (Tekir/Tekfūr Daghi̊ [*q.v.*]) on the Ottoman "route of the left hand" (*ṣol ḳol*) from Istanbul to Greece and Albania.

In the oldest surviving Turkish narrative sources for the conquest of Eastern Thrace, the apparently uncontested (and possibly temporary) first Turkish seizure of Malḳara is linked with that of Bizye/Vize (which incontestably occurred between September 1357 and August 1358, cf. Schreiner, i, 9, 42; ii, 287-8), and of Kypsela/Ipsala, and with the name of Sulaymān Pasha b. Orkhan [*q.v.*] (Aḥmedī, *Iskender-nāme*, 120, 11. 117-119: *Wize wü Mighalkara wü Ibṣala/fetḥ oldi̊ aña* [sc. Sulaymān Pasha] *bu üči* [*sic:* ? *udji̊*] *bile/anda leshkeri oldi̊ zebūn*). In a different, *taḳwīm*-derived tradition, the fall of Malḳara is linked with Dimetoḳa [*q.v.*], Keshan and, dubiously, Edirne [*q.v.*; but see now Beldiceanu-Steinherr, *Recherches*, and *Travaux et mémoires*, i]. Other sources, some of which are reflected in later recensions (e.g. Saʿd al-Dīn, *Tādj al-tawārīkh*, i, 57-8), attribute to the *udj-begi* Ḥādjdjī Ilbegi the "extinction of the rites of polytheism" in Malḳara, while Murād I's tutor and commander Lālā Shāhīn Pasha is also linked with grants of land in the vicinity of Malḳara (cf. Babinger, *Beiträge*, 47). This process of Ottomanisation of territory originally conquered and controlled by the virtually autonomous *udj-beg*s probably took place after *ca.* 777/1376, from which time the other great *udj-begi* family of the Turakhan-oghullari̊, which also had its original seat in Rumeli in and around Malḳara (Beldiceanu-Steinherr, *Recherches*, 47-8), found more lasting possessions in the new *udj* being opened up by then in Thessaly.

Despite this uncertainty in matters of chronology, evidence, such as the listing of a number of villages in the *nāḥiye* of Malḳara as forming part of the *waḳf* of Sulaymān Pasha, and the names of some of them (e.g. Ṣarukhanlu, Ḳasṭamonlu, Tatarlar, Ḳarā Akhī, Ḳara Yakhshi; cf. Gökbilgin, *op. cit.*, 167-8; Beldiceanu-Steinherr, *op. cit.*, 142-3), suggests both the origin and the rapidity of Turkish colonisation in that part of Thrace. Malḳara, indeed, from the earliest period of Turkish rule, seems to have been a place of particular resort for *akhīs* and dervish elements (cf. the numerous 9th/15th and 10th/16th century foundations of minor *tekkes* and *zāwiyas* in and around Malḳara, Gökbilgin, *op. cit., passim*). Conversely, the *yürük* element in the population appears to have been scanty in comparison with districts more to the north and north-west (Gökbilgin, *Yürükler*, 262).

In the later centuries of Ottoman rule, the history of Malḳara appears to have been both obscure and uneventful. In the reign of Meḥemmed II, Malḳara possessed 938 Muslim hearths, but there was still a Christian element in the population, not only at the end of the 9th/15th century (cf. Barkan, *Belgeler*, i/1 [1964], Ek cedvel I), but also in the 19th century (150 Armenian houses and one chapel; 100 Greek houses and one church (*Journals* of Benjamin Barker [1823], cf. R. Clogg, in *Univ. Birmingham Historical Journal*, xii/2 [1971], 259; *Sāl-nāme-i wilāyet-i Edirne 1311*, 223 f.). In the 11th/17th century Malḳara formed a *ḳaḍāʾ* in the *sandjaḳ* of Gallipoli (Gelibolu [*q.v.*]); a rather meagre description of the town at this time is given by Ewliyā Čelebi [*q.v.*], *Seyāḥat-nāme*, v, 325). At the end of the 11th/17th century, it figures as a relay-station (*menzil-khāne*) on the above-mentioned *ṣol ḳol*, between Tekir Daghī and Keshan (Istanbul, Başbakanlık Arşivi, Kepeci 3006).

Bibliography: Given in the text; cf. also Sh. Sāmī Bey, *Ḳāmūs al-aʿlām*, vi, Istanbul 1316, 4329.

(C. J. Heywood)

MALKOM KHĀN, Mīrzā, Nāẓim al-Dawla (1249-1326/1833-1908). Perso-Armenian diplomat, journalist and concession-monger, important in the history of 19th-century Iran for his early advocacy of governmental reform and thorough-going westernisation, themes he expounded first in a series of privately-circulated treatises and then in the celebrated newspaper *Ḳānūn*.

He was born in the Iṣfahān suburb of Djulfā [*q.v.* in Suppl.] to an Armenian family whose ancestors had been transplanted there by Shāh ʿAbbās from Ḳarabāgh [*q.v.*] in the southern Caucasus. His father, Mīrzā Yaʿḳūb, was converted to Islam some time after the birth of Malkom, but the profession of Islam sat lightly on the shoulders of father and son; both appear to have believed in a "religion of humanity", inspired by freemansonry and the theories of Auguste Comte. Recognising the importance of Islam in Iranian society, Malkom generally took care to present his proposals in Islamically-acceptable terms (see H. R. Haweis, *Talk with a Persian statesman*, in *Contemporary Review*, lxx [1896], 74-7), a stratagem imitated by other secular reformists of the time.

After preliminary studies in Djulfā, Malkom received his further education at the Samuel Moorat College in Paris, an Armenian institution operated by the Mechitarist Fathers. The seven years which he spent studying in Paris were the first of his many residences in Europe, which far exceeded in total the years he spent in Iran. He returned to Iran in 1267/1850, entering government service in two capacities: as interpreter for European instructors at the newly-established Dār al-Funūn, the first institution of modern, secular learning in Iran, and as personal translator for Nāṣir al-Dīn Shāh. At the same time, he began composing his earliest treatises on the necessity of westernising reform, notably the *Kitābča-yi ghaybī* ("The Booklet inspired from the Unseen"). In 1273/1856, he acquired his first diplomatic experience, accompanying Mīrzā Farrukh Khān's mission to Paris and London. After his return the following year, Malkom established a *farāmūsh-khāna* (lit. "house of forgetfulness") [*q.v.* in Suppl.] in Tehran, the first masonic lodge to be set up in Iran. Numerous courtiers, merchants and even religious scholars joined the organisation, the purpose of which appears to have been twofold: the propagation of ideas of governmental reform, and the building up of a personal following for Malkom Khān. Fearing that the *farāmūsh-khāna* might be the centre of a republican conspiracy, Nāṣir al-Dīn Shāh ordered its dissolution in October 1861, and soon after banished Malkom to Arab ʿIrāḳ. After Malkom had spent a few months in Baghdād, the Ottoman authorities, responding to Iranian pressure, had him transferred to Istanbul.

There he was able to acquire the friendship of Mīrzā Ḥusayn Khān, the Iranian ambassador, and to enter his service. With his livelihood thus assured, he resumed writing his treatises, and also began to take an interest in alphabet reform, corresponding extensively on the subject with the ʿAdharbāydjānī playwright Fatḥ ʿAlī Ākhūnd-zāda [*q.v.*].

In 1288/1871, Mīrzā Ḥusayn Khān was recalled to Iran and appointed prime minister, and the following year he invited Malkom to join him as special adviser. Malkom accepted, and his influence is to be seen on the measures of governmental reorganisation that Mīrzā Ḥusayn Khān undertook. But a new emphasis had emerged in the thinking and aspirations of both men: the attraction of foreign capital to Iran, for the sake of personal profit as well as economic development. Thus Malkom became profitably involved in the negotiations surrounding the notorious Reuter concession, and it was partly in connection with the unfinished business of the concession that he left Iran early in 1873 to take up an appointment as Iranian envoy in London. He was now destined to spend the rest of his life in Europe, with the exception of four brief return visits to Iran, later in 1873, in 1881, in 1887 and in 1888.

His sixteen years as minister in London were spent chiefly in fruitless attempts to promote various concessions, above all for the construction of railways in Iran, and to interest Britain more closely in Iran, in the hope that she would provide a counterweight to Russia and would encourage reform in Iran. Despite his relative ineffectiveness in these areas, Malkom exerted some influence on events through correspondence with numerous princes and politicians, the most important of whom were Mīrzā ʿAlī Khān Amīn al-Dawla, a confidant of Nāṣir al-Dīn Shāh and later prime minister; Mīrzā Yūsuf Khān Mustashār al-Dawla, Iranian ambassador in Paris; Masʿūd Mīrzā Ẓill al-Sulṭān, the governor of Iṣfahān; and Muẓaffar al-Dīn Mīrzā, the heir-apparent. He also continued to compose treatises on the problems of government and reform, and took up again the question of alphabet reform (the scheme he finally elaborated is set forth in *Namūna-yi khaṭṭ-i ādamiyyat*, London 1303/1885).

The most important period of Malkom's career began after his dismissal from his diplomatic post in December 1889. The preceding year, he had obtained from Nāṣir al-Dīn Shāh a concession for the institution of a national lottery and the construction of casinos in Iran. The concession was swiftly rescinded, but Malkom deftly sold it to European investors before they had a chance to realise it was worthless. He invoked diplomatic immunity and escaped legal condemnation, but the profitable venture cost him his post of ambassador. Partly to avenge himself for his dismissal, he embarked on the publication of a newspaper, *Ḳanūn* ("The Law"), in which he castigated the Iranian government—particularly Amīn al-Sulṭān, the prime minister of the day—for its corruption, and hinted at the existence of a vast revolutionary network in Iran, owing allegiance to himself. It is unlikely that such a nework did exist, although an association called *Madjmaᶜ-i Ādamiyyat* ("The League of Humanity") did operate under Malkom's general and remote supervision, chiefly for the purpose of distributing *Ḳanūn*. Malkom also attempted to implicate the Bahāʾīs in his activities, almost certainly without foundation (see the letter of ᶜAbd al-Bahāʾ to E.G. Browne quoted in Browne, *Materials for the study of the Bábí religion,* Cambridge 1918, 296). Despite these ambiguities, it is certain that the newspaper was widely-circulated and avidly-read in Iran. Its strictures on tyranny struck a responsive chord, and it is indeed the impact made by *Ḳanūn* during the years preceding the constitutional revolution that is Malkom's chief claim to a place of importance in modern Iranian history. In keeping with its agitational purposes, *Ḳanūn* contained little systematic discussion of the changes Malkom proposed; noteworthy, however, is the demand, put forward in no. 35 of the newspaper, for the institution of a bicameral legislature, with the lower house to be elected by popular vote.

The contents of *Ḳanūn* appear to have been written almost exclusively by Malkom himself. Nonetheless, during the years of its publication he had extensive contact with other notable opponents of the Tehran government: Sayyid Djamāl al-Dīn Asadābādī ("Afghānī") [*q.v.*], who met Malkom in London in 1891; Mīrzā Āḳā Khān Kirmānī, a formerly Azalī freethinker resident in Istanbul, who helped in the distribution of *Ḳanūn* in the Ottoman Empire; and Shaykh al-Raʾīs Abu 'l-Ḥasan Mīrzā, a Ḳādjār prince of unconventional views living in India.

When Nāṣir al-Dīn Shāh was assassinated in 1896 and it appeared to Malkom that his political fortunes might be restored, the insurrectional tone which had marked *Ḳanūn* was abruptly abandoned. Two years later, in anticipation of his appointment to the Iranian embassy in Rome, Malkom ceased publishing *Ḳanūn* altogether. He retained his diplomatic post in Italy until the end of his life in July 1908, and no longer seriously involved himself in Iranian politics. Another organisation operating under this supervision, the *Djāmiᶜ-i Ādamiyyat* ("The Society of Humanity"), did, however, play a role of marginal importance in the struggles over the constitution in 1907 and 1908, and, more importantly, many of those active in promoting its cause can be shown to have belonged to the readership of *Ḳanūn*.

Most of those who knew Malkom personally—even those who can be termed his collaborators—seem to have had a low opinion of his personal qualities, regarding him as venal, arrogant and inconstant, despite his obvious talents as writer and thinker. Subsequent Iranian historiography accorded him a more honorable mention, emphasising his role as a pioneer of reform and modernisation. Of late, with the growing rejection in Iran of westernisation as a panacea, critical voices have again begun to be raised (Djalāl Āl-i Aḥmad, for example, ridiculed Malkom as "a homegrown Montesquieu" in his *Gharb-zadagī* (new, uncensored edition, Tehran 1357 *sh.*/1978, 80; for a similar, but more detailed critique, see Humā Nāṭiḳ, *Mā wa Mīrzā Malkom Khānhā-yi mā,* in her book *Az māst ki bar māst,* Tehran 1354 *sh.*/1975, 165-99).

Bibliography: (1) Published works of Malkom: *Kulliyyāt-i Malkum,* ed. Hāshim Rabīᶜ-zāda, Tabriz 1328/1908 (this collection contains 13 treatises, including one, *Risāla-yi Ghaybiyya,* falsely ascribed to Malkom); *Madjmūᶜa-yi āthār-i Mīrzā Malkom Khān,* ed. with introd. by Muḥīṭ Ṭabāṭabāʾī, Tehran 1327 *sh.*/1948 (the contents of this collection overlap with those of the preceding one); *Persian civilisation,* in *Contemporary Review,* lix (1891), 238-44; *Ḳanūn,* 42 issues, London 1890-8. (2) Unpublished works of Malkom: manuscript collection dated 1295/1878 containing 11 treatises, Central Library, University of Tehran 3257; *Risāla-yi Farāmūsh-khāna,* Malik Library, Tehran 3116; manuscript treatises in the library of Firīdūn Ādamiyyat, Tehran. (3) Letters written and received by Malkom: Fatḥ ᶜAlī Ākhūnd-zāda, *Alifbā-yi djadīd wa maktūbāt,* ed. Ḥamīd Muḥammad-zāda and Ḥamīd Ārāslī, Baku 1963 (contains letters exchanged between Malkom and Ākhūnd-zāda on the alphabet question); B. N. Paris, supplément persan 1986-91, 1995-7 (a collection of letters received by Malkom and donated by his widow in 1924; contents described in Blochet, *Catalogue des manuscrits persans,* iv, 284-91). (4) Studies of the life and ideas of Malkom: Hamid Algar, *Mirza Malkum Khan. A Study in the history of Iranian modernism,* Berkeley and Los Angeles 1973; Firishta Nūrāʾī, *Taḥḳīḳ dar afkār-i Mīrzā Malkom Khān,* Tehran 1352 *sh.*/1973; A. Piemontese, *Per una biografia di Mīrzā Malkom Xān,* in *AIUON,* n.s. xix (1969), 361-85; Ismāᶜīl Rāʾīn, *Mīrzā Malkom Khān. Zindagī wa kūshishhā-yi siyāsī-yi ū,* Tehran 1350 *sh.*/1971. (5) Works containing substantial mention of Malkom: Firīdūn Ādamiyyat, *Andīsha-yi taraḳḳī wa ḥukūmat-i ḳanūn dar ᶜaṣr-i Sipahsālār,* Tehran 1351 *sh.*/1972; idem, *Fikr-i āzādī wa muḳaddima-yi nihḍat-i Mashrūṭiyyat,* Tehran 1340 *sh.*/1961 (esp. 94-181); Mīrzā ᶜAlī Khān Amīn al-Dawla, *Khāṭirāt-i siyāsī,* ed. Ḥāfiẓ Farmānfarmāʾiyān, Tehran 1341 *sh.*/1962; W. S. Blunt, *Secret history of the English occupation of Egypt,* London 1903 (pp. 82-4 contain a fanciful autobiographical fragment of Malkom relating to the episode of the *farāmūsh-khāna*); Mīrzā Muḥammad Ḥasan Khān Iᶜtimād al-Salṭana, *Rūz-nāma-yi khāṭirāt,* ed. Īradj Afshār, Tehran 1345 *sh.*/ 1967; Humā Nāṭiḳ and Firīdūn Ādamiyyat, *Afkār-i idjtimāᶜī wa siyāsī wa iḳtiṣādī dar āthār-i muntashir nashuda-yi dawra-yi Ḳādjār,* Tehran 1356 *sh.*/1976 (contains numerous references to the unpublished treatises of Malkom); Djahāngīr Ḳāʾimmaḳāmī, *Rawābiṭ-i Ẓill al-Sulṭān wa Mīrzā Malkom Khān,* in *Barrasīhā-yi Tārīkhī,* iii/6 (Bahman-Isfand 1347/January-February 1969), 83-120; Ismāᶜīl Rāʾīn, *Farāmūsh-khāna wa frāmāsūnrī dar Īrān,* 3 vols., Tehran 1348 *sh.*/1968 (i, 487-568), contains a detailed account of Malkom's *farāmūsh-khāna*); Ibrāhīm Ṣafāʾī, *Rahbarān-i Mashrūṭa,* Tehran 1344 *sh.*/1966 (41-63 are devoted to Malkom); Khān Malik Sāsānī, *Siyāsatgarān-i dawra-yi Ḳādjār,* i, Tehran 1337 *sh.*/1958 (esp. 127-47).

(Hamid Algar)

MALLĀḤ, "Jewish quarter in Morocco". The institution of *mallāḥ/mellāḥ* is essentially linked to the history of Jewish settlement in the major cities of Morocco and to the distribution of their communities within the frontiers of the Sharīfian Empire. In

Morocco, it is the name given to the place of residence assigned to the Jewish *dhimmīs*.

At the outset, it is necessary to distinguish the urban *mallāḥ* from the rural *mallāḥ*. The former, as it exists in several large towns, is a quarter adjacent to the Muslim city, integrated within it or shifted to the nearby periphery, yet enclosed within a separate enclave defended by a wall and a fortified gateway. It is most often situated close to the *ḳaṣaba* (citadel), the residence of the king or the governor, in order to guarantee the security of its inhabitants, some of whom occupy senior positions in the civil administration or carry out important functions in the royal palace and must therefore remain close at hand in order to answer the summons, should their presence be required. The latter, the rural *mallāḥ*, that of the mountains and valleys of the Atlas and the Rīf, the southern and eastern plains as far as the fringes of the Sahara, is an "open" village exclusively inhabited by Jews, situated some distance from the nearest Muslim *ḳṣar* or the fortress of the protector *ḳāʾid*). Also to be noted is the existence, in some towns, of an old and a new *mallāḥ, mallāḥ ḳdīm* and *mallāḥ jdīd*. The reason may be a transfer of the Jewish population from one to the other, in order to move it away from an already existing site of Muslim culture or for purposes of construction (here we may note the religious scruples of the pious sultan Mawlāy Slīmān/Sulaymān, with reference to Tetouan and Salé), or it may be an extension of the former quarter on account of its over-population (al-Sawīra and Meknès/Miknās).

Not all towns necessarily possess a *mallāḥ*, and with those that do have one, it has not always been so. The institution of the *mallāḥ* was only imposed on some communities at a relatively recent date, as their history testifies. Whereas, in Christian cultures, segregation was the rule (although originally, here too, there was a preference for living together in the same quarter for reasons of security or simply for convenience, in order to facilitate the practice of ritual and the communal observance of religious laws, customs and usages), in Islamic lands the Jews coexisted for a long time, and almost everywhere, in the towns as well as in the country, with their Muslim fellow-citizens, in peaceful proximity in the same quarters and the same streets. Very often, and this predates the Arab conquest, there is evidence of a deliberate choice on the part of ethnic, religious and professional groups, to live together in the same space, with their own streets and quarters. Jewish quarters are called *ḥāra* in Algiers, Tunis and Tripoli; *ḳāʿa* in the Yemen; *maḥalla* in Persia, or quite simply *darb al-yahūd* "the street of the Jews" or *al-sharʿ* "the avenue".

The etymology of the term *mallāḥ* is closely associated with the history of the Jewish community of Fās and with what might be called its "ghettoisation". At the end of the 7th/13th century, the Marīnids founded, alongside Fās al-Bālī ("Old Fez"), Fās al-Jdīd ("New Fez"), and close by, a little later (first half of the 8th/14th century), the town of Ḥimṣ, which was initially allocated to the *Ghuzz* archers and the Christian militia; then, at the beginning of the 9th/15th century, in 1438 according to the Jewish chronicles (*Kisse ha-melakhim* "Throne of the Kings", by Raphael Moise Elbaz; *Yaḥas Fās* "Genealogy of Fās" by Abner Hassarfati), the Jews were compelled to leave their homes in Fās al-Bālī and to settle in Ḥimṣ, which had been built on a site known as *al-Mallāḥ* "the saline area". From toponymy (derived from the root *m-l-ḥ* with the connotations "salt", "to salt", etc.), this term is extended in a generic sense, becoming a common name which, passing from Fās to the other towns of Morocco, ultimately designated the Jewish quarter. All the other proposed etymologies are to be rejected, in particular that which maintains that *mallāḥ* is "salted, cursed ground" and that the Jews are "those appointed to the task of salting the heads of decapitated rebels". It should be noted that originally there was nothing derogatory about this term: some documents employ the expression "*mallāḥ* of the Muslims" and conversely, the Jewish quarter contained large and beautiful dwellings which were favoured residences for "the agents and ambassadors of foreign princes". But for the Jews, these transfers from one quarter to the other were resented as a bitter exile and as the manifestation of a painful segregation, often accompanied by the conversion to Islam of those who refused to submit to the exodus imposed by the royal edicts and to abandon their homes and their shops. This was what happened at Fās in 1438 and, much later, at Salé in 1807.

The *mallāḥ* of Fās is, in every respect, the oldest in Morocco and, for a long time, remained the only and the most important one. It is only in the second half of the 10th/16th century (*ca.* 1557) that the term *mallāḥ* appears in Marrakesh, with the settlement there of Jewish and Judaised populations from the Atlas and, in particular, from the city of Aghmāt where there had lived, since time immemorial, an important Jewish community. G. Mouette, a French captive in Morocco from 1670 to 1681, writes (*Histoire des Conquestes de Moulay Archy*, Paris 1683): "In Fās and in Morocco (= Marrakesh), the Jews are separated from the inhabitants, having their own quarters set apart, surrounded by walls of which the gates are guarded by men appointed by the King ... In the other towns, they are intermingled with the Moors." It was not until 1682, or more than a century later, that a third *mallāḥ* was founded; it was that of the town of Miknās, new capital of the kingdom of Mawlāy Ismāʿīl (1672-1727). At the beginning of the 19th century, *ca.* 1807, the "ghettoisation" of the Jews was undertaken by the pious sultan Mawlāy Sulaymān in the towns of the coastal region, at Rabat and Salé, at al-Sawīra (Mogador) and at Tetouan. With the exception of Tetouan, where the Spanish word *juderia* is used, elsewhere it is the term *mallāḥ* which designates the new Jewish residential areas.

In Rabat, the Jews were living alongside the Muslims in the Bḥīra quarter when, in 1807, the sultan ordered the construction of a *mallāḥ* at the eastern extremity of the town, buying the land with his own money, building houses, kilns, mills and shops, all in the space of one year. In Salé, the New Mallāḥ, built in 1807, is a long avenue extending from the Gate of the Mallāḥ to the old monumental gate dating from the Marīnid period; in the alleyways which open out on this avenue there are 200 houses, 20 shops and trading booths, two kilns and two mills.

The Jewish community of Mogador deserves a special mention: the Jews were for a long time a majority in this town which was familiar with intense commercial activity and uninterrupted international relations (with the United States and Europe) from its recent foundation, in 1765, on ancient sites (the Purple Islands in the time of Juba II, the Portuguese Castello Real) until the beginning of the 20th century. When Muḥammad b. ʿAbd Allāh set about building the town, there were Jews living in the village of Dyābāt on the Oued Ḳsob, some 2 km. to the south of the town. To populate the new city, designed to replace Agadir as a centre of international commerce, the sultan appealed to the wealthieth and most dynamic Jews of other Moroccan communities, conferring upon them, along with the title of *tudjdjār al-sulṭān* "the King's merchants", special privileges such as tax exemptions and other immunities, assigning them comfortable homes in the quarter known as *ḳaṣaba al-ḳdīma* which was the residence of the governor, the higher functionaries and the consuls. The other Jews and Christian traders lived, with the Muslims, in the *madīna*. As in Tetouan, Rabat and Salé, it was in 1807 that orders were given for the separation of Jews from Muslims and for the construction of the present-day "old *mallāḥ*", with a surrounding wall and a fortified gate. Becoming overpopulated (8,000 souls in 1865), it was permitted to extend into the quarter known as Shabanāt where it took the name of *al-mallāḥ al-jdīd* "the new *mallāḥ*".

On the topography of the *mallāḥ*, administrative organisation, commercial and manufacturing activities, intellectual and cultural life, see in the *Bibl.* the works which the author of the present article has devoted to these various themes.

Bibliography: M. Gaudefroy-Demombynes, *Marocain: mellah*, in *JA*, ii (1914), 651-8; J. Goulven, *Les mellahs de Rabat-Salé*, Paris 1927; L. Brunot and E. Malka, *Textes judéo-arabes de Fès*, Rabat 1939; J. Benech, *Essai d'explication d'un mellah*, Marrakech 1940 (?); R. le Tourneau, *Fès avant le Protectorat*, Casablanca 1949; G. Vajda, *Un recueil de textes judéo-marocains*, in *Hespéris*, xii (1951); H. Z. Hirschberg, *Histoire des Juifs d'Afrique du Nord* (in Hebrew, see also the English version, Leiden 1974, i), Jérusalem 1965; D. Corcos, *Studies in the History of the Jewish Morocco*, (collection of articles in Hebrew, French and English), Jerusalem 1976; H. Zafrani, *Les Juifs du Maroc. Vie sociale, économique et religieuse. Etude de Taqqanot et Responsa*, Paris 1972; idem, *Poésie juive en Occident Musulman*, Paris 1977; idem, *Littératures populaires et dialectales juives en Occident Musulman*, Paris 1980; idem, *Mille ans de vie juive au Maroc, culture et histoire, religion et magie*, Paris 1983; see also G. Colin, *Mellāḥ*, in *EI*[1] and D. Corcos, *Jewish Quarter*, in *Encyclopaedia Judaica*, Jerusalem 1971. (H. ZAFRANI)

MALLŪ IḲBĀL ḴHĀN, Indian military leader of the Tughluḳ period.

The decade of decadence following the death of Sultan Fīrūz Shāh of Dihlī in 790/1388 is marked by the manoeuvrings of the princes, intrigues of the nobles and sufferings of the people. According to Firishta, the vast kingdom of the Tughluḳs fell to pieces and the central administration lost all authority over the outlying provinces. Confusion reached such a point that there occurred an unprecedented spectacle of two sovereigns within a radius of 12 miles of Dihlī, i.e. Nuṣrat Shāh at Fīrūzābād and Maḥmūd Shāh at Djahānpanāh, like two kings in the game of chess, to use Badāʾūnī's words. Both the monarchs were no more than puppets in the hands of their ambitious but unscrupulous patron-nobles; and Mallū Iḳbāl Khān was one such noble who emerged as the strongest out of this internecine mêlée.

Mallū was one of the three sons of Daryā Ḵhān, better known as Ẓafar Ḵhān Lodī II, the influential Afghān chief under Fīrūz Shāh Tughluḳ. Along with his elder brother Sārang Ḵhān, who was governor of Dīpālpūr, he obtained ascendancy over all other *amīrs* of Sultan Maḥmūd, who gave him the title Iḳbāl Khān and the command of the fortress of Siri, modern Shahpur Jat, east of the Dihlī-Ḳuṭb road. He owed his rise also to the Sultan's minister, Muḳarrab Ḵhān, another member of the ruling military oligarchy of that time. Perfidious as he was by nature, Iḳbāl Ḵhān

gradually got rid of those whom he regarded as rivals. He first aligned himself with the other king, Sultan Nuṣrat Shāh, whom he deceitfully dislodged from Fīrūzābād, which he immediately occupied in 800/1398. He followed it up by treacherously killing his benefactor Muḳarrab Ḵhān and securing complete control of Dihlī. Annexation of Pānipāt a little later made Iḳbāl Ḵhān undisputed master of the region.

His triumph proved short-lived, as Tīmūr's sudden invasion of the Dōʾāb country caught him unawares. He confronted the Mongol invaders, but had to flee in order to avoid complete annihilation. He escaped to Baran (modern Bulandshahr), while Sultan Maḥmūd fled to Gudjarāt.

After Tīmūr's onslaught ended, Iḳbāl Ḵhān again took possession of the ruined city of Dihlī. Though he had the capital of the sultanate under his sway, his writ did not extend beyond a part of the Dōʾāb and some districts round Dihlī. In 804/1401, he invited thither the fugitive Sultan Maḥmūd Shāh and accorded him a warm reception, without however parting with the reality of power. Not content with a limited sovereignty, Iḳbāl Ḵhān was bent upon extending the boundaries of his suzerainty. But he felt frustrated by the powerful Sharḳī rulers of Djawnpur [q.v.] in the east and the influential governor of Multān, Khiḍr Ḵhān, in the west. Accompanied by Sultan Maḥmūd, Iḳbāl Ḵhān undertook an expedition against Djawnpur, where Ibrāhīm Shāh Sharḳī had lately ascended the throne. At a time when battle lines were being drawn, Sultan Maḥmūd secretly deserted Iḳbāl's camp and went over to the ruler of Djawnpur with a view to securing his assistance to extricate himself from tutelage of Iḳbāl Ḵhān. On failing there, the Sultan went to Kanawdj [q.v.], an appendage of the Sharḳī kingdom, where he was allowed to live with the status of a local king as long as Iḳbāl lived. Iḳbāl returned to Dihlī in 805/1402 disappointed.

Iḳbāl Ḵhān now decided to try his luck in the west, an attempt which brought about his downfall. He first marched to Samana, which was ruled by Bahrām Ḵhān Turkbačča, who was in league with Khiḍr Ḵhān. Though Iḳbāl managed to have Bahrām Ḵhān murdered, he had to face the challenge of Khiḍr Ḵhān, and in a fierce engagement by the river Dahinda in Adjodhan (modern Pakpattan in Pakistan), Iḳbāl Ḵhān was defeated and killed by Khiḍr Ḵhān's army in 808/1405. His severed head was presented to Khiḍr Ḵhān, who sent it to Fatḥpūr, the latter's native town, where it was fixed on the gate of the city. According to the *Ṭabaḳāt-i Akbarī*, the family and dependents of Iḳbāl Ḵhān were expelled from Dihlī and sent to Kol, but none of them was harmed in any way.

A Persian inscription of Iḳbāl Ḵhān, fixed on the southern bastion of an old ʿīdgāh at Kharera village near Dihlī, describes him as Mallū Sulṭānī, indicating that he insisted on being called a slave or servant of the Sultan. It must be said to his credit that in spite of possessing what were in effect the absolute political and administrative powers of a king, Iḳbāl Ḵhān never assumed royal prerogatives, such as striking coins in his name and inserting his name in the *khuṭba*. The epitaph referred to above also reveals his religious zeal in having erected the place of worship with his own money, and condemns the destruction and desolation wrought by the Mongol marauders.

Bibliography: *Proceedings of the Indian History Congress, Second Session*, 1938; *History and culture of the Indian people*, vi. *The Delhi Sultanate*, Bombay 1960; K. S. Lal, *Twilight of the Sultanate*, Bombay 1963; Mahdī Ḥusain, *The Tughluq dynasty*, Calcutta 1963;

A comprehensive history of India. v. *The Delhi Sultanate*, Bombay 1970. (ABDUS SUBHAN)

MALTA (ancient Melita; Ar. Māl(i)ṭa; French Malte), the name of the main island of a Mediterranean archipelago which is situated around 100 km from Sicily and about 300 km from Tunisia and which also includes Gozo, Comino, Cominotto, Filf(o)la and some unimportant rocks, measuring 47 km. from the north-west to the south-east. The island of Malta measures 27 km in length and 14 km in breadth; its main town is Valletta (Fr. La Valette), the capital of what has been since 21 September 1964 an independent state included however in the British Commonwealth. In 1968, the total population was around 320,000. Malta is exclusively Christian, and owes its mention in the *EI* solely because it was occupied for more than two centuries by the Muslims and because its official language derives from an Arabic dialect.

1. History. Malta was inhabited in ancient times by a Mediterranean race, whose megalithic monuments are preserved at Hagiar Kim ("standing stones"), Hal Tarxen and Hal Saflieni. It was colonised very early, certainly before the 10th century B.C., by the Phoenicians, and formed a base for their trading ships. It is not certain that the name of Malta is derived from the Phoenician, while the Phoenician origin of Gaulos (Gozo), meaning "a merchant boat of round shape", seems certain.

The Carthaginians became masters of the island in the 7th-6th century B.C. and kept it for four or five centuries. The Romans conquered it in 218 B.C., and for the next ten centuries Malta remained under Roman and Greek influence, being situated near Eastern Sicily. Gozo had only Greek coins, and Greek and Roman coins in great number were minted in Malta. Very early, with St. Paul in the 1st century A.D., the island was converted to Christianity; during the Western Empire's decay the Byzantines established themselves in it; after their conquest of Northern Africa, the possession of Malta became indispensable to them.

The Muslim conquest of Malta is generally fixed in 256/870, but it is possible that the island was the goal of at least a reconnaissance raid in 221/835-6, if one considers it probable that the island was included amongst those against which the Ag͟hlabid Ibrāhīm sent a fleet in that year. E. Rossi (in *EI*[1] s.v.) thought that it would not be too bold to adopt the view of Malta's falling under Muslim domination even before 184/800, and added that de Goeje shared his opinion (in *ZDMG*, lviii, 905 n. 2), but there is nothing to confirm this hypothesis. What seems certain is that in 256/870 a squadron left Sicily under the command of Aḥmad (called Ḥabas͟hī) b. ʿUmar b. ʿAbd Allāh b. Ibrāhīm b. al-Ag͟hlab in order to relieve Malta, which was being invested by a Byzantine fleet (Ibn al-At͟hīr, vi, 307, and al-Nuwayrī, ed. Remiro, ii, 81, do not give the exact year). This shows that the island was already occupied by the Muslims before that date, and the year 255/869 indicated notably by Ibn K͟haldūn (*ʿIbar*, iv, 430) and al-Ḳalḳas͟handī (*Ṣubḥ*, vi, 121) should probably be retained. The retreat, without a fight, of the Byzantine fleet on 28 Ramaḍān 256/29 August 870 seems to have given the signal for ill-treatment inflicted on the Greek population of the island, the arrest of its bishop, who was then sent into captivity at Palermo, and the destruction of the church, the materials from which were re-used at the time of the construction of the Ḳaṣr Ḥabas͟hī at Sousse.

In Malta, the Muslim occupation was certainly more permanent and strongly established than in Sicily; the narrow island was completely subjugated by the conquerors, who made it a strategic base; this helps us to understand how the Arab-Berber Muslims of Africa succeeded in forcing upon Malta the Arabic language, from which the modern Maltese dialect is derived (see below, 2).

Besides the Arabic language and place-names, the Muslims have left in Malta a few coins and a considerable number of inscriptions on tombstones; one of them, the celebrated inscription called of Maymūna, dated 568/1173, was published more than a century ago, and repeatedly studied by orientalists (Italinski, Lanci, Amari, Nallino, etc.); another one, found in Gozo, is to be seen in the Malta Museum. About twenty more have been found in the excavations in 1922-5 at Rábato (near the place called Notabile); they are preserved in the Museum of the Villa Romana, near the place of the excavations.

The Muslims lost Malta in 483/1090, when the Normans conquered it; they were however allowed to live on the island under the Norman government until 647/1249, the date when Frederick II expelled them. From 1530 to 1798 Malta was the seat of the Order of St. John of Jerusalem, which the Turks had expelled from Rhodes in 1522. The Order organised there an important war fleet. The island was in constant relations with the East and with Barbary; thousands of Muslim slaves were taken to Malta; the Maltese ships had repeated encounters with those of the Porte and the Levantine and Barbary pirates. The Turks attempted to occupy Malta in 1565, with their well-known expedition, which ended in disaster, and again in 1614; more than once, they threatened to invade it under Sultan Meḥemmed IV.

A few Arabic manuscripts and nautical charts, of no great value, are preserved in the Public Library of Malta and in its Museum.

Bibliography: S. Gsell, *Histoire ancienne de l'Afrique du Nord*, Paris 1918-20, i-iv; A. Mayr, *Die Insel Malta im Altertum*; G. A. Abela, *Descrittione di Malta, isola nel mare siciliano*, Malta 1647 (repr. with additions by G. A. Ciantar 1722); M. Miège, *Histoire de Malte*, Paris 1840, 20-1; Th. Nöldeke, review of H. Stumme's works, in *ZDMG*, lviii, 903 ff.; R. Paribeni, *Malta, un piccolo paese dalla grande storia*, Rome 1925; I. Zammit, *Malta: the Maltese islands and their history*, Malta 1954; M. Talbi, *Aghlabides*, index; B. Blouet, *The story of Malta*, Malta 1967; A. A. Vasiliev, *Byzance et les Arabes*, tr. M. Canard, ii/1, Brussels 1968, 25.

(E. ROSSI*)

2. The Maltese language. Maltese is the language of the inhabitants of the Maltese Islands (Malta, Gozo, and Comino; *ca.* 330,000 speakers). It is to some extent a mixed language, for its basic structure, together with much of the vocabulary for the more basic features of life, are derived from Arabic—mainly North African Arabic—while an important Romance adstratum (mainly [Siculo-] Italian) comprises, in particular, vocabulary linked with more advanced civilisation. The relation between the two constituent elements is comparable to that between the Anglo-Saxon and Norman French elements in English. For several centuries mainly a medium of oral communication, Maltese became a literary language chiefly during the 19th and 20th centuries; it gained official recognition in 1933, and became the national language of Malta in 1964. It is written in a modified form of the Latin alphabet (29 letters; see table), being the only Semitic language thus written; the present system, officially adopted in 1934, follows

experimentation influenced by Italian and Arabic models from the 18th century onwards. The language has thus been subject to standardising influences only for a comparatively brief period, and it is still actively developing in response to modern needs. Several variants of contemporary Maltese can be distinguished. Literary Standard Maltese, used in *belles lettres*, tends to aim at a mainly Semitic diction. Journalistic Maltese tends to differ from it slightly in spelling, phonology, morphology and syntax, but substantially in vocabulary and phraseology (many foreign loanwords and *calques*). Colloquial Standard Maltese is intermediate between the two, varying in composition according to socio-linguistic factors such as the social standing of individual speakers. In addition, there is dialectal Maltese, varying from town to town and from village to village, but essentially to be divided into urban and rural. Dialectal Maltese is now under threat, owing to the levelling effects of compulsory education and the news media.

Any attempt to offer a description of present-day Maltese, and still more of the past history of the language is faced with some difficulties. Grammars and dictionaries of Maltese were indeed being made at least by the 18th century: notably early works are Agius de Soldanis' grammar *Della lingua Punica presentemente usata dai Maltesi* (Rome 1750), and his unpublished dictionary surviving in manuscript *Damma tla Kliem Kartaginis Mscerred Fel Fom tal Maltin u Ghaucin*, followed by M. A. Vassalli's dictionary *Lexicon Melitense-Latino-Italum* (Rome 1796) and his two grammars, *Mylsen Phoenico-Punicum sive grammatica Melitensis* (Rome 1791), and *Grammatica della lingua Maltese* (Malta 1827). Understandably, the Maltese described by them differs somewhat from that of today. Correct present usage as taught in schools is given in A. Cremona's *Tagħlim fuq il-Kitba Maltija* (2 vols. Malta 1934-8; many reprints), and in the grammars by E. Sutcliffe and J. Aquilina listed in the bibliography below. However, Maltese is at present not yet completely covered descriptively; thus no complete comprehensive dictionary on modern lines is available: the one by E. Serracino Inglott, *Il Miklem Malti* (Maltese-Maltese, Malta 1975 ff.) is still proceeding, while the Maltese-English dictionary by J. Aquilina is still to be published. There is also as yet no complete and comprehensive description of Maltese dialects, though work is proceeding.

Historically, Maltese is at present practically undocumented before the 15th century, and very badly known up to the 18th. To the 15th century belongs the earliest known Maltese literary text, the *Cantilena* by Peter Caxaro published by G. Wettinger and M. Fsadni (*Peter Caxaro's Cantilena, a poem in medieval Maltese*, Malta 1968; for a discussion, see the literature quoted by G. Wettinger, in *Jnal. of Maltese Studies*, xii [1978], 88 ff., and R. Bin Bovingdon, in *ibid.*, 106 ff.), as well as Maltese phrases and names of persons and places contained in notarial documents, all written in varying and often ambiguous transcriptions into the Latin alphabet. More texts of this nature are available from the 16th and 17th centuries (cf. G. Wettinger, in *Oriental studies presented to Benedikt S. J. Isserlin*, Leiden 1980, 173 ff.; idem, in *Procs. of the First Congress of Mediterranean Studies of Arabo-Berber influence*, Algiers 1973, 484 ff.), as well as a 16th-century word list gathered by the German traveller H. Megiser, published in his *Propugnaculum Europae* ... (Cracow 1611; discussed by W. Cowan in *Journal of Maltese Studies*, ii [1964], 217 ff.). Of 17th century date is another word list compiled by the English traveller Philip Skippon (cf. A. Cremona, *A historical review of the Maltese language*, Malta 1945, 14), as well as a sonnet by G. P. Bonamico (*ca.* 1672). From the 18th century, a few prose texts also survive, such as popular dialogues by de Soldanis, sermons and other devotional work, the Lord's Prayer (1718) and the first catechism in Maltese (1752)—brief bibliographical notes concerning all of which can be found in Wettinger and Fsadni, *op. cit.*, 8 ff. Broadly speaking, however, Maltese prose literature postdates the age of the early grammarians and lexicographers, though the origins of Maltese folk literature (songs, ballads, tales, proverbs) are earlier. Confronted with this scarcity of data, scholars attempting to trace the development of Maltese, and to explain its character and relations to Arabic dialects, have been compelled to work back from the present state of the language, to some extent, through theoretical reconstruction.

It can, however, be said that Maltese contains, according to present information, no recognisable linguistic elements going back to the pre-Phoenician prehistoric period. Though Phoenician or Punic was both spoken and written in Malta from *ca.* 800 B.C. to the Roman conquest of 218 B.C. and probably afterwards, the once popular opinion that Maltese is a direct descendant from Phoenician or Punic is now antiquated (cf. P. Grech, *Journal of Maltese Studies,* i [1961], 130 ff.).

The persistence of Phoenician substratum influences in Maltese has been suggested by J. Cantineau with reference to the realisation of *ā* as *ō* in Maltese rural dialects (*Cours de phonétique arabe,* Paris 1960, 100), and other scholars have suggested morphological or lexical survivals; but all this remains hypothetical at present. The existence of Latin elements in Maltese vocabulary going back to the period of Roman rule there is also disputed (cf. J.Aquilina, *Papers in Maltese linguistics,* Malta 1961, 8 ff.), and Greek terms which should date from the time of Byzantine supremacy, like *lapsi* (from Greek *analepsis* "Ascension Day") are remarkably few. The linguistic board appears in fact to have been wiped clean to an astonishing extent by the Arab conquest of A.D. 870, which brought in the North African dialectal (pre-Hilālian) Arabic which is still the basis of Maltese. This included some Berber elements in vocabulary (cf. G. S. Colin, in *Mémorial André Basset (1895-1956),* Paris 1957, 7-16; J. Aquilina, *Maltese linguistic surveys,* Malta 1976, 25 ff.). Possible links with Eastern Arabic, like the Maltese realisation of *ḳ* as a glottal stop, are less cogent, though *bitāʿ*, recently identified in transcription in 15th century Maltese lists as the ancestral form of present Maltese *ta* "of" (G. Wettinger, *Journal of Maltese Studies,* vi [1971], 37 ff.), links Malta with Egypt rather than the North African dialect region, which has *mtaʿ*. Eastern Arabic-derived religious terms were possibly brought to Malta by Maronite clergy (J. Aquilina, *Maltese linguistic survey,* 19 ff.). The essentially Western Arabic dialect ancestry of Maltese is in fact sufficiently evident from two morphological features: the formation of the first persons singular and plural of the imperfect of verbs according to the pattern *nḳtl/nḳtlu* as against Classical and Eastern Arabic *ʾḳtl/nḳtl,* and the replacement of the verbal form derived from IX by a modified XI, with a resultative meaning (like *hmar* (*ḥmār*) "to redden"). See further on the whole question, Ph. Marçais, ARABIYYA. 3. Western dialects.

Nevertheless, classical literary Arabic was used in Malta as well, down to *ca.* 1200 A.D. at least, as is shown by tombstones and surviving quotations from three 12th century Maltese poets writing in Arabic. This must have kept dialectal tendencies in check at least among the educated. However, the Norman conquest of A.D. 1090, followed by the expulsion of the Arabs in 1249, gradually separated Malta from the Arabic-speaking world of Islam and linked her with the Romance-speaking part of the Christian West. This would have involved the removal of the linguistic control up to then exercised over Maltese Arabic by the Arab scribal and grammatical tradition, and allowed dialectal tendencies and local linguistic development to progress unchecked. With this one may link grammatical impoverishment, such as the loss of derived form IV of verbs (not all of which can still form perfect, imperfect and participle), or the loss of the feminine plurals of adjectives, besides a reduction and modification in the stock of broken plurals (e.g. merging of type *faʿālīlᵘ* with *faʿālilᵘ*, spread of *faʿālī*), as well as the survival and development of aberrant forms, like mixed verbal forms derived from forms VII and VIII (such as *intharat* as well as normal *inħarat* "was ploughed"—Arabic root *ḥ-r-th̲*), or of forms X and II (like *stkerraħ* "he loathed"—Arabic root *k-r-h*, besides normal forms X of type *staktab*). There are analogies to such developments in dialectal Arabic, including North African Arabic. This is partly true also where the development of auxiliaries is concerned, Maltese *giegħed/qed* corresponding to dialectical Arabic *ḳāʿid* followed by the imperfect, indicating the actual present.

Lexically, Maltese underwent progressive shrinkage of its Semitic stock—even basic Semitic terms, like "father", "much, many" have disappeared. The former was replaced by Romance *missier*, the latter by Semitic terms changed in meaning, like *ħafna* (Arabic "a handful"), or *wisq* (Arabic "a load"). Changes in meaning are indeed not uncommon: thus, e.g., in Maltese *ħalq* means "mouth", not "throat" as in Arabic. This loss of contact with Literary Arabic also meant that Maltese was not much affected later by the Arabic renaissance of the 19th and 20th centuries; its vocabulary of abstract and technical terms has remained non-Semitic to a considerable extent, the use e.g. of verbal nouns, or of nouns ending in *-iyya* (Maltese *-ija*) for such purposes being much rarer than in Arabic. The replacement of Arabic as a written language first by Latin, then in the 15th century by Siculo-Italian and from the 16th onwards by Italian, the close connection with Sicily which continued during the rule of the Knights (1530-1798), and the influx of Romance speakers (administrators, merchants, artisans, sailors and fishermen) into Malta, all explain the importance which the Romance, and in particular the Siculo-Italian, element then acquired in Maltese. Standard Italian became the language of law and administration, literature and culture, up to the 20th century. The coming of British rule (1813-1964) added an English element to the language, which is noticeable now particularly in such semantic fields as sport, commerce and administration, and in professional and technical vocabularies. The English component in Maltese is still developing, owing to the importance of English as an international medium and also because it is taught in Maltese schools. On the other hand, recent interest in Malta's Arab connections has not so far found much linguistic reflection.

The present condition of the language thus evolved can be summarised as follows. While the Semitic vocabulary in Maltese may be limited, it is quantitatively very strong where actual use is concerned. In literary and ecclesiastical texts it may amount to over 90% of the total, according to word statistical investigation. In spoken Maltese the percentage is smaller, but even in newspapers with their tendency to use foreign loan words the Semitic element comes to over two-thirds, the Romance element to not quite one-third; similarly also in other texts dealing with political, social, and economic matters (cf. F. Krier, *Le maltais au contact de l'italien*, in *Forum phoneticum*, xv, Hamburg 1976, 110 ff.; E. Fenech, *Contemporary journalistic Maltese*, Leiden 1978, 216-17 and *passim*). The growth of this Romance component can be followed to some extent over the centuries: in Peter Caxaro's *Cantilena* there is one single purely Romance term, but by the mid-18th century de Soldanis' dictionary shows the Romance constituent in Maltese vocabulary was fairly substantial. English words in most contexts on the other hand amount to less than 5% of the total.

Phonetically, the Semitic stock of Maltese has undergone considerable changes. Among consonants, the emphatics, primary or secondary, have become fused with the corresponding non-emphatics: *ṭ* > *t*, *ḍ* > *d*, *ẓ*> *d*, *ṣ* > *s* (*ṛ* > *r*, etc.). However, the former presence or absence of emphasis may still be responsible for the different colouring of adjoining vowels: contrast Maltese *sajf* "summer" (Arabic *ṣayf*) with *sejf* "sword" (Arabic *sayf*). Interdental fricatives *d̲h̲*, *t̲h̲* have become stops *d*, *t*. Arabic *ḳ* is normally replaced in Standard Maltese pronunciation by glottal stop (occasionally by *g*; and in some dialect pronunciations by *k*). *K̲h̲* has become fused with *ḥ*, and *g̲h̲* with ʿ (but *k̲h̲* and *g̲h̲* survive as allophones in some dialects). ʿ itself, while still written, is no longer pronounced: it has left traces of various kinds (pharyngalisation, colouring, or lengthening of neighbouring vowels); in some contexts it is replaced by *ḥ*. *H* in standard Maltese is mostly silent (in which case it may cause compensatory lengthening in neighbouring vowels); in certain conditions it may become *ḥ*. Many of these changes seem to have occurred after the 15th or 16th century, when ʿ, *d̲h̲*, *t̲h̲* may still have existed (though the fusion of *d̲h̲* and *t̲h̲* with *d* and *t* may have gone some way in pre-Hilālian Arabic, from which Maltese descended, and *d̲h̲* had become *d* in Muslim Sicily); *k̲h̲* and *g̲h̲* were still fairly widely used in the 18th century. The diminishing Semitic consonantal répertoire was on the other hand augmented by the inclusion of Romance phonemic consonants *p*, *v*, *č*, *ts*, *dz*, and Romance influence is reponsible for a much wider use of *g*. The devoiced pronunciation of voiced consonants, an occasional feature in Arabic dialects, became regular in word final position or before voiceless consonants (thus *bieb* "door" is pronounced approximately *biep*, and *libsa* "suit" *lipsa*). *Vice versa*, voiceless consonants before voiced consonants become voiced. Consonant assimilation, fairly frequent, also affects the verbal prefix *t-* (e.g. *iġġib* (for Arabic *tad̲j̲īb* "you/she bring(s)" (via *itjīb*). As for vowels, the various realisations of phonemic vowels (*a*, *i*, *u*:*ā*, *ī*, *ū* inherited from Arabic are supplemented by the phonemic vowels *e*, *o*:*ē*, *ō* taken over from Romance. Since there is pronounced stress in Maltese, short unstressed vowels may disappear. Original Arabic *i* and *u* in open syllable before stress normally vanish, but short *a* is preserved near former emphatics and after ʿ or *g̲h̲*; since in some environments it may have gone into *i* before disappearing, Maltese may originally have been a "differential" dialect in Cantineau's terminology (*a* in the feminine singular ending *-a* once seems to have undergone *imāla*—15th century transcriptions not rarely give it as *-e*, but present Standard Maltese again has *-a*; the reasons for this change are not clear. *Imala* of *-a* may still occur in rural dialects). Among long vowels, Arabic *ā* is now mostly represented by *ie* (*ī*) in Maltese, rarely by *ē*—

except near former emphatics, velars, and pharyngals, where it may survive as *ā*. This *ie* is very typical of Maltese; it seems to have spread at the expense of *ē* during the last four centuries. Diphthongs mostly survive with some modification, though Arabic *ay* may be represented by *ī*, and *aw* by *ū*, as in *xitan* (Arabic *s̲h̲ayṭān*) "devil", or *mulud* (Arabic *mawlūd*) "born". Vowel harmony, and the formation of prosthetic and epenthetic vowels, are all noticeable features.

Maltese morphology remains essentially that of dialectal Arabic, somewhat modified and reduced. Foreign loan words may be fitted into this framework: thus, among nouns, *spalla* "shoulder" is given the dual ending *-ejn* (*spallejn* "two shoulders"), and sound or broken plurals are often given to loan words. On the other hand, foreign plural endings may be preserved: Italian *-i* (standing also for Italian *-e*), and English *-s*, the latter in recent loans. Incorporation often involves restructuring of loan words. In the case of Romance loan terms, this has most recently been studied by F. Krier (*Le maltais au contact de l'Italien*, following J. Aquilina, *The structure of Maltese*, Malta 1959; *Papers in Maltese linguistics*. Italian vowels may undergo the impact of Sicilian: cf. Maltese *munita* with Italian *moneta*. Nouns may lose vocalic endings but receive prosthetic prefixes (cf. Maltese *istess* with Italian *stesso*). Unstressed short vowels, but also some consonants, may be lost (cf. Maltese *storbju* with Italian *disturbo*, archaic variant *disturbio*). Early Romance loan words in particular may show a replacement of Romance by corresponding Semitic consonants (cf. Sicilian *palla* with Maltese *balla*). English loan words, recently studied by E. Fenech (*Contemporary journalistic Maltese*) have undergone similar restructuring: cf. e.g. Maltese *kitla*, plural *ktieli*, for English *kettle*. Verbs of both Romance and English derivation are similarly adapted, e.g. by internal modifications, or the addition of prefixes or suffixes; cf. e.g. *ikkopja* "copied" *jibbrajba* "bribes".—The Romance element has in turn affected the Semitic by the incorporation of endings—*azz* (from Sicilian - *acciu*) and *-un* (Italian *-one*) cf. *sakranazz* "addicted to drunkenness" and *darun* "big house", from Semitic *sakrān* and *dār*, respectively.

This substantial influx of foreign terms has led to many Romance-Semitic doublets, such as *hu stessu/hu nnifsu*, both meaning "he himself". Sometimes there are different shades of meaning. The occurrence of numerous *calques* derived from Italian and English expressions is a related feature. On the other hand, foreign influence in syntax is rather less marked, though e.g. the frequence of the sentence structure in which the verbal predicate follows rather than precedes the subject may owe something to European models.

Dialectal Maltese has received attention since the 18th century, when Vassalli recognised the existence of five regional dialects in the Maltese Islands and outlined their respective characteristics. H. Stumme's *Maltesische Studien* (*Leipziger Semitische Studien*, i/4, Leipzig 1904) made an outstanding contribution of permanent value; within the last decade, study has received a renewed impetus (cf. works by P. Schabert, J. Aquilina and B. S. J. Isserlin *et alii*, and A. Borg listed in the *Bibl.*). While urban dialects may be nearer to Standard Maltese, rural dialects show some archaic features: *k̲h̲* and *g̲h̲* are still sounded in some Gozitan villages, and the *imāla* of Arabic *ā* into *ē* (or *ī*—the latter found especially in Gozo) recalls 15th century transcriptions. The realisation of the *ā*, preserved as *ā* in standard Maltese, as *ō* is typical of country dialects; so is a tendency towards the diphthongisation of simple vowels, such as *ū* into *eo* or *eu*. The age of the former phenomenon is unclear—up to now, it has not been attested in early transcriptions—but the latter may have spread during the past few centuries. A greater tendency to use rare or archaic terms and broken plurals, and to employ Semitic rather than Romance vocabulary, are shared also by some oral folk literature. All in all, rural dialectal Maltese may represent to some extent a strain parallel to Standard Maltese, but one which is less far removed from the Western Mediterranean Arabic ancestry of the Maltese language than the latter.

Bibliography: (in addition to works mentioned in the text above): Grammars: E. F. Sutcliffe, *A grammar of the Maltese language*, Oxford 1936, reprints in Malta; J. Aquilina, *Teach yourself Maltese*, London 1965; Dictionaries: E. D. Busuttil, *Kalepin (Dizzjunarju) Malti-Ingliż*, 3rd ed., Malta 1964; idem, *Kalepin (Dizzjunarju) Ingliż-Malti* 2nd ed. Malta 1968; C. Psaila, *Dizzjunarju Ingliż u Malti*, Malta 1947, reprints; C. L. Dessoulavi, *A Maltese-Arabic word list*, London 1938; D. G. Barbera, *Dizionario Maltese-Arabo-Italiano*, Beirut 1939-40; Other works: J. Aquilina, *Maltese linguistic surveys*, Malta 1976; idem, and B. S. J. Isserlin (eds.), *A survey of contemporary dialectal Maltese*, i, Leeds 1981; A. Borg, in *Israel Oriental Studies*, vi (1976), vii (1977); D. Cohen, *Études de linguistique sémitique et arabe*, Janua linguarum, Series practica 81, The Hague-Paris 1970; W. Cowan, *A reconstruction of proto-colloquial Arabic*, University Microfilms. Ann Arbor 1975; J. Cassar Pullicino, *Kitba w Kittieba tal Malti*, 3 vols, Malta 1962; P. Schabert, *Laut- und Formenlehre des Maltesischen anhand zweier Mundarten*, Erlanger Studien 16, Erlangen 1976; A. J. Borg, *A study of aspect in Maltese*, Linguistica extranea, Studia 15, Ann Arbor 1981. Numerous additional references will be found in issues of the *Journal of Maltese Studies* and works listed here; and bibliographical detail may be found in G. Mangion, in *Atti. XIV Congresso Internazionale di linguistica e filologia romanza, Napoli 1974*, 612-41; idem, in *Onoma*, xxv (1981), 303-4; idem, in *Rivista Italiana di dialettologia*, ii-iv (1979-80), 489-96. See also his *Appunti di storia linguistica Maltese*, in *Atti del IX Convegno por gli studi dialettali Italiani*, Pisa 1974, 389-415. (B. S. J. Isserlin)

3. Maltese literature.

The literature of the small Maltese archipelago emanates from a culture which may still be defined today as Christian, and more specifically as Roman Catholic, in all its essential aspects. The very early Christianisation of the island of Malta (which its inhabitants trace back to a visit made there by Saint Paul—Acts, xxviii, 1-10) was able to resist a Muslim domination of almost four centuries, and Islam does not seem to have exerted a significant influence.

Until the 19th century, Italian, the official and administrative language, the language of education, was the vehicle of Maltese literature, just as it was the language of social relations among the educated classes. But alongside this learned literature, written in a foreign language, there existed, and still exists, an oral and genuinely national literature. At the festival of *Imnarja*, a great popular gathering in the woods of Buskett attended by peasants and artisans from all the villages of the island, among other displays there take place, on the night of 28-9 June, poetical contests and improvisations, some forms of which are approved by public acclamation.

On the other hand, since the end of the 19th cen-

Table showing the Maltese alphabet and corresponding Arabic and Romance sound values
(Rare correspondences are shown in brackets, occasional ones mostly omitted)

Maltese letter		sound value	corresponding Arabic sound[s]	corresponding Romance (Italian and Sicilian sound[s])
A	a	a	a, i	a
B	b	b	b (f)	b (p)
Ċ	ċ	č	s̲h̲, d̲j̲ (k)	č (k)
D	d	d	d, d̲h̲, ḍ, z̧	d (t)
E	e	e	a, i	e (i)
F	f	f	f	f
Ġ	ġ	d̲j̲	d̲j̲	d̲j̲, č
G	g	g	k, q (d̲j̲)	g
H	h	- (h, ħ)	h	-
Ħ	ħ	ḥ	ḥ, k̲h̲ (ʿ)	-
I	i	i	i (a, u)	i (e)
J	j	y	y	y (d̲j̲)
K	k	k	k	k
L	l	l	l	l
M	m	m	m	m
N	n	n	n	n
Għ	għ	(see text)	ʿ, g̲h̲	-
O	o	o	u (a, i)	o, u
P	p	p	b, f	p (b, v)
Q	q	hamza	ḳ (ʿ, k)	k
R	r	r	r	r
S	s	s	s, ṣ	s
T	t	t	t, t̲h̲, ṭ	t (d)
U	u	u	u	u, o
V	v	v	w	v, b
W	w	w	w	w (k)w, (g)w
X	x	s̲h̲	s̲h̲ (s)	s̲h̲, s
Ż	ż	z	z	z, ʒ
Z	z	ts	t and s in disjunction	ts, č

Note: Long and short vowels are not distinguished in Maltese writings; e.g. *dar* stands for *dār*.

tury, collections of oral literature have been made by foreigners, including the German Stumme, and also by Maltese: Nawel Magri (1851-1907) published collections of popular tales, including *Ħrejjef misserijietna* ("Stories of our ancestors", 1902). Gużè Cassar-Pullicino (b. 1921) wrote a number of volumes dealing with f o l k l o r e ; one of these, *Femmes de Malte dans les chants traditionnels* (1981), in collaboration with Micheline Galley, specifically studies the feminine repertoire.

These collections reveal the basic forms of this literature: stories which are generally short, very vivid and colourful, little quatrains which are usually satirical or amorous, also lullabies, prayers and ballads of which the most renowned is *L-Għarusa tal-Mosta* ("The wife of Mosta"), the tale of the kidnapping of a girl by Turks on her wedding day.

Similarly, p r o v e r b s have been collected since a very early date. In the 18th century, de Soldanis had already made an extensive collection, *Apoftegmi e proverbi maltesi*. He was followed in this course by M. A. Vassalli, whose *Motti, aforismi e proverbi maltesi* dates from 1828, and by G. Aquilina, whose *Comparative dictionary of Maltese proverbs* appeared in 1969.

Despite the cultural domination of Italian, there are available some items written in Maltese dating from before the 19th century. The oldest is a *Cantilena* of twenty verses attributed to Peter Caxaro, dating from the 15th century. Unfortunately, difficulties of reading and a syntax sometimes unfamiliar to modern scholars make its interpretation problematical. Moreover, the system of transcription lacks consistency, since a single phoneme may have two or even three

graphical equivalents, and the converse applies. However, analysis of this text shows that certain phonetic evolutions, characteristic of Maltese as currently spoken, have not yet taken place; in particular the pharyngeals and the velars have not disappeared. Also worthy of mention are a short poem by the writer G. F. Bonamico (1639-80) composed *ca.* 1672 and dedicated to the Grand Master Nicholas Cottoner; humorous verses concerning the Carnival composed by Dun Felic Demarco in 1760; religious hymns and also some prose works, including a collection of sermons of Father Ignazio Saverio Mifsud (1739), in a rather feeble oratorical style, and a catechism (*Tagħlim Nisrani*) of F. Wzzino, published in 1752. It was also in the middle of the 18th century that de Soldanis composed his *Djalogi*; this consists of eight short dialogues which were discovered in the manuscript of his grammar and published in 1947 by Ġ. Cassar-Pullicino. The majority of their protagonists are common people, whom the author makes talk in a very idiomatic manner, from which it may be supposed that these dialogues are a faithful reflection of the popular language of the period. Moreover, they contain a great deal of sociological and historical interest. Also available to us is an acrostic poem (1758) by the same author, in honour of Dr Ludovico Coltellini, secretary of the Academy of Botany and Natural History of Cortona, a documentary rather than literary curiosity.

Maltese p r o s e - w r i t i n g began quite modestly. Over a long period, the main concern of writers was to translate religious works, as well as Italian, English or French works. M. A. Vassalli himself made an excellent Maltese version of the Gospels (1823-9). Richard Taylor (1818-68) produced in 1846 a translation of *Robinson Crusoe* which is still highly regarded today. But all these works had the merit of showing that the Maltese language, unjustly scorned by the educated classes, was capable of serving literature of the highest quality.

It is only in the last quarter of the 19th century that an original prose is seen to emerge. The first novels, described as "Gothic" by the Maltese, enjoyed considerable popular success, in spite of their somewhat mediocre quality. *Neriku u Guditta* ("Henry and Judith", 1872), by M. German, *Ġorġ il-Bdot* ("George the Pilot", 1880) by Ninu Muscat Fenech and *Ermelinda u l-vendetta tal-Konti* ("Ermelinde and the vengeance of the Count", 1894) by A. Adam are nothing more than somewhat pale imitations of popular foreign novels. However, some works testify even at this time to a greater degree of independence, such as *Fernandu Montagnes* (1896) by Alwig Vella, or the stories of V. Busuttil, *Il-Ħabib tal-familji* ("The friend of the families", 1893-4). Here too the phraseology is of Italian type, but the reader is no longer aware of the awkwardness of a language of translation. In fact, it should not be forgotten that all these authors began their writings in Italian, a situation still applying at the beginning of the 20th century, before Italian was displaced in favour of English, which became an official language in 1934, at which time Maltese achieved the same status.

Two authors succeeded particularly well in defying the ascendancy of Italian, an achievement which earns them a special place in the history of Maltese literature. The first, A. E. Caruana, is distinguished by the purity of his language and the facility with which he expresses complex notions in spite of a vocabulary remarkably deficient in abstract terms. These features are especially evident in his historical novel *Ineż Farruġ*, which appeared in 1889 and of which the action is set in the 15th century during the Spanish occupation, but which denounces by implication all the foreign powers who have ruled the archipelago. The second, Ġużè Muscat Azzopardi (1853-1927), was concerned above all to give to the Maltese language a literary syntax of its own. It may be said that he achieved his purpose with *Nazju Ellul* (1909), a historical work describing the Maltese resistance to the occupation by Napoleonic troops.

But the Maltese novelists of this period, guided by concern for purity and nobility of expression, were generally unable to avoid the pitfalls of an excessively neutral language, of a frigid style dominated by the taste for oratorical eloquence. A further four decades were to elapse before they were able to rid themselves of the shackles of Italian romanticism.

However, their ambitious works exerted only a limited influence on the authors of the 20th century. The stories composed by F. M. Galea (1861-1941), *Mogħdija taż-żmien* ("Entertainments"), between 1899 and 1915, provided a model for a popular literature; written in a simple and living language, dealing with issues of daily and local life, they enjoyed immediate success. But it is to Temi Zammit (1864-1935) that there belongs the privilege of being considered the founder of the Maltese short story, idiomatic and concise. His writings were collected by Cremona in *Stejjer, ħrejjef u kitba oħra* ("Stories, tales and other works") and *Stejjer u kitba oħra* ("Stories and other works") in 1961.

The historical and patriotic vein continued predominant in the inter-war period. Among the works produced at this time and worthy of mention are *Imħabba u mibegħda* ("Love and hate", 1927) and *Helsien* ("Liberty", 1940) by Ġużè Bonniċi (1907-40), *Żmien l-Ispanjoli* ("The time of the Spanish", 1938) by Ġużè Galea (1901-78) and *Anġli tan-niket* ("Angels of sadness", 1938) by Ġino Muscat Azzopardi (1899-1982), the son of Ġużè Muscat Azzopardi.

But, at the same time, new tendencies are taking shape. There is observed the appearance of an ironical tone, hitherto absent from Maltese literature, and Ġwann Mamo (1886-1941) is its initiator. His novel *Ulied in-Nann Venut fl-Amerka* ("The children of Grandmother Venut in America", 1930) is described by the author himself as a "satirico-descriptive, contemporary, semi-political novel". *Leli ta' Ħaż-Żgħir* ("Christmas of Ħaż-Żgħir", 1938) by Ġużè Ellul Mercer (1898-1961) is written in the same vein.

Some clear social preoccupations also begin to be observed, as in *Tejbilhom ħajjithom* ("To improve their life", 1937) by John Francis Marko (1894-1954) or in *Is-Salib tal-fidda* ("The cross of silver", 1939) by Henry Wistin Born (b. 1910).

However, the novel which is still today considered the masterpiece of modern prose belongs to the historical vein. The work in question is *Taħt tliet saltniet* ("Under three dominations"), published in 1937 by Ġużè Aquilina, then only 26 years old. But historical anecdote is here only the pretext for a more general social critique which goes far beyond the scope of the traditional historical novel. Furthermore, the work contains neither melodramatic plot nor rudimentary psychology. In addition, the work is distinguished by a great virtuosity of writing, Aquiline possessing perfect knowledge of the language and its popular usages.

Although under increasing competition, the historical novel was to remain an important genre until the decade of the 1970s. Example include *Manwel Gellel* (1961) by Ġużè Cardona (b. 1922), *Il-Qassis li rebaħ* ("The victorious priest", 1970) by Ġorġ Scicluna (1923-74), or *Beraq u qawsalli* ("Lightning and rainbow", 1976) of Ġorġ Pisani (b. 1909).

The "ironical" novel was also to be developed by M. C. Spiteri (b. 1917) in *L-Għafrid* ("The devil", 1975), and Trevor Zahra (b. 1947) in *Is-Surmast* ("The master", 1973).

But two European movements were to give rise to a new literary genre, the "social" genre, after the Second World War; these were the expressionist movement, which reached the archipelago at a late stage, and the theories of existentialism. The Maltese novel began to turn more and more towards contemporary social reality. Numerous authors achieved renown in this genre, notably Ġużè Chetcuti (b. 1914) who was the pioneer with *Nirien ta' mħabba* ("The fires of love", 1961). He was followed in particular by Victor Apap (b. 1913) and Alfred Massa (b. 1938). The former published *F' bieb il-ħajja* ("At the doors of life") in 1975, the latter *It-Tfajla tal-bikini vjola* ("The girl in the violet bikini") in 1979.

However, this movement only really began to be taken seriously under the pen of J. J. Camilleri (b. 1929). Thus *Aħna sinjuri* ("We are rich", 1965) is a political diatribe against certain aspects of Maltese life.

Finally, since the end of the decade of the 1960s, it has been the psychological novel which has dominated. The characters are no longer out-of-the-ordinary heroes; they are simple individuals, confronted by daily reality. The way was opened in 1968 by Frans Sammut (b. 1945) with his stories *Labirint u stejjer oħra* ("Labyrinth and other tales"). But it was especially in his first novel *Il-Gaġġa* ("The cage",

1971) that he showed himself a writer of talent, confirming this four years later with *Samuraj* ("Samurai"). Alfred Sant (b. 1948) for his part shows more philosophical preoccupations in *L-Ewwel weraq tal-bajtar* ("The first leaves of the fig-trees"), which appeared in 1969. Also worthy of mention are J. J. Camilleri for *Is-Sejħa tal-art* ("The call of the earth", 1974), T. Zahra for *Ħdejn in-nixxiegħa* ("Close to the source", 1975). Anton Grasso (b. 1952) for *Aħjar nibqa joħlom* ("Better continue to dream", 1975), and Oliver Friggieri (b. 1947) with *L-Istramb* ("The strange one", 1980).

Unlike the novel, dramatic art had a long time to wait before attaining a position of prestige. With Italian opera exerting a strong attraction upon the educated classes, theatre was relegated to a status of simple entertainment designed for the people, who had to be content with mediocrity.

It is to Luigi Rosato (1795-1872) that Maltese literature owes its first dramatic work, *Katarina* (1836), a historical and patriotic drama written in verse. But most of the works produced in the 19th century were nothing other than farces and melodramas, without much psychology or technical originality, and served by feeble, barely natural dialogues and excessively conventional situations.

The only dramatist of distinction of this period was Ġużè Muscat Azzopardi, who composed several pieces of romantic inspiration, or of social character, for example *X' Inhuma l-fatati* ("What phantoms are"), a comedy in two acts dating from 1874. Later, his son Ġino also wrote numerous dramatic works of some merit, including *Huwa* ("He").

Later still, certain authors distinguished themselves by sound knowledge of scenic technique and by vivid dialogue. Cremona set the example with a versified drama in five acts, *Il-Fidwa tal-bdiewa* ("The redemption of the farmers"), written in 1913, published in 1936. Subsequently added to the repertoire were some pieces by A. Born (b. 1901), whose main concern was in adapting French or Italian vaudeville, and by E. Sarracino Inglott (1904-83), in whose work the formal influence of the Classical Greek theatre is clearly perceived (*Il-Barrani*, "The stranger", 1942). A. Cassola (1915-74) was renowned in particular for a comedy in three acts, *Il-Vizzju tal-vjaggi* ("The vice of journeys"), and Ġorġ Pisani for four comedies of social nature derived directly from the expressionist trend: *Is-Sengħa tal-imħabba* ("The art of love", 1945). *Għanja tar-rebbiegħa* ("Song of spring", 1947), *Il-Kewkba* ("The star", 1949), and *Is-Sigriet ta' Swor Kristina* ("The secret of Sister Christina"), written in 1958 and published in 1978. Ġ. Chetcuti is also known for his two dramas, *Il-Kerrejja* ("The Reformatory", 1963), and *Imħuħ Morda* ("Sick spirits", 1966), in which he studies the effects of social environment on individuals.

But four authors have been especially esteemed by critics; these are Ġużè Diacono (b. 1912). Ġużè Aquilina, Francis Ebejer (b. 1925) and Oreste Calleja (b. 1946).

Ġużè Diacono is a realist author whose works are both a document and a study of the life of his contemporaries. His most ambitious piece, *Erwieħ marbuta* ("Enslaved souls", 1965) is a transposition to the period of the Second World War of the Biblical story of Samson and Delilah. There also exists in his work a "naturalist" tendency, after the pattern of Zola, especially in relation to the problems of heredity, as emerges from *L-Ewwel jien*! ("I am the first!", 1963).

The works of Ġużè Aquilina show real, and often courageous, moral and sociological preoccupations, as in *L-Ikkundannata* ("The condemned woman", 1969), the plot of which revolves around the drama of an unmarried mother. In 1962, he published a collection of one-act plays, intitled *Fit-teatru* ("In the theatre"), which deal with both serious and humorous themes in a very brisk and masterly style. In 1981, there appeared a collection of three plays: *Xafra mill-borża* ("The knife of the sack"), *Il-Każ taz-Zija Olga* ("The case of aunt Olga") and *Coqqa u dublett* ("Hood and petticoat"), of a very different style which Ġ. Aquilina defines as "the exploration of the mystic aspects of pathological crime".

Francis Ebejer is for his part considered the leading light of the new Maltese dramatic art. His theatre, very philosophical and symbolic, has been strongly influenced by the "Theatre of the absurd" of Ionesco, although he lacks the latter's pessimism, since he always endows his characters with a certain willingness to change. In *Boulevard*, he denounces the absurdity of stereotyped and mechanical human language, as an image of the alienating ascendancy of society over the individual. In *Menz*, a more overtly political play, he contrasts the romantic hero, a positive and revolutionary figure, with the anti-hero, a man without qualities or illusions. These two plays were published in 1970.

Belonging to the same vein is the work of Oreste Calleja, whose four *Drammi* ("Dramas"), appearing in 1972, were favourably received by critics.

With the exception of Dwardu Cachia (1858-1907), whose poems were for the most part based on the octosyllabic metre of popular verse, a form of which M. A. Vassalli was a leading advocate, Maltese poetry, since its beginnings in the 19th century, has been much influenced by the Italian school, copying the metre, the accentual rhythm and strophic forms of classical and romantic poetry.

It was initially in the field of translations that the efforts of the first versifiers, who at this stage can hardly be called poets, were deployed. At around the middle of the 19th century, Dun Dovik Mifsud Tommasi (1796-1879) translated the hymns of the Breviary (1853), as well as the original compositions of a Salvatore Cumbo (1810-77) or of an Indri Schembri (1805-72); Richard Taylor also provided a version of the *Psalms* (1846), then adapted a canto of the *Divine Comedy* in 1864.

Ġan Anton Vassallo (1817-67) has left a corpus that is more personal, although considerably less spontaneous, in which he has experimented extensively in metrical forms. His epic *Il-Ġifen Tork* ("The Turkish galley"), based on the folklore tradition of piracy, written in 1844 and published in 1853, is still widely known.

These authors had opened the way, at least in part, and all that was lacking was a poet of real quality. This was found in the person of Ġużè Muscat Azzopardi. By means of pure and simple language, he was able to avoid the stiffness and monotony of his predecessors, and to adapt an original content to a borrowed form. His poetry, essentially religious, like all Maltese poetry, sought to express the preoccupations of his contemporaries. To him belongs the credit of having removed poetry from servile imitation of classical Italian forms. His influence on the following generation, of which Dun Karm is the most eminent representative, was essential.

The reputation of Dun Karm, considered the national poet, has extended beyond the frontiers of the archipelago, as is attested by the study devoted to him jointly by the Maltese P. Grech and the Englishman A. J. Arberry. He wrote one work of great lyrical inspiration which has led him to be compared with Foscolo and Leopardi. In its entirety, it is a long meditation on nature (*Dell u dija*, "Shadow and Light"), history (*Lil Malta*, "To Malta"), the condition of Man, especially in his relationship to God (*Zjara lil Ġesù*, "Visit to Jesus"), and on the destiny of the poet himself (*Non omnis moriar*). Although very romantic in its inspiration and sentiments, the versifying of Dun Karm remained classical and in conformity with the model of Azzopardi, although no constraint is perceptible since the writing is smooth and fluent. The major part of his works was published in 1940 by G. Bonnici in three volumes: *X' Ħabb u x' kaseb il-poeta* ("What the poet likes and thinks"), *X' Emmen il-poeta* ("What the poet believes"), and *X' Ħamel izjed il-poeta* ("What the poet does most"). O. Friggieri devoted a critical edition to him in 1980: *Dun Karm, il-poeżiji miġbura* ((Dun Karm, collected poems").

Among his contemporaries, Anastasju Cushieri (1876-1962) and Ninu Cremona showed the greatest audacity in prosodic and rhythmic style. Cushieri's poem *Il-Millied* ("Christmas") contains no less than six different metres within a very complex structure. Cremona has adopted the rhythms and the lightness of popular poetry in his recent *Għana Malti* ("Maltese songs"), after going somewhat astray in attempts at complicated syntax. A collection of his poems was edited in 1970 under the title *Mis-Siġra ta' ħajti, weraq mar-riħ* ("From the tree of my life, leaves in the wind").

All of this poetry is characterised chiefly by a very serious and relatively objective manner of approaching religious, patriotic or narrative subjects, which is found in such diverse works as those of Ġorġ Pisani, who gives the impression of being an Epicurean (*Il-Għid taż-żgħożija*, "The feast of youth", 1945), Ġorg Zammit (b. 1908), Ġ. Aquilina, Mary Meylaq (1905-75), a poetess of nature as is shown by her collection *Pleġġ il-hena* ("The promise of joy", 1945) and *Villa Mejlaq* (1947), Anton Buttigieg (1912-83), or Ġużè Delia (1900-80), renowned as the poet of legends following the appearance in 1958 of his collection *Leġġendi*.

But even among the poets of this generation there is already a perceptible change, with the deepening of poetic sentiment. "Religious fervour is tainted by pessimism and often has the object of questioning the norms of social life. Patriotic exaltation yields to philosophical or poetic satire. Lyricism becomes more personal" (David Cohen, *La littérature maltaise*, in *Encyclopedie de la Pléiade*). The work of a certain Karmenu Vassallo (b. 1913) takes this new tendency to the extreme. His collections, *Nirien* ("Flames, 1938), *Kwiekeb ta' qalbi* ("Stars of my heart", 1944), *Ħamien u sriep* ("Doves and serpents", 1959) and *Tnemnim* ("Flickerings", 1970) give the impression of a man disgusted with his century. Even Ružar Briffa (1906-63), in spite of the elegance and the musicality which characterise his work, is not immune from existential pessimism (*Jien ma naf xejn*, "I know nothing", 1957) and from social and political indignation (*Milied atomiku*, "Atomic Christmas", 1957).

His influence, as well as that of Wallace Gulia (b. 1926) who has greatly diversified his source of inspiration, has exerted a powerful influence on contemporary poetry. Indignation and lyricism, despair and hope, are intermingled in the world of young Maltese poetry, and there has been a revival of amorous poetry. Moreover, unlike their elders who were moulded by the influence of the Italian school, contemporary poets turn rather towards English poetry (that of T. S. Eliot for example) or French, abandoning classical versification. However, there has not been a crucial break with tradition, since Roman Catholicism still maintains the link with the preceding generation, and the same Christian perception of the world is evident.

Nevertheless, the independence of the country in 1964 induced among many young Maltese writers a new awareness of the restraint which the British occupation had constituted; this sense was accompanied by a reaction against the scholasticism of ancient poets. But this national awareness was combined with a desire to set poetry on the level of modern European literature. This was expressed in a kind of "dispute of the Ancients and the Moderns". Out of this controversy there was born in November 1966 the *Moviment Qawmien Letterarju* ("Movement for Literary Revival"), of which the first efforts materialised, under the inspiration of Victor Fenech (b. 1935), in publications to which all young authors contributed: *Kwartett* ("Quartet") in 1965, *Dħaħen fl-imħuh* ("Smoke in the brains") in 1967, *Prizmi* ("Prisms") and *Antenni* ("Antennae") in 1968 and *Kalejdoskopju* ("Kaleidoscope") in 1969. In 1973 P. Serracino Inglott (b. 1936) devoted an authoritative anthology to this movement, *Linji godda* ("New lines").

Numerous authors illustrate this "revival": J. J. Camilleri, Marjan Vella (b. 1927) and Bernard Mallia (b. 1941) have succeeded in creating in various genres a synthesis between tradition and modernity. Ġorġ Borġ (b. 1946), greatly influenced initially by R. Briffa, has subsequently shown an occasional affinity with modern Arabic poetry in poems that are for the most part very short and melodious (*Solitudni fir-ramla*, "Solitude in the bay", 1978). Achille Mizzi (b. 1936), in *L-Għar tal-enimmi* ("The cave of the enigma", 1964) attempts a new metrical system. A poet of dreams and of mythology, he appeals to the mind rather than to the feelings. Daniel Massa (b. 1937), while being very close to the last-named, showed greater audacity in the treatment of themes.

Mario Azzopardi (b. 1944) expresses with great violence the protest of the individual against society in *Il-Qniepen nhar ta' ġimgħa* ("The bells of Friday", 1971); he is also a poet of sensuality. But his stylistic experiments sometimes lead him to copy foreign phraseologies.

Victor Fenech is also one of the most rare "committed" poets, but his vision is more analytical than that of M. Azzopardi. Worthy of mention, finally, are Joe Friggieri (b. 1946); Lilian Sciberras (b. 1946); Kenneth Wain (b. 1943); Philip Sciberras (b. 1945), an autobiographical author; and O. Firggieri, whose cold style conceals a deep despair.

These are some of the names which attest to the vitality of this poetry, the finest flower of Maltese literature.

The history of Maltese literature, barely a century old, is closely linked with the development of a literary language, the objective of several generations of writers. Today, the objective seems to have been attained. Works such as those of Dun Karm or Aquilina show that, after the ideological barriers, the linguistic obstacle has also been overcome. Furthermore, the Maltese writers, while succeeding in preserving their national identity, increasingly show a desire and a real capacity to exert a universal appeal.

For their part, the Europeans have begun to take an interest in this young literature, through the medium of anthologies and translations, of which the most recent are devoted to Dun Karm, Ġużè Galea (in English), Anton Buttigieg (in Italian) and Oliver Figgieri (in Serbo-Croat).

It may be agreed with the writer Ġużè Cardona that

"the effort represented by the flowering of Maltese language and literature, coming from a small nation of 320,000 souls, is such as to fill us ... with astonishment and admiration".

Bibliography: Studies: H. Stumme, *Maltesische Studien*, Leipzig 1904; idem, *Maltesische Märchen, Geschichte und Rätsel*, Leipzig 1904; A. J. Arberry and P. Grech, *Dun Karm, poet of Malta*, Cambridge 1961; Ġ. Aquilina, *Papers in Maltese linguistics*, Valetta 1961; idem, *Maltese*, London 1965; idem, *Die maltesische Literatur*, in *Die Literaturen der Welt*, Zurich 1968; K. Vassallo, *"Vatum Consortium" jew Il-Poezija bil-Malti*, Malta 1969; M. Galley, *L'Imnarja à Malte*, in *Bulletin de littérature orale arabo-berbère*, Paris 1970; O. Friggieri, *Kittieba ta' Żmienna*, Malta 1976; Ġ. Cassar-Pullicino, *Studies in Maltese folklore*, Malta 1976; D. Cohen, *Littérature maltaise*, in *Histoire des littératures, Encyclopédie de la Pléiade*, Paris 1977; G. Cassar-Pullicino and M. Galley, *Femmes de Malte dans les chants traditionnels*, Paris 1981; — Anthologies: L. Bonelli, *Saggi del folklore dell'Isola di Malta*, Palermo 1895; B. Ilg, *Maltesische Märchen und Schwänke*, Leipzig 1906; E. Magri, *Ħrejjef Misserijietna*, Malta 1906; L. Ropa, *Poètes maltais*, Tunis 1937; Arberry, *A Maltese anthology*, Oxford 1960; Aquilina, *Il-Muża Maltija, Antoloġija ta' poeti Maltin*, Malta 1969.

(MARTINE VANHOVE)

AL-MAᶜLŪF, a Lebanese family name which became renowned throughout the Arab world through the literary and other intellectual efforts of at least ten of its members, both in Lebanon and in the *Mahdjar* [*q.v.*], during the past 150 years. The best known members are Nāṣīf (1823-65), Lūwīs (1867-1947), Yūsuf (1870-1956), Amīn (1871-1943), the three brothers Ḳayṣar (1874-1964), Djamīl (1879-1950) and Mīshāl (1889-1942) and ᶜĪsā Iskandar (1869-1956) and his sons Fawzī (1899-1930) and Shafīḳ (1905-76).

According to ᶜĪsā Iskandar, who wrote the history of the family, the Maᶜlūf family are descendants of the Ghassānids [*q.v.*] who had their centre at Dāma al-ᶜUlyā in the Ḥawrān. They gave armed support to the four Rightly-Guided caliphs and so won exemption from paying the poll-tax. The same services were rendered to the Umayyads, who likewise exempted them from payment of the poll-tax. They called themselves Banu 'l-Maᶜyūf, because of the *iᶜfā*ʾ (exemption) which they enjoyed. The ᶜAbbāsids did not prolong this privilege for the supporters of their adversaries, and then the name was changed into Banu 'l-Maᶜlūf.

The Ḥawrān became less secure for Christians when a new round of fights between the Ḳays and the Yaman [*q.v.*] had begun at the beginning of the 15th century. Some members of the Maᶜlūf clan left the Ḥawrān. One of those who left was Ibrāhīm al-Maᶜlūf, called Abū Nātiḥ because of his large offspring. He settled in Sirᶜīn not far from the Baᶜalbakk. His descendants split up after a fight in 1572 and settled in Nazareth, Djūni, al-Muḥaydatha and above all in Kfar ᶜAḳāb. The descendants of those who settled in Kfar ᶜAḳāb again spread over Syria and Lebanon with Zaḥla as their main city (see *al-Machriq*, viii, ix).

Muslim branches of the family are mentioned by ᶜĪsā Iskandar in his *Riḥlatī ilā Miṣr* (*al-Adīb* [March 1964], 58-9). He describes his visit in 1934 to the shrine of al-Shaykh Aḥmad al-Maᶜlūf in Shubrā al-Khayma, Cairo, to which he refers as a place of pilgrimage and of a *mawlid*. Among his other discoveries is a manuscript in the National Library in Cairo, with the title *Riyāḍ al-nufūs*, by Abū Bakr ᶜAbd Allāh al-Mālikī. This manuscript mentions the *Āl al-Maᶜlūf al-muslimīn fī Siḳilliyya wa 'l-Ḳayrawān wa-Sūsa*. The oldest Maᶜlūf mentioned is Abū ᶜUmar Ibn Maymūn b. ᶜAmr b. al-Maᶜlūf, who died in 316/928 (see *al-Adīb, loc. cit.*).

I. NĀṢĪF al-MAᶜLŪF (Nassif Mallouf), born in Zabbūgha (Lebanon) 20 March 1823, died near Smyrna 14 May 1865.

He received his first educational lessons at Bayt al-Dīn, where he went with his father, *ᶜāmil* of the *amīr* Bashīr II (1788-1840). He met there the poets and the scholars who were invited to Bayt al-Dīn by Amīr Bashīr, among whom he met Nāṣīf al-Yāzidjī. Languages attracted his prime interest. He was engaged by a merchant from Smyrna to instruct his sons in Arabic and to teach them the basic rules of French in 1843. Part of his time was reserved for the business of the merchant. In 1845 he was nominated teacher of eastern languages at the school of the Propaganda of the Lazarists at Smyrna. From then on, he used his spare time for the study of Turkish, Italian and modern Greek. He was Dragoman to Lord Raglan, the supreme commander of the English forces during the Crimean War, whom he accompanied from August 1855 to September 1856. His travels with Lord Raglan brought him to London, where he stayed until the end of the year. During this stay, he was elected a member of the Athenaeum Club. He then became Dragoman to Sir Henry Bulwer, whom he accompanied from Bucharest to Istanbul. In 1858 he went back to Smyrna to become the first Dragoman of the English consul. He died in 1865 from yellow fever.

All his chroniclers make mention of the fact that Nāṣīf al-Maᶜlūf was a member of both the English and the French Asiatic Societies. He is listed as a member of the Société Asiatique from 1854, and the Royal Asiatic Society has his name on its lists of members from 1860 until 1867. A *curriculum vitae* was published in French in the *Courrier d'Orient*.

His most renowned works are his French-Turkish and Turkish-French dictionaries. The first was printed in Smyrna in 1849 and reprinted in 1856 by Maisonneuve in Paris and listed as Nassif Mallouf, *Dictionnaire français-turc*. The companion volume *Turc-français* was first published in 1863. Most of his polyglot and two-language conversation books had at least one reprint edition. His *Grammaire élémentaire de la langue turque* was published by Maisonneuve.

Bibliography: *Maṣādir al-dirāsa al-adabiyya*, Beirut 1957, iii, 1258-61; Y. A. Dāghir, in *al-Machriq*, viii, ix; Ziriklī, *al-Aᶜlām*⁴, vii, 350; *Philologiae turcicae fundamenta*, i, Wiesbaden 1959.

2. LŪWĪS AL-MAᶜLŪF, SJ (Louis Maᶜlūf), born in Zaḥla 18 October 1867, died in Beirūt, 7 August 1947. He was baptised with the name Ẓāhir, which he changed into Louis upon his entry into the Jesuit Society. He studied at the Jesuit College in Beirut, went to England to study philosophy and studied theology in France, where he stayed for ten years. He is best known for his *al-Mundjid fi 'l-lugha wa 'l-adab wa 'l-ᶜulūm*, the first edition of which dates from 1908 and which has since been reprinted and expanded in many editions.

From 1906-32 he was director and editor of the Catholic weekly *al-Bashīr*. Its annual supplement *Taḳwīm al-Bashīr*, the almanac, was made by him into a useful instrument of information on matters of calendar, church and state, in that order. His *Maḳālāt falsafiyya ḳadīma li-baᶜḍ mashāhir falāsifat al-ᶜarab, muslimīn wa-naṣārā* was first published in Beirut in 1911 by the Imprimerie Catholique and then republished at Frankfurt in 1911 with the French title *Traités inédits d'anciens philosophes arabes musulmans et chrétiens, publiés dans la revue al-Machriq par L. Malouf, E. Eddé et L. Cheikho.* He edited *Taʾrīkh ḥawādith al-Shām wa-Lubnān min sanat 1197 ilā sanat 1257 (1782-1841)* of Mikhāyil al-Dimashkī, Beirut 1912. His *Riyāḍa rūḥiyya li 'l-kahana ḥasab ṭarīkat al-kiddīs Ighnāṭiyūs* was published in 1937 in Beirut.

Bibliography: Dāghir, *Maṣādir,* ii, 727-9; Ziriklī, *al-Aᶜlām*⁴, v, 247; Riyād al-Maᶜlūf, *Shuᶜarāʾ al-Maᶜālifa*, Beirut 1962, 85.

3. YŪSUF NUᶜMĀN AL-MAᶜLŪF, born at Zaḥla 1870, died at New York, 18 June 1956. He emigrated to North America, settled in New York and founded the newspaper *al-Ayyām*, which survived for ten years from 1897 to 1907. He enlisted the help of his nephew Djamīl (no. 6), who migrated for this purpose. Through their newspaper they made propaganda for Arab independence, and thus earned the displeasure of the Ottoman government. Both were condemned to death under Djamāl Pasha, the military governor of Syria from 1915 until the end of the Syrian campaign of the combined Arab-English forces. Yūsuf, however, never came within reach of the Ottoman authorities. Together with Djamīl he published *Kitāb Khizānat al-ayyām fī tarādjim al-ᶜiẓām*, New York 1899, a biographical dictionary of important men, Arabs and Turks. Another joint publication is *Asrār Yildiz aw al-ᶜakd al-thamīn fī taʾrīkh arbaᶜat salāṭīn*, New York 1900. His other publications were *Lāʾiḥat Ismāᶜīl Bek*, and *Ḥikāyat Abi 'l-Hudā*.

Bibliography: Dāghir, *Maṣādir*, iii/2, 1262-3; Ṣaydaḥ, *Adabunā wa-udabāʾunā fi 'l-Mahādjir al-Amīrkiyya*², Beirut 1957, 21, 307; al-Badawī al-Mulaththam, *al-Nāṭiķūn bi 'l-ḍād fī Amīrkā*, New York 1946, 36; Ziriklī, *al-Aᶜlām*⁴, viii, 255; Riyāḍ Maᶜlūf, *Shuᶜarāʾ al-Maᶜālifa*, 88.

4. AMĪN FAHD AL-MAᶜLŪF, born in al-Shwayfāt (Lebanon), 1871, died in Cairo, 21 January 1943.

Amīn al-Maᶜlūf studied medicine at the Medical Faculty of the University of Beirut until 1894 and then went to Istanbul to obtain his *idjāza.* He served as a physician in the Egyptian army and took part in the Sudan expedition, the battle of Khartoum and the occupation of Bahr al-Ghazāl. An account of the Baḥr al-Ghazāl occupation by his hand was published in ten instalments in *al-Muktafaf* in 1911 and 1912.

He was active during the Balkan war and during the battle of the Dardanelles in the First World War, and then joined the Arab forces of Sharīf Ḥusayn. He taught biology at the Maᶜhad al-Ṭibbī al-ᶜArabī in Damascus after the capture of that city. When the French put an end to the rule of Fayṣal over Syria and the British offered him ᶜIrāķ instead, Amīn also went to ᶜIrāķ to serve in the ᶜIrāķī army. He returned to Egypt when his time of retirement had come.

He wrote a large number of articles on Arabic scientific terms, especially on the names of plants. His *Muᶜdjam al-ḥayawān* was published in instalments in *al-Muķtaṭaf*, from 1908 onwards, giving the English names in alphabetical order, followed by the scientific names, the Arabic equivalents and the current Arabic names. It was republished in book-form by *al-Muķtaṭaf* and given to the subscribers as the annual present in 1932. A supplement was published not long after, possibly in 1933. His *al-Muᶜdjam al-falakī* appeared in Cairo, 1935. Studies about plant-names appeared in the *Madjallat al-Madjmaᶜ al-ᶜIlmī al-ᶜArabī*, but reasons of health prevented the author from developing these studies into a dictionary of plant names. Medical terms in Arabic were another field of study for him. He started the translation of *Webster's Dictionary*, reaching the letter F. An obituary by Fuʾād Ṣarrūf appeared in the magazine of the Overseas Services of the BBC, *Hunā London*, no. 75 (Febr. 1963), 30.

Bibliography: *al-Adīb*, 55-6; Dāghir, *Maṣādir*, ii, 713-15; Ziriklī, *al-Aᶜlām*⁴, iii, 19; *al-Muķtaṭaf*, lxxxvii (1935), 245, cii (1943), 186, 418, 479.

5. KAYṢAR IBRĀHĪM AL-MAᶜLŪF, born in Zaḥla 1874, died in Beirut, 25 April 1961; brother of Djamīl and Mīshāl, brother-in-law of ᶜĪsā Iskandar and nephew of Yūsuf, his paternal uncle.

In 1895 he emigrated to São Paulo, Brazil. In 1898 he became editor of the newspaper *al-Barāzīl*, which had been founded in Santos in 1896 and had been moved to São Paulo in 1897. He continued to work for this paper until 1903, when it was absorbed by the paper *al-Afkār.* He was one of the founding members of an Arabic literary circle among emigrants *al-Nahḍa al-adabiyya* and of the literary club *Riwāķ al-Maᶜarrī*, both in São Paulo. The *Riwāķ al-Maᶜarrī* was quite popular, having many itinerant merchants among its members. Their main activity was the recitation of newly-received poems by Aḥmad Shawķī and Khalīl Muṭrān, followed by comments and imitations along well-known lines of the *muᶜāraḍa* (Ṣaydaḥ, 151). The activities of the *Riwāķ* came to an end during the First World War, when preference for nationalistic content to the detriment of literary value drove the better poets out (Ṣaydaḥ, 316). Ķayṣar had meanwhile, in 1906 (Riyāḍ al-Maᶜlūf, *Shuᶜarāʾ*, 45) or 1914 (Ziriklī, *Aᶜlām*⁴, v, 209 f.) returned to Lebanon.

The list of his publications opens with a play in verse, *Riwāyat Nīrūn*, Zaḥla 1894. His *dīwān, Tidhkār al-Mahādjir*, was published in São Paulo in 1904, as were his novels: *al-Ghāda al-Sūriyya fi 'l-diyār al-Amīrkiyya*, São Paulo 1907; *Fidyat al-ḥubb*, São Paulo 1907 and *Midḥat Bāshā*, São Paulo 1907. *Djamāl bilādī* is an epic poem which appeared in Beirut in 1939. The *Dīwān Ķayṣar al-Maᶜlūf* was published in Beirut in 1958.

Bibliography: F. dī Ṭarrāzī, *Kurrās al-nasharāt al-dawriyya al-ᶜarabiyya*, Beirut 1933, 450-1; Riyāḍ Maᶜlūf, *Shuᶜarāᶜ al-Maᶜālifa*, 45; Dāghir, *Maṣādir*, iii/2, 1256 f.; Ziriklī, *al-Aᶜlām*⁴, v, 209 f.; Ṣaydaḥ, *Adabunā wa-udabāʾunā*, 151, 316, 454.

6. DJAMĪL AL-MAᶜLŪF, born at Zaḥla, 15 February 1879, died 30 December 1950; brother of Ķayṣar and Mīshāl, brother-in-law of ᶜĪsā Iskandar and nephew of Yūsuf Nuᶜmān, his paternal uncle.

He learned Turkish in Beirut and then, in 1896, answering the call of his uncle, he migrated to the United States and helped in editing the newspaper *al-Ayyām.* He became a member of the literary circle *al-Ḥalka al-Afghāniyya.* Part of his time he spent travelling between New York, São Paulo and Lebanon. In 1908 he went to Paris and made contact with the Turks who were working for the deposition of ᶜAbd Ḥamīd II. The following year, after ᶜAbd Ḥamīd's reign had come to an end, Djamīl travelled via Istanbul to Beirut. The coming of Djamāl Pasha as military governor of Syria turned out to be a direct threat against his life. He was condemned to death, but escaped from being hanged as his family knew how to hide him from Turkish eyes. An incurable disease put him in hospital before the First World War ended, and there he remained until his death in 1950.

He wrote a large number of articles for the newspaper *al-Iṣlāḥ* in Brazil with the title *Kayf tatḥūr al-umam.* With his uncle Yūsuf he published *Khizānat al-ayyām fī tarādjim al-ᶜiẓām*, New York 1899, in which publication he wrote the part concerning the Turkish notables. His *Turkiya al-djadīda wa-ḥuķūķ al-insān*, São Paulo, is said to have served Kemāl Pasha as a handbook, but the catalogue of Atatürk's library does not mention the book. Djamīl advocated turcification of the country, the separation of church and state, unified schooling programmes, the adoption of the European dress, etc.

His further publications include *Waṣiyyat Fuʾād Bāshā*, Sao Paulo 1908, and *Ḳānūn al-ṣiḥāfa al-ᶜarabiyya*, also 1908, which he translated from the Turkish.

Bibliography: *Madjallat al-ᶜUṣba*, xi/4 (April 1951), 297-308; *al-Adīb*, x/4 (April 1951), 55 ff.; Riyāḍ al-Maᶜlūf, *Shuᶜarāʾ al-Maᶜālifaʾ*, 21-2; Dāghir, *Maṣādir*, ii, 716-19; Ṣaydaḥ, *Adabunā wa-udabāʾunā*, 308; Ziriklī, *al-Aᶜlām*[4], ii, 137; *Atatürk'ün özel kütüphanesinin kataloğu (Anıtkabir ve Çankaya bölümleri)*, Ankara 1973.

7. MĪSHĀL AL-MAᶜLŪF, born in Zaḥla, 1889, died in Beirut, 3 June 1942; younger brother of Ḳayṣar and Djamīl, brother-in-law of ᶜĪsā Iskandar, and nephew of Yūsuf Nuᶜmān al-Maᶜlūf, his paternal uncle.

His fame chiefly rests on the fact that he was one of the founding-members and the first chairman of *al-ᶜUṣba al-Andalusiyya* from 1932 to 1938, being one of the sponsors who made the publication of the monthly *al-ᶜUṣba* possible. In 1938 he returned to Lebanon.

His contribution to Arabic poetry was limited. Some of his poems are reprinted as an appendix to the memorial volume *Fī haykal al-dhikrā*, containing the commemorative speeches and the elegies of the members of *al-ᶜUṣba al-andalusiyya*, as well as the "In memoriam"'s which had appeared in *Djarīdat Zaḥla al-Fatāt* and in the monthly *al-Adīb*. A play by his hand, *Sadjīn al-ẓulm*, was printed at Zaḥla in 1910.

Bibliography: *Fī haykal al-dhikrā*, São Paulo 1944; Riyāḍ al-Maᶜlūf, *Shuᶜarā al-Maᶜālifa*, 51.

8. ᶜĪSĀ ISKANDAR AL-MAᶜLŪF, born at Kfar ᶜAḳāb, 23 April 1869, died 2 July 1956. He married in 1897 ᶜAfīfa Maᶜlūf, the daughter of Ibrāhīm Bāshā al-Maᶜlūf. Out of this marriage were born Fawzī (1899-1930) and Shafīḳ (1905-76), for whom see below, nos. 9 and 10.

ᶜĪsā Iskandar received his education at the Scottish Missionary school in his home village and at the Scottish Missionary school in al-Shuwayr. Circumstances forced him to leave this last school and to pursue his studies privately. In 1890 he was nominated teacher at the Patriarchal Orthodox school in Damascus. Almost simultaneously, he began to contribute historical articles to the periodical *al-Niᶜma*, and in December of the same year he started to work as the editor, secretary and proof-reader of the newspaper *Lubnān*. He exchanged Damascus for Zaḥla in 1898 to teach Arabic, English and Mathematics at al-Kulliyya al-Sharḳiyya (al-Badawī al-Mulaththam, *ᶜĪsā Iskandar*, 49). His articles in *al-Machriq* in this period have his name followed by the words *mudarris ādāb al-lugha al-ᶜarabiyya wa 'l-khiṭāba*. At al-Kulliyya al-Sharḳiyya he edited and printed the paper *al-Muhadhdhib* from 1901 onwards, and, after an absence from the college for one year, 1908-9, he produced the paper *al-Sharḳiyya*. Both papers were produced on a forerunner of the stencil-machine. In 1903 he founded the *Djamᶜiyyat al-nahḍa al-ᶜilmiyya* for his students as a training-ground on which they could develop their eloquentia and where they could indulge into literary research. He was its chairman until 1921. He made an important contribution in the field of humanities when in 1911 he founded *al-Āthār*, a periodical devoted to history, archaeology and literature, to which many scholars of fame throughout the Arab world contributed. The periodical continued to appear until 1928, with an interruption of three years during the First World War.

His efforts in the field of learning were so much appreciated that he became a member of the learned societies in Syria, Lebanon and Egypt on the very first day of their existence. On 8 January 1918 the *Shuᶜbat al-tardjama wa 'l-taʾlīf* was formed during the reign of Fayṣal in Syria. It was transformed into the *Madjlis al-maᶜārif* and then in 1919 into *al-Madjmaᶜ al-ᶜilmī al-ᶜarabī*. He was a member of these societies from the first day, as also of *al-Madjmaᶜ al-ᶜilmī al-Lubnānī*, founded on 20 February, 1928. The *Madjmaᶜ al-lugha al-ᶜarabiyya* Egypt counted him among its members on its foundation-day, 6 October 1933. In 1936 he was nominated corresponding member of the Brazil Academy of History and Literature in Rio de Janeiro.

He was a very prolific writer. Ṭarrāzī, *Taʾrīkh al-Ṣiḥāfa*, ii, 234-8, lists almost 40 journals and magazines to which he contributed his articles on a wide variety of subjects. Larger works were often serialised in magazines and then printed in book-form. Dāghir lists 22 printed works and more than 50 titles of works which did not pass the manuscript-stage. During his lifetime he acquired a large library of about 1,000 manuscripts and 10,000 printed works. Some 500 manuscripts were purchased by the American University in Beirut and catalogued.

The following is a list of works published in book-form or serialised in the periodicals *al-Adīb, al-Machriq* and *al-Muḳtaṭaf:*

—*al-Kitāba*—a volume of studies on script, language and writing (84 pp.), 1895—*Lamḥa fi 'l-shiᶜr wa 'l-ᶜaṣr* (40 pp.) 1902—*al-Akhlāḳ. Madjmūᶜ ᶜādāt*, Zaḥla 1902—*al-Mubkiyāt*, a collection of elegies in memory of Mrs. Mahība bint Yūsuf Abī ᶜAlī al-Maᶜlūf, the wife of Ibrāhīm al-Aswad, proprietor of the newspaper *Lubnān*, 1903—*al-Iḥtiḍārāt wa-ḳabariyyāt*, about last words and epitaphs. A series of articles in *al-Muḳtaṭaf*, xxx-xxxi (1905-6)—*Nāṣīf al-Maᶜlūf wa-usratuhu*, a series of articles on the origins of the al-Maᶜluf family and a short biography of Nāṣīf al-Maᶜlūf, in *al-Machriq*, viii-ix (1905-6)—*al-Khūrī Djirdjis ᶜĪsā al-Lubnānī*, 2 parts, in *al-Machriq*, ix, (1906)—*Nukhba min dīwān Ibrāhīm al-Ḥakīm al-Ḥalabī*, 4 parts, in *al-Machriq*, x (1907)—*Dawānī al-ḳuṭūf fī sīrat Banī Maᶜlūf*, al-Maṭbaᶜa al-ᶜUthmāniyya, Baᶜabda 1908. Apart from being a family history of the Maᶜlūfs, other families are also followed. The book is a history of Lebanon, Syria and Palestine with information about customs. Asad Rustum, in *al-Machriq*, lvii (1963), 518-20, describes the book as an encyclopaedia of the situation in Lebanon in the first half of the 19th century as it survived in the memories of the old people at the end of that century. The subtitle is *A general socio-historical book, being a description of facts, morals and customs and cultural affairs.*—*Nukhba min amthāl al-ḳiss Ḥanānyā al-Munīr*, 5 parts, in *al-Machriq*, xii, (1909)—*al-Shuᶜarāʾ wa 'l-sirḳāt wa 'l-maʾākhidh al-shiᶜriyya*, 16 parts, in *al-Muḳtaṭaf*, xxxvii-xxxix, xliv-xlvi (1910-15)—*Taʾrīkh madīnat Zaḥla*, 298 pp., Zaḥla 1911 and 1912—*Taʾrīkh Lubnān*, printed during World War I, it is said.—*Muᶜāraḍāt Yā layl al-ṣabb*, a collection of *muᶜāraḍāt* and the original poem by al-Ḥuṣrī al-Ḳayrawānī [see Abu 'l-Ḥasan al-Ḥuṣrī al-Ḳayrawānī, ed. of M. Marzūḳī and Dj. b. al-Ḥādjdj Yaḥyā, Tunis 1963, 143-9 and *muᶜāraḍāt*, 150-201, containing César al-Maᶜluf (177-9), ᶜĪsā Iskandar (182-4), Fawzī al-Maᶜluf, (185-6) and a *muᶜāraḍa* by ᶜĪsā Iskandar 1921, also published in *al-Muḳtaṭaf*, lix, (1921)]—*Taʾrīkh al-ṭibb ḳabl al-ᶜarab*, 55 pp., 1924—*Taʾrīkh al-ṭibb ᶜind al-ᶜarab*, Damascus 1922—*al-Ḳilāᶜ wa l-ḥuṣūn fī Sūriyya*, in *al-Muḳtaṭaf*, lxi-lxiii, lxv, (1922-4)—*Ṣināᶜāt Dimashḳ al-ḳadīma*, Damascus 1924—*Taʾrīkh ḳaṣr Āl al-ᶜAẓm bi-Dimashḳ*, Beirut 1926. This was serialised in *al-Machriq*, xxiv

(1926) with the title *Ḳaṣr Asᶜad Bā̲s̲h̲ā al-ᶜAẓm fī Dimas̲h̲ḳ—al-Ḳaḍāʾ fī Lubnān bi-zaman al-umarāʾ al-S̲h̲ihābiyyīn*, in *al-Machriq*, xxxi (1933)—*Taʾrīk̲h̲ al-Amīr Fak̲h̲r al-Dīn al-Maᶜnī al-t̲h̲ānī ḥākim Lubnān min sanat 1590 ilā sanat 1635*, 468 pp., Beirut 1934 and 1966, also published in *al-Machriq* until vol. xxx (1932)—*al-Usar al-ᶜarabiyya al-mus̲h̲tahira bi 'l-ṭibb al-ᶜarabī wa as̲h̲har al-mak̲h̲ṭūṭāt al-ṭibbiyya al-ᶜarabiyya* (60 pp.), Beirut 1935—*al-G̲h̲urar al-taʾrīk̲h̲iyya fi 'l-usra al-Yāzid̲j̲iyya*, two parts of 128 and 142 pp., Sidon 1944 and 1945—*Taʾrīk̲h̲ Mas̲h̲āyik̲h̲ al-Yāzid̲j̲iyyīn wa-as̲h̲ᶜārihim*, Dayr al-Muk̲h̲alliṣ 1945, which is an abridged edition of *al-G̲h̲urar al-taʾrīk̲h̲iyya*—*Muᶜd̲j̲am al-alfāẓ al-ᶜāmmiyya al-ᶜarabiyya wa 'l-dak̲h̲īla*, serialised in 9 parts in *al-Adīb*, iii (1944), iv (1945). The introduction gives a survey of Arabic colloquial words and expressions from ancient until modern times.—*Muᶜd̲j̲am taḥlīl asmāʾ al-as̲h̲k̲h̲āṣ*, serialised in *al-Machriq*, lix-lx (1964-6)— *Muᶜd̲j̲am taḥlīl asmāʾ al-amākin fi 'l-bilād al-ᶜarabiyya*, serialised in *al-Machriq*, liii-lvii (1959-63)—*Taʾrīk̲h̲ Ṣaydnāyā*, written in 1924 but not published till 1973 at Bikfāyā—*al-Ak̲h̲bār al-marwiyya fī taʾrīk̲h̲ al-usar al-s̲h̲arḳiyya*, only partly published in periodicals.

Bibliography: *al-Adīb*, xvi/1 (January 1957), 56-7; *al-Machriq*, lvii (1963), 518-20; al-Badawī al-Mulat̲h̲t̲h̲am, *ᶜĪsā Īskandar al-Maᶜlūf: al-muʾarrik̲h̲, al-mawsūᶜī, al-adīb*, Cairo 1969; Riyāḍ al-Maᶜlūf, *al-ᶜAllāma al-Marḥūm ᶜĪsā Iskandar al-Maᶜlūf, ᶜuḍw al-Mad̲j̲āmiᶜ al-ᶜilmiyya al-ᶜarabiyya: ḥayātuhu, āt̲h̲āruhu, baᶜḍ maḳālātihi*, in *MMIA* (1957); Dāg̲h̲ir, *al-Maṣādir*, iii/2, 1246-55; Riyāḍ al-Maᶜlūf, *S̲h̲uᶜarāʾ al-Maᶜālifa*, 37-8; Ziriklī, *al-Aᶜlām*[4], v, 101; Ṭarrāzī, *Taʾrīk̲h̲ al-Ṣiḥāfa*, i, 25, ii, 234-8.

9. S̲h̲afīḳ al-Maᶜlūf, born at Zaḥla, March 1905, died at São Paulo 1976; son of ᶜĪsā Iskandar and brother of Fawzī.

S̲h̲afīḳ studied at al-Kulliyya al-S̲h̲arḳiyya in Zaḥla. In 1922 he went to Damascus and joined the editorial staff of the newspaper *Alif-Bāʾ*. His first *dīwān* of poetry, *al-Aḥlām*, was completed in 1923 but not printed till 1926 in Beirut. The *dīwān* called forth many disputes and comments, including those of Anṭūn Saᶜāda, published in his *al-Ṣirāᶜ al-fikrī fi 'l-adab al-Sūrī*, Beirut 1947. S̲h̲afīḳ left for São Paulo in 1926 to join his brothers Fawzī and Iskandar, who had set up a textile factory there. With his uncle Mīs̲h̲āl and others, he took an active part in founding *al-ᶜUṣba al-Andalusiyya* in 1932 and its monthly *al-ᶜUṣba* in 1933, which survived until 1952. He served Arab literary life in São Paulo by giving weekly dinners, at which he and his wife Rūz received writers and poets, with literary discussions before and after the meals (al-Badawī al-Mulat̲h̲t̲h̲am, *al-Nāṭiḳūn bi 'l-ḍād fī Amīrkā al-D̲j̲anūbiyya*, part 2, Beirut 1956, 747).

In 1936 he produced the first version of *ᶜAbḳar*, or a visit to the land of the D̲j̲inn, S̲h̲ayṭāns, Ḥūrīs, etc., in six cantos. This work was immediately hailed as an important innovation in Arabic literature, and a solemn meeting in honour of its author was held shortly after its publication. Speeches and poems read at this meeting were published in a special issue of *al-ᶜUṣba* (ii, December 1936). The second edition with six new cantos added was published in 1949.

From 1951 onwards he published five new *dīwāns*: *Li-kull zahra ᶜabīr*, São Paulo 1951; *Nidāʾ al-mad̲j̲ād̲h̲īf*, São Paulo 1952; *Wa-ᶜaynāki mihrad̲j̲ān*, 1960; *S̲h̲umūᶜ fi 'l-adāb* and *ᶜAlā sindān al-k̲h̲ayl*. A selection from the last two *dīwāns* was republished in a new *dīwān* with the title *Sanābil Rāᶜūt̲h̲* (= Ruth), Beirut 1961. *Ḥabbat zumurrud*, Damascus 1966, consists of two longer essays and a collection of shorter essays. *Saṭāʾir al-hawdad̲j̲*, containing poetry and prose, was published in Damascus 1975. His *Laylā al-Ak̲h̲aliyya* is a *riwāya*.

A commemorative meeting was held in Zaḥla on 26 June 1977.

Bibliography: Īliyyā al-Ḥāwī, *S̲h̲afīḳ al-Maᶜlūf, s̲h̲āᶜir ᶜabḳar*, Beirut 1978; *al-Adīb*, xxxv (Jan.-Dec. 1976); xxxvii (7 July 1978), 37; *al-Machriq*, lxiv (1970), 719; Riyāḍ al-Maᶜlūf, *S̲h̲uᶜarāʾ al-Maᶜālifa*, 34-6; Ṣaydaḥ, *Adabunā wa-udabāʾunā*, 351-6; al-Badawī al-Mulat̲h̲t̲h̲am, *al-Nāṭiḳūn bi 'l-ḍād fī Amīrkā al-D̲j̲anūbiyya*, part 2, Beirut 1956, 747; *al-ᶜUṣba*, xi/3 (1951), 247-8; xi/5-6, 481-3; xi/9-10, 781-90; ii (Dec. 1936), *ᶜAdad mumtāz*; ᶜĪsā al-Nāᶜūrī, *Adab al-Mahd̲j̲ar*[1], Cairo 1959, 516-22; ᶜUmar al-Daḳḳāḳ, *S̲h̲uᶜarāʾ al-ᶜUṣba al-Andalusiyya fi 'l-Mahd̲j̲ar*, Beirut 1973. (C. Nijland)

10. Fawzī al-Maᶜlūf, born at Zaḥla, 21 May 1899 (*D̲h̲ikrā*, 4; *Dawānī al-ḳuṭūf*, 288; *Dīwān*, 127), died at Rio de Janeiro 1930; son of ᶜĪsā Iskandar and brother of S̲h̲afīḳ.

Of the primary constituent elements of his development, mention may be made of the influence of his father (see *al-Ḍād*, v [1935]; Aoun, 28-9) and the dual cultural background that he acquired in the two clerical institutions of al-S̲h̲arḳiyya (in Zaḥla) and of the Brothers of the Christian Schools (Beirut 1914-15). The World War and the severe famine in Lebanon forced him to interrupt his studies; in 1916 he was employed by the Wheat Commission (*Biḳāᶜ*, ms. Jan. 1916), then, in 1919, he was appointed bursar of the teachers' training college in Damascus, and secretary to the Dean of the School of Medicine (*al-Maᶜhad al-ṭibbī*, vii, 127; *D̲h̲ikrā*, 4; Aoun, 33-4). It is to this period that his literary first-fruits belong (*D̲h̲ikrā*, 5-6, 8-11, 39), and in 1921 his poem *al-Firdaws al-mustaᶜād* won him a literary prize. On 17 September of the same year, apparently under compulsion (*D̲h̲ikrā*, 30; *Dīwān*, 25-28), he emigrated to Brazil and settled in São Paulo, where he joined his maternal uncle and engaged in commerce (*al-S̲h̲arḳ*, iv [March 1931]; *D̲h̲ikrā*, 186-8).

In 1922, he founded *al-Muntadā al-Zaḥlī* (*al-Ittiḥād*, 18 January 1930; *al-Rābiṭa*, 10 January 1930; *D̲h̲ikrā*, 4-5, 185), which led to a redoubling of both social and literary activity, and Spanish-Portuguese culture came to be grafted on to his original Arabic-French background (*D̲h̲ikrā*, 37). Although well-known in emigré society from the year 1923 onward, his name only began to arouse the interest of Brazilian literary circles after the appearance, in 1926, of his poem *ᶜAlā bisāṭ al-rīḥ*.

Details concerning his short life, his generous nature, his illness (20 November 1929) and his death in the English Hospital in Rio de Janeiro (7 January 1930) have been carefully collected by his father (*D̲h̲ikrā, passim*): *al-Adīb*, xxxii (March 1973), 53d, reprints a letter of S̲h̲afīḳ to ᶜĪsā al-Nāᶜūrī saying that Fawzī had not died of appendicitis but of an inflamation of the duodenum, but that he had told his parents at the time that Fawzī was suffering from an appendicitis in order to allay their worries. The letter was written after ᶜĪsā al-Nāᶜūrī had written in *al-Adīb*, xxi/11 (Nov. 1972), 46, that Fawzī had possibly died of a venereal disease or of tuberculosis.

The rare unedited works preserved in his father's library (fragments of poetry, the first issue of a monthly revue, *al-Adab*, intended to be distributed in the school—ms. January 1914—assorted meditations, proverbs and aphorisms translated from French, two panegyrics—ms. 1914-15) display tendency towards an elegant and elaborate prose (*al-Adab*, preface), a quasi-traditional prosody, a romantic taste and a concern for the collation or insertion of items of wisdom.

His first novellas, including *Salmā* and *ʿAlā difāf al-kawthar* (*Dhikrā*, 5-6, 39) recall the romantic genre of Djabrān (d. 1931 [*q.v.*]). In 1916 he completed the composition of *Ibn Ḥamīd aw sukūṭ Gharnāṭa* (*Dhikrā*, 39, 107-9), a romantic drama in five acts (published in Brazil by *al-ʿUṣba*, 1952). The subject is borrowed from Andalusian Muslim history and the action is set in Granada. Attention has been drawn to analogy between this drama and the novel of Florian, *Gonzalve de Cordoue* (*Ibn Ḥāmid*, preface; Aoun, 59-74) which the poet, while still an adolescent, is said to have translated into Arabic (*Dhikrā*, 10). A closer analysis, however, shows the precise similarity between the drama and the novel by Chateaubriand, *Le dernier des Abencérages*, translated into Arabic by Shakīb Arslān (1870-1946) as *Ākhir Banī Sirādj* (ed. *al-Manār*, 1920, in *Khulāṣat taʾrīkh al-Andalus*). The dialogue is a poetic-prosodic mixture of a high level. There are, however, a number of weaknesses regarding theatrical technique, plot, analysis of characters (Act iv, sc. 2) and strict observation of local colour (Act iii, sc. 3, pp. 66, 69). Lyrical effusions have the effect, here and there, of hindering the rhythmic evolution of the action (*passim*; and Act v, sc. 7).

In its incomplete form, the *Dīwān* is a collection of 46 fragments and poems. It shows numerous omissions (see tentative outline, Aoun, 35-53, and appendix, 166-8; thesis, AUB 1967, appendix) and a chronological classification of the poems has still to be made. The three main titles (*Taʾawwuhāt al-rūḥ*: 12 poems; *Aghānī al-Andalus:* 12 *muwashshaḥāt*; *Shuʿlat al-ʿadhāb*; 6 cantos with a seventh incomplete) denote a set of varying correspondences within classical conformism (in the themes, *Elegy of Sulaymān al-Bustānī*, the *Muwashshaḥāt*, the occasional borrowings from al-Maʿarrī and al-Mutanabbī).

The influence of the two poets Shawḳī (d. 1932; see Firʿawn, in *Dīwān*, 9-15) and Kh. Muṭrān (d. 1949; see Ṣaydaḥ, 348-9) and a lyricism charged with childhood memories, nostalgia, love, dreams, mingled with the thought of death and the disillusionment of a bitter pessimism (his poems *Baʿlabakk, ʿalā shāṭiʾ Rio, al-Lifāfa*), are typical of the literary output of his generation and that of émigré poets in particular.

His position in contemporary Arabic poetry rests, however, on *ʿAlā bisāṭ al-rīḥ*. This long poem (218 verses, in *khafīf* metre) contains fourteen cantos each with fourteen lines and originally modelled on the French sonnet (see the 1st ed., published in São Paulo, 28 June 1926, by al-Djāliya (*Dhikrā*, 74; *al-Āthār*, viii [October 1927], 387-400). In a 2nd ed. (1929) which was to give the poem its definitive form, the author fixes the number of lines at sixteen, except in the last three cantos. A two-line preamble, in the guise of a musical leitmotif (*madjzāʾ al-khafīf* = *fāʿilātun, mustafʿilun*) defines the respective phases of the poem. The illustrated edition (1929, 1931) is accompanied by a long introduction by F. Villaespasa, responsible for the Spanish version. Venturelli Sobrinho undertook the Portuguese version and seven other translations followed (*MSOS*, xxxi, 158-65; Aoun, 93-4; Dāghir, *Maṣādir*, ii, 722-3; *Dīwān*, 139-40). The poetic form, erratic in the *Dīwān*, more accomplished in the later poems, is to a large extent free from earlier imperfections and represents a harmonious fusion of restraint and simplicity. In this freely-flowing acoustic style, ideas, often common ones, take on a new and larger potential. The imaginary escape to the astral plane and the "Land of the Souls" is stimulated by the dualism of a divorce between the soul and the body. Faced by his insoluble dilemma, the divided and shattered being searches for its lost unity. The transitory tends towards immortality and the finite towards infinity. Thanks to his imaginative power, the poet, a stranger in the material world, seeks deliverance from his terrestrial imprisonment and project himself into space (cantos i, ii, iii). The stellar journey is marked out with dialogues, notably that of the winged and planetary race. These passages nevertheless bear the melancholic accent of a broken and lonely poet facing his implacable destiny (cantos vi, vii, viii). The spatial distance opens up a vertical perspective on the world; seen from these spiritual altitudes, controversies deepen, life takes on the appearance of a thin flux of ephemeral beings and there is a proliferation of meditations on the passions of mankind, his vanity and the destructive materialism of a perverse and perfidious civilisation ruled by the spirit of evil (cantos x to xiii). The poet's expiation is achieved by purificatory inspiration, and original unity is regained by the fusion of the two unyielding elements. But this state of grace attained through the mystery of love is dissipated like "the brightness of a dream" and the flesh is seen to fail. Only the pen, the poet's beloved harp, remains as the sole instrument of consolation and deliverance (canto xiv).

His poetic style takes as its starting-point the neo-classicism of his contemporaries, where the new professes to be the epiphenomenon of a traditionalist prosody. Then he frees himself from this genre so as to integrate himself with the emigrant literary movement. We may recall, in this connection, the elaborate themes, the nature of the imagery, the dimensions of the poetic state, the system of evocative language, which form common ground with the pleiad of *al-Rābiṭa al-ḳalamiyya*. Other reminiscences seem to recall the Arabic version of the *Rubāʿiyyāt* of ʿUmar Khayyām (tr. W. Bustānī, 1912) and Djabrān's poem *al-Mawākib* (New York 1918). Imbued with French romanticism, a desperate idealist, fleeing from confusion, an uprooted emigrant, his lyrical impulse is characterised by an authentic and personal accent within an incomplete poetic corpus.

Bibliography: ʿI. I. al-Maʿlūf, *Dhikrā Fawzī al-Maʿlūf*, Zaḥla 1931; G. Kampffmeyer, in *MSOS*, xxxi, 158-65; Mgr. I. Dīb, *Rūḥ shāʿir fī ṭayyāra*, 1935; F. Fāris, *Risālat al-minbar ilā al-Shark al-ʿArabī*, Alexandria 1936; F. Aoun, *Fawzī Maʿlūf et son oeuvre* (thesis), Paris 1939; Brockelmann, S III; P. G. Abū Saʿda, *Fawzī al-Maʿlūf*, St.-Sauveur (Lebanon) 1945; Dāghir, *Maṣādir*, ii,; Y. Awdāt, *Shāʿir al-ṭayyāra*, Cairo 1953 ; G. Ṣaydaḥ, *Adabunā wa-udabāʾunā*; R. al-Maʿlūf, *Shuʿarāʾ al-Maʿalifa*; ʿĪ. al-Nāʿūrī, *Adab al-Mahdjar*², Cairo 1967, 465-72; Ṭaha Ḥusayn, *Ḥadīth al-arbiʿāʾ*, ii, Cairo 1968; Kaḥḥāla, *Muʿdjam al-muʾallifīn*, viii, 83-4; see also the journals *al-Āthār*, ii-v (1912-28); *al-Ḍād*, v (June, July, August 1935), (May, June 1959); *al-Iṣlāḥ*, iv (1932), 417-22; *al-Kitāb*, v/3 (1948); *al-Muktaṭaf*, lxxv/4 (1928), lxxvi/3 (1929), lxxviii/3 (1931); *al-Shark*, São Paulo ii, iv, vii, viii, xii (1929-40). (A. G. KARAM)

11. DJŪRDJ ḤASSŪN MAʿLŪF, born at Bikfayā 1893, died in São Paolo 1965. He visited the English school at Shuwayr and then studied law at the Jesuit College in Beirut. Yaʿḳūb al-ʿAwdāt, who knew him well in later years, relates that Djūrdj Ḥassūn joined the Jesuit College in 1907 to study law and that he practised as a barrister for two years before he left Lebanon for Argentine in 1911. There he worked as the secretary to the Ottoman Consulate at Buenos Aires for one year and then he went to Brazil. He became

one of the founding-members of *al-ᶜUṣba al-andalusiyya.* Though he had an astounding knowledge of Arabic poetry, prose held his chief interest. He translated from French, Spanish and Portuguese, and composed some stories himself, apart from numerous articles. He wrote a long introduction (32 pp.) to the *Dīwān* of Ilyās Farḥāt in 1932. *Al-ᶜUṣba* published a volume of stories, partly translated, partly original, with the title *Aḳāṣīṣ* in 1954. The first instalment of a book on the literature of the *Mahdjar* was published in *al-Marāḥil.* He died in 1965 in a car accident.

Bibliography: al-Badawī al-Mulaththam (= Yaᶜḳūb ᶜAwdāt), *al-Nāṭiḳūn bi 'l-ḍād fī Amīrkā al-Djanūbiyya*, part 1, Beirut 1956, 338-9.; ᶜĪsā al-Nāᶜūrī, *Adab al-Mahdjar,*[2] Cairo 1967.

(C. NIJLAND)

MAᶜLŪLĀ, a place in Syria.

1. The locality. Maᶜlūlā is situated 38 miles/60 km. to the south-east of Damascus, 6 miles/10 km. to the west of the main Damascus-Ḥimṣ road, on the second plateau (5,000 feet/1,500 metres altitude) of the Djabal Ḳalamūn, the last chain of the Anti-Lebanon. The agglomeration is constructed in the form of an amphitheatre, inside a wide and deep gap; access to it is protected, from the side of the third plateau, by two defiles which open on to its flanks. There is access by one of these defiles to the monastery of St. Sergius, whose church with a cupola supported on pendentives is of Byzantine date; at the entrance to the other defile there is built, partly on the rock, the monastery of St. Thecla. The parish church of St. Leontius has no features of interest, but a mosaic from the 4th century A.D. has been found in the church of St. Elias.

Maᶜlūlā is mentioned by George of Cyprus as Magloula and as forming part of Lebanese Phoenicia; Yāḳūt gives it as a district (*iḳlīm*) of the environs of Damascus. It is known to have been the seat of a Melkite Orthodox bishopric in the 17th century, and in 1724 was attached to Ṣaydnāyā. At the time of the rebellion of the *amīr* of Baᶜlabakk, Muḥammad Ḥarfūsh, in 1850, Maᶜlūlā was sacked by the Turkish troops of Muṣṭafā Pasha chasing the rebels who had taken shelter in the village against the desires of the local population. In 1860 and 1925, Maᶜlūlā was again attacked and besieged.

The fame of this picturesque place comes from the fact that its inhabitants (about 2,000), who have remained Christians, mainly Melkite Catholics, still speak a Western Aramaic dialect, just like the people of two other nearby villages, Djubbaᶜdīn and Bakhᶜa, which became Muslim in the 18th century. Since the time of the first notes on the Aramaic or Maᶜlūlā published by Cl. Huart in 1878, this speech has been the subject of several important works by Dom J. Parisot, G. Bergsträsser, S. Reich and A. Spitaler (see below, 2. The language).

Since the Aramaic of Edessa was formerly the liturgical language of these Christians of Byzantine rite, a certain number of Syriac manuscripts from the monasteries and churches of Maᶜlūlā have come down to us, but most were burnt on the orders of a bishop in the 19th century.

Bibliography: *EI*[1] art. s.v. (E. Honigmann); R. Dussaud, *La topographie historique de la Syrie antique et médiévale*, Paris 1927, 264, 270, 281; S. Reich, *Études sur les villages araméens de l'Anti-Liban*, in *Docs. d'Études Orientales de l'Institut Français de Damas*, vii (1938), 5-9; B. Poizat, *Bibliographie du néo-araméen*, in *Comptes-rendus du GLECS*, xviii-xxiii (1973-9), 379-80.

(G. TROUPEAU)

2. The language. Maᶜlūla and its Aramaic-speaking neighbouring villages, Bakhᶜa and Djubb ᶜAdīn-Ghuppa ᶜŌdh are bilingual, and use varieties of dialectal Arabic more or less rapidly assimilating to the regional prestige speech of the city of Damascus—a process already completed for Maᶜlūla itself—in all outside relations. Hence it is not astonishing that there is a strong Arabic influence on their Aramaic vernacular, especially in the field of vocabulary: a random count will yield an average of about 20% and even more of words of Arabic origin in any given text. Loan translations abound. Nevertheless, the Aramaic language of Maᶜlūla and Djubb ᶜAdīn is still in full vigour, while at Bakhᶜa there seems to be a marked tendency, especially among the younger generation, to supplant it entirely by Arabic, which, of course, in due time will lead to its extinction there; in 1971 people of less than forty years' age were, according to information by inhabitants of the village, no longer able to use the vernacular correctly, although they had no difficulties in understanding it. Understandability among the three villages is mutual, except for smaller details which on the whole will not impair the comprehension of any utterance.

The characteristics of Maᶜlūla Aramaic (or, to be more exact, Western Neo-Aramaic) include:

General. MA is a descendant of the western branch of Aramaic (*yiḳṭul, yḳuṭlenn-e, inter alia*), its closest relationship being to Judaeo-Aramaic and Syro-Palestinian.

Phonology. Long vowels of Older Aramaic have been preserved under stress; *ā* > *ō*. In unstressed position, they appear shortened *-ā* > *a* - and partially merged, e.g. *ḥōmi* < *ḥāmē*, *páyṯī* < *bayṯī*. Short vowels in a stressed syllable seem to continue the former state, while, when unstressed, they too have undergone, at least phonologically, certain mergers (*e* ~ *i*, *o* ~ *u* against *a*, pre-tonic even *e i o u* > *ə* against *a*). Stress is usually on the penult, and may hit even originally prosthetic vowels: *ébra* < *brā* via *əbrā.* Voiced plosive consonants have been devoiced (*b d g* > *p t k*), voiceless plosive consonants except *p* palatalised (*ṯ ḵ* > *č k*; Dj. ᶜA. *k* > *č*), *p* has become *f*, *ḇ* > *b*. *Begadkefat* laws are no longer operating, although they have left many traces; roots containing susceptible consonants will appear either unified: *irkheb* "he mounted (a horse)" from *rkeḇ*: *arkhep* "he put somebody on horseback" corresponding to older *arkeḇ* which, except for palatalisation and *ḇ* > *b*, should have remained unchanged (for *p*, see below); or there exists a so-called root-variant: *irkheb* as above: *rikhpiṯ* "I mounted", the *p* having been generalised in the causative (see above example). Initially, in general the spirant version of these consonants has been perpetualised (original context pronunciation after final vowel).

Morphology. On the whole, the older system has changed very little, much less than in eastern Neo-Aramaic. This is doubtless to be attributed to a certain preserving force exerted by the structurally very similar surrounding Arabic dialects. Salient innovatory features out of Aramaic material are the development by fusion of analytical constructions of obligatory verbal forms to show the definiteness of a following direct or indirect nominal object (*iḳṭal ghabrōna* "they hit a man": *ḳaṭlull ghabrōna* "they hit the man", < *ḳaṭlunn-eh l-*) and the personal inflexion of predicative adjectives by prefixes formally identical with those of the imperfect (*ana n-ifḳer* "I'm poor"), as well as the strongly extended use of old *ḳṭīl* and *ḳaṭṭīl* participles as a resultative or perfect. Arabic has contributed in addition to a good many of verbal stems (III, V, VI, VII—the normal expression of the passive voice—, VIII, X), which, with the exception of VII, of course may be regarded as a special kind of lexical innovation, above all its construction of *ʿamma* + *b*-imperfect (this latter being represented in Aramaic by the present participle) to render continuous action or state. This fact has led to at least a partial restructuring of the verbal system, the simple participle in main clauses being restricted to the function of a general present. Besides, mention should be made of the free possibility of forming an elative even of Aramaic roots on the model of Arabic (*awrab* "bigger", from *yrb*: Ar. *aḥsan*).

Syntax. For category syntax, see the preceding section. Clause and sentence connection is realised on the one hand to a large extent by intonation alone (asyndesis), while on the other hand there is, as far as clause adverbials of time are concerned, a real profusion of incessantly reappearing temporal conjunctions. Very remarkable is the introduction from Arabic of the asyndetic relative clause (the *ṣifa*) to be used in exactly the same circumstances (indefinite clause-head) as in the tongue of origin.

The value of western Neo-Aramaic for the clarification of difficult problems raised by our not always complete understanding of the intricacies of the grammar of Older Aramaic has not yet been fathomed; there is still a grave lack of studies of this kind.

Bibliography: Specifically linguistic studies: A. Spitaler, *Grammatik des neuaramäischen Dialekts von Maʿlūla (Antilibanon)*, Leipzig 1938, repr. Nendeln 1966; V. Cantarino, *Der neuaramäische Dialekt von Ǧubb ʿAdin (Texte und Übersetzung)*, diss. Munich 1961; Chr. Correll, *Materialien zur Kenntnis des neuaramäischen Dialekts von Baḫʿa*, diss. Munich 1969; idem, *Untersuchungen zur Syntax der neuwestaramäischen Dialekte des Antilibanon (Maʿlūla, Baḫʿa, Ǧubb ʿAdīn). Mit besonderer Berücksichtigung der Auswirkungen arabischen Adstrateinflusses. Nebst zwei Anhängen zum neuaramäischen Dialekt von Ǧubb ʿAdīn*, Wiesbaden 1978. General: S. Reich: *Études sur les villages araméens de l'Anti-Liban* Damascus 1937. (Chr. Correll)

MĀLWĀ proper is an inland district of India bordered on the south by Vindhyās, and lying between lat. 23° 30′ N. and long. 74° 30′ E.

To this tract, known in the age of the *Mahābhārata* as Nishadha, and later as Avanti, from the name of its capital, now Udjdjayn, was afterwards added Akara, or eastern Mālwā, with its capital, Bhīlsā, and the country lying between the Vindhyās and the Sātpūras. Primitive tribes like Ābhīras and Bhīls have been dwelling among the hills and jungles of Mālwā since ancient times, some of whom still cling to their primitive way of life. The province formed part of the dominions of the Mauryas, the Western Satraps, the Guptas of Magadha, the white Huns, and the kingdom of Kanawdj [*q.v.*], and then passed to the Mālawās, from whom it has its name since about the 5th century A.D. These when Hinduised formed the Paramāra tribe of Rādjpūts, which bore sway in Mālwā from 800 to 1200, but from the middle of the 11th century onward their power was increasingly challenged by a confederacy of the Čālukyas of Anhilvada and the Kalačuris of Tripurī.

Mālwā, at the crossroads between northern India and the Dakhan, and between the western provinces and the seaports of Gudjarāt [*q.v.*], always occupied a position of great strategic and commercial importance. It was therefore only a matter of time for the territory to attract the attention of the Sultans of Dihlī. In 632/1234-5 Shams al-Dīn Iltutmish [*q.v.*] of Dihlī invaded Udjdjayn, demolished the temple of Mahākāl, and sacked Bhīlsā. This, however, was no more than a predatory raid and did not lead to annexation. Sultan ʿAlāʾ al-Dīn Khaldjī [see KHALDJĪS]—who as governor of Karā had led a successful raid on Bhīlsā in 691/1292—sent his commander ʿAyn al-Mulk Multānī [*q.v.* in Suppl.], "a master of pen and sword" (Amīr Khusraw), in 705/1305 to conquer Mālwā. It now became a province of Dihlī, and, with interludes of Hindu revolt, remained so until, in 804/1401-2, on the disintegration of the Kingdom of Dihlī after Tīmūr's invasion, the Afghān governor Dilāwar Khān Ghūrī made it an independent kingdom. On his death in 809/1406-7 (evidence of his having been poisoned by his son Alp Khān is inconclusive), Alp Khān succeeded him under the title of Hūshang Shāh. He transferred the capital from Dhār to Māndū [*q.v.*] and founded Hūshangābād. To him goes the credit for the consolidation of the newly-established kingdom. He followed an active foreign policy, extended his territory wherever possible, maintained friendly relations with his southern neighbours and succesfully withstood the pressure of Gudjarāt. He favoured a policy of toleration towards his Hindu subjects and encouraged Rādjpūts to settle in his kingdom. Mālwā prospered under his benign rule, and his patronage of letters attracted many scholars. On his death in 838/1435 he was succeeded by his son Ghaznī Khān, entitled Muḥammad Shāh, who after a reign of less than a year was poisoned by his ambitious *wazīr* and brother-in-law Maḥmūd Khaldjī.

Attempts by *amīrs* loyal to the Ghūrī dynasty to raise Muḥammad Shāh's thirteen-year old son Masʿūd were foiled by Maḥmūd who, in 839/1436, ascended the throne as Maḥmūd I, and whose reign of thirty-three years was the most glorious in the annals of Mālwā [see MAḤMŪD I KHALDJĪ]. He waged war successfully against the kings of Gudjarāt, the Dakhan, and Djawnpūr, against the small state of Kālpī, and against Rana Kūmbhā of Čitor; he retired, but without disgrace, before the superior power of Dihlī; and he extended the frontiers of his kingdom on the north, east and south. Maḥmūd followed a policy of "perfect toleration" (Jain). He protected the interests of the peasantry and encouraged extension of cultivation; trade and industry flourished, since he succeeded in establishing law and order throughout the realm. Robbery and theft were said to be almost unknown in his kingdom (Firishta). He was interested in the welfare of his subjects, and established hospitals, dispensaries, schools and colleges. Maḥmūd was known outside India, and had diplomatic relations with the titular ʿAbbāsid caliph of Cairo as well as with the Tīmūrid Abū Saʿīd Mīrzā of Khurāsān.

On his death in 873/1469 he was succeeded by his son ʿAbd al-Ḳādir Ghiyāth al-Dīn. Though Ghiyāth al-Dīn was well-versed in warfare, he had the sagacity to shift the emphasis from conquest to consolidation. He gave up his father's aggressive foreign policy and tried to maintain friendly relations with his neighbours. His reign was a period of peace and plenty and of cultural development. Having a large harem to look after, he increasingly associated his son Nāṣir al-Dīn in state affairs. In the event, Nāṣir al-Dīn removed all rivals from the throne, forced abdication on his father and himself ascended the throne (906/1500). His cruel reign ended with his death in 916/1510, leaving the kingdom in disarray and beset with grave problems. He was succeeded by his son Maḥmūd II [*q.v.*], who, though personally brave, was a poor general. With the help of Muẓaffar II of

Gudjarāt he rid himself of his powerful Rādjpūt minister, Mednī Raī, but in doing so embroiled himself with Sangrāma Rānā of Čitor, who defeated him in the field and took him prisoner, but generously released him. He then, with inconceivable folly and ingratitude, bitterly offended Bahādur Shāh of Gudjarāt, who invaded Mālwā and, after giving Maḥmūd every opportunity of atoning for his error, carried Māndū by assault in Shaʿbān 937/March 1531. Maḥmūd and his sons were sent in custody towards Čāmpāner, but the officer in charge of them, apprehending a rescue, put them to death.

Mālwā now became a province of Gūdjarāt, and in 941/1535 the emperor Humāyūn [*q.v.*], invading that kingdom, defeated Bahādur Shāh at Mandasor and captured Māndū, but was recalled to Hindūstān in the following year by the menacing attitude of Shīr Khān in Bengal; hence Mallū Khān, an officer of Maḥmūd II, established himself in Mālwā and assumed the title of Ḳādir Shadjāʿat Khān and Ḥādjdjī Khān, two officers of Shīr Shāh, drove him from Mālwā and assumed the government of the province. Shadjāʿat Khān died in 962/1554-5, and was succeeded by his son Malik Bāyazīd, known as Bāz Bahādur, who, during the decline of the power of the Sūr emperors, became independent. A severe defeat at the hands of the queen of the Gond Kingdom of Garha Mandla engendered in him a distaste for warlike enterprise, and he devoted himself to music and to the embraces of the beautiful Rūpmatī. In 968/1561 Akbar's army under Adham Khān surprised Bāz Bahādur at Sārangpūr, defeated his troops, put him to flight, and captured his mistress, who took poison rather than become the conqueror's paramour. Bāz Bahādur fled into Khāndēsh [*q.v.*] and Pīr Muḥammad Khān, second-in-command of Akbar's army, who followed him thither, was defeated by Mubārak Khān of Khāndēsh and drowned in the Narbadā. Bāz Bahādur returned and again reigned in Māndū, but in 969/1562 another Mughal army under ʿAbd Allāh Khān the Uzbek invaded Mālwā and compelled him to flee to Čitor. He remained a fugitive until 978/1570, when he submitted to Akbar and entered his service. Abu 'l-Faḍl mentions him among the musicians of Akbar's court.

Mālwā flourished under Mughal rule, and made notable progress in agricultural and industrial production. It became one of the best revenue-yielding provinces of the empire. The Marāthās [*q.v.*] started raiding the province during the closing years of Awrangzīb ʿĀlamgīr's [*q.v.*] reign. The province suffered greatly under their recurring depredations. In 1154/1741 the Mughal emperor Muḥammad Shāh, with his authority greatly shaken by Nādir Shāh's invasion, was compelled by increasing Marāthā pressure to appoint the Peshwā as deputy-governor of Mālwā and virtually to hand over the province to the Marāthās. They failed, however, to restore Mālwā as a unified and settled province, and it soon "became a jumble of principalities ruled over by Marāthā generals and officers, Rajput princes and Afghan adventurers" (Raghubir Sinh).

It was afterwards divided between the great Marāthā generals whose descendants, Sindhya of Gwalior, Holkar of Indore, and the Ponwārs of Dhār and Dewas, still held most of it till 1947.

From 1780 until 1818, when British supremacy was firmly established, the province was one of the principal arenas in which Muslim, Marāthā and European contended for empire. Since then, its history has been uneventful, but sporadic risings took place at six military stations during the great rebellion of 1857.

Bibliography: Amīr Khusraw, *Khazāʾin al-futūḥ*, ʿAlīgaŕh 1927; idem, *Dawal-Rānī-Khiḍr-Khān*, ʿAlīgaŕh 1917; ʿAlī b. Maḥmūd al-Kirmānī, alias Shihāb Ḥakīm, *Maʾāthir-i Maḥmūd Shāhī* (completed 872/1467-8), ms. no. Elliott 237, Bodleian, Oxford (also see an abridged version of the work, edited by Nūr al-Ḥasan Anṣārī, Dihlī 1968); Ḍiyāʾ al-Dīn Baranī, *Taʾrīkh-i Fīrūz Shāhī*, Calcutta 1860-2; Abu 'l-Faḍl ʿAllāmī, *Āʾīn-i Akbarī*, Calcutta 1867-77; idem, *Akbar-nāma*, Calcutta 1873-87; Niẓām al-Dīn Aḥmad, *Ṭabaḳāt-i Akbarī*, iii, Calcutta 1935; ʿAbd al-Ḳādir Badāyūnī, *Muntakhab al-tawārīkh*, Calcutta 1864-9; Firishta, *Gulshan-i Ibrāhīmī*, Bombay 1832; Ḥādjdjī al-Dabīr, *An Arabic history of Gujarat*, ed. E. D. Ross, London 1921-8; A. B. M. Habibullah, *The foundation of Muslim rule in India*, Lahore 1945; K. S. Lal, *History of the Khaljīs*, revised ed. New Dehli 1980; K. C. Jain, *Malwa through the ages*, Dihlī 1972; P. N. Day, *Medieval Malwa*, Dihlī 1965; Ishwari Prasad, *The life and times of Humayun*, Calcutta, etc., revised ed. 1956; Raghubir Sinh, *Malwa in transition*, Bombay 1936; G. C. Grant Duff, *History of the Mahrattas*, London 1921; *Cambridge hist. of India*, i.

(T. W. Haig - [Riazul Islam])

MALZŪZA, an ancient Berber people belonging to the branch of the Butr, and to the family of Ḍarīsa, who most probably lived in Tripolitania.

If we are to believe Ibn Khaldūn (8th/14th century) and his sources, the Berber genealogists, the Malzūza were descendants of Fāṭin, son of Tamzīt, son of Ḍarī (eponym of the Ḍarīsa) and were the sister-tribe of the important Berber tribes of the Maṭghara, the Lamāya, the Ṣadīna, the Kūmiya, the Madyūna, the Maghīla, the Maṭmāṭa, the Kashāna (or Kashāta) and the Dūna. The majority of these peoples have survived until the present day, except for three, sc. the Malzūza, Kashāna and Dūna, who became extinct at an early date and whom the mediaeval Arab historians knew only by name. According to Ibn Khaldūn, all the nine peoples above-mentioned occupied, before the 8th/14th century, "an exalted rank among the Berber populations and were distinguished by their great exploits". One should add that, according to another passage of the *History of the Berbers* of Ibn Khaldūn, the Malzūza were not a sister-tribe of the Maghīla [*q.v.*], but rather a clan of this latter people. Another genealogy of the Malzūza, quite different from that of Ibn Khaldūn, was given by Ibn al-Aḥmar in his monograph on the Marīnids entitled *Rawḍat al-nisrīn fī dawlat Banī Marīn*. According to this author, the Malzūza belonged, together with the Maghīla, the Maṭghar (*sic*), the Madyūna, the Kashāshāna (or Kashāna), the Maṭmāṭa and the Lamāya, and also the people of Fāṭin, not to the descendants of Ḍarī, but to the great Berber branch of the Zanāta.

It seems that the majority of the Malzūza were annihilated by the ʿAbbāsid general Yazīd b. Ḥātim b. Ḳabīṣa b. al-Muhallab during the great massacre of the Berber peoples of Tripolitania which took place after the defeat and death of the Ibāḍī *imām* Abū Ḥātim al-Malzūzī [*q.v.*]. The Malzūza, his fellow tribesmen, were to suffer in particular after his fall. However, it is not impossible that a clan of the Malzūza survived until the 4th/10th century. Indeed, one would be tempted to link the name of مزورة Malzūza with that of ملزوزة Mazūra whom Ibn Ḥawḳal, who was writing during this century, mentions in his list of Berber tribes as among the peoples of Tripolitania belonging to the great branch of the Mazāta.

Bibliography: Ibn Khaldūn, *Histoire des*

*Berbères*², i, 172, 236, 248; Abū Zakariyyā᾽ b. Yaḥyā Ibn Khaldūn, *Histoire des Beni ᶜAbd al-Wād*, ed. A. Bel, i, Algiers 1903, 123, n. 4; Ibn Ḥawḳal, *Kitāb Ṣūrat al-arḍ*, ed. J. H. Kramers, Leiden 1938, i, 107, Fr. tr. Kramers-Wiet, i, 104.

(T. Lewicki)

AL-**MALZŪZĪ**, Abū Ḥātim Yaᶜḳūb b. Labīd, famous Ibāḍī *imām*. He is mentioned in the *Kitāb al-Sīra wa-akhbār al-a᾽imma*, an Ibāḍī chronicle written shortly after 504/1110-11 by Abū Zakariyyā᾽ Yaḥyā b. Abī Bakr al-Wardjlānī. Abū Ḥātim was also known by other names. In the chronicle (which is at one and the same time a collection of biographies of famous Ibāḍī-Wahbī *shaykhs*) composed by Abu 'l-ᶜAbbās Aḥmad al-Shammākhī towards the beginning of the 10th/16th century and entitled *Kitāb al-Siyar*, the *imām* concerned is called Abū Ḥātim Yaᶜḳub b. Ḥabīb al-Malzūzī al-Nadjīsī; he was, according to this author, a *mawlā* of the Arab tribe of Kinda. Al-Shammākhī used, in the paragraph of his work concerning Abū Ḥātim, the historical work written by Ibn Salām b. ᶜUmar, a scholar who is the first Ibāḍī historian known from the Maghrib and who lived in the 3rd/9th century. Similarly, the form of the name of the *imām* Abū Ḥātim mentioned in the *Kitāb al-Siyar* is the oldest known and may be correct. As for the *nisba* al-Nadjīsī, which is added by al-Shammākhī, following Ibn Salām b. ᶜUmar, to the name of Abū Ḥātim al-Malzūzī, it most probably originates from the Berber tribe of Nadjāsa, which is known to us from the table of Berber peoples of Ibn Ḥawḳal (4th/10th century). The latter author cites the Nadjāsa among the peoples belonging to the branch of the Mazāta who lived in Tripolitania. Similarly, the tribe of the Malzūza seem to have belonged to the Mazāta and not to the Ḍarīsa or Zanāta, as it would appear from the evidence of the works of Ibn Khaldūn and Ibn al-Aḥmar.

Another Ibāḍī historian and biographer of the Maghrib who has transmitted to us several details concerning Abū Ḥātim al-Malzūzī, that is, Abu 'l-ᶜAbbās Aḥmad b. Saᶜīd al-Dardjīnī (7th/13th century), calls him Abū Ḥātim Yaᶜḳūb b. Labīb al-Malzūzī al-Hawwārī. The tribe of the Hawwāra, the largest part of which lived, in the first centuries of Islam, in the vicinity of the city of Tripoli, had, in the 2nd/8th century, played a major role in the history of the Ibāḍīs of Tripolitania. Also, it is not impossible that this tribe may have headed the confederation of Ibāḍi Berber people of the Maghrib who supported Abū Ḥātim al-Malzūzī, giving its tribal name to this confederation. It is very likely that Abū Ḥātim, being the supreme head of the confederation in question, added the name of Hawwāra to that of the tribe into which he was born, Malzūza [*q.v.*].

To conclude our discussion of the Ibāḍī sources, let us add that Abū Ḥātim is also mentioned in an anonymous document called *Tasmiyat mashāhid al-Djabal*, published by R. Basset under the title *Sanctuaires du Djebel Nefousa*. It is a list of the places venerated on Djabal Nafūsa, probably composed in the 9th/15th century, and was written as an autograph in an appendix to al-Shammākhī's *Kitāb al-Siyar* (ed. Cairo, 598-600). At the end of this list, we read that "one faces towards the oratory opposite the tomb of Abū Ḥātim". No doubt this is Abū Ḥātim al-Malzūzī who was killed, as we shall see, in a battle with the ᶜAbbāsid army in the Djabal Nafūsa and buried in a place in this district. Finally, a distinguished Ibáḍī writer of the 9th/15th century, Abu 'l-Ḳāsim al-Barrādī, calls the leader in question Abū Ḥātim Yaᶜḳūb b. Labīd al-Malzūzī al-Hawwārī.

As for the orthodox Arabic sources, only three authors tell us of Abū Ḥātim al-Malzūzī: Ibn ᶜIdhārī al-Marrākushī (7th/13th century), al-Nuwayrī (8th/14th century) and Ibn Khaldūn, who lived in the same century. Ibn ᶜIdhārī calls him simply Abū Ḥātim, except in a passage where he cites al-Ṭabarī and where this *imām* is called Abū Ḥātim al-Ibāḍī. Al-Nuwayrī says that this leader bore the name Abū Ḥātim b. Ḥabīb and that he was also called Abū Ḳādim. He adds that Abū Ḥātim was a *mawlā* of the Arab tribe of Kinda. Sometimes he is named by al-Nuwayrī quite simply as Abū Ḥātim. Ibn Khaldūn gives the Berber leader the name of Abū Ḥātim Yaᶜḳūb b. Ḥabīb b. Midyan Ibn Īṭūwafat. According to Ibn Khaldūn, he also bore the name Abū Ḳādim; this historian also makes him an *amīr* of the tribe of the Maghīla [*q.v.*]. It should be noted that the tribe into which Abū Ḥātim was born, the Malzūza, was regarded by Ibn Khaldūn and the Berber genealogists on whom he depended as the sister tribe of the Maghīla or, indeed, as a clan of this latter tribe.

Let us now turn to Abū Ḥātim's political and military activity. It is not impossible that he played a certain role, as *amīr* of the powerful tribe of the Maghīla who professed Khāridjī, Ibāḍī and Ṣufrī doctrines, as early as the imāmate of Abu 'l-Khaṭṭāb ᶜAbd al-Aᶜlā al-Maᶜāfirī (140-4/757-61). In fact, if we are to believe Abū Zakariyyā᾽ al-Wardjlānī (6th/12th century), he was governor of the city of Tripoli during this *imām*'s rule. He survived the great massacre of the Ibāḍī populations of Tripolitania by the ᶜAbbāsid general Ibn al-Ashᶜath which followed the defeat and death of Abu 'l-Khaṭṭāb in the battle that took place at Tawargha between the Ibāḍī forces and the ᶜAbbāsid army (Ṣafar 144/May-June 761). In 151/768-9, when the ᶜAbbāsid caliph al-Manṣūr sent a new governor to Ifrīḳiya in the person of a distinguished Arab general called ᶜUmar b. Ḥafṣ, also known as Hazārmard, the Ibāḍī Berber tribes of Tripolitania, already recovered after the defeat of Tawargha, were ready to rise again against Arab domination. ᶜUmar b. Ḥafṣ established himself in Ḳayrawān, capital of Ifrīḳiya, but soon received orders from the caliph al-Manṣūr to go to the Zāb and rebuild the strong fortress of Ṭubna which was to be the main base of the Arab armies in the central Maghrib. He was anxious to confront the powerful Ṣufrī leader of the central Maghrib, Abū Ḳurra, who was supported by two great Berber tribes of this land, the Banū Īfran and Maghīla, and who was proclaimed caliph by his followers in 148/765. Abū Ḳurra had created a powerful state with Tilimsān (Tlemcen) as his capital. Making for Ṭubna, ᶜUmar b. Ḥafṣ entrusted the government of Ḳayrawān (already depleted, like the whole of Ifrīḳiya, of Arab troops, most of whom had gone to Ṭubna, following the new governor), to his cousin Ḥabīb b. Ḥabīb b. Yazīd b. al-Muhallab. ᶜUmar b. Ḥafṣ was entirely assured of the attitude of the Berbers of Tripolitania and Ifrīḳiya who had been, in 144/761-2 so severely punished by Ibn al-Ash ᶜath. But this peace was only apparent. In fact, the Ibāḍīs of this land were already prepared to rebel against the Arabs. Indeed, immediately after the departure of the ᶜAbbāsid forces commanded by ᶜUmar b. Ḥafṣ in the central Maghrib, where they had difficulty in dealing with Abū Ḳurra, the Ibāḍī Berbers of the area around the city of Tripoli rebelled, in 151/768-9, against the Arab governor of the city of Tripoli. The rebels chose as their leader Abū Ḥātim. Under the command of their leader, they challenged the forces that the ᶜAbbāsid governor of this city had sent against them, and seizing Tripoli, they went on to lay siege to Ḳayrawān. Later, Abū Ḥātim al-

Malzūzī moved against Ṭubna, at the head of the Ibāḍī insurgents of Tripolitania and Ifrīḳiya, who then joined with the other Ibāḍī and Ṣufrī groups besieging ᶜUmar b. Ḥafṣ. The latter put up a brave defence, at the head of 15,000 soldiers. As for the besieging forces, they formed a huge army, in which Abū Ḳurra stood out at the head of 40,000 Ṣufrīs. Another band of Ṣufrīs numbering 2,000 soldiers was commanded by ᶜAbd al-Malik b. Sakardīd. Several Ibāḍī forces, commanded by different leaders, were independent of one another. The sources mention among these latter troops: Abū Ḥātim at the head of a considerable number of warriors; ᶜAbd al-Raḥmān b. Rustam, with 15,000; ᶜĀṣim al-Sadrātī at the head of 6,000 warriors and al-Miswar b. Hāniʾ with 10,000. The army under the command of Djarīr b. Masᶜūd al-Madyūnī was also composed of Ibāḍīs. During the siege of Ṭubna, Abū Ḥātim al-Malzūzī was only one of the leaders of the Ibāḍī groups and not the commander-in-chief of the Ibāḍī armies who besieged ᶜUmar b. Ḥafṣ. The latter, threatened by the great Khāridjī army, whose total strength was about four times that of his own army, bought the neutrality of Abū Ḳurra for 40,000 *dirhams*. After this, the latter's warriors left Ṭubna. Similarly, ᶜAbd al-Raḥmān b. Rustam, whose troops had been routed by a detachment of the garrison of ᶜUmar b. Ḥafṣ, hastened to lead back to Tāhart, his capital, the remnants of his army. It was only from this time that Abū Ḥātim al-Malzūzī took charge of the besieging forces. ᶜUmar b. Ḥafṣ, seeing that the forces of the Ibāḍīs surrounding Ṭubna were very much weakened, succeeded in escaping from this fortress and making haste to Ḳayrawān, which was also besieged by the Ibāḍīs. The Ibāḍī army which was besieging this city was already commanded by Abū Ḥātim, who had abandoned the siege of Ṭubna to make an end of the capital of Ifrīḳiya and its governor in the name of the ᶜAbbāsids, ᶜUmar b. Ḥafṣ Hazārmard. This army was at this moment 350,000 men strong, of whom 35,000 were horsemen. It may be that, during the siege of Ḳayrawān, Abū Ḥātim al-Malzūzī had been proclaimed *imām* of all the Ibāḍīs of the Maghrib with the title of *imām al-difāᶜ* (Abu 'l-Khaṭṭāb ᶜAbd al-Aᶜlā al-Maᶜāfirī bore the title of *imām al-ẓuhūr*). The siege of Ḳayrawān lasted for a long time and ended with the death of ᶜUmar b. Ḥafṣ (who was killed by the Ibāḍīs during a sortie) and with the surrender of Ḳayrawān, whose population and garrison were already totally starved.

But Arab help was near. Indeed, a large ᶜAbbāsid army was heading for Tripolitania under the command of the new Arab governor Yazīd b. Ḥātim. At the news of the approach of this army, Abū Ḥātim al-Malzūzī set out for Tripoli, from where he headed for the Nafūsa Mountains, whose inhabitants were particularly attached to the Ibāḍī doctrine. But other Ibāḍī Berber tribes also gathered around Abū Ḥātim, in anticipation of the final battle which would decide the future of Ibāḍism in the Maghrib. Among Abū Ḥātim's faithful followers, apart from the Nafūsa, may be counted the Hawwāra and Ḍarīsa. Abū Ḥātim held out in the Djabal Nafūsa in an almost impregnable place, according to certain sources, in Djanbī, where, however, he died, with his companions, despite their brave defence (155/772). Abū Ḥātim's tomb, which is situated in the same part of the Djabal Nafūsa and which is one of the holy places of this land, was surrounded with legends. After his death, the dignity of the Ibāḍī *imām* of the Maghrib passed to ᶜAbd al-Raḥmān b. Rustam and his descendants, who succeeded in maintaining what was left of the Ibāḍī imāmate of Tāhart until the beginning of the 4th/10th century.'

Bibliography: Ibn Khaldūn, *Histoire des Berbères*², i, 221-3; Nuwayrī, *Conquête de l'Afrique septentrionale par les musulmans, apud* Ibn Khaldūn, *op. cit.*, i, 379-85; Ibn ᶜIdhārī, *Bayān*², i, 75-8; *Chronique d'Abou Zakaria*, Fr. tr. E. Masqueray, Algiers 1878, 41-9; Shammākhī, *Kitāb al-Siyar*, Cairo 1301/1883-4, 133-8; Dardjīnī, *Kitāb Ṭabaḳāt al-mashāyikh*, ed. Ṭallāʾi, Blida 1394/1974, i, 36-40; Barrādī, *Djawāhir al-muntaḳāt*, ed. Cairo 1302/1884-5, 172-3; *Tasmiyat mashāhid al-Djabal*, ed. R. Basset, in *JA* (May-June 1899), 423-36, (July-August 1899), 115-20; H. Fournel, *Berbers*, i, 371-80.

(T. LEWICKI)

AL-**MĀMAḲĀNĪ**, ᶜABD ALLĀH B. MUḤAMMAD ḤASAN B. ᶜABD ALLĀH AL-NADJAFĪ (b. at Nadjaf 15 Rabīᶜ I 1287/15 June 1870, d. 15 Shawwāl 1351/11 February 1933), Imāmī Shīᶜī scholar of *fiḳh* and *uṣūl*, and author of some 30 works to which the bibliographical guides devote in general only a few lines.

He is very well-known among the Imāmīs for his *Tanḳīḥ al-maḳāl fī ᶜilm al-ridjāl* (lith. Nadjaf, i, 1349/1930-1, ii, 1350/1931-2, iii, 1352/1933-4), one of the last works in the tradition of *ᶜilm al-ridjāl* [*q.v.*], of which al-Kashshī, al-Nadjāshī and al-Ṭūsī are the most eminent representatives. This is a collection in which the persons who were witnesses and/or transmitters of the *sunna* of the Prophet and the Twelve Imāms are arranged in alphabetical order. It gathers together 13,365 persons, enumerated by the author, and it is also possible to glean information about his own life from the *tardjama* which he devotes to himself, to follow his scholarly career, i.e. his studies, his travels and pilgrimages and the bibliography of his works, and to discover some important dates of his life, such as that of 14 Ramaḍān 1314/16 February 1897 when he received from his father the *idjāza* to function as a *mudjtahid*. The *Tanḳīḥ* can certainly be considered as his main work, and can be judged as the widest repertory existing of *ridjāl*. At the same time, it has been the object of various criticisms, both for the author's numerous errors and also for his particular way of using the term *madjhūl*. Among the specialists in this field, the term indicates a transmitter concerning whom the *aʾimmat al-ridjāl* (i.e. the chief authorities in this matter) have asserted *djahāla* "ignorance about the degree of confidence to be placed in him", but al-Māmaḳānī uses it in a wider sense, so that the *madjhūl* becomes merely a person whose biography he is ignorant about. This is why, on reading the *Tanḳīḥ*, and even more the *Natāʾidj al-Tanḳīḥ*, the index in which are set forth the "results" of the *Tanḳīḥ*, the impression is given that the transmitters of Imāmī *ḥadīth* were very largely *madjhūl*, unknown persons. These deficiencies led the contemporary scholar Muḥammad Taḳī al-Tustarī to write a final dictionary, the *Ḳāmūs al-ridjāl*, which puts itself forward as definitive in this particular sphere.

Bibliography: Mamaḳānī, *Tanḳīḥ*, ii, 208-11; Āghā Buzurg Ṭihrānī, *al-Dharīᶜa*, iv, Nadjaf 1360/1941, 466-7; idem, *Muṣaffā 'l-maḳāl fī muṣannifī ᶜilm al-ridjāl*, Tehran 1378/1959, 250; Muḥammad ᶜAlī Tabrīzī Khiyābānī, *Rayḥānat al-adab fī tarādjim al-maᶜrūfīn bi 'l-kunya aw al-laḳab*, iii, 1369/1949-50, 430-3; Muḥammad Taḳī al-Tustarī, *Ḳāmūs al-ridjāl*, i, Tehran 1379/1959-60, 2-4; Kaḥḥāla, *Muʾallifīn*, iv, 116. General references: A. Arioli, *Introduzione allo studio del* ᶜilm ar-riğāl *imamita: le fonti*, in *Cahiers d'onomastique arabe*, Paris 1979, 77-8; B. Scarcia Amoretti, *L'introduzione al*

Qāmūs al-riğāl *di Tustarī: per una guida alla lettura dei testi prosopografici imamiti*, in *ibid.*, 37-49.

(A. Arioli)

AL-**MĀMĪ**, AL-SHAYKH MUḤAMMAD (d. 1282/1865-6), traditional Mauritanian scholar of a highly individualistic nature, whose reputation is founded less upon his considerable qualities as a poet and a Mālikī jurist than upon some of his statements, which caused a sensation in their time.

Thus, for example, he claimed to know the number of grains of sand contained by the earth, by means of a calculation which he reveals in a poem in *ḥassāniyya* Arabic, although he refrains from giving the precise result of his computations. He caused something of a scandal by declaring the principle of the roundness of the earth, something of which his compatriots, adhering to the letter of the Ḳurʾān: "The earth, We have stretched it out ..." (XV, 19), were still unaware in the 19th century. He is also credited with having predicted the existence of the rich mineral deposits which are exploited today in Mauritania. Legend has it that from his reading of all the books currently available (except two!) he acquired original knowledge which is revealed particularly in his poems in dialectal Arabic. He employed this same mode of expression to declare grammatical rules or to formulate prayers, but he resorted to classical Arabic for anything that could be described as didactic poetry; the latter includes in particular the *ḳaṣīdas* intitled *al-Mīzābiyya* on the art of debate, and *al-Dulfīniyya* which express the essence of his judicial teaching.

Concerned to adapt law in such a way as to legitimise the practices of his time, he naturally rejects *taḳlīd*, blind imitation, and reveals himself an advocate of *idjtihād*, personal effort; while not going to far as to claim for himself the status of a *mudjtahīd*, he skilfully recommends recourse to the practice of *takhrīdj*, which consists in formulating general rules on the basis of the teaching of a particular school, in his case, Mālikism.

A practical problem which engaged the attention of al-Māmī is that of the *zakāt* [*q.v.*] of animals owned by the tributaries of a Mauritanian tribe; he considers that they should be relieved of this obligation and bases his conclusion on substantial arguments. Otherwise, in a general fashion, he makes it his business to give legal foundation, in conformity with the *sharīʿa*, to all the customs rooted in his social milieu and, in his principal work entitled, significantly, *Kitāb al-Bādiya*, he addresses himself to the specific problems of nomadic societies: the open-air mosque, the valuation of objects according to a monetary system constituted by non-financial items (a block of salt, a sheep or a piece of fabric), the treatment of *waḳf*s among nomads, etc. At the beginning of the *Kitāb al-Bādiya*, he deals at length with custom (*ʿurf* or *ʿāda*), stressing its continuance and normative value, and he reveals the fundamental role that it has played in the judicial system of Islam, especially among the Mālikīs. He is thus led to sanction practices current in his time and considered contrary to the *sharīʿa: wangala* (the slaughtering and sharing, each day, of a sheep within a given group), force-feeding of women, ear-piercing, *iḥsān* (contract for the loan of a lactiferous animal, the hiring of young camels for the purpose of following a she-camel so that she continues to give milk), gifts offered by merchants to sellers of gum, *faskha* (dowry supplied by the family of the bride when she joins the conjugal home), consumption of tobacco, etc., all these being topics treated in a very liberal fashion. It is this spirit which characterises the teaching of al-Māmī in the judicial sphere; it appears more exacting in the context of politics, and this author is observed deploring the absence of any administrative structure corresponding to the requirements of the authentic Islamic city and regretting to some extent that he has never found the opportunity to exploit his talents as a statesman, in spite of his prestige, his wealth and his personal connections with sultans of Morocco, to whom he dedicated many of his poems.

The literary corpus of al-Māmī is quite significant, but is yet to be edited. It comprises in particular, besides the *K. al-Bādiya* and the verse writings to which reference has been made, a rendering in verse of the *Mukhtaṣar* of al-Khalīl and several commentaries on judicial works.

Bibliography: The only study is that of Mohamed El Mokhtar Ould Bah, *La littérature juridique et l'évolution du Mālikisme en Mauritanie*, Tunis 1981, 82-96, 112-13 (list of works) and index.

(M. M. Ould Bah)

MAMLAKA (A.), which may be considered (*LA*, s.v.) either as *maṣdar* or *ism al-makān* of the root *m-l-k* "to hold, possess", denotes in its first sense absolute power over things and especially over beings: to begin with, that of God over creation as a whole, and then, that of any individual, in certain circumstances. In a second sense, the word is applied to the place either in origin or by application, of the power under consideration: in the first case, it can refer e.g. to an all-powerful minister (Dozy, *Supplément*, s.v.); in another case, it can denote the spatial entity under the control of the above-mentioned power—the human one (whence: a free man who has become a slave, above all, by reason of war) or the natural one (notably: the middle of a road). But the most current denotation of the word, in this latter sense, is that of a piece of territory under the control of some authority—in the modern meaning of the term, a kingdom.

Arabic geographical literature provides some interesting developments of the word. It adopts it, on one hand, in its plural form *mamālik*, as it attested by the titles of several works of the type of geography called "that concerned with roads and kingdoms" (*Kitāb al-Masālik wa 'l-mamālik* [*q.v.*]), made popular by Ibn Khurradādhbih. But it is the singular form, *mamlaka*, which merits attention here. One of the pioneers of Arab geography, al-Djāḥiẓ, distinguishes in his *K. al-Amṣār wa-ʿadjāʾib al-buldān* between the *mamlakat al-ʿArab* and the *mamlakat al-ʿAdjam*, which was a classic distinction in the framework of the Shuʿūbiyya controversies. About 70 years later, around 316-20/928-32, another pioneer of the genre, representing administrative geography, Ḳudāma b. Djaʿfar, want beyond the controversy and reunited the two *mamlaka*s into a single one, the *mamlakat al-Islām* or, more simply, *al-mamlaka*. This course of evolution ended with the geographers of the Balkhī school, that of the so-called "atlas of Islam" who devoted themselves to depicting the Islamic world and that world only. The *mamlakat al-Islām* from this time onwards monopolises geographical description in al-Iṣṭakhrī, Ibn Ḥawḳāl and above all al-Muḳaddasī, who opposes, en bloc, this *mamlaka* to the whole of the remainder of the world, calling it, according to the needs of the context, *mamlakat al-Islām, al-mamlaka* or *al-Islām*. The feeling of unity, based on economic links and the sense of belonging to the same civilisation, here transcends the political cleavage inherent in the existence of two caliphates at Cordova and Cairo, rivals of the one in Baghdād. But the appearance of the Turks in the 5th/11th century en masse, and the decline of the caliphate were to justify this vision;

political divisions were to make this vision disappear, at a single blow, after the year 1000 A.D., from the works of the geographers.

Bibliography: Given in A. Miquel, *La géographie humaine du monde musulman jusqu'au milieu du XIe siècle*, Paris-The Hague 1963 (new ed. 1973) - 1980, index (see esp. i, 99, ii, 525-8, iii, pp. x-xi).

(A. Miquel)

MAMLŪK (a.), literally "thing possessed", hence "slave" [for which in general see ᶜabd, ḳayna and khādim], especially used in the sense of military slave"; for these last in various parts of the Islamic world, with the exception of those under the Mamlūk sultanate of Egypt and Syria [see next article], see ghulām. Although for many centuries the basis of several Islamic powers, the institution of military slavery can in many ways best be studied within the framework of the Mamlūk sultanate of Egypt and Syria (648-922/1250-1517) since the latter is so richly documented in the historical sources, many of them contemporary to the events which they describe and containing definitions and descriptions of that sultanate's institutions. Although differences of circumstances and the need to handle the Mamlūk sources with care (since many of them are partial or inaccurate or valid only for the author's own time) call for caution in making a comparative study, it is nevertheless true that an examination of Mamlūk military slavery is bound to shed much light on other Islamic societies in which the institution played a leading rôle.

Of all the slave societies which should be examined in connection with that of the Mamlūks, it is obvious that those immediately preceding and following it (in the Ayyūbid period and in Ottoman Egypt) should have first priority.

1. *Countries of origin and racial composition.*

We know quite a lot about the racial composition of the Mamlūks of the Mamlūk sultanate and their countries of origin (called quite often simply *al-bilād*; see e.g. Ibn al-Dawādārī, ix, 71, 11. 12-13). By contrast, though we know that the greater part of the Ayyūbids' Mamlūks were Turkish, we do not know their exact lands of origin, with the certain exception of al-Malik al-Ṣāliḥ Nadjm al-Dīn Ayyūb's reign, the direct precursor of the Mamlūk period, and with the possible exception of the reigns of one or two of his Ayyūbid contemporaries or immediate predecessors.

The source evidence on the characteristics of the peoples supplying the Mamlūks and on the various factors which brought about those Mamlūks' sale and importation into the sultanate, clarifies the reasons for the creation of a military slave institution and explains its unparalleled success and durability as the major military force for its time in the lands of Islam.

A most important description of the Ḳîpčaḳ steppe [see dasht-i ḳîpčaḳ in Suppl.] and its people, the major source of military slaves for the Mamlūk sultanate in the first part of its existence, is that of Ibn Faḍl Allāh al-ᶜUmarī, who based it on the evidence of persons who visited the Golden Horde (K. Lech, *Das Mongolische Weltreich*, Wiesbaden 1968, 68-71 of the Arabic text, which is an excerpt of the *Masālik al-abṣār*; al-Ḳalḳashandī, *Ṣubḥ al-aᶜshā*, iv, 456-8). There the author stresses both the very harsh circumstances in which the inhabitants of that steppe live, their primitiveness (including that of their pagan religion), as well as their military ability, faithfulness and loyalty (see also al-Dimashḳī, *Nukhbat al-dahr*, 264, 11. 4-11, 279, 11. 9-12), a combination of qualities which made them highly suitable raw fighting material. The sources attest a unanimous conviction that the Mamlūks of Egypt and Syria had been the decisive factor in saving Islam both from the Frankish and the Mongol threats since the battles of al-Manṣūra (647/1249) and ᶜAyn Djālūt (658/1260) [*q.v.*] to the later battles against the Ilkhāns of Persia and ᶜIrāḳ (al-ᶜUmarī, *op. cit.*, 70, 1.7-71, 1.12; *Ṣubḥ*, iv, 458. See also D. Ayalon, *The transfer of the ᶜAbbāsid caliphate*, 58-9, and n. 1; idem, *The European-Asiatic steppe*, 47-52; idem, *The Great Yāsa*, part C_1, 117-130, part C_2, 148-56; idem, *From Ayyūbids to Mamlūks*). This unanimous and repeated evidence is crowned by Ibn Khaldūn's evaluation of the Mamlūk phenomenon in the lands of Islam in general and in the Mamlūk sultanate in paticular (*ᶜIbar*, v, 369-73; Ayalon, *Mamlūkiyyāt*, 340-3). The resultant prestige greatly helped the Mamlūks in overthrowing the Ayyūbids, in firmly establishing their rule, and in thoroughly incorporating in their realm an undivided Syria, as a region with a status very inferior to that of Egypt.

The factors which led to the sale of slaves by the inhabitants of the Ḳîpčaḳ steppe and their rulers were the following ones: the general destitution of the population, which forced it, in certain years, to sell its children (ᶜUmarī, 70, 11. 2-4; *Ṣubḥ*, iv, 458, 1.2; al-Maḳrīzī, *Sulūk*, i, 942, 11. 10-12); the need to sell the children in lieu of taxes to the ruler (*Ṣubḥ*, iv, 476, 11. 11-16); the ruler's capturing and selling the children and women of his subjects (ᶜUmarī, 69, 11.6-10; *Ṣubḥ*, iv, 474, 1.10-475, 1.1). It was not, however, only under duress and such pressures that those children were sold. The high sums paid for them constituted an immense incentive. In the third reign of al-Nāṣir Muḥammad b. Ḳalāwūn (1309-40 [*q.v.*]), who was exceptionally lavish in his buying of Mamlūks, the Mongols competed so fiercely with each other in selling their boys, girls and relatives to the slave-merchants, that it marred their internal relations (*Sulūk*, ii, 525, 11.6-10).

It is true that the Mongol attacks on the Ḳîpčaḳ steppe filled the slave markets with Turks from there, thus facilitating their purchase by the later Ayyūbids and particularly by al-Ṣāliḥ Nadjm al-Dīn Ayyūb, and indirectly contributing to the establishment of the Mamlūk state (see e.g. Ayalon, *Le régiment Bahriya*, 133-4; idem, *The Great Yāsa*, part C_1, 117 ff.). However, prisoners of war captured by any kind of external enemy, or even by a Muslim ruler, could not guarantee the uninterrupted supply of Mamlūks, particularly children below military age, without the constant co-operation of local elements, whether the ruler, or the heads of the tribes, or above all, the parents and relatives of those children. Furthermore, that co-operation in selling their own flesh and blood was not confined to the subjugated peoples, but included as well the conquering and subjugating Mongols, and we are even informed as well that the subjugated peoples of that region used to steal the children of their Mongol conquerers and sell them to the slave-dealers (ᶜUmarī, 72, 11.16-17).

The Islamisation of the Mongol dynasty of the Golden Horde and many of its constituent peoples must have contributed, in the long run, to the diminution of military manpower for the lands of Islam from the Ḳîpčaḳ steppe and especially for the Mamlūk sultanate. In the short run, however, it is quite doubtful whether the adoption of Islam had a considerable effect on the slave-trade from that region. For many years, those who became Muslims retained many of their old pagan habits, and numerous others remained pagan (ᶜUmarī, 72, 11.12-19; *Ṣubḥ*, iv, 457, 1. 19-458, 1.3). Both sellers and buyers had a very strong interest in the continuation of the slave-trade, which meant that new converts to Islam were not necessarily excluded from becoming Mamlūks (*ibid.*). For the effects of conversion to Judaism or Christianity of nomads of the Eurasian steppe at an earlier period on their readiness to sell their children, see al-Iṣṭak͟hrī, 223, 11.11-15.

One of the major drawbacks of the Mamlūk system, from which almost all the Muslim states suffered, was that they had little or no control on their sources of supply (the outstanding exception being the Ottoman empire, which recruited most of its *ḳullar* from the Christian peoples living within its boundaries). The states which were not contiguous to those sources of supply had an additional major problem, that of being dependent on favourable factors concerning the routes leading to the sources in question (be they sea or land-routes) (see e.g. Ayalon, *Aspects of the Mamlūk phenomenon*, i, 207-9). The Mamlūk sultanate was, in this respect, completely dependent on foreign factors both on land and on sea; hence its attempts to diversify its routes (and very probably its sources) of supply as far as it could.

The main route was by sea through the Bosphorus and the Dardanelles, and this was under the complete command of Byzantium, and later the Ottomans, and the Franks. In the Byzantine period there is no complaint in the Mamlūk sources about Byzantine interference with the ordinary flow of slaves to the Mamlūk sultanate, in spite of Byzantium's ambivalent policy in its relations with the Mongols of the Golden Horde, the Ilk͟hāns of Persia and ᶜIrāḳ and the Mamlūks. In the correspondence between Michael Palaeologus and Ḳalāwūn in 680/1281 concerning the conclusion of a pact between the two states, the slave traffic figures quite prominently. The emperor promises, *inter alia*, safe passage of Mamlūks and slave girls, on the condition that there will be no Christians among them, but demands the release of all the Christian Mamlūks already in the sultanate to Byzantium. The sultan agrees, in his answer, to most of the emperor's suggestions, and stresses the importance of granting safe conduct to the merchants coming from Ṣūdāḳ and the Ḳïpčaḳ steppe, but completely ignores the emperor's demand about the Christian Mamlūks (Ibn al-Furāt, vii, 229, 1.20-230, 1.16, 232, 11.15-22, 233, 11.3-6).

Even more important was the attitude of the Ottoman empire, now in the ascendant. With the deterioration of Mamlūk-Ottoman relations from the beginning of Ḳāyitbāy's reign onwards, the Ottomans had an excellent means of weakening the Mamlūks by cutting off the supply of military manpower to them, and they do seem to have used that weapon to some extent. In 895/1490, when the Ottomans wanted to conclude peace with the Mamlūks, one of Ḳāyitbāy's two major stipulations was the release of the merchants of Mamlūk slaves (Ibn Iyās, iii, 267). In 922/1516, on the eve of the destruction of Mamlūk sultanate's independence, Sultan Selīm writes to Sultan Ḳānṣawh al-G͟hawrī a conciliatory letter in which he states that al-G͟hawrī's claim that the Ottomans prevent the slave merchants from coming to his empire is wrong; those merchants avoided bringing Mamlūks to the Mamlūk sultanate because of its debased currency (Ibn Iyās, v, 43, 11.17-17). Considering the sizes of the Mamlūk regiments of Ḳāyitbāy and Ḳānṣawh al-G͟hawrī, it would appear that the Ottoman embargo, as far as it existed, was not very thorough.

There were two additional land routes. One ran through Eastern Anatolia, about which we do not know much, but which seems to have been quite important. In using this route, the Mamlūks had to surmount two formidable obstacles: their enemies, the Ilk͟hānid Mongols, and the Mongols' staunch allies, the Christians of Little Armenia (*Bilād Sīs*). The attitude of the Mongols is unknown (for a single exception, see below), but that of the rulers of Little Armenia, as well as the importance of the route, is revealed in the truce (*hudna*) concluded between Ḳalāwūn and King Leon III in Rabīᶜ II 684/June 1285, which included the following stipulation; the merchants bringing Mamlūks and slave-girls to the Mamlūk sultanate will be permitted to pass through King Leon's territory without hindrance, and those of them already stopped or imprisoned will be freed and allowed to pursue their journey (Ibn ᶜAbd al-Ẓāhir, *Tas͟hrīf al-ayyām wa 'l-ᶜuṣūr*, Cairo 1960, 99, 11.7-11,15, and especially 100, 1.19-101, 1.1). In all probability, Sultan Baybars I, who had been bought together with others in Sīwās, arrived in the Mamlūk realm by this Eastern Anatolian route.

The other land route seems to have been through the very heart of the Ilk͟hānid empire, and the slave-trade here apparently centred round a great merchant, named Mad͟jd al-Dīn Ismāᶜīl al-Sallāmī (or al-Mad͟jd al-Sallāmī), a native of that empire, who was born in the vicinity of Mawṣil, described as al-Nāṣir Muḥammad b. Ḳalāwūn's "slave-dealer of the Privy Purse" (*tad͟jir al-k͟hāṣṣ fi 'l-raḳīḳ*) and very influential at the Ilk͟hānid court. He is said to have been the main instrument in the conclusion of a peace treaty between the Mamlūks and the Mongols (723/1323), but even before that date, he used to go repeatedly to Tabrīz and other places in the Ilk͟hānid realm and bring slaves from there. One of the stipulations of the Mamlūk sultan in that treaty was the free purchase of Mamlūks in the Ilk͟hānid dominions (*Esclavage*, 3; al-Ṣafadī, *al-Wāfī bi 'l-wafayāt*, ix, Wiesbaden 1974, 220, 1.9-221, 1.6; Ibn al-Dawādārī, *Kanz al-durar*, ix, 312, 1.16-313, 1.10; al-Maḳrīzī, *Sulūk*, ii, index, p. 1020b), and it is thus very probable that the flow of Mamlūks through Ilk͟hānid territory increased as a result of the treaty. It is true that Dimurdās͟h b. D͟jūbān, the Ilk͟hānid governor of Anatolia (*Bilād al-Rūm*), prohibited, after 1323, the dispatch of Mamlūks to Egypt from or through that area (*sulūk*, ii, 293, 11.1-8), but the attitude of that highly controversial ruler, for which he paid with his life, should be considered as exceptional. How the slave trade from the Ilk͟hānid empire went on after its disintegration in 736/1336 is unknown.

In the third reign of al-Nāṣir Muḥammad b. Ḳalāwūn, the purchase of Mamlūks reached, perhaps, its peak. He is said to have imported Mamlūks and slave girls from "the Golden Horde (*Bilād Uzbak*), Anatolia (*al-Rūm*), Tabrīz and Bag͟hdād and other countries" (*Sulūk*, ii, 524, 11.13-15); clearly, at this time all the three main routes connecting his realm with the Mamlūks' countries of origin were in use.

In summing up the problem of the routes through which military manpower was supplied to the Mamlūk sultanate, it can be said that interference with the flow of slaves into it, be it by Byzantines, Ottomans, rulers of Little Armenia, Ilk͟hānid Mongols or Christian Europeans, never seriously affected the military strength of that sultanate; only an effective embargo on this item alone might have broken that strength.

One of the major events in the history of the Mamlūk sultanate, which transformed the racial composition of its military aristocracy, was the supplanting of the Ḳïpčaḳ Turks by the Circassians. The

Mamlūk sources attribute that transformation solely to internal causes (Ayalon, *Circassians*, 135-6). There are, however, good reasons to suggest that the situation in the Mamlūks' countries of origin had some share in bringing about that result. There is a considerable amount of evidence about the comparatively flourishing situation and the dense population of the Ḳîpčaḳ steppe in *ca.* 1200-1350 (*ibid.*, 136, and n. 2), although the process of its decline seems to have started with the Mongol occupation (al-ᶜUmarī, 71, 11.15-18). Ibn ᶜArabs̲h̲āh gives quite a detailed description of how it had been devastated and depopulated by internal wars and the attack of Tīmūr (*Ak̲h̲bār Tīmūr*, 113, 1.5-115, 1.4, 122, 1.2, 126, 1.2-127, 1.4; see also A. N. Poliak, in *REI* [1935], 241-2; *idem*, in *BSOS*, x, 864-7). The very fact that the area had been a major source for the supply of Mamlūks must have contributed considerably to its depopulation and perhaps even to the military devaluation of its human material, since the slave traffic was confined mainly to a particular section of a special age group, namely, the cream of adolescent boys and girls who still had all the reproductive years ahead of them, and this must have adversely affected the future generations in the steppe. Although the number of the Royal Mamlūks (*al-mamālīk al-sulṭāniyya*) was not very great, it should be remembered that many of the commanders, both in Egypt and in Syria, had their own Mamlūks, and that the owning of white slaves existed in sections of society well beyond the military aristocracy. Furthermore, the Ḳîpčaḳ steppe supplied slaves to countries outside the Mamlūk sultanate as well. Finally, the rate of mortality among those Mamlūks in the countries to which they had been imported was very high, especially in times of epidemics, necessitating the more or less constant need for the replenishment of their thinning ranks. The long-range effects of the islamisation of the peoples of the Ḳîpčaḳ steppe have already been mentioned.

Before enumerating the races of the Mamlūks, the term *Turk* must be discussed. It had two meanings; one very wide, the other much narrower. We shall start with the wider meaning, leaving the other to the enumeration of the races. *Turk* or *Atrāk* in the wide sense embraced all the Mamlūk races, and was practically synonymous with Mamlūks. The Mamlūk sultanate was called *Dawlat al-Turk* or *Dawlat al-Atrāk* or *al-Dawla al-Turkiyya.* The commonest designation of the Mamlūk sultans was *Mulūk al-Turk.* But whereas the sultans of the Ḳîpčaḳ period had only this designation, each of the sultans of the Circassian period had a double designation; thus Sultan D̲j̲aḳmaḳ was the thirty-fourth of "*Mulūk al-Turk* and their sons" and the tenth of the "*D̲j̲arākisa* and their sons"; and so on.

To compile a list of the various races represented in Mamlūk military society is quite easy. But to evaluate the respective weight of the various racial groups, with the exception of the two major ones (the *Turk* and the *D̲j̲arkas*) is very difficult. This is because it is quite rare that the sources refer to the racial affiliation of individual Mamlūks, who were usually given Turkish names, irrespective of their racial origin; moreover, the mention of racial groups taking an active part in a certain event or struggle (again with the exception of the two main races) is even much rarer (some lists of Mamlūk racial groups do however exist). This is in glaring contrast to the extremely rich and varied data furnished by those sources about the groups (*ṭawāʾif*, sing. *ṭāʾifa*) based on slave and patron relations, like the Ẓāhiriyya of Baybars, Manṣūriyya of Ḳalāwūn, Nāṣiriyya of Farad̲j̲, As̲h̲rafiyya of Ḳāyitbāy, etc. Therefore, our picture of these groups and their relations (on whom see below) is far clearer than that of the racial groups (*ad̲j̲nās*, sing. *d̲j̲ins*). The racial struggle comes into prominence mainly in connection with the Circassians and from a comparatively early date in the Turkish-Ḳîpčaḳ period, reaching its peak in the closing decades of the 8th/14th century. After the almost total victory of the Circassians, it is brushed aside, with the exception of some flickers of antagonism on the part of other races, and of repeated expressions of haughtiness towards and discrimination against those races on the part of the Circassians.

In Ottoman Egypt, the racial factor is even more subdued than the Mamlūk one. Furthermore, at least as far as the chronicle of al-D̲j̲abartī [*q.v.*] is concerned, practically the only data we possess about the racial composition of the military aristocracy are that source's mentioning of the racial affiliation of a certain number of individual Mamlūks.

From the data in the sources of the Mamlūk period (including the lists of races), the following general list can be reconstructed: *Turk* (or *Atrak*), *Ḳifd̲j̲āk, Tatar, Mug̲h̲ul* (or *Mug̲h̲ūl*), *K̲h̲iṭāʾiyya, Rūs, Rūm, Arman, Āṣ, Abaẓa, Lāz* and *D̲j̲arkas.*

By far the two dominant races were the *Turk* and the *D̲j̲arkas*, if the whole Mamlūk period is considered. The *D̲j̲arkas* seem to have constituted an important element already in the *Burd̲j̲iyya* [*q.v.*] regiment created by Ḳalāwūn, and are the only ones mentioned as repeatedly challenging the supremacy of the *Turk.* The *Ḳifd̲j̲āḳ* are rarely referred to in the above-mentioned data and lists, and are an obvious synonym of *Turk.* The case of the *Mug̲h̲ul* and the *Tatar* is more complicated. The *Mug̲h̲ul*, who are mentioned only in the Ḳîpčaḳ period, seem to have been distinct from the *Turk*, although perhaps with a certain degree of overlapping. The *Tatar*, on the other hand, especially under the Circassians, were very often synonymous with *Turk.* This can be proved in two ways: (a) *Turk* and *Tatar* are never mentioned together in the same list, or in connection with the same event; and (b) a good number of individual Mamlūks in the Circassian period are said to have been *Turkī al-d̲j̲ins* on one occasion and *Tatarī al-d̲j̲ins* on another. The reason for that alternation is obvious. The more the Tatars advanced in the steppe, the greater was the Turkish element which they subjugated and incorporated in their armies; and since the Turks were much more numerous, it was they who absorbed their conquerors. Already Ibn Faḍl Allāh al-ᶜUmarī says that the Tatars were completely assimilated by the Ḳîpčaḳīs and lost their own identity (*op. cit.*, 73, 11. 17-20).

The *Rūm* were third in importance. There is no sufficient information for establishing the relative importance of the other racial groups. The *Rūs* are never mentioned as a racial group outside the lists, and there are hardly any individual Mamlūks who are said to have belonged to that race (the best-know individual is Baybug̲h̲ā Rūs, or Urus or Urūs).

The Franks (*Farand̲j̲, Ifrand̲j̲*) are never mentioned in the Mamlūk sources as a racial group. There are, however, a fair number of Mamlūks who are said to have been of Frankish origin; and since the Mamlūks, as already stated, did not preserve their original infidel names—especially if they had not been Turks—and since the origin of many of them is not mentioned, the number of the Franks amongst them might well have been considerably higher. Yet the sources' absolute silence about the Franks as a separate body does not support the claim of some mediaeval European writers about the very great proportion of Franks in the Mamlūk army. One should, however, take into consideration the possibility that there might have been a certain degree of overlapping between *Farandj* and *Rūm*.

There were some Muslim-born people, even from within the boundaries of the Mamlūk sultanate, or from the neighbouring countries (particularly the areas inhabited by the Turcomans), or from regions lying further away, who managed to join the Mamlūk military aristocracy either by fraudulent means (such as an arrangement with the slave dealer), or because they were taken prisoners and found the status of a Mamlūk too good to give up by admitting that they were in reality Muslims. Some of these whose bluff had been called were ousted from the military aristocracy, deprived of their Mamlūk names and forced to bear again their original names. These Muslim-born Mamlūks constituted, however, only a very marginal element in Mamlūk society. A few of the Turcomans who became Mamlūks were called *Rūmīs* as well.

2. *The arrival and early training of the Mamlūk*

The crucial stage in the Mamlūk's career, from his leaving his country of origin, through his education and upbringing, and up to his manumission, can be reconstructed fairly well in the Mamlūk sultanate, despite numerous gaps which affect the sureness of the general picture; even so, this picture is far superior to what we know at present about the parallel careers of military slaves in the rest of the mediaeval Muslim world, including the Ottoman empire, up to the beginning of the 10th/16th century.

In the life story of each Mamlūk, his slave merchant, and especially the one who brought him over from his country of origin, figured most prominently. He was his first patron and protector from the hardships and dangers during the long voyage to his adopting country. He also served as the most usual link between him and his original homeland, so that Mamlūk was usually bound with strong ties of affection and veneration to that merchant. All of those merchants were Muslim civilians from outside the Mamlūk sultanate, and some of them became very influential in that sultanate. They should not be confused with the "merchant of the Mamlūks" (*tādjir al-mamālīk*, or fully, *tādjir al-mamālīk al-sulṭāniyya*), who was generally a low-ranking Mamlūk *amīr* (*amīr* of ten) and whose function was to supervise the commerce of the Mamlūks; this personage usually stayed within the boundaries of the sultanate.

While we know very little about the slave-market and its functioning, we know much more about how the sultans bought their Mamlūks; they in fact usually bought them from the *Bayt al-Māl* [*q.v.*] or treasury. Those of them who had not yet been manumitted before the death or dismissal of the reigning sultan were returned to the *Bayt al-Māl* and bought from there by the new sultan.

The sultan's Mamlūks were brought up in a military school situated in the barracks (*ṭibāk*, *aṭbāk*, sing. *ṭabaḳa*) of the Cairo citadel, of which there were 12. It would appear that each of those barracks had a special (probably separate and secluded) section assigned to the Mamlūk novices (*kuttābiyya*, or possibly *kitābiyya*, sing. *kuttābī* or *kitābī*), since (a) after having finished their period of training, and as long as they had not been driven out of the citadel, the Mamlūks continued to stay in those barracks and belong to them, bearing their respective names; and (b) the barracks accommodated far bigger numbers of Mamlūks than the number of novices staying there at any given moment.

The education of the novice was divided into two main parts: first, the study of the elements of Islam and afterwards the military training (*anwāʿ* (or *funūn*) *al-ḥarb* (or *al-furūsiyya*)). The first part was most essential; for, in spite of its unavoidable elementary character, it inculcated in him the conviction that he had been led in the right path from the darkness of heathendom to the light of Islam (see also Baybars al-Manṣūrī, *Zubdat al-fikra*, B.L. ms. no. 23325, fol. 51b, 11.5-16). This kind of gratitude of the Mamlūk, even if later in his career he did not lead a very strict religious life, was at least as important as his other kinds of gratitude to the Muslim environment in general, and to his patron in particular, for raising him from poverty to richness and from anonymity to fame and high position. As al-Maḳrīzī aptly puts it in his well-known passage on the Mamlūk's upbringing, the combination of his identification with his new religion, and a great proficiency in the art of war (more precisely, in horsemanship) were the targets of the Mamlūk's education. "[Until] the glorification of Islam and its people had been merged in his heart, and he became strong in archery, in handling the lance and in riding the horse" (*Khiṭaṭ*, ii, 214, 11.1-2). Curtailing the religious education, or dropping it altogether, because of the need or desire to shorten the period of apprenticeship, was always a symptom of decline in the Mamlūk sultanate or elsewhere.

3. *The role of the eunuchs*

The overwhelming dominant element in the personnel of the military school was that of the eunuchs [see KHAṢĪ], who took part in the upbringing of the novices (even in the religious field, in addition to the theologians), as well as in keeping very strict discipline among them. A major reason for manning the school with eunuchs was to use them as a buffer between the young and adult Mamlūks to prevent pederasty [see LIWĀṬ]. A novice proved to have been the object of sodomy could be sentenced to death (*Khiṭaṭ*, ii, 214, 11.6-8).

The eunuchs in the military school formed a kind of a pyramid, at the basis of which were the simple eunuchs called *khuddām* (or *ṭawāshiyat*) *al-ṭibāḳ*. At the head of each barracks was a eunuch called *muḳaddam al-ṭabaḳa*, and all the barracks were commanded by a eunuch who was called *muḳaddam al-mamālīk al-sulṭāniyya* and who had a deputy (*nāʾib*), also a eunuch.

There does not seem to have been a separation between eunuchs serving in the school and in other military or administrative capacity and those of them serving in the harem or in religious institutions. It would appear, however, that they did not usually perform those different functions simultaneously.

The eunuchs as a body were extremely strong and influential under the Mamlūk sultans. It is difficult to compare their power with that of the eunuchs in other Muslim mediaeval states, because the eunuch hierarchy of those other states cannot be reconstructed to the same degree. What is certain, however, is that individual eunuchs in the Mamlūk sultanate could not rise to the highest ranks or be as powerful as those in other Muslim states, including under the Ayyūbids and in the very early decades of the Mamlūk sultanate; neither could they be commanders in the field of battle, as happened so often in earlier Muslim states. The highest rank that a eunuch could reach under the Mamlūks was the middle one, namely, *amīr* of forty, and even to this rank only one single eunuch could be appointed, the *Muḳaddam al-Mamālīk al-*

Sulṭāniyya. Only in the chaotic conditions prevailing in the years immediately following al-Nāṣir Muḥammad b. Ḳalāwūn's third reign, to a very great extent as a result of that reign, the eunuchs, together with the women and slave-girls of the court, accumulated unprecedented power. This kind of power could not have lasted for long, for in addition to its running counter to the basic concepts of Muslim society, it would have destroyed the very foundations of Mamlūk aristocracy. Other evils originating from that reign (usually believed to be good and great, with only partial justification) lasted much longer (see below).

The eunuchs in the Mamlūk sultanate belonged mainly to four races, the *Rūm, Ḥabash, Hind* and *Takrūr*, the two first-named being the predominant races. Thus only one race, the *Rūm*, was common to them and to the Mamlūks. Like the Mamlūks, each one of them was considered to be Ibn ʿAbd Allāh (thus shrouding his infidel past in obscurity). Unlike them, however, they bore a special kind of Muslim names, representing the pleasant and beautiful (gems, perfumes, etc.; see LAḲAB). Only a few of them bore Turkish names.

With all the differences between them and the Mamlūks, the eunuchs of the court formed a very essential part of the aristocracy, and without them, the early stage of the Mamlūk's career, which affected so decisively his subsequent one, would have been fundamentally different.

4. *Completion of training and manumission*

There is no evidence indicating the average length of the period which the novice had to stay in the military school. There is, however, much proof to show that, on the whole, that period was considerably shortened in the later period, a curtailment which adversely affected the proficiency of the Mamlūk soldier. Each single Mamlūk attending the school was manumitted on finishing his period of apprenticeship. The ceremony was a communal one, carried out in the presence of the sultan in a passsing-out parade called *khardj*, in which 150 to 500 "graduates" took part. Each one of them received a manumission certificate, called *ʿitāḳa*, which attested, at the same time, his being a fully-fledged soldier.

The *amīrs* did not have at their disposal facilities even remotely similar to those of the sultan for upbringing and training their Mamlūks, a fact which was reflected in their comparative military inferiority. There are, however, certain indications that the Mamlūks of the great *amīrs* were brought up according to principles resembling those which were applied in the case of the sultan's Mamlūks (see e.g. *Zubdat al-fikra*, fols. 51b, 11.5-16, 99b, 11.13-100a, 1.4).

The Mamlūks, on their manumission, were simple soldiers. Thus they were given an equal start. However, they had a real chance to rise to the highest ranks only if they had been manumitted by a sultan and not merely by an *amīr*, and this chance was greatly improved if the Mamlūk was included in the sultan's personal guard (*al-khāṣṣakiyya* [*q.v.*]). There was no school for training officers; these rose from the rank of simple soldier without having to undergo a special kind of training.

In a most illuminating passage, where al-Maḳrīzī contrasts the attitude of al-Nāṣir Muḥammad b. Ḳalāwūn to his Mamlūks with that of the sultans who preceded him, the correct principles for creating a healthy and successful Mamlūk military body, as against the wrong ones, come to the fore: The earlier sultans, besides giving the Mamlūk the proper upbringing (already described earlier), used to dress him in comparatively simple costumes, raise his salary gradually and promote him slowly in rank and position. A Mamlūk thus treated, when reaching the top, will know how valuable is his new status, acquired with such efforts, and will be able to make the right comparison between his previous wretchedness (*shaḳāʾ*) and his present well-being (*naʿīm*) (*Sulūk*, ii, 524 1.3-525 1.15).

5. *The Mamlūk and his patron*

The period of the Mamlūk's slavery, terminated by his manumission, did not only affect his career (i.e. his chances of rising in the socio-military ladder), but also determined for life his close affiliations. He was bound by loyalty, on the one hand, to his manumitting patron (*muʿtiḳ, ustādh*), and, on the other, to his colleagues in servitude and manumission (*khushdāshiyya*). The intensity of the Mamlūks' feelings of loyalty to their patron is revealed in those cases when things did not work according to plan. It happened that a patron-sultan died or was dismissed shortly before the date fixed for the manumission of a certain group of his Mamlūks. This group refused sometimes to be manumitted by their new patron-sultan in spite of the fact that by doing so they practically dealt a death blow to their chances of becoming part of the uppermost stratum of the military aristocracy. The patron and his freedmen developed relations very similar to those of a family. He was considered to be their father (*wālid*), and they his sons (*awlād*, sing, *walad*), and the freedmen amongst themselves were regarded as brothers (*ikhwa*, sing. *akh*), with special relations between senior and junior brothers (*aghawāt*, sing. *agha*, and *iniyyāt*, sing. *inī*).

The ties binding the patron to his own freedmen and the same freedmen to each other constituted the pivot upon which Mamlūk internal relations hinged. These ties continued to be binding after the dismissal or death of the patron. That cohesive factor, most formidable in itself, was supplemented and strengthened by a rejective one: a freedman of patron A, who had been transferred to the service of patron B, would never be accepted by him and his own freedmen on an equal footing. He would always be considered as a stranger (*gharīb, adjnabī*). A Mamlūk "family" or group or faction (*ṭāʾifa*, pl. *ṭawāʾif*) kept outsiders serving their patron at arm's length. Such a faction, if and when separated from its patron, could either be broken by killing its members, putting them in prison, sending them into exile and transferring them to the service of other patrons, under whom they were given an inferior status, or else remain intact and carry on until the death of the last of its members. In the Mamlūk sultanate, a new sultan quite often broke up part of his immediate predecessor's freedmen and let the other part stay on until it petered out after several decades. Under the Circassians, where the attempts to create a dynasty failed constantly, and sultans followed each other in quick succession, numerous factions, owing allegiance to different sultans, existed simultaneously. Many combinations of short-lived coalitions between those factions were constantly forming and dissolving. A very instructive case in point is Ibn Taghrībirdi's account of the change in sultan Khushḳadam's position from almost complete shakiness to comparative stability as a result of the varying attitudes of the Mamlūks of the sultans who preceded him, both in their relations among themselves and with the Mamlūks of the reigning sultan, al-Ẓāhiriyya Khushḳadam. The Mamlūks of the sultans who preceded Khushḳadam were, in the order of their seniority, al-Muʾayyadiyya Shaykh, al-

A<u>sh</u>rafiyya Barsbāy, al-Ẓāhiriyya <u>Dj</u>aḳmaḳ and al-A<u>sh</u>rafiyya Aynāl (*Ḥawādi<u>th</u> al-duhūr*, 442, 1.7-444, 1.10, 550, 11.4-9). They formed ephemeral coalitions which changed kaleidoscopically.

The particular ties existing between the patron and his slave soldiers go back to the very beginning of military slave society in Islam and always constituted one of that society's mainstays. However, they clashed quite often with interests wider than those of the specific ruler and his military slaves, thus constituting a source of weakness as well. Yet on balance, they had, from a Muslim point of view, a positive value. The great drawback of the whole system was that it had outlived its purpose; it could not cope properly with the progress of technology and with the unavoidable military changes which it brought about, as was so decisively demonstrated in the annihilation of the Mamlūk army and empire by the Ottomans [see BĀRŪD. iii. The Mamlūks]. In Ottoman Egypt, the antiquated character of the art of war as practised by the Mamlūks was only accentuated. At the same time, the internal dissensions within Mamlūk society were greatly intensified, through a strange merging of hereditary and one-generation nobilities in that society. Hence Mamlūk "houses" (*buyūt*, sing. *bayt*) did not peter out as they did in the Mamlūk sultanate, but went on living indefinity as long as they were not crushed by a factor external to the specific "house". The longer they lived, the more deep-rooted and vehement became their mutual hatreds. The incidents necessitating the taking of blood revenge (*al-a<u>kh</u>d<u>h</u> bi 'l-<u>th</u>aʾr*) grew in number, ultimately leading to the unflinching determination of annihilating physically (*ḳaṭʿ, izāla*) the rival "house". When the Fiḳāriyya wiped out the Ḳāsimiyya in 1142/1729, the causes which brought about the inevitably uncompromising struggles within the Mamlūk society were not removed; the "houses" which grew out of the Fiḳāriyya continued their fights according to the old pattern.

6. *Mamlūk society*

Mamlūk society in the sultanate was a very exclusive one. In order to become a member of it, one had to fulfill very definite requirements. One had to be fair-skinned; to be (in most cases) an inhabitant of the area stretching to the north and to the north-east of the lands of Islam; to be born an infidel; to be brought into the Mamlūk sultanate as a child or young boy (preferably at the age of puberty); and to be bought, brought up and manumitted by a patron who was a member of the military aristocracy (preferably a Mamlūk as well, and most preferably the sultan himself). The chances of a Mamlūk who had been bought and manumitted by a civilian of joining the aristocracy, and particularly of rising high within it, were very meagre indeed.

What greatly helped in making the Mamlūks such an easily distinguishable, distinct and exclusive caste was a practice which started long before the creation of the Mamlūk sultanate, namely, that all of them, with but a few exceptions, bore Turkish names, irrespective of their origin. This was also the case of the Circassians when they came to constitute the major factor in the military aristocracy. The fact that most of the Mamlūks' sons (*awlād al-nās* [*q.v.*]) bore Muslim names greatly helped in their smooth ousting from that aristocracy, thus facilitating its preservation as a one-generation aristocracy. In Ottoman Egypt, the adoption of Muslim names by the overwhelming majority of the Mamlūks was an important factor in the creation of a society in which hereditary and one-generation nobilities merged into one.

Another important aspect of the exclusiveness of that society was that its members married mainly slave-girls from their own countries of origin or daughters of Mamlūks. Most of their concubines were also from the same region, although black girls were by no means excluded from that category. Marriages between Mamlūk *amīrs* and local girls (mainly the daughters of high-ranking officials, great merchants or distinguished *ʿulamāʾ*) were quite rare. This meant that the number of slave-girls imported from the areas which served as the source for military slaves was at least as great as the number of Mamlūks. Marriages between the sons of the Mamlūks and local girls were much more numerous, and this represents one facet of the assimilation of the Mamlūks' offspring in the local population.

The Mamlūks were also distinguished by their dress, which was considered to be much more respectable than that of any other class. This distinction goes back to the Mamlūk regiment of the ʿAbbāsid caliph al-Muʿtaṣim (al-Masʿūdī, *Murū<u>dj</u> al-<u>dh</u>ahab*, vii, 118 = § 2801).

The owning of Mamlūks was the prerogative of the Mamlūks (although cases of Mamlūks owned by civilians were quite frequent), as was the riding of horses. Orders prohibiting civilians from buying Mamlūks were rarer than those forbidding them to ride horses (some of the highest civilian officials were explicitly exempted from the riding prohibition).

The language which the Mamlūks used predominantly among themselves was Turkish. The knowledge of Arabic of most of them seems to have been very superficial, although a more systematic study of this question may change that impression to a certain extent. Their Islamic awareness, however, was very strong. It was expressed, *inter alia,* in the numerous religious institutions which they built. This activity had also its material aspect, as stated by Ibn <u>Kh</u>aldūn; in order to assure the future of the Mamlūks' descendants, who could not join the military upper class, they appointed them as administrators or superintendents of the *waḳfs* assigned to those institutions for their maintenance (*al-Taʿrīf bi-Ibn <u>Kh</u>aldūn,* 279).

The main body of the Mamlūk sultanate's army, namely, all the Royal Mamlūks (*al-mamālīk al-sulṭāniyya*)—who formed the backbone of the Sultanate—and most of the armies of the first-ranking *amīrs* were stationed in Cairo. It was very difficult to make any part of the Royal Mamlūks serve as a garrison anywhere outside the capital. Units of the corps which were forced to stay in Syria, for example, soon declined in power and importance, and some minor exceptions to this rule do not affect the general picture. Considering the comparatively limited number of the Mamlūks, keeping their élite element together must have been the only way of preserving its military might. This, in its turn, considerably increased the already great preponderance of the capital vis-à-vis the rest of the realm. Nothing could move the Royal Mamlūks, of their own choice, from Cairo, not even epidemics, which wrought havoc among them.

This concentration in the capital had its grave drawbacks. Any serious revolt of the Bedouins or Turcomans anywhere in the realm could not be quelled without the participation of the Royal Mamlūks, who were often stationed far away from the scene of the revolt. Worse still, all the major wars of the Mamlūk sultanate took place in its northern part or beyond it, a great distance from the main centre of military might, and this became critical in the closing decades of Mamlūk rule, when the Mamlūks had to cope with the Turcomans beyond their borders, who lived contiguously to the Turcomans of their own realm, and who were supported by the ominously growing power of the Ottoman empire.

7. *Mamlūks in other Islamic states*

The Mamlūk sultanate served as an example to other Muslim states, including in the reliance on Mamlūk soldiers, many of whom were acquired in Egypt. For the ruler of Yanbuᶜ, see Ibn al-Furāt, ix, 43, 11.6-9; for the ruler of Mecca, see *Ḍawʾ al-ṣubḥ*, 332; Ibn Iyās, iv, p. 456, 11.10-12; *Nudjūm*, ed. Popper, vi, 117, 11. 18-23; Ibn al-Furāt, ix, 208, 11.12-15, 308, 11. 7-20; for the ruler of Yemen, see *Ṣubḥ*, v, 35, 11. 15-17; Nudjūm, v, 81, 11.1-2; for the ruler of Bidjāya, see *Ṣubḥ*, v, 137, 1.9; and for the sultan of Takrūr, see *Ṣubḥ*, v, 300, 11.7-9.

In 869/1464-5 the army of the ruler of Shīrwān and the adjacent areas, whose capital was Shamākhī, was estimated at 20,000 combat soldiers (*muḳātila*), of whom 1,000 were Circassian Mamlūks (*Ḥawādith al-duhūr*, 579, 1.16-580, 1.13). This does not necessarily imply direct influence from the Mamlūk sultanate, but what it certainly reflects is the great competition from other Muslim states which that sultanate had to face in drawing manpower from the same sources, and especially from states situated much nearer to those sources.

The character, structure and development of military slavery in the Mamlūk sultanate can be more properly understood if it is studied in connection with its Ayyūbid predecessor. The Kurdishness of the Ayyūbid régime and its army has been greatly exaggerated. The Turkish, and even more so the Turkish Mamlūk element in its armed forces was the dominant one throughout its history, as was only natural for a dynasty whose founders came from the ranks of the Zangid army. Shīrkūh's private army, the Asadiyya, who numbered 500, and who were, most probably, the main factor which enabled Ṣalāḥ al-Dīn to succeed his uncle, were—contrary to what students of the Ayyūbids have written about them—a pure Mamlūk unit (see e.g. Abū Shāma, i, 173, 1.1-2; al-Maḳrīzī, *Ittiᶜāẓ al-ḥunafāʾ*, iii, 308, 11. 9-10), as were the other private armies of the Ayyūbid sultans, like the Kāmiliyya of Muḥammad, the Ashrafiyya of Mūsā, the Nāṣriyya of Yūsuf, etc.

The reign of al-Malik al-Ṣāliḥ Nadjm al-Dīn Ayyūb, the founder of the Baḥriyya regiment which toppled the Ayyūbids and established the Mamlūk sultanate, strengthened the Ayyūbid impact on that sultanate. That sultan was venerated by his Baḥriyya, who looked upon him as the example which should be followed. It was very rare that a ruler belonging to a deposed dynasty should leave such an impress on its deposers; it took the Baḥriyya quite a long time to disconnect themselves from the direct heritage of their patron, and from their general Ayyūbid heritage they disconnected themselves only partly.

Mamlūk military slavery certainly shows an evolution in comparison with its Ayyūbid prototype, but the changes were quite slow and each of them has to be traced and identified separately.

Bibliography: That given here is restricted to studies dealing in some detail with Mamlūk military slavery and with a few related subjects discussed above; works based on European sources are only perfunctorily mentioned.

G. Wiet, *L'Égypte arabe ... 642-1517*, in *Histoire de la nation égyptienne*, iv, Paris 1937, 387-636 (esp. 387-92); M. M. Ziada, *The Mamluk sultans*, in Setton and Baldwin, eds., *History of the Crusades*, ii, Philadelphia 1962, 735-58; iii, 1975, 486-512, passim; S.ᶜA. ᶜĀshūr, *Miṣr fī ᶜaṣr dawlat al-Mamālīk al-Baḥriyya*, Cairo 1959; I. ᶜA. Tarkhān, *Miṣr fī ᶜaṣr dawlat al-Mamālīk al-Djarākisa*, Cairo 1960; ᶜA. M. Mādjid, *Dawlat al-salāṭīn al-mamālīk wa-rusūmuhum fī Miṣr*, Cairo 1964; E. Quatremère, *Histoire des Sultans Mamlouks de l'Égypte*, Paris 1837-42 (the notes on Mamlūk terms are still very useful; see indices); M. Van Berchem, *CIA, Égypte*, Paris 1894-1929 (many relevant terms, indices); W. Björkman, *Beiträge zur Geschichte der Staatskanzlei im islamischen Ägypten*, Hamburg 1928 (much relevant terminology, index); M. Gaudefroy-Demombynes, *La Syrie à l'époque des Mamelouks*, Paris 1923, esp. pp. XIX-CXIX; W. Popper, *Egypt and Syria under the Circassian Sultans*, Berkeley 1955; M. Mostafa, *Beiträge zur Geschichte Ägyptens zur Zeit der türkischen Eroberung*, in *ZDMG*, lxxxix (1935), 194-224, esp. 208-24; J. Sauvaget, *La poste aux chevaux dans l'empire des Mamelouks*, Paris 1941; idem, *La chronique de Damas d'al-Jazari*, Paris 1949 (terms in the index); idem, *Noms et surnoms de Mamelouks*, in *JA*, ccxxxviii (1950), 31-58; A. N. Poliak, *Le caractère colonial de l'état mamelouk dans ses rapports avec la Horde d'Or, in REI*, ix (1935), 231-48; idem, *The influence of Chingiz-Khān's Yāsa upon the general organization of the Mamlouk state*, in *BSOS*, x (1940-2), 862-76; idem, *Some notes on the feudal system of the Mamluks*, in *JRAS* (1937), 97-107; idem, *Feudalism in Egypt, Syria, Palestine and Lebanon (1250-1900)*, London 1939; S. B. Pevzner, art. in Russian on the *iḳṭāᶜ* analysed by M. Canard in *Arabica*, vi-vii (1960-1); L. A. Semenova, *Salakh al-Dīn i Mamlūku v Egipte*, Moscow 1966; M.C.S. Tekindağ, *Berkuk devrinde Mamluk sultanliği*, Istanbul 1961, 151-7 *et passim*; A. Darrag, *L'Égypte sous le régime de Barsbay 825-841/1422-1438*, Damascus 1961, 33-55; P. M. Holt, *The sultanate of al-Manṣūr Lāchīn (696-8/1296-9)*, in *BSOAS*, xxxvi (1973), 521-32; idem, *The position and power of the Mamluk sultan*, in *BSOAS*, xxxviii (1975), 237-49; I. Lapidus, *Muslim cities in the later Middle Ages*, Cambridge, Mass. 1967, index, 301; H. M. Rabie, *The financial system of Egypt 564-741/1169-1341*, Oxford 1972 (numerous relevant terms, index); idem, *The training of the Mamlūk Fāris*, in *War, technology and society in the Middle East*, London 1975, 153-63; R. S. Humphreys, *The emergence of the Mamluk army*, in *SI*, xlv (1977), 67-99, xlvi (1977), 147-82; idem, *From Saladin to the Mongols*, Albany 1957, passim; B. Flemming, *Literary activities in Mamlūk halls and barracks*, in *Studies in Memory of Gaston Wiet*, Jerusalem 1977; 249-60, and the studies quoted there; U. Haarmann, *Alṭun Ḫān and Čingiz Ḫān bei den ägyptischen Mamluken*, in *Isl.*, li (1974), 1-36; D. P. Little, *Notes on Aitamiš, a Mongol Mamlūk*, in *Die islamische Welt zwischen Mittelalter und Neuzeit, Festschrift für H. D. Roemer*, Beirut-Wiesbaden 1979, 387-401; G. Guémard, *De l'armement et de l'équipement des mamelouks*, in *BIE*, viii (1926), 1-19; L. A. Mayer, *Saracenic heraldry*, Oxford 1933 (esp. 1-43); idem, *Mamlūk costume*, Geneva 1952; M. Meinecke, *Die Bedeutung der mamlukischen Heraldik für die Kunstgeschichte*, in *ZDMG* (1974), 213-40; G. T. Scanlon, *A Muslim manual of war*, Cairo 1961; J. D. Latham and W. F. Paterson, *Saracen archery*, London 1970; S. H. Labib, *Handelsgeschichte Ägyptens im Spätmittelalter*, Wiesbaden 1965 (index s.vv. Sklaven, Sklavenhandel, etc.); W. Heyd, *Histoire du commerce du Levant*, Leipzig 1885-6 (index s.vv. *Esclaves, Mamelouks*); A. Schaube, *Handelsgeschichte der romanischen Völker des Mittelmeergebiets bis zum Ende der Kreuzzüge*, Munich 1906 (index s.v. Sklaven, Sklavenhandel); G. I. Bratianu, *Recherches sur le commerce génois dans la mer Noire au XIIIe siècle*, Paris 1929, passim; R. S. Lopez and W. Raymond, *Medieval trade in the Mediterranean world*, New York 1955 (index s.vv. slaves, slave trade); P.-H. Dopp, *Traité d'Emmanuel Piloti sur le passage en Terre Sainte (1420)*, Louvain-Paris 1958, esp. 51-6; D. Ayalon, *Studies on the Mamlūks of Egypt (1250-1517)*, London 1977; idem, *The Mamlūk military society*, London 1979 (two collections of studies); idem, *Gunpowder and firearms in the Mamlūk kingdom - a challenge to a mediaeval society*, London 1978; idem, *The Great Yāsa of Chingiz Khān—a reexamination*, in *SI*, esp. parts C_1, xxxvi (1972), 113-58, and C_2, xxxviii (1973), 107-56; idem, *Mamlūkiyyāt, part I*, in *Jerusalem Studies in Arabic and Islam*, ii (1979), 321-49; idem, *The Mamlūk army in the first years of the Ottoman conquest* [in Hebrew], in *Tarbiz*, Jerusalem 1952, 221-6; idem, *From Ayyūbids to Mamlūks*, in *Muqarnas*, Cambridge, Mass.; idem, *Egypt as a dominant factor in Syria and Palestine during the Muslim period*, in *The history of relations between Egypt and Palestine*, Jerusalem; arts. BAḤRIYYA. II. The navy of the Mamlūks; BURDJIYYA; ḤARB. iii; ḤIṢAR. iv; M. Sobernheim, *EI*[1], art. MAMLŪKS; A. S. Ehrenkreutz, *Strategic implications of the slave trade between Genoa and Mamlūk Egypt in the second half of the thirteenth century*, in A. L. Udovitch, ed., *The Islamic Middle East. Studies in economic and social history*, Princeton 1983; W. M. Brinner, *A chronicle of Damascus 1389-1397*, Berkeley and Los Angeles 1963, esp. i, 341-3. (D. AYALON)

MAMLŪKS, the Mamlūk sultanate, i.e. the régime established and maintained by (emancipated) *mamlūks* [see preceding article] in Egypt from 648/1250 to 922/1517, and in Syria from 658/1260 to 922/1516; and with the role of their successors, the neo-Mamlūks, in Ottoman Egypt. It surveys (i) political history, and (ii) institutional history. On military history, see the relevant sections by D. Ayalon of the articles BAḤRIYYA (i.e. navy), BĀRŪD, ḤARB, ḤIṢĀR; on the bureaucracy, see DĪWĀN, ii. Egypt (H. L. Gottschalk).

(i) POLITICAL HISTORY

(a) *Origins of the Mamlūk sultanate*

The Mamlūk sultanate had its origins in the Baḥriyya [*q.v.*], a military household of Ḳïpčaḳ [*q.v.*] Turkish *mamlūks*, which belonged to the bodyguard (*ḥalḳa* [*q.v.*]) of al-Ṣāliḥ Ayyūb (637-47/1240-9). The Baḥriyya superseded the Ayyūbids [*q.v.*] in Egypt and Syria less by a deliberate process of usurpation than under the constraint of two military crises: the crusade of St. Louis (647-9/1249-50) and the Mongol invasion of Syria (657-8/1259-60). Their seizure of power in Egypt resulted directly from the preference shown by the new sultan, Tūrān<u>sh</u>āh, for his own household at the expense of the Baḥriyya. A group of the Baḥriyya murdered Tūrān<u>sh</u>āh on 27 Muḥarram 648/1 May 1250. The rise of the Baḥriyya to political dominance was assisted by their outstanding part in the resistance to the crusade, and probably also by the death of the last non-*mamlūk* commander, Fa<u>kh</u>r al-Dīn Ibn <u>Sh</u>ay<u>kh</u> al-<u>Sh</u>uyū<u>kh</u>, who had handled the affairs of state when al-Ṣāliḥ Ayyūb died, but was himself killed before the arrival of Tūrān<u>sh</u>āh. The Baḥriyya sought to preserve the appearance of Ayyūbid sovereignty by installing as sultan al-Ṣāliḥ Ayyūb's widow, Umm <u>Kh</u>alīl <u>Sh</u>a<u>dj</u>ar al-Durr, herself of Turkish slave origin, but the shift of power was indicated by the appointment of a Mamlūk commander (*atābak al-ʿasākir*), Aybak al-Turkumānī. Al-Nāṣir Yūsuf, the Ayyūbid ruler of Aleppo, refused to recognise the sultanate of <u>Sh</u>a<u>dj</u>ar al-Durr, and captured Damascus. The Baḥriyya thereupon deposed <u>Sh</u>a<u>dj</u>ar al-Durr, and raised Aybak to the sultanate as al-Malik al-Muʿizz (28 Rabīʿ II 648/11 July 1250). A few days later he resumed his former command, and a child, al-A<u>sh</u>raf Mūsā, descended from the Ayyūbids of the Yaman, was recognised as nominal sultan. This device failed to appease al-Nāṣir Yūsuf, who undertook more than one campaign against Egypt in the following decade. Aybak resumed the sultanate in 652/1254. At some time he married <u>Sh</u>a<u>dj</u>ar al-Durr, thus following Sal<u>dj</u>ūḳid precedents for the marriage of an *atabeg* to the widow of his former lord. Meanwhile, hostility was developing between the Baḥriyya and the household of Aybak, the Muʿizziyya. The leading Baḥrī, Fāris al-Dīn Aḳṭāy al-<u>Dj</u>amadār, assumed the royal insignia, contracted a political marriage with an Ayyūbid princess, and demanded that she should reside in the Citadel of Cairo. Aybak procured Aḳṭay's assassination by his *mamlūk*, Ḳuṭuz al-Muʿizzī. This coup broke the power of the Baḥriyya, many of whom fled to Syria and entered Ayyūbid service. Among these was Baybars al-Bunduḳdārī [*q.v.*], who now emerged as their leader.

Ironically, another political marriage led to Aybak's death. His intention to marry a daughter of the *atabeg* of Mosul, Badr al-Dīn Luʾlu [*q.v.*], aroused the jealousy of <u>Sh</u>a<u>dj</u>ar al-Durr, who had him murdered on 23 Rabīʿ I 655/10 April 1257. The dispersal of the Baḥriyya had, however, left her without an adequate power-base. The Muʿizziyya had her put to death, and installed as sultan ʿAlī, a youthful son of Aybak by another wife, Ḳuṭuz being the most important of the magnates. When the Mongol invasion of Syria began in 657/1259, Ḳuṭuz usurped the sultanate and effected a reconciliation with Baybars, who returned to Egypt. They led an expeditionary force into Palestine, and defeated the Mongols at ʿAyn <u>Dj</u>ālūt [*q.v.*] on 25 Ramaḍān 658/3 Sept. 1260. The Mongol evacuation of Syria rapidly ensued. Al-Nāṣir Yūsuf being a captive of the Mongols, the two major Ayyūbid principalities of Damascus and Aleppo fell under direct Mamlūk control, although the three minor lordships of Ḥimṣ, Ḥamāt and al-Karak retained their autonomy. With the ending of this crisis, the inveterate rivalry of the Mamlūk households reappeared. Baybars headed a group of conspirators who murdered Ḳuṭuz. He then usurped the sultanate after undertaking to help his brothers-in-arms, the Baḥriyya.

(b) *The embattled sultanate*

Al-Ẓāhir Baybars, rather than his predecessors, was the effective founder of the Mamlūk sultanate. In his comparatively long reign (658-76/1260-77), a high degree of internal stability, contrasting with the political vicissitudes of the previous decade, allowed the establishment of the characteristic political structure and institutions of the régime. Nevertheless, during his reign and those of his immediate successors, the Mamlūk sultanate was an embattled power, threatened by the Mongol Īl<u>kh</u>āns [*q.v.*] in the east, and by the remains of the Frankish states on the Syro-Palestinian coast. Of the two, the Mongols were by far the greater danger. A few months after ʿAyn <u>Dj</u>ālūt, a second Mongol invasion of Syria was stopped by the Ayyūbids of Ḥimṣ and Ḥamāt at the first battle of Ḥimṣ (Muḥarram 659/December 1260). Another critical encounter was at the second battle of

Ḥimṣ [*q.v.*] in 680/1261, during the reign of Ḳalāwūn [*q.v.*], while the last invasion took place as late as 712/1313, early in the third reign of al-Nāṣir Muḥammad b. Ḳalāwūn. The Frankish states were by comparison militarily insignificant: the danger was that they might provide a base for a crusade from Europe, which would make possible a pincer-movement of Crusaders and Mongols against the Mamlūks. This fear seemed about to be realised when the Lord Edward, son of the English King Henry III, brought a crusading force to Acre in 669/1271, and obtained the limited co-operation of the Īlkhān Abaḳa. This combined operation, the first and last of its kind, accomplished nothing. The security of Muslim Syria as a salient in enemy territory was thus one of Baybars's chief preoccupations. He strove with much success to strengthen his control there. At the beginning of his reign, his comrade Sandjar al-Ḥalabī, whom Ḳuṭuz had appointed governor of Damascus, proclaimed himself sultan, perhaps hoping for autonomy under Baybars's overlordship, somewhat on the Ayyūbid pattern. His bid for power was, however, quickly terminated, as was that of a war-lord in Aleppo, Āḳūsh (for Āḳ-ḳūsh) al-Burunlī (or al-Barlī). In 661-2/1263, two of the remaining Ayyūbid principalities fell into Baybars's hands: al-Karak by the treacherous capture of its lord, al-Mughīth ʿUmar (whom Baybars had served when in exile), and Ḥimṣ by the death without an heir of Shīrkūh's last descendant. The Ismāʿīlīs were reduced to submission, and between 669/1271 and 671/1273 their castles were taken over by Baybars. The reduction of the Frankish states was equally one of his objectives, and his aggressive policy contrasts with the general acceptance of co-existence by the Ayyūbids after Saladin. Baybars campaigned almost annually in Syria, and captured many of the remaining Frankish cities and castles: Caesarea, Haifa and Arsūf fell in 663/1265, Jaffa and Antioch in 666/1268. These towns were forthwith demolished, to deny them as bases to Crusaders. Inland fortresses, however, such as Ṣafad (captured in 664/1266) and Ḥiṣn al-Akrād (Crac des Chevaliers, taken in 669/1271) were restored and provided with Muslim garrisons. Warfare alternated with uneasy truces, in which the Frankish frontiers were eroded by the establishment of condominia (*munāṣafāt*). Against the Mongols Baybars remained on the defensive, seeking to weaken them by diplomacy rather than force of arms. He exploited the hostility between the Īlkhāns and Berke [*q.v.*], the *khān* of the Golden Horde (reigned 654-64/1256-66), a convert and the ruler of the Ḳïpčaḳ steppes [see DASHT-I ḲÏPČAḲ in Suppl.], the Mamlūk recruiting-ground. The alliance with Berke promoted a flow of Mongol tribal warriors (*wāfidiyya*) from Īlkhānid territories to Baybars. Only at the end of his reign did Baybars invade the Īlkhānid sphere of influence by an expedition into the sultanate of Rūm. He defeated a Mongol army in the frontier-region of Elbistan [*q.v.*] in Dhu 'l-Ḳaʿda 675/April 1277, and was enthroned in Kayseri (Ḳayṣariyya), but withdrew without achieving a lasting conquest.

Two of Baybars's internal aims were to legitimise his rule and to establish a dynasty. He succeeded in the former by installing an ʿAbbāsid prince as caliph in Cairo, and receiving from him a formal delegation of plenary powers as the universal sultan of Islam (Radjab 659/June 1261). When this caliph (al-Mustanṣir bi 'llāh) shortly afterwards died in a forlorn hope against Baghdād, Baybars installed a successor, al-Ḥākim bi-amri 'llāh, whose descendants were recognised as caliphs in Egypt and Syria until (and even beyond) the Ottoman conquest. This translation of the caliphate assisted Baybars in his negotiations with Berke, in view of the social disparity between a *mamlūk* and a Čingizid. In regard to the second aim, Baybars early took steps to ensure the succession of his son, Baraka (i.e. Berke) Khān, named after his maternal grandfather, a Khʷārazmian warrior-chief. In Shawwāl 662/August 1263, Baraka Khān, aged about four years, was duly invested as joint-sultan with his father.

Baybars's dynasty did not long survive, the essential cause of its downfall being the hostility between the veteran magnates of Baybars's household, the Ẓāhiriyya, and the *khāṣṣakiyya*, i.e. the court-*mamlūks* of his son. The leading opponent belonged to an older generation, and was Ḳalāwūn al-Alfī, a comrade of Baybars. Having deposed Baraka Khān, the magnates installed his seven-year-old brother Salāmish (Süleymish) as nominal sultan. A few weeks later, Ḳalāwūn usurped the throne (Rabīʿ II 678/August 1279), and exiled the sons of Baybars to al-Karak.

Al-Manṣūr Ḳalāwūn was responsible for an important military innovation, viz. the recruitment of a Circassian *mamlūk* regiment, known (from its quarters in the towers of the Citadel) as the Burdjiyya [*q.v.*]. This was the first indication of a threat to the ascendancy of the Ḳïpčaḳ Turkish *mamlūks*. In other respects, Ḳalāwūn continued the policies of Baybars. Syria remained a central preoccupation. The governor of Damascus, Sunḳur al-Ashḳar, proclaimed himself sultan like Sandjar al-Ḥalabī before him. He was defeated after some difficulty in Ṣafar 679/June 1280, but succeeded in establishing himself in the former crusader-castle of Ṣahyūn, whence he controlled the fortresses in the mountainous hinterland of Latakia. Finally, he joined Ḳalāwūn in operations against a Mongol force sent by the Īlkhān Abaḳa, which was routed at the second battle of Ḥimṣ (Shaʿbān 680/November 1281). Abaḳa died in the following year, and his successor, Tegüder Aḥmad, a convert to Islam, sought good relations with the sultan. Ḳalāwūn was thus left free to pursue the *djihād* against the Frankish states. Tripoli fell in Rabīʿ II 688/April 1289, and like the other coastal towns was demolished. Ḳalāwūn was about to lead an expedition against Acre when he died (Dhu 'l-Ḳaʿda 689/November 1290). Like Baybars, he endeavoured to establish a dynasty, but his intended successor, his son al-Ṣāliḥ ʿAlī, predeceased him. The throne passed to another son, al-Ashraf Khalīl [*q.v.*], for whom was reserved the crowning mercy of the capture of Acre (Djumādā I 690/May 1291) and the extinction of the Latin kingdom. In the following year, Khalīl took the Armenian patriarchal see of Ḳalʿat al-Rūm (Radjab 691/June 1292), but in Muḥarram 693/December 1293 he fell a victim to a conspiracy of magnates who had belonged to his father's military household (the Manṣūriyya), and who felt themselves threatened.

The murder of al-Ashraf Khalīl inaugurated seventeen years of political instability, during which magnates with the support of *mamlūk* factions dominated the sultanate. Twice in this period, in 693-4/1293-4 and 698-708/1299-1309, another son of Ḳalāwūn, al-Nāṣir Muḥammad, was installed as sultan. Aged less than ten at his first accession, he was no more than a figurehead, and he was twice set aside by usurpers; between 694/1294 and 698/1299 by Kitbughā and Lāčīn (Lādjīn [*q.v.*]), and in 708-9/1309-10 by al-Muẓaffar Baybars al-Djāshnikīr [*q.v.*]. It is significant that this last usurper was a Circassian, originally recruited into the Burdjiyya. The part played by the Burdjiyya added a further comlication to the factional struggles after the death of l-Ashraf Khalīl. In 709/1310, however, al-Nāṣir Auḥammad, now mature in political experience and vith a *mamlūk* household of his own, emerged from exe in al-Karak, and, with the support of the governors f Aleppo, Ḥamāt and Tripoli, marched on Egypt nd overthrew al-Muẓaffar Baybars.

(c) *The autocracy of al-Nāṣir Muḥammad*

During the long third reign of al-Nāṣir Muḥammad 709-41/1310-41) the Mamlūk sultanate was no longer hreatened by external enemies. The Frankish states vere gone, and with them any serious danger of a rusade from Europe. The last Mongol invasion, ommanded by the Ilkhān Öldjeytü in the winter of 12/1312-13, was abortive. Thus the Sultan did not eed to divide his time between Syria and Egypt, and l-Nāṣir Muḥammad was free to concentrate on inernal problems, and to establish an autocratic overnment.

He had first to secure his own position. The usurper Baybars and his colleague Salār were put to death vithin a few months of the restoration. The three yrian governors who, as kingmakers, might become langerous were the next to go. One died naturally, he second was arrested, while the third fled to Öldjeytü. Meanwhile, with consummate political kill, al-Nāṣir Muḥammad carried out the operation vhich had been fatal to several earlier sultans—the ubstitution of his own *mamlūks* for veteran magnates n key positions. Outstanding among his servants was Tankiz al-Ḥusāmī, appointed governor of Damascus n 712/1312, and in effect governor-general of Syria wo years later. Another, Arghūn al-Dawādār, reeived similar extensive powers as vicegerent in Egypt *nā'ib al-salṭana bi 'l-diyār al-Miṣriyya*). Early in the eign, the sultan carried out a fiscal reorganisation (*alawk al-Nāṣirī*), which greatly strengthened his own osition against the magnates. Such a reform had een attempted in 697/1298 by Lāčīn, and had been principal cause of his murder. Al-Nāṣir Muḥammad roceeded with his habitual caution, commissioning irst a cadastral survey and redistribution of assignnents of landed revenue (sing. *iḳṭā'* [*q.v.*]) in the less olitically sensitive province of Damascus (713/1313). This was followed in 715/1315 by the cadastral survey f Egypt, after which the sultan sat in full court to listribute warrants of assignments to the eneficiaries. In consequence of the *rawk*, the share of evenue assigned to the sultan's fisc (*al-khāṣṣ*) was aised from one-sixth to five-twelfths at the expense of he other holders of assignments. At this time also he bolished a wide range of uncanonical taxes (*mukūs* see MAKS]), many of them abusive. This was a opular act, which probably had little effect on the ultan's own resources but worked to the detriment of he tax-farmers.

Al-Nāṣir Muḥammad's third reign was thus a eriod of autocratic and sometimes arbitrary rule. His enure of power was so secure that on three occasions 712/1313, 719/1320, 732/1332) he was able to absent iimself from Cairo for the Pilgrimage—thereby also lemonstrating his suzerainty over the Holy Cities. His relations with his magnates, although apparently lose and cemented by political marriages, were liable o sudden rupture. Even Tankiz al-Ḥusāmī was lisgraced and put to death, after nearly thirty years' ervice in Syria. In the last months of the sultan's life, ival court-factions were forming around two of his avourites, Ḳawṣūn (who had married a daughter of he sultan) and Bashtak, although on his deathbed he obtained the semblance of a reconciliation between them. He died in Dhu 'l-Ḥidjdja 741/June 1341, having nominated his son, Abū Bakr, to succeed him.

(d) *The ascendancy of the magnates*

Although three generations of al-Nāṣir Muḥammad's descendants succeeded him in the sultanate, the fact that twelve sultans reigned in less than half a century indicates their weakness. They were mostly young and inexperienced, some of them mere children, who lacked the essential power base of *mamlūk* households. Behind these figureheads, the magnates controlled the state, and struggled among themselves for the ascendancy. The period also saw a rise in Circassian recruitment after an intermission during the reign of al-Nāṣir Muḥammad. Political instability appeared immediately after al-Nāṣir Muḥammad's death. Three weeks later, Ḳawṣūn obtained Abū Bakr's approval for the arrest of Bashtak and the sequestration of his vast wealth and assignments. The fallen *amīr* was sent to Alexandria, where shortly afterwards he was put to death. Then in Ṣafar 742/August 1341, Ḳawṣūn forestalled a plot against himself by the sultan, whom he deposed, substituting an infant son of al-Nāṣir Muḥammad, named (or perhaps nicknamed) Kudjuk, i.e. Küčük. The new sultan was certainly not more than seven years old, and Ḳawṣūn was the effective ruler until he was overthrown, and his puppet-sultan deposed, in Radjab 742/January 1342. It would be otiose in this article to recount in detail the political history of the later Ḳalāwūnids. The one sultan in this period who showed some promise of repeating the success of his father, al-Nāṣir Muḥammad, was al-Nāṣir Ḥasan. Eleven years old when he was first raised to the throne after the killing of his brother and predecessor (Ramaḍān 748/December 1347), he was deposed in favour of another brother in Djumādā II 752/August 1351. Restored in Shawwāl 755/October 1354, he succeeded in ridding himself of the kingmaker and regent, Ṣarghatmush al-Nāṣirī, in Ramaḍān 759/August 1358. He then promoted his own *mamlūks*, chief among them being Yalbughā al-ʿUmarī, and tried to create a power-base of a new kind by conferring high amīrates and provincial governorships on *awlād al-nās* [*q.v.*], i.e. descendants of the *mamlūks*, a socially privileged group who nevertheless did not normally form part of the military and ruling establishment. This experiment inevitably aroused the mistrust of the *mamlūks*, and an opposition faction appeared, headed (against the traditions of *mamlūk* loyalty to the founder of the household) by Yalbughā al-ʿUmarī. The sultan was defeated, captured, and put to death (Djumādā I 762/March 1361). Yalbughā acted as regent until his own overthrow and death in Rabīʿ II 768/December 1366. Sixteen years later, Barḳūḳ b. Anaṣ [*q.v.*], a Circassian nurtured in his military household, the Yalbughāwiyya, deposed the last Ḳalāwūnid and usurped the sultanate.

(e) *The Circassian Mamlūk sultanate*

The Circassian Mamlūk sultanate, which begins with al-Ẓāhir Barḳūḳ's usurpation in Ramaḍān 784/November 1382, follows a regular and almost invariable pattern of succession. A magnate would usurp the throne, which on his death would pass to his son. Within a few years at most, the latter would be deposed by another usurper, and the cycle of events would be repeated. But the sultanate was not a prize open to all comers: the usurpers emerged from specific circles, namely the military households of previous sultans. The two principal nurseries of sultans were the households of Barḳūḳ and of Ḳā'it Bāy [*q.v.*], each of which produced five rulers. Since Ḳā'it Bāy was a *mamlūk* of Barsbāy [*q.v.*], who was himself a *mamlūk* of Barḳūḳ, the Circassian sultans may be regarded as constituting a dynasty by *mamlūk* clientage rather than blood descent (cf. Table 2).

The Circassian sultanate faced in its early years a threat comparable to that which al-Ẓāhir Baybars had confronted in the later 7th/13th century—the danger of annihilation by the Turco-Mongol forces of Tīmūr Leng. Barḳūḳ responded by offering asylum in 796/1394 to Aḥmad b. Uways the Ḏjalāyirid [*q.v.*] expelled from Baghdād by Tīmūr, by establishing a common front with the Ottomans and the Golden Horde, and by replying defiantly to Tīmūr. The storm did not break until 803/1400-1, during the reign of Barḳūḳ's son, Faraḏj [*q.v.*]. He and his forces were compelled to evacuate Syria, which Tīmūr occupied and devastated. He did not, however, attempt to invade Egypt. In Sha'bān 803/March 1400, he began to withdraw from Damascus, having secured his flank for an advance on the Ottomans.

Although throughout the 9th/15th century the Mamlūk sultanate continued to present the appearance of a great power, it was undergoing a prolonged economic and military decline. Its growing economic weakness has usually been ascribed to political factors—the factional conflicts of the magnates, resulting in enfeebled administration, and hence in the decay of agriculture. These disorders were probably rather symptomatic than causative, and the basic reason for the economic decline may lie in the heavy mortality occasioned by successive epidemics of plague. The most serious of these (the Black Death of European history) occurred in 749/1348-9, during the first reign of al-Nāṣir Ḥasan, and there were twelve severe epidemics during the last century of the sultanate. Since mortality was particularly high among the *mamlūk*s, this must have necessitated very heavy expenditure by the sultans and magnates to keep up their military households. Even so, there seems to have been a marked fall in recruitment. The Royal Mamlūks dropped from about 12,000 in the third reign of al-Nāṣir Muḥammad to less than half the number under the Circassian sultans. The plague, however, inflicted its severest damage by its inroads upon the agrarian and industrial workforce. Villages were deserted, irrigation works neglected, and cultivated land went back to waste. The landed revenue of Egypt shrank in the last century of the sultanate from over 9 milion *dīnār*s to less than 2 million. Alexandria, the centre of the textile industry, suffered badly from the Black Death, and its decline continued in the Circassian period. Both in Egypt and Syria, the weakening of administration and the decline of the sedentary population were reflected in growing tribal pressure on the cultivable areas and the routes. It is in this period that a fraction of Hawwāra [*q.v.*], settled by Barḳūḳ in Upper Egypt, established a domination there which they retained into the Ottoman period.

As the landed revenue decreased, the magnates and sultans made growing depredations upon commerce; e.g. they compelled merchants to buy goods at an artificially-enhanced price (*ṭarḥ*, *rimāya*), an abuse for which there had been sporadic precedents. The transit-trade, especially in spices, from the Indian Ocean, which had been handled since the 6th/12th century by the group known as the Kārimīs [*q.v.*], was brought under strict control by Barsbāy (825-41/1422-38). Ḏjudda, under Mamlūk customs-administration from 828/1425, became in effect the staple for oriental trade in the Red Sea, and its revenue was shared between the sultan and the Sharīf of Mecca. In 832/1428 Barsbāy established a monopoly of the pepper trade, forcing up the price at Alexandria to the detriment of the Venetian merchants. His interest in the transit-trade between the Red Sea and the Mediterranean explains two other developments in his reign. Three campaigns against Cyprus, culminating in the conquest of the island (829/1426) and the reduction of its king to a vassal of the sultan, ended the danger to Muslim shipping from this Frankish outpost. The campaigns are of interest as being the only major naval operations undertaken by the Mamlūks. Furthermore, Barsbāy's refusals, repeated over ten years (828-38/1424-34), to allow Shāhrukh the formal privilege of providing a veil for the Ka'ba indicate a determination to deny the Tīmūrid any *locus standi* within the Mamlūk commercial sphere of interest.

Between the reign of Barḳūḳ at the beginning of the Circassian period, and that of Ḳānṣawh al-Ghawrī [*q.v.*] at its end, the Mamlūk sultanate was involved in only one major land-war, that fought with the Ottomans between 890/1485 and 896/1491. The underlying cause of this war in the reign of Ḳā'it Bāy 872-901/1468-96) was the threat offered by the Ottomans to the marcher-principalities, particularly Elbistan, which since its foundation by the ruling dynasty (Dulḳadir, see DHU 'L-ḲADR) in the first half of the 8th/14th century had been a Mamlūk protectorate. This localised conflict of interests was aggravated by considerations of high policy when, on the accession of Sultan Bāyazīd II [*q.v.*] in 886/1481, Ḳā'it Bāy gave asylum to his brother and rival, Ḏjem [*q.v.*]. Although in appearance the Mamlūks confronted the Ottomans on equal terms, the outcome of the war was merely to maintain the *status quo* on the frontiers.

Bāyazīd had been unable to commit all his forces to the war, and the next conflict between the two powers was to reveal the inherent military and political weakness of the Mamlūks. As a fighting-force they were obsolescent. Unlike the Ottomans, they had failed to take advantage of the development of firearms, the conservative Mamlūk cavalry showing particular reluctance to adopt the crude hand-guns of the period. Even the traditional equestrian exercises and games were neglected, and the insubordination of newly-recruited *mamlūk*s (*djulbān*) is a feature of the later 9th/15th century. A principal cause of the overthrow of Ḳā'it Bāy's son and successor, al-Nāṣir Muḥammad (901-4/1496-8) was his recruitment of a force of black arquebusiers. Ḳānṣawh al-Ghawrī attempted to restore the military effectiveness of his state. An arquebus unit (*al-ṭabaḳa al-khāmisa*) was set up in 916/1510, but the old prejudice remained, and it was dissolved in 920/1514. He paid attention to the casting of cannon, which had been used by the Mamlūks (but for siege-warfare only) since the later 8th/14th century, and he made efforts to revive the traditional cavalry-training.

At the beginning of Ḳānṣawh al-Ghawrī's reign (906-22/1501-16), the Mamlūk sultanate was hemmed in by three great powers. To the north was the Ottoman state, which was now confronted on the east by the new military monarchy of the Ṣafawid Shāh Ismā'īl [*q.v.*]. To the south, dominating the Indian Ocean and threatening the Red Sea, was the naval power of the Portuguese. The Mamlūks lacked the maritime traditions and experience to deal with this danger. They received supplies of material and personnel for a naval expedition from the Ottomans in 520/1514. Ottoman-Ṣafawid hostilities, however, inolved the Mamlūks when Sultan Selīm I invaded yria, probably to safeguard his flank, and defeated ānṣawh (who died during the battle) at Mardj Dābiḳ 25 Radjab 922/24 Aug. 1516). He subsequently adanced into Egypt, and inflicted a second defeat on he Mamlūks at al-Raydāniyya (29 Dhu 'l-Ḥidjdja 22/23 January 1517). Cairo fell, and the last Mamlūk sultan, al-Ashraf Ṭūmān Bāy, was subseuently captured and hanged. Egypt thus became a rovince of the Ottoman Empire, and was separately dministered from Syria.

(f) *The Neo-Mamlūks of the Ottoman period*

The Ottoman conquest of Egypt was not followed y the extirpation of the *mamlūks*. Indeed, from one oint of view, it may be regarded as an episode in Mamlūk factional politics, since Selīm's victories were acilitated by Mamlūk collaborators in opposition to ānṣawh al-Ghawrī and Ṭūmān Bāy. The leaders of his faction were the governors of Aleppo and Damascus, Khāʾir Bay and Djānbirdī al-Ghazālī q.v.], who received their reward from the conqueror, Khāʾir Bey being appointed viceroy in Cairo (where e maintained much of the state of the sultans, his redecessors), and Djānbirdī being restored to Damascus. These arrangements marked, however, a ransitional phase. On Selīm's death in 926/1520, Djānbirdī attempted to make himself independent, ut his revolt was suppressed, and he himself killed 927/1521). Khāʾir Bey died in 928/1522, and hereafter Ottomans were appointed to both Damascus and Cairo. A last Mamlūk rising headed y the *kāshifs* Djānim and Īnāl was suppressed shortly fterwards.

Mamlūk recruitment and the formation of *mamlūk* nilitary households nevertheless continued, and proided part of the armed forces of Egypt beside, but istinct from, the seven corps of the Ottoman garrison roops, the most important of which were the anissaries and the *ʿazabs* [*q.v.*]. The heads of the Mamlūk establishment, nominally 24 in number, ore the Ottoman designation of *sandjaḳ beyi* (whence n the Arabic chronicles *sanādjik/ṣanādjiḳ* is used as the lural of *bak/beg*; the modern *bakawāt* is a neologism), ut they differed in their functions from their omonyms elsewhere in the Ottoman empire. After ontinuing in obscurity during the remainder of the 0th/16th century, the beylicate emerged as a factor of reat political importance in the middle decades of the 1th/17th century (a period of Ottoman weakness), nd the old pattern of Mamlūk factionalism reapeared with the inveterate hostilities between the two ouseholds of the Dhu 'l-Faḳāriyya (usually Faḳāiyya) and the Ḳāsimiyya [*q.vv.*]. The former attained s apogee with Riḍwān Bey, who was *amīr al-ḥādjdj* for ver 20 years until his death in 1066/1656. The Faḳārī scendancy was broken in 1071/1660 by the āsimiyya in collusion with the Ottoman viceroy, but vith the assassination of their chief, Aḥmad Bey the osniak, in 1072/1662, they too sank into impotence. revival of the political power of the beylicate, and f factional rivalry, may be observed in the early 2th/18th century. By this time, complex webs of proection and patronage were linking the Mamlūk ouseholds with the officers and troops of the Otoman garrison, the urban population of Cairo and ne Arab tribes, and a new polarisation appears in the actional struggles. There was a manifestation of this n 1123/1711, when the ambition of a Janissary boss, Afrandj Aḥmad, produced a split between Janissaries nd *ʿazabs*, and between Faḳāriyya and Ḳāsimiyya, vhich culminated in a battle outside Cairo. Although in 1142/1730 the Faḳāriyya finally obtained the supremacy over the Ḳāsimiyya, they were soon overshadowed by a younger household, the Ḳāzdughliyya [*q.v.*], which (a significant indication of the assimilation of Ottoman military society in Egypt to Mamlūk norms) had been founded, and was for some decades headed, by officers of the garrison. *Mamlūks* from this household began to enter the beylicate after 1161/1748. Its most famous member was ʿAlī Bey [*q.v.*], known as *Bulūṭ Ḳāpān*, who as *shaykh al-balad* (i.e. premier bey) dominated the affairs of Egypt between 1173/1760 and 1186/1772. He was ruthless in extirpating his rivals and opponents, and gave signs of an intention to make himself independent in Egypt. After his overthrow, his former *mamlūk*, Muḥammad Bey Abu 'l-Dhahab, enjoyed a brief supremacy until he died on campaign against Shaykh Ẓāhir al-ʿUmar in 1189/1775. Thereafter factional struggles continued among the leading beys, the most notable of whom were two of Abu 'l-Dhahab's *mamlūks*, Ibrāhīm Bey al-Kabīr [*q.v.*] and Murād Bey, whose uneasy duumvirate was threatened by the expedition of Djezāʾirli Ghāzī Ḥasan Pasha [*q.v.*] in 1200-1/1786-7, and destroyed by Bonaparte's occupation of Egypt in 1213/1798. The massacre and proscription of the Mamlūk chiefs by Muḥammad ʿAlī Pasha in 1812 marked the end of their ascendancy in Egypt.

(ii) INSTITUTIONAL HISTORY

(a) *Institutions of the sultanate*

The central and essential institution of Mamlūk society under both the sultanate and the Ottomans was the military household. This consisted of the *mamlūks* obtained, trained and emancipated by a master (*ustādh*), to whom they remained attached by loyalty and more formally by legal clientage (*walāʾ*). This link was indicated by the *mamlūk*'s *nisba*. The loyalty felt towards the *ustādh* was narrowly personal; during the sultanate, it extended, if at all, only in a very attenuated form to his sons or other members of his family. The second bond of loyalty created by the Mamlūk household was the comradeship (*khushdāshiyya*) existing among the *mamlūks* as brothers-in-arms (sing. *khushdāsh*). The constant propensity of each generation of magnates to recruit new households of *mamlūks* virtually excluded their blood-descendants (*awlād al-nās*) from military functions, and hence from political power. The second and later generations of immigrant origin thus became absorbed into the Arabic-speaking Muslim society of Egypt and Syria, to the culture of which they made notable contributions.

The principal households were those of the sultans (the Royal Mamlūks), designated from the *laḳab* of the founding *ustādh*, e.g. the Ṣāliḥiyya of al-Malik al-Ṣāliḥ Ayyūb, the Ẓāhiriyya of al-Malik al-Ẓāhir Baybars etc. Since the *mamlūks* were immigrants, recruited at any one time principally from a single ethnic group (originally the Ḳïpčaḳ Turks, subsequently the Circassians), they formed in effect a synthetic alien tribe. The factional struggles among the different households, which form a recurrent feature of Mamlūk history, bear some analogy to clan warfare. The *mamlūks* depended upon their *ustādh* for patronage and advancement, while the *ustādh* depended upon his *mamlūks* for the maintenance of his own power and security. This was clearly the case as regards the royal household. The short reigns of many sultans, e.g. the later Ḳalāwūnids and the sons of Circassian usurpers, may largely be explained by their lack of *mamlūk* households recruited before their accession. Even if a sultan began his reign with an effective household, as did most of the usurping magnates, his position was not secure until he had ousted the great office-holders who were his potential rivals (often his khushdāsh-comrades), and installed his own mamlūks in their places. It was this situation which produced recurrent succession-crises from the time of Tūrānshāh onwards, and it resulted in continual tension between the two constituent groups of the Royal Mamlūks—those recruited by the reigning sultan (djulbān, adjlāb, mushtarawāt) and the veterans of his predecessors' recruitment (karānisa, karānīs).

The nature of the sultanate in the Mamlūk period is obscured by our sources, which present the ruler in accordance with traditional Islamic stereotypes. During the early decades, the sultan was primarily a war-leader, seen by his khushdāsh-comrades as first among equals, and presented as the supreme mudjāhid in the royal biographies. On the other hand, there is an anxiety to assert the Islamic legitimacy of the sultans, at first as the successors to the Ayyūbids. In his biography, Ibn ʿAbd al-Ẓāhir shows Baybars as the true successor to al-Ṣāliḥ Ayyūb by mamlūk clientage and qualities of character, rather than Tūrānshāh, the heir by blood-descent. The need for these somewhat specious arguments was ended, however, when Baybars, by his translation of the caliphate to Cairo, placed the supreme legitimating authority in Sunnī Islam under the control of himself and his successors. Thereafter the caliph played an essential, if formal, part in the accession observances of the Mamlūk sultans. When the danger from the Frankish states and the Mongols came to an end, and the sultans became sedentary in Cairo, their governmental functions became more important than leadership in war—a development demonstrated in the autocracy established by al-Nāṣir Muḥammad in his third reign (709-41/1310-41), and reasserted by the effective usurping sultans during the Circassian period.

The distinctive characteristic of the administrative system was the over-riding control exercised by the sultan through Mamlūk amīrs. The amīrates that had existed under the Ayyūbids were organised, probably in Baybars's reign, into three principal ranks. At the top was that of amīr miʾa wa-muḳaddam alf, i.e. the commander of a household force of 100 horsemen and head of a company of 1,000 warriors of the ḥalḳa. With the differentiation of the Baḥriyya from the ḥalḳa which had been its matrix, the latter sank into being an honourable but archaic formation of declining military significance, latterly recruited largely from awlād al-nās. In theory there were 24 amīrs of the highest rank. The second rank was that of amīr ṭablkhānāh, who had the privilege of a military band, and came to be equated with the commander of 40 household troopers. The third rank, amīr ʿashara, had a military household of ten horsemen. This was a hierarchy of rank; it did not imply a chain of command, nor was there any kind of subinfeudation, although it usually provided a cursus honorum. The military households, including that of the sultan, were maintained by assignments of landed revenue (sing. iḳṭāʿ [q.v.], khubz), which as mentioned above were reorganised by al-Nāṣir Muḥammad in 715/1315, thereby laying the fiscal basis of his autocracy. It was the Royal Mamlūks who were promoted to amirates and appointed to the great offices at court and in the provinces. Although their tenure of office was individually precarious, and their assignments were never in this period hereditary or life-tenures, these magnates were always potential opponents of the sultan. Repeated attempts to establish a species of

contractual relationship by obtaining an accession-compact at the installation of a sultan were never effective in practice; hence many reigns ended in factional revolt, and the deposition (or even murder) of the ruler.

A noteworthy instance of the development of offices in this period, and of the extension of Mamlūk control over the administration, is provided by the history of the vizierate. Under the Ayyūbids, as under previous régimes, the greatest officer of state had been the wazīr, a civilian usually trained as a jurist, who served during the ruler's pleasure as his omnicompetent minister. The erosion of the wazīr's powers began with the establishment of the office of vicegerent (nāʾib al-salṭana), held by a mamlūk, as a permanent post, not an ad hoc appointment during the sultan's absence on campaign. This development may be dated to the reign of Baraka Khān (676/1277). The close relationship which had existed between the ruler and the wazīr was further weakened in 678/1280 when Ḳalāwūn promoted the civilian head of the chancery (ṣāḥib dīwān al-inshāʾ) to the confidential post of secretary (kātib al-sirr) to himself. The secretaryship was held by a succession of civilian officials down to the end of the Mamlūk sultanate. The wazīr then was restricted to being the head of the state treasury (al-dawla al-sharīfa, dīwān al-wizāra), but on several occasions Mamlūk amīrs were appointed to the office until it was abolished by al-Nāṣir Muḥammad in 728/1328. A professional financial official, the controller of the treasury (nāẓir al-dawla) was jointly responsible with the wazīr, and handled its affairs directly when his colleague was an inexpert military officer. On the abolition of the vizierate, the controller continued to administer the treasury. A new financial department, dīwān al-khāṣṣ, created by al-Nāṣir Muḥammad to administer his fisc, was also placed under a civilian controller (nāẓir al-khāṣṣ), who absorbed many of the wazīr's financial functions as the secretary had taken over his chancery functions. Although the vizierate was restored after the reign of al-Nāṣir Muḥammad, it was restricted to a limited financial field. Barḳūḳ created two new personal treasuries, al-dīwān al-mufrad and dīwān al-amlāk, which were managed by a Mamlūk great officer of the household, the high steward (ustādār al-ʿāliya from ustādh al-dār al-ʿāliya).

The militarisation of household offices, and the acquisition by some of state functions, were characteristic developments of the Mamlūk sultanate. In contrast to the Ayyūbids, under whom only four court offices were normally held by the military, the Mamlūks beginning with Baybars quickly developed a hierarchy of such offices. The dawādāriyya was militarised, and its holder rose from being the bearer of the royal ink-well to being the channel of communication between the sultan and the chancery. Not until the 8th/14th century, however, was this office usually given to an amīr of the highest rank. Another officer who acquired public functions was the chamberlain (ḥādjib [q.v.]), who obtained jurisdiction in disputes between the amīrs and the soldiery. Originally, he acted in conjunction with the vicegerent, hence his importance increased when al-Nāṣir Muḥammad left the vicegerency vacant after 727/1326. During the first half of the 9th/15th century, the chamberlain's jurisdiction was abusively extended to ordinary subjects, to the detriment of the Sharīʿa courts. A proliferation of offices took place; e.g. by the end of Barḳūḳ's reign there were six chamberlains, Faradj raised the number to eight, and by the mid-9th/15th century their numbers had increased still more.

An important military office, which went back

through Ayyūbid and Zangid antecedents to a Saldjūḳid institution, was that of the *atābak* [*q.v.*], i.e. *atabeg*. From the start of the Mamlūk sultanate, it was held exclusively by officers of *mamlūk* origin, whereas under the Ayyūbids, free-born Muslims, and even princes of the blood, had also been appointed. The Mamlūk *atābakiyya* was originally a tenure of the supreme military command by delegation from a sultan who could not exercise it in person, e.g. Shadjar al-Durr, ʿAlī b. Aybak. Hence the specific title of *atābak al-ʿasākir* becomes standard form. The regency, which had been exercised by the *atabeg* under previous régimes, is usually separately designated as *tadbīr al-mamlaka* (or equivalent term), although this function was often combined with the *atābakiyya*. The four decades of the last Ḳalāwūnids, during which *atābak*s and *mudabbir*s flourished at the expense of the feeble sultans, saw the absorption of another title, that of *amīr kabīr*. In the Ayyūbid period and during the first century of the Mamlūk sultanate, this meant simply and literally a senior *amīr*, until in 756/1355-6, during the second reign of al-Nāṣir Ḥasan, Shaykhūn al-ʿUmarī annexed the title to his office of *atābak al-ʿasākir*, and the two terms were thenceforth synonymous. This was, however, itself an indication that the *atābakiyya* was coming to imply pre-eminence in rank rather than specific functions. From about the same time also, the title of *atābak al-ʿasākir* comes to be held by *amīr*s in the Syrian provinces, and so loses its uniqueness.

In contrast to the loose Ayyūbid family confederacy of autonomous principalities, the provinces of the Mamlūk sultanate were under close central control, being administered by governors of *mamlūk* origin serving as the sultan's delegates (sing. *nāʾib al-salṭana*). In Egypt, this title was originally held solely by the vicegerent (*al-nāʾib al-kāfil*), who (as indicated above) was in some respects the functional successor to the *wazīr*. The title of *nāʾib* was extended in 767/1365 to the governor of Alexandria (after the brief occupation of the city by King Peter I of Cyprus), and by Barḳūḳ to the governors of Upper and Lower Egypt. The vicegerency was characteristically allowed to lapse by al-Nāṣir Muḥammad in 727/1326. Restored after his death, it was overshadowed by the *atābakiyya*. The last appointment was made by Faradj in 808/1405. The Syrian *nāʾib*s held the title of *malik al-umarāʾ*, which had been used by the Saldjūḳs of Rūm [see BEGLERBEGI], and which continued to be borne by Khāʾir Bey as viceroy of Egypt after the Ottoman conquest. Pre-eminent among them was the governor of Damascus. Although the Syrian governors seemed like kinglets in their provinces, they were subject to various controls, both from the arbitrary will of the sultan and of an administrative nature. Grants of assignments could only pass under the sultan's signature, or sometimes that of the vicegerent. Several of the principal provincial officials, e.g. the governor of the citadel at Damascus and the chamberlain there, were appointed by the sultan, as was the governor's secretary, who served as a spy on him. Governors of the Egyptian provinces bore the inferior titles of *kāshif* or *wālī*.

(b) *Neo-Mamlūk institutions*

The extinction of the Mamlūk sultanate ended the recruitment of Royal Mamlūks, but the formation of *mamlūk* households continued until the time of Muḥammad ʿAlī Pasha. Detailed information on their structure is only available from the early 12th/18th century with the copious data provided by al-Djabartī. By this time the households (sing. *bayt*) had developed into complex patronage-systems comprising the following elements: (1) the head (*ustādh*) of the household, who might be a *bey*, an Ottoman garrison-officer, or even a native civilian (e.g. Ṣāliḥ al-Fallāḥ, d. before 1161/1748). (2) Children of the *ustādh*. By contrast with the normal practice under the sultanate, sons of an *ustādh* were members of the military household, and might succeed to its headship. Daughters or widows of an *ustādh* might marry *mamlūks* of the household. (3) True *mamlūks*. The immigration (especially of Circassians) continued as under the sultanate, but there is some evidence of the recruitment for military purposes of black slaves (*ʿabīd sūd*). (4) Free retainers recruited in Anatolia and Rumelia. They served chiefly as mounted bodyguards (sing. *sarrādj*), and were subsequently, it appears, enrolled in the Ottoman garrison-corps as clients (sing. *čiraḳ*, whence *ishrāḳ* or *djirāḳ*) of their former employers. They were thus largely excluded from the advancement open to true *mamlūk*s, although the Bosniaks who appear in the Ḳāsimiyya in the 11th/17th century, and the future Djazzār Aḥmad Pasha, may have started their careers in this way. (5) Allies among the native urban population and the tribes, where Mamlūk factionalism tended to link up with an indigenous division into the rival groupings of Saʿd and Ḥarām.

With the disappearance of the Royal Mamlūks, the old factional polarisation between *ḳarāniṣa* and *djulbān* ceased, but factionalism reappeared (perhaps not before the later 11th/17th century) basically to obtain high office and the control of the revenues of Egypt. Although the old *iḳṭāʿ*s had been abolished after the Ottoman conquest, their place was soon taken by a system of tax-farms (sing. *iltizām* [*q.v.*]), many of which were appropriated by the neo-Mamlūks. The *sandjaḳ beyi*s (an Ottoman term which almost certainly conceals their continuity with the *amīr*s of the highest rank under the sultanate) were at one and the same time the leading *multazim*s and the chiefs of the neo-Mamlūk establishment. Although they formed a military élite, the *bey*s were outside the cadres of the Ottoman garrison. Their lack of specific duties enabled them to assume a wide range of functions and to develop into a self-perpetuating ruling group. Their principal functions were: (1) the command as *serdār* of forces levied for service inside Egypt (e.g. against nomadic incursions) or outside in the Ottoman sultan's wars. (2) The command of the annual tribute-convoy sent by land to Istanbul, held by the *amīr al-khazna*. (3) The command of the annual Pilgrimage-caravan to Mecca, held by the *amīr al-ḥādjdj* (the form *amīr al-ḥadjdj*, which might be expected, is not found in mediaeval or later sources), who accompanied the *maḥmal*, sent, as during the Mamluk sultanate, in token of sovereignty. (4) The headship of the financial administration as *daftardār*. The earliest *daftardār*s after the conquest were Ottomans, but from the later 10th/16th century the post was held by a *bey*. (5) Service as acting viceroy (*ḳāʾim-maḳām* [*q.v.*]) in the interim between the withdrawal of a viceroy and the arrival of his successor. In the factional struggles, such an appointment was a means of legitimating the position of the dominant group. In addition, during the 12th/18th century, *bey*s served as military governors of the sub-provinces of Egypt, thus reducing the status of the former governors, the *kāshif*s, who were also *mamlūk*s by origin. They became in effect subordinates of the *bey*s. An important new office which emerged during the 12th/18th century was that of *shaykh al-balad*, which institutionalised the primacy (*riʾāsa*) held by military and political leaders. The title

TABLE 1

THE TURKISH MAMLŪK SULTANS

Continuous line: blood descent
Broken line: *mamlūk* clientage

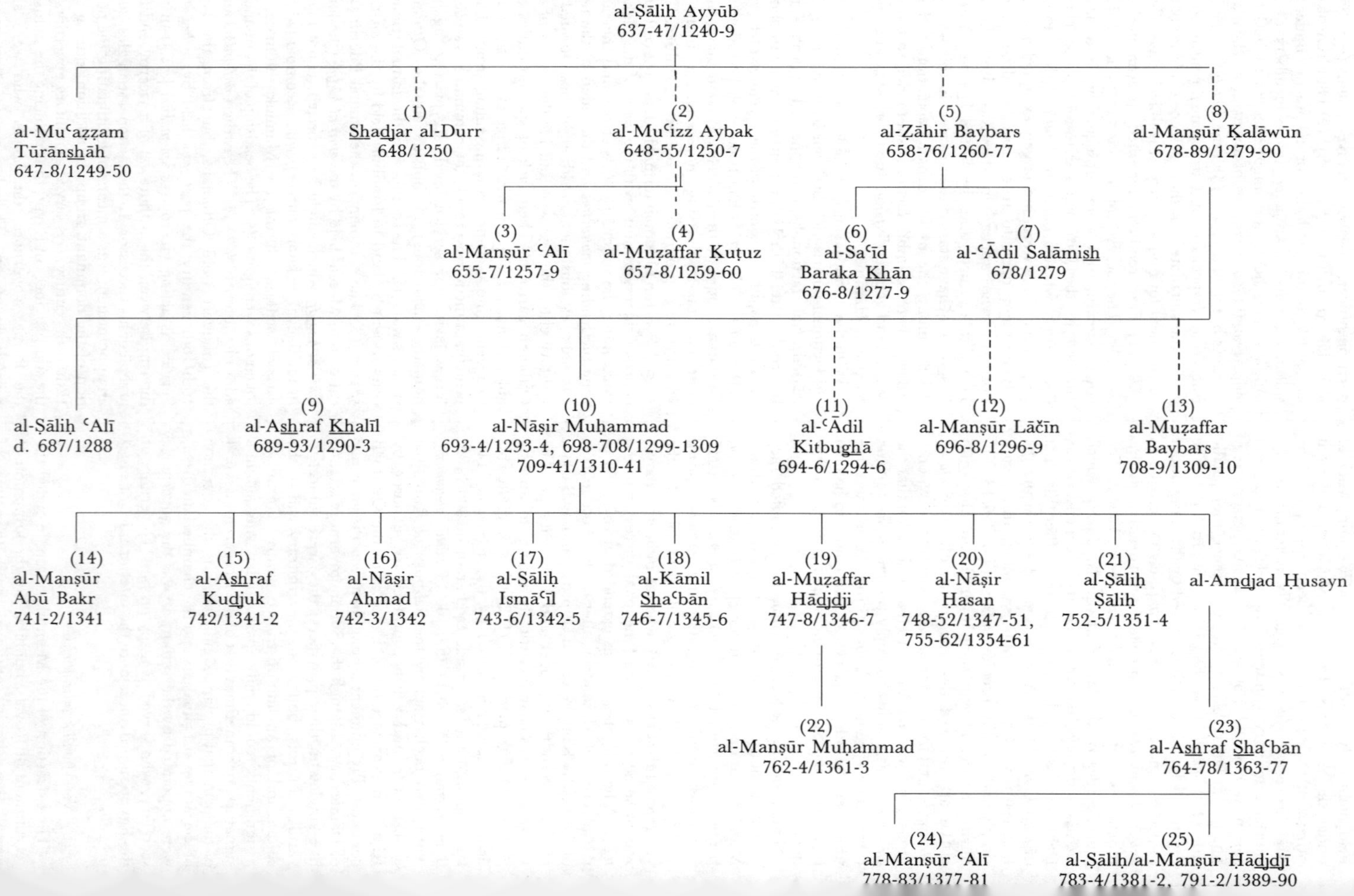
al-Ṣāliḥ Ayyūb 637-47/1240-9
al-Muʿaẓẓam Tūrān<u>sh</u>āh 647-8/1249-50
(1) <u>Sh</u>a<u>dj</u>ar al-Durr 648/1250
(2) al-Muʿizz Aybak 648-55/1250-7
(5) al-Ẓāhir Baybars 658-76/1260-77
(8) al-Manṣūr Ḳalāwūn 678-89/1279-90
(3) al-Manṣūr ʿAlī 655-7/1257-9
(4) al-Muẓaffar Ḳuṭuz 657-8/1259-60
(6) al-Saʿīd Baraka <u>Kh</u>ān 676-8/1277-9
(7) al-ʿĀdil Salāmi<u>sh</u> 678/1279
al-Ṣāliḥ ʿAlī d. 687/1288
(9) al-A<u>sh</u>raf <u>Kh</u>alīl 689-93/1290-3
(10) al-Nāṣir Muḥammad 693-4/1293-4, 698-708/1299-1309 709-41/1310-41
(11) al-ʿĀdil Kitbu<u>gh</u>ā 694-6/1294-6
(12) al-Manṣūr Lāčīn 696-8/1296-9
(13) al-Muẓaffar Baybars 708-9/1309-10
(14) al-Manṣūr Abū Bakr 741-2/1341
(15) al-A<u>sh</u>raf Ku<u>dj</u>uk 742/1341-2
(16) al-Nāṣir Aḥmad 742-3/1342
(17) al-Ṣāliḥ Ismāʿīl 743-6/1342-5
(18) al-Kāmil <u>Sh</u>aʿbān 746-7/1345-6
(19) al-Muẓaffar Ḥā<u>dj</u>dji 747-8/1346-7
(20) al-Nāṣir Ḥasan 748-52/1347-51, 755-62/1354-61
(21) al-Ṣāliḥ Ṣāliḥ 752-5/1351-4
al-Am<u>dj</u>ad Ḥusayn
(22) al-Manṣūr Muḥammad 762-4/1361-3
(23) al-A<u>sh</u>raf <u>Sh</u>aʿbān 764-78/1363-77
(24) al-Manṣūr ʿAlī 778-83/1377-81
(25) al-Ṣāliḥ/al-Manṣūr Ḥā<u>dj</u>djī 783-4/1381-2, 791-2/1389-90

TABLE 2

THE CIRCASSIAN MAMLŪK SULTANS

Continuous line: blood descent
Broken line: *mamlūk* clientage

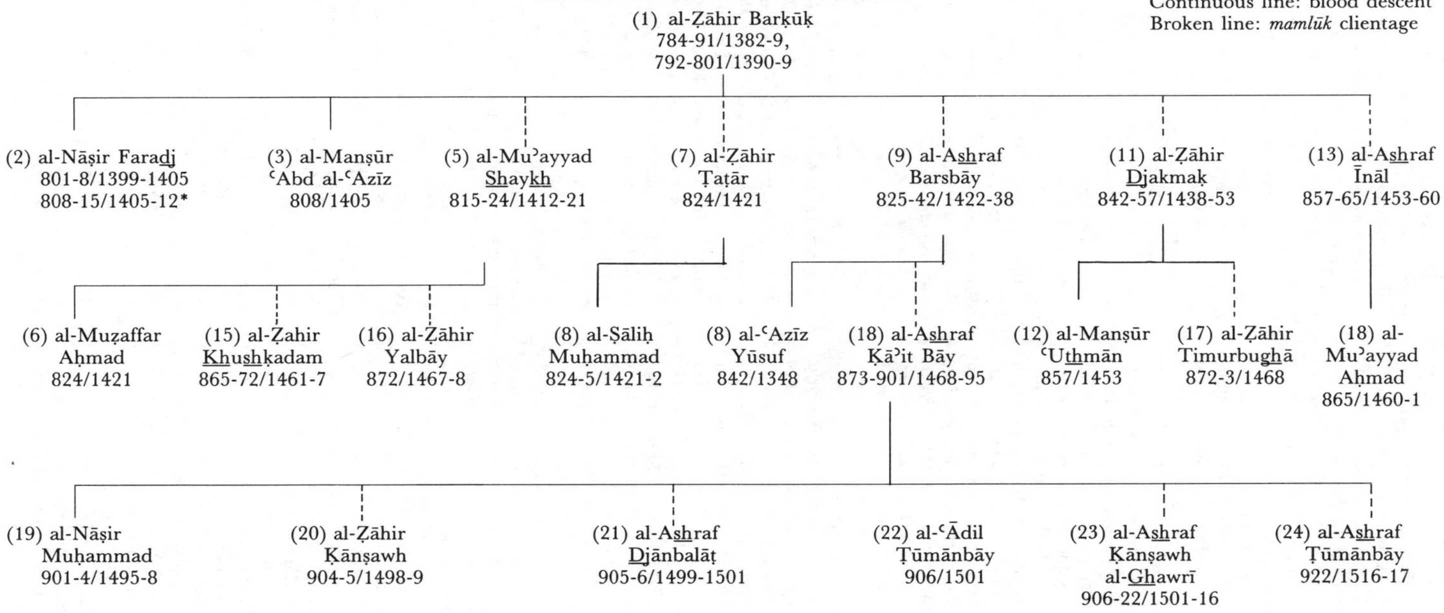

* al-Mustaᶜīn, caliph and sultan: 815/1412.

seems to have been held only by members of the beylicate. With the administrative reorganisation carried out by Muḥammad ᶜAlī Pas̲h̲a as the autonomous viceroy of Egypt, the neo-Mamlūk titles and offices became obsolete.

Bibliography: (i) *Primary sources*: (a) Archival. For documentary material preserved in the monastery of St. Catharine in Sinai, see H. Ernst, *Die mamlukischen Sultansurkunden des Sinai-Klosters*, Wiesbaden 1960; S. M. Stern, *Petitions from the Mamlūk period*, in *BSOAS*, xxix (1966), 233-76. For other documents extant in various European archives, see Aziz Suryal Atiya, *Egypt and Aragon*, in *Abh. K. M.*, 1938; J. Wansbrough, *A Mamluk ambassador to Venice*, in *BSOAS*, xxvi (1963), 503-30; idem, *Venice and Florence in the Mamluk commercial privileges*, in *BSOAS*, xxviii (1965), 482-523; idem, *A Mamlūk commercial treaty concluded with the republic of Florence 849/1489*, in S. M. Stern (ed.), *Documents from Islamic chanceries*, Oxford 1965, 39-79. Various documents are reproduced in al-Ḳalḳas̲h̲andī, *Ṣubḥ al-aᶜs̲h̲ā*, Cairo 1331-8/1913-20; e.g. treaties with the Frankish states and other Christian powers, on which see P. M. Holt, *Qalāwūn's treaty with Acre in 1283*, in *English Historical Review*, xci, no. 361 (1976), 802-12; idem, *Qalāwūn's treaty with Genoa in 1290*, in *Isl.* lvii (1980), 101-8; idem, *The treaties of the early Mamluk sultans with the Frankish states*, in *BSOAS*, xliii (1980), 67-76.

(b) Literary. There is extant a very considerable amount of material, particularly chronicles, royal biographies and biographical dictionaries, a number of which have been published. The following is a representative sample only. (1) The four major chronicles for the period are: Ibn al-Dawādārī (d. after 736/1335), *Kanz al-durar*, viii, ed. U. Haarmann, Freiburg 1391/1971; ix, ed. H. R. Roemer, Cairo 1379/1960; al-Maḳrīzī (d. 845/1442), *K. al-Sulūk*, ed. M. Mustafa Ziada *et alii*, Cairo 1956- Ibn Tag̲h̲rībirdī (d. 874/1470), vii-xvi, Cairo 1348-92/1929-72, ed. W. Popper, Berkeley-Leiden 1908-36; Ibn Iyās (d. *ca.* 930/1524), *Badāʾiᶜ al-zuhūr*, ed. Mohamed Mostafa, Wiesbaden 1379-95/1960-75. Among Syrian chroniclers may be mentioned Abu 'l-Fidāʾ (d. 732/1332), *al-Mukhtaṣar fī taʾrīkh al-bashar*, various edns., iv, for memoirs of his own times; Ibn Ṣaṣrā (d. after 801/1399), *A chronicle of Damascus 1389-1397*, ed. and tr. W. M. Brinner, Berkeley and Los Angeles 1963; Ibn Ṭūlūn (d. 953/1546), *Mufākahat al-k̲h̲illān fī ḥawādit̲h̲ al-zamān*, ed. Mohamed Mostafa, Cairo 1381/1962, 1384/1964. The principal published royal biographies are: (Baybars), Ibn ᶜAbd al-Ẓāhir, *al-Rawḍ al-zāhir fī sīrat al-Malik al-Ẓāhir*, ed. ᶜAbd al-ᶜAzīz al-K̲h̲uwayṭir, al-Riyāḍ 1396/1976; S̲h̲āfiᶜ b. ᶜAlī b. ᶜAbbās (d. 730/1330), *Ḥusn al-manāḳib al-sirriyya al-muntazaᶜa min al-sīra al-Ẓāhiriyya*, ed. al-K̲h̲uwayṭir, al-Riyāḍ 1396/1976; (Ḳalāwūn), Ibn ᶜAbd al-Ẓāhir, *Tas̲h̲rīf al-ayyām wa 'l-ᶜuṣūr fī sīrat al-Malik al-Manṣūr*, ed. Murād Kāmil, Cairo 1961; (K̲h̲alīl), A. Moberg (ed. and tr.), *Ur ᶜAbd Allâh b. ᶜAbd Eẓ-Ẓâhir's biografi över Sultanen El-Melik El-Aśraf Ḫalîl*, Lund 1902. Among biographical dictionaries, a recent important publication is Ibn al-Ṣuḳāᶜī (d. 726/1326), *Tālī kitāb wafayāt al-aᶜyān*, ed. and tr. Jacqueline Sublet, Damascus 1974.

(2) Much less has been published on the Ottoman period. Chronicles available are: al-Isḥāḳī (*fl. ca.* 1032/1623), *Kitāb Ak̲h̲bār al-uwal fī man taṣarrafa fī Miṣr min arbāb al-duwal*, various edns.; Aḥmad S̲h̲alabī b. ᶜAbd al-G̲h̲anī (d. 1150/1737), *Awḍaḥ al-is̲h̲ārāt fī man tawallā Miṣr al-Ḳāhira min al-wuzarāʾ wa 'l-bās̲h̲āt*, ed. ᶜAbd al-Raḥīm ᶜAbd al-Raḥmān ᶜAbd al-Raḥīm, Cairo 1978; ᶜAbd al-Raḥmān b. Ḥasan al-D̲j̲abartī (d. 1825-6), *ᶜAd̲j̲āʾib al-āt̲h̲ār*, Būlāḳ 1297/1879-80. Two important documents are: S. J. Shaw, *Ottoman Egypt in the eighteenth century* [i.e. the *Niẓām-nāme-yi Mîṣîr* of D̲j̲azzār Aḥmad Pas̲h̲a], Cambridge, Mass. 1962; S̲h̲afīḳ G̲h̲urbāl, *Miṣr ᶜinda mafraḳ al-ṭuruḳ* [i.e. the answers of Ḥusayn Efendi to Estève in 1216/1801], in *Mad̲j̲allat Kulliyyat al-Adab* [Cairo], iv (1936), 1-71; tr. and annotated Shaw, *Ottoman Egypt in the age of the French Revolution*, Cambridge, Mass. 1964.

(ii) Secondary sources: (a) Political history. There is no recent large-scale study of the Mamlūk sultanate. The pioneer work is that of Gustav Weil, *Geschichte der Chalifen*, iv-v, Stuttgart 1860-2. Its derivative, W. Muir, *The Mameluke or slave dynasty of Egypt*, London 1896, is inadequate. The period is presented in wider historical surveys by S. Lane-Poole, *A history of Egypt in the Middle Ages*, London 1901; and by G. Wiet, *L'Egypte arabe ... 642-1517* [= G. Hanotaux (ed.), *Histoire de la nation égyptienne*, iv, Paris 1937]. On individual sultans, see G. Schregle, *Die Sultanin von Ägypten*, Wiesbaden 1961 (for S̲h̲ad̲j̲ar al-Durr); Abdul-Aziz Khowaiter, *Baibars the First: his endeavours and achievements*, London 1978; P. M. Holt, *The sultanate of al-Manṣūr Lāc̲h̲īn (696-8/1296-90)*, in *BSOAS*, xxxvi (1973), 521-32; Shah Morad Elham, *Kitbuġā und Lāǧīn*, Freiburg 1977; Aḥmad Darrag, *L'Égypte sous le règne de Barsbay 825-841/1422-1438*, Damascus 1961. The establishment of the Circassian ascendancy is studied in Ḥākīm Amīr ᶜAbd al-Sayyid, *Ḳiyām dawlat al-Mamālīk al-t̲h̲āniya*, Cairo 1966. Some account of the neo-Mamlūks of Ottoman Egypt is given in Holt, *Egypt and the Fertile Crescent 1516-1922*, London 1966; see also idem, *Studies in the history of the Near East*, London 1973. A. Raymond, *Artisans et commerçants au Caire au XVIIIe siècle*, Damascus 1973, deals widely with political as well as social and economic history.

(b) Social, economic and institutional history. Data (chiefly from al-Ḳalḳas̲h̲andī) on the institutions of the Mamlūk sultanate are presented in the introduction to [M.] Gaudefroy-Demombynes, *La Syrie à l'époque des Mamelouks*, Paris 1923. Most of the illuminating articles of D. Ayalon on many aspects of Mamlūk society are now conveniently assembled in *Studies on the Mamlūks of Egypt (1250-1517)*, London 1977, and *The Mamlūk military society*, London 1979; idem, *Gunpowder and firearms in the Mamluk kingdom*, London 1956, is a seminal monograph on military and social history. The transition from Ayyūbid institutions is examined by R. Stephen Humphreys, *The emergence of the Mamluk army*, in *SI*, xlv (1977), 67-99; xlvi (1977), 147-82. A general survey is provided by Saᶜīd ᶜAbd al-Fattāḥ ᶜĀs̲h̲ūr, *al-Mud̲j̲tamaᶜ al-Miṣrī fī ᶜaṣr al-salāṭīn al-mamālīk*, Cairo 1962. On economic and social history, E. Ashtor, *A social and economic history of the Near East in the Middle Ages*, London 1976; idem, *Histoire des prix et des salaires dans l'orient médiéval*, Paris 1969; Hassanein Rabie, *The financial system of Egypt A.H. 564-741/1169-1341*, London 1972; H. Halm, *Ägypten nach den mamlukischen Lehensregistern. I. Oberägypten und das Fayyūm*, Wiesbaden 1979, *II. Das Delta*, Wiesbaden 1982. On governmental institutions, Holt, *The position and power of the Mamlūk sultan*, in *BSOAS*, xxxviii (1975), 237-49;

and *The structure of government in the Mamluk sultanate*, in Holt (ed.), *The eastern Mediterranean lands in the period of the Crusades*, Warminster 1977, 44-61. For urban society during the sultanate, I. M. Lapidus, *Muslim cities in the later Middle Ages*, Cambridge, Mass. 1967; C. F. Pekry, *The civilian elite of Cairo in the later Middle Ages*, Princeton 1981; in the Ottoman period, A. Raymond (as above).

(P. M. HOLT)

MAʿMAR B. AL-MUTHANNĀ [see ABŪ ʿUBAYDA].

AL-**MAʾMŪN** [see AL-BAṬĀʾIḤĪ; DHU 'L-NŪNIDS].

al-**MAʾMŪN**, ABU 'L-ʿABBĀS ʿABD ALLĀH B. HĀRŪN AL-RASHĪD, seventh ʿAbbāsid caliph. Born on 15 Rabīʿ I 170/14 September 786, "the night of the three caliphs" (death of al-Hādī, accession of al-Rashīd, birth of the future al-Maʾmūn), he was the eldest of the eleven sons of al-Rashīd. His mother, Marādjil, a concubine originally from Bādhghīs, died soon after his birth and he was brought up by Zubayda, the grand-daughter of al-Manṣūr, wife of al-Rashīd and mother of Muḥammad (the future al-Amīn) who was born in Shawwāl 170/April 787. He received a classical education in Arabic, tutored by al-Kisāʾī [*q.v.*], in *adab* (as a pupil of Abū Muḥammad al-Yazīdī), in music and in poetry (where his tastes were classical). In religious sciences, he was trained in *ḥadīth* (and became a transmitter himself) and in *fiḳh* (taught by al-Ḥasan al-Luʾluʾī), where he excelled in Ḥanafī jurisprudence. He was distinguished by his love of knowledge, making him the most intellectual caliph of the ʿAbbāsid family, which accounts for the way in which his caliphate developed.

In 177/794, in response to the wishes of members of his family, al-Rashīd named as his first successor Muḥammad (al-Amīn), the only caliph born to parents both of whom were ʿAbbāsids; proclaimed initially in Khurāsān by his guardian al-Faḍl b. Yaḥyā al-Barmakī [*q.v.*], he subsequently received the *bayʿa* in Baghdād. As for ʿAbd Allāh (al-Maʾmūn), he had to wait until the age of puberty to be declared second heir of al-Rashīd, in 183/799, under the guardianship of Djaʿfar b. Yaḥyā al-Barmakī, the caliph's favourite. While reviving the Marwānid tradition of appointing two heirs to the throne in order to guarantee the stability of the régime and the future of the dynasty, al-Rashīd made an innovation in accepting the appointment of a third successor, al-Ḳāsim (al-Muʾtamin), the son of a concubine, sponsored by his ʿAbbāsid guardian ʿAbd al-Malik b. Ṣāliḥ [*q.v.*].

The protocol was solemnly proclaimed, during the pilgrimage of 186/802, in Mecca: the unity of the empire was re-affirmed by the existence of a single caliph-designate, Muḥammad (al-Amīn), residing in Baghdād, supported by his two heirs who were given charge of key-provinces: greater Khurāsān, the heartland of the ʿAbbāsid régime since the success of the *daʿwa hāshimiyya* (132/750), was entrusted to ʿAbd Allāh (al-Maʾmūn) and the war-front in the struggle against the Byzantine Empire (al-Djazīra and northern Syria), a major pre-occupation of al-Rashīd, placed under the authority of al-Ḳāsim (al-Muʾtamin). This interdependence between the different groupings of the empire conferred autonomy on Ifrīḳiya, where the authority of the Aghlabids was recognised in 184/800, with the purpose of containing the Khāridjīs, the ʿAlids and the Umayyads who had succeeded in founding principalities in the Maghrib and in al-Andalus, in the second half of the 2nd/8th century.

On his return from the pilgrimage, al-Rashīd rid himself of the patronage of the Barmakids, ordering the execution of Djaʿfar b. Yaḥyā on the night of 1 Ṣafar 187/29 January 803, and arresting al-Faḍl and his brothers, who were imprisoned at al-Rāfiḳa. Henceforward, ʿAbd Allāh (al-Maʾmūn) had as his guardian al-Faḍl b. Sahl, son of a Zoroastrian from a village near Kūfa, who entered the service of the Barmakids and ultimately converted to Islam, in 190/806, assuming the role of *kātib*-tutor, thus becoming qualified for the post of future vizier on the accession of al-Maʾmūn.

At the age of eighteen, ʿAbd Allāh married his cousin, Umm ʿĪsā, daughter of Mūsā al-Hādī, who bore him two sons (Muḥammad al-Aṣghar and ʿAbd Allāh), and had numerous concubines. In 192/808, having stabilised the war-front with the Byzantine empire, al-Rashīd took personal charge of the situation in Khurāsān, which was disturbed by the revolt of Rāfiʿ b. Layth, grandson of Naṣr b. Sayyār (the last Umayyad governor of Khurāsān), against the centralising policy of the governor ʿAlī b. ʿĪsā b. Māhān, who represented the *abnāʾ al-dawla* (Khurāsānians resident in ʿIrāḳ). Accompanied by ʿAbd Allāh (al-Maʾmūn) and al-Faḍl b. Sahl, but also by the *ḥādjib*-vizier al-Faḍl b. al-Rabīʿ, successor to the Barmakids at the head of the central administration, he set out, but died at Ṭūs on 3 Djumada II 193/24 March 809, al-Maʾmūn having preceded him to Marw with a part of the army. Immediately, the new caliph in Baghdād began to take measures designed to reinforce the position of the central power in opposition to the autonomist aspirations of greater Khurāsān, in line with the policy that had been in force for fifty years; he ordered the return of the army and of the treasury to Baghdād, which deprived the prince-governor al-Maʾmūn of the means to "pacify" rapidly and completely the troubled regions (Transoxania; Sīstān-Kirmān, disturbed by the revolt of the Khāridjī Ḥamza since 179/795; etc.). Nevertheless, al-Maʾmūn did not lack the ingenuity to consolidate his position in confrontation with the caliphate, and following the example of his father, he devolved his responsibilities upon the Sahlids, who received full powers to manage affairs and to safeguard his rights of inheritance to the caliphate, which were sealed in the Kaʿba. A process of pacification and mobilisation of the forces of the eastern provinces was achieved by means of the recognition of the autonomy of local chieftains, the support of the aristocracy, which saw in the potentialities of the empire an opportunity of gaining unprecedented wealth and prestige, an increase in the wages of the army, the reduction of the *kharādj* by a quarter, the restoration of the efficiency of the administration and recourse to the *maẓālim* [*q.v.*], regularly presided over by al-Maʾmūn. Particular efforts were applied in the direction of the *fuḳahāʾ* and *mutakallimūn* suffering persecution in ʿIrāḳ (the Muʿtazila), whose opinions were canvassed. These various concessions, following the line of the Barmakid policy of al-Faḍl b. Yaḥyā, as practised at the time of his recruitment of an *ʿAbbāsiyya* army (in 177/794), had the expected effects in regard to the maintenance of the territorial integrity of the provinces subject to the authority of al-Maʾmūn (ending the various insurrections, except that of the Khāridjī Ḥamza in Sīstān) and the rallying of local populations to the "son of their sister" and a member of the Family of the Prophet whose rights to the *imāma* of the *umma* had been endorsed by the *daʿwa hāshimiyya*, installed at Marw.

Similarly, in the West, supported by his *ḥādjib*-vizier al-Faḍl b. al-Rabīʿ b. Yūnus, chief of the *mawālī* of the caliph, whose role had been augmented at the expense of the *kuttāb* of the administration (represented by the Barmakids), his confidential ally Bakr b. al-Muᶜtamir (the holder of the Seal), his chief of police, al-Sindī b. S̲h̲āhak, *mawlā* of the caliph, al-Amīn enlarged his circle of partisans; he ordered the release of ᶜAlī b. ᶜĪsā b. Māhān, chief of the *Abnā᾿* (determined to preserve their privileges at the expense of the autonomist aspirations of K̲h̲urāsān), and the surviving Barmakids, including Mūsā b. Yaḥyā, who rallied to his cause, while Muhammad rejoined the camp of al-Ma᾿mūn. ᶜAlī b. ᶜĪsā b. Māhān was promoted leader of the caliph's bodyguard, while ᶜAbd al-Malik b. Ṣāliḥ, the principal supporter of al-Mu᾿tamin, was arrested. Rule over Syria was entrusted to T̲h̲ābit b. Naṣr, grandson of Mālik b. al-Hayt̲h̲am al-K̲h̲uzāᶜī (one of the twelve *nuḳabā᾿* of the *daᶜwa hās̲h̲imiyya*, who became the confidential ally of Abū Muslim al-K̲h̲urāsānī), while Egypt, governed by ᶜAbd al-ᶜAziz b. ᶜAbd al-Raḥmān al-Azdī (descended from a Hās̲h̲imite *dāᶜī*, former governor of K̲h̲urāsān), was potentially dissident. Only the Ḥid̲j̲āz, which had benefited from irrigation projects and from the riches of Zubayda, was firmly behind al-Amīn (at the expense of the ᶜAlids). This bipolarisation has been the object of a historical misunderstanding, with the eastern provinces being identified with "Iran" and the western provinces with the contemporary Arab countries. In fact, greater K̲h̲urāsān extended only as far as Rayy and Hamad̲h̲ān (in the west), while Fārs was detached from it following the assassination of Abū Muslim (137/755), and the most advanced centres of Islamisation and Arabisation in the period of al-Ma᾿mūn were situated in the former Sāsānid empire (divided between al-Amīn and al-Ma᾿mūn) rather than in the former Roman-Byzantine empire (Syria-Egypt); cf. R. W. Bulliet, *Conversion to Islam in the medieval period: an essay in quantitative history*, Cambridge, Mass.-London 1979. Likewise, the rivalry between al-Amīn and al-Ma᾿mūn is not explained by the origin of their mothers (Arab and Iranian), in view of the patrilineal system of the ᶜAbbāsid family, recalled by al-Manṣūr, son of a Berber concubine, to Muḥammad al-Nafs al-Zakiyya (who prided himself on being of pure and free descent on both the paternal and maternal side) to refute the legitimising pretensions of the ᶜAlids (in 144/762; cf. al-Ṭabarī, iii/1, 211-15). Al-Amīn attempted to copy the example of al-Manṣūr (in regard to ᶜĪsā b. Mūsā), of al-Mahdī (in regard to the same ᶜĪsā b. Mūsā), and of al-Hādī (in regard to his brother al-Ras̲h̲īd), seeking to institute a direct line of succession, at the expense of his brothers (al-Mu᾿tamin and al-Ma᾿mūn). This attempt to modify the pre-established order had its supporters, the *mawālī* of the caliph and the *abnā᾿ al-dawla* of ᶜIrāḳ, whose privileges were threatened by the success of regional autonomism, beginning in the Mag̲h̲rib and extending to greater K̲h̲urāsān, the pillar of the ᶜAbbāsid régime. Under these circumstances, it comes as no surprise to find the eastern provinces supporting the defender of their aspirations. This was the first time that their status was officially defined (by the "Meccan Documents") and that their representative was not only an ᶜAbbāsid prince but also an heir to the caliphate. In other words, if victorious, the K̲h̲urāsānians would win their autonomy and be assured of an influential position in the structure of the state. As for al-Ma᾿mūn, it was his good fortune to reside beyond the jurisdiction of the reigning caliph, thus avoiding the fate undergone by ᶜĪsā b. Mūsā (obliged to abdicate in favour of the sons of al-Mahdī) or that all but suffered by al-Ras̲h̲īd (imprisoned by his brother al-Hādī). His brother al-Mu᾿tamin did not have the same opportunity and his case confirmed *a contrario* the lot of al-Ma᾿mūn.

The conflict began in 194/810, sparked off by the addition of the name of Mūsā, the young son of al-Amīn, to the list of heirs to the caliphate: al-Ma᾿mūn and al-Mu᾿tamin. A delegation was sent to Marw to persuade al-Ma᾿mūn to return to Bag̲h̲dād, where he was to take on the role of adviser of the caliph. Offended by his refusal, al-Amīn attempted to re-assert his authority over the whole of the empire; he demanded the sending of the surplus revenues of certain provinces (Rayy, Ḳūmis and western K̲h̲urāsān, then the nomination of fiscal agents and finally the appointment of a chief of postal services or intelligence officer at Marw, al-Ma᾿mūn's capital. The perspicacity of al-Faḍl b. Sahl, and the determination of the K̲h̲urāsānians to defend the autonomy that they had finally acquired, helped al-Ma᾿mūn to refuse any modification of the letter of "Meccan Documents" and thus to avoid any involvement with the mechanism set in motion by the advisers of al-Amīn with the object of threatening his position. The rift opened wide in 195/811, with the removal of the caliph's name from the coinage and the *ṭirāz* of K̲h̲urāsān. Taking advantage of the strength of his position, al-Amīn resolved to settle the question of relations between the central power and K̲h̲urāsān, while there was still time. He proclaimed his son Mūsā (son of a concubine) first heir (at the expense of al-Ma᾿mūn) and ᶜAbd Allāh (son of another concubine) second heir (at the expense of al-Mu᾿tamin), in flagrant violation of the "Meccan Documents". Al-Ma᾿mūn replied by taking the title of *Imām*, following the example of the *Imām* Ibrāhīm, son of Muḥammad b. ᶜAlī, heir of Abū Hās̲h̲im (son of Muḥammad b. al-Ḥanafiyya). This return to the principles of the first *daᶜwa hās̲h̲imiyya* at Marw was further underlined by appeals sent to the various Arab tribal factions of K̲h̲urāsān, exalting the role of the *nuḳabā᾿*: Abū Dāwūd K̲h̲ālid b. Ibrāhīm al-D̲h̲uhlī al-S̲h̲aybānī (confidential ally of Abū Muslim), Ḳaḥṭaba b. S̲h̲abīb al-Ṭā᾿ī (commander of the revolutionary army), Mūsā b. Kaᶜb al-Tamīmī, Mālik b. al-Hayt̲h̲am al-K̲h̲uzāᶜī, etc. In addition, the authority of the *Imām* is of a more religious nature than that of the *Amīr al-Mu᾿minīn*, this prefiguring the "imperial-papal" policy of al-Ma᾿mūn. Communications between ᶜIrāḳ and K̲h̲urāsān were cut, and the frontiers guarded to prevent the sending of intelligence to Bag̲h̲dād, while al-Ma᾿mūn's intelligence service was in action at the court itself (through the efforts of al-ᶜAbbās, son of the former heir to the caliphate ᶜĪsā b. Mūsā, and other informers recruited by al-Faḍl b. Sahl).

The "Meccan Documents" were undermined and then revoked at the behest of al-Amīn, who finally ordered his brother to recognise his complete authority over K̲h̲urāsān. The rupture became total with the appointment of ᶜAlī b. ᶜĪsā b. Māhān, the deposed former governor of K̲h̲urāsān, as governor of D̲j̲ibāl (the provinces of Ḳumm, Nihāwand, Hamad̲h̲ān, Iṣfahān) with the mission of restoring the caliph's authority over K̲h̲urāsān (D̲j̲umādā II 195/March 811). The caliph's army was composed of the *abnā᾿* "sons" of the K̲h̲urāsānian army garrisoned in ᶜIrāḳ, of whom some were supporters of the conflict with K̲h̲urāsān (notably ᶜAlī b. ᶜĪsā b. Māhān), while others showed themselves loyal, in spite of the reservations of some (in particular K̲h̲uzayma, son of K̲h̲āzim b. K̲h̲uzayma al-Tamīmī, governor of the region bordering on the Byzantine empire, the *ᶜAwāṣim* [*q.v.*] of al-D̲j̲azīra and of northern Syria). Consequently, it is not appropriate to identify the partisans of al-Amīn with Arabs bent on vengeance, since this leads to a flagrant contradiction: after all, the Khurāsānian army (composed of Arabs and of *mawālī*) had destroyed the Ḳaysī army of al-Djazīra to establish equality between Muslims, conquering Arabs or conquered *mawālī*, and to solve the social problems of the empire. The politico-military "establishment" was divided on the question of centralisation as oppossed to the autonomy of provinces, whose supporters were likewise of Arab and non-Arab origin. It is for this reason that a certain number of *abnāʾ al-dawla* are found in the camp of al-Maʾmūn, including Harthama b. Aʿyan, a *mawlā* of the Banū Ḍabba, a native of Balkh; this former supporter of ʿĪsā b. Mūsā (who accepted the idea of a partial autonomy for Khurāsān), having espoused the cause of al-Hādī and become a confidential ally of al-Rashīd, took the part of al-Maʾmūn, who appointed him chief of his bodyguard (although his son Ḥātim was governing Egypt in the name of al-Amīn); Zuhayr, son of al-Musayyib b. Zuhayr al-Ḍabbī (who was a deputy of the *naḳīb*), put himself on the side of al-Maʾmūn (who appointed him governor of Sīstān), as did his brother al-ʿAbbās, retained as chief of police by al-Maʾmūn (although another brother, Muḥammad, was an army officer in Baghdād in the service of al-Amīn); Shabīb, grandson of Ḳaḥṭaba b. Shabīb al-Ṭāʾī, took the part of al-Maʾmūn (who appointed him head of the Ḳūmis), although the rest of his family supported al-Amīn; Muḥammad b. al-Ashʿath al-Khuzāʿī, whose family was resident in a village of Bukhārā, supported al-Maʾmūn, while the grandsons of his namesake (who was a deputy of the *naḳīb*) were in the camp of al-Amīn.

The reserved attitude of ʿAbd Allāh, son of the *naḳīb* al-Haytham al-Khuzāʿī, who refused a post in the administration (the other members of his family were on the side of al-Amīn), as well as Yaḥyā b. Muʿādh b. Muslim, a *mawlā* of the Banū Dhuhl, a veteran of the army of al-Rashīd, opened the way to the promotion of Ṭāhir b. al-Ḥusayn, of Būshandj, descendant of Abū Manṣūr Ṭalḥa b. Ruzayḳ, a *mawlā* of the Khuzāʿa, one of the twelve *nuḳabāʾ* of the *daʿwa hāshimiyya*, in charge of relations with the *Imām* Ibrāhīm. As governor of his native city. Ṭāhir had taken part in the revolt of Rāfiʿ b. al-Layth against the governor ʿAlī b. ʿĪsā b. Māhān, until his deposition at the hands of Harthama b. al-ʿAyan (192/808). Promoted governor of Djibāl, Ṭāhir was sent to Rayy with a small army, to oppose the advance of ʿAlī b. ʿĪsā b. Māhān, commander of the main army of the caliph (40,000 men against 4,000-5,000 under the orders of Ṭāhir).

The composition of al-Maʾmūn's army was Transoxanian, thus extending recruitment to the ʿAbbāsid army to the populations of Soghdia, of Khwārazm and of other principalities of Central Asia. Only the chiefs were dignified with the title of *mawālī* of al-Maʾmūn, in the sense of supporters (singular *muwālī*) of the heir to the caliphate, this permitting them to acquire a majority of key posts in the event of victory. The confrontation with the caliph's army took place near Rayy and, with odds of ten against one, the result of the battle seemed a foregone conclusion. Nevertheless, Ṭāhir b. al-Ḥusayn succeeded in killing ʿAlī b. ʿĪsā b. Māhān (7 Shawwāl 195/3 July 811). This surprise victory earned him the honorific title of *Dhu 'l-Yamīnayn* and restored the situation in favour of al-Maʾmūn, saved by this feat of arms. Ṭāhir occupied Ḳazwīn and marched against Hamadhān, where the remnants of the caliph's army were entrenched. He was obliged to confront an army of reinforcements (20,000 *abnāʾ* based at al-Anbār) commanded by ʿAbd al-Raḥmān b. Djabala, who had borne a grudge against al-Maʾmūn since the latter ordered the sending of the army of al-Rashīd and the treasury to Marw, in 193/809. Once more, Ṭāhir was victorious, and ʿAbd al-Raḥmān was killed (196/812). The whole of the province of Djibāl was now conquered, opening the road to ʿIrāḳ. To block the route of the Khurāsānian army, al-Amīn mobilised two new armies, one of 20,000 *abnāʾ* under the orders of ʿAbd Allāh b. Ḥumayd, grandson of the *naḳīb* and commander of the revolutionary army Ḳaḥṭaba b. Shabīb al-Ṭāʾī [*q.v.*], and the other of 20,000 Arabs commanded by the Ḳaysī Aḥmad b. Mazyad al-Shaybānī, representing the Rabīʿa of al-Djazīra. Once more, Ṭāhir skilfully succeeded in playing these two sections of the army against each other by exploiting their rivalries (Ḳaysīs cheated of their rights by the Khurāsānians for 60 years!). These repeated reverses suffered by the *abnāʾ* of ʿIrāḳ and the impracticability of mobilising the Arabs of al-Djazīra forced al-Amīn to attempt to raise levies in Syria, in spite of the recent revolt of the Sufyānid against him (195/811). ʿAbd al-Malik b. Ṣāliḥ was reinstated as governor of the *ʿAwāṣim* of al-Djazīra and Syria, and Ḥusayn son of ʿAlī b. ʿĪsā b. Māhān, his lieutenant, was sent on a recruiting mission to Syria. However, the divisions between Ḳaysīs and Kalbīs (Yemenis) did not constitute a propitious climate, all the more so in that the Arabs of Syria had learned lessons from their participation in the struggle for the caliphate, and the support given to the ʿAbbāsid ʿAbd Allāh b. ʿAlī against the caliph al-Manṣūr (136/754). Finding his task impossible, al-Ḥusayn organised a *coup d'état* at Baghdād; in Radjab 196/March 812, he ordered the arrest of al-Amīn and proclaimed his brother al-Maʾmūn caliph. Nothing better illustrates the divisions of the *abnāʾ* than the counter-coup which restored the caliphate of al-Amīn, while al-Ḥusayn was sent away to fight the army of Ṭāhir, but was killed in retribution. Henceforward, the *ḥādjib*-vizier al-Faḍl al-Rabīʿ, one of the leading instigators of the conflict with al-Maʾmūn, sensing the cause of al-Amīn to be finally lost, decided to make provision for the future by leaving the political scene and plunging into obscurity. He was replaced by the *kātib al-sirr* of al-Amīn, Ismāʿīl b. Ṣubayḥ al-Ḥarrānī, who had little to say regarding the opening of further hostilities with al-Maʾmūn.

On the same date, al-Maʾmūn was officially proclaimed caliph at Marw, while al-Faḍl b. Sahl was endowed with the title of *Dhu 'l-Riʾāsatayn* (a dual civil and military command), and Ṭāhir b. al-Ḥusayn received orders to march on Khuzistān, which was defended by a Muhallabid, Muḥammad b. Yazīd b. Ḥātim, resident at Ahwāz. Ṭāhir won the battle, and this forced the Muhallabid of Baṣra, Ibn Abī ʿUyayna, to assure the position of his family by rallying to the new caliph al-Maʾmūn. In return, he was appointed governor of Eastern Arabia (Baḥrayn, Yamāma and ʿUmān), while an ʿAbbāsid prince, Ismāʿīl b. Djaʿfar, was charged with the government of Baṣra. Ṭāhir's troops marched on Kūfa, where they encountered some resistance; then they set out towards al-Madāʾin, which they occupied, and finally arrived at a point west of Baghdād. A second Khurāsānian army, commanded by Harthama b. al-Aʿyan, one of the leading military chiefs under al-Rashīd, was sent by al-Maʾmūn to invest the capital from the east (Dhu 'l-Ḥidjdja 196/August 812). The siege of Baghdād lasted thirteen months, prolonged by the popular resistance of the *ʿayyārūn* [*q.v.*], people of humble origin, who exploited the situation to their advantage. This urban guerilla warfare checked the advance of the regular army of Ṭāhir b. al-Ḥusayn, who began a destructive bombardment of the "City of Peace". The provinces situated to the west of ʿIrāḳ recognised the authority of al-Maʾmūn in 197/813: the Ḥidjāz (where the pilgrimage was under the supervision of al-ʿAbbās, son of Mūsā b. ʿĪsā, an early ally of al-Maʾmūn); Egypt, where the *abnāʾ* were divided between partisans of *al-Makhlūʿ* (al-Amīn) and those allied to al-Maʾmūn, supported by the Yemeni Arabs (against the Ḳaysīs); Ifrīḳiya, autonomous under the Aghlabids, recognised the established power; northern Syria and al-Djazīra, which had lost their governor ʿAbd al-Malik b. Ṣāliḥ (d. 196/812), took advantage of the situation to establish their autonomy, an example followed by Ādharbāydjān and Armenia.

As for al-Amīn, after squandering the resources of the public treasury (several hundreds of millions of *dirhams*), he lost his supporters, who negotiated with Ṭāhir b. al-Ḥusayn in order to safeguard their interests. Finally, he was obliged to seek the protection of Harthama b. al-Aʿyan. But Ṭāhir captured him and ordered his execution on the night of 24-5 Muḥarram 198/24-5 September 813; this was the first time that an ʿAbbāsid caliph was thus humiliated and put to death by rebel soldiers, whose conduct contrasted with the more respectful and conciliatory attitude of the veteran Harthama b. al-Aʿyan.

The government of ʿIrāḳ was entrusted to al-Ḥasan, brother of al-Faḍl b. Sahl, while Ṭāhir b. al-Ḥusayn was charged with securing the front in the war against Byzantium, starting with al-Djazīra, where Naṣr b. Shabath al-Laythī, grandson of one of the leading Kayṣī chiefs, had made his base at Kaysūm (in Diyār Muḍar). The conqueror of al-Amīn underestimated this adversary (whose resistance lasted until 210/825), while in Ādharbāydjān Arab chieftains took control of the towns in which they were established (their autonomy lasted until 206/821). In order to subjugate Baghdād, al-Ḥasan b. Sahl did not spare the conquered *abnāʾ*, and this had the effect of re-kindling their resistance under the leadership of the family of the Banū Khālid, *mawālī* of the Banū ʿĀmir b. Luʾayy, originally from Marw al-Rūdh, who took over the role of the family of ʿAlī b. ʿĪsā b. Māhān (it may be noted that Aḥmad b. Abī Khālid allied himself with al-Maʾmūn and held high office in the administration of Marw). This unrest, encouraged by the demobilisation of the *abnāʾ* and fiscal problems in Baghdād, was exploited by the ʿAlids, of Zaydī tendency, who sought to seize power at the very heart of the empire: on 10 Djumādā 199/26 January 815, Muḥammad b. Ibrāhīm Ṭabāṭabā [*q.v.*], a descendent of al-Ḥasan b. ʿAlī and of Fāṭima, was proclaimed *al-Riḍā min āl Muḥammad* (in accordance with the *daʿwa hāshimiyya*) at Kūfa. He was supported by Abu 'l-Sarāyā al-Sirrī b. Manṣūr al-Shaybānī, who had left the army of Harthama b. al-Aʿyan; the troops of al-Ḥasan b. Sahl, sent to suppress this revolt, were repulsed, but Ibn Ṭabāṭabā died of his wounds (February 815). A new Ḥusaynid *Imām* was proclaimed in the person of Muḥammad b. Muḥammad b. Zayd. The movement sought to spread throughout ʿIrāḳ: at Baṣra, the Ḥusaynid Zayd, son of Mūsā al-Kāẓim, set upon the ʿAbbāsids of this metropolis to avenge the execution of his father (in 183/799) on the orders of al-Rashīd, as did the victims of the revolt of 145/762-63 which had been organised by Ibrāhīm b. ʿAbd Allāh, brother of Muḥammad al-Nafs al-Zakiyya [*q.vv.*], against al-Manṣūr. The same occurred at Kūfa, where the property of ʿAbbāsids was attacked. Emboldened by these successes, the Shīʿīs marched on Baghdād, forcing al-Ḥasan b. Sahl to appeal for help to the veteran Harthama b. Aʿyan, who put an end to the revolt of his former lieutenant Abu 'l-Sarāyā (executed in Rabīʿ I 200/October 815 [*q.v.*]). Kūfa was recaptured, as was Baṣra (where Zayd al-Nār "the Firebrand" was arrested and sent to Marw). Other Shīʿī centres were established in the Ḥidjāz and the Yemen: at Mecca, the envoy of Abu 'l-Sarāyā succeeded in organising the proclamation of Muḥammad al-Dībādj, grandson of the *Imām* Djaʿfar al-Ṣādiḳ, in Rabīʿ I 200/ November 815. The suppression of the uprising was entrusted to Ḥamdawayh, son of ʿAlī b. ʿĪsā b. Māhān, leading a force of those *abnāʾ* who had supported al-Maʾmūn in the civil war. Mecca was recaptured and Muḥammad al-Dībādj was spared (he eventually went into exile in Djurdjān). There was still the Yemen, where Ibrāhim, son of Mūsā al-Kāẓim succeeded in taking power in a bloodthirsty fashion (which earned him the epithet of al-Djazzār "the Butcher"), from Ṣafar 200/September 815. Ḥamdawayh succeeded in suppressing this movement (then attempted, in his turn, to make himself independent!).

These outbursts of hatred on the part of the ʿAlids for the ʿAbbāsids, who were accused of violating the "rights" of the descendents of ʿAlī and Fāṭima, drove al-Maʾmūn to effect a spectacular reconciliation between the two branches of the Family of the Prophet, ʿAlids and ʿAbbāsids, by means of a return to the principles of the first *daʿwa hāshimiyya,* which did not in any way prohibit the choice of an ʿAlid *Imām,* in accordance with the interpretation of the first vizier Abū Salama al-Khallāl [*q.v.*] (who, on the death in 132/749 of the ʿAbbāsid *Imām* Ibrāhīm had offered the caliphate to the Ḥusaynid Djaʿfar al-Ṣādiḳ, then to the Ḥasanid ʿAbd Allāh b. al-Ḥasan, as well as to ʿUmar b. ʿAlī b. al-Ḥasan). In addition, not only did he spare the ʿAlids who had recently been proclaimed anti-ʿAbbāsid caliphs, but most significant of all, he went further than his grandfather al-Mahdī in choosing as his successor another son of the martyr Mūsā al-Kāẓim, ʿAlī, brother of Zayd the rebel in Baṣra and of Ibrāhīm the rebel in the Yemen, who was given the title of *al-Riḍā min āl Muḥammad.* This initiative by al-Maʾmūn ran counter to the policy pursued for a century, and in particular, since the support given by the Khurāsāniyya to the ʿAbbāsid branch, with the proclamation of al-Saffāḥ, brother of the *Imām* Ibrāhīm, in preference to the ʿAlid candidates. The Sahlids, who controlled the machinery of state, were forced to identify with this etymologically revolutionary policy in order to avoid suffering disgrace analogous to that of the Barmakids (when they did not share the anti-ʿAlid policy of al-Rashīd). Nevertheless, the relative strengths of ʿIrāḳ and of Khurāsān did not permit the realisation of this attempt to broaden the social base of al-Maʾmūn's régime. In fact, the threat of an inversion of roles at the expense of ʿIrāḳ led its aristocracy, far from enfeebled by the war between partisans of al-Amīn and of al-Maʾmūn, to resist the Sahlids whose policy in ʿIrāḳ was judged dangerous for the caliphate itself by such veterans as Harthama b. Aʿyan. The latter did not hesitate to present himself in person at Marw, to inform al-Maʾmūn of the reality of the situation in ʿIrāḳ, instead of taking up his post as governor of Syria and the Ḥidjāz, to which he had been appointed on the eve of the revolt of Kūfa. Taking advantage of his influence over the caliph, al-Faḍl b. Sahl succeeded in turning al-

Maʾmūn against him and ultimately he had him executed in Dhu 'l-Ḳaʿda 200/June 816. In consequence, Ḥātim, son of Harthama b. al-Aʿyan and governor of Armenia, raised a revolt. Allying himself with other local chieftains of Ādharbāydjān, Bābak al-Khurramī [*q.v.*] went into action in 201/816 at Badhdh [*q.v.* in Suppl.] in the mountainous region to the south of the Araxes.

The struggle for power in Baghdād and the attempt to impose ʿAlī al-Riḍā as successor to al-Maʾmūn granted a respite to the autonomists of Ādharbāydjān, of Armenia, of the *ʿAwāṣim* of northern al-Djazīra and Syria, of Syria and of Egypt. In fact, the resistance of the *abnāʾ* forced al-Ḥasan b. Sahl to abandon the capital. A triple power was established there with the appointment of al-Manṣūr b. al-Mahdī, son of a Persian concubine, as delegate of al-Maʾmūn, from 25 Djumādā II 201/18 January 817 onwards. In addition, the urban lower classes supported the movement of Sahl b. Salāma al-Anṣārī, a native of Khurāsān, in the quarter of al-Ḥarbiyya; "[the command] *al-amr bi 'l-maʿrūf wa 'l-nahy ʿan al-munkar* became identified more or less with political independence and with the self-government of small social groups" (J. van Ess, *Une lecture à rebours de l'histoire du muʿtazilisme,* in *REI,* xlvii/1 [1979], 68 = Extrait hors série 14, Paris 1984, 127), while Abu 'l-Hudhayl and al-Naẓẓām, who had introduced Muʿtazilism to the court of al-Maʾmūn, worked, on the contrary, for a policy of reconciliation with the ʿAbbāsid power. In other words, the process of recovery of the second half of the reign of al-Maʾmūn, was beginning to evolve. In the meantime, on 2 Ramaḍān 201/24 March 817, al-Maʾmūn proclaimed ʿAlī b. Mūsā al-Kāẓim as his successor (at the expense of al-Muʾtamin, his brother), with the title of *al-Riḍā min āl Muḥammad,* and abandoned the black colour of the ʿAbbāsids in favour of the green colour (the *Katība al-khaḍrāʾ* of the Prophet). Henceforward, the choice of caliph-*Imām* was to be made from among the descendents of Hāshim, common ancestor of Muḥammad and of his uncles al-ʿAbbās and Abū Ṭālib the father of ʿAlī (a census taken in 201/816 counted 30,000 Hāshimites, who had their own *naḳīb*). When the news reached ʿIrāḳ four months later, the ʿAbbāsids and their supporters reacted against this assault on their "acquired rights": the ʿAbbāsid governor of Baṣra Ismāʿīl b. Djaʿfar b. Sulaymān b. ʿAlī refused to wear green, while in Baghdād, the sons of al-Mahdī led the opposition. When al-Manṣūr (whose mother was al-Buḥturiyya, daughter of the Dābūyid *ispahbadh* of Ṭabaristān, Khurshīd) refused to be proclaimed caliph, his half-brother Ibrāhīm b. al-Mahdī (whose mother was Shakla, daughter of the Maṣmughān of Damāwand, deposed at the time of the conquest of this district) accepted the title (28 Dhu 'l-Ḥidjdja 201/17 July 817) and chose his nephew Isḥāk b. Mūsā al-Hādī, brother-in-law of al-Maʾmūn, as heir to the throne. He was supported by the ʿAbbāsid princes, notably Ibrāhīm b. Muḥammad b. ʿAbd al-Wahhāb b. Ibrāhīm al-Imām (known as Ibn ʿĀʾisha), Abū Isḥāḳ the future al-Muʿtaṣim, the *mawālī* of the preceding caliph al-Amīn, al-Faḍl b. al-Rabīʿ (who returned to his post of *ḥādjib* at the court), al-Sindī b. Shāhak, reappointed chief of the police, and the *abnāʾ*, comprising the sons of both ʿAlī b. ʿĪsā b. Māhān and of Abū Khālid, and even of former partisans of al-Maʾmūn, including al-Muṭṭalib b. ʿAbd Allāh, grandson of the *naḳīb* Mālik b. al-Haytham al-Khuzāʿī, or Nuʿaym b. Khāzim b. Khuzayma al-Tamīmī (who joined his brother Khuzayma, who had remained loyal to al-Amīn). In other words, this was the revival of the war between the two camps, dormant since 198/813. The fact that al-Amīn was the son of an Arab wife, and Ibrāhīm b. al-Mahdī that of a Persian concubine, like al-Maʾmūn, did not affect the way that the conflict was waged, in terms of the relations between ʿIrāḳ, (capital Baghdād) and Khurāsān (capital Marw).

The new caliph Ibrāhīm b. al-Mahdī succeeded in extending his authority over the capital by putting and end to the activities of Sahl b. Salāma al-Anṣārī in the quarter of al-Ḥarbiyya. Then he sought to take control of Kūfa, from which the ʿAlid governor al-ʿAbbās, brother of ʿAlī al-Riḍā, was expelled (Djumādā I 202/November 817). But Wāsiṭ served as a headquarters for al-Ḥasan b. Sahl, who regained control of Baṣra. The governor of Egypt, ʿAbd al-ʿAzīz b. ʿAbd al-Raḥmān al-Azdī, rallied to Ibrāhīm b. al-Mahdī, while the autonomous *amīr* of Ifrīḳiya remained neutral as before. The gravity of the situation was hidden from al-Maʾmūn by al-Faḍl b. Sahl, until ʿAli al-Riḍā disclosed to him that Ibrāhīm b. al-Mahdī had been proclaimed caliph, rather than *amīr*, in Baghdād. Henceforward, at the age of thirty-one years, al-Maʾmūn decided to take personal control of affairs; he recognised that a military solution was not appropriate and that only agreement between the social elements of the empire was capable of saving the régime, by enlarging its social base as a means of gaining control of the different provinces. A first concession to the aristocracy of ʿIrāḳ was effected by the announcement of his return to Baghdād, whose rôle as capital of the empire was thus assured; on 10 Radjab 202/22 January 818 al-Maʾmūn left Marw with the court, the administration and the army, leaving Ghassān b. ʿAbbād, a cousin of the Sahlids, as governor of Khurāsān at Marw. At Sarakhs, al-Faḍl b. Sahl, who had attempted to usurp the authority of the caliph, suffered the same fate as the Barmakids; he was assassinated at the instigation of al-Maʾmūn (2 Shaʿbān 202/13 February 818), but unlike the Barmakids, the other Sahlids were spared; besides controlling Khurāsān and southern ʿIrāḳ, they held influential posts in the central administration, with the promotion of al-Ḥasan b. Sahl to the post of vizier-*amīr* which had been held by his brother al-Faḍl. A matrimonial alliance was concluded to consolidate this situation, with the betrothal of al-Maʾmūn to Būrān, daughter of al-Ḥasan b. Sahl (the marriage was to be celebrated in Ramaḍān 210/December 825). Two months later, al-Maʾmūn left Sarakhs for Ṭūs, making no attempt to hasten the issue. As for Ibrāhīm b. al-Mahdī, he was hampered by lack of financial resources and was obliged to combat opposition movements: on the part of Asad, who raised a revolt in the quarter of al-Ḥarbiyya (suppressed by ʿĪsā b. Muḥammad b. Abī Khālid); on the part of Mahdī b. ʿAlwān al-Shārī (al-Ḥarūrī) in the region between Baghdād and Madāʾin (the headquarters of Ibrāhīm b. al-Mahdī), who was defeated by Abū Isḥāḳ (al-Muʿtaṣim); and on the part of certain *abnāʾ* who sought to come to terms with the generals of al-Ḥasan b. Sahl. Alerted to this conspiracy, in which al-Manṣūr b. al-Mahdī was implicated, Ibrāhīm b. al-Mahdī returned to Baghdād (14 Ṣafar 203/21 August 818) and had his half-brother arrested, as well as Khuzayma b. Khāzim al-Tamīmī, although al-Muṭṭalib b. ʿAbd Allāh al-Khuzāʿī succeeded in escaping. It was then that the army of al-Ḥasan b. Sahl captured al-Madāʾin and the Nahr Diyālā. Meanwhile, in Khurāsān, ʿAlī al-Riḍā met his death in the village of Sānabād, near Ṭūs, on 29 Ṣafar 203/5 September 818, and the Shīʿīs were convinced that al-Maʾmūn had had him poisoned (whence the name of *Mashhad* [*q.v.*], given to this place). Not only was a heavy taxation levied, but in Bāghdād, certain *abnāʾ* conspired against Ibrāhīm b. al-Mahdī; ʿĪsā b. Abī Khālid was supposed to capture him and hand him over on Friday 29 Shawwāl 203/29 April 819, but his plan was revealed and he was imprisoned. To free him, the family of the Banū Khālid entered into conflict with Ibrāhīm b. al-Mahdī and rallied to the cause of al-Maʾmūn (Dhu 'l-Ḳaʿda 203/May 819), who was in Djurdjān at this date (in other words, it had taken him sixteen months, since leaving Marw, to cover the twenty journey-stages which separated this town from Djurdjān). Feeling the cause lost, once more, the *ḥādjib* al-Faḍl b. al-Rabīʿ deserted his caliph and his post and plunged again into obscurity. As for Ibrāhīm b. al-Mahdī, he was reduced to using his rival Sahl b. Salāma al-Anṣār in an attempt to mobilise the lower classes of Baghdād. After two years as caliph, Ibrāhīm decided to leave the political scene, at the same time escaping from a conspiracy of some of his military chiefs who had plotted to hand him over to al-Ḥasan b. Sahl (16 Muḥarram 204/13 July 819). The authority of al-Maʾmūn was restored in Baghdād, while al-Ḥasan b. Sahl withdrew from political life (on account of his ill-health). In other words, the way was clear when al-Maʾmūn arrived at Ḥulwān, which separates ʿIrāḳ from the Iranian plateau. Ṭāhir b. al-Ḥusayn, who had withdrawn to Raḳḳa, received orders to return to Baghdād, where al-Maʾmūn made a triumphal entry on 17 Ṣafar 204/August 819 (after ten years of absence). One month later, he re-adopted the colour black, but retained the title of *Imām* (which all his successors were to bear) with the object of consolidating his role as guide of the *umma*, following the example of the ʿAlid *Imāms*.

Henceforward, the attempt to control the empire and to guide the *umma* was the personal responsibility of al-Maʾmūn, advised by the Muʿtazilīs and the *ḳāḍī* Aḥmad b. Abī Duʾād [*q.v.*]. To apply the new policies of the *Imām*, the *kuttāb* of the previous administration were first disbanded but then reinstated as advisers on the administrative staff which was recalled from Khurāsān. Aḥmad b. Abī Khālid, kinsman of the *abnāʾ* of ʿIrāḳ, was the personal secretary of al-Maʾmūn, and acted as principal adviser and as agent for rallying the *abnāʾ* of Baghdād (until his death in 211/826). The chiefs of the *dīwāns*, most of whom were former protégés of the Barmakids, were controlled directly by the caliph, who took personal charge of recourse to the *maẓālim*. For the maintenance of order, supervision of the police was entrusted to Ṭāhir b. al-Ḥusayn, while yesterday's adversaries were pardoned in the interests of communal reconciliation: thus al-Faḍl b. al-Rabīʿ and then Ibrāhīm b. al-Mahdī (in 210/825) benefited from the *ḥilm* of al-Maʾmūn (who executed only the recalcitrant Ibrāhīm Ibn ʿĀʾisha, descendent of the *Imām* Ibrāhīm, in 210/825). The central army combined numerous bodies of troops, and privileged status reverted to the supporters of al-Maʾmūn, of Transoxanian and Khurāsānian origin, at the expense of the *abnāʾ* who had been defeated on two occasions, in 198/813 and then in 204/819. Since the empire was only now emerging from a civil war that had lasted ten years, al-Maʾmūn confined himself to supporting the revolt of Thomas the Slav in Asia Minor (820-3), while awaiting the opportunity to renew the campaign against the Byzantine empire (which he did from 215/830 onwards). As for the government of the provinces, he entrusted the holy cities of the Ḥidjāz to an ʿAlid, while al-Djazīra, troubled by the revolt of Naṣr b. Shabath at Kaysūm, received as its ruler the veteran Yaḥyā b. Muʿādh b. Muslim, who was also required to act with restraint.

In 205/820, a number of troublesome incidents occurred in the marshlands of lower ʿIrāḳ, where the Zuṭṭ [*q.v.*] controlled the routes of communication (until 219/834), but also and especially in Khurāsān. It was in response to these problems that there was established a dynasty of Ṭāhirid governors, in accordance with the conditions granted to al-Maʾmūn by the "Meccan Documents" (in 186/802), this representing a durable compromise solution. This was the first time that the ʿAbbāsids made use of governors to rule the eastern half of the empire and to support the policies of the caliphate (similar methods had been practised under Muʿāwiya with Ziyād b. Abīhi, and under ʿAbd al-Malik b. Marwān with al-Ḥadjdjādj b. Yūsuf al-Thaḳafī). In fact, Ṭāhir b. al-Ḥusayn ruled greater Khurāsān, while his cousin Isḥāḳ b. Ibrāhīm b. Muṣʿab deputised for him as commander of the police in Baghdād, and his son ʿAbd Allāh b. Ṭāhir was responsible for extending the caliph's authority over the autonomous provinces by means of the central army, which was recruited principally from the eastern provinces.

In other words, the autonomy of the Ṭāhirids was of a different nature from that of the Aghlabids in Ifrīḳiya, and, contrary to the views of some "Jacobin" historians, the power of the state was not conceived in terms of centralisation, representing a very high cost and uncertain results, but in the co-operation of different provinces which, in exchange for a degree of autonomy, were prepared to mobilise and to employ the energies and creative abilities of their inhabitants in the service of the *umma*. It was by this means that the integration of the former Sāsānid empire was achieved, assisting al-Maʾmūn in his task of restoring the unity of the empire on new cultural bases. In fact, Muʿtazilism seemed to represent a compromise solution which would conciliate the ʿAlids and would adapt Islam to the economic and social evolution of the empire, seeing that the rural communities were unfairly oppressed by the scale of land-taxes levied by the aristocracy of the towns, while the urban proletariat, by frugal living, managed after a fashion to support a non-Ḳurʾānic burden of taxation (whence its support for Ḥanbalism, favouring a strict adherence to the Ḳurʾān and to the *Sunna* of Muḥammad and his Companions). The political implications of Muʿtazilism, elaborated by the *mawālī* of Kūfa (including Bishr b. al-Muʿtamir) and of Baṣra (including Abu 'l-Hudhayl al-ʿAllāf and his nephew al-Naẓẓām), explain the interest of al-Maʾmūn in this school of *kalām*, which supplemented the Arabic literary tradition by recourse to Greek philosophy as a means of arguing in favour of the oneness of God (whose shadow on the earth is the *Imām*). In other words, the "son of the Persian" al-Maʾmūn, far from hallowing the influence of the Sanskrit and Pahlavi cultural and scientific heritage, was the promoter of the cultural watershed of the 3rd/9th century, encouraging the translation into Arabic from Greek (and from Syriac) of the philosophy, astronomy, mathematics and medicine of the Hellenistic period (cf. R. Walzer, *Greek into Arabic*, 1962; G. E. von Grünebaum, *Islam and medieval Hellenism*, London). The foundation of the *Bayt al-Ḥikma* [*q.v.*] in Baghdād (217/832) confirmed his interest in the development of a new culture, Arabic in expression and Islamic in inspiration, integrating the contributions of the various peoples of the Orient, including the neighbours of the ʿAbbāsid empire, whether they were commercial partners (India) or political enemies (Byzantium). Scholars of all persuasions (Muslims, Christians, Jews, Zoroastrians and Ṣābians) and from different provinces of the empire (Khʷārazm, Farghāna, Khurāsān, Ṭabaristān, al-Djazīra and ʿIrāḳ) contributed to the advancement of Arab science, heir to the sciences of antiquity, adopted and adapted according to the requirements of Arab-Islamic civilisation.

These borrowings from various foreign cultures were not to the taste of the traditionists (*muḥaddithūn*) who adhered to the Ḳurʾān and the *Sunna* as sources of the law. While certain *fuḳahāʾ* were supporters of *raʾy* in questions of jurisprudence (particularly the Ḥanafīs of ʿIrāḳ), the majority tended to distrust divergences of opinion and, to maintain the purity of religion, re-affirmed the authority of the Ḳurʾān completed by the *Sunna* (at that time being edited in textual form, a process begun by Mālik. b. Anas). Al-Maʾmūn applied himself to encouraging politico-religious controversies, on the one hand between representatives of different religions (cf. G. Tartar, *Dialogue islamo-chrétien sous le calife al-Maʾmūn. Les épitres d'al-Hāshimī et d'al-Kindi*, doctoral thesis, Univ. of Strasbourg, ii, 1977, repr. in the Bulletin *Evangile-Islam*, special issue, October 1982; *Gudjastak Abalish*, ed. and tr. A. Barthélemy, Paris 1887; the subject is a polemic between a Zoroastrian converted to Islam and the leader of the Mazdaeans of Fārs); on the other hand, and most of all, between *ʿulamāʾ* of the different tendencies with regard to the interpretations of Islam. Aware of the gulf between Muʿtazilī concepts (hitherto classed as *zandaḳa*) and those of the *fuḳahāʾ* and *muḥaddithūn*, opposed to the notion of the created Ḳurʾān, al-Maʾmūn was at pains, over the years, to promote the Muʿtazilī point of view, of which the political implications were obvious: the *Imām*, seeking to correct the inequitable effects of the established order (particularly in terms of the taxation levied on citizens) borrowed from the Muʿtazilīs that which he judged necessary for his purpose, this being the dogma of the created Ḳurʾān (only God is uncreated and eternal), which he was able to use in rectifying the order himself, by means of his knowledge (*ʿilm*). This perspicacity brought him close to the example of ʿAlī, the first of the Companions of Muḥammad to have understood that a practical interpretation of Islam was necessary after the upheavals set in motion by the success and the extent of the Arab conquests (634-44). Furthermore, with the object of wooing the support of the Shīʿīs, ʿAlī was proclaimed "the best of the Companions after the Prophet" (in 211/826, re-affirmed in 212/827).

Scientific work, especially in the realms of astronomy and of mathematics, as well as cartography, conducted alongside the theological discussions of the decade beginning in 820, coincided with the restoration of the authority of the caliphate over the autonomous provinces with the regions situated to the north of ʿIrāḳ. Through the efforts of ʿAbd Allāh b. Ṭāhir, the revolt in al-Djazīra of Naṣr b. Shabath was suppressed (surrender in 210/825), while in Ādharbāydjān, ʿĪsā b. Abī Khālid put an end to the autonomy of the chieftains in the principal cities, but failed to subdue the mountainous region held by Bābak, who controlled the principalities of Siounik and Baylaḳān, situated in Arrān (on the other side of the Araxes). The various expeditions entrusted to Ṣadaka b. ʿAlī al-Azdī (in 209/824), then to Muḥammad b. Ḥumayd al-Ṭāʾī or al-Ṭūsī (212-14/827-9) were unable to stamp out a mountain guerilla force, strongly based and particularly effective against a regular army. These repeated failures cost the caliphate very dear, but did not impede the extension of the caliph's control over other mountainous regions; in 207/822, after arranging the succession of Ṭāhir b. al-Ḥusayn at Marw, Aḥmad b. Abī Khālid succeeded in integrating the principality of Ushrūsana into the empire, through the help of Ḥaydar b. Ḳāwūs, son of al-Afshīn [*q.v.*], who had taken refuge with al-Maʾmūn. Another local prince, Māzyār b. Ḳārin, driven out of his mountainous principality in the Elburz, was employed by al-Maʾmūn as co-governor of Ṭabaristān, of Rūyān and of Dunbāwand which were under the control of the Ṭāhirids (cf. M. Rekaya, *Māzyār*, in *Studia Iranica*, ii/2 [1973], 143-92, and ḲĀRINIDS). All these local princes who rallied to al-Maʾmūn were converted to Islam and were honoured with the title of *mawālī Amīr al-Muʾminīn* as a reward for their support of his policies. As for the Yemen, it was the base for the outbreak of a new ʿAlid revolt, fomented in 207/822 by ʿAbd al-Raḥmān b. Aḥmad, but al-Maʾmūn succeeded in obtaining his surrender, thus salvaging the desired reconciliation. However, the revolt of the citizens of Ḳumm, discontented by the refusal to reduce the *kharādj*, had to be suppressed (in 210/825, again in 216/831).

Once the pacification of the empire had been almost achieved, with the return of Egypt under the control of the caliphate (in 210-11/825-6), and the confirmation of the autonomous status of Aghlabid Ifrīḳiya, al-Maʾmūn felt sufficiently strong to proclaim Muʿtazilism as the official doctrine (in 212/827). He thus announced an "imperial-papal" policy, the application of which had been deferred until the consolidation of the new régime. In fact, the *Imām* undertook to reorganise the central army in order to provide himself with a powerful and effective striking force which would serve under his guidance. In 213/828 he took control of the armed forces, and divided them into three main army groups (each comprising a company of *abnāʾ*, troops of the *ʿAwāṣim* and recruits drawn from the eastern provinces): the first under the command of Isḥāḳ b. Ibrāhīm (charged with the maintenance of order in ʿIrāḳ and in Djibāl and Fārs, adjoining greater Khurāsān, which was entrusted to Ṭalḥa b. Ṭāhir); the second under the orders of al-ʿAbbās b. al-Maʾmūn (responsible for the war-front in the struggle against the Byzantine empire in al-Djazīra and northern Syria); and the third entrusted to Abū Isḥāḳ Muḥammad (al-Muʿtaṣim, successor to al-Maʾmūn) and charged with the government of Egypt, where the situation was explosive. In fact, from 214/829, the Muslims and the Copts fomented a revolt against the system of taxation and inflicted a defeat upon the forces of al-Muʿtaṣim. In northern Ādharbāydjān, Bābak al-Khurramī succeeded in killing Muḥammad b. Ḥumayd al-Ṭūsī (214/829) and repelling his army, forcing al-Maʾmūn to charge ʿAbd Allāh b. Ṭāhir, veteran of the pacification of al-Djazīra and then of Egypt, with the suppression of this movement. However, before being able to intervene against Bābak, ʿAbd Allāh b. Ṭāhir was transferred to Khurāsān on the death of his brother Ṭalḥa (214/829), this coinciding with the end of the revolt of the Khāridjī Ḥamza b. Ādarak (which had lasted for a third of a century in Sīstān-Kirmān). The task of pacifying Djibāl, Ādharbāydjān and Armenia was then entrusted to ʿAlī b. Hishām, one of al-Maʾmūn's leading generals, who did not however succeed in changing the territorial *status quo*.

This policy of restoring the unity of the empire preceded the resumption of war against Byzantium, already under way with the settlement of Andalusians in Crete (from 210/826) and the conquest of Sicily by the Aghlabids of Ifrīkiya (a campaign launched in 211/827). In addition, deserters from the Byzantine empire were gathered together and posted in frontier sites (cf. P. Lemerle, *L'histoire des Pauliciens d'Asie mineure d'après les sources greques*, in *Travaux et Mémoires du Centre de recherches d'histoire et civilisation de Byzance*, v [1973]; H. Gregoire, *Manuel et Théophobe*, in *Byzantion*, ix [1934]; M. Rekaya, *Mise au point sur Théophobe et l'alliance de Bâbek avec Theophile*, in *ibid.*, xliv [1974]).

The first campaign began in 215/830 under the personal command of al-Ma'mūn, who thus intended to prove himself worthy of his title of *Imām*, according to the Zaydī definition which then obtained, meaning a guide endowed with great knowledge (*ʿilm*) and with tried and tested political and military courage. On the way, al-Ma'mūn made the discovery of the Sabaeans of Ḥarrān, some of whom were obliged to convert to a Religion of the Book, while a *fatwā* proclaimed a formal accord between Islam and this religious community (then assimilated to the Ṣābi'ūn of the Ḳur'ān, II, 59/62, V, 73/69, XXII, 17), which produced many scholars and translators of the Greek heritage into Arabic. The outcome of this campaign was the capture of a number of fortresses in Cappadocia (in Arabic: al-Maṭāmīr [see MAṬMŪRA]. In response, the Byzantine emperor Theophilus attacked the fortresses of al-Maṣṣīṣa and Tarsus, provoking the second campaign of al-Ma'mūn (216/831) in which he was accompanied by his son al-ʿAbbās (the conqueror of Theophilus) and by his brother and successor Abū Isḥāḳ (al-Muʿtaṣim). After a series of victories in Asia Minor, al-Ma'mūn rejected the proposal for an exchange of prisoners and a five-year truce. The caliph withdrew to Damascus and from here he was obliged to make his way in person to Egypt to put an end to the revolt of the Copts and the Muslims against the burden of taxation. After the subjugation of the rebels, al-Ma'mūn undertook a fiscal reform; the system of *ḳabāla* replaced the former method of collection, and the state showed itself willing, in case of need, to take account of difficult circumstances. In addition, relations with the Nubians were improved, enabling the Muslims to exert better control of the lands of the Nile.

With the pacification of Egypt achieved, al-Ma'mūn returned to the Byzantine front in 217/832, with the object of gaining control over the ports of Cilicia beyond the Taurus. The siege of the fortress of Lu'lu'a (which controlled access to Tyana) ended with its capitulation, and once more the emperor Theophilus called unsuccessfully for a truce and an exchange of prisoners.

In spite of his preoccupation with the Byzantine war-front, and the political difficulties aroused by the persistent rebellions of the Zuṭṭ (of lower ʿIrāḳ), of Bābak al-Khurramī in the north of Ādharbāydjān, complicated by the sedition of ʿAlī b. Hishām, governor of Djibāl, of Ādharbāydjān and of Armenia (executed in Djumādā I 217/June 832), al-Ma'mūn did not neglect cultural matters (foundation of the *Bayt al-Ḥikma* in 217/832) and did not lose sight of his objective of having his "imperial-papal" policy recognised by the Sunnī *ʿulamā'*. While preparing for the major campaign of 218/833 (of which the objective was Amorium, the natal city of the current Byzantine dynasty and thus the heart of Byzantium itself), al-Ma'mūn engaged in a trial of strength with the *ʿulamā'* in the Islamic sciences, instituting the *miḥna* [*q.v.*] (Rabīʿ I 218/April 833), four months before his death. Henceforward, Muʿtazilism was to be adopted by all the *ʿulamā'*, whether in the service of the state or independent of the ʿAbbāsid power. A struggle for influence over the *ʿāmma* took place between the *Imām* al-Ma'mūn who claimed for himself the right to interpret the law (and to change the established rules in the name of social justice), and the *ʿulamā'* and *fuḳahā'*, traditionalists who refuted this pretension on the part of the caliphate (and believed that the changes would be, in fact, carried out in the interest of the *khāṣṣa*, the least of whose concerns was the general interest, represented by the *ʿāmma'*). The majority of the *ʿulamā'* conceded the claims of the *Imām*, whether through loyalty or through fear of reprisals. A minority refused his directive, forming the nucleus of a resistance movement which received the support of the urban proletariat of Baghdād (cf. W. M. Patton, *Aḥmed ibn Ḥanbal and the Miḥna*, Leiden 1897). The social conflict between the *khāṣṣa* and the *ʿāmma* of the capital was revived (leading the successor of al-Ma'mūn to found a new capital at Sāmarrā).

Shortly before his death, al-Ma'mūn chose as his successor not his son al-ʿAbbās, who was in charge of the *ʿAwāṣim* (in the manner of al-Mu'tamin, who was to be the third heir of al-Rashīd), but his brother al-Muʿtaṣim who was responsible for the new recruits from Transoxania. His political testament recommended the pursuit of his politico-religious work, incomplete in Radjab 218/August 833, the date of his death near Tarsus.

In conclusion, it is not inappropriate to compare al-Ma'mūn with ʿAbd al-Malik b. Marwān (65-86/685-705), both of whom restored unity to the empire after a long civil war and promoted a political and cultural upheaval (of the 2nd/8th century in the case of ʿAbd al-Malik, and of the 3rd/9th century in the case of al-Ma'mūn). Their successors benefited from their work (built up over twenty years) and developed its main points of policy during their reign (of ten years); al-Muʿtaṣim put an end to various centres of persistent revolt (the Khurramiyya of Djibāl in 218/833, the Zuṭṭ of the marshlands of lower ʿIrāḳ in 219/834; the Khurramiyya of Bābak in Ādharbāydjān in 222/837; the *abnā'* favourable to al-ʿAbbās b. al-Ma'mūn in 223/838; and the Sufyānid al-Mubarḳaʿ in Syria in 226/841). He endorsed the Ṭāhirids, the pillars of the régime, going so far as to suppress the autonomist revolt of Māzyār, the prince-governor of Ṭabaristān (225/840) and to sacrifice one of his leading supporters, al-Afshīn of Ushrūsana (225/840), in order to put an end to his rivalry with the Ṭāhirids. He surrounded himself with the same Muʿtazilī advisers as had been chosen by al-Ma'mūn, in particular the chief *ḳāḍī* Aḥmad b. Abī Du'ād, a native of Ḳinnasrīn, and pursued the *miḥna* inaugurated in 218/833. He made new campaigns against the Byzantine empire, achieving in 223/838 the project undertaken by al-Ma'mūn in 218/833. The stimulus given to translations and to scientific works under al-Ma'mūn continued unabated, permitting the tutor of the sons of al-Muʿtaṣim, al-Kindī, to achieve the integration of Neo-Platonism into Muʿtazilī theology. In spite of this continuity there were some changes, exemplified by the transfer of the capital to Sāmarrā [*q.v.*] (from 221/836), in order to preserve the strength of the strike force constituted by the army, dominated by Transoxanians, among whom the rôle of the Turkish guard was growing in importance.

Bibliography: Sources. These embrace practically all the categories of documents, cf. Cl. Cahen, *Introduction à l'histoire du monde musulman médiéval (VIIe-XVe siècle)*, Paris 1982. The section of Ṭabarī on al-Ma'mūn's reign has been translated into English by C. E. Bosworth, *The caliphate of al-*

Ma'mūn 198-213 (813-33), Albany 1986. 2. Studies. There is no work of synthesis on al-Ma'mūn (the subject however of the present writer's thèse d'état, in preparation). The 3 vols. of A. al-Rifāʿī, *ʿAṣr al-Ma'mūn*, Cairo 1928, are a compilation from the Arab sources; M. M. Haddāra, *al-Ma'mūn, al-khalīfa al-ʿālim*, Cairo n.d. [1966], has no scholarly pretentions. F. ʿUmar touches on this period only in certain articles collected together in his *Buḥūth fi 'l-ta'rīkh al-ʿAbbāsī*, Baghdād 1977, and *al-Ta'rīkh al-islāmī wa-fikr al-ḳarn al-ʿishrīn*, Beirut 1980. Chapters are devoted to al-Ma'mūn's age in recent works on the ʿAbbāsids: M. A. Shaban, *Islamic history, a new interpretation. 2. A.D. 750-1055 (A.H. 132-448)*, Cambridge 1976; H. Kennedy, *The early Abbasid caliphate. A political history*, London 1981; D. Sourdel, *Le vizirat ʿabbāside*, Damascus 1959, i; P. Crone, *Slaves on horses*, Cambridge 1980; O. Racine, *L'aristocratie au premier siècle ʿabbāside* (doctorat du 3e cycle), Univ. of Toulouse II 1984. One should also mention F. Gabrieli, *La successione di Hārūn al-Rašīd e la guerra fra al-Amīn e al-Ma'mūn*, in *RSO*, xi (1926-8), 341-97; S. B. Samadi, *The struggle between the two brothers Al-Amin and Al-Mamun*, in *IC*, xxxii (1958), 99-120; Barbier de Meynard, *Ibrâhîm fils de Mahdî*, in *JA* (1869); A. Arioli, *La rivolta di Abū Sarāya*, in *Ann. Fac. Ling. Lett. stran. Ca' Foscari*, v (1974); S. Hamdi, *The pro-alid policy of Ma'mun*, in *Bull. Coll. Arts Sc.*, Baghdad, i (1959); D. Sourdel, *La politique religieuse du calife ʿabbāside al-Ma'mūn*, in *REI*, xxx/1 (1962), 26-48; F. Gabrieli, *al-Ma'mūn e gli ʿAlidi*, in *Morgenländische Texte und Forschungen*, Leipzig ii, 1929; L. Veccia Vaglieri, *Le vicende del ḫāriǧismo in epoca ʿābbaside*, in *RSO*, xxiv (1949), 31-44; M. Rekaya, *Le khurram-dīn et les révoltes khurramites jusqu'à Bābak (m. 837)*, Paris 1985; M. Kaabi, *Les Ṭāhirides au Ḫurāsān et en Iraq (IIIe/IXe siècle)*, Tunis 1983; D. Sourdel, *Les circonstances de la mort de Ṭāhir Ier au Ḫurāsān en 207/822*, in *Arabica*, v (1958), 66-9; E. L. Daniel, *Iran's awakening: a study of local rebellions in the eastern provinces of the islamic empire, 126-227 A.H. (743-842 A.D.)*, Ph. D. thesis, Univ. of Texas, Austin 1978 (publ. by University Microfilms International, Ann Arbor 1982); idem, *The political and social history of Khurasan under Abbasid rule 747-820*, Minneapolis-Chicago 1979; C. E. Bosworth, *The Ṭāhirids and Arabic culture*, in *JSS*, xiv (1969), 445-79; idem, *An early Arabic mirror for princes: Ṭāhir Dhū l-Yamīnayn's epistle to his son ʿAbdallāh* (206/821), in *JNES*, xxix (1979); D. M. Dunlop, *A diplomatic exchange between al-Ma'mūn and an Indian King*, in *Medieval and Middle Eastern Studies*, Leiden 1972; A. A. Vasiliev, *Byzance et les Arabes. I. Relations politiques de Byzance et les Arabes au temps de la dynastie d'Amorium (820-67)*, Fr. edn. H. Grégoire and M. Canard, Brussels 1935, repr. 1959; H. Ahrweiler, *L'Asie mineure et les invasions arabes (VIIe-IXe siècle)*, in *Revue Historique*, ccxxvii (1962), 1-32; M. M. Ahsan, *Social life under the Abbāsids (170-289/786-902 A.D.)*, London-New York 1976; Cl. Cahen, *Mouvements populaires et autonomisme urbain dans l'Asie musulmane du Moyen Age*, in *Arabica*, v (1958), 225-50, vi (1959), 25-56; *Baġdād*, special no. of *Arabica*, ix (1962); G. Le Strange, *Baghdad during the ʿAbbāsid caliphate*. Oxford 1924; S. Sabari, *Mouvements populaires à Bagdad à l'époque ʿabbasside, IXe-XIe siècles*, Paris 1981; E. Ashtor, *Histoire des prix et des salaires dans l'Orient médiéval*, Paris 1969; idem, *A social and economic history of the Near East in the middle ages*, London 1976; M. ʿAwīs, *al-Mudjtamaʿ al-ʿabbāsī min khilāl kitābāt al-Djāḥiẓ*, Cairo 1977; M. R. al-Nadjdjār, *Ḥikāyāt al-shuṭṭār wa'l-ʿayyārīn fi 'l-turāth al-ʿarabī*, Kuwait 1981; J. Pradines, *Recherches sur le rôle des chrétiens à la cour des Umayyades et des premiers ʿAbbāsides (661-861)*, thèse de 3e cycle, Univ. of Toulouse II, 1975; Y. Eche, *Les bibliothèques arabes publiques et semi-publiques en Mésopotamie, Syrie, Egypte au Moyen Age*, Damascus 1967; R. Arnaldez, *Sciences et philosophie dans la civilisation de Baġdād sous les premiers ʿAbbāsides*, in *Arabica*, ix (1962), 357-73; Ch. Pellat, *Etudes sur l'histoire socio-culturelle de l'Islam (VIIe-XVe s.)*, London 1976; J. E. Bencheikh, *Poétique arabe*, Paris 1975.

(M. REKAYA)

AL-**MA'MŪN**, ABU 'L-ʿALĀ' IDRĪS B. YAʿKŪB AL-MANṢŪR B. YŪSUF B. ʿABD AL-MU'MIN B. ʿALĪ, ninth sovereign of the Almohad dynasty, born in 581/1185-6 in Málaga, of the marriage of his father with the Spanish princess Ṣafiyya, daughter of the *amīr* Abū ʿAbd Allāh b. Mardanīsh (Martinez). The Arab historians pay high tributes to the good qualities of this prince, who was very well-read, and equally well-versed in profane and religious learning. At a time when the Almohad dynasty was much troubled by the strife stirred up by pretenders, he was able by his energy to postpone for several years its final collapse.

At first, al-Ma'mūn served in Spain as the lieutenant of his brother Abū Muḥammad ʿAbd Allāh al-ʿĀdil, then on the throne. The latter had soon to leave the Peninsula and return to Morocco without having been able to subdue the rebel leader Abū Muḥammad al-Bayyāsī, who was supported by Ferdinand III of Castile, but he was soon betrayed by his own men in his own land and assassinated in 624/1127. This murder was followed by the almost simultaneous proclamations of al-Ma'mūn and another Almohad pretender, nephew of the preceding, Yaḥyā b. al-Nāṣir b. al-Manṣūr, who took the honorific *laḳab* of al-Muʿtaṣim bi'llāh. On his accession and without leaving Spain, al-Ma'mūn was soon able to make himself recognised in the greater part of his empire and to get rid of the rebel al-Bayyāsī. But almost immediately, a rebellion broke out in the east of al-Andalus, in which Muḥammad b. Yūsuf of the powerful family of the Banū Hūd [*q.v.*] was proclaimed caliph in the town of Murcia. At the same time, the prestige of Yaḥyā al-Muʿtaṣim increased in Morocco and his partisans became more and more numerous. Feeling himself powerless in Spain and forced to turn his eyes towards Africa, al-Ma'mūn was forced to seek an alliance with the king of Castile. The latter agreed to support al-Ma'mūn under very harsh terms, including the surrender of ten Muslim strongholds of the *frontera* and the building of a church in Marrākush and the granting of freedom of worship. In return, al-Ma'mūn received a body of 500 Christian mercenaries with whom he at once went to the Maghrib. He was soon able to enter Marrākush in triumph, after having defeated the army of al-Muʿtaṣim (627/1230), and to open the chapel of St. Mary for his Christian troops.

Enraged at the defection of the Almohad *makhzan* [*q.v.*] so devoted to his predecessors, al-Ma'mūn took a decision at Marrākush that was quite unprecedented in the annals of the dynasty. He stigmatised the memory of the Mahdī Ibn Tūmart, denied him "impeccability" (*ʿiṣma*) and had a large number of Almohad *shaykhs* executed whom he suspected of having betrayed him. The rest of the reign of al-Ma'mūn was spent in trying to put down several rebellions in the Maghrib; but he did not succeed in bringing al-Muʿtaṣim to terms, for the latter was able to take Marrākush, to massacre the Christians and destroy their church and to plunder the town. On hearing this, al-Maʾmūn, then busy with the siege of Ceuta, hurried off to the capital at once but fell ill and died on the way in the valley of the Wādi 'l-ʿAbīd at the end of Dhu 'l-Ḥidjdja 629/October 1232.

Bibliography: Ibn Abī Zarʿ, *Rawḍ al-ḳirṭās*, ed. Tornberg, *Annales regum Mauritaniae*, Upsala 1843, 166-9; *al-Ḥulal al-mawshiyya*, Tunis 1329, 123-5, ed. Allouche, 137, tr. Huici Miranda, 192; Ibn Khaldūn, *ʿIbar, Histoire des Berbères*, ed. de Slane, i, 342-4, tr. idem, ii, 233-7; al-Nāṣiri al-Salāwī, al-*Istiḳṣāʾ*, Cairo, ii, 197-200, tr. I. Hamet, in *Archives Marocaines*, xxxii (1927), 213-25; R. Millet, *Les Almohades*, Paris 1923, 145-50; A. Huici Miranda, *Colección de crónicas árabes de la reconquista*, ii, 313 ff.; G. Deverdun, *Marrakech des origines à 1912*, Rabat 1959, index; R. Le Tourneau, *The Almohad movement in North Africa in the twelfth and thirteenth centuries*, Princeton 1969, 94-7. (E. LÉVI-PROVENCAL)*

MAʾMŪN B. MUḤAMMAD, ABU 'L-ʿABBĀS, founder of the short-lived line of Maʾmūnid Khwārazm-Shāhs in Khwārazm [*q.v.*].

Maʾmūn was governor, probably as a nominal vassal of the Sāmānids [*q.v.*], in the town of Gurgandj [*q.v.*], which during the 4th/10th century had been prospering commercially at the expense of the ancient capital Kath [*q.v.*], seat of the old-established line of Afrīghid Khwārazm-Shāhs [see KHWĀRAZM-SHĀHS]. In 385/995 the Afrīghids were overthrown and their dynasty extinguished, so that Maʾmūn became ruler of a unified Khwārazm.

Very soon he was drawn into the struggle between the last Sāmānid *amīrs*, in particular, Nūḥ b. Manṣūr, and the rebellious Turkish slave commanders Abū ʿAlī Sīmdjūrī and Fāʾiḳ Khāṣṣa, arranging a peace between the two sides in 386/996, in the face of the threat of a renewed Ḳarakhānid invasion [see ILEK-KHĀNS]. In the following year, however, Maʾmūn was assassinated in an internal turmoil, and was succeeded on the throne by his son Abu 'l-Ḥasan ʿAlī.

Bibliography: E. Sachau, *Zur Geschichte und Chronologie von Khwârizm*, in *SBWAW*, lxxiv (1873), 290-2; Barthold, *Turkestan*, 261-3; Zambauer, *Manuel*, 208. (C. E. BOSWORTH)

AL-**MAʾMŪNĪ**, ʿABŪ ṬĀLIB ʿABD AL-SALĀM B. AL-ḤASAN, Arabic poet of the 4th/10th century, whose name indicates his descent from the caliph al-Maʾmūn. He was born in Baghdād after 343/953, left the capital in his youth and went to Rayy, where the famous Ṣāḥib Ibn ʿAbbād [*q.v.*] made him a member of his learned circle. However, "the scorpions of envy from the part of the boon-companions of the Ṣāḥib were creeping around him", so he decided to move and went to Nīshāpūr, where he was introduced to Ibn Sīmdjūr, a high-ranking military commander of the Sāmānids, who recommended him to the court in Bukhārā. The brilliant young poet having arrived there, al-*wazīr* Abu 'l-Ḥusayn al-ʿUtbī and his successor Abū Naṣr showered gifts and honours upon him. Al-Maʾmūnī seems to have dreamt of regaining—or usurping—the ʿAbbāsid caliphate by the aid of a Khurāsānian army; at least, this is what he intimated to al-Thaʿālibī (cf. below). However, his poetry shows him to have been rather an epicure and pleasure-lover than a warrior. He died of hydropsy in 383/993.

The main source for his life and poetry is al-Thaʿālibī's *Yatīmat al-dahr* (vol. iv, part. 4, ch. 3, Damascus 1304/1886-7,iv,84-112; Cairo (1352/1934), iv, 149-79). In addition to this, a number of verses are scattered in various sources including al-Djurdjānī's *Asrār al-balāgha* and al-Nuwayrī's *Nihāyat al-arab*. Most of his poems are short specimens of *waṣf*, descriptive epigrams on buildings, various utensils (e.g. for writing), fruits, and dishes. His art of description makes ample use of metaphors, metonymy, periphrasis, and the attribution of human characteristics to objects, e.g. showing a pair of scissors as two inseparable spouses, a basket as a devout, reliable servant, and so on. With its still somewhat clumsy mannerism, this poetry forms an interesting document for the development of the sophisticated Persian style, showing it at an early stage and in Arabic guise, as already pointed out by Bertels.

Bibliography: E. Barthold, *Turkestan down to the Mongol invasion*³, 258; E. Bertels, *Persidskaya noeziya v Bukhare—X vek* (Trudī Instituta vostokovedeniya, 10), Moscow 1935; J. C. Bürgel, *Die ekphrastischen Epigramme des Abū Ṭālib al-Maʾmūnī—Literaturkundliche Studie über einen arabischen Conceptisten*, in *Abh. Ak. W.Gött.*, Phil.-hist. Kl. 14, (1965), detailed review by W. Heinrich, in *ZDMG*, xcci (1971), 166-90. (J. C. BÜRGEL)

MAʾMUNIDS [see KHWARAZM-SHĀHS]

MAʾMŪR (A), in the usage of the late Ottoman empire and Turkish republic, "civil official".

Roughly at the end of the 18th century, this term began to appear in Ottoman Turkish, not only as a passive participle designating "one who is ordered or commissioned" to do something, but also as a substantive referring to an "official", normally a "civil official". As far as one can tell from research done to date, the change was a matter of gradual transition, and not the result of any clearly-marked shift in governmental practice. This was, however, a period when traditional scribal institutions were undergoing extensive change, and scribal officials were being used increasingly for assignments or missions *(meʾmūriyyet)* other than those evoked by such traditional designations for scribal roles as *kātib* [*q.v.*], *kalfa* (from *khalīfe*, normally applied to scribal officials only in the plural form *khulefāʾ*), or *khwādje* (also normally applied to officials only in the plural form *khwādjegān* [see KHWĀDJEGĀN-Ī DĪWĀN-Ī HÜMĀYŪN]; Findley, 64-6, 106-11). Usage in historical works of this period suggests that repeated references to individuals who were "ordered" (*meʾmūr*) to perform a particular mission (*meʾmūriyyet*) gradually caused these terms to float free of association with specific persons or duties and acquire the general meanings of "official" and "official position or appointment". In the *History* of Wāṣīf, published in 1219/1804, and in that of ʿĀṣīm [*q.v.*], written about five years later, there are numbers of section headings containing the terms *meʾmūr* or *meʾmūriyyet* (e.g. Wāṣīf, i, 148, 155, 184, ii, 110, 116, 119, 147, 154, 185, 207, 266, 268, 272, 294; ʿĀṣīm, i, 62, 155, 174, 223, ii, 20, 26, 166). At some points, the word *meʾmūr* appears with meanings approaching that later conventional in Turkish. *Meʾmūrs* go to Egypt and return (Wāṣīf, i, 172-3); the *meʾmūrs* of the naval arsenal (*tersane*) are accused of negligence (ʿĀṣīm, i, 51); Russian consuls behave inappropriately toward government officials (*dewlet meʾmūrlarī, ibid.*, i, 178-9).

From roughly the 1830s onwards, the term *meʾmūr* began to be associated in Ottoman official usage with the term *mülkiyye*, which was then coming into use as a noun meaning "civil administration" or "civil service". Eventually, a civil official came to be known as a *mülkiyye meʾmūrī*, a compound that contrasted both the man and his branch of service with the scribe (*kātib*, etc.) of the scribal service (*ḳalemiyye*), as it had been known prior to the beginning of reform. Since ıe terms *mülkī* and *mülkiyye* convey associations with oth land ownership and sovereignty, generalised use f the new nomenclature may have been a result of the rowing association of civil officials with provincial dministration, thus with a vast domain of employ-ıent external to the bureaux in the capital city, in ɾhich most scribal officials had historically served. When Maḥmūd II [*q.v.*] reorganised the central of-ces as a series of ministries, the first title of the new ıinister of the interior was, in fact, *umūr-ï mülkiyye āẓiri*, or "Minister of Civil Affairs". The title was onferred in 1251/1836 (Luṭfī, v, 29-31), but was hanged to Minister of the Interior (*dā<u>kh</u>iliyye nāẓiri*) year later. Ultimately, however, the term *mülkiyye ıeʾmūrī* and its variations, such as the common plural *ıeʾmūrīn-i mülkiyye*, clearly referred, not just to local dministrators but to civil officials in general Findley, 65-6, 140, 364, n. 66). Despite some incon-istency in usage, this fact became clearer as a ystematic personnel policy emerged for this branch of ervice (*ibid.*, 140-7, 194-7, 270-9, 326-33). In the Turkish of the republican era, *meʾmūr* remains, first nd foremost, a noun that means "official" and refers specially to the civil service.

Nineteenth-century lexicographical works were low to register the use of *meʾmūr* in this sense. This act no doubt reflects the tendency of the authors to re-y on earlier written works; but it is probably also an-ther sign that the shift in usage was not clearly ıarked. Works that do not mention the new usage in-lude Alexandridis (1812), Bianchi (*Vocabulaire*, 1831, *vv.* "fonction", "fonctionnaire", "officier"), Hin-oglu (1838, *s.v.* "*meʾmūr*"), and Handjéri (1841, *vv.* "fonction", "fonctionnaire", "officier"). Even Redhouse, whose long years in Ottoman service made im a great authority, gave only conservative defini-ions in his first lexicographical publication, the *Müntakhabāt-i lughat-i ʿothmāniyye*, prepared by the ear-y 1840s and first published in 1269/1852-3 (see the rinting of 1285/1868-9, 88). Even in his last dic-ionary, he gave the traditional meanings first, as was is wont (*Turkish and English Lexicon*, 1890, *s.vv. ıeʾmūr, meʾmūriyyet*). By then, however, indications of he new usages had long since appeared in Rhasis 1828, *s.vv.* "fonctionnaire" and "civil", giving as ne translation of the latter term *milkī* [*sic*], with the xample "troubles civils, *i<u>kh</u>tilālāt-ï milkiyye* ou *ā<u>kh</u>iliyye*"), Bianchi (*Dictionnaire français-turc*, 1843, *v.* "fonctionnaire"), and in Guzel-oglou (1852, *s.v.* "fonction"). In 1835, Bianchi and Kieffer (*Diction-aire turc-français*, s.vv. *meʾmūr, meʾmūriyyet, mülkī*) had iven the new meanings, but had associated them ɾith Egyptian usage.

The reference to Egypt does reflect usage there, at east in Ottoman Turkish, under Muḥammad ʿAlī Pa<u>sh</u>a. In Ottoman-language Egyptian documenta-ion of that period, one finds *meʾmūr* as a general term or "official" (Deny, 106); by the 1820s, *mülkiyye* was lso in use in Egypt with essentially the meaning "civil affairs" (e.g. *dīwān-ï mülkiyye*, as opposed to *īwān-ï d<u>j</u>ihādiyye*; *ibid.*, 108, 111-5). From this period lso dates the use of the term *meʾmūr* as a title for the hief officer of a given type of local administrative istrict (*ibid.*, 130, 565); this usage has survived in Egypt. In general, *muwaẓẓaf*, rather than *maʾmūr* has een the common term for "civil official" in modern Arabic.

Bibliography: D. Alexandridis, *Grammatiké graikiko-tourkiké*, Vienna 1812 (reference supplied by A. Tietze); Aḥmed ʿĀṣim, *ʿĀṣim taʾrī<u>kh</u>i*, 2 vols., Istanbul n.d.; T.-X. Bianchi, *Dictionnaire français-turc*, 2 vols., Paris 1843-6; idem, *Vocabulaire français-turc*, Paris 1831; T. X. Bianchi and J. D. Kieffer, *Dictionnaire turc-français*, 2 vols., Paris, 1850 (also an earlier edn., 1835-7); J. Deny, *Sommaire des archives turques du Caire*, Cairo 1930; C. V. Findley, *Bureaucratic reform in the Ottoman empire: the Sublime Porte. 1789-1922*, Princeton 1980; E. Guzel-oglou, *Nouveaux dialogues français-turcs précédés d'un vocabulaire*, Constantinople 1852 (reference supplied by A. Tietze); A. Handjéri, *Dictionnaire français-arabe-persan et turc*, 3 vols., Moscow 1840-41; A. Hindoglu, *Dictionnaire abrégé turc-français*, Vienna 1838; Aḥmed Luṭfī, *Taʾrī<u>kh</u>-i Luṭfī*, 8 vols., the 8th edited by ʿAbd ul-Raḥmān <u>Sh</u>eref, Istanbul 1290-1328/1873-1910; anon. [by J. W. Redhouse], *Müntakhabāt-ï lughat-ï ʿothmāniyye*, Istanbul 1285/1868-9; idem, *A Turkish and English lexicon*, Constantinople 1921; G. Rhasis, *Vocabulaire français-turc*, St. Petersburg 1828; Aḥmed Wāṣīf, *Maḥāsin ül-ā<u>th</u>ār we ḥaḳāʾiḳ ül-a<u>kh</u>bār*, 2 vols., Istanbul <u>Sh</u>aʿbān 1219/November 1804.

(C. V. FINDLEY)

MAʿMŪRAT AL-ʿAZĪZ, a town in eastern Anatolia, modern Turkish Elaziğ, now the chef-lieu of a *vilayet* of the latter name.

The area around the town is rich in evidence of prehistoric and protohistoric settlement. Bronze Age sites have been investigated at Ağin, Norşuntepe, Tepecik and Han İbrahim Şah, whilst traces of Hellenistic and later occupation have been found at Aşvankale and Kalecikler. Thus a more or less continuous occupation of the Elaziğ area since Chalcolithic times seems likely, even though it is not certain exactly at what periods the site of Elaziğ town was inhabited. In classical and mediaeval times, the main settlement of the region was at <u>Kh</u>artpert (Latin name Ziata Castellum, Arabic Ḥiṣn Ziyād, <u>Kh</u>artabird or <u>Kh</u>artabirt, Classical Armenian <u>Kh</u>arberd, mediaeval French Quart-Pierre, vulgar Armenian Kʾarpʾut, Byzantine Greek Χαρπότε, Ottoman Turkish <u>Kh</u>arpurt, <u>Kh</u>arpurd, or as in ʿAynī ʿAlī Efendī's *Ḳawānīn risālesi*, repr. Istanbul 1979, 30: <u>Kh</u>arbrūt, modern Turkish Harput). For its history in classical and Byzantine times, see *EI*[1] art. <u>KH</u>ARPŪT, and for the mediaeval Islamic and Ottoman periods, see <u>KH</u>ARTPERT). It survives as a village and as a recreational area for the inhabitants of Elaziğ.

Although <u>Kh</u>arpūt's location on its hilltop made it splendidly defensible, during the 19th century the difficulty of access came to be considered a liability rather than an asset. Hence early in that century, the governors of the *sand<u>j</u>aḳ* of <u>Kh</u>arpūt in the *eyālet* of Diyārbakr, moved their residence to the plain to the little town of Mezere. The name of this settlement is probably derived from the word *mazraʿa, mezraʿa* "sown area, hamlet", which has not infrequently entered into the formation of Anatolian place names (compare in this context the articles *Harput* and *Elâziz* in *İA*, by Besim Darkot, also the different editions of TC Dahiliye Vekâleti, *Köylerimiz*. For an alternative, but less likely, suggestion, connecting the name with Μαξάρα as apparently found in Ptolemy, see H. Hübschmann, *Die altarmenischen Ortsnamen*, in *Indogermanische Forschungen*, xvi [1904]). Visitors of the 19th and early 20th centuries such as von Moltke and Gertrude Bell still record the name of the new settlement as Mazraa.

The new settlement gained importance in 1250/1834 when Ra<u>sh</u>īd Meḥmed Pa<u>sh</u>a, after a tour of inspection through the provinces of eastern Anatolia, suggested Mezere as the seat for the local governor. Barracks and a hospital were accordingly constructed, and von Moltke saw them on his visit in

1254/1838. In 1278/1862, upon a suggestion from the local governor Ismāʿīl Pasha, the settlement was renamed Maʿmūrat al-ʿAzīz in honour of the reigning sultan ʿAbd al-ʿAzīz [*q.v.*]. The name was extended to the *sandjak* and then in 1296/1879 to a new *wilāyet* formed on these upper reaches of the Euphrates. It was soon transformed in popular parlance into al-ʿAzīz/Elaziz, and the present name Elaziğ adopted in 1937.

Until the end of World War II, the growth of Elaziğ was somewhat irregular. While the town probably consisted of about 10,000 to 12,000 inhabitants at the beginning of World War I, the first census conducted by the Turkish Republic in 1927 recorded 20,052 inhabitants. In 1940, this figure had risen to 25,465, but the shortages of the war years led to an exodus of population, so that in 1945 only 23,695 inhabitants were counted. However, from then onward, the city has gone through a period of dramatic and uninterrupted growth (1950: 29,317; 1955: 41,667; 1960: 60,289; 1965: 78,605; 1970: 107,364; 1975: 131,415).

The most important factor determining the growth of Elaziğ in recent years has been the construction of the Keban power plant at a distance of only 45 km. from the town (lake area: 68,000 ha., productive capacity 5,871,000 kwh/year). Throughout the construction period, building workers employed on the Keban dam generally lived in the city, so that during the nineteen-sixties and seventies, Elaziğ was inhabited by many more males than females (1960: 32,449 males, 27,840 females; 1975: 69,797 males, 61,681 females).

Among the factories constructed in the area, some of the more important ones are connected more or less directly with the Keban dam project. Thus a cement factory belonging to the public sector of the Turkish economy was founded in the city, possessing a capacity of 400,000 ton/year. In addition, the city is located close to an important mining area, in which chrome is extracted; this situation accounts for the relatively high percentage of miners in the Elaziğ district (2.5% of the active population in 1965). Due to these activities, the level of urbanisation in the district of Elaziğ (40.2% in 1970) has surpassed the average not only for eastern Anatolia, but even for Turkey as a whole (38.7% in 1970).

The growth of Elaziğ has also been stimulated by a side effect of the Keban dam, namely the total flooding of close to a hundred villages. In addition, over a hundred others have lost a large part of their agricultural lands. Among the 20,000 people who were forced to move, many apparently chose to settle in Elaziğ and to invest the indemnities paid by the government in houses and small business. Some of the recipients of major indemnities were encouraged to invest their money in a holding company, which by 1972 had built a factory producing plastic pipes and tubes, and by 1977 had also erected a leather factory employing 260 workers. State offices and enterprises also absorbed some of the migrants, mainly in subordinate capacities. However, just as the electricity produced by the Keban dam is mainly consumed outside of the area, it appears that a considerable percentage of the money received as indemnities was invested in the large cities of western Turkey.

Bibliography: Helmuth von Moltke, *Briefe über Zustände und Begebenheiten in der Turkei*, Berlin 1877, 212 etc.; *Ḳāmūs al-aʿlām*, iii, 2032, vi, 4330; V. Cuinet, *La Turquie d'Asie, Géographie administrative, statistique descriptive et raisonnée de chaque province de l'Asie Mineure*, Paris 1892, 355-7; Gertrude Bell, *Amurath to Amurath*, London 1911, 329-32; E. Banse, *Die Türkei, Eine moderne Geographie*, Brunswick 1916, 227; T. C. Başvekaleti, Istatistik Umum Müdürlüğü, *1946-1954 zirai bünye ve istihsal*, Ankara 1955; METU Department of Restoration, *Doomed by the dam. A survey of the monuments threatened by the Keban Dam flood area ...*, Ankara 1967; *[Keban Projesi] 1968 yaz çalışmaları*, ODTÜ Keban Projesi yayınları 1/1, Ankara 1970; Devlet Istatistik Enstitüsü, *Tarımsal yapı ve üretim 1969*, Ankara 1971; *Keban Projesi 1969 çalişmaları*, same series, 1/2, Ankara 1971; *Keban Projesi 1970 çalışmaları*, same series 1/3, Ankara 1972; *Keban Projesi 1971 çalışmaları*, same series 1/3, Ankara 1974; Devlet Istatistik Enstitüsü, *Genel nüfus sayımı, idari bölünü* 25.10. 1970. Ankara 1973; Devlet Su Işleri, *Keban barajı ve hidroelektrik santralı*, Ankara 1973 (folder); *Cumhuriyetin 50. yılında Sümerbank 1933-1973*, n.p., n.d.; O. Silier, *Keban köylerinde sosyo ekonomik yapı ve yeniden yerleşim sorunları*, Ankara 1976; Devlet Istatistik Entitüsü, *Genel nüfus sayımı, idari bölünüş*, 25.10.1970, Ankara 1973, 26.10.1975, Ankara 1977; *Türkiye deri ve deri mamulları rehberi*, Ankara 1977; Devlet Istatistik Enstitüsü, *Tarımsal yapı ve üretim 1969*, Ankara 1971, *1976-78*, Ankara 1979.

(SURAIYA FAROQHI)

MĀN SINGH, Mahāradjā of Amber, outstanding general of the Mughal armies under Akbar, later governor of Mughal provinces.

He was born in 1607 V.S. = 975/1550, the son of Bhagwant Dās, eldest son and heir apparent of the reigning Mahārādjā Bhārah Mali, a Rādjpūt [*q.v.*] of the Kaččhwāha clan; the Muslim sources (Niẓām al-Dīn, Badāʾūnī, Firishta, Abu 'l-Faḍl, and Djahāngīr in his *Tūzuk*) garble the names and confuse Mān Singh's parentage, but there seems no reason to doubt the contemporary Rādjpūt records. After a young martial training, he entered the Mughal service (together with his father Bhagwant Dās) in 970/1562 on the occasion of Akbar's marriage with the daughter of Bhārah Mall, the first of those alliances which were to strengthen Mughal-Rādjpūt relations. He was with the Mughal armies at the capture of Ranthambor in 976/1569 (Tod, ii, 472-3, casts Mān Singh as mediator in the surrender, but the assertion is without evidence and inherently improbable); his first command seems rather to have been in the Gudjarāt campaigns in 980/1572 against the Mīrzās [*q.v.*], before the campaign against Dāwūd Khān Kararānī [*q.v.*] two years later. He was, though, sent as a mediator to Pratāp Singh who had succeeded as Mahārāṅā of Mewār on the death of Uday Singh, the knowledged senior ruler of the Rādjpūt tribes. Pratāp continued his father's arrogance and hostility to the Mughals, and gratuitously insulted Mān Singh, which resulted in the latter's being chosen to lead the Mughal army against him at the battle of Haldīghāt, 35 km. north-west of Udaypur, in 984/1576; he inflicted a devastating defeat, but his chivalrous orders that the Rāṅā was not to be pursued and that Mewār was not to be looted lost him Akbar's favour for a while. He next cleared Mālwā of Mīrzā disaffection, and was rewarded with a *manṣab* [*q.v.*] of 3,500. Sent against the disaffected Afghān and Balūčī elements in the Pandjāb, he acquitted himself well, and was placed in charge of operations in the north-west against Akbar's half-brother Mīrzā Muḥammad Ḥākim [*q.v.*], then ruling Kābul; after the Mīrzā's death in 993/1585, he occupied Kābul, brought the district to order, and was officially its governor, his principal occupation being to control the threat from the Rawshanāʾīs [see RAWSHANIYYA] and Yūsufzays. In 995/1587 Mān Singh was transferred to the governorship of the *ṣūba* of Bihār, where he pursued a vigorous policy against both recalcitrant Hindū *rād̲j̲ās* and disaffected local Afg̲h̲ān chiefs. He had succeeded to the Ambēr *gaddī* "cushion of state", i.e. throne in 998/1589, receiving the Mug̲h̲al title of Rād̲j̲ā with his *manṣab* confirmed as 5,000. In two campaigns he next brought Orissa (Uṛīsā, [*q.v.*]) under Mug̲h̲al suzerainty, its local Afg̲h̲ān chieftains fleeing to eastern Bengal. His campaigns against them were continued in his next appointment, as *ṣūbadār* of Bengal, in 1002/1594. He built a new capital at Agmahal which he renamed Akbarnagar (Akbarī mint-town; later renamed Rād̲j̲mahal [*q.v.*]), with fort, palace and large mosque (see Catherine B. Asher, *Inventory of key monuments*, in G. Mitchell (ed.), *The Islamic heritage of Bengal*, UNESCO-Paris 1984, 120-1). Further chastisement of dissident Afg̲h̲āns, and the conquest of Kuč̣h-Bihār, occupied him until 1014/1605, when he returned to the imperial court at Āgrā with the *manṣab* of 7,000. He was less successful as a courtier than as a military commander, for he urged the claims of K̲h̲usraw against those of D̲j̲ahāngīr; when the latter succeeded to the Mug̲h̲al throne a couple of months later, Mān Singh was sent first to Bengal again, then on the Deccan campaign, accomplishing nothing of note in either. He died a natural death in Iličpur in 1023/1614. His contributions to building are important. Among much temple building and restoration, irrelevant here, stands the Govindadeva temple at Mathurā, which marries the Muslim use of arch and dome to traditional Hindū forms; Mān Singh's palace at Ambēr is largely in frank imitation of the buildings of Āgrā fort; various buildings at Akbarnagar [see RĀD̲J̲MAHAL]; especially repairs to fortifications at Rohtās [*q.v.*] with gateways and imposing palace, and originally a garden in the Mug̲h̲al style.

Bibliography: Career details especially in Abu 'l-Faḍl, *Akbar-nāma*; Badāʾūnī, *Muntak̲h̲ab al-tawārīk̲h̲*; Niẓām al-Dīn Aḥmad, *Ṭabaḳāt-i Akbarī*, all *passim*, and information concerning "Mancinus" in Fr A. Monserrate, *Mongolicae legationis commentarius*, and de Laet, *De imperio magno Mongoli*, Leiden 1631. Valuable additional information, often correcting the above, in *D̲j̲aypur Vansāvalī* in State Archives of Jaipur. R.N. Prasad, *Raja Man Singh of Amber*, Calcutta 1966, is very useful for the Hindū sources quoted. (J. BURTON-PAGE)

MAᶜN, BANŪ, an Arab family of chiefs of the Druse district of the S̲h̲ūf, in the southern parts of Mount Lebanon, who enjoyed a special political prominence in Syria in the 10th/11th and 11th/17th centuries.

The origin of the house of Maᶜn remains unclear, what is related about it by the traditional Lebanese historians being without foundation. The first Maᶜn whose historicity is beyond question was Fak̲h̲r al-Dīn ᶜUt̲h̲mān b. al-Ḥād̲j̲d̲j̲ Yūnis who died in 912/1506. Another, possibly Fak̲h̲r al-Dīn ᶜUt̲h̲mān's son, was a Yūnis Maᶜn who died a young man in 917/1511. Ḳurḳumāz b. Yūnis Maᶜn, possibly a son of this Yūnis, was established as a *muḳaddam* (local chief) in the S̲h̲ūf in 922-3/1516-17, when the Ottomans conquered Syria and Egypt. At least two other Maᶜns, a ᶜAlam al-Dīn Sulaymān and a Zayn al-Dīn (thus known by his *laḳab*, with no *ism* mentioned), were recognised chiefs in the S̲h̲ūf at the same time. While the Maᶜns of the 10th/16th and 11th/17th centuries comprised Ḳurḳumāz and his descendants, it appears that the ᶜAlam al-Dīns, who feature as the rivals of the house of Ḳurḳumāz in the S̲h̲ūf at the time, were also Maᶜns descended from ᶜAlam al-Dīn Sulaymān.

Of the career of Ḳurḳumāz b. Maᶜn, not much is known, beyond the fact that he was reportedly residing in the village of al-Bārūk in 934/1528 and being deeply involved in the factional politics of the mountain. A second Ḳurḳumāz, possibly the grandson of the first, died in 993/1585 while Ottoman forces were invading the Druze districts. This Ḳurḳumāz left two sons, Fak̲h̲r al-Dīn and Yūnis. By the 1590s, his son Fak̲h̲r al-Dīn (d. 1044-5/1635), commonly believed to have been the older of the two, was already set on a career of political success which was to make him the dominant figure in the politics of Syria during the first three decades of the seventeenth century.

From small beginnings as a *muḳaddam* and Ottoman *multazim* (tax farmer) in the S̲h̲ūf, Fak̲h̲r al-Dīn rose by 1011/1602-3 to become the *sand̲j̲aḳ-beyi* of Sidon-Beirut and of Ṣafad, under the *beylerbeyi* of Damascus. He had already taken possession of Beirut, along with the southern parts of the district of Kisrawān, as far north as Nahr al-Kalb (the Dog River), in 1006/1598. In 1014/1605, he took possession of the whole of the Kisrawān. He next became involved in the rebellion of ᶜAlī D̲j̲ānbūlād, the usurper Pas̲h̲a of Aleppo, by coming to his support against the *beylerbeyis* of Tripoli and Damascus. This aroused the suspicion of the Porte against him for the first time.

As the master of two *sand̲j̲aks*, Fak̲h̲r al-Dīn established himself in Sidon. He recruited a mercenary army of *levends* [*q.v.*] and *sokmans*, whom he used to garrison old Crusader fortresses in his territory which were restored for military use. By 1017/1608 he had reached an agreement with the Medicis of Tuscany, who had ambitions in Syria at the time, which increased the Ottoman suspicious against him. Attacked by the Ottomans in 1022/1613, Fak̲h̲r al-Dīn fled to Tuscany, but was permitted to return home in 1027/1618, to resume office as *sand̲j̲ak-beyi* of Sidon-Beirut and Ṣafad. During the years that followed, he crushed rival chiefs in every direction, at first with Ottoman support and approval, until most of rural Syria fell under this control. Alarmed by the growth of his power, the Ottomans organised an expedition against him in 1042/1633. In the face of the Ottoman offensive, his power rapidly collapsed; his eldest son, ᶜAlī, was killed in battle, and he and his remaining sons were captured and taken to Istanbul in 1045/1635. There Fak̲h̲r al-Dīn was put to death by strangulation in that year, along with his son Manṣūr. His youngest son, Ḥusayn Maᶜn-zāda [see MAᶜN-ZĀDA], survived him to become chamberlain to the Sultan and Ottoman ambassador to India. This Ḥusayn was an informant of the Ottoman historian Nāᶜīmā [*q.v.*], and the author of a book of *adab* literature entitled the *Kitāb al-Tamyīz*.

At home, Fak̲h̲r al-Dīn was survived by a nephew, Mulḥim, whose political claims in the S̲h̲ūf (the Sidon hinterland) and the other Druze districts (the G̲h̲arb, D̲j̲urd and Matn, in the Beirut hinterland) were challenged by the ᶜAlam al-Dīns—as already mentioned, probably the descendants of ᶜAlam al-Dīn Sulaymān b. Maᶜn. At various times, Mulḥim held the *sand̲j̲aḳ* of Ṣafad, or the *sand̲j̲aḳ* of Batrūn, the latter in the *eyālet* of Tripoli. Upon his death, reportedly in 1068/1658, he was survived by a son, Aḥmad, who succeeded in expelling the ᶜAlam al-Dīns from the Druze districts and the Kisrawān in 1078/1667 and in installing himself in their place as the local *multazim*, in subordination to the *beylerbeyi* of Sidon (an *eyālet* since 1070/1660). By holding this position without interruption for thirty years (1078-1108/1667-97), Aḥmad Maᶜn became, *de facto*, the founder of the autonomy enjoyed by the territory in question (today part of Lebanon) until the 19th century.

With the death of Aḥmad Maᶜn, the direct Maᶜnid male line became extinct, and the *iltizām* of his territory passed over to his nephew (sister's son) Ba<u>sh</u>īr I <u>Sh</u>ihāb (1109-1118/1697-1706), then to his grandson (daughter's son) Ḥaydar <u>Sh</u>ihāb, Sunnī Muslim chiefs from Wādī al-Taym, in the Anti-Lebanon. The ᶜAlam al-Dīns, apparently as Maᶜns in the indirect line, rose to challenge this <u>Sh</u>ihāb succession sometimes by intrigue, sometimes by military action, until they were defeated in battle and killed to a man in 1123/1711.

In the modern Republic of Lebanon, the Banū Maᶜn have become a national legend, and their tenure of their mountain territory in the southern Lebanon, as *multazims* for the Ottoman State, has come to be regarded as a precursor to the modern Lebanese State. Fa<u>kh</u>r al-Dīn, in particular, is regarded as a Lebanese national hero, although Lebanon in his time was no more than a geographical expression. The real achievements of the Banū Maᶜn are of a different order. By controlling the predominantly Maronite district of Kisrawān alongside the Druze districts of the <u>Sh</u>ūf, <u>Gh</u>arb, <u>D</u>jurd and Matn, Fa<u>kh</u>r al-Dīn and his Maᶜn successors, more by accident than by design, laid the foundations of a political symbiosis between Maronites and Druzes in the *san<u>dj</u>aḳ* of Beirut-Sidon (after 1660, part of the *eyālet* of Sidon). This became, in its turn, the mainstay of the *de facto* autonomy enjoyed by the same territory in subsequent Ottoman times. By encouraging silk production, and protecting foreign traders, the Maᶜns furthermore secured for their territory a modest properity unknown in other rural parts of Syria in Ottoman times.

Bibliography: Hasan al-Bīrūnī, *Tara<u>dj</u>īm al-aᶜyān min abnāʾ al-zamān*, ms. Vienna, Cod. Arab. 1190, Mixt. 346; Iṣṭifān al-Duwayhī, *Taʾrī<u>kh</u> al-azmina*, 1095-1699, ed. Taoutel, Beirut 1951; Na<u>dj</u>m al-Dīn Muḥammad al-<u>Gh</u>azzī, *Luṭf al-samar wa-ḳaṭf al-<u>th</u>amar min tarā<u>dj</u>im al-ṭabaḳāt al-ūlā min al-ḳarn al-ḥādī ᶜa<u>sh</u>ar*, ed. Kamāl al-<u>Sh</u>ay<u>kh</u>, Damascus 1981-2; Ḥamza Ibn Sibāṭ, *Taʾrī<u>kh</u>*, ms. American University of Beirut, 956.9, I 13t; <u>Sh</u>ams al-Dīn Muḥammad Ibn Ṭūlūn, *Sall al-ṣārim ᶜalā atbāᶜ al-Ḥākim bi-amr Allāh*, no. 79, Taymūriyya Library, ff. 247-60; Aḥmad al-<u>Kh</u>ālidī, *Taʾrī<u>kh</u> al-Amīr Fa<u>kh</u>r al-Dīn al-Maᶜnī*, ed. Asad Rustum and Fuad A. Bustani, Beirut 1936; al-Muḥibbī, *<u>Kh</u>ulāṣat al-a<u>th</u>ar fī aᶜyān al-ḳarn al-ḥādī ᶜa<u>sh</u>ar*, Beirut n.d.; Muna<u>dj</u><u>dj</u>im Bā<u>sh</u>ī, *<u>Dj</u>āmiᶜ al-duwal*, ms. Topkapı Saray, no. 5966; Muṣṭafā Naᶜīmā, *Rawḍat al-Ḥusayn fī <u>kh</u>ulāṣat a<u>kh</u>bar al-<u>kh</u>āfiḳayn*, Istanbul 1282/1865-6; Abu 'l-Wafāʾ, *Maᶜādin al-<u>sh</u>ahāb fī al-ri<u>dj</u>āl al-mu<u>sh</u>arrafa bi-him Ḥalab*, ms. British Museum Or. 3618; G. Minadoi, *Historia della guerra fra Turchi e Persiani*, Venice 1594; George Sandys, *A relation of a journey, an. Dom. 1610*, London 1615; R. Knolles and P. Rycaut, *The Turkish History from the Original of that Nation to the Growth of the Ottoman Empire, with a continuation to this present year 1687*, London 1687. (K.S. Salibi)

MAᶜN b. **AWS** al-**MUZANĪ,** Arab poet belonging to the tribe of the Muzayna (see Ibn al-Kalbī-Caskel, *<u>Dj</u>amhara*), Tab. 88), which was established in a fertile region between Medina and Wādī 'l-Ḳurā.

He was considered to have been a *mu<u>kh</u>aḍram* poet, but was probably born shortly before the mission of Muḥammad and lived most of his life under Islam. He lost his sight towards the end of his life, which came about no earlier than 64/684, at least if the verses in which he complains about the hospitality offered by ᶜAbd Allāh b. al-Zubayr [*q.v.*] in Mecca are authentic. Although probably converted along with his tribe before the capture of Mecca, he does not seem to have participated in the conquests, and his poetry barely reflects the situation created by the new religion, which is mentioned only occasionally. Moreover, the available biographical information is sparse and is mainly concerned with his private life, his wives and his daughters (whom he by no means considered insignificant persons). Closely attached to an estate which he owned not far from Medina, and to the Bedouin life-style which he followed in his home-territory, he nevertheless visited Baṣra, where he is said to have met al-Farazdaḳ [*q.v.*] and to have married a woman of his tribe, also of Syria, the country of origin of another of his wives. He wrote eulogies of a number of Muslim personalities, including ᶜUbayd Allāh b. al-ᶜAbbās, ᶜAbd Allāh b. <u>D</u>jaᶜfar, ᶜĀṣim b. ᶜUmar b. al-<u>Kh</u>aṭṭāb and Saᶜīd b. al-ᶜĀṣ, without deviating from the Bedouin tradition. Although Ibn Sallām and Ibn Ḳutayba appear to ignore him, he is considered a talented poet, regarded by Muᶜāwiya as almost the equal of his fellow-tribesman Zuhayr b. Abī Sulmā. The fact is that his poetry contains, alongside personal references, passages of a moralistic nature. His name does not feature in the lists of *dīwāns*, collected by the early *ruwāt*, but P. Schwarz discovered in the Escurial an incomplete manuscript, with a commentary the contents of which go back to al-Ḳālī [*q.v.*] and published it under the title *Gedichte des Maᶜn ibn Aus* (Leipzig 1903) with an introductory account of the poet (cf. Nöldeke, in *ZA* [1903], 274 ff.; Reckendorf, in *OLZ* [1904], 138-40; R. Geyer, in *WZKM*, xvii, 246-70). Kamāl Muṣṭafā reprinted the Schwarz edition, with some additions and omissions, under the title *Maᶜn b. Aws, ḥayātuh, <u>sh</u>iᶜruh, a<u>kh</u>bāruh*, Cairo 1927; these collections could probably be enriched by the use of new sources. O. Rescher partially translated the *dīwān* in his *Beiträge zur arab. Poesie*, vi/2, Istanbul 1956-8, 1-28, and M.R. al-Nadawī has devoted a study to the poet, *Maᶜn b. Aws al-Muzanī*, in *Ma<u>dj</u>allat al-Ma<u>dj</u>maᶜ al-ᶜIlmī al-Hindī*, i/l (1396/1976), 107-25. A new edition of the *Dīwān*, based on Muṣṭafā's edition plus a combing of *adab* works, etc., is by ᶜUmar Muḥammad Sulaymān al-Ḳaṭṭān, <u>D</u>judda 1403/1983. *<u>Sh</u>iᶜr Muᶜn b. Aws al-Muzanī* (47 poems and fragments).

Bibliography: In addition to the references cited, see <u>D</u>jāḥiẓ, *Bayān*, index; idem, *Bu<u>kh</u>alāʾ*, ed. Ḥā<u>dj</u>irī, 205, 379; Abū Tammām, *Ḥamāsa*, ii, 2-4; Buḥturī, *Ḥamāsa*, index; *A<u>gh</u>ānī*, x, 154-8, ed. Beirut, xii, 50-9; *Naḳāʾiḍ*, ed. Bevan, 819; Ḳālī, *Amālī*, ii, 234; ᶜAskarī, *Ṣināᶜatayn*, 55-6; Ḥuṣrī, *Zahr al-ādāb*, 816-7 (cf. Ibn Abi 'l-Ḥadīd, *<u>Sh</u>arḥ Nah<u>dj</u> al-balā<u>gh</u>a*, ii, 125); Marzubānī, *Muᶜ<u>dj</u>am*, 399; Ibn Ḥa<u>dj</u>ar, *Iṣāba*, no. 8451; Ba<u>gh</u>dādī, *<u>Kh</u>izāna*, ed. Būlāḳ, iii, 258; Yāḳūt, *Buldān*, index; Ṣafadī, *Nakt al-himyān*, 294; Abkāryūs, 272-3; Brockelmann, S I, 72; O. Rescher, *Abriss*, i, 107; R. Blachère, *HLA*, 320-1; Sezgin, *GAS*, ii, 269-70, ix, 275. (M. Plesser - [Ch. Pellat])

MAᶜN b. **MUḤAMMAD,** b. Aḥmad b. Ṣumādiḥ al-Tu<u>dj</u>ībī, Abu 'l-Aḥwas, founder of a branch of the dynasty of the Tu<u>dj</u>ībids [*q.v.*] in the little principality of Alméria [see al-mariyya] in eastern Spain in the middle of the 5th/11th century. The principality had been founded in *ca.* 416/1025 by the two ᶜĀmirid *fatās* <u>Kh</u>ayān and Zuhayr. On the latter's death in 428/1037, their overlord ᶜAbd al-ᶜAzīz b. Abī ᶜĀmir, king of Valencia, declared it his property and in 432 or 433/1041-2, placed his brother-in-law Maᶜn b. Ṣumādiḥ as governor there. The latter belonged to a noble family of Arab origin; his father had been one of the generals of the celebrated *ḥādjib* al-Manṣūr [*q.v.*] and was governor of the town Huesca [see WASHKA]. Maᶜn remained loyal to the king of Valencia for nearly four years, then cast off his allegiance and declared himself independent. He reigned at Alméria for a few years longers and died in Ramaḍān 443/January 1052.

Bibliography: Ibn ᶜIdhārī, Bayān, iii, 167; Ibn al-Abbār, *al-Ḥulla al-siyarā*ʾ, ed. Ḥ. Muʾnis, Cairo 1964, ii, 81; R. Dozy, *Recherches sur l'histoire et la littérature de l'Espagne pendant le Moyen-âge*, Leiden 1881, i, 241 and appendices xix, xx; A. Prieto Vives, *Los reyes de taifas*, Madrid 1926, 40, 44, 61.

(E. Lévi - Provençal)

MAᶜN b. ZĀʾIDA, Abu 'l-Walīd al-Shaybānī. military commander and governor of the late Umayyad and early ᶜAbbāsid period. He came from the *ashrāf* of the Shaybān tribe and rose to importance with the patronage of Yazīd b. ᶜUmar b. Hubayra (see IBN HUBAYRA], the last Umayyad governor of ᶜIrāḳ. He fought against the advancing ᶜAbbāsid armies when they reached ᶜIrāḳ in 132/749, and was said to have killed the enemy commander, ḳaḥṭaba b. Shabīb [*q.v.*]. He joined his master Ibn Hubayra in the defence of Wāsiṭ and was one of the few leaders not to be executed, apparently because he was in Ḳūfa, conveying Ibn Hubayra's oath of allegiance to al-Saffāḥ. Thereafter he remained in hiding until the rebellion of the Rāwandiyya in the newly-founded capital of Hāshimiyya (variously dated 139 to 141/756-9), when he was able to rescue the caliph from the rebels and so earn his forgiveness. Al-Manṣūr appreciated his value as a man with a strong tribal following, and sent him as governor to Yaman in 142/759-60. In this post he pacified the country brutally but successfully, and in 151/768 he was recalled and sent on another difficult mission to Sīstān. It was here that he came into conflict with the local Khāridjīs, who were defeated in battle but succeeded in killing him in his winter quarters at Bust by disguising themselves as workmen (152/769-70). He left at least four sons, but his position in the tribe of Shaybān and at the ᶜAbbāsid court was inherited by his nephew, Yazīd b. Mazyad, who also continued the feud with the Khāridjīs. Maᶜn was remembered in the Arab literary tradition as a fierce warrior, but also for his extreme generosity and as a patron of poets, notably Marwān b. Abī Ḥafṣa [*q.v.*], who wrote a famous elegy on Maᶜn.

Bibliography: Ibn al-Kalbī, *Djamhara*, ed. Caskel, i, table 146; Yaᶜḳūbī, *Historiae*, ii, 389-400, 448, 462-3; Balādhurī, *Futūḥ*, ed. Munadjdjid, 493-4; idem, *Ansāb*, iii, ed. Dūrī, 96-8, 138, 145-6, 235-8; Ṭabarī, ii, 1978-80, iii, 16, 63-5, 130-3, 368-9, 394-7; Masᶜūdī, *Murūdj*, vi, 45-6, 168-70 = §§ 2272, 2380-1; *Aghānī* (tables) iii, 642; Ibn al-Athīr, v, 284, 309, 336-7, 383-5, 464, vi, 15-6; Ibn Khallikān, ed. Wüstenfeld, no. 742, ed. Iḥsān ᶜAbbās, v, 244-54, tr. de Slane, iii, 398-408.

(H. Kennedy)

MAᶜN-ZĀDA, Ḥusayn b. Fakhr al-Dīn al-Maᶜnī (Maᶜn-oghlu) son of the famous Druze *amīr*, Fakhr al-Dīn II [*q.v.*]; [see also MAᶜN, BANŪ], born on 14 Dhu 'l-Ḥidjdja 1030/29 October 1621, his mother being the niece of Yūsuf Pasha Sayfa, the Sunnī Turkoman chieftain in the regions of ᶜAkkār and Tripoli. When he was an infant, his father sent him several times in delegations to receive senior Ottoman officials passing via the Syrian coast. Through bribery and other cunning methods, his father was in 1031/1621 able to get an imperial order entrusting Ḥusayn with the *sandjaḳ* of ᶜAdjlūn, replacing the established Ghazzāwī family who were confidants of the Ottomans and the leaders of the Ḳaysī faction in southern Syria. Fakhr al-Dīn deputed one of his men to administer the *sandjaḳ* on behalf of Ḥusayn, but two years later delegated the job to a certain Bashīr al-Ghazzāwī.

Very little is know about the childhood of Ḥusayn and his youngest brother Ḥasan. However, when Sultan Murād IV in 1043/1634 commissioned the governor of the province of Damascus, Küčük Aḥmad Pasha, to eradicate the Maᶜnids, Fakhr al-Dīn instructed Ḥusayn to take shelter in al-Marḳab citadel situated in the neighbourhood of Lādhiḳiyya. Ḥusayn was arrested and sent to Aleppo, whence he was eventually dispatched to Istanbul. In 1044/1635, his father and two of his sons were put to death, but the life of Ḥusayn was spared because of his youth. He was sent to the Palace pages' school. After graduating from there, he served at the Ottoman court in the *Khāṣṣ odası*. It appears that he showed competence, because he was promoted to be a private secretary to Sultan Meḥemmed IV (1058-99/1648-87). Later on, he held the post of chief assistant at the treasury, *khazīne ketkhüdāsī*, and then in 1066/1656 that of *ḳapīdjī bashī* or head of the Sultan's guards. Later in the same year, he was sent as the Sultan's special envoy (*elči*) to the Mughal sultan in India Shāh Djahān (1037-68/1628-57), travelling by land to Baṣra in the company of an ambassador sent by Shāh Djahān, and from there they sailed to India; Ḥusayn refers to this journey in his only surviving work *al-Tamyīz*. Arriving in Dihlī, he found that the emperor had died and that fighting had broken out between his sons. It seems that his stay there did not last long, and he went back to Istanbul carrying a message of good wishes from Murād Bakhsh, son of the deceased sultan. It is possible that he was not on good terms with the new Grand Vizier Meḥmed Köprülü (1656-61) [see KÖPRÜLÜ], since he was not appointed to any official post, although fortunately his property was not confiscated. This enabled him to devote ample time to his work *al-Tamyīz*, for which he made use of his own rich library and other private libraries in Istanbul. During this period of his life, it seems that the court historian, Muṣṭafā Naᶜīmā [*q.v.*] (d. 1128/1716) came to acquaint himself with Ḥusayn and to make use of his knowledge and of his library; on several occasions, Naᶜīmā acknowledges his indebtedness to him, praising his vast knowledge, his modesty and *zuhd*. He states that his information about both Sultan Ibrāhīm and Sultan Meḥemmed IV was taken orally from Ḥusayn, but a recent study doubts this role accredited to Ḥusayn by Naᶜīmā.

The *Tamyīz* comprises 26 *bābs* with a *faṣl* (section) appended to each chapter. In the *bāb* he mentions the merits of the subject he is analysing, whereas in the *faṣl* he relates what other learned sages have said for or against that particular subject. His citations came from innumerable sources, but mainly from the Ḳurʾān, *Ḥadīth*, the *Nahdj al-balāgha* and the *Iḥyāʾ ᶜulūm al-dīn*. Naᶜīmā states that on the request of Ḥusayn, he made several copies of the *Tamyīz*, which were presented by the author to the dignitaries of Istanbul, and particularly to the Grand Vizier Ḥusayn Köprülü. It appears that he finished the first final copy in 1686.

Naᶜīmā places Ḥusayn's death in 1102/1690, while Muḥammad Khalīl al-Ḥusaynī al-Murādī (d. 1206/1791) mentions that this took place in 1109/1697, and this last report was accepted by some Lebanese historians such as the Patriarch Iṣṭifān al-Duwayhī (d. 1704), Ḥaydar al-Shihābī (d. 1835) and

Ṭannūs al-S̲h̲idyāḳ (d. 1859), who claim that Ḥusayn intervened with Ottoman officials in 1697, when the Ma'nid family came to an end. According to this, he succeeded in persuading the Ottomans to appoint Ḥaydar al-S̲h̲ihābī, the grandson of amīr Aḥmad al-Ma'nī, the last Ma'nid amīr, rather than amīr Bas̲h̲īr al-S̲h̲ihābi, to govern al-S̲h̲ūf. If Na'īmā is accurate in reporting the date of Ḥusayn's death (1102/1690), then this aspect of local Lebanese history clearly needs further investigation.

Bibliography: Aḥmad b. Muḥammad al-K̲h̲ālidī al-Ṣafadī, Ta'rīk̲h̲ al-Amīr Fak̲h̲r al-Dīn al-Ma'nī, ed. Asad Rustum and Fu'ād Afrām al-Bustānī², Beirut 1969, 105, 110, 112, 116-17, 119, 120, 123, 125-6, 137, 155, 160, 166; Nad̲j̲m al-Dīn al-G̲h̲azzī, al-Kawākib al-sā'ira fī a 'yān al-mi'a al-'āshira, ed. D̲j̲. D̲j̲abbūr, Beirut 1945-59, iii, 201-2; Muḥammad K̲h̲alīl al-Murādī, Silk al-durar fī a 'yān al-ḳarn al-hādī a 'shar, Būlāḳ ii, 59-60; Muḥammad Amīn b. Faḍl Allāh al-Muḥibbī, K̲h̲ulāṣat al-at̲h̲ar fī a 'yān al-ḳarn al-ḥādī 'ashar, repr. Beirut 1970, i, 365-8, iii, 266-9, 299-303; Iṣtifān al-Duwayḥī, Ta'rīk̲h̲ al-Azmina, ed. Ferdinand Taoutel al-Yasū'ī, Beirut 1961, 312, 314, 327, 329, 382-3; Muṣṭafā Na'īmā Efendī, Ta'rīk̲h̲ Na'īmā. Rawḍat al-Ḥusayn fī k̲h̲ulāṣat ak̲h̲bār al-k̲h̲āfiḳayn, Istanbul 1967-9, iii, 1229-30, v, 2373-5, 2471, vi, 2698; tr. Ch. Fraser, Annals of the Turkish empire from 1591 to 1659, London 1832, 422-5; Ḥaydar Aḥmad al-S̲h̲ihābī, al-G̲h̲urar al-ḥisān fī ak̲h̲bār abnā' al-zamān, i, ed. Asad Rustum and Fu'ād Afrām al-Bustānī, Beirut 1969, 3-5; Ṭannūs al-S̲h̲idyāḳ. Kitāb Ak̲h̲bār al-a'yān fī D̲j̲abal Lubnān, ed. Fu'ād Afram al-Bustānī, Beirut 1970, i, 170, 266, 268-9, 277-9, 287; Ismā'īl Pas̲h̲a al-Bag̲h̲dādī, Hadiyyat al-'ārifīn, asmā' al-mu'allifīn wa-āt̲h̲ār al-muṣannifīn, Istanbul 1951, i, 324; 'Isā Iskandar al-Ma'lūf. Kitāb al-Ta'bīr fi 'l-muḥāḍarāt: mak̲h̲ṭūṭ li 'l-Amīr Ḥusayn b. al-Amīr Fak̲h̲r al-Dīn al-Ma'nī, in al-Mac̲h̲riḳ, xxvii (1929), 811-15; idem, Ta'rīk̲h̲ al-Amīr Fak̲h̲r al-Dīn al-Ma'nī al-T̲h̲ānī, Beirut 1966, 162, 169-70, 179, 188, 205, 210, 249; Meḥmed T̲h̲üreyyā, Sidjill-i 'ot̲h̲mānī, ii, 73-119, 286; L. Thomas, A study of Naima, ed. N. Itzkowitz, Albany 1972, 22-4, 142-5, 147; Kamal S. Salibi, Ta'rīk̲h̲ Lubnān al-ḥadīt̲h̲², Beirut 1972, 31-2; idem. EI² art. Fak̲h̲r al-Dīn; M. Cavid Baysun, İA, art. Naima. A text of the Tamyīz, edited by M.A. Bak̲h̲īt from eleven Istanbul mss. and the Yale one, is being printed in Beirut.   (M.A. BAK̲H̲ĪT)

MA'NĀ (A.), a term whose sense needs to be defined according to the discipline in which it is used.
1. In grammar. Etymologically, ma'nā is what the speaker intends to say ('ibāra 'an al-s̲h̲ay' allad̲h̲ī 'anāhu 'l-'ānī, al-Rāzī, Mafātīḥ, i, 24,16); it is then almost synonymous with terms such as maḳṣūd, niyya and murād. As a technical term, ma'nā indicates the semantic counterpart of lafẓ. Each word has an aṣl, i.e. the radicals that constitute the consonantal structure of the word, which is realised in a pattern (binya). For each aṣl there is a correlating ma'nā, as well as for each binya, the latter ma'nā being the primary concern of the grammarian.

The terminological pair ma'nā/lafẓ is already found in Sībawayhi's Kitāb (according to Troupeau, Lexique-index, 891 and 215 times respectively). This early popularity shows the importance of the use of ma'nā in grammar and the need to take the grammatical data into account for any theory which tries to explain its origin in other disciplines, e.g. by pointing out analogies with the Stoic term lektón.

Although according to some authors there exists a correlation between the phonic and the semantic part of a word (Ibn D̲j̲innī, K̲h̲aṣā'iṣ, ed. Nad̲j̲djār, ii, 245

ff., iii, 264 ff.), there is an inherent discrepancy between the two entities, in that one expression may stand for several meanings, and vice-versa (cf. already Sībawayhi, Kitāb, ed. Būlāḳ, i, 7, 22-8, 3). On other level, one may say that the lafẓ never expresses the complete meaning, which can only reconstructed by means of a grammatical analysis, called taḳdīr. Through this method, the grammarian re-establishes, for instance, those governing words which are necessary for the meaning, but do not appear in the actual sentence ('āmil ma'nawī).

A special use of ma'nā in grammatical writings is found in the expression ḥarf ma'nā "particle" as against ḥarf "consonant, letter" (connected with the controversial definition of the ḥarf d̲j̲ā'a li-ma'nan, Sībawayhi, Kitāb, i, 2, l); and ism ma'nā "abstract noun" as against ism 'ayn "concrete noun" (e.g. al-Zamak̲h̲s̲h̲arī, Mufaṣṣal, 5, 3).

In the debate between logicians and grammarians in the period after the first translations of Greek logical writings had appeared, the difference between lafẓ and ma'nā was used by the logicians to define the different subjects of the two disciplines; grammar was to occupy itself solely with the alfāẓ, whereas the study of the ma'ānī was restricted to logic (e.g., al-Sid̲j̲istānī, apud al-Tawḥīdī, Muḳābasāt, ed. Sandūbī, 169, 21 ff.). The two terms are not synonymous with the pair ism/musammā, which is often used in logical and philosophical discussions, because ism denotes the entire linguistic symbol., whereas musammā is either the correlating thought or the object in the outer world.

The opposition between alfāẓ as the linguistic expression, and ma'ānī as the underlying meaning, was common in rhetorics and poetics, where one of the much-debated questions concerned the status of these two entities. For al-D̲j̲āḥiẓ, for instance, the alfāẓ of the poet are more essential for an evaluation of his qualities than the ma'ānī (Bayān, ed. Sandūbī, i, 98 ff.). The numerous books with titles such as Kitāb Ma'ānī 'l-s̲h̲i'r, Kitāb Ma'ānī 'l-Ḳur'ān, etc., contain primarily discussions of the meaning of words and phrases and are, therefore, lexicographical rather than grammatical writings.

In Ibn Ḥazm's grammatical theory, finally, there is a strict distinction, contrary to the generally-accepted usage, between the intention of the speaker and the inherent signification of the word.

Bibliography: A fundamental analysis is given by G. Bohas, Contributions à l'étude de la méthode des grammairiens arabes en morphologie et en phonologie d'après des grammairiens "tardifs", thèse d'état Paris III, 1979, 33-42, 64 ff., 167 f.; cf. also C. Versteegh, Greek elements in Arabic linguistic thinking, Leiden 1977, 178-90; N. Anghelescu, 'Sensul' în gîndirea linguisticâ arabâ, in I. Coteanu and L. Wald (eds.), Semanticâ și semioticâ, Bucharest 1981, 166-77. Lafẓ/ma'nā in rhetorics: W. Heinrichs, Arabische Dichtung und griechische Poetik, Beirut 1969, 62-82; L. Bettini, Studi sulla teoria letteraria araba, Florence 1981, esp. 9-14. Lafẓ/ma'nā in the debate between logic and grammar: M. Mahdi, Language and logic in Classical Islam, in G.E. von Grunebaum (ed.), Logic in Classical Islamic culture, Wiesbaden 1970, 51-83; G. Endress, al-Munāẓara bayn al-manṭiḳ al-falsafī wa 'l-naḥw al-'arabī fī 'uṣūr al-k̲h̲ulafā' (with English summary), in Jnal. for the history of Arabic Science, i (1977), 339-51; Versteegh, Logique et grammaire au dixième siècle, in Histoire, Epistémologie, langage, ii (1980), 39-52. Ma'nā in Ibn Ḥazm's and Ibn Maḍā's Ẓāhirī system: R. Arnaldez, Grammaire et théologie chez Ibn Ḥazm de Cordoue, Paris 1056, 56-61, 90-6.   (C. H. M. VERSTEEGH)

2. In philosophy. This term is used to translate a number of Greek expressions. *Maᶜnā* is frequently used as a synonym of *maᶜḳūl*, corresponding to the Greek *noéma*, a concept, thought or idea. Sometimes *maᶜḳūl* is used to translate the term "concept" (as in al-Fārābī's commentary on Aristotle's *De Interpretatione*) and sometimes *maᶜnā* (as in his commentary on Aristotle's *De Intellectu*). Isḥāḳ b. Ḥunayn uses *maᶜnā* in his translation of the *De Interpretatione*, but he also translated Aristotle's use of *prágmata* (real things) by *maᶜānī*. (For an argument against the Latin translation of *maᶜnā* by *intentio*, see Gyeke). Al-Ghazālī uses *maᶜānī* to represent meaning, a general usage, and it has been argued that this sense of the expression is Stoic in origin, representing *lectón* (Shehaby). Al-Ḥasan b. Suwār, in his notes on Aristotle's *Categories*, identifies *maᶜānī* with *āthār* (affections produced by natural things in the soul) and identical to the forms (*ṣuwar*) of the actual things (*umūr*). It is in a similar sense that Ibn Sīnā identifies a form in the soul with a *maᶜnā*, a meaning or notion, which in mediaeval epistemology has the technical sense of "natural sign in the soul". Ibn Sīnā's distinction between *maᶜānī* of the first and second understanding probably stems from Porphyry's distinction between terms of first and second imposition. The latter, *maᶜānī* of second understanding, are abstract notions which are applied to the notions of first understanding. The expressions *maᶜānī maᶜḳūla*, intelligible notions, or *maᶜānī* or just *maᶜḳūlāt*, are often found in Ibn Sīnā, all frequently translated as *intellecta*. These terms are important for his argument of the complex relationship between logic and language (see Sabra).

Muᶜammar b. ᶜAbbād al-Sulamī, the Baṣran Muᶜtazilī philosopher, is undoubtedly the chief exponent of the use of the term *maᶜnā* as a vital part of a metaphysical system. According to him, every *maᶜnā* (entity) is brought about by another entity, which itself has its origin in a third entity, and so on ad infinitum. Muᶜammar speaks of an infinite chain of determinant *maᶜānī*, the first determinant of which is God, and through which God is indirectly the real cause for the accidental external appearance of substances. For example, he talks of God creating countless *maᶜānī* of colour, the final effect of which is the accident "colour". The infinite chain of *maᶜānī* are causes of creating, and the occasionally evil accidents brought about thereby are caused by the subtance through the real features of nature, not God. *Maᶜnā* is used by Muᶜammar to represent the principle of individuation of one substance from another. Horovitz identifies *maᶜānī* with Plato's ideas, while Horten thinks they originate in the Indian system of categories. Watt identifies *maᶜnā* with Aristotelian *eidos* and Plato's ideas, as a real determination of a substance. Wolfson relates it to Aristotle's concept of nature as the cause of motion and rest, a claim hotly contested by Frank. The latter describes it as an intrinsic causal determinant, a Stoic notion which certainly seems to be present in Muᶜammar's distinction between primary and secondary causal determinants. Frank criticises the accounts of Muᶜammar's use of *maᶜnā* provided by al-Rāzī and al-Shahrastānī and insists that *maᶜānī* in the original system inhere in the material substrate of atoms, not with the accidents (references in Frank). Daiber, in the fullest account of *maᶜānī* in Muᶜammar's system yet to appear, on the contrary stresses their relational properties as opposed to their property of inherence in substance.

Bibliography: Fārābī, *Risāla fī 'l-ᶜaḳl*, in *Philosophische Abhandlungen*, ed. F. Dieterici, Leiden 1890, 43, 11. 17-18, 44, 11. 6-7; S. Horovitz, *Über den Einfluss der griechischen Philosophie auf die Entwicklung des Kalam*, Breslau 1908, esp. 44-54; M. Horten, *Die Ideenlehre des Muᶜammar*, in *Archiv für systematische Philosophie*, xv (1909), 469-84; idem, *Was bedeutet m-ᶜn-y als philosophischer Terminus?*, in *ZDMG*, lxiv, 391-6; Ghazālī, *Maḳāṣid al-falāsifa*, Cairo 1912, 25, 64, 70, 71; Ibn Sīnā, *Kitāb al-Nadjāt*, Cairo 1938, 3; O. Pretzl, *Die frühislamische Attributenlehre*, in *SB Bayr. Ak.* (1940), 37-43; Ibn Suwār, ed. and tr. Kh. Georr, *Les catégories d'Aristote dans leurs versions syro-arabes*, Beirut 1948, 361-86, esp. 361, ll. 1-4; Ibn Sīnā, *al-Shifāʾ, al-Manṭiḳī. i. al-Madkhal*, ed. G. Anawātī, M. El-Kohdeiri and F. El-Ahwānī, Cairo 1952, esp. 17, 22-3; Aristotle, *Arisṭūṭālis, Fī al-Nafs*, etc., ed. A. Badawī, Cairo 1954, 79; Ibn Sīnā, *al-Shifāʾ, al-Ilāhiyyāt*, ed. G. Anawātī and S. Zāyed, i, Cairo 1960, 10-11; *Al-Fārābī's commentary on Aristotle's De Interpretatione*, ed. W. Kutsch and S. Marrow, Beirut 1960, esp. 24; W. M. Watt, *The logical basis of early Kalām*, in *IQ*, vi (1961), 3-10; H. Wolfson, *Muᶜammar's theory of maᶜnā*, in *Arabic and Islamic Studies in honour of H.A.R. Gibb*, ed. G. Makdisi, Leiden 1965, 673-88; N. Rescher, *The concept of existence in Arabic logic and philosophy*, in his *Studies in Arabic philosophy*, Pittsburgh 1966, 80; R. Frank, *Al-Maᶜna: some reflections on the technical meanings of the term in the Kalām and its use in the physics of Muᶜammar*, in *JAOS*, lxxxvii (1967), 248-59; K. Geyke, *The terms "prima intentio" and "secunda intentio" in Arabic logic*, in *Speculum*, xlvi (1971), 32-8; H. Daiber, *Das theologisch-philosophische System des Muᶜammar ibn ᶜAbbād as-Sulamī*, Beirut 1975, esp. 78-89, 350-9 (excellent bibl.); N. Shehaby, *The influence of Stoic logic on al-Jassas's legal theory*, in *The cultural context of medieval learning*, ed. J. Murdoch and E. Sylla, Boston 1975, 61-86, esp. 80-5; A. Sabra, *Avicenna on the subject matter of logic*, in *Jnal. of Philosophy*, lxxvii (1980), 746-63.

(O.N.H. Leaman)

3. In poetry. Marked out to serve as a reflection on the language and to take its place in a cultural synthesis, poetry, after the preaching of Islam, assumed its role under the surveillance of academic phraseology. Scholars began to derive arguments from it to support their theories. Thus called upon by morpho-phonology, syntax, lexicography and even exegesis and historiography, poetry was turned into an instrument and reduced to being just a speech practice meant for providing arguments for the basic disciplines of language and thought. Hence one should not be surprised at the lack, until the 4th/10th century, of a true theory of meaning visualised as starting from poetical experience. Until then the word *maᶜnā* had only two meanings:

(1) The meaning of a word or proposition in a *certain given verse*. This meaning limits the reading to a purely contextual explanation. The *Kitāb Maᶜānī al-shiᶜr* of Abū ᶜUthmān Saᶜīd al-Ushnandānī, transmitted by Ibn Durayd, gives an example of these courses and monographs devoted to verses considered difficult. Lexically, attention is concentrated on terms which have become rare in usage (*gharīb*) or culturally marginal (*waḥshī*), but also on those syntactic expressions which leave the expressions ambiguous. Numerous works devoted to poetry are subsumed under this pragmatic aim and the elucidation of meaning.

(2) The meaning of a trope. The procedure here is similar, that of a clarification of the meaning, but the specific nature of the figurative expressions opens up perspectives which were later to become a semantics of poetry.

In this way, a fragmentary poetical text, reduced to citations, finds a place in lexicography, syntax and rhetoric. The school exercise of explaining it corresponds to a demand of criticism. The latter, born out of philology, requires the fitting of the maʿnā to the maḳṣad or g̲h̲araḍ, with the supposition that what is said corresponds exactly to what it was intended to say. Every displacement between the intention and the statement betrays the poet's inability to express what is correct with complete exactitude and shows up an inadequacy in the tools of the language. The maʿnā is a target which may be missed in two ways: either by not respecting the established correlations between the word and its referent, or between the syntactic expression and the logical distribution of its meanings; or else by disturbing the rules of construction of such figurative expressions as comparison, metaphor, metonymy, etc. The divergence between what is said and what it was intended to say (buʿd) is the measure of the ambiguity in the meaning (g̲h̲umūḍ). Criticism of meaning remains, within this framework, a criticism of effectiveness.

This enterprise ends up by updating the cultural codes prevailing in the language and makes an important contribution to the study of an archaeology of meaning. But one must note carefully that the works devoted to classification of meanings and tropes (Ibn Ḳutayba, al-Mubarrad, T̲h̲aʿlab, Ibn al-Muʿtazz in the 3rd/9th century) do not have poetry in view in the first place, or else they do not make the tropes analysed there a specific phenomenon of poetic writing. Moreover, even the terms connected with a single poetic genre such as madīḥ, hid̲jā̲ʾ, rit̲h̲āʾ or nasīb are not fashioned by means of a reflecting on the genres and themes. Till the end of the 3rd/9th century, it is quite wrong to consider the ʿilm al-maʿānī as an analysis of thematic forms, even with an author like Ibn Ḳutayba, who devotes a chapter of his Kitāb Maʿānī al-s̲h̲iʿr to marāt̲h̲ī.

It is Ḳudāma b. D̲ja̲ʿfar [q.v.] in his Naḳd al-s̲h̲iʿr who puts forward a general theory on the nature of poetry. This theory aims at defining an aesthetic, hence at regulating taste (d̲h̲awḳ) by setting out the rules of a science of what is good in poetry. Since the latter is an art (ṣināʿa), its actualisation can be placed on a scale of values which it is possible to draw up by reference to established canons of taste. Ḳudāma brings forward these canons of the connections existing between the constituent elements of poetic writing (lafẓ, maʿnā, wazn and ḳāfiya). The maʿnā here does not mean signification, since the latter is a fact of language, but the register of expression. There are six maʿānī in poetry: madīḥ, hid̲jā̲ʾ, marāt̲h̲ī, tas̲h̲bīh, waṣf and nasīb. Four of these names denote a semantic field relatively clearly delimited. Ḳudāma is here remaining within the track traced by his forerunners. He is an innovator in that he included tas̲h̲bīh in this list; he considers it as a general way of proceeding for the production of poetical statements, and all his attention is concentrated on the figures of thought. Waṣf brings in the general problem of the relationship of the statement to the object described. We can discern here a trace, small but clear, of the Greek theory of mimesis. The dialectic of kad̲h̲ib and ṣidḳ is thus here set aside, for Ḳudāma himself clearly, on this occasion, distances himself from all moralistic purposes.

Maʿnā is definitively that particular form (ṣūra) which poetry sketches out in a general sense. What is good may be measured by the amount of the conforming of the statement produced to an ideal statement (g̲h̲araḍ) The progress of poetry is contained in this movement which leads towards the perfect forms.

In fact, reflection about meaning in poetry eluded the udabāʾ, who remained fixed on the need of philological and lexical explanations, and had no theoretical system which could enable them to go further ahead. Work on the maʿnā became the preoccupation of the rhetoricians who had evolved the required tools for analysis. But it was the task of the logicians to put forward an attempt at definition, no longer of poetry, but of poetic theory, i.e. the ways of achieving the specific meanings required in poetry. Since al-Kindī's commentary on Aristotle's Poetics has not come down to us, we have to consider al-Fārābī [q.v.] as the first to have turned his attention and thought to al-aḳāwīl al-mukh̲ayyila. The problem of tak̲h̲yīl was to remain as a subject of thought for the analysts, especially for Ibn Sīnā, ʿAbd al-Ḳādir al-D̲j̲urd̲jā̲nī, Ibn Rus̲h̲d and Ḥāzim al-Ḳarṭād̲j̲annī. Our point of departure is a re-interpretation of the Aristotelian mimesis, which al-Ḳarṭād̲j̲annī in the end separates completely from speculative discourse. Tak̲h̲yīl denotes "the imaginary representation of the object which mimetic discourse (i.e. poetry) fixes in the speaker's imagination. The meaning is thus contained in a relationship of the object with its aesthetic representation as the producer of an effect". In this way, a fresh posing of the problem of meaning is formulated, and "the specificness and autonomy of poetry is circumscribed". The poet, as the creator of images, thus throws off the task of being truthful to life and becomes consequently free to project on to the object chosen all the features which his imagination pictures for him. The theory of the poetic uslūb set forth by Ibn K̲h̲aldūn in his Muḳaddima is actually a theory of the genuine poetic image. The uslūb is the abstract form of the meaning which becomes fixed in the poet's imagination. The latter realises it in statements made up of a thing signified (maʿnā) contained within a framework of the phrase (tarkīb). The nomenclature put forward by Ibn K̲h̲aldūn stems from this: kalām/fann (poetry, in contrast to prose)/mad̲h̲āhib (madḥ, rit̲h̲āʾ, nasīb)/ asālīb/ag̲h̲rāḍ or maʿānī and tarākīb. Ibn K̲h̲aldūn in this way completes his predecessors' analysis by studying the mechanism of production of maʿānī.

Bibliography: Texts: Since the texts utilised are well-known and amply cited in the articles on the respective authors, it is enough to say that the logicians' developments of the topic of poetic theory are given in ʿAbd al-Raḥmān Badawī's Arisṭūṭālīs, fann al-s̲h̲iʿr¹, Cairo 1954, with a better ed. of Ibn Rus̲h̲d's commentary and a 1st ed. of al-Fārābī's D̲ja̲wāmiʿ al-s̲h̲iʿr by M. Salīm Salīm, Cairo 1971; the part of Ibn Sīnā's K. al-S̲h̲ifāʾ devoted to the commentary on Aritotle's Poetics has been tr. with an English commentary by I. M. Dahiyat, Avicenna's commentary on the Poetics of Aristotle, a critical study with an annotated translation of the text, Leiden 1974. Studies: J. E. Bencheikh, Poétique arabe, Paris 1975; D̲j̲. A. ʿUsfūr, Mafhūm al-s̲h̲iʿr, Cairo 1978; K. Abu Deeb, Al-Jurjani's theory of poetic imagery, Warminster 1979; Bencheikh, Min al-ḳawālib al-lisāniyya ilā 'l-asālīb al-s̲h̲iʿriyya, Ibn K̲h̲aldūn wa-māhiyyat al-s̲h̲iʿr, in Aʿmāl nadwat Ibn K̲h̲aldūn, Casablanca 1981, 47 ff.; ʿA. al-Msaddī, al-Tafkīr al-lisānī fi 'l-hadar al-ʿarabiyya, Tripoli and Tunis 1981; Ḥ. Ṣammūd, al-Tafkīr al-balāg̲h̲ī ʿind al-ʿArab, ususuhu wa-taṭawwuruhu ilā 'l-ḳarn al-sādis, Tunis 1981; H. Foda, La formule due sens, essai sur al-Nuḳaṭ fī iʿg̲h̲āz al-Qurʾān d'al-Rummānī, in Analyses-Théorie (1982), no. 1, 43-70; idem, La rhétorique au coeur des enjeux. art. Littérature arabe, in Encyclopaedia Univer-

salis, new ed. (the definition of *takhyīl* is borrowed from here). (J. E. Bencheikh)

MANĀF, name of a deity of ancient Arabia. This IVth form *maṣdar* from the root *n-w-f* is connected with the Qatabanite *nwfn* "the exalted", an epithet describing ᶜAthar-Venus at its zenith, as opposed to *shrḳn* "the eastern" and *ghrbn* "the western". From the same root is derived *tanūf* "that which climbs high in the firmament", an epithet of the sun, as opposed to *mshrḳtym* "that which rises", and *tadūn* "that which sets" (cf. A. Jamme, *Le panthéon sud-arabe préislamique d'après les sources épigraphiques*, in *Le Muséon*, lx [1947], 88 and n. 225, 102, 106; on the meaning of this root and the vocabulary which is derived from it, cf. *TA*, s.v.).

"Manāf was one of the greatest deities of Mecca", states al-Ṭabarī (i, 1092). Such a statement is nevertheless surprising, bearing in mind how little information we have on the subject. Only Ibn al-Kalbī (*K. al-Aṣnām*, ed. and Fr. tr. W. Atallah, Paris 1969, 26) devotes a few lines to it, repeated by al-Ṭabarī (i, 1091-2) and Yāḳūt (iv, 651); however, going by the inscriptions, the name was known in Thamudic (A. van den Branden, *Les inscriptions thamoudéennes*, 48 (Huber, 12), 225 (Huber, 696), in Ṣafaitic and in Liḥyanitic (G. Ryckmans, *Les noms propres sud-sémitiques*, i, Louvain 1934, 18; *idem*, *Les religions arabes préislamiques*², Louvain 1953, 17), and altars were dedicated to him in the Ḥawrān (cf. P. Mouterde, *Inscriptions grecques conservées à l'Institut Français de Damas, no. 33*, in *Syria*, vi [1925], 246-52) and at Volubilis in Morocco (cf. L. Robert, in *Revue des études grecques* [1936], 3-8).

Probably of South Arabian origin, the cult of this deity was widespread among the Ḳurayshites, Hudhayl and Tamīm, as is shown by the theophoric names composed with his name (cf. Ibn al-Kalbī, *Aṣnām, loc. cit.*; Ibn Durayd, *Ishtiḳāḳ*, 143, l. 16, 66; *TA*, iii, 470, l. 7 f. *a fine*). One of the most famous is that of ᶜAbd Manāf, one of the four sons of Ḳuṣayy, reformer of the cult in Mecca. His mother had promised him to the god, so as to protect him from the evil eye, for he was so handsome that he was surnamed *al-ḳamar* "the moon" (al-Ṭabarī, *loc. cit.*).

Ibn al-Kalbī, reproduced by Yāḳūt, notes a practice common to all the idols, mentioned by G. Ryckmans (*Les religions arabes préislamiques*, 17) as being peculiar to Manāf; menstruating women did not touch them as a token of blessing and kept at a distance from them. Two verses, one by Balᶜā᾽ b. Ḳays, relating to Manāf, the other Bishr b. Abī Khazīm, relating to Isāf, allude to this (Ibn al-Kalbī and Yāḳūt, *locis citatis*; Yāḳūt, i, 235).

Bibliography: Apart from the references cited, see J. Wellhausen, *Reste*², Berlin 1897, 57; T. Fahd, *Le Panthéon de l'Arabie centrale à la veille de l'hégire*, Paris 1968, 122-3. (T. Fahd)

MANĀḲIB (a.), plural substantive (sing *manḳaba*) featuring in the titles of a quite considerable number of biographical works of a laudatory nature, which have eventually become a part of hagiographical literature in Arabic, in Persian and in Turkish.

To define this term, the lexicographers make it a synonym of *akhlāḳ*, taken in the sense of "natural dispositions (good or bad), innate qualities, character", and associate it with *naḳība*, explained by *nafs* "soul", *khalīḳa* or *ṭabīᶜa*, likewise signifying "trait of character, disposition", but also with *nafādh al-ra᾽y*, "perspicacity", in such a way that the connection with the radical *n-ḳ-b*, which is particularly expressive and implies especially the concrete sense of "perforate, pierce (a wall, for example)", thus, in an abstract sense, "succeed in penetrating a secret", becomes perfectly clear. Perhaps it should be approached as is suggested by Ibn Manẓūr (*LA*, sub radice *n-ḳ-b*), via *naḳīb* "chief", thus named because he is privy to "the secrets of his fellow-tribesmen (*dakhīlat amr al-ḳawm*) and to their *manāḳib*, which is the means of knowing their affairs"; in short, *manāḳib* would signify almost simultaneously both "traits of character" and "acts and deeds", and its use to introduce a biography centred not only on the actions, but also on the moral qualities of an individual, would be entirely legitimate. Finally, also worth consideration is an alternative meaning of the verb *naḳaba*, "walk, follow a narrow path", and a subtle connection may be observed between two senses of the singular *manḳaba*: on the one hand, "narrow street between two houses", or "difficult path on the mountain" (cf. Yāḳūt s.v. al-Manāḳib; *Sīra*, ii, 468) and, on the other hand, "noble action", in contrast to *mathlaba* "villainy, subject of shame" [see MATHĀLIB], as is supported by the evidence of numerous titles, particularly that on the *Kitāb al-Manāḳib wa 'l-mathālib* by Hibat Allāh Ibn ᶜAbd al-Wāḥid (Brockelmann, S II, 908), where the two antithetical terms possess the added advantage of mutual rhyme. If the last explanation suggested is correct, one is entitled to consider that a semantic evolution has occurred comparable to that of *sīra* [*q.v.*].

However, although this last term may be accompanied by a depreciative epithet (e.g. *sayyi*᾽), *manāḳib*, sometimes made more precise, sometimes not, by a qualificative (*djamīl, karīm*, etc.), is always taken in a good sense; the term may be rendered approximately by "qualities, virtues, talents, praiseworthy actions", and introduces a laudatory biography in which the merits, virtues and remarkable deeds of the individual concerned are given prominence. It will be observed that, immediately following the development of mysticism and the cult of saints, it is the marvellous aspects of the life, the miracles or at least the prodigies (*karāmāt*) [*q.v.*]) of a Ṣūfī or of a saint believed to have been endowed with miraculous powers, which are the subjects preferred, and *manāḳib* ultimately acquires the sense of "miracles" or "prodigies". It is perhaps a reminiscence of this last sense that is used to form an abstract applied even to the army by ᶜAzīz al-Aḥdab in his *Djaysh Lubnān wa-manāḳibiyyatuh al-ᶜaskariyya*, Beirut 1975.

Such is, schematically outlined, the apparent evolution of this concept, although it is not easy, in reality, to follow it with precision. In fact, the most ancient texts bearing the title of *manāḳib* have in general hardly survived at all, and their existence is only known to us thanks to the biographers and bibliographers of the Middle Ages; on the other hand, that which could be called "the *manāḳib* genre" is hard to isolate, since it is practically impossible, on account of constant interference, to establish a neat classification according to the etiquettes affixed by authors to the account of the life and enumeration of the virtues of the individual or the group chosen. The nomenclature in fact comprises a full gamut of titles which must be examined.

—*tardjama* [*q.v.*], quite neutral, implies no particular quality and introduces any biography; it may be said, however, that this term features in titles where another would be expected, for example *Tardjamat Aḥmad b. Ḥanbal* or *Tardjamat al-Shāfiᶜī* by al-Dhahabī (see Ṣ. al-Munadjdjid, *Muᶜdjam al-mu᾽arrikhīn al-dimashkiyyīn*, Beirut 1398/1978, 445), while the founders of judicial schools are most often entitled to *manāḳib* (see below).

—*taᶜrīf*, likewise neutral, but already used by ᶜIyāḍ

(see below) for the Prophet, appears in the title of lives of saints, possibly for reasons of discretion, in a period where *manāḳib* seems to be confined to the hagiographical sphere. For example, ʿAbd al-Salām al-Ḳādirī (d. 1110/1698 [see AL-ḲĀDIRĪ]) devoted *al-Maḳṣad al-aḥmad fī 'l-taʿrīf bi-Sayyidinā Ibn ʿAbd Allāh* to Ibn Maʿn al-Andalusī (see E. Lévi-Provençal, *Les historiens des Chorfa*, Paris 1922, 278), while the monograph on the same saint by Muḥammad al-Mahdī al-Fāsī (d. 1109/1698 [see AL-FĀSĪ in Suppl.]) is intitled *ʿĀrif/ʿAwārif al-munna bi-manāḳib Sayyidī (Sīdī) Maḥammad b. ʿAbd Allāh muḥyī 'l-sunna* (*Chorfa*, 275; ms. in Leiden, see P. Sj. van Koningsveld, *Ten Arabic manuscript-volumes of historical contents acquired by the Leiden Univ. Libr. after 1957*, in E. van Donzel (ed.), *Studies on Islam*, Amsterdam-London 1974, 95). Similarly, Maḥammad al-Masnāwī al-Dilāʾī (d. 1136/1724 [see AL-DILĀʾ in Suppl.]), is the author of *al-Taʿrīf bi 'l-shaykh Abi 'l-ʿAbbās al-Yamanī* (*Chorfa*, 302), ʿAbd al-Madjid al-Zabādī (d. 1163/1750; see *Chorfa*, 314) wrote the *Ifādat al-murād bi 'l-taʿrīf bi 'l-shaykh Ibn ʿAbbād* (d. 792/1390) and al-Darʿī (12th/18th century), *al-Rawḍ al-zāhir fī 'l-taʿrīf bi 'l-shaykh Ibn Ḥusayn wa-atbāʿih al-akābir*, on the saint of Tamgrūt named al-Ḳabbāb (d. 1045/1635-6; see *Chorfa*, 315). This term, adopted by Ibn Khaldūn for his autobiography, seems to be particularly common in Morocco, where hagiographical literature is especially prolific.

—*akhbār*, also neutral, tends to be applied to collections of historical traditions, even of simple anecdotes, concerning individuals of ethnic or social groups (see e.g. *Akhbār Abī Nuwās*, *Akhbār al-ḳiyān*, etc.). Nevertheless, one encounters, again from the pen of al-Dhahabī (d. 748/1347 [*q.v.*]), the *Akhbār Umm al-Muʾminīn ʿĀʾisha* (Munadjdjid, 445), which does not necessarily imply a greater concern for objectivity than is found in the *Manāḳib Ḥaḍrat Umm al-Muʾminīn ʿĀʾisha*. (Ḥādjdjī Khalīfa, *Kashf al-ẓunūn*, ed. Istanbul 1941, ii, col. 1843) by Muḥibb al-Dīn al-Ṭabarī (d. 694/1294-5 [*q.v.*]) or in the *Kitāb al-Albāb al-ṭāʾisha fī manāḳib Umm al-Muʾminīn ʿĀʾisha* by the Moroccan Muḥammad b. ʿAlī al-Wadjdī al-Ghammād (d. 1033/1624; see M. Hajji, *L'activité intellectuelle au Maroc à l'époque saʿdide*, Rabat 1976, 487). For his part, Aḥmad Adfāl gave the title *Akhbār* to his biography of Aḥmad b. Mūsā al-Samlālī (d. 971/1564; see Hajji, 181, 650; al-Sūsī, *al-Maʿsūl*, Casablanca 1380-3/1960-3, 20-43), whereas that of the same Sūsī saint by Yibūrk al-Samlālī (Hajji, 181) bears the title of *Manāḳib al-Sayyid Aḥmad b. Mūsā*. A further example: ʿAbd al-Raḥmān al-Fāsī (d. 1096/1685 [see AL-FĀSĪ in Suppl.]) celebrated the memory of his father in two works: *Bustān al-azāhir fī akhbār al-shaykh ʿAbd al-Ḳādir* and *Tuḥfat al-akābir fī manāḳib ʿAbd al-Ḳādir* (*Chorfa*, 267).

—*sīra*, as is known, is not reserved for the Prophet, and a considerable number of biographies (and even stories, such as the *Sīrat ʿAntar*) bearing this title are mentioned in the repertoires; it will be noted only, for the sake of example, that al-Dhahabī (yet again) wrote a *Sīrat al-Ḥallādj* (Munadjdjid, 446), and the Ṣūfī Ḥiṣnī (d. 829/1426; see Munadjdjid, 231), a *Siyar al-nisāʾ al-ʿābidāt*, just as Ḳāsim al-Ḥalfawī (d.after 1000/1591; see Hajji, 181) entitled his monograph on the santon of Marrakesh known as Abū ʿAmr al-Ḳaṣṭallī *Shams al-maʿrifa fī sīrat ghawth al-mutasawwifa* (mss. in Rabat and Marrakesh).

—*faḍāʾil*, "virtues", is closer to the sense of *manāḳib* and even serves as its equivalent, although covering a much more extensive range [see FAḌĪLA].While the "*faḍāʾil* genre" is in part reserved for the vindication of towns and of countries, Ibn al-Djawzī (d. 597/1200 [*q.v.*]) wrote the *Manāḳib Baghdād* (ed. Baghdād 1921; see Brockelmann, S I, 917), he merely used *faḍāʾil* for Bishr al-Ḥāfī (d. 226 or 227/840-2 [*q.v.*]). The two terms are set in parallel and applied with exactly the same meaning to the people of Cordova by al-Idrīsī [*q.v.*] in his *Opus geographicum* (written in 548/1154), v, 574. *Faḍāʾil* is used by authors anxious, as was al-Ṭabarī (d. 310/923 [*q.v.*]), to celebrate the virtues of the Companions and of the Orthodox Caliphs (see Yāḳūt, *Udabāʾ*, xviii, 80-1); otherwise it had already been adopted by al-Madāʾinī (d. 226/840 [*q.v.*]) for Djaʿfar b. Abī Ṭālib, al-Ḥārith b. ʿAbd al-Muṭṭalib and Muḥammad Ibn al-Ḥanafiyya (*Udabāʾ*, xiv, 132) and by al-Bukhārī (d. 256/870), who dedicates a *bāb* to the *faḍāʾil aṣḥāb al-Nabī*, following it however with a *bāb manāḳib al-Muhādjirīn* and a *bāb m. al-Anṣār* (v, 2-47); as late as the 5th/11th century, Ibn al-ʿUshārī (d. 441/1049; see Brockelmann, S I, 601) wrote a *Kitāb Faḍāʾil Abī Bakr al-Ṣiddīḳ*, and, in the 7th/13th century, Amīn al-Dawla Ibn ʿAsākir (d. 686/1288), *Faḍāʾil Umm al-Muʾmimīn Khadīdja* (Munadjdjid, 120). However, the anonymous ms. 8273 of the British Museum is called *Manāḳib al-Ṣaḥāba*, and, in Spain, al-Ghāfiḳī (d. 540/1146; see Brockelmann, S I, 629) wrote *Manāḳib al-ʿashara wa-ʿammay Rasūl Allāh*, while ʿAbd al-Ghanī al-Maḳdisī (d. 600/1203; see Munadjdjid, 68-9) left for posterity *Manāḳib al-Ṣaḥābiyyāt* (ms. Ẓāhiriyya 3754), and Madjd al-Dīn Ibn al-Athīr (d. 606/1210; see IBN AL-ATHĪR), *al-Mukhtār fī manāḳib al-akhyār* (cf. O. Spies, in *MO*, xxiv [1930], 1-15) on the pious men and women of early Islam; al-Ḍiyāʾ al-Maḳdisī (d. 643/1245; see Munadjdjid, 86, 442) eulogised the *manāḳib* of Djaʿfar b. Abī Ṭālib (ed. M.H. Āl Yāsīn, Baghdād); the afore-mentioned Muḥibb al-Dīn al-Ṭabarī, has, like al-Ghāfiḳī, celebrated the "ten assured of Paradise" in *al-Riyāḍ al-naḍira fī manāḳib al-ʿashara* (ed. Cairo 1372/1953); al-Dhahabī is himself credited with *al-Tibyān fī manāḳib ʿUthmān* (Munadjdjid, 445) and Ibn ʿAbd al-Hādī (d. 909/1503; see Munadjdjid, 274, 276) even wrote a *Maḥḍ al-ikhlāṣ fī manāḳib Saʿd b. Abī Waḳḳāṣ* (ms. Ẓāhiriyya 3248). If, for ʿAlī b. Ṭālib and his descendants, the use of *manāḳib* is fully justified in the works of those authors who particularly revere their memory (see below), and if the same can to a certain extent be said of ʿUmar b. 'Abd al-ʿAzīz, thus eulogised by Ibn al-Djawzī, it is hard to say why the last-named (*Kashf*, iv, col. 560; Brockelmann, S I, 916-17) and, for example, al-Barzandjī (Brockelmann S II, 934) gave the title *Manāḳib* to their biographies of Abū Bakr and of ʿUmar b. al-Khaṭṭāb. It is true that it is impossible to find the explanation in the variation which manifests itself in the *Djamʿ al-fawāʾid min Djāmiʿ al-uṣūl* [of Ibn al-Athīr] *wa-Madjmaʿ al-zawāʾid* [of al-Haythamī], Medina 1381/1961, in which *ḥadīth*s concerning the Companions as a group are given under the title of *faḍāʾil* (ii, 490-500), whilst those relating to the same Companions considered individually are given under that of *manāḳib* (ii, 500-81).

—*maʾāthir* and *mafākhir*, "exploits, objects of pride", normally feature in the titles of collections of traditions in favour of tribes, peoples or groups and are the reverse of *mathālib*; they are also encountered, as is sometimes *maḥāsin*, in those of monographs of individuals who have played an eminent political, politico-religious or military role. An example which may be mentioned, from Morocco, is a *Rawḍat al-taʿrīf fī mafākhir Mawlānā Ismāʿīl b. al-Sharīf* by al-Ifrānī (d. 1156 or 1157/1743-5 [*q.v.*]), which concerns a sultan (*Chorfa*, 275); *al-Muntaḳā 'l-maḳṣūr ʿalā maʾāthir khilāfat al-Manṣūr* (ms. in Leiden, see van Koningsveld, 94;

Brockelmann, S II, 679) by Ibn al-Ḳāḍī (d. 1065/1616 [*q.v.*]), where *ma'āthir* is sometimes replaced by *maḥāsin*, is a panegyric of the sultan al-Manṣūr al-Dhahabī; on the other hand, the *Rawḍat al-maḥāsin al-zahiyya bi-ma'āthir al-shaykh Abi 'l-Maḥāsin al-bahiyya*, by the afore-mentioned Muḥammad al-Mahdī al-Fāsī, is the biography of a religious man (*Chorfa*, 114), and the same al-Ifrānī who is cited above gave the title *Durar al-hidjāl fī ma'āthir "sab'at ridjāl"* (*Chorfa*, 115) to a hagiography of the "seven saints" of Marrakesh (see G. Deverdun, *Marrakech*, Rabat 1959, 571-5), whereas *manāḳib* would more naturally be expected.

—*akhlāḳ*: Ibn Fāris (d. 395/1004 [*q.v.*]) is credited with a *Kitāb Akhlāḳ al-Nabī (Udabā'*, iv, 84) which justifies the assimilation, by Ibn Manẓūr (see above), of *manāḳib* to *akhlāḳ*, for it seems likely that in choosing this latter term, the author of the *Ṣāḥibī* wished to signal his intention of dealing with the character and moral qualities of the Prophet, as al-Tirmidhī (d. *ca.* 275/888-9 [*q.v.*]) had done in his *Shamā'il al-Nabī* (ed. Cairo 1306). In the 6th/12th century, the *ḳāḍī* 'Iyāḍ (d. 544/1149 [*q.v.*]) chose a more neutral title, *al-Shifā bi-ta'rīf al-Muṣṭafā* (numerous editions), not suspecting that this biography of the Prophet was destined to be accorded "throughout North Africa, supernatural virtues" (M. Talbi, *Biographies aghlabides*, Tunis 1968, 19); Ibn Ḥabīb al-Dimashḳī (d. 779/1377; see Munadjdjid, 449), who is said to have imitated the *Shifā*, showed less discretion, since he entitled his work *al-Nadjm al-thāḳib fī ashraf al-manāḳib*. Ibn 'Arabī (d. 638/1240 [*q.v.*]) for his part, is the author of a *manḳabat mawlid al-Nabī* (this is the only attestation of the singular in a title), which is a "presentation of the life of the Prophet from the point of view of his metaphysical reality, that is to say in his capacity of representing the Perfect Man upon the earth" (O. Yahia, *Histoire et classification de l'œuvre d'Ibn 'Arabī*, Damascus 1964, 358; the singular is not attested in any Arabic title, but it may be noted that in Urdu *manḳabat* indicates a poem in honour of 'Alī and the Shī'ī *Imāms*. [see MADĪḤ. 4. In Urdu]). *Shamā'il* is almost synonymous with *akhlāḳ* when the latter is taken in good a sense, and 'Abd al-'Azīz b. 'Abd al-Sulamī al-Dimashḳī (d. 660/1262; see Munadjdjid, 97) associates this term with *manāḳib* in his *Manāḳib al-Muṣṭafā wa-shamā'iluh*. There is however a fundamental difference between *akhlāḳ* and *manāḳib*, as is clearly revealed by al-Djāḥiẓ (d. 255/868 [*q.v.*]), who is the author of a *Madḥ* ... and of a *Dhamm akhlāḳ al-kuttāb*, where the key-word remains neutral, and of a *Risāla fī manāḳib al-Turk/al-Atrāk wa-'āmmat djund al-khilāfa*, in the title of which no further proof is needed of the desire to depict in the most favourable colours the natural dispositions, the merits and the characters of the Turkish troops and of other elements in the army. It appears from this example that in the 3rd/9th century, under the pen of a writer of the calibre of al-Djāḥiẓ, *akhlāḳ* and *manāḳib* may again be practically synonymous, on condition that the former be given clearer definition by means of a favourable term, except, of course, where no doubt is possible as to the intentions of the writer, as when the subject of discussion is the Prophet.

—*manaḳib*: R. Sellheim [see FAḌĪLA] considers that the *Faḍā'il* of al-Ḥasan al-Baṣrī by Ibn al-Djawzī belongs to the literature of *manāḳib*, but one may wonder why this author chose *faḍā'il* for the title of his eulogy of the famous preacher, whereas he opted for *manāḳib* when he sought to glorify Baghdād, 'Umar b. Khaṭṭāb or 'Umar b. 'Abd al-'Azīz, and the most appropriate usage of the word in question is found in his *Kitāb Manāḳib al-imām Ibn Ḥanbal* (ed. Cairo 1349/1931), as will be observed in due course. Study of a long series of titles in fact leaves the impression that, for many writers, there was scarcely any difference in conception and in method of exposition according to the terminology employed; in effect, the latter seems to be to a large extent interchangeable, and although R. Sellheim is probably correct in thinking that the lives of saints were to exercise a sort of monopoly over the use of *manāḳib*, the fact remains that a degree of fluctuation in the choice of terms demands constant vigilance.

While the *Manāḳib* of 'Alī b. Abī Ṭālib by Aḥmad b. Ḥanbal (d. 241/855 [*q.v.*]) which Ḥadjdjī Khalīfa (ii, col. 1843-4) mentions, saying that later authors have to a large extent exploited this biography, and perhaps also that by al-Kūfī (d. 300/931; Brockelmann, S I, 209), are probably no more than collections of traditions relating the virtues of the Prophet's son-in-law, this probably does not apply to the *Manāḳib 'Alī b. 'Abī Ṭālib* by al-Khwārazmī (d. 568/1172; Brockelmann, S I, 623; there is said to be a ms. of it at Nadjaf (al-Samāwī library), which further possesses others; see *RIMA*, iv, 237), to the *Manāḳib Āl Abī Ṭālib* (ed. Telmay 1317; Nadjaf 1376/1956), by Ibn Shahrāshūb (d. 588/1192 [*q.v.*]), *al-Arba'īn fī manāḳib sayyidat al-nisā' Fāṭima al-Zahrā'* by the same author or the *Manāḳib Fāṭima al-Zahrā'* by al-Suyūṭī (d. 911/1505 [*q.v.*]), to which reference is made in the *Kashf* (ii, col. 1843). These last-named works are in fact closer to hagiography, like those, in a more general sense, which are devoted to the family of the Prophet, such as the *Dhakhā'ir al-'uḳbā fī manāḳib dhawi 'l-ḳurbā* (ed. Cairo 1356) by Muḥibb al-Dīn al-Ṭabarī (d. 694/1294-5) or the *Maḥāsin al-azhār fī manāḳib al-'itra al-aṭhār* by Ḥamīd al-Maḥallī (d. after 652/1254; see A. Fu'ād Sayyid, *Sources de l'histoire du Yémen à l'époque musulmane*, IFAO, Cairo 1974, 127, 128) or even the *Nūr al-abṣār fī manāḳib Āl Bayt al-Nabī al-mukhtār* by Mu'min al-Shablandjī (ed. Cairo n.d.).

There is no doubt as to the legitimacy of associating with this category a *Kitāb al-Manāḳib* of a 4th/10th century Imāmī Shī'ī named 'Alī b. Ibrāhīm b. Hāshim al-Ḳummī (*Fihrist*, ed. Cairo, 311; cf. *Udabā'*, xii, 215), but there is certainly no justification for including in the corpus of hagiographical literature *the K. al-I'lām bi-manāḳib al-Islām* (ed. Cairo 1968) by the Persian philosopher al-'Āmirī (d. 381/992 [*q.v.*]) "a philosophical defence of Islam" or the *Manāḳib al-a'imma* by al-Bāḳillānī (d. 403/1013 [*q.v.*]), which are designed to defend "the Sunnī position with regard to the imāmate". In fact, a number of other titles are encountered which testify to the imprecision of the nomenclature, for example the *Manāḳib al-ma'ārif* by Ibn 'Arabī (O. Yahia, *op. cit.* no. 406; Brockelmann, S I, 801, no, 175) or *Kitāb Manāḳib al-kuttāb* by Ibn Kuthayyir al-Ahwāzī (*Fihrist*, ed. Cairo, 200; cf. *Udabā'*, iv, 244) which must have been a simple vindication of government secretaries; it is hardly likely that 'Ubayd Allāh b. Djibrīl (d. 450/1058) described miraculous cures in the *Manāḳib al-aṭibbā'* (*Kashf*, ii col. 1842), and attention may be drawn to *Manāḳib* of poets in Persian by Abū Ṭāhir al-Khātūnī (*Kashf*, ii, col. 1842) and, in Turkish, the *Manāḳib-i hünerverān* (ed. Istanbul 1926) by 'Ālī (d. 1008/1599-1600 [*q.v.*]), in which "he collected important material on several hundred calligraphers, miniaturists, illuminators and book binders". Also, *al-Kawkab al-thāḳib fī akhbār al-shu'arā' wa-ghayri-him min dhawī 'l-manāḳib* of 'Abd al-Ḳādir b. 'Abd al-Raḥmān al-Salawī (written 1176/1762-3) contains some 129 biographies of poets (ms. Royal Library of Rabat 925; see 'Abd Allāh al-Yāsimī, in *al-Fikr*, xxvii/10 [1982], 121-32).

Dynasties, families, distinguished individuals, also have their compilations of *manāḳib* which are apparently nothing more than glorious deeds or achievements. Thus al-Yazīdī al-Naḥwī (d. 313/925) gathered together those of the Banu 'l-ʿAbbās (*Kashf*, ii, col. 1841) and al-Ṣūlī (d. 335/946-7 [*q.v.*]), those of Ibn al-Furāt (d. 312/924 [*q.v.*]), as is noted by Ḥādjdjī Khalīfa (iv, col. 559), while Ibn al-Samāʿī (d. 674/1275-6 wrote a *Kitāb Manāḳib al-khulafāʾ* (*Kashf*, ii, col. 1841) and Ṣadr al-Dīn al-Baṣrī (7th/13th century) dedicated to Baybars (d. 676/1277 [*q.v.*]) *al-Manāḳib al-ʿabbāsiyya wa 'l-mafākhir al-mustanṣiriyya* (Brockelmann, S I, 457), where the two terms used in parallel are evidently regarded by the author as synonymous. This Mamlūk sultan was himself the subject of a biography by Shafiʿ b. ʿAlī b. ʿAbbās (d. 730/1330), *Ḥusn al-manāḳib al-sirriyya al-muntazaʿa min al-sīrā al-ẓāhiriyya*, ed. al-Khuwayṭir, Riyāḍ 1396/1976. The *Manāḳib Banī Hāshim wa-mathālib Banī Umayya* (Sezgin, *GAS*, i, 577) and the *Kitāb Manāḳib al-ḥikam fī mathālib al-umam* by a somewhat presumptuous author known as Shumaym al-Ḥillī (d. 602/1204; see *Udabāʾ*, xiii, 72) testify once more to the use of *manāḳib* as an antonym of *mathālib* and as a synonym, here too, of *faḍāʾil* or of *maʾāthir*/*mafākhir*. These latter terms could without inconvenience be substituted for *manāḳib* in the titles of those works written in praise of the ʿAbbāsids which have just been mentioned, and of the following, which celebrate ruling families or political figures: *al-Kawākib al-durriyya fi 'l-manāḳib al-Badriyya*, a *maḳāma* [*q.v.*] written in 791/1389 by al-Ḳalḳashandī [*q.v.*] for his master Badr al-Din (see C.E. Bosworth, *A maqāma on secretaryship*, in *BSOAS*, xxvii [1964], 291-5); *al-Ḥadāʾiḳ al-wardiyya fī manāḳib (wa-dhikr tarādjim) al-aʾimma al-Zaydiyya* by the already-mentioned Ḥamīd al-Maḥallī (Fuʾād Sayyid, 127), *al-Durr al-thamīn fī manāḳib Nūr al-Dīn* by Badr al-Dīn Ibn Ḳadī Shuhba (d. 874/1470 [see IBN ḲĀḌĪ SHUHBA]), of which numerous mss. exist (Brockelmann, S II, 25; Munadjdjid, 252-3), *al-Mashraʿ al-rawī fi manāḳib al-sādāt Āl Abī ʿAlwī* (ed. Cairo 1319) by al-Shillī (d. 1093/1682; see Fuʾād Sayyid, 246), *Fatḥ al-Raḥmān fī manāḳib Sayyidī ʿAbd al-Raḥmān b. Sulaymān*, written in 1263/1847 in honour of a member (d. 1250/1834-5) of the al-Ahdal [*q.v.*] Yemeni family by Saʿd b. ʿAbd Allāh Suhayl (Fuʾād Sayyid, 294), or indeed *al-Durr al-thamīn fī dhikr al-manāḳib wa 'l-waḳāʾiʿ li-Amīr al-Muslimīm ʿIyāḍ* (Fuʾād Sayyid, 305), a history of the revolt against the Ottomans of this *amīr* and his descendants up until the year 1288/1871, by Ḥasan b. Aḥmad al-Yamanī. Also to be mentioned, in this context, are the *Manāḳib-i Maḥmūd Pasha-yi Welī* on an Ottoman Grand Vizier (d. 879/1474 [*q.v.*]) and al-*Manāḳib al-Ibrāhīmiyya wa 'l-ma ʾāthir al-khidīwiyya* (ed. Cairo 1299/1882) by Abkāryūs (d. 1885 [see ISKANDER AGHA]) on the viceroy of Egypt Ibrāhīm Pasha [*q.v.*]. The natural gifts of the Yemenis are celebrated by al-Afḍal al-Rasūlī (d. 778/1377) in *al-ʿAṭāyā 'l-saniyya wa 'l-mawāhib al-haniyya fi 'l-manāḳib al-Yamaniyya* (Fuʾād Sayyid, 148), and reference is also made to a work of al-Ghazzī (d. 1061/1651), *al-Kawākib al-sāʾira bi-(manāḳib) a ʿyān al-mi ʾa al-ʿāshira*, ed. Dj. S. Djabbūr, Beirut 1945-9 (cf. Munadjdjid, 319-20).

To the examples of this genre others could be added which would only further complicate the preceding survey, involved as it is already, and intentionally so, since the titles are an indication of a constant fluctuation of the terminology. What emerges from them is simply a clear desire on the part of the authors to emphasise the remakable qualities of the persons whose lives they describe and the superior merits of the groups concerned. Conversely, there are a good many works which could be entitled *manāḳib*, for they con tain laudatory biographies and even belong to a literature of hagiographic type, starting with th *Ḥilyat al-awliyāʾ* by Abū Nu ʿaym (d. 430/1039 [*q.v.*]) Nevertheless, two important tendencies come to ligh in the usage of the term which is the subject of th present article.

Biographies of the founders of *madhāhib*.

Regarding the first of these tendencies, we are for tunate in that a connoisseur of Arabic literature in general of the calibre of Ḥādjdjī Khalīfa (d. 1067/165 [see KĀTIB ČELEBI]), can help us to a clearer view of th subject by offering his own interesting conclusions. I happens that this bibliographer not only supplies th researcher with a long list of *manāḳib* (*Kashf*, ii, col 1836-43; see also iv, 559-60), but also declares, referr ing to the authors of works belonging to this category that the disciples of the different legal schools need t know, in order to imitate them, the *manāḳib*, th qualities (*shamāʾil*), the virtues (*faḍāʾil*), the behaviou (*sīra*) and the truth of the sayings (*aḳwāl*) of thei founders, besides information regarding thei genealogy, places of birth etc. Although in thi passage, *manāḳib* could no doubt be rendered simpl by "natural dispositions, character", it is plain that for Ḥadjdjī Khalīfa, the term has a specialised mean ing in its application to a genre composed of de tailed, edifying and exemplary biographie of the great *imāms*. In fact, although *faḍāʾil* i employed from time to time, notably by al-Maghām (d. 288/900) for Mālik b. Anas (see al-Maḳḳarī, *Naf al-ṭīb*, Cairo 1949, iii, 274-5) and by Abu 'l-ʿArab (d 333/945 [*q.v.*]) for the same *imām* and for Saḥnūn (se below), and although al-Dhahabī preferred *tardjam* for Abū Yūsuf, Aḥmad b. Ḥanbal and al-Shāfi ʿī (se Munadjdjid, 445), it is nevertheless *manāḳib* whic prevails in this category for:

—Abū Ḥanīfa (d. *ca.* 150/767 [*q.v.*]): the im pressive list contained in the *Kashf* (ii, cols. 1836-9) also includes compilations in Persian (ii, col. 1839 and in Turkish (iv, col. 560). Those of Brockelman (S I, 285) and more especially of Sezgin (*GAS*, i, 411 12) are likewise well-stocked; their most significan contents are the works of al-Muwaffaḳ b. Ahmad al Makkī (d. 588/1192) and Muḥammad b. Muḥamma al-Kardarī (d. 827/1424), *Manāḳib al-imām al-aʿẓa* (ed. Ḥaydarābād 1321) and of al-Suyūṭī, *Tabyīḍ al ṣaḥīfa fī manāḳib Abī Ḥanīfa* (ed. Ḥaydarābād 1307) Also to be mentioned are al-Ṭaḥāwī (d. 321/93 [*q.v.*]); al-Zamakhsharī (d. 538/1144 [*q.v.*]), *Shaḳāʾi al-nuʿmān ...fī manāḳib al-imām Abī Ḥanīfa al-Nuʿmā* (*Udabāʾ*, xix, 135); al-Bakrī (d. 568/1172; Brockel mann, S I, 549); Ibn al-Djawzī (d. 597/1200); al Shāmī (d. 942/1536), *ʿUḳūd al-djumān fī manāḳib Ab Ḥanīfa al-Nuʿmān* (numerous mss. in Cairo, Istanbu and Damascus; see Munadjdjid, 287-8); Ibn Ṭūlū al-Ṣāliḥī (d. 953/1546 [*q.v.*]) *al-Amānī 'l-laṭīfa manāḳib Abī Ḥanīfa* (Munadjdjid, 291); Ibn Ḥadjar al Haythamī (d. 973/1565 [*q.v.*]) see Brockelmann, S II 528): al-ʿAdjlūnī (d. 1162/1749), *ʿIḳd al-laʾālī wa ' mardjān fī manāḳib Abī Ḥanīfa al-Nuʿmān* (ms. Princeto 4225; see Munadjdjid, 351-2); anon., ms. Yale 1202 Abu 'l-Kāsim b. ʿAbd al-ʿAlīm al-Ḥanafī, *Manāḳi Abī Ḥanīfa wa-ṣāḥibayhi* (ms. ʿAbd al-Wahhāb, se *Ḥawliyyāt al-Djāmiʿa al-Tūnisiyya*, vii [1970], 153, no 76).

—al-Awzāʿī (d. 157/774 [*q.v.*]): Ibn Zayd (d 870/1465; see Munadjdjid, 248), *Maḥāsin al-masāʿī manāḳib al-Awzā ʿī*, ed. Shakīb Arslān, Cairo 1352 (se Brockelmann, S I, 308; O. Spies, in *ZS* [1935], 18 ff.; for the identification of the author, see *MMIA*, x [1947], 187).

—Mālik b. Anas (d. 178/795 [*q.v.*]): besides the *Ta*

yīn of al-Suyūṭī (Brockelmann, S I, 297; Sezgin, GAS, i, 458), one may mention al-Dīnawarī al-Miṣrī (d. 310/922; *Kashf*, ii, col. 1841), al-Zawāwī (Brockelmann, S II, 961) and al-Ḥanbalī (d. 909/1503; Sezgin, *GAS*, i, 458).

—al-Shāfiʿī (d. 204/820 [*q.v.*]) has benefited from a large number of collections of *manāḳib*; Ḥādjdjī Khalīfa alone (ii, cols. 1839-40) lists thirteen: al-Subkī (*Ṭabaḳāt*, i, 185), Brockelmann (S I, 304) and Sezgin (*GAS*, i, 480) mention several others. One of the most ancient is probably that of Abu 'l-Husayn al-Rāzī (d. 347/958; see Munadjdjid, 17-18), whose death Ḥādjdjī Khalīfa places in 454/1063, while Sezgin (*GAS*, i, 480; cf. Brockelmann, S I, 921) attributes the *Manāḳib al-Shāfiʿī* (ed. Cairo 1372/1953) to Fakhr al-Dīn al-Rāzī (d. 606/1209 [*q.v.*]). It is also appropiate to mention Ibn al-Nadjdjār (d. 643/1245; see *Udabāʾ*, xix, 50; *Dāʾirat al-maʿārif*, iv, 102-3); Ibn al-Ṣalāḥ (d. 643/1245; Munadjdjid, 83-4), *Ḥilyat al-Shāfiʿi* (ms. Ẓāhiriyya 3795), the title of which recalls that of Abū Nuʿaym; al-Nawawī (d. 676/1277 [*q.v.*]), *Manāḳib al-Shāfiʿī wa 'l-Bukhārī* (ms. Ulu Cami 2462; Munadjdjid, 113-4); Ibn Kathīr (d. 774/1373 [*q.v.*]), *Tardjamat* (or *Manāḳib*) *al-imām al-Shāfiʿī* (ms. Chester Beatty 3390; Munadjdjid, 204, 206-7); Badr al-Dīn al-Hāshimī (d. 826/1423; *Kashf*, iv, col. 560); Ibn Ḥadjar al-ʿAskalānī (d. 852/1449 [*q.v.*]), *Tawālī 'l-taʾsīs bi-maʿālī Ibn Idrīs fī manāḳib ... al-Shāfiʿī* (ed. Būlāk 1301/1884).

—Aḥmad b. Ḥanbal (d. 241/355 [*q.v.*]) has been the subject of fewer collections than al-Shāfiʿī, but some are encountered (*Kashf*, ii, col. 1836; Brockelmann, S I, 309); Sezgin, *GAS*, i, 503-4), among which the following may be mentioned: al-Bayhaḳī (d. 458/1066 [*q.v.*]), *Manāḳib al-imām Ibn Ḥanbal wa 'l-imām al-Shafiʿī* (*Kashf*; cf. Brockelmann, S I, 619, nos. 11-12; Sezgin, i, 503), al-Harawī (d. 481/1088), Ibn al-Djawzī (d. 597/1200), *Manāḳib al-imām Aḥmad b. Ḥanbal* (ed. Cairo 1349/1931) and al-Maḳrīzī (d. 845/1442 [*q.v.*]), *Manāḳib Aḥmad b. Ḥanbal* (Brockelmann, S II, 37; Sezgin, *GAS*, i, 504).

To these monographs may be added the biographical dictionaries devoted to the disciples of a school. They usually start with an account of the founder, and most often bear the classical title *Ṭabaḳāt* [*q.v.*], but one encounters nevertheless, by al-Sharīf al-Ḥusaynī (d. 776/1374), *al-Makātib al-ʿaliyya fī manāḳib al-Shāfiʿiyya* (ms. Feyzallah 1525; see Munadjdjid, 211) and, by Taḳī al-Dīn Ibn Ḳāḍī Shuhba (d. 851/1448 [see IBN ḲĀḌĪ SHUHBA]), *Manāḳib al-Shāfiʿī wa-aṣḥābih* (= *Ṭabaḳāt al-Shāfiʿiyya*), drawn from the *Taʾrīkh al-Islām* by al-Dhahabī (numerous mss.; see Munadjdjid, 238-9).

It has been observed (see above) that al-Bukhārī (d. 256/870 [*q.v.*]) was associated with al-Shāfiʿī by al-Nawawī, although he belonged to no particular *madhhab*, and it will be noted not without interest that al-Dhahabī, whose capricious choice of titles has already been established, entitled *manāḳib* the biographies of the author of the *Ṣaḥīḥ* and of Sufyān al-Thawrī (d. 161/778 [*q.v.*]), but *tardjama* those of the founders of the legal schools (see *Kashf*, iv, col. 560; Munadjdjid, 446).

On account of the specialisation of the *manāḳib* genre and the proscribing of *iʿtizāl*, one would hardly expect to find compilations of this type composed in honour of the Muʿtazilīs. On the other hand, partisans of al-Ashʿarī (d. 324/935-6 [*q.v.*]) were entitled to the *Manāḳib al-Ashʿariyya* (*Kashf*, ii, col. 1835) by ʿAlī Ibn ʿAsākir (d. 571/1176 [see IBN ʿASĀKIR] and to the *Manāḳib al-miʾa min al-aʾimma al-Ashʿariyya* (*Kashf*, ii, col. 1841) by a certain al-Yāfiʿī (d. 868/1464).

Among the Ḥanbalīs, Ibn Taymiyya (d. 728/1328 [*q.v.*]) was not slow to benefit from a favourable treatment, as three of his contemporaries dedicated compilations of *manāḳib* to him: Ibn ʿAbd al-Hādī (d. 744/1343; see Munadjdjid, 157), *al-ʿUḳūd al-durriyya fī manāḳib shaykh al-Islām Ibn Taymiyya* (ed. Cairo 1356), Ibn Ḳudāma al-Maḳdisī (d. 745/1344; see Brockelmann, S II, 119) and al-Bazzār (d. 749/1349), *al-Aʿlām al-ʿaliyya fī manāḳib shaykh al-Islām Ibn Taymiyya*, ed. Munadjdjid, Beirut 1396/1976.

The Mālikism which prevails in North Africa owes much to one of its interpreters, Saḥnūn (d. 240/854 [*q.v.*]), founder of a local legal school, to whose memory al-Khushanī (d. 371/981 [*q.v.*]) dedicated a compilation of *manāḳib*, after Abu 'l-ʿArab gave the title *faḍāʾil* to his biography and to that of Mālik, while he had written a *Kitāb Manāḳib Banī Tamīm*. Among the eminent representatives of Mālikism in Ifrīḳiya, al-Ḳābisī (d. 403/1012 [*q.v.*]) was the object of *manāḳib* (ed. H.R. Idris, Algiers 1959) on the part of Abū ʿAbd Allāh Muḥammad al-Mālikī (d. 438/1046); a similar honour was awarded to his disciple Abū Bakr Aḥmad b. ʿAbd al-Raḥmān (d. 432 or 435/1040-3; see Idris, *Deux maîtres de l'école kairouanaise*, in *AIEO Alger*, xiii [1955], 30-41) by a pupil of the latter, Ibn Saʿdūn (d. 485 or 486/1092-3; see Idris, *ibid.*, 35-6). It is appropriate in this context to stress the importance of biographical works relating to this Mālikī school which was so active in the Maghrib, especially *al-Iftikhār fī manāḳib fuḳahāʾ al-Ḳayrawān* by ʿAtīḳ al-Tudjībī (d. 422/1030; see Idris, *Deux juristes kairouanais*, in *AIEO Alger*, xii [1954], 153), the *Tartīb al-Madārik wa-taḳrīb al-masālik bi-maʿrifat aʿlām madhhab Mālik* (ed. A. Bakīr, Beirut 1967) by the *ḳāḍī* ʿIyāḍ (d. 544/1149 [*q.v.*]), which begins with a lengthy biography of Mālik and in which the articles on the leading *fuḳahāʾ* contain a paragraph entitled *faḍāʾiluh* (= *manāḳibuh*), and the *Maʿālim al-īmān fī maʿrifat ahl al-Ḳayrawān* by Ibn Nadjī (d. 839/1435 [*q.v.* in Suppl.]), who took up (see ed. Tunis, iii, 262, 263) the *Maʿālim al-īmān fī manāḳib al-mashhūrīn min ʿulamāʾ al-Ḳayrawān* of al-Dabbāgh (d. 699/1300 [*q.v.* in Suppl.]), already continued by Ibrāhīm al-ʿAwwānī (d. 720/1320), and is also furnished with Ḳayrawānī *manāḳib* such as those of Sīdī Abū Yūsuf al-Dahmānī or of Abū 'Ali al-Ḳadīdī. R. Brunschvig (*Ḥafṣides*, ii, 382), who quotes these last-named authors, reckons that the biographies of the *Maʿālim* "are closely linked to the *manāqib* genre", meaning that they tend towards hagiography.

Hagiography

This second tendency appears all the less astonishing as certain of these Ḳayrawānī jurists were drawn, from the beginning of the 4th/10th century, into the ascetic movement which held sway in Ifrīḳiya and died more or less in an odour of sanctity or as "martyrs" in the ranks of the insurgents led by Abū Yazīd (d. 336/947 [*q.v.*]): it is thus in this period that the *manāḳib* genre begins in the Maghrib to take on a gradually more marked hagiographical tone. Featuring prominently among these persons is al-Rabīʿ b. al-Ḳaṭṭān (d. 334/946 who, having renounced his activities as a *faḳīh*, withdrew from the world but was one of the instigators of the revolt and attained the accolade of martyrdom (see Idris, *Deux juristes*, 129-30) in such a way that his *manāḳib* were gathered together by al-Ḥusayn b. ʿAbd Allāh al-Adjdābī (d. 432/1040) who dedicated monographs of the same type to another "martyr", al-Mammasī (d. 333/944), also to al-Sabāʾī (d. 356/966) whose piety and asceticism has been noticed (see Idris, *op. laud.*, 126-7, 133-4). Two other Ifrīḳiyans whose merits are widely celebrated, al-Djabanyānī (d. 369/979) and the patron saint of Tunis, Muḥriz b. Khalaf (Sīdī Maḥrez, d. 413/1022 [*q.v.*]), have been the object, through the offices of, respectively, al-Labīdī (d. 440/1048) and al-Fārisī (d. *ca.* 440-50/1048-58), of hagiographies which have been published and translated by H.R. Idris (*Manāqib d'Abū Isḥâq al-Jabanyânî par Abû l-Qāsim al-Labîdî et Manâqib de Muḥriz b. Ḫalaf par Abû Ṭâhir al-Fârisî*, Tunis 1959, 111-20; one can also find there a short exposé on the genre studied in the present article and a description of several mss. containing various collections of *manāḳib*, as well as the text and the translation of those concerning (161-2, 329-30) Ibn al-Nafīs (d. 479/1086) and (163-7, 331-3) Abū Zayd al-Manāṭiḳī; see also Yūsuf al-Ḥanāshī, *Kutub al-manāḳib wa-maẓāhir min al-ḥayāt al-idjtimāʿiyya bi-Ifrīḳiya fi 'l-ḳarn al-rābiʿ li 'l-hidjra/al-ʿāshir mīlādī*, in *al-Fikr*, xxvii/6 [1982], 111-20).

From that time onward, the development of hagiolatry, then of religious orders, favoured in the Muslim world as a whole the evolution and the rich proliferation of a specialised *manāḳib* genre, and there is scarcely a single famous ascetic, venerated saint, founder of a *ṭarīḳa* [*q.v.*] or eminent Ṣūfī who did not earn his own monograph or at very least an article in general works, the titles of which do not necessarily contain the word *manāḳib*; this is the case, as has been observed, of the *Ḥilyat al-awliyāʾ* by Abū Nuʿaym or of the Indian and other *Tadhkira*s [*q.v.*], or indeed, in a later period, the *Akhbār al-akhyār* (ed. Dihlī 1309/1891) by ʿAbd al-Ḥaḳḳ Dihlawī (d. 1052/1642 [*q.v.*]). But reference may be made to, for example, the *Manāḳib al-abrār min maḥāsin al-akhyār* by Ibn Khamīs al-Mawṣilī al-Shāfiʿi (d. 552/1157; Brockelmann, S I, 776), the *Manāḳib al-abrār fī maḳāmāt al-akhyār* by Muḥammad b. al-Ḥasan al-Shāfiʿī (d. 676/1277-8; *Kashf*, iv, col. 559), the *Manāḳib al-ʿibād min ṣulaḥāʾ al-bilād* by al-Ṣayrafī, of whom Ḥadjdjī Khalīfa says (ii, col. 1843) that he took some of his biographies from the *Ṣafwat al-ṣafwa* by Ibn al-Djawzī, the *Manāḳib al-aṣfiyāʾ* (ed. Calcutta 1895) by Shuʿayb b. Djalāl al-Dīn Manīrī (after the 8th/14th century) and, in Turkish, the *Manāḳibi-awliyāʾ* of Sharīfī-zāde (d. 1040/1630-1; *Kashf*, iv, 560).

The eminent eastern saint Uways al-Ḳaranī (d. 37/657 [*q.v.*]), who is not lacking in biographies (see for example Abū Nuʿaym, *Ḥilya*, ii, 79-87), has, omissions excepted, only at a late stage been the object of a monograph, and in Turkish, by al-Lāmiʿī (d. 938/1531-2 [*q.v.*], *Manāḳib-i Ḥaḍrat-i Uways al-Ḳaranī*; for mss. see G. K. Alpay, *Lāmiʿī Chelebi and his works*, in *JNES*, xxxvi [1976], 82, no. 9. The legend of Abū Ayyūb (d. 52/672) is recounted by Ḥadjdjī ʿAbd Allāh in *al-Āthār al-madjīdiyya fi 'l-manāḳib al-khālidiyya* (ed. Istanbul 1257/1841), and Ibn al-Djawzī celebrates the *manāḳib* of Maʿrūf al-Karkhī (d. 200/815-16 [*q.v.*]), ed. Ṣ.M. al-Djumaylī, in *al-Mawrid*, ix/4 (1401/1981), 609-80. On Dhu 'l-Nūn (d. 246/861 [*q.v.*]) we are aware of *al-Kawkab al-durrī fī manāḳib Dhi 'l-Nūn al-Miṣrī*, attributed to Ibn ʿArabī (d. 638/1240), but not mentioned by O. Yahya (*Histoire et classification de l'oeuvre d'Ibn ʿArabī*; a ms. of this work exists in Leiden, see van Koningsveld, 108), while Ibn ʿArabī himself has *manāḳib* composed in his honour (*Kashf*, ii, col. 1843), in particular by al-Suyūṭī (d. 956/1549) according to Ḥādjdjī Khalīfa (ii, col. 1835). The great saint ʿAbd al-Ḳādir al-Djīlānī (d. 561/1166 [*q.v.*]) naturally has his place in the hagiographical dictionaries, and it is even said that the *Mirʾāt al-zamān* by Sibṭ Ibn al-Djawzī supplied al-Yūnīnī (d. 726/1326) with the material for a collection of his *manāḳib* (*Kashf*, ii, col. 1842), which would be a further indication of the close links that have already been observed between general biography and hagiography when religious persons are concerned. Ḥādjdjī Khalīfa lists numerous other monographs on the eponymous founder of the Ḳādiriyya [*q.v.*], notably *Asnā 'l-mafākhir fī manāḳib al-shaykh ʿAbd al-Ḳādir* by al-Yāfiʿī (d. 768/1367 [*q.v.*]). Another founder of an order, Abu 'l-ʿAbbās Aḥmad b. ʿAlī al-Rifāʿī (d. 578/1183 [see AL-RIFĀʿĪ]) soon earned his *manāḳib* from the pen of al-Wāsiṭī (d. 589/1194; see Brockelmann, S I, 781, who also mentions the compilation by Djaʿfar al-Barzandjī, 1179/1765). For their part, the Mawlawiyya [*q.v.*], and in particular their first *shaykh*, Djalāl al-Dīn Rūmī (d. 672/1273 [*q.v.*]) and his successors, quickly inspired Aflākī (8th/14th century [*q.v.*]) to compose, in Persian, the *Manāḳib al-ʿārifīn wa-marātib al-kāshifīn* (French tr. Cl. Huart, *Les saints des derviches tourneurs*, Paris 1918-22; ed. T. Yazıcı, Ankara 1959); numerous other religious persons have their *manāḳib* written in Turkish (see *Kashf*, ii, col. 1842, iv, col. 560); for instance, Ahmet Yaşar Ocak presents in *JA*, cclxvii/3-4 (1979) a Turkish *mathnawī* of Elwān Čelebī (after 761/1360), Menāḳib 'ul-ḳudsīya fī menāṣib 'il-unsīya: *une source importante pour l'histoire religieuse de l'Anatolie au XIII*[e] *siècle*, devoted to Baba Ilyās and his descendants. The saint so much respected in Egypt, Aḥmad al-Badawī (d. 675/1276 [*q.v.*]), has been honoured by various compilations (see Brockelmann, S I, 808), but ʿAbd al-Ṣamad Zayn al-Dīn (d. 1028/1634-5), no doubt judging *manāḳib* insufficiently expressive, entitled his *al-Djawāhir al-saniyya fi 'l-karāmāt al-Aḥmadiyya* (numerous editions). Ibn Ḳiwām (7th/13th century) owes to his grandson the *Manāḳib al-shaykh Abī Bakr Ibn Ḳiwām* (mss. Ẓāhiriyya 5398, 6951), while Ibn Ṭūlūn (d. 953/1546 [*q.v.*]) is content to entitle his biography *Tuḥfat al-kirām fi tardjamat Abī Bakr Ibn Ḳiwām* (Munadjdjid, 291). Naḳshband (d. 791/1389 [*q.v.*]), eponymous founder of the Naḳshbandiyya, speedily acquired his *manāḳib* through the offices of al-Sharīf al-Djurdjānī (d. 816/1413; *Kashf*, ii, col. 1841), while the Khalwatiyya [*q.v.*] have been honoured by Muḥammad b. al-Makkī in *al-Nafaḥāt al-raḥmāniyya fī manāḳib ridjāl al-Khalwatiyya* (Istanbul 1927) and by Ibn ʿAzzūz al-Tūnisī (*Kashf*, iv, col. 560). Ibn al-Bazzāz al-Ardabīlī (8th/14th century [*q.v.* in Suppl.] wrote a biography of Ṣafī 'l-Dīn, founder of the Ṣafawiyya order and eponymous ancestor of the Ṣafawids, *al-Mawāhib al-saniyya fī manāḳib al-Ṣafawiyya*, or *Ṣafwat al-ṣafāʾ* (lith. Bombay 1329/1911). The patron saint of Aden or ʿAdan, Abū Bakr Ibn Aydarus (d. 914/1508 [see ʿAYDARUS]), found his panegyrist in the person of his contemporary Ḥusayn b. Ṣiddīḳ al-Ahdal (d. 903/1497 [see AL-AHDAL]), author of the *Mawāhib al-ḳuddūs fī manāḳib Ibn ʿAydarūs*. Al-Djaʿfarī (d. after 1157/1744) wrote *al-Ṭabīb al-mudāwī bi-manāḳib al-shaykh Aḥmad al-Nahlawī* on a saint who died in 1157/1744 (see Munadjdjid, 347), and *mullā* Niẓām al-Dīn is the author of the *Manāḳib-i Razzāḳiyya* in honour of the *pīr* Sayyid ʿAbd al-Razzāḳ [see FARANGĪ MAḤALL in Suppl.]. In the 13th/19th century, the vogue for *manāḳib* was perpetuated in the east. The Egyptian Ṣūfī saint Ahmad al-Ṣāwī (d. 1241/1825) inspired a collective work, *al-Nūr al-waḍḍāʾ fī manāḳib wa-karāmāt ʿumdat al-awliyāʾ Sayyidī Aḥmad al-Ṣāwī* (ed. Cairo 1347/1928), al-Duwayhī (d. 1874 [*q.v.* in Suppl.] has left behind a biography of his master Aḥmad b. Idrīs, partially reproduced in a compilation of Ṣāliḥ b. Muḥammad al-Madanī, *al-Muntaḳā al-nafīs fī manāḳib Ḳuṭb dāʾirat al-taḳdīs Aḥmad b. Idrīs*, Cairo 1960, Khalīfa al-Safṭī (d. 1296/1879) is the author of the *manāḳib al-shaykh* ʿAbd al-Laṭīf al-Ḳayātī (d. 1258/1842; ms. Yale 1209), and Ḥusayn al-Djisr dedicated the *Nuzhat al-fikr fī manāḳib mawlānā 'l-ʿārif bi-llāh taʿālā ḳuṭb zamānih wa-ghayth awānīh al-shaykh Muḥammad al-Djisr* (ed. Beirut 1306) to his father, who was a Syrian Ṣūfī (d. 1262/1846) and a disciple of al-Ṣāwī. Al-Ḥiṣāfī (d. 1910 [*q.v.* in Suppl.], founder of the *ṭarīḳa ḥiṣāfiyya*, has found his hagiographer in the person of ʿAlī al-Djaʿfarāwī, author of *al-Manhal al-ṣāfī fī manāḳib al-Sayyid Ḥasanayn al-Ḥiṣāfī*, Cairo 1330/1911-12.

Rich though the list of Ḥādjdjī Khalīfa is, it is still incomplete, for it is highly probable that many hagiographies of a more or less popular nature, which must have circulated in Ṣūfī circles, have escaped this conscientious bibliographer, without counting, of course, those which appeared at a later time. Whatever the reason, he makes scant reference to the collections of *manāḳib* composed in North Africa and particularly in Morocco, which was a breeding-ground of saints and marabouts. Just as hitherto there has been no attempt to cite all the relevant titles or to go beyond the 19th century, so we will confine ourselves to discussion of those Maghribī works which appear to be the most characteristic.

The earliest compilations of Ifrīḳiyan *manāḳib* have already been mentioned. The Moroccan saint al-Sabtī (d. 601/1205 [*q.v.*]), whose memory has remained very much alive in the Maghrib, inspired a number of them (mss. in Rabat, Algiers, Tunis, Paris etc.; see E. Lévi-Provençal, *Les manuscripts arabes de Rabat*, Paris 1921, no. 403; Brockelmann, S II, 1013). ʿAbd al-Salām b. Mashīsh (d. 625/1227-8 [*q.v.*]) has been honoured by al-Warrāḳ; Abū Sa ʿīd Khalaf al-Bādjī (d. 629/1230) enjoyed the same distinction, after 633/1235, through the offices of Abu 'l-Ḥasan al-Hawwārī (see the catalogue of the mss. left by H.H. ʿAbd al-Wahhāb, in *Ḥawliyyāt al-Djāmi ʿa al-tūnisiyya*, vii [1970], no. 205; Public Library of Tunis, ms. ar. no. 30). Al-Shādhilī (d. 656/1258 [*q.v.*]), his disciples and even his grotto situated in the Djabal al-Zallādj (ms. ʿAbd al-Wahhāb, no. 655), have been the object of collections of *manāḳib* which have survived (mss. ʿAbd al-Wahhāb nos. 45, 321, 655). In the same period (7th/13th century), there lived in Tunis the saint ʿĀʾisha al-Mannūbiyya [*q.v.*], whose *manāḳib* have been published (Tunis 1344/1925). To a Tunisian saint of a later time, Sīdī Ben ʿArūs (d. 868/1463; see R. Brunschvig, *Ḥafṣides*, ii, 341-50), ʿUmar al-Rashīdī dedicated the *Ibtisām al-ghurūs wa-washy al-ṭurūs bi-manāḳib al-shaykh Abi 'l-ʿAbbās Aḥmad b. ʿArūs* (ed. Tunis 1303); to a member al-Asmar (d. 981/1574 [*q.v.*]), of the order of the ʿArūsiyya founded by the above-named, numerous compilations have likewise been dedicated, among which that of Muḥammad b. Muḥammad al-Munastīrī, *Tanḳīḥ rawḍat al-azhār ... fī manāḳib Sīdī ʿAbd al-Salām al-Asmar*, was published in Tunis in 1325/1907-8. A large number of monographs on Tunisian saints have yet to be published. Two mss. of the Great Mosque of Tunis (nos. 1697 and 3875) contain some fifteen of them, and in the catalogue of ʿAbd al-Wahhāb manuscripts more than half-a-dozen *madjmūʿas* are to be found (nos. 45, 205, 321, 519, 520, 541, 655) comprising a total of some 45 texts (some of them in duplicate or triplicate); it is likely that private libraries have also preserved a certain number of them.

On writings of this genre dating from the Ḥafṣid period (627-982/1229-1574), R. Brunschvig (*op. laud.*, i, 381) makes a judgement which is capable of wider application: "Numerous and of living and of varying dimensions, often anonymous, are these lives of saints or *manāḳib*, a genre which is, moreover, fairly monotonous, where virtues and miracles are complacently enumerated on the testimony of witnesses, living or dead, who are named. Works of panegyrists or of devotees, they should not be expected to show any critical tendency, and some of the historical information that they purport to contain is to be treated with caution. Often composed by the semi-literate who address a poorly-educated public, they are written in simple language, as close as possible to the spoken idiom ... In this sense, they constitute linguistic documents of some interest. Similarly, the insights that they supply, unwittingly, on the toponomy and the 'realia' of their period are by no means to be disregarded, but above all they throw a useful light on the mentality and customs of these people, insignificant folk who congregated around the mystical shaikhs, eager to benefit from their *baraka*."

In the course of the ensuing period, the cult of saints did not weaken in Tunisia, but the activity of the hagiographers seems to have declined somewhat. A Abdesselem (*Les historiens tunisiens des XVIIe, XVIIIe et XIXe siècles*, Tunis 1973, 495) notes that this literary genre "contains very few works", and, although monographs were probably still being composed, in addition to *al-Fatḥ al-munīr fī taʿrīf al-ṭarīḳa al-shābbiyya* by Muḥammad al-Masʿūdī al-Shābbī (10-11th/16th-17th century), the third chapter of which contains the miracles and prophecies of the founder of the Shābbiyya fraternity and of his sons, he points out and analyses only two hagiographical works: the first (149-53) is the *Nūr al-armāsh fī manāḳib Sayyidī (Sīdī) Abu* (sic) *'l-Ghayth al-Ḳashshāsh* (d. 1031/1621) written in 1032 by al-Muntaṣir b. Abī Liḥya of Gafsa, who put together a number of miracles (*karāmāt*) "all of them equally implausible" (according to Ḥādjdjī Khalīfa, ii, col. 1835, a certain Muḥammad b. Sha ʿbān al--Ṭarābulusī, d. 1020/1611, had already recorded the *manāḳib* of this saint); the second (385-6) is the *Takmīl al-ṣulaḥāʾ wa 'l-aʿyān li-maʿālim al-īmān fī awliyāʾ al-Ḳayrawān* (ms. Paris ENLOV, 452) by ʿĪsā al-Kinānī al-Ḳayrawānī (d. 1292/1875), which purports to be a sequel to the *Maʿālim al-īmān* by Ibn al-Nādjī (see above) and contains "material borrowed from earlier *manāqib*".

Travel narratives of a later period [see RIḤLA] are not lacking in hagiographical tendencies, but this does not apply to that of al-Sanūsī (d. 1318/1900 [*q.v.*]), who is nevertheless the author of numerous texts which A. Chenoufi (*Un savant tunisien du XIXe siècle: Muhammad al-Sanūsī, sa vie et son œuvre*, Tunis 1977, 181-6) classifies under the heading "works of a hagiographical nature"; they do not bear the title *manāḳib*, but the *Tuḥfat al-akhyār bi-mawlid al-Mukhtār*, where there is an account of "the miraculous happenings which attended the birth of the Prophet, and those which characterised his youth", and *al-Mawrid al-maʿīn fī dhikr al-arbaʿīn*, which contains the laudatory biographies of the forty companions of al-Shādhilī (see above) testify to the permanence of this literary genre in Tunisia.

In Morocco, hagiolatry made its appearance at approximately the same time as in Ifrīḳiya, thus well before the springing-up, in the 9th/15th century, of the wave of mysticism which was to spread throughout North Africa and before the evolution of maraboutism as a characteristic of religious activity. In fact, the first elements of Moroccan hagiography appear as early as the 7th/13th century in the form of dictionaries such as the *Tashawwuf ilā [ma ʿrifat] ridjāl al-taṣawwuf* (ed. A. Faure, Rabat 1958) of Ibn al-Zayyāt al-Tādlī (d. 627/1229-30) which contains 277 biographies of san-tons and Ṣūfīs of the 5th-7th/11th-13th centuries, or *al-Maḳṣad al-s͟harīf ... fī d͟hikr ṣulaḥāʾ al-Rīf* (tr. G.S. Colin, in *AM*, xxvi [1926]), of al-Bādisī (d. after 722/1322 [*q.v.*]), which describes the lives of some forty saints of the Rīf, of whom the majority are now forgotten; among this number, one who features (88-93) is an Andalusian named Abū Marwān ʿAbd al-Malik b. Ibrāhīm al-Ḳaysī al-Yuḥānisī (7th/13th century), who was the master of al-S͟hād͟hilī and to whom is dedicated the *Tuḥfat al-mug͟htarib bi-bilād al-Mag͟hrib fī karāmāt al-s͟hayk͟h Abī Marwān* by Aḥmad al-Ḳas͟htālī (ed. Madrid 1974, under the title *Milagros de Abū Marwān al-Yuḥānisī*, by F. de la Granja, who stresses the rarity of words of this type in Spain). In the 8th/14th century, Abū ʿAbd Allāh al-Ḥaḍramī dedicated to the Marīnid sultan Abu 'l-Ḥasan (767-74/1366-72) *al-Salsal al ʿad͟hb wa 'l-manhal al-aḥlā* on the forty saints revered in Fez, Meknès and Salé (*Chorfa*, 222-3; ms. in Leiden, see van Koningsveld, 94). Aḥmad b. ʿĀs͟hir al-Ḥāfī (d. 1163/1750; see *Chorfa*, 313-14) is the author of a hagiographical work on his homonym, the patron saint of Salé (d. 764 or 765/1362) or 1363), the *Tuḥfat al-zāʾir bi-baʿd manāḳib Sayyidī (Sīdī) al-Ḥād͟jd͟j Aḥmad b. ʿĀs͟hir al-Ḥāfī* (ms. in Leiden, see van Koningsveld, 96). Ibn Ḳunfud͟h al-Ḳusanṭīnī (d. 810/1407-8 [*q.v.*]) uses *manāḳib* in the sense of "prodigies" when he gives the title *Taḥṣīl al-manāḳib fī takmīl al-maʾārib* (ms. in Rabat) to a commentary on his astronomical treatise, the *Taysīr/Tashīl al-maṭālib fī taʿdīl al-kawākib*, but curiously, he refrains from employing the term in the *Uns al-faḳīr wa- ʿizz al-ḥaḳīr*, which is a biography of the patron saint of Tlemcen Abū Maydan (d. 594/1197 [*q.v.*]) and of his disciples (ed. M. al-Fāsī and A. Faure, Rabat 1965).

On account of the often-quoted *ḥadīt͟h: bi-d͟hikr al-ṣulaḥāʾ tanzil al-raḥma* "mention of the virtuous (= saints) makes mercy descend", biographical literature developed to a considerable extent in Morocco under the S͟harīfian dynasties, and the *manāḳib* genre, even though this term is not always used, plays a significant role in the form both of hagiographical dictionaries and of monographs of saints or at least of persons whose memory is revered. To become familiar with the extent of the phenomenon, it is sufficient to peruse *Les historiens des Chorfa* by Lévi-Provençal (from p. 220); numerous works of this type have been mentioned at the beginning of this article, and we confine ourselves here to reference to those which seem particularly representative.

A relatively ancient hagiography, dating from the 8th/14th century, bears a title devoid of ambiguity (*Chorfa*, 221); *al-Minhād͟j al-wāḍiḥ fī taḥḳīḳ karāmāt Abī Muḥammad Ṣāliḥ*, by the great-grandson of this disciple (d. 631/1234) of Abū Madyan. The term *manāḳib* is observed as appearing to introduce an account of the lives of two saints of Ag͟hmāt [*q.v.*] by al-Hazmīrī al-Marrākus͟hī (*Chorfa*, 223); *It͟hmid al-ʿaynayn wa-nuzhat al-nāẓirayn fī manāḳib al-ak͟hawayn Abī Zayd wa-Abī ʿAbd Allāh al-Hazmīriyyayn* (d. respectively in 706 or 707/1306-8 and 678/1280). In the 10th/16th century, the D͟jazūlī [*q.v.*] movement, of which the spiritual line stretches back to ʿAbd al-Salām b. Mas͟hīs͟h (see above), found its historian in the person of Ibn ʿAskar (d. 986/1578; [*q.v.*]), author of the *Dawḥat al-nās͟hir li-maḥāsin man kān bi 'l-Mag͟hrib min mas͟hāyik͟h al-ḳarn al-ʿās͟hir*, (lith. Fās 1309/1892; ed. M. Ḥād͟jd͟jī, Rabat 1396/1976), which is a catalogue of *s͟hayk͟hs* to whom, as a group, "was allotted a particle of sanctity" (*Chorfa*, 234); another catalogue, from which was drawn the *ʿArif al-munna* of the above-mentioned Muḥammad al-Mahdī al-Fāsī, was moreover entitled *Mumtiʿ al-asmāʿ bi-manāḳib al-s͟hayk͟h al-D͟jazūlī wa-man lahu min al-atbāʿ*. The great Moroccan saint Abū Yaʿazzā (d. 572/1177 [*q.v.*]), who was the subject of a long article in the *Tas͟hawwuf* (195-205), inspired another al-Tādlī (d. 1013/1604), to write a monograph, the *Kitāb al-Mu ʿzā fī manāḳib Abī Ya ʿzā* (ms. in Rabat; see *Chorfa*, 239-40). Ibn Raysūn al-ʿAlamī (d. 1055/1645) is the author of the *Manāḳib al-Raysūniyyīn* on his father and his paternal uncles (Hajji, 520). To Ibn ʿAys͟hūn al-S͟harrāṭ (d. 1109/1697) is attributed *al-Rawḍ al-ʿāṭir al-anfās fī ak͟hbār al-ṣāliḥin min ahl Fās* (ms. in Rabat; see Hajji, 712). The *Ṣafwat man intas͟har min ak͟hbār ṣulaḥāʾ al-ḳarn al-ḥādī ʿas͟har* (lith. Fās n.d.) by al-Ifrānī (d. 1151/1738-9 [*q.v.*]) is a catalogue of Moroccan saints, forming a sequel to the *Dawḥa* of Ibn ʿAskar. A Syrian emigré in Morocco, Aḥmad al-Ḥalabī (d. 1120/1708) is the author of *al-Durr al-nafīs wa 'l-nūr al-anīs fī manāḳib al-Imām Idrīs b. Idrīs* (lith. Fās 1300, 1304; see *Chorfa*, 287). ʿAbd al-Raḥmān al-Fāsī, who has already been mentioned on account of the fact that, like al-Ifrānī, he preferred *ak͟hbār* to *manāḳib*, nevertheless also wrote the *Bustān al-ad͟hhān fī manāḳib al-s͟hayk͟h Abī Muḥammad ʿAbd al-Raḥmān* ;(ms. in Rabat) on the saint and poet in *malḥūn* al-Mad͟jd͟hūb [*q.v.*]. Also to be mentioned is *al-Murḳī/Muraḳḳī fī baʿd manāḳib al-ḳuṭb al-Sayyid Maḥammad al-S͟harḳī* (12th/18th century?) by his descendant ʿAbd al-K͟hāliḳ al-S͟harḳī (ms. in Rabat); and *al-D͟hahab al-ibrīz fī manāḳib al-s͟hayk͟h ʿAbd al-ʿAzīz* by al-Lamaṭī (d. 1156/1743 [*q.v.*]) devoted to the Fāsī saint called al-Dabbāg͟h (d. 1131/1719), lith. at Cairo in 1278/1861, printed at Būlāḳ in 1292/1875 and at Cairo in 1304/1886. The Ḳādirīs [*q.v.*] left to posterity numerous monographs of saints and prominent members of their family. One of them, ʿAbd al-Salām (1110/1698), is the author of the *Muʿtamad al-rāwī fī manāḳib walī Allāh Aḥmad al-S͟hāwī*, on a popular saint of Fās (d. 1014/1605), and of the *Nuzhat al-fikr fī manāḳib al-s͟hayk͟hayn Sayyidī (Sīdī) Maḥammad wa-wālidih sayyidī (Sīdī) Abī Bakr*, on the founder of the *zāwiya* of al-Dilāʾ [*q.v.* in Suppl.] and his son (see *Chorfa*, 278); the wonderful history of this *zāwiya* is recorded by al-Tāzī (d. 1247/1831-2) in the *Nuzhat al-ak͟hyār al-marḍiyyīn fī manāḳib al-ʿulamā al-Dilāʾiyyīn al-Bakriyyīn* (ms. in Rabat). The As͟hrāf (S͟hurafāʾ) of Wazzān [*q.v.*] have, in their own right, been the object of several complications: ʿAbd al-Salām al-Ḳādirī, *al-Tuḥfa al-Ḳādiriyya fī manāḳib al-Wazzāniyyīn wa 'l-S͟hād͟hiliyyīn* (ms. in Rabat); Ḥamdūn al-Ṭāhirī (d. 1191/1777), *Tuḥfat al-ik͟hwān bi-baʿd manāḳib s͟hurafāʾ Wazzān*, lith. Fās 1324/1906, with, in the margins, *al-Kawkab al-as ʿad fī manāḳib Sayyidinā wa-Mawlānā ʿAlī b. Muḥammad* [*al-Wazzānī*] (d. 1226/1811), of a 19th century author, Abū Allāh Muḥammad b. Ḥamza al-Miknāsī (see *Chorfa*, 327), Muḥammad al-Ruhūnī (d. 1230/1815) likewise collected the *manāḳib* of this last-named *s͟harīf* (see M. Lakhdar, *Vie littéraire*, 279). As early as 1214/1799, Ḥarāzim was commending the merits of the founder of the Tīd͟jāniyya [*q.v.*] in the *Bulūgh al-amānī fī manāḳib al-s͟hayk͟h al-Tīd͟jānī* (d. 1230/1815) which was published in Cairo in 1345/1926-7, with a different title. To conclude, attention may also be drawn to the *Manāḳib al-s͟hayk͟h Abī ʿAbd Allāh Muḥammad al-Ḥadīkī* by Muḥammad b. ʿAbd Allāh al-Ḥadīkī al-D͟jazūlī (d. 1189/1775), the *Manāḳib al-ṣulaḥāʾ* (see Lakhdar, 259) by Muḥammad al-Tāwudī Ibn Sūda (d. 1209/1795) and the *Manāḳib al-ʿAkkārī* (d. 1118/1707) by one of his descendants (d. 1304/1886); a ms. of it exists in Rabat. Finally, it will be noted that Ḥamdūn b. al-Ḥād͟jd͟j (d. 1232/1817 [see IBN AL-ḤĀD͟JD͟J in Suppl.]) who was in no sense a saint, also earned his *Manāḳib* (ms. in Rabat), which proves that this key-word was not always felt, even in the 19th century, necessarily to imply the accomplishment of miracles.

As may be observed through a perusal of the intentionally-abridged list which precedes, several hagiographers are descendants of a saint or a *shaykh*; possessing sufficient education, they were no doubt able by themselves to put into shape the oral or written testimony as well as assembled family documents. On the other hand, many poorly-educated Moroccans devoted themselves to similar researches, but were obliged to entrust the dossier thus compiled to some learned individual, with instructions to compose the monograph which they wished to dedicate to the memory of their ancestor; E. Lévi-Provençal (*Chorfa*, 49, n. 1) cites an example of the latter procedure of which he has had direct knowledge, but it is known that others exist. Thus the libraries, especially the private ones, contain, among others, a number of these lives of saints which R. Brunschvig finds monotonous because the portraits of the individuals whom they honour are repeated without any great regard for originality. In general, writes Lévi-Provençal (50), although one may encounter "some accounts of events which seem distorted and tending towards the miraculous, it should be recognised that, in the majority of cases, the men whose lives are presented here are quite ordinary mortals. The true legend of the saint is not found in the written hagiographies, so to speak; it resides in the spirit of the uneducated masses. Popular hagiolatry often has little in common with compilations of *manâqib*. In the latter, the saint is above all a very orthodox, devout and ascetic Muslim; his biographers endow him with the nature of an intercessor; he sometimes has the ebullient spirit of a mysticism which brings him close to unity with the divine ... It is in the social role which they play in the land that the Moroccan marabouts gradually appear through the monographs. It is precisely here that the interest of the latter resides. This general observation also provides an explanation as to why female saints, who enjoy a widespread popular cult in Morocco, are almost ignored by the learned national hagiography". It will be noted, however, as exceptions confirming the rule, that a number of articles relating to Moroccan women, often anonymous, feature in the hagiographical dictionaries, particularly in the *Tashawwuf*, that there exist in the Sūs the *Manāḳib* of al-Sayyida Maryam bint Mas ʿūd al-Sūsī al-Samlālī (d. 1165/1751) by Abu 'l-ʿAbbās Aḥmad b. Ibrāhīm al-Adrīzī (d. 1168/1754) and that al-Kuntī (d. 1224/1810 [see KUNTA]) honoured both his parents in one tribute, *al-Ṭarīfa wa 'l-tālida min karamāt al-shaykhayn al-wālid wa 'l-wālida* (ms. B.N. Paris 5511).

At the end of this inevitably limited catalogue of works which may be regarded as belonging in general to the *manāḳib* genre, it is possible to summarise its evolution as follows.

Since the earliest centuries of Islam, *manāḳib*, which is not yet a key-word, appears, concurrently with other terms which may be neutral *(tardjama, akhbār, taʿrīf)* or more expressive (*faḍāʾil, mafākhir, maʾāthir*), in the titles of individual biographies or of biographical compilations whose principal aim is to offer to the reader a moral portrait and information on the noble actions of the individuals who constitute their subject or on the superior merits of a certain group. This concurrence is perpetuated over the centuries, although *manāḳib* clearly tends towards specialisation. In fact, from the 4th/10th century onwards, both in Ifrīḳiya and in other Islamic countries this term is quite regularly applied to laudatory biographies of the *imāms* who founded the great legal schools and played a fundamental role in the elaboration of the *Sharīʿa*. Like the *faḍāʾil* of the Companions of the Prophet, the *manāḳib* of the *imāms* and of their leading disciples are aimed towards the edification of the community, which is thus invited to acquire their real or supposed virtues and scrupulously to follow their example. However, hagiolatry which begins to emerge at this time and subsequently expands to a considerable extent, is concerned to recount the lives of saints whose memory has not yet been effaced, while the gradual foundation of religious orders, a gradual process over the years, leads to the proliferation of *shaykh*s who are to a greater or lesser extent tinged with an aura of sanctity; thus the *manāḳib* genre takes on an increasingly marked hagiographical nature, and the term which designates it, having been applied to the qualities and actions and behaviour of any human being, however little virtuous, becomes synonymous, in the public mind, with prodigies, even more with miracles performed by a saint recognised as such, or by a Ṣūfī, a marabout or indeed by a simple mortal to whom, rightly or wrongly, miraculous gifts are attributed.

Systematic research into the bibliographical catalogues, of biographical works and of general histories of Islamic literature, as well as a more detailed examination of texts bearing the title *manāḳib*, would certainly serve to bring into sharper focus the preceding outline. Just as the study of the *ṭabaḳāt* genre undertaken by I. Hafsi (in *Arabica*, xxiii/3 [1976], 227-65 and xxiv/1-2 [1977], 1-41, 150-86) has shown how a term as simple as the plural of *ṭabaḳa* has undergone, in the sphere of biographical literature, an astonishing semantic evolution, so parallel researches into the *manāḳib* genre deserve to be undertaken, seeing that it involves a delicate and ultimately quite complex concept.

Bibliography : The principal sources have been cited in the article. What is offered here is a simple reminder of the titles of a few works to which reference has repeatedly been made: E. Lévi-Provençal, *Les historiens des Chorfa*, Paris 1922; R. Brunschvig, *La Berbérie orientale sous les Ḥafṣides*, Paris 1940-7; A. Fuʾād Sayyid, *Sources de l'histoire du Yémen à l'époque musulmane*, IFAO, Cairo 1974; P. Sj. van Koningveld, *Ten Arabic manuscript-volumes acquired by the Leiden University Library after 1957*, in E. van Donzel (ed.), *Studies on Islam*, Amsterdam-London 1974; M. Hajji, *L'activité intellectuelle au Maroc à l'époque sa ʿdide*, Rabat 1976; S. al-Munadjdjid, *Mu ʿdjam al-muʾarrikhīn al-dimashḳiyyīn*, Beirut 1398/1978.

(CH. PELLAT)

AL-**MANĀMA,** the capital city of the amirate of Baḥrayn [*q.v.*] in the Persian Gulf. The city is located at latitude 26° 13′ N and longitude 50° 35′ E, on the north-eastern coast of the island of Baḥrayn, which was formerly known as Awāl. The shallow waters between Manāma and the neighbouring island of Muḥarraḳ [*q.v.*] have long been used to provide good shelter for native craft. It has been suggested that the name Manāma (A. "a place of resting, sleeping") may reflect the proximity of a number of prehistoric burial mounds.

The early history of Manāma remains obscure, for reliable references are few and their topographical nomenclature is both vague and confusing. When the Portuguese seized Baḥrayn in the 10th/16th century, they built their major fortification on the coast at Ḳalʿat al-ʿAdjādj, some 4 miles west of Manāma. The Persians, who wrested control from the Portuguese in 1011/1602, held the archipelago for much of the following turbulent period of 180 years, during which time they erected a defensive position on the current side of Manāma. In 1197/1783 the Āl Khalīfa [*q.v.*] clan of the ʿUtūb tribe invaded the islands from Zubāra in Ḳaṭar, and after a siege of some 2 months the Persians were expelled from that fort. The Āl Khalīfa — who remain the ruling dynasty — did not, however, enjoy an unchallenged accession to power, and the Āl Bū Saʿīd [*q.v.*] rulers of ʿUman mounted a series of expeditions against Baḥrayn between 1214/1799 and 1244/1828 during which time the small town was attacked and occupied on several occasions.

Over the next century, Manāma gradually became an important entrepôt port serving much of eastern Arabia, though its fortunes fluctuated in response to the vagaries and violence of local and regional political rivalries. Although Manāma was becoming the commercial centre of the archipelago, the Āl Khalīfa usually resided at Muḥarraḳ, which was also the harbour used by the island's large pearling fleet. The ruling family used the fort at Manāma only during the hottest months of the year, and it was not until the second decade of the 20th century that the town became the true capital of the amirate.

European activities had, however, been concentrated at Manāma since the end of the 19th century. In 1893 the Dutch Reformed Church of America established a mission in the town, and in 1902 that organisation built a hospital and a dispensary. A British Assistant Political Agent was appointed and took up residence in 1900; four years later the post was upgraded to a Political Agency. According to Lorimer, the population of Manāma in 1905 was approximately 25,000, of whom 60% were Shīʿī and 40% Sunnī Muslims. There were, in addition, a small number of Hindu, Jewish and Christian residents.

The development of the modern city began after the First World War. In 1920 a municipal administration was established, educational facilities at the primary school level were created, and electricity supplies were inaugurated in 1930. The discovery of oil at Djabal al-Dukhkhān in 1932, and the subsequent development of that resource, helped to stave off the otherwise serious economic and social consequences of the decline in pearl fishing. In 1935 the British established a naval base at Raʾs al-Djufayr, some 2 miles southeast of Manāma, following withdrawal from the Persian island of Handjām. This base later became the major centre of British naval activity in the Gulf. In 1942 a causeway road was built linking Manāma with Muḥarraḳ. In 1946 the British Political Residency was transferred from Būshahr to Manāma. By 1950, the population of the town had grown to over 40,000 and the following three decades have seen even greater expansion and development. By 1981 the population was believed to be over 121,000, and Manāma had become an important regional centre for banking, commerce and communications.

Bibliography: As there are no works devoted exclusively to Manāma, the reader is referred to the bibliographical sections of the entries for BAḤRAYN and ĀL-KHALĪFA, which list the standard sources. The following recent monographs contain some additional information. E.A. Nakleh, *Bahrein: political development in a modernizing society*, Lexington 1976; M.G. Rumaihi, *Bahrain: social and political change since the First World War*, London 1976; Fuad I. Khuri, *Tribe and state in Bahrein: the transformation of social and political authority in an Arab state*, Chicago 1980 and Mahdi Abdalla al-Tajir, *Language and linguistic origins in Bahrain: the Baḥārnah dialect of Arabic*, London 1982. (R.M. BURRELL)

MANĀR, MANĀRA (A), "lighthouse", an elevated place where a light or beacon is established; the means of marking (with fire, originally) routes for caravans or for the army in war; lampstand ("candelabrum", archaic meaning); minaret (in this sense normally in the fem., *manāra*, whereas for "lighthouse", in both the masc. and fem., *manār*, *manāra*). In some modern Arabic dictionaries we also find *fanār*. It is by chance that this latter word resembles *phare* (French), *faro* (Italian, Spanish, which derive their origin from Pharos = the islet situated at the entrance to the port of Alexandria, on which formerly stood the famous lighthouse; see below). *Fanār* has no doubt come into Arabic via Turkish *fanār/fener*, which comes from the Greek *pharos*, whose diminutive *phanarion* was used, for example in Byzantine Greek; in a parallel fashion, in mediaeval Latin *fanarium* = lantern, lighthouse, beacon light, French *fanal* (cf. von Hammer-Purgstall and *İA*, s.v. *Fenerliler*; but the *Türk Ansiklopedisi*, 1968, xvi, 230, confuses *phanòs* and Pharos). From Turkish, the word has also passed into Persian.

Classical Arabic literature describes several uses of fire among the ancient Arabs (*nīrān al-ʿArab* = "fires of the Arabs"; see al-Djāḥiẓ, *Ḥayawān*, iv, 461-91, v, 123, 133-4; al-Nuwayrī, *Nihāya*, i, 109-13; T. Fahd, *Le feu chez les anciens Arabes*, in *Le feu dans le Proche-Orient antique*, Leiden 1973, 43-61). Some of them were intended to guide caravans, convoys and individuals who were travelling, by night, indicating the route for them, or the beginning of it (*irshād al-sārī*). The roads were shown with "landmarks" (stones, etc., with fire; then the meaning was extended to those even without fire); the historical legends give the ruler of Pre-Islamic South Arabia, Abraha, the title "the man of the *manār*", for he was the first to mark out the routes, in time of war (see al-Suyūṭī, *al-Wasāʾil*, ed. al-ʿAdawī and ʿUmar, 146). But among these clearly recorded fires, we find no mention of maritime lighting (see also Yāḳūt, s.v. *manāra*; al-Nuwayrī, *Ilmām*, iv, 3: *manāra* of ʿĀd).

The word *manāra* designates several objects (or buildings) which facilitated lighting; for example the candelabrum in the sense outlined above, and which supported the lamp (*misradja*; see al-Djāḥiẓ, *Bukhalāʾ*, ed. al-Ḥādjirī, 19; al-Bīrūnī, *K. al-Djawāhir*, 227: *manāra* in porcelain; and the iconographic evidence in a miniature of the illustrated ms. Paris BN, Ar. 5847, fol. 13b; Leningrad, Acad. of Sc., Or. S. 23, fol. 30; cf. in the Cairo Geniza, e.g. Camb. T-S.J.1, 15 and Ox. 2821 [16], fol. 56a [and see E. Ashtor, in *JESHO*, vii, 179; *idem*, *Histoire des prix*, Paris 1969, under "chandelier"]), and even certain kinds of "arms" (arm-rests of seats, thrones, etc. (Sadan, *Mobilier*, 39, 126). The commonest word to designate the tower standing alongside (or on top of) a mosque and which is used to call the faithful to prayer, is *miʾdhana* [*q.v.*], but *manāra* is also found. This word has produced, in the European languages, forms such as *minaret* and *minareto* (A. J. Butler, *The Arab conquest of Egypt*, thinks that the connection between *manāra*-lighthouse and *manāra*-minaret is much more than a pure and simple etymological connection; the lighthouse of Alexandria influenced, in his view, the creation and form of the minaret in Islamic architecture; in the new ed. of Butler-Fraser, pp. LXXIV-LXXV, other references have been added, for, in fact, there is no unanimity among researchers; cf. H. Thiersch, *Pharos*, 98-201; Creswell, *A short account of Muslim architecture*, Beirut 1968, 14; and see MASDJID).

The research published on the pre-Islamic Arabs bears witness to the existence among them of a certain knowledge of maritime life; however, they did not have very substantial experience. If we add that the "fires of the Arabs" do not contain anything on maritime lighting, we may assume that it is especially after the expansion of Islam that interest in this genre was awakened. It seems that in the east of the Islamic world (Persian Gulf, Indian Ocean), the Arabs had discovered the sporadic use of fires, and only the more durable "lighthouse" of the *khashabāt* [*q.v.*], near Baṣra, is mentioned in the description of Arab geographers.

Some sporadic uses of fire are even confirmed in the information about the only fixed and noteworthy lighthouse, properly speaking, that of Alexandria: communication by signalling with fires on the departure of Muslims' ships towards the Alexandria lighthouse which, in its turn, gave warning of the arrival of an enemy (by lighting the fire in the direction of the town); some fires were lit on the Mediterranean coast from Alexandria as far as the regions of North Africa, so as to give notice of enemies and direct ships. It is even recorded that opposite the Palestinian coast an exchange of signals of this kind was made between ships and the coast (see, apart from the *Bibl.* below, M. Gaudefroy-Demombynes, *La Syrie*, 258-61; RIBĀṬ, in *EI*[1], and especially ʿA. Elʿad, *Coastal cities*, in *The Jerusalem Cathedra*, ii, 146-67, which summarise (following G. Marçais and others) information taken from al-Balādhurī, al-Muḳaddasī, Ibn Marzūḳ (according to E. Lévi-Provençal, in *Hespéris*, v, 31 and al-Maḳrīzī, and cf. al-Ḳalḳashandī *Khiṭaṭ* ch. iv of *maḳāla* 10). It was a system of lighted fire signals, rather than fixed lighting, but nothing prevented them from profiting from this use of fires for the security of maritime pilotage (see al-Ḥamawī, in the *Bibl.*). These fires and their sites, near the sea, are called *nīrān*, *mawāḳīd*, *maḥāris* and *manāẓir*; al-Muḳaddasī even uses the word *manāra* for a kind of "lighthouse" or beacon-light and even for a tower (minaret of a *ribāṭ*?) being used as a lighthouse. Arabic geographical literature, and especially that of the maritime guides, e.g. in the 9th/15th century (Ibn Mādjid) and in the 10th/16th (Sulaymān al-Mahrī), clearly reflects the dangers presented by reefs and other maritime obstacles and the various means used to avoid them, as if the existence of lighthouses was rare (see I. Y. Kračkovskiy, *Geografičeskaya literatura*, Ar. tr., Cairo 1963-5, ii; G. R. Tibbetts, *Study*, Leiden and London 1979, *passim*; A. M. ʿAṭiyya, *Adab al-baḥr*, Cairo 1981, 79-98).

The famous lighthouse of Alexandria was inherited by the Arabs from the civilisation which had preceded theirs; it had been built, at the entrance to the port, on the islet of Pharos (which is connected today to the coast by a causeway), by Ptolemy Philadelphus, around 279 A.D. Since then and until the conquest of Alexandria by the Arabs (in 21/642), it had undergone some modifications and it has been concluded that its functioning and structure deteriorated successively. There is a tendency to accuse, often moreover without reason, the conquerors and change of régime of being the cause of deterioration, and the assumption that two centuries after the conquest, the lighthouse had fallen completely into ruin (G. F. Hourani, *Seafaring*, 61: "The wonderful Pharos fell to ruin and no one could be found who knew to repair it") seems exaggerated; for several centuries the lighthouse was indeed used, although its functioning was not as perfect as before Islam.

It is logical to suppose that during the first years of the Islamic régime, maritime traditions persisted as before. It is to the Umayyad period that certain historian-geographers attribute its first deterioration; the legend relates that a Christian, pretending to be a Muslim, was able to convince the caliph al-Walīd (d. 87/705) to allow him to look for treasure near (and underneath) the lighthouse and that the sabotage carried out at that time caused some damage to the upper part of the tower. But the Muslims continued to light the fire on the lighthouse, and only the Arab writers (geographers, etc.) allude to the fact that, in the past, the technique used in its functioning (the lantern) was more perfected, in recounting to their readers that in earlier times it was equipped with mirrors (or a mirror); by concentrating the sun's rays, these mirrors could burn the enemy ships (the historical fact which is hidden here is, perhaps, the existence in ancient times of a reflector or another technical method; the technique consisting of adding a reflector to a lantern was not completely unknown in the Islamic world (see al-Maḳḳarī, *Rawḍa*, 13-14),but it was probably more difficult to repair the damage undergone by a proper lighthouse). In the 3rd/9th century, the governor Ibn Ṭūlūn had the upper part of the lighthouse repaired, but the work was often in wood which was not strong and durable. The use of the lighthouse by the Arabs (lighting the fire on top, at night, by means of special custodians, who even had rooms intended for their lodging) continued until the 5th/11th century. In 578/1182-3 the lighthouse was only 50 cubits high; this diminution of its height was due to a deterioration of the construction and to an earthquake (which was neither the first nor the last experienced by the lighthouse), so that the upper parts had been destroyed. At the beginning of the 8th/14th century, it was no more than a ruin, despite the efforts made by certain sultans (for example, Baybars I (d. 676/1277) and Baybars II (d. 709/1310), some time earlier to repair it a little. Already al-Malik al-Kāmil (d. 635/1238) had built on this site a mosque, and the fort which is to be found there today (and which now houses the maritime museum of Alexandria) was constructed by the sultan Ḳāʾit Bay (d. 901/1496).

As for the form of the lighthouse of Alexandria, it is often described by the mediaeval Arab authors, who strive to accentuate its splendour in the past (one of the "Seven Wonders of the World"); but it is hard to deduce what were its original dimensions, especially because the upper parts (a statue of Poseidon, on top, and the lantern) no longer existed in the Islamic period; some conclude that, during the major part of its history, after the birth of Islam, the lighthouse only reached two-thirds of its original height. Three attempts have been made to record its form and dimensions according to the description of the Muslim historians and geographers by H. Thiersch, Asín Palacios (who also discovered a description of the 7th/13th century) and E. Lévi-Provençal (who added a source drawing on the description of the geographer al-Bakrī in the 5th/11th century). The latter is the most recent and may also be summarised. The rectangular base of 320 cubits was surmounted by a narrower, octagonal section of 80 cubits, then by another narrower, rectangular section (until the discovery of this description it was considered to be cylindrical) of 50 cubits; no more of it was in existence.

Manār and *fanār* have given their names to some neighbouring quarters, e.g. in Istanbul (see Fanar-[a]ki = Fener + köy, J. von Hammer-Purgstall, *Constantinopolis und der Bosporus*, 1822, 270, 279 and the Istanbul miniature of the 17th century, in B. Lewis, *Istanbul*, Norman, Oklahoma 1963, 99, on the left; see also *Fenerliler* in *İA*; however, the lighthouse—or rather the signalling tower, KIZ KULESI, at the entrance to the Bosporus—dates almost from our own times). With or without a direct connection with maritime illumination, some trading places, an important journal [see AL-MANĀR], etc., are called "lighthouse".

The modern age has witnessed several improvements and constructive efforts in the maritime field, including the building of lighthouses (e.g. in Morocco in 1865 [see MUḤAMMAD B. ʿABD AL-RAḤMĀN]), of a more organised nature, in the necessary places.

Bibliography: Apart from the works cited in the article, see A.J. Butler and P.M. Fraser, *The Arab conquest of Egypt*, pp. lxxiv-lxxv, 389-400; E.M. Forster, *Alexandria—history and guide* (new ed.), 17-18, 106-7, 144-50; Le Strange, *Lands*, 49; H. Thiersch, *Pharos*, Leipzig-Berlin 1909; Asīn Palacios, *Una descriptión nueva*, in *al-And.*, i/l (1933), 242 ff.; E. Lévi-Provençal, *Une description arabe*, in *Mélanges Maspero*, iii, Cairo 1940, 161-71; G. Ferrand, *Les monuments*, in *ibid.*, 58-60; P. Kahle, *Katastrophe*, in *ibid.*, 150; A.M. Fahmy, *Muslim seapower*, London 1950, 29-30; G. F. Hourani, *Arab seafaring*, Princeton 1951, 60-1, 69; F. Faradj, *al-Iskandariyya*, Cairo n.d. (e.g. 20); *Türk Ansikl.*, 1966, xiii, 45-51; Dj. D. al-Shayyāl, *Taʾrīkh al-Iskandariyya*, Alexandria 1967, 53 ff., 70, 85-6; Ḥammawī, *Taʾrīkh al-usṭūl*, Damascus 1975, 76, 81-3; M. Brill, *Pharos*, in *Cairo Today* (January 1984), 20-4; Univ. of Alexandria, *Taʾrīkh al-baḥriyya*, Alexandria 1973-4, geog. index s.vv. *fanār* and *manār*.

(J. SADAN AND J. FRAENKEL)

AL-**MANĀR,** a journal of Muslim thought and doctrine which appeared in Cairo from 1898 to 1940. Its work was the counterpart of that of a printing-house, of the same name, which, besides its other publications, re-issued articles previously published in the review, such as the famous modern commentary on the Ḳurʾān (*Tafsīr al-Manār*). Without forming part of any particular school, the *Manār* subscribed to the reformist line of the *salafiyya* [*q.v.*]; this movement of cultural resistance towards colonial encroachment sought to restore to Islam its former power and to re-establish confidence in its traditional values, starting with the Arabic language, while employing modern techniques. It elaborated an apologetic which is still widely known and influential today.

The *Manār* was the personal work of one man, Sayyid Rashīd Riḍā [*q.v.*], born in 1865 near Tripoli (Lebanon). At the end of 1897, the same year as the death of Djamāl al-Dīn al-Afghānī [*q.v.*], with whom he had dreamed of collaborating, he travelled to Cairo in order to work in partnership with the *Imām* Muḥammad ʿAbduh [*q.v.*]. Resolved, from the outset, to found a journal which he entitled the *Manār* ("The Beacon"), he published the first issue at the end of Shawwāl 1315/March 1898. He was, over the course of the years, to include in it a number of articles by al-Afghānī, Muḥammad ʿAbduh, al-Kawākibī, Djamāl al-Dīn al-Ḳāsimī, and others. Scientific questions were tackled by Dr. Tawfīḳ Ṣidḳī. After the war of 1914-18, the *amīr* Shakīb Arslān sent him copy from Geneva. But the bulk of the material was drawn from him own tireless pen.

As H. Laoust writes in his article *Le réformisme orthodoxe des "Salafiya"*, "Its discreet expertise, its Islamic internationalism and the reliability of its general documentation, direct the *Manār* towards a liberal, cultured minority. The publication of the commentary of ʿAbduh gives it the prestige of a great name. Its leading articles perfectly convey the progressive orthodox view, always well-argued and a balanced in form, of the major contemporary Islamo-Arab questions." In addition, its judicial discussions, its criticism of books and its news of the Muslim world made it into a link between correspondents, writing from Indonesia as well as from India, Syria, North Africa and even some European countries.

From being at the outset a weekly periodical numbering eight pages, later distributed at longer intervals (once a fortnight, then once a month), the journal very rapidly built up an annual total of 960 pages, a figure which declined during the war of 1914-18 and then rose back to 800 (ten issues per year). Each of its 35 volumes possesses either a detailed table of contents, or alphabetical indices, the form of which evolved over the years. The first 34 volumes covered a period of 37 years (1898-1935). As a result of the death of Rashīd Riḍā in 1935, the next volume (no. 35) had its ten issues spread over a period of six years (July 1935 - September 1940). The Muslim Brothers [see AL-IKHWĀN AL-MUSLIMŪN] had guaranteed its revival, but they preferred to concentrate their efforts on journals of their own. Initially printed in an edition of 1,500, then of 1,000, its circulation rose after the fifth volume with subscriptions from students. The figure of 300 subscribers henceforward guaranteed it a stable, basic readership. There were sometimes temporary difficulties in the distribution of the issues: these were later solved (cf. Turkish censorship in Syria in the first year of publication).

The collected corpus of the *Manār* provides a mine of information on the attitudes, the focuses of interest, the hopes and disappointments of reformists over a period of nearly forty years. It reflects the major events of the Muslim world seen from Cairo, as well as the personal development of Rashīd Riḍā. The judicial discussions have been separately reprinted in Beirut.

Being centred on the religious and social reform (*iṣlāḥ*, [*q.v.*]) of the Islamic *umma*, the *Manār* vindicates the *salafi* heritage of al-Afghānī and of ʿAbduh, extolling a return to the Ḳurʾān and to the Sunna with a view to a purer *tawḥīd*. It is concerned with the unity of the community, and makes appeals for the surmounting of divisions. It opposes those Europeans who seek to efface the last vestiges of the Muslim law. It teaches the compatibility of Islam with science and with reason, in the best interests of mankind at all times and in all places. Following the expression of H. Laoust, "The canonical legitimacy of the sciences, the incorporation into the primitive conception of Islam of the most contemporary social and political ideas to which Muḥammad ʿAbdūh had attached his name", have the right of free entry into the *Manār*. But Rashīd Riḍā remained cautious with regard to what was later to be called *al-tafsīr al-ʿilmī* which seeks to discover in the Ḳurʾān all the modern sciences (cf. *Manār*, xxx, 514-16, on the *tafsīr* of Shaykh Ṭanṭāwī Djawharī [*q.v.* in Suppl.]).

Diverging from the Ḥanafism-Māturīdism of ʿAbduh, the *Manār* turned towards Ḥanbalism. The journal's continual attacks on culpable practices, contrary to the *tawḥīd (mawlid, bidaʿ*, etc.) are based on Ibn Taymiyya and certain of his *fatwās*. This paved the way for the reconcilation which was realised through the eulogy of Wahhābism and the transformation of the *Manār* publishing-house into an active centre of Wahhābī propaganda, beginning after the war of 1914-18 and especially following the conquest of the Ḥidjāz by Ibn Saʿūd (1924-6). In the *Manār* there is insistence on the need for Muslim propaganda and for guidance (*al-daʿwa wa 'l-irshād*). Many lines are devoted to these topics, particularly to the idea of founding a seminary designed to train enthusiasts for this task. There are articles on Arab nationalism, on relations between Turks and Arabs and on the need to ensure for the Arabic language a land of freedom where it may flourish; Islam cannot in fact survive without it, especially at a time when the Turks are adopting a hostile linguistic policy. Similarly, the *Manār* enables us to follow the affair of the caliphate and the upheavals caused by its suppression by the Turks in 1924 [see KHILĀFA].

There are articles describing various personalities of the Muslim world, mostly Arab. Attitudes towards Shīʿism are discussed. Polemic is directed as much against liberal Muslims (cf. that against the *Siyāsa*, which supported Ṭāhā Ḥusayn, etc.) as against al-Azhar. There is news relating to the pilgrimage, the construction of the Ḥidjāz railway, the wars in Tripolitania, in the Rīf, etc., as well as European colonial policy, particularly in regard to the Syrian question after 1918, the Coptic Congress in Asyut in 1911, the Muslim Congresses of Cairo, of Mecca, etc.; relations with the Christians, their doctrine, missions of Western Christians, Western writers sympathetic to Islam, studies on the greatness and decadence of nations, on pedagogy, on the role of the *ʿulamāʾ* in the Muslim renaissance, etc. Literary and cultural Arab news items are not lacking. The judicial discussions tackle various difficulties, some of them relevant to the modern world, mentioning the position of Muḥammad ʿAbduh (cf. for example the question of the Savings Bank). In short, the periodical contained material suitable for learned and illuminating monographs.

The commentary on the Ḳurʾān published from the third year onward was the work of Rashīd Riḍā; it included lengthy extracts from the commentary expounded by Muḥammad ʿAbduh in evening lectures at al-Azhar, and the respective contributions of the two men were clearly distinguished. ʿAbduh went no further than v. 125 of sūra IV *(al-Nisāʾ)* whereas Riḍā continued to the end of sūra XII, (*Yūsuf*, v. 107). Some of the positions adopted were daring: ʿAbduh maintained that the texts of the Jewish Scriptures and of the Gospels were authentic and that only their interpretation had been false (Riḍā denied their authenticity); he claimed that the execution of the Muslim apostate was a measure dating from a time of war during which apostasy constituted desertion in the face of the enemy—today this is not the case and the apostate who does not attack Islam should not be put to death; it is for God to punish him. These examples and other show how ʿAbduh sought to re-open the door of *idjtihād*. Reference to all these allusions are to be found in the studies mentioned in the bibliography.

Although a positive and very important work in the context of the modern Muslim awakening, it should be noted that the *Manār* sometimes confined itself to schematic views of an apologetic nature, simplifying in extreme fashion certain historical problems, notably those of the causative influences which helped to bring about the Renaissance of Europe. It also used its influence on behalf of the Gospel of Barnabas, "this undoubtedly apocryphal work" according to L. Massignon, edited for the first time in the 14th century and later in the 16th, sponsoring its translation into Arabic in 1908. This apologetic must have responded to a deeply-felt need, for it enjoyed, and still enjoys, enormous success, even if it contributed little to imparting a sense of objectivity and of history to those who studied it. Similarly, the *Manār* seems to have ignored a fundamental question: did the adoption of Western techniques not also entail a certain change of mentality, and if so, what? It thus remained silent on one of the key problems posed by the very existence of technological civilisation.

Bibliograpy: Rashīd Riḍā, *Taʾrīkh al-Ustādh al-Imām*, 3 vols., Cairo; the 35 volumes of the review al-*Manār* itself, as well as texts reprinted separately, such as *Fatāwā 'l-Imām Muḥammad Rashīd Riḍā*, 6 vols., Beirut 1961-2, or from Cairo, *al-Manār* printing house: *Tafsīr al-Manār*, 12 vols.; *al-Manār wa 'l-Azhar*, 1353/1934-5; *al-Khilāfa aw al-Imāma al-ʿuẓmā*, 1341/1923. Numerous references to *al-Manār* articles are to be found in the notes accompaying the translation of the latter work by H. Laoust, under the title *Le califat dans la doctrine de Rashīd Riḍā*, Beirut 1938. The most important study of the subject is H. Laoust, *Le Réformisme orthodoxe des "Salafiya"*, in *REI* (1932), 175-224. See also J. Jomier, *Le Commentaire coranique du Manār*, Paris 1954; idem, *Les raisons de l'adhésion du Sayyed Rashīd Riḍā au nationalisme arabe*, in *Bulletin Inst. d'Egypte*, liii-liv, 53-61; idem, *L'Imam Mohammad ʿAbdoh et la Caisse d'Épargne (1903-1904)*, in *Revue de l'Occident Musulman et de la Méditerranée* (1973), 99-107. For the influence of *al-Manār* on the *ʿulamāʾ* of Algeria, see Ali Merad, *Le Réformisme musulman en Algérie de 1925 à 1940*, Paris 1967. (J. JOMIER)

MANĀRA, MANĀR (A.) minaret.

1. In the Islamic lands between the Maghrib and Afghanistan.

Unlike the other types of Islamic religious building, such as the mosque and the *madrasa*, the minaret is immediately and unambiguously recognisable for what it is. The reasons for this are worth investigating. It seems on the whole unrelated to its function of the *adhān* [*q.v.*] calling the faithful to prayer, which can be made quite adequately from the roof of the mosque or even from a house-top. During the lifetime of the Prophet, his Abyssinian slave Bilāl [*q.v.*], was responsible for making the call to prayer in this way. The practice continued for another generation, a fact which demonstrates that the minaret is not an essential part of Islamic ritual. To this day, certain Islamic communities, especially the most orthodox ones like the Wahhābīs in Arabia, avoid building minarets on the grounds that they are ostentatious and unnecessary. Others are content with the so-called "staircase" minarets which consist simply of a few broad external steps leading to a diminutive kiosk a little above roof level. These perpetuate a practice common in the first century of Islam. While such structures are obviously functional, it is very doubtful whether the same can be said for any minaret much more than 15 m. high. Without mechanical amplification, the human voice simply cannot make itself heard, especially in a noisy urban setting, from the top of such celebrated minarets as the Giralda in Seville [see ISHBĪLIYA: 2. Historic buildings] or the Ḳuṭb Minār [*q.v.*] in Dihlī.

If then, the ostensible function of the minaret is somewhat misleading, what other purposes might it have served? If the investigation confines itself in the first instance to the early minarets of the Islamic world —i.e. those predating 1000 A.D.—three possible approaches may be suggested. One is to examine the role of the very earliest minarets in their particular historical setting, on the theory that these examples laid down guidelines for the further development of the form. Another is to see what clues lie in the Arabic words used for minaret, and in their etymology. A third approach would focus on the forms of these early minarets and on their immediate sources, and would thus involve the assumption that at least traces of the earlier functions associated with these forms survived into the Islamic period. It must be remembered, however, that throughout the mediaeval period, the rôle of the minaret oscillated between two polarities: as a sign of power and as an instrument for the *a<u>dh</u>ān*. These functions were not mutually exclusive.

It will be convenient to begin by studying the circumstances in which the earliest minarets were built. According to the literary evidence, the first minaret was erected in *ca.* 45/665 by the governor of ʿIrāḳ Ziyād b. Abīhi [*q.v.*]: a stone tower (*manāra*) was added to the mosque at Baṣra. Soon afterwards, orders were given by the caliph Muʿāwiya to the governor of Egypt, and the mosque of ʿAmr at Fusṭāṭ was given a quartet of *ṣawāmiʿ*, whilst these were also added to other mosques in Egypt. Although nothing remains of these structures, this literary evidence is important in showing that the impetus to build was not a matter of local initiative but came from the highest power in the land, the idea emanating from Syria, where minarets were presumably added to at least some Syrian mosques at this time. It is hard not to see religio-political motives at work here. Christian Syria, within which the Muslims formed a few small enclaves, was lavishly endowed with fine stone churches whose most striking external feature was a tall tower. At the top of these towers was struck the *simandron*—the Orthodox equivalent of the church bell—to summon worshippers for divine service. Some attribute the change in the *a<u>dh</u>ān* to ʿUmar, but Muʿāwiya, sensitively attuned as he was to the discrepancies between Christian and Muslim culture, and to the need to reconcile them wherever possible, can scarcely have failed to compare this Christian practice with its simpler Islamic equivalent. It would have been wholly in character for him to have decided to secure for the *a<u>dh</u>ān* a dignity and formality it had not hitherto possessed by giving it monumental expression. Typically, too, that expression borrowed a Christian form but imbued it with a new Muslim meaning. The slightly later case of the Dome of the Rock leaps to mind as the obvious parallel. The intrusion of political concerns into the forms of early Islamic religious architecture was to be a hallmark of the Umayyad period.

The arguments set out above are susceptible to more than one interpretation. They could support the theory that these early, essentially redundant, minarets were intended simply to demonstrate to the local non-Muslims that the new faith was no less capable than its rivals of devising monumental architecture to glorify itself. However, they could also imply the conclusion that from its very beginning the minaret was intended to function as an outward sign of Islam. A usage formulated in response to a hostile environment would then gradually have become canonical and would have persisted even when circumstances had overtaken the need for it. These two interpretations will be considered in more detail below in the context of the form of the earliest minarets.

The second possibly approach to the original function of the minaret is through the etymology of the words used in Arabic to describe this kind of building. It is perhaps significant that the three words most commonly used - *manāra, ṣawmaʿa* and *miʾ<u>dh</u>ana* - all arguably refer to quite separate functional aspects of the building. Thus the notion that the minaret served multiple functions is embedded in the Arabic language itself. These functions quite naturally generated appropriate terms for themselves. Whether the prevalence of a given term in a given geographical area reflects the predominance of one function over another is, however, doubtful.

By far the commonest of the three terms is *manār(a)*, the source via Turkish of English and French "minaret", lit. "place of fire" (*nār*), a word used in pre-Islamic Arabia to denote an elevated place from which signals of fire or smoke were made. Whence the frequent education of the minaret with the lighthouse [see preceding article MANĀR]; the cylindrical towers attached to Islamic fortresses along parts of the North African littoral, e.g. in Tunisia, not only served as beacons and lighthouses but were actually called *manāras*. One should, on the other hand, avoid any temptation to connect *manār(a)* with *nūr* "light" and to discern a basis for symbolic interpretation of the minaret as an emanation of divine light or as an image of spiritual illumination. The original term *manār(a)* soon lost its necessary connection with fire, and became used to designate signposts, boundary stones or markers, and watch-towers when no particular association with fire was intended. Hence there emerges that *manār(a)* came to involve the two distinct notions of fire and of a marker, neither of which, however, had a specific role in Islamic ritual. The lighting of a fire on the minaret of a mosque was an event of utmost rarity in early Islam (it is recorded as having occured in the case of the Manārat al-ʿArūs in the Damascus mosque), though it is self-evident that the minaret had a value as marker of the principal building of the Islamic community. It seems therefore safe to assume that, in the context of religious architecture, the association between the minaret and fire is irrelevant.

The second term frequently used to designate the minaret—indeed, it is the standard usage in North Africa—is *ṣawmaʿa*. The word means the cell in which a person (usually a monk) secludes himself, with the particular gloss that the cell has a slender pointed apex. Such cells were a regular feature of pre-Islamic Byzantine architecture; they were incorporated into the tall rectangular towers with which churches, monasteries and houses were furnished. Once again, however, as in the case of *manāra*, the etymology is apt to mislead—for while the basic meaning of *ṣawmaʿa* is indeed "hermitage", the word has come to designate, by a process of *pars pro toto*, the entire structure of which the cell was a small part. The specific connotation of *ṣawmaʿa* in the present context is perhaps a "sentry-box" minaret, and eventually a tall, rectangular minaret, rather than the minaret genre itself. For this reason, it is an entirely appropriate term for the minarets of North Africa. Moreover, unlike the word *manāra*, its connotations are religious, albeit with a Christian tinge. Possibly as a result of its association with the minaret, the word is also used more generally to mean "a higher place" or even "a high building", and in this less specific since its connection with *manāra* in the sense of signal tower or marker is plain. In North Africa, however, a distinction clearly exists, for *manāra* is used for signal towers and lighthouses. Appropriately enough in view of its Christian connotations, *ṣawmaʿa* has found a lodging in Europe, in the Spanish word *zoma* meaning "minaret".

It is a challenging reflection that the two Arabic words most frequently used to designate the minaret give no clue to the ritual function commonly associated with the building. Instead, they evoke respectively pre-Islamic and Christian associations. The term that does accurately render the ritual function of the building—*miʾ<u>dh</u>ana*—is, ironically enough, much rarer than the other two, suggesting, perhaps, that earlier "minarets"/*manāras* had functions not exclusively ritual. It derives of course from *adhān*, hence literally "place from which the call to prayer is made", whose root further gives *muʾadhdhin* "muezzin, he who gives the call to prayer". Even this last has pre-Islamic connections, for in the Djāhiliyya the herald who made important announcements was known as the *muʾadhdhin*. Before leaving the problem of etymology, it may be worth noting that several other words occur sporadically in literary or epigraphic texts as synonyms for at least some of the meanings of *manāra*: *ʿalam*/*ʿalama* ("signpost", "boundary maker", "standing stone", "flag"), *mīl* (possibly derived from the Greek *miliarion*, "milestone") and *ʿasās*, "a place of watching", a term especially popular in the Maghrib. The mere mention of these words in the context of the foregoing discussion is enough to emphasise yet again that etymology is a somewhat treacherous guide in determining the function of the minaret. It can safely be asserted, however, that the review of Arabic terminology given above establishes that the minaret performed not one function but several in the mediaeval Islamic world. Whilst the rarer Arabic words for "minaret" may well reflect the function of the building in the particular context concerned, the most commonly employed word, *manāra*, was obviously a blanket term which does not readily lend itself to precise elucidation, unless the context offers further, more specific, clues.

The third possible approach to determining the function of the minaret in the early centuries of Islam is by way of morphology. The briefest survey of the formal characteristics of mediaeval minarets is enough to yield one very significant result: that virtually the whole body of surviving minarets belongs to one of two categories. One category comprises minarets with ample interior space; the other, minarets in which the interior space is reduced to the bare minimum required for a spiral staircase to ascend the structure. Minarets with external staircases obviously belong in neither category. Useful as this division is, it cannot shed light on the crucial first century of Islam. Any attempt to explain the function of the minaret by means of its form has to take some account of the earliest recorded minarets, even though none of these has survived. The interpretation placed on the tantalising brief literary accounts which refer to the earliest minarets is therefore crucial.

These accounts are unfortunately either ambivalent or too short to throw any light on the problem. For example, the historian al-Balādhurī refers to the minaret at Baṣra as a stone minaret. Since stone is specified and the rest of the mosque was of mud brick, it seems legitimate to conclude that the minaret was important enough to have special care taken over its construction. This, then, seems to be a fairly straightforward case. The same cannot be said for the minarets of the mosque of ʿAmr at Fusṭāṭ. The source here is the 9th/15th century author al-Maḳrīzī, who states that Muʿāwiya ordered the building of four *ṣawāmiʿ* (pl. of *ṣawmaʿa*) for the call to prayer, and that Maslama placed four *ṣawāmiʿ* in the corners of the mosque. Since this is not, in all probability, the first word for minaret that would have come naturally to the Mamlūk historian's mind, its use in this passage needs some explanation. It is possible that al-Maḳrīzī used it deliberately because it connoted to him tall, rectangular minarets of the Syrian or Maghribī type (very unlike those which he saw all around him in Egypt). His choice of word would in that case have reflected either his own or his source's precise knowledge of the form which these early Umayyad minarets took; or he may have been quoting an earlier text. Alternatively, he may have used the word *ṣawāmiʿ* with one of his other meanings in mind, such as a high place. In that case, the sense of the passage might be more accurately rendered by translating the key passage as "Maslama heightened the four corners of the Friday Mosque". Such an interpretation would find further support in the literary accounts dealing with the construction of the Damascus mosque.

The key point to bear in mind in a discussion of the Damascus minarets is that there is no evidence that they were the work of any early Muslim patron. Indeed, the geographer Ibn al-Faḳīh, writing at the opening of the 10th century A.D., states specifically that the minarets (*miʾdhana*) in the Damascus mosque "were originally watch towers in the Greek days, and belonged to the Church of John. When al-Walīd turned the whole area into a mosque, he left these in their old condition". Similarly, al-Masʿūdī writes that in this rebuilding "the *ṣawāmiʿ* were not changed, they serve for the *adhān* at the present day". Thus strictly speaking, there is no clear evidence even that these pre-Islamic towers were used for the call to prayer in Umayyad times, and one may especially doubt that they served this function before the reign of al-Walīd, when the Muslims shared the site of the future Great Mosque with the Christians. Nevertheless, the significant use of the word *ṣawāmiʿ* by the ʿIrāḳī al-Masʿūdī pinpoints the connection between Damascus and Fusṭāṭ, a connection which would make sense anyway because Damascus was Muʿāwiya's capital. Conversely, one might justifiably use the evidence of Fusṭāṭ to conclude that in all probability the corner towers at Damascus were indeed used for the *adhān* after the mosque had been built.

Reasonable grounds therefore exist for assuming that the corners of the mosque of ʿAmr at Fusṭāṭ looked very like those of the Damascus *temenos*. Such *ṣawāmiʿ* could be no more than abrupt excrescences at roof level, possibly articulated a little further by crenellations. They would indeed resemble Christian towers, but only in a somewhat stunted fashion. They could not aspire to dominate the skyline or indeed make any marked physical impact on the urban landscape. If this motive had loomed large in the mind of al-Walīd at the time that he was building the Damascus mosque, it would have been a simple process to heighten the existing corner towers accordingly. That he chose not to do so is clear evidence that the symbolic role of the minaret was not yet generally accepted. Indeed, the mosques of Baṣra and Fusṭāṭ are more prophetic of later developments, even though they were built earlier. At Baṣra, the minaret, whatever its form may have been, was clearly distinguished by its different material of construction, while at Fusṭāṭ the *ṣawāmiʿ* were solid up to roof level, necessitating access by ladders. While this detail reflects the early Islamic practice of delivering the *adhān* from the roof, it is also conceivable that such corner *ṣawāmiʿ* had an architectural function as buttresses for the whole building. Their location and strength in turn invites a symbolic interpretation of their function as cornerstones of the faith. The impact of their placing can be gauged from the statement of al-Maḳrīzī that, at the time of the dawn prayer, a muezzin was stationed at each *ṣawmaʿa* and that their combined *adhān* resounded like thunder through the silent city. It might fairly be said, then, that despite the probably rather truncated nature of their resemblance to Christian towers, the *ṣawāmiʿ* of the Mosque of ʿAmr did operate as markers of the mosque. This function was certainly performed more effectively and elegantly by later minarets, but the crucial point is that it is already implicit in the earliest buildings of this genre.

As evidence of the relationship between the Christian towers of Syria and the early minaret, the earliest surviving Islamic monument, at Boṣrā [*q.v.*] in southern Syria, is often cited and certainly its minaret fits naturally into a long series of similar towers erected in pre-Islamic times as part of Christian churches, monasteries and houses, often with a defensive function. Yet, this Boṣrā minaret, notable for its bold projection from the otherwise regular perimeter wall of the mosque, a feature not explicable by e.g. any peculiarity of the site or structural consideration, is actually Mamlūk. The Umayyad *miʾdhana*, according to recent research by Jonathan Bloom, is the staircase minaret along the west wall.

Hence already in the first Islamic century, the religious role of the minaret had been defined in essentials; later times were to bring refinements, but after this first century, the development of the minaret proceeded rather on the lines of variations in form and new secular functions.

For some time, the square form, already well established in Syria, continued to dominate in the Islamic world. Recent excavations have confirmed that the square substructure of the minaret of the Mosque of Sīdī ʿUḳba at al-Ḳayrawān in Tunisia is of Aghlabid date though some of the upper parts are later (thus weakening a once-popular theory that this minaret reflects the influences of the Pharos of Alexandria, which had a three-tier elevation, each tier smaller than the previous one), but it is quite possible that in its original form the minaret looked much as it does now. Lézine suggested that the lighthouse at Salakta was the formal model, but it is also possible that the Arab conquerors of North Africa, coming westwards as they did from Egypt, should have used the most celebrated tower of Egypt as a model for the minaret of the first mosque built in the newly-Islamised territory. In this mosque of al-Ḳayrawān, the minaret was placed opposite the *muṣallā*, and it was only a matter of time before the last refinement was added and the minaret aligned exactly with the *miḥrāb* [*q.v.*] (the Great Mosque at Sāmarrā is the earliest and best surviving example of this culminatory process). The substantial enclosed space of the al-Ḳayrawān minaret (base *ca.* 10m. square and height *ca.* 35m.) encouraged the possibility of provision of chambers within the minaret. For some reason, this was not done there, hence the minaret has inordinately thick walls; but later Maghribī and Andalusian minarets, such as the Almohad examples in Seville, Rabat and Marrakesh, employed such chambers and also gave them decorative vaults in stone or brick.

These three minarets of the later 6th/12th century mark the zenith of this genre in Western Islam, perpetuating the outer shell of pre-Islamic and early Islamic Syrian towers, and of the minaret at Cordoba, but they are much larger than their distant Syrian models (approaching 65m. in height) and display rich decoration on all four sides, with cusped, horseshoe or multifoil arches, often generating a lattice-work design, and also with single or paired windows on each storey. Eventually, too, the Andalusian minarets were to exert an influence on the campaniles of Spanish churches of the period—the wheel coming full circle, as it were, after these towers' Syrian Christian origins. So strong was the tradition of the tall, square-shafted minaret in the Maghrib, that in the eastern Maghrib it survived the coming of the Ottomans; and in Ottoman Tunis, a novel type of octagonal minaret, with each face richly tiled and the whole crowned by a projecting balcony and steepled pavilion, enjoyed special popularity.

An unexpected and distant by-product of the Syrian tradition is the Saharan or West African minaret. The Saharan type, often very high (e.g. the fairly recent example of the Walad Djalal at Zibane) has a marked batter to its walls—a feature which had occurred at al-Ḳayrawān but had not been exploited subsequently in the mediaeval period—and is crowned by an open-plan kiosk. In West African minarets, most of which date from the last four centuries (e.g. Timbuktu and Agadès), the latter is so pronounced that the minaret resembles a truncated cone, studded with projecting palm beams. These facilitate the constant repairs that such mud-brick structures require. Similar minarets are found as far north as the Mzāb region in Algeria.

The minarets of the Maghrib and Andalusia form a school unique in the Islamic world for its fidelity to an imported model and for its innate conservatism, which maintained a broadly consistent form throughout a vast area for over a millennium. The history of the minaret in the rest of the Islamic world, sc. in Egypt and Turkey and in the area to the east of them, is somewhat more varied. It embraces a very wide range of forms, of alien influences, and of functions both secular and religious.

This wider canvas is immediately apparent in the immediately post-Umayyad minarets which survive in the eastern Islamic world. These are principally to be found in ʿIrāḳ. Possibly the earliest among them is the so-called Manārat al-Mudjīda, which departs from the norms of the first century by being a slender cylindrical structure of baked brick, with a winding interior stair and sparing external decoration in baked brick; hence it is prophetic of the minarets erected in Iran during the Saldjūḳ period. Moreover, it is entirely freestanding, with no sign of there ever having been a building adjoining it. It lay strategically on the route between the ʿAbbāsid princely palace of al-Ukhayḍir [see ARCHITECTURE and pl. XIV there] and Kūfa, hence may have had the funtion of a marker, with its peculiar form a reflection of watchtowers which apparently stood along the former Sāsānid *limes* against the Arabs in ʿIrāḳ.

The most celebrated of early ʿAbbāsid minarets are of course the helicoidal towers attached to the Great Mosque of Sāmarrā (234-7/848-52) and the mosque of Abū Dulaf (245-7/859-61) [see ARCHITECTURE and Pls. XVII-XVIII there]. Although their precise origin is a matter of dispute, the question of a classical or Christian source does not arise. Their forms are deeply rooted in ancient Near Eastern architecture. In both cases, a square base carries an external ramp which spirals upwards, at first gently but then with increasing steepness, around a solid central cylinder. In the case of the minaret at Sāmarrā (the *malwiyya*) the ramp ends after five complete revolutions at an arcaded kiosk. A similar aedicule probably crowned the minaret of the Abū Dulaf mosque after the ramp had completed four revolutions. The Sāmarrā minaret is therefore substantially larger, and with a height of 53m. is indeed one of the highest minarets in the Islamic world. As befits its importance, the minaret has a new and imposing location. It is placed some 30m. outside the mosque and is precisely on the axis of the *miḥrāb*. By this means, its integration with the mosque and its liturgical function in relationship to the rest of the building is adequately stressed, while its isolation is sufficiently marked for the minaret to invite attention as a separate structure. The practice of placing the minaret on the *miḥrāb* axis was copied throughout the Islamic world.

There seem to be two possible origins for this bizarre helicoidal form for a minaret. Firstly, an Iranian one. There survives at Fīrūzābād in Fārs, the first capital of the Sāsānids, a square-shafted tower with the remains of an external ramp winding round it (called a *tirbāl* by the Arabs), and this monument has been interpreted as a Zoroastrian one, which had a fire burning at its summit; and we have noted the Arabs' readiness to take over architectural forms sanctified by earlier faiths. Secondly, there is the ancient Mesopotamian form of the ziggurat or tower-temple. Whilst most of these had stepped elevations made up of superimposed squares of decreasing size, a few had a square base which carried a huge central cylinder encircled by a rising ramp; a four-storeyed building of this type has been excavated at Khorsābād [*q.v.*] in northern ʿIrāḳ. To have adopted either of these types as a basis for minarets would have accorded with the anti-Syrian attitudes of the ʿAbbāsids. In the event, however, the *malwiyya* form seems to have been too eccentric to serve satisfactorily as a minaret, and it remained virtually without progeny.

The sole important descendant of the ʿIrāḳī *malwiyya*, specifically that of the Mosque of Abū Dulaf, was indeed the minaret of the mosque built by a servant of the ʿAbbāsids in ʿIrāḳ, Aḥmad b. Ṭūlūn, in Egypt (263-5/876-9) [see ARCHITECTURE and Pls. XXI-XXIV there]. Unfortunately, the present minaret is a reconstruction of the late 7th/13th early 8th/14th century, but earlier historians agree that its original form was spiral.

But these spiral minarets, though fascinating, represent a by-way in the history of the minaret. In the eastern Islamic world, the dominating tradition was henceforth to be that of Iran, where an entirely different form, that of the lofty, cylinder type, developed; this obviously owed nothing to Syria, but might well have owed something to the regions on Iran's northern and eastern fringes, sc. India, Central Asia and even China (E. Schroeder speculated that the pillar form is an immemorial symbol of "the axis of the universe, and the direct way to Heaven"). Even so, such fragmentary evidence as survives suggest that the very earliest Iranian minarets, e.g. at Dāmghān and Sīrāf, followed the Umayyad square-towered form, but judging by the minaret of the Nāyin mosque, which has a square, ground-level format surmounted by an octagonal shaft merging into a tapering cylinder, this form was soon modified. The Nāyin minaret seems to be pre-Saldjūḳ, and the literary evidence confirms that, by the 4th/10th century, extremely tall minarets were a feature of Iranian towns.

The tally of surviving 5th/11th and 6th/12th century buildings in Iran shows that this was a time of unprecedented building activity, with mosques being, like *madrasas* [*q.v.*], expressions of official Saldjūḳ patronage often executed by their *amīrs* (as at e.g. the mosques of Ḳazwīn and Burudjird). These soaring Saldjūḳ minarets—often around 30m. high, with a pronounced taper which accentuates their height, internal stairways, and lavish external brick geometric or calligraphic decoration contrasting with the plainness of the mosque walls—are of such assurance and completeness in their form that a previous period of development must surely be postulated. Within this context of Saldjūḳ patronage, one notes that the rich decoration of such minarets testified to its patron's munificence. Moreover, as an architectural project it was substantially smaller in scope—despite its ostentation—than a mosque. This would obviously recommend it to less wealthy patrons. That these minarets did not necessarily have a straightforward liturgical function is suggested by the case of 6th/12th century Iṣfahān. Given that it is only the Friday mosque that according to custom (not dogma) requires a minaret, it is remarkable to note that this city, one of the Saldjūḳ capitals of Iran, had over a score of minarets in this period. In nearly every case, the mosque for which the minaret was originally intended has vanished. It is tempting to speculate that these mosques were very much simpler and humbler structures which had earlier not had minarets. One may justifiable assume that some evidence besides the minarets themselves would have remained if these minarets had been built contemporaneously with their adjoining mosques as integrated building projects.

The case of the mausoleum traditionally associated with the Sāmānid Ismāʿīl b. Aḥmad at Bukhārā shows that by *ca.* 900 A.D. the effectiveness of brick decoration as a mantle for a building, one of relatively small surface area and therefore cheap, had been discovered, and was now transposed to the minaret (overall brick decoration on contemporary tomb towers, with their much larger diameters, occurs only on smaller buildings of that genre). The cylindrical Iranian minaret generated a surprising variety of forms, mostly in the 6th/12th century, with variations in the proportion of the plinth, octagonal or square, and the cylindrical shaft; two or three tiers of tapering cylinders (e.g. at Ziyar near Iṣfahan and at Djam in Ghūr in central Afghanistan); staircases might revolve round a central column or be built into the thickness of the exterior wall and carried on small vaults. Paired minarets probably date from this period, as a means of lending extra importance to the entrance gate of a building (e.g. at Ardistān and Nakhčiwān), eventually to be brought into the mosque proper in order to flank the entrance to the *muṣallā*. There seems to have been no consistent practice governing the location of single minarets within the mosque. When the minaret was erected as an integral component of the mosque, provision was often made for it to be entered not at ground level but from the roof of the mosque. The otherwise puzzling existence of such doorways comparatively high up the shaft of minarets which are now free-standing are clear evidence that they were originally intended to be part of a mosque.

A few minarets of this period raise searching problems of function. Some are located along major routes or at the edge of the desert (Khusrawgird; Ziyār; Mīl-i Nādirī), which would lend support to the theory that they served, no doubt *inter alia*, as signposts. Since much caravan travel was by night, a lamp at the top of a minaret would allow the building to serve as a landlocked lighthouse. A chance literary reference establishes that in 581/1185 the practice of placing a lamp at the top of a minaret was sufficiently familiar in Khurāsān to occasion no comment. Perhaps the most enigmatic, as well as the most splendid, minaret of the period is that of Djam, with a height of *ca.* 60m. unprecedented among Iranian minarets, and its main lower shaft principally decorated by a whole Ḳurʾānic sūra (XIX, *Maryam*) plus other, mainly historical, inscriptions, lauding the achievements of the Ghūrid sultan Ghiyath al-Dīn Muḥammad b. Sām [see GHŪRIDS]; clearly, there is a motive here of prestige and victoriousness, with the Ḳurʾānic text perhaps emphasising the Islamic faith in a land which had not long emerged from paganism.

In later periods, the Iranian minaret never recovered the importance it had had under the Saldjūḳs, but even so, new uses and new types of decoration were found for it. In Il-Khānid times, the device of paired minarets flanking an important *īwān* [*q.v.*]—usually the entrance to a building—was enthusiastically employed (Abarḳūh, Ashtardjān, Ḳarābāghlar and two buildings in Iṣfahān). There was a new emphasis on lavishly-applied tilework, and this was a crucial factor in a change of emphasis, the deliberate highlighting of the lower stages of the minaret. Under the Tīmūrids, the separateness of the minaret was stressed by the technique of enveloping the shaft with a lozenge grid in brick whose interstices were each filled with a medallion of high-quality tilework (e.g. the minarets of the Masdjid-i Shāh and the Mosque of Gawhar Shād, both in Mashhad). In Ṣafawid times, the topmost storey of the minaret was standardised in the form of a tapering shallow-domed cylinder which, like the rest of the minaret, was entirely sheathed in glazed tilework, with, occasionally, much of the shaft gilded (e.g. at the shrines of Ḳum and Mashhad). Under the Ḳādjārs, architects signalled the increasingly secular function of the minaret by using it to punctuate entrance portals to bazaars (Yazd), towns (Ḳazwīn, Simnān) and places (Ṭihrān); minarets, formerly single or in pairs, now proliferated and became trivial.

The influence of the Saldjūḳ minaret is clearly discernable in Muslim India, carried thither by the Ghūrids and their epigoni; see below, 2. India.

There remains to examine the architectural genre of the minaret in Egypt and Turkey, two areas where it enjoyed great popularity. Turkey has had a distinguished though shorter tradition of minaret construction than Egypt, beginning with the very numerous minarets erected by the Saldjūḳs of Rum, in which we find a use of paired portal minarets, of massive strength, all of brick in their upper sections, contrasting with the ashlar stone façades below, all of this showing their ultimate Iranian origins.

Rather more individual, perhaps, was the Anatolian interpretation of what had long been a standard device of Islamic architects, namely employing a single minaret as an integral part of a mosque deserving special attention in its own right. The novelty lay in reducing the surface area of the mosque and thereby giving the minaret much more prominence. Nowhere in the Islamic world is the familiar silhouette of a compact mosque with a low dome and cylindrical minaret encountered as regularly as in Turkey. This is a schema which has attained well-nigh symbolic status, and was in Anatolia extended to *madrasa*s and *ʿimāret*s. Their sturdiness and their location at a corner of the building lends these minarets the air of a bastion, well exemplified in the ʿAlāʾ al-Dīn mosques at Konya and Niğde or the Ulu Cami at Divriği (all 7th/13th century) and, in the following century or so, in the mosques of ʿĪsā Bey at Selçuk 777/1375) or Ilyās Bey at Miletus (806/1404). Such buildings kept the tradition alive and ensured that it became canonical under the Ottomans from the time of their earliest buildings at Iznik (Yeşil Cami) and Bursa (Yeşil Cami and the Hüdavendigâr mosque among others). In the mature Ottoman masterpieces of Istanbul, two or more minarets are standard equipment for mosque complexes; but in the provinces the old tradition continued unchanged, as mosques in Elbistan, Diyarbakir, Gebze and elsewhere testify.

Although a variety of forms were used in pre-Ottoman Anatolia, these minarets give little hint of the unique role which the minaret was to play in Ottoman architecture, one which became largely fixed, with its slender and elegant form, like a sharpened pencil, after the capture of Istanbul. In the Ottoman minaret, the main cylindrical shaft rises from a square or polygonal base and is punctuated by one, two or even three circular balconies carried on *muḳarnas* [*q.v.*] vaulting, the whole being capped by elongated conical roofs, sheathed in lead and ending in finials. Muezzins on each balcony would deliver the call to prayer in the form of a canon; and the acoustic impact of these many voices would of course be significantly intensified in a mosque with multiple minarets, the voices interweaving in different sonorities depending on the height and distance separating the muezzins. Whether such musical refinements were entirely audible is another matter.

Perhaps the most celebrated feature of Ottoman minarets was not their outward form but their use in pairs, quartets or sextets as a device to proclaim the royal status of the building—for it seems that only a reigning sultan could erect more than one minaret per mosque. There can be little doubt that these mosques represent the most sustained attempt in all of Islamic architecture to reconcile the divergent aims of royal and religious iconography. These gigantic, needle-sharp lances clustered protectively, like a guard of honour, around the royal dome, have a distinctly aggressive and ceremonial impact, largely dependent on their almost unprecedented proportions; the pair of minarets flanking the Süleymaniye dome are each some 70m. high. Such minarets function simultaneously to enrich the exterior silhouette of the mosque—in the case just cited, for instance, the outer minarets flanking the principal façade of the building are shorter than those flanking the dome. Thus a pyramidal effect is achieved which is still further emphasised by the choice of a sloping site. The gently rolling skyline of Istanbul, with its rural views, was ideally suited for this kind of display, and the political significance of the city as the Ottoman capital may partly have motivated this new use of the minaret as a component of urban design on a mammoth scale. Such minarets were also used in a more symbolic way as markers of the courtyard of the *muṣallā*, or of the entire mosque, staking out the boundaries of the religious domain within a secular environment. Dome chamber and minaret alike thus acquire extra significance as symbols of the faith. This development was not new, but only in Ottoman architecture is it pursued with such singlemindedness. It is therefore entirely appropriate that these minarets should, like the domes over the *miḥrāb*, also bear the emblem of the crescent, supported on a series of superposed orbs.

If conservatism is the hallmark of the Ottoman minaret, its counterpart in Egypt is above all varied. This variety is all the more remarkable because the Egyptian school is to all intents and purposes concentrated on the buildings of Cairo, though it is represented in some small measure in the provincial towns of Egypt and in the architecture of the Mamlūks in Syria and the Levant. Unfortunately, very few surviving pre-Mamlūk minarets have escaped extensive alternation. Moreover, the most important examples to fall within this category are not metropolitan work at all but are found in various provincial towns—Esna, Luxor, Aswan and nearby Shellal, all dating from the late 5th/11th century and already displaying the characteristic Egyptian division of the minaret into separately conceived superimposed tiers, though Ḥidjāzī influences are at work also.

Interesting as these minarets are stylistically, they are insignificant in comparison with the great corner towers marking the main façade of the Mosque of al-Ḥākim in Cairo, built between 380/990 and 401/1010. With their massive—but later—embattled square bases, whose taper, like that of an ancient Egyptian pylon, is so pronounced that it is almost a slope, they have all the appearance of bastions. That this military quality was to some degree present in the original layout is shown by the façade of the Mahdiyya mosque, built in Tunisia early in the previous century, which too had the corners of its main façade heavily emphasised by bastions which matched the main entrace of the mosque in projecting some 3m. from it and moreover projected a full 7m. from the lateral walls. In its original layout, the Ḥākim mosque maintained the consonance between corner projections and portal already established at Mahdiyya, though the projection was twice as marked. Very soon, however—by 401/1010—each minaret was enclosed by a huge salient some 17m. square which allotted it a revolutionary and portentous role. Finally, in 480/1087, Badr al-Djamālī enlarged the northern salient to gigantic proportions—some 25m. square. He thereby not only incorporated the principal façade of the mosque into the expanded fortifications of the city—a clear indication of the essentially military flavour of this mosque—but managed to make the minarets play a major part in this process without noticeable strain or incongruity.

Since the minarets of al-Ḥākim survive only in an altered state, it is not easy to see where they belong in the corpus of Egyptian minarets. This is all the more regrettable in view of the once-vigorous controversy over the role of the Pharos of Alexandria, which stood intact until it was partially ruined by an earthquake in 180/796-7, in the evolution of the Egyptian minaret. *Pace* Creswell, who argued against any connection between the two building types, it can scarcely be overlooked that the surviving Egyptian minarets which date before 1100 all attest a pronounced multipartite division of the elevation. Since this feature is absent alike in the Syrian, Iranian and Maghribī traditions (with two significant exceptions), some rationale for this unusual feature must be proposed, and a probability here seems to be the Pharos, with the Egyptian minarets as free variations on the Pharos theme. (One should note that the Pharos was repeatedly rebuilt by the Muslims until its final disappearance between the early 7th/13th and the mid-8th/14th century. Indeed, as Butler noted, the account of ʿAbd al-Laṭīf indicates that in *ca.* 1200 the Pharos comprised successively square, octagonal and round storeys and was crowned by a lantern or small cupola. It may well be, therefore, that this semi-Islamic Pharos rather than the original buiding was the means of establishing the tradition of the multi-staged minaret in Egypt.)

But if the Pharos did, in one or other of its successive guises, exert some influence on early Egyptian minarets, this does not seem to have been continuous. In the early versions of certain towers, the emphasis was on a tall, square shaft of Syrian type, which may be very plain (mausolea of Abu 'l-Ghaḍanfar, 552/1157, and Fāṭima Khātūn) or richly decorated (minaret in *madrasa* of Sultan al-Nāṣir Muḥammad), with the so-called *mabkhara* (because it resembled the top of an incense burner), a two-storey octagonal pavilion, crowning it. Subsequently, the *mabkhara* was accorded more emphasis, and its interior divisions made more marked, with differing ground plans, octagonal and circular, and decorative patterns.

In later times, the principle persisted of altering the ratio of the component tiers. The main shaft was reduced to the point where it was lost in the surrounding walls of the mosque, leaving the visible part of the minaret as an octagonal shaft with a cylindrical superstructure (minarets of Shaykhūn and Sarghatmish, both mid-8th/14th century). The transitions between the tiers were often marked by multiple balconies on *muḳarnas* corbelling, recalling Ottoman minarets, and these were indeed used to secure the same antiphonal effects in the chanting of the *adhān* as in Turkey. There was an emphasis on absolute height, with the southeastern corner minaret of the Sultan Ḥasan mosque soaring to 90m., the tallest in Cairo. The *mabkhara* was now replaced by the *ḳulla*, so-called because of its resemblance to the upper half of the typical Egyptian water container, pear-shaped and with at least two bronze finials whose crescents are orientated towards the *ḳibla*. In the final decades of Mamlūk rule, the minaret is crowned by a pair of square-plan pavilions crowned by a cluster of *ḳulla*s (funerary complex of Ḳānṣūh al-Ghūrī).

Finally, the popularity of the minaret in Mamlūk architecture invites explanation. In the 8th/14th and 9th/15th centuries, the main building type in Cairo appears to have been the composite ensemble. Its constituent parts could vary from one ensemble to another, but their main functional elements were the mosque, *madrasa, khānḳāh* and mausoleum. Similar complexes had already become popular in Saldjūḳ Anatolia. In Egypt, however, unlike Anatolia, the minaret was from the first regarded as an integral part of such complexes. Whether this was entirely for functional reasons may be doubted. In the dense urban fabric of Cairo, nothing could more appropriately designate such a complex from afar than a minaret; and in this sense, it could be regarded as a public affirmation of its patron's munificence. Their placing varied. Sometimes they were located at the two corners of the principal façade, or flanking a gateway (e.g. Bāb Zuwayla); these were traditional locations. But many of the locations were unusual or even unprecedented. The *madrasa* of al-Ṣāliḥ has a single minaret above the central porch of the façade, and the two minarets in the mosque of al-Nāṣir Muḥammad on the citadel are at the corner of the *ḳibla* wall and to one side of the main entrance. The latter location recurs in the funerary complex of Ḳāʾit Bay. In this unpredictable positioning of the minaret, one may recognise similar concerns to those of Ottoman architects. Now the minaret was, it seems, valued less for its actual or symbolic religious function and more for its role as a marker or articulating feature, both within the complex to which it belonged and more broadly within the cityscape itself. Once again, then, the flexibility of the forms developed by Islamic architects asserted itself.

Bibliography : E. Doutté, *Les minarets et l'appel à la prière*, in *RAfr.*, xliii (1899), 339-49; H. Thiersch, *Pharos in Antike, Islam und Occident*, Leipzig and Berlin 1909; R. Hartmann, *Manāra*, in *Memnon*, iii, (1910), 220-2; idem, *Zum Thema: Minaret und Leuchtturm*, in *Isl.*, i (1910), 388-90; H. Lammens, *Phares, minarets, clochers et mosquées: leur origine, leur architecture*, in *Revue des Questions Historiques,* N.S. xlvi (1911), 5-27; F. Sarre and E. Herzfeld, *Archäologische Reise im Euphrat- und Tigrisgebiet,* Berlin 1911-20, 4 vols.; K. A. C. Creswell, *The evolution of the Minaret, with special reference to Egypt*, in *The Burlington Magazine*, xlviii (1926), 134-40, 252-8, 290-8; E. Diez, *Manāra*, in *EI*[1]; M. B. Smith, *The Manārs of Iṣfahān*, in *Athār-é Īrān*, i/2 (1936), 313-58; E. Schroeder, *The Iranian mosque form as a survival*, in *Proceedings of the Iran Society*, i (1936-8), 82-92; J. Schacht, *Ein archäischer Minaret-Typ in Ägypten und Anatolien*, in *Ars Islamica*, v (1938), 46-54; S. Hassid, *The Sultan's turrets, a study of the origin and evolution of the minaret in Cairo*, Cairo 1939; J. Sourdel-Thomine, *Deux minarets d'époque seljoukide en Afghanistan*, in *Syria*, xxx (1952), 108-36; Creswell, *The Muslim architecture of Egypt*, i-ii, Oxford 1952-9; G. Marçais, *L'architecture musulmane d'Occident*, Paris 1954; Schacht, *Sur la diffusion des formes d'architecture religieuse musulmane à travers le Sahara*, in *Travaux de l'Institut de Recherches Sahariennes*, xi (1954), 11-27; idem, *Further notes on the staircase minaret*, in *Ars Orientalis*, iv (1961), 137-41; G. R. Moḥammad *The minaret and its relationship to the mosque in early Islam*, Ph.D. thesis, Univ. of Edinburgh 1964, 2 vols., unpubl.; Creswell *Early Muslim architecture*², i/1, Oxford 1969, 59-61; D. Whitehouse, *Staircase minarets on the Persian Gulf*, in *Iran*, x (1972), 155-8; A. M. Hutt, *The development of the minaret in Iran under the Saljūqs*, M. Phil. thesis, Univ. of London 1974, 2 vols. unpubl.; F. Hernández Giménez, *El alminar de ʿAbd al-Rahman III en el mezquita mayor de Córdoba. Genesis y repercusiones*, Granada 1975; Hutt, *The Central Asian origin of the eastern minaret form*, in *Asian Affairs*, N.S. viii/2 (1977), 157-62; J. M. Bloom, *The Mosque of al-Ḥākim in Cairo*, in *Muqarnas*, i (1983), 15-36; *idem*, *Five Fatimid minarets in Upper Egypt*, in *Journal of the Society of Architectural Historians*, xliii/2 (1984), 162-7; B. O'Kane, *Salǧūq minarets: some new data*, in *Annales Islamologiques*, xx (1984), 85-101, with full bibl. covering recent work on Saldjūḳ minarets; D. Behrens-Abouseif, *The minarets of Cairo*, Cairo 1985; Bloom, *The minaret before the Saljūqs*, in *The art of the Saljūqs in Iran and Anatolia*, ed. R. Hillenbrand (in the press).

(R. Hillenbrand)

2. In India.

The *manāra* in India, commonly referred to by the *imāla* form *mīnār*, may be either (a) free-standing or (b) an integral part of a mosque or other building. In the second category, it is convenient to distinguish the (actually or potentially) functional from the non-functional forms. With rare exceptions, in some regional styles [see hind. vii. Architecture] no form of the *mīnār* is used at all; Djawnpur; Mālwā; the Dihli sultanates and the pre-Mug͟hal Pandjāb; Sind; Kas͟hmīr; the ʿImād S͟hāhī, Niẓām S͟hāhī and Barīd S͟hāhī sultanates in the Deccan. (It might be objected that the non-functional forms do not properly qualify to be called *mīnārs* at all; but these forms, with others to be mentioned below, are certainly derived from *mīnār* prototypes, and there is no other recognised term by which they may conveniently be described. The term *mīnār* is regularly applied to towers of many types and functions.)

(a) The free-standing *mīnār* first appears in India as an adjunct to the earliest mosque ("Ḳuwwat al-Islām") in Dihlī, standing outside the original mosque compound, commenced by Ḳuṭb al-Dīn Aybak (whence, possibly, its sobriquet of "Ḳuṭb Mīnār" [*q.v.*]) about 595/1199, and completed before 634/1236 by Iltutmis͟h [*q.v.*] to a height of some 230 feet. The taper of its profile is very pronounced, nearly 5° from the vertical and it was divided into four stages by encircling balconies supported by *muḳarnas* corbels; the three lower stages show different designs of vertical fluting, the flutes on the lowest stage being alternately rounded and angular, those in the second all rounded, those in the third all angular (the original fourth stage was rebuilt into two storeys in 770/1368 under Fīrūz S͟hāh the Tug͟hluḳid). The occurrence of the Ḳurʾān, LXII, 9-10, in an inscription on the second storey affords presumptive evidence for the use of the *mīnār* as a *miʾd͟hana*. The assertions s.v. dihlī (II, 260) and hind (III, 441) above, that the fluted storeys develop the polygonal outline of the *mīnārs* of G͟hazna, taken as the prototype of the Dihlī *mīnār*, now need modification in the light of later research: A. Hutt, in *Three minarets in the Kirman region*, in *JRAS* (1970), 172-80, shows that the section of the base of the minaret of the Masdjid-i Djāmiʿ of Zarand shows precisely the same disposition of alternate rounded and angular flutes; this is therefore a more exact exemplar for the Ḳuṭb Mīnār than the *mīnārs* at G͟hazna, whose section is stellate, based on two interlaced squares. A *mīnār* in the Sīstān region, described by K. Fischer in *Afghanistan*, xxii/3-4 (1970), 91-107, of similar form, suggests a nearer prototype on the probable line of transmission to India. (There is thus now even less need to cite the form of the Doddabasappa temple in Dambal, Dharwar district, as a possible prototype of the Ḳuṭb Mīnār plan, as has been advocated by some Hindū enthusiasts.) The characteristic taper of the Kirmān examples, and of the minaret of Djām in Afg͟hānistān, is also closer to that of the Ḳuṭb Mīnār than are the G͟hazna examples. These details are emphasised here because of their persistence in certain aspects of mosque architecture, described under (b) below. Other free-standing *mīnārs* stand or stood at Kōʾil (ʿĀlīgarh) (inscr. 652/1254; erected by Balban as governor to commemorate victories of the sultan Nāṣir al-Dīn Maḥmūd; tapering with square base and external galleries supported by cornices, with internal spiral stair, but demolished in 1862 without adequate record; Bayānā, cylindrical with slight entasis but unfinished, in city near Ukhā mandir and Ukhā masdjid, 9th/15th century, and tall *mīnār* in hilltop fort, tapered with corbelled balcony, inscr. 871/1466 (?), possibly with a double staircase (entrance blocked on my visit in 1972); Dawlatābād, "Čānd Mīnār" in inner city, *ca.* 849/1445, three encircling galleries supported by elaborate brackets, similar profile to *mīnārs* of *madrasa* in Bīdar, see below; Bīdar town, "Čawbāra", low cylindrical tower at crossing of main thoroughfares, early 9th/15th century; Čhoṭā Panḍuʾā Bengal: massive *mīnār* 50m. from Bafī masdjid, early 8th/14th century, five diminishing tiers resembling half-drawn-out telescope, lowest three fluted; Gawŕ: Fērōz Mīnār, *ca.* 895/1490, no taper, polygonal section. Both Hiran *mīnār* at Fatḥpur Sīkrī and "Nīm safāʾī" *mīnār* at old Māldā, Bengal, tapered with stone projections resembling elephant tusks (on which to display heads of rebels?), Mug͟hal, late 10th/16th century; Dihlī "Čōr Mīnār", early 9th/15th century, many holes for same purpose; S͟hayk͟hūpūra, Pandjāb, Hiran Mīnār, 30m., tapering 1044/1635, popularly sometimes supposed to commemorate Djahāngīr's favourite elephant, but often attributed to Dārā S͟hukōh. Finally, the Kōs Mīnārs of the early Mug͟hal period, solid towers of similar profile to the Ḳuṭb Mīnār but only 6-8 m. high, were set at intervals of a *kōs* [see miṣāha. 2. India] along the major thoroughfares. Many purposes are involved in the above: *miʾd͟hana*; observation post to command dead ground; possibly, following Hindū examples, "victory tower"; other commemoration; platform for shooting or observation game; execution displays; distance markers. The purposes are frequently combined.

(b) *Mīnārs* attached to a mosque or other building, however, are provided primarily as *miʾd͟hanas*, although since they are almost always multiplied symmetrically, they obviously have also an important aesthetic function (the single *mīnār* in the south-east corner of the courtyard of the Bahmanī Ék mīnār kī masdjid at Rāyčur [*q.v.*] is a striking exception). Only in Gudjarāt under the Aḥmad S͟hāhī sultanate, and in Burhānpur in K̲h̲āndēs̲h̲, are paired functional *mīnār*s used regularly before the Mug̲h̲al period; here they are cylindrical, their internal staircases opening on to one or more encircling balconies supported on heavy corbels as well as to the mosque roof, and are capped by conical roofs with no suggestion of an open turret. The earliest Aḥmad S̲h̲āhī examples flank the central arch of the *līwān*, although later they may be placed at the north and south ends of the façade. The latest mosques of the Aḥmad S̲h̲āhī period, e.g. Rānī Sabarī's mosque and the Īsānpur one, have solid pseudo-*mīnār*s at the ends of the façade.

This sudden reintroduction of the *miʾd̲h̲ana-mīnār*, with an immediate secondary aesthetic function, is not fully explained. Gudjarāt mosques in Dihlī Sultanate times such as Hilāl K̲h̲ān's one at Dhōlkā, the Djāmiᶜ mosque at Cambay, have only solid conical or cylindrical pillars over the parapet flanking the central bay of the *līwān*; but earlier Dihlī Sultanate examples outside Gudjarāt may show the connection with the Ḳuṭb Mīnār; e.g. the Arhāʾī din ká djompfá mosque at Adjmēr carries two cylindrical turrets, solid and some 2m. tall, over the *maḳṣūra* arch, with vertical flutes alternately circular and angular exactly as on the lowest storey of the Ḳuṭb Mīnār (similar fluting occurs on the external corner buttresses of the mosque courtyard). In Dihlī itself, the Ḳuṭb Mīnār profile is perpetuated in the solid buttresses which flank mosque gateways, the central bay of the *līwān* façade, the external *miḥrāb*-projection, and external corners of courtyards, in the Tug̲h̲luḳ and Lōdī periods; these show at least one band of Ḳuṭb Mīnār-like fluting, and their profile is carried up above parapet level to end in a *guldasta*; especially when flanking the central propylon-like arch of the *līwān* façade, these suggest paired *miʾd̲h̲ana* towers, and may thus have a psychological purpose. This would seem to be the explanation for many of the examples which follow. In the Bahmanī Sultanate, the *mīnār* is not used regularly with mosques; that al Rāyčūr mentioned above is an exception, and the Čānd Mīnār at Dawlatābād is doubtless sited with the old Djāmiᶜ mosque in mind although physically separated by some 100 metres—doubtless also to enable a view of broken ground to the east. The profile of both resembles that of the remaining one *mīnār* of two at the ends of the entrance façade of the *madrasa* of Maḥmūd Gāwān [*q.v.*] at Bīdar, inscr. 877/1472, although the balconies of the latter are carried out from the main shaft in a curvilinear form rather than being supported on brackets in the usual Indian manner. All are crowned with a dome-shaped cap, with no open room at the top. The old brick *mīnār*s attached to the courtyard of the much later Makkā Masdjid at Bīdjāpur, also of Bahmanī date, have lost their upper parts; their balconies seem to have been supported on wooden brackets. Other Bahmanī *mīnār*s, all of similar profile, are the pairs flanking the gateways of the *dargāh* of S̲h̲aykh Sirādj al-Dīn Djunaydī and the so-called house of Gēsū Dārāz, both in Gulbargā, and those flanking both the outer and inner gateways of the *dargāh* at Āland; but these are crowned with foliated domes of three-quarter sphere shape, as in the ᶜĀdil S̲h̲āhī and Ḳuṭb S̲h̲āhī styles, and those of the outer gateway have moreover an encircling band of open arches in the Ḳuṭb S̲h̲āhī manner. Of possible relevance to the designs in north India referred to above are the *guldasta*s which stand at the corners of the parapets of Bahmanī tombs, starting with the very earliest at Gulbargā: these are fluted, although fluting does not extend to the *mīnār*s. The *mīnār* proper is not used at all in the

Bahmanīs' successor states. The skylines of mosques and tombs of the ᶜĀdil S̲h̲āhīs in Bīdjāpur and elsewhere are so liberally provided with vertical pillars as to resemble a burgeoning asparagus bed, but these are at best pseudo-*mīnār*s which may psychologically suggest the *miʾd̲h̲ana-mīnār* but whose real function is merely artistic. Turrets, *čhatrī*s and *guldasta*s are also freely used, but the relation between these forms cannot be pursued here. The *mīnār*-like structures of the Ḳuṭb S̲h̲āhīs of Ḥaydarābād and Golkondā, similarly, are usually solid shafts, cylindrical, with characteristic encircling arcaded galleries, although in a late offshoot of the Ḳuṭb S̲h̲āhī style in the Djāmiᶜ mosque of Srīrangapaṭṭana [*q.v.*] ("Seringapatam") an internal staircase is provided. That the bases of the pseudo-*mīnār*s of the Tōlī Masdjid (1082/1671) outside Ḥaydarābād city stand in pot-shaped bases should not be taken as representing any connexion with ancient Indian pillars.

Under the Mug̲h̲als, the functional *mīnār* returns to north India; this is possibly inspired by Gudjarāt examples, since other typically Gudjarātī features are introduced into Mug̲h̲al architecture after the conquest of Gudjarāt in 980/1573. The first example is that of the four *mīnār*s at the corners of the gateway of Akbar's tomb at Sikandra, completed in the early years of the 11th/17th century: tapering, white marble (the lowest stage fluted), two intermediate balconies supported on corbel brackets, topped by an open *čhatrī* with slender columns. With some variation in the patterns of the intermediate balconies, and of the material, section and decoration of the shaft, this type is the model for the major later *mīnār*s: at Djahāngīr's tomb in Lāhawr; the Djāmiᶜ mosque (S̲h̲āhdjahānābād) Dihlī; the Tādj Maḥall at Āgrā (but not the Djāmiᶜ mosque); the mosque of Wazīr K̲h̲ān at Lāhawr; the Bāds̲h̲āhī mosque of Lāhawr, which has also short *mīnār*-like corner turrets; the tomb of Rābi ᶜa Dawrānī ("Bībī kā maḳbara") at Awrangābād; Awrangzīb's mosques in Banāras, Mathurā, etc.; short corner staircased *mīnār*s also at the tomb of I ᶜtimād al-Dawla at Āgrā, little more than turrets, seem to be the model for engaged corner turrets at e.g. the tomb of Safdar Djang at Dihlī, and Mug̲h̲al mosques in Bengal e.g. Dhakā, Murs̲h̲idābād, etc. Since there is no necessity for the *ād̲h̲ān* at tombs, many of these Mug̲h̲al *mīnār*s are thus also principally decorative.

Bibliography: In addition to references in the text, see for the Ḳuṭb Mīnār, J. A. Page, *Historical memoir on the Qutb* (= *MASI*, 22), Calcutta 1926, and its abridgement *Guide to the Qutb, Dehli*, Calcutta 1927; cf. also A. Maricq and G. Wiet, *Le minaret de Djam*, Paris 1959. For Kōʾil: *Aligarh gazetteer*, 1902, 165 ff.; A. Rashid, *Koil minar—who built?*, in *Proc. Ind. Hist. Congr.*, vi, 1943, 395-7 (not seen). For Bīdar: G. Yazdani, *Bidar: its history and monuments*, Oxford 1947, 90-100 and Plates L-LVI, LXIV. For Bengal: short descriptions, photographs and bibliographical notes in Catherine B. Asher, *Inventory of key monuments*, in G. Michell (ed.), *The Islamic heritage of Bengal*, UNESCO Paris 1984, 53, 73, 108; for Chofā, Panduā, also H. Blochmann, in *Proc. ASB* (1870), 122, and *JASB* (1870), plates. For Gudjarāt, see *Bibl.* to HIND, vii. For the Bahmanī structures mentioned: illustrations in E.S. Merklinger, *Indian Islamic architecture: the Deccan 1347-1686*, Warminster 1981 (text very unreliable); for Rāyčūr also *Ann. Rep. Arch. Dept. Hyderabad*, 1339F. Illustrations of Ḳuṭb S̲h̲āhī (pseudo)-*mīnār*s: Čār Mīnār, *Ann. Rep. Arch. Dept. Hyderabad*, 1328F., 3-4, and Pl. III-IV; Tōlī masdjid, *ibid.*, 1326F., 3-5,

Plates II-III, IX-X., and see also SRĪRANGAPAṬṬANA. For the ʿĀdil Shāhī decorative forms, see *Bibl.*. to BĪDJĀPUR. Monuments. For the Mughal *mīnārs* and associated structures, see MUGHALS. Architecture. A fully-illustrated study by the author of *mīnārs*, *guldastas* and associated structures is in preparation. (J. BURTON-PAGE)

3. In East Africa, the word (Swahili, *mnara*, pl. *minara*), has three connotations:

(1) Before the late 19th century minarets were of extreme rarity. The Great Mosque of Kilwa in Tanzania, the largest of all, did not have one. The only examples are the Great Mosque (1238) and the Mosque of Arbaʿa Rukūn (1268) at Mogadishu, and the Friday Mosque at Merca (1609), all in Somalia and dated by inscriptions; a late 14th century mosque at Ras Mkumbuu, Pemba Island; and the Malindi Mosque in Zanzibar Town built in 1831, of which the minaret is reputedly of greater age. Many mediaeval mosques, however, possess an external staircase, sometimes part of the structure of the ablutions, from which the call to prayer was given. The earliest such example is at Kaole, near Bagamoyo, Tanzania, while the Great Mosque at Kilwa, Tanzania, has two such staircases outside the mosque proper in its north and south courts respectively.

(2) The word is also used, both in Arabic and Swahili, for the pillar tombs which are an architectural peculiarity of the eastern African coast. Situated generally on the north of *ḳibla* side—for Mecca lies almost due north of the eastern African coast—these tombs are formed by a roofless square or rectangular walled structure, providing space for two up to five or six burials, the distinguishing pillar being cylindrical or tapered, square, hexagonal or octagonal, and usually with a string course or some other form of decoration near the top that markedly suggests a phallic origin. (In this connection it should perhaps be noted that at Mtitimira, some 12 miles north of Kilwa, a representation of a phallus the size of a man's forearm surmounts the *miḥrāb* arch in a mosque that was abandoned in the 14th century.) The height of the pillars varies greatly from some 10 to 20 feet, but at Mombasa an extreme example reaches some 60 feet and has a base which actually spans the entire tomb. It is alleged today by some Sunnī Muslims amongst the Swahili that these pillar tombs are the work of Shīʿīs, but this has never been confirmed. The only reference to a pillar tomb in literature is in the Arabic *History of Kilwa*, B.L. Or. ms. 2666, which refers to the burial *ca.* 1364 of sultan Ṭālūṭ b. al-Ḥusayn of Kilwa in a pillar tomb on Mafia Island which was already occupied by the burials of two *faḳīhs*. This is the earliest date that we possess for these structures, but regrettably the tomb in question seems to have fallen into ruin and disappeared. Pillar tombs are distributed from as far north as Koyama in the Bajun Islands off the east coast of Somalia to as far south as Mboamaji, a few miles south of Dar es Salaam, Tanzania. Their walls are frequently panelled and often elaborately decorated with different motifs sculptured in coral, and sometimes inlaid with plates of Chinese porcelain, rarely celadon, but chiefly blue-and-white of the Ming dynasty. This practice already existed in the 14th century, as witness Yüan porcelain inlaid in the pillar of a pillar tomb at Kaole, near Bagamoyo, Tanzania. In 1954 the Zumbe (chief) of Mkwaja regretted to the present writer that no porcelain plates of Chinese origin were available for the decoration of the Zumbe's father's tomb. In default of porcelain, a group of early 20th century tombs at Moa, Tanzania, is decorated with blue enamel plates.

(3) A structure on Songo Mnara Island near Kilwa, which gives the island its name, is built on a platform of four steps some sixteen yards offshore. Visiting it in 1950, the late Gervase Mathew found the skeletal remains of a goat which had apparently been sacrificed on top of it. It is described by P. S. Garlake as a mosque, but an Arabic treaty between the then Sultan of Kilwa and a French slave-trader, Jean-Vincent Morice, dated 12 Shaʿbān 1190/4 November 1776, clearly refers to it as *bayt manār (sic)*. Garlake prints a plan of the structure showing a small mosque with a ruined *miḥrāb*, but H.N. Chittick, who partly cleared the building in 1961, founds it to be "a truncated pyramid with stepped sides, surmounted by a rectangular chamber", with doors at the north and south. The present writer did not distinguish the remains of a *miḥrāb* when he visited it in 1955. Morice's two maps of *ca.* 1776 show it as a three-storeyed building, the three storeys tapering towards the top; he refers to is as *la pagode*. Chittick found only two storeys remaining, the second storey being decorated with numerous late 15th century celadon bowls. J. Crassons de Medeuil, another slave-trader, writing in 1784, says that *la pagode* which "was very curious looking", had fallen down at some time during the preceding three years. This sentence follows immediately upon the description of a mosque, thus clearly differentiating it therefrom. M. H. Dorman thought it to have been a lighthouse, but this is unlikely because these are unknown in eastern Africa at the period indicated by the celadon bowls, and indeed until the later 19th century. The elaborate decoration suggests rather that the building was domestic, even if the lowest of the three rooms was used for prayer, and that perhaps it was a tower kiosk built so as to take advantage of the evening breeze on what is a hot sticky island. This explanation would satisfy the meaning both of *mnara* and that of *pagode* in 18th century French.

Bibliography: H. N. Chittick, *Tanganyika, Annual report of the Antiquities Division, 1961*, 1963, 5; M. H. Dorman, *The Kilwa civilisation and the Kilwa ruins*, in *Tanganyika Notes and Records*, no. 6 (1938), 68; G. S. P. Freeman-Grenville, *Medieval history of the coast of Tanganyika*, London 1962, 116; idem, *The East African coast: select documents*, Oxford 1962; idem, *The French at Kilwa Island*, Oxford 1965, 72-5, 202, 206; idem and B. G. Martin, *A preliminary handlist of the Arabic inscriptions of the Eastern African coast*, in *JRAS* (1973), 103, 107; P. S. Garlake, *The early Islamic architecture of the East African coast*, Nairobi 1966, 84, 91; V. L. Grotanelli, *I pescatori dell'Oceano Indiano*, Roma 1955, 29; J. S. Kirkman, *Men and monuments on the East African coast*, 1964, numerous references, esp. 90-1; S. A. Strong, *The History of Kilwa*, in *JRAS* (1895), 417; anon., *A guide to Zanzibar*, Government Printer, Zanzibar 1952, 49 (historical sections compiled by Sir J. M. Gray).

(G.S.P. FREEMAN-GRENVILLE)

MANAS, the name of the paramount hero of the Kirghiz oral epic tradition and also of the totality of the epics which accreted about him and his kindred by the process of cyclisation, in this case very marked.

Some 4,000,000 lines of *Manas* are said to have been recorded in Kirgizia in this century, but not one scholarly edition of a self-contained performance has appeared, or, if it has, has yet reached the West. A recording of an episode from *Manas* was made by R Dor in the Pamir in 1973, of which a philological edition, with translation and commentary, is imminent and recordings of *Manas* in Xinjiang by members of the Institute for Minorities, Peking, are reported t have been made during the last decade. In 1911-12, G. von Almásy published 72 lines critically, with translation and commentary. Thus the importance of the 15,705 lines of *Manas* recorded by W. Radloff (V. V. Radlov) and Ch. Ch. Valikhanov between 1856 and 1869 cannot be overestimated: it is obligatory in method that the earliest extant specimens of an heroic tradition be studied before the later, and the later Kïrghïz epics can scarcely be available in acceptable editions within a hundred years from now.

What follows here is largely based on close study of the mid-19th century recordings. The disordered renarration from *Manas* in the Tādjīk *Madjmū*ᶜ *al-tawārīkh* of Sayf al-Dīn, attributed to the 16th century, has been accepted as evidence of the flourishing of *Manas* at that time; yet the two mss. of the *Madjmū*ᶜ so far cited are dated respectively 1792-3 and 19th century, so that the (very likely) possibility that the *Manas* passage was interpolated to serve the political ends of Khoḳand requires convincing disproof before it can be considered as evidence for *Manas* in Kïrghïz at so early a date. However, *Manas*, as it appears in Kïrghïz verse for the first time in the Valikhanov recording of *Kökötöydün ashï* ("The memorial feast for Kökötöy") in 1856, reflects a mature and truly epic tradition which is obviously the product of many generations. Surprisingly, if one goes back to this earlier tradition from the patriotic and at times stridently nationalistic material of the 20th century, one finds that the heroes are not Kïrghïz but Noghay; on the very rare occasions when "Kïrghïz" are named, it is with irony. Nevertheless, the connection between the mid-19th century epic tradition and the life of the Kïrghïz as then lived is supplied by the situation of Manas, his son Semetey and his grandson Seytek: all are only sons forming a fragile line of *khāns* that is threatened with extirpation in manhood, boyhood, in the very womb. And such, *mutatis mutandis*, was the situation of the scattered Kïrghïz tribes themselves, dangerously hemmed in as they were on their high pastures by the Chinese, the Kalmïk, the Khoḳanders and the Russians. The "Noghay" of mid-19th century Kïrghïz epic are, as were the Kïrghïz themselves, only superficially touched by Islam, their treacherous Kalmïk antagonists even less by Lamaist Buddhism. The plots of the various self-contained episodes of the abstraction *Manas* that were recorded in 1856-69 are clear-cut, stark and existential. The style is rapid, graphic and abounding in beautifully-structured epithets and formulae aimed at connoisseurs. It provides a touchstone by which the published 20th-century material, despite its enrichment by Persian narrative poetry and the European novel, must be pronounced inflated, distorted and, *qua* epic, decadent.

Bibliography: See for pre-1966 references, ḤAMĀSA. iv. Central Asia. Since 1966: (i) Mid-19th-century. (Edition) A.T. Hatto, *The memorial feast for Kökötöy-khan (Kökötöydün ašï). A Kirghiz epic poem edited for the first time from a photocopy of the unique manuscript with translation and commentary*, London Oriental Series, 33, Oxford 1977. (Interpretation) [All by A.T. Hatto] *The birth of Manas*, in *Asia Major*, N.S., xiv (1969), 217-41; Kukotay *and* Bok Murun: *a comparison of two related heroic poems of the Kirgiz*, in *BSOAS*, xxxii (1969), 344-78, 541-70; *Almambet, Er Kökčö and Ak Erkeč*, in *CAJ*, xiii (1969), 161-98; *Köz-kaman*, in *CAJ*, xv (1971), 81-101, xv (1972), 241-83; *The Kirgiz original of Kukotay found*, in *BSOAS*, xxxiv (1971), 379-86; *Semetey*, in *Asia Major*, xviii (1973), 154-80, xix (1974), 1-36; *Germanic and Kirgiz heroic poetry. Some comparisons and contrasts*, in *Deutung und Bedeutung. Studies ... presented to Karl-Werner Maurer*, ed. Brigitte Schludermann *et alii*, The Hague-Paris 1973, 19-33; *The catalogue of heroes and heroines in the Kirgiz Joloi-kan*, in *Tractata altaica. Festschrift for Denis Sinor*, Wiesbaden 1976, 237-60; *Plot and character in mid-nineteenth-century Kirghiz epic*, in *Die mongolischen Epen*, Asiatische Forschungen, Bd. 68, Wiesbaden 1979, 95-112; *The marriage, death and return to life of Manas: a Kirghiz poem of the mid-nineteenth century*, in *Turcica*, xii (1980), 66-94 (= Pt. I; Pt. II in 1981); *Zyklische Anspielungen und Epitheta in der altkirghisischen Heldenepik*, in *Asiatische Forschungen*, lxxii (1981). (Survey) *Kirghiz. Mid-nineteenth century*, in *Traditions of heroic and epic poetry*, gen. ed. A.T. Hatto, London, i (1980), 300-27. (ii) 20th century. (Miscellaneous) *Manas. Geroičeskiy épos kirgizskogo naroda*, ed. S. Musaev, Frunze 1968 (= Reprints of in part-inaccessible essays); J. Hein, *Epik altaischer Völker (passim)*, in *Volksepen der uralischen und altaischen Völker*, ed. W. Veenker (= Ural Alaische Bibliothek, xvi), Wiesbaden 1968, 55-65; S. M. Musaev, *Problemï naučnoy publikatsii tekstov "Manasa"*, in *Fol'klor: izdanie éposa*, ed-in-chief A.A. Petrosyan, Moscow 1977, 223-9; İ. Başgöz, *The epic tradition among Turkic peoples*, in *Heroic epic and saga*, ed. F. Oinas, Bloomington and London 1978, 318-22; S. Musaev, *Épos "Manas": naučno-populyarnïy očerk*, Frunze 1979, 1-205.

(A.T. HATTO)

AL-**MANĀṢIR**, BANŪ (sing. AL-MANṢŪRĪ), the name of half-a-dozen tribes, or branches of a single tribe, residing in eastern and southern Arabia, ᶜIrāḳ, Jordan, the Sudan and Algeria. The Arabian tribe or branch, at least, claim descent from Ḳaḥṭān through Ghuwaynim, and they are thus, in the Arabic genealogical scheme, *al-ᶜArab al-ᶜāriba*, or true Arabs. Both they and the Jordanian branch boast of having been originally Christian, hence the derivation of the name from Naṣārā. Presumably therefore, the tribe originated in the Yemen, although the name does not appear in any of the South Arabian genealogical works.

Little has been written about those residing in the Fertile Crescent or in the Sudan, aside from the statements that those in Jordan (al-Balḳāʾ) are affiliated with the Banū Djarūmiyya and those in ᶜIrāḳ with the large and important Banū Shammar. In Algeria, the al-Manāṣīr, living along the coast between Ténès and Cherchell, have apparently been Berberised.

In eastern and southern Arabia, the Banu 'l-Manāṣīr share the entire southern edge of the Rubᶜ al-Khālī from the border of ᶜUmān to Nadjrān, a distance of about a thousand miles, with the Banū Murra, noted, until modernisation, for their particularly fine herds of camels. Although supporters of the Suᶜūdī family, the al-Manāṣīr are not Wahhābīs and follow the Mālikī school of law.

Bibliography: ᶜUmar Riḍā Kaḥhāla, *Muᶜdjam ḳabāʾil al-ᶜArab*, Damascus 1948, iii; H.St. J.B. Philby, *The Empty Quarter*, New York 1933; A. Hamilton, *The Kingdom of Melchior*, London 1949; Frauke Heard-Bey, *From Trucial States to United Arab Emirates*, London 1982. (C.L. GEDDES)

MANĀSTİR. The name Manāstïr (Greek *monastírion*) is not an uncommon toponym (cf. Goljam Manastir in Bulgaria and Manastïr near Beyşehir in Turkey). However, it usually occurs as the Turkish designation for the modern town of Bitola in the Socialist Republic of Macedonia in Yugoslavia. Bitola is situated near the site of the ancient town of

Heraclea where the eastern foothills of the 2,601m. high Mt. Pelister merge with the Pelagonian Plain. The town, already mentioned as an episcopal see in the 5th/11th century, had developed into an important urban centre as a result of its advantageous situation on the old Via Egnatia even before it was conquered by Tīmūrtas̲h̲ Pas̲h̲a in the eighth decade of the 8th/14th century. While documents pertaining to the history of the town under Ottoman rule are extant from as early as the first half of the 9th/15th century (H. Kaleši, *Najstarija arapska vakufnama u Jugoslaviji*, in *POF*, x-xi [1961], 55-75), statistical data reflecting the development of Manāstir are extant only since the seventh decade of the century, and only last (as far as is known) until the seventh or eighth decade of the following 10th/16th century (M. Sokoloski, *Turski izvorni podatoci od XV i XVI vek za gradot Bitola*, in *Glasnik INI*, vii/l [1963], 127-56; idem (ed.), *Turski dokumenti za istorijata na makedonskiot narod. Opširni popisni defteri od XV vek*, ii, *Turksi dokumenti za makedonskata istorija*, 5 vols. Skopje 1973, 141-5). The *sid̲j̲ills* of the *ḳāḍīs* of Manāstir, which offer a penetrating view into almost all aspects of urban life, document the period from 1016/1607 to the end of Ottoman rule in Macedonia (1912) and beyond. They also witness the development of Manāstir first into a residence of the *wālīs* of Rūmeli (in the course of the second half of the 12/18th century), and then to the official seat of the provincial government of the *eyālet* of Rūmeli which was redefined in 1836 (M. Sokoloski, A, Starova, V. Boškov and F. Ishak (eds.), *Turksi dokumenti za istorijata na makedonskiot narod, Serija prva: 1607-1699*, 4 vols. Skopje 1963-72: i (1607-23), ii (1627-35), iii (1636-9), iv (1640-2); A. Matkovski (ed.), *Turski izvori za ajdutstvoto i aramistvoto vo Makedonija*, 5 vols. Skopje 1961-80: i (1620-50), ii (1650-1700), iii (1700-25), iv (1725-75), v (1775-1810); P. Džambazovski, and A. Starova (eds.) Skopje 1951-8: i (1800-3), ii (1803-8), iii (1809-17), iv (1818-27), v (1827-39)). In addition, documents from the archives of the metropolitan of Manāstir pertaining to the first half of the 13th/19th century have been published (I. Snegarov, *Grăcki kodeksi na Pelagonijskata mitropolija/Griechische Kodexe der Pelagonischen Metropolie*, in *Godišnik na Sofiskija universitet, Bogoslovski fakultet*, xxv [Sofia 1948], 2-58). Since the middle of the 13th/19th century, when numerous European consulates were established in Manāstir, consular reports comprise one of the most important historical sources. As a result of its importance, Manāstir became the capital of a *wilāyet* of the same name in 1874 and again in 1879 (A. Birken, *Die Provinzen des Osmanischen Reiches*, Wiesbaden 1976, 71 f.). Its population in 1900 was 37,000, and in 1971, 65,035 (M. Panov, *Geografija na SR Makedonija*, i, Skopje 1976, 303).

Bibliography: A first, uncritical, sketch of the history of Manāstir from its beginning is given by Meḥmed Tewfīḳ, *Manāstir wilāyetiniñ tārīk̲h̲česi ve istātistīḳ-i ʿumūmīsi*, Manāstir 1327/1909, Serbo-Croat tr. Gliša Elezović, *Kratka istorija bitolskog vilajeta*, in *Bratstvo*, xxvii (1935), 190-244. Although no comprehensive, scientific treatment of Manāstir's history has been undertaken as yet, a general abstract, based in part on more recent research, has been undertaken by Apostolos E. Vacalopoulos, *History of Macedonia 1354-1833*, Thessaloniki 1973 (cf. index s.v. "Monastir"). The first, tentative, contributions to a bibliography of "Bitola and environs up to World War I" have been begun by Kočo Sidovski, *Prilog kon bibliografijata za Bitola i Bitolsko do prvata svetska vojna*, in *Istorija*, ix/l (Skopje 1973), 264-70; x/l (1974), 405-8; x/2 (1974), 571-5; xii/1-2 (1976), 323-7. (M. Ursinus)

MANĀSTİRLİ MEḤMED RIFʿAT (1851-1907), Ottoman Turkish officer, writer, poet and playwright of the younger *Tanẓīmāt* generation. Born in Monastir [see manāstir], son of a regimental secretary, Res̲h̲īd Efendi, who had migrated from Athens and settled there, he attended the local military school and then was trained at the War College (*Mekteb-i Ḥarbiyye*) in Istanbul and graduated in 1872 as a staff captain. He and his class mate, a close friend (and future collaborator in many plays) Ḥasan Bedreddīn (Bedr al-Dīn) were both appointed teachers at the War College where they attracted the attention of Süleymān Pas̲h̲a [*q.v.*], director general of military schools (*makātib-i ʿaskeriyye nāẓiri*) who thought highly of them and protected them.

When Ḥüseyn ʿAwnī Pas̲h̲a, the Minister of War (*Serʿasker*) and his close friends in the government (including the great liberal Midḥat Pas̲h̲a [*q.v.*]) who strongly disapproved of Sultan ʿAbdülʿazīz (ʿAbd al-ʿAzīz)'s régime, decided to dethrone the Sultan, they secured the help of their trusted man, Süleymān Pas̲h̲a, a convinced liberal and prominent soldier-scholar. On the night of 30 May 1876, the Dolmabahçe Palace was surrounded by troops led by Süleymān Pas̲h̲a. They consisted of two battalions of War College cadets commanded by Meḥmed Rifʿat and his colleague and friend Ḥasan Bedreddīn respectively. ʿAbdülʿazīz commited suicide on 5 June, six days after his dethronement.

During the Russian-Turkish War of 1877-8, Meḥmed Rifʿat, now a major, was sent to the Eastern Anatolian front and fought under G̲h̲āzī Aḥmed Muk̲h̲tār Pas̲h̲a [*q.v.*]. He was taken prisoner, sent to Russia and returned home after the peace (July 1878). But the new absolutist régime which was inaugurated after the dissolution of Parliament (13 February 1878) marked down Meḥmed Rifʿat and Ḥasan Bedreddīn as *persona non grata*, having collaborated with "dangerous" liberals.

When in 1882 ʿAbdülḥamid II (ʿAbd al-Ḥamīd) decided to get rid of Midḥat Pas̲h̲a, "the Father of the Constitution" (*Eb-i Mes̲h̲rūṭiyyet*) who was at the time in Izmir as governor of the *wilāyet* of Aydin, he accused him of having arranged the "assassination" of Sultan ʿAbdülʿazīz in 1876, had him arrested and sent to the Yildiz Palace, where he and fourteen others were sentenced. All soldiers and civil servants involved in the dethronement, or simply thought to have liberal ideas, were banished from Istanbul. True to Ḥamīdian methods of dealing with undesirable soldiers and civil servants, Meḥmed Rifʿat was first promoted to lieutenant-colonel, then posted to a division in Damascus and later transferred to Aleppo, whence he never returned. He died in Aleppo in this same rank, in 1907, one year before the restoration of the Constitution.

A prolific writer, Manāstirli Rifʿat was both an author and also the translator of more than thirty books: text-books on mathematics, military science, religion, poetics, letter writing, Arabic and Persian grammar and plays, particularly during the theatre boom of the 1870s. While teaching in the War College, he founded the periodical *Čanta* ("Satchel, bag") in which he published mainly epic-patriotic essays, largely for the benefit of the cadets and his fellow officers, which prompted enthusiastic response from the great patriot Nāmiḳ Kemāl [*q.v.*] from his prison at Famagusta in Cyprus (for the text of his letter, see Ebüzziya (Abu 'l-Ḍiyāʾ) Tewfīḳ, *Nümūne-yi edebiyyāt-i ʿOt̲h̲māniyye*[1], Istanbul 1292/1875).

Manāstirli Rifʿat's poems, written mostly in the old style and published in various newspapers and periodicals, his *sīra* and *Ḳiṣaṣ-i enbiyāʾ* in verse and his verse translations of many Arabic and Persian *ḳaṣīdas*, etc., have not been collected into book form. His other poems, mostly of a personal nature, which he collected in a small *dīwān* (*dīwānče*) remain unedited.

Manāstirlī Rifʿat is mainly remembered because of his remarkable contribution to the Turkish theatre in writing, translating and adapting many plays. Some of these plays were written in collaboration with this close friend, Ḥasan Bedreddīn (later Pas͟ha) [*q.v.* in Suppl.].

Although it is customary to begin the modern Turkish theatre with Ibrāhīm S͟hināsī's *S͟hāʿir evlenmesi* (1859), there are many indications that an earlier date should be adopted (see Fahir Iz, *Pabuççu Ahmed'in garip maceraları*, Istanbul 1961, and Metin And, *100 soruda Türk tiyatrosu*, Istanbul 1970), However, modern Turkish theatre had a speedy development soon after S͟hināsī's play, and reached the proportions of a boom, particularly in the late 1860s and early 1870s, one which lasted until the inauguration of the anti-liberal, reactionary period after 1878. Nāmiḳ Kemāl, S͟hemseddīn (S͟hems al-Dīn) Sāmī, ʿAlī Bey, Aḥmed Wefīḳ Pas͟ha, Teodor Ḳaṣāb and others contributed to this activity. Early modern plays were considerably inspired by the Turkish traditional or folk theatre (Karagöz, Orta oyunu, Meddāḥ [*q.vv.*]) and used, to some extent, the techniques of French comedy and farce (Molière being the favourite author). Often Western (mainly French) plays were translated or adapted.

Manāstirlī Rifʿat and Ḥasan Bedreddīn joined this movement and published together, in fascicules, between 1875 and 1879, 16 plays, under the general title *Temās͟hā* ("Spectacle"), which eventually made up two volumes (Vol. i, fasc. 1-9. vol. ii, fasc. 1-7) of nearly a thousand pages. The majority of these plays, including two comic-operas and one opera-bouffe, of little interest, are translations from the French or via French. The following 7 plays are original: Vol. i, Fasc. 2, *Delīle yāhūt ḳanlī intiḳām* ("Delīle or bloody vengeance"), 1875, an historical drama of Eastern Anatolia; fasc. 4, *Ebu 'l-ʿAlā yāhūt mürüwwet* ("Abu 'l-ʿAlāʾ or humaneness"), 1875, a play on Islamic history; fasc. 6, *Ebu 'l-Fidā* ("Abu 'l-Fidā"); a comic opera, in three acts, 1975; fasc. 7, *Nedāmet* ("Repentance") 1875, a comedy; Vol. ii, fasc. l, *Kölemenler*, a historical drama in five acts; fasc. 4, *Faḳīre yāhūt mükāfā-ī ʿiffet* ("The poor girl, or the reward of virtue"), 1876; fasc. 6, *Aḥmed-i yetīm yāhūt natīd͟je-yi ṣadāḳat* ("Aḥmed the orphan, or the result of loyalty"), 1879, an historical drama of the Egypt under the Ṭūlūnids.

All these plays were performed in the famous Gedik Pas͟ha Theatre in Istanbul. Apart from these plays, written in collaboration, Manāstirlī Rifʿat published the following plays independently: *Görenek* ("Social practice, custom"), 1873, social criticism satirising over-lavish weddings, where families try to outdo one another; *ʿOt͟hmān G͟hāzī*, 1873, *Yā g͟hāzī yā s͟hehīd*, 1874, two patriotic plays, possibly inspired by the enthusiastic reception of the performance of Nāmiḳ Kemāl's famous *Waṭan* ("Fatherland"), which caused such a furor at the time; and *Pākdāmen* ("The chaste one") which seems to have been inspired by Red͟jāʾi-zāde Ekrem's [*q.v.*] *ʿAfīfe Anz͟helik* (1870), with non-Turkish dramatis personae, about a married woman's resistance to the valet's overtures during her husband's absence. Manāstirlī Rifʿat's other works worth mentioning include: *Med͟jāmiʿ el-edeb*, in four volumes, 1890, a detailed treatise on the art of literature, rhetoric, poetics, prosody, etc., and *Ḥikāyāt-ī müntak͟habe* ("Selected stories"), 1876, a striking example of the spoken Turkish of the time used as written Turkish.

Bibliography: İbnülemin Mahmud Kemal İnal, *Son asır Türk şairleri*[2], Istanbul 1969, 157-60, 1455-61; Fehmi Edhem Karatay, *Istanbul Üniversitesi Türkçe basmalar alfabetik kataloğu*, Istanbul 1956, ii, 670-3; Ibrahim Alaettin Gövsa, *Türk meşhurları ansiklopedesi*, Istanbul n.d. [1946], s.v.; Behçet Necatiğil, *Edebiyatımızda isimler sözlüğü*[10], Istanbul 1980, s.v.; Agâh Sırrı Levend, *Türk dilinde gelişme ve sadeleşme evreleri*[3], Ankara 1972, 168, 215, 258; Metin And, *Tanzimat ve İstibdat döneminde Türk tiyatrosu, 1839-1908*, Istanbul 1972, 261.

(Fahir İz)

MANĀT, name of one of the most ancient deities of the Semitic pantheon, who appears in the Pre-Sargonic period in the form Menūtum and constitutes one of the names of Ishtar (J. Bottéro, *Les divinités sémitiques anciennes en Mésopotamie*, in S. Moscati (ed.), *Le antiche divinità semitiche*, 30; Tallqvist, *Götterepitheta*, 373-4); the Ḳurʾānic *scriptio* of her name preserves the primitive *w*, which also appears in the Nabatean *mnwtw* (Lidzbarski, *Handbuch*, 313; Wellhausen, *Reste*[2], 28). The *w* changes to *i* in the Bible (Isa. lxv, 11), as in the Sallier IV papyrus, *verso*, i, 5-6 (in J.B. Pritchard, *Ancient Near Eastern Texts relating to the Old Testament*, Princeton 1950, 250), where Meni is presented as a Semitic deity forming part of "the Ennead which is in the house of Ptaḥ". The difference of gender poses no obstacle to this identification, due to the fact that the *t* is not radical in the two forms and that the Arabic sources regard it as a feminine termination referring to *ṣak͟hra*, the stone or rock embodying the deity (cf. Yāḳūt, iv, 652, 1. 15; *TA*, x, 351 *in fine*; Ibn al-Kalbī speaks of Manāt in the masculine (*K. al-Aṣnām*, ed. and Fr. tr. W. Atallah, Paris 1969, 9), thinking in this case of *ṣanam*). Originally, the two names had the root *mnw/y* which is to be found in all Semitic languages with the meaning of "to count", "to apportion", being applied in particular to the idea of "to count the days of life", hence death (*maniyya*), and "to assign to each his share", hence, lot, destiny (cf. C. Bezold, *Babylonisch-Assyriches Glossar*, ed. Götze, Heidelberg 1926, 176; Gesenius-Buhl, *Hebräisches und aramaïsches Handwörterbuch über das Alte Testament*[17], Berlin 1949, 436 ff.; *TA*, x, 347 ff.; Yāḳūt, iv, 652.

The Greco-Roman equivalents given to Manāt testify to this meaning, since she is identified with Τύχαι or the Fortunae, the dual reflecting the form Manawāt (a false plural used for the dual *manawān* (Yāḳūt, iv, 652, 1.12), as in Thamudic, where she is called *st slm* "the Lady of Peace", see A. van den Branden, *Les inscriptions thamoudéennes*, 110 (Huber, 193), and in Nabatean (CIS 198). In Palmyra she is represented on a mosaic, seated and holding a sceptre in her hand, after the fashion of Nemesis, goddess of destiny (J. Starky, *Palmyre*, Paris 1952, 103 and pl. xii, nos. 5 and 6).

Like al-Lāt [*q.v.*] and al-ʿUzzā [*q.v.*] who form with her the Arab triad (Ḳurʾān, LIII, 19-20), Manāt was worshipped by all the Arabs". It was [originally] a rock for Hud͟hayl in Ḳudayd" (Yāḳūt, iv, 652, 1.15 f.). ʿAmr b. Luḥayy [*q.v.*], who substituted for the cult of betyls that of idols, erected for her, in Ḳudayd, a statue imported from the north, like that of Hubal [*q.v.*]. The sacred site of al-Mus͟hallal in Ḳudayd, about 15 km. from Yat͟hrib, became the gathering place of the Aws and K͟hazrad͟j, who were the most ardent worshippers of Manāt, to such an extent that they considered their pilgrimage to Mecca as incomplete if they had not been to her to shave their heads. All the tribes of the surrounding area took part in her cult. Before the arrival of the Aws and Khazradj, coming from the south, she was worshipped by the Hudhayl who led a nomadic life in the region of Yathrib and by the Khuzāʿa in that of Mecca.

Also, from being a simple rock in Ḳudayd, the third divinity of the Arab triad, following the normal evolutionary process, ended up by being sculpted to suit the root from which she derives her name, representing one of the faces of the Asiatic Venus, i.e. Fortune, who, according to the testimony of Pausanias (vi, 2,4), was worshipped by the Syrians on the banks of the Euphrates. Al-Lāt, with whom Manāt shared the title of Ṭāghiya (Yāḳūt, i, 236, 1.11), and al-ʿUzzā represented the two others volets of the triptych.

The destruction of the sanctuary of Manāt in Ḳudayd gave rise to a legend of the same interpretation as that which is associated with the destruction of al-ʿUzzā (cf. T. Fahd, *Panthéon*, 173).

Saʿd b. Zayd al-Ashhalī (Ibn Saʿd, ii/1, 106, and al-Ṭabarī, i^3, 1649, whereas Yāḳūt states that it was ʿAlī b. Ṭālib who found in his treasury the two famous swords, Mikhdham and Rasūb, which Ibn Saʿd, ii/1, 118, places in the treasury of al-Fals), ordered by the Prophet to go to destroy Manāt, in the year 8/629, accompanied by twenty horsemen, appeared before the *sādin* and announced to him his intention to destroy her. "Go on", he said to him in an ironic tone. Saʿd went towards her and at once saw a nude black women rise up with her hair dishevelled, uttering curses and beating her breast. The *sādin* called out: "Come on! O Manāt, show the anger of which you are capable!". Saʿd began to beat her to death; then he approached the idol with his companions and they destroyed it.

Bibliography: The principal sources are: Ibn al-Kalbī, *K. al-Aṣnām*, ed., Ger. tr. and introd. by Rosa Klinke-Rosenberg, Leipzig 1941 *(Sammlung Orientalischer Arbeiten*, 8), ed. Atallah, index; Yāḳūt, s.v. The principal studies are: T. Fahd, *Le panthéon de l'Arabie centrale à la veille de l'hégire*, Paris 1968: J. Wellhausen, *Reste*^{2}, Berlin 1897 (cf. 29 on the theophoric names formed with Manāt); J.H. Mortmann, *Mythologische Miscellen. V. Tyche-Gad Menî*, in *ZDMG*, xxxix (1885), 44-6; D. Nielsen, *Der Dreieinigegott in religions-historischer Beleuchtung*, i-ii/1, Copenhagen 1922, 1942; G. Ryckmans, *Les religions arabes préislamiques*^{2}, Louvain 1953; G.A. Barton, *The Semitic Ištar cult*, in *Hebraica*, ix (1892-3), 131-66, x (1893-4), 1-74. (T. Fahd)

MANĀZGERD [see malāzgird]

al-**MANĀZIL** (A.) or more fully *manāzil al-ḳamar*, the lunar mansions, or stations of the moon (sing. *manzil* or *manzila*), a system of 28 stars, groups of stars, or spots in the sky near which the moon is found in each of the 28 nights of her monthly revolution.

The system seems to be of Indian origin (see Scherer; Pingree [1] and [2]; Billard). Babylonian origin has sometimes been suggested (cf. Hommel), but could never be established from the documents. The "stars in the moon's path", in the ^{mul}APIN text (cf. van der Waerden [1], 77; recently re-dated to 2300 B.C., cf. van der Waerden [2]) are 17 or 18 in number and rather represent an early stage in the development of the zodiac. The system of the lunar mansions was adopted by the Arabs, through channels as yet unknown, some time in the pre-Islamic period, since the term *manāzil* is already mentioned in the Ḳurʾān (X, 5; XXXVI,39). To the single mansions, the Arabs applied names already found with them previously, and originally used to designate their *anwāʾ* [see anwāʾ]. A complete list of the 28 mansions is reported by ʿAbd al-Malik b. Ḥabīb (d. 238/852) on the authority of Mālik b. Anas (d. 179/795); nearly contemporary to this is the list drawn up by the astronomer al-Farghānī. Items of information concerning the lunar mansions were collected by the Arabic philologists in their *kutub al-anwāʾ* (see the printed works of Ibn Ḳutayba al-Marzūḳī, Ibn Sīda, Muḥammad al-Muḳriʾ, al-Ḳazwīnī, Ibn al-Adjdābi, Ibn Manẓūr/al-Tīfāshī, and Aḥmad b. Mādjid), and by astronomers, who took pains in identifying these mansions astronomically (see al-Farghānī, al-Battānī, al-Ṣūfī, al-Bīrūnī [1], [2], and [3]). Whereas the scientific astronomers of the Arabic-Islamic period did not actually use the lunar mansions, these apparently were of some importance for the distribution of the ecliptic (besides of the zodiac) in earlier times. Later, they were often used by astrologers and others for different systems of divination (see e.g. *Picatrix*, and ʿAlī b. Abi 'l-Ridjāl; cf. also Savage-Smith, for the lunar mansions in relation to geomancy). Hence they were engraved, together with other calendric and astrological items, on the back of many Islamic and some western astrolabes (cf. Hartner, 2549 f.; Michel, 42; Mayer, pls. XV, XVIB, XX, XXII-XXV). Through Latin translations of Arabic works, the list of the 28 lunar mansions and their Arabic names known to mediaeval Europe from the late 10th century onwards (see Millās, 251 ff.), and, later, were much used for divinatory purposes (see e.g. Steinschneider, Vian, Svenberg, Weidemann, Lutz and Müller). Lists of the 28 lunar mansions, with their Arabic names, have also penetrated Byzantine astrological texts (see CCAG).

The names of the 28 mansions, and their astronomical identifications, are as follows (for the names, see the individual entries in Kunitzsch [1], where sources and further details are given):

1. *al-sharaṭān* (also: *al-naṭḥ*), βγ, or βα Arietis.
2. *al-buṭayn*, εδρ Arietis.
3. *al-thurayyā*, the Pleiades.
4. *al-dabarān*, α Tauri.
5. *al-haḳʿa*, λφ$^{1.2}$Orionis (according to the *Almagest*, one nebulous object, the first star of Orion; but registered as three individual stars by al-Bīrūnī [3]). Alternatively also, *al-maysān*, which properly would be one of the two stars of no. 6.
6. *al-hanʿa*, γξ Geminorum; also *al-taḥāyī*, ημν Geminorum (either separately, or together with γξ Geminorum). Al-Bīrūnī [3] has it νγξ Geminorum.
7. *al-dhirāʿ*, αβ Geminorum. There is confusion in the sources as to whether this *dhirāʿ* is *al-dhirāʿ al-maḳbūḍa* or al-*dhirāʿ al-mabsūṭā*.
8. *al-nathra*, ε Cancri, or εγδ Cancri (Ibn Ḳutayba, and al-Bīrūnī [3]).
9. *al-ṭarf*, δ Cancri + λ Leonis.
10. *al-djabha*, ζγηα Leonis (included with this station is the star α Leonis, "Regulus", which had no individual name in the classical Arabic star lore).
11. *al-zubra* (also: *al-kharātān*), δθ Leonis.
12. *al-ṣarfa*, β Leonis.
13. *al-ʿawwāʾ*, βηγε Virginis, sometimes δ Virginis is also added to these.
14. *al-simāk* (i.e. *al-simāk al-aʿzal*), α Virginis.
15. *al-ghafr*, ικλ Virginis (al-Bīrūnī [3] has ικ only).
16. *al-zubānā*, αβ Librae.
17. *al-iklīl*, βδπ Scorpii.
18. *al-ḳalb*, α Scorpii.
19. *al-shawla*, λυ Scorpii. Sometimes, *al-ibra*, or *ibrat al-ʿaḳrab*, is given as an alternative designation, but some authors refer this name to a different ob-

ject, viz. the nebulous cluster following behind *al-shawla*, i.e. M 7 Scorpii.

20. *al-naʿāʾim*, the two groups of four stars each, γδεη + σφτζ Sagittarii; alternatively, *al-waṣl*, the space between these two groups.
21. *al-balda*, a region void of stars, between stations nos. 20 and 22.
22. *saʿd al-dhābiḥ*, $\alpha^{1,2}$ νβ Capricorni.
23. *saʿd bulaʿ*, με Aquarii, to which some authors add Fl. 7, or ν Aquarii, as a third star.
24. *saʿd al-suʿūd*, βξ Aquarii + c^1 Capricorni.
25. *saʿd al-akhbiya*, γπζη Aquarii.
26. *al-fargh al-muḳaddam* (also *al-fargh al-awwal*), αβ Pegasi.
27. *al-fargh al-muʾakhkhar* (also *al-fargh al-thānī*),γ Pegasi + α Andromedae.
28. *baṭn al-ḥūt* (also *al-rishāʾ*). β Andromedae.

Some authors additionally register the names of some stars, or spots in the sky, near which the moon is seen when failing to reach her proper mansion, whereas the interstices between two mansions, generally, are called *furdja* (see Ibn Ḳutayba, 86; al-Marzūḳī, 196 f.; Ibn Sīda, 12; Ibn Manẓūr, 1800 = al-Tīfāshī, 205; al-Bīrūnī [1], 351 f., tr. 353 f.).

The knowledge of the 28 lunar mansions has lived on into modern times, and agricultural calendars formed according to them are still today found in various regions of the Arabic-speaking world and its neighbourhood (cf. Landberg, Cerulli, Monteil, Serjeant, Hiskett, Galaal, and the literature cited there; less so consistent are the observations reported by C. Bailey, *q.v.*). Such calendars are already known from mediaeval times (see *Liber anoe* [= *Kitāb al-anwāʾ*, Spain, 961 A.D.; translated into Latin by Gerard of Cremona], and Ibn al-Bannāʾ); they appear to continue older astro-agricultural traditions as paralleled in Ptolemy's *Phaseis* and the Babylonian mulAPIN texts.

Bibliography: 1. Arabic sources: ʿAbd al-Malik b. Ḥabīb, *Risāla fī maʿrifat al-nudjūm*, ms. Ait Ayach, Ḥamzawiyya 80/4, p. 188 (cf. F. Sezgin, *GAS*, vii, 346, 373); Aḥmad b. Mādjid, *Kitāb al-Fawāʾid fī uṣūl ʿilm al-baḥr wa 'l-ḳawāʿid*, ed. I. Khoury, Damascus 1971, 31 ff., Eng. tr. G.R. Tibbetts, *Arab navigation in the Indian Ocean before the coming of the Portuguese*, London 1971, 79 ff.; ʿAlī b. Abi 'l-Ridjāl, *Kitāb al-Bāriʿ fī aḥkām al-nudjūm*, Latin tr. *Praeclarissimus liber completus in iudiciis astrorum*, Venice 1485, see pars vii, cap. 101; al-Battānī, *Opus astronomicum*, ed. and tr. C.A. Nallino, i-iii, Milan 1899-1907, see ch. 51 (text, iii, 187 ff.; tr., i, 124 ff.; comm., i, 295 ff.); Latin tr., printed Nuremberg 1537, and Bologna 1645; in the Old Spanish tr. this chapter is missing, cf. G. Bossong (ed.), *Los Canones de Albateni*, Tübingen 1978, 84; al-Bīrūnī [1]: *al-Āthār al-bāḳiya*, ed. E. Sachau, Leipzig 1878, 336 ff., Eng. tr. E. Sachau, *The chronology of ancient nations*, London 1879, 335 ff.; idem [2]: *Kitāb al-Tafhīm li-awāʾil ṣināʿat al-tandjīm*, ed. and tr. R.R. Wright, London 1934, §§ 164-6; idem [3]: *al-Ḳānūn al-Masʿūdī*, i-iii, Hyderabad 1954-6, see ix, 8 (pp. 1139 ff.); al-Farghānī, *Elementa astronomica*, ed. J. Golius, Amsterdam 1669, see ch. 20; two Latin translations, by Johannes Hispalensis (A.D. 1135), ed. F.J. Carmody, *Al-Farghānī, Differentie scientie astrorum*, Berkeley 1943, and by Gerard of Cremona, ed. R. Campani, *Alfragano: Il "libro dell'aggregazione delle stelle"*, Città di Castello 1910; Ibn al-Adjdābī, *al-Azmina wa 'l-anwaʾ*, Damascus 1964, 60 ff. (lacuna in the ms., supplied from other sources); Ibn al-Bannāʾ, *Le Calendrier d'Ibn al-Bannâʾ de Marrakech*, ed. and tr. H.P.J. Renaud, Paris 1948; Ibn Ḳutayba, *Kitāb al-Anwāʾ*, Hyderabad 1956, 16 ff.; Ibn Manẓūr, *Kitāb Nithār al-azhār fī 'l-layl wa 'l-nahār*, Constantinople 1298, 174 ff., re-edited, under the name of the original author Aḥmad b. Yūsuf al-Tīfāshī, *Surūr al-nafs bi-madārik al-ḥawāss al-khams*, Beirut 1980, see 199 ff.; Ibn Sīda, *Kitāb al-Mukhaṣṣaṣ*, ix, Cairo 1319, 9 ff.; al-Ḳazwīnī, *Kosmographie*, ed. F. Wüstenfeld, i, Göttingen 1849, 41 ff.; German tr. H. Ethé, *Zakarija ... el-Kazwîni's Kosmographie*, Leipzig 1868, 87 ff.; *Liber anoe: Le Calendrier de Cordoue*, ed. R. Dozy, Leiden 1873, new ed. Ch. Pellat, Leiden 1961; al-Marzūḳī, *Kitāb al-Azmina wa 'l-amkina*, i-ii, Hyderabad 1332, see i, 184 ff. and 310 ff.; Muḥammad al-Muḳriʾ (cf. Brockelmann, S II, 364: Abū Miḳraʿ al-Baṭṭūwī), *Les mansions lunaires des arabes*, ed. and tr. A. de C. Motylinski, Algiers 1899; *Picatrix* (Ps.-Madjrīṭī, *Kitāb Ghāyat al-ḥakīm*), ed. H. Ritter, Berlin-Leipzig 1933, see i,4; German tr. H. Ritter and M. Plessner, *"Picatrix". Das Ziel des Weisen*, London 1962; al-Ṣūfī, *Kitāb Ṣuwar al-kawākib...*, Hyderabad 1954.

2. Modern studies: C. Bailey, *Bedouin star-lore in Sinai and the Negev*, in *BSOAS*, xxxvii (1974), 580-96; R. Billard, *L'astronomie indienne*, Paris 1971, 15, 18, 40; *CCAG* (= *Catalogus codicum astrologorum graecorum*, i-xii, Brussels 1898-1953), see v, 3, pp. 90 f. and 91 f.; viii, 1 p. 217 f.; ix, 1 p. 138 ff.; E. Cerulli, *Le stazioni lunari nelle nozioni astronomiche dei Somali e dei Danākil*, in *RSO*, xii (1929-30), 71-8, xiii (1931-2), 76-84; M.H.I. Galaal, *The terminology and practice of Somali weather lore, astronomy, and astrology*, Mogadishu 1968; W. Hartner, *The principle and use of the astrolabe*, in A.U. Pope (ed.), *A survey of Persian art*, Oxford 1938-9, iii, 2530 ff. (repr. separately as *Astrolabica*, no. 1, Paris 1978); M. Hiskett, *The Arab star-calendar and planetary system in Hausa verse*, *BSOAS*, xxx (1967), 158-76; F. Hommel, *Ueber den Ursprung und das Alter der arabischen Sternnamen und insbesondere der Mondstationen*, in *ZDMG*, xlv (1891), 592-619; P. Kunitzsch [1], *Untersuchungen zur Sternnomenklatur der Araber*, Wiesbaden 1961; idem [2], *Arabischen Sternnamen in Europa*, Wiesbaden 1959, 53-7; C. von Landberg, *Glossaire Daṯînois*, ii, Leiden 1923, 1092 ff.; B.F. Lutz, *Das Buch "Alfadol"*, diss. Heidelberg 1967, 131, 321 ff. (appendix by P. Kunitzsch); L.A. Mayer, *Islamic astrolabists and their works*, Geneva 1956; H. Michel, *Traité de l'astrolabe*, Paris 1947, repr. Paris 1976; J.M. Millás Vallicrosa, *Assaig d'història de les idees fisiques i matemàtiques a la Catalunya medieval*, i, Barcelona 1931; V. Monteil, *La toponymie, l'astronomie et l'orientation chez les Maures*, in *Hespéris*, xxxvi (1949), 189-219; U. Müller. *Deutsche Mondwahrsagetexte aus dem Spätmittelalter*, diss. Berlin 1971; C.A. Nallino, *Raccolta di scritti*, v, Rome 1944, 175 ff.; Ch. Pellat, *Dictons rimés*, anwāʾ *et mansions lunaires chez les arabes*, in *Arabica*, ii (1955), 17-41; D. Pingree [1], in *Isis*, liv. no. 176 (1963), 229 f.; idem [2], in *Viator*, vii (1976), 144, 146, 174 ff.; L. de Saussure, in G. Ferrand, *Instructions nautiques et routiers arabes et portugais des XVe et XVIe siècles*, iii, Paris 1928, 143 ff.; E. Savage-Smith and M.B. Smith, *Islamic geomancy and a thirteenth-century divinatory device*, Malibu, Calif., 1980; A. Scherer, *Gestirnnamen bei den indogermanischen Völkern*, Heidelberg 1953, 151 ff.; R.B. Serjeant, *Star-calendars and an almanac from South-West Arabia*, in *Anthropos*, xlix (1954), 433-59; M. Steinschneider, *Über die Mondstationen (Naxatra) und das Buch Arcandam*, in *ZDMG*, xviii (1864), 118-201, with addi-

tions in xxv (1871), 378-428; E. Svenberg, *Lunaria et zodiologia latina*, Göteborg 1963 (esp. 45 ff.); B.L. van der Waerden [1], *Erwachende Wissenschaft*, ii, *Die Anfänge der Astronomie*, Basel-Stuttgart 1968; idem [2], *On pre-Babylonian mathematics. II*, in *Archive for History of Exact Sciences*, xxiii (1980), 36 (confirming the theory of W. Papke, in his unpublished doctoral diss. of 1978, Tübingen); R. Vian, *Ein Mondwahrsagebuch*, Halle 1910; B. Weidemann, *"Kunst der Gedächtnüss" und "De Mansionibus", zwei frühe Traktate des Johann Hartlieb*, diss. Berlin 1964; Ph. Yampolsky, *The origin of the twenty-eight lunar mansions*, in *Osiris*, ix (1950), 62-83.

(P. Kunitzsch)

MANĀẒIR, or **ʿILM AL-MANĀẒIR**, the science of optics. The term *al-manāẓir* (pl. of A. *manẓar* or *manẓara*, from *naẓara*, "to look at") was used by the Arabic translators of Greek scientific writings as equivalent to τὰ ὀπτικά, optics or the theory of vision. The feminine *manẓara* in the sense of "aspect" or "appearance" (the way a thing or a group of things looks) is attested in *al-S͟hāmil fī uṣūl al-dīn* of Abu 'l-Maʿālī al-D͟juwaynī (d. 478/1085), where the plural *manāẓir* is also used in the same sense (ed. ʿA.S. al-Nas͟hs͟hār *et alii*, Alexandria 1969, esp. 476-7, 479, 483-4).

The *kalām* literature, to which al-D͟juwaynī's *al-S͟hāmil* belongs, adopted *s͟huʿāʿ* both for the light rays emanating, for example, from the sun, and for the visual rays (i.e. rays emanating from the eye) which, according to Muʿtazilī and As͟hʿarī *kalām*, were the vehicles of vision (see the relevant sections in al-Ḳāḍī ʿAbd al-D͟jabbār's *al-Mug͟hnī*, iv (*Ruʾyat al-Bāriʾ*), ed. M.M. Ḥilmī and Abu 'l-Wafāʾ al-Taftāzānī, Cairo 1965, esp. 59-79). However, in the medical literature deriving from Galen, we find the word *manāẓir* used in the sense of visual rays (Galen's ὄψεις), and it is in this sense that Ḥunayn b. Isḥāḳ speaks of "the reflexion (*inkisār*) of *al-manāẓir*" (cf. M. Meyerhof, *The book of the ten treatises of the eye ascribed to Hunain ibn Is-hâq (809-977 A.D.)*, Cairo 1928, Ar. text 109; Meyerhof translated *manāẓir* here as "images" — see p. 36 of his English translation in the same volume — but cf. the Arabic version of Galen's *De usu partium*, Escorial ms. 850, fol, 29b). It may be noted that the Greek writers on optics, including Euclid, Hero and Theon, used ὄψεις and ἀκτῖνες interchangeable to designate visual rays (cf. A. Lejeune, *Euclide et Ptolémée*, Louvain 1948, 18-21).

In the scheme of the sciences inherited by mediaeval Islamic scholars from the Greeks, optics was considered a mathematical science. But Aristotle had already characterised optics as one of "the more physical of the mathematical disciplines", a group of enquiries which also included astronomy and harmonics (*Physica*, II.2). And although Euclid's book on *Optics* (*ca.* 300 B.C.) was formulated almost exclusively in geometrical terms, physical, physiological and even psychological elements tended increasingly to mingle with geometrical considerations in the writings of later Hellenistic mathematicians. Thus for example, Hero of Alexandria (1st century A.D.) compared the reflexion of visual rays to the behaviour of projectiles when they strike a hard surface (cf. his *Catoptrica*, iii, in *Herons von Alexandria Mechanik und Katoprik*, ed. and German tr. L. Nix and W. Schmidt (*Heronis Alexandrini opera quae supersunt omnia*, i/1, Leipzig 1900), 322-5). The (lost) first book of Ptolemy's *Optics* (2nd century A.D.) expounded a theory of luminous radiation as distinguished from the emission of visual rays; the same work dealt with binocular as well as monocular vision; and it mentioned a *virtus discernitiva* (or *regitiva*), a psychological faculty to which was assigned a certain vague role in visual perception (cf. *L'Optique de Claude Ptolémée dans la version latine d'après l'arabe de l'émir Eugène de Sicile*, édition critique et exégétique par Albert Lejeune, Louvain 1965, index and 22, n. 22; and 62, n. 81).

In the Islamic period, this tendency shows itself early in a work by Abū Yūsuf Yaʿḳūb b. Isḥāḳ al-Kindī (3rd/9th century [*q.v.*]), which survives in a 12th century Latin translation entitled *De aspectibus* (*Al-Kindi, Tideus und Pseudo-Euclid: drei optische Werke*, ed. A.A. Björnbo and S. Vogl, Leipzig and Berlin 1912 [= *Abhandlungen zur Geschichte der Mathematischen Wissenschaften mit Einschluss ihrer Anwendungen*, Heft, XXVI. 3]). Here al-Kindī considers optics to be a mathematical science (*ars doctrinalis: ʿilm taʿlīmī*), but one which must satisfy physical as well as geometrical principles (*ibid.*, 3); and he opens his book with a treatment of rectilinear *light* radiation and the formation of shadows, thus departing from Euclid's presentation but in agreement with Ptolemy and, it appears, Theon of Alexandria (see the Introduction to Theon's *Recension* of Euclid's *Optics in Euclidis Optica, Opticorum recensio Theonis, Catoptrica, cum scholiis antiquis*, ed. I. L. Heiberg, Leipzig 1895, 144 ff.; French. tr. P. Ver Eecke, in *Euclide: l'Optique et la Catoptrique*, Paris 1959, 53 ff.).

With Ibn al-Hayt͟ham [*q.v.*] in the 5th/11th century, we reach an entirely new stage in the conception of the nature of optics. His great *Kitāb al-Manāẓir* ("Book of Optics", of which several manuscripts are extant) begins with the assertion that optics is a synthetic branch of inquiry that combines mathematical and physical considerations. But this was not merely to continue the trend that had already started in late antiquity. Ibn al-Hayt͟ham's position implied a complete break with the visual-ray hypothesis which had been consistently maintained by the entire mathematical tradition from Euclid to al-Kindī and by the medical tradition of Galen and his Islamic followers. Ibn al-Hayt͟ham opted instead for the view of "physicists" (*ṭabīʿiyyūn*) or natural philosophers, according to which vision consisted in the eye's reception of a form (*ṣūra*) emanating from the object seen. But again, this was not a mere imitation, and his theory was the first attempt to treat this view mathematically. The result was, therefore, not only a new doctrine of vision, but also a new methodology. In other words, Ibn al-Hayt͟ham was led to formulate problems which either would not have made sense from the standpoint of the visual-ray theory or had been ignored by philosophers aiming primarily to give an account of *what* vision is rather than an explanation of *how* it takes place.

Ibn al-Hayt͟ham was also convinced that an intromission explanation of visual perception was essentially incomplete without a theory of the psychology of perception, and he accordingly devotes a considerable part of his *K. al-Manāẓir* to such a theory. His argument is that since the eye can only receive impressions of the light and colour in the visible object, all other properties of the object, including the fact that it is situated in outer space, must somehow be "inferred" from the received visual material. His theory then consists in describing the models of inference (*ḳiyās*) which the "faculty of judgement" (*al-ḳuwwa al-mumayyiza*) employs in achieving the perception of such visual properties (*maʿānī mubṣara*) as distance, size, shape, opacity, transparency, beauty—in fact, all properties other than light and colour as such.

Ibn al-Hayt͟ham wrote substantial treatises on the burning sphere and burning mirrors of various shapes, on the formation of shadows, on *camera obscura* phenomena and on the halo and the rainbow. Yet none of these phenomena is treated in the *K. al-Manāẓir*. The book thus illustrates a restricted conception of optics as primarily a theory of vision by means of direct, reflected or refracted light rays. (A discussion of the rainbow would not have been out of place in a book on optics in this narrow sense, since the phenomenon depends on the position of the eye. But the rainbow had been traditionally treated since Aristotle in books on meteorology—*aḥdāth al-djaww* or *al-āthār al-ʿulwiyya* [*q.v.*]. The force of this tradition continued into the 17th century: Descartes, for example, offered his explanation of the rainbow in a work entitled *Météores*, and not in his *Dioptrique*.) But since these are luminous (not visual) rays, Ibn al-Haytham's explanations are presented on the basis of an experimental examination (*iʿtibār*) of the relevant properties of light as objective phenomena existing independently of a seeing eye. Because of its highly-sophisticated character, combining physical, mathematical, experimental, physiological and psychological considerations in a methodically-integrated manner, the influence of Ibn al-Haytham's book upon later writers on optics both in the Muslim world and (through a mediaeval Latin translation) in the West can hardly be exaggerated.

It is remarkable that two centuries-and-a-half had to elapse before the *Optics* of Ibn al-Haytham began to exert any appreciable influence in the Islamic world, by which time the book had already made a deep impression in Europe (especially on Roger Bacon, John Pecham and Witelo). Towards the end of the 13th century, the Persian Kamāl al-Dīn al-Fārisī [*q.v.*] rescued the *Optics* from near oblivion by writing a large and critical commentary on it, entitled *Tanḳīḥ al-Manāẓir li-dhawi 'l-abṣār wa 'l-baṣāʾir*, which survives in many manuscript copies testifying to its wide use (printed at Hyderabad, Dn., in two volumes in 1347-8/1928-9). In this work, Kamāl al-Dīn went beyond discussion of the matters treated in the *K. al-Manāẓir*, adding, among other things, recensions (sing. *taḥrīr*) of Ibn al-Haytham's treatises "On the halo and the rainbow", "On the burning sphere", "On the formation of shadows" and "On the shape of the eclipse". We have here, then, a book on optics that is not entirely restricted to questions related directly or indirectly to vision. And yet the book does not include a discussion of burning mirrors, a subject which Ibn al-Haytham had thought fit to include in a (non-extant) treatise "On optics, according to the method of Ptolemy". (As for gnomon shadows, these were generally considered a separate subject to be treated in a separate category of writings sometimes referred to as *Kutub al-Aẓlāl*, "books on shadows".) But the narrower conception of optics proved tenacious; when in the 10th/16th century Taḳī al-Dīn Ibn Maʿrūf (d. 993/1585) wrote his *Nūr ḥadaḳat al-ibṣār wa-nūr ḥadīḳat al-abṣār* (Bodleian ms. Marsh 119) for the Ottoman sultan Murād III, he based himself directly on Kamāl al-Dīn's *Tanḳīḥ*. But rather than include the topics appended by the Persian mathematician to his commentary on Ibn al-Haytham's *K. al-Manāẓir*, he limited himself to the subjects treated in the earlier work.

Bibliography: In addition to works, cited in the article, see the bibls. to the articles on Ibn al-Haytham, Kamāl al-Dīn al-Fārisī and al-Kindī in *Dictionary of scientific biography*, ed. C. Gillispie, New York: vi (1972), 189-210; vii (1973), 212-19 and xv (1978), 261-7. The mediaeval Latin translation of Ibn al-Haytham's *K. al-Manāẓir* was published in 1572 by Friedrich Risner at Basel in a volume entitled *Opticae thesaurus*, which also included Witelo's *Perspective* and a treatise on dawn and twilight which is wrongly attributed in this volume to Ibn al-Haytham. An edition of the Arabic text of *K. al-Manāẓir* is in progress; see A. I. Sabra, ed., *Kitāb al-Manāẓir I-II-III* (*On direct vision*), Kuwait 1982. This includes an introduction, Arabic-Latin glossaries and concordance tables for comparing the Arabic and Latin texts. An English translation is forthcoming. (A. I. Sabra)

MANBIDJ, an ancient town of Syria which was situated to the north-east of Aleppo.

It appears that an urban settlement with the name Nappigi or Nampīgi existed on this site in the Assyrian period. In the time of Shalmaneser, it was known as Lita Ashūr. The Syriac appears to refer back to the Assyrian root; in fact the name became Mabbog or Mambog which signifies "gushing water", linked, according to Yāḳūt, to the root *nabadja* "to gush", which would hardly be surprising in a region of abundant springs. The following spellings are encountered: in the Greek texts of the Byzantine period βέμπετξ, Μέμπετξε (Leo the Deacon, iv), βαμσύχη; elsewhere Manbadj (*Subḥ*, iv, 127), Manbidj (Yāḳūt, v, 205), Mambedj (Volney, 279), Mambidj (Honigmann), Menbidj (Dussaud, *Topographie*, 474), Meenbidj (Baedeker and Wirth), Membîdj (*Guide Bleu*, 1932). On the origin and orthography of the name, see E. Honigmann, *Ostgrenze*, 16; K. Ritter, *Erdkunde* 1057 ff.; E. Honigmann, *EI*[1], s.v. On the various traditions regarding the origin of Manbidj, see Pauly-Wissowa, Suppl., iv, 732-42 and *Der kleine Pauly*, ii, 1130.

The Arab geographers are agreed in placing Manbidj in the middle of the fourth climatic region to the north-east of Ḥalab; on the other hand, there are variants for the geographical coordinates. Yāḳūt (s.v.), quoting Baṭlamiyūs [*q.v.*] gives the longitude of 71°15′ and presents the horoscope of the town, then he mentions the *Zīdj* of al-Battānī, where the longitude is 63°45′ and the latitude is 35°. In the *Taḳwīm al-buldān* of Abu 'l-Fidāʾ, the corresponding figures are 62°50′ and 36°50′.

This oasis is situated at an altitude of 1310 feet (398 m) in a zone of annual rainfall greater than 250 mm, bordering on two contrasting economies: to the north-north-east, a region of sedentary inhabitants, crop-growers or craftsmen; to the south-south-west, the domain of the nomadic shepherd or stock-breeder.

To the north of Manbidj, along the Sadjūr, the plateaux are covered with flints from the Acheulian and Middle Palaeolithic epochs which enabled prehistoric man to manufacture tools; the presence of numerous springs permitted, as early as the Assyrian period, the organisation of a system of irrigation (*saḳya*) and the installation of *ḳanāts* [*q.v.*] which established the renown of the region (*ʿamal*) to the west of the elbow of the Euphrates in Syria and of which, some 15-20 m. under ground, numerous remains have been found and are mentioned by all the Arab or foreign geographers and travellers who have visited the area.

The abundant supply of water also facilitated the development of the cultivation of cereals (corn and barley), as well as cotton and hemp, and the exploitation of orchards and plantations of mulberries for the rearing of silk-worms from the early Middle Ages. To the south of Manbidj, there also exists a hot water spring marked by a cupola in a place called "Hama".

For the demography of the region from Neolithic times to the birth of Islam, see the results of two archeological excavations conducted in the region of the

Nahr Sadjūr and on the Syrian Higher Euphrates, published in *Holocene settlement in North Syria* by Paul Sanlaville and others in the *BAR International Series*, Oxford 1985, no. S 238. Under the Umayyads, a section of the Banū Taghlib [*q.v.*] settled on the east bank of the Euphrates and led a nomadic existence near Manbidj, although the bulk of the tribe was established between the Khābūr [*q.v.*], the Euphrates and the Tigris. They were to distinguish themselves at the end of the 7th/13th century in the struggle against the Tatars. Palgrave (*Narrative*, London 1865, i, 118) mentions in the region the presence of a modern tribe, the Shammār, who are said to be related to the Banū Taghlib. According to A. Musil (*Middle Euphrates*, 281), the tribe of the Tarleb (*sic*) was still leading a nomadic existence at the beginning of the 20th century in the arid plain between Manbidj, Ruṣāfa and the heights of the Djabal Bishrī.

After having been "the mustering point of the Roman expeditions directed against the Sāsānid Empire which followed the route of the Euphrates", the latter being a military communication route parallel to the river on the western bank, Manbidj was an important centre of the *limes* of Chalcis, linked to Aleppo by a Roman causeway, before becoming the capital of the *ʿAwāṣim* in the ʿAbbāsid Golden Age. In the Middle Ages, it continued to play an important strategic and commercial role in north-south and east-west communications, the town being not only a staging-post, but also a major road-junction to the west of the Euphrates, on the route which maintained connections between the Mediterranean world and the Asiatic world, between the valley of the Orontes and that of the Euphrates.

Manbidj, of which mention is made in the *Antonine itinerary*, features on the 16th century *Tabula* of Peutinger. It was a military base of the Romans against the Persians, of the Byzantines under Justinian and his successors against the Sāsānids, of the ʿAbbāsid caliphs and the Syrian princes against the Crusaders, and a stronghold against Turkish invasions from the east. Its role was not only to safeguard the frontier posts (*thughūr*), but also to watch over the Syrian desert to the south as far as the region of Bālis-Maskana. Situated in a fertile plain furrowed with ravines, placed in the centre of a *ghūṭa* [*q.v.*], Manbidj also owes its importance to the presence there of abundant drinkable water for caravans. The site was of vital significance, because it controlled all the access routes from northern Syria towards the Djazīra [*q.v.*] and ʿIrāḳ and, in particular, three junctions leading to crossing-points (ζεῦγμα, *djisr*) on the great bend of the Middle Euphrates: to the north, up-stream from Biredjik [*q.v.*], a crossing protected by the Ḳalʿa Bayḍāʾ; or downstream from the confluence of the Sadjūr, opposite Tell Aḥmar, at Djarāblus, the ancient Caeciliana; or 29 km. to the north-east, at Ḳalʿat Nadjm [*q.v.*], which protected Djisr Manbidj, the bridge of boats permitting access to the Upper Djazīra. A further crossing-point was further south at Sūriya, opposite Ḳalʿat Djaʿbar [*q.v.*].

In the time of al-Muḳaddasī (4th/10th century), Manbidj was reached from Ḥalab in two days' journey, passing through Bāb and crossing the Wādī Buṭnān [*q.v.*], a distance of ten *farsakhs* [*q.v.*] (approximately 80 km.); from this point a single stage (*marḥala*) remained to be covered; Yāḳūt gives a figure of three *farsakhs* to arrive at Djisr Manbidj, where the Euphrates could be crossed by means of a bridge of boats, a crossing made today by ferry-boat. From Manbidj, ʿAynṭāb or Ḳūrūsh (Cyrrhus) could be reached in two days and Malaṭiya in four.

It seems that the *darb sulṭāniyya*, which passed through Manbidj on the way to ʿIrāḳ, changed direction at the end of the 8th/14th century, crossing the Euphrates at the latitude of Ṣiffīn and Raḳḳa [*q.v.*], and the route was shifted further to the south. At the beginning of the 20th century, as Franz Cumont testifies, "caravans or *ʿarabas* [*q.v.*] setting out towards Ourfa (Edessa) and Mossoul still pass through Manbidj towards the same crossing, where ferry-boats transport them to the left bank of the Euphrates".

There also existed in the Ayyūbid period a route from Ḥamā towards the north-east. Protected against the Franks by Bārin, Fāmiya and Kafar Ṭāb, it permitted access to Djazīra by way of Manbidj, avoiding Ḥalab.

Today, the road from Ḥalab to Manbidj via Bāb (78 km.) is well-asphalted, as is that leading from Manbidj to Djarāblus (37 km.), where the Euphrates is crossed by a metal bridge.

Shortly before the reign of Alexander the Great, in the 4th century B.C., the town was in the hands of a dynast surnamed ʿAbd Ḥadad (= worshipper of Ḥadad, the god of thunder), who had coinage struck there. For a long period of Antiquity, Manbidj was a religious centre dedicated to the cults of Atargatis and her consort Ḥadad.

In the Hellenistic period, Manbidj played an important military role in countering invasions from the east. The Greeks endowed it with a double rampart and a temple owning an important treasure, which Crassus sacked before setting out with his legions to fight the Parthians and dying, the victim of an assassin, in 53 B.C.

From the 3rd century onwards, through the good offices of Septimus Severus, the town became, in its role as a bulwark against the Sāsānid Persians, one of the principal bases of the "*limes* of Chalcis". From there, in 363, Julian the Apostate led an expedition against Ctesiphon, in the course of which he was mortally wounded.

Manbidj was part of the Cyrrhestian province, before being promoted by Constantine II, in the middle of the 4th century, to the status of capital of Euphratesian Syria. In 451, the metropolitan of Manbidj was Stephen of Hieropolis. At the end of the 5th century there lived there an innovative theologian, the Monophysite bishop Philoxenus of Mabbugh, who had a Syriac translation made of the New Testament and published a commentary to it; he died in exile in Thrace in 523. In April 531, Kawādh, Emperor of Persia, occupied Hierapolis; Belisarius arrived to resist the invasion and in the same year inflicted a defeat on the Sāsānid army at Callinicos, near the confluence of the Balīkh and the Euphrates. In 532, Kisrā Anūshirwān, the new Persian sovereign, offered Justinian a treaty of "permanent peace" which was to be commemorated by a monument at Manbidj, but in 540 he attacked the town, which was obliged to pay a ranson for its liberation. It was in this period that a temple of fire was built in the town by the Sāsānid Emperors. Kisrā gave the town the name of Manbik, which was arabised into Manbidj.

During the 5th and early 6th centuries, the Byzantine emperors, including Justinian, maintained Hierapolis/Manbidj as a front-line stronghold against the East. In 612, the Persians invaded Syria, took Jerusalem on 5 May 614 and occupied Alexandria (617-19). Heraclius reacted and succeeded in restoring the situation and, in March 630, he came to Manbidj to receive the True Cross which the Persians had carried off from Jerusalem in 614. The chronicler

Pseudo-Dionysius mentions in Manbidj a church of Saint Mary and a church of Saint Thomas. According to Ibn Khurradādhbih, in the 3rd/9th century there was there a very fine church built of wood.

In the time of the caliphs ʿUmar and of ʿUthmān, after the conquest of Syria, Manbidj was one of the *ʿawāṣim*, fortified posts which marked the frontier between the *Dār al-Islām* and the Byzantine province of Antioch.

In 16/637, the inhabitants of Manbidj were attacked by ʿIyāḍ b. Ghānim, who had been sent as vanguard by Abū ʿUbayda b. al-Djarrāḥ [*q.v.*]. They capitulated, and the treaty was ratified by Abū ʿUbayda when he appeared before the town. The surrounding areas of the town were at this time occupied by Yemeni tribes and, in particular, the Banū Taghlib.

Under the Umayyads, according to the testimony of the Monophysite Christian poet al-Akhṭal (20-92/640-710), the Banū Taghlib, his own tribe, were settled between the Tigris, the Euphrates and the Khābūr and led a nomadic existence towards the west as far as the fertile region of Manbidj. Situated in the frontier zone of northern Syria, Manbidj seems to have enjoyed a degree of independence, in view of the fact that its inhabitants had requested permission from ʿUmar to practise commerce in the interior of the caliphate. When Yazīd b. Muʿāwiya constituted the *djund* of Ḳinnasrīn, he incorporated Manbidj into it. In 131/748 the town was devastated by a violent earthquake in the course of which the church of the Jacobites (Monophysites) collapsed during a service, entombing the faithful. In 170/786, Hārūn al-Rashīd reorganised the northern frontier of the ʿAbbāsid caliphate with the intention of reviving *djihād*. He detached Manbidj from the *djund* of Ḳinnasrīn and made it the capital of the new zone of *ʿawāṣim*, which combined the frontier posts of Syria and of the Upper Djazīra. From 173/789-90, the caliph appointed as local governor ʿAbd al-Malik b. Ṣāliḥ b. ʿAlī [*q.v.*], an ʿAbbāsid who was later (196/811-12) to be promoted governor of Syria and of Upper Mesopotamia by al-Amīn, who had many new buildings constructed in Manbidj. It was henceforward to serve as a starting base for summer expeditions (*ṣāʾifa*) directed against the Byzantines by the caliph of Baghdād. The good condition of its fortifications in this period contributed to its designation as capital. "A vast area of land was attached to it, stretching from the limits of the territory of Ḥalab to the Sadjūr and the Euphrates".

Implicated in an abortive plot against his uncle, the caliph al-Muʿtaṣim, a pretender to the ʿAbbāsid caliphate, al-ʿAbbās b. al-Maʾmūn, died in the prison of Manbidj in 223/838. Forty years later, in 264/877-8, Aḥmad b. Ṭūlūn occupied Syria under the pretext of conducting *djihād*, and Manbidj then passed under Egyptian domination. In the 4th/10th century, under the Ḥamdānids, Manbidj owed its importance to its agricultural wealth, to its location in the region forming the junction of the Mesopotamian and Syrian frontiers and also to its proximity to Ḥalab and the Euphrates close to a crossing over that river, Djisr Manbidj or Ḳalʿat Nadjm. In the middle of this century, the region was subjected to raids on the part of the ʿUḳayl, Kalb, Kilāb and Numayr tribes [*q.v.*]. According to al-Hamadhānī, Manbidj was shared between the Kalb and the Kilāb.

In 334/945 the Ḥamdānid prince Sayf al-Dawla signed a peace treaty with the Ikhshīdid [*q.v.*] ruler of Egypt and took possession of a vast area comprising the *ʿawāṣim* of Anṭākiya and of Manbidj. Two years later, the eastern part of this zone was entrusted to the poet Abū Firās [*q.v.*], a cousin of the prince of Ḥalab, who was, in 336/947, only sixteen years of age. In 343/late summer 954, a major expedition was launched from Manbidj with the object of combating the Nizārī tribes of Diyār Muḍar [*q.v.*] and of the Syrian Desert. In 351/962, Nicephorus Phocas seized Manbidj from Sayf al-Dawla's viceroy, Abū Firās, and took him prisoner. The latter was obliged to spend seven years in captivity in Constantinople, evoking Manbidj in his *Rūmiyyāt*.

In 355/966, Nicephorus Phocas, who had now become emperor, camped before Manbidj from where he removed the sacred tile bearing the portrait of Christ (*al-Ḳirmīda*, κεραμέδιον). According to Leo the Deacon, it was John Tzimisces who is said to have procured this "portrait of Christ" when in 363/974 he took the citadel of Manbidj, where he found the sandals of Christ and some hairs of St. John the Baptist, which he carried away as relics to Byzantium. During the second half of the 4th/10th century, Manbidj was to remain one of the primary objectives of the Byzantines.

At the end of the 4th/10th century, Ibn Ḥawḳal writes: "Not far from Bālis is situated Manbidj, a fertile and fortified town where there are numerous very ancient markets, rich in Greek relics. One of the local products is a kind of nougat (*nāṭif*) of dried grapes, made with nuts, pistachios and sesame ... Spread among the farms of Manbidj there is a very great number of non-irrigated vineyards. The dried grapes are exported to Ḥalab and to other places. This town is located in a desert plain without water-courses, but its soil is humid, red in colour and turning yellow saffron-colour, and the greater part of its land is not artificially irrigated. It is surrounded by an ancient rampart". Already at this time, thanks to water mills on the Ṣadjūr, manufactured paper could be found there.

Although the Fāṭimids were occupying northern Syria in 406/1015, Ṣāliḥ b. Mirdās became master of Ḥalab in 414/1023; he took Manbidj in the autumn of the following year. An agreement having been made between the Mirdāsid Rashīd al-Dawla Maḥmūd and his uncle Abū Duʿāba ʿAṭiyya, lord of Raḳḳa, Manbidj reverted to the latter between 456/1063 and 457/1064. In early 461/late 1068, Romanus IV Diogenes took possession of Manbidj and reinforced the citadel, thus securing communications between Anṭākiya and al-Ruhā [*q.v.*]. Subsequently, the town was to be entrusted to the Armenian prince Philaretos. Taken prisoner after his defeat at Malāzgird [*q.v.*] (Mantzikert) in Dhu 'l-Ḳaʿda 463/August 1071, Romanus ceded Manbidj to Alp Arslān [*q.v.*], who was already occupying the town. A small mosque was built there in the same year by Ṣāliḥ, son of Muḥammad Sharīf al-Adhamī. In 468/1075, under the caliphate of al-Muḳtadī, Manbidj was entrusted to Saldjūḳ Turkish *amīr*s who are said to have restored the citadel. Ten years later (477/1085), it formed part of the territory subject to the authority of the ʿUkaylid *amīr* Sharaf al-Dawla Muslim b. Ḳuraysh [*q.v.*], a domain which extended from al-Mawṣil to the Euphrates, including the districts of Diyār Rabīʿa and of al-Djazīra.

In 479/1086, the Saldjūḳ sultan Malik Shāh placed Manbidj under the authority of Abū Saʿīd Āḳ-Sunḳur ʿAbd Allāh Ḳasīm al-Dawla al-Ḥadjib, one of his Turkish officers, who, the following year, took over the government of Ḥalab, of Ḥamāt and Lādhiḳiya. In 485/1092, on the death of Malik Shāh, the situation changed; two years later, his brother Tādj al-Dawla Tutush defeated Āḳ Sunḳur, whom he put to death, and occupied Manbidj in his turn.

In the early years of the 6th/12th century, Manbidj

was to be coveted by the Atabeg of al-Mawṣil, Djawālī, by Riḍwān b. Tutush of Ḥalab and by the Franks. In Ṣafar 502/September 1108, after Djawālī seized Bālis from the prince of Ḥalab, the latter appealed to Tancred for aid. Baldwin and Joscelin restored Djawālī to Manbidj where Ṣadaḳa, chief of the Banū Mazyad Bedouins, was also present. In 503/1110, at the time of the attack on the principality of Antioch by Riḍwān, the troops of Joscelin descended from Tell Bashīr, attacking Manbidj and Bālis. The following year, the Franks seized and ravaged Manbidj; they joined it to the archbishopric of Tell Bashīr, subject to the Latin Patriarchate of Antioch. Shortly afterwards, the Franks lost the town, to which they were never to return, but there was to be for a long time a Latin prelate consecrated bishop of Manbidj *in partibus*.

In 514/1120, the territory of Manbidj was attacked from Tell Bashīr by Joscelin who, barely released from captivity by Djawālī, had crossed the Euphrates on his way to Antioch and, arriving at Manbidj, was unable to resist pillaging the lands belonging to Riḍwān of Ḥalab. In spring 517/1123, after the *amīr* Ḥassān b. Gümüshtigin, a Turkish lieutenant of Balak at Manbidj, had taken prisoners in the territory of Edessa, Joscelin returned to pillage the region by way of reprisal. In 518/1124, the Artuḳid Nūr al-Dawla Balak b. Bahrām b. Artuḳ [*q.v.*], the nephew of Il-Ghāzī, having become master of Ḥalab on the death of the latter in Ramaḍān 516/November 1122, resolved to attack Tell Bashīr. He entrusted an army to his cousin Ḥusām al-Dīn Tīmūr-Tāsh and asked him to invite Ḥassān to accompany him. Suspicious of Ḥassān's lukeward response, Tīmūr-Tāsh arrested him and occupied Manbidj, while ʿĪsā, the brother of Ḥassān, took refuge in the citadel of Manbidj and appealed for help to Joscelin of Edessa, offering him the town in return for driving away the troops of Balak. Joscelin marched towards Manbidj with Geoffrey the Monk, lord of Marʿash, and in Ṣafar 518/March-April 1124, was confronted by Balak as the latter was preparing to attack Manbidj. The Franks suffered a grave defeat; Geoffrey was killed, Joscelin fled and took refuge at Tell Bashīr. Balak occupied Manbidj and tried to take possession of the citadel, which he wished to hand over to his cousin Tīmūr-Tāsh, but on 19 Rabīʿ I 518/6 May 1124 an arrow shot from the citadel wounded him fatally. His troops disbanded, Tīmūr-Tāsh brought the body back to Ḥalab and took power there, while Ḥassān, released from detention, returned to Manbidj.

In 520/1126, the Atabeg Bursuḳī of al-Mawṣil, on a journey through Syria, passed beneath the walls of Manbidj. The following year, in Rabīʿ I 521/April 1127, ʿImād al-Dīn Zangī, having become Atabeg of al-Mawṣil and master of Ḥalab, did not hesitate to seize the important road junction of Manbidj. In 525/1131 Joscelin de Courtenay besieged Tell ʿArān, a site between Ḥalab and Manbidj. Injured by a collapsing undermining, he was carried to Tell Bashīr, where he died. The governor of Manbidj, accompanied by the *amīr* Sawār of Ḥalab, took advantage of the situation by attacking the knights of Edessa.

When the Byzantine John Comnenus attacked the region of Manbidj in 536/1142, he did not take the town. Two years later, Manbidj contributed a contingent of Turkomans to the army of Zangī. On the death of the latter, in 541/1146, his son Nūr al-Dīn, on his way from Ḥalab to lay siege to al-Ruhā, passed through Manbidj with his siege machinery. It was the *amīr* of Manbidj, Ḥassān, loyal ally of Nūr al-Dīn, who by taking Tell Bashīr in 546/1151, put an end to the County of Edessa.

In 553/1158 Madjd al-Dīn Abū Bakr, foster-brother of Nūr al-Dīn, governor of the province of Ḥalab, warned by the *amīr* in command of Manbidj of a conspiracy against Nūr al-Dīn, foiled the plot which had been hatched during the illness of the latter and was to have been put into effect in Muḥarram 554/February 1150. When Ḥassān al-Manbidjī died (562/1167), Nūr al-Dīn gave Manbidj in *iḳṭāʿ* to Ghāzī b. Ḥassān, but the latter rebelled and the sovereign then came in person with Madjd al-Dīn Abū Bakr b. al-Dayā and Asad al-Dīn Shirkūh, in spring 563/1168, to take the town after a full-scale siege. He deposed Ghāzī and gave the place in *iḳṭāʿ* to Ḳuṭb al-Dīn Ināl b. Ḥassān, the rebel's brother. Nūr al-Dīn consolidated the defences of Manbidj, constructing there, as at Ḥalab, a protective outer wall. After 563/1167 he also built there a Shāfiʿī *madrasa* for Ibn Abī ʿAṣrūn, while Ḳuṭb al-Dīn built one for the Ḥanafīs.

On 14 Shawwāl 571/April 1176, Ṣalāḥ al-Dīn (Saladin) launched an offensive in northern Syria against Sayf al-Dīn of Ḥalab. He headed towards the north-east, in the knowledge that Manbidj was held by Ḳuṭb al-Dīn Ināl b. Ḥassān, a resolute enemy of the Ayyūbid sovereign; the siege-engineers had already begun their work when Ināl offered to surrender, giving up his citadel and his treasury, in exchange for safe-conduct. The prospect of taking Manbidj without bloodshed and gaining precious time persuaded Ṣalāḥ al-Dīn, who permitted Ināl to make his way to al-Mawṣil. Manbidj was taken on 29 Shawwāl 571/11 May 1176, and the victor found significant spoils there. Ṣalāh al-Dīn recalled his nephew Taḳī al-Dīn ʿUmar b. Ṭurān Shāh, who was seeking to impose his authority in Egypt, and gave him fiefdoms in Syria, including Manbidj. In 577/1181, Taḳī al-Dīn al-Muẓaffar ʿUmar, prince of Ḥamāt, while in Manbidj, attempted to bar the road from Ḥalab to ʿIzz al-Dīn Ibrāhīm Ibn al-Muḳaddam, but he failed and was forced to retreat to Ḥamāt. In Ramaḍān 579/June 1179, Ṣalāḥ al-Dīn appointed his brother al-Malik al-ʿĀdil governor of Manbidj and, two years later, he added a minaret to the Great Mosque.

It was during this period (Rabīʿ I 580/June 1184) that Ibn Djubayr, coming from Ḥarrān, mentioned the purity of the air, the beauty of the landscape, the abundance and quality of the water of Manbidj. He described its broad streets and markets, noted the piety of the Shāfiʿī inhabitants, mentioned the ancient defensive wall as well as the remains of Roman buildings, and referred to the separate and isolated citadel.

In 586/1190, Manbidj, then ruled by Nāṣir al-Dīn, son of al-Muẓaffar Taḳī al-Dīn ʿUmar, was an important rallying-point for troops setting out to fight Frederick Barbarossa.

In 588/1192, al-Malik al-Ẓāhir, third son of Ṣalāḥ al-Dīn, sought to assert control of Manbidj, appealing to al-Malik al-Manṣūr of Ḥamāt to lend him his support against al-Malik al-ʿĀdil. But al-Manṣūr refused to give up the town which controlled the communication routes towards the north-east, the valley of the Upper Euphrates and Diyār Muḍar. In Radjab 589/April-May 1193, al-Malik al-Ẓāhir and al-Malik al-Afḍal attacked Manbidj; al-Ẓāhir destroyed the citadel to prevent it being used by an enemy and the town, deprived of defences, was given in *iḳṭāʿ*.

In 591/1195, Manbidj was dependent on al-Manṣūr of Ḥamāt; al-Malik al-Ẓāhir came from Ḳinnasrīn to attack it, but he was obliged to return in haste to Damascus and he abandoned the operation. In Dhu 'l-Ḳaʿda 595/September 1199, al-Malik al-Manṣūr

Muḥammad took Bārin from ʿIzz al-Dīn Ibrāhīm Ibn al-Muḳaddam and gave him Manbidj by way of compensation. Several months later, at the request of al-Malik al-ʿĀdil, he also gave Fāmiya and Kafar Ṭāb to ʿIzz al-Dīn in recompense for Bārin. Meanwhile, ʿIzz al-Dīn Ibrāhīm died at Fāmiya, and Manbidj reverted to his younger brother Shams al-Dīn ʿAbd al-Malik. In 598/1202, al-Malik al-Ẓāhir undertook restoration work on the Great Mosque.

Ca. 600/1204, Manbidj was a much-frequented place of pilgrimage. At the end of the 6th/12th century, al-Harawī refers to "the tomb, no longer to be seen, of al-Ḥakam b. al-Muṭṭalib b. ʿAbd Allāh b. al-Muṭṭalib", an eminent KuraS̲h̲ī who lived at the end of the Umayyad period and is said to have died in Syria. This author mentions the *mashhad* of al-K̲h̲aḍir and "the *mashhad* of the light (*mashhad al-nūr*), where it is claimed that there lies the tomb of some prophet". Ibn S̲h̲addād (*Aʿlaḳ*, 57) confirms the existence of this monument; "*Mashhad* with the cenotaph of K̲h̲ālid b. Sinān al-ʿAbsī" [*q.v.*], a personage of the *fatra* [*q.v.*]; this tomb was situated to the east of Manbidj. There was also a *masdjid al-mustadjāb*, an oratory where vows were fulfilled. Also mentioned is a "Temple of the Moon which was a place of pilgrimage for the Sabians".

In 597/1201 al-Malik al-Ẓāhir G̲h̲āzī who, like al-Malik al-Afḍal, did not recognise the authority of al-Malik al-ʿĀdil, sent al-Mubāriz Aḳdjā, one of his senior *amīr*s of Ḥalab, with troops to take possession of Manbidj and of Ḳalʿat Nadjm. Shams al-Dīn was taken prisoner and incarcerated in the citadel of Ḥalab. Henceforward, Manbidj was incorporated among the territories of Ḥalab, and the domination of the Banu 'l-Muḳaddam came to an end.

Al-Malik al-Ẓāhir was not slow to acknowledge al-Malik al-ʿĀdil as overlord, and the latter, in 598/-1202, granted Manbidj in *iḳṭāʿ* to ʿImād al-Dīn b. Sayf al-Dīn ʿAlī Aḥmad b. al-MaS̲h̲ṭūb. Soon afterwards, al-Malik al-Ẓāhir, who struck coinage at Ḥalab, took it back from al-MaS̲h̲ṭūb in Djumādā II 598/March 1202 and dismantled the walls and the citadel, while ʿAbd al-Malik b. ʿAlī b. ʿAbd al-Malik b. Abī S̲h̲aybā contributed to the restoration of the Great Mosque. Manbidj was the object of numerous attacks on the part of al-Malik al-Ẓāhir, who died in 613/1216.

In Rabīʿ II 615/July 1218, the vanguard of the troops of the Saldjūḳ Kaykāwūs b. Kayk̲h̲usraw [*q.v.*] having invaded the territory of Manbidj, the town opened its gates to him. But the Saldjūḳ sultan of Rūm was forced to evacuate the place, which was taken by al-Malik al-Afdal; the latter spared the population and appointed as governor of the town one of his officers, Ṣārim al-Dīn al-Manbidjī, who restored the defensive walls. At the approach of al-Malik al-AS̲h̲raf, who had succeeded al-Malik al-ʿĀdil as head of the Ayyūbids, Ṣārim al-Dīn advanced against the Ayyūbid army, suffered a decisive defeat and lost the town. In 625/1228, the army of Djalāl al-Dīn K̲h̲wārazm-S̲h̲āh [*q.v.*] advanced to Manbidj, but withdrew at the approach of winter. In 631/1234, al-Malik al-ʿAzīz Muḥammad received orders from the Ayyūbid supreme ruler al-Malik al-Kāmil to muster troops at Manbidj in preparation for an assault on Tell BaS̲h̲īr; as a result, the chieftains assembled on the plain of Manbidj included al-Malik al-AS̲h̲raf Mūsā, Kayḳubād b. Kayk̲h̲usraw, al-Malik al-Mug̲h̲īt̲h̲ of Ḥimṣ, al-Malik al-Muẓaffar of Ḥamāt and al-Malik al-Nāṣir of Karak; the commander of the operation was al-Malik al-Muʿaẓẓam Ṭūrān S̲h̲āh, cousin of the prince of Ḥalab, who was responsible for bringing these leaders together.

In 634/1236-7, at the end of the reign of al-Malik al-ʿAzīz ʿUt̲h̲mān, further construction work was done to the Great Mosque of Manbidj. In 636/1238, al-Muʿaẓẓam Ṭūrān S̲h̲āh brought his army to occupy the town, which gave shelter to refugees from Raḳḳa and Bālis fleeing before the K̲h̲wārazmians. In 637/1240-1, the latter, crossing the Euphrates once more, routed the troops of Ḥalab and marched against Manbidj; on Thursday 20 Rabīʿ II/8 November 1240, the population took refuge within the fortifications, but the town was taken by assault three days later and burnt. The K̲h̲wārazmians massacred a great many of the inhabitants before recrossing the Euphrates. Al-Malik al-Manṣūr retrieved the town. In Djumādā I 640/November 1242, on their way from Ḳalʿat Djaʿbar, al-Malik al-Manṣūr and al-Malik al-Muẓaffar stopped at Manbidj before reaching Ḥalab.

When the Mongols of Hūlāgū [*q.v.*] crossed the Euphrates in their turn, in the course of their headlong invasion of the West, having taken Bālis in Dhu 'l-Ḥidjdja 657/November-December 1259, they turned towards the north and sacked Manbidj, and then attacked Tell BaS̲h̲īr before returning to their base at al-Ruhā.

With the arrival of the Mamlūk sultans, the post of *ḳāḍī* of Manbidj, which had been occupied by Awḥad al-Dīn, was entrusted to Shams al-Dīn Abū ʿAbd Allāh Muḥammad b. Maḥmūd al-Iṣfahānī (616-88/1219-89).

In the treaty which the sultan Ḳalāwūn concluded with Leo of Armenia on 1 Rabīʿ II 684/6 June 1281, Manbidj is mentioned among the "Egyptian" towns. According to Ibn al-S̲h̲iḥna, it contributed to the sultan's *dīwān* a sum of approximately 500,000 *dirham*s per year, composed of various levies.

At the end of 699/1299, Manbidj was destroyed by the Tatars, but in the vicinity, numerous pastures and gardens were still to be seen; the majority of the trees were mulberries.

In the period of Abu 'l-Fidāʾ (first half of the 8th/14th century) Manbidj was replaced by Anṭākiya as capital of the *ʿAwāṣim*. It became a small *niyāba*, but remained an important place in the region of the Syrian Upper Euphrates. It is known from al-Ḳalḳas̲h̲andī (1418), who summarised the *Taḳwīm* (1321), that the region was dependent then upon the *nāʾib* of Ḥalab and that its governor was a *djundī*, *mukaddam* of the *ḥalḳa* [*q.v.*], appointed by *tawḳīʿ karīm* and enjoying an *iḳṭāʿ*. In Dhu 'l-Ḥidjdjâ 721/November 1321, the place became the objective of the Turkoman *amīr* Mintās̲h̲, who came to attack it; the siege lasted several days, and finally Manbidj was taken and burnt, and a large section of the population massacred. A few weeks later, *the amīr* of al-Ruhā joined battle with Mintās̲h̲, who was defeated, taken prisoner and sent to Djulbān, viceroy of Ḥalab (early 722/late 1321).

In 748/1349, a major plague of locusts infested the region, which, the following year was to be smitten by a serious outbreak of the Black Death. In this period, the town had as its *wālī* the poet and historian ʿUmar b. Muẓaffar al-Maʿarrī Zayn al-Dīn al-Wardī, author of a sequel to the chronicle of Abu 'l-Fidāʾ. In the 8th/14th century, following changes to the road network, Manbidj played no further part in the postal system (*barīd*); Ibn Baṭṭūta did not pass this way, and the mail between Ḥalab and the Euphrates, routed furhter to the south, crossed the river opposite Ḳalʿat Djaʿbar.

At the beginning of the 9th/15th century, Manbidj, like many other places, suffered great damage as a result of the invasion of the Tīmūr Lang. However, in the middle of this century, according to Ibn al-Shiḥna of Ḥalab (in his *al-Durr al-muntakhab*), it was contributing 40,000 *dīnārs* in annual taxation to the sultan's treasury, a fact which testifies to a degree of economic activity. For his part, the Egyptian Khalīl al-Ẓāhirī, in his survey of the province of Ḥalab in the *Zubdat kashf al-mamālik* (mid-9th/15th century), makes no mention of Manbidj.

In 922/1516, Syria passed under the authority of the Ottoman sultans; the re-organisation of the eastern provinces of the empire and changes in the road network placed Manbidj on the periphery of the major commercial processes.

In 1784 Volney visited the *pashalïk* of Ḥalab, and wrote: "Two days' travel to the north-east of Aleppo is the small town of Manbidj, formerly renowned under the name of Bambyce and Hierapolis. There remains no trace of the temple of that great goddess, whose cult is described by Lucian."

For the 19th century, two important sources of evidence are worthy of mention, those of Chesney and of Yanovski. In his account of an exploration of the valley of the Euphrates, Chesney provides valuable information concerning the state of Manbidj at the beginning of the century. He refers to the town and the castle, which were then called Kara Mambuche or Büyük Munbadj, and mentions remains of surrounding walls, square Arab towers and a trench which marked the limits of the Muslim city. He describes four large cisterns, a fine sarcophagus and the sparse ruins of the acropolis, the remains of two temples, in the smaller of which were an enclosure and the traces of seven columns. In the larger, which could be that of Atargatis, there are, he mentions specifically, traces of massive architecture: eleven arches alongside a paved court, in which there lie the shafts of columns and lotus-shaped capitals. Slightly to the west of the defensive walls there is a necropolis containing many Turkish tombs as well as some which are pagan, Saldjūḳ and Syriac, the last-named bearing inscriptions with illegible characters. Two roads leave this site, leading to two bridges of boats (ζεῦγμα). Towards Sādjūr, there are the remnants of a *ḳanāt*, partially abandoned, which has supplied Manbidj with water perhaps since the Assyrian, if not the Persian period. To the east of the town there is an aqueduct carrying water from the hills of the Djabal Dana Tagh situated 7 miles to the south-south-east. Two miles to the south is the encampment of the Banū Saʿīd Bedouins, whose herds roam the pasture-lands stretching from Bālis to the Sādjūr.

Some years later, J. Yanovski and J. David note that "as throughout the pachalik of Aleppo, subterranean water-courses abound in the territory of Mambidj, relayed by communication channels and thousands of reservoirs". In this region, Yanovski stresses the contrast between "the natural magnificence and the human squalor." From Manbidj to the southern limits of the land of Ḥalab, the author describes "massive plains, which although laid out in the form of fertile steppes, already resemble desert and which are variegated only by a series of low hills with derelict citadels on their summits". Yanovski also speaks of "once luxuriant prairies ruined by the disorderly encampments of nomadic tribes."

As for the remaining vestiges of the ancient Manbidj at the beginning of the 20th century, according to Baedeker (French edition, 1912, 411), "the extensive ruins of the ancient town are barely visible above the surface of the ground; however, it is possible to recognise the contours of a theatre and of a stadium". The *Guide Bleu* (1932 edition, 165) states for its part: "besides the perimeter wall, nothing is visible of the remains of the ancient town, the ruins of which have been used as a stone quarry of centuries". In the first third of the century, there still existed there a large pool, still stocked with carp similar of those which had been dedicated in Antiquity to the cult of Atargatis. This was, in fact, an ancient sacred lake which, like its equivalent at Marathus (Amrīt) on the Syrian coast, was originally flanked by a rectangular stone wall, and in the centre of which there rose an altar of marble, (*maʿābid*). In the middle of the 20th century all that remained of it was a deep unwalled depression without water, the dried-up sacred pool being used as a playground, while its spring supplied a bathing pool from which water was also drawn off to irrigate gardens. Of the successive ramparts surrounded by a broad trench which, since Antiquity had protected the town, there remained nothing but a circular earth embankment and a few vestiges on the north-west side.

Since the 16th century, Manbidj had been incorporated into Ottoman Turkey. At the beginning of the 20th century it was a regional centre of a *ḳaḍāʾ* of the *wilāyet* of Ḥalab, joined to the latter since 1913 by a telegraph cable. The region was then inhabited by groups of Kurdish and arabised Turkish families, among whom there were settled, after the Treaty of San Stefano put an end to the Russo-Turkish war of 1877-8, a number of Circassians, Ḥanafī Muslims [see ČERKES]. In 1915, at the time of the Russian offensive against eastern Turkey, the Circassians were obliged, as a precautionary measure, to join their kinsmen established at Khanāzīr, 50 km to the south-south-east of Ḥalab at the northern limit of the Syrian desert.

In 1921, after the imposition of French authority in the Levant, Manbidj was incorporated into the third region of the provincial government of Ḥalab.

In 1924, the agricultural zone of Manbidj was part of the *sandjaḳ* of Ḥalab; later, it was to contribute one of the seven *minṭaḳas* of the *muḥāfaẓa* of Ḥalab. In this region, in the first half of the 20th century, there existed a tripartite association between the owner of the land, the owner of the irrigation equipment and the farmer, the supply of water being linked to the exploitation of the land. In this period, irrigation was still operated by the system of *ḳanāṭs*. Since before 1914, Manbidj had been an important staging-post for the convoys of humped cattle which, coming from al-Mawṣil, made a halt there, which explains the presence in the town, from this period onwards, of a veterinary surgeon who inspected the beasts before they set out for Ḥalab by way of Bāb. In the region of Manbidj itself, there was livestock, comprising in 1924, according to Ch. Parvie, 386 oxen, 414 calves and 4,182 cows, which made the town an important centre of dairy production. There were also herds of sheep and goats.

In 1930, Manbidj, where there existed a police station and a magistrate's court, was incorporated into the *ḳaḍāʾ* of the Djabal Samaʿān, which was dependent on Ḥalab. Two years later, the population of the town numbered 2,000, including 800 Circassians and 100 Armenians. In 1945, a census counted 4,653 inhabitants, including the population of the regional centre of the *ḳaḍāʾ*. According to the official statistics of the Syrian Arab Republic (1982), the population of the town was estimated in 1960 at 8,577, in 1970 at 14,635 (the *minṭaḳa* or district then numbered 102,730), and in 1981 at 30,844. The significant demographic growth of the region in the course of the last decade is due to electrification made possible by the barrage of Tabḳa on the Euphrates, to the improvement of the road network and to a re-structuring of the hydraulic system, measures which have led to a spectacular development of agriculture in the region and to an improvement of the habitat.

Bibliography: 1. Arabic authors: Akhṭal, *Dīwān*, ed. Sālḥānī, Beirut 1891-2, 134; Ibn Khurradādhbih, 75, 98, 117, 162, 228, 229, 246, 254; Balādhurī, *Futūḥ*, 132, 150, 188, 191; Ibn Rusta, 83, 97, 107; Ya ᶜḳūbī, *Buldān*, 161; Ṭabarī, i, 959, ii, 779, 1876, iii, 47, 654, 694, 1103, 1265; Battānī, *al-Zīdj al-ṣābī, ed.* Nallino, ii, 41 (no 154), iii, 238; Iṣṭakhrī, 62, 65, 67; Masᶜūdī, *Murūdj*, §§ 228, 2644; idem, *Tanbīh*, 44, 152; Ḳudāma, 228-9, 246, 254; Abū Firās, *Dīwān*, ed. S. Dahan, Damascus 1944, 326-9; Ibn Ḥawḳal, 187 (tr. Kramers-Wiet, 164, 178, 184-6, 206); Muḳaddasī, 54, 60, 154, 190 (tr. A. Miquel, Damascus 1963, 132, 159, 240, 302); Nāṣir-i Khusraw, *Safar-nāma*, ed. Ch. Schefer, 31; Idrīsī, *Opus geographicum*, 378, 643, 651, 652. ᶜImad al-Dīn al-Iṣfahānī, *al-Fatḥ al-ḳussī fi 'l-fatḥ al-ḳudsī*, tr. H. Massé, Paris 1972, 231; Harawī, *Kitāb al-Ziyārāt*, ed. and tr. J. Sourdel-Thomine, Damascus 1953-7, 101, 237; Ibn Djubayr, *Riḥla*, tr. M. Gaudefroy-Demombynes, Paris 1949-65, 286-7; Yāḳūt, ed. Beirut 1957, v, 205-7; Ibn al-Athīr, see index ii, 813; Ibn al-ᶜAdīm, *Zubdat al-Ḥalab fī taʾrīkh Ḥalab*, ed. Dahan, Damascus 1951-4, i and ii, index; Abu 'l-Fidāʾ, *Taḳwīm*, 271; Ḳalḳashandī, *Ṣubḥ al-a ᶜshā*, iv, 127-8; Ibn Shiḥna, *al-Durr al-muntakhab fī ta'rīkh mamlakat Ḥalab*, ed. Sarkīs, Beirut 1909, 191 ff.; Ibn Ṣaṣrā, *al-Durra al-muḍīʾa. A chronicle of Damascus 1389-1397,* ed. and tr. W.M. Brinner, Berkeley 1963, 132a, 204b.

2. Non-Arabic sources: Leo the Deacon, *Historiae*, in *Patrologia Migne*, cxvii, 102; Matthew of Edessa, *Armenian chronicle*, tr. E. Dulaurier, Paris 1858, 311-12, 373, 384, 426, 450, 463, 468; Michael the Syrian, *Chronicle*, ed. and tr. J.-B. Chabot, Paris 1899-1914; Pseudo-Dionysius, *Chronicle*, ed. Chabot, Paris 1895, 47, 68;

3. Western works: Volney, *Voyage en Égypte et en Syrie*, 1799, new ed. by J. Gaulmier, Paris 1959, 279; J. Yanovski, *Syrie ancienne et moderne*, Paris 1848, 19-21; F. Chesney, *Expedition for the survey of the rivers Euphrates and Tigris*, London 1850, 420, 421, 510; H. Guys, *Statistique du Pachalik d'Alep*, Marseilles 1853; K. Ritter, *Erdkunde*, viii.2 = Teil 14-17, Berlin 1852-5, 1057 f.; Palgrave, *Narratives*, London 1865, i, 128; E. Sachau, *Reise im Syrien und Mesopotamien*, Leipzig 1883. 146-52, 154; G. Le Strange, *Lands*, 107; idem, *Palestine*, Cambridge 1890, 500-2; D.G. Hogarth and J.A.R. Munro, *Modern and ancient roads in Eastern Asia Minor*, R. Geog. Soc. Suppl. Papers, London 1893, iii, 643; V. Cuinet, *Syrie, Liban, Palestine*, Paris 1898; D.G. Hogarth, *Carchemish and its neighbourhood*, in *Annals of Archaeology and Anthropology*, ii, Liverpool 1909, 166, 183; K. Baedeker, *Palestine et Syrie*, 4th Fr. ed. 1912, 410, 411; Fr. Cumont, *Études Syriennes*, Paris 1917, 23-6, 358; M. Gaudefroy-Demombynes, *La Syrie à l'époque des Mamelouks,* Paris 1923, p. xxxlv, 9, 10, 92, 219, 281; L. Caetani, *Annali dell'Islam*, Milan 1905-26, iii, 792, 794, 797, 816; C. Pavie, *État d'Alep. Renseignements agricoles*, Aleppo 924; R. Dussaud, *Topographie historique de la Syrie*, Paris 1927, viii, 187, 450 ff., 462, 468, 470, 474 f. map XIII h; A. Musil, *The Middle Euphrates*, New York 1927, 281; Guide Bleu, *Syrie-Palestine*, Paris 1932, 165; Cl. Cahen, *Chronique de Djazīra d'après Ibn Shaddād*, in *REI*, viii (1934), 109-28; idem, *La Syrie du Nord*, Paris 1940, index; R. Grousset, *Histoire des Croisades*, Paris 1934-7, index; E. Honigmann, *Die Ostgrenze des byzantinischen Reiches*, Brussels, 1935, 142, 462 ff.; A. Latyon, *La vie rurale en Syrie et au Liban*, Beirut 1936, 78; Goossens, *Hierapolis de Syrie. Essai de monographie historique*, Louvain 1943; R. Mouterde et A. Poidebard, *Le limes de Chalcis*, Paris 1945, 21, 66, 127, 230; M. Canard, *Hamd'ânides*, Algiers 1951 (see index in *Arabica*, xviii [1971] 309); S. Runciman, *A history of the Crusades*, Cambridge 1952, ii, 113, 165, 170, 312, 330, 385, 409; K.M. Setton, *A history of the Crusades*, Philadelphia, 1955, i, see index, ii, 1962, 696, 708, 775; L. Dillemann, *Haute Mésopotamie*, Paris-Beirut 1962, 131, 177-84; N. Elisséeff, *Nūr al-Dīn*, Damascus 1967, index, map 2-D; E. Wirth, *Syrien*, Darmstadt 1971, 103, 180, 296, 390; A. Ehrenkreutz, *Saladin*, Albany, N.Y. 1972, 146, 147; D.E. Pitcher, *An historical geography of the Ottoman Empire*, Leiden 1972, map xxxxii A.2; E. Ashtor, *A social and economic history of the Near East in the Middle Ages*, Los Angeles 1976, 100; R.S. Humphreys, *From Saladin to the Mongols*, Albany N.Y. 1977, index; *Syrian Arab Republic, Statistical abstract*, Damascus 1982; J. Lauffray, *Halabiye*, Paris 1984, 27, 32; P. Sanlanille et al., *Holocene settlement in North Syria*, BAR Intern. series, Oxford 1905, no. S 238; *RCEA*, nos. 2673, 2970, 3402, 4123, 4124, 4125. (N. Elisséeff)

MĀND (Mūnd, Mund), the longest river in Fārs (*Nuzhat al-ḳulūb*; 50 *farsakhs*; E.C. Ross: over 300 miles in length).

The name. As a rule in Persia, sections of a river are called after the districts through which they flow. Mānd is the name of the last stretch near its mouth. The name seems to appear for the first time in the *Fārs-nāma* (before 510/1116), but only in the composite Māndistān (cf. below).

The old name of the river is usually transcribed in Arabic characters Sakkān (al-Iṣṭakhrī, 120; Ibn Ḥawḳal, 191; al-Idrīsī, tr. Jaubert, i, 401), but the orthography varies: Thakān, *Fārs-nāma*, GMS, 152; *Nuzhat al-ḳulūb*, 134; Zakkān or Žakkan, *Nuzhat al-ḳulūb*, 217; Sitāragān, *Djihān-numā*, 247; cf. also Ṣayhkān in Ḥasan Fasāʾī.

The identification of the Sakkān with the Σιταxός mentioned in the *Periplus* of Nearchus (Arrian, *Indica*, xxxviii, 8) is generally recognised. The identity of Sitakos with the Sitioganus (Sitiogagus) mentioned by Pliny, *Nat. Hist.*, vi. 26, is also usually admitted (Weissbach, 1927), but Herzfeld (1907) relying on the existence of another river, the Shādhkān (= Sitioganus?), has suggested doubts about the identification of the Sitakos with the Sitioganus. Now according to al-Iṣṭakhrī, 119, the Shadhkān flows into the Persian Gulf at Dasht al-Dastaḳān (north of Būshīr?). This Shadhkān must be identified with the river Shāpūr. The *Fārs-nāma*, ed. Le Strange, 163, mentions Rūdbāl-i Sittadjān ("the banks of the S.") as a station on the road from Shīrāz to Tawwadj. From this fact and especially from the name, Sittadjān seems to have applied to the left bank tributary of the Shāpūr. Pliny, who follows Onesicritos, adds that by the Sitioganus one reaches Pasargades in 7 days. Whatever be the identity of the Sitioganus, the exaggeration in this statement is evident (especially in the direction of the sea to Pasargades) and the waters of Pasargades (Mashad-i Murghāb) do not flow into the Persian Gulf. But there is nothing to prove the absolute impossibility of using the Sakkān as a subsidiary means of transport in the season of floods (the winter). According to Arrian, Nearchus found at the mouth of the Sitakos large quantities of corn which Alexander had brought there for the army. Al-Iṣṭakhrī, 99, places the Sakkān among the rivers of

Fārs which are navigable at need (*al-anhār al-kibār allatī taḥmil al-sufuna idhā udjriyat fī-hā*).

Another question is the phonetic identity of the names Sitakos (Sitioganus?) and Sakkān. According to C.F. Andreas, Σιταχός is a nominative restored from a supposed genitive *Σιταχων (Sitakān); Sitiogan-us is a mistake for Sittagan-us; lastly, the peculiarity of the Arabic script could explain the change of Sittakān to Sakkān. Here we may add that Ḥasan Fasāʾī gives one of the stretches of the river the strangely written form Ṣayḥkān (*Stkān?). Al-Iṣṭakhrī, however, derives the name of the river from that of the village of Sakk (*Nuzhat al-ḳulūb*: Zakān) in the district of Karzīn considerably below the Ṣayḥkān stretch of the river.

To sum up, the identification of the Sitakos with the Sitioganus does not seem sufficiently established.

The course of the river. The Sakkān (Mānd) describes a great curve. At first it runs in the direction N.W.-S.E., to the northern base of the Kūh-i Marra-yi Shikaft, which separates it from the valley of the river Shāpūr. It follows this direction (*ca.* 100 miles) to the end of the Āsmāngird mountains around which it makes a bend and turns south (70 miles). It then meets the parallel ranges which run along the Persian Gulf and continues its winding course to the sea in a westerly direction (140 miles).

The Sakkān (Mānd) and its tributaries drain and irrigate a considerable area (the Kūh-i Mānd and the Kūh-i Darang). Al-Iṣṭakhrī says that its waters contribute the largest share to the fertility of Fārs (*aktharu ʿimāratin*).

The sources of the river (Kān-i Zand, Čihilčashma and Surkh-rag) rise in the mountains of Kūh-i Nār and Kūh-i Marra-yi Shikaft to the northwest and west of Shīrāz. These streams unite before Khan-i Zinyān in the district of Māṣarm on the great Shīrāz-Kārrūn-Būshīr road. Al-Iṣṭakhrī, 120, places the sources of the Sakkān near the village of Shādhfarī (?) in the district of Ruwaydjān (?). In the same author, 130, Khān al-Asad on the Sakkān corresponds to the modern Khān-i Zinyān. The *Fārs-nāma* (and the *Nuzhat al-ḳulūb*) places the sources of the Sakkān near the village of Čatrūya (?). Under the Turkish name of Ḳara aghač, i.e. "[the river of] the elm", the combined streams flow through the districts of Māṣarm (= Kūh-i Marra-yi Shikaft), Siyākh (al-Iṣṭakhrī, 120: Siyāh) and Kawār. In this last district, Rivadaneyra, iii, 81, going from Shīrāz to Fīrūzābād, crossed the river by a "substantial bridge". It is in the district of Kawār that Ḥasan Fasāʾī gives the river the name of Ṣaykhān. In Kawār (Ḥasan Fasāʾī) there used to be the barrage of Band-i Bahman, where by a subterranean channel (*ḳanāt*) part of the water was led into reservoirs (*čāh*) and then to the fields. In the *bulūk* of Khafr (al-Iṣṭakhrī, 105: Khabr), which must be distinguished from the district of the same name in the *kūra* of Iṣṭakhr, the river turns south. Aucher-Eloy, who crossed the river on the road from Fīrūzābād to Djarrūn (Djahrum) calls it "Tengui Tachka" (= Tang-i Ḳashḳay?) and speaks of its "beautiful valley". Rivadaneyra continuing his journey from Fīrūzābād to Dārāb crossed the river by a ford between the villages of Tadwān and "Assun-Dscherd" (Āsmāngird?). He also admires the pleasant and flourishing aspect of Khafr. Below the latter, the river enters the *bulūk* of Ṣimkān where, near the village of Sarḳal, it receives on its left bank, the brackish (*shūr*) river of Djahrum, and then flows through the ravine of Kārzīn, and waters the *bulūk* of Ḳīr-wa-Kārzīn. Abbott coming from Fasā crossed the river by a ford between ʿAlī-ābād and Lifardjān (cf. the name of the *ramm* of Kurds in Fārs al-Liwāldjān, al-Iṣṭakhrī, 113), where it was 100 yards wide and the water rose up to the horse's belly. Farther down below the ford, Stack, going from Ḳīr to Kāriyān crossed the river, here 60 yards broad, by the bridge of ʿArūs, built in a zig-zag and in two stories ("the queerest structure in the way of a bridge"). Near the village of Nīm-dih, the river enters the *bulūk* of Afzar. After having wound round the fort of Ḳal ʿa-yi Shahriyār the river receives (near the place called Čam-i Kabkāb) the name of Bāz and then irrigates the *bulūk* of Khundj (cf. Ibn Baṭṭūṭa, ii, 241: Khundjbāl = Khundj + Bāl). In the district of Diz-gāh of the *bulūk* of Galla-dār, the river has two tributaries: near the village of Gabrī, the Dār al-Mizān, and two *farsakhs* lower, that of Dihram. The Dār al-Mīzān comes from the left (east) side of the *bulūk* of Asīr. The Dihram, much more important, comes from the right side after watering the historic district of Fīrūzābād (the ancient Gūr, capital of Ardashīr-Khurra; cf. the details in Le Strange, 256, and also FĪRŪZĀBĀD). Al-Iṣṭakhrī, 121, makes this tributary come from Dārdjān (of Siyāh) and water first Khunayfghān and then Gūr (in place of the name of the river Tirza, al-Iṣṭakhrī, 99, 121, one should probably read Burāza; cf. the *Fārs-nāma*, 151, *Nuzhat al-ḳulūb*, 117-18: Ḥakīm Burāza was the sage who dried up the Lake of Gūr).

After Diz-gāh, the river enters the district of Sanā-wa-Shumba of the *bulūk* of Dashtī, and near the village of Bāghān receives on the right bank the river Čanīz which comes from the district of Tasūdj-i Dashtī. Finally, near the village of Dūmānlū the river enters the coast district of Māndistān and receives the name of Mānd. It flows into the sea near the village of Ziyārat, halfway between the old harbours of Nadjīram (to the north and Sirāf (to the south).

Māndistān. The district forms part of the *bulūk* of Dashtī (which is to be distinguished from Dashtistān to the north of Dashtī up to Būshīr). Dashtī (36 × 18 *farsakhs*) is composed of 4 districts: 1. Bardistān, the part of the coast in which is the port of Dayyir. 2. Māndistān in the coast to the north of Bardistān and the two banks of the river Mānd. 3. Sanā and Shumba on the river above Māndistān. 4. Tasūdj-i Dashtī, a very narrow valley (11 × ½ *farsakhs*), watered by the Čanīz and separating Sanā and Shumba from the *bulūk* Arbaʿa (on the lower course of the river of Fīrūzābād).

The whole of the *bulūk* belongs to the torrid zone (*garmsīr*) of Fārs. Māndistān (12 × 5 *farsakhs*) includes lands so flat that the current of the river is imperceptible and the water cannot be used for irrigation. Agriculture (wheat, barley, palm-trees) is dependent on the winter floods. The district has 40 villages. The capital of the district and of the *bulūk* is Kākī. There used to be two rival families in Māndistān: the Shaykhiyān and the Ḥādjdjiyān. During the disturbances under Afghān rule (1722-9) the Ḥādjdjī Raʾīs Djamāl exterminated the Shaykhiyān and founded a little dynasty of hereditary governors, who were able to annex the district of Bardistān through matrimonial alliances. One of his descendants, Muḥammad Khān (d. at Būshir in 1299/1881), was noted as a poet under the pen-name of Dashtī.

Ḥasan Fasāʾī explains the name Māndistān by a popular etymology: "the place where the water flows slowly (*wāmānda*)". Names in *-stān* are common in Fārs (Lāristān, Bardistān), but even if such a formation was possible in a river-name, the element Mānd would still be a puzzle. It is curious that Ḥasan Fasāʾī sometimes writes it Mānd (read Mūnd) and sometimes Mund (read *Mŏnd*). It might be suggested as a

ISBN 90 04 08659 5

PRINTED IN THE NETHERLANDS

Studies in Islamic History and Civilization

in Honour of

Professor David Ayalon

Edited by

M. SHARON

1986. (611 p., 18 pl., frontisp.)
ISBN 965 264 014 X *bound* **Gld. 145.—**

Contents

Distributed in Israel by Cana Ltd., P.O.B. 1199, Jerusalem

E.J. Brill — P.O.B. 9000 — 2300 PA Leiden — The Netherlands

THE ENCYCLOPAEDIA OF ISLAM

NEW EDITION

PREPARED BY A NUMBER OF
LEADING ORIENTALISTS

EDITED BY

C. E. BOSWORTH, E. van DONZEL, B. LEWIS and Ch. PELLAT
ASSISTED BY F. Th. DIJKEMA AND Mme S. NURIT

UNDER THE PATRONAGE OF
THE INTERNATIONAL UNION OF ACADEMIES

VOLUME VI

FASCICULES 105-106

MĀND — MARʿASHĪS

LEIDEN
E. J. BRILL
1988

EXECUTIVE COMMITTEE:

All correspondence on editorial matters should be addressed to the Editorial Secretaries, whose addresses are:

For the English Edition

Dept. of Near Eastern Studies,
The University of Manchester,
Manchester,
England M13 9PL.

For the French Edition

Centre Universitaire
94, avenue des Grésillons
92600 Asnières
France

AUTHORS OF ARTICLES IN THESE FASCICULES

Haleh Afshar, University of Bradford. 488.
M. Ajami, Princeton University. 409.
P. A. Andrews, University of Cologne. 457.
Ghaus Ansari, Kuwait University. 490.
R. Arnaldez, University of Paris. 452.
[W. Barthold, Leningrad. 420, 433.
W. Björkman, Uppsala. 424.
J. R. Blackburn, University of Toronto. 437.
P. N. Boratav, Centre National de la Recherche Scientifique, Paris. 421.
C. E. Bosworth, University of Manchester. 419, 421, 498, 505.
Yu. Bregel. Indiana University, Bloomington. 417, 418, 419, 420.
J. Burton-Page, Church Knowle, Dorset. 410.
P. Chalmeta, University of Madrid. 432.
J. Chelhod, Centre National de la Recherche Scientifique, Paris. 481, 491.
J. W. Clinton, Princeton University. 453.
D. C. Conrad, Stinson Beach, California. 422.
Yolande Crowe, London. 408.
F. Dachraoui, University of Tunis. 435.
E. van Donzel, Netherlands Institute for the Near East. Leiden. 434.
T. El-Achèche, University of Tunis. 438.
N. Elisséeff, University of Lyons. 456, 457.
J. van Ess, University of Tübingen. 458.
Suraiya Faroqhi, Middle East Technical University, Ankara. 510.
G. S. P. Freeman-Grenville, University of York. 385.
Y. Friedmann, Hebrew University, Jersualem. 440.
Adnan Güriz, University of Ankara. 498.
U. Haarmann, University of Freiburg-im-Breisgau. 414.
H. Halm, University of Tübingen. 440, 454.
Angelika Hartmann, University of Hamburg. 430.
D. R. Hill, Great Bookham, Surrey. 406.
[E. Honigmann, Brussels. 508.
F. de Jong, University of Utrecht. 454.
H. Kennedy, University of St. Andrews. 428.
Ann K. S. Lambton, Kirknewton, Northumberland. 485, 496.
J. M. Landau, Hebrew University, Jerusalem. 400.
J. D. Latham, University of Edinburgh. 405.
Linda Y. Leach, Richmond, Surrey. 426.
T. Lewicki, Cracow. 453.
K. McPherson, Western Australian Institute of Technology, Bentley. 504.
W. Madelung, University of Oxford. 436, 439, 442.
[G. Marçais, Algiers]. 427, 441.
R. E. Miller, University of Regina. 466.
[V. Minorsky, London]. 385, 503, 505.
Ch. Pellat, University of Paris. 406.
J. F. Richards, Duke University, Durham. 423.
F. Rosenthal, Yale University, New Haven. 403.
Maya Shatzmiller, University of Western Ontario, London, Ontario. 441.
Nada Tomiche, University of Paris. 472.
Ch. Vial, University of the Provence, Aix-en-Provence. 415.
D. Zahan, University of Paris. 402.

Names in square brackets are those of authors of articles reprinted or revised from the first edition of this Encyclopaedia.

pure hypothesis that there is a connection with the people Mnd (cf. Mēd) of which there might have been a colony in Māndistān.

Bibliography : Weissbach, *Sitakos*, in Pauly-Wissowa, *Real-Encyclopädie*[2], 2nd Ser., v, 1927, 377; Iṣṭak̲h̲rī, 120; Ibn Ḥawḳal, 191; Ibn al-Balk̲h̲ī, *Fārs-nāma*, GMS, 156; *Nuzhat al-ḳulūb*, GMS, 134; Ḥādjdjī K̲h̲alīfa, *Dj̲ihān-numā*, 247; Ḥasan Fasāʾī, *Fārs-nāma-yi Nāṣirī*, Tehran 1314, ii, 210, 328-9; the author of this excellent work published separately a map of Fārs which is now very rare. Aucher-Eloy, *Relations*, Paris 1843, ii, 520; Keith Abbott, *Notes on a journey eastwards from Shiraz*, in *JRGS* (1857), 149-84; Haussknecht, *Routen im Orient*, map no. iv: *Centrales und südliches Persien*; Rivandaneyra, *Viaje al interior de la Persia*, Madrid 1880, iii, 110; Stack, *Six months*, London 1882, ch. xvi, p. 111; E.C. Ross, *Notes on the river Mand, or Kara Aghatch*, in *Proc. RGS*, v (1883), December, 712-16 with a map (the article reproduces the learned note by C. F. Andreas); Stolze, *Persopolis, Bericht über meine Aufnamen*, in *Verh. d. Gesell. f. Erdk.*, Berlin, x (1883), 251-76; Tomaschek, *Topogr.Erläuterung d. Küstenfahrt Neuarchs*, in *SB Ak. Wien*, cxxi, (1890), no. vii, 58-61; Schwarz, *Iran*, i, 1896, 8; Le Strange, *The lands of the eastern caliphate*, Cambridge 1905, 252, 255; Herzfeld, *Pasargadae*, Inaugural-Dissertation, 1907, 9-10 (with a sketch based on Ḥasan Fasā ʾī); *Admiralty handbook, Persia*, London 1945, 70-1, 126, 372, 374-5; *Cambridge history of Iran*, i, 29-30.

(V. Minorsky)

MANDA, an island off the coast of Kenya. It lies in approximately 2° 12′ S, 41° E, on the east side of Lamu Island [*q.v.*] in the Lamu Archipelago. There is a small modern settlement at Takwa Milinga, near the ruins of the ancient walled town of Takwa in the centre of the island, a small, deserted and allegedly ancient settlement at Kitau at the south-west corner of the island, and, in the extreme north, not far from a small modern settlement, the remains of the ancient walled town of Manda, which gives the island its name. It was finally destroyed by Fumo Luti, Sultan of Pate, in 1806. Its sole mention in Arabic literature is as Mandak̲h̲ā or Manda K̲h̲ā in the *History of Kilwa* [see KILWA], as one of the settlements at which a son of the founder was set up; the Arabic form presumably represents the Swahili Manda Kuu, or Great Manda, recorded by A. Voeltzkow. Al-Idrisi's reference *M.l.n.da.* more probably refers to Malindi [*q.v.*]. According to the traditional *Habari za Pate* ("History of Pate"), it was founded earlier than Pate, by which it was conquered later. However, it was of sufficient importance to pay tribute to the Portuguese separately from Pate, and it was its failure to do so that led to reprisals by the Portuguese in 1569, when many houses and some 2,000 palm trees were destroyed. In 1637 it was required to demolish its defensive walls.

H.N. Chittick carried out excavations at the site between 1966 and 1982. (These have been entirely filled in, and there is scarcely anything to be seen, other than the remains of two mosques.) There are massive stone walls on the western and northern sides abutting on the shore, and the remains of later walls on the south-west and south-east of the site. These walls are distinguished by Chittik as mega-walls and maxi-walls: the mega-walls are of blocks of stone weighing up to one ton each. The stone used, in both cases, is coral, quarried from a nearby reef which can still be identified. The walls provided stability for the sand dunes, so that houses could be built on the resulting terraces. These constructions are similar to ones ob-

served by the writer at S̲h̲iḥr in South Yemen. The houses were built of coral, but also used brick. Very similar bricks have been found at Ṣuḥār, ʿUmān, and were probably brought from there as ships' ballast unloaded here in order to take on cargoes of mangrove timber. Certain houses have brick cisterns, and one, with a sunken courtyard, is similar to one known in Sīrāf. *Per contra*, the lay-out of the houses, however, is compared by M.C. Horton rather to types known from the Red Sea. Glazed and unglazed imported Islamic pottery, in which the earliest period of the site abounds, can be paralleled closely in D. Whitehouse's excavations at Sīrāf [*q.v.*], and some was certainly made in the Sīrāf vicinity. It need not be concluded, however, that Manda was a colony of Sīrāf. Rather, its connections with the Red Sea, and also with Ṣuḥār, suggest that it served both the Red Sea and the Persian Gulf as a trading port, already in existence in the mid-8th century, busied chiefly in the ivory and mangrove trades, in a region in which they abound naturally. A curiosity is an arcaded building with open sides, probably of the 13th-14th centuries, and most likely to have been a covered market, albeit it has been fancifully described as a "kiosk". There is a Friday mosque and another mosque, of 14th-15th century date. Only six coins have been found, two of them Fāṭimid, and apparently from Sicilian mints, an illustration of the wide dispersal of coinage. (The plate published by Chittick is illegible.) There is no trace of there having been a local currency.

At Takwa there is a well-preserved Friday Mosque and quite a number of houses in what was a walled town of some 12½ acres. The mosque appears to be of the late 15th or early 16th century, and was cleared by J.S. Kirkman, *Pace* the latter author, the pillar that rises above the roof of the *miḥrāb* is not of religious significance. Examination of the side walls discloses stumps of what were a series of pillars that originally provided an open clerestory below the roof, a feature still perpetuated in domestic architecture on Pate Island. A curiosity in the mosque ablutions is the decoration of the cistern with three plates: that in the place of honour in the centre is of Portuguese manufacture, and bears the Cross that is the emblem of the Portuguese Order of Christ. Outside the walls an inscription on a pillar tomb is read by Kirkman *ʿAbd Allāh Muḥammad ʿAlī al-mutawaffā sana 1094*. Local tradition, nevertheless, claims it as the tomb of S̲h̲ayk̲h̲ Aḥmad Manṣūr b. Aḥmad or "S̲h̲ayk̲h̲ Fakīhi Manṣūr", honouring it with an annual pilgrimage from Shela on Lamu Island. The Friday Mosque also enjoys the reputation of being a place of sanctuary. The inability to read the inscription can be taken as an indication of the local level of literacy in Arabic.

Bibliography : (H.) N. Chittick, *Manda, excavations at an island port on the Kenya coast*, Nairobi, 1984; G.S.P. Freeman-Grenville, *The East African coast: select documents*[2], Oxford 1975, 248-53 (Swahili *History of Pate* in English tr.); P.S. Garlake, *The Early Islamic architecture of the East African Coast*, Nairobi 1966, 65-6 and figs. 31, 34; J.S. Kirkman, *Takwa—The Mosque of the Pillar*, in *Ars Orientalis*, iii (1957); J. Strandes, *The Portuguese period in East Africa* (1899), ed. J.S. Kirkman, Nairobi 1968; A. Voeltzkow, *Die Witu-Inseln und Zanzibar-Archipel*, Stuttgart 1923; personal communications by M.C. Horton and by D. Whitehouse, and personal visit, 1982. (G.S.P. Freeman-Grenville)

MANDATES. The mandate (Arabic *intidāb*; Turkish *manda*, from the French) was essentially a system of trusteeship, instituted by the League of Nations after the end of the First World War, for the administration of certain territories detached from the vanquished states, chiefly the Ottoman and German Empires. The concept of the mandate has been variously understood as either a new world order or, contrariwise, merely as a façade for neo-colonialism, with other interpretations ranging between these two extremes. Essentially, the option of establishing mandates in conquered territories was largely intended to defuse (if not quite resolve) three foci or conflict: (1) Among the Powers themselves, particularly the victorious Allies, regarding domination of areas formerly administered by the vanquished - according to their respective global and regional interests and in consideration of secret agreements drawn up during the war years. (2) Between each Mandatory Power and the populations of the to-be-mandated territories — whose élites had become at least partially suffused with assertive patriotism — in an attempt to find methods of fulfilling promises expressed during the war. (3) Among rival sectors within each of these populations, some of which rejected mutual accommodation.

The mandate was not only a response to the real or potential threat of the above conflicts, but also a compromise between the desire of the victors — chiefly France and Great Britain — to maintain their hold on certain territories and the demand for self-determination raised by idealists, among whom President Woodrow Wilson and General Jan Smuts were most prominent. The guiding principle essentially agreed upon was to adopt a system of Great Power administration, intended to foster not only material welfare and cultural advancement but also progressive development of the mandated territory towards independence and statehood as well. The degree of development varied among the territories, which were classified accordingly into three categories. Category A, the highest level, comprised three mandates (out of a total of fourteen), all in ex-Ottoman territories: ᶜIrāḳ; Syria and Lebanon; and Palestine and Transjordan. We will consider only these mandates herein, as they included sizeable Muslim populations (mandates in Category B were located in Africa and those in Category C in Africa and the Pacific area; for both, a more paternal type of rule was envisaged). For a brief while (1918-19) there was some discussion of a British and then an American mandate over Anatolia — the latter mooted separately by K͟hālide Edīb [*q.v.*] in Turkey and Henry Morgenthau, former U.S. ambassaor of Istanbul, in *The New York Times*. These projects were soon dropped, however, due to the Turkish nationalists' flat rejection, at the Sivas Congress (1919) of any mandate idea and their success in Turkey's war of independence. Similarly, projects of mandates for Armenia and Albania failed to materialise (the United States Senate debated the former, which received insufficient support because of majority opposition to the Treaty of Versailles. Furthermore, no other state was willing to assume a mandate over Armenia).

The victorious Allies first agreed in principle about mandates, in a formal manner, in a resolution of the Council of Ten on 30 January 1919, which became Article 22 of the Covenant of the League of Nations signed in Paris in April 1919 and incorporated into the Versailles Peace Treaty two months later. Concerning the "A" areas, the Covenant stated, in part, that "Certain communities formerly belonging to the Turkish Empire have reached a state of development where their existence as independent nations can be provisionally recognised, subject to the rendering of administrative advice and assistance by a Mandatory until such time as they are able to stand alone. The wishes of these communities must be a principal consideration in the selection of the Mandatory."

The above formulation reflected the feelings of humanity and justice prevalent in the wake of the First World War and well suited the principle of efficiency in public administration, better served by a defined Mandatory state whose commitment to the local population could be safeguarded by the control and criticism of international public opinion. However, not all the above principles were fully acceptable to France and Great Britain; hence the final texts of the mandates introduced certain modifications (e.g. in allowing local populations a share in selecting "their" Mandatory). At the San Remo Conference, in April 1920, the Allies definitively allotted ᶜIrāḳ and Palestine to Great Britain, and Syria and Lebanon to France. The final versions of the mandates and the respective specifications of each were worked out within the League of Nations and approved in July 1922 for Palestine and Syria; those relating to ᶜIrāḳ, however, were never ratified as such and consisted instead of a British-ᶜIrāḳī Treaty — a modified version of the original draft of the mandate — signed on 12 October 1922 and approved by the Council of the League of Nations in September 1924. The mandates became valid only since September 1923, after the Republic of Turkey (at the Lausanne Conference) had officially renounced all claims on the non-Turkish territories of the defunct Ottoman Empire. Even then, certain frontier issues remained to be ironed out subsequently.

From a legal point of view, the appointment of a Mandatory took the form of an agreement between the League of Nations and the relevant Power, in which the latter was enjoined to promote the interests of the population in the mandated territory and prepare it for self-rule, under the control of the international body — a new conception in political science. The Mandatory had to report annually to the League of Nations' Permanent Mandates Commission, whose Constitution was approved by the League's Council in December 1920. The Commission was first appointed in February 1921 and formally supervised the application of the mandates. This Commission, numbering at first nine members (the number subsequently varied), comprised a majority of representatives from countries other than the Mandatory. It usually met in Geneva twice a year, diligently examining reports from the Mandatory and petitions by the local population, generally insisting upon the presence of representative officials of the Mandatory for cross-examination. Consequently, the commission's functions were simultaneous control of and collaboration with each of the Mandatories. It was hampered, however, by the lack of direct contact with people in the Mandated territories and by an absence of any power other than that of relaying observations to the Council of the League of Nations, whose duties included overall observance of the system and its modification where required. In addition, the International Court of Justice at the Hague served as a court of appeals, in certain cases, for the people of the mandated territories.

On a practical basis, the Mandatory thus had considerable latitude in its day-to-day governing and even in much of its decision-making. Nevertheless, there remained certain basic juridical differences between mandates and colonies. The Mandatory lacked exclusive rights and possessed merely a delegated — and consequently limited — authority; hence it was not the sovereign power of the mandated territory, nor even its protector, in an international sense. Rather, it constituted merely a trustee for international society and a tutor appointed by the League of Nations to take care of the interests of the country's population. Legally, this implied both rights and obligations for the Mandatory. In actual practice, much depended upon the interests involved and the forces applied in each case.

ʿIrāḳ. The mandates offered differing degrees of autonomy to the local populations — to ʿIrāḳ the most, to Palestine the least, and to Syria an intermediate degree — apparently dependent upon the level of homogeneity of the population (assuming that too much autonomy might be unsuitable for a heterogeneous population). The case of ʿIrāḳ is rather special, however, on other grounds as well. In 1921, even before final approval of the mandate, the British, who had already assumed effective control, invited Fayṣal b. Ḥusayn (who had been ejected from Syria by the French) to reign over ʿIrāḳ under their aegis, assisting him in setting up the institutions of government [see FAYṢAL I]. True to their conception of the mandate, the British created directors' posts at the top level of every Ministerial office and appointed advisers in various administrative departments, as well as local judges. In 1921, an ʿIrāḳī army was set up; in 1923, a Constituent Assembly was elected, which met in March of the following year and approved ʿIrāḳ's constitution of July 1924. The assembly also approved the October 1922 British-ʿIrāḳī Treaty which, without explicitly supplanting the Mandate, constituted official legal recognition by Great Britain of ʿIrāḳ's sovereignty, provided the former offered binding advice in international and financial matters. Great Britain indeed successfully represented and defended ʿIrāḳ's interests in the delicate negotiations held with Turkey since 1925 concerning the area of Mawṣil [*q.v.*] which the League of Nations eventually allotted to ʿIrāḳ. Although the 1922 Treaty did not mention the mandate at all, it was nonetheless approved by the Council of the League of Nations, on 27 September 1924, as the instrument of mandate.

These moves only satisfied the ʿIrāḳī nationalists for a brief while, however, if at all. Largely due to their pressures, a new British-ʿIrāḳī treaty was signed in 1930, one which practically terminated the mandate; Great Britain reserved for itself certain rights, largely in the military domain, for another twenty-five years. The League of Nations, however, was the only institution which could terminate a mandate officially — and this was the first time the issue had arisen. Thus the Permanent Mandates Commission set up five pre-requisites for ending a mandate: a settled government and administration capable of running all public services; ability to maintain territorial integrity and political independence; capability of keeping internal peace and order; adequate financial resources for governmental requirements; and a legal and judicial system affording regular and equal justice to all. The Commission had some doubts about the suitability of conditions in ʿIrāḳ for ending the mandate, primarily those relating to the judicial system and minority rights. After lengthy debates, however, in autumn 1932 the Permanent Mandates Commission voted to recommend termination of the mandate for ʿIrāḳ to the Council of the League of Nations. The Council approved and in October 1932 admitted ʿIrāḳ to the League of Nations (the first Arab state to join); thus the 1930 Treaty came into force and the mandate ended definitively. All formal restrictions on ʿIrāḳ as a sovereign state were abrogated, although Great Britain did exercise its rights to intervene in crucial state and security matters until the end of the Second World War.

Syria and Lebanon. The French mandate in Syria and Lebanon, also imposed in 1922, continued to exist for a much longer period that that of ʿIrāḳ, ending only in 1945. The Mandatory was charged with framing an organic law for Syria and Lebanon within three years and then to lead them into developing as independent states. It was further enjoined to levy taxes, develop natural resources, and establish judicial and educational systems, as well as military forces, these last to be eventually handed on to the local people. All this was conditional on the Mandatory's promoting the well-being of the population and refraining from granting monopolies and concessions to its own nationals to the detriment of the local people or those of those states. The French in Syria accordingly allowed Arab Syrians and Lebanese to staff the administration — although it was headed (as in ʿIrāḳ) at its highest echelons by advisers delegated by the Mandatory. The French had a parallel organisation of their own, led by the High Commissioner; furthermore, they not only managed foreign and military affairs themselves, but often intervened in internal matters as well, through their officials. As with the British in ʿIrāḳ, the French in Syria and Lebanon found Francophile Arabs willing to cooperate with them, simultaneously incurring the hostility of the nationalists.

On the whole, the Mandatory had greater success in Lebanon than in Syria. In the former, a representative council was prompted to prepare an Organic Law, in 1925, which was adopted by the Mandatory in the same year; in the following year, Lebanon became a republic with its own constitution, president and government — supervised by the Mandatory (as in ʿIrāḳ). In Syria, however, a serious uprising (called a "revolt" by the nationalists and an "insurrection" by the French) occurred in the Druze region 1926-7, probably brought about by a combination of local grievances and patriotic aspirations; this uprising spread and the Mandatory forces put it down stronghandedly. An attempt to set up a Constituent Assembly, 1928, to prepare a constitution, foundered largely because of tensions between the above groups. In 1930, the assembly was dissolved and the French authorities unilaterally proclaimed a constitution, with the proviso that it could not contradict the responsibilities entailed in the Mandate. In principle, it resembled the Organic Law in ʿIrāḳ, although it was republican rather than monarchical in intent and comprised variations for Syria's different units. An assembly was elected two years later and, in 1936, a French-Syrian treaty was agreed upon. This would have recognised Syria's sovereign independence (in three years' time), while allowing France to maintain its military forces there. However, the Government and Parliament in France did not ratify the treaty and Syria reverted to Mandatory rule, with the French High Commissioner increasing his authority.

All this exasperated the nationalists who, although divided among themselves, were antagonised by the French division of the mandated territory into separate units and by the changes repeatedly introduced. The nationalists were particularly irritated by what they interpreted as the Mandatory Power's actions to increase autonomy in Druze and ʿAlawī districts, carve out a "Great Lebanon" and hand over the *sandjak* of Alexandretta (Hatay) to Turkey. Even the declaration of General Catroux (commander of the Free French forces which entered Syria, together with the British, in June 1941), in September 1941, that the French mandate had ended hardly convinced the Syrian nationalists, as France insisted on a "predominant position" there. Only at the end of the war, in 1945, did France recognise Syria's independence, thus ending the mandate (the League of Nations had been inactive during the war and was considered defunct, for practical purposes; hence it had no part in this decision).

The mandate in Lebanon developed along parallel although not identical lines. As early as August 1930, the French carved out a "Great Lebanon" which did away with the area's former Christian hegemony and turned Lebanon into an even more complicated mosaic of religious communities. The division of the main official positions, as well as the composition of the elected representative assemblies since 1926, have reflected and institutionalised this complexity. The 1926 Constitution accorded a high degree of home rule to the Lebanese, while granting France important decision-making privileges. A Franco-Lebanese treaty, similar to the Franco-Syrian one of 1936, was drawn up during the same year, but likewise failed to obtain ratification in France. Nevertheless, the difference between Lebanon and Mandatory France led to less violence in Lebanon than in Syria; Lebanon's independence (and termination of the mandate), attained in 1945, demanded fewer struggles that did Syria's.

Palestine and Transjordan. The mandate for Palestine was *sui generis* in several respects. Unlike the drafts of the mandates for ʿIrāḳ and for Syria and Lebanon, the text of the mandate for Palestine did not charge the Mandatory with drafting an organic law, but rather with promoting political, administrative and economic conditions to ensure the establishment of a national home for the Jewish people, while protecting the civil and religious rights of the rest of the population. The Balfour Declaration of 2 November 1917 was inserted into the preamble of this text and certain privileges were granted to the Jews, sc. the formation of an official Jewish Agency to represent them as well as provisions concerning land settlement, Palestinian nationality, the establishment and operation of public works, services and utilities, the development of national resources and the recognition of Hebrew as an official language (along with English and Arabic)

Considering the terms of the mandate and, even more so, the increasing rivalries between Arabs and Jews in Palestine, the British authorities found it difficult to accommodate communities; many official measures antagonised one community, or the other, or both. One of the first such British decisions was to separate Transjordan from Palestine, in 1922, and endow it with a separate administration (to be headed, however, by the same High Commissioner). Relations between the Mandatory and Transjordan were then formalised, in 1928, by a treaty and a Constitutional Law, both patterned on British-ʿIrāḳī ones and confirmed by the Permanent Mandates Commission.

In both Palestine and Transjordan, the British instituted an administration essentially differing from the colonial ones they had established elsewhere. Its legal authority was based on *The Palestine Order in Council, 1922*, providing the British administration in Palestine with executive, legislative and judicial powers. The administration was led by the High Commissioner, assisted by a Chief Secretary and other British heads of various departments. Some of the middle-rank positions and most of the lower ones were staffed by local Arabs and Jews — one of their few and highly competitive meeting grounds. All British efforts to establish joint Arab-Jewish bodies, such as a Legislative Council, were doomed to failure. Even when reluctance was overcome, mutually acceptable terms could not be agreed upon: the Arabs wanted such bodies to reflect their statistical majority, while the Jews wished guarantees that they would not be voted down on every single issue. In consequence, both Arabs and Jews in Palestine developed their own separate systems for self-rule, the latter enjoying greater success in virtually developing "a state within a state" in such domains as education, self-defence, elections, trade unions, religious, social and cultural affairs. Many of these were taken care of within an "Assembly of Israel" (*Kneset Israʾel*) and co-ordinated by its elected "National Council" (*Vaʿad Lʾūmī*). The Arabs, on the other hand, were more divided among rival factions, of which the most important was the "Arab Higher Committee" (*al-Hayʾa al-ʿArabiyya al-ʿulyā*), led by the Muftī al-Ḥādjdj Amīn al-Ḥusaynī [*q.v.* in Suppl.], which succeeded in co-opting a number of Christian Arabs as well.

The 1920-1 and 1929 flare-ups, directed mostly against the Jews, culminated in a large-scale Arab uprising which continued sporadically during 1936-9, against both the Jews and the British. Each was followed by British Commissions of Inquiry, which resulted in official White Papers duly laid before both the British Parliament and the Permanent Mandates Commission. The Royal Commission headed by Lord Peel proposed the partition of Palestine, but this was rejected by both Arabs and Jews. The 1939 White Paper limited Jewish immigration and restricted land sales to Jews, thus appeasing the Palestinian Arabs during the Second World War. After the war, however, it was the Palestinian Jews who acted against the 1939 White Paper policy: in steps initiated by the Jewish Agency and the National Council, they smuggled in Jewish immigrants from amongst the survivors of the Nazi Holocaust, while small groups, disobeying the above bodies, physically attacked British officials and soldiers in Palestine. When neither strong military reprisals nor additional commissions proved to be of any avail, the British, undergoing a process of decolonisation in any case, bowed to local wishes and world opinion. American pressure played a particularly prominent role in this respect, as did the United Nations, before which the issue had been brought in 1947 (and which had decided on partition). Thus the British terminated the mandate for Palestine on 15 May 1948. They had already granted Transjordan formal independence by a treaty concluded in March 1946 and amended in March 1948 in Transjordan's favour (equalising relations, although, in practice, Great Britain remained the new state's preferred ally).

Conclusion: The mandate system was far from a signal success; nor was it a total failure, however. First of all, it succeeded in providing a formula, acceptable to both idealistic statesmen and *Realpolitik* partisans, for dividing the spoils of the First World War; and, secondly, it represented a *modus operandi* for the victorious Allies, chiefly Great Britain and France, to maintain their interests in the Middle East without blatantly contradicting their mutual agreements during the war and their promises to Arabs, Jews and others. On the other hand, it failed to provide either a solution to tensions between local nationalists and the respective Mandatories, or a permanently satisfactory *modus vivendi* among the various local population groups within each of the mandates. It was nationalist pressure, escalating into violence, which hastened termination of the physical presence of the

Mandatories in ʿIrāḳ, Syria and Lebanon, Palestine and Transjordan. The process itself was part of the new world order following the Second World War, one which witnessed decolonisation and the founding of numerous new states, not unrelated to the political, military and economic relinquishing of Great Power status by the British and French. The tensions between Arabs and Kurds, Sunnīs and S͟hīʿīs in ʿIrāḳ, various ethnic and religious coomunities in Syria and Lebanon, Arabs and Jews in Palestine, or Bedouins and other groups in Transjordan, erupting into violence or even war, were among the more unfortunate aspects of the unresolved legacies of the mandates.

It may be that the Mandatories had neither the time nor the opportunity required to tackle these tensions and to set up a lasting accomodation. They were too busy with forging unitary countries and nations in the mandated territories, which had been disparate units in the sprawling Ottoman Empire. Although the Mandatories' fostering of local culture was tempered by a desire to export their own civilisation, they did succeed in encouraging education, setting up a more impartial judiciary, instilling law and order, promoting a national economy, establishing a more adequate taxation system, improving agriculture and irrigation and assisting with public health, roads and communications — all of which led to significant advances towards modernisation.

Bibliography : *Publications issued by the League of Nations*, n.p. [Geneva] 1935, and its supplements list materials about the mandates. Updated bibliographical information is in A.C. de Breycha-Vauthier's *La Société des Nations centre d'études et source d'information*: *ce que contiennent ses publications*, Paris 1937. The League's Permanent Mandates Commission regularly published its *Minutes*, 4 Oct. 1921 to 21 Dec. 1939, which, with their detailed subject-indexes, form a voluminous body of primary sources; so does *The League yearbook*. Among other League publications: League of Nations — Mandates, *Statistical information regarding territories under mandate* (also in French: Société des Nations, Mandats, *Reneignements statistiques relatifs au territoires sous mandat*), Geneva 1933; Nachrichtenabteilung — Sekretariat des Völkerbundes, *Der Völkerbund und das Mandatssystem*, Geneva n.d. [1926]; The League of Nations, *The mandate system*, Geneva 1927; idem, *The mandate system*: *origin, principles, application*, Geneva 1945 (of particular interest, as it summed up the whole issue before dissolving). Considerable archival materials on the Mandates are located in the Public Record Office (London), especially the Foreign Office and Colonial Office series, the various Cabinet files, and the private correspondence and papers of key personalities; and the Ministère des Affaires Etrangères (Paris), particularly the series E-LEVANT 1918-1929 and E-LEVANT 1930-1940, sub-series SYRIE-LIBAN, as well as E-LEVANT, sub-series TURQUIE, vols. 262-77. Many others are located in the states which were formerly mandated territories (see below). Some important American materials, both manuscript and printed, are listed in S.R. Dorr's *Scholar's guide to Washington, D.C. for Middle Eastern studies*, Washington, D.C. 1981. A useful general bibliography on the countries under mandate is the American University of Beirut's *A post-war bibliography of the Near Eastern mandates*: *a preliminary survey of publications on the social sciences dealing with Iraq, Palestine and Trans-Jordan and the Syrian states, 1919-1930*, i-viii, Beirut 1932-6. More updated are Jalal Zuwiyya's *The Near East*, Metuchen, N.J. 1973, and G. Feuer's *Le Moyen Orient contemporain. Guide de recherches*, Paris 1975. For a detailed chronology of events, see M. Mansour, *Arab world. Political and diplomatic history 1900-1967*: *a chronological study*, Washington, D.C. 1972, i (for 1900-41), ii (for 1942-52). A selection of additional materials follows (first the general ones and then by country), with bibliographies and primary materials preceding, respectively, a sample of the more representative among the numerous studies available, scholarly or political-minded.

General (in addition to the sources mentioned above): K.T. Khairallah, *Le problème du Levant*: *les régions arabes libérées — Syrie — Irak — Liban. Lettre ouverte à la Société des Nations*, Paris 1919; H. Morgenthau, *Mandates or war? The New York Times*, 9 Nov. 1919, repr. in Morgenthau's *All in a lifetime*, London 1923, 423-37; *Franco-British convention of December 23, 1920, and certain points connected with the mandates for Syria and the Lebanon, Palestine and Mesopotamia*, London 1921 (= Cmd. 1195); *La Nation Arabe*: *revue mensuelle politique, littéraire, économique et sociale*, Geneva 1933 (monthly of the Syro-Palestinian lobby at the League of Nations); P. Mantoux, *Les délibérations du Conseil des Quatre* (*24 mars-29 juin 1919*). *Notes de l'officier interprète*, i-ii, Paris 1955. See also F. Pollock, *The League of Nations*, London 1920; A. Sweetser, *The League of Nations at Work*, New York 1920, 122-34 ("Mandates"). A. Acito, *L'Oriente arabo*: *Odierne questioni politiche (Siria — Palestina — Libano — Irak*), Milan n.d. [1921]; G. Cioriceanu, *Les mandats internationaux*, Paris 1921; L. Bourgeois, *L'oeuvre de la Société des Nations (1920-1923)*, Paris 1923, 303 ff.; Th. H. Dickinson, *The United States and the League*, New York 1923, ch. 8; P. Furukaki, *Les mandats internationaux de la Société des Nations*, Lyons 1923; J. de V. Loder, *The truth about Mesopotamia, Palestine and Syria*, London 1923, 135 ff. ("Mandates, treaties and conclusions"); P. Pic, *Le régime du mandat d'après le traité de Versailles*: *son application dans le Proche Orient*: *Mandats français en Syrie, anglais en Palestine et Mésopotamie*, in *Revue Générale de Droit International Public* (Paris), xxx (1923), 321-71; A. Vallini, *I mandati internazionali della Società delle Nazioni*, Milan 1923; Ch. Ayoub, *Les mandats orientaux*, Paris 1924, 87-182; M. Bileski, *Die entwicklung des Mandatssystem*, in *Zeitschrift für Völkerrecht* (Breslau), xiii/1 (1924), 77-102; G. Menassa, *Les mandats A et leur application en Orient: il faut convoquer les assemblées constituentes*, Paris 1924, 54 ff.; A. Millot, *Les mandats internationaux*: *étude sur l'application de l'article 22 du Pacte de la Société des Nations*, Paris 1924; W.R. Batsell, *The United States and the system of mandates*, Worcester, Mass. 1925; L.B. Guryevič, *Siriya, Palyestina, Myesopotamiya (mandatniye strani*): *političyeskiy očyerk*, Leningrad 1925; J. Stoyanovsky, *La théorie générale des mandats internationaux*, Paris 1925; Rās͟hid Ṭabāra, *al-Intidāb wa-rūḥ al-siyāsa al-Inklīziyya*, Beirut 1925; W. Schneider, *Das völkerrechtliche Mandat in historisch-dogmatischer Darstellung*, Stuttgart 1926; Freda White, *Mandates*, London 1926, 7-82; V.A. Kuri, *L'évolution du mandat A*, Paris 1927; M. Pernot, *Deux expériences: L'Irak et la Syrie*, in *Revue des Deux Mondes* (Paris), xcvii (1 April 1927), 530-59; D.F.W. van Rees, *Les mandats internationaux: le contrôle international de l'administration mandataire*, Paris 1927; idem, *Les mandats internationaux*: *les principles généraux du régime des mandats*, Paris 1928; H. Gilchrist, *Imperialism and the mandates system*, New York 1928; J.M. Gortázar, *Los man-*

datos internacionales en la política colonial, Madrid 1928; F. Gsell-Trümpi, *Zur rechtlichen Natur der Völkerbundmandate*, Glarus 1928; E.G. Mohr, *Die Frage der Souveränität in den Mandatsgebieten*, Leipzig 1928; L. Palacios, *Los mandatos internacionales de la Sociedad de Naciones*, Madrid 1928, 161-287; *La politique du mandat français: Irak et Syrie*, in *L'Asie Française* (Paris) xxviii (Feb. 1928), 60-7; Sch. Milkonowicki, *Das Mandatssystem in Völkerbund mit besonderer Berücksichtigung der A-Mandate*, Berlin 1929; R. Pahl, *Das völkerrechtliche Kolonial-Mandat*, Berlin 1929; E. Topf, *Die Staatenbildungen in der arabischen Teilen der Türkei seit dem Weltkriege nach Entstehung, Bedeutung und Lebensfähigkeit*, Hamburg 1929; Freda White, *The mandate system*, in J. Epstein (ed.), *Ten years' life of the League of Nations*, London 1929, 148-56; N. Bentwich, *The mandates system*, London 1930; D.C. Blaisdell, *Representation of minorities and guarantees of minority rights in the former Ottoman Empire, Cyprus, Egypt, the Ottoman Sanjak of Lebanon and the mandates of Syria and the Lebanon, Irak, and Palestine*, New York, 1930; B. Gerig, *The open door and the mandates system: a study of economic equality before and since the establishment of the mandates system*, London 1930, chs. 4-8; S.F. Kyečyekʾyan, *Mandati ligi natsiy v stranakh Arabskogo Vostoka*, Baku 1930; A.A. Margalith, *The international mandates*, Baltimore 1930, esp. 124-44; D.P. Myers, *Handbook of the League of Nations since 1920*, Boston 1930, 192-207; S.D. Myres, *The Permanent Mandates Commission and the administration of mandates*, in *Southwestern Political and Social Science Quarterly* (Austin, Texas), xi/3 (Dec. 1930), 1-34; H. Roth, *Das Kontrollsystem der Völkerbundmandate*, Berlin 1930; Q. Wright, *Mandates under the League of Nations*, Chicago 1930; E. Jung, *Les Arabes et l'Islam en face des nouvelles Croisades et Palestine et Sionisme*, Paris 1931; E. Marcus, *Zur Theorie und Praxis des Mandatssystem*, in *Zeitschrift für Völkerrecht*, xvi/2 (1931), 314-30; A. Peltzer, *Die völkerrechtlichen Mandate und die Mandatskommission*, Würzburg 1931; F.M. Zeineddine, *Le régime du contrôle des mandats de la S.D.N.*, Paris 1932; A. Giannini, *I mandati internazionali*, Rome 1933; K. Grunwald, *Le finanze statali dei territori sotto mandato nel Vicino Oriente durante il loro primo decennio*, Rome 1933; L. Jovelet, *L'évolution sociale et politique des 'Pays Arabes' (1930-1933)*, in *REI*, vii/4 (1933), 425-644; J. Achkar, *La France et l'Angleterre dans le Proche-Orient. L'évolution politique de la Syrie et du Liban, de la Palestine et de l'Irak*, Lyons 1934; L. Comisetti, *Mandats et souveraineté*, Paris n.d. [1934], 77-153; J. Alcandre, *Le mandat colonial: analyse juridique et critique politique*, Paris 1935, 43 ff.; F. Fischer, *Die formelle Natur der völkerrechtlichen Mandate insbesondere ihre Verteilung, Endigung und Änderung*, Tübingen 1935; E. Yapou, *De la non-discrimination en matière économique notamment en pays de protectorat et sous mandat*, Paris 1935; C.A. Boutant, *les mandats internationaux*, Paris 1936, esp. 93-114; Ali Akbar Akhavi, *L'échec de la S.D.N. dans l'organisation pratique de la paix: ses causes, son avenir*, Paris 1937; N. Feinberg, *La jurisdiction et la jurisprudence de la cour permanente de justice internationale en matière de mandats et de minorités*, Paris 1937, 10 ff.; N. Macaulay, *Mandates: reasons, results, remedies*, London 1937; H.H. Cumming, *Franco-British rivalry in the post-war Near East: the decline of French influence*, London 1938, 68-120; [A.] von Freytagh-Loringhoven, *Das Mandatsrecht in den deutschen Kolonien: Quellen und Materialien*, Munich 1938; J. Pichon, *Le partage de l'Orient*, Paris 1938, 184 ff, 253 ff.; G. Venturini, *Il protettorato internazionale*, Milan 1939; E. E. Reynolds, *The League experiment*, London 1940; *Pays sous mandat*, n.p. [Paris] 1943, mimeographed (= no. 2508 in the library of the Centre des Hautes Etudes Administratives sur l'Asie et l'Afrique Modernes, Paris); P. de Azcárate, *League of Nations and national minorities: an experiment*, Washington, D.C. 1945, index; R. W. Logan, *The Senate and the Versailles mandate system*, Washington, D.C. 1945 H.D. Hall, *Mandates, dependencies and trusteeship*, Washington, D.C. 1948; M.V. Seton-Williams, *Britain and the Arab states: a survey of Anglo-Arab relations, 1920-1948*, London 1948, index; J. Kimche, *Seven fallen pillars: the Middle East 1915-1950*, London 1950, index; E.B. Haas, *The reconciliation of conflicting colonial policy aims: acceptance of the League of Nations mandate system*, in *International Organization* (Boston), vi/4 (Nov. 1952), esp. 525-36; A. Homont, *L'application du régime de la tutelle aux territories sous mandat*, in *Revue Juridique et Politique de l'Union Française* (Paris), vi/2 (April-June 1952), 149-88; C.L. Upthegrove, *Empire by mandate*, New York 1954, chs. 5-6; R.N. Chowdhuri, *International mandate and trusteeship systems: a comparative study*, The Hague 1955, esp. 103-12; J. Mulenzi, *La tutelle internationale et le problème des unions administratives*, Louvain and Paris 1955, 11 ff.; E.F. Çelik, *Manda ve vesayet rejimleri hakkında milletlerarası adalet divanının istişarî mutalaâsı*, in *İstanbul Üniversitesi Hukuk Fakültesi, Muammer Reşit Seviğ'e armağan*, Istanbul 1956, 263-75; R. Furon, *Le Proche Orient*, Paris 1957, 178 ff. ("Le système des mandats"); F.P. Walters, *A history of the League of Nations*, London 1960, index; J.A. DeNovo, *American interests and policies in the Middle East, 1900-1939*, Minneapolis 1963, index; L. Evans, *United States policy and the partition of Turkey, 1914-1924*, Baltimore 1965, 89-107 ("Establishing the mandate system"), 292-322 ("The United States and the mandates"); Djalāl Yaḥyā, *al-ʿĀlam al-ʿArabī al-ḥadīth: al-fatra bayn al-ḥarbayn al-ʿālamiyyatayn*, Cairo 1966; B. Dexter, *The years of opportunity: the League of Nations, 1920-1966*, New York 1967, index; M.A. Gannon, *The influence of the Permanent Mandates Commission in the administration of the class A mandate*, unpubl. Ph.D. diss., St. John's Univ., New York 1969; J. Nevakivi, *Britain, France and the Arab Middle East, 1914-1920*, London 1969, ch. 12 ("San Remo and after"); S.K. Garrett, *Aspects of Anglo-French rivalry over the question of the Middle East mandates*, unpubl. M.A. thesis, Keele Univ. (U.K.) 1970; H.K. Jacobson, *Quincy Wright's study of the mandates system*, in *Journal of Conflict Resolution* (Ann Arbor, Mich.), xiv/4 (Dec. 1970), 499-503; E. Monroe, *Round Table and the Middle Eastern peace settlement, 1917-1922*, in *The Round Table* (London), 1x/240 (Nov. 1970), 479-90; G. Scott, *The rise and fall of the League of Nations*, New York 1973; E. Bendiner, *A time for angels: the tragicomic history of the League of Nations*, New York 1975, index; Yaacov Shimoni, *Mĕdīnōt ʿArav: pirḳey hisṭōriyya mĕdīnīt* (Hebrew, *The Arab states: chapters of political history*), Tel-Aviv 1977, index; J.A. Joyce, *Broken star: the story of the League of Nations (1919-1939)*, Swansea 1978; A.J. Crozier, *The establishment of the mandates system 1919-25: some problems created by the Paris Peace Conference*, in *Jnal. of Contemporary History* (London), xiv/3 (July 1979), 483-513.

For the projected mandate over a part of Turkish Anatolia, see Armenian National Union of America, *Should America accept a mandate for Armenia?*, New York 1919. G. van Horn Morseley, *Mandatory over Armenia*, Washington, D.C. 1920 (= 66th Congress, 2nd session, Senate Document no. 281); J.

Harbord, *American military mission to Armenia*, in *International Conciliation* (New York), 151 (June 1920); Halide Edib, *The Turkish ordeal: being the further memoirs of Halide Edib*, New York 1928, 15-6; Gazi Mustafa Kemal, *Nutuk*, i, Istanbul 1934, 5, 64, 80-2; Ahmed Emin Yalman, *Turkey in my time*, Norman, Oklahoma 1956, 71-9; Uluğ İğdemir (ed.), *Sivas Kongresi tutanakları*, Ankara 1969, index. See also E. Blyth, *Australia and the mandate for Armenia*, in *The Near East* (London), xvii/477 (24 June 1920), 903-4; *No mandate for Armenia*, in *Current History* (New York), xii/4 (July 1920), 710-3; Ph.M. Brown, *The mandate over Armenia*, in *American Jnal. of International Law*, xiv (1920), 396-7; Vehbi Cem Aşkun, *Sivas Kongresi*, Istanbul 1963; G. Jäschke, *Ein amerikanisches Mandat für die Turkei?* in *WI*, N.S., viii (1963), 219-34; Th. A. Bryson, *Woodrow Wilson, The Senate, public opinion and the American mandate, 1919-20*, unpubl. Ph.D. diss., Univ. of Georgia 1965, 40 ff.; G. Jäschke, *Ein Angebot Mustafa Kemals an die Engländer vom November 1918*, in *WI*, N.S., x (1965), 69; J.B. Gidney, *A mandate for Armenia*, n.p. [Kent, Ohio] 1967, 168-255; Mahmut Goloğlu, *Sivas Kongresi*, Ankara 1969, 87-97; Mine Erol, *Türkiye' de Amerikan mandası meselesi 1919-1920*, Giresun 1972; S.L. Meray, *Lozan'ın bir öncüsü: Prof. Ahmet Selâhattin Bey*, Ankara 1976, 11-20; İnci Enginün, *Halide Edib Adıvar'ın in eserlerinde Doğu ve Batı meselesi*, Istanbul 1978, 44-51; H.A. Reed, *Atatürk, the Turkish nationalists and the United States: a neglected prospect for peace in 1919*, in *Jnal. of the American Institute for the Study of Middle Eastern Civilization* (Kew Gardens, N.Y.), i/3-4 (Autumn-Winter 1980-1), 99-111; Secil Akgün, *General Harbord'un Anadolu gezisi*, Istanbul 1981.

ʿIrāḳ. For bibliographies, see *Publications issued by the League of Nations*, 159, 172-3, 190; National Library, Cairo, *A bibliography of works about Iraq*, Cairo 1960; Abdul Jabbar Abdulrahman, *A bibliography of Iraq*, Bag͟hdād 1977. The Permanent Mandates Commission's *Minutes*, 1921-39, are important, as are the Société des Nations' *La question de Mossoul à la 35me session du Conseil de la Société des Nations*, Lausanne 1925, and its *L'activité politique*, Geneva n.d., ii, 7-53 ("Affaire de Mossoul"). For archival material in ʿIrak, see references in Diana Grimwood-Jones *et alii* (eds.), *Arab Islamic bibliography*, Hassocks, Sussex and Atlantic Highland, N.J. 1977, 194. The draft of the text of the mandate was printed as a British parliamentary paper, *Draft mandates for Mesopotamia and Palestine as submitted to the approval of the League of Nations*, London 1921 (= Cmd. 1176). The final text of the mandate may be found in *ibid.*, London 1921 (= Cmd. 1500). It was reprinted several times, e.g. in Q. Wright, *Mandates....*, 593 ff. Instead of the mandate, a series of treaties was entered into by the British and ʿIrāḳīs. The most important of these, published as preliminary papers and presented to the League of Nations (and approved by it) are the following: *Iraq. Treaty with King Feisal*, London 1922 (= Cmd. 1757); *ʿIraq. Protocol of the 30th of April, 1923 and the agreements subsidiary to the treaty with King Feisal, signed 10th of October, 1922*, London 1924 (= Cmd. 2120); *Treaty of alliance between Great Britain and Irak signed at Bagdad, October 10, 1922; and protocol to treaty of alliance between Great Britain and Irak of October 10, 1922, signed at Bagdad, April 30, 1923*, London 1925 (= Treaty Series no. 17 (1925), Cmd. 2370); *ʿIraq. Treaty with King Feisal, signed at Bagdad, 13th january, 1926, with explanatory note*, London 1926 (= Cmd. 2587); *Treaty between the United Kingdom and Iraq regarding the duration of the treaty between the United Kingdom and Irak of October 10, 1922, signed at Bagdad, January 13, 1926*, London 1926 (= Treaty Series, no. 10 (1926), Cmd. 2662); *ʿIraq. Treaty between the United Kingdom and ʿIraq, signed at London, December 14, 1927*, London 1927 (= Cmd. 2998); *Treaty of alliance between Iraq and Great Britain, signed on 30th June, 1930*, Bag͟hdād 1930, whose Arabic title is *Muʿāhadat al-taḥāluf bayn al-ʿIrāḳ wa-Barīṭāniya al-ʿUẓmā*. Of special relevance is yet another British parliamentary paper, *ʿIraq. Papers relating to ʿIraq of the principles of article 22 of the Covenant of the League of Nations*, London 1925 (= Cmd. 2317). The British official reports, first entitled *Report on ʿIraq administration*, were later issued annually by the Colonial Office, as *Report by his Britannic Majesty's Government to the Council of the League of Nations on the administration of ʿIraq*, London 1920-31. A general 330-page report by the Colonial Office appeared as *Special report by His Majesty's Government in the United Kingdom of Great Britain and Northern Ireland to the Council of the League of Nations on the progress of ʿIraq during the period 1920-1931*, London 1931 (= Colonial no. 58). Special documents were published as Command Papers, which included *Reports to the Council of the League of Nations*. Several relevant documents appeared in Arabic in the officials *al-Waḳāʾiʿ al-ʿIrāḳiyya* (published since 1922), then in Fārūḳ Ṣāliḥ al-ʿUmar's *al-Muʿāhadāt al-ʿIrāḳiyya wa-at͟haruhā fi 'l-siyāsa al-dāk͟hiliyya*, Bag͟hdād 1977. Other primary sources are Fahmī al-Mudarris, *Maḳālāt siyāsiyya, taʾrīk͟hiyya, id͟jtimāʿiyya*, Bag͟hdād 1351/1932, esp. 117 ff.; H. Bowman, *Middle-East window*, London 1942, 163-248; Mudīriyyat al-Diʿāya al-ʿĀmma, *Fayṣal b. Ḥusayn fī k͟huṭabihi wa-aḳwālihi*, Bag͟hdād 1945, 231-325; C.J. Edmonds, *Kurds, Turks and Arabs: politics, travel and research in Near-Eastern Iraq, 1919-1925*, London 1957, chs. 26-7 ("The Mosul Commission"); ʿAbd al-ʿAzīz al-Ḳaṣṣāb, *Min d͟hikrayātī*, Beirut 1962; Muḥammad Mahdī Kubba, *Mud͟hakkirātī fī ṣamīm al-aḥdāt͟h, 1918-1958*, Beirut 1965, 26ff.; Ṭaha al-Hās͟himī, *Mud͟hakkirāt 1919-1943*. Beirut 1967; Abū K͟haldūn Sāṭīʿ al-Ḥuṣarī, *Mud͟hakkirātī fi 'l-ʿIrāḳ*, 1921-1941, i, Beirut 1967; Tawfīḳ al-Suwaydī, *Mud͟hakkirātī: niṣf ḳarn min taʾrīk͟h al-ʿIrāḳ wa 'l-ḳaḍiyya al-ʿArabiyya*, n.p. [Beirut] n.d. [1969], 53 ff. See also Khairallah, *Le problème....*; Acito, 49 ff.; D.C. Lee, *The mandate for Mesopotamia and the principle of trusteeship in English law*, London 1921; Muḥammad al-Mahdī al-Baṣīr, *Taʾrīk͟h al-ḳaḍiyya al-ʿIrāḳiyya*, Bag͟hdād 1342/1923, 325-609; B.H. Bourdillon, *The political situation in Iraq*, in *Jnal. of the British Institute of International Affairs* (London), iii (Nov. 1924), 273-87; Menassa, *Les mandats A ...*, 204-15; J. van Ess, *The Mesopotamia mandate*, in *MW*, xiv/1 (Jan. 1924), 54-7; R. Coke, *The heart of the Middle East*, London 1925, 216 ff.; Guryevič, 13 ff.; F. Hesse, *Die Mosul Frage*, Berlin 1925; *La question de Mossoul et la signature du traité d'armistice de Moudros, 30 Octobre 1918 au 1er Mars 1925*, Constantinople 1925; V.A. Gurko-Kryadz͟hin, *Arabskiy Vostok i impyerializm*, Moscow 1926, 104-42; F. White, *Mandates*, 38-61; Q. Wright, *The government of Iraq*, in *The American Political Science Review*, xx/1 (Nov. 1926), 743-60 (tr. by Ikrām al-Rukābī as *Ḥukūmat al-ʿIrāḳ*, n.p. n.d. [1345/1927]); Ch.A. Hooper, *L'Irak et la Société des Nations: application à l'Irak des dispositions de l'article 22 du Pacte de la Société des Nations*, Paris 1927, 13-97; idem, *The constitutional law of Iraq*, Bag͟hdād 1928; P.E.J. Bomli, *L'affaire de Mossoul*, Amsterdam 1929; Mikonowicki,

The mandates system, 52 ff., 173-9; Blaisdell, *Representation...*, 47-53; A. Giannini, *La costituzione dell' Irak*, in *OM*, x/11 (Nov. 1930), 525-46; Kyečyekʾyan, *Mandati ...*, 56-62; H. Kohn, *Das Königreich Irak: sein erstes Jahrzehnt*, in *Zeitschrift für Politik* (Berlin), xx/4 (July 1930), 246-84; Q. Wright, *Mandates ...*, index; Muḥammad D̲j̲amīl Bayham, *al-Intidābān fi 'l-ʿIrāḳ wa-Sūriya: Inklitrā-Fransā*, Sidon 1931, 42-95; H.U. Hoepli, *England im Nahen Osten: das Königreich Irak und die Mossulfrage*, Erlangen 1931, 63-159; A. de Farkas, *Irak Királyság* (in Hungarian: *The Kingdom of ʿIrak*), Paris 1931; G. Ambrosini, *Irak, Gran Bretagna e Società delle Nazioni: considerazioni sulla fine del mandato*, in *Atti della R. Academia di Scienze, Lettere e Belle Arti di Palermo*, xviii/1 (1932), 3-34; L.H. Evans, *The emancipation of Iraq from the mandates system*, in *The American Political Science Review*, xxvi/6 (Dec. 1932), 1024-49; Abdel Halim El Gammal, *La fin des mandats internationaux et l'expérience irakienne*, Dijon 1932; W.L. Williams, *The state of Iraq: a mandatory attains independence*, in *Foreign Policy Reports* (New York), viii/16 (12 Oct. 1932), 184-94; N. Davidson, *The termination of the Iraq mandate*, in *International Affairs* (London), xii/1 (Jan.-Feb. 1933), 60-78 (tr. by ʿAd̲j̲d̲j̲ād̲j̲ Nuwayḥiṣ as *al-ʿIrāḳ aw al-dawla al-d̲j̲adīda*, Jerusalem 1351/1932). R. Tritonj, *La fine del mandato sull' Iraq è una preoccupazione per l'Italia*, in *OM*, xiii/4 (Apr. 1933), 169-77; (Mrs.) Steuart Erskine, *King Faisal of ʿIraq: an authorised and authentic study*, London 1933, 119 ff.; Aounoullah El-Djabri, *L'évolution et la fin du mandat en Irak*, Geneva 1934; Chafik Djeroudi, *Application des mandats internationaux à l'Irak*, Toulouse 1934; Amīn al-Rayḥānī, *Fayṣal al-awwal*, Beirut 1934, 28-211; E. Main, *Iraq from mandate to independence*, London 1935, 78-112; al-Sayyid ʿAbd al-Razzāḳ al-Ḥasanī, *al-ʿIrāḳ fī dawray al-iḥtilāl wa 'l-intidāb*, i-ii, Sidon 1354-7/1935-8; Boutant, *Les mandats....*, 95-9; H.A. Foster, *The making of the modern Iraq*, London 1936, 87 ff.; ʿUmar Abū al-Naṣr, *al-ʿIrāḳ al-d̲j̲adīd*, n.p. 1937; P.W. Ireland, *Iraq: a study in political development*, London 1937, 201-453; Rachad Kodsi, *Le mandat anglais sur l'Irak: son origine, son évolution, sa fin*, Strasbourg 1937; G. Antonius, *The Arab awakening: the story of the Arab national movement*, London 1938, 358-68; W.H. Ritsher, *Criteria of capacity for independence*, Jerusalem 1934, 15-40 (tr. into Arabic as *Maḳāyīs li 'l-kafāʾa li 'l-istiḳlāl*, Beirut 1938; Muḥammad ʿAbd al-Fattāḥ al-Yāfī, *al-ʿIrāḳ bayn inḳilābayn*, Beirut 1938; Hassan Aaref, *La Grande-Bretagne en Égypte et en Irak, étude comparée*, Beirut 1939; F. Cataluccio, *Storia del nazionalismo arabo*, Milan 1939; J. Robinson *et alii*, *Were the minority treaties a failure?* New York 1943, index; *Strani Blidz̲h̲nyego i Sryednyego Vostoka*, n.p. [Moscow] 1944, 100-18; al-Sayyid ʿAbd al-Razzāḳ al-Ḥasanī, *Taʾrīk̲h̲ al-ʿIrāḳ al-siyāsī al-ḥadīt̲h̲*, i-iii, Sidon 1367/1948; Seton-Williams, 17-47; Kimche, 83-99; Āl Firʿawn, *al-Ḥaḳāʾik al-nāṣiʿa fi 'l-t̲h̲awra al-ʿIrāḳiyya sanat 1920 wa-natāʾid̲j̲ihā*, Bag̲h̲dād 1371/1952; S.H. Longrigg, *Iraq 1900-1950: a political, social and economic history*, London 1953, chs. 4-7; Upthegrove, *Empires...*,, 125-42; J.M. Salih, *Anglo-Iraq relations (1925-1932)*, unpubl. Ph.D. diss., Univ. of Chicago 1957; al-Sayyid ʿAbd al-Razzāḳ al-Ḥasanī, *al-ʿIrāḳ fī ẓill al-muʿāhadāt*[2], Sidon 1377/1958 (for the years 1920-30); Longrigg and F. Stoakes, *Iraq*, London 1958, 78-94; Lord Birdwood, *Nuri al-Said: a study in Arab leadership*, London 1959, index; E. Kedourie, *Réflexions sur l'histoire du royaume d'Irak 1921-1958*, in *Orient* (Paris), xi (1959), 55 ff.; M. Montserrat, *L'affaire de Mossoul*, in *ibid.*, ix (1959), 23-30; J. Morris, *The Hashemite kings*, London and New York 1959, 67-86; Ali Ghalib al-Ani, *La vie parlementaire en Irak (de 1921 à 1957)*, Neuchâtel 1960, 17 ff.; ʿAbd al-Raḥmān al-Bazzāz, *Muḥāḍarāt min al-iḥtilāl ḥattā al-istiḳlāl*[2], n.p. [Cairo] 1960, 26 ff.; Aḥmad Saʿīd, *ʿUrūs̲h̲ ṣināʿa Briṭāniyya*, Cairo n.d. [1960], 17 ff.; G. de Gaury, *Three kings in Baghdad, 1921-1958*, London 1961, 15-93; A.A. al-Marayati, *A diplomatic history of modern Iraq*, New York 1961, 12 ff.; J.A. DeNovo, 347-54; M. Gdański, *Arabski wschód: historia, gospodarka, polityka*, (in Polish, *The Arab world: history, economics, politics*), Warsaw 1963, 212-28; *Novyeys̲h̲aya istoriya stran Azii i Afriki*, Moscow 1965, 397 ff.; F. Cataluccio, *La questione arabe dopo la prima guerra mondiale: i mandati britannici in Iraq e Palestina*, in *Archivio Strorico Italiano* (Florence), cxxv (1967), 291-351, 443-87; Ph.A. Marr, *Uasin al-Hashimi: the rise and fall of a nationalist*, unpubl. Ph.D. diss., Harvard Univ, 1967; *Novyeys̲h̲aya istoriya Arabskik̲h̲ stran (1917-1966)*, Moscow 1968, 159-73; Gannon, *The influence...*, 293-332; Rasheeduddin Khan, *Mandate and monarchy in Iraq*, in *IC*, xliii/3 (July 1969), 189-213: xliii/4 (Oct. 1969), 255-76; A.M. Myentyes̲h̲as̲h̲vili, *Irak v godi Angliyskogo mandata*, Moscow 1969, 90-248; Salih Tuğ, *İslam ülkelerinde anayasa hareketleri (xiv ve xx. asırlar)*, Istanbul 1969, 294 ff.; D.E.B. Fuleihan, *The development of British policy in Iraq from 1914 to* 1926, unpubl. Ph.D. diss., London Univ. 1970; A.F. Fyedčyenko, *Irak v bor'bye za nyezavisimost' (1917-1969)*, Moscow 1970, 13-47; A.S. Klieman, *Foundations of British policy in the Arab world: the Cairo conference of 1921*, Baltimore 1970, 139-70; H.J.F. Mejcher, *The birth of the mandate idea and its fulfilment in Iraq up to 1926*, unpubl. Ph.D. diss., Oxford Univ. 1970; Ayad al-Qazzaz, *Power elite in Iraq, 1920-1958*, in *MW* lxi/4 (Oct. 1971), 267-83; J.Sh. Yaphe, *The Arab revolt in Iraq of 1920*, unpubl. Ph.D. diss., Univ. of Illinois, Urbana 1972; Khadim Hashim Niama, *Anglo-Iraqi relations during the mandate*, unpubl. Ph.D. diss., Univ. College of Wales 1974; G. Warner, *Iraq and Syria in 1941*, London 1974, 78-121; Zāhiya Ḳaddūra, *Taʾrīk̲h̲ al-ʿArab al-ḥadīt̲h̲*, Beirut 1975, 134 ff.; Kh. S. Husry, *King Faysal I and Arab unity, 1930-33*, in *Jnal of Contemporary History*, x/2 (April 1975), 323-40; N.T. al-Hasso, *Administrative politics in the Middle East: the case of monarchical Iraq, 1920-1958*, unpubl. Ph.D. diss., Univ of Texas, Austin 1976; Habib Ishow, *L'enseignement technique en Irak du mandat à la première décennie de la république*, in *L'Afrique et l'Asie Modernes* (Paris), cviii (1976), 19ff.; G.N. Landenmann, *Establishment of the Iraqi government in 1921*, unpubl. Ph.D. diss., Johns Hopkins Univ., Baltimore 1976; N.D. Oganyesyan, *Natsional'no-osvobodityel'noye dvidz̲h̲yeniye v Irakye (1917-1958 gg.)*, Erevan 1976, 139-238; Sarah Reguer, *Winston Churchill and the shaping of the Middle East, 1919-1922*, unpubl. Ph.D. diss., Columbia Univ., New York 1976, 254-82; P. Sluglett, *Britain in Iraq, 1914-1932*, London 1976, 67-299; H. Mejcher, *Iraq's external relations, 1921-26*, in *Middle Eastern Studies*, xiii/3 (Oct. 1977), 340-58; Edith and E.F. Penrose, *Iraq: international relations and national development*, London 1978, 41-78; W.A. Stivers, *The mastery of Iraq: Anglo-American politics of primacy and oil, 1918-1930*, unpubl. Ph.D. diss., Johns Hopkins Univ. 1978; Abbas Kelidar (ed.), *The integration of modern Iraq*, London 1979, index; N.W. Spencer, *The diplomatic history of Iraq, 1920-1932*, unpubl. Ph.D.

diss., Univ. of Utah, Salt Lake City 1979; D. Pool. *From elite to class: the transformation of Iraqi leadership, 1920-1939*, in *IJMES*, xii/3 (Nov. 1980), 331-50; P.J. Beck, *"A tedious and perilous controversy": Britain and the settlement of the Mosul dispute, 1918-1926*, in *MES*, xvii/2 (Apr. 1981), 256-76; L.I. Yusupov, *Natsional'-no-osvobodityel'naya bor'ba i lityeratura Iraka v pyeriod medzhdu mirovimi voynami*, in *Arabskiye strani: istoriya i sovryemyennost'*, Moscow 1981, 241-7; Amīn Saʿīd, *al-Thawra al-ʿarabiyya al-kubrā*, ii/2, Cairo n.d., 1 ff.; Muḥammad Ṣubayḥ, *Fayṣal al-awwal*, n.p. n.d.

Syria and Lebanon. For bibliographies, see *Publications issued by the League of Nations*, 158-60, 172-5; R. Patai, *Jordan, Lebanon and Syria: an annotated bibliography*, New Haven, Conn. 1957; National Library, Cairo, *A bibliographical list of works about Syria*², Cairo 1965; C.H. Bleaney (ed.), *Modern Syria: an introduction to the literature*, Durham n.d. [1978]; Shereen Khairallah, *Lebanon*, Oxford 1979; Maurice Saliba, *Index Libanicus: Analytical survey of publications in European languages on Lebanon*, Beirut 1979; The Permanent mandates Commission's *Minutes*, 1921-32, are important, as is the Ligue des Nations, *La France en Syrie et au Liban: le mandat devant les faits*, n.p. n.d. [1921] (documents sent to the League and to France's High Commissioner). For the text of the mandate, see League of Nations, *Mandate for Syria and the Lebanon*, Geneva 1922. This has been reprinted several times, e.g. by Q. Wright, *Mandates...*, 607 ff., and Hourani, *Syria and Lebanon*, 308-14. For archival materials in Syria and Lebanon, see the references in Grimwood-Jones *et alii* (eds.), 1932; and, for Lebanon, M.H. Chéhab, *Les archives historiques du Liban*, in A. Raymond (ed.), *Les Arabes par leurs archives*, Paris 1976, 57-62. Essential sources are also the official Haut Commissariat de la République Française en Syrie et au Liban, *La Syrie et le Liban en 1922*, Beirut 1922, 46 ff., followed by République Française, Ministère des Affaires Etrangères, *Rapport à la Société des Nations sur la situation de la Syrie et du Liban*, annual, 1924-39 (for 1923-38). This is supplemented by Haut Commissariat de la République Française en Syrie et au Liban, *Recueil des actes administratifs du Haut Commissariat de la République Française en Syrie et au Liban*, i-xiv, Beirut 1919-32. An official general survey of the mandate's early years is [France, Haut Commissariat en Syrie et au Liban], *La Syrie et le Liban sous l'occupation et le mandat français, 1919-1927*, Nancy n.d., 26 ff. Useful collections of documents are Alfred Tabet (ed.), *Les actes diplomatiques intéressant les États du Levant sous mandat français*, Beirut 1935; [France] Ministère de l'Information, Directions des Informations, *La France et les États du Levant*, Paris 1945 (= Notes Documentaires et Études, 74, Série Internationale, xxvi); the magazine *Correspondance d'Orient*'s *Le Livre jaune sur la crise syrienne et libanaise*, Paris 1945; and Munīr Taḳī al-Dīn (ed.), *al-Djalāʾ: wathāʾiḳ khaṭīra tunshar li-awwal marra takshif al-niḳāb ʿan asrār djalāʾ al-ḳuwwāt al-adjnabiyya ʿām 1946*, Beirut 1946. Other primary sources are Adib Pacha, *Le Liban après la guerre*, Paris 1918-19; Comité Central Syrien, *La Syrie devant la conférence: mémoire à Monsieur Georges Clemenceau... et à MM. les délégués des puissances aliées et associées à cette conférence*, Paris 1919; G. Gautherot, La France en Syrie et en Cilicie, Courbevoie, Seine, 1920; Association de la Jeunesse syrienne, *Ce que tout Français doit savoir de la Syrie*, Paris 1922; Catroux, *Le mandat français en Syrie, son application à l'état de Damas*, in *Revue Politique et Parlementaire* (Paris), cx (10 Feb. 1922), 199-227; Emir Chekib Arslan, *Syrian opposition to French rule*, in *Current History* (New York), xx/2, (May 1924), 239-48; P. La Mazière, *Partant pour la Syrie*, Paris 1926; J. Harvey, *With the Foreign Legion in Syria*, London n.d. [1928]; Alice Pouleau, *A Damas sous les bombes: journal d'une Française pendant la révolte syrienne, 1924-1926*, Yvetot n.d. [1928]; E. Rabbath, *L'évolution politique de la Syrie sous mandat*, Paris 1928, 47-277; R. de Beauplan, *Où va la Syrie? le mandat sous les cèdres*, Paris 1929, 44-220; V. de Saint Point, *La vérité sur la Syrie par un témoin*, Paris 1929; *Dix ans de mandat. L'oeuvre française en Syrie et au Liban*, Paris 1931; A. Keyali, *Réponse à M. Ponsot*, Haut-Commissaire de la République Française en Syrie et au Liban, au sujet de ses déclarations à la Commission des Mandats de la Société des Nations, Aleppo 1933; ʿAbd al-Raḥmān al-Shahbandar, *al-Thawra al-Sūriyya al-waṭaniyya*, Damascus 1352/1933; Madjīd Khaddūrī, *al-Masʾala al-Sūriyya*, n.p. 1934, 92-176; E. Rabbath, *Unité syrienne et devenir arabe*, Paris 1937; Jérôme et Jean Tharaud, *Alerte en Syrie*! Paris 1937, 1-108; Office National Arabe de recherches et d'informations, *Syrie 1938: la situation en Syrie après la conclusion du traité franco-syrien*, Damascus n.d. [1938-9]; *La proclamation de l'indépendance de la Syrie*, Damascus 1941; Freya Stark, *Letters from Syria*, London 1942, 19-191 (for 1927-9); M. Chiha, *Liban d'aujourd'hui (1942)*, Beirut 1949; R. Pearse, *Three years in the Levant*, London 1949, 1-178; G. Puaux, *Deux années au Levant: souvenirs de Syrie et du Liban, 1939-1940*, Paris 1952; Général Catroux, *Deux missions en Moyen-Orient (1919-1922)*, Paris 1958, 1-176; *Mudhakkirāt Sāmī Bek al-Ṣulḥ*, n.p. n.d. [1958-9], 39ff.; E. Spears, *Fulfilment of a mission: the Spears mission to Syria and Lebanon, 1941-1944*, London 1977. See also Khairallah, *Le problème* ...; Acito, 31 ff., 59 ff.; Testis, *L'oeuvre de la France en Syrie*, in *Revue des Deux Mondes* (Paris), xci (15 Feb. 1921), 801-40; (1 March 1921), 97-136; XXX, *L'organisation de la Syrie sous le mandat français*, in *ibid.*, xci (1 Dec. 1921), 633-63; L. Bergasse, *L'œuvre française en Syrie*, Marseilles 1922; Ihssan El Cherif, *La condition internationale de la Syrie: analyse juridique du mandat Syrien*, Paris 1922, 44-126; R. de Gontaut-Biron, *Comment la France s'est installée en Syrie (1918-1919)*, Paris 1922, H.J.E. Gouraud, *La France en Syrie*, Corbeil 1922; Abdallah Sfer, *Le mandat français et les traditions françaises en Syrie et au Liban*, Paris 1922 (also in Arabic, *al-Intidāb al-Fransāwī wa 'l-taḳālīd al-Fransāwiyya fī Sūriya wa-Lubnān*, Cairo 1922); J. Luquet, *Le mandat A et l'organisation du mandat français en Syrie*, Paris 1923; A. Joffre, *Le mandat de la France sur la Syrie et le Grand Liban*, Lyons 1924; Menassa, *Les mandats A* ...; B. Aboussouan, *Le problème politique syrien*, Paris 1925, 135 ff., 166 ff., 286 ff., 312 ff.; Ch. Burckhardt, *Le mandat français en Syrie et au Liban: la politique et l'oeuvre de la France au Levant*, Nîmes 1925; R.V. Giscard, *La Syrie et le Liban sous le mandat français (mai 1923-nov. 1924)*, in *Revue des Deux Mondes*, xcv (15 Apr. 1925), 838-65; D. McCallum, *The French in Syria, 1919-1924*, in *Jnal. Central Asian Society* (London), xii/1 (1925), 3-25; Guryevič, 13 ff.; J. Makarczyk, *Przez Palestyne i Syrie: szkice z podrózy* (Polish, *Through Palestine and Syria: travel notes*), Warsaw 1925, 52 ff., 105 ff.; H.Ch. Woods, *The French in Syria*, in *Fortnightly Review* (London), cxviii (Oct. 1925), 487-98; *Le contrôle par la Société des Nations du mandat pour la Syrie et le Liban*, in *L'Asie Française* (Paris), xxvi/241 (May 1926), 178-87; H. Froideveaux, *Quelques causes du* *malaise syrien*, in *ibid.*, xxvi/237 (Jan. 1926), 6-9; R. de Feriet, *L'application d'un mandat: la France puissance mandataire en Syrie et au Liban comment elle a compris son rôle*, Paris 1926 (2nd edition, 1927); [Colonel] Clément Grandcourt, *La tactique au Levant*, Paris 1926; Gurko-Kryadzhin, *Arabskiy Vostok...*, 75-103; al-Ladjna al-tanfīdhiyya li 'l-muʾtamar al-Sūrī al-Filasṭīnī, *al-Ḳaḍiyya al-Sūriyya: maẓālim al-Fransāwiyyīn wa-faẓāʾiʿihim*, Cairo 1926; *Thawrāt al-Durūz wa-ḥawādith Sūriya*, Cairo 1926, 25-80; F. White, *Mandates*, 62-72; Q. Wright, *Syrian grievances against French rule*, in *Current History*, xxiii/5 (Feb. 1926), 678-93; P. Bonardi, *L'imbroglio syrien*, Paris 1927; R. de Gontat-Biron, *Sur les routes de Syrie après neuf ans de mandat*, Paris 1928; E.P. MacCallum, *The nationalist crusade in Syria*, New York 1928, 3-15, 226-61; *La politique syrienne: le mandat et la Société des Nations*, in *L'Asie Française*, xxviii/264 (Nov. 1928), 363-9; H. Ch. Woods, *Syria yesterday and today*, in *Contemporary review* (London), cxxxiv (Sept. 1928), 295-303; Būlus Masʿad, *Lubnān wa Sūriyā ḳabl al-intidāb wa-baʿdahu*, i, Cairo 1929, 60-129; Milkonowicki, *Das Mandatssystem...*, 60-3; J. -A. Sorel, *Le mandat français et l'expansion économique de la Syrie et du Liban*, Paris 1929; H. Kohn, *Die staats- und verfassungsrechtliche Entwicklung der Republik Libanon*, in *Jahrbuch des Öffentlichen Rechts* (Tübingen), xvii (1929), 386-411; idem, *Der Staat Libanon: das erste Jahrzehnt seines Bestandes*, in *Zeitschrift für Politik*, xx (1930), 645-56; Bentwich, *The mandates system*, 21-51, 69-86, 166-72; Blaisdell, *Representation...*, 27-45; B.-G. Gaulis, *La question arabe: de l'Arabie du roi Ibn Saʿoud à l'indépendance syrienne*, Paris 1930, 99-275; A. Giannini, *La costituzione della Siria e del Libano*, in *OM*, x/12 (Dec. 1930), 589-615; Kyečyekʾyan, *Mandati...*, 50-6; N. Maestracci, *La Syrie contemporaine: tout ce qu'il faut savoir sur les territoires placés sous mandat français*², Paris 1930; Santi Nava, *Il mandato francese in Siria dalle sue origine al 1929*, Padua 1930, 62-261; Wright, *Mandates ...*, index; Bayham, *al-Intidāb ...*, 96-137; *al-Ḥukūma al-Sūriyya fī thālāth sinīn 15 shubāṭ 1928 ilā 15 shubāṭ 1931*, Damascus 1349/1931, 1-58; A. Megglé, *La Syrie terre française*, Paris 1931, 34 ff.; P. Pic, *Syrie et Palestine, mandats français et anglais dans le Proche Orient*, Paris 1931 (1st edition, Paris 1924). R. O'Zoux, *Les états du Levant sous mandat français*, Paris 1931, 57-302; A. Bruneau, *Traditions et politique de la France au Levant*, Paris 1932, 302-69, 403 ff.; G. Ambrosini, *Sulla transformazione del mandato francese in Siria*, in *OM*, xiii/5 (May 1933), 221-31; *Taḳrīr al-ladjna al-tanfīdhiyya li 'l-muʾtamar al-Sūrī al-Filasṭīnī bi-Miṣr ilā djamʿiyyat al-umam ʿan al-ḥāla al-siyāsiyya wa 'l-iḳtiṣādiyya fī Sūriya li-sanat 1933*, Cairo 1933; P. Amory, *Le régime administratif au Liban avant et depuis l'institution du mandat international de la France sur ce territoire*, Lyons 1934; Antonius, *Syria and the French mandate*, in *IA*, xiii/4 (July-Aug. 1934), 523-39; A. Armellini, *La Francia in Siria*, Lanciano n.d. [1934], 37-256; Choucri Cardahi, *Le mandat de France sur la Syrie et le Liban* (*son application au droit international public et privé*), Paris 1934; Omar Djabry, *Le Syrie sous le régime du mandat*, Toulouse 1934, 33-151; L. Jalabert, *Syrie et Liban: réussite française?*, Paris 1934; Tritonj, *L'unità della Siria e l'indivisibilità del suo mandato*, Rome 1934; idem, *L'inversione degli scopi del mandato in Siria*, in *OM*, xiv/6 (June 1934), 257-64; Muḥammad Saʿīd al-ʿĀṣṣ, *Ṣafḥa min al-ayyām al-ḥamrāʾ 1925-1927: kitāb yabḥath ʿan al-thawra al-Sūriyya wa-taṭawwurātihā*, Jerusalem 1354/1935; P. Bazantay, *Les états du Levant sous mandat français*, Beirut 1935; Boutant, *Les mandats...*, 99-106; R. Favre, *Les problèmes politiques des Etats du Levant sous mandat français*, Paris 1936; J. Lapierre, *Le mandat français en Syrie: origines, doctrines, exécution*, Paris 1936; *Quinze ans de mandat: L'oeuvre française en Syrie et au Liban*, Beirut n.d. [1936]; Général Andréa, *La révolte druze et l'insurrection de Damas 1925-1926*, Paris 1937, 43-241 (Arabic tr., *Taʾrīkh al-Durūz wa-tamarrud Dimashk*, Beirut 1971, 65 ff.); Nader Kuzbari, *La question de la cessation du mandat français sur la Syrie*, Paris 1937; Macaulay, *Mandates...*, 167-9; Antonius, *The Arab awakening...*, 368-86; Alessandro Ausiello, *La Francia e l'indipendenza della Siria e del Libano*, Rome 1938; J. Morgan-Jones, *La fin du mandat français en Syrie et au Liban*, Paris 1938; B. Vernier, *Qédar: carnets d'un méhariste syrien*, Paris 1938; Cataluccio, *Storia...*, 131-98; Mesud Fani Bilgili, *Manda idaresinde Hatay kültür hayatı*, Antioch 1939; Santi Nava, *La questione de Hatay (Alessandretta) e la sua soluzione*, Florence 1939; Ch. Schultz-Esteves, *Syriens Freiheitskampf*, Leipzig 1939, 43-123; P. Viénot, *Les relations de la France et de la Syrie*, Mars 1939, n.p. n.d. [1939]; Irfan Jabry, *La question d'Alexandrette dans le cadre du mandat syrien*, Grenoble 1940; P. Richard, *Frankreich in Syrien*, Berlin 1940; K. Weiss, *Frankreichs Verrat an Syrien: Tatsächen und Berichte*, Berlin 1940, 11-53; I. Zingarelli, *Vicino e Lontano Oriente*, Milan 1940, 109-70; E. Samy, *I partiti e le associazioni politiche in Siria e nel Libano visti da un Siriano (1921-1929)*, in *OM*, xxi/3 (March 1941), 101-23; *Strani Blidzhnyego...*, 119-40; Union des Ingénieurs et Techniciens de la France Combattante, Section du Levant, *Vingt cinq ans d'efforts français au Levant, 1920-1944*, Beirut 1944; Rifʿat al-ʿAsalī, *al-Siyāsa al-irtidjāliyya fī awḍāʿ Sūriyā wa-Lubnān wa-Filasṭīn*, n.p. n.d. [1946], 17 ff.; Hourani, *Syria and Lebanon: a political essay*, London 1946, 163-384; P. Rondot, *Les institutions politiques du Liban: des communautés traditionnelles à l'état moderne*, Paris 1947, 10 ff.; E.E. Abouchdid, *Thirty years of Lebanon and Syria (1917-1947)*, Beirut 1948, 29 ff.; D. Censoni, *La politica francese nel Vicino Oriente: Siria e Libano dal mandato all'indipendenza (1919-1946)*, Bologna n.d. [1948]; Rondot, *L'expérience du mandat français en Syrie et au Liban (1918-1945)*, in *Revue Générale de Droit International Public*, lii/3-4 (1948), 387-409; Seton-Williams, 89-120; A. Fabre-Luce, *Deuil au Levant*, Paris 1950, 69-239; G. Haddad, *Fifty years of modern Syria and Lebanon*, Beirut 1950, 68-152; Kimche, 100-7; Nizar Kayali, *Syria: a political study (1920-1950)*, unpubl. Ph.D. diss., Columbia Univ., New York 1951, 12-180; Khadduri, *Constitutional development in Syria*, in *MEJ*, v/2 (Spring 1951), 137-48; idem, *Ḳaḍiyyat al-Iskandarūna*, Damascus n.d. [1953]; Aḥmad Muṣṭafā Ḥaydar, *al-Dawla al-Lubnāniyya, 1920-1953*, Beirut 1953; Munīr Taḳī 'l-Dīn, *Wilādat istiḳlāl*, Beirut 1953, 9 ff.; Nadjīb al-Armanāzī, *Muḥāḍarāt ʿan Sūriyā min al-iḥtilāl ilā al-djalāʾ*, Cairo 1954; A.K. Sandjian, *The Sanjak of Alexandretta (Hatay): a study in Franco-Turco-Syrian relations*, unpubl. Ph.D. diss., Univ. of Michigan, Ann Arbor 1956; L. Evans, *The United States policy in the Syrian mandate, 1917-1922*, unpubl. Ph.D. diss., Johns Hopkins Univ. 1957; N.A. Ziadeh, *Syria and Lebanon*, New York 1957, 46-92; Muḥammad Djamīl Bayham, *Sūriya wa-Lubnān 1918-1922*, Beirut 1958; Longrigg, *Syria and Lebanon under French mandate*, London 1958; L.M.-T. Meo, *The separation of Lebanon from Greater Syria: a case study in Lebanese politics*, unpubl. Ph.D. diss., Indiana Univ., Bloomington 1961; al-Rāʾid Iḥsān Hindī, *Kifāḥ al-shaʿb al-ʿArabī al-Sūrī, 1908-1948, dirāsa ʿaskariyya taʾrīkhiyya*, Damascus 1962,

50 ff.; Wizārat al-Thaḳāfa wa 'l-Irshād al-Ḳawmī, *Ḳiṣṣat al-djalā' ʿan Sūriya*, n.p. (Damascus?) 1962; DeNovo, 322-37; Gdański, *Arabski wschód...*, 198-211; I. Lipschits, *La politique de la France au Levant, 1939-41*, Paris and Amsterdam 1963; J. Nantet, *Histoire du Liban*, Paris 1963, 248-84; V.B. Lutskiy, *Natsional' no-osvoboditel'naya voyna v Sirii (1925-1927 gg.)*, Moscow 1964, index; Ẓāfir al-Ḳāsimī, *Wathā'iḳ djadīda ʿan al-thawra al-Sūriyya al-Kubrā*, Beirut 1965; L.M.-T. Meo, *Lebanon, improbable nation: a study in political development*, Bloomington, Ind. 1965, 40 ff.; *Novyeyshaya istoriya stran Azii i Afriki*, 380-95; K.S. Salibi, *The modern history of Lebanon*, London, 1965, 164-95; Wadjīh ʿAlam al-Dīn, *Marāḥil istiḳlāl dawlatay Lubnān wa-Sūriya, 1922-1943*, Beirut 1943; W.C. Bandazian, *The crisis of Alexandretta*, unpubl. Ph. D. diss., The American Univ., Washington, D.C. 1967, 49 ff.; M.-C. Davet, *La double affaire de Syrie*, Paris 1967; Nadjib Dahdah, *Évolution historique du Liban*[3], Beirut 1968, 243-80; *Novyeyshaya istoriya Arabskikh stran ...*, 45-62, 94-8; N.O. Oganyesyan, *Obrazovaniye nyezavisimoy Sirikskoy Ryespubliki (1939-1946)*, Moscow 1968; Rabbath, *Constitution et indépendance au Liban: un cas de genèse conjointe*, in *Orient*, xlvii-xlviii (1968), 9-96; A. Bleckmann, *Die französische Kolonialreiche und die Gründung neuer Staaten, Die Rechtsentwicklung in Syrien, Libanon, Indochina und Schwarzafrika*, Cologne 1969, 5-76; Gannon, *The influence ....*, 99-183; W. Skuratowicz, *Liban* (Polish, *Lebanon*), Warsaw 1969, esp. 117-47; H.H. Smith *et alii*, *Area handbook of Lebanon*, Washington, D.C. 1969, 38-43 and index; A.L. Tibawi, *A modern history of Syria including Lebanon and Palestine*, London 1969, 338-78; Tuğ, 285 ff.; Pierre Ziadé, *al-Ta'rīkh al-diblūmāsī li-istiḳlāl Lubnān wa-madjmūʿāt min al-wathā'iḳ*, Beirut 1969; J. Couland, *Le mouvement syndical au Liban (1919-1946), son évolution pendant le mandat français*, Paris 1970; J.L. Miller, *Henry de Jouvenel and the Syrian mandate*, unpubl. Ph.D. diss., Bryn Mawr College 1970; R.F. Nyrop *et alii*, *Area handbook for Syria*, Washington, D.C. 1971. 42-7; E. Baldissera, *La composizione dei governi siriani dal 1918 al 1965*, in *OM* lii/11-12 (Nov.-Dec. 1972), 617-25; Tabitha Petran, *Syria*, London 1972, 61-79; Nadjīb al-Armanāzī, *Sūriya min al-iḥtilāl ilā 'l-djalā'*[2], Beirut 1973; E. Burke III, *A comparative view of French native policy in Morocco and Syria, 1912-1925*, in *MES*, ix/2 (May 1973), 175-86; Rabbath, *La formation historique du Liban politique et constitutionnel: essai de synthèse*, Beirut 1973, 330-563; Massoud Daher, *L'histoire sociale de l'État du Grand Liban, 1920-1926*, unpubl. Ph.D. diss., Univ. of Paris 1973; Christine Giappesi, *Structures communautaires et idéologie politique au Liban à l'époque du mandat français*, unpubl. Ph.D. diss., Univ. of Paris 1974; M. Maʿoz, *Sūriyya ha-ḥadasha* (Hebrew, *New Syria*), Tel-Aviv 1974, ch. 6; Warner, *Iraq and Syria...*, 67 ff., 122-58; Ḳaddūra, *Ta'rīkh...*, 260 ff., 307 ff.; Y.M.H. Chaherly, *L'évolution politique en Syrie de 1936 à 1939*, unpubl. Ph.D. diss., Univ. of Grenoble 1976, 19 ff.; A. Mockler, *Our enemies the French: being an account of the war fought between the French and the British, Syria 1941*, London 1976; M.P. Zirinsky, *France, Syria and Lebanon: the treaties of 1936*, unpubl. Ph.D. diss., Univ. of North Carolina, Chapel Hill 1976; W.L. Browne, *The political history of Lebanon, 1920-1950*, i-iv, Salisbury, N.C. 1976-80; Saffiuddin Joarder, *Syria under the French mandate: the early phase, 1920-27*, Dacca 1977 (= Asiatic Society of Bangladesh Publications, 31); J.L. Miller, *The Syrian revolt of 1925*, in *IJMES*, viii/4 (Oct. 1977), 545-63; D.A. Makyeyev, *Iz istorii economičyeskikh svyazyey SSSR s Siriyey i Livanon (20-30g.)*, in *Narodi Azii i Afriki* (Moscow), 1977, part 2, 27-35; Abed al-Hafiz Mansur, *Great Britain and the birth of Syrian and Lebanese independence*, in *International Studies* (New Delhi), xvi/2 (Apr. -June 1977), 245-73; Cl. Palazzoli, *La Syrie: le rêve et la rupture*, Paris 1977, 133-45; Z.N. Zeine, *The struggle for Arab independence: Western diplomacy and the rise and fall of Faisal's kingdom*, Delmar, N.Y. 1977; Lyne Lohéac, *Daoud Ammoun et la création de l'état libanais*, Paris 1978, 71-181; I. Rabinovich, *Compact minorities and the Syrian state, 1918-45*, in *Jnal. of Contemporary History*, xiv/4 (Oct. 1979), 693-712; J.M. Landau *et alii* (eds.), *Electoral politics in the Middle East: issues, voters and elites*, London and Stanford 1980, index; Ph.S. Khoury, *The tribal shaykh, French tribal policy, and the nationalist movement in Syria between two world wars*, in *MES*, xviii/2 (April 1982), 180-93; Djamʿiyyat al-muhādana al-Turkiyya al-ʿArabiyya, *al-Muhādana al-Turkiyya al-ʿArabiyya*, Cairo n.d., also a Turkish version, *Türk-Arap muhadeneti* (about the Alexandretta-Hatay issue); Amīn Saʿīd, *al-Thawra al-ʿArabiyya*, iii, 288 ff.; Karīm Khalīl Thābit, *al-Durūz wa 'l-thawra al-Sūriyya wa-sīrat Sulṭān Bāshā al-Aṭrash*, n.p. n.d.

Palestine and Transjordan. Bibliographies in *Publications issued by the League of Nations*, 158, 160, 172-3; Patai, *Jordan, Lebanon...*; National Library, Cairo, *A bibliographical list of works about Palestine and Jordan*[2], Cairo 1964; Walid Khalidi and Jill Khadduri, *Palestine and the Arab-Israel conflict: an annotated bibliography*, Beirut 1974; *Palestine and Zionism*, New York, i-viii (1946-53), is a detailed bibliography, published periodically, of books, pamphlets and magazine articles. A recent review article by R.W. Zweig, on *The Palestine mandate*, appeared in the *Historical Jnal.* (Cambridge), xxiv (1981), 243-51. For archival materials in Israel, see P.A. Alsberg (ed.), *Guide to the archives in Israel*, Jerusalem 1973; for others, particularly in Britain, but also in Jordan and elsewhere, the best guide is by P. Jones (ed.), *Britain and Palestine, 1914-1918: archival sources for the history of the British mandate*, Oxford 1979. See also references in Grimwood-Jones *et alii* (eds.), 193. For the draft of the text of the mandate, see *British Parliamentary Papers*, *Draft mandates for Messopotamia and Palestine as submitted to the approval of the League of Nations*, London 1921 (= Cmd. 1176). For its final draft, see *ibid.*, London 1921 (= Cmd. 1500); for the definitive text, see *ibid.*, London 1922 (= Cmd. 1785) and in the League of Nations' *Mandate for Palestine and memorandum by the British Government relating to its application to Transjordan, approved by the League of Nations of September 16th, 1922*, Geneva 1926. The last comprises an official French version as well, Société des Nations, *Mandat pour la Palestine et Mémorandum du gouvernement britanique relatif à l'application de ce mandat à la Transjordanie, approuvé par le Conseil de la Société des Nations le 16 septembre 1922.* The text itself has been reprinted frequently, e.g. in Wright, *Mandates...*, 600 ff., and J.C. Hurewitz, *Diplomacy in the Near and Middle East*, Princeton, N.J. 1956, ii, 106-11. A Hebrew translation appeared, e.g., in M. Medzini (ed.), *Ḳōveṣ mismakhīm bĕ-tōlĕdōt ha-mĕdīna* (Hebrew, *A collection of documents in the history of the state*), Jerusalem 1981, 23-7; an Arabic one in Ṭabāra, *al-Intidāb...*, 240-52; a German one as *Das Mandat für Palästina, vom Völkerbundsrat am 24. Juli 1922 genehmigter geltender Text*, Berlin n.d. [1922], and an Italian one as *Il mandato inglese per la*

Palestina, tradotto dal testo ufficiale publicato dal ministero degli esteri inglese, Florence 1921. The Permanent Mandates Commission's *Minutes*, 1921-39, comprise firsthand material. The British have published numerous papers, both Parliamentary and non-Parliamentary ones, some as *Reports* in the 1920s, *Statements of policy* during the 1930s, and *Proposals for the future of Palestine* in the 1940s. The first appeared as Government of Palestine, *Report on Palestine administration, July 1920-December 1921*, London 1922; later ones as Colonial Office, *Report by his Majesty's government in the United Kingdom of Great Britain and Northern Ireland to the Council of the League of Nations on the administration of Palestine and Transjordan*, annually, London, until 1939. Among the others, the following are particularly important: *Palestine. Correspondence with the Palestine Delegation and the Zionist Organization*, London 1922 (= Cmd. 1708); *Report of the High Commissioner on the administration of Palestine*, London 1925 (= Colonial no. 15); *Report of the commission on the Palestine disturbances of August, 1929*, London 1930 (= Cmd. 3530); *Report of the Palestine royal commission* (*July 1937*), Geneva 1937; *The political history of Palestine under British administration* (*memorandum by His Britannic Majesty's Government presented in July, 1947, to the United Nations Special Committee on Palestine*), Jerusalem 1947; Government of Palestine, *Memorandum on the administration of Palestine under the mandate*, Jerusalem 1947; *Proposals for the future of Palestine*, London 1947 (= Cmd. 7044); *Palestine: Termination of the mandate, 15th May 1948. Statement prepared for public information by the Colonial Office and Foreign Office*, London 1948. For Transjordan, see *Agreement between His Majesty and the Amir of Trans-Jordan, signed at Jerusalem, February 20, 1928*, London 1930 (Treaty Series, no. 7) (= Cmd. 3488); *Treaty of alliance between His Majesty in respect of the United Kingdom and His Highness the Amir of Trans-Jordan, London 22nd March, 1946*, (= Cmd. 6779). For the Order-in-Council of 1922 and others, ordinances, proclamations and regulations of the Mandatory, see N. Bentwich (ed.), *Legislation of Palestine 1918-1925*, i-ii, Alexandria 1926. For Transjordan, see C.R.W. Seton (ed.), *Legislation of Transjordan 1918-1920, translated from the Arabic, including the laws, public notices, proclamations, regulations, etc.*, London n.d. [prob. 1931]. For some official documents of the Arab case, see The Executive Commitee, Palestine Arab Congress, *Report on the State of Palestine during four years of civil administration submitted to the mandate commission of the League of Nations through H.E. the High Commissioner for Palestine*, Jerusalem n.d. [1947]; idem, *Two memoranda submitted to the Council & Permanent Mandates Commission of the League of Nations respectively through the High Commissionner for Palestine*, Jerusalem 1925; idem, *Spoliation in Palestine*, Jerusalem 1925 (also in Arabic, *Ig̲h̲tiṣāb ḥukūmat Filasṭīn*); idem, *Memorandum on the Palestine white paper of October 1930*, Jerusalem 1930; *Ḥukm Allāh taʿālā fī 'l-bāʿa wa 'l-samāsira: Mad̲j̲mūʿat al-fatāwī al-k̲h̲aṭīra allatī aṣdarahā ʿulamāʾ al-Muslimīn fī Filasṭīn wa-fī g̲h̲ayrihā min al-aḳṭār al-Islāmiyya*, Jerusalem n.d. [A.H. 1353-4]; The Arab Higher Committee, *A sample of the methods adopted by the government of Palestine in the administration of the country*, Jerusalem n.d. [1936]; idem, *Memorandum submitted to the Permanent Mandates Commission and the Secretary of State for the Colonies*, n.p. 1937; idem, *The Palestine Arab case*, Cairo 1947; The Arab Office, London, *The future of Palestine*, London 1947, 12-166. For some official documents of the Jewish case, see Zionist Organisation, *The mandate for Palestine: memorandum submitted to the Council of the League of Nations*, n.p. 1922 (also in French, *L'organisation sioniste, Le mandat sur la Palestine, mémorandum soumis à la Société des Nations*, s.p. 1922); Waad Leumi (National Council) of the Jews in Palestine, *Memorandum submitted to the Permanent Mandates Commission of the League of Nations*, Jerusalem 1926; The Jewish Agency for Palestine, *Memorandum on the "Report of the Commission on the Palestine disturbances of August 1929", submitted to the Secretary-General of the League of nations, for the information of the Permanent Mandates Commission*, London 1930; idem, *Memorandum submitted to the Palestine Royal Commission on behalf of the Jewish Agency for Palestine*, London 1936; idem, *The Jewish case against the Palestine White Paper: documents submitted to the Permanent Mandates Commission of the League of Nations*, London 1939; idem, *Documents relating to the Palestine problem, London 1945;* idem, *Reply to the Government of Palestine's memorandum on the administration of Palestine under the mandate*, Jerusalem 1947; idem, *The Jewish case before the Anglo-American committee of inquiry on Palestine*, Jerusalem 1947. For representative collections of documents, see Department of State, Division of Near Eastern Affairs, *Mandate for Palestine*, Washington, D.C. 1927; *Kas̲h̲f al-ḳināʿ: mad̲j̲mūʿat muʿāhadāt wa-ḥaḳāʾiḳ ʿan aḥwāl al-iḍṭirābāt al-ak̲h̲īra fī Filasṭīn*, Haifa 1937; M.M. Laseron (ed.), *On the mandate: documents, statements, laws and judgements relating to and arising from the mandate for Palestine*, Tel-Aviv 1937; *British labour policy on Palestine: a collection of documents, speeches and articles, 1917-1938*, London 1938; Mamun al-Hamui (ed.), *Die britische Palästina-Politik*, Berlin 1943; M. Moch (translator), *La Palestine de Balfour à Bevin: déclarations et documents*, Paris n.d. [1946]; Moshe Atias (ed.), *Sefer ha-tĕʿūdōt s̲h̲el ha-Vaʿad ha-Lĕʾūmī li-Kneset Israʾel bĕ-Erets-Israʾel, 1918-1948* (Hebrew), *The book of documents of the National Council of Kneset Israel in Palestine, 1918-1948*), Jerusalem 1963; Doreen Ingrams (ed.), *Palestine Papers 1917-1922: seeds of conflict*, London and New York 1973, esp. 88-183; *Seeds of Conflict*, i-vi, Nedeln (Lichtenstein), 1974; Division of Near Eastern Affairs, U.S. Department of State, *The Palestine mandate. Collected United States documents relating to the league of Nations mandate for Palestine, to the possible future independence of Palestine and to the need for the creation of a separate Jewish state*, Salisbury, N.C. 1977. For others primary sources, see B. Pullen-Burry, *Letters from Palestine, February-April 1922*, London n.d. [1922]; C.R. Ashbee, *A Palestine notebook, 1918-1923*, New York 1923, 92-278; Yūsuf Tūmā al-Bustānī, *ʿĀmān fī ʿAmmān: mud̲h̲akkirāt ʿāmayn fī ʿāṣimat S̲h̲arḳ al-Urdunn*, Cairo 1925; *al-Kitāb al-aswad fī 'l-ḳaḍiyya al-Urduniyya al-ʿArabiyya*, Jerusalem n.d. [prob. 1928-9]; H.B. Samuel, *Unholy memories of the Holy Land*, London 1930, index; Herbert Samuel, *Great Britain and Palestine*, London 1935; C. Arlosoroff, *Leben und Werk*, Berlin 1936, 39-284; L. Farago, *Palestine on the eve*, London 1936; G. Mansur, *The Arab worker under the Palestine mandate*, Jerusalem 1936; L. Rosner *Szkice Palestyńskie* (Polish, *Palestine sketches*), Cracow 1936; F.H. Kisch, *Palestine diary*, London 1938; *Mud̲h̲ākkirāt al-malik ʿAbd Allāh b. Ḥusayn*, n.p. n.d. [1938-9], 158 ff.; R. Courtney, *Palestine policeman*, London 1939. H. Bowman, *Middle-East window*, 249-340; Sir Herbert Samuel, *Memoirs*, London 1945, 139-84; Sir Ronald Storrs, *Orientations*, London 1945, 273-440; R. Crossman, *Palestine mission: a personal record*, London n.d.

[1946-7]; B.C. Crum, *Behind the silken curtain: a personal account of Anglo-American diplomacy in Palestine and the Middle East*, New York 1947 (French, *Derrière le rideau de soie*, Paris 1948); J. García-Granados, *The birth of Israel: the drama as I saw it*, New York 1948, index; J. B. Glubb, *The story of the Arab Legion*, London 1948, 37 ff.; R.M. Graves, *Experiment in anarchy*, London 1949; Pearse, *Three years...*, 179 ff.; Chaim Weizmann, *Trial and error*, London 1949, 747-589; R.D. Wilson, *Cordon and search: with 6th airborne division in Palestine*, Aldershot (U.K.) 1949; B.S. Vester, *Our Jerusalem: an American family in the holy city, 1881-1949*, n.p. [Beirut] 1950, 305-81; Menahem Begin, *The revolt: story of the Irgun*, New York 1951 (also in French, *La révolte d'Israël*, Paris 1953); D.V. Duff, *Bailing with a teaspoon*, London 1953; *al-Takmila min muḏhakkirāt... al-malik ʿAbd Allāh b. al-Ḥusayn*, Amman 1951 (Eng. tr., King ʿAbdallah of Jordan, *My memoirs completed*, Washington, D.C. 1954); Hāshim al-Sabʿ, *Ḏhikrayāt ṣuḥufī muḏtahad*, i, Jerusalem 1951; D. Horowitz, *State in the making*, New York 1953, index; David Ben Gurion, *Rebirth and destiny of Israel*, New York 1954; Sir Alec Kirkbride, *A crackle of thorns: experiences in the Middle East*, London 1956, 18-168; Glubb, *A soldier with the Arabs*, London 1957, 41 ff. (French tr., *Soldat avec les Arabes*, Paris 1958); H.H. Bodenheimer (ed.), *So wurde Israel: Erinnerungen von Dr. M.I. Bodenheimer*, Frankfurt a/M 1958, 266-75 ("Die Mandatspolitik") (Eng. tr., *The memoirs of M.I. Bodenheimer: prelude to Israel*, New York and London 1963, 340-53). Hazzāʿ al-Madjdjālī, *Muḏhakkirātī*, n.p. [Jerusalem] 1960, 11-80; R. Meinertzhagen, *Middle East diary, 1917-1956*, New York 1960, ch. 5; E.M. Epstein, *Jerusalem correspondent, 1919-1958*, Jerusalem 1964, index; N. and Helen Bentwich, *Mandate memories, 1918-1948*, London 1965; O. Tweedy, *Gathering moss: a memoir*, London 1967, index; G. Furlonge, *Palestine is my country: the story of Musa Alami*, London 1969, 76 ff.; C. Mitchell, *Having been a soldier*, London 1969, 50-66; *Ben Gurion looks back in talks with Moshe Pearlman*, New York 1970, 66 ff.; R. John and Sami Hadawi, *The Palestine diary*, i-ii, Beirut 1970; E. Samuel, *A lifetime in Jerusalem: the memoirs of the Second Viscount Samuel*, Jerusalem 1970, 26-251; Ben Gurion, *Igrōt* (Hebrew, *Letters*), i-iii, Tel-Aviv 1971-4; idem, *Zikhrōnōt* (Hebrew, *Memoirs*), i-v, Tel-Aviv 1971-82. A. Ruppin, *Memoirs, diaries, letters*, London 1971, 183-314; Emīl al-Ghūrī, *Filasṭīn ʿibrat sittīn ʿāman*, i-ii, Beirut 1972-3; Iskandar al-Khūrī, *Ḏhikrayātī*, Jerusalem n.d. [1973], 77 ff.; Golda Meir, *My life*, London 1975, chs. 4-8 (German tr., *Mein Leben*, Hamburg 1975, 75 ff.); Christina Jones, *The untempered wind: Forty years in Palestine*, London 1975, 1-144; Moshe Dayan, *Story of my life*, New York 1976, 29-148; Kirkbride, *From the wings: Amman memoirs, 1947-1951*, London 1976, 1-119; Moshe Sharett, *Yōman mĕdīnī* (Hebrew, *A political diary*), i-v, Tel-Aviv 1976-9; M.W. Weisgal (ed.), *The letters and papers of Chaim Weizmann*, Series A: Letters, x-xxiii, New Brunswick, N.J. and Jerusalem 1977-80; Mūsā ʿAdīl Baymirzā Shardan, *al-Urdunn bayn ʿahdayn*, n.p. n.d., 12 ff. See also F. Ruffini, *Sionismo e Società delle Nazioni*, Bologna 1919; E.L. Langton, *The British mandate for Palestine and its significance*, London 1920; Acito, 39 ff.; Federazione Sionistica Italiana, *Mandato per le Palestine e la sede nazionale ebraica*, Rome 1922; H.C. Luke and E. Keith-Roach, *The handbook of Palestine*, London 1922; L. Stein, *The mandate for Palestine: some objections answered*, London n.d. [1922]; P.

Graves, *Palestine, the land of three faiths*, London 1923, 62-286; P. Appel, *Das Palästina-Mandat*, in *Mitteilungen der Deutschen Gesellschaft für Völkerrecht* 7 June 1924, 81-8; Menassa, *Les mandats A...*, 215 ff.; Guryevič, 12 ff.; Makarczyk, *Przez Palestyne...*, 5 ff.; W.B. Worsfold, *Palestine of the mandate*, London 1925, index; Gurko-Kryaḏzhin, *Arabskiy Vostok...*, 49-74; H.J. Seidel, *Der britische Mandatstaat Palestina im Rahmen der Weltwirtschaft*, Berlin 1926; F. White, *Mandates...*, 78-82; Q. Wright, *The Palestine problem*, in *Political Science Qtly.* (New York), xli (1926), 384-412; A. Krämer, *Das völkerrechtliche Mandat unter besonderer Berücksichtigung des Palästina-Mandates*, Heidelberg 1927; Lord Melchett *et alii*, *Report of the joint Palestine survey commission*, London 1928; I.R. Moreno, *Teoría general de los mandatos: el mandato Británico en Palestina*, Buenos Aires 1928; M. Spiegel, *Das völkerrechtliche Mandat und seine Anwendung auf Palästina*, Vienna 1928; J. Stoyanovsky, *The mandate for Palestine: a contribution to the theory and practice of international mandates*, London 1928; Bentwich, *The mandate for Palestine*, in *The British Year Book of International Law* (London, etc.), x/2 (1929), 137-43; idem [signed N.B.], *The mandate for Transjordan*, in *ibid.*, 212-13; A. Besozzi, *Italia e Palestina*, Milan 1929, 197-283; Kohn, *Die staats- und verfassungsrechtliche Entwicklung des Emirats Transjordanien*, in *Archiv des öffentlichen Rechts* (Tübingen), N.F.., xvi/2 (1929), 238-67; E. Marcus, *Palästina - ein werdender Staat*, Leipzig 1929 (= *Frankfurter Abhandlungen zum modernen Völkerrecht*), 23-318; Milkonowicki, *Das Mandatssystem...*, 63-73; M. Samuel, *What happened in Palestine: the events of August, 1929, their background and their significance*, Boston 1929; G. Schwarzenberger, *Das Völkerbunds-Mandat für Palästina*, Stuttgart 1929 (= *Tübinger Abhandlungen zum Öffentlich Recht*, 21); H. Sidebotham, *British policy and the Palestine mandate*, London n.d. [1929]; Blaisdell, *Representation...*, 55-62; J.H. Kann, *Some observations on the policy of the mandatory government of Palestine*, The Hague 1930; Kyečyekʾyan, *Mandati...*, 39-50; S.E. Soskin, *Problèmes sionistes vus de Genève (l'oeuvre de la Commission des Mandats)*, Paris 1930; Wright, *Mandates...*, index; F.F. Andrews, *The Holy Land under mandate*, i-ii, Boston 1931; A. Baumkoller, *Le mandat sur la Palestine*, Paris 1931, 67 ff.; J. Cohn, *England und Palästina: ein Beitrag zur Britischen Empire-Politik*, Berlin 1931, 104-96; G.T. Garrat, *The future of Palestine*, in *Political Qtly.*, ii (1931), 46-58; A. Giannini, *La constituzione della Transgiordania*, in *OM*, xi/3 (March 1931), 117-31; Bentwich, *England in Palestine*, London 1932, index; A. Bonne, *Palästina: Land und Wirtschaft*, Leipzig 1932, index; S. Ficheleff, *Le statut international de la Palestine orientale (la Transjordanie)*, Paris 1932, 23-108; M. Moch, *Le mandat britannique en Palestine*, Paris 1932, 41-376; Anis Saghir, *Le sionisme et le mandat anglais en Palestine*, Paris 1932; H. Viteles and Khalil Totah (eds.), *Palestine: a decade of development*, Philadelphia 1932 (= *Annals of the American Academy of Political and Social Sciences*, 164); A. Granowsky, *The fiscal system of Palestine*, Jerusalem 1933; M. Burstein, *Self-government of the jews in Palestine*, Tel-Aviv 1934; B.S. Erskine, *Palestine of the Arabs*, London 1935, 69 ff.; Boutant, *Les mandats*, 106-14; Wadīʿ al-Bustānī, *al-Intidāb al-Filasṭīnī bāṭil wa-muḥāl*, Beirut 1936 (also in English, W.F. Boustany, *The Palestine mandate, invalid and impracticable*, Beirut 1936); T. Canaan, *The Palestine Arab cause*, Jerusalem 1936; D. Duff, *Palestine picture*, London 1936; N. Feinberg, *Some problems of the Palestine mandate*, Tel-Aviv 1936, 65-

115; Emile Ghoury, *An Arab view of the situation in Palestine*, in *IA*, xv/4 (July-Aug. 1936), 684-99; J. Gottlieb, *Juden und Araber im Mandat*, Tel-Aviv n.d. [1936]; E. Ovazza, *L'Inghilterra e il mandato in Palestina*, Rome 1936; A. Revusky, *Les Juifs en Palestine*, Paris 1936, 28 ff. (Eng. tr., *Jews in Palestine*, New York 1945, 20 ff.); E. Sereni and R.E. Ashery (eds.), *Jews and Arabs in Palestine: studies in a national and colonial problem*, New York 1936; F.H. Beck, *The case of the Palestine Arab*, n.p. [London] 1937, 4-28; Fr. Friedmann, *Das Palästina Mandat*, Prague 1937; M. Le Guillerme, *Bagarres en Palestine*, Paris 1937, 34 ff.; Macaulay, *Mandates* ..., 161-7; E. Main, *Palestina at the crossroads*, London 1937, 91 ff.; M.E.T. Mogannam, *The Arab woman and the Palestina problem*, London 1937,123 ff.; The Royal Institute of International Affairs, *Great Britain and Palestine, 1915-1936*, London 1937, 17-111; ᶜĪsā al-Safarī, *Filasṭīn al-ᶜArabiyya bayn al-intidāb wa 'l-Ṣahyūniyya*, i-ii, Jaffa 1937; H.J. Simson, *British rule and rebellion*, Edinburgh and London 1937, 131-320; D.J. Tosević, *Palestine v bouři* (Czech, *Palestine in storm*), Prague 1937, index; H.L. Weisman, *The future of Palestine: an examination of the partition plan*, New York 1937; A. Musil, *Zaslíbená Země: Nova Palestina* (Czech, *The Promised Land: New Palestine*), Prague n.d. [1937-8], 21-217; J. Schechtmann, *Transjordanien im Bereiche des Palästinamandats*, Vienna n.d. [1937-8], 68-262; Antonius, *The Arab awakening* ..., 386, 412; Bentwich, *Fulfilment in the Promised Land, 1917-1937*, London 1938, 12 ff.; S. Bissiso, *La politique anglo-sioniste en Palestine: étude juridique et critique du sionisme et du mandat anglais*, Paris 1938; I. Hazan, *Palestina la răspântie* (Rumanian, *Palestine at the crossroads*), Bucharest 1938, 3-77; Office of Statistics, Jerusalem, *Statistical abstract of Palestine, 1937-38*, Jerusalem 1938, Giselher Wirsing, *Engländer, Juden und Araber in Palästina*, Jena 1938, 47 ff.; B. Akzin, *The Palestine mandate in practice*, in *Iowa Law Review* (Iowa City), xxv (1939), 32-77; M. Buchwaje, *Mandat ligi narodów nad Palestyna* (Polish, *The mandate of the League of Nations over Palestine*), Cracow 1939, 8-161; Cataluccio, *Storia*..., 199-258; J.M.N. Jeffries, *Palestine: the reality*, London 1939, 336-712; The Royal Institute of International Affairs, *Great Britain and Palestine, 1915-1939*, London 1939; A. Lourie, *Britain and Palestine: an examination of present British policy in the light of the mandate for Palestine*, New York n.d. [1940?]; J. Cohen-Megouri, *La Palestine sous le régime des Ordres en Conseil*, Caen 1940; P.M. Hanna, *British policy in Palestine*, Washington, D.C. 1942, 39-169; A.M. Hyamson, *Palestine: a policy*, London 1942, 126-209; Celâl Tevfik Karasapan, *Filistin ve Şark-ül-Ürdun*, ii, Istanbul 1942; E. Marton, *Palesztina és a nagyvilág* (Hungarian, *Palestine and the wide world*), Koloszvar 1943; P. van Paassen, *The forgotten ally*, New York 1943, 105 ff.; Shmuel Ben Eliezer Zvi, *Palestine is mandated, not British territory: British white paper 1939 violates mandate*, New York 1943; R. Fink, *America and Palestine*, New York 1944, 37 ff.; E. Frankenstein, *Justice for my people*, New York 1944, 51 ff.; C.J. Friedrich, *American policy toward Palestine*, Washington, D.C. 1944, 5-103; S.S. Perry, *Britain opens a gateway*, London 1944; A. Abrahams, *Background of unrest: Palestine journey, 1944*, n.p. [London?] n.d. [1945]; Santi Nava, *Termini vecchi e nuovi del problema palestinese*, in *OM*, xxv/1-12 (Jan.-Dec. 1945), 1-8; B.A. Toukan, *A short history of Tranjordan*, London 1945, 44-9; N. Zackai, *Trans-Jordan 1914-1939*, unpubl. Ph.D. diss., Northwestern Univ. 1945; Frankenstein, *Palestine in the light of international law*, London 1946, 9-54; Hashomer Hatzair Workers' Party of Palestine, *The case for a bi-national Palestine*, Tel-Aviv 1946, 7 ff.; S. Katznelson, *The Palestine problem and the solution: a new scheme*, Jerusalem 1946; A. Konikoff, *Transjordan: an economic survey*, Jerusalem 1946; J. Marlowe, *Rebellion in Palestine*, London 1946, 43-269; Ṣādiḳ Saᶜīd, *Filasṭīn bayn maḵẖālib al-istiᶜmār*, Cairo n.d. [1946?]; Nad̲j̲īb Ṣadaḳa, *Ḳaḍiyyat Filasṭīn*, Beirut 1946, index; N. Barbour, *Nisi Dominus: a survey of the Palestine controversy*, London 1946, 88-234; idem, *Palestine: star or crescent?*, New York 1947; M.F. Abcarius, *Palestine through the fog of propaganda*, London n.d. [1947]; Arab Office, London, *The future of Palestine*, London 1947, 14 ff.; Muḥammad D̲j̲amīl Bayham, *Filasṭīn Andalus al-s̲h̲arḳ*, n.p. n.d. [1947], index; Nadīm Bayṭār, *Ḳaḍiyyat al-ᶜArab al-Filasṭīniyya*, Beirut 1947, 39 ff.; Essco Foundation for Palestine, *Palestine: a study of Jewish, Arab and British policies*, i-ii, New Haven, Conn. 1947; J.L Magnes *et alii*, *Palestine — divided or united? The case for a bi-national Palestine before the United Nations*, Jerusalem 1947; M. Picard, *Palestine carrefour brûlant*, Paris 1947, 9 ff.; Muḥammad Rifᶜāt, *Ḳaḍiyyat Filasṭīn*, Cairo 1947; J. Robinson, *Palestine and the United Nations: Prelude to solution*, Washington, D.C. 1947, index; Y. Shimoni, *ᶜAravey Ereṯs-Israʾel* (Hebrew, *The Arabs of Palestine*), Tel-Aviv 1947; H. Valentin, *Problemet Palaestina* (Swedish, *The problem of Palestine*), Copenhagen 1947, 38 ff.; J. Waschitz, *Ha-ᶜAravīm bĕ-Ereṯs-Israʾel* (Hebrew, *The Arabs in Palestine*), Merhavya 1947; A. Cunningham, *Palestine — the last days of the mandate*, in *IA*, xxiv/4 (Oct. 1948), 481-90; B. Joseph, *British rule in Palestine*, Washington, D.C. 1948, index; Seton-Williams, 121-79; P. Tábori, *Palesztina* (Hungarian, *Palestine*), Budapest n.d. [1948], 39 ff.; Daphne Trevor, *Under the white paper: some aspects of British administration in Palestine from 1939 to 1947*, Jerusalem 1948, index; W.B. Ziff, *The rape of Palestine*, London 1948, 84-528; Bentwich, *The legal system of Palestine under the mandate*, in *MEJ*, ii/1 (Jan. 1948), 33-46; idem, *The present and future of Palestine*, in *Political Quarterly*, xx (1949), 247-56; Musa Alami, *The lesson of Palestine*, in *MEJ*, iii/4 (Oct. 1949), 373-405; A. Koestler, *Promise and fulfilment: Palestine 1917-1949*, London 1949; L.L. Leonard, *The United Nations and Palestine*, in *International Concilation*, 454 (Oct. 1949), 607-786; F.E. Manuel, *The realities of American-Palestine relations*, Washington. D.C. 1949, chs. 6-8; Hurewitz, *The struggle for Palestine*, New York 1950; A.M. Hyamson, *Palestine under the mandate, 1920-1948*, London 1950; chs. 4-16; Kimche, 137-273; Mis̲h̲el Ilyās Rag̲h̲īb, *al-Mamlaka al-Urdunniyya al-Hās̲h̲imiyya: lamḥa taʾrīḵẖiyya ᶜan al-awḍāᶜ al-ḳadīma wa 'l-ḥadīt̲h̲a*, i, Beirut 1950; D.J. Simpson, *British Palestine policy, 1939-1949*, unpubl. Ph.D. diss., Stanford Univ. 1950; E. Wright, *Abdallah's Jordan*, 1947-1951, in *MEJ*, v/4 (Autumn 1951), 439 ff.; J.J. Zasloff, *Great Britain and Palestine: a study of the problem before the United Nations*, Geneva 1952, 6-128; al-Mudīriyya al-ᶜāmma li 'l-maṭbūᶜāt wa 'l-iᶜlām wa 'l-nas̲h̲r,*al-Urdunn al-ḥadīt̲h̲: maḳālāt*, Amman n.d. [1953]; W.E. Goldner, *The role of Abdullah Ibn Husayn*, King of Jordan, in Arab politics, 1914-1951, unpubl. Ph.D. diss., Stanford Univ. 1954; Upthegrove, *Empire* ..., 143-63; H.F. Frischwasser-Raᶜanan, *The frontiers of a nation*, London 1955, ch. 5 ("Frontiers of mandatory Palestine"); G. Lias, *Glubb's legion*, London 1956 (French tr., *Légionnaires de Glubb-Pacha*, Paris 1959); *Ye*.. A. Lyebyedyev,

Iordaniya v bor'bye za nyezavisimost', Moscow 1956, 6 ff.; I. Oder, *The United States and the Palestine mandate*, unpubl. Ph.D. diss., Columbia Univ., 1956. J. Bowle, *Viscount Samuel: a biography*, London 1957, 167-236; Ṣawwān al-Djāsir and Nuʿmān Abū Bāsim, *al-Urdunn wa-muʾāmarāt al-istiʿmār*, Cairo 1957, 7-33; Ann Dearden, *Jordan*, London 1958, 41-79; E.E. Gutmann, *The development of local government in Palestine: background to the study of local administration in Israel*, unpubl. Ph.D. diss., Columbia Univ. 1958; G.L. Harris *et alii*, *Jordan: its society, its culture*, New York 1958, index; Patai, *The kingdom of Jordan*, Princeton, N.J. 1958, ch. 2 and index; H.G. Peake, *History and tribes of Jordan*², Coral Gables, Fla. 1958, 104-10 (Arabic tr., *Taʾrīkh Sharkī al-Urdunn wa-ḳabāʾilihā*, Jerusalem n.d. [1935-6]); R.E. Gabbay, *A political study of the Arab-Jewish conflict*, Geneva and Paris 1959, 24 ff.; Munīb al-Māḍī and Sulaymān Mūsā, *Taʾrīkh al-Urdunn fi 'l-ḳarn al-ʿishrīn*, n.p. [Amman] 1959, 88-533; Marlowe, *The seat of Pilate: an account of the Palastine mandate*, London 1959; J. Morris, *The Hashemite kings*, 86-122; B. Shwadran, *Jordan: a state of tension*, New York 1959, chs. 8-15; Muḥammad ʿIzzat Darwaza, *al-Ḳaḍiyya al-Filasṭīniyya fī mukhtalif marāḥilihā*², i-ii, Sidon 1959-60; Ṣubḥī Yāsīn, *al-Thawra al-ʿArabiyya al-kubrā, 1936-1939*, n.p. [Damascus] n.d. [1959-60]; Ali al-Abdallah, *Les relations anglo-jordaniennes de 1921 à 1957*, unpubl. Ph.D. diss., Univ. of Paris [1960], esp. i, chs. 1-3; *L'affaire Palestinienne: documents de source arabe*, in *Orient*, xvi (1960), 183-209; Muḥammad al-ʿIzbī, *Kayfa ṣanaʿa al-Indjilīz al-Urdunn? al-Mufāwaḍāt al-sirriyya bayn al-Ṣahyūniyya wa 'l-bayt al-Hāshimī*, n.p. n.d. [1960]. Saʿīd, *ʿUrūsh...*, 71 ff.; A. Razak Abdel-Kader, *Le conflit judéo-arabe: Juifs et Arabes face à l'avenir*², Paris 1962, 31 ff.; L.N. Kotlov, *Iordaniya v novyeyshyeye vryemya*, Moscow 1962, 13-99; De Novo, *American interests* ..., 337-47; Niḳūlā al-Durr, *Hākadhā ḍaʿat wa-hākadhā taʿūd*, Beirut 1963, 16 ff.; Gdański, *Arabski wschód* ..., 228-45; Sami Hadawi, *Palestine: loss of a heritage*, San Antonio, Texas 1963, 12-49; L. Hirszowicz, *Nazi Germany and the Palestine partition plan*, in *MES*, i/1 (Oct. 1964), 40-65; Y.S. Brenner, *The "Stern gang" 1940-48*, in *ibid.*, ii/1 (Oct. 1965), 2-30; F.A. Sayegh, *Zionist colonialism in Palestine*, Beirut 1965; C. Sykes, *Cross roads to Israel*, London 1965, index; Y. Bauer, *From cooperation to resistance: the Haganah, 1938-1946*, in *MES*, ii/3 (April 1966), 182-210; G.B. Doxee, *British policy toward Palestine, 1914-1949*, unpubl. Ph.D. diss., Harvard Univ. 1966; Ingrid Mährdel, *Die britische Mandatsherrschaft über Palästina (1922-1936)*, unpubl. Ph.D. diss., Karl-Marx-Univ., Leipzig 1966; J.B. Schechtman, *The United States and the Jewish state movement: the crucial decade, 1939-1949*, New York 1966, index; M. Asaf, *Tōlĕdōt ha-ʿAravīm bĕ-Erets-Israʾel w-bĕrīḥatam* (Hebrew, *History of the Arabs in Palestine and their flight*), Tel-Aviv 1967, 93-182; M. Bar-Zohar, *The armed prophet: a biography of Ben-Gurion*, London 1967, index; F. Cataluccio, *La questione* ...; A.M. Goichon, *Jordanie réelle* [Paris] 1967, i, 119-289; Hadawi, *Bitter harvest: Palestine between 1914-1967*, New York 1967, 55-115; P.J. Vatikiotis, *Politics and the military in Jordan: a study of the Arab legion, 1921-1957*, London 1967, chs. 2-3; F.J. Khouri, *The Arab-Israel dilemma*, Syracuse, N.Y. 1968, 16-101; W.Z. Laqueur (ed.), *The Israel Arab reader*, New York 1968, 44-122; H. Marcus, *"Middle East" ce nid d'intrigues: politique mandataire, camps d'internement*, Jerusalem n.d. [1968], 6 ff.; Ben Gurion, *Mĕdīnat Israʾel ha-mithaddeshet* (Hebrew, *The renovated State of Israel*), Tel-Aviv 1969, i, 52-87; *Novyeyshaya istorya Arabskikh stran* ..., 113-43; E. Atiyah and H. Cattan, *Palestine: terre de promesse et de sang*, n.p. [Paris] 1969, 53-104; Ḥasan al-Djalbī, *Ḳaḍiyyat Filasṭīn fī ḍawʾ al-ḳānūn al-duwalī*, n.p. 1969, 53-61. 135-67; Furlonge, *Palestine is my country: the story of Musa Alami*, London 1969, 67-163; Gannon, *The influence* ..., 184-292; Kedourie, *Sir Herbert Samuel and the government of Palestine*, in *MES*, v/1 (Jan. 1969), 44-68; U. Dann, *The beginnings of the Arab Legion*, in *ibid.*, v/3 (Oct. 1969), 181-91; Tuğ, 303 ff.; E. Weisband, *The Sanjak of Alexandretta, 1920-1939: a case study*, in R.B. Winder (ed.), *Near Eastern round table*, New York 1969, 156-224; ʿAwda Buṭrus ʿAwda, *al-Ḳaḍiyya al-Filasṭīnıyya fi 'l-wāḳiʿ al-Arabī* , n.p. 1970 ; Y. Bauer, *From diplomacy to restistance: a history of Jewish Palestine, 1939-1945*, Philadelphia 1970, index; S.L. Hattis, *The bi-national idea in Palestina during mandatory times*, Haifa 1970: A.S. Klieman, *Foundations* ..., 171-235; Abdel Wahhab Ahmed Abdel Rahman, *British policy towards the Arab revolt in Palestine, 1936-1939*, unpubl. Ph.D. diss., London Univ. 1971; Ibrahim Abu Lughod (ed.), *The transformation of Palestine: essays on the origin and development of the Arab-Israeli conflict*, Evanston, Ill. 1971; A. Elon, *The Israelis: founders and sons*, London 1971, index; D.E. Knox, *The development of British policy in Palestine, 1917-1925*, unpubl. Ph.D. diss., Michigan State Univ. 1971; Sulaymān Mūsā, *Taʾsīs al-imāra al-Urdunniyya, 1921-1925*, Amman 1971; G. Sheffer, *Policy-making and British policies toward Palestine, 1929-1939*, unpubl. Ph.D. diss., Oxford Univ. 1971; Annamarie Adé, *Winston S. Churchill und die Palästina-Frage, 1917-1948*, unpubl. Ph.D. diss., Zürich Univ. 1972, 21-254; N.A. Aruri, *Jordan: a study in political development (1921-1965)*, The Hague 1972, 18-88; W. Khalidi, *Die Palästinaproblem*, Rastatt-Baden 1972, 26 ff.; Laqueur, *A history of Zionism*, London 1972, index; Amin Abdullah Mahmud, *King Abdullah and Palestine: an historical study of his role*, unpubl. Ph.D. diss., Georgetown Univ. 1972; P. Ofer, *The role of the High Commissioner in British policy in Palestina*, unpubl. Ph.D. diss., London Univ, 1972; Ann Sinai and I.R. Sinai (eds.), *Israel and the Arabs: Prelude to the Jewish state*, New York 1972, index; Adnan Mohammed Abu-Ghazaleh, *Arab cultural nationalism in Palestine during the British mandate*, Beirut 1973, 20 ff.; Ben Gurion, *My talks with Arab leaders*, New York 1973; Dann, *The political crisis of the summer of 1924 in Transjordan*, Tel-Aviv 1973; N. Grant, *The partition of Palestine, 1947: Jewish triumph, British failure, Arab disaster*, New York 1973; W.B. Quandt *et alii*, *The politics of Palestinian nationalism*, Berkeley, Calif. 1973, 5-42; N.A. Rose, *The gentile Zionists: a study of Anglo-Zionist diplomacy*, London 1973; S.R. Silverburg, *Organization and violence: the Palestinian Arab nationalistic response, 1920-1948*, unpubl. Ph.D. diss., The American Univ., Washington, D.C. 1973; N. Katzburg, *Mi-ḥalūḳa la-sefer ha-lavan: mĕdīniyyūt Bĕrīṭanya be-Erets-Israʾel, 1936-1940* (Hebrew, *From partition to white paper: Britain's policy in Palestine, 1936-40)*, Jerusalem 1974, index; Kāmil Maḥmūd Khilla, *Filasṭīn wa 'l-intidāb al-Briṭānī, 1922-1939*, Beirut 1974, 51 ff.; J.J. Mc Tague, *British policy in Palestine, 1917-1922*, unpubl. Ph.D. diss., SUNY, Buffalo 1974; Y. Porath, *The Palestinian Arab national movement*, i-ii, London 1974; idem, *The political organization of Palestinian Arabs under the British mandate*, in M. Maʿoz (ed.), *Palestinian Arab politics*, Jerusalem 1975, 1-20; T. Bowden, *The politics of the Arab rebellion in Palestine, 1936-39*, in *MES*, xi/2 (May 1975), 147-74; M.J. Cohen, *Direction of policy in Palestine*, in *ibid.*, xi/3 (Oct. 1975), 237-61; M. Curtis *et alii* (eds.), *The Palestinians: people, history, politics*, New Brunswick, N.J. 1975, 21-50; Cl. Lo Jacono, *I governi transgiordanici dal 1921 al 1948*, in *OM*, lv/1-2 (Jan.-Feb. 1975), 67-78; Y.N. Miller, *From village to nation: government and society in rural Palestine, 1920-1948*, unpubl. Ph.D. diss., U.C. Berkeley 1975; Aida Ali Najjar, *The Arabic press and nationalism in Palestine*, unpubl. Ph.D. diss., Syracuse Univ. 1975; G. Cohen, *Ha-Ḳabīneṭ ha-Bĕriṭī w-shĕʾelat Ereṯs-Israʾel, 1943* (Hebrew, *The British Cabinet and the question of Palestine, 1943)*, Tel-Aviv 1976; Dann, *The United States and the recognition of Transjordan 1946-1949*, in *Asian and African Studies* (Jerusalem), xi/2 (1976), 213-39; B. Litvinoff, *Weizmann: last of the patriarchs*, London 1976, 127 ff.; Reguer, *Winston Churchill...*, 283-317 ("Policy for Palestine"); H.M. Sachar, *A history of Israel from the rise of Zionism to our time*, New York 1976, 116-353; B. Wasserstein, *Herbert Samuel and the Palestine problem*, in *English Historical Review*, xci/361 (Oct. 1976), 753-75; T. Bowden, *The breakdown of public security: the case of Ireland 1916-1921 and Palestine 1936-1939*, London and Beverly Hills 1977, 143 ff.; O. Carré, *Le mouvement national palestinien*, Paris 1977, 39-107; M.J. Cohen, *Secret diplomacy and rebellion in Palestine, 1936-1939*, in *IJMES*, viii/3 (July 1977), 379-404; Ph. Daumas, *La Palestine et le mandat brittanique*, in J. Bauberat *et alii*, *Palestine et Liban: promesses et mensonges de l'Orient*, Paris 1977, 106-30; M. Gilbert, *Britain, Palestine and the Jews: the evolution of the 1939 white paper, 1891-1939*, Oxford 1977; Ann Sinai and A. Pollack (eds.), *The Hashimite kingdom of Jordan and the West Bank: a handbook*, New York 1977, 21-8 and index; Tibawi, *Anglo-Arab relations and the question of Palestine, 1914-1921*, London 1977, 387-503; A.W. Kayyali, *Palestine: a modern history*, London n.d. [1977-8], 84 ff.; G. Ben-Dor (ed.), *The Palestinians and the Middle East conflict*, Ramat-Gan 1978; N. Caplan, *Palestine Jewry and the Arab question, 1917-1925*, London 1978; M.J. Cohen, *Palestine: retreat from the mandate: the making of British policy, 1936-45*, London 1978, index; R.H. Eisenman, *Islamic law in Palestine and Israel*, Leiden 1978, 73-151; M. Gilbert, *Exile and return: the emergence of Jewish statehood*, London 1978, 119-309; D. Horowitz and M. Lissak, *Origins of the Israeli polity: Palestine under the mandate*, Chicago and London 1978; B. Wasserstein, *The British in Palestine: the mandatory government and the Arab-Jewish conflict, 1917-1929*, London 1978, 73-241; N. Bethell, *The Palestine triangle: the struggle between the British, the Jews and the Arabs, 1935-1948*, London 1979; N. Feinberg, *Die völkerrechtliche Grundlagen der Palästinensischen Staatsangehörigkeit*, repr. in idem, *Studies in International Law*, Jerusalem 1979, 385-400; idem, *The problem of the legislative council — its legal aspect*, repr. in *ibid.*, 401-13; idem, *The interpretation of the Anglo-American convention on Palestine, 1924*, repr. in *ibid.*, 414-29; Z. Ganin, *Truman, American Jewry and Israel, 1945-1948*, New York and London 1979, index; A. Ilan, *Ameriḳa, Bĕriṭanya ve-Ereṯs-Israʾel* (Hebrew, *America, Britain and Palestine*), Jerusalem 1979; W. Kazziha, *The political evolution of Tranjordan*, in *MES*, xv/2 (May 1979), 239-57; A.S. Klieman, *Divisiveness of Palestine: Foreign Office versus Colonial Office on the issue of partition, 1937*, in *Historical Jnal.*, xxii/2 (June 1979), 423-41; A.M. Lesch, *Arab politics in Palestine, 1917-1939: the frustration of a nationalist movement*, Ithaca and London 1979, 79 ff.; Fallāḥ K͟hālid ʿAli, *Filasṭīn wa 'l-intidāb al-Briṭānī*, 1919-1948, Beirut 1980; Sarah Graham-Brown, *Palestinians and their society 1880-1946: a photographic essay*, London 1980; J. Jankowski, *Egyptian responses to the Palestine problem in the interwar period*, in *IJMES*, xii/1 (Aug. 1980), 1-38; R.L. Jasse, *Zion abandoned: Great Britain's withdrawal from the Palestine mandate, 1945-1948*, unpubl. Ph.D. diss., Catholic Univ. of America, Washington, D.C. 1980; Shmuel Dotan, *Ha-Maʾavaḳ ʿal-Ereṯs-Israʾel* (Hebrew, *The struggle for Palestine)*, Tel-Aviv 1981, index; Kedourie, *The Bludan congress on Palestine, September 1937*, in *MES*, xvii/1 (Jan. 1981), 107-25; M.J. Haron, *The British decision to give the Palestine question to the United Nations*, in *ibid.*, xvii/2 (Apr. 1981), 241-8; H. Mejcher and A. Schölch (eds.), *Die Palästina Frage 1917-1948: historische Ursprünge und internationale Dimensionen eines Nationenkonflikts*, Paderborn 1981, 47-216; A. Nachmani, *British policy in Palestine: The Anglo-American committee of inquiry into the problems of European Jewry and Palestine, 1945-1946*, unpubl. Ph.D. diss., Oxford Univ. 1981; M.J. Cohen, *Palestine and the Great Powers, 1945-1948*, Princeton 1982; N. Gross, *The economic policy of the Mandatory Government in Palestine*, Jerusalem 1982 (= Falk Institute's Discussion Paper 816); Y. Porath and Y. Shavit (eds.), *Ha-Māndāṭ wĕ-ha-bayit ha-lĕʾūmī (1917-1947)* (Hebrew, *The mandate and the national home, 1917-1947)*, Jerusalem 1982; Yūsuf Haykal, *al-Ḳaḍiyya al-Filasṭīniyya: taḥlīl wa-naḳd*, Jaffa n.d.; idem, *Mas͟hrūʿ taksīm Filasṭin wa-ak͟htāruhu*, n.p. n.d.; Amīn Saʿīd, *al-T͟hawra al-ʿArabiyya...*, iii, 5 ff.; M. Sarkīs and D. G͟halī, *al-Ṣahyūniyya wa 'l-ittiḥād wa-d͟jalāʾil aʿmāliha fī Filasṭīn*, Cairo n.d.; Aziz B. Shihadeh, *A.B.C. of the Arab case in Palestine. An exposition of the Arab case in concise and readable form*, Jaffa n.d. (J.M. Landau)

MANDE, a term which simultaneously possesses geographical, political and ethnic connotations. Mande is a region situated between the upper Niger to the East, Beledougou to the North and the upper Bakhoy to the West. Mande is also applied, however, to the whole of an enormous ethnic family comprising, according to some West African traditions (Dogon, Bambara, Malinke in particular), more than forty population groups currently inhabiting the Republics of Guinea, the Ivory Coast, Ghana, Mali, Upper Volta, Niger and even Nigeria (see D. Zahan, *Aperçu sur la pensée théogonique des Dogon*, in *Cahiers Internationaux de Sociologie*, vi [1949], 113-33; S. de Ganay, *Notes sur la théodicée bambara*, in *RHR*, cxxxv [1949], 212-13; G. Dieterlen, *Essai sur la religion bambara*, Paris 1951, 13; the same, *Mythe et organisation sociale au Soudan français*, in *Journal de la Société des Africanistes*, xxv/1-2 [1955], 40-2).

More precisely, Mande designates the "motherland" of one of the ethnic groups which originated there, the Mandingos. According to dialectal variants, the latter pronounce the term *Mande* or *Mandeng*, *Mandi*, or *Manding*, while the Bambara of Ouassoulu (South of Bamako) say *Mane* or *Mani*, the Soninkes *Malle* or *Malli*, the Foulbe *Melle* or *Melli* (cf. M. Delafosse, *Haut-Sénégal-Niger* (*Soudan français*), 1st series, i, 121). All these forms constitute variants of one word which in phonetic notation should be transcribed as *Mãdẽ* or Mãdẽ.

This phonetic rendering illustrates the uncertain etymology of the morpheme, *Mãdẽ* could signify either "child" (*dẽ*) of the mother *ma*", i.e. uterine issue or "child (*dẽ*) of the master of the soil (*mã*)", i.e. indigenous (cf. M. Delafosse, *La Langue mandingue et ses dialects* (*Malinké, Bambara, Dioula*), Bibl. de l'ENLOV,

Paris 1929, i, 11). There is no basis for deciding in favour of either of these hypotheses.

In the current state of knowledge, little is known of the early history of the Mande. The first written information on this subject derives from Arabic sources, it being understood that the first scholars to transmit in writing their knowledge of sub-Saharan Africa lived in North Africa and were directly or indirectly in contact with the negroes of the Sudan of their period. Among the latter, the Mandingos were, doubtless from an early period, the suppliers of gold (the *tibr* of the Arab authors, signifying "unrefined gold" and "gold dust") to the Italian, Portuguese and Spanish merchants who acquired it in North Africa through the intermediary of local traders. But it is logical to suppose that the tracks crossing the Sahara and bearing this precious metal towards the Mediterranean did not become "trade routes" until after the conquest of North Africa by the Arabs. Furthermore, it was subsequent to this invasion that there appeared the first written testimonies relating to the Mande.

The earliest in date, known today, is given by al-Ya^c^ḳūbī (d. 284/897) in his *Ta^ɔ^rīkh*, 28: "There is also another kingdom called Mallal, which is at war with the sovereign of Kānim (Kanem). Their king is called Mayusī (Mai Wasī?)" (cf. J.M. Cuoq, *Recueil des sources arabes concernant l'Afrique Occidentale du VIIIe au XVIe siècle* (*Bilād al-Sūdān*), Paris 1975, 48). Mallal is in fact Mali [*q.v.*], the future rival, then destroyer, of Ghāna [*q.v.*]. Al-Ya^c^ḳūbī knew of it only by hearsay, never having travelled himself in the Bilād al-Sūdān. If his orthography is to be believed, the information that he provides is without doubt of Soninké origin, the Soninkés (or Sarakolés) constituting the predominant group, from a political and economic point of view, in the kingdom of Ghāna, situated between the Maghrib and the valleys of Senegal and of the upper Niger (otherwise known as the "Nile" by the Arab historians and geographers).

It is difficult to say what was the nature of Mallal at the time of this ancient historical testimony; a modest local chiefdom, no doubt, situated in the region of the confluence of the Niger and the Sankarani, but one which was beginning to make itself known because of its deposits of gold, coveted by the Arabs and the peoples living to the north of the Mediterranean.

Some time ago, having understood the cultural importance of the historical evidence, traditional story-tellers (*griots*) or minstrels of the present-day Republic of Mali began to reveal their knowledge concerning Mali. Certainly, this information is to be taken with the caution appropriate to oral testimonies separated from the events that they describe by a considerable period of time. But caution is not the same as rebuttal, far from it. According to these story-tellers, then, at the time of the foundation of the empire of Mali (beginning of the 13th century), the Manding comprised 34 clans, lineages and socio-professional groups: 16 clans of warriors (Konâté, Coulibaly, Traoré, Koné, Doumbya (or Koroma, or Kourouma, or Sissoko, or Fakoly), Kamara-Komagara, Bagayogo-Sinayogo, Dèrèba-Kamissoko, Dannyoko, Magassouba, Diawara, Dâbo, Diallo, Diakité, Sidibé and Sangeré); 5 Keïta lineages belonging to the family of Soundyata, founder of the empire; 5 maraboutic families (Cissé, Touré, Berété, Diâné and Sânogo)(according to some, the Kouma constituted the fifth maraboutic family of the Manding); 4 Dyâbi families, related to the afore-mentioned maraboutic families; 4 families of people of "caste": the *griots* or minstrels (Kwaté (Kouyaté), Kamissoko, Dyabaté, Soumano); the blacksmiths: Doubya, Bagayogo, Sinayogo, Sinaba, Kanté; the shoemakers: Kamare, Garanké; the descendants of slaves and slaves themselves (SCOA, *L'Empire du Mali*, 1976, 413).

Originally, however, the number of Manding clans was smaller. The memories of the story-tellers mention twelve of them, as having constituted the nucleus of what was later to become the Manding "world", the difference (between this number and 34) consisting of new elements coming in from the exterior, either from the empire of Ghāna, or from Sosso Mande, in fact, attracted these "immigrants", as they would now be called, for two reasons: first, the gold of Bouré, with all that this metal offered in terms of opportunity for work and wealth, and second, the paganism of the animist religion which was seen as virgin territory for Islamic missionary effort. The first of these attractions was more of a lure to the inhabitants of Sosso, almost all of whom practised the extraction and casting of iron; the second appealed to natives of the kingdom of Ghāna, among whom Islam was already beginning to be implanted on a wide scale and who were seeking, at the same time, to migrate towards the south, as a result of increasingly frequent droughts.

It is evident that available knowledge concerning Mande before the foundation of the empire represents fragments of little importance. If to these there is added an item from al-Bakrī (*K. al-Masālik wa 'l-mamālik*, tr. de Slane, 1965, 333, quoted by Cuoq, *op. cit.*, 102-3), mentioning the conversion to Islam of a king of Mallal (*ca.* 442/1050) with the aim of putting an end to the drought which was devastating his country, then in a passage from al-Idrīsī (548/1154) on the subject of Mallal, "a small town without walls (*Opus geographicum*, i, Naples-Rome 1970, 22; Cuoq, *op. cit.*, 132), the sensation of "historicity" may perhaps be reassuring, but our knowledge relating to Mande gains nothing in substance. It is not until the beginning of the 13th century, and again with recourse to the oral tradition relayed by the minstrels, that a "history" is discovered in which Mande becomes a kind of stage, upon which actors, half-real and half-mystical, play a role in events of interest and significance.

At this period there was in Mande a certain Naré-Famaghan, who was only one of forty or more Manding princelings all of whom bore the title of *mansa* (chief). He had twelve sons, his potential successors, of whom the youngest, Soundiata (the Mari-Diata of Ibn Khaldūn) was to have a historic destiny: it was he who was soon to found the empire of Mali. Meanwhile, Mande was tributary to the neighbouring kingdom of Sosso.

This destiny was, in reality, dependent on three factors: (a) the decline of the neighbouring empire to the north, Ghāna, threatened by the king of Sosso, as well as by Arabo-Berbers descending from the north who were ultimately to destroy it (469/1076-7); (b) the lack of unity in Mande, where each princeling was master of his own territory; and (c) the victory of Soundiata over his rival Soumangourou Kanté, king of Sosso.

This last factor constitutes a remarkable example of the oral history of Mande. The narration of the events which took place in the confrontation between the two protagonists takes the form of an epic account in which the real, the miraculous, the serious and the comic are mingled in an apparently inextricable manner, but where a guiding thread is detectable throughout. The story-tellers have seized with relish on these events and, in general, accord little importance to the other two factors.

The plot of the account in question may be summarised in the following manner. Soumangourou, king of Sosso and suzerain of Mande, massacres the eleven sons of Soundiata. The latter is spared only on account of his disability, which renders him inoffensive in the eyes of his suzerain. His disability is significant and makes him the opposite of his rival, the blacksmith of Sosso, the archetypal "man of action", dressed in garments of iron; he has crippled legs, as a result of which he lives for seventeen years in a hole in the ground, only his head and shoulders being visible. But Soundiata is cured of his infirmity in an equally significant manner: with the aid or two enormous bars of iron (used by him successively), of which the first becomes his bow and the second his royal sceptre, he hoists himself out of his "hole", permanently cured, takes to arms, rallies his warriors and goes to fight Soumagourou in a decisive battle, at Krina. The latter escapes from his pursuer only by disappearing into a cave, at Koulikoro, the opening of which is blocked by a slab of stone immediately after the entry of the unlucky hero. Traditionists and historians agree in making these events coincide with the foundation of the Manding empire, *ca.* 1235, and the dispersion of the blacksmiths across West Africa, subsequent to the destruction of their "empire".

It has not been possible to include all the details of the famous encounter between the two protagonists. The elements of the account supplied here have the purpose only of giving an impression of the structure of the narrative and an "introduction" to its eventual interpretention.

This structure and its interpretation have as their starting point the idea that the status of the hunter-cultivator is superior to that of the blacksmith; but this superiority only emerges and becomes evident from the moment that the first masters the products of the technology of iron possessed by the second. Soundiate is in subjection to Soumangourou until the day that he takes possession of arms, of which the raw material has been supplied to him by his rival, the blacksmith. This could, conceivably, be translated into more modern terms as an assertion that strategy and skill in the manipulation of arms (traits characteristic of the hunter-cultivator) represent a knowledge more profound than that which concerns metallurgy and the science of the armourer. The story summarised above also refers, undoubtedly, to the type of knowledge acquired through initiation. The blacksmith is, on account of his skill, a "natural" and it could be said, initiated being. The hunter-cultivator, on the other hand, acquires this knowledge only after a long period of initiation corresponding to a "death". Soundiata remains "buried" for seventeen years, and emerges from his "hole" to conquer. Soumangourou, on the contrary, is the archetype of life and strength, but, beaten, he descends into bowels of the earth. One comes out of the earth to defeat his adversary, the other enters the earth, vanquished by his enemy. This gives an explanation not only of the dispersal of blacksmiths across Africa, but especially of their place in society.

Soundiata, rich in exploits and in wisdom, occupies a position of eminence in the memory of Malinké story-tellers. He has no equal in the history of Mande other than in the person of one of his successors at the beginning of the 8th/14th century, Mansa Mūsā [*q.v.*], whose reign marked the highest point of the Manding empire. In his time, this extended from Gao to the estuary of the Gambia, and from Oualata (in the north) to the jungles of Guinea. But Mansa Mūsā owes his place of honour in the work of Arab historians, particularly in that of al-ʿUmarī (*Masālik al-abṣār fī mamālik al-amṣār*, quoted by Cuoq, *op. cit.*, 275-9), to the pilgrimage which he made to Mecca and to the fast which he observed during the journey. This sovereign dominated the whole of the 8th/14th century in West Africa. Even Europe was aware of him and he was featured on the Catalan maps of Dulcert (1339) and of Cresques (1375). Ibn Baṭṭūṭa (iv, 376-48), who passed through Mande in 753/1352-3, was unable to make the acquaintance of the Manding emperor who died *ca.* 1337, but his journey coincided with the last years of prosperity of the great empire. From about the year 1380 onwards, this empire entered upon a period of decadence concerning which Ibn K͟haldūn gives some interesting information (cf. Cuoq, *op. cit.*, 339-50). The 15th century marked the beginning of the death-throes of Mande, harassed by the Touareg, the Songhai and the Mossi; the second half of the 17th century saw its disappearance. In 1670, Mande, as a political entity, was reduced, under the onslaught of the Bambara kings of Segou, to the small province from which it had originated, in the region of the Upper Niger; it had survived for approximately three and a half centuries.

Situated in a zone of commercial contacts between North Africa and Black Africa, Mande has, on account of its rich gold deposits, throughout its history attracted much covetousness, on the part of its immediate neighbours as well as of the Arabo-Berber tribes of the Mediterranean coast. In view of the facts, it is quite astonishing that this great kingdom, born out of the victory of strategy over technology, could have lasted so long. This would not, in the opinion of the present writer, have been possible had not those who presided over the affairs of the country, as well as the people themselves, been particularly conscious of the values which permit the realisation of human potential. The initiatic societies of the Malinkés, so closely linked to the monarchy, are instructive in regard to the "spiritual" preoccupations of the kings of Mande. Such concerns are not rare in African history, but in this case they take on a particular dimension in view of the zone of insecurity in which the Manding empire was located from the very beginning of its existence.

Bibliography: In addition to references given in the article, see J.J. Trimingham, *A history of Islam in West Africa*, Oxford 1962, index; *L'Empire du Mali. Un récit de Wa Kamissoko de Krina*, set down, transcribed and annotated by Youssouf Tata Cisse, Premier Colloque International de Bamako (27 January-1 February 1975), Fondation SCOA, Paris 1975; Colloque de Bamako, 1975, *Actes*, Fondation SCOA, Paris 1975; *L'Empire du Mali. Un récit de Wa Kamissoko de Krina*, set down, transcribed, translated and annotated by Youssouf Tata Cisse, Deuxième Colloque International de Bamako, (16 February-22 February 1976), Fondation SCOA, Paris 1977; Colloque de Bamako 1976, *Actes*, Foundation SCOA, Paris 1977; *Actes du Colloque de Niamey*, Paris 1980. (D. Zahan)

MANDĪL, normalised *mindīl*, from Latin/Greek *mantēl(e, -um, ium)*, entered Arabic speech in pre-Islamic times, presumably through Aramaic, and has remained in use to this day. Its principal meanings were those of handkerchief, napkin, and towel. *Mandīl* was, however, understood generally as "piece of cloth" and used for many other purposes, such as covering or carrying something or serving, attached to the body, as an untailored part of dress. Numerous other words were available in Islamic languages as synonyms of *mandīl* in both its specific and its generalised meanings. Arabic thus had _mashūsh_ and _minshafa_, while _khirḳa_ was often substituted as an inferior sort of _mandīl_. Persian had _dastār_ (dimin. _dastārča_), _rūmāl_, and many other words; some were used in Arabic contexts such as _shustadja_ (al-Ṭabarī, i, 1048, also Glossary, CCCXI, and below) and _dastadja_ (Kushādjim, below, although the meaning of handkerchief for _dastadja_ seems unusual, read _shustadja_?). Turkish _buḳča_ was frequent in later Arabic texts (_buḳdja_, for instance, al-Djawbarī, _Kashf_, Cairo 1316, 24; Ibn Abī Uṣaybiʿa, ii, 178). The diminutive _munaydi/īl_ is attested (Ibrāhīm b. Yaʿḳūb [_q.v._], in al-Bakrī, _Masālik_ in connection with Prague; Ibn Sūdūn, _Nuzhat al-nufūs_, ms. Brit. Mus. or. 6517, fols. 70a, 110a). Philologists invented _kunyas_ for _mandīl_: Abu 'l Hānī, Abū Ṭāhir, Abu 'l-Naẓīf (Ibn al-Athīr, _Muraṣṣaʿ_, Baghdād 1972, 230, 323, 344, 373). Construct formations indicated function, such as _m. al-ghamar_ ("grease"), _al-ṭaʿām_ ("food"), _al-sharāb_ ("drink"), _al-wadjh_ ("face"), _al-ʿudhra_ ("virginity"), _al-amān_ ("safe conduct"). _M. al-kumm_ (cf. German _Taschentuch_) got its designation from the wide sleeve in which it was carried.

_Mandīl_s were made of many textile fibres. Often they were outstanding products of the weaver's and embroiderer's craft. This applied in particular to handkerchiefs, but also, in a more modest way, to napkins and towels. Handkerchiefs were praised for their sheerness and beauty. The qualities of their different makes were compared (al-Mubarrad, _Kāmil_, repr. Cairo _ca._ 1968, ii, 146). They came in many colours and had colourful embroidered borders. Many localities, especially in Iran and Egypt, produced, and gave their names to, special kinds of _mandīl_s. Depending on quality, they could be very costly; even badly worn _mandīl_s could still be sold for cash (al-Tanūkhī, _al-Faradj baʿd al-shidda_, Cairo 1357/1938, i, 55 f., cf. also _Nishwār_, Cairo 1391-3/1971-3, iii, 67). They shared with other textiles the fact that they were often not within the reach of the poor. Not having a _mandīl_ was part of the definition of poverty (al-Ghazālī, _Iḥyāʾ_, Cairo 1352/1933, i, 198). Conversely, the wealthier classes took considerable pride in them and counted them among their prized possessions, to which a person might become unduly attached (_Iḥyāʾ_, iv, 426, 1. 23) and which had to be taken good care of. But even among ordinary people, it was customary to carry a handkerchief when going out, as is shown, for instance, by the curious story of the trained donkey in al-Ghuzūlī, _Maṭāliʿ al-budūr_, Cairo 1299-1300, ii, 183 (for the use of _mandīl_s in tricks, cf. also al-Djawbarī, 16, etc.). A complete outfit of clothing (_Iḥyāʾ_, iv, 185, 200) or a proper trousseau would include _mandīl_s. Since they were thought to be indispensable, they were assumed to exist in Paradise (according to the _ḥadīth_, cf. also Abu 'l-Layth al-Samarḳandī, _Ḳurrat al-ʿuyūn_, on the margins of al-Shaʿrānī, _Mukhtaṣar_, Cairo 1358/1939, 159; Ibn Ḳayyim al-Djawziyya, _Ḥādī al-arwāḥ_, Cairo 1381/1962, ch. 50). Angels had _mandīl_s of fire (al-Nuwayrī al-Iskandarānī, _Ilmām_, Hyderabad 1388-96/1968-76, i, 123, 1. 6). Fire-resisting _mandīl_s in this world were described as curiosities.

Many uses of _mandīl_s are attested, for instance: covering the face to conceal crying (al-Yūnīnī, _Dhayl_, Hyderabad 1374-80/1954-61, i, 364; al-Djawbarī, 23, speaking of a trained monkey); wiping off tears (_Taʾrīkh Baghdād_, xi, 185) or sweat (al-Ṣābiʾ, _Rusūm dār al-khilāfa_, Baghdād 1383/1964, 75, using _shustadja_, tr. Salem, Beirut 1977, 61); blowing the nose, which had to be done in a refined manner, and the _m. al-ṭaʿām_ was not to be used for it (al-Nuwayrī, _Nihāya_, iv, 126, 1. 18; al-Ghuzūlī, i, 146, 1. 3); stilling a nose bleed al-Yūnīnī, i, 354); cleaning hands and mouth after

eating and drinking; wiping off spittle, to be done delicately with the end (_dhuʾāba_) of a folded _mandīl_, as was the custom of the great al-Ṭabarī (Yāḳūt, _Udabāʾ_, vi, 459); drying parts of the body; covering the loins (_izār_) after bathing (cf. H. Grotzfeld, _Bad_, Wiesbaden 1970, 67, 93); wrapping it around the body like a _wishāḥ_ (al-Shābushtī, _Diyārāt_, Baghdād 1951, 133; al-Ṣanawbarī, _Dīwān_, Beirut 1970, 486); covering the head as _ʿimāma_ (al-Zadjdjādjī, _Amālī_, Cairo 1382, 171 f.); covering dishes and tables; carrying practically anything, money, sandals (Ibn al-Sukāʿī, _Tālī_, Damascus 1974, 111), the medicines of a visiting physician (Ibn Abī Uṣaybiʿa, i, 158, 1. 28, and, using _shustadja_, i, 217, 1. 2); massaging and serving as hot compresses (al-Rāzī, _Tadjārib_, ms. Istanbul, Topkapısarayı Ahmet III 1975, fols. 72a, 93a); wrapping objects, even heavy ones in large _mandīl_s; strangling (al-Mubarrad, _Kāmil_, iv, 8) or poisoning (al-Masʿūdī, _Murūdj_, viii, 211 = § 3354); using it in _futuwwa_ installation ceremonies (cf. F. Taeschner, _Zünfte und Bruderschaften_, Zürich-Munich 1979, 222), etc., etc.

Literature speaks of handkerchiefs as convenient for writing on, or concealing in, billets-doux (Ibn al-Djawzī, _Dhamm al-hawā_, Cairo 1381/1962, 532 f.). In general, littérateurs considered them worthy of notice as art objects whose mention conveyed special moods and aesthetic impressions. A poem by Kushādjim [_q.v._] mourning a _mandīl_ of his that had been pilfered by a lover gives a graphic description of their use and the esteem in which they were held (_Dīwān_, Baghdād 1390/1970, 86-8; al-Ḥuṣrī, _Zahr al-ādāb_, Cairo 1389/1969, 868 f.). Blood covering a wolf's head from between the ears to the shoulder blades suggested a _mandīl_ to the _mukhaḍram_ poet Ibn Muḳbil [_q.v._ in Suppl.] (Ibn Ḳutayba, _Maʿānī_, Hyderabad 1368-69/1949, i, 184). The elephant's ear was compared to it (al-Djāḥiẓ, _Ḥayawān_, ed. Hārūn, vii, 173), as was the flame of a candle spread by the wind's blowing (Diyāʾ al-Dīn Ibn al-Athīr, as quoted by al-Ghuzūlī, i, 81). _Mandīl_ was used metaphorically to indicate low status, commonness, and abuse (al-Tawḥīdī, _Akhlāḳ al-wazīrayn_, ed. al-Ṭandjī, 232; al-ʿImād al-Rāghib al-Iṣfahānī, _Muḥāḍarāt_, Cairo 1287, i, 313; al-ʿImād al-Iṣfahānī, _Kharīda_, iv, Cairo _ca._ 1951, ii, 134; see also al-Rāʿī al-Numayrī, _Dīwān_, ed. Weipert, Beirut 1980, 235, Steiger and Keller, 126 f.). All this shows that the _mandīl_ was always an object that engaged the human fancy.

Most, if not all, of the uses of _mandīl_s antedated Islam (cf. H. Kindermann, _Über die guten Sitten_, Leiden 1964, 99-102). The widespread use of handkerchiefs, however, shows a high degree of general cultural refinement, much in advance of mediaeval Europe (cf. N. Elias, _The civilizing process_, Eng. tr. New York 1978, 143 ff.).

Bibliography: The few selected references in the article are meant to be in addition to those in F. Rosenthal, _Four essays on art and literature in Islam_, Leiden 1971, 63-99. Fundamental earlier studies are R.B. Serjeant, _Material for a history of Islamic textiles_, in _Ars Islamica_, ix-xvi (1942-51), repr. as _Islamic textiles_, Beirut 1972, and A. Steiger and H.-E. Keller, _Lat. Mantēlum_, in _Vox Romanica_, xv/1 (1956), 103-54, where _mandīl_ is followed in its forms and uses through the European languages and Arabic. More recently, Geniza studies have enriched our knowledge of the _mandīl_, cf. the publications by S. D. Goitein and, especially, Y. K. Stillman, for instance, _The wardrobe of a Jewish bride in Medieval Egypt_, in _Studies in marriage customs_, iv (1974), 297-304. See also LIBĀS.

(F. ROSENTHAL)

MANDĪL, Awlād or Banū, a chiefly family of the Maghrāwa [*q.v.*], prominent in what is now western Algeria in the 7th-8th/13th-14th centuries, taking its name from Mandīl, grandson of one Abū Nās, a scion of the Banū Khazrūn, rulers of Tripoli (391-540/1000-1 to 1145-6) and descendants of the 10th-century Spanish Umayyad Maghrāwī chief, Khazrūn b. Falfūl.

Abū Nās, whose forbear from Tripoli had made his way to kin in the Chélif (Shalaf) basin and finally established himself among the local Maghrāwa, had received an *ᶜiḳṭāᶜ* there for his services to the Almohads in ᶜAbd al-Muʾmin's [*q.v.*] day. His son ᶜAbd al-Raḥmān thereafter united the Maghrāwa behind him and garnered the rewards of loyalty to the Almohads. On his death, he was succeeded by Mandīl, the elder of two sons, whose expansionism won him the Ouarsenis (Wansharīs), Médéa (al-Madiyya) and the fertile Mitidja (Matīdja) plain, which he devastated with unswerving pro-Almohad zeal. Subsequently he lost Mitidja itself [see BULAYDA] to Yaḥyā, the last of the Banū Ghāniya [*q.v.*], and around 623/1226 Yaḥyā had him killed. Mandīl was the founder of the stronghold of Marāt on the Riou (Wādī Rahyū), a tributary of the Chélif.

Mandīl's eldest son, al-ᶜAbbās, was accepted by his brothers as the new chief. As such, he looked to his father's example, but in fact lost all Mandīl's gains to his rivals, the Banū Tūdjīn, and fell back with his tribe on their heartlands in the lower Chélif. There he remained for a time as ruler of a modest principality. A change came with the intervention of the Ḥafṣids [*q.v.*] in the Central Maghrib following the repudiation of Almohad authority by the ᶜAbd al-Wādid [*q.v.*] Yaghamrāsan, *de facto* ruler of Tlemcen. Tribal appeals to the Ḥafṣid Abū Zakariyyāʾ for aid against Tlemcen's aggression met with success: in 640/1242 Tlemcen was taken and Yaghamrāsan made a Ḥafṣid vassal. On his way back, the Ḥafṣid set up, on the basis of tribal support for him, three small buffer dependencies, each with an accredited ruler. One such ruler was al-ᶜAbbās, chief of the Maghrāwa with sway over Miliana (Milyāna), Ténès (Tanas), Brechk (Barishk) and Cherchell (Sharshāl). During the chieftaincy of al-ᶜAbbās, the Maghrāwa founded Mazouna (Māzūna). On his death in 647/1249-50 he was succeeded by his brother Muḥammad. The latter's assassination in 662/1263 by his brothers Thābit and ᶜĀʾid disrupted family unity, With ᶜAbd al-Wādid aid, their brother ᶜUmar eventually won the day (668/1269-70) and, till his death in 676/1277-8, remained chief to the Maghrāwa. Thereafter the chieftaincy reverted to Thābit.

From Muḥammad's murder to Thābit's death the salient feature of the family's history is its involvement with Tlemcen, ending with its début on the Marīnid stage in Fez. Briefly, the facts are as follows. After an accord with Tlemcen, then a quarrel that cost him Miliana, Muḥammad regained the town with the aid of the Ḥafṣid Mustanṣir and ruled it in his name. But ᶜUmar, resenting Thābit's position as chief of the Maghrāwa, conspired with Yaghamrāsan to put Miliana under Tlemcen's suzerainty in return for its governorship and command of the Maghrāwa. To spite ᶜUmar and to curry favour with Yaghamrāsan, Thābit and ᶜĀʾid then sold to the latter Ténès (672/1273-4). Thābit's attempts after ᶜUmar's death to retrieve Miliana for himself and his tribe, though initially successful, ended in disaster. Tlemcen did not allow his disloyalty and rebellion to go unpunished: Yaghamrāsan began a campaign which, after his death, his son ᶜUthmān was to complete. Within a few years, ᶜUthmān had taken Médéa, Mazouna and Ténès and finally forced the Maghrāwa to take to the mountains. Thābit tried in vain to hold Brechk and sailed for Morocco (694/1294-5) to enlist Marīnid support. In his absence, his son Muḥammad usurped his chieftaincy of the Maghrāwa, but did not live long to enjoy it. Thereafter, the Awlād Mandīl of the Central Maghrib disintegrated in a welter of fratricidal and internecine quarrels.

For his part, Thābit was warmly welcomed by the Marīnid sultan Yūsuf b. Yaᶜḳūb, but died in an unfortunate incident in Fās before attaining his goal. His family, however, was cared for by Yūsuf, who in fact came to marry the sister of Thābit's grandson, Rāshid b. Muḥammad. The alliance gave Rāshid reason to hope for the retrieval of his birthright in the Maghrāwa homeland. But it was not to be: during the long Marīnid siege of Tlemcen (689-706/1290-1306), it was to ᶜUmar b. Wīghran b. Mandīl that Yūsuf assigned chieftancy of the Maghrāwa and, later, command of the army that was to take Miliana, Ténès and Mazouna in 699/1299-1300. Resenting his kinsman's preferment, Rāshid deserted the Marīnids. From the Mitidja mountains he won a Maghrāwa following, provoked a rising in Mazouna, and, having eliminated his rival ᶜUmar, gained united Maghrāwī support. Leaving Mazouna strongly garrisoned, he entrenched himself in the mountain fastness of the Banū Bū Saᶜīd between Mazouna and Ténès. For the Marīnids he was a scourge: it took them two years to regain Mazouna, and in 704/1304-5 they sustained heavy losses in attempting to dislodge him. After his withdrawal to the Mitidja mountains they regained control of Maghrāwī territory, but readily agreed to end their pursuit of Rāshid when he sued for peace.

Peace between Tlemcen and Fās came in 706/1307 on terms restoring to the former all that the latter had taken. Thinking to retrieve his homeland, Rāshid marched on Miliana, but, finding the ᶜAbd al-Wādids in control, banished the thought. Around 707/1307-8 he took up with Abu 'l-Baḳāʾ, the Ḥafṣid ruler of Bougie (Bidjāya) and, later, of Tunis. An initially successful and promising alliance between Rāshid and his Maghrāwa, on the one hand, and the Ḥafṣid and the Ṣanhādja, on the other, collapsed a few years later with the death of Rāshid in a heated personal quarrel with a new chief of his allies, the Ṣanhādja (between 709 and 711/1309 and 1311; date unclear). Dismayed at Rāshid's death, the Maghrāwa left their Chélif heartlands, and many took refuge in places as far apart as Andalusia and Ifrīḳiya. Rāshid's young son, ᶜAlī, found safety with his aunt in Fez, the sultan's wife, and the Awlād Mandīl migrated to Marīnid soil and married into Marīnid tribes.

ᶜAlī b. Rāshid grew up at court as a Marīnid by adoption and, in adult life, took part in the sultan Abu 'l-Ḥasan's ambitious campaigns that toppled Tlemcen, but on the sultan's defeat at Kairouan (al-Ḳayrawān) in 749/1348 he took over Miliana, Ténès, Brechk and Cherchell and re-established his ancestors' principality. He requested, but was refused, Marīnid recognition in return for support against ᶜAbd al-Wādid resurgence. ᶜAlī's subsequent reliance on the ᶜAbd al-Wādids to respect his principality proved misplaced, and brought him to disaster and suicide (752/1351-2). His young son, Ḥamza, was taken to Fās and, like ᶜAlī, was reared as a Marīnid.

As an adult, Ḥamza deserted the Marīnids on the grounds of an alleged injustice when in the field against Tlemcen (772/1370). Taking to the mountains of the Banū Bū Saᶜīd, he won Maghrāwa support and held out till a vast Marīnid army terrified his allies into surrender. With few followers he next established himself among the Arab tribe of Ḥuṣayn, then in revolt against the Marīnids with ʿAbd al-Wādid backing. His style "ruler of Titteri" suggests that the tribe's *ḥiṣn Tīṭarī* was his stronghold. His subsequent failure to rally the Banū Bū Saʿīd drew him into a rash exploit at Timzought (Tīmzūghat), north-west of Miliana, which ended in disaster. Both he and his friends were captured, and the Ḥuṣayn fled to the Titteri mountains from their plain below. From the fortress they made their last stand—an event actually witnessed by Ibn Khaldūn. Ḥamza and his friends were executed, and early in 1372 their headless corpses were crucified outside Miliana. Thereafter the Awlād Mandīl disappear from history.

Bibliography: Ibn Khaldūn, *ʿIbar*, vii, 63-71 (text often corrupt) = de Slane, iii, 310-26 (translation not always accurate); on the places mentioned see "Table géographique", *ibid.*, iv, 489 ff., under the French spellings; Ibn Khaldūn, *al-Taʿrīf bi-Ibn Khaldūn*, Cairo 1951, 29, 139; Yaḥyā b. Khaldūn, *Bughyat al-ruwwād*, ed. and tr. A. Bel, *Hist. des Beni ʿAbd al-Wâd*, Algiers 1903-13, i, 128 f. = tr. 173; 146 f., 154 ff. = tr. 195, 206 ff. (the translation carries very informative notes on the places mentioned; see index); M. Gaspar Remiro, ed. and tr., *Correspondencia diplomática entre Granada y Fez (siglo XIV)*, etc., Granada 1916, 42, 82, 118; Lévi-Provençal, *Hist. Esp. mus.*, ii, 261 (on Khazrūn); J. D. Latham, *Ibn al-Aḥmar's* Kitāb Mustawdaʿ al-ʿalāma, in *Studia Arabica et Islamica: Festschrift for Iḥsān ʿAbbās*, ed. W. al-Ḳāḍī, Beirut 1981, 329 f. (see n. 127 on Titteri); J. M. Abun-Nasr, *A history of the Maghrib*², London 1975, 152, 156. R. Brunschvig, *La Berbérie orientale sous les Ḥafṣides*, Paris 1940-7, i, 48, 128, ii, 77. All the chronicles of the Marīnids, ʿAbd al-Wādids and Ḥafṣids should be consulted. (J.D. LATHAM)

MANDINGO [see MANDE]

MANDJANĪḲ, (A., ultimately from Greek μαγγανικόν, via Aramaic, cf. Fraenckel, *Die aramänische Fremdwörter*, 243, passing into Spanish as *almajaneque*, cf. Dozy and Engelman, *Glossaire*, 153), a general term for any kind of stone-throwing siege-engine. The expressions *mandjanīḳ* and *ʿarrāda* [*q.v.*] are both used for this kind of machine, and although the *ʿarrāda* may have been the smaller of the two, the expressions often seem to be interchangeable. *Mandjanīḳ* occurs more frequently than *ʿarrāda*, but their presence at a siege is often confined to a mere mention, without any description of the machines being given. The earliest reference to the *mandjanīḳ* in Muslim times is the machine used to bombard the walls of al-Ṭāʾif when the town was besieged by the Muslims in 8/630 (al-Balādhurī, *Futūḥ*, 55). We are not told what kind of machine this was; it may well have been of the type used by the Greeks and Romans, which was operated by the release of energy stored in twisted fibres or large bows. These weapons were characterised by the high velocity and low trajectory of the missiles, which were fairly light. They were therefore of more use on the battlefield than against the strong walls of cities and fortresses. From some time in the 1st/7th century onwards, however, the siege-engines used by the Muslim armies were of beam-operated type, first the traction trebuchet and, much later, the counterweight trebuchet.

The traction trebuchet originated in China no later than the 4th century B.C. and was in common use in Chinese armies from that time onwards (J. Needham, *China's trebuchets, manned and counterweighted*, in *Lynn White Festschrift, Humana civilitas*, i [1976], 107-45). It consisted of a beam, composed of a single spar, or of several spars bound together, which was supported on a fulcrum on top of a timber tower. The tower was often provided with wheels, to assist in the emplacement and aiming of the weapon. The beams were from 5.60 to 8.40 m. in length, with diameters at the extremities of 12.5 and 7 cm. At the narrower end was a copper "nest", attached to the beam by iron wires, thus forming a short sling. The missile, which could weigh up to 60 kg. was placed in the sling. At the other end of the beam there was a special attachment to which a number of ropes were attached. A team of men, ranging in number from 40 to 250 or more, pulled in unison on these ropes to discharge the missile, to distances of up to 150 metres (D.R. Hill, *Trebuchets*, in *Viator*, iv [1973], 99-114). Although the range of these machines was less than that of the classical weapons, the greater weight of the missiles made them much more effective against fortifications.

The traction trebuchet was diffused from China, through the Turkish areas, to the Middle East during the 1st/7th century. At the siege of Mecca in 64/683 there was a *mandjanīḳ* called *Umm Farwa* ("Mother of the hair"). This description may well have been derived from the appearence of the ropes hanging down from the end of the beam. A poet added his own description: "swinging its tail like a foaming [camel] stallion" (al-Ṭabarī, ii, 426). At the siege of Daybul in Sind in 92/711-12, the Muslims had a siege-machine called *al-ʿArūs* ("The Bride"). It was operated by 500 men, and was under the control of a skilled operator who took charge of the aiming and shooting (al-Balādhurī, *Futūḥ*, 437). There was a battery of machines at the siege of Baghdād in 261/865-6: men were assigned to every *mandjanīḳ* and *ʿarrāda*, and pulled on ropes to discharge the missiles (al-Ṭabarī, iii, 1551 f.).

The counterweight trebuchet, which came into use at the end of the 6th/12th century, was a much heavier machine. It consisted of a heavy wooden beam resting on a fulcrum, which was supported on a massive timber tower. The beam, typically about 20 m. long, was divided by the fulcrum in the ratio of 5:1 or 6:1. At the end of the short arm, the box containing the counterweight was suspended, and filled with lead, iron or stones; the total weight was from 10 to 30 tonnes. A long sling—about as long as the beam itself—was attached to the end of the long arm, with a pouch to contain the missile. The trebuchet was spanned by a winch, whose rope was attached to the long arm at about the mid-point. When the release mechanism was pulled, the beam rotated and the sling accelerated to a greater velocity than that of the beam. The missile was released when the end of one of the ropes slipped from a hook, at an instant when the combined effect of the sling's velocity and the angle of discharge gave maximum range to the missile. Ranges were of the order of 300 m., and the missiles could be very heavy. During the 8th/14th century sieges of Tlemcen, the *mandjanīḳs* were capable of bombarding the town with balls made of marble, some of which have been found there, the largest with a circumference of 2 m. and weighing 230 kg. (see ḤIṢĀR, ii; for characteristics of both kinds of trebuchet, see Hill, *op. cit.*, *passim*).

The question of the point of origin of the counterweight trebuchet has not yet been resolved. The earliest unambiguous description of the machine in Europe refers to its use in northern Italy in A.D. 1199 (Lynn White Jr., *Medieval technology and social change*, Oxford 1962, 102-3). In a treatise on weapons written a few years earlier than this, Murḍā b. ʿAlī devotes a section to trebuchets, all except one of the traction type. The exception is called a "Persian" *mandjanīķ*, and although the passage is obscure, it is possible that this was a counterweight machine (Cl. Cahen, *Un traité d'armurerie composé pour Saladin*, in *BEO*, xii [1947-8], 16-18). On present data, we can only locate the origin of the counterweight trebuchet somewhere in Mediterranean Christendom or western Islam, towards the end of the 6th/12th century. Its spread thereafter was very rapid, both in Europe and in the Muslim world. The first report we have of its use in Islam refers to the siege of Ḥimṣ in 646/1248, where the machine in question is referred to as a *mandjanīķ maghribī*, a western or a North African trebuchet (Abu 'l-Fidāʾ, *Mukhtaṣar taʾrīkh al-bashar*, in *RHC*, *Historiens orientaux*, i, 1872, 125). Counterweight trebuchets were used in great numbers by the Muslims at the siege of ʿAkkā in 690/1291 (al-Maķrīzī, *K. al-Sulūk*, ed. Quatremère, *Histoire des sultans Mamlouks*, Paris 1837-42, ii, 125). Almost certainly, the counterweight trebuchet was introduced to China by the Muslims. Two Muslim engineers, ʿAlāʾ al-Dīn and Ismāʿīl, are honoured by a biography in the official history of the Yuan dynasty. They constructed the machines for Ķubilay for the siege of Fan-chhêng towards the end of A.D. 1272. Thus the counterweighted trebuchets acquired the name of "Muslim phao", by which they were long afterwards known (Needham, *op. cit.*, 114).

Bibliography: In addition to the works mentioned in the text, see K. Huuri, *Zur Geschichte des Mittelalterlichen Geschützwesens aus orientalischen Quellen*, Helsinki 1941; information about the construction of traction trebuchets is to be found in Abu ʿAbd Allāh al-Khʷārazmī, *Mafātīḥ al-ʿulūm*, ed. van Vloten, 247-9. (D. R. Hill)

AL-**MANDJŪR**, ABU 'L-ʿABBĀS AḤMAD B. ʿALĪ AL-MIKNĀSĪ AL-FĀSĪ, a learned Moroccan scholar and teacher, from a family originally from Meknès, born in Fās 926/1520 and died there 16 Dhu 'l-Ķaʿda/18 October 1587. Endowed with vast learning and a great power of verbal expressiveness, he spent his life teaching, with the methods in use at the time, various Islamic topics, in particular, theology and law, and was considered one of the greatest masters of his age at the Karawiyyīn [*q.v.*]. Between 987 and 993/1579-85, he stayed frequently for periods in Marrakesh, where his most eminent disciple was the sultan al-Manṣūr al-Dhahabī [*q.v.*].

He was the author of commentaries and glosses on well-known and esteemed works of theology and law (see Lévi-Provençal, *Chorfa*, 91), of which various manuscripts are extant (see Hajji, *Activité intellectuelle*, 164-77, *passim*), but above all he has left behind a *Fahrasa* [*q.v.*] of great documentary interest which has not however yet been made the object of a critical edition. It was written in Radjab 989/August 1581 at the request of al-Manṣūr, who wished to get from his master a general *idjāza* [*q.v.*] theoretically authorising him to teach all the topics studied under his direction and further containing the names of his own masters, with biographical notices and items of information of a literary nature. Several manuscripts of al-Mandjūr's *Fahrasa* exist (see Hajji, *op. cit.*, 27, no. 72), which was written in two versions, a long and a short one, according to the author's own practice.

Independently of the sultan, this teacher oversaw the intellectual formation of several pupils, who themselves became more or less distinguished subsequently and who filled the office of *ķāḍī* in various Moroccan towns, unlike their master who, despite his great learning, piety and exalted protection and patronage, never exercised any religious office at all because of his distant Jewish ancestry [see MAYYĀRA]; he was even barred from leading the prayer when he had been thus designated by al-Manṣūr (al-Ifrānī, *Nuzhat al-ḥādī*, 155).

Bibliography: Ibn ʿAskar, *Dawḥat al-nāshir*, ed. M. Ḥadjdjī, Rabat 1396/1976, 59; Ibn al-Ķāḍī, *Djadhwat al-iķtibās*, lith. Fās 1309, 65; idem, *Durrat al-ḥidjāl*, Cairo 1390/1970, i, 153-63, ii, 221; Aḥmad Bābā, *Nayl al-ibtihādj*, Cairo 1352/1932, 95, Maķķarī, *Rawḍat al-ās*, Rabat 1383/1964, 285-6; Muḥammad Makhlūf, *Shadjarat al-nūr*, Cairo 1349/1930, 287; Ifrānī, *Ṣafwat man intashar*, lith. Fās n.d., 4-6; M. Ben Cheneb, *Étude sur les personnages mentionnés dans l'idjâza du cheikh ʿAbd al-Qâdir el-Fâsy*, in *Actes du XVIe Congr. des Or.*, iv, 1907, § 28; Nāṣirī, *Istiķṣāʾ*, v, 191; Lévi-Provençal, *Chorfa*, 88-92; Brockelmann, S II, 697; M. Hajji, *L'activité intellectuelle au Maroc à l'époque saʿdide*, Rabat 1976-7, index. (CH. PELLAT)

MĀNḌŪ, fortress and town of Central India.

1. History. Once the fortress-capital of Mālwā [*q.v.*] and now a village 34 km. south of Dhār in Madhya Pradesh, in lat. 22° 21' N and long. 75° 26' E. The first rulers took full advantage of a natural outcrop of the Vindhya range, overlooking the Nimar plain to the south. A deep and jagged ravine, the Kakra Khoh, isolates it on the sides. The plateau, well-supplied with lakes and springs, stretches unevenly over 5 km. and more from north to south, and 6 to 7 km. from east to west, at an average altitude of 600 m. with the remains of the inner fort of Songaŕh as one of the more prominent landmarks to the west. *Maṅḍapika* is mentioned on an inscription found at Pratapgadh in Rādjasthān and dated to the equivalent of 946 A.D. *Maṅḍapa-durga* appears on a copper-plate grant of Jayavamadeva dated 1261 A.D. Thus Mānḍū could be a corruption of *Maṅḍapa* or even of *Mānḍava*.

In the early Islamic days of the subcontinent, the Paramāra king Bhoja deflected Maḥmūd, the Ghaznawid sultan [*q.v.*], from the area. Iltutmish himself did not reach as far as Mānḍū in his conquests, but Djalāl al-Dīn Khaldjī sacked the neighbouring lands in 1293, and the fort fell to ʿAlāʾ al-Dīn Khaldjī's general Āʾīn al-Mulk in 1303. Thereafter, the local governors ruled from Dhār, where Maḥmūd Shāh Tughluķ took refuge from the chaos engendered by Tīmūr's onslaught; after his return to Dihlī in 804/1401, Dilāwar Khān Ghūrī proclaimed himself independent, and at his death in 808/1405, his eldest son Alp Khān ascended the throne of Mālwā under the name of Hūshang Shāh, and moved the capital to Mānḍū. On his coins and until the end of the century, Shādīābād, the "city of joy", appears as the name for the new capital. Although much involved in warfare with the rulers of Gudjarāt, Djawnpur, Dihlī, Uŕisā and the Dakhan, he fully restored and strengthened the ancient fortifications protecting the access to the extensive plateau, as shown on the inscriptions on the Bhagwānīya *darwāza* (809/1416-17) and the Dihlī *darwāza* (820/1417). he also embarked on the ambitious construction of his Djāmiʿ Masdjid besides, no doubt, an impressive building programme over the 30 years of his liberal reign, in order to enhance the new capital and to rival with his neighbours. After his death, the cruelty of his own son led the son of his trusted relative and *wazīr* Malik Mughīth to accept the throne in 839/1436 under the name of Maḥmūd I Khaldjī [*q.v.*]. During the 36 years of his reign, the fame of Mānḍū spread abroad as far as Cairo as well as to Samarḳand; scholars and holy men called at the capital, sometimes on their way to the Bahmanī court of S̲h̲ams al-Dīn Muḥammad III at Bīdar [q.v.]. The buildings of his reign reflect the ever-expanding size of his realm; besides palaces and hospitals, Maḥmūd ordered the start of Hūs̲h̲ang S̲h̲āh's tomb in 843/1439, his own *madrasa* and victory tower in 846/1443 after his victories over Chitor (Čitawr), and the completion of the Djāmiᶜ Masd̲j̲id in 858/1454. In 871/ 1467 the lunar calendar replaced the solar one. Under the generous if orderly rule of sultan G̲h̲iyāt̲h̲ al-Dīn, the town of Māndū was further enhanced, one may imagine, by buildings to fit his desire "to open the door of peace and rest, and pleasure and enjoyment on me and those depending on me" after the "34 years at the stirrups" of his father. His large and somewhat eccentric harem never deterred him from his religious duties and from a sober life, unlike his son Nāṣir al-Dīn (906-16/1500-10), who was a dipsomaniac, although for a time a sound ruler, a lover of the arts and a great builder of palaces such as the so-called Bāz Bahādur palace dated 914/1508. During the troubled reign of his son Maḥmūd II, Muslim and Hindu nobles were rivals for power at court, especially Mēdinī Rāy [q.v.]. Notwithstanding its architectural highlights, his rule came to a brutal end in 937/1531, when Māndū fell to Bahādur S̲h̲āh of Gud̲j̲arāt and the S̲h̲āh was taken prisoner, with his seven sons, and later killed. In 941/1534, the Mug̲h̲al Humāyūn [q.v.] broke into the fort near the Tārāpūr gate, but not before Bahādur S̲h̲āh had been lowered with horses from the inner fort of Songaṛh down into the deep Kakra Khoh. Two years later Mallū K̲h̲ān, an officer of the defunct K̲h̲ald̲j̲ī retinue, seized Māndū and ruled for 6 years under the name of Ḳādir S̲h̲āh until submitting in 949/1542 to S̲h̲īr S̲h̲āh Sūr, who replaced him by his relative S̲h̲ud̲j̲āᶜ K̲h̲ān as governor of Mālwā. In 963/1555 his son Baz Bahādur seized power, although unable to assert himself for long; when Akbar's general Adham K̲h̲ān overran Māndū in 968/1560, Bāz Bahādur escaped while his favourite Rupmati, of poetical fame, chose poison rather than servitude. He managed to recapture Māndū briefly, but finally submitted to Akbar in 978/1570. The latter first visited the fort in 991/1573; further visits were connected with expeditions to the Dakhan. Two inscriptions dated 1008/1600 and 1009/1601 recall the hospitality given by his governor S̲h̲āh Budāg̲h̲ K̲h̲ān in his palace now called Nīl Kanth. On Akbar's order, the southern Tārāpūr *darwāza* was re-orientated to the west in 1014/1605 and Maḥmūd K̲h̲ald̲j̲ī's tomb was roughly repaired at the same time. D̲j̲ahāngīr [q.v.], according to his memoirs, spent seven months in Māndū during the rainy season in 1026/1617; buildings were restored and the whole court enjoyed hunting and feasting; his birthday celebrations took place in Bāz Bahādur's garden next to his palace with the future S̲h̲āh D̲j̲āhān and Sir Thomas Roe in attendance. Four years later, the young prince spent another rainy season there and held a conference to induce reconciliation between two Jain factions. Awrangzīb [q.v.] is represented in Māndū by only one inscription on the northern ᶜAlamgīr *darwāza* dated 1079/1668-9. After his death 1118/1707, a rapid deterioration of the empire lead to the supremacy of Marāt̲h̲ā [q.v.] power. In 1734 A.D. Pēs̲h̲wā Bād̲j̲i Rao was appointed governor of Mālwā. His deputy Anand Rāo Pūar and his descendants ruled thereafter from Dhār. Māndū reverted to its first vocation of a hunting ground until basic restoration was started early this century; it has continued to this day.

2. Architecture. As in Gud̲j̲arāt, D̲j̲awnpur and Bīdar [q.vv.] throughout the 9th/15th century, the newly-independent state of Mālwā competed not only on the battlefield but also in setting up an imposing new capital. It was imperative to modernise the walls and the ten complex gates and to make good use of the expanses of water and springs, as well as to plan the town along a north-south axis with the new D̲j̲āmiᶜ Masd̲j̲id sited at the central east-west crossing. As in Dhār, the master-builders at first drew on the Gud̲j̲arātī tradition by adapting Hindu proportions and style to the Dilāwar K̲h̲ān D̲j̲āmiᶜ (808/1405-6) measuring about 37 by 45 m., and the Malik Mug̲h̲īt̲h̲ D̲j̲āmiᶜ (835/1432), about 42 by 46 m. In both cases, spoils from temples were used to implement an Arab mosque plan, with three domes over the prayer hall in the later building. The D̲j̲āmiᶜ Masd̲j̲id, built of red ochre sandstone like the rest of Māndū, was completed by the mid-9th/15th century to include the revered marble tomb of Hūs̲h̲ang S̲h̲āh. An inscription dated 1070/1659 recalls the reverential visit of four master builders of the Mug̲h̲al court. An exalting plinth emphasises the 85m. façade of the mosque, with its eastern domed entrance of metropolitan quality. A similar dome over the *miḥrāb* rests on competent corner arches. A total 150 smaller domes line the *ṣaḥn*. Opposite, the one-time *madrasa* (As̲h̲rafiyya Maḥall) of Maḥmūd I K̲h̲ald̲j̲ī, with its tower of victory once seven storeys high, was changed into a marble-lined imposing tomb, with impressive inscriptions, before his death; but it soon became derelict. A large number of lesser tombs are scattered along the approach road to Māndū and across the plateau. Always on a plinth and at most times following a square plan, the domed chamber usually belongs to a complex including a prayer hall also on a plinth, and a tank, as with the Daryā K̲h̲ān mausoleum (10th/16th century). Geometric bands of glazed tiles enhance the base of drums inside domes, as in the D̲j̲āmiᶜ Masd̲j̲id, as well as outside some of the tombs; they are chiefly turquoise and white, of mediocre quality when compared with those on buildings in Bīdar. Stone carving on elegant projecting windows, arched walls and *d̲j̲āli*s are far more successful.

In secular architecture, an attractive balance is struck between palaces and water expanses: the D̲j̲ahāz ("ship") Maḥall, on two levels, extends to about 115 m. between the Mund̲j̲a Talaō and the Kapūr Talaō. Each level has an original stepped bath; moreover, the long terrace of the upper level is dominated by elegant domed pavilions. In the more austere, T-shaped Hindolā ("swing") Maḥall, the broad buttressing outer walls (at an angle of 77° from the horizontal) contain an imposing audience hall with five double and one single-pointed arches. By the north wall of the royal enclosure, a large palace complex once dominated the Mund̲j̲a Talaō, including a special well, the Champa *bāolī*, with adjacent underground rooms for the summer. Further afield, the Ud̲j̲ālā (bright) *bāolī* and the Andherī (dark) *bāolī* recall the elaborate wells of Gud̲j̲arāt and Rād̲j̲asthān. Both the Gadā (beggar) S̲h̲āh's shop and house hint at a later audience hall and palace. Beyond the large Sāgar Talaō to the south, the so-called Bāz Bahādur palace overlooks the waters of the Rīwā Kund. Once a complex of barracks, the so-called Rupmati pavilions dominate the whole scene. The last important palace to be built was the Nīl Kanth ("blue throat"); it faces westward on the edge of the cliff by a spring. At present it is used as a Hindu temple.

3. Painting. As in architecture, painting in manuscripts for the court evolved along original lines, but drew on two main sources, relating to neighbouring

states. A Jain minister of the Paramāra king Jayasimha founded in Maṇḍapa-durga one of his six *Jnāna-bhaṅḍāras* ("storage of knowledge"), a specifically Jain library, in 1263; the books always contained an important pictorial element. The Māndū *kalpa sutra* of 1439 illustrates the continuity in production. On the other hand, illustrated Islamic texts of the time blend this traditional draughtmanship and vivid colours with the conventions from the 9th/15th century schools of Shīrāz and Harāt, to produce a recognisable Mālwā style; the few manuscripts discovered so far relate to the early part of the 10th/16th century: the *Niʿmat-namā* (a book of delicacies), (Ethé 2775, India Office Library), the *Miftāḥ al-fuḍalāʾ* (a Persian glossary of rare words), (BL Or. 3299), the *Bustān* of Saʿdī dedicated to Nāṣir al-Dīn before 916/1510 (National Museum of India, New Delhi, no. 48.6/4), *ʿAdjāʾib al-ṣanāʾiʿ* (a Persian translation of al-Djazarī's book on the knowledge of mechanical devices [see AL-DJAZARI and ḤIYAL in Suppl.]) (BL Or. 13718).

Bibliography: *Taʾrīkh-i Firishta*, Eng. tr. J. Briggs, *History of the rise of the Mahomedan power in India till the year A.D. 1612*, iv, London 1910; *Ṭabaḳāt-i Akbarī*, Eng. tr. B. De, revised B. Prashad, iii/2, Calcutta 1939; *Tūzuk-i Djahāngīrī*, Eng. tr. A. Rogers and H. Beveridge, London 1909-14; *The embassy of Sir Thomas Roe*, ed. W. Foster, Hakluyt Society; H.N. Wright, *Catalogue of coins in the Indian Museum, Calcutta*, ii, Oxford 1907; J. M. Campbell, *Māndū*, in *JBBRAS*, xix (1896), 154-201; Capt. E. Barnes, *Dhār and Māndū*, in *JBBRAS*, xxi (1904), 339-91; Z. Hasan, *The inscriptions of Dhār and Māndū*, in *Epigraphia Indo-Moslemica* (1909-10), 6-29, 110-1; G. Yazdani, *Remarks on the inscriptions of Dhār and Māndū*, in *Epigraphica Moslemica* (1911-12), 8-11; G. Yazdani, *Māndū, the city of joy*, Oxford 1929; P. Brown, *Indian architecture (Islamic period)*, Bombay 1942; H. Goetz, *An irruption of Gothic style forms into Indo-Islamic architecture*, in *Artibus Asiae*, xxii (1959), 33-8; *In praise of Māndū*, in *Marg*, xiii/3 (1959: articles by R. Ettinghausen, G. Yazdani, R. Skelton, P. Chandra and L. M. Crump with plans and sections; D. R. Patil, *Mandu*, New Delhi 1971; W.G. Archer, *Central Indian painting*, London 1958; N.M. Titley, *An illustrated Persian glossary of the sixteenth century*, in *BMQ*, xxix (1964-5), 15-9; M. Chandra, *New documents of Jaina painting*, Bombay 1975; arts. HIND. vii. Architecture. v. Mālwā, and MAḤALL.

(YOLANDE CROWE)

MANDŪB (A.) "meritorious and recommended action", term of Islamic law; see SHARĪʿA.

MANDŪR, MUḤAMMAD B. ʿABD AL-ḤAMĪD MŪSĀ (1907-65), the *shaykh* of modern Egyptian and Arab literary critics, was born in Kafr Mandūr, near Minyā al-Ḳamḥ, in Egypt's Sharḳiyya Province, to a rather wealthy family. His semi-literate father was a devout and tolerant Muslim who belonged to the Naḳshbandī dervish order. Mandūr learned many Ḳurʾānic verses from his father, and his religious upbringing in a rural milieu instilled in him moral and spiritual values that he preserved all his life. At the age of five, he was sent to the village *kuttāb* [*q.v.*], and the following autumn he entered the elementary school in Minyā al-Ḳamḥ. In 1921 he transferred to the secondary school in Ṭanṭā, where he studied English and earned the Baccalauréat Littéraire in 1925. He then enrolled in the law school of the newly inaugurated Egyptian University, hoping to become a public prosecutor. He was persuaded by Ṭāhā Ḥusayn [*q.v.*] and another teacher to enrol also in the Departments of Arabic and Sociology. In 1929 he obtained a *Licence* in Arabic Literature, and in 1930 a *Licence* in Law. Immediately afterward, Mandūr was offered a position as a public prosecutor, but he declined it in order to accept a government scholarship to study at the Sorbonne.

After studying for nine years in France, Mandūr graduated both in classical languages and literatures and in law and political economy. The turbulent political situation in France before World War II discouraged him from finishing his doctorate and hastened his return to Egypt in 1939. Without a doctorate, he could not assume a university teaching position in Egypt. Hence he spent the years 1940-1 translating and teaching translation from French and English into Arabic. In 1942, the University of Alexandria was established and Mandūr was appointed a professor of Arabic literature. There the eminent scholar and educator Aḥmad Amīn (d. 1954) encouraged Mandūr to finish his doctorate, which he did in 1943. His dissertation, "Arabic critical trends in the fourth century A.H." (*Tayyārāt al-naḳd al-ʿArabī fi 'l-ḳarn al-rābiʿ al-hidjrī*), supervised by Aḥmad Amīn, was later published under the title "Methodical criticism among the Arabs" (*al-Naḳd al-manhadjī ʿind al-ʿArab*), 1946, and has since become the most celebrated single work in Arabic on mediaeval Arabic literary criticism.

He resigned his post at the University of Alexandria in 1944 in order to accept a position as Editor-in-Chief of the newspaper *al-Miṣrī*, thus embarking on a tumultuous career of political and literary journalism in the vanguard of opposition to the government of Ṣidḳī Pasha and the British. Mandūr was discharged after only three months, and for a short while he contented himself with publishing a few articles and teaching at the newly-founded (1944) evening Institute of Drama. In 1945 he was appointed Editor-in-Chief of the evening newspaper *al-Wafd al-Miṣrī*, which, with the assistance of some rebellious avant-garde writers, he gradually transformed into a daily revolutionary manifesto against the British and their Egyptian collaborators. Despite his socialist writings and his leadership of the liberal progressive wing within the Wafd party, Mandūr was never a communist. His deep involvement in national politics and his vehement opposition to the Ṣidḳī-Bevin Treaty brought him imprisonment twenty times in 1945 and 1946, and cost him the closing of his own six-months-old newspaper, *al-Baʿth* ("Resurrection"), as well as eleven other newspaper and magazines. With the fall of Ṣidḳī's cabinet, Mandūr assumed the editorship of the new Wafd newspaper, *Ṣawt al-Umma* ("The voice of the Nation"), where he pursued his political struggle against "colonialism and Western exploitation of Egypt's national resources". Mandūr operated a successful law office from 1948 to 1954, and at the same time continued to write and edit the newspaper *Ṣawt al-Umma*. He was elected to the Egyptian parliament in 1950, and served on several parliamentary committees. In 1953 he embarked on yet another teaching and writing career at the Arab League's Institute of Higher Arabic Studies, and continued until some time before his death in 1965.

Mandūr's copious œuvre consists of specialised and general books treating one or several related subjects or literary genres; translations of diverse works, mostly from French into Arabic; book reviews; hundreds of political and literary articles; some elementary attempts at poetry; and one screenplay.

Despite his prominence as a journalist, political activist and translator, Mandūr's reputation is principally that of eminent literary critic, surpassing in

1. Malik Mug̲h̲īt̲h̲ D̲j̲āmiʿ, 835/1432, east façade.

2. Malik Mug̲h̲īt̲h̲ D̲j̲āmiʿ, *Ḳibla riwāḳ*s and *ṣahn*.

3. Hūshang Shāh's tomb, started 843/1439.

4. Daryā Khān's mausoleum, early 10th/16th century (photographs: Y. Crowe).

intellectual vigour and critical insight his teacher Ṭāhā Ḥusayn, but without his fame and versatility. His literary works encompass three basic fields: criticism, theoretical and practical; poetry and poets; and theatre, in both its prose and verse forms. Most notable and enduring of his critical books are *Fi 'l-mīzān al-d̲j̲adīd* ("In the new balance"), in which Mandūr expounded his theory of *al-s̲h̲iʿr al-mahmūs* ("whispered poetry"), inspired by the title of Mik̲h̲āʾīl Nuʿayma's [*q.v.*] poetry collection *Hams al-d̲j̲ufūn*, n.d. ("The whispering of eyelids"); and *al-Naḳd al-manhad̲j̲ī ʿind al- ʿArab* ("Methodical criticism among the Arabs"), 1946. Some other books in this category are: *Fi 'l-adab wa 'l-naḳd* ("On literature and criticism"), 1949; *al-Adab wa-mad̲h̲āhibuh* ("Literature and its schools"), 1958; and *al-Adab wa-funūnuh* ("Literature and its genres"), 1963. Mandūr's major works on poetry and poets comprised a theoretical work on poetry, *Fann al-s̲h̲iʿr* ("The art of poetry"), 1960, and a renowned series of critical studies on Syro-American poets, Egyptian modernist poets, and the poets of the *vers libre* movement. His principal works on the theatre include *al-Masraḥ* ("The theatre"), 1959; *al-Klāsīkiyya wa 'l-uṣūl al-fanniyya li 'l-drāmā* ("Classicism and the artistic roots of drama"), n.d.; and applied studies of the verse plays of Aḥmad S̲h̲awḳī (d. 1932) and the prose theatre of Tawfīḳ al-Ḥakīm (born 1898).

The most distinguished of Mandūr's translations are the two acclaimed critical treatises which greatly influenced his early critical thought and which punctuated his critical writings throughout his career: Georges Duhamel's *Défence des lettres* (1943) and Gustave Lanson's *La Méthode de l'histoire littéraire* (1946), which he appended to the fifth edition of *al-Naḳd al-manhad̲j̲ī ʿind al-ʿArab*. The other translated works encompass a whole range of literary disciplines, from Flaubert's *Madame Bovary* to E.A. Poe's "The Raven".

His political and ideological writings comprise one major book, *al-Dīmūḳrāṭiyya al-siyāsiyya* ("Political democracy"), 1952?, and innumerable articles, some of which were published in two books.

Mandūr's training in the French critical tradition, especially the then-predominant approach of *l'explication de textes*, was inculcated in his critical writings and eventually evolved into an eclectic theory that underwent, according to him, three distinct stages:

(1) Aesthetic impressionistic, in which precedence is accorded to aesthetic values. This approach is adopted in his two earlier and much celebrated works, *al-Naḳd al-manhad̲j̲ī ʿind al-Arab* and *Fi 'l-mīzān ad-d̲j̲adīd*, which also includes his famous theory of *al-s̲h̲iʿr al-mahmūs* ("whispered poetry"). Mandūr acclaimed poetry that "whispers", that communicates with the listener is an undertone, *à mi-voix*, poetry that is devoid of elocutionary bombast, florid rhetoric and effete sentimentality. Emigré poetry [see MAHD̲J̲AR] (especially Nuʿayma's) and Free Verse were grand examples of "whispered poetry" in his judgement.

(2) Descriptive analytic. Here Mandūr undertakes an objective method that strives more for analysis, identification and instruction than for guidance. He generally applied this approach in the thirteen books on poetry and the theatre, including the renowned series "Egyptian poetry after S̲h̲awḳī", which he wrote for the Arab League's Institute of Higher Arabic Studies.

(3) Ideological criticism, which conceives of a well-defined social function for literature. His application of this approach was a consequence of his socialist beliefs and of his involvement in national politics, and is attributed to his diversified activities in journalism, law, parliament, and his enduring interest in Egyptian rural life. Ideological criticism, embedded in socialist (New) realism, is equivalent to committed literature, or as Mandūr called it, purposive literature (*al-adab al-hādif*), which he propounded more than he applied it to poetry in his critical works.

Despite the multiplicity of approach, Mandūr's fundamentally eclectic theory espouses the pursuit of beauty in any given literary work, and the ultimate judgment, in his reckoning, lay with cultivated personal taste reinforced by vast and diversified knowledge. He defined criticism as the art of distinguishing between literary style and its function as interpretation, evaluation and guidance. Criticism as such has the capacity to participate in re-creating a literary work.

Mandūr's remarkable literary presence, fecundity, originality and vibrant intellect earned him endless and brutal literary battles with his contemporary critics, especially with al-ʿAḳḳād [*q.v.* in Suppl.] (d. 1964), and with the opponents of modern Free Verse. Both the critics and their psychological, positivistic and dogmatic approaches were the subject of his learned and astute criticism.

Mandūr's precise, elegant and unembellished style enhanced the comprehensibility and accessibility of his rather original writings. Mandūr introduced into modern Arabic critical lore such concepts as whispered poetry, poetic pantheism, purposive literature, objective romanticism, and methodical criticism. Despite his political and socialist undertakings, Mandūr remained all his life a literary, but not an ideological critic.

Bibliography: Mandūr wrote upwards of thirty books and hundreds of articles and book reviews, the majority of which remain uncollected. In 1964, he granted an elaborate and informative interview which was published in Fuʾād Dawwāra's book *ʿAs̲h̲rat udabāʾ yataḥaddat̲h̲ūn*, Cairo 1965. Another interview was published in the Lebanese literary journal *al-Ādāb* (January 1961), by Fārūḳ S̲h̲ūs̲h̲a. Scores of articles about his life and critical writings have been written after his death in such major Arab literary journals as *al-Ādāb*, *al-Ṭalīʿa* and *al-Mad̲j̲alla*. The most detailed and penetrating expositions of Mandūr's criticism in English are presented by D. Semah in his book, *Four Egyptian literary critics*, Leiden 1974, and in his *Muḥammad Mandūr and "New Poetry"*, in *JAL*, ii (1971). Major Arabic studies of Mandūr include Henri Riyāḍ's *Muḥammad Mandūr*, *Rāʾid al-adab al-is̲h̲tirākī*, Khartoum 1965 and Beirut 1967; and K̲h̲ayrī ʿAzīz, *Udabāʾ ʿalā ṭarīḳ al-niḍāl al-siyāsī*, Cairo 1970. Works published posthumously, such as *Kitābāt lam tuns̲h̲ar*, Cairo n.d., and more recent editions of Mandūr's work, feature representative lists of his publications.

(MANSOUR AJAMI)

MANĒR, a former town, now no bigger than a village, 22 miles/32 km. west of Paṭnā [*q.v.*] in Bihār state, India, by the junction of the rivers Sōn and Ganges (it was reported to be at the junction in 1722, 3 miles/5 km. south of it by 1812, 7 miles /10 km. south by 1907); it had therefore some strategic and mercantile advantage, and was one of the earliest and most important sites of Muslim colonisation in this part of India.

By Mug̲h̲al times, it had become the chief town of a *pargana* of some 80,000 *bīghas* [see MISĀḤĀ 2. India] in the *ṣūba* of Bihār (*Āʾīn-i Akbarī*, tr. Jarrett, Calcutta 1891, ii, 151, 153). A copperplate grant from a Hindu king of Kanawdj (ed. and tr. Pt. R. Sharma, in *JBORS*, ii/4 [1916]) of 1126 A.D. requires its Brahman recipient in "Maniyāra" to pay the tax called *turushka ḍanḍa* "Turk's duty", which seems to imply that tribute was being paid some seventy years before the Muslim conquest of north India, presumably to a Ghaznawid agent; the early date is strengthened by local tradition, which holds one grave in the great *dargāh* to be that of Tādj al-Dīn Khandgāh, the nephew of Maḥmūd of Ghaznī (local traditions in eastern India may refer to other putative kinsmen of the Ghaznawid rulers; but other early 6th/12th century Sanskrit inscriptions also mention the *turushka-ḍanḍa*, and references in Bayhaḳī point to sporadic trans-Gangetic Muslim settlement; see K.A. Nizami, *Some aspects of religion and politics in India during the thirteenth century*, Bombay, etc. 1965, 76 ff.). The consolidation of Islam is, however, thus explained: a Yamanī saint Muʾmin ʿĀrif (still of great local repute) had settled in Manēr, but was harassed by the local *rādjā*; he went back to Medina and returned with a raiding party led by Ḥaḍrat Tādj Faḳīh which defeated the local *rādjā* in a pitched battle, destroyed the temple (chronogram, *shud dīn-i Muḥammad ḳawī* = 576/1180) and dismantled the riverside fort. Many "*shahīd*s' graves" in Manēr are said to date from this time. Tādj Faḳīh returned to Medina, leaving his kinsmen to rule Manēr; but the rule seems to have been a spiritual one, for his grandson Shaykh Yaḥyā Manērī, d. 690/1291 (chronogram: *makhdūm*!), was the most celebrated saint of Bihār, progenitor of a distinguished line of local saints, whose shrine (in the Baṛī Dargāh; see below) was visited by Sikandar Lodī, Bābur, Humāyūn and Akbar, though his fame has been eclipsed by (and sometimes conflated with) that of his son Sharaf al-Dīn Aḥmad Manērī [see MAKHDŪM AL-MULK, SHARAF AL-DĪN] of Bihār Sharīf, *murīd* of Nadjīb al-Dīn Firdawsī. Eighth in descent from Shaykh Yaḥyā was Abū Yazīd, commonly known as Makhdūm Shāh Dawlat, d. 1017/1608-9, whose tomb (the Čhōṭī Dargāh) is the finest Muslim building in Bihār.

The *khānḳāh* forms a complex of buildings disposed around a vast rectangular tank (*ḥawḍ*), its stepped masonry sides equipped centrally with *ghāṭ*s and *bārādarīs*, drawing its water from the river Sōn by a subterranean channel. The tank is said to have been rebuilt in stone at the same time as the Baṛī and Čhōṭī Dargāhs were erected in the early 11th/17th century by Ibrāhīm Khān Kākar (*not* by Ibrāhīm Khān Fatḥ Djang, *ṣūbadār* of Bihār 1023-5/1615-17, as Horn and others assert). The Baṛī ("great") Dargāh west of the tank, on the site of the temple mound, is great in sanctity rather than magnificence. It consists of a great boundary wall enclosing a graveyard and a small mosque, standing to the west of a railed platform containing the simple open grave of Shaykh Yaḥyā (inscription of Ibrāhīm Khān Kākar, 1014/1605-6); also odd stone pillars, and a mutilated statue at the entrance presumably from the old temple. The Čhōṭī ("small") Dargāh is a high square platform in a fortress-like brick enclosure north of the tank, on which stands the square sandstone mausoleum of Makhdūm Shāh Dawlat (inscription with decease chronogram 1017/1608-9, and two construction chronograms 1025/1616), a superb specimen of provincial Mughal architecture. The central square chamber is domed, with lower and upper verandahs (fine carved ceilings: floral, geometric and Ḳurʾānic designs) running round all sides, each corner formed into a square room with arched openings below and an open domed *čhatrī* of similar size above. The lower verandah and the *čhatrīs* are built on the beam-and-bracket principle, and heavy stone corbels support both the lower and upper *čhadjdjā*, contrasting with the arches of the tomb chamber which also has finely carved stone screen openings. A local tradition asserts that the stone was brought from Gudjarāt; certainly, features of Gudjarāt tomb design are apparent here [see further MUGHALS. Architecture.]. West of the mausoleum is a small mosque with curvilinear roof, centrally situated between stone verandahs running along the entire western wall of the enclosure; inscription dated 1028/1619, quoting Ḳurʾān, III, 97-8. An underground chamber in the south-west corner is identified as the *čilla* of Shāh Dawlat. A fine entrance gate, in a more conventional Mughal style, bears two chronograms of 1022/1614-15 and 1032/1622-3. Other minor buildings around the tank are in grave disrepair. The earliest inscription of Manēr, 798/1395-6, records the reconstruction of an older mosque, now disappeared. The Djāmiʿ mosque of Manēr, itself undistinguished, bears two records of renovations, of 1103/1691-2 and 1283/1866 (the last on a marble slab carved in Medina), both mosques thus testifying to a vigorous Muslim population over the centuries; but the grounds around the Manēr tank are also the scene of a doubtfully Islamic fair on the ʿ*urs* of Ghāzī Miyān [*q.v.*].

Bibliography: P. Horn, *Muhammadan inscriptions from Bengal*, in *Epigr. Ind.*, ii, 1894, 280-96; T. Bloch, *Report, ASBengal Circle*, 1901-2, 19 ff.; Syed Zahiruddin, *History and antiquities of Manair*, Bankipore 1905; Farīd al-Dīn Aḥmad (Sadjdjāda-nishīn of the *dargāh* in 1918), untitled Urdu ms. on the history of the *dargāh*, author's collection; Hafiz Shamsuddin Ahmad, *Maner and its historical remains*, in *Procs. and Trans. of 6th All-India Oriental Conference*, Patna 1933, 123-41; Yusuf Kamal Bukhari, *Inscriptions from Maner*, in *Epigr. Ind. Arabic and Persian Suppl. 1951 and 1952* [1956], 13-24, and pls. viii-x; Qeyamuddin Ahmad, *Corpus of Arabic and Persian inscriptions of Bihar*, Patna 1973, 67, 162, 182-5, 214-15, 294-7, 391-2; Muhammad Ḥamīd Ḳuraishī, *List of ancient monuments protected ... in Bihar and Orissa* = *ASI*, N.I.S., li, Calcutta 1931. Excellent aquatint in T. Daniell, *Oriental scenery*, 1st series, xii: "The mausoleum of Mucdoom Shah Dowlut, at Moneah [*sic*], on the river Soane," London 1795; A. Casperz, in *Jnal. Photogr. Soc. India* (June 1902). For the Firdawsiyya order, see TAṢAWWUF. India. For Ibrāhīm Khān Kākar, see *Maʾāthir al-ʿulamāʾ*, Bibl. Ind. text, ii, 9-14, and *Tūzuk-i Djahāngīrī*, ed. Rogers and Beveridge, i, 29-30, 49, 59, 62, 77, 105, 248, 286, 298. See also the *Bibls.* to BIHĀR, PAṬNĀ.

(J. BURTON-PAGE)

MANF, Memphis, the capital of the Egyptian Old Kingdom, situated on the west bank of the Nile opposite modern Ḥulwān [*q.v.*] about twelve miles south of Fusṭāṭ [*q.v.*], plays a pivotal rôle in mediaeval Arabic geographical and historical writing on Egypt.

Al-Ḳalkashandī (*Ṣubḥ al-aʿshā*, iii, 316, 6-8; German tr. F. Wüstenfeld, *Die Geographie und Verwaltung in Ägypten*, Göttingen 1879, 41) presents the climate (= the third) and the geographic coordinates of Manf. The Muslims knew about the great antiquity (*madīna ... azaliyya*; *K. al-Istibṣār fī ʿadjāʾib al-amṣār*, Alexandria 1958, 83, French tr. 68) of the formerly huge city (cf. Ibn Zūlāḳ, quoted by al-Ḳazwīnī, *Āthār al-bilād wa-akhbār al-ʿibād*, Beirut 1399/1979, 274). The great scholar and most prominent mediaeval authority on Manf, ʿAbd al-Laṭīf al-Baghdādī (*al-Ifāda wa 'l-iʿtibār*, in Kamal Hafuth Zand *etalii*, *The eastern key*, London 1965, 136-7) speaks of over 4,000 years, a surprisingly exact estimate. Manf was destroyed when ʿAmr b. al-ʿĀṣ conquered Egypt and presented itself to mediaeval visitors in ruins (*kharāb*, cf. e.g. al-Yaʿḳūbī, *K. al-Buldān*, 331,9, and Abu 'l-Fidāʾ, *Taḳwīm al-buldan*, 117), unlike ʿAyn Shams [*q.v.*] (Heliopolis), Manf's traditional rival in the eyes of mediaeval Muslim authors (al-Idrīsī, *Nuzhat al-mushtāḳ*, 135, 4-5; *Opus geographicum*, 326, l. 2; Ibn Ḥawḳal, *K. Ṣūrat al-arḍ*, 160, French tr. J.H. Kramers and G. Wiet, Beirut-Paris 1964, i, 158). The two cities are often mentioned together—as in a poem ascribed to the caliph al-Maʾmūn (cf. Ps.-Ibn Ẓahīra/Ibn Ẓuhayra = Abū Ḥāmid al-Ḳudsī, *al-Faḍāʾil al-bāhira fī maḥāsin Miṣr wa 'l-Ḳāhira*, ed. Muṣṭafā al-Saḳḳā and Kāmil al-Muhandis, Cairo 1969, 69; on the author, see now M. Cook, *Abū Ḥāmid al-Qudsī* (d. 888/1483), in *JSS*, xxviii [1983], 85-97)—and are sometimes confused (Ibn Ḥawḳal, as cited by Ibn al-Djawzī, *Mirʾāt al-zamān*, in Ibn al-Dawādārī, *Kanz al-durar*, i, ed. B. Radtke, Cairo 1982, 124, 1-5).

Despite its decay, however, Manf continued to denominate the northermost *kūra* (district or country) of Upper Egypt for some centuries (see e.g. Ibn Khurradādhbih, *al-Masālik wa 'l-mamālik*, 81; Ibn al-Faḳīh, *Mukhtaṣar Kitāb al-Buldān*, 73; al-Dimashḳī, *K. Nukhbat al-dahr fī ʿadjāʾib al-barr wa 'l-baḥr*, 231-2; and the tables in J. Maspero and G. Wiet, *Matériaux pour servir à la géographie de l'Égypte*, Cairo 1919, 173-84, and A. Grohmann, *Studien zur historischen Geographie und Verwaltung des frühmittelalterlichen Ägypten*, Vienna 1959, appendix ii). Many, though certainly not all, mediaeval authors (e.g. al-Dimashḳī, 232) merge the districts of Manf and of Wasīm-Awsīm into one. A papyrus of 133/750-1 explicitly mentions the *kūrat Manf* (Grohmann, 40b). Al-Dimashḳī counts 54 villages in the district of Manf (232). As late as the early 7th/13th century, Abū Djaʿfar al-Idrīsī [*q.v.*] speaks of a village like Būṣīr as belonging to the *aʿmāl madīnat Manf*, the vicinity of Manf (*Anwār ʿulwiyy al-adjrām*, ms. Munich, fol. 47b). By that time, Djīza [*q.v.*], the provincial capital (*ḳaṣaba*, cf. Ibn Duḳmāḳ, *K. al-Intiṣār li-wāsiṭat ʿiḳd al-amṣār*, iv, 130), had succeeded Manf as the regional centre (ʿAbd al-Laṭīf, 134-5). Until the 4th/10th century at least, Manf remained the see of a bishop (Severus of Ushmūnayn, in *Patr. orient.* vi, 490 [26]; Abū Ṣāliḥ al-Armanī, in B. T. A. Evetts and A. J. Butler, *The churches and monasteries of Egypt and some neighbouring countries*, Oxford 1895, 199), though only a few generations later (al-Idrīsī, *Nuzha*, 135-2, *Op. geog.*, 32b, *l.*2), it is labelled a village (*ḳarya*).

The Nile posed a constant threat to the fields and pastures around Manf in pre-Islamic and in Islamic times; Ibn ʿAbd al-Ḥakam (*Futūḥ Miṣr wa-akhbāruhā*, 6,8) still speaks of the canal of Manf as one of the seven *khuludj* of Egypt; for al-Wāḳidī (see Ibn al-Zayyāt, *al-Kawākib al-sayyāra fī tartīb al-ziyāra*, 6,8 ff.) it was one out of six. In al-Ḳalḳashandī's time this canal had disappeared, unlike the six others (*Ṣubḥ*, iii,, 297-302). The Christian author Abū Ṣāliḥ al-Armanī (early 7th/13th century), in his remarkably vivid and original chapter on Manf, mentions that since antiquity the Nile gradually changed its bed towards the city (*Churches*, 19; see also Sibṭ b. al-Djawzī, in Ibn al-Dawādārī, *Kanz* , i, 124). In the 9th/15th century finally, the village of Badrashayn (Umm ʿĪsā) flourished, either exactly where (Ibn Duḳmāḳ, 130), or close to where (al-Ḳalḳashandī, iii, 316,14) the old Memphis had stood (see also H. Halm, *Ägypten nach den mamlukischen Lehensregistern*. i, Wiesbaden, 211).

Manf is the accepted rendering of the name of the city (al-Ḳalḳashandī, ii, 316,5), although one also reads Minf (Abu 'l-Fidāʾ, 116), Munf (a variant reading in Ibn ʿAbd al-Ḥalam, 6,5), Munayf (Abū Ṣāliḥ, 200), Manfish (Abū ʿUbayd al-Bakrī, *al-Masālik wa 'l-mamālik*, 21, 11; al-Bakrī was an expert of Greco-Latin toponyms, cf. 21, 10 and 13) and, wrongly, Manūf al-ʿulyā (Ibn Taghribīrdī, *al-Nudjūm al-zāhira*, i, 49, 11 ff). On the confusion of Manf and Manūf [al-ʿulyā/al-suflā], see Maspero-Wiet, 200, 202-4). Ibn ʿAbd al-Ḥakam (8-9), on the authority of his prestigious informants, was the first of many subsequent authors to connect the Arabicised form Manf with Coptic *māfa* (= *maab, maave*), "thirty"; al-Ḳalḳashandī (iii, 316,10) quotes al-Ḥimyarī, *al-Rawḍ al-miʿṭār*, stating a Syriac root. We also find the forms Māf (Ibn al-Zayyāt, 7,6-7) and Manāfa (Abū Ṣāliḥ, 199). As an explanation for this etymology, we learn that the first inhabitants of Manf—in one case described as unruly rogues *djabābira*; cf. al-Maḳrīzī, *al-Khiṭaṭ*, ed. G. Wiet, iii, 29, quoting from Ibn Waṣīf Shāh's legendary history of Egypt—numbered thirty (e.g. al-Nuwayrī, *Nihāyat al-arab*, xv, 44, 8 ff.).

The seventeenth-century Turkish traveller Evliyā Čelebi (*Seyāḥatnāme*, x, 11, 18) vacillates, in his interpretation, between a Coptic (*menûf* = a bride) and an Hebrew etymology ("place of purity").

The Muslims regard Manf as the first settlement (Ibn Duḳmāḳ, 130, offers as an alternative the city of B.d.w. in the province of al-Sharḳiyya) and as the capital city (*miṣr*, *ḳāʿida*) of postdiluvian Egypt, epitomising Egypt as a whole (al-Nuwayrī al-Iskandarānī, *K. al-Ilmām*, iii, 367) until it was destroyed by Nebuchadnezzar (Ibn Khaldūn, *al-ʿIbar*, Cairo 1355/1936, i, 113; *Khiṭāṭ*, iii, 26). He took the city because its king Ḳūmis (Abū Ḥāmid al-Ḳudsī, 69) had given shelter to the Jews who had fled from his oppressive régime (ʿAbd al-Laṭīf, 134-5). According to Ibn Duḳmāḳ (130), there had been an antediluvian settlement named M.z.na in the location of Manf. The earlier Egyptian capitals, Amsūs, off the Mediterranean coast, and B.r.sān (of uncertain location), had perished in the Flood (al-Ḳalḳashandī, iii, 315, 14-20).

There is no consensus about the identity of the founder of Manf. We hear of Bayṣar b. Ḥām (Ibn ʿAbd al-Ḥakam, 9,3) who was the first to be buried in Egyptian soil (Abū Ṣāliḥ, 199), i.e. in the terrain of St. Jerome's—still visible—monastery (*Dayr [Abī] Hirmīs*) in the vicinity of Manf (Maspero-Wiet, 96). Symbolising the continuity of Egyptian history beyond the dividing line of the Flood, Bayṣar married the daughter of Philemon or Polemon al-Kāhin (*al-Khiṭaṭ*, iii, 29-30), the antediluvian sage of Egypt who had warned king Sūrīd of the imminent carastrophe and advised him to erect the Pyramids as a shelter for the secret knowledge of Egypt (cf. Ibn Waṣīf Shāh/al-Waṣīfī—on this latter form, see Ṣāʿid al-Andalusī, *Ṭabaḳāt al-umam* ed. L. Cheikho, Beirut 1912, 39; Abū 'l-Ṣalt, *al-Risāla al-miṣriyya*, ed. ʿA. Hārūn, in *Nawādir al-makhṭūṭāt*, i, 24, 14 ff.; *K. al-Istibṣār*, 62; Abū Djaʿfar al-Idrīsī, fols. 22a, 23a *et alia*—in Ps.-Masʿūdī's *Akhbār al-zamān*, ed. ʿA. al-Ṣāwī[3], Beirut 1978, 134-5; on Waṣīfī's hermetic history of pre-Islamic Egypt, see M. Cook, *Pharaonic history in medieval Egypt*, forthcoming in *SI*). Other authors (e.g. al-Dimashḳī, 229) claim Bayṣar's son Miṣr[īm/āyim] to have been the first to leave the security of the Muḳaṭṭam mountain (*al-Khiṭaṭ*, iii, 27) in the company of his grandfather Ḥām b. Nūḥ (Ibn Duḳmāḳ, 130) and to settle in the plains on the other bank of the Nile that could be reached by the clement east winds (ʿĀbd al-Laṭīf, 26-7). Abū Ṣāliḥ (199) also mentions another legendary king, Manfā'ūs b. ᶜAdīm, as founder of Manf. In Ps.-al-Madjrīṭī's famous manual of the arcane sciences, Ghayāt al-ḥakīm, the inventor of the Indian amulet, Kanka al-Hindī al-Munadjdjim, is presented as the founder of the city where he built castles for his daughters, equipped with wondrous appliances that produced whistling and other sounds (H. Ritter and M. Plessner, *"Picatrix". Das Ziel der Weisen von Pseudo-Mağrīṭī*, London 1962, 285-6; Arabic ed. 278; cf. also Ibn al-Dawādārī, i, 213-14).

The explicit and implicit information on Pharaonic Egypt given in the Ḳur'ān and in the stories of the prophets was the indispensable repertory for mediaeval Muslim reports on the history of the country in pre-Islamic times. The ubiquitous archeological remains of Pharaonic period were eagerly identified with items familiar from the sacred text and the commentaries. In a similar fashion, Manf was given its well-defined and prominent place within salvation history. The reports of traditionists such as Ibn Lahīᶜa [*q.v.*], recorded by early historians like Ibn ᶜAbd al-Ḥakam and ᶜUmar al-Kindī, remained the main corpus of information on Manf well into the modern period. Even in the 19th century the truths of the *ḳiṣaṣ al-anbiyā'* were not easily superseded by the results of enlightened empirical and historical research. ᶜAlī Mubārak Pasha's lengthy chapter on Manf is introduced and, so it seems, legitimised by a long verbatim quotation from al-Maḳrīzī's *Khiṭaṭ*, i.e. by an intrinsically Islamic text. Only then does there follow what European scholarship has found out about the factual history of the city (see his *al-Khiṭaṭ al-Tawfīḳiyya al-djadīda*, xvi, 2-8).

Three verses of the Ḳur'ān are interpreted as referring directly to the city of Manf: xxviii, 15, "And he [= Mūsā] entered the city at a time of carelessness of its folk" (cf. also ᶜUmar al-Kindī, *Faḍā'il Miṣr*, ed. Ibrāhīm Aḥmad al-ᶜAdawī and ᶜAlī Muḥammad ᶜUmar, Cairo-Beirut 1391/1971, 25); xxviii, 21, "So he [= Mūsā] escaped from thence, fearing, vigilant"; and xliii, 51, "Is not mine the sovereignty (*mulk*) of Egypt and these rivers flowing under me? Can ye not then discern?" (cf. Ibn ᶜAbd al-Ḥakam, 6,5; al-Nuwayrī al-Iskandarānī, *Ilmām*, iii, 363, on Hārūn al-Rashīd's symbolic defiance of Pharaoh's claim to the *mulk Miṣr*; Ibn Khaldūn, *ᶜIbar*, i, 115). The latter verse posed particular problems to historical and geographical commentators. What to do with the rivers in the plural? It was Manf, 12 miles long, the city of iron (Ibn al-Dawādārī, *Kanz*, i, 124 writes "copper") and brass walls (Ibn al-Faḳīh, 73; Ibn Khurradādhbih, 161 [not 81, as in *EI*¹ art. MANF]) and of 70—or, alternatively, 30 (Abū Ṣāliḥ, 199-200—gates from which the four great rivers of the earth flowed. The numerous dams and bridges (*ḳanāṭir wa-djusūr*) of the lowlands of Manf (Ibn ᶜAbd al-Ḥakam, 6,3; *al-Khiṭaṭ*, iii, 27) are also directly linked to this Ḳur'ānic verse.

The dominant Islamic stereotype associated with Manf is its role as the seat of Pharaoh (*madīnat Firᶜawn*, see e.g. Ibn al-Faḳīh, 73). Other familiar epithets are *dār al-mamlaka* (*al-Istibṣār*, 83; al-Ḥimyarī, *al-Rawḍ al-miᶜṭār*, ed. I. ᶜAbbās, Beirut 1975, 551a), *dār al-mulk* (Ibn ᶜAbd al-Ḥakam, 20, 14; Abu 'l-Ṣalt, 29; *al-Khiṭaṭ*, iii, 29), *dār al-mulk wa 'l-ᶜilm* (Ibn al-ᶜIbrī, *Ta'rīkh mukhtaṣar al-duwal*, Beirut n.d. [1978-9], 20, 10), *madīnat al-iḳlīm* (Abū Ḥāmid al-Ḳudsī, 69), *miṣr al-iḳlīm* (Ibn Duḳmāḳ, 130) and, last but not least, *Miṣr al-ḳadīma* (Abū Djaᶜfar al-Idrīsī, fol. 34a; al-Ḳalḳashandī, iii, 316, 14). At least five Pharaohs resided there (al-Dimashḳī, 229). Al-Maḳrīzī (*al-Khiṭaṭ*, iii, 25-70) integrates the complete story of Egypt between Mūsā and Nebuchadnezzar into his chapter on Manf. Eight prophets, from Idrīs to Yūshaᶜ, lived to see it as the Egyptian capital (Abū Djaᶜfar al-Idrīsī, fol. 12b). The famous stories of Mūsā and Yūsuf b. Yaᶜḳūb took place in and around Manf (see e.g. Yāḳūt, *Muᶜdjam al-buldān*, Beirut 1397/1977, v, 214b, s.v. *Manf*). Miscellaneous monuments are identified with Yūsuf's granary and prison, with Zalīkhā/Zulaykhā's tomb and with the mosques of Yaᶜḳūb and Mūsā (see e.g. al-Ḳalḳashandī, iii, 317, 4-12). The village of al-ᶜAzīziyya north of Manf is said to go back to Potiphar, the *ᶜazīz Miṣr* [*q.v.*]. It was at Manf that Yūsuf's coffin was lowered into the floods of the Nile (only in al-Masᶜūdī, *Murudj al-dhahab*, i, 90 = § 83). Manf becomes an important scene of Jewish history. From there the Jews were banished to ᶜAyn Shams, as one source maintains (Abū Djaᶜfar al-Idrīsī, fol. 57a). Al-Ḥimyarī goes so far as to claim Jewish rule over Egypt after the demise of Pharaoh's troops in the Red Sea (*al-Rawḍ al-miᶜṭār*, 551a, cf. the footnote of the editor). According to ᶜAbd al-Laṭīf (134-5) and Abū Djaᶜfar al-Idrīsī (fol. 35a), both writing in the Ayyūbid era, Mūsā took refuge in the neighbouring hamlet of Dunūh/Dumūya/Dumuwayh. This place remained sacred to the Jews, who erected a synagogue there (ᶜAbd al-Laṭīf) and made it a place of public veneration (Abū Djaᶜfar al-Idrīsī).

The women's régime established in Egypt after the Pharaoh of Moses had perished in the Red Sea together with the soldiers of the country provided the "historical" nucleus for the hen-pecked predicament of the Egyptian male, to be encountered among non-Egyptian writers from the days of Herodotus to the time when Muṣṭafā ᶜĀlī, at the end of the 10th/16th century, visited Cairo. Manf too has an important part to play in this context. The main temple (*birbā/barbā* [*q.v.*]) of Manf, with its four doors, built by the valiant Queen Dalūka, had an apotropaic function in those sad days when Egypt was bereft of men and seemed an easy prey to foreign invaders. If we follow Ibn ᶜAbd al-Ḥakam and his sources (27, 16-28, 8), the sorceress Tadūra had prepared images of the riding beasts and of the vessels on which the numerous potential enemies could enter Egypt. In voodoo-like magical substitution, the destruction of the image entailed, whenever the situation arose, the destruction of the object depicted. With the extinction of Tadūra's offspring in Manf, this magic knowledge was irretrievably lost (Ibn Duḳmāḳ, 130; Ibn al-Zayyāt, 11, 14-22). In another tradition of obscure origin, cited by Abū Ḥāmid al-Ḳudsī in his *faḍā'il Miṣr* work (70), it was not the animals and vehicles but rather the enemy kings themselves who were depicted in Manf and who could thus be annihilated from afar whenever they were tempted to attack Egypt. We are reminded of one of the immortal stereotypes connected with Egypt: whomever God wishes to destroy, He lures into Egypt. In our story, Nebuchadnezzar contrived to gain knowledge of the secret, to have his own effigy in the tower (*ḳubba*) of Manf soaked with the blood of pigs, and thus to break the spell and conquer the city and the country. Al-Maḳrīzī, in his chapter on Manf (*al-Khiṭaṭ*, iii, 27), brings Manf into the orbit of Muḥammad's miraculous telepathic powers; the pagan monuments of Manf collapsed at the precise moment when the Prophet victoriously entered Mecca, destroyed the idols and proclaimed the advent of truth from east to west, all around the world.

As we have seen in the case of Manf's epithet "capital city of the Egyptian kings", historical veracity and pious legend are inevitably and inextricably mixed. Some of the miraculous buildings of the Manf of the magicians may well have had their less conspicuous counterparts in historical reality. Thus we hear of sophisticated gears (*al-daradj al-mudjawwafa, al-Khiṭaṭ*, iii, 28) engineered to lift water to the highest buildings on Manf in early postdiluvian times. Manf is—truly or falsely?—mentioned as the location of Egypt's first Nilometer [see MIḲYĀS], (al-Masʿūdī, *Murūdj* ii, 365 = §781; a slightly altered version in al-Ḳazwīnī, 265, who cites al-Ḳuḍāʿī, and in Sibṭ Ibn al-Djawzī, as quoted by Ibn al-Dawādārī, *Kanz*, i, 196, 18-20). Al-Ḳalḳashandī (iii, 317,14) speaks of a place in Manf that up to his own time, the 9th/15th century, was known under the name of *al-miḳyās*. Al-Masʿūdī (*loc. cit.*) and Abū Ṣāliḥ (200) tell us that Yūsuf erected it, together with the Pyramids, and "was the first who measured the Nile in Egypt by the cubit" (see also Ibn ʿAbd al-Hakam 16, 17 on the *miḳyās Manf*). The Nilometers of Ikhmīm or Akhmīm [*q.v.*] and in the "extreme Ṣaʿīd"—the latter, presumably referring to the Nilometer on the island of Elephantine, mentioned only by al-Masʿūdī—were built as the second and third ones much later by Queen Dalūka. Of equally indeterminable historicity is the widespread report of an observation post (*marḳab*) on the Muḳaṭṭam between Manf and ʿAyn Shams (Ibn ʿAbd al-Ḥakam, 157,18 - 158,5, on the authority of Saʿīd Ibn ʿUfayr, quoting Kaʿb al-Aḥbār). Whenever, according to legend, Pharaoh set out from Manf to ʿAyn Shams, his other favourite abode (al-Idrīsī, *Opus geogr.*, 376, l.3), or vice versa, his departure could immediately be signalled to the other city so that the people there had enough time for an appropriate to their ruler. This station on the Muḳaṭṭam was allegedly equipped with a mobile mirror (*mirʾāt tadūr ʿalā lawlab*, al-Idrīsī, *op. cit.*, 326 l.6). Later on, this place became known as "Pharaoh's oven" (*tannūr Firʿawn*) (cf. e.g. al-Idrīsī, *loc. cit.*; Yāḳūt, v, 214b). Ibn Ṭūlūn had a mosque erected there (cf. Zaky Mohamed Hassan, *Les Tulunides. Étude de l'Égypte musulmane à fin du IXᵉ siècle 868-905*, Paris 1933, 295). Ibn Khaldūn's remark that Manf was one of the residences of the Muḳawḳis is also at the borderline of legend and historical truth (*ʿIbar*, I, 114).

The vast and fabulous ruins of Manf—according to ʿAbd al-Laṭīf (176-7) another Bābil—left profound impressions on mediaeval visitors, some of whom declared the city as a whole one of the *ʿadjāʾib* of Egypt (cf. Ibn al-Zayyāt, 11, 13-14). It took ʿAbd al-Laṭīf (134-5) half a day to tour the site of Manf, which is often closely connected with the adjacent Pyramids (sc. of Saḳḳāra, Būṣīr and Djīza), Egypt's greatest *uʿdjūba* (Abū Ṣāliḥ, 200; Abū Djaʿfar al-Idrīsī, fol. 34a, speaking of Manf as the "settlement" [*khiyām*] belonging to the Pyramids). A visit to the Pyramids and to Manf seems to have been the minimum programme for visitors to the area who were interested in Pharaonic archaeology (cf. Abū Djaʿfar al-Idrīsī, 45a, on the envoy of Frederick II to the court of al-Malik al-Kāmil). In striking unanimity, most authors mention the prevalence of the indelible green colour (sc. of the granite monuments) in the ruins of Manf (see Abu 'l-Fidāʾ, 117).

Certain monuments are singled out in the descriptions available to us, though it is not always easy to identify them and to differentiate between their legendary function—in such cases as Joseph's abode or Pharaoh's palace—and the archaeological reality as seen and recorded by the authors. Therefore the detailed scholarly observations of ʿAbd al-Laṭīf al-Baghdādī are of particular value. One building, not mentioned by ʿAbd al-Laṭīf, is the magnificent, monolithic, so-called "bishop's church" (*kanīsat al-usḳuf*); Abū Ḥāmid al-Ḳudsī (150) lists it even as the first among the *ʿadjāʾib* of Egypt. It is not all clear whether this church, the church "spread with mats" mentioned by Abū Ṣāliḥ (200), and, thirdly, the monolithic Dār Firʿawn, with its many halls, rooms and roofs, about which an ʿAlid authority reports full of awe (*al-Istibṣār*, 83; Yāḳūt, v, 214a; al-Ḥimyarī, 55a; al-Nuwayrī al-Iskandarānī, *Ilmān*, iii, 367), all mean the same building or not.

There was certainly one other *kanīsa*—since we have to do with Pharaonic buildings, rather to be rendered as "temple" than "church"—in Manf. It was noted for its small size, for which a hieroglyphic inscription, deciphered by ʿUthmān b. Ṣāliḥ (d. 217/832), the "sage of Egypt" and one of Ibn ʿAbd al-Ḥakam's main authorities, gives a very convincing financial explanation: building with granite on a large scale was just too expensive (ʿUmar al-Kindī, *Faḍāʾil*, 52, quoting Ibrāhīm b. Munḳidh al-Khawlānī; modified in Yāḳūt, v, 214a-b, quoted by al-Ḳazwīnī, 274-5, and Abū Ḥāmid al-Ḳudsī, 70). This temple was allegedly erected on the spot where the irate young Mūsā, at Satan's instigation, had killed an Egyptian (*al-radjul al-ḳibṭī* [!], cf. Ḳurʾān, XXVIII, 15). Again we have the problem of identification. Is this monument the famous monolithic green chapel that was located within the precinct of the great temple of Manf and is described in detail by ʿAbd al-Laṭīf (138-9), al-Ḳalḳashandī (iii, 316, 19-317,3) and al-Maḳrīzī (*al-Khiṭaṭ*, iii, 28)? Its weight was legendary (*ibid.*). Both from the inside and the outside it was covered with hieroglyphic inscriptions (*al-ḳalam al-birbāwī, aḳlām al-birbāwiyya*, Abū Djaʿfar al-Idrīsī, fol. 42a), with pictures of the sun, of stars, men in different postures, snakes and other animals—for ʿAbd al-Laṭīf, important proof to his conviction that the old Egyptians used the pictograms not for simple decorative purposes (138-9). The fundament of this building had already been destroyed in his days by some, as he complains, foolish treasure-hunter (*loc. cit.*). Sultan Ḥasan b. Muḥammad b. Ḳalāwūn's generalissimo, the *amīr* Shaykhū, tried to transport the chapel to Cairo after the year 750/1350. It broke into pieces; Shaykhū had them polished and re-used them as sills and thresholds in his *khānaḳāh* and his Friday mosque in the vicinity of the mosque of Ibn Ṭūlūn south of the Fāṭimid city of Cairo (*al-Khiṭaṭ*, iii, 29; al-Ḳalḳashandī, iii, 317, 1-3; see the still important comments by Silvestre de Sacy, *Relation de l'Égypte par Abd-allatiph médecin de Bagdad*, Paris 1810, 248, n. 65; G. Wiet, *L'Égypte de Murtadi*, Paris 1953, 93, n. 2; U. Haarmann, *Die Sphinx. Synkretistische Volksreligiosität im spätmittelalterlichen islamischen Ägypten*, in *Saeculum*, xxix [1978], 377). There they can still be seen in our time. The astronomical reliefs on the green chapel attracted particular attention; Abū Ḥamid al-Ḳaysī al-Gharnāṭī (*Tuḥfat al-albāb*, ed. G. Ferrand, in *JA*, ccvii [1925], ii, 78) mentions them, and according to al-Maḳrīzī (*al-Khiṭaṭ*, iii, 28), the Sabians maintained that this building was dedicated to the moon as one of originally seven such houses, each of which pertained to one of the seven planets. Also, Ps.-Madjrīṭī's remark (286) about a sanctuary dedicated to the planets by the Indian Kanka should be linked with the green chapel at Manf. ʿAbd al-Laṭīf (140-55) goes on to describe the sad remains of the temple terrain within which the green chapel still stood in his time. He displays an expertise on the sophisticated techniques and materials of Pharaonic masonry and on the harmonious proportions of the huge human statues of limestone and red granite, one of which undoubtedly represents Isis with the child Horus (154-5). Al-Ḳalḳashandī (iii, 316, 16-18) speaks of two idols of 20 cubits length each which lie precipitated in the mud as being made of "white granite". Al-Maḳrīzī (*al-Khiṭaṭ*, iii, 28) attributes them (or two other, similar, monuments) to Potiphar. One of the two statues could well be identical with the monument mentioned by Abū Ṣāliḥ (199) with the surprising name of Abu 'l-Hawl (see Haarmann, *Die Sphinx*, 373) and with the famous statue of Rameses II that was transported from Manf to the Cairo railway staion at the Bāb al-Ḥadīd in this century.

Bibliography: (in addition to the works quoted in the article): Else Peitemeyer, *Beschreibung Ägyptens im Mittelalter aus den geographischen Werken der Araber*, Leipzig 1903, 129-36; *L'Égypte de Murtadi*, 90-3 (both works containing German or, alternatively, French translations of the passages referring to Manf in Abū Ḥamīd al-Ḳaysī al-Gharnāṭī, ʿAbd al-Laṭīf al-Baghdādī, al-Maḳrīzī's *al-Khiṭaṭ* and al-Ḳalḳashandī); Maspero-Wiet, *Matériaux*, 200.

(U. HAARMANN)

AL-**MANFALŪṬĪ**, MUṢṬAFĀ LUṬFĪ (1293-1343/1876-1924), Egyptian writer and poet.

Born in al-Manfalūṭ (Upper Egypt), then going to live in Cairo, al-Manfalūṭī never attended any teaching institutions except al-Azhar. He later composed poems which appeared in the press; one was published in 1904 by Faraḥ Anṭūn's magazine *al-Djāmiʿa*. By the very traditional character of his art, he belongs among the great Egyptian poets of the age. Like them, he cultivated the still flourishing genre of occasional poetry. His composition of epic poems cannot even be regarded as original, since Khalīl Muṭrān, Aḥmad Shawḳī and Ḥāfiẓ Ibrāhīm had distinguished themselves in this field. (He left no *dīwān*, but only an anthology, *Mukhtārāt al-Manfalūṭī*, 1912, in which some prose texts accompany several poems.)

Finally, his true originality derived from his doctrinal commitment, and from its quite unexpected literary corollary. His Islamic faith appears strong in the face of any test. For him, Islam is not an old system of values in which he will seek refuge, but a dynamic religion whose constantly renewed force should animate the faithful, allowing them to view the future with optimism. He also believes that everything capable of favouring this dynamism should be encouraged. Thus he took the side of the great reformist Muḥammad ʿAbduh [*q.v.*] and even went to prison for supporting him against the Khedive. His support for the companion of al-Afghānī is often evident in his poems, but being as he is above all a moraliser, he found a more convenient form in which to express himself in the collection of essays in the shape of edifying stories which he published in the weekly *al-Muʾayyid* under the title of *al-Naẓarāt* ("Sketches"). Death, misfortune and tears, represent the essential ingredients of these narratives. At times, destiny, cruel and unjust, besets pure and defenceless beings. But often it is the evolution of society which brings on catastrophes; at the end of the last century and beginning of the present one, the rash Egyptians have repudiated their sound traditions and turned their back on the wise precepts of Islam in order to imitate blindly the European example. This is the message to be drawn from al-Manfalūṭī's fables. We must believe that the content and form of these writings matched the expectations of the public of the period, since they were reprinted in three volumes in 1910, 1912 and 1920.

But in 1915 our author published another collection with the evocative title *al-ʿAbarāt* ("Tears"). The dominant tone remains one of pathos, but it is to be noted that the stories are of two kinds. Only three of them are the original work of al-Manfalūṭī, while the eight others have been translated by him from French or—in one case—from American English. For, paradoxically, despite his admonitions against the Western life style, he admired the literature which it produced. Chateaubriand and Alexandre Dumas the Younger are translated here, and later it was to be the turn of Alphonse Karr (*Sous l'ombre des tilleuls* ["In the shade of the linden trees"], 1919), Bernardin de Saint-Pierre (*Paul et Virginie*) and François Coppée (*Pour la couronne* ["For the crown"], 1920). Are we not to suppose that this pitiful picture of disasters, to which venal, unshared or impossible love leads, constitutes the most eloquent condemnation of the society which attaches such importance to this sentiment? Furthermore, one of the three original stories in *al-ʿAbarāt*, entitled *al-Ḥidjāb* ("The veil") shows how a young Egyptian, returned from Europe where he has studied, brings on his own misfortune by allowing his wife to spend time in the company of his best friend. However, this interpretation is not always justified. It is clear that the narrator is little concerned to explain the avalanche of misfortunes which befall his heroes. His main concern is to place them in a desperate situation, which he knows how to turn to the best advantage in order to move his readers. For here we have an artist who excelled in appealing to the emotions. The instrument that he used was the Arabic language, on which he played to perfection because he kept it in the register which suited him best: ample periods, sonorities balanced with majesty and the theatrical expression of powerful feelings. All his contemporaries and even some of his successors bore witness to the quality of his style, which they regarded as enchanting. But, quite obviously, the conclusions that they reached could be diametrically opposed.

The novelist Maḥmūd Taymūr [*q.v.*], in the preface of one of his first collections (*al-Shaykh Sayyid al-ʿAbīṭ*, 1926), believed that the subjects and characters imagined by al-Manfalūṭī lacked consistency, but he did not cease to write eulogies on the quality of his vocabulary and the absolutely classical purity of his language. This testimony is worth bearing in mind when one realises how great an audience at this period in the Arab world such a writer enjoyed. On the other hand, the equally famous Ibrāhīm ʿAbd al-Ḳādir al-Māzinī [*q.v.*] proceeded, for his part, to a definitive execution of al-Manfalūṭī in the book of literary criticism which he published in collaboration with ʿAbbās Maḥmūd al-ʿAḳḳād [*q.v.* in Suppl.] (*al-Dīwān*, 1921). His intrigues, he says, are a tissue of improbabilities, and his pretended virtue is only shoddy sentimentalism nourishing women's fiction; as for the style, let us speak about it in detail! It is characterised by artifice, accumulation of *mafʿūl muṭlaḳs*, abuse of synonyms, i.e. of tinsel and eye shadow, whereas the art of the real writer resides in the care taken in significant and subtle composition, in the choice of the "mot juste".

Even if al-Manfalūṭī's works are constantly being republished, there is no doubt that from now on they will be merely of historical interest. But at any rate, this interest is undeniable. At a time when Arabic romantic literature was still sought after, al-Manfalūṭī contributed to winning a public for it. In fact, this well-known foreign genre became acclimatised on Arab soil. It did so in the first place thanks to the quality of its language, although some Syro-Lebanese and Egyptian translators of the period wrote in very mediocre Arabic. It must be noted that, never having left Egypt or studied seriously any foreign language, his expression did not risk being contaminated and debased by foreign idioms. Also, his supposed translations were actually adaptations of pre-existing translations. Thus it is to be understood that they were, probably, not very faithful, and that his original works and translated works might be closely related. Furthermore, the kind of story which he preferred is the same in both cases. This was, moreover, along with the language, the second method of luring the reader. The *romantic*, in the technical and literary sense of the word, had to use the romantic in the emotional and popular sense of the word. He believed that, like himself, his compatriots might have a passion for the unhappy love stories in Europe, while they also might have a passion for the life stories of those who had died or had been driven mad by love, of whom Arab collective memory had preserved the remembrance. It is significant that the modernist al-Māzinī had mentioned, in the above-mentioned work, what a danger al-Manfalūṭī's literature presented for lovers of bad novels, those who put nothing above Platonic love (*al-ḥubb al- ʿudhrī*), i.e. the pure love which made the Ḥidjāzī tribe of the Banū ʿUdhra famous from the 2nd/8th century onwards.

Bibliography : Apart from the references given in the text: S. Bencheneb, *Deux sources d'al-Manfalūṭī*, in *RAfr.*, lxxxv (1941), 260-4; Brockelmann, S III, 195-202; H. Pérès, *Le roman arabe dans le premier tiers du XXe s.: al-Manfalūṭī et Haykal*, in *AIEO Alger*, xvii (1959), 145-68; A. al-Djindī, *Adab al-marʾa al-ʿarabiyya ... Taṭawwur al-tardjama*, Cairo n.d., 59-60. (Ch. Vial)

MANGIR [see sikka].

MANGĪSHLAK, a mountainous peninsula on the eastern shores of the Caspian Sea. The northern part of Mangīshlak (the Buzači peninsula) is a lowland covered with small salt-marshes. In the central part, the Mangīstau mountains stretch from northwest to southeast for *ca.* 100 miles; they consist of three ranges, Southern and Northern Aktau and Karatau, the last one running between the first two. The highest peak (in the Karatau) is only 1,824 feet. To the south of the mountains lies the Mangīshlak Plateau. From the east, the peninsula borders the Üst-Yurt Plateau. Mangīshlak is now one of the most arid areas of Central Asia, without permanent rivers and with an annual precipitation of *ca.* 150 mm. The most often suggested etymology of the name is from Turkish *ming ḳishlaḳ* "the thousand winter quarters"; another one derives the name from Turkish *man* (*mang*) "four-year-old sheep" (Maḥmūd al-Kāshgharī, iii, 157; cf. *mang* "three-year-old sheep" in Čaghatay and modern Turkmen), so that Mangīshlak is, presumably, "sheep's winter quarters". Neither etymology is proven; other etymologies trying to connect the word with its present Ḳazaḳ form Mangīstau or with the name of a subdivision of the Nogays, Mang (?), are unacceptable, since the term was registered in the sources long before the emergence of both the Ḳazaḳ and the Nogays with their languages.

The region was first mentioned under the Persian name Siyāh-Kūh ("Black Mountain"; see al-Iṣṭakhrī, 218; *Ḥudūd al-ʿālam*, 60), which, probably, is a translation of the Turkic name Ḳaratau (or Ḳaratāgh) mentioned above. The same name Siyāh-Kūh was given to the mountains (*djabal*; apparently, the steep scarp of the plateau of Üst-Yurt) west of the Sea of Aral (Ibn Rusta, 92). In mediaeval Muslim works, the localisation of the Siyāh-Kūh mountains was not always clear, and sometimes they were located also on the northern shore of the Caspian Sea and even as stretching along the whole eastern shore of this sea.

According to al-Iṣṭakhhrī (219), the peninsula used to be uninhabited; it was only shortly before his time (or that of his predecessor al-Balkhi, i.e. in the first half or by the beginning of the 10th century A.D.) that Turks, who had quarrelled with the Ghuzz [*q.v.*], i.e. with their own kin, had come here and found springs and pastures for their flocks. Ships which were wrecked on the cliffs of the peninsula used to be plundered by these Turks, A short mention of the Ghuzz Turks on Siyāh-Kūh in *Ḥudūd al-ʿālam* goes back most probably to the same account of al-Iṣṭakhrī. Al-Muḳaddasī mentions the mountain of Binḳishlah as marking the frontier between the land of the Khazars and Djurdjān [*q.v.*] (see *BGA*, iii, 355); this is, apparently, the earliest mention of the name in literature. The name in its present form appears in the 5th/11th century in the dictionary of Maḥmūd al-Kāshgharī (i, 387, vocalised Mānḳishlāgh), where it is explained somewhat vaguely as "name of a place in the country of the Ghuzz". In almost the same form (B.n.kh.sh.lāgh) the name is mentioned in the *Ḳānūn* of al-Bīrūnī as a harbour, or port (*furḍa*), of the Ghuzz, belonging to the region of the Khazar (see *Bīrūnī's picture of the world*, ed. A.Z.V. Togan, New Delhi 1941, 67; cf. Bīrūnī, *al-Ḳānūn*, ii, Ḥaydarābād 1955, 575, with the spelling Y.n.ḥ.sh.lāgh. The interchangeable initial *m/b* probably supports the etymology *ming/bing ḳishlaḳ*).

Mangīshlak as a region of the Saldjūḳ empire, apparently subordinate to the governor of Māzandarān, was mentioned in Persian documents compiled in the Saldjūḳ chancery in the middle of the 6th/12th century (where the spelling M.n.ḳ.sh.lāḳ and M.n.k.sh.lāgh is given; see Muntadjab al-Dīn Badīʿ, *ʿAtabat al-kataba*, ed. by M. Ḳazwīnī and ʿA. Iḳbāl, Tehrān 1329/1950, 19, 85); here also some unbelievers (*kuffār*) were mentioned in the desert of Mangīshlak and the regions of Dihistān [*q.v.*], and the governor of Djurdjān was instructed to wage *djihād* on them. In the very early 7th/13th century, Mangīshlak was mentioned by Ibn al-Athīr and Yāḳūt (both vocalised as Manḳashlāgh) and by Muḥammad Bakrān in his *Djahān-nāma* (vocalised Manḳishlāgh). Ibn al-Athīr (x, 183) tells about a Turkic principality on Manḳashlāgh, with a town (*madīna*) of the same name, at the end of the 5th/11th century. In 490/1097 the Manḳashlāgh Turks (their tribal affiliation is not mentioned) unsuccessfully interfered in the fight between the Khwārazmshāh Ḳuṭb al-Dīn Muḥammad and Toghrīl Tegin, son of Ekinči b. Ḳočḳar [*q.v.* in Suppl.]. According to Ibn al-Athīr, the son and successor of Ḳuṭb al-Dīn Muḥammad, the Khwārazmshāh Atsïz, conquered the town of Manḳashlāgh when he commanded the army of Khwārazm during the reign of his father (i.e. before 521/1127 or 522/1128). Yāḳūt (iv, 670) describes Manḳashlāgh not as a region, but only as a strong fortress (*ḳalʿa ḥaṣīna*) near the sea between Khwārazm [*q.v.*], Saḳsīn [*q.v.*] and the land of the Rūs; he cites verses by Abu 'l-Muʾayyad al-Muwaffaḳ b. Aḥmad al-Khwārazmī, where Manḳashlāgh and its conquest by Atsïz are mentioned. Muḥammad Bakrān, a contemporary of Ibn al-Athīr and Yāḳūt, first mentions Manḳīshlāgh in his description of the Caspian Sea, as a region lying between Siyāh-Kūh and the Balkhān [*q.v.*] region in the south and the region of the Khazar in the north (*Djahān-nāma*, ed. Yu. Borshčevskiy, Moscow 1960, fol. 5b). In another place (fol. 17a) he explains Manḳishlāgh as a name of a tribe (*ḳawm*) of Turks who left their former place because of an enmity between them and the Ghuzz and came to live in the region of Siyāh-Kūh near the Caspian Sea, where they found springs and pastures (cf. the account of al-Iṣṭakhrī-al-Balkhī above); they were called the "People of Manḳishlāgh" (*ahl-i Manḳishlāgh*), and their ruler was called *khān*. Immediately after this, speaking about the Turkic tribe (*ḳawm*) Yazīr which lived in the Balkhān mountains, Bakrān adds that two other tribes, one from Manḳishlāgh and the second from Khurāsān, joined the Yazīr, after which the latter became numerous and strong, and at the time of writing (*aknūn*) they consisted of three parts: the Yazīr proper, those of Manḳishlāgh (*Manḳishlāghī*) and of Fārs.

As one can conclude from all accounts cited above, Mangīshlak became inhabited by some Turkic (apparently Oghuz) tribe of tribes about the first half of the 4th/10th century, and the migration of these Turks to Mangīshlak was connected with the internal strife in the Oghuz confederation. The Mangīshlak Turks were apparently hostile to the Oghuz tribes involved in the Saldjūḳ movement, and they were considered pagan as late as in the middle of the 6th/12th century; in the early 7th/13th century they (or at least a part of them) were included into the Yazīr group of the Oghuz, the centre of which was in northern Khurāsān. No permanent settlement on Mangīshlak is again mentioned in the sources after the account of the campaign of Atsïz, and Barthold assumed that the "town" mentioned by Yāḳūt was destroyed by the Khwārazmians (see *EI*[1], iii, 243). However, it is quite possible that the "fortress of Mangīshlak" was in fact not a town, but rather a fortified place where the Oghuz nomads could find refuge in time of danger.

The accounts of written sources are to some extent corroborated by the Turkmen genealogical tradition as rendered by Abu 'l-Ghāzī (*Shadjara-yi Tarākima*, ed. Kononov, text, 61-2), which also connects the migration of the Oghuz to Mangīshlak with the great disturbances in the *el* of the Oghuz in the time of ʿAlī Khān and Shāh Malik (Oghuz rulers, contemporaries of the first Saldjūḳs). It is to this time that the Turkmen tradition relates the migration to Mangīshlak of all those tribes which were also later found on the peninsula, as attested in other sources. The most numerous among these tribes was the Salor [*q.v.*], which in the 10th/16th century was divided into the "inner" (*ičkï*) Salor" who lived on the coast, and the "outer (*tashkï*) Salor" who lived farther to the east, on the road from the coast to Khwārazm (see Bartol'd, *Sočineniya*, viii, 148). The "outer Salor" was, in fact, a group of tribes affiliated with the Salor proper, and it was found also in the Balkhān and Khurāsān; among them the tribe Ersarī [*q.v.* in Suppl.] lived partly on Mangīshlak. Other tribes mentioned in *Shadjara-yi Tarākima* as those who came there with the Salor included the Čawdor [*q.v.*] and Igdir, which remained on the peninsula also later.

According to the Turkmen tradition, in the middle of the 8th/14th century Mangīshlak belonged to the Golden Horde, together with the Balkhān and the northern part of Khwārazm (see Abu 'l-Ghāzī, *Shadjara-yi Tarākima*, ed. Kononov, text, 72). Nothing is known about the region in Tīmūrid times. The available sources only clearly indicate that after the Mongol conquest, Mangīshlak remained for several centuries one of the main regions inhabited by the Turkmens, together with the Balkhān and the western part of the Ḳaraḳum desert (see Yu. Bregel, in *CAJ*, xxv/1-2 [1981], 20-2). With the conquest of Khwārazm by the Uzbeks in the early 10th/16th century, the ʿArabshāhid khāns subdued also the Turkmen tribes of Mangīshlak, which were divided between the Uzbek *sulṭāns* as part of their appanages (see Abu 'l-Ghāzī, *Shadjara-yi Turk*, ed. Desmaisons, text, 201, 202, 206; tr., 216, 220). In the 11th/17th century, however, the Turkmens of Mangīshlak seemed to be mostly independent, and the region sometimes served as a refuge for the Uzbek *sulṭāns*, who fled from Khwārazm during internal strife there. Via Mangīshlak there ran a trade route from the Volga basin to Khwārazm. Goods were unloaded in the Ḳabaḳlī landing-place on the Buzači peninsula and taken to Khwārazm by caravans through the plateau of Üst-Yurt. The route became especially important after the conquest of Astrakhan [*q.v.*] by the Russians (1556). Turkmens also profited from this trade, supplying camels and protection to the caravans, extorting presents from the merchants and occasionally plundering them. Mangīshlak also served as the starting point of a sea-route to Shīrwān [*q.v.*], in the late 10th/16th and early 11th/17th centuries used by Central Asian merchants and pilgrims to Mecca wishing to avoid travel through Shīʿī Irān (see Abu 'l-Ghāzī, *Shadjara-yi Turk*, ed. Desmaisons, text, 257, 273; tr., 275, 294). In 1558 the first English traveller to Central Asia, Anthony Jenkinson, passed through Mangīshlak to Khwārazm (see *Purchase his Pilgrimes*, xii, Glasgow 1906, 10-13).

Both the Turkmen tribes on Mangīshlak and the trade caravans were endangered by the raids from the north of the Mangīt [*q.v.*], or Nogays, in the 10th/16th century and of the Kalmuk [*q.v.*] in the 11th/17th century. The Kalmuk raids in 1620s and 1630s caused the transfer of the landing-place from the Ḳabaḳlī Bay to the Ḳaragan Bay, near the Sarī-Tash Mountain, farther to the south (see A. Čuloshnikov, in *Materialī po istorii Uzbekskoy, Tadzhikskoy i Turkmenskoy SSR*, pt. 1, Leningrad 1932, 74-6, and the map attached to the book). Already the Mangīt raids forced a part of the Turkmens to leave Mangīshlak. Another cause of emigration was, apparently, the growing desiccation of the steppe which began at the same time (see Yu. Bregel, *op. cit.*, 29-30). Later, the Kalmuk pressure had the same effect. In the middle of the 11th/17th century, the Ersarī tribe totally abandoned Mangīshlak, together with a part of the Salor; another part of the Salor probably remained there till the early 12th/18th century. The Kalmuks under Ayuka (1670-1724), or as early as the reign of Puntsuk-Mončak (1667-70) deported parts of the tribes of the Čawdor and Igdir as well as the whole tribe of the Soyinadji to the Volga basin (from where they moved to the Caucasus). In the first half of the 12th/18th century, most of the remaining Čawdors and Igdirs migrated to Khwārazm, and in the early 19th century several groups of the same tribes migrated via the Volga to their tribesmen in the Caucasus; but Mangīshlak was finally abandoned by the Turkmens only in 1840s (a small section of the Čawdor has continued to dwell near the Caspian shore till the present time). The Turkmens were replaced on Mangīshlak by the Ḳazaḳs, who belonged to the clan Aday of the Bayulī tribe (of the Little Horde). There seems to be no historical evidence of the time of this migration; Ḳazaḳ legends relate this movement to the middle or the second half of the 12th/18th century. Assertion of some modern Ḳazaḳ scholars trying to connect the Aday with the ancient Dahae, and thus trying to prove that the Ḳazaḳs were the most ancient inhabitants of Mangīshlak, are totally unfounded. For the Aday, Mangīshlak was the region of their winter pastures, their summer pastures being about 600 miles from there to the north.

As early as the 1670s, the khān of Khīwa, Anūsha, asked the Russian government to build a fortress on Mangïshlak to protect the trade route between Russia and Central Asia; but the first Russian attempt at establishing a permanent position on the peninsula was made only under Peter the Great, when three fortresses were built near the Caspian coast by the ill-fated expedition of Bekovič-Čerkasskiy (1716); the fortresses were abandoned the next year. During the 12th/18th and early 19th centuries a number of Russian expeditions studied Mangïshlak, and in 1834 the Russians founded a fortress on the southern shore of the Mertvïy Kultuk Bay, named Novo-Aleksandrovskoye, with a permanent garrison. The establishment of Russian power on the Mangïshlak shore was one of the reasons of tensions between her and the Khānate of Khīwa which led to the unsuccessful Russian military campaign of 1839-40. Mangïshlak remained a bone of contention between Russia and Khīwa for another decade, both sides trying to use against one another the Aday Ķazaķs, but neither actually extending its sovereignty over the peninsula until in 1846 the Russians built a fortress on Cape Tüp-Karagan, named first Novo-Petrovskoye and then in 1859 renamed Fort Aleksandrovskiy. But the final incorporation of Mangïshlak into the Russian Empire occured only after the occupation of the Krasnovodsk region in 1869 and the submission of Khīwa in 1873.

According to the imperial decree of 1870, the district (*pristavstvo*) of Mangïshlak was subordinated to the Russian vicegerent of Caucasus, and after the Russian conquest of Turkmenia in 1881 this district was incorporated, as an *uyezd*, in the newly-organised Transcaspian region (*Zakaspiyskaya oblast'*). After the revolution of 1917, Mangïshlak (except for its southernmost part around the Ķara-Boghaz Bay) was separated from the land of the Turkmens and included in the republic of Kazakhstan. Since 1973 it has formed a separate Mangïshlak region (*oblast'*) of Kazakhstan, including also a part of the Üst-Yurt plateau, with an area of 100,000 square miles and its centre at Shevčenko (built only in 1960s; until 1964 Aktau); the population of the *oblast'* was 256,000 in 1978, of which the population of Shevčenko was almost a half (110,000 in 1979); 92% of the inhabitants of the *oblast'* live in cities (see *Sovetskiy éntsiklopedičeskiy slovar'*, Moscow 1980, 1522). The present economic and strategic importance of Mangïshlak is determined by its mineral riches, especially petroleum and natural gas (discovered in 1961) and uranium; details about the uranium mines are kept secret by official Soviet sources, but this uranium is used, apparently, by the atomic power station in Shevčenko.

Bibliography: In addition to the works mentioned in the text, see S. P. Polyakov, *Etničeskaya istoriya Severo-Zapadnoy Turkmenii v sredniye veka*, Moscow 1973; R. Karutz, *Unter Kirgizen und Turkmenen. Aus dem Leben der Steppe*, Leipzig 1911; V. V. Vostrov, M.S. Mukanov, *Rodoplemennoy sostav i rasseleniye kazakhov (konets XIX - načalo XX v.)*, Alma-Ata 1968, 248-54; M. S. Tursunova, *Iz istorii kazakhov Mangïshlaka v pervoy polovine XIX veka*, in *Voprosï istorii Kazakhstana XIX - načala XX veka*, Alma-Ata 1961, 173-202; M.S. Tursunova, *Kazakhi Mangïshlaka vo vtoroy polovine XIX veka*, Alma-Ata 1977. On the present geographical conditions, see V. Ya. Gerasimenko, *Poluostrov sokrovishč*, Alma-Ata 1968; *Kazakhstan* (series *Sovetskiy Soyuz*), Moscow 1970, 274-9; *BSE*³, xv, 317-18.

(Yu. Bregel)

MANGÏT, the name of Mongol and Turkic tribes.

It first appears in Rashīd al-Dīn (in the transcription Mangķūt; Rashīd al-Dīn, i/l, ed. Romaskevič *et alii*, 87, 501-15, Russ. tr., 78, 184-6; i/2, Russ. tr., 29, 125) and the *Secret history* (§ 46) as one of the tribes belonging to the Nirun branch of the Mongols; its genealogy went back to Djaksu, the first son of Tumbine Khān (the great-great-grandfather of Čingiz-Khān). The Mangït were subjugated by Čingiz Khān together with the tribes of the Tayčiʾut. Later they belonged to both right and left wings of the army of Čingiz Khān (Rashīd al-Dīn, Russ. tr., 1/2, 208, 272), and parts of this tribe were found in all major Mongol *uluses*. The Mangït tribe (since the 14th century the name appears in the sources in the forms Mangķit, Manghūt, Mānghīt, Manghīt; in later Central Asian sources mainly Manķit and Manghit) became especially important in the *ulus* of Djoči (the "Golden Horde"), where it was completely Turkicised, along with the other Mongol tribes, apparently already by the 14th century. From the 15th century onwards, the Mangïts inhabited the territory in the lower Volga basin and farther to the east, at least to the Emba. At the same time they began to be called in Russian sources Nogai (according to N.G. Volkova, *Etnonimï i plemennïye nazvaniya Severnogo Kavkaza*, Moscow 1973, 78, not earlier than the 1380s). It is believed that this ethnic name was connected with the name of the famous Noķay Noyan [see NOGAY], a *tümen-begi* and an actual ruler of the *ulus* of Djoči in the end of the 13th and the beginning of the 14th century (cf. on him B. Spuler, *Die Goldene Horde*², Wiesbaden 1965, 56-77, with further references). According to this view, the Mangït was the predominant Turkic tribe in the *ulus* of Noķay. However, there seems to be no evidence of the tribal composition of the *ulus* of Noķay, which possessed the territory to the west of the Dnieper and formed the right wing of the *ulus* of Djoči, while the later Mangïts, between the Volga and the Emba, belonged to the left wing of the same *ulus*. Thus the connection between these two Turkic groupings remains unclear. The people known to the Russians as Nogai was known in Central Asia and Iran only as Mangït; on the other hand, Crimean and Ottoman sources of the 16th-18th centuries know only the Nogay. In the 14th and 15th centuries, this was a large tribal confederation in the central part of Dasht-i Ķipčāķ [*q.v.* in Suppl.] which included, besides the Mangït proper, also a number of other Turkic tribes. Since at least the second half of the 14th century, the confederation was ruled by the chiefs of the Mangït tribe. The most famous among them was the founder of this dynasty Edigü (Yedigey of the Russian sources), a contemporary and adversary of Toķtamish and Tīmūr and for a long time an actual ruler of the Golden Horde (d. 822/1419). In the middle of the 15th century, the Mangït (under Edigü's grandson Waķķāş Biy) played an important role in the nomadic state of Abu 'l-Khayr Khān [*q.v.*]. After the dissolution of this empire, the Mangït dominated the western part of Central Asian steppe till the end of the 15th century.

With the decline of the so-called "Great Horde" (the Golden Horde's successor in the lower Volga basin) in the late 15th and early 16th century, a part of the Mangït migrated to the Crimean Khānate, where their chiefs became the senior *begs* (on the Mangït in Crimea, see V. Ye. Sïroyečkovskiy, *Mukhammad-Geray i ego vassalï*, in *Učeniye zapiski Moskovskogo Gosudarstvennogo Universiteta*, lxi [Moscow 1940], 32-4, 36-7). At the same time another part of the Mangït tribe joined the Uzbek confederacy restored by Shaybānī Khān [see SHAYBĀNIDS] and participated in his conquest of Transoxania; the Mangïts in the troops of Shaybānī Khān are mentioned in the *Shaybānī-nāma* by Muḥammad Ṣāliḥ (ed. Vámbéry, Budapest 1885, 272, 276). Yet the bulk of the Mangït confederacy still remained between the Volga and the Emba rivers for another century, until they were driven from this territory by the Kalmuks [*q.v.*] in the 1620s. After this, the greater part of the confederacy moved to Northern Caucasus, where they have been known only as the Nogays (about the Mangït as one of the tribal units of the Caucasin Nogays, cf. N.G. Volkova, *op. cit.*, 80-3), while another part migrated to the Khānate of Khīwa, where they first established themselves in the Āmū-Daryā delta. Abu 'l-Ghāzī mentions the Mangïts only outside Khwārazm, in their old territory, and as distinct from the Uzbeks (see *Shadjara-yi Turk*, ed. Desmaisons, text, 212-13, 230, 267, 270, 290; tr., 228-9, 246-7, 286, 289, 311). However, the same Abu 'l-Ghāzī is said to have divded all the Uzbek tribes of Khwārazm into four groups, one of which was formed by the tribes Mangït and Nukuz (Muʾnis, *Firdaws al-iḳbāl*, ms. of the Leningrad Branch of the Institute of Oriental Studies, C-571, fol. 65b). Probably, the migration of the Mangïts and other Turkic groups of the Mangït *ulus* to Khwārazm happened in the reign of Abu 'l-Ghāzi (1053-74/1643-63), and it was perhaps this movement that caused the redistribution of the Uzbek tribes and their territories in the khānate.

In Khwārazm, the Mangït tribe contended for power with the tribe of Ḳongrat [see KUNGRAT]; the historian of the Ḳongrat dynasty Muʾnis [*q.v.*] traced this rivalry back to the time of Noḳay Noyan (see *Firdaws al-iḳbāl*, ms. cit., fol. 94b). At the end of the 17th and the 18th centuries, the Mangït who inhabit the central part of the Āmū-Daryā delta (Aral) with the fortresses Mangït-ḳalʿa and Shāh-Temir, together with several other Uzbek tribes of the same region, had their local rulers who did not recognise the authority of the khāns of Khīwa. In their struggle with the Ḳongrats, the Mangïts of Khwārazm were supported by their tribesmen in Transoxania, whose chiefs founded a new dynasty in Bukhārā in the middle of the 18th century [see MANGÏTS]. After some success in 1740s (when two chiefs of the Mangït, Artūḳ Ïnaḳ and then his brother Khuraz Bek, were the actual rulers of the khānate), the Mangït were finally overcome by the Ḳongrat and lost any political importance in Khwārazm. Since the beginning of the 19th century, they have inhabited mainly a region to the south of the Āmū-Daryā delta, where the town Mangït was founded in 1215/1800 (see Muʾnis, *Firdaws al-iḳbāl*, ms. cit., fol. 156b) on a canal of the same name (Mangït-arnā).

In Transoxania, the Mangïts were much more numerous and powerful than in Khwārazm; their main territory was the oasis of Ḳarshi [*q.v.*], in the Ḳashḳa-Daryā basin, but a greater number of them lived also in the oasis of Bukhārā, as well as near Samarḳand and Ḳatta-Kurghan. It is not clear, whether they all were descendants of the Mangïts who came with Shaybānī Khān, or whether some of them arrived later, as in Khwārazm (and, probably, through Khwārazm), with the dissolution of the Mangït *ulus* (cf. above). According to statistical data of 1923, the total number of the Mangïts in Transoxania was 99,200 (of whom 44,000 were near Bukhārā and 31,000 in the region of Ḳarshi), and in Khwārazm, 10,435. There seem to be no later data.

The Karakalpaks [*q.v.*] also include the Mangït as one of their major tribal subvisions (see T.A. Zhdanko, *Očerki istoričeskoy étnografii Karakalpakov*, Moscow-Leningrad 1950, 123-4; *Dokumentï arkhiva khivinskikh khanov po istorii i étnografii karakalpakov*, ed. Yu. Bregel, Moscow 1967, see index). This may go back to the 15th-16th centuries, when the Karakalpaks were apparently included in the *ulus* of the Mangït.

Bibliography: in addition to the works mentioned in the text, see M.G. Safargaliyev, *Raspad Zolotoy Ordï*, Saransk 1960, 225-31; M. Kafali, *Altın Orda Hanlığının kuruluş ve yükseliş devirleri*, Istanbul 1976, 41-2, 132; A.D. Grebenkin, *Uzbeki*, in *Russkiy Turkestan. Sbornik izdannïy po povodu Politekhničeskovy vïstavki*, i, Moscow 1872, 87-9; *Territoriya i naseleniye Bukharï i Khorezma*, Tashkent 1926, pt. 1. Bukhārā (*Materialï po rayonirovaniyu Sredney Azii*, 1), 185-6; pt. 2. *Khorezm* (*Materialï* ..., 2), 98; G. P. Snesarev, in *Khozyastvenno-kul'turnïye traditsii narodov Sredney Azii i Kazakhstana*, Moscow 1975, 83.

(YU. BREGEL)

MANGÏTS, a Turkish dynasty which reigned in Bukhārā [*q.v.*] from 1166/1753 to 1339/1920.

It was founded by the chiefs of the Uzbek tribe Mangït [*q.v.*], which was dominant in the central regions of Transoxania after the Uzbek conquest of the 16th century. Khudāyār Biy, the grandfather of the founder of the dynasty Muḥammad Raḥīm, became an *atalïḳ* [*q.v.* in Suppl.] in 1126/1714 under the Djānīd khān Abu 'l-Fayḍ (*Taʾrīkh-i Abu 'l-Fayḍ-Khānī*, Russ. tr. A.A. Semenov, 3). His son Muḥammad Ḥakīm Biy was appointed to the same post in 1134/1722 (*ibid.*, 67), and he became an all-powerful minister of Abu 'l-Fayḍ Khān. He was instrumental in securing the peaceful surrender of Abu 'l-Fayḍ Khān to Nādir Shāh in 1153/1740 and therefore enjoyed special favour of the latter, and began to style himself *amīr-i kabīr*. His son Muḥammad Raḥīm Biy served as the head of a detachment of Bukhāran troops with the army of Nādir Shāh. After the death of Muḥammad Ḥakīm Atalïḳ in 1156/1743 and the subsequent disturbances in the country, Muḥammad Raḥīm was sent by Nādir Shāh to Bukhārā with Iranian troops to restore order. Having firmly established his authority in Bukhārā, he ordered Abu 'l-Fayḍ Khān to be killed several days after the assassination of Nādir Shāh in Mashhad in 1160/1747. During the first years of his actual rule, he enthroned puppet khāns (the first of whom, ʿAbd al-Muʾmin, the son of Abu 'l-Fayḍ, was killed as early as 1161/1748), officially remaining only an *atalïḳ*; but after 1166/1753 he apparently reigned alone with the same title, and in 1170/1756 he was proclaimed khān. After his death in 1172/1758, his uncle and successor Dāniyāl Biy Atalïḳ (1172-99/1758-85; according to some sources, the correct name was Dāniyār; however, the coins give Dāniyāl) again enthroned puppet khāns, grandsons of Abu 'l-Fayḍ. Only Dāniyāl's son Shāh Murād (nicknamed "Amīr-i Maʿṣūm", 1199-1215/1785-1800) finally deposed the Djānīds and acceded the throne himself. The latest known silver coin with the name of the last Djānīd khān Abu 'l-Ghāzī is dated 1203/1788-9 (see Davidovič, *Istoriya monetnogo dela*, 51-2; Burnasheva, *Monetï* [I], 120). However, Shāh Murād did not adopt the title *khān*, and instead of this called himself *amīr*, as did all his successors. Shāh Murād ascribed this title even to his father Dāniyāl on the coins which he minted in the name of the latter. The implied meaning was that of *amīr al-muʾminīn* (this title actually appears on the coins of *amīr* Ḥaydar, 1215-42/1800-26), which had to show that the Mangīt rulers considered themselves Muslim kings par exellence and not continuators of the nomadic state tradition.

A characteristic feature of Mangīt rule was a sharp decline of power of the Uzbek tribal chiefs, with a parallel strengthening of the central government in Bukhārā. The Mangīts could achieve this because of the support which they received from the urban population as well as because of the creation of a small standing army. The tribal aristocracy was finally smashed by the seventh ruler of the dynasty, Naṣr Allāh (1242-77/1827-60), who in a relentless struggle against the aristocratic clans killed many of their members, including those of his own family, and well deserved the nickname "the butcher *amīr*" (*amīr-i ḳaṣṣāb*). As a result, the Khānate of Bukhārā became a despotic monarchy, where the *amīr*, enjoying practically unlimited power, ruled through a huge bureaucratic apparatus. Persons of a mean or at least non-Uzbek origin (former Persians slaves, Turkmens, etc.), tied to the sovereign by personal loyalty, held the key positions in this bureaucracy.

Despite the incessant wars with their neighbours and some military successes, the most important of which were the conquest of Marw by Shāh Murād in 1204/1789-90 and the temporary capture of Khoḳand in 1258/1842, the Mangīts were unable to impose their authority on all the territories which had been included into the Khānate of Bukhārā under the previous dynasties. The regions to the south of the Āmū-Daryā in Afghān Turkestān were lost already under Shāh Murād, and Marw passed under the control of Khīwa in 1238/1823; the principality of Shahr-i Sabz remained independent, under hostile chiefs of the Keneges tribe, until 1272/1855-6; the principality of Ura-Tübe was a bone of contention between Bukhārā and Khoḳand, but mostly was either independent or under Khoḳand rule; and the mountain principalities of the Pāmir also remained mostly independent until the Russian conquest.

Under Naṣr Allāh's son, *amīr* Muẓaffar al-Dīn (1277-1302/1860-85), the Khānate of Bukhārā was defeated by the Russians and in 1285/1868 lost its independence. Samarḳand and its province were annexed by Russia; the *amīr* was slightly compensated by establishing, with Russian help, his firm control over the mountainous regions in the upper Zarafshān valley (1870); in 1895 principalities of the Western Pāmir were also annexed by Bukhārā. The Mangīts retained their throne as the vassals of the Russian Empire. The last two *amīrs*, ʿAbd al-Aḥad (1303-28/1885-1910) and Sayyid ʿĀlim Khān (1328-39/1910-20), maintained close relations with the imperial court in St. Petersburg. They were granted Russian honorary military ranks and high orders, were frequent visitors to Russia and used to spend summer in their villa in Crimea; the last *amīr* was educated during his teens at a Russian cadet corps in St. Petersburg. All this little affected the character of their reign, which remained no less despotic than that of their predecessors. ʿĀlim Khān was deposed and the khānate was formally abolished on 6 October 1920 as a result of a revolution orchestrated by Soviet Russia. ʿĀlim Khān fled to the mountainous regions of Eastern Bukhārā and from there to Kābul (beginning of 1921), where he died in 1934; it is reported that his descendants were living in Kābul in great misery (see B. Hayit, *Turkestan zwischen Russland und China*, Amsterdam 1971, 258, n. 57).

Bibliography: For the historical works in Persian on the history of the Mangīts, see Storey-Bregel, 496-9, nos. 361-2, and 1150-82, nos. 1007-41. On the coins of the Mangīts, see V. V. Vel'yaminov-Zernov, *Monetī bukharskiye i khivinskiye*, in *Trudī Vostočnogo Otdeleniya Russkogo Arkheologičeskogo Obshčestva*, iv (St. Petersburg 1859), 409-27; E. A. Davidovič, *Istoriya monetnogo dela Sredney Azii XVII-XVIII vv.*, Dushanbe 1964, 163-8, 176-97; R. Burnasheva, *Monetī Bukharskogo khanstva pri Mangītakh (seredina XVIII - načalo XX v.)* in [III] *Epigrafika Vostoka*, xviii (1967), 113-28, [I] *ibid.*, xxi (1972), 67-80. For the general history of the Khānate of Bukhārā under the Mangīts, see V.V. Bartol'd, *Istoriya kul'turnoy zhizni Turkestana*, in his, *Sočineniya*, ii/1, Moscow 1963, 278-83, 290-2, 400-11, 416-33; P. P. Ivanov, *Očerki po istorii Sredney Azii*, Moscow 1958, 117-47; *Istoriya narodov Uzbekistana*, ii, Tashkent 1947, 119-24, 162-8; *Istoriya Uzbekskoy SSR*, i/2, Tashkent 1956, 32-41, 43-5, 47-9; *Istoriya tadzhikskogo naroda*, ii/2, Moscow 1964, 57-114; S. Becker, *Russia's protectorates in Central Asia: Bukhārā and Khīva, 1865-1924*, Cambridge, Mass. 1968 (all these with extensive bibliographies). Also still useful is H.H. Howorth, *History of the Mongols*, ii/2, London 1880, 765-816; A. Vámbéry, *History of Bokhara*, is however outdated and should not be used. For valuable information on the personalities of the last Mangīt *amīrs*, court life and the administration of Bukhārā in the early 20th century, see A. A. Semenov, *Očerk ustroystva tsentral' nogo administrativnogo upravleniya Bukharskogo khanstva pozdneyshego vremeni* (*Materialī po istorii tadzhikov i uzbekov Sredney Azii*, ii), Stalinabad 1954, and M.S. Andreev and O. D. Čekhovič, *Ark (kreml') Bukharī v. kontse XIX - načale XX vv.*, Dushanbe 1972 (esp. pp. 89-127: "The day of an *amīr* of Bukhārā"). (Yu. Bregel)

MANGRŌL, the name of two places in India.

1. A port on the southwestern coast of the Kāthiāwāṛ peninsula, in lat. 21° 28' N. and long 70° 14' E., formerly coming within the native state of Djunāgaṛh [*q.v.*] and with a Muslim local chief there tributary to the Nawwāb of Djunāgaṛh; the mosque there carries a date 785/1383.

Bibliography: *Imperial gazetteer of India*², xvii, 180.

2. A town in the former British Indian territory of Rajputana, within the native state of Kotah, in lat. 25° 20′ N. and long. 70° 31′ E. and 44 miles/70 km. to the northeast of Kotah city. Here there took place on 1 October 1821 the battle between two rival Rajput powers, that of the Maharao Kishōr Singh of Kotah and that of the aged regent of Kotah, the *fawdjdār* [*q.v.*] Ẓālim Singh (1740-1826), the latter aided by British troops, which resulted in a decisive victory for Ẓālim Sing and the retreat of the Maharao to Baroda.

Bibliography: J. Tod, *Annals and antiquities of Rajast' han*, Madras 1880, ii, 5-43; *Imperial gazetteer of India*², xviii, 180-1. (C.E. Bosworth)

MANGŪ-TĪMŪR (thus on his coins: Mong. Möngke-Temür, sometimes written also Mūngkā (e.g. Rashīd al-Dīn, ed. Blochet, 109); in Russian annals Mengutimer and Mengutemer, called also Külük "Glorious", "Famous"), khān of the Golden Horde (665-79/1267-80), grandson of the khān Bātū [*q.v.*] and son of Toḳūḳān (Toghon).

His predecessor Berke [*q.v.*] died, according to al-Dhahabī, in Rabīʿ II 665/30 Dec. 1266 - 27 Jan. 1267 (see Tiesenhausen, 210-2; other Egyptian sources mention only the year). In Ṣafar 666/Oct.-Nov. 1267), an embassy left Cairo which was to bring the new khān an expression of sympathy and congratulations from Sultan Baybars I [*q.v.*]. In 667/Sept. 1268-Aug. 1269, an embassy from the khān arrived in Egypt. The exchange of embassies was maintained throughout the whole of the khān's reign. When in 670/1271-2 an embassy on the way to Egypt was captured by a Frankish ship from Marseilles, the ambassadors and all their goods had to be released on the sultan's demand. When in 680/April 1282 an Egyptian embassy left for the Golden Horde, nothing was yet known of the death of the khān. Only later did they learn that he was no more, having died in Rabīʿ I 679/July 1280 in the district of Aḳlūḳiyā (apparently nowhere else mentioned; cf. P. Pelliot, *Notes*, 62); his death is said to have been caused by the unskilful removal of a boil on the neck.

The Egyptian state tried to induce the khān to resume the war against the Persian Mongols begun by his predecessor Berke; but already in 667/1268-9 Mangū-Tīmūr concluded a peace with Abāḳā and never again attacked Persia. At the same time, Mangū-Tīmūr interfered in the affairs of Central Asia, sending an army of 50,000 men under Berkečār, a brother of Bātū, to help his ally Ḳaydū against Baraḳ [*q.vv.*]; as a result of the *ḳuriltay* of 667/1269 on the Talas river under Ḳaydū, one-third of Transoxania (probably one-third of its income) was secured for Ḳaydū and Mangū-Tīmūr together (Rashīd al-Dīn, iii, ed. A. Ali-zade, Baku 1957, text, 108-11). The alliance between Mangū-Tīmūr and Ḳaydū is also mentioned later; when in 1277 two sons of the emperor Ḳubilay Khān were taken prisoner in the war with Ḳaydū; the latter had the princes sent to the court of Mangū-Tīmūr, from which they were later sent back to their father (Rashīd al-Dīn, ed. Blochet, 8; d'Ohsson, *Hist. des Mongols de la Perse*, ii, 452-3).

In Russia, Mangū-Tīmūr continued the policy of his predecessor Berke. Under him a second census of Russian population was taken in the 1270s for tax purposes. The Russian princes of Rostov were close to Mangū-Tīmūr and enjoyed his favour; prince Fedor Rostislavovič of Yaroslavl' was married to his daughter. In winter 1277, a great number of Russian troops, especially those under the Rostov princes, participated in the Tatar campaign against the Alāns [*q.v.*] in the northern Caucasus, during which the Alān city of Dedyakov was captured and destroyed. In 1279 Lev of Galicia received assistance from Mangū-Tīmūr against the Lithuanians and Poles, but the Tatar auxiliaries proved a great burden not only to his enemies, but also to their protégés. From Mangū-Tīmūr dates the earliest extant edict of a khān of the Golden Horde on the privileges of the Greek Orthodox clergy; it is dated in the year of the hare (probably 1267; see M.D. Priselkov, *Khanskiye yarlïki russkim mitropolitam*, Petrograd 1916, 58-9, 83-5, 96-8). The Bishop of Saray, Theognostes, was sent by Mangū-Tīmūr as an ambassador to Constantinople in 1279. This was probably done to counterbalance the growing influence and involvement in Byzantine and Russian affairs of Mangū-Tīmūr's army commander and the chief of the Tatar tribes of the right wing, *amīr* Noḳāy [*q.v.*], who became all-powerful after the khān's death. However, under Mangū-Tīmūr, in contrast to the last two decades of the 13th century, the Golden Horde was a great power, free from internal troubles. Coins were still struck mainly in the old commercial city of Bulghār [*q.v.*] and some also in Crimea, but, unlike those of his predecessors, in his own name and not in that of the Great Khān. On his coins, the seal (*tamgha*) of the Golden Horde appears for the first time.

Mangū-Tīmūr apparently did not embrace Islam as his predecessor Berke had done, despite the facts that Islamic formulae were used on his coins and that some Egyptian historians praised him for "having followed the path" of Berke. On his attitude towards Islam there seems to be no direct evidence; a story is told, however, about his attempt to make the Saldjūḳ prince of Rūm Masʿūd marry his stepmother upon the death of his father ʿIzz al-Dīn Kay-Kāwūs, according to the Mongol customary law and in contradiction to the *Sharīʿa*.

Bibliography: H. Howorth, *History of the Mongols*, London 1880, ii, 125-34; J. Hammer-Purgstall, *Geschichte der Goldenen Horde*, Pesth 1840, 248-59; B. Spuler, *Die Goldene Horde*², Wiesbaden 1965, 52-63; A.N. Nasonov, *Mongolï i Rus'*, Moscow-Leningrad 1940, 47, 60-8; M. G. Safargaliyev, *Raspad Zolotoy Ordï*, Saransk 1960, 52-5; M. Kafalı, *Altın Orda Hanlığının kuruluş ve yükseliş devirleri*, Istanbul 1976, 59-62. All of these works contain further references to primary sources. For the Egyptian references, see esp. W. Tiesenhausen, *Sbornik materialov otnosyā shčikhsya k istorii Zolotoy Ordï*, i, St. Petersburg 1884. On the correct forms of the name and the nickname of Mangū-Tīmūr, see P. Pelliot, *Notes sur l'histoire de la Horde d'Or*, Paris 1949, 58-62. (W. Barthold - [Yu. Bregel])

MĀNI (<A. *maʿnā*), a form of Turkish popular poetry.

The *mani* is, most usually, a piece of poetry made up of heptasyllabic verses rhymed on the pattern *a a b a*; each quatrain may be sufficient to fulfil a certain function or to transmit a certain message. This norm of a self-sufficient unity, as well as those in regard to the ordering of the rhymes, the number of verses and the metre, does not impose an absolutely watertight rule. The use of the *māni*, in certain circumstances, to form a song in dialogue shape (see below) can give it a polystrophic nature. Moreover, a considerable number of folk songs—which are not in dialogue shape—as well as certain lullabies (the *ninnis* of Anatolia and the *lay-lays* of Ādharbāydjān) are made up of a stringing-together of *mānis*, with however the adding of refrains which provide a thematic unity and give them their generic character. There are also *mānis* rhymed *b a c a*, notably those of the northeastern littoral of Anatolia. In the texts of certain poems, the first verse is shortened to 3 or 4 syllables (words which simply set forth the rhyme) or disappears completely; the piece thus reduced to the schema *a b a* is called *kesik māni* "truncated *māni*", a form which is found most frequently in the *mānis* with *djinās*, i.e. in the pieces which play upon the rhyme words of the second and fourth verses. There are also cases where the quatrain is made longer by means of several distichs in *a a b a c a* ... or in *b a c a d a* ... A kind of *māni*, sung by nightwatchmen at the time of their rounds from door-to-door during the nights of Ramaḍān, is octosyllabic. This form, with its variant in *b a c a*, is also that of another genre of popular poetry, the *aghïts* (funeral dirges) of the peoples of Avshar origin in central and southern Anatolia.

The term *māni* is used to denote this form and these poetical genres in Anatolia, amongst the Turkish-speaking Balkan peoples, amongst the Crimean Tatars, in Ādharbāydjān and amongst the Gagaouz of Bessarabia, sometimes with variant forms: in Anatolia, *māna* at Denizli and *maʿāni* at Urfa; in Ādharbāydjān, *mahni*; and in the Crimea, *māne*. Other terms are also used to denote poetic pieces with the same thematic and formal characteristics: *bayatï* in the two parts of Ādharbāydjān and in the Ādharī-influenced provinces of easter Anatolia; *khoyrat* at Urfa and Diyarbakir; *djïr* amongst the Crimean and Kazan Tatars; and *čïn* amongst the Misher.

On the basis of their themes and the circumstances

in which they are cited or sung, *mānis* can be classified as follows:

(1) *Mānis* about foretelling the future and divination recited at the festival of *hidrellez* [see KHIḌR-ILYĀS], on the occasion of other festivities and on winter evenings by womenfolk;

(2) Work *mānis* recited by women in the course of communal activities, such as the preparation of provisions for the winter, fruit-gathering, hay-making, etc. On the occasion of the latter two types of activity, *mānis* are adressed to passers-by, who are required to reply in the same fashion in order to avoid mockery by the womenfolk;

(3) Declamatory *mānis*, sung by boys and girls at the time of certain festivals and excursions into the countryside;

(4) *Mānis* of the watchmen of town quarters sung during the nights of Ramaḍān;

(5) *Mānis* of certain itinerant sellers of sweetmeats and delicacies who sing out to announce their appearance in the streets;

(6) *Mānis* of café singers in the tradition of old Istanbul;

(7) *Mānis* of letters, inserted as sentimental messages in letters exchanged between relatives, friends or couples; and

(8) *Mānis* of certain *ʿāshiḳs* [*q.v.*] or reciters and story-tellers, which they improvise and insert between the strophes of the poems which make up the sung part of their prose narratives (see P.N. Boratav, *Halk hikâyeleri ve halk hikâyeciliği*, Ankara 1946, 239-42, 291).

Concerning the origin of the *māni*, one may suggest as a hypothesis an adaption of the model of the *rubāʿī* to the heptasyllabic and octosyllabic metres peculiar to the Turkish languages; a first stage in this process of adaptation of would be the *tuyugh*, another type of quatrain peculiar to Turkish classical poetry, composed in the *ʿarūḍ* metre and rhymed according to the same schema as the *rubāʿī* and *māni*.

Bibliography: For publication up to 1964, see Boratav, *Littérature orale*, in *PTF*, ii, Wiesbaden 1964-5, 107-13, 126-7; idem, art. *Māni* in *İA*. For more recent publications, see Hikmet Dizdaroğlu, *Halk şiirinde türler*, Ankara 1969, 51-68; S. Djāwīd, *Nomonāhā-ye folklor-e Āzärbāydjān*, Tehran 1344/1965, 14-21; İsmail Hakkı Acar, *Zara folkloru*, Sivas 1975, 47-55 (83 *māni* texts); Ferruh Arsunar, *Gaziantep folkloru*, Istanbul 1962, 302-13 (131 texts); M. Hasan Göksu, *Mânilerimiz*, Istanbul 1970 (2,796 texts); Hayriye Süleymanova and Emil Boef, *Rodop mânileri*, Sofia, 1st ed. 1962, 2nd ed. 1965 (2,000 texts classified in themes); Ata Terzibaşı, *Kerkük hoyrat ve mânileri*, Istanbul 1975 (2,490 texts). For the subject in general, studies and collections of texts, see also the following bibliographical works: *Türk folklor ve etnografya bibliyografyası*, i-iii, Ankara 1971, 1973, 1975; East Bozyiğit, *Mâni üzerine bir bibliyografya denemesi*, in *Türk folklor araştırmaları*, no. 264 (July 1971); Tuncer Gülensoy, *Anadolu ve Rumeli ağızları bibliyografyası*, Ankara 1981. (P.N. BORATAV)

MĀNĪ B. FĀTTIK or FĀTIK, the form found in mediaeval Islamic sources (e.g. al-Masʿūdī, *Murūdj*, ii 164, 167-8, vii, 12-16, viii, 293, = §§ 589, 594, 2705-7, 3447) for the founder of the dualist religion of Manichaeism, Mani son of Pātik, born in southern Mesopotamia in 216 A.D. and martyred under the Sāsānid Bahrām I in 274, 276 or 277, and whose faith spread from the Persian empire in the 7th century as far as Central Asia, eastern Turkestan (where after 762 it was the chief religion of the Uyghur Turks [*q.v.*]) and northern China. In Islamic sources, the adherents of Manichaeism appear as the Manāniyya (Mānawiyya), as in the important section on them in al-Nadīm's *Fihrist*, ed. Riḍā Tadjaddud, Tehran 1350/1971, 391-402, tr. Dodge, ii, 773-805, and in al-Khʷārazmī's *Mafātīḥ al-ʿulūm*, 37, where both forms are however registered.

Although Manichaeism was in the early Islamic centuries largely pushed into Central Asia (thus the *Ḥudūd al-ʿālam*, tr. Minorsky, 113, § 113.25, mentions a "convent of the Manichaeans", *khānagāh-i Mānawiyān*, in Samarḳand in 982, with *nighūshāk* or *auditores*) and beyond, it had an important part in the general phenomenon of *zandaḳa* "heresy, unbelief" in early ʿAbbāsid ʿIrāḳ; for a general consideration of this, see ZINDĪḲ, and meanwhile, Spuler, *Iran*, 206-9.

Bibliography: Older references are given by Spuler, *op. cit.* Of more recent ones, see G. Widengren, *Mani und der Manichäismus*, Stuttgart 1961, Eng. tr. *Mani and Manichaeism*, London 1965; Mary Boyce, *H. der O.*, Abt. 1, Bd. 4. *Iranistik*, Abschn. 2. *Literatur*, Lief. 1, *The Manichaean literature in Middle Iranian*, Leiden-Cologne 1968, eadem, *Acta Iranica IX. A reader in Manichaean Middle Persian and Parthian*, Leiden 1975, Introd., 1-14; W. Foerster, *Die Gnosis. III. Der Manichäismus*, ed. J. P. Asmussen, tr. A. Böhlig, Zürich-Munich 1980. (C. E. BOSWORTH)

MANISA [see MAGHNISA].

MANŌHAR, MANŌHARGÁRH, a fortress on a lofty rock, some 2,500 feet/770 m. high, in lat. 16° N. and long. 74° 1' E., in the Western Ghats range of peninsular India. Formerly in the southernmost part of the British Indian province of Bombay, it is now just within the southwestern corner of the Maharashtra state of the Indian Union.

Bibliography: *Imperial gazetteer of India*², xvii, 200. (ED.)

MANSA MŪSĀ, king (*mansa*) of Mali (712-38/1312-37).

He was apparently the grandson of Abū Bakr (Manding Bori), who was the brother of Mārī Jāta (Sunjata), the legendary hero credited with the establishment of Mali in the 14th century [*q.v.*] as a powerful empire. Mansa Mūsā reigned at the pinnacle of Mali's prosperity, and is remembered in the Arabic sources as a pious and virtuous sovereign. Following the example of several earlier Malian rulers, and having appointed his son Maghā (Muḥammad) to rule in his absence, he made a pilgrimage to Mecca in 1324 that made a profound impression on the Egyptians and was chronicled by Arab writers. According to the 17th-century Timbuktu chronicles *Taʾrīkh al-Sūdān* and *Taʾrīkh al-Fattāsh*, whose authors relied extensively on oral sources, Mansa Mūsā was accompanied by an entourage of thousands, including his favourite wife, Inari Konte, and he travelled via Timbuktu, where he caused to be built one of several mosques constructed during his journey. In Cairo, he flooded the market with so much gold that its value fell throughout Egypt. One of al-ʿUmarī's informants, Ibn Amīr Ḥādjib, was often in the company of Mansa Mūsā when he was in Egypt, and among the things told him him by Mansa Mūsā himself was that he came to power when his predecessor (Muḥammad, of a different branch of the same family) appointed him deputy before leaving on a seafaring expedition, from which he never returned, to discover the limits of the Atlantic Ocean. While on pilgrimage, Mansa Mūsā also met the Andalusian poet and architect Abū Isḥāḳ Ibrāhīm al-Sāḥilī, who accompanied him back to Mali where, according to Ibn Khaldūn's friend Khadīdja, Abū Isḥāḳ constructed for the *mansa* an elaborately decorated domed building that may have been the first of its kind in that country. Also accompanying Mansa Mūsā were four *shurafā*ʾ from Ḳuraysh who settled in Mali with their families. Upon his return, Mansa Mūsā continued his policy of diplomatically furthering the interests of Mali in the greater Islamic world by corresponding with the sultan at Cairo, sending *ʿulamā'* to study in Fās, and exchanging embassies and gifts with the Marīnid ruler of the Maghrib, Abu 'l-Ḥasan. Al-ʿUmarī claims that Mansa Mūsā had returned to Mali from his pilgrimage with the intention of handing over his sovereignty to his son and returning to Mecca to live near the sanctuary; but he died before he could carry out his plan.

Viewed from the local African perspective, Mansa Mūsā and his pilgrimage engendered a western Sudanic oral tradition, the hero of which is Makanta Jigi (Fajigi), "Father of hope who went to Mecca". As an oral record of the local Sudanic interpretation placed on Mansa Mūsā's pilgrimage by his subjects and their descendants, the Fajigi legend reveals attitudes that helped make it possible for an accommodation between indigenous religious practices and Islam to be achieved. The basic narrative line of the legendary oral account tells how Mansa Mūsā/Fajigi was motivated to make the pilgrimage because he was responsible for a regrettable incident involving his mother Gongo (Kankan), possibly resulting in her death. Making a pilgrimage to Mecca, he acquires the most important of the spiritually powerful altars (*boliw*) used in traditional Manding religious ritual, including those of the prestigious Komo society. As Fajigi returns through the land of the Manding, he distributes some of the altars, as well as various potions and amulets to people who help him. When he reaches the rivers of Mali, he uses a magic canoe to transport the altars. The canoe encounters rough waters and some of the cargo falls into the water, where it is transformed into several life forms such as fish and scorpions. On arriving home, the location of which varies according to the informant, the canoe sinks to the bottom of a lake or river where it remains to this day, itself a powerful altar that receives periodic offerings. The most significant feature of this legend is the paradoxical claim that the *mansa* most famous for his devotion to Islam was at the same time the one who provided his subjects with the essential paraphernalia of the ancestral non-Islamic Manding religion. Thus, from the traditional non-Muslim point of view, Mansa Mūsā and his pilgrimage emerge, not as examples of faithful Islamic endeavour and early Sudanic statesmanship, but as the source of an oral narrative that provided a framework on which descendants of the *mansa*'s subjects based their claim that certain features of their autochthonous religion were rooted in the same soil that nurtured the foundations of Islam.

Bibliography: ʿUmarī, *Masālik al-abṣār* (written Cairo 737 or 738/1337-8), French tr. Gaudefroy-Demombynes, *L'Afrique moins l'Egypte*, Paris 1927; Ibn Baṭṭūṭa, *Riḥla* (written Fās 757/1356); Ibn Khaldūn, *Kitāb al-ʿIbar* (written 776-80/1374-8, but information about Mali recorded in 796/1393-4, partially ed. de Slane as *Kitāb Taʾrīkh al-duwal al-islāmiyya bi 'l-Maghrib*, 2 vols. Algiers 1847-51, 7 vols. Cairo 1867, tr. idem, *Histoire des Berbères*, 4 vols. Paris 1852-6; al-Saʿdī, *Taʾrīkh al-Sūdān* (written Timbuktu *ca.* 1655), Arab text and French tr. O. Houdas, Paris 1911, repr. 1964; Ibn al-Mukhtār, *Taʾrīkh al-Fattāsh* (written Timbuktu *ca.* 1664), Arab text and French tr. Houdas and M. Delafosse, Paris 1913, repr. 1964; N. Levtzion, *The thirteenth- and fourteenth-century kings of Mali*, in *Jnal. of African History* (1963); idem, *Ancient Ghana and Mali,* London 1973; J.M. Cuoq, ed. and tr. *Recueil des sources arabes concernant l'Afrique occidentale du VIIIe au XVIe siècle (Bilād al-Sūdān)*, Paris 1975; J. F. P. Hopkins and Levtzion, ed. and tr. *Corpus of early Arabic sources for West African history*, Cambridge 1981; arts. MALI, MANDE.

(D.C. CONRAD)

MANṢAB and **MANṢABDĀR,** terms of the military system of the Mughals in India.

The Mughal empire possessed a graded official hierarchy of officers with military and civil duties. The emperor, his *dīwān* or other high officials, assigned to each officer a rank or *manṣab*. The holder of this rank was termed a *manṣabdār*. Personal or *dhāt* rank was expressed numerically in even-numbered decimal increments. Ranks could vary from as low as 20 *dhāt* to a maximum of 7,000 *dhāt* for the highest nobles (*amīrs*). Princes of the blood held *dhāt* ranks as high as 20,000 *dhāt* when they reached maturity. The emperor, or a high-ranking noble acting with the emperor's approval, raised or lowered all *dhāt* ranks on the basis of perceived performance as well as favour at court. *Dhāt* determined the *manṣabdār's* relative status and his pay. Personal rank also set approximate limits upon official assignments, honorific titles and influence. Those five or six hundred *manṣabdārs* who, in the mid-11th/17th century held *dhāt* rank of 1,000 or above, were officially classified as nobles or *amīrs*. This small group comprised the ruling élite of the empire. Usually, lesser-ranked *manṣabdārs* served as subordinates to one of the *amīrs*.

A second numerical ranking system existed alongside that of *dhāt* ranks. *Manṣabdārs* could simultaneously hold trooper or *suwār* ranks. The latter was expressed in multiples of five from as low as five to as much as 7,000 *suwār*. Those *manṣabdārs* receiving *suwār* rank received extra pay. In return, they were obliged to recruit, command and pay a body of heavy cavalry acceptable to imperial standards. The actual number of horsemen brought to the muster in a *manṣabdār's* contingent was not equal to the nominal *suwār* rank, but was instead a fraction determined by a complex series of imperial regulations. All cavalrymen employed by *manṣabdārs* to meet *suwār* rank obligations were subject to periodic inspection and identification. Cavalrymen were identified in muster rolls by name and physical appearance; horses by description and imperial brands. Special *du-asbah suwār* rank obliged the *manṣabdār* to employ men bring two, rather than merely one mount to the muster [see further DĀGH U TAṢḤĪḤA in Suppl.].

Most *manṣabdārs* obtained payment for their fixed *dhāt* and *suwār* ranks in the form of salary assignments known as *djāgīrs* [*q.v.*]. Under this arrangement, the empire transferred to the *manṣabdār* the right of collection of its share of the land tax from a specified area—a village or portion thereof; or a *pargana* [*q.v.*] or portion thereof—in an amount equivalent to his pay claim. Assignment of a *djāgīr* ordinarily did not carry with it any administrative rights or responsibilities in the area assigned. Many lesser-ranked *manṣabdārs* were paid directly in cash from the provincial or central treasuries.

The *manṣabdārī* system formally expressed the uniformity and cohesiveness and discipline of the Mughal administrative and military élites. *Manṣabdārs* were the instruments of imperial unification and expansion. The honorific ranking system tied all the nobles and lesser *manṣabdārs* to the person and the preference of the emperor. All advancement (and punishment) came directly from the throne. Thus the loyalty of the *manṣabdārs* was bound to the house of Bābur alone. But *manṣabdārs* were also bound by established policies, by precedent, and by written regulations in their conduct of official business.

It is important to note that another body of middling and lesser officers also served the empire without benefit of *manṣabdārī* status or rank. Many private servants of the *amīrs* employed within the massive households and military camps of their masters held responsible positions. Some were slaves; many were free Muslims or Hindu officers in private employ. Acting under the supervision of their master—an *amīr*—and the *manṣabdārs* attached to him, these men performed the essential functions of imperial administration and military service. It is difficult to estimate their numbers, but they must have been at least as numerous as the lesser and middle-ranking *manṣabdārs*.

Between 1119/1707 and 1136/1724 discipline and the integrity of the *manṣabdārī* system began to detoriorate. Ranks rapidly became inflated and, if not meaningless, were very much distorted. By the late 12th/18th century, the *manṣabdārī* ranks so freely given or so readily coerced from the Mug̲h̲al emperor were merely a travesty of what they had once implied.

Bibliography: It is not possible to find a truly useful or synoptic account of the *manṣabdārī* system in the original sources apart from the passages in the *Āʾīn-i Akbarī*. But these last do not reflect the growth and change of the institution in the 11th/17th century. The student may see the working of the ranking system and the active role of the emperor in such works as the memoirs of D̲j̲ahāngīr, the *Tūzuk-i D̲j̲ahāngīrī*, tr. A. Rogers, ed. H. Beveridge, Dihlī 1909-14, 2nd ed. Dihlī 1968. For a similar impression later in the century, see the *Maʾāt̲h̲ir-i ʿĀlamgīrī* of Mustaʿid K̲h̲ān, ed. Maulawī Ag̲h̲ā Aḥmad ʿAlī, Bibliotheca Indica no. 66, Calcutta 1870-3, Eng. tr. Jadunath Sarkar, Bibliotheca Indica no. 269, Calcutta 1947. Those large archival collections of Mug̲h̲al documents which have survived are filled with references to promotions, demotions, transfers and *d̲j̲āgīr* assignments for *manṣabdārs*. Any official reference to an individual *manṣabdār* invariably appended his numerical *d̲h̲āt* and *suwār* rank. See Yusuf Husain Khan, ed., *Selected documents of Aurangzeb's reign, 1659-1706*, Hyderabad-Deccan 1958, for a sampling of these documents. The indispensable modern discussion of the *manṣabdārī* system, although focussed on the nobility, is M. Athar Ali, *The Mughal nobility under Aurangzeb*, Aligarh 1966. Another systematic description may be found in I. H. Qureshi, *The administration of the Mughal empire*, Karachi 1966. For a discussion of the role of *manṣabdārs* in a particular province, see J. F. Richards, *Mughal administration in Golconda*, Oxford 1975.

(J. F. Richards)

MANS̲H̲ŪR (A.) means literally "spread out" (as in Ḳurʾān, XVII, 14, and LII,3: opposite, *maṭwī* "folded"), or "not sealed" (opposite, *mak̲h̲tūm*) hence it comes to mean a certificate, an edict, a diploma of appointment, and particularly, a patent granting an appanage (pl. *manās̲h̲īr*).

In Egypt in the early Arab period, *mans̲h̲ūr* seems to be a name for the passes which the government compelled the *fellāḥīn* to have in order to check the flight of colonists from the land, which threatened to become overwhelming (*d̲j̲āliya*). In any case, in the *Führer durch die Ausstellung* (*Papyrus Erzherzog Rainer*), no. 631 (cf. also nos. 601-2), such a certificate of the year 180/796 is called a *mans̲h̲ūr*, and in al-Maḳrīzī, *K̲h̲iṭaṭ*, ii, 493, we are told of the period of the financial controller Usāma b. Zayd al-Tanūk̲h̲ī (104/722-3) that Christians who were found without identification papers (*mans̲h̲ūr*) had to pay 10 *dīnārs* fine (cf. Becker, *Beiträge zur Gesch. Ägyptens*, 104). In the texts of such passports themselves (cf. Becker, *Papyr. Schott-Reinhardt*, i, 40, l.1) however, we have, so far as I can see, not the word *mans̲h̲ūr* but only *kitāb*.

Mans̲h̲ūr seems also to have a quite general meaning of "pass", when we are told in al-Ḳalḳas̲h̲andī, *Ṣubḥ al-aʿs̲h̲āʾ*, xiii, 142, that it was written on an ʿAbbāsid grant of a fief dating from the year 373/983-4) that no one could demand for the holder that he should show a *ḥud̲j̲d̲j̲a* or a *tawḳīʿ* or a *mans̲h̲ūr*.

The Egyptian Fāṭimids usually called all state documents, appointments, etc., by the general term *sid̲j̲ill*, but they had also special terms for partcular diplomas of appointment, including *mans̲h̲ūrs*.

Thus among the examples of Fāṭimid documents given by al-Ḳalḳas̲h̲andī, x, 452-66, there are several which in their texts are described as *mans̲h̲ūrs*. Among these are for example, appointments to the supervision of inheritants (*mus̲h̲ārafat al-mawārīt̲h̲ al-has̲h̲riyya*), of the poll-tax (*mus̲h̲ārafat al-d̲j̲awālī*), to a professorship (*tadrīs*), etc. A grant of an appanage could also be called *mans̲h̲ūr* at this time, as in al-Ḳalḳas̲h̲andī, xiii, 131 [see IBN K̲H̲ALAF, in Suppl.] from the Fāṭimid *Mawādd al-bayān* of ʿAlī b. K̲h̲alaf; and the regulation that the *manās̲h̲īr* must not have an address (*ʿunwān*) and that in place of this, the head of the *Dīwān* must write the date with his own hand, seems to be first found in Ibn al-Ṣayrafī, *Ḳānūn Dīwān al-Rasāʾil*, 113 = al-Ḳalḳas̲h̲andī, vi, 198.

Under the Ayyūbids also, *mans̲h̲ūr* had quite a general meaning. Thus in *ibid.*, xi, 49 f., a "marshall of the nobles" (*naḳīb al-as̲h̲rāf*) is appointed by a *mans̲h̲ūr*, and in 51 ff., governors (*wulāt*) of different provinces. In the text of it, the name *mans̲h̲ūr* is given to the edict on the equation of taxation and lunar years (*taḥwīl al-sinīn*) which is quoted from the *Mutad̲j̲addidāt* of the Ḳāḍī al-Fāḍil for the year 567/1171-2) in al-Maḳrīzī, i, 281, ed. Wiet, iv, 292 (cf. also al-Ḳalḳas̲h̲andī, xiii, 72 ff.), and according to a further quotation, for the year 584/1188 (al-Maḳrīzī, i, 269 = Wiet, iv, 248) the so-called "lord of the new year" (*amīr al-nawrūz*) issued his *manās̲h̲īr*.

The term *mans̲h̲ūr* became limited and specialised in the Mamlūk period, for which we have very full sources. The increasingly complicated system of the administration brought a minute distinction between and special names for the various diplomas of appointment, edicts, etc., and the term *mans̲h̲ūr* was henceforth used exclusively of the grants of appanages. These *manās̲h̲īr* were always written in Cairo in the chancellery (*dīwān al-ins̲h̲āʾ*) in the name of the sultan; only in exceptional cases might they be in the name of the *al-nāʾib al-kāfil* (see al-Ḳalḳas̲h̲andī, iv, 16; xiii, 157). According to the very full description in al-Ḳalḳas̲h̲andī, xiii, 153 ff., and al-Maḳrīzī, ii, 211, the procedure in granting a fief was as follows: if a fief became vacant (*maḥlūl*) in a provincial town, e.g. in Damascus, the governor there (*nāʾib*) proposed a new holder and had a document (*ruḳʿa*, also called *mit̲h̲āl* or *murabbaʿa*) drawn up about his proposal by the inspector of the army (*nāẓir al-d̲j̲ays̲h̲*; cf. al-Ḳalḳas̲h̲andī, iv, 190; xii, 97) in the military *Dīwān* (*dīwān al-d̲j̲ays̲h̲*) of his town. This document was then sent by courier (*barīdī*) or pigeon post (*ʿalā ad̲j̲niḥat al-ḥamām*) to the government (*al-abwāb al-s̲h̲arīfa*) in Cairo. Here it was received by the postmaster (*dawādār*), later by the private secretary (*kātib al-sirr* = *ṣāḥib dīwān al-inshā*ʾ) who placed it before the sultan in audience (*djulūs fī dār al-*ʿ*adl*) for approval, receive the sultan's signature (*khaṭṭ sharīf*) and the note *yuktab* ("let it be written out"; see al-Ḳalḳashandī, iv, 51). The document then went to the Military *Dīwān* in Cairo (*dīwān al-djaysh*, occasionally also called *dīwān al-iḳṭā*ʿ), where it was filed, after what was called the *murabba*ʿ*a* had been made out. The latter was sent to the *dīwān al-inshā*ʾ, and the private secretary, the head of this *Dīwān*, wrote his requisition (*ta* ʿ*yīn*) for the *inshā*ʾ writer concerned; now finally the patent of the appanage (*manshūr*) proper could be made out in the *dīwān al-inshā*ʾ in Cairo, while the *murabba*ʿ*a* of the army *Dīwān* remained filed in the *dīwān al-inshā*ʾ as *shāhid* (proof) (cf. al-Ḳalḳashandī, vi, 201).

Full particulars are given of the formulae used in these *manāshīr* and of their external form in Shihāb al-Dīn b. Faḍl Allāh, *al-Ta*ʿ*rīf bi 'l-muṣṭalaḥ al-sharīf*, 88 f.; al-Ḳalḳashandī, xiii, 153 ff., and Quatremère, *Histoire des Sultans Mamlouks de l'Egypt*, i/1, 200 f., n. 82. There are many variants of format (*ḳaṭ*ʿ [*q.v.*]) and script according to the military rank of the recipient. Thus *manāshīr* for the *muḳaddamū 'l-ulūf* were written on *ḳaṭ*ʿ *al-thulthayn*, for *the umarā*ʾ *al-ṭablkhānā* on *ḳaṭ*ʿ *al-niṣf*, for the *umarā*ʾ *al-*ʿ*asharāt* on *ḳaṭ*ʿ *al-thulth* and for the *mamālīk al-sulṭāniyya* and *muḳaddamū 'l-ḥalḳa* on *ḳaṭ*ʿ *al-*ʿ*āda*. Many rules were laid down for the wording to be used; the text is to be shorter and less florid than in the other appointments and there are none of the usual rules about service (*waṣāyā*); an original "virgin" (*mubtakarat al-inshā*ʾ) is recommended as the finest form of a *manshūr*. Special formulae are further required for grants of appanages which were concerned with renewal (*tadjdīdāt*), addition (*ziyādāt*) or substitution (*ta* ʿ*wīḍāt*). A regular signature of the sultan, such as is usual on appointments as confirmation (*mustanad*), is not found on the *manāshīr*; instead of this, the sultan writes formulae like "God is my hope" (*Allāh amalī*), "God is my protector" (*Allāh waliyyī*), "God is sufficient for me" (*Allāh ḥasbī*), "To God belongs the rule" (*al-mulk li 'llāh*), or "God alone has grace" (*al-minna li 'llāhi waḥdahu*).

Occasionally, the *manāshīr* for the highest ranks (*muḳaddamū 'l-ulūf* and *muḳaddamū 'l-ṭablkhānā*) had a *ṭughrā* [*q.v.*] at the top. The *ṭughrās* were prepared by a special official beforehand and gummed on to the finished diplomas. In al-Ḳalḳashandī, xiii, 165 f., the *ṭughrās* of al-Nāṣir Muḥammad b. Ḳalāwūn (693-741 with interruptions) and Ashraf Shaʿbān b. Ḥusayn (764-78) are reproduced and described; they differ considerably from the better-known form of the *ṭughrā* of the Ottoman sultans. After Ashraf Shaʿbān, *ṭughrās* were no longer used on the *manāshīr*; these were only used for purposes of representation on letters to infidel rulers.

The completed *manshūr* was then again taken back by a courier from Cairo to the town concerned, e.g. Damascus, and handed over to the tenant of the appanage. The inspector of the army there (*nāẓir al-djaysh*), however, first entered it in his register, for he had to keep a roll of the holders of fiefs in his province. Al-Ḳalḳashandī, xiii, 167-99, gives as examples of *manāshīr* no fewer than 26 texts, beginning with one drawn up by Muḥyī 'l-Dīn b. ʿAbd al-Ẓāhir in the reign of Ḳalāwūn for the latter's son al-Nāṣir Muḥammad, which for its remarkable beauty he calls a regular *sulṭān al-manāshīr*. The other texts are of the above-mentioned military ranks, as well as for sons of *amīrs* (*awlād al-umarā*ʾ) and for *amīrs* of the Arabs, Turkomans and Kurds.

In the Ottoman Empire, certain patents of appointment were called *menshūr*. The *menshūrs* for a vizier, *beylerbeyi* and *sandjaḳbeyi* were issued by the Grand Vizier (*ṣadr-i a*ʿ*ẓam*). But they were also written for the *Ser* ʿ*asker, Baḥreyn ḥākimi*, the *mufti*, and even for Christian patriarchs and bishops. All *menshūrs* were controlled and if necessary corrected by the chancellor (*nishāndji*) and registered in the *menshūr defteri* of the *Dīwān-i humāyūn*.

In Persia, many documents, of a great diversity of subject matter, were called *manshūr*, sometimes with additions as *manshūr-i taḳlīd* or *manshūr-i tafwīḍ*. In modern Lahore, Pakistan, the *Manshūrāt-i Iḳbāl* are edited by the Bazm-i Iḳbāl.

In modern Egypt, edicts of the government are called *manshūr*, cf. some texts in *Ma*ʿ*riḍ al-khuṭūṭ al-*ʿ*arabiyya*, 1912, nos. 44, 69, 76, 78, 79, and *Taḳwīm*, 1937, 278, *madjmū* ʿ*at ḳarārāt wa-manshūrāt al-ḥukūma al-miṣriyya*, and 279, *madjmū* ʿ*at al-ḳawānīn wa 'l-ḳarārāt wa 'l-manshūrāt al-khāṣṣa bi-tasdjīl al-*ʿ*uḳūd*. In many Arabic states, serial publications now are called *manshūrāt*. In conclusion, it may be mentioned that *manshūr* in mathematical language means "prism" (varieties: e.g. *M. mā*ʾ*il* "oblique prism", *M. ḳā*ʾ*im* "straight prism", *M. mutawāzi 'l-adlā*ʿ "parallel prism", *M. muntaẓam* "regular prism", *M. muthallathī* "triangular prism", *M. nāḳiṣ* "truncated prism"), and that in the language of the Persian poets, the nightingales are called "the *manshūr*-writers of the garden" (*manshūr-niwīsān-i bāgh*).

Bibliography: In addition to the passages quoted, cf. Ibn Shīth, *Ma*ʿ*ālim al-kitāba*, 43; Khalīl al-Ẓāhiri, *Zubdat kashf al-mamālik*, 100, 102; M. Gaudefroy-Demombynes, *La Syrie à l'époque des Mamlouks*, index; W. Björkman, *Beiträge zur Geschichte der Staatskanzlei im islamischen Ägypten*, index 1; İ.Ḥ. Uzunçarşılı, *Osmanli devletinin saray teşkilâtı*, Ankara 1945, 285; idem, *Osmanlı devletinin merkez ve bahriye teşkilâtı*, Ankara 1948, 180; J. Reychman and A. Zajączkowski, *Handbook of Ottoman Turkish diplomatics*, The Hague 1968, 137, 140; H. R. Roemer, *Staatsschreiben der Timuridenzeit*, Wiesbaden 1952, 35, 47. (W. Björkman)

MANSŪKH [see Nāsikh].

MANṢŪR, miniature painter of the Mughal period in India.

Manṣūr had a highly successful career of at least 45 years in the Mughal studio, achieving the distinction of being the only artist who made his reputation by nature painting. His progress is interesting as he was one of few painters whose fortune was improved by changes in the atelier when the amateur naturalist and aesthete Djahāngīr (1014-37/1605-27 [*q.v.*]) succeeded his father Akbar [*q.v.*] as emperor. His evolution demonstrates the fact that the Mughal artist was moulded by his patron's requests, since the painter's earlier work shows he had a proclivity for rendering animals or plants; however, although his talent was apparently known, as this type of subject matter was relatively undeveloped in the 10th/16th century, his ability was without particular significance. Djahāngīr made animal portraiture one of his primary interests and because he had a strong scientific curiosity, he demanded realistic renderings of a very high standard from his artists. Around the time of his accession, it appears from the number of animal portraits signed by other artists that the emperor widely awarded such commissions, but after a few years Manṣūr seems to have been singled out consistently. The painter had to deal particularly with exotic specimens of animals, birds or flowers brought to Djahāngīr's attention in the course of extensive travels or through embassies and presentations.

Although nothing is known of the painter's origins,

Manṣūr was working in Akbar's studio by about 988/1580, when he co-operated as a colourist for many natural history vignettes from the now dispersed earliest *Bābur-nāma* manuscript (E. Smart, *Paintings from the Baburnama*, Ph.D. diss., London University 1977, 327). Since his last dated painting is a work of 1033/1624 (see A. Das, *Ustad Mansur*, in *Lalit Kala*, xvii), it can be ascertained that Manṣūr was probably one of those recruits who began grinding pigments and colouring designs during his teenage years. The memoirs of the Mug̲h̲al dynasty's founder Bābur [*q.v.*] that record the strange flora and fauna of his adopted country were among the few early outlets for Manṣūr's talent; he definitely contributed to three of the four copies of this manuscript and probably also to the remaining volume (now in Baltimore and Moscow) which no longer has artist attributions (Smart, *loc. cit.*). Manṣūr's greatest achievement for the 10th/16th century Mug̲h̲al manuscripts is the colouring of a scene filled with animals which shows Akbar hunting in a *ḳamarg*; this is one of the most spirited miniatures in the *Akbar-nāma* manuscript (998-1003/1590-5), intended to be a uniquely powerful and impressive volume glorifying the dynastic position of the reigning sovereign. Although Manṣūr did not produce the design, much of the painting's impact can be attributed to him and indicates that he may have attracted some attention in the studio by this time.

The animal paintings of the four *Babūr-nāmas* are quite precise, but the challenge of anatomical studies on a small scale was perhaps not significant; a larger picture done about 998/1590 of two birds (rosy pastors, *sturnus roseus* Linnaeus) arranged in front of an imaginary landscape shows the limitations of Akbarī naturalism (E. Kühnel and H. Goetz, *Indian book painting*, London 1926, pl. 10). It is clear that in this period Manṣūr uneasily applied flesh and feathers over a lumpish inner structure without the kind of anatomical knowledge that he had derived from observation of European paintings by about 1021/1612. Manṣūr was not a draughtsman; he acquired modelling skills with more difficulty than some other artists, and throughout his career there are indications in his work that he was forced to master formulae concerning structure. He does produce a few free and imaginative studies of animals poised in motion, such as that of a chameleon on a branch (S. C. Welch, *Indian drawings and painted sketches*, New York 1976, no. 15), but his greatest innate skill seems to be in transcribing patterns or textures. In this 10th/16th century compositions of birds, however, he does not render textures with as much illusionistic ability as he later did under the influence of Renaissance art.

Manṣūr did both the design and colouring of four political and courtly scenes for the first portion of an *Akbar-nāma* begun in 1912/1603. Such commissions indicate that artists were expected to be versatile during the Akbarī period in order to maintain their places in the studio; these compositions, which were the most usual types in an era devoted to historical illustration, were expected to be within the scope of all painters. Manṣūr is just able to manage the figural groups competently. The painter was apparently inconsistent in his ability to render figures, perhaps succeeding in revealing character only when he felt particular interest in his subjects. Of two portraits done in *ca.* 1003/1595, one of a *vina* player skilfully reveals an easy, jocular individual, while the other of a prince on a throne demonstrates the artist's decorative talent (*vina* player in Welch, *Art of Mughal India*, New York 1963, no. 18; prince on throne, private collection, Hyderabad). Since an ornate portrait of D̲j̲ahāngīr seated on a low throne is inscribed to both Manṣūr and his fellow artist Manōhar, who was primarily a portraitist, it is probable that Manṣūr contributed the details of costume and throne which are as intricately as his later bird pictures (A. Ivanova *et alii*, *Albom indiyskik̲h̲ i persidskik̲h̲ miniatur*, Moscow 1962, pl. 17).

D̲j̲ahāngīr began his commissions of hunting and probably animal subjects while still a prince; it is possible that the picture of rosy pastors mounted in an extensive *muraḳḳa*ᶜ or album prepared for D̲j̲ahāngīr had also been commissioned by him before 1008/1600. No specific evidence, however, remains to show how Manṣūr's special association with the emperor developed. By the time of D̲j̲ahāngīr's accession, Manṣūr had commenced signing pictures Ustād Manṣūr or Manṣūr Naḳḳās̲h̲ (N. Titley, *Miniatures from Persian manuscripts*, London 1977, 4), but despite this assertion of mastery there were many other painters, some younger than Manṣūr, who were more prominent and who had undoubtedly attracted the emperor's attention (e.g. Manōhar, Abu 'l-Ḥasan and Bis̲h̲ndas). There are only a few pictures which stylistically appear to have been done early in D̲j̲ahāngīr's reign because of the combination of delicate drawing and tentative modelling. These compositions are notably Manṣūr's green chameleon creeping along a leafy branch and his portrait of a Himalayan blue-throated barbet (S. C. Clarke, *Indian drawings*, London 1922, pl. 15). The latter composition has very sensitive details, but the bird is awkwardly posed, indicating an early date. By 1021/1612, Manṣūr had acquired a more exact scientific knowledge. In that year, D̲j̲ahangir records that he received several exotic creatures, including a turkeycock, which he ordered to be painted together in a special durbar scene by an unspecified artist (D̲j̲ahāngīr, *The Tuzuk-i-Jahangiri, or Memoirs of Jahangir*, tr. A. Rogers, ed. H. Beveridge, repr. New Delhi 1968, i, 215-17). A single portrait of the rare turkey which has crisp, very sophisticated, decorative details was probably painted by Manṣūr in this same year and demonstrates the evolution of his mature abilities (Clarke, pl. 15).

Both this composition and that of the barbet deserve attention because they are inscribed with Manṣūr's title *Nādir al-ᶜAṣr* ("Wonder of the age") which was given to him by the emperor at some indeterminate date. Though such an inscription may have been placed on these miniatures—which are here presumed to be early—at any time, it is worth noting the doubtful possibility that such a tribute had been awarded by *ca.* 1021/1612. The most reasonable assessment, however, seems to be that the encomium was given after this date because the painter has left a large body of consistent work which is slightly more advanced and complex than the turkeycock; it therefore seems logical to assume that it is this corpus which would have won such singular praise from D̲j̲ahāngīr. When in 1027/1618 D̲j̲ahāngīr himself mentions the title in his diary, it is clear from the context that he had bestowed it some time previously, perhaps in *ca.* 1024/1615 (*Tuzuk*, ii, 20). In the diary, the emperor begins with a discussion of Abu 'l-Ḥasan, whom he had also selected for the reception of a similar title and whom he asserts to be his best painter. An implicit comparison of the two artists is made by the emperor as the foremost in two artistic categories; it is apparent from the passage that D̲j̲ahāngīr's appreciation of natural history drawing was profound and that he had elevated the subject by his interest in it.

Of the five artists mentioned by name in Djahāngīr's memoirs (Abu 'l-Ḥasan, Āḳā Riḍā, Bishndas, Farrukh Beg and Manṣūr), Manṣūr receives most attention because the emperor discusses animal portraiture in great detail. Several interesting points emerge from his reminiscences, including the fact that the Djahāngīrī studio functioned with noteworthy artists like Manṣūr on call and ready to be summoned in the manner of news photographers for recording unusual occurences, such as the sighting of a novel bird species. Djahāngīr additionally mentions his habit of taking artists on trips like the 1029/1620 spring journey to Kashmīr during which he requested Manṣūr to paint more than one hundred flowers (*Tuzuk*, ii, 145). Since the artist also seems to have sketched a fish that is found in Gudjarāt (now in the Red Fort Museum, New Delhi), it appears that he accompanied the emperor on this long trip in 1026-7/1617-18 and probably on other journeys, as the studies of birds like the Himalayan barbet, Himalayan cheer pheasant and Bengal florican may imply.

Because of the demand for strict scientific accuracy, Manṣūr generally concentrates on his subjects with only rudimentary landscape forms or with no background. Since he often reconstructed dead animals and was not requested to focus on movement or behavioural patterns, his compositions are generally very still. His work can be divided into slightly different styles which are really treatments suggested by the animal or bird species itself. Among the most sophisticated and decorative of his paintings are those of birds such as the Himalayan cheer pheasant with striking contrasts of feather texture. An attributed painting of a *nilgai* is a much softer study with the fur of the animal done in small slurred brush strokes that create a hazy effect (L. Ashton, *The art of India and Pakistan*, London 1947, pl. 139). A picture of peafowl that is unsigned but attributable to the artist embodies in its design, colour and composition all the exhibitionist, majestic and coldly intense qualities of the species (M. Beach, *The Grand Mogul*, Williamstown, Mass. 1978, no. 47).

The date of Manṣūr's death or retirement is unknown, but it is doubtful that he would have continued in the atelier much beyond 1033/1624; no study done for Shāh Djahān is known by inscription. Most of the painter's work were mounted in the great royal albums commenced in Djahāngīr's reign and continued into Shāh Djahān's one, indicating the esteem in which the painter was held, as the albums include the most significant royal commissions from these two periods. Many of the miniatures originally in these album groups that each contained 60 pictures have been lost; in addition, in the early 19th century, these groups were rearranged and adulterated with copies by contemporary imperial artists. Manṣūr's remaining works can, however, be distinguished by the small folio numbers applied to the original leaves of the Minto and Wantage albums (V. and A., London) and the Kevorkian one (Met. Museum, New York), sometimes before the copies were inserted in the 19th century.

A painting of red tulips which is almost the sole survivor from the Kashmīrī flower group that Manṣūr painted is mounted on an album page like those of the Kevorkian, Wantage and Minto album groups (Red Tulips and Butterfly (Aligarh University) published in N. C. Mehta, *Studies in Indian painting*, Bombay 1928, pl. 31); however, the folio number which appears on the reverse is not positioned as those of the other album leaves, and it thus seems possible that the Kashmīrī flowers were originally placed together in a book of their own very similar to the other albums that were mainly portraits. In the composition of tulips, Manṣūr has blended the colour of the blooms very subtly to express their fragile, waxy quality which he then contrasts with the powdery wings of a butterfly. Clearly, by the end of his career he was interested in the nature of substances and in how the imagination reacts to sensation.

Other paintings by Manṣūr not previously mentioned include early work in the *Djāmiʿ al-tawārīkh*, Tehran; the *Khamsa* of Dihlawī (fol. iv), Baltimore, and Djahāngīr's *Muraḳḳaʿ gulshan* (fol. 53a), Tehran. Additional flowers and birds include an iris and narcissus (Y. Godard, *Un album de portraits des princes timurides de l'Inde*, in *Āthār-è-Īrān*, ii (1937), nos. 80 and 81 (fig. 113), goldfinch (M.A. Alvi and A. Rahman, *Jahangir the naturalist*, New Delhi 1968, pl. XVIIA), falcon (R. Krishnadasa, *Mughal miniatures*, New Delhi 1955, pl. IV) and pheasant (G. Marteau and H. Vever, *Miniatures persanes*, Paris 1932, no. 259, pl. CLXXVII). Unfortunately, because of Manṣūr's reputation, most unsigned flower and bird paintings done in the first half of the 11th/17th century have been ascribed to him without stylistic consideration. Manṣūr's work is quite bold, his compositions are generally simple with few objects, and the atmosphere is often somewhat static, so that it is to great extent possible to distinguish his mannerisms from those of other painters. Not only have inferior unrelated miniatures been atttributed to him, but deliberate copies of Manṣūr's work were done by admiring artists of the 12th/18th and 13th/19th centuries. In a few instances, since it was customary for Djahāngīr to ask several artists to paint the same subject or to request an artist to produce more than one version of a miniature, there are two or more excellent pictures from Djahāngīr's reign that should be equally appreciated; these include another version of the turkeycock, probably by Manṣūr, and two others of the cheer pheasant—one perhaps by Manṣūr's fellow artist Payag. Since Djahāngīr's memoirs show that Manṣūr produced a vast number of paintings that have disappeared, what is known of his output should be evaluated as an accurate but limited indication of his abilities. It is clearly unfortunate that such a large percentage of his work should have been lost.

Bibliography (in addition to references given in the article): T. Ahmad, *Nadiru l'Asr Mansur*, in *Indo-Iranica*, xxv (1972), 51-5; Beach, *The Grand Moghul* 137-43; Das, *Lalit Kala*, xvii, 32-9, xix, 40; Djahāngīr, *Tuzuk*, ii, 20-1, 107-8, 145, 157.

(LINDA Y. LEACH)

AL-**MANṢŪR**, the sixth ruler of the Ḥammādid dynasty, succeeded his father al-Nāṣir in the year 481/1088. The latter had witnessed the rise to the height of its power of the dynasty and the somewhat artificial development of the Ḳal ʿa of the Banī Ḥammād [see ḤAMMĀDIDS], as a result of the destruction of al-Ḳayrawān by the Arabs. Two years after the accession of al-Manṣūr, the Arabs, who had advanced towards the West and who had spread over all the region adjoining the Ḳal ʿa, began to make existence there difficult. The prince moved his capital from the Ḳal ʿa to Bougie, which he considered less accessible to the nomads; it should be mentioned that his father al-Nāṣir had already made preparation for this exodus by transforming a little fishing port into a regular town, which was called al-Nāṣiriyya but which was to assume the name of Bougie [see BIDJĀYA], while on the other hand, the Ḳal ʿa was not completely abandoned by al-Manṣūr and he even embellished it with a number of palaces. The Ḥammādid kingdom had therefore at this time two capitals joined by a royal road.

After taking up his quarters at Bougie, al-Manṣūr had in the first place to quell the revolt of one of his uncles, Balbār, the governor of Constantine. He sent against the rebel another Ḥammādid *amīr*, Abū Yaknī. The latter after his victory was given the governorship of Constantine, but shortly after, he in his turn, together with his brother, who had been given the governorship of Bône, rebelled. These risings over which al-Manṣūr, thanks to his energy, was triumphant, brought to the side of the rebels of the Ḥammādid family the Zīrids of al-Mahdiyya, who wished to get back some power in Barbary, the Almoravids of the Maghrib, who wished to extend towards the east, and the Bedouins, who were, always ready to join in the feuds of their powerful neighbours.

Al-Manṣūr was, on the other hand, led to oppose the advance of the Almoravids who were, somewhat curiously, allied with the traditional opposition of the Zanāta [*q.v.*]. With the probable object of disarming the opposition, al-Nāṣir and al-Manṣūr had married two sisters of Māk̲h̲ūk̲h̲, the chief of the Banū Wamānū, at that time the most powerful of the Zanāta group. This alliance did not hinder the time-honoured feud from breaking out again. It became more acute when al-Manṣūr murdered his wife, the sister of his enemy. The latter then asked for support from the Almoravids.

From Tlemcen, where they had been installed for more than twenty years, the Almoravids had, after many attempts, endeavoured to expand towards the east at the expense of their brethen of the same race, the Ṣanhādja Banū Ḥammād. Al-Manṣūr had twice reduced them to impotence. It was at this time that the murder of the sister of Māk̲h̲ūk̲h̲ by al-Manṣūr drove the Wamānū chief into an alliance with the Almoravids of Tlemcen. The alliance formed in this way was a great blow to the Ḥammādid kingdom. Algiers was besieged for two days; As̲h̲īr was taken.

The fall of the latter fortress, the oldest stronghold of the family, was bitterly resented by al-Manṣūr. He got together an army of 20,000 men, composed of Ṣanhādja, Bedouins and even Zanāta; he marched against Tlemcen, met the governor Tās̲h̲īn b. Tīn-ʿamer to the north-east of the town and put him to flight. Tlemcen was spared at the supplication of Tās̲h̲fīn's wife, who invoked the ties of relationship uniting them with the Ṣanhādja (496/1102).

After the defeat of the Almoravids, al-Manṣūr severely punished the Zanāta and the rebel tribes of the Bougie district, whom he forced to flee into the mountains of Kabylia.

Thus al-Manṣūr seems on the eve of his death (498/1105) to have thoroughly re-established the power of the Ḥammādids. According to a tradition, which is not above suspicion, recorded by Ibn Khaldūn, the two capitals owed very important buildings to him: Bougie, the Palace of the Star and the Palace of Salvation; the Ḳalʿa, the government palace and the Ḳaṣr al-Mannār, the beautiful donjon of which is still in part extant.

Bibliography: Ibn K̲h̲aldūn, *Hist. des Berbères*, i, 227-8, tr. de Slane, ii, 51-5; Ibn al-At̲h̲īr, x, 110; tr. E. Fagnan, *Annales du Maghreb et de l'Espagne*, 448; E. Mercier, *Hist. de l'Afrique septentrionale*, ii, 53-6; L. de Beylié, *La Kalaa des Beni Hammad*, 38 ff., 99 ff. (doubtful traditions relating to the mosque of Bougie which was enlarged by al-Manṣūr); G. Marçais, *Manuel d'art musulman*, i, 105, 121-3, 129-30.   (G. MARÇAIS)

AL-MANṢŪR, ABŪ D̲J̲AʿFAR ʿABD ALLĀH B. MUḤAMMAD B. ʿALĪ, the second ʿAbbāsid caliph,

reigned 136-58/754-75. He was born in *ca.* 90-4/709-13 at al-Ḥumayma [*q.v.*] to the east of the Jordan, where the ʿAbbāsid family were living. His mother, Sallāma, was a Berber slave girl. In 127-9/744-6 he joined the unsuccessful revolt of the Ṭālibid ʿAbd Allāh b. Muʿāwiya [*q.v.*] against the Umayyads in western Iran. He then returned to al-Ḥumayma and took no part in the early stages of the ʿAbbāsid revolution, coming to al-Kūfa with his brother Abu 'l-ʿAbbās (soon to be the caliph al-Saffāḥ) as the ʿAbbāsid armies were approaching from the east.

After the establishment of his brother as caliph, he was sent to conduct the siege of Wāsiṭ where the last Umayyad governor of ʿIrāḳ, Yazīd b. ʿUmar b. Hubayra [see IBN HUBAYRA], was holding out. There he made contact with K̲h̲urāsānī generals, including al-Ḥasan b. Ḳaḥṭaba, who was to be one of his most loyal supporters. He also tried to reach an agreement with Ibn Hubayra but was thwarted by Abū Muslim, who demanded that the Umayyad leader be executed. After the fall of Wāsiṭ, he was appointed governor of al-D̲jazīra and Armenia, where he succeeded in winning the loyalty of some of the most important Umayyad generals, including Isḥāḳ b. Muslim al-ʿUḳaylī. When al-Saffāḥ died in D̲h̲u 'l-Ḥid̲j̲d̲j̲a 136/June 754, he had already considerable political experience and had attracted a powerful body of supporters.

His brother designated Abū D̲j̲aʿfar as his heir, to be succeeded in turn by his nephew ʿĪsā b. Mūsā, the governor of al-Kūfa; Abū D̲j̲aʿfar, who was on the *ḥad̲j̲d̲j̲* with Abū Muslim at the time, quickly returned to take control. However, until the defeat of the ʿAlid rebellions of 145/762-3, he faced a series of challenges to his rule.

The first threat came from his uncle ʿAbd Allāh b. ʿAlī, who at the time of al-Saffāḥ's death was preparing to attack the Byzantine Empire with a large army of Syrians and K̲h̲urāsānīs, and he decided to use this force to make a bid for the caliphate. Al-Manṣūr was obliged to seek the support of Abū Muslim, who, against his better judgment, was persuaded to lead a large K̲h̲urāsānī army against the rebel, and ʿAbd Allāh's army, by this time composed almost exclusively of Syrians, was defeated near Niṣībīn in D̲jumādā II 137/November 754. ʿAbd Allāh spent the rest of his life in disgrace in ʿIrāḳ, but the caliph typically, was careful to be reconciled to the Syrian leaders who had supported him.

The defeat of the rebels left al-Manṣūr free to deal with Abū Muslim [*q.v.*]. Tension between the two men had been growing since the death of Ibn Hubayra, and a visit by al-Manṣūr to Abū Muslim's court at Marw before he became caliph had convinced him that Abū Muslim was too powerful to be allowed to survive. The conflict was not simply about personalities, but concerned the whole direction of the caliphate: Abu Muslim wished that eastern Iran should be effectively independent, under his rule, and that its revenues should be assigned to his K̲h̲urāsānī supporters, while al-Manṣūr insisted that the caliph should appoint governors and collect taxes from the area. The presence of Abū Muslim in ʿIrāḳ made him vulnerable, and he was murdered at al-Madāʾin in the caliph's presence (S̲h̲aʿbān 137/February 755). His murder was followed by disturbances in Iran, notably the strongly anti-Muslim revolt of Sunbād̲h, but in the end, al-Manṣūr asserted his control over K̲h̲urāsān.

The last major challenge which al-Manṣūr faced was the threat of an ʿAlid uprising which eventually broke out in Rad̲jab 145/September 762 in Medina, led by Muḥammad b. ʿAbd Allāh [*q.v.*]. Attempts to spread the revolt to Syria and Egypt failed, whilst al-Kūfa, the traditional centre of ʿAlid support, was closely watched by the caliph and his troops. Al-Manṣụr ordered that food supplies from Egypt be cut off and Muḥammad, now isolated in Medina, was easily defeated and killed by an ʿAbbāsid force led by ʿĪsā b. Mūsā (Ramaḍān 145/November 762).

Shortly before Muḥammad's death, his brother Ibrāhīm led a rising in al-Baṣra which attracted widespread support in the city. Having taken over the town, he began to march on al-Kūfa, but was met by ʿĪsā b. Mūsā with an ʿAbbāsid army and was defeated and killed at Bākhamrā after a fierce battle (Dhu 'l-Ḳa-ʿda 145/February 763).

The failure of the revolt left al-Manṣūr free to consolidate his rule in comparative peace. He was a political planner of great skill and had a clear vision of the development of the caliphate. His policy was to establish a centralised, largely secular state, based on a reliable, salaried army and an efficient revenue-gathering system. His models were the great Umayyad rulers ʿAbd al-Malik and Hishām, and he rejected the demands of those groups like the Rāwandiyya [*q.v.*] who launched a short-lived but dangerous revolt in 141/758-9 and who wanted to assume a more messianic role.

His main support came from the Khurāsāniyya, who had formed the army which overthrew the Umayyads and who now became a privileged military group; governors of Khurāsān were always chosen from among their number, and they were appointed to important posts in other parts of the Caliphate. In ʿIrāḳ, garrison cities were established for them at Baghdād and al-Raḳḳa. Al-Manṣūr also relied heavily on members of his own family. They were frequently given key governorates in ʿIrāḳ and in the western half of the caliphate, and some, like Sulaymān b. ʿAlī in al-Baṣra and Ṣāliḥ b. ʿAlī in Syria, came near to establishing semi-autonomous sub-dynasties. The Syrian leaders with whom the caliph had made contact during al-Saffāḥ's reign also proved an important source of support, notably during the ʿAlid rising of 145/762-3. Finally, al-Manṣūr also recruited some leaders of the Yamanī faction in the Umayyad state, notably the Muhallabī family, who were given governorates in Egypt, Ifrīḳiya and Ādharbāydjān as well as their native al-Baṣra. This broadly-based coalition of supporters meant that the caliph retained considerable political autonomy within the system, since he was never dependent on any one group; and it also assured a broad base of support for the régime.

The government of Khurāsān remained a problem, and demands for local autonomy led to a series of rebellions. After the rebellion of ʿAbd al-Djabbār al-Azdī in 140/757-8, al-Manṣūr solved the problems of the province by sending his son Muḥammad, later the caliph al-Mahdī [*q.v.*], to al-Rayy as viceroy. This allowed Khurāsān a wide measure of autonomy while ensuring overall ʿAbbāsid control. There were still sporadic rebellions in the remoter parts of the province, notably that of Ustādhsīs in Bādhghīs [*q.v.*] from *ca.* 147/764 to 151/768, but they did not seriously threaten ʿAbbāsid power.

Other frontier areas of the caliphate also saw continuing disturbances. In 147/764 the Khazars [*q.v.*] attacked through the Caucasus and briefly took Tiflis before being driven out. The Byzantine frontier was the scene of settlement and fortification rather than important campaigns. In North Africa, Ifrīḳiya was threatened by continuous Khāridjī uprisings, until in 155/772 Yazīd b. Ḥātim al-Muhallabī finally established ʿAbbāsid rule. In al-Andalus, power was seized by a member of the Umayyad family, ʿAbd al-Raḥmān b. Muʿāwiya [*q.v.*], who established an independant amīrate in 138/756

Al-Manṣūr's most lasting achievement was the foundation of the new ʿAbbāsid capital at Baghdād. Al-Saffāḥ and al-Manṣūr lived at a variety of sites in central ʿIrāḳ until in 145/762, the caliph decided to build a new capital at Baghdād. Part of the reason for this was the need for security, and the outbreak of the Rāwandiyya had shown how vulnerable the caliph was to even small-scale rebellions. Baghdād was also developed as a centre for the Khurāsānī soldiers who had come westwards and could not be settled in existing cities like al-Kūfa without arousing the hostility of the local population. At first, the city was essentially administrative and military in character, but the building of the al-Karkh commercial district to the south from 151/768 onwards and settlement on the east bank of the Tigris meant that, by the end of his reign, the new capital was already a thriving metropolis. On the Euphrates in al-Djazīra, al-Raḳḳa was also developed from 155/772 onwards, as a Khurāsānī base to supervise the affairs of Syria and the Byzantine frontier.

In 147/764, al-Manṣūr forced the resignation of ʿĪsā b. Mūsā from his position as heir apparent and designated his own son Muḥammad al-Mahdī, who enjoyed the support of the bulk of the Khurāsāniyya, who now obliged ʿĪsā to content himself with being heir to al-Mahdī.

Al-Manṣūr died on the road to Mecca in Dhu 'l-Ḥidjdja 158/October 775 in his mid-sixties. The twenty-one years of his reign had seen the establishment of the ʿAbbāsid caliphate as a centralised state under the caliph's control. He was a politician of genius who pursued his aims with a single-minded but prudent determination. He cannot be considered a popular ruler; he was noted for his hard work and his almost proverbial meanness (cf. his nickname Abu 'l-Dawānīḳ "Father of farthings"), and many felt that his autocratic style of government had betrayed the hopes of the ʿAbbāsid Revolution. Yet without his firm hand, the Muslim world might well have become prematurely fragmented in the mid-2nd/8th century.

Bibliography: 1. Texts. Ṭabarī, iii, 85-451; Yaʿḳūbī, *Taʾrīkh*, ii, 409, 420-5, 430, 433, 436-75; Khalīfa b. Khayyāṭ, *Taʾrīkh*, ed. ʿUmarī, 415-36; Balādhurī, *Ansāb al-ashrāf*, iii, ed. Dūrī, 182-275; Masʿūdī, *Murūdj*, vi, 156-233 = §§ 2370-2434; Djahshiyārī, *Kitāb al-Wuzarāʾ*, ed. al-Saḳḳāʾ, 96-140; Iṣfahānī, *Maḳātil al-Ṭālibiyyīn*, ed. Ṣaḳr, 178-399; *Aghānī*, *Tables*; Thaʿālibī, *Laṭāʾif al-maʿārif*, ed. Abyārī and Ṣayrafī, 19-22, tr. Bosworth, 48-51 and index. 2. Studies. T. Nöldeke, *Orientalische Skizzen*, Berlin 1892, 113-51; S. Moscati, *La rivolta di ʿAbd al-Ǧabbār contro il califfo al-Manṣūr*, in *Ren. Lin.* ser. 8, ii (1947), 613-5; idem, *Studi su Abū Muslim*, in *Ren. Lin.* ser. 8, iv (1949-50), 323-35, 474-95, v. (1950-1), 89-105; A. Dietrich, *Das politischen Testament des zweiten ʿAbbāsiden Kalifen al-Manṣūr*, in *Isl.*, xxx (1952), 33-65; D. Sourdel, *La biographie d'Ibn al-Muqaffaʿ d'après les sources anciennes*, in *Arabica*, i (1954), 307-23; idem, *Le vizirat ʿabbāside*, Damascus 1959-60; F. Omar, *The ʿAbbasid caliphate*, Baghdād 1969; idem, *Aspects of ʿAbbasid-Husaynid relations*, in *Arabica*, xxii (1976), 170-9; E. Daniel, *Khurasan under ʿAbbasid rule*, Minneapolis 1979; J. Lassner, *The shaping of ʿAbbāsid rule*, Princeton, 1980; H. Kennedy, *The early ʿAbbasid caliphate*, London 1981. (H. KENNEDY)

AL-**MANṢŪR** [see YAʿḲŪB AL-MANṢŪR]

AL-**MANṢŪR, AḤMAD** [see AḤMAD AL-MANṢŪR]

AL-**MANṢŪR** (MADINAT-) [see BAGHDĀD]

AL-**MANṢŪR**, AL-MALIK MUḤAMMAD B. ʿUMAR B. SHĀHANSHĀH, local ruler of Ḥamāt [*q.v.*], historian and patron of letters, b. 567/1171-2 (al-Maḳrīzī, *Sulūk*, i, 205), son of Ṣalāḥ al-Dīn's nephew al-Malik al-Muẓaffar Taḳī al-Dīn ʿUmar [*q.v.*], and paternal grandfather of Abu 'l-Fidā [*q.v.*] (but not Tūrānshāh's grandchild, as in vol. i, 805, above).

According to autobiographical remarks in his *Miḍmār* (see below), al-Manṣūr was still a child when taking part in campaigns and sieges of Ṣalāḥ al-Dīn and Taḳī al-Dīn. When in 579/1183 the latter was appointed governor of Egypt by Ṣalāḥ al-Dīn, al-Manṣūr accompanied him (*Miḍmār*, 158, 227), and in Alexandria he studied *ḥadīth* with Abū Ṭāhir al-Silafī [*q.v.*] (al-Ṣafadī, *Wāfī*, iv, 259, no. 1790), and with Abū Ṭāhir b. ʿAwf [*q.v.*] (al-Dhahabī, *ʿIbar*, v, 71). Already in 580/1184, when his father had to leave Cairo temporarily (*Miḍmār*, 200), he became his official representative in Egypt. After his father's death in Ramaḍān 587/September-October 1191, he became ruler of the city state of Ḥamāt and its dependencies, Ma ʿarrat al-Nuʿmān, Manbidj, Ḳalʿat al-Nadjm and Salamiyya [*q.vv.*]. The fiefs on the eastern side of the Euphrates, however, which Ṣalāḥ al-Dīn had granted to his father in 586/1190, he had to restore to the sultan, who passed them on to his brother al-ʿĀdil [*q.v.*] (Ibn al-Athīr, xii, 82-3; Ibn al-ʿAdīm, *Zubda*, iii, 121-3; Abu 'l-Fidā, *Mukhtaṣar*, iii, 85). Eight years later in 595/1199, al-Manṣūr conquered the fortress of Bārīn (*mons ferrandus*) (Ibn Wāṣil, *Mufarridj*, iii, 101), but was forced by al-ʿĀdil to substitute for this fortress Manbidj and Ḳalʿat al-Nadjm (Ibn al-ʿAdīm, *Zubda*, iii, 148; Ibn Wāṣil, *Mufarridj*, iii, 114; Abu 'l-Fidā, *Mukhtaṣar*, iii, 132). Thus his territory was at least a compact unit.

Ḥamāt and its surroundings held a key position against the Crusaders on the one hand, and on the other they were, after Ṣalāḥ al-Dīn's death, a buffer state between the main opposing rulers of the Ayyūbids, especially between al-Malik al-Ẓāhir Ghāzī in Aleppo and al-Malik al-ʿĀdil in Damascus (see AYYŪBIDS].

Al-Malik al-Manṣūr succeeded in maintaining his sovereignty and keeping his territory together through all the dangers of the internal struggles of the Ayyūbids. Moreover, for thirty years to come, i.e. until his death in 617/1220, he made it into a centre of *adab* and the sciences. In and around Ḥamāt he engaged in a busy building activity (Abu 'l-Fidā, *Mukhtaṣar*, iii, 132; Yāḳūt, *Muʿdjam*, ii, 300), and made the town into an almost impregnable fortress. The results of these activities proved useful during his victorious battles against the Crusaders (599-601/1203-4), as well as during the difficulties with his father's cousin and his temporary overlord al-Ẓāhir. For the battles against the Crusaders and the relations with them, see F. J. Dahlmanns, *al-Malik al-ʿĀdil*, 118 f.; Ibn Wāṣil, *Mufarridj*, iii, 141-50; Abu 'l-Fidā, *Mukhtaṣar*, iii, 111-2; al-Maḳrīzī, *al-Sulūk*, i, 164; Ibn al-Furāt, *Taʾrīkh*, v/1, 22-4. The sources do not agree in the details: Ibn Wāṣil, *Mufarridj*, iii, 163 f.; Ibn al-Athīr, xii, 195; Ibn Naẓīf, *al-Taʾrīkh al-Manṣūrī*, 15 (= Gryaznevič, Moscow 1960, fol. 122b); Sibṭ b. al-Djawzī, *Mirʾāt*, viii/2, 523. For his difficulties with al-Ẓāhir, see Ibn Wāṣil, *Mufarridj*, iii, 121-3; Abu 'l-Fidā, *Mukhtaṣar*, iii, 99; Ibn al-ʿAdīm, *Zubda*, iii, 149. Differing from each other are: Ibn al-ʿAdīm, *Zubda*, iii, 152; Ibn Naẓīf, *al-Taʾrīkh al-Manṣūrī*, 8 (= Gryaznevič, fol. 111b); Ibn Wāṣil, *Mufarridj*, iii, 132, and after him Sibṭ b. al-Djawzī, *Mirʾāt*, ms. Topkapı Sarayı Ahmed III 2907 /xiii, fol. 292b, l. 11 (this line lacking in ed. Ḥaydarābād, viii/2, 510).

During the unrest after Ṣalāḥ al-Dīn's death, al-Manṣūr officially took the part of al-Ẓāhir. In 595-6/1199-1200, he even declared himself ready to enter into a loose alliance with the latter against al-ʿĀdil (Ibn al-ʿAdīm, *Zubda*, iii, 144. Ibn Wāṣil, *Mufarridj*, iii, 101). However, at an early stage he had also recognised the political advantage of an alliance with Ṣalāḥ al-Dīn's brother; already in 590/1194 he openly showed his sympathy for al-ʿĀdil (al-Maḳrīzī, *al-Sulūk*, i, 124). But this again did not prevent him from playing the Ayyūbid rivals off against each other to his own advantage. Both al-ʿĀdil and al-Ẓāhir wanted control over northern Syria, while al-Manṣūr was able alternately to promote or to foil their plans. In 596/1200, after al-ʿĀdil had become sultan of Egypt, al-Manṣūr swore allegiance to him (Ibn Wāṣil, *Mufarridj*, iii, 114) and the sultan confirmed him as ruler of Ḥamāt. In 598/1201-2 he married one of al-ʿĀdil's daughters, and in 603/1206 and 606/1209 he supported the sultan in his attacks on the Crusaders' territory and in al-Djazīra (Ibn Wāṣil, *Mufarridj*, iii, 172 f., 192; Ibn al-Furāt, *Taʾrīkh*, v/1, 86-90).

In politics, al-Manṣūr did not have much room for direct manoeuvring. However, his decision not to engage in politics on his own account whenever possible, but rather to keep a balance between the competing forces of the Ayyūbids, benefited not only his own city state but in the end also the state as a whole. He was the first ruler of Ḥamāt to have copper coins struck with his own name (Balog, *The coinage*, 249-52). They also bear the name of the ʿAbbāsid caliph al-Nāṣir li-Dīn Allāh [*q.v.*], whose *futuwwa* [*q.v.*] he had joined with great pomp (Ibn al-Furāt, *Taʾrīkh al-duwal*, in *JA*, 5th ser., vi [1855], 285 f.) His escort (*mawkib*) was so large that it was compared with the ones of al-ʿĀdil and al-Ẓāhir (Ibn Wāṣil, *Mufarridj*, iv, 81). The ruler of Ḥamāt was not only an important Maecenas and an *ʿālim* in his own right (Abu 'l-Fidā, *Mukhtaṣar*, iii, 132) but also *imām* and *muftī* in several fields (al-Maḳrīzī, *al-Sulūk*, i, 205). His illness and death in 617/1220 threw the whole state considerably out of balance (see Gottschalk, *al-Malik al-Kāmil*, 103-4, 167-70). The pretender to the succession, al-Manṣūr's middle son Ḳilīdj Arslān, as well as the crown prince, his elder son al-Muẓaffar, who in the end secured his rights, were no more than dependents on al-ʿĀdil's son al-Malik al-Muʿaẓẓam of Damascus and al-Malik al-Kāmil of Egypt [*q.vv.*].

Works. 1. *Miḍmār al-ḥaḳāʾiḳ wa-sirr al-khalāʾiḳ*, a chronicle originally in ten volumes, preserved in parts (see *Bibl.*). The full title is given by Shihāb al-Dīn al-Ḳūṣī (d. 653/1255), one of the author's pupils who studied part of the work with him (al-Ṣafadī, *Wāfī*, iv, 259-60, no. 1790), as well as by Ibn Wāṣil who knew a part of the *Miḍmār* which is lost today (*Mufarridj*, iv, 78,84), and by Ḥādjdjī Khalīfa, who apparently saw only a *mukhtaṣar* of the *Miḍmār* (*Kashf al-ẓunūn*, ii, 1713). Ḥādjdjī Khalīfa's remark that some historians were sceptical about the authorship of this chronicle is refuted by al-Ḳūṣī's direct information. The exact size of the *Miḍmār* cannot be determined, the preserved part apparently being only a final section of the whole work (see *Miḍmār*, 4). The text starts with the year 575/1180 and ends abruptly in 582/1186, and there are moreover lacunae (see 41, 115, 208). The text shows (38, 72) that the work was to be continued at least until 583/1187 (*Miḍmār* 122, 144). The *Miḍmār* was composed after the siege of Jerusalem (Radjab 583/ Oct. 1187), or even after the death of Ṣalāḥ al-

Dīn (Ṣafar 589/Feb. 1193), with the purpose of glorifying the deeds and character of the Ayyūbid sultan. It thus stands in the tradition which began with ʿImād al-Dīn al-Iṣfahānī, was continued by Ibn Shaddād and came to its completion in the work of Abū Shāma [*q.vv.*], in whose eyes Ṣalāḥ al-Dīn played the role of a saviour in Islamic history.

The *Miḍmār* is one of the principal primary sources of its time. It contains numerous autobiographical data as well as reports of eye-witnesses, which are also of importance for the biography of the author's father al-Malik al-Muẓaffar [*q.v.*], to whom the son devoted two chapters. He explaines why his father was unable to take part in the battle of Mardj ʿUyūn (*Miḍmār*, 18 ff.) and deals with his nomination as governor of Egypt (*ibid.*, 154-8). Here (*ibid.*, 155-8) the certificate of investiture (*taḳlīd*) as granted by Ṣalāḥ al-Dīn is for the first time edited in its full context. The work contains numerous official documents, several of which can only be found here. Amongst them are letters of Ṣalāḥ al-Dīn's famous secretaries al-Ḳāḍī al-Fāḍil and ʿImād al-Dīn al-Iṣfahānī [*q.vv.*] (*Miḍmār*, 114, 149 f., 224 f.). The main figures are al-Nāṣir li-Dīn Allāh, Ṣalāḥ al-Dīn and Ḳarāḳūsh [*q.vv.*], to each of whom the author assigns a section for every year. Ṣalāḥ al-Dīn's politics are described as exemplary, with the caliph as his direct antagonist. In this context, al-Manṣūr's anti-Shīʿī attitude supports the claim to legitimacy which was so important for the usurper Ṣalāḥ al-Dīn.

Two different groups of sources, an ʿAbbāsid one and an Ayyūbid one, may underly the *Miḍmār*, although there are only scanty indications of informants (see A. Hartmann, *an-Nāṣir*, 14-17, and Index, *s.v.* Miḍmār; L. Richter-Bernburg, in *JAOS*, cii/2 [1982], 278 f.; A. Hartmann, *al-Malik al-Manṣūr*, in *ZDMG* cxxxvi (1986), 570-606). For the events in Baghdād, Ibn al-Māristāniyya is mentioned once (*Miḍmār*, 122), while the informants for Ṣalāḥ al-Dīn and Ḳarāḳūsh remain anonymous (139, 226), although al-Manṣūr received some information on the last-mentioned from himself or from participants in his campaigns (e.g. 54). A direct source for much of the information on Ṣalāḥ al-Dīn in the *Miḍmār* is found in ʿImād al-Dīn al-Iṣfahānī's *al-Barḳ al-Shāmī*. Since the *Barḳ* exists only in ms., with its greater part lost anyway, the *Miḍmār* is of interest for the reconstruction of several passages of the *Barḳ*, together with the text of al-Bundārī and Abū Shāma (see Hartmann, *al-Malik al-Manṣūr*). The author must have been in very close contact with the state chanceries, but his sources have still to be investigated, as does also the influence of the *Miḍmār* on later chronicles. The work was denied a large circulation, as remarked by Ḥādjdjī Khalīfa (*Kashf al-ẓunūn*, ii, 1713) who calls it something precious which could only have been composed by someone who belonged to the learned men of his time.

2. *Akhbār al-mulūk wa-nuzhat al-mālik wa 'l-mamlūk fī ṭabaḳāt al-shuʿarāʾ*, a lexicon in 10 volumes on poets from the Djāhiliyya period down to the author's time (*GAL* I, 324; S I, 558; Ḥādjdjī Khalīfa, *Kashf al-ẓunūn*, ii, 1102, ll. 27-9). Only the ninth volume, composed in 602/1205-6, has been preserved (ms. Leiden, Or. 639). It contains selections from poems and very short biographies of poets from ʿIrāḳ, Syria, Egypt, Transoxania and al-Andalus of the 4th-6th/10th-12th centuries. The poets are arranged according to their functions: kings, *amīrs*, viziers, judges and secretaries (see M. ʿAwīs, *Kitāb Ṭabaḳāt al-shuʿarāʾ li-'l-Manṣūr b. Shāhanshāh Ṣāḥib Ḥamāt*, al-Minyā: Dār Ḥirāʾ [1983]).

3. *Durar al-ādāb wa-maḥāsin dhawī 'l-albāb*, an *adab* anthology, composed in 600/1203-4, preserved only in fragments (ms. Leipzig 606; Brockelmann, I, 324; S I, 558; not mentioned in Ḥādjdjī Khalīfa).

Bibliography : Maḳrīzī, *al-Sulūk*, i, Cairo 1934; Ṣafadī, *Wāfī*, iv, Wiesbaden 1959 (Bibl. Isl., 6d); Dhahabī, *ʿIbar*, v, Kuwait 1966; Ibn al-Athīr, *al-Kāmil*, xii, Beirut 1966; Ibn al-ʿAdīm, *Zubda*, iii, Damascus 1968; Abu 'l-Fidā, *Mukhtaṣar*, iii, Istanbul 1286/1869-70; Ibn Wāṣil, *Mufarridj*, iii, Cairo 1960; Yāḳūt, *Muʿdjam*, ii, Beirut 1955; F. J. Dahlmanns, *al-Malik al-ʿĀdil*, Ph.D. thesis, Giessen 1975; Ibn al-Furāt, *Taʾrīkh*, v/i, Baṣra 1390/1970; the same work in ms. Vienna 814, rendered by J. v. Hammer-Purgstall, in *JA*, 5th ser., vi (1855), 285 f.; Ibn Naẓīf, *al-Taʾrīkh al-Manṣūrī*, ed. and tr. B. Doudou, Ph.D. thesis Vienna, 1961, facs. edn. after the Leningrad unicum by P. A. Gryaznevič, Moscow 1960, ed. B. Dudu, Damascus 1401/1980-1; Sibt b. al-Djawzī, *Mirʾāt*, viii/2, Ḥaydarābād 1952; P. Balog, *The coinage of the Ayyūbids*, London 1980, Plate xl; H. Gottschalk, *al-Malik al-Kāmil von Egypten*, Wiesbaden 1958; *Miḍmār al-ḥaḳāʾiḳ wa-sirr al-khalāʾiḳ*, ed. Ḥasan Ḥabashī, Cairo 1968, after the unicum Aḥmadiyya 4938, Tunis, probably to be dated shortly after Ramaḍān 589/Aug.-Sept. 1193.—For al-Ḳūṣī: Ṣafadī, *Wāfī*, ix, Wiesbaden 1974 (Bibl. Isl, 6 i), 105-6, no. 4021; J. van Ess, *Ṣafadī-Splitter II*, in *Isl.*, liv (1977), 85, no. 108; J.C. Garcin, *Qūṣ*, Cairo 1976, 154.—Ḥādjdjī Khalīfa, *Kashf al-ẓunūn*, ii, Istanbul 1941-3.—For Ibn al-Māristāniyya as historian: A. Hartmann, *an-Nāṣir li-Dīn Allāh*, Berlin-New York 1975, 12-13, 184-86, 258, resumed by L. Richter-Bernburg, *Ibn al-Māristāniyya*, in *JAOS*, cii/2 (1982), 276-8.—Bağdatlı Paşa, *Hadiyyat al-ʿārifīn*, ii, Istanbul 1955, 110; al-Ziriklī, *al-Aʿlām*, iii, Beirut[3] 1969, 958-9; Wüstenfeld, *Geschichtsschreiber der Araber*, in *Abh. Ak. W. zu Göttingen*, xxviii (1881), 108-9; H.-P. Kalbhenn, *Studien zur Geschichte der Ayyūbiden nach der Chronik Miḍmār al-ḥaqāʾiq ...*, unpubl. thesis, Freiburg [1974]; Cl. Cahen, *Some new editions of oriental sources about Syria in the time of the crusades*, in *Outremer: studies in the history of the crusading kingdom of Jerusalem presented to Joshua Prawer*, Jerusalem 1982, 324, 329-31; A. Hartmann, *al-Malik al-Manṣūr (gest. 617/1220, ein ayyubidischer Regent und Geschichtsschreiber*, in *ZDMG*, cxxxvi (1986), 570-606.

(ANGELIKA HARTMANN)

AL-**MANṢŪR** BI'LLĀH (Almanzor in the mediaeval Spanish chronicles) is the name by which is known the man who was, *de facto*, the real master of al-Andalus from 368/978 to 392/1002. Since no new source is available, except as regards the military campaigns, to expand upon the major features of the biography of ABŪ ʿĀMIR MUḤAMMAD B. ʿABD ALLĀH B. MUḤAMMAD B. ABĪ ʿĀMIR AL-MAʿĀFIRĪ, as revealed through the works of R. Dozy (*Histoire des musulmans d'Espagne*) and E. Lévi-Provençal (*Histoire de l'Espagne musulmane*), this article will be confined to a summary of this material.

Born in 326/938 into a minor aristocratic family which had settled after the conquest at Torrox, in the district of Algeciras, and which had fulfilled various posts in the judicial administration, Ibn Abī ʿĀmir studied, in Cordova, *ḥadīth* and *fiḳh* as a pupil of Abū Bakr b. Muʿāwiya al-Ḳurashī, and Arabic language and literature as a pupil of Abū ʿAlī al-Ḳālī and of Ibn al-Ḳūṭiyya [*q.vv.*]. He began his career in the service of the *ḳāḍī* of Cordova, Muḥammad b. al-Salīm, and subsequently, in 356/967, became steward of the eldest son of *al-Sayyida al-kubrā*, the sultana Ṣubḥ [*q.v.*]. He skilfully acquired the friendship and support of the latter, according to some accounts, through the giving of presents and according to others, through the exercise of his personal charm. This relationship was by no means unconnected with the rapid advance of his distinguished administrative career: director of the *sikka* [*q.v.*], treasurer, curator of intestate property, *ḳāḍī* of Seville and Niebla, etc. After a brief interlude (he had embezzled from the coffers of the mint, but his friend Ibn Ḥudayr made good the loss before the enquiry), he continued his advance and was appointed to the functions of chief of *al-s̲h̲urṭa al-wusṭā* [see SHURṬA] in 361/972. The construction of his palace at al-Ruṣāfa dates from this period, and it was also at this time that he set out to court popularity among the Cordovans. The fact that he had been sent, as inspector of finances, to verify the sums by G̲h̲ālib [*q.v.*] during his campaign against Ḥasan b. Gannūn enabled him to forge solid links with the army.

The death of al-Ḥakam II [*q.v.*], in 366/976, opened a new phase. The caliph had named as his successor his son His̲h̲ām II [*q.v.*], who was only eleven years old, under the tutelage of the vizier al-Muṣḥafī. The party of palace slaves (*ṣaḳāliba* [*q.v.*]) wished to appoint his uncle, al-Mug̲h̲īra. Al-Muṣḥafī, foreseeing that this would be the end of his political career, sent Ibn Abī ʿĀmir to strangle the latter. The ʿĀmirid was already closely linked to the vizier, through his personal ambitions and through his relationship with Ṣubḥ. It was thus that there fell to him the task of drafting the act of allegiance (*bayʿa* [*q.v.*]) to al-Muʾayyad bi 'llāh and of accepting the oaths of various Cordovan social groups. The new caliph appointed al-Muṣḥafī as *ḥād̲j̲ib* [*q.v.*] and Ibn Abī Āmir as vizier. These two succeeded totally in destroying the political influence of the slaves' party and declared a remission of taxes as a means of ensuring popular support.

In 366/977, Ibn Abī ʿĀmir left to repel an attack by the Christians and captured the suburb of al-Ḥamma (Baños of Ledesma, in the province of Salamanca). The campaign was of little importance but, skilfully exploited, it served to increase the prestige of the new vizier, attracting to him the sympathy of military men and especially that of the commander in chief of the Middle March (*al-t̲h̲ag̲h̲r al-wusṭā* [*q.v.*]), G̲h̲ālib, who soon afterwards received the title of *d̲h̲u 'l-wizāratayn*. As the popularity of al-Muṣḥafī declined on account of his lack of political vision and his nepotism, Ibn Abī ʿĀmir succeeded in taking to wife the daughter of the old general, appointed himself *ṣāḥib al-madīna* [*q.v.*], accused the *ḥād̲j̲ib* of malpractice, imprisoned him in 978 and caused his disappearance.

Having become *ḥād̲j̲ib*, Ibn Abī ʿĀmir foiled a conspiracy against him but was forced to make concessions to the opinion of the *ʿulamāʾ* who criticised his conduct, private and public, under the pretext of lack of orthodoxy. He therefore decided to "censor" the splendid library of al-Ḥakam II, and works of philosophy, astronomy, etc., were destroyed. It was in the same spirit of ostentatious piety that he made his own manuscript copy of the Ḳurʾān and ordered the final expansion of the Great Mosque of Cordoba in 377/987. In order to strengthen his control of the administration of the state, he transferred the offices of Madīnat al-Zahrā [*q.v.*] to his new residence at Madīnat al-Zāhira and obtained from the young caliph a "delegation of all his powers, so as to permit him to devote himself to pious observances". He took advantage of these powers to seclude the latter in his palace and to prevent all contract with him. This delegation thus supplied him with legal ratification of his *de facto* authority. But thereby he overstepped the limits and he was obliged to confront G̲h̲ālib, who died at Torre Vicente in 371/981. The *ḥād̲j̲ib* then took the title of al-Manṣūr bi 'llāh.

Al-Manṣūr conducted 52 expeditions against the Christian states of Spain (a partial list—the first 25—with dates of departure and return is given in the *Tarṣīʿ al-ak̲h̲bār* of al-ʿUd̲h̲rī; a list of 56—including two enagements at Algeciras, but undated—is given in the *D̲h̲ikr bilād al-Andalus*). On these campaigns, the reader is referred to the substantial and well documented article by Ruiz Asensio, *Campañas de Almanzor* (for the sake of completeness, attention is also drawn to the very unreliable and presumptuous article by L. Molina, *Las campañas de Almanzor*) and only the principal ones are mentioned: Zamora 981, Simanacas 983, Sepúlveda 984, Bracelona 985, Coimbra 987, Léon 988, Clunia 994, St. James of Compostella 997 and Cervera 1000. The last, in 392/1002, destroyed San Millan de la Cogolla; but on the return journey, al-Manṣūr fell ill and died at Medinacelli, and it was this which gave rise, two centuries later, to the legendary "defeat of Calatañazor".

The king of Léon, Ramiro III, was forced to surrender to him in 984; Sancho Garcès Abarca of Navarra had been his client since 982; Vermudo II of Léon asked and obtained from the ʿĀmirid an army which helped him to re-establish his authority; and the Castilian Count Garci Fernandez surrendered in 990. Sancho Garcès and Vermudo II gave their daughters in marriage to al-Manṣūr, who became the true arbiter of the Spanish situation. It is equally certain that these campaigns ruined a major part of the work of "reconquest" and almost the entire effort of repopulating Léon in the 9th century; the whole of Estramadura was devastated. The effects seem to have been still more in those eastern states which had no "frontier" (cf. P. Bonnassié, *La Catalogne du milieu du Xe à la fin du XIe siècle*, Toulouse 1978).

The *Mafāk̲h̲ir al-Barbar* [*q.v.*], which reproduces the chapter of Ibn Ḥayyān [*q.v.*] on Hispano-Mag̲h̲ribi relations, is the principal source for the study of his North African activity. Al-Manṣūr inherited the policy of ʿAbd al-Raḥman III [*q.v.*] and of al-Ḥakam II; rather than seeking conquests, he preferred to obtain submissions and vassalages. This had the double advantage of not immobilising too many troops while allowing the recruitment of large numbers of colonial troops for the purposes of his Spanish campaigns. There were numerous dangerous moments: when the pro-Fāṭimid Buluggīn b. Zīrī [*q.v.*] advanced as far as the gates of Ceuta in 980; the insurrection of Ḥasan b. Gannūn in 985 (he was executed in defiance of the guarantee of security given by Ibn ʿAsḳalād̲j̲a, which aroused a considerable degree of resentment); and the rebellion of Zīrī b. ʿAṭiyya [*q.v.*] in 998, suppressed by ʿAbd al-Malik al-Muẓaffar [*q.v.*], who went on to install a sort of "viceroyalty" of Fās.

Almost all the authors stress the politico-military activity of al-Manṣūr, which was brilliant, and pass too quickly over his internal policy. The famous military reforms have not been correctly assessed and are generally considered an innovation, whereas they were in fact simply a systematic application of the policy inaugurated by the caliph al-Nāṣir, when the latter drew conclusions from the disaffection and subsequent rout of his troops during the campaign of 327/939, that of al-K̲h̲andaḳ (on this expedition and its setbacks, see Chalmeta, *Simancas y Alhandega*, in *Hispania* [1976], 397-464). Al-Manṣūr confined himself—in regard to the ethnic basis of recruitment—to intensifying the policy already applied by al-Nāṣir in 328/939-40 (see Chalmeta, *Simancas-Alhandega: al-año siguiente*, in *Actas Jordanas Cultura Arabe* [1978]) and to enlisting only non-Andalusians. This was therefore an army without attachment to the country, or to its people; a "neutral" force, a "Foreign Legion". These professional warriors, mercenaries, required payment and were expensive to maintain. The ʿĀmirid novelty consisted in taxing heavily *all* the Andalusians, even the Arab *adjnād*. The desired effects were achieved. Powerful opponents were estranged from the army (thus deprived of prestige, of command, of access to information and to weapons), the considerable sums raised compensated the troops, who could be mobilised at 24 hours notice and who were entirely in his pay. The effect of his action was, primarily (*Tibyān*), 17) to forge for himself an instrument of internal repression and, subsequently, an army which by its very nature constituted an offensive machine of quality, but whose numbers and composition made it unsuitable for use as an occupying force (hence for the consolidation of captured positions). This policy also had unforeseen and undesirable effects in the long term: the impoverishment of the local population; its indifference towards the government; and its lack of military training. The otherwise incomprehensible phenomenon of the collapse of the caliphate, when confronted by the Christians of the north at the time of the *fitna* [*q.v.*], thus becomes understandable and almost inevitable.

The impact of the orthodox "purge" of the library of al-Ḥakam II on the intellectual life of Arab Spain is difficult to assess. It seems inevitable that it took a heavy toll. Many volumes must have been unique in al-Andalus, and their destruction must have prevented, or at the very least delayed, their dissemination. In an indirect fashion, the library of al-Ḥakam also performed, in part, the function of a public library, and it was dispersed during the siege of Cordova; furthermore, the economic crisis which accompanied the *fitna* was hardly propitious for the constitution or enrichment of private libraries.

The campaigns of al-Manṣūr, which assumed a change in relations between al-Andalus and the Christian kingdoms, were to bring about, in the long term, the birth of a new attitude, a new sense of unity in the popular Christian consciousness. Hitherto the Muslim campaigns had only been responses to Christian initiatives. In order to avoid conflict, it was sufficient to abstain from provocation. These campaigns had also been relatively benign, without too drastic effects in terms of destructions and death. After all, the frontier-dwellers had relatives on the other side; they could be caught unawares in their turn; etc. The Christian states had hardly ever struck in any depth, and the danger had never affected the majority of the population. However, the ʿĀmirid raids were not responses, but attacks, and thus difficult to foresee. They were conducted with a ferocity unprecedented in the Spanish context, and left behind a long trail of destruction, of death and of rancour. The Muslims were no longer Hispano-Arabs, but foreigners, different people. These campaigns affected the hinterland, it was no longer simply a matter of frontier-dwellers, of people who had chosen, in exchange for certain fiscal and social advantages, to "live dangerously". All sectors of the population, including those people who preferred a peaceful existence, far from the exposed territories, were affected, capital cities were plundered, etc. Since survival was at stake, any likelihood of coexistence must have seemed absurd. These destructive raids provoked a defensive reflex and a much greater sense of solidarity between the various Spanish Christian kingdoms—Cervera is the proof of this—faced with what was coming to be regarded as a common enemy.

The ʿĀmirid campaigns, which employed a number of Christians, either as mercenaries or as vassal troops, for example in the famous raid against St. James of Compostella, enabled the latter to acquire, from the inside, a useful knowledge of the roads, the resources and the structure of the Cordovan state. This was to prove advantageous, some years later, when the Christians put into effect, in the reverse direction, the ʿĀmirid policy. By this time the damage had been done. The bitterness accumulated as a result of al-Manṣūr's 52 expeditions had engendered the notion that it was essential at the earliest possible opportunity to settle accounts with the adversary, an adversary whose lack of reaction aroused contempt. The new identification between the concepts of Christendom and Spain required the expulsion of the "other Spain" (Chalmeta, *Historiografiá hispana y arabismo: biografía de una distorsion*, in *Rev. Infor. Esp. UNESCO* [1982]).

The systematic policy of infiltration, destabilisation and then reconstruction of the Cordovan state which had enabled al-Manṣūr to seize power and above all to sustain it, led to the annihilation of all the structures constituting a system: political, economic, social, ethnic, cultural, etc. After him, there was to be no more caliphate, great families, surplus budgets, social or ethnic coexistence. The Andalusians were henceforward aware of only one enemy: the Berbers. They forgot the Christians, or saw them as their allies. In view of the fact that al-Andalus did not constitute a feudal society, its chances of resisting the advance of a society which had the necessary mechanics for waging war were limited. According to the *Chronicle of Silos*, "In the year 1002, Almanzor died; he was entombed in Hell". Such was the Christian verdict. It could be extended to the whole of Muslim Spain, for the policies of al-Manṣūr engendered the mental attitude which spelled the doom of Hispano-Arab Islam.

Bibliography: 1. Sources: Ibn ʿIdhārī, *al-Bayān al-mughrib*, ii, 267-321; Ibn Bassām, *al-Dhakhīra fī maḥāsin ahl al-djazīra*, vii, 56-78; ʿUdhrī, *Nuṣūṣ ʿan ... Tarṣīʿ al-akhbār*, 74-80; Ibn al-Athīr, *Kāmil*; Ibn al-Khaṭīb, *K. Aʿmāl al-aʿlām*, 59-73, 97-104; idem, *K. al-Iḥāṭa*; Ibn Darrādj Ḳasṭallī, *Dīwān*, ed. M. Makkī, Damscus 1961; *Mafākhir al-Barbar: fragments historiques...*, ed. E. Lévi-Provençal, Rabat 1934; Makkarī, *Nafḥ al-ṭīb*, i, 257-72; anon., *Dhikr bilād al-Andalus wa-faḍlihā wa-ṣifatihā*; one should add the details to be gleaned from Ibn al-Abbār, *al-Ḥulla al-siyarā*ʾ; Ibn Saʿīd al-Maghribī, *al-Mughrib fī ḥulā 'l-Maghrib*; Ḥumaydī, *Djadhwat al-muktabis*; Ibn Khaldūn, *K. al-ʿIbar*; Nuayrī, *Nihāyat al-arab*; etc. 2. Studies. The basic works are still the *Histoire des Musulmans d'Espagne*, of R. Dozy, ed. Lévi-Provençal, Leiden 1932, and the *Histoire de l'Espagne musulmane* by Lévi-Provençal, Paris 1950-3, to be completed by R. Menéndez Pidal, *Historia y epopeya*, Madrid 1934, 1-27; J. Pérez de Urbel, *Historia del Condado de Castilla*, Madrid 1945, 667-802; M. Makki, *La España cristiana en el dīwān de Ibn Darrāŷ*, in *B.R. Acad. Buenas Letras Barcelona*, xx (1963-4), 63-104; J. M. Ruiz Asensio, *Campañas de Almanzor contra el reino de León (981-986)*, in *An. Est. Med.*, v (1965), 31-64; L. Seco de Lucení, *Acerca de las campañas militares de Almanzor*, in *MEAH*, xiv-xv (1965 ff.), 7-29; M. Lachica Garrido, *Almanzor en los poemas de Ibn Darrāŷ*, Saragossa 1979.

(P. CHALMETA)

MANṢŪR B. NŪḤ, the name of two *amīrs* of the Sāmānid dynasty of Tranoxania and Khurāsān.

1. MANṢŪR B. NŪḤ I, Abū Ṣaliḥ, ruler of Khurāsān and Transoxania (350-65/961-76), succeeded his brother ʿAbd al-Malik b. Nūḥ I. Ibn Ḥawḳal is able

to describe the internal conditions of the Sāmānid kingdom under Manṣūr as an eye-witness; cf. especially BGA, ii, 341: *fī waḳtinā hādhā*; 344 on the character of Manṣūr "the justest king among our contemporaries, in spite of his physical weakness and the slightness of his frame". On the vizier Abū ʿAlī Muḥammad Balʿamī, see BALʿAMĪ, where also information is given about the Persian version of al-Ṭabarī's history composed in 352/963 by or by orders of this vizier. On the rebellion of the commander of the Sāmānid bodyguard, Alp-Tegīn, and the independent kingdom founded by him in Ghazna and on the establishment of Sāmānid rule there in the reign of Manṣūr and the son and successor of Alp-Tegīn, Isḥāḳ (or Abū Isḥāḳ Ibrāhīm) see ALP-TEGĪN and GHAZNA; in Barthold, Turkestan, 251, n. 4, Abū Isḥaḳ Ibrāhīm should be read for Isḥāḳ b. Ibrāhīm (this passage is misunderstood in the Russian original). In other directions also in this reign, the Sāmānid kingdom prospered in its foreign affairs; the fighting with the Būyids [see BUWAYHIDS] and Ziyārids [*q.v.*] was as a rule successful.

2. MANṢŪR B. NŪḤ II, Abu 'l-Ḥārith, ruler in Transoxania only (387-9/997-9). His father Nūḥ II b. Manṣūr, to whom out of all the Sāmānid empire only a portion of Transoxania was left, died on Friday, 14 Radjab 387/July 23, 997 but it was not till Dhu 'l-Ḳaʿda/November that homage was paid to Manṣūr as his successor. The Ghaznawid historian Bayhaḳī, ed. Morley, 803, ed. Ghanī and Fayyād, 640, Russian tr. Arends[2], 776, talks highly of his courage and eloquence; on the other hand, he is said to have been feared by every one for his extraordinary severity. During his brief and impotent reign he was hardly able to instil terror into any one. The last Sāmānids were quite helpless against the rulers and generals who were quarrelling over the inheritance of the dying dynasty. One of these generals, Fāʾiḳ, succeeded even in taking Bukhārā at the head of only 3,000 horsemen; Manṣūr had to fly to Āmul [*q.v.*], but was called back by Fāʾiḳ. The last months of his reign were devoted to fruitless efforts to settle peacefully the question of the governorship of Khurāsān, which was claimed by various parties; but before the problem had been settled by force of arms, Manṣūr was dethroned on Wednesday, 12 Ṣafar 389/1 February 999, by his generals Fāʾiḳ and Begtūzūn, blinded a week later and sent to Bukhārā.

Bibliography: W. Barthold, *Turkestan down to the Mongol invasion*, London 1928, 251-2, 264-6; Narshakhī, *The history of Bukhara*, tr. R.N. Frye, Cambridge, Mass. 1954, 98-9; Frye, in *Cambridge history of Iran*, iv, 152-9; C.E. Bosworth, *The Ghaznavids...*, Edinburgh 1963, 45-6; art. SĀMĀNIDS. For the chronology of these reigns, see Zambaur, *Manuel*, 202-3. (W. BARTHOLD)

AL-**MANṢŪR BI'LLĀH** ʿABD ALLĀH b. ḤAMZA b. SULAYMĀN b. ḤAMZA, Zaydī Imām of the Yemen. Born in Rabīʿ I 561/January 1166, he became *Imām* in 583/1187-8 (some sources have 593/1196-7). He was not a direct descendant of al-Hādī ilā 'l-Ḥaḳḳ Yaḥyā [see ZAYDIDS], but of the latter's grandfather al-Ḳāsim al-Rassī b. Ṭabāṭabā (Kay, *Yaman*, 184-5, 314; Van Arendonk, *Débuts*, 366). Between 532/1137-8 and 566/1170-1, the *Imām* al-Mutawakkil ʿalā Allāh Aḥmad b. Sulaymān had tried to assure Zaydī power over al-Djawf, Nadjrān, Ṣaʿda, al-Ẓāhir and Zabīd (Kay, *Yaman*, 317; *EI*[1] s.v. AL-MAHDĪ LI-DĪN ALLĀH AḤMAD), but his influence had been seriously challenged by Ḥamīd al-Dawla Ḥātim and his son ʿAlī b. Ḥātim [see HAMDĀNIDS] (Smith, *Ayyūbids*, 71-5). When al-Manṣūr bi'llāh was proclaimed *Imām* in Maʿīn al-Djawf (Smith, *Ayyūbids*, ii, 94-5), according to Tritton [*EI*[1] s.v. RASSIDS] after a year of probation, the Ayyūbids had already started to interfere in Yemeni affairs. Tūrānshāh [*q.v.*] had arrived from Egypt in 569/1173-4 and had left in 571/1175-6, while his brother Ṭughtakīn [*q.v.*] had entered the country in 579/1183-4. He came to Ṣan ʿāʾ in 585/1189-90, thus limiting the influence of the *Imām* to the north-west. Al-Manṣūr bi'llāh took up his residence in Ṣaʿda, then moved southwards and succeeded in entering Ṣan ʿāʾ in 594/1197-8 or the beginning of 595/1198. In the same year, he took possession of Dhamār [*q.v.*] and its neighbourhood, but in 597/1200-1 he was defeated by al-Mu ʿizz Ismā ʿīl, son of Ṭughtakīn, and forced to retreat northward (Ibn al-Athīr, xii, 113). He nevertheless extended his power into the Ḥidjāz, and in 600/1203-4 he restored the fortress of Ẓafār. In 601/1204-5 he ordered Sayyid Ḳatāda b. Idrīs (cf. al-Ḥabshī, *Muʾallafāt*, 47, no. 77) to restore the *mashhad* of al-Ḥusayn (Van Arendonk, *Débuts*, 58/65). About 611/1214, Badr al-Dīn al-Ḥasan b. ʿAlī, grandson of Rasūl (Muḥammad b. Hārūn) who gave the Rasūlid dynasty its name (see Smith, *Ayyūbids*, ii, 85 ff.), made contact with the *Imām*, who had occupied Ṣanʿāʾ for a second time, in an attempt to dislodge the Ayyūbid al-Muʿaẓẓam Sulaymān, grandson of Tūrānshāh. In the end, however, the Rasūlid came to terms with the Ayyūbid. Meanwhile, the *Imām* had also regained possession of Dhamār, and was trying to subject the *Muṭarrifiyya*. According to Kay (*Yaman*, 318, repeated in *Ghāyat al-amānī*, i, 371, n. 4; cf. *ibid.*, 390), this term, very generally accompanied by the epithet *shaḳiyya* "vile", may designate the Sunnīs (cf. B. L. Suppl. 210 II, IV), but see also R. Strothmann, *Die Literatur der Zaiditen*, in *Isl.*, ii, 67-9. Ibn Khaldūn—whose statements on the Yemen need some caution (Kay, *Yaman*, 284)—relates that al-Manṣūr bi'llāh displayed a hostile demeanour towards the ʿAbbāsid caliph al-Nāṣir li-dīn Allāh [*q.v.*], with whom he affected a tone of equality. He sent his *dāʿīs* to the Daylamī [see DAYLAM] and to Djīlān [*q.v.*], with the result that the *khuṭba* was recited among these people in his name (the Caspian Zaydiyya had been merged into the Nuḳtawiyya [see ṬABARISTĀN and AL-ZAYDIYYA in *EI*[1], and cf. *EI*[2], art. ḤURŪFIYYA]. The caliph al-Nāṣir endeavoured to raise the Arabs of the Yemen against the *Imām* by means of subventions, and in 612/1215-16 al-Masʿūd, the last Ayyūbid in the Yemen (see on him Smith, *Ayyūbids*, ii, 88 ff.), sent Kurdish and Turkish troops, headed by ʿUmar b. Rasūl, to meet the Hamdānīs and Khawlānīs of the *Imām*. Al-Manṣūr bi'llāh retreated to the neighbourhood of Kawkabān, where he built a substantial house for himself and quarters for his followers, and even set up a mint. After frequent engagements, a truce was agreed upon in 613/1216-17. Having removed to Kawkabān and then to Ẓafār, al-Manṣūr bi'llāh died in Muḥarram 614/April 1217 in Kawkabān (Redhouse, *El-Khazraji*, 80). For a more detailed survey of the intricate situation in the Yemen during the life of al-Manṣūr bi'llāh, see *Ṣanʿāʾ*, ed. Serjeant, 61-3.

Al-Ḥabshī, *Muʾallafāt*, 37, mentions four *sīra*s of al-Manṣūr bi'llāh: one anonymous, one by Muḥyī al-Dīn Muḥammad b. Aḥmad al-Walīd, a third one by ʿAlī b. Nashwān b. Saʿīd al-Ḥimyarī, and a fourth one by Abū Firās Daghtham (= Duʿaym) al-Ṣanʿānī, the *Imām*'s secretary (see Smith, *Ayyūbids*, ii, 8, 78 n. 4, 98). Al-Manṣūr bi'llāh is also the last *Imām* treated by his companion Ḥamīd b. Aḥmad al-Muḥallī in his *Kitāb al-Ḥadāʾiḳ al-wardiyya fī dhikr (manāḳib) aʾimmat al-Zaydiyya* (Brockelmann, I, 325; S I, 560; Strothmann, *Die literatur*, in *Isl.*, i, 361).

Like many other Zaydī *Imāms* before and after him,

al-Manṣūr bi'llāh developed a great literary activity. Besides the 21 titles mentioned in Brockelmann (*GAL*, I, 403, S I, 701; cf. also Ahlwardt, *Verzeichnis*, iv, 4950, XI), al-Ḥabs̲h̲ī, *Muʾallafāt*, 38-48, lists 62 other titles, some of which may be the same as those summarised in B.L. Suppl. nos. 210, 211, 1230 IV-VII. In his *Kitāb al-S̲h̲āfī* (Brockelmann, I, 403, S I, 701; al-Ḥabs̲h̲ī *Muʾallafāt*, 44, no. 53), the *Imām* often quotes from the *Kitāb al-ʿUmda* by al-Ḥillī al-Wāsiṭī (Brockelmann, S I, 710; Van Arendonk, *Débuts*, 15/17 n. 1) and makes use of the *kutub al-ʿāmma*, i.e. collections of traditions favourable to the descendants of Fāṭima and ʿAlī (Strothmann, *Die Literatur*, in *Isl.*, i, 358, ii, 64). Of historical interest might be the following numbers, mentioned by al-Ḥabs̲h̲ī, *Muʾallafāt*. No. 23 is a *daʿwa* to Sunḳur of the year 599/1202-3. This Sunḳur is probably the *atābeg* Sayf al-Dīn Sunḳur, a *mamlūk* of Ṭug̲h̲takīn (cf. Smith, *Ayyūbids*, 97, 98; *G̲h̲āya*, i, 356 ff.). No. 24 is a *daʿwa* to the ʿIrāḳī *amīr al-ḥad̲j̲d̲j̲* Ṭas̲h̲kīn (= Ṭas̲h̲tikīn? cf. A. Hartmann, *an-Nāṣir*, 146), while no. 64 is a *kitāb* to (the same?) *amīr ḥād̲j̲d̲j̲ al-ʿirāḳī*. No. 25 is a *daʿwa* of the *Imām* to (al-Muʿizz) Ismā ʿīl b. Ṭug̲h̲takīn when the latter came down (*ḥaṭṭa*) to Kawkabān, of the year 599/1202-3. (According to *Ṣanʿāʾ*, ed. Serjeant, 62, al-Muʿizz was murdered in 598/1201-2, but see *G̲h̲āya*, i, 380). No. 56 is a *ṣūra kitāb* to the *ʿāmil* of the Banū ʿAbbās in the Yemen, and no. 60 is a *ḳaṣīda* sent to the ʿAbbāsid caliph = al-Nāṣir li-dīn Allāh (see *G̲h̲āyat*, i, 400 n. 1). According to al-Ḥabs̲h̲ī, part of this *ḳaṣīda* is mentioned in Muḥammad Yaḥyā Zabāra, *Aʾimmat al-Yaman*, Taʿizz 1375/1955-6, (but see *Ṣanʿāʾ*, ed. Serjeant, 572), 139-41, and there is a commentary on it by Ḥamīd b. Aḥmad al-Muḥallī, d. 652/1254, entitled *Maḥāsin al-azhār* (Brockelmann, I, 325, S I, 560). No. 63 is a *kitāb* to al-Malik al-ʿĀdil Abū Bakr b. Ayyūb [*q.v.*] of the year 598/1201-2, while no. 79 contains correspondence between the *Imām* and the Banū Rasūl.

Bibliography: H.K. Kay, *Yaman, its early mediaeval history*, London 1892; C. van Arendonk, *Les débuts de l'Imamat Zaidite au Yémen*, Leiden 1960; G.R. Smith, *The Ayyūbids and early Rasūlids in the Yemen (567-694/1173-1295)*, 2 vols., GMS London 1978; Sayyid ʿAbd Allāh Muḥammad al-Ḥabs̲h̲ī, *Muʾallafāt ḥukkām al-Yaman. The works of the rulers of Yemen*, ed. Elke Niewöhner-Eberhard, Wiesbaden 1979; R. Strothmann, *Die Literatur der Zaiditen*, in *Isl.*, i (1910), 354-68; ii (1911), 49-78; Sir J. Redhouse and Muhammad Asal, *El-Khazrají's History of the Resúli Dynasty of Yemen*, GMS, 5 vols., Leiden-London 1906-18; Angelika Hartmann, *an-Nāṣir li-Dīn Allāh (1180-1225). Politik, Religion, Kultur in der späten ʿAbbasidenzeit*, Berlin-New York 1975; *Ṣan ʿāʾ, an Arabian Islamic city*, ed. R. B. Serjeant and R. Lewcock, London 1983; Yaḥyā b. al-Ḥusayn, *G̲h̲āyat al-amānī fī ak̲h̲bār al-ḳuṭr al-Yamānī*, ed. S. A. F. ʿĀs̲h̲ūr, 2 vols. Cairo 1388/1968.

(E. VAN DONZEL)

AL-**MANṢŪR BI'LLĀH**, ISMĀʿĪL, third caliph of the Fāṭimid dynasty in Ifrīḳiya (334-41/946-53). His personality shines with an unparalleled brilliance under the pens of the Ismāʿīlī authors, who, as also the Sunnī chroniclers, show great wonder in relating his exalted deeds and who dwell at length on giving accounts of the battles, rebellions and other bloody events, especially as his name is linked with the defeat of the "man on the donkey", the celebrated K̲h̲ārid̲j̲ī rebel Abū Yazīd [*q.v.*], whose remarkable revolt almost put an end to the caliphate and the ʿAlid line.

Sunnī and Ismāʿīlī authors are at one in acknowledging his exemplary bravery and tenacity in the face of all odds, shown by him during the long and dangerous campaign which he had to lead, at the head of his troops, against the rebel leader, as far as the massif of the Zāb. According to their accounts, Ismāʿīl possessed only good qualities: he was generous and benevolent, level-headed and perspicacious; above all possessing a brilliant eloquence; since his youth, he had devoted himself to piety and study, and was deeply conscious of his high calling as impeccable *Imām* and of his grandeur as a monarch.

Ismāʿīl was born at Raḳḳāda in the first ten days of Ramaḍān 301 January 914, the son of an Ifrīḳiyan slave concubine called Karīma, who had been left by the last Ag̲h̲labid *amīr* Ziyādat Allāh III [*q.v.*] and received as his share by his father, the second Fāṭimid caliph al-Ḳāʾim bi-amr Allāh [*q.v.*]. He was thus an Ifrīḳiyan Arab, for there was as much Ifrīḳiyan blood in his veins through his mother as eastern blood. It was at the death of his grandfather al-Mahdī bi'llāh [*q.v.*] that, in accordance with a rule of Ismāʿīli doctrine, he was secretly designated successor (*ḥud̲j̲d̲j̲a*) of al-Ḳāʾim. He had accordingly to wait a dozen years with no involvement in the great civil and military responsibilities before he became heir presumptive; his public designation took place only on 7 Ramaḍān 334/12 April 946, a mere five weeks before his father's death, with great suffering, in an al-Mahdiyya besieged by Abū Yazīd.

Thus he had to face up to, immediately, the heaviest responsibilities without having served any apprenticeship as ruler. He did not wait for his father's death to engage with ardour in the task awaiting him, sc. to defeat the "accursed one", the K̲h̲ārid̲j̲ī rebel; he sent reinforcements to Sousse, which was undergoing siege, on 11 S̲h̲awwal 334/16 May 946. Two days later, his father died, but Ismāʿīl concealed his death for fear lest Abū Yazīd derive profit from the news and, without announcing his own accession, buried his father secretly, and then, on 19 S̲h̲awwāl 334/24 May 946, began his campaign against the rebel. His lieutenant Kābūn b. Taṣūla soon relieved Sousse, whose siege Abū Yazīd had to relinquish in order to fall back towards al-Ḳayrawān. Encouraged by this victory, Ismāʿīl decided to undertake personally the pursuit of his enemy; he required less than five months to subjugate him.

Having reached the southern part of the town, whose shame-faced notables had rushed out to meet him and to ask for *amān* and pardon for support which they had given to the K̲h̲ārid̲j̲ī chief, Ismāʿīl deployed his troops behind the shelter of a trench (*k̲h̲andaḳ*), from which he doggedly repelled the repeated attacks of the enemy, undertaken from the time of his camp being set up at Mams. Abū Yazīd, accustomed for two years to fighting dispirited troops led by timorous officers, found himself now up against a young *amīr* full of fighting spirit, always ready to expose himself to danger under his ceremonial parasol at the head of troops still weak, but determined to fight fiercely.

The battle for al-Ḳayrawān began at the end of S̲h̲awwāl 334/beginning of June 946, and ended after two months of fierce fighting in the crushing defeat of the K̲h̲ārid̲j̲ī leader, now driven to retreat into the region of the Zāb, the original seat of his revolt. But even though this batle allowed the Fāṭimid ruler to save his kingdom, it did not mean the end of the revolt, but only the beginning of the decline of K̲h̲ārid̲j̲ism. It remained for the Fāṭimid ruler, in order to extirpate the roots, to continue and subjugate its adherents the Kamlān, Birzāl, Huwwāra and other Zanāta elements in their fastnesses of the Aurès and the Zāb. Also, he still had to kill Abū Yazīd. But to put an end to his formidable enemy, Ismāʿīl was going to need less than one year of untiring warfare.

Thus after an interval of two months used to regroup his forces and to take suitable measures for restoring a country ravaged by war,—sc. a tax holiday for the current year, exemption of his subjects, including the tributaries, from all legal and extraordinary levies, and the undertaking by the state only to levy, during the ensuing years, the tithe and the *ṣadaḳa* in kind—Ismāʿīl went off in pursuit o the enemy. On the spot of his encampment marked off by the trench, in order to immortalise his brilliant victory, he had just marked out a new city, appropriately called Ṣabra al-Manṣūriyya, his future capital.

The rebel had withdrawn into the massif of Sālāt, so that Ismāʿīl had to dislodge him from there and force him to fall back to the north of the Zāb mountains, into the massif of ʿUḳbār, the Djabal Maʿādid. Thus harassed, Abū Yazīd retired into the strongholds of Shākir and Kiyāna. It was in this last, which was taken by storm, that he was at last taken prisoner, before dying of his wounds a few days later, in the night of Wednesday-Thursday 28 Muḥarram 336/ August 947. Having suppressed the rebellion and killed the "accursed" Khāridjī, Ismāʿīl could now make public his father's death and his own accession to the throne with the title of al-Manṣūr bi 'llāh. Then having pacified the Zāb from Masīla [*q.v.*] onwards, where the Banū Kamlān, previously uncompromising participants in the revolt but now submissive, had come to give him their submission, he proceeded to Tāhart in order to re-establish his authority there and to punish the rebellious tribes, notably the Lawāta [*q.v.*]. Did he then dream of leading his troops still further towards the central Maghrib with the intention of making an impression of his rival in al-Andalus, ʿAbd al-Raḥmān III and his Zanāta allies? Some Ismāʿīlī sources suggest this. In any case, a serious illness reduced him to inactivity, and when he at last recovered, he took the road towards Ifrīḳiya, on Saturday, 18 Rabīʿ II 336/6 November 947. He only arrived there two months later after a long stay at Sétif amongst his faithful adherents the Kutāma, from whom 14,000 families now accompanied him in order to settle in the new capital al-Manṣūriyya.

It was on Thursday, 27 Djumādā II 336/13 January 948 that Ismāʿīl entered there. His return was celebrated with great pomp, and in his presence was held a parade in the course of which the crowd was amused by the comic spectacle of the "man on the donkey", his skin stuffed with straw and hoisted on to the back of a camel and handed over to the tricks of an ape and monkey.

Thus only 15 months had been necessary for al-Manṣūr to finish off the leader of the Khāridjī insurrection. But hardly had he got back when he had to go personally to pacify the provinces of the Ḳasṭīliya region and the southern part of the Aurès and to reduce to obedience the Manāwa, Maghrāwa, Ḳalāla and other Yafran tribal elements stirred up by Faḍl, a son of Abū Yazīd. The death of Faḍl put an end to all Ibāḍī threats to the Fāṭimid kingdom. For the remainder of his all-too-short reign, less than seven years, al-Manṣūr devoted himself to dealing with internal and external affairs of his realm, which had suffered considerably from the revolt of the "man on the donkey". He resumed the wars of prestige undertaken by his predecessors in the central Maghrib against the Muslim Spanish ruler, who had not failed to support Abū Yazīd; and also in Sicily against Byzantium, which had, during the opening stages of the revolt, caused a deterioration of the authority of the Fāṭimids there. Order was soon re-established in Sicily, and rule there was entrusted to the faithful family of the Kalbids [*q.v.*], whilst in the farthest Maghrib, the influence of the Spanish Umayyads was contained and the Zanāta held in check by the tragic death of Abū Yazīd, which intimidated them. In the east, al-Manṣūr endeavoured equally to re-establish the prestige of his dynasty; he found time, before his demise, to give further weight to the Ismāʿīlī *daʿwa* against his ʿAbbāsid rivals and in support of its supporters in the Yemen and amongst the Ḳarāmiṭa of al-Aḥsā. It was on his orders that the chief of these last, Aḥmad al-Djannābī, was made in 340/951 to restore to Mecca the Black Stone which his father had carried off after seizing Mecca.

Before dying in his capital, hardly having reached the age of 40, on 28 Shawwāl 341/18 March 953, Ismāʿīl al-Manṣūr could justly pride himself on having restored in a short period of time, the tottering edifice of the Fāṭimid caliphate in Ifrīḳiya.

Bibliography: The main sources for the campaign of al-Manṣūr against Abū Yazīd are Ibn ʿIdhārī, *Bayān al-mughrib*, i, ed. G.S. Colin and E. Lévi-Provençal, Leiden 1948-51; the chronicle of Ibn Ḥammādo, ed. and tr. Vonderheyden as the *Histoire des rois Obeidites*, Algiers 1927; Maḳrīzī, *Ittiʿaẓ al-ḥunafāʾ*, Cairo 1948; Ibn Khaldūn, *Kitāb al-ʿIbar*, tr. de Slane as *Histoire des Berberes*, ii, 355 ff., iii, 209 ff.

The Sunnī and Ibāḍī sources have been used by R. Le Tourneau, in an exhaustive fashion, in *La révolte d'Abū Yazīd au Xᵉ siècle*, in *CT*, no. 2, Tunis 1953. For his part, S.M. Stern has the advantge of having utilised the Ismāʿīlī sources ignored by Le Tourneau in his *EI²* art. *Abū Yazīd.* F. Dachraoui has used all these sources in his *Le Califat fatimide au Maghreb. Histoire politique et institutions*, Tunis 1981, 183 ff., and has especially used the works of the Ḳāḍī al-Nuʿmān, *K. al-Madjālis wa 'l-musāyarāt*, at that time in ms., now ed. Chabbouh, Fequih and Yaalaoui, Tunis 1983, and *K. Iftitāḥ al-daʿwa*, ed. Dachraoui. But the basic source remains the *K. ʿUyūn al-akhbār wa-funūn al-athār* of the *dāʿī* Idrīs, from which Dachraoui has published extracts from vol. v as *Taʾrīkh al-dawla al-fāṭimiyya bi 'l-Maghrib*, Tunis 1981, and M. Yaʿlāwī has published a complete edition of the section devoted to the Maghrib, Tunis 1985. (F. DACHRAOUI)

AL-**MANṢŪR BI'LLĀH** AL-ḲĀSIM B. ʿALĪ AL-ʿIYĀNĪ (d. 393/1003), Zaydī *imām* of Yaman, and a descendant of al-Ḳāsim b. Ibrāhīm al-Rassī [see RASSIDS] but not of the latter's grandson al-Hādī ilā 'l-Ḥaḳḳ, the founder of the Zaydī imāmate in Yaman.

The dates given by late sources for his birth (310/922 or 316/928) are unreliable. More likely he was born between 330/941 and 340/951. Before his arrival in Yaman, he lived in Tardj, south of Bīsha, in the country of Khathʿam [*q.v.*]. He gained early a reputation as a religious scholar and was visited for over twenty years by Zaydīs from Yaman urging him to revolt. In 383/993 he rose in the Ḥidjāz, claiming the imāmate. The revolt was quickly subdued by the *amīr* of Makka, ʿĪsā b. Djaʿfar al-Ḥasanī, who arrived together with the rebel in Cairo in Muḥarram 384/February-March 994. The Fāṭimid caliph al-ʿAzīz treated him well, and after a few months permitted him to return to the Ḥidjāz together with the *amīr* (al-Maḳrīzī, *Itti ʿāẓ al-ḥunafāʾ*, ed. al-Shayyāl, i, Cairo 1967, 278, 281-2). In his first invasion of Yaman, which occured probably in 387/997 or 388/998, he occupied Ṣaʿda, the stronghold of the descendants of al-

Hādī, and brought Nadjrān and the territories of Khawlān, Wādaᶜa and Bakīl under his control. After his departure to Tardj, however, his administration quickly crumbled. In Muḥarram 389/January 999 he returned permanently to Yaman. During the next two years, he extended his sway over much of the highlands of Yaman. In the heyday of his reign, his rule extended from the Bilād Khathᶜam to Ṣanᶜāʾ and Dhamār, and included the territory of Khawlān al-ᶜĀliya, ᶜAns, Alhān, Ḥimyar with Shibām Aḳyān, Kuḥlan, Lāᶜa, Djabal Maswar and Djabal Tays. His extensive kingdom, however, had no outlet to the sea, and his hopes to gain control of the Red Sea port of ᶜAththar, ruled by two, presumably Ziyādid, slave *amīrs*, by diplomacy or military means, came to nought. For his residence in Yaman he came to prefer the town of ᶜIyān, a two days' trip south-east of Ṣaᶜda, in the territory of the Banū Salmān, who were among his most loyal supporters. He also acquired an estate which he brought newly under irrigation in Wādī Madhāb, between ᶜIyān and Ṣaᶜda, and built a castle there. In Ṣaᶜda he restored the ruined castle of the *Imām* Aḥmad al-Nāṣir, son of al-Hādī, which lay outside the town, for his own use.

His position in the old capital of the Zaydī state was, however, precarious, as the population and the tribes of the neighbourhood were predominantly loyal to the descendants of al-Hādī, whose allegiance to his imāmate proved to be fickle. After his failure to reduce the rebellious Banu 'l-Ḥārith in Nadjrān to obedience in two successive campaigns, the latent opposition came out into the open, led by Ibrāhīm al-Malīḥ b. Muḥammad b. al-Mukhtār b. Aḥmad al-Nāṣir and Yūsuf b. Yaḥyā b. Aḥmad al-Nāṣir. The latter had claimed the imāmate before the arrival of al-Manṣūr with the regnal name al-Dāᶜī ilā 'l-Ḥaḳḳ and had relinquished his claim only under duress. Al-Manṣūr's cause was lost when his governor of Dhamār, al-Ḳāsim b. Ḥusayn al-Zaydī, turned against him and captured his son Djaᶜfar, governor of Ṣanᶜaʾ, in Dhu 'l-Ḥidjdja 391/October 1001. When al-Zaydī voluntarily released his son, al-Manṣūr consented to a peace agreement in Ṣafar 392/January 1002. He declined al-Zaydī's offer to let him keep the rule over Bakīl and Wādaᶜa because of the lack of support he had received from them, and withdrew to private life in Madhāb and ᶜIyān. Al-Zaydī now supported the imāmate of Yūsuf al-Dāᶜī, who gained wide recognition, As al-Manṣūr's qualifications for the imāmate were now impugned by many, he wrote an "Answer to the rejectors" (*Radd ᶜalā 'l-rāfiḍa*) against his critics. After a severe illness, he died on 9 Ramaḍān 393/11 July 1003 in ᶜIyān. His shrine there was left unharmed in the razing of the town of ᶜIyān by the *Imām* al-Manṣūr al-Ḳāsim b. Muḥammad [*q.v.*], in Dhu 'l-Ḳaᶜda 1026/November 1617. Later Zaydīs generally recognised him as a full *imām*, no doubt on account of his scholarship, and denied this title to his rival Yūsuf al-Dāᶜī.

Of his writings, only excerpts from his *Kitāb al-Tafrīᶜ*, a collection of legal opinions, are known to be extant, besides letters and poems quoted in his *Sīra*. Other works are known by title (see A. M. al-Ḥibshī [al-Ḥabshī], *Muʾallafāt ḥukkām al-Yaman*, Wiesbaden 1979, 21-3). In his teaching, he generally followed the doctrine of al-Ḳāsim b. Ibrāhīm and al-Hādī, although strict followers of the doctrine of al-Hādī like the *faḳīh* ᶜAbd al-Malik b. Ghiṭrīf accused him of deviation and stirred up opposition to him.

Bibliography: al-Ḥusayn b. Aḥmad b. Yaᶜḳūb al-Hamdānī, *Sīrat al-imām al-Manṣūr bi 'llāh al-Ḳāsim b. ᶜAlī*, ms. Brit. Mus. Or. 3816; Ḥumayd al-Muḥallī, *al-Ḥadāʾiḳ al-wardiyya*, ii, mss., biography of al-Manṣūr; al-Ḥadjūrī, *Rawḍat al-akhbār*, iv, ms. Paris 5982 (see *JNES*, xxxii [1973], 179-80), fol. 240; Ibn al-Daybaᶜ, *Ḳurrat al-ᶜuyūn*, ed. Muḥammad al-Akwaᶜ al-Ḥiwālī, Cairo n.d., i, 228-31; Yaḥyā b. al-Ḥusayn, *Ghayāt al-amānī*, ed. S. ᶜA. ᶜĀshūr and M. M. Ziyāda, Cairo 1968, 227-34; W. Madelung, *Der Imam al-Qāsim ibn Ibrāhīm*, Berlin 1965, 194-7. (W. MADELUNG)

AL-MANSŪR BI'LLĀH AL-ḲĀSIM B. MUḤAMMAD, the *imām* and eponymous founder of the Ḳāsimī dynasty (*al-dawla al-ḳāsimiyya*) of Zaydī *imāms* which dominated much of Yemen from the early 11th/17th century to the outbreak of the republican revolution in 1962. Like almost all recognised Rassī *imāms*, he was descended from al-Hādī ilā 'l-Ḥaḳḳ Yaḥyā b. al-Ḥusayn b. al-Ḳāsim al-Rassī (d. 298/911), who established the temporal authority of the Zaydī imāmate in Yemen. Their aristocratic pedigree notwithstanding, al-Ḳāsim's forbears from the death of Yūsuf al-Dāᶜī, the great-grandson of al-Hādī Yaḥyā, kept a low political profile, while members of other branches of al-Hādī Yaḥyā's descendants filled the imāmate. Al-Ḳāsim's greatest claim to history is his initiation of the lengthy but sporadic rebellion against Ottoman rule in Yemen, which rule had been continuous since 945/1538-9 and ended in 1045/1645 with the expulsion of the last Turks from Yemen by al-Ḳāsim's son, Imām al-Muʾayyad bi'llāh Muḥammad.

Al-Ḳāsim was born during Ṣafar 967/November 1559, probably in the northwestern Zaydī district of al-Sharaf. Recognising a strong *imām*-like potential in his noble origins and his marked propensity for scholarship, and having for some time forestalled any serious claimant to the imāmate, the Turks pursued the young al-Ḳāsim into a peripatetic life of secluded study, authorship and preparation for leadership. Formal proclamation of his claim to the imāmate (*daᶜwa*) in late Muḥarram or early Ṣafar 1006/September 1597 occured at Ḥadīd (possibly Djadīd) al-Ḳāra, a village in the northern district of Ḥudjūr. It was coupled with an appeal to all Yemenis to rebel against the Ottoman Turks for their irreligious and corrupt rule. At the time, Yemen was governed by Ḥasan Pasha, during whose remarkably long term (989-1013/1581-1604) local Ottoman fortunes had reached a high point: he had secured the loyalty of several Zaydī aristocrats, especially among those descendants of Imām al-Mutawakkil ᶜalā 'llāh Sharaf al-Dīn Yaḥyā (d. 965/1558) who survived the mass exile of their family to Istanbul in 994/1586.

The rebellion began modestly in the Zaydī heartlands northwest of Ṣanᶜāʾ, in the districts of Ḥudjūr, al-Ahnūm and Ḥadjdja, and spread quickly southwards into the regions of al-Ḥayma, Sanḥān and Ānis, as local chiefs joined, if often more out of personal grievance with the Ottomans than loyalty to the new *imām*. After about a year of demoralising reverses, however, the Turks and their native allies, led principally by Ḥasan Pasha's capable commander, the *ketkhudā* Sinān, regained their balance and turned the tables on al-Ḳāsim. The latter lost all of his earlier gains, including Shahāra, his principal base, where he was besieged for 15 months before escaping to Baraṭ, in the remote north, leaving his eldest son Muḥammad to surrender it and to enter Ottoman captivity at Kawkabān (Muḥarram 1011/June-July 1602). When local support for the Turks was eroded during the governorship of the harsh Sinān Pasha (1013-6/1604-8), al-Ḳāsim resumed the offensive and recaptured many places.

Matters became settled for a time after 11 Dhu 'l-Ḥidjdja 1016/28 March 1608, when, on petition from Dja^cfer Pasha, Sinān Pasha's successor, al-Ḳāsim agreed to a ten-year peace treaty, by which the Ottomans recognised his control over much of northern Yemen and undertook to release his son Muḥammad.

Serious disorders within the Ottoman ranks during 1022/1613 induced al-Ḳāsim to breach the peace with a new offensive in the northern sector. Although at first it succeeded, with even Ṣa^cda falling to the *imām* for a time, Dja^cfer Pasha was able to restore Ottoman unity and achieve some modest gains, including the capture of al-Ḥasan, another of al-Ḳāsim's sons. Thereafter, each party tasted victory and defeat, until Dja^cfer Pasha, learning of his recall and wishing to depart with his province in order, obtained from al-Ḳāsim a one-year truce by which each side recognised the other's gains (1 Radjab 1025/15 July 1616). Hostilities recommenced the following year when Meḥmed Pasha, Dja^cfer's overconfident replacement, declined al-Ḳāsim's offer to extend the truce. Nevertheless, by Djumādā I 1028/April-May 1619 the Turks, dismayed at how well supplied with firearms were the *imām*'s supporters, agreed with al-Ḳāsim to another ten-year peace based upon the mutual recognition of each party's possessions and the release of all prisoners except al-Ḥasan b. al-Ḳāsim.

When the Imām al-Ḳāsim died and was buried at Shahāra in mid-Rabī^c I 1029/February 1620, he controlled substantial territories in almost all directions from Ṣan^cā^ɔ, the Ottoman provincial capital. At least five of his sons survived him, and two of them succeeded as *imām*—al-Mu^ɔayyad bi'llāh Muḥammad (1029-54/1620-44) and al-Mutawakkil ^calā 'llāh Ismā^cīl (1054-87/1644-76). It was during al-Ḳāsim's time that English and Dutch ships first secured limited commercial privileges in Yemen, although negotiations were conducted with Ottoman rather than imāmic officials.

In view of his numerous impressive military gains against four Ottoman governors over more than two decades, it is hardly surprising that most accounts of Imām al-Ḳāsim dwell on his role as a warrior *imām*, so much so that one of his biographers (al-Djurmūzī) arranged the history of his imāmate according to his four "risings (*nahaḍāt*)" against the occupying power. But this should not obscure the fact that he commanded wide respect among fellow-Zaydīs for his scholarly attainments and extensive knowledge of Islamic law and religious practice. Al-Ḥabshī's study of the literary output of the various *imāms* attributes to al-Ḳāsim's authorship some 41 works, a productivity surpassed apparently by only four of his peers. His compositions, both in poetry and in prose, range in length from one or two folios to several hundred and deal mainly with jurisprudence and Zaydī dogma. Although some were produced prior to the proclamation of his *da^cwa*, others must have been composed during the military off-season in his wars with the Turks. Among the more frequently mentioned are *al-I^ctiṣām*, a substantial work on *ḥadīth* uncompleted at his death; *al-Asās li-^caḳā^ɔid al-akyās*, concerning the fundamental principles of the faith and widely commented upon; *al-Irshād ilā sabīl al-rashād*, a collection of articles; and several compilations of his answers to questions regarding law and dogma.

Bibliography : The principal source for the life of al-Ḳāsim is a biography by Aḥmad b. Muḥammad al-Sharafī (d. 1055/1645-6), an early supporter of the *imām* and one of his officials. A ms. of the second part of this *sīra* (title unknown) at Edinburgh formed the basis for A. S. Tritton's *The rise of the Imams of Sanaa*, London 1925; it is possible that this *sīra* and another title attributed to the same author, *al-La^ɔālī al-muḍiyya fī akhbār a^ɔimmat al-zaydiyya*, are one and the same. However, the best known account of al-Ḳāsim's imāmate remains *al-Durra al-muḍiyya fi 'l-sīra al-Ḳasimiyya* (and its abridgement, *al-Nubdha al-mushīra*) by al-Djurmūzī (d. 1077/1667), who freely acknowledges his debt to al-Sharafī. Yet a third biography is the anonymous *Sīrat al-Manṣūr bi 'llāh al-Ḳāsim* described by Ayman Sayyid (*Maṣādir ta^ɔrīkh al-Yaman*, Cairo 1974, 332) as a history of Yemen 985-1085/1577-1674. Also rich in details are the *Rawḥ al-rūḥ* by ^cĪsā b. Luṭf Allāh b. al-Muṭahhar (d. 1048/1638), *Ghāyat al-amānī* by Yaḥyā b. al-Ḥusayn (d. *ca.* 1100/1688), al-Ḳāsim's grandson (ed. Sa^cīd ^cAbd al-Fattāḥ ^cĀshūr, Cairo 1968, ii, 770-814), and *al-Iḥsān* by al-Mawza^cī (d. *ca.* 1031/1621), unique among these accounts for its anti-Zaydī bias. For other ms. source materials, especially those of the 12th/18th century, consult al-Ḥabshī, *Mu^ɔallafāt ḥukkām al-Yaman*, Wiesbaden 1979, 127 f., which work also identifies, describes and locates the mss. of all works attributed to al-Ḳāsim's authorship (pp. 128-36). Ottoman archival materials for al-Ḳāsim's era are extensive.

An important monograph on this figure is by al-Maddāḥ, *al-^cUthmāniyya wa 'l-Imām al-Ḳāsim*, Djudda 1982. Other published secondary materials include Muḥibbī, *Khulāṣat al-athar*, Cairo 1284/1867-8, i, 485-7, ii, 73-6, 217 f., iii, 293-7, iv, 296-9; Aḥmed Rāshid, *Ta^ɔrīkh-i Yemen we Ṣan^cā^ɔ*, Istanbul 1291/1874-5, i, 170-223; Wüstenfeld, *Jemen im xi (xvii) Jahrhundert*, Göttingen 1884, 38-48; ^cĀṭif Pasha, *Yemen ta^ɔrīkhi*, Istanbul 1326/1908, 86-96; Zabāra, *Ithāf al-muhtadīn*, Ṣan^cā^ɔ 1343/1924-5, 78 f.; Shawkānī, *al-Badr al-ṭāli^c*, Cairo 1348/1929-30, ii, 47-51; Djurāfī, *al-Muktaṭaf min ta^ɔrīkh al-Yaman*, Cairo 1951, 141-4; ^cArshī, *Bulūgh al-marām*, ed. al-Karmalī, Cairo 1939, 65 f.; Muṣṭafā Sālim, *al-Fatḥ al-^cUthmānī*, Cairo 1969, 338-69; Bayḥānī, *Ashi^{cc}at al-anwār*, Cairo 1391/1971-2, ii, 244, n.l.

(J. R. Blackburn)

MANṢŪR al-NAMARĪ, Arab poet of the 2nd/8th century.

1. *Life.* Abu 'l-Faḍl or Abu 'l-Ḳāsim Manṣūr [b. Salama] b. al-Zibriḳān al-Namarī, from the Namir b. Ḳāsiṭ, one of the tribes of Rabī^ca b. Nizār, was born at Ra's al-^cAyn probably at the beginning of the 2nd/8th century. Since the sources give no precise information regarding the various stages of life, it is useful, indeed essential, to examine his relations with the poets and leading political figures of his time. In fact, Manṣūr al-Namarī knew Muslim b. al-Walīd (d. 208/823) whom he met at a poetry symposium at the home of al-Faḍl b. Yaḥyā b. Khālid al-Barmakī (d. 193/808), Marwān b. Abī Ḥafṣa (d. 182/797), Salm al-Khāsir (d. 186/802) and al-Khuraymī (d. 214/829), whom he met at the court of the caliph Hārūn al-Rashīd (d. 193/809). Two other poets should be mentioned here: the first is a certain Manṣūr b. Bādja, who was sufficiently wealthy to avoid the need to court and praise the great and who, according to some sources, was allegedly the author of the *ḳaṣīda ^cayniyya* dedicated to al-Rashīd by al-Namarī. The second, who is far the most important in the life of al-Namarī is Kulthūm b. ^cAmr al-^cAttābī (d. 220/835 [*q.v.*]). In fact, it is stated in the sources, and notably in the *Ṭabaḳāt* of Ibn al-Mu^ctazz and in the *Aghānī*, that al-^cAttābī was the "teacher in verse composition" of al-Namarī, who admired him "for his sobriety, his dedication, his vast knowledge and his general erudi-

tion in literary subjects''. Moreover, these contacts were not limited to the poetic sphere. It was al-ʿAttābī who introduced al-Namarī to al-Faḍl b. Yaḥyā, who persuaded him to come from al-Djazīra to Baghdād and introduced him to al-Rashīd. Subsequently, rivalry broke out between the two poets, and it was through the good offices of the celebrated Ṭāhir b. al-Ḥusayn (d. 207/822 [*q.v.*]) that they were reconciled.

Besides these poets, Manṣūr al-Namarī was acquainted with numerous political figures. In addition to the Barmakids and especially al-Faḍl Yaḥyā and his brother Djaʿfar (d. 187/803) and the afore-mentioned Ṭāhir b. al-Ḥusayn, he knew al-Faḍl b. al-Rabīʿ b. Yūnus (d. 208/824 [*q.v.*]), an enemy of the Barmakids and himself the vizier of al-Rashīd. Al-Faḍl b. al-Rabīʿ intervened with the caliph to secure the release of the poet, who had been imprisoned for his proclaimed Shīʿī tendencies. A similar intervention was was assured him, we are told, by Yazīd b. Mazyad al-Shaybānī (d. 185/801), the governor of Ādharbāydjān. Al-Namarī knew al-Maʾmūn (d. 218/833) then heir to the throne, at whose court he met numerous poets. But according to all the evidence, it was the caliph al-Rashīd who influenced the life and who signed the death warrant of the poet. In fact, al-Rashīd invited al-Namarī to his court, where the latter addressed eulogies to him and received gifts from him. However, when the caliph became aware of his pro-ʿAlid tendencies, he cast him into disgrace, imprisoned him and ordered Abū ʿIṣma, a pro-ʿAbbāsid Zaydī, to torture and execute him. But the latter was only able, on arriving in Mecca, to attend the obsequies of the poet, probably in 190/805.

2. *Works*. Of the hundred-page *Dīwān* attributed by Ibn al-Nadīm (d. 385/995) to the poet and of the anthology or *Ikhtiyār shiʿr al-Namarī* attributed by Yāḳūt (d. 622/1225) to Aḥmad b. Ṭāhir, it has been possible to assemble only 57 fragments totalling 386 verses gleaned from various historical or literary sources, of which the most important are the *Aghānī* (14 pieces), the *Amālī* of al-Ḳālī (d. 356/979) and *al-Tibyān* or *Sharḥ dīwān al-Mutanabbī* by al-ʿUkbarī (d. 616/1219) (10 pieces), the *Ṭabaḳāt* of Ibn al-Muʿtazz, the *Zahr al-adab* of al-Ḥuṣrī (d. 413/1022), the *Muwāzana* of al-Āmidī (d. 371/981) and the *K. al-Ṣināʿatayn* of al-ʿAskarī (d. 395/1005) (7 pieces). On the other hand, two modern authors, al-Rifaʿī in *ʿAṣr al-Maʾmūn* (10 pieces) and especially al-ʿĀmidī in the *Aʿyān al-Shīʿa* (15 pieces) have taken an interest, among many others, in Manṣūr al-Namarī.

These 57 fragments, of which 14 may be disregarded since they are also attributed to other poets, are of unequal length; only 15 contain 7 verses or more and may thus be considered *ḳaṣīdas*, 16 others contain one verse, 11 others three verses, and 8 two verses.

The poet uses 10 different metres and, in particular, *ṭawīl, basīṭ, kāmil* and *wāfir* (respectively 20, 8, 8 and 6 fragments) which are the ''noble'' classical metres; *ramal*, *munsariḥ*, *hazadj* and *mutaḳārib*, the ''light'' metres, are used only once. For rhyme, al-Namarī uses 14 of the 28 letters of the alphabet: most prominently used are *lām, bāʾ*, *rāʾ*, *mīm, dāl* and *nūn* (respectively 14, 9, 8, 5 and 4 times), a common phenomenon in Arabic poetry. *Hamza, hāʾ*, *fāʾ*, *ḳāf* and *kāf* are used only once.

Moreover, in his poetry (or in that portion of it which is available to us) al-Namarī makes use of the principal poetic genres. While he reserves for satire (*hidjāʾ*), description (*waṣf*), boastfulness (*fakhr*) and lament (*rithāʾ*) only respectively 1, 2, 3 and 4 pieces, on the other hand he devotes to erotic poetry (*ghazal*) 17 fragments which are in fact nothing more than amorous preludes, where the poet evokes youth and looks forward with foreboding the old age. But, according to all the evidence, it was laudatory poetry (*madḥ*) which al-Namarī practised most prominently, In fact, 20 pieces or 200 verses are devoted to *madḥ*, 6 of them for the above-mentioned viziers and governors and 14 for al-Rashīd; noble lineage, munificence, courage, dedication, competence in handling the affairs of the state, in other words the socio-politico-religious qualities commonly recognised, are the principal themes of the laudatory poems and especially of those which are dedicated to the caliph. However, some authors make the remark that al-Namarī is not at all pro-ʿAbbasīd and that he only praises al-Rashīd with prudent dissimulation (*taḳiyya*) as do many poets. Moreover, he displays his Shī-ʿism in 9 pieces totalling 69 verses, emanating exclusively, admittedly, from Shi-ʿī sources. The poet expresses his deep affection for the ʿAlids, mourns al-Ḥusayn (d. 61/681), displays his hatred of the Umayyads and the ʿAbbāsids to whom he denies all merit, and calls for armed revolt with the purpose of avenging the sons of Fāṭima.

In conclusion, in poems of classical structure and in a pure language and a sometimes quite virulent style, al-Namarī practises the principal genres, distinguishing himself in ''political'' or ''opposition'' poetry in spite of the contradictions which the majority of classical Arab poets display.

Bibliography: In addition to the works mentioned in the article, see T. al-ʿAshshāsh, *Shiʿr Manṣūr al-Namarī*, Publications of the Arab Academy of Damascus, 1401/1981, and the reviews by Shākir al-Faḥḥām, in *MMIA*, lvi (Oct. 1981), and M. Yaʿlawī, in *Ḥawliyyāt al-Djāmiʿa al-Tūnisiyya*, xxi (1982). (T. EL-ACHÈCHE)

MANṢŪR AL-YAMAN ABU 'L-ḲĀSIM AL-ḤASAN B. FARADJ B. ḤAWSHAB B. ZĀDHĀN AL-NADJDJĀR AL-KŪFĪ, often known as IBN ḤAWSHAB, was the founder of the Ismāʿīlī *daʿwa* in Yaman. Other forms of his name and genealogy are less well attested; later Ismāʿīlī tradition considered him a descendant of Muslim b. ʿAḳīl b. Abī Ṭālib.

He was a Kūfan Imāmī Shīʿī, probably from Nars, a canal near Kūfa, learned in the religious sciences, and was won for the Ismāʿīlī cause by a *dāʿī*, who is identified in a Fāṭimid source as the chief *dāʿī* Fīrūz and by the Ḳarmaṭī account as Ibn Abi 'l-Fawāris, an assistant of ʿAbdān, the chief *dāʿī* in ʿIrāḳ. According to his own account, as related by Ḳāḍī al-Nuʿmān, he was introduced by the *dāʿī* to the *imām* who, after a training period, sent him together with the Yamanī ʿAlī b. al-Faḍl al-Djayshānī to Yaman. They arrived there early in 268/late summer 881 and separated. Ibn Ḥawshab passed through Ṣanʿāʾ and Djanad and stayed some time in ʿAdan before establishing himself, allegedly in accordance with the instructions of the *imām*, in the village of ʿAdan Lāʿa in territory under the rule of the Ḥiwālids (Yaʿfurids). In 270/883-4 he began his mission, publicly proclaiming the imminent appearance of the Mahdī, and quickly attracted a large following. After an attack on his followers by a local Ḥiwālid garrison he occupied the stronghold of ʿAbr Muḥarram on a mountain below Djabal Maswar (*ca.* 272/885-6). Later, he captured Bayt Fāʾis on Djabal Tukhlā and fortified Bayt Rayb on Djabal Maswar as his residence. He sent the *dāʿī* Abu 'l-Malāḥim as governor to Djabal Tays and conquered Bilād Shāwir, ʿAyyān and Ḥumlān. His first campaign against Shibām, the residence of the Ḥiwālids, failed. Later, he took the town aided by the treason of a Ḥiwālid client, but was soon forced to leave again. These events took place before 290/903, though their exact dates are unknown. It is evident, however, that he was firmly established before 278-9/892-3 when the *dāʿī* Abū ʿAbd Allāh al-Shīʿī [*q.v.*] was sent to him from ʿIrāḳ to be trained for his mission in the Maghrib. He sent *dāʿīs* also to other countries: al-Haytham, cousin of his wife who was the daughter of a local Shīʿī, to Sind; ʿAbd Allāh b. al-ʿAbbās al-Shāwirī to Egypt; Abū Zakariyyāʾ al-Ṭamāmī (al-Ẓamāmī?) to al-Baḥrayn; and others to al-Yamāma and Hind (presumably Gudjarāt). His *laḳab* al-Manṣūr or Manṣūr al-Yaman, which he was given after his early successes, implied ideas both of a restorer of Yamanī glory and a precursor of the Mahdī (see B. Lewis, *The regnal titles of the first Abbasid caliphs*, in *Zakir Husain presentation volume*, Delhi 1968, 16-18).

In 282/905 ʿAlī b. al-Faḍl, who had initially established himself further south in the Bilād Yāfiʿ, seized the territories of Djaʿfar b. Ismāʿīl al-Manākhī, including the mountain stronghold of al-Mudhaykhira, and thus became a powerful rival of Ibn Ḥawshab. He had acted independently of the latter from the outset, and doubts about his loyalty to the Fāṭimid cause seem to have induced ʿUbayd Allāh al-Mahdī to go to the Maghrib rather than to Yaman as previously planned. ʿAlī's conquest of Ṣanʿāʾ from the Ḥiwālid Asʿad b. Abī Yaʿfur in Muḥarram 293/November 905 gave Ibn Ḥawshab the opportunity to occupy Shibām. ʿAlī came to meet him there; reports that Ibn Ḥawshab met him in Ṣanʿāʾ seem unreliable. The meeting was evidently uneasy, and Ibn Ḥawshab warned his rival against overextending himself by further campaigns. The latter did not heed the advice and had to be rescued by Ibn Ḥawshab when he ran into troubles in a raid to al-Bayāḍ. Ibn Ḥawshab lost Shibām during the occupation of Ṣanʿāʾ by the Zaydī *imām* al-Hādī and his allies, but regained the town before the end of 293/906. He held it during the following years while Ṣanʿāʾ was under the rule of ʿAlī b. al-Faḍl. In Shawwāl 297/June-July 910 his followers briefly entered Ṣanʿāʾ after the withdrawal of the army of al-Hādī, but left again because of their small number. Asʿad b. Abī Yaʿfur occupied Ṣanʿāʾ and repeatedly raided Shibām, but failed to dislodge the followers of Ibn Ḥawshab permanently. In Muḥarram 299/August 911, ʿAlī b. al-Faḍl retook Ṣanʿāʾ and publicly repudiated his allegiance to the Fāṭimid caliph al-Mahdī. He wrote to Ibn Ḥawshab demanding his allegiance. When the latter reproached him for his break with the Fāṭimid cause, he marched against him, taking Shibām and Djabal Dhukhār. After a few battles, he besieged Ibn Ḥawshab in Djabal Maswar for eight months. In Ramaḍān 299/April 912, Ibn Ḥawshab was forced to sue for peace and to surrender his son to ʿAlī b. al-Faḍl as a token of his submission. The latter returned the son to him a year later with a golden necklace. Ibn Ḥawshab died on Djabal Maswar on 11 Djumādā II 302/December 914. This date, given by the continuation of the *Sīrat al-Hādī*, is to be preferred to accounts of later sources suggesting dates two or three decades later. The dispute about the succession which these accounts describe as immediately following Ibn Ḥawshab's death was evidently considerable later.

Ismāʿīlī tradition ascribes to Manṣūr al-Yaman a *Kitāb al-Rushd wa 'l-hidāya*, of which fragments are extant, and a *Kitāb al-ʿĀlim wa 'l-ghulām* also ascribed to his son Djaʿfar. The authenticity of both, and especially the latter, must be considered uncertain, although both appear to belong to pre-Fāṭimid Ismāʿīlī literature. A *Risāla* of an otherwise unknown Ibn Ḥamdūn which "he ascribed to Manṣūr al-Yaman" is quoted by the Yamanī *dāʿī* Ibrāhīm al-Ḥamidī (d. 557/1162).

Bibliography: al-ʿAbbāsī al-ʿAlawī, *Sīrat al-Hādī ilā 'l-Ḥaḳḳ*, ed. Suhayl Zakkār, Beirut 1972, 389-402; al-Nuʿmān b. Muḥammad, *Iftitāḥ al-daʿwa*, ed. Wadād al-Ḳāḍī, Beirut 1970, 32-62; Ibn Malīk al-Ḥammādī, *Kashf, asrār al-Bāṭiniyya*, in al-Isfarāyinī, *al-Tabṣīr*, ed. M. Z. al-Kawtharī, Baghdād 1955, 201-14; al-Maḳrīzī, *Ittiʿāẓ al-ḥunafāʾ*, ed. al-Shayyāl, i, Cairo 1967, 166-7; Idrīs b. al-Ḥasan, *ʿUyūn al-akhbār*, iv, ed. Muṣṭafā Ghālib, Beirut 1973, 396-403, vi, ed. M. Ghālib, Beirut [1979], 31-44; Ibn al-Daybaʿ, *Ḳurrat al-ʿuyūn*, ed. Muḥammad al-Akwaʿ al-Ḥiwālī, Cairo n.d., i, 181-213; Yaḥyā b. al-Ḥusayn, *Ghāyat al-amānī*, ed. S.ʿA. ʿAshūr and M. M. Ziyāda, Cairo 1968, 191-202, 219; C. van Arendonk, *Les débuts de l'imamat Zaidite au Yemen*, tr. J. Ryckmans, Leiden 1960, 119-24, 237-48; Ḥ. F. al-Hamdānī, *al-Ṣulayḥiyyūn*, Cairo 1955, 30-49; I. K. Poonawala, *Biobibliography of Ismāʿīlī literature*, Malibu 1977, 34, 74; H. Halm, *Die Sīrat Ibn Ḥaušab: die Ismailitische daʿwa im Jemen und die Fatimiden*, in *WO*, xii (1981), 108-35.

(W. Madelung)

AL-MANṢŪRA, the principal city of the province of Sind under the Arabs. It was founded by ʿAmr b. Muḥammad b. al-Ḳasim, the son of the celebrated conqueror of Sind, in 120/738 or shortly afterwards (al-Balādhurī, *Futūḥ*, 444; al-Yaʿḳūbī, ii, 389; Caetani, *Chronographia Islamica*, 1507), 47 miles to the north-east of modern Haydarabad [see HIND]. i. Geography, at iii, 407], Al-Bīrūnī's statement, according to which Manṣūra is merely a Muslim name given by Muḥammad b. al-Ḳāsim to the ancient city of Brahmanābād at the time of its conquest (*al-Djamāhir fī maʿrifat al-djawāhir*, Ḥaydarābād, Deccan 1355, 48; *al-Ḳānūn al-Masʿūdī*, Ḥaydarābād, Deccan 1954, 552), is at variance with the earlier traditions, though the sites of the two cities were certainly close to each other. The attribution of the founding of Manṣūra to the Umayyad governor and adventurer Manṣūr b. Djumhūr (Hidayet Hosain, in *EI*[1], s.v.; al-Masʿūdī, *Murūdj*, i, 379; Yāḳūt, *Muʿdjam al-buldān*, s.v.) or to the ʿAbbāsid caliph Abū Djaʿfar al-Manṣūr (al-Yaʿḳūbī, *Buldān*, 238; al-Idrīsī, *Opus geographicum*, Naples-Rome 1970, i, 169; al-Ḳazwīnī, *Āthār al-bilād*, ed. Wüstenfeld, Göttingen 1848, ii, 83; Elliot and Dowson, *The history of India as told by its own historians* London 1867, i, 136; M. Ikram, *Āb-i kawthar*, Lahore 1968, 28-9) stems from the desire to forge a connection between the name of the city and the name of its founder. There is, however, no need to seek such a connection: Abu 'l-Fidāʾ correctly observed that numerous cities were named Mansūra "as an omen for victory and durability" (*tafāʾulan lahā bi 'l-naṣr wa 'l-dawām*) (Abu 'l-Fidāʾ, *Taḳwīm al-buldān*, ed. Schier, Dresden n.d, 194; cf. al-Bīrūnī, *al-Ḳānūn al-Masʿūdī*, *loc. cit.*) Manṣūra was founded in order to provide the Arab conquerors with a secure base from which they could attempt to expand their rule in the hostile Hindu environment.

Classical Arab geographers of the 3rd/9th and 4th/10th centuries describe Manṣūra as a flourishing city, which served as a centre for a number of smaller towns. It was surrounded by a branch of the Indus and therefore looked like an island. Its land was fertile, and it was the scene of both agricultural and commercial activity. The ruler, who is said to have been a scion of Ḳuraysh, bore allegiance to the ʿAbbāsid caliphs and during the second half of the 4th/10th century also recognised the authority of the Buwayhids (al-Muḳaddasī, 485). It seems, however, that the central government was unable to exercise effective control over Sind and the rulers of Manṣūra therefore enjoyed considerable independence.

The importance of Manṣūra diminished in later periods. It is briefly mentioned in connection with the conquests of Maḥmūd of Ghazna [*q.v.*] (in 416/1025-6; Ibn al-Athīr, ix, 243) and with the Khwārazmian incursions into India in 623/1226 (Djūzdjānī, *Ṭabaḳāt-i Nāṣirī*, Calcutta 1864, 143). Abu 'l-Fidāʾ, who completed his *Taḳwīm al-buldān* in 721/1321, says that all cities called Manṣūra, including that in Sind, were in ruins despite their auspicious name (*loc. cit.*, cf. Badāyūnī, *Muntakhab al-tawārīkh*, Lucknow 1868, 154; tr. W. H. Lowe, Patna 1973, ii, 70). Though this is a reflection on the futility of human endeavour rather than a statement of reliable historical fact, Manṣūra was indeed ruined around Abu 'l-Fidāʾ's period. The fact that it is not mentioned by Ibn Baṭṭūṭa is an indication in this direction.

The exact location of Manṣūra, the question whether it was built on the site of Brahmanābād or at some distance from it, as well as the precise date and circumstances of its destruction and abandonment, are inconclusively discussed by several authors. (see *Bibl.*).

Bibliography: Balādhurī, *Futūḥ*, 439, 445; Ṭabarī, ii, 1895, iii, 80, 491; Masʿūdī, *Murūdj*, i, 207, 378; Iṣṭakhrī, 35, 175, 177; Ibn Ḥawḳal, 320-2; Muḳaddasī, 53, 476, 479, 480, 485; Buzurg b. Shahriyār, *ʿAdjāʾib al-Hind*, Leiden 1883-6. 2-3, 103; Bīrūnī, *Taḥḳīḳ mā li 'l-Hind*, Haydarabad, Deccan 1958, 16; ʿAllāmī, *Āʾīn Akbarī*, Calcutta 1948, i, 465, ii, 330, iii, 67 (identifying Manṣūra with Bhakkar; a view disputed by Bazmee Ansari in *EI*[2] art. BHAKKAR). J. McMurdo, *Dissertation on the river Indus*, in *JRAS*, i (1834), 20-44; Elliot and Dowson, *The history of India*, i, 368-74 and index; M.R. Haig, *On the sites of Bramanābād and Manṣūra in Sind*, in *JRAS*, xvi (1884), 281-94; S. Razia Jafri, *Description of India (Hind and Sind) in the works of al-Iṣṭakhrī, Ibn Ḥauqal and al-Maqdisī*, in *Bull. of the Institute of Islamic Studies (Aligarh)*, v (1961), 8-9, 13, 19-20, 35-6 and passim; I. H. Qureshi, *The Muslim community in the Indo-Pakistan subcontinent*, The Hague 1962, 43; H. T. Lambrick, *Sind. A general introduction*. Ḥaydarabād, Sind 1964, index (including extensive bibliography); Mumtaz Husain A. Pathan, *Foundation of al-Manṣūra and its situation*, in *IC*, xxxviii (1964), 183-94; idem, *Present ruins of al-Manṣūra*, in *IC*, xlii (1968), 25-33; Y. Friedmann, *A contribution to the early history of Islam in India*, in M. Rosen-Ayalon, ed., *Studies in memory of Gaston Wiet*, Jerusalem 1977, 314-15.

(Y. FRIEDMANN)

AL-**MANṢŪRA**, a town in Lower Egypt near Damietta (Dimyāṭ [*q.v.*]), and chief place of the *mudīriyyat al-Daḳahliyya*. The town was founded in 616/1219 by the Ayyūbid sultan al-Malik al-Kāmil [*q.v.*] as a fortified camp against the Crusaders, who had conquered Dimyāṭ in Shaʿbān 616/November 1219. Situated at the fork of the branches of the Nile near Dimyāṭ and Ushmūm Ṭannāḥ, the town dominated the two most important waterways of the eastern delta and served as an advanced outpost of Cairo. In July/August 1221, the advance of the Crusaders under King John of Jerusalem and the Cardinal-Legate Pelagius was checked before al-Manṣūra. When al-Malik al-Kāmil ordered the dikes to be pierced and the land flooded, the Franks, who had pitched their camp in the angle between the two branches of the Nile, were forced to surrender and to purchase an unhampered retreat by giving up their Egyptian conquests (7 Radjab 618/27 August, 1221).

During the reign of the last Ayyūbid Tūrānshāh, the Crusade of Louis IX of France came to its end before al-Manṣūra in exactly the same way. In December 1249 the Franks, approaching from Dimyāṭ, appeared before the town and pitched camp again in the angle between the branches of the Nile. On 5 Dhu 'l-Ḳaʿda 647/10 February, 1250, they forced the crossing of the Baḥr Ushmūm and penetrated into al-Manṣūra, but were driven back after heavy street fighting. During the ensuing battle before the gates of the town, King Louis found himself facing Baybars I al-Bunduḳdārī [*q.v.*]. After hesitating for several weeks, the Franks beat a retreat, but did not reach Dimyāṭ. On 3 Muḥarram 648/7 April 1250, the King and the remainder of his army were taken prisoner, and on 3 Ṣafar/7 May of the same year were ransomed in exchange for Dimyāṭ.

During the reign of the Mamlūk sultans, the town belonged to the province of al-Daḳahliyya, whose chief place was Ushmūm Ṭannāḥ, the present Ushü mūm al-Rummān (Ibn Duḳmāḳ, *Intiṣār*, ed. Vollers, v, 71; Ibn al-Djīʿān, *Tuḥfa*, ed. Moritz, 50; Halm, *Ägypten nach den mamlukischen Lehensregistern*, Wiesbaden 1982, ii, 728). In 933/1527, the ottoman *wālī* of Egypt, Sulaymān Pasha al-Khādim, transferred the provincial court (*dīwān al-ḥukm*) from Ushü mūm to the more conveniently situated al-Manṣūra, and made this town into the capital of the al-Daḳahliyya province, which it has remained until today. In 1826, al-Manṣūra also became the centre of a *ḳism* (an administrative subdivision of a *muḥāfaẓa*, renamed *markaz* in 1871) with 60 villages. As a staple place of cotton, harvested in the Delta, al-Manṣūra witnessed an important increase in population: 27,000 inhabitants in 1900: 49,000 in 1917; and 218,000 in 1970.

Bibliography: Yāḳūt, *Muʿdjam*, s.v.; Maḳrīzī, *Khiṭaṭ*, ed. Būlāḳ, i, 231 f. (ed. Wiet, iv, 103 ff.); ʿAlī Pasha Mubārak, *al-Khiṭaṭ al-djadīda* xv, 88 ff.; Muḥammad Ramzī, *al-Ḳāmūs al-djughrāfī li'l-bilād al-Miṣriyya*, Cairo 1954-5, ii/1, p. 26 of the introduction and 215 ff.; Maspěro-Wiet, *Matériaux*, Cairo 1909, 198 ff. For the 1249-50 crusade: Ibn al-Athīr, xii, 213 ff.; Ibn Wāṣil, *Mufarridj al-kurūb*, iv, ed. Rabīʿ-ʿĀshūr, Cairo 1972, 94 ff.; H. L. Gottschalk, *Al-Malik al-Kāmil von Egypten und seine Zeit*, Wiesbaden 1958, 87, 109 ff. For the crusade of Louis IX: Jean de Joinville, *Histoire de St. Louis*, ed. N. de Wailly, [2]Paris 1874; Ibn Wāṣil, *Mufarridj al-kurūb*, ms. Paris B. N. ar. 1702, fol. 357 ff. (Italian tr. F. Gabrieli, *Storici arabi delle Crociate*, Turin 1963, 281 ff.; Engl. tr.: *Arab historians of the Crusades*, Berkeley-Los Angeles 1969, 286 ff.; French tr. : *Chroniques arabes des Croisades*, Paris 1977, 314 ff.; German tr.: *Die Kreuzzüge aus arabischer Sicht*, Zürich-Munich 1973, 346 ff.).

(H. HALM)

AL-**MANṢŪRA**, the name of a town, now in ruins, constructed on two occasions by the Marīnid sultans about 3 miles/5 km. west of Tlemcen, during the sieges of that town. The desire to control the commerce in gold from Black Africa terminating at Tlemcen was a continuing concern of the North African policy of the Marīnids and explains their efforts to control this place. The account given by Ibn Khaldūn enables us to reconstruct the history of this typical camp-town. In the year 698/1299, the Marīnid Abū Yaʿḳūb Yūsuf, who had come to lay siege to the capital of Banū ʿAbd al-Wād [*q.v.*], which he closely surrounded with entrenchments, set up his camp on the plain which stretches to the west. As it was a long drawn-out blockade, he built a few dwellings for himself and the leaders of his army and laid the foundation of a mosque. In the year 702/1302 the "Victorious Camp" (*al-Maḥalla al-Manṣūra*), was given the form of a regular town by the construction of a rampart. In addition to the mosque, the dwelling of the chiefs, the storehouses for munitions and the shelters for the army, there were baths and caravanserais. As Tlemcen was inaccessible to caravans, al-Manṣūra, or New Tlemcen, as it was called naturally attracted the business of the besieged town. Documents in the archives of the Crown of Aragon attest to the fact that it was visited by Christian merchants, and that a Majorcan consul lived there. After a siege of eight years and three months, the Marīnids in 706/1307 withdrew from Tlemcen following the death of sultan Yaʿḳūb, and al-Manṣūra was methodically evacuated under the direction of Ibrāhīm b. ʿAbd al-Djalīl, the vizier of the sultan Abū Thabit. The people of Tlemcen were compelled, by the terms of the treaty made by the Marīnids, to respect the rival town for some time later; then, when the entente between the two empires had collapsed, they demolished its building and rendered uninhabitable the entrenchments left at their gate by their hereditary enemy.

The second phase of al-Manṣūra's existence began 30 years afterwards, in 735/1335, with the Marīnid drive eastwards under the great ruler Abu 'l-Ḥasan ʿAlī. Tlemcen, once more besieged, was compelled to surrender (27 Ramaḍān 737/1337). Al-Manṣūra was splendidly restored, according to the indications of Ibn Marzūḳ, Abu 'l-Ḥasan's historian, who had accompanied him to the town, and provided with a *ḳaṣba* and mosque, a *meshwar*, a house of justice, palaces, baths and caravanserais. It was probably at this time that the great mosque was completed and that the "Victory Palace" was built (747/1344-5). The Marīnid court installed itself there and conducted the affairs of state thence until the defeat of al-Ḳayrawān and the re-installation of the Banū ʿAbd al-Wād at Tlemcen (Djumādā II 749/September 1348).

After the retreat of the Marīnids, al-Manṣūra, once more abandoned, fell gradually into ruins. Today the rampart of terre pisée flanked by square towers is still comparatively intact, but the interior is land under cultivation. There still exists, however, the ruins of a palace, no longer distinct, a section of a paved street, and probably the surrounding wall in terre pisée of the mosque with half of the great stone minaret which rose above the principal entrance. Although the inlaid ceramic work has almost entirely disappeared, the façade of the square tower, which is 120 feet high, is one of the finest pieces of Maghribī art of the 8th/14th century that survives. The columns and the capitals in marble of the mosque are preserved in the Museums of Tlemcen and Algiers.

Bibliography: Ibn Khaldūn, *Histoire des Berbères*, ed. de Slane, ii, 136, 332 ff., 379 ff.; tr. iii, 375; iv, 414 ff., 221 ff.; Yaḥyā Ibn Khaldūn, *Bughyat al-ruwwād*, ed. Bel, i, 121, 141; tr. i, 164, 189; Ch.-E. Dufourq, *L'Espagne catalane et le Maghrib aux 13e et 14e siècles*, Paris 1966, 133-6 351, 354-5, 360-3, 365, 372-5, 519; Ibn Marzūḳ, *Musnad*, ed. Lévi-Provençal, 25, 35, ed. M. J. Viguera, Algiers 1981, 125-6, 173, 230-5, 447-8, 491-2, Spanish tr. Madrid 1977, 109-10, 148, 192-6, 369-70, 406-7; M. Shatzmiller, *Un texte relatif aux structures politiques mérinides*, in *REI*, xlvii (1979), 239-47; Bargès, *Tlemcen, ancienne capitale*, 249 ff.; Brosselard, *Inscriptions arabes de Tlemcen*, in *RAfr*, iii (1895) 322-40; W. and G. Marçais, *Monuments arabes de Tlemcen*, 192-222; G. Marçais, *Manuel d'art musulman*, ii, 485-9, 549-50, 568-70, 625-9.

(G. Marçais - [M. Shatzmiller])

MANṢŪRIYYA, an extremist Shīʿī sect of the 2nd/8th century named after its founder Abū Manṣūr al-ʿIdjlī. The latter is also called al-Mustanīr in some sources, but the reading is uncertain.

Abū Manṣūr was a native of the *sawād* of Kūfa and, a tribesman rather than a peasant, grew up in the desert. Later, he owned a house in Kūfa. The statement of some sources that he belonged to ʿAbd al-Ḳays is not necessarily wrong, since ʿIdjl is often counted as a branch of ʿAbd al-Ḳays. His following came chiefly from he traditionally Shīʿī tribes of ʿIdjl, Badjīla and Kinda, and included also *mawālī*. Initially, Abū Manṣūr supported the imāmate of Muḥammad al-Bāḳir, exalting him and the *imāms* preceding him to the rank of divinely-inspired Messenger prophets. He taught that the line of such Messengers could never be interrupted. After the death of al-Bāḳir (*ca.* 117/735), he claimed to be his successor and justified this claim, asserting that the Family of Muḥammad were heaven and the Shīʿa, earth, while he, Abū Manṣūr, was the miraculous "fragment" (*kisf*) fallen from heaven which is mentioned in Ḳurʾān, LII, 44; thus he belonged spiritually to the Banū Hāshim. He identified those who, according to the Ḳurʾānic verse, would not recognise the miracle and claimed that it was merely "piled up clouds", with the followers of al-Mughīra b. Saʿīd, his chief rival among the Shīʿī *ghulāt*. He claimed that he had been raised to heaven and that God had wiped his head with his hand and had told him in Syriac or Persian, "My son, go and teach on my behalf". Abū Manṣūr taught that the first being to be created by God was Jesus and the next ʿAlī. The rest of mankind was composed of light and darkness. He maintained that God had sent Muḥammad with the revelation (*tanzīl*) of the Ḳurʾān and himself with its interpretation (*taʾwīl*). Like other Shīʿī *ghulāt*, he interpreted the Ḳurʾān allegorically, identifying heaven and hell, religious commandments and prohibitions with man, friends and enemies of God in the struggle between good and evil, and repudiating all religious laws.

Abū Manṣūr was vainly sought by Khālid al-Ḳasrī, governor of Kūfa, during his campaign of repression against Shīʿī extremists. He was seized and killed by Khālid's successor, Yūsuf b. ʿUmar al-Thaḳafī (120-6/738-44). After his death, the Manṣūriyya split into two groups. One of them, known as the Ḥusayniyya, recognised his son al-Ḥusayn as his designated successor. They seem to have held that the imāmate would continue among his descendants, since there were to be seven prophets from Ḳuraysh and seven from ʿIdjl. the other group, known as the Muḥammadiyya, recognised the Ḥasanid Muḥammad b. ʿAbd Allāh al-Nafs al-Zakiyya (d. 145/762) as their *imām*. They maintained that al-Bāḳir had appointed Abū Manṣūr to succeed him merely as a temporary depositary (*mustawdaʿ*) in order to forestall discord between the descendants of al-Ḥasan and al-Ḥusayn, just like Moses had appointed Joshua before the succession reverted to the offspring of his brother Aaron. They reported that Abū Manṣūr had stated "I am only a depositary, and have no right to transfer the imāmate to anyone else. The Ḳāʾim is Muḥammad b. ʿAbd Allāh." Al-Ḥusayn b. Abī Manṣūr was captured under the caliph al-Mahdī (158-69/775-85) and put to death by him. Much money was confiscated from him, and many of his followers were now sought out and killed. The sect evidently disintegrated quickly.

The Manṣūriyya were particularly notorious as stranglers of their religious opponents. They are said to have considered murdering them a meritorious act and to have used the method of strangling or stoning, because they held that iron weapons must not be employed before the coming of the Mahdī. They considered all belongings of their victims as booty and turned over a fifth (*khums*) to their leader. Al-Djāḥiẓ describes them as living and travelling together in groups and acting together, beating their drums and tambourines and making their dogs bark in order to cover up the cries of their victims. Abū Manṣūr's "foster mother" (*ḥāḍina*), Maylā³, is named as a head of the stranglers in a poem of Ḥammād al-Rāwiya.

Bibliography: Djāḥiẓ, *Ḥayawān*, ed. ʿAbd al-Salām Hārūn, Cairo 1965, ii, 264-71, vi, 389-91 (cf. Pellat, in *Oriens*, xvi [1963], 102, 104-6); Ibn al-Faḳīh, 185, 191; Nāshiʾ, *Masāʾil al-imāma*, ed. J. van Ess, Beirut 1971, 39-40; Nawbakhtī, *Firaḳ al-shīʿa*, ed. H. Ritter, Istanbul 1931, 34-5; Saʿd b. ʿAbd Allāh al-Ḳummī, *al-Maḳālāt wa 'l-firaḳ*, ed. M. Dj. Mashkūr, Tehran 1963, 46-8; Ashʿarī, *Maḳālāt al-Islāmiyyīn*, ed. H. Ritter, Istanbul 1929-33, 9-10, 24-5; Kashshī, *Ikhtiyār maʿrifat al-ridjāl*, ed. Ḥasan al-Muṣṭafawī, Mashhad 1349, 303-4; Baghdādī, *Farḳ*, 214-5, 234-5; Ibn Ḥazm, *Fiṣal*, Cairo 1317-21, iv, 185-6 Shahrastānī, 135-6; Nashwān al-Ḥimyarī, *al-Ḥūr al-ʿīn*, Cairo 1367/1948, 168-70; I. Friedländer, *The heterodoxies of the Shiites*, in *JAOS*, xxviii (1907), 62-4, xxix (1908), 89-93; W. H. Watt, *The formative period of Islamic thought*, Edinburgh 1973, 46-7, 51-2; W. Tucker, *Abū Manṣūr al-ʿIjlī and the Manṣūriyya: a study in medieval terrorism*, in *Isl.*, liv (1977), 66-76.

(W. MADELUNG)

MANṬIḲ (A.), a technical term denoting logic.

1. Etymology.

The *LA* gives *manṭiḳ* as a synonym of *kalām* in the sense of "language"; a book is described as being *nāṭiḳ bayyin* as if it does itself speak; God says in the Ḳurʾān (XXII, 62): "And before Us is a Book which tells the truth (*yanṭiḳu bi 'l-ḥaḳḳ*)". This telling of the truth also has a quality of judgment; thus (XLV, 29): "This is Our Book; it pronounces against you in all truth (*yanṭiḳu ʿalaykum bi 'l-ḥaḳḳ*)". Metaphorically, *manṭiḳ* expresses the language of all things, for example the language of birds (Ḳurʾān, XXVII, 16: *manṭiḳ al-ṭayr*). But idols do not speak (XXI, 63, 65). On the Day of Judgment, the accused will not speak (*lā yanṭiḳūn*, LXXVII, 35). It is God who makes every thing speak (*anṭaḳa kulla shayʾ*, cf. XLI, 20-1). It is thus seen that the Ḳurʾān uses this root with a normative quality; it is linked to the expression of truth and to justification. Although man can speak in order to tell lies and nonsense, this is not the case of the Prophet and of those to whom God gives the power of telling the truth. God says of the Messenger (LIII, 3): "And he does not talk through passion (*lā yanṭiḳu ʿan al-hawā*)". The man who has received wisdom (*ḥikma*) speaks according to reason. It is understandable that this root should have been chosen to translate the Greek λόγος (word, reason) and λογικός (reasonable). Man is defined as *ḥayawān nāṭiḳ*, a reasonable animal, although the *LA* gives a broader sense to the word *nāṭiḳ*, opposing it to *ṣāmit* (that which is silent): every thing which has a voice (*ṣawt*) is *nāṭiḳ*. But it is certain that the articulate language of man distinguishes him from all other animals on the vocal level, just as reason distinguishes him on the spiritual level.

2. Definition of logic (*ʿilm al-manṭiḳ*).

Al-Tahānawī, in his *Dictionary of technical terms*, comments that this is also called the science of balance (*ʿilm al-mīzān*), "because this is a means of weighing arguments (*ḥudjadj*) and demonstrative proofs (*barāhīn*)". Ibn Sīnā calls it "the servant of the sciences" (*khādim al-ʿulūm*), "because it is not a science in its own right, but a means (*wasīla*) of acquiring sciences". But al-Fārābī called it the "mistress" (*raʾīsa*) of sciences "on account of its efficacity (*nafādh*) in the practice of them". This science, al-Tahānawī continues, "was called *manṭiḳ* because the root *nuṭḳ* (action of speaking, elocution) applies in a general fashion to statement (*lafẓ*), to the perception of universals (*idrāk al-kulliyyāt*) and to the reasonable soul (*al-nafs al-nāṭiḳa*); since this art reinforces the first of these concepts, through the second it follows the path of rectitude (*sadād*), and by its means the perfection of the soul is realised, a word has been derived from this root to designate it, sc. the word *manṭiḳ*. It is the science of rules (*ḳawānīn*) which explains the methods for passing from that which is known to that which is unknown, and the conditions that they pose (*sharāʾiṭ*) so that error (*ghalaṭ*) will not survive in thought (*fikr*). The known extends to the necessary truths of intuition (*ḍarūriyyāt*) and to speculative truths". It may be noted that this distinction corresponds to that made by Aristotle (*Anal. Pr.* i, 10, 76 b 10) between "common axioms" and "entirely demonstrated conclusions".

As for the unknown, "it extends to that which is derived from concepts and to that which is derived from judgments (*taṣawwuriyyāt* and *taṣdīḳiyyāt*)". This definition is, according to al-Tahānawī, preferable to that which holds that the rules of logic "supply knowledge of the methods permitting a passage from the necessary truths of intuition to speculative truths, because this expression at first sight gives the impression of a passage which is effected [directly] by itself (*intiḳāl dhātī*), while the more general sense is that this is a passage which is either made directly by itself or through an intermediary (*bi 'l-dhāt aw bi 'l-wāsiṭa*)". This being so, al-Tahānawī points out the difference between logic and grammar (*naḥw*) on the one hand, and logic and geometry (*handasa*) on the other. Grammar "only explains the general rules which apply to the quality of elocution in Arabic terms, and that in general manner; when one wishes to propound a discourse appropriate to a particular subject (*makhṣūṣ*) in a correct fashion, there is a need for particular modalities (*aḥkām djuzʾiyya*) which are drawn from these rules as are normally the derivations (*furūʿ*) of principles (*uṣūl*). But this does not apply in the passage of thought from a known to an unknown. Grammar is of absolutely no assistance in making passages of this kind. The name is true of geometry; it is in posing normative problems (*masāʾil ḳānūniyya*) that it tackles objects of research on configurations, in the sense that it makes these problems the principles of the demonstrations whereby it reasons on these objects. As for the particular notions which intervene in these demonstrations, geometry does not in any way contribute to their understanding." Al-Tahānawī is no doubt thinking here of the Euclidian method which proceeds from problems to arrive at theorems: the given data of the problems serving as a base for the demonstrations. As for the particular notions, they relate to the terms of the syllogism, in particular the middle term which is the cause of the conclusion in the minor. Thus Aristotle writes (*Anal. Post.*, ii, 11, 94 a 27-34): "Why is the angle drawn in the semi-circle a right-angle? Or, from what given information does it follow that is is a right angle?" J. Tricot explains Aristotle's argument in these terms: "We have here the following *Barbara* syllogism, in which B, the middle term, is the cause of the conclusion: Every angle which is the half of two right-angles (B) is a right-angle (A); Every angle drawn in the semi-circle (r) is the half of two right-angles (B); Every angle drawn in the semicircle (r) is a right-angle (A)." But it is evident that the role of geometry is precisely to show that every angle drawn in the semi-circle is the half of two right-angles. Although it implicitly uses the preceding syllogism, it is not by means of the syllogism that it achieves the end which it seeks. Consequently, the science of logic is different from the demonstrative science of geometry. Logic is definitely defined as one of the instrumental sciences (*min al-ʿulūm al-āliyya*). But if it plays a role in the treatment by each particular science of its own object, what is the object of logic itself?

"It is said," al-Tahanāwī states, "that it has its object (*mawḍūʿ*) concepts (*taṣawwurāt*) and judgments (*taṣdīḳāt*)". It is a process of passing from known concepts or judgments to unknown concepts or judgments, by short or long steps: short when a concept is defined through *ḥadd* or through *rasm*, or when judgment is by analogy (*ḳiyās*), induction (*istiḳrāʾ*), or comparison (*tamthīl*); long, when there is the added consideration that a concept is universal or particular, essential or accidental, or when a judgment is proved by a contrary or contradictory judgment (*ḳaḍiyya wa-ʿaks ḳaḍiyya wa-nāḳiḍuhā*). The logician also enquires into concepts in as much as they give access to judgment when they are considered as subjects (*mawḍūʿāt*) and attributes (*maḥmūlāt*). Those who are concerned with the precise meaning of words (*ahl al-taḥḳīḳ*) reckon that the object of logic is constituted by secondary intelligibles (*al-maʿḳūlāt al-thāniya*) not as such and taken in themselves, nor as existing in thought, for it then becomes an issue to be dealt with by philosophy; but in as much as they give access to the unknown. "In fact, when the universal intelligible notion (*al-mafhūm al-kullī*) exists in thought and it is compared with particular things which are beneath it, it becomes either essentiality (*al-dhātiyya*) because it becomes a part of their quiddity, or accidentality (*al-ʿaraḍiyya*) because it is exterior to them, or specificity (*al-nawʿiyya*) because it is their quiddity itself. That which becomes essentiality is the genre (*djins*) relative to its different individuals, and the specific difference (*faṣl*) relative to another thing. Similarly, that which becomes accidentality is either an attribute (*khāṣṣa*), or a common accident (*ʿaraḍ ʿāmm*), according to two differing points of view". These "intentions" (*maʿānī*), i.e. the fact that the universal notion is essential, accidental or specific, do not belong to exterior entities; they are what becomes of the universal natures (*al-ṭabāʾiʿ al-kulliyya*) when they are found in thought. The same applies to the fact that a judicative proposition is attributive or conditional, that an argument is an analogy, an induction or a comparison, for this is what becomes of the nature of particular relation (*al-nisab al-djuzʾiyya*) in thought. Consequently, these secondary intelligibles are indeed the object of logic. Finally, al-Tahānawī comments that logic is also concerned with "intelligibles of the third degree" (*al-maʿḳūlat al-thālitha*) which are essentially what becomes of secondary intelligibles. Thus the judicative proposition (*ḳaḍiyya*) is a secondary intelligible. But inquiry can be made as to its divisibility (*inḳisām*), on the fact that it contradicts another (*tanāḳuḍ*), or that it is convertible (*inʿikās*), or that a conclusion may be drawn from it (*intādj*); these are intelligibles which fall to the third rank (*al-daradja al-thālitha*). These questions are tackled by Aristotle in *De Interpretatione* and the *Prior Analytics*, whence this separation of intelligibles into three degrees seems to be derived. As for the purpose (*gharaḍ*) of logic, it is the discernment of truth and falsehood (*tamyīz al-ṣidḳ wa 'l-kidhb*) in speech, of true and false (*al-ḥaḳḳ wa 'l-bāṭil*) in beliefs (*fi 'l-iʿtiḳādāt*), of good and bad in actions (*al-khayr wa 'l-sharr fi 'l-aʿmāl*). Its utility (*manfaʿa*) is thus to give access to the theoretical sciences (*al-ʿulūm al-naẓariyya*) and to the practical sciences (*al-ʿamaliyya*).

Such is the survey of logic made by al-Tahānawī at a late date (12th/18th century). It shows the ideas which were current in the Muslim world, following a long history in the course of which it was both attacked and defended, and cultivated in a more or less fruitful fashion. It is necessary now to go further back in time.

3. Discussions of logic among Arab-Muslim thinkers.

A. *Grammar and logic*. It is undeniable, and the work of Aristotle proves this, that there is a connection between logic and language in general, and with the spoken language and its grammar in particular. But can logic, which aspires to be universal to all men, be reduced to the grammar of a language spoken by a particular people? This question was posed in the course of a famous debate described by Abū Ḥayyān al-Tawḥīdī, between the Christian logician Abū Bishr Mattā b. Yūnus and the grammarian and commentator of Sībawayh, Abū Saʿīd al-Sīrāfī. Mattā defines the purpose and utility of logic in the same terms as those employed by al-Tahānawī. Logic is an instrument comparable to a balance, giving awareness of "healthy" discourse (*kalām ṣaḥīḥ*) and distinguishing it from "sick" discourse (*saḳīm*). Abū Saʿīd replies then that, for the Arabic speaker, the quality of discourse is known by the laws of grammar; but if enquiry is to be made by means of intelligence (*ʿaḳl*), it is through reason that that which is false in an idea (*fāsid al-maʿnā*) is to be distinguished from the genuine (*ṣāliḥ*): As for the balance, it gives awareness of what weighs the most, but not the nature of that which is weighed. Furthermore, in bodies, not everything is evaluated by weights; there are measures other than weight. The same applies to intelligibles. This reply is evidently an argument *ad hominem* which does not explain how, alongside the grammar which regulates discourse, reason would pronounce, in intellectual problems, on the truth and falsehood of ideas.

Whatever the case, Abū Saʿīd returns to his thesis: it was a Greek who instituted logic according to the language of his people, on the basis of the technical terminology (*iṣṭilāḥ*) applied to it by the grammarians and of knowledge of the traits which characterise it. How could this logic be imposed upon Turks, Indians, Persians and Arabs? Mattā replies that logic is concerned with intelligibles and ideas; on this level all men are equal. For all men, two and two make four; the same applies to the rules of logic, which is denied by Abū Saʿīd, who declares that these intelligibles are only reached by the language with its nouns, verbs and particles. To preach the study of logic is to preach the study of the Greek language, seeing that the people who spoke it have disappeared and it is known only through translations into Syriac, then into Arabic. But, Mattā replies, the translations preserve intentions and ideas. Abū Saʿīd does not insist and does not pose the problem of the difficulties of translation, unlike al-Djāḥiẓ (*K. al-Ḥayawān*, i, 75-9). Even admitting, he says, that these translations may be accurate, there is no reason to think "that there is no proof other than the intelligence of the Greeks". To claims of the importance of their contribution to the sciences, he replies that "knowledge of the world is dispersed throughout the world among all the inhabitants of the world", without perceiving that by this reasoning there could be a logic common to all.

If the Greeks do not occupy a privileged position, it is also true that Aristotle is not the whole of Greece; he borrowed from his predecessors, and moreover, not all Greeks are in agreement with him. Here Abū Saʿīd touches on a central problem. Logic should suppress differences in opinions and in speculation; it should, as certain *falāsifa* (including al-Fārābī) believed, form a basis of agreement for all philosophers. How could a single man suppress all these differences "which are fundamental and natural"? It seems that Abū Saʿīd has not seen the gravity of his words, for they pose the question of knowing if there are diverse mentalities irreconcilable in their diversity, and if there are among men one or several truths. Should the existence be admitted of as many logics as there are languages and grammars and people? Whatever the implications, he concludes: "The world has remained the same after the logic of Aristotle as it was before." This being so, he attempts to explain that it is by grammar and not by logic that one can understand, for example, all the uses of the particle *wa* (and), which is undeniable, but proves nothing. Mattā replies that the logician has no need of grammar, although the grammarian needs logic: it is by accident that the logician is concerned with words, as it is by accident that the grammarian hits upon an idea (*maʿnā*); but the idea is more noble than the word. On the contrary, for Abū Saʿīd, "grammar is a logic, but it is derived from Arabic; logic is a grammar, but it is included in the language". The difference between the word and the meaning (*maʿnā*), is that the word is a "natural reality" which is effaced with time, while the meaning is a "reality of intelligence" which remains fixed across time. He then shows that, in order to express his logic, Mattā needs the Arabic language and its grammar; ignorance of the meanings of a single particle can invalidate any kind of reasoning.

This being so, Abū Saʿīd leaves the consideration of words in order to turn towards the intellectual content of their meanings. What is to be made of the statement "Zayd is the most virtuous of *his* brothers"? Mattā believes that this is correct. Abū Saʿīd retorts that he is mistaken and that the statement should be: "Zayd is the most virtuous of *the* brothers". Zayd is one of the brothers, but he is not one of his brothers. In fact, "the brothers of Zayd are other than Zayd, and Zayd is exterior to their group." Abū Saʿīd claims that Mattā does not know why one of the propositions is correct and the other false. But he himself does not explain how grammar demonstrates this, and his own explanation, based on the logical notions of inclusion and exclusion, has nothing grammatical about it. It is true that Aristotle does not deal directly with this type of proposition. Nevertheless, Mattā should have been able to reply, for the notion of a brother is relative and according to Aristotle (*Categories*, 7, 6 a 36) relatives "refer to another thing." Zayd, as a brother, is thus the brother of his brothers who are other than him: he is not one of them.

Finally, Abū Saʿīd criticises the logicians for having done nothing more than "frighten people" with the technical terms of genre, type, specific difference, attribute, accident, individual, and especially with the neologisms in *iyya*, such as *ḥalliyyà*, *ʿayniyya*, *kayfiyya*, *kammiyya*, *dhātiyya*, *ʿaraḍiyya*, *djawhariyya*, etc. Ibn Ḳutayba had already made a similar critique in the *Adab al-kātib*. Abū Saʿīd mocks the "magical" formulae of the syllogism and concludes, "All of this is nonsense, trifles, incomprehensible and confused propositions. Anyone possessing fine intelligence, good discernment and refined insight, can do without it altogether."

This critique poses more problems than it resolves, in particular that of a grammatical logic. Abū Saʿīd's performance is that of a debater seeking only to have the last word, unperturbed by his self-contradictions and avoidance of questions. But his critique is interesting, in that it shows the existence of a certain Arabism opposed to all things Hellenic, based no doubt on the religious belief that God has revealed the Ḳurʾān in clear Arabic language (XVI, 103).

B. *The doctrine of Ibn Ḥazm*. The Ẓāhirī views of Ibn Ḥazm leads him to deliberate on the nature of languages and to lay the foundations of a Ẓāhirī grammar which takes account only of the linguistic intentions expressly contained in the forms of the language and the speech which makes use of them. He excludes any psychological intention which might remain implied, having no clear indication (*dalīl*) in what is said or written. His object is to understand precisely the Word of God, without the intervention in the exegesis of any consideration, any human interpretation. The reason given to Man has no other purpose than to identify and attest to the revealed truth. Under these conditions, what role remains for logic? In the *K. al-Taḳrīb li-ḥadd al-manṭiḳ*, Ibn Ḥazm justified logic by means of Ḳurʾānic testimonies, in particular the verse LV, 3: "And the Merciful has created man; He has taught him *bayān*". *Bayān*, Ibn Ḥazm explains with reference to the verse II, 31, "And he taught Adam all the names", is "the exposition of all existing beings according to their different manners of being (*wudjūh*), and the account of their meanings (*maʿānī*), the differences of which are the cause that their names necessarily differ; it is the awareness of the way in which the denominated things are allotted their names". It is by this that God distinguishes Man from the beast: "He that does not know the qualifications (*ṣifāt*) of the denominated things which make necessary the distinction of the names, he that does not define all things by their definitions (*ḥudūd*), ignores the greatness of this precious gift... From him that ignores logic, the structure (*bināʾ*) of the language of God remains hidden". Thus the utility of logic is to make understood the Word of God and , thereby, the works of God in creation. However, Ibn Ḥazm recognises that there were formerly sages who wrote books on the connection between denominated things and their names, names "on the meanings of which all peoples are in agreement, even though they use different names to express them, for [human] nature is unique, but the choice [of words] is diverse and varied". Ibn Ḥazm also cites the eight books which constitute the *Organon* of Aristotle, among which he includes the *Rhetoric* and the *Poetics*, giving precedence to the *Isagoge* of Porphyry. But he declares at once, "As for us, our resolution is that of the man who wishes to have his Creator, the Unique and First One, to guide him, who attributes to himself no power or strength except through Him, and who has no knowledge except that which He has taught him". With regard to these books, men are divided into four groups. The first are those who, without having read and studied them, judge them as impious and tending towards heresy. The second see in them nothing but nonsense, but censure those who ignore them. In third place are those who have read them, but with defective intelligence and poor understanding. The fourth group includes those who study them with clear intelligence and with impartial ideas. They establish the oneness of God by necessary demonstrative proofs (*bi-barāhīn ḍarūriyya*); they see the diversity of creators and the action of the Creator in them. The last-mentioned group find that these books have a worth and a utility like that of a "friend of good counsel" (al-ḳhadīn al-nāṣiḥ). Unfortunately, translations render them in obscure terms and arcane usage: "Nor every expression is right for every notion." Consequently, "we shall discuss these meanings in simple, not complex terms, equally comprehensible to the common man and the educated, to the scholar and the ignorant, in the same measure as we have understood them".

This being so, Ibn Ḥazm surveys the eight books of logic. As regard the *Isagoge*, it is sufficient to mention what he says of names which can designate several individuals, or a single one, as the case is presented in Arabic. For example. God says (CIII, 2): "In truth, man is in distress". Here, the name indicates the species (*nawʿ*). A phrase such as "The man whom you know has come to see me", refers to an individual. But the ambiguity can be removed by the use of the collective: *al-nās* instead of *al-insān* (the man), *al-ḳhayl* instead of *al-faras* (the horse). This reference to the Ḳurʾān and to Arabic is worthy of note. Ibn Ḥazm then tackles the works of Aristotle: first the book "of isolated names" (*al-asmāʾ al-murfrada*), i.e. the *Categories* (*Ḳāṭāg̲h̲ūriyās*); these are the ten *maḳālāt*.

He begins by defining synonyms (*al-asmāʾ al-mutawāṭiʾa*) and homonyms (*al-asmāʾ al-mus̲h̲tarika*), for example, *naṣr* which denotes the vulture, a star of the constellation of the Eagle and the shoe of a horse. In this he follows Aristotle, but he gives a different definition to paronyms which he calls "derivations" (*al-asmāʾ al-mus̲h̲taḳḳa*), the word πτῶσις used by Aristotle having the sense of a word formed from another. It is thus that one speaks of several denominated things, such as white-clothing, white-bird, white-man. "Each of these denominated things has a definition other than that of the other, and a name which, in its kind, is other than the name of the other; but they are associated in that they are all called "white". They thus concur in one of their qualifications which unites them "in a name derived from these denominated things". To these three types of names, Ibn Ḥazm adds "different names" (*al-asmāʾ al-muḳhtalifa*) when the things denominated differ although their meanings concur, as is the case with *sinnawr*, *daywār* and *hirr* which all signify the cat. These names are distinguished from synonyms which are, according to Aristotle, "that which has both community of name and identity of notion, for example, the animal which is both man and ox (*Cat.* 1, 1 a 5)". Then Ibn Ḥazm develops in an independent fashion what Aristotle says about expressions that bear a liaison (*Cat.* 2, 1 a 16 ff.) and which he calls "composed discourse" (*kalām murakkab*). He introduces the very Arab notion of *ḳhabar* (cf. below), as an informative or enunciatory discourse to which corresponds only imperfectly the predicative judgment, and he adds other forms of discourse: the interrogative, the vocative, the optative and the imperative (a useful point of view for the interpretation of the legislative texts of the Ḳurʾān). For example, in order to determine the *aḥkām* of the Law, it is important to know that an enunciative, in the form of a promise or a threat, can have the weight of a command or a prohibition. It is necessary also to distinguish the different qualities of verbal imperatives: the obligatory and constraining imperative (*al-wād̲j̲ib al-mulzim*); the imperative of incitement (*al-maḥdūd ʿalayhi*) which is not constraining; in addition, the imperative which gives an accord (*al-masmūḥ fīhi*); that which leaves the subject free (*al-tabarruʾ*) as in "Do as you wish"; threat (*waʿīd*) as in the verse (XII, 40): "Do as you wish: truly God sees that which you do"; irony (*tahakkum*), as when God mocks the damned in Hell with the

words (XLIV, 49): "Taste [the boiling water]: you are the powerful, the noble one"; the imputation of powerlessness (*taʿd̲j̲īz*), as in "Be stone or iron" (XVII, 50); and the prayer, the request, the appeal (*duʿāʾ*). Finally, there is the imperative *kun* (Be!) which brings beings into existence and which is the prerogative of the Creator. On the other hand, where Aristotle speaks of the affirmed or not-affirmed beings of a subject, existing or not existing in a subject, Ibn Ḥazm speaks of a division of names into four groups: bearers (*ḥāmila*) and qualifiers (*nāʿita*), bearers and qualified (*manʿūta*), born and qualified, born and qualifying. "Things" (*as̲h̲yāʾ*) of which the names belong to the first group, are like Man as a universal or taken in general (*al-insān al-kullī al-muṭlaḳ*). It is the bearer of all its attributes and it qualifies all the individuals denominated by it; but it is never "born", for "the substance (*d̲j̲awhar*) bears and is not born ". Here there is estblished the ambiguity which results from the substitution of names for beings. Aristotle had stated clearly, "Among beings, some are affirmed by a subject, while not being in any subject' (*Cat.*, 2 1 a 20). Ibn Ḥazm should have specified that Man, in the sense of a secondary substance (cf. *Cat.*, 5, 2 a 10 ff.) is not in a subject, but as a universal, he can be the predicate of an individual subject: Zayd is a man. The names of the second group are the "substantial individuals" (*al-as̲h̲ḳhāṣ al-d̲j̲awhariyya*) who bear their qualifications or attributes, but are not born, for example Zayd. The names of the third group are like the knowledge of such a man; it is born in his soul and is qualified by knowledge. The names of the fourth group are like the knowledge which is a kind of quality relative to the soul and which includes such studies as medicine, jurisprudence, etc., particular types of knowledge which it qualifies. What is of interest to Ibn Ḥazm is names, their meanings and their relationship within the language and their usage. The thing denominated is only considered in terms of the name which renominates it.

Turning to the ten categories, Ibn Ḥazm follows Aristotle, while simplifying him. With regard to the substance which is that which exists in itself, he does not say that the primary substance is neither in a subject (ʾεν ῾νποχειμένῳ), not attributable to a subject (χαθʾ ῾νποχειμένον), while the secondary substance, once it has been seen, is not in a subject, but is attributable to a subject. He insists above all on the fact that the substance has no contrary (*ḍidd*). When two substances are taken to be contraries, the contrariety derives from their qualities (*kayfiyyāt*). Consequently, God, having no qualities, is in no sense contrary to His creation. It is no longer possible to talk of more and of less: an ass is not more than another ass in "the-nature-of-the-ass" (*fi ʾl-ḥimāriyya*), nor is a goat more than another goat in "the-nature-of-the-goat (*fi ʾl-taysiyya*): it is interesting to note this use of abstract terms in -*iyya* which in principle Ibn Ḥazm rejects since they evoke ideas of the Platonic type existing in reality. But here there is little risk of "realism", since the context shows quite clearly that *ḥimāriyya* and *taysiyya* are nothing more than conventional terms which designate the ass and the goat in the sense of secondary substances. Without pursuing further this analysis of the categories, it is evident that logic has so far been presented as a means of classifying words, of specifying their usage and thus developing a method of explaining the Ḳurʾānic text which is often quoted to illustrate, or to support, such-and-such a signification. Nevertheless, in his chapter on the *De Interpretatione*, which he calls "Book of Enunciations" (*K. al-Aḳhbār*), where there is a discussion of "names joined to express a new signification (*al-madjmūʿa ilā ghayrihā*)'', in other words ''composites'' (*al-murakkaba*), he denounces pure ''nominalism''. ''All qualifications and enunciations bear on the things denominated, not on the names, for the things denominated are the significations (*al-maʿānī*) and the names are the expressions of them (*al-ʿibārāt ʿanhā*): it is thus well established that the name is other than the thing denominated.'' Those of a contrary opinion seek support from the verse (LXXXVII, 1), ''Praise the Name of your Master...''. But they are mistaken, since a thing denominated can only be reached through the name which expresses it; these are the two inseparable relatives.

It is worth paying attention to what Ibn Ḥazm says concerning speech, in order to show how he understands Aristotle in relating him to the notions of Arabic grammar. He renders the word ῥῆμα by *kalima* and says that it is what the grammarians call qualifications (*naʿt*) and the theologians attribute (*ṣifa*). The Greek word in fact primarily signifies speech and discourse (and in second place ''verb'' in the grammatical sense). J. Tricot writes (*De l'Interprétation*, 81, n. 1), ''In the language of Aristotle and also that of Plato (cf. *Sophist*, 262 c; *Cratylus*, 399 b), the word ῥῆμα espresses the act of qualifying a subject or the qualification which is given to it, in a more general sense that which is stated on a subject.'' The Arab grammarians describe it as ''a name derived from a verb (*fiʿl*)''. For example: *ṣaḥḥa, yaṣiḥḥu, fa-huwa ṣaḥīḥ* (sense of being in good health). *Kalima* indicates a determined time. Thus *ṣaḥīḥ* is a statement (*ikhbār*) on the present state of health of a person; *ṣaḥḥa* indicates an action in the past (*fi 'l-māḍī*); *yaṣiḥḥu*, a future action (*mustakbal*). The word *ṣiḥḥa* (act of being in good health) is a name (*ism*), not a *kalima*. It is what the grammarians call *maṣdar* (verbal noun). These are of two types: (1) the *maṣdar* can express the action of an agent (*fāʿil*) or the movement of a mobile, for example the blow (*ḍarb*) of one who strikes (*ḍārib*); or (2) that which is a qualificative for what is qualified, for example the fact of being in good health (*ṣiḥḥa, maṣdar* or *ṣaḥḥa*) for someone who is in good health and is one of his qualificatives''. There are thus two enunciative propositions: (1) Zayd strikes (*ḍaraba*), and (2) Zayd is in good health (*ṣaḥḥa*), which means that Zayd is the agent-subject of the act of striking which is his effectiveness (*taʾthīr*), and that he is the qualified-subject of the fact of being in good health which is ''borne'' *maḥmūl*) on him. With this incursion into Arabic grammar, Ibn Ḥazm deviates considerably from what Aristotle says.

In his study of the first part of the *Prior Analytics*, Ibn Ḥazm follows Aristotle fairly closely. He speaks of defined propositions (*kaḍāyā maḥṣūra*), ''those which are preceded by a word (*lafẓ*, cf. below: *sūr*) which explains that they are intended to signify a global extension (*al-ʿumūm*): these are universal propositions; or else a limited extension (*al-khuṣūs*): these are particular propositions. Next come undefined propositions (*muhmala*), ''in which the one who enunciates them does not state explicitly that he means a part (*baʿḍ*) of what is offered by the sense of the noun which they contain, or in which nothing prevents them from receiving a signification of global extension''. It is evident that it is always the verbal expression (*lafẓ, ism*) which interests Ibn Ḥazm, where Aristotle speaks of attribution to such or such a subject (ὑποκειμένῳ). Furthermore, when he employs the words *mawḍūʿ* (subject) and *maḥmūl* (predicate), he always explains them by terms borrowed from Arabic grammar: *mukhbar ʿanhu* (that on which an enunciation bears) and *khabar* (enunciative). He stresses the means of concluding in an always true and necessary fashion (*intādj*^an^ *ṣaḥīḥ*^an^ *abad*^an^). Logical necessity has posed a problem for theologians (cf. below). But here it is reduced to evidence supplied by the sense of words themselves. If the noun ''man'' denotes living beings, and if the noun ''substance'' is applied to living and to inanimate beings, it is evident that the noun ''substance'' applies to man. If this is formalised, the result is a first-figure syllogism of the *Barbara* type: Every living being is substance; man is a living being; thus every man is substance. (N.B. This syllogism is giving in the order major, minor, conclusion, whereas Arab logicians enunciate first the minor, then the major.)

Ibn Ḥazm devotes several paragraphs to judgments and to conditional syllogisms (*sharṭiyya*). Aristotle does not deal with these in the *Prior Analytics*. As in the case of al-Fārābī and Ibn Sīnā, a Stoic influence is evident here. The conditional proposition is either conjunctive (*muʿallaka*), or disjunctive (*mukassama*). Conjunctives are divided into connected propositions (*muttaṣila*): if A, therefore B; and into propositions with exception (*istithnāʾ*) : A (or not A) unless if B. The disjunctive enumerates cases, two or several, exclusive of one another, in a manner which is exhaustive (therefore perfect) or non-exhaustive (therefore imperfect): either A, then B; or C. then D...; now A, thus B. Ibn Ḥazm gives examples, well-known as instruments of the Stoics: if the sun has risen, it is day. The rising sun is the cause (*sabab*) of the day. But he also gives judicial examples, which is to be expected since in the *K. al-Muḥallā*, among other texts, he stresses the obligation to take account of the conditions which are in the Book of God (*al-shurūṭ fī Kitāb Allāh*), without excision or addition. Thus a fornicator who is married, adult and healthy of mind, is punished by flogging; that which intoxicates is forbidden; now the wine of figs, when (*idhā*) it is fermented, intoxicates; thus the wine of figs if fermented is forbidden. The conditional particles are if (*in*), as soon as (*matā mā*), when (*idh mā*), whenever (*mahmā, kullamā*). This being so, Ibn Ḥazm examines the different conditional syllogisms, according to whether their premisses are universal or particular, affirmative or negative.

This brief appraisal shows that, without rejecting logic in general, and that of Aristotle in particular, Ibn Ḥazm reduces it to an instrument for the evaluation of names and of their meanings, whether they are isolated or connected in speech. By this means, genres, types, differences, particulars and accidents serve first to classify names, then, through them, the things denominated, to define the relations between names, and thereby between things denominated. While laying the foundations of a Ẓāhirī grammar, he has transformed the logic of Aristotle into a Ẓāhirī logic. It makes no attempt to advance a theory of quiddities and essences, being designed above all to serve in commentaries on Ḳurʾānic and prophetic texts, and the truth that it propounds is that of legal maxims and of *aḥkām*. It is for this reason that it is illustrated essentially by examples drawn from ''Islamic law'', and the nature of the work in question is clearly indicated by the full title, *al-Taḳrīb li-ḥadd al-manṭiḳ wa 'l-madkhal ilayhi bi'l-alfāẓ al-ʿāmmiya wa'l-amthila al-fiḳhiyya*.

C. *The theologians and logic.* (a) The Ḥanbalīs. Very attached to the notion that all knowledge comes from God, they admit however that reason (*ʿaḳl*), being a gift of God, is something of which use should be made. This is stated, for example, by al-Barbaharī [*q.v.*], although he denounces personal and arbitrary use of reasoning. He attacks innovations (*bidaᶜ*) as also does Ibn Baṭṭa [*q.v.*], who denounces those "who take ignorant and deluded beings as their masters, although the Lord has given them knowledge" and thus adopt "ideas which have no proof in the Book of God" (*Profession de foi*, introd., ed. and tr. H. Laoust, Damascus 1958). There is no doubt that logic is envisaged in this attack on *bidaᶜ*.

But the most important text written by a Ḥanbalī on this subject is the "Refutation of Logicians" (*K. al-Radd ᶜalā 'l-manṭiḳiyyīn*) by Ibn Taymiyya [*q.v.*]. The author is at pains to show the uselessness of the logic of Aristotle. For example, a theory of definition teaches nothing about the defined object to those who do not already have knowledge of it: "There is nothing more clear than 'man', but his definition as a reasonable animal encounters objections". There is no need for a definition in forming a concept (*taṣawwur*) of the defined object and of its reality. "All men of good sense in all nations know the realities of things without being taught them by the school of Aristotle." However, Ibn Taymiyya admits nominal definitions which "distinguish between the defined object and that which is other than it". But he reproaches al-Ghazālī for having introduced Greek logic into the *uṣūl al-dīn* and *fiḳh*; he denounces his works *al-Mustaṣfā, Miḥakk al-naẓar, Miᶜyar al-ᶜilm* and *al-Ḳisṭās al-mustaḳīm*. On the other hand, when the logicians declare that knowledge of judgments can only be formed by the syllogism (*ḳiyās*), this is a negative proposition (*ḳaḍiyya salbiyya*) which is not known through evident intuition (*badīha*), and they have no proof (*dalīl*) of this negation. How can they claim that no man can acquire knowledge of a non-intuitive judgment except through the intermediary of a logical syllogism based on the universal (*bi-wāsiṭat al-ḳiyās al-manṭiḳī al-shumūlī*)? The difference between the intuitive and the speculative is relative. A judgment is intuitive when it is sufficient to observe the two terms (subject and attribute) in order to recognise that it is true. But in this men are very different from one another. Some are capable of understanding a conceptual representation with great rapidity. "In such cases the two terms of a perfectly accomplished representation are presented so well that it serves to clarify the concomitants (*lawāzim*) which are not clarified by any other..." It is an error to believe that the medium (*wasaṭ*) is in the thing qualified itself and that it is through its intermediary that the concomitant qualifications are actually established. This logical realism is evidently diametrically opposed to Ḥanbalī doctrine. But if by *wasaṭ* is meant the proof (*dalīl*) on which the conviction of thought (*al-thubūt al-dhihnī*) is based, not a conviction bearing on that which is exterior to thought, the differences between men are seen to reappear. "There is no doubt that the thing by which one shows (*mā yustadall bihi*) can be the cause (*ᶜilla*) in thought of an affirmation of existence bearing on the thing itself, whether this demonstration is called *ḳiyās* [*q.v.*] or *burhān* [*q.v.*] or any other name; it is then what is called *ḳiyās al-ᶜilla* or *burhān al-ᶜilla*, or *burhān limā*." But it can be otherwise, and it is then indication pure and simple (*dalīl muṭlaḳ*), called *ḳiyās* or *burhān al-dalāla* and *burhān inna*. "It is a reasoning based on verification by evidence." As Ibn Sīnā expressed it, "it gives the why of judgment, not the why of being" (*Ishārāt*, 84). But in this too men differ. It is an error to claim that every speculative item of knowledge must have two premisses: a *dalīl* can have only one, or two, or more than two "according to the need of the one who speculates and demonstrates". In short, logical operations which are the operations of thought in the interior of thought, even when they form judgment of things, are relative to the strength or weakness of the faculty of thought of different individuals. In this sense, the logic of Aristotle, indeed all logic, will be nothing other than methods of exposition of known truths, not rules for transference from a known to an unknown.

In matters of religious tradition, there may be a need for unversal propositions. If, for example, the prohibition of *nabīdh* is to be explained, the statement will be that *nabīdh* is an intoxicating drink and every intoxicating drink is prohibited (or, *nabīdh* is a form of *khamr* (fermented drink), and all *khamr* is prohibited). Each of these propositions is known through a text (Ḳurʾānic or prophetic) or through consensus (*idjmāᶜ*). It there is objection to the minor premiss, the reply will be that it is established in the *Ṣaḥīḥ* of Muslim that the Prophet said, "All intoxicating drink is fermented drink, and all intoxicating drink is forbidden". Those who believe that there is a demonstration by means of two premisses display enormous ignorance, "for the Prophet is of too eminent a rank to have recourse to such a method in the dissemination of knowledge". But it appears that this method may be applied to the purpose of those whose intelligence is of a less eminent rank.

Furthermore, universal propositions are known, in a general manner, not by demonstrative proof (*burhān*), but by an analogy of comparison (*ḳiyās tamthīlī*). If the demonstration of the logicians requires a universal proposition, the knowledge that is had of them must have a cause. If one advances the consideration of that which is absent by that which is present (*iᶜtibār al-ghāʾib bi 'l-shāhid*, cf. below), or the principle that the judgment borne on a thing is identical to that which is borne on a similar thing, then one has recourse to the analogy in question. If it is said that at the time of particular perceptions, there is produced in the soul a universal knowledge by the grace of the Giver of Intellect (*Wāhib al-ᶜaḳl* = *Wāhib al-ṣuwar, dator formarum*; cf. the theory of the Intellect of al-Fārābī) who is the Agent Intellect (*al-ᶜaḳl al-faᶜᶜāl*), or further, that in perceiving particular things, the soul is "disposed" to receive from the Agent Intellect the influx of the universal, the reply will be that it is discourse (*kalām*) on particular things which shows that the universal judgment is knowledge and not opinion or ignorance. Finally, if demonstrative proof supplies only a knowledge of the universal, as the universal is only in thought and there is nothing at the exterior but the determined existent (*mawdjūd muᶜayyan*), it follows that, through *burhān*, no existent can be absolutely known. The above are a few of the many criticisms levelled by Ibn Taymiyya against the logicians.

(b) The Ashᶜarīs. In his *K. al-Tamhīd*, al-Bāḳillānī distinguishes between various kinds of demonstrations (*istidlāl*): (1) those which divide a thing in the intelligence (*fi 'l-ᶜaḳl*) into two or more parts which cannot all be true or all false; proof (*dalīl*) shows that these divisions are false, except one; the intelligence judges as necessarily true that which remains; (2) that which states in that which is presently given (*fi 'l-shāhid*), that it is necessary to judge and to qualify a thing by reason of a cause: it must therefore be judged that that which has the same qualification in that which is not presently given (*al-ghāʾib* = the absent), must have it by reason of this cause (cf. Gardet and Anawati, *Introduction à la théologie musulmane*, 365 and n. 3). "In fact it is impossible (*mustaḥīl*) to establish a proof which shows that which justifies the qualification by an attribute in the absence of that which renders this attribute necessary." Thus it is known that a body is qualified as a body only by reason of the fact that it is composite; it must therefore necessarily be judged that everything qualified as a body has a composition; (3) that which demonstrates the truth or the falsehood of a thing according to (*ʿalā*) the truth or the falsehood of another thing which is similar to it and included in the same notion. For example, it is shown that God can give back life to the dead by the fact that this is the same thing as giving it to the living. Other types of demonstration depend on the exigencies of lexicography, or on the Ḳurʾān, the Sunna, *idjmāʿ* and the analogical reasoning of jurists (*al-ḳiyās al-sharʿī*) which, likewise, is linked to a "cause" (*ʿilla*, cf. below). "All these traditional proofs (*adilla samʿiyya*) have the same role in the unveiling of truth through *ḳiyās* as have judgments based on reason."

In his *Irshād*, al-Djuwaynī defines just reasoning (*al-naẓar al-ṣaḥīḥ*) as "everything which leads to an understanding of the manner in which the proof proves (*al-ʿuthūr ʿalā 'l-wadjh alladhī minhu yadull al-dalīl*)". As for proofs, "they are that which, through just reasoning with regard to them, lead to the knowledge of that which is not known in a necessary manner by deep-rooted practice." Muslim theologians are confronted here by an important problem, which al-Djuwaynī explains clearly. "Reasoning (*naẓar*) does not engender knowledge as a derived effect (*lā yuwallid al-ʿilm*); it does not necessitate it (*lā yūdjibuhu*) in the way that the efficient cause (*ʿilla*) necessitates its effect. "He thus expresses, on the one hand, the opposition of the Ashʿarīs to the Muʿtazilī doctrine of *tawallud*, and on the other hand, their opposition to the doctrine of the *falāsifa* who, following Aristotle, consider that the minor clause of a syllogism is the cause of its conclusion by the route of essential necessitation. According to the Ashʿarīs, it is God who immediately creates knowledge of the conclusion as soon as the premisses have been posed. This is an application to logic of the doctrine of occasional causes. Logical laws, like the laws of nature, are for God a custom (*ʿāda*), a rule of conduct (*sunna*) which He freely decides to observe, and the correlation between premisses and conclusion is purely *ʿādī*. Nevertheless, for al-Djuwaynī this correlation is rational (*ʿaḳlī*) in the sense that God has created reason and its necessary principles; they cannot be incumbent on Him, since He creates them freely, and it is by the same free act that, having created them, He decides to observe them habitually. (On this question, cf. Luciani, *El-Irchad*, ed. and tr. Paris 1938, 14-15, n. 2.) This problem of logical necessity (*al-ḍarūrī*) is of prime importance to theologians. According to al-Bāḳillānī, in his *Tamhīd*, a knowledge is necessary in two senses. First, it is a knowledge which is attached to the creature itself "by a connection (*luzūm*) of which it cannot rid itself". Doubt is not possible; here there is an act of violence done to the one who knows, for, in the language, the word *iḍṭirār* signifies *ikrāh* (violence), i.e. *ildjāʾ* (constraint). It is in this sense that there is talk of a necessary knowledge. Subsequently, a knowledge can be said to be necessary when there is a need for it, for, in the language, *ḍarūra* signifies *ḥādja* (need). In the first sense, sensible knowledges are necessary, since they are imposed on the five senses. But there is a sixth necessity "which has been originally created in the soul", arriving through none of the senses, such as the knowledge that the soul has of itself, and the knowledge of the principles of necessary intuition, such as that a statement is true or false; two statements posing two contrary objects cannot be simultaneously true or simultaneously false; and this applies in all cases where the intelligence makes a division by which is applied the principle of the excluded third. It is this necessity which renders the conclusion necessary. Here, too, there is recourse to the notion of the *ʿaḳlī* connection. (On the tripartite division of knowledge, cf. *Irshād*, 25, and n. 1.)

In his *Munḳidh min al-ḍalāl*, al-Ghazālī writes that questions of logic have no reference to religion, either to refute it or to prove it. "They are a rational examination (*naẓar*) of methods of proof and of criticism, of conditions relating to the premisses of the demonstrative syllogism (*burhān*) and the manner of disposing them, of the conditions of correct definition and the manner of organising it." However, misuse of this science leads to the belief that the conditions of demonstrative proof necessarily engender certitude (*al-yaḳīn*). On the level of religious problems, it is not possible to unite these conditions in an exhaustive manner. If al-Ghazālī thus warns the theologian against the dangers of logic, he does not fail to recognise in the *Iḥyāʾ ʿulūmʾ al-dīn* that logic, as "enquiry into the manner and conditions of proof and of definition", enters into the science of *kalām*. A branch of philosophy, it is placed in the second rank, after mathematics and before metaphysics (*al-ilāhiyyāt*) and the philosophy of nature (*al-ṭabīʿiyyāt*). In *al-Ḳisṭās al-mustaḳīm*, al-Ghazālī has shown that there are syllogistic demonstrations in the Ḳurʾān, which he is concerned to set in form.

4. The logic of the *falāsifa*.

(a) *Preliminary comment.* The logic of Aristotle depends on judgments of attribution which express the inherence of the predicate in the subject (*omne praedicatum inest subjecto*) when it is a case of essential attributes, or its simple presence in the subject, when the predicate is accidental. The link between the predicate and the subject is marked by the copula "is" ('εστι). But the Arabic language disregards the copula. The verb *kāna* indicates a state at which the subject has arrived, a manner of being; this is why it is followed by the direct case (*naṣb*) such as a *ḥāl*. Grammarians recognise only the relation of the *mubtadaʾ* (inchoative) and of the *khabar* (enunciative). In his commentary on the *Mufaṣṣal* of al-Zamakhsharī, Ibn Yaʿish [*q.v.*] explains that the *mubtadaʾ* is definite in order to show that it is known to the two interlocutors who are in accord in discussing it, while the *khabar* is indefinite in order to show that one of the two is ignorant of that which the other intends to tell him regarding the *mubtadaʾ*. It is thus not a case of a discussion expressing the relation of a predicate to a subject, but of an informative discourse (*ikhbār*) of one who addresses a second person regarding something which is the object of the information (*al-mukhbar ʿanhu*). This concept is close to that of the Stoics in regard to the λεκτόν, that which can be said of a thing. Their dialectic concerns true or false statements relating to things; these statements or judgments ('αξιώματα) comprise a subject (substantive or pronoun) and an attribute expressed by a verb. They never express the relation of two concepts. Although the *khabar* can be something other than a verb (even an entire proposition, e.g. Zayd, his father has come) there is evident kinship between the notions of the Stoics and those of the Arab grammarians. There is even a relic of this where Muslim thinkers, especially in matters of *fiḳh* (cf. below) adopt formulae of the Aristotelian type. It may further be noted that for Ibn Yaʿīsh, the true agent of a proposition is not the grammatical subject, but the one who enunciates it: before every statement, there is an understood "I say that". Now the verb *ḳāla* (say) is constructed with the particle *in* or *inna* (that). Consequently, it may be said that phrases commencing with *inna*, the particle normally introducing the consecutive of *ḳāla*, testify to the reality of this understood preface.

This being so, the *falāsifa*, under the influence of Aristotle, were obliged to find an equivalent of the copula. The particle adopted for this purpose was *huwa* (he; Zayd, he [is] wise), although its copulative usage is incorrect. As is shown by A. Taha (*Langage et philosophie*, Rabat 1979, 25), "in its ordinary usage, the pronoun *huwa* serves to establish a relating of identity between the subject and the noun (or rather the nominal description) attributed to it, for example, *Ibn Khaldūn huwa muʾallif al-Muḳaddima* (Ibn Khaldun is the author of the *Prolegomena*)". But it is also admitted, for example by al-Fārābī in his commentary on *De Interpretatione* (*Sharḥ K. al-ʿIbāra*, Beirut, 103) that the copula is "potentially" contained in the statement, since the verb to be is "either expressed in a word, or contained in the idea" (*ibid*, 46).

(b) *The commentaries.* The work of the *falāsifa* rests on translations and commentaries on a major, medium and minor scale, of the books of the *Organon*. In the article *Manṭiḳ* in *EI*[1], Van den Bergh wrote, "The Arabic philosophers did not develop this logic, but they have summarised, reproduced and commented on it, often with felicity". But this judgment assumes a positive contribution on their part. It should first be stated, with N. Rescher, that the first generations of Arab writers on logic, including al-Kindī, Abū Zakariyyāʾ, al-Rāzī and al-Fārābī, were in a true sense "the products of Syriac schools". "The Arab logicians thus continue the tradition of the Greeks of the Hellenistic period, and the Muslim Aristotelians, like al-Fārābī and Averroes, are the last link in a chain of which the first members are the masters of the Greek language, such as Alexander of Aphrodisias, Porphyry, Themistius, Ammonius and Joannes Philoponus" (*Al-Fārābī's Short Commentary on Aristotle's Prior Analystics*, Pittsburgh 1963, Introd., 23). Nor should the influence of Galen, and through him of Stoic ideas, be forgotten. Thus in his Short Commentary on the Prior Analytics, al-Fārābī introduces the conditional syllogism which Aristotle does not discuss, although he has promised to do so (*Pr. Anal.* 50a 40 - B 1). On the other hand, the theory of propositions- and modal syllogisms to which Aristotle devotes more than a half of his treatise, is entirely ignored (cf. Rescher, *ibid.*, 38). It is true that al-Fārābī has dealt with this in his *Major Commentary*. In his disdain for modal syllogisms, Rescher sees the influence of the Syriac theologian-logicians. It may be noted that Galen, in his *Institutio Logica*, does not speak of them either.

One original step taken by al-Fārābī in this short commentary is the use of ecthesis (ἔκθεσις: *iftirāḍ*, *apax*, which D. M. Dunlop suggests should be amended to *iftirāḍ* or *ifrāḍ*) in the reduction to the first figure of syllogisms of the second of the Baroco system and the third of the Bocardo. The following is an example of the Baroco system (with the major moved to the head):

Every mobile (M) is corporel (C) Major A
Some existent (X) is not corporel (C) Minor O
Some existent (X) is not mobile (M) Conclusion O.

If some C is not C, it may be said that a part of the Xs is not C. Let this part be called P. We then have: No P is C (E), which provides a second figure syllogism of the Camestres type:

All M is C Major A
No P is C Minor E
No P is M Conclusion E.

But "no P is C" is converted into "no C is P", and by inverting the premisses the result is a definitive reduction from Camestres to Celarent of the first figure, with the second concluding:

No C is P Major E
All M is C Minor A
No P is M Conclusion E.

It is thus proved by this reduction to the first figure that no P is M. But it is given that P is some X. Therefore, it is true that some X is not M.

Rescher also draws attention to the originality of the chapter on analogy or transfer, in relation to what Aristotle says (*Pr. Anal.* ii, 25, 69 a 20 f.) on this reasoning which he calls 'απαγωγή. Of the latter, the following is typical: there is an evident major and a minor which is uncertain, but more probable or at least no less probable than the conclusion which is to be demonstrated. For example: Every science can be taught; justice is a science, therefore justice can be taught (syllogism of the first figure in the Barbara system). But al-Fārābī's analysis is different. He revives the distinction between *shāhid* and *ghāʾib* (cf. above). Rescher analyses this reasoning as follows: when A and B are two similars relative to S, and when T is present in A, it may be concluded that T is present in B. Thus experience seems to teach us that bodies, such as animals and plants, are created. This character of being created is transferred from these bodies to the celestial bodies. But al-Fārābī adds, the resemblance must be "relative to that which characterises animals as created," in other words, "a similarity between animals and the heavens on a point which gives truth to the judgment that the character of being created belongs to all these beings", for example the fact that they are all contingent. This requirement recalls a passage in the *Topics* concerning resemblance (i, 17, 108 a 14-17): "it is in the measure that they possess an identical attribute that things are similar." Therefore the bodies of animals and plants are created because they have this character of being contingent. The result is a first figure syllogism of the Barbara type:

All contingent bodies are created
The celestial bodies are contingent bodies
Therefore the celestial bodies are created.

Al-Fārābī is not the only one to achieve originality in his commentaries. Ch. E. Butterworth has also drawn attention to the originality of Ibn Rushd, although the latter is reputed to have followed Aristotle to the letter. He had "the onerous task of introducing the thought of a pagan philosopher to a somewhat closed Muslim community..." And, since he conceives that "teaching by means of demonstration is the apogee of what Aristotle has said on the art of logic, he sees no objection to presenting everything which precedes the exposition of this teaching as preliminaries based on general opinion, provided that this tactic induces his readers to revise their attitude towards the philosophy ... of Aristotle" (*La valeur philosophique des commentaires d'Averroès sur Aristote*, in *Multiple Averroès*. Paris 1978, 117-26). Also worth consulting is the same author's very interesting introduction to the edition of the Middle Commentary on the *Topics* (*Averroes' Middle Commentary on Aristotle's Topics*, Cairo 1979).

(c) *The original treatises.* It is with Ibn Sīnā that logic is genuinely detached from commentary to become an integral part of the great treatises. The *Shifāʾ*, the *K. al-Nadjāt* and the *Ishārāt* all begin with a section devoted to logic. In the *Shifāʾ*, moreover, Ibn Sīnā follows the order of the treatises of the *Organon* while making them precede the *Isagoge* (*al-Madkhal*), then moving on from the Categories as far as the *Poetics*. Ibrahim Madkour has well demonstrated that this treatise is not a commentary in the manner of those of Ibn Rushd; it presents an original development with "personal hypotheses and analyses of great breadth" (*Le Shifâʾ*, ed. Cairo, General Introd. 16-17). The connections between the *Shifāʾ* and the *Nadjāt* are close. Both respond to the same principal idea: " to combine together logic, physics and metaphysics" (*ibid.*, 19). The *Ishārāt*, which are subsequent to them, further display "the originality and the personality of Avicenna. This is why the work is associated with the ʿOriental Philosophyʾ" (*ibid.*, 22). There has been much discussion of this philosophy, which Ibn Sīnā himself evokes at the beginning of the *Madkhal*. That which remains of the *Manṭiḳ al-Mashriḳiyyīn* (the Logic of the Orientals) offers no new ideas in relation to the other works. Ibn Sīnā shows himself here closely attached to Aristotle. But he himself indicates the sense in which this philosophy is different. "We have revealed in this book the philosophy conforming to that which is in the nature of the spirit (*fi 'l-ṭabʿ*) and to that which expresses the correct point of view (*al-raʾy al-ṣaḥīḥ*) without concessions to those who are associated in this discipline. There is no hesitation in diverging from their authority, as there is hesitation in other books" (*Madkhal*), 10). In fact, he specifies that the *Shifāʾ* is more in agreement with the Peripatetics (*al-Mashshāʾūn*). It could thus be considered, as a result of the works of S. Pinès on the *K. al-Inṣāf*, that the Orientals are the thinkers of Khurāsān who are represented by Ibn Sīnā and that the Occidentals are the Peripatetics of Baghdād; it is the latter that Ibn Sīnā opposes and it is their interpretation of Aristotle that he criticises, on account of the fact that it is marked by the influence of "those Christian simpletons of Baghdād". It is certainly a fact that these Christians, Nestorians in the main, had pursued their studies of logic "in close association with their theological studies, since Greek philosophy provided a rational conceptual analysis, in which the theology of these churches found its articulation" (*The development of Arabic logic*, Pittsburgh 1964, 16).

Nevertheless, in the *Shifāʾ*, there is already a debate conducted with various logicians. Nabil Shehaby (*The propositional logic of Avicenna*, Dordrecht 1973) has sought to discover whether these are Ancient Greeks, contemporary Muslims or Christian Arabs. The author refers to Aristotle, to the Stoics (Chrysippus), to Galien, and he uses information supplied by Diogenes Laertius, Sextus Empiricus, etc. In the posterity of Avicenna, Fakhr al-Dīn al-Rāzī [*q.v.*] and Naṣīr al-Dīn al-Ṭūsī, who both commented on the *Ishārāt*, differ on their interpretation. Al-Rāzī wrote numerous critiques of Avicenna, while acknowledging the scale of his debt to him. Rescher writes with reference to him: "In principle, Fakhr al-Dīn was not only a critic, but also an interpreter and a continuer of the work of Avicenna. He may, nevertheless, be considered the founder of an important 'western school' of Persian logicians ... since it constitutes a focus of opposition to the tradition of Avicenna" (*Development*, 184). On the other hand, al-Ṭūsī (597-672/1201-74) criticised the writings of the "westerners", specifically those of al-Rāzī (*ibid.*, 197). In Spain, the influence of al-Fārābī was dominant, and there are seen perpetuated there the concepts of the school of Baghdād which had been introduced by Muḥammad b. ʿAbdūn (4th/10th century). Worthy of mention among the logicians of this country are Abu 'l-Ṣalt [*q.v.*] and Ibn Ṭumlūs [*q.v.*]. Many of these logicians had maintained an ancient tradition dating back to the Syrians, that of associating the study of logic with that of medicine.

Among the successors of Ibn Sīnā, mention should also be made of Abu 'l-Barakāt al-Baghdādī [*q.v.*] who constructed his *K. al-Muʿtabar* on the tripartite division of logic, physics, metaphysics. He sometimes follows Ibn Sīnā and sometimes attacks him. His method is based on immediate, evident *a priori* forms of knowledge, which, as S. Pinès writes, "disparage the *a posteriori* theses" accepted by the Peripatetics.

This arrangement of treatises poses the problem of deciding whether logic forms an integral part of philosophy (the Stoics), or is only a methodological introduction to it (the Peripatetics). Many Arab logicians support the latter point of view. Ibn Sīnā and the Muslim Neoplatonists reconcile these two concepts: logic is a part of philosophy to which it constitutes an introduction.

There is room here only to draw attention to the interest in the study of logic on the part of scholars of the Arabo-Muslim world in the Middle Ages. Thus it is known that the great mathematician, astronomer, [optical] physicist and physician, Ibn al-Haytham (d. 430/1039 [*q.v.*] wrote on the "seven books". Al-Bīrūnī, a centemporary of Avicenna, considered that the perfect language of science was the mathematical language characterised by the bi-univocity of signifiers and signified. Nevertheless, he mentions in the introduction to his *Pharmacopoeia*, the interesting quality of the *Isagoge* and the four treatises, from the *Categories* to the *Secondary Analytics*. It may be wondered what use would have been made of it in cases where the mathematical language does not apply. In these matters, much research remains to be done.

(d) The logic of the Ikhwān al-Ṣafāʾ. It is from the 10th to the 14th Epistle that questions of logic are dealt with, after mathematics (arithmetic and geometry), astronomy, geography and music. The Ikhwān speak of the *Isagoge* and the first four books of the *Organon*. Men, being tied to a body, require for its comprehension an elocution formed of articulated words (*nuṭḳ lafẓī*). But, having access to intelligibles, they also possess an elocution formed of thought (*nuṭḳ fikrī*). There are thus two logical sciences to be distinguished: (1) *ʿilm al-manṭiḳ al-lughawī*. and (2) *ʿilm al-manṭiḳ al-falsafī*. It is necessary to start with the first in order to make the second comprehensible; this is the object of the *Isagoge*, the *Madkhal*. Then the logic of thought (*al-manṭiḳ al-fikrī*) is approached. "Terms (*alfāẓ*) are only the signs which designate ideas, which are in the thought of souls: they have been instituted between men, so that each may express to other men what he has in his soul". These ideas are forms which are given to the individual soul by the Creator, through a series of intermediary emanations: from God to the Agent Intellect, then to the universal Soul, then to the primary Matter, then to the human soul. "They are that by which men express themselves in their thought relative to knowable things, having seen material testimony to them by means of the senses." Logical philosophy is thus fundamentally linked to a cosmology in which man is a microcosm (*ʿālam ṣaghīr*) and the world a *makros anthropos* (*insān kabīr*). But he requires verbal logic (*manṭiḳ lafẓī*) in order to convey knowledge to others and to question them. This logic is thus not an art of discovery, but an art of revealing and of answering questions. Its object is to inform and to "popularise" (Rescher).

Lexicographers recognise several senses for the word "genre". For the philosophers, there is only one: that which is applied "to the ten terms studied in the categories (*al-ʿas͟hrat al-alfāẓ allatī fī Ḳāṭīg͟huriyās*)", which they call *maḳūlat*. Each of these terms is the name of one of the existent genres. All ideas belong within these ten terms. From the starting-point of sensible experience, the philosophers define as matter the things anterior in existence, and as form the posterior things (this is evidently a case of logical anteriority and posteriority; if there is no matter, there is no form for a matter). Then they perceive that form is of two kinds, the one constitutive (*mukawwina*), the other perfective (*mutammima*); they call the first substance and the second accident. They declare that substances, having a unique status (*ḥukm*), constitute a single genre, unlike accidents which vary according to nine genres corresponding to the nine unities. Thus the logical expression of the reality of beings is in harmony with their arithmological expression, fundamental among the Ik͟hwān. Furthermore, this presentation of categories is intimately linked to sensible experience on the one hand, to the terms of the language which express it on the other.

On the *De Interpretatione*, the Ik͟hwān follow Aristotle only approximately. They abridge the work considerably and even mutilate it. On the other hand, they present some original features. E.g. their analysis of propositions which "enunciate universally of a universal" (*De Int.*, 7. 17, a 36-17 b 15); they speak of enunciations of which the truth or falsehood is manifest, and which do not lend themselves to interpretation (*taʾwīl*), as opposed to those which require this, an important issue in Ḳurʾānic exegesis. A proposition is not subject to *taʾwīl*, "when it is delimited (*maḥṣūr*); delimited things are those which are determined by a *sūr*". This word denotes an enclosing wall. Al-Tahānawī explains that it indicates the quantity (*kammiyya*) of individuals in an attributive judgment, such as "every" or "some". This is the προσδιορισμός of Aristotle. This *sūr* can be universal or particular. Thus: Every man is animal (evidently true); no man is animal (evidently false), etc. Propositions which do not have a *sūr* are either indefinite (*muhmal*), for example, the man is (or is not) a writer, or specific, for example, Zayd is (or is not) a writer; the latter is neither true or false, since it is not known which Zayd is being discussed. These ideas (which have already been encountered above) can be traced back to the *Topics* (iii, 6, 120 a 5 f.). It is worth quoting further from this typically Muslim passage, which no doubt refers to what Aristotle says of future contingents, "things which do not yet exist, but have only the potential of being or not being" (*De Int.*, 9, 19 b 2); in this case, affirmation and negation are mutually exclusive, they can be united in the true or the false when care is taken to say for example, of a young child, that he is potentially a writer but not so in fact. This is the sense which is to be given to the statement of the Messenger of God, "I was a prophet when Adam was between the water and the clay". He was a prophet in potential, but not in fact.

As for the syllogism, the Ik͟hwān note that from two judgments united as premisses, a conclusion can only result if there is a common middle term, and they use the analogy of sexual union (*izdiwād͟j*), the conclusion being like the child which is the object and the result. But the presence of a middle term does not suffice; hence the existence of inconclusive modes. The Ik͟hwān explain the syllogism (*ḳiyās*) on the basis of the root *ḳāsa*, which means to measure a thing by using a yardstick of the same type. Thus the scales measure that which has weight (*t͟hiḳl*) with weights (*ṣand͟jāt*). It is the combination of two planes, of an axis, of threads and weights. The same applies to the logical balance which is demonstrative reasoning (*burhān*). What it is composed of and what it is capable of weighing are both shown in the *Categories*; then in the *De Interpretatione*, how it is arranged and adjusted to form a balance and a scale of measure (*miḳyās*); then in the *Prior Analytics*, how this balance should be observed in such a way that it will not be falsified and twisted; finally, in the Secondary Analytics, how the weighing is to be performed and used, with the aim that it will be just and faultless.

In more than one respect, the ideas of Ibn Sabʿīn [*q.v.*] on logic are close to those of the Ik͟hwān. Like them, he insists on term and names. Ideas are that which is produced in the spirit as a result of sensible perceptions. But the absolute monism of Ibn Sabʿīn condemns their plurality; knowledge thus obtained cannot be other than inadequate. In *Budd al-ʿārif*, the beginning of which is devoted to a critical survey of Aristotelian logic, he takes issue with the plurality of terms used by the logicians, in relation to the plurality of perceptions, those of genre, type, difference, particular, accident, and *a fortiori*, of individual. Thus, definition serves no purpose in the acquisition of genuine knowledge, that of the *ʿārif*. "There is no need of it for explaining to another that which one knows". If there is removed from definition everything which belongs to discourse expressed between men, all that remains is the affirmation of an existence. Thus, the defined is the existent (*fa 'l-maḥdūd huwa 'l-mawd͟jūd*). Now existence cannot be defined, at least, Ibn Sabʿīn adds ironically, "unless one wishes to call existence definition; we do not discuss these expressions, we seek only true realities". In a word, logic is in relation with the thought of men enclosed in a multiple world, with their awarenesses which bear on the multiplicity of finite and defined beings. But it is useful, as are the sciences which follow its rules, to show the inadequacy of this type of knowledge and the need to pass beyond it to acquire the awareness of the Absolute One which is sought by the *mustars͟hid* under the guidance of his master.

5. Logic in the judicial sciences.

There developed very early in Islam a science of the principles of law (*ʿilm uṣūl al-fiḳh*) of which it could be said that its function in the law was the same as that of logic in philosophy and the sciences. There is thus already a doctrine of reasoning among the *uṣūliyyūn*. From the Ḳurʾānic verse IV, 83, there has been drawn the notion of *instinbāṭ*, elucidation of the divine word, closely related to *istik͟hrād͟j* with the sense of deduction. The commandment in LIX, 2, *fa- ʿtabirū yā ulī 'l-abṣār* ("Draw the lesson from this, you who are of clear vision") is also interpreted in the sense of an obligation to reflect by means of analogy. There has thus been from the start the practice of informal modes of reasoning which constitute what is called in a general fashion *id͟jtihād* (personal effort). The great problem was to apply the revealed Law, often "approximately" (*ʿalā 'l-id͟jmāl*), to detailed questions and to particular cases. First to be used were the *ḥadīt͟hs* of the Prophet which gave clear guidance in detail (*ʿalā 'l-tafṣīl*). But when this was insufficient, there was recourse to analogy.

It is with the *Imām* al-S͟hāfiʿī that analogy (*ḳiyās*) was properly constituted as a form of reasoning more rigorous than the simple comparison of similar cases (*tamt͟hīl*). Al-S͟hāfiʿī proceeds from the notion that every order given by God has a cause (*ʿilla*), which is more general than the order itself. When a case is presented on which there is no particular text, if it resembles a case dealt with by a text, it falls under the name judgment on account of this same cause. In his *Risāla*, al-S̲h̲āfiʿī employs the word *maʿnā* in the sense of cause or reason; the *ḳiyās* which is not based on a simple resemblance is that which rests on the fact that "God or his Messenger have in a text (*manṣūṣan*) forbidden or permitted some thing *li-maʿnā* (for a reason). Consequently, when we find some thing similar to this *maʿnā* in a case which in itself is the object of no text of the Book or of the Sunna, we permit it or forbid it, because it is in the *maʿnā* of the permitted of the forbidden" (*Risāla*, ed. A. M. S̲h̲ākir, Cairo 1357/1938, 40). In order to extend the application of the Law, there are disinctions drawn between reasonings *a minori ad majus* (*ḳiyās al-adnā*), *a majori ad minus* (*ḳiyās al-awlā*), *a pari* or *a simili* (*ḳiyās al-musāwāt* or *al-mit̲h̲l*) and *a contrario* (*dalīl al-k̲h̲iṭāb*). But these first elaborations of a judicial logic are contemporaneous with the translation of Greek philosophy. Also no doubt perceptible, in this distinction of arguments, is the influence of the *Topics*, ii, 10 and iii, 6, for example, "An argument may be drawn from more or from less or from the same degree (119 b 16)". The influence of the methodology of Roman law is indisputable, and comparisons could also be drawn with the methods of Rabbinic law.

It is with al-G̲h̲azālī, in his introduction to the *Mustaṣfā*, that Greek logic is genuinely introduced into judicial speculations. For him there is no logic peculiar to the science of law, and therefore use is made of categorical syllogisms as well as conjunctive and disjunctive conditional syllogisms. Jurists reason only on texts or on cases which may be subjected to texts. The conclusion must demonstrate under which of the *aḥkām* (prescribed, forbidden, advisable, inadvisable and permitted) the case being considered falls. But on this point there is a certain parallelism between the logic of the jurists and that of the philosophers. Thus the modality of necessity corresponds to that of obligation; that of the impossible to that of the forbidden; and that of the possible to that of the permitted.

The *uṣūliyyūn* accept other principles such as *istiḥsān* and *istiṣlāḥ* [*q.vv.*]. There is debate on the one hand as to their value (some reject them), and on the other as to whether these are forms of reasoning or simply more or less subjective principles of evaluation without genuine logical foundation. In a thoroughly documented article, based in particular on the testimony of the Ḥanafīs al-Bazdawī and al-Sarak̲h̲sī and of the Ḥanbalī Ibn Taymiyya, G. Makdisi has arrived at the conclusion that "*istiḥsān* can be the abandonment or modification of reasoning by analogy, being based either on a disposition in the Ḳurʾān, the *sunna* or consensus which is opposed to it, or on another reasoning by analogy which contradicts it" (*Legal logic and equity in Islamic law*, in *The American Journal of Comparative Law*, xxxiii/1 [1985]). *Istiḥsān* is thus not a subjective preference in favour of what is considered equitable; it is a preference based on an *ʿilla* which is either a text, or the fact that one analogical reasoning has more force than another. But this point is controversial.

Bibliography: In addition to the works mentioned in the text, attention is due above all to the work of N. Rescher, *The development of Arabic logic*, Pittsburg 1964, of which the second part consists of a list of the Arab logicians, with biographical data, lists of logical works, bibliography and assessment of their status in Arab logic. By the same author, who is in fact the chief promotor of studies in Arabic logic, see also *Studies in the history of Arabic logic*, Pittsburg 1964; *Studies in Arabic philosophy*, Pittsburg 1966; *Galen and the syllogism* (containing the Arabic text with an annotated English translation of *Treatise on the fourth figure of the syllogism* by the mathematician Ibn al-Ṣalāḥ), 1966; *Al-Farabi, an annotated bibliography*, Pittsburg 1962; R. Arnaldez, *Grammaire et théologie chez Ibn Ḥazm de Cordoue*, Paris 1956; *La raison et l'identification de la vérité selon Ibn Ḥazm de Cordoue*, in *Mélanges Louis Massignon*, Damascus 1956, i, 110-21; R. Brunschvig, *Logique et droit dans l'Islam classique*, in *Études d'Islamologie*, Paris 1976, ii, 347; idem, *Valeur et fondement du raisonnement juridique par analogie d'après al-Ghazālī*, in *ibid.*, 363; idem, *Rationalité et tradition dans l'analogie juridico-religieuse chez le muʿtazilite ʿAbd al-Ǧabbâr*, in *ibid.*, 395; idem, *Pour ou contre la logique grecque chez les théologiens jusristes de l'Islam*: *Ibn Ḥazm, al-Ghazālī, Ibn Taymiyya*, in *ibid.*, 303; Ch. Chehata, *Logique juridique et droit musulman*, in *SI* (1965), 5; G. Deledalle, *La logique arabe et ses sources non aristotéliciennes*, in *Les Études philosophiques*, iii (1969), 299-318; F. Jadaane, *L'influence du stoïcisme sur le pensée musulmane*, Beirut 1968; Hassan Abdel-Rahman, *La logique des raisonnements juridiques*, thesis, Service de reproduction des thèses, Lille 1976; idem, *L'argument* a maiori *et l'argument par analogie dans la logique juridique musulmane*, in *Rivista Internazionale di Filosofia del Diritto* (1971), 127; A. M. Goichon, *La démonstration de l'existence dans la logique d'Avicenne*, in *Mélanges Henri Massé*, Tehran 1963, 168-84; I. Madkour, *L'Organon d'Aristote dans le monde arabe*, Paris 1934; idem, *Le traité des Catégories du Shifāʾ*, in *MIDEO*, v (1958), 253-78; A. Turki, *Polémique entre Ibn Ḥazm et Baǧī sur les principes de la loi musulmane*, Algiers; E. Tyan, *Méthodologie et sources du droit en Islam*: *istiḥsān, istiṣlāḥ, siyāsa šarʿiyya*, in *SI* (1959), 79; J. van Ess, *The logical structure of Islamic theology*, in *Logic in Classical Islamic culture*, Wiesbaden 1970, 21-50.

(R. Arnaldez)

MĀNŪ (and also Ḳaṣr Mānū or Tīn Mānū), ancient locality situated on the Mediterranean coast, in the western part of the plain of D̲j̲afāra, between Ḳābis (Gabès) and Aṭrābulus (Tripoli), and on the old route leading from Ifrīḳiya to Egypt.

In our opinion it should be identified with *[Ad] Ammonem* of the Ancients, a place situated about 30 km. west of the town of Sabratha, Ṣabra of the old Arabic sources. It was here that there took place, in 283/896-7, a great battle between the army of the Ag̲h̲labid *amīrs* and that of the great Ibāḍī Berber tribe of Nafūsa [*q.v.*]. The latter people who lived in the D̲j̲abal Nafūsa to the south-west of Tripoli (it was already called Nauusi by Corippus towards the middle of the 6th century A.D.), were already dominating the western part of the D̲j̲afāra before the Arab conquest, having their main centre in the town of Sabratha. The Nafūsa, being Christians in this period, made their influence felt as far as Tripoli, whose inhabitants appealed for their help, in the year 22/642-3, against the Arab general ʿAmr b. al-ʿĀṣ. Later on, after the Arab conquest of Tripolitania, the Nafūsa, who became orthodox Ibāḍī Muslims and transferred their political centre to the D̲j̲abal Nafūsa, continued to extend their domination over the plain of the Western D̲j̲afāra, thus assuring themselves of control of the communication routes running along the coast between Ifrīḳiya and Egypt. In 267/879-80 Abū Manṣūr Ilyās, chief of the Nafūsa and at the same time governor of this tribe nominated by the Rustamid *imāms* of Tāhart, was called upon for help, as the true master of the hinterland of Tripoli, by the inhabitants of this town, which was besieged by the Ṭūlūnid al-ʿAbbās b. Aḥmad b. Ṭūlūn [*q.v.* in Suppl.]. Sixteen years later, in 283/896-97, the Nafūsa barred near Mānū the passage of the Aghlabid *amīr* Ibrāhīm b. Aḥmad who was leading an expedition against Egypt. In the bloody battle between the two armies, the troops of Nafūsa were annihilated, and the power of his people broken. From this time onwards, they were to withdraw into the mountains of the Djabal Nafūsa.

Bibliography : E. Masqueray, *Chronique d'Abou Zakaria*, Algiers 1878, 194-202; Dardjīnī, *Ṭabaḳāt al-mashāyikh*, ed. Ibrāhīm Ṭallāʾī, Blida 1394/1974, i, 87-9; Ibn ʿIdhārī, *al-Bayān al-mughrib*, ed. G.S. Colin and E. Lévi-Provençal, i, 117-18, 129; Tidjānī, *Riḥla*, ed. Ḥ.Ḥ. ʿAbd al-Wahhāb, Tunis 1377/1958, 239; Ibn Khaldūn, *Histoire des Berbères*, Fr. tr. de Slane², i, 226-7; Shammākhī, *K. al-Siyar*, Cairo 1301, 267, 268; H. Fournel, *Les Berbères*, Paris 1876-81, i, 563-5, 575; T. Lewicki, *La repartition géographique des groupements ibāḍites dans l'Afrique du Nord au moyen âge*, in *RO*, xxi (1957), 329-30; S. Reinach, *Atlas de la province romaine d'Afrique*, Paris 1888, pl. xiv; M. Talbi, *L'émirat aghlabide*, Paris 1966, 14, 301-2. (T. Lewicki)

MANŪČIHRĪ, Abu 'l-Nadjm Aḥmad b. Ḳawṣ b. Aḥmad, Dāmghānī, was the third and last (after ʿUnṣurī and Farrukhī [*q.vv.*]) of the major panegyrists of the early Ghaznawid court.

Very little is known of his life, and that little is derived exclusively from his poetry. Later *tadhkira* writers have expanded and distorted this modicum of information with a few, readily refuted speculations. What can be ascertained with reasonable certainty is that he spent his youth, presumably in Dāmghān, acquiring an encyclopaedic knowledge of Persian and Arabic poetry and otherwise honing his poetic skills in preparation for a career as a court panegyrist. Nineteenth-century scholars speculated that Manūčihrī's first patron was the Ziyārid prince Falak al-Maʿālī Manūčihr (d. 420/1029 [see ziyārids]), from whose name the poet took his own pen name. Yet there is no mention of Falak al-Maʿālī in what survives of Manūčihrī's *dīwān*, nor any evidence that he was ever a patron of poets.

Between the years 422/1031 and 424/1033 he dedicated poems to deputies of Sultan Masʿūd then at Ray, and he appears to have gone to the court of Ghazna some time after Aḥmad b. ʿAbd al-Ṣamad Shīrazī had replaced Aḥmad b. Ḥasan Maymandī [*q.v.*], who died in the spring of 424/1033, as Masʿūd's vizier. He remained at Ghazna until the death of Masʿūd in 432/1041, subsequent to his defeat at Dandānḳān [*q.v.* in Suppl.] at the hands of the Saldjūḳs. He may himself have died about this time. Certainly, no poems of his survive that refer to events or persons after that date. (There is a detailed examination of Manūčihrī's biography in ch. 2 of J.W. Clinton, *The Divan of Manūchihrī Dāmghānī*, see Bibl.).

The latest and best modern edition of Manūčihrī's works (Dabīr-Siyāḳī, Tehran 1347/1968) contains some 2,800 *bayts*, of which the majority are in the form of panegyric *ḳaṣīdas* (57) and *musammaṭs* (11) — the latter a form which Manūčihrī introduced to the canon of Persian forms — and the remainder make up a handful of *ghazals*, *rubāʿīs*, brief fragments and individual lines. There are no indications that Manūčihrī ever attemped the *mathnawī*. Of the panegyrics, roughly a third are addressed to Masʿūd, and most of the remainder to major officials of his court. A few of Manūčihrī's patrons cannot be identified, or can be identified only with difficulty, and several of his poems either identify no patron at all or do so only with the ambiguous *shahriyār* "ruler" (Dabīr-Siyāḳī, introd.).

Manūčihrī's poetry has several qualities which distinguish it from the work of his contemporaries. His enthusiasm for Arabic poetry, expressed in imitations of *djāhiliyya* style *ḳaṣīdas* and frequent allusions to Arab poets, was unknown among the Persian-writing poets of his day. Even more distinctive, however, is his delight and great skill in depicting the paradisial beauty of the royal garden at *Nawrūz* and *Mihrgān*, and the romantic and convivial scenes associated with them, in the exordium (*naṣīb*, *tashbīb*) of the *ḳaṣīda*. Moreover, he displays a gift for mythic animation in elaborating such concepts as the battle of the seasons (poem 17) and wine as the daughter of the vine (poems 20, 57, 58, 59 and 60). Though it is not unique to him, Manūčihrī's engaging lyricism is remarked upon by all commentators.

Bibliography : *Dīwān*, ed. Muḥammad Dabīr-Siyāḳī, 3rd ed., Tehran 1347/1968; J. W. Clinton, *The Divan of Manūchihrī Dāmghānī: a critical study*, Minneapolis 1972 (contains an extensive bibliography); Viktor al-Kīk, *Taʾthīr-i farhang-i ʿarab dar ashʿār-i Manūčihrī Dāmghānī*, Beirut 1971; C.-H. de Fouchecour, *La description de la nature dans la poésie lyrique persane du XIe siècle*, Paris 1969; Muḥammad Riḍā Shafīʿī-Kadkanī, *Ṣuwar-i khiyāl dar shiʿr-i pārsī*, Tehran 1350/1971.

(J. W. Clinton)

MANŪF, name of two towns in the Nile delta.

1. Manūf al-Suflā, near the present Maḥallat Manūf in the *markaz* of Ṭanṭā, in Byzantine times a bishopric in Coptic Panouf Khīt, in Greek Ὀνοῦφις ἡ κάτω. After the Arab conquest, the town became the centre of a *kūra* [*q.v.*] (Ibn Khurradādhbih, 82; Ibn al-Faḳīh, 74; al-Yaʿḳūbī, 337), but seems to have disappeared already in the Fāṭimid period (cf. al-Ḳalḳashandī, *Ṣubḥ*, iii, 384). It was replaced by Maḥallat Manūf which, since the administrative reform of the caliph al-Mustanṣir and the latter's vizier Badr al-Djamālī [*q.vv.*], has belonged to al-Gharbiyya province (Ibn Mammātī, *Ḳawānīn*, ed. ʿAṭiyya, 183). In Mamlūk times, the tax-farm lands of the town were given as *iḳṭāʿ* [*q.v.*] to Mamlūks of the sultan and to officers of the guard (Ibn Duḳmāḳ, *Intiṣār*, ed. Vollers, v, 97), but later revoked in favour of the *dīwān al-mufrad* (Ibn al-Djīʿān, *Tuḥfa*, ed. Moritz, 91; Halm, *Ägypten nach den mamlukischen Lehensregistern*, Wiesbaden 1982, ii, 523 and map 34).

2. Manūf al-ʿUlyā, the modern Manūf/Minūf, in Byzantine times a bishopric, in Coptic Panouf Rīs, in Greek ʾΟνοῦφις. After the Arab conquest, the town became the centre of a *kūra* (Ibn Khurradādhbih, 82; Ibn al-Faḳīh, 74). According to Ibn Ḥawḳal (*BGA*, ii, 128) there was a tax official (*ʿāmil*) and a *ḳāḍī* in the town in early Fāṭimid times. At the administrative reform of the caliph al-Mustanṣir and Badr al-Djamālī, the *kūras* were united into greater provinces (*aʿmāl*, sing. *ʿamal*). The southern point of the Delta then became the *aʿmāl al-Manūfiyya*, with the town of Manūf as the residence of the *wālī* (Ibn Mammātī, 188; Yāḳūt, *Muʿdjam, s.v.*). During the Mamlūk period, the municipal lands of the town were divided into several *iḳṭāʿs* (Ibn al-Djīʿān, 100; Halm, *Lehensregister*, ii, 372 and map 23). Al-Ḳalḳashandī gives the name "Munūf", and mentions the ruins of the older town to the west of the new settlement (*Ṣubḥ*, iii, 405; cf. iv, 66). Under the jurisdiction of the *wālī* of al-Manūfiyya, there came also the small province of Ibyār (Djazīrat Banī Naṣr), neighbouring on the north-west. In 1826, under Muḥammad ʿAlī Pasha, the town was replaced by the larger Shibīn al-Kūm as chief place of the *mudīriyyat al-Minūfiyya*. At present, Manūf is the centre of the *markaz* of the same name.

Bibliography : ʿAlī Pasha Mubārak, *al-Khiṭaṭ*

al-djadīda, 47 ff.; Muḥammad Ramzī, *al-Ḳāmūs al-djughrāfī li 'l-bilād al-Miṣriyya*, Cairo 1954-5, ii/2, 107 f., 190, 222 ff.; Maspéro-Wiet, *Matériaux*, Cairo 1909, 202 ff. (H. Halm)

al-**MANŪFĪ**, a *nisba* referring to the Egyptian town of Manūf [*q.v.*]. The vocalisation of the name of the town and the *nisba* varies. In the older texts (cf. Mubārak, *Khiṭaṭ*, xvi, 47) the name is vocalised as Manūf. The recent official vocalisation is Minūf; cf. Wizārat al-Māliyya (Maṣlaḥat al-Misāḥa), *al-Dalīl al-djughrāfī li-asmā' al-mudun wa 'l-nawāḥī al-miṣriyya*, Cairo [Būlāḳ], 1941, 220, and Muḥammad Ramzī, *al-Ḳāmūs al-djughrāfī li 'l-bilād al-miṣriyya*, Cairo 1958, i/2, 222. The biographical dictionaries of Kaḥḥāla and al-Ziriklī give the old vocalisation, and this is adopted here. Many persons carried the *nisba* of al-Manūfī, of whom, in chronological order, the following deserve mention:

1. ʿAbd Allāh al-Manūfī al-Mālikī (d. 7 Ramaḍān 748/11 December 1347), alleged founder of al-Manūfiyya (al-Manāyifa) al-Aḥmadiyya, one of the oldest branches of the Aḥmadiyya order [*q.v.*], which are collectively known as *al-bayt al-kabīr* (F. De Jong, *Ṭuruq and ṭuruq-linked institutions in nineteenth-century Egypt*, Leiden 1978, 14 f.). He was the nephew of Ramaḍān al-Ashʿath al-Manūfī, one of the disciples of Aḥmad al-Badawī [*q.v.*], and appears third in the *silsila* [*q.v.*] of the present-day Manāyifa order. His shrine is in the Ḳarāfat al-Mudjāwirīn, near the mosque of Sultan Ḳāyitbāy (ʿAbd al-Wahhāb al-Shaʿrānī, *Ṭabaḳāt*, ii, 2; Yūsuf b. Ismāʿīl al-Nabhānī, *Djāmiʿ karāmāt al-awliyā'*, ii, 119; Mubārak, *Khiṭaṭ*, xvi, 48).

2. Muḥammad b. Ismāʿīl b. Ibrāhīm b. Mūsā b. Saʿīd b. ʿAlī al-Shams b. Abi 'l-Suʿūd al-Manūfī (d. 856/1452), head (*shaykh al-mashāyikh*) of the important *khānaḳāh* Saʿīd al-Suʿadā' [*q.v.*] in Siryāḳūs near Cairo. Later in his life, he became head of the *khānaḳāh* al-Shaykhūniyya (cf. Mubārak, *Khiṭaṭ*, xvi, 49 f.) which is also known as *takiyyat* Shaykhūn (cf. De Jong, *op. cit.*, 17).

3. Abu 'l-ʿAbbās Aḥmad b. Muḥammad b. Muḥammad b. ʿAbd al-Salām b. Mūsā Shihāb al-Dīn al-Manūfī (847-927/1443-1521), once head of the *khānaḳāh* al-Ẓāhir Baybars (al-Ẓāhiriyya). He was born and died in Manūf, where he was for some time *ḳāḍī*, and lived and studied in Cairo and in Mecca. On his works, see Brockelmann, I, 380, S II, 406. For a French translation of sections of his *al-Fayḍ al-madīd fī akhbār al-Nīl al-sadīd*, by the Abbé Bargès, see *JA*, iii/3 (1837) 97-164; iv/7 (1846), 485-527; ix/9 (1849) 101-31 (compilatory; contains fragments from lost texts). For short biographies and additional references, see al-Ghazzī, *Kawākib*, i, 154; al-Ziriklī, i, 232; and Kaḥḥāla, *Muʿdjam*, ii, 184.

4. Abu 'l-Ḥasan ʿAlī b. Naṣr al-Dīn b. Muḥammad... b. Khalaf b. Djibrīl al-Manūfī al-Mālikī al-Shādhilī (857-939/1453-1532), author of a number of tracts of Mālikī *fiḳh* (Brockelmann, II, 316; S II, 434; Sarkīs, *Muʿdjam*, 1807). He was born in Cairo, where he studied under ʿAlī al-Sanhūrī [*q.v.*] and Djalāl al-Dīn al-Suyūṭī [*q.v.*]. He also wrote on *ḥadīth* and grammar. For additional biographical data, see Mubārak, *Khiṭaṭ*, xvi, 49, and al-Ziriklī, v, 11.

5. ʿAbd al-Djawwād b. Muḥammad b. Aḥmad al-Manūfī al-Makkī (d. 5 Shawwāl 1068/6 July 1658), once *ḳāḍī* and *muftī* of Mecca and author of numerous tracts in the fields of the traditional sciences (*ʿulūm naḳliyya*). He was born in Manūf and lived for prolonged periods of time in Mecca, where in his later life he became the protégé of its ruler and attained high office. He died in al-Ṭā'if; cf. Mubārak, *Khiṭaṭ*, xvi, 48; al-Muḥibbī, *Khulāṣat al-athar*, ii, 303.

6. Manṣūr b. ʿAlī b. Zayn al-ʿĀbidīn al-Manūfī al-Baṣīr al-Shāfiʿī (d. 1135/1722-3), jurist and *ḥadīth* scholar who studied, and later taught, at al-Azhar mosque in Cairo. He was born and died in Manūf (al-Djabarī, i, 74; Mubārak, *Khiṭaṭ*, xvi, 50; Kaḥḥāla, *Muʿdjam*, xiii, 16).

7. Maḥmūd Abu 'l-Fayḍ al-Manūfī (1892-1972), founder of al-Fayḍiyya, a Shādhiliyya [*q.v.*] branch, and author of more than a dozen books on Islam and Islamic mysticism in the modern age. He was a disciple of Ḥasanayn al-Ḥiṣāfī [*q.v.* in Suppl.] and had also been initiated into al-Fāsiyya, a branch of al-Madaniyya [*q.v.*]. In 1918 he founded the Djamʿiyyat al-Fayḍiyyīn al-Mubashshirīn al-Islāmiyyīn, which was active in combating Christian missionary activity in Egypt, and from around 1920 he presented himself as head of his own distinct *ṭarīḳa* [*q.v.*], al-Fayḍiyya al-Shādhiliyya (cf. Maḥmūd Abu 'l-Fayḍ al-Manūfī, *Maʿālim al-ṭarīḳ ilā Allāh*, Cairo 1969, 445-7; and *idem*, *Djamharat al-awliyā' wa-aʿlām ahl al-taṣawwuf*, Cairo 1967, i, 323-5). His early writings, which were published and distributed under the aegis of the Djamʿiyya, present a modernist conception of Islam in conjunction with a reformist version of Shādhilī mysticism. In the main works, all written after 1950, he elaborates an intellectualised conception of Islamic mysticism which is presented as Islam itself. He was the original founder, owner and editor-in-chief of the Cairene monthly *Liwā' al-Islām*, which was later bought from him by Aḥmad Ḥamza (d. 1980), and of the monthly *al-ʿĀlam al-Islāmī* which appeared from 1949 until his death in 1972. For further references and additional details, see De Jong, *Aspects of the political involvement of Ṣūfī orders in 20th-century Egypt (1907-1970). An exploratory stock-taking*, in G. Warburg and U. Kupferschmidt (eds.), *Islam, nationalism and radicalism in Egypt and Sudan*, New York 1983; and idem, *The Ṣūfī orders in post-Ottoman Egypt, 1911-1981* (in preparation), ch. 4.

Bibliography: Given in the article. For the biographies of other, but insignificant, scholars from Manūf, see Mubārak, *Khiṭaṭ*, xvi, 47-8.

(F. de Jong)

MANZIKERT [see malāzgird]

MANZIL (a., pl. *manāzil*), noun of place and time from the root *n - z - l*, which expresses the idea of halting, a temporary stay, thence stage of a journey.

1. In the central and western Islamic lands.

In the Ḳur'ān (X,5; XXXVII, 39), it appears only in the plural, designating the lunar mansions (*manāzil* [*q.v.*]). *Manzil* may also be a stage in the spiritual journey of the soul, in the mystical initiation, see e.g. in the title of ʿAbd Allāh al-Anṣārī al-Harawi's *K. Manāzil al-sā'irīn*.

According to the *LA*, it is the place where one halts (*mawḍiʿ al-nuzūl*), where the traveller dismounts after a day's march (*marḥala*, pl. *marāḥil*), of from 6 to 8 *farsakhs* [*q.v.*], sc. *ca.* 35 to 48 km. A stage through the desert could reach 60 km, with a travelling span of 11 hours. In the terminology of itineraries given by Arab authors, *manzil* corresponds to the *mansio* of Latin texts, "halting place, resting place", not to be confused with *mutatio*, "place where one changes mounts, staging-post".

In setting up a *manzil*, a place of transit, on a road (*darb* [*q.v.*]), account has to be taken of the topography and relief for the distances between the *manāzil*, the presence of a watering-place, spring, well (*bi'r* [*q.v.*]) or cistern (*birka* [*q.v.*]) and the possibilities of pasture [see marʿā] for the beasts and camping for the men. In the *1001 Nights*, the *manzil al-ḳabā'il* is the place where the tent [see KHAYMA] are erected, and in general, this term is a synonym for the encampment of nomadic Arabs and then for the halting place of caravans.

In the geographical works and travel accounts of Arabic authors from the mediaeval period, this term is used for the site or encampment of caravans on the fringes of some settlement or equally, at the side of a *khān* [*q.v.*] along the highway which might be fortified to a greater or lesser degree according to the needs for security. At the opening of the 7th/13th century, the Ayyūbid al-Malik al-Muʿaẓẓam built a lodging-place (*maḳām*) at each *manzil* on the Pilgrimage Road (*darb al-ḥadjdj* [*q.v.*]), according to Aḥmad b. Ṭūlūn in his *Ḳalāʾid*. Ibn Baṭṭūṭa mentions a *funduḳ* [*q.v.*] at each stop (*manzil*) along the Cairo-Damascus road; these must be the foundations of Nāṣir al-Dīn, Tankiz's *dawādār*. According to Sauvaget, there was, during the Mamlūk period, a lodging-place (*manzila*) at each posting-stage (*manzil*) of the *barīd* [*q.v.*] network. It could also happen that a *manzil* could be the origin of a village, as at Khān Shaykhūn in central Syria.

Manzil is thus the equivalent of a *dār al-manzila*: a house where one halts, whence a place where one offers hospitality, a "hospice", for travellers. Along the routes through Arabia used by the pilgrims, the *manzil* was often a pious foundation, with a *waḳf*; this is probably why Niebuhr mentions the "free hostelries" in his *Description of Arabia*, and why Burckhardt says, in his *Travels in Syria*, that these existed all through the countryside to the south of Damascus and that they did great credit to the Turks' sense of hospitality.

At the end of the Mamlūk period, at certain stages there were fortified caravanserais, with kitchens and farriers attached, which could accomodate military detachments. In the Ottoman period, Lālā Muṣṭafā Pasha, governor of Damascus, built in 971/1563-4 to the north of the citadel, in the Taḥt al-Ḳalʿa quarter, a *khān* and also independent lodging-places in its vicinity; the *manzil* in this way became an inn meant for travellers without either mounts or merchandise. Al-Khiyarī (d. 1083/1672), who in 1080/1669 travelled from Medina to Istanbul, states that there was, at one stage (*marḥala*) from al-Ḳunayṭira [*q.v.*] in the Djawlān, a *manzil* where one could stay in tents in summer but live in a *khān* during the winter. In 1081/1671, the stage of Madāʾin Ṣāliḥ [see AL-ḤIDJR], one of the centres where the pilgrims assembled on the Pilgrimage Road to the south of Tabūk [*q.v.*], suffered a serious attack by the Bedouins. The frequency of such attacks against this *manzil* led Asad Pasha to construct, in the middle of the 12th/18th century, a fort in order to protect the religious caravans. At the end of the Ottoman period, there were, according to Tibawi, two types of hostelries: the *maḍāfa*, which was communal, and the *manzil*, which was private. In the first, lodging and food were offered free to travellers by the better-off members of the community, on a rota system. In the second, similar hospitality was given in private houses situated along the roads constantly used by travellers; the owners who offered this hosptality had to pay reduced taxes.

At the present time, *manzil* denotes a lodging, a house and even an appartment. It is sometimes accompanied by a term which pinpoints its function more exactly, e.g. *manzil al-ṭālibāt* "home for female students", the title of a work by Fawziyya Mahrān which appeared in Cairo in 1961.

The term *manzil* forms part of certain place names. We find mention of the main halting-places considered to be *manāzil* in such authors as Ibn Khurradādhbih (272/885), al-Yaʿḳūbī (287/900), Ibn Ḥawḳal (366/977) and al-Muḳaddasī (390/1000), or later, the Andalusian ones al-Bakrī (487/1094) and al-Idrīsī (561/1166), who give us the itineraries of the main commercial routes of the *Dār al-Islām* and the Pilgrimage ones. Thus along the *darb al-ḥadjdj* of Egypt, between Fusṭāṭ and Mecca, one finds the Manzil Ibn Bunduḳa (BGA, vi, 111, 149, 190, vii, 183), which al-Muḳaddasī (215, 249) and al-Idrīsī (*Opus geographicum*, 345) call Manzil Ibn Ṣadaḳa, between Buwayh and ʿAdjrūd; at the next stage, there was a *manzil* at Biʾr al-Hudhā, but with merely a well and no provision for travellers. Going westwards from Egypt, Ibn Khurradādhbih (223) mentions in Cyrenaica, on the track connecting Barḳa with Sulūḳ, in the Wādī 'l-ʿArab, the Manzil Shaḳīḳ al-Fahmī, which de Goeje translated as "territoire". Amongst the best-known *manāzil* of mediaeval Ifrīḳiya should be mentioned Manzil Bashshū [*q.v.*]; the Manzil of Ḳābis [*q.v.*] (Brunschvig, *Ḥafṣides*, i, 313), which in the 7th/13th century was outside the walls and which Victor Guérin visited in the mid-19th century in the course of his travels through the Regency of Tunis; and on the coast, at the end of the 7th/13th century, to the north of Sousse, Manzil Abī Naṣr and Manzil Tamīm, a fishing port with a fertile hinterland [see DJAZĪRAT SHARĪK]. The dependencies of al-Mahdiyya [*q.v.*] included Manzil Khayra and Manzil Banī Maʿrūf (Brunschvig, *op. cit.*, i, 309). In Sicily, there existed a Manzil al-Amīr which al-Harawī (55/125) calls Ḳaṣr al-Amīr (the present Misilmeri), a famed pilgrimage place, where, according to some, was the tomb of Galen (Ḳabr Djālīnūs) and according to others, that of Aristotle. Numerous place names in al-Andalus recorded by al-Idrīsī as being in the 4th clime are made up of Manzil followed by a proper noun, e.g. Manzil Aban (573), Manzil al-Amīr (603), Manzil Yūsuf (606) and Manzil Maldjaʾ Khalīl (615) in a fertile and populous region. In the province of Valencia, one finds Manzil ʿAṭāʾ (= Mislata) and Manzil Naṣr (= Masanasa); Lévi-Provençal (iii, 318) mentions a *manzil* at Diezma and one at Mondújar, these being "kinds of inns". In the province of Cordova, there was a lodging-place at one of the stages, Manzil Hānī, two days' journey from the capital (*ibid.*, i, 478); and on the nearby site of Manzil Ibn Badr was to be constructed, from 368/979 onwards, al-Madīna al-Zāhira [*q.v.*].

Bibliography: (in addition to references given in the article): Aḥmad b. Ṭūlūn, *al-Ḳalāʾid al-djawhariyya*, ed. A. Duhmān, Damascus 1949, 147; Balādhurī, *Futūḥ*, Cairo 1932, 228; al-Harawī, *K. al-Ziyārāt*, ed. and tr. J. Sourdel-Thomine, Damascus 1957, 34/78 and n. 9, 55/125 and n. 5; Ibn Baṭṭūṭa, *Riḥla*, i, 151, 152, tr. Gibb, i, Cambridge 1958, 97-8; Ibn Ḥawḳal, tr. Kramers-Wiet, 117, 158; Ibn al-Ḳalānisī, *Dhayl T. Dimashḳ*, ed. Amedroz, Leiden 1908, 298-309; Ibn al-Kathīr, *Bidāya*, Cairo 1929, xiv, 17; Ibn Khurradādhbih, 111-12, 149-51, 190, 223; Muḳaddasī, 215, 249, tr. Miquel, 108, 109, 237; Yaʿḳūbī, *Buldān*, 183; Buṭrus al-Bustānī, *Muḥīṭ*, i, 608; Khalīl Mardam, *Waḳf al-Wazīr Lālā Muṣṭafā Bāshā*, Damascus 1342/1925, 216; S. Munadjdjid, *Madīnat Dimashḳ*, Beirut 1967, 18, 20, 197; Ḥ.Ḥ. ʿAbd al-Wahhāb, *Villes arabes disparues*, in *Mélanges William Marçais*, Paris 1950, J. L. Burckhardt, *Travels in Syria and the Holy Land*, London 1822, 169, 188, 194, 650-1; R. Brunschvig, *A propos d'un toponyme tunisien au Moyen Age: Nūba-Nūbiya*, in *Rev. Tun.* (1935), 149-54; R. L. Devonshire, *Relations du voyage du sultan Ḳaitbay*, in *BIFAO*, xx (1922), 23; M. Gaudefroy-Demombynes, *La Syrie à l'époque de Mamelouks*, Paris 1923,

p. XCVI; V. Guérin, *Voyage archéologique dans la Régence de Tunis*, Paris 1862, i, 190-7; H. Laoust, *Les gouverneurs de Damas*, Damascus 1952, 186; E. Lévi-Provençal, *Hist. Esp. mus.*, i, 424, 478, iii, 318; A. Musil, *The middle Euphrates*, New York 1927, 281; idem, *Palmyrena*, New York 1928, 175; idem, *Arabia deserta*, New York 1927, 523, 524; C. Niebuhr, *Description de l'Arabie*, Paris 1779, i, ch. XI, 67-9; A. Raymond, *Artisans et commerçants au Caire*, Damascus 1973, 255; J. Sauvaget, *Caravanserails ottomans du Hadjdj de Constantinople*, in *AI*, iv (1937), 98-121; idem, *Caravanserails syriens du Moyen Age, I* and *II*, in *AI*, vi (1939), 48-55. vii/1 (1940), 1-19; idem, *La poste aux chevaux au temps des Mamelouks*, Paris 1941, 22 n. 101; A.L. Tibawi, *A modern history of Syria*, London 1969, 55.

(N. Elisséeff)

2. In the eastern Islamic lands.

In Iran and, especially, in Hindūstān, it came to designate a camp, characteristically the royal camp, with corresponding verbs like *nuzūl kardan* and *manzil giriftan* meaning "to encamp".

This usage is distinct from the sense of *urdū* [*q.v.*], properly "the royal precinct in camp" from Mongolian *ordo*, and of *yūrt* [*q.v.*] meaning "camp site, territory" as in Turkic, from the time of Djuwaynī onwards. The camp centre had already been organised as a rectangle by the Kʾi-tan, with the emperor's screened precinct differentiated into an outer and an inner area, as a mobile extension of the palace. The concept appears to have been inherited by the Mongols, but with the orientation shifted from east to south. The sides were defined by lines of carts and tents, the royal guard was quartered to the rear, forming the battle guard, *yeke ḳol,* and in front stood the standards, drums and ceremonial drinkling vessels (*tuḳ*, *güʾürge*, *ayaḳa saba*); a horse park, *kirüʾe*, for visitors was set at a considerable distance on the approach, while the khān's own horses were probably behind his tents. The remaining disposition reflected the division into right wing, *baraʾun ḳar*, and left wing, *djewün ḳar*. This corresponds to the late Īlkhānid arrangement described by Nakhčiwānī (see *Bibl.*) ii, 62-3, where a further distinction appears in the placing of princes, *umarāʾ-yi ulūs*, and Turanian nobles close to the ruler on the right, and viziers, chancellors and Iranian (*Tāzīkī*) nobles on the left. The select company of *īnāḳs* [*q.v.*] remained in his immediate neighbourhood. A *masdjid-i djāmiʿ* had supplanted the earlier shamans' tents opposite his own site, i.e. to the south, with its complement of clerics and secretaries. Al-ʿUmarī (see *Bibl.*), 98-100, adds that so many scholars, jurisconsults and students accompanied Abū Saʿīd's camp that they were known as the "travelling academy", *mudarrisī 'l-sayyāra*; there were all kinds of craftsmen and tradesmen, a fully stocked market, *urdū-bāzār*, and tents could even be hired by travellers. At the head of the approach was the court gate, *bāb al-kiryās* or *bāb al-khān*, where the *amīrs* assembled daily. The administration of this establishment required special officers, notably the quartermaster, *yūrtčī*, and the lost-property keeper, *bulārghūčī*, whose tent was placed conspicuously. The early 7th/13th century *Ādāb al-ḥarb* (see *Bibl.*), 286, provides comparative plans of camps, including one of "the infidels of Khiṭā"which may represent the Mongol form. Behind the stables are the kitchens, to their right the treasury, and to their left the wardrobe; the market is at the very rear. The wings curve out like bull's horns, a formation later referred to in the *Altan tobči*, 116, as *buḳa*. The Iranian (*ʿAdjam*) form differs mainly in grouping the wings compactly on either side of the royal enclosure and bedchamber, *sarāy-parda wa khʷabgah*, and placing the *ḥaram* behind it, with treasury and wardrobe to the right, and saddlery and amoury to the left; the bazaar is now in front, beyond a triangular area for stables, standards, and drums. A rather similar Indian form groups the treasury and wardrobe with the *ḥaram*, with the armoury on its right and the saddlery to its left, and after an interval, musicians and vintners to the rear: the chief divergence is in an advance guard placed forward of the bazaar, with ranks of infantry and sentinels on either side. In spite of this, it seems that by the 10th/16th century, the usual Indian camp enclosure was rounded, and Humāyūn made a point of demonstrating a *sarāparda* to Ṭahmāsp "like a watermelon" in 951/1544, in contrast to the Iranian practice of leaving it open behind (Gülbadan, see *Bibl.*, 58b). The arrangements under Akbar, described in detail by Abu 'l-Faḍl (*ʿAʾīn*, bk. i, nos. 16, 17, with plan datable to *ca.* 1006-13/1597-1605), shows an arrangement closer to the Iranian plan (*ʿAdāb al-ḥarb*) than the Indian: the basis is strictly rectangular, with a highly elaborated system of service departments on either flank of the royal enclosure, and a new defence for the private area consisting of a folding wooden trellis, the *gulāl-bār*, covered with red sheeting (red tentage had remained a royal prerogative since Saldjūḳ times). The guard was still behind the royal enclosure, as in the Mongol plan, and indeed much of the camp terminology was still Mongol-Čaghatay, as in *urdū*, *yūrt*, *ḳol, barānḳār, djuwānghār*, and *keshik-dār* for the guard itself, though the terms for tentage were by now Persian, as in *bargāh*, *khargāh*, *khayma* [*q.v.*], *sarāparda* and *sarāča*. Akbar's main innovation was probably the combination of bazaar streets along the perimeter of his own precinct with diagonal ones at its corners, dividing the army into manageable corps corresponding to tactical units. The space required for the centre alone was 1,530 *gaz* (1,275 metres if *ilāhī gaz*) [see misāḥa. 2. India], with a security zone around the precinct 300 *gaz* (250 m.) wide. European reports confirm the huge size of such camp cities, at about 3 *ḳos* across, or 6 English miles, and 20 miles circuit; even so, they could be pitched in four hours, the tents of the nobility being pitched in advance of their arrival as a *pīsh-khāna* or duplicate set. The movement on royal progresses was relatively slow, at 4-5 *ḳos* or 10 miles a day, or every other day (Roe, see *Bibl.* 324-5, 329, 334, 341, *et passim*). The camp defences were later modified by Ṣalābat Khān for Awrangzīb, to protect the precinct as much from the vast number of camp followers in moments of panic as from the enemy. Such numbers (Gemelli-Careri claims half-a-million at Bīdjāpūr in 1695, iii, 153) led to self-destruction through the inadequacy of supplies, and immobility, as at the defeat of Muḥammad Shāh at Karnāl in 1151/1739. In the earlier Mughal period, a high degree of order had been maintained by the *mīrān-i manzil* or *khʷush-manzilān*, with inspectors (*ṣāḥib-i ihtimāmān*), a superintendent (*dārūgha*), an auditor (*mushrif*), and workmen and labourers from the tent department, *farāsh-khana*, who levelled the ground and built platforms for the main tents (Čandar-Bhān, see *Bibl.*, fol; 155b). Royal tentage was carried on elephants, camels, and mules; eight mules were loaded with tents for meals and short rests while on the move. The mobility achieved through such camps, though nomadic in origin, came to be essential to the administration of an ever-expanding empire, yet moves remained seasonal, and Shāhdjahān regularly moved northward in summer for a change of climate alone.

In the nomadic camps of Central Asia, the greatest

change was from the cart tents which had been characteristic of the Golden Horde and were still used as *köterme üy* (Mongol *ger tergen*) by the Ḳazaḳ in 915/1509, but survived to this century only among the Noghay, with their auxiliary baggage carts, *küyme araba*; elsewhere, they have been supplanted by trellis tents. The protective circular camping formation is already defined by Rashīd al-Dīn (Mongol *güreʾen*) (see *Bibl.*, i, 21).

Bibliography: For the references given above, see Muḥammad b. Hindūshāh Nakhčiwānī, *Dastūr al-kātib fī taʿyīn al-marātib*, ed. A. A. Ali-zade, Moscow 1964-76; Ibn Faḍl āllāh al-ʿUmarī, *Masālik al-abṣār fī mamālik al-amṣār*, ed. K. Lech as *Das mongolische Weltreich*, Wiesbaden 1968; Muḥammad b. Manṣūr Mubārakshāh, Fakhr-i Mudabbir, *Ādāb al-ḥarb wa 'l-shadjāʿa*, ed. A. Suhaylī Khʷānsārī, Tehran 1346/1967-8; *The Mongol chronicle Altan Tobči*, ed. C. R. Bawden, Wiesbaden 1955; Gülbadan Begam, *The history of Humāyūn*, ed. A.S. Beveridge, London 1902; Abu 'l-Faḍl b. Mubārak ʿAllāmī, *Āʾīn-i Akbari*, ed. H. Blochmann, Calcutta 1872-7, and plans in B. L. mss. Add. 7652, Add. 6552 and Add 6546, etc; Sir Thomas Roe, *The embassy*, ed. W. Foster, London 1926; G. F. Gemelli-Careri, *Giro del mondo*, Naples 1699-1700; Čandar-Bhān Brahman, *Ḳawāʿid al-salṭanat*, in I. O. ms. 3760; Faḍl Allāh Rashīd al-Dīn, *Djāmiʿ al-tawārīkh*, ed. I. N. Berezin as *Sbornik letopisey: istoriya Čingiz Khana*, i, St. Petersburg 1868. For further exploration of the subject, see W. Irvine, *The army of the Indian Moghuls*, London 1903, and P. A. Andrews, *The felt tent in Middle Asia*, unpublished Ph.D. thesis, London University 1980 (forthcoming in the *Kölner ethnologische Mitteilungen*)

(P. A. Andrews)

MANZIL BASHSHŪ, a place in Ifrīḳiya whose site has been identified as the place called Djadīda.

Under the Aghlabids [*q.v.*] it was the chief town of the administrative district of the peninsula of Cape Bon or Djazīrat Sharīk [*q.v.*], which al-Idrīsī (*Opus geographicum*, 293, 302) calls moreover Djazīrat Bashshū. In the 4th/10th century, it was "an extensive and fertile region", concerning which Ibn Ḥawḳal (tr. Kramers-Wiet, 69-70) further says: "... The tax yield and the population are both numerous. A small province is attached to it; there are various kinds of harvests there, and the merchants come there to get supplies. At more than one spot, there are polluted waters, whose impurity is obvious; hence all outsiders entering the town fall ill, with the exception of Blacks, who retain their good health. These Blacks can be used in all conditions and perform their tasks with good humour. All sorts of fruit are to be found there. Each month, Bashshū has a market which is held on a fixed day".

A century later, al-Bakrī mentions at Bashshū a place, the Ḳaṣr Ibn Abī Aḥmad, probably constructed in dressed stone, according to the remains still on the site, and whose marble columns were re-used in the Djāmiʿ al-Ḳaṣaba in Tunis in 630-4/1232-6. The town had a Great Mosque, baths, three open places (*riḥāb*) where the markets and bazaars were situated, but it lacked ramparts, even though it occupied a strategic site on the ancient highway linking Tunis to the main centres of the Sahel and the south. This urban centre was destroyed in 582/1186-7 by the governor of Mayūrḳa [*q.v.*] ʿAlī b. Isḥāḳ b. Ghāniya. Al-Tidjānī, who in 706/1306-7 visited this *manzil* one stage away (*marḥala*) from Tunis, gives a description of it in his *Riḥla*. The region remained abandoned from the end of the 6th/12th century to the opening of the 11th/17th one.

Bibliography: Bakrī, *Description de l'Afrique Septentrionale*, ed. and tr. de Slane, Paris 1859, 96/45 and index; Muḳaddasī, 227; Tidjānī, *Riḥla*, ed. Ḥ.Ḥ. ʿAbd al-Wahhāb, Tunis 1958, 13; ʿAbd al-Wahhāb, *Villes arabes disparues*, in *Mélanges William Marçais*, Paris 1950, 5-10; R. Brunschvig, *A propos d'un toponyme tunisien au Moyen Age: Nūba-Nūbiya*, in *Rev. Tun.* (1935), 153-4; idem, *Ḥafṣides*, i, 306, 344; V. Guérin, *Voyage archéologique dans la Régence de Tunis*, Paris 1892, i, 190-7; P. Hubac, *Tunisie*, Paris 1948, 9-18; M. Talbi, *L'emirat aghlabide*, Paris 1966, 294, 698. (N. Elisséeff)

AL-MANZILA BAYN AL-MANZILATAYN, a theological term used by Wāṣil b. ʿAṭāʾ [*q.v.*] and the later Muʿtazila [*q.v.*] for designating the salvational status of the mortal sinner (*fāsiḳ* [*q.v.*]). The word *manzila* alone is attested, in the technical sense of "salvational status", in *Ḥadīth* (cf. Muttaḳī al-Hindi, *Kanz al-ʿummāl*, i, 28, no. 519) and, later than Wāṣil, in the *K. al-ʿĀlim wa 'l-mutaʿallim* which was probably composed by Abū Ḥanīfa's pupil Abū Muḳātil Ḥafṣ b. Salm al-Samarḳandī in the second half of the 2nd century (cf. ed. Hyderabad 1349, 20, 11. 4 ff. and Schacht, in *Oriens*, xvii [1964], 111). It was used together with, and perhaps derived from the corresponding verb *anzala* (cf. a story told in Murdjiʾī circles at Kūfa where Nāfiʿ b. al-Azraḳ asks somebody: "Where do you locate [*ayna tunzilu*] the unbelievers in the Hereafter?" and gets the answer: "In Hell"; Abū Ḥanīfa, *Risāla ilā ʿUthmān al-Battī*, ed. Kawtharī, Cairo 1368/1949, 38 n.). The dual *al-manzilatānⁱ* is used, with respect to Paradise and Hell, in a *ḥadīth* preserved by Ibn Ḥanbal (*Musnad*, iv, 438, 1. 7 from bottom; for the context, cf. Van Ess, *Zwischen Ḥadīṯ und Theologie*, 47 ff.). The idea of a *manzila bayn al-manzilatayn* is prepared in a saying attributed to the Baṣran ascetic Yazīd al-Raḳāshī (d. between 110/729 and 120/738): *laysa bayn al-djanna wa 'l-nār manzila* (in the presence of ʿUmar II; cf. Ibn ʿAbd al-Ḥakam, *Sīrat ʿUmar b. ʿAbd al-ʿAzīz*, ed. Aḥmad ʿUbayd, Damascus 1374/1953, 90, 1. 9). The Muʿtazilī phrase appears for the first time in the title of one of Wāṣil's books (cf. Ibn al-Nadīm, *Fihrist*, ed. R. Tadjaddud, Tehran² 1393/1973, 203, 1. 5). But whether he coined it for the purpose of his own theology must remain doubtful, for all the reports which we possess agree that, in reality, he did not dissociate from two positions only, namely those who regarded the *fāsiḳ* as a "believer" and those who called him an "unbeliever", but from three, he equally rejecting Ḥasan al-Baṣrī's definition of the *fāsiḳ* as a "hypocrite" (*munāfiḳ*) which was taken over by numerous Baṣran ascetics and especially by the so-called Bakriyya, the adherents of Bakr b. Ukht ʿAbd al-Wāḥid b. Zayd (*fl.* probably in the second third of the 2nd century). It is possible that this third standpoint did not become relevant, and also vexing, through explicit opposition, for the early Muʿtazila, until the Bakriyya entered the scene, for even they—and *a fortiori* Ḥasan al-Baṣrī—ultimately considered the *munāfiḳ* as a "believer", though as a believer who will be eternally punished in Hell (cf. al-Ashʿarī, *Maḳālāt al-Islāmiyyīn*, 286, 11. 2 ff.).

The discussion about the different *manzil*s had always been connected with an attempt to specify the juridical or theological consequences attached to them. This is how the Muʿtazilī position is proven in most of our testimonies (which are all much later than Wāṣil: cf. al-Djāḥiẓ, *Risāla fi 'l-ḥakamayn*, in *Mashriḳ*, lii (1958), 460, 11. 5 ff.; al-Khayyāt, *Intiṣār*, ed.

Nader, 118, 11. 2 ff.; Pseudo-Ḳāsim b. Ibrāhīm, *K. al-ʿAdl wa 'l-tawḥīd*, in *Rasāʾil al-ʿAdl wa 'l-tawḥīd*, ed. Muḥammad ʿImāra, i, Cairo 1971, 125, 11. 4 ff.): the unbeliever must be fought and cannot be inherited from, the believer is loved by God, the *munāfiḳ* should be summoned to do penance or otherwise be executed; all this cannot be said about the *fāsiḳ*. Therefore, since these juridical regulations (*aḥkām*) cannot be applied to him, the corresponding designations (*asmāʾ*) are not valid in his case either. In this presentation of the problem which became common in the future, the term *manzila* was replaced by *ism*; thus it slowly lost its significance for the theological vocabulary. Ḍirār b. ʿAmr (2nd century [*q.v.*]) and Bis͟hr. b. al-Muʿtamir (d. 210/825 [*q.v.*]) still wrote treatises about the *manzila bayn al-manzilatayn* (cf. *Fihrist*, 215, 1. 13 and 205, 11. 23 f.). Abu 'l-Hud͟hayl included it among the *uṣūl al-k͟hamsa*; Ibn al-Rēwandī [*q.v.*] refuted the Muʿtazila in this point (cf. *Fihrist*, 217, 1. 10). The terms *ism* and *ḥukm* are already found, though perhaps not yet systematically linked with each other, in Abū Ḥanīfa's *Risāla ilā ʿUt͟hmān al-Battī* (ed. Kawt͟harī, 35, 1. 16 and 36, 11. 12 f.). The disputation between Wāṣil and ʿAmr b. ʿUbayd preserved by al-S͟harīf al-Murtaḍā (*Amālī*, ed. Muḥammad Abu 'l-Faḍl Ibrāhīm, Cairo 1373/1954, i, 165, 11. 8 ff.) where Wāṣil uses *ism* but not *ḥukm*, is apparently a retrojection or a recast possibly taken from the *K. Mā d͟jarā baynahū* [sc. *bayna Wāṣil*] *wa-bayna ʿAmr b. ʿUbayd* (cf. *Fihrist*, 203, n. 1) which may have been composed in the second half of the 2nd century; nevertheless, it remains our oldest testimony for the Muʿtazilī position and shows archaic features in part of its argumentation.

Similarities with Christian speculations about penitence have been pointed out by E. Gräf (in *OLZ*, iv [1960], 397; cf. also R. Strothmann, in *Isl.*, xiv [1931], 215). There is, however, to date no proof for any influence.

Bibliography: Given in the article. Cf. also W. Madelung, *Der Imam al-Qāsim ibn Ibrāhīm und die Glaubenslehre der Zaiditen*, Berlin 1965, 10 ff.; W. M. Watt, *The formative period of Islamic thought*, Edinburgh 1973, 213; J. van Ess, in *REI*, xlvii (1979), 51 ff.; M. Cook, *Early Muslim dogma*, Cambridge 1981, 94. See also FĀSIḲ and MUʿTAZILA.

(J. VAN ESS)

MAPPILA, standard Western form of Malayalam Māppila, the name of the dominant Muslim community of southwest India, located mainly in the state of Kerala, primarily in its northern area popularly known as Malabar, Significant numbers of Mappilas are to be found also in southern Karnataka and western Tamil Nad, as well as in diaspora groups scattered throughout India, including the Laccadive Islands, Pakistan, the Gulf States and Malaysia. In 1971 there were 4,162,718 Muslims in Kerala, almost all Mappilas, and of these 2, 765,747 (est.) were concentrated in Malabar. Mappila growth in the past century has considerably outpaced that of the general population. If the rate of increase in the decade 1961-71 (37.5 %) was maintained, the size of the community in 1981 would exceed 5,700,000. Mappilas share the language (Malayalam) and the culture of the inhabitants of Kerala (Malayalis), as well as the unique religious blend of its 25 million people (59,5% Hindu, 21.0% Christian, 19,5% Muslim). Not only because of its size but also because of its particular historical experience, the Mappila community represents a significant segment of Indian Islam.

1. *The Name*

The name Māppiḷa (= Māppila, Moplah) is a direct transliteration of the current Malayalam term. Its origin is not settled, but it appears to have been a title of respect formed by a combination of *mahā* "great" and *piḷḷa* "child"; it was referred to visitors and immigrants from abroad, both Christians and Muslims, either in the broad sense of "honoured ones" (Logan, i, 191; Innes, 186; Hameed Ali, 265; Kareem, 61) or in the more specific meaning of "bridegroom" and "son-in-law" (Miller, 33; Thurston, iv, 458; Gough, 442; Gundert, *A Malayalam and English dictionary*). The latter meaning points to a process of intermarriage and is supported by contemporary usage in colloquial Malayalam and Tamil. Other derivations, including Arabic, have been suggested, but none so persuasive as the above. In time, the term became the distinctive appellation of the indigenous Muslim community of Malabar, although it is still occasionally applied also to Syrian Christians in South Kerala.

2. *The origin of the Mappilas*

Mappila culture is the Malayalam culture of Kerala with an Arabian blend, a fact that points to the ancient intercourse between Kerala and southern Arabia, founded on the great spice trade. The Mappila community traces its origin to that well-documented relationship. Arab trade with Malabar [*q.v.*] was going on for centuries prior to the advent of Islam, becoming particularly energetic from the 4th century A.D. and continuing until the European era. Islamicised Arab traders brought their faith with them to Kerala, where some settled and intermarried with the native Malayalis. The earliest generally accepted epigraphic evidence of Muslim presence in Kerala is represented by the Tarisapally copper plates dated 235/849 (Kunjanpillai, 370), which contain Muslim names in Kūfic script; however, a Muslim tombstone at Irikkalur dated 50/670 was observed by Mappila scholar C.N. Ahmed Moulavi before it was washed away, and another tombstone inscription at Pantalayini-Kollam dated 166/782 was legible in the 19th century (Logan, i, 197; but note the criticism of Burgess in Logan, i, p. ix). Because of the Kerala climate and the impermanence of palm leaf writing materials, there are no known literary manuscripts in Malayalam predating the 14th century. Nevertheless, despite the paucity of material proof, I.H. Qureshi's (p. 11) balanced opinion that Islam entered Kerala "within a few years of the proclamation by the Prophet of his mission" is very probably correct and Mappilas, in that light, may be regarded as the first settled Muslim community of South Asia.

Another view favouring a later 3rd/9th century dating for Mappila beginnings is dependent on an unreliable passage of the *Ak͟hbār al-Ṣīn wa 'l-Hind* [*q.v.* in Suppl.]. Arab geographers, who provide the available materials for the 3rd-6th/9th-12th centuries of Mappila history, were compelled to rely on such reports (only al-Masʿūdī travelled to India, and he to the north; cf. Nainar, 3 ff.). The point of view, however, is also related to the persistent and much-debated tradition of the conversion of an important Hindu ruler, Čēraman Perumāl. The form of the tradition that is generally accepted by Mappilas is that reported by S͟hayk͟h Aḥmad Zayn al-Dīn (904-89/1498-1581) (referred to as Zainuddin), who was the earliest known Kerala Muslim to deal with the subject of Mappila origins and whose *Tuḥfat al-mud͟jāhidīn* became the basis for later Indian Muslim writings on the subject (Firis͟hta, iv, 531). Zainuddin dates the conversion event to 207/822, but most Mappilas prefer an earlier dating, that of 3/624. According to the story, Čēraman Perumāl's missionary followers led by Mālik b. Dīnār established a series of mosques, thus facilitating the expansion of Islam. While there is no historical evidence for the strongly-held tradition, there can be little doubt of the hospitality and toleration of native Hindus toward the Arab visitors and their faith.

The direct relation of Mappilas with Arabian Islam is as significant as their relative isolation from Indo-Persian Islam. That original relationship continued over the years, furthered in recent times by the extensive employment of Mappilas in the Gulf region, and it has affected the Mappilas more profoundly than any other Indian Muslims.

3. *Mappila development to 1921*

(i) Beginnings to 1498

Through eight centuries from their origin to 1498, the Mappilas and Islam in Kerala experienced an apparently calm and peaceful development. Mutual economic interest and religious tolerance, expressed in the direct support of Arab traders by the Zamorin of Calicut, the leading figure in Malabar commerce, paved the way. Immigration, intermarriage and missionary activity were inter-woven strands in the Mappila growth. While occasional stress must be assumed, there is no record of overt abrasiveness or militant encounter between the religious communities; the long period of harmonious relationships, including as it did the delicate areas of religion and marriage, stands as a model development in the history of the subcontinent. Mappilas flourished under these conditions, especially in coastal areas, as noted by Ibn Baṭṭūṭa (704-79/1304-77) during his three stops in Malabar; Zainuddin estimates that 10% of the population of Malabar was Muslim by the midpoint of the 10th/16th century (p. 59).

(ii) The European period

Vasco da Gama's arrival in Calicut in 1948 ushered in the European era and signalled a sharp change in Mappila fortunes. A participant in the events, Duarte Barbosa (p. 78), summed up the history when he said: "Thus they continued to thrive until the Portuguese came to India". The imperialist aims of the newcomers, embracing both economic and religious interests and exercised through military means, introduced a new tone into Kerala life. They succeeded in cutting off the Arab trade, and Mappilas who had been prevented from becoming landowners by the hereditary system of land tenure and who depended on commerce, were cast into reduced economic straits which eventually became a pattern of poverty. As new alliances developed the warm relationships between Hindus and Mappilas were also disturbed, and in the end cordiality was replaced by antipathy. Extreme cruelty, chiefly on the part of the Portuguese, produced an inevitable reaction. The Portuguese attitude reflected the mediaeval European tradition and was well represented by the governor of Goa, Afonso Albuquerque (d. 1515), who dreamt of destroying Mecca and who bitterly persecuted his Mappila opponents.

The volatile combination of commercial rivalry and religious animus produced long-lasting negative effects on the Mappila community: economic retrogression, estrangement from Hindus, bitterness against Christians and a new spirit of militancy. These trends continued in the ensuing period of "pepper politics" as the Portuguese were replaced by the Dutch (1656), the British (1662) and the French (1725). Power remained in the hands of a coalition of Christian foreigners and their Hindu allies, while the Mappilas gradually became a society of small traders, landless labourers and poor fishermen. The Mappila community experienced psychological gloom and distress, and defensive attitudes developed.

During the period 1755-99 the Muslim leaders of neighbouring Mysore [see MAHISUR], Ḥaydar ʿAlī (d. 1782) and Tīpū Sulṭān (d. 1799) [*q.vv.*] briefly interrupted the European hegemony over Malabar. Their suzerainty provided fresh hope for the Mappilas, who for the first time in their history were under Muslim rule. Mappilas were now able to obtain some land rights and administrative positions. There was a sharp increase in the community's growth, especially through accessions from the outcaste society. The fanatical religious policy of the Mysore rulers, however, served to intensify the spirit of militancy in the whole region, and the Muslim-Hindu alienation that had been born in the Portuguese period now became an established pattern.

The British assumed full power in 1792 (continuing till 1947), and the newly-raised Mappila hopes were dashed. The British restored the old order, adopting a policy of deference to Hindu leadership and maintaining a wary eye toward the Mappilas. The latter, disappointed and embittered, displayed their resentment in a series of 51 militant outbreaks during the century 1821-1921. The formal causes of the outbreaks included agrarian discontent, poverty, religious zeal and resentment toward the rulers, but underlying these was the emotion of an oppressed people, who responded to a seemingly hopeless situation with often unreasoned and self-destructive violence. Not all Mappilas shared in the depression-agression syndrome, and only a small portion of the populace actively participated in the outbreaks. Those who did participate, however, did so in the tradition of militant *d̲j̲ihād*, resulting in violent activities against those whom they perceived as their oppressors, whether British administrators or Hindu landlords (*jenmis*), and they very willingly accepted martyrdom.

This course of events reached its final dénouement in the Malabar Rebellion of 1921, frequently called the Mappila Rebellion. This was a spontaneous uprising (not one of "systematic preparation", as stated by T.W. Arnold, *EI*[1], MĀPPILAS) that included the establishment of a temporary "Moplastan" in Ernad, South Malabar, under V.K. Kunyahamad Haji. The new factor that helped to provoke this major upheaval was Mappila involvement in the K̲h̲ilāfat movement [*q.v.*], an organised effort within Indian Islam and the Non-cooperation Movement, to help restore the caliphate in Turkey [see K̲H̲ALĪFA]. This ill-fated cause had helped to generate temporary Hindu-Muslim unity in the Indian freedom struggle. The message that came to the Mappila community through the visits of leaders such as M.K. Gandhi and S̲h̲awkat ʿAlī was clear: only a free India could effectively plead this cause, and Malabar must join the struggle. Their intention to promote a non-violent cooperative effort of Hindus and Mappilas was initially honoured, but the message had an explosive effect and a sudden violent uprising resulted. Distressed by the violence, most Malabar Hindus withdrew from the struggle which, by default, became the Mappila revolt. A minority of Mappilas continued the hopeless battle against superior British forces, particularly in South Malabar. Disappointed and resentful they also vented their anger of the Hindu community in several ways, including vendettas against landlords and forced conversions (estimates vary widely from "a few" to 2,500). In wider India, this series of events helped to sunder the newly-established Hindu-Muslim entente.

The immediate results for the Mappila community

were disastrous. The Rebellion was put down after six months of bitter fighting in which thousands lost their lives. Severe reprisals followed: 252 Mappilas were executed, 502 were sentenced to life imprisonement, thousands were jailed or transported to the Andaman Islands, and large fines were levied. A special force named "The Malabar Special Police" was organised to provide a permanent solution to the "Mappila problem". The community was recumbent in defeat, ist relations with Hindu neighbours at an all-time low, its reputation for uninformed zealotry unparalleled on the sub-continent. The fundamental implication was that Mappilas were at the end of the kind of road that had been followed; a fresh philosophy needed to be developed, and a new life forged. Contemporary evaluation within India tends to the view that the Malabar Rebellion was a war of liberation, and in 1971 the Kerala Government granted the remaining active participants in the revolt the accolade of *Ayagi*, "freedom fighter".

4. *From 1921 to the present*

Subsequent events have dramatically altered the shape of the Mappila community from a defeated and closed society to a community marked by recovery, change and positive involvement in the modern world. Factors producing the change include: the new political situation in India, involving Mappilas in the democratic process; the necessity to deal with economic problems, as well as the Communist challenge to traditional forms or belief and response; the development of modern education and the growth of a new generation of leaders who press for dynamic progress; and theological reform movements that provide a basis for conservative rapprochement with the modern spirit. This reshaping of the Mappila community has involved it in severe inner conflicts and has introduced a series of unresolved dilemmas. In the process, however, Mappilas have been transformed from a negative symbol to a positive force in contemporary Indian Islam.

(i) The political factor

In the post-Rebellion period, 1921-47, Mappilas began to draw away from the Congress Party, although Mappila leaders such as the highly-esteemed Muhammad Abdurrahiman Sahib and E. Moidu Moulavi continued to struggle for the nationalist cause. Most Mappilas were convinced that a Muslim party must speak for them, and they aligned with the Muslim League. They were led by the inspirational K. M. Seethi Sahib (1898-1960), the chief architect of the Mappila revival. In the Partition controversy, these Mappilas upheld the two-nation theory and put forward an abortive proposal for a separate Muslim-majority province in the Malabar region, to be called "Moplastan". Although the Muslim League suffered a demise in the rest of India, it continued to remain a serious political factor in Malabar, and Mappilas eventually provided the leadership for its resurgence on a national level.

It was after the linguistic state of Kerala was formed in 1956 (including Malabar District, formerly part of Madras State) that Mappilas became a strong political force, giving the community a new sense of confidence and importance. Mappila political views covered a broad spectrum, and Mappilas were associated with every major party. Under its able leaders Syed Abdurrahiman Bafaki Tangal (d. 1973), P. M. S. A. Pukkoya Tangal (d. 1975) and C. H. Muhammad Koya (b. 1928), the state Muslim League, however, held the allegiance of the majority of Mappilas, and it played a king-making role in the state. Although never gaining more than 14 seats in the legislature, through clever alignments it participated in several governments. This success not only created a taste for power politics, but also encouraged the conviction that the welfare of the Mappila community depended on political prowess. Their participation in Kerala politics further gave rise to a psychology of accommodation that took Mappilas into co-operative relationships with all segments of society, including coalitions with Marxist parties. The strong Mappila support for a Muslim party, however, gave rise to the charge of "communalism", a criticism that rose from both within and outside the Mappila community. It was noted that Pukkoya Tangal, much revered for his saintly qualities, was at the same time the President of the Samastha Kerala Jamiat-ul-Ulema and President of the Kerala Muslim League. The criticisms increased when the Marxist-led state government granted the wish of the League for the formation of a Muslim-majority district in 1969 (Malappuram District, 64% Muslim, the fifth largest Muslim-populated district in India), over vigorous protests of the Jan Sangh and other right-wing Hindu organisations. In 1975 the contention of the Muslim League that it represented the sole legitimate Muslim voice was seriously weakened when the party, largely as the result of personality conflicts, split into a continuing division. In 1983, the two Muslim parties held 12.8% of the seats in the state assembly (Indian Union Muslim League, 14; All India Muslim League, 4).

(ii) The economic factor

Mappila material strength recovered very slowly during the period 1921-47 and there was only slight improvement thereafter. Economic disabilities were keenly felt (e.g. by 1947, only 3% of *taluk* officers in Malabar were Muslim, though one-third of the population was Muslim; in 1971 Muslims held only 30% as many state government posts as did Hindu Nayars, whose numbers they exceeded). The problems of poverty and unemployment, endemic in densely-populated Kerala, were felt in a special way by the educationally-backward Mappilas. The situation produced within the community an emphasis on material concerns, self-critical attitudes, a thirst for education, and an open door to the influences of Communism.

Traditional Mappila leaders appeared baffled by the magnitude of their community's problems, and many disadvantaged Mappilas were gradually attracted to the arguments of Comunists that promised a better life. Communist parties, strong in Kerala, had down-played religious issues and had become accepted as ordinary political alternatives. As did many Hindus and Christians, Mappilas began to mark their ballots "Communist" without any sense of contradiction. It has been suggested (by Mappilas; precise data unavailable) that more than a fifth of Mappila voters may have made this choice at one time or another. For most, it was a statement of protest rather than a affirmation of ideology; some, however, were influenced by the ideas of the Communist movement, others became doctrinaire proponents of Marxism, and a few became prominent Party leaders and officials. Typifying the latter is Ayesha Bai, the first Muslim woman to rise to public fame in modern Kerala, who illustrates the startling impact of Communism on this conservative Islamic society. Joining the Communist Party in 1953, she became Deputy Speaker of the Kerala Assembly (1957), an organiser of the State Women's Society (Mahila Samajum), and an aggressive advocate for the forward progress of Mappila women.

Within the past five years, a dramatic turn-around has taken place in Mappila prospects as a result of the great influx of funds from the earnings of Mappilas employed in the oil production centres of the Middle East. The sudden and unevenly distributed wealth is creating a new set of circumstances, within which the interplay of economics and religion will take new forms.

(iii) The educational factor

Pre-independence governments had made special efforts to advance Mappila education, but Mappilas had maintained a generally suspicious attitude toward those efforts (the community's literacy rate was only 5% in 1931). By the 1950s, however, the Mappila community had accepted the state programme of universal education, especially at the elementary level, and by 1960 nearly half the eligible Mappila children in Kerala were attending schools: by 1972 almost all were enrolled. Higher education experienced slower growth. In 1922, the Aikya Sankhum society was founded in Cochin State to promote higher education, and it provided strong impetus for the establishment of Mappila-managed schools. In 1936 a special Mappila high school was founded at Malappuram under the pioneering C.O.T. Kunyipakki Sahib. Another significant event was the founding of Farook College in 1948, through the efforts of Maulavi Abussabah Ahmedali (d. 1971) who had spent some years in Egypt in association with Taha Husayn. The Islamic context was deliberately maintained in the College, but modern disciplines were placed in the foreground. Under the leadership of K.A. Jaleel (b. 1922), later Vice-Chancellor of Calicut University, the institution had great impact on the Mappila community. By 1974 there were over 700 elementary schools, 36 high schools, nine first-grade colleges, and several technical institutions conducted under Muslim management. The spirit of modern education was still the subject of controversy in the Mappila community, but not the value of schools.

The explosion of education fostered an increasing sense of individual independence and intellectual freedom. The Muslim Educational Society (MES), founded in 1964 by a group of Mappila professionally trained men, headed by P. K. Abdul Ghafoor, a professor of medicine, typified the new Mappila spirit and brought into sharper focus the increasing conflict between the old and the new. The MES was characterised by intense dissatisfaction with the slowness of the community's forward progress, by the call for "revolutionary change", by its attack on what it regarded as superstition, and by a burst of philanthropic activity. In addition to promoting new colleges and providing support for students, it began social service activities, including the founding of 14 hospitals. Its influential periodical, *MES Journal*, led the cry for change. The response of the Mappila community was broadly supportive, and the success of the MES gave it a wiser prominence in Indian Islam. The movement, however, came into conflict with traditional approaches, and major controversies within the Mappila community followed in its wake. After initially supporting the new dynamism, the Muslim League and Jamiat-ul-Ulema each issued calls to Mappilas to dissociate themselves from the popular cause, charging it with advocating changes in the *S̲h̲arīʿa*. As a result, Mappilas began to be polarised between progressive and conservative views, but did not break into sharp and formal division. The MES itself, however, experienced a schism in 1982; dissatisfied with its leadership some members formed a new, parallel organisation called the Muslim Service Society.

5. *Mappila theology*

(i) General features

Mappila theological development followed a path independent of trends in other areas of Indian Islam, a phenomenon accounted for by the origins of the community and by its linguistic and geographical situation. It was the conservative pattern of Arabian Sunnī orthodoxy that provided the major external influence. Mappila development has not been merely imitative, however, but it has been affected by its living experience in the Malayalam cultural context, especially after 1947.

Mappila isolation from Urdu-speaking Islam is notable, although never total. Contacts in the post-Independence period have increased significantly as Mappilas assumed leadership roles in the Indian Union Muslim League, as well as in other all-India Muslim organisations, but these have been primarily of a political and social rather than theological nature. The only Malayalam translation (1967) of a major Indian Muslim work on theological themes is that of Sayyid Amīr ʿAlī's *Spirit of Islam*. The views of Sir Sayyid Aḥmad K̲h̲ān, of Sir Muḥammad Iḳbāl, and even of Mawlānā Abū 'l Kalām Āzād, remain relatively unknown. Mawlānā Abū 'l ʿAlāʾ al-Mawdūdī's work is better known as a result of the translation efforts of the D̲j̲amāʿat-i-Islām. A few Mappilas have studied at Aligarh or Osmania universities, and Urdu is offered as a language option in Kerala schools. These factors, combined with societal mobility, indicate a probable deepening of relationships in the future.

The basic Mappila theological orientation is summed up in the two statements: All Mappilas are Sunnis ... The majority of Mappilas are Sunnīs. Both statements may be understood correctly. The former refers to the absence of S̲h̲īʿa in the Mappila community. The latter refers to ordinary Mappila usage of the term Sunnī: in common parlance it signifies the traditionally orthodox in contrast to adherents of other movements. Chief among the latter are the Mud̲j̲āhids; the D̲j̲amāʿat-i-Islām party has some influence, and there are a few Aḥmadiyya. In this secondary connotation, about two-thirds of the community are Sunnīs, who represent popular Mappila religious belief marked by conventional doctrine and practice, and alligiance to S̲h̲āfiʿī law.

(ii) Mappila religious leaders

The major categories of authoritative religious figures are maulavis, mullas, tangals and *ḳāḍīs*. Maulavis (= musaliar, the earlier term) are the true leaders, combining in effect the functions of *imām* and *k̲h̲aṭīb*, and to some extent those of *faḳīh* and *muftī*, the latter being dependent on the community's esteem. A maulavi must have graduated from an acceptable training program. Mullas are religious workers of lesser standing and slight education, whose functions are primarily Ḳurʾān reading and home visitation. Tangals (Mal. pers. pron.; honorific) are individuals descended from saintly families; not necessarily engaged in religious vocations, they are generally respected and occasionally revered. *Ḳāḍīs* are fewer in number, and though their sphere of influence is limited, they are well regarded; they may be hereditary tangals or appointed.

Mappila theological progress is closely related to the pattern of maulavi training. The older form was set by the S̲h̲ayk̲h̲ Mak̲h̲dūm institution at Ponnani. Said to have been founded in the 6th/12th century, it reached its peak under S̲h̲ayk̲h̲ Zayn al-Dīn b. S̲h̲ayk̲h̲ ʿAlī

(872-928/1467-1521), known as the "senior Makhdūm", who wrote religious treatises, and his famed grandson, Shaykh Aḥmad Zayn al-Dīn b. Shaykh Muḥammad al-Ghazālī, historian and legal scholar. The office of the Makhdum was hereditary, the style of education personal and the curriculum narrowly traditional. Although the institution has lost its earlier importance, its spirit lives on. It houses the Maunathul-Islam Sabha, whose key purpose is "instructing new converts to Islamism" (*The Maunathul-Islam Association—Articles of Association*, Ponnani 1949, 1).

Contemporary maulavi training follows two paths. The Ponnani tradition is carried forward by the Djamīʿa Nūriyya College at Pattikad (founded 1965) led by T.K. Abu Bekr Musaliar, which has rapidly become the premier Sunnī training college for Mappilas. Some Mappilas still attend al-Bāḳiyat-us-Ṣāliḥat College at Vellore, Tamil Nad, and a few have gone to Deoband. The curriculum at Djamīʿa Nūriyya follows the Deoband model, substituting Shāfiʿī law for Ḥanafī; theological authorities studied include al-Bayḍāwī, al-Maḥallī, al-Nawawī and al-Ghazālī. The basic intent of this educational stream is that the student becomes a true proponent of *taḳlīd* and obtain basic vocational skills, and the educational style combines the lecture method with memorisation. The narrow and concentrated learning experience instils the dedication for which the Mappila maulavi is noted, and assures that he will remain the symbol of continuity. Its lack of foundation in modern knowledge, however, has also made the system the focus of vehement criticism from within the Mappila community, and many Mappilas regard the reform of religious education as the key to Mappila forward progress. Reflecting this view a second track of maulavi training has developed that emphasises a basis in modern education. A high school degree, and desirably a college degree in Arabic is a prerequisite, in addition to the traditional Islamic disciplines. Within this stream the Rouzathul-Uloom at Feroke is a representative institution; the Djāmiʿa-i-Dār-us-Salaam College at Umerabad, Tamil Nad, has long served the Mudjāhid movement, while the Djamāʿat-i-Islām maintains its separate centre at Shantapuram Pattikad.

(ii) Mappila theological reform

Mappila theology remained in a fairly constant mould until the present century when Wakkom Muhammad Abdul Khader Maulavi (1873-1932) of Quilon sparked the beginning of the modern reform movements. He was influenced by the Egyptian reform of Muḥammad ʿAbduh and Rashīd Riḍā through *al-Manār* [*q.v.*], and was to some degree aware of the ideas of Djamāl al-Dīn al-Afghānī [*q.v.*] and Muḥammad b. ʿAbd al-Wahhāb [see IBN ʿABD AL-WAHHĀB]. Wakkom Maulavi exhorted Kerala Muslims to abandon un-Islamic practises, to respect reason, to adopt English education, and to develop progressive movements. He spread his views through the short-lived but influential Arabic-Malayalam periodical, *al-Islām* (1919) and by his Malayalam books *A literary view*, *Progress and literature* and *The rights of man*. He inspired a group of students at Trivandrum who carried forward his ideals, including K.M. Seethi Sahib in the socio-political realm and Khatib Muhammad Maulavi (1886-1964) in the religious field. A Malabar scholar respected for his skill in *tafsīr* and *fiḳh*, for his important *fatwās*, and for his efforts to establish the all-Kerala Jamiat-ul-Ulema, Khatib Muhammad's integrity and personality enabled him to transmit the southern reform to the more traditional north. To help express the spirit of the reform, "K.M." also joined with his colleagues, E. K. Maulavi and M. K. Haji, in establishing the major Mappila orphanage at Tirurangadi.

The *iṣlāḥ* initiated by Wakkom Maulavi and carried forward by his followers was basically a conservative reform, marked by an insistent call to return to the fundamentals of Islam and a positive reaching out to the new world. It is this fact, taken together with the quality of its leaders and their effective teaching and writing, that accounts for its wide impact. In the end, the movement affected a broad spectrum of Mappila leaders: orthodox maulavis, teachers and other professionals, and business men. It took on an organisational form in 1952 when some Mappilas formed the Nadvat-ul-Mujahideen as "a progressive" organisation to enlighten the Muslim masses "on scientific lines," to further "the true injunctions of Islam" and to promote harmonious relationships" with other religionists" (cf. imprints on Mudjāhid invitations). Sunnī leaders felt compelled to resist many of the new trends; they called the Mudjāhids "Wahhābīs" as a term of reproach and criticised the Mudjāhid practice of establishing separate mosques. Mappila Mudjāhids place strong emphasis on *tawḥīd*, accompanied by severe criticism of saint veneration and other "superstitious" practices. They lay stress on the Ḳurʾān in contrast to Ḥadīth, and they argue for the validity of translations and the use of the vernacular in mosque and *madrasa*. They support the use of reason in the interpretation of the Ḳurʾān ("how it promotes thinking and discourages imitation", C.N. Ahmed Moulavi, *Religion of Islam*, Calicut 1979, 53) and its appropriate application to modern conditions. In that connection, the principles of *idjmāʿ* and *taḳlīd* are attacked, and *idjtihād* is affirmed. Modern education is to be promoted and should include women. C.N. Ahmed Moulavi (b. 1906), the premier Mudjāhid scholar and the most profilic Mappila theologian writing today, represents this approach. His six-volume translation of the Ḳurʾān (1951-61) was the first in Malayalam. His translations and other interpretative works (cf. *Bibl.*) comprise an important body of reformist literature and have made "C.N." the subject of controversy in the Mappila community.

The final stream in the contemporary Mappila theological development was added by the social reformers represented by such organisations as the MES (see above). Communist Mappilas had criticised what they viewed as "other-wordly" religion, but the orthodox tendency was to resist the critique in view of the source. The lay leaders of the Mappila social reform from a stronger base declared in effect that theology must be judged by its ability to respond to human problems. Their treatment of *zakāt*, which produced a major controversy, is illustrative. Traditional charitable giving practices should be altered, and a portion of *zakāt* should be diverted to revolving funds that will help establish productive enterprises and so deal with the roots of economic hardship. Science is to be respected, for there is no conflict with religion, and co-operation with people of other faiths for mutual uplift is enjoined. The fundamental emphasis of the Mudjāhids and MES is the same: it is not Islam but Muslims that need change and reform.

As a result of these influence, Mappila theology displays an increasingly divided face. Sunnī theology, which has both resisted and absorbed, is no longer a solid block. There is considerable inner movement and diversity of approach. The possibility of a new theological synthesis exists, but may be difficult to realise.

6. *Mappila religious and social custom*

(i) Religious practice

Formal religious life centres on the mosque, of which there are 5, 350 in Kerala, an estimated one for every seventy Muslim homes (*Kērala Muslīm Directory*, 668). The architecture is unique, following the general pattern of Kerala Hindu temples, with peaked roofs and no minarets, Mappilas believe that the oldest mosques were originally Hindu temples, setting the pattern for later construction. Newer mosques tend to an amalgam of style; the explosion of mosque construction in the early 1980s reflected both Arab cultural and financial influence. A defined geographical area will include a *djamā^cat* mosque, other mosques and a number of small prayer halls (*niskarapalli*). Each mosque has a maulavi assisted by a *mukri* (= *muʾadhdhīn*), and other staff, depending on its size and affluence. Arabic continues to be the primary language of the *khuṭba*, with Malayalam making some inroads. Women do not ordinarily attend mosque services. The popular Ramaḍān night services, however, are open to all and are well attended. Since only a minority of Mappilas attend the Friday mosque service, religious leaders look to a combination of Ramaḍān programmes and *madrasa* instruction to nurture the community.

Advanced Arabic studies are conducted at the more than 25 Arabic Colleges in the state. The majority follow the older method of rote instruction, but seven are chartered to grant the Afzal-ul-Ulama degree which is based on modern language study and which qualifies the bearer to teach the subject in secondary schools. The art of chanting has been drawn into public rhetoric and has created a special Mappila art form. The *iʿdjāz* of the Ḳurʾān is taken with great seriousness, and it has led to the protective use of Ḳurʾānic phrases in amulet form, usually blessed by a person possessing the grace of *karāmāt*, and used especially to ward off sickness.

Mappilas commonly observe the basic practices of *dīn*, and a disproportionately high percentage of the annual pilgrims from India to Mecca are Mappilas. *Mawlūd* readings are common in Mappila homes. Even more important are the Arabic-Malayalam *mālas*, religious song-stories, which celebrate the lives of Muslim saints or heroic events in the history of the community. The most popular is the *Moideen Māla* representing the life of al-Djīlānī (470-561/1078-1167), closely followed by *Rifaʿīn Māla* commemorating al-Rifāʿī (500-78/1106-83). Sunnī Muslims also revere local saints, who are regarded as having miraculous powers, although the practice of shrine visitation is falling into some disrepute as the result of community criticism and the relentless pressure of modern views. The best-known is Syed Alavi of Mambram (1749-1843), whose shrine is still frequently visited; "by the foot of the Mambram Tangal" is a sacred verbal seal to a Mappila agreement. Other important shrines are those of Shaykh Zainuddīn at Ponnani and the Kondotti shrine of Muḥammad Shāh Tangal. The latter was an 18th century saint, possibly an itinerant Ṣūfī, whose followers have always denied the Sunnī allegation that he was a Shīʿī. In addition to Baḳr ʿĪd and ʿĪd al-Fiṭr, special festivals called *nerčas* are connected with particular localities. The most famous of these, the Malappuram *nerča*, recalls the deaths of 44 Mappila martyrs (1141/1728). These celebrations were traditionally accompanied by much fanfare and with very high emotional expression, but are increasingly regarded by the educated populace as outmoded expressions of religious fervour. A number of Sunnī leaders are waging a determined battle to validate the concept of *waliyat*, which is the most hotly debated issue in contemporary Mappila religion.

(ii) Social custom

Mappila social custom is governed by the *Sharīʿa*, subject to the retraints of national law and the conditioning influences of Malayalam culture. Mappilas have generally stood for the inviolability of the *Sharīʿa* in the area of personal law. Birth, marriage and burial ceremonies are strongly traditional, but in other areas, Mappila customs have been relatively open to change, including the area of family planning. Mappila women are experiencing a quiet revolution; some are joining professional vocations and assuming leadership roles. Polygamy was never common, but the divorce rate is high. Social classes in the Mappila community are nor sharply defined, but there is a continuing distinction of Mappilas of Arab descent, which is maintained through marriage practice and special regard for descent from the Prophet's line.

Mappila adaptation from the Hindu environment is not pronounced. The most striking example is the matrilinear system called *marumakkathayām*, indigenous to the Nayar caste, which played an influential role in Mappila history. Although in South Malabar accessions to Islam were primarily from outcaste groups, in North Malabar many Nayars joined Islam through conversion or intermarriage. Through this process, *marumakkathayām* took its place alongside the patrilinear system in Mappila Islam. The practice traces descent through the female side, assigns authority to the eldest sister, and controls property through the joint family system. This pattern, unusual in Islam (but cf. the Minangkabau Muslims of Sumatra) is progressively yielding to the development of nuclear families and to the pressure to conform to the more traditional Islamic order.

Other elements of Kerala culture, ranging from dress habits to architecture, have become part of the Mappila tradition. It is not possible, however, to speak of a fundamental cultural inter-penetration between Mappilas, Hindus and Christians. Mappila religious practice and theology, in particular, remaining relatively unaffected. The notable example of syncretistic practice—that associated with the Muslim saint, Vāvār, at the Hindu Sabarimala shrine in South Kerala—is an isolated exception to the general rule.

7. *Mappila character*

The key element in Mappila character is devotion to Islam. Although there is controversy within the community over the answer to the question "What is Islamic?", the importance of the issue is not doubted. The intensity of this commitment has given rise to the Mappila reputation for excessive religious fervour. The assessment that Mappilas are "religious fanatics" has followed as a more or less accepted assumption in many scholarly writings, particularly Western, contributing to the development of a caricature that bears little resemblance to reality.

As a result of the stress and reverses of the European period, Mappila reactions were extreme from time to time. The emotional and untutored response of some Mappilas to conditions that seemed hostile to Islam, however, did not represent an innate disposition characterising the entire community, which for centuries had co-existed with Hindu and Christian neighbours in practical harmony. Even those who maintained the "fanatic" assessment were forced to recognise variations between Mappilas of north and south Malabar, and in the south between coastal and inland Mappilas; these generalisations were too broadly sweeping, however, to be accurate or helpful. Since 1947, Mappilas have turned their backs on the kind of reactions that produced the caricature; nothing so clearly illustrates that fact as the Mappila restraint in the anti-Muslim riots that took place in Cannanore District in 1971.

Mappilas share the emotional traits of Malayali personality, but Mappila character is especially marked by simplicity of faith; loyalty to friends, Muslim and non-Muslims; fortitude and patient endurance; honest and frugality; industriousness, marked ability in commerce; a sense of community pride and oneness; and the readiness to follow recognised leaders. Various influences are modifying the traditional character. Community loyalty is no longer blindly granted, and there is a new sense of individual freedom, as well as more impatience with unsolved problems. Although displaying remarkable vitality, religious faith is neither so simple nor so stable as it once was, and as the public attention is more and more directed to social progress, there is a growing tendency to view it as a purely private matter.

8. *Mappila literature*

For much of Mappila history, the number of Mappila writers and their influence upon the community was severely limited by the lack of education. As Mappila literature developed, religious publications dominated the field. These continue to increase rather than decrease in quantity, and the Ḳurʾān itself remains as the best-seller. More recently, however, Mappila writers have expanded their interests to general themes, and secular literature is being written and published in abundance.

The special, and still largely hidden, Mappila literary achievement is the Arabic-Malayalam body of religious materials, narrative poetry and songs. It is estimated (P. Seyd Muhammad, *Farook College Annual*, 1974, 56) that less than 10% of these materials are translated into Malayalam. This literary form emerged about five centuries ago as a complex blend of Malayalam language, Arabic script with special orthographic features, and some Arabic, Tamil, Urdu and Persian vocabulary. Particularly loved are the *khissa pattukal*, comprising a series of romantic ballads and battle songs. These heroic epics represent the private Mappila folk annals, which are memorised and sung on special occasions, particularly by women. The poet laureate of the Arabic-Malayalam song literature is Moyinkutty Vaidyar (1857-91). With the rise of general education, the Arabic-Malayalam literary genre is on the decline, although religious literature is still being produced in considerable quantities at the publishing centre of Parappanangadi for use in *madrasas*.

Mappila periodical literature is extensive and wisely read, and is especially influential in the religious sphere. Almost one hundred periodicals have appeared during the past half-century, the majority in Malayalam, but many have died an early death. There are currently about a dozen significant publications, representing different points of view. A Mappila newspaper which played a significant role in the community's development is the *Chandrika* (founded 1934). For a more natural picture of Muslim life and emotion, the works of contemporary Muslim novelists must be considered. They represent Mappila culture, views and feelings with realism, freshness, honesty and a sense of humour. Generally uninterested in politics, the novelists also tend to be secular in spirit and deal lightly with religion, showing little hesitation to smile at its pretensions or to mock its idiosyncrasies. Drawing on universal human issues, they project a paradoxical mood of hope and pessimism. Leading authors include U.A. Khader, K.T. Muhammad, N.P. Muhammad and Moidu Padiyath, but the outstanding Mappila novelist is the widely honoured Vaikom Muhammad Basheer (b. 1910). His most noted work, *Nduppuppakkoranentarnnu* ("My grandfather had an elephant", 1951), follows the interaction between a conservative and progressive Mappila family, the elephant symbolising unrealistic traditionalism; the story illustrates a dilemma that faces Mappilas both in the present and in the future.

Bibliography (the non-English titles listed are Malayalam publications): Full studies of the Mappilas are rare; the only work in English that seeks to treat critically the whole Mappila tradition is Roland E. Miller, *The Mappila Muslims of Kerala. A study in Islamic trends*, Madras 1976. The single major investigation of the community's history by a Mappila is P.A. Syed Mohammad, *Kērala Muslīm charitrum* ("Kerala Muslim history"), Trichur 1961; other useful (uncritical) studies are C.N. Ahmed Moulavi, *Mahattāya Māppila sāhitya pārambariyum* ("The illustrious literary tradition of the Mappilas"), Trichur 1976, and K. Muhammad's thoughtful *Māppilamār engottu* ("Whither the Mappilas"), Trichur 1956. V. Abdulla, *The Moplahs*, in *The Illustrated Weekly*, 1 Feb. 1970, is an example of a popular presentation by a knowledgeable Mappila leader. *The Kerala Muslim directory* (Mal.), ed. P. A. Syed Mohamed, Cochin 1960, assembles a mass of information of varying quality. I. H. Qureshi, *The Muslim community of the Indo-Pakistan sub-continent*, New York 1962, correctly positions the Mappilas in the wider Indian Muslim context. Brief older articles include T. W. Anold, *EI*[1], iii, 250 f., who uses mainly British sources, while Hamid Ali, *The Moplahs*, in *Malabar and its folk*, ed. T. K. Gopal Panikkar, Madras 1929, and G. Tokinam, *Moplah-Nad*, Calicut 1924, represent Muslim and Hindu points of view respectively. For Mappila statistics, see India Census Reports, 1891-1971, especially the useful *Census of India, 1961, Paper no. 1 of 1963, Religion*, Delhi 1963; the statistical tables in Miller, Appx. A; H. A. Gleason, Jr., *Religious communities in the Indias*, a regional survey, Fancy Gap, Va. 1946; and N.A. Siddiqui, *Population geography of Muslims in India*, New Delhi 1976.

In general, western studies of the Mappilas from the British period must be used with great care because of frequent bias and inadequate sources, but see P. Holland-Pryor, *The Mappilas or Moplahs*, Calcutta 1904, a caste handbook of the Indian Army; W. Crooke, *The Moplahs of Malabar*, in *Edinburgh Review* (1922), 181-93; G. MacMunn, *The martial races of India*, London 1933. Much more useful are the Madras and Kerala government-published *District gazeteers*, and of these the best is William Logan's oft-quoted *Malabar manual*, 3 vols., Madras 1887, a mine of information, meticulously gathered by a relatively objective civil servant, and generally reliable; C. A. Innes, *Malabar*, ed. F. B. Evans 1933, is an up-dating of this classic. E. Thurston, *Castes and tribes of Southern India*, Madras 1909, iv, 455-501, provides ethnographic information, much of which is now outdated.

For the immediate cultural context, cf. A. Sreedhara Menon, *A survey of Kerala history*, Kottayam 1967. K. P. P. Menon, *A history of Kerala*, ed.

T. K. K. Menon, 4 vols., Ernakulam 1934-7, and L. K. Anantha Krisha Iyer, *The Cochin tribes and castes*, 2 vols., Madras 1912, include materials for central Kerala; *Travancore State manual*, ed. K. K. Velu Pillai, 4 vols., Trivandrum 1940, and *The Travancore castes and tribes*, Trivandrum 1937-9, deal with the southern area. L. W. Brown, *The Indian Christians of St. Thomas*, Cambridge 1956, studies the parallel "Mappila" community. A. Basham, *The wonder that was India*, London 1954; H. G. Rawlinson, *Intercourse between India and the Western world*, Cambridge 1916; A. Das Gupta, *Malabar in Asian trade*, Cambridge 1967; and G. Hourani, *Arab seafaring in the Indian Ocean in ancient and early medieval times*, Princeton 1951, study commercial relationships between Malabar and Arabia. H. Yule, *Cathay and the way thither*, rev. H. Cordier, iv, 72 ff., provides an exhaustive note on Malabar ports. T. W. Arnold, *The preaching of Islam*, London 1913, and S. Nadvi, *Religious relations between Arabia and India*, in *IC*, vi, 129-39, 200-11, and idem, *The Muslim Colonies in India before the Muslim conquests*, in *IC*, viii, 478-89, are dependable sources for the Arab Muslim expansion and Mappila origins. For Ḥaḍramawt, especially Tarim, to which many Mappilas trace their origins, cf. D. Van Der Meulen, *Aden to the Hadhramaut*, London 1947, and Van Der Meulen and H. von Wissmann, *Hadramaut, some of its mysterious unveiled*, Leiden 1932, and ḤAḌRAMAWT in Suppl. For the Tarisapally plates, see E. Kunjanpillai, *Studies in Kerala history*, Kottayam 1970. S.M.H. Nainar, *Arab geographers*, Madras 1942, is a valuable outline of references to Malabar; see also *Ibn Baṭṭūṭa, Muḥammad ibn Abd Allāh, Travels in Asia and Africa*, 1325-1354, tr. H.A.R. Gibb, New York 1929. The Čeraman Perumāl conversion tradition was first reported by Barbosa, *The Book of Duarte Barbosa*, tr. M. Dames, London 1918; for the form accepted by Mappilas, cf. Shaykh Zaynu'd-Dīn, *Tohfut-al-Mujahidin*, tr. S. M. H. Nainar, Madras 1942. K. P. P. Menon, i, 429 f., criticises the tradition, and K. V. Krishna Ayyar, *The Zamorins of Calicut*, 1938, treats it as legendary.

The Portuguese incursion into Kerala is surveyed by K. M. Panikkar, *Malabar and the Portuguese*, Bombay 1929; F. C. Danvers, *The Portuguese in India*, 2 vols., London 1894; R. S. Whiteaway, *The rise of Portuguese power in India*, London 1899; Barbosa, *op. cit.*; and G. Correa, *The three voyages of Vasco da Gama*, tr. H. Stanley, London 1849. The Dutch period is dealt with by Panikkar, *Malabar and the Dutch*, Bombay 1931; T. I. Poonen, *A survey of the rise of Dutch power in Malabar (1603-1675)*, Tiruchirapalli 1947; and P. Baideaus, *A true and correct description of the most celebrated East India coasts of Malabar and Coromandel*, tr. A. and J. Churchill, London 1745. Scholarly writing on the Mysorean interlude tends to widely differing interpretations. For the Muslim perspective, cf. C. K. Kareem, *Kerala under Haidar Ali and Tipu Sultan*, Cochin 1973, which includes a helpful bibliography, and M. H. Khan, *History of Tipu Sultan*, 2nd ed., Calcutta 1971; for the variation in European views, see *Reports of a Joint Commision ... Malabar in the years 1792-1793*, 3 vols., Bombay *ca.* 1794; M. Wilks, *Historical sketches of South India*, 3 vols., Madras 1869; and M. De La Tour, *The history of Haydar Ali Khan*, London 1784; C.H. Rao, *History of Mysore*, 2 vols., Bangalore 1946, is a standard gazetteer.

The complex Malabar land tenure system that has played a major role in Mappila history is introduced in Sreedhara Menon, *The evolution of the Jenmi system in Kerala, op. cit.*, 325-69 and P. N. Kunyan Pillai, *Jenmi systems in Kerala*, Kottayam 1966. For observation of the Mysorean impact, cf. F. Buchanan, *A journey from Madras through the countries of Mysore, Canara and Malabar*, 3 vols., London 1807. The development through the British period may be traced in the *Guide to the records of the Malabar District, 1714-1935*, 9 vols., Madras 1936. For a British opinion favourable toward Mappilas, see Logan, i, 621-70, while Innes, 304-72, summarises the different types of land rights. L. Moore, *Malabar law and custom*, Madras 1905, and A. Mayer, *Land and society in Malabar*, Oxford 1952, provide systematic overviews. M. A. Oomen, *Land reforms and socio-economic change in Kerala*, Madras 1971, outlines the recent dramatic changes.

Aspects of the British period are analysed by S. F. Dale, *Islamic society on the South Asian frontier: the Mappilas of Malabar, 1498-1922*, London 1981, with special attention to the 1921 Rebellion and with notes on similar Muslim communities. For another view, stressing economic factors, cf. C. Wood, *The Moplah Rebellion of 1921-22 and its genesis*, unpubl. Ph.D. diss., University of London 1975. Cf. also Wood-Dale, *Correspondence of the Moplah outbreaks*, in *Journal of Asian Studies*, xxxvi (1977), 391-400. Pertinent materials are found in the Kozhikode (Calicut, Kerala) and Madras (Tamil Nad) Archives, in the Madras Record Office, and in the Record Department of the India Office, London; but for the British viewpoint, cf. especially *Correspondence on Moplah outrages in Malabar, 1848-1853*, 2 vols., Madras 1863, while *Proceedings of the Legislative Council of the Government of Madras*, 1921-2, report a broader range of views. On the Rebellion itself, Mappila sources include K. M. Maulavi, *Khilāfattu anusmarana kurippukal* ("Khilafat reminiscences") Caliçut 1981; K. Koyatty Maulavi, *1921 Malabār lahaĺa* ("Malabar Rebellion"), Calicut 1953, and C.K. Kareem, ed., *Charitrum: Malābar lahala* ("History: Malabar Rebellion"). Trivandrum, 1971; Hindu observers were: K. Madhaven Nair, *Malābar kalapūm* ("Malabar Rebellion"), Manjeri 1971, and K. P. Kesava Menon, *Karinya kālum* ("The Past"), Calicut 1969; a Marxist opinion is found in E. M. S. Namboodiripad, *The national question in Kerala*, Bombay 1952; the primary British source is R.H. Hitchcock, *A history of the Malabar Rebellion*, Madras 1925; see also J. J. Banninga, *The Moplah Rebellion of 1921*, in *MW*, xii (1923), 379-89. The post-Rebellion period is treated by E. Moidu Maulavi through a biography of Muhammad Abdurrahiam, *Ende Kūttukūran* ("My companion") Calicut 1964. Raza Khan, *What price freedom?* Madras 1969, traces the Muslim League and Partition questions, see also *Debates of the Madras Legislative Assembly*, 1947, Madras 1947, Aboosidique, *Seethi Sahib*, Calicut 1966 (Mal.). Miller, *op. cit.*, 158-314, outlines the contemporary development.

Orthodox Sunnī beliefs are found in short Malayalam or Arabic-Malayalam writings such as *Muslim prārambha čatangl* ("Basic Muslim tenets") Ponnai, 1950; Madrasa textbook, *Classes I to V.* Parappanangadi 1972; K. Umar Maulavi, *Tarjumān-ul-Khurān*, Tirurangadi 1971; and the *al-Munir Annual*, publication of the Dj̲āmiʿa Nuriyya College. The classic *S̲h̲arīʿa* manual is Shaikh Ahmed Zainuddīn, Fathul Muīn, Trichur 1968. Uncritical hagiologies of Muslim saints include M.A.

Kareem, *Sayyid Alavi Tangal*, Tirurangadi 1970, and I. Mitankutty, *Hazrat Muhammad Shah Tangal*, Kondotti 1964. For Wakkom Abdul and Khader's views, cf. his *Islāmile čintāprasthanangl* ("The progress of ideas in Islam") Perumbavoor 1954, and for his impact, cf. Muhammad Kannu *Vakkam Maulavi*, Calicut 1981. For the development of the Mudjāhid reform, see *K.M. Maulavismāraka grantham* ("K. M. Maulavi Memorial volume"), Tirurangadi *ca.* 1965, and the biographies of Seethi Sahib. The extensive writings of C. N. Ahmed Moulavi include his translation and commentary of the Ḳurʾān, *Pariśuddha Khurān*, 6 vols., Perumbavoor 1951-61, and of al-Bukhārī, *Saheelhul Bukhāri*, 2nd ed., Calicut 1970; idem, *Islām, oru samagrapāthanum* ("Islam, a comprehensive study"), Calicut 1979; idem, *Principles and practice of Islamic economy*, tr. K. Hassan, Calicut 1964. Vernacular publications such as *Chandrika* (League-oriented newspaper), *Al-Amīn* (Congress-oriented tabloid), *Sunni Times* (traditionalist weekly), *Muslim Education Society Journal* (progressive monthly), and *Prabōdhanum* (Djamāʿat-Islām journal), report on the clash of views on an broad range of subjects.

Neither Mappila religious practice nor social custom are well documented. For both, cf. *Kerala Muslim Directory* (*op. cit.*). The unique Mappila mosque architecture is studied by J. Fergusson, *History of Indian and Eastern architecture*, London 1876. The Malappuram *nĕrča* is reported on in *Manōrama*, 7 April 1972, p. 8. See also S.F. Dale and M.G. Menon, *Nĕrccas: saint martyr worship among the Muslims of Kerala*, in *BSOAS*, xli/3 (1978), 523-38. For Mappila songs, cf. K. K. Abdul Kareem's introduction to *Moyinkutty Vaidyar, Malappuram khissa pāttukal* ("Malappuram ballads"), Alwaye n.d.; O. Abdu, *Mappila pāttukal* (Mappila songs"), Chandrika Republic Day Edition, Calicut 1961; F. Fawcett, *A popular Mappila song*, in *Indian Antiquary*, xxviii (1899), 64-71; *idem, War songs of the Mappillas of Malabar*, in *IA*, xxx (1901), 499-508, 528-37; and C. N. Ahmed Moulavi, *Mahattāya Māppila Sāhitya Pārambariyum*, *passim*. Mappila marriage practice is treated in V. S. D'Souza, *A unique custom regarding Mahr (Dowry) observed by certain Indian Muslims of South India*, in *IC*, xxix (1955), 267-74, and *Kinship organization and marriage customs among the Moplahs on the south-west coast of India*, in Imtiaz Ahmad, ed. *Family, kinship and marriage among Muslims in India*, Columbia, Mo. 1976, 141-67; see also D. M. Schneider and K. Gough, *Matrilinear kinship*, Berkeley 1961. Mappila literature is discussed in K. Chaitanya, *A history of Malayalam literature*, New Delhi 1971, and in I. V. Ittiavar, *Social novels in Malayalam*, Bangalore 1968. In 1983 Farook College, Kerala inaugurated a Mappila Studies cum Research Centre, issuing a draft version of *Mappila Muslims of Kerala, a select bibliography*, ed. A.P. Abdurahiman, with the intent of developing a complete bibliography of Mappila materials.

(R.E. Miller)

AL-**MARʾA** (A) Woman.

1. In the Arab world.

For a long time, the problem of woman has been avoided or dealt with only partially or in a biased way, but now a general twinge of conscience has brought it to the focus of our attention. Not just one but many different problems confront the Arab woman and affect how she is seen by society. There is the legal aspect, defining the precise relationship between divine and human law; there is the collection of "distorted pictures" (the expression used by Etiemble) with which literature in particular presents the "myth" of woman; and there is feminine behaviour reported by contemporary witnesses since the beginning of the *Nahḍa*, to which she adds her own version.

Woman and the law. Problems arise within the systematic framework of law because of the ambiguity of legal phraseology and because of the growing confusion over the centuries between human and divine law with regard to the personal status of women. The major principles are outlined in the Ḳurʾān, two sūras of which are especially relevant: the one concerned with women (IV, *al-Nisāʾ*), and the other to divorce (LXV, *al-Ṭalāḳ*). Other verses deal with different problems such as adultery, modesty and inheritance (II, V, VII, XXIV, 31, 60/59, XXXIII, 30-3, 55, 59, XLIX, 11). Most of the hierarchies of human relationships are established in the Ḳurʾān; for Muslims it is a revealed morality rather than a *corpus iuris*. "Men have authority over women ... reprimand those you fear to be unmanageable! Confine them to their sleeping quarters! Beat them! If they then obey, you do not look for any other method [of constraint]! "(IV, 34/38) "Men have pre-eminence over them" (II, 228). A woman is "worth" approximately half a man, and there must be two female witnesses where one man will suffice (II, 282). The woman's share of an inheritance is generally half that of a man who has the same rights of succession (IV, 11-12/12-13). Polygamy is lawful (IV, 3). Great divine indulgence is promised to men, for "you could not be fair in your dealings with your women even if you wanted to; but do not be too partial!" (IV, 129, 128). But there are limits: "Do not force your slaves into prostitution....!" and certain taboos: "Your mothers your daughters, your sisters .... are unlawful for you [to have as wives]" (IV, 23-4, 26-7).

A free wife is described as a "field for ploughing (*ḥirth*); come to your ploughing as you wish!" (II, 223). In the hierarchy, she is placed along with children and the weak in need of protection. Over the centuries she has been kept in a state of almost total subjection by Ḳurʾānic "paternalism". Her attitude ("lowered eyes"), her gait and the chaste attire are all defined whether she is young (XXIV, 31) or old (XXIV, 60). Even more strict attention is paid to the "wives of the prophet", *yā nisāʾ al-nabī* (XXXIII, 30-3, 55, 59), and, as models of reference, caused women to be more rigorously restricted, through the veil and certain other prohibitions.

Rigorous interpretation has made the Ḳurʾān very severe. For example, according to the Ḳurʾān, marriage dowries, *ṣadukāt* in Ḳurʾān, IV, 4/3, translated *muhūr* in the *Tafsīr* of al-Bayḍāwī (Cairo 1947, 102), had to be paid "spontaneously" (*niḥlat^an^*) to the woman, but in practice this did not happen. The act of marriage, in origin stripped of all religious overtones, and purely "a civil act" concluded by *īdjāb* and *ḳabūl*, offer and acceptance, without any obligatory presence of a religious authority, according to Santillana, Schacht and Chehata, acquired a sacralised aura in law and became for the population at large an act subject to the divine law, contrary to the principles stressed by legal historians.

The constraints on women have become progressively worse. Adultery (*zinā*) punished in the Ḳurʾān (XXIV, 2) by a hundred lashes of the whip, applied to the offending woman and also to the man, eventually acquired legal sanction for the stoning of the women to death. What is perhaps even worse is that the Ḳurʾān stipulated that there should be four witnesses to an act of adultery before punishment could be authorised (XXIV, 4, 13 and IV, 15/19), but later practice allowed the husband or the brother to put the suspected woman to death more expeditiously. Divorce (II, 226-32 and LXV *in toto*) is an absolute right reserved to the husband (LXV, 2), who must nevertheless refer to "the evidence of honest men among you" at all times. But in practice, this control has been neglected over the centuries. In the end, a new legal right evolved, allowing a man to use the police authorities to bring back a wife who has left the conjugal home (*bayt al-ṭāʿa*). Nevertheless, there had been constant reference to the Ḳurʾān even when irrelevant (*bayt al-ṭāʿa*, stoning the adulterous woman) and this was used as an argument for "sacralising" the status imposed on a woman.

This sacralising of her inferiority is perhaps the main reason for the problems of the Arab woman. She is regarded from an ontological point of view as a second-rate human being, coming after man in the order of God's creatures. She submits to her duties, is limited in her powers and is mistress neither of her own development nor of her own body. Everything about her is considered taboo, so that "marriage is dealt with in the same way as a man thinks about correct behaviour"

However, in the early stages of Islam "correct behaviour" was still flexible. Verses were revealed at the appropriate time to allow the Prophet to marry the divorced wife of his adopted son (XXXIII, 37) or, according to the exegetes, to expose the depraved character to public abuse for having accused ʿĀʾis̲h̲a of adultery (XXIV, 11-19; see note in Blachère's translation). Later, after the death of the Prophet, the conquests increased the number of marriages between Muslims and Jews and Christians. Although there was clear authorisation for this in the Ḳurʾān, the caliph ʿUmar temporarily prohibited this type of marriage for the sake of the welfare of the state. The revealed text was distorted or even contradicted to justify the need of the moment (cf. Muḥammad Muṣṭafā S̲h̲alabī, *Taʿlīl al-aḥkām*, 244).

In fact, the law was to become the battleground for two opposing factions. There were the literalists with their rigorous interpretation, who claimed to take their stand on the Ḳurʾān and the Sunna (*al-tafsīr bi 'l-manḳūl*) as well as on "consensus" (*id̲j̲māʿ*) and "precedent" (*taḳlīd*), methods essentially formalist or literalist. On the other hand, there was a body of rationalist or liberal opinion from the Muʿtazilīs to Avicenna and to K̲h̲ālid Muḥammad K̲h̲ālid in the 20th century who have tried to take into account the original historical setting of the statutes and the development of individual interpretation, especially concerning woman. However, over the period of the Arab-Muslim evolution, it has been the literalist tendency which has carried weight, even where in one region or another of the Muslim world some traditional customs favoured women's rights (cf. G.-H. Bousquet, 161 ff.).

In modern times, Muslims jurists, influenced by reformist ideas, have tried to make a distinction between "human law" and "divine law"; the "*ʿibādāt*, religious acts which bring the creature into contact with his creator", and the "*muʿāmalāt*, relations between individuals" (Chehata, 11). Since 1897, the institution of marriage (which is included in the *muʿāmalāt*) has been a written contract in Egypt and, therefore, has implied some means of protection for women, even though traditionally "it is not advisable to write it down" (Linant de Bellefonds, ii, 40). It has become more and more the general rule to draw up a legal document (in Ottoman law, 1911; in the Tunisian statute book, 1956; in Morocco, 1958; etc.). By borrowing from articles drawn up by the most liberal judicial schools, the modernists have followed a parallel course and tried legally to restrain the practice of polygamy; they include a "monogamy clause" taken from the Ḥanbalī school. This is why the Ottoman law of 1917 allows a wife to obtain the annulment of her marriage contract if her husband marries someone else. The Jordanian legal code of 1951 is similar. The Syrian (art. 14.3) and the ʿIrāḳī (art. 3.4) codes do not include the monogamy clause, but insist that the second marriage is given preliminary authorisation by a judge. The Tunisian code of 1959 (art. 18) was the first in an Arabic-speaking country, and until now (1982) the only one, to prohibit polygamy completely. As with marriage, there has been a gradual tendency to embody the procedure in a written document. It happened in Egypt in 1931 and in Syria in 1953 where, as also in Morocco, the judge may sentence the husband to pay costs and alimony. Several Islamic countries have forbidden "triple repudiation" in any circumstances. There has been a complete break with tradition in Tunisia, where (arts. 31 ff.) the act of repudiation is not reserved just for the husband, but it is possible to have "legal divorce", granted by the court "at the request of either husband or wife", each having equal statutory rights.

In Syria the law of 31 December 1975 (art. 60) stipulates that "the dowry must be paid to the woman herself" and almost everywhere, legal limits are imposed on the minimum age of marriage for young women and young men.

Although in most Arab-Muslim countries, it remains true that the witness of two women is worth that of one man; a marriage between a Muslim woman and a non-Muslim is null and void; and rights of inheritance are always regulated in an unjust way, improvements cannot be systematically denied. The wishes of a woman herself about her own future are now being taken into account. For example, the woman who marries a man with a different nationality is no longer obliged to lose her own nationality if she acquires that of her husband. In ʿIrāḳ (*J.O.* no. 2217. 1973), she may choose the nationality she wishes. In Lebanon (document dated 11 January 1968), she may have dual nationality and will lose her own only if she makes an official request to have her name removed from the registers of her native country. In Libya (Law no. 7, 1963), she keeps her nationality unless she is able and wishes to assume that of her husband; it is the same for Egyptian women (Nationality law, 1958) and for Syrian women (1969, art. 12). In Tunisia and the Sudan, the husband's nationality has no effect on that of the wife, who always keeps her own. It is also of note that in two decrees by the Supreme Court of Appeal in Egypt, in 1972 and 1975, equal weight was given to the testimony of women and men, and thereby the principle of the charter of 1962, "Woman must be equal with man", was introduced into the judicial system. Such examples indicate the tendency in recent times to concede a much greater autonomy in legal matters to a woman.

Distorted images of women in literature. From earliest times to the *Nahḍa*, poetic and literary compositions present their heroines with two sides to their character. Poetry of the archaic type always praises the hard life of the Bedouin with their historical records of events, their virtue and their sweethearts, who were not only ravishingly beautiful but were sometimes perfidious, were small-waisted and heavy-hipped, mendacious and inconstant (cf. Kaʿb b. Zuhayr's

Bānat Suʿād). They were always moving about, wandering with their tribes, seeking watering places as fleeting as the mirages. Later, love poetry evolved with society and a new image was added to the traditional one; there appeared the townswomen of the holy cities of Islam, Mecca and Medina, and of the Islamic capitals like Damascus and Baghdād. Pilgrims from Byzantium and Persia, both conquered territories, brought with them the first musical slave-girls, who were to play a considerable role in the creation of a new female image [see ḲAYNA]. Though them and the popular story-tellers [see ḲĀṢṢ], foreign influences reached different circles of Muslim society. The inspired stories from the Bible and from folklore frequently described queens like Zenobia, queen of Palmyra, and Bilḳīs [*q.v.*], queen of Sheba. The poets describe her as a silhouette surrounded by social prohibitions. The love aroused by woman in one group (Djamīl) is chaste and sad because it is always thwarted. For others (like ʿUmar b. Abī Rabīʿa), love has become a game which is always spurred on by desire. It is played outside marriage with a woman who is conversant with the art of teasing. She becomes the object of a demanding "courtship", she must set aside her inferiority and inflame the man's passion, using her mind, her beauty and her talents. Since a wife has become the property of her husband (his "field"), she cannot be his equal and has lost this power, which is why in literature love affairs outside marriage were seen to be necessary. Ribald and mischievous poetry portrays a gallery of free-mannered women, even libertines. There were two types of women that could be described in this way in the early centuries of Islam. There were the beautiful, cruel slave-singers, and the so-called "free" women who tried first to imitate the free manner of the former and then allowed much more boldness in their behaviour than their successors under the ʿAbbāsid régime were able to tolerate (Lammens, *Moʿâwia Ier*, 259, 440). Both groups display strong intellectual qualities, for countless passages from the *Kitāb al-Aghānī* represent free-women and slaves as being wise and good, firm advisers as well as well as mocking, insolent and cunning (i, 75, 76, 89, 126; ii, 86; viii, 133-4, 135, etc.). Again, this shows the dual image of woman described.

With the development of cities, these two female types finished on opposite sides of the social hierarchy. The urban Arabs adopted the values and ways of life of the peoples with whom they mixed, but they wanted to "preserve" their wives from them. This policy resulted in the practice of shutting up the so-called free townswomen of the wealthy and generally better-off social groups, especially after the transfer of the capital to ʿIrāk. Consequently, the influence of the slave singer became greater since she alone could mix with the men of the élite classes. She was shrewd, witty, cultured and often a poetess. She frequented all the places of social entertainment and constituted herself as a civilising influence on the sensitivity, the mind and the tastes of an expanding society throughout the Muslim empire, from al-Andalus to Persia.

Perhaps it was under the influence of the Manichaean beliefs of Persia or of Śatkism and Tantrism in Hindu and Buddhist India, that these same women of such great cultural importance gradually became a source of spiritual joy and a way of salvation. Such an apotheosis is evident in Shīʿī poetry which hails Fāṭima, the daughter of the Prophet, as "the mother of her father", according to her *kunya* [see FĀṬIMA], "an angel of knowledge"; thus al-Suhrawardī says, referring to the *ḥadīth*, "He who knows Fāṭima as she is, knows himself". Now "he who knows himself, knows his God".

When she is transformed into such an icon, woman is the idealisation of the qualities of the slave-singer as well as those of the inaccessible free-woman. Poetry and prose alike express the sexual frustrations experienced by writers who have accepted the social prohibitions and who respect the traditional hierarchies. In love with his goddess, (whose social standing has been questioned by biographers), al-ʿAbbās b. al-Aḥnaf claims only to "adore" a free woman. He says, "Only slaves can love servants" (*Dīwān*, ed. Khazradjī, 86, poem 161, verses 3, 4, 5). The same contempt was expressed later by al-Djāḥiẓ concerning slave prostitutes (cf. Ch. Pellat, *Le milieu baṣrien*, 253-4).

Theologians were appalled at the sacralisation of woman before she became this symbol of mystery. Al-ʿAbbās b. al-Aḥnaf is said to have "added apostasy to debauchery in his poetry" (*yaʿḳud al-kufr wa 'l-fudjūr fī shiʿrihi*), according to Abu 'l-Hudhayl al-ʿAllāf, the Muʿtazilī (*Aghānī*, viii, 15; concerning Ibn al-Aḥnaf, the poet at the court of Hārūn al-Rashīd, and his love poetry, see N. Tomiche, *Réflexions sur la poésie de ʿAbbās b. al-Aḥnaf*, in *Arabica*, xxviii/3 [1981], 275-99). In fact, poetic writing had become an expression of submission to social prohibitions and a sublimation of unattainable romantic desire. A poet like Ibn al-Aḥnaf really tortured himself in order to tell of his desire in a way that none of his predecessors had. Probably it was at this stage of literary development that the myth of Madjnūn, "the fool of love", became established (see Blachère, *HLA*, i, 122) and was anachronistically projected back to the beginnings of Islam. The poet makes an ideal of his frustration, and through his metamorphoses (the ground trodden on by the feet of the beautiful woman, or the linen encircling her beautiful body) he declares an impossible love.

Despite an apparent sacralisation, this poetry also carries the connotation of the suppression of the "game" of love and of reciprocal pleasure. It undoubtedly represents the woman as an idol beyond man's reach, but also as an erotic yet passive object, flattering the fantasies of the poet and of the story teller. This is why she was also a passive object of physical pleasure for poets like Abū Nuwās or Ibn al-Ḥadjdjādj, who spoke of her in less mystical and less guarded terms. There was, therefore, an adoration and total submission of one group before woman, and a libertine attitude, an ethical debauchery and a revolt against social prohibitions of another; all these characteristics feature in the "man of high birth", the *ẓarīf*, the ideal man of the most illustrious centuries of the empire.

For centuries there has been a fixed dual image of woman as angel and demon. In Arab literature of the modern era, since the beginning of the *Nahḍa* and in later audio-visual media, feminine characters retain some of their traditional aspects. In current art forms, like modern novels and the theatre, the mediaeval contrast between angel and demon appears in familiar guise with the mother and wife on the one hand, and on the other, the "femme fatale", with eroticism aroused by the female form. Sexuality may, of course, be used to stimulate a wider circulation (magazine stories and films taken from the works of Iḥsān ʿAbd al-Ḳuddūs or Yūsuf al-Sibāʿī). In the avant-garde novels, however, or in the new poetry, it may also convey a message of revolt against Society and the Establishment. Eroticism has a structural function just like that of violence in works like those of Ghīṭānī or Madjīd Ṭūbiyā in Egypt or Ḥaydar Ḥaydar and Zakariyyā Tāmir in Syria.

Old feminine images still persist. Sometimes they are used to guarantee the old established order (proud, strong mothers and wives who keep the man on the right path in social behaviour); but they may also have an evil effect, threatening the dominant position of man, his virility, the family and the social structure (mistresses of restaurants, and brothels, treacherous women, real Delilahs capable of stripping any Samson of his vigour). Details are borrowed from real life and known events in order to bring these images up-to-date and to allow the stereotypes to be used again and again. New images show the changing life experience of women and enrich the discussion of novels, poetry, theatre and the cinema. There is the woman who has regained part of her independence by working and becoming entirely responsible for her own affairs. Her autonomy is accompanied by portraying a sexual emancipation in the artistic image of her, which is on the whole badly tolerated by the writer and the media. There is also the female student who is potentially emancipated and who often preaches looser morals than she practises. In contrast, there is the peasant woman, the worker and the servant, who have left their familiar countryside, are exploited for their work and their sex, and are all fighting to survive. And there is the freedom fighter, who struggles beside men for the liberation of the homeland in Palestinian literature. No judgment is made on her sexual behaviour, usually.

When issues of daily political and social life are involved, these images of woman are moulded to suit the artistic work in which they are used. Real events are set in a fictional world and then become symbolic elements within it. It is often difficult to discern what is true experience and what has been imagined, so they should not be taken seriously as historical documents. They do remain as important disclosures of their authors' aspirations and ultimately of the attitudes of their social groups, but not as a real description of the situation of woman in the Arab-Muslim society to-day.

Woman in real life. It is hard for official laws and idealising images in literature to reveal the true life style of Arab women. We can obtain a much better description by observing how historians and biographers from the past portray her, and then how the press and audio-visual media of to-day continue to do so. In ancient texts, she only appeared when some noteworthy event occurred, like her being expelled from the harem. But in early Islam she could win a measure of respect and even evoke fear. There were frequent political alliances made between the powerful to ensure the loyalty of influential tribes; and when wives were selected from a tribe, it gave the woman a distinctive prestige and respect (see Lammens, *Moʿāwia*, i, 324, 318). There seems to have been no need for her to be confined or veiled for several decades. One Amazon, who exposed the calves of her legs, took part in the horse racing at Medina, and women with uncovered faces received strangers and went out at night to visit friends or to discuss poetry within the precinct of the mosque (see *Aghānī*, x, 58, i, 150). Khadīdja, the Prophet's wife, would not allow her illustrious husband to marry again while she was alive, and his daughter, Fāṭima, imposed the same restriction on ʿAlī. These two men became polygamous only after the death of their first wives. The Ḳur'ān imposed the wearing of the veil only on the wives of the Prophet (XXXIII, 53, 59), for originally it was a mark of flattery and distinction.

In the course of time, after the conquests and the beginning of urbanisation, confining women and obligatory wearing of the veil became general among the leisured classes. Generally speaking, women ceased to participate in social life and only rare glimpses of a woman's life are provided. Some of the most suggestive scenes are found in the autobiography of Usāma b. al-Munḳidh (see H. Derenbourg, *Femmes musulmanes et chrétiennes de Syrie au XIIe s., épisodes tirés de la biographie d'Ousāma*, in *Mélanges Julien Havet*, Paris 1895, 305-16; also N. Tomiche, *La femme en Islam*, 136-7). There women are seen who exemplify the poetic myth of the "brave woman"; they help warriors in their struggles against the Crusaders and they help to maintain the social order. These are, of course, exceptional exploits, and apart from them, women make only rare appearances, whilst their slaves had less restrictions on their freedom and could be followed for a longer time in their movements.

In ʿIrāḳ, Syria, Egypt, and even in al-Andalus, in the large towns of the Muslim empire of ʿAbbāsid times, higher-class women ceased to appear in public, and they concealed themselves under copious layers of diaphanous material. The female world retracted into a fringe society and escaped observation. It was only common women that went about unveiled. They were no longer accepted in mosques under the pretext that they would defile them in their periods of impurity or that they would distract the minds of men who were over-sensitive to the gracefulness of their form and movement.

As the Ottoman Empire expanded, the confinement of free, well-to-do women became severe from the 14th century onwards, and woman's position in society weakened. Isolated in the harem, she deployed remarkable qualities in order to dominate her husband (see Creasy, *History of the Ottoman Turks*, repr. 1961, 225-6, 230-1; M. Gaudefroy-Demombynes, *Le monde musulmane*, 387; Clot, i, 331). There was a mystery surrounding woman, her underhand activities and her ambitions, which produced in man a deep distrust of her and an imperious insistence on her local submission.

Lower-class women were not considered worthy of interest until the 19th century and afterwards. Then, many European travellers, especially in Egypt, gave precise information about their situation (see Mengin, *Histoire de l'Égypte*, ii, 305; Michaud and Poujoulat, *Correspondance d'Orient*, v, 13; vii. 83; 85-6; P.-S. Girard, in the monumental *Description de l'Égypte*, xvii, 36; Schoelcher, *L'Égypte en 1845*, 160-1, 305; Clot; etc.). Such a woman seemed lively and active, working in the factories of Muḥammad ʿAlī or as an *almeh*, "dancing girl". She endured "a type of circumcision" performed in Egypt (Clot, i, 321-3) [see KHAFḌ], and in the Sudan, infibulation, probably through the influence of pagan practices from black Africa. Following the occupation of Egypt by the French (1798-1801), the growing influence of the West, the development of the Arab bourgeoisie, the modernisation of towns and reformist ideas all had a disturbing effect on the family and social structures as well as on general attitudes. Any attempt to defend the earlier *status quo* brought about a deterioration in female segregation and increased restrictions. However, crises are sometimes salutary in the way they precipitate a liberation movement.

The year 1839 saw the beginning of the *Tanẓīmāt* [*q.v.*], a period of social reform when many schools were opened for girls in Turkey, but not in the other Arab regions of the empire. There had been a school for girls in Beirut opened by the American missionaries in Beirut in 1835, but it was the only one of its kind for a long time. The first primary school for girls in Egypt was opened in 1876, and in ʿIrāḳ in 1899; tuition was given in Turkish.

The First World War brought about a growing need for labour, especially female labour, in these countries: they worked in the spinning and weaving industries, in companies manufacturing cigarettes and in factories making preserves, matches, etc. Women used to work side-by-side with men for the same pittance. In 1921 the first proto-trade union organisations demanded equality for men and women before the law. These rights, though often only existing in theory, like the nine-hour day and maternity leave on half pay, were granted from 1933 onwards. They led in turn to the setting up of a legal labour code in Iraq (1936), Syria and Lebanon (1946). These laws and guarantees, rarely respected at first, gradually and slowly are becoming customary.

It was not only in industry that women were employed. They worked in greater numbers (as they always have done) in craft and family enterprises. The patriarchal structure of the family favours an almost closed economy, and there the woman's fight for independence has almost no room to develop. The development of female education and the formation of a female consciousness has undoubtedly been made possible because of the wealth generated by oil and commerce.

The Arab woman's evolution was inevitably accompanied by a development of conscience, in the absence of which, in spite of lengthy periods of common conflict, she finds herself excluded from trade union activities through what is in effect discrimination. Furthermore, because of ignorance she did not avail herself of the rights which the law allowed her. Perhaps the quickest stirring of female consciousness was brought about by the fruitful activities of the feminist organisations. They were formed after the First World War and were mostly philanthropic, although some were definitely political; they were constantly active despite the sarcasm of the media.

Of all the Islamic countries, Turkey had the largest population of literate women, and it led the way in major changes. Developments in female education led to the propagation of more liberal thought. With the revolution of Atatürk in 1923, the country was laicised, and the wildest dreams of female liberation were realised—a model for other Arab states. At the end of the 19th century in Egypt, the first theorist of eastern feminism, Ḳāsim Amīn [*q.v.*], published a book entitled *Taḥrīr al-marʾa*, "The emancipation of the [Egyptian] woman" which, in the name of the law of the Ḳurʾān itself, protested against the breaking of the law, the obligatory wearing of the veil, unjustified polygamy, and repudiation without the arbitration of a judge. He claimed equality of teaching for both sexes. Egyptian feminists supported him. From 1911 Bāḥithat al-Bādiya demanded that women should have free access to the mosques and that there should be compulsory primary education for everyone. After the First World War, Hudā Shaʿrāwī, a member of the Turkish aristocracy, opened her salon in Cairo and in 1923 appeared in public with an uncovered face.

At the end of the last century, feminist claims were expressed only by some women of the aristocracy, but now they have become increasingly urgent. They have been taken up by the upper and middle classes, by writers and journalists of both sexes and they have been organised into various unions or associations. The right to vote is now denied only to women in the Arabian peninsula, and since this right has become general, women's groups have assumed an electoral significance and have been recognised by the political authorities. In Egypt, the "Organisation of Arab Women" was formed by the female Minister of Social Affairs in 1962. In Syria, in 1968, the "General Union of Women" was directed by the Baʿth. The "Women's Union" was created by law in Libya in 1975 and in ʿIrāḳ the "General Federation of ʿIrāḳī Women" is one of the organisations (*munaẓẓamāt*) of the Baʿth party.

Trade unions and feminist activity have a value, but a general spread of education provides a much more favourable climate for female consciousness. Laws established after the achieving of independence have democratised education. The Declaration of Human Rights signed by the United Nations (art. 26) decreed that primary education should be free. Despite this, compulsory education is far from being generally accepted. Little schooling is available in the rural areas (in Morocco, Jordan, ʿIrāḳ and even Egypt, for example), but elsewhere only half the population of female school age reaches a primary school. In Saudi Arabia, the proportion is a third, with absolute segregation of the sexes (cf. *Maghreb-Machrek*, Paris, Doc. française, no. 78 (Oct.-Dec. 1977); *L'Islam*, Doc. fr. photogr. 27). The situation is the same in Syria. These difficulties arise because of an insufficient number of schools and qualified teaching staff. There are added problems because families use their children to work in the fields, in small industries, or in the home to eke out their resources.

Even when they are given the chance of a place at school and they pursue their studies, girls are subconsciously moulded by the cultural outlook fostered by the school and their view of the world is not necessarily different from that of their society, at least not until the final stages of secondary school. Official Syrian statistics for 1975 can act as a guide for the rest of the Arab world. In 1970, out of a population of 65,925 women who held certificates of primary education, 8,758 were pursuing an occupation other than that of housewife (= 13.4%); for secondary-modern (secondary and technical levels combined) diploma holders, the figures were 7,176 out of 8,059 (= 89.03%); for higher education diploma holders it was 3,365 out of 4,482 (= 75.07%); and for doctorate holders it was 108 out of 151 (= 71.5%) most of whom came from the middle classes or were the wives of diplomats living abroad. Very often (in 38% of the cases), the women were working for relatives or private individuals without receiving any payment. In 1970, this was the situation for 64,088 of them. It is also interesting to compare figures for married and unmarried women in the same year; there were 1,067,073 married women and 515,751 single, divorced or widowed, but although there were nearly twice as many married women, the number of active unmarried women (71,996) was well over the number of active married ones (58,886).

Often women agree to sacrifice their career in order to respond to the wishes of a husband or family. Such behaviour cannot simply be explained as due to the state of her mind, but must be influenced by the almost complete lack of necessary social infrastructures like crèches, canteens, etc. Pedagogic activity, therefore, cannot exist without educational activity, and they must complement each other. At the present time, there is insufficient integration of the different claims for equality of the sexes and for the liberation of women. Deep disturbances can be felt even in the socialist universities of Damascus and Mawṣil concerning the actual segregation of women and concerning the wearing of the veil on the head or over the face. It has been an erratic path of development, and any progress that has been achieved by the work of cultured women, heroines in the fight for freedom, and trade unionists have been followed by some spectacular steps backwards, even in the so-called progressive countries.

The struggle goes on in the Arab-Muslim world between those who used to be called "literalists" but now "integrists" and the liberals; old arguments have been rekindled. The rise of Muslim "integrationism" has been made possible by the new-found power of the *āyatallāhs* in Iran through the success of their revolution against the Shah's régime, and above all by their resistance against the unfortunate ʿIrāḳī aggression. Even if the Arab-Muslim world accepts modern techniques in the hope of bettering its way of life, it still remains attached to the values and religious beliefs by which it hopes to preserve its identity. The threats and fulminations of the *ʿulamāʾ* conservatives of Syria, ʿIrāḳ, Egypt and Algeria exploit this religious attachment and encourage the observance of passivity and submissive attitudes in the societies concerned. This has led to a spectacular return to the veil and long dress, the symbols of female submission.

Once they had given up the signs of their bondage, the cultured middle-class heroines of the Arab resistance movement became submerged in the fear of "integrationist" opposition. In Egypt, the law upholds the right of the husband to beat his wife and a legal official will even go so far as to stipulate what length of stick to use. In Kuwayt, members of the assembly have refused to grant women the right to vote in February 1982, even though the Dean of the Faculty of Law at Kuwayt University was a woman (*Le Monde*, 14 February 1982). The project for a "family code" in Algeria maintains the legal inferiority of the woman: she is always considered a minor and must pass from the guardianship of her father to that of her husband, brother or uncle, or even to that of her eldest son. Polygamy and repudiation are allowed and any professional activity a woman undertakes must be sanctioned by her husband (*Le Monde*, 9 January 1982). In the Assembly, Algerian officals have had to face up to the disagreements between those of the liberal tendency, who recognise the equality of men and women, and the traditionalists, who are faithful to the "Arab-Muslim heritage".

When the conflict moves to the political level, "progressive" and "modernist" tendencies within Arab socialism are opposed by totalitarian and theocratic tendencies, legitimised by religious tradition. Because of the overlap between politics and social life, the degree of freedom a present-day Muslim woman enjoys can be seen as an accurate indication of the degree of political change the society in which she lives has undergone. In the past, she was given a role which allowed her to consolidate the family unit and to perpetuate habits, modes of thought and the cultural heritage; even so, to-day she has a role which, depending on whether it is in a society reflecting archaic attitudes or one belonging to the secular liberal viewpoint, indicates a stagnant stage of civilisation or a modern attitude in harmony with the principles of the "rights of man"—and of woman. A solution will have to be found, but it is hardly likely to consist of a total victory for either side, or in its complete crushing. Too many political interests and deep-seated attachments are involved. Dialogue between the "integrationists" and the modernists will probably have to be re-established. To reach this end, however, it is essential for the liberal debate no longer to be resented as a much-hated innovation.

Bibliography: The *Kitāb al-Aghānī*, ed. Shanḳīṭī, 21 parts in 7 vols., Cairo n.d., and four parts in two vols. of index, Cairo 1323, has been used. Although it would be impossible to record all the poets, prose writers and theorists from the classical period of Arab-Muslim writing who have discussed love and women, the following should be mentioned: Anṭāḳī, *Tazyīn al-aswāḳ*; Djāḥiẓ, *Risāla fi l-ʿishḳ wa ʾl-nisāʾ* and *Risālat al-Ḳiyān* (see Ch. Pellat, *al-Djāḥiẓ wa ʾl-marʾa*, in *Ḥawliyyāt al-Djāmiʿa al-Tūnusiyya*, 1986); Ibn Dāwūd, *Kitāb al-Zuhra*; Ibn Ḥazm, *Ṭawḳ al-ḥamāma*; Ibn Ḳayyim al-Djawziyya, *Rawḍat al-muḥibbīn* and *Kitāb Akhbār al-nisāʾ*; Masʿūdī, *Murūdj al-dhahab*; Washshāʾ, *Kitāb al-Muwashshā*. The 19th-century writers that have been mentioned are A.B. Clot, *Aperçu général sur l'Égypte*, 2 vols., Paris 1840; E. W. Lane, *An account of the manners and customs of the modern Egyptians*, London 1830; Mengin, *Histoire de l'Égypte*, 2 vols., Paris 1823; Michaud and Poujoulat, *Correspondence d'Orient*, 7 vols., Paris 1835; Schoelcher, *L'Égypte en 1845*, Paris 1846; Volney, *Voyage en Égypte et en Syrie*[1], 1789. These sources, as well as the monumental *Description de l'Égypte* compiled by scholars in Bonaparte's army, second ed., Paris 1822 (xi-xxi) and *ʿAdjāʾib al-āthār* by Djabartī, 4 vols., Cairo 1879-80, have been used exhaustively by N. Tomiche in *The situation of Egyptian women in the first half of the nineteenth century*, in W. R. Polk and R. L. Chambers (eds.), *The beginnings of modernisation in the Middle East*, Chicago 1968. More recent important works of reference are: Blachère, *HLA*; M. Borrmans, *Statut personnel et familie au Maghreb de 1940 à nos jours*, Paris 1977; G.H. Bosquet, *La morale de l'Islam et son éthique sexuelle*, Paris 1953; idem, *Le droit musulmane*. Paris 1963; C. Chehata, *Études de droit musulmane*, Paris 1971; E. Doutté, *Magie et religion dans l'Afrique du Nord*, Paris 1909; *Femmes et politiques* [collective work] Paris 1980; R. Höll, *Die Stellung der Frau im Zeitgenössischen Islams: dargestellt am Beispiel Marokkos*, Frankfurt 1979; Kaḥḥāla, *Aʿlām al-nisāʾ fī ʿālam al-ʿArab wa ʾl-Islām*, 3 vols., Damascus 1959; Ḳāsim Amīn, *Taḥrīr al-marʾa*, Cairo 1899; H. Lammens, *Études sur la règne du calife omayyade Moʿâwia Ier*, Paris-Beirut 1908; Y. Linant de Bellefonds, *Traité de droit musulmane comparé*, ii, Paris 1965; L. Milliot, *Introduction à l'étude du droit musulman*, Paris 1953; J. Minces, *La femme dans le monde arabe*, Paris 1980; Ṣ. Munadjdjid, *Amthāl al-marʾa ʿind al-ʿArab*, Beirut 1401/1981; R. Paret, *Zur Frauenfrage in der arabisch-islamischen Welt*, Stuttgart-Berlin 1934, repr. in *Schriften um Islam*, ed. J. van Ess, Stuttgart, etc. 1981; Ch. Pellat, *Le milieu baṣrien et la formation de Ǧāḥiẓ*, Paris 1953; idem, *Les esclaves chanteuses de Ǧāḥiẓ*, in *Arabica*, x/2 (1963); M. Shakankiri, *Loi divine, loi humaine et droit dans l'histoire juridique de l'Islam*, in *Revue historique de droit français et étranger*, lix (1981); M.M. Shalabī, *Taʿlīl al-aḥkām*, Cairo 1947; Afaf Lutfi al-Sayyid-Marsot (ed.), *Society and the sexes in medieval Islam*, Malibu, Calif. 1979; G. Stern, *Marriage in early Islam*, London 1939; Ṭāhir al-Ḥaddād, *Imraʾatunā fi ʾl-sharīʿa wa ʾl-mudjtamaʿ*, Tunis 1930; G. Ṭarabīshī, *Ramziyyat al-marʾa fi ʾl-riwāya al-ʿarabiyya*, Beirut 1981; G. Tillion, *Le harem et les cousins*, Paris 1966 Aïcha Lemsine, *Ordalie des voix. Les femmes arabes parlent*, Paris 1983; N. Tomiche, *La femme en Islam*, in *Histoire mondiale de la femme*, 4 vols., Paris 1965-6, iii; J.-C. Vadet, *L'esprit courtois en orient dans les cinq premiers siècles de* *l'hégire*, Paris 1968; Ch. Vial, *Le personnage de la femme dans le roman et la nouvelle en Egypte de 1914 à 1960*, Damascus 1979; G.E. von Grunebaum, *Avicenna's Risāla fi l-ʿišq and courtly love*, in *JNES* (Oct. 1952); Wiebke Walther, *Die Frau im Islam*, Leipzig-Stuttgart-Berlin 1980 (good bibl.); E. Westermarck, *Marriage ceremonies in Morocco*, London 1914; *Women of the fertile crescent* [collective work], Washington, D.C. 1978; *Women in the Muslim world* [collective work], Cambridge, Mass. - London 1978; N.H. Youssef, *Women and work in developing societies*, Westport, Conn. 1974.

(N. Tomiche)

2. The Arab woman in customary law and practice.

a. *The material and the problems raised.*

The noun *marʾa* is relatively rarely used in the Qurʾān. Although it occurs only 26 times, women are frequently alluded to as believers, wives, mothers, daughters, sisters, aunts, cousins, slaves, or simply as "females", *unthā*. Traditional usages and customs about women are often mentioned in the *ḥadīth* as well as in pre- and post-Hidjra poetry. Research by ethnographers into both ancient and modern Arab societies has produced much information on the rights and obligations of a woman, her social status, her daily life and her conduct on important occasions in her life. From the rich and varied material available, from pre-Islamic sources to contemporary Arab societies, we can present a reasonably precise account of her status as it emerges from an analysis of customs and usages.

Unfortunately, the material is not all of the same value, and what is found in pre-Islamic poetry must be treated with special care. It is even more important to remember that there is a serious gap in the material. Whereas the different sources all provide, by a sort of complicity between informants, information on the women of the North (the Bedouin), there is hardly any mention of the women of the South (sc. the Yemeni) ones), who have grown up in an environment appreciably different from that of Mecca or the desert, in religious texts, literature or ethnographic research work. Here and there references to customs presumably of South Arabian origin can probably be found in pre-Islamic sources, but these can be identified in one way only, the origin of the tribes where they were practised. Such information was collected well after the Hidjra when most of the Yemeni tribes, like the Ṭayyiʾ, ʿAws, Khazradj, Madhhidj, Murād, ʿUdhra, Kinda, Ḥaḍramawt, etc., had adopted customs which were fundamentally Bedouin. To judge from their poetry, they also spoke the same language as the Arabs from the North.

It would thus be unwise to consider as Yemeni one particular custom which does not fit into a group of well-established customs, just because it was observed in a society which originated in the South of Arabia. It could easily have arisen through the external influence on a tribe in the course of its many wanderings, or it could be the relic of behaviour characteristic of earlier social conditions and subjected to internal evolution within the tribe. Starting out from this hypothesis, the most plausible and generally accepted one, one could artificially bring into a unity an essentially disparate group of customs, which will then appear as landmarks in a long cycle of evolution.

That is how Robertson Smith suggested, under the influence of 19th century evolutionary theory, that family relationships among the ancient Arabs were primarily polyandrous. This system gave way to matriarchy, which was in turn followed by patriarchy. It is true that just before the birth of Islam, relationships were centred on the males of the family, although the old matriarchal system had not disappeared and many relics of it persisted. It is proper to mention this idea in the introduction to this article because of the role it gives to women in the evolution of the Arab kinship system; it has been the cause of much discussion and is still accepted by more than one orientalist. It assumes that the whole of the Arabian peninsula before the Hidjra enjoyed a cultural and linguistic unity and consequently a unity of behaviour patterns also. There is a reason to believe that the theory of evolution devised by this distinguished British scholar strays noticeably from the facts; the cultural unity of Arabia probably emerged only during the first century of Islam.

It is well known that Southern Arabia was regarded as a separate region from the rest of the country for a long time. Though moderately influenced by the desert, it developed a civilisation based on agriculture and commerce with more leanings to India and the Mediterranean than to the steppes of the interior. It seems certain that, before Islam, an area of Arabia experienced a system based on maternal rights. But this régime must have existed somewhere in *Arabia felix* rather than in *Arabia deserta*, where exogamy would seem incompatible with the warring nomads. It would have reached to other parts of the peninsula through Southern tribes emigrating, then gradually being absorbed by the customs of the Bedouin, and ultimately abandoning their traditional behaviour which had survived until just before the Hidjra. The cultural and linguistic unity, which came much later than Robertson Smith suggested, would have followed the decline of the kingdoms of the South and the progress of desertification. The language of the North, close to but different from the South Arabian which it ended up by supplanting, finally imposed itself on the whole peninsula, spreading with itself the customs and manners of the desert.

Robertson Smith's serious error has finally led to a regrettable confusion. At the time of the Hidjra, Classical Arabic (that of the Ḳurʾān) although not prevalent, was understood in almost all areas of Arabia. From this fact, he assumed that there was a linguistic unity long before Islam. Furthermore, having identified the relics of the old matrilinear customs in particular tribes, he concluded that these customs were prevalent in the whole of Arabia, without taking into account the question of migration.

What was the status of Arab women prior to Islam? It is quite clear from what has been said that the inhabitants of Southern Arabia (the "Southern Arabs") must be distinguished from those of the North. Even so, it is not necessary to agree with the genealogists who suggest a double lineage, Ḳaḥṭānī for the one and ʿAdnānī for the other, for they have merely translated into the language of their own particular discipline the ever-present rivalry between cultivators and pastoralists. Nonetheless, there were the well-established agricultural traditions of the southern Arab farmers. The Northern Arabs were traditionally dependent on a pastoral economy for their sustenance; they developed for themselves a distinctive nomadic civilisation marked by the stamp of the desert. Research into the South Arabian area has proceeded, but there is still only fragmentary and inadequate information on many aspects of social life. On the other hand, the abundance of information about the Arabs of the steppes is such that it is extremely difficult to synthesise.

b. *The status of the South Arabian woman*

Little is known about the customary status of woman (*ʾ n th t, m r ʾ t*) in South Arabia before Islam.

In a recently discovered inscription, anyone of the Dhū Matāra is forbidden to kill their daughter (Chr. Robin, *Mission archéologique et épigraphique française au Yémen du Nord en automne 1978*, 185, *CRAIBL*, April-Jule 1979: this scholar has helped to provide some of the bibliography in this study of the South Arabian woman). This practice may quite properly be compared with *waʾd*. It always denotes an inferior attitude to girls as compared to boys. In the same text, it is similarly forbidden to hand over girls by way of reparation, which leads one to suppose that the man had control of the woman. As in other Semitic societies, so here it is probable that the husband regards his wife as a chattel. Some inscriptions group wives and possessions together (A. F. L. Beeston, *The position of woman in pre-Islamic South Arabia*, in *Proceedings of the 22nd Congress of Orientalists, Istanbul, 1951*, ii, Leiden 1957, 104). However, it would not be correct to infer from this that the wife was in a state of slavery.

In other inscriptions, it is stated that she had a rôle in questions of inheritance. Rhodokanakis even dared to suggest that in South Arabia, the women were financially independent. Beeston does not share this point of view, but he does admit that the widow could acquire economic independence in certain conditions, as, for example, when the male heirs were too young to exercise their rights (Beeston, *op. cit.*, 105). He also draws attention to the fact that the woman could assume high office, especially that of priestess, a role in which she would have practised sacred prostitution (idem, *The so-called harlots of Hadramawt*, in *Oriens*, [1952]; cf. J. Ryckmans, *Les "hierodulenlisten" de Maʿin et la colonisation minéenne*, 152). She also had access to high administrative offices. In one inscription a woman bore the title *maḳtawiya*, fem. of *maḳtawī*, a senior official who came under the direct orders of the king. Could it be that a woman may even have held the office of the highest magistrate, as suggested by the legend of the Queen of Sheba? However, the inscriptions do not mention the name of any sovereign or *ḳayla*. Nevertheless, after the *ridda*, the Banū Mūʿāwiya in the Ḥaḍramawt, who were called the royal Kinda, were ruled by four brothers as joint kings in association with their sister, the famous al-ʿAmarrada, who was a famous and despotic as they (Ibn Ḥazm, *Djamharat ansāb al-ʿArab*, Cairo 1962, 428).

Information provided by the inscriptions about the system of family relationships might well lead to confusion. In most cases, the line of descent is through the father. However, in every age there are isolated instances of descent through women. In one text there is even a case of both types of descent side-by-side (see the inscription on the statue in Chr. Robin, *L'Arabie du sud antique*, in *Bible et Terre Sainte*, 177 [Jan. 1976], 19). Two other inscriptions record a concession granted by a king to men and women of the same class Now it seems that the transmission of the concession was made by the women to their descendants (Ahmed Fakhry, *An archaeological journey to Yemen*, ii, *Epigraphical texts*, Cairo 1952, inscrs. 3 and 76). In other inscriptions, women are mentioned only in terms of their lineage; even their ascendants are considered from the point of view of the female line. From there to the conclusion of the existence of a system of matriliny in South Arabia before Islam is one step only, easily made. One can even go on to affirm that polyandry may also have been known to the South Arabians. The observations of Strabo already mentioned are relevant here, and certain scholars like Glaser, Winckler and more recently Müller, consider that the views of the Greek geographer have been confirmed by the inscriptions (for further discussion and bibliography, see J. Chelhod, *Du nouveau à propos du matriarcat arabe*, in *Arabica*, xxviii [1981], 99 ff.; Chr. Robin has drawn our attention to a Hasaean inscription where the line of descent is traced exclusively through women; it reads "Burial place and tomb of Ghabya, daughter of Mālikat, daughter of Shibām, daughter of Ahadhat, of the lineage of Yankhāl"). However, documents where this type of union is mentioned are rare so that it is wise to treat them with caution. On the other hand, it is clear that polygamy was practised in ancient Yemen and, according to Beeston, they even practised temporary marriage (*Temporary marriage in pre-Islamic South Arabia*, in *Arabian Studies*, iv [1978], 21-5).

The inscriptions so far discovered do not contain any reference to the existence of a system of maternal rights in ancient Yemen before Islam, but the discussion must necessarily remain open, for ethnographers have produced several examples of matrilinear succession in contemporary Yemen society. Some sexual freedom before and after marriage has also been noted as prevalent in some tribes in Yemen. This is no recent innovation but, as will be shown, has its roots in the past.

c. *The status of women in customary law in modern South Arabia.*

As a rule, the *sharīʿa* governs the status of both men and women in the whole of South Arabia, with slight modifications in the case of South Yemen. Its successful application relies on the central government maintaining effective control. Outside the large urban societies of Ṣanʿāʾ, Taʿizz, ʿAdan, Sayʾūn, Shibām, etc. it is well known that the semi-sedentary and village Yemenis observe customs which do not always conform to Islamic law. Girls are often disinherited and marriages are contracted by exchange. This customary practice is known as *ṭāghūt*, or also *aḥkām al-salaf*. It is inspired by strongly-held desert values, and in accordance with Bedouin customs promotes an idea of honour among the Yemenis, related to the "whiteness of the face".

The law decrees that woman should be completely submissive to the will of the man; father, brother, husband, uncle, paternal cousins, and even her own adult children. She is considered to be a feeble being, whose defence depends entirely on the man. In his eyes, she symbolises his own virility: every thoughtless action is interpreted by her strong protector as a challenge to his power, an outrage to his dignity. A whole mystique has grown up around the concept of honour which decrees that the modesty of the women whom he guards should be a sacred object. Any assault or attempted assault on their chastity is classed as murder and may be punished extremely severely. This is the conventional attitude to the love life of Yemeni women. Among the Ḥumūm of the Ḥaḍramawt, however, despite her unfavourable position, the woman enjoys a certain amount of sexual liberty. Indeed, tradition even permits a girl to conceive a child outside marriage. If the child is not recognised by its natural father it will take the name of its mother or that of its maternal uncle. Even a married woman can take a lover without fear of her life and without the risk of being molested.

A girl wanting to take a lover would have to take him from among the people of her tribe. As a rule, the lucky man should exhibit all the physical and moral qualities which a woman would like to find in the father of her child. The aim of such a liaison is, presumably, to produce an ideal child, but the custom is disappearing; it is called *kasb* or *iktisāb*. A similar type of union was known to the Arabs before Islam by exactly the same name. The Arabs were supposed to do this to raise children of pure Arab stock, so that the man who was to father the child should be especially good. There is some similarity between the two customs, but here it was the husband who asked the wife to have relations with another man, whereas among the Ḥumūm it is the girl who takes the initiative. Within this tribe, as among the ancient Arabs, no one is at all embarrassed to announce the birth of a child conceived outside marriage. The child born this way is called *al-farkh*, "the chicken", a harmless nickname which indicates the "illegitimate" nature of his birth, even if his father recognises him as his own. If he does not, he will take the name of his mother and be raised by her. She may subsequently be sought in marriage, and the intentions of her suitor will be judged by asking him if he will take her *bi-ḥamli-hā wa-shamlihā*, "with her burden and her coat". If he takes both mother and child, then the dowry would be more significant; but if he will take only the girl, the child will be brought up by her maternal uncles.

Custom likewise allows to Ḥumūm married women the right to have affairs during the prolonged absence of their husbands; when a husband returns, he cannot inflict reprisals on the unfaithful spouse. He has the choice of accepting the situation or repudiating his wife. If he nevertheless ill-treats his wife, he risks legal proceedings by his parents-in-law, and this appears to be an old custom. According to Ibn al-Mudjāwir, a woman among the Saru could take a lover called a *mukhlif*, "a replacement", when her husband was on a journey (Ibn al-Mudjāwir, *Taʾrīkh al-mustabṣir*, Leiden 1951-4, 26).

Whatever the cause of trouble, the Ḥumūm never punish an adultress; but a woman who takes a lover while her husband is at home is severely condemned. Despite this, she is generally in a favourable position, for she can ask her husband to repudiate her so that she can start a new life, and he cannot deny her this privilege. All that is necessary is for the dowry and any wedding expenses to be returned. If she is repudiated at her own request, the unfaithful wife has no rights regarding her children; they will remain with their father and keep his name. Despite this freedom enjoyed by women in Ḥumūm society, the family is patrilocal and patrilinear, as elsewhere in Yemen.

How can these obviously matrilinear customs be reconciled with the prevailing patriarchal way of life? They seem to be the relics of a system of matrilinear rule which once was to some extent normal in South Arabia. It seems that neither virginity nor chastity was considered as important as modern Arabs unusually consider them. Ibn al-Mudjāwir states that among the Bahīmiyya, the "fiancée" was tried out by her suitor. If he was satisfied, he left his sandals behind at her father's house and the marriage could then be settled; if he were to put them on when leaving the house, it meant that he did not want the girl (Ibn al-Mudjāwir, *op. cit.*, 54). The custom of giving a traveller a girl for the night goes back to the 3rd/9th century. The founder of the Zaydī state opposed certain sexual liberties practised in the village of al-Aʿsūm. It was situated in the high plateaux, and there a host would honour his guest by offering him his daughter or his sister after he had dressed her up in her most beautiful clothes. She would then be subjected to the most intimate caressing but not extreme sexual behaviour (C. van Arendonck, *Les débuts de l'imamat zaydite au Yemen*, 165). Similar observations were made by Ibn Mudjāwir, but in his account the wife was offered to the traveller (Ibn al-Mudjāwir, *op. cit.*, 53). After fourteen centuries of Islam, it is only recently that a similar custom was observed in Yemen in the region of Mārib, though it is true that the guest there was made to respect his partner under the threat of reprisals (private investigation. Cf. K. al-Iryāni, *L'organisation social de la tribu des Hashid*, in *COC*, lxx [1968], 8).

This sexual liberty has ensured that sufficient scholarly attention has been paid to women in Yemen, and it seems that in some areas she has been able to impose her will on her husband. It is public knowledge among the Yemenis that in the Djabal Ṣabir, the pleasant mountain overlooking Taʿizz, the village women rule the roost in financial matters. They have even gone so far as to send back lazy husbands. It is still only the man who has the right to repudiate, but he must nevertheless obey his wife's commands. Among the Dihm in the region of the Djawf, a woman will put a piece of red cloth on the entrance to her tent when she is displeased with her husband. He knows from this that he is in disgrace, and does not dare to cross the threshold of his home until his wife has removed the sign of the quarrel with her own hand (A. Fakhrī, *al-Yaman māḍīha wa-ḥāḍiruhā*, Cairo 1970, 110). A similar custom existed among the Ṭayyʾin pre-Islamic Arabia. To show Ḥātim that he should leave, Māwiya simply moved the entrance to the tent (*Aghānī*, Beirut 1956, xvi, 207). She was thus mistress of her own fate, since she could separate at will from her husband when the latter displeased her. Among the ancient Arabs, a number of high-society ladies seem to have enjoyed the same privilege. There is, for example the case of Salma bint ʿAmr from Medina, who belonged to the Nadjdjār, originally from Yemen. The chroniclers say that she agreed to marry her husband only on condition that she could leave him if she wished.

Other accounts confirm how common these matrilocal customs were. Ezzé, Botta's guide, entered into a marriage contract, the principal clause of which stated that the wife could live with her own people and not follow the husband to his village (Botta, *Relation d'un voyage dans le Yémen*, Paris 1880, 125). According to Ibn Baṭṭūṭa, at Zabīd marriage to a stranger was freely accepted, but if the husband decided to leave the town the wife would not follow him under any circumstances (Ibn Baṭṭūṭa, *Riḥla*, ii, 168). The child of such a marriage would be brought up by his mother or some other relative. Ibn al-Daybaʿ of Zabīd, the Yemeni historian, was abandoned by his father in his infancy and entrusted to his maternal grandfather. When this relative died, the boy was looked after by his maternal uncle (Ibn al-Daybaʿ, *al-Faḍl al-mazīd ʿalā bughyat al-mustafīd fī akhbār madīnat Zabīd*, ed. J. Chelhod, Ṣanʿāʾ 1983, 217).

When this discussion is analysed, the following facts emerge:

(a) A Yemeni woman is not required to follow a strict sexual morality, as is generally the case in the Arab East.

(b) The sexual freedom enjoyed by the women of the Ḥumūm dates back to ancient times.

(c) In some tribes, the woman controls her own destiny, having the right to take a lover and to dismiss her husband.

(d) Children conceived apart from the husband belong to the maternal side of the family.

(e) Such matrilocal customs are still to be observed in some parts of Southern Arabia.

Although it cannot be assumed at all that South

Arabia exerted an influence on North Africa (Helfritz, *L'Arabie heureuse*, Paris 1961, 116), there are certain similarities between the customs described above and those observed in Kabylia. The Berber woman is generally known to enjoy more sexual freedom than the Arab woman, and many monographs have been devoted to describing her love life. Its luxuriance and diversity of customs make any attempt at synthesis problematical. Prenuptial chastity is certainly not expected of any girl, but once married they must be faithful to their husbands. But if they are freed from their marriage ties by widowhood, repudiation or the prolonged absence of the husband, they are allowed to take lovers. Their sexual freedom is even more marked than that of the Ḥumūm. Many of them still work as prostitutes, and this is not thought in any way dishonourable. Many courtesans belong to high-class families and subsequently end up with good marriage arrangements (E. Dermenghem, *Le pays d'Abel*, Paris 1960, 69). Children born of these temporary unions belong to the mother's line.

When the life of the Yemeni woman is compared to that of her sister in the North, it seems very similar, except for the sexual freedom, limited in any case to certain districts, she enjoys. The Northern girl is also married very young (often before the age of ten) and her paternal cousin holds the right of preemption. She will not usually be consulted initially about her choice of husband; only after she has been widowed or divorced will she be free to reject a suitor. Analogies between her situation and that of the Bedouin women will be discussed later.

d. *The Arab woman in traditional law just before the Hidjra and during the first century of Islam.*

The status of women in Western Arabia before the Hidjra again raises the question of different customs in different areas. Clear differences in male attitudes can be detected, when comparing evidence from nomadic tribes, from the sedentary population, from a trading city or from a village community, even though at this particular time almost the whole peninsula was Bedouin in character. The word Bedouin clearly refers not only to the Arab of the steppe, *al-aʿrābī*, but also to anyone who follows the desert customs and conforms to its code of honour. Poets like al-Akhṭal and Djarīr called themselves Bedouin (*Aghānī*, vii, 134), and from this point of view, just before the Hidjra, the Meccans practised Bedouin customs.

Most of those Arab tribes which, by their nomadic and war-like life style set great store by their virility, consider that women are feeble and almost irresponsible beings and in need of constant help. At the same time, she embodies man's ideals and is sometimes almost venerated as sacred. This ambivalence naturally leads to the paradoxical description of her as *ʿawra*, nude, shameful and needing concealment and *ḥurma*, sacred, to be defended and protected. This two-fold attitude gives rise to a series of prohibitions for women and obligations on men, and failure to observe them casts a slur on their honour. Female chastity together with conjugal fidelity, *inter alia*, constitute *ʿirḍ* [*q.v.*]. Licentiousness is severely punished and brings disgrace to a family and to a tribe. In satirical poetry, the mother of the person being mocked is often spoken of disparagingly (for examples, see the *dīwān* of Ḥassān b. Thābit; cf. *Aghānī*, iv, 8,10,11,81). Even the custom of *waʾd* is attributed to the fear of dishonour (*Aghānī*, iv, 248). In attempting to safeguard the rights of the female believer from an economic point of view, Islam confirms the pre-Islamic arrangements in everything touching her love life.

In fact, it would be unwise to make generalisations. Epinal's picture of a humble Arab woman submissive to the wishes of her *baʿl*, her lord and master, might well be the masculine ideal for a wife, but this is not the picture painted by our evidence. Many tales of the pre-Islamic and even the Islamic period show woman as a refined but mischievous creature, resisting supervision and enjoying sufficient freedom to enable her to embark on a few amorous adventures. The belief in the child sleeping peacefully in his mother's bosom is the incontestable proof of this. We shall see later that, in sexual matters, traditional customs are not adhered to so rigidly as is often believed.

The birth of a daughter was not welcomed at all, for families believed it could bring dishonour (*Aghānī*, iv, 248) or even poverty (Ḳurʾān, VI, 151; XVII, 31). Fathers sometimes buried their daughter alive, even though this custom was condemned in the Ḳurʾān (XVI, 58; LXXXI, 8). Among the Ḳuraysh, this custom was common, and they buried their daughters at a place called Abū Dulāma, a hill above Mecca (*Aghānī*, xi, 246). But for the most part, fathers seemed to accept the inevitable and to find consolation in counting up how much the infant girl would bring him on the occasion of her marriage.

Khafḍ [*q.v.*] "excision" was practised everywhere. It is not certain whether this happened soon after birth or just before marriage, but if the latter, it can be seen as a rite of passage. The girl would be married when she was scarcely nubile, and often she was promised from birth; sometimes her father or brother would exchange her for a wife without spending any money. This type of union was known as *shighār* (*LA*, s.v. *sh.-gh.-r*) and even applied to married women. A man would repudiate his wife and exchange her for another man's (*Aghānī*, xviii, 356). Marriage by exchange was forbidden in Islam (Muslim, *Ṣaḥīḥ*, Cairo 1334, iv, 136), but nonetheless practised even to the present day. This emphasises the lack of real concern shown for the girl's own wishes, regarding her future partner. Her father, brother or guardian would draw up an agreement without even consulting her (*Aghānī*, x, 104; xix, 131-2, 275) which is not surprising considering how young she was when first married. ʿĀʾisha was married to the Prophet at the age of six, and the marriage was consummated when she was nine (Muslim, *Ṣaḥīḥ*, iv, 142). A widow or a divorced woman (*thayyib*), not so much in demand as a virgin (*bikr*), would generally make her own arrangements. This was probably what happened when a woman offered herself to Muḥammad (Ḳurʾān, XXX, 50); he declined the offer. The Ḳurʾānic reforms tried to protect the young girl when her parents abuse the right to be consulted (but see DJABR in Suppl.).

Arab dictionaries use the same word *nikāḥ* to denote stable and temporary unions, which often do not last long and border on prostitution. According to a *ḥadīth*, attributed to ʿĀʾisha and recorded by al-Bukhārī, pre-Islamic society recognised four forms of marriage. (1) A man may marry the daughter or sister of another man on payment of a dowry. (2) A man asks his wife, after her menstruation, to have intercourse with someone he names so that she can have a child of good pedigree. He himself avoids all contact with her until her pregnancy is evident. (3) A group of less than ten men assemble at a woman's house and all have intercourse with her. For the child which is subsequently born, the mother chooses one of the ten she prefers to be the official father. (4) A woman gives herself to any man as a prostitute. If she becomes pregnant, she waits until the child is born and then consults a physiognomist to decide which of her clients is to be the father of the child. Once he has been selected, that man must accept paternity. To these four types, others can now be added. (5) *shighār*, a marriage by exchange described above. (6) *nikāḥ al-maḳt*, a marriage to the father's widow, which was prohibited by the Ḳurʾān (IV, 22). (7) *nikāḥ al-mutʿa*, temporary marriage, which was authorised at the beginning of Islam but forbidden by the *sunna*, apparently on the initiative of the caliph ʿUmar; tolerated however by the Shīʿa. (8) *nikāḥ al-khidn*, concubinage, which is also prohibited by the Ḳurʾān (IV, 25, V, 5).

On examination, the various types of "marriage" listed show two different attitudes to the relationship. Types 1,2,5 and 6 clearly betray the influence of the patriarchal system. The woman is completely subjugated to the man and has apparently little freedom. He may use her as he wishes, even to the point of making her share another man's bed; this is done either to honour the man or to raise a child of good stock. Moreover, he can "reserve for himself" a close relation (a sister or a daughter for example), not to marry himself but to exchange for a wife. The domination of women by men in this family system is absolute, and it is nowhere illustrated better than in the Arab preferential marriage. Now as before, it occurs between a man and the daughter of his paternal uncle, the well-known *bint ʿamm*, a word which has now become synonymous with "wife". Similarly *ibn ʿamm* means both paternal cousin and "husband" (*Aghānī*, xv, 263, 275). The son of a father's brother has by tradition a preemptory right over the daughter of his uncle. He is therefore required only to pay a symbolic dowry imposed by Islam. The *mahr* [*q.v.*] recouped by the father is in inverse proportion to the degree of the relationship. Strangers to the tribe pay more than fellow tribesman who are in an unfavourable position in regard to the *ḥamūla*; the *ibn ʿamm* would be absolved from payment and could even compel his uncle to give him his daughter. More distant cousins were equally favoured, but could not press their demands. Nevertheless, this unwritten right is not absolute; the more sedentary the community, the more it is contested. In literature, there are many examples of an uncle refusing his nephew through greed. The fear of weak progeny is an equally common reason for advising against marriage to the *bint ʿamm*. But the woman who is called to live in a strange tribe naturally evokes sympathy. She will be far away from her agnates, her natural protectors. Once relieved of the constraints imposed on her, the girl need no longer submit to the will of her cousin. When the poet al-Farazdaḳ became the guardian of his *bint ʿamm* Nawār, he had to devise a plan to get her to marry him after she had refused many times (*Aghānī*, xix, 12ff.).

Though the nomadic life, which condemns its followers to an indrawn existence, may favour endogamy, it does not explain a man's domination of his *bint ʿamm*. Robertson Smith likens this type of marriage to the right of inheritance. It is as though the woman forms part of the patrimony and many other customs confirm this point of view.

Marriage to the step-mother was quite widespread among the ancient Arabs. Al-Shahrastānī tells the story of three brothers who succeeded to their father's widow. It was recorded in both Medina and Mecca, and can be connected with the levirate, which was known to the Arabs then and is known now. Greed was the main reason for marrying a father's widow. The Ḳurʾān considered it an abominable practice (IV, 22), and contemporaries of Muḥammad maligned anyone who resorted to it; they called him a *ḍayzan*, which means one who is callous to his father and, not content to have his goods, wants to have his wife as well. On this point the Ḳurʾān expressly says: "O you who have believed! You are forbidden to inherit wives against their wishes, or to prevent them marrying in order that you may appropriate from them a part of what you gave them" (IV, 19). Commentators have observed that when a man dies, leaving a widow, his heir covers her with his cloak to show the right he has over her. Having done this, he may either keep her for himself without spending any money, for the dowry was paid by the deceased; or he can marry her off on condition that a new dowry is paid, which will come to him. He can also prevent her from marrying until she has bought back her freedom with what she received from her husband; if she does not, she will remain in his possession until she dies, and he will become her heir. Such a greedy attitude is found not only in the son but in the other male agnate relations, especially when the deceased left behind very young daughters. Here again the Ḳurʾān (IV, 127) plainly refers to orphaned girls whose guardians refuse to give them what has been bequeathed to them; they would rather keep them in order to marry them or force them to buy their freedom. In the same way, the paternal cousin, who is the first claimant able to marry the girl without committing incest, tries to seize what will ultimately come to him by inheritance, even during the lifetime of his uncle. Al-Wāḥidī, in his commentary on verse xix of the Sūra on Women, refers to this. A woman called Kubaysha complained to Muḥammad about the behaviour of her stepson who had inherited her; he did not support her financially, he did not cohabit with her nor would he grant her her freedom. Once they knew of her complaint, all the women of Medina searched for the Messenger of Allāh and told him, "All of us are in the same situation as Kubaysha, except that the right to marry us is not inherited by our sons but by the children of our paternal uncles" (al-Wāḥidī, *Aṣbāb al-nuzūl*, Cairo 1315, 108). Thus in the minds of the women of Medina, marriage to a parallel cousin was similar to that of a son to his father's widow, sc. a right of succession. In neither case did the woman have any free will; at one time, she could belong to her husband's heir, and at another to her father's future heir.

All this raises the question of the status of the Arab woman regarding inheritance before Islam, a much-debated issue. It is generally thought that at Medina she was disinherited for the same reason as children: "Only those who fight and defend property can inherit." At Mecca. a trading town, the system of succession may have been more favourable, although the sources contradict each other. The words of the caliph ʿUmar are often quoted: "We Ḳurayshites dominate our wives; at Medina we find the men are dominated by their wives" (al-Bukhārī, *Ṣaḥīḥ*, Cairo 1376, vii, 25). Obviously, the writer here is not concerned so much with the system of inheritance as with e.g. the behaviour of the women. It is difficult to imagine that a woman who behaves like a virago to her husband will display docility when her property is under attack. In any case, whether the woman was from Mecca or Medina, she would receive presents from her *khidn* "friend", her husband, and her relatives. She could even have a personal fortune and administer it as she pleased, as did Khadīdja, who ran her own business. She might even receive part of the inheritance by will.

Many orientalists feel that the reforms introduced by the Ḳurʾān to help women were inspired by the system of inheritance used in Mecca; but that thesis cannot be discussed here. We shall simply observe that in several verses of the Ḳurʾān it clearly states that the woman, be she mother or wife, had wealth which on her death reverted to her husband or children (IV, 12,37,175). In the circumstances, the Ḳurʾān must only have recorded what was a known fact. It would be difficult to explain in any other way the compulsion brought to bear on a widow to make her buy back her freedom by giving up part or all of what she had received from her husband. Besides what money she could earn from her own work (weaving, husbandry, beauty care, singing and dancing), she had other opportunities to be materially independent, thanks to matrimonial customs approaching free unions.

The four other types of marriage mentioned above (types 3,4,7 and 8) could assure the woman of a more or less comfortable existence. They are rooted in a matrilinear conception of relationship, and assume that the woman enjoys a fairly large amount of sexual freedom. In a society founded on the code of honour of the desert, even prostitution would be interpreted as a sign of tolerance in sexual matters, since the woman can indulge in this activity without fearing for her life. Furthermore, she is able to take a *k͟hidn* who pays for the services thus rendered by a *ṣadāḳ*. Group marriage and *mutʿa* also confirm the existence of matrilinear customs. In a temporary union, while still living within the group of relations, she grants her favour to a man and receives a payment in kind (a dress, a measure of dates or flour), and it lasts for a fixed time, usually three days (Muslim, *Ṣaḥīḥ*, iv, 130 ff.). The texts say nothing about any child born of this union; probably he would belong to his mother's clan and take her name, as was the case with the child born to a prostitute. The famous Ziyād b. Abīhi [*q.v.*] was better known by the name Ibn Sumayya in Arab literature, and many men used their mother's name. One cannot for certain whether they were all born from cohabitation; it simply implies that the system of matriliny was well-known to the ancient Arabs. There are several examples: the king ʿAmr b. Hind, the poets Sulayk b. Sulaka, Ibn al-Dumayna (*Ag͟hānī*, xv, 350), Ibn al-Ṭat͟hriyya (*ibid.* xv, 385), Ibn al-Ḥaddādiyya (*ibid.* xiii, 3), Ibn Ḍabba (*ibid.*, vi, 307), etc.

Very many tribes have a woman as eponymous ancestor, such as the ʿĀmila, Bad͟jīla. K͟hindif and Ḳayla. There are also numerous examples of matrilocality. The poet Maʿn b. Aws [*q.v.*] took advantage of a visit to Baṣra to marry a woman whose guest he was. He spent a year with her and then asked her permission to go back to his first wife (*Ag͟hānī*, x, 352).

Whatever interpretation is put on these customs, they certainly show that the pre-Islamic Arab woman enjoyed much more freedom, even in sexual matters, than is generally supposed. Whenever the outcome of a battle seemed uncertain, the chief would place his daughter in a litter among the warriors in the hope that it would stimulate their excitement, and the prospect of such a marvellous reward would lead to victory. On the day of *taḥāluk*, the two daughters of Find al-Zimmānī, like she-devils, undressed among the warriors and sang love songs to give them more courage (*Ag͟hānī*, xx, 345). On the day of Uḥud, the same song was taken up by Hind bint ʿUtba among the ranks of Ḳurays͟h (*Ag͟hānī*, xi, 238).

It was the custom, especially for the tribes from the South, like the Kinda, the D͟jarm and the Banū ʿUd͟hra, to let a man speak to the girl he loved of his sentiments (e.g. *Ag͟hānī*, vii, 218, 219, 234, 263). However, when the suitor pressed his claim, the girl's father, fearing a scandal, might ban him from the house and decline his offer of marriage. The most famous example is that of Tawba b. al-Ḥumayyir and Laylā al-Ak͟hyaliyya [*q.v.*]. Imruʾ al-Ḳays celebrated his love affairs in his *Muʿallaḳa*. Al-Farazdaḳ once surprised some girls bathing in a pool and exclaimed, "By God! It's like the day of *d͟jārat d͟juld͟jul*" (*Ag͟hānī*, xix, 52). Men and women might meet on many occasions, in the pasture lands, at wells and even in the tents. A woman would converse with men and have guests when the master of the house was away. The big annual fairs, which served well for arranging marriages, were frequented by women, poetesses, tradeswomen, inquisitive women and those eager for a sexual relationship, whether regular, temporary or licentious. In the first century after the Hid͟jra, while pursuing beauty, ʿUmar b, Abī Rabī ʿa took advantage of the pilgrimage season to embark on some amorous adventures. On the question of the veil, see ḤID͟JĀB. Not only could the pre-Islamic woman converse with men (cf. *Ag͟hānī*, xix, 306) but by tradition she had the right to protect them. Fugitives from the battle of the Fid͟jār found sanctuary in the tent of Subayʿa bint ʿAbd S͟hams (*ibid.*, 161). When hard-pressed and in danger of his life, the well-known *ṣuʿlūk* Sulayk b. Sulaka sought refuge with a woman who belonged to his enemy's clan. Without hesitation, she defended him from his pursuers, covered him with her mantle and took up a sword to drive off those pursuing him; but, being outnumbered, she uncovered her hair and called her brothers to the rescue. The fugitive thus escaped death (*Ag͟hānī*, xviii, 320; cf. xx, 380 ff.).

However a man might behave himself towards his wives and female relatives, he expected strangers to show them the greatest respect. To cast a slur on a woman's honour was to throw down the gauntlet. Chroniclers say that the cause of the war of the Fid͟jār (*Ag͟hānī*, x, 152) can be attributed to a joke in very bad taste. The victim of the joke was a woman of the Banū ʿĀmir who let herself be courted by the young men at the *sūḳ* of ʿUkāẓ.

There is considerable evidence of a considerate attitude to women, but nevertheless they did not escape the hazards of war with the risk of captivity. Her conqueror would rarely spare her the ultimate humiliation of making her grace his bed (*Ag͟hānī*, xix, 340 ff.). Islam permits sexual relations with prisoners of war (Muslim, *Ṣaḥīḥ*, iv, 158; 170; cf. *Ag͟hānī*, xii, 370); married women are not excluded (*Ag͟hānī*, xix, 25, supported by a verse of al-Farazdaḳ); but pregnant women must not be approached (Muslim, iv, 161).

Even before Islam repudiation (*ṭalāḳ*) was known to the Arabs. A man could send away his wife simply by unilateral decision. All he had to do was to recite the formula *anti ṭāliḳa*. Another formula, with incestuous overtones, lent more gravity to the situation, but it belonged to the *ẓihār* and was forbidden by Islam (Ḳurʾān, LVIII, 2). The man would say to his wife, *anti ʿalayya ka-ẓahri ummī*, "To me you are like my mother's back". When the woman desired to separate, the man had recourse to *k͟hulʿ*; he would agree to restore her freedom on condition that she gave him back all or most of the property he had given her (cf. Ḳurʾān, II, 229; the arrangement is not prohibited provided the financial agreement is mutually acceptable). There were two other ways, rather more exigent, by which a man could force a woman to return to him what she had been given by him. The *īlāʾ* was a temporary interruption of the marriage and could last for up to two years. The Ḳurʾān reduced the period to four months (II, 226). There was also the *ʿaḍl*, which was prohibited by the Ḳurʾān (IV. 9).

In the face of all this oppression the woman seemed helpless, yet there are records of women wanting to safeguard their independence, who only agreed to marry if they were granted the right to leave their husbands. Such women appear to have belonged to the higher social levels, and appear at Medina as well as at Mecca, among the sedentary communities as well as among the nomads. One cannot speak in this connection of polyandry, but they certainly changed their husbands very frequently. Al-Maydānī has recorded the names of some of them, the most famous one being Umm Khāridja, who is said to have married about forty times and whose hastiness in marriage became proverbial (*Amthāl*, proverb no. 1871, Cairo 1959, i, 348; according to Ibn Ḥabīb, *Muḥabbar*, 436, she married only about eight times).

Islam, it is true, allowed only men the right of repudiation, but the women of the Ḳuraysh aristocracy sometimes behaved like their independent sisters of the old régime. Because of their nobility, they were much in demand, and so they married many times; in this way, they were able to amass large fortunes (*Aghānī*, xiv, 37; x, 110 ff.) and make life hard for their husbands (*Aghānī*, xviii, 468). One of these women, the famous ʿĀʾisha bint Ṭalḥa [*q.v.*], even repudiated her husband by using the ancient formula of the *ẓihār*; she would not go back on her oath until she was convinced that it was invalid (*Aghānī*, x, 106).

In the pre-Islamic period, a widow would observe a delay before remarrying. When her husband died she would be shut away, wear her oldest clothes and use no perfume. After a year, she would come out from her place of withdrawal and throw a clod of mud. From that time onwards, she could lead a normal life (al-Bukhārī, *Ṣaḥīḥ*, vii, 52). This period was shortened by Islam to four months and ten days (Ḳurʾān, II, 234), during which she might not use perfume or *kuḥl*. When she received condolences, if she wished to remarry she remained seated; otherwise she would stand (*Aghānī*, x, 114).

These details have been given so that the status of women during the period of the Hidjra can be understood in the light of tradition, but these customs do not necessarily have any legal force. There are many problems still to be solved about the position of women in traditional law, and the pre-Islamic material is too scanty to help in solving them. The Ḳurʾān and the early *fiḳh* accord a considerable part to traditional customs, but Islam also provided a new outlook here by giving women a legal position, even though it is a diminished one, for she only counts as half the value of a man. It is not clear whether this is new legislation, or merely an adaption of old customs. Rather than waste time in conjecture, it seems worthwhile to study the behaviour of present-day Arab nomads.

Being Muslims, they have probably been influenced by that faith, notably in regard to what concerns their personal status, even though its influence may not be very deep. More than one modern custom is in direct contravention of the *sharʿ*. Woman is systematically disinherited and her evidence is often disregarded; marriage by exchange is frequently practised, and in blood revenge, equality is demanded. Clearly, the permanence of pre-Islamic customs here proves the lasting influence of the *ṭāghūt*. Traditional rights are still decided this way in the Yemen. Not all the pre-Islamic customs still thrive in Bedouin society, but the prevailing legal framework observed by them has been inspired by that tradition. They bear the mark of the desert, the same influence that has shaped all the Semitic nomads.

e. *The legal status of Bedouin women*.

The birth of a daughter is no cause for rejoicing. She is of so little account that if a Bedouin is asked how many children he has, he deliberately misses out the females. For the same reason, the strength of a tribe is measured purely by the number of warriors it can muster.

A girl's education is left entirely in the hands of her mother. From the time she is able to be of the smallest service, she is made to help with the domestic chores. From infancy onwards, excision is practised; sometimes it occurs just before marriage, which can take place when the girl is very young, often before she is ten. This occasion is of great importance for the father, for it falls to him to fix the amount of the dowry which he generally keeps for himself. It usually happens that the girl, whose opinion is rarely sought, has been promised from birth to an agnate relative, notably to her first paternal cousin, who has a pre-emptory right over her. He often uses this right and abuses it, for he can carry off his *bint ʿamm* on the day she is married to someone else if he disapproves of the union. He also has the right to "reserve" her for himself, although he is not required to follow up his expressed matrimonial intention. There is only one restriction to this excessive right, that is, the prohibition of marriage by exchange, *badal*, when the girl's father or her brother try to get themselves a wife thus. One should add that the traditional prerogatives of the *ibn ʿamm* are being contested more and more.

Because she is regarded as a source of wealth, the woman is jealously guarded, if not for the members of her *ḥamūla*, at least for own clan. Marriage outside the tribe is rare; generally it will take place only for political reasons or to stifle revenge. Of all the different types of union mentioned above, there remain only the marriage union as it is practised by the Muslims, marriage by exchange, profit, and finally, a special type of matrilocal union which will be discussed below.

Marriage by exchange, though condemned by Islam, is much practised, even among the sedentary Yemeni people. To conform to the *sharīʿa*, each side must offer the other exactly the same *mahr*. But things become complicated when one of the husbands repudiates his wife, since the other is then pledged to follow his example or to pay back a suitable dowry. It is not hard to envisage that law suits and angry scenes are bound to follow as a consequence of this custom in a society where the husband has only to repeat a set formula in order to dissolve his marriage.

Abduction must be carefully distinguished from taking captive. It is severely condemned in Bedouin society, even when it is done with a view to marriage. When it becomes known that a woman has been taken off, all the agnate relatives set off in pursuit of the culprit. If they catch him, he does not usually escape death, and the ravished woman may suffer the same fate. In fact, the treatment they each receive depends on the intentions of the abductor and the civil status of the woman he has taken.

A man who wishes to marry may encounter opposition from the girl's parents, and so he may, with her consent, resort to abduction. Provided it is carried out in good taste, his actions are looked on somewhat indulgently, but it must take place in the presence of a trustworthy witness who has been enlisted to help in the operation. He must guard the girl, bring her to a safe place and vouch for the fact that everything was conducted honourably. With such pressure on the father, the latter will usually give his consent but ask for a high dowry. If the abduction is followed by illicit sexual relations, the man and the girl will be punished with the same severity as lovers who are caught in the act. If the abduction has been carried out against the wishes of the girl, the action is treated as rape. The man must offer to make amends by marrying the girl, and considers himself lucky if he is accepted. A dowry will then be required of him equal to the price of her blood. In addition, he is required to offer in marriage a girl who is a close agnate relative to the father, brother or paternal cousin of his future wife without a dowry.

To abduct a married woman, even with her consent, brings severe disapproval from Bedouin society. It can lead to reprisals, often violent from the husband in the first place, but also, and above all, from the agnate relatives of the unfaithful wife. Death awaits the lovers. They will escape their fate only if they can find refuge with some powerful person or influential leader. In order to save his guests, this person must bring the husband to recite the repudiation formula in exchange for the dowry he paid. He must also gain the parents' consent to the marriage. The abductor in turn must give one or more girls in exchange for the wife.

If any woman is suspected of having an illicit sexual relationship, whether she is a girl or a married woman, widowed or divorced, she finds herself in great danger. If gossip about her continues, she runs the risk of being killed by a close agnatic relative, her brother, cousin or uncle. Absence of proof of the alleged misconduct is not regarded as proof of innocence. It is customary to exonerate her or to condemn her by adopting one of the following procedures. Her father or guardian may request that a court of justice summon her lover, about whom the rumours are circulating, and that they make him swear that the accusations being made against him are untrue. It is remarkable that the woman stays away from this judicial action, even though her life depends on it. Her presumed partner must stand before the judge, and it is he who must take the oath. Women are considered to be legally incapable, and so are seldom authorised to appear before a Bedouin court even as simple witnesses. Certainly, if it should happen that there are no male witnesses in a particular case, a judge might agree to hear a woman's evidence, but solely for his own information. A woman's evidence is only acceptable in law when it concerns another woman. A quicker way to judge a woman's guilt is by subjecting her to the ordeal of *bas̲h̲ʿa*. If the evidence according to this procedure is against her, it is not uncommon for her to be put to death by a close agnatic relative.

The reputation of a woman for whom he is responsible evokes an uncompromising attitude among the Bedouin. Abduction, adultery and rape all taint her honour, and their guilt can be washed away only by a blood-bath. But it always appears to be the woman who pays the price, and there is a quick, private system of justice to punish any girl who has compromised her reputation. Traditional Bedouin law relating to illicit love affairs is so complex that it is impossible to survey the main features briefly and accurately. Consideration must be given to the civil status of the woman or girl, whether she is married, widowed or divorced, her religious status, her connivance with or opposition to her ravisher, the resistance she displaced, the circumstances under which the crime occurred, and the time and place of the rape or attempted rape. It would obviously be tedious to dwell on these points. However, the culprits caught in the act are generally put to death. Their blood has been spilled, which means that the one exacting justice will not be pursued for that action and the *diya* will not have to be paid. The agnate relations may be less severe with a young girl who is seduced, and may let her off with her life, but the abductor must then marry her and must give a girl from his close family without asking for a dowry. He will also be forbidden to repudiate his wife because of these special circumstances.

It is probably unnecessary here to struggle through the labyrinthine procedure of the *ʿurf* on matters of illicit love affairs, but two of the previously-mentioned points are worthy of note: the place and the time of the crime. It may have been committed near the camp at dusk after the flock had returned; or in grazing land when the shepherdess was naturally far away from her family. In the first case, the woman is described as *ʿāḳibat al-sarḥ*, "the one who returns behind the livestock" and she is entirely responsible for what has occurred. At that time of day, it is thought that she should be at home, and the fact that she was far from her house proves that she was conniving with her seducer. But if she was away at her place of work, then her guilt is somewhat lessened, but she must cry for help (hence the expression *muṣayyihat al-ḍuḥā* "the girl who cries in the morning"). She is therefore spared by her family.

In several places previously, we have mentioned that an abductor must hand over a girl from his close family, without a dowry, to a member of the injured family. This custom is sometimes observed in a case of murder, when the blood relative forgoes his right of vengeance and accepts a compromise. The wergeld that the family of a murderer must give as compensation may include a young girl, called a *g̲h̲urra* in these circumstances. She must be a virgin, white and free. She is given in marriage without *mahr* to a near relative of the victim, and is reduced in effect to a state of semi-slavery. Although she is legally united to the man whose life she shares, she is not completely granted the status of a wife. She is liable to all the oppressions that a husband metes out to his womenfolk and endures his ill-treatment without being able to have recourse to the protection of her family. The most she can do is to seek refuge with an influential person and ask for his help. Her role is to correct the wrong inflicted on the injured family, by giving birth to a male child to replace the deceased. When the boy is old enough to bear arms, her mission is completed. At that time she ceases to be a *g̲h̲urra*, a servant, and becomes *ḥurra*, free. She can leave her husband, who has no further right over her; if he tries to keep her he must pay the dowry. She is not thought of as belonging permanently to the man who takes her, but is handed over by her family against a guarantee that she will be returned to them when she has finished her task. Even when the conditions of a woman's marriage are perfectly normal, she is still legally dependent on her own family. It is their responsibility to defend her, and it also falls on them in the end to avenge her blood.

One point of interest here is often passed over in silence, but deserves to be mentioned. Although by marriage a woman must be entirely submissive to her new master's will and must follow him and live together with him, for all that, she is not his property.

She is like a precious investment placed in his hands and which is entirely at his disposal. He may rebuke her, he may even hit her, but he is not allowed to injure her or to atttempt to take her life, for he is answerable to his parents-in-law for his conduct. He is perfectly within his rights to kill her if he actually catches her in the act of adultery, but then he may not ask for the return of the dowry he has paid. He would be entitled to a return of the dowry if he simply repudiated her, and he would then leave her relatives to wash away their shame in the culprit's blood.

The married woman depends, legally speaking, on her own family in most situations. It falls to her father, brother, uncle or paternal cousin to chastise her if she is at fault, and to avenge her blood if she is a victim of murder. Unless the husband is also the paternal cousin, he must restrain himself from any violent action and be content to have the dowry paid back to him.

The Bedouin woman is not handed over defenceless to the despotism of her husband. It is even probable that she often exerts a good influence on him. In his absence, she may offer hospitality and shelter to a fugitive. Even if her natural defenders, her agnatic close relatives, disappear or are at a distance, she is not left entirely without defence. If she is ill-treated by her husband she can put herself in the protection of a distinguished person as a *da<u>kh</u>īla*, a refugee. It is then up to her husband to ask her if she will resume married life. To do this, he arranges a delegation of at least three witnesses to inform her of his wishes. This procedure can be repeated three times. If, despite his insistence, his wife remains obstinate in her refusal the husband then has the right not to support her financially any more, if he does not want to dissolve the marriage. If he does not make any of these customary approaches, a Bedouin court can condemn him to pay his wife substantial financial compensation.

The dissolution of a marriage contract may occur in two different ways: repudiation or widowhood. Only the man has the right to divorce his spouse. If he does this without an adequate motive, he cannot reclaim the dowry, as custom enables him to if the fault is the wife's. This financial aspect to marriage plays an important role when the woman seeks to regain her independence and her husband refuses to recite the liberating formula on his own. There is, however, one circumstance where he is obliged to grant her her freedom, sc. in the case of his impotency. Since a woman's legal incapacity forbids her to appear before a law court, a relative representing her brings the action against her husband. The latter then has the right to only one-half of the dowry he paid. The divorced woman, like the widow, must observe a period of restraint before remarrying. The *ʿidda* for the Jordanian Bedouin is normally one hundred nights, but often the woman is put back into circulation before the expiry of the minimal legal delay, for she is considered a source of wealth.

Like repudiation, widowhood grants a woman some freedom in her choice of further husband. She may return to her own family, leaving behind all the property left by her husband, or she may stay with her husband's family and her children. If she is of remarriageable age, the dead man's brother may marry her. But if the widow has the role of guardian according to the wishes of the *de cujus*, in which case she can neither rejoin her paternal home nor remarry. It is her responsibility to remain at home looking after the children and administering the property which she inherited and which will pass to them when they attain the age of majority. Since remarriage is unavailable, she may ensure that she enjoys a normal sexual life by taking a *zaw<u>dj</u> musarrib* "visiting husband" This type of union is very rare and runs counter to the principle of patrilocality on which Bedouin society is built. Instead of following her new partner, the widow receives him at her house almost as a guest. Whether the man is married or single, he must have his own home to which he returns after visiting her. In this way, the woman retains her freedom since she can dismiss her visiting husband if she no longer wants him. However, it is still he who has the right of repudiation. This is one of the very rare times that a Bedouin woman enjoys much economic independence.

The *ʿurf* is very strict with women in financial matters. It especially disregards the teaching of the Ḳurʾān which decrees that a daughter shall inherit exactly half the portion inherited by a son. It says that the only people who are allowed to inherit are the agnate males. On the father's death, the sons possess the property. The heirs must first attend to the needs of the mother and the widows of the deceased. Daughters are in their brother's care until their marriage. They must also help their sister both financially and morally if she is divorced, widowed or ill-treated. In return for these services, not only do these brothers exclude them from the inheritance but they also keep their dowries and exchange their sisters when they barter for wives. Custom is no more favourable to daughters in the case of a subsequent inheritance from the mother's side. No matter how important the total, they receive only the jewelry and the clothes. Even if the price of their mother's blood is involved, they do not receive anything more.

The problem of the *diya* for the murder of a woman brings many related complexities. From a purely formal point of view, the *ʿurf* decrees that a woman's blood is worth half of a man's. It is exactly the *diya* of an unemancipated slave. In reality, this applies when the murder was committed by a person of the same sex or when it happened purely by accident and not as the result of war or raid. A complete *diya* is required when a woman is unfortunately hit by a stray bullet in a brawl between two families or clans. On the other hand, the blood money can in effect quadruple in nominal value, i.e. double that for a man, when the death follows a struggle with a man, even if that man was only defending himself. If a woman dies at or after an attempted rape, the *diya* becomes from eight to twelve times its original value. In addition, the *ʿurf* makes a subtle distinction between a single and a married woman. In the latter case, it seeks to establish whether she is pregnant or not. If her pregnancy is confirmed, the sex of the foetus must be determined. Whatever the cause of death, a pregnant woman counts as two people. The culprit will have to pay either the *diya* for two women or for a man and a woman; of course, the case can be made worse depending on the circumstances and prevailing conditions at the time of the crime.

In conclusion, two comments should be made on the legal status of the Bedouin woman. First, it would be erroneous to pretend that the situation is the same for all the desert Arabs. Customs more or less local may vary, and important variations may be seen from one region to another. But there is good reason to suppose that these variations reflect differences in the letter of the traditional law rather than in its spirit, the perpetuity of the law being firmly guaranteed by its environment. The *ʿurf* represents one kind of mentality, that of the nomadic Semite, and there are many similar customs to those described above attested among the ancient Hebrew nomads. Secondly, it would be equally wrong to suggest that this law, even where women are concerned, is as alive today to the extent it was at the opening of this century. The evolutionary process, less or more active according to the different regions, seems to develope in two directions. There is a marked return to the *shar*ᶜ, and many persons have tried to prove, in a contradictory fashion, that there is no break in the continuity of tradition between ᶜ*urf* and *shar*ᶜ. On the other hand, central governments have, in a rather more discreet manner, endeavoured to move towards a more modern conception of justice to accord with the general trends in the country. Despite all this pressure, there appears to be a part of ᶜ*urf* which seems secure against all modern reforms: that of whiteness of the face, honour and ᶜ*irḍ*, which in its very essence is symbolised by woman.

Bibliography: As well as the references in the text see in general: ᶜAfīfī, *al-Mar'a al-ᶜarabiyya*, Cairo n.d.; Ālūsī, *Bulūgh al-arab fī maᶜrifat aḥwāl al-ᶜArab*, Cairo 1342; Hāshimī, *al-Mar'a fi 'l-shiᶜr al-djāhili*, Baghdād 1960; Ibn Ḳayyim al-Djawziyya, *Akhbār al-nisā'*, Beirut 1964; I. Lichtenstädter, *Women in the Aiyam al-ᶜArab*, London 1935; A. El-Yafi, *La condition privée de la femme dans le droit de l'Islam*, Paris 1928; W. Walter, *Femmes en Islam*, Paris 1981. Kinship and marriage: W. Robertson Smith, *Kinship and marriage in early Arabia*, Cambridge 1885; B. Z. Seligman, *Studies in Semitic kingship*, in *BSOS*, iii (1923), 51-68, 263-80; G. Stern, *Marriage in early Islam*, London 1936; R. F. Spencer, *The Arabian matriarchate: an old controversy*, in *Southwestern Journal of Anthropology*, viii (1952); J. Henninger, *Polyandrie im vorislamischen Arabien*, in *Anthropos*, xlix (1954); idem, *Le problème du totémisme chez les arabes après quatre-vingt ans de recherche*, in *Actes du VIᵉ congrès des sciences anthropologiques et ethnologiques*, Paris 1960; J. Lecerf, *Note sur la famille dans le domaine arabe et islamique*, in *Arabica*, iii (1956); W. Montgomery Watt, *Muhammad at Medina*, Excursus J. Oxford 1956; J. Chelhod, *Le mariage avec la cousine parallèle dans le système arabe*, in *L'Homme*, v (1965), 113-74; F. Peltier and G. H. Bousquet, *Les successions agnatiques mitigées*, Paris 1935; Ethnography: J. Chelhod, *Le droit dans la société bédouine*, Paris 1971 (with an important bibl.); idem, *La parenté et le marriage au Yémen*, in *L'Ethnographie*, n.s., lxvii (1973); idem, *L'Arabie du Sud*, iii, Paris 1985, 63-123. (J. Chelhod)

3. In Persia. a. Before 1900.

The following will not be concerned with the legal position of women—this has been discussed above in sections 1 and 2—but will focus on their position and role in society. The sources are meagre. Women did not normally leave written accounts of their lives. We know little of their motives and characters from their own accounts, and it is not to be expected that others should write of them except in very general terms. So far as women are mentioned, they belong for the most part either to the ruling classes or to those who are believed to have made some contribution to the religious life of the community. Among the latter are women of the family of the Prophet and saints. Their lives are recorded in biographical dictionaries and hagiographical works. Their characters are seldom delineated in any but the broadest terms, and the virtues ascribed to them are usually characteristic Islamic virtues. This is to some extent true of the women of the ruling class also. They are mentioned in histories and chronicles because they either played a prominent part in events as regents or in some other capacity and because marriage alliances were an important element in state policy. Women of the middle and lower classes are seldom mentioned and peasant women are virtually ignored. Much incidental information on women is, however, to be found in the historical literature of the 5th-8th/11th-14th centuries. The anonymous *Tārīkh-i shāhī-i Ḳara-Khiṭā'iyān* written in the 7th/13th century (ed. Muḥammad Ibrāhīm Bāstānī Pārīzī, Tehran Shāhinshāhī 2535/1976-7), and the *Simṭ al-ᶜulā* of Nāṣir al-Dīn Munshī, written between 715/1315-16 and 720/1320-1 (ed. ᶜAbbās Iḳbāl, Tehran AHS 1327/1949-50) contain lively accounts of the women of the Ḳara-Khiṭay (Ḳutlugh-Khānid) dynasty of Kirmān, and the *Djāmi*ᶜ *al-tawārīkh* of Rashīd al-Dīn Faḍl Allāh gives much information on the women of the Īlkhānid family. The sources for the later centuries are less rich, until the 19th century, when there are several important works which give a picture of the activities of women of the ruling class, notably the *Tārīkh-i ᶜAḍudī* of Sulṭān Aḥmad Mīrzā ᶜAḍud al-Dawla b. Fatḥ ᶜAlī Shāh (ed. ᶜAbd al-Ḥusayn Nawā'ī, Tehran Shāhinshāhī, 2535/1976-7) *Yāddāsht-hā'ī az zindagānī-i khuṣūṣī-i Nāṣir al-Dīn Shāh* by Dūst ᶜAlī Muᶜayyir al-Mamālik, who grew up as a page in the Ḳādjār court (Tehran n.d.); and vol. i of *Sharḥ-i zindagī-i man* by ᶜAbd Allāh Mustawfī (3 vols., Tehran AHS 1324-5/1945-6), which gives an intimate picture of life in an upper class family in Tehran; while Tādj al-Salṭana, the daughter of Nāṣir al-Dīn Shāh, who was born in 1301/1883-4, wrote an autobiography entitled *Khāṭirāt-i Tādj al-Salṭana* in 1343/1924-5) (ed. Manṣūra Ittiḥādiyya and Sīrūs Saᶜdwandiyān, Tehran AHS 1361/1982). From the 10th/16th century onwards, Persian sources are supplemented by the accounts of European travellers. These, by the nature of things, are the accounts of outsiders, but as intercourse increased in the 19th century and European women began to come to Persia, the information on the position of women and their daily life becomes fuller.

At all periods, there was a difference between townswomen, peasant women and tribal women. The general consensus of the settled population was against the participation of women in public affairs. Townspeople were secluded and played no part in public life; and little is revealed of their influence in family affairs. All houses, other than those of the very poor, were divided into the women's apartments, the *andarūn*, public apartments, the *bīrūn*, where business was transacted and male guests entertained. In the richer houselholds, it was customary for eunuchs and female slaves to be employed in the *andarūn*. Peasant women worked in the fields. They did not, however, usually appear unveiled in public before the opposite sex.

In tribal society, great weight was given to the bond of blood relationship, and the woman's role in establishing this was of great, perhaps paramount, importance. Marriage alliances consolidated tribal federations and marked the entry of new tribes into existing federations. The exchange of women was also a method of terminating blood feuds. The nature of tribal society was such that women enjoyed a status and function which was, on the whole, denied to them in settled society. Tribeswomen did not normally veil. They played an active part in the daily life of the tribe and often in the management of tribal affairs (cf. Sir John Malcolm, *Sketches of Persia*, London 1845, 154-5).

In all classes and sectors of society, child marriage and the marriage of cousins were normal practice.

Among the richer classes, polygamy was common. Rivalry between the inmates of the *ḥaram* to secure favour for their own sons was of frequent occurence. Remarriage of widows and divorced women was also common [see MUTʿA and NIKĀḤ].

With the rise of the Saldjūḳs [*q.v.*] in the 5th/11th century, women of the ruling class began to play a more active role in political life. The reason for this is probably to be sought in their Turkic tribal background, even though the Saldjūḳs were to some extent separated from this once they had become the rulers of an empire. From the time of Ṭoghrïl Beg onwards, marriage alliances with local ruling families and with the caliphate were an important aspect of Saldjūḳ policy. This was also true of the succession states. The sons of Saldjūḳ mothers do not appear to have had precedence over the sons of other wives, nor, in general do the sons of free women appear to have had precedence over the sons of slave women or concubines. Some of the wives of the sultans had their own *dīwān*s and establishments; some held *iḳṭāʿ*s [*q.v.*] and landed property; and some disposed of considerable wealth. The office of *wazīr* to the wife of the sultan was sometimes a stepping-stone to important office under the sultan. Several "royal" women played a prominent part in public life. Ṭoghrïl Beg is reported to have consulted his chief wife Altun Djan in affairs, Sibṭ b. al-Djawzī states that she was a religious woman, much given to charitable works, of good judgement and firm determination (*Mirʾat al-zamān*, ed. Ali Sevim, Ankara 1968, 75; cf. also Ibn al-Djawzī, *al-Muntaẓam*, Ḥaydarābād, Deccan 1938-40, viii, 218). Terken Khātūn, the chief wife of Malikshāh, was a masterful and ambitious woman. She and Zubayda Khātūn, another of Malikshāh's wives, vied with each other in order to secure the succession of their respective sons after the death of Malikshāh. The former appears to have had a sizeable force of military slaves at her disposal.

Some of the wives of the *amīr*s and atabegs were also women of character; and several of them were noted for their charitable benefactions. One such was Zāhida Khātūn, who ruled Fārs for twenty-one years after the death of her husband Boz Aba in 541/1146-7. Another was the mother of Arslan b. Ṭoghrïl b. Muḥammad, who was married after the death of Ṭoghrïl to Ildegüz, the Atabeg of ʿĀdharbāydjān, under whose tutelage Arslan was installed as nominal ruler in Hamadān in 556/1161. Recording her death, which occurred in 571/1175-6, Ẓahīr al-Dīn Nīshāpūrī states that "it was as if the good order of the kingdom and the dynasty depended upon the existence of that lady" (*Saldjūḳ-nāma*, Tehran AHS 1332/1953-4, 82). Abish Khātūn, the daughter of the Atabeg Saʿd of Fārs, had a lively though short life. After the death of the last of the Atabegs of Fārs, Saldjūḳ-Shāh b. Salghur-Shāh b. Saʿd in 662/1263-4, she was put on the throne with the support of the Shūl and Turkoman *amīrs*, although she was only 4 or 5 years old, because no direct male descendant of the Atabegs survived. She had apparently already before that been betrothed by her mother to Tash Möngke, Hülegü's son. In due course, she became his chief wife. Her daughter Kürdüdjin received a contract (*muḳāṭaʿa*) in 719/1319-20 for the taxes of Fārs from Abū Saʿīd, the last Īlkhān. She was married first to Soyurghatmïsh, the Ḳutlugh-Khānid ruler of Kirmān, and secondly and thirdly to Mongol *amīrs*.

In Khwārazm, Terken Khātūn, the wife of the Khwārazmshāh Tekesh, played a turbulent role in the politics of Khwārazm during the reign of her son Muḥammad (596-617/1199-1220). She finally fell into the hands of the Mongols, and was sent to Ḳaraḳorum where she died in 630/1232-3 (see Barthold, *Turkestan*, index under *Turkān-Khātūn*). Another Terken Khātūn, who was also known after her marriage in 632/1235 to Ḳuṭb al-Dīn Muḥammad, the Ḳara Khiṭay (Ḳutlugh-Khānid) ruler of Kirmān, by her *laḳab* Ḳutlugh Terken, was an outstanding woman. She ruled Kirmān after her husband's death in 655/1257 because her two sons, Soyurghatmïsh and Ḥadjdjādj Sulṭān, were minors. She was a capable and vigorous woman, who in addition to her attention to affairs of state, was also given to charitable works and generous patronage of the *ʿulamāʾ*. Her daughters Pādishāh Khātūn and Bībī Khātūn also played a prominent part in the political affairs of the day; the former was married to the Īlkhān Abaḳa (see *Tārīkh-i shāhī-i Ḳara Khiṭāʾiyān* and Nāṣir al-Dīn Munshī, *Simṭ al-ʿulā, passim*).

The Mongol conquest brought changes in the position and status of women of the ruling class. The Īlkhāns for the most part appear to have taken their wives from the Mongol tribes, and through them to have retained their links with the Mongols in Central Asia and China. They also concluded marriage alliances with local ruling families, whose daughters they took into their *ḥarams*. Such alliances had benefits for both parties: the local rulers assured their own positions, even if only temporarily, while the Īlkhāns were able through such unions to bring outlying provinces more closely under their control. But while local women were taken into the establishments of the Īlkhāns, women of the Īlkhānid family and of Mongol *noyans* are seldom recorded as having been given to local rulers. The women of defeated enemies, so far as they escaped massacre, were regarded as part of the booty and were taken into the establishment of the Mongol princes and army commanders.

The wives and daughters of the Īlkhāns and Mongol princes enjoyed a privileged position vis-à-vis the rest of society. They received a share of the booty and took part in the *ḳuriltay*s [*q.v.*] held to acclaim or appoint a new Īlkhān. Many of them accumulated great wealth. Ögedey's chief wife Töregene and Güyük's chief wife both acted as regent on the death of their respective husbands, pending the appointment of a new Great Khān. There are no instances of women acting as regents in the Īlkhānate, but after the death of Abū Saʿīd, the last Īlkhān, his sister Sati Beg was put on the throne with the help of Shaykh Ḥasan, the grandson of the Amīr Čopan, in 799/1338-9, on the grounds that the right of the throne was hers since no male member of the house of Hülegü remained. In fact, however, the kingdom passed to the Čopanids and the Djalāʾirids. In spite of the prestige and authority enjoyed by the women of the Īlkhānid house, their freedom was limited by custom and their position was, in many respects, one of subjection. On the death of an Īlkhān, his wife passed to his successor or to one of his uncles, brothers or sons. If accused of plotting against the Īlkhān or of some other misdemeanour, Īlkhānid women were not immune from trial by *yarghu* [*q.v.*], the bastinado and even execution, whether guilty of the crime of which they were accused or not.

The senior wives of the Īlkhānids had their own *ordus*. Junior wives were often placed in the *ordu* of a senior wife. Imperial concubines were distributed among the *ordus* of the Īlkhān's wives. Some were in due course promoted to the status of a "full" wife. On the death (or disgrace) of one of his wives, the Īlkhān would give her *ordu* to another of his wives. It is difficult to determine exactly the composition and size of the *ordus* of the Mongol princesses. By the time of Ghazan, many of them were large and powerful establishments. The Mongol princesses also took part in the activities of the trading and money-lending partnerships known as *ortak̲s*. Ghazan apparently sought to bring the *ordus* of the princesses under control and to use their revenues for military and other expenditure (see further Lambton, *Continuity and change in medieval Persia: aspects of administrative, economic and social history 5th/11th to 8th/14th century*, forthcoming; Spuler, *Die Mongolen in Iran³*, Berlin 1968, see index under *Frau*; S̲h̲īrīn Bayānī, *Zan dar Īrān-i ʿahd-i Mug̲h̲ul*, Tehran AHS 1352/1974).

The position of women under the Tīmūrids resembled in many ways their position in the Īlk̲h̲ānate. Tīmūr himself seems to have chosen wives mainly of Mongol origin for himself and his family (H. Hookham, *Tamburlaine the conqueror*, London 1962, 72). They had their own quarters in the royal camp (*Clavijo: embassy to Tamerlane*, tr. G. Le Strange, London 1928, 242-3, 268, 271). They appeared in public at royal feasts and on occasion gave banquets themselves, at which they appeared only lightly veiled before their male and female guests (*ibid.*, 237, 244 ff., 275; cf. also Muʿīn al-Dīn Natanzī's account of a great feast given by Tīmūr in 806/1403-4 at which women were present, *Muntak̲h̲ab al-tawārīk̲h̲* ed. J. Aubin, Tehran AHS 1336/1957, 398 ff.).

Under the Ḳara Ḳoyunlu and Aḳ Ḳoyunlu, women of the ruling class continued to play an influential role, especially through the establishment of kinship links (see J. E. Woods, *The Aqquyunlu: clan, confederation, empire*, Minneapolis and Chicago 1976). Marriage alliances in the early Ṣafawid period also were an important means of consolidating the ruler's influence. Ṭahmāsp was allied in this way with powerful *amīr*s and local rulers (see Iskander Muns̲h̲ī, *ʿĀlamārā-yi ʿAbbāsī*, Tehran AHS 1334/1956, 2 vols., i, 125 ff., for mention of his wives); his sister was married to the religious leader, Islām S̲h̲āh Ni ʿmat Allāh Yazdī, and a daughter of this union was married to Ṭahmāsp's son, Ismā ʿīl Mīrzā (*ibid.*, 132). Zaynab Begum, one of Ṭahmāsp's daughters, whose mother was a Georgian woman, was, according to Iskandar Muns̲h̲ī, highly intelligent and acquired great influence with ʿAbbās I, into whose *haram* she passed. She was known for many charitable works and benefactions (*ibid.*, 135). Parī K̲h̲ān K̲h̲ānum, another of Ṭahmāsp's daughters, played an influential part on her father's death in promoting the accession of Ismāʿīl Mīrzā. After his accession, she fell from favour, but after his death, on the accession of Muḥammad Mīrzā, she exercised great influence in the government of the country. Great rivalry existed between her and Muḥammad S̲h̲āh's wife, Mahd Awliyāʾ K̲h̲ayr al-Nisāʾ Begum. Parī K̲h̲ān K̲h̲ānum's high handed behaviour aroused the enmity of the Ḳizilbas̲h̲ *amīr*s and she was eventually murdered by them. K̲h̲ayr al-Nisāʾ Begum then took upon herself the government of affairs because of her husband's defective eyesight. She too was murdered by the Ḳizilbas̲h̲ *amīr*s, who resented her interference (see *ibid.*, index under *Parī K̲h̲ān K̲h̲ānum* and *Mahd Awliyāʾ K̲h̲ayr al-Nisāʾ Begum*, and *Maḥmūd b. Hidāyat Allāh Afus̲h̲taʾī, Naḳāwat al-āt̲h̲ār*, ed. Iḥsān Is̲h̲rāḳī, Tehran AHS 1350/1971-2, 21, 72, 250). K̲h̲adīdja, another of Ṭahmāsp's daughters, was married to Djams̲h̲īd b. Sulṭān Aḥmad, the ruler of Biyā Pas in Gīlān (see ʿAbd al-Fattāḥ Fūminī, *Tārīk̲h̲-i Gīlān*, ed. M. Sotoodeh, Tehran AHS 1349/1970, 54-6).

As the Ṣafawids moved away from their tribal background, the influence of their women was increasingly confined to *haram* intrigues. Already under Ṭahmāsp, large numbers of concubines and slaves, especially Georgians and Circassians, were introduced into the royal *haram*. This trend continued, and with it the power of the eunuchs of the palace greatly increased. The general deterioration in the position and status of the royal women in all probability spread among other ranks of society also (cf. Jean-Baptiste Tavernier, *Voyages en Perse*, Geneva 1970, 282-4; Du Mans, *Estat de la Perse*, Paris 1890, repr., 1969, 27-8; Chardin, *Sir John Chardin's travels in Persia* with an introduction by Brig. General Sir Percy Sykes, London 1927, 222). The status of the mother appears to have had little influence on the choice of the *walī ʿahd*. The mother of the shah was the most important lady in the *haram*; after her came the shah's wives and then his favourite concubines (E. Kaempfer, *Am Hofe des persischen Grosskönigs 1684-1685*, tr. W. Hinz, Tübingen and Basel 1977, 232). When the ladies of the royal *haram* went out, the district through which they were to pass was declared *k̲uruk̲* (a reserve), and those who inadvertently strayed into the road were beaten and sometimes done to death by guards and eunuchs (cf. Tavernier, *op. cit.*, 284; Du Mans, *op. cit.*, 95-6; Chardin, *The coronation of Solyman the III*, published with *The travels of Sir John Chardin into Persia and the East Indies*, London 1691, 77; Thévenôt, *The travels of Monsieur de Thévenôt into the Levant*, London 1687, repr. 1971, pt. 2, 99). The practice of *k̲uruk̲* continued in a modified form under the Ḳādjārs. Males were expected to turn their faces to the wall when the royal women passed by (see Curzon, *Persia*, 2 vols., London 1892, i, 404).

The accession of S̲h̲āh Sulṭān Ḥusayn (1105-55/1694-1722), the last of the Ṣafawids, was largely secured by his great aunt Maryam Begum, a masterful lady who exercised great influence. The shah took an inordinate pride in his *haram*, the scale and magnificence of which became a drain on the treasury. It was not uncommon for beautiful women to be seized by his officers and sent to his *haram*, as they had been in the reign of his predecessor, S̲h̲āh Sulaymān (L. Lockhart, *The fall of the Ṣafavī dynasty and the Afghan occupation of Persia*, Cambridge 1958, 36, 41, 47-8). Muḥammad Hās̲h̲im Āṣaf Rustam al-Ḥukamāʾ alleges that there were nearly 1,000 beautiful girls of varying provenance in S̲h̲āh Sulṭān Ḥusayn's *haram* (*Rustam al-tawārīk̲h̲*, ed. Muḥammad Mus̲h̲īrī, Tehran AHS 1348/1969-70, 70-1).

Āḳā Muḥammad K̲h̲ān (1193-1211/1779-97), the first of the Ḳādjārs, took the daughters and women of defeated enemies and rebels into the royal *haram* as hostages to lessen the likelihood of rebellion and to consolidate his rule. He also sought to heal the breach which had occurred between the Ḳoyunlu branch of the Ḳādjār tribe, to which he himself belonged, and the Develu branch, by the marriage of his nephew and successor Fatḥ ʿAlī to the daughter of Fatḥ ʿAlī K̲h̲ān Develu [see ḲĀDJĀR]. On one occasion, when Āḳā Muḥammad K̲h̲ān, was absent from Tehran, it was arranged that his sister should receive an envoy from one of the k̲hāns of Turkistān, sitting behind a curtain to do so. This, however, gave great offence to the head of the Afs̲h̲ār tribe, either because of its supposed impropriety or because he had not been consulted (Mustawfī, *op. cit.*, i, 23-4).

From the reign of Fatḥ ʿAlī S̲h̲āh onwards, there was a great increase in the size and expenses of the royal *haram* and in the number of black and white eunuchs employed in the palace (ʿAḍud al-Dawla, *op. cit.*, 54 ff. See also Malcolm, *Sketches of Persia*, 220; J.

Morier, *A journey through Persia, Armenia, and Asia Minor to Constantinople, in the years 1808 and 1809*, London 1812, 225, 239; Mustawfī, *op. cit.*, i, 40-1). Muʿayyir al-Mamālik puts the inmates of the *ḥaram* of Nāṣir al-Dīn S̲h̲āh (1848-96) at over 3,000; when the shah moved to summer quarters in the hills near Tehran, he was accompanied by a vast cavalcade (*Yāddās̲h̲t-hāʾī az zindagānī-i k̲h̲uṣūṣī-i Nāṣir al-Dīn S̲h̲āh*, 106, 127. See also Docteur Feuvrier, *Trois ans à la cour de Perse*, Paris 1906, 142). Fatḥ ʿAlī apparently abandoned the practice of ranking the princes in his audience according to their mother's birth (ʿAḍud al-Dawla, *op. cit.*, 47). As in Ṣafawid times, the mother of the ruler was the most important lady in the royal *ḥaram*. The mothers of Fatḥ ʿAlī S̲h̲āh, ʿAbbās Mīrzā, Muḥammad S̲h̲āh and Nāṣir al-Dīn S̲h̲āh were, in succession, known as *mahd awliyāʾ*. Fatḥ ʿAlī's mother attempted in vain to mediate between Fatḥ ʿAlī and his full brother Ḥusayn Ḳulī K̲h̲ān after the former's accession (Fasāʾī, *Fārs-nāma-yi nāṣirī*, Tehran lith. 1895-6, 2 vols. in 1, i, 245-6). ʿAḍud al-Dawla describes the hierarchical order in the royal *ḥaram* and the rivalries of the royal ladies (*Tārīk̲h̲-i ʿAḍudī*, 12 ff. Cf. also Malcolm, *History of Persia*, 2 vols., London 1829, ii, 394, 396; Morier, *op. cit.*, 369. See also the introduction by ʿAbbās Iḳbāl to *S̲h̲arḥ-i ḥāl-i ʿAbbās Mīrzā Mulk-Ārā*, ed. ʿAbd al-Ḥusayn Nawāʾī, Tehran AHS 1325/1946-7, pp. iii ff., on the jealousy and rivalry between the mother of Nāṣir al-Dīn and the mother of his half-brother Mulk-Ārā).

The female establishment of Fatḥ ʿAlī S̲h̲āh is in some ways reminiscent of that of the Īlk̲h̲āns. One of his wives, the daughter of Imām Ḳulī K̲h̲ān Afs̲h̲ār Urūmī, gave Fatḥ ʿAlī several of her serving maids with appropriate outfits and in due course they bore him children (ʿAḍud al-Dawla, *op. cit.*, 15). Lady Sheil relates how one of the wives of Muḥammad S̲h̲āh, when he was still *walī ʿahd*, bought a Circassian slave-girl as a present for her husband (*Glimpses of life and manners in Persia*, London 1856, 203-4). Several of Fatḥ ʿAlī S̲h̲āh's wives were very rich and had their separate establishments outside and independent of the royal *ḥaram*, notably Tād̲j̲ al-Dawla Ṭāwūs K̲h̲ānum Iṣfahānī (ʿAḍud al-Dawla, *op. cit.*, 18-19) and Ḍiyāʾ al-Salṭana. The latter's mother, Maryam K̲h̲ānum, was a Jewess. She had been in the *ḥaram* of Āḳā Muḥammad K̲h̲ān, and after his death was married to Fatḥ ʿAlī. Ḍiyāʾ al-Salṭana was a good calligrapher and copied many books of prayers and *ziyārat-nāmas*. She enjoyed Fatḥ ʿAlī's confidence, and during his lifetime remained unmarried. She often acted as his scribe and wrote his secret letters (*ibid.*, 25). Another of Fatḥ ʿAlī's wives, Sunbul K̲h̲ānum, was among the prisoners taken by ʿĀḳā Muḥammad K̲h̲ān during his Kirmān campaign. She enjoyed great favour with Fatḥ ʿAlī, and repeatedly interceded with him for the subjects (*ibid.*, 20). Her daughter, Ḥusn D̲j̲ahān K̲h̲ānum, was a poetess and a Ṣūfī. She was married to Amān Allāh K̲h̲ān, the governor of Kurdistān, and for several years exercised great authority in that province (*ibid.*, 67). Another of Fatḥ ʿAlī S̲h̲āh's daughters, Zubayda, who was married to ʿAlī K̲h̲ān Nuṣrat al-Mulk Ḳara Güzlü, was also a Ṣūfī. She lived for many years in Hamadān, where she enjoyed great authority. She went on the pilgrimage and made several visits to shrines in ʿIrāḳ and Mas̲h̲had. She gave many gifts to the poor, *sayyids* and *mullas*, and was noted for her charitable benefactions. Every year, she set aside a sum for her personal expenses from the income of her estates and gave the rest to the poor and orphans (*ibid.*, 30-2). Badr-i D̲j̲ahān K̲h̲ānum, the mother of Fatḥ ʿAlī S̲h̲āh's sons Ḥasan ʿAlī and Ḥusayn ʿAlī, the former of whom became governor of Fārs and the latter governor of Tehran, lived principally in S̲h̲īrāz, where she exercised great influence over her son, interfering in the administration of affairs and enriching herself greatly by commerce and monopolies. She was believed to have made a corner in corn with an accomplice in *ca.* 1810. Nevertheless, she was reputed to be charitable to the poor and ready to do justice for the oppressed. From time to time, she negotiated a visit to the capital, for which she was generally obliged to make a considerable present to the king, who then permitted her to return and reside with him as a wife (Morier, *A second journey through Persia, Armenia, and Asia Minor to Constantinople, 1810-16*, London 1818, 61; idem, *A journey through Persia ... in the years 1808 and 1809*, 154-5).

Mustawfī describes in detail the *ḥaram-k̲h̲āna* of Nāṣir al-Dīn S̲h̲āh and the discipline exercised in it (*op. cit.*, i, 510 ff.). Nāṣir al-Dīn's mother, who presided over it, was a capable woman. She was a granddaughter of Fatḥ ʿAlī S̲h̲āh; her father was Muḥammad Ḳāsim K̲h̲ān b. Sulaymān Ḳād̲j̲ār (see Muʿayyir al-Mamālik, 172-6; Sheil, *op. cit.*, 9). Munīr al-Dawla, one of Nāṣir al-Dīn S̲h̲āh's wives, used to hold a feast for women in Tehran on the birthday of Fāṭima, after her son Kāmrān Mīrzā Nāʾib al-Salṭana became governor of the city in 1277/1860-1 (Abu 'l-Ḥasan Buzurg Umīd, *Az māst kih bar māst*, Tehran ASH 1335/1957, 79). On the occasion of Nāṣir al-Dīn's first journey to Europe, which took place in 1873, it was finally agreed that only one of his wives should accompany him. In the event, the lady returned to Persia from Moscow. The only other of his wives to go to Europe was Amīna Aḳdas, one of his favourite wives, who went blind towards the end of her life. She was sent to Vienna for treatment, which, however, proved fruitless. She was accompanied by the eunuch Bahrām K̲h̲ān K̲h̲ʷād̲j̲a and several women nurses and attendants (Muʿayyir al-Mamālik, *op. cit.*, 159; Feuvrier, *op. cit.*, 185).

Although women might exercise great authority within the *ḥaram*, their liberty outside was gravely circumscribed. However, Lady Sheil remarks that the practice of veiling enabled them to move freely in the streets, the princess being indistinguishable from the peasant (*Glimpses*, 212; cf. also Feuvrier, *op. cit.*, 144). She also notes that the mission doctor's door and house was crowded with women of all ages and ranks (*Glimpses*, 212-13). Women, other than tribal women, when they went on journeys normally travelled in panniers carried by mules or in litters suspended between two mules. The panniers carrying women of the higher classes were canopied by semi-circular tops covered with cloth hanging down like a curtain (Sir Robert Ker Porter, *Travels in Georgia, Persia, Armenia, ancient Babylon ... during the years 1817, 1818, 1819, and 1820*, 2 vols., London 1821-2, i, 398-9). Tribal women and some of the royal women rode and were often accomplished horsewomen (cf. *ibid.*, 259; Muʿayyir al-Mamālik, *op. cit.*, 127).

There was in general opposition to the education of women. So far as provision existed, it was of a rudimentary kind, though some women achieved competence in religious studies and were known for their learning. Girl's schools were not founded until the 20th century, apart from the small girls' school opened by the American Board of Foreign Missions of the Presbyterian Church in the United States in Tehran in 1874, in Tabriz (1879) and Hamadan (1885) (R.E. Waterfield, *Christians in Persia*, London 1973, 135, 136, 137). Some girls were educated at home by private tutors (cf. Mustawfī, *op. cit.*, i, 296-7, 298). Girls up to the age of seven were allowed to attend a *maktab*, but the number who did so was small; when they were then too old to go unveiled, their education was sometimes finished at home by female *mullās*. Girls in well-to-do households were taught to sew and embroider and such other accomplishments as were necessary for the running of the *ḥaram*. Spinning was the ubiquitous occupation of the poorer classes. Carpet weaving was also carried on by women and children, mainly as a house industry, in many districts, and also in tribal areas. Textiles were also woven by women in many towns and villages. Little is known of the condition of those so employed until modern times [see BISĀṬ, in Suppl.].

The recreation of women was largely confined to visiting relatives. Marriages, births, deaths and other anniversaries also broke the daily round. The weekly visit to the bath was an occasion which offered the opportunity of intercourse with female friends. Visits to shrines and cemeteries, especially on Thursday evenings, were other recognised outings (see Du Mans, *op. cit.*, 93-4; Sheil, *op. cit.*, 145 ff.; Morier, *A second Journey....*, 137, 166). *Rawḍa-ḵẖʷānī*s, especially in Ṣafar and Muḥarram, were other occasions for visiting and recreation. Female *rawḍa-ḵẖʷān*s usually conducted those held for women (Mustawfī, *op. cit.*, i, 373, 711-12) and also the assemblies for women in Ramaḍān (Muʿayyir al-Mamālik, *op. cit.*, 111, 113). So far as women attended mosques, they sat curtained off from the men. They were also segregated at *taʿziya*s. In the Tikiya-yi Dawlat in Tehran, the shah's women and women of the upper classes had their own separate boxes, while poorer women sat in a separate part of the "pit" (Sheil, *op. cit.*, 127-8; Buzurg Umīd, *op. cit.*, 157-8, and see p. 106 for a description of the procession taking the shah's standard (*ʿalam*) from the royal *ḥaram* to the Tikiya-yi Dawlat). Women of the Prophetic family figured prominently in several of the passion plays, but their roles were normally played by men and boys (see P.J. Chelkowski, ed., *Taʿziyeh: ritual and drama in Iran*, New York 1976).

Gradually in the second half of the 19th century, changes took place in the position of women, partly as a result of increased intercourse with Europe. Emancipation was slow, but women began from time to time to take part in public demonstrations (cf. the account of a bread riot in Tehran in 1861 during the famine, E.B. Eastwick, *Journal of a diplomat's three years' residence in Persia*, London 1864, repr. Tehran 1976, 2 vols., i, 288-91). The most notable case was their participation in the movement against the Tobacco Régie in 1891. They supported the boycott declared against the use of tobacco, and urged their menfolk to do the same; some also took part in public protests against the Régie. It is reported that the movement spread even to the shah's *ḥaram* (Muʿayyir al-Mamālik, *op. cit.*, 177). New trends among women were also to be found in the Bābī movement [*q.v.*], who numbered among their leaders the beautiful and brilliant woman Ḳurrat al-ʿAyn [*q.v.*], who was martyred in their cause in 1852.

Bibliography (in addition to references given in the article): Spuler, *Iran*, 381-3; J. Atkinson, *Customs and manners of the women of Persia*, London 1832. The accounts of most European travellers have some information on the composition of women, but it has not been possible to quote them all. On Nādir Shāh's women, see Jonas Hanway, *Historical account of the British trade over the Caspian Sea*, London 1762, 2 vols., i, 169. On women's dress, see LIBĀS; see also Tavernier, *op. cit.*, 282;

Thévenôt, *op. cit.*, pt. 2, 293-4; Ker Porter, *op. cit.*, i, 202, 259. 396, 499; Scott Waring, *A tour to Sheeraz*, London 1807, 61-2; Morier, *A second journey ...* 61; Kay Kāwūs b. Iskandar, *Ḳābūs-nāma*, ed. Ghulām Ḥusayn Yūsufī, Tehran 1967, 129-31; Naṣīr al-Dīn Ṭūsī, *Aḵẖlāḳ-i Nāṣirī*, ed. M. Mīnovī and ʿAlī Riḍā Ḥaydarī, Tehran ASH 1356/1976, 215-22, 229-30; Faḵẖrī Ḳawīmī, *Kārnāma-yi zanān-i mashhūr-i Īrān*, Tehran AHS 1352/1973-4; Dhabīḥ al-Dīn Maḥallātī, *Rayāḥīn al-sharīʿa dar tardjuma-yi dānishmandān-i bānūwān-i shīʿa*, 5 vols., Tehran 1375/1955-6; Abu 'l-Ḥasan Buzurg Umīd, *op. cit.*, 21-2, 39-40; Mustawfī, *op. cit.*, i, 689 ff. On marriage customs see MUTʿA and NIKĀḤ; see also Ker Porter, *op. cit.*, i, 345; Malcolm, *History of Persia*, ii, 426-8, 440-3; Sheil, *op. cit.*, 143 ff.; ʿAḍud al-Dawla, *op. cit.*, 59, 68-9; Mustawfī, *op. cit.*, i, 287 ff., 456 ff.　　　(A.K.S. LAMBTON)

b. After 1900

The end of the 19th century marked the beginning of a long struggle for emancipation by Iranian women, which culminated in a short-lived success in the 1970s. The participation of women in the public demonstration against the Tobacco Concessions in 1893 was a watershed for their political activities; for the first time women, a hitherto invisible sector of society, had taken part in Iranian street politics. In these demonstrations, women proved themselves valuable to the ʿulamāʾ, who subsequently encouraged them to participate in the uprisings that led to the 1906 constitution. Women mobbed Nāṣir al-Dīn Shāh's carriage, organised public meetings and even marched to the *Madjlis* brandishing guns and weapons. But although their activities provided actual and moral support, women were not granted the vote by the ensuing constitution. The opposition of the ʿulamāʾ to female suffrage was extreme: when Ḥādjdjī Wakīl al-Raʿāyā proposed their enfranchisement in 1911, the President of the *Madjlis* moved that no record be made "of this unfortunate incident" (Mangol Bayat 1978).

The active participation of women in the constitutional revolution, however, served to heighten their political consciousness and in the years that followed, women formed a number of secret societies and organisations seeking three main objectives: access to education, freedom from the *ḥidjāb* (veil) and suffrage. It was in the field of education that women had their first success.

Since women were physically and socially confined to the sphere of domesticity, few had had the opportunity of obtaining any formal schooling before 1900. There were, however, exceptional women, some related to the ʿulamāʾ, who had been educated at home, or, in a few cases, attended schools and were thus able to educate other women. In 1910 one of these, Mrs Ṭūbā Azimūda, opened the first private girls' school in Iran, Nāmūs. Three years later Mrs Yazdī, the wife of a leading *mudjtahid*, opened a second girls' school, ʿIffatiyya. Despite considerable hostility and repeated attacks by mobs, more schools were set up, and finally in 1918 the government capitulated and opened ten state schools for girls as well as a women's training college, the *Dār al-Muʿallimāt*. This college was subsequently expanded and its courses extended from three to five years. In 1934 it was renamed the Preliminary Teachers' Training College for Girls, *Dānishsārā-yi Muḳaddimatī-yi Dukẖtarān*. Much of the material taught in the 1920s at the college was subsequently compiled in text books and used for teaching in secondary schools (Badr-ol-Moluk Bamdad, *From darkness to light*, ed. and tr,

F.R.C. Bagley, New York 1977, 60). The increasing secularisation of education and the growing power of the state administration in this sector was an important factor in enabling women to gain access to education. The next major campaign was directed against compulsory seclusion and the veil.

In the 30 years that followed the constitutional revolution, many dedicated women participated in the prolonged battle for emancipation. Middle-class and upper-class women, some of whom had been educated at the foreign schools in Iran and many of whom were taught by their male relatives at home, formed secret societies and women's groups such as *Andjuman-i Āzādī Zanān* ("Women's Freedom Society"), which included a member of the royal family. In 1910, one of these groups published the first journal to be edited by a woman, *Dānish*, and other journals followed. Some, such as *Shukūfa*, edited by Maryam Umīd Muzayyin al-Sulṭān, which began publishing in 1913, were devoted to literature and education. Others were more overtly committed to political emancipation. One such was *Zabān-i zanān* edited by Ṣiddīḳa Dawlatābādī which began publication in Iṣfahān in 1919. Despite repeated threats to her life and attacks on her newspaper, Dawlatābādī remained a powerful force in the women's movement.

By 1930 there were a number of women literary figures, the best known among whom were Parwīn Iᶜtiṣāmī [*q.v.*] (1906-41) and Sīmīn Dānishwar, as well as more than 10 women publishers and journalists. In the face of hostility, exile and imprisonment, women such as Shahnāz Āzād, editor of *Nāma-yi banūwān* ("Women's letter") and Āfāḳ Pārsā, publisher of *Djahān-i zanān* ("Women's world"), continued to oppose the religious establishment and its more restrictive dicta, and in the event, finally found an unexpected ally in Riḍā Shāh Pahlawī. (For a detailed discussion of women journalists and writers, see Parī Shaykh al-Islāmī, *Zanān-i rūznāmanigār wa andīshmandī-yi Īrān* ("Women journalists and women intellectuals of Iran"), Tehran 1351/1972, and in Elizabeth Sansarian, *The Women's rights movement in Iran*, New York 1982, 32-7).

After the overthrow of the Ḳādjārs in 1924, Riḍā Shāh embarked on an extensive programme which initially did not benefit women very much. For example, the Civil codes of 1930, although intended to curtail the judicial control of the *ᶜulamā³*, in fact incorporated much of the Twelver Shīᶜa *Sharīᶜa* laws (Bagley, *The Iranian Family Protection Laws*, in C.E. Bosworth (ed.), *Iran and Islam*, Edinburgh 1971, 50). women continued to inherit only half as much men on the death of a spouse and that of parents. Paternal consent was needed for marriage of spinsters; the husband remained the legal head of household and his formal consent was required before a wife could take employment or travel abroad. Men also retained their right to polygamy and temporary *ṣīgha* marriages, as well as the right to divorce their wives at will with the custody of their sons at the age of two and daughters at seven. Divorced women were required to keep the *ᶜidda* and remain unmarried for two months in case of *ṣīgha* and three for permanent wives. The only departure from the *Sharīᶜa* was the stipulation of a minimum age for marriage: 15 for girls and 18 for boys.

The Penal Code of 1940, though almost wholly European in conception, retained the *Sharīᶜa* laws for adultery. The killing of one's wife, daughter or sister caught *in flagranti delicto*, is not considered murder and carries either no sentence at all or a short discretionary term of imprisonment. Retribution against an adulterous husband, father or brother, however, is not sanctioned in the same way.

Nevertheless, by 1936 Riḍā Shāh felt sufficiently confident to include women's education and the banning of the veil in his modernisation process. He began in 1935 by giving state recognition to women's groups and setting up a women's centre, *Ḳānūn-i bānuwān*, with a budgetary allocation from the Ministry of Culture and under the patronage of his daughters Ashraf and Shams, and headed by Ḥadjar Tarbiyat. In 1937 Ṣiddīḳa Dawlatābādī was appointed as the head of the *Ḳānūn* and it was reorganised into an educational and craft training centre for women. In 1936, Tehran University began admitting women. It was, however, the outlawing of the veil in the same year and rigorous enforcement of this measure until Riḍā Shāh's abdication in 1941 which proved a historical landmark for Iranian women. Along with access to education, the abolition of the *ḥidjab* finally ended their physical and mental segregation and enabled them to participate openly in the public sphere (see Bamdad, *op. cit.*, 80-3; Sansarian, *op. cit.*, 62-6; Avery, *Modern Iran*, London 1965, 291-2).

After the departure of Riḍā Shāh, there was something of a backlash against women. Nevertheless, organisations such as the Women's League, *Djamᶜiyyat-i Zanān*, and the Tūdeh (Communist) party's *Tashkīlat-i Zanān-i Īrān*, continued to agitate for legal reforms and female suffrage. In this, they met with the resolute opposition of the *Madjlis*, which in 1934 had voted and again in 1959 was to vote against the emancipation of women. Middle-class Iranian women, many of whom had been educated abroad, saw the religious establishment as the main opposition and sought to circumvent the legislature by taking to the streets. In this they had the tacit support of the Shāh's twin sister, Ashraf Pahlawī, who headed the influential High Council of Women's Organisation, *Shūrā-yi ᶜĀlī-yi Djamᶜiyyat-i Zanān*.

In January 1963, women organised a widely-publicised and well-supported one-day strike, refused to celebrate the anniversary of the unveiling of women, marched to the Senate and insisted on voting in the Shah's White Revolution referendum. Although their vote was counted separately, the high turnout, the extensive publicity given to the women's protests and royal patronage finally enabled them to obtain the vote in February 1963. A year later, there were two women senators and four women deputies in the *Madjlis*. In the struggle between the secular and the religious establishment, the state scored a temporary gain and acquired the wholehearted support of middle-class women.

Once enfranchised, the campaign for legal reforms was intensified. Assisted by the Women Lawyers' Union and the newly formed Iranian Women's Organisation (*Sāzamān-i zanān*) headed by members of the royal household, Iranian women succeeded in securing radical changes. By 1978 abortion was legalised and, through the Family Protection Laws of 1967 and 1975, the husband's right to *ṣīgha* and polygamous marriages was curtailed, as was his discretionary right of divorce and custody of children. Family Courts were set up and empowered to allow divorced women to claim an alimony over and above the customary *mahr*. Conditions for working women were also improved, and they gained an entitlement to twelve weeks' maternity leave and nurseries in work places with more than ten nursing mothers.

On the whole, it was the urban middle-class women who benefited from these measures; rural women, though theoretically entitled to nurseries and legal protection, were generally unaffected by these laws and were unable to get to such law enforcement agencies as the town-based Family Courts. There were, however, a number of programmes intended specifically for rural women. For example, the Literacy Corps, the Extension Corps and the Health Corps, were set up in 1968, and despatched women conscripts to teach village women respectively to read, produce handicrafts and instruct them in family planning. Of these, by far the most successful was the Extension Corps which taught women to improve on their traditional crafts of weaving and sewing and embroidery and which facilitated the marketing of these products through a network of urban shops. Ironically, the ability of rural women to gain their livelihood as craft workers reinforced the parental reluctance to allow them to go to school, since schooling merely deprived the family of their daughter's all-too-valuable labour without giving them any substantial returns (for a case study on this, see Haleh Afshar, *The position of women in an Iranian village*, in *Feminist Review*, no. 9 [Autumn 1981], 76-8). Thus despite numerous literary campaigns, nearly 95% of rural women remained illiterate (J. Rudolph Touba, *Relationship between urbanisation and the changing status of women in Iran*, in *Iranian Studies*, v/1 [Winter 1972], 29, and *Bārrassī sōsialistī*, in *Asnād-i Djunbish-i Trotski-yi Īrān* [New York, Summer 1357/1978], 191).

Even for urban women, successes of the 1970s were short-lived. Although the Shāh appointed one women minister, an ambassadress and nearly 40 women judges, his modernisation policies did not benefit the mass of the poor rural and urban dwellers, male and female. Welfare legislation remained unimplemented and the bulk of Iranian women continued working in the informal sector without security and for minimal wages. It was the combination of poverty and illiteracy that made poorer women so responsive to the extensive campaigns waged by the religious establishment against the Shāh. In the early seventies, Āyatallāh Khumaynī emerged as the charismatic leader of this opposition. Khumaynī appealed directly to women to abandon their unrewarding tasks given to them by the Shāh and return to the sphere of domesticity, reminding them that the Muslim husband must fulfil his duty of supporting his wife and family "whether he has the means or not" (Āyatallāh Rūḥ Allāh Khumaynī, *Tawḍīḥ al-masāʾil*, ed. Ḥawza-yi ʿIlmī, Ḳum n.d., *masʾala* 2412).

The prospect was an alluring one for the many women who earned a pittance and often supported an idle husband or son. Some middle-class women among the intelligentsia also feared the total breakdown of the family. The high rate of divorce—Īrān ranked fourth in the world (*Iran Almanac*, published by *Echo of Iran*, Tehran 1974, 434)—and the predominance of divorce among working women, (40%), were seen by this group as evidence of social disintegration, and they espoused the cause of Islamic fundamentalism. They expected the Islamic Republic to bestow the dignity of motherhood and domesticity on women (Zahrā Rāhnaward, *Ṭulūʿ-i zan-i muslimān*, Nashr-i Maḥbūba n.d., 85). In the event, women appear to have lost everything but the vote. Their wholehearted support of Khumaynī and active participation in the street demonstrations marked women as an important support base and secured them the vote (H. Afshar, *Khumayni's teachings and their implications for Iranian women*, in A. Tabari and N. Yeganeh (eds.), *In the shadow of Islam*, London 1982, 75-90). But all women judges were dismissed, and women were expelled from the Faculty of Law. Female education has been segregated; given that only about 3% of women had any tertiary education, this measure has condemned them to an inferior education. In addition, the reversion to the *Sharīʿa* laws has meant that husbands have gained the discretionary right to polygamous and *ṣīgha* marriages as well as the custody of children on divorce. Women are now required to wear the *ḥidjāb*, and the implementation of the new *ḳaṣāṣ* laws has deprived them of equality before the law. A man who murders a woman has a *khūnbahā*, blood money; this must be paid by the woman's guardian before the murderer is punished. Women have a *khūnbahā* only half that of a man. Iranian women have opposed these measures with street demonstrations, a refusal to wear the *ḥidjāb* and collaboration with the resistance movement. It is too early to judge whether the restriction placed on women will prove any more long lasting than the liberalisation of the Pahlawīs; what is certain is that Iranian women will not easily concede defeat.

Bibliography (in addition to the references given in the article): 1. *General*. Maryam Mirhādī, *Zindigān-i zan*, Tehran 1334/1955; C. Colliver Rice, *Persian women and their ways*, London 1923; Olive Hapburn Suratgar, *I sing in the wilderness, an intimate account of Persia and Persians*, London 1951. 2. *Legal position*. Ḳudsiyī Ḥidjāzī, *Arzash-i zan yā zan az naẓar-i ḳaḍāʾī wa idjtimāʿī*, Tehran n.d.; Siyid Ali Rida Naghavi, *Family laws of Iran*, Islamabad 1971; Ḥasan Ṣadra, *Ḥuḳūḳ-i zan dar Islām wa Ūrūppā*, Tehran 1319/1940. 3. *Marriage*. Muḥammad ʿAlī Afghānī, *Shawhar-i Āhū Khānum*, Tehran 1341/1968 (a novel about marriage marred by polygamy; the setting is a merchant family in the 1930s); J. Behnam, *Population*, in *The Cambridge history of Iran*, i, 479-83; Ruyā Khusrawī, *Kār-i Khānigī wa-maḳām-i khanawī-yi zan*, Tehran 1358/1979; Āyatallāh Murtaḍā Muṭahharī, *Ḥuḳūḳ-i zan, taʿdād-i zawdjāt, izdiwādj-i muwaḳḳat*, Fārs wa Khūzistān n.d.; Manučihra K. Muḥibbattī, *Shārik-i mard*, Tehran 1325/1946; Sayyid Riḍā Pāknizhād, *Izdiwādj wa rawūsh-i zan dar Islām*, Tehran 1360/1981. 4. *Women and religion*. Shirin Mahdavi, *Women and the Shii Ulama in Iran*, in *MES*, xix/1 (January 1983), 17-27; Āyatallāh Murtaḍā Muṭahharī, *Masʾala-yi ḥidjāb*, Ḳum nd.; Mujahedin Khalk, *On the question of Hijab*, in *In the shadow of Islam, the women's movement in Iran*, ed. Azar Tabari and Nahid Yeganeh, London 1982, 126; M.H. Shahīdī (ed.), *Ḥurmat wa ḥuḳūḳ-i zan dar Islām*, Tehran 1358/1979; ʿAlī Sharīʿatī, *Zan-i muslimān* (text of a speech on Muslim women), n.p. n.d.; Azar Tabari, *Islam and the struggle for emancipation of Iran's women*, in *In the shadow of Islam*, 5-25; Āyatallāh Ṭāliḳānī, *On ḥijāb*, English tr. in *op. cit.*, 103-7; Nahid Yeganeh, *Women's struggle in the Islamic Republic in Iran*, in *op. cit.*, 26-74. 5. *Women's movements*. Ṭalʿat Bāsarī, *Zandukht pīshāhang-i nizhāt-i āzādī-yi bānuwān-i Īrān*, Tehran 1345/1967; Kūmitīʾ bārāʾ-i āzādi-yi zan dar Īrān, *Mubārizī bārāʾ-i āzādi-yi zan dar Īrān*, London, Summer 1357/1978; Maryam Mirhādī, *Zindigān-i zan*, in *op. cit.*, (ch. 3 includes a detailed discussion of the activities of a number of women's groups from 1297/1918 to 1325/1946; the *Ḳānūn-ī bānuwān* is discussed on 93-9); Azar Tabari and Nahid Yeganeh (eds.), *In the shadow of Islam* (present women's organisations are discussed in part 4, 143-230). 6. *Women in tribal areas*. Lois Beck, *Women among Qashqai nomadic pastoralists in Iran*, in Lois Beck and Nikki Keddie (eds.), *Women in the Muslim world*, 351-73; Erika Friedl, *Islam and tribal women in a village in Iran*, in Nancy Falk and Rital M. Gross (eds.), *Unspoken world*, New York 1980, 159-73;

Nancy Tapper, *The women's sub-society among the Shahsavan nomads of Iran*, in *ibid.*, 374-98; R. Tapper, *Pasture and politics*, in G. Stober, *Die Afshar. Nomadismus in Raum Kermans*, Marburg/Lahn 1978.
7. *Women in literature.* Bozorg Alavi, *Geschichte und Entwicklung der Modernen Persischen Literatur*, Berlin 1964; Sayyid Muḥammad ʿAlī Djamālzāda, *Taṣwīr-i zan der farhang-i Īrānī*, Tehran 1357/1978; Nuṣrat Allāh Fatḥī, *Āʾīnī-yi Parwīn*, introd. Tehran 1355/1976; Erika Friedl, *Women in contemporary Persian folktales*, in *Women in the Muslim world*, 629-50; G. Tikku, *Furūgh-i Farrukhzād: a new direction in Persian poetry*, in *SI*, xxvi, 149-73.

(HALEH AFSHAR)

4. In Turkey [see Supplement].

5. In the Indo-Pakistan sub-continent. The evolution of Muslim social polity in India, from the earliest date of advent of Islam in the subcontinent in the 2nd/8th century, has been constantly affected and acculturated by the indigenous cultural environment. In this process, the status and role of Muslim women also underwent significant changes throughout the ages. The earliest accounts indicate that among the Turkish settlers women enjoyed a respectable position; they even took an active part in state affairs. Seclusion was not strictly enforced during the earlier centuries, but began as a rigid practice after the 4th/10th century.

During the Dihlī Sultanate period (7th/13th century), despite strict seclusion of women, ambitious ladies of royal households often played decisive roles in intricate affairs of succession to the throne. Shāh Turkān (wife of Iltutmish and mother of Rukn al-Dīn Fīrūz Shāh I) and Malik-yi Djahān (wife of Djalāl al-Dīn Fīrūz Shāh II) had succeeded in effectively outmanoeuvring the male-dominated courts by installing on thrones the princes of their choice and wielding absolute power in their behalf. Iltutmish's daughter, Raḍiyya Sulṭāna, even succeeded in ascending to the throne herself and ruled for four years (634-7/1236-40). The records of the Tughluḳ and Lōdī dynasties are also full of accounts of royal ladies often playing leading roles in state politics.

The harem life from the Sultanate period down to the Lōdī dynasty (i.e. in the pre-Mughal era) was centred around the ladies of royal households. with their dependents, maids, slaves and eunuchs. Seniority in rank among royal ladies was a major factor in commanding both respect and power. Seclusion was so strictly observed that even outside women were not permitted to enter the harem enclosures. The princesses and girls of higher classes received Ḳurʾānic and literary education at home from learned tutors (ladies as well as elderly men). In regard to literary and artistic talents, there are numerous instances of outstanding achievements by ladies. Raḍiyya Sulṭāna was a noted poetess; Dukhtar Khāṣṣa, Nuṣrat Bībī and Mihr Āfrūz had mastered the art of dancing; Futūḥa and Nuṣrat Khātūn were famous musicians of their times.

During the Mughal period (932-1161/1526-1748), although the practice of seclusion had become more intensive and was considered as a sign of respect—even royal decrees were issued for observing strictly the rules of *parda*/*purdah* (seclusion)—women of the royal households and upper classes played perceptible roles in state politics and achieved high merits in literary accomplishment. On occasion, Nūr-i Djahān (wife of Djahāngīr) broke the *purdah* convention and did not mind coming out in public. In fact, she was the real power behind the Djahāngīrī throne. She also led an army expedition against Mahābat Khān [*q.v.*]. In southern India, during the same period, Sulṭāna Čand Bībī personally defended the fort of Aḥmadnagar against the mighty forces of Akbar, and Makhdūma-yi Djahān ruled the Deccan as a regent on behalf of Niẓām Shāh of the Bahmanī family.

In literary achievement, the Mughal period provides a long list of ladies of distinction. Djahānārā (second wife of Shāhdjahān) was a noted biographer; Gulbadān Begam was the author of the *Humāyūn-nāma*. and Djān Begam (daughter of Khān-i Khānān) wrote a commentary on the Ḳurʾān, for which she received from Akbar an award of 50,000 *dīnārs*. Among the famous poetesses of this period, Salīma Sulṭāna, Nūr-i Djahān, Sitt al-Nisāʾ and Zīb al-Nisāʾ (eldest daughter of Awrangzīb) were outstanding.

The decline of the Mughal dynasty towards the middle of 12th/18th century heralded the emergence of the modern era in Indian history. The incoming European powers (Portugese, Dutch, British) were in the process of consolidating in the subcontinent their political and military powers, which eventually weakened the power bases of Muslim courts in northern as well as southern India. With this shift of power, new socio-economic groups gradually emerged in which the élites of the long-established courts lost their hold and their dominant status. The centralised feudal power fragmented into the holdings of local feudal lords, who started aligning themselves with the European powers. This basic shift in social organisation ultimately had its impact on women's rôle in society. The central harems of the past gradually lost their hold on political manoeuvrings, whilst the artistic and literary pursuits of these élite ladies also lost much of their significance as the popularity of Western-type education gradually spread. For almost a century, virtually all contributions of Muslim women in art and literature, and their active participation in education or politics, came to a standstill. It was not until the second half of the 19th century that a gradual revival of Muslim women's participation in active life of education and artistic and literary manifestations became visible.

In 1886 Sir Syed Ahmad Khan [see SAYYID AḤMAD KHĀN] founded the Anglo-Mohammedan Educational Conference for the general advancement of Western education among Muslim in India. Under the auspices of this organisation, the provision of Western education for Muslim girls was envisaged also. At the beginning of this century, the first Muslim women's college was established at ʿAlīgaṛh (now a constituent college of the Muslim University); the basic aim of this college was to provide facilities for higher Western education for Muslims girls under the strict rules of seclusion. Almost at the same time, Ḥakīm Adjmal Khān opened an exclusive section for women in his Yūnānī College (centre of Greco-Arab medical education) at Dihlī. The ʿAlīgaṛh College, in particular, contributed a great deal in giving a new direction to the role of Muslim women in modern India. It was followed by the establishment of educational institutions for Muslim girls in Bombay in the 1920s, and in other parts of the subcontinent in the 1930s.

During the 1920s, two monthly magazines in Urdu for Muslim women started their publication: *ʿIṣmat* from Dihlī and *Tahdhīb-i-Niswān* from Lahore. The objectives of both these periodicals were to publish reformist material for the average, middle-class Muslim woman. Their circulation was throughout the Urdu-speaking region of the subcontinent. The main themes on which the contributors (male and female) concentrated were: the stability of family life, children's upbringing, women's role as wives and mothers, religious education, domestic economy, and light social fiction. Ḥidjāb Imtiyāz ʿAlī was the first Muslim woman writer of the modern era who earned an all-India fame in the late 1920s; most of her writings appeared in *Tahdhīb-i-Niswān*.

The 1935 Government of India Act had awarded separate electorates for Hindus and Muslims; female members of the two communities were also given the franchise. According to the terms of the new Act, general elections were held in 1936. By this time, a few Muslim women of the upper middle class had come out of seclusion and were actively participating in various fields: politics, medicine, education, social welfare, literary pursuits, etc. Thus they had demanded and were granted a reserved seat for Muslim women in the United Provinces legislature. In the 1936 elections, Begam Ḥabībullāh won the reserved seat and entered the U.P. Legislative Assembly as the first Muslim woman member.

During the Second World War, India witnessed an unprecedented political upheaval which had its bearing on Muslim women's increasing participation in political activities and literary expressions. Saleha Abid Husain, Rasheed Jahan and Ismat Chughtai emerged as leading Urdu writers of that time. Begam Mohammad Ali, maintaining her seclusion, fought and won a seat in U.P. legislature in 1946. Rasheed Jahan and Hajira Begam were Communist activitists; both of them were among the organisers of several industrial strikes, and were imprisoned for a considerable time in 1949.

In 1947, after Partition, two separate commonwealth states came to exist: India with Hindu majority provinces, and Pakistan consisting of Muslim majority regions, sc. the North-West Frontier Province, Sind, West Punjab (as the western wing) and East Bengal (as eastern wing). Among the remaining Muslim population in India, after independence, Muslim women came out of seclusion in greater number; they started entering the institutions of higher education in ever-increasing numbers and competed for specialised jobs. Although up to higher secondary level, seclusion of sexes has been maintained in college and university education, the predominant majority of Muslim girls have been enrolling in institutions of co-education. Their participation in active educational, professional and political fields has been of great significance. At ʿAlīgaṛh Muslim University, several Muslim women professors have chaired various academic departments. There have been a number of Muslim women holding administrative positions in various government establishments. In the political sphere, the traditions of Muslim women's participation have been continuous. Begam Anis Kidwai was the first Muslim female minister appointed in the 1970s in the Uttar Pradesh cabinet, and later on she was elected as President of Congress (I) of the U.P. Branch. In Assam, during the most politically troubled period, in the early 1980s, Begam Anwara Taimur took up the charge as Chief Minister of that state and headed the Congress (I) cabinet for several months.

At present, Muslim women are found throughout India as eminent medical practitioners, educationists, administrators, and political activists. In all these fields their status for all practical purposes is equal to men without significant discrimination.

Soon after the establishment of Pakistan as a Muslim state in 1947, women's emancipation became a key factor in all walks of life and especially in the provinces of West Punjab and Sind. Muslim women of the Punjab were already far advanced in education; a large number of well-educated families from the U.P. and Hyderabad had migrated after the partition to Sind province, and women of these families were demanding better opportunities for themselves in the newly-established state. Muslim women in the North-West Frontier Province and East Bengal had not been able to advance beyond average primary education in those early years. Thus the establishment of the All-Pakistan Women's Association (APWA) during early 1950s drew upon female activists mostly from Lahore and Karachi. It remained a middle-class dominated organisation which aimed at a better deal for women: it organised meetings and demonstrations against polygamy and the maltreatment of women, and it presented a mild programme of social reforms in favour of women. But any active participation of women in politics was at least two decades away.

In literature, however, several women writers rose to prominance: Hajira Masroor, Khadija Mastoor, and Jilani Bano in short story writing; Qurat-ul-Ain Hyder as a novelist and Zohra Nigar as a poet. During the early 1960s, Begam Liaquat Ali Khan was appointed as the first woman ambassador of Pakistan; she was accredited to Belgium. Her appointment was not due to her own active participation in political or social life; she was honoured as the widow of the assassinated first Prime Minister of Pakistan, Sahibzada Liaquat Ali Khan [see LIYĀḲAT ʿALĪ KHĀN].

It was mostly during the 1970s that woman came to prominence in Pakistani politics. Begam Nasim Wali Khan had emerged, side-by-side with her husband, Khan Abdul Wali Khan, as a political activist against the rule of Zulfiqar Ali Bhutto. Soon after Bhutto's execution, his widow—Begam Nusrat Bhutto—and daughter—Benazir Bhutto—took up the leadership of the Pakistan People's Party and have become the focal point of opposition to the Martial Law Authority. More and more women are becoming involved in political activity; thus Hinda Gilan, a lawyer by profession, has recently emerged in Lahore as a dynamic political activist.

Bibliography: Most of the works referring to the status and role of Muslim women in the Indo-Pakistan subcontinent from the earliest times down to the end of the Mughal period comprise the standard historical sources, see the Bibls. to HIND. iv. History and vi. Islamic culture. For a summary treatment of the status of Muslim women in pre-Mughal times, see I.H. Qureshi, *Administration of the Sultans of Delhi*[4], n.d. Karachi, 150; Rekha Misra, *Women in Mughal India*, Delhi 1967, 5-15; R. P. Tripathy, *Some aspects of Muslim administration*, Allahabad 1936, 29; and Ishwari Parasad, *History of Qaraunah Turks in India*, Allahabad 1936, 132. Accounts of the status of Muslim women during the Mughal period are available, mostly written in Persian: Gulbadan Begam, *Humāyūn-nāma*, tr. A. S. Beveridge, London 1902, provides an elaborate account of female life inside harems. Other important references to Muslim women's life can be found in ʿAbd al-Ḳādir Badāʾūnī, *Muntakhab al-tawārīkh*, Calcutta 1884, 404-6; Abu 'l-Faḍl, *Akbar-nāma*, tr. H. Beveridge, Calcutta 1912, i, 43, 114, ii, 39-41, 149-51, 212, 230, 288-93, 317-19, 324-30, iii, 212-13, 215, 536, 1140; Muʿtamid Khān, *Iḳbāl-nāmā-yi Djahāngīrī*, tr. Elliot and Dowson, Calcutta 1865, 345-6, 424-8, 430-1, 435-6. There are numerous studies in English on this period; see Rakha Misra, *op. cit.*, chs. 2-8; P. N. Chopra, *Society and culture during the Mughal age*, Agra 1963, ch. 5, 103-31; B. Andrea, ed. L. Binyon, *The life of a Mughal princess — Jahanara Begum*, London 1931. On the status of Muslim women in modern times, intensive study is still very much needed; however, two works which have dealt with this theme should be mentioned, Cora Vreede de Stuers, *Parda: a study of Muslim women's life in Northern India*, Assen 1968, and Zarina Bhatty, *Status of Muslim women and social change*, in *Indian women: from purdah to modernity*, New Delhi 1976. (GHAUS ANSARI)

MARʿĀ (A.), pasture. 1. In nomadic Arab life.

The word *marʿā* is used only twice in the Ḳurʾān, where it has the purpose of praising the divine power (LXXIX, 31, and LXXXVII,4). In *ḥadīth* there are also two uses of this substantive to be noted (cf. Wensinck, *Concordance*); one of them touches incidentally on the problem of the exploitation of pastures, but *ḥadīth* is more explicit with reference to *kalaʾ*, dry and green forage. In fact, a tradition asserts that "the Muslims are united (*shurakāʾ*) in three things: water, forage and fire"; it is the principle of the primitive collectivism of the Arab tribe which is stressed here. Another tradition conforms this point of view: "three things cannot be withheld: water, forage and fire". According to a third tradition, "it is forbidden to refuse excess water with the purpose of thereby denying forage" (*lā yumnaʿ faḍl al-māʾ li-yumnaʿ bi-hi 'l-kalaʾ*), since cattle eating without drinking will die of thirst (cf. Muslim, *Ṣaḥīḥ*, Cairo 1334, v, 34; *LA*, s.v. *k-l-ʾ*).

Besides these somewhat vague pieces of information, neither *ḥadīth* nor even the works of *fiḳh* seem to be concerned with the manner in which pastures were exploited among the Arabs of the open plains. On the other hand, tracts of religious jurisprudence are often concerned with the problem of the sharing of water and its utilisation among riverside communities. One of the most important sources, in this context, is presumably the work, still in manuscript form, intitled *al-Marʿā al-akhḍar fī fatāwī al-Bakrī wa-bn Ḥadjar* (in the library of Tarīm).

In accounts describing the *ayyām al-ʿArab*, the contest for pastures is frequently evoked. Each tribe has its own, where only its members enjoy grazing rights. If a *sayyid* considers himself sufficiently powerful to appropriate pasture land, he then declares it *ḥimā* [*q.v.*] and forbids even his fellow-tribesmen access to it. The violent war of Basūs between the sister-tribes of Bakr and of Taghlib came about as a direct result of trespass on the reserve of Kulayb by a camel belonging to the Tamīmi Basūs.

The romantic tales of Arab chivalry, such as the story of ʿAntara, often describe heroic, warlike exploits in the conquest or defence of pastures. A clan whose lands are blighted by drought sets out to seek other grazing land belonging to friendly or allied tribes, but it cannot proceed there without having asked for and obtained authorisation from the proprietors. This approach is usually accompanied by gifts presented to the chief whose goodwill is sought; if he consents, the agreement is made conditional on terms, the most important of which is the duration of the grazing facilities. The clan which accepts then takes the visitors und its protection (*dhimām*), but it may revoke its decision and insist on the latter leaving its reserves on the grounds that their presence has caused friction. This breach of promise can degenerate into armed conflict.

It is a fact that the information supplied by the classical Arabic sources on the question of pastures among the Bedouin is far from satisfactory. To examine this subject it is necessary to turn to another source, sc. ethnography.

The Bedouin economy is based essentially on animal husbandry, sometimes linked with land cultivation of a more or less intermittent nature. These two activities could not be developed without at the same time creating a certain number of rules, determined by custom and relating in particular to the ownership of land and of wells. It might be supposed that the desert, on account of its aridity and particularly severe living conditions, is free territory belonging to anyone who has the courage to dwell there. This is not at all the case. An expert on the subject, T. E. Lawrence, states correctly in this regard:

"Men have looked upon the desert as barren land, the free holding of whoever chose; but in fact each hill and valley in it had a man who was its acknowledged owner and would quickly assert the right of his family or clan to it, against agression. Even the wells and trees had their masters, who allowed men to make firewood of the one and drink of the other freely, as much as was required for their need, but who would instantly check anyone trying to turn the property to account and to exploit it or its products among others for private benefit. The desert was held in a crazed communism by which Nature and the elements were for the free use of every known friendly person for his own purposes and no more" (*The seven pillars of wisdom*, London 1935, 83-4).

Each tribe, even the most itinerant, possesses a fixed centre which serves it as a place of resort and as a rallying centre where its various clans assemble during the months of greatest heat. At this time of the year, everything in the desert has been scorched by the sun. Then the Bedouin returns to his summer camp, situated close to an oasis or a major source of water. When the ferocity of the climate is alleviated, with the signs of the first rains, he goes back to his natural habitat in search of grazing for his flocks. But he cannot wander at will. Each tribe has its pastures which it frequents periodically. The vast extent of its nomadic range enables it, in a good or a bad year, in spite of the rigours of the severest climate, to find adequate nourishment for its livestock. In this manner, the Ruwāla spend the summer, especially the months of July and August, in Syria, to the south of Damascus. With the alleviation of the temperature, they travel to their winter pastures situated in Saudi Arabia, crossing the Jordanian desert by way of Wādī Sirḥān.

It can happen, however, that a persistent drought consumes the hardy desert vegetation, roots and all, in spite of its legendary resilience. The Bedouin is then constrained to leave his ancestral territory in search of a more fertile zone. But he is evidently obliged to take into account the attitude towards him of the lawful owner of the coveted pastures. The latter, however, can in fact refuse to accede to his request or may offer him grazing rights only in exchange for the payment of rent. If the supplicant considers himself strong enought to confront him with force, he will be inclined to reject any compromise. Otherwise, he must submit to the conditions prescribed, or search elsewhere. In Jordan, a nanny-goat, known as *shāt al-ritāʿa*, is offered to the owner of the pastures.

The territory of a Bedouin tribe is jointly owned; it is communal property, the exploitation and tenure of which are reserved for its occupants alone, the members of the group and their protégés. It is divided into lots, of unequal size, corresponding to the number of clans belonging to this group. Friends, even strangers properly introduced, may move about there freely and use the wells. But the grazing right is accorded only to fellow-tribesmen and their clients.

Even at this level of social organisation, pastures are a cause of dispute, the best being appropriated by the strongest clans. Consanguinity and solidarity impose upon all an obligation to accept here, with apparent enthusiasm, the least prosperous among them, especially in times of drought. But the latter would be wrong to consider an acquired right what is in fact a duty for mutual aid. The collectivism of the desert is located essentially at the level of the *ḥamūla*, the members of which may pasture their livestock in any part whatsoever of the communal lot. The members of another *ḥamūla* are admitted to it only with the authorisation of the *shaykh*, and by reason of their links of kinship, geographical proximity and good relations with the titular proprietors.

Among the Ḳabīlīs of the high plateaux of the Yemen, although this people has long been sedentarised, the pastures of a tribe are reserved for its members, but also for those who are admitted on account of being refugees: *rabīʿ*, *matīʿ* or *ḳaṭīr*. The stranger who ventures there without authorisation is tolerated for three days; this is the right of tenure (*mutʿa*) accorded to a friendly clan. Once this interval is passed, pressure is exerted on the unwelcome visitor to force him to leave. He is harassed, he is threatened, his mount may even be seized. But no attempt is made on his life, even if he insists on remaining; it will be enough to notify his *shaykh*. The latter is obliged to compensate the proprietors and force his subordinate to leave the place. If the demand is refused, serious conflict may erupt. To avoid this, the group of outsiders which has suffered drought must come to an understanding with more fortunate neighbours to pasture its livestock on their territory, in a place and for a period of time prescribed, in exchange for the payment of an indemnity in kind or in cash. Henceforward it will not be troubled. Furthermore, it enjoys the right of protected neighbour status (*djiwār* [*q.v.*]), according to which the lessors are required to act as official protectors.

There also exist in the Yemen, as among the Arabs of the desert, treaties of friendship between tribes which allow each contracting party to use the pastures of the other if the need arises. This is the case e.g., with the alliance known as *ṣuḥba* or *ṣaḥāb* which is based on a kind of fraternal relationship (*taʾākhī*). It is an agreement, both defensive and offensive, by which two tribes undertake to take up arms on one another's behalf. To conclude the agreement, there is no need for bloody sacrifices, except for the purpose of celebrating the event, nor for oaths; this is a pact that goes beyond sworn pledges. The agreement is set out in writing and signed by the leading *shaykhs*. Such documents (*marāḳīm*) state explicitly that the contracting parties consider themselves henceforward "as a single member, a single arm, sharing the same fear and the same tranquillity, sharing the loss and the gains, however meagre they may be, accruing from a common action against the enemy" (al-Hamdānī, *Iklīl*, ed. Khaṭīb, x, 70). Henceforth, the members of a tribe may go to live on the territories of the other and also take advantages for its pastures. Excluded from this treaty are the fornicator and the thief.

It will be understood that here it is the perspective of an essentially nomadic tribe that is under discussion. When the process of sedentarisation is initated, the community of proximity tends to take the place of consanguinity. Arabs residing in the same region exploit the pastures in common, even where they belong to different tribes. But a group from a different area which seeks to install itself there cannot do so before obtaining the consent of the leading *shaykhs*. The latter can even exact the payment of tribute.

The ownership of land, among the Arabs of the desert, is controlled by the law of the strongest. For this reason, it is never definitive. Until recent times, the Bedouin, even if sedentarised, despised any kind of bureaucratic administration of land and seldom had recourse to it. To defend his rights, he trusted his sword. The demarcation of territories operated in the most rudimentary fashion, since each clan knew its own domain, as well as that of its neighbour. For marking boundaries, very simple means were employed: a shallow ditch, stakes, mounds, piles of stones and, more recently, barrels. Those who occupied themselves with agriculture planted strips of onions to mark boundaries. Such an administrative system, clearly precarious and imprecise, often gave rise to disputes. Litigation was submitted to the jurisdiction of an *ʿārifa*.

Bibliography: A. Jaussen, *Coutumes des Arabes au pays de Moab*, 235-40; J. Chelhod, *Le droit dans la société bédouine*, ch. viii; idem, *Le droit intertribal dans les hauts plateaux du Yémen*, in *Al-Bahit* (sic), *Studia Instituti Anthropos*, xxviii (1976), 49-76; Ruks al-ʿUzayzī, *Ḳāmūs al-ʿādāt ... al-urduniyya*, ʿAmmān 1973, i, 339.

(J. Chelhod)

2. In Persia.

The terms *martaʿ* (pl. *marātiʿ*), *ʿalafzār*, *ʿalafkhʷār*, *ʿalafčar*, *marghzār*, and *čarāgāh* are used interchangeably in Persian literature to mean pasture. In early works, *giyāh-khʷār* is also found (cf. *Ḥudūd al-ʿālam*, tr. Minorsky, 94, 85 and Ibn al-Balkhī, *Fārs-nāma*, ed. G. Le Strange, London 1921, 155). *Marghzār* is also used to mean meadow-land, while the word *čaman* is restricted to this meaning. *Marāʿī*, *ʿalafkhʷār* and *ʿalafčar* are also used in the sense of pasture tax.

The wide variation in temperature in Persia is highly important in shaping the general plant geography, and coupled with the variations in the annual distribution of precipitation is responsible for the differences of Persia's plant cover and pasturage. Relief is also a decisive factor and affects both climate and soils; and a striking feature of Persia, especially the central plateau, is its micro-relief. The bulk of Persia's surface, apart from the Caspian region, receives its rains in autumn, winter and spring: summer rains are negligible in most regions. This affects the development of pastures and results in their exploitation being largely seasonal. In Islamic times the phytogeographical boundaries have probably continued broadly the same. Changes in micro-climates may have been experienced, but the over-all macro-climate has probably remained unaltered.

Millenia of human activity have left their impress through the cutting of trees and grazing. In many regions it is probable that the primary vegetation was a kind of *Artemisietum* which included perennial grasses. Centuries of overgrazing and steady grazing would appear to have reduced the original vegetation of much of the plateau to a state of barrenness. In some places, it has led to the disapppearance of perennial grasses from the steppe vegetation and their replacement by anti-pastoral non-palatable components, such as *Amygdalus*, *Anabasis*, *Astragalus*, and *Artemisia herba-alba*. The movement of flocks has also resulted in the severe cropping of trees, as, for example, in the oak forests of Luristān, Pusht-i Kūh, Īlām and Kurdistān, and the disappearance of *Quercus brantii* from hillsides in the neighbourhood of Kirmānshāh. The natural vegetation along the travel routes of nomad and semi-nomad tribes has also been disturbed in recent centuries.

Another factor which has led to change in the make-up of vegetation is the collection of plants for industry, fuel, drugs and food. Fuel collection, especially, has affected not only the forest regions but also the steppes and led to the occurence of some barren, almost unvegetated areas. At the higher altitudes on the plateau, the climate is often too cold and water too scanty to produce anything more than a thin vegetational cover of short grass and low scrub. Large areas of the country are sterile or almost sterile hammadas due to very low rainfall or to an excess of salt in the soil or both. The ecology of hillsides varies greatly with respect to latitude, altitude, exposure and soil. Many slopes of low ridges and hills are bare because of their exposure to wind, heat and drought. Perennial grasses survive only in the high mountains beyond the limits of agriculture and in places inaccessible to grazing, on slopes too steep for agriculture and in those districts which have a long snow cover (approximately at an altitude of 2,400 m. to 2,600 m.). Seasonal grasses are found in the steppe areas and a periodic or episodic growth of grasses in some semi-desert regions (see further E. Ehlers, *Iran: Grundzüge einer geographischen Landeskunde*, Darmstadt 1980, 63-127).

Drought, demographic movements, disease, invasian and war have all at different times affected the local distribution of arable and pastoral land and dead lands—sometimes temporarily and sometimes permanently. Frontier regions, in particular, tended frequently to be laid waste, presumably with the destruction of, or damage to, local pastures. In the predominantly pastoral regions the maintenance of a balance between pastures, animal population and human population was maintained, on a short term, by the dispersal or concentration of flocks according to the productivity of the pastures and the utilisation of widely separated pastures at their different periods of productivity. If the balance between pastures, flocks and human population was upset, conflicts between different groups over pastures and encroachment upon neighbouring arable land would be likely to occur. If the settled population increased and productivity rose, more land would be brought under cultivation and grazing land would be restricted. Changes in land use, usually on a small scale and sometimes of a temporary nature, have also occurred from time to time when nomad tribes have adopted a settled life.

Since most pastures were exploited seasonally, it is difficult to arrive at any realistic estimate of the number of animals carried per acre in the different regions. Masson Smith's estimate that "a sheep required something like 10 acres of steppe pasture" (*Turanian nomadism and Iranian politics*, in *Iranian Studies*, xi [1978], 62) does not appear to take the seasonal factor into consideration. B. Spooner puts the stocking rate in the Tūrān district, east of Simnān, which was declared a biosphere reserve in 1977 and in which pastoralism of various types was the dominant form of land use, at 8.6 acres per animal for the period October/November to May (*The Turan programme*, in Margaret R. Biswas and Asit K. Biswas (eds.), *Desertification*, Oxford 1980, 192). Similarly, it is difficult to determine the relative distribution of sheep and goats. The matter is to some extent obscured by the fact that the term *gūsfand* in Persian literature covers both. In modern times sheep predominate; they probably did so in the past also. Goats are numerous, especially in areas where the vegetation is less abundant. They voraciously crop all green plants and are largely responsible for the deforestation and decrease in plant and grass cover which has taken place. Oxen are widely used as draught animals, but herds of cattle are not important except in a few, mainly lowland, districts. Herds of camels are put out to pasture in the tragacanthic steppes, often in areas where the vegetation is unpalatable or too sparse for either sheep or goats. Herds of horses are (or were) bred and turned out to pasture in some tribal districts (cf. Sardār Asad, *Tārīkh-i Bakhtiyārī*, lith. 1333 AH, 20-1). Rulers needed large numbers of horses for their armies. Royal herds and army remounts were grazed in special reserves and elsewhere (see Sir John Chardin, *Travels in Persia*, London 1927, 169-70, on the horses of the Ṣafawid shah). Flocks of sheep kept to provision the royal establishments were similarly pastured in royal reserves.

Seasonal pastures in cool upland regions (*sardsīr, yaylāḳ*) are exploited mainly by tribal groups. Some of them make long-range migrations from their winter quarters in lowland regions (*garmsīr, ḳishlāḳ*); others travel short distances, sometimes only from valley bottoms to the upper mountain slopes. Most villages are surrounded by many square miles of waste land in which the villagers are able to keep a few sheep and goats and donkeys. Some, in the more fertile regions, keep flocks which they take to graze either in the neighbourhood of their villages or farther afield. Stubble grazing is an important form of land use. In many upland regions, notably in the Alburz, villagers practise a limited form of transhumance, sending their flocks to summer pastures in the neighbourhood of their villages. There is also some winter migration of village flocks to the coastal plains of the Caspian from higher regions (see also A.K.S. Lambton, *Landlord and peasant in Persia*, Oxford 1953, 354-5, and ĪLĀT).

With the contraction of the frontiers of Persia in the 19th century, the Mughān steppe in the north-west and the Turkoman steppe in the north-east, both regions in which there were good pastures, became frontier districts and tribal groups migrated annually across the Perso-Russian frontier. The Perso-Ottoman frontier in Kurdistān also traversed pasture land and seasonal migration across it took place, and continued in the 20th century after the creation of ʿIrāḳ.

A survey made by H. Pablot in 1967 shows 25% of the total land as range-land (*Pasture development and range improvement through botanical and ecological studies*, in *Report to the government of Iran*, FAO 3211, Rome 1967, quoted by E. Ehlers, *Agriculture in Iran*, in *Encyclopaedia Iranica*, i, fasc. 6, 613). It would, however, be rash to assume that this percentage was constant throughout Islamic times, but because of the inadequacy of the sources for a historical survey it is not possible to discuss changes in the extent of the land under agriculture and pasture land at different periods except in the most general terms.

Pasture was an important resource for villagers, and for nomads it was vital, while for those dynasties which relied on the support of tribal and nomadic forces the ability to ensure the availability of pasture for their followers was also of critical importance. This was especially the case during and after the Mongol invasions, which resulted in a large and permanent increase in the number of nomads. Throughout the Īlkhānate (654-736/1256-1335), the demand for pastures was insatiable. The wars between the Īlkhānate and the Golden Horde were, in part, over the acquisition of the rich pastures of Ādharbāydjān (C.J. Halperin, *Russia in the Mongol empire in comparative perspective*, in *HJAS*, xliii [1983], 250-1). The war which broke out between the Īlkhānate and the Mongols of Central Asia in A.D. 1270 was in part over the pastures of Bādghīs (W. Barthold, *An historical geography of Iran*, tr. S. Soucek and ed. C.E. Bosworth, Princeton 1984, 49). The possession of pastures was also important for the succession states to the Īl<u>kh</u>ānate, with the possible exception of the Muẓaffarids, who observed, to some extent, the traditions of settled government. It was also the case under Tīmūr (d. 807/1405), the Turkoman dynasties of the Aḳ Ḳoyunlū and the Ḳara Ḳoyunlū and the Ṣafawids when they first came to power in the early 10th/16th century; while one of the reasons which led Āḳā Muḥammad <u>Kh</u>ān Ḳād<u>j</u>ār to choose Tehran as his capital was that it was within easy reach of Gurgān, where the pasture grounds of the Ḳad<u>j</u>ār tribe were situated.

A comparison of the accounts of the early Islamic geographers with later accounts will reveal some changes in the distribution of pasture land. The accounts of later writers must, however, be used with reserve unless they are known to be writing from personal experience. Sometimes they merely repeat the information available in the works of their predecessors. What an author records does not necessarily refer to the time he was writing.

There is little evidence that the Arab invasion had much effect on the distribution of pastures, though there probably was some displacement of those who had previously exploited them. There are references to the collective reserves of tribes (*ḥimā*, *ḥimāya* [*q.v.*]) and to reserves in which the cattle and flocks of the caliphs and their governors and army remounts grazed. Al-Balā<u>dh</u>urī mentions the pastures of the flocks of the caliph al-Mahdī (158-69/775-85) in the neighbourhood of Hamadān (*Futūḥ al-buldān*, 310-11). The *Tārī<u>kh</u>-i Ḳumm* also mentions that pastures (*čirāgāhhā wa ^calafzārhā*) were reserved in every village in the neighbourhood of Nihāwand and Karad<u>j</u> for the beasts (*dawābb*) of the caliphs and were called *ḥiyāzāt* (Ḥasan b. Muḥammad b. Ḥasan Ḳummī, *Tārī<u>kh</u>-i-Ḳumm*, Persian tr. by Ḥasan b. ^cAlī b. Ḥasan b. ^cAbd al-Malik Ḳummī, ed. <u>D</u>jalāl al-Dīn Ṭihrānī, Tehran AHS 1313, 185).

It is perhaps significant that Dīnawar, the centre of Māh Kūfa, was within easy reach of rich pastures. Kirmān<u>sh</u>āh, also part of Māh Kūfa, was similarly a district with plentiful pastures. Ibn Ḥawḳal, writing in the second half of the 4th/10th century mentions that it had abundant pastures where numerous flocks grazed and much water (*K. Ṣūrat al-arḍ*, ii, 359). Similarly, the availability of pastures in <u>Kh</u>urāsān would have facilitated the settlement of large numbers of Arabs in that province and may perhaps have influenced the choice of the centres where they established garrisons. Even if they were not accompanied by flocks and herds, they would have required pastures for their remounts and baggage animals (on Arab settlement in <u>Kh</u>urāsān, see further M. A. Shaban, *The ^cAbbāsid revolution*, Cambridge 1970). Elsewhere, so far as the Arabs settled in Persia as tribal groups, they would have required pastures for their flocks. But on the whole, there do not appear to have been many conflicts with local groups over pastures. The *Tārī<u>kh</u>*-i *Ḳumm*, 243-4, states that the A<u>sh</u>^carī leaders ^cAbd Allāh and Aḥwaṣ complained in 102/720-1 to Yazdānfā<u>dh</u>ār, who had allocated to them the villages of Mamad<u>j</u>ān and <u>D</u>jamar near Ḳumm in 99/717-18, saying that the pastures were too small for their camels, horses and sheep. Yazdānfā<u>dh</u>ār accordingly allocated to them the village of Farāba also.

The geographers of the 3rd/9th and 4th/10th centuries give, on the whole, a picture of a prosperous countryside practising arable and pastoral farming. There is mention of pastures and meadow lands in some districts and of the presence of large flocks in various regions, which implies the existence of pastures and grazing land [see ĪLĀT]. Transhumance was practised in Fārs, and al-Iṣṭa<u>kh</u>rī puts the number of nomads at 500,000 tents (*Masālik al-mamālik*, 97-9; ĪLĀT), which suggest that pasturage was extensive. Yāḳūt, writing in the early 7th/13th century, also states that they were estimated at 500,000 tents (Barbier de Meynard, *Dictionnaire géographique et historique de la Perse*, Paris 1868, 412). It seems likely that he was merely copying al-Iṣṭa<u>kh</u>rī, unless it is to be assumed that the pastures, flocks and tribal population were in a state of absolute equilibrium.

There were extensive pastures and grazing grounds on the borders of the *dār al-islām* occupied by the <u>Gh</u>uzz (cf. *Ḥudūd al-^cālam*, 100, and GHUZZ). One of the factors behind their migration in the 5th/11th century into the *dār al-islām* may have been pressure on pastures in Central Asia and tribal movements which resulted therefrom. One of their needs on entering Persia was to secure pasturage for their flocks. However, the numbers of the <u>Gh</u>uzz coming into Persia, first as independent groups and then under the leadership of the Sal<u>dj</u>ūḳs, were not large, and there is little evidence of major displacements by them of those exploiting existing pastures (see further Lambton, *Aspects of Saljūq-<u>Gh</u>uzz settlement in Persia*, in D.S. Richards (ed.), *Islamic civilisation 950-1150*, Oxford 1973, 121 ff.), nor, with the exception of Gurgān, does there seem to have been much change in the distribution of arable land and grazing land as a result of their advent into Persia. Whereas Gurgān in the 3rd/9th and 4th/10th centuries appears to have been a well-cultivated countryside, in Sal<u>dj</u>ūḳ times much of it was pasture land. By the reign of San<u>dj</u>ar (511-52/1118-57), large numbers of Turkomans occupied pastures in Gurgān, Dihistān and the neighbourhood of Marw (*ibid.*, 110), and pasture land was probably encroaching on arable land.

Fārs continued to be rich in pastures in the Sal<u>dj</u>ūḳ period. Ibn al-Bal<u>kh</u>ī, who wrote in the reign of Muḥammad b. Malik<u>sh</u>āh (498-511/1104-18), mentions by name extensive pastures in Fārs, and states "From end to end Fārs was valleys and mountains. The whole of it was pasture land (*giyāh-<u>kh</u>^{w}ār*)" (*Fārs-nāma*, 155). The pastures of Sīkān, Da<u>sh</u>t-i Ar<u>zh</u>an and Kāmfīrūz were associated with woodland, in which were found lions (*ibid.*, 154-5). Ibn al-Bal<u>kh</u>ī gives the interesting information that the grass of the Ḳālī pasture was beneficial in winter but that in summer it was harmful for animals (*ibid.*, 154). Afḍal al-Dīn Kirmānī, writing in the second half of the 6th/12th century, mentions the excellence of the pastures in Rūdbār (in the district of <u>D</u>jīruft), and states that animals thrived in them (*^cIḳd al-^culā li 'l-mawḳif al-a^clā*, ed. ^cAlī Muḥammad ^cĀmirī Nā^ɔīnī, Tehran AHS 1311, 70), Earlier, the *Ḥudūd al-^cālam*, which was composed in 372/982-3, had mentioned the woods, trees and meadows of Rūdbār (124). Afḍal al-Dīn makes no mention of woods. When the <u>Gh</u>uzz invaded Kirmān after the death of San<u>dj</u>ar, there appears to have been a temporary contraction in arable land. Afḍal al-Dīn mentions that land in the Rāwar district was not cultivated because of the encroachment of nomads (*^cIḳd al-^culā*, 29) and that crops were grazed by the flocks of the <u>Gh</u>uzz (*al-Muḍāf ilā badāyi^c al-azmān*, ed. ^cAbbās Iḳbāl, Tehran AHS 1331, 19-20).

The Mongol invasions in the 7th/13th century resulted in widespread destruction and depopulation. Standing crops were ruthlessly grazed by the Mongol hordes; much land went out of cultivation. There was a permanent increase in the numbers of the nomadic population and the flock population and consequently in the demand for pastures; it is likely that much arable land was converted into pasture. Hülegü, according to D̲j̲uwaynī, when preparing his expedition to Persia, declared pastures in the districts through which it was expected that the army would march to be reserves (*ḳuruḳ*) and forbade any grazing in them other than by the army (*Tārīk̲h̲-i D̲j̲ahāngus̲h̲ā*, ed. Muḥammad Ḳazwīnī, London 1912-32, iii, 93). Later rulers also sometimes declared pastures to be *ḳuruḳ*. After their invasion of Persia, the Mongol hordes continued to practise transhumance. Al-ᶜUmarī, who lived in Mamlūk territory in the first half of the 8th/14th century, states that their summer residence was in the Ḳarabāg̲h̲ region, which had many pastures, and that their winter quarters were in Ūd̲j̲ān, which also had extensive pastures, and sometimes in Bag̲h̲dād (*Masālik al-abṣār wa-mamālik al-amṣār*, ed. and tr, K. Lech, Wiesbaden 1968, Ar. text, 86). Many of the Mongol settlements in Persia were within easy, or fairly easy, reach of rich pastures. Marāg̲h̲a, the first Īlk̲h̲ānid capital, had good pasture in the neighbourhood and further afield at Us̲h̲nū and other districts in Kurdistān. Tabrīz, the capital of Abaḳa (663-80/1265-81) and later of G̲h̲azan K̲h̲ān (694-703/1295-1304), had good pastures nearby in Ūd̲j̲ān and summer pastures in Mt. Sablān and Mt. Sahand. G̲h̲azan also built a city, Maḥmūdābād, in the Mug̲h̲ān steppe, where the Mongols pastured their flocks and herds in winter (see Le Strange, *Lands of the eastern caliphate*, 176). Arg̲h̲un (673-80/1284-91) founded the city of Sulṭāniyya, which was completed by Öld̲j̲eytü (703-16/1304-16) where there were very rich spring pastures. Another foundation built by Öld̲j̲eytü was Sulṭānābād-i Čamčamāl at the foot of Bīsutūn, which, because of its excellent pastures, was a regular camping ground of the Mongol establishments (Ḥamd Allāh Mustawfī, *Nuzhat al-ḳulūb*, ed. Le Strange, London 1915, 107).

One of the biggest changes in the distribution of pasture land brought about by the Mongols was the expansion of land under pasture in the Mug̲h̲ān steppe and in the country round Sulṭāniyya. Some of this had formerly probably been under cultivation. Both regions continued to afford pasture to nomadic groups and army remounts down to modern times. Marco Polo on his journey south-east from Alamūt towards Yazd and Kirmān wrote, "When you leave this castle (sc. Alamūt), you ride across beautiful plains and valleys and charming hill-slopes, rich in fine grass and excellent pasture, and with abundance of fruits, and all other good things. Armies are glad to stop there on account of the great plenty" (*Travels*, tr. A. Ricci, London 1931, 53). Pastures in Gurgān, on the other hand, do not appear to have been important in Īlk̲h̲ānid times: Mustawfī states that Gurgān and Kabūd D̲j̲āma were in a state of ruin (*Nuzhat al-ḳulūb* 160). It is possible that, apart from the destruction brought about by the Mongol invasion, they had been overgrazed. The pastures in Fārs of which Mustawfī gives a list were still extensive. He follows Ibn al-Balk̲h̲ī's account but adds one or two details. He remarks that the pasture of Bīd and Mis̲h̲kān was extremely large (135) and that the grass of the Shīdān pasture was beneficial (*ibid.*). He omits any reference to the pasture of Darābd̲j̲ird, but mentions an extensive spring pasture near Kāzirūn (136). Mustawfī also mentions that there were excellent pastures in K̲h̲alk̲h̲āl (82) and a large pasture near Karad̲j̲-i Abū Dulaf (69). He states that the pastures of Ḳazwīn were especially rich in fodder for camels (58), and that the pasture lands of Iṣfahān were good for fattening animals (49). Round Tustar and in the neighbourhood of Dizful there were also many excellent pastures (110, 111). Curiously, he does not mention the pastures of Ūd̲j̲ān or Us̲h̲nūya.

There is not much information on the pastures of Luristān [*q.v.*] in the early Islamic centuries. There was presumably some exploitation by transhumant herding, but this may have been more regularly organised in Īlk̲h̲ānid times with benefit to the pastures. Muᶜīn al-Dīn Natanzī state that when Hülegü gave the governorate of Luristān to the Atabeg S̲h̲ams al-Dīn Alp Arg̲h̲un (d. 670/1271-2), the province was in a state of ruin and the subjects dispersed. The Atabeg brought the province back to prosperity by various measures. One reason for its renewed prosperity was, according to Mu ᶜīn al-Dīn, the fact that S̲h̲ams al-Dīn adopted the custom of the Mongols of moving from summer to winter quarters, spending the winter in S̲h̲ūs̲h̲ and Īd̲h̲ad̲j̲ and the summer in the Zarda Kūh (*Muntak̲h̲ab al-tawārīk̲h̲-i muᶜīnī*, ed. J. Aubin, Tehran 1957, 43-4).

Initially, the basis of the Mongol economy was the produce of their flocks and herds, hence their primary need was for pastures; but once they had become the rulers of a settled empire some more stable basis was required. G̲h̲azān K̲h̲ān, towards the end of his reign, sought to bring about an agricultural revival, and his efforts may well have restricted the availability of pasture. One of the measures he took to provide for the upkeep of the military forces of the state was to issue a *yarlig̲h̲* in 703/1303-4 to allocate *iḳṭāᶜ*s to the soldiers. One of its provisions forbade the ploughing up of permanent pasture (Ras̲h̲īd al-Dīn, *Tārīk̲h̲-i mubārak-i g̲h̲āzānī*, ed. K. Jahn, 306). The reason for this prohibition can only be guessed at; perhaps, since land capable of cereal growing gave a higher yield in terms of foodstuffs per unit of area than land under pasture, it was due to a fear that the soldiers might plough up all the land allocated to them and as a result would not be able to keep their horses. G̲h̲azan's reforms were shortlived and the agricultural revival ephemeral. With the emergence of new federations of tribes at the end of the Īlk̲h̲ānid period and the apparent resurgence of nomadism in K̲h̲urāsān from about 747/1346 (see Mu ᶜīn al-Dīn Natanzī, *op. cit.*, 197 ff.), it is likely that the need for pasture again became paramount.

Tīmūr and his successors appear to have been in the habit of allocating pastures to their followers (cf. ᶜAbd al-Razzāḳ Samarḳandī, *Maṭlaᶜ al-saᶜdayn*, ed. Muḥammad S̲h̲afīᶜ, Lahore 1360-8 AH, ii, 1337). From the account of Clavijo, who travelled through Persia in the time of Tīmūr, there does not seem to have been undue pressure on pastures, in spite of the new influx of nomads. He states that a certain Čag̲h̲atay tribe, who served as Tīmūr's bodyguard, was allowed by him to seek pasture and to sow its crops in all districts, and he mentions meeting between Andk̲h̲ʷuy and Balk̲h̲ parties of Čag̲h̲atay nomads in search of pasture, who encamped in all places where there was pasture and water (*Embassy to Tamerlane*, 1403-1406, tr. Le Strange, London 1928, 196). He also describes extensive pastures in the neighbourhood of K̲h̲ʷuy (148), meadow lands in Lār in the Alburz (169), rich pastures along the Ted̲j̲en River (186-7) and round Samarḳand (233) and the winter pastures of the plains of Ḳarabāg̲h̲ (309). We know from the *Maṭlaᶜ al-sa ᶜdayn* that in 866/1461-2 the D̲j̲alāyirid tribe [see D̲J̲ALĀYIR, D̲J̲ALĀY IRID] had "long since" (*az dīr bāz*) had its *yurt*, or tribal pastures, in Astarābād and had innumerable flocks (*op. cit.*, ii,

1253), which suggests that there had been an improvement in the pastures there since Īlkhānid times.

The period from the 8th/14th to the early 10th/16th centuries was one of tribal movement and resurgence under the Aḳ Ḳoyunlu, Ḳara Koyunlu and the early Ṣafawids, and it is unlikely that there was any reduction in the land under pasture, with the possible exception of the reign of Uzun Ḥasan (871-83/1466-78). With the consolidation of the power of the central government under Shāh ʿAbbās (966-1038/1587-1629), more land may have been brought under cultivation. Already before this in the reign of Ṭahmāsp (930-84/1524-76) one of the Ṣāʾin Khānī Turkoman tribes from Khwārazm, who had come from there to Astarābād, are said by Iskandar Munshī to have engaged in agricultural activity along the Gurgān River (*ʿĀlamārā-yi ʿAbbāsī*, Iṣfahān AHS 1334, i, 530). The pastures of ʿArabistān, Luristān, Bakhtiyārī, Kurdistān and many of the frontier regions, which were under provincial governors and *beglarbegs*, were presumably exploited by their tribal followers. The shahs themselves owned large herds of horses and sheep, for which they needed pasture in the neighbourhood of the capital and elsewhere. Tavernier, who visited Persia several times between 1632 and 1668, states that the shah kept 40,000 horses (*Voyages en Perse*, introd. by V. Monteil, Geneva, 1970, 231; cf. also *The travels of Monsieur de Thévenôt into the Levant*, London 1687, repr. 1971, ii, 121) and large flocks of sheep (Tavernier, 258). The movement of tribes to border districts and elsewhere by the Ṣafawids and later by Nādir Shāh and Āḳā Muḥammad Khān Ḳādjār may have resulted in some minor changes in land use. The Turco-Persian frontier in Ādharbāydjān was deliberately laid waste during part of the Ṣafawid period, presumably with damage to its pasture also.

During the 12th/18th century, there is little information on the state of grazing land or the relative extent of arable and pastoral land. The numbers of various tribal groups were apparently increasing [see ĪLĀT], and this may have resulted in pressure on pastures. The disorders and disturbances which broke out on the fall of the Ṣafawids, on the death of Nādir Shāh in 1160/1747 and after the death of Karīm Khān in 1193/1779, were in any case not conducive to prosperity in regions of either arable or pastoral farming. We have more information on the condition of pasture land in the 19th century, thanks to the accounts of European travellers. Much of this is to be found in the pages of the various editions of the *Gazeteer of Persia* compiled for the Government of India (this information is also to be found in L. W. Adamec (ed.), *Historical gazeteer of Iran*, Graz 1976-, of which two volumes have so far appeared).

In Khurāsān there appears to have been excellent pasture in the 19th century. It is possible that the more stable conditions which prevailed compared to the 18th century may have resulted in an improvement in the pastures, but in the absence of information on their condition in the 18th century this can only be conjecture. There was good grazing in spring in the Djām valley, round Sarakhs, in the Gurgān plains and along the Gurgān and Atrek Rivers. Parts of the Gurgān steppe were, however, again converted into arable land. The Yamut, who inhabited the land south of the R. Atrek up to Astarābād, are recorded as regularly firing grass and undergrowth for grazing purposes (*Historical gazeteer of Iran*, ii, 665). There were fine pastures at Činārūd at the head of the R. Kashaf, and in the mountains of Ḳūčān and Budjnurd. In Darra Gaz there was good pasture in the plain and luxuriant herbage on the slopes of the Darra Gaz mountains. The plains of Farīmān also had excellent pasture. Along the Afghān, border there was abundant grass in spring and in a good year it lasted well into the summer. In the Hastādān district of Bākharz, there was plentiful grass in winter and spring. In Rādkān there were also good but not very extensive pastures. In the region round Mashhad, Turbat-i Ḥaydarī and Bīrdjand, short-lived spring grass fattened quantities of sheep.

In the north-west and the south-west there was probably little change in the distribution of pastures, which continued to be exploited by various tribal federations. Kinneir mentions the rich pasture lands of Sulṭāniyya (*A geographical memoir of the Persian empire*, London 1813, 124), the rich soil and pastures of Mughān (153) and the luxuriant pasture of Luristān (138). In Kirmānshāh the pasture was very good but inferior to that of Ardalān (141).

Failure of rains resulting in a partial or total lack of pasture occurred frequently in different localities. In the late 1860s and early 1870s there was widespread drought. From the winter of 1863-4, the rains were below average for some nine years, with the exception of 1865-6. In 1869-70, hardly any snow or rain fell in the valleys. In the south, particularly, there was little or no grass on the lower plains and there were heavy losses in flocks and herds (O.B. St. John, *Narrative of a journey through Baluchistan and Southern Persia*, in F. J. Goldsmid (ed.), *Eastern Persia, an account of the journeys of the Persian Boundary Commission 1870-1-2*, repr. London 1976, i, 95). From 1869-72, there was severe famine in almost all regions, accompanied by a country-wide outbreak of cholera; but what the effect of the resulting decline in population was on the distribution of arable and grazing land is not well documented.

In the last decades of the 19th century, there appears to have been some sedentarisation of nomads, on a fairly small scale, which may have resulted in the conversion of pasture land into arable land in some districts (see G. G. Gilbar, *Demographic developments in late Qajar Persia 1870-1906*, in *Asian and African Studies*, xi [1976], 146-7). In the latter part of the 19th century, there was also an expansion of cultivation in the piedmont zone round Tehran and Karadj; as a result of this, various tribal groups which had formerly grazed this land were forced to extend their annual migration farther and farther south towards the heart of the Central Lūṭ, in order to make use of very inferior and short-lived flushes of pasture that follow sporadic rainfall (W. B. Fisher, *Physical geography*, in *Camb. hist. of Iran*, i, 58). Similar events may have taken place elsewhere.

It will have become clear from the foregoing that much grazing land was situated either in the *ḥarīm* of villages, i.e. in the land surrounding the cultivated lands of a village, or in waste or dead land, and so far as the law books discuss pastures they do so chiefly under the headings of *ḥimā* and *mawāt* [*q.vv.*]. A *ḥadīth* of the Prophet is recorded to the effect that all Muslims are partners in water, fire and grass. In the light of this, Abū Yūsuf lays down that although the meadows belonging to a village were similar to other private property, their owners could not prevent others from the free use of water and grass unless they had no pasturage apart from such meadows and unless no common land was available to them in which they could graze their flocks (*Le livre de l'impôt foncier*, tr. E. Fagnan, Paris 1921, 155 ff.; see also N. P. Aghnides, *Mohammedan theories of finance*, repr.

Lahore 1961, 513-14). Most Mālikīs and Ḥanafīs, however, apparently gave the villagers the exclusive use of the pasture lands in the *ḥarīm* of their village, but they nevertheless granted the *Imām* the right to make concessions of such lands to individuals should the public interest required it (*ibid.*, 514). In practice, a wide variety of usage seems to have prevailed. In modern times, the pastures round a peasant proprietor village were usually held in common by the villagers, while in landlord villages the villagers usually had a customary right to graze their animals in the village pastures (Lambton, *Landlord and peasant*, 355-7).

In privately-owned land (*milk, mulk*), the pastures followed the ownership of the rest of the land and could be transmitted by sale, gift or inheritance in the same way. Many pastures constituted, or were situated in, crown lands [see KHĀLIṢA], and could be granted to individuals as permanent, temporary or life grants like other crown land. Ibn al-Balkhī states that the pastures of Daṣht-i Rūn in the Kūhgīlūya were partly *iḳṭāʿī* and partly *milkī* (*mulki*) (*Fārs-nāma*, 124, 155). At different times and in different regions there were considerable variations in the ownership of pastures and grazing rights, particularly in tribal districts. The allocation of grazing rights within the tribal areas was largely based on custom. Sometimes, rights were held jointly by households or tribes, sometimes individually. In some cases they were transmitted by inheritance, but in others they were subject to re-allotment by the chief of the tribe. Information on these matters is to be found in modern anthropological studies (see especially R. L. Tapper, *Pasture and politics*, London 1979, on the S̲h̲ahsivan of Ād̲h̲arbāyd̲j̲ān; F. Barth, *Nomads of South Persia: the Basseri tribe of the Khamseh confederacy*, London 1961; W. G. Irons, *The Yomut Turkmen: a study of social organisation among a Central Asian Turkic-speaking population*, Anthropol. papers, Museum of Anthropology, no. 58, University of Michigan, Ann Arbor 1975; idem, *The Turkmen nomads*, in *Natural history*, lxxvii [1968], 44-51; and G. R. Garthwaite, *Khans and shahs: a documentary analysis of the Bakhtiari in Iran*, Cambridge 1983).

On the basis of the *ḥadīt̲h̲* of Muḥammad quoted above, al-Māwardī states that no governor could exact anything for the use of pastures in dead or reserved land (*al-Aḥkām al-sulṭāniyya*, Cairo 1966, 187, tr. Fagnan, *Les statuts gouvernementaux*, Algiers 1915, 401). In practice, however, there was a wide variety of usage in the matter of pasture taxes generally, and they are not always easily distinguishable from flock taxes [see KHARĀD̲J̲. ii. In Persia]. The owners of pastures also levied dues on those who grazed their flocks in them (for modern usage, see *Landlord and peasant*, 290, 355-8).

Bibliography (in addition to references given in the article): H. E. Wright, Jr., J. H. McAndrews and Willem van Zeist, *Modern pollen rain in Western Iran, and its relation to plant geography and quaternary vegetational history*, Contribution no. 50, Humanological Research Center, University of Minnesota; H. Bobek, *Die natürlichen Wälder in Geholzflüren Irans*, in *Bonn. Geogr. Abh.*, viii (1951), 1-62; idem, *Klima und Landschaft Irans in vor-und frühgeschichtlicher Zeit*, in *Geogr. Jahresberichte aus Österreich*, xxv (1953-4), 1-42; M. Zohary, *On the geobotanical structure of Iran*, in *Bull. Research Council Israel*, Sect. D. (Botany), 11 D, Suppl. (1963); idem, *Man and vegetation in the Middle East*, in W. Holzner, M. J. A. Werger and I. Ikusima (eds.), *Man's impact on vegetation*, The Hague, Boston,

London 1983, 287-95; P.D. Moore and A. C. Stevenson, *Pollen studies in dry environments*, in B. Spooner and H. S. Mann (eds.), *Desertification and development: dryland ecology and social perspectives*, London and New York 1982, 429-67; J. Pullar, *Early cultivation in the Zagros*, in *Iran*, xv (1977), 15-38; W. B. Fisher, *The Middle East*, London and New York 1950; E. Ehlers, *Man and the environment—probems in rural Iran*, tr. J. T. Craddock, *Tübingen, Institut für wissenschaftliche Zusammen-Arbeit*, Applied geography and development, xix (1982), 108-25; idem, *Bauern-Hirten-Bergnomaden am Alvand-Kuh/Westiran. Junge Wandlungen bäuerlich-nomadischer Wirtschaft and Sozialstruktur in iranischen Hochgebirgen*, in *40th Conference of German Geographers, Innsbruck 1975, conference reports and papers*, 775-94; idem and G. Stöber, *Entwicklungstendenzen des Nomadismus im Iran*, in *Abh. des geogr. Instituts' Anthropogeographie*, xxxiii: *Nomadismus—ein Entwicklungsproblem*, Berlin 1982, 195-205 (with a comprehensive bibliography); A. Pour-Fickoui and M. Bazin, *Élevage et vie pastorale dans le Guilân (Iran septentrional)*, Publs. du Départm. de Géogr. de l'Université de Paris-Sorbonne, vii, 1978; Garthwaite, *Pastoral nomadism and tribal power*, in *Iranian Studies*, xi, 173-97; Tapper, *Individual grazing rights and social organization among the Shahsevan nomads of Azerbaijan*, in *Pastoral production and society*, Cambridge-Paris (Ed. de la Maison des sciences de l'homme), 95-114; Taḳī Bahrāmī, *D̲j̲ug̲h̲rāfiyā-yi kis̲h̲āwarzī yi-Īrān*, Tehran AHS 1333, 614-76, for a list of pastures in modern Iran. (A. K. S. LAMBTON)

3. In Turkey.

The legal practice on the pastures appears, from the ancient legal texts, to have been influenced by custom and tradition. The Aydîn Edict of 935/1528, issued during the reign of Süleymān the Magnificent, states in its 8th clause that farming in areas that have been used from time immemorial as pasture is forbidden as being against public interest. Likewise, the 13th clause of the Kütahya Edict of the same year indicates that the ploughing and private ownership of areas where cattle are pastured is forbidden, in the interests of both the urban as well as rural population.

In fact, similar provisions existed even earlier: the 16th clause of the Bursa Edict of 892/1487 suggests that the arrangements concerning pastures were much the same previously. It says that "It is forbidden to cultivate and to establish private property on pastures where both city and village dwellers graze their herds because it brings harm to the public."

Hence we conclude from these measures of the 9th/15th and 10th/16th centuries that:

(1) acceptance of a given stretch of land as pasture is contingent upon its being used for this purpose from very old times and its having been allocated as a pasture for a certain town or village; (2) pasture lands should not be used for grain production, and frequent references to this prohibition in the laws of different periods show that this rule was implicitly admitted by society as an unchanging principle; (3) pastures cannot become private property; and (4) only the dwellers of the village or town to which the pasture is allocated may use it for this purpose.

The Land Edict of 1274/1858 is by far the most significant Ottoman legal text on this subject of the 19th century. Though it was a product of the *Tanzīmāt* [*q.v.*] era when western influence was being felt in an increasing degree, this Edict combined custom and tradition with the tenets of the formal Islamic land law. Articles 91 to 102 of this Edict contained provi-

1. Open semi-desert-like vegetation in Adharbāydjān having been browsed extensively for millennia by sheep, goats, horses and camels and dominated by antipastoral plants. (Photograph by M. Zohary, published in W. Holzner, M. J. A. Werger and I. Ikusima (eds.), *Man's impact on vegetation*, The Hague - Boston - London 1983, 292.)

2. Same formation as shown in Fig. 1 but in a still hotter and drier area near Iṣfahān. Dominants are antipastoral and antipyric plant species (*Artemisia* spp., *Astragalus* spp.). The white dots are plants of *Tulipa polychroma*; the flowering shrub to the right in the foreground is a thorny species of *Amygdalus*. (Photograph by M. Zohary, *ibidem*, 292.)

3. Slope grazed by sheep and goats near Kirmān*sh*āh originally covered by a low forest of *Quercus brantii*. (Photograph by M. Zohary, *ibidem*, 290.)

4. Detail from Fig. 2: *Artemisia*, probably *herba-alba*. (Photograph by M. Zohary, *ibidem*, 293.)

5. Another detail from Fig. 2: *Astragalus sect. Tragacantha*. (Photograph by M. Zohary, *ibidem*, 293.)

sions regarding the *arāḍī-yi matrūka* "assigned lands", though the normal term of Islamic law in which such stretches which are allocated to the use of town or village dwellers as pastures and winter grazing [see ḲĪSHLAḲ] is *arāḍī-yi maḥmiya* "protected lands". Now according to this new law, there were two kinds of *arāḍī-yi matrūka*. The first included areas of public utility such as roads, and recreational areas, while the second covered pasture, summer and winter grazing grounds, and scrubland where firewood might be gathered. Their salient features may be summarised as follows: (1) title deeds cannot be released for such lands; (2) they are not subject to taxation; (3) prescription is not applicable to them; (4) *ex officio* settlements of conflicts on these areas are not admissible; (5) such areas cannot be increased or decreased; (6) they cannot be made the subject of gifts; and (7) proof of collective use of such areas prevails over that of individual use in conflicts regarding their allocation.

Article 97 of the law defines pastures, concerning which the following points may be noted: (1) allocation is the *conditio sine qua non* for any area to be considered as pasture; (2) where allocation does not exist, it must have been used as a pasture from time immemorial; (3) the town or village dwellers to whom the allocation has been made alone can utilise a pasture for their herds; (4) pastures cannot be bought or sold; (5) buildings cannot be constructed on and trees cannot be planted in pastures, nor can they be converted into vineyards and fruit farms; (6) the surface areas of pastures may not be increased or decreased; (7) pastures cannot become private property through prescription; (8) the nature of the pasture cannot be altered, thus it cannot be used as arable land; (9) the offspring of animals grazing in the pasture are allowed there also; (10) summer and winter grazing grounds are accessible to dwellers of other town and cities, while the pastures are exclusive to urban or rural population to whom they are allocated; and (11) the use of summer and winter grazing grounds requires the payment of a certain fee, although the pastures are at the free disposal of the herds of towns and villages to which they are allocated.

There has been much debate among the Turkish jurists on whether the provisions regarding pastures of the 1274/1858 Land Edict were annulled by the 1926 Turkish Civil Code modelled on its Swiss counterpart. Though article 641 of this Code stated that *ad hoc* provisions would be introduced regarding the administration and utilisation of property for public use, such provisions have yet to be adopted, particularly concerning the pastures. Likewise, article 912 states that immovable property allocated for public use and not owned by individuals is in general not subject to the registration procedure. This does not appear to contradict the spirit of the 1274/1858 Land Edict or the practical implementation of the provisions concerning pasture lands. Article 43 of the Law on the Implementation of the Turkish Civil Code states unequivocally that the *Medjelle-yi aḥkām-i ʿadliyye* is rescinded, but without making any reference to the Land Edict; it merely mentions in a general fashion that the provisions of the previous laws contradictory to those of the Civil Code are deemed to have been repealed. Due to this uncertainty, the status of pastures has largely been governed by existing law and the Land Edict, even after the entry into force of the Civil Code in 1926.

Some of the laws passed after the proclamation of the Republic in 1923 nevertheless contain a number of provisions on pastures. Law no. 442 of 1340/1924 on Rural Administration declares in its article 6 that the rural population will continue utilising pastures as in the past and article 8 indicates that infringements of the arrangements regarding pastures will entail action appropriate to those usurping State property. Law no. 1580 of 1930 on Municipal Administration declares in its article 4 that the right to use the pastures within city limits is reserved to their previous users, and article 15 charges the municipalities with protecting such pastures.

During the period of its implementation, Law no. 4753 of 1945 on Land Distribution to Farmers has introduced some modifications to the law on pastures. Article 8 (b) permits the distribution to landless peasants of such areas of common village, town or city property as may be declared redundant by the Ministry of Agriculture. This Law has been rescinded, however, by no. 1757 of 1973 on Land and Agrarian Reform. Formally, Law no. 66 of 1966 on Cadastral Surveys empowers the national cadastral survey organisation to determine the boundaries of pastures and their areas (article 35). Law no. 1757 of 1973 mentioned above did not introduce a system different from that established by the Land Edict and existing legal practice. Its article 140, however, was important in that it foresaw the estalishment of a registry for pastures and winter and summer grazings as an expression of the state's determination to get a firm grip on the pasture land and to keep it from being nibbled away. At the same time, as a distinct departure from the previous principles of free use of pastures, article 151 required users to pay a certain fee to the village administration or to the municipality. This Law was in fact cancelled in 1976 by the Constitutional Court on procedural grounds, with effect from 1977. Consequently, it may be contended that the Turkish pasture law is governed today by the 1274/1858 Land Edict and the existing legal practice.

Statistics show that there has been a continuous decrease of pasture areas in Turkey:

Years	*Pastures* (in 1000 ha)
1928	46.298
1938	42.370
1948	38.330
1952	34.789
1957	29.748
1962	28.598
1967	26.135

Under article 639 of the Civil Code governing the acquisitive extraordinary prescription, any person who holds immovable property not entered on the land registry for an uninterrupted and legally unchallenged 20 years may request the registration of such property in his possession. Though this provision was used in a rather limited fashion in Switzerland, whence the Civil Code was borrowed, widespread use had been made of this article in Turkey in order to establish private ownership of land under state control and possession, including of pastures. This has been to some extent facilitated by the inadequacy of the land registry system and by the incompleteness of the cadastral survey work, not to mention the rapid population growth and the accelerating rate of agricultural mechanism. Finally, when the matter appeared to have attained significant proportions, the legislative power felt the need to take action, and a modification was made to article 639 of the Civil Code concerning the acquisitive extraordinary prescription whereby requests for registry were to be directed to the treasury and the relevant public corporation. In 1972, Law 1617 limited the areas for which registration as private property could be requested under acquisitive extraordinary prescription to 20 *donums*. Meanwhile, the over-use of pastures far beyond their possibilities of natural regeneration has caused major problems, such as soil erosion. Accordingly, the introduction of a new legal framework for the regulation of pasture lands in Turkey should yield considerable benefits in developing livestock production and in making the existing pasturelands more productive.

Bibliography: Anon., *Arāḍī Ḳānūnnāme-yi Hümayūn sherḥi*², Istanbul 1330/1914; Ömer Lütfi Barkan, *XV ve XVI asırlarda Osmanlı imparatorluğunda zirai ekonominin hukukî ve malî esasları*, i, Istanbul 1943; Ebül'ûlâ Mardin, *Toprak hukuku dersleri*, Istanbul 1947; Bülent Köprülü, *Toprak hukuku dersleri*, i, Istanbul 1958; Zerrin Akgün, *Mer'a hukuku*³, Ankara 1959; Şakir Berki, *Toprak hukuku*², Ankara 1960; *Tarim istatistikleri özeri*, 1967; Suat Aksoy, *Tarim hukuku*, 1970; Mustafa Reşit Karahasan, *Mülkiyet hukuku*, Istanbul 1970; *Anayasa Mahkemesi Kararlar Dergisi*, xiv (1977); Halil Cin, *Türk hukukunda mer'a, yaylak ve kışlaklar*, Ankara 1980. (Adnan Güriz)

MARABOUT [See ḲUBBA, MURĀBIṬ and WALĪ].

MARĀFIḲ (A.), sing, *marfiḳ*, "bribes, douceurs", literally, "benefits, favours". In mediaeval Islamic society, various terms in addition to this are found, such as *rashwa/rishwa*, *manāla*, *djaᶜāla*, *hadiyya*, etc., with varying degrees of euphemism, for the inducements given either directly to a potential bestower of benefits or as an inducement for a person's intercession or mediation (*shafāᶜa*, *wasāṭa*).

In the ᶜAbbāsid caliphate, this form of bribery became institutionalised in the caliphate of al-Muḳtadir (295-320/908-32 [*q.v.*]), when the vizier Ibn al-Furāt [*q.v.*] instituted a special office, the *dīwān al-marāfiḳ* [see DĪWĀN. i] in which were placed bribes and money from commissions collected from aspiring candidates for office, above all for the lucrative financial ones, in return for a grant of such an office. Naturally, the vizier himself benefited from this, and among the accusations against Ibn al-Furāt at his fall was the one that he had kept back a proportion of the monies received from confiscations (*muṣādarāt* [see MUṢĀDARA]) and bribes for the grant of an office (presumably above the level at which it was recognised that a vizier or secretary might by convention keep back some part of the payment as a recognised commission, the *ḥaḳḳ al-istithnā*ʾ). Even a vizier with a reputation for probity and avoidance of the grosser forms of corruption like ᶜAlī b. ᶜĪsā [*q.v.*] was not averse to accepting *marāfiḳ* as a normal perquisite of office.

Bibliography: Material in such sources as Ṭabarī, Miskawayh and Hilāl al-Ṣābiʾ is utilised in H. F. Amedroz, *Abbasid administration in decay, from the Tajarib al-umam*, in *JRAS* (1913), 828-9, 834-5; F. Lokkegaard, *Islamic taxation in the classic period*, Copenhagen 1950, 190-1; D. Sourdel, *Le vizirat ᶜabbāside*, Damascus 1959-60, ii, 408, 510-11, 594, 610-13, 636, 741. See also HIBA and for a more detailed treatment of bribery, RASHWA. (C. E. Bosworth)

MARĀGHA, the old capital of Ādharbaydjān.

Position. The town lies in lat. 37° 23' N. and long 46° 15' E. at a height of 5,500 feet above sea-level on the southern slope of Mount Sahand (11,800 feet high) which separates it from Tabrīz [*q.v.*]. This explains the very considerable difference in climate between the two towns, which are only 50 miles apar as the crow flies (by the high road 80 miles). Th climate of Marāgha is mild and rather moist (Ḥam Allāh and Mecquenem, 1904). The plentiful wate supply makes the vegetation rich. The fruit o Marāgha is celebrated in Persia and a good deal of i is exported to Russia via Ardabīl. The district i watered by the stream which comes down from th Sahand and then turns west to Lake Urmiya which i 20 miles from Marāgha. The town is built on the lef bank of the river Ṣāfī (Sofi)-čay which then water Bināb. A little distance to the east runs the paralle river Murdi-čay which waters the district to whicl Mecquenem gives the name Pahindur (Bayandur?) on the left bank rise the heights of Mandīlsar (= "with head bound"). The next stream is the Laylā which flows into the Djaghatu [cf. SĀWDJ-BULĀḲ]. Th rivers farther east (Ḳaranghu and its sources, whicl water the Hashtarūd district) belong to the system o the Safīd-rūd [*q.v.*], i.e. the basin of the Caspian Sea

From the geographical point of view, Marāgha i quite independent of Tabrīz. It lies a little off the grea road from Tabrīz to Kirmānshāh which runs neare Lake Urmiya (via Bināb). The direct bridle-patl Tabrīz-Marāgha by the passes of the Sahand is onl practicable in summer. There is also a direct rout along the Sahand on the south and southeast side joining Marāgha to Ardabīl and Zandjān. This roa has always been of importance whenever Marāgh was the capital of Ādharbāydjān. The important plac on the route was Kūlsara (cf. below).

At the beginning of the 19th century, Marāgha ha 6,000 families (*Bustān al-siyāḥat*); in 1298/1880 it ha 13,259 inhabitants, of whom 6,865 were men an 6,394 women (H. Schindler). Mecquenem (1904 gives Marāgha 15-20,000 inhabitants.

At the present day, the inhabitants speak Ādhär Turkish, but in the 14th century they still spok "arabicised Pahlawī" (*Nuzhat al-ḳulūb*: *pahlawi-y muᶜarrab*) which means an Iranian dialect of the north western group.

The walls of the town are in ruins. Its gates have th following names: Aḥmadī, Kūra-Khāna, Aḳdash Pul-i Bināb (or Gilaslik) and Ḥādjdj-Mīrzā. Th quarters are: Agha-Beg, Maydān, Darwāza an Sālār-Khāna.

Prehistory. The valley of the Murdi-čay i famous for its deposits of fossil vertebrates discovere by Khanikov in 1852. Excavations have bee conducted by Goebel (Russia), Straus, Rodler, Pohli (Austria), Günter (England) and Mecquenen (France). On the Murdi-čay have been found remain of the hipparion, of the rhinoceros, etc., dating fron the period before the eruption of the volcano o Sahand. Cf. J.F. Brandt, *Über die von A. Goebel .... be der Stadt Maragha gefundenen Säugethierreste*, in *Denkschr d. Naturforscher-Vereins zu Riga* (1870), and th bibliography in Mecquenem, *Contribution à l'étude d gisement des vertébrés de Maragha*, 1908; cf. another arti cle of the same author and title in *Annales de paléon tologie* (1924), 133-60.

The name. According to al-Balādhurī, the tow was at first called Aḳrā-rūdh (Ibn al-Faḳīh, 284 Afrah-rūdh; Yāḳūt, iv, 476: Afrazah-rūdh). Thi name which means in Persian the "river of * Afrāh' recalls very much the name of the town τὰ Φράατ which Mark Antony besieged in this region on hi campaign against the Parthians in 36 B.C. (Plutarch *Vita Antonii*, ch. xxxviii, Paris 1864, 1113, and Pseud Appian, *Parthica*, ed. Sweighäuser, Leipzig 1785, iii 77, 99). It has long been supposed that the names c Οὔερα in Strabo xi, ch. xiii, and Index, 935, Φαράσπα

Ptolemy, vi, ch. ii, τοῖς Πραάσποις, Dio Cass., xlix, 25, are variants of the same name, which was probably that of the ancient capital of Atropatene; cf. Ritter, *Erdkunde*, ix, 770. If the identification of Γάζακα (summer capital, Strabo) with Tak̲h̲t-i Sulaymān suggested by Rawlinson has been accepted (cf. Hoffmann, *Auszüge aus syrischen Akten*, 252; Marquart, *Ērānšahr*, 108; A.V. Williams Jackson, *Persia, past and present*, 136), the identification of Θράατα is still uncertain. On general principles, it is improbable that a town like Marāg̲h̲a so advantageously situated by nature was not in existence in Roman times, as the ancient name of Marāg̲h̲a increases the probability of the identification Φράατα = Marāg̲h̲a (of course with a reservation as to the exact site of the ancient town).

A place-name Marāg̲h̲a is mentioned in Arabia (Yāḳūt) and a little town of the same name is in Egypt near Ṭanṭā. The etymology "place where an animal rolls" (from *m-r-g̲h̲*) proposed itself to the Arabs here, but in Ād̲h̲arbāyd̲j̲ān (cf. also the village of Marāg̲h̲a near Abarkūh, *Nuzhat al-ḳulūb*, 122) the name is rather a popular Arab etymology of some local name. It is to be observed that Ptolemy, vi, ch. 2, calls Lake Urmiya Margiane (μέχρι τῆς Μαργιανῆς λίμνης) and gives the same name to the country along the coast of Assyria. Lastly, Marquart in *Ērānšahr*, 143, 221, 313, retains the variant Μαρτιανή, but Μαργιανή seems also to be based on a good tradition (cf. Ptolemy, ed. Wilberg, 1838, 391).

The Arabs. Marāg̲h̲a must have been among the towns of Ād̲h̲arbāyd̲j̲ān conquered by al-Mug̲h̲īra b. S̲h̲uʿba al-T̲h̲aḳafī in the year 22 (al-Balād̲h̲urī, 325; al-Yaʿḳūbī, *Buldān*, 271). Marwān b. Muḥammad returning from his expedition to Mūḳān and Gīlān in 123/740 (cf. al-Yaʿḳūbī, *Historiae*, ii, 365) stopped here. As the place was full of dung (*sird̲j̲īn* < Pers. *sirgīn*) the old village (*ḳarya*) was given the name of Marāg̲h̲a (cf. above). Marwān did some building there. The town later passed to the daughters of Hārūn al-Ras̲h̲īd. On the rebellion of Wad̲j̲nāʾ b. Rawwād, lord of Tabrīz [*q.v.*], K̲h̲uzayma b. K̲h̲āzim, who was appointed governor of Ād̲h̲arbāyd̲j̲ān and Armenia (probably in 187/803, cf. R. Vasmer, *K̲h̲ronologia namestnikov Armenii*, in *Zap. Kolleg. Vostokovedov* [1925], i, 397), built walls round Marāg̲h̲a and put a garrison in it. When Bābak rebelled in 201/816-17, the people sought refuge in Marāg̲h̲a. Al-Maʾmūn sent men to restore the walls and the suburb (*rabaḍ*) became inhabited again (al-Balād̲h̲urī, *loc. cit.*). In 221/836 Marāg̲h̲a is mentioned as the winter quarters of Afs̲h̲īn in his campaign against Bābak (al-Ṭabarī, iii, 1186).

In 280/893 the Sād̲j̲id Muḥammad Afs̲h̲īn b. Dīwdād seized Marāg̲h̲a from a certain ʿAbd Allāh b. Ḥusayn, who was killed (al-Ṭabarī, iii, 2137; al-Masʿūdī, *Murūd̲j̲*, viii, 143 = § 3281). In 296/908 the caliph confirmed Yūsuf b. Dīwdād in possession of Marāg̲h̲a and the whole of Ād̲h̲arbāyd̲j̲ān. A *dirham* is known of this year struck by Yūsuf at Marāg̲h̲a (Vasmer, *O monetak̲h̲ Sadjidov*, Bākū 1927, 14). According to Ibn Ḥawḳal, 238, there was at Marāg̲h̲a a military camp (*muʿaskar*), a governor's palace (*dār al-imāra*), a treasury (*k̲h̲izāna*) and government offices (*dawāwīn al-nāḥiya*), but Yūsuf razed the walls of Marāg̲h̲a and transferred the capital to Ardabīl (cf. al-Iṣṭak̲h̲rī, 181). Marāg̲h̲a is only mentioned as the place where the last Sād̲j̲id Abu 'l-Musāfir al-Fatḥ was killed in 317/929 (ʿArīb, *Ṭabarī continuatus*, ed. de Goeje, 145).

The Daylamīs. In 332/943 (during the rule of the Daylamī Musāfirids) the Russians (Rūs) had taken Bard̲h̲aʿa [*q.v.*]. Ibn Miskawayh (GMS, vi, 100) speaks of the diseases which decimated them because they ate too much fruit in Marāg̲h̲a. This reference to Marāg̲h̲a is quite unexpected in the text, and Margoliouth has rightly proposed to read برذعة in place of مراغة. A coin struck at Marāg̲h̲a in 337/948-9 by Muḥammad b. ʿAbd al-Razzāḳ is a record of the brief conquest of Ād̲h̲arbāyd̲j̲ān by the general of the Būyid Rukn al-Dawla (Vasmer, *Zur Chronologie d. Ǧastāniden*, in *Islamica*, iii/2 [1927], 170). Of 347/958 we also have *dirhams* of Marāg̲h̲a in the names of the two sons of the Daylamī Marzubān, Ibrāhīm and D̲j̲astān (*ibid.*, 172).

The Rawwādīs and the Sald̲j̲ūks. After the disappearance of the Daylamīs, we find in Tabrīz the family of Rawwādī Kurds who seem to have been related to the Musāfarids by marriage only. On the other hand, it is very likely that the Rawwạdīs are the descendants of the Arab al-Rawwād al-Azdī, lord of Ād̲h̲arbāyd̲j̲ān (al-Balād̲h̲urī, 331) who became assimilated by their neighbours in Ād̲h̲arbāyd̲j̲ān. The best-known of these Rawwādīs is Wahsūdān b. Mamlān (= Muḥammad; the change of *d* to *l* in Kurdish is common) who is mentioned between 420/1029 and 446/1054 (Ibn al-At̲h̲īr, ix, 279, 351, 410), and who in addition to Tabrīz possessed other strongholds in the mountains (Sahand). When in 420/1029 the G̲h̲uzz reached Marāg̲h̲a and executed there a great number of Had̲h̲bānī Kurds, the latter united under Wahsūdān and drove out the G̲h̲uzz (Ibn al-At̲h̲īr, ix, 270-2). This incident shows that the district of Marāg̲h̲a was within the sphere of influence of Wahsūdān. In 446/1054 Wahsūdān became a vassal of the Sald̲j̲ūks, but Ibn al-At̲h̲īr, ix, 410, says nothing about the extent of his possessions around Sahand.

In 497/1104 the peace between the sons of Malik-S̲h̲āh, Barkiyaruḳ and Muḥammad, was signed near Marāg̲h̲a, and in 498/1105 Muḥammad visited Marāg̲h̲a.

The Aḥmadīlīs. In 505/1111-12 we have for the first time mention of the Āmīr Aḥmadīl b. Ibrāhīm b. Wahsūdān al-Rawwādī al-Kurdī, lord of Marāg̲h̲a and Kūtab (Kūlsara?) (Ibn al-At̲h̲īr, x, 361). He was the founder of a little local dynasty, which lasted till about 624/1227. We know very little of the history of the Aḥmadīlīs [*q.v.*], which has never been closely studied.

Aḥmadīl was certainly the grandson of Wahsūdān b. Mamlān of Tabrīz (cf. above), and this explains the insistence with which the Atābegs of Marāg̲h̲a tried to retake Tabrīz. Only imprescriptible hereditary rights can explain the strange fact of the presence of a Kurd among the *amīrs* of the Sald̲j̲ūḳs. The name Aḥmadīl is a peculiar formation; the name of Maḥmadīl, a village to the south of Marāg̲h̲a, belongs to the same category of diminutives. The Aḥmadīls, however, very soon adopted Turkisch names.

Aḥmadīl with a large army took part in the Counter-Crusade of 505/1111-12. During the siege of Tell Bās̲h̲ir, Joscelin came to terms with him (*taṭāraḥa*) and he withdrew from the town (Kamāl al-Dīn, *Taʾrīk̲h̲ Ḥalab*, in *Rec. des hist. des croisades*, iii, 599). Aḥmadīl soon abandoned Syria entirely, for he coveted the lands of the S̲h̲āh-i Arman Sukmān who had just died. We know that Sukmān had extended his sway over Tabrīz, and the reference is probably to this town. According to Sibṭ b. al-D̲j̲awzī, in *ibid.*, 556, Aḥmadīl had 5,000 horsemen and the revenues from his fiefs amounted to 400,000 *dīnārs* a year. In 510/1116-17 (or 508/1114-15) Aḥmadīl was stabbed in Bag̲h̲dād by the Ismāʿīlīs, to whom he had done much injury (*ibid.*, 556; Ibn al-At̲h̲īr, x, 361).

Aḳ-Sunḳur I. In 514/1120 Malik Masʿūd, governor of Mawṣil and Ādharbāydjān, rebelled against his brother Maḥmūd and gave Marāgha to his Atābeg Ḳasīm al-Dawla al-Bursuḳī, but the rebellion collapsed and in 516/1122 Aḳ-Sunḳur al-Aḥmadīlī (client of Aḥmadīl?), lord of Marāgha, who was in Baghdād, was authorised by Sultan Maḥmud to return to his fief. As the *amīr* Kün-toghdï, Atābeg of Malik Ṭughrïl (lord of Arrān; Ibn al-Athīr, x, 399), had died in 515/1121, Aḳ-Sunḳur expected to get his place with Ṭughrïl. The latter ordered Aḳ-Sunḳur to raise 10,000 men in Marāgha and set out with him to conquer Ardabīl, in which enterprise, however, they failed. In the meanwhile, Marāgha was occupied by Djuyūsh Beg, sent by Sultan Maḥmūd. The Georgian Chronicle (Brosset, i, 368) mentions under 516/1123 the defeat of Aḳ-Sunḳur (whom he calls "Aghsunthul, Atābeg of Ran" = Arrān) during a demonstration against the Georgians carried out by Ṭughrïl from Shīrwān. In 522/1128, Aḳ-Sunḳur took a part, but not a very active one, in the suppression of the intrigues of the Mazyādid Dubays [see MAZYADIDS]. In 524/1130 he was one of the promoters of the election of Sultan Dāwūd, whose Atābeg he was. In 526/1132 Ṭughrïl, uncle of Dāwūd, defeated the latter and occupied Marāgha and Tabrīz (al-Bundārī, ed. Houtsma, 161). Dāwūd, along with his uncle Masʿūd and Aḳ-Sunḳur, sought refuge in Baghdād. With the support of the caliph and the assistance of Aḳ-Sunḳur, Masʿūd reoccupied Ādharbāydjān. After the capture of Hamadān, Aḳ-Sunḳur was killed there by the Ismāʿīlīs (527/1133), instigated by Ṭughrïl's vizier (al-Bundārī, 169).

Aḳ-Sunḳur II. The name of Aḳ-Sunḳur's son is transmitted in different forms. Ibn al-Athīr, xi, 166, 177, calls him, Aḳ-Sunḳur (II); cf. also *Taʾrīkh guzīda*, 472. Al-Bundārī, 231, calls him al-Amīr al-Kabīr Nuṣrat al-Dīn Khāṣṣbek and, 243, Nuṣrat al-Dīn Arslān Āba (cf. al-Kāshghari, *Dīwān lughat al-Turk*, i, 80). The *Rāḥat al-ṣudūr*, 241, 244, 262, gives him the name of Atābeg Arslān Āba. Al-Bundārī treats him as an equal of the great *amīr* Ildeñiz [*q.v.*], whose family finally triumphed over the lords of Marāgha. Aḳ-Sunḳur II's adversary was the *amir* Khāṣṣbek b. Palang-eri (?), who was the favourite of Sultan Masʿūd and sought to establish himself in Arrān and Ādharbaydjān. This Khāṣṣbek had besieged Marāgha in 541/1146-7 (al-Bundārī, 217). In 545/1150-1 Sultan Masʿūd took Marāgha and destroyed its walls (*bāra*), but a reconciliation later took place between Khāṣṣbek and Aḳ-Sunḳur II under the walls of Rūyīn-diz (cf. below). The execution of Khāṣṣbek in 547/1153 by Sultan Muḥammad alienated Ildeñiz and Aḳ-Sunḳur II and they installed Sulaymān on the throne of Hamadān. Muḥammad on his return to power sent an embassy to restore good relations with the two lords of Ādharbāydjān (*ṣāḥibay Ā.*). Peace was concluded in 549/1154, and the two great *amīrs* shared Ādharbāydjān between them (al-Bundārī, 243). On his deathbed (554/1159), Muḥammad entrusted his young son Malik Dāwūd, (cf. the genealogical tree in the *Rāḥat al-ṣudūr*) to Aḳ-Sunḳur. As Ildeñiz was furthering the interests of his ward Sultan Arslān, Pahlawān b. Ildeñiz advanced against Aḳ-Sunḳur II, but the latter with the help of Shāh-i Arman defeated him on the Safīd-rūd. In 556/1161 Aḳ-Sunḳur sent 5,000 men to the help of the governor of Ray, İnandj, who was fighting Ildeñiz. The latter gained the upper hand, and in 557/1162 Aḳ-Sunḳur II took part in the expedition of Ildeñiz against the Georgians (Ibn al-Athīr, xi, 189). In 563/1168, however, Aḳ-Sunḳur II obtained recognition for his ward from Baghdād. Pahlawān b. Ildeñiz at once besieged Aḳ-Sunḳur in Marāgha (*ibid.*, 218), but a peace put an end to hostilities.

In 564/1168-9, the *amīr* of Ray, İnandj, was killed (Ibn al-Athīr, xi, 230). The *Taʾrīkh-i guzīda*, 72, seems to suggest that the rebellion in Marāgha of Ḳutlugh (?), brother of Aḳ-Sunḳur (II?), was due to İnandj's influence. He was punished by the Atābeg Pahlawān b. Ildeñiz, and Marāgha was given to his brothers ʿAlāʾ al-Dīn and Rukn al-Dīn.

Under 570/1174-5, Ibn al-Athīr (xi, 280) mentions at Marāgha Falak al-Dīn, son of Ibn Aḳ-Sunḳur (i.e. son of Aḳ-Sunḳur II), to whom his father had bequeathed his estates. Pahlawān besieged the fortress of Rūyīn-diz and Marāgha. On this occasion, peace was concluded on the cession of Tabrīz to the family of Ildeñiz. This important detail shows that down to 570 the fief of the Aḥmadīlīs comprised all the country round Mount Sahand, including Tabrīz.

In 602/1205-6 the lord of Marāgha ʿAlāʾ al-Dīn came to an agreement with the Atābeg of Arbīl, Muẓaffar al-Dīn Gök-büri, to deprive the Ildeñizid Abū Bakr of Ādharbāydjān of power, on the pretext that he was incapable of ruling. From Marāgha they marched on Tabrīz, but Abū Bakr called to his aid the former slave of his family Ay-doghmïsh (cf. Defrémery, *Recherches sur quatre princes d'Hamadan*, in *JA* [1847], i, 160). Gökbüri returned to his own lands and Abū Bakr with Ay-doghmïsh came to Marāgha. ʿAlāʾ al-Dīn had to surrender the fortress which was the bone of contention, but was given in compensation the towns of Urmiya and Ushnū. In 604/1207-8 ʿAlāʾ al-Dīn, whom Ibn al-Athīr, xii, 157, 182, here calls Ḳara-Sunḳur, died and left one son, a minor. A brave servant of ʿAlāʾ al-Dīn assumed the guardianship of the child, but the latter died in 605/1208-9. Abū Bakr then took possession of all the lands of the Aḥmadīlīs except Rūyīn-diz, where the servant already mentioned had entrenched himself with his late master's treasures.

It is not clear if ʿAlāʾ al-Dīn Ḳara-Sunḳur is identical with the brother of Aḳ-Sunḳur II mentioned in 564/1168-9. For the date of his accession and his importance we have a hint. According to the preface of the *Haft-paykar* of Niẓāmī [*q.v.*], this poem (finished in 593/1197) was composed at the request of ʿAlāʾ al-Dīn K.r.b (?) Arslān (the Rūm and the Rūs paid him tribute [*kharādj*]; the Georgians suffered reverses at his hands). This *mamdūḥ* was definitely identified by Rieu, *Catalogue*, ii, 567 and *Supplement*, 1895, 154, with ʿAlāʾ al-Dīn of Marāgha. Niẓāmī mentions two sons of ʿAlāʾ al-Dīn, Nuṣrat al-Dīn Muḥammad and Aḥmad; but to reconcile this with Ibn al-Athīr we should have to suppose that both died before their father.

The family of the Aḥmadīlīs was continued for some time in the female line. In 618/1221 the Mongols arrived before Marāgha, and the town was stormed on 4 Ṣafar/30 March. The Mongols sacked and burned the town and massacred the inhabitants (*ibid.*, xii, 246, 263), but the lady of Marāgha (daughter of ʿAlāʾ al-Dīn?), who lived in Rūyīn-diz escaped the catastrophe.

Djalāl al-Dīn. In 622/1225, the Khʷārazmshāh Djalāl al-Dīn came to Marāgha via Daḳūḳā. He entered it without difficulty, for the inhabitants were complaining of all kinds of oppressions and raids by the Georgians (Nasawī, *Sīrat Djalāl al-Dīn*, ed. Houdas, 110). Djalāl al-Dīn tried to restore the prosperity of Marāgha; cf. Ibn al-Athīr, xii, 280, 282.

In 624/1227, while Djalāl al-Dīn was in Persian ʿIrāḳ, his vizier Sharaf al-Mulk was forced to reconquer Ādharbāydjān. In the course of his campaign he besieged Rūyīn-diz, the lady of which was a granddaughter (*min ḥafadāt*) of the Atābeg ʿAlāʾ al-Dīn Karāba (?) (Nasawī, 129). This princess was married to the deaf-mute Khamūsh, only son of the Ildeñizid Özbek. The Atābeg Nuṣrat al-Dīn, son of Khamūsh, mentioned incidentally by Djuwaynī, *GMS*, ii, 242, must have been his son. As a way out, she offered her hand to Sharaf al-Mulk. Djalāl al-Dīn suddenly arrived from ʿIrāḳ and married the princess himself. Rūyīn-diz was given to a certain Saʿd al-Dīn. The citadel contained some thousands of houses (*ulūf min dūr*) occupied by the former inhabitants of the town (*ḳudamāʾ*). Saʿd al-Dīn decided to evacuate them, but as a result of his tactlessness, the fortress closed its gates again (to Saʿd?) (Nasawī, 129, 157). Ibn al-Athīr, xii, 322, seems to deal with the course of these events. Under 627/1230 he says that the troops of Djalāl al-Dīn besieged Rūyīn-diz for some time. The fortress was about to capitulate when some malcontents summoned the assistance of a Turkoman *amīr* Sewindj (Ṣwndj) of the tribe of Ḳush-yalwa. The domination of this chief and his relatives who succeeded him only lasted two years.

Rūyīn-diz. This fortress lay "near Marāgha" (Ibn al-Athīr, xii, 322). According to Zakariyyā Ḳazwīnī, who gives a very accurate description of Rūyīn-diz, it was 3 *farsakhs* from Marāgha. Its proverbially impregnable position (*ḍuriba bi-ḥiṣānatiha al-mathal*) suggests that is was built on the side of Sahand. The Russian map marks on the Sofiča 10 miles (*ca.* 3 *farsakhs*) above Marāgha a place called Yay-shähär (in Turkish = "summer town") besides which two streams flow into the Sofi-ča (on the left bank) and between them is written the corrupted name "Res or Eris". It is very probable that this is the site of the famous fortress, on either side of which there was a stream (*nahr*); for *Res* one should read *Dez*, i.e. Rūyīn-diz. The date of the final destruction of Rūyīn-diz unknown. As late as 751/1350 the Čobanid Ashraf imprisoned his vizier there (von Hammer, *Geschichte der Ilchane*, ii, 337) but the *Nuzhat al-ḳulūb*, in 740/1340, only knows the other Rūyīn-diz, that of Sawalān (there is still a Rūyīn-dizak 4 *farsakhs* north-east of Ardabīl).

Kūlsara. Ibn al-Athīr, x, 340, calls Aḥmadīl "lord of Marāgha and of Kūtab". This last name (كوتب) seems to be a corruption of Kūlsara (كولسره) or Kūsara, a little town well-known to the Arab geographers on the Marāgha-Ardabīl road (10-12 *farsakhs* from Marāgha and 20-7 from Ardabīl); cf. Ibn Khurradādhbih, 120; Ḳudāma, 213; al-Iṣṭakhrī, 194; Ibn Ḥawḳal, 252, in particular from his own experience talks of the importance of Kūlsara and its flourishing commerce. This place may correspond to the village of Kül-täpä "hill of cinders" (polular Turkish etymology) which lies on the Ḳaranghu about 35 miles (ca. 10 *farsakhs*) east of Marāgha. The fort of Ḳalʿa-yi Zohāk, notable ruins of which were discovered by Monteith, *ca.* 15 miles below Kül-täpä (cf. Morier , *op. cit.*, 296), must have been a bulwark for Kūlsara and Marāgha against invasion from the northeast. Rawlinson, in *JRGS* (1841), 120, saw a Sāsānid fortress in Ḳalʿa-yi Zohāk.

The Mongols. Marāgha was definitely taken by the Mongols in 628/1231 (Ibn al-Athīr, xii, 324). After the taking of Baghdād in 656/1258, Hülegü took up his quarters in Marāgha and ordered an observatory to be built there from the plans of Naṣīr al-Dīn Ṭūsī (who had as advisers four astronomers, one of whom, Fakhr al-Dīn, was a native of Marāgha) (Rashīd al-Dīn, ed. Quatremère, 324). The observatory was built on a fortified hill to the west of the town, where only traces of foundation of the walls are still to be seen. According to Schindler's plan (1883), the levelled area on the hill measures 137 x 347 metres. On the observatory, cf. Jourdan, *Mémoire sur les instruments employés à l'observatoire de Maragah*, in the *Magasin encyclop, rédigé par A. L. Millin*, Paris 1809, vi, 43-101 (tr. of an Arabic *risāla* belonging to the Bibl. Nationale and attributed to Naṣīr al-Dīn's colleague Muʾayyid al-Dīn al-ʿArḍī); Ritter, *Erdkunde*, ix, 839-43; D. Wilber, *The architecture of Islamic Iran. The Il Khānid period*, Princeton 1955, 107-8, no. 9. To contain his treasures, Hülegü built a castle on the island of Shāhī, 1-2 days distant from the capital. Here he was buried. On the fortifications of Shāhī, cf. al-Tabarī, iii, 1171. The handsome sepulchral towers, of which there are four at Marāgha (Mecquenem, 1908), date from Hülegü or his immediate successors: (1) the one at the entrance to the bridge of Ṣāfī-čay is built of red brick on a square foundation and with a vaulted cellar (*Gunbad-i ḳirmiz*?); (2) a similar one, situated in the gardens to the south of the town on the road from Khānägä; (3) and (4) near the old cemetery in the interior of the town, the octagonal tower (3) being of red brick overlaid with blue enamelled faience (*Gunbad-i kābūd*), and (4) being round, covered with plaster which is decorated with arabesques (*Ḳoy-burdj* "Tower of the Ram"). There is a photograph of (1) in de Morgan (1894), 337, and Sarre, *op. cit.*, text, 15-16; of (3) in Sarre, *ibid.*, and of (4) in the Morgan, *ibid.*, 340. According to Sarre, (4) is later than 751/1350. The monuments require to be again studied on the spot. Lehmann-Haupt says that inscriptions can still be seen in their interiors. See now on the Gunbad-i Ghaffāriyya, apparently the tomb of Shams al-Dīn Ḳara-Sunḳur, governor of Ādharbāydjān under Abū Saʿīd, A Godard, *Les monuments de Marāgha*, Paris 1934; idem, *Notes complémentaires*, in *Athār-é Īrān*, i/l (1936), 125-60; and Wilber, *op. cit.*, 171-2, 175-6, nos. 78, 82.

The early Mongol Īlkhāns led a semi-nomadic life, which explains the absence from Marāgha of any other kind of memorial. It was only with Ghazan that a regular capital was built at Tabrīz. Marāgha continued to be of some importance on account of its pastures, and was a station on the road between Ādharbāydjān and Mesopotamia. Its name continually appears in the history of the ʿIlkhāns. In 703/1304 Öldjeytü received at Marāgha the ambassadors from the Ḳāʾān of China and installed at the observatory the son of Naṣīr al-Dīn Ṭūṣī.

In 712/1312 Ḳara-Sunḳur, *amīr al-umarāʾ* of Aleppo, fearing the wrath of the sultan of Egypt al-Nāṣir Muḥammad, sought an asylum in Persia with Öldjeytü, who gave him Marāgha. Ibn Baṭṭūṭa, who tells this (i, 179), adds that this town was known as "Little Damascus" (*Dimishḳ al-ṣaghīra*). Ḳara-Sunḳur died in 728/1328 (d'Ohsson, *Hist. des Mongols*, iv, 699).

The geographers of the Mongol period. Zakariyyā Ḳazwīnī (673/1275) seems to be personally acquainted with the town. According to him, there were in the town memorials of the pre-Islamic period. He describes the mineral springs (near the village of Ḳiyāmatābād) and a cave which must correspond to the Čay-bāghī visited by Morier, Lehmann-Haupt, Minorsky, etc. Ḳazwīni also mentions the mountain of Zandjaḳān with a calcareous spring, the village of Djnbdḳ (Gunbadak) with a bottomless well (350) and gives a description of Rūyīn-diz (358).

The *Nuzhat al-ḳulūb* (written in 740/1340), ed. Le Strange, 27, estimates the revenues of Marāgha paid to the treasury at 70,000 *dīnārs* (Ardabīl paid 85,000) and those of its *wilāyat* at 185,000 *dīnārs*. The *tuman* of Marāgha comprised all the southern part of Ādharbāydjān; in the north it was bounded by the *tuman* of Tabrīz, in the west by that of Khoy (Urmiya), in the south by the lands of Kurdistān (Dīnawar) and in the east by ʿIrāḳ-i ʿAdjam (Zandjān, Sudjās). All the lands now under the modern Sāwdj-Bulāḳ or Mahābād [*q.vv.*] were then ruled from Marāgha. As dependencies of Marāgha, Ḥamd Allāh gives the towns of Dih-i Khʷāraḳān (in popular Turkish, Tukhorghan) to the south of Tabrīz, Laylān on the right bank tributary of the Djaghatu (cf. Rawlinson, 1841, 39: the ruins of Ḳalʿa-yi Bākhta) and Paswē in Lāhidjān, in the valley of the Tigris [cf. SĀWDJ-BULĀḲ]. The *tuman* comprised six cantons (the names are much mutilated): Sarādjūn (?): Niyādjūn (?); Dūzakhrūd (? cf. the mountain Dūzakh on the middle course of the Djaghatu); Gāwdūk (at the confluence of the river of Laylān with the Djaghatu (the name is also read Gāwdūl, Gāwdawān. It is remarkable that Firdawsī (ed. Mohl, vii, 141, 151) mentions in these regions a Dash-i Dūk and Kūh-i Dūk where Bahrām Čūbīn was defeated by Khusraw); Bīhistān (probably the district of Bāhī on the Tatawu); and Hashtarūd (to the east of Sahand on the Karanghu). The district of Angūrān on the Ḳizil-üzen was also a dependency of Marāgha.

Christianity at Marāgha. In the Mongol period, Marāgha had become an important centre of Christianity. The celebrated Mār Bar Hebraeus [see IBN AL-ʿIBRĪ] (Jacobite *Maphrian*) lectured in 1268 on Euclid and in 1272 on Ptolemy in the "new monastery" of Marāgha; there he wrote the *Kitāb al-Duwal*. When he died on 30 July 1286, as a sign of mourning the Greeks, Armenians and Nestorians closed their shops in the market-place (Assemani, *Bibl. Orientalis*, ii, 266; Wright, *A short history of Syriac literature*, Oxford 1894, 267, 271, 276, 279). The history of Mār Yahbalāhā III (patriarch of the Nestorians [1281-1317], tr. Chabot, Paris 1895) contains valuable notes on Marāgha. Yahbalāhā rebuilt the already existing church of Mār Shalīṭā and built a house beside it. In 1289 Arghūn had his son baptised in Marāgha. In 1294 the patriarch laid the foundations of the monastery of John the Baptist two-thirds of a *farsakh* north of Marāgha. After the accession of Ghazan (694/1295), the persecution of the Christians began, instigated by the *amīr* Nawrūz. The mob plundered the residence of the patriarch and the church of St. George built by the monk Rabban Ṣawmā (it had been furnished with articles from the portable church of Arghūn's camp). The patriarch sought refuge in the suite of the Armenian king Haiton. On his return to Marāgha, Ghazan punished the formenters of the troubles. In 1298 Yahbalāhā was confirmed in his rights. In September 1301 he finished the monastery of St. John, authorised by Gaykhatu (see Wilber, *op. cit.*, 14). His biographer and contemporary gives an account of the beautiful buildings, the numerous relics and riches of the monastery (Chabot, *op. cit.*, 133). The village of Dahlī (?) to the east of Marāgha was purchased to serve as a *wakf* of the monastery (to the north-east of the town there is still a village of Kilisä-kändi "village of the church"). Ghazan and his successor Öldjeytü visited the monastery. Yahbalāhā died and was buried there in 1317.

On the south side of the hill of the observatory there are chambers carved out of the rock (3 rooms, 12 feet high, communicating with one another, and a corridor). Inside there are niches in the shape of altars. Local tradition sees a church in these (perhaps of the Sāsānid period); cf. Macdonald Kinneir; Houtum-Schindler; Lehmann-Haupt; and Minorsky, in Zvoirao, xxiv (1917), 167.

After the Mongols. In 737/1337 the Djalāyirid Shaykh Ḥasan inflicted a defeat on Tugha-Tīmūr near Marāgha (or at Hashtarūd). The pretender Muḥammad was buried at Marāgha in 738/1337-8 (*Shadjarat al-Atrāk*, 315). Later, the political struggles of the Turkmens had their pricipal arena in the northern part of Ādharbāydjān. In the same period, the Kurdish elements of the districts south of Lake Urmiya became consolidated and received reinforcements from the districts of Mawṣil (*Sharaf-nāma*, i, 288). The Mukrī Kurd *amīrs* extended their influence over Marāgha and even as far as Dih-Khʷāraḳān. The Turks during their rule over Ādharbāydjān included Marāgha with Tabrīz and levied 15 *kharwārs* of gold per annum on it, which caused its inhabitants to go away (*ibid.*, 294). In 1002/1593 the name of the fortress of Saru-ḳurghan (demolished in 795/1393 by Tīmūr; cf. *Ẓafar-nāma*, i, 628 and rebuilt by the Mukrīs) in the regions of Marāgha often occurs in the *Sharaf-nāma*, 294-6; this name recalls that of the Sārūḳ, the right bank tributary of the Djaghatu.

During the second Ottoman occupation (1137/1725), Marāgha was governed by ʿAbd al-ʿAzīz Pasha; this administrative unit consisted of 5 *sandjaks*, of which 2 were hereditary and 3 granted by the government (von Hammer, *GOR*, iv, 228, according to Čelebizāde). In 1142/1729 Nādir defeated the Ottomans at Miyān-dū'āb on the Djaghatu and occupied Dimdim, Sāwdj-bulāḳ, Marāgha and Dih-Khʷāraḳān (Mahdī-Khān, *Taʾrīkh-i Nādirī*, Tabrīz 1284, 66; tr. Jones, i, 104). According to the recently-discovered history of Nādir, the monarch transplanted 3,000 inhabitants from Marāgha to Kalāt (Barthold, in Zvoirao, xxv, 88).

The Muḳaddams. As early as the time of Nādir, the Turkish tribe of Muḳaddam is mentioned as settled in the region of Marāgha (Macdonald Kinneir: 15,000 men). Aḥmad Khān Muḳaddam played a considerable part in the affairs of Ādharbāydjān. Jaubert, *Voyage*, 160, knew him in 1805 as *beglerbegi* of Ādharbāydjān under prince ʿAbbās Mīrzā. In 1810 he exterminated the Bilbās chiefs whom he had invited to Marāgha [see SĀWDJ-BULĀḲ]. According to Morier, *Second journey*, 293, this patriarch was aged 90 in 1815 (cf. Brydges, *Dynasty of the Kajars*, 90). The governor of Marāgha Ṣamad Khān, a partisan of Muḥammad ʿAlī Shāh who besieged Tabrīz in 1909, was of the family of Aḥmad Khān. At the present day, the Muḳaddams are concentrated round Miyān-dūʾāb.

In 1828 Marāgha was occupied by Russian troops. In 1881, the Kurdish invasion by Shaykh ʿUbayd Allāh reached the gates of Marāgha. The town was not taken, but the whole country round was in ruins when Houtum-Schindler visited it in 1882. During the Great War of 1914-18, Marāgha was within the zone of the Russo-Turkish operations [see TABRĪZ].

Marāgha is today a town of 54,106 people (*ca.* 1970 figure) in the province (*ustān*) of Eastern Ādharbāydjān. It is also the centre of a district (*shahrastān*) of the same name which stretches as far west as Lake Urmiya and contains four component sub-districts (*bakhshs*), Huma, ʿAdjabshīr, Bunāb and Malik Kardī, the total population of the *shahrastān* being 252,067. As well as Sunnīs and Shīʿīs, in the main Turkish-speaking, the district also has some ʿAlī-Ilāhīs [see AHL-I ḤAḲḲ], mainly Kurdish; see *Farhang-i djughrāfiyā-yi Īrān*, iv, 489-91, and L. Adamec,

Historical gazetteer of Iran. i. Tehran and north-western Iran, Graz 1976, 434-5.

Bibliography: In addition to the indigenous sources quoted in the text: Samʿānī, *Kitāb al-Ansāb, GMS*, xx, fol. 519a, ed. Hyderabad, xii, 171-5 (he also derives the *nisba* Marāg͟ha from the clan al-Marāg͟h of the tribe of al-Azd); Ḥādjdjī K͟halīfa, *Djihān-nümā*, 389; Ewliyā Čelebi, *Siyāḥat-nāma*, iv, 333 (confused and of doubtful value); Zayn al-ʿĀbidīn, *Bustān al-siyāḥa*, 555; Ḥāfiẓ-i Abrū, *D͟hayl-i Djāmiʿ al-tawārīk͟h*, i, ed. K͟h. Bayānī, Tehran 1317/1938, 95.

The European descriptions of Marāg͟ha (only since the 19th century) are not very numerous and do not exhaust the subject: Macdonald Kinneir, *Geogr. memoir*, London 1813, 155-5; S. Morier, *A second journey*, London 1818, 281-97 (Tabrīz-Marāg͟ha-Gultapa[Kül-täpä?]-Säräskänd); R. Ker Porter, *Travels*, London 1822, ii, 493; Monteith, *Journal of a tour*, in *JRGS* (1833), 4 (Sahand-Säräskänd-Kalʿa-yi Zohak); H. Rawlinson, *A march from Tabrīz*, in *JRGS* (1841), 39 (Miyān-dūʾāb); Ritter, *Erdkunde*, ix, 828-52; G. Hoffmann, *Auszüge aus syrischen Akten*, Leipzig 1880, 248, etc. (important historical and geographical notes); A. Houtum-Schindler, *Reisen im nord-west Persien*, in *Zeitschr. d. Gesell. d. Erdkunde*, Berlin (1883), 334 (cf. the article *Marāg͟ha* in the *Encycl. Britannica*, 11th ed., 1911); J. De Morgan, *Mission scientifique. Études géographiques*, i, Paris 1894, 337-40 (several views); Zugmayer, *Eine Reise d. Vorderasien*, Berlin 1905, 123-8; S.G. Wilson, *Persian life*, London 1890, 71-80; Le Strange, *The lands of the eastern caliphate*, 164-5; R. de Mecquenem, *Le lac d'Ourmiah*, in *Annales de Géogr.* (1908), 128-44; C. Lehmann-Haupt, *Armenien*, i, (1910, 208-16; de Mecquenem, *Contribution à l'étude du gisement des vertébrés de Maragha*, in *Ministère Instr. Publique, Délégation en Perse, Annales d'Histoire naturelle*, i/2, 1908, 1-79 (with a geographical introduction); Ismāʿīl Dībādj, *Bināhā-yi taʾrīk͟hī-yi bāḳīmānda dar Ād͟harbāydjān az dawra-yi Ilk͟hānān-i Mug͟hul*, in *Barrasīhā-yi taʾrīk͟hī*, ii/5, 133-50; idem, *Rāhnamā-yi āt͟hār-i taʾrīk͟hī-yi Ād͟harbāydjān-i s͟harḳī wa Ād͟harbāydjān-i g͟harbī*, Tabrīz 1343/1964, 35-42; M. Dj. Mas͟hkūr, *Naẓarī ba-taʾrīk͟h-i Ād͟harbāydjān wa āt͟hār-i bāstānī wa djamʿiyyat s͟hināsī-yi ān*, Tehran 1349/1970, 19-21; D. Krawulsky, *Īrān, das Reich der Īlhāne, eine topographisch-historische Studie*, Wiesbaden 1978, 536-7.

(V. Minorsky*)

MARAKKAYAR (Tamil corruption of A. *markab* "boat"), an endogamous Tamil-speaking Muslim group of South India located mainly in the coastal districts of Tamil Nadu State in the Indian Union. Major concentrations are found in the districts of Thanjavur, South Arcot, Tiruchi-rapalli and Tirunelveli, particularly in the ports of Nagappattinam, sc. Nagor, Porto Novo, Adirampatnam, Muttupet and Pottalpudar.

No population figures exist, but the Marakkayar probably number under 100,000. They are Sunnīs of the S͟hāfiʿī *mad͟hhab* and read the Ḳurʾān in a Tamil translation written in Arabic characters. Descent is claimed from Arab traders, and certainly Nagappattinam was known to early Arab merchants as Malifattan and was an important port of call en route to the Malay peninsula and Sumatra by the 15th century A.D.

The division between the Labbai [*q.v.*] and the Marakkayar is obscure. In the 19th century, the term was used in Thanjavur district amongst wealthy Labbai shipowners and traders to distinguish them from their poorer co-religionists, and in the 18th century records of the English East India Company similar usage is found particularly for Muslims trading out of ports in the Thanjavur district. As late as the early 20th century the title was freely adopted in Tirunelveli district by Labbais engaged in the rice export trade to Ceylon.

Despite such loose usage, there was by the 19th century a clear division between Labbai and Marakkayar in larger ports such as Nagappattinam. The division was most clearly based on wealth, with the Marakkayar comprising the more prosperous section of the Muslim community and dominating indigenous seaborne trade with Burma, Malaysia, Singapore, Indonesia and Ceylon. The Marakkayar Tamil dialect in Nagapattinam also included a smattering of Arabic words, and socially they followed fewer Hindu practices than the Labbai. In part, the division between Labbai and Marakkayar was probably confirmed by occupational and wealth differentiation which occurred during the 18th century and 19th with wealthy Muslim shipowners and overseas traders separating themselves socially from the larger and poorer Labbai community.

By the mid-19th century the Marakkayar were stereotyped as the wealthiest and most orthodox section of the Tamil Muslim community. Their women were unique in observing *gos͟ha* (*purdah*), intermarriage with other Muslim groups was discouraged, and they deliberately attempted to eliminate Hindu practices from their social and religious life. In the late 19th century, under the influence of north Indian *ʿulamāʾ*, and propagandists from ʿAlīgarh, there was a shortlived movement to abandon Tamil in favour of Urdu.

Despite the tightening of group boundaries in the 19th century, the Marakkayar remain a cosmopolitan community. Communities exist abroad today in Malaysia, Sri Lanka, Singapore and Indonesia, and formerly in Burma. During the 20th century, they have broadened their economic base in southern India to include shopkeeping, hotel development and industrial development.

The most important Marakkayar religious centre, which is shared by other Muslim groups and Hindus, is the nationally-famous tomb of S͟hāh al-Ḥamīd ʿAbd al-Ḳādir (d. 1600), commonly known as Ḳādir Walī or Mīrān Ṣāḥib, at Nagappattinam-Nagore. The tomb was endowed at foundation by the Hindu Raja of Thanjavur, and until the late 19th century it was patronised by the princesses of that family. Similar centres of pilgrimage patronised by the Marakkayar exist at Adirampatnam (the tomb of S͟hayk͟h ʿAlāʾ al-Dīn Ṣāḥib Andavār) and Muttupet.

Bibliography: The first references to Marakkayars are found scattered amongst the voluminous records of the English East India Company. G.A. Herklots, *Islam in India*, London 1832, details the history and practice of the Nagore shrine. E. Sell, *The faith of Islam*, Madras 1880; E. Thurston, *Castes and tribes of Southern India*, Madras 1909, and Kadir Hussain Khan, *South Indian Mussalmans*, Madras 1910, provide the first modern descriptive and anthropological analysis of the group. *The census of India*, xv (1901), xii (1911), xiv (1931), provides details of occupation, distribution and social practices, but no statistics; the records of the Madras Presidency are similar. District Gazetteers provide local information concerning the group: L. Moore, *Trichinopoly*, Madras 1878; T. Venkasami Row, *Tanjore*, Madras 1883; F. R. Hemingway, *Tanjore*, Madras 1906 and Trichinopoly Madras 1907; W.

Francis, *South Arcot*, Madras 1906; and H. R. Pate, *Tinnevelly*, Madras 1917. S. Playne and W. Bond, *Southern India, its history, people, commerce and industrial resources*, London 1914, provides biographical and descriptive data of the groups' economic interests; S. M. Fossil, *The Islamic South*, Madras 1942, provides further biographical details. J. Dupuis, *Madras et le nord du Coromandel*, Paris 1960, details group economic diversification. K. McPherson, *The political development of the Urdu- and Tamil-speaking Muslims of the Madras Presidency, 1901 to 1937*, M.A. thesis, University of Western Australia 1969, unpublished, and idem, *The social background and politics of the Muslims of Tamil Nad, 1901-1937*, in *The Indian Economic and Social History Review*, vi (1969), provide accounts of the group in their regional context. M. Mines, *Muslim merchants*, New Delhi 1972, describes the economic behaviour of Muslim merchants in a changing, industrialising Tamil urban community. (K. McPherson)

MARAND 1. Town in the Persian province of Ādharbāydjān.

Position. The town lies about 40 miles north of Tabrīz, halfway between it and the Araxes or Aras in lat. 38° 25' 30″ N. and 45° 46" E. at an altitude of *ca.* 4,400 feet/1,360m. (it is 42 miles from Marand to Djulfā). The road from Tabrīz to Khoy also branches off at Marand. A shorter road from Tabrīz to Khoy follows the north bank of Lake Urmiya and crosses the Mishowdagh range by the pass between Tasūdj [*q.v.*] and Ḍiyā al-Dīn. Marand, which is surrounded by many gardens, occupies the eastern corner of a rather beautiful plain, about 10 miles broad and sloping slightly to the west. To the south, the Mishow range (western continuation of the Sawalān) separates it from the plain of Tabrīz and from Lake Urmiya. The pass to the south of Marand often mentioned by historians is called Yam (Mongol = "post-station"). The pass between the plain of Marand and Tasūdj takes its name from the village of Waldiyān. To the east of Marand lies the wild and mountainous region of Ḳaradja-dagh (capital: Ahar). To the north, the plain of Marand is separated from the Araxes by a range, a continuation of the central heights of the Ḳaradja-dagh which is crossed by the defile of the Därädiz. The plain of Marand is watered by the river of Zunūz, the southern arm of which called Zilbīr runs quite near Marand. The combined waters of Zunūz and Zilbīr flow into the Ḳotur-čay (an important right-bank tributary of the Araxes) about 20 miles north-east of Khoi. The length of the Zunūz is about 40 miles (Ḥamd Allāh Mustawfī: 8 *farsakhs*).

History. A lofty *tell* which rises besides the town is evidence of the great antiquity of this as an inhabited site; it must have existed in the time of the Vannic (Urartian) and Assyrian kings. Its Greek name Μοροῦνδα is perhaps connected with the people Μαροῦνδαι who, according to Ptolemy, vi, 2, occupied the lands as far as Lake Urmiya. A legend of Armenian origin based on the popular etymology *mair and* "mater ibi" locates in Marand the tomb of Noah's wife (Hübschmann, *Die altarmenischen Ortsnamen*, Leipzig 1904, 346, 415; Ker Porter, *Travels*, i, 217). Moses of Chorene places Marand (ch. 60) in the district of Bakurakert. There was another Marand mentioned by the Armenian historian Orbelian (*ca.* 1300) in the province of Siunikh (north of the Araxes) and a village of Marand still exists east of Tīghnīt in the khānate of Mākū [*q.v.*].

Ibn Baʿīth. After the Arab conquest, a certain Ḥalbas of the tribe of Rabīʿa took Marand. His son Baʿīth, a soldier of fortune (*ṣuʿlūk*) in the service of Ibn al-Rawwād, ruler of Tabrīz, fortified Marand. Muḥammad b. Baʿīth erected castles there (*kuṣūr*) (al-Balādhuri, 330; cf. *Camb. hist. of Iran*, iv, 227). This chief had acquired considerable notoriety. In 200/815 he had taken from the family of Rawwād the strongholds of Shāhī and Tabrīz (al-Ṭabarī, iii, 1171). (In another passage, al-Ṭabarī, iii, 1379, mentions Yakdur [?] in place of Tabrīz). Ibn Baʿīth lived at Shāhī, which stood in the centre of Lake Urmiya (the peninsula of Shāhī, where at a later date the Il-Khānid Hülegü kept his treasure and where he was buried). Ibn Baʿīth was at first on good terms with the Khurramī Bābak [*q.v.*], whose authority must have prevailed in the Ḳaradja-dagh in particular, in the north-eastern corner of which was his residence al-Badhdh [*q.v.* in Suppl.]. Ibn Baʿīth suddenly changed his tactics and seized by a ruse ʿIṣma, one of Babāk's generals, whom he sent to the caliph al-Muʿtaṣim. In 221/836 Ibn Baʿīth accompanied Bughā on his expedition against al-Badhdh (al-Ṭabarī, iii, 1190, 1193). Under the caliphate of al-Mutawakkil, Ibn Baʿīth committed some crime (*khālafa*) and was imprisoned in Sāmarrā or Surra-man-raʾa. On the intercession of Bughā al-Sharābī, 30 people of repute became guarantors of Ibn al-Baʿīth's good behaviour, and he must have been allowed considerable liberty, for in 234/848 he escaped to Marand. Ibn Khurradādhbih, who wrote in 234/848-9, mentions Marand as being Ibn Baʿīth's fief. Al-Ṭabarī, iii, 1379-89, gives a very graphic account of the expedition sent against this town. The wall which enclosed Marand and its gardens was 2 *farsakhs* in circumference. There were springs within it. The dense forest outside was a further protection to the town. Ibn Baʿīth collected 2,200 adventurers who were reinforced by a number of non-Arabs (*ʿulūdj*) armed with slings. He had ballistas constructed to repel the assailants. During the 8 months that the siege lasted, 100 individuals of note (*awliyāʾ al-sulṭān*) were killed and 400 wounded. When Bughā al-Sharābī (al-Balādhuri, 330: Bughā al-Ṣaghīr) arrived, he succeeded in detaching the men of the Rabīʿa tribe from Ibn Baʿīth. Ibn Baʿīth and his relatives were seized and his house and those of his partisans plundered. In Shawwāl of 235/April-May 850, Bughā arrived with 180 prisoners at the caliph's court. Al-Mutawakkil ordered Ibn Baʿith to be beheaded, but the latter recited verses in Arabic and the caliph was astonished by his poetic gifts (*inna maʿahu la-adab^{an}*) and gave him his life. Ibn Baʿīth died in prison and his sons entered the corps of mercenaries (*al-shākiriyya*). According to one of al-Ṭabarī's authorities (iii, 1388), the *shaykhs* of Marāgha who praised the bravery and literary ability (*adab*) of Ibn Baʿīth also quoted his Persian verses (*bi 'l-fārisiyya*). This important passage, already quoted by Barthold, *BSOS*, ii (1923), 836-8, is evidence of the existence of the cultivation of poetry in Persian in northwestern Persia at the beginning of the 9th century. Ibn Baʿīth must have been Iranicised to a considerable extent, and, as has been mentioned, he relied for support on the non-Arab element in his *rustāks* (*ʿulūdj rasātīkihi*).

Later history. The Arab geographers of the 4th/10th century (al-Iṣṭakhrī, 182; Ibn Ḥawḳal, 239; cf. Le Strange, *Lands*, 166-7) mention Marand among the little towns of Ādharbāydjān where the trouser-bands called *tikak* were manufactured. Al-Muḳaddasī, 51, 374, 377, puts Marand under Dabīl and notes its gardens, its flourishing suburb and a cathedral mosque in the centre of the market. The same author, 382, mentions a direct road from Marand to Marāgha (via Nūrīn [?], somewhere west of Tabrīz?). Later,

Marand must have shared the fate of Tabrīz [*q.v.*]. According to Yāḳūt, iv, 503, the town had begun to decline after it was plundered by the Georgians (Kurdj), who carried off its inhabitants. This is valuable confirmation of the Georgian expedition to Persia, a detailed account of which is given in the Georgian Chronicle for 1208-10 (605-7) [see TABRĪZ and AL-KURDJ].

Among the theologians born in Marand, Yāḳūt mentions one who died in 216/831 and another who had studied in Damascus in 433/1041-2. In 624/1226, Marand, which had not sufficient defences, was occupied by the *ḥādjib* ^cAlī al-Ashrafī of Akhlāt. Sharaf al-Mulk, governor for the Kh^wārazmshāh, retook the town and wrought great slaughter in it (Nasawī, ed. Houdas, 166).

The only historical monument in Marand is the old mosque, Saldjūḳ in origin, now in ruins, with a *miḥrāb* in stucco bearing the dates of rebuilding 730/1330 (reign of the Il-Khānid Abū Sa^cīd) and 740/1339 by Kh^wādja Ḥusayn b. Maḥmūd (Cf. Sarre, *Denkmäler persischer Baukunst*, Berlin 1910, 24-5 and pl. xvii; the observations by E. Herzfeld, *Die Gumbadh-i ^cAlawiyyan*, in the *Volume ... presented to E. G. Browne*, Cambridge 1922, 194-5; and D. Wilber, *The architecture of Islamic Iran. The Il Khānid period*, Princeton 1955, 172-3, no. 79. A caravanserai some 8 miles/13 km. to the north of Marand dates from *ca.* 730-5/1330-5 but is known locally as "the caravanserai of Hülegü (Wilber, *op. cit.*, 176-7, no. 85).

Around this time, Ḥamd Allāh Mustawfī describes the excellent fruit and cereals of Marand and mentions that to the south of the town was found the *ḳirmiz* insect (*kermes ilicis*) for crimson dye. There were 60 villages in the district, and the revenues of the town and its dependencies amounted to 24,000 *dirhams*. The walls of the town were 8,000 paces round, but the town itself occupied only half this area (*Nuzhat al-ḳulūb*, 88, tr. 89). In the Tīmūrid period, Marand appears as a mint-town (in 832/1428-9), see E. von Zambaur, *Die Münzpragungen des Islams, zeitlich und örtlich geordnet*, i, Wiesbaden 1968, 238.

Marand is several times mentioned in connection with the Turco-Persian wars. According to Ewliyā Čelebi (in 1647), *Siyāḥat-nāma*, ii, 242, Marand was a hunting-resort of the Tīmūrid Shāhrukh. In spite of the damage done by the invasion of Sulṭān Murād, the town looked prosperous and had 3,000 houses. Ewliyā enumerates a number of celebrated theologians buried north of Marand.

In the autumn of 1724 ^cAbd Allāh Pasha Köprülü sent the Kurdish Khān of Bitlīs Muḥammad ^cĀbid to occupy Marand, the inhabitants of which had fled. Resistance centred round the town of Zunūz (10 miles north of Marand) which had 7,000 (?) houses and a castle called Diza by the Persians. To dispose of the threat to their flank, the Janissaries, before advancing on Tabrīz, fought a battle here in May 1725 with the Persians, of whom a large number were slain. Diza was taken and dismantled (cf. von Hammer, *GOR*², iv, 226, following Čelebi-zāde).

Marand has often been mentioned by European travellers since the time of Hans Chr. von Teufel (1589), cf. the notices by Chardin (ed. 1811, i, 318) and by Ker Porter, Jaubert, Morier, Ouseley and Monteith, of which a résumé is given in Ritter, *Erdkunde*, ix, 907. Marand has recently gained in importance since it lies on the modern high road from Tabrīz to Djulfā built by the Russians in 1906 and replaced by a railway in 1915-16.

In contemporary Iran, Marand comes within the third *ustān* of Ādharbāydjān, and is the centre of a *shahrastān* (1951 pop. 128,762) containing three *bakhshs*; the town itself had a population of almost 14,000 in 1951 and about 24,000 some years later (see Razmārā, *Farhang-i Djughrāfiyā-yi Īrān*, iv, 493; L. Adamec, *Historical gazetteer of Iran. i. Tehran and north-western Iran*, Graz 1976, 435-7).

Bibliography: Given in the article.

2. Town in the district of Khuttal. On this town to the north of the Oxus, cf. al-Muḳaddasī, 49, 290-1. (V. MINORSKY-[C. E. BOSWORTH])

MAR^cASH, a town in the Taurus Mountains region of southern Anatolia, falling within modern Turkey and now the chef-lieu, as Maraş, of the *il* (formerly *vilayet*) of Maraş.

It lies about 2,000 feet/610 m. above sea-level on the northern edge of the hollow (^cAmḳ of Mar^cash; now Čaḳal Owa and south of it Shēker Owa or Mar^cash Owasī) which lies east of the Djayḥān and is watered by its tributary, the Nahr Ḥūrīth (Aḳ-Ṣū). As a result of its situation at the intersection of the roads which run to Anṭākiya, to ^cAyn Zarba and al-Maṣṣīṣa, to Albistān (Abulustain) and Yarpūz, via Göksün (Kokussos) to Ḳaysāriyya, via Behesnī (Bahasnā) to Sumaysāṭ and via al-Ḥadath and Zibaṭra to Malaṭya, Mar^cash was from the earliest times one of the most important centres of traffic in the Syrian frontier region. It is repeatedly mentioned as early as the Assyrian texts as Marḳasi, capital of the kingdom of Gurgum [see DJARĀDJIMA], and several Hittite monuments have been found there (cf. Unger, *Marqasi*, in Ebert's *Reallexik. d. Vorgesch.*, viii, 1927, 48).

1. History up to the Ottoman period. In the Roman imperial period it was called Germanikeia in honour of Caligula (on the coins, Ceasarea Germanikē; cf. Grégoire, in *Rev. de l'instr. publ. en Belg.*, li [1908], 217 ff.). The identity of Germanikeia and Mar^cash is certain from numerous literary, especially Syriac, references. The Armenians probably knew, but probably from learned tradition only, the name Germanik (Kermanig in Vahram; cf. Matthew of Edessa, ed. Dulaurier, 487 below; St. Martin, *Mém. sur l'Arm.*, i, 200). The statement in a description of the district of Ḥalab (B.N. ms. Arab., no. 1683, fol. 72a) that the Armenian name of the town was Nākinūk (Blochet, *ROL*, iii, 525-6, 6) is wrong; this is a mistake for Göynük, a name later given to the neighbouring al-Ḥadath [*q.v.*]. The Emperor Heraclius passed through the town in 626 (Theophanes, *Chron.*, ed., de Boor, 313; Ramsay, in *Classical Review*, x, 140; Gerland, in *Byz. Zeitschrift*, iii [1894], 362). The Emperor Leo III came from Mar^cash (Germanikeia); later authors (like Theophanes, *op. cit.*, 391) wrongly called him the "Isaurian" (a confusion with Germanikopolis; cf. K. Schenk, in *Byz. Zeitschr.*, v [1896], 296-8).

In the year 16/637 Abū ^cUbayda sent Khālid b. al-Walīd from Manbidj against Mar^cash, and the Greek garrison surrendered the fortress on being granted permission to withdraw unmolested; Khālid then destroyed it (Caetani, *Annali dell' Islām*, iii, Milan 1910, 794, 806). Sufyān b. ^cAwf al-Ghāmidī in 30/650-1 set out from Mar^cash against the Byzantines. Mu^cāwiya rebuilt Mar^cāsh and settled soldiers in this "Arab Cayenne" (as Lammens, in *MFOB*, vi [1913], 437 calls it). After Yazīd I's death, the attacks of the Greeks on the town became so severe that the inhabitants abandoned it.

After Muḥammad b. Marwān in 74/693-4 had broken the truce concluded by ^cAbd al-Malik with the Greeks, in Djumādā I of the following year the Greeks set out from Mar^cash against al-A^cmāḳ (= ^cAmḳ of

Antāḳiya; cf. Le Strange, *Palestine under the Moslems*, 391) but were again driven back in the ᶜAmḳ of Marᶜash. Marᶜash was restored by al-ᶜAbbās, son of al-Walīd I, and fortified and repopulated; a large mosque was also built there.

The people of Ḳinnasrīn [*q.v.*] (i.e. probably of the djund of Ḳinnasrīn) had to send troops every year to Marᶜash. During Marwān II's fighting against Ḥimṣ, the Emperor Constantine again besieged Marᶜash, which had finally to capitulate (129/746) and was destroyed (al-Balādhurī, 189; Theophanes, *Chron.*, ed.de Boor,422; Georgios Kedrenos, ed. Bonn, ii, 7). The inhabitants emigrated to Mesopotamia and the *djund* of Ḳinnasrīn. After the capture of Ḥimṣ, Marwān sent troops to Marᶜash, who rebuilt the town in 130/747; the castle in the centre of the town was henceforth called al-Marwānī after him (Yāḳūt, iv, 498-9). But by 137/754 the Greeks again sacked the town. Al-Manṣūr then had it rebuilt by Ṣāliḥ b. ᶜAlī (d. 150/767) and gave it a garrison which al-Mahdī strengthened and supplied with ample munitions (al-Balādhurī, *loc. cit.*; Theoph., *op. cit.*, 445: ὁ Σάλεχ .... μετεποιήθε Γερμανικείαν ἐις Παλαιστίνην). The Arabs in 769 (1080 Sel.) entered the ᶜAmḳ of Marᶜash and deported the inhabitants of the region who were accused of espionage on behalf of the Byzantines, to al-Ramla (Michael the Syrian, *Chron.*, ed. Chabot, ii, 526). According to the Syriac inscription of ᶜEnesh on the Euphrates, in 776-7 A.D. (1088 Sel.) the people of the hollow (*ᶜumkā*) of Marᶜash invaded Asia Minor (Bēth Rhōmāyā) to plunder (Chabot, in *JA*, ser. 9, vol. xvi [1900], 286-7; Pognon, *Inscr. semit. de la Syrie et de la Mésopotamie*, 148-50, no. 84). A Greek army of 100,000 men in 161-2/778-9 under Michael Lachanodrakon besieged Marᶜash, which was defended by ᶜĪsā b. ᶜAlī (Ἰσβααλί in Theophanes, *op. cit.*, 451), grand-uncle of the Caliph al-Mahdī, destroyed al-Ḥadath and laid waste the Syrian frontier (Weil, *Gesch. d. Chalifen*, ii, 98). In 183/799 Hārūn al-Rashīd built the town of al-Hārūniyya near Marᶜash (al-Balādhurī, 171; Yāḳūt, iv, 498, wrongly calls it a suburb of Marᶜash); he also raised the prosperity of Marᶜash and al-Maṣṣīṣa (al-Masᶜūdī, *Murūdj*, viii, 295 = § 3449). The *amīr* Abū Saᶜīd Muḥammad b. Yūsuf in 226/841 invaded Asia Minor; the Greeks drove him back, however, and took al-Ḥadath, Marᶜash and the district of Malaṭya (Michael the Syrian, iii, 102; Weil, *Gesch. d. Chalifen*, ii, 315-16, n. 1, considers this story unhistorical). The emperor Basil I in 877 passed via Κουκουσός (Göksün) and the Taurus passes (στενὰ τοῦ Ταύρου) against Marᶜash (Γερμανίκεια), but could not take it and had to be content with burning and plundering the suburbs; the same thing happened at al-Ḥadath (Ἄδατα; Georgios Kedrenos [Bonn], ii, 214; Theophanes continuatus, ed. Bonn, 280). According to the Περὶ παραδρομῆς πολέμου (*De velitatione bellica*, Migne, Patrol. Graec., cxvii, 1000), shortly before the attack on Germanikeia he crossed the Παράδεισος ποταμός (cf. Pliny, *Nat. Hist.*, v. 93: one of the *intus flumina* of Cilicia, probably the Aḳ-Ṣū, Arabic Nahr Djūrīth or Ḥūrīth; the location by Tomaschek in *SBAḳ Wien*, cxxiv [1891], Abh. viii, 66, is therefore presumably wrong). The Byzantine Andronicus in 292/904-5) invaded the region of Marᶜash, defeated the garrisons of Ṭarsūs and Maṣṣīṣa and destroyed Kūrus (Ibn al-Athīr, vii, 378; al-Ṭabarī, iii, 2298, Weil, *op. cit.*, ii, 533; Vasiliev, *Vizantiya i Arabî*, i, 1902, 154). The Armenian Mleḥ (Arab. Malīḥ) plundered Marᶜash in 916; 50,000 prisoners were carried off from it and Ṭarsūs (Weil, *op. cit.*, ii, 634; Vasilev, *op. cit.*, 203). In the fighting against Sayf al-Dawla, the Greeks under John Kurkuas took Marᶜash in the spring of 337/949 (Kamāl al-Dīn, in Freytag, *ZDMG*, xi, 187; Weil, *op. cit.*, iii, 14, n. 1; Vasiliev, *op. cit.*, 268). In 341/952 the Ḥamdānid defeated the Domestikos at Marᶜash, and in June rebuilt the defences of the town (Freytag, *op. cit.*, 191; Vasiliev, *op. cit.*, 291). When the Ḥamdānid Abu 'l-ᶜAshāʾir in 345/956 was taken prisoner by the Byzantines, his father-in-law Abū Firās followed as far as Marᶜash in the attempts to rescue him, but could not overtake his captors (Dvořák, *Abû Firâs*, Leiden 1895, 31; Vasiliev, *op. cit.*, 297). Nicephorus Phocas in Rabīᶜ I 351/August 962 occupied Marᶜash, Dulūk and Raᶜbān (Freytag, *op. cit.*, 199; Rosen, in *Zapiski Imp. Akad. Nauk*, xliv, 152, n. 100). Bandjūtakīn in 382/992 carried out a raid on Marᶜash and came back with prisoners and great booty (Freytag, 248; Rosen, 250, 263). The Armenian Philaretos Brachamios (Filardūs al-Rūmī) who in the second half of the 5th/11th century, as a leader of a robber band and ally of the Byzantine emperor, conquered a little kingdom for himself on the Syrian frontier, belonged to the village of Shīrbaz in the district of Marᶜash (Michael the Syrian, iii, 173, 173 n.*).

After the Franks under Godfrey de Bouillon had taken Marᶜash in 490/1097, they installed a bishop there (Michael the Syrians, iii, 191). Bohemund of Antioch was taken prisoner in June 1100 in the *ᶜamḳ* of Marᶜash in the village of Gafinā (*ibid.*, iii, 188) on his campaign against Malaṭya by Gümüshtegīn b. Dānishmand (*Recueil des hist. or des crois.*, iii, 589; Röhricht, *Gesch. des Königr. Jerus.*, 9; Weil, *op. cit.*, iii, 179). The emperor Alexius later sent the general Butumites against Marᶜash (τὸ Μάρασιν) who took the town, fortified the surrounding small towns and villages and gave them garrisons and left Monastras there as ἡγεμῶν (Anna Comnena, *Alexiad*, ed. Reifferscheid, ii, 132, 11 ff; F. Chalandon, *Les Comnène*, i, Paris 1900, 234). The town of Marᶜash was placed under the Armenian prince Thathul, who had distinguished himself in its defence against Bohemund (Matthēos Uṛhayecᶜi, ed. Dulaurier, ch. clxvi, 229-30; Chalandon, *op. cit.*, i, 104-5). But by 1104 he had to abandon it and surrender it to Joscelin de Courtenay, lord of Tell Bāshir (Matthēos, *op. cit.*, 257, ch. clxxxvi; Raoul of Caens, ch. 148; Röhricht, *op. cit.*, 49, n. 8, 52, n. 4). This Thatful is perhaps the same Armenian as had given his daughter in marriage to Godfrey's brother Baldwin (in William of Tyre, x, 1, he is called Tafroc; in Albert of Aix, iii, 31, v, 18: Taphnuz; cf. Chalandon, *op. cit.*, 103). By 1105 Tancred of Antioch seems to have been in possession of Marᶜash (Röhricht, 56), to whom it was allotted in the treaty of September 1108 (ἡ Γερμανίκεια καὶ τὰ ὑπὸ ταύτην πολίχνια: Anna Commena, ed. Reifferscheid, ii, 217; Röhricht, 66). In 1114 the widow of the recently-deceased Armenian prince Kogh Vasil (= "Basil the thief") of Marᶜash submitted to Aḳ Sunḳur of Mawṣil (Weil, *op. cit.*, iii, 199); on 28 Djumādā II 508/27 November 1114, Marᶜash was devastated by a disastrous earthquake in which 40,000 lost their lives (Michael the Syrian, tr. Chabot, iii, 200; *Recueil hist. or. crois,*, iii, 607; Matthēos Uṛhayecᶜi, 289, ch. ccvii). King Baldwin granted a monk named Godfrey (*Goisfridus Monachus*) a fief consisting of Marᶜash, Kaysūm and Raᶜbān (Michael the Syrian, iii, 211; Röhricht, *op. cit.*, 161); in 1124 Godfrey was killed at the siege of Manbidj in the train of Joscelin of Edessa. The Dānishmandid Muḥammad b. Amīr Ghāzī in 531/1136-7 laid waste the villages and monasteries near Marᶜash and Kaysūm (Matthēos, 320, ch. ccliii). The Saldjūḳ sulṭān Masᶜūd in 532/1138 advanced as far as Marʿash, plundering the country as he went (Michael the Syrian, iii, 246) as did Malik Muḥammad of Malaṭya in 535/1141 (*ibid.*, iii, 249) and Ḳilidj Arslan II in 541/1147 ibid., iii, 275). The town then belonged to Raynald, son-in-law of Joscelin II of Edessa, who fell in 1149 at Innib (Röhricht, *op. cit.*, 260). On 5 Djumādā I 544/11 September 1149, Ḳilidj Arslan and his father Masʿūd set out from Albistān against Marʿash, plundered the country around and besieged the town. The Frankish garrison capitulated on being promised a safe retreat to Anṭākiya; but the sultan sent a body of Turks after them, who fell upon them on the road and slew them. On this occasion, all the treasure of the churches of Marʿash was lost, which the priests who had rebelled against the bishop had appropriated (Michael the Syrian, iii, 290; Matthēos Uṛhayecʿi, 330, ch. cclix; Chalandon, *op. cit.*, 421; Röhricht, *op. cit.*, 263). After the capture of Joscelin, Nūr al-Dīn of Ḥalab in 546/1151-2 took a large part of the country of Edessa including the towns of Marʿash, Tell Bāshir, ʿAyntāb, Dulūk, Kūrus, etc. (*Recueil hist. or crois.*, i, 29, 481, ii, 54; Weil, *op. cit.*, iii, 296; Röhricht, *op. cit.*, 265, n. 5). The district was then divided: the sultan received Marʿash, Barzamān, Raʿbān, Kaysūm and Bahasnā; the Arṭuḳid Ḳara Arslan of Ḥiṣn Ziyād got Bābūlā, Gargar, Kʸākhta and Ḥiṣn Mansūr; Nūr al-Dīn kept the rest (Michael the Syrian, iii, 297; William of Tyre, xvii, 16). When Masʿūd's son Ḳilidj Arslan, lord of Marʿash (Michael the Syrian, iii, 318), attacked an Armenian village, the Armenians under Stephan, brother of the prince Thoros, in 1156 revenged themselves by setting Marʿash on fire and carried off the whole population into captivity, during the absence of the sultan and his Turks (*ibid.*, ii, 314 [expanded from Barhebraeus, *Chron. syr.*]; differently in Abū Shāma, *Rec. hist. or. crois*, iv, 92;F. Chalandon, *Les Comnène*, ii, Paris 1912, 434). Among those carried off was the bishop Dionysios bar Ṣalībī, who escaped to the monastery of Kālsiūr (according to Chabot, *loc. cit.*, the κάστρον Καλιζίεριν of Anna Comnena, ed. Reifferscheid, ii, 219) and wrote three *mēmrē* about the devastation of his former diocese of Marʿash (Michael the Syrian, *loc. cit.*; Baumstark, *Gesch. d. syr. Litt.*, 298). Thoros of Little Armenia in 1165 plundered Marʿash (Barhebraeus, *Chron. syr.*, ed. Bedjan, 331; Röhricht, *op. cit.*, 319, n. 8; Chalandon, *op. cit.*, ii, 531, n. 1). Nūr al-Dīn again took Marʿash from Ḳilidj Arslan II when he was on a campaign against the Dānishmandid Dhu 'l-Nūn (Michael the Syrian, iii, 350) in the beginning of Dhu 'l-Ḳaʿda 568/14 June 1173) and Bahasnā in Dhu 'l-Ḥidjdja (*Rec. hist. or. crois.*, i, 43, 592, iv, 158, Matthēos Uṛhayecʿi, ed. Dulaurier, 360; Abu 'l-Fidāʾ, *Annal. musl.*, ed. Reiske, iv, 4; Röhricht, *op. cit.*, 303, who is followed by Chalandon, *Les Comnène*, ii, 463, wrongly puts these events as early as 1159).

Nūr al-Dīn perhaps handed Marʿash over to his ally Mleḥ of Little Armenia. When the dynast of Marʿash raised the district of Raʿbān, al-Malik al-Ẓāhir in 592/1195-6 took the field against him, whereupon the lord of Marʿash sought forgiveness and recognised his suzerainty (Kamāl al-Dīn, tr. Blochet, in *ROI*, iv, 212). The Armenian ruler Rupen III took Bohemund III of Anṭākiya prisoner in 1185 and forced him to cede the territory from the Djayḥān up to Kastūn (Michael the Syrian, ii, 396-7; Röhricht, *op. cit.*, 403, n. 7, 661). Ghiyāth al-Dīn Kay-Khusraw, son of Ḳilidj Arslan II, in 605/1208, when on a campaign against Little Armenia, took Marʿash (Abu 'l-Fidāʾ, *Annal. musl.*, ed. Reiske, iv, 232), and made Ḥusām al-Dīn Ḥasan governor of the town. He was succeeded in this office by his son Ibrāhīm, who in turn was succeeded by his son Nuṣrat al-Dīn, who ruled Marʿash for 50 years. The long reign of his son Muẓaffar al-Dīn was followed by that of his brother ʿImād al-Dīn who however in 656/1258 abandoned the town, which was much harassed by the Armenians and Georgians, after failing to find support either from ʿIzz al-Dīn Kay-Kāwūs of Rūm or al-Malik al-Ṣāliḥ of Egypt. The town then surrendered to the Armenians (Ibn al-Shiḥna, Beirut 1909, 192).

Marʿash did not escape during the great Mongol invasion of Asia Minor. Baybars I of Egypt in his campaign against them in 670/1271 sent from Ḥalab a division under Ṭaybars al-Wazīrī and ʿĪsā b. Muhīn to Marʿash, who drove all the Tatars from there and slew them (*Rec. hist. or. crois.*, ii, 246; al-Maḳrīzī, ed. Quatremère, *Hist. de Sultans Mamlouks*, i/2, 101). In the wars with the rulers of Little Armenia, troops from Ḥalab went as far as Marʿash in 673/1274 and destroyed the gates of the outer town (Weil, *Gesch. d. Chal.*, iv, 7). In the next few years, Baybars negotiated with envoys from Sīs, from whom he demanded the surrender of Marʿash and Bahasnā; but he was satisfied instead with a considerable sum of money (al-Maḳrīzī, *op. cit.*, i/2, 123 [year 673/1274]; ii/l, 104 [688/1289]). It was not till 692/1292 that sultan Khalīl by a treaty received Bahasnā, Marʿash and Tell Ḥamdūn (Mufaḍḍal b. Abi 'l-Faḍāʾil, *Hist. des Sultans Mamlouks*, ed. Blochet, in *Patrol. Orient.*, xiv, 557; Weil, op. cit., iv, 186; S. Lane-Poole, *History of Egypt in the Middle Ages*, London 1901, 287). But the Armenians must have retaken the two last-named towns not long afterwards (Weil, iv, 213, n. 1), for in 697/1297 Marʿash was again taken by the *amīr* Bilban Tabakhī, *nāʾib* of Ḥalab, for Lādjīn. A treaty was then concluded with the ruler of Little Armenia, by which the Djayḥān was to be the frontier between the two countries; Ḥamūs, Tell Ḥamdūn, Kūbarā, al-Nukayr (for its position, cf. L. Alishan, *Sissouan*, 493-6), Ḥadjar Shughlān, Sirfandakār and Marʿash thus passed to Egypt (al-Maḳrīzī, *op. cit.*, ii/2, 63; Abu 'l-Fidāʾ, *Ann. musl.*, v, 140).

In the second half of the 8th/14th century, Zayn al-Dīn Ḳaradja and his son Khalīl, the founders of the house of the Dhu 'l-Ḳadr-oghlu, conquered the lands along the Egyptian Asia Minor frontier with Malaṭya, Albistān, Marʿash, Bahasnā and Kharpūt [see DHU 'L-ḲADR]. In the mosque of Marʿash, one of his successors, Malik Arslān, was murdered in 870/1465-6; his portrait with the inscription "Sulṭān Arslān" and that of his sister Sittī Khātūn with the legend ἡ μεγάλη χάτω are painted in the Codex Venetus 516 of the *Geography* of Ptolemy, which he apparently intended to dedicate to this father-in-law Meḥemmed II (Olshausen, in *Hermes*, xv [1880], 417-42)

Bibliography: Iṣṭakhrī, 55-6, 62, 67-8; Ibn Ḥawḳal, 108-10, 120, 127, 153; Muḳaddasī, 154; Ibn Khurradādhbih, 97; Ḳudāma, 216, 253; Idrīsī, ed. Gildenmeister, in *ZDPV*, viii, 27; Ibn Rusta, 107; Masʿūdī, *Tanbīh*, 58; idem, *Murūdj*, viii, 295; Abu 'l-Fidāʾ, *Taḳwīm al-buldān*, tr. Guyard, ii/2, 2, 39; Dimishḳī, ed. Mehren, 206, 214; Yāḳūt, iv, 498; Ṣafī al-Dīn, *Marāṣid al-iṭṭilāʿ*, ed. Juynboll, iii, 81; Balādhurī, 150, 188-9; Ibn al-Athīr, index, ii, 806; Ṭabarī, indices, 774; Ḥamd Allāh Muṣtawfī, ed. Le Strange, 268; Michael the Syrian, *Chronicle*, ed. Chabot, index, 48; Matthēos Uṛhayecʿi, tr. Dulaurier, Paris 1858, 532; Le Strange, *Palestine under the Moslems*, 502-3; idem, *The lands of the eastern caliphate*, 128-9; Tomaschek, in *SBAk. Wien* (1891),

Abh. viii, 86; V. Cuinet, *La Turquie d'Asie*, ii, Paris 1891, 240-7; H. Grothe, *Meine Vorderasienexpedition 1906 u. 1907*, ii, 312, index; Besīm Atalāʾī, *Marᶜas̲h̲ taʾrīk̲h̲ī wa-d̲j̲ug̲h̲rafiyāsī*, Istanbul 1339/1920-1; E. Honigmann, *Die Ostgrenze des byzantinischen Reiches*, index; Canard, *Hʾamdânides*, 270. On the ancient town, cf. *Germanikeia*, in Pauly-Wissowa, Suppl.-vol., iv, cols. 686-9. (E. Honigmann)

2. In Ottoman and modern times.

In Ottoman times, Marᶜas̲h̲ lay on one of the major routes to Syria: in the early 11th/17th century, Polonyalī Simeon passed through the city when returning from Aleppo to Istanbul by way of Kayseri. The pre-Ottoman or else 10th/16th century bridge, which still crosses the Ceyhan somewhat to the west of Marᶜas̲h̲, must have served this traffic. If the surviving bridge is identical with the bridge mentioned in an Ottoman tax register of the second half of the 10th/16th century, this structure should been the site of a toll gate. According to the *ḳānūn* applied in the region, nomads travelling with their flocks were exempted from toll payment, which was only demanded from traders.

Marᶜas̲h̲ was considered as lying on a *ḥad̲j̲d̲j̲* or pilgrimage route, even though the "diagonal road" crossing Anatolia by way of Konya and Adana seems to have been much more popular. Ewliyā Čelebi passed through Marᶜas̲h̲ on his way to the Ḥid̲j̲āz, and the suppression of robbery in the district of Marᶜas̲h̲ was always treated with particular urgency because of the danger it presented to pilgrims (cf. Başbakanlık Arşivi, Istanbul, Mühimme defterleri, 40, p. 42, no. 88, 987/1579-80). Probably for the same reason, a number of guarded mountain passes (*derbend*) was instituted in the area in the course of the 11th/17th and 12th/18th centuries.

In the second half of the 19th century, the old thoroughfare passing through Marᶜas̲h̲ had apparently lost much of its importance, for in 1891 Cuinet reported that no road suitable for wheeled vehicles existed in the entire *sand̲j̲aḳ*. As a result, not much of an outlet existed for local industries. Only in 1948 was Marᶜas̲h̲ linked up with the Malatya-Fevzipaşa railway, which in certain sections follows the area's historical routes. In addition, asphalted roads were built, so that by 1960, Marᶜas̲h̲ was easily accessible from Adana, Iskenderun, Gaziantep and Malatya.

Administrative structure and population. After the Ottomans had conquered the D̲h̲u 'l-Ḳadr principality in 921/1515, the area was first governed by D̲h̲u 'l-Ḳadrlī ᶜAlī Beg b. S̲h̲āhsuwār under Ottoman suzerainty. However, after the latter had been killed in 928/1522, surviving members of the D̲h̲u 'l-Ḳadrlī family were appointed to governorships in the European provinces of the Ottoman Empire, and the Ottoman *wilāyet-sand̲j̲aḳ* structure was established in the lands which this dynasty had formerly ruled. A tax register (*taḥrīr*) dating from the early years of Sultan Ḳānūnī Sulaymān's reign (after 931/1525-6) refers to a *wilāyet* of D̲h̲u 'l-Ḳadriyya, governed by two *sand̲j̲aḳ begis* and divided into five *ḳaḍāʾ*s (Marᶜas̲h̲; Elbistān; Ḳarş or modern Kadirli, also referred to as a *liwā-sand̲j̲aḳ*; Şamanto; and Bozok). This *wilāyet* consisted of 523 villages, 665 nomadic tribes, and 3,412 *mezraᶜas* (sown, but not necessarily inhabited, agricultural land). The total adult male population of the *wilāyet* amounted to 76,181 men. Among the latter, 9, 644 were exempt from the payment of *ᶜawāriḍ* [*q.v.*] taxes, either because of their former position under the D̲h̲u 'l-Ḳadr dynasty or because of services rendered to the Ottoman administration. Total population registered in the *wilāyet* can thus be estimated at 230,000 to 300,400 persons.

During those years, the town of Marᶜas̲h̲ appears as an administrative centre with an unusually high proportion of tax-exempt inhabitants. Of the 1,557 adult males recorded in the town (this should have corresponded to a population of about 7,500, since only 85 persons were recorded as unmarried), 836 men were *sipāhī*s and *sipāhīzāde*s, in addition to the usual contingent of tax-exempt religious functionaries. This would have left the town with a tax-paying population of only about 550 adult males, an anomalous situation which can be explained only by the fact that the count must have been prepared a short time after the conquest. At this time, Marᶜas̲h̲ was inhabited only by Muslims.

During Ḳānūnī Sulaymān's reign, the number of adult males registered in the *taḥrīr* as resident in Marᶜas̲h̲ almost doubled, and before 972/1564-5 had reached the level of 3,054 men. Of these, 370 were recorded as unmarried. Thus a total population of 13,000-14,000 is probable, apart from certain tax-exempt families which may have gone unregistered. This figure placed Marᶜas̲h̲ among the large towns of contemporary Anatolia. According to Ewliyā Čelebi, who passed through Marᶜas̲h̲ in 1058/1648 and again in 1082/1672-3, the town consisted of 11,000 houses, which would seem to point to a much larger settlement than that described in the 10th/16th century tax registers. However, the town seems subsequently to have lost population. Texier, who refers to Marᶜas̲h̲ as it was in the early 19th century, estimates its population at 5,000-6,000 inhabitants. Struggles between the family factions of the D̲h̲u 'l-Ḳadrlī and the Bāyezīdli were brought to an end only during the reign of Sultan Maḥmūd II (1223-55/1808-39), and seem to have contributed to a decline in urban population. However, according to a British Foreign Office source, between 1830 and 1840 Marᶜas̲h̲ had again reached the level of 23,000 inhabitants.

Administrative structure between the late 10th/16th and the early 19th century showed relatively slight variations. According to a register containing appointments to provincial governorships between 975-82/1568-74, the *wilāyet* of D̲h̲u 'l-Ḳadriyya consisted of the *sand̲j̲aḳ*s of Marᶜas̲h̲, Malāṭya, ᶜAyntāb, Sis and Ḳarş (modern Kadirli). In 1041-6/1632-41, this *wilāyet* had been much reduced, and now consisted only of the *sand̲j̲aḳ*s of Marᶜas̲h̲, ᶜAyntāb and Ḳarş. ᶜAynī ᶜAlī, who wrote during the reign of Sultan Aḥmed I (1012-26/1603-17) mentions the *sand̲j̲aḳ*s of Marᶜas̲h̲, Malāṭya, ᶜAyntāb, Ḳarş and Samīṣād as forming part of the *wilāyet* of D̲h̲u 'l-Ḳadriyya. This list has also been reproduced in the *D̲j̲ihān-numā* of Kātib Čelebi (p. 598). Thus the *wilāyet* was apparently soon restored to its former size. Writing at the end of the 11th/17th century, Ewliyā Čelebi enumerates the following: Marᶜas̲h̲, Malāṭya, ᶜAyntāb, Ḳarş, Samṣad and Niğde.

During the Ottoman-Egyptian conflict of the 1830s, the troops of Ibrāhīm Pas̲h̲a, Muḥammad ᶜAlī's son, temporarily held Marᶜas̲h̲, which was returned to the Ottoman realm in 1840. Administrative structure as it existed during the second half of the 19th century has been described by Cuinet: the *sand̲j̲aḳ* of Marᶜas̲h̲ then formed part of the *eyālet* of Aleppo and consisted of the *ḳaḍāʾ*s of Marᶜas̲h̲, Elbistān, Andīrīn, Pazārd̲j̲īḳ and Zeytūn (modern name: Süleymanlı). According to the same author, the total *sand̲j̲aḳ* population amounted to 179,853, of whom 52,000 lived in the town of Marᶜas̲h̲ proper (32,000 Muslims, 20,000 non-Muslims). These figures indicate that a substantial number of non-Muslims must have immigrated into the town, probably mainly during the 19th century.

For the early days of World War I, Besim Atalay reports 32,700 inhabitants for the town of Mar^cash proper including 8,500 non-Muslims. In 1927, when the first census of the Turkish Republic was undertaken, the impact of the World War, the occupation of 1919 (first British, then French), and the War of Independence had reduced population to 25,672. From this low point, the city expanded continuously (1940: 27,744; 1945: 33,104; 1950: 34,641; 1960: 54, 447, 1970: 110,761; 1980: 178,557), without experiencing the temporary contraction that many Anatolian towns went through during and immediately after World War II. Between 1960 and 1980, the *vilâyet* (later *il*) consisted of the following *kazas* (later *ilçe*): Maraş-merkez, Afşin, Andırın, Elbistan, Göksün, Pazarcık and Türkoğlu. In 1980, the *il* of Kahramanmaraş contained a total population of 738,032, of which 281, 382 (38%) lived in towns and cities.

Economic activities. From the dues recorded in the tax register compiled before 972/1564-5, the importance of textile manufacture becomes apparent. Apart from a sizeable dyehouse, we hear of a tax payable by bleachers or fullers. The provincial governor claimed the right to tax the weavers' pits, (*djullāh čuḳuru*); at the end of the 11th/17th century, complaints on this score were addressed to the Ottoman central administration. In the late 12th/18th century, red cottons were particularly esteemed among locally manufactured textiles. Even in the last years of the 19th century, Mar^cash still possessed a reputation as a textile centre. Although by that time many looms lay idle, 281 workshops were still active in this sector. Apart from fabrics intended for everyday use, Cuinet mentions the manufacture of textiles embroidered in gold and silver thread. A certain revival has taken place in the second half of the 20th century; in 1960 a state factory for the manufacture of poplin and other cottons (Sümerbank) began to operate in Mar^cash.

Throughout the Ottoman period, the Mar^cash area produced ironware; in 983/1575-6, anchors for a flotilla to be constructed in Baṣra were being ordered from Mar^cash. This iron must have been mined in the *ḳaḍā*^ʾ of Süleymānlī, for Cuinet records that, in the second half of the 19th century, soft iron from this district was being employed by local farriers and blacksmiths. From the tax register of Ḳānūnī Sulaymān's early years, we learn that silver was being mined in Göksun; this latter mine, whose existence was also known to Cuinet, was apparently not exploited during the 1890s. In addition, salpetre mines were worked and powder was manufactured; during the Cyprus campaign of the 10th/16th century, the Ottoman armies were using powder from Mar^cash. However, in the second half of the 20th century, the most important mines of the province of Kahramanmaraş are in Elbistan, where abundant lignite has been discovered, and power plants for the conversion of this raw material into electric energy are in the course of being completed.

Mar^cash possesses an ample source of wood in the forests which are still fairly abundant in the district; in the 10th/16th century, this wood was used by the Ottoman central administration for the construction of a Euphrates flotilla in Bīredjik. According to Cuinet, in the second half of the 19th century wood was employed particularly in the manufacture of European-style furniture, whose quality and cheapness the author praised highly.

Agriculture in the Mar^cash area during the 10th/16th century was dominated by the cultivation of wheat and barley; but in addition, a wide variety of garden cultures was present. Among the latter, the vine was particularly prominent, as it also was in Cuinet's time and still is today. Apparently fruit cultivation even by the reign of Ḳānūnī Sulaymān had given rise to processing activities; for the tax register compiled before 972/1564-5 specifically mentions the existence of helva and paste manufacturers. By the second half of the 19th century, rice had turned into a major commercial crop of the Mar^cash area; it was traded mainly within the Ottoman Empire. On the other hand, fruit, dyestuffs, and other garden and forest products were at this time also being exported to Europe, primarily through the port of Iskenderun.

By the middle of the 1970s, the continued importance of fruit and vegetable cultivation (163, 194 tons of fruit in 1975) had given rise to a certain number of processing industries, particularly the manufacture of dried red pepper. Furthermore, since World War II, agriculture has benefited from a number of state-sponsored projects for irrigation and swamp drainage.

Throughout the Ottoman period, the nomadic tribes which were particularly numerous in the Mar^cash district and in the province of Dhu 'l-Ḳadriyya as a whole practiced a pastoral economy. In the 10th/16th century, the province was not infrequently called upon to provide sheep so that Istanbul could be supplied with meat. Records of the 11th/17th century also refer to the raising of water buffaloes. But in the late 19th century, the most widely present animal was the goat, which particularly in the Mar^cash *ḳaḍā*^ʾ, by far outnumbered sheep. By the mid-1970s, however, this pattern had changed, and throughout the *vilâyet* of Kahramanmaraş, sheep now substantially outnumbered goats. In addition, the state has been encouraging cattle raising by the establishment of the Maraş Inekhanesi.

Pious foundations and public buildings. The long reign of ^cAlā^ʾ al-Dawla Bozḳurd (884-921/1479-1515) marks the period during which the Dhu 'l-Ḳadr principality moved from the Egyptian into the Ottoman orbit. This period is of special importance in the history of Mar^cash, for it was ^cAlā^ʾ al-Dawla Beg who established the capital of his principality in this town, after Elbistan, the previous seat of the dynasty, had been sacked and destroyed by the Ṣafawid Shāh Ismā^cīl I in 913/1507. A construction programme of some importance was undertaken by the ruling dynasty. ^cAlā^ʾ al-Dawla Beg's name appears most frequently in this context, but certain structures were equally erected in the name of his wife Shams-Māh (also Shams) Khātūn and other members of the ruling family. Among the surviving buildings, one might name the Ulu Djāmi^c, the Tash *madrasa* with the grave of (possibly) ^cAlā^ʾ al-Dawla's son Meḥmed, the Khaznadārlī Djāmi^c, the mausoleum of Iḳlīme Khātūn and the Khātūniyya Djāmi^c. In an Ottoman list of pious foundations compiled before 972/1564-5, we also find a Djāmi^c-i Sulaymān Beg, which had possibly been established by ^cAlā^ʾ al-Dawla's father (846-58/1442-54), and which Ewliyā seems to ascribe to Sultan Ḳānūnī Sulaymān. This foundation is not mentioned in the secondary literature of the 20th century, and the same applies to the mosque of Shādī Beg, although Ewliyā knew of its existence; this latter foundation had been established at an unknown date. During the later years of the 10th/16th century, a *madrasa* called the Maktūbiyya also flourished in Mar^cash, but nothing is known about the founder.

According to an Ottoman *idjmāl* register going back

to the early years of Ḳānūnī Sülayman, Marʿas̲h̲ at the time also possessed three *zāwiyas*. However, in actual fact the number must have been greater, for a later register (before 972/1564-5) refers to six dervish foundations as having benefited from the D̲h̲u 'l-Ḳadrlī rulers' generosity. Among the latter, the *zāwiya* of Čomaḳ Baba continued to function at least until the late 12th/18th century, and during this latter period of its existence was inhabited by Bektās̲h̲ī dervishes.

The Ottoman tax registers of the 10th/16th century also refer to the existence of a covered market or *bedestān*, which had been constructed by ʿAlāʾ al-Dawla Beg. This latter ruler had also established a *kerbānsaray* and an *ārāsta*. It is possible that the last-named building survived in one of the three covered streets, lined with shops, which still exist, or until recently existed, in the centre of Marʿas̲h̲. In the early Ottoman period, further business structures were added, for it is very probable that Ferhād Pas̲h̲a, who caused his rival ʿAlī Beg b. S̲h̲āhsuwār to be killed upon Sultan Ḳānūnī Sulaymān's order in 928/1522, is identical with the Ferhād Pas̲h̲a who (at sometime before 972/1564-5) had a *ḥammām* and *kerbānsaray* constructed in Marʿas̲h̲. The citadel, which is said to go back to Hittite times, was according to Ewliyā Čelebi adorned with an inscription bearing the date 915/1509-10 (*sic*) and bore the name of Sultan Ḳānūnī Sulaymān (926-74/1520-66), who had ordered a complete reconstruction of the fortress.

Bibliography: Sources, unpublished: Başbakanlık Arşivi, Istanbul, Tapu Tahrir 998, pp. 408-638; Tapu Kadastro Genel Müdürlüğü Kuyudu kadime 101 (inc. *ḳānūn-nāme and waḳf*); Başbakanlık Arşivi, Istanbul, Mühimme defterleri series; a *s̲h̲ikāyet defteri* from 1085-86/1674-5, in the National Library at Vienna, catalogued as "Procolle des divers Fermans Turcs" and in the course of being published.

2. Sources published: See the *Bibls.* to 1. above and *Maraş* in *İA*; cf. also the arts. *Dulkadırlılar* in *İA* and *D̲h̲u 'l-Ḳadr* in *EI*², and also Ewliyā Čelebi, *Seyāḥat-nāme*, iii, Istanbul 1314/1896-7, 170-1, ix (= Anatolia, Syria, Ḥid̲j̲āz), Istanbul 1935, 545-50; Kātib Čelebi, *D̲j̲ihān-numā*, Istanbul 1145/1732; ʿAyn-i ʿAlī Efendi, *Ḳawānīn risālesi, 1018 senesi*, repr. as *Kavânîn-i Âl-i Osman der hülâsa-i mezâmin-defter-i dîvân*, introd. by M. Tayyib Gökbilgin, Istanbul 1979, 50-1; *Polonyalı Simeon'un Seyahatnâmesi*, 1608-1619, tr. Hrand D. Andreasyan, Istanbul 1964, 157 (inc. summary of Inciciyan's description).

3. Modern studies: C. Texier, *Asie Mineure*, i, Paris 1872, 586; Shams al-Dīn Sāmī, *Ḳāmūs al-aʿlām*, vi, Istanbul 1316/1898, 4262-4; E. Banse, *Die Türkei, eine moderne Geographie*, Berlin-Brunswick-Hamburg 1916, 222-3; Besīm Atalāʾī, *Marʿas̲h̲ tārīk̲h̲i ve D̲j̲ug̲h̲rāfyāsī*, Istanbul 1339/1920-1; Ismail Hakkı Uzunçarşılı, *Anadolu beylikleri ve Akkoyunlu, Karakoyunlu devletleri*, Ankara 1937, 42-5; Ömer Lütfi Barkan, *XV ve XVI ıncı asırlarda Osmanlı imparatorluğunda zirai ekonominin hukuki ve mali esaslarlı. i. Kanunlar*, Istanbul 1943, 114-24; Hasan Reşit Tankut, *Maraş yollarında*, Ankara 1944; Hadiye Tuncer, *Osmanlı imparatorluğunda toprak taksimi ve asar*, Ankara 1948, 107-8, 139-40; Faruk Sümer, *Anadolu'da yaşayan bazı Uçoklu Oğuz boylarına mensup teşekküler, in Istanbul Üniversitesi, Iktisat Fakültesi Mecmuası*, xi/1-4 (1949-50), 446, 462-4; Cengiz Orhonlu and Turgut Işıksal, *Osmanlı devrinde nehir nakliyatı hakkında araştırmalar: Dicle ve Firat nehirlerinde nakliyat*, in *Tarih Dergisi*, xiii, 17-18 (1962-3), 81, 96; Mustafa Akdağ, *Celâlî isyanları* Istanbul 1963, 4, 138, 228, 253-4, 268, 275; Orhonlu, *Osmanlı imparatorluğunda aşiretleri iskan teşebbüsü, 1691-1696*, Istanbul 1963, 22, 37, 78, 91, 92; Lord Kinross, *Atatürk, a biography of Mustafa Kemal, father of modern Turkey*, London and New York 1965, 235; Hanna Sohrweide, *Der Sieg der Ṣafaviden in Persien und seine Rückwirkungen auf die Schiiten Anatoliens im 16. Jahrhundert*, in *Isl.*, xli (1965), 95-223; *Maraş il yıllığı 1967*, Ankara n.d.; Orhonlu, *Osmanlı imparatorluğunda derbend teşkilatı*, Istanbul 1967, 16, 62, 97, 103, 104; Metin Sözen, *Anadolu medreseleri, Selçuklular ve Beylikler devri*, ii, Istanbul 1972, 168-70; M. Zafer Bayburtluoğlu, *Kahramanmaraşa'ta bir gurup Dulkadiroğlu yapısı*, in *Vakıflar Dergisi*, x (1973), 234-50; Devlet Istatistik Enstitüsü, *Genel nüfus sayimı, idari bölünüş, ... 25.10.1970*, Ankara 1973; Cevdet Çulpan, *Türk taş köprüleri, ortaçağdan Osmanlı devri sonuna kadar*, Ankara 1975, 152; Başbakanlık Devlet Istatistik Enstitüsü, *Tarımsal yap, ve üretim 1974-76*, Ankara 1978; Metin Kunt, *Sancaktan eyalete, 1550-1650 arasında Osmanlı ümerası ve il idaresi*, Istanbul 1978, 138-9, 173-4, 188-9; Huricihan Islamoğlu and Suraiya Faroqhi, *Crop patterns and agricultural production trends in sixteenth-century Anatolia*, in *Review*, ii/3 (1979), 401-36; Charles Issawi, *The economic history of Turkey 1800-1914*, Chicago and London 1980, 35, 273, 299, 316; Başbakanlık Devlet Istatistik Enstitüsü, *Genel nüfus sayımı, idari bölünüş, 12.10.1980*, Ankara 1981; Halil *İnalcık, Rice cultivation and the Çeltükci - Reʿâyâ system in the Ottoman empire*, in *Turcica*, xiv (1982), 82, 136-7.

(Suraiya Faroqhi)

al-**MARʿAS̲H̲Ī** [see nūr allāh al-s̲h̲us̲h̲tarī].

MARʿAS̲H̲IS, a line of *sayyids* originally from Marʿas̲h̲ [*q.v.*], whose *nisba* became well-known on account of their dynasty which dominated Māzandarān [*q.v.*] for most of the period between 760/1358-9 and the second half of the 10th/16th century. The Ṣafawids [*q.v.*] were related to them by matrimonial alliances (see Table B and below, 2). Their descendants, offspring of the various branches of the Marʿas̲h̲īs, have continued to bear this *nisba* by which they are generally known (see below, 3). It was also attributed over the course of the centuries to various *sayyid* and non-*sayyid* individuals. Concerning the *laḳab* Marʿas̲h̲, another explanation of the origin of the Marʿas̲h̲i *sayyids*, see Table A.

1. The dynasty of the Marʿas̲h̲ī *sayyids* of Māzandarān. (a) The first phase. Founded by Sayyid Ḳawām al-Dīn al-Marʿas̲h̲ī, known by the name of Mīr-i Buzurg, this dynasty is sometimes called *Silsila-yi mulūk-i ḳawāmiyya-yi marʿas̲h̲iyya* (*Rayḥānat*, iii, 323). Its historical context is the vacuum of political power which—in post-Ilk̲h̲ānid Iran—enabled *sayyids* and dervishes to impose their influence. Ḳawām al-Dīn traced his lineage to the Imām ʿAlī Zayn al-ʿĀbidīn. However, the connection between his Marʿas̲h̲ī ancestors and Zayn al-ʿĀbidīn remains unclear (see M. Sutūda, ed., *TDG, Muḳaddima*). His genealogy, as featured in the work of Ẓahīr al-Dīn (*TTRM*) has been disputed by ʿA. S̲h̲āyān, who established an "exact" genealogy with which the biographers of the Marʿas̲h̲ī family concur. A genealogy, different from the two afore-mentioned. seems to have been current in the Ṣafawid period (see Table A.).

The family of Mīr-i Buzurg resided at Dābū, a village near Āmul [*q.v.*] where he studied religious sciences. He made a pilgrimage to the tomb of the Imām ʿAlī b. Mūsā al-Riḍā at Mas̲h̲had [*q.v.*] and

Table A
THE LINE OF MĪR ḲAWĀM AL-DĪN MARʿASHĪ "MĪR-I BUZURG"

After:

Ẓahīr al-Dīn Marʿashī[1]	*The Ṣafawid sources*[3]	*ʿAbbās Shāyān*[5]
Imām ʿAlī Zayn al-ʿĀbidīn	Zayn al-ʿĀbidīn	Zayn al-Ābidīn
Ḥusayn al-Aṣghar	Ḥusayn al-Asghar	al-Ḥasan Abū Muḥammad
Ḥasan al-Marʿashī	Ḥasan	Muḥammad Abu 'l-Karām
Muḥammad	Muḥammad al-Akbar	ʿAbd Allāh Abū Muḥammad
Ābd Allāh	ʿAbd Allāh	ʿAlī al-Marʿashī Abu 'l-Ḥasan
ʿAlī	Ālī al-Marʿash[4]	al-Ḥusayn Abū ʿAbd Allāh
Ḥusayn	Ḥasan	ʿAlī Abu 'l-Ḥusayn
ʿAbd Allāh	ʿAlī	Abū Hāshim
Ṣādiḳ	Abū Hāshim	Muḥammad Abū ʿAbd Allāh
Muḥammad[2]	Muḥammad	ʿAbd Allāh Abū Ṣādiḳ
ʿAbd Allāh	Abd Allāh	al-Ṣādiḳ
Ḳawām al-Dīn	Ṣādiḳ	Ḳawām al-Dīn
	Ḳawām al-Dīn	

Notes to Table A

(1) *TTRM*, ed. Tasbīḥī, 166.
(2) Muḥammad absent from *TTRM*, ed. Shāyān, 236.
(3) *Djahān-ārā*, 88; Yazdī, fol. 2a; Shūshtārī, *Madjālis*, ii, 380.
(4) The *laḳab* al-Marʿash (a kind of pigeon) is said to have been given in the first place to ʿAlī Marʿash, the eponym of the Marʿashi *Sayyids* (*Rayḥāna*, iv, 10). In Yazdī, ʿAlī al-Marʿash and his son Ḥasan are made into a single "al-Marʿash".
(5) *TTRM. Muḳaddima* (approved by the Āyatallāh Marʿashī-Nadjafī, *TTRM*, ed. Tasbiḥī, *Muḳaddima*, 39-40, with typographical errors).

frequented the *khānḳāh* of the *sayyid* ʿIzz al-Dīn Sūghandī, one of the three influential Ṣūfī *shaykh*s of Khurāsān, disciple of Shaykh Ḥasan Djūrī, founder of the Shaykhiyya-Djūriyya *ṭarīḳa*, promotor of the Sarbadār movement in Khurāsān (see J. Aubin, in *Studia Iranica*, v [1976], 217-24). Having obtained the *idjāzat* of ʿIzz al-Dīn, Ḳawām al-Dīn founded his own *khānḳāh* at Dābū where he attracted numerous disciples. The control of Ṭabaristān-Māzandarān was then the object of keen competition between local powers. After the reconciliation concluded between the Kiyā-i Čulāb and the Kiyā-i Djalāl, in 750/1349, Fakhr al-Dawla Ḥasan, last representative of the third branch of the Bāwandids [*q.v.*], was assassinated by a son (or by two sons?) of Kiyā Afrāsiyāb, former *sipahsālār* and brother-in-law of Fakhr al-Dawla, eponym of the Kiyā-i Čulāb who were also known as Afrāsiyābids [*q.v.*]. Having thus obtained a precarious control over Āmul and Māzandarān, Kiyā Afrāsiyāb attempted to strengthen his popularity by becoming a disciple of Mīr-i Buzūrg, who conferred on him the *laḳab* of *shaykhī*. But the other disciples of Mīr-i Buzurg harassed Afrāsiyāb and his followers. Afrāsiyāb imprisoned Mīr-i Buzūrg, but the latter was freed by his furious disciples. Having appealed in vain for the aid of the Kiyā-i Djalāl, Afrāsiyāb was defeated at Djalālakmār-parčīn, near Dābū, by three hundred dervishes under the command of Kamāl al-Dīn b. Ḳawām al-Dīn (760/1358-9). Afrāsiyāb and four of his sons were killed; another, Muḥammad, the assassin of Fakhr al-Dawla, was killed by the *malik* of Rustumdār; another, Sayf al-Dīn, died of *kūlandj*, i.e. some abdominal illness (an act attributed to the supernatural powers of Mīr-i Buzurg); the only survivor was an infant, Iskandar-i Shaykhī (according to Rabino, in *JA* [1943-5], 236, three sons were killed at Djalālakmār-parčīn and ʿAlī in the same battle as Muḥammad: *TTRM*, 250 ff.; Mahdjūrī 15 ff.). The Marʿashīs then turned on the Kiyā-i Djalāl, Fakhr al-Dīn and Vishtāsp, who held respectively Sārī and Tūdjī (a fortress near Bārfurūsh-dih = Bābul). After the first battle, Ḳawām al-Dīn and Kamāl al-Dīn entered Bārfurūsh-dih as victors. With some former followers of Afrāsiyāb, Vishtāsp assassinated ʿAbd Allāh b. Ḳawām al-Dīn. Fakhr al-Dīn and four of his sons perished in a battle near Bārfurūsh-dih. Vishtāsp took refuge with his family and close associates in the fortress of Tūdjī, which was reduced by the Marʿashīs after a long siege, in the course of which Vishtāsp and his seven sons were killed (763/1362). Kamāl al-Dīn married the daughter of Vishtāsp by the daughter of Ḥasan Fakhr al-Dawla Bāwand, grandmother of the historian Ẓahīr al-Dīn (see below, 2). Then he undertook the restoration and enlargement of Sārī.

From the outset, Mīr-i Buzurg had indicated his intention to devote himself exclusively to pious activities. He entrusted the government of Māzandarān to his sons, and it was only in a non-combattant capacity that he accompanied them on their expeditions. The elder son, ʿAbd Allāh (see above) having refused to assume power, this was exercised in the name of Mīr-i Buzurg by his second son Kamāl al-Dīn, who shared responsibilities with his brothers. In 763/1361-2, he entrusted the government of Āmul to Riḍā al-Dīn (*TTRM*, 255 ff.). With control of Āmul, Bārfurūsh-dih and Sārī thus assured, the Marʿashīs extended their power over Sawādkūh and Fīrūzkūh, which were held by the representatives of the last Bāwandids. In the conquest of the fortress of Fīrūzkūh, and seizure of the treasury of Fakhr al-Dawla, they were assisted by their allies, the Malātī *sayyid*s of Gīlān (*TTRM*, 261 ff.). The conquest of Rustamdār as far as Nātil-rustāḳ was the operation of Sayyid Fakhr al-Dīn (782/1380-1). His conquest of Kudjūr having given to the Marʿashis control over the whole of Māzandarān, Kamāl al-Dīn entrusted Rustamdār to him. Henceforward, he undertook to subdue the fortresses of Kudjūr, of Kalā-rustāḳ and of Nūr; he conquered Ṭāliḳān and Lawāsān, as well as part of Lārīdjān fortresses of Kuhrūd or Kahrūd in Dayla-rustāḳ, from Lawandar to Rayna (*TTRM*, 271 ff.). Fakhr al-Dīn took possession of Ḳazwīn—then being contested between Ādharbāydjān and ʿIrāḳ-i ʿAdjam—a brief control interrupted by the death of Mīr-i Buzurg (see below). Subsequently, he reoccupied the town, levied taxes there, went to Ṭālikān, and then pillaged Alamūt (*TTRM*, 290 ff.).

At the end of a long retreat to Bārfurush-dih, Mīr-i Buzurg died of an illness (781/1379). For a period of twenty years, by his charismatic leadership, he controlled Māzandarān through his sons, among whom there was then a fair degree of unity (four of his fourteen sons died in infancy). Kamāl al-Dīn held Sārī and had entrusted Āmul to Riḍā al-Dīn, Rustamdār to Fakhr al-Dīn and Karaṭughan to Sharaf al-Dīn. The power of the Marᶜashīs extended to the west as far as the frontiers of Kazwīn; with their support, the Malāṭī *sayyids* controlled a large part of Gīlān. But their position was threatened in the east by Mīr ᶜImād al-Dīn, founder of the small dynasty of the Murtaḍāʾī *sayyids* of Hazārdjarīb and in Astarābād by Amīr Walī, who attempted to have Kamāl al-Dīn assassinated. The latter conquered Astarābād, where he left a garrison (781/1379). Fearing lest Amīr Walī would join forces with Tīmūr Lang, he restored Astarābād to him; similarly, he handed over Rustamdār to Malik Ṭūs (794/1391-2; *TTRM*, 293 ff.; Mahdjūrī, 23 ff.). But soon after Tīmūr's conquest of Khurāsān and Harāt, Iskandar-i Shaykhī, younger son of Afrāsiyāb, who had campaigned in Khurāsān, joined forces with him. Twice, Tīmūr took possession of Astarābād. The second time, he appointed as governor there Pīrak, with whom Kamāl al-Dīn maintained amicable relations. Kamāl al-Dīn also sent his son Ghiyāth al-Dīn to Tīmūr on three occasions with suitable presents, in the hope of persuading him to protect the Marᶜashīs from persecution by Iskandar. But animosity towards the Marᶜashīs (Imāmī and Rāfiḍī Shīᶜīs) was rife among the predominantly Sunnī military chieftains of Tīmūr. It was fostered in the west, in Rustamdār, by Malik Ṭūs and in the east, in Astarābād, by Pīrak, who, inwardly, supported Iskandar-i Shaykhī (Mahdjūrī, 27 ff.).

Tīmūr had given orders to open up the route through the forests of Māzandarān, and he sent Ghiyāth al-Dīn, held as a hostage, with his vanguard force. Kamāl al-Dīn had a fortified camp built on a promontory in the lagoon of Māhānasar. Besides some property concealed at Sārī, the greater part of the wealth of Māzandarān, including that of merchants, foreigners and dignitaries, as well as funds seized from the Čulābīs, Djalālis, Sawādkūhīs, etc., was hoarded at Māhānasar. Informed of Tīmūr's advance, Kamāl al-Dīn and his supporters left Māhānasar and took up a position at Karaṭughan, where the confrontation with the Tīmūrid forces took place on 6 Dhu 'l-Kaᶜda 794/24 September 1392. Although inflicting losses, the Marᶜashīs were defeated by numerical superiority and withdrew to Māhānasar. after two months and six days of siege, Kamāl al-Dīn sent *ᶜulamāʾ* to Tīmūr to request *amān* or quarter for himself and his associates. They left the fortress of Māhānasar on 22 Ramaḍān 795/2 August 1393 and escaped persecution at the hands of Iskandar-i Shaykhī due to the efforts of Malik Ṭūs, who interceded with Tīmūr on their behalf. All the non-*sayyid* occupants of Māhānasar were executed (*TTRM*, 300 ff.).

Tīmūr is said to have obtained the most important spoils ever conceded to him by a king. Massacres and pillage continued in all the urban centres from Māhānasar to Āmul as well as at Sārī, to where the *sayyids* were brought. He then despatched them to Khwārazm and to Transoxiana by sea and river routes, and compelled them to reside in these mutually isolated places. Before embarkation, three *sayyids* were able to take refuge in Gīlān: ᶜAbd al-Muṭṭalib b. Riḍā al-Dīn, ᶜAbd al-ᶜAẓīm b. Zayn al-ᶜĀbidīn and ᶜIzz al-Dīn Ḥasanī Rikābī. Two sons of Kamāl al-Dīn (ᶜAlī and Ghiyāth al-Dīn) were in the service of Tīmūr, who entrusted Sārī to Djamshīd Ḳarīn Ghawrī and Āmul to Iskandar-i Shaykhī. In spite of their efforts towards repopulation and economic restoration, these towns did not regain their former prosperity. Iskandar destroyed the mausoleum of Mīr-i Buzurg at Āmul, which numerous inhabitants left for Sārī. ᶜIzz al-Dīn Rikābī, returning from Gīlān, was pursued and killed with his five sons. Iskandar accompanied Tīmūr in his campaigns, before leaving him in Ādharbāydjān and setting out for Āmul (802/1399-1400). Subsequently, he rebelled and fortified the fortress of Fīrūzkūh, which he entrusted to his son Ḥusayn Kiyā. ᶜAlī and Ghiyāth al-Dīn Marᶜashī took part in Tīmūr's operations against Iskandar (805/1402-3), whose son ᶜAlī Kiyā, coming to his rescue, was captured. Overtaken in the forest, Iskandar fought valiantly against the troops of Hazārasf Muḥammad and was killed at Shīr-rūd-dūhazār. His severed head was displayed to his sons, the prisoners ᶜAli Kiyā and Ḥusayn Kiyā, who surrendered the fortress of Firūzkūh. Both sons were pardoned by Tīmūr, who then assigned the governorship of Āmul to ᶜAlī b. Kamāl al-Dīn, with his brother Ghiyāth al-Dīn as his deputy, and promised him the liberation of the *sayyids* upon his return to Transoxiana. At Sārī, Djamshīd Ḳārīn died and was replaced by his son Shams al-Dīn. who did his utmost to discredit Sayyid ᶜAlī (*TTRM*, 313 ff.; Mahdjūrī, 29 ff.).

(b) The second phase: return to power and decline. On the death of Tīmūr (Shaᶜbān 807/February 1405), four sons of Mīr-i Buzurg were living in Transoxania (Zayn al-ᶜĀbidīn, ᶜAlī, Yaḥyā and Sharaf al-Dīn). Kamāl al-Dīn and Fakhr al-Dīn had died at Kāshghar and three others (Riḍā al-Dīn, Ẓāhir al-Dīn and Naṣīr al-Dīn) in Transoxiana. The four surviving sons travelled with other *sayyids* to Harāt for an audience with Shāhrukh, who permitted them to return to Māzandarān. At Astarābād, Pīrak did not believe in the validity of their *idjāza* and detained them in order to protect Shams al-Dīn Ḳārin Ghawrī. The latter was then attacked and killed by dervishes, who informed ᶜAlī b. Kamāl al-Dīn of their intention of marching on Astarābād. But Pīrak freed the *sayyids* who, joined by numerous partisans, entered Sārī in triumph. Having controlled Āmul for three years, ᶜAlī b. Kamāl al-Dīn (ᶜAlī Sārī) took over the government of Sārī and of Mazandarān (809/1406-7 to 812/1409-10). He retained Yaḥyā and Sharaf al-Dīn at Sārī and entrusted Bārfurūsh-dih to Ghiyāth al-Dīn. The descendants of Riḍā al-Dīn wanted to install ᶜAbd al-Muṭṭalib as ruler of Āmul, but ᶜAli Sārī preferred Ḳawām al-Dīn b. Riḍā al-Dīn (Ḳawām al-Dīn II), replaced in 810/1407-8 by ᶜAlī b. Ḳawām al-Dīn (ᶜAlī Āmulī) who governed equitably (*TTRM*, 317 ff.; ḤS, iii, 347; Mahdjūrī, 33 ff.). Ghiyāth al-Dīn sowed discord between ᶜAlī Āmulī and ᶜAlī Sārī who, defeated by a coalition of elements from Rustamdār and from Hazārdjarib (Amīr ᶜIzz al-Dīn and his son-in-law Sayyid Murtaḍā) was forced to flee to Astarābād. His only ally in this business was his brother Naṣīr al-Dīn, whom he sent to Harāt to anticipate Shāhrukh.

After their victory, the people of Āmul set Murtaḍā b. Kamāl al-Dīn in control at Sārī where, in spite of the threats of Shāhrukh, he continued to hold sway for almost a year (812-13/1409-10) before being deposed by the populace on account of his drinking habits. ᶜAlī Sārī regained control of Sārī and of Māzandarān

ADDENDA AND CORRIGENDA

VOLUME I

P. 194[b] **A<u>DH</u>RUḤ,** *add to Bibliography* A. G. Killick, *Udhruh and the early Islamic conquests*, in *Procs. of the Second Symposium on the history of Bilād al-Shām during the early Islamic period (English and French papers)*, Amman 1987, 73-8.

VOLUME III

P. 293[b] **ḤAWRĀN,** *add to Bibliography* M. Sartre, *Le Hawran byzantin à la veille de la conquête musulmane*, in *Procs. of the Second Symposium on the history of Bilād al-Shām during the early Islamic period (English and French papers)*, Amman 1987, 155-67.

P. 367[a] **HI<u>DJ</u>RA,** *add to Bibliography* Z. I. Khan, *The origins and development of the concept of* Hijrah *or migration in Islam*, Ph. D. thesis, Manchester 1987, unpublished.

VOLUME IV

P. 834[a] **ḲAYS ʿAYLĀN,** *add to Bibliography* Chang-kuan Lin, *The role of internecine strife and political struggle in the downfall of the Umayyad dynasty*, M. Phil. thesis, Manchester 1987, unpublished.

P. 1100[a] **MA<u>DJ</u>MAʿ ʿILMĪ,** l. 32, *instead of* statues *read* statutes

VOLUME VI

P. 262[a] **MALIK,** *at end of Bibliography add* A. Ayalon, *'Malik' in modern Middle Eastern literature*, in *WI* xxiii-xxiv (1984), 306-19.

P. 334[a] **MAʿN,** *at end of Bibliography add* Abū 'l-Wafaʾ al-Urḍī, *Maʿādin al-<u>dh</u>ahab fī 'l-ri<u>dj</u>āl al-mu<u>sh</u>arrafa bi-him Ḥalab*, MS B.M. Or. 3618.

P. 358[a] AL-**MANĀMA,** l. 3, *instead of* side *read* site
Add to Bibliography Mahdi Abdalla al-Tajir, *Bahrain 1920-1945, Britain, the Shaikh and the administration*, London 1987.

P. 374[b] AL-**MANĀZIL,** l. 8, *after* Ibn Ḳutayba *insert a comma*
l. 27, *after* names *insert* became
No. 5 of the list, *instead of* $\lambda\psi^{12}$. Orionis *read* $\lambda\varphi^{1,2}$ Orionis
No. 9 of the list, *instead* of δ *read* κ

P. 375[a] No. 28 of the list, instead of *al-hūt* read *al-ḥūt*
l. 23, *instead of* 1800 *read* 180.

ISBN 90 04 08825 3

PRINTED IN THE NETHERLANDS

The Supreme Muslim Council

Islam under the British Mandate for Palestine

by

URI M. KUPFERSCHMIDT

1987. (xvi, 297 p., 7 fig.)
ISBN 90 04 07929 7 *cloth* **Gld. 96.—/US$ 48.—**

The Supreme Muslim Council was a unique administrative body, established by the British Mandatory to shift responsibility for the management of Muslim religious affairs to the Palestinian Muslims themselves. Under the presidency of Hajj Amin al-Husayni, the Grand Mufti, however, it evolved into what was to be for years the most powerful political body in the Palestinian-Arab community. In 1937, following the outbreak of the Arab Rebellion in Palestine and Hajj Amin having been ousted from his powers, the British finally imposed a measure of supervision over the Council.

The present work provides an outline of the development and activities of the Supreme Muslim Council. Special emphasis is laid on organizational and socio-religious aspects. Much attention is also paid to the *waqfs* (pious foundations), which were controlled by the Council and which Hajj Amin fully exploited for his political ambitions. The book also draws a picture of the Shari'a (religious) Courts, the *qadis* and the *muftis* serving in Palestine. Two chapters elaborate on ideological aspects of the Council's activities; one of these contains a detailed description and analysis of the General Muslim Congress which convened in Jerusalem in 1931 under the auspices of Hajj Amin al-Husayni. Comparisons with the neighbouring countries supplement this case study of Islam under the specific circumstances of the British Mandate for Palestine.

E. J. Brill — P.O.B. 9000 — 2300 PA Leiden — The Netherlands

THE ENCYCLOPAEDIA OF ISLAM

NEW EDITION

PREPARED BY A NUMBER OF
LEADING ORIENTALISTS

EDITED BY

C. E. BOSWORTH, E. van DONZEL, W. P. HEINRICHS and Ch. PELLAT

ASSISTED BY F. Th. DIJKEMA AND Mme S. NURIT

UNDER THE PATRONAGE OF
THE INTERNATIONAL UNION OF ACADEMIES

VOLUME VI

FASCICULES 107-108

MARʿA<u>SH</u>ĪS — MĀSAR<u>DJ</u>AWAYH

LEIDEN
E.J. BRILL
1989

EXECUTIVE COMMITTEE:

All correspondence on editorial matters should be addressed to the Editorial Secretaries, whose addresses are:

For the English Edition

Dept. of Near Eastern Studies,
The University of Manchester,
Manchester,
England M13 9PL.

For the French Edition

Centre Universitaire
94, avenue des Grésillons
92600 Asnières
France

AUTHORS OF ARTICLES IN THESE FASCICULES

R. Arnaldez, University of Paris. 571.
R. W. J. Austin, University of Durham. 614.
J. E. Bencheikh, University of Paris. 626.
the late J. Bosch Vilá, University of Grenade. 577.
C. E. Bosworth, University of Manchester. 539, 542, 557, 618, 621, 623, 628.
J. T. P. de Bruijn, University of Leiden. 633.
[F. Buhl, Copenhagen]. 575.
J. Burton-Page, Church Knowle, Dorset. 534, 536, 537.
J. Calmard, Centre National de la Recherche Scientifique, Paris. 518, 556.
[P. de Cenival, Rabat]. 598.
the late E. Cerulli, University of Rome. 628.
P. Chalmeta, University of Madrid. 521.
A. Cohen, Hebrew University, Jerusalem. 544.
Patricia Crone, University of Oxford. 640.
H. Daiber, Free University, Amsterdam. 639.
G. Delanoue, University of Aix-Marseille. 602.
A. Dietrich, Göttingen. 557.
E. van Donzel, Netherlands Institute for the Near East, Leiden. 628.
N. Elisséeff, University of Lyons. 546, 548, 583.
Barbara Flemming, University of Leiden. 610.
W. J. Griswold, Colorado State University, Fort Collins. 613.
A. H. de Groot, University of Leiden. 532.
W. L. Hanaway, Jr., University of Pennsylvania, Philadelphia. 609.
P. Hardy, Fulford, York. 536.
G. R. Hawting, University of London. 625.
J. A. Haywood, Lewes, Sussex. 612.
[W. Heffening, Cologne]. 558.
Carole Hillenbrand, University of Edinburgh. 627.
[E. Honigmann, Brussels]. 544.
Penelope Johnstone, Oxford. 632.
F. de Jong, University of Utrecht. 627.
D. A. King, University of Frankfort. 598.
J. Knappert, London. 613.
[H. J. Kramers, Leiden]. 633, 634.
Ann K. S. Lambton, Kirknewton, Northumberland. 529.
[E. Lévi-Provençal, Paris]. 568.
[V. Minorsky, London]. 541, 542.
S. Moreh, Hebrew University, Jerusalem. 617.
M. Morony, University of California at Los Angeles. 634.
W. W. Müller, University of Marburg. 567.
S. Munro-Hay, London. 575.
[R. A. Nicholson, Cambridge]. 614.
Ch. Pellat, University of Paris. 608, 628, 636, 640.
[M. Plessner, Jerusalem]. 543.
J. Rikabi, Constantine. 539.
M. Rodinson, Ecole Pratique des Hautes Etudes, Paris. 587.
[E. Rossi, Rome]. 613.
J. Samsó, University of Barcelona. 543, 602.
Paula Sanders, Harvard University, Cambridge, Mass. 520.
R. Sellheim, University of Frankfort. 635.
Maya Shatzmiller, University of Western Ontario, London, Ont. 574.
S. Soucek, Princeton, New Jersey. 588.
Nada Tomiche, University of Paris. 599.
F. Viré, Centre National de la Recherche Scientifique, Paris. 537.
[A. J. Wensinck, Leiden]. 632.
[A. Yu. Yakubovskii, Moscow]. 621.

Names in square brackets are those of authors of articles reprinted or revised from the first edition of this Encyclopaedia.

(814-20/1411-17). Ghiyāth al-Dīn took refuge at Āmul under the protection of ᶜAlī Āmulī and then at Rustamdār under the protection of Malik Gayūmarth, and finally returned to Bārfurūsh-dih with his son Zayn al-ᶜĀbidīn. Aided by the sons of Riḍā al-Dīn, ᶜAlī Sārī expelled ᶜAlī Āmulī from Āmul; the latter took refuge at Rustamdār and then at Gīlān under the protection of Sayyid Riḍā Kiyā (*TTRM*, 321 ff.). ᶜAlī Sārī sent his brother Naṣīr al-Dīn to Harāt with *pīshkash* or presents. Under the pretext of the agitation maintained by ᶜAlī Āmulī and his supporters over a period of two years, he refused to pay the annual tribute and expelled the envoy of Shāhrukh, having cut off his beard. By chance, the punitive expedition mounted by Shāhrukh was obliged to make a detour towards Samarḳand, at which time, on the instructions of Naṣīr al-Dīn, who was being held hostage, Murtaḍā b. Kamāl al-Dīn came to offer apologies to Shāhrukh (816/1413). This same year, when ᶜAlī Sārī was suffering from an attack of gout, Malik Gayūmarth (of Rustamdār) brought ᶜAlī Āmulī back from Gīlān and sent him to Āmul with an army in pursuit of Ḳawām al-Dīn II.

Once returned to power, ᶜAlī Sārī decided to come to terms with Malik Gayūmarth, to whom he entrusted some territories (Namā-rustāḳ. Daylā-rustāḳ and Tartiya-rustāḳ). The union was sealed by matrimonial alliances (his son Murtaḍā married the daughter of Gayūmarth; the daughter of his nephew Ḳawām al-Dīn II (Āmulī) married Kāwūs b. Gayūmarth). After a temporary refuge at Tunukābun, ᶜAlī Āmulī regained Āmul from Ḳawām al-Dīn II (*TTRM*, 331 ff.).

Before dying, ᶜAlī Sārī named his son Murtaḍā as successor (820/1417). His brother Naṣīr al-Dīn promised to support the legitimacy of Murtaḍā, which Ghiyāth al-Dīn did not accept. Thus Naṣīr al-Dīn installed his nephew at Sārī (820-37/1417-33). He obtained from ᶜAlī Āmulī a guarantee not to rebel and strengthened ties with Malik Gayūmarth. But when Murtaḍā took power into his own hands, he made strenuous efforts to eliminate his uncle Ghiyāth al-Dīn and his two sons (whom he held as hostages), using for this purpose a former officer of Ghiyāth al-Dīn, Iskandar Rūzafzūn, whom he had made his *sipahsālār*. Disapproving of this conduct, Naṣīr al-Dīn left Murtaḍā. Prompted by Iskandar, Murtaḍā sent pursuers after Naṣīr al-Dīn, who reached Harāt by way of Čulāw, Sawādkūh and Dāmghān. He returned with Shāhrukh's army and a contract for the taxation of Māzandarān, but Murtaḍā made a higher bid and retained Māzandarān. After a fierce battle, Naṣīr al-Dīn was defeated by Murtaḍā and levies (*čarīk*) from Rustamdār. He was forced to flee to Nūr by way of Lārīdjān, then to Nātil-rustāḳ, and took up residence in the region of Rūdsar in Gīlān. Murtaḍā expelled ᶜAlī Āmulī and Naṣīr al-Dīn tried in vain to recapture Āmul. ᶜAlī Āmulī returned to Tunukābun, and Naṣīr al-Dīn to Rūdsar (824/1421). After a further attempt, ᶜAlī was wounded and died (825/1421-2). Naṣīr lived as a beneficiary of the ruler of Lāhidjān (Sayyid Riḍā Kiyā died in 829/1425-6 and was replaced by his brother Sayyid Ḥusayn Kiyā) until his death in 836/1433. The same year, Ghiyāth al-Dīn died in prison at Sārī (*TTRM*, 336 ff.).

Malik Gayūmarth sought to extend his domain towards Tunukābun and Daylamistān, and Murtaḍā was thus drawn, with his ally Amīr Ilyās, governor of Ḳūm, into a conflict from which he emerged victorious (832/1428-9). After governing firmly and fairly, Murtaḍā died (837/1433) and was succeeded by his son Shams al-Dīn Muḥammad (837-56/1433-52). Although a drinker, the latter was a decent and peace-loving man, regularly paying the annual revenue to Shahrūkh. On the death of Ḳawām al-Dīn II, the governorship of Āmul passed to his son Kamāl al-Dīn, who conscientiously paid tribute to Sārī. But Muḥammad had five sons, including two favourites, ᶜAbd al-Karīm and Kamāl al-Dīn, to whom he wanted to award governorships. His *sipahsālār* Bahrām Rūzafzūn suggested that Kamāl al-Dīn and the other descendants of Riḍā al-Dīn should be deprived of control of Āmul. Muḥammad expelled Kamāl al-Dīn and established ᶜAbd al-Karīm at Āmul, which was soon retaken by Kamāl al-Dīn with the aid of the people of Tunukābun. Muḥammad then sought to install Murtaḍā b. Riḍā al-Dīn (uncle of Kamāl al-Dīn) at Āmul. When Murtaḍā was put to flight by Kamāl al-Dīn in alliance with Ẓahīr al-Dīn b. Naṣīr al-Dīn, Muḥammad allied himself with Amīr Hindūka of Astarābād. This coalition expelled Kamāl al-Dīn and Ẓahīr al-Dīn, who sought refuge with Malik Gayūmarth at Rustamdār and then at Gīlān. Kamāl al-Dīn proceeded to regain from his uncle control of Āmul, which he retained until his death (849/1445-6). Murtaḍā (a pious and just man) then returned from exile in Rustamdār and was established in power at Āmul by the inhabitants and by dervishes (*TTRM*, 350 ff.).

On the death of Shāhrukh (850/447) the Tīmūrid Abu 'l-Ḳāsim Bābur b. Baysunghur undertook the conquest of Khurāsān and fought with Muḥammad for control of Māzandarān. In spite of the losses which he inflicted, Muḥammad was obliged to come to terms with Bābur, and gave him his daughter in marriage. Subsequently, he was forced to confront him again and was killed by one of his own officers acting on behalf of Babūr who, with the murder of his brother Muḥammad, controlled Khurāsān (Mahdjūrī, 465-6, according to *MS* and *RS*).

On the death of Muḥammad (865/1452), his son ᶜAbd al-Karīm was held hostage at Harāt (in the army of Djahān Shāh Ḳara-Ḳoyunlu, according to *ḤS*, iii, 352). A month after the temporary enthronement of his son ᶜAbd Allāh, ᶜAbd al-Karīm I arrived to take over the government of Sārī and of Māzandarān (856/1452 to 864/1459-60). Soon afterwards, Murtaḍā died and was replaced at Āmul by his son Shams al-Dīn, an incompetent drunkard. To obtain payment of the revenue, Bābur was obliged to send an expedition against ᶜAbd al-Karīm, who experienced difficulties with rival families claiming to be his *sipahsalar*: the Bābulkānī *sayyids* (ᶜAzīz and later Shams al-Dīn) to the east of Sārī, and Bahrām b. Iskandar Rūzafzūn to the west of Sārī. Killed at the instigation of Shams al-Dīn Bābulkānī, Bahrām was replaced by his brother ᶜAlī Rūzafzūn. ᶜAbd al-Karīm entrusted Āmul to Asad Allāh b. Ḥasan b. Riḍā al-Dīn (*TTRM*, 367 ff.).

After the death of Bābur (861/1457), Sulṭān Ibrāhīm and Maḥmūd competed for control of Māzandarān. Out of patience with the tyranny of Amīr Bābā Ḥasan, the Tīmūrid governor of Astarābād, Abd al-Karīm and the leading citizens of Māzandarān appealed to Djahān Shāh Ḳara Ḳoyunlu (d. 872/1467) to come and intimidate them (Mahdjūrī, 48, according to *MS* and *RS*). But the Tīmūrid took control of Khurāsān (863/1459), then, on two occasions, of Māzandarān which he gave in *suyūrghāl* to his son Maḥmūd. ᶜAbd Allāh b. ᶜAbd al-Karīm (ᶜAbd Allāh I) succeeded his father (865/1461 to 872/1467-8). Under this ruler, an ineffectual man and a drunkard, the Rūzafzūn and the Bābulkānī carried on their vendettas. The Bābulkānī replaced ᶜAbd

Allāh I with his uncle Kamāl al-Dīn even more of a drunkard and more ineffectual than this nephew, who returned to power. ᶜAbd Allāh I had another uncle, Mīr Ḳawām al-Dīn, a simple and virtuous man who went to live in Āmul, then governed by Asad Allāh. As he gained influence, ᶜAlī Rūzafzūn made him return to Sārī. But disorder erupted in Māzandarān following the elimination of ᶜAlī Rūzafzūn by the Bābulkānī *sayyids*. ᶜAbd Allāh I eliminated his rivals. He had his cousin Murtaḍā castrated and put his uncle Kamāl al-Dīn in prison where he died. Zayn al-ᶜĀbidīn avenged his father by killing ᶜAbd Allāh, whose son and heir, ᶜAbd al-Karīm was only four years old and lived in the *urdū* of Abū Saᶜīd. The majority of leading citizens pledged alliance to Zayn al-ᶜĀbidīn, but the Pāzavārī *sayyids* took pains to overthrow him. The supporters of ᶜAbd Allāh attempted to enthrone his son ᶜAbd al-Karīm, whom they brought back from Ādharbāydjān, but when Asad Allāh refused them entry to Āmul, Ābd al-Karīm was taken by his mother to the court of Ḥasan Beg Aḳ Ḳoyunlu (Uzun Ḥasan [*q.v.*]) with some *pishkashs*. Ḥasan Beg appointed one of his officers, Shiblī, who, with levies from Gīlān, Rustamdār and Māzandarān, established ᶜAbd al-Karīm at Sārī. But Zayn al-ᶜĀbidīn retained allies, including Sayyid Haybat Allāh Bābulkānī, who betrayed ᶜAbd al-Karīm and joined him. Hiding in the forest, he defied Shiblī's confederation and recaptured Sārī, then helped Ibrāhīm to drive his uncle Asad Allāh from Āmul. But on the orders of Malik Djahāngīr b. Kāwūs Pādūspānī, he reinstated Asad Allāh at Āmul. In the interval before acceding to power, ᶜAbd al-Karīm lived at Gīlān under the protection of Kār Kiyā Muḥammad (end of 878/1474) and spent seven months at Ḳum as the guest of Ḥasan Beg. Sayyid Ḥasan, one of the sons of Asad Allāh, left Āmul and went to Sārī to serve Zayn al-ᶜĀbidīn, who ordered the detention of Asad Allāh and his younger son Ḥusayn and installed Ḥasan at Āmul. Asad Allāh was imprisoned at Bārfurūsh-dih, but was freed by the inhabitants and, when reinstated at Āmul, urged ᶜAbd al-Karīm to join him in opposing Zayn al-ᶜĀbidīn. But the latter attacked Asad Allāh at night, had him executed and regained temporary control of Sārī (880/1476). ᶜAbd al-Karīm went to Āmul and then, with numerous supporters, took Sārī and control of Māzandarān, but was expelled once more by Zayn al-ᶜĀbidīn and was forced to take refuge for the third time at Lāhīdjān under the protection of Sayyid Muḥammad and then of his son ᶜAlī Kiyā, who sent him back to Māzandarān with a force commanded by Sayyid Ẓahīr al-Dīn Marᶜashī. Zayn al-ᶜĀbidīn fled to Sawādkūh and sent his brother Shams al-Dīn to appeal to Yaᶜḳūb Beg Aḳ Ḳoyunlu, who sent an army to confront Mīrzā ᶜAlī at Gīlān and another army to Māzandarān. Ẓahīr al-Dīn installed ᶜAbd al-Karīm at Sārī, but the latter fled once more to Gīlān at the approach of the army of Yaᶜḳūb Beg. In the disorder which ensued, a fiscal officer of Yaᶜḳūb Beg was killed (888/1483) when he tried to establish himself as independent sovereign at Sārī (*TG*, 443-4; Woods, 147, n. 38). The continuing agitation led to an Aḳ Ḳoyunlu invasion of Māzandarān and to a threat posed to ᶜAlī Kiyā, required to pay a heavy indemnity, and to his protégé ᶜAbd al-Karīm, who was extradited to Tabriz. Even after his annexation of Māzandarān, control remained difficult for Yaᶜḳūb Beg (Woods, 147, n. 40).

On the death of Zayn al-ᶜĀbidīn, his brother Shams al-Dīn succeeded him at Sārī (892/1486-7 to 905/1499-1500). Further bloody battles took place between ᶜAbd al-Karīm with the army of Gīlān (reinforced by Malik Bisutūn) and the army of Sārī. Temporally ousted, Shams al-Dīn regained Sārī through the good offices of his *sipahsālār*, Āḳā Rustam Rūzafzūn, who captured twelve *sardārs* of the army of Gīlān (*TKh*, 48 ff.). Faced by the unwillingness of Shams al-Dīn and Āḳā Rustam to return the prisoners, ᶜAlī Kiyā made his way towards Māzandarān (899/1493-4), and was joined by forces from Tunukābun, Rustamdār and Fīrūzkūh. These forces linked up at Tunukābun with an army from Astarābād sent by Badīᶜ al-Zamān Mīrzā. In spite of initial successes, the Gīlān confederacy was obliged to accept a compromise: Sārī and Āmul reverted to Shams al-Dīn and Bārfurūsh-dih to ᶜAbd al-Karīm (*TKh*, 65 ff.).

After the death of Shams al-Dīn, Āḳā Rustam enthroned the son of the former, Mīr Kamāl al-Dīn (905/1499-1500 to 908/1502-3). ᶜAbd al-Karīm made a further attempt, with the army of Gīlān, to regain Māzandarān. Defeated by Rustam Rūzafzūn, he went to Harāt, allied himself with the Tīmūrid Ḥusayn Bāyḳarā, and returned several times with the army of Khurāsān. Finally, Rustam (initially governor of Sawādkūh) assigned to him half of the revenue of Āmul and then, having eliminated Kamāl al-Dīn, firmly controlled Māzandarān and maintained good relations with the neighbouring powers. He admired Shaybak Khān Uzbek and died, it is said, when Shāh Ismāᶜīl Ṣafawī sent him the latter's hand after killing him (*Ilčī*, 78-9, *AAA*, 38-9, tr. 62-3).

After the death of Rustam, ᶜAbd al-Karīm was obliged to negotiate with his sons (Suhrāb and Muḥammad) and with the Ṣafawid power in order to regain a precarious control over Māzandarān (916/1510-11 to 932/1525-6). Having squandered his patrimony, Suhrāb attempted an alliance with ᶜAbd al-Karīm who eliminated him. Compelled by the Ṣafawid power to share the government of Māzandarān with Muḥammad Rūzafzūn (who maintained amicable relations with the leading Ṣafawid dignitary Čūha Sulṭān Tekkelu), ᶜAbd al-Karim regained his throne by force and subsequently reigned with benevolence and equity. A learned man, in spite of his stammer, he was eloquent and conversed with the *ᶜulamāʾ*. He was protected by Shāh Ismāᶜīl, whose commensal he was. But under Ṭahmāsp (1524-76), Čūha Sulṭān obtained the release of Muḥammad Rūzafzūn (imprisoned under Shāh Ismāᶜīl) and established him at Sārī. Ābd al-Karīm returned to Bārfurūsh-dih, where he died at about 24 years old after an unsuccessful attack on Muḥammad.

The *sayyids* and leading citizens were divided into two groups regarding the succession, some favouring the son and heir designate Amīr Shāhī (932/1525-6 to 938/1531), others his brother Sulṭān Maḥmūd. Placed in power by one faction, Maḥmūd was quickly deposed and sought refuge with Muḥammad Rūzafzūn who eliminated him (*Ilčī*, 86). Amīr Shāhī led a licentious life, and delegated official business to Amīr ᶜAlī Ḥusaynī who was soon eliminated by the partisans of Maḥmūd. Out of patience, the leading citizens turned towards Muḥammad Rūzafzūn. Others allied themselves with ᶜAbd Allāh b. Sulṭān Maḥmūd. Amīr Shāhī joined Ṭahmāsp's retinue in Khurāsān, and Muḥammad Rūzafzūn had him assassinated on his return to Māzandarān, at Āhūsar (near Fīrūzkūh) by Muẓaffar Beg Turkamān. Muḥammad also eliminated some of the Marᶜashī princes (Sulṭān Murād b. Mīr Shāhī, then in Gīlān, escaped the massacre), then dominated Māzandarān and maintained its security (939/1533-4 to 952/1545-

6; *Ilčī*, 86 ff.). He entrusted military affairs to Ḥasan-mat, a leading citizen of Sawādkūh, who appointed his brother Surhāb-mat to the *wikālat* of Āḳā Rustam, elder son of Muḥammad, and his other brother Gustahm to the governorate of Sawādkūh. In gradual stages, all districts of Māzandarān came under the control of his relations, but jealous parties impelled Muḥammad to depose Ḥasan-mat and his associates and disorder ensued. S̲h̲āh Ṭahmāsp sent an expedition (in 952/1545-6) to avenge the blood of Amīr S̲h̲āhī. But Muḥammad maintained a longstanding friendship with the *wakīl* Ḳāḍī D̲j̲ahān, who was able to pacify the S̲h̲āh. Mīr ᶜAbd Allāh b. Sulṭān Maḥmūd came to Rustamdār to avenge his father, and defeated the army commanded by Āḳā Rustam near Barfūrūsh-dih. Almost a year after this defeat, Āḳā Rustam died (*Ilčī*, 89 ff.).

After killing Farāmarz b. Muḥammad—who was in the Ṣafawid *urdū*—at the time of his father-in-law's death, and expelling Suhrāb, nephew of Muḥammad (enthroned at Sārī for a brief period)—ᶜAbd Allāh b. Māhmūd ruled over the whole of Māzandarān. Ignoring the demands of S̲h̲āh Taḥmāsp to pay tax and to restore the funds of Muḥammad Rūzafzūn, he was deposed in favour of Sulṭān Murād b. Amīr S̲h̲āhī who, under Muḥammad Rūzafzūn, was part of the retinue of S̲h̲āh Taḥmāsp at Ḳazwīn. Summoned to repay the funds of Muḥammad, ᶜAbd Allāh was tortured by Murād and put to death in the course of a collective execution involving *sayyids* and other leading citizens of Māzandarān (969/1561-2). Shortly afterwards, Murād died, leaving the government (in part, see below) of Māzandarān to his son "Mīrzā K̲h̲ān" Sulṭān Maḥmūd (*Ilčī*, 90-6). Two sons of ᶜAbd Allāh and their sister took refuge at the court of S̲h̲āh Taḥmāsp. The elder of the two, Ibrāhīm, died after consuming opium. Taḥmāsp married the daughter of ᶜAbd Allāh, K̲h̲ayr al-Nisāʾ Begum (Mahd-i ᶜUlyā), to his eldest son, Sulṭān Muḥammad K̲h̲udābanda (see below). Mīrzā K̲h̲ān was obliged to share the government of Māzandarān with the elder son of Muḥammad K̲h̲udābanda, Ḥasan Mīrzā, accompanied by a *wakīl*, Mīrak Dīv, whom he caused to be assassinated at the instigation of Mīr ᶜAzīz K̲h̲ān, another son of ᶜAbd Allāh (*AAA*, 210, 240, tr. 312-13, 358-9). After the death of S̲h̲āh Taḥmāsp (984/1576), control of Māzandarān reverted in entirety to Mīrzā K̲h̲ān, through the good offices of S̲h̲ams al-Dīn Dīv, but in order to avenge the death of her father ᶜAbd Allāh, Mahd-i ᶜUlyā had Mīrzā K̲h̲ān assassinated and replaced him with her uncle Mīr ᶜAlī K̲h̲ān b. Maḥmūd, who died soon afterwards (*AAA*, 210-11, 240-1; tr. 312-13, 358-9; on the campaigns of Mīr ᶜAlī K̲h̲ān against Mīrzā K̲h̲ān and his "reign", see Mīr Taymūr, 201-2; on the successors of ᶜAbd Allāh K̲h̲ān, see also *D̲j̲ahān-ārā*, 91-2; S̲h̲āyān, *Māzandarān*, 230-1).

In the chaos which ensued, Mahd-i ᶜUlyā was assassinated in her turn. While *ḳizilbās̲h̲* factionalism enfeebled Ṣafawid power, Māzandarān was the object of competition between various local potentates. After the death of Mīr ᶜAlī K̲h̲ān, his control was shared between Sayyid Muẓaffar Murtaḍāʾī (of Hazārd̲j̲arīb, d. 1005/1596-7) and Alvand Dīv, but the descendants of the various branches of the Marᶜas̲h̲ī family continued to struggle for power. Notable among the latter were Mīr Ḥusayn K̲h̲ān, cousin of Mīr ᶜAlī K̲h̲ān (Mīr Taymūr, 282-3) and especially Mīr Sulṭān Murād II b. Mīrza K̲h̲ān (*ibid.*, 316-17). This unstable situation persisted until annexation to the Ṣafawid crown (see below). At Iṣfahān, distant descendants of Mīr-i Buzurg were influential at the centre of Ṣafawid power (below, 2).

Political, religious and cultural activity. In pre-Ṣafawid Iran, the Marᶜas̲h̲ī movement represents an interesting case of political aspirations from which "Mahdism" is apparently absent. Unlike the militant messianism professed by the "S̲h̲īᶜī republic" of the Sarbadārs of Sabzavār (1338-81), it remains, although S̲h̲īᶜī, within the framework of Ṣūfism (Arjomand, 68-9, 83; on the Marᶜas̲h̲īs in the context of "popular" movements, see Petrushevsky, *Islām dar Īrān*, tr. K. Kis̲h̲āvarz, Tehran 1354, 379-80). Few indications are available, however, as to the doctrine of the Marᶜas̲h̲īs between the 8th/14th and 10th/16th centuries, preoccupied as they were with the extension or defence of their power (very few theological or literary works have survived, see below). Their immunity as *sayyids* saved them from the extermination inflicted by Tīmūr on the Sarbadārs and other local potentates, but the charisma enjoyed by the founders—Mīr-i Buzurg and his sons—suffered from the erosion of power.

During the "second phase", after the death of Tīmūr, their descendants divided into rival groups competing for control of Sārī, Āmul, Bārfurūs̲h̲-dih and the frontier zones (in the east, Ḳaraṭug̲h̲an; in the west, Rustamdār; in the south, the foothills of the mountains) which, with Gīlān, often provided refuges for claimants temporarily deprived of power. Control of Sārī, entailing that of Māzandarān, was the most hotly-contested. Essentially, it belonged to the descendants of Kamāl al-Dīn, while Āmul was controlled in the 8th/14th-9th/15th centuries by Riḍā al-Dīn and his descendants. But claimants from both branches remained in a state of constant rivalry.

Limited to the east by Tīmūrid control of Astarābād, the influence of the Marᶜas̲h̲īs was more easily extended on the side of their allies in Gīlān, especially at Lāhīd̲j̲ān [*q.v.*], where they assisted Sayyid ᶜAlī Kiyā to establish himself as master of Biyā-pīs̲h̲ and to extend his control as far as Ḳazwīn, Ṭārum and S̲h̲amīrān. The rivalries between claimants were complicated by the fact that some were supported by contemporary powers (Tīmūrids, Ḳara Ḳoyunlu, Aḳ Ḳoyunlu and Ṣafawids), while others asserted to varying degrees a refusal of allegiance or independence. Increasingly threatened by local powers, they sought alliances and even, after the end of the 8th/14th century, marriages with influential families (Kiyā-i D̲j̲alāl, Kār Kiyā, Pāzavārī, Rustamdārī, etc.). Eclipsed in their domains by the Rūzafzūn of Sawādkūh in the early 10th/16th century, the Marᶜas̲h̲īs were in no position to compete with the increasing power of the Ṣafawids. It was another S̲h̲īᶜī power, that of Amīr Ḥusayn Kiyā Čulāwī, which was obliged to tackle S̲h̲āh Ismāᶜīl I (1501-24) in order to establish a precarious control over Māzandarān in 909/1504 (Savory, *Consolidation*, 73-4). It was to assert his hereditary rights as grandson of Mīr ᶜAbd Allāh K̲h̲ān Marᶜas̲h̲ī (through his mother) that S̲h̲āh ᶜAbbās took control of Māzandarān in 1005/1596; local non-Marᶜas̲h̲ī chieftains (Sayyid Muẓaffar Murtaḍāʾī, Alvand Dīv and especially Malik Bahman Lārīd̲j̲ānī) were obliged to defeat or subdue his general Farhād K̲h̲ān Ḳaramanlu (*AAA*, 518 ff.; tr. 693 ff.).

Some important vestiges of the Marᶜas̲h̲ī domination have survived in Māzandarān, a region subject to frequent earthquakes. The mausoleum (sometimes called mosque) of Ḳawām al-Dīn Mīr-i Buzūrg at Āmul, constructed in 781/1379-80, destroyed under Iskandar-i S̲h̲ayk̲h̲ī, rebuilt after the death of Tīmūr, decorated with *kās̲h̲ī*s [*q.v.*] and embellished with gold under S̲h̲āh ᶜAbbās I, was in a quite dilapidated state in the mid-19th century (Stuart, quoted by Rabino,

Māzandarān, 37; drawings from photographs in the Morgan (1307/1890) reproduced in Mahdjūrī, 24; Rabino, *Le Guilan*, Illustrations, 87). The Gunbad-i Naṣīr al-Ḥaḳḳ or Naṣīr al-Kabīr (i.e. of the *dāᶜī* Ḥasan b. ᶜAlī al-Uṭrush) was built (or restored?) at Āmul by Sayyid ᶜAlī b. Kamāl al-Dīn (*TTRM*, 328 ff.; Mahdjūrī, 36, 339). Among the monuments of Sārī, the *Imām-zāda* Zayn al-ᶜĀbidīn shelters the tombs of Zayn al-ᶜĀbidīn and Shams al-Dīn, son of Kamāl al-Dīn b. Muḥammad (Rabino, Māzandarān, 55; Mahdjūrī, 340; photograph in Rabino, *Le Guilan*, Illustrations, 89). On the monuments of Māzandarān and the tombs of the Marᶜashīs, see Sutūda, *Astārā*, iv, v (photographs and numerous indices).

2. Some descendants of the Marᶜashī Sayyids of Māzandarān. Although all related to Ālī al-Marᶜash/al-Marᶜashī or to Ḥasan al-Marᶜashī, the Marᶜashī *sayyids* are divided into various branches (in Māzandarān, at Ḳazwīn, Iṣfahān, Shūshtar, Mashhad, Nadjaf, etc.) in which the lines of kinship are sometimes hard to trace. The only ones to be mentioned here are the best-known, in the period subsequent to the foundation of the dynasty (on other Marᶜashīs, see below, 3).

In spite of their charisma and their acknowledged status as *sayyids*, very few of the Marᶜashīs of the dynasty gained renown as *ᶜulamā*ʾ or *udabā*ʾ. Besides Kamāl al-Dīn b. Mīr-i Buzurg, a prolific author and poet (*Rayḥānat*, iv, 12), two historians have left vivid accounts of their family. The best-known, Ẓahīr al-Dīn b. Naṣīr al-Dīn, spent the greater part of his life at Gīlān, where he had taken refuge with his father. Becoming one of the senior officers of the sovereigns of Biyā-pīsh (Lāhīdjān), he participated with the army of the Gīlānīs in numerous operations in Māzandarān (see above). Two important works of this author are available (*TTRM*, *TG*, in *Bibl.*). The date of his death must have been close to the last events described in *TG* (894/1488-9); on the author, his brothers and sons, his works, see *TTRM* (ed. Shāyān, *Muḳaddima*, where there is reproduction of an article by Kasravī and a translation of the Preface of Dorn's edition; ed. Tasbīḥī, with reproduction of an article by Kasravī; *TG*, *Muḳaddima*, by M. Sutūda). Little is known of the works of the second historian, Mīr Taymūr, identified by M. Sutūda as a son of ᶜAbd al-Karīm b. ᶜAbd Allāh. His only known work (see *Bibl.*, s.v. Mīr Taymūr) constitutes a kind of supplement to the *TTRM*, which comes to an end in 881/1476-7, and recounts the history of the family until 1075/1664-5.

Beginning at the start of the 9th/15th century, the migration of the Marᶜashī *sayyids* beyond the bounds of Māzandarān accelerated with their decline. Under the Ṣafawids, many of them settled at Shūshtar, Iṣfahān, Shīrāz, and then in India, at Nadjāf, etc. These migrations sometimes took the form of deportations. Among the descendants of representatives of the dynasty, Shāh Mīr b. Mīr Ḳawām al-Dīn, grandson of Mīr ᶜAlī Khān, deported to Iṣfahān, was followed by a group of Marᶜashī *sayyids* deported to Shīrāz in 1039/1629 (Mīr Taymūr, 377 ff.).

The Marᶜashī *sayyids* of Shūshtar were related to ᶜAlī Marᶜash/Marᶜashī and to the *sayyids* of Māzandarān. Mīr Nadjm al-Dīn b. Aḥmad, coming from Āmul on a pilgrimage to the *ᶜatabāt*, settled in Shūshtar where he was *naḳīb* at the beginning of the 9th/15th century. When Shāh Ismāᶜīl took the town (914/1508), he confirmed in office his fourth descendant, the *naḳīb* Mīr Nūr Allāh, who disseminated Imāmī Shīᶜism there. While the Marᶜashīs of Shūshtar tended to an increasing extent to migrate towards Shīrāz and India, the Imāmī Shīᶜī *ᶜālim* Ḳāḍī Nūr Allāh b. Mīr Sharīf b. Mīr Nūr Allāh (965-1019/1549-1610), author of numerous works (including the *Madjālis* and *Iḥḳāḳ*, see *Bibl.*), held the office of *ḳāḍī* at Lāhawr, under Akbar. On the instigation of Sunnī *ᶜulamā*ʾ, he was executed at the orders of Djahāngīr. Imāmī Shīᶜīs conferred on him the title of Third Martyr. His son, ᶜAlāʾ al-Mulk Ḥusaynī Shūshtarī Marᶜashī, was the author of the *Firdaws*; his descendants ultimately settled at Nadjaf (*Firdaws*, 16 ff.; see also *Muḳaddima* and *Taᶜlīḳāt*; *Tadhkira-yi Shūshtar*, 33 ff.; *Rayḥānat*, ii, 436-9). Amīr Asad Allāh b. Mīr Zayn al-Dīn Marᶜashī Shūshtarī (d. 963/1555-6) was appointed *ṣadr* under Shāh Ṭahmāsp in 943/1536-7. His son, Mīr Sayyid ᶜAlī, shared the *ṣidāra* with Muḥammad Yūsuf Astarābādī, and later performed the *tawliya* of the sanctuary of Imām Riḍā at Mashhad (*AAA*, 144, 316, tr., 251, 450; *AT*, 362, 510-11; *KhT*, 435. 797; *Firdaws*, 21-2 and *Taᶜlīḳāt*, 195 ff.). Another descendant, Amīr Zayn al-Dīn, received the *ṣidāra* of Shīrwān, of Khurāsān and of Ādharbāydjān in 970/1562-3 (*AT*, 538).

At Iṣfahān, descendants of Mīr-i Buzurg formed the influential family of the Khulafāʾ Sayyids, of which the most eminent representative was the *ᶜālim* Khalīfa Sulṭān Ḥusayn b. Muḥammad b. Maḥmūd al-Ḥusaynī, son-in-law of Shāh Abbās I, appointed *wazīr-i-dīwān-i aᶜlā* (1033/1624), while his father Mīrzā Rafīᶜ al-Dīn held the post of *ṣadr*. Under Shāh Ṣafī (1629-42), he was exiled to Ḳūm, and his four sons were blinded (as were some Ṣafawid princes). He returned to the *wizāra* under Shāh ᶜAbbās II (1642-66) and died at Ashraf in 1064/1653-4 (*AAA*, 1013, tr. 1234 sq.; Mahdjūrī, 15; Shāyān, *Māzandarān*, 233).

Other Marᶜashis enjoyed the favour of Ṣafawid sovereigns. Under Shāh Ṭahmāsp, Mīr ᶜAlāʾ al-Mulk Marᶜash, *ḳāḍī-i ᶜaskar*, was appointed *ṣadr* of Gīlān (*AAA*, 155, tr. 234). The *ᶜālim* Sayyid Asad Allāh Ḥusaynī Marᶜashī "Shah Mīr" (d. 984/1576-7)—who also exercised the *ṣidāra*—was appointed *mutawallī* of the sanctuary of Imām Riḍā at Mashhad (*Rayḥānat*, iv, 10-11). Other Marᶜashīs continued to exercise this important function at the shrine-town of Mashhad [*q.v.*]. Their descendants were even able to claim double Ṣafawid and Marᶜashī lineage on account of Mīrza Sayyid Muḥammad Mutawallī (1126-76/1714-63), crowned under the name of Shāh Sulaymān II at Mashhad in January 1740 (on this "forty days' king" and his genealogy, see Gulistāna, *Mudjmal al-tawārīkh*, ed. Mudarris Raḍawī, Tehran 2536/1977, 396 ff. and index; *Madjmaᶜ al-tawārīkh*, 90 ff.). His grandson, Mīrzā Muḥammad Khalīl Marᶜashī Ṣafawī (who died in Bengal *ca.* 1220/1805-6) was the author of the *Madjmaᶜ al-tawārīkh* (ed. ᶜA. Iḳbāl, Tehran 1328 A.S.H.; see *Muḳaddima*; *Rayḥānat*, iv, 12-13).

Many other Marᶜashīs have played important roles in the religious or political domain since the time of the Ṣafawids (Marᶜashī-Nadjafī, in *TTRM*, ed. Tasbīḥī, *Muḳaddima*, 41-2; Fischer, 94-5). The *ᶜālim* Sayyid Aḥmad b. Muḥammad b. ᶜAlī Musawī Marᶜashī was a close associate of Faṭh ᶜAlī Shāh Ḳādjār (*Rayḥānat*, iv, 10). Scion of an *ᶜulamā*ʾ lineage, Mīr Muḥammad Ḥusayn Shahristānī Ḥāʾirī b. Mīr Muḥammad ᶜAlī b. Muḥammad Ḥusayn Ḥusaynī Marᶜashī (*mardjaᶜ-i taḳlīd* at Karbalā) was the author of numerous works, as was his son Ḥādjdj Shaykh Mīrzā 'Alī Shahristānī, who settled at Ḳum (*ibid.*, 362-3). Currently, the most eminent *ᶜālim* of the family is the *āyatallāh* Shihāb al-Dīn Muḥammad Ḥusayn b. Maḥmūd Ḥusaynī Marᶜashī Nadjafī (born at Nadjaf in 1315/1897). Having arrived at Ḳūm in 1924, he is best known as *mutawallī* of numerous *madrasas*, of which one, endowed with a wealthy library, bears his name (brief biography in *Rayḥānat*, iv, 11-12; Fischer, index; Momen, 317). Although

TABLE A
THE LINE OF MĪR ḲAWĀM AL-DĪN MARʿASHĪ "MĪR-I BUZURG"

	After:	
Ẓahīr al-Dīn Marʿashī[1]	*The Ṣafawid sources*[3]	*ʿAbbās Shāyān*[5]
Imām ʿAlī Zayn al-ʿĀbidīn	Zayn al-ʿĀbidīn	Zayn al-Ābidīn
Ḥusayn al-Aṣghar	Ḥusayn al-Asghar	al-Ḥasan Abū Muḥammad
Ḥasan al-Marʿashī	Ḥasan	Muḥammad Abu 'l-Karām
Muḥammad	Muḥammad al-Akbar	ʿAbd Allāh Abū Muḥammad
Ābd Allāh	ʿAbd Allāh	ʿAlī al-Marʿashī Abu 'l-Ḥasan
ʿAlī	Ālī al-Marʿash[4]	al-Ḥusayn Abū ʿAbd Allāh
Ḥusayn	Ḥasan	ʿAlī Abu 'l-Ḥusayn
ʿAbd Allāh	ʿAlī	Abū Hāshim
Ṣādiḳ	Abū Hāshim	Muḥammad Abū ʿAbd Allāh
Muḥammad[2]	Muḥammad	ʿAbd Allāh Abū Ṣādiḳ
ʿAbd Allāh	Abd Allāh	al-Ṣādiḳ
Ḳawām al-Dīn	Ṣādiḳ	Ḳawām al-Dīn
	Ḳawām al-Dīn	

Notes to Table A

(1) *TTRM*, ed. Tasbīhī, 166.

(2) Muḥammad absent from *TTRM*, ed. Shāyān, 236.

(3) *Djahān-ārā*, 88; Yazdī, fol. 2a; Shūshtārī, *Madjālis*, ii, 380.

(4) The *laḳab* al-Marʿash (a kind of pigeon) is said to have been given in the first place to ʿAlī Marʿash, the eponym of the Marʿashi *Sayyids* (*Rayḥāna*, iv, 10). In Yazdī, ʿAlī al-Marʿash and his son Ḥasan are made into a single "al-Marʿash".

(5) *TTRM*, *Muḳaddima* (approved by the Āyatallāh Marʿashī-Nadjafī, *TTRM*, ed. Tasbiḥī, *Muḳaddima*, 39-40, with typographical errors).

more and more involved in the world of politics and public affairs, the Marʿashīs of Iran regard themselves predominantly as religious "specialists" (*rūḥāniyyūn*), with the religious line contracting matrimonial alliances among the élite of the *ʿulamāʾ*. Alongside the major branch constituted by the family of the *āyatallāh* Marʿashi-Nadjafī—one of the seven leading *mardjaʿ-i taḳlīds* in 1975 (a position still held in 1985: Momen, 249)—there exists a junior branch of Marʿashī *mardjaʿ-i taḳlīds* at Shīrāz (see Fischer, tables, 90, 92, 94).

Like other Imāmī *ʿulamāʾ*, the Marʿashī *sayyids* have established themselves in various parts of the Muslim world (Iran, ʿIrāḳ, Syria, Turkey and Egypt) and in countries of the Indian Ocean fringes (East Africa (Zanzibar) and Java (*Rayḥānat*, iv, 12)). Sayyid ʿAbd al-Ḥusayn Marʿashī Shushtarī was sent to Zanzibar in 1885 as *mullā* to guide the newly-established Imāmī community there (Momen, 317).

3. Other Marʿashīs. In the genealogies of descendants of ʿAlī Marʿash/Marʿashī (or Ḥasan Marʿashī), mention is found of titles or functions such as *muḥaddith*, *faḳīh*, *naḳīb al-ashrāf*, *wazīr*, etc., which indicate that previous to Mīr-i Buzurg, some of them must have held office or wielded a certain influence in ʿIrāḳ and later in Iran, in the capacity of *ʿulamāʾ* or *naḳībs* of the *sayyids*, or in administration. Among the other *sayyid* or non-*sayyid* Marʿashīs, whose lines of kinship with the various branches of the Marʿashīs are uncertain, the following are worthy of mention: Sayyid Ḥasan b. Ḥamza b. Alī Marʿash, Abū Muḥammad Ṭabarī Marʿashī, *ʿālim* of Ṭabaristan who went to Baghdād in 356/966-7 and died there two years late (*Rayḥānat*, iv, 11); Ḥusayn b. Muḥammad Marʿashī, Abū Manṣūr (d. 421/1030), historian and close associate of Sulṭān Maḥmūd of Ghazni (*ibid.*); Sayyid Aḥmad b. ʿAlawī Marʿashī (d. 539/1144-5) extremist Shīʿī *ʿālim* (*ghuluwwī*) who travelled widely before settling at Sārī where he died (*ibid.*, 10); and Shibāb al-Dīn Aḥmad b. Abū Bakr b. Ṣāliḥ b. ʿUmar Marʿashī, Abū al-ʿAbbās, Ḥanafī *faḳīh* (d. 872/1467-8) (see Dihkhudā, *Lughat-nāma*, s.v. Marʿashī).

Bibliography and abbreviations: *AAA* = Iskandar Beg Munshī, *Tārīkh-i ʿālam-ārā-yi ʿabbāsī*, ed. Īradj Afshār, Tehran 1334-5/1956-7, tr. R. Savory, *History of Shah ʿAbbas the Great*, Boulder, Col. 1978 (notes unpubl. variants); Āmulī, *Tārīkh-i Rūyān*, ed. M. Sutūda, Tehran 1348 sh.; *AT* = Ḥasan Beg Rumlu, *Aḥsan al-tawārīkh*, ed. ʿA. Nawāʾī, Tehran 1357 sh.; S. A. Arjomand, *The shadow of God and the Hidden Imam*, Chicago 1984; *Djahān-ārā* = Ḳāḍī Aḥmad Ghaffārī, *Nusakh-i Djahān-ārā*, ed. H. Narāḳī (*Tārīkh-i Djahan-ārā*), Tehran 1343 *sh.*; *Firdaws* = ʿAlāʾ al-Mulk Shushtarī, *Firdaws dar tārīkh-i Shūshtar wa barkhī az mashāhir-i ān*, ed. Muḥaddith Urmawī, Tehran 1352 sh.; M. J. Fischer, *Iran. From religious dispute to revolution*, Cambridge, Mass. and London 1980; "The Qum Report" (Fischer 1976) which contains unpubl. biographical information; Mullā Shaykh ʿAlī Gīlānī, *Tārīkh-i Māzandarān*, ed. M. Sutūda, Tehran 1352 sh.; ḤS = Khwāndmīr, *Ḥabīb al-siyar*, ed. Dabīr-Siyāḳī, 4 vols., Tehran 1333 sh.; *Iḥḳāḳ* = Nūr Allāh Shushtarī, *Iḥḳāḳ al-ḥaḳḳ*, Tehran 1376/1956; *Ilčī* = Khūrshāh b. Ḳubād Ḥusaynī, *Tārīkh-i Ilčī-i Niẓāmshah*, cited after ed. Schefer, *Chrestomathie persane*, ii, Paris 1885, 56/104; *KhT* = Ḳāḍī Aḥmad Ḳumī, *Khulāṣat al-tawārīkh*, ed. Ishrāḳī, Tehran, i, (1359 sh.), ii (1363 sh.); *Madjālis* = Nūr Allāh Shushtarī, *Madjālis al-Muʾminīn*, 2 vols., ed. Islāmiyya, i, Tehran 1375 A.H., ii, 1354 pp.; Ismāʿīl Mahdjurī, *Tārīkh-i Māzandarān*, ii, Sārī 1345 sh.; Mīr Taymūr Marʿashī, *Tārīkh-i khāndān-i Marʿashī-i Māzandarān*, ed. M. Sutūda, Tehran 2536/1977; Moojan Momen, *An introduction to Shiʾi Islam. This history and doctrine of Twelver Shiʾism*, New Haven-London 1985; *MS* = ʿAbd al-Razzāḳ Samarḳandī, *Maṭlaʿ al-saʿdayn wa-madjmaʿ al-baḥrayn*, 2 vols., ed. Lāhawr 1941-9, ed. Tehran 1353 sh.; Sayyid Ḥusayn Mudarrisī Ṭabāṭabāʾ ī, *Bargī az tārīkh-i Ḳazwīn*, Ḳum 1361 *p.* (contains material on the Marʿashī *sādat* acting as *mutawallīs* and *muḥtasib* in Ḳazwīn); H. L. Rabino, *Les provinces caspiennes de la*

Perse, Le Guilan, in *RMM*, xxxii (1916-17), *Illustrations*; idem, *Les dynasties alaouites du Māzandarān*, in *JA* (1927), 253-77; idem, *Māzandarān and Astarābād*, GMS, n.s., VII, London 1928; idem, *Les dynasties du Māzandarān*, in *JA* (1936), 397-474; idem. *L'Histoire du Mazandarān*, in *JA* (1943-5), 211-45; *Rayḥānat* = Muḥammad ʿAli Mudarris Tabrīzī, *Rayḥānat al-adab*, 5 vols. (see also Samʿānī, *Ansāb*, 13 vols., Hyderabad 1963-81; M. Tihrānī, *Ṭabaḳāt aʿlām al-shīʿa*, 2 vols., Nadjaf 1954, 5 vols., Beirut 1971-5; R. Savory, *The consolidation of Safawid power in Persia*, in *Isl.*, xli (1965), 71-94; *RṢ* = Mīrkh-wānd, *Rawḍat al-ṣafā*, 7 vols., Tehran 1338-9 sh.; ʿAbbās Shāyān, *Māzandarān. Djughrāfiyī-i tārīkhī wa iḳtiṣādī*, I, Tehran 1336 sh.; M. Sutūda, *Az Astārā tā Astarābād*, 7 vols., Tehran 1349-56 sh.; idem, *Darvīshān-i Māzandarān*, in *Tārīkh*, ii (2536/1977), 7-29; Shāh Ṭahmāsp Ṣafawī, *Tadhkira*, ed. P. Horn, in *ZDMG*, xliv (1890), 563-649; Sayyid ʿAbd Allāh al-Ḥusaynī, *Tadhkira-yi Shūshtar*, Calcutta 1343/-1924; TGD = Ẓahīr al-Dīn Marʿashī, *Tārīkh-i Gīlān wa Daylamistān*, ed. Sutūda, Tehran 1347 sh.; *Tkh* = Lāhīdjī, *Tārīkh Khānī*, ed. Sutūda, Tehran 1352 sh.; *TTRM* = Ẓahīr al-Dīn Marʿashī, *Tārīkh-i Ṭabaristān wa Rūyān wa Māzandarān*, ed. B. Dorn, St. Petersburg 1850, ed. ʿA. Shāyān, Tehran 1333 sh.; ed. M. Tasbīḥī, Tehran 1345 sh.; (cited in ed. Shāyān); J. Woods, *The Aqquyunlu*, Minneapolis-Chicago 1976; Yazdī = Djalāl al-Dīn Munadjdjim Yazdī, *Rūz-nāma*, ms. B.L. Or. 6263; Sharaf al-Dīn ʿAlī Yazdī, *Ẓafar-nāma*, ed. M. ʿAbbāsī, 2 vols, Tehran 1336 sh.

(J. Calmard)

MARĀSIM (A), official court ceremonies, both processional and non-processional. The whole range of ceremonial, including protocol and etiquette, is called also *rusūm*; other terms found frequently are *mawsim* [*q.v.*] and *mawkib*. *Mawākib* [*q.v.*] refer specifically to solemn processions, but seem also to have had the more general meaning of audiences (for the ʿAbbāsids, see references in D. Sourdel, *Le vizirat ʿabbāside de 749 à 946*, Damascus 1960, ii, 684, n. 3; for the Fāṭimids, see e.g. al-Ḳalḳashandī, *Ṣubḥ*, iii, 494: *djulūs* [*al-khalīfa*] *fi 'l-mawākib*; *ayyām al-mawākib*).

1. Under the caliphate and the Fāṭimids.

The caliph presided over court ceremonies seated on a throne (*kursī*, *sarīr*), a custom dating back to the Umayyads, surrounded by the insignia of sovereignty (*shiʿār al-khilāfa*), and veiled by a curtain (*sitr*). The insignia, according to al-Ḳalḳashandī, *Ṣubḥ*, iii, 269-72, are: the seal (*khātam* [*q.v.*], the mantle of the Prophet (*burda* [*q.v.*], the staff (*ḳaḍīb* [*q.v.*]), the caliphal garments (*thawb* [see khilʿa and libās]), and [the dynastic] colour displayed in banners and robes of honour [see ʿalam and khilʿa]. Most of these insignia can be traced back to the Prophet himself. To these, the prerogatives of the *khuṭba* and *sikka* [*q.vv.*] can be added. For further discussion of insignia of sovereignty, see Ibn Khaldūn, *Muḳaddima*, tr. Rosenthal, New York 1957, ii, 48 ff.

Clear distinctions were made between ceremonial costume and ordinary wear. When summoned to the palace by al-Muḳtadir shortly before his arrest in 306/918, the vizier Ibn al-Furāt enquired, *bi-thiyāb al-mawkib am bi-durrāʿa*? ("in ceremonial dress or the *durrāʿa* [everyday costume of the scribal class]?", al-Ṣābī, *Kitāb al-Wuzarāʾ*, 264).

The ʿAbbāsid caliph wore a black *ḳabāʾ* and black *ruṣāfiyya* (a *ḳalansuwa*-type turban), and red boots. He girded himself with the sword of the Prophet. To his left, another sword was kept, and in front of him, the Ḳurʾān of ʿUthmān. He wore the *burda* and held the *ḳaḍīb* (al-Ṣābī, *Rusūm dār al-khilāfa*, ed. Mikhaʾīl ʿAwwād, Baghdād 1383/1964, 90-8, tr. Elie A. Salem, *The rules and regulations of the ʿAbbasid court*, Beirut 1977). Dignitaries, *arbāb al-marātib*, wore black *ḳabāʾ*s and black robes of honour (*khilaʿ*) were conferred on army commanders and honoured notables (al-Ṣābī, *op. cit.*, 90-4).

For the Fāṭimids, the sources on caliphal costume are more plentiful. The *dār al-kiswa* (see al-Maḳrīzī, *Khiṭaṭ*, i, 409-13) provided magnificent costumes to the caliph and his entourage for each ceremony, as well as the *khilʿ*as bestowed on innumerable occasions. The Fāṭimid colour was white, and the caliph's garments were often made of white *dabīḳī*, a fine silk stuff [see dabīḳ]. The most common term for Fāṭimid court apparel is *badla*, an outfit consisting of eleven pieces (al-Maḳrīzī, *op. cit.*, i, 413: *badla mawkibiyya*). The caliphs adopted the white *ṭaylasān* of lawyers and judges during Ramaḍān and the two festivals (*ibid.*, i, 413; ii. 227. 280).

The prerogative of wearing the dynastic colours was reserved to the caliphs, their families, their retinue and the highest officials of the bureaucracy and court. Red was also a royal colour. We read of a Fāṭimid vizier upon whom the caliph bestowed his own red garment (Ibn Taghrībirdī, *al-Nudjūm al-zāhira*, iv, 99), as well as a warning against wearing red in the caliph's residence "[because it] is the colour of the caliph's dress as well as those who rebel against him" (al-Ṣābī, *Rusūm*, 75).

The most frequent of all ceremonies were caliphal audiences (*madjlis*; *djulūs*, used in the general sense as well as for accession) which took place in the palace (for discussion, see Sourdel, *Questions de cérémonial ʿabbāside*, in *REI* [1960], 121-48, and M. Canard, *Le cérémonial fatimite et le cérémonial byzantin: essai de comparaison*, in *Byzantion* [1951], 408 ff.). Al-Ḳalḳashandī lists three categories of audiences for the Fāṭimids: *al-madjlis al-ʿāmm ayyām al-mawākib* (general audiences), the *djulūs* held expressly for the *ḳāḍī* and *shuhūd* on the four *layālī al-wuḳūd* ("nights of lights"), and the *djulūs* on the *mawlid al-nabī* [see mawlid] and several other *mawlid*s.

Even these audiences had some processional elements, manifested primarily in the formal arrival of the vizier at the palace riding his mount. After the audience hall had been prepared by covering the walls and the *sarīr* in fine fabrics (*dībādj* in the winter, *dabīḳī* in the summer), the *ṣāḥib al-risāla* summoned the vizier and rode with him, in customary haste, to the palace (*ʿalā al-rasm al-muʿtād fī surʿat al-ḥaraka*). The vizier wore ceremonial costume and rode with his entourage in the same order as that of the procession of the New Year (*fa-yarkabu fī ubbahatihi wa-djamāʿatihi ʿalā 'l-tartīb al-muḳaddam dhikruhu fī dhikr al-rukūb awwal al-ʿām*); cf. al-Maḳrīzī, *Khiṭaṭ*, i, 448-9 ff., for details of the vizier's arrival at the palace on the New Year.

The prerogative of mounts, even in a non-processional setting, was an important symbol of authority. Caliphs maintained large stables [see iṣṭabl], and horses were often distributed as gifts to particularly honoured officials. Even within the palace walls, caliphs were expected to ride from one point to another. Similarly, gates and doors were symbols of sovereignty and authority and were the sites of important ceremonial activity. The caliph and vizier usually mounted and dismounted at a gate or door (see e.g. al-Maḳrīzī, *Khiṭaṭ*, i, 389-90), and officials sometimes dismounted at a gate of the palace and kissed it even when the caliph was not present (idem, *Ittiʿāẓ al-ḥunafāʾ*, Cairo 1967, ii, 71-2).

Under both the ʿAbbāsids and the Fāṭimids, the

vizier enjoyed the privilege of entering the palace walls while riding his mount, a prerogative normally reserved to the caliph himself (idem, *Khiṭaṭ*, i, 387) Even the high-ranking *ḳāḍī al-ḳuḍāt*, accorded so many other ceremonial privileges (see below), dismounted at the avenue running between the two Fāṭimid palaces (*bayn al-ḳaṣrayn*, see *ibid.*, i, 433). The Fāṭimid vizier dismounted at the first *dihlīz* (vestibule of columns) of the palace, which is referred to in texts as his *makān* (*ibid.*, i, 386, 389). Upon his investiture with the *laḳab* [*q.v.*] of *Tādj al-milla* in 367/977, the Būyid *amīr* ʿAḍud al-Dawla [*q.v.*] requested permission to enter the courtyard of the palace (*ṣaḥn al-salām*) mounted on his horse, as a special mark of distinction by which his honoured position would be known. The caliph granted the audacious request, but took the precaution of having a barrier of baked brick and clay built across the door to the courtyard, forcing the vizier to dismount before entering (al-Ṣābī, *Rusūm*, 80).

Caliphal ceremonies in the palace required keen attention to rank and dignity. In this sense, the position of each person in attendance with respect to the caliph can yield important information about social and political order. The responsibility for ordering the participants according to rank, presenting them to the caliph, and observing protocol in general, rested with the chief chamberlain (*ḥādjib* [*q.v.*]). He controlled access to the caliph and shielded him from those unworthy of his attention. He also supervised the retinue of the caliph and a corps of assistant chamberlains.

In addition to the *ḥādjib*, several other functionaries supervised the preparations and conduct of caliphal audiences. The ʿAbbāsids, for whom such information is sparse, employed a *ṣāḥib al-sitr* (master of the curtain, known already in the Umayyad period) and *ṣāḥib al-marātib* (master of the ranks). For the Fāṭimids, we are somewhat better informed. The *ṣāḥib al-bāb* (master of the door) was recruited from the *arbāb al-suyūf* (men of the sword) and fulfilled many of the functions of the chamberlain. He, along with the *isfahsālār* of the army [see ISPAHSĀLĀR], had duties in processional ceremonies as well.

The caliph's private service was provided by an élite corps of eunuchs (*al-ustādhūn al-muḥannakūn*) [see FĀṬIMIDS], who performed a wide range of ceremonial duties. From this corps were drawn the *shādd al-tādj* (the official charged with winding the caliph's turban in the prescribed manner), and the *ṣāḥib* (or *mutawallī*) *al-madjlis* (master of the audience hall), who placed people in their assigned places and informed the vizier when the caliph was seated on his *sarīr*, also called *ṣāḥib al-sitr*, master of the curtain. The *ṣāḥib al-risāla* (messenger), *ṣāḥib* (or *mutawallī*) *bayt al-māl*, the *ḥāmil al-dawāt* (bearer of the inkwell) and *ṣāḥib al-māʾida* (master of the table) performed ceremonial duties (for enumeration of these functions, see al-Maḳrīzī, *Khiṭaṭ*, i, 386, 411; al-Ḳalḳashandī, *Ṣubḥ*, iii, 484-5; and explanations in Canard, *Cérémonial fāṭimite*, 365 ff.).

The protocol for both ʿAbbāsid and Fāṭimid audiences was much the same. The caliph was concealed behind a *sitr* until all those in attendance were in their assigned places, according to their rank (*ʿalā ṭabaḳātihim*, *ʿalā marātibihim*). The *sitr* was then raised to reveal the caliph, who was saluted first by the vizier and then in descending order of rank by the highest officials of the state. The salute (*al-adab fi 'l-salām*, *adab al-khidma*) consisted in greeting the caliph with the formula *al-salām ʿalā* [or: *ʿalayka*] *amīr al-muʾminīn wa-raḥmat Allāh wa-barakātuh*. Under the Fāṭimids, however, this formula seems to have been reserved exclusively for the *ḳāḍī al-ḳuḍāt* (*Khiṭaṭ*, i, 386, and *Ṣubḥ*, iii, 496). The second element, *taḳbīl al-arḍ*, kissing the ground, was acknowledged to be a late introduction. Previously, high-ranking officials (viziers and *amīrs*) used the verbal salute only. As an honour to a favoured official, the caliph might offer his hand, covered by his sleeve, to be kissed. The custom of kissing the ground seems to have been thoroughly engrained and observed, regardless of rank, by the ʿAbbāsid period. Variations included kissing the caliph's hand and foot, kissing his stirrup, and kissing the *martaba* in front of his *sarīr*.

Those attending a caliphal audience were exhorted to stand straight and still, not to fidget, to maintain absolute silence unless spoken to by the caliph, and then to answer in a low and clear voice. They were to fix their attention upon the caliph to refrain from laughing even if there was cause for it, and to avoid slander, calumny, and criticism at all costs. The caliph's mistakes were not to be corrected, nor was his name or that of his wives to be used. One approached the caliph only if summoned and in that case, advanced a few steps at a time, stopped with bowed head, and waited for the caliph's command to proceed. Even the vizier, who was permitted to approach the caliph to speak about matters of state with him, was advised to retreat to a distance of five cubits upon completion of his business.

The *djulūs* for the four *layālī al-wuḳūd* (at the beginning and middle of Radjab and Shaʿbān) took place in the belvedere (*manẓara*) overlooking the Bāb al-Zumurrud. The high point of the ceremony occurred when the caliph opened one of the windows of the *manẓara* and revealed his head and face. On of his *muḥannak* eunuchs put his head and right hand, covered by his sleeve, out of another window and proclaimed: "The Commander of the Faithful returns your greeting." The *ḳāḍī al-ḳuḍāt* and the *ṣāḥib al-bāb* were then greeted personally.

The Fāṭimids celebrated six (according to some sources four) different *mawlids*: those of the Prophet, al-Ḥasan and al-Ḥusayn, ʿAlī, Fāṭima, and the present *imām* (*mawlid al-khalīfa* [or *al-imām*] *al-ḥāḍir*). The *mawlids* took place under the *manẓara* surmounting the *Bāb al-dhahab*, and included much of the same ceremony as the *layālī al-wuḳūd*, with the addition of distribution of *ṣadaḳāt* and an impressive quantity of food prepared in the *Dār al-fiṭra*. The powerful vizier al-Afḍal b. Amīr al-Djuyūsh annulled the observance of these *mawlids* at the height of his power, but the caliph al-Āmir, encouraged by his *muḥannak* eunuchs, restored them when he regained power.

Both the Fāṭimids and the ʿAbbāsids prepared elaborate receptions of ambassadors, in particular of the Byzantine embassies. Ambassadors rode to the palace and dismounted at its gate, then entered the audience hall through a column of soldiers. The *ṣāḥib al-bāb* and his *nāʾib* flanked the caliph, who was seated on his *sarīr*, surrounded by his vizier and high-ranking members of his retinue. Al-Maḳrīzī describes two such embassies in *Khiṭaṭ*, i, 403, 461, and al-Ṣābī, *Rusūm dār al-khilāfa*, describes in detail the reception of the Byzantine ambassador Ward, 14-17. See also S.M. Stern, *An embassy of the Byzantine emperor to the Fāṭimid caliph al-Muʿizz*, in *Byzantion*, xx (1950), 425 ff.

The caliphs (at least theoretically) held an audience every evening for redress of grievances (*al-djulūs li 'l-maẓālim*). The Fāṭimids conducted these *djulūs* in the *saḳīfa* of the palace.

Investitures of high officials with robes of honour

(*khilʿas*) and titles (*alḳāb* [see LAḲAB]) abound in the historical literature. These investitures generally occurred in the context of an audience, and the same protocol was observed.

Banquets (*simāṭ*, pl. *asmiṭa*) were some of the most elaborate and impressive ceremonial occasions. They occurred during Ramaḍān and on the two *ʿīds* (*ʿīd al-fiṭr* and *ʿīd al-aḍḥā* or *al-naḥr*), at the New Year, and at the *mawlid al-nabī*. The *simāṭ* of the Fāṭimids extended across the entire length of the audience hall, and was filled with all manner of delicacies, including sugar figurines and castles made entirely of confectionery. During Ramaḍān, the *amīrs* would rotate in attending the banquet every night, although their presence was not required. They were, as usual, seated according to their ranks. A significant feature of all banquets was the permissibility of taking food out of the palace and distributing (and even selling) it among one's family and friends. Descriptions of these banquets are found in Ibn Taghbirdī, *al-Nudjūm al-zāhira*, iv, 97-8; al-Maḳrīzī, *Khiṭaṭ*, i, 387-8. For further information about ceremonies on Ramaḍān and the two *ʿīds*, see MAWĀKIB.

Bibliography: (in addition to the works mentioned in the text): for the Umayyads and ʿAbbasids, pseudo-Djāḥiẓ, *Kitāb al-Tādj fī akhlāḳ al-mulūk*, ed. Ahmed Zaki Pasha, Cairo 1914, tr. Ch. Pellat, *Le livre de la couronne*, Paris 1954; Ibn al-Zubayr, *Kitāb al-Dhakhāʾir wa 'l-tuḥaf*, ed. Muḥammad Ḥamīd Allāh, Kuwait 1959, for extensive information on the treasuries of Islamic dynasties; for the Fāṭimids in the North African period, important data on ceremonial in Muḥammad b. Muḥammad al-Yamanī, *Sīrat Djaʿfar al-Ḥādjib*, ed. W. Ivanow in *Mudhakkirat fī ḥarakat al-Mahdī al-Fāṭimī*, in *Bull. of the Fac. of Letters, The Egyptian University* (1936); for prescriptive literature on court etiquette as well as general theory of the Fāṭimid imāmate, al-Ḳāḍī al-Nuʿmān, *Kitāb al-Himma fī ādāb atbāʿ al-aʾimma*, ed. Muḥammad Kāmil Ḥusayn, Cairo n.d.; important sources are also *al-Madjālis al-Mustanṣiriyya*, ed. Muḥammad Kāmil Ḥusayn, Cairo n.d., and *Dīwān al-Muʾayyad fi 'l-dīn, dāʿī al-duʿāt*, ed. Muḥammad Kāmil Ḥusayn, Cairo 1949. Secondary literature: O. Grabar, *Notes sur les cérémonies umayyades*, in *Studies in Memory of Gaston Wiet*, Jerusalem 1977, 51-60; idem, *Ceremonial and art at the Umayyad court,* unpublished PhD thesis, Princeton University 1954; K. Inostransev, *La sortie solennelle des califes Fatimides*, St. Petersburg 1905 [in Russian]; P. Kahle, *Die Schätze der Fatimiden*, in *ZMDG*, xiv (1935), 329 ff.; A. Mez, *The renaissance of Islam*, Eng. tr. Patna 1937, chs. ix and xiii; Zakī Muḥammad Ḥasan, *Kunūz al-Fāṭimiyyīn*, Cairo 1937; M. Canard, *La procession du nouvel an chez les Fâṭimides*, in *AIEOAlger*, x (1952), 364-98; A.M. Mādjid, *Aṣl ḥafalāt al-Fāṭimiyyīn fī Miṣr*, in *Ṣaḥīfat al-Maʿhad al-Miṣrī li 'l-Dirāsāt al-Islāmiyya fī Madrid*, ii/1-2 (1954), Ar. Section 253-57; idem, *Le personnel de la cour fāṭimide en Égypte*, in *Ann. Fac. of Arts*, *ʿAin Shams*, iii (1955), 147-60; A. M. Mādjid (Magued), *Nuẓum al-Fāṭimiyyīn wa-rusūmuhum fī Miṣr*, ("Institutions et cérémonial des Fāṭimides en Égypte"), Cairo 1973; E. Tyan, *Institutions de droit public musulman*, Paris 1954-6, ii, 495-545. (P. SANDERS)

2. In Muslim Spain.

In al-Andalus, as elsewhere, *rusūm* is used, in the same manner as *marāsim*, to denote court etiquette and procedure. On this subject, no treatise is available comparable to the *De Caeremoniis* composed by the Byzantine Emperor Constantine Porphyrogenitus, or to the *Rusūm dār al-khilāfa* of Hilāl al-Ṣābī; there is no alternative therefore other than to attempt to reconstruct Hispano-Arab court etiquette by means of the meagre information preserved by the chronicles and to have recourse to descriptions of official acts (*bayʿa*, [*q.v.*]), signings of agreements, receptions, processions (*mawākib* [*q.v.*]).

When, in 138/756, ʿAbd al-Raḥmān al-Dākhil [*q.v.*] transformed al-Andalus into an independent amīrate, he was the initiator of the (embryonic) Cordovan etiquette. It is in this sense that the dispositions of his entourage are best understood. According to al-Maḳḳarī (*Nafḥ*, ii, 25), "he was obliged to maintain a certain distance and not to mingle to an excessive degree with the people, nor to show himself in public". But it was ʿAbd al-Raḥmān II [*q.v.*] who (influenced by Ziryāb [*q.v.*]?) instituted Andalusian etiquette. According to al-Maḳḳarī (*Nafḥ*, i, 223), "he was the first to isolate himself, behind a tapestry, from the public". Ibn Ḥayyān (*Muḳtabas*, ii, 91) is still more explicit: "It was he who organised the hierarchy of the court (*rattaba rusūm al-dawla/al-khidma*)". This information is confirmed by Ibn ʿIdhārī (*Bayān*, ii, 91) and Ibn Saʿīd (*Mughrib*, i, 45); the *Dhikr bilād al-Andalus* (117) makes of him "the first to clothe himself in the pomp of the caliphs". The separation of the functions of the *shurṭa* [*q.v.*] and of the *ṣūk* [*q.v.*] which all authors attribute to him are to be seen in the same sense.

At the time of his *bayʿa*, in 206/822, his brothers, his uncles, his kinsmen, his "men" (the senior functionaries of the court), the judges and the *fuḳahāʾ*, military officers of every rank, the dignitaries and the people, pledged allegiance to him (*Dhikr*, 117). This order reflects a hierarchy, since the text clearly distinguishes six "groups" or "categories". The same regulation recurs (with minor variations) throughout the whole of the caliphate. It is observed in the allegiance pledged, in 300/912, to ʿAbd al-Raḥmān III al-Nāṣir [*q.v.*] (*Chron. anón.*, 29-30) and in the list of witnesses who applied their signatures to the act of surrender of Saragossa in 326/937 (Ibn Ḥayyān, *Muḳtabas*, v, 277-9). The same hierarchy appears in the description of the feasts of the Breaking of the Fast in the years 360-4 and in that of the Sacrifices in the years 360-4, preserved by the *Muḳtabas* of Ibn Ḥayyān. Lévi-Provençal (*Hist. Esp. Mus.*, ii, 117) speaks of pomp and ostentation, of a rigid etiquette: "The reverential fear (*hayba*) which is inspired by the august person of the caliph and the magnificence (*fakhr*) which presides over all the manifestations of his official life encompass him in the manner of a halo".

It does not seem that al-Manṣūr b. Abī ʿĀmir [*q.v.*] introduced any changes into the organisation of the caliphate. He was obliged to co-exist with the *mulūk al-ṭawāʾif* [*q.v.*], judging by the comments of the *amīr* ʿAbd Allāh [*q.v.*], when he examines, in his *Memoirs*, the various groups capable of supporting him.

Nothing is known of the norms of Almoravid etiquette. In the Almohad period, there is no demonstrative proof of the effective application of the complex and discordant order described by Ibn al-Ḳaṭṭān, *al-Ḥulal al-mawshiyya* and the *K. al-Ansāb fī maʿrifat al-aṣḥāb* (13 categories according to the former, 18 according to the *K. al-Ansāb*; cf. the observations of J.F.P. Hopkins, *Medieval Muslim government in Barbary*, London 1958). The actual gradation was that relfected by Ibn Ṣāḥib al-Ṣalāt (*al-Mann bi 'l-imāma*, 232, 420, 437, 445, 457, 511), similar to the Hispano-Umayyad pattern.

In 558/1163, at the time of his proclamation, Abū Yaʿḳūb b. ʿAbd al-Muʾmin was recognised by the *shaykh* Abū Ḥafṣ, the Almohads and the *ashyākh* of the tribes. In the course of the formal audience at Marrākush in 1170, the hierarchical order was: Almohad *ashyākh*, *ṭalaba* [*q.v.*] *ashyākh* and viziers. In 1171, at the time of his entry into Rabat-Salé, he was followed by the Almohad *ashyākh*, the vizier, the *kuttāb*, the *ṭalaba* and the Bedouin. During the Feast of Sacrifices, at Cordova, the "great Almohad *ashyākh*, the *abnāʾ al-djamāʿa* [*q.v.*], and their followers, the *ṭalaba* of the capital, the *fuḳahāʾ*, the judges, the *kuttāb*, the governors, delegations and notables of the town, were introduced according to their rank." At the time of the Feast of Sacrifices of 568/1172, at Murcia, a development is observed: "First to present themselves were his brothers, followed by the Almohad *ashyakh* and the great men of the state". A further development is attested by ʿAbd al-Wāḥid al-Marrākushī (*al-Muʿdjib*, 239); in 610/1213, the proclamation of Abū Yaʿḳūb Yūsuf "took place first—on the Thursday—in private, attended by his close relatives; on the Friday, he was recognised by the Almohad *ashyākh*; and on the Saturday, by the people".

The hierarchy of the Naṣrids [*q.v.*] was probably close to the Hispano-Umayyad tradition. This is merely a hypothesis, for although Ibn al-Khaṭīb (*Lamḥa*, 38) makes of the second sultan, Muḥammad b. Muḥammad (672-701/1273-1302), "the initiator of the State, the organiser of its administration and its hierarchy... the creator of the royal protocol (*mumahhid al-dawla waḍaʿa alḳāb khidmatihā wa-ḳaddara marātibihā... wa-aḳāma rusūm al-mulk*)" this tells us nothing of its components.

Bibliography: Given in the article.

(P. Chalmeta)

3. In Iran.

Persian society in most, if not all, periods was intensely formal: the demeanour, manners, dress and mode of speech of each class was minutely regulated by custom. The court set the pattern. Respect for age and position was ubiquitous. An extensive *adab* [*q.v.*] literature, which sought to regulate all aspects of social life and behaviour, grew up (cf. al-Ghazālī, *al-Adab fi 'l-dīn*; Kāwūs b. Iskandar, *Ḳābūs-nāma*; and see J.S. Badeau, *They lived once thus in Baghdad*, in Sami A. Hanna (ed.), *Medieval and Middle Eastern Studies in honor of Aziz Suryal Atiya*, Leiden 1972, 38-49).

Persian ceremonial was designed to emphasise both the awe in which the ruler was held and his separation from the rest of the population. Its influence was felt already in Umayyad times and became marked under the ʿAbbāsids. Much of the ceremonial of later times can be traced back to the early centuries. There was a long continuity of tradition in respect of the insignia of sovereignty. The parasol or *čatr* [see MIẒALLA] held over the ruler's head was an ancient custom going back at least to Achaemenid times, while the *liwāʾ* or standard was an old symbol of royalty going back to Parthian and Sāsānid times (see Spuler, *Iran*, 348), though neither were confined absolutely to the rules, but might also be attached to high offices. The beating of kettle-drums [see NAWBA] in honour of the ruler and those elevated to important governorships was also a practice of great antiquity, the origins of which are possibly to be found in Mithraism. The office charged with this ceremony was known as the *naḳāra-khāna* [*q.v.*]. Drums, trumpets and other instruments were played daily at sunset and sunrise and on religious festivals, on the ruler's birthday and at feasts given by him. If the ruler was in camp or on a journey, his musical instruments accompanied him. The *naḳāra-khāna* survived in Tehran until 1937. Considerable importance attached also to the throne. In the early centuries this was placed on a *ṣuffa*, or dais, which was often a considerable structure, consisting sometimes of a portico or pavilion open in the front in which the dais was situated. Sometimes on the throne itself there was another chair or seat on which the ruler sat. Apart from these ancient insignia, there were also insignia of Islamic provenance, such as the right of the ruler to have his name mentioned in the *khuṭba* [*q.v.*] and on coins [see SIKKA].

The grant of robes of honour [see KHILʿA] though not specifically one of the insignia of royalty, was a practice followed by all rulers and one attended in Ṣafawid and Ḳādjār times, if not earlier, by special ceremonies. The purpose of the grant was partly to honour the recipient, but partly also to fill the ruler's coffers, since the recipient was often expected to make gifts to the ruler in return, and if the recipient was in the provinces, to whoever brought the *khilʿa*. Another practice was the distribution of bags of gold and silver coins by the monarch on the occasion of his accession to those who were present at his court (H.L. Rabino, *Coins, medals, and seals of the Shahs of Iran, 1500-1941*, London 1945, 87). The distribution of scattering (*nithār*) of coins. jewels and precious objects, both by the ruler and by his subjects, was also customary on festive occasions such as the Naw Rūz (the Persian New Year). The canonical festivals of the *ʿīd al-aḍḥā* and the *ʿīd al-fiṭr* [*q.vv.*] were the occasion for public celebration. It was customary for the ruler to go out to the the *muṣallā* outside the town where the *ʿīd* prayers were performed and to take part in them (see further MAWĀKIB. 2. In Iran).

The ruler was expected, especially if his followers were largely drawn from tribal groups, to keep open table. Feasting was especially common under the Ghaznawids, the Īlkhāns and the Tīmūrids. Masʿūd b. Maḥmūd, the Ghaznawid, used to have a large leather table-cloth (*khʷān*) laid out on the dais on which he sat to hold audiences, on in some neighbouring garden or pavilion, and to invite the great men of the state to sit with him at the *khʷān* (cf. Abu 'l-Faḍl Bayhaḳī, *Tārīkh-i Masʿūdī*, ed. ʿAlī Akbar Fayyāḍ Mashhad A.H.S. 1350/1971, 439, 734-5). Wine flowed freely at these feasts (see *ibid.*, *passim*). Niẓām al-Mulk considered it indispensable for the ruler to keep an open table and he claims that Ṭoghrïl Beg entertained his followers thus in the early morning (*Siyāsat-nāma*, ed. Schefer, Paris 1891, 115). The court astrologer, though not essential to court ceremonial, nevertheless played an important role, especially under the Ṣafawids and Ḳādjārs, in deciding the most auspicious moment for the coronation of the ruler or for some movement such as when the entry into a town should take place, or even for the proper hour "to sit, to rise, to depart, to eat, to go to bed" (Du Mans, *Estat de la Perse en 1660*, ed. Schefer, Paris 1890, repr. 1969, 30).

The Ziyārid Mardāwīdj [*q.v.*] (d. 323/935), when he sat on a golden throne and wore a crown (*tādj*), was imitating Sāsānid (or what he believed to be Sāsānid) custom (Miskawayh, *Tadjārib al-umam*, v, 489, and see A. Mez, *Die Renaissance des Islams*, Heidelberg 1922, 17). In subsequent centuries, the throne and the *tādj* continued to be important elements in royal ceremonial. The Būyid ʿAḍud al-Dawla [*q.v.*] was surrounded by great magnificence when holding audiences. Like the caliph, he sat on a throne on a dais. High-standing visitors sat on stools or chairs (*kursī*) in front of his throne. As in the caliph's court, the right hand side was the place of honour (see further H. Busse, *Chalif and Grosskönig*, Beirut 1969, 222 ff., and ʿAlī Aṣghar Faḳīhī, *Shāhinshāhī-i ʿAḍud al-Dawla*, Ḳumm n.d., 215 and *passim*). Hilāl al-Ṣābī describes the caliph al-Ṭāʾiʿ's reception of ʿAḍud al-Dawla in Baghdād in 367/977-8 and the royal insignia which he gave to him in 368/978-9 (Faḳīhī, *op. cit.*, 62 ff. See also al-Suyūṭī, *History of the caliphs*, tr. H.S. Jarrett, Calcutta 1881, 427).

The Sāmānids and Ghaznawids both evolved an elaborate ceremonial, which was influenced by what was assumed to be Sāsānid practice and by practice at the caliph's court. In the Ghaznawid court, every effort was made to enhance the glory of the ruler. On formal occasions, the greatest deference was exacted from all, even the caliph's envoys. It was Masʿūd b. Maḥmūd's custom to hold court, sitting on a dais (*ṣuffa*), in one or other of his palaces or gardens (cf. Bayhaḳī, 438). It seems that his throne was originally made of wood. This was replaced in 429/1038 by a golden throne of great magnificence, which had taken three years to make. When it was finished, it was placed on a dais in the new palace which Masʿūd had built and surmounted by a parasol. Bayhaḳī describes the splendour of the scene when Masʿūd, wearing a red satin cloak shot with gold, mounted the throne for the first time on 21 Shaʿbān 429/8 July 1038. Ten richly dressed *ghulāms* stood on the dais on the right side and ten on the left, with rows of *ghulāms*, also finely dressed and bearing arms and the *martabadārān* standing in a body the hall. (The meaning of *martabadār* is uncertain. The term may have been applied to a *farrāsh* who held a switch or some such implement, whose duty was to keep back the crowds. On the other hand, one of the meanings of *martaba* was a cushion on a dais, see Ibn Baṭṭūṭa, *Travels*, tr. H.A.R. Gibb, Cambridge 1956-71, iii, 660, 18n., and *martabadār* may, thus, have been the bearer of the royal cushion.) The notables from the provinces and the great men sat on the dais. The "pillars of the state" and the great men of Masʿūd's entourage scattered innumerable gifts before him. The ceremony apparently began early in the morning, for Bayhaḳī states that Masʿūd sat until breakfast time (*čāstgāh*). At the close of the audience, Masʿūd's boon companions (*nadīmān*) came forward and scattered their gifts, after which Masʿūd mounted and rode off to a garden. Having changed his clothes, he went again on horseback to another palace or pavilion (the Spring House) where a feast was held for the great men and the "pillars of the state". After this Masʿūd went to another garden where he drank wine with his boon companions until the time of the afternoon prayer (Bayhaḳī, 714-15).

Masʿūd's reception in Muḥarram 423/December 1031-January 1032 in Balkh of an envoy sent by the caliph was marked, according to Bayhaḳī's description, by much splendour. Four thousand palace *ghulāms*, splendidly dressed and equipped, were drawn up in ranks on either side of the palace. Two hundred royal *ghulāms*, in full regalia, stood in rows near Masʿūd, while the great men of the court, the provincial governors and chamberlains, in their court dresses, gathered in the assembly. Masʿūd sat on a dais. The only other person to be seated was the chief minister, Aḥmad b. Ḥasan al-Maymandī [*q.v.*]. When the caliph's envoy was brought in, he greeted Masʿūd and was led to a seat by the chamberlain, Bū Naṣr. Masʿūd then asked after the health of the caliph, and the envoy told him of the death of al-Ḳādir. After Aḥmad b. Ḥasan had said a few words to the envoy in Arabic, he gave him a signal to give the caliph's letter to Masʿūd. The envoy got up, took the letter, which was in a black brocade bag, gave it to Masʿūd and went back to his seat. Masʿūd then called to Bū Naṣr to come up to the throne. He took the bag, opened it and read the letter and then at Masʿūd's command translated it into Persian. The following day, a mourning assembly for the caliph al-Ḳādir was held. Masʿūd and all his court were dressed in white. The bazaars were closed and the *dīwān* shut for three days. When they were reopened, drums were played and on the following Friday the *khuṭba* was read in the name of the new caliph. Masʿūd sat close to the *minbar*, which was covered with cloth of gold (*dībā-yi zar-bāft*). The chief minister and the notables of the court sat nearby, with ʿAlī Mīkālī and the caliph's envoy rather further off. After the *khuṭba* had been read, the royal treasures placed 10,000 *dīnārs* and five silken purses at the foot of the *minbar* as a present for the caliph. The gifts of Masʿūd's sons, the chief minister, the great chamberlain, and others were then brought, after which Masʿūd departed, while the treasurers' scribes and *mustawfīs* took the gifts to the royal treasury. Some days later, the envoy was given a *khilʿa*, a mule and two horses, and sent back with the presents to the caliph. The chief minister also sent him a mule, with a rug (*djul*) and hood (*burḳaʿ*), 500 *dīnārs*, and ten garments (*ibid.*, 383 ff.). Similarly, in later times, the exchange of presents was also not confined to the two principal parties on the occasion of ambassies: ministers also expected to receive presents from envoys and sometimes made gifts themselves to envoys.

In the following year, 424/1033, another envoy accompanied by a eunuch (*khādim*) brought a diploma and *khilʿa* from the caliph for Masʿūd, who was then in Ray. When the envoy was taken to Masʿūd, he kissed the latter's hand, while the *khādim* kissed the ground. On this occasion, after Masʿūd had enquired for the health of the caliph, Bū Naṣr took the envoy under the arms and seated him near the throne on the dais, on which the army commander ʿAlī Dāya and the *ʿāriḍ*, the head of the military department [see ISTIʿRĀḌ] were also sitting—the chief minister was absent (*ibid.*, 471-2). This custom of taking envoys under the arms when bringing them near to the presence of the ruler also prevailed in the Tīmūrid, Ṣafawid and Afshārid courts (see below). Bū Naṣr then came forward and told the envoy to rise and take the diploma, which was rolled up in black brocade, and put it on the throne. The envoy, standing up, told Masʿūd to come down from the throne in order to put on the caliph's *khilʿa*. Masʿūd ordered a prayer rug (*muṣallā*) to be brought. As he turned to the *ḳibla*, drums were beaten and trumpets blown in the garden and at the gate of the palace. Bilge Tegīn and other military leaders ran forward to help Masʿūd down from the throne to sit on the prayer rug. The caliph's envoy then called for the box with the *khilʿa* and brought out seven robes and other garments. Masʿūd kissed them and performed two *rakʿas* of prayer and remounted the throne. A jewelled crown, necklace and bracelet were then brought forward, kissed and placed on the throne at Masʿūd's right hand, while the *khādim* advanced with a turban, which Masʿūd kissed and placed on his head. A standard (*liwāʾ*) had also been brought by the envoy, and this Masʿūd held in his right hand. He also put on the sword and sword-belt which the envoy had brought and then, having kissed them, put them aside. Finally, Bū Naṣr read and translated into Persian the caliph's letter and the diploma, after which those present began to scatter coins, jewels and rarities (*ibid.*, 473-4).

Mihragān and Naw Rūz appear to have been regularly celebrated by Mas^{c}ūd. In 426/1035 Mihragān fell on the 16 Dhu 'l-Ḳa^{c}da. Bayhaḳī states that on this occasion coins and jewels were scattered before Mas^{c}ūd and presents made to him. After prayers, wine was passed round and the "the customs of Mihragān were performed" (*ibid.*, 643, cf. also 655, 697, 743). When recording the celebration of Mihragān in 430/1039, Bayhaḳī states that poets and singers were not given presents on that occasion because there had been a shortage of rain (*ibid.*, 789-90). Under later rulers, the festival of Mihragān fell into desuetude. Bayhaḳī mentions that in 429/1038 Mas^{c}ūd observed the customs of the Naw Rūz and gave presents and that wine flowed (*ibid.*, 705, cf. also 815). After the Ghaznawids, Naw Rūz was celebrated as a popular rather than a public festival; under the Ṣafawids and Ḳādjārs it was again celebrated as a public festival (see below). Bayhaḳī also mentions the celebration of Sada, the festival of fire, in 426/1035, but this was probably not a public celebration. He states that Mas^{c}ūd sat in a tent pitched beside a stream with his boon companions. Musicians were also present and a fire of wood was lit (*ibid.*, 572). (On Sada, see *Cambridge History of Iran*, iii/2, *The Seleucid, Parthian and Sasanian periods*, ed. E. Yarshater, Cambridge 1983, 800-1.) The Ziyārid Mardāwīdj had before this made an abortive attempt to revive the feast of Sada. He prepared a great bonfire in Iṣfahān in 323/935, but was murdered before the ceremony could take place (Faḳīhī, *op. cit.*, 20). The recovery of the ruler from illness was another occasion for the offering of presents to him. On 1 Rabī^c 428/22 December 1036 Mas^{c}ūd, who had just recovered from an illness, held a court in Bust. His entourage and the great men of the city came and scattered coins and presents, while the people offered prayers for him and sacrificed animals, giving the meat with bread to the poor (Bayhaḳī, 278).

It would appear from the *Tārīkh-i Mas^{c}ūdī* that Mas^{c}ūd b. Maḥmūd frequently granted *khil^{c}as* to his subjects. These appear to have differed according to the rank of the recipient. A large stock was presumably held in the royal wardrobe (*djāma-khāna*). Thus ^{c}Alī Dāya on 1 Djumādī I 432/6 January 1041 was "clothed with a *sipahsālārī khil^{c}a*, such as was customary for army commanders" (*op. cit.*, 436), while the *khil^{c}a* given to the caliph's envoy in 423/1031-2 was "such as is given to the *fuḳahā*ʾ" (*ibid.*, 390). When the *ḥādjib* Sübashī was made chief minister (*kh^{w}ādja-i buzurg*) on 10 Ṣafar 427/13 December 1036, he was given a "complete" *khil^{c}a* with a banner, standard, drum and kettle drum, suits of clothes (*takht-hā-yi djāma*), bags of silver and other things which went with this office (*ibid.*, 648). A special horse was also the mark of certain offices. Tāsh Farrāsh, the army commander, when setting out for ^{c}Irāḳ in 422/1030-1 was presented with "the horse of the army commander (*sipahsālār*) of ^{c}Irāḳ" (*ibid.*, 373). Bayhaḳī also mentions "the horse of the leader (*sālār*) of Hindustān" (*ibid.*, 355). Horses played a special part in royal processions [see MAWĀKIB].

The Saldjūḳs, when they came into Khurāsān, took over some of the ceremonial forms they found in existence. When Ṭoghrïl Beg came to Nīshāpūr in 429/1073-8 he sat on Mas^{c}ūd b. Maḥmūd's throne, which was in the front part of a dais, to receive the welcome of the population. His personal apparel was modest compared to that affected by Mas^{c}ūd. Bayhaḳī states that on his entry into Nīshāpūr he wore a woven cloak (*ḳabā-yi mulḥam*), a *tawwazī* turban and felt boots, and was fully armed, and carried on his arm a strung bow with three wooden arrows (*ibid.*, 732). It is not without interest that a bow and arrows were part of the insignia of the Ḳādjārs (see below). Even after the rule of the Saldjūḳs had become firmly established, their court remained less minutely regulated and less luxurious than that of the Ghaznawids. This may have been due in part to a survival of tribal tradition (so far as this survived), and in part to the fact that the Saldjūḳ sultans were frequently engaged in military expeditions and spent much time travelling about their empire. Rāwandī states that Malikshāh was not cut off from the people by a curtain (*ḥidjāb*) and that if someone came to him for redress he would speak to him face to face (*Rāḥat al-ṣudūr*, ed. Muḥammad Iḳbāl, London 1921, 131).

Niẓām al-Mulk believed that fixed procedures in ceremonial matters enabled the subjects to regulate their conduct. Accordingly, he lays down rules in the *Siyāsat-nāma* for the holding of audiences by the sultan (110, 84, 86). These may well have represented his ideal rather than actual practice. He obviously felt that the Saldjūḳ sultans had failed to maintain the pomp necessary to preserve the awe in which he believed the monarch ought to be held. However, on occasion the Saldjūḳ sultans did observe an elaborate ceremonial (cf. the marriage of the daughter of Malikshāh to al-Muḳtadī [see MAWĀKIB]). Niẓām al-Mulk also lays down rules for the reception of foreign envoys. They were to be accompanied by an officer of the sultan as soon as they crossed the frontier. The reason for this was not only to honour the envoy but also to find out the aims and power of his patron (*ibid.*, 86). The practice of appointing an official, known in later times as the *mihmāndār* [*q.v.*], to conduct important personages through the country is also found under the Ṣafawids and Ḳādjārs.

Bundārī and Ibn al-Athīr both give the impression that Ṭoghrïl Beg held the caliph in great veneration, though this did not prevent him from demanding the same honours as had been accorded to the Ghaznawids and in insisting on his own marriage to the caliph's daughter (see G. Makdisi, *Ibn ^{c}Aqīl et la résurgence de l'Islam traditionaliste au XIe siècle*, Damascus 1963, 78 ff. and *passim*; idem, *The marriage of Tughril Beg*, in *IJMES*, i [1970], 259-75). In 449/1057-8 when he was granted an audience by the caliph, he dismounted at the gate of the caliph's palace and went in on foot. On seeing the caliph sitting on his throne, he kissed the ground several times. He was then seated on a chair (*kursī*) in front of the caliph's throne. The caliph, addressing him through the *raʾīs al-ruʾasā*ʾ, gave him a *khil^{c}a*, standard and diploma and girded him with a sword (Sibṭ b. al-Djawzī, *Mirʾāt al-zamān*, ed. Ali Sevim Ankara 1968, 24-6; Ibn al-Athīr, *al-Kāmil*, ix, 436; see also MAWĀKIB). The caliph's envoy when he came in Sha^{c}bān 453/August-September 1061 to Tabrīz for the conclusion of the *^{c}aḳd* between the caliph's daughter and Ṭoghrïl Beg, appears to have been treated with great respect. When he entered the sultan's presence the latter was sitting on his throne, around which were standing the *amīrs* and *maliks* according to their ranks. After the envoy had saluted the sultan, ^{c}Amīd al-Mulk al-Kundurī [*q.v.*], Ṭoghrïl Beg's *wazīr*, approached him and greeted him; under both the Ghaznawids and the Saldjūḳs it appears to have been the function of the chief minister to speak on such occasions on behalf of the sultan. The caliph's envoy then stood up and took out his deed of proxy (*kitāb al-wikāla*). The whole company rose and when he came to the passage stating the "exalted ceremonies which were to be performed" he bowed, and those present, including the sultan and ^{c}Amīd al-

Mulk, also bowed. When details of the marriage portion (*mahr*) were mentioned, voices were raised in prayer for the caliph. The *khuṭba* was read by a certain Masᶜūd al-Khurāsānī, after which ᶜAmīd al-Mulk scattered pearls and *dīnārs* before the throne (Sibṭ b. al-Djawzī, *Mirʾāt al-zamān*, ed. Sevim, 93-4).

Whereas the Ghaznawid Masᶜūd b. Maḥmūd distributed *khilᶜas* in great profusion, the Saldjūḳ sultans seem to have been more sparing in their grants. When Alp Arslan took oaths of allegiance from his *amīrs* for his son Malikshāh as his heir apparent, he gave them *khilᶜas* (Ibn al-Athīr, x, 34). Similarly, when Sandjar came to Rayy in 543/1148-9 and renewed Masᶜūd b. Muḥammad's diploma, he gave Masᶜūd and all the *amīrs* of ᶜIrāḳ valuable *khilᶜas* (Rāwandī, 175). Whereas Masᶜūd b. Maḥmūd appears to have espected his subjects to present him with gifts on all occasions, under the Saldjūḳs the practice was less common. The Salduḳs adopted the various insignia of royalty which had prevailed under earlier rulers. They added to them the *ghāshiya* [*q.v.*, and see also MAWĀKIB]. They apparently had special tents when on expeditions. When Maḥmūd b. Muḥammad spent one month with his uncle Sandjar in 521/1127 after he had rebelled against him, he was not allowed a red *djahrumī* tent. When he was restored to the government of ᶜIrāḳ at the end of the month, Sandjar again accorded to him the customary marks of royalty and a special garment (*kiswat-i khāṣṣ*), as well as a bejewelled cloak, a special horse (*asb-i nawbat*) with harness set with jewels and an elephant with a howdah also set with jewels (Rāwandī, 170). Pīr Muḥammad, Tīmūr's grandson, also had a red tent (Clavijo, *Embassy to Tamerlane 1403-1406*), tr. from the Spanish by G. Le Strange, London 1928, 254), and so too did Fatḥ ᶜAlī Shāh (Feuvrier, *Trois ans à la cour de Perse*, Paris 1906, 44).

The Īlkhāns brought with them new ceremonial from Central Asia, some but not all of which survived their conversion to Islam. On the death of an Īlkhān, after the mourning ceremonies had been held, the Mongol princes and princesses and the great *amīrs* used to hold a *ḳuriltay* [*q.v.*], or council, to elect (or acclaim) a new Īlkhān. The procedure was similar to that held on the enthronement of the Great Khan (for a description of the enthronement of Güyük, see Simon de Saint-Quentin, *Histoire des Tartares*, ed. J. Richard, in *Documents relatifs à l'histoire des Croisades*, viii, Paris 1965, 90-2; see also Spuler, *Die Mongolen in Iran*³, Wiesbaden 1968, 264). The decision to confer the throne on one of the princes was followed by feasting and celebrations. During the reign of Ḳubilay (d. 1294), confirmation of the election by the Great Khan was considered necessary. Ghazan had a golden tent (*khargāh*) and a golden throne which, like the throne of the Ghaznawid Masᶜūd, also had taken three years to make. It was set up in Ūdjān in 701/1301-2 and a seat, set with jewels, placed on it. After three days, during which religious celebrations were held, Ghazan gave a great feast, at which he put on garments of gold brocade, placed on his head a jewelled crown and girded on a belt of similar splendour to the crown (Rashīd al-Dīn, *Tārīkh-i mubārak-i ghāzānī*, ed. K. Jahn, London 1940, 137-8, 139). Mongol customs pertaining to the recognition of the ruler appear to have been adopted in Fārs by the Atabeg Abū Bakr Saᶜd b. Zangī. Rashīd al-Dīn relates that the *umarāʾ*, when offering allegiance to him, "took off their girdles and put them on their necks" (ed. Blochet, ii, 36, quoted by Spuler, *op. cit.*, 264). Subordinate rulers were given, together with the *yarligh* or *farmān* entrusting them with their governments (which was sealed with a special seal or *tamgha*), some or all of the following insignia: a parasol (*čatr*), a sword, a *pāʾiza* or tablet of authority in gold, silver or wood, according to the rank of the recipient, a standard, kettle-drums and a *khilᶜa*. Some *pāʾizas* were written in red and had a falcon at their head (cf. Naṣīr al-Dīn Munshī, *Simṭ al-ᶜulā*, ed. ᶜAbbās Iḳbāl, Tehran A.H.S. 1328/1949-50, 79, 89; *Tārīkh-i Sīstān*, ed. Malik al-Shuᶜarāʾ Bahār, Tehran A.H.S. 1314/1935-6, 406; see also Marco Polo, *Travels*, tr. A. Ricci, London 1931, 17, 113). The birthday of the ruler, at least during the reign of Ghazan Khān, was celebrated with great splendour and presents were given to him (see Spuler, *op. cit.*, 264). There were apparently special ceremonies concerned with the presentation of drink to the Īlkhān. These, too, were modelled on the practice of the court of the Great Khan (cf. *Travels*, 132 and also *Tārīkh-i shāhī-i Ḳarā-Khitāʾīān*, ed. Muḥammad Ibrāhīm Bāstānī Pārīzī, Tehran Shāhinshāhī 2535/1976-7, 139). One of the features which differentiated the ceremonies of the Īlkhānid and Tīmūrid courts from earlier and later courts was the participation, on occasion, of women of the royal house in public ceremonies. The Īlkhān's chief wife sometimes sat on the throne with him. The Īlkhāns were lavish in their grant of *khilᶜas*. They and their wives held large stocks of precious garments. Some of these were made in royal workshops (cf. Rashīd al-Dīn, *Tārīkh-i mubārak-i ghāzānī*, 333; Kāshānī, *Tārīkh-i Öljeytü*, ed. Mahīn Hambly, Tehran A.H.S. 1348/1969, 121-2). Rashīd al-Dīn states that Ghazan gave away on one occasion 20,000 garments (*Tārīkh-i mūbarak-i ghāzānī*, 185);

Much of the ceremony of earlier times continued to be found under the Tīmūrids. Clavijo, in his account of Tīmūr's reception of foreign ambassadors in Samarḳand, describes how they were taken under the armpits by a series of waiting officials as they advanced through the palace and its grounds. First they came to Tīmūr's nephew, a very old man, seated on a dais, to whom they made obeisance; then they came to several of Tīmūr's grandsons, who were also seated on a dais and to whom they paid their respects. Three of the young princes got up, asked for the letter which the envoys had brought from the king of Castile and took it to Tīmūr. The envoys followed and found Tīmūr sitting on a dais in the portal at the entrance of the palace. He was dressed in a cloak of plain silk, wearing a tall white hat, ornamented with pearls and jewels, with a balas ruby on the crown, and sat on a mattress covered by an embroidered silk cloth with cushions behind him. On sight of Tīmūr, the envoys bowed and put their right knees to the ground, crossing their arms over breasts. Advancing another step, they again bowed, and on the third occasion remained kneeling. Tīmūr then commanded them to rise and approach him. Three chamberlains came forward, took them under the armpits, led them up to Tīmūr until they stood immediately before him, and again made them kneel. At the end of the audience a feast was held (*Embassy of Tamerlane*, 220 ff.). Clavijo describes another feast given by Tīmūr which was attended by numerous men and women (ibid., 227 ff.). At the end of it "one of the lords in waiting came forward with a silver bowl full of small pieces of silver money ... and of this money he proceeded to throw handfuls over us ambassadors as also over the other guests present, and gathered up all the rest of the coins that remained in the bowl and threw them into the skirt of the cloaks we ambassadors were wearing, this being a gift to us" (*ibid.*, 232). Tīmūr then presented each of them with a robe of honour. They bowed in acknowledgement three times and then knelt before him (*ibid.*, cf. also the reception of the Spanish envoys by Pīr Muḥammad, Tīmūr's grandson, 254). At various other times the ambassadors were given robes of honour—on one occasion they each received not only a robe of kincob, but also a skirt to match, a hat and a horse for riding (*ibid.*, 236), and on another they were each given a robe of honour of kincob and for wearing underneath it a close fitting jacket of silk cloth lined with skins, with a high collar made of the fur of two marten skins, a hat and a wallet containing 1,500 silver pieces (*ibid.*, 276-7).

Once when Tīmūr received the envoys in the Great Pavilion in Samarḳand, he was accompanied by a great crowd of his imperial kinsmen and many foreign ambassadors, all of whom took their seats in due order of precedence. Elephants then were brought in and performed tricks, and minstrels played their instruments. Round about there stood some 300 wine jars for the guests and two tripods made of wooden staves painted red, with a great leather sack hanging on each filled with cream and mares' milk. These the attendants kept stirring and threw in many loaves of sugar. Tīmūr's chief wife appeared at the feast, taking her place beside Tīmūr but slightly behind him on a low dais, three of her ladies sitting beside her. Seven others of his wives, and the wife of one of his grandsons also took their allotted places (*ibid.*, 257 ff.). Describing the ceremonies connected with drinking that took place at the feast (which appear to have resembled customs at the court of the Īlkhāns), Clavijo states, "Those who are given to drink at the hands of Timur have to do so ceremoniously and after this fashion. They come forward and bending the right knee kneel, once at some distance before approaching: then they rise and step forward nearer to him (Timur) and kneel with both knees on the ground, receiving the offered cup from his hand. Then they stand up and go backwards a little distance, taking care always to face his highness, and they kneel again and then drink at a draught all that is in the cup, for to leave any wine undrunk would be against good manners. Then having swallowed the draught they rise again and salute, placing the hand to the head. When we ambassadors were thus called up for presentation, two of the lords in waiting seized each of us under the arms and did not let us loose until we had been subsequently brought back to our seats .... All round and about there were pitched many smaller tents and awnings where sat the various other ambassadors who had come to attend the court of his Highness but who were not deemed of sufficient rank to warrant a seat in the Great Pavilion where Timur himself had his place" (*ibid.*, 262).

Under the Ṣafawids court ceremonial was more tightly controlled. The *Dastur al-mulūk* of Mīrzā Rafīʿā gives an account of the duties of court officials and of the precedence of civil and military officials and where they stood or sat in the royal assembly and of the robes of honour and other insignia given to them on appointment to office. This manual appears to have been written in the reign of S̲h̲āh Sulṭān Ḥusayn, the last of the Ṣafawids, but the practices which it describes probably go back to earlier reigns, and some of them were later revived under Fatḥ ʿAlī S̲h̲āh and his successors (Muḥammad Taḳī Dānis̲h̲-Paz̲h̲ūh, *Dastūr al-mulūk-i Mīrzā Rafīʿā wa Tad̲h̲kirat al-mulūk-i Mīrzā Samīʿā*, in *Tehran University*, *Rev. de la Faculté des Lettres et des Sciences Humaines*, xv/5-6 [1967], 62-93, xvi/1-6 [1968-9], 298-322, 416-40, 475-504; see also V. Minorsky, *Tad̲h̲kirat al-mulūk*, London 1943). The *is̲h̲ikaḳasi-bas̲h̲i*, the chief chamberlain, was charged with the supervision of court ceremonial. He normally belonged to the military classes and was one of the four "pillars of the state", the others being the *ḳurči-bas̲h̲i*, the *ḳullar-aḳasi* and the *tufangči-aḳasi*. His insignia of office was a mace (*daganak*). He regulated the proceedings of the Bihis̲h̲tāʾīn assembly. It was his duty after repasts and feasts to recite the *takbīr* Dānis̲h̲paz̲h̲ūh, *Dastūr al-mulūk*, in *op. cit.*, xvi [1968], 82-3). Great splendour prevailed in the court. The reception of envoys was accompanied by banquets and the giving and receiving of presents.

When Humāyūn, the Mug̲h̲al emperor, took refuge in Persia in 951/1544-5, S̲h̲āh Ṭahmāsp welcomed him warmly. Many banquets were held, and at the final one Ṭahmāsp showered gifts on Humāyūn (Iskandar Muns̲h̲ī, *Tārīk̲h̲-i ʿālamārā-yi ʿabbāsī*, Tehran A.H.S. 1334/1956, 99). Similarly, when Bāyazīd, the son of the Ottoman sultan, took refuge in Persia, having been dismissed by his father from the governorship of Kütahya, Ṭahmāsp arranged a magnificient reception for him in Ḳazwīn (*ibid.*, 102). The Mug̲h̲al emperor and the Ottoman sultan were the greatest of the contemporary Muslim rulers, but the lavishness of Ṭahmāsp's reception of Humāyūn and Bāyazīd was probably due to the fact that he hoped through them to extend his own influence in India and the eastern provinces of the Ottoman empire respectively.

Great importance was attached to the custom of kissing the ground before the ruler (*pābūsī, zamīnbūsī*), his throne and the gates of his palace; not only was it a means of showing honour to the ruler, but the action was believed to confer honour also upon the one who performed it. When the D̲j̲alālīs, who had defected to Persia from the Ottoman empire, came to Iṣfahān in 1016/1607-8 they had, Iskandar Muns̲h̲ī states, "the good fortune of kissing the shah's stirrups" in the audience hall of the Naḳs̲h̲-i D̲j̲ahān palace, and the supports of the shah's throne (*ibid.*, ii, 777). William Parry records that Sir Robert Sherley and his companions, on their arrival in Ḳazwīn, were brought by the shah's steward (the shah being absent on an expedition) to the gate of the palace "to offer that homage that all strangers do—that is to kiss the entrance of the palace three times" (*Sir Antony Sherley and his Persian adventure, including some contemporary narratives relating thereto*, ed. E.D. Ross, London 1933, 116). Sir John Chardin describes the ceremony which took place when a foreign ambassador was presented to the shah in the following words: "The ambassador or other person is conducted to within four paces of the king, and right against him where they stop him, and make him kneel, and in that posture he makes three prostrations of his body and head to the ground, so low that his forehead touches it. This done, the ambassador rises and delivers the letter he had for the king to the captain of the gate, who puts it in the hands of the first minister, and he presents it to the king, who puts it on his right side without looking into it: after this the ambassador is conducted to the place appointed for him" (*Sir John Chardin's travels in Persia*, with an introduction by Sir Percy Sykes, London 1927, 84-5).

Exaggerated respect was shown to any communication received from the shah. The recipient of a letter or *farmān* would kiss the document and raise it to his eyes and head, "a ceremony all Persians religiously observe" (*The journal of Robert Stodart*, with an introduction and notes by E.D. Ross, London 1935, 29). If a *k̲h̲il ʿa* was sent to a provincial governor, the recipient would go out to a set distance beyond the city gates to meet the *k̲h̲ilʿa*, which he would then put on and return to the city accompanied by a concourse of the local officials and inhabitants (*The travels of Monsieur de Thevenôt*, London 1687, repr. 1971, ii, 72, 104; Jean-Baptiste Tavernier, *Voyages en Perse*, Geneva 1970, 273). This was also the case under the Afs̲h̲ārs and Ḳād̲j̲ārs (cf. Jonas Hanway, *An historical account of the British trade over the Caspian Sea*, London 1762, i, 101; Malcolm, *History of Persia*, London 1829, ii, 407, 408; ʿAbd Allāh Mustawfī, *S̲h̲arḥ-i zindagānī-i man*, Tehran A.H.S. 1324/1945-6, i, 546-7). Prior to taking leave of the shah, envoys were given *k̲h̲ilʿa*s, which they wore at the farewell audience. The quality of the person regulated the value of the *k̲h̲ilʿa*. Some consisted of a whole suit of clothing, even to the shirt and shoes. Some were taken out of the king's own wardrobe from amongst the garments he had worn. The common ones consisted of a vest, an upper vest, a scarf and a turban. The value of *k̲h̲ilʿa*s varied enormously. One given to an ambassador from the Mug̲h̲al emperor was valued at 100,000 crowns and consisted of a garment of gold brocade with several upper vests, lined with marten furs and enriched by a clasp of precious stones, 15,000 crowns in money, forty very fine horses, their trappings garnished with precious stones, a sword and a dagger covered with the same and two large boxes filled with rich brocade of gold and silver, and several chests of dried fruits, liquors and essences (Chardin, ed. Sykes, 112-13). *K̲h̲ilʿa*s were also given to ministers, provincial governors and others, especially on their appointment to office and on the accession of the shah (cf. *Dastūr al-mulūk*, in *op. cit.*, xvi/1-2 [1968], 71 and *passim*). In the latter case, the grant of a *k̲h̲ilʿa* indicated that the repicient was to continue to hold the office which he had held under the previous shah. Iskandar Muns̲h̲ī states that sultan Muḥammad S̲h̲āh (985-96/1578-87) gave the large stocks of robes of honour which had been accumulated over the years to officials and others and that never a day passed without him giving ten or twenty robes of honour to unknown persons (Iskandar Muns̲h̲ī, i, 228). Chardin records that when S̲h̲ayk̲h̲ ʿAlī K̲h̲ān, Ṣafī II's first minister, was restored to favour after he had been in disgrace, he was sent a *k̲h̲ilʿa*, a horse with a saddle and trappings of gold, a sword and a dagger both set with diamonds, with an inkhorn, letters patent and other marks which denoted the post of prime minister. The next day, ʿAlī K̲h̲ān, clothed in the *k̲h̲ilʿa*, came to kiss the shah's feet. Three days later he entertained the shah (Chardin, ed. Sykes, 8-9). Minor rulers also gave *k̲h̲ilʿa*s to their followers and to each other (cf. ʿAlī b. Shams al-Dīn, *Tārīk̲h̲-i k̲h̲ānī*, ed. M. Sotoodeh, Tehran A.H.S. 1352/1973-4, 87, 129, 135).

Olearius, describing an audience given by the shah in 1656, mentions that the ambassadors were held under the arms by officials as they approached the shah, and notes that the purpose was both to honour the envoy and to ensure the security of the shah. At the end of the audience there was a feast at which dancers and singers performed (*Vermehrte Newe Beschreibung der Muscowitischen und Persischen Reyse*, Schleswig 1656, ed. von Dieter Lohmeier, repr. Tübingen 1971, 510-12). Du Mans, who gives a detailed description of court ceremonial, does not mention the practice of taking envoys under the arms. He states that the ambassador, with his hands crossed on his chest, would be led by the *is̲h̲iḳaḳasi-bas̲h̲i*, holding a kind of mace in his hand, to the shah to perform his obeisance. As they approached the shah, the *is̲h̲iḳaḳasi-bashi* would press his hand on the ambassador's shoulder to make him kneel. Then in that posture he would kiss the feet of the shah, after which he would retreat backwards to the place asigned to him by the *is̲h̲iḳaḳasi-bas̲h̲i* (*Estat de la Perse en 1660*, ed. Schefer, 30). Whenever an ambassador presented his letters and kissed the shah's feet, it was customary for him to eat with the king and his court and to sit in his assembly (*ibid.*, 32). According to the *Dastūr al-mulūk*, it was the duty of the *wazīr* of the supreme *dīwān* to read the *Fātiḥa* after meals in the royal assembly (*mad̲j̲lis-i bihis̲h̲tāʾīn*) (in *op. cit.*, xvi/1-2 [1968], 77). Thevenôt states that in audiences given to Christian ambassadors or others there was always much drinking (*op. cit.*, ii, 100). Kaempfer describes in detail the farewell audience given by the shah in Iṣfahān to the Swedish ambassador Ludwig Fabritius in 1684 (*Am Hofe des persischen Grosskönigs 1684-1685*, tr. W. Hinz, Tübingen-Basel 1977, 252 ff.). Twenty-two eunuchs stood behind the shah in a half-circle and six Georgian pages on his right side. One of them fanned the shah, another looked after the water-pipe (*ḳaliyān*), a third the spittoon, and a fourth had charge of a censer. One of the black eunuchs held the shah's dagger, and others held his gun, quiver, and bow, etc. (*ibid.*, 259). The various officials, who had their allotted places, stood in two rows, one on the right and the other on the left; the bodyguard stood four paces behind them (*ibid.*, 259-60). After the audience a sumptuous banquet was held (*ibid.*, 260 ff., 277 ff.).

On the shah's birthday the *amīr*s, "pillars of the state", the intimates of the court and the retinue, each according to his rank and status, gave the shah a sum of money. Some of this was handed over to the chief astrologer (*munad̲j̲d̲j̲im-bas̲h̲i*) to give to the deserving (*arbāb-i istiḥḳāḳ*). The garments that the shah wore on his birthday were given as a *k̲h̲il ʿa* to the *munad̲j̲d̲j̲im-bas̲h̲i* (*Dastūr al-mulūk*, in *op. cit.*, xvi/3 [1968], 309). The Naw Rūz was also an occasion for the giving of presents (*pīs̲h̲kas̲h̲*) to the shah (*Dastūr al-mulūk*, in *op. cit.*, xvi/1-2 [1968], 71 and *passim*). It was the duty of the *malik al-s̲h̲uʿarāʾ* [*q.v.*] to write a *ḳaṣīda* in praise of the shah, or in description of spring, and to read it at the public audience held on the Naw Rūz (*ibid.*, in *op. cit.*, xvi/4 [1969], 424). When the shah was in Iṣfahān, the Naw Rūz was celebrated by a great banquet held usually in the Čihil Sutūn palace or in the Naḳs̲h̲-i D̲j̲ahān gardens. In 1004/1595-6, the celebrations went on for several days and there was a public holiday for ten or twelve days. The bazaars were decorated and in the Saʿādatābād Square there were polo matches and archery contests (Iskandar Muns̲h̲ī, i, 506, cf. also 518, 532). In 1011/1602-3 the Naw Rūz celebrations were held in the Naḳs̲h̲-i D̲j̲ahān gardens, which were brilliantly lit for the occasion. The celebrations lasted three days (*ibid.*, ii, 634). In 1017/1608-9 the celebrations were again held in the Naḳs̲h̲-i D̲j̲ahān gardens. The space round the large pond (*ḥawḍ*) in the middle of the garden was reserved for the *amīr*s, *wazīr*s, pillars of the state, and intimates of the court, while the great men and notables of Iṣfahān and its districts (*bulūkāt*), the people of K̲h̲urāsān and Tabrīz, merchants and different groups who happened to be in Iṣfahān, were given places along the banks of the irrigation canals according to their different ranks (*ibid.*, ii, 780). In 1022/1613-14 also, celebrations were held in the Naḳs̲h̲-i D̲j̲ahān gardens, but they did not begin until the third day of the Naw Rūz because the shah did not return to Iṣfahān from Farahābād until then. On this occasion, he gave tax remissions to the people of the province of Iṣfahān (*ibid.*, ii, 861). If the shah was in the provinces, the celebrations of the Naw Rūz were of a minor character. In 1009/1600-1 he was in Mas̲h̲had and the celebrations took the form of games of polo and archery contents in the *maydān* of the city (*ibid.*, i, 598). Sometimes owing to the exigencies of war, the Naw Rūz was not celebrated officially, as was the case in 1025/1616-17 when the shah was en route for Georgia (*ibid.*, ii, 897-8).

Sir John Chardin gives an eye-witness account of the coronation of S̲h̲āh Ṣafī II (1077-1105/1667-94). His father S̲h̲āh ʿAbbās II having died in Ṭabaristān without designating his successor, his chief ministers decided to put Sulaymān (who later took the name Ṣafī) on the throne. They sent the k̲urči-bas̲h̲i to Iṣfahān to bring Sulaymān out of the *ḥaram* where he had been confined on the orders of his father, and to give him a letter announcing their decision. Every effort was meanwhile made to conceal the late shah's death, to which purpose the chief ministers, other than the k̲urči-bas̲h̲i remained in Ṭabaristān, sending only their deputies to Iṣfahān. Sulaymān was informed of the decision to place him on the throne and preparations for the coronation were immediately made. The k̲urči-bas̲h̲i, attended by the chief eunuch and a train of other persons, conducted the prince to the audience hall, where the deputies of the ministers of state made their three usual prostrations in the name of the ministers of state as also did the *munad̲j̲d̲j̲im-bas̲h̲i*, who had come with them from Ṭabaristān (for a description of the hall, see *The travels of Sir John Chardin into Persia and the East Indies .... to which is added The coronation of the present king of Persia Solyman the III*, London 1691, *Coronation*, 37 ff.). The prince then went to the bath to purify himself and put on new clothes. Meanwhile, the *munad̲j̲d̲j̲im-bas̲h̲i* and another astrologer who had come with him from Ṭabaristān set themselves to observe the most favourable moment for the coronation to take place. The s̲h̲ayk̲h̲ al-islām, who was to perform the ceremony, was sent for and the hall prepared for the coronation. Four articles needed for the coronation were placed in the middle of the hall. The first was the throne or *kursī*, "a little square cushion stool, three geometrical feet in height, the feet of the pillars that supported the corners being fashioned like so many great apples". These and the pillars were plated with gold and set with rubies and emeralds. When not in use, the throne was kept in the royal treasury and was so weighty that it needed two men to carry it (Chardin, *Coronation*, 39-40). The second article was the *tād̲j̲* or crown (for a description of this see *ibid.*, 40-1). The third was a sword and the fourth a dagger, both of which were set with precious stones (*ibid.*, 41). The three last mentioned articles were placed near the throne. When all was ready, Sulaymān came in and sat down (not on the throne) and the assembled company ranged themselves in their appointed places (*ibid.*, 42-3). When the *munad̲j̲d̲j̲im-bas̲h̲i* gave notice that the propitious moment had arrived, the prince and those present rose to their feet. The k̲urči-bas̲h̲i, after throwing himself at the shah's feet, rose to his knees, opened the bag in which was the letter he had brought from Ṭabaristān, took it out, kissed it, raised it to his forehead, and presented it to the prince and then rose to his feet. The prince, having received it, returned it to him and commanded him to open it and read it. When he had finished reading, the prince ordered him to send for the s̲h̲ayk̲h̲ al-islām. The latter, approaching the prince, threw himself at his feet, rose after the usual prostrations, and took the letter from the k̲urči-bas̲h̲i. Having laid it on his head, he read it and examined the seals, and then fell upon his knees before the prince and made three bows to the ground, thus declaring the authenticity of the letter and the elevation of the prince to the throne. The k̲urči-bas̲h̲i on

the left and the s̲h̲ayk̲h̲ al-islām on the right then conducted the prince to the golden chair or throne in the middle of the hall. The s̲h̲ayk̲h̲ al-islām, kneeling, said a prayer, blessed the *tād̲j̲*, the sword and the dagger, girded the sword on the shah's left side and hung the dagger on his right side. Then having made a sign to the k̲urči-bas̲h̲i to take off the shah's bonnet, he put on the *tād̲j̲*, reciting as he did so verses from the Ḳurʾān, which he also did when he girded him with the sword and the dagger. He then gave way to the k̲haṭīb, who read the k̲huṭba. As the latter ended the k̲huṭba by praying for the long life of the shah and the increase of his conquests, those present loudly repeated five or six times the words *in s̲h̲āʾ allāh*. The s̲h̲ayk̲h̲ al-islām then bowed his forehead to the ground three times, pronounced a second benediction and bowed again three times, after which those present, according to their rank, came forward and made the three customary prostrations. This concluded the ceremony (*ibid.*, 42 ff.). Subsequently, as a result of an illness which attacked the shah, a shortage of foodstuffs, an outbreak of pest and various other infelicitous events, it was believed that the coronation had taken place under an unfavourable constellation. Accordingly, a second coronation was decided upon at what was hoped would be a more favourable hour. This took place in the Čihil Sutūn palace, and the shah took the name of Ṣafī (*ibid.*, 132-3).

Under Nādir S̲h̲āh, court ceremonial was inevitably much reduced, since he spent much of his life in camp and on military expeditions. Hanway describes his camp and the pavilion tent in which he gave audience and transacted business. Sometimes he used to sit cross-legged on a large chair or dais and sometimes on the floor. There was nothing sumptuous in the pavilion; the front was always open even in the worst weather; in very cold weather charcoal braziers were placed in the middle. Behind the pavilion were his private apartments, to which he retired at meal-times. His officers of state and those having business with him stood in the open air forming a semi-circle in front of the tent. If anyone was brought to answer for his conduct, he was held under the arms by officers to prevent his escape or committing an act of violence. "The same ceremony with very little difference", Hanway continues, "was observed towards foreign ambassadors, of great men, being made on the pretence of respect but in reality to prevent an accident" (*op. cit.*, i, 166-7). He mentions that there were two standards in Nādir's camp when he visited it in 1743. One was in stripes of red, blue and white and the other in red, blue, white and yellow, without any ornament. They were very large and extremely heavy (*ibid.*, i, 169).

Nādir's coronation was also a break with tradition. When he had decided to assume the crown, he summoned governors, ḳāḍīs, ʿulamāʾ and provincial notables to a *ḳuriltay* in the Mūg̲h̲ān steppe ostensibly to choose their ruler, but in fact to acclaim him as their ruler. Those who assembled were too numerous to be received simultaneously and so were divided into groups, each being given a separate audience. Finally, on 24 S̲h̲awwāl 1148/8 March 1736, after several days of charade, Nādir having signified his readiness to accept the crown subject to certain conditions, the umarāʾ and other persons of consequence clad in robes of honour assembled, and Mīrzā Zakī placed a golden crown, adorned with magnificent jewels, on Nādir's head. All those present knelt down and prayed, except the deputy chief *mullā*, who intoned the prayer. While this was being uttered, all kept their arms above their heads; afterwards, while the *Fātiḥa* was being read, they bowed their faces to the ground. When the *Fātiḥa* was finished, everyone rose and seated himself in his appointed place according to his rank (see further, L. Lockhart, *Nadir Shah*, London 1938, 96 ff.). Among the spoils that Nādir brought back to Persia from his Indian expedition in 1739 was the Peacock Throne. This was lost in the troubles after Nādir's death. The modern Peacock Throne is of Ḳādjār manufacture (see Amīr Gīlāns͟hāh, *Yak ṣad u pandjāh sāl-i salṭanat dar Īrān*, n.d. Tehran, 28-9 ʿAlī Aṣg͟har Ḥikmat, *Tak͟ht-i ṭāwūs*, in *FIZ*, viii, 138-52).

Āḳā Muḥammad K͟hān (1193-1211/1779-97), like Nādir S͟hāh, spent much of his life in military expeditions and had little use for court ceremonial. Under his successor Fatḥ ʿAlī S͟hāh (1211-50/1797-1834), traditional ceremonies were revived. No court, according to Sir John Malcolm, paid more rigid attention to forms and ceremonies, the maintenance of which were deemed essential to the power and glory of the monarch. Looks, words, and the motions of the body were all regulated by the strictest forms. When the king was seated in public, his sons, ministers and courtiers stood erect, with their hands crossed over their chests, and in the exact place belonging to their rank (*History of Persia*, ii, 400). James Morier also remarks that the king was never approached by his subjects without frequent inclinations of the body; and when the person introduced to his presence had reached a certain distance, he would wait until the king ordered him to proceed; upon which he would leave his shoes and walk forward to a second spot and wait there until the king directed him to advance further. No one sat before the king except relations of kings, poets, learned and holy men and ambassadors; his ministers and officers of state were never permitted this privilege (*A journey through Persia, Armenia, and Asia Minor*, London 1812, 286).

The insignia of royalty consisted of the following articles, all of which were set with jewels and pearls: the crown (of which there appear to have been several), the sword of state, a dagger, the royal bow and its arrows, a shield and staff or mace. These were held on ceremonial occasions by pages (*g͟hulāms*) or other officials, or by the princes (cf. W. Ouseley, *Travels in various countries of the east....*, London 1819, iii, 130-1; Morier, *op. cit.*, 192, 214-15; Muʿayyir al-Mamālik, *Yāddās͟ht-hā-ī az zindagānī-i Nāṣir al-Dīn S͟hāh*, Tehran n.d., 25). On the front of the crown was placed an aigrette (*djīg͟ha*). A similar ornament was also worn on the headdress of the shah and princes. On state occasions, special bracelets were worn by the shah and his sons (Morier, *A second journey through Persia, Armenia, and Anatolia*, London 1818, 173). A variety of standards were in existence, some with religious symbols, such as D͟hu 'l-Fiḳār, the sword of ʿAlī, on them. The royal standard usually had on it the figure of a lion couchant with the sun rising behind it, which sign was also commonly sculptured upon the royal palaces (Malcolm, *History of Persia*, ii, 406-7). Hanway mentions that this emblem was to be found on the palace built by S͟hāh ʿAbbās at As͟hraf (*op. cit.*, i, 199). It was a sign of some antiquity; the Saldjūḳ of Rūm, G͟hiyāt͟h al-Dīn Kay Ḳubād (634-42/1236-44) had it on one of his coins (Malcolm, *op. cit.*, ii. 406 n.).

The arrival of a foreign embassy was deemed one of the occasions when the king ought to appear in all his grandeur. Fatḥ ʿAlī vied with the most magnificent of his predecessors in this respect. The exact procedure differed, however, in that ambassadors were no longer required to kneel and kiss the ground in front of the monarch, but merely to bow at intervals as they approached his presence (Malcolm, *op. cit.*, ii, 400-1); those who escorted them into the royal presence no longer took them under the arms; and banquets were no longer held after audiences. Only ambassadors and the representatives of sovereign princes were allowed the distinction of being seated in the presence of the king at public audiences (Sir Robert Ker Porter, *Travels in Georgia, Persia...*, London 1821, i, 356). There is a curious reference in the account of the negotiations for the reception of Sire Gore Ouseley, the British envoy, who brought a letter from King George III addressed to Fatḥ ʿAlī S͟hāh, in 1811. Ouseley wished to present the letter personally. The Persian ministers insisted that it should be transmitted through them according, as they alleged, to Persian usage; and Fatḥ ʿAlī himself said that he could not possibly receive the letter directly from Ouseley at a public audience. A compromise was reached, by which the shah agreed to receive the letter at a private audience (W. Ouseley, *op. cit.*, iii, 123).

It was the custom in early Ḳādjār times for foreign envoys, when they were received in audience by the shah or a prince governor, to wear red cloth stockings under green leather slippers with high heels, which they removed on entering the audience hall (Ker Porter, *op. cit.*, i, 249-50; cf. also Morier, *A journey through Persia*, 186; Ouseley, *op. cit.*, ii, 10-11, 222, iii, 129-30). In the early years of the 19th century, if *k͟hilʿas* had been sent to the envoy and his suite by the shah or prince governor, they would wear these when attending his audience. The practice of sending New Year presents to foreign envoys was discontinued, at least so far as the British mission was concerned, from about the middle of the century (Great Britain, Public Record Office, F.O. 60.130.Sheil to Palmerston, No. 46, Tehran, 23 April 1847).

The Naw Rūz was the most important of the public festivals celebrated by the shah. Fatḥ ʿAlī appears always to have returned to Tehran or Sulṭāniyya for it. To each of the chief men and officers of the court he would send a *k͟hilʿa*, consisting of a complete suit of brocade with a shawl, and sometimes he would add to this a horse with its trappings and caparisons (see further Morier, *op. cit.*, 205; idem, *A second journey through Persia, Armenia and Asia Minor*, 93). Malcolm states that it was the custom for the shah to march out of his capital on the Naw Rūz, attended by his ministers, nobles, and as many of his army as could be assembled. The ceremonies of the day would commence with a review, after which the tribute and presents of all the rulers and governors of the different provinces would be laid at the foot of the throne, which was placed in a magnificent tent pitched for the purpose in an open plain. The shah would remain in camp for several days. Horse-races were among the amusements. (*History of Persia*, ii, 405; cf. also Morier, *op. cit.*, 208). Often, however, the Naw Rūz audience took place in the capital (see Ker Porter for a detailed account of Fatḥ ʿAlī S͟hāh's Naw Rūz audience in Tehran in 1818, *op. cit.*, 320 ff., also quoted by R.G. Watson, *History of Persia*, London 1866, 138 n.). Under Nāṣir al-Dīn S͟hāh also, the Naw Rūz was celebrated with great magnificence. Three audiences were held; the first (the *salām-i taḥwīl*) took place when the sun passed into Aries and was held in the hall in which Fatḥ ʿAlī's throne was kept. A large white cloth for the Haft Sīn stretched from near the door of the hall to the edge of the dais on which the throne was placed. The Ḳādjār princes, military officers, civil officials, and religious dignitaries proceeded to their places an hour before the sun entered Aries. Three quarters of an hour later, a curtain was raised and the shah in a blaze of jewels, preceded by the *is̲h̲iḳaḳasi-bas̲h̲i* and the Iʿtimād al-Ḥaram, advanced slowly towards the throne, but out of respect for the *ʿulamāʾ*, he did not sit on the throne; instead he sat on a chair (*masnad*) covered with gold brocade, placed beside the throne, holding the sword of Nādir S̲h̲āh on his knees. The first minister (the *ṣadr-i aʿẓam*), with his cloak and sword of office, and his subordinates stood near the throne. The *imām d̲j̲umʿa* and the great *ʿulamāʾ* sat beside the *masnad* of the shah, while the less distinguished *ʿulamāʾ* stood at the foot of the throne. The *k̲h̲aṭīb al-mamālik* and the *munad̲j̲d̲j̲im-bas̲h̲i* stood facing the throne. The former, approaching the throne, read a *k̲h̲uṭba* and at the mention of the names of the prophet, ʿAlī and the shah all heads bowed. The *munad̲j̲d̲j̲im-bas̲h̲i* then came forward and after a moment or two announced that the sun had entered Aries. Immediately the trumpeters, who were drawn up outside, sounded their trumpets and guns were let off in the Maydān-i Mas̲h̲ḳ. The shah offered his congratulations to the *ʿulamāʾ* and then to the rest of the company. Taking the Ḳurʾān in his hands he reverently read a passage, after which Ḥād̲j̲d̲j̲ī Niẓām al-Islām knelt before the shah and put a little dust from a packet into water and gave it to him to drink. Having drunk it, the shah began to give New Year presents (*ʿīdī*) consisting of purses full of gold coins, to the *ʿulamāʾ*. When this was finished and the *ʿulamāʾ* had left, the bands which were drawn up outside, hitherto silent out of respect to the *ʿulamāʾ*, would begin to play. The shah then got up from his *masnad* and sat on a chair and gave purses full of gold coins first to the princes, then to the army leaders and *mustawfī*s and finally to the rest of those present, saying a few words to each one in turn. The recipients, on receiving their presents, kissed them and raised them to their heads. The assembly lasted some two or three hours, after which the shah withdrew into the garden, and thence into the *andarūn*, where the ladies of the *ḥaram* vied with each other in kissing his feet (Muʿayyir al-mamālik, *op. cit.*, 70 ff.).

On the second day of the Naw Rūz, a public audience was held in the *dīwān-k̲h̲āna*, attended by the Ḳād̲j̲ār princes and leaders of the Ḳād̲j̲ār tribe, military officers, civil officials and foreign envoys. When all were assembled, the shah entered the *dīwān-k̲h̲āna*, mounted the marble throne and sat on a chair, set with jewels, which was placed on it. Bands then played the special music for the *salām* (*muzīḳ-i salām-i īrān*), trumpeters sounded their trumpets, guns were fired, and the instruments of the *naḳāra-k̲h̲āna* were played. When this was over the *k̲h̲aṭīb al-mamālik* read the *k̲h̲uṭba*, and the court poet recited a *ḳaṣīda*, after which the *ḥakīm al-mamālik* brought the special *ḳāliyān* kept for audiences on a tray set with jewels and placed it at the feet of the shah, who, according to custom, began to smoke it. At this audience presents were given only to the military and the bureacracy; the *muns̲h̲ī al-mamālik*, with two others, took round large trays of coins and each person to whom it was offered took a handful (*ibid.*, 82 ff.). The audience held on the third day was of an informal nature; the *mustawfī*s and military officers were not present, only the shah's intimates. On this occasion he would watch the various activities which went on in the grounds and streets around the palace. These included ram fights, cock-fighting, bear-dancing, performances by conjurers, wrestlers and members of *zūr-k̲h̲āna*s. The shah would distribute largesse to the performers and a special armlet to the champion wrestler (*ibid.*, 86-7). On the eve of the Naw Rūz there was a firework display, which the shah would watch with his ladies from one of the palaces. On the thirteenth day of the *ʿīd*, the shah would go to one of the royal gardens with his *ḥaram* (*ibid.*, 89).

On the shah's birthday, three receptions were given in the reign of Nāṣir al-Dīn S̲h̲āh. One was given by Anīs al-Dawla, the shah's chief wife, to which the wives of ambassadors and other European women resident in Tehran would be invited, together with wives of ministers and notables. The shah would appear at the reception and give the guests presents of gold coins. A lunch would then be held for the princes, after which Nāṣir al-Dīn would sit in the portico of the S̲h̲ams al-ʿAmāra palace and give them presents (*ʿīdī*). In the evening the Nāʾib al-Salṭana, the shah's son, who was governor of Tehran, would hold a reception at which he would make a speech in honour of the shah's birthday, after which the foreign envoys who were present would also make speeches; before each of these the national anthem of the country which the envoy represented would be played. The shah would watch the proceedings with members of his *ḥaram* from a window looking on the audience hall (*ibid.*, 91).

The other major festivals celebrated by Nāṣir al-Dīn S̲h̲āh were the religious festivals of the *ʿīd al-aḍḥā*, the birthdays of the prophet Muḥammad, the Imām ʿAlī and the Hidden Imām, the *ʿīd-i g̲h̲adīr* [see G̲H̲ADĪR K̲H̲UMM], the *mabʿat̲h̲* and the *ʿīd al-fiṭr*. Muẓaffar al-Dīn added to these the birthday of Ḥusayn (*ibid.*, 73).

The Ḳād̲j̲ārs, influenced by European precedent, made various innovations in ceremonial matters. In addition to the playing of national anthems on state occasions, various orders were instituted. One of the first was the Order of the Sun which Fatḥ ʿAlī gave to the French envoy General Gardane; shortly afterwards he instituted the Order of the Lion and the Sun for Malcolm (see Kaye, *Life and correspondence of Major-General Sir John Malcolm*, London 1856, ii, 31 ff.). Nāṣir al-Dīn S̲h̲āh introduced the custom of giving his picture (*timt̲h̲āl-i humāyūn*) adorned by one, two or three rows of diamonds to favoured recipients. The first class with three rows of diamonds was given only to foreign rulers (Muʿayyir al-Mamālik, *op. cit.*, 83-4).

Bibliography: Given in the article.

(A.K.S. LAMBTON)

4. In the Ottoman Empire.

In the Ottoman Empire, ceremonial, protocol and etiquette are generally referred to as *Tes̲h̲rīfāt. Alay* [*q.v.*] "procession", "parade", forms an integral part of most ceremonies held by the court, in the residence of the sultans as well as those organised by provincial governors who, in a lesser way, were expected to display the splendour of their monarch's régime.

The same purpose was served by military ceremonial and display. Splendid occasions were the mustering of the army setting out on campaign when the "horsetails" were planted in the field of Davudpaşa or outside Üsküdar. Likewise, the fleet of the *ḳapudān-pas̲h̲a* lay at anchor in front of the tomb of K̲h̲ayr al-Dīn Barbarossa at Beşiktaş before putting to sea on its yearly tour in the Mediterranean (see BAḤRIYYA. iii, and TUG̲H̲).

Popular entertainment (modern *şenlik*) often had a processional character as well. Ceremonial festivities of the sultan's court, such as weddings, circumcisions of princes and anniversaries, were coupled as a rule with extensive popular entertainments like illuminations (*donanma*) and theatricals.

The great Islamic festivals [see ʿĪD], especially those

during Ramaḍān, were occasions of general enjoyment. Special dress and the distribution of presents by the sultan, as well as to his person, by his subjects and by foreign princes belong to the ceremonial sphere [see HIBA; KHILʿA; LIBĀS, iv; PĪSHKASH]. Ottoman ceremonial derives on one hand from the ancient traditions of world rule cultivated by the Mongol and Turkish empires in Central Asia and the Middle East. On the other hand, the traditions of leadership in Islam begun in Medina and developed in the historical seats of the caliphate in Syria and ʿIrāḳ which had adopted much from the pre-Islamic Persian kingdoms and from elements of provincial Byzantine administrations, were formative elements. The Mamlūk sultanate played an important role in the transmission of prevalent Islamic political culture to the Ottomans. Some scholars maintain that the greater part of Ottoman court ceremonial was in direct imitation of imperial Constantinople, but recent research in Islamic history has shown that such a hypothesis is no longer tenable. The pioneering studies here of M.F. Köprülü have been confirmed by the work of modern scholars such as A.K.S. Lambton and H.İnalcık.

The rules of ceremonies and protocol set by the Ottoman government were applied within the frame of Islamic legal usage and custom (*ʿörf*) [see ʿURF] and laid down in so-called "law codes" *Ḳānūn-nāme*s [*q.v.*]. Hardly any sources can be dated with certainty before the reign of Bāyazīd II (886-918/1481-1512). Dilger's (1967) and Heyd's (1973) researches have shown that the mss. of *Ḳānūn-nāme*s used and published by von Hammer and Meḥmed ʿĀrif were composites or pious frauds of later date than the years of Sultan Meḥemmed II (second reign 855-86/1451-81). Hence the so-called "Ottoman *Ḳānūn-nāme*" is unreliable as an unqualified source, and the use made of these texts by von Hammer and, *a fortiori* by İ. H. Uzunçarşılı, is therefore flawed.

Court ceremonial, appropriately enhanced by Islamic ritual, was designed to emphasise the awe in which the ruler was to held by means of a show of splendour to be seen as evidence of his power. As a consequence, his separation from the rest of the population followed. A protective seclusion was a characteristic of the Ottoman sultans, with their forerunners in the Islamic Middle East. A reliable source, Bertrandon de la Brocquière (1433) describes already the isolation of the reigning sultans, e.g. Murād II still dining with the companions, but his successor sitting at table alone. The increased elevation of the sultan's person and his gradual disappearance from the public eye led to heightened ceremonial on the rare event of the ruler showing himself at appointed occasions.

The audience maintained the link between the separate spheres of authority of the sultan and of his ministers united in the *Dīwān-i hümāyūn* [*q.v.*] presided over by the Grand Vizier [see ṢADR-I AʿẒAM]. In the early days of the Ottoman monarchy, the meetings of the *dīwān* were still public audiences. Probably during the reign of Selīm I (918-26/1512-20), the public audience was instituted in front of the *Bāb-ï Seʿādet* in the Palace of Istanbul, when a throne was placed there under an awning. The appearance of the ruler was formally applauded under the guidance of the Chief Applauder or *Alḳïshčï Bashï. Alḳïsh* (applause), accompanied by exclamations like "*pādishāhïmïz čoḳ yasha*" intonated by the *Selām Čavūsh* or *Duʿādjï*, is a ceremonial known already in Saldjūḳ times. The audience proper (*ʿarḍ*) implied kissing hands (*destbūs*) or kissing the hem of the ceremonial kaftan of the sultan seated on his throne placed on a dais (*ṣofa*) on such occasions. *Ca.* 1525 the throne was replaced in a room specially built for audiences just inside the gate, the *ʿarḍ odasï* still to be seen in the Topkapı Sarayı today. The protocol is well-known from numerous reports of foreign ambassadors thus received. The guests were led to the sultan while held by their arms. The traditional explanation that it was a measure of security originating in the assassination of Murād I [*q.v.*] in 1389 is rendered doubtful by the earliest sources mentioning this protocol dating from 1518. In fact, this rigid guidance is known from Saldjūḳ times and the Mamlūk court (Dilger, 1967, 58-9 and n.; Lambton).

As tokens of favour, precious kaftans were presented to those persons received as *khilaʿ* or robes of honour. In times of decline, according to diplomatic sources of the 17th and 18th centuries, these robes were actually bought back by the Ottoman Porte to be given out another time. Since the days of Selīm I, the ruler would remain immobile and practically silent during audiences. An exceptional favour was a compliment on a speech of an ambassador in the guise of a word or two, e.g. "*güzel*" or a mere gesture of the hand. Bāyāzīd II and Meḥemmed II still seem to have entered upon some civil conversation on such occasions. The throne (*Takht-i hümāyūn, serīr*) did not have an important ceremonial significance in itself apart from being of luxury manufacture. The newly-succeeding sultan would receive the homage or oath of allegiance of his subjects (*bayʿa* [*q.v.*], *biʿat* in Ottoman usage).

The actual accession to rule was the subject of the great ceremony of the *djulūs*. The ruler proceeded in state on horseback (or boat) to the shrine of Eyyūb on the Golden Horn, where took place the Girding of the Sword (*taḳlīd-i sayf, ḳïlïc kushatmasï* in Turkish) in lieu of a coronation in Western style. According to tradition, this took place for the first time in 824/1421 at Bursa, where the venerable Sheykh Emīr Bukhārī girded Murād II. Since Meḥemmed II, the ceremony was held at the Eyyūb *türbe* till the accession of the last Ottoman Meḥemmed VI, on 3 July 1918, when the Sheykh Sayyid Aḥmad Sanūsī [*q.v.*] performed it. It is a persistent but erroneous notion that the sword was fastened by the Grand Sheykh of the Mawlawiyya [*q.v.*] dervish order.

An imperial astronomer had to appoint the exact date, which was to fall between the third and seventh day after the actual accession. On the return journey, the sultan passed the Janissary Barracks of Eski Odalar. There, this corps offered *sherbet*, and the traditional intention for the next campaign of holy war was formulated by the ruler's words "We shall meet at the Red Apple" (*Ḳïzïl Elma*, in Turkish the symbol of distant Christian capitals such as Rome and Vienna). A distribution of money to the Janissary Corps became usual (*Djulūs bakhshīshi*) as was also customary at the reception of foreign ambassadors by the sultan and separately by the *dīwān* in full session, a so-called *Ulūfe Dīwānï* ("Salary Council"). The swords used formed part of the collection of the Holy Relics of the Prophet Muḥammad, *emānāt-i mubāreke*, still kept in the room in the Palace appointed for that purpose, the *khïrḳat-i sherīf odasï*. These relics acquired by Selīm I comprised *inter alia* the Holy Mantle itself (*burda*), the Holy Banner (*sandjaḳ-i sherīf*), a fragment of a tooth of the Prophet (*dendān-i seʿādet*), hairs of the Prophet's beard (*lihya-yi seʿādet*), a print of his footstep (*ḳadem-i seʿādet*) and swords which belonged to the Prophet, to the caliphs Abū Bakr, ʿUmar and ʿUthmān and to six of his Companions.

These *eshyāʾ-i müteberrike* were in a way the insignia of government for the Ottoman sultans in their role as leaders of Islam, and during the 19th century, especially from the time of ʿAbd Ḥamīd II (1293-1327/1876-1909) became symbolic of Ottoman pretentions to the caliphate. The true regalia and symbols of recognition as Muslim ruler were for the Ottomans as for all others, the right of coinage (*sikka* [*q.v.*]); the mention of the sultan's name in the Friday Prayers (*khutba* [*q.v.*]); the seal stamp (*mühür*); the monogram, i.e. the prestigious *ṭughra* [*q.v.*], the hallmark of Ottoman rule par excellence; on some occasions, the dressing of the Imperial Tent (*oṭāgh-i hümāyūn*, also *čadïr*); and accompanying most ceremonies, the military music of the Janissaries (*mehterkhāne* [*q.v.* and also NAḲĀRA-KHĀNA and NAWBA]).

The other sovereign ceremony with religious significance was the expedition of the annual "holy" caravan to Mecca and Medina carrying the concrete embodiment of Ottoman devotion toward the Holy Places. The *sürre-yi hümāyūn* was organised around the date of 12 Radjab by the *Dār al-seʿādet aghasï* [*q.v.*] in the Harem apartment of the Palace. The first sending of the *ṣadaḳāt-i rūmiyye* was ordered by Meḥemmed I. Selīm I for the first time received the holy relics, together with the keys of the Kaʿba. ʿAbd al-Ḥamīd II sent a sum of 3,503,610 *ghurush* with the *Maḥmal-ï Sharīf* the "Holy Camel", thus called by Western observers. The end of the Ramaḍān saw a regular series of splendid religious ceremonials at court and in the capital. The congratulations on the occasion of the principal Islamic holidays took place in the sultan's palace in the form of a great audience in front of the *Bāb-i Seʿādet* (the *muʿāyede*). The traditional public visit to the mosque by the sultan for the Friday *ṣalāṭ al-ẓuhr* each week remained one of few ceremonies during which a great number of subjects, and also foreign visitors, had the opportunity to see if the ruling sultan was alive and well. This so-called *selāmlïḳ* is the Ottoman ceremony most widely described (and photographed) through the ages, and was the symbol of the religious as well as the secular sovereignty exercised by the Ottoman dynasty.

Ceremonial and protocol were maintained according to traditional standards by a number of court officials. The *Čavūsh-Bashï* was in charge of protocol of the *Dīwān* and the sultan's audiences in the Palace. The *Mīr ʿAlem(Emīr-i ʿAlem)* or standard bearer, an officer of the "Outside Service" of the palace, was custodian of the regalia, e.g. the *aḳ ʿalem*, *čadïr* [see MIẒALLA], the *mehter* and the "Horse tails" (*tugh* [*q.v.*]). He had to distribute standards and banners to newly-appointed *beylerbeys* and lesser provincial governors. The office of Master of Ceremonies, *teshrīfātčï bashï*, was instituted according to traditional opinion by Süleymān I. Registers were kept of all expenses and receipts related to ceremonial occasions. A journal of day-to-day events at court or at the headquarters of the Commander-in-Chief (*Serdār-ï Ekrem*) seems to have been kept by these officials (also see R.F. Kreutel and K. Teply, *Kara Mustafa vor Wien 1683*, Graz, etc. 1982, 103-210). This office by 1683 or at least by 1703 fell under the authority of the Grand Vizier rather than that of the palace service (see K. Kepeci, *Tarih lûgati*, Istanbul 1952, s.v. *teşrifatçılık*).

The reforms begun by Sultan Maḥmūd II (1223-55/1808-39), and completed under the *Tanẓīmāt* [*q.v.*], brought about changes in ceremonial and protocol: if not in principle and terminology, then certainly in size, luxury and uniforms. The setting of many occasions was changed completely by the moving of the sultans' residence and court out of Top Kapı Sarayı to palaces outside town along the Bosphorus near Beşiktaş and even across the water, notably the palaces of Çiragan, Dolmabahçe and the vast complex of Yıldız, the last one built upon the initiative of ʿAbd-Ḥamīd II.

On the whole, tradition was maintained in a more sober form. To the ever-increasing number of foreign visitors to the Ottoman capital, ceremonies nevertheless still made a deep impression, as is evident from the mass of travel accounts, private memoirs and observations of diplomatists. ʿAbd al-Ḥamīd reputedly took a great interest in keeping alive the great traditions, and promoted the study and restoration of institutions from the Ottoman and Islamic past, for ceremonial was still considered a useful means to enhance the pretentions of the Ottoman Sultan-caliph to great power status and to paramount leadership of the Islamic world.

During the second half of the 19th century, we see in ceremonial a blend of ancient oriental and modern European styles. The *Teshrīfātčī* remained an official attached to the Grand Vizerate, i.e. the *Dīwān-i Hümāyūn*. The newly-created Ottoman Foreign Office employed its own Chef-de-Protocole (*Khāridjiyye Teshrīfātčïsï*). Official titles and ranks are systematically arranged into a hierarchy. The *sālnāme* of 1323/1905-6 (164) mentions a *Teshrīfāt-i ʿUmūmiyye Nāẓïrï*, ranking as a vizier of second class attached to the Grand Vizier's office. Next to him functioned a *Teshrīfātī-yi Dīwān-i Hümāyūn* carrying the *ūlā* rank of civil servants (*ibid.*, 164). In the Yıldız Palace, a *Merāsim Dāʾiresi* functioned. The ancient office of *Alḳïshčï Bashï* leading a group of official "applauders" still survived. The classical *mehterkhāne*, however, was replaced by a western-style military band playing martial music at all occasions.

A remarkable innovation *alla franga* was the introduction at public ceremonies, such as the *muʿāyede*, *selāmlïḳ* or the visit to the *Khïrḳa-yi Sherīf*, on 15 Ramaḍān, of the prominent female members of the Sultan's household and family. The Wālide Sulṭān [*q.v.*] princesses, high-ranking consorts and female officials of the Harem had to take part in a great number of ceremonies and to watch the military parades in front of the *Taʿlīmkhāne Köshkü* inside Yıldız Park, which was the successor, in a way, of the *Alay Köshkü* on the wall of the Topkapı Sarayı facing the Sublime Porte (*Bāb-i ʿAlī* [*q.v.*]). As of old, the births, circumcisions and weddings of princes and princesses were occasions for court ceremonies and public entertainments. The collective circumcision of princes took place three times during ʿAbd al-Ḥamīd II's reign. The first days of the great Islamic holidays were celebrated with splendid ceremonial audiences in the Dolmabahçe palace. Foreign ambassadors could watch proceedings from balconies opened for that purpose. The *destbūs* was performed by a long row of dignitaries. The *Sheykh al-Islām* performed the ritual prayer first but (a sign of the reforms!) was followed by the Orthodox Patriarch and the Chief Rabbi in congratulating the Sultan.

The last time Ottoman ceremonial was watched by multitudes in the streets of Istanbul was the accession to the throne by the last Ottoman sultan, Meḥemmed VI, in 1918. The Grand Vizier Aḥmed Tewfīḳ Pasha [*q.v.*] was the last one to leave the sultan's palace in stately procession (*alay*) to proceed to the Sublime Porte, this time in a carriage instead of on horseback, on 4 November 1922 (see A. F. Türkgeldi (a former *Mabeyn*, Chief Secretary to the last sultan) *Görüp işittiklerim* [= Memoirs], Ankara 1951², 165).

Bibliography: 1. Archival sources: BBA Teşrifatçılık nos. 1-17 (955-1240) (KPT); Teşrifat Kalemi (B) 1-15 (988-1194/1580-1780 (KPT); Yıldız Arsivi (Yıldız Esas Evrakı 32), Hukumdaran-i ecnebiyyenin vurudunda ve sur-i humayunlara ve sâire merasimde icra kılınan teşrifât muamelâtına dair evrak. 2. Ms. sources; Meḥmed b. Aḥmed Te<u>sh</u>rīfātizāde, *Defter-i Te<u>sh</u>rīfāt*, mss. Vienna Kons. Akad. 283 and ÖNB 1136 (cf. *GOW*, no. 200). 3. Printed sources: *Sālnāme* 1296 (1878-9), 50; *ibid.*, 1323 (1905-6) 164, 218; Tewḳīʿī ʿAbdurraḥmān Pa<u>sh</u>a, ed. *ʿO<u>th</u>mānlī ḳānūnnāmeleri*, in *MTM*, i, 49-112, 305-48, 497-544; Aḥmed Rāsim, *Resimlī we <u>kh</u>arīṭalī ʿO<u>th</u>mānlī taʾrī<u>kh</u>ī*, Istanbul 1326-30, 4 vols. (*Fāʾideler* in vols. i, ii, iii); Ali Seydi Bey, *Teşrifât ve teşkılâtımız*, ed. N. Banoğlu, Istanbul 1972 (unscholarly ed.); ʿAṭāʾ Bey, *Taʾrī<u>kh</u>-i ʿAṭāʾ*, Istanbul 1291/1874, 5 vols., i, 59 f., 221, 253 f., 269 f.; İ. Artuk, *Alay Köşkü*, in *TED*, xii (1981-2), 587-92; A. Berker, ed., *Teşrifati Naim Efendi tarihi*, in *TV*, iii (1949); K. Dilger, *Untersuchungen zur Geschichte des osmanischen Hofzeremoniells in 15. und 16. Jahrhundert*, Munich 1967 (important, bibl.); J. Fletcher, *Turco-Mongolian monarchic tradition in the Ottoman Empire*, in *Eucharisterion. Essays presented to O. Pritsak*, Cambridge, Mass. 1981, 236-51; Gibb and Bowen, i, 120, 152; O.Ş. Gökyay, *Osmanlı donanması ve Kapudan-i derya ile ilgili teşrifat hakkında belgeler*, in *TED*, xii (1981-2), 25-84; idem, *Kızıl Elma üzerine*, in *Tarih ve Toplum* [Istanbul] (1986), ix (425), xiv (430), xx (84), xxv (89); H. İnalcık, *The problem of the relationship between Byzantine and Ottoman taxation*, in *Akten... XI. Int. Byzantinisten Kongresses 1958*, Munich 1960, 237-42; Hammer-Purgstall, *Staatsverfassung*, i, 434 f., ii, 131 f.; U. Heyd, ed. V. L. Ménage, *Studies in Old Ottoman criminal law*, Oxford 1973; H. İnalcık, *The Ottoman Empire. The classical age 1300-1600*, London 1973; M.F. Köprülü, new ed. by O.F. Köprülü, *Bizans müesseselerinin osmanlı müesseselerine tesiri*, Istanbul 1981; R. F. Kreutel, tr. and ed., new ed. by K. Teply, *Kara Mustafa vor Wien. 1683*, Graz etc. 1982; R. van Luttervelt, *De "Turkse" Schilderijen van J. B. Vanmour en zijn School* [Leiden-] Istanbul 1958; Meḥmed Esʿad Ṣaḥḥāflar<u>sh</u>ey<u>kh</u>īzāde, *Te<u>sh</u>rīfāt-i ḳadīme*, Istanbul 1287, new ed. Y. Ercan, *Osmanlılarda töre ve törenler*, Istanbul 1979 (unscholarly ed.); Ö. Nutku, *IV. Mehmet'in Edirne şenliği (1675)*, Ankara 1972; Ayşe Osmanoğlu, *Babam Abdülhamid*, Istanbul 1960; A. Özcan, *Fâtih' in teşkilât kanunâmesi ve nizam-i âlem için kardeş katlı meselesi*, in *TD*, xxxiii (1980-1, publ. 1982), 7-56; T. Reyhanlı, *İngiliz gezginlerine göre XVI yüzyılda Istanbul'da hayat (1582-1599)*, Ankara 1983, 49-80; Leylâ Saz, *Harem'in içyüzü*, ed. S. Borak, Istanbul 1974; M. Sertoğlu, *Resimli Osmanlı tarihi ansiklopedisi*, Istanbul 1958; B. Spuler, *Die europäische Diplomatie in Konstantinopel bis zum Frieden von Belgrad (1739)* (= *Jahrbücher für Kultur und Geschichte der Slaven* (1935), 53-115, 171-222, 313-66; *Jahrbücher für Geschichte Osteuropas*, i (1936), 229-62, 383-440); Ç. Uluçay, *Harem II*, Ankara 1971; İ. H. Uzunçarşılı, *Osmanlı devletinin saray teşkilâtı*, Ankara 1945[1], 1984[2]; idem, *Osmanlı devletinin merkez ve bahriye teşkilâtı*, Ankara 1948[1]; Halid Ziya Uşaklığil, *Saray ve ötesi. Son hatıralar*, Istanbul, 2 vols., 1940-1, 1965[2]; A. Tezbaşar, *Mehter tarihi teşkilâtı ve marşları*, Istanbul-Erenköy 1975; C. Türkay, *Osmanlı saray ve idare teşkilâtından örnekler padişahların kılıč kuşanmaları*, in *Belgelerle Türk Tarihi Dergisi*, xxiv (Istanbul 1969), 3-10; A. Vandal, *Une ambassade française en Orient sous Louis XV. La mission du Marquis de Villeneuve 1728-1741*, Paris 1887[2], 360-7.

(A.H. de Groot)

5. In Muslim India.

Ceremonial at the Muslim courts in India, while deriving much from Islam elsewhere, especially Iran, has also continued and adapted indigenous traditions. The pomp and ceremonial of Hindū courts is of considerable antiquity, and the grandeur of kings is a favourite theme of Hindū literature and Indian folklore; no Muslim ruler could have allowed the splendour of Hindū ceremonial to exceed his own! The psychological value of state ostentation is of course considerable, as tending to emphasise the power of the sovereign, his distance from his subjects, and the awe in which he is held. This ceremonial is most in evidence in the state audiences, and in the royal processions; for the latter, see MAWĀKIB.

Ceremonial in the earliest days of the Dihlī sultanate must be presumed, from the fact that the earliest records of the administration of the sultanate show such a close connection with that of the <u>Gh</u>aznawids whose power in the Pan<u>dj</u>āb it inherited, to have been modelled on that of the <u>Gh</u>aznawids, for whom see section 3 above; through them came ʿAbbāsid connections also, which were undoubtedly strengthened in the time of Iltutmi<u>sh</u> when Fa<u>kh</u>r al-Dīn ʿIṣāmī, who had served as a *wazīr* at Ba<u>gh</u>dād, was appointed the Dihlī *wazīr*. However, the prestige of the sultanate declined after the death of Iltutmi<u>sh</u>, when real power was in the hands of a confederacy of Turkish *amīrs* ("the Forty")—with the result that the sultan was prevented from being adequately distanced from his subjects—and was not restored until the reign of Balban who "introduced the Persian ceremonial" (Ḍiyāʾ al-Dīn Baranī, *Taʾrī<u>kh</u>-i Fīrūz-<u>Sh</u>āhī*, Bibl. Ind. text, 27-9, 30-2). Ibn Baṭṭūṭa (iii, 217-29, tr. Gibb, Cambridge 1971, 658-64), an eyewitness, describes that of the court of Muḥammad b. Tu<u>gh</u>luḳ; the entrance to his palace (the Hazār Sutūn at <u>Dj</u>ahānpanāh: see DIHLĪ. 2. Monuments) was approached by three gates, each guarded by men-at-arms and equipped with a band of musicians [see NAḲḲĀRA-<u>KH</u>ĀNA, and also NAWBA]. At the second gate was the *naḳīb al-nuḳabāʾ* (principal usher; for his functions see NAḲĪB), whose headdress was surmounted with peacock feathers (a borrowing from Hindū practice); he and his assistants scrutinised all who entered. At the third gate, beyond the antechamber, the names of all visitors were recorded, and none who had not the sultan's permission were permitted to proceed to the *darbār* within. Here the ceremonial was under the direction of the *amīr ḥā<u>dj</u>ib* (also called *bārbek* in the Dihlī sultanate). In Ibn Baṭṭūṭa's description this was the sultan's nephew Fīrūz b. Ra<u>dj</u>ab, who later succeeded to the throne as Fīrūz <u>Sh</u>āh; but it was common for the *amīr ḥā<u>dj</u>ib* to be of royal blood. His duty was, with the *nāʾib bārbek* and his assistant *ḥā<u>dj</u>ibs*, to marshall those attending the *darbār* according to their precedence and seniority, to present all petitions to the sultan, and to transmit the royal commands to subordinate officials and to any petitioners; one *ḥā<u>dj</u>ib* (*ḥā<u>dj</u>ib-i faṣl*, *ḥā<u>dj</u>ib-i faṣṣāl*) had the special duty of making an inventory of all gifts received by the sultan [see further, ḤĀ<u>DJ</u>IB]. The sultan sat in the daily *darbār* on a cushioned seat (golden bejewelled thrones were in use only at *darbārs* on feast days), the *wazīr* and his secretaries standing before him, followed by the various *ḥā<u>dj</u>ibs*, and about a hundred *naḳībs*. The noble appointed to carry the fly-whisk stood immediately behind the sultan, who was flanked to left and right by his special armed bodyguard, the *silāḥdārs*.

ranged in order down the *darbār*-hall were the *ḳāḍīs*. the *khaṭīb*, the principal jurists and other *ʿulamāʾ*, the *shaykh*s of the Ṣūfī brotherhoods in the capital, the sultan's relations by blood and marriage, and then the principal *amīrs* and other commanders. When all these were in place, some sixty caparisoned horses of the royal stable, and fifty adorned war-elephants, were brought in. If anyone waiting at the third gate had brought a gift for the sultan, this was reported to him by the *ḥādjib*s; if the sultan approved, the donor and his gift were brought in, and welcomed by the sultan who might recompense the donor by a *khilʿa* [*q.v.*] and a purse of money "for washing the head" (*sar-shustī*); Ibn Baṭṭūṭa describes a more elaborate ceremonial in the case of gifts and revenues presented by one of the provincial officers (*ibid.*, iii, 226-7, tr. Gibb, iii, 663). When an audience was held on a feast day, the palace was spread with carpets and the hall was enclosed beneath vast awnings; on the first day of a feast the sultan sat on a cushioned seat on the large golden throne, with heavily jewelled legs, and a jewelled parasol was held over him; on later days of feasts smaller golden thrones were in use. All attending the court would salute the sultan individually, in descending order of precedence; then revenue-holders would bring present, and all would be entertained to a great banquet, again being served in order of precedence, while a large golden brazier would fill the hall with the smoke of different kinds of incense and fragrant woods, and those present would be sprinkled with rose-water. The dishes were escorted from the kitchens by *naḳīb*s, and a eulogy of the sultan would be pronounced by the *naḳīb al-nuḳabāʾ* before those present were assigned to their places. Ibn Baṭṭūṭa describes some of the dishes presented; last comes *pān* (betel-leaves containing chopped areca-nut with lime and a bitter gum). (This is an indigenous custom, and the presentation of *pān* is still used at Indian meals as a gracious sign of dismissal.) Ibn Baṭṭūṭa further describes the special ceremonies at the reception at court of the son of the ʿAbbāsid caliph; since these involved a processional entry, they are described s.v. MAWĀKIB.

Ibn Baṭṭūṭa (iii, *passim*) refers often to the insignia of rulers and *amīrs*; for these see MARĀTIB. Shams-i Sirādj ʿAfīf, whose *Taʾrīkh-i Fīrūz Shāhī* is richer in administrative details than most chronicles, lists twenty-one royal prerogatives (*sikkahā-yi tādj-dārān*) maintained by Fīrūz Shāh, including the *khuṭba* [*q.v.*], the throne (*takht*), the royal seal cut in agate, use of a *tughra* [*q.v.*], the right to the fly-flap (*magas-rān*), the royal saddlecover [see GHĀSHIYA], a white quiver, encampments outside the gate, the black umbrella, the royal headdress (*kulāh-i malik*; a crown is not specified), and others. The right to strike coin [see SIKKA] is, curiously enough, not included here, and also *ṭirāz* [*q.v.*] finds no mention, although the practice is not unknown in India. For the umbrellas (*recte čhatra*, though commonly also *čatr* in Indian Persian texts) see MIẒALLA; for the special spear used in the royal escort see DŪRBĀSH. Another common royal prerogative is the scattering of small coin (and also small golden stars, arrowheads, etc.) among the populace at festivals, sometimes by catapult (*mandjānīḳ*); for this see NITHĀR. Possession of royal slaves (usually *bandagān* in Indian histories; but see GHULĀM, iii, and also ḤABSHĪ), and the overlordship of the state treasuries and workshops (*kārkhānas*) should also be mentioned.

There is little definite information on ceremonial in the later Dihlī sultanate and in the provincial dynasties, but there is no ground for supposing it to be different other than in detail (for example, the vast number of slaves, both male and female, in the later stages of the sultanate of Mālwā) from that already described. With the coming of the Mughals in the 10th/16th century, however, there are notable innovations, and also many more sources of information: autobiographies by Bābur, Gulbadan Bēgam and Djahāngīr, extensive dynastic histories (many produced under the stimulation of the millennium) and administrative accounts such as the *Āʾīn-i Akbarī* and part of the *Mirʾāt-i Aḥmadī*, accounts by European travellers, and the valuable contributions to social history of contemporary Mughal painting.

The *naḳḳāra-khāna* was extended both in the number and the variety of its instruments (*Āʾīn-i Akbarī, āʾīn* 19). The ruler in *darbār*, whether in the hall of general or special audience, was always seated on one of the thrones, which were of several kinds and of different shapes; some, in the Mughal forts, were permanent structures of marble, with or without a canopy. That in the *dīwān-i ʿāmm* of the Red Fort at Dihlī is a marble baldachino (*nishēman-i ẓill-i ilāhī*) under a marble "Bengali" roof, all inlaid with precious stones; Bernier describes a railed space round it, reserved for the *umarāʾ*, the Hindū *rādjās* at court, and foreign ambassadors; further space within the *dīwān* was reserved for other officials, and the general public awaiting audience were accommodated in the outer courtyard; he gives a full account of *darbār* ceremonial in *Travels*, 261-3. The elaborate golden thrones were in use in the halls of special audience (*dīwān-i khāṣṣ*), including the magnificent Peacock Throne (*takht-i ṭāwūs*) which was later looted by Nādir Shāh in 1152/1739 (description in *Bādshhāh-nāma*, i, 78-81; Bernier, *Travels,* 269 ff.; Tavernier, *Travels*, i, 384 ff.; for its fate, see G. N. Curzon, *Persia and the Persian question*, i, 321-2). Besides the appearance of the ruler in audience, there had been introduced under Akbar his appearance on a balcony on the wall of his palace so that he might be seen by the populace at large; for this adoption of a Hindū practice, see DARSHAN. The emperor here and in *darbār* was usually accompanied only by the *magas rān* and a single veiled sword; outside the palace he was invariably accompanied by the royal umbrella and the *ḳur*, a variety of arms wrapped in bags of scarlet cloth (other colours also appear in Mughal painting), the hilts of the swords often showing, together with *ʿalams* and the *čhatrtōḳ*, and *tumāntōḳ*, standards resembling the common *ʿalam* but with their shafts adorned with Tibetan yak-tails. The *magas rān* was commonly a switch of yak-tails (*čamarī, čawnrī*; see Hobson-Jobson, s.v. *Chowry*), although the folded towel is not unknown in Mughal painting; in contemporary Deccan painting, however, the folded towel is invariably depicted. *Darbār* paintings of Shāhdjahān often show the fly-whisk in the hands of a Hindū *rādjā* at court. Together with these trappings was carried a flat oval shield-like screen on a long pole, the *āftābgīr* (also called *sāyabān*), to shade the royal person from the rays of the sun. Other insignia also might be carried; see further MARĀTIB.

The dignities of the *čhatrtōḳ* and *tumāntōḳ*, the *māhī-marātib*, the right to an umbrella and to the use of elephants, might be conferred on royal princes and favoured nobles. The emperors took the title *bahādur* [*q.v.*] to themselves, only very rarely conferring it on distinguished generals; they used also the title *bādshāh*; it would seem that *mīrzā* might also be awarded as a title, as it is found appended to the names of those not of noble birth, and even to Hindūs [see MĪRZĀ]; royal princes were generally called *sulṭān*.

To the privilege of striking coin was added the

minting of pieces bearing the royal portrait, perhaps starting with the "symbols of faith"—the likeness of the emperor and the motto *Allahu Akbar*—presented by Akbar to his *murīds* in the Dīn-i Ilāhī (*Āʾīn-i Akbarī*, i, 160), and a *shast wa shabīh* were given by Djahāngīr to favoured members of his court circle—including Roe, the English ambassador (*Embassy of Sir Thomas Roe*, ed. Foster, Hakluyt Socy., i, 244-5). Austin de Bordeaux ("Hunarmand") was similarly honoured. Other portrait medals were presented to nobles (S. H. Hodivala, *Historical studies in Mughal numismatics*, xi: "Portrait muhrs" of Jahāngīr, 147-70, Calcutta 1923). Gigantic minted pieces of Mughal emperors are also known, some intended as presents, but more generally retained as treasury pieces. Small coin was also struck specially for the *nithār* [*q.v.*], together with gold and silver fruits and flowers following Čaghatay practice, and was continued at least as late as the reign of Farrukh-siyar. Royal seals [see MUHR] were cut in steel as well as in cornelian and agate, for use on *farmāns* and for accessioning additions to the royal libraries (*Āʾīn-i Akbarī*, *āʾīn* 20).

As well as royal attendance at the public mosques and at the *ʿīd* ceremonies (described s.v. MAWĀKIB), new ceremonies were introduced within the Mughal courts: Djahāngīr writes of his own regular weighing against gold, silver and other commodities, on the lunar and solar anniversaries of his accession, and the scenes are represented in Mughal painting. He also writes of the golden chain outside his palace, attached to a bell, which any suppliant for justice could ring (but *zandjīr pīsh-i dākhūl* already occurs in ʿAfīf's list of prerogatives of Fīrūz Shāh). The *nawrūz* and *āb-pāshān* ceremonies were also observed with great pomp in the palaces, again with painting confirmation available. Plate 7 of the Leningrad Album shows the scene of Djahāngīr's investiture (sometimes called "coronation": but there was no Mughal crown, merely a jewelled headband worn on the cap): foreign emissaries and Jesuit priests are distinguished by their attire (including perhaps Roe?), wrestlers and dancing-girls perform, ushers carry trays of money-bags, a courtier scatters coin, kettledrums are played from the back of an elephant which blocks a gateway, while *karnās* are blown from the palace walls. Plate 32 shows a *darbār* scene of Djahāngīr, painted by Abu 'l-Ḥasan: Djahāngīr wears a jewelled band round his turban, behind him are the *āftābgīr* and a small *čhatr* with the *ḳur* in a pink cloth; many of the courtiers are named, and indeed Rādjā Bīr Singh Dēv acts as his chowry-bearer (Leningrad Album publ. as *Al'bom indiiskikhi persidskikh miniatyur xvi-xviii vv.*, Moscow n.d.).

Bibliography: In addition to references in the text, see I. H. Qureshi, *Administration of the sultanate of Dehli*[4], Karachi 1958, esp. ch. 4; Shams-i Sirādj ʿAfīf, *Taʾrīkh-i Fīrūz Shāhī*, Bibl. Ind. text, Calcutta 1890, 107-8; Abu 'l-Faḍl ʿAllāmī, *Āʾīn-i Akbarī*, and ʿAbd al-Ḥamīd Lāhawrī, *Bādshāh-nāma*, cited from Bibl. Ind. texts; F. Bernier, *Travels in the Mogul empire*, ed. London 1901; *Tavernier's travels in India*, ed. V. Ball, London 1889. (J. BURTON-PAGE)

MARĀTHĀS, the name of the "caste-cluster of agriculturalists-turned-warriors" inhabiting the north-west Dakhan, Mahārāshtra "the great country", a term which is extended to all Marāthī-speakers. The Marāthā homeland stretched between 15° N. and 23° N., nearly equidimensional with the main mass of the Dakhan lavas north of the Malaprabha river and south of the Sātpūras. It lies within the rain-shadow of the Western Ghāts, a plateau compartmented by mesas and buttes between which valleys of black soil, watered by a 20" to 30" annual rainfall, yielded cereals, oilseeds and cotton. The significance of the Marāthās in Islamic Indian history is that they stopped the Mughal empire in its prime.

Marāthā fighters and revenue agents became indispensable to the sultanates of Aḥmadnagar [see NIẒĀM-SHĀHĪS] and Bīdjāpur [see ʿĀDIL-SHĀHĪS]. Hereditary local notables, *deśmukhs*, *deśpāndes* and *desājīs*, and village headmen, *pātīls*, dominated rural society with their armed followings and family connexions as *waṭandārs* with rights to land revenue. *Deśmukh* families, often ensconced in hill forts, became *ṣardārs*, cavalry captains, for Muslim rulers, receiving *muḳāsa* or (additional) revenue assignments. One such, Shāhdjī Bhōnslē (1002-74/1594-1664) father of Śivādjī (1036 or 1040/1627 or 1630 to 1680), the creator of Marāthā *rādj*, helped, along with other Marāthā *deśmukh* families, Malik ʿAnbar [*q.v.*] to preserve Aḥmadnagar against the Mughals in the 1620s. Following the final Mughal absorption of Aḥmadnagar in 1035/1636, Shāhdjī served Bīdjāpur in South India. In Shādjī's absence, Śivādjī from 1056/1646 onwards used the resources of his father's *djāgīr* of Pūna to extend his own control over the strongholds of neighbouring, often hostile, *deśmukh* families. By 1066/1656, Śivādjī was sufficiently important and free from Bīdjāpurī control for Awrangzīb, then governor of the Mughal Dakhan and attacking Bīdjāpur, to make overtures. In 1070/1659, Śivādjī's slaying of the Bīdjāpurī commander Afḍal Khān drew more Marāthās to himself. Hitherto, Śivādjī had been a Marāthā chief among many, taking advantage of the agriculturally-destructive wars between the Mughals and the Dakhan sultanates, and the dearths that accompanied them, to recruit larger Marāthā war bands for service under Muslim paymasters. Afḍal Khān, however, had desecrated the shrine of Tuldjapur and Pandharpur, the latter a major centre of Marāthā pilgrimage as "the focus of a specifically Maharashtrian *bhaktī* movement". By 1073-4/1663-4, during which time Śivādjī humiliated the Mughals by successfully raiding their chief commander's camp at Pūna (Shaʿbān 1073/April 1663) and the port of Sūrat (Djumādā II 1074/January 1664), Śivādjī had created a distinctively non-Muslim political authority in the Dakhan.

The massive Mughal campaign under Rādja Djay Singh in 1075/1665, together with the bait of a future joint Śivādjī-Djay Singh campaign against Bīdjāpur, led to the treaty of Purandar by which Śivādjī was to surrender 23 of his 35 forts. Śivādjī's attendance upon Awrangzīb at Āgra in 1076-7/1666 and his escape in a fruit basket illumine the obstacles to his becoming loyal to the Mughals at the price which they could pay. Rādjput refusal to accord Śivādjī *kśātriya* status, Mughal anger over the sack of Sūrat, and reluctance to reward defiance, limited Awrangzīb's freedom of action, while the decay of Bīdjāpur offered Śivādjī more opportunities than Mughal service could have done.

Śivādjī's coronation in 1085/1674 according to "Hindu" rites as *chatrapatī* symbolised the repudiation of an Indo-Muslim ethos, but not of the administrative structure of the Dakhan Muslim sultanates. He tried to curb the larger *deśmukhs* and assignees in his own territory (*svarādjya*) and his successful military and political activity furthered upward social movement among Marāthā and Kunbi *djātīs* and the tribal Kolis.

Prince Akbar's rebellion in 1091-2/1681 against

Awrangzīb, and his joining Śivādjī's successor Śambhadjī (1067-1100/1657-89) following on a Śivādjī-Golkondā alliance from 1084-5/1674 and the experience of only temporary accommodations with Śivādjī before the latter's death in 1091/1680, determined Awrangzīb to destroy Bīdjāpur and Golkondā and to force Marāṭhā submission. By 1100/1689, with the capture and brutal execution of Śambhadjī, following the seizure of Bīdjāpur (1097/1686) and Golkondā (1098/1687), Awrangzīb appeared triumphant. But Rādjarām, Śivādjī's younger son, migrated to Marāṭhā outposts at Tandjūr and Djindjī in South India, and the Mughals were faced with a mounted guerrilla campaign in the western and southern regions of the peninsula. Although Djindjī was taken in 1109/1698, several hill forts in Śivādjī's former *svarādjya* occupied, and many Marāṭhā chiefs apparently won over by the award of Mughal *manṣabs*, "the Mughal peace" was, south of the Narmadā, only established (temporarily) in Golkondā. The Mughals indeed succeeded in shattering authority and in splintering allegiances; they did not weaken Marāṭhā self-consciousness. At Awrangzīb's death in 1118/1707, there was no chief Marāṭhā with whom to conclude an agreement by which all Marāṭhās would abide, but only Marāṭhā chiefs to be cajoled into a personal and temporary submission. Śambhadjī's son Shāhū (1093-1163/1682-1749) was being raised in Awrangzīb's camp. In 1111/1700 Rādjarām's widow Tarabai installed her young son Śivādjī II as *chatrapatī* in one of the Marāṭhā camps.

After Awrangzīb's death, Mughal-Marāṭhā relations became a function of inter-Marāṭhā and inter-Mughal rivalries. Shāhū was allowed to escape: he was installed as *chatrapatī* at Satara in 1119/1708. In 1121/1709, the Mughal *pādshāh* Bahādur Shāh granted both Shāhū and Śivādjī II rights to *sardeśmukhī* (a notional 10% of the land revenue assessment as *deśmukh*) from the Mughal Dakhan. In 1130/1718, Ḥusayn ʿAlī, governor of the Mughal Dakhan, promised Shāhū *čawth* (a notional 25% of the land revenue assessment), *sardeśmukhī* and recognition of his *svarādjya* in return for 15,000 Marāṭhā horse for use against the Mughal *pādshāh* Farrukh-siyar, private concessions which were formally confirmed by the puppet *pādshāh* Rafīʿ al-Daradjāt in 1131/1719. Earlier, Ḥusayn ʿAlī's rival, Čīn Ḳilič Khān, had intrigued with Tarabai's faction while resisting raids upon the Mughal Dakhan by Marāṭhās obedient to Shāhū. In 1137/1724, Shāhū's *pēshwā*, Bādjī Rāo, assisted Čīn Ḳilič Khān to retain by force (against the Mughal *pādshāh* Muḥammad Shāh [1131-61/1719-48]) the governorship of the Dakhan. However, fear of encirclement by Bādjī Rāo's Marāṭhās raiding northwards into Gudjarāt and Mālwā and southward into the Karnātak induced Čīn Ḳilič Khān to treat with Shāhū's rivals (how headed by Rādjarām's second son Śambhadjī II [1109-74/1698-1760] at Kolhāpur). Defeat by Bādjī Rāo in 1140/1728 at Palkhed, and the treaty of Mungi Śivgaon, tilted the balance in the Dakhan permanently towards the Satara Marāṭhās.

In 1125/1713, Shāhū, struggling to assert authority over leaders of raiding bands unused to control, and faced with a rival *chatrapatī* at Kolhāpur, had appointed Bālādjī Rāo Visvanāth (d. 1132/172) as *pēshwā* or chief minister. A systematic policy of raiding Mughal territories and of dealing with local Mughal officers enabled the *pēshwā* to bind chiefs to him and to acquire resources for a Marāṭhā central direction. Under Bālādjī Rāo's son Bādjī Rāo (1132-53/1720-40), the Satara Marāṭhās secured Mughal recognition of their claim to *čawth* and *sardeśmukhī* (supplemented by *rāhdārī* or transit dues) from Gudjarāt (by 1143-4/1731), and from Mālwā (by 1154/1741)—this following a decisive victory over the Mughals at Bhopal in 1150/1737. Between 1154/1741 and 1164/1751, the forces of Raghudjī Bhōnslē plundered Bihār, Bengal and Orissa, forcing the granting of *čawth* from Bengal and the loss of Orissa. In the 1740s, the Marāṭhās were ready to intervene in the Gangetic region, over which Mughal authority had been fatally weakened by Nādir Shāh's [*q.v.*] sack of Dihlī in 1151/1739.

Although in wars against the *niẓām* of Ḥaydarābād in 1164-5/1751-2, 1171/1757 and 1173/1760, the Marāṭhās acquired the cities of Aḥmadnagar, Bīdjāpur, Dawlatābād and Burhānpur, their gains further south proved insecure. After 1145-6/1732, the Marāṭhā possessions centred upon Tandjūr often became tributary to the *nawwābs* of Ārkāt (Arcot), and in 1156/1743 the then *niẓām* of Ḥaydarābād (Čīn Ḳilič Khān) captured Tiruchirapallī (Trichinopoly). In 1174/1760-1, Ḥaydar ʿAlī [*q.v.*] seized power in Mahisūr (Mysore) [*q.v.*] and closed off the south to Marāṭhā exploitation. Even in the Marāṭhā homeland, the treaty of Varana (Warna) in 1143/1731 between Shāhū and Śambhadjī II of Kolhāpur, giving Shāhū control of the latter's diplomatic relations but recognising his *svarādjya*, indicated the segmentary character of Marāṭhā polity.

Under the *pēshwā* Bālādjī Rāo II (1153-74/1740-61) the Marāṭhās led by Malhar Rāo Holkar, Djayappa Śīndhīyā and Raghunnāth Bādjī Rāo, supported now Ṣafdar Djang of Awadh [*q.v.*], now Ghāzī al-Dīn ʿImād al-Mulk (grandson of Čīn Ḳilič Khān), and now the puppet *pādshāhs* Aḥmad Shāh (1161-7/1748-54) and ʿĀlamgīr II (1167-73/1754-9) in return for promises of *čawth* from the Pandjāb or from the Gangā-Djamnā *dō-āb*, and of Mughal offices and subventions. In 1171/1758 Raghannāth Rāo moved to Lāhawr against the invading Afghān ruler Aḥmad Shāh Durrānī [*q.v.*]. In Djumādā I-II 1173/January 1760 Aḥmad Shāh's forces expelled the Marāṭhās from Dihlī, provoking a grand military riposte under Sadaśiv Rāo, the *pēshwā's* uncle. In Djumādā II 1174/January 1761 the Afghāns savagely defeated the Marāṭhās at Pānīpat, decimating their military leadership.

The death of many of the *pēshwā*'s principal aides and a succession of feeble *pēshwās* after the early death of Madhav Rāo in 1186/1772, dispersed authority among the Marāṭhās to the regional military chiefs, the Gāikwārs of Barōda, the Holkars of Indore, the Śīndhīyās of Gwāliyar and the Bhōnslēs of Nagpur. The military power of the Marāṭhās as an uneasy confederacy was sufficient for Mahādadjī Rāo Śīndhīyā (1139-40 to 1208/1727-94) to instal in 1185/1772 the Mughal *pādshāh* Shāh ʿĀlam in Dihlī as a dependent: it was sufficient for the Marāṭhās to defeat the East India Company's army at Talegaon in 1192/1779 and to repulse it from Pūna in 1195/1781, during the indecisive Anglo-Marāṭhā wars of 1192-96/1778-82; it was sufficient for Tukodjī Rāo Holkar and Dawlat Rāo Śīndhīyā in 1209/1795 to defeat the *niẓām* of Ḥaydarābād's forces at Kharda.

But Dawlat Rāo Śīndhīyā and Djaswant Rāo Holkar fell to struggling for control of the *pēshwā* Bādjī Rāo II (1211-33/1796-1818) and, in desperation, the latter turned to the East India Company. Wellesley's subsidiary treaty of Bassein (1217/1802) took away the *pēshwā*'s independence. Raghudjī Bhōnslē and Dawlat Rāo Śīndhīyā resorted to arms and in 1218/1803 the latter lost Dihlī, the *dō-āb* and territories in Gudjarāt and the Dakhan. Djaswant Rāo Holkar belatedly intervened in 1219/1804, inflicting a major defeat on the Company's troops near Kotah, a further inducement for Wellesley's recall to England. A revised settlement with Śindhīyā restored to him territories south of the Čambāl; Holkar was left free in central India. But in 1233/1817, British pressure on the Pindarī freebooters was recognised as pressure on the Marāthā leaders, so the *pēshwā*, the Bhōnslēs and Holkar made one last effort by war to retain their independence, but were defeated piecemeal. The peace settlements of 1233/1817-18 incorporated the Marāthā home territories into the Bombay Presidency and reduced the *pēshwā* and the principal Marāthā chiefs to pensionaries or to mediatised princes under British paramountcy.

The Marāthās had hollowed out the Mughal empire, diverting its resources to themselves and distressing its peoples. But by accepting Mughal privileges, grants of revenue and titles, conferred in due form, they had preserved Mughal "sovereignty". Shāhū accepted the title of *rādjā* and Mughal *farāmīn* granting *čawth* and *sardeśmukhī*; in 1154/1741 the *pēshwā* accepted the *nā'ib-ṣūbadārī* of Mālwā; in 1198/1784 Mahādadjī Rāo Śindhīyā received the title of *wakīl-i muṭlaḳ* from Shāh ʿĀlam. Mughal political and military defeats were accompanied by Mughal ideological successes. The Marāthās behaved like *arrivistes* with no faith in themselves. This was not inevitable. By 1091/1680, Śivādjī had created an independent polity with (against the backcloth of Awrangzīb's Islamising aspirations as expressed in the formal imposition of *djizya* and some temple destruction) an alternative religio-political symbolism (to be represented in Marāthā historiography). Śivādjī moved to protect cultivators in his *svarādjya* against his own kind—the overmighty *deśmukh* and *muḳāsa* holder. But by 1118-19/1707, Awrangzīb had occupied sufficient of Śivādjī's *svarādjya* to force Marāthā warrior bands to live off the Mughal countryside by plunder, unable to dominate and rule it from the urban centres that formed the nuclei of Mughal power. Wide-ranging Marāthā raids estranged the rural notables, the *zamīndārs*, from the Mughals, without attaching them to the Marāthās.

Among the Marātha chiefs, respect for Śivādji's family, the success of the *pēshwās* against the *niẓām* of Ḥaydarābād and the Mughals north of the Narmadā, and the pride of confounding the Mughals, provided sufficient cohesion before Shāhū's death in 1163/1749. Thereafter, the centrifugal possibilities opened up both by the practice of the chiefs operating in Mughal territory receiving the larger proportion of *čawth* and *sardeśmukhī* collections, and also by their being granted hereditary assignments and tax farms in the Marāthā homelands, proved to be beyond thwarting by a succession of sickly and feeble minors installed as *pēshwās*. How in fact the emergence of regional and local Marāthā chiefdoms affected the welfare of those living under them remains to be fully investigated.

Bibliography: Records in Marāthī, Persian and English—N.N. Gidwani and K. Navalani, *A guide to reference materials on India*, Jaypur 1974, ii, 1066-72; J.C. Grant Duff, *A history of the Mahrattas*, 2 vols., Oxford 1921; G.S. Sardesai, *New history of the Marathas*, 2 vols., Bombay 1946-8; Jadunath Sarkar, *Fall of the Mughal empire*, 4 vols., Calcutta 1932-50; idem, *Shivaji and his times*, Calcutta 1920; V.G. Dighe, *Bajirao and Maratha expansion*, Bombay 1944; Satish Chandra, *Parties and politics at the Mughal court 1707-1740*, Aligarh 1959; A.R. Kulkarni, *Maharashtra in the age of Shivaji*, Poona 1969; S.N. Sen, *Military system of the Marathas*, Calcutta 1928; idem, *Administrative system of the Marathas*, 2nd ed., Calcutta 1925; Percival Spear, *The Oxford history of modern India 1740-1947*, Oxford 1965, 43-129 *passim*; Hiroshi Fukazawa, *A study of the local administration of Ādilshāhī sultanate (A.D. 1489-1686)*, in *Hitotsubashi Journal of Economics (June 1963)*, 37-67; Satish Chandra, *The Maratha polity and its agrarian consequences*, in *Ideas in history*, ed Bisheshwar Prasad, London 1968, 173-89; idem, *Social background to the rise of the Maratha movement during the 17th century in India*, in *The Indian Economic and Social History Review* (Sept. 1973), 209-17; idem, *Shivaji and the Maratha landed elements*, in *Indian Society: historical probings*, ed. R.S. Sharma, New Delhi 1974, 248-63; S.N. Gordon, *The slow conquest: administrative integration of Malwa into the Maratha empire, 1720-1760*, in *Modern Asian Studies* (1977), 1-40; M. A. Nayeem, *The working of the* chauth *and* sardeshmukhi *system in the Mughal provinces of the Deccan (1707-1803 A.D.)*, in *The Indian Economic and Social History Review* (April-June 1977), 153-91; *The Cambridge economic history of India. i. c.1200-c.1750*, ed. Tapan Raychaudhuri and Irfan Habib, Cambridge 1982, 193-203, 249-60, 471-7; A. Wink, *Land and sovereignty in India: agrarian society and politics under the eighteenth-century Maratha Svarajya*, Cambridge 1986. (P. Hardy)

MARĀTHĪ, the main Indo-Aryan language [see hind. iii. Languages] spoken by some 40 million in Bombay and the surrounding state of Mahārāshtrā. It differs from the "central" Hindī-Urdū language especially by its retention of the three genders of Old Indo-Aryan, by retroflex *-n-* and *-l-* consonants, by the presence of a past tense with *-l-* infix, and by a vocabulary more dependent on Sanskrit than on Arabic and Persian. As the chief language of Barār and the north-west Deccan, it was the regular demotic language for the populations of the old Niẓām Shāhī, ʿImād Shāhī and part of the ʿĀdil Shāhī sultanates, and later for much of the Niẓām's dominions in the old Ḥaydarābād [*q.v.*] state, as bilingual (Marāthī-Persian) and trilingual (Marāthī-Kannada-Persian) inscriptions, as well as monoglot ones, testify. These are particularly directed to conveying official orders (*ḳawl-nāmas*, *farmāns*, etc.) in the country districts, Marāthī has however been little cultivated as a literary language by Muslims, except for a few productions of "Sant" poets, i.e. local Ṣūfīs aiming at reaching the local population, often by reinterpreting well-known Hindū religious or philosophical works.

Bibliography: J. Bloch, *La formation de la langue marathe*, Paris 1920; for the linguistic relations of Marāthī, see *Bibl.* to hind. iii. Languages. For the Muslim contribution to Marāthī literature, see S. Dhere, *Musulmān Marāthī santa-kavi*, Poona 1967 (in Marāthī). Useful comment on the bilingual inscriptions is in Z.A. Desai, *Arabic and Persian epigraphy*, in H.K. Sherwani (ed.), *History of Medieval Deccan*, ii, 378, Hyderabad 1975; see also M.K. Dhavalikar, *Marathi epigraphy*, in *ibid.*, ii, 398-9, 401-2. (J. Burton-Page)

MARĀTIB (a.), literally "ranks, degrees" (sing. *martaba*), a term applied especially in Muslim India to the "honours" or "dignities", *aṭbāl wa- ʿalamāt*, drums and standards, borne by the sultan or conferred by him on the great *amīrs* (Ibn Baṭṭūṭa, iii, 106; tr. Gibb (1971), iii, 599), later elaborated (ibid., iii, 110; tr. iii, 601) as "standards, kettledrums, trumpets, bugles and reedpipes" as carried by two ships among the fifteen of the governor of Lāharī Bandar. The practice of Fīrūz Shāh's troops marching with 90,000 cavalry under 180 *marātib* and *nishāna-yi har djins* (ʿAfīf, *Taʾrīkh-i Fīrūz Shāhī*, Bibl. Ind. text 144), i.e. two such insignia per thousand troops, indicates that the *marātib* could function as battle ensigns. (One per thousand troops were employed in Čingiz Khān's army, cf. Djuzdjānī, *Ṭabaḳāt-i Nāṣirī*, Bibl. Ind. text, 338; tr. Raverty 968.) A phrase in ʿAfīf, *op. cit.*, 374, *ʿalamhā wa nishānhā-yi marātib hamīsha ṣūrat taṣwīr mīkardand* seems to indicate that "standards and banners among the *marātib*" were painted with pictures, although Fīrūz Shāh ordered their removal. The practice of using the *marātib* as battle ensigns continued in Mughal times, as is demonstrated profusely in Mughal painting; but there is no lack of painted (or embroidered) pictures here, including conspicuously the Persian Lion-and-Sun device (Sol in Leo?); see SHĪR WA KHURSHĪD. This device is known elsewhere in Indian Muslim art, e.g. among the Bahmanī buildings at Bīdar [*q.v.*], with no evidence however, to connect it with the *marātib*.

A special dignity, especially but not exclusively of Mughal times, is the *māhī-marātib*, "fish banner", the institution of which has been attributed to Khusraw Parvīz, Sāsānid emperor of Persia 591-628, from whom it passed to the house of Tīmūr, especially to the Mughal emperors, as a symbol of sovereignty or of authority emanating from the sovereign (W. H. Sleeman, *Rambles and recollections of an Indian official*, ed. V.A. Smith, London 1915; the editor states that he "has been unable to discover the source of the author's story"). Originally there was a golden fish carried upon a long staff, flanked by two metal balls (*kawkaba*) similarly carried (possibly commemorating the inception of a royal reign when the moon was in Pisces); later the two emblems were separated and the fish used independently: the fish alone passed through Mīrzā Muḳīm Abu 'l-Manṣūr Khān, Ṣafdār Djang, governor of Awadh under Muḥammad Shāh, to the sultans of Awadh, becoming the badge of the royal house and used freely on their buildings in Laknaʾū. "Possessors of [*djāgīrs*], collectors of districts, etc., have permission to use the fish in the decorations on their flags ... In Oude the fish is represented in many useful articles—pleasure boats, carriages, etc. Some of the king's chobdaars [*čūbdār*, "mace-bearer"] carry a staff representing a gold or silver fish." (Mrs Meer Hassan Ali, *Observations on the Mussulmauns of India...*, 1832; ed. W. Crooke, Oxford 1917, 43; her account is based on 12 years' residence in Laknaʾū). The *māhī-marātib* was among the favours conferred by Shāh ʿĀlam II on Lord Lake in 1803 after the latter had delivered Dihlī from the Marāthās.

The *marātib* are also mentioned by Djaʿfar Sharīf (*Ḳānūn-i Islām*, ed. W. Crooke as *Herklots' Islam in India*, Oxford 1921), 159 ff., among the standards carried in procession at the Muḥarram [*q.v.*] ceremonies, later to be laid up at the Imāmbāŕā; his list, however, does not specifically distinguish *marātib* from other emblems. He says the *marātib* "is [sic] also a standard fixed on a bamboo, decorated with a rich cloth. These are carried on elephants, like colours". Certainly banners may bear such signs as the Prophet's sword Dhu 'l-Faḳār [*q.v.*], the lion, the hand of ʿAlī, the shield or *dál ṣāḥib*, the shoe of Ḥusayn's horse at the battle of Karbalā (*naʿl ṣāḥib*); many of these are also represented as metal objects, and are then called simply *ʿalam* [*q.v.*]. Djaʿfar also remarks that "in all Shīʿa houses the fish standard is conspicuous"; this practice persists today in Ḥaydarābād. For the possible connexion of the common device in Bīdjāpur building of the rosette-on-bracket with the fish symbol, see J. Burton-Page, review of E. S. Merklinger, *Indian Islamic architecture: the Deccan. 1347-1686*, in *Marg*, xxxvii/3 (Bombay 1986), 89.

Other "dignities" and emblems of sovereignty or nobility such as the *čhatr* [see MIẒALLA] and *dūrbāsh* [*q.v.*], the *aftābgīr* and the veiled swords of state do not seem to be included in the term *marātib*, although treated similarly in practice, as Mughal art shows; for these see MARĀSIM. 5. India. For the use of flags and banners in the central Islamic lands, see ʿALAM.

Bibliography: Given in the article.

(J. BURTON-PAGE)

MARBAṬ, MARBIṬ (A., pl. *marābiṭ*), the noun of place from the root *r-b-ṭ* in the sense of "to fasten, attach, tie", which denotes first of all the place where domestic animals (members of the camel, equine, canine, and more rarely, of the goat and sheep families) are tethered. Among the nomads, the *marbaṭ* simply involves tying the animal's halter to some bush or, failing that, tying the two ends of a rope (*ribāṭ*, pl. *rubuṭ*, *mirbaṭ* or *ākhiyya*) to a large stone which is buried in the sand and letting the loop emerge as a ring for tethering, in the shade of a tent; the beast thus tethered is called *rabīṭ* (for *marbūṭ*). With the same association of ideas, in Saʿūdī Arabia and the United Arab Emirates, *marbaṭ* and *mirsal* are also the names of the "leash" which holds the falcon down to its perching-block (*wakar*) or on the falconer's gauntlet (*mangala*).

In regard to the Ḳurʾānic expression (VIII, 62/60) "... *min ribāṭ al-khayl* ... (horses held in readiness)", the philogist al-Bayḍāwī [*q.v.*] in his commentary (*Anwār al-tanzīl*, ed. H. L. Fleischer, Leipzig, 1896, i, 372) is hesitant about the exact nature of this term *ribāṭ*, proposing to interpret it either as a singular, or as a *maṣdar*, or as a plural of *rabīṭ*; this last seems most logical, even though the lexicographers do not give a plural for this singular.

For sedentary and urban populations, the *marbaṭ* takes the form of a kind of shelter, made from palm leaves or from straw thatching, beneath which animals can shelter from the sun.

By extension, *marbaṭ* very soon imposed itself, in the towns of the East, on *iṣṭabl* [*q.v.*] and, in the Maghrib, on *riwā/rwa* in the general sense of stables, i.e. the building intended for the guard and the housing of horses in the palaces; for garrisons, for postal relays [see BARĪD] and for the open spaces used for equestrian exercises and racing [see MAYDĀN].

Already in the 5th/11th century, the hagiographer al-Thaʿlabī [*q.v.*] in his "History of the Prophets" (*K. ʿArāʾis al-madjālis fī ḳiṣaṣ al-anbiyāʾ*), describing the fabulous flying city of King Solomon, mentions the following nomenclature: ... *wa-fī asfali-hā marābiṭ wa-iṣṭablāt wa-awārī wa-awākhī li-khayli-hi wa-dawābbi-hi* "and in the lower part [of this city] were shelters, stables, tethering-posts and rings for attaching there his horses and beasts of burden". There is hardly anything one could add to these four terms for defining means of restraining domestic beasts.

Bibliography: In addition to references given in the article, see those in FARAS and KHAYL.

(F. VIRÉ)

MARCHES [see THUGHŪR].

MARDAITES [see DJARĀDJIMA].

MARDAM, name of an affluent and distinguished Syrian family, two of whose members, the cousins Djamīl and Khalīl, achieved renown in the first half of the 20th century, the former in the realm of politics, the latter in that of literature.

1. Djamīl, born in Damascus in 1894, received his primary and secondary education in various schools in his native city, in particular that of the Lazarist Fathers, and pursued higher studies in law and political sciences in Paris and Switzerland. For this reason, he was residing in Paris when the First World War broke out. His political activities began in 1913 with his involvement in the Arab Congress which was convened in Paris to defend the interests of the Arabs and of which he was elected Secretary-General. In 1919, after making a tour of South America, he returned to Damascus where he was appointed adviser to the *amīr* Fayṣal. In 1920, he became adviser to the Ministry of the Interior in the Cabinet of Hāshim al-Atāsī.

Having participated in the Syrian Revolution (1925-6), he escaped to Jaffa in Palestine, but was arrested and handed over to the French Mandatory authorities. He spent two months imprisoned at Arwād/Ruwād, a small island situated close to the Syrian coastal city of Ṭarṭūs. In 1928, he was sent to Paris to negotiate on behalf of the Constituent Assembly which had recently been instituted in Syria. Elected deputy for the city of Damascus to the Syrian Parliament in 1932, Djamīl Mardam was subsequently appointed Minister of Finance. In April 1933 he resigned and became involved again in the politics of resistance.

From January to March 1936, he was placed under house-arrest by the French authorities at Ḳirḳ-Khān, a little town belonging to the *sandjaḳ* of Alexandretta. On his return to Damascus, he was received with enthusiasm. Subsequently he was a member of the Syrian delegation which travelled to Paris to discuss the term of the Franco-Syrian Treaty.

In December 1936 he formed the first Nationalist cabinet and served as Prime Minister until February 1938. During this period, he travelled to Paris and to Geneva to defend the Syrian position in the question of the *sandjaḳ* of Alexandretta and to continue discussions relating to the Franco-Syrian Treaty. In the early part of the Second World War, he lived in ʿIrāḳ and in Saudi Arabia, not returning to Damascus until 1941. In 1943, he was again elected deputy for his native city and became successively Minister of Foreign Affairs (1943-4) and Minister of National Defence and of the National Economy (1944-5).

After the proclamation of Syrian independence in 1945, Djamīl assumed the functions of Minister Plenipotentiary to the Kingdom of Egypt and to the Kingdom of Saudi Arabia. In November 1946, he returned to Damascus and formed a Syrian Cabinet for the second time (from January 1946 to October 1947). In July 1947, he was re-elected deputy for Damascus and was charged for the third time with the task of forming a Syrian Cabinet which lasted from October 1947 to summer 1948. Having resigned, he was recalled to form yet another Cabinet, and he remained at its head until the *coup d'état* of Colonel Ḥusnī al-Zaʿīm (30 March 1949). Djamīl Mardam then left Syria and made his way to Egypt, where he stayed until the end of his life. He died in Cairo in 1961, and his remains were conveyed to Damascus and interred in the cemetery of Bāb al-Ṣaghīr.

A veteran activist of the Nationalist Bloc (*al-kutla al-waṭaniyya*), a political party linking the eminent Syrian personalities who led Syria to independence, Djamīl Mardam was a skilful and far-sighted statesman. Fervent in his speeches, which were sometimes improvised, he was not lacking in eloquence.

Bibliography: Ziriklī, *Aʿlām*[4], ii, 138; Georges Faris, *Man hum fi 'l-ʿālam al-ʿarabī*, i (Syria), Damascus 1957; Archives of the Syrian Ministry of Foreign Affairs and of the Syrian Parliament.

2. Khalīl, born in Damascus in 1895, received his primary and secondary education in the schools of his native city, then studied *fiḳh*, *ḥadīth* and the Arabic language as a pupil of the great masters of his time, including the *shaykh* ʿAṭāʾ al-Ḳasm, *muftī* of Damascus, the great scholar of tradition *shaykh* Badr al-Dīn al-Ḥasanī and the *shaykh* Saʿīd al-Bānī.

After the establishment of the Arab government in Damascus (1918-9), he was appointed, at a very early age, editor-in-chief of the Bureau of Communication (*dīwān al-rasāʾil*), and then a teacher at the school for journalists which had recently been founded by the authorities, but he left his post when French troops entered Damascus (1920).

In 1921 he founded, with a group of eminent contemporary scholars, a "literary league" (*al-Rābiṭa al-adabiyya*), of which he was elected president. This association published a review bearing the same name, to which he contributed his first poems as well as his first articles. This review was also the forum for numerous well-known writers of the period. But the league was disbanded and its organ ceased to appear after its ninth issue.

In 1925 Khalīl Mardam was elected a member of the Arab Academy of Damascus after presenting a monograph on "The Syrian poets of the 3rd century of the Hidjra". The following year he travelled to Alexandria where he stayed four months, associating with certain eminent Egyptian literary figures, in particular, the poet Ḥāfiẓ Ibrāhīm. Then, deciding to pursue his studies in the West, he made his way to England where, for four years, he studied literature at the University of London. This journey to the West and his knowledge of English literature exerted a profound influence on his poetry.

In 1929, returning to Damascus, he composed a fine poem entitled "Hail Damascus!", which was received enthusiastically by scholars who recognised in him a great poet. He was subsequently professor of Arabic Literature in a college renowned in Syria at that time, *al-Kulliyya al-ʿilmiyya al-waṭaniyya*, for a period of nine years (1929-38). Many of his pupils subsequently became respected literary figures.

In 1933, he published a review entitled *al-Thaḳāfa* with the aid of some well-known teachers and men of letters, including Djamīl Ṣalībā, Kāmil Dāghistānī and Kāmil ʿAyyād. Serious literary articles, short stories and poems were published in this review, which unfortunately was short-lived.

In 1941 he became Secretary-General of the Arab Academy of Damascus and in 1953 he was appointed President of the Academy, a post which he held until the end of his life. He was also elected a corresponding member of numerous Arab and European Academies, notably those of Cairo (1948) and of Baghdād (1949), the Mediterranean Academy of Palermo (1952) and the Moscow Academy of Sciences (1958).

Besides his literary activity, Khalīl Mardam participated in the political life of his country, serving as Minister of Public Education in 1942, ambassador of the Syrian Republic to Baghdād in 1951 and Minister of Foreign Affairs in 1953. Then he abandoned political life and devoted his energies to literature and to the Arab Academy. He died in Damascus on 21 July 1959, and was buried in the plot reserved for his family in the cemetery of Bāb al-Ṣaghīr.

His principal works are: a *dīwān* (edited after his death by the Arab Academy of Damascus in 1960 in collaboration with his son, the poet ʿAdnān Mardam);

and studies of al-Djāḥiẓ, Ibn al-Muḳaffaᶜ, Ibn al-ᶜAmīd, al-Ṣāḥib Ibn ᶜAbbād and al-Farazdaḳ (published, undated, in Damascus in the *Aʾimmat al-adab* collection). He also established and published in the series of the Arab Academy of Damascus the texts of the *dīwāns* of Ibn ᶜUnayn (1946), ᶜAlī b. al-Djahm (1949), Ibn Ḥayyūs (1951) and Ibn al-Khayyāṭ (1958). Some biographical works were published in Damascus and Beirut after his death; most worthy of mention are *Djamharat al-mughannīn* (the singers), *al-Aᶜrābiyyāt* (the Bedouin women), *ᶜAyān al-ḳarn al-thālith ᶜashar*, (the notables of the 13th century A.H.) and *Yawmiyyāt al-Khalīl* (his diary).

The poetry of Khalīl Mardam comprises the traditional genres and is distinguished by its lyrical tone. In his description of nature and in his love poems, the poet displays extreme sensibility and remarkable finesse. His patriotic poetry is sincere, and his cultivated style is always fluent and clear and reflects the lucidity of his mind.

Bibliography: Khalīl Mardam, *Dīwān*, ed. Damascus 1960; Ziriklī, *Aᶜlām*[4], ii, 315; Kaḥḥāla, *Muᶜdjam al-muʾallifīn*, Damascus 1961, xiii, 384; Georges Fāris, *Man hum fi ʾl-ᶜālam al-ᶜarabī*, i (Syria), Damascus 1957; S. al-Dahhān, in *MMIA*, xxxiv/4 (1949); a collection of speeches in memory of Khalil Mardam, published by the Ministery of Culture in Damascus, 1960. (J. Rikabi)

MARDANĪSH [see ibn mardanīsh].

MARDĀWĪDJ b. Ziyār b. Wardānshāh, Abu ʾl-Ḥadjdjādj, founder of the Ziyārid dynasty [*q.v.*] in the Caspian regions of Persia.

Mardāwīdj's rise as a soldier of fortune in northern Persia is bound up with the decline of direct caliphal control there, seen already in the independent role of the Sādjid governors [*q.v.*] in Ādharbāydjān towards the end of the 3rd/9th century and in the general upsurge of hitherto submerged indigenous Iranian elements, Daylamī, Djīlī and Kurdish, forming what has been called the "Daylamī interlude" of Persian history [see daylam, and also buwayhids, kākūyids, musāfirids, rawwādids, shaddādids, etc.].

On his father's side, Mardāwīdj (literally, "man-assailant", see Justi, *Iranisches Namenbuch*, 194) sprang from the royal clan of the Djīlīs, and on his mother's from the *ispahbadhs* of Rūyān. He served the Ḥasanid Shīᶜī rulers of Ṭabaristān and then the Djīlī condottiere Asfār b. Shīrūya or b. Shīrawayh [*q.v.*] until the latter's tyranny impelled Mardāwīdj, with the support of the ruler of Ṭārum, Muḥammad b. Musāfir, to rebel against Asfār, killing him in 319/931 and then rapidly capturing Hamadān, Dīnawar and Iṣfahān in western Persia from their caliphal governors. He now clashed with a rival Daylamī commander, Mākān b. Kākī [*q.v.*], who had held Ṭabaristān, Gurgān and western Khurāsān since 318/930. Mardāwīdj conquered Ṭabaristān and attacked Mākān, but since Mākān obtained the backing of the Sāmānid *amīr* Naṣr b. Aḥmad, Mardāwīdj agreed to a peace treaty, retaining only Ray as tributary to Naṣr. It was at this time that the three Būyid brothers ᶜAlī, Ḥasan and Aḥmad transferred to his service from that of Mākān, and Mardāwīdj appointed ᶜAlī (the future ᶜImād al-Dawla) governor of Karadj. Since Mardāwīdj was able to overrun most of Djibāl almost to Ḥulwān, the ᶜAbbāsid caliphs al-Muḳtadir and al-Ḳāhir were compelled to recognise him as governor there, on condition that Mardāwīdj evacuate Iṣfahān, now governed by his brother (and eventual successor) Wushmgīr.

By the end of 322/934, Mardāwīdj's forces had even occupied the province of Ahwāz. But the ambitions attributed to him in the (generally hostile) sources of planning to conquer Baghdād, overthrow the caliphate and proclaim himself ruler of a renewed Persian empire, were frustrated by his murder at Iṣfahān in Ṣafar 323/January 935, whilst celebrating the Zoroastrian festival or Sadhak, by his Turkish *ghulāms*, whom he had treated with contempt and harshness. Minorsky has described Mardāwīdj as "fantasque et barbare", and al-Masᶜūdī imputes to him delusions of grandeur and the assumption of a messianic role as the awaited "man with yellow-marked legs" who would rule the world. His brother Wushmgīr and his descendants kept the Ziyārids as a force in the Caspian region for a further century, but the main southwards impetus of the Daylamī *Völkerwanderung* was to be spearheaded by the Būyids.

Bibliography: 1. Sources: Masᶜūdī, ix, 15-30 = §§ 3578-3603; Miskawayh, in *Eclipse of the ᶜAbbasid caliphate*, i, 161-3, tr. iv, 181-4; Gardīzī, ed. Nāẓim, 30, ed. Habībī, 84-5, 153; ᶜArīb, 154; Hamadhānī, *Takmila*, ed. Kanᶜān, i, index; Ibn Isfandiyār, tr. Browne, 214-17; Ibn al-Athīr, Beirut 1385-7/1965-7, viii, 227-9, 246-7, 263, 267-72, 285-7, 298-303; Ẓahīr al-Dīn Marᶜashī, ed. Dorn, 171 ff. 2. Studies. Cl. Huart, *Les Ziyarides*, in *Mems. de l'Acad. des Inscrs. et Belles-Lettres*, xlii (1922), 357 ff.; H. L. Rabino, *Mázandarán and Astarábád*, London 1928, 141; idem, *L'histoire du Mâzandarân*, in *JA*, ccxxxiv (1943-5), 229 ff.; B. Spuler, *Iran*, 89-92; V. Minorsky, *La domination des Daïlamites*, in *Iranica, twenty articles*, Tehran 1964, 17-19; W. Madelung, in *Camb. hist. of Iran*, iv, 212-13. (C. E. Bosworth)

MĀRDĪN (written in Arabic as Māridīn, in Greek as Μάρδης, Μάργδις, in Syriac as Mardē and in modern Turkish as Mardin), a town in what was in mediaeval Islamic times Upper Mesopotamia or al-Djazīra, in the region of Diyār Rabīᶜa [*q.v.*] lying on a slope rising to an altitude of 3780 ft./1152 m. in lat. 37° 18' N. and long. 40° 44' E. The modern town, in southeastern Turkey near the Syrian border, is the chef-lieu of the *il* (formerly *vilayet*) of the same name.

Position. In Upper Mesopotamia, the watershed between the Tigris and Euphrates is formed by the heights which culminate in Ḳaradja-dagh (5,000 feet) to the south-west of Diyār Bakr. This basalt massif is continued eastwards in the direction of Djazīrat Ibn ᶜUmar by the limestone chain known in ancient times as Masius and later as Izala (Ἰζαλᾶς). The eastern part of this ridge forms the district of Djabal-Ṭūr or Ṭūr ᶜAbdīn [*q.v.*], the capital of which is Midyāt. From the southern slopes of the Masius descend numerous watercourses, the majority of which join one another before flowing between the mountains of ᶜAbd al-ᶜAzīz or Elaziğ (in the west) and Tell Kawkab and Sindjār (in the east); their combined waters form the river Khābūr [*q.v.*].

Mārdīn lies near the point where there is an easy pass through the Masius from the lands south of the Tigris (the rivers Gök-su and Shaykhān) to the lands round the sources of the Khābūr (the stream called Zuwārak which rises north of Mārdīn), in other words, Mārdīn commands the Diyār Bakr-Niṣībīn road (which then turns towards Djazīra Ibn ᶜUmar and Mawṣil). On the other side towards the west, several (Ritter, xi, 356, gives three) direct roads connect Mārdīn via Urfa with Bīredjik (on the Euphrates); to the south-west, a road runs from Mārdīn to Raʾs al-ᶜAyn and to Ḥarrān. The direct distances are as follows: Mārdīn-Diyār Bakr 55 miles: Mārdīn-Niṣībīn 30 miles; Mārdīn-Sawur-Midyāt 75 miles; Mārdīn-Bīredjik 160 miles; Mārdīn-Adana (by rail) 450 miles.

The advantages of this position at the intersection

of important roads are enhanced by the very strong natural situation of the town, built on an isolated eminence, on the top of which is a fort 300 feet above the town (cf. the sketch in Černik, *Technische Studien-Expedition*, in *Peterm. Mitt.*, Ergänzungsheft, x [1875-6], Heft, 45, pl. ii, no. 17). J.S. Buckingham compared its position with that of Quito in South America. All travellers (cf. Ibn Ḥawḳal, 152) have been struck by the unique spectacle of the vast Mesopotamian plain which from the height of the town is seen to stretch southwards as far as the eye can see. Only a hundred years ago, Mārdīn was still considered impregnable, but the difficulty of access sensibly affected its commerce. According to Černik, loaded camels could not ascend right up to the town. A branch line 15 miles in length now connects Mārdīn with the station of Derbesiye on the Adana-Nusaybin section of the Istanbul-Baghdād railway, but the station for Mārdīn is five miles from the town.

1. In pre-Ottoman times.

Ancient history. It is noteworthy that in spite of its remarkable situation, Mārdīn does not seem to be mentioned in the cuneiform sources. Ammianus Marcellinus (xix, 9,4) is the first to mention two fortresses "Maride and Lorne" between which the road passed from Āmid (Diyār Bakr) to Nisībīn. Theophanes Simocatta (ii, 2, 19) mentions τοῦ Μάρδιος φρουρά and (v. 3,17) το Μάρδες 3 parasangs from Dārā. Procopius, *De Aedificiis*, (ii, 4) mentions Σμάργδις (or Σμάρδις) and Δούρνης and Georgius Cybrius, ed. Gelzer, 1820, 46, Μάρδης Δόρνης. The name Μάρδη in Ptolemy, vi, l, however, refers to another place in Assyria to the east of the Tigris.

The Muslim conquest. The Muslims under ʿIyāḍ b. Ghanm occupied the fortress of Mārdīn along with Ṭūr ʿAbdīn and Dārā in 19/640 (al-Balādhurī, *Futūḥ*, 176). In 133/750-1 Mārdīn is mentioned in connection with a rebellion in Upper Mesopotamia. The town formed part of the possessions of Burayka, chief of the Rabīʿa, who was defeated by the ʿAbbāsid Abū Djaʿfar (Ṭabarī, iii, 53). In 279/892, Aḥmad b. ʿĪsā took Mārdīn from Muḥammad b. Isḥāḳ b. Kandādj (*ibid.*, iii, 2134). The Ḥamdānid Ḥamdān b. Ḥamdūn after his accession in 260/873 seized Mārdīn. In 281/894, the caliph Muʿtaḍid marched on the town. Ḥamdān fled and left Mārdīn to his son. The latter surrendered the fortress which was dismantled (*ibid.*, iii, 2142). The "grey fortress" (*al-bār al-ashhab*) was later restored, for Ibn Ḥawḳal (in 366/976-7) attributes its erection to Ḥamdān b. al-Ḥasan Nāṣir al-Dawla b. ʿAbd Allāh b. Ḥamdan. On the death of his father 358/969, Ḥamdān was dispossessed by his brother Faḍl Allāh Abū Taghlib [*q.v.* in Suppl.]. By the peace of 363/794, concluded between the Būyid Bakhtiyār and Abū Taghlib, Ḥamdān recovered his possessions with the exception of Mārdīn (Ibn Miskawayh, ed. Amedroz, ii, 254, 319.

The Arab geographers give few details about Mārdīn, but they emphasise its importance. According to Ibn al-Faḳīh, 132, 136, the *kharādj* of Mārdīn was equal to that of Mayyāfarīḳīn (865,000 *dirhams*). Al-Iṣṭakhrī, 76 n. *k*, says that it is a large town on the summit of a peak, the ascent of which is a *farsakh* in length; Dunaysar [*q.v.*] was one of its dependencies. Ibn Ḥawḳal, 143, gives the ascent at two *farsakhs*. The quarter of Mārdīn itself was flourishing, thickly populated with large markets. The water supply was brought by subterranean canals from the springs to the town. The rain-water was also collected in cisterns (*ṣahāridj wa-birak*). Yāḳūt, iv, 390 (cf. al-Ḳazwīnī, 172), speaks of the splendour of the quarters outside Mārdīn (i.e. below the town itself) and its many *madrasas*, *khānḳāhs*, etc.; as to the *ḳaʿla*, there was nowhere in the world so strong a defence; its dwelling-houses rose in terraces one above the other.

The Marwānids and the Saldjūḳs. It is probable that Mārdīn was within the sphere of influence of the Marwānids, for according to their historian (cf. Amedroz, in *JRAS* [1904], their ancestor Bādh (d. 380/990) had extended his power over Diyār Rabīʿa (Niṣībīn, Ṭūr ʿAbdīn). The Saldjūḳs ruled here next. After the death of Malikshāh [*q.v.*] Tutush b. Alp Arslan seized for a time all the lands as far as Niṣībīn. Under Berk-yaruḳ, Mārdīn was given to his old bard (*mughannī*).

The Artuḳids. At this time arose the dynasty whose fortunes are especially associated with Mārdīn. The Artuḳ grandson called Yāḳūtī took by stratagem the fortress in which he had been imprisoned, but it was taken from him by his brother Sukmān b. Artuḳ, who died in 498/1104-5. In 502/1108-9, we find at Mārdīn Īl-Ghāzī b. Artuḳ (Ibn al-Athīr, x, 269, 321), whose line ruled there till 811/1408. (On their coins struck at Mārdīn in 599, 600, 634, 637, 648, 655, 656, etc., cf. Ghālib Edhem, *Catalogue des monnaies turcomanes*, Constantinople 1894, and S. Lane Poole, *Catalogue of oriental coins in the British Museum*, iii, x, index, s.v. Mardin.)

In 579/1183 Ṣalāḥ al-Dīn came to Ḥarzam (6 miles to the south-west of Mārdīn) but was unable to take the town. In 594/1198, al-Malik al-ʿĀdil b. Ayyūb seized the outer suburb, which was pillaged, but the siege of the town itself was abandoned in the following year. In 599/1202-3, al-ʿĀdil sent against Mārdīn his son al-Ashraf, who appointed governors (*shaḥna*) in its dependencies. The Ayyūbid of Aleppo al-Ẓāhir b. Ṣalāḥ al-Dīn offered his good offices, and al-ʿĀdil was content with an indemnity of 150,000 *dinars* and the acknowledgement of his suzerainty by the Artuḳid of Mārdīn (cf. Abu 'l-Faradj Barhebraeus, *Mukhtaṣar*, ed. Pococke, 412, 425, 427).

The Mongols. In 657/1259, the Mongol Hūlāgū Khān demanded the homage of the prince of Mārdīn, Nadjm al-Dīn Ghāzī Saʿīd, who sent his son Muẓaffar to him but maintained a neutral attitude. In 658/1260 the town was besieged for 8 months by the troops of Yashmut, son of Hūlāgū. Famine and an epidemic raged in the town. According to Rashīd al-Dīn (ed. Quatremère, 375), Muẓaffar killed his father in order to put an end to the sufferings of the inhabitants (Abu 'l-Faradj and Waṣṣāf give different versions, cf. d'Ohsson, iii, 308, 358). Muẓaffar was confirmed as lord of Mārdīn; his descendants also received from the Mongols the insignia of royalty (crown and parasol). In the reign of Ṣāliḥ b. Manṣūr (769/1367), whose sister Dunyā Khātūn was the wife of the Īlkhān Muḥammad Khudābanda, Ibn Baṭṭūṭa (ii, 142-5) visisted Mārdīn; he mentions the fine garments made there from goats' hair wool (*mirʿizz*).

Tīmūr. The Artuḳid sultan ʿĪsā (778-809/1376-1406) was the king of Mārdīn at the invasion of Tīmūr in 796/1394. Malik ʿĪsā came to pay his homage to the conqueror, but the citizens attacked those of Tīmūr's men who ventured into the town. Malik ʿĪsā was put in chains and taken to Sulṭāniyya (*Ẓafar-namā*, i, 663, 671-2). In Shawwāl 803/April 1401, Tīmūr returned to the attack and the town was taken by storm. Then the siege of the upper fortress (*al-ḳalʿa al-shahbāʾ*) was begun, but it was never taken. Tīmūr was content with presents and promises of *kharādj*, and returned to the plain (*ibid.*, i, 676-9). The people of Mārdīn obtained an amnesty on the birth of Ulūgh Beg. Ṣāliḥ was appointed at Mārdīn in place of his brother, ᶜĪsā (*ibid.*, i, 676-81), but three years afterwards the latter was pardoned and restored to his fief (*ibid.*, i, 787). When in 803/1400-1 Tīmūr reappeared in Mesopotamia, ᶜĪsā shut himself up in Mārdīn. As the siege would have taken some time and supplies were short, Tīmūr did not stop before the town, but ordered Ḳara ᶜUthmān Aḳ-Ḳoyunlu to besiege Mārdīn (*ibid.*, ii, 354).

The Aḳ-Ḳoyunlu. This was the beginning of Aḳ-Ḳoyunlu interference in Mārdīn, but Ḳara ᶜUthmān's forces were not yet equal to this task. In 805/1402-3, ᶜĪsā came of his own accord to Tīmūr and was pardoned (*ibid.*, ii, 51).

For a brief period, the Ḳara-Ḳoyunlu tried to resist the extension of the power of the Aḳ-Ḳoyunlu to Mārdīn. When, after the death of Tīmūr, Ḳara Yūsuf left Egypt to re-enter into possession of his territory he joined ᶜĪsā and advanced against Ḳara ᶜUthmān. The battle lasted 20 days and was settled by agreement. As soon as Ḳara Yūsuf had left for Ādharbaydjān, Ḳara ᶜUthmān returned to the attack, defeated ᶜĪsā near Djawsaḳ (there is a Djawsat 10 miles to the west of Mārdīn on the road from Derek) and besieged Mārdīn, but once more without success (Münedjdjim-bashî, ii, 685). It is not clear what connection these hostilities have with an expedition against Diyār Bakr conducted by Djakīm or Djakūn (governor of Aleppo, a former *mamlūk* of Barḳūḳ's) in which Malik ᶜĪsā took part. In the battle which Muḥammad (?) son of Ḳara Ilik (= Ḳara ᶜUthmān) fought against the allies on 15 Dhu 'l-Ḳaᶜda 809/23 April 1407, ᶜĪsā was slain (cf. the Egyptian sources consulted by Rieu for Howorth, iii, 685). Ṣāliḥ succeeded a second time to ᶜĪsā, but the Aḳ-Ḳoyunlu continued to harass him and finally in 811/1408, he ceded Mārdīn to the Ḳara-Ḳoyunlu, who gave him Mawṣil in exchange.

We do not know the exact course of subsequent events, but according to Münedjdjim-bashî, Ḳara ᶜUthmān's successor ᶜAlī Beg (832-42/1429-39, cf. Aḥmed Tewḥīd, *Musée Imp. Ottoman, monn. musulmanes*, part iv, Constantinople 1903) gave his brother Ḥamza the task of establishing the Turkomans in the vicinity of Mārdīn. Djihāngīr (848-57/1444-53), son of ᶜAlī, was already master of the town. In the reign of Uzun Ḥasan, Josafa Barbaro visited Mārdīn and was lodged in the hostel (*ospedale*) built by Djihāngīr Beg (*Ziangir*). We have coins struck at Mārdīn by Uzun Ḥasan (875/1470-1) and his son Yaᶜḳūb. After the death of Yaᶜḳūb, ᶜAlāʾ al-Dawla, prince of the Dhu 'l-Ḳadr Turkomans [*q.v.*], seized the land of Diyār Bakr but, as the anonymous Venetian merchant shows, the Aḳ-Ḳoyunlu retained Mārdīn. In 903/1498, Abu 'l-Muẓaffar Ḳāsim b. Djihāngīr dated his *firmān* in the name of the prince of Egīl from his capital (*dār al-salṭāna*) Mārdīn; cf. Basagić, *Der älteste Firman der Čengić-begs*, in *Wissensch. Mitt. aus Bosnien*, vi, Vienna 1899, 497. The coins of Ḳāsim come down to 908/1502-3. The *takiya* of Ḳāsim-Padshāh which Niebuhr mentions must date from the same ruler.

The Persian conquest. In 913/1507, all the lands as far as Malaṭya were conquered by Shāh Ismāᶜīl [*q.v.*], who appointed his general Ustadjlu Muḥammad over them. According to the Venetian merchant who travelled there in 1507 (*Travels*, 149), Mārdīn was occupied without bloodshed. The same traveller mentions the fine palace and mosques of the town; there were more Armenians and Jews in Mārdīn than Muslims. The battle of Čāldirān [*q.v.*] in 920/1514 shook the power of the Persians. In place of Ustadjlu Muḥammad, killed at Čāldirān, his brother Ḳara Khan was appointed and established his headquarters at Mārdīn. Soon the Ottomans occupied Diyār Bakr, and then the town of Mārdīn, but the Persians, who never lost the fortress, restored the status quo.

Bibliography: Idrīsī, tr. Jaubert, ii, 142; Ibn Djubayr, ed. Wright-de Goeje, 240-1, tr. R. J. C. Broadhurst, London 1952, 250-1; Ibn Baṭṭūṭa, ii, 142-7, tr. Gibb, ii, 352-5; Abu 'l-Fidā, tr. Reinaud, Paris 1848, ii/2, 55 = Arabic text, 279; *The travels of Josafa Barbaro* (1431) and *The travels of a merchant in Persia* (1517), Hakluyt Society, London 1873; E. Sachau, *Reise in Syrien und Mesopotamia*, Leipzig 1883, 404-7; Pauly-Wissowa, xiv/2, col. 1648, art. *Mardē* (Weissbach); Le Strange, *The lands of the eastern caliphate*, 96; E. Honigmann, *Die Ostgrenze des byzantinischen Reiches von 363 bis 1071*, Brussels 1935, index; M. Canard, *Histoire de la dysnastie des H'amdânides*, Algiers 1951, 989 and index (in *Arabica*, xviii/3 [1971], 309).

(V. Minorsky*)

2. The Ottoman and modern periods

Finally, in 922/1516, the Persian commander Ḳara Khān was defeated and slain in battle at Karghandede near the old town of Ḳoč-ḥiṣār, 10 miles to the southwest of Mārdīn. Persian domination in Upper Mesopotamia thus collapsed, but the fortress of Mārdīn still remained in the hands of Sulaymān Khān, brother of Ḳara Khān. The siege lasted a year, and not till Meḥmed Bîyîklî Pasha [*q.v.*] arrived from Syria with reinforcements was it stormed and its valiant defenders put to the sword (Iskandar Munshī, *Taʾrīkh-i ᶜālam-ārā*, 24, 32, tr. Savory, i, 72; this Persian source mentions Oläng-i Ḳurūḳ in place of Ḳoč-ḥiṣār) (von Hammer, *GOR*², i, 7367-40, quoting Abu 'l-Faḍl, son of Ḥakīm Idrīs and continuer of his *Hasht-bihisht*).

In the Baghdād campaign of 941/1534, Mārdīn was created a *sandjaḳ* and included in the *eyālet* of Diyārbakr (for the history of the region at this time, see Nejat Goyunç, *XVI. Yüzyılda Mardin sancağı*, Istanbul 1969). Ewliyā Čelebi, iv, 59, gives Mārdīn 36 *zi ᶜāmets* and 465 timāriots; Mārdīn could put in the field 1,060 armed men (*djebeli*) In the 18th century, Mārdīn became a dependency of the Pashas of Baghdād; Otter (1737) found at Mārdīn a *voyvoda* appointed by Aḥmed Pasha. As late as the time of Kinneir (1810), Mārdīn was the frontier town of the *pashalîḳ* of Baghdād and was governed by a *müteselli̇m* sent from Baghdād.

The reforms of Sultan Maḥmūd II were badly received in Upper Mesopotamia. In 1832 (Ainsworth), Mārdīn rebelled. Power in Mārdīn had passed to the Kurdish beys. Southgate (1836) speaks of a hereditary (?) family who ruled in Mārdīn. The two brothers of the "ruling bey" seized power and refused to recognise the authority of the Porte. (It may be asked if these beys were not of the Millī tribe; on their chiefs cf. Buckingham, *Travels in Mesopotamia*, London 1827, 156.) Rashīd Pasha, the pacifier of Kurdistān, besieged the town and blew up the great mosque (Ainsworth). Order was temporarily restored. Considerable works were undertaken to improve the road giving access to the town. Rashīd Pasha died in January 1837 (Poujoulat). When the Egyptians under Ibrāhīm b. Muhammad ᶜAlī Pasha invaded Syria, their partisan Timawī b. Ayyūb of the Millī tribe seized Mārdīn (Sir Mark Sykes, *The Caliphs' last heritage*, 320) but was killed. The defeat of the Ottomans at Nizīb (June 1839) brought matters to a head. The Porte entrusted Mārdīn to Saᶜd Allāh

Pas̲h̲a of Diyārbakr, but the inhabitants preferred to submit to Ibrāhīm Pas̲h̲a of Mawṣil, who was opposed to the *Tanẓīmāt* reforms. This Pas̲h̲a appointed a governor to Mārdīn, but the rebels still held the citadel (Ainsworth 1840), and the governor soon perished in a rising.

By the *"wilāyet* law" of 1287/1870, Mārdīn became a *sand̲j̲aḳ* of the *wilāyet* of Diyārbakr. It had 5 *ḳaḍā*ʾs: Mārdīn, Nīṣībīn, D̲j̲azīra, Midyāt and Avine. The area of the *sand̲j̲aḳ* was 7,750 square miles and the number of towns and villages 1,062. The *sand̲j̲aḳ* was mainly agricultural. The town of Mārdīn produced a small quantity of silk, wool and cotton, leather, shawls, etc., but in spite of the excellence of the work these articles were mainly used for local consumption (Cuinet). By the reforms of 1921, Mārdīn formed a *wilāyet* with 6 *ḳaḍā*ʾs, 1,018 towns and villages, and 125,809 inhabitants (*Türkiyye D̲j̲emhüriyeti 1925-1926 sāl-nāmesi*). In the present-day Turkish Republic, Mārdīn is also the name of one of the 12 component *ilčes* or counties of the Mārdīn *il*. The modern town lies on the main road from Diyarbekir to Nusaybin and the Syrian frontier, and is also the terminus of a railway spur from Şenyurt on the Konya-Adana-Nusaybin-Bag̲h̲dād line.

Population. Niebuhr (1766) counted 3,000 houses in Mārdīn (of which 1,000 were Christian) with 60,000 inhabitants. Dupré (1808) estimated the population at 27,000, of whom 20,000 were Turks (i.e. Muslims), 3,200 Jacobites, 2,000 Armenians and 800 S̲h̲amsiyya. The statements of other travellers are as follows: Kinneir (1814): 11,000, of whom 1,500 were Armenians; Southgate (1837): 3,000, of whom 1,700 were Muslims, 500 Armenian Catholics, 400 Jacobites, 250 Syrian Catholics, 100 Chaldaeans; Mühlbach (1838): 12-15,000 inhabitants; Sachau (1879): 20,000; Cuinet (1891): 25,000, of whom 15,700 were Muslims. By 1955, the town had an estimated population of 24,306, and according to the 1970 census, the town had 33,251 inhabitants, the *ilçe* of Mārdīn 66,197, and the whole *il* 456,415.

According to Southgate, Arabic and Kurdish were the predominating languages in the town. The rural population of Ṭūr ʿAbdīn speaks the Ṭorānī dialect of Neo-Aramaic; cf. E. Prym and A. Socin, *Der neu-aramäische Dialect des Ṭūr ʿAbdīn*, Göttingen 1881; H. Ritter, *Die Volkssprache der syrischen Christen des Ṭūr ʿAbdīn*, Beirut-Wiesbaden 1967-79; on the Kurdish dialect, cf. Makas, *Kurdische Texte aus der Gegend Mârdîn*, Leningrad 1924.

Among the religious sects of Mārdīn, the S̲h̲amsiyya would merit a special study. In the time of Niebuhr (1766), there were about a hundred families in the town, and Buckingham (*op. cit.*, 192) and Southgate (1837) also mention them. The S̲h̲amsiyya probably represent the last survivors of a local pagan cult. Towards the middle of the 18th century, they were led to declare themselves Jacobite Christians, but only formally (cf. Ritter, *Erdkunde*, xi, 303-5).

Christianity at Mārdīn. The district of Mārdīn has played an exceptionally important part in the development of Eastern Christianity. A brilliant period of the Nestorian church which began in 755 is closely associated with Mārdīn. Towards the end of the 8th century, numerous monasteries were established round the town by the bishop John of Mardin. In 1171 the Jacobite patriarchate was transferred from Diyār Bakr (Āmid) to Mārdīn. In 1207 it was moved to Dayr al-Za ʿfarān, an hour's journey from Mārdīn, to return to Mārdīn in 1555 (Assemani, *Bibl. Orient.*, ii, 110, 221, 470; W. Wright, *A short history of Syriac literature*, Oxford 1891, index). On the position of the Christians before 1914, cf. the works of Southgate, Parry, Cuinet, etc.

Monuments. Niebuhr noted many Arabic inscriptions at Mārdīn. Those of the buildings of the Artuḳids and the *waḳfiyyas* of their principal buildings were studied by ʿAlī Emīrī [*q.v.* in Suppl.], himself a native of the Diyār Bakr region; see his edn. of Kātib Ferdī (wrote 944/1537-8), *Mārdīn mulūk-i Artuḳiyye taʾrīk̲h̲i*, Istanbul 1331/1931. The citadel of the town was built or rebuilt in Ḥamdānid times. Numerous mosques were erected by the Artukid beys from the time of Nad̲j̲m al-Dīn Īl-G̲h̲āzī in the early 6th/12th century onwards, including the great mosque, and an Artuḳid *ḥammām* remains. They constructed the Zind̲j̲īriyya and K̲h̲ātūniyya or Sitt Riḍwiyya *madrasas*, whilst the imposing Ḳāsim Pas̲h̲a *madrasa* was built in 849/1445 by the Aḳ-Ḳoyunlu Ḳāsim b. D̲j̲ihāngīr. There are many interesting churches and monasteries in the town and the surrounding countryside, including the Dayr al-Zaʿfarān, where numerous Syrian Christian patriarchs and metropolitans are buried. See A. Gabriel, *Voyages archéologiques dans la Turquie orientale*, Paris 1940, i, 3-44, ii, pls. a-d, I, XXIV; *İA*, art. *Mardin*, addition on *Eski eserler* by T.H.; Metropolit Hanna Dolapönü, *Tarihte Mardin, Itr-el-nardin fi tarih Merdin*, Istanbul 1972, 128 ff.

Bibliography: (in addition to references given in the article): P. della Valle, *Viaggi*, Brighton 1843, i, 515 (the traveller's wife was a native of Mārdīn); J. B. Tavernier (1644), *Les six voyages*, 1692, i, 187; C. Niebuhr (1766), *Reisebeschreibung*, Copenhagen 1778, ii, 391-8, and plate xlvii; G. A. Olivier (1795), Voyages, Paris 12 (rep.), iv, 242; A. Dupré (1808), *Voyage*, i, 77-82; J.M. Kinneir, *A geogr. memoir of the Persian Empire*, London 1813, 264-5; idem (1814), *Journey through Asia Minor*, London 1818, 433; J.S. Buckingham, *Travels in Mesopotamia*, London 1827, 188-94 (with a general view of the town); H. Southgate (1837), *Narrative of a Tour through Armenia*, London 1840, ii, 272-88; W.K. Ainsworth (1840), *Travels and Researches*, London 1842, ii, 114-16; C. Defrémery, *Observations sur deux points de l'histoire des rois d'Akhlath et de Mardin*, in *JA* (1843); Southgate, *Narrative of a visit to the Syrian church of Mesopotamia* (1841), New York 1844, 215-42; K. Ritter, *Erdkunde*, xi (1844), 150-3, 379-97 (very detailed résumé); F.J. Goldsmith, *An overland journey from Bagdad*, in *Trans. Bombay Geogr. Soc.* xvii (1868), 29 (the population of Mārdīn is 22,000, half of whom are Christians); Černik, *Technische Studien-Expedition*, in *Peterm. Mitt.*, Ergänzungsheft, x (1875-6), Heft 45, 15-18; H. Howorth, *History of the Mongols*, iii, 683-6; Socin, *Zur Geogr. des Ṭūr ʿAbdīn*, in *ZDMG*, xxxv (1881), 237-69 (map), 327-415; Sachau, *Reise in Syrien und Mesopotamien*, 404-7, 428; V. Cuinet, *La Turquie d'Asie*, Paris 1895, ii, 494-519; Tomilov, *Otčet o poyězdkě 1904*, St. Petersburg 1907, i, 263-7; Sykes, *The Caliphs' last heritage*, London 1915, index.

(V. Minorsky-[C.E. Bosworth])

al-**MĀRDĪNĪ**, the *nisba* of three mathematicians and astronomers, for whose life and work we have up to now little information.

1. Abu 'l-Ṭāhir Ismāʿīl b. Ibrāhīm b. G̲h̲āzī al-Numayrī, S̲h̲ams al-Dīn, known as Ibn Fallūs. He probably came from Mārdīn [*q.v.*]) in al-D̲j̲azīra, and was born in 590/1194, dying in *ca.* 650/1252. He made the pilgrimage to Mecca, and was the author of works on arithmetic (see Suter, 143-4, no. 359, and *Nachträge*, 227; Brockelmann, I², 622, S I, 860).

2. ʿAbd Allāh b. K̲h̲alīl b. Yūsuf, D̲j̲amāl al-Dīn

(d. 809/1406-7), disciple of the great astronomer Ibn al-Shāṭir (d. 777/1375), perhaps at Damascus; he later became a *muwaḳḳit* at Cairo (list of works in Suter, 170, no. 421; Brockelmann, II², 218, S II. 218). A good number of these are treatises on the use of various kinds of astronomical quadrants (*dastūr* quadrant, almucantarat quadrant and sinus quadrant). W.H. Worrell and W. Carl Rufus have translated the introduction to the *K. al-Durr al-manthūr fī 'l-ᶜamal bi rubᶜ al-dastūr* (*Maridini's introduction to the use of the quadrant*, in *Scripta mathematica*, x [1944], 170-80); this introduction is a brief, independent treatise in which the author sets forth the basic ideas (mainly definitions) of geometry and spherical astronomy. The rest of the work (60 chapters) is mostly concerned with problems regarding the transformation of coordinates with the *dastūr* quadrant. D.A. King has edited, translated and studied his *R. fi- 'l-ᶜamal bi-rubᶜ al-shakkāziyya (An analog computer for solving problems of spherical astronomy*, in *AIHS*, xxiv [1974], 219-42). This is a treatise on the use of a double quadrant, probably an evolved version of a similar instrument invented, in the second half of the 8th/14th century, by the astronomer of Aleppo Ṭaybughā al-Biklimishī or by his son ᶜAlī. All these instruments derived from the *ṣafīḥa shakkāziyya* of the Spanish astronomer of the 5th/11th century al-Zarḳālluh or from the universal plate of his contemporary ᶜAlī b. Khalaf. King has also edited and translated the introduction to his *R. fi 'l-ᶜamal bi 'l-djadāwil al-maᶜrūfa bi 'l-shabaka*, a work in which Djamāl al-Dīn tabulates three functions of spherical astronomy and elaborates three auxiliary tables similar to those of Ḥabash al-Ḥāsib (d. perhaps between 250 and 260/864-74 [*q.v.*]), Abū Naṣr Manṣūr (d. between 416 and 427/1025-36) or al-Khalīlī (*ca.* 766/1365), although less useful.

3. Muḥammad b. Muḥammad b. Aḥmad Abū ᶜAbd Allāh, Badr al-Dīn, known as Sibṭ al-Māridīnī (826-912/1423-1506), grandson of no. 2 and disciple of the astronomer Ibn al-Madjdī (d. 850/1506); he became *muwaḳḳit* at the Azhar Mosque in Cairo (list of works in Suter, 182-4, no. 445, and 222 n. 90; Brockelmann, II², 216-18, S II, 215-17; see also II,² 468, S II, 484). Like his grandfather, he wrote on the use of the almucantarat quadrant and the *dastūr* and sinus ones (cf. P. Schmazl, *Zur Geschichte des Quadranten bei den Arabern*, Munich 1929, 34-5, 63, 68, 72, 84). He also compiled a collection of tables, computed for the latitude of Cairo, in order to trace the curves of a solar quadrant (cf. K. Schoy, *Sonnenuhren der späterarabischen Astronomie*, in *Isis*, vi [1924], 332-60). He was also interested in arithmetic, algebra, the division of inheritances (*farāʾiḍ* [*q.v.*]) and mental arithmetic (*al-ḥisāb al-hawāʾī*), further writing commentaries on the works of the Egyptian mathematician Ibn al-Hāʾim (d. 815/1412), as well as on those of the Maghribī mathematician Ibn al-Yāsmīn (d. 601/1204; cf. Mohammed Souissi, *Ibn al-Yāsamīn, savant mathématicien du Maghreb*, in *Actas del VI Coloquio Hispano-Tunecino*, Madrid 1983, 217-25). In a work on the arithmetic of degrees and minutes, he brings out the periodicity of the sexagesimal fraction (cf. B. Carra de Vaux, *Sur l'histoire de l'arithmétique arabe*, in *Bibliotheca mathematica*, ser. 2, xiii [1899]). His works on the *mīḳāt* [*q.v.*] and the astronomical instruments became very popular, and were still in use as textbooks at the Azhar in *ca.* 1800, according to the testimony of the Egyptian historian al-Djabartī (d. 1237/1822).

Bibliography: In addition to references in the text, see King, *The astronomy of the Mamluks*, in *Isis*, lxxiv (1983), 531-55.

(M. Plessner - [J. Samsó])

al-**MARDJ** [see barḳa].

MARDJ BANĪ ᶜĀMIR, "the plain of the Banū ᶜĀmir", the largest of its kind in Palestine, named after the Arabian tribe ᶜĀmir b. Ṣaᶜṣaᶜa [*q.v.*], parts of which reached Palestine after the Arab conquests and settled there. Stretching between the mountains of Nābulus and those of Galilee, it constituted an important link on the Cairo-Damascus highway. Ever since the Neolithic era, it has encompassed fortified urban centres, some of which (e.g. Megiddo) flourished in biblical times. Its strategic location turned it into a scene of crucial battles in pre-Islamic periods and after; Ṣalāḥ al-Dīn and other Ayyūbids against the Crusaders, the Mamlūks Baybars and Ḳutuz against the Mongols in the 7th/13th century, and Allenby against the Ottomans in 1918.

Mediaeval geographers usually referred to it rather by its most famous historical site, ᶜAyn Djālūt [*q.v.*], or by the administrative centres to its east (Baysān) and south (Djinīn and Nābulus). The term occurs, however, occasionally in texts from late Mamlūk times in various forms: "*Wilāyat* Djinīn and Mardj Banī ᶜĀmir" or as a separate administrative sub-unit (*ᶜamal*) of the province of Ṣafad.

Early Ottoman *taḥrīrs* point to a formalisation of the term and its status: as part of the newly-set administrative system, a *nāḥiya* by this name was designated, consisting of 38 villages bordering on Baysān in the east, Nazareth in the north, Ḳabāṭiyya in the south, and extending towards the Mediterranean. The 74 uninhabited *mezraᶜas* included in it indicate the extent of ruin caused to the population and economy during the late Mamlūk period. In order to restore law and properity, it was granted to the local Bedouin *amīrs* of Ṭurabāy, who continued to rule it during the 16th and 17th centuries. The decline of Ottoman rule in Palestine meant once more a loss of any central control over this area, which became increasingly infested with Bedouins and gradually deserted by its sedentary population. "The whole of this country is in a state of insecurity... at present almost entirely deserted" is a description by Burckhardt which was invariably repeated by dozens of travellers who visited the place in the 18th and 19th centuries.

In the second half of the 19th century, most of its land was registered in the name of a few urban *aᶜyān* [*q.v.*] families, of which the Christian Sursuḳs of Beirut had the lion's share. Jewish philanthrophic societies anxious to purchase lands in Palestine conducted elaborate negotiations with the Sursuḳs during the late 19th century, but actually bought only a small fraction. In the wake of First World War, the Jewish National Fund acquired from these *aᶜyān* 250,000 dunams, compensated the 700 tenants living there, and proceeded with similar purchases in later years when this became a major bone of contention between Jews and Arabs. The drainage of the infectious swamps that covered most of the plain, the establishment of Jewish collective settlements and the intensive cultivation that resulted there, turned it into most fertile part of Palestine during the British Mandate. Ever since, both under the British and in the State of Israel, the term Mardj Banī ᶜĀmir fell into disuse and was replaced by the biblical equivalent, "the valley of Jezreel".

Bibliography: Ibn al-Furāt, *Taʾrīkh*, vii, 191; Yāḳūt, *Muᶜjam*, ii, 180; Ḳalḳashandī, *Ṣubḥ al-aᶜshā*, iv, 154; Maḳrīzī, *Kitāb al-Sulūk*, i, 683; Muḥammad ᶜAdnān Bakhīt, *al-Usra al-ḥārithiyya fī Mardj Banī ᶜĀmir*, in *al-Abḥāth* (1980), 55-78; B. Lewis, *An Arabic account of the province of Safad*, in *BSOAS*, xv,

483; M. al-Dabbāgh, *Bilādunā Filasṭīn*, i, Beirut 1965, 50-2 ff.; Y. Porath, *From riots to rebellion, the Palestinian-Arab national movement 1929-1939*, Tel Aviv 1978, 105-27; K. Stein, *The land question in Palestine 1917-1939...*, Chapel Hill and London 1984, 52-60, ff. (A. Cohen)

MARDJ DĀBIḲ, a plain near Dābiḳ [*q.v.*] on the Nahr al-Ḳuwayḳ in northern Syria. The town of Dābiḳ, was known to the Assyrians as *Dabigu* (Sachau, *ZA*, xii, 47) and is called Δάβεκον by Theophanes (*Chron.*, ed. de Boor, 143, 451 ff.).

For convenience in his campaigns against the Byzantines, Sulaymān b. ʿAbd al-Malik moved the headquarters of the Syrian troops from Djābiya [*q.v.*] to Dābiḳ. In 717 with an army under ʿUbayda he set out from Mardj Dābiḳ for Asia Minor and on his return died there in Ṣafar 99/September-October 717 (al-Masʿūdī, *Murūdj*, v, 397 = §2151; *Chronica minora*, ed. Guidi, in *GSCO*, *Scr. Syri*, ser. iii., vol. iv., text, 234, tr. 177). Hārūn al-Rashīd also encamped in 191/807 on this plain (Syr. *Margā Dābeḳ*) and composed the differences between the Syrian bishops (Michael Syrus, *Chron.*, ed. Chabot, iii, 19; Barhebraeus, *Chron. eccles.*, ed. Abbaloos-Lamy, i, 339). The Mirdāsid Maḥmūd in Radjab 457/ June 1065 defeated his uncle ʿAṭiyya on the field of Dābiḳ and then took Ḥalab (Ibn al-ʿAdīm, *Zubda*, ed. Dahan, i, 296.

When in 491/1098 the Franks conquered Anṭākiya, Kerbōghā of Mawṣil assembled a large army on Mardj Dābiḳ, with which he laid siege to Anṭākiya. (Ibn al-Athīr, x, 188; Abu 'l-Fidāʾ, Ibn al-ʿAdīm, etc., in *Rec. hist. or. crois.*, i, 3, 194; iii, 580). In the spring of 513/1119, Īl-Ghāzī on his campaign against the Franks crossed the Euphrates at Baddāyā (now Beddāī on Sachau's map) and Sandja and advanced via Tell Bāshir [*q.v.*], Tell Khālid, Mardj Dābiḳ and Muslimiyya against Ḳinnasrīn (Ibn al-ʿAdīm, ii, 187 *Rec. hist. or. crois.*, iii, 616). In Radjab 518/September 1124, Dubays b. Ṣadaḳa was defeated by Ḥusām al-Dīn Timūrtāsh on the field of Dābiḳ (*Rec. hist. or. crois.*, v, 645). On his campaign against Leo II of Little Armenia, al-Malik al-Ẓāhir encamped in 602/1305-6 on Mardj Dạbiḳ (*Rec. hist. or. crois.*, v, 155). On Sayf al-Dīn Tungur's campaign against the Tatars to Malaṭya [*q.v.*], in which Abu 'l-Fidāʾ of Ḥamā took part, a halt was made on the way back on the plain of Dābiḳ from 3 Ṣafar to 2 Rabīʿ II 715/9 May-6 July 1315) (Abu 'l-Fidāʾ, in *Rec. hist. or. crois.*, i, 3).

On 25 Radjab 922/24 August 1516 was fought at Mardj Dābiḳ the battle which gave Selīm I a decisive victory by which Syria passed for the next four centuries under Ottoman rule (H. Jansky, *Mitteil. z. osman. Geschichte*, ii [1923-6], 214-25) [see also dābiḳ and ḳānsawḥ al-ghawrī].

Bibliography: The geographical texts are gathered together in Le Strange, *Palestine under the Moslems*, 503; cf. R. Dussaud, *La topographie de la Syrie antique et médiévale*, Paris 1927, 474, to which should be added ʿIzz al-Dīn Ibn Shaddād, *Aʿlāḳ*, ed. S. Dahan, tr. A. M. Edde-Terrasse, index. The main historical references are: Masʿūdī, *Murūdj*, index; Yaḥyā al-Anṭākī, ed. Kratchkovsky and Vasiliev, in *Patr. or.*, 442; Ibn al-Athīr, ix, 160, x, 188; Ibn al-Adīm, *Zubda*, ed. S. Dahan, index. (E. Honigmann)

MARDJ RĀHIṬ, the name of a plain near Damascus famous in Islamic history on account of the battles which took place there.

According to Ibn Ḥawḳal, "a *mardj* is a wide expanse of land with numerous estates where large and small cattle and beasts are raised". For M. Canard (*H'amdânides*, 204), a *mardj* is "the place where agriculture and gardens cease to be found". Beyond the *mardj* lies the *ḥamād*, the sterile terrain.

Mardj is a term which, in reference to Damascus, denotes a semicircular zone situated between the Ghūṭa [*q.v.*] and the marches of ʿUṭayba and Hidjdjāna, and the desert steppe which extends eastwards. In the north, the *mardj* is bounded by the foothills of the first chain of the Ḳalamūn, in the west by the slopes of Mt. Hermon, and in the south by the lava bed of the Ladjāʾ [*q.v.*] and the Ṣafā. At the present time, this plain forms parts of the *muḥāfaẓa* of Damascus. Certain part of the *mardj* have special names; amongst these, certain ones have played a great rôle in the history of Syria, sc. the Mardj ʿAdhrāʾ or Mardj Rāhiṭ in the north-east, and the Mardj al-Ṣuffar [*q.v.*] in the south.

The climate of the *mardj* is identical with that of Damascus; at an elevation of 700 m. above sea level on average, it receives each year between 300 to 400 mm of rain. In February, after the winter rains, the region is swollen with water, and it is more difficult to get around, since the roads and tracks are impassable. In the spring, the springs situated at the foot of the first lines of the Ḳalamūn allow the agglomeration of ʿAdhrāʾ to be irrigated and give enough water to Mardj Rāhiṭ for the grass and flowers to grow in April. Towards mid-May, the Bedouin come to camp and to pasture their flocks on the eastern border of the *mardj*. In August, the grass has disappeared, and the region is dusty until the first rains of autumn.

According to certain authors, like Muḥammad Kurd ʿAlī, Mardj Rāhiṭ is identical with Mardj ʿAdhrāʾ, but for others, Mardj Rāhiṭ is situated near ʿAdhrāʾ, which Yāḳūt mentions as one of the villages in the vicinity of Damascus. This settlement, which sometimes give its name to the neighbouring *mardj*, is situated between the modern village of Shafūniyya and the Khān al-Ḳuṣayr at the foot of the Hill of the Eagle (Thaniyyat al-ʿUḳāb) on the road from Damascus to Ḥimṣ. When going northwards, one passes by the Ḳubbat al-ʿAṣāfīr, the Khān ʿAyyāsh—identified with the Khān of Lādjīn [*q.v.*] built in 690/1291—and the Khān of al-Ḳuṣayr. It is to the south-east of this district that Musil fixes the Mardj Rāhiṭ.

In Muḥarram 13/March-April 634, the general Khālid b. al-Walīd [*q.v.*] left ʿIrāḳ in order to take part, with two other Arab contingents, in the conquest of Syria. After their defeat at al-Adjnādayn [*q.v.*], the Byzantines fell back on Damascus, where they shut themselves up in Muḥarram 14/March 635. Khālid b. al-Walīd, having arrived himself at the beginning of spring in the region of Damascus, drove out the Ghassānids who were there and installed himself at Mardj Rāhiṭ, to the north-east of the city, which fact has led some people to think that he had come via Tadmur. Some others think that he took the southern road via Dūmat al-Djandal [*q.v.*]. Whilst Khālid encamped to the north-east, the general Abū ʿUbayda b. al-Djarrāḥ [*q.v.*] deployed his troops to the south-west in order to besiege Damascus, which had to surrender in Radjab 14/September 638.

In 64/684 Mardj Rāhiṭ was the scene of a great battle involving an internal struggle of the Arabs. On the death of Muʿāwiya II b. al-Yazīd [*q.v.*], a complex crisis ensued over the succession to the caliphate. The community became divided into two, with the Ḳaysīs, partisans of ʿAbd Allāh b. al-Zubayr [*q.v.*] on one side, and the Kalbīs, supporters of Marwān b. al-Ḥakam [*q.v.*] on the other. Whilst an assembly convoked to choose a successor to Muᶜāwiya II met at al-D̲j̲ābiya [*q.v.*], al-Ḍaḥḥāk b. Ḳays al-Fihrī [*q.v.*], head of the Ḳays and supporter of ᶜAbd Allāh b. al-Zubayr, who had made him governor of Damascus, concentrated the Ḳaysī forces at Mard̲j̲ al-Ṣuffar. Marwān, having become caliph, had as his prime aim the dislodging and breaking-up of the forces of al-Ḍaḥḥāk, who had rallied to Ibn al-Zubayr, in turn proclaimed caliph at Mecca. A first engagement took place in the middle of D̲h̲u 'l-Ḥid̲j̲d̲j̲a 64/mid-August 684 at Mard̲j̲ al-Ṣuffar; the Ḳaysīs fell back towards Damascus, but their opponents were in place to the north-east of Damascus at the foot of the T̲h̲aniyyat al-ᶜUḳāb; this was "the encounter (*waḳᶜa*) of Mard̲j̲ Rāhiṭ". After some 20 days ("nights", according to Ibn al-At̲h̲īr) of skirmishes, the final struggle, called "the day (*yawm*) of Mard̲j̲ Rāhiṭ", took place on 1 Muḥarram 65/18 August 684. If certain sources are to be believed, Marwān is supposed to have had 13,000 men under the command of ᶜAbbād b. Ziyād [*q.v.*], whilst al-Ḍaḥḥāk had as many as 30,000. Can the death of al-Ḍaḥḥāk in battle, and the sight of his severed head presented to Marwān, alone explain the débâcle for the Ḳaysīs, whose main leaders were killed, only Zufar b. al-Ḥārit̲h̲ al-Kilābī finding safety in flight northwards? Amongst the dead are mentioned 80 *as̲h̲rāf* of Damascus. According to al-Harawī and Ibn S̲h̲addād, at Mard̲j̲ Rāhiṭ in the 6th-7th/12th-13th centuries there were to be found the tombs of two Companions of the Prophet, Zumayl b. Rabīᶜa and Rabīᶜa b. ᶜAmr al-D̲j̲aras̲h̲ī, both killed fighting Marwān; it was, accordingly, a place of pilgrimage.

The success of the Kalb party may be explained by the rallying to Marwān, in the course of the manoeuvres, of elements allied to Ḳays, as well as the fact that the Umayyads, having succeeded by means of a coup-de-main in seizing the state treasury (*bayt al-mal*) at Damascus and a store of arms, had at their disposal means for redressing the balance of forces. Only the defection, to Marwān's profit, of an important part of the Syrian tribes, anxious to preserve their hegemony, seems able to explain the overwhelming success of the Umayyad army.

After this victory, Marwān undertook the conquest of the lands where allegiance had been given to ᶜAbd Allāh b. al-Zubayr. One result of the battle was to accentuate the rivalry of the Ḳays and the Kalb. The victorious Kalb and the family of Baḥdal [*q.v.*] acquired a preponderance which the Ḳays, with the support of Bāhila and G̲h̲anī [*q.vv.*], were to contest strongly.

The "encounter at Mard̲j̲ Rāhiṭ" was much mentioned in poetry of the Marwānid period, in particular by al-Ak̲h̲ṭal [*q.v.*]; and al-Masᶜūdī cites in his *Tanbīh*, in connection with this Umayyad victory, verses by al-Farazdaḳ [*q.v.*].

In D̲h̲u 'l-Ḥid̲j̲d̲j̲a 334/July 946, the Ḥamdānid Sayf al-Dawla [*q.v.*] broke the treaty which he had made with the Ik̲h̲s̲h̲īdid regent Kāfūr [*q.v.*] and seized Damascus, but the ruler in Cairo sent troops to regain the city. The Ḥamdānid army was put to flight by the Ik̲h̲s̲h̲īdid troops near Nāṣira in D̲j̲umādā I 335/December 946, and retreated towards Damascus; it encamped at Mard̲j̲ Rāhiṭ and then reached Ḥimṣ in D̲j̲umādā II 335/January 947, whilst Kāfūr's forces reoccupied Damascus. In spring 335/947, Sayf al-Dawla returned to Damascus, but he was beaten at Mard̲j̲ Rāhiṭ, whose terrain was suitable for warfare, and fled towards Aleppo, pursued by the Ik̲h̲s̲h̲īdid forces.

In 381/991 the Fāṭimid caliph al-ᶜAzīz [*q.v.*] dismissed Munīr al-K̲h̲ādim, the governor of Damascus, and sent as his replacement the Turkish general Mangūtakīn, who took up his position initially at ᶜAd̲h̲rāᵓ at Mard̲j̲ Rāhiṭ before making his entry into Damascus.

In D̲j̲umādā I 529/mid-February 1135, the Atabeg ᶜImād al-Dīn Zangī arrived from Aleppo and went to encamp at Mard̲j̲ Rāhiṭ between ᶜAd̲h̲rāᵓ and al-Ḳuṣayr with the aim of occupying Damascus. Whilst the city organised its defence, the Atabeg left Mard̲j̲ Rāhiṭ and took up a position to the south at the ᶜAḳabat al-Ḳibliyya on the road to Ḥawrān [*q.v.*]. On 7 D̲h̲u 'l-Ḳaᶜda 535/22 June 1141, Zangī appeared again on the outskirts of Damascus in order to cut off food supplies from the city. A sortie by the defenders compelled Zangī to lift the siege and beat a retreat; he then fell back to Mard̲j̲ Rāhiṭ in order to await his troops. When these last returned, loaded with plunder, he joined them on the road northwards.

A few years later, in spring 544/1149, Nūr al-Dīn in turn established his camp at ᶜAdhrāᵓ in the western part of Mard̲j̲ Rāhiṭ whilst he was besieging Damascus. Two years later, on 13 Muḥarram 546/2 May 1151, Nūr al-Dīn's vanguard set up its tents at ᶜAd̲h̲rāᵓ in Mard̲j̲ Rāhiṭ, but then the army, endeavouring to keep up the pressure on the city, changed camp several times before falling back at the approach of the Franks from Jerusalem who had come to the aid of the Damascenes. When Nūr al-Dīn came back a third time to lay siege to Damascus, in the second half of Muḥarram 549/beginning of April 1154, he set up his camp at Mard̲j̲ al-Ḳaṣṣāb to the north of the Bāb Tūma.

Ibn al-Furāt [*q.v.*] tells us that in 680/1280, "al-Manṣūr (sc. the Mamlūk sultan Ḳalāwūn [*q.v.*]) got together his troops in the *mard̲j̲* and left with his army for Ḥimṣ"; assuming that the sultan journeyed northwards, this must be Mard̲j̲ Rāhiṭ.

In 698/1298-9, the Mongol troops of the Il-K̲h̲ān G̲h̲azan [*q.v.*] entered Syria, passed by Ḥamāt [*q.v.*] and marched on Damascus. In Ramaḍān 698/June 1299, they regrouped at Mard̲j̲ Rāhiṭ before embarking on the attack on Damascus. Fighting between the Mongols and Mamlūks was fierce. The city was burnt, the suburbs destroyed, the G̲h̲ūṭa sacked, and Sayf al-Dīn Ḳïpčaḳ al-Manṣūrī who, with the *amīr* Baktimur al-Silāḥdār had passed into the Mongol service, was appointed governor of Damascus by G̲h̲azan. But after the retreat of the troops commanded by Ḳuṭlūs̲h̲āh, Sayf al-Dīn Ḳïpčaḳ once more submitted to the Sultan al-Nāṣir Muḥammad b. Ḳalāwūn, and D̲j̲amāl al-Dīn Aḳḳus̲h̲ al-Afram re-assumed the office which he had abandoned when the Mongols had appeared.

In 702/1303, the Mongols crossed Mard̲j̲ Rāhiṭ in order to reach Mard̲j̲ al-Ṣuffar, where they went to take up positions at S̲h̲aḳḥab before confronting the Mamlūk army.

From the 8th/14th century onwards, the name Mard̲j̲ Rāhiṭ seems to disappear in local toponomy in favour of the designation Mard̲j̲ ᶜAd̲h̲rāᵓ.

Bibliography: 1. Arabic texts: Ṭabarī, ii, 472-4, 480, 482, 483, 485, 486, 643; Masᶜūdī, *Tanbīh*, 309-11; Ag̲h̲ānī, ix, 37; x, 161; xiv, 119, 124; xvii, 111, 112, 114; xix, 109; xx, 124, 126; Ibn al-Ḳalānisī, *D̲h̲ayl*, ed. Amedroz, Leiden 1908, 40, 273; Harawī, *K. al-Ziyārāt*, ed. and tr. J. Sourdel-Thomine, Damascus 1953, 12/28; Yāḳūt, *Buldān*, Beirut 1957, iii, 625; iv, 91; v, 101; Ibn al-At̲h̲īr, *Kāmil*, Cairo 1930, iii, 326-8; Ibn al-ᶜAdīm, *Zubda*, ed. S. Dahhān, Damascus 1951, I, 44, 118; Ibn S̲h̲addād, *al-Aᶜlāḳ al-k̲h̲aṭīra* (*Dimas̲h̲ḳ*), ed. S.

Dahhān, Damascus 1956, 181 and n. 7; Ibn Kat͟hīr, *Bidāya*, viii, 242-4; Ibn al-Furāt, *Taʾrīk͟h*, ed. Ḳ. Zurayḳ, Beirut 1942, vii, 213; Ibn Tag͟hrībirdī, *Nud͟jūm*, i, 281, viii, 159; M. Kurd ʿAlī, *K͟hiṭaṭ al-S͟hām*, Damascus 1925, i, 146-7; idem, *G͟hūṭat Dimas͟hḳ*², Damascus 1952, 218 ff.—2. Geography and topography: G. Le Strange, *Palestine*, 69, 503; H. Sauvaire, *Description de Damas*, in *JA*, c. (1894-6), 476, n. 3, 479, n. 24; R. Dussaud et F. Macler, *Mission scientifique dans les régions désertiques de la Syrie Moyenne*, Paris 1903, 447 n. 2; R. Dussaud, *Topographie historique de la Syrie*, Paris 1927, 294, 299, 306 and n. 12, 317, map XIV B-4; A. Musil, *Arabia Deserta*, New York 1927, 546, 554, 558, 560-5, 571-3; idem, *The Middle Euphrates*, New York 1927, 303; idem, *Palmyrena*, New York 1928, 225, n. 73; R. Thoumin, *La géographie humaine de la Syrie Centrale*, Tours 1936, 56, 70, 232-3; N. Elisséeff, *Description de Damas d'Ibn ʿAsākir*, Damascus 1959, 239, n. 1; E. Wirth, *Syrien*, Darmstadt 1971, 403, 405; G. Cornu, *Atlas du monde arabo-islamique d'époque classique*, Leiden 1983, 12, map I, D -4.—3. History. J. Wellhausen, *Das arabische Reich und sein Sturz*, Berlin 1902, 107 ff., Eng. tr. *The Arab kingdom and its fall*, 171 ff.; F. Buhl, *Zur Krisis der Umayyadenherrschaft im J. 684*, in *ZA*, xxvii (1912), 50-64; M. Gaudefroy-Demombynes, *La Syrie à l'époque des Mamelouks*, Paris 1923, 33; H. Lammens, *L'avènement des Marwanides et le califat de Marwan*, in *MFOB*, xii/2, (1927), 57-75; J. Sauvaget, *Caravansérails syriens du Moyen Age*, in *Ars Islamica*, vii (1940), 1-19; idem, *La Poste aux Chevaux dans l'Empire des Mamelouks*, Paris 1941, 89 and 337; M. Canard, *H'amdânides*, Algiers 1951, i, 204, 586, 587; R. Le Tourneau, *Damas de 1075 à 1154*, Damascus 1952, 259; R. Dussaud, *La pénétration des Arabes en Syrie avant l'Islam*, Paris 1955, 28-9; N. Elisséeff, *Nūr ad-Dīn*, Damascus 1967, 237, 250, 253, 371, 464, 783; A. A. Dixon, *The Umayyad caliphate, 65-86/664-705*, London 1971, 83 ff.; K. Salibi, *Syria under Islam*, New York 1977, 60, 96 and n. 27; F. M. Donner, *The early Islamic conquests*, Princeton 1981, 124-6; G. Rotter, *Die Umayyaden und die zweite Bürgerkrieg (680-692)*, Wiesbaden 1982, 133-50; H. Zotenberg, *Les Omeyyades* (*Chronique de Tabarī*), re-impr. Paris 1983, 61-2.

(N. Elisséeff)

MARD͟J AL-ṢUFFAR, the plain stretching from the south of the G͟hūṭa and falling within the administrative district of Damascus (*arḍ Dimas͟hḳ*). It holds an important position in the history of Syria because of the many battles occurring there over the centuries and the frequent crossings of it by pilgrims. It provides a convenient stopping place south of Damascus, and because of the good water supply there and excellent grazing, it makes an ideal encampment for any army travelling from the north or the south.

To the north it is bounded by the right bank of the Nahr al-Aʿwad͟j, which drops down from Hermon to disappear to the east in the Baḥr al-Hid͟jd͟jāna, and to the east by the railway line from Damascus to Darʿa (Ad͟hriʿāt [*q.v.*]) and Amman (ʿAmmān [*q.v.*]). In the south-east, the Mard͟j ends in the volcanic area of the Safā, and in the south the boundary is the lava field of the Lad͟jā [*q.v.*], which is roughly situated between Umm al-Ḳuṣūr and G͟habāg͟hib. To the west, the village of Kanākir marks the boundary, while in the north-west it is marked by the lava flow (*waʿr*) of Zakiya.

The Syrian Darb al-Ḥad͟jd͟j crosses the Mard͟j al-Ṣuffar from north to south after going through the S͟huḥūra pass, the D͟jabal Aswad and the Nahr al-Aʿwad͟j. In its course it passes through Kiswa, K͟hān Danūn, S͟hakḥab and G͟habag͟hib, before entering the Ḥawrān [*q.v.*].

Here on the Mard͟j al-Ṣuffar one of the historically famous battles in the Syrian campaign of the caliph Abū Bakr was fought, in D͟jumādā 13/August 634. After the victory of Ad͟jnādayn [*q.v.*], the Prophet's Companion K͟hālid b. Saʿīd b. al-ʿĀṣ [*q.v.*], who had been put under the command of S͟huraḥbīl b. Ḥasana, arrived in the advance party on his way from D͟jawlān [*q.v.*] and camped here with his troops. He was taken by surprise by the Byzantines under Theodore, the brother of the emperor Heraclius, who was supported by the G͟hassānid troops of al-Ḥārit͟h b. Abī S͟hām. K͟hālid b. Saʿīd was killed in battle and buried on the spot. His newly-married wife Umm Ḥakīm bint al-Ḥārit͟h b. His͟hām b. al-Mug͟hīra, who had been the widow of ʿIkrima b. Abī D͟jahl, plunged into the conflict and killed his enemies. In memory of this exploit, the bridge on which she fought was named Ḳanṭarat Umm Ḥakīm. With the arrival of Arab reinforcements, the Byzantines fell back and shut themselves in Damascus, which was besieged by the Muslims shortly afterwards.

After his victory over the G͟hassānids at Mard͟j Rāhiṭ [*q.v.*], K͟hālid b. al-Walīd [*q.v.*] headed southwards and stayed for some time at the Mard͟j al-Ṣuffar before returning to Boṣrā [*q.v.*] by way of Ḳanawāt.

In Ramaḍān 64/May 684, partisans of the Umayyads met at al-D͟jābiya [*q.v.*] to nominate a successor to Muʿāwiya II [*q.v.*]. The governor of Damascus, al-Ḍaḥḥāk b. Ḳays al-Fihrī [*q.v.*], the leader of the Zubayrid party, was also invited to the meeting and promised to be there. He left Damascus with a considerable number of troops, but when he came to the Mard͟j al-Ṣuffar, half-way to al-D͟jābiya, he decided to stop there to await the outcome of the meeting, whilst at the same time making his way towards a meeting of the Ḳays [*q.v.*] of Syria, who were in rebellion against the Umayyads.

On 3 D͟hu 'l-Ḳaʿda 64/22 June 684, after forty days of deliberation, the Kalb [*q.v.*] and the Umayyad partisans elected to the caliphate by acclamation Marwān b. al-Ḥakam [*q.v.*]. Immediately, he started out for Damascus and arrived at the Mard͟j al-Ṣuffar in the middle of D͟hu'l-Ḳaʿda/the beginning of July. The Ḳays were unable to hold their position, and in an effort to avoid combat al-Ḍaḥḥak set off hastily towards Mard͟j Rāhiṭ, to the north of Damascus. In the battle which followed, the Ḳaysī leader and a large number of his men lost their lives.

In 476/1083, while the Sald͟jūḳ Tutus͟h [*q.v.*] was away leading an expedition against the Byzantines in the Anṭākiya region, Muslim b. Ḳurays͟h, the leader of the Banū ʿUḳayl and ruler of Ḥalab [*q.v.*] decided to besiege Damascus. The troops of Ḥalab, joined by the Banū Numayr [*q.v.*] and the Banū S͟haybān [*q.v.*] as well as some Turkmen elements, came to lay siege to the town. The Ḳays and some Yemenis joined them there. Muslim hoped for aid from Egypt promised by the Fāṭimids, but he hoped in vain. Tutus͟h was recalled by the townsmen of Damascus, but they had defeated their attacker before he could get back. The ʿUḳaylid was betrayed by some of his troops, and leaving the walls of the city, he went to make camp on the Mard͟j al-Ṣuffar. From there he took the road eastwards across the Ḥamād and reached the district of Salāmiyya.

Riḍwān b. Tutus͟h [*q.v.*], the ruler of Ḥalab, came to besiege Damascus in 489/1096, supported by Suḳmān b. Artuḳ. When he heard that S͟hams al-

Mulūk Duḳāḳ was returning to Damascus with his troops, Riḍwān raised the siege and fell back to the Mardj al-Ṣuffar, and then went on to pillage the Ḥawrān. Duḳāḳ arrived in Damascus, and set out in pursuit of Riḍwān's army. As Duḳāḳ began to close in on him, Riḍwān broke away, took a northerly route through the Syrian desert and returned to Ḥalab at the end of Dhu 'l-Ḥidjdjā 489/mid-December 1096.

In 11 Muḥarram 507/28 June 1113, the Saldjūḳ troops of the Amīr Sharaf al-Dīn Mawdūd of Mawṣil and of the Atabeg Tughtakīn [*q.v.*] of Damascus won a resounding victory over the Franks at al-Ṣinnabra, the former winter residence of the caliph Muʿāwiya, south of Lake Tiberias. The Franks retreated to some rising ground to the west of Tiberias, whilst the Muslims camped at the foot of the hill. After thirty-six days under siege, debilitated by the extreme heat and the lack of provisions, they were obliged to surrender their position on Rabīʿ I 507/16 April 1113. Heading north through Baysān, they reached the Mardj al-Ṣuffar, where Mawdūd paid off his troops and they dispersed. He then accompanied the Atabeg Ṭughtakīn to Damascus, arriving there on 21 Rabīʿ I 507/5 September 1113.

At the end of 519/1125, Baldwin II of Jerusalem decided to launch a surprise attack on Damascus in reprisal for a raid during the previous autumn by the Atabeg Ṭughtakīn. He intended to reach the area by way of the Mardj al-Ṣuffar and Sharkhub. The Atabeg positioned his troops on the Mardj al-Ṣuffar and advanced as far as Tell al-Shaḳḥab. On 27 Dhu 'l-Ḥidjdja 519/25 January 1127, the two armies confronted each other and fought a little battle which has become of great interest to military historians, as noted by Charles Oman, relying upon the accounts of Fulcher of Chartres and William of Tyre. This was, in fact, the first time that the Turks had used infantry to support their cavalry. The Franks were split into twelve field units each composed of cavalrymen and footsoldiers. Opposed to them was the Muslim army made up of Turkmen cavalrymen supported by young recruits, who were mounted behind the riders and ready to leap down and fight on foot when the enemy was near. On the Damascene side also were thousands of men on foot, for the most part citizens who had very little military training. It was only in respect of the irregular foot-soldiers that the Damascenes had a clear numerical superiority. Although the battle was extremely hard-fought, the casualties were not excessive. The Franks were first surprised by a hail of arrows and yielded ground, but then rallied, and the Damascus troops retreated at nightfall, falling back as far as Djabal Aswad, near Kiswa. Finally, both sides returned home.

In the first half of Shawwāl 523/the second half of September 1129, the Franks launched a new offensive against Damascus after the massacre of the Bāṭiniyya [*q.v.*]. Tadj al-Mulūk Būrī in vain solicited the help of the Fāṭimid caliph. The Franks encamped at the entrance to the Mardj al-Ṣuffar before Djisr al-Khashab and foraged on the plain between Tell Shaḳḥab and Kiswa. The Muslim army, now enlarged by Turkmens and Bedouins, halted in front of the Franks, who clustered round their tents while one group of them continued foraging in the Ḥawrān. After launching several attacks the Muslims were at last able to achieve a decisive victory, taking much booty and leaving many dead.

During the reigns of Nūr al-Dīn [*q.v.*] and Ṣalāḥ al-Dīn [*q.v.*], we find hardly any mention of the Mardj al-Ṣuffar in contemporary chronicles. The *Nudjūm* of Ibn Taghrībirdī makes no mention of any conflict on this plain which the armies used to cross on the way from Cairo to Damascus. In Djumādā II 590/May 1194, the Ayyūbid of Egypt al-ʿAzīz camped at Kiswa, on the banks of the Nahr al-Aʿwadj on the northern edge of the Mardj al-Ṣuffar, on his way to Damascus to hold discussions with his eldest brother al-Afḍal.

During the battle between al-ʿĀdil and al-Afḍal in 595/1199, al-Afḍal went to encamp on the Mardj al-Ṣuffar several times before resuming the siege of Damascus in Ramaḍān/July. In the following year (596/1200), it was the turn of al-Malik al-Ẓāhir to encamp on the Mardj al-Ṣuffar during the rainy season before reaching to Ḥalab.

In 614/1217 al-ʿĀdil [*q.v.*], the younger brother of Ṣalāḥ al-Dīn, was hard pressed by the Crusaders, and fell back from Palestine to the north. He travelled through Baysān, crossed the Jordan, passed through ʿAdjlūn [*q.v.*] and then turned northwards to follow the track of Raʾs al-Māʾ in order to get the Mardj al-Ṣuffar. From there he appealed for help to the Ayyūbid princes, but only al-Mudjāhid Shīrkūh of Ḥimṣ came to his camp. While al-ʿĀdil was in the Mardj al-Ṣuffar, his elder son, who was governing Egypt on his behalf, had to confront the Fifth Crusade when it disembarked at Damietta (Dimyāṭ [*q.v.*]) on Rabīʿ I 615/28 May 1218. As soon as al-ʿĀdil had heard that the Franks had set foot on Egyptian soil, he left for Damietta. After a day's forced march he arrived at ʿAliḳīn where he fell ill, shocked by the defeat at Damietta. He died in his camp on Friday, Djumādā II/31 August 1218. He was buried in Damascus, firstly in the citadel and then in his own *turba*. Whenever al-ʿĀdil stayed at Damascus during the rose blossom season, he would have his tent erected in the Mardj al-Ṣuffar, being allergic to the smell of the flowers, and then go back to the city later.

When al-Kāmil died in Radjab 635/March 1238, there was trouble among the Ayyubīd princes, and al-Nāṣir Dāwūd [*q.v.*] had to leave his post as governor of Damascus. For a time, he took refuge in Ḳabūn, some 4 km. north of Damascus. But he felt himself threatened there, so sought refuge in the Mardj al-Ṣuffar in the old Umayyad castle of Umm Ḥakīm, from where he fled to Ḳalʿat al-Rabaḍ, the castle of ʿAdjlūn.

In Shaʿbān 702/end of March or beginning of April 1303, the Mongols of Persia again crossed the Euphrates and marched towards Ḥamāt [*q.v.*]. Damascus had been occupied for a short while by the Tatars in 699/1300, and they now went out to wait for the enemy in the Mardj al-Ṣuffar, where they were to be joined by the Mamlūk sultan of Egypt al-Nāṣir Muḥammad. The troops of the Ilkhānid Ghazan Maḥmūd [*q.v.*] took up their position near Shaḳḥab, to the west of the Mardj al-Ṣuffar. They launched their attack on 2 Ramaḍān 502/21 April 1303 and were repulsed by the Mamlūks, who sustained heavy losses. The *amīrs* ʿIzz al-Dīn Aydamur al-ʿIzzī al-Naḳīb, together with ʿIzz al-Dīn Aybak al-Turkī al-Ẓāhirī, the governor of the province of Ḥimṣ, and also the *ḥādjib* [*q.v.*] Djamāl al-Dīn Aḳḳūsh al-Shāmī, all fell "as martyrs" on that day.

In 791/1359 and 792/1390, the Mardj al-Ṣuffar was the theatre for violent fighting between Muslims. Barḳūḳ, the sultan who had been stripped of his position, left al-Karak [*q.v.*] where he had just been released from captivity, in Shawwāl 791/September-October 1389, and he arrived in Mardj al-Ṣuffar on 22 Shawwāl with, it is said, 500 men, some Mamlūks and some Bedouins. He clashed with the troops from Damascus near Shaḳḥab on 10 Dhu 'l-Ḥidjdja/30

October 1389, and went on to lay siege to Damascus. The *amīrs* of the main towns of the north of Syria banded together and came to the help of the city, but on the way, some of them decided to go over to Barḳūḳ. When, at the beginning of Muḥarram 792/end of December 1389 a warning was given of the approach of Tīmūrbughā Minṭāsh, Barḳūḳ left Damascus after a violent battle at Bāb al-Djābiya, within the eastern area of the city. He fell back towards the Mardj al-Ṣuffar, passed through Kiswa, and went on to camp at Shaḳḥab. According to Ibn Ṣaṣrā, the two armies confronted one another on 17 Muḥarram/5 January 1390. In this critical situation, Barḳūḳ was looking for cover when he suddenly came face to face with the sultan al-Manṣūr Ḥādjdjī, the caliph of Cairo al-Mutawakkil I, and the great *ḳāḍīs* who, since they had only a feeble escort, quickly surrendered. Hence at that point, the situation was reversed. Minṭāsh tried three times to release Ḥadjdjī and his companions but without success, since a violent storm of hail and rain forced the adversaries to abandon their conflict. Though the number of dead on both sides was less than 50, it was nevertheless a battle important for history. While Minṭāsh sought refuge in Damascus, Barḳūḳ went back to Cairo with the caliph and the *amīrs* who had joined his cause, and was restored to the office of sultan in Ṣafar 792/February 1390, whilst al-Manṣūr (al-Muẓaffar) Ḥadjdjī disappeared without any more trouble.

One may note that during the 8th/14th century, *khāns* [*q.v.*] were built in the Mardj al-Ṣuffar, a sign of a certain prosperity in the district. One *khān* was built to the north-west of the Ladjāʾ at Shaḳḥab in 716/1316-17 by the *amīr* Tankiz b. ᶜAbd Allāh al-Nāṣirī, the viceroy of Damascus. In 725/1325 another was built between Kiswa and Ghabāghib in the *nāḥiya* of al-Katf al-Buṣrī (?) in the Mardj al-Ṣuffar, at the expense of al-Amīr al-Kabīr ᶜIzz al-Dīn Khaṭṭāb b. Maḥmūd b. Murtaᶜish (?) al-ᶜIrāḳī al-Ghazakī, and it attracted many travellers. The Khān Danūn, a very large *khān*, built 5 km. south of Kiswa on the road to Adhriᶜat, was completed in 778/1376 during the reign of sultan al-Ashraf Shaᶜbān. One should also mention a *khān* at Ghbāghib, north of Ṣanamayn, on the Pilgrimage route, and another, the Khān al-Zayyāt, to the south-west of Kiswa and north-east of Shaḳḥab.

In 1941, during the course of hostilities between the Free French forces (supported by the British and Commonwealth troops) and the Vichy troops, there was a battle on the Mardj al-Ṣuffar, which took place on the very spot where the Byzantines had been forced to yield ground to the Arabs 1300 years before, and this later battle allowed the Allies to enter the Syrian capital.

Bibliography: Arabic texts. Masᶜūdī, *Tanbīh*, 261, 286; Ibn Ḥawḳal, tr. Kramers-Wiet, 210-11; Ibn al-Ḳalānisī, *Dhayl* (Ibn al-Azraḳ al-Fāriḳī), Beirut 1908, 115/10, 132/35, 213/65; Harawī, *K. al-Ziyārāt*, ed. and tr. J. Sourdel-Thomine, Damascus 1953, 12/28; Yāḳūt, *Buldān*, Beirut 1957, iii, 413; v, 101; Ibn al-Athīr, *Kāmil*, Cairo 1930, ii, 276-78; viii, 132, ix, 216; Ibn al-ᶜAdīm, *Zubdat*, ed. S. Dahhān, Damascus 1968, iii, 146; Ibn Shaddād, *al-Aᶜlāḳ al-khaṭīra (Dimashḳ)*, ed. Dahhān, Damascus 1956, 182; Ibn Kathīr, *Bidāya*, vii, 4; xiii, 76, 78; xiv, 21, 24; Ibn al-Furāt, *Taʾrīkh*, ed. K. Zurayḳ, Beirut 1936-9, viii, 205; ix, 152-3, 185-6; Maḳrīzī, *Khiṭāṭ*, iii, 58, 92; Ibn Ḳāḍī Shuhba, *Taʾrīkh*, ed. A. Darwīsh, Damascus 1977, index, s.v.; Ibn Taghrībirdī, Cairo, vi, 121, 122, 149, 222, 223, 304, vii, 267, viii, 159, 204-6, xi, 260, 355, 367, 371.—Geography and topography. G. Le Strange, *Palestine*, 482, 503, 504; H. Sauvaire, *Description de Damas*, in *JA* (1894-6), ii, 402, iii, 469 n. 139, n. 140, viii, 285, 307 n. 83, xi, 249, 251, 283 n. 59 bis, C, 477 n. 8, O.T. 409 n. 20; R. Dussaud, *Topographie historique de la Syrie*, Paris 1927, 218, 306, 317-22, 334, 340, map II; A. Musil, *Palmyrena*, New York 1928, 71 n. 17, 100; R. Thoumin, *La géographie humaine de la Syrie centrale*, Tours 1936, 56, 232; N. Elisséeff, *Description de Damas d'Ibn ᶜAsākir*, Damascus 1959, 97 n. 5; E. Wirth, *Syrien*, Darmstadt, 1971, 403-5; G. Cornu, *Atlas du monde arabo-islamique*, Leiden 1983, 12, map I.—History. Ibn Ṣaṣrā, ed. W.M. Brinner, *A chronicle of Damascus 1389-1397*, Los Angeles 1963, 25 (37) b. 26 (38) a, 49 (15) b, 51 a, 51 b, 55 b, 95 a; N. Elisséeff, *Nūr ad-Dīn*, Damascus 1967, 264, 308, map: 5 - c; R. Grousset, *Hist. des Croisades*, Paris 1934-6, i, 275, 637-44, 663, iii, 203; R. S. Humphreys, *From Saladin to the Mongols*, New York 1977, 111-13, 157, 159, 160, 176, 243; H. Lammens, *L'avènement des Marwanides et le califat de Marwān*, in *MFOB*, xii/1 (1927), 39-40, 42, 61-3; R. Le Tourneau, *Damas de 1075 à 1154*, Damascus 1952, 10 and n. 3, 35, 123-5, 165-7, 184-7, 213; Ch. Oman, *A history of the art of war in the Middle Ages*, London 1924, i, 302-4; J. Prawer, *Royaume Latin de Jérusalem*, Paris 1969, i, 293, 309; J. Sauvaget, *Caravansérails syriens du Moyen Age*, in *Ars Islamica*, vii (1940), 1-19; K. M. Setton, *History of the Crusades*, Philadelphia 1955-62, i, 401-3, 426, 430, ii, 390, 398, 775; C. Thubron, *Mirror to Damascus*, London 1967, 201. (N. ELISSÉEFF)

MARDJAᶜ-I TAḲLĪD (pl. *marādjiᶜ-i taḳlid*, Pers. for Ar. *mardjaᶜ/marādjiᶜ al-taḳlīd*), title and function of a hierarchal nature denoting a Twelver Imām Shīᶜī jurisconsult (*mudjtahid, faḳīh*) who is to be considered during his lifetime, by virtue of his qualities and his wisdom, a model for reference, for "imitation" or "emulation"—a term employed to an increasing extent by English-speaking authors—by every observant Imāmī Shīᶜī (with the exception of *mudjtahids*) on all aspects of religious practice and law. As in the case of other institutions, the history of this function (called *mardjaᶜiyyat-i taḳlīd* or simply *mardjaᶜiyyat*, the term *mardja ᶜi- taḳlīd* often being abbreviated as *mardjaᶜ*, pl. *marādjiᶜ*) is to be understood in the context of the protracted doctrinal development of Imāmism. Although the Arab element played and continues to play an important part in this development, historical circumstances prevalent in Iran since the establishment of Imāmi Shīᶜīsm as the state religion under the Ṣafawids (907-1135/1501-1722 [*q.v.*]) were ultimately responsible for giving to the Imāmī *mudjtahids* a dominant spiritual and temporal influence. Under the Ḳādjārs (1794-1925 [*q.v.*]), the Imāmī *ᶜulamāʾ* developed or re-interpreted various concepts or points of doctrine (*niyābat, aᶜlamiyyat, mardjaᶜiyyat, wilāyat*) which contributed to the increase of their power. Having undergone an eclipse since the 1920s—a period corresponding with the renaissance of Ḳum [*q.v.*] as a theological centre—the influence of the Imāmī *mudjtahids* and the role of the *mardjaᶜ-i taklid* were seriously reexamined in the early 1960s as a result of doubts concerning the succession to Āyatullāh al-ᶜUẓmā Burūdjirdī (d. 1961 [*q.v.* in Suppl.]), sole *mardjaᶜ-i taḳlīd* since 1367/1947. Discussions and debates were held by members, religious and lay, of the Islamic societies (*andjumanhā-yi islāmī*) concerning the method of selection and the functions of the *mardjaᶜ-i taḳlīd* and the institution of *mardjaᶜiyyat* in general, the position of Imāmism with regard to *idjtihād, taḳlīd* and the various problems posed by the relations between religious and political authorities, the forms and the degrees of power which could be exercised by the *mudjtahids*, etc. It was especially after the publication of these discussions (*Baḥthī*, 1341/1962; cf. Lambton (1964), 120), of which the authors, Āyatullāh Ṭāliḳānī (d. 1979) and Mihdī Bāzargān, were arrested and imprisoned following the demonstrations of spring 1963 against the "white revolution" of the Shāh (in which Āyatullāh Khumaynī played a prominent role) that abroad there ensued a wide-ranging debate concerning these questions, of which the salient points are summarised below in their historical context.

1. Discussions of *idjtihād* and *taḳlīd*. The evolution of Imāmī attitudes towards *idjtihād* and *taḳlīd* may be analysed in the context of what has been called, sometimes retrospectively and anachronistically, the conflict between the Akhbārīs/Akhbāriyya [*q.v.* in Suppl.] and the Uṣūlīs/Uṣūliyya [*q.v.*]. The eminent scholars of the period of the Būyids [see BUWAYHIDS] who formulated the Imāmī *uṣūl al-fiḳh* (al-Mufīd, d. 413/1022; al-Murtaḍā, d. 436/1044; Shaykh Ṭūsī, d. 460/1067) reject both *ḳiyās* and *idjtihād* (although al-Murtaḍā acknowledges a subordinate role for *idjtihād*: Brunschvig, 210; Arjomand (1984), 53). Even while employing its techniques, the Imāmī *ʿulamāʾ* continue to reject *idjtihād*. At the same time, Shaykh Ṭūsī describes the traditionists as literalists (*aṣḥāb al-djumal*, cf. Kazemi Moussavi (1985), 36). Akhbārīs and Uṣūlīs appear as opposing factions in the *Kitāb al-Naḳḍ*, an anti-Sunni polemical work written by the fervent Uṣūlī ʿAbd al-Djalīl al-Ḳazwīnī al-Rāzī (d. 565/1170; on this source, see Calmard (1971), Scarcia Amoretti (1981)). In the Ilkhānid period, al-Muḥaḳḳiḳ al-Ḥillī (d. 726/1325) admits that—although rejecting *ḳiyās*—the Imāmī *ʿulamāʾ* have practised *idjtihād*. His pupil Ibn al-Muṭahhar al-ʿAllāma al-Ḥillī (d. 726/1325) formulated the methods of Imāmī *idjtihād*. According to Muṭahharī (*Baḥthī*, 42), he was the first Imāmī jurist to use the term *mudjtahid* to describe one who derives religious precepts (*ḥukm-i sharʿī*) on the basis of authentic articles of the *sharīʿat*. According to other opinions, al-Mufīd is said to have been the first Imāmī *faḳīh* to practise *idjtihād*, al-Ṭūsī having given him a definitive formulation (J. M. Hussain, 150, quoting M. Ramyar, 88, 92).

Like *idjtihād*, *taḳlīd* is rejected by the first Imāmī theologians, notably al-Kulaynī (cf. Arjomand (1984), 139) and al-Mufīd (cf. McDermott, 257 ff.). For al-Murtaḍā, the disciple of al-Mufīd, the *taḳlīd* of an *ʿālim* is permitted (with reservations). He is followed three centuries later by Ibn al-Muṭahhar al-Ḥillī who—while no longer basing the competence of the *mudjtahid* on the entirety of the *sharīʿat*—draws a distinction between *idjtihād al-mukallafīn* and *idjtihād al-mudjtahidīn* or indeed between the *muftī* and the *mustaftī*, i.e. between the jurisconsult and the simple believer (Arjomand (1984), 139 f.; Kazemi Moussavi (1985), 37).

2. Basis and extent of the influence of the Imāmī *mudjtahids*. According to Imāmī tradition, the world cannot exist for a single moment without a *ḥudjdja* ("proof" or "guarantee" of God), this function being supplied, after the Prophet, by the Imāms. During the Minor Occultation (*ghaybat al-ṣughrā*, 260-329/874-941), the *fuḳahāʾ* were able to consult the Twelfth Imām through the intermediacy of his four *safīrs* or *wakīls*. On the instructions of the Imām, the fourth *wakīl* did not appoint a successor (Madelung, (1982), 163 ff.). During the Major Occultation (*ghaybat al-kubrā*, after 329/941), the Imāmī community therefore lived in a state of messianic expectation which compelled it to seek out solutions for its spiritual and temporal organisation. Unlike the Sunnīs, the Imāmī *fuḳahāʾ* generally denied the legitimacy of powers established *de facto* during the *ghayba* (the basis and the logic of this attitude have been questioned by Arjomand (1979) who criticises the interpretations of N.R. Keddie, A.K.S. Lambton, H. Algar etc.; cf. Calmard (1982), 255, Calder (1982 A), 3, n. 2).

In the acknowledged absence of an infallible guide or of a just sovereign, or of transmitters of traditions (*muḥaddithūn*), the Imāmī *fuḳahāʾ* became scholastic theologians (*mutakallimūn*) before extending their prerogatives in the capacity of *mudjtahidūn* (J. Hussain, 150). Their influence increased under the Būyids (who professed Shīʿism), with whom they felt able to collaborate without sacrificing their loyalty to their Imām (Kohlberg (1976 A), 532 f.). Numerous Imāmīs, including some *ʿulamāʾ*, collaborated with Sunnī authorities and occupied senior posts in the service of the ʿAbbāsids and the Saldjūḳs (Calmard (1971), 55 f.). The theologian Naṣīr al-Dīn Ṭūsī (d. 672/1274) and the Shīʿī vizier Ibn al-ʿAlḳamī promoted, in varying degrees, the accession to power of the Mongol Ilkhāns (Calmard (1975), 145 ff.). The Ilkhān Öljeytü/Uldjaytū (1304-17) showed favour to eminent Imāmī *ʿulamāʾ* such as Ibn al-Muṭahhar al-Ḥillī and his son Fakhr al-Muḥaḳḳiḳīn (d. 771/1369-70): *ibid.*, 150 ff.; Arjomand (1984), 57 f.).

Whether accepting or contesting the powers established *de facto*, the Imāmī *ʿulamāʾ* continued to seek, within the structural limits of the *sharīʿa*, a means of coming to terms with their existence. According to a theory elaborated under the Būyids, during the *ghayba* certain parts of the *sharīʿa* (such as *djihād* or *ḥudūd*, legal penalties) are inapplicable (this is the doctrine of the *suḳūṭ*: cf. Calder (1982 A), 4, quoting the same (1979 A), ch. 3). Points of doctrine concerning especially *djihād* and the duties incumbent (such as *amr bi 'l-maʿrūf wa-nahy ʿan al-munkar*, ordering the good and forbidding the bad) are thoroughly discussed (Arjomand (1984), 61 ff., see also Kohlberg (1976 B)). But the Imāmī political ethic expounded especially by al-Murtaḍā (and adopted by his successors) recommends in judicial and administrative matters "a positive and ethically responsible involvement in the existing political order" (Arjomand (1984), 65; see also Madelung (1980)).

With the rise of Ṣūfism in the post-Ilkhānid period (14th-16th centuries), Shīʿī themes began to permeate the *ṭarīḳāt* and the thought of various messianic or millenarian politico-religious movements inspired by charismatic chieftains or miracle-workers who seized power (the Sarbadārs, the Mushaʿshaʿīs, the Ṣafawids, etc.). Various Ṣūfī movements threatened the existence of the existing established powers or compromised with them (Kubrāwiyya, Dhahabiyya, Nūrbakhshiyya, Niʿmatullāhiyya, Ḥurūfiyya, etc.). The case of the Shīʿī order of the Marʿashī Sayyids [*q.v.*] constitutes a separate example of politicisation of Ṣūfism from which Mahdism is absent (for a socio-historical study of these movements, see Calmard (1975), 154 ff; Arjomand (1984), 66 ff.). Although these socio-political changes were unconnected with the efforts of the *ʿulamāʾ* to formulate and practise the Imāmī doctrine, their advice was sometimes solicited by politico-religious chiefs, as in the case of the "Shīʿī republic" of the Sarbadārs which created a precedent regarding the functions which could henceforward be exercised by Imāmī *ʿulamāʾ* in a Shīʿī state.

It was in this context of Ṣūfism and extremism that there came about the rise of the Ṣafawiyya and its transformation in the course of the 15th century into a militant order exercising an increasingly extravagant messianic hold over the Turkoman dervish-g͟hāzis, the ḳizilbas͟h [*q.v.*]. The imposition of Imāmī S͟hīᶜism as the state religion by S͟hāh Ismāᶜīl (1501-24 [*q.v.*]) had the notable consequence of incorporating into the Ṣafawid state Persian dignitaries who were men of high religious or administrative rank and the owners of large properties (Aubin, 39). Since Ṣafawid "imperio-papism" was based simultaneously on the ethos of Iranian nationalism and on S͟hīᶜism, state policy led to the ruthless suppression of messianic and Ṣūfī tendencies both outside and inside the Ṣafawid movement and to the persecution of Sunnīs. With the appeal to the dogmatic principles of S͟hīᶜism, this situation favoured the establishment and the ascendancy of a hierocracy of Imāmī *ᶜulamā*ʾ who, from the outset, under S͟hāh Ismāᶜīl, were subject to the hostility of Persian religious dignitaries (Glassen, 262; Arjomand (1984, 133). The decisive initiative for the establishment of an Imāmī hierocracy was taken by S͟hāh Ṭahmāsp (1524-76). A devout Imāmī, professing no messianic pretensions, he favoured the installation of Imāmī *ᶜulamā*ʾ, "imported" from the Arab countries (Syria, mainly the D̲j̲abal ᶜĀmil, Arab ᶜIrāḳ and Baḥrayn). With their Persian students or colleagues recruited from the hostile camp of the Persian religious dignitaries, they ultimately constituted a "brotherhood" of religious specialists. The *farmān* through which S͟hayk͟h ᶜAlī al-Karakī al-ᶜĀmilī (d. 940/1534), the "Propagator of Religion" was awarded the titles of *Nā*ʾ*ib* (deputy) of the Imām and of *K͟hātam al-mud̲j̲tahidīn* ("seal of the *mud̲j̲tahids*") could be considered both as the ratification of the establishment of the Imāmī hierocracy in Iran and as the definitive transition from extremism to Imāmism (Arjomand (1984), 129 ff., 133 f.).

The principles on which the authority of the Imāmī *ᶜulamā*ʾ rests were redefined under the Ṣafawids. The combination of the concepts of *taḳlīd* and *id̲j̲tihād* is expressed in various works (*Zubdat al-bayān*, by Mullā Muḥammad Ardabīlī al-Muḳaddas, d. 983/1585; *Zubdat al-uṣūl*, by Bahāʾ al-Dīn ᶜĀmilī "S͟hayk͟h-i Bahāʾī", d. 1030/1621; *Maᶜālim al-uṣūl*, by Ḥasan b. Zayn al-Dīn, d. 1011/1602). Although the "Mud̲j̲tahid al-zamānī" al-Karakī fulminates against the prospect of imitating a dead *mud̲j̲tahid* (*taḳlīd al-mayyit*), the general competence of the *mud̲j̲tahids* in all areas of the *s͟harīᶜa* (*id̲j̲tihād muṭlaḳ*) is confirmed, sometimes with the intention of restricting its performance to one or a few jurists, as recommended by Mīr Dāmād [see AL-DĀMĀD], d. 1041/1631-2 (*ibid.*, 138 ff.).

The authority of the *mud̲j̲tahids* during the *g͟hayba* is also redefined around the concept of *niyāba ᶜāmma*, Pers. *niyābat-i ᶜāmma* ("deputed authority") of the Hidden Imām exercised, in principle, collectively (Madelung (1982), 166). The prerogatives attached to this concept vary according to the *mud̲j̲tahids*. While al-Karakī limits their applications, ᶜAlī b. Zayn al-Dīn al-ᶜĀmilī, called *al-S͟hahīd al-t͟hānī* (d. 765/1557), introduces a terminological innovation in describing the *faḳīh* as the *Nā*ʾ*ib ᶜāmm* or *Ḥākim-i s͟harᶜī* of the Hidden Imām. Among the important implications of the *niyāba ᶜāmma* is the right given to the *mud̲j̲tahids* to collect and administer legal taxes (*zakāt*, *k͟hums*) which, with the management of mortmain property, enjoyed with other religious dignitaries, gives them financial autonomy (*ibid.*, 141 f.; Calder (1982 A), 4 f.; on the development of the doctrine of *niyāba ᶜāmma*, see Calder (1979 A), chs. 4-6; on *zakāt* and *k͟hums*, see idem, (1981), (1982 B); Sachedina (1980)). The authority of the *mud̲j̲tahids* also derives formally from various *ḥadīt͟hs*, including a declaration by the Twelfth Imām which describes the *ᶜulamā*ʾ as the proof (*ḥud̲j̲d̲j̲a*) of the proof of God (i.e. of the Hidden Imām) for all the faithful. The *ᶜulama*ʾ are also said to be the heirs of the Prophet (Hairi (1977), 59).

Although formulation of the concept of deputed authority was not pursued systematically in the Ṣafawid period, some of the attributes of the Imāms were then transferred to the *mud̲j̲tahids* (Arjomand (1984), 143). But the Imāmī hierocracy lacked an independent "clerical" organisation and needed political power in order to consolidate its position in relation to the religious dignitaries, especially the *sayyids*, who also enjoyed a certain mystique and wielded politico-economic influence. Claiming to represent the Hidden Imām, but incapable of assuming the heritage of Ṣafawid extremism, it legitimised the Ṣafawid dynasty only as a purely temporal power (this was the prudent attitude of Muḥammad Bāḳir Mad̲j̲lisī [*q.v.*], d. 1111/1699; cf. *ibid.*, 184). But in spite of its efforts and the support of S͟hāh Ṭahmāsp, the hierocracy did not succeed in taking over the important religious and administrative function of the *ṣadr* (*ṣidārat*), which was increasingly. The mystique of the *nā*ʾ*ib ᶜāmm* did not fuse with that attached to the most learned *mud̲j̲tahid* to constitute a hierocratic institution. These setbacks were due in part to the fact that in addition to its rivalries with the religious dignitaries, the new Imāmī hierocracy experienced internal dissensions due to the diversity of its geographical origins and the diverse attitudes of its *ᶜulamā*ʾ, some of whom directed their attention to worldy matters, while others sought refuge in philosophy (*ibid.*, 132 f.). Despite the considerable influence enjoyed by al-Karakī in the 16th century, it was only at the end of the 17th century, with Muḥammad Bāḳir Mad̲j̲lisī, that there were established the bases of the future influence of the Imāmīᶜ *ᶜulāmā*ʾ, with solid popular roots rendering them independent of the State (*ibid.*, 159 and below).

3. Ak͟hbārī resurgence and Uṣūlī reaction. After being dormant since the Sald̲j̲ūḳ period, the opposition of the Ak͟hbārīs towards the Uṣūlī school was renewed at the beginning of the 17th century, when Mullā Muḥammad Amīn b. Muḥammad S͟harīf Astarābādī (d. 1036/1626-7), encouraged by his teacher Mīrzā Muḥammad b. ᶜAlī Astarābādī (d. 1028/1619), formulated the Ak͟hbārī doctrine in his *K-al-Fawāʾid al-madaniyya*, the basis of the neo-Ak͟hbārism which flourished in Iran and in ᶜIrāḳ in the 17th and 18th centuries (on Ak͟hbārism, notably in this period, see E. Kohlberg, AK͟HBĀRĪYA, in *Encyclopaedia Iranica*, i, 716-18). Both teacher and pupil belonged to the clique of Persian religious dignitaries. Neo-Ak͟hbārism was embraced by two eminent representatives of gnostic S͟hīᶜism, the elder Mad̲j̲lisī, Muḥammad Taḳī (d. 1070/1660), and Mullā Muḥsin Fayḍ Kās͟hānī (d. *ca.* 1091/1680). The *s͟hayk͟h al-Islām* of Mas͟hhad, al-Ḥurr al-ᶜĀmilī (d. 1120/1708-9) was a fervent propagandist on its behalf. Rejecting the *id̲j̲tihād* and the *taḳlīd* of anyone who is not infallible (i.e. other than the Imām), Ak͟hbārism reflects the thought of religious dignitaries who prefer philosophy, hermeneutism and mysticism. By extolling reverence for the Imāms, it constituted, for the simple believers, an attractive element of S͟hīᶜism which gained in popularity. But with the anti-clerical policies of S͟hāh Ṣafī (1629-42) and of S͟hāh ᶜAbbās II (1642-66) and the resurgence of Ṣūfism in the mid-17th century, this tendency was to in part restored

before being rejected by the Imāmī hierocracy (*ibid.*, 146 ff. and below).

In fact, despite the advance of Akhbārism at the time of the decline and collapse of the Ṣafawids and throughout periods of disorder and instability (Afghan conquest and domination, 1722-9; reign of Nādir Shāh, 1736-47; Afshāri-Zand interregnum, until 1763), an Uṣūlī reaction emerged in the very bosom of the Madjlisī family, under Shāh Sulṭān Ḥusayn (1694-1722). In an effort to destroy popular devotion to Akhbārī-inspired Imāms, thus regaining it for himself, and to isolate the Ṣūfi and mystical trend of the élite, as a prelude to attacking it, Muḥammad Bāḳir Madjlisī adopted Uṣūlism. This reversal and this strategy (adopted by other *ᶜulamā*ʾ), had decisive consequences for the consolidation of an Imāmī hierocracy (*ibid.*, 151 ff.; on the Madjlisī family and its descendants see Cole (1985), 6 ff.).

During the years 1722-63, neo-Akhbārism was dominant in ᶜIrāḳ, especially among converts from Uṣūlism coming from Baḥrayn or Iran. But it was not long before in Iran and even in ᶜIrāḳ, Imāmī *ᶜulamā*ʾ were observed moving discreetly from Akhbārism to Uṣūlism. After a difficult period for the *ᶜulamā*ʾ, involving a kind of Sunni-Shīᶜī ecumenism (1736-51) imposed by the religious policy of Nādir Shāh, the Uṣūlī resurgence came about under the Zands, when Karīm Khān moved his centre of government to Shīrāz (1763-79). However, Karīm Khān had little regard for the *ᶜulamā*ʾ (Perry, 220 ff.) and the decisive struggles took place at the *ᶜatabāt* [*q.v.* in Suppl.], the Shīᶜī holy places of ᶜIrāḳ, where the Akhbārīs exploited alliances with wealthy financiers and even with heads of criminal gangs (the *lūṭīs* [*q.v.*]). The leading figure in this resurgence of Uṣūlism was Āḳā Sayyid Muḥammad Bāḳir Waḥīd al-Bihbahānī (d. 1208/1793-4 [*q.v.*]), considered the "renovator" (*mudjaddid*) of the 13th century of the Hidjra or as the founder (*muʾassis*) of Imāmī jurisprudence. He was linked both spiritually and genealogically to Muḥammad Bāḳir Madjlisī. Like other *ᶜulamā*ʾ of ᶜIrāḳ, he enjoyed the support of the merchant-artisan class (through the intermediary of family alliances). Forcibly imposing a reformulation of the Uṣūlī doctrine and refuting Akhbārism (*K. al-Idjtihād wa 'l-akhbār*), he went so far as to proclaim *takfīr* (excommunication) against the Akhbārīs, sending armed men (his *mirghaḍabs*) to harry them, and persecuted the Niᶜmatullāhī Ṣūfī order (Cole (1983), 39 ff.; idem, (1985), 13 ff.). Bihbahānī and his followers succeeded in "converting" to Uṣūlism numerous Akhbārīs, some of whom migrated towards Iran (in part on account of political tensions between Iran and the governor ᶜUmar Pasha concerning Iranian pilgrims, instability and outbreaks of plague). Some *ᶜulamā*ʾ of Northern India were then trained in the Uṣūlī doctrine, which they proceeded to canvass in India (Cole (1985), 21 ff.). The resurgence of Uṣūlism, which developed during the 1760s in the *ᶜatabāt*, was spread in Iran during the 1770s (*ibid*)., 26).

In the final phase of the conflict, the last important representative of the Akhbārī school, the *muḥaddith* Muḥammad b. ᶜAbd al-Nabī al-Nishābūrī al-Akhbārī, was discredited in the eyes of Fatḥ ᶜAlī Shāh Ḳādjār (1797-1834), who was at that time sympathetic towards Akhbārism, by the Shaykh Djaᶜfar Kāshif al-Ghiṭāʾ [*q.v.*] who declared him an infidel. In spite of the protests of the Shāh, he was expelled to ᶜIrāḳ and killed by the mob at al-Ḳāzimayn in 1233/1818 (Algar (1969), 65 ff.). Although the situation of the Akhbārīs subsequently declined rapidly, some groups survived and aspects or concepts of their doctrinal positions remained, especially in Shaykhism (generally considered as being founded by Shaykh Aḥmad al-Aḥsāʾī [*q.v.*], d. 1241/1826; see also McEoin, art. AL-AḤSĀʾĪ in *Encyclopaedia Iranica*, i, 674-9). According to Shaykhism, each believer has, in principle, a vocation to *idjtihād*, the only authority to be followed or imitated (*taḳlīd*) being that of the Hidden Imām (Corbin, iv, 252 f.).

4. The institution of *mardjaᶜiyyat-i taḳlīd*. Under the Ḳādjārs, relationships of power with the Imāmī hierocracy were ambiguous. Since Nādir Shāh, the state had lost the "imperio-papal" character on which Ṣafawid power had been based. Despite the continuation of the "separation-collaboration", Fatḥ ᶜAlī Shāh sought and obtained confirmation of a certain degree of legitimisation on the part of eminent *ᶜulamā*ʾ such as Mīrzā Abū 'l-Ḳāsim Ḳumī (d. 1233/1817-18), and Āḳā Sayyid Bihbahānī, grandson of Waḥīd Bihbahānī, who extolled Āḳā Muḥammad Khān and Fatḥ ᶜAlī Shāh as Ẓill Allāh ("Shadow of God") (Arjomand (1984), 221 ff.).

While continuing to express themselves through *fatwā*s or *takfīr*s against one or other hostile or rival tendency or person (Akhbārī, Shaykhī, Ṣūfī), the Imāmī *mudjtahid*s were consulted by the temporal authority regarding important issues. Anxious to assure himself of their support, Mīrzā ᶜĪsā Ḳāʾim-Maḳām, vizier of the crown prince ᶜAbbās Mīrzā, consulted them in connection with the threat of invasion on the eve of the first Irano-Russian conflict (1810-13). Their attitudes and their *fatwā*s which he collected in his *Risāla-yi djihādiyya* testify to their influence. The most significant initiative came from Shaykh Djaᶜfar Kāshif al-Ghiṭāʾ who—in the capacity of *niyābat-i ᶜāmma* of the *mudjtahid*s—authorised Fatḥ ᶜAlī Shāh to conduct the *djihād* in the name of the Hidden Imām (on the parallels and divergencies between the *Risāla-yi djihādiyya* and the positions adopted by Shaykh Djaᶜfar, see Lambton (1970 A), 187 ff.; cf. also Kohlberg (1976 B), 82 ff., Calder (1982 A), 6, and Arjomand (1984), 224 f.). This was also a time of re-assessment of the notion of *niyābat-i khāṣṣa*. Relating, in principle, to the only representatives of the Imāms (initially to the four *sufarā*ʾ), it became, with the endorsement of the *fuḳahā*ʾ, applicable to the just sovereign. Although the system of taxation had little connection with *djihād*, the subject was discussed at this time, with the *mudjtahid*s re-affirming their rights concerning *kharādj* and especially *khums* of which a half, considered to be *sahm-i Imām* ("the Imām's share"), should revert to them after the period of the *djihād* (Arjomand (1984), 229 f.).

The sharing of prerogatives between the *ᶜulamā*ʾ and the temporal power is well defined by Djaᶜfar Kashfī in his *Tuḥfat al-mulūk*. His dualist theory of legitimate authority, recalled by eminent *mudjtahid*s under Nāṣir al-Dīn Shah (1848-96), permitted the *ᶜulamā*ʾ to acquire financial autonomy and judicial rights independent of the state (*ibid.*, 225 ff.). But it was especially the reformulation of concepts or doctrines regarding the powers and functions of the *mudjtahid*s which led to a structuralisation of their leadership. Long discussions of *idjtihād* and *taḳlīd* culminated in establishing the competence of the *mudjtahid*s in guiding the *muḳallid*s ("imitators") in matters of *furūᶜ-i dīn* (i.e. the "branches" derived from "roots", *uṣūl*), the *taḳlīd* of a dead *mudjtahid* being definitively ruled out. The problem of the application of the *ḥudūd* during the *ghayba* continued to be thoroughly debated (*ibid.*, 231 ff.). The faithful

S̲h̲īʿī "being unable to understand the code" must entrust himself to the instructions of a jurist (Scarcia (1958 A), 237). The need for recourse to authorised interpreters of the *s̲h̲arīʿa*, in the name of the *niyābat-i ʿāmma*, is energetically reformulated by Mullā Aḥmad Narāḳī (d. 1245/1829-30) in *ʿAwāʾid al-ayyām*, where he employs the terms *wilāyat-i ʿāmma* and *wilāyat-i k̲h̲āṣṣa* to describe the delegation of devolved authority to the *mud̲j̲tahid*s in the name of the Hidden Imām (Kazemi Moussavi (1984); idem (1985), 40 ff.). Although making of the government of the jurisconsult (which he calls *salṭanat al-s̲h̲arʿiyya*) an independent subject of Imāmī *fiḳh*, he does not seem to have considered the latter obliged to supplant the existing power or to function in parallel with it (*ibid.*, 43 ff.).

A new and decisive step was taken, however, with the doctrinal formulation of the concept of *aʿlamiyyat* according to which the Imāmī community must follow or imitate the precepts of the most learned jurisconsult. Its premisses may be traced back to the Īlk̲h̲ānid period (it was then applied to the Imāms, but one celebrated *mud̲j̲tahid* then bore the title of "ʿAllāma" al-Ḥillī). Under the Ṣafawids, the term *aʿlam* is clearly applied to the Imāmī *mud̲j̲tahid*s (Ḥasan b. Zayn al-Dīn ʿĀmilī, *Maʿālim al-uṣūl*, quoted by Kazemi Moussavi, *ibid.*). When, after many cautious and hesitant attempts, the politico-religious context forced the Imāmī hierocracy to adopt a hierarchy, the rehabilitation of the concept of *aʿlamiyyat* took on its full importance, since the title of *mard̲j̲aʿ-i taḳlīd* was given to the most learned *mud̲j̲tahid*. In view of the obscurity surrounding the birth of the concept of *mard̲j̲aʿiyyat*—the initial signs of which may be traced back to the Ṣafawid period—the greatest *mud̲j̲tahid*s of the past have recently been reinstated, *a posteriori*, as prototype *mard̲j̲aʿ-i taḳlīd*s (on the lists, beginning with al-Kulaynī, d. 328/939, generally including sixty-three names and ending with Burūd̲j̲irdī, see Bagley (1970), 31; Hairi, 62 f.; Fischer, Appx. 2, 252 ff.). This tendency to reassess, in regard to a concept or a doctrine, the great figures of the past is also found in the tradition according to which the beginning of each century of the Hid̲j̲ra should be marked by a renewer of the religion (cf. a provisional list of S̲h̲īʿī *mud̲j̲addid*s in Momen, 206, Table 7).

Having been in a process of gestation since the rebirth of Uṣūlism with Waḥīd Bihbahānī, the concept of *mard̲j̲aʿiyyat* took on precise form under his successors. But neither Bihbahānī nor Aḥmad Narāḳī bore the title of *mard̲j̲aʿ-i taḳlīd* (although Bihbahānī and his immediate successor Sayyid Muḥammad Mahdī Ṭabāṭabāʾī "Baḥr al-ʿulūm", d. 1212/1797, are currently called *mard̲j̲aʿ-i taḳlīd* in S̲h̲īʿī biographical works: cf. McChesney, 168). For numerous *mud̲j̲tahid*s and ordinary worshippers in Iran and ʿIrāḳ, the first to have secured this title and this function was Ḥād̲j̲d̲j̲ī S̲h̲ayk̲h̲ Muḥammad Ḥasan Nad̲j̲afī, d. 1266/1849-50, known by the name of Ṣāḥib al-D̲j̲awāhir (i.e. the author of *D̲j̲awāhir al-kalām*, "The jewels of scholarship", the most remarkable post-Ṣafawid work of *fiḳh* (Cole (1983), 40 f.; McEoin (1983), 157). When the Imāmī community was riven by the rise of Bābism, Muḥammad Ḥasan Ṣāḥib al-D̲j̲awāhir appointed S̲h̲ayk̲h̲ Murtaḍā Anṣārī (d. 1281/1864) as his successor. Having initially offered it to Saʿīd al-ʿUlamāʾ Māzandarānī who refused it, Anṣārī occupied this function for fourteen years and became the single *mard̲j̲aʿ-i taḳlīd* (*mard̲j̲aʿ al-taḳlīd al-muṭlaḳ*) for the entire S̲h̲īʿī world. He encouraged Uṣūlī studies to a considerable extent and arranged direct payment of contributions (*sahm-i Imām*) to local centres of education. With him, the institution of *mard̲j̲aʿiyyat* attained its zenith. He defined its functions in the manual of ritual practice entitled *Sīrat al-nad̲j̲āt* ("The Way of Salvation"). All the Imāmī S̲h̲īʿī communities (Iran, ʿIrāḳ, India, the Caucasus and the Ottoman Empire) sent contributions to him representing considerable sums of money, yet he led a pious, simple and ascetic life. His political attitudes were moderate and he adopted a conciliatory policy towards the Bābīs, who treated him with respect. Some of his works became manuals (*Farāʾiḍ al-uṣūl*, *al-Makāsib*), and many of his pupils became *mud̲j̲tahid*s and even *mard̲j̲aʿ-i taḳlīd* (see Algar (1969), 162 ff.; Hairi, art. ANṢĀRĪ, in Suppl.; idem (1977), 63; Cole (1983), 40 ff.; Murtaḍā al-Anṣārī, list of his works, 131-4). Besides the piety and the wisdom of al-Anṣārī, the emergence of a single *mud̲j̲tahid* to occupy the supreme function of *mard̲j̲aʿiyyat* owes much to the disappearance of major Imāmī potentates as well as to the decline of Iṣfahān and the rise of Nad̲j̲af as an Imāmī religious centre (art. ANṢĀRĪ, in Suppl.; Kazemi Moussavi (1985), 45 f.).

Henceforward, it was in the *ʿatabāt*, especially at Nad̲j̲af, but also at Sāmarrā (site of the "catacomb" of the Hidden Imām), places of residence and instructions of the major *marād̲j̲iʿ-i taḳlīd*, that resistance was organised to Ḳād̲j̲ar autocracy and foreign domination. Although not political at the outset, the institution of *mard̲j̲aʿiyyat* became so, as a consequence of historical circumstances and the respective attitudes of each of the *mud̲j̲tahid*s. Unlike his predecessor, Anṣārī issued no directives concerning his succession. But his definition of the institutional and ideological role of *mard̲j̲aʿ-i taḳlīd aʿlā* ("supreme model") offered opportunities for the exercise of political prerogatives of which his followers took advance, beginning with his immediate successor, Mīrzā Muḥammad Ḥasan S̲h̲īrāzī (d. 1312/1894), who assumed the responsibility of issuing the *fatwā* to revoke a concession on Iranian tobacco awarded to a British company (the Excise Affair, *fatwā* of December 1891; cf. Bibl. in Hairi (1977), 111, n. 8).

The essential characteristic of the institution of *mard̲j̲aʿiyyat* in the 19th century is that the office was occupied successively by a single *mard̲j̲aʿ-i taḳlīd*. After the death of Mīrzā S̲h̲īrāzī, a number of *mud̲j̲tahid*s, equally qualified and unable to choose among themselves, were recognised as single *mard̲j̲aʿ* only after the demise of their colleagues. This tendency towards selection by longevity—working to the disadvantage of numerous highly-qualified *mud̲j̲tahid*s—was continued until the death of Burūd̲j̲irdī. Since the beginning of the institution, the list of *marād̲j̲iʿ-i taḳlīd* who exercised the function in a sole capacity for a greater of shorter period of time until their death is summarised as follows:

1. Ḥād̲j̲d̲j̲ī S̲h̲ayk̲h̲ Muḥammad Ḥasan Iṣfahānī Nad̲j̲afī, "Ṣāḥib al-D̲j̲awāhir" (d. at Nad̲j̲af 1266/1850).
2. S̲h̲ayk̲h̲ Murtaḍā Anṣārī (d. at Nad̲j̲af 1281/1864).
3. Mīrzā Ḥasan S̲h̲īrāzī, *mud̲j̲addid* of the 14th century of the Hid̲j̲ra (d. at Sāmarrā 1312/1895).
4. Mullā Muḥammad Kāẓim K̲h̲urāsānī, "Āk̲h̲und K̲h̲urāsānī" (d. at Nad̲j̲af, 1329/1911).
5. Ḥud̲j̲d̲j̲at al-Islām Sayyid Muḥammad Ḳāẓim Ṭabāṭabāʾī Yazdī (d. at Ḥuways̲h̲, near Nad̲j̲af, 1337/1919).
6. Mīrzā Muḥammad Taḳī Ḥāʾirī S̲h̲īrāzī (d. at Karbalā, 1338/1920).
7. S̲h̲ayk̲h̲ Faḍl Allāh Iṣfahānī "S̲h̲ayk̲h̲ al-S̲h̲arīʿa" (died 1338/1920, surviving his predecessor by only four months).
8. Ḥād̲j̲d̲j̲ī Sayyid Abu 'l-Ḥasan Mūsawī Isfahānī (d. at Kāẓimayn, 1365/1946).
9. Sayyid Āḳā Ḥusayn b. Muḥammad Ṭabāṭabāʾī

"Āyatullāh Ḳumī" (d. at Karbalā, 1366/1947, surviving his predecessor by only three months).
10. Āyatullāh al-ᶜUẓmā Ḥādjdjī Āḳā Ḥusayn Burūdjirdī (d. at Ḳum, 1380/1961).

After the death of Mīrzā Shīrāzī, religious leadership was shared between eminent *mudjtahids* of Nadjaf: Mullā Muḥammad Kāẓim Fāḍil Sharabyānī (d. 1322/1904); Shaykh Muḥammad Ḥasan b. ᶜAbd Allāh Mamaḳānī (d. 1323/1905); and Mīrzā Muḥammad Kāẓim Ākhund Khurasānī, who became sole *mardjaᶜ* after the death of Ṭihrānī. A disciple of Mīrzā Shīrāzī, Khurasānī was a fervent supporter of the constitutional revolution of 1905/11. With the *mudjtahids* Ṭihrānī and Māzandarānī, he issued *fatwās*, manifestos and telegrams and took part in the deposition of Muḥammad ᶜAlī Shāh (July 1909). He also campaigned against foreign influences and supported the Young Turk revolution (cf. Hairi, art. KHURĀSĀNĪ idem (1976) and (1977), 98 ff. and index; Momen, 246 f.). His successor, Sayyid Kāẓim Yazdī, abstained from political activity, refused to cooperate with the constitutionalist *ᶜulamāʾ* and cultivated amicable relations with the British after their occupation of ᶜIrāḳ (Hairi (1977), 96 ff., 117 ff. and index; Momen, 247). Mīrzā Muḥammad Taḳī Hāʾirī, resident at Karbalā, declared that he had no part in the constitutional revolution. He was a determined opponent of the British in ᶜIrāḳ, against whom he decreed a *djihād* in collaboration with other *ᶜulamāʾ* (Hairi (1977), 122 ff. and index).

With the revival of the centre of theological studies (*ḥawḍa-yi ᶜilmiyya*) of Ḳum, at the initiative of Shaykh ᶜAbd al-Karīm Yazdī Ḥāʾiri (d. 1937 [*q.v.* in Suppl.]), there was during the 1920s a period in which several high-ranking *mudjtahids* were considered as *mardjaᶜ-i taḳlīd*. For Iran, the rôle was entrusted, at Ḳum, to Ḥāʾirī; for Nadjaf, to Shaykh ᶜAbd Allāh Mamaḳānī (d. 1933), Shaykh Muḥammad Ḥusayn Nāʾīnī (d. 1936) and Shaykh Abu 'l-Ḥasan Iṣfahānī (d. 1946), who became sole *mardjaᶜ* after the death of the others. On the death of Āyatullāh Ḳumī (1947), Āyatullāh Burūdjirdī [*q.v.* in Suppl.] was recognised as sole *mardjaᶜ-i taḳlīd* (cf. below). Ḳum thus became the leading centre of Shīᶜī studies, although many students, especially those from Arab countries and the Indian subcontinent, continued to frequent Nadjaf. Following the example of Yazdī Ḥāʾirī and other *mudjtahids*, Burūdjirdī pursued a passive rôle in political matters. He occasionally collaborated with temporal authorities, especially from 1953 to 1958, and supported the anti-Bahāʾī campaign of 1955. It was not until shortly before the end of his life (1960) that he declared his opposition to the agrarian reforms proposed by the Shāh (see Algar (1972) 242 ff.; Akhavi (1980), 24, 77 ff., 102). Despite his title of Āyatullāh al-ᶜUẓmā (see below), and although his name has been mentioned as a *mudjaddid*, Burūdjirdī seems to have been acknowledged as the supreme *mardjaᶜ* in an organic rather than a charismatic sense (Binder, 132, MacEoin (1983), 161 f.). He succeeded no more than other *mudjtahids* in structuring the religious leadership to resist the initiatives of the Pahlavī régime which favoured as his successor Āyatullāh Shaykh Muḥsin al-Ḥakīm (d. 1970), an Arab *mudjtahid* resident at Nadjaf (Algar (1972), 244).

In the reformist religious movements of the "Islamic societies" (cf. above), besides discussion of doctrinal issues (*idjtihād, taḳlīd*, religious taxes, etc.), the idea was expressed that the function of *mardjaᶜiyyat* had become too heavy to be entrusted to a single *mudjtahid* and should be exercised by a "council for religious decrees" (*shūrā-yi fatwā*): M. Ṭāliḳānī, in *Baḥthī*, 201-13; M. Djazāʾirī, *ibid.*, 215-30. It was also proposed (by M. Muṭahharī) that, in accordance with the wishes of ᶜAbd al-Karīm Yazdī Hāʾirī, each *mudjtahid* should be "imitated" in the field of his speciality (cf. Lambton (1964), 127; Akhavi, 122 ff.). But the application of the ideas of this movement, revived in part in the 1970s by various reformist trends, did not open the way to a harmonious restructuring of the religious leadership, which henceforward became progressively more influenced by politics.

On the death of Burūdjirdī, the disintegration of the institution of *mardjaᶜiyyat* led to a dispersal of *mardjaᶜ*s: at Ḳum, the Āyatullāhs Sharīᶜatmādarī, Gulpāygānī and Marᶜashī-Nadjafī; at Mashhad, Āyatullāh Mīlānī (d. 1975); at Tehran, Āyatullāh Aḥmad Khwānsārī (d. 1985); at Nadjaf, the Āyatullāhs Khūʾī, ᶜAbd al-Hādī Shīrāzī (d. 1961), Kāshif al-Ghiṭāʾ and Muḥsin al-Ḥakīm. Other less important *mudjtahids* were also considered as *mardjaᶜ* (Momen, 248, n. 2).

While Mashhad [*q.v.*] for some rivalled Ḳum in importance, the events of 1963 catapulted Āyatullāh Khumaynī into pre-eminence in the capacity of *mardjaᶜ* (at Nadjaf, from 1965 onwards). With Mīlānī and Sharīᶜatmādarī, he was regarded as heir to Burūdjirdī (Algar (1972), 245), at least in Iran, since some consensus on the *mardjaᶜiyyat-i kull* of Muḥsin al-Ḥakīm seems to have been reached in about 1966 (Bagley (1970), 78, n. 7). In 1975 there were six *mardjaᶜ*s of senior rank: Khūʾī and Khumaynī at Nadjaf; Gulpāygānī, Sharīᶜatmādarī and Marᶜashī-Nadjafī at Ḳum; Khwānsārī in Tehran (Mīlānī died at Mashhad in August 1975). But there are also numerous lines of *mardjaᶜ-i taḳlīd*s linked by matrimonial alliances to the most important branches (see Fischer (1980), 88 ff., Fig. 3. 1. ff.).

After the death of Burūdjirdī, the Imāmī *ᶜulamāʾ*, together with the laity, were divided into various groups: radicals wishing to establish Islamic justice; social reformers; conservative heirs to the line of Burūdjirdī; collaborators with the Pahlavī régime (Akhavi, 199 ff.). The three first tendencies are to be found in the Islamic Republic of Iran (since February 1979), where rivalries have rent the religious leadership. The concept of *wilāyat-i faḳīh* reformulated by Āyatullāh Khumaynī could be considered as the logical conclusion to the development of Imāmī religious institutions since the Ṣafawids, absolute political power being regained and reverting *de facto* to the *mardjaᶜ-i taḳlīd*, supporters of the idea of collective *mardjaᶜiyyat* (including Āyatullāh Ṭāliḳānī, d. 1979) thus being defeated (Fragner, 98; see also the analysis of Calder (1982) regarding Khumaynī's position regarding Shīᶜī jurisprudence; F. Rajaee (1983) on Khumaynī's attitude towards man, the state and international politics etc.; see also Rose (1983)). But this new situation has in fact led to another schism in the institution of *mardjaᶜiyyat*; the most influential of the *marādjiᶜ* before the Islamic revolution, Āyatullāh Sharīᶜatmādarī, a man of moderate tendency who retained numerous supporters, especially among the people of Ādharbāydjan, his native region, was progressively isolated and then, accused of subversion, deposed from his position as Āyatullāh al-ᶜUẓmā in April 1982 (Momen, 296, 320). Some pious Imāmīs follow the leader of the revolution in political matters and that of one or other of the *marādjiᶜ* in religious practice (the one with the largest following now, in 1986, apparently being Āyatullāh Khūʾī who also enjoys a large following in the Arab world, India and Pakistan). It seems, however, that for the new generation of Imāmī *ᶜulamāʾ*, the doctrine of *wilāyat-i faḳīh* has ultimately prevailed (Momen, 296 ff.). It is in this context that there is taking place the muted struggle over succession to Āyatullāh/Imām Khumaynī, the Assembly of Experts (*madjlis-i khibrigān*, created at the end of 1982, a group of seventy-two experts chosen to appoint the future supreme *mardjaᶜ*) having recently (October 1986) criticized the "heir-apparent", Āyatullāh Muntaẓirī; Ḥudjdjat al-Islām Rafsandjānī, President of Parliament, now appears to be a possible successor.

5. Qualifications, selection, functions, consultative rôle and titles of the *mardjaᶜ-i taḳlīd*. Among the conditions necessary for assuming the position of *mardjaᶜ-i taḳlīd*, six are judged indispensable: maturity (*bulūgh*), intelligence (*ᶜaḳl*), faith (*īmān*), justice (*ᶜadālat*), being of legitimate birth (*ṭahārat-i mawlid*) and of the male sex (*dhukūrat*; some women may, under exceptional circumstances, attain the level of *idjtihād*, but they cannot be *mardjaᶜ-i taḳlīd*). Other conditions are sometimes required: literacy, possession of hearing and sight, and being free, i.e. not a slave (Algar (1969), 8 f., following Burūdjirdī, Sanglādjī). In addition to these preliminary conditions, the future *mardjaᶜ* must be qualified to practice *idjtihād*, receive the *idjāza* from *ᶜulamāʾ* of repute and demonstrate his knowledge through his teaching, his sermons, his discussions, his writings, etc. The *mardjaᶜ* must be generally acknowledged as the most learned (*aᶜlam*) person of his time. However, this title cannot be awarded to him through appointment, selection or election. His authority can only be confirmed by the universal recognition of the Imāmī community (Hairi (1977), 62; it seems however that there was at Ḳum a kind of "college of cardinals" deciding on the choice of the supreme *mardjaᶜ*, the Āyatullāh al-ᶜUẓmā; see Binder, 134).

The essential function of the *mardjaᶜ-i taḳlīd*—also called *muḳallad*—is to guide the community of those who "imitate" his teaching and follow his precepts, in particular concerning the following: application of the rules of the *sharīᶜa* (*furūᶜ-i dīn*); judicial solutions or legal qualifications (*aḥkām*) in regard to the problems of contemporary life. Imitation or emulation of the *mardjaᶜ* has no connection, in principle, with the *uṣūl-i dīn* which are derived from faith (*īmān*) and from inner conviction (*yaḳīn*). The *mudjtahid* established as *mardjaᶜ* must pronounce judicial decisions (*fatwās*) and write one or more books to guide his *muḳallids* (*risāla-yi ᶜamaliyya*, a kind of practical treatise; *tawḍīḥ al-masāʾil*, "explanation of problems" etc.).

For his part, the *muḳallid* has particular duties, especially as regards consultation of the *mardjᶜ-i taḳlīd* to whom access is sometimes difficult. The rules of conduct in this respect are explained at length by Anṣārī who forbids *taḳlīd* of a dead *mudjtahid* and stresses the role of the most learned (*aᶜlam*) *mudjtahid* in sanctioning worship and ritual. Every *muḳallid* is obliged to consult him, to follow or to "imitate" him, either directly, or in a case of obvious impossibility, through the intermediacy of an honest man who has himself witnessed to conduct of the *mardjaᶜ*, or through consultation of a book of rules of behaviour written by the latter. In cases of doubt or contradiction, prudence (*iḥtiyāṭ*) is recommended (on these complicated rules for consultation of the *mardjaᶜ*, see the analysis in the *Sīrat al-nadjāt* of Anṣārī, in Cole (1983), 42 ff.). These criteria represent only general principles, no specific process having been established for the choice of a *mardjaᶜ* (cf. Algar (1969), 10).

With the development of the concept of *mardjaᶜiyyat*, the economic power enjoyed by the *mudjtahids* has been concentrated in the hands of one man or of a small group of men. Besides the collection and distribution of *zakāt* and *khums*, the administration of *waḳf/awḳāf* (taken under state control by the Pahlavīs), the *mudjtahids* have economic and family ties with the merchant-artisan class of the *bāzār*. Imāmī *ᶜulamāʾ* have also sometimes taken advantage of threats posed to political authority by movements such as the Ṣūfīs, Shaykhīs, Bābīs, etc. In fact, they have taken the initiative in countering or representing the doctrines and activities of groups seeking to find alternative solutions to the prolonged absence of the Hidden Imām (*wilāyat-i ṣūfī*, *shīᶜa-yi kāmil, rukn-i rābiᶜ* ("fourth pillar" of Shaykhism), *bāb*, etc.). Despite periods of tension or confrontation, *mudjtahids* and *marādjiᶜ* claiming the *niyābat-i ᶜāmma* have in varying degrees given a certain amount of support to the existing temporal power and have formulated a "variable approach" towards accommodation with an illegal régime established *de facto* (cf. Calder (1982), 6). However, remaining generally mistrustful of both spiritual and temporal powers, the *marādjiᶜ* claimed for themselves an important role in the political life of Ḳādjar Iran (see especially Algar (1969)). Although abstaining from political activity, Anṣārī formulated the notion of *mardjaᶜ-i taḳlīd-i aᶜlā* which offers the potential for political utilisation (cf. Cole (1983), 46 and below). Some of his successors have strongly resisted foreign economic, cultural and political influences favoured by the international context and by the political choices of the Ḳādjārs. They nevertheless held extremely diverse opinions regarding the events of the constitutional revolution of 1905-11 (cf. Lambton (1970 B); Hairi (1976-7), (1977), 55 ff.; Arjomand (1981)). In fact, neither the supporters nor the opponents of the constitution have ever preached the establishment of a government directly controlled by the *mudjtahids*. It is quite clear that recent events in the Middle East (in particular the seizure of power by the religious in Iran (1979), the Iran-ᶜIrāḳ war (since 1980) and the situation in Lebanon) have added to the difficulties of Shīᶜī believers, increasingly preoccupied with political choices and economic problems.

Since the Ḳādjār period, the number of titles and functions, civil as well as religious, has increased considerably in Iran. This has given rise to abuses, especially as regards the title of Āyatullāh [*q.v.* in Suppl.], often used to denote a *mardjaᶜ-i taḳlīd*. Although the distinctions remain somewhat fluid, current usage seems to describe a *mardjaᶜ-i taḳlīd* by the epithet *Āyatullāh al-ᶜUẓmā*, the term *Āyatullāh* alone being used to describe a *mudjtahid* and *Ḥudjdjat al-Islām* an aspiring *mudjtahid* (Momen, 205 f.). According to a recent decree of Khumaynī (September 1984), certain *ᶜulamāʾ* who used to call themselves *Āyatullāh* are henceforward to bear the title of *Ḥudjdjat al-Islām* (Momen, 298 f.; the two titles having been used interchangeably until the creation of the *ḥawḍa-yi ᶜilmiyya* of Ḳum in the 1920s: Djalāl Matīnī, 583 ff.). The question may be asked whether the replacement of the title of *Āyatullāh* by that of *Imām* to designate Khumaynī implies a change in the religious hierarchy (i.e. the creation of a title superior to that of *Āyatullāh al-ᶜUẓmā*) or is simply an indication of political function (Momen, *ibid.*; on these problems of Shīᶜī titles and their historical precedents, see Djalāl Matīnī; on the epithet *Imām* for Khumaynī, 603 f.).

Bibliography and abbreviations: Concerning the abundant literature on the Imāmī *uṣūl*, see H. Löschner, *Die dogmatischen Grundlagen des šīᶜitischen Rechts*, Cologne, Berlin, etc. 1971; Brunschvig [1970]; Abu 'l-Ḳāsim Gurdjī, *Nigāhī bi taḥawwul-i ᶜilm-i uṣūl*, in *Maḳālāt wa barrasīha*, xiii-xvi, 1352; H. Mudarrisī Ṭabāṭabāʾī, *An introduction* to Shiʿi law. A bibliographical study*, London 1984 (presentation of the great, classical treatises plus a list of the modern ones and their various divisions; takes Ṭihrānī, *al-Dharīʿa*, into account); among the numerous Imāmī biographical works, see ʿAlī Shāh, *Ṭarāʾiḳ al-ḥaḳāʾiḳ* (on the Ṣūfīs and *ʿulamāʾ*), 3 vols., Tehran n.d.; Muḥsin al-Amīn, *Aʿyān al-Shīʿa*, Beirut, from 1960; Muḥammad ʿAlī Muʿallim Ḥabībābādī, *Makārim al-āthār*..., 5 *djilds* in 4 vols., Isfahan n.d.; Muḥammad Bāḳir Khʷānsārī, *Rawḍat al-djannāt fī aḥwāl al-ulamāʾ wa 'l-sādāt*, Tehran 1367/1947 (new ed., 8 vols. 1970); Shaykh ʿAbbās al-Ḳumī, *Fawāʾid al-riḍāwiyya fī aḥwāl ʿulamāʾ al-madhhab al-djaʿfariyya*, Tehran n.d.; Nūr al-Dīn ʿAlī Munʿal-i Ḳumī, *Tadhkira-yi mashāyikh-i Ḳum*, Ḳum 1353; Muḥammad ʿAlī Mudarris Tabrīzī, *Rayḥānat al-adab*, 8 vols., Tabrīz 1967; Āḳā Buzurg Ṭihrānī, *al-Dharīʿa ilā taṣānīf al-Shīʿa*, 25 vols., Tehran and Nadjaf 1355-98/1936-78; idem, *Ṭabaḳāt aʿlām al-Shīʿa*, Nadjaf and Beirut, from 1373/1953-4; Muḥammad Tunakābunī, *Ḳiṣaṣ al-ʿulamāʾ*, Tehran n.d.; see also detailed bibls. in the works cited below, esp.: Algar [1969], Arjomand [1984], Calder [1979], Cole [1984] and [1985], Fischer, McChesney, MacEoin [1979], Momen, etc.).

Sh. Akhavi, *Religion and politics in contemporary Iran*, New York 1980; H. Algar, *Religion and state in Iran 1795-1906*, Berkeley and Los Angeles 1969; idem, *The oppositional role of the Ulama in twentieth-century Iran*, in *Scholars*, 1972, 231-55; idem, *Shiʿism and Iran in the eighteenth century*, in *Studies in eighteenth century Islamic history*, ed. Th. Naff and R. Owen, London and Amsterdam 1977, 288-302; Murtaḍā al-Anṣārī, *Zindagānī wa shakhṣiyyat-i Shaykh Anṣārī*, (Ahwāz?) 1380/1960-1; S. A. Arjomand, *Religion, political action and legitimate domination in Shiʾite Iran: fourteenth to eighteenth centuries A.D.*, in *Archives Européennes de Sociologie*, xx (1979), 59-109; idem, *The Ulama's traditionalist opposition to Parliamentarism 1907-1909*, in *MES*, xvii/2 (1981), 174-90; idem, *The office of Mulla-bashi in Shiʿite Iran*, in *Stud. Isl.*, vii (1983), 135-46; idem, *The Shadow of God and the Hidden Imam. Religion, political order and social change in Iran from the beginning to 1890*, Chicago and London 1984 (numerous articles taken from this work in *Archives Européennes de Sociologie* [xx, 1979; xxii, 1981], *Journal of Asian History* [xv, 1981], *JESHO*, xxviii/2 [1985]); J. Aubin, *Etudes Safavides. I. Šāh Ismāʿīl et les notables de l'Iraq persan*, in *JESHO*, ii (1959), 27-81; F.R.C. Bagley, *Religion and the state in modern Iran. I*, in *Actes du Ve Congrès international d'arabisants et d'islamisants*, Brussels 1970, 75-88; idem, *ibid. II*, in *Procs. of the VIth Congress of Arabic and Islamic Studies*, Visby-Stockholm 1972 (ed. F. Rungren, Uppsala 1975), 31-44; *Baḥthī* = Ṭabāṭabāʾī *et alii*, *Baḥthī dar bāra-yi mardjaʿiyyat wa rūḥāniyyat*, Tehran 1341/1962, new ed., n.p., n.d. 1979); Hanna Batata, *Shiʿi organizations in Iraq; al Da'wah al-Islamiyah and al-Mujahidin*, in R.I Cole and N.R. Keddie, eds, *Shiʿism and social protest*, New Haven and London, 1986, 179-200; M. Bāzargān, *Intiẓārāt-i mardum az marādjiʿ*, in *Baḥthī*, 103-27; M. Bihishtī, *Rūḥāniyyat dar Islām wa dar miyān-i Muslimīn*, in *Baḥthī*, 131-61; L. Binder, *The proofs of Islam: religion and politics in Iran*, in *Arabic and Islamic studies in honor of Hamilton A.R. Gibb*, ed. G. Makdisi, Leiden 1965, 118-40; R. Brunschvig, *Les uṣūl al-fiqh imâmites à leur stade ancien (X^e et XIe siècles)*, in *Shīʿisme imâmite*, Paris 1970, 201-13; N. Calder, 1979A = *The structure of authority in Imami jurisprudence*, London Univ. Ph.D. thesis, 1979 unpubl.; idem, 1979B = *Judicial authority in Imami jurisprudence*, in *Bull. British Society for Middle Eastern Studies*, vi (1979), 104-8; idem, *Zakāt in Imāmī Shīʿī jurisprudence from the tenth to the sixteenth century A.D.*, in *BSOAS*, xliv/3 (1981), 468-80; idem, 1982A = *Accommodation and revolution in Imami Shiʿi jurisprudence: Khumayni and the classical tradition*, in *MES*, xviii (1982), 3-20; idem, 1982B = *Khums in Imami Shiʿi jurisprudence from the tenth to the sixteenth century A.D.*, in *BSOAS*, xlv/1 (1982), 39-47; J. Calmard, *Le chiisme imamite en Iran à l'époque seldjoukide d'après le Kitāb al-naqḍ*, in *Le monde iranien et l'Islam*, i (1971), 43-67; idem, *Le culte de l'Imām Ḥusayn. Étude sur la commémoration du drame de Karbalā dans l'Iran pré-safavide*, diss. Paris 1975; idem, *Les olamâ, le pouvoir et la société en Iran: le discours ambigu de la hiérocratie*, in *Le cuisinier et le philosophe. Hommage à Maxime Rodinson*, ed. J. P. Digard, Paris 1982, 253-61; J. R. Cole, *Imami jurisprudence and the role of the Ulama: Morteza Ansari on emulating the supreme exemplar*, in *Religion and Politics* (1983), 33-46; idem, *Imami Shiʿism from Iran to North India 1722-1856: state, society and clerical ideology in Awadh*, UCLA Ph.D. thesis 1984, unpubl.; idem, *Shiʿi clerics in Iraq and Iran: The Akhbari-Usuli conflict reconsidered*, in *Iranian Studies*, xviii/1 (1985), 3-34; H. Corbin, *En Islam iranien. Aspects spirituels et philosophiques*, 4 vols., Paris 1971-2; M. Djazāʾirī, *Taḳlīd-i aʿlam ya shūrā-yi fatwā*, in *Baḥthī*, 215-30; J. Eliash, *The Ithna ʿAshari-Shiʿi juristic theory of political and legal authority*, in *Stud. Isl.*, xxix (1969), 17-30; idem, *Misconceptions regarding the judicial status of the Iranian ʿUlamāʾ*, in *IJMES*, x/1 (1979), 9-25; M. M. J. Fischer, *Iran. From religious dispute to revolution*, Cambridge, Mass. and London 1980; B. Fragner, *Von den Staatstheologen zum Theologenstaat. Religiöse Führung und historischer Wandel im schiʿitischen Persien*, in *WZKM*, lxxv (1983), 73-98; C. Frank, *Über den schiitischen Mudschtahid*, in *Islamica*, ii (1926), 176-92; E. Glassen, *Schah Esmāʿīl und die Theologen seiner Zeit*, in *Isl.*, xlviii (1972), 254-68; K. H. Göbel, *Moderne Schiitische Politik und Staatsidee*..., Opladen 1984; Abdul-Hadi Hairi, *Why did the ʿulama participate in the Persian Constitutional Revolution of 1905-1909?*, in *WI*, xvii (1976-7), 124-54; idem, *Shiʿism and constitutionalism in Iran*, Leiden 1977; J. M. Hussain, *The occultation of the Twelfth Imam*, Cambridge 1982; S. A. Kazemi Moussavi, *Zindagī wa nakhsh-i fiḳāhatī-yi Mullā Aḥmad Narāḳī*, in *Nashr-i dānish*, iv/3 (1363/1984), 4-8; idem, *The establishment of the position of marjaʿiyyat-i taklid in the Twelver-Shiʿi community*, in *Iranian Studies*, xviii/1 (1985), 35-51; N. R. Keddie, *The roots of the Ulama's power in Modern Iran*, in *Scholars* (1972), 211-29 (also in *St. Isl.*, xxix [1969], 31-53); E. Kohlberg, 1976A = *From Imamiyya to Ithna-ʿashariyya*, in *BSOAS*, xxxix (1976), 521-34; idem, 1976B = *The development of the Imami Shi'i doctrine of Jihad*, in *ZDMG*, cxxvi (1976), 64-86; A. K. S. Lambton, *Quis custodiet custodes? Some reflections on the Persian theory of government*, in *St. Isl.*, v (1955), 125-48, vi (1955), 125-46; eadem, *A reconsideration of the position of the marjaʿ al-taqlīd and the religious institution*, in *St. Isl.*, xx (1964), 115-35; eadem (1970A) = *A nineteenth century view of Jihād*, in *St. Isl.*, xxiii (1970), 181-92; eadem, (1970B) = *The Persian ʿulamā and constitutional reform*, in *Le Shiʿisme imâmite*, 245-69; R. D. McChesney, *The life and intellectual development of an eighteenth century Shiʿi scholar Sayyid Muhammad Mahdī Ṭabāṭabāʾī "Baḥr al-ʿulūm"*, in *Folia Orientalia*, xxii (1981-4), 163-84; M. J. McDermott, *The theology of Shaikh al-Mufid (d. 413/1022)*, Beirut 1978; D. M.

MacEoin, *From Shaykhism to Babism: a study in charismatic renewal in Shiʿi Islam*, Cambridge Univ. Ph.D. thesis 1979, unpubl.; idem, *Changes in charismatic authority in Qajar Shiʿism*, in *Qajar Iran 1800-1925. Studies presented to Professor L. P. Elwell-Sutton*, ed. E. Bosworth and C. Hillenbrand, Edinburgh 1983; W. Madelung, *A treatise of the Sharīf al-Murtaḍā on the legality of working for the government*, in *BSOAS*, xliii (1980), 18-31; idem, *Shiʿite discussions on the legality of the Kharaj*, in *Procs. of the Ninth Congress of the Union Européenne des Arabisants et Islamisants*, Leiden 1981; idem, *Authority in Twelver Shiʿism in the absence of the Imam*, in *La notion d'autorité au Moyen Age. Islam, Byzance, Occident*, ed. G. Makdisi, Paris 1982, 163-73; Djalāl Matīnī, *Baḥthī dar bāra-yi sabiḳa-i tarīkhī-yi alḳāb wa ʿanāwīn-i ʿulamāʾ dar madhhab-i shīʿa*, in *Iran Nameh*, i/4 (1983), 560-608; H. Modarresi Tabatabaʾi, *Kharaj in Shiʿi law*, Oxford Univ. Ph.D. thesis 1982, unpubl.; M. Momen, *An introduction to Shiʿi Islam*, New Haven and London 1985; R. Mottahedeh, *Loyalty and leadership in an early Islamic society*, Princeton 1980; M. Muṭahharī, *Idjtihād dar Islām*, in *Baḥthī*, 35-68; idem, *Mushkil-i asāsī dar sāzmān-i rūḥāniyyat*, in *ibid.*, 165-98; idem, *Mazāyā wa khidmāt-i marḥūm Āyatullāh Burūdjirdī*, in *ibid.*, 223-49; J. R. Perry, *Karim Khan Zand. A history of Iran 1747-1779*, Chicago 1979; F. Rajaee, *Islamic values and world view. Khomeyni on Man, the State and International Politics*, Lanham, New York and London 1983; M. Ramyar, *Shaykh Ṭūsī*, Edinburgh Univ. Ph.D. thesis, 1977, unpubl.; *Religion and politics in Iran*, ed. N. R. Keddie, New Haven and London 1983; G. Rose, *Velayat-e Faqih and the recovery of Islamic identity in the thought of Ayatollah Khomeini*, in *Religion and politics* (1983), 166-88; A. Sachedina, *al-Khums. The fifth in the Imami Shiʿi legal system*, in *JNES*, xxxix/4 (1980), 275-89; idem, *Islamic messianism: the idea of the Mahdi in Twelver Shiʿism*, Albany 1981; G. Scarcia, *A proposito del problema della sovranità presso gli Imamiti*, in *AIUON*, N.S. vii (1957), 95-126; idem, *Stato e dottrine attuali della setta sciita imamita degli Shaikhi in Persia*, in *Studie e Materiali di Storia della Religioni*, xxix/2 (1958), 215-41; idem, (1958A) = *Intorno alle controversie tra Aḫbārī e Uṣūlī presso gli Imamiti di Persia*, in *RSO*, xxxiii (1958), 211-50; idem, *Kermān 1905: La "guerra tra šeiḫī e bālādsarī"*, in *AIUON*, N.S. xiii (1963), 195-238; B. Scarcia Amoretti, *L'imamismo in Iran nell'epoca Seldgiuchide: a proposito del problema della "communita"*, in *La Bisaccia dello Sheikh. Omaggio ad Alessandro Bausani*, Venice 1981, 127-40; *Scholars* = *Scholars, saints and Sufis*, ed. N. R. Keddie, Berkeley and Los Angeles 1972; *Shiʿisme imâmite* = *Le Shiʿisme imâmite*, ed. T. Fahd, Paris 1970; A. Tabari, *The role of the clergy in modern Iranian politics*, in *Religion and Politics* (1983), 47-72; M. H. Ṭabāṭabāʾī, *Idjtihād wa taḳlīd dar Islām wa Shīʿa*. in *Baḥthī*, 13-22; idem, *Wilāyat wa ziʿāmat*, in *ibid.*, 71-99; M. Ṭāliḳānī, *Tamarkuz wa ʿadam-i tamarkuz dar mardjaʿiyyat wa fatwā*, in *ibid.*, 201-11; idem, *Mālikiyyat dar Islām*, n.p., n.d.; idem, *Djihād wa shihādat*, Tehran 1385/1965; W. M. Watt, *The significance of the early stages of Imami Shiʿism*, in *Religion and Politics* (1983), 21-32; Abu 'l-Faḍl Mūsawī Zandjānī, *Sharāʾiṭ wa waẓāʾif-i mardjaʿ*, dans *Baḥthī*, 25-31. (J. Calmard)

MARDJĀN (A.), coral. As a rule, red coral (*Corallium rubrum*) is used as a piece of jewelry; the black and white coral are also mentioned. The Persian term *bussadh*, often employed as a synonym, strictly speaking is the root of the coral "which grows as a stone in the sea in the same way as a tree on land" (al-Ḳazwīnī, *Cosmography*, i, 212,7), as well as the subsoil to which it is stuck.

With the pearl (*luʾluʾ* [*q.v.*]) and amber (*kahrubā* [*q.v.*]), the coral belongs to the organic products which were however, as in our time, mostly associated with the precious stones (*djawāhir*), i.e. the minerals (*maʿādin*). The most detailed information on the coral is given by al-Tīfāshī (see *Bibl.*), according to which the coral belongs to the mineral kingdom on the one hand because of its petrification (*taḥadjdjur*), and to the vegetable one on the other because it grows on the bottom of the sea like a tree with branches and twigs. For the rest, descriptions are taken over from Antiquity. According to Theophrastus, the coral, which grows in the sea, is like a stone, red and round like a carrot (*De lapidibus*, 38). Pliny (*Historia naturalis*, xxxii, 11) repeats a number of older tales on the way coral is won. He describes it as a shrub which, on green stalks, sprouts green, soft berries which petrify, turn red the moment they come out of the water and look like cornelians. According to Aristotle, the coral is "a red-coloured stone which grows in the sea. If put in dung and putrescent material, it is often used [chemically]" (al-Ḳazwīnī, *Cosmography*, i, 238, 5-6). According to the so-called "Stone-book of Aristotle", the coral grows in the way branches do, and puts forth thin or thick twigs (*Kitāb al-Aḥdjār*, see *Bibl.*).

As opposed to these relatively sober statements, Ps.-Apollonius of Tyana [see BALĪNŪS] enlarges and speculates upon the double vegetable-mineral nature of the coral: "It resembles the waterplants; it originates from fire and earth through the intermediary of water... its body is mineral-like because hot fire and dry earth combine in it with the help of water, but its spirit is vegetable-like because water acts as a mediator... when water, warmed by the sun, absorbs the dryness of the earth, it becomes able, in its turn, to attract the warmth and dryness of the sun, and so the coral grows gradually like a plant; in cold air however it petrifies... its vegetable character is shown by the fact that it grows and branches in proportion to the warmth which the water, mixed with dryness, causes to mount in it as nourishment", see *Sirr al-khalīḳa wa-ṣan ʿat al-ṭabīʿa. Buch über das Geheimnis der Schöpfung und die Darstellung der Natur*, ed. Ursula Weisser, Aleppo 1979, 348, 7-351,8; cf. also the shortened translation by the same author in *Das "Buch über das Geheimnis der Schöpfung" von Pseudo-Apollonius von Tyana*, Berlin-New York 1980, 120 f. (*Ars medica*, iii, 2). In al-Tīfāshī, who in general quotes Apollonius extensively, the same passage is found on p. 178 f.

Coral is repeatedly said to be won at Marsā 'l-Kharaz (= La Calle in Algeria); from a boat, a wooden cross, weighted with a stone, is sunk on a rope to the bottom of the sea; the boat sails up and down so that the corals get caught at the extremities of the cross, which then is weighed with a jerk. Then emerges a body with a brown crust, branched like a tree. On the markets, these corals are abraded until they shine and show the desired red colour, then are sold in great quantities at a low price. Spain, Sicily and "the Frankish" i.e. probably the European, coast are given as other finding places. From the western Mediterranean, still nowadays the main deposit area of coral, it is shipped to the Orient, the Yemen, India and East Asia. At the finding places, coral is put on the market in quantities of 10.5 Egyptian *raṭls*, costing, in Egypt and ʿIrāḳ, 1,020 *dirhams* if polished, 1,100 *dirhams* if unpolished. Otherwise, prices fluctuate greatly according to the market situation (al-Dimashḳī, *Kitāb al-Ishāra ilā maḥāsin al-tidjāra*, in Wiedemann, *Aufsätze*, i, 858).

In medicine, coral is used above all in collyria against eye diseases (full description by al-Tamīmī, see *Bibl.*). Dioscurides deals with it under κουράλιον, var. κοράλλιον (in the Arabic translation, *kūrāliyūn*), and mentions the λιθόδενδρον "stone-tree" as a synonym because of the above-mentioned vegetable-mineral double nature of the coral. It is astringent and cooling, reduces proliferations, is effective against haemorrhage, softens the spleen and is a proved remedy against blockage of the urinary tracts. The curative property of the branches and roots is heightened if they are crushed, put in a clay jar, burned overnight in an oven and then baked. Mixed with tooth-powder, pounded coral cleanses and whitens the teeth, purifies the interstices between them, strengthens the gums and removes cavities in the roots. Until today, pulverised coral serves in the Orient as an anti-epilepticum and as a remedy against dysentery.

Bibliography: Dioscurides, *De materia medica*, ed. M. Wellmann, lib. V 121 = tr. Stephanos-Ḥunayn, *Hayūlā 'l-ṭibb*, ed. C. Dubler and E. Terés, Tetuán-Barcelona 1952-57, v, 102; Jutta Schönfeld, *Über die Steine. Das 14. Kapitel aus dem "Kitāb al-Muršid" des ... at-Tamīmī*, Freiburg 1976, 71-7, and commentary 164-7 (thorough and stimulating); Bīrūnī, *K. al-Djāmāhir fī maʿrifat al-djawāhir*, Ḥaydarābād 1355, 137 f., 189-93; Ibn Biklarish, *K. al-Mustaʿīnī*, ms. Naples, Bibl. Naz. III, F. 65, fol. 23b,9; Ibn Hubal, *Mukhtārāt*, Ḥaydarābād 1362, ii, 42; Mūsā b. ʿUbayd Allāh, *Sharḥ asmāʾ al-ʿuḳḳār. Un glossaire de la matière médicale composé par Maïmonide*, ed. M. Meyerhof, Cairo 1940, no. 227; Ibn al-Bayṭār, *Djāmiʿ*, Būlāḳ 1291, i, 93,20-94,18 (= Leclerc no. 282); Tīfāshī, *K. Azhār al-afkār fī djawāhir al-aḥdjār*, ed. M. Yūsuf Ḥasan and M. Basyūnī Khafādjī, Cairo 1977, 178-85; cf. J. Clément-Mullet, *Essai sur la minéralogie arabe*, new impr. Amsterdam n.d. 173-7; Yūsuf b. ʿUmar al-Ghassānī, *Muʿtamad*, ed. Muṣṭafā al-Saḳḳā, Beirut 1395/1975, 24 f.; Ḳazwīnī, *K. ʿAdjāʾib al-makhlūḳāt wa-gharāʾib al-mawdjūdāt. Kosmographie*, ed. F. Wüstenfeld, Göttingen 1848/49, i, 212, 238, tr. J. Ruska, *Das Steinbuch aus der Kosmographie des... al-Ḳazwīnī*, 9, 36 f. (*Beilage zum Jahresbericht 1895/96 der prov. Oberrealschule Heidelberg*); Ibn al-Ḳuff, *ʿUmda*, Ḥaydarābād 1356, i, 220, cf. H.G. Kircher, *Die "Einfachen Heilmittel" aus dem "Handbuch der Chirurgie" des Ibn al-Quff*, Ph.D. thesis Bonn 1967, no. 40; Anṭākī, *Tadhkira*, Cairo 1371/1952, i, 75, 4-20; *Tuḥfat al-aḥbāb, glossaire de la matière médicale marocaine*, ed. H. P. J. Renaud and G. S. Colin, Paris 1934, no. 73; Dozy, *Suppl.* ii, 578 f.; W. Heyd, *Histoire du commerce du Levant au Moyen-Age*, Leipzig 1885-6, ii, 609 f.; M. Berthelot, *La chimie au Moyen Age*, i, 1893 (new impr. Osnabrück-Amsterdam 1967), 14, 75, 187, 200, 208, 211, 263 (based on Latin sources); *K. al-Aḥdjār li-Arisṭāṭālīs. Das Steinbuch des Aristoteles*, ed. and tr. J. Ruska, Heidelberg 1912, no. 53; M. A. H. Ducros, *Essai sur le droguier populaire arabe de l'Inspectorat des Pharmacies au Caire*, Cairo 1930, no. 215; E. Wiedermann, *Aufsätze zür arabischen Wissenschaftsgeschichte*, ed. W. Fischer, Hildesheim-New York 1970, i, 858, 868 f. (A. Dietrich)

MARDJUMAK AḤMAD [see MERDJÜMEK, AḤMED B. ILYĀS].

MAREA [see MĀRYĀ].

MARGHELĀN [see MARGHĪNĀN].

MARGHĪNĀN, later form Marghelān, a town of Farghāna [*q.v.*] in Central Asia, situated to the south of the Sīr Daryā [*q.v.*] or Jaxartes, on a small river now called the Margelan Say.

It was a place of modest importance in the first Islamic centuries as one of the main towns, with *inter alia* Andidjān [*q.v.*], of the district of Farghāna known as Lower Nasyā; according to al-Mukaddasī, 272 (see also Le Strange, *Lands*, 479; Ibn Ḥawḳal[2], 513-14, tr. 491; al-Samʿānī, *Ansāb*, facs. ed. f. 522a), it had a Friday mosque and markets. Coins were first minted there under the Sāmānids. Then under the Ḳarakhānids [see ILEK-KHĀNS], coins were occasionally minted by members of the eastern branch of the dynasty, e.g. at Marghīnān and the neighbouring towns of Akhsikath and Tūnkath by the son of Yūsuf Ḳadīr Khān, Maḥmūd Ṭoghrīl Ḳara Khān (451-67/1059-75) and then by the latter's son ʿUmar Ṭoghrīl Tigin (467/1074-5), see G. C. Miles, in *Camb. hist. of Iran*, v, 374, 376; E. von Zambaur, *Die Münzprägungen des Islams zeitlich und örtlich geordnet*, i, Wiesbaden 1968, 233. It was in the later Ḳarakhānid or Ḳara Khiṭay [*q.v.*] period that the famous Ḥanafī jurist Burhān al-Dīn al-Marghīnānī [see next article] was born.

Marghīnān appears on a Chinese map of the 14th century as Ma-rh-i-nang (Bretschneider, *Mediaeval researches*, ii, 54). Under the Mongols, Tīmūrids and Özbegs it continued to play a certain role, e.g. in the fighting of rival contenders for power amongst the Tīmūrids' epigoni in the opening years of the 10th/16th century, recorded in Mīrzā Ḥaydar Dughlāt's *Taʾrīkh-i Rashīdī*, see tr. N. Elias and E. D. Ross, London 1895, index. Bābur gives a description of Marghīnān as it was at this time in the *Bābur-nāme*, tr. Beveridge, 6-7. The town was famed for its fruits, including a special variety of pomegranates; the population was mainly of Sarts, i.e. sedentary Tādjīks, who were rough and turbulent. It was probably under the Özbeg Turks, who replaced these Sarts, that the form Marghīlān/Marghelān appeared, giving the Russian form Margelan.

It subsequently came within the khānate of Khoḳand [*q.v.*], and just prior to the Russian occupation was already a centre for textile production, including silk and cotton; the American traveller E. Schuyler described it in 1873 as an unfortified place, with a population of *ca.* 30,000 (*Turkistan. Notes of a journey in Russian Turkistan, Khokand, Bukhara, and Kuldja*, London 1876, ii, 49-50). When General Skobelev marched into the region, Marghīnān was occupied without resistance (8/20 September 1875). A settlement, called New Margelan, was founded two years later as the capital of the *oblast* of Fergana in the Governor-Generalship of Turkestan, some 7 miles/12 km. south of Old Marghīnān, and the new town was renamed Skoblev from 1907 till 1924. When the Bolsheviks began to impose their rule in Russian Central Asia, Margelan became a centre of Basmači [*q.v.*] resistance from January 1918 till 1922 (see G. R. Wheeler, *The modern history of Soviet Central Asia*, London 1964, 108 ff.). Old Margelan is still a place of significance, with nearly 48,000 inhabitants, but has been outstripped in growth by New Margelan, now called Fergana, the administrative centre of the Fergana *oblast* of the Uzbek S.S.R., which already in 1951 had a population of *ca.* 50,000.

Bibliography: Given in the article; see also Barthold, *Turkestan*, 158-9, 315.

(C. E. Bosworth)

AL-**MARGHĪNĀNĪ**, the name of two families of Ḥanafī lawyers; the *nisba* comes from their native town and the scene of their activities, Marghīnān [*q.v.*] in Farghāna.

I. 1. The most important was Burhān al-Dīn Abu 'l-Ḥasan ʿAlī b. Abī Bakr b. ʿAbd al-Djalīl al-Farghānī al-Marghīnānī, the author of the

al-Bidāya
|
author's own commentary
|
al-Hidāya

comm. by al-Sighnākī,
al-Nihāya
(written in 700/1300)

comm. by al-Bābartī
(d. 786/1384),
al-ʿInāya

comm. by al-Kurlānī
(8th/14th century),
al-Kifāya

synopsis by Maḥmud b. Ṣadr al-Sharīʿa I
(7th/13th century),
al-Wiḳāya

comm. by Ṣadr al-Sharīʿa II
(d. 747/1346),
Sharḥ al-Wiḳāya
(written in 743/1342-3)

synopsis by
Ṣadr al-Sharīʿa II,
al-Nuḳāya
|
comm. by al-Kūhistānī
(d. 950/1543),
Djāmiʿ al-rumūz

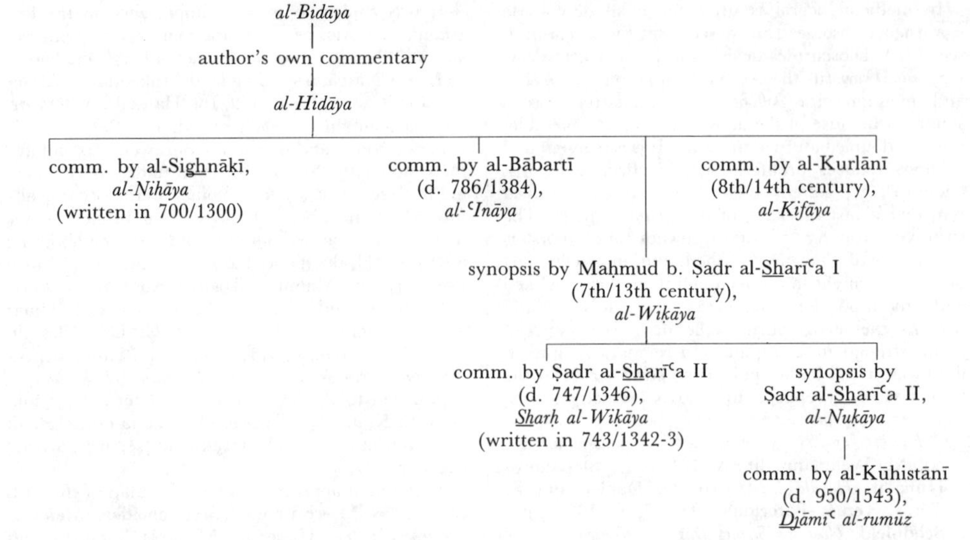

celebrated *Hidāya*. He acquired his knowledge on his travels, then still the usual way of studying in Islam. His principal teachers were Nadjm al-Dīn Abū Ḥafṣ ʿUmar b. Muḥammad b. Aḥmad al-Nasafī (d. 537/1142-3), al-Ṣadr al-Shahīd Ḥusām al-Dīn ʿUmar b. ʿAbd al-ʿAzīz b. ʿUmar b. Māza (d. 536/1141-2) and Abū ʿAmr ʿUthmān b. ʿAlī al-Baykandī (d. 552/1157), a pupil of al-Saraḵẖsī. He studied al-Tirmidhī's work on tradition under Ḍiyāʾ al-Dīn Abū Muḥammad Ṣāʿid b. Asʿad with the *isnād* given in al-Ḳuraẖsī, i, 259, no. 679, and also with al-Ḥasān b. ʿAlī al-Marghīnānī (al-Ḳuraẖsī, i, 198, no. 487). He himself, as was often done at this time, wrote a record of his studies, but it does not appear to have survived. He far surpassed his teachers and won recognition in his native town also, where he died in 593/1197. Of his works, the following are known, some surviving in manuscript and others only known from literary references: 1. *Naṣhr al-madhhab* (Ḳur., Lak., in Ḥādjdjī Khalīfa, no. 13,790, probably wrongly, *al-Madhāhib*); 2. *K. Manāsik al-ḥadjdj* (Ḳur., Lak., H. Ḵẖ., no. 12,943); 3. *K. fī 'l-Farāʾid* (Ḳur., Lak.), also called *Farā ʾid al-ʿUthmānī* (Ḥ. Ḵẖ., no. 8,989); 4. two collections of *fatwās*: *K. al-Tadjnīs wa 'l-mazīd* (Ḳutl., Lak., H. Ḵẖ., no. 2,467; mss. in Brockelmann) and 5. *Muḵẖtārāt al-nawāzil* (Lak.; in Ḳutl., called *K. Muḵẖtār Madjmūʿ al-nawāzil*, and in H. Ḵẖ., no. 11586, called *Muḵẖtār al-fatāwā*; mss. in Brockelmann); 6. *Mazīd fī furūʿ al-Hanafiyya* (Ḥ Ḵẖ., no. 11,838; identical with no. 4?); 7. a commentary on al-Ṣhaybānī's *al-Djāmiʿ al-kabir* (Ḥ. Ḵẖ., ii, 567); 8. his principal work is the legal compendium, *K. Bidāyat al-mubtadī* (mss. in Brockelmann), based on al-Ḳudūrī's *Muḵẖtaṣar* and al-Ṣhaybānī's *al-Djāmiʿ al-ṣaghīr*. On this work, he himself wrote a large commentary in 8 volumes, the *Kifāyat al-muntahā*. But before he had completed it, he thought it was much too diffuse and decided to write a second commentary, the celebrated *Hidāya*, which later writers repeatedly edited and annotated. The most important commentaries and synopses are given in the table below.

For the manuscripts and printed texts of these commentaries and synopses and of many supercommentaries and glosses, see Brockelmann, II², 466-9, S I, 644-9; a printed edition of the *Hidāya* appeared in 4 vols., Cairo 1326/1908.

Bibliography: al-Ḳuraẖsī, *al-Djawāhir al-muḍīʾa*, Ḥaydarābād 1332, i, 383, no. 1058: ʿAbd al-Ḥayy al-Laknawī, *al-Fawāʾid al-bahiyya*, Cairo 1324, 141 ff. (synopsis of the *Ṭabaḳāt* of Kafawī); Ibn Ḳutlūbughā, *Tādj al-tarādjim*, ed. Flügel, Leipzig 1862, no. 124; Brockelmann, *loc. cit.*, and the literature there given.

His sons and pupils were:

2. ʿIMĀD AL-DĪN AL-FARGHĀNĪ; cf. al-Laknawī, 146.

3. ʿUMAR NIẒĀM AL-DĪN AL-FARGHĀNĪ. Two works by him are recorded: 1. *Fawāʾid* (Ḥ. Ḵẖ., no. 9305); 2. *Djawāhir al-fiḳh*, which he compiled from the *Muḵẖtaṣar* of al-Ṭaḥawī and other works (Ḥ. Ḵẖ., no, 4,291; mss. in Brockelmann, S I, 649; cf. al-Ḳuraẖsī, i, 394; al-Laknawī, 149).

4. MUḤAMMAD ABU 'L-FATḤ DJALĀL AL-DĪN AL-FARGHĀNĪ; cf. Ḳutl., 137 and al-Laknawī, 182; in al-Ḳuraẖsī, ii, 99, apparently identical with no. 2.

5. A son of no. 2 and grandson of no. 1: ABU 'L-FATḤ ZAYN AL-DĪN ʿABD AL-RAḤĪM B. ABĪ BAKR ʿIMĀD AL-DĪN B. ʿALĪ BURHĀN AL-DĪN B. ABĪ BAKR B. ʿABD AL-DJALĪL AL-FARGHĀNĪ AL-MARGHĪNĀNĪ. He wrote the work on legal procedure in civil cases entitled *al-Fuṣūl al-ʿimādiyya*, which he completed in Ṣhaʿbān 651/October 1253 in Samarḳand. Cf. Ḥ. Ḵẖ., no. 9,094; Lak., 93; Brockelmann, I², 475-6, S I 656, where the mss. are given.

II. Another family of Ḥanafī lawyers goes back to ʿABD AL-ʿAZĪZ B. ʿABD AL-RAZZĀḲ B. NAṢR B. DJAʿFAR B: SULAYMĀN AL-MARGHĪNĀNĪ, who died in 477/1084-5 in Marghīnān at the age of 68. Of his six sons who attained fame as *muftī*s, we may mention ABU 'L-ḤASAN ẒAHĪR AL-DĪN ʿALĪ (d. 506/1112-13). His son and pupil was ẒAHĪR AL-DĪN AL-ḤASAN B. ʿALĪ ABU 'L-MAḤĀSIN. Four works by him are recorded: *al-Aḳdiya*, *al-Fatāwa*, *al-Fawāʾid* and *al-Shurūṭ*, of which only the last survives in manuscript. He was the teacher of the famous Faḵẖr al-Dīn Ḳādiḵẖān (d. 592/1196) and of Burhān al-Dīn al-Marghīnānī [*q.v.*].

Bibliography: Samʿānī, *K. al-Ansāb*, fol. 522a; Ḳuraẖsī, nos. 487, 850, 1010; Laknawī, 62, 97, 121; Flügel, *Classen der hanaf. Rechtsgelehrten*, Leipzig 1860, 309; Brockelmann, I², 471, S I, 651.

(W. Heffening)

MARḤALA (a.), pl. *marāḥil*, in mediaeval Islamic usage, a stage of travel, normally the distance which a traveller can cover in one day; it was, therefore, obviously a variable measurement of length, dependent on the ease or difficulty of the terrain to be crossed. The classical Arabic geographers frequently use the term. Al-Muḳaddasī [*q.v.*] in one place (206) gives as his norm 6 to 7 *farsakhs* or parasangs (the *farsakh* [*q.v.*] being roughly 6 km.), and has an ingenious orthographical notation for *marāḥil* of less than 6 or more than 7 *farsakhs* (cf. A. Miquel, *La géographie humaine du monde musulman jusqu'au milieu du 11e siècle*, Paris-The Hague 1967-80, i, 328 n. 1). But elsewhere (64 n. *c*), his *marḥala* works out at an average of 8.6 *farsakhs* = 50 km. (cf. Miquel, *Aḥsan at-taqāsīm* ... (*La meilleure répartition* ...), Damascus 1963, 139 n. 6).

Bibliography: Given in the article. (Ed.)

MĀRIB, Maʾrib (*mryb* or *mrb* in the ancient South Arabian inscriptions), in classical antiquity, capital of the Sabaean realm in South-West Arabia, now the chef-lieu of the *muḥāfaẓa* of the same name in the Yemeni Arab Republic, lying some 135 km. to the east of Ṣanʿāʾ. At the last census in 1975, the *muḥāfaẓa* of Mārib counted 70,000 inhabitants, and the *ḳaḍāʾ* of Mārib—with a population density of 2.4 inhabitants per km.^{2}—13,000 inhabitants, consisting of about 10,000 residents, 2,000 Bedouins and 1,000 refugees. The *ʿuzla* of Mārib counted 1,900 residents, and the place Mārib itself only 292 inhabitants, of whom 270 were men and 22 women, in 48 houses.

The ancient town of Mārib lies in a plain which rises 1,160-1,200 m. above sea level, and which forms the dry delta of the great Adhana wadi (now pronounced Dhana). The latter drains an extensive area of over 10,000 km.^{2} in the north-eastern highlands of the Yemen which has an abundant rainfall. Since the Mārib region lies at the fringe of the desert in an arid zone which has an annual rainfall of less than 100 mm., agriculture is only possible by way of irrigation through flooding. The Adhana wadi carries water twice a year, namely for some two weeks in spring and some six weeks in late summer. Before reaching the oasis of Mārib, this wadi forces its way through a narrow passage between the Balaḳ mountains. By constructing a dam, extensive irrigation became possible and the deposition of fertile clay easier, so that conditions for a lush vegetation were created. The Ḳurʾānic statement in *Sūrat Sabaʾ* about a "good land" (*baldat^un^ ṭayyibat^un^*: XXXIV,15) is rightly applied to Mārib and its surroundings (al-Hamdānī, *Iklīl*, viii, 57,1). The land of Sabaʾ around Mārib is said to have been one of the most fertile and best irrigated regions of the Yemen (al-Masʿūdī, *Murūdj*, iii, 366, 9-367,2 = § 1252), with irrigation creating the possibility of three sowings per year (Yāḳūt, *Muʿdjam*, iv, 383,10). The actual place of the same name stands inside the ancient urban area on a great hill of ruins which is increased by the débris of successive cultures. It lies at 15° 26′ N. and 45° 16′ E., about as far from the Red Sea as from the Gulf of ʿAdan. By its favourable position in an oasis between the highland on the one side and the desert on the other, Mārib was predestined to be the capital of the Sabaean realm, the core of which was formed by the urban district of Sabaʾ with Mārib as its centre. Besides, Mārib was one of the most important halting-places on the ancient caravan-route which linked the regions producing incense with the Mediterranean Sea and which, along a chain of water-places, skirted the spurs of the wadis on the eastern slope of the range of hills between the mountains and the sandy plain of the desert. Arriving from Shabwa in Ḥaḍramawt or Timnaʿ in Ḳatabān respectively, two different routes of the incense-road led on from Mārib, one north-westward through the Djawf, the other first northward, to unite again before Nadjrān [*q.v.*], the next important destination on the route. Information about the course of these routes and their halting-places can in many cases be gained from later Arabic itineraries, because the Islamic pilgrim roads often followed the ancient trade-routes.

In antiquity, Mārib was a large, walled town with an area of about 110 hectares/275 acres. According to Pliny (*Naturalis historia*, vi, 32, 160), it is said to have had a circumference of six miles. From the shape of its ruins, still perceptible in our days, the town formed an irregular quadrangle, with a maximum extension of 1,430 m. in length and 1,070 m. in breadth. The remains of the ancient town, such as blocks of stone from the citywall and other constructions as well as fragments of columns, have disappeared almost completely in the last decades through unauthorised diggings. Consequently, since no scientific archaeological excavations have been carried out, for the description of ancient Mārib we still depend upon the information of the European travellers who, in the 19th century, succeeded in penetrating as far as Mārib under adventurous and dangerous circumstances. These were the two Frenchmen Th.J. Arnaud (1843) and J. Halévy (1870), and the Austrian E. Glaser on his third journey to South Arabia (1888). It is to the latter that we owe the most detailed, accurate and valuable observations.

More recent investigations in the Mārib oasis, carried out by the German Archaeological Institute in Ṣanʿāʾ, have led to the conclusion that the irrigation sediments in places reach as high as 30 m. At a rate of sedimentation of 1.1 cm. per year, this height would lead to an irrigation period of *ca.* 2,700 years, i.e., if irrigation ended around the end of the 6th century A.D. or the first part of the 7th century, its beginning would reach back as far as the later period of the third millennium B.C. As for inscriptions, Mārib is mentioned in one of the earliest Sabaean texts which names a ruler, namely in Gl 1719 + 1717 + 1718 = MAFRAY-al-Balaḳ al-Djanūbī 1, a rock-inscription in which one of the governors (*ʾḳyn*) of Mārib (*mryb*), the governor (*ʾḳyn*) of Yadaʿ ʾil Yanūf, dedicates some stone-hewn basins to a deity. H. von Wissmann, whose investigations into the chronology of ancient Sabaean texts is largely utilised in the following, dates this text to around 755 B.C.; its ductus belongs to the oldest paleographic stage of ancient South Arabian script. But already before this period, Mārib may well have become the capital of the Sabaean realm and the centre of South Arabia. The earliest Sabaean inscription bearing directly upon the town of Mārib is probably the three-line boustrophedon inscription (Ga 46), published by G. Garbini in *Oriens Antiquus*, xii (1973), 143. Here Yithaʿʾamar Bayyin, son of Sumhuʿalī, relates that he has walled in *mryb ḥwkw*. The Mukarrib of Sabaʾ named here is most probably to be dated to around 715 B.C., while Ḥawkāwu, which figures after the name of the town of Mārib, is likely to indicate a part of the town or a section of its fortifications.

Rock-inscriptions dating from the same period or even earlier, and likewise originating from the Mārib region, mention the oasis area of the town. These inscriptions, containing probably the oldest Sabaean texts, inform us in ever recurring formulaic phrases that, during the priesthood of their founder, the god ʿAthtar drenched Sabaʾ with rain in high summer and spring. Occasionally the word "Gaww" is added to Sabaʾ, or the variant "Adhana from Yahwir to

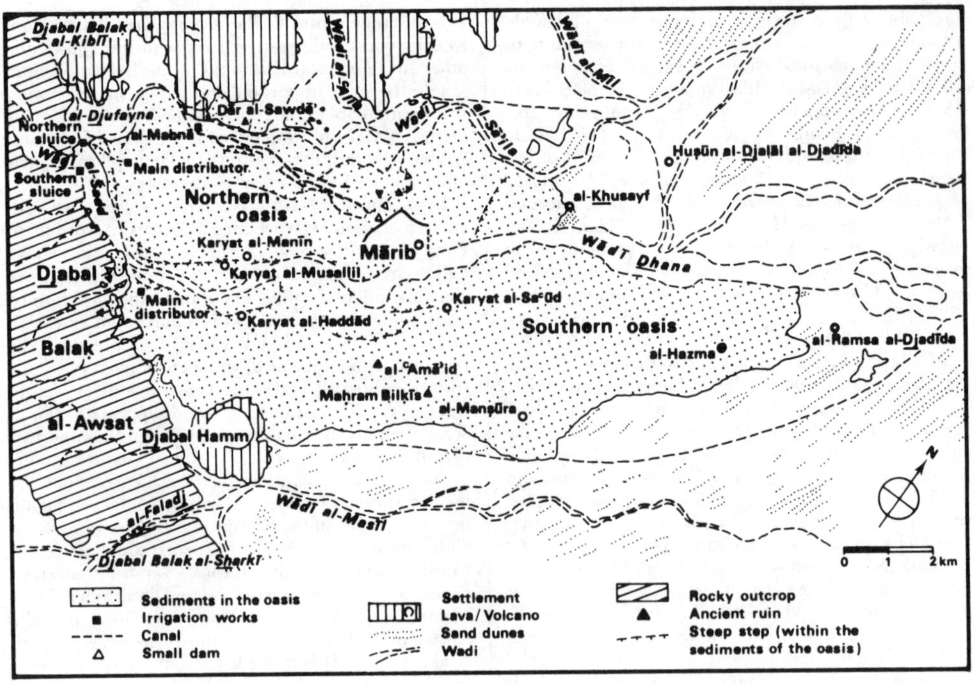

Fig. 2. The Mārib oases: physical geography.

Ḥimārum''. Gaww indicates the lowland, i.e. the lower course of the wadi Adhana, while the expression ''Adhana from Yahwir to Ḥimārum'' probably also describes the area of the Mārib oasis. The name Sabaʾ, emerging here as the name of the region in which Mārib was situated, is originally the name of a tribe which in the inscriptions is more than once named together with Mārib. So we find e.g. ''the tribe of Sabaʾ, the lords of the town of Mārib and its valleys'' (*shᶜbn/sbʾ/ʾbᶜl/hgrn/mrb/wʾsrrhw*: RES 3910, 2), or ''the Sabaeans, the inhabitants of the town of Mārib'' (*ʾsbʾn/ḥwrw/hgrn/mryb*: Ga 9,3-4 with a reading corrected after F. Bron, in *AION*, xli [1981], 163). Still in Arabic tradition, Mārib is indicated as Maʾrib Sabaʾ (e.g. al-Hamdānī, *Ṣifa*, 26, 22) i.e. the Mārib which lies in Sabaʾ. After Sabaʾ, as a byname of ᶜAbd Shams, had been personified as the alleged ancestor of the Sabaeans, and had been inserted into a pedigree by Arab genealogists, Mārib could thus become the town of Sabaʾ, that is to say of Sabaʾ b. Yashdjub b. Yaᶜrub b. Ḳaḥṭān, who allegedly founded it or after whom it also occasionally may have been named (see e.g. Yāḳūt, *Mushtarik*, ed. F. Wüstenfeld, 239, 17-8; Ibn Saᶜīd al-Maghribī, *Nashwat al-ṭarab*, 87, 1-2; Ibn al-Mudjāwir, *Taʾrīkh al-mustabṣir*, 199, 1-2).

Line 4 of the fragmentary inscription RES 3943 relates that the ruler constructed both gates of Mārib and surrounded the town with towers, that is bastions of limestone (*blḳ*). The ruler, whose name is not retained in the text, may be Yithaᶜʾamar Bayyin, son of Sumhuᶜalī Yanūf, whose reign can be fixed around 510 B.C. When the Sabaean realm reached the zenith of its power and founded a colony in Abyssinia, there were among the colonists also emigrants from Mārib, as is shown by the indications of their origin *dh-mryb*, found in Sabaean inscriptions in Yeha and Melazo. By its geographical position at the eastern side of the mountains, Mārib was protected only slightly by nature: to the south, plains stretched out as far as Timnaᶜ, the capital of Ḳatabān, to the east as far as Shabwa, the capital of Ḥaḍramawt, and to the north as far as the towns of the Minaean realm. With the rise and strengthening of these other ancient South Arabian realms, fortification of Mārib became an urgent necessity. The town was not only the capital, but had also become the eastern fortress of the land-locked Sabaean realm: its frontier with Ḳatabān was only some 25 km. south of Mārib, and that with the Minaeans only some 40 km. to the north. The improvement of the traffic connections with the Yemeni highlands and their maintenance became all the more urgent through the danger threatening from the south. Inscription CIH 955 + 418, dating from the period of Sumhuᶜalī Yanūf around 390 B.C., mentions the construction of a road from Mārib to Ṣirwāḥ, the second important town of the Sabaean realm, to which refuge could be taken in case of necessity. ''The town which is revered'' (*hgrn/thrgb*) in CIH 375,2, very probably also indicates Mārib. From this inscription, dealing with the construction of the Awām temple, we learn that an attack from Ḳatabān against Sabaʾ could be repelled and that its founder brought peace to Mārib. CIH 37, an inscription of the vassal of Sumᶜay in the Yemeni highlands drawn up under king Karibʾil Watar at the beginning of the 3rd century B.C., speaks about the Sabaean overlords as kings of Mārib (*ʾmlk/mryb*). The next information about the construction of a wall of Mārib cannot be fitted in accurately, since only the name of the king's father, Yithaᶜʾamar Watar, has been preserved (RES 4452, CIH 626, Gl 1110). The latter, however, cannot be identified with either of the other rulers of this name. On palaeographic grounds, the three fragments belonging to this text can be dated to the middle of the 2nd century B.C. The kings of Sabaʾ repaired the walls of their capital, above all at the time in which danger from the outside was threatening. At that time, this may still have been the encirclement by Ḳatabān in the south and Maʿīn in the north, which ended only when Sabaʾ conquered the Minaean realm in the last quarter of the 2nd century B.C. A monumental inscription, occurring in at least nine homonymous versions and compiled by H. von Wissmann from more than fifty fragments (RES 2669, Fa 91 + 92, Gl 1103 and many others), reads as follows: "Yadaʿ ʾil Watar, king of Sabaʾ, son of Sumhuʿalī Yanūf, walled Mārib (*mryb*) in at the order and promise of ʿA<u>th</u>tar and Hawbas and Almaḳah". Unfortunately, the name of this ruler is not known from other inscriptions either, although von Wissmann plausibly dated him to around 30 B.C.

Shortly after the latter date, in 25-24 B.C., a Roman army under Aelius Gallus, the proconsul of Egypt, invaded South Arabia, escorted by Nabataeans, and reached, as Strabo relates, the gates of the Sabaean capital Mārib. Although assaulted during a period of six days, Mārib was able to resist, for the Romans were forced to withdraw because of scarcity of water and disease among their troops. Pliny is certainly not correct in counting Mārib among the destroyed cities. While besieging Mārib, the Romans probably laid waste the neighbourhood of the town and destroyed the irrigation works of the oasis. After their retreat, the most urgent task of the inhabitants of Mārib may well have been the reconstruction of the dam, the sluices and the water-distributors. Numerous fragments of Yadaʿ ʾil Watar's inscription about the construction of the wall were found to have been used again as building material near the northern sluice and its distributor installations. From this, it may be concluded that ashlars were removed from the city-wall, probably destroyed for the greater part, in order to set up the irrigation works anew and to revitalise the oasis of Mārib. Is is not known at what time the city-wall was reconstructed, because no inscriptions about the construction of the wall are known from a later period. At the time of E. Glaser's sojourn in Mārib, the ancient city-wall, only one metre thick and probably provided with eight gates, was still preserved almost entirely. Air photographs of recent years show on the western and northern side only a few ruins of the ancient city-wall with its bastions.

During the decades after the Roman campaign against South Arabia, a period of decline set in for Mārib. The traditional dynasty of the kings of Sabaʾ in Mārib was pressed hard by rulers of four other dynasties rising in the Yemeni highland. All of them assumed also the title of king of Sabaʾ and controlled Mārib alternately. Sabaʾ and Ḥimyar, which had grown strong, were hostile to each other, each claiming the realm of the other. Henceforth, the kings of both states bore the title "King of Sabaʾ and <u>Dh</u>ū Raydān", the latter being the royal castle in the Ḥimyarite capital of Ẓafār. In the same period, Bedouins from the desert steppes also pressed forward from the north and the east into the region of Mārib, and were admitted into the army as contingents. In an inscription, the Bedouins of Mārib (*ʾʿrb/mrb*: CIH 353, 10) are explicitly mentioned among the troops participating in a campaign. But even after South Arabia, towards the end of the 3rd century A.D., had come almost entirely under the domination of the Ḥimyar, and the highlands had become the centre of the united Sabaeo-Ḥimyarite realm, Mārib still retained a certain importance as the site of the central sanctuary of the realm. The fact that Mārib and its inhabitants are mentioned even later on in Sabaean inscriptions leads to the conclusion that the town still enjoyed prestige and influence. Notwithstanding the fact that caravan traffic had declined and trade had been transferred to the sea-route, the prosperity of the town had by no means disappeared. This is shown, to a certain extent, by inscription Fa 74, erected in the year 614 of the Ḥimyarite era (= 499 A.D.), according to which a citizen of Mārib had ordered a stately house with two bronze statues of lions and other bronze statuettes to be erected for himself. The fragments of columns, capitals, friezes and relief-slabs, and above all the perfectly executed inscriptions on stones preserved in Mārib, bear eloquent witness of the high level which artistic and manual skill had reached in this town during antiquity. It had struck al-Hamdānī, too, that elsewhere in Yemen columns dating from ancient times were not of such beauty and value as those in Mārib (*Iklil*, viii, 151, 11-2). After the Abyssinian conquest of the Yemen in 525, a Christian church was also built in Mārib, as we learn from an inscription set up under king Abraha (*bʿt/mrb*): CIH 541, 66-7). One of the new churches, consecrated in South Arabia according to the *Vita Sancti Gregentii*, is said to have been in the middle of Δανα, which probably means Wadi <u>Dh</u>ana, and thus the oasis region of Mārib.

The royal castle of Mārib was Salḥīn, which is also the building of ancient South Arabia most frequently mentioned in Sabaean inscriptions. If we admit that the most ancient form of the name was Salḥum (*slḥm*), the castle is already mentioned in the ancient Sabaean inscription RES 3946, set up by Karibʾil Watar probably around 685 B.C. Line 5 relates that he constructed the upper storey of his house Salḥum. From this statement it may even be concluded that the stronghold was founded in a still earlier period. Salḥīn is mentioned with special frequency in the inscriptions of the 2nd and 3rd centuries A.D. which originate from the Awām temple near Mārib, the place of ruins now called Maḥram Bilḳīs. They mostly relate that the king or one of his commanders returned safely to Salḥīn, or happiness is implored for the house of Salḥīn and its lords. Salḥīn was also the place where indigenous coins were minted on behalf of the Sabaean realm.

Next to Salḥīn, al-Hamdānī mentions Ha<u>dj</u>ar and al-Ḳa<u>sh</u>īb as other castles of Mārib (*Iklīl*, viii, 99, 10). From epigraphic tradition, these two are not known so far. The name al-Ha<u>dj</u>ar, "the town", is unusual for a fortress, and may already raise doubts for that very reason. According to al-Hamdānī (*Iklīl*), viii, 100, 2), al-Ḳa<u>sh</u>īb was built by a member of the <u>Dh</u>ū Ḥazfar, i.e. of that ancient eponymous kin of the <u>Kh</u>alīl tribe resident in and around Mārib. According to Yāḳūt (*Muʿ<u>dj</u>am*, iv, 104, 6), the castle al-Ḳa<u>sh</u>īb is said to have been built at the order of king <u>Sh</u>uraḥbīl bin Yaḥṣib. Such a ruler, is, however, not attested epigraphically. The name <u>Sh</u>urahbīl would fit in with <u>Sh</u>uraḥbiʾil Yaʿfur and the father's name Yaḥṣib with Il<u>sh</u>araḥ Yaḥḍib, with a faulty rendering of the surname Yaḥḍib. However, the defective title of a "king of Sabaʾ and the Tihāma and their Bedouins" which is also mentioned (Yāḳūt, *Muʿ<u>dj</u>am*, iv, 104, 7-8), points to a king of the later period, i.e. rather to <u>Sh</u>uraḥbiʾil Yaʿfur who reigned in the middle of the 5th century A.D. than to Il<u>sh</u>araḥ Yaḥḍib who lived more than two centuries earlier. Since *ḳa<u>sh</u>īb* means "new", both in Sabaean and Arabic—an explanation given by al-Hamdānī himself in another place (*Iklil*, ii, 317,7)—the name of the fortress may correspond to names like Newcastle, Neufchâteau or Neuburg.

The most important temple of ancient Mārib was the sanctuary of Awām of the god Almaḳah, now called Ḥaram Bilḳīs or Maḥram Bilḳīs. It lay at the eastern edge of Yasrān, the southern part of the oasis, at the other side of the wadi and at a distance of 3.5 km. south-east of the town. Partly excavated in 1952 by an American expedition under Wendell Phillips, it produced hundreds of dedicatory inscriptions, often quite extensive, which were erected in the entrance hall between the middle of the 1st and the 4th centuries A.D. They are our most important source for the history of that turbulent period. The sanctuary consists of a large, oval construction with a spacious courtyard, surrounded by a high, thick circular wall. The latter is made up of two mantles, an outer one and inner one consisting of ashlars, kept together by lateral walls, the hollow spaces being filled up with débris. The longitudinal axis between the north-western gate and the mausoleum on the opposite side measures about 105 m., while the latitudinal axis, which runs from the inner gate of the rectangular entrance hall, constructed before the circular wall, to the south-west, measures about 75 m. The temple court-yard thus had a surface of *ca.* 6,000 m². The construction, with its strongly fortified courtyard was originally perhaps also conceived as a refuge fortress, as is suggested by the name of the temple, *ʾwm*, which very probably means "place of refuge". The inscription CIH 957, placed in the wall of the temple, relates that Yadaʿ ʾil Dharīḥ, son of Sumhuʿalī and Mukarrib of Sabaʾ, erected the wall of the Awām, the house of Almaḳah. According to von Wissmann, this ruler is to be dated around 670 B.C. The concept of the entire construction presumably reaches back to this ruler, who is known as a temple builder, even if the works were transformed and changed in later times. Thus the oval enclosing wall, originally no doubt as high as 29 layers of ashlars i.e. 8.70 m. without the frieze, was, since the first quarter of the 4th century B.C., raised by 13 more layers of ashlars (cf. CIH 375). This was done in order to make up for the heap of sand and deposit which had accumulated in the precinct of the wall since the time of foundation and to raise the wall to its original height.

The last constructional renovation which is attested epigraphically was undertaken in the second half of the 1st century A.D. under king Karibʾil Watar Yuhanʿim "for the prosperity of the house of Salḥīn and the town of Mārib" (*hgrn*/*mryb*: CIH 373). It was also in this sanctuary that the tribe of Sabaʾ, i.e. the inhabitants of the town and oasis of Mārib, offered thanks for the fertility granted to their land through the water of wadi Adhana (cf. e.g. Sh 18); or they went there in a rogation procession when rain held off unduly (cf. Ja 735). Until the period of the beginning of monotheism in the second half of the 4th century A.D., hence during a whole millennium, the Awām temple of the god Almaḳah was the central place of worship of the Sabaean realm, to which people came in pilgrimage from afar (cf. e.g. RES 4176, 1-2).

Another large, sacred building in the area of the southern oasis, second only to the Awām sanctuary, was the Barʾān temple (*mḥrmn*/*brʾn*: CIH 400,2), likewise dedicated to the god Almaḳah. Nowadays it is called al-ʿAmāʾid, "the columns", because five pillars with capitals and a pillar stump still rise up from the débris of the construction so far unexcavated. With reference to Ḳurʾān, XXVII,23, these columns are occasionally also called *ʿarsh Bilḳīs* "throne of Bilḳīs", a designation which is however also used for a colonnade in Ṣirwāḥ (see R. G. Stiegner, *Die Königin von Sabaʾ in ihnen Namen*, 73).

In Mārib itself there was also a temple of the god Almaḳah. As proved by an epigraphical discovery in 1982 (Schmidt, *Mārib*, 24), the sanctuary Ḥarūnum (*ḥrwnm* or *ḥrnm*), already known from numerous Subaean inscriptions, was situated inside the area of the ancient town.

The oldest epigraphical evidence of the construction of irrigation works in the oasis area of Mārib is found in inscription RES 3946, an account of the activities of Karibʾil Watar, the son of Dhamarʿalī, probably dating from 685 B.C. Lines 5 and 6 relate that the ruler constructed in the wadi Adhana the foundation Tafīsh and the overflow-basin of the main canal of Yasrān, as well as the foundation of Yaliṭ and the overflow-basin of the main canal of Abyan; that for Yasrān, he further erected Ẓarib and Milkān and, in their midst, the construction works of Yasrān and Abyan. In an inscription which unfortunately has been copied deficiently and published inadequately, namely text ZI 71 = Sh 6, Sumhuʿalī Yanūf, son of Yadaʿ(ʾ)il Dharīḥ, a ruler who, according to von Wissmann, is to be dated around 660 B.C., already proclaimed an instruction which more or less reads as follows: the water, allotted to a certain area which has been prepared for sowing, should not be limited if one lets it flow on that section of Yasrān which is irrigated by opening [the storage works], so that Mārib property (*mlk*/*mryb*) can be fertilised by water supply. Yasrān is the ancient name of the half of the Mārib oasis which lies south of the river bed of wadi Adhana, while Abyan indicates the northern half of the oasis, at whose further lower end the town of Mārib lay. In the Sabaean inscriptions, both oases are occasionally indicated as "Mārib and its two valleys" (*mryb*/*wsryhw* in Sh 18,3 and *mrb*/*wsryhw* in Fa 71,6), which survives in the Ḳurʾān as "the two gardens to the right and to the left" (*djannatānⁱ ʿan yamīnⁱⁿ wa-shimālⁱⁿ*; Sūra, XXXIV,15). Recent investigations by the German Archaeological Institute have shown that downstream on the southern bank and in the middle of wadi Adhana, remains of constructions and works are to be found in the rocks. They belong to the ancient irrigation systems and functioned as constructions for damming up and distributing the water. A natural lava-barrier served as a dam for the builders of these ancient reservoirs. There are three ruins in all, two of which can be labelled, with a fair amount of certainty, as the oldest damming and distributing constructions in the Mārib oasis. They are perhaps the irrigation works which are mentioned epigraphically in the beginning of the 7th century B.C. as the first northern and southern oases. These ruins of water works, lying in the wadi bed, must be considered as forerunners of the great dam of later date between the Djabal Balaḳ al-Ḳiblī and Balaḳ al-Awsaṭ. This dam only came into existence when the two halves of the oasis had already risen considerably above the wadi level through sedimentation. Originally, the irrigation works of Yasrān and Abyan were separated from each other, for the possibility of building one single great dam for the two halves of the oasis was only created much later, due to the difficult constructions at the southern sluice. The building of this dam and its sluices was realised under Sumhuʿalī Yanūf, son of Dhamarʿalī, who according to von Wissmann is to be dated approximately around 528 B.C. In Gl 513 and Gl 514 = CIH 623, two identical rock-inscriptions placed almost opposite one another, this Mukarrib of Sabaʾ announces that he has hewn out in the rock the opening for the reservoir Raḥābum of the main canal of Yasrān, i.e. by cutting through the contiguous limestone rock of the Djabal Balaḳ al-Awsaṭ he has built the southern sluice, so that the southern half of the Mārib oasis can be irrigated from a higher water-level. Although no inscription *in situ* is known at the northern sluice which led to Abyan, the northern half of the Mārib oasis, it can be concluded from the construction of the southern sluice that the great dam and the northern sluice too were built by the same Mukarrib, since the entire complex can only have been executed as a whole, and since the hewing out of the storage canal Raḥābum at the southern sluice presupposes the construction of the dam which held back the waters of the wadi. This dam, which lay about 8 km. west-south-west of ancient Mārib, consisted of sediments heaped on the rocky, solid stratum. At the surface, it was covered with small, unhewn stones, strongly joined by mortar; it was at least 16 m. high, at the bottom at least 60 m. broad, and about 620 m. long. The dam served less to create a storage reservoir than to raise the water, brought down twice a year by the *sayl*, to a level from which the fields could be irrigated. So it was in fact a diverting dam, blocking the total breadth of the wadi, one which made it possible to irrigate regularly a defined acreage. The northern sluice too may well have been constructed at the same period in an analogous way. From the sluice, a main canal of 1,120 m. led to the principal distributor at the western edge of the northern oasis, from where the mass of water, through 15 sluice-like openings and 121 secondary distributors, was directed to the canal systems of the various arrays built on the fields which had to be irrigated. The complicated irrigation works of the northern oasis, with its constructions of water-distributors and remains of the network of canals, is partly still discernible. The next ruler who ordered the canal of the southern sluice to be hewn further through the rock of the Djabal Balaḳ al-Awsaṭ was Yithaᶜʾamar Bayyin, the son of Sumhuᶜalī Yanūf. From him has also been preserved a boustrophedon inscription of two lines, recorded in two versions on the smoothened contiguous rock of the walls of the southern sluice, namely Gl 523 and Gl 525 = CIH 622. This inscription related that Yithaᶜʾamar Bayyin hewed out the opening in the rock for the storage reservoir Ḥabābiḍ of the main canal of Yasrān. The incision of the southern sluice, which has been hewn out of the rock, divides after some 30 m. towards the east in a northern and a southern branch. The northern one, which lies closer to the wadi, belonged to the Raḥābum basin, as is recorded in the two versions of rock inscription CIH 623, mounted there. Consequently, the southern branch could be the Ḥabābiḍ basin, although the two versions of inscription CIH 622 which relate its construction have been chiselled on both sides of the entrance to the sluice on the west-side. Since Yithaᶜ ʾamar Bayyin, through this main canal which branched off to the right, enlarged the construction of the southern sluice, a still greater acreage could probably be irrigated through the distributing constructions in the Yasrān oasis which were fed by this canal. Line 5 of the fragmentary, ancient Sabaean inscription RES 3943, preserved without the name of a ruler, mentions the hewing out of the storage reservoir Ḥabābiḍ (the text wrongly has *ḥ b ḍ ḍ* instead of *ḥ b b ḍ*). Hence it may be concluded that the text was set up under Yithaᶜ ʾamar Bayyin. Besides, the enlargement of the storage reservoir Raḥābum and the building of further irrigation works in Yasrān and Abyan are also recorded. The constructions of the southern sluice have been best preserved. According to Glaser, the inhabitants of Mārib called them Marbaṭ al-Dimm "place where the cat was tied", because a cat was said to have been tied there once on a long chain in order to catch the rat which undermined the dam, and to prevent thus the calamity of a bursting of the dam.

North-north-east of the great dam lies a smaller dam construction, probably built relatively late and called Mabnā al-Ḥashradj. Water, also supplied from the great dam, was stored here and, through a canal system, was used to irrigate the fields of Dār al-Sawdāʾ, lying to the east, as far as the town of Mārib.

According to the calculations of U. Brunner, the entire surface irrigated at the lower end of the dam amounted to 9,600 hectares/24,000 acres, 5,300 hectares/13,250 acres belonging to the southern oasis and 3,750 hectares/10,740 acres to the northern one. The rest of the fields lay north-west and north of the northern oasis near al-Djufayna and Dār al-Sawdāʾ. If the results of the census of 1975, according to which 13,000 people were living in the *ḳaḍāʾ* of Mārib, is taken as a basis, the number of inhabitants in and around Mārib in antiquity may be calculated at 30,000 at the least estimate and 50,000 at the most.

From the later Sabaean period, several dam-bursts have been recorded epigraphically. From text RES 4775, until today to be found on a wall near the northern sluice, we learn that, during the reigns of Dhamarᶜalī Yuhabirr and his son Thaʾrān, at some time or other in the first two decades of the 4th century A.D., the storage basin Dhū-Amīr, in the Abyan oasis, was repaired after it had been destroyed and swept away by the rain flood. Inscription Ja 788 + 671 from the Awām temple mentions that, at the time of the kings Thaʾrān Yuhanᶜim and Malik-karib Yuʾmin, in the beginning of the second half of the 4th century A.D., the dam broke at the storage basins Ḥabābiḍ and Raḥābum; the whole wall of the middle section between the two basins mentioned was destroyed, as well as 70 *shawāḥiṭ*, i.e. 350 ells or some 180 m. of the dam. Repair of the constructions took three months. The first of the two great inscriptions on the dam works, CIH 540, erected at the northern sluice constructions, relates that in the year 564 of the Ḥımyarite era (= 449 A.D.), under Shuraḥbiʾil Yaᶜfur, the dam was restored after it had broken down as a result of the floods after late summer rain, but that in the next year heavy damage occurred again, which had to be made good through great expense of people and material. The main victuals are said to have been flour made from wheat, barley and *dhura* (*ṯḥnm/dhbrm/wshᶜrm/wgdhdhtm*: CIH 540, 86-7; in another sequence in CIH 540, 39-40), i.e. from the three most important kinds of cereals which in the Mārib region nowadays still constitute about three-quarters of cultivation. The same king Shuraḥbiʾil Yaᶜfur testifies in an inscription (Garbini, *AION*, xxix [1969], 560 = ZM 1) to the building of a castle in the capital Ẓafār in the year 572 of the Ḥimyarite era (= 457 A.D.). It is also said there that at the same time, repairs were executed at the dam in Mārib and constructions carried out at the storage basin Raḥābum; the first activity involved the removal of the mud deposits. The second great inscription on the construction of the dam, CIH 541, set up under king Abraha, relates to a dam-burst in the year 657 of the Ḥimyarite era (= 542 A.D.), which again could only be repaired after enormous efforts. It remains undecided whether by the newly-built construction, erected as high as 35 ells (CIH 541, 107-8), the dam proper is meant or another part of the storage works. The last inscription which mentions the great Mārib dam is the rock-inscription Ja 547 which is certainly to be united with Ja 545, the latter being dated in the year 668 of the Ḥimyarite era (= 553 A.D.). The authors of the text were again engaged, under great exertion, in removing the mud deposits at the dam. Researches by U. Brunner on the discordances which occur in the sediments of the storage area have revealed that another dam-burst must have taken place some 35 years after the one described in inscription CIH 541. It was again repaired. The final catastrophe apparently occurred only at the beginning of the 7th century. It is the event which is mentioned in the Ḳurʾān as the dam-flood (*sayl al-ʿarim*: Sūra XXXIV, 16), i.e. the flood which broke the dam (Sabaean *ʿrm*). Afterwards, the Mārib oasis became desolate and, in the words of the Ḳurʾān, produced only briar fruits, tamarisks and a few Zizyphus trees (*loc. cit.*). Only small fields which lie at the edge of the wadi bed, and to which the high water can be directed through diverting dams, are cultivated. Al-Hamdānī already relates how in Mārib the pieces of land are irrigated from the *sayl*, and *ṭahaf* and *dukhn* are sown there until finally, the harvest is reaped and ploughing prepares the soil for the next sowing (*Ṣifa*, 199, 19-22). In more recent times, more and more extensive areas have been added, especially in the section lying to the south of the Adhana wadi; they are irrigated by subsoil water which has, however, to be brought up by pumps from as deep as 45-50 m.

Considering that, after a dam-burst, the sediments deposited by the floods had to be cleared away each time until the original level of the wadi was reached, it follows that each rebuilding of the dam became more difficult. Since the level of the oasis meanwhile had risen further, the dam had to be built higher each time. The mud which was carried along with the floods, and which raised the fields and was precipitated on to the dam and the storage basins, must have played an essential role in the dam construction being completely abandoned in the end.

Air photographs of the neighbourhood of Mārib show so called "dotted fields" standing out prominently. These accumulations of sediment clods lying in the ancient fields of the oasis, are relics of ancient tree and shrub plantations, widely spread, especially in the southern oasis. This observation is confirmed by the inscriptions. Text CIH 375 enumerates by name 13 palm-groves in the area of the Yasrān oasis alone, which is irrigated by the water of the Adhana wadi by means of sluices and canals conducting the waters of the dam. Al-Hamdānī, too, relates that, during a visit to the Mārib oasis, he saw a sunken *arāk* shrub, at whose root was a black palm trunk. One of his companions was of the opinion that this was a remnant of palms from pre-Islamic times (*Iklīl*, viii, 96, 2-4). In his time, date-palms remained only in Ruḥāba (*Ṣifa*, 102, 21), the region lying beyond the dam on both sides of the Adhana wadi.

The reasons which led to the neglect of the dam constructions and to their being left continuously to decay, and which finally reached a point so that they could not be renewed any more, may also have had a political and social background. The constant disputes between the individual principalities and dynasties of ancient South Arabia resulted in the loss of a strong central power and the disintegration of a well-organised society. This led to the growing influence of foreign powers, namely of Ethiopia and later of Sāsānid Persia. Moreover, the intensified penetration of North Arabian tribes brought about an increasing bedouinisation and a decline of rural culture based on agriculture and irrigation. A decrease of the population as a whole was probably connected with this. The Arab authors of the early Islamic period hold the same view. The fact that the last dam-burst is mentioned in the Ḳurʾān as *sayl al-ʿarim*, and the significance of this event for the town of Mārib and its surroundings, have caused Islamic tradition to deal in detail with this catastrophe and its consequences. Occasionally, information about the dam and the oasis themselves crept in, even if distorted and exaggerated. According to the Arab authors, too, events which had happened before the dam-burst, and the bursting of the dam itself, led to the Mārib oasis being abandoned by its inhabitants. The migration of entire South Arabian tribes towards the north is to be connected with it. Thus e.g. the Banū Ghassān and the Azd are said to have come from there and to have spread over various regions of the Arabian peninsula. The Banū Ghassān are even said to have established their era after the year of the dam-burst (*ʿām al-sayl*) (al-Masʿūdī, *Tanbīh*, ed. de Goeje, Leiden 1894, 202, 14-15). This would admittedly mean that the *sayl al-ʿarim* event has to be dated much earlier than it in fact took place. Through late Sabaean inscriptions we meanwhile know, however, that dating this last catastrophe in the 3rd, 2nd or 1st centuries A.D., or even earlier, as assumed by many Muslim authors and also some European scholars of the 18th and 19th centuries, is untenable. The Arab author who comes closest to the real date is Yāḳūt, who relates that the bursting of the dam took place in the period of the sovereignty of the Abyssinians (*Muʿdjam*, iv, 383, 20). Only al-Masʿūdī dares to attribute the bursting to natural causes, when he writes that the water gradually undermined the dam constructions built by man (*Murūdj*, iii, 370, 9-371, 2 = § 1254). To be sure, it cannot be completely excluded that traditions about a catastrophic bursting of the dam of a much earlier date have also crept into the legends which attached themselves to the *sayl al-ʿarim*. The most current version of the legend of the migration from the Mārib oasis is the following: a ruler of Mārib, ʿAmr b. ʿĀmir of the Azd, nicknamed al-Muzayḳiyāʾ, was married to Ẓarīfa, who had visions and dreams which she was also able to interpret. Evil omens being communicated to her, she warned ʿAmr, and one day she sent him to the dam, where he saw how a giant rat with iron teeth and big claws, called Khuld, was about to trundle away boulders and to undermine the dam. Thus warned and informed about the coming catastrophe of the bursting of the dam, ʿAmr decided to sell his possession at the lower end of the dam and to leave the country. However, in order to hide the real motive, he simulated a brawl with his son during which the latter slapped his face openly. This feigned defamation of the family presented him with the pretext of giving up his possessions, which could then be sold satisfactorily. After that, ʿAmr, with numerous followers, migrated from the Mārib oasis still in good time before the bursting of the dam set in (according to other versions, he only left after the event). His descendants spread over extensive parts of Arabia. After ʿAmr al-Muzayḳiyāʾ had left, the people of Mārib agreed upon a new king, who is, however, said not to have been designated as *tubbaʿ*. (For examples of detailed and embellished versions of this legend, see e.g. Wahb b. Munabbih, *Kitāb al-Tīdjān*, Ṣanʿāʾ 1979, 273-97; al-Masʿūdī, *Murūdj*, iii, 378, 2-392, 7 = §§ 1264-76; Yāḳūt, *Muʿdjam*, iv, 383, 20-385, 10; Ibn Saʿīd al-Maghribī, *Nashwat al-ṭarab*, 114, 13-117, 10, 16; al-Khazradjī, *al-ʿUḳūd al-luʾluʾiyya*, 9, 1-15, 3; a version which is divergent in some respects is given by Ibn al-Mudjāwir, *Taʾrīkh al-Mustabṣir*, 195, 5-197,

15, where the dam, as in al-Hamdānī, *Ṣifa* 110, 26, is called *sadd al-maʾzimayn* "the dam of the two closely joining places".)

The name of the ancient Sabaean capital has been transmitted in two forms in the ancient South Arabian inscriptions. The early inscriptions up to the 2nd century A.D., have always the form *mryb*; after that time, the form *mrb* appears. Two texts from the 2nd century A.D. still have both forms side by side. Inscriptions Fa 71 has *mryb* in lines 17-18, but *mrb* in line 6, while inscription Ja 576 has *mryb* in line 3, but *mrb* in line 2. The place-name *mryb* may originally have been a *nomen loci* of a root *ryb* of unknown meaning, which possibly has a parallel in Hebrew Mərībā, a spring in the desert (Exodus, xvii, 7, and repeatedly), in as much as one does not admit the meaning "quarrel", given in the Old Testament. For the pronunciation of *mryb* as Maryab, reference can be made to the rendering by ancient authors: Μαρίαβα as Μητρόπολις in Strabo, xvi, 4, 768, after Erastosthenes, and *ibid.*, xvi, 4,778, after Artemidoros, as well as Μαρούαβα, *ibid.*, xvi, 4, 782, distorted either from Μαρύαβα or from Μαρίαβα or Σάβα, and also the *regia tamen omnium Mareliabata*, probably miswritten from Mareiaba, in Pliny, *Naturalis historia*, vi, 32, 155. The pronunciation Marīb may be inferred from the renderings Maribba in Pliny, *Naturalis historia*, vi, 32, 157, Mariba, *ibid.*, vi, 32, 160, and Mariba or, in the Greek version, Μαρίβα in the *Monumentum Ancyranum* = *Res gestae divi Augusti*, 26,5. In his *Introduction* to *Geography*, Book vi, ch. 6, Ptolemy has the name Μάρα μητρόπολις, but in his *Canon of the noteworthy cities* he has Μάραβα. A transition from a form Marīb to Mārib or Maʾrib is easier to explain than a change from Maryab to Mārib. When describing Mārib, al-Hamdānī too (*Iklīl*, viii, 104, 1-3) still gives both names Marīb and Maʾrib side by side, but explains them as being the names of two Arabian tribes, on the basis of a line of poetry which he transmits. In one of the fragments of the Ethiopian inscriptions from Mārib, the name of the town occurs as Mārəb (DJE 1 + 2, 13; see W.W. Müller, *Zwei weitere Bruchstücke der äthiopischen Inschrift aus Mārib*, in *Neue Ephemeris für Semitische Epigraphik*, i [1972], 62-3 and 66). Remarkable are the forms in which Mārib evidently appears in Syriac sources, namely *mrʾb* (*b-mrʾb m<u>dh</u>ittā*, in the town of Mārib; see A. Moberg, *The Book of the Himyarites*, Lund 1924, 5b, 8-9), and *mwrb* (*men mwrb*, from Mārib; see I. Shahîd, *The Martyrs of Najrân. New documents*, Brussels 1971, xxix, 4). *Mrʾb* is certainly not the rendering of the *mryb* of the inscriptions, as Moberg, *op. cit.*, pp. xcii-xciii, seems to admit, for at that time the latter had not been in use for a long period. It is rather a miswriting for *mʾrb*, while *mwrb* could reflect a Syriac pronunciation Mōrib for Mārib. In Arabic tradition, the placename always appears as Maʾrib, which is probably formed secondarily from Mārib. The Arab lexicographers seem indeed undecided as to the root under which to put the name. The *Lisān al-ʿArab* and the *Tā<u>dj</u> al-ʿarūs* give the name Maʾrib both under *ʾrb* and *mrb*, while Na<u>sh</u>wān al-Ḥimyarī gives it only under *mrb* (see ʿAẓīmuddīn Ahmad, *Die auf Südarabien bezüglichen Angaben Našwān's im Šams al-ʿulūm*, Leiden 1916, 96,19). Yāḳūt (*Muʿ<u>dj</u>am*, iv, 382, 17-20) even tries, unsatisfactorily, to give three explanations at a time for the name Maʾrib, namely as *nomen loci* of *arab* or of the verbs *aruba* and *ariba*. Immediately afterwards he remarks (*ibid.*, iv, 382, 20-1) that Mārib is the name of each of the Sabaean kings. In this connection, one might think of the ancient South Arabian word *mrʾ* "lord", especially as a designation of the king in his quality of sovereign of the founders of dedicatory inscriptions, the more so because Na<u>sh</u>wān al-Ḥimyarī transmits a gloss according to which *mārī* means "lord" in the Ḥimyaritic language (see O. Blau, in *ZDMG*, xxv [1871], 591, n. 7).

After the death of the Persian governor Bā<u>dh</u>ān [*q.v.* in Suppl.], the Prophet Muḥammad appointed representatives for the various towns of the Yemen, among them Abū Mūsā al-A<u>sh</u>ʿarī [*q.v.*] as representative for Mārib (see al-Ṭabarī, i, 1852, 19-20 and 1983, 9). From then on, Mārib is enumerated as a separate *mi<u>kh</u>lāf* under the *ma<u>kh</u>ālīf* of the Yemen (al-Hamdānī, *Ṣifa*, 102, 19). For al-Hamdānī, in the first half of the 4th/10th century, Mārib is still a town full of curiosities (*Iklīl*, viii, 95, 5). He counts it among the places to which God has shown mercy (*Iklīl*, viii, 191, 7-8), and names it among the towns where treasures are said to be hidden (*Iklīl*, viii, 194, 3-7). Certainly, the dam had been destroyed so that the two halves of the oasis, having been raised too high to be reached by the floods of the *sayl*, had become desolate (*Iklīl*, viii, 95, 7-96, 1). But the distributing constructions, which led the water from the reservoirs of the dam to the fields, were still standing there as if their builders had finished their work only the day before (*Iklīl*, viii, 96, 6-7). Moreover, even of the dam itself a piece had survived on the left-hand side; at the lower part it is said to have been 15 ells wide (*Iklīl*, viii, 96,10-97,1). This, however, was probably not the former lowest part of the dam. According to the words of al-Hamdānī, the dam was based on the foundation-wall which, between the side-walls, was joined to the reservoirs with mighty ashlars hewn from the rocks, and to the base by molten lead (*Iklīl*, viii, 99, 1-2). The building of such wonderful works as the dam constructions was therefore ascribed to the legendary Luḳmān b. ʿĀd, according to some (*Iklīl*, viii 99, 3; al-Masʿūdī, *Murū<u>dj</u>*, iii, 366, 3-4 = § 1251; al-Bakrī, *Muʿ<u>dj</u>am*, 1171, 2; Yāḳūt, *Muʿ<u>dj</u>am*, iv, 383, 1), while others were of the opinion that they had been erected by Ḥimyar b. Sabaʾ and al-Azd b. al-<u>Gh</u>aw<u>th</u>, a descendant of Kahlān (*Iklīl*, viii, 99, 3 ff.). According to other traditions, the dam was begun by Ya<u>sh</u><u>dj</u>ub b. Yaʿrub and finished by Ṣaʿb <u>Dh</u>u 'l-Ḳarnayn al-Ḥimyarī (Wahb b. Munabbih, *Kitāb al-Tī<u>dj</u>ān*, 58, 15 and 273, 19-274, 8), or built by ʿAbd <u>Sh</u>ams Sabaʾ b. Ya<u>sh</u><u>dj</u>ub (Yāḳūt, *Muʿ<u>dj</u>am*, iv, 382, 22-3), who are said to have directed there 70 rivers and floods from far away (Ibn Saʿīd al-Ma<u>gh</u>ribī, *Na<u>sh</u>wat al-ṭarab*, 86, 16-7). It is also said that the dam was begun by ʿAbd <u>Sh</u>ams, continued by Ḥimyar and finished by Ṣaʿb (al-<u>Kh</u>azra<u>dj</u>ī, *al-ʿUḳūd al-luʾluʾiyya*, 7, 6-9). The building of the Mārib dam is occasionally also ascribed to Bilḳīs [*q.v.*], the legendary queen of Sabaʾ (al-Damīrī, *Ḥayāt al-ḥayawān*, Cairo 1309/1892, i, 270, 31), or she is said to have repaired it (see R.G. Stiegner, *Die Königin von Sabaʾ in ihren Namen*, 75). Finally, the irrigation works are said to have been built by a king, not mentioned by name, after he had consulted wise men (Masʿūdī, *Murū<u>dj</u>*, iii, 369, 3-370, 7 = § 1254). As al-Hamdānī rightly observed, the *sayl* of the A<u>dh</u>ana wadi collected its water from many places and numerous sites of the Yemen (*Iklīl*, viii, 97, 10; detailed information in *Ṣifa*, 80, 12-23). Other authors even relate that the plantations in the Mārib oasis were so extensive that a horseman needed more than a month to cross them and that, in doing so, he found himself continuously in the shadow of the trees (al-Masʿūdī, *Murū<u>dj</u>*, iii, 367, 2-5 = § 1252; Ibn Saʿīd al-Ma<u>gh</u>ribī, *Na<u>sh</u>wat al-ṭarab*, 114, 20-115,1; it is even said that it took him six months (al-<u>Kh</u>azra<u>dj</u>ī, *al-ʿUḳūd al-luʾluʾiyya*, 8,9-10). If a woman or servant walked under the trees of the two gardens with a basket on the head, it used to fill of itself with fruits in a short time, without it being necessary to pluck them by hand or to pick them up from the ground (Ibn Rusta, *al-Aᶜlāḳ al-nafīsa*, 114, 7-10; Ibn Saᶜīd al-Maghribī, *Nashwat al-ṭarab*, 115, 9-10; al-Khazradjī *op. cit.*, 8, 5-7). According to a tradition, when shown the kingdom of heaven, Abraham asked for two earthly items only, namely the Ghūṭa of Damascus and the two gardens of Sabaʾ in Mārib (Ibn ᶜAsākir, *Taʾrīkh madīnat Dimashḳ*, ii, 195, 11-2; Aḥmad al-Rāzī, *Taʾrīkh madīnat Ṣanᶜāʾ*, Damascus 1974, 191 and 407, 17-408, 2). The fame and vanished glory of Mārib are also sung in numerous lines of poetry (see al-Hamdānī, *Iklīl*, viii, 98 ff.; Nashwān al-Ḥimyarī, *al-Ḳaṣīda al-ḥimyariyya*; *et alii*), and until today the former capital of the Sabaeans has remained an inexhaustible theme for Yemeni poets, as is shown e.g. by the anthology published by ᶜAbduh ᶜUthmān and ᶜAbd al-ᶜAzīz al-Maḳāliḥ under the title *Maʾrib yatakallamu* "Maʾrib speaks" (Taᶜizz 1971).

According to al-Hamdānī, there lies, to the east of Mārib in the desert of Ṣayhad, the *Djabal al-milḥ*, the salt mountain (*Ṣifa*, 102, 25-6), which he mentions once again among the wonders of the Yemen because its equal is not found throughout the world and its salt is rich and pure like crystal (*Ṣifa*, 201, 8-9). The Prophet Muhammad had given the salt of Mārib as a fief to Abyaḍ b. Ḥammāl when the latter came to him with a delegation and requested it as such (Abū Dāwūd, *Sunan*, ch. *Imāra, bāb* 36; al-Tirmidhī, *Sunan*, ch. *Aḥkām, bāb* 39). What is meant here is the salt-mine at the Djabal Ṣāfir, which can be reached from Mārib with camels in three days' journey along a waterless road. In earlier times, the Banū ᶜAbīda supplied from there almost the entire Yemeni highlands with salt. Since the salt traffic passes through Mārib, this commodity is called in the Yemen Mārib salt (*milḥ Māribī*; Ḥayyim Ḥabshūsh, *Ruʾyat al-Yaman*, 116, 16) until today. Among the products of the Mārib region, al-Hamdānī calls special attention to the sesame, whose oil is quite bright, pure and of good quality (*Ṣifa* 199, 9-10). Until today it is considered as the best in all Yemen.

In later Islamic times, the place Mārib which already al-Muḳaddasī (*Aḥsan al-taḳāsīm*, 89, 2) quotes only as *ḳaryat Mārib*, did not play a rôle of importance. Its name emerges sporadically in Yemeni chronicles, mostly in combination with warlike events, as when troops of the *Imām* moved from Ṣaᶜda through the Djawf to Mārib, or opponents of the *Imām* settled there. In 418/1027 there appeared in Nāᶜiṭ a man who claimed the imāmate. He went to Mārib where he was received, and proclaimed himself *imām* under the title al-Muᶜīd li-dīn Allāh. He succeeded even in obtaining entrance into Ṣanᶜāʾ and in winning adherents in various parts of the Yemen until he was killed by people from ᶜAns (Yaḥyā b. al-Ḥusayn, *Ghāyat al-amānī*, 243-4). Around 1050/1640, Mārib came under the sovereignty of Sharīf Ḥusayn b. Muḥammad b. Nāṣir who, at the head of a cavalry unit of the Dhū Ḥusayn, the Dhū Muḥammad and the Yām, had helped to expel the Turks from the Yemen. He adopted the title of *amīr* and ruled in Mārib, which remained a more or less independent principality. C. Niebuhr, who also collected in 1763 in Ṣanᶜāʾ information about Mārib, called it "the as yet most prominent town in the Djawf" (*Beschreibung von Arabien*, Copenhagen 1772, 277). Although consisting of only 300 houses, most of which were in wretched condition, it was still surrounded by a wall with three gates. A poor Sharīf was in power, who, apart from Mārib, commanded only a few villages and was hardly able to defend this area against his neighbours. When E. Glaser visited Mārib in 1888, the place counted hardly more than 600 inhabitants in some 80 houses of several storeys. In 1350/1932, Mārib was occupied by the *Imām* Yaḥyā's troops, commanded by ᶜAbd Allāh al-Wazīr, and the last *amīr* of the reigning *Ashrāf*, Muḥammad b. ᶜAbd al-Raḥmān, was deposed.

In cultural and scientific life in Islamic times, Mārib was hardly of any significance either. The *nisba* al-Māribī occurs only very sporadically. Apart from Abyaḍ b. Ḥammāl already mentioned, it is borne only by an informant who transmitted the request to leave the Mārib salt as a fief, namely Yaḥyā b. Ḳays al-Māribī (al-Dhahabī, *Mushtabih*, ed. de Jong, Leiden 1881, 465, 5; according to this source, *al-Māribī* should be read instead of *al-Māzinī* in al-Balādhurī, *Futūḥ*, 73, 7). Other scholars, mostly traditionists, who bore the *nisba* al-Māribī in the early Islamic period, are mentioned by Yāḳūt (*Muᶜdjam*, iv, 388, 9-21). For the later time, ᶜAbd Allāh al-Ḥibshī, *Maṣādir al-fikr al-ᶜarabī al-islāmī fi 'l-Yaman*, Ṣanᶜāʾ 1978, 316, was able to name only one bearer of the *nisba* al-Māribī.

During the Yemeni civil war of 1962-6, Mārib's fate was uncertain. Already in the beginning of October 1962 it was captured by the Royalists, but in March 1963 it was conquered by the Republicans who received Egyptian air support. In summer 1965, the Royalists succeeded in occupying Mārib again. During these combats, the houses of Mārib, which stand closely together on the ancient site, were largely destroyed by air attacks. Most of the inhabitants left the place and settled down in the neighbourhood, which explains the astonishingly low present number of the population. Until the present day, numerous houses of Old Mārib lie in ruins. At the foot of the hill of the old town lie in the *Masdjid* Sulaymān (with ancient columns), the residence of the governor (*muḥāfiẓ*), the police station, the military garrison, a water-pump installation, a number of huts covered with sheet-iron, shops and a restaurant. Formerly, Mārib could only be reached from Ṣanᶜāʾ by means of cross-country vehicles after an eight to twelve hours' difficult drive on tracks and through passes by three different routes, with a length between 170 and 220 km. Since 1981 the place has been linked with the capital Ṣanᶜāʾ by a road of about 150 km. length. After this convenient connection had been established, the flights between Sanᶜāʾ and Mārib with obsolete DC-3 aeroplanes, which had existed for years with occasional interruption, could be discontinued.

Bibliography: Wahb b. Munabbih, *Kitāb al-Tīdjān fī mulūk Ḥimyar*, Ṣanᶜāʾ 1979; Hamdānī, *Ṣifat Djazīrat al-ᶜArab*, ed. D.H. Müller, Leiden 1884-91; idem, *al-Iklīl*, viii, ed. M. al-Akwaᶜ al-Ḥiwālī, Damascus 1979, 95-107; Ibn Rusta, *Kitāb al-Aᶜlāḳ al-nafīsa*; Masᶜūdī, *Murūdj al-dhahab*, iii, 365-93 = §§ 1250-77; idem, *al-Tanbīh wa 'l-ishrāf*; Muḳaddasī, *Aḥsan al-taḳāsīm*; Bakrī, *Muᶜdjam ma 'staᶜdjama min asmāʾ al-bilād wa 'l-mawāḍiᶜ*, Cairo 1945-54, 1170-2; Yāḳūt, *Muᶜdjam al-buldān*, iv, 382-8; idem, *Kitāb al-Mushtarik*, ed. F. Wüstenfeld, Göttingen 1846; al-Rāzī al-Ṣanᶜānī, *Taʾrīkh madīnat Ṣanᶜāʾ*, Damascus 1974; Nashwān al-Ḥimyarī, *al-Ḳasīda al-ḥimyariyya*, ed. R. Basset, Algiers 1914; ᶜAẓīm-uddīn Aḥmad, *Die auf Südarabien bezüglichen Angaben Našwān's in Šams al-ᶜulūm*, Leiden 1916; Ibn Saᶜīd al-Maghribī, *Die Geschichte der "reinen Araber" vom Stamme Qaḥṭān. Aus dem Kitāb Našwat aṭ-ṭarab fī taʾrīḫ ǧāhiliyyat al-ᶜArab*, ed. M. Kropp, Frankfurt 1982;

Ibn al-Mudjāwir, *Taʾrīkh al-mustabṣir*, ed. O. Löfgren, Leiden 1951-4, 195-200; Damīrī, *Ḥayāt al-ḥayawān*, Cairo 1309/1891; ʿAlī b. al-Ḥasan al-Khazradjī, *al-ʿUḳūd al-luʾluʾiyya fī taʾrīkh al-dawla al-rasūliyya*, ed. M. ʿAsal, Leiden-London 1913; Ibn ʿAbd al-Munʿim al-Ḥimyarī, *al-Rawḍ al-miʿṭār fī khabar al-aḳṭār*, ed. I. ʿAbbās, Beirut 1975, 515-16; Yaḥyā b. al-Ḥusayn, *Ghāyat al-amānī fī akhbār al-ḳuṭr al-yamānī*, Cairo 1968; C. Niebuhr, *Beschreibung von Arabien*, Copenhagen 1772, 277-9; J.J. Reiske, *De Arabum epocha vetustissima, Sail ol-Arem, id est, ruptura catarrhactae Marebensis dicta*, Leipzig 1779; F. Fresnel, *Études sur l'histoire des Arabes avant l'Islamisme*, Paris 1836; Th.J. Arnaud, *Relation d'un voyage à Mareb (Saba) dans l'Arabie méridionale, entrepris en 1843*, in *JA*, ser. 4, vol. v (1845), 211-45, 309-45; A. P. Caussin de Perceval, *Essai sur l'histoire des Arabes*, Paris 1847-8; A. von Kremer, *Über die südarabische Sage*, Leipzig 1866; J. Halévy, *Rapport sur une mission archéologique dans le Yémen*, in JA, ser. 6, vol. xix (1872), 5-98; Th. J. Arnaud, *Plan de la digue et de ville de Mareb*, in *JA*, ser. 7, vol. iii (1874), 1-16; A. Sprenger, *Die alte Geographie Arabiens*, Bern 1875; D.H. Müller, *Die Bürgen und Schlösser Südarabiens nach dem Iklīl des Hamdânî*, Vienna 1879-81 (= *SB Ak. Wien*, xciv, xcvii); *Corpus inscriptionum semiticarum*, Pars iv, *Inscriptiones ḥimyariticas et sabaeas continens*, i-iii, Paris 1889-1929; E. Glaser, *Zwei Inschriften über den Dammbruch von Mârib* (*Mitteilungen der Vorderasiatischen Gesellschaft*, 1897, 6); *Eduard Glasers Reise nach Mârib*, ed. D. H. von Müller and N. Rhodokanakis, Vienna 1913 (*Sammlung Eduard Glaser*, i); Rhodokanakis, *Studien zur Lexikographie und Grammatik des Altsüdarabischen*, ii, Vienna 1917 (*SB Ak. Wien*, CLXXXV/3); *Répertoire d'Épigraphie Sémitique*, v-vii, Paris 1929-50; A. Grohmann, *Mariaba* in Pauly-Wissowa, xiv (1930), 1713-44; N.M. al-ʿAẓm, *Riḥla fī bilād al-ʿarabiyya al-saʿīda*, Cairo 1938; Ḥ. Ḥabshush, *Travels in Yemen. An account of Joseph Halévy's journey to Najran in the year 1870*, ed. S.D. Goitein, Jerusalem 1941; A. Fakhry, *An archaeological journey to Yemen*, i-iii, Cairo 1951-2; H. von Wissmann and M. Höfner, *Beiträge zur historischen Geographie des vorislamischen Südarabien*, Wiesbaden 1953 (*Akad. d. Wissensch. u.d. Literatur, Abh. d. geistes- und sozialwiss. Kl.*, Jg. 1952, 4); A. Jamme, *Inscriptions des alentours de Mâreb*, in *Cahiers de Byrsa*, v (1955), 265-81; R. Le-Baron Bowen, *Irrigation in ancient Qatabân (Beiḥân)*, in *Archaeological discoveries in South Arabia*, Baltimore 1958 (*Publications of the American Foundation for the Study of Man*, ii), 43-131; J. M. Solá Solé, *Las dos grandes inscripciones sudarábigas del dique de Mârib*, Barcelona-Tübingen 1960; J. Pirenne, *Le royaume sud-arabe de Qatabân et sa datation d'après l'archéologie et les sources classiques*, Louvain 1961 (*Bibliothèque du Muséon*, xlviii); A. Jamme, *Sabaean inscriptions from Maḥram Bilqîs (Mârib)*, Baltimore 1962 (*Publications of the American Foundation for the Study of Man*, iii); A. K. Irvine, *A survey of Old South Arabian lexical materials connected with irrigation techniques*, unpubl. D.Phil. thesis, Oxford Univ. 1962, 230-320; M. W. Wenner, *Modern Yemen 1918-1966*, Baltimore 1967; A. Ḥ. Sharaf al-Dīn, *Taʾrīkh al-Yaman al-thaḳāfī*, Cairo 1967, ii, 17-56; H. Dequin, *Eine Wasser-Kultstätte am Staudamm von Maʾrib im Jemen*, in *Orient*, ix/5 (October 1968), 164-7; G. Garbini, *Una nuova iscrizione di Šaraḥbiʾil Yaʿfur*, in *AION*, xxix (1969), 559-66; idem, *Antichità yemenite*, in *AION*, xxx (1970), 537-48; M. al-Akwaʿ al-Ḥiwālī, *al-Yaman al-ḥaḍrāʾ mahd al-ḥaḍāra*, Cairo 1971, 281-5, 293-303; D. B. Doe, *Building techniques in ancient South Arabia*, unpubl. Ph.D. thesis, Cambridge Univ. 1971; A.G. Loundine, *Qui a bâti le mur de Marib?*, in *AION*, xxxi (1971), 251-5; J. Ryckmans, *Un rite d'istisqâʾ au temple sabéen de Mârib*, in *Annuaire de l'Institut de Philologie et d'Histoire Orientales et Slaves*, xx (1968-72), 379-88; G. Garbini, *Un nuovo documento per la storia dell'antico Yemen*, in *Oriens Antiquus*, xii (1973), 143-64; A. G. Loundine, *Deux inscriptions sabéennes de Mârib*, in *Le Muséon*, lxxxvi (1973), 179-92; W. W. Müller, *Aus dem antiken Jemen (V.): Marib und Saba*, in *Jemen-Report 6* (1975), 10-13; idem, *Neuinterpretation altsüdarabischer Inschriften: RES 4698, CIH 45 + 44, Fa 74*, in *AION*, xxxvi (1976), 55-67; H. von Wissmann, *Die Mauer der Sabäerhauptstadt Maryab. Abessinien als sabäische Staatskolonie im 6. Jh. v. Chr.*, Istanbul 1976 (*Uitgaven van het Nederlands Historisch-Archaeologisch Instituut te Istanbul-Leiden*, 38); idem, *Die Geschichte des Sabäerreichs und der Feldzug des Aelius Gallus*, in *Aufstieg und Niedergang der römischen Welt. Geschichte und Kultur Roms im Spiegel der neueren Forschung*, ed. H. Temporini und W. Haase, ii, 9,1 (1976), 308-544; *Final report on the airphoto interpretation project of the Swiss Technical Cooperation Service, Berne, carried out for the Central Planning Organisation, Ṣanʿāʾ. The major findings of the population and housing census of February 1975*, Zürich 1978; R. Schoch, *Die antike Kulturlandschaft des Stadtbezirks Sabaʾ und die heutige Oase von Maʾrib in der Arabischen Republik Jemen*, in *Geographica Helvetica, xxxiii (1978), 121-9; Gazeteer of Arabia. A geographical and tribal history of the Arabian peninsula*, ed. Sh. A. Scoville, i, 1979, 45-6; R. G. Stiegner, *Die Königin von Sabaʾ in ihren Namen. Beitrag zur vergleichenden semitischen Sagenkunde und zur Erforschung des Entwicklungsganges der Sage*, Ph.D. thesis, Graz Univ. 1979; J. E. Dayton, *A discussion on the hydrology of Marib*, in *Proceedings of the Seminar for Arabian Studies*, ix (1979), 124-9; J. Ryckmans, *Le barrage de Marib et les jardins du royaume de Saba*, in *Dossiers de l'Archéologie*, xxxiii (March-April 1979), 28-35; R. Wade, *Archaeological observations around Marib*, 1976, in *PSAS*, ix (1979), 114-23; idem, *Taḳrīr maydānī ʿan Maʾrib*, in *al-Iklīl*, i/2 (1980), 207-11; Ḥ.A. as-Sayāghī, *Maʿālim al-āthār al-yamaniyya*, Ṣanʿāʾ 1980, 49-54; W. W. Müller, *Altsüdarabische Miszellen* (I), in *Raydān*, iii (1980), 63-73; J. E. Dayton, *Marib visited, 1979*, in *PSAS*, xi (1981), 7-26; J. Schmidt, *Mārib. Erster vorläufiger Bericht über die Forschungen des Deutschen Archäologischen Instituts in der Umgebung der Sabäerhauptstadt. With contributions by U. Brunner, M. Gerig, W. W. Müller and R. Schoch*, in *Archäologische Berichte aus dem Yemen*, i (1982), 5-89, Tables 1-34; Chr. Robin and J. Ryckmans, *Dédicace de bassins rupestres antiques à proximité de Bāb al-Falağ (Mârib)*, in *ibid.*, 107-15; W.W. Müller, *Bemerkungen zu einigen von der Yemen-Expedition 1977 des Deutschen Archäologischen Instituts aufgenommenen Inschriften aus dem Raum Mārib und Barāqiš*, in *ibid.*, 129-34; A.H. al-Scheiba, *Die Ortsnamen in den altsüdarabischen Inschriften (mit dem Versuch ihrer Identifizierung und Lokalisierung)*, Ph.D. thesis, Marburg Univ. 1982, 133-4; U. Brunner, *Die Erforschung der antiken Oase von Mārib mit Hilfe geomorphologischer Untersuchungsmethoden*, Mainz 1983 (= *Archäologische Berichte aus dem Yemen*, ii) Y. M. ʿAbd Allāh, *Ḥadīth fī ḥaḍārat Sabaʾ wa-ramzihā sadd Maʾrib*, in *al-Yaman al-Djadīd*, xi/7 (July 1982), 9-20; von Wissmann, *Die Geschichte von Sabaʾ. II. Das Grossreich der Sabaer bis zu seinem Ende im frühren 4. Jh. v. Chr.*, ed. W. W. Müller, Vienna 1982 (= *SB Ak. Wien*, ccccii); Ü. Brunner, *Die Erforschung der antiken Oase von Mārib mit Hilfe geomorphologischer Untersuchungsmethoden*, Mainz 1983.

(W. W. Müller)

MĀRIDA, Spanish Mérida, from the Latin Emerita, a town in the south-west of Spain, in the modern province of Badajoz, where it is the capital of a *partido*, on the right bank of the Guadiana. Now somewhat decayed, it has only about 35,000 inhabitants. It is on the Madrid-Badajoz railway and is also connected by rail with Cáceres in the north and Seville in the south.

The ancient capital of Lusitania, Augusta Emerita, was founded in 23 B.C., and under the Roman empire attained remarkable importance and prosperity. Numerous remains of Roman buildings still testify to the position it held in the Iberian peninsula in those days: a bridge of 64 arches, a circus, a theatre, and the famous aqueduct of *los Milagros*, of which there are still standing ten arches of brick and granite. Merida under the Visigoths became the metropolis of Lusitania and, according to Rodrigo of Toledo, was fortified and strongly defended, which explains why the Muslim conquerors led by Mūsā b. Nuṣayr [*q.v.*] had some difficulty in taking it. The Arab leader on landing in Spain in Ramaḍān 93/June 712 first took Medina-Sidonia and Carmona, then Seville. He next laid siege to Mérida, before which he stayed for several months; but the inhabitants in the end capitulated and the town surrendered on 1 Shawwāl 94/30 June 713. From Mérida, Mūsā b. Nuṣayr continued his advance to Toledo.

Under the Arab governors, Mérida seems to have very soon become a rallying point for a large number of rebels of Berber and Spanish origin. It was there that Yụsuf al-Fihrī endeavoured to organise a movement against that organised for his own benefit by ʿAbd al-Raḥmān al-Dākhil in 141/758. At a later date, a Berber named Aṣbagh b. ʿAbd Allāh b. Wānsūs rebelled there against al-Ḥakam I in 190/805 and the *amīr* of Cordova had for the next seven years to undertake summer campaigns against him before bringing him to reason. Another rebellion broke out in Mérida in 213/828, and the town had to be besieged in 217/832 and again in 254/868. In the reign of the *amīr* ʿAbd Allāh it was the headquarters of ʿAbd al-Raḥmān b. Marwān al-Djillīkī ("the Galician"), an Arabic name which concealed that of a Christian nationalist leader. Mérida definitely returned to its allegiance in the reign of ʿAbd al-Raḥmān III al-Nāṣir, when it submitted in 316/928 to the *ḳāʾid* Aḥmad b. Ilyās.

From the 5th/11th century, Mérida began to decline in favour of Badajoz, especially when the latter town became the capital of the independent little kingdom of the Afṭasids [*q.v.*]. It remained in the hands of the Muslims till the beginning of the 7th/13th century. In 625/1228 it was retaken by Alfonso IX of Léon, but never recovered its former importance.

The Arab geographers who mention Mérida describe its Roman ruins in detail; they also mention the Muslim citadel, the foundation inscription of which has been preserved. It was built in 220/835 by the governor ʿAbd Allāh b. Kulayb b. Thaʿlaba by order of the Umayyad ʿAbd al-Raḥmān II.

Bibliography: The Arabic historians of Umayyad Spain (*Akhbār madjmūʿa*; Ibn ʿIdhārī, *Bayān*; Ibn al-Athīr; Nuwayrī; Maḳḳarī, *Analectes, passim*); Idrīsī, *Description de l'Afrique et de l'Espagne*, ed. Dozy and de Goeje, text, 175, 182, tr. 211, 220; Yāḳut, iv, 389-90; Ibn ʿAbd al-Munʿim al-Ḥimyarī, *al-Rawḍ al-miʿṭār*, 210-13; E. Fagnan, *Extraits inédits relatifs au Maghreb*, Algiers 1924, index; Dozy, *Histoire des Musulmans d'Espagne*, ii, 37, 40, 62, 96; idem, *Recherches*³, i, 54-6; Codera, *Inscription árabe del Castillo de Mérida*, in *Bol. R. Acad. Hist.*, Madrid 1902, 138-42; E. Lévi-Provençal, *Inscriptions arabes d'Espagne*, Leiden-Paris 1931, 39-40; idem, *Hist. Esp. mus.*, iii, 350-1 and index.

(E. Lévi-Provençal)

MĀRIDĪN [see mārdīn].

al-**MĀRIDĪNĪ** [see al-mārdīnī].

MAʿRIFA (a.) "Knowledge, cognition".

1. As a term of epistemology and mysticism

I. Lexicographical study. Like *ʿirfān*, the word *maʿrifa* is a noun derived from the verb *ʿarafa*. According to the lexicographers, it is a synonym of *ʿilm* [*q.v.*]. Ibn Manẓūr (*LA*) notes that *ʿarafa* may be used in place of *iʿtarafa* ("to recognise"), in the sense that *maʿrifa* is that which enables a person to recognise, to identify a thing. On the other hand, *iʿtarafa* signifies "to ask somebody for information (*khabar*) regarding something". It is the reply which makes recognition of this thing possible. When an animal is lost, "a man comes who recognises it (*yaʿtarifu-hā*), that is to say, he describes it by an attribute (*ṣifa*) which makes known (*yuʿlimu*) that it belongs to him". According to a tradition related by Ibn Masʿūd, people were asked if they knew their Lord. They replied: "If He makes Himself recognised to us, we know Him." Consequently, from a philological point of view, the *maʿrifa* which causes recognition and which thereby gives knowledge (*ʿilm*) of its subject, always contains the indication of an attribute through which its subject is identified. The *ḥadīth* of Ibn Masʿūd is explained thus: "If God describes Himself by means of an attribute through which we can authenticate Him, then we know Him."

In his *Dictionary of technical terms*, al-Tahānawī lists several senses of the word *maʿrifa*, which he identifies with the word "knowledge" while noting particular connotations which are sometimes given to it to distinguish it from *ʿilm*. (1) In the first place, *maʿrifa* is knowledge, in the absolute sense of perception (*idrāk*), whether in the form of a concept, or in the form of a judgment. (2) It is the perception of a concept; in the case of a judgment it is called knowledge. (3) It is the perception of what is simple (*basīṭ*), whether it is a concept of the quiddity or a judgment regarding the conditions of this quiddity; or it is the perception of something which is composite (*murakkab*), whether it be a concept or a judgment. But according to technical terminology, perception of the composite is specifically called knowledge. In addition, according to the lexicographers, the correct statement is "I have cognition of God (*ʿaraftu 'llāh*)" and not "I have knowledge of God (*ʿalimtu-hu*)", because God is a simple entity. Consequently, that which is in relation to *maʿrifa* is simple, whereas that which is in relation to knowledge is multiple (*mutaʿaddid*) and thus composite. (4) It is the perception of the particular, notion (*mafhūm*) or verdict (*ḥukm*); or the perception of the universal, notion or sentence. But the perception of universals is more specifically called knowledge or speculation (*naẓar*). According to al-Tahānawī, it is most probable that in principle, the word *maʿrifa* is used to apply to a concept, and the word knowledge to apply to a judgment. Then there are ramifications. Thus it may be considered that definitions (2) and (4) are ramifications of definition (3), since the particular and the concept resemble the simple, and the universal and the judgment resemble the composite. (5) It is the perception of a particular by means of a proof or indication (*dalīl*); this is called *maʿrifat istidāliyya*, cognition by proof. This is reminiscent of what the *LA* states regarding cognition by *ṣifa*. The language itself clearly marks the connection between *dalīl* and cognition; it is said *dalaltu bi 'l-ṭarīk* in the sense of "I have made the way known (*ʿarraftuhu*), as the *LA* notes. One also considers the meaning that grammarians give to the word *maʿrifa* to indicate the determination of a noun, as opposed to *nakira*. It is the condition of a noun applied to a thing taken in itself (*bi-ʿaynihi*) and the article which determines it (by *taʿrīf*) acts in such a way that the object that it signifies may be pointed to (*mus̲h̲ār bihi*) with a positive designation (*is̲h̲āratan waḍʿiyya*). The noun is furthermore, in a general sense, that which is indicated by a meaning (*mā dalla ʿalā 'l-maʿnā*). It thus seems that there is indeed a connection between *maʿrifa*, in the sense of the perception of a particular by means of *dalīl*, and *maʿrifa* in the sense of determination of a noun which makes known an "essence" definable in itself. (6). It is the perception that comes after ignorance (*d̲j̲ahl*). Thus it cannot be said that God is cognisant (*ʿārif*); it must be said that He is knowing (*ʿālim*). In this sense, the word *ʿilm* has a general meaning, and the word *maʿrifa* a particular meaning. (7) It is a technical term employed by Ṣūfis.

II. *Maʿrifa* in mystical thought. Al-Tahānawī relates that it is usually (*ʿurfan*) considered to be the knowledge (*ʿilm*) which precedes ignorance (*nakara*). The use of the word *nakara* in place of *d̲j̲ahl* is interesting (cf. above, *nakira*). It is the knowledge (*ʿilm*) which does not admit doubt (*s̲h̲akk*) since its object, the *maʿlūm*, is the Essence of God and his attributes. Cognition of the Essence consists in knowing (*an yuʿlama*) that God is existent (*mawd̲j̲ūd*), one (*wāḥid*), sole and unique (*fard*); that He does not resemble any thing; and that nothing resembles Him. Cognition of the attributes consists in knowing Him as living, omniscient, hearing, seeing, speaking, etc. It is thus seen how regularly the word "knowledge" or the verb "to know" intervene in definitions of *maʿrifa* among the mystics.

It is necessary to distinguish *maʿrifa* based on proving indications which, by means of "signs" (*āyāt*) constitute the proof of the Creator. Certain people see things, then see God through these things. In reality, *maʿrifa* is realised only for those to whom there is revealed something of the invisible (*al-g̲h̲ayb*), in such a way that God is proved simultaneously by manifest and by hidden signs. Such is the *maʿrifa* of men "anchored in knowledge" (*al-rāsik̲h̲īn fī 'l-ʿilm*; cf. Ḳurʾān, III, 7; IV, 162). Then there is the *maʿrifa* of direct testimony (*s̲h̲uhūdiyya*) which asserts itself as evidence (*ḍarūriyya*); it is this which gives cognition of the signs through Him who has instituted them, and this is the prerogative of the just (*al-ṣiddīḳīn*, cf. Ḳurʾān, LVII, 19: *hum al-ṣiddīḳūn wa 'l-s̲h̲uhadāʾ ʿinda rabbihim*). These are the men of contemplation (*aṣḥāb al-mus̲h̲āhada*).

III. Definitions given by the Ṣūfis, and the mystical tradition. It is related that God said to David in a revelation. "Do you understand what it is to know Me? Cognition of Me is the life of the heart in the contemplation which it has of Me." Al-S̲h̲iblī said, "When you are attached to God, not to your works, and when you look at nothing other than Him, then you have a perfect *maʿrifa*." Cognition has been compared to the sight of God in the Other Life; "Just as He is known here below without perception, so He will be seen in the other life without perception (*idrāk*)" (al-Tahānawī), for it is said in the Ḳurʾān (VI, 101), "Vision will not comprehend Him, but He, He will comprehend vision." The Ṣūfis cite the following *ḥadīt̲h̲* of the Prophet, "If you knew God by a true *maʿrifa*, the mountains would disappear at your command." Cognition is linked to various conditions (*aḥwāl*) with which *taṣawwuf* deals. Thus Abū Yazīd al-Biṣṭāmī [*q.v.*] said, "True *maʿrifa* is life in the memory of God (*d̲h̲ikr*)." Similarly, al-Tahānawī quotes Abū ʿAlī (perhaps al-D̲j̲uzd̲j̲ānī, 3rd/9th century), "The fruit of *maʿrifa* is that one bears with patience (*ṣabr*) proofs when they come; that a man gives thanks (*s̲h̲ukr*) when he receives a benefit; and that he gives his consent (*riḍā*) to God, when he is struck with a hateful evil." The father-in-law of al-Ḳus̲h̲ayrī [*q.v.*], Abu 'l-Daḳḳāḳ, said, "One of the signs of the cognition that a man has of God, is the entry into him of reverential fear (*hayba*). One of the signs that it is growing, is that this fear grows. *Maʿrifa* necessarily entails quietude (*sakīna*) as knowledge entails rest." *Maʿrifa* assumes not only the abolition of the consciousness of self at the level of the soul, the empirical self, but an absence of self at the level of the heart and the spirit. Abū Ḥafṣ (ʿUmar b. Maslama al-Ḥaddād, born near Nīs̲h̲āpūr, d. *ca.* 260/874) said, "Since I have cognition of God, there enters into my heart neither truth nor falsehood. Cognition necessarily entails for the man his absence (*g̲h̲ayba*) from himself, in such a way that the memory of God reigns exclusively in him, that he sees nothing other than God and that he turns to nothing other than to Him. For, just as the man who reasons has recourse to his heart, to his reflection and to his memories, in every situation which is presented to him and in every condition which he encounters, so the *ʿārif* has his recourse in God. Such is the difference between him who sees through his heart and him who sees through his Lord." In the same context, al-Bistāmī said, "The creature has its conditions, but the *ʿārif*, the cognisant one, does not have them, because his traits are effaced and his ipseity (*huwiyya*) is abolished in the ipseity of One Other than him (God). His features become invisible beneath the features of God." Also worthy of quotation is al-Wāsiṭī (pupil of D̲j̲unayd and of al-Nūrī, d. 320/932), "*Maʿrifa* is not authentic when there remains in the man an independence which dispenses with God and the need for God. For to dispense with God and to have need of Him are two signs that the man is awake and that his characteristics remain, and this on account of his qualifications. Now the *ʿarīf* is entirely effaced in Him whom he knows. How could this—which is due to the fact that one loses his existence in God and is engrossed in contemplation of Him—be true, if one is not a man devoid of any sentiment which could be for him a qualification, when one approaches existence?" The following are other conditions which are related to *maʿrifa*. Ibn Abi 'l-Ḥawwārī (3rd/9th century) said, "He who knows God best and he who fears Him the most." Ibn ʿAṭāʾ, the friend of al-Ḥallād̲j̲, thought that *maʿrifa* depends on three things: reverential fear, modesty (*ḥayāʾ*) and intimacy with God (*uns*). In fact, he who has cognition of God is in intimacy (*anasa*) with Him. The following are some definitions and qualifications of the one who knows God. It has been said, "The *ʿārif* is he who acts for the pleasure of his Lord, without gaining anything for himself by this action." Seeing that some teachers taught that having once arrived at cognition, man no longer acts, al-D̲j̲unayd took issue with this opinion: "Those who have the cognition (*al-ʿārifūn*) of God, draw their actions from God and turn to God in their actions. If they needed to last for a thousand years, acts of piety would not be diminished by a jot." The same D̲j̲unayd said, "That man is not truly an *ʿārif*, so long as he is not like the earth which is trodden by the pious man and the licentious alike, like the cloud which extends its shade over all things, and like the rain which drenches the one that it likes and the one that it does not like." In some instances, the definition adopts a dialectical twist. Thus Yaḥyā b. Muʿā*dh* (a native of Rayy, who settled and died in Nī*sh*āpūr in 248/872), said, "The *ʿārif* is the man who is there without being there." Al-*D*junayd added, "who is distinct without separation."

In general, it is to be noted that all these conceptions, while placing *maʿrifa* above demonstrative and speculative knowledge, do not absolutely imply an esoteric vision. All or most depend on certain features which make of *maʿrifa* an illuminative cognition whose brightness has the power to stun. Thus Ruwaym, a Ṣūfī of Ba*gh*dād (d. 303/915), said, "For the *ʿārif*, *maʿrifa* is a mirror; when he looks at it, his Lord shines there for him (*tadjallā lahu*)", and Sahl b. ʿAbd Allāh al-Tustarī notes that "the final stage of *maʿrifa* consists in two things: amazement (*dahash*) and confusion (*ḥayra*)". The same notion is found in the writings of *Dh*u 'l-Nūn al-Miṣrī.

Some interesting analyses, and important conclusions, are to be found in the work of Farid Jabre, *La notion de maʿrifa chez Ghazālī*, Beirut 1958. Comparing al-*Gh*azālī with Plotinus, he writes (p. 134), "The former aspires towards an abstract ideal world, the 'well-guarded Table', archetype of revealed knowledge, the latter seeks to lose himself ontologically in the One... It is here that *maʿrifa* and *gnosis* diverge fundamentally: the latter is achieved in ecstasy... which is not simply vision... but unitive vision, and the former in the loss of consciousness of the self." Al-*Gh*azālī indeed belongs to the line of mystics whose conceptions have been related in this article.

IV. *Maʿrifa* in the thought of Ibn ʿArabī. It seems that Ibn ʿArabī makes no distinction in usage between the words "knowledge" and "cognition". For him, there is one *maʿrifa* which is attained through the light of intelligence (*bi-nūr al-ʿaḳl*): this is cognition of the divine nature (*maʿrifat al-ulūhiyya*) and of what is necessary, impossible, possible and not impossible for it. It is evident therefore that what is in question is a rational cognition, in other words, knowledge. On the other hand, there is a *maʿrifa* which is attained by the light of faith (*bi-nūr al-īmān*), by means of which intelligence (*al-ʿaḳl*) seizes the Essence and the qualifications which God ascribes to Himself. It is this second *maʿrifa* which has to be that of the mystics (cf. *Futūḥāt*, ed. ʿU*th*mān Yaḥyā, i, 203, no. 289). Ibn ʿArabī devoted ch. 177 of the *Futūḥāt* to "cognition of the status of cognition." Nobody has knowledge (*ʿilm*) except He who knows (*ʿarafa*) what is through its essence. Whoever knows what is through some thing which is added to its essence, is a *muḳallid* who intimates that which is added thus by means of that which he receives from it. Every cognisant being that is not God thus has cognition through *taḳlīd* in conforming to the data of the senses and of reason. Since he is compelled to imitate, the man of good judgment (*al-ʿāḳil*) who wishes to know God, must imitate Him in that which He has made known (*akhbara*) of Himself in His Books and through the mouths of His Messengers. When he wishes to know things, not relying on his own faculties but through force of obedience (*bi-kathrat al-ṭāʿāt*), he comes into a state where God is his hearing, his sight and all his faculties. Then he knows all things through God, and God through God. This was the answer given by *Dh*u 'l-Nūn when he was asked by what means he knew his Lord: "I know my Lord through my Lord; without Him, I would not know Him." Those who rely on their own senses, know that senses and reason can be mistaken (as al-*Gh*azālī pointed out in the *Munḳidh*). They seek to distinguish the cases where they are mistaken and the cases where they are justified. But since they make this distinction with faculties which can be mistaken, they can never know whether what they classify as true is not false and *vice versa*. Here there is a serious malady (*dāʾ ʿuḍāl*), which can be avoided only by those who in all things have knowledge only through God. As for knowing what it is that causes such men to have knowledge from God, this is something which our error-prone faculties are incapable of establishing. Since we see that we can have knowledge only through *taḳlīd*, all that remains for us is to imitate "him who is called the Messenger and that which is designated as the Word of God." We conform to these models to the point at which God becomes the totality of our faculties. We will thus be able to determine the cases where we shall take possession of truth. The man who arrives at this state is then, as the Ḳurʾān expresses it (XII, 108; LXXV, 14), *ʿalā baṣīratⁱⁿ*. *Maʿrifa*, in its highest degree, is thus this *baṣīra*, this interior view of realities which neither the senses nor reason are capable of attaining.

Ibn ʿArabī distinguishes three ranks of categories of knowledge (*marātib al-ʿulūm*). The first is that of the knowledge of intelligence, founded on necessary principles and the demonstrations based on them. This is not under discussion here. The second is that of the knowledge of states (*ʿilm al-aḥwāl*), to which the only access is through taste (*dhawḳ*), such as the knowledge of the sweetness of honey or the bitterness of bile. This definition also accords with the taste-oriented cognition of the Ṣūfīs. The third rank is that of knowledge of secret things (*ʿulūm al-asrār*). It is superior to the category of intelligence (*fawḳ ṭawr al-ʿaḳl*); it is the knowledge of the infusion of the breath of the Spirit of Holiness in the human spirit (*ʿilm nafth Rūḥ al-Ḳuds fi 'l-rawʿ*). It is the prerogative of the prophet (*al-nabī*) and of the saint (*al-walī*). It includes two types. The first is apprehended by the intelligence, as in the first rank of knowledges, but not as a result of speculation (*naẓar*). The second type is of two kinds. One is linked to knowledge of the second rank, to *dhawḳ*, but is superior (*ashraf*). The other is a knowledge of information (*min ʿulūm al-akhbār*). This is evidently concerned with information the veracity (*ṣidḳ*) of which is guaranteed; this is the information given by the prophets (cf. *Futūḥāt*, ed. Yaḥyā, i, 138-40, nos. 64-8). Consequently, *maʿrifa* in its highest degree, where *baṣīra* is exercised, seems to accord well with the different aspects of the *ʿulūm al-asrār*.

A further division is found (*ibid*., i, 153, no. 100): "The axis of the knowledge which belongs to men of God (*ahl Allāh*) consists of seven questions. For whosoever knows them (*ʿarafa-hā*), there is nothing in the knowledge of Realities (*ʿilm al-ḥaḳāʾiḳ*) which presents a difficulty. These are: cognition (*maʿrifa*) of the Names of God; the cognition of epiphanic emanations (*tadjalliyāt*); cognition of the Word addressed by God to man in the form of the language of the Law; cognition of disclosure through imagination (*al-kashf al-khayālī*); and cognition of sicknesses and remedies. A detailed study of these *maʿārif* forms the object of ch. 177 of the *Futūḥāt*, to which the reader is referred. All that is noted here is that it seems that among all these cognitions, there is one which is distinct in the sense that is operates in all the others; this is the cognition of disclosure through imagination. In particular, that which Ibn ʿArabī says concerning cognition of the Names of God depends on a symbolic vision which is the act of the imagination. Here we refer to the work of H. Corbin, *L'imagination créatrice dans le soufisme d'Ibn ʿArabi*,[2] Paris 1977.

V. The Yazdān-shanākht of al-Suhrawardī. This Persian title is the equivalent of *maʿrifat Allāh*. Corbin has analysed it in his *Oeuvres philosophiques et mystiques d'al-Suhrawardī*, Tehran-Paris 1970, ii, 117-31. Here the author examines the development of human cognition, estimative and intellective. Corbin writes in this context: "There is certainly a measure of Avicennism in all this, but it is possible in addition to discern the premisses of the philosophy of Ishrâq." In fact, this treatise which aspires towards prophetic cognition, towards mystical charismas and visions in dreams or in states of trance, is definitely less original than Corbin suggests. It calls to mind the *Kitāb al-Fawz al-aṣghar* of Miskawayh (tr. Arnaldez, Tunis 1986). But it is in relation to the philosophy of *ishrāḳ* that Corbin defines true *maʿrifa*: "In contrast to *representative* cognition, which is cognition of the abstract or logical universal (*ʿilm ṣūrī*), this is a case of *presential* cognition, which is unitive and intuitive, of an essence absolutely true in its ontological singularity (*ʿilm ḥuḍūrī ittiṣālī, shuhūdī*), a presential illumination (*ishrāḳ ḥuḍūrī*) which the soul, the being of light, brings to bear on its object; it makes itself present in making itself present to itself" (*Histoire de la philosophie islamique*, in the series *Idées*, NRF, Paris 1964, 291).

VI. Conclusion. *Maʿrifa* has frequently been translated as gnosis. The Greek γνωσίς probably denotes purely and simply cognition. But the word "gnosis" has taken on a particular sense; it denotes, not one, but several systems which undoubtedly have common features, but which differ considerably from one another. There are thus several *gnoses*: Basilidian, Valentinian, Ismāʿīlī, *Ishrāḳī*, Shīʿī, etc. Corbin has written (*Avicenne et le récit visionnaire*, Berg International, 1979, 23), "But ultimately it remains a case of a spiritual attitude which is fundamentally the same: a deliverance, a salvation of the soul obtained not merely through cognition, but through cognition which is precisely gnosis." But this is nothing more than a nominal definition. The notion of salvation through cognition is certainly present in the gnoses, but it is also to be found in the systems inspired by Plato and by Neo-Platonism, in which it is taught that the cognition of intelligibles by the human intellect liberates man and even assures his survival after physical death. Yet there is nothing gnostic in these systems. In criticising the gnostics, Plotinus characterises the gnoses by other features entirely, in particular by the multiplicities of intermediaries, standing as so many entities between the First Principle and the world below, according to a succession of manifestations whose link with the mythologies is apparent. Thus it is undoubtedly true that there is a *maʿrifa* in the gnoses, and that *maʿrifa* can be of gnostic type, esoteric and initiatory. But it is definitely a misuse to translate *maʿrifa* automatically as "gnosis". Were it not so, it would be necessary to render the plural *al-maʿārif* by "the gnoses" (listed above), which would obviously be unacceptable.

Bibliography: Given in the text.

(R. Arnaldez)

2. As a term denoting secular knowledge

Hence opposed to *ʿilm* and almost synoymous with *adab*, see ʿilm.

MARĪNIDS (Banū Marīn), a Berber dynasty of the Zanāta group, which ruled the western Maghrib (Morocco) from the middle of the 7th/13th century to the middle of the 9th/15th.

A considerable number of contemporary sources, chronicles, literary works, inscriptions, collections of judicial decisions (*fatwās* and *nawāzil*), Italian, Aragonese and French archive documents make it possible to paint a fairly complete picture of the history of Morocco under the Marīnid dynasty. The historian Ibn Khaldūn, their most famous contemporary, reproduced in his *Kitāb al-ʿIbar* the genealogical descent, largely mythical, of the Marīnid tribes in the context of the Zanāta family, and designates the desert between Figuig and Sidjilmāsa as the terrain which they originally frequented. It is to be believed that the arrival of Arab tribes in the region from the south during the 5th and 6th/11th-12th centuries was the cause of various demographic mutations which obliged the Marīnid tribes to proceed towards the north and to settle in the plains of the north-west of what is now Algeria. Nomadic shepherds and breeders of sheep, the Banū Marīn gave their name to the wool (merino) that they produced and which, being of superior quality, was, as early as the beginning of the 8th/14th century, exported to Europe through the agency of Genoese merchants. An Italian document which tells of 49 consignments of wool called "merinus", purchased in Tunis in 1307, also supports the theory that the dynasty was not unconnected with the introduction of the sheep of this name in the Iberian peninsula.

The appearance of the Marīnids in the works of Arab chroniclers dates from the 6th/12th century, first in reference to local conflicts, then as a political factor, from the time of their participation in the battle of Alarcos, in Spain, alongside the Almohads (591/1195) [see al-muwaḥḥidūn]. After 610/1213-14, they maintained a slow but persistent penetration into the inhabited areas of the zone which they had habitually frequented, where the Almohad régime was in the process of rapid disintegration. At the start, their activity consisted only in claiming dues from the towns and charging protection dues, and the Almohads conducted an ambiguous policy towards them, fighting them at times and collaborating with them at others. By the middle of the 7th/13th century, the Almohads were no longer able to resist forcibly the physical occupation and settlement of the Marīnids in the large towns. United under the leadership of the house of ʿAbd al-Ḥaḳḳ, which at this point became the dynastic family, they captured Meknès in 642/1244, Fās in 646/1248, Sidjilmāsa in 653/1255 and finally Marrakesh, the capital, in 668/1269. Only recently converted to Islam, the Marīnids showed no particular reformatory zeal at the time of their occupation of Morocco, unlike their Almoravid and Almohad predecessors. They did, however, as a result of their encounters with jurists and city dwellers, cultivate a sense of mission which had a religious ingredient, wishing to provide the Muslims with just and prosperous government, which the Almohads were no longer able to offer (M. Shatzmiller, *Islam de campagne et Islam de ville: le facteur religieux à l'avènement des Merinides*, in *SI*, li [1980], 123-36).

Following the seizure of Marrakesh, the history of the Marīnids is divided into two periods of approximately equal length, corresponding to two phases: a first phase (668-759/1269-1358) characterised by military exploits, urban expansion and governmental stability, and a second phase (759-870/1358-1465) which sees a slow erosion of the political structures, a territorial regression and internal division. Almost all the Marīnid sovereigns of the first phase (see the dynastic list) were distinguished by the vigour of their military campaigns and the length of their reigns. From the start, the Marīnids displayed a remarkably dynamic military strength: with a series of campaigns conducted in Spain against Castile (674/1275, 676/1277, 682/1283), the sultan Abū Yūsuf Yaʿḳūb established the central position which the Marīnid factor was to occupy in the diplomatic scene of the western Mediterranean basin during the 7th and 8th/13th and 14th centuries. For their Maghribī co-religionists, this constant *Drang nach Osten* of Marīnid policy constituted a permanent threat which was realised from time to time, the most violent episode being the prolonged siege of Tlemcen under the sultan Abū Yaʿḳūb Yūsuf (698-706/1299-1307). The high point of Marīnid history was reached under the sultan Abu 'l-Ḥasan ʿAlī with the seizure of Tlemcen (737/1337) and of Tunis (748/1347) and the temporary subjection of the entire Maghrib (R. Thoden, *Abu 'l-Hasan ʿAli. Merinidenpolitik zwischen Nordafrika und Spanien in den Jahren 710-725H/1310-1351*, Freiburg 1973).

The chroniclers of the period, al-ʿUmarī and Ibn Marzūḳ, supply numerous details regarding the composition, the routine, the equipment and the pay of the army. Composed of regular and irregular units, its striking force seems to have been constituted by Zanāta horsemen (40,000 in the time of Abu 'l-Ḥasan). The Arab tribes also supplied horsemen, while Andalusians were recruited as unmounted archers. In addition to its numerical importance, the army was frequently engaged in training exercises and equipped with catapults and fire-throwers. A Christian militia, commanded by an "alcayt" and recruited in Aragon, Castile and Portugal from 1306 onwards, with other non-indigenous elements including Kurds and negroes, constituted the regular army and the personal bodyguard of the sovereign. The Christians, between 2,000 and 5,000 at the time of Abu 'l-Ḥasan, were paid once every three months at the rate of 5 to 50 gold *dīnārs* per month, part of their salary being paid to their respective sovereigns. In the turbulent years of the second phase, this militia took an active part in the increasingly numerous palace revolutions. The remainder of the army was also registered in the *Dīwān* and paid in kind. Only the chieftains of tribes received land in *iḳṭāʿ*.

The only point of weakness was constituted by the fleet, which, in spite of the abundant supply of wood and the existence of ship-building yards at Ceuta and Salé, was never large enough to compete with the Aragonese fleet. The archives of the court of Aragon testify, in fact, that for naval battles, such as the seizure of Ceuta in 678/1279, Catalan ships were hired at a high price by the Marīnid sovereigns. On the other hand, a Marīnid unit of Zanāta horsemen participated in 1285 in the European campaign against France and in 1307, 7,000 Marīnids were in the service of the Naṣrids of Granada.

The first phase of Marīnid history was also an age of major architectural activity, and the Marīnid monuments of the early period reflect the energy and the material wealth of the time. These consist primarily of three new urban conurbations, New Fez, al-Binya near Algeciras and al-Manṣura near Tlemcen; of *zāwiyas*; of the necropolis of Chella; of the arsenals of Ceuta and Salé; of a *ḳaṣaba* at Meknès; of mosques at al-ʿUbbād, al-Manṣūra and Taza; of fortifications; of a hospital for the insane at Fās; of hydraulic wheels in numerous towns, of fountains and gardens; but most of all, of magnificent *madrasas*, four at Fās and one at Salé, which, renowned for the beauty of their decoration and their Hispano-Moorish style, remain the Marīnid monuments *par excellence*. The material prosperity of the Marīnid state and the image that it adopted at this time, as champion of Maghribī Islam, explains the large number of pious donations (*waḳf khayrī*) made by members of the dynasty to the benefit of public institutions in their own towns and in captured towns, as well as those of the holy cities of the East. The chronicles, the *fatwās* and the inscriptions of *waḳfs* all attests to the donation of goods, property and land by the sultans Abū Saʿīd, Abu 'l-Ḥasan and Abū ʿInān to the benefit of *madrasas*, mosques and libraries.

Like its two contemporary dynasties, the ʿAbd al-Wādids and the Ḥafṣids [*q.vv.*], the Marīnid state maintained the demographic, social and governmental structures of the Almohads, as well as the physical aspects of their civilisation. In addition to the Arab and Berber ethnic variety—the human wealth of the Marīnid state—the demographic composition of the countryside, still agrarian and tribal, was coloured by the distinction between the sedentary population of the plains and that of the mountain regions. While the countryside remained linguistically and socially, even religiously, almost entirely Berber, the nomadic shepherds, islamised to a small extent, became more and more arabised. In the towns, largely arabised and absolutely islamised, tribal loyalty gave way to familial aristocracy. Under the Marīnids, the towns gathered in Andalusian elements in ever-increasing numbers. The ethnic variety was completed by the existence of Jewish and Christian communities in the urban centres. While the Christians were merchants, priests and soldiers, more numerous in the coastal towns but still a small minority, the Jews, an indigenous element reinforced by immigrants from Spain, were more numerous and more active in all aspects of the life of the country.

The Marīnid court resided at Fās, which replaced Marrakesh as the seat of the administrative apparatus. A Marīnid sultan, bearing the title of *amīr al-muslimīn*, and later also that of *amīr al-muʾminīn*, was the supreme sovereign of his country, his involvement in government varying largely according to his personal inclination. Thus the sultan Abu 'l-Ḥasan was involved in all the bureaucratic activities of his state, especially the administration of the army, taxation—he even introduced a landownership and fiscal reform in the Maghrib—intellectual and religious activity, and even the administration of justice to citizens who complained of abuses on the part of his agents.

The responsibilities of the vizier, who was at certain times subordinate to the chamberlain, were on a day-to-day basis in the charge of various functionaries; head of finances, head of chancellery, chief of police, admiral, town governor, head of *ḳaṣaba*, senior *ḳāḍī*, head of the mint and head of the *muḥtasibs*. The Berber democratic and consultative nature of the Marīnid government was maintained by the existence, throughout its history, of the council of chiefs of the Marīnid tribes, which was convened at the invitation of the sovereign and mainly discussed military affairs. The economic life of Morocco under the Marīnids attests to a prosperity which was unconnected with the rise, in the 8th/14th century, of the kingdom of Mali [*q.v.*] and the development of the gold trade. This prosperity was reflected in three sectors: agriculture, urban industry and trade with Africa and Europe. Agriculture was dominated by a system of land-ownership largely similar to that of the Ḥafṣids: land was classified into three categories, these being public land (*djazāʾ*), from which territory was leased to individuals and granted as *iḳṭāʿ*; *mulk* (private property); and land endowed for religious institutions and individuals (*ḥubus*).

According to al-ᶜUmarī, the revenues of *iḳṭāᶜ* land were reserved for senior chiefs of the army, high dignitaries of the court, palace secretaries, *ḳāḍīs* and Ṣūfī *shaykhs*. The Marīnid *fatwās* attest to the existence of small and medium-sized plots of land, cultivated by the owner with one or more tenant-farmers. There is no indication of the existence of large agricultural holdings, except those in the possession of members of the reigning family. All co-operation in this regard was regulated by one of three agricultural contracts agreed upon by Muslim jurists, *muzāraᶜa, mughārasa* and *musāḳāt*; *khamāsa* also existed. The sources speak of abundant yields of fruit and vegetables, cultivated in the countryside but also in the proximity of towns, wheat being the major exported product.

The local industries of the towns, textiles, tanneries, building, metal-working, ceramics, food-stuffs and glassware, gave rise to an important craft milieu which achieved prominence in the 8th/14th century with its participation in royal processions, where members of each profession marched in a group displaying a flag showing the tools of its trade, as well as written texts. Commerce with Christian countries passed especially through the town of Ceuta, but other Atlantic ports were also frequented from the 7th/13th century (660/1262), Salé, Safi, Arzila and Anfa, where in 705/1305 an agent was in residence, acting on behalf of Majorcan merchants. The duties levied by Marīnid customs on imported and exported goods varied from one port to another. Christians imported into Marīnid Morocco wine, cotton, pepper, flour, finished silk, camphor, cinnamon, metals, cloth, linen, fine fabrics, ropes, tackle, gum, lac, cloves, gall-nuts, brazil wood, jewellery. They exported copper, wax, cotton goods, coral, wool, salt, leather, and above all wheat, which was cheaper than in Ifrīḳiya and held as a monopoly by the palace administration. No less important for Marīnid Morocco was trade with Black Africa across the Sahara, whence caravans brought salt, ivory, ostrich-feathers, gum and incense, musk, Guinea pepper, ambergris, and above all gold from the Sudan in ingot and powder form, which arrived through the town of Sidjilmāsa. The vigour of external commerce explains the importance of Ceuta and of Sidjilmāsa throughout the Marīnid period, as well as the aggressive Maghribī policy of the Marinids, which had the object of gaining control of the revenues of the Oriental, Saharan and European trade which converged in the coastal cities of the Maghrib. An abundance of yellow metal characterises the Marīnid economy, as is manifested by the payments in gold (*dīnārs*) made by Marīnid sovereigns especially to Spanish monarchs and recorded in their archive documents. Silver was scarce. The Marinids struck gold *dīnārs* of high quality; they followed the tradition introduced by the Almohads in minting a double *dīnār*, the *dīnār dhahabī* of the sources, of a weight of 4.57 gr., alongside the traditional *dīnār* with inscription in *naskhī* and *kūfī*, the *dīnār fiḍḍī* or *ᶜashrī* of the Marīnid sources, of 2.26 g., thus called because it was worth ten *dirhams*. Coins found indicate the existence of halves, quarters and eighths for *dīnārs* and *dirhams*. The Marīnids also maintained the square shape of the Almohad *dirham*, with an inscription also in Almohad style and in *naskhī* script. The quality of the striking seems, however, inferior. Marīnid coinage was struck at Azemmour, Ceuta, Sidjilmāsa, Fās, Marrakesh, and Salé, as well as in Maghribī towns occupied by the Marīnids: Tlemcen, Algiers, Bougie, Tunis and Tarifa. The taxes levied on the subjects of the Marīnid state were usually numerous, for the most part non-Ḳurʾānic and, except during the reform introduced under Abu 'l-Ḥasan, leased out to *wulāt*. In addition to *maghārim* and *mukūs* of all kinds [see MAKS], three major taxes were in evidence: the rural population paid the *khiras*, which corresponded to the canonical *kharādj* [*q.v.*], also imposed on citizens who cultivated fruit trees; city and country dwellers also paid the *ḳānūn*, a capital tax similar to the *djizya* [*q.v.*] levied on the Jews; shepherds paid the *ḥukr*, a tax on the lands used for pasture, and each user of the irrigation systems also paid a tax on the water.

The diverse manifestations of religious and intellectual life and of literary production under the Marīnids were to a large extent conditioned by the changes undergone by urban society and by the development of new political and social structures. Thus from the earliest days of the dynasty, the sovereigns had to deal with a numerically strong and powerful religious establishment, which claimed for itself the role of spokesman of society and was in evidence especially at Fās. The popular revolts which took place in this city obliged the Marīnids to confront the opposition of an autonomist urban movement to their régime, and to neutralise it by the creation of their own religious and intellectual circles. In order to achieve this aim, there was introduced into Morocco for the first time the institution of the *madrasa* [*q.v.*], which led to the creation of a body of Zanāta *fuḳahāʾ* whose loyalty to the régime could not be doubted. At the same time, because of the hostility of the city dwellers, even the administrative and literary circles of the court had to be recruited from among the new immigrants from Andalusia, from Ifrīḳiya, from the central Maghrib and even from the countryside (Shatzmiller, *Les premiers Mérinides et le milieu religieux de Fès: l'introduction des médersas*, in *SI*, xliii [1976], 109-18).

In general, the religious life of the period was marked by the restoration of Mālikism as an official rite, a process which had been well advanced under the last Almohads, but even more by the diffusion of Ṣūfism which, spreading to the countryside and practised in a particularly Maghribī form, degenerated into maraboutism. In the towns, Ṣūfism was also practised, but in a more refined form, with the participation of the sultans, the dignitaries and the men of letters.

Literary production under the Marīnids was multiple and varied, with Oriental and Andalusian elements of style and structure playing a dominant role. The areas cultivated were classical: *fiḳh*, biography, hagiography, poetry, geography (Ibn Baṭṭūṭa and al-ᶜAbdarī) at the same time as philosophy and natural sciences (Ibn al-Bannāʾ). Only history experienced an extraordinary development in this period, both in general and in detail, a phenomenon illustrated by the composition of the great regional histories of the mediaeval Maghrib (Ibn ᶜIdhārī and Ibn Khaldūn) and the appearance of local history, of towns and of dynasties, the mouthpiece of the social milieu and of territorial nationalism. The Marīnid sovereigns encouraged the writing of their history, driven by a desire for legitimisation which their authority lacked.

The decline which struck the Marīnid dynasty, immediately after its period of greatest prosperity, continued throughout the second phase of its history. This process was characterised by a crisis of succession of which the *Kitāb al-ᶜIbar* provides the details: a multitude of children of the Marīnid family were successively placed in power by innumerable revolts on the part of Arab and Berber tribes and by palace revolutions, while real power passed into the hands of viziers. The absence of a strong central authority provoked a movement of political and territorial disintegration in the regions far from the capital, especially in the south, but also in the north, where the activity of pirates provoked Castilian and Portuguese attacks on Tetuan and Ceuta. The weakening of the authority of the Marīnid dynasty was accelerated by socio-religious changes, which took place in proximity to the major towns and disrupted their stability. Since the dynasty was extinguished, in 870/1465, not by a palace revolution but by a popular uprising led by the *sharīfs*, which was nothing other than a renaissance of the cult of Idrīs, it is necessary to credit these movements with real importance. The fact that the country passed once again under the domination of a Berber family, the Waṭṭāsids, related to the Marīnids, demonstrates that in spite of its development, urban autonomism was not sufficiently powerful to check the demographic and military might of the tribal countryside. It remains true, however, that under the Marīnid dynasty there were introduced into Morocco, for the first time, the idea and the political structures of national and geographical unity which were to become modern Morocco.

Bibliography: Vol. iii of the *Bayān* of Ibn ʿIdhārī, Tetuan 1963, supplies useful information on the beginnings of the dynasty, but the most complete account of its history is given by Ibn Khaldūn in the *Kitāb al-ʿIbar*, of which the section dealing with the Maghrib has been edited and translated into French by M.G. de Slane under the title of *Histoire des Berbères*, 2 vols., Algiers 1852-6 (new ed., i-iii, Paris 1925-34, and iv, containing the history of the Marīnids and the index, 1956); two other chronicles which provided source material for the *Histoire des Berbères* are the anonymous *al-Dhakhīra al-saniyya*, ed. M. Ben Cheneb, Algiers 1921, and the *Rawḍ al-ḳirṭās* of Ibn Abī Zarʿ, ed. and Latin tr. C.J. Tornberg, Uppsala 1843 (ed. Rabat 1972); the history of the town of Fās which occupies the first part of the *Rawḍ al-ḳirṭās* is the theme of the chronicle intitled *Zahrat al-ās*, of al-Djaznāʾī, ed. and French tr. A. Bel, Algiers 1923; an almanac of the Marīnid sovereigns was composed at about the end of the 8th/14th century by Ibn al-Aḥmar and is preserved in his two chronicles which are almost identical: the *Rawḍat al-nisrīn*, French ed. and tr. G. Bouali and G. Marçais, Paris 1917, and the *al-Nafḥa al-nisrīniyya*, still in manuscript form. Two chronicles describe Marīnid Morocco under the reign of Abu 'l-Ḥasan: *al-Musnad al-ṣaḥīḥ al-ḥasan* of Ibn Marzūḳ, ed. and Spanish tr. M. J. Viguera, Algiers 1981 and Madrid 1977 respectively, and the *Masālik al-abṣār* of al-ʿUmarī, French tr. M. Gaudefroy-Demombynes, Paris 1927, 137-223; historical sources on the Marīnids are examined in M. Shatzmiller, *L'historiographie mérinide, Ibn Khaldūn et ses contemporains*, Leiden 1982, where there is a more complete bibliography for this period. A general history of the Marīnids was composed by H. Terrasse in his *Histoire du Maroc*, Casablanca 1950, ii, 3-99; Ch.-E. Dufourq described and analysed the relations of the first Marīnids with Aragon in *L'Espagne catalane et le Maghrib au XIIIe et XIVe siècles*, Paris 1966; J. Caille included a chapter intitled *Les Marseillais à Ceuta au XIIIe siècle*, in *Mélanges d'histoire et d'archéologie de l'Occident Musulman*, Algiers 1957, ii, 21-31; on Fās under the Marīnids, see R. Le Tourneau, *Fès avant le Protectorat*, Casablanca 1949; Marīnid coinage is described by H. Hazard, *The numismatic history of late medieval North Africa*, New York 1952, 192-227, 275-8; and the architecture by G. Marçais, *L'architecture musulmane d'Occident*, Paris 1954, 261-361, and A. Bel, *Inscriptions arabes de Fès*, in *JA* (1915-19). A quite uncritical catalogue of the literary production of the period is given by M, Benchekroun, *La vie intellectuelle marocaine sous les Mérinides et les Waṭṭāsides*, Rabat 1974; equally uncritical and based exclusively on Arab authors are the articles of M. al-Manūnī collected in *Waraḳāt ʿan al-ḥaḍra al-maghribiyya fī ʿaṣr Banī Marīn*, Rabat 1980. The Jewish communities of Marīnid Morocco are studied by D. Corcos, *The Jews of Morocco under the Marinids*, in *JQR*, liv, 271-87, 55, 55-81, 137-150; Shatzmiller, *An ethnic factor in a medieval social revolution: the role of Jewish courtiers under the Marinids*, in *Islamic society and culture, essays in honour of Professor Aziz Ahmed*, New Delhi 1983, 149-65; and M. Garcia-Arenal, *The revolution of Fās in 869/1465 and the death of sultan ʿAbd al-Ḥaqq al-Marīnī*, in *BSOAS*, xli, 43-66. On the Marīnid *waḳf*, see Shatzmiller, *Some social and economic aspects of "waḳf khayrī" in fourteenth century Fez*, in *Internat. Seminar on Social and Economic Aspects of the Muslim Waḳf*, Jerusalem 1979. On Ṣūfism, see P. Nwyia, *Ibn ʿAbbād de Ronda (1332-1390)*, Beirut 1961. Finally to be noted is a new study of the history of the Marīnids by M. Kably, *Société, pouvoir et religion au Maroc à la fin du Moyen Âge*. Paris 1986.

(MAYA SHATZMILLER)

AL-**MARĪS**, the term applied to the area of the ancient kingdom of Nobatia, northernmost of the Nubian Christian kingdoms, and occasionally also to its people.

Broadly, it encompassed the area from Aswān to the northern border of al-Muḳurra [*q.v.*], and was under the control of the king of Dunḳula [see DONGOLA], the "Lord of Muḳurra and Nubia". The northern frontier, according to al-Manūfī, quoting al-Djāḥiẓ, was indicated by two rocks jutting into the Nile five miles beyond Aswān; the southern limit was at Bastū (and variants) where al-Muḳurra proper began. The capital was at Faras, and there were also important forts, including Ḳaṣr Ibrīm. The administration was vested in the "Lord of the Mountain" (*Ṣāḥib al-Djabal*, or "Lord of the Horses", *Ṣāḥib al-Khayl*, in Ibn al-Furāt), the Eparch of Nobatia, under the authority of the king at Dunḳula. This official's duties were to receive correspondence and visitors destined for the king, and to control passage southward into Nubia. The population of al-Marīs contained an admixture of Arabs, and al-Masʿūdī mentions a case in 218/833 between the king of Nubia and the Muslim citizens of Aswān who owned estates in al-Marīs. The king held that land could not be sold since it was his property, worked by his subjects only in their capacity as his slaves. The case was judged in favour of the purchasers. According to Yūsuf the Egyptian, there was a bishop of al-Marīs (perhaps the bishop of Pachoras (Faras)). The provinces of al-ʿAlī and al-Djabal, part of al-Marīs, were apparently ceded to Egypt by the treaty of 674/1276, and the Muslim Banu 'l-Kanz [*q.v.*] gradually became prominent in the region, eventually taking the throne at Dunḳula. Several of the Arab writers tell of the Marīsī wind, which brought a pestilence to Egypt, so that people began, when the wind arrived, to buy ointments and shrouds for their funerals. The designation "Maurotania" in Abba Mina's Coptic *Life of the patriarch Isaac* (*ca.* 700 A.D.), would appear to refer to al-Marīs. The term al-Marīs is found in Arabic texts from at least the 1st/7th to the 10th/16th centuries.

Bibliography: Abba Mina, *Vie d'Isaac*, in *Patr. Or.*, xi, 1916, 3, 377-8; Ibn al-Faḳīh, 75; Masʿūdī, *Murūdj*, iii, 32, 42-3, vi, 273 = §§ 874, 880-1, 886, 2479; Ibn Ḥawḳal, 58; Abū Ṣāliḥ, tr. Evetts, *Churches and monasteries of Egypt*, 266; Ibn Khallikān, Beirut, i, 228; Yūsuf, in *Mon. Cart.* 1150b; Nuwayrī, *Nihāya*, Cairo ms. xxviii, f. 259, Paris ms 1578, f. 88b; Ibn al-Furāt, ed. Beirut, vii, 44 ff, 51; Ibn Khaldūn, v, 922, vi, 10; Ibn Sulaym al-Uswānī, in al-Manūfī, ch. I; *idem*, in Maḳrīzī, *Khiṭaṭ*, iii, 252 ff., 298-9, 303; Ibn Taghrībirdī, Cairo, vii, 188-9; Y. F. Hasan, *The Arabs in the Sudan*, Edinburgh 1967, index; G. Vantini, *Oriental sources concerning Nubia*, 1975, index.

(S. MUNRO-HAY)

MĀRISTĀN [see BIMĀRISTĀN].

MARITSA [see MERIČ].

MĀRIYA, a Copt maiden, according to one statement, daughter of a man named Shamʿūn, who was sent with her sister Sīrīn by the Muḳawḳis [*q.v.*]in the year 6 or 7/627-9 to Muḥammad as a gift of honour (according to another authority there were four of them). The Prophet made her his concubine, while he gave Sīrīn to Ḥassān b. Thābit [*q.v.*]. He was very devoted to her and gave her a house in the upper town of Medina, where he is said to have visited her by day and night; this house was called after her the *mashraba* of the mother of Ibrāhīm. To the great joy of the Prophet, she bore him a son whom he called Ibrāhīm, but he died in infancy. According to tradition, an eclipse of the sun took place on the day of his death, an interesting statement by which we can get the date exactly—if the story is true—as 27 January 632, that is, only a few months before Muḥammad's death. Māriya's beauty and Muḥammad's passionate love for her excited such jealousy among his other wives that, to pacify them, he promised to have nothing more to do with the Copt girl, a promise which he afterwards withdrew. Abū Bakr and ʿUmar honoured her and gave her a pension which she enjoyed till her death in Muḥarram 16/February 637. There is no reason to doubt the essential correctness of this story, as there is no particular bias in it and it contains all sorts of details which do not look in the least like inventions, so that it is exaggerated scepticism when Lammens supposes that the "mother of Ibrāhīm", after whom the *mashraba* was called, was some Jewess. On the other hand, in view of the fact that all the marriages of Muḥammad after the *hidjra* were childless, it would have been surprising if evil-minded people had not cast suspicions on the paternity of Ibrāhīm, and that this actually happened is evident from some traditions, the object of which is to defend Māriya from this suspicion.

On the other hand, it is not so easy to justify the part which Ḳurʾānic exegesis makes Māriya play in the exposition of sūra LXVI. In this sūra, the Prophet speaks in a very indignant tone against one of his wives, because she has betrayed a secret to another, which he had imparted to her under a promise of the strictest secrecy. At the same time, Allāh blames him, because, in order to please his wives, he had bound himself by oath to refrain from something which is not definitely stated and because he does not use the right granted him by Allāh to release himself from his oath. In addition, there is a word of warning to the two women who had disobeyed him and a threat to all his wives that he might divorce them in order to marry more pious ones (cf. XXXIII, 28-9). According to the usual explanation, the two wives are Ḥafṣa and ʿĀʾisha, and the revelation is said to have been provoked by the fact that Ḥafṣa, on returning unexpectedly to her house, found Māriya and the Prophet in an intimate tête-à-tête and that on a day which by rotation belonged to her (or ʿĀʾisha). In his embarrassment, he pledged himself by oath to have no more relations with the Copt girl. But after Ḥafṣa's breach of faith, Allāh tells him to release himself from his oath. This explanation fits very well in some respects, and that the promise of continence is connected with marital complications is illuminating. That there are *ḥadīths*, which explain his quarrel with his wives quite differently, does not mean very much, for they are no doubt invented to drive out of currency the popular, less edifying version. But, on closer examination, there is one flaw which makes the latter uncertain, for it does not answer the question how Muḥammad could call the situation in which Ḥafṣa caught him and Māriya a secret that he is said to have entrusted to her.

Bibliography: Ṭabarī, i, 1561, 1686, 1774, 1781-2; Ibn Saʿd, i/2, 16-17; viii, 131-8, 153-6; the commentaries on sūra LXVI; Nöldeke-Schwally, *Geschichte des Qorāns*, i, 217; Caetani, *Annali dell' Islam*, ii, 211-12, 237, 311-12; Lammens, *Fāṭima et les filles de Mahomet*, Rome 1912, 2-9. F, Buhl, *Das Leben Muhammeds*, Leipzig 1930, 297; W.M. Watt, *Muhammad at Medina*, Oxford 1956, 286, 396; M. Gaudefroy-Demombynes, *Mahomet*², Paris 1969, 228, 230-2; M. Rodinson, *Mohammad*, Harmondsworth 1973, 279-83. On the eclipse of the sun, see Rhodokanakis, in *WZKM*, xiv, 78 ff.; Mahler, in *ibid.*, 109 ff.; K. Öhrnberg, *Māriya al-Qibṭiyya unveiled*, in *Studia orientalia, Finnish Oriental Society*, xi/14 (1984), 297-303.

(F. BUHL).

AL-**MARIYYA** is the Arab name for the Spanish town of Almería. According to some authors, it was originally called Mariyyat Badjdjāna, for it had been the port or maritime suburb of Pechina (Badjdjāna) [*q.v.*], the ancient Roman Urci. Today, Almería is the chief town of the province (which has the same name) in the most easterly part of Andalusia on the Mediterranean coast. It is surrounded by bare mountains with steppe-like vegetation, and this means that its countryside is very similar to that of some parts of the North African coastline opposite. The only part not surrounded by rocky mountains is the area towards Cape Gata, and it has always been a region of low rainfall. The land is very eroded and marked by numerous *ramlas*, which have been hollowed out by raging torrents during the times when it does rain. By contrast, the Rio de Almería valley, the Andarax (Andarash), is a green fertile zone producing an abundance of fruit. This land of violent contrast has been witness to many splendid years of the Islamic era and has been described often in great detail by Arab writers, from East and West alike.

The Islamic history of Almería is closely linked with that of Pechina which, thanks to its own location on the coast, existed before Almería, gave it birth and saw it develop. Soon after its rapid conquest from 93/713 to 95/715, it was populated mainly by Yemeni Arabs throughout a large area extending almost as far as the Guadix (Wādī Ash), but there were also several Berber settlements, especially in the region of the lower Almerian Alpujarra. During its 765 years of Islamic history, this territory of Almería experienced various changes of fortune.

The small village and port of al-Mariyya became

more important than the neighbouring Aguilas, and it was an administrative dependency of the *kūra* (the *iḳlīm*, according to al-Idrīsī) of Pechina. Before they were controlled by al-Mariyya, the towns of Berja (Bardja) and Dalías (Dalāya) were also dependent on Pechina. Dalías was the birthplace of al-ʿUdhrī, the well-known geographer of the 5th/11th century, who provided a careful description of al-Mariyya with much interesting information (see *Tarṣīʿ al-akhbār*, ed. ʿAbd al-ʿAzīz al-Ahwānī, Madrid 1965, index). Other towns are Adra and the fortresses of Vélez Rubio (Bālīsh), Belicena (Balisāna), Purchena (Barshāna), Senés (Shanish), Andarax (Andarash), to name but a few mentioned by al-Idrīsī (*Opus geographicum*, v, 537, 562-4) and by Abu 'l-Fidā. All these towns, as well as Vera (Bayra) and some others, were taken as dependencies of Naṣrid Granada during the last centuries of Islamic rule.

The region of al-Mariyya is surrounded by steeply sloping sierras which make overland communications difficult. The town was established in 344/955 by order of ʿAbd al-Raḥmān III al-Nāṣir [*q.v.*]; its special maritime importance arises from the fact that it faces the North African ports of Ténès and other Algerian and Tunisian ports, as well as Alexandria and the extreme Eastern Mediterranean. Arab geographers, therefore, chose an apt name for it, "the gateway to the East" and "the key to commerce and trade of every kind". The name of al-Mariyya (*sic*, not al-Māriyya) has given rise to various explanations. The idea of "watch-tower" could have come from the time when men reported there for guard duty, for it was a look-out post during the raids by the Normans, and later by the Maghribīs, which occurred in the mid-3rd/9th century and the 4th/10th century. A number of defensive towers (*maḥāris*) were built then along the coast to house garrisons and where people could lead a life of service in *ribāṭs* [*q.v.*]. Al-Rābiṭa, which is mentioned by al-Idrīsī, is only a day's journey away. Yāḳūt, *s.v.*, gives free rein to his imagination when he considers the original meaning of this town name.

All writers seem to agree that this city was a recent one (*muḥdatha*), and not, like the others, from the distant past (*azaliyya*), founded by the Arabs as a place in which "to practise the life of service in a *ribāṭ*", according to al-ʿUdhrī and the anonymous *Dhikr al-Andalus* (Rabat ms.). Al-Nāṣir turned it into the main port and arsenal for all the country's ships and also into a *madīna*. He gave it a fortress on a very rocky hill to the west, at the bottom of which was the district of al-Ḥawḍ; this was an area enclosed by a series of walls with a great number of markets, inns and baths. The population of Pechina, situated several kilometres inland, was absorbed by al-Mariyya, and it was used as a naval base and the point of embarkation for maritime raids against Chistian countries. During the period of the caliphate, it was a defensive bastion against the threat of the Fāṭimids. There was more commercial activity here than in any other port of al-Andalus, and it was open to the influence of all kinds of travellers to and from North Africa and the Eastern Mediterranean. According to L. Torres Balbás (*Almería islámica*, in *al-And.*, xxii [1957], 411-53, which includes a plan of the town in the 14th century) at the end of the 4th/10th century the *madīna* comprised a rectangle of a little more than 19 hectares in area, excluding the fortress which was called *ḳalʿat Khayrān*, enlarged by the ʿĀmirid *fatā* Khayrān in 410/1019-20. He had also had a wall constructed from Mt. Laḥam, to the north of the town, to the sea. Within this area, the city was able to shelter about 27,000 people, according to L. Torres Balbās (*Extensión y demografía de las ciudades hispano-musulmanas*, in *SI*, iii [1955], 55-6). The town grew and became even more splendid during the time of Khayrān (d. 429/1038) and Zuhayr, the two slaves who seized Almería and its territory at the time of the *fitna*, and during that of the *mulūk al-ṭawāʾif*.

Shortly after the assassination of Zuhayr in 429/1037-8, al-Mariyya passed to ʿAbd al-ʿAzīz b. Abī ʿĀmir of Valencia, who controlled it from Dhu 'l-Ḳaʿda 429/Sept. 1038 to Radjab 433/Feb.-March 1042. According to Ibn ʿIdhārī (*Bayān*, iii, 191-2), the *amīr* of Valencia was also the ruler of Tudmīr (Murcia) and he sent his son ʿAbd Allāh to be the governor of al-Mariyya. But he stayed only a short time; he soon died and was replaced by Abu 'l-Aḥwaṣ Maʿn b. Ṣumādiḥ al-Tudjībī. In 433/1042 he revolted against the ʿĀmirid ruler of Valencia, declared his independence and ruled the town as his own territory until his death in 443/1052. The town certainly prospered under him, but it prospered even more so under his son Abū Yaḥyā Muḥammad b. Maʿn b., Ṣumādiḥ, who took the title of al-Muʿtaṣim; it became a centre of culture, with one of the most famous of the literary courts of al-Andalus until the time of the Almoravids (see R. Dozy, in *Recherches*[3], 211-81). During the period of the *mulūk al-ṭawāʾif*, al-Mariyya maintained relations (though not always friendly ones) with the neighbouring *taifas* of Granada (see H.R. Idris, *Les Zīrīdes d'Espagne*, in *al-And.*, xxix [1964], 39-145), with Denia, Valencia, and even with Cordova and Seville. This had the effect of reducing the extent of the territorial possessions of the Banū Ṣumādiḥ.

Under the Almoravids, al-Mariyya achieved its fullest economic potential. It can be argued that it prospered most in the second half of the 5th/11th century and the first half of the 6th/12th century; then it suffered the first Christian conquest, in 1147, by Alfonso VII of Castile, which is celebrated in the *Chronica Adephonsi Imperatoris*. Its economic development and its military and naval importance showed itself in the commercial and industrial ventures that were undertaken and its growth as a city and artistic centre. Beginning with al-Idrīsī, many geographers from the 6th/12th to the 8th/14th centuries, including the compiler al-Maḳḳarī, agree that the cloth and brocade (*dībādj*) produced there were as fine as the products of Cordova; the town became highly renowned for this and without rival in al-Andalus. Among the materials and brocades which had built up the reputation of the town's industry were cloth of gold (*washy* [*q.v.*]) (which was also made at Malaga) [*q.v.*], siglaton, baldachin, and all sorts of silk, which was known to be better (and more expensive) than that from other areas. There was an obvious eastern influence on the manufacture of textiles, as can be seen from the names given to some of the cloths, like *iṣfahānīs* and *djurdjānīs*, which sound Persian, and *ʿattābī*, which was probably ʿIrāḳī. Al-Zuhrī (*Kitāb al-Djaʿrāfiya*, ed. M. Hadj-Sadok, in *BEO*, xxi [1968], 101/206) mentions other white-coloured fabrics brocaded with gold, which, according to many sources, were favoured by the women of al-Mariyya for their garments. Other reliable authorities claim that there were 800 or 1,000 factories for *ṭirāz* in the town, and that there were as many looms for producing other fabrics as well. Naturally, this would have given employment to a considerable number of weavers.

Beside textiles, other industries included the building of warships (in the *dār al-ṣināʿa*) and the manufacture of tools and weapons from copper and iron. Agricultural products of the region came especially from the valleys of the Andarax and the Almanzora (*wadī 'l-Manṣūra*) where there were olive trees, vineyards, a large variety of fruit trees, banana plantations and sugar-cane. The marble from the Macael quarries in the Sierra Filabres was particularly famous because it was used for covering plinths and for paving palaces, especially the one called *al-ṣumādiḥiyya* (see L. Seco de Lucena, *Los palacios del taifa almeriense al-Muᶜtaṣim*, in *Cuadernos de la Alhambra*, iii [1967], 15-20; J. Bosch Vilá, *Mocárabes en el arte de la taifa de Almería?*, in *Cuad. Hist. Isl.*, viii [Granada 1977], 156). Mine-working in the area was to produce silver and gold; some writers say there were precious stones. The marble was also used to make columns, capitals, tombstones (*maḳbariyya*) and fountains.

From the time when the town was taken by the Christians in 1147 and its recapture by the Almohads in 1157, the commercial and cultural prosperity there dwindled. The most eminent citizens emigrated to North Africa, and several of the more densely populated and busier areas of the town were destroyed. Muḥammad b. Yaḥyā al-Ramīmī (or Rumaymī), who had recognised the authority of Ibn Hūd [see HŪDIDS], was to be assassinated in al-Mariyya. These factions and subsequent internal political struggles considerably weakened the influence of the capital and, after it had been incorporated into the kingdom of Granada by Muḥammad I in S̲h̲awwāl, 635/May-June 1238, it ended its Islamic life under the Naṣrids. There was a major attack on the town in August 1309 when it was besieged by the Aragonese of James II (see R. Basset, *Le siège d'Alméria en 709*, in *JA*, 10th ser., x [1907], 275 ff.; I.S. Allouche, *La relation du siège d'Alméria en 709 (1305-1310) d'après de nouveaux manuscripts de la Durrat al-ḥijāl*, in *Hespéris*, xvi [1933], 122-38; E. Lévi-Provençal, *Un "zaŷal" hispanique sur l'expédition aragonaise de 1309 contre Alméria*, in *al-And.*, vi [1941], 377-99). It continued to suffer from internal troubles and was involved in the dynastic rivalries and civil wars which weakened the kingdom of Granada and cast a shadow over the future of the Muslims of al-Andalus. Al-Zag̲h̲al, the uncle and enemy of Boabdil, took refuge there, and it was delivered into the hands of the kings of Castile on 22 December 1489.

Bibliography: References have been given in the text to Arab authors and the principal geographical and historical sources relevant to al-Mariyya and Mālaḳa. See also S. Gilbert, *La ville d'Alméria à l'époque musulmane*, in *CT*, xviii/69-70 (1970), 61-72; J.A. Tapia Garrido, *Almería musulmana (711-1147 y 1147-1482)* = vols. ii and iii of *Historia General de Almería y su provincia*, [Almería] 1976-8; and finally, E. Molina López, *Algunas consideraciones sobre la vida socio-económica de Almería en el siglo XI y primera mitad del XII*, in *Actas del IV coloquio hispano-tunecino de Mallorca en 1979*, Madrid 1982. There is also ᶜAbd al-ᶜAzīz Sālim, *Algunos aspectos del florecimiento económico de Almería islámica durante el periodo de los Taifas y de los Almorávides*, Madrid 1979; *idem*, *Taʾrīk̲h̲ madīnat al-Mariyya al-islāmiyya*, Beirut 1969. (J. BOSCH VILÁ)

MARḲAB, observatory [see MARṢAD].

AL-**MARḲAB**, a fortress situated on the Syrian coast.

The name of al-Marḳab, from the root *raḳaba* "observe, watch", denotes any elevated site from which it is possible to see and observe, such as the summit of a mountain, of a fortified castle or of a watch-tower (*LA*, ed. Beirut 1955, i, 424-8; Yāḳūt, ed. Beirut 1957, v, 108-9). Arab authors generally call this stronghold al-Marḳab; also found are Ḳalᶜat Marḳab and Ḥiṣn Marḳab. There are also Arabic transcriptions such as Mār Kābūs for Markappos, Mār Kābān for Marckapan, Mār G̲h̲ātūm for Margathum or Mārg̲h̲at for Margat. In western works various spellings are encountered, including El-Marcab, Margat and Margath, Markab or Marqab.

1. Geography of the site. On current maps, the castle is situated at 35°27' E. by 35°10' N., between Lād̲h̲iḳiyya [*q.v.*] and Ṭarṭūs, standing at an altitude of 1,187 ft./362 m. at the summit of a broad and steeply-sloping basalt promontory, separated from a plateau of lava deposits. This barely accessible summit is one of the western foothills of the D̲j̲abal Anṣāriyya range which extends towards the north, evidence of very ancient volcanic activity marked by streams of basalt in the regions of al-Marḳab.

The castle affords a unique panorama towards the east over land consisting of calcareous hills with outcrops of quaternary and pliocene clay, the territory of the Assassins or Ḥas̲h̲īs̲h̲iyya [*q.v.*], and towards the west over the coastal plain which is fringed by basaltic sand and intended with small coves. At the foot of the castle there is a cove which is sheltered from the wind and capable of accommodating ships of limited tonnage; Walpole (*Travels*, iii, 289) noticed here in the 19th century some remains of masonry, possibly relics of mediaeval harbour installations. At this latitude the coast is one-and-a-half days' sailing distance from Cyprus.

The castle overlooks the main coastal road, at the point where the coastal expanse is narrowest. It is also at the foot of al-Marḳab that the road from Ḥamāt [*q.v.*] by way of Masyaḍ [*q.v.*] reaches the sea.

The barrier constituted by the basalt mass of al-Marḳab is skirted to the north by the Nahr Bāniyās, which is swollen by a prolific water-source upstream from Bāniyās, and to the south by the Nahr Markiya, which flows between al-Marḳab and K̲h̲irāb Markiya (ruins of Maraclea, Marachea); this coastal stream, according to *The initerary from Bordeaux to Jerusalem*, constituted the northern frontier of Phoenicia. According to William of Tyre, this place marked the frontier between the Principality of Antioch and the County of Tripoli.

2. History. Among the early Arab geographers and travellers who made mention of al-Marḳab, al-Idrīsī (*Opus geographicum*, 644, tr. Jaubert, 130) says that "it is a fortress built on a mountain inaccessible from all directions"; Yāḳūt says in his *Muᶜd̲j̲am* that "it is a town and a castle overlooking the shore of the Syrian Sea. It protects the city of Bulunyās and the coast of D̲j̲abala [*q.v.*]. All those who have passed by it say that they have never seen anything of comparable might." At the beginning of the 8th/14th century, Ibn Baṭṭūṭa (i, 183) visited al-Marḳab and mentions it as one of the great castles of Syria constructed on the summit of a high mountain and recalls that Sultan Ḳalāwūn [*q.v.*] captured it from the Christians (in 684/1285). His contemporary al-Dimas̲h̲ḳī (ed. Mehren, 208) says that "Ḥiṣn al-Marḳab is an impregnable fortress on a 'tongue of land' overlooking the sea". Abu 'l-Fidāʾ is more laconic, saying only that "al-Marḳab and Buluniyās are situated on the coast of Ḥimṣ; al-Marḳab is the name of the castle overlooking the sea". Finally, al-Ḳalḳas̲h̲andī, in the 9th/15th century, stresses that "al-Marḳab is mentioned neither in the *Taᶜrīf* nor the *Masālik al-abṣār*"; he used material from Abu 'l-Fidāʾ in his *Ṣubḥ* (iv, 145-6), saying that "it is a fortress near the coast of "the Roman Sea" (*al-Baḥr al-Rūmī*) in the

fourth region and according to the *Zīdj*, (corrective tables of the Ptolemaic measures, one dating from 360/961, the other from 691/1292) situated at long. 60°, lat. 34°45'. It is a powerful and finely-constructed fortress overlooking the sea; at a distance of about one parasang, the town of Bilinyās (sic = Bāniyās) is located."

According to the chronicle of Abū Ghālib Humām b. al-Faḍl al-Muhadhdhib al-Maᶜarrī, quoted in Yāḳūt, and according to the *Taʾrīkh ak-Ḳilāᶜ wa 'l-ḥuṣūn* of Usāma b. Munḳidh quoted in Abu 'l-Fidāʾ (ed. Reinaud and de Slane, 255), the fortress was built by the Muslims in 454/1062. Al-Dimashḳī (ed. Mehren, 208) states that al-Markab was constructed with stones from previous ruins, often with well-cut blocks found on the site, and attributes its foundation to al-Rashīd. It is hardly probable that the person in question is Hārūn al-Rashīd, considered by Van Berchem (*Voyage*, 304, n. 4) to be a proverbial expression, and even less likely is the opinion of G. Le Strange (*Palestine*, 506) that the reference is to Rashīd al-Dīn (Sinān) a contemporary of Ṣalāḥ al-Dīn. It is not impossible that the Rashīd mentioned by Usāma b. Munḳidh and then by al-Dimashḳī could be Rashīd [al-Dawla Maḥmūd b. Naṣr], who was Mirdāsid *amīr* of Ḥalab in 452-3/1060-1 and again from 454/1062 to 468/1075, a supposition which is not contradicted by the secondary use of ancient materials and which is confirmed by the presence of relics dating back to the 5th/11th century. The citadel was intended to block the advance of the Byzantines, who controlled the province of al-Anṭākiya, towards the south.

In 494/1101, al-Marḳab and its hinterland were in the hands of the Banū Muḥriz, who were also in command of the castle of Ḳadmūs. In the course of an expedition conducted in 497/1104 by the Byzantines against the Syrian coast, the Admiral Cantacuzenus, having been repulsed before the citadel of Lādhiḳiyya, disembarked at Buluniyās (Bāniyās) and took possession, according to Anna Comnena in the *Alexiad* (ᶜΑλεξίας, ed. B. Leib, III, liv, XI, 48), of the important strategic point known as al-Marḳab (τὸ χαλουμενον Μαρχαπιν, the Marchapin of the historians) and of other fortified sites in the region such as Sāfīthā (τό τε 'Αργυρόκαστρον) and Djabala (τὰ Γάβαλα).

In 506/1116-17 the heights of al-Marḳab represented the frontier of the principality of Antioch. In 510/1116-17 the crops failed as a result of inclement weather and drought and the situation was aggravated by financial inflation; Ibn Muḥriz, master of al-Marḳab, was placed in an increasingly difficult position, in that he did not have the means to maintain the citadel and was threatened by the Franks. He even went to the extent of offering to cede the castle to Ṭughtakīn. The Atabeg of Damascus sent the *ḳāḍī* Ibn Ṣulayḥa, the former master of Djabala, to his aid. On the advice of Ṭughtakīn, Ibn Ṣulayḥa took possession of the fortress and allowed the family of the Banū Muḥriz to remain there. The same year, Roger of Antioch, having concluded a treaty with the eunuch Luʾluʾ who governed Aleppo, marched against al-Marḳab. Pons de Saint-Gilles, Count of Tripoli, came to his aid, but following a quarrel, they abandoned the siege.

Soon afterwards the Atabeg of Damascus negotiated an agreement with the Franks, ceding al-Marḳab in exchange for Rafanea and the cessation of their attacks on Ḥamāt and Ḥimṣ. Ibn Muḥriz resisted the attacks of Renaud Mazoyer, the master of Bulunyās/Bāniyās, eventually negotiating with him in 511/1117-18. Renaud took possession of the castle, promising Ibn Muḥriz that he would be allowed to remain, but the new castellan expelled him twenty-five days later, allotting to him in exchange the fortress of Manīḳa in the Djabal Baḥra.

Thus Renaud Mazoyer, High Constable of the principality of Antioch, belonging to an important family mentioned in the *Lignages*, became the first Frankish governor of al-Marḳab, with territory embracing the mountainous hinterland as far as Abū Ḳubays, which overlooked the valley of the Ghāb [*q.v.*]. Frankish and Armenian settlers were established at al-Marḳab.

After the death of Roger of Antioch at the battle of Ager Sanguinis at Sarmada on 17 Rabīᶜ I 513/28 June 1119, the situation in the principality became tense, and the Mazoyers had difficulty retaining control of the stronghold.

If the Syrian historian al-ᶜAẓīmī [*q.v.*] is to be believed, it seems that the Muslims occupied al-Marḳab between 525/1130 and 534/1140 during the dispute between the Franks of Antioch and the Franks of Tripoli. The situation caused anxiety to the Franks, as freedom of movement in the coastal area was threatened. According to the Genoese historian Caffaro (d. 1166), the castle of al-Marḳab was taken from the Muslims by trickery in 534/1140 and seized by Renaud II Mazoyer, who proceeded to undertake fortifications, the relics of which may be found among the construction works of 582/1186. These fortifications had been demanded of him by the Prince of Antioch, anxious to reinforce the southern frontier of his domain.

In 551/1156 and 552/1157 several earthquakes affected the Syrian coast, but the most violent was that of 12 Shawwāl 565/29 June 1170 which was felt throughout Syria and in Cyprus and which, having damaged the castles of the Djabal Anṣāriyya, cannot have spared al-Marḳab.

In 577/1181 Bohemond III, excommunicated by the Latin Patriarch of Antioch Aimery de Limoges, was obliged to deal with a revolt on the part of the latter's partisans, among whom was Renaud II Mazoyer, who seems to have received the Patriarch at al-Marḳab. In order to meet the cost of maintaining the castle and its garrison, the castellan of al-Marḳab was obliged to sell, piecemeal, to the Order of the Hospitallers, his huge domains, part of which lay in the Rūdj between Anṭākiya and Afāmiya [*q.v.*]. After the death of Renaud II, his son Bertrand Mazoyer, having insufficient resources at his disposal, renounced his claims to the castle; on the advice of the Patriarch Aimery and with the consent of the Prince of Antioch, he ceded to Roger de Moulins, Grand Master of the Hospitallers, by an act of donation concluded at al-Marḳab on 9 Dhu 'l-Ḳaᶜda 581/1 February 1186, the castle with all its territories and dependencies including Bāniyās, Ḳadmūs, ᶜUlayḳa and Abū Ḳubays. On 30 June 1186 Pope Urban III appointed Brother Henry as castellan.

"The fief of Marḳab corresponded approximately to the bishopric of Boulouniyas (Valania); after 1188 the bishop of Valania and his hierarchical superior, the archbishop of Apamea, were constrained by the military situation to take refuge within the walls of Marḳab" (Cl. Cahen, *Syrie*, 519).

After the victory of Ḥiṭṭīn [*q.v.*], Ṣalāḥ al-Dīn was intent on the reconquest of Syria. In Djumāda I 584/July 1188, coming from Ṭarṭūs, he was obliged to pass by the foot of al-Marḳab on the narrow coastal road dominated by the Burdj al-Ṣabī, linked to the castle by a wall. In his advance along the coast he had been followed by the Norman fleet of Sicily commanded by the Admiral Margaritus of Brindisi. The ships moored in the cove of al-Marḳab, and their crews showered missiles on the Ayyūbid army, which was only able to continue its northward march with the protection of a veritable palisade erected along the sea-shore, as described by ʿImād al-Dīn al-Iṣfahānī (tr. Massé, 125-6). In the principality of Antioch, only the city itself and the fortress of al-Marḳab remained in the hands of the Crusaders at the end of Ṣalāḥ al-Dīn's campaign.

The Prince Isaac Comnenus, who became the independent ruler of Cyprus in 1184, gave the Crusaders an unfriendly reception on his island and was taken prisoner, at the battle of Tremithoussia on 5 Djumāda I 587/31 May 1191, by Richard Cœur-de-Lion, who incarcerated him at al-Marḳab, where he remained until his death in 591/1195.

By means of the tribute levied on the Assassins of Djabal Bahra and their own resources, the Hospitallers were able, after 588/1192, to restore the defences of al-Marḳab. This site, with Ḥiṣn al-Akrād, became one of the most important items in the defensive apparatus of the Crusaders against the Muslim domain, an apparatus comprising ʿAkkār, ʿArḳa, Ḳulayʿat, Sāfīthā (Chastel Blanc), ʿUrayma, Ḳalʿat Yaḥmūr (Chastel Rouge) and Ṭarṭūs, in addition to the towers and subsidiary points linking these various places.

In 601/1204, a general chapter of the Order of the Hospitallers was held at al-Marḳab under the presidency of the Grand Master. From the beginning of the 7th/13th century, the garrison of al-Marḳab was in a state of constant conflict with the chieftain of Aleppo. In 601/1204-5, al-Malik al-Ẓāhir Ghāzī [*q.v.*], whose domain bordered on that of al-Marḳab, sent an army to attack the castle; several towers were destroyed but when its leader was killed by an arrow the army withdrew.

In the account of his travels in Syria in 1212, Wilbrand von Oldenburg gives the most complete description available of al-Marḳab: "A huge and very strong castle, defended by a double wall and surrounded by numerous towers. It stands on a high mountain. This castle belongs to the Hospitallers and is the most powerful defence of the whole country... The "Old Man of the Mountains" and the Soudan of Aleppo pay to it every year a tribute of 2,000 marks. Each night, four Knights of the Hospital and twenty-eight soldiers mount guard. In addition to the garrison, the Hospitallers maintain 1,000 persons there. The territory surrounding the fortress yields every year crops in excess of 500 loads of sheaves. The provisions gathered there are sufficient to last five years." (Laurent, *Peregrinatores*, 170). The same author informs us that "for quite a long time, Margat has been an episcopal seat" and that the bishop of Valania (Bāniyās) had transferred his residence there. In this period, pilgrims embarked from al-Marḳab en route for Suwaydiyyya in the Principality of Antioch, with the aim of avoiding the Muslim towns and territories of the coast.

On the eve of the Fifth Crusade, in 613/1216, Pope Honorius III, successor to Innocent III, sent Jacques de Vitry to preach the Holy War in Syria, where he visited all the Crusaders' strongholds and praised especially the might of al-Marḳab. In the same period, Yāḳūt wrote that al-Marḳab "is a castle such that all men declare that they have never seen its equal" (v, 108).

The following year, in Djumāda II 614/September 1217, Andrew II, king of Hungary, disembarked at ʿAkkā with a Crusader army; at the beginning of Ramaḍān 614/early December 1217 he suffered a defeat before Mount Tabor (Djabal Thawr) and subsequently returned to Europe. Before leaving Syria, he halted at al-Marḳab; he was impressed by its defences and made a substantial donation towards their maintenance. At the end of 614/early 1218, the castellan of al-Marḳab enlarged his territory and made himself master of Djabala, whose ruler and inhabitants were obliged to perform an act of allegiance to the Hospitallers.

Having refused Frederick II, the excommunicated German Emperor, any support for his crusade in 1229, the Hospitallers received no aid from him towards the upkeep of al-Marḳab and Ḥiṣn al-Akrād.

In Rabīʿ II 628/February 1231, the troops of Aleppo began once more to pillage the neighbourhood of al-Marḳab; a truce was concluded at the end of spring 628/1231. In 639/1242, the truce was revoked and the Grand Master of the Order, Pierre de Vieille Bride, resumed a campaign of harassment against the territory of Aleppo from al-Marḳab.

Towards the middle of the 7th/13th century, al-Marḳab became an official episcopal seat when the bishop of Valania (Bāniyās) transferred his residence there.

From 659/1261, Sultan Baybars [*q.v.*] launched offensives against the strongholds of the Hospitallers, who paid a heavy price for their defence. The frantic appeals of the Grand Master of the Order, Hugues Revel, went unanswered. But, inasmuch as the Mamlūk sultans feared a revival of the Crusades and an expedition of Christians from Cyprus or from the West, al-Marḳab, like Ḥiṣn al-Akrād, retained its strategic value. An agreement was reached between the Hospitallers and the Templars regarding the possessions of the Hospitallers in the region of al-Marḳab.

In 665/1267, a treaty was concluded between Baybars and Hugues Revel in regard to these two fortresses for a period of ten years, ten months and ten hours; the enforcement of his treaty, accompanied by considerable sums of money, was supervised by the *nāʾib* of the sultan at Ḥimṣ. In 666/1268, Baybars took possession of Antioch, and seized Djabala and Lādhiḳiyya. In 1270, the sultan pillaged the neighbourhood of al-Marḳab and of Ḥiṣn al-Akrād. In Shaʿbān 669/March-April 1281, after the capture of Ḥiṣn al-Akrād by Baybars, the Hospitallers were left with only one fortress, al-Marḳab; the Grand Master of the Order was only able to obtain a truce of ten years and ten days—negotiated through the intermediary of the *amīr* Sayf al-Dīn Balabān al-Dawādār (*Manhal*, no. 689)—in exchange for the cession of half of the coastal region (*ṣāḥil*) of Ṭarṭūs, al-Marḳab and Bāniyās and on condition that no new fortresses were to be constructed.

In Djumāda II 678/October 1279, taking advantage of the unrest which broke out in Syria with the accession of Sultan Ḳalāwūn, the Hospitallers launched a raid in the direction of Buḳayʿa [*q.v.*], but withdrew when attacked by the Muslims. On reaching the coast, they turned and routed the Muslims. After the defeat of the Armeno-Mongolian troops, the sultan commanded the *amīr* Sayf al-Dīn Balabān al-Ṭabbākhī (*Manhal*, no. 692), governor of Ḥiṣn al-Akrād, to lay siege to al-Marḳab. In Shawwāl 679/February 1281, the Hospitallers made a sortie and repelled the Muslims, inflicting heavy losses. On 22 Muḥarram 680/13 May 1281, a truce of ten years and ten months was concluded between Ḳalāwūn and Nicholas Lorgne, the Grand Master of the Hospitallers.

In autumn 680/1281, the latter appealed in writing for help from Edward I, King of England; in September 1281 a Mongol invasion took place in Syria. Ḳalāwūn succeeded, in Djumāda II/October, in repelling the Mongols near Ḥimṣ, whither the Hospitallers of al-Marḳab had sent a contingent to aid the Ilkhān.

In 682/1283, the pilgrim Burchard de Mont Sion mentions in his account the "castrum Margath"—whose defensive might he extols—as belonging to the Hospitallers of St. John and as the residence of the Bishop of Valania (Laurent, *Peregrinatores*, 30, 70).

In 1285, the sultan sought to punish the Hospitallers of al-Marḳab for the assistance that they had provided to the Mongols. Having assembled at Damascus, in great secrecy, a considerable quantity of siege materials, Ḳalāwūn appeared before al-Marḳab on 10 Ṣafar 684/17 April 1285. The siege lasted 38 days, and was especially remarkable for the work of the Muslim sappers and miners who dug numerous tunnels under the walls. An exploding mine caused the collapse of the angle of the salient (*bashūra*) near the Ram Tower at the southern extremity and sowed panic among the attackers, who withdrew on 17 Rabīʿ I/23 May. Discovering the number of tunnels dug around the castle, the Hospitallers abandoned the struggle; the *amīr* Fakhr al-Dīn Muḳrī received the surrender, and Ḳalāwūn entered the castle on 19 Rabīʿ I/25 May, having given *amān* to the vanquished. Aware of the strategic importance of al-Marḳab, the sultan, after installing a strong garrison, repaired the defences as is indicated by the large inscription on white marble (cf. *RCEA*, xiii, no. 4858). Among the eye-witnesses to the siege were Abu 'l-Fiḍā', then eleven years old, and his father, as well as the historian Ibn ʿAbd al-Raḥīm, who completed the *Chronicle* of Ibn Wāṣil. The best account of the capture of al-Marḳab is to be found in the biography of Ḳalāwūn entitled *Tashrīf al-ayyām wa 'l-ʿuṣūr bi-sīrat al-sulṭān al-Malik al-Manṣūr* (see the text in M. van Berchem and Fatio, *Voyage*, 310-15, where the French translation by Reinaud is also provided).

In the treaty concluded on 1 Rabīʿ II 684/6 June 1285 between Ḳalāwūn and Leo III of Armenia, al-Marḳab is mentioned among the possessions of the Mamlūk sultan; the district (*niyāba*) of al-Marḳab is the sixth dependency of the *mamlaka* of Ṭarābulus. The maintenance of the fortress was charged to the private resources of the sultan. Curiously, al-Marḳab is mentioned neither in the *Masālik* of al-ʿUmarī (mid-8th/14th century), nor in the *Taʿrīf*. When Ibn Baṭṭūṭa visited al-Marḳab, he found there outside the walls a suburb used as a stopping place by foreign travellers, who were not permitted to enter the castle.

At the end of the 8th/14th century and the beginning of the 9th/15th (*Ṣubḥ*, xii, 463, 464) the *nā'ib* of Ḳalʿat al-Marḳab was an *amīr* of twenty; he was *wālī* of the eastern regions and had the duty of ensuring night and day the defence of the coast, the maintenance of observation-posts (*adrāk*) and guard-towers (*shawānī*) and was also required to deter potential enemies, the place being only a day's sailing time from Cyprus.

In the 9th/15th century, in the *Zubda* (ed. J. Gaulmier, 71), Khalīl al-Ẓāhirī mentions among the important sites of the province of Ṭarābulus, "the fortress of Marḳab which is clearly impregnable and controls a territory containing numerous villages".

In the course of his travels in Palestine and Syria in 842/1476, the sultan Ḳāʾitbāy passed by the foot of al-Marḳab in Djumādā II/mid-October (Devonshire, 10), but did not halt there.

From the time of the period of the Burdjiyya Mamlūks [*q.v.*], al-Marḳab is primarily mentioned in the texts in its capacity as a state prison. Among the unwilling guests of this castle were: Sayf al-Dīn Aynabak al-Badrī, *atabak al-ʿasākir* (*Manhal*, no. 622; Ibn Taghrībirdī, *Nudjūm*, xi, 154) and his kinsman Sayf al-Dīn Ḳaratāy Ibn ʿAbd al-ʿAzīz al-Ashrafī (*Manhal*, no. 1850), both imprisoned in 778/1376-7. Djardamur, known as Akhū Ṭāz (*Manhal*, no. 831; Ibn Ḳāḍī Shuhba, 84) was sent there on the order of Ḳidjmās in Shaʿbān 784/October 1382, an experience which did not prevent him becoming governor of Damascus in 791/1389 (Laoust, *Governeurs*, 16). In 785/1383, Sayf al-Dīn Aḥmad Aḳbughā b. ʿAbd Allāh al-Dawādār (*Manhal*, no. 478; Ibn Ḳāḍī Shuhba, 106, 113; *Nudjūm*, xi, 202, 303) joined him there and was freed a few months later at the same time as the former.

In 791/1389, three *amīrs* were incarcerated there: Naṣr al-Dīn Ibn al-Hadhbānī, *nāʾib* of Ḥamāt (Ibn Ḳāḍī Shuhba, 291), Timurbughā known as Mintāsh (*Manhal*, no. 722) and Bahādur al-Shihābī al-Ṭawāshī (*Manhal*, 702) who arrived there in Djumādā II/June.

In 800/1397-8, Sayf al-Dīn Shaykh Ibn ʿAbd Allāh al-Ṣafawī al-Khāṣṣakī (*Manhal*, no. 1184) arrived as a prisoner at the castle and died there a year later. The *amīr akhūr kabīr* Īnāl Bay b. Ḳidjmās al-Ẓāhirī (*Manhal*, no. 621) was imprisoned there in 805/1402-3. In the same year, Sūdūn min ʿAlī Bak al-Ẓāhirī known as Ṭāz (*Manhal*, no. 1126; *Nudjūm*, xii, 177, 298) was transferred from the prison of al-Iskandariyya to al-Marḳab. Sayf al-Dīn Baktimur Djillak al-Ẓāhirī, *nāʾib* of Ṭarābulus (*Manhal*, no. 676) was present there for a short period; imprisoned in 810/1408, he was freed the same year. Sayf al-Dīn Manku Bāy al-Azdamūrī (H. Sauvaire, *Description de Damas*, in *JA* [1895], xi, 308, no. 135) was interned there for a period of time on the orders of al-Malik al-Muʾayyad Shaykh and then released in 818/1415. The *amīr* Ḳānī-Bay b. ʿAbd Allāh al-Muḥammadī (*Manhal*, no. 1811; Darrag, *L'Égypte sous Barsbay*, 14) governor of Damascus who, following a rebellion in 818/1415 was recalled to Cairo, was appointed governor of Tripoli in Rabīʿ II 821/May 1417; shortly after this he suffered a defeat at the hands of the Turcomans, was dismissed and imprisoned at al-Marḳab, where he stayed for two years before being freed. Finally, in Rabīʿ II 905/November 1499 (Ibn Iyās, *Mamelouks*, 466), the sultan al-Malik al-Ẓāhir Ḳānsawḥ ordered the imprisonment at al-Marḳab of the *amīr* Khayr-Bak, prefect of the province of al-Gharbiyya, but then released him.

After his return from Florence, in autumn 1027/1618, the *amīr* Fakhr al-Dīn b. Maʿn [*q.v.*] took steps to strengthen his power in Syria; he succeeded in gaining the support of a number of places which had belonged to Yūsuf Ṣayfā, including al-Marḳab.

Among the travellers of the 18th century, Richard Pococke, who passed through Syria *ca.* 1740, noted in his *Description* (ii, 200) that the castle of al-Marḳab, of which he gives a good description, was the residence of the governors of the region and that it could be reached from Bāniyās in an hour and a half by way of a steep incline, in a south-easterly direction. In his *Voyage* (ed. Gaulmier, 284), Volney mentioned, in the Syrian coast "various villages, which were formerly fortified towns" including "the precipitous site of Merkab". He gives no description of it and in fact does not seem to have seen it.

3. Description of the fortress. Numerical and alphabetical references are those of the plan drawn up by E. G. Rey (*Arch. milit.*), copied by Max

van Berchem and Ed. Fatio (*Voyage*) and by P. Deschamps (*Terre Sainte Romane*, 140-1).

The configuration of the terrain is responsible for the plan of the castle, which is shaped like an isosceles triangle with its base line facing north. The latter measures 350 m., while the east and west walls each measure 400 m.; the area is more than three hectares. In the southern part is the "body of the site" separated from the remainder of the surface by a wall; the space located to the north of this internal defence is the "bailey", used as a farmyard and containing some outbuildings, enabling the population and the livestock of the immediate vicinity to be gathered within the walls in the event of hostilities.

On the west from of the perimeter wall of al-Marḳab, some 50 m. above the southern point of the triangle, is a rectangular tower (1), in the short southern side of which a door is located, giving access to the castle; further along are two square towers (2,3) both typical of the architecture of the period between 1140 and 1186. At approximately the mid-point of this slightly concave face, is a large square barbican (A) to which access is gained by a stepped north-south ramp, then turning at a right-angle, by a small west-east bridge with three arches above the ditch. This entrance permitted access to the "bailey" which extended towards the north and east and to the entrance giving access to the "body of site", the castle as such. It is fitted with a loggia supported by four corbels; the door is framed with two archery apertures and provided with a trap-door and a portcullis. Continuing towards the north, are found four semi-circular towers (4,5,6,7) lacking their battlements and curtains and in a poor state of repair. In the north-west angle is a large tower (8) which was restored after the siege of 1285. The north face of the perimeter, slightly concave, measures 350 m. This face is in a badly ruined state, with the relics of two towers, one in about the centre and the other (9) further east, 75 m. from the larger tower in the angle (10).

The eastern face is convex as far as tower 16. As on the remainder of the diagram, the perimeter wall with its archery apertures is double; it overlooks quite steep inclines and juts out at this point over a ditch, both sides of which are bricked from a depth of 5 to 7 m. There are the remains of five towers (11 to 15). It is from tower 16 that there began the east-west wall which separated the "body of the site" from the huge expanse of the "bailey", and the stones of which were used in the 19th century by local peasants for the construction of their houses.

The semi-circular tower R, 11.2 m. in diameter, constructed astride the double perimeter wall, comprises several stories. On its defensive front it has a stone "jacket" 17 m. in diameter (16). With the donjon (L), it is the finest construction of al-Marḳab. To the north of this tower, there was a defensive emplacement (Q) and a square tower (P). In 1211 the perimeter towers of al-Marḳab greatly impressed Wilbrand von Oldenburg, who said of them that they were "built to support the heavens rather than to provide defence".

By the entry A, there is access to the "bailey"; proceeding further east, a second door (O) is found, also provided with solid defensive structures and its right-angled passage opening on the courtyard (G). The latter is surrounded by a "series of buildings suitable for the accommodation and subsistence of a large garrison"; its southern side was limited by the "body of the site".

To the west, there is a building with a large vaulted hall (J), and on the first floor is a room (F). "From the window of this room," wrote P. Deschamps (*Terre Sainte*, 169), "there is an excellent view of the sea." Opposite the large hall, on the facing side of the court-yard, are some buildings "which were places of domestic use. In one of them, are two bread-ovens" and two millstones. The castle maintained five years' reserve of food.

Built on to the south-east wall of these premises (I), there is a building (S) with two superimposed stories, cradle-vaulted and 46 m. long to correspond with the tower (R).

To the south of the "body of the site" are located a chapel (H), a donjon (L), a hall (K) and two other halls (M, N).

The Gothic chapel (H) dates from 1186. It is of rectangular shape with two doors, the one to the north opening on the courtyard (G), the other an ogival portal opening to the west and allowing descent to the parvis by way of a flight of steps. The nave, 23 x 10 m., with walls more than 5 m. thick, has two spans of arched ribs; it is larger than that of Ḥiṣn al-Akrād. Two small sacristies open on the sides of the chancel, that on the north side apparently showing the remnants of a fresco. This chapel has retained foliated capitals which resemble those of the first stage of construction of the cathedral of Ṭarṭūs [*q.v.*]. Following the Muslim occupation, a *miḥrāb* was constructed in the south wall.

The donjon (L), built on the southern angle of the castle, is a powerful tower with circular south front facing a nearby and potentially threatening escarpment. This tower is 21 m. high with basalt walls 5 m. thick, and in the interior are the remnants of a great hall.

Lower down, before the donjon, is a projecting structure (C) the base of which is protected by a "batter". The south face, 21 m. in breadth, is rounded in its central section—hence, by allusion to the prow of a ship, its technical name of "Ram Tower". At the top, under the watch-posts of this tower, a monumental inscription (*RCEA*, xiii, no. 4858), on a long band of white marble, written in enormous Mamlūk *naskhī* characters, commemorates its construction by sultan Ḳalāwūn in 684/1285.

A huge building (K) in three stories was constructed at the same time as the donjon (L), as is proved by "the common staircase which serves their upper rooms". This structure, shaped like a parallelogram, has three archery apertures opening towards the south-east and three doors, including a small one opening to the west on a triangular space giving access to the donjon or to the parvis of the church and the courtyard.

To the west of the donjon and the building (K), there are two buildings in two stories of vaulted rooms: M, in which there is a room "decorated with finely sculpted marble capitals", and N, closely linked to the donjon with which it shares a partition and a common passage.

The *birka* at al-Marḳab, as in many other places, is located outside the perimeter wall. In this case it is a stone-built reservoir 40 m. long and 10 m. wide; currently, it is less than 4 m. deep. Laid out on a north-south bearing, it was fed with water from mountain springs situated to the north. In times of peace, it supplied the needs of the men and livestock living within the perimeter of al-Marḳab. During sieges, the garrison made use of a reservoir and above all a well in the interior of the castle.

Ernest Renan, in 1863, referring to the testimony of his two colleagues, Thobois and Lockroy, wrote (*Mission*, 106) in regard to al-Marḳab: "Here there is no sculpture or fine decoration, the design is that of a French 12th century castle. It is evident that in Syria the Crusaders did not have a uniform style of construction. Each of the nations which took part in its building followed its own taste, and all were subject to the constraints of the materials which they found."

According to the testimony of W. N. Thomson, to which Ritter (*Erdkunde*, xvii, 883) and M. van Berchem (*Voyage*, 305 n.), refer, "it seems that the fortress was still in a good state of repair before the middle of the 19th century".

4. The village of al-Marḳab. In an assessment of tithes, dating from 589/1193, it is noted that al-Marḳab exported must, wine, sumac, almonds, figs and pottery. The same products are mentioned in an agreement signed between the Order of the Hospital and the Templars in 630/1233. The "wine of Margat" was extolled by the traveller Burchard de Mont Sion at the end of the 13th century.

This is probably the suburb, built to the north and east at the foot of the slopes of the castle, which is mentioned by Ibn Baṭṭūṭa (i, 183). It was in the spring of 726/1325 that the latter, coming from Lād̲h̲iḳiyya, passed before the fortress of al-Marḳab, of which he said that it resembled Ḥiṣn al-Akrād, constructed on a high eminence; he noted that it was forbidden to enter the castle and that foreigners were obliged to halt in an exterior suburb.

In the early 19th century, the castle of al-Marḳab does not seem to have greatly attracted the interest of travellers. When George Robinson visited Syria and Palestine in 1828, he took the coastal road and passed through Bāniyās on his way to Tripoli; he marked al-Marḳab on his map, but made no mention of it in the text of his account (ii, 94).

The Ottoman *ḳāʾimmaḳām* resided in the castle of al-Marḳab, administrative centre of the district of the same name which comprised some 1,500 inhabitants, for the most part Nuṣayrīs. In 1884, at the request of the *Ḳāʾimmaḳām*, the seat of government was transferred to Bāniyās.

In 1893, according to V. Cuinet, the *ḳaḍāʾ* of al-Marḳab was situated to the south of the *sand̲j̲aḳ* of Lād̲h̲iḳiyya; it was then bounded to the north by the *ḳaḍāʾ* of D̲j̲abala, to the east by the *vilāyet* of Syria, to the south by the *sand̲j̲aḳ* of Tripoli and to the west by the Mediterranean. This *ḳaḍāʾ* was divided administratively "into three nahiés which are *Marqab*, *Qadmous* and *Ghaouabi*. It contains 393 towns, villages and hamlets. The nahiés are administered directly by the caïmakam (deputy governor), with the exception of that of Qadmous which has a resident mudir in a fort of the nahié of Ghaouabi" (Cuinet, 169-70).

The total population of the *ḳaḍāʾ* rose to 39,671 inhabitants, including 27,121 Anṣāriyya. There were almost 200 schools there for 2,060 pupils. The main agricultural products were olives and onions, tobacco and silk which was sold for the most part to merchants in Beirut. Also found in the *ḳaḍāʾ* of al-Marḳab was the raising of livestock, especially goats.

In 1895, Max van Berchem and Ed. Fatio noted (*Voyage*, i, 308) that "the mosque, recognised from a distance by a cupola and a minaret-lantern white-washed with lime, contains some Arabic inscriptions. The most important are two decrees announcing the abolition of taxes, promulgated by two governors of the province of Tripoli, one under Sultan Barqūq in 795/1393, the other under Sultan Jaqmaq in 868/1463" (Wiet, *Décrets*, nos. 8, 166).

In 1914 al-Marḳab was the regional centre, as it was again in 1920. Between 1920 and 1937, this *ḳaḍāʾ* comprised three *nāḥiya*s: al-Marḳab, Ḳadmūs and Ennaya. In 1938 there were, between Bāniyās and al-Marḳab, five Sunnī villages. of which one, close to the foot of the castle comprised 832 inhabitants in 1945. These villages were dependent upon the *ḳaḍāʾ* of Bāniyās. In the neighbourhood there were Maronite, Greek Catholic and Greek Orthodox villages.

Since 1968 this region has experienced considerable economic prosperity with the development of the I.P.C. pipeline and the petroleum port of Bāniyās.

5. The isolated tower. At a distance of 1,500 m. in a direct line from the castle, in the coastal plain, on an isolated hillock, stands a tower called Burd̲j̲ al-Ṣabī ("Tower of the Boy").

This is a massive square guard-tower, 15 m. high, constructed of blocks of black basalt, held together with white mortar. On each face are constructed five archery apertures 2 m. high in walls 2.8 m. thick. A low door opens in the south-west face, giving access to a groin-vaulted hall; in one of the walls a staircase is constructed, leading to an upper room and thence to a terrace. This guard-tower was closely linked to the castle; its role was to watch over the small bay of the port of al-Marḳab and to control the coastal road. It is possible that there was a tunnel linking the tower to the castle, permitting the garrison, in time of siege, an outlet to the road or to the port.

The traces of a long defensive wall, which was covered over, are still visible; apparently in the Middle Ages it linked the coast to the castle. The road passed through a gate in the wall and, in all probability, there would have been a customs-post here.

6. The place of pilgrimage. Nearby, 150 m. from the goat to the south of the castle of al-Marḳab, is a cave called "el Basiyeh" where, according to popular belief, the Virgin Mary sheltered with the Infant Jesus. At the end of the 19th century this was a place of pilgrimage much visited by the Christian and Muslim inhabitants, especially on 8 September, feast of the Nativity of the Virgin.

Bibliography: ʿImād al-Dīn al-Iṣfahānī, *al-Fatḥ al-ḳussī*, ed. Landberg, Leiden 1888, 485, ed. Cairo 1322/1904, 110-11, tr. H. Massé, *Conquête de la Syrie*, Paris 1972, 125-6; Yāḳūt, iv, 500 = ed. Beirut 1952, v, 108-9; Ibn al-ʿAdīm, *Taʾrīk̲h̲ Ḥalab*, ed. S. Dahhān, Damascus 1968, iii, 140; Abū S̲h̲āma, *K. al-Rawḍatayn*, in *RHC Hist. Or.*, iv, 352-7, ed. Cairo 1288/1871, ii, 127; Dimas̲h̲ḳī, ed. Mehren, 114, 108; Abu 'l-Fidāʾ, ed. Reinaud, 255; Mufaḍḍal Ibn Abi 'l-Faḍāʾil, text and tr. E. Blochet, *Histoire des Sultans Mamelouks*, in *Patrologia Orientalis*, xii/3, Paris 1911, 536; Ibn Baṭṭūṭa, i, 183, new edn. Paris 1982, i, 155; Ibn al-Furāt, *Taʾrīk̲h̲*, Cambridge 1971, ii, tr., index s.v.; Ḳalḳas̲h̲andī, *Ṣubḥ al-aʿs̲h̲ā*, iv, 145-6, xii, 463, xiv, 382-5; Maḳrīzī, tr. Quatremère, *Sultans Mamelouks*, ii/1, 79-85; K̲h̲alīl al-Ẓāhirī, *Zubdat kas̲h̲f al-mamālik*, Fr. tr. Venture de Paradis, ed. J. Gaulmier, Beirut 1950, 71; Ibn Ḳāḍī S̲h̲uhba, *Taʾrīk̲h̲*, ed. ʿA. Darwīs̲h̲, Damascus 1977, 84, 106, 291, 293; Ibn Tag̲h̲rībirdī, *Manhal*, tr. G. Wiet, Cairo 1932; Ibn Iyās, *Histoire des Mamelouks Circassiens*, ii, tr. G. Wiet, Cairo 1945, 466; Ibn Iyās, *Journal d'un bourgeois du Caire*, tr. Wiet, Paris 1955, i, 79, 297; Anna Comnena, *Alexiad*, ed. B. Leib, Paris 1937-45, iii, xi, 148; Caffaro, *De Liberatione civitatum Orientis Liber*, in *RHC Hist. Or.*, v, 67; Wilbrand von Oldenburg, *Itinerarium Terrae Sanctae*, in J. C. M. Laurent, *Peregrinatores medii aevi quattuor*, Leipzig 1864, 170; Burchard de Mont Sion, *Descriptio Terrae Sanctae*, in *ibid.*, 12, 19, 70; Jacques de Vitry, *Historia Hierosolymitana*, chs. 32-3, in Bongars, *Gesta Dei per Francos sive Orientalis*, i, Hanover 1611,

1068 ff.; R. Pococke, *A Description of the East and some other countries*, London 1743-5, ii/1, ch. 25, pp. 199-201; Volney, *Voyage en Égypte et en Syrie*[1], Paris 1787; ed. J. Gaulmier, Paris-The Hague 1959, 284; G. Robinson, *Travels in Palestine and Syria*, Fr. tr. Paris 1837, i; F. R. Chesney, *The expedition for the survey of the rivers Euphrates and Tigris*, London 1850, i, ch. 19, p. 452; F. Walpole, *The Ansayrii and the Assassins. Travels in the Further East in 1850-1851*, iii, 289 ff.; C. Ritter, *Erdkunde*, xvii, 917; E. G. Rey, *Étude sur les monuments de l'architecture militaire des Croisés en Syrie....*, Paris 1871, 19-38. Pls. II, III; idem, *Les Périples des côtes de Syrie...*, in *Archives de l'Orient Latin*, ii, 1882, 334-5; E. Reclus, *Géographie de l'Asie Antérieure*, Paris 1884, 775; W. Heyd, *Histoire du commerce du Levant au Moyen-Âge*, Leipzig 1885, i, 373; G. Chester, *Notes on a journey from Iskanderun to Tripoli*, in *PEF. Quarterly* (April 1888), 74-5; G. Le Strange, *Palestine under the Moslems*, London 1890, 504-5; H. Sauvaire, *Description de Damas*, in *JA* (1895), xi, 308, n. 135; V. Cuinet, *Syrie, Liban et Palestine*, Paris 1896-1901, 169-74; Sir Ch. Oman, *A history of the art of war in the Middle Ages*[1], London 1898, 3rd ed. 1978, 51-2; M. van Berchem, *Inscriptions arabes de Syrie*, en *MIÉ*, iii (1900), 486-9; idem, and Ed. Fatio, *Voyage en Syrie*, in *MIFAO*, xxxvii, Cairo, i, 1913, 94-6, 281-325, ii, 1914, Pls. LXIII to LXIX; R. L. Devonshire, *Relation d'un voyage du Sultan Qayt-bay en Palestine et en Syrie*, in *BIFAO*, xx (1922), 10-12; M. Gaudefroy-Demombynes, *La Syrie à l'époque des Mamelouks*, Paris 1923, 114, 227-8; R. Dussaud, *Topographie historique de la Syrie*, Paris 1927, 94, 127-31, 147, map VIII, B2; Guide Bleu, *Syrie-Palestine*, Paris 1932, 250-3; Guide Bleu, *Moyen Orient*, Paris 1956, 350-2; E. Honigmann, *Die Ostgrenze des byzantinischen Reiches*, Brussels 1935, 114, 117, 125; R. Grousset, *Histoire des Croisades*, Paris 1934-6, index s.v.; G. Wiet, *Répertoire des décrets mamlouks de Syrie*, in *Mélanges Syriens R. Dussaud*, *BAH*, xxx (1939), 522, 537; Cl. Cahen, *La Syrie du Nord à l'époque des Croisades et la principauté d'Antioche*, Paris 1940, index s.v.; J. Weulersse, *Le pays des Alaouites*, Tours 1941, index s.v.; M. Canard, *Histoire de la dynastie des H'amdanides*, i, Algiers 1951, 206; R. Mantran and J. Sauvaget, *Règlements fiscaux ottomans. Les provinces syriennes*, Damascus 1951, 73, 77; S. Runciman, *A history of the Crusades*, ii, Cambridge 1952, 11, 54, 134, 190, 490, iii, Cambridge 1954, 47, 103, 220, 344, 348, 390-1, 395-6, 423; H. Laoust, *Les gouverneurs de Damas*, Damascus 1952, v. index M. Dunand, *De l'Amanus au Sinaï, sites et monuments*, Beirut 1953, 53-56; J. Sourdel-Thomine, *Deux décrets mamelouks de Marqab*, in *BEO*, xiv (1952-4) 61-4; P. Deschamps, *Terre Sainte Romane*, Paris 1964, 138-51; L.A. Mayer, *Une lettre sur le tremblement de terre de 1212*, in *Studies for A. S. Atiya*, ed. S. A. Hanna, Leiden 1972, 295-310; R. Breton, *Monographie du Château de Markab*, in *MUSJ*, x/vii (1972), 253-74; Deschamps, *Les châteaux des Croisés en Terre Sainte. iii. La défense du Comté de Tripoli et de la Principauté d'Antioche*, *BAH*, xc (1973), 258-5, et index s.v.; R. C. Smail, *The Crusaders in Syria*, London 1973, 38, 56, 113-15, 152; T. S. R. Boase, *Military architecture in the Crusader states in Palestine and Syria*, in K. M. Setton, ed., *A history of the Crusades*, Madison 1977, iv, ch. 4, pp. 140-64; Aḥmad Fā'iẓ al-Ḥumṣī, *Ḳal'at al-Marḳab* (guide book in Arabic), Damascus 1982, 38 pp. (N. Elisséeff)

MĀRK(I)SIYYA, Marxism.

1. *Terminology*. Marxism is denoted in numerous Islamic languages by a pure borrowing from Anglo-French forms, already adopted by the Russian: *marksizm* (or *marksism*) in Turkish, Persian, Pus̲h̲tu, Uzbek, etc. (Albanian *marksízëm*). Elsewhere, an abstract form has been derived from the name of Karl Marx: Arabic *mārksiyya* (often *mārkisiyya* on account of the antipathy of the phonological system to a succession of three consonants), Urdu *mārks-vād* ("tendency of Marx"). In some languages there is a distinction, as there is in Russian, between an individual Marxist, *mārksist*, and a Marxist concept or practice, *mārksīstī* in Persian, Pus̲h̲tu etc., *marksīstīk* in Uzbek (Russian *marksistski* as opposed to *marksist*). In Arabic, both adjective and substantive are *mārksī*. On the same model, more recently terms have been coined for "Marxism-Leninism", "Marxist-Leninist" etc.

2. *The concept*. In the Muslim world as elsewhere, that which is called Marxism is most often conceived as a complete doctrine claiming to explain the world and society, upheld by a school of thought and by a social and political movement designed to bring into reality the conclusions which it draws from this doctrine. There are orthodox forms of the doctrine and of the movement, in other words forms consistent with the thought of the founders (Karl Marx, 1818-83 and Friedrich Engels, 1820-95) and with the reality of things, as opposed to deviant, heretical and erroneous forms. This orthodox concept, official doctrine in the USSR, is almost universally adopted, among other places, in the Muslim world, following the tradition of religious or classical religious tendencies attached to a particular founder (cf. *mānawiyya, ḥanafiyya*, etc.). But its supporters ultimately make of "Marxism" a particular (though very general) science, like physics.

Specialists without affiliation to a "Marxist" organisation tend towards a quite different vision. "Marxian" ideas (those of Marx and Engels) in questions of sociology, economics, philosophy, politics, etc., qualified, fluctuating and often recast by themselves, have formed the basis of multiple doctrinal syntheses, starting with Engels himself. Groupings of political and social campaigners have set themselves up, declaring that they take as their guide one of these syntheses which they claim to be the sole legitimate interpretation, a "scientific", complete and consistent doctrine. One of these groupings, the Communist Bolshevik Party of Russia, on coming to power in Russia in November (October in the Julian calendar) 1917, codified under the title of Marxism-Leninism the interpretation propounded by its leader Vladimir Ilič Ulyanov, known as Lenin (1870-1924). Under its direction, a large number of Communist Parties were formed, united in the Communist International (Komintern according to the abbreviated Russian form) between 1919 and 1943, and some of these gained power after 1945. Differences of interpretation have continued to appear in these parties (whether in power or not), with dissident groups and parties seceding from them.

It is not to be denied that there are common traits in all these doctrinal syntheses, in certain ideas which are the basis of them or which derive from them. It is only in this sense that it is possible to speak of a "Marxism" which would encompass the many variants. On the level of history, it is also possible to speak of a Marxist ideological movement, comprising numerous branches, derived in the final analysis from the ideas and activities of Marx. Clearly, these terms should be used with caution.

3. *Knowledge of Marx and of Marxism before 1917*. In the 1890s, when there was for the first time talk of "Marxism" or "Scientific Socialism" as a complete and coherent doctrine, there emerged, within the vast

European socialist movement, organisations calling themselves "Social Democrats" (united after 1889 in the Second International) which claimed inspiration from this doctrinal synthesis and tolerated numerous variations.

In the first decade of this century, a few isolated intellectuals from the Muslim world became aware of these ideas in Europe, through reading or through contact with organisations. Thus, in Paris, the Tatar student from Simbirsk, Yūsuf Akčura, who published in 1902 in the Young Turk periodical *Shūrā-yi ümmet* (Cairo-Paris) an economic analysis of the Eastern question with reference to Marx, and the Copt Salāma Mūsā in 1908. For them, as for many others, Marx was an eminent socialist thinker alongside others.

In the Russian empire, the Russian Social Democratic Labour Party, founded in 1898, encompassed or influenced Marxist factions and study groups among Muslim intellectuals and workers, at Kazan from 1902 (among Tatars) and at Baku from 1904 onwards (with Iranians, Armenians, Georgians, etc.). At Baku, one group adopted the name of "Muslim Social Democratic Party *Hümmet*" (with the sense of energy, effort, co-operation, from the Arabic *himma*). In Iran itself, a social-democratic group was in existence at Tabrīz already in 1905 (with many Armenian members at least), requesting advice from the Marxist theoreticians Georgii V. Plekhanov and Karl Kautsky. At about this date, another group adopted the name of Social Democratic Party of Iran (*firḳa-yi idjtimāᶜiyyūn-ᶜāmmiyyūn-i Īrān*). In the course of the Iranian Revolution, the latter seems, through the intermediary of a more substantial clandestine organisation, the *mudjāhidīn*, to have taken action aimed at a profound social revolution, invoking the Ḳurᶜān and the *Sharīᶜa*.

In the Ottoman empire, tendencies of the same order existed within the Christian minorities. From 1911 to 1914, Yūsuf Akčura, who resided there after having been one of the leaders of the movement of the Muslims of Russia during the revolution of 1905, appointed the German Marxist economist of Russian Jewish origin Alexander Helphand, known as Parvus, to edit (with personal editorial responsibility) the economic column of his journal *Türk Yurdu* at Istanbul.

The more radical social democrats of the colonising countries sometimes supported the nationalists of the Muslim lands and guided them in the direction of social struggle. An outstanding example was the Dutch social-democrat H. J. F. M. Sneevliet who, taking up residence in 1913 in the Dutch East Indies, founded there in 1914 the Indian Social Democratic Association (Indische Sociaal Democratische Vereeniging) whose members included other Dutchmen, Eurasians and a few Indonesians.

4. *Knowledge of Marx and Marxism after 1917*. Within the Russian Social Democratic Labour Party and the Second International, V. I. Lenin defended his own stance and defined the other tendencies as "an anti-Marxist current in the bosom of Marxism". He thus made the struggle for an exclusive orthodoxy a primary pre-occupation for his own tendency, that of the majority (Russian *bolsheviki*) in the Party (a temporary majority in this case), which became virtually an autonomous party in 1912 and seized power in Russia in October/November 1917.

The new Soviet power, endowed with considerable means and considering itself the first territorial resort of a world-wide revolution, consequently saw as a priority the diffusion of the works of Marx and Engels, as well as those which condensed their doctrine according to the canonical interpretation, the writings of Lenin in the first instance.

The same applied to all the communist parties (united in the Third International from 1919 to 1943) which were founded throughout the world on the model and the inspiration of the Russian Communist (Bolshevik) Party and of the parties and groups produced by schisms within the communist movement. Each grouping added to the so-called "classic" works of the founders other texts, those of the successive supreme leaders of the Soviet Union (especially Lenin and Stalin), those of the leaders of the various national parties, those of heads of groups of tendencies (above all Leon Trotsky), those of certain theoreticians considered particularly orthodox, or text-books defining the various orthodoxies. Meanwhile the Second ("Socialist") International continued to attempt a parallel diffusion of texts, but on a much smaller scale and with much less exclusive reference to a Marxist orthodoxy.

This massive activity of editing and diffusion was naturally performed in the languages relevant to each party or group. The Soviet state also published translations of selected texts into the many languages of the Union or of the outside world. In the Muslim countries, parties, groups and sub-groups undertook the diffusion of works published in Soviet (and later Chinese) editions and (often in association with the latter) in editions emanating from the Communist publishers of the major western countries. Often, in times of isolation or difficulty, they produced and diffused, by improvised means, their own translations and the texts of local leaders.

There exists no general bibliography of this immense literature, written in so many languages. Only a bibliography of bibliographies of editions of the "classics" of Marxism, edited in the USSR and elsewhere in the Azeri, Albanian, Bashkir, Kazakh, Tatar and Uzbek languages, is to be found in L. Levin, *Bibliografiya bibliografiy proizvedeniy K. Marksa, F. Éngel'sa, V. I. Lenina*, Moscow 1961 (see index by language).

For the purposes of a typical example, it may be noted that one of the texts most widely translated and distributed in the Stalinist era was the second section of Chapter iv of the *Istoriya vsesoiuznoy kommunističeskoy partiy (bolshevikov), kratkii kurs*, "History of the Party of the Soviet Union (Bolshevik), short course", Moscow 1938. The sub-title was "course composed by a commission of the Central Committee of the C(b)P of the USSR, approved by the Central Committee of the C(b)P of the USSR, 1938". The section in question (it was leaked out that the author was Stalin himself) entitled "Historical materialism and dialectical materialism", set out to summarise (in 30 pages in the French edition of Moscow) "the theoretical basis of communism, the theoretical principles of the Marxist Party". Every communist group considered it a duty to distribute this text, reckoned to be fundamental. Cf. for example, in Arabic, Yūsuf Stālīn, *al-Māddiyya al-dāylaktīkiyya wa 'l-taʾrīkhiyya*, Baghdād, Maṭbaᶜat al-Rashīd, 1944, 50 pp., in the collection *Rasāʾil al-baᶜth* "Essays of the Renaissance" (there was no connection here with the still embryonic Baᶜth Party).

5. *The Marxist groupings*. Bearing in mind that which has been stated above, it is difficult to characterise a group as Marxist unless (directly or indirectly) it expressly declares itself so. On the other hand, it is not possible here to give a complete list of the many Marxist groupings in the Muslim world. Such a list would have to include: (a) Marxist study

groups; (b) groups and parties which called themselves "social democrats" before 1919 (some of them continuing to do so today), those which declared themselves "communists" (Arabic *shuyūʿī*, in other languages usually transcriptions of the European or Russian word) after this date; (c) groups and parties which adopt other designations, but which declare themselves inspired by Marxism and whose ideological and political programmes are to be identified with those of social democratic and communist parties, such as the *Tūda* ("Masses") Party of Iran; (d) trade unions and so-called mass or popular organisations (of women, students, youth, peace campaigners, etc.), such as communist parties customarily create around themselves, in order to be assured permanently of a number of sympathisers, when it is established that these "popular" groups closely follow the line of a Marxist movement, mostly of a communist movement; (e) groups, parties or organisations which declare themselves "socialist", groupings or association which are attached to them, but only when they state categorically that their main inspiration is from Marxism.

6. *Attitudes to Marxism*. In the Muslim world, attitudes in regard to what is known and understood from Marxist ideas have varied as much as have attitudes in regard to organisations, and then states, which declared themselves Marxist or were supposed to be so, the whole being most often considered as constituting a coherent unity.

The attitude of men of religion has been influenced above all by the atheism which they considered to be the corner-stone of Marxist thought and even to be the major innovation of Marx, thus displaying their ignorance of the irreligious tendencies of European thought before Marx and alongside the Marxists. The anti-religious policies and atheistic propaganda of the Soviet State have inevitably reinforced this concept, still very widespread. The connection in actual fact of this philosophical atheism with Marxist economic and social principles has evoked memories of Muslim religious history: the Ismāʿīlī heresy being especially perceived on the basis of accounts of the Carmathian [see ḲARMAṬĪ] "communism" and the Nizārī terrorism [see ISMĀʿĪLIYYA], with its supposedly non-Muslim instigators, the "communists" Plato and Mazdak. Against these ideas, prominence was given to the right of private property guaranteed by the Ḳurʾān and the *Sunna*.

A quite different attitude, developed especially in certain circles after the Second World War, has seen in Marxism a kind of encyclopaedic scientific and philosophical synthesis giving sure guidance on action in the social sphere. Its role has been compared with that played by the Aristotelian encyclopaedia in the mediaeval Muslim world (cf. A. Laroui, *L'idéologie arabe contemporaine*, Paris 1967, 152 f.).

Attitudes have been particularly influenced by the policies of states claiming to be Marxist. During the 1920s and again after the Second World War, a series of states and movements have seen in them allies against Euro-American imperialism. In many cases, the sympathy engendered by this alliance was extended into attraction towards the doctrine reckoned to be basic to the general attitude of Marxist states and movement. In other cases, alliance of the external level has been able to coincide with the persecution of local Marxists.

Nationalists of Muslim countries have been able to denounce the internationalism which is an essential principle of the Marxist movement, with its antipathy towards total and unhesitating adherence to purely national objectives. Similarly, they have denounced the nationalisms which could be disguised by this theoretical internationalism: the Russian nationalism of the Soviet State, the nationalism of the communist parties of the colonialist countries (France, Britain, etc.), Zionist Jewish nationalism, etc.

7. *Influence of Marxist ideas*. The Marxist movement, most often indirectly, has diffused in the Muslim world ideas and elements of *Weltanschauung* which, although alien in many cases, it has systematised and popularised in its own way. They have been widely adopted, even in circles hostile to theories and political initiatives emanating from the Marxist movement.

This applies in the case of appeal in a voluntarist vein for the structural transformation of the social sphere, the traditional structures being judged to constitute permament causes of exploitation and oppression. Dissatisfaction with the established order and the demand for justice are given a great value at the expense of the traditional attitude of Islam (among other religions and philosophies), which sees in this a culpable rebellion against the order willed by God. Transformation cannot be achieved by a moral change, by conversion, but by an organised struggle on the part of the disadvantaged against the privileged, by pressures exerted by strikes, demonstrations, electoral campaigns and the like (reformism) or by a genuine civil war, a revolution. Circumstances having favoured the revolutionary options, the term "revolution" (Ar. *thawra*) and its synonyms (*inḳilāb*, etc.) have acquired a quasi-mystical quality.

The Marxist movement, born in Europe, had given the primary role to the transformation, reformist or revolutionary according to the tendencies, of industrial European society. In its communist branch, it had however also appealed for the revolt of colonised or dependent peoples, reckoned to be exploited and oppressed by the western ruling classes just like the proletarians of the industrial world. This appeal was taken up to the point of a complete inversion of priorities. Some doctrinarians, starting with the Tatar Mīr Saʿīd Sulṭān Ghaliev (see below) in Soviet Russia in the 1920s, placed on the primary level the struggle of "proletarian nations" against the totality of industrial nations, reckoned to exploit and oppress them with the complicity of and for the partial benefit of their own proletarians.

This theme of the exploitation of the colonial world by the industrial capitalist world which robbed it of its riches had been developed by Lenin as an appendix to the primary doctrine of internal exploitation. It had enormous success in all circles of the Islamic world. The term of imperialism which expressed this process, often confused with that of "colonialism" (Ar. *istiʿmāriyya*), was taken up by the most anti-Marxist elements and became a *leitmotif* (with some conceptual efforts to distinguish in a more precise fashion between "colonialism" and "imperialism" *imbiryāliyya*, etc.).

The diffusion of these dynamic ideas has been combined with an internal evolution, complex in origin, which tended towards a veiled secularisation, a recoil from specifically religious values (the quest for salvation, etc.) in favour of the primacy of earthly activism (which has always been regarded as important in Islam). This activism is often invested in the defence and promotion of the Muslim *umma* or one of its parts, but this objective henceforward takes precedence over piety and religious observance. Biographies of Muḥammad place far greater emphasis on his earthly works than on his rôle as a messenger of the divine will.

There are limits to the influence exerted by concepts more or less Marxist in source in the world of Islam. The nationalism which is such a dominant force in this world (including the form of nationalism attached to the Muslim *umma* [see KAWMIYYA]) inspires distrust, to say the least, of any analysis of the classical Marxist type which identifies, within the struggling nation itself, exploiters and oppressors to be resisted. The vision of an end of history and an egalitarian classless society has not easily taken root, traditional Islam with its hierarchies of wealth and power being considered to constitute already a society without classes as such. Similarly, the internationalism which is fundamental to Marxism (although often abandoned in practice) could hardly be expected to tempt a public opinion moulded by nationalism.

A very widespread moralism also spurns the essential determinism of Marxism (even though Marxists have often been inconsistent on this subject in practice). Finally, in spite of the logical possibility of dissociating from atheism the political, sociological, social and strategic conclusions of historical Marxism, in spite of the sporadic efforts by communist parties to emphasise this dissociation, there is avoidance of any affiliation which could be interpreted as a public proclamation of atheism or (perhaps even more repugnant) a calling into question of the supra-human origin of the sacred books, the Ḳurʾān in particular. Atheistic propaganda, often amounting to restraint of religion in the communist states (without going in general to the extreme lengths of Albania, which has radically suppressed churches and mosques), causes unease, even among the leaders of movements or states which have chosen for strategic reasons to ally themselves with the former in a given period.

8. *Marxist view of Islam and the Muslim world.* Marx and Engels were not greatly interested in Islam as a religion, and as such it was subject to their general criticism of religious consciousness. Only the late reading by Engels of a book by the Anglican priest and orientalist Charles Forster, *The historical geography of Arabia* (London 1844) awakened in him reflections communicated to his friend and briefly commented upon by the latter (Marx and Engels, *Briefwechsel*, i, Berlin 1949 (= Moscow 1935), 568-90, letters of 18 (?) May, 2, 6 and 14 June 1853. At the end of his life, Engels, inspired by the revolt of the Sudanese *Mahdī* [see AL-MAHDIYYA], compared Muslim revolts to the religous uprisings of the Christian Middle Ages, more "progressive" in his opinion (*Zur Geschichte des Urchristentums*, in *Die Neue Zeit*, xiii/1 (1894-5), 4 ff., 36 ff. = Marx-Engels, *Werke*, Berlin 1963, xxii, 446-73, at p. 450). In general, both authors tend to explain the religious phenomena of Islam in terms of historical sociology and insist on the "stagnant" character of the "Orient" in general (cf. also *Marxisme et Algérie*, texts edited by R. Gallissot and G. Badia, Paris 1976).

The two founders followed much more closely the international events affecting the Ottoman Empire, the "Eastern Question". A favourable attitude towards the Ottoman Empire, inspired by their hatred of Russia, Turkey's enemy and supposedly the bastion of international reaction, led them to take a certain interest in Ottoman institutions following the example of their ally against Russia, the passionately Turcophile (and Turcophone) British parliamentarian, David Urquhart (1805-77), a conservative romantic. Towards the end of his life, Engels was at pains to dampen the enthusiasm ("sentimentalist" and "poetic") of French Marxists (the Guesdists) for the revolt of ʿUrābī, in his opinion a *pas̲h̲a* like any other (cf. his letter to E. Bernstein, 9 August 1882, in Marx-Engels, *Werke*, Berlin 1967, xxxv, 349 ff.).

The Marxist theoreticians of the Second International showed even less interest in the world of Islam, with the exception of Parvus (see above) and some examples of the destruction of the "natural economy" by capitalism in Kabylia mentioned Rosa Luxemburg, quoting the Russian sociologist M.M. Kovalevskiy. Indignation at the traumas wrought by colonisation was counter-balanced, as it had been among the founders, by the conviction that socialist revolution could only be produced in the industrialised world as a result of the maximum development of capitalism. Only subsequently would the event have world-wide repercussions.

After the Russian Revolution, the Third International included in its strategy the insurrection of colonies against the capitalist metropolises, while maintaining the priority of revolution conducted by the proletariat in these metropolises themselves. This often led to more or less elaborated attempts at analysis, both on the part of communist parties (and eventually dissident factions) established in the colonial and dependent countries, including Islamic countries, and on the part of those of the metropolises whose duty it was to support, even encourage, the revolt of their colonies.

In Soviet Russia itself (subsequently transformed into the Union of Soviet Socialist Republics), the Tatar Mīr Saʿīd Sulṭān G̲h̲aliev and his companions, originally from nationalist and reformist [see IṢLĀḤ. 5. Central Asia, in Suppl.] circles but impregnated with Marxist ideas, adhered to the Bolshevik Communist Party and initially collaborated with the new power. Sulṭān G̲h̲aliev then elaborated his doctrine on the specificity and the globally "proletarian" nature of Muslim society, the primacy of the Muslim East in the struggle against world capitalism, the "progressive" and "democratic" nature of the Muslim religion. Expelled from the Party in 1923, his ideas evolved still further. He drew up plans for a Colonial Communist International and for a Socialist State of Tūrān, researching Muslim and Turco-Mongolian sources for Marxist concepts. He was forced to go underground and finally eliminated.

Studies of Islam and of the Muslim peoples have been developed in the USSR, naturally on Marxist lines as soon as the level of somewhat generalised conclusions has been reached. Particular attention is paid to the Muslim peoples of the Union, from among whom specialists have emerged. Advantage has been taken of the pre-revolutionary tradition of Russian orientalism which took a special interest in problems of economic and social history. In the communist states of Eastern Europe, studies have followed the same model on the basis of somewhat different academic orientalist traditions. In addition to numerous detailed studies, attempts at synthesis have been hampered by the ideological monopoly of the Party which reserves for itself the right to any general conclusion, however minor. Interpretations have also been required to follow the lines inspired by fluctuations of official ideology in general and above all by successive strategic attitudes adopted in relation to Islam, the Muslim populations of the interior and the Muslim states of the exterior.

The communist parties of the capitalist countries or of the Third World have undertaken virtually no general study of Islam. But they have sometimes encouraged their members to study a particular Muslim country or patronised their works. Outside or on the margin of the orbit of communist states and parties, Marxist or quasi-Marxist studies have been published in increasing numbers with, in general, a great deal more originality.

Among the most interesting studies are economics-based analyses of contemporary developments in the Muslim world, some of them written by natives of these countries. More generally, intellectuals of the Muslim world tend to take as their guide in numerous domains the neo-Marxist synthesis codified in the Soviet Union, presented as "*the* authentic Marxism" and regarded as a kind of new science throughout the Third World. For this reason there is frequent recourse to the works inspired by this synthesis even in circles hostile to the political, social and ideological options of the states and parties laying claim to Marxism.

Bibliograpy: M. Rodinson, *Marxisme et monde musulman*, Paris 1972; W. Z. Laqueur, *Communism and nationalism in the Middle East*, London 1956; H. Bräker, *Kommunismus und Weltreligionen Asiens. i. Kommunismus und Islam*, Tübingen 1969-71, 2 vols.; F. Georgeon, *Aux origines du nationalisme turc, Yusuf Akçura*, Paris 1980; K. S. Abu Jaber, *Salāmah Mūsā: precursor of Arab socialism*, in *MEJ*, xx/2, 196-206; A. Bennigsen and Ch. Lemercier-Quelquejay, *La Presse et le mouvement national chez les Musulmans de Russie avant 1920*, Paris-The Hague 1964, 120 ff.; eidem, *Lex mouvements nationaux chez les Musulmans de Russie. i. Le "sultangaliévisme" au Tatarstan*, Paris-The Hague 1960; A. Bennigsen and E. S. Wimbush, *Muslim national communism in the Soviet Union, a revolutionary strategy for the colonial world*, Chicago-London 1979; Kh. Shakeri, *Le Parti communiste iranien*, unpubl. thesis, E.H.E.S.S., Paris 1980, 50 ff.; C. Chaqueri, *La Social-démocratie en Iran*, Florence 1979; J.S. Mintz, *Mohammed, Marx and Marhaen, the roots of Indonesian socialism*, London-Dunmow 1965; J. Th. Petrus Blomberger, *Le communisme aux Indes néerlandaises*, Paris 1929; *Le bolchevisme et l'Islam*, in *RMM*, li-lii (1922); P. Dumont, *Un économiste social-democrate au service de la Jeune Turquie*, in *Mémorial Ö. L. Barkan*, 75-80; H. Batatu, *The old social classes and the revolutionary movement of Iraq,* Princeton 1978; H. Carrère d'Encausse and S. Schram, *Le marxisme et l'Asie 1854-1964*, Paris 1965; G. Haupt, *Le début du mouvement socialiste en Turquie*, in *Le mouvement social*, xiv (1963) 121-37; M. S. Sfia, *Le socialisme dans les pays musulmans au début du XXe siècle, aperçu bibliographique*, in *ibid.*, 139-42; G. Haupt and M. Rebérioux (ed.), *La Deuxième Internationale et l'Orient*, Paris 1967; J. Thrower, *Marxist-Leninist "Scientific Atheism" and the study of religion and atheism in the U.S.S.R. today*, The Hague 1983 (exhaustive material on the study of Islam in the USSR and amongst Marxists); R. Gallissot (ed.), *Mouvement ouvrier, communisme et nationalisme dans le monde arabe*, Paris 1978; K. E. Pabst, *Zu einigen Übersetzungen der Klassiker des Marxismus-Leninismus ins Arabische*, in *Hallesche Beiträge zur Orientwissenschaft*, i (1979), 21-31.

(M. Rodinson)

MARMARA DEÑIZI, the Turkish name of the Sea of Marmara.

1. The Sea itself.

(a) *Geography*. This is a small sea within the borders of Turkey, communicating with the Aegean Sea through the Dardanelles [see čanaḳ-ḳalᶜe boghazî] and with the Black Sea through the Bosphorus [see boghaz-iči]. Istanbul is the most prominent city on its shore.

The Sea has a surface area of 11,350 km.²; its greatest length, from the Dardanelles to the end of the Gulf of Izmit, is 260 km; its width between Silivri on the Thracian side and Bandirma on the Anatolian side is 80 km. Its greatest depth reaches 1,355 m.roughly in its geographical centre, but it is much shallower around the central depression, mostly under 200 m. The salinity of its water is relatively low, from 22/1000 near the surface to 38.5/1000 at 30 m. and deeper. A surface current flows towards the Dardanelles, while a deeper counter-current moves in the opposite direction.

In antiquity, it was called Propontis, and was thus distinguished from the Dardanelles and the Bosphorus; this distinction was continued by mediaeval European authors, but not by the Muslim ones, who usually bracketed all three phenomena under the term al-Khalīdj "The Strait", often specified as that of Constantinople: Khalīdj al-Ḳusṭanṭīniyya or al-Khalīdj al-Ḳusṭanṭīnī. This lack of terminological discrimination on the part of early Muslim authors was symptomatic of their unfamiliarity with the exact configuration of the area, although some seem to have been aware of the considerable variation in the width of this "Strait"; thus al-Masᶜūdī, writing in 345/956 (*Tanbīh*, 66) states that the width at "Filās" is 40 miles. A hint of this sea appears on al-Idrīsī's map of A.D. 1154, although there too we find the usual single name of Khalīdj al-Ḳusṭanṭīniyya. The attempts by the Arabs to conquer Constantinople, especially those of 97-9/715-17, during which their fleets sailed through the Sea of Marmara, were obviously too brief and transitory to leave a clearer idea of this sea. The difficulty of sailing through the Dardanelles, and the fact that armies and travellers usually crossed from Anatolia to Thrace through this strait, may also have attracted the Muslims' attention thither and have obscured the small sea between it and Constantinople. A better understanding of the actual geographical nature of the area appears in Abu 'l-Fidāʾ's *Taḳwīm al-buldān*, composed by 721/1321, where the Sea of Marmara is described without, however, being assigned a name: "When travellers have entered it [i.e. the Khalīdj al-Ḳusṭanṭīniyya], it widens and resembles a lake (*birka*)..." Abu 'l-Fidā's lack of any specific name for the Sea of Marmara is also illustrated by a reference to the Marmara Island as "one of the islands of the Mediterranean (Baḥr al-Rūm)", with the remark that "it is in the midst of al-Khalīdj al-Ḳusṭanṭīnī" (*Taḳwīm*, 34, 188-9).

(b) *History*. The Sea of Marmara came permanently within the Dār al-Islām with the Turkish conquest of Byzantine territory. The *beylik* of Ḳarasî [*q.v.*] was the first Turkish principality to reach the Sea of Marmara, occupying, during the first half of the 8th/14th century, its southern shore from the Ḳapîdaghî peninsula to the Dardanelles. Ḳarasî, extending also along the Anatolian side of the Dardanelles and along the adjacent part of the Aegean shore, became a maritime power: its principal naval base was Edindjik on the Gulf of Erdek. The experience of Ḳarasî sailors, gained in their encounters with the Byzantines, proved useful to the Ottomans after the latter had absorbed Ḳarasî towards the middle of the 8th/14th century and after they had further extended Turkish domination to the remaining, eastern part of the Anatolian coast of the Sea of Marmara. At that point, the arsenal of Edindjik was joined by other naval installations such as Mudanya, Ḳaramürsel and Izmid. Although these shipyards and bases were eventually eclipsed by those of Gallipoli [see gelibolu] and Ḳāsîmpasha, those on

Marmara's southern shore, so significant in the incipient period of Turkish maritime history, retained their importance, some of them to this day.

In contrast to the southern, Anatolian shore of the Sea of Marmara, the northern, Thracian shore was occupied by the Turks more gradually and as a by-product of the Ottoman penetration into the Balkans and of the eventual conquest of Constantinople. Lacking the bays and natural or man-made harbours characteristic of the southern shore, the northern shore never played a similar role in Turkish maritime affairs, except for Istanbul itself, of which the Ḳadïrgha Limanï was developed by Meḥemmed II and had some importance until Selīm I founded the arsenal of Ḳāsïmpasha on the Golden Horn.

After the Ottomans had established themselves in Rumelia and had taken Constantinople, the Sea of Marmara became a Turkish lake and has remained so to this day; a certain limitation on Turkish sovereignty over this sea, however, has existed since the 19th century, for the special status of the Straits of the Dardanelles and the Bosphorus affects Marmara as well. Its secure domination by the Ottomans was in part responsible for the relatively uneventful place this sea had in Ottoman naval history, and for the neglect it received in Ottoman literature. The Sea of Marmara is not described in the text of the *Kitāb-i Baḥriyye*, the 10th/16th century Turkish portolan by Pīrī Reʾīs [*q.v.*], although the first, "draft" version does include brief chapters on the Marmara Island and the Princes' Islands, and its map does appear in some manuscripts. It is still anonymous in the *Tuḥfat al-kibār fī asfār al-biḥār* by the 11th/17th century author Kātib Čelebi (*q.v.*]: "It (i.e. the Mediterranean) ends at Bozdja-ada (= Tenedos). Between the inner side of the Strait (i.e. the Dardanelles) and Istanbul, there is a small sea whose circumference amounts to 700 miles... There are islands in it: Marmara, Imralï, Ḳïzïl adalar (= the Princes' Islands)..." (1729 ed., p. 2b). In the *Djihān-nümā*, the cosmography by the same author, however, there is already a reference to this sea as "Baḥr-i Marmara" (1732 ed., p. 667). This name, derived from that of the Marmara Island, had begun to appear since the 16th century on European maps and in atlases in such forms as Mar de Marmora, and Kātib Čelebi, whose *Djihān-nümā* was in part a translation of such works, may have followed their example.

2. The island after which the Sea of Marmara is named.

Marmara, the classical Proconnesos, is the largest island in this sea, with an area of 200 km.[2] It is the principal one in a cluster that includes Avsha (also called Türkeli), Pashalimanï, and a few other smaller ones, near the Ḳapïdaghï peninsula, the latter originally also an island but eventually linked to the southern shore by a process of marine sedimentation. Marble quarries, exploited on Marmara Island since antiquity, gave rise to its later name. The population of these islands was until the recent exchange chiefly Greek-speaking, but was then replaced by Turkish immigrants from Crete and Bulgaria. While fishing, fruit and olive growing, and vegetable gardening (and until recently, lumber exportation, which has disappeared with the completion of deforestation), were the traditional occupations of the population, tourism has now taken precedence as the main industry of these islands, with regular boat service between Istanbul, Marmara (the chief town and harbour on Marmara Island) and Avsha. Administratively, the Marmara Islands form a *bucak* within the *ilçe* of Erdek of the *il* of Balıkesir.

The second group of islands within the Sea, the Princes' or Prince Islands, in Turkish simply Adalar or Kızıl Adalar, is a cluster situated between 13 and 22 km. to the south-east of Istanbul and about 5 km. from the Anatolian coast. They consist of four larger islands (Kınalı, Burgaz, Heybeli and Büyükada) and five small ones. Together they form an *ilçe* within the *il* of Istanbul; Büyükada, Heybeli, and Burgaz-Kınalı form individual *bucak*s within this *ilçe*. The largest of these, Büyükada, lit. "the large island", was called in Byzantine times Prinkipo, but its classical name as mentioned by Pliny, that of Megale (*Naturalis historiae...*, v, 151) was a semantic ancestor of the Turkish name. In the Byzantine period, these islands were the occasional place of banishment or seclusion for members of the ruling family or for other important persons; in recent times, they have been the favourite resort of Istanbul's wealthier citizens. Heybeli harbours two establishments which train officers for the Turkish navy: the preparatory Deniz Lisesi, and the higher Deniz Harp Okulu, the latter the continuation of an older school at Ḳāsïmpasha, whence it had moved in 1851.

Aside from these two groups of islands, there is the isolated Imralı, Byzantine Kalolimni, an elongated island near the beginning of the Gulf of Gemlik. After the departure of its Greek-speaking population during the population exchange in the early years of the Turkish Republic, the island remained uninhabited until in 1935 a penitentiary was placed on it, the inmates practising some of the traditional occupations of the former inhabitants.

3. Administrative organisation.

In administrative terms, during the Ottoman period the greater part of the coasts of the Sea of Marmara was usually within the *eyālet* of Djazāʾir-i Baḥr-i Safīd [*q.v.*], the special province under the Ḳapudan Pasha [*q.v.*] administered from Gallipoli.

Today, these shores are distributed among six *ils*, named after their administrative centres: Istanbul, Izmit (also called by its historical name of Kocaeli), Bursa, Balıkesir, Çanakkale and Tekirdağ.

Bibliography: In addition to references given in the text, see *BGA*, iv, 57 and viii, 418 (indices for Khalīdj al-Ḳusṭanṭīniyya); Pauly-Wissowa, s.vv. Propontis, Proconnesos; *Türk Ansiklopedisi*, s.vv. Marmara Denizi, Marmara Adaları, Adalar, Imralı; G. Schlumberger, *Les Îles des Princes*[2], Paris 1925; O. Erdenen, *Istanbul adaları*, Istanbul 1962; W. Tomaschek, *Zur historischen Topographie von Kleinasien im Mittelalter*, in *SBWAW*, Phil.-Hist. Cl., cxxiv (1891), 1-18; D. E. Pitcher, *An historical geography of the Ottoman Empire*, Leiden 1972; J.B. Lechevalier, *Voyage de la Propontide et du Pont-Euxin*, Paris 1800, i, 1-40; Ali Tanoğlu, Sırrı Erinç and Erol Tümertekin, *Türkiye atlası*, Istanbul 1961, map 1/a and *passim*; Ankara, Coğrafya Encümeni, *Marmaradenizi havzası*, Ankara 1934; K. Miller, *Mappae arabicae*, Stuttgart 1926; K. Kretschmer, *Die italienischen Portolane des Mittelalters*, Berlin 1909, 639-40, 650-2; İ. H. Uzunçarşılı, *Osmanlı devletinin merkez ve bahriye teşkilâtı*, Ankara 1948, 389-90; M. Canard, *Les expéditions des Arabes contre Constantinople dans l'histoire et dans la légende*, in *JA*, ccviii (1926), 61-121; H. N. Howard, *Turkey, the Straits, and U.S. policy*, Washington 1974. (S. Soucek)

MARRĀKUSH (popular pronunciation *Merrāksh*, in French Marrakech, English Marrakesh) a town in Morocco, and one of the residences of the sovereign.

The form Marrakech, adopted by the administration of the protectorate, is of recent origin. Down to about 1890 the town was always known as Morocco. The kingdom of Morocco, distinct in origin from those of Fās and the Sūs, finally gave its name to the whole empire. At one time it only consisted of the country south of the wādī Umm Rabīᶜ as far as the range of the Great Atlas.

Marrakesh is situated in 31° 37' 35 '' N. lat. and 7° 59' 42'' E. long. (Greenw.). Its mean height above sea-level is about 1,510 feet. The town is 150 miles south of Casablanca. It is through the latter that almost all the traffic with the coast passes at the present day. It used to go via Safi which is the nearest port (100 miles). Sīdī Muḥammad b. ᶜAbd Allāh [*q.v.*] in 1765 tried to supplant it by Mogador (115 miles) where he built a town and harbour through which at the end of the 18th century most of the trade between Marrakesh and Europe passed.

The temperature which is very mild in winter is very hot in summer. The average maxima of 39°6 in the month of August 1927 have nothing unusual and imply extreme temperatures reaching or passing 50° on certain days. Rainfall is low (284.5 mm. in 1927, against 706.5 in Rabat and 1,007.3 in Tangier). But water fed by the snows of the Atlas is found at no great depth. It is collected by a system of long subterranean tunnels (*k͟haṭṭāra*, plur. *k͟haṭāṭīr* [see ḲANĀT] which bring it to the surface by taking advantage of the very slight slope of the surface. This method of obtaining water has enabled the vast gardens which surround the town to be created. The Almohads and the dynasties which succeeded them also built aqueducts and reservoirs to supply the town with water from the springs and streams of the mountains.

Contrary to what was until quite recently believed, Marrakesh has for long been the most thickly populated town of the empire. The census of 7 March 1926 gave 149,263 as the total population, 3,652 Europeans, 132,893 Muslims, 12,718 Jews. In 1936 the figures were respectively 190,314, 6,849, 157, 819 and 25,646; in 1947, the city had a total of 241,000 inhabitants. The probable growth of the population is not sufficient to explain the difference between the present-day figures and the old estimates, almost all far below the truth and varying greatly among themselves: from 20,000 (given by Diego de Torres in 1585 and Höst in 1768), 25,000 (Saint Olon, 1693), 30,000 (Ali Bey al-Abbassi, 1804), 40 to 50,000 (Gatell, 1864, and E. Aubin, 1902), 50,000 (Lambert, 1868), 60,000 (Beaumier, 1868), 80 to 100,000 (Washington, 1830) up to the obviously exaggerated figure of 270,000 given by Jackson in 1811.

About 40 miles north of the Atlas, the vast silhouette of which, covered by snow for eight months of the year fills the background, Marrakesh is built in a vast plain called the Ḥawz which slopes very gently towards the wādī Tansift, which runs 3 miles north of the town. The extreme uniformity of the plain is broken only in the north-west by two rocky hills called Gillīz (1,700 feet) and Kudyat al-ᶜAbīd. In 1912 at the time of the French occupation, there was built a fort which commands Marrakesh. The European town called the Gueliz lies between this hill and the walls of the old town.

The wādī Issīl, a left-bank tributary of the Tansift, a stream often dried up but transformed into a raging torrent after storms, runs along the walls of the town on the east. To the north of Marrakesh as far as the Tansift and to the east stretches a great forest of palm-trees, the only one in Morocco north of the Atlas. It covers an area of 13,000 hectares and possesses over 100,000 palm-trees but the dates there only ripen very imperfectly.

The town is very large. The ramparts of sun-dried mud which run all round it measure at least 7 miles in length. The town in the strict sense does not occupy the whole of this vast area. The part built upon forms a long strip which starting from the *zāwiya* of Sīdī bel ᶜAbbās in the north runs towards the *ḳaṣaba* (*ḳaṣba*) which stands at the southern end of the town. On the two sides lie great gardens and estates among which we find in the neighbourhood of the chief gates inside the walls, isolated quarters grouped like so many villages around their *sūḳ* and the mosque.

The town consisted mainly of little low houses of reddish clay, often in ruins, among which were scattered huge and magnificent dwellings without particularly imposing exteriors built either by the viziers of the old Mak͟hzen (e.g. the Bāhiya, the old palace of Bā Ḥmād [*q.v.* in Suppl.], vizier of Mawlāy al-Ḥasan) or by the great *ḳāʾids*, chiefs of the tribes of the country around. The narrow and overhung streets in the central area broaden towards the outskirts into sunny and dusty squares and crossroads. The colour, the picturesque architecture, the palm trees, the branches of which appear over the walls of the gardens, the presence of a large negro population, all combine to give the town the appearance of a Saharan *ḳṣar* of vast dimensions.

The centre of the life of the city is the D͟jāmaᶜ al-Fnā, a vast, irregular, ill-defined open space, surrounded in the early years of this century by wretched buildings and reed huts, overshadowed by the high minaret of the Kutubiyya Mosque. Its name comes, according to the author of the *Taʾrīk͟h al-Sūdān*, from the ruins of a mosque which Aḥmad al-Manṣūr had undertaken to build there; "As he had planned it on a wonderful scale, it had been given the name of mosque of prosperity (*al-hanā*); but his plans being upset by a series of unfortunate events, the prince was unable to finish the building before his death and it was therefore given the name of mosque of the ruin (*d͟jāmiᶜ al-fanāʾ*)". This origin having been forgotten; an attempt was later made to explain the name of the square from the fact that the heads of rebels used to be exposed there. It was there also that executions took place. Lying on the western edge of the principal agglomeration of buildings at its most thickly populated part, close to the *sūḳ*, connected with the principal gates by direct and comparatively quiet roads, D͟jāmaᶜ al-Fnā is the point of convergence of the roads. At all hours swarming with people, it is occupied in the morning with a market of small traders: barbers, cobblers, vendors of fruit and vegetables, of medicines, of fried grasshoppers, of tea and of soup (*ḥarīra*); in the evening, it is filled with acrobats and jugglers (Awlād Sīdī Aḥmad ū Mūsā of Tazerwalt), sorcerers, story-tellers, fire-eaters, snake charmers and *s͟hlūḥ* dancers. The audience consists mainly of people from the country who have come into town on business and want to enjoy the distractions of the town for a few hours before going home. These visitors are always very numerous in Marrakesh. Besides the regular inhabitants there is a floating population, the number of which may be of the order of 10,000 persons. For Marrakesh is the great market for supplying not only the Ḥawz but also the mountain country, the Sūs and especially the extreme south, Dādes, Darᶜa (Draᶜ) and the Anti-Atlas. Marrakesh used to be the starting-point for caravans going through the Sahara to trade with Timbuktu. They brought back chiefly Sudanese slaves for whom Marrakesh was an important market. The conquest of the Sudan by France put an end to this traffic.

To the north of the D̲jāmaʿ al-Fnā begin the *sūḳ*s, which are very large. As in Fās and in the other large towns, the traders and artisans are grouped by trades under the authority of the *muḥtasib* [*q.v.*] The most important *sūḳ*s are those of the cloth merchants (*ḳīsāriyya*), of the sellers of slippers, of pottery, of basket work, of the embroiderers of harness, of the dyers and of the smiths. An important Thursday *sūḳ* (*al-k̲h̲amīs*) is held outside and inside the walls around the old gate of Fās which has taken the name of the market (Bāb al-K̲h̲amīs). This *sūḳ* was already in existence in the 10th/16th century.

There is no industry to speak of in Marrakesh. The most important is the making of leather (tanning). The manufacture of slippers occupied 1,500 workmen who produce over 2,000 pairs each working day. There are the only articles manufactured in the town that are exported. They are sold as far away as Egypt and West Africa. For the rest, Marrakesh is mainly an agricultural market. The whole town is a vast fondouk (*funduḳ*) in which are warehoused the products of the country, almonds, carraway seeds, goat-skins, oils, barley, wool, to be exchanged either for imported goods (sugar, tea, cloth) or for other agricultural produce (wheat, oil, which the tribes of the mountains and of the extreme south for example do not have).

The town is divided into 32 quarters, including the *mellāḥ* or Jewish quarter. We may further mention outside the walls near the Bāb Dukkāla a quarter called al-Ḥāra where the lepers lived. Until the 1920s, the gates of the town were closed during the night. The superintendents of the quarters (*muḳaddamīn*) had watchmen (*ʿassāsa*) under their orders. The old custom long survived of firing a salvo at midnight on the D̲jāmaʿ al-Fnā as a curfew.

Marrakesh being an imperial town, the sultan, who only stayed there at long intervals, was represented in his absence by a *k̲h̲alīfa*, a prince of the imperial family (usually the son or brother of the sovereign). The role of this *k̲h̲alīfa* was not purely representative, for he was a true viceroy, who formerly governed the territories to the South. The governor of the town is today a *pas̲h̲a*, assisted by a delegate (*nāʾib*) and several *k̲h̲alīfa*s. One of the latter supervises the prisons and the administration of justice. Another has the title of *pas̲h̲a* of the *ḳaṣba*. He governs the southern part of the town which includes the imperial palace and the Jewish quarter. Formerly, the *pas̲h̲a* of the *ḳaṣba* was independent of the *pas̲h̲a* of the town and served to counterbalance the power of the latter. He commanded the *gīs̲h̲*, an armed contingent furnished by the warlike tribes (Ūdāya, Ayt Immūr, etc.) settled in the vicinity of the town by the sultans of the domain lands. The *pas̲h̲a* of the *ḳaṣba* only retains of his former powers certain rights of precedence and honorary privileges.

Muslim law is administered in Marrakesh by three *ḳāḍīs*: one is established at the mosque of Ibn Yūsuf; the other at the mosque of al-Mwāsīn and the third at the mosque of the *ḳaṣba*. The latter's competence does not extend beyond the limits of his quarter. That of the others extends over the whole town and even over the tribes of the area governed from it who have no local *ḳāḍīs*.

Marrakesh is not numbered like Fās, Rabat and Tetuan among the *ḥaḍariyya* towns, i.e. it has not, like them, an old-established citizen population, of non-rural origin, with a bourgeoisie whose tone is given by the descendants of the Moors driven from Spain. In the 10th/16th century, however, Marrakesh did re-receive a colony of Moriscoes large enough to give one quarter the name Orgiba D̲jadīda, a reminiscence of Orgiba, a town of Andalusia from which they came. The foundation of the population consists of people of the tribes for the most part Berbers or Arabs strongly mixed with Berber blood. S̲h̲lūḥ (*tas̲h̲elḥit*) is much spoken in Marrakesh although the language of the tribes around the town (Rḥāmma, Ūdāya) is Arabic. The movements of the tribes, the coming and going of caravans, the importation of slaves from the Sudan have resulted in a constant process of mixing in the population, and the old Maṣmūda race which must, with the Almoravids, have been the primitive population of Marrakesh is only found in combination with amounts difficult to measure of Arab, Saharan and negro blood. Even to-day this process is going on: the newcomers come less from the valleys of the Atlas than from the Sūs, the Draʿ and the Anti-Atlas, from the extreme south which is poor and overpopulated. The greater number of these immigrants soon become merged in the population of the town; but the *Enquête sur les corporations musulmanes*, conducted by L. Massignon in 1923-4 (Paris 1925) yielded some very curious information about the survival in Marrakesh of vigorous groups of provincials, specialising in particular trades: the makers of silver jewellery (at least those who are not Jews) owe their name of *tāgmūtiyyīn* to the fact that they originally came from Tagmut in the Sūs; the Mesfīwa are charcoal-burners and greengrocers, the G̲h̲īg̲h̲āya, salters; the people of the Ṭodg̲h̲a, gatherers of dates and *k̲h̲aṭāṭīriyya*, i.e. diggers of wells, who specialise in water-channels (*k̲h̲aṭāṭīr*); those of Tafilalt, porters and pavers; those of Warzarāt, watercarriers and of Tattaʿ (Anti-Atlas), restaurateurs; of the Draʿ, water-carriers and *k̲h̲aṭāṭīriyya*, etc. This division is not the result of specialisation in their original home nor of privileges granted by the civic authorities but arises from the fact that artisans once settled in Marrakesh have sent for their compatriots when they required assistance. Thus groups grew up, sometimes quite considerable. The list of the corporations of Marrakesh gives a total of about 10,000 artisans. These corporations lost much of their power under the pressure of the Mak̲h̲zen. Some of them, however, still retained a certain social importance: in the first place that of the shoemakers which is the largest (1,500 members); then come the tanners (430), the cloth (237) and silk (100) merchants; the *Fāsī* wholesalers, then some groups of skilled artisans, highly esteemed but of less influence, embroiderers of saddles, makers of mosaics, carpenters, sculptors of plaster, etc.

Religious and intellectual life. Mosques are numerous in Marrakesh. Some of them will be the subject below of brief archaeological studies. Those which play the most important part in the religious life of the city are the mosque of al-Mwāsīn, the mosque of ʿAlī b. Yūsuf, both close to the *sūḳ*s, that of Sīdī bel ʿAbbās and that of the *ḳaṣba*. Then come the Kutubiyya, the mosque of the Bāb Dukkāla, of the Bāb Aylān, of Berrīma, and the D̲jāmaʿ Ibn Ṣāliḥ. There are also many little mosques in the various outlying quarters. But although it can claim illustrious men of learning, Marrakesh is not like Fās, a centre of learning and of teaching. The Almohads built schools and libraries there, brought the most illustrious scholars, philosophers and physicians from Spain, like Ibn Ṭufayl, Abū Marwān Ibn Zuhr (Avenzoar) and Abu 'l-Walīd Ibn Rus̲h̲d (Averroes) who died at Marrakesh in 595/1198. These great traditions did nor survive the dynasty. At the beginning of the 10th/16th century, in the time of Leo Africanus, the library of the Almohad palace was used as a poultry house and the *madrasa* built by the

Marīnids was in ruins. In the inter-war period, in the town of the Kutubiyya there was not a single bookseller. A certain number of *ṭolba* still live in the *madrasas* (Ibn Yūsuf, Ibn Ṣāliḥ, Sīdī bel ʿAbbās, Berrīma, Ḳaṣba) but the teaching in Marrakesh has neither the prestige nor the traditions which still give some lustre to the teaching at al-Ḳarawiyyīn in Fās, much decayed as it is. Although they attempt to imitate the customs of Fās (they celebrate notably the "festival of the sultan of the *ṭolba*" [see FĀS] every spring), the students are far from holding in Marrakesh the position their comrades enjoy in Fās, even though a dahir of 1357/1938 established a *madrasa* of Ibn Yūsuf intended, like the Ḳarawiyyīn, for the training of *ḳāḍīs*. One should note that the city now possesses a modern university.

The devotion of the people of Marrakesh expends itself particularly on the cult of saints, not at all orthodox but dear to the Berbers. Their town has always been famous for the great number of *walīs* who are buried in its cemeteries and who justify the saying: "Marrakesh, tomb of the saints". But in the time of Mawlāy Ismāʿil, the S͟hayk͟h Abū ʿAlī al-Ḥasan al-Yūsī by order of the prince organised, in imitation of the old established cult of the Sabʿatu Rid̲j̲āl (the seven saints of the Ragrāga, around the D̲j̲abal al-Ḥadīd, among the S͟hyāḍma), a pilgrimage to the Sabʿatu Rid̲j̲āl of Marrakesh, including visits to seven sanctuaries and various demonstrations of piety. The following are the names of the seven saints in the order in which they ought to be visisted: (1) Sīdī Yūsuf b. ʿAlī al-Ṣanhād̲j̲ī, a leper, d. 593/1196-7, buried outside the Bāb Ag͟hmāt on the spot where he had lived; (2) the *ḳāḍī* ʿIyāḍ, 476-544/1083-1149 [*q.v.*], *ḳāḍī* of Ceuta, then of Granada, a learned theologian, author of the *S͟hifāʾ*, buried beside the Bāb Aylān; (3) Sīdī bel ʿAbbās al-Sabtī, patron saint of Marrakesh and the most venerated of the saints of the region, 542-601/1130-1204. He came to Marrakesh when the town was being besieged by the Almohads and settled there, at first in a hermitage on the D̲j̲abal Gillīz where a *ḳubba* dedicated to him can still be seen. But the principal pilgrimage is to his tomb at the northern end of the town over which Abū Fāris b. Aḥmad al-Manṣūr built a *zāwiya* and an important mosque at the beginning of the 11th/17th century; (4) Sīdī Muḥammad b. Slīmān al-D̲j̲azūlī, d. in 870/1465 at Afug͟hal among the S͟hyāḍma, a celebrated Ṣūfī, founder of the D̲j̲azūlī brotherhood. His body was brought to Marrakesh in 930/1523 by Aḥmad al-Aʿrad̲j̲ the Saʿdian; (5) Sīdī ʿAbd al-ʿAzīz al-Tabbāʿ, a pupil of al-D̲j̲azūlī, d. 914/1508; (6) Sīdī ʿAbd Allāh al-G͟hazwānī, popularly called Mawlā (Mūl) ʾl-Ḳṣūr, d. 935/1528; (7) Sīdī ʿAbd al-Raḥmān al-Suhaylī, called the Imām al-Suhaylī, a native of the district of Malaga, d. 581/1185, and buried outside the Bāb al-Rabb.

It is quite an arbitrary choice that these seven individuals have been chosen as the Sabʿatu Rid̲j̲āl. Others could equally well have been chosen, as the town of Marrakesh and the cemeteries which stretch before it, contain a very large number of other venerated tombs. The principal ones are mentioned in the article by H. de Castries, *Les Sept Patrons de Merrakech*, in *Hespéris* (1924). Legend of course plays a great part in the cults of the various saints. We may mention for example the sayings and songs which perpetuate the memory of Lallā ʿŪda, mother of the sultan Aḥmad al-Manṣūr, a real personage much transformed by the popular imagination. The various trade corporations have chosen patron saints. Thus Sīdī Yaʿḳūb is the patron of the tanners, Sīdī bel ʿAbbās of the soapmakers and lacemakers, Sīdī Masʿūd "slave" of Sīdī Muḥammad b. Slīmān is the patron of the masons, Sīdī ʿAbd al-ʿAzīz al-Tabbāʿ of the dyers, etc. The majority of the artisans are also affiliated to the religious brotherhoods. In Massignon's investigation may be found details of the attraction which some of the latter had for certain trades.

The Jews. At the foundation of Marrakesh, the Jews had no permission to settle in the town. They came there to trade from Ag͟hmāt Aylān where they lived. Al-Idrīsī relates that under ʿAlī b. Yūsuf they had not even the right to spend the night in Marrakesh and that those who were caught within the walls after sunset were in great danger of losing their lives and property. They settled there at a later date. At the beginning of the 10th/16th century there was, according to Marmol, in Marrakesh a ghetto of over 3,000 houses. It lay near the *sūḳ* on the site now occupied by the mosque of al-Mwāsīn. When this mosque was built by sultan ʿAbd Allāh al-G͟hālib, the more scrupulous refused to pray there for some time on the pretext that it occupied the site of a Jewish cemetery. It was ʿAbd Allāh al-G͟hālib who, in about 967/1560, settled the Jews on the site they occupied lately, along the wall of the *ḳaṣba* to the east, where the stables of the palace had been. At the beginning of the 11th/17th century, there was here, according to the French traveller Mocquet, "like a separate town, surrounded by a good wall and having only one gate guarded by the Moors; here live the Jews who are over 4,000 in number and pay tribute". A century later, there were about 6,000 Jews and many synagogues. The Jewish quarter, called *mellāḥ* [see MALLĀḤ] after the example of the Jewish quarter of Fās (the name *mellāḥ* is attested for Marrakesh as early as the end of the 10th/16th century), was placed, as regards policing, under the authority of the *pas͟ha* of the *ḳaṣba* but otherwise is administered by an elected Jewish committee. Questions of personal law were judged by a rabbinical tribunal of three members nominated and paid by the Mak͟hzen. The Jews of Marrakesh early began to leave the bounds of the *mellāḥ*. The older ones wore the ritual costume: gaberdine, skullcap and black slippers, but the younger generations emancipated themselves from this dress. The Jews have little influence on the corporations of Marrakesh. They are limited to certain trades (jewellers, tinsmiths and embroiderers of slippers) and share with the people of Fās the wholesale trade. They trade particularly with the S͟hlūḥ of the mountains.

History. The Roman occupation never extended so far as the region of Marrakesh. It is quite without probability that some writers, following the Spanish historian Marmol, have sought at Ag͟hmāt or at Marrakesh the site of *Bocanum Emerum* (Βόκχανον ῾Ημεροσκοπεῖον of Ptolemy), a town of Tingitana, the site of which is now unknown. The earliest historians agree that the place where Marrakesh was built by the Almoravids was a bare marshy plain where only a few bushes grew. The name Marrakesh gives no clue to the origin of the town. The etymologies given by the Arab authors are quite fanciful (see Deverdun, *Marrakech*, 64 ff.). It was, it appears, in 449/1057-8 that the Almoravids advanced from Sūs north of the Atlas and took Ag͟hmāt Urīka. It was there that they settled at first. But after the campaign of 452/1060 in the course of which they conquered the country of Fazāz, Meknès and of the Lawāta near Fās, they wanted to make their position more permanent and independent by creating a kind of camp, which could be used as a base for their further campaigns and would threaten the Maṣmūda of the mountains and could be used as a connecting link between the south from which they came and the kingdom of Fās. Yūsuf b. Tas̲h̲fīn therefore purchased from its owner an estate on the frontier between two Maṣmūda tribes, the Haylāna and the Hazmīra, and pitched his camp there. So far was he from thinking of founding a great capital, a thing for which this Saharan nomad felt no need, that at first he lived in a tent here, beside which he built a mosque to pray in and a little *ḳaṣba* in which to keep his treasures and his weapons; but he did not build a surrounding wall. The native Maṣmūda built themselves dwellings surrounded by palisades of branches beside the Almoravid camp. The town grew rapidly to a considerable size, if it is true, that, in the reign of ʿAlī b. Yūsuf it had at least 100,000 hearths, but it did not lose its rural character until Ibn Tūmart appeared and the threat of the Almohad movement revived by him forced ʿAlī b. Yūsuf to defend his town and surround it by a rampart which was built in eight months, probably in 520/1126. Some historians give the date 526/1132, but it is certain that the walls were already built in 524/1130, when the Almohads attacked Marrakesh for the first time. Marrakesh, the creation and capital of the Almoravids, was to be the last of their strongholds to yield. When Ibn Tūmart had established his power over the tribes of the mountains he tried to attack Marrakesh; he then sent an Almohad army under the command of the *s̲h̲ayk̲h̲* al-Bas̲h̲īr, who, after defeating the Almoravids in the vicinity of Ag̲h̲māt, pursued them to the gates of Marrakesh. The Almohads could not enter the town but established themselves before its walls. After 40 days' siege, ʿAlī b. Yūsuf received reinforcements and made a successful sortie which forced the attackers to retreat. This was the battle of al-Buḥayra (D̲j̲umādā I-II 524/May 1130 from the name of a large garden, *Buḥayrat al-Raḳāʾiḳ*, near which it was fought. It lay to the east of the town before the Bāb Dabbāg̲h̲ and the Bāb Aylān. Al-Bas̲h̲īr was slain and Marrakesh respited for 17 years. Ibn Tūmart died a few months later. It is hardly likely that ʿAbd al-Muʾmin should have made soon after his accession, as the *Ḳirṭās* says, a new attempt to take Marrakesh. The memoirs of al-Bayd̲h̲aḳ which give such full details of all the events of this period make no mention of it. They show on the contrary the Almohad armies busied at first in conquering the country before occupying the capital, taking Tadla, Salé, Taza, Oran, Tlemcen and Fās and only returning to lay siege to Marrakesh after the whole country had been occupied and the capital alone held out as the last stronghold of the doomed dynasty. It was in the summer of 541/1146 that ʿAbd al-Muʾmin laid siege to Marrakesh. He made his headquarters at Gillīz and, seeing that the siege would be a long one, at once had houses built in which to instal himself and his army. The siege lasted eleven months. An unsuccessful sortie by the Almoravids seems to have hastened the fall of the town. Disgusted by lack of success and by famine, a number of chiefs of the besieged went over to the enemy. ʿAbd al-Muʾmin had scaling-ladders made and distributed them among the tribes. The assault was made and, according to Ibn al-At̲h̲īr, the defection of the Christian soldiery facilitated its success. The Almoravid sultan Isḥāḳ, a young boy who had sought refuge in the fortress, was slain, along with a large number of the Almoravids. This event took place in 541/S̲h̲awwāl 6 March-3 April 1147, according to the majority of the historians.

The Almohad dynasty which came from the south naturally took Marrakesh as its capital. It was here that ʿAbd al-Muʾmin and his successors usually resided when they were not in the country. The town prospered exceedingly under their rule. They gave it many important public buildings: the *ḳaṣba*, mosques, schools, a hospital, aqueducts and magnificent gardens. During this period of prosperity, there were very few events of particular interest in the history of Marrakesh. In 547/1152-3 according to Ibn K̲h̲aldūn, in 549/1154-6 according to al-Bayd̲h̲aḳ and the *Ḳirṭās*, the Banū Amg̲h̲ār, brothers of the Mahdī Ibn Tūmart, entered the town and tried to raise the inhabitants against ʿAbd al-Muʾmin who was away at Salé. The rising was speedily put down and ended in the massacre of the rebels and their accomplices. But on the decline of the dynasty, i.e. after the battle of Las Navas de Tolosa (609/1212 [see AL-ʿIḲĀB]) and the death of al-Nāsir, son of al-Manṣūr, Marrakesh became the scene of the struggle between the royal family descended from ʿAbd al-Muʾmin and the Almohad *s̲h̲ayk̲h̲*s descended from the companions of Ibn Tūmart who, quoting traditions of the latter, claimed the right to grant investiture to the sultans and to keep them in tutelage. Abū Muḥammad ʿAbd al-Wāḥid, brother of al-Manṣūr, was strangled in 621/1224. His successor al-ʿĀdil was drowned in a bath in the palace (624/1227) and the Almohad *s̲h̲ayk̲h̲*s appointed as his successor the young Yaḥyā b. al-Nāṣir, while Abu 'l-ʿUlā Idrīs al-Maʾmūn, brother of al-ʿĀdil, was proclaimed in Spain. The whole country was soon in the throes of revolution. Yaḥyā, fearing the defection of the fickle Almohads, fled to Tinmal (626/1228). Disorder reigned in Marrakesh, where a governor named by al-Maʾmūn was finally appointed. But four months later, Yaḥyā returned to Marrakesh with fresh troops, put al-Maʾmūn's governor to death and after staying seven days in the town was forced to go to Gillīz to fight a battle (627/1230), for al-Maʾmūn had arrived from Spain to take possession of his kingdom. Ferdinand III, king of Castile, had given in return for various concessions, a body of 12,000 Christian horsemen with whose assistance al-Maʾmūn defeated Yaḥyā and his followers, entered Marrakesh and installed an anti-Almohad regime there, marked not only by a terrible massacre of the *s̲h̲ayk̲h̲*s and their families but by a new orientation in religious matters quite opposed to that of the preceding reigns. On his arrival in Marrakesh, al-Maʾmūn mounted the pulpit of the mosque of the *ḳaṣba*, recited the *k̲h̲uṭba*, solemnly cursed the memory of Ibn Tūmart and announced a whole series of measures, some of which are given by the *Ḳirṭās* and Ibn K̲h̲aldūn and which show he intended to do everything on opposite lines to his predecessors. His innovations revived the discontent so that two years later (629/1232) while al-Maʾmūn and his militia were besieging Ceuta, Yaḥyā again occupied Marrakesh and plundered it. Al-Maʾmūn at once turned back to the rescue of his capital but died on the way (30 D̲h̲u 'l-Ḥid̲j̲d̲j̲a 629/17 October 1232). His widow, al-Ḥabāb, succeeded in getting her son al-Ras̲h̲īd, aged 14, proclaimed by the leaders of the army, including the commander of the Christian mercenaries. In return she gave them Marrakesh to plunder if they could reconquer it. But the people of the town, learning of this clause in the bargain, made their own terms before opening their gates to the new sultan. The latter had to grant them *amān* and pay the Christian general and his companions the sum they might have expected from the plunder of the capital—according to the *Ḳirṭās*, 500,000 *dīnār*s.

In 633/1235-6, a rebellion of the K̲h̲loṭ [see KHULṬ] drove al-Ras̲h̲īd out of Marrakesh, and he took refuge in Sidjilmāsa while Yaḥyā recaptured Marrakesh. Al-Rashīd, however, succeeded in retaking it and Yaḥyā finally was assassinated. It was in the reign of the Almohad al-Saʿīd (646/1242-8) that the Marīnids who had arrived in the east of the country in 613/1216, seized the greater part of the kingdom of Fās. His successor ʿUmar al-Murtaḍā proclaimed in 646/1248, found himself in 658/1260 reduced to the solitary kingdom of Marrakesh, to the south of the Umm al-Rabīʿ. In 660/1261-2, the Marīnid Abū Yūsuf Yaʿḳūb b. ʿAbd al-Hāḳḳ came to attack Marrakesh. He encamped on mount Gillīz, whence he threatened the town. Al-Murtaḍā sent his cousin, the *sayyid* Abu 'l-ʿUlā Idrīs, surnamed Abū Dabbūs, to fight him. The *amīr* ʿAbd Allāh b. Abū Yūsuf was slain in the battle and his father lost heart, abandoned his designs on Marrakesh and returned to Fās at the end of Radjab 661/beginning of June 1262.

From this time, one feels that the dynasty was lost although peace was made, which moreover showed the humiliation of the Almohads who consented to pay tribute; but they were to destroy themselves. Falling into disfavour with his cousin al-Murtadā, Abū Dabbūs, this great-grandson of ʿAbd al-Muʾmin, who in the preceding year had defended Marrakesh against the Marīnid sultan, sought refuge with the latter and obtained from him the assistance necessary to overthrow al-Murtaḍā, on condition that he shared the spoils. Victorious and proclaimed sultan in Muḥarram 665/October 1266, Abū Dabbūs forgot his promises. Abū Yūsuf Yaʿḳūb came in person to remind him of them. He laid siege to Marrakesh in 665-6/1267, but Abū Dabbūs had a stroke of good fortune, for the Marīnid had to raise the siege to go and defend the kingdom of Fās against an attack by the sultan of Tlemcen, Yaghmurāsen. The campaign being over, Abū Yūsuf Yaʿḳūb returned to Marrakesh. He entered it in Muḥarram 668/Sept. 1269. The *Ḳirṭās* tells us that he gave *amān* to the inhabitants and to the surrounding tribes, whom he overwhelmed with benefits and ruled with justice and remained seven months to pacify and organise the country. By accepting Marīnid rule, however, Marrakesh lost for two-and-a-half centuries its position as a capital. The new dynasty made Fās its capital.

Its sultans however, did not neglect Marrakesh, especially during this period (end of the 7th/13th and first half of the 8th/14th century). The chronicles record many sojourns made by them there but its great days were over. The town began to lose its inhabitants. Abu 'l-Ḥasan ʿAlī was the only Marinid to undertake buildings of any importance at Marrakesh (a mosque and a *madrasa*). In the absence of the sovereign, the government of the town and district was entrusted to powerful governors as befitted a large town remote from the central authority. For nearly 20 years, from 668 to 687/1269-88, this office was held by Muḥammad b. ʿAlī b. Muḥallī, a chief greatly devoted to the Marīnids, says Ibn Khaldūn, and allied by marriage to the family of their ruler. But in Muḥarram 687/ February 1288, fearing treachery from Muḥammad b. ʿAlī, Abū Yaʿḳūb Yūsuf threw him into prison and gave his office to Muḥammad b. ʿAṭṭū al-Djānātī, a client and confidant of the royal family, to whom the sultan further entrusted his son Abū ʿĀmir. Abū Yaḳūb had not left Marrakesh six months when the young prince Abū ʿĀmir rebelled there and proclaimed himself sovereign at the instigation of the governor Ibn ʿAṭṭū (Shawwāl 687/November 1288). Abū Yaʿḳub hastened to Marrakesh which he took after several days siege. The young Abū ʿĀmir had time to escape and seek refuge in the mountains among the Maṣmūda tribes, after plundering the treasury.

The custom of giving the governorship of Marrakesh to a prince of the ruling family was kept up. Towards the end of Dhu 'l-Ḳaʿda 706/May 1307, under the walls of Tlemcen, the sultan Abū Thābit gave his cousin Yūsuf, son of Muḥammad b. Abī ʿIyāḍ b. ʿAbd al-Ḥaḳḳ, the governorship of Marrakesh and the provinces depending on it. By the end of the year, Yūsuf rebelled and proclaimed himself independent at Marrakesh after putting to death the governor of the town, al-Hādjdj Masʿūd. Defeated by the imperial troops on the banks of the Umm al-Rabīʿ, the rebel fled to the mountains, plundering Marrakesh on his way (Radjab 707/January 1308). The punishment inflicted on the rebels was severe. Yūsuf b. Abī ʿIyāḍ, handed over by a *shaykh* with whom he had taken refuge, was put to death and the heads of 600 of his followers went to adorn the battlements of the town. Abū Saʿīd ʿUthmān stayed at Marrakesh on several occasions. He did much rebuilding in 720/1320. Peace and comparative prosperity seem to have reigned there under the rule of Abu 'l-Ḥasan until this prince, as a result of reverses suffered in his struggle with the Ḥafṣids, found his own son, the ambitious Abū ʿInān, rebelling against him. During the troubles which now broke out, Ibn Khaldūn tells us, the town was seriously threatened with being sacked by the Maṣmūda of the mountains led by ʿAbd Allāh al-Saksīwī. Abū ʿInān was able to consolidate his power and avert this danger. The struggle between father and son ended in the region of Marrakesh. Abu 'l-Ḥasan, defeated at the end of Ṣafar 757/May 1350, near the town, sought refuge in the mountains with the *amīrs* of the Hintāta and died there just after becoming reconciled to his son and designating him his successor (Rabīʿ II 753/June 1352).

During the course of the 8th/14th century, the *amīrs* of the Hintāta played a very important part in the country. The position of the tribe on an almost inaccessible mountain, from which it commanded Marrakesh, gave its chiefs comparative independence and predominating influence among the other Maṣmūda. Abū ʿInān took no steps against the *amīr* ʿAbd al-ʿAzīz who had given asylum to the fugitive Abu 'l-Ḥasan. He retained him in the command of his tribe, which he gave a few years later to his brother ʿĀmir. In 754/1353 the latter, becoming chief of all the Maṣmūda tribes and sufficiently powerful to keep under his thumb the governor of Marrakesh al-Muʿtamid, son of Abū ʿInān, very soon succeeded in making himself completely independent. He received and for a time held as hostages two rebel Marīnid princes Abu 'l-Faḍl, son of the sultan Abū Sālim, and ʿAbd al-Raḥmān, son of sultan Abū ʿAlī. Quarrelling with his protégé Abu 'l-Faḍl whom he had made governor of Marrakesh, he retired into his mountains and for several years defied the armies of the sultan. He was in the end captured and put to death in 771/1370.

After the death of ʿAbd al-ʿAzīz, the pretender Abu 'l-ʿAbbās, son of Abū Sālim, had himself proclaimed in Fās with the help of his cousin ʿAbd al-Raḥmān b. Abī Ifellūsen, himself a pretender to the throne. The latter as a reward for his services was given the independent governorship of Marrakesh and the country round it (Muḥarram 776/June 1374). The empire was thus completely broken up. The two rulers soon began to quarrel but then signed a treaty of peace in 780/1378. There was a new rupture and a new truce two years later after Marrakesh had been besieged for two months without result. Abu 'l-Abbās in the end took Marrakesh in Djumādā 784/July-August 1382, and ʿAbd al-Raḥmān was slain. Abu 'l-ʿAbbās, dispossessed in 1384 and exiled to Granada, succeeded in reconquering his kingdom in 789/1387 and sent to Marrakesh as governor his son al-Muntaṣir. This event is the last recorded by Ibn Khaldūn. From the time when his record ceases and throughout the 9th/15th century, we are incredibly poor in information about the history of Marrakesh. The south appears to have continued to form a large governorship in the hands of princes of the royal family. The only information at all definite that we have comes from a Portuguese historian who records that during the three years which followed the capture of Ceuta by the Portuguese (1415-18), Morocco was a prey to the struggles among the pretenders. While Abū Saʿīd ʿUthmān was ruling in Fās, Mawlāy Bū ʿAlī, king of Marrakesh, was fighting against another Marīnid prince called Fāris. The "kingdom" or governorship of Marrakesh does not seem to have completely broken the links which bound it to the kingdom of Fās, for the governors of Marrakesh supplied contingents to the army which tried to retake Ceuta. But they very soon ceased to take part in the holy war in the north of Morocco, and their name is not found among the opponents of the Portuguese. Marrakesh by 833/1430 seems to have become *de facto* if not *de jure* independent but we do not know within fifty years at what date the Hintāta *amīrs* established their power; they were descended from a brother of ʿĀmir b. Muḥammad. They were "kings" of Marrakesh when in 914/1508 the Portuguese established themselves at Safi, taking advantage of the anarchy prevailing, for the power of the Hintāta *amīrs* hardly extended beyond the environs of their capital and they could not effectively protect their tribes against the attacks of the Christians. By 1512 the Portuguese governors of Safi had succeeded in extending their power over the tribes near Marrakesh (Awlād Mṭāʿ) and the town lived in fear of the bold raids which on several occasions brought the Portuguese cavalry and their Arab allies into the district. The king of Marrakesh, overawed, entered into negotations in 1514, but the terms were nothing less than his paying tribute as vassal and the building of a Portuguese fortress at Marrakesh. Agreement could not be reached. The occupation of Marrakesh remained the dream of the Portuguese soldiers. An attack on the town led by the governors of Safi and Azemmūr failed (9 Rabīʿ I 921/23 April 1515). This was the period when in reaction against the anarchy and foreign invasions the Saʿdian *sharīfs* began to come to the front in Sūs. Aḥmad al-Aʿradj, who appeared in 919/1513 to the north of the Atlas, had himself recognised as leader of the holy war and accepted as such by the local chiefs, even by al-Nāṣir, king of Marrakesh. In Ṣafar 920/April 1514, it is recorded that he was in Marrakesh with the king. At the end of 927/1521, al-Aʿradj established himself peacefully in Marrakesh which he found partly depopulated by famine and married the daughter of the king Muḥammad b. Nāṣir called Bū Shenṭūf. The latter in 930/1524 having tried to kick against the tutelage of his too powerful son-in-law al-Aʿradj and his brother Maḥammad al-Shaykh, seized the *ḳaṣba*, which seems till then to have been held by Bū Shenṭūf. They disposed of the latter by having him assassinated in the following year (932/1525). Marrakesh became the Saʿdian capital. The king of Fās, Aḥmad al-Waṭṭāsī, tried unsuccessfully to take it in Ramaḍān 933/June 1527. It remained in the hands of al-Aʿradj till 961/1554, when it was seized by his brother Maḥammad al-Shaykh, up till then king of Sūs. After the assassination of Maḥammad al-Shaykh in 964/1557, al-Aʿradj was put to death at Marrakesh with seven of his sons and grandsons, so as to secure the crown for Mawlāy ʿAbd Allāh al-Ghālib. The whole of the latter part of the century was for Marrakesh a period of great prosperity. ʿAbd Allāh al-Ghālib built a series of important public works: rearrangement of the palace and of the provision storehouses in the *ḳaṣba*; in the town, the *madrasa* Ibn Yūsuf and the al-Mwāsīn mosque, etc. Aḥmad al-Manṣūr finished his brother's work by building in the *ḳaṣba* from 986 to 1002/1578 to 1594 the famous al-Badīʿ palace. The sultan, enriched by several years of peace and good government, and by the gold brought from the conquest of the Sūdān (1000/1591-2), lived almost continually in Marrakesh, to which he restored a splendour and a prosperity that it had not enjoyed since the end of the 6th/12th century. But the death of al-Manṣūr opened a period of trouble and civil war "sufficient to turn white the hair of an infant at the breast", to use the expression of the historian al-Ifrānī. While Abū Fāris, son of al-Mansūr, was proclaimed at Marrakesh, another son, Zaydān, was chosen sultan at Fās. A third brother, al-Shaykh, came and took Fās, then sent against Marrakesh an army led by his son ʿAbd Allāh, who seized the town on 21 Shaʿbān 1015/22 December 1606. But Zaydān, who sought refuge first in Tlemcen, then made his way to the Sūs, via Tafilalt and coming suddenly to Marrakesh, had himself proclaimed there while ʿAbd Allāh b. al-Shaykh, while escaping with his troops, was attacked in the midst of the gardens (*jnān Bekkār*) and completely defeated (29 Shawwāl 1015/25 February 1607). In Djumādā II/October of the same year, ʿAbd Allāh returned after defeating Zaydān's troops on the Wādī Tifālfalt (10 Djumādā II/2 October, 1607), fought a second battle with them at Rās al-ʿAyn (a spring in Tansift), regained possesion of the town and revenged himself in a series of massacres and punishments so terrible that a portion of the population having sought refuge in the Gillīz, proclaimed as sultan Muḥammad, great-grandson of Aḥmad al-Aʿradj. ʿAbd Allāh was forced to fly (7 Shawwāl 1016/25 January 1608). Zaydān, recalled by a section of the populace, regained possession of his capital in a few days. The struggle between Zaydān and his brother al-Shaykh, in the year following, centred round the possession of Fās. Zaydān failed in his plans to retake it and henceforth Fās, given over completely to anarchy, remained separate from the kingdom of Marrakesh. On these happenings, a marabout from Tafilalt, named Abū Maḥallī [*q.v.* in Suppl.], attempted to intervene 1020/1611) to put an end to the fighting among the pretenders, which was inflicting great suffering on the people. His intervention only made matters worse. He took Marrakesh on 19 Rabīʿ I 1021/20 May 1612. Zaydān took refuge in Safi and succeeded in again gaining possession of his capital with the help of an influential marabout in Sūs, called Yaḥyā b. ʿAbd Allāh. After a battle near Gillīz, Zaydān withdrew into Marrakesh on 17 Shawwāl 1022/30 November 1613. But Yaḥyā, succumbing to ambition, rebelled himself at the end of 1027/1618, against the ruler whose cause he had once so well sustained. Zaydān had again to take refuge in Safi. He was soon able to return to Marrakesh, taking advantage of the discord that had broken out in the enemy ranks. ʿAbd al-Malik, son and successor of Zaydān, has left only the memory of his cruelty and debauchery. He was murdered in Shawwāl 1040/May 1631. The renegades, who killed him, also disposed of his brother and successor al-Walīd in 1636. A third brother, Maḥammad al-Shaykh al-Aṣghar, succeeded him but had only a semblance of power. He managed however to reign till 1065/1655, but his son Aḥmad al-ᶜAbbās was completely in the hands of the Shabbāna, an Arab tribe who assassinated him and gave the throne to his *ḳāʾid* ᶜAbd al-Karīm, called Ḳarrūm al-Ḥādjdj, in 1659. "The latter", says al-Ifrānī, "united under his sway all the kingdom of Marrakesh and conducted himself in an admirable fashion with regard to his subjects". His son Abū Bakr succeeded him in 1078/1668, but only reigned two months until the coming of the Fīlālī sultan al-Rashīd, already lord of Fās, who took Marrakesh on 21 Ṣafar 1079/31 July 1668. Called to Marrakesh by the rebellion of his nephew Aḥmad b. Muḥriz, al-Rashīd met his death there in the garden of al-Agdāl, his head having been injured by a branch of an orange tree against which his horse threw him when it stumbled.

Mawlāy Ismāᶜīl had some difficulty in getting himself proclaimed at Marrakesh, which preferred his nephew, Aḥmad b. Muḥrīz. Ismāᶜīl forced his way in on 9 Ṣafar 1083/4 June, 1672. In the following year, Marrakesh again welcomed Aḥmad b. Muḥriz. After a siege of more than two years (Dhu 'l-Ḥidjdja 1085-Rabīᶜ II 1088/March 1675-June 1677), Ismāᶜīl reoccupied Marrakesh and plundered it. He passed through it again in 1094/1683 on his way to the Sūs to fight Aḥmad b. Muḥriz who was still in rebellion. Marrakesh was no longer the capital. Mawlāy Ismāᶜīl took an interest in it and destroyed the palaces of the *ḳaṣba* to use the materials for his works in Meknès. In Ramaḍān 1114/February 1703, a son of Mawlāy Ismāᶜīl, Muḥammad al-ᶜĀlim, rebelled against his father, seized Marrakesh and plundered it. Zaydān, brother of the rebel, was given the task of suppressing the rising, which he did, plundering the town once more.

Anarchy again broke out after the death of Ismāᶜīl. Its centre was Meknes. Mawlāy al-Mustaḍī, proclaimed by the ᶜAbīd in 1151/1738, was disowned by them in 1740 and replaced by his brother ᶜAbd Allāh. He sought refuge in Marrakesh. His brother al-Nāṣir remained his *khalīfa* in Marrakesh till 1158/1745, while al-Mustaḍī tried in vain to reconquer his kingdom. Marrakesh finally submitted in 1159/1746 to Mawlāy ᶜAbd Allāh, who sent his son Sīdī Muḥammad there as *khalīfa*. The governorship and then the reign of the latter (1171-1204/1757-90) formed one of the happiest periods in the history of Marrakesh. Sīdī Muḥammad completely restored the town, made it his usual residence, received many European embassies there, including a French one led by the Comte de Breugnon in 1767, and developed its trade. Peace was not disturbed during his long reign except for a riot raised by a marabout pretender named ᶜUmar, who at the head of a few malcontents tried to attack the palace in order to plunder the public treasury. He was at once seized and put to death (between 1766 and 1772, according to the sources). On the death of Sīdī Muḥammad b. ᶜAbd Allāh, the situation remained very unsettled for several years. After taking the oath of allegiance to Mawlāy Yazīd (18 Shaᶜbān 1204/ 3 May 1790), the people of Marrakesh took in his brother Mawlāy Hishām and proclaimed him. On hearing this, Yazīd abandoned the siege of Ceuta, returned to Marrakesh, plundered it and committed all kinds of atrocities (1792). Hishām, supported by the ᶜAbda and the Dukkāla, marched on Marrakesh. Yazīd, wounded in the battle, died a few days later in the palace (Djumādā II 1206/February 1792). Marrakesh remained faithful to the party of Mawlāy Hishām, but very soon the Rḥāmna abandoned him to proclaim Mawlāy Ḥusayn, brother of Hishām. He established himself in the *ḳaṣba* (1209/1794-5). While the partisans of the two princes were exhausting themselves in fighting, Mawlāy Slīmān, sultan of Fās, avoided taking sides in the struggle. The plague rid him at one blow of both his rivals (Ṣafar 1214/ July 1799), who had in any case to submit some time before. The last years of the reign of Mawlāy Slīmān were overcast by troubles in all parts of the empire. Defeated at the very gates of Marrakesh, he was taken prisoner by the rebel Shrārda. He died at Marrakesh on 13 Rabīᶜ I 1238/28 November 1822. Mawlāy ᶜAbd al-Raḥmān (1824-59) did much for the afforestation of Agdāl and restored the religious buildings. His son Muḥammad completed his work by repairing tanks and aqueducts. These two reigns were a period of tranquillity for Marrakesh. In 1862, however, while Sīdī Muḥammad b. ᶜAbd al-Raḥmān was fighting the Spaniards at Tetwan, the Rḥāmna rebelled, plundered the Sūḳ al-Khamīs and closely blockaded the town, cutting off communications and supplies, until the Sulṭān, having made peace with Spain, came to relieve the town (Dhu 'l-Ḥidjdja 1278/June 1862). Mawlāy al-Ḥasan hardly ever lived in Marrakesh, but he stopped there on several occasions, notably in October 1875, to punish the Rḥāmna and the Bū 'l-Sbaᶜ, who had rebelled, and in 1880 and 1885, to prepare his expeditions into the Sūs.

During the last years of the reign of Mawlāy ᶜAbd al-ᶜAzīz (1894-1908), it was at Marrakesh that the opposition to the European tastes and experiments of the sultan made itself most strongly felt. The xenophobia culminated in the murder of a French doctor named Mauchamp (19 March 1907), and the spirit of separatism in the proclamation as sultan of Mawlāy ᶜAbd al-Ḥafīẓ, brother of ᶜAbd al-ᶜAzīz and governor of the provinces of the south (24 August 1907). But ᶜAbd al-Ḥafīẓ becoming ruler of the whole empire (24 August 1907) and having signed the treaty of 24 March 1912 establishing the protectorate of France and of Spain over Morocco, the anti-foreign movement broke out again in the south. The Mauritanian marabout al-Ḥība [see AḤMAD AL-HĪBA in Suppl.] had himself proclaimed and established himself in Marrakesh. He only held out there for a brief period. His troops having been defeated at Sīdī Bū ᶜUthmān on 6 September 1912, the French troops occupied Marrakesh the next day.

Relations with Europe. Five minor friars sent by St. Francis were put to death at Marrakesh on 16 January 1220, for having attempted to convert Muslims and having insulted the Prophet Muḥammad in their discourses. Their martyrdom attracted the attention of the Holy See to Marrakesh. A mission and a bishopric were established by Honorius III in 1225 to give the consolations of religion to the Christians domiciled in Morocco: merchants, slaves and mercenaries in the sultan's army. In the Almoravid period, the sultans had Christian mercenaries recruited from prisoners reduced to slavery or from the Mozarab population of Spain whom they had from time deported to Morocco by entire villages. In 1227, Abu 'l-ᶜUlā Idrīs al-Maʾmūn, having won his kingdom with the help of Christian troops lent by the king of Castile, found himself bound to take up quite a new attitude to the Christians. He granted them various privileges, including permission to build a church in Marrakesh and worship openly there. This was called Notre Dame and stood in the *kaṣba*, probably opposite the mosque of al-Manṣūr: it was destroyed during a rising in 1232. But the Christian soldiery continued to enjoy the right to worship, at least privately, and the bishopric of Marrakesh supported by a source of income at Seville, existed so long as there was an organised Christian soldiery in Morocco, i.e. to the end of the 8th/14th century. The title of Bishop of Marrakesh was borne till the end of the 10th/16th century by the suffragans of Seville (cf. Father A. Lopez, *Los obispos de Marruecos desde el siglo XIII*, in *Archivo Ibero-Americano*, xlii [1920]). A Spanish Franciscan, the prior Juan de Prado, who came to re-establish the mission, was put to death in 1621 at Marrakesh. A few years later (1637), a monastery was re-established beside the prison for slaves in the *kaṣba*. It was destroyed in 1659 or 1660 after the death of the last Saᶜdian. Henceforth the Franciscans were obliged to live in the *mellāḥ* where they had down to the end of the 18th century a little chapel and a monastery. As to the Christian merchants, they had not much reason to go to Marrakesh in the Middle Ages. Trade with Europe was conducted at Ceuta from which the Muslim merchants carried European goods into the interior of the country. In the 16th century, ᶜAbd Allāh al-Ghālib had a *fondak* or "bonded warehouse" built in the *sūk* where the Christian merchants were allowed to live; but the majority of those who came to Marrakesh preferred to settle in the Jewish quarter. It was here also that foreign ambassadors usually lodged, at least when they were not made to encamp in one of the gardens of the palace.

Monuments. The present enceinte of Marrakesh is a wall of clay about 20 feet high, flanked with rectangular bastions at intervals of 250 to 300 feet. Bāb Aghmāt, Bāb Aylān and Bāb Dabbāgh which still exist more or less rebuilt, are mentioned in the account of the attack on Marrakesh by the Almohads in 524/1130. Bāb Yīntān and Bāb al-Makhzen, mentioned at the same time, have disappeared. Bāb al-Ṣāliḥa (no longer in existence: it stood on the site of the *mellāḥ*) and Bāb Dukkāla (still in existence) figure in the story of the capture of the town by the Almohads (542/1147). The plan of the wall has therefore never changed. It has been rebuilt in places from time to time, as the clay crumbled away, but it may be assumed that a number of pieces of the wall, especially on the west and south-west, are original, as well as at least three gates all now blocked up, to which they owe their survival, but have lost their name. According to Abu 'l-Fidāᵓ (8th/14th century), there were in Marrakesh seventeen gates; twenty-four at the beginning of the 10th/16th century, according to Leo Africanus. It would be very difficult to draw up an accurate list, for some have been removed, others opened, since these dates or the names have been altered. Ibn Faḍl Allāh al-ᶜUmarī (beginning of the 8th/14th century) adds to the names already mentioned those of Bāb Nfīs, Bāb Muḥriḳ, Bāb Messūfa, Bāb al-Raḥā, all four of which have disappeared, Bāb Taghzūt, Bāb Fās (now Bāb al-Khamīs) and Bāb al-Rabb, which still exist. The only important changes, which have been made in the walls of Marrakesh since they were built, have been the building of the *kaṣba* in the south and in the north the creation of the quarter of Sīdī bel ᶜAbbās. The *zāwiya* which as late as the 10th/16th century stood outside the walls beyond the Bāb Taghzūt, was taken into the town with all its dependencies.

The *Kaṣba*. The little *kaṣba* and the palace of Dār al-ᶜUmma built by Yūsuf b. Tashfīn, lay north of the present "Mosque of the Booksellers" or Kutubiyya. ᶜAlī b. Yūsuf added in the same quarter other palaces called Sūr al-Ḥadjar, or Ḳaṣr al-Ḥadjar because they were built with stones from the Gillīz, while all the other buildings in the town were of brick or clay. It was here that the first Almohads took up their quarters. According to a somewhat obscure passage of the *Istibṣār*, Abū Yaᶜḳūb Yūsuf seems to have begun the building of a "fort" in the south of the town but it was Yaᶜḳūb al-Manṣūr who built the new *kaṣba* (585-93/1189-97); that is to say he joined to the south wall of the town a new walled area within which he built palaces, a mosque, and a regular town. Nothing remains of the Almohad palaces, but from pieces of wall and other vestiges one can follow the old wall, at least on the north and the east side. There also the line of the wall has hardly changed. The magnificent gateway of carved stone by which the *kaṣba* is now entered, must be one of al-Manṣūr's buildings. Its modern name of Bāb Agnaw (the dumb mute's = Negro's Gate) is not found in any old text. It probably corresponds to Bāb al-Kuḥl (Gate of the Negroes?), often mentioned by the historians.

Ibn Faḍl Allāh al-ᶜUmarī, in the 8th/14th century, Leo Africanus and Marmol in the 10th/16th have left us fairly detailed descriptions of the *kaṣba*, in spite of a few obscure passages. In the Almohad period, the *kaṣba* was divided into three quite distinct parts. One wall in the northwest, around the mosque of al-Manṣūr which still exists, contained the police offices, the headquarters of the Almohad tribes and the barracks of the Christian soldiery. From this one entered through the Bāb al-Ṭubūl a second enclosure in which around a huge open space, the "Cereque" of Marmol (*asārāg*), were grouped the guard houses, the offices of the minister of the army, a guest-house, a *madrasa* with its library and a large building called *al-saḳāᵓif* (the porticoes), the "Acequife" of Marmol, occupied by the principal members of the Almohad organisation, the "Ten", the "Fifty", the *ṭolba* and the pages (*ahl al-dār*). The royal palace, sometimes called the Alhambra of Marrakesh, in imitation of that of Granada, was entered from the Asārāg and occupied the whole area east of the *kaṣba*. The palaces of al-Manṣūr were still in existence at the beginning of the 10th/16th century when the Saᶜdians took possession. ᶜAbd Allāh al-Ghālib incorporated them in the new palaces which he was building. Aḥmad al-Manṣūr added, in the gardens to the north, the famous al-Badīᶜ palace celebrated for its size and splendour. Only a few almost shapeless ruins remain of it, but its plan is perfectly clear. Mawlāy Ismāᶜīl had it destroyed in order to use its materials. The *kaṣba* remained so completely in ruins that Sīdī Muḥammad b. ᶜAbd Allāh, when he became governor of Marrakesh in 1159/1746, was obliged to live in a tent until his new buildings were finished. It is to him that we owe an important part of the present palace with its inner garden, ᶜArṣat al-Nīl. Other works were later undertaken by Mawlāy Slīmān and his successors. Some large unfinished buildings date only from Mawlāy ᶜAbd al-Ḥafīẓ. A number of gates, in addition to the Bāb Agnaw, give admittance to the *kaṣba*: these are Bāb Berrīma and Bāb al-Aḥmar in the east, Bāb Ighlī and Bāb Ḳsība in the west. The palace has vast gardens belonging to it: Jnān al-ᶜAfīya, Agdal, Jnān Riḍwān, Maᵓmūniyya and Manāra. The latter, two miles west of the town, contained in the 10th/16th century a pleasure house of the sultans. The palace of Dār al-Bayḍāᵓ, situated in the Agdal, took the place of a Saᶜdian palace. It was rebuilt by Sīdī Muḥammad b. ᶜAbd Allāh and has since been restored. As to the gardens of the Agdal, they seem to have been created in the 6th/12th century by ᶜAbd al-Muᵓmin.

Mosques. Nothing remains of the early Almoravid mosques, in the building of one of which Yūsuf b. Tas͟hfīn himself worked along with the masons as a sign of humility. But the Friday mosque of ᶜAlī b. Yūsuf, where Ibn Tūmart had an interview with the sultan, although several times rebuilt, still retains its name. The Almohads, on taking possession of Marrakesh, destroyed all the mosques on the pretext that they were wrongly oriented. The mosque of ᶜAlī b. Yūsuf was only partly destroyed and was rebuilt. ᶜAbd Allāh al-G͟hālib restored it in the middle of the 10th/16th century. The present buildings and the minaret date from Mawlāy Slīmān (1792-1822).

Kutubiyya. When the Almohads entered Marrakesh, Abd al-Muᵓmin built the first Kutubiyya of which some traces still remain and it has been possible to reconstruct its plan. As it was wrongly oriented he built a new mosque, the present Kutubiyya, in prolongation of the first but with a slightly different orientation. It takes its name from the 100 booksellers' shops which used to be around its entrance. It is a very large building with seventeen naves, which with its decoration in carved plaster, its stalactite cupolas, the moulding of its timberwork, its capitals and magnificent pulpit (*minbar*) of inlaid work, is the most important and the most perfectly preserved work of Almohad art. The minaret, begun by ᶜAbd al-Muᵓmin, was only finished in the reign of his grandson al-Manṣūr (591/1195). It is 230 feet high and its powerful silhouette dominates the whole town and the palm groves. It is the prototype of the Giralda of Seville and of the tower of Ḥassān at Rabat. It is decorated with arcatures the effects of which were formerly heightened by paintings still visible in places, with a band of ceramic work around the top.

The mosque of the *ḳaṣba* or mosque of al-Manṣūr is the work of Yaᶜḳūb al-Manṣūr. It was begun in 585-91/1189-95 and built in great splendour. It has been profoundly altered, first by ᶜAbd Allāh al-G͟hālib the Saᶜdian, then in the middle of the 18th century by Muḥammad b. ᶜAbd Allāh, then more recently by Mawlāy ᶜAbd al-Raḥmān (1822-59). The minaret of brick is intact and magnificently ornamented with green ceramics. The lampholder supports a *d̲j̲āmūr* of three bowls of gilt copper, which occupy a considerable place in the legends of Marrakesh. They are said to be of pure gold and to be enchanted, so that no one can take them away without bringing on himself the most terrible misfortunes. This legend is often wrongly connected with the *d̲j̲āmūr* of the Kutubiyya.

Among the religious monuments of Marrakesh of archaeological interest may also be mentioned the minarets of the mosque of Ibn Ṣāliḥ (dated 731/1331) and of the sanctuary of Mawlā 'l-Ḳṣūr, built in the Marīnid period in the Almohad tradition, and two Saᶜdian mosques: the mosque of al-Mwāsīn or mosque of the S͟harīfs, which owes its origin to ᶜAbd Allāh al-G͟hālib, and that of Bāb Dukkāla, built in 965/1557-8 by Lālla Masᶜūda, the mother of the sultan Aḥmad al-Manṣūr.

Madrasas. An Almohad *madrasa*, built "to teach the children of the king and others of his family in it", formed part of the buildings of Yaᶜḳūb al-Manṣūr. This royal school was presumably different from what were later the Marīnid *madrasas*. It stood on the great square in front of the palace and was still in existence in the time of Leo Africanus. The Marīnid Abu 'l-Ḥasan in 748/1347 built another *madrasa*, also described by Leo. It lay north of the mosque of the *ḳaṣba*, where traces of it can still be seen. The *madrasa* of Ibn Yūsuf is not, as is usually said, a restoration of the Marīnid *madrasa*. It was a new building by ᶜAbd Allāh al-G͟hālib, dated by an inscription of 972/1564-5 and the only surviving example of a Saᶜdian *madrasa*.

Saᶜdian tombs. The two first founders of the dynasty rest beside the tomb of Sīdī Muḥammad b. Slīmān al-D̲j̲azūlī in the Riyāḍ al-ᶜArūs quarter. Their successors from 964/1557 were buried to the south of the mosque of the *ḳaṣba*. There was a cemetery there, probably as early as the Almohad period, which still has tombs of the 8th/14th century. The magnificent *ḳubbas* which cover the tombs of the Saᶜdian dynasty must have been built at two different periods. The one on the east under which is the tomb of Maḥammad al-S͟hayk͟h seems to have been built by ᶜAbd Allāh al-G͟hālib. The other, with three chambers, seems to have been erected by Aḥmad al-Manṣūr (d. 1012/1603) to hold his tomb.

Bibliography: Arab writers: see the indexes to the editions of Bakrī (tr. de Slane, 1859); Idrīsī (ed. tr. and Dozy and de Goeje, 1866); Ibn al-At͟hīr (tr. Fagnan, 1901); *Documents inédits d'histoire almohade* (ed. and tr. E. Lévi-Provençal, 1928); *Chronique almohade anonyme* (ed. and tr. E. Lévi-Provençal, in *Mélanges René Basset*, ii, 1925); Zarkas͟hī (tr. Fagnan, 1895); Marrākus͟hī (tr. Fagnan, 1893); Abu 'l-Fidāᵓ (tr. Solvet, 1839); Ibn Faḍl Allāh al-ᶜUmarī, *Masālik* (tr. Gaudefroy-Demombynes, 1927); Ibn K͟haldūn, *ᶜIbār* (tr. de Slane, 1852); Ifrānī, *Nuzhat al-ḥādī* (ed. and tr. Houdas, 1889); Zayyānī (ed. and tr. Houdas, 1886); Naṣīrī, *Istiḳṣāᵓ* (part tr. in *AM*, ix, x, xxx, xxxi); *Extraits inédits relatifs au Maghreb* (tr. Fagnan, 1924); see also: *Kitāb al-Istibṣār* (tr. Fagnan, 1899); *al-Ḥulal al-maws͟hiyya*, Tunis 1329, Ibn Abī Zarᶜ, *Rawḍ al-ḳirṭās* (ed. Tornberg, 1846, tr. Beaumier, 1860); Leo Africanus (tr. Épaulard, Paris 1956); Ibn al-Muwaḳḳit, *al-Saᶜādat al-abadiyya*, Fās 1336; al-ᶜAbbās b. Ibrāhīm al-Marrākus͟hī, *Iẓhār al-kamāl*, Fās 1334.

European authors: Damião de Góis, *Crónica do felicissimo Rei D. Manuel*, ed. D. Lopes, Coimbra 1926, tr. R. Ricard, *Les Portugais au Maroc*, Rabat 1937; Marmol Carvajal, *Descripción general de Affrica*, ii, Granada 1573, French tr. 1667; H. de Castries, *Sources inédites de l'Histoire de Maroc, passim*, cf. the indexes to the French and Dutch series; Matias de S. Francisco, *Relación del viage... que hizo à Marruecos el Ven. P. Fr. Juan de Prado*, Madrid 1643, 2nd ed. Tangier 1945; G. Höst, *Nachrichten von Marokos und Fes*, Copenhagen 1781; L. de Chénier, *Recherches historiques sur les Maures*, iii, 1787; Jackson, *Account of the Empire of Morocco*, 1809; Ali Bey el Abbassi, *Voyages*, i, 1814; P. Lambert, *Notice sur la ville de Maroc*, in *Bull. de la Soc. de Géogr.* (1868); Gatell, *Viages por Marruecos*, Madrid 1869; E. Doutté, *Merrakech*, 1905; P. Champion, *Rabat et Marrakech, Les villes d'art célèbres*, 1926; H. de Castries, *Du nom d'Alhambra donné au palais du souverain à Marrakech et à Grenade*, in *JA* (1921); P. de Cénival, *L'Eglise chrétienne de Marrakech*, in *Hespéris* (1927); H. Basset and H. Terrasse, *Sanctuaires et forteresses almohades*, in *Hespéris* (1925-7); Gallotti, *Le Lanternon du minaret de la Koutoubia de Marrakech*, in *ibid.* (1923); G. Rousseau and F. Arin, *Le mausolée des princes saᶜdiens à Marrakech*, 1925; de Castries, *Le Cimetière de Djama el-Mansour*, in *Hespéris* (1927); G. Aimel, *Le Palais d'el Bediᶜ à Marrakech*, in *Archives Berbères* (1918); Ch. Terrasse, *Medersas du Maroc*, 1928; Capt. Begbéder, *Notes sur l'organisation administrative de la Région de Marrakech*, in *Bull. de la*

Soc. de Géogr. du Maroc (1921); Voinot, *Les tribus guich du Haouz de Marrakech*, in *Bull. de la Soc. de Géogr. et d'Archéologie d'Oran* (1928); in *France-Maroc*, 1919-21, a number of articles signed Aimel, Doutté, Guichard, etc.; Doctoresse Légey, *Contes et légendes populaires recueillis à Marrakech*, 1926; *Guides Bleus, Maroc*. There is a detailed list of the archival, manuscript, cartographic and iconographic sources, followed by an exhaustive bibliography (works in both Arabic and European languages), in G. Deverdun's monograph, *Marrakech des origines à 1912*, 2 vols., Rabat 1959-66, complemented by the work of idem, *Inscriptions arabes de Marrakech*, Rabat 1956. (P. de Cenival)

al-**MARRĀKUSHĪ** [see ʿAbd al-Wāḥid; Ibn al-Bannāʾ].

al-**MARRĀKUSHĪ**, Abū ʿAlī al-Ḥasan b. ʿAlī, astronomer of Maghribī origin who worked in Cairo. In *ca.* 680/1281-2, he compiled a compendium of spherical astronomy and astronomical instruments entitled *Kitāb Djāmiʿ al-mabādiʾ wa 'l-ghāyāt fī ʿilm al-mīḳāt*, which is perhaps the most valuable single source for the history of Islamic astronomical instrumentation.

In this work, which exists in several manuscript copies, al-Marrākushī presented a detailed discussion of the standard problems of spherical astronomy [see mīḳāt. 2. Astronomical aspects], and then dealt with different kinds of plane sundials, the armillary sphere, the planispheric astrolabe, the universal plate known as the *shakkāziyya*, the trigonometric grid called *al-rubʿ al-mudjayyab*, and a variety of aquadrants for determining time from solar altitude [see aṣṭurlāb and rubʿ]. Most of the material was apparently culled from earlier sources which are not identified by the author and which have not yet been established. Those earlier scholars whom he does mention do not appear to be his major sources. The compendium does contain several tables computed specifically for Cairo, and these appear to be original to al-Marrākushī. Rather surprisingly, he makes no reference to and does not exploit the *Zīdj ḥākimī* of the 4th/10th century Egyptian astronomer Ibn Yūnus [*q.v.*], which included an exhaustive account of spherical astronomy and also contained numerous tables for Cairo.

Al-Marrākushī's work was highly influential in later Islamic astronomy in Rasūlid Yemen, in Mamlūk Egypt and Syria, and in Ottoman Turkey. Most of the surviving manuscripts are of Egyptian, Syrian or Turkish provenance. His work was apparently unknown in the Maghrib and the Islamic East.

The first half of al-Marrākushī's treatise dealing with spherical astronomy and sundials was translated by J.J. Sédillot, and the second half dealing with instruments summarised by L.A. Sédillot. Al-Marrākushī's sundial theory has been studied by K. Schoy. A detailed study of this work, and an investigation of its sources, has yet to be conducted. An uncritical edition was prepared by the late Egyptian scholar Shaykh Ḥasan al-Bannāʾ, but this has not been published.

Al-Marrākushī is usually described as a Maghribī scientist because of his *nisba*. Unfortunately, we have no biographical information on him of any consequence. Whatever his origin, his *magnum opus* was clearly compiled in Cairo. Apparently neither of the Sédillots realised that he was writing there, and Sédillot *père* misdated him to 660/1261-2 in spite of the fact that his solar tables and star catalogue are computed for 680/1281-2.

Bibliography: See H. Suter, *Die Mathematiker und Astronomen der Araber und ihre Werke*, in *Abh. zur Gesch. der mathematischen Wissenschaften*, x (1900) (repr. Amsterdam 1982), no.363; M. Krause, *Stambuler Handschriften islamischer Mathematiker*, in *Quellen und Studien zur Geschichte der Mathematik Astronomie und Physik*, iii/4 (1936), 437-532, no. 363; Brockelmann, I², 625, S I, 866; L. A. Mayer, *Islamic astrolabists and their works*, Geneva 1956, 46 (on an unusual astrolabe made by him); and D. A. King, *A survey of the scientific manuscripts in the Egyptian National Library*, Malibu, Calif. 1985, no. C17. See also idem, *The astronomy of the Mamluks*, in *Isis*, lxxiv (1983), 531-55, esp. 539-40.

Studies of his works: J. J. Sédillot, *Traité des instruments astronomiques des Arabes...*, 2 vols., Paris 1834-5; L. A. Sédillot, *Mémoire sur les instruments astronomiques des Arabes*, in *Méms. de l'Acad. Royale des Inscrs. et Belles-Lettres de l'Inst. de France*, i (1844), 1-229; K. Schoy, *Die Gnomonik der Araber*, Band I, Lieferung F, of E. von Bassermann-Jordan (ed.). *Die Geschichte der Zeitmessung und der Uhren*, Berlin-Leipzig 1923. (D. A. King)

MARRĀSH, Fransīs b. Fatḥ Allāh b. Naṣr, Syrian scholar and publicist of the *Nahḍa* (1835-74 according to M. ʿAbbūd and S. al-Kayyālī, or 1836-73 according to Brockelmann, Dāghir and al-Ziriklī).

He was born and died at Aleppo, coming from a Melkite Christian family of literary men (Brockelmann, S II, 755), and in the opening stages of the modern Arabic literary renaissance, the *Nahḍa* [*q.v.*], tried to introduce "critical reasoning" into a sphere at that time in a state of cultural effervescence. For this, he employed pseudo-scientific terms in order to prove, in his early works, the need for freedom and peace in the world, and then in his later works, the existence of God and the divine law (the *sharīʿa* which, in his eyes, goes beyond the sphere of the Islamic law alone). In order to free human thought from the yokes of tradition and respect for the ancients, he used extra-literary methods, the discoveries of the botanical, geological and zoological sciences; but, so as not to frighten off his public, he did not endeavour to free himself from traditional forms of expression (*sadjʿ*, the *maḳāma* genre, numerous poetic citations). The whole of his work involved religion and history in an epistemological revision, and in this, he contributed with Faris al-Shidyāḳ and Faraḥ Anṭūn [*q.vv.*] in the development of critical reasoning, fed by multi-disciplinary aspects of knowledge, in contemporary Arab thought.

He was aided in this by his milieu. Aleppo was at that time a lively centre of thought about the Arab future, within a society still under Ottoman rule. It was in the French religious schools that the Marrāsh family learnt Arabic with French and other foreign languages (Italian and English). The father, Fatḥ Allāh, and the brother, ʿAbd Allāh, achieved a certain literary fame. A young sister, Maryāna, born in 1848 (Brockelmann, S II, 756, erroneously calls her "daughter"; Dāghir, ii, 697), was to conduct a literary salon and seems to have been the first Arab woman to write in the daily newspapers (*al-Djinān* and *Lisān al-ḥāl*).

Since he was 4 years old, as a consequence of measles, Fransīs Marrāsh began to lose his sight. He studied science and learnt medicine with an English physician in Aleppo. He continued his studies in 1867 at Paris, where he had already been in 1850 for treatment for his eyes. But as his sight deteriorated, he had to return to Aleppo completely blind. During the last years of his life, he was able to dictate a relatively abundant body of work.

His biographers reproach him for using a linguistic style at times incorrect and inelegant (Dāghir, ii, 693; al-Ziriklī; Ḳusṭākī; M. ʿAbbūd, 115), but they speak with appreciation of the quality of his personal thought and insight (*kātib mabādiʾ wa-tafkīr... min al-ṭirāz al-awwal*, Dāghir, ii, 693) at a time when *bidʿa*, innovativeness and originality, were still viewed with disfavour by traditional cultural circles. From the titles onwards, his works reveal a clearly marked-out form and a new range of contents: *Dalīl al-ḥurriyya al-insāniyya* "Guide to human liberty", Aleppo 1861, 24 pp.; *al-Mirʾāt al-ṣafiyya fi 'l-mabādiʾ al-ṭabīʿiyya* "The clear mirror of natural principles", Aleppo 1861, 60 pp. of pseudo-scientific text; *Taʿziyat al-makrūb wa-rāḥat al-matʿūb* "Consolation of the anxious and repose of the weary one", Aleppo 1864, a philosophical and pessimistic discourse on nations of the past; *Ghābat al-ḥakk* "The forest of truth" (Brockelmann, S II, 756: *Ghāyāt al-ḥakk*), Aleppo 1865, Cairo 1298/1881, Beirut 1881, his most famous and most often printed work, "almost a novel" (Dāghir, ii, 695; ʿAbbūd, 131; Kayyālī, 57), a kind of apocalyptic vision and pleading for the liberty of peoples and for peace; *Riḥla ilā Bārīs*, a description of his trip to Paris, Beirut 1867; *al-Kunūz al-fanniyya fi 'l-rumūz al-maymūniyya* "Artistic treasures concerning the symbolic visions of Maymūn", a poem of almost 500 verses, a kind of symbolic vision whose hero is called Maymūn; *Mashhad al-aḥwāl* "The witnessing of the stages of human life", Beirut 1870, 1883 (Brockelmann, S II, 756, gives an edition of 1865 [?]), these editions testifying to the work's success, as confirmed by ʿAbbūd—with its 130 pp. (this in the 1870 edition, 75 being in verse and 55 in prose), the book sets forth the author's philosophical ideas on beings and things: minerals, vegetable and plant life, animals and human kind; *Durr al-ṣadaf fī gharāʾib al-ṣadf* "The pearl of nacre concerning the curious aspects of change", a social narrative which appeared at Beirut in 1872; *Mirʾāt al-ḥasnāʾ* "The mirror of the beautiful one", Beirut 1872, 1883, a collection of poems; and his posthumous work, *Shahādat al-ṭabīʿa fī wudjūd Allāh wa 'l-sharīʿa* "The proofs of nature for the existence of God and the divine law", Beirut 1892.

In his articles published in *al-Djinān*, Buṭrus al-Bustānī's journal [see AL-BUSTĀNĪ, 2., in Suppl.], he reveals himself as favourable to women's education, which he limited however to reading, writing, and a little bit of arithmetic, geography and grammar. He wrote that it is not necessary for a woman "to act like a man, neglect her domestic and family duties, or that she should consider herself superior to the man" (*al-Djinān*, 1872, 769-70, cited by A. al-Maḳdisī, 268-9). He nevertheless closely followed his sister Maryāna's studies not suspecting that the first poem which she would publish in the public press—actually in *al-Djinān*—would be her elegy on him (ʿAbbūd, 173).

Bibliography: Mārūn ʿAbbūd, *Ruwwād al-nahḍa al-ḥadītha*, Beirut 1966, 115, 121, 123-36, 173, 193, 208; Brockelmann, II², 646, S II, 755; Y.A. Dāghir, *Maṣādir al-dirāsa al-adabiyya*, Beirut 1956, ii, 693-6; S. al-Kayyālī, *al-Adab al-ʿarabī al-muʿāṣir fī Sūriya (1850-1950²*, Cairo 1968, 53-9; Ḳusṭākī al-Ḥimṣī, *Udabāʾ Ḥalab dhawu 'l-athar fi 'l-ḳarn al-tāsiʿ ʿashar*, Aleppo 1925, 20-30; Anīs al-Maḳdisī, *al-Ittidjāhāt al-adabiyya fi 'l-ʿālam al-ʿarabī al-ḥadīth²*, Beirut 1967, 205, 268-9, 275 (on Maryāna); Sarkīs, *Muʿdjam al-maṭbūʿāt al-ʿarabiyya wa 'l-muʿarraba*, Cairo 1346/1928, col. 1730; L. Cheikho, *al-Ādāb al-ʿarabiyya fi 'l-ḳarn al-tāsiʿ ʿashar*, Beirut 1926, ii, 45; Ṭarrāzī (Philippe de Tarrazi), *Taʾrīkh al-ṣiḥāfa al-ʿarabiyya*, Beirut 1913-33, i, 141; Dj. Zaydān, *Tarādjim mashāhīr al-shark fi 'l-ḳarn al-tāsiʿ ʿashar*, Cairo 1900, ii, 152; idem, *Taʾrīkh ādāb al-lugha al-ʿarabiyya*, Cairo 1913-14, iv, 237; Ziriklī, *Aʿlām³*, v, 344b.

(N. TOMICHE)

MARRIAGE [see ʿMAHR, MARʾA, NIKĀḤ, ʿURS].

MARS [see AL-MIRRĪKH].

MARSĀ [see MĪNĀʾ].

MARSĀ ʿALĪ [see ṢIḲILLIYYA].

MARṢAD (A.) originally means a place where one keeps watch, whence comes the meaning of o b s e r v a t o r y, also described by the word *raṣad*.

The first astronomical observations carried out in the Islamic world seem to date back to the end of the 2nd/8th century, i.e. to the period when Indo-Persian astronomical materials were introduced and the first Ptolemaic data appeared. According to Ibn Yūnus (d. 399/1009), Aḥmad b. Muḥammad al-Nihāwandī (174/790) made some observations in Djundīshāpūr in the time of the minister Yaḥyā b. Khālid b. Barmak (d. 190/805) and used their results in his *Zīdj mushtamil*, unfortunately lost. The same Ibn Yūnus informs us, on the other hand, that in 159/776 the first determination of the obliquity of the ecliptic was made with a result of 23°31', but he does not cite the one responsible for these observations, who may have been al-Nihāwandī himself.

The first systematic programme of observations concerning which we have solid information is that which was implemented under the patronage of the caliph al-Maʾmūn [*q.v.*] (198-218/813-33) who gave an impulse to this research, perhaps because of his own interest in astronomy or his desire to achieve a permanent solution of the problem presented by the contradictory parameters used by the three astronomical schools known to Muslims: Indian, Persian and Greek (D. Pingree, *The Greek influence on early Islamic mathematical astronomy*, in *JAOS*, xciii [1973], 38-9). This second hypothesis would also explain the careful measurement of a meridian degree undertaken on al-Maʾmūn's order, in the Syrian desert (between the towns of al-Raḳḳa and Palmyra) and in ʿIrāḳ (between Baghdād and Kūfa and on the Sindjar plain; see T. Bychawski, *Measurement of one geographical degree undertaken and carried out by the Arabs in the IXth century*, in *Actes du IXᵉ Congrès International d'Histoire de Sciences*, Barcelona-Paris 1960, 635-8). The observations encouraged by al-Maʾmūn were undertaken in Baghdād and Damascus, not simultaneously, it seems, but consecutively, although we possess a reference to the collation of the results of an observation of the autumnal equinox carried out in the two towns. In Baghdād, the observations took place in al-Shammāsiyya quarter, but the sources do not say if there was an observatory, properly speaking, in a building reserved for this purpose; in any case, the insistence in the introduction of the *zīdj* attributed to Hayḥā b. Abī Manṣūr (d. *ca.* 215/830) on the use of the "circle" (*dāʾira*) of al-Shammāsiyya makes us think of a large scale instrument requiring a fixed installation and a minimal permanent space (cf. J. Vernet, *Las "Tabulae Probatae"*, in *Homenaje à Millás Vallicrosa*, ii, Barcelona 1956, 508, repr. in *Estudios sobre historia de la ciencia medieval*, Barcelona-Bellaterra 1979, 198). The situation was the same in Damascus, where the observations took place in the monastery of Dayr Murrān on Mount Ḳāsiyūn [*q.v.*]; a sun-dial ten cubits high (about 5 m.) was built there and a marble wall dial, whose interior radius also measured ten cubits. In any case, it was not necessary for the installations to be of a permanent character, for the programmes were brief; in Baghdād the observations were carried out in 213/828 and 214/829 under the direction of Yaḥyā b. Abī Manṣūr with the collaboration of Sanad b. ᶜAlī and al-ᶜAbbās b. Saᶜīd al-Djawharī. They had to be interrupted for a year, to be repeated later in Damascus, where they took place at the end of a solar year between 216 and 217/831-2, under the direction of Khālid b. ᶜAbd al-Malik al-Marwarrūdhī, perhaps with the assistance of Sanad b. ᶜAlī and ᶜAlī b. ᶜĪsā al-Asṭurlābī. The question as to whether Ḥabash al-Ḥāsib (d. between 250 and 260/864-74) was involved in these observations, especially as head of the team in Damascus, has been much discussed, but there does not seem to be sufficient proof and Ḥabash himself, in the introduction of his *zīdj* where he alludes to these observations, does not say that he took part personally. The caliph's death, in 218/833, interrupted, according to some sources, the programme of observations, but the matter is not clear, for, on the one hand, some evidence shows that this work preceded al-Maʾmūn's death and, on the other, we possess some references to later observations carried out by al-Maʾmūn's astronomers in Damascus (Khālid in 219/834) and in Baghdād (Khālid, ᶜAlī b. ᶜĪsā al-Ḥarrānī and Sanad b. ᶜAlī in 230-1/843-4). It is furthermore possible that the observations in question survived to be followed up by a later imitator or that the latter to which allusion is to be made (such as those of Ḥabash in Baghdād between 210 and 220/825-33 and in 250/864) were carried out on the fringe of the official programme laid down by the caliph.

The observers of al-Maʾmūn's time seem to have given themselves to the systematic observation of the sun and moon, although observations were also made of the fixed stars and no doubt of the planets. The results of these labours were recorded in a certain number of *zīdj*s, outstanding among which are those attributed to Yaḥyā b. Abī Manṣūr and Ḥabash. As far as the sun is concerned, these *zīdj*s improve upon the Ptolemaic parameters, and it is also known that al-Maʾmūn's astronomers established a new method, which offers some advantages as against that of Ptolemy, for establishing the parameters of the solar (W. Hartner and M. Schramm, *Al-Bīrūnī and the theory of the solar apogee: an example of originality in Arabic science*, in A.C. Crombie (ed.), *Scientific change*, London 1963, 208-9). Various calculations of the obliquity of the ecliptic (see al-Bīrūnī, *Taḥdīd nihāyāt al-amākin*, ed. P. Boulgakov, in *RIMA*, viii [1962], 90-1) and of the duration of the tropical year were undertaken. However, the observation of the moon, stars and planets proved to be less fruitful, and we can only say, by way of example, that the estimation of the precession of the equinoxes (1 every 66 years) obtained by Yaḥyā b. Abī Manṣūr (following an observation of the autumnal equinox carried out on the 27 Radjab 215/19 September 830) is suspect, for D. Pingree (*Precession and trepidation in Indian astronomy before A.D. 1200*, in *Jnal. of the Hist. of Astronomy*, iii [1972]), has demonstrated that the parameter cited above is of Sanskrit origin.

The status given to astronomical observations by al-Maʾmūn's patronage was to be followed by a period during which the same work had to be pursued, on a lower level, in small private observatories: this is the case with the brothers Muḥammad and Aḥmad b. Mūsā b. Shākir who observed the sun and fixed stars between 225 and 225/840-69, principally in Baghdād, but also in Sāmarrā and Nīshāpūr. This activity of the Banū Mūsā is easily explained, for they had at their disposal a considerable fortune and became patrons of other scholars, among whom figured Thābit b. Ḳurra [*q.v.*] (d. 288/901), who also made observations himself, but is distinguished essentially by his use of the results of those which dated back to antiquity and al-Maʾmūn's period. Between the 3rd and 4th/9th-10th centuries, attention should be drawn to the work undertaken by al-Mahānī (observation of conjunctions and eclipses of the sun and moon between 239 and 252/853-66), the 30 years (273-305) of systematic observations of al-Battānī [*q.v.*] in al-Raḳḳa which are crystallised in his famous *zīdj* (edited by C.A. Nallino, Milan 1899-1907) and the labours of the Banū Amādjūr in Baghdād between 271 and 321/885-933, who made observations not only of the sun but also of the moon and planets.

The 4th/10th century had already begun when the interest of the Buwayhid dynasty in astronomy brought a revival of official patronage which facilitated the undertaking of very extensive work; Abu 'l-Faḍl Ibn al-ᶜAmīd [*q.v.*], minister of the ruler of al-Rayy, Rukn al-Dawla (d. 366/977), subsidised the construction of a large-scale instrument with which Abu 'l-Faḍl al-Harawī and Abū Djaᶜfar al-Khāzin [*q.v.*] made solar observations in 348/950. This same minister also had in his service ᶜAbd al-Raḥmān al-Ṣūfī (d. 376/986), who was also patronised, in Iṣfahān, by another Buwayhid, ᶜAḍud al-Dawla (d. 372/983). Al-Ṣūfī's important stellar observations resulted in a systematic revision of Ptolemy's catalogue of stars; simultaneously, Ibn al-Aᶜlam, also for ᶜAḍud al-Dawla, made some planetary observations which are recorded in his famous *zīdj* (cf. E. S. Kennedy, *The astronomical tables of Ibn al-Aᶜlam*, in *JHAS*, i [1977], 13-21). This work was further developed under Sharaf al-Dawla (372-9/982-9), who commanded Abū Sahl al-Ḳūhī to observe the seven planets, which resulted in the construction of an observatory in the royal palace garden at Baghdād where some large-scale instruments were used. Astronomers such as Abu 'l-Wafāʾ al-Būzdjānī [*q.v.*] and Aḥmad b. Muhammad al-Ṣāghānī must have taken part in the first observations, which took place in 378/988. Unfortunately, this Baghdād observatory had an ephemeral existence, for its activities ended with the death of Sharaf al-Dawla. Even so, the patronage of Fakhr al-Dawla (366-87/977-97) supported the solar observations of al-Khudjandī [*q.v.*] (d. 390/1000) carried out in Rayy with the help of a large sextant called *al-sudus al-fakhrī*. The Buwayhids' example must obviously have awakened a desire to emulate it among members of other dynasties, and this was the case with the Kākwayhid ᶜAlāʾ al-Dawla Muḥammad (d. 433/1041-2) who supplied Ibn Sīnā [*q.v.*] (370-428/980-1037), with funds to carry out observations of the planets in Hamadān around 414/1023-4, and with Maḥmūd of Ghazna (d. 421/1030), under whose patronage al-Bīrūnī [*q.v.*] (362-442/973-1050) also made certain observations and wrote a main part of his astronomical work.

From the 4th/10th century onwards, observations began to take place further west. In Egypt, there emerges the remarkable figure of Ibn Yūnus (d. 399/1009), despite the fact that the account according to which this astronomer is said to have had at his disposal a well-equipped observatory, thanks to the patronage of the Fāṭimid caliph al-Ḥākim (386-411/996-1021), appears entirely legendary; he probably had at his disposal only a private observatory, although a number of his observations (described in the introduction to his *zīdj*) were carried out in various places in the town between 367/977 (or 380/990) and

398/1007), such that we may assume that he used essentially portable instruments and obtained excellent results. In al-Andalus, the first observations known from documents are those of Maslama al-Madjrīṭī [*q.v.*] (d. *ca.* 398/1107; see J. Vernet and M. A. Catalá, *Las obras matemáticas de Maslama de Madrid*, in *al-And.*, xxx [1965], 15-47; repr. in *Estudios sobre historia de la ciencia medieval*, Barcelona-Bellaterra 1979, 241-71), while far more remarkable work in this respect was carried out by Azarquiel/al-Zarḳālī (d. 493/1100), of whom we know that, with the assistance of several collaborators, he made observations of the sun, moon and fixed stars for more than 25 years, first in Toledo, then in Cordoba (J. M. Millás-Vallicrosa, *Estudios sobre Azarquiel*, Madrid-Granada 1943-50, 279); yet there does not seem to be any proof of an organised observatory.

The observatory as an institution, if not permanent, at least longer lasting than the examples mentioned until now, seems to be an Eastern development dating from the later Middle Ages. The most obvious antecedent, although not well-known, is the observatory founded by Malik Shāh (465-85/1072-92) around 467/1074, perhaps in Iṣfahān and where ʿUmar al-Khayyām [*q.v.*] (440-526/1048-1131), in collaboration with other astronomers, completed a *zīdj* and effected the reform of the Persian solar calendar [see further, DJALĀLĪ]. This observatory stayed active for about 18 years, until the death of the ruler, whose son, Sandjar b. Malik Shāh, patronised the planetary observations carried out in Marw by al-Khāzinī (between about 509 and 530/1115-35). With regard to the observatory of Malik Shāh, there appears for the first time the idea that the minimum time necessary to complete a programme of observations is 30 years (a revolution of Saturn). Naṣīr al-Dīn al-Ṭūsī [*q.v.*] (597-672/1201-74) was to recall this minimum period in the course of his negotations with the Mongol sultan Hülegü with a view to creating the Marāgha observatory; facing resistance from the ruler, the astronomer agreed to complete the same work in twelve years (a revolution of Jupiter). In the 9th/15th century, al-Kāshī (d. 833/1429), the principal astronomer of the Samarḳand observatory, was also to speak of a minimum period of between 10 and 15 years.

Hülegü Khān (d. 663/1265) founded, at the suggestion of Naṣīr al-Dīn al-Ṭūsī, the Marāgha observatory, on a hill situated near the town. It is the first large-scale Islamic observatory whose organisation and structure we know about in detail; it contained several buildings, including a residence for Hülegü, a mosque and a rich library (the sources speak of 400,000 volumes, which is a traditional figure). It had large-size instruments and was financed by the official revenues of pious foundations (*awḳāf*); this is the first time that we see an observatory subsidised in a manner ordinarily reserved for schools, hospitals and libraries. The motives behind this undertaking seem to have been, for Hülegü, basically astrological. The most important astronomers of the age, whose names are mainly associated with important modifications to the Ptolemaic system and undertakings, before the observatory's foundation, by Muʾayyad al-Dīn al-ʿUrḍī (d. 666/1266; see the work of G. Saliba, in *JHAS*, iii [1979], 3-18 and iv [1980], 220-34, and in *Isis*, lxx [1979], 571-6), participated in the observatory's work. Outstanding among them, apart from al-Ṭūsī and al-ʿUrḍī, are Muḥyī 'l-Dīn al-Maghribī (d. between 680 and 690/1281-91) and Ḳuṭb al-Dīn al-Shīrāzī [*q.v.*] (634-710/1236-1311). The observatory, founded in 657/1259, survived Hülegü. On the death of al-Ṭūsī (672/1274), the *Zīdj-i īlkhānī* had already been composed, i.e. some astronomical tables which constitute the basic result of the work completed in Marāgha. The observations thus lasted more than 12 years, and we know that they were pursued after al-Ṭūsī's death, until the end of the period of 30 years corresponding to a revolution of Saturn: following these new observations (around 672-703/1274-1304) some corrections were made to the *Zīdj-i īlkhānī*. It seems, on the other hand, that there was some activity at the observatory until around 715/1316 and that it was in ruins in 740/1339. So it was the first Islamic observatory to enjoy a remarkable longevity (55 or 60 years) and give birth not only to al-Ṭūsī's *zīdj* but also to that of Muḥyī 'l-Dīn al-Maghribī.

Marāgha provided a model for several imitations among which may be cited the observatory of Sham (a suburb of Tabrīz) which was built by the ruler Ghāzān Khān (694-703/1295-1304) and survived 15 or 16 years (*ca.* 701-17/1300-17). However, no observatory of the size of that at Marāgha appears before the 9th/15th century. Thanks to the patronage of the great prince Ulugh Beg [*q.v.*], governor of the Samarḳand region, in 823/1420 an important *madrasa* was founded in that town. It specialised in the teaching of astronomy at the heart of what constituted the nucleus of a scientific circle frequented by Ulugh Beg, who was himself a mathematician and astronomer of note (see A. Sayılı, *A letter by al-Kâshî on Ulugh Bey's scientific circle in Samarquand*, in *Actes du IXe Congrès Intern. d'Hist. des Sciences*, Barcelona-Paris 1960, ii, 586-91; E.S. Kennedy, *A letter of Jamshīd al-Kāshī to his father. Scientific research and personalities at a fifteenth century court*, in *Orientalia*, xxix [1960], 191-213, republ. in *idem* (ed.), *Studies in the Islamic exact sciences*, Beirut 1983, 722-44). It was in this same year that the observatory of Samarḳand was to be founded, situated on a hill near to the town, consisting of several buildings and equipped with huge instruments such as a large meridian axis, remains of which were excavated in 1908. The principal astronomers who made observations in Samarḳand were Ghiyāth al-Dīn al-Kāshī [*q.v.*] (d. *ca.* 833/1429), Ḳāḍīzāda al-Rūmī (d. between 840 and 850/1436-46) and ʿAlī b. Muḥammad al-Ḳūshdjī (d. 879/1474). Ulugh Beg was assassinated in 853/1449, but the observatory continued to function under his son and successor ʿAbd al-Laṭīf, and the building remained standing for the 50 years which followed the death of its founder. Some systematic observations were carried out there, at least during the key period of 30 years, and it was then that the *Zīdj-i gurgānī* or *zīdj* of Ulugh Beg was prepared (see L. Sédillot, *Prolégomènes des tables astronomiques d'Oloug Beg*, Paris 1847, 1853).

The Samarḳand observatory was twice imitated, firstly in the 10th/16th century, in Istanbul, where Taḳī 'l-Dīn b. Maʿrūf b. Aḥmad (932-93/1525-85) founded one in 982/1575 thanks to the patronage of Sultan Murād III (982-1004/1574-95); the building was completed in 985/1577. This establishment is said to have been a large observatory in a category analogous to those of Marāgha and Samarḳand, but an unfortunate astrological prediction about a comet carried out by Taḳī 'l-Dīn in this same year 985/1577, as well as the hostility of the most conservative sectors of society, made the sultan order the destruction of the buildings in 988/1580.

The last large Islamic observatories are those which were founded by Djay Singh (Savai Jayasiṁha II), *mahāradjā* of Ambēr from 1111/1699 (d. 1156/1743) who, wishing to bring up to date the astronomy of his time, dedicated himself to collecting manuscripts of Sanskrit, Persian and Arabic astronomical works, as well as European printed books of astronomy (D. Pingree, *Islamic astronomy in Sanskrit*, in *JHAS*, ii [1978], 315-30; D. A. King, *A handlist of the Arabic and Persian astronomical manuscripts in the Maharaja Mansingh II Library in Jaipur*, in *ibid.*, iv [1980], 81-6). Not satisfied with the results obtained with the *zīdj*s of Ulugh Beg and Ibn al-Shāṭir (705-77/1306-75), he constructed five observatories in Djaypūr (the capital which he had founded in 1141/1728), Dihlī, Banāras, Mathurā and Udjdjayn. Those of Banāras and Mathurā seem to have been built after 1147/1734. These observatories were equipped with large metal and stone instruments (the stone ones are mostly still standing), conforming to their models in Marāgha and Samarḳand. Djay Singh also patronised the preparation of astronomical tables with rules in Persian, which were dedicated to the Mughal Emperor Muḥammad Shāh in 1141/1728 and were given the title *Zīdj-i djadīd-i Muḥammad Shāhī*. This *zīdj* was later to be rewritten (the introduction was written after 1147/1734) and we are not clear as to their relationship with the work carried out in the observatories, which were abandoned on the death of their founder (see G. R. Kaye, *The astronomical observatories of Jai Singh*, Memoirs of the Archeological Survey of India. Imperial series, Calcutta 1918, repr. Varanasi 1973; *idem, A guide to the old Observatories at Delhi, Jaipur, Ujjain and Benares*, Calcutta 1920; W. A. Blanpied, *The astronomical program of Raja Sawai Jai Singh II and its historical context*, in *Jap. Stud. Hist. of Science*, xiii [1974], 87-126).

Bibliography: Given in the article. The basic monograph which has been quite extensively drawn upon is the work of A. Sayılı, *The observatory in Islam and its place in the general history of the observatory*, Ankara 1960. On the connections between observatories and *zīdj*s, see E. S. Kennedy, *A survey of Islamic astronomical tables*, in *Transactions of the American Philosophical Society*, N.S., xlvi (Philadelphia 1956), 123-75; A. Bausani, *The observatory of Marāghe*, in *Quaderni del Seminario di iranistica*, ix (Venice 1982), 125-51. (J. Samsó)

al-**MARṢAFĪ**, al-Ḥusayn, Egyptian scholar and teacher (1815-90) from a family originating from the village of Marṣafā, near Banha; his father taught at the al-Azhar Mosque. Al-Ḥusayn became blind at the age of three; however, he underwent the programme of studies usual for boys destined to teach at al-Azhar and reached the rank of master in 1840-5. He was remarkable for the interest that he showed in his classes in belles-lettres, something rare among teachers at that period in Egypt. In 1872, ʿAlī Pasha Mubārak [*q.v.*] Minister of Public Education, appointed him professor of Arabic linguistic disciplines in the Dār al-ʿUlūm [*q.v.*], the school that he founded for teachers, with a more modern orientation than al-Azhar. Al-Marṣafī taught there until 1888. His importance as a teacher and author stems from the fact that he is regarded as the first to have formulated what was to become the attempt at a renaissance (*nahḍa*) in regard to literature. His lectures were first published in the review *Rawḍat al-Madāris*, then in a separate work, *al-Wasīla al-adabiyya ilā ʾl-ʿulūm al-ʿarabiyya* (i, 216 + 7 pp., 1289/1875; ii, 704 pp., 1292/1879); a second work on the art of writing remains unpublished: *Dalīl al-mustarshid fī fann al-inshāʾ*; it was described and analysed by Muḥammad ʿAbd al-Djawād in his study on al-Marṣafī (see *Bibl.*).

The thought of Ḥusayn al-Marṣafī is entirely favourable to the spread of the European "enlightenment"; in this he is very close to men such as Rifāʿa al-Ṭahṭāwī [*q.v.*] and ʿAlī Mubārak, who enlivened the new schools' system founded and developed in Egypt by Muḥammad ʿAlī [*q.v.*] and his successors. A revival of the art of writing (*inshāʾ*) is necessary for the use of the élite of modern Egypt, after the centuries of decadence, and in view of the catastrophic situation of this art in the 19th century. Al-Marṣafī takes as his guide Ibn Khaldūn, in the chapters of his *Muḳaddima* where he speaks of teaching language and belles-lettres; in *al-Wasīla*, he presents both a synthetic, clear account of the disciplines of the Arabic language (*lugha, ṣarf, naḥw, balāgha, badīʿ, ʿarūḍ* [*q.vv.*]), stripped of the commentaries and glosses which until then almost always accompanied them, and also a choice of relatively numerous examples, referring especially to Umayyad and ʿAbbāsid prose. Al-Marṣafī's teaching was regarded as formulating the general programme to be followed, if one wished to revive Arabic language and letters, by a great number of Egyptian writers and teachers who had a diffuse but effective influence on the educational system. The best known are ʿAbd Allāh Fikrī and Ḥifnī Nāṣif. This programme for reviving the language was gradually spread through almost all the Arab countries—with or without reference to al-Marṣafī—from the last years of the 19th century, thanks to the efforts of the reformists [see iṣlāḥ. i and muḥammad ʿabduh].

Al-Marsafī was also interested in the history of political ideas; in October 1881, he published an essay, the *Risālat al-Kalim al-thamān* (Cairo 68 pp.) on eight words of political vocabulary in frequent use, he said, in modern debates; *umma*, nation or community according to language, territory or religion; *waṭan*, fatherland; *ḥukūma*, government; *ʿadl*, justice; *ẓulm*, injustice; *siyāsa*, politics; *ḥurriyya*, liberty; and *tarbiya*, education. If it is read in the light of the debates of the time, his position appears to be that of a moderate, an advocate of a reasonable modernity, legitimised by constant reference to moral and cultural examples from the glorious ages of Islam; the author seems reserved and anxious about the haste of some (doubtless the partisans of ʿUrābī, officers, groups of intellectuals and notables) who would like to modify institutions prematurely to create a true parliamentarianism. The matter of greatest urgency for al-Marṣafī is the spreading among the élite as well as the masses of a reformed education (*tarbiya, adab*), modern in some of its forms, but based on an Islam whose faith and practices would be purified of the innovations (*bidaʿ*, sing. *bidʿa* [*q.v.*]) accumulated during the ages of decadence. This essay was re-published in 1903 by Muḥammad Masʿūd, one of the men involved in editing al-*Muʾayyad*, the journal with a moderate Islamic bias run by Shaykh ʿAlī Yūsuf; this is an indication that he could still represent those expressing a moderate, stable opinion.

Bibliography: Muḥammad ʿAbd al-Djawād, *al-Shaykh al-Ḥusayn al-Marṣafī*, Cairo 1952, 160 p.; G. Delanoue, *Moralistes et politiques musulmans dans l'Egypte du XIXᵉ siècle (1798-1882)*, Cairo 1982, ii, 357-79, 650-1; for the political debates of the period, see A. Schölch, *Ägypten den Ägyptern! Die politische und gesellschaftliche Krise der Jahre 1878-1882 in Ägypten*, Zürich-Fribourg 1973 (Eng. tr. *Egypt for the Egyptians! The socio-political crisis in Egypt 1878-82*, London 1981). (G. Delanoue)

MARTHIYA or *marthāt* (A., pl. *marāthī*) "elegy", a poem composed in Arabic (or in an Islamic language following the Arabic tradition) to lament the passing of a beloved person and to celebrate his merits; *ri*<u>*th*</u>*ā*ʾ, from the same root, denotes both lamentation and the corresponding literary genre.

1. In Arabic literature.

The origin of the *mar*<u>*th*</u>*iya* may be found in the rhymed and rhythmic laments going with the ritual movements performed as a ritual around the funeral cortège by female relatives of the deceased, before this role became the prerogative of professional female mourners (cf. M. Gaudefroy-Demombynes, *Ibn Qotaiba. Introduction au Livre de la poésie et des poètes*, Paris 1947, pp. xvii-xviii). It was in fact customary for the mother, a sister or a daughter of the deceased, originally perhaps with the intention of appeasing his soul, and in any event as a means of perpetuating his renown, to commemorate his noble qualities and exploits and to express the grief of the family and the tribal group, in a short piece composed in *sa*<u>*dj*</u>ᶜ, normalisation in verse form being a later development. These improvisations, probably of a rather stereotyped nature, have not been handed down to posterity, but one fairly scanty specimen (see J. Wellhausen, *Skizzen und Vorarbeiten*, i, 1884, 47), said to be the work of the mother of Taʾabbaṭa <u>Sh</u>arr[an] [*q.v.*] has survived.

With the transition from *sa*<u>*dj*</u>ᶜ to verse, it seems that women retained their role in the lamentation and the celebration of the deceased, and there are many *marā*<u>*th*</u>*ī* traditionally credited to more or less obscure pre-Islamic poetesses; outstanding examples are Da<u>kh</u>tanūs, mourning the death of her father Laḳīṭ b. Zurāra [*q.v.*] in the <u>Sh</u>iᶜb <u>D</u>jabala (*A*<u>*gh*</u>*ānī*, ed. Beirut, xi, 137-8) and al-<u>Kh</u>irniḳ, who was responsible for a number of elegies, most of them concerning her brother Ṭarafa [*q.v.*] and her husband, preserved by the *ruwāt* (see L. Cheikho, <u>*Sh*</u>*u* ᶜ*arā*ʾ *al-Naṣrāniyya*, 321-7); the most renowned is unquestionably al-<u>Kh</u>ansāʾ [*q.v.*], who gave *ri*<u>*th*</u>*ā*ʾ a polished form and to this very day enjoys unanimous admiration (see N. Rhodokanskis, *al-Ḫansāʾ und ihre Trauerlieder*, Vienna 1904).

In the early years of Islam, Laylā al-A<u>kh</u>yaliyya [*q.v.*] enhanced her reputation with elegies, much appreciated by local critics, in which she mourns the death of Tawba b. al-Ḥumayyir (*A*<u>*gh*</u>*ānī*, ed. Beirut, xi, 212-20) and even that of ᶜU<u>th</u>mān b. ᶜAffān (Ibn Ḳutayba, <u>*Sh*</u>*i*ᶜ*r*, ed. Cairo, ii, 123, 417-8). On account of their extreme sensivity (and, according to Ibn Ra<u>sh</u>īḳ, ᶜ*Umda*, ii, 123, their low capacity for endurance), women are able to express unreservedly their grief at the death of a member of the family and to celebrate merits which ultimately reflect upon the entire group; they give to their compositions a passionate tone of such intensity and spontaneity that the expert connoisseur of Arabic poetry, Père Cheikho, did not hesitate to gather together the more or less authentic works of these poetesses in his *Riyāḍ al-adab fī marā*<u>*th*</u>*ī* <u>*sh*</u>*awā*ᶜ*ir al-*ᶜ*Arab*, Beirut 1897.

Men were also active in this area, and without entirely taking the place of women, composed verse pieces of various lengths which offer variations on the common themes. It is worthy of note that a number of pre-Islamic poets, Mutammim b. Nuwayra [*q.v.*] for example, owe their reputations almost entirely to their elegies, and that among the four compositions regarded as most successful by the critics, there figures, alongside the *marā*<u>*th*</u>*ī* of Ibn al-Rūmī, al-<u>Sh</u>arīf al-Raḍī and Mihyār al-Daylamī (see below), an ᶜ*ayniyya* which has become proverbial (although it is probably in part apocryphal on account of the Ḳurʾānic influence discernible in it) by a poet of the last years of the <u>D</u>jāhiliyya, Labīd [*q.v.*], who mourns his half-brother Arbad, killed by lightning (Ibn Ḳutayba, <u>*Sh*</u>*i*ᶜ*r*, ed. Cairo, 236-7; *A*<u>*gh*</u>*ānī*, ed. Beirut, xv, 300-1). Some authors, no doubt sensitive to the sincere expression of profound emotions, go so far as to place the *marā*<u>*th*</u>*ī* of the Bedouin above their other poetic works; al-<u>D</u>jāḥiẓ (*Bayān*, ed. Hārūn, ii, 320) quotes without comment the reply given by one of them when asked why their elegies were the best of their poems: "Because we speak [our verses], as our hearts burn [with grief]". This affirmation of the sincerity and the poignancy of their feelings does not however explain the fact (judging from the texts currently available, which probably reflect the true position) that these poets continue to refrain from expressing their sorrow at the death of a mother, a wife, a daughter or a sister (the lines of a Bedouin on his wife in the ᶜ*Iḳd* of Ibn ᶜAbd Rabbih, ed. Cairo 1348/1926, ii, 181, are perhaps of a later date).

In fact, it is to a male parent or member of the group that the *marā*<u>*th*</u>*ī* are addressed; the intention is to exalt the deceased by presenting his death as a loss felt by the entire clan or tribe; there is, on the other hand, the hope of continuing to benefit from his protection, and to this end he is implored not to go far away (*lā tab*ᶜ*ad*; the reading *lā tab*ᶜ*ud*, in *LA*, root *b*ᶜ*d*, is inappropriate since it would mean "do not perish"), he is promised revenge if he has been a victim of murder, and there are forceful expressions of hatred for his enemies. In spite of the repetition, in the prologue, of clichés and hackneyed themes ("weep, mine eye"; the impossibility, since the event, of finding sleep; etc.), the lyrical passages are not of a solely conventional nature, and images of some originality are sometimes to be found.

In the guise of consolation, the themes of lamentation and eulogy are supplemented by a *leitmotif* concerning the unavoidable and irreparable nature of death. The fact that nobody, neither man nor animal, is capable of escaping it, is sometimes illustrated by the imagery of the hunt; outstanding examples are three episodes inserted in the masterpiece ascribed to the *mu*<u>*kh*</u>*aḍram* poet Abū <u>Dh</u>uʾayb [*q.v.*], a sixty-seven verse elegy of questionable authenticity in which the poet mourns the passing, in the same year (or the same day), of five of his sons, in variously described circumstances (see *Dīwān al-Hu*<u>*dh*</u>*aliyyīn*, Cairo 1384/1965, i, 1-21).

It might be expected that a radical change would affect the concept of the *mar*<u>*th*</u>*iya* following the birth of Islam, but the teachings of the Ḳurʾān inspire only minor additions and slight differences in tone which do not significantly alter the content of the poems, except perhaps where the author mourns the death of a group rather than that of an individual or members of the same family. During the wars and expeditions which took place in the lifetime of the Prophet, there were many poets, in both camps, who mourned the deaths of their comrades and hurled defiance at their adversaries. This applies, for example, to Ḍirār b. al-<u>Kh</u>aṭṭāb, giving to the Ḳuray<u>sh</u>ites notice of the death of Abū <u>D</u>jahl [*q.v.*] at Badr and calling upon his fellow-tribesmen to avenge him (Ibn Hi<u>sh</u>ām, *Sīra*, ed. Saḳḳā *et alii*, ii, 27-8), also to Umayya b. Abi 'l-Ṣalt [*q.v.*] who, after the same battle, mourns the Ḳuray<u>sh</u>ites slain by the Muslims, against whom he likewise incites the members of his tribe (*Sīra*, ii, 30-3; Ibn ᶜAbd Rabbih, ᶜ*Iḳd*, Cairo 1346/1928, ii, 194-5); the Prophet is said to have forbidden the circulation of this poem (*A*<u>*gh*</u>*ānī*, ed. Beirut, iv, 126). Jewish poets did not hesitate to lament the massacre of their co-religionists and to threaten their enemies (e.g. Sammāk, in *Sīra*, ii, 198, 200, after the death of Kaᶜb b. al-A<u>sh</u>raf [*q.v.*]).

Compositions of this type are sometimes ripostes addressed to Muslim poets, who were not slow to reply in their turn; the *Sīra* echoes these exchanges, while it gives prominence to the poems of Muslims, significant among whom are Kaᶜb b. Mālik, Ibn Rawāḥa and in particular Ḥassān b. Thābit [*q.vv.*]. The *Dīwān* of the last-named contains a number of *marāthī* inspired by the death of Ḥamza b. ᶜAbd al-Muṭṭalib [*q.v.*], also by the deaths of the combatants who fell at Biᵓr Maᶜūna and at Muᵓta (*Dīwān*, ed. W. ᶜArafāt, *GMS*, xxv/1, London 1971, respectively 321, 450 and 504 (?); 207; 98, 295, 323). Among some thirty elegies which figure in this *Dīwān*, it is to be noted that one of them (234) breaks with tradition in that it concerns the poet's daughter, that two or possibly three, where Ḳurᵓānic inspiration is more clearly discernible, are dedicated to the Prophet (269, 272, 455), one to Abū Bakr (125), two to ᶜUmar (273, 499), eight to ᶜUthmān (96, 120, 122, 311, 319, 320, 511) and the others to various individuals, but a large part of this enormous composition is definitely apocryphal. In general, it may be said that the difference between the works of the early Muslim poets and those of their pagan predecessors consists in the fact that they refrain from calling for vengeance and confine themselves to promising the fires of Hell to their adversaries killed in combat, while they stress the consolation gained by the certain knowledge that the Muslims who have achieved the status of martyrdom are already in Paradise (e.g. Ḥassān, *Dīwān*, 338, vv. 17-18; tr. R. Blachère, in *HLA*, 432). The expression *ṣallā l-ilāh ᶜalā...* "May God bestow his blessing upon (the deceased)" would also appear to be characteristic. To all these elements, and to the eulogy addressed to the departed, there is added a sense of the superiority of Islam, a concept belonging to the *mufākhara* [*q.v.*] which to some extend takes the place of the glorification of the group typical of the work of pre-Islamic poets.

Thus *rithāᵓ* may become an instrument of politico-religious propaganda. Following the defeat of the pagans, it is the opponents of established authority, Shīᶜīs and Khāridjīs, who make use of it. Conversely, the Umayyads and, later, the ᶜAbbāsids, also have recourse to this medium, in their case as a means of self-defence. In a brief survey it is impossible to take account of all the poems inspired by dramatic incidents such as the execution, for the crime of proclaiming his Shīᶜī beliefs in Mecca, of a certain Khandaḳ (see the two eulogies dedicated to him by Kuthayyir [*q.v.*] in *Aghānī*, ed. Beirut, xii, 170-1, 173-5; *Dīwān*, ed. H. Pérès, ii, 148-54, 156-66). The assassination of ᶜAlī b. Abī Ṭālib understandably gave rise, over the centuries, to a considerable number of *marāthī*, but a drama which deeply affected the Shīᶜī poets was the murder of his son al-Ḥusayn and his companions at Karbalāᵓ [*q.v.*]; this tragic event, which later inspired the emergence of the genre known as the "passion play" (*taᶜziya* [*q.v.*]) has been evoked by poets relatively close, chronologically, to the deed itself, for example, al-Aᶜshā of Hamdān [*q.v.*] (see R. Geyer, *K. al-Ṣubḥ al-munīr*, London 1928, no. 5); one Ibn al-Aḥmar author of a piece on the episode (a piece of popular verse? see R. Blachère, *HLA*, 514); Sulaymān b. Ḳatta (see Muṣᶜab al-Zubayrī, *Nasab Ḳuraysh*, 41; al-Masᶜūdī, *Murūdj*, § 1910 and ref.); al-Sayyid al-Ḥimyarī [*q.v.*], who hopes that the grave of the martyr will be well-tended, according to the pure pre-Islamic tradition (*Dīwān*, Beirut, n.d., 470-2) or even Muslim b. Ḳutayba (*Murūdj*, § 1906); the tradition was preserved by later poets, the most prominent being Diᶜbil (*Shiᶜr Diᶜbil*, ed. Ashtar, Damascus 1384/1964, 141) and al-Sharīf al-Raḍī [*q.v.*], who appeals for vengeance in five lengthy and highly-regarded poems. Diᶜbil [*q.v.*] bemoans the fate of the Ahl al-Bayt [*q.v.*] in a poem which has enjoyed wide acclaim (rhyme *-ātī*, metre *ṭawīl*; *op. laud.*, 71-7), while in his *rithāᵓ*, al-Riḍā takes the opportunity to recall the misfortunes of members of the Prophet's family, celebrating their merits and abusing their enemies rhyme *-arī*, metre *basīṭ*; (*op. laud.*, 110-13). However, the *Maḳātil al-Ṭālibiyyīn* of Abu 'l-Faradj al-Iṣfahānī (Cairo 1949, ²1970) constitutes a long lament studded with verses borrowed from various elegies. Contrary to these, one may point out the poem of al-Ṣanawbarī (d. *ca.* 334/945-6 [*q.v.*]) on the pilgrims killed by the Carmathians [see ḲARMAṬĪ] in 317/930 discussed and translated by C.E. Bosworth in *Arabica*, xix/3 (1972), 222-39.

The Khāridjīs, far from mourning the losses that they have suffered, celebrate their dead in often-improvised pieces, rejoicing in the idea that the slain have earned the palm of martyrdom in the course of heroic action and include in their poetry passages from the Ḳurᵓān which testify to their religious fervour (see Iḥsān ᶜAbbās, *Shiᶜr al-Khawāridj*, Beirut 1963, 32-3, 79 and *passim*).

To a certain extent, these compositions are reminiscent, with the sincerity of the feelings expressed, of the *marāthī* of the Bedouin. The latter are also perpetuated in the works of the major poets of the Umayyad era; thus some twenty elegies of classical construction are to be found in the *Dīwān* of al-Farazdaḳ [*q.v.*] and in that of Djarīr [*q.v.*]; the latter, however, breaks with tradition—much to the indignation of the former (*Dīwān*, ed. Ṣāwī, Cairo 1354/1936, 465-74, in particular 471)—in devoting several verses to the death of his wife Khālida, at the beginning of a rather mixed but nonetheless moving poem (*Dīwān*, ed. Ṣāwī, Cairo n.d., 199-210; tr. Blachère, *HLA*, 579); it is for mourning the passing of a woman and not for expressing his own grief that al-Farazdaḳ rebukes Djarīr, for he himself has no scruples about lamenting the demise of his father (*Dīwān*, 210, 611, 674, 676) and of his two sons (270-3, 764-5, 885-6), besides various individuals and the victims of an epidemic (491). It is nevertheless possible to discern the presence of a number of women among the departed loved ones of poets (see e.g. Ibn ᶜAbd Rabbih, *ᶜIḳd*, ed. Cairo 1346/1928, ii, 179-81; Abu Tammām, *Ḥamāsa*, Cairo n.d., i, 380: poetry of a certain Mālik/Muwaylik al-Mazmūm), and at a slightly later date a Muslim b. al-Walīd [*q.v.*] is observed refusing to drink wine after the death of his wife, an event which he evokes in a few discreet verses (*Dīwān*, ed. S. Dahhān, Cairo n.d., 341).

The 2nd/8th century sees the birth of the poetic genre known as "ascetic poems" (*zuhdiyyāt* [*q.v.*]), which involves reflection on death and no doubt influences *rithāᵓ*, in which gnomic themes, present since the pre-Islamic period, become increasingly numerous. Abū Nuwās [*q.v.*], himself the author of *zuhdiyyāt* (see ᶜA.A. al-Zubaydī, *Zuhdiyyāt Abī Nuwās*, Cairo 1959), has left no less than twenty *marāthī* in memory of distinguished persons, scholars and poets, friends and parents (although in some cases the individuals mourned were not yet dead), and even including himself (*Dīwān*, ed. Ghazālī, Cairo 1953, 572-95; cf. E. Wagner, *Abū Nuwās*, Wiesbaden 1965, 349-60). It is often, in fact, the natural or violent death of an eminent person, the death in battle of an acquaintance or the demise of a distinguished scholar which inspires the poets. Thus Ibn Durayd [*q.v.*] writes funeral orations for al-Shāfiʿī and al-Ṭabarī [*q.vv.*] and for his relatives slain in battle, demanding that they be avenged (*Dīwān*, ed. Ibn Sālim (A. Ben Salem), Tunis 1973, 67-72, 89-97). Being unable to revive the classic themes, the poets of the 3rd/9th century concentrate their efforts on the form, but they are not the first to act in this manner, since the fact that many of their predecessors, beginning with Ḥassān, dedicated more than one elegy to the same person would seem to prove that they were at pains to revise their compositions. Nevertheless, we may still find some masterly works which are appreciated by Arab critics. Ibn al-Rūmī [*q.v.*], in his *marāthī*, allows his sentiments to overflow, gives expression to his sensivity and develops his own philosophy of existence; in particular, he mourns his wife, his mother, his brother, his sons (see *Dīwān*, ed. K. Kaylānī, Cairo 1924, 13, 80, 97, 104, 224, 326, 351), and his *dāliyya* (*ibid.*, 29) on the death of his younger son is regarded as one of the finest examples of the genre.

It is worth noting in passing that from the 2nd/8th century onwards, even more so from the 3rd/9th century onwards, a new form becomes frequent, the letter of condolence (*taʿziya* [*q.v.*]) addressed to the parents of the deceased; when it is in verse, it is virtually indistinguishable from the *marthiya* proper, but it is often written in prose (see e.g. Ibn ʿAbd Rabbih, *ʿIkd*, ed. cit., ii, 197-202), even when produced by the pen of poets like Ibn al-Muʿtazz [*q.v.*] (see al-Ṣūlī, *Awrāḳ*, ii, 288 ff.), and it should be noted that at least one writer composed a true *marthiya* in prose form; in fact, in the course of his campaign aimed at opposing the supremacy of poetic composition in Arabic literature, al-Djāḥiẓ [*q.v.*] wrote a long *risāla* on the death of Abū Ḥarb al-Ṣaffār in which free prose, albeit blended with poetic reminiscence, permits an extent of detail and an expression of feelings which the constraints of metre would render impossible (ed. Ṭ. al-Ḥādjirī, in *al-Kātib al-Miṣrī*, iii/9 [1946], 38-44; translated in Pellat, *The life and works of Jāḥiẓ*, 116-24 = *Arabische Geisteswelt*, 187-97).

The theorists of poetry (Ḳudāma, *Naḳd al-shiʿr*, ed. S. A. Bonebakker, Leiden 1956, 49-55; Ibn Rashīḳ *ʿUmda*, ii, 117-26; etc.) do not give inordinate attention to the *marthiya*, essentially because they regard it as comparable with panegyric [see MADĪḤ], in the sense that it is a celebration of one or several individuals. It is in fact a kind of bipartite *ḳaṣīda* [*q.v.*], of which the dominant characteristic is the absence of the *nasīb* [*q.v.*] which would in effect have been out of place. There exist, however, a few exceptions, of which the most significant is a *ḳaṣīda* by Durayd b. al-Ṣimma [*q.v.*] where he mourns the death of a murdered brother (in *Aṣmaʿiyyāt*, ed. Ahlwardt, Leipzig 1902, 23-4); however, Ibn Rashīḳ (*ʿUmda*, ii, 121-2) justifies this deviation from the rule on the grounds that the poem was composed a year after the murder and that in the meantime the victim had been avenged. Further examples are supplied by Ibn al-Zibaʿrā (*Sīra*, ii, 141-2), al-Aʿshā of Hamdān and a few others.

Laments over the remains of an abandoned encampment are thus replaced by a prologue, in which sorrow ignites and tears flow freely, also by more or less banal observations concerning the fragility of human life, the cruelty of destiny (*dahr*), the patience (*ṣabr*) which is necessary and always displayed, and other clichés among which the equivalents of "a single person is lacking and all is desolate" or "ubi sunt qui ante nos in mundo fuere" are not uncommon (see Becker, *Ubi sunt....*, *Festschrift E. Kuhn*, Munich 1916, 87-105; M. Lidzbarski, *Ubi sunt...*, in *Isl.* viii [1918], 300; cf. P. Keseling, *Ubi sunt...*, in *ibid.*, xvii [1928], 97-100). The *raḥīl* is similarly omitted, sometimes being replaced by an account of the circumstances of the death, especially of a violent death, but it is virtually impossible to delineate an overall scheme, since the various elements overlap one another, and reflections on death intrude on more than one occasion into the posthumous eulogy. The latter effectively resembles the *madīḥ*, to the point of confusion with it, not however without certain differences of detail. Ḳudāma (*op. laud.*, 49) in fact recommends the use of the past tense to indicate that the portrait drawn by the poet is no longer a present reality, not however saying, for example, "he was generous" but employing expressions such as "generosity has vanished", "after his passing, generosity is no more", etc. (this dictum does not inhibit Muḳātil b. ʿAṭiyya from saying of Niẓām al-Mulk "the vizier was (*kān*) a jewel...", al-Ibshīhī, *Mustaṭraf*, Cairo n.d., ii, 365). There is no rule that forbids lamentations over the destruction of an object (see below, with regard to cities) or the loss of an animal (the funeral eulogy of a cat figures in *Madjānī 'l-adab*, v, 135), and the poet is entitled to make reference to the sadness of Nature and of domestic animals; but he must beware of committing blunders, saying for example that a horse subjected by his master to harsh treatment in the course of his exploits is saddened by the latter's passing, whereas in fact this is for him liberation. It is the moral qualities of the deceased which should be celebrated: intelligence, courage, generosity, decency. Thus Ḳudāma approves particularly of three verses by Aws b. Ḥadjar [*q.v.*], who enumerates generosity, valour, energy, strength (or munificence, since the reading *al-tuḳā* cannot be accepted) and perspicacity (see the *Dīwān* of Aws, ed. M.Y. Nadjm, Beirut 1381/1960, 53-5). It need hardly be said that the poets do not restrict themselves to these qualities, but the rule enunciated by the critic proves that, even in the context of *rithāʾ*, spontaneity is bridled, or tends to be so. The anthologists of the Middle Ages (see *Bibl.*) reserve an important amount of space for *marāthī*, but, always inclined to include only poems which are to their own personal taste, they adopt a system which precludes an overall judgment of the real structure and content of compositions arranged separately and often in the form of brief fragments, quite insufficient to allow generalisation without excessive risk of error.

The disintegration of the ʿAbbāsid empire brought virtually no change to the various aspects of *marthiya*, which seems however to become more and more influenced by "professional" exigencies. It is at the beginning of the 5th/11th century that Mihyār al-Daylamī [*q.v.*] achieves renown with his successful *rithāʾ* of ʿAlī or of al-Ḥusayn (see *Dīwān*, Cairo 1344-50/1925-31, ii, 259-62, 367-70, iii, 109, etc.) and especially with the *mīmiyya* in which he mourns the death of his master al-Sharīf al-Raḍī (*Dīwān*, iii, 366-70), regarded as a masterpiece. Previously, the proliferation of provincial dynasties had increased the number of occasions for the composition of elegies of a nature more formal and elaborate than personal and spontaneous; a tendency which has already been seen to emerge takes on a definitive form in the work of al-Mutanabbī [*q.v.*], who revives the classical theme of destiny, pays tribute to the deceased and adds a panegyric in praise of an heir from whom he expects some reward, but without making mention of his own qualities (see R. Blachère, *Motanabbî*, 46, 119, 250). This is not unlike the approach to the family of the deceased noted by ᶜAlī Dj. al-Ṭāhir in the poetry of the Saldjūḳ period (*al-Shiᶜr al-ᶜarabī fi 'l-ᶜIrāḳ wa-bilād al-ᶜAdjam fi 'l-ᶜaṣr al-saldjūḳī*, Baghdād 1958-61, ii, 108-113). This author holds in high regard a *rāʾiyya* and a *ḳāfiyya* of al-Ṭughrāʾī [*q.v.*] dedicated, respectively, to the memory of a wife and of a concubine (see *Dīwān al-Ṭughrāʾī*, ed. ᶜA. Dj. al-Ṭāhir and Y. al-Djabūrī, Baghdād 1396/1976, 151-5, 264-5), and rightly criticises the *maṭlaᶜ* of the famous elegy of Djarīr (see above), who in his long *ḳaṣīda* manages to devote only a few verses to the memory of his wife. Otherwise, the *marthiya* continues to be largely conventional in character, and ᶜUmar Mūsā Bāshā (*Adab al-duwal al-mutatābiᶜa: ᶜuṣūr al-Zankiyyīn wa 'l-Ayyūbiyyīn wa 'l-Mamālīk*, Beirut 1386/1967, 579) finds nothing new that is worthy of note in traditional *rithāʾ*; he does however make one honourable exception in the case of Usāma Ibn Munḳidh [*q.v.*], who mourns, in a moving *ḳaṣīda*, the demise of members of his family who were victims of an earthquake at Shayzar (*Dīwān*, Cairo 1953, 304-5, 307-9). This same literary historian lays emphasis on the *marāthī* of Muslim warriors slain during the Crusades and is appreciative of certain poems by ᶜImād al-Dīn al-Iṣfahānī [*q.v.*] on the death of ᶜImād al-Dīn Zangī, the death of Nūr al-Dīn and in particular that of Ṣalāḥ al-Dīn (Abū Shāma, *K. al-Rawḍatayn*, Cairo 1287-8, i, 45-6, 244-5, ii, 215-6) which lack neither emotion nor vigour in the description of events (*Adab al-duwal al-mutatābiᶜa*, 505-12). As with the Khāridjīs of former times, warriors are impelled to seek the palm of martyrdom (*talab al-shahāda*) which is the supreme reward (cf. E. Sivan, *L'Islam et la Croisade*, Paris 1968, 62). But this is not the only theme to be developed by the poets of the period, who engage in a propaganda whose elements E. Sivan (*op. laud.*) has analysed on the basis of a meticulous study of the poetry of the time; they reveal their fear of seeing recaptured cities falling again into the hands of the Christians, criticise those in authority for not having foreseen the defeats and mourn the loss of places seized from the Muslims.

The characteristic feature of this type of *marthiya* is the introduction, as objects of lamentation, on the one hand, of cities destroyed or damaged by wars and conquests, on the other, of local dynasties which are overturned. Omissions excepted, the oldest specimen of this type is the long *ḳaṣīda* of 135 verses in which Abū Yaᶜḳūb al-Khuraymī [*q.v.*] describes in pathetic terms the desolation of Baghdād during the war which saw the confrontation between al-Amīn and his brother al-Maʾmūn (see al-Ṭabarī, iii, 873-80; *Dīwān al-Khuraymī*, ed. ᶜA. Dj. al-Ṭāhir and M. Dj. al-Muᶜaybid, Beirut 1971, 27-37); this poet is also the author of several interesting elegies, for his brother (*Dīwān*), 24), for Khuraym (40-4, 44-6, 55) and for his own son (56-8). Another well-known *ḳaṣīda* is the *mīmiyya* which begins, conventionally, with the evocation of sleeplessness and tears, and was dedicated by Ibn al-Rūmī to Baṣra, describing the condition of the town following its sacking by the Zandj (*Dīwān*, ed. K. Kaylānī, 419). The conquest of Baghdād by the Mongols and the death of the caliph al-Mustaᶜṣim were also to inspire compositions in similar vein, in particular two *ḳaṣīdas* in which Shams al-Dīn Maḥmūd al-Kūfī bewails the tragic fate of the capital (see Ibn Shākir al-Kutubī, *Fawāt*, ed. ᶜAbd al-Ḥamīd, Cairo n.d., i, 497-501).

Previous to this, in Ifrīḳiya, where traditional *rithāʾ* was extensively cultivated (and still by women; see Ḥ. Ḥ. ᶜAbd al-Wahhāb, *Shahīrāt al-Tūnisiyyāt*, Tunis 1353, 25), the invasion by the Banū Hilāl and the destruction of al-Ḳayrawān (Kairouan) gave rise to the composition of poems describing "the pitiable lot of the people of Kairouan, the ruin of the once glorious city, the emotion inspired by the disaster" (Ch. Bouyahia); the best-known of these poems are the work of poets contemporary with the events: Ibn Sharaf (in Ibn Bassām, *Dhakhīra*, iv/1, 177-9); Ibn Rashīḳ (*Dīwān*, ed. Yāghī, Beirut n.d., 204-12) and al-Ḥuṣrī (*Dīwān*, ed. M. Marzūkī and al-Djilānī b. al-Ḥādjdj Yaḥyā, Tunis 1963, 125-7); all three have been the object of a study by Ch. Bouyahia, in *La vie littéraire en Ifriqiya sous les Zirides*, Tunis 1972, 332-40.

In al-Andalus, where the tradition of classical *rithāʾ* remained strong and vigorous, it is again the collapse of dynasties and the loss of towns to the Christians during the *reconquista* which inspire poems much appreciated by critics and enthusiasts. Quite apart from descriptions of the dramatic events in Cordova during the *fitna* which preceded the fall of the Umayyads (such as e.g. Ibn Shuhayd, *Dīwān*, ed. Pellat, Beirut 1963, 64-6 (authenticity of attribution suspect), 154-6, vv. 54 ff.) and from a series of elegies collected by H. Pérès (*Poésie andalouse*, 99 ff.), notably those by Ibn al-Ghassāl on the conquest of Barbastro by a Norman army, by al-Waḳḳāshī (preserved in a Spanish translation only) on the conquest of Valencia by the Christians (to the references in Pérès, 107 add A. R. Nykl, *La elegía árabe de Valencia*, in *Hispanic Review*, viii [1940], 9-17) or by Ibn Khafādja [*q.v.*] on the burning of that city by the Cid, three poems deserve particular attention. The first comes from the pen of Ibn al-Labbāna [*q.v.*] and concerns the exile of al-Muᶜtamid and the end of the ᶜAbbādids (in Ibn Khāḳān, *Ḳalāʾid al-ᶜiḳyān*, ed. Paris, 25-6; cf. 32-5); the second was composed by Ibn ᶜAbdūn [*q.v.*] after the fall of the Afṭasids, and the historical allusions which it contains inspired Ibn Badrūn to compile a lengthy commentary on it (ed. Dozy, Leiden 1846); finally, the greatest significance is accorded to the *nūniyya* of al-Sharīf al-Rundī (d. 584/1285), on the fate of al-Andalus after the loss, in 664/1266, of several places in the provinces of Murcia and Jerez (see al-Maḳḳarī, *Azhār al-riyāḍ*, i, 47-50). However, a poem well-known in North Africa was inspired by the capture of Granada in 897/1492, the work of an anonymous poet who describes the advance of the Christians and the progressive loss of the last places occupied by Muslims, while evoking the hardships suffered by citizens under siege and the feelings of sadness of those Andalusians driven from their land (see M. Soualah, *Une élégie andalouse sur la guerre de Grenade*, Algiers 1914-19). This work is largely documentary in character, as is also another (anonymous) *ḳaṣīda* composed in 1501 and appealing for aid to the Ottoman Sultan Bāyazīd II (886-918/1481-1512) and depicting the dramatic predicament of the Moriscoes after the reconquest (text in al-Maḳḳarī, *Azhār al-riyāḍ*, i, 108-15, edited and translated with commentary by J.T. Monroe, *A curious Morisco appeal to the Ottoman Empire*, in *al-And.*, xxxi/1-2 [1966], 281-303).

In general, when the lamentation is applied to places, the poets mourn over the *aṭlāl*, ruins not to be regarded with greater significance than in the pre-Islamic period; they bewail the destruction of buildings (mosques in particular), atrocities committed by the enemy and the slaughter of peoples condemned to exile; the emotions experienced by the survivors give rise to lyrical developments which are supplemented by the nostalgia of émigrés and their desire to return to their lost homeland, where life was so enjoyable. Mustapha Hassen (*Recherches sur les poèmes inspirées par la perte ou la destruction des villes dans la littérature arabe du IIIe/IXe siècle à la prise de Grenade en 897/1492*, unpubl. thesis, Sorbonne 1977) has, in the course of his analysis of the poetical texts, noted a total of 96 items, containing slightly fewer than 2,000 verses, of which almost half were composed by Andalusians, a little more than a quarter by easterners, and the rest by Ifrīḳiyans. No doubt it would be possible to find a number of specimens of the same type dating back to a period earlier than the conquest of Granada, but the total collected so far is quite sufficiently instructive. It would be appropriate at this stage to add to the list more recent poems which the end of Islamic domination in al-Andalus has continued to inspire.

In Morocco, the destruction of the *zāwiya* of al-Dilāʾ [*q.v.* in Suppl.] inspires to this very day (see M. Ḥadjdjī, *al-Zāwiya al-dilāʾiyya*, Rabat 1384/1964, 270-2) occasional poems, having been lamented by numerous poets, whose number probably includes al-Yūsī [*q.v.*], who has the most compelling of nuances (see ʿA. Gannūn, *al-Nubūgh al-maghribī*[2], Beirut 1964, 80, 277-8; Lakhdar, *Vie littéraire*, 101-2).

Still in the Maghrib, there is also a *ḳaṣīda* by a Tunisian, Aḥmad al-Ḳlībī, on the conquest of Algiers by the French (see Ḥ.Ḥ. al-Ghazzī, *al-Adab al-tūnisī fi 'l-ʿahd al-ḥusaynī*, Tunis 1972, 54-62). This event was also to be bewailed in poems of dialectical Arabic [see MALḤŪN], specimens of which are reproduced by, for example, Gen. E. Daumas, *Mœurs et coutumes de l'Algérie*[3], 1858, 160-74. In dialectical Algerian Arabic, an interesting poem is the *Complainte arabe sur la rupture du barrage de Saint-Denis-du-Sig* (in 1885), published and translated by G. Delphin and L. Guin, Paris-Oran 1886. The popular poetry of the Maghrib, which is so full of panegyrics of the Prophet, some of which are sung at funeral ceremonies along with the *Burda* [*q.v.*], are hardly *marāthī* proper; the most remarkable is probably that which ʿAbd al-ʿAzīz al-Maghrāwī composed on the death of the sultan al-Manṣūr al-Dhahabī in 1012/1603 (see Abū ʿAlī al-Ghawthī, *Kashf al-ḳināʿ ʿan ālāt al-samāʿ*, Algiers 1322/1904, 85). The review *Hunā 'l-Djazāʾir = Ici-Alger*, in its 19th issue (1953), 14-5, published an elegy of 162 verses, also in *malḥūn*, by Muḥammad Ibn Gīṭūn on the death of his wife, but this piece appears quite exceptional.

We thus arrive at the contemporary period, in the course of which the tradition has been perpetuated in Arabic-speaking circles. More or less improvised pieces of verse are still recited over the grave of the deceased, even in the countryside (see e.g. P.A. Jaussen, *Coutumes des Arabes au pays de Moab*[2], Paris 1948, 96-7, who gives an idea of what the pre-Islamic conventions may have been), while more polished poems are published in newspapers and periodicals or prepared with a view to public recitation at ceremonies taking place forty days after the demise (*ḥaflat al-arbaʿīn*) or on the occasion of its anniversary (*taʾbīn al-faḳīd*). Some celebrated individuals in the Muslim world have inspired a host of *marāthī* (about twenty, for example in memory of Muḥammad ʿAbduh) and it is to be noted that the *Dīwān* of the ʿIrāḳī poet al-Zahāwī [*q.v.*] contains several pages of lamentation over the death of Saʿd Zaghlūl [*q.v.*]. This politician has also been celebrated by a considerable number of poets, prominent among whom is Aḥmad Shawḳī [*q.v.*], a remarkably prolific writer of *rithāʾ*; in fact, he has left a legacy of no fewer than 53 elegies (the whole of vol. iii of the *Shawḳiyyāt*, ed. Maḥmūd Abu 'l-Wafāʾ, Cairo 1384/1964) relating to parents, personalities of Egypt, the Muslim world and even of Europe (Hugo, Tolstoy, Verdi); as in classical *marthiya*, gnomic themes dominate the prologue and are followed by an appeal to the deceased, then by a eulogy in his honour; these compositions also convey an echo of the major political, cultural and social events of the time (see A. Boudot-Lamotte, *Aḥmad Šawqī, l'homme et l'œuvre*, Damascus 1977, 158-77). A similar point is made by J. Majed (*La presse littéraire en Tunisie de 1904 à 1955*, Tunis 1979, 350-1) with reference to the funeral tributes paid to poets by their colleagues, who take advantage of the occasion to proclaim their determination to maintain the struggle in the literary, political or social domain. Finally, with the *marthiya* may be associated the laments on the hardships of the times, on the deterioriation of morals and on the deplorable situation in the world to be found in such prose works like the *Dhamm al-zamān* by al-Djāḥiẓ or such verse works like the *Marthiyat al-ayyām al-ḥāḍira* by Adonis.

From this brief survey, it emerges that *rithāʾ* occupies a position of importance in Arabic literature, both on account of its volume and its content and in spite of distinct differences, belongs to the same overall scheme as panegyric, to which it is subsidiary. Many poets, major or minor, have cultivated this genre which has enabled some of them to express sentiments all the more sincere because, in most cases, they had no reason to expect reward from the heirs of the deceased. No doubt attention should be drawn to the role of convention and of "professionalism"—which is by no means scanty—but the impression is often gained that of all verse, *marāthī* contain the greatest essence of true poesy.

Bibliography: More or less complete *marāthī* figure in a large number of *dīwāns*, some published, others unpublished, and the present article has been able to give only an imperfect idea of them; some editors have taken the trouble to classify the poems by genre or at the very least to indicate separately, in the table of contents (which is otherwise of no great importance) those which belong to *ghazal, madīḥ*, etc., with the result that the task of researchers is made much easier. Furthermore, the anthologists of the Middle Ages (Abū Tammām, Buḥturī, Ibn al-Shadjarī, Ḳurashī, etc.) have generally reserved a special section for *rithāʾ* (and it is worth noting that the *Bāb al-marāthī* follows immediately after the *Bāb al-ḥamāsa* which gives its name to Abū Tammām's selection). Ibn ʿAbd Rabbih, in his *ʿIḳd* (ed. Cairo 1346/1928, ii, 158-202) classes the chosen specimens according to the nature of the deceased: son, brother, husband, concubine, wife, daughter, *ashrāf*, and he includes epitaphs and *taʿāzī*. Several scholars have even devoted monographs to *marāthī*, among which that of Ibn al-Aʿrābī survives in part (ed. W. Wright, *Opuscula arabica*, Leiden 1859, 97-136); the *K. al-Taʿāzī wa 'l-marāthī* of Mubarrad is said to exist in ms. in the library of Maḥmūd Muḥammad Shākir. Some texts figure in collections of biographies (Ibn Sallām, Ibn Ḳutayba, *Aghānī*, Ibn Khallikān, Ibn Shākir al-Kutubī, etc.), in works of criticism, *adab*, and also in historico-literary works (see e.g. Masʿūdī, *Murūdj*, ed. Pellat, Ar. index, root *r-th-y*). To the works of criticism and literary history mentioned in the article may be added A. Trabulsi, *La critique poétique des Arabes*, Damascus 1955, 226-8. General histories of Arabic literature do not reserve a separate place for *rithāʾ*, but useful information is to be found in R. Blachère, *HLA* (index, s.v. *thrène*). Finally, a very exhaustive study, of which much profitable use has been made in the present article, is that of M. Abdesselem, *Le thème de la mort dans la poésie des origines à la fin du IIIe/IXe siècle*, Tunis 1977. (CH. PELLAT)

2. In Persian literature.

The term *marthiya* in Persian is used primarily to designate poems in memory of someone who has died, wherein that person's good qualities are mentioned and regret is expressed at his death. This discussion will include *marthiyas* written for secular public figures, those written for family members and close friends, and those written for religious figures, especially for al-Ḥusayn. Sometimes included in the category *marthiya* but not discussed here are poems lamenting old age and the loss of youth, poems complaining about the unfortunate state of the times, conventional gravestone inscriptions and chronograms.

Unlike the classical elegy, the *marthiya* is not a genre defined by its form. It is a thematic category of Persian poetry, appearing principally in the monorhyme forms of the *ḳaṣīda*, the *ḳiṭʿa*, the *rubāʿī* and the *ghazal*; the strophic forms of *tarkīb-band* and *tardjiʿ-band*; and the *mathnawī* form of rhyming hemistiches. After 1500, the popular religious *marthiya* began to develop certain formal characteristics of its own. In general, the language and style of *marthiyas* followed the language and style of the times in which they were written. The conventional imagery differs, however, among the public, private, and religious *marthiyas*.

The earliest known *marthiya* in New Persian is a *ḳaṣīda* in Manichaean script reconstructed by Henning (*A locust's leg*, London 1962, 98-104) and dated before the first half of the 3rd/9th century. It shows a blending of Islamic and Manichaean elements and is probably a crypto-Manichaean allegory. It is spoken from the grave by the deceased himself. The poem that established many stylistic characteristics of the Persian *marthiya* is Farrukhī Sīstānī's [*q.v.*] striking *ḳaṣīda* of 69 lines for Sultan Maḥmūd of Ghazna [*q.v.*] (*Dīwān*, ed. Dabīr-Siyāḳī, Tehran 1335/1956, 90-3). The poem begins with the speaker describing the changed look of Ghazna as he walks about the city after a years's absence. He notices the grief expressed by different classes of society, questions an anonymous companion about what has happened, and begins to imagine reasons why the ruler has not appeared that morning. Not until line 21 does he allude to Maḥmūd's death. He expresses his own grief at the loss, calls upon the dead ruler to arise and resume his normal activities, finally becomes reconciled to the situation, and concludes by mentioning Maḥmūd's successor and praying for the dead sultan's happiness in heaven.

Some specific characteristics of Farrukhī's poem that often appear in later *marthiyas* are (1) the device of the speaker questioning a companion, or posing rhetorical questions about what has happened; (2) the use of euphemisms for dying, such as "he has gone"; (3) the speaker addressing the deceased directly as if he were still living; (4) the speaker making excuses for the absence of the deceased; (5) the frequent use of words such as *dardā* and *darīghā* meaning "alas"; (6) the use of images appropriate to the status of the deceased, often as a means to enumerate the subject's praiseworthy qualities; (7) descriptions of man and nature grieving for the dead; (8) the frequent use of anaphora; (9) the mention of the successor to the deceased; and (10) the use of a prayer for the happiness of the deceased in heaven.

The influence of Farrukhī can be seen in *marthiyas* written up to the 20th century. For example, Masʿūd Saʿd Salmān [*q.v.*] (d. 515/1121-2) in a *marthiya* for ʿImād al-Dawla Abu 'l-Ḳāsim has the speaker refuse to believe the bad news, address the deceased directly, praise his successor and wish the subject well in heaven. The theme of the infidelity and unpredictability of fortune, which becomes very common in *marthiyas* after this, is used prominently in this poem (*Dīwān*, ed. R. Yāsimī, Tehran 1339/1960, 215-18) Amīr Muʿizzī [*q.v.*] (d. 519-21/1125-7) in a *marthiya* for Niẓām al-Mulk, has the speaker ask questions in disbelief, uses anaphora, addresses the deceased directly and wishes him well in heaven (*Dīwān*, ed. ʿA. Iḳbāl, Tehran 1318/1939, 476). Anwarī [*q.v.*] begins his *marthiya* for Madjd al-Dīn b. Abī Ṭālib b. Niʿma, the *naḳīb* of Balkh, by stating that the city of Balkh is in an uproar because Madjd al-Dīn did not hold his audience that day. The speaker questions a chamberlain, thinks up excused for the *naḳīb*'s absence, blames fortune for this loss, uses anaphora and the word *darīghā*, and prays for his well-being in heaven (*Dīwān*, ed. Mudarris Raḍawī, Tehran 1337/1958, i, 46-8). Among other famous *marthiyas* that display these conventions one can mention Saʿdī's *marthiya* for Saʿd b. Abū Bakr, Muḥtasham Kāshānī's for Shāh Ṭahmāsp and Abu 'l-Ḳāsim Lāhūtī's for Lenin.

A variation of this form of public *marthiya* is the poem which combines mourning for the deceased and congratulations to the successor in approximately equal proportions. The earliest example is by Abu 'l-ʿAbbās Rabindjanī (*fl.* 331/942-3) where he mourns the death of the Sāmānid ruler Naṣr b. Aḥmad and congratulates his successor Nūḥ b. Naṣr (text and tr. in G. Lazard, *Les premiers poètes persans*, 2 vols., Paris and Tehran 1964, i, 87; ii, 68). Other examples may be found in the *dīwāns* of Djamāl al-Dīn Muḥammad b. ʿAbd al-Razzāḳ Iṣfahānī, Khwādju Kirmānī, and ʿUrfī Shīrāzī.

The *marthiyas* written for relatives and close friends are very personal in tone, in contrast with the more formal and distant tone of those written for public figures. Less emphasis is placed on the universal mourning of man and nature and more on the poet's own feelings. The poet does not adopt the persona of a puzzled observer who must discover what has caused the public grief, although other themes and devices typical of Farrukhī may be present, such as the use of anaphora, the direct address of the deceased, words meaning "alas", and prayers for well-being in heaven. Fate is often blamed for the untimely death, and if the deceased died young, much use is made of images of gardens, flowers, young shoots, and the seasons of spring and autumn. An early example is Firdawsī's [*q.v.*] *marthiya* for his son which comes at the beginning of the story of Bahrām Čūbīn in the *Shāh-nāma*. Masʿūd Saʿd Salmān's *marthiya* for his son is apparently the first use of the *tarkīb-band* form for a *marthiya* (*op. cit.*, 543-8). The most moving expressions of grief for the loss of a relative in all of classical Persian poetry are those of Khāḳānī Shīrwānī [*q.v.*] for his son Rashīd al-Dīn. Khāḳānī was one of the most prolific writers of *marthiyas* before the Ṣafawid period, and his *Dīwān* (ed. M. ʿAbbāsī, Tehran 1336/1957) contains over 50 of these poems. In three of his *marthiyas* for his son, Khāḳānī displays his mastery of language and the poetic tradition, and his freedom from the restraints of conventional imagery. He begins one (*Dīwān*, 147-50) with the son's illness and ends with his death. The father orders many preparations to cure the boy, but when he dies, Khāḳānī demands these back. In a powerful use of the *radīf* "*bāz dihīd*" ("give back") the poet proceeds through a long list of folk medicines and spells, and ends by asking for his son back. Another (*op. cit.*, 142-6) begins with 33 lines containing imperative verbs expressing the sense "weep and mourn and contemplate this tragedy". He then orders various parts of his house and articles of clothing to be destroyed, his hair to be cut, and his face scratched. The abundant use of images of death and mourning and imperative verbs constitutes an unusual and striking innovation within the poetic tradition. Equally as compelling is a third *marthiya* (*ibid.*, 371-4) cast in the words of the dying son to his father. This is reminiscent of the crypto-Manichaean poem mentioned above, and also anticipates certain characteristics of the post-Ṣafawid religious *marthiyas*, especially the motif of a speaker anticipating his own death and describing the mourning that will follow it.

Some other particularly moving *marthiyas* of this sort are Kamāl al-Dīn Ismāʿīl's for his son who was drowned (*Dīwān*, ed. H. Baḥr al-ʿUlūmī, Tehran 1348/1969, 429-32), and Humām Tabrīzī's cycle of 16 short *ghazals* on the death of his beloved (*Dīwān*, ed. R. ʿAywaḍī, Tabrīz 1351/1972, 170-6). Djāmī's [*q.v.*] *marthiya* for his brother in the form of a *tarkīb-band* of seven stanzas (*Dīwān*, ed. H. Raḍī, Tehran 1341/1962, 115-18) echoes closely in the first stanza a line from Saʿdī's *marthiya* for Abū Bakr b. Saʿd Zangī (*Hanūz dāgh-i nakhustīn durust nā-shuda būd...*), and includes (*taḍmīn*) a *ghazal* written by his brother. Muḥammad Taḳī Bahār's [*q.v.*] *marthiya* for his father (*Dīwān*, Tehran 1344/1965, i, 1-2) with its images of the setting sun, night, dark mourning clothes, and of poetry and writing, shows a clear departure from convention.

A special category of "personal" *marthiyas* consists of the poems that poets write on the death of other poets. Among these may be mentioned Rūdakī's short *marthiya* for Shahīd Balkhī, Labībī's for Farrukhī (with invective against ʿUnṣurī), Sanāʾī's for Muʿizzī, Bahār's for Djamīl Ṣadīḳī al-Dhahāwī, Īradj Mīrzā, Parwīn Iʿtiṣāmī and ʿIshḳī, and the collection of *marthiyas* by twelve contemporary poets for Furūgh Farrukhzād which were published in *Djāwidāna-yi Furūgh Farrukhzād* (Tehran 1347/1968).

An unusual exception to the rule that *marthiyas* are composed in verse is the prose *marthiya* for Muḥammad b. Ghiyāth al-Dīn Balban (d. 683/1284-5) by Ḥasan Dihlāwī [*q.v.*] (in M.A. Ghani, *Pre-Mughal Persian in Hindūstān*, Allahabad 1941, 428-34). This begins with a complaint about the tyranny of fate, then recounts the circumstances of Muḥammad's death, describes all nature as mourning and ends with prayers for his happiness in heaven. It uses many of the conventional images of verse *marthiyas*, and has poetry interspersed throughout.

With the spread of Shīʿī Islam in the early Ṣafawid period came the mourning ceremonies associated with the month of Muḥarram and centring on *ʿāshūrāʾ*, the day of al-Ḥusayn's death. The religious *marthiyas* that were written to recall the events at Karbalāʾ developed in two directions: long courtly poems in the classical tradition, and various less formal popular genres.

Just as Farrukhī had established a model for writing secular courtly *marthiyas*, so Muḥtasham Kāshānī (d. 996/1587-8) created the model for the courtly religious *marthiya* with his famous twelve-stanza *tarkīb-band* on the death of al-Ḥusayn (*Dīwān*, ed. M. ʿA. Kirmānī, Tehran 1344/1965, 280-5). Reminiscent of Farrukhī's *marthiya*, Muḥtasham's begins with questions asking why the world and the heavens are in tumult. Anaphora are used prominently. Important images are those of shipwreck, floods of tears, waves and seas of blood, thirst, date palms and gardens, and the world and the heavens weeping. These images, and those of light and darkness which later became common in the *taʿziya* [*q.v.*], are the basic images of the religious *marthiya* in Persian. A great number of *tarkīb-bands* were written after the example of Muḥtasham, and this remained the principal courtly form for the religious *marthiya* until the 20th century. *Ḳaṣīdas* were also written, the most strikingly original being that of Ḳāʾānī [*q.v.*] for al-Ḥusayn. Employing the device, first used by Rūdakī, of short questions and answers in each line, Ḳāʾānī produced a powerful, ritual-like poem describing and lamenting the tragedy at Karbalāʾ (text and tr. in Browne, *LHP*, iv, 178-81).

The popular forms of the Shīʿi *marthiya* are the *taʿziya*, the *rawḍa* and *nawḥa*. The *rawḍa* takes its name from Kamāl al-Dīn Ḥusayn b. ʿAlī Kāshifī's [*q.v.*] *Rawḍat al-shuhadāʾ*, from which readings and recitations, called *rawḍa-khʷānī*, were given. The *marthiyas* in *rawḍa-khʷānī* sometimes involve considerable oral improvisation on well-known Karbalāʾ themes, and thus do not necessarily follow a prescribed literary form. Two popular 19th century books of *marthiyas* and Karbalāʾ accounts which have been reprinted many times are the *Ṭūfān al-bukāʾ* of Muḥammad Ibrāhīm b. Muḥammad Bāḳir Harawī Ḳazwīnī "Djawharī" (d. 1253/1837-8) and Muḥammad Ḥusayn b. ʿAbd Allāh Shahrābī Ardjastānī's *Ṭarīḳ al-bukāʾ*. The latter seems to have been written especially for *naḳḳāls* and *rawḍa-khʷāns*.

The *nawḥas*, which are sung on occasions involving breast-beating (*sīna-zanī*) of self-flagellation with chains (*zandjīr-zanī*), are a genre of strophic poems in classical metres which often have unconventional rhyme-schemes and arrangements of lines and refrains within the stanza. The number and placement of stresses in each line are important in *nawḥas*, those for breast-beating having a more rapid rhythm than those for chain-flagellation.

Bibliography (in addition to references given in the text): a popular anthology of *marthiyas* was compiled by Ḥ. Kūhī Kirmānī under the title *Sūgwarīhā-yi adabī dar Īrān*, Tehran 1333/1954 (uncritical); Zayn al-ʿĀbidīn Muʾtaman, *Shiʿr wa adab-i Fārsī*, Tehran 1346/1967, 74-106; Zahrā Iḳbāl (Nāmdār), *Elegy in the Qajar period*, in P. Chelkowski, ed., *Taʿziyeh: ritual and drama in Iran*, New York 1979, 193-209 (uncritical).

(W. L. Hanaway, Jr.)

3. In Turkish literature.

Funeral laments, inscribed in stone or recorded in Uyghur manuscripts, belong to the pre-Islamic heritage of the Turks. For the *marthiya* proper to Islamic Turkish literature, the poetic forms were the *ḳaṣīda*, or among the Ottoman Turks, preferably the stanzaic *tardjīʿ-band* or *tarkīb-band*. Ottoman *marthiyas* present the same varied and cultivated style which we know from *dīwān* poetry. Bāḳī's (d. 1008/1600) elegy on sultan Süleymān is regarded as the classical masterpiece, but it has behind it a long tradition of formal *marthiyas* by Aḥmedī, Sheykhī, Ḳiwāmī, Aḥmed Pasha, Nedjātī, Kemālpashazāde and Lāmiʿī, who composed "parallels" in the same metre and with the same *radīf* (N. M. Çetin, art. *Terci*, in *İA*, xii, 172). Underneath the high-flown imagery, a current of real feeling could flow. Closeness to the sultan could give power, office, and wealth; it was small wonder that the death of a sovereign caused real anxiety. The favour of the princes, too, potential successors to the throne, could raise poets to high positions. When a prince or a high dignitary died, the poets in his entourage lost not only a friend but often their livelihood. Nedjātī (d. 915/1509), who mourned two princes in moving *marthiyas*, lived on a pension, but survived his last patron prince Maḥmūd by only two years. The abolition of the princes' courts in the 10th/16th century removed from the Anatolian countryside many centres of culture. At the central court in Istanbul, fear and flattery did not always prevail. When the much-loved prince Muṣṭafā was executed (960/1533), poets and prose writers expressed their grief, and Tashlîdjalî Yaḥyā (d. 990/1582) in his famous *marthiya* took some risk when he openly accused the Grand Vizier.

Ghazālī (d. 942/1535 [*q.v.*]) lived in retirement in Mecca after he had written in praise of the executed Iskender Čelebi. In the grand tradition of Ottoman *marthiyas*, but in a different vein, is the *Marthiya-yi gurba*, in which the urbane Meʾālī [*q.v.*] (d. 942/1535-6) commemorates his deceased cat with a mock solemnity in stanzas, from which also genuine affection emerges. In this way, the imagery of the *marthiya*, steeped in the panegyric convention, could be used for a deeper vein of feeling, for political criticism or for gentle irony. The form was in use until the end of the 19th century. The elegy written by Ghālib Dede [*q.v.*] on the death of his friend Esrār Dede belongs to the last great examples of Turkish *dīwān* literature. ʿĀkif Pasha (d. 1845) wrote a short moving *marthiya* on the death of his child. The lyrical poem *Maḳber*, written by ʿAbdülḥaḳḳ Ḥāmid Tarhan upon the death of his young wife in 1885, has been classed as the greatest *marthiya* after Bāḳī's elegy (S. E. Siyavuşgil, in *İA*, i, 71). Not completely removed from the urban tradition, the unlettered and the peasants have *marthiyas* of their own. In Turkish folklore, lyrical compositions expressive of grief, *aghît*, have survived; they commemorate the deceased, treat of general aspects of death or express sorrow over collective calamities (P. N. Boratav, in *PhTF*, ii, cf. *chanson funèbre*). Whereas the sufferings caused by the Russo-Turkish war of 1877-8 inspired Namîḳ Kemāl [*q.v.*] to write his impassioned *Waṭan merthiyesi*, popular poets had already since 1683 turned to elegies upon the loss of Rumelian cities to the Christian enemy, such as Buda, Belgrade, Sarajevo, Banyaluka and Bügürdelen. The popular *aghît* lives to this day; about twenty such compositions lamenting Atatürk's death are known. Religious *marthiyas* on the martyrs of Karbalāʾ belong to the *maḳtal* genre.

Bibliography: H. A. Yücel, *Ein Gesamtüberblick über die türkische Literatur* (tr. O. Reşer), Istanbul 1941. Several *marthiyas* are printed in F. İz, *Eski türk edebiyatında nazım*, i/l, Istanbul 1966. On the genre and the writers of religious *marthiyas*, K. E. Kürkçüoğlu, ed., *Tahir'ül-Mevlevi, Edebiyat lügatı*, Istanbul 1973. F. K. Timurtaş, *Bakî'nin Kanunî mersiyesi*, in *TDED*, xii (1962), is a philological analysis. Kemālpashazade on the death of Sultan Selīm I: Ş. Turan, introduction to *Defter* vii of the *Tevarih-i Al-i Osman*, Ankara, p. xviii. On the princes' courts, P. Kappert, *Die osmanischen Prinzen und ihre Residenz Amasya im 15. u. 16. Jahrhundert*, Istanbul 1976; E. Ambros, *Candid penstrokes. The lyrics of Meʾālī, an Ottoman poet of the 16th century*, Berlin 1982, 35-9, 175-80. On Tanẓīmāt *merthiyes*, M. Kaplan, İ. Enginün and B. Emil, *Yeni türk edebiyatı antolojisi*, i, Istanbul 1974, 324, ii, Istanbul 1978, 169-75. On *saz* poets: S. Plaskowicka-Rymkiewicz, *Les lamentations ou agıtlar dans la création populaire turque*, in *Zagadnienia Rodzajów Literackich*, viii (1965), 89-107; K.-D. Wannig, *Der Dichter Karaca Oğlan*, Freiburg 1980; V. Boşkov, *Türk edebiyatında şehir şiirleri ve şehir mersiyeleri*, in *Atatürk Üniv. Edeb. Fak. Araştırma Dergisi*, xii (1980), 69-76. *Aghîts* on Atatürk: cf. M. Fuad Köprülü, *Türk sazşairleri*, iii, Istanbul n.d., 729 (Aşık Süleyman); P. N. Boratav, *La guerre de libération et Atatürk dans la tradition populaire*, in *Turcica*, xiv (1982), 274.

(B. Flemming)

4. In Urdu literature.

Marthiya (pls. in Urdu, *marthiyē*, *marāthī*) is one of the oldest forms of Urdu poetry. Two types exist, secular and religious, but the second is by far the more important; indeed, it is almost always assumed whenever Urdu writers mention *marthiya*. Moreover, it is usually about the Karbalāʾ martyrs, especially the *Imām* al-Ḥusayn b. ʿAlī b. Abī Ṭālib. Shorter poems on this theme may be termed *nawḥa* or *salām*, the latter normally containing a word such as *salām*, *salāmī*, *mudjrā* or *mudjrāʾī* in the first few verses. Urdu critics often begin their accounts with the pre-Islamic Arabic *marthiya*, and also postulate some slight debt to Persian elegists such as Muḥtashim (Shiblī, *Muwāzana*, 1-9). Yet they regard the form it took in 19th century Lucknow as peculiarly Indian—perhaps the only truly indigenous major Urdu poetical genre.

Its early development goes back to Dakkani, that form of Urdu used in southern India, which is related to the literary language which emerged in northern India somewhat as Chaucer's English is to that of Shakespeare. The ʿĀdil Shāh [*q.v.*] sultans of Bīdjāpūr (895-1047/1489-1686) and the Ḳuṭb Shāhs [*q.v.*] of Golkondā (901-1098/1496-1687) were Shīʿīs, patrons of poetry, and sometimes poets themselves. They encouraged the reciting of *marthiyē* in Muḥarram, and even had ʿ*Āshūrā-khānas* built specially for the purpose. Thus though, like other Urdu poetical forms, it was at first court poetry, because of its religious nature it was taken by princes to the people, to form a corporate religio-literary and social activity. It probably played an important part in the development of the *mushāʿara* (public poetical recital or competition) which became—and still remains—a phenomenon of Indo-Pakistani literary and social life. In the Deccan, from the 10th/16th century onwards, numerous poets composed *marthiyas*; some specialised in it. The researches of Naṣīr al-Dīn Hāshimī and Muḥyī al-Dīn Ḳādirīzōr (see *Bibl.*) have brought hundreds of examples to light from manuscripts in the Subcontinent and Europe, including an important two-volume collection in Edinburgh University Library. Thus the Dakkanī *marthiya* can now be seen as the ancestor of the north-Indian *marthiya* which reached its apogee in the works of Anīs and Dabīr in the mid-19th century. Its spread northward was a by-product of the subjugation of the Deccan sultanates by the armies of the Emperor Awrangzīb (1097-8/1686-7).

Nevertheless, the 19th century Lucknow *marthiya*, varied in content but invariably in *musaddas* form, and frequently extending to between 100 and 200 stanzas (300-600 vv.), is a far cry from the modest elegies of early Dakkanī poets. To begin with, *musaddas* was rarely used in the Deccan. An isolated exception by Yatīm Aḥmad (Hāshimī, 379, gives two stanzas) dates from the Mughal period. It would appear that in Bīdjāpūr and Golkondā, the great majority of *marāthī* were in "*ghazal* form"—that is, monorhyme, the rhyme also coming at the end of the first hemistich of the first verse. Among other forms occasionally used were *mathnawī* and quatrains. To take an early poet, Sultan Muḥammad Ḳulī Ḳuṭb Shāh (976-

020/1568-1611) wrote 5 *marāt͟hī* (*Kulliyyāt*, $\frac{56}{1}$ - $\frac{56}{8}$, ;7-60), one in *mat͟hnawī*, the rest in *g͟hazal* form. Of the atter, the longest, no. 5, has a good deal of internal hyme, usually in the middle of the hemistich, thus uggesting quatrains. After the Mug͟hal conquest, juatrains gained ground, and this trend continued in iorthern India in the 18th century. But *g͟hazal* form vas not completed eliminated, as can be seen from the *narāt͟hī* of Sawdāʾ (1125-95/1713-81) (*Kulliyyāt*, ii, 34-333) and Mīr Taḳī Mīr (1135-1223/1722-1810) *Kulliyyāt Mīr*, 1203-1325). The quatrains used in *nart͟hiya* differed from *rubāʿiyyāt* in their rhyme cheme, which was *aaaa, bbba, ccca*, etc., that is *tarkīb-and*. They are called *murabbaʿ* or *čaw-maṣraʿ*. By the nd of the 18th century, this was considered the iormal verse-form for *mart͟hiya*.

Certainly, both Sawdāʾ and Mīr tried out *musaddas* of various kinds in about 10% of their elegies; but it vas in Lucknow, where both poets gravitated late in ife, that *mart͟hiya* became inextricably associated with *nusaddas*, with the rhyme scheme *aaaabb, ccccdd, eeeeff*, tc. The credit is usually given to Mīr Ḍamīr, of the generation before Anīs. It may be that Anīs' father, Mīr K͟halīḳ, also had a hand in it, if only we could late poems attributed to him and could be sure they vere not composed by his celebrated son (see S͟hiblī, *p. cit.*, 15).

The disturbed situation in Dihlī, due to Afg͟hān and Marāt̤hā incursions, attracted many of its poets to ucknow, whose Nawwābs were poets and patrons of poetry; and as they were also S͟hīʿīs, they encouraged legiac poetry. In its progress from the Deccan via Dihlī to Lucknow, the *mart͟hiya* changed in length, cope and content, as well as in prosody. In the Deccan, it began as a short lament, ranging from 5 verses (10 hemistiches) to 20—rarely 30, even allowing for the possibility that some examples which have urvived may be mere fragments. Nor did its length ncrease significantly in the early Mug͟hal era. In fact, t resembled the *nawḥa* or *salām* of northern India. The poet's task was *rōna awr rulāna* (lit. "to weep and cause veeping"). Thus the rhyme often included repeated nterjections of sorrow, such as *wāʾē*, *wā*, *waylā*, *āh*, *āʾē* and *ḥayf*: other evocative words such as *Ḥusayn*, *Ḥusaynā*, *Karbalā* and *muṣībatā* were also used in hyme. The effect was heightened by the chanting (*sōz k͟hʷānī*) in which elegies were recited. There were also ealistic, if brief, descriptions of the blood-stained body or shroud or the martyr. Heaven and earth were aid to be thunderstruck by his death. Yet despite its mall compass, the Dakkanī *mart͟hiya* foreshadows, pasmodically, almost all the elements in the content of that of the 19th century. The various characters, heir words, their feelings, and their exploits, are to be ound. For example, the unhistorical marriage of al-Ḥusayn's daughter Sakīna to his nephew Ḳāsim is alluded to by Hās͟him ʿAlī (d. after 1169/1756) and his contemporary G͟hulāmī (Ḳādirī, 293, 297).

Brevity inhibited the development of these themes. But some long *mathnawīs* on the Karbalāʾ martyrdoms vere written in the Deccan, predating the 19th century Lucknow "epic" *mart͟hiya*. Whether they had any direct influence on it is hard to say. Both S͟hāh Muḥammad's *Djang-nāma* and Walī Wēlūrī's *Rawḍat al-s͟huhadāʾ* date from around 1730. However, the atter, which begins with the Prophet's death and ends vith Karbalāʾ, might better be described as a equence of separate elegies. Another *Rawḍat al-s͟huhadāʾ*, by a certain Muḥkam, dates from 1806.

Sawdāʾ was a major elegist, and composed 91 *narāt͟hī*. Though their average length is only about ifty verses, he was able to extend the battle-scenes, characterisation and dramatic content. He seems an obvious half-way house between the *mart͟hiya* of the Deccan and that of Lucknow. He was often been criticised for his lack of sincerity in lamentation.

The Lucknow "epic" *mart͟hiya* may be said to have begun with Mīr Ḍamīr and reached its climax with Mīr Babar ʿAlī Anīs (1802-74) and Mīrzā Salāmat ʿAlī Dabīr (1803-75), who composed more than a thousand *marāt͟hī* each. *Sōz-k͟hʷānī* often gave way to declamation (*taḥt al-lafẓ*), thus enhancing the dramatic impact. Despite the great length of many elegies, which has already been mentioned, so varied and extended was the content that no one *mart͟hiya* told the whole Karbalāʾ story in full. This was doubtless necessitated by the circumstances and the popularity of the form which led the poets to go on writing *mart͟hiyē*. Variety was achieved by the selection of incidents as well as variation in treatment. Yet some readers may regret that no full-fledged Karbalāʾ epic resulted. Characterisation, dialogue, description of scenes and nature, battle preparation and the battle itself, all played their part, without neglecting the original aim of lamentation. From the literary point of view, no devices of *faṣāḥat-o-balāg͟hat* were neglected, with rich vocabulary and telling similes and metaphors. Critics have analysed the content-sequence as follows (Riḍwī, *Rūḥ-i-Anīs*, Introd., 14-15: Afḍal Ḥusayn, *Ḥayāt-i-Dabīr*, i, 137-40):

1. *čihra* (*maṭlaʿ/tamhīd*) - introductory verses setting the tone, with no restriction at to details.
2. *ruk͟hṣat* - the martyr-hero's farewell to his nearest and dearest.
3. *sarāpā* - a description of the hero from head to foot.
4. *āmad* - the army's preparation for battle, perhaps including a detailed description of the hero's horse.
5. *radjaz* - the hero's battle oration.
6. *djang* (*laŕāʾī*) - the actual battle, stressing the hero's valour, often including a description of his sword.
7. *s͟hahādat* - the death of the martyr, either al-Ḥusayn or some member of his family.
8. *bayn* - the lamentation of the martyr's family and friends, of the poet himself, and of all believers.

But the above scheme was not mandatory: there were really only two thematic essentials to qualify a poem as a *mart͟hiya*—it must be a lament, and must involve the martyrs of Karbalāʾ.

There was both mutual influence and intense rivalry between Anīs and Dabīr. Lucknow split into two camps, and a considerable literature of comparison was generated. Both were outstanding poets, and some consider Anīs the greatest of all Urdu poets. If he is preferred to Dabīr, it may be because on the whole he exhibits less pedantry and straining after effect. Two such giants were hard to equal; and before their deaths, the Lucknow principality ended with the exile of Nawwāb Wādjid ʿAlī to Calcutta after the Indian Mutiny (1857-8). Though *mart͟hiya* continued into the present century, with encouragement at other courts such as Rampur and Hyderabad, its great days were over. Those interested in the contemporaries and successors of Anīs may consult Ṣiddīḳī, 713-39, and Saksena, 137-9. To the present writer, the *marāt͟hī* of Anīs's brother Muʾnis seem to merit reassessment.

The importance of *mart͟hiya* in Urdu literary history has been widely recognised. Ḥālī (*Muḳaddima-yi-s͟hiʿr-o-s͟hāʿirī*, 182-91) describes Anīs's *mart͟hiya* as "the creation of a new form which greatly extended the range of Urdu poetry, increasing its vocabulary, ending its stagnation and breathing new life into it." It is also said to have demonstrated the suitability of *musaddas* for long poems, Ḥālī's famous *musaddas*, *Madd-o-jazr-i-Islām*, being a prime example.

Secular *marthiya* has existed alongside the religious type throughout its history, but it has received scant attention, and examples are hard to come by. Zōr (130-31, 258) gives an elegy on Awrangzīb in 5 verses of mixed Dakkanī-Persian *mathnawī*. The poet, Mīr Djaʿfar ʿAlī (1068-1125/1658-1713), was born in north India, but accompanied the Emperor's son to the Deccan.

In the 19th century, the ʿAlīgaṙh Movement revived interest in secular *marthiya*. Ḥālī himself composed five of them plus two shorter elegiac pieces (*Kulliyyāt-i-naẓm-i-Ḥālī*, Lahore 1968, i, 327-62), in various verse-forms. His elegy of the poet Ghālib in ten stanzas of ten verses each is an often-quoted masterpiece. Among others often praised are that of Shiblī Nuʿmānī (1857-1914) on his brother and that of Munshī Nawbat Rāʾe Naẓar on his son. Nationalism and independence in the Subcontinent have led to a proliferation of the form in newspapers and magazines.

Bibliography: For general accounts, Ram Baku Saksena, *A history of Urdu literature*, Allahabad 1927, 123-39; Muhammad Sadiq, *A history of Urdu literature*, London 1964, 145-63, contains useful extracts with English translations, including two Dakkanī elegies; ʿAbd al-Salām Nadwī, *Shiʿr al-Hind*, Aʿẓamgaṙh n.d., ii, 353-68, concentrates on generalities and the secular *marthiya*; most studies of individual poets and introductions to *dīwāns* contain short histories of the form; for Dakkanī elegy, Naṣīr al-Dīn Hāshimī, *Dakkan mēn Urdū*, 6th enlarged edition, Lucknow 1963, 62-4, 90-7, 183-5, 287-319 (fundamental), 321-45, 362-84, 489-98, 545-6; Sayyid Muḥyī al-Dīn Ḳādirī Zōr, *Urdū shāhpārē*, Hyderabad, Deccan n.d., i, 130-1, 137-8, 144-6 (on Walī Wēlūrī), 152-71, 258, 264-79, 293-316; both these two books give the Urdu texts of many *marāthī*, those in the second being more substantial, especially for Dakkanī elegists of the early Mughal period; for individual Dakkanī elegists, Muḥammad Ḳulī Ḳuṭb Shāh, *Kulliyyāt*, ed. Sayyid Muḥyī al-Dīn Ḳādirī Zōr, Hyderabad, Deccan 1940, $\frac{56}{1}$ - $\frac{56}{8}$, 57-60; Shāhī (Sultan ʿAlī ʿĀdil Shāh II) *Kulliyyāt Shāhī*, ed. Sayyid Mubāriz al-Dīn Rifʿat, ʿAlīgaṙh 1962, 90, 192-215, though of 16 *marāthī* included, only one, no. 16 in 28 vv., can confidently be attributed to this poet; Baḥrī, *Kulliyyāt Baḥrī*, ed. Muḥammad Ḥāfiẓ Sayyid, Lucknow 1939, 96-7, including the text of 5 *marāthī* for the 18th century northern Indian elegy; Shaykh Čānd, *Sawdā*ʾ, Hyderabad n.d., 282-315; *Kulliyyāt Sawdā*ʾ, ed. ʿAbd al-Bārī Āsī, Lucknow 1932, i (Introd.) 17, ii, 134-333; Mīr Taḳī Mīr, *Kulliyyāt Mīr*, ed. ʿIbādat Brēlwī, Karachi-Lahore 1958, 1203-1333; Afsōs, *Kulliyyāt Afsōs*, ed. Sayyid Ẓahīr Aḥsan, Patna 1961, 262-86; for the 19th century Lucknow *marthiya*, Abu 'l-Layth Ṣiddīḳī, *Lakhnāʾō kā dabistān-i shāʿirī*, Lahore 1955, 661-743; Shiblī Nuʿmānī, *Muwāzana-yi-Anīs-o-Dabīr*, Lucknow 1924; Mīr Ḍamīr, *Madjmūʿa-yi-marthiyē-yi-Ḍamīr*, i, Cawnpore 1898; art. *Anīs*, by Sayyid Amdjad Alṭāf, in *Urdu Encyclopaedia of Islam*, iii, 500-5; which lists editions of this poet's works from the Lucknow five-volume ed. of 1876 onwards; Sayyid Masʿūd Ḥasan Riḍwī's *Rūḥ-i-Anīs*, Allahabad n.d., contains selected *marāthī* and a useful introduction; art. *Dabīr*, by Muḥammad Shafīʿ, in *Urdu Encyclopaedia of Islam*, xii, 208-10; Afḍal Ḥusayn, *Ḥayāt-i-Dabīr*, i, Lahore 1913, ii/l, 1915; Muʾnis, *Madjmūʿa-yi-marāthī-yi-Muʾnis*, 3 vols., Cawnpore 1912; for an account of Lucknow in the era of Anīs and Dabīr, Abdul Halim Sharar, *Lucknow: the last phase of an oriental culture*, tr. and ed. E. S. Harcourt and Fakhir Hussain, London 1975, esp. 83-4, 147; for the ʿAlīgaṙh attitude to *marthiya*, see Alṭāf Ḥusayn Ḥālī, *Mukaddima-yi-shiʿr-o-shāʿirī*, Lahore 1950, 180-93. (J. A. Haywood)

5. In Swahili literature.

The word *marthiya* is not used in Swahili literature; the word for an elegy is *lalamiko* "lament". It is very much a living tradition among Swahili men of letters to compose praising poems for great men who have died. The custom is well-known in Bantu Africa outside the sphere of Islamic influence, so that it may well have been in use among the Swahili before the advent of Islam in the late Umayyad period. Among the Bantu peoples, songs of lament have been recorded by De Rop, Rycroft, Van Wing and others.

Few songs of lament in Swahili have come down to us from any earlier period than the present century, except the *Inkishafi*, which laments in eighty stanzas the fall of the ancient city of Pate (the ruins of which have not yet been excavated) written probably before 1232/1820, by Sayid Abdallah bin Ali bin Nassir, a Swahili of Arabic origin. His contemporary Muyaka bin Hajji al-Ghassaniy (whose family name also betrays his Arabic ancestry) (d. *ca.* 1250/1837) wrote secular verse on personal as well as political subjects, and quatrains on love and philosophy. One of his poems may be called an elegy. It begins thus:

"Do not remind me of that time
when both my parents were alive
when friends and kinsmen filled the house...
Today I have remained alone
with none to help or counsel me
alone with thoughts that no-one shares..."

In Tanga, Hemedi al-Buhriy, who also wrote in the second quarter of the 19th century, composed the *Utenzi wa Kutawafu Nabii*, the Epic on the Death of the Prophet, in which he inserts a few lines of what may have been an elegy on Muḥammad, see J. W. Allen's edition, p. 39. In Lamu, Muhammad bin Abu Bakari Kijumwa wrote an elegy on the death of Professor Alice Werner, of the School of Oriental Studies in London, whom he had served as an informant in 1913. The poem is dated 1354/1935-6. It begins:

"The hearts are full of grief and their
sadness cannot be measured..."

Mohamed Bin Nasor Shaksi wrote an elegy on the death of the Governor of the Kenya Coast, Sir Mbaraka Ali Hinawy, in 1959. It begins: "We pray to Thee, O Majesty, O Lord without a peer..." Some of the best elegies were written in the last twenty years, first at the death of the author Shaaban Robert (1962), then at the death of the poet and Minister of Justice in Tanzania. Sh. Amri K. Abedi, in 1964. The latter had himself composed a now famous lament at the death of his friend Shaaban Robert, which begins thus: *Hae msiba mzito* "Woe! A grave misfortune..". The complete text was published, together with many other elegies that were composed by Swahili poets in both Kenya and Tanzania for the same sad occasion, by the present writer in *Swahili. Journal of the East African Swahili Committee*, xxxiii (1963), in Dar es Salaam. The same journal published the elegies written at the death of Amri Abedi (*Swahili*, xxxv/1 [1965], 4-18).

It is evident that the majority of Swahili elegies which have been published belong to the secular tradition of mourning the death of great men. Some of the finest pieces of Swahili lyric are among them, which is all the more remarkable since very little real lyric verse in the Western sense has been written in

Swahili; there is for instance hardly any nature-lyricism. The probable reason for the excellence of elegiac poetry in Swahili is the popular predilection for nostalgia common not only among the Swahili but also among other Bantu-speaking peoples, notably the Zulu. The mood of feeling that in the past everything was better, when good men and great leaders were still alive, is a natural one for people who are so deeply attached to their parents, their grandparents, their aunts and uncles, that they will always go to their elders for advice and guidance. The demise of such senior friends creates a mood of loneliness and aimlessness which explains the refrains of several of the elegies, e.g. Amri Abedi's on Shaaban Robert (tr. in the original metre): "Our language is still tender/who will be its foster father? Now that Shaaban has departed,/he that nursed it like an infant!"

In the purely Islamic elegies, these feelings of nostalgia and solitude are projected on the demise of the Prophet Muḥammad, as in the elegiac hymn probably composed by Sharifu Badruddini in Lamu, which begins: "Longing fills the hearts of people..." The people need guidance in all matters of daily life and so, in Swahili literature, the time when the Holy Prophet walked on earth is described as one of happiness, since all men knew then what to do.

Bibliography: On songs of lament in a Bantu language, see especially A. de Rop, *Gesproken Woordkunst der Nkundo*, Tervuren 1956, 62-85. On the *Inkishafi*, see Knappert, *Four centuries of Swahili verse*, London 1979, 127-37; on Muyaka bin Hajji, see *op. cit.*, 146, where the full text and translation of this elegy are given; for text and full translation of Amri Abedi's elegy on Shaaban Robert, see *op. cit.*, 285-7. The same work gives a bibliography of Swahili poetry, including the works of J. W. T. Allen, on 314-16. For Ahmad Basheikh Husayn's elegy on Sir Mbarak Ali Hinawy, written in 1959 a few years before his own death, see Knappert, *op. cit.*, 258-60.

(J. KNAPPERT)

MARTOLOS, a salaried member of the Ottoman internal security forces, recruited predominantly in the Balkans from among chosen land-owning Orthodox Christians who, retaining their religion, became members of the Ottoman *ʿaskerī* caste [*q.v.*]. The word almost certainly originated from the Greek, either *amartolos* (ἁμαρτωλός), "corrupt", "gone astray", or *armatolos* (ἁρματολός), "armed", "weapon-carrying". It was shortened to *martolos* (sometimes *martuloz*, with the occasional plural *martulosān*, مارتلوسان) in Ottoman Turkish, whence it entered Bulgarian and then Serbian. By the end of the 9th/15th century it had entered Hungarian and was often used by Europeans to describe Christian sailors on the Danube River who served the Ottomans as rowers on light wooden barques called *nassad*. Its use by the Ottomans, however, was much broader.

In the mid-9th/mid-15th century, the conquering Turks assigned *martolos* in the Balkans as armed police, mounted and foot, who occasionally participated in war, but usually acted in their locales as peacetime border patrols, castle guards, security forces for important mines, guards for strategic passes (*derbend*) and, occasionally, tax collectors. Because of their military positions, *martolos* were able to keep their lands within the *tīmār* system [*q.v.*], *Martolos* were not limited to the Balkans, however, as some were used as spies and messengers as early as the 8th/14th century conquest of western Anatolia (see Anhegger, in *İA*, vii, 342). *Martolos* in the Balkans were almost always led by Muslims (*martolos bas̲h̲ī*, *martolos ag̲h̲asī*, *martolos bas̲h̲bug̲h̲u*). They remained loyal to the Sultan for more than two centuries because the Ottomans rewarded them with daily-wage *ʿaskerī* status, though they remained Christian; their positions were heritable; and they were exempt from the *d̲j̲izya* [*q.v.*] and various local taxes.

When in the 11th/17th century local Balkan antagonisms against Ottoman rule increased, Christian *martolos* serving against rebellious haiduks caused hostility, some *martolos* joining with the anti-Ottoman revolutionaries. By 1104/1692 Istanbul no longer allowed Christians to serve as *martolos* in the Balkans, and by 1135/1722 the Rumeli governor, ʿOt̲h̲mān Pas̲h̲a, merged the institution of *martolos* with the Muslim *pandor* (local security police) (Orhonlu, 89). By the 13th/19th century, a few *martolos* persisted in northern Macedonia, but these were effectively replaced by new institutions brought about by the *Tanẓīmāt* reforms.

Bibliography: The term is briefly explained in Pakalın, s.v. *Martulos*, ii, 409-10, and Midhat Sertoğlu, *Resimli Osmanlı tarihi ansiklopedisi*, Istanbul 1958, 197. It exists in numerous western language studies, e.g. S. Kakuk, *Recherches sur l'histoire osmanlie des XVI*[e] *et XVII*[e] *siècles, les éléments osmanlis de la langue hongroise*, Budapest 1973, 268. References to the institution in standard sources for Ottoman history may be found in E. Rossi's *EI*[1] article and in his addition in *EI*[1] *Suppl.* The most extensive bibliography on the formation of the institution is in R. Anhegger, *Martolos*, in *İA*, vii, 341-4, and in C. Orhonlu, *Osmanlı imparatorluğunda derbend teşkilâtı*, Istanbul 1967, 79-90. For the Balkans, see M. Vasić, *Die Martolosen im Osmanischen Reich*, in *Zeitschr. für Balkanologie*, Jahrgang ii (1964), 172-89, or the Turkish translation, M. Vasiç, *Osmanlı imparatorluğunda martoloslar*, in *TD* xxxi (1977), 47-64; and M. Vasich, *The Martoloses in Macedonia*, in *Macedonian Review*, vii/1 (1977), 30-41.

(E. ROSSI - [W. J. GRISWOLD])

MARTYR, MARTYRDOM [see S̲H̲AHĪD; S̲H̲AHĀDA].

MAʿRŪF AL-KARK̲H̲Ī, ABŪ MAḤFŪẒ B. FĪRŪZ or FĪRŪZĀN, d. 200/815-16, one of the most celebrated of the early ascetics and mystics of the Bag̲h̲dād school.

While it is possible that the *nisba* al-Kark̲h̲ī may be connected with the eastern ʿIrāḳī town of Kark̲h̲ Bād̲j̲addā, it is more likely that it derives from his association with the Kark̲h̲ area of Bag̲h̲dād. It is generally thought that his parents were Christians, although Ibn Tag̲h̲rībirdī (ed. Juynboll and Matthes, i, 575) maintains that they were Ṣābians of the district of Wāsiṭ. Among his teachers in the tenets of Ṣūfism were Bakr b. K̲h̲unays al-Kūfī and Farḳad al-Sabak̲h̲ī (al-Makkī, *Ḳūt al-ḳulūb*, Cairo 1310, i, 9). He himself was an important influence on another famous Ṣūfī of the earlier period, Sarī al-Saḳaṭī [*q.v.*], who was in turn the teacher and master of one of the most famous exponents of Ṣūfism, al-D̲j̲unayd [*q.v.*]. The story of his conversion to Islam at the hands of the S̲h̲īʿī *Imām* ʿAlī b. Musā al-Riḍā and his attempt to persuade his parents to the same course is now generally regarded as untrue. Among the sayings attributed to him are: "Love cannot be learned from men; it is in God's gift and derives from His Grace"; "Saints may be known by three signs; their concern for God, their preoccupation with God and their taking refuge in God"; and "Ṣūfism means recognising the divine realities and ignoring that which bears the mark of created beings". Maʿrūf has always been venerated as a saint, and his tomb at Bag̲h̲dād, on the west bank of the

Tigris, is still an object of pious resort and pilgrimage. Al-Ḳus̲h̲ayrī relates that prayer at his tomb was generally regarded as propitious in obtaining rain. Maʿrūf's name appears in many of the *silsila*s of the Ṣūfī orders.

Bibliography: Ḳus̲h̲ayrī, *Risāla*, Cairo 1319, 11; Hud̲j̲wīrī, *Kas̲h̲f al-maḥd̲j̲ūb*, ed. Z̲h̲ukovski, Leningrad 1926, 141, tr. Nicholson, 113; Sulamī, *Ṭabaḳāt al-Ṣūfiyya*, Cairo 1953, 83-90; Abū Nuʿaym, *Ḥilyāt al-awliyāʾ*, Cairo 1932-8, viii, 360-8; K̲h̲aṭīb, *Taʾrīk̲h̲ Bag̲h̲dād* 1931, xiii, 199-209; ʿAṭṭār, *Tad̲h̲kirat al-awliyāʾ*, ed. Nicholson, i, 269 ff., tr. Arberry, *Muslim saints and mystics*, London 1966, 161-5; Ibn K̲h̲allikān, *Wafayāt*, Cairo 1948, iv, no. 700, tr. de Slane, ii, 88; Yāfiʿī, *Mirʾāt al-d̲j̲anān*, Hyderabad 1337-9, i, 460-3; D̲j̲āmī, *Nafaḥāt al-uns*, ed. Nassau Lees, Calcutta 1859, 42; Ibn al-ʿImād, *S̲h̲ad̲h̲arāt al-d̲h̲ahab*, Cairo 1350-l, i, 360; R. A. Nicholson, *The origin and development of Sufism*, in *JRAS* (1906), 306, and *A saying of Maʿrūf al-Kark̲h̲i*, in *JRAS* (1906), 999; L. Massignon, *Essai sur les origines du lexique technique de la mystique musulmane*, 207.

(R. A. NICHOLSON - [R. W. J. AUSTIN])

MAʿRŪF AL-RUṢĀFĪ (1875-1945), leading poet of modern ʿIrāḳ and one extremely audacious and outspoken in expressing his political views. He was born in Bag̲h̲dād in 1875 to his father ʿAbd al-G̲h̲anī Maḥmūd, of Kurdish descent and from the D̲j̲abbāriyya tribe (between Kirkūk and Sulaymāniyya in N. ʿIrāḳ), who was a pious man and worked as a gendarme outside Baghdad; for this reason, Maʿrūf was brought up and educated by his devoted mother Fāṭima bint D̲j̲āsim at her father's house (she was of the Ḳarag̲h̲ūl Arabic tribe, a branch of S̲h̲ammar, who inhabited the Ḳarag̲h̲ūl quarter in Bag̲h̲dād).

Maʿrūf was sent to a *kuttāb* in Bag̲h̲dād where he learnt reading and reciting the Ḳurʾān by heart. After three years of primary school, he joined al-Rus̲h̲diyya al-ʿAskariyya school. In his fourth year there, he failed his examinations and was unable to continue his secular studies which would have paved him the way for high military or government service. Hence he switched to religious studies under the supervision of the celebrated scholar Mahmūd S̲h̲ukrī al-Ālūsī (1857-1924 [*q.v.*]), and others such as S̲h̲ayk̲h̲ ʿAbbās al-Ḳaṣṣāb and Ḳāsim al-Ḳaysī, for twelve years. He was a distinguished student and became a devoted Ṣūfī. In appreciation of this, his master al-Ālūsī gave him the name of Maʿrūf al-Ruṣāfī, in contrast to the name of the celebrated Ṣūfī scholar Maʿrūf al-Kark̲h̲ī (which derived from the name of the western bank of the river Tigris), and thus Maʿrūf's family name became attributed to the eastern bank of the river.

There is no indication in the various biographical sources as to how he sustained himself during these years of his religious and literary studies and how he became a completely secular poet. What is known is that he was compelled to work as a teacher in two primary schools in Bag̲h̲dād until he left for a third school in Mandalī in Diyālā because of a higher wages.

Later, he attempted to return to Bag̲h̲dād and passed there an examination in Arabic language and literature with distinction, so that he was appointed a teacher at a secondary school until 1908. During these years, he published poems in well-known Egyptian periodicals such as *al-Muʾayyad* and *al-Muḳtaṭaf*, as did other famous poets of ʿIrāḳ, e.g. al-Zahāwī [*q.v.*], there being no periodical of distinction in ʿIrāḳ at that time. He became well-known in other Arab countries as well as among the Arab emigrants in America.

However, by this stage of his life, his poetry was already devoid of religious tendencies and completely secular, favouring freedom of thought, against tyranny, urging his people into scientific and cultural revival following the European model, describing and praising modern inventions, defending the victims of social injustice and lamenting the deteriorating conditions to which the Ottoman Empire, and especially ʿIrāḳ, was reduced. He also supported the slogan of the French Revolution, adopted by the Committee of Union and Progress (C.U.P.) as *Ḥurriyya. ʿAdāla, Musāwāt* ("Liberty, Justice and Equality"), as it appears in his poems published in *Dīwān al-Ruṣāfī*, Beirut 1910.

After the Young Turk Revolution of 10 July 1908, he translated into Arabic the rallying-song of their poet Tewfīḳ Fikret, which became a school song in many Arab countries. It seems that his sympathy with the ideology of the C.U.P. induced the Bag̲h̲dād branch of C.U.P. headed by Murād Bey Sulaymān (the brother of Maḥmūd S̲h̲ewḳat [*q.v.*]), to invite him to edit the Arabic part of the bilingual political and cultural journal (*Bag̲h̲dād* (6 August 1908) which was the party's bulletin.

Al-Ruṣāfī celebrated the declaration of the *Dustūr* (or Constitution of 10 July 1908) with both poetry and action. According to Ḳāsim al-K̲h̲aṭṭāt (*Maʿrūf al-Ruṣāfī, s̲h̲āʿir al-ʿArab al-kabīr*, Cairo 1971, 52-5), al-Ruṣāfī with a group of his Jewish and Christian friends entered the al-Wazīr mosque on a Friday and removed forcibly the Muslim preacher from his pulpit and delivered a speech in favour of the C.U.P. ideology. Al-Ruṣāfī's behaviour roused tremendous anger among the religious and conservative circles of Bag̲h̲dād, who demanded that he be hanged and who demonstrated in front of the *Wālī* or governor Nāẓim Pas̲h̲a, so that the latter, out of fear for al-Ruṣāfī's life, put him in preventive custody.

However, at the beginning of 1909, at the request of Aḥmed D̲j̲ewdet, the editor of the newspaper *Iḳdām*, al-Ruṣāfī arrived in Istanbul via Beirut in order to produce an Arabic version of his periodical, which it was hoped would create a new understanding between the two main groups of the Ottoman Empire, the Turks and the Arabs, and would serve as the voice of the C.U.P. Al-Ruṣāfī was disappointed to learn that the editor had not been able to get the financial support needed to publish the Arabic part. So he left for Salonika, and there Maḥmūd S̲h̲ewḳat, the commander of the 3rd Army Corps of Macedonia, marched with his army on Istanbul, deposed the Sultan ʿAbd al-Ḥamīd II [*q.v.*] on 13 April 1909, and removed his supporters, the reactionaries headed by Darwīs̲h̲ Waḥdatī, who had been raised to power on 31 March 1909. In his poem *Ruḳyat al-ṣarīʿ* ("An incantation for the fallen victim") (*Dīwān*, 6th ed., Beirut (?) 1958, 162-4), al-Ruṣāfī rebuked the Ottoman government for its tyranny, as being against Islamic tradition, and he called for a republican government (*d̲j̲umhūriyya*), in order to achieve progress and freedom as in Europe. In his poem *Fī Silānīk* (*ibid.*, 382-8), he described the revolution and his journey with the army to Istanbul againt the Sultan. In his poem *Tammūz al-ḥurriyya* ("July, the month o freedom") (*ibid.*, 388-9) he greeted the Young Turk Revolution, and expressed his joy at the deposition o ʿAbd al-Ḥamīd.

On his return to ʿIrāḳ via Beirut, where he wa received with courtesy by men of letters headed b Amīn al-Rīḥānī, he became short of money, bu fortunately the owner of al-Maktaba al-Ahliyy helped him by buying his *Dīwān*. The poems wer edited and rearranged by Muḥyī al-Dīn K̲h̲ayyāṭ an provided with a preface (Beirut 1910). This edition as well as the following ones were full of printing errors. The edition of Dār al-ᶜAwda, Beirut 1970, contains less errors, but the new edition annotated by Muṣṭafā ᶜAlī, al-Ruṣāfī's close friend and disciple, published in 4 vols. by the ᶜIrāḳi government, Bag͟hdād 1974, is the only authorised and complete edition. The pornographic poems of al-Ruṣāfī, except his poem *Badāᶜa lā k͟halāᶜa* (*Dīwān*, 6th edn., 283-5), are excluded from all editions, and the ᶜIrāḳi authorities never allowed their publication. In the former editions many verses and poems which were against King Fayṣal I, his officials, and against the Regent ᶜAbd al-Ilāh, Nūrī al-Saᶜīd and others, were not included.

Back home he resumed his work at the newspaper *Bag͟hdād*, but soon, in 1909, he reviewed a new invitation, this time from "The Arab Friends' Association" headed by al-Zahāwī and Fahmī al-Mudarris in Istanbul, to edit their daily newspaper *Sabīl al-ras͟hād* ("The Path of Reason"). In Istanbul he also gave lectures in two high schools on Arabic language and literature (collected in *Nafḥ al-ṭīb fī 'l-k͟hiṭāba wa 'l-k͟haṭīb*, Istanbul 1331/1917), and taught Ṭalᶜat Pas͟ha, a leading member of C.U.P., the Arabic language. It may be that his connection with Ṭalᶜat helped him to be elected as a deputy in the Ottoman Chamber of Deputies on behalf of the Muntafiḳ district of ᶜIrāḳ from 1912 onwards. He also married a widow named Balḳīs, but they had no children. He mentions her twice in his *Dīwān* (78, 244): in the first poem, when she is asking him "not to depart, while his ambitions forced him to", and in the second poem dedicated to the al-D̲jamīl family, asking them for support to be able to travel to Turkey in order to see "the person whom his heart is longing for". It seems that he later divorced her officially in 1925 because he was not able to sustain her.

Al-Ruṣāfī's main concern was the maintenance of the unity of the Ottoman Empire through the unity of all its religious and national groups, as well as its revival according to the ideology of the C.U.P. For this reason, he attacked the Arab Congress in Paris (17-23 June 1913) and censured its members in his satiric poem *Mā hākad͟hā* ("Not in this way") (*Dīwān*, 402-5, cf. also 405-7), accusing them of jeopardising the unity of the Empire, besides encouraging French ambitions in Syria and causing enmity between Christians and Muslims. In fact, al-Ruṣāfī was a great defender of the Arab spiritual and cultural revival within the framework of the Ottoman Empire, and a vehement critic of the European powers who were aiming at its destruction. When World War I broke out, he composed a poem *al-Waṭan wa 'l-d̲jihād* ("The homeland and the holy war") (*Dīwān*, 489-91) calling all the Muslims to defend Islam and criticising the Egyptians for backing the British, and he expressed his hope that ᶜIrāḳ would defeat the approaching enemy. This solidarity with the Ottoman Empire explains also why al-Ruṣāfī, in his poetry, did not lament those Arab nationalists who were hanged by D̲jamāl Pas͟ha (1916). On the other hand, he attacked the S͟harīf Ḥusayn of Mecca for his revolt against the Ottomans (10 June 1916); he neither celebrated an Arab government being established in Damascus and headed by Prince Fayṣal b. al-Ḥusayn (1918) nor lamented the latter's expulsion from Syria (1919); and in his poetry he did not as much as mention the ᶜIrāḳī revolt against the British in 1920.

After the war ended in 1918, al-Ruṣāfī left Istanbul for Damascus, where Prince Fayṣal formed his Arab government, but he was given the cold shoulder because of his former satirical poems against Fayṣal's father the S͟harīf Ḥusayn and the Arab nationalists. In fact, al-Ruṣāfī did not expect a reception of this kind from his former colleague in the Ottoman Parliament Prince Fayṣal, and was disappointed, because he considered his stand as having been honest and proper in the interests of the Ottoman Empire (*Dīwān*, 420-3).

For this reason, he accepted a job at the Teachers' Training College (*Dār al-Muᶜallimīn*) in Jerusalem (1918-21), where he became the focus of social and literary activities together with the Palestinian writers Isᶜāf Nas͟hās͟hībī, K͟halīl Sakākīnī and ᶜĀdil D̲jabr (*Dīwān*, 141, 428, 515). In 1921 the Director of the College, K͟halīl Ṭūṭaḥ, published al-Ruṣāfī's collection of 17 school songs with their musical settings under the title *Mad̲jmūᶜat al-anās͟hīd al-madrasiyya* (lith., Jerusalem 1921, with an introduction by Isᶜāf al-Nas͟hās͟hībī).

Safa Khulusi in his article *Maᶜrūf al-Ruṣāfī in Jerusalem* (in *Arabic and Islamic garland ... Studies presented to Abdul-Latif Tibawi* ... London 1977, 147-52) has discussed this period in the life of al-Ruṣāfī. Khulusi thinks that the poem which al-Ruṣāfī composed after attending a lecture which Prof. A. Sh. Yehuda gave on Arab civilisation at the invitation of Rāg͟hib Nas͟hās͟hībī, the Mayor of Jerusalem, and which was attended by Sir Herbert Samuel, the British High Commissioner for Palestine, succeeded in diverting the attention from the resolutions of the Palestinian Arab Congress held at Haifa in December 1920 and deflated the opposition to Samuel's policy. In this poem, al-Ruṣāfī praised the lecturer and the speech of Sir Herbert Samuel, as well as the Arab-Jewish blood ties, denying the accusation of their mutual enmity, and finally expressing the Arab's fear of being expelled from their homeland *Ilā Herbert Samuel*, *Dīwān*, 429-37). The poem evoked strong protests from Arab nationalists, and the Lebanese Maronite poet Wadīᶜ al-Bustānī, who lived in Haifa, composed a poem rebuking al-Ruṣāfī. This strong campaign against him persuaded al-Ruṣāfī to accept an invitation to return to Bag͟hdād in order to become the editor of a newspaper in support of Ṭālib Pas͟ha al-Naḳīb, who claimed the throne of ᶜIrāḳ.

One of the main questions asked by some Arab writers, and especially by the ᶜIrāḳi writer Hilāl Nād̲jī in his *al-Ḳawmiyya wa 'l-is͟htirākiyya fī s͟hiᶜr al-Ruṣāfī*, Beirut 1959, 108-9, is why al-Ruṣāfī did not deal with the Palestinian question and why he did not attack in his poetry the Zionist Movement in Palestine. The answer may be that al-Ruṣāfī was a great supporter of science, progress, socialism, woman's liberation, equality, freedom of thought and self-determination, as Hilāl Nād̲jī himself observed in his work and as is clear from several poems in al-Ruṣāfī's *Dīwān* (see e.g. *Yawm Sing͟hāfūra*, 473). It seems that he found all these qualities among the Jewish settlers in Palestine, hence admired them and did not criticise their projects.

Al-Ruṣāfī left for ᶜIrāḳ, but the expulsion of al-Naḳīb to India by the British in order to pave the way for Prince Fayṣal to become King of ᶜIrāḳ put an end to the publication of the newspaper. Instead, al-Ruṣāfī was appointed a deputy director of the office of translations, which he considered below his capability and his glorious previous career. He felt that he was being neglected and humiliated, at the time when what he called "flatterers and those devoid of talents" were attaining high and influential positions (*Dīwān*, 426-8). At the end of 1922 he left for Beirut and decided not to return to ᶜIrāḳ, but when he heard of the elections to the first ᶜIrāḳi Parliament he returned to Bag̲h̲dād. There he published his daily newspaper *al-Amal* (1 October-20 December 1923) whose editorials were his own, flattering British policy in ᶜIrāḳ. He also tried to make peace with King Fayṣal I, but to his great disappointment was not elected as an M. P. At the end of 1923 he was appointed Inspector of Arabic language in the Ministry of Education and gave lectures at the Teachers' College in Bag̲h̲dād on Arabic Literature, lectures that were partly published in *Durūs fī taʾrīk̲h̲ ādāb al-lug̲h̲a al-ᶜArabiyya*, Bag̲h̲dād 1928.

During this period he was in bad financial circumstances, and wrote the most vicious poems against King Fayṣal I, his government (especially against officials of the Ministry of Education) and the British (*Dīwān*, 448-50, 460-71); some of these poems remained unpublished and circulated orally or in handwriting. In his poem *Ḥukūmat al-intidāb* ("The Mandatory Government") (*Dīwān*, 461), he satirised the ᶜIrāḳi government as "False flag, constitution and parliament", and affirmed that the government was enslaved by the British. In a poem, not included in his *Dīwān* (see K̲h̲aṭṭāt, *Ruṣāfī*, 139, and Hilāl Nād̲j̲ī, *Ṣafaḥāt min ḥayāt al-Ruṣāfī*, Cairo 1962, 80), he accused King Fayṣal I of doing nothing but "counting days and receiving his salary" and cursed him and his palace, imploring its destruction. In order to escape from his poverty, he wrote panegyrical poems to ᶜAbd al-Muḥsin al-Saᶜdūn and others, asking for financial support.

By the help of Saᶜdūn, he succeeded in being elected as a member of the ᶜIrāḳi Chamber of Deputies (19 May 1928), but Saᶜdūn's suicide on 13 November 1929 was a great loss to him, and he elegised him in several poems (*Dīwān*, 318-26). Later on, however, al-Ruṣāfī succeeded several times in being elected for a period of eight years in all between 11 November 1930 and 22 February 1939.

Between 1933-4 al-Ruṣāfī lived in Fallūd̲j̲a in Diyāla; there he wrote his work *al-S̲h̲ak̲h̲ṣiyya al-Muḥammadiyya, aw ḥall al-lug̲h̲z al-muḳaddas* ("Muḥammad's personality, or the solving of the holy mystery"). S. A. Khulusi called it a *magnum opus*, adding that "according to his closest friends, he advised that it should not be published before the year A.D. 2000," and stated that the book was described as "heretical and ... that it abounds in many objectionable views" (*Maᶜrūf ar-Ruṣāfī*, in *BSOAS*, xiii/3 [1950], 619). A microfilm of the ms. is kept in the Irāḳī Academy of Sciences.

From the middle of 1941, after the *coup d'état* of Ras̲h̲īd ᶜĀlī al-Kīlānī, he returned to Bag̲h̲dād, where he lived in poverty. He supported the *coup* with his poetry, satirising the British and the Regent ᶜAbd al-Ilāh, as well as Nūrī al-Saᶜīd and other officials whom he accused of corruption. With the failure of the *coup*, followed by a massacre of the Jews known as the *Farhūd*, the British occupied Bag̲h̲dād (2 June 1941). Later on, al-Kīlānī's four lieutenant-colonels ("The Golden Square") were caught and hanged. Al-Ruṣāfī composed a long elegy on the failure of the *coup* and the hanging of some of its leaders, and threatened that a day would come and that the royal family would be destroyed by the army (K̲h̲aṭṭāṭ, 159-60; Nād̲j̲ī, *al-Is̲h̲tirākiyya*, 44-5). However, he was not arrested, and was left without support until he was forced to sell cigarettes in a small shop.

In 1944 he published his *Rasāʾil al-taᶜlīḳāt* (Bag̲h̲dād 1944), which contained three refutations of two of Zakī Mubārak's works *al-Taṣawwuf al-Islāmī* (1938) and *al-Nat̲h̲r al-fannī* (1934), and a third one of Caetani's work on the life of Muḥammad in his *Annali de l'Islam* (Milan 1905). Al-Ruṣāfī's views on monism expressed in his refutation of *al-Taṣawwuf al-Islāmī* caused tremendous criticism and anger and he was accused of blasphemy. *Fatwās* were given against him and for the banning of his book. It seems that these attacks induced him to write his will, in which he affirmed that he was a Muslim who believed in God and in Muḥammad, and that he believed in the essence of the religion but not in its trivialities (Muṣṭafā ᶜAlī, *al-Ruṣāfī, ṣilatī bihi, waṣiyyatuhu, muʾallafātuh*, Cairo 1948, 43, and K̲h̲aṭṭāṭ, 188-9).

By the end of 1944, he was allotted 40 ᶜIrāḳī *dīnār*s a month by a rich and influential political personality, Muẓhir al-S̲h̲āwī (d. 1958), to the end of his life, which came on 16 March 1945.

The great fame of al-Ruṣāfī is based upon his political and social poetry. The 6th edn. of *Dīwān al-Ruṣāfī* (Beirut ?1958) is divided into 11 sections of different length: (1) On the universe (8 poems); (2) Social topics (63 poems); (3) Philosophy (9 poems); (4) Descriptions (59 poems); (5) Conflagrations (3 poems); (6) Elegies (24 poems); (7) On women (8 poems); (8) History (11 poems); (9) Politics (42 poems); (10) War (8 poems); (11) Short Poems (111 poems, the shortest being of 2 verses, some of them improvised at receptions and parties and the longest being of 29 verses). These sections contain altogether 346 poems. The longest poem is of 104 verses of monorhyme, a biographical poem on Abū Bakr al-Rāzī (*Dīwān*, 358-66), and a narrative poem (Poverty and illness) (*ibid.*, 94-102) in 51 quintets. However, the division of the poems into these precise sections is arbitrary. Most poems are of monorhymes, in which each verse is divided into two hemistichs, and in the opening ones, both hemistichs are rhymed. A few poems are of stanzaic form, such as one poem in couplets; one poem is of three hemistichs to each stanza; two in quartets; four in quintets, and three *muwas̲h̲s̲h̲aḥ*s in the classical ten hemistichs form. Of the four quintets, one is a versification according to the modern theory of the formation of the universe entitled *al-Arḍ* ("The globe") (*Dīwān*, 27-32), and the second is a narrative poem on the consequence of poverty in ᶜIrāḳ (*ibid.*, 94-102). He composed poems in difficult rhymes which are avoided by other poets such as *z,ṣ,ẓ,ḍ,ṭ* and *n*, and at least eight poems, in the last hemistichs of which the numerical value of letters gives the date of their composition (*ᶜalā ḥisāb al-d̲j̲ummal*), a method which was used in the post-classical period. However, most of his poems are undated. Others were composed on the metre and rhyme of well-known classical examples, especially those of al-Mutanabbī and al-Maᶜarrī [*q.vv.*], and some have even quotations from pre-Islamic poets and others.

At the end of his life, he became free of this classical influence on style and metaphors and was able to use in his political poetry a spontaneous and more flexible style. The influence of al-Mutanabbī is clear also in his personal behaviour, his pride, his honesty and his endearing way in expressing his ideas. Like al-Mutanabbī, he used proverbial sayings, and boasted of his character and poetry in his panegyrics in which he asked for alms, while the influence of al-Maᶜarrī on him was clear in his philosophical outlook and his ideas on religion and God, including his scepticism and monism. Unlike Ibn Sīnā [*q.v.*], al-Ruṣāfī was sceptical about the eternity of the soul and its ascent to heaven (*Dīwān*, 182, 116, 189) and about religion as a divine revelation: for him, religion was, rather, an invention of wise thinkers for the benefit of mankind (*ibid.*, 187, 189). But like William Blake, he believed in the harmony and unity of body and soul (*ibid.*, 192-3), and even if the soul was supposed to be eternal, he would be inclined to think that it had no awareness of life. On the other hand, he urged on the Arabs the need for a scientific and cultural revival, for unity and liberty, and he defended the freedom of women, especially of Muslim ones, in his poems on women's affairs and in others. He also defended freedom of thought, behaviour and the press, and held that it was up to a free man to violate customs and traditions if he felt it necessary. He backed the oppressed, the persecuted and the victims of society, poverty and illness, and called for social security and equality. He rebuked the Arabs for their stagnation and apathy and for boasting of their old and glorious history. A unique poem which shows his attitude towards the oppressed and against religious fanaticism is his poem "The orphan's mother" (*Dīwān*, 39-42). In this, he relates the story of an Armenian widow and her orphaned son, both victims of religious fanaticism and racial hatred, her husband having been killed in the massacre of the Armenians in Turkey in 1915, and he declares that Islam is innocent of such cruelty. He also described new technical inventions such as the telegraph, the railway, the car, the watch, etc., and admired the inventions of the steam engine and of electricity.

He favoured long metres which suited his declamatory and rhetorical tone, such as *ṭawīl*, *wāfir*, *kāmil*, *basīt* and *khafīf*. Thought, not the emotions, dominated his poetry. He expressed his ideas in a direct and denotative style, not metaphorically or symbolically, and was fond of a classical vocabulary.

In his scientific works, he witnessed to his wide and profound knowledge of Arabic language and literature as well as of Islam and its history; yet he depended more on his talent and what he had studied during his youth. His published works, according to the chronological order of appearance are as follows:

(1) *al-Ruʾyā* [a novel] by Nāmiḳ Kemāl, tr. from Turkish into Arabic by al-Ruṣāfī, Baghdād 1909.
(2) *Dīwān al-Ruṣāfī*, Beirut 1910, 2nd ed. Beirut 1932, 6th ed. Beirut (?) 1958, with new poems added. New edn., Beirut, Dār al-ᶜAwda 1971, with new poems added. Also Baghdād, Maṭbaᶜat al-Ḥukūma 1974, 4 vols. ed. and annotated by Muṣṭafā ᶜAlī.
(3) *Madjmūᶜat al-anāshīd al-madrasiyya*, lith., with notes, Jerusalem 1921.
(4) *Dafᶜ al-hudjna fī irtiḍākh al-lukna*, Istanbul 1331/1912 (Arabic vocabulary used in the Turkish language and vice versa).
(5) *Nafḥ al-ṭīb fi 'l-khiṭāba wa 'l-khaṭīb*, Istanbul 1336/1917.
(6) *Tamāʾim al-tarbiya wa 'l-taᶜlīm*, Beirut 1924 (versified didactic and scientific subjects, for school children).
(7) *Muḥāḍarāt al-adab al-ᶜarabī*, Baghdād 1339/1921.
(8) *Muḥāḍara fī ṣalāḥ al-lugha al-ᶜarabiyya li 'l-tadrīs*, Baghdād 1926.
(9) *Durūs fī taʾrīkh al-lugha al-ᶜarabiyya*, Baghdād 1928.
(10) *Rasāʾil al-taᶜlīḳāt*, Baghdād 1944.
(11) *ᶜAlā bāb sidjn Abī al-ᶜAlāʾ*, Baghdād 1946 (a commentary on Ṭaha Ḥusayn's *Maᶜa Abī al-ᶜAlāʾ fī sidjnih*).
(12) *ᶜĀlam al-dhubāb*, Baghdād 1945 (a commentary on *Risālat ᶜālam al-dhubāb* by Dr. Fāʾiḳ Shākir).
(13) *al-Adab al-rafīᶜ fī mīzān al-shiᶜr*, Baghdād 1968 (on Arabic prosody—metre and rhyme).

There are 6 other unpublished works which are still in ms., the most important of which is *al-Shakhṣiyya al-Muḥammadiyya*.

Bibliography: The first detailed biography on al-Ruṣāfī was written by the Egyptian scholar Badawī Ṭabāna, *Ma ᶜrūf al-Ruṣāfī, dirāsa adabiyya li-shāᶜir al-ᶜIrāḳ wa-bīʾatihi al-siyāsiyya wa 'l-idjtimāᶜiyya*, Cairo 1947. Muṣṭafā ᶜAlī, al-Ruṣāfī's close friend, corrected many details of this book which he thought wrong in his work *Adab al-Ruṣāfī*, Baghdād 1947. Later on, Muṣṭafā ᶜAlī wrote another book, *al-Ruṣāfī, ṣilatī bihi, waṣiyyatuhu, muᶜallafātuh*, Cairo 1948, and his lectures in the Maᶜhad al-Dirāsāt al-ᶜĀliya in Cairo were published in his book *Muḥāḍarāt ᶜan Maᶜrūf al-Ruṣāfī*, Cairo 1953. Other friends of al-Ruṣāfī wrote also about him, including Nuᶜmān Māhir al-Kanᶜānī and Sa ᶜīd al-Badrī, *al-Ruṣāfī fī aᶜwāmihi al-akhīra*, Baghdād 1950; Saᶜīd al-Badrī, *ᶜĀrāʾ al-Ruṣāfī*, Baghdād 1951; ᶜAbd al-Ṣāḥib Shukr, *ᶜAbḳariyyat al-Ruṣāfī*, Baghdād 1958; Saᶜīd al-Badrī, *Dhikrā al-Ruṣāfī*, Baghdād 1959; Ṭālib al-Sāmarrāʾī, *al-Ruṣāfī dhālika al-insān*, Baghdād 1959. Other books on Ruṣāfī are Hilāl Nādjī, *Ṣafaḥāt min ḥayāt al-Ruṣāfī wa-adabih*, Cairo 1962, which contains poems and letters by al-Ruṣāfī praising the generosity of ᶜAbd al-Madjīd and Muẓhir al-Shāwī. Another important book by Nādjī is *al-Ḳawmiyya wa 'l-ishtirākiyya fī shiᶜr al-Ruṣāfī*, Beirut 1959. See also ᶜAbd al-Laṭīf Sharāra, *al-Ruṣāfī*, Beirut 1964; Djalāl al-Ḥanafī, *al-Ruṣāfī fī awdjih wa-ḥaḍīḍih*, Baghdād 1962; and Ḳāsim al-Khaṭṭāṭ, Muṣṭafā ᶜAbd al-Laṭīf al-Saḥartī and Muḥammad ᶜAbd al-Munᶜim Khafādjī, *Maᶜrūf al-Ruṣāfī shāᶜir al-ᶜArab al-kabīr, ḥayātuh wa-shiᶜruh*, Cairo 1971; at the end of this last book there is a comprehensive bibliography of books and articles in Arabic language only (381-9). Beside the two articles in English by Safa Khulusi mentioned above in the text, see Brockelmann, S III, 488-9; L. Massignon, *EI*[1], art. s.v.; Y. A. Dāgher, *Maṣādir al-dirāsa al-adabiyya, ii/*1: *al-Rāḥilūn (1800-1955)*, Beirut 1956, 388-92; Yūsuf ᶜIzz al-Dīn *Shuᶜarāʾ al-ᶜIrāḳ fī 'l-ḳarn al-ᶜishrīn* Baghdād 1960, 17-28, where he gives an interview made by Kāmil al-Djādirdjī with al-Ruṣāfī before his death; Salma Kh. Jayyusi, *Trends and movements in modern Arabic poetry*, Leiden 1977, i, 188-93. (S. MOREH)

MĀRŪN AL-NAḲḲĀSH [see AL-NAḲḲĀSH].

MĀRŪT [see HĀRŪT WA-MĀRŪT].

MARW AL-RŪDH, a town on the Murghāb river in mediaeval Khurāsān, five or six stages up river from the city of Marw al-Shāhidjān [*q.v.*], where the river leaves the mountainous region of Gharčistān [see GHARDJISTĀN] and enters the steppe lands of what is now the southern part of the Ḳara Ḳum [*q.v.*]. The site seems to be marked by the ruins at the modern Afghān town of Bālā Murghāb (in lat. 35° 35' N. and long 63° 20' E.) described by C. E. Yate in his *Northern Afghanistan or letters from the Afghan Boundary Commission*, Edinburgh and London 1888, 208; the modern settlement of Marūčak or Marw-i Kūčik apparently marks the dependency of Marw al-Rūdh mentioned by the mediaeval geographers as-Ḳaṣr-i Aḥnaf. At present, Bālā Murghāb falls within the post-1964 administrative reorganisation Bādghīs province of Afghānistān.

Marw al-Rūdh's name, "Marw on the river", or that of "Little Marw" served to distinguish it from the larger centre of Marw al-Shāhidjān. The pre-Islamic name of the place was in MP Marvirōt, Armenian Mṛot, later, giving the Arabic *nisbas* of al-Marwarrūdhī and al-Marrūdhī. The foundation of the town was attributed to Bahrām Gūr. In 553 a

Nestorian bishopric of Marw al-Rūdh is mentioned, and at the time of the Islamic conquest in 32/652 the local governor Bādhām became a client of the Arabs (Marquart, *Ērānšahr*, 75-6; Markwart-Messina, *A catalogue of the provincial capitals of Ērānshahr*, Rome 1931, 44; M.A. Shaban, The *ʿAbbāsid revolution*, Cambridge 1970, 21-2). In the early ʿAbbāsid period, *ca.* 160/777, in the governorships of Ḥumayd b. Ḳaḥṭaba and ʿAbd al-Malik b. Yazīd, Marw al-Rūdh, Ṭālaḳān and Gūzgān were in the hands of the Khāridjite rebel Yūsuf al-Barm al-Thaḳafī (Gardīzī, *Zayn al-akhbār*, ed. Ḥabībī, 126).

The geographers of the 4th/10th century describe it as being in a flourishing agricultural region, with dependent settlements such as Diza and Ḳaṣr (or Diz)-i Aḥnaf and with its Friday mosque built on wooden columns in the middle of the covered market. Al-Muḳaddasī states that in his time (*ca.* 370/980) it depended administratively on the local rulers, the Shīrs, of Gharčistan and that the appearance and speech of the local people resembled that of the mountain peoples of Gharčistān (314; see also al-Iṣṭakhrī, 269-70; Ibn Ḥawḳal², 441-2, tr. Kramers and Wiet, 427; *Ḥudūd al-ʿālam*, 105, comm. 328, spelling the name as Marūd). The district flourished under the Saldjūḳs. Malik-Shāh built defences at the nearby town of Pandj-dih, and Sandjar built Marw al-Rūdh's wall, 5,000 paces in circumference and still standing in Mustawfī's time (158-9, tr. 155). The area was much fought-over in the warfare of the Ghūrids and Khʷārazm-Shāhs, and a sharp battle took place near Marw al-Rūdh between the Ghūrīd rivals for supremacy in Khurāsān Ghiyāth al-Dīn Muḥammad and Sulṭān-Shāh (Djuwaynī-Boyle, i, 298). Marw al-Rūdh must accordingly have escaped the devastations which the Mongols wrought at Marw al-Shāhidjān, but appears to have become ruinous in Tīmūrid times.

Bibliography (in additions to references given in the article): Le Strange, *Lands*, 404-5; Barthold, *Merverrud*, in *ZVOIRAO*, xiv (1902), 028-032; idem, *Istoriko-geografičeskiy obzor Irana*, St. Petersburg 1903, 25, Eng. tr. S. Soucek, *An historical geography of Iran*, Princeton 1984, 35-6; Barthold, *Turkestan*³, 79.

(C. E. BOSWORTH)

MARW AL-SHĀHIDJĀN or simply MARW, the city which dominated the rich but notoriously unhealthy oasis region of classical and mediaeval Islamic times along the lower course of the Murghāb river on the northeastern fringes of Persia, also called "Great Marw". Formerly within the historic province of Khurāsān [*q.v.*], the seat of pre-Islamic wardens of the marches and often of provincial governors in Islamic times, its site ("Old Merv") and the nearby modern settlement of Bairam Ali (see below) fall today within the Turkmenistan SSR. The name Marw al-Shāhidjān "Royal Marw" clearly relates to Marw's role as the seat of representatives of royal authority, guarding this bastion of the Iranian world against barbarians from the Inner Asian steppes, and is contrasted with the name of the smaller town of Marw al-Rūdh [*q.v.*] "Marw on the river", situated further up the river. Concerning the basic element of the name, Marw, we find in Avestan Moᵘry-, and in OP Marghu, MP Marv, indicating the existence of both a labialised form like Marv and a spirantised one like Margh (see Markwart-Messina, *A catalogue of the provincial capitals of Ērānshahr*, Rome 1931, 45-6). The Arabic *nisba* is *al-Marwazī*, cf. al-Samʿānī, *Ansāb*, facs. ed. Margoliouth, f. 523b.

As a result of the work of V. A. Zhukovski (*Razvalinï starogo Merva*) and W. Barthold (*K istorii oroshenïya Turkestana*, reprinted in *Sočineniya*, iii, Moscow 1965, see 136-56), we are better informed on the history of Marw than on that of any other town in Persia or Central Asia. Literary sources alone are not sufficient to enable us to fix the date to which history goes back in the valley of the Murghāb. Archaeology alone could supply the information, but the archaeology of this region has not yet adequately been studied. We are therefore only able to give the following facts. In the Achaemenid period (6th-4th centuries B.C.), we find a highly developed agricultural community in the region of the Murghāb incorporated in the Persian state. Details on this point are given by Greek writers of antiquity, in particular, the geographers and historians of the campaigns of Alexander the Great (336-323 B.C.). The Greeks found in this region not only a settled population but also a rural society practising agriculture on a very high level. They grew the vine and made good wine.

Classical sources refer to the Murghāb as the Margus river and to the region of Marw as Margiana; authors like Pliny attribute the foundation of the city to Alexander, but it seems that we are on surer ground in attributing this, or conceivably its refounding, to the slightly later Seleucid king Antiochus I Soter (280-261 B.C.). To this same period belongs the building of the wall intended to protect the agricultural zone from the nomads of the steppe, then inhabited by the predecessors of the Turkish people. There is no reason, it seems, to doubt the date of the foundation of Marw, but only archaeology can settle the question definitely. To what date does the earliest building in the area of Marw, that is, the citadel, belong? The fact that already several centuries before our era we find agriculture highly developed shows that the valley of the Murghāb had a system of artificial irrigation. The rapid development of the oasis of Marw was due not only to this but also to the fact that in the Parthian period the great caravan route which linked Western Asia with China passed through Marw. The caravan from Western Asia went from Marw to Balkh, thence via the Darwāz and the northern part of Badakhshān, then on to the Alāy, Kāshgar and finally to China. In the Sāsānid period, the trade-route was moved further north. Caravans went from Marw to Čardjūy, Samarḳand and Semirečye or the land of the Seven Rivers. Marw was not only an emporium on the trade-route but a great industrial city. It is, however, only after the Arab conquest that history gives us ample details of the life of the city.

By utilising the information supplied by the Arab historians and geographers, we can obtain a fair picture of what Marw was like in their period and in antiquity. To understand the part played by Marw in the economic life of Western Asia and Central Asia, we have to study all that the Arab geographers and administrative historians of the 4th/10th century tell us about the system of irrigation. These sources record a highly-organised system of supervision and upkeep of the irrigation canals, under a *mutawallī* or *muḳassim al-māʾ*, corresponding to the general Persian term for a local irrigation official, *mīr-āb* [see MĀʾ. 6. Irrigation in Persia]. Ibn Ḥawḳal and al-Muḳaddasī report that this chief of irrigation had an extensive staff to keep the channels in repair, including a group of divers (*ghawwāṣūn*). There was a dam across the Murghāb above the city, and the supply of water from this store was regulated and measured by a metering device, called by al-Muḳaddasī a *miḳyās* on analogy with the famous Nilometer [see MIḲYĀS], comprising essentially a wooden plank with intervals marked at each shaᶜīra. An office called the *dīwān al-kastabzūd* (< Pers. *kāst u afzūd* "decrease and increase") kept a record of all those entitled to shares in the water. See on all this, E. Wiedemann, *Beitrag X. Zur Technik bei den Arabern*, in *SBPMS Erlg.*, xxxviii (1906), 307-13 = *Aufsätze zur arabischen Wissenschaftsgeschichte*, i, Hildesheim 1970, 272-8; C.E. Bosworth, *Abū ᶜAbdallāh al-Khwārazmī on the technical terms of the secretary's art*, in *JESHO*, xii (1969), 151 ff.

It is to the 2nd-7th/8th-13th centuries that the great economic prosperity of the oasis of Marw belongs, with a highly developed system of exchanges. Numerous technical and agricultural methods of cultures were developed, except the cultivation of wheat, which was imported from the valleys of Kashka-Daryā and Zarafshān. The people cultivated the silkworm. Shortly before the coming of the Mongols, there was at Kharaḳ to the south-west of Marw a "house" called al-Dīwakush, where sericulture was studied. Al-Iṣṭakhri, 263, says that Marw exported the most raw silk; its silk factories were celebrated. The oasis was also famous for its fine cotton which, according to al-Iṣṭakhrī, was exported, raw or manufactured, to different lands; see on the textiles of Marw, R.B. Serjeant, *Islamic textiles, material for a history up to the Mongol conquest*, Beirut 1972, 87-90. The district of Marw also contained a number of large estates which assured their owners considerable revenue. According to al-Ṭabarī (ii, 1952-3), in the 2nd/8th century whole villages belonged to one man. In the absence of legal documents, little is known of the life of the peasants. It is evident, however, that they were bound by feudal bonds to their lords (*dihḳāns*), and paid them at the time of the Arab conquest in kind and in the 2nd-4th/8th-10th centuries in kind and money. No evidence of the amount of these payments has come down to us. The town, built in the centre of a highly cultivated area, was destined to have a brilliant future. If we also remember that it had become one of the great emporiums on the caravan routes between Western and Central Asia and Mongolia and China, we can easily realise how the city grew so rapidly with its manufactures, markets and agriculture. At the present day, within the area of the old region of Marw, we can see three sites of ancient towns: 1. Gavur-Ḳaᶜla, corresponding to the town of Marw of the Sāsānid and early Muslim period; 2. Sulṭān-Ḳalᶜa quite close to the preceding on the west side. This is the Marw of the 2nd-7th/8th-13th centuries, which was destroyed by the Mongols in 1221; and lastly 3. ᶜAbd Allāh-Khān-Ḳalᶜa south of Sulṭān-Ḳalᶜa-Marw, rebuilt by Shāh Rukh in 812/1409. This is all that remains of the famous city, including its nearer environs.

The citadel of Marw, contemporary with the town built on the Gavur-Ḳalᶜa area, goes back to a date earlier than that of the town itself. The latter (Gavur-Ḳalᶜa) must be recognised as the earliest site (called *shahristān*); it grew up around the castle of a great lord (*dihḳān*), i.e. around the citadel itself. The *shahristān* can hardly be earlier than the beginnings of the town of Marw, but it will only be by excavation that the problem of the date of the earliest habitations in the citadel will be settled.

The Arabs on their arrival found the western quarter so much increased that it was by then the most important part of the town. It is to this part that the Arab geographers give the name of *rabaḍ*. The market was at first on the edge of the *shahristān* near the "Gate of the Town", not far from the western wall, and one part of it extended beyond this wall as the Razīḳ canal. The great mosque was built by the Arabs in the middle of the *shahristān* (al-Muḳaddasī, 311). Little by little, with the moving of the life of the town towards the *rabaḍ*, the administrative and religious centre of the town was moved thither also. On the bank of the Razīḳ Canal was built the second mosque which at the beginning of the 3rd/9th century was allotted by al-Maʾmūn to the Shāfiᶜīs. In the middle of the 2nd/8th century, in the time of the revolutionary leader Abū Muslim, the centre was moved still farther westward to the banks of the Mādjān Canal. At this date, the town was gradually occupying the site of the *rabaḍ*. The town of Marw in the 2nd-7th/8th-13th centuries was therefore no longer Gavur-Ḳalᶜa, but the town of which ruins still exist to the west of the latter, now known as Sulṭān-Ḳalᶜa. But the *shahristān* did not lose its importance at once. The site of the old town on Sulṭān-Ḳalᶜa is in the form of a triangle, elongated from north to south with an area equal to that of Gavur-Ḳalᶜa. It is surrounded by a fine wall built of unbaked brick, with several towers and other buildings belonging to the fortress. The latter was rebuilt by order of Sultan Malik-Shāh [*q.v.*] in 462-72/1070-80. It is one of the most splendid buildings of the period.

In the time of the Arab geographers, the two towns with their suburbs were surrounded by a wall, remains of which still exist. As regards the wall built in the time of Antiochus I, its remains were still visible in the 4th/10th century and are mentioned by al-Iṣṭakhrī, 260, under the name of al-Rāy.

The social structure of the town of Marw in the period when it took the place of Sulṭān-Ḳalᶜa changed a great deal, like the social and economic life of Western and Central Asia generally. The growth of cities, the development of urban life, the exchange of city products for those of the country and those of the nomads of the steppes, the expansion of caravan traffic, now no longer limited to the trade in luxuries, all these encouraged the growth of new classes of society. It was no longer the *dihḳans* who were the great lords of the town of Marw in the 2nd-7th/8th-13th centuries, although in Gavur-Ḳalᶜa, however, their *kūshks* existed down to the end of the 6th/12th century; it was the rich merchants and an aristocracy of officials who were masters. Although both were connected with the local aristocracy, it was no longer agriculture but trade and property in the town which were their sources of wealth. Similarly, a change was taking place in the position of the artisans who had long ceased to be the serfs of the *dihḳans*. Down to the 3rd/9th century, a number of men still paid feudal dues to the *dihḳans*. From then onwards, they seem to have been free. The appearance of the town also changed as regards both topography and buildings. While in the *shahristān* (Gavur-Ḳalᶜa) the bazar was at the end of the town and in part outside of it, when the *rabaḍ* attracted urban life to it, the markets and workshops became the centre of the town. Marw (Sulṭān-Ḳalᶜa) became in the 5th/11th century a commercial city of the regular oriental type. It was traversed by two main streets, one running north and south, and the other east and west; where they intersected was the *čārsū*, the centre of the market, roofed by a dome; the shops had flat roofs. It was there also that were to be found the little shops of the artisans, and although the literary sources only mention the money-changers', the goldsmiths' and the tanners' quarters, there also must have been the quarters of the weavers, coppersmiths, potters, etc. It was not only the administrative and religious centre, for it also contained the palaces, the mosques, *madrasas* and other buildings. For example, to the north of the *čārsū* was the great mosque, already built in the time of Abū Muslim, which survived till the Mongol invasion, if we may believe Yāḳūt. It must, however, have been frequently rebuilt. Yāḳūt also says that beside the great mosque was a domed mausoleum, built on the tomb of Sultan Sandjar; its mosque was separated from it by a window with a grill. The great dome of the mausoleum of turquoise blue could be seen at a distance of a day's journey. Within the walls which surrounded the mosque was another mosque built at the end of the 6th/12th century which belonged to the Shāfiʿīs. In the period of Yāḳūt, it seems that the domed building erected by Abū Muslim in baked brick, 55 cubits in height, with several porticoes—which is said by al-Iṣṭakhrī to have served as a *dār al-imāra* or "house of administration"—no longer existed. It used to stand close to the great mosque built by Abū Muslim. The town of Marw in this period—in addition to its great wall—had inner ramparts which separated the different quarters of the town. The city was famous for its libraries, and Yāḳūt spent nearly two years there just before the Mongol cataclysm working in these libraries (on the topography of mediaeval Marw, see Le Strange, *Lands*, 397-403).

Regarding the history of Marw, the city was under the Sāsānids the seat of the *Marzbān* of the north-eastern marches, Marw being the farthest outpost of the empire, beyond which lay the city-states of Soghdia, the kingdom of Khʷārazm and steppe powers like the Western Turks. Marw may be the Homo (for Mo-ho) of the Chinese Buddhist traveller Hiuen-tsang, and on a Chinese map of the early 14th century it appears as Ma-li-wu (Bretschneider, *Mediaeval researches*, ii, 103-4). Nestorian Christianity flourished there until the Mongol period, and its ecclesiastical leaders are often mentioned as present at synods; before 553 it was a bishopric, and thereafter a metropolitanate (see Marquart, *Ērānšahr*, 75-6). It was the metropolitan Īlīyā who buried the body of the slain Yazdigird III at Pā-yi Bābān (al-Ṭabarī, i, 2881, 2883), and there was a monastery of Masardjasān lying to the north of Sulṭān-Ḳalʿa (*ibid.*, ii, 1925; Yāḳūt, *Buldān*, ii, 684).

The last Sāsānid Yazdigird fled before the invading Arabs to Marw and was killed there in 31/651 by the *Marzbān* Māhūī Sūrī, so that the city acquired in Persian lore the opprobrious name of *khudāh-dushman* "inimical to kings" (al-Ṭabarī, i, 2872). It was conquered in this year for the Arabs by the governor of Khurāsān ʿAbd Allāh b. ʿĀmir b. Kurayz [*q.v.*], who made a treaty with Māhūī on the basis of a large tribute of between one and two million *dirhams* plus 200,000 *djarībs* of wheat and barley; the local *dihḳāns* of the oasis were to be responsible for the tribute's collection, and the soldiers of the Arab garrison were to be quartered on the houses of the people of Marw. There was thus from the start a basic difference in settlement pattern from that in the great *amṣār* of ʿIrāḳ and Persia, where the Arabs built distinct encampments as centres of their power. ʿAbd Allāh b. ʿĀmir left a garrison of 4,000 men in Marw, and then in 51/671 Ziyād b. Abīhi [*q.v.*] sent out 50,000 families from Baṣra and Kūfa, who were then settled in the villages of the oasis by the governor al-Rabīʿ b. Ziyād al-Ḥārithī. A process of assimilation with the local Iranian population now began, especially as some Arabs began to acquire taxable land in the countryside, and so became financially subject to the *dihḳāns*. These atypical social conditions of the Marw oasis may have contributed to Marw's role in the later Umayyad period as the focal point in the east for the ʿAbbāsid *daʿwa*, for the propaganda of the Hāshimiyya *duʿāt* seems early to have made headway among the settled and assimilated Arab elements. Some ʿAbbāsid agents were discovered there and executed in 118/736, and soon afterwards, a committee of twelve *nuḳabāʾ*, headed by Sulaymān b. Kathīr al-Khuzāʿī, was formed. Abū Salama al-Khallāl [*q.v.*] was in Marw in 126/746, and two years later Abū Muslim [*q.v.*] arrived as representative of the ʿAbbāsid *imām* Ibrāhīm b. Muḥammad b. ʿAlī b. ʿAbd Allāh b. ʿAbbās. Abū Muslim took advantage of the tribal strife of Ḳays and Yaman, and the assimilated population of Arabs, whose fiscal grievances had not been fully redressed by the tentative reforms of the Umayyad governor Naṣr b. Sayyār [*q.v.*] in 121/739, aided by Yamanīs against Naṣr and his North Arab supporters, so that by early 130/748, Abū Muslim was in control of Marw (thus the interpretation of M.A. Shaban, *The ʿAbbāsid revolution*, Cambridge 1970, 129 ff., 138 ff.; idem, *Islamic history A.D. 600-750 (A.H. 132), a new interpretation*, Cambridge 1971, 84-5, 173-5, 177, 182-5).

Under the early ʿAbbāsids, Marw continued to be the capital of the east, despite a humid and unpleasant climate (it was notorious for the guinea worm, *filaria medinensis*), and was for instance the seat of al-Maʾmūn whilst he was governor of the eastern provinces and whilst he was caliph until the year 202/817, when he left for Baghdād. The Ṭāhirid governors of Khurāsān, however, followed here by their supplanters the Ṣaffārids, preferred to make their capital at Nīshāpūr, although Marw remained the chief commercial centre of Khurāsān, and continued to flourish under the Sāmānids. Nevertheless, the disorders in Khurāsān during the last decades of Sāmānid rule, when power was disputed by ambitious military commanders, seem adversely to have affected Marw's prosperity. Al-Muḳaddasī, writing *ca.* 980, says that one-third of the *rabaḍ* or outer town was ruinous, and the citadel too had been destroyed; moreover, the city was racked by the sectarian strife and factionalism which seems to have been rampant in the towns of Khurāsān at this time (311-12; on the Shāfiʿī *madhhab* in Marw—where the Ḥanafīs in fact had a preponderance—see H. Halm, *Die Ausbreitung der šāfiʿitischen Rechtsschule von den Anfängen bis zum 8./14. Jahrhundert*, Wiesbaden 1974, 83-90).

But under the Saldjūḳs, the fortunes of Marw revived. It transferred its allegiance from the Ghaznawids to the Türkmens in 428/1037, and became the capital of Čaghrī Beg Dāwūd [*q.v.*], ruler of the eastern half of the newly-established Saldjūḳ empire, and from *ca.* 1110, that of Sandjar [*q.v.*], viceroy of the east. The latter's father Malik-Shāh had built a wall of 12,300 paces round the city, which in Sandjar's time underwent attack from various of the Saldjūḳ's enemies, such as the Khʷārazm-Shāh Atsïz [*q.v.*], who in 536/1141-2 raided Marw and carried off the state treasury. It was at Marw that Sandjar built his celebrated mausoleum, 27 m. square in plan and called the *Dār al-Ākhira* "Abode of the hereafter" (see on this, G. A. Pugačenkova, *Puti razvitiya arkhitekturī Yuzhnogo Turkmenistana*, Moscow 1958, 315 ff.). Under Sandjar's rule, the Türkmens of the steppes around Marw were under the control of a Saldjūḳ *shiḥna* or police official, but when in 548/1153 these Oghuz or Ghuzz rebelled against this control and defeated Sandjar, Marw fell under the nomads' control, and the latter held on to it, together with Balkh and Sarakhs, until the Khʷārazm-Shāhs imposed their rule in northern Khurāsān. Marw suffered terribly in the time of the first Mongol invasions, when Kh^wārazmian rule was overthrown. It was savagely sacked by Toluy's followers (beginning of 618/1221). According to Ibn al-Athīr, xii, 256, 700,000 people were massacred, and according to Djuwaynī, tr. Boyle, i, 163-4, 300,000; even if one allows for the customary hyperbole, it nevertheless remains true that Marw's prosperity was dealt a blow from which it took two centuries to recover. Mustawfī found Marw still largely in ruins in the mid-8th/14th century, and with the sands of the Ķara Ķum encroaching on the arable lands of the oasis (*Nuzha*, 156-7, tr. 153-4).

What then remains of the town of the 2nd-7th/8th-13th centuries—in addition to the wall already mentioned? The whole site of Sulṭān-Ķalʿa is covered with mounds and hillocks, formed on the sites of ancient buildings. Everywhere one sees great piles of bricks, whole and broken, and fragments of pottery, plain and glazed. In the centre, like a memorial of the great past, rises the domed mausoleum of Sultan Sandjar mentioned by Yāķūt, one of the finest buildings of the 6th/12th century. The question arises whether it had any connection with the "house of administration" with a dome and several porticoes mentioned by al-Iṣṭakhrī. The Marw of this period contains numerous buildings within the area of Sulṭān-Ķalʿa, as well as outside its walls, especially the western suburb, the subject since 1946 of archaeological investigations by M.E. Masson. In 808/1406 the Tīmūrid ruler Shāhrukh endeavoured to restore prosperity to this region, which had at one time been a flourishing oasis. Ḥāfiẓ-i Abrū gives us details of his scheme. The dam was rebuilt on its old site and the water restored to its old channel; but only a portion of the oasis could be irrigated. The town was rebuilt, but not on the old site because water could not be brought in sufficient quantity to Sulṭān-Ķalʿa. The town of Marw of this period corresponds to the old town of ʿAbd Allāh-Khān-Ķalʿa (popular legend wrongly attributing its building to the Shaybānid ʿAbd Allāh b. Iskandar (991-1006/1583-98 [*q.v.*]), the area of which was much less than that of Marw of the Mongol period, covering about three hundred square poles. The town of Marw of this period cannot be compared with that of the pre-Mongol period. In time, Marw and its oasis declined more and more. In the period of the Ṣafawid kingdom, it was the object of continual attacks on the part of the Özbegs, which could not help affecting it.

An almost mortal blow was dealt it at the end of the 18th century. Maʿṣūm Khān (later called Shāh Murād), son of the *atalīķ* [*q.v.* in Suppl.] Dāniyāl Biy of the newly-founded Mangīt [*q.v.*] dynasty of *amīrs* in Bukhārā, attacked the Ķādjār Türkmen local lord of Old Marw, Bayram ʿAlī Khān, killing him in 1785. Shāh Murād also destroyed the Sulṭān-Band, the dam across the Murghāb 30 miles/48 km. above Marw, and thereby reduced the economic prosperity of the region (F.H. Skrine and E.D. Ross, *The heart of Asia, a history of Russian Turkestan and the Central Asian khanates from the earliest times*, London 1899, 206). Consequently, the traveller Alexander Burnes found Marw in ruins and the surrounding district in complete neglect (*Travels into Bokhara*, London 1834, ii, 23 ff., 37-8, 258-60).

In 1884 the Marw oasis was occupied by the Russian army, and secured in the following year from an Afghān threat by General Komarov's victory. From 1887 onwards, attempts were made, with considerable success, to revive the agricultural prosperity of the devastated region by the building of two dams on the Murghāb, that of Hindū-Kush and that of Sulṭān-Band. The Transcaspian railway line from Krasnovodsk to Bukhārā, Samarķand and Tashkent passed through ʿAshķābād and Marw, and from Marw a branch was built southwards to Kushka on the Afghān frontier. In Tsarist times within the *oblast* of Transcaspia, Marw has since 1924 come within the Turkmenistan S.S.R. In 1935 the modern settlement of Bairam Ali was founded in the Marw region, and this town is now the chef-lieu of the *rayon* of the same name. In 1969 it had a population of 31,000, with flourishing cotton textile and dairy products industries (see *BSE*[3], ii, 534).

Bibliography (in addition to references given in the article): E. O'Donovan, *The Merv oasis. Travels and adventures east of the Caspian during the years 1879-80-81*, London 1882; V. A. Zhukovskii, *Razvalinï starogo Merva*, St. Petersburg 1894; W. Barthold, *K istorii Merva*, in *ZVORAO*, xix (1910), 115-38 = *Sočineniya*, iv, 172-95; idem, *Istoriko-geografičeskii obzor Irana*, St. Petersburg 1903, ch. 2 = *Sočineniya*, vii, 60-9, Eng. tr. Princeton 1983, 35-46; idem, *Turkestan down to the Mongol invasion*, index; E. Cohn-Wiener, *Die Ruinen der Seldschuken-Stadt von Merv und das Mausoleum Sultan Sandschars*, in *Jahrb. der Asiatische Kunst*, ii (1925), 114-22.

(A. Yu. Yakubovskii - [C. E. Bosworth])

AL-**MARWA** [see AL-ṢAFĀ].

MARWĀN I B. AL-**ḤAKAM** B. ABI 'L-ʿAṢ, Abu 'l-Ķāsim and then Abū ʿAbd al-Malik, first caliph of the Marwānid branch of the Umayyad dynasty [*q.v.*], reigned for several months in 64-5/684-5.

Marwān, born of al-Ḥakam's wife Āmina bt. ʿAlķama al-Kināniyya, stemmed from the same branch of the Umayyad clan of Ķuraysh, sc. Abu 'l-ʿĀṣ, as the Rightly-guided caliph ʿUthmān, and was in fact ʿUthmān's cousin. The sources generally place his birth in A.H. 2 or 4 (*ca.* 623-6), but it may well have occurred before the *Hidjra*; in any case, he must have known the Prophet and was accounted a Companion. He became secretary to ʿUthmān when he already had a considerable reputation for his profound knowledge of the Holy Book (al-Madāʾinī, in al-Balādhurī, *Ansāb*, v, 125: *min aķraʾ al-nās li'l-Ķurʾān*), and doubtless helped in the recension of what became the canonical text of the Ķurʾān in that caliph's reign [see ĶURʾĀN. 3]. Also during this reign, he took part in an expedition into North Africa, and it was apparently his share of the rich plunder from this which laid the foundations of Marwān's extensive personal fortune, invested in property in Medina; and it is further mentioned that he was for a while a governor in Fārs. He was wounded at the *Yawm al-dār*, the defence of ʿUthmān's house in Medina against the insurgents of the Egyptian army in 35/656, and fought at the Battle of the Camel with ʿĀʾisha and her allies [see AL-DJAMAL], but seized the opportunity personally to slay Ṭalḥa, whom he regarded as the most culpable person in the murder of ʿUthmān. Somewhat surprisingly, he then gave allegiance to ʿAlī after the battle.

During Muʿāwiya's caliphate, Marwān was governor of Baḥrayn and then had two spells as governor of Medina, 41-8/661-8 and 54-7/674-7, alternating with his kinsmen Saʿīd b. al-ʿĀṣ and al-Walīd b. ʿUtba. It was during these years that he acquired from the caliph the estate, with its lucrative palm groves, of Fadak [*q.v.*], which he subsequently passed on to his sons ʿAbd al-Malik and ʿAbd al-ʿAzīz. It is possible that Muʿāwiya latterly grew suspicious of Marwān's ambitions for his family, especially as the family of Abu 'l-ʿĀṣ was perceptibly more numerous than that of Ḥarb, Muʿāwiya's grandfather; Marwān himself had, according to al-Balādhurī, *Ansāb*, v, 164, ten sons and two daughters, and al-Thaʿālibī, *Laṭāʾif*, 136, tr. 107-8, states that he further had ten brothers and was the paternal uncle of ten of his nephews. It may have been fears of the family of Abu 'l-ʿĀṣ that impelled Muʿāwiya to his adoption (*istilḥāḳ*) of his putative half-brother Ziyād b. Sumayya [see ZIYĀD B. ABĪHI] and to the unusual step of naming his son Yazīd as heir to the caliphate during his own lifetime. There was certainly a lack (with the exception of al-Walīd b. ʿUtba, Muʿāwiya's nephew) of mature, experienced Sufyānids to succeed Muʿāwiya, whereas at the time of the expulsion of the Umayyads from the Ḥidjāz (see below), Marwān was the most senior of the Umayyads and the only one whom the Prophet had known (*shaykh kabīr* in the sources, probably referring as much to his prestige and authority as to his age).

When the difficulties arose in 60/680 over Yazīd b. Muʿāwiya's succession, involving a refusal of allegiance by the cities of the Ḥidjāz, Marwān advised the governor of Medina, al-Walīd b. ʿUtba, to use force against the rebels. After the withdrawal of the expeditionary force of Muslim b. ʿUḳba al-Murrī and its return to Syria (beginning of 64/autumn 683), the Umayyads and their clients who had been previously expelled but had returned with Yazīd's troops, comprising principally members of the lines of al-ʿĀṣ under ʿAmr b. Saʿīd al-Ashdaḳ [*q.v.*] and of Abu 'l-Āṣ under Marwān, were forced by the partisans of the anti-caliph ʿAbd Allāh b. al-Zubayr [*q.v.*] to abandon their properties in the Ḥidjāz and flee to Syria for a second time. Marwān was back in Syria by the beginning of 684, and some accounts say that he went in the first place to Palmyra rather than to the court of the ephemeral caliph Muʿāwiya II b. Yazīd [*q.v.*] at Damascus. With the latter's death, and in face of the widespread support, even in Palestine and northern Syria, for a Zubayrid caliph, Marwān despaired of any future for the Umayyads as rulers, and was himself inclined to give his allegiance to ʿAbd Allāh b. al-Zubayr. But heartened by the urgings of ʿUbayd Allāh b. Ziyād b. Abīhi [*q.v.*], Marwān allowed his own candidacy to go forward at the meeting of Syrians at al-Djābiya [*q.v.*] convoked to hail a successor to Muʿāwiya II, and with the support of the leader of Djudhām, Rawḥ b. Zinbāʿ, was hailed as caliph, with Khālid b. Yazīd b. Muʿāwiya [*q.v.*] and ʿAmr b. Saʿīd al-Ashdaḳ named as next heirs. With this acclamation and the support of the Kalb under Ibn Baḥdal [see ḤASSĀN B. MĀLIK], Marwān was able to defeat the Ḳays under al-Ḍaḥḥāk b. Ḳays al-Fihrī [*q.v.*] at the battle of Mardj Rāhiṭ [*q.v.*], probably to be placed in July or early August 684. Then shortly after his installation as caliph in Damascus, Marwān married Umm Hāshim Fākhita bt. Abī Hāshim b. ʿUtba, the widow of Yazīd I and mother of his two sons; this diplomatic alliance gave him a link with the Sufyānids.

Marwān was now able to consolidate his position in Syria and Palestine. His short reign was filled with military activity, beginning with the expulsion of the Zubayrid governor, ʿAbd al-Raḥmān b. ʿUtba al-Fihrī, called Ibn Djaḥdam, from Egypt. Marwān seems to have secured that province by Radjab 65/February-March 685, leaving there as governor his son ʿAbd al-ʿAzīz. Although the sources are confused here, it seems that Marwān's forces also repelled a Zubayrid attack on Palestine led by Muṣʿab b. al-Zubayr [*q.v.*]. It is possible, but not certain, that a Marwānid army itself invaded the Ḥidjāz under Ḥubaysh b. Duldja, but was repelled at al-Rabadha [*q.v.*] to the east of Medina. Marwān certainly took steps to secure ʿIrāḳ, which had declared for the Zubayrid cause, sending an army under ʿUbayd Allāh b. Ziyād which by-passed the hostile Ḳaysī centre of Ḳirḳīsiya in al-Djazīra and had reached al-Raḳḳa when the news of Marwān's death arrived.

This last event took place in the spring of 65/685, possibly as a result of a plague which was affecting Syria at this time. The date of Marwān's death is variously given in the sources: Elias of Nisibin has 7 May, and the Islamic historians such dates as 3 Ramaḍān/13 April (al-Masʿūdī, *Tanbīh*) and 29 Shaʿbān-1 Ramaḍān/10-11 April (Ibn Saʿd, al-Khalīfa b. Khayyāṭ, al-Ṭabarī). The place of his death is given by several authorities as Damascus (Ibn Saʿd, al-Ṭabarī, al-Masʿūdī, *Tanbīh*), but by al-Yaʿḳūbī and al-Masʿūdī, *Murūdj*, as al-Ṣinnabra on the Lake of Tiberias, a place used, it seems, as a winter residence by the early Umayyads. The length of his reign is placed at between six and ten months. Even less certain is Marwān's age when he died; the sources make him at least 63, but he may well have been over 70.

On the occasion of the successful outcome of the Egyptian expedition, Marwān had taken the opportunity to vest the succession in his own sons ʿAbd al-Malik and ʿAbd al-ʿAzīz [*q.vv.*], and it was accordingly the former who succeeded to the caliphate in Damascus after Marwān's death, apparently without opposition (at least, at this moment) from the two heirs designated at al-Djābiya, ʿAmr b. Saʿīd and Khālid b. Yazīd, but now set aside.

Marwān's life had been crowded with action, above all in its later years, filled with military campaignings and the negotiations surrounding his succession to the caliphate. He seems to have suffered severe after-effects from various wounds, and his tall and emaciated frame earned him the nickname of *khayṭ bāṭil* "insubstantial, gossamer-like thread" (see al-Thaʿālibī, *Laṭāʾif*, 35-6, tr. 56). His brusqueness and lack of the social graces resulted in his being described as *fāḥish* "uncouth". Later, anti-Umayyad tradition stigmatised him as *ṭarīd ibn ṭarīd* "outlawed son of an outlaw", associating him with his father al-Ḥakam who was allegedly exiled by the Prophet to Ṭāʾif, and as *abu 'l-djabābira* "father of tyrants" because his son and five of his grandsons subsequently succeeded to the caliphate. But he was obviously a military leader and statesman of great skill and decisiveness, amply endowed with the qualities of *hilm* [*q.v.*] and *dāhiya*, shrewdness, which characterised other outstanding members of the Umayyad clan. His attainment of the caliphate, starting from a position without many natural advantages beyond his own personal qualities (for he had no power-base in Syria and had spent the greater part of his career in the Ḥidjāz), enabled his successor ʿAbd al-Malik to place the Ummayyad caliphate on a firm footing so that it was able to endure for over 60 years more.

Bibliography: 1. Sources. The main historical sources for early Islam all contain relevant material. See al-Khalīfa b. Khayyāṭ, *Taʾrīkh*, index; Yaʿḳūbī, *Taʾrīkh*, ii, 304-6 and index; Ṭabarī, index; Kindī, *Wulāt Miṣr*, ed. Guest, 42-8; Masʿūdī, *Murūdj*, iv, 271-4, 277-9, v, 197-209 = §§ 1596-7, 1601-2, 1961-72 and index; idem, *Tanbīh*, 292, 304, 307-12, tr. Carra de Vaux, 383, 395, 399-404. There are biographical sections devoted to Marwān in Ibn Saʿd, v, 24-30; Balādhurī, *Ansāb al-ashrāf*, v, ed. Goitein, 125-64; Ibn Ḳutayba, *Maʿārif*, ed. ʿUkkāsha, 353-5; Ibn al-

Athīr, *Usd al-ghāba*, ii, 33-5 (al-Ḥakam), iv, 348-9 (Marwān). *Adab* works like Ibn ʿAbd Rabbihi's *ʿIḳd*, Iṣfahānī's *Aghānī* and Thaʿālibī's *Laṭāʾif al-maʿārif* (here cited ed. Abyārī and Ṣayrafī, and Eng. tr. Bosworth, *The book of curious and entertaining information*) contain much anecdotal material.

2. Studies. Th. Nöldeke, *Zur Geschichte der Omajjaden*, in *ZDMG*, lv (1901), 683-91; H. Lammens, *Études sur le règne du calife Moʿâwia Iᵉʳ*, in *MFOB*, i (1906), 27-9, 34-9, ii (1907), 94-132; idem, *Le califat de Yazîd Iᵉʳ*, in *MFOB*, iv (1910), 294-5, v (1911-12), 88-9, 93, 115; F. Buhl, *Zur Krisis der Umajjadenherrschaft im J. 684*, in *ZA*, xxvii (1912), 50-64; Lammens, *Moʿâwia II ou le dernier des Sofiânides*, in *RSO*, vii (1915), 37-8; idem, *L'avènement des Marwānides et le califat de Marwān Iᵉʳ*, in *MFOB*, xii (1927), 43-147; A. A. ʿAbd Dixon, *The Umayyad caliphate 65-86/684-705 (a political study)*, London 1971, 17-19; G. Rotter, *Die Umayyaden und der zweite Bürgerkrieg (680-692)*, Wiesbaden 1982, 115-26, 135-65; G. R. Hawting, *The first dynasty of Islam: the Umayyad caliphate A.D. 661-750*, London and Sydney, 1986, 46-8.   (C. E. Bosworth)

MARWĀN II b. Muḥammad b. Marwān b. al-Ḥakam, the last of the Ūmayyad caliphs of Syria (reigned 127/744 to 132/749-50) was, on his father's side, a grandson of the caliph Marwān I [*q.v.*], but there are variant accounts concerning his mother and the year of his birth. It is frequently reported that his mother was a non-Arab woman (sometimes specified as a Kurd) who passed into the possession of Marwān's father Muḥammad after ʿAbd al-Malik's defeat of Muṣʿab b. al-Zubayr and his general Ibrāhīm b. al-Ashtar in 72/691. Some reports say that the woman was already pregnant when Muḥammad took possession of her and that she gave birth to Marwān "on the bed of Muḥammad". A number of the *nasab* works fail to refer to Marwān's mother, a fact which perhaps confirms that at least she was not known to belong to one of the important Arab families. If his mother was indeed pregnant when taken from the Zubayrids, then 73/692 would be a likely year for his birth, but al-Ṭabarī, ii, 940, has a specific reference to it under 76/695-6. Statements of his age at the time of his death in 132/750 vary between 58 and 69. In tradition two *laḳab*s, again variously explained, are attached to Marwān's name: al-Djaʿdī and Ḥimār al-Djazīra (or simply al-Ḥimār, "the ass"). The former is usually said to be derived from the *ism* of Djaʿd b. Dirham [see IBN DIRHAM] who, it is asserted, acted as Marwān's tutor (*muʾaddib*; see *Fihrist*, i, 337-8; cf. Ibn al-Kalbī, *Djamharat al-nasab*, Kuwayt 1983, 156-7). The explanation of the name al-Ḥimār is equally uncertain; in modern works it is often claimed that it refers to Marwān's resolution and bravery in battle, but Bar Hebraeus (*Chronography*, tr. Wallis Budge, i, 111) says that it referred to Marwān's fondness for "the ass's flower" (for the *ward al-ḥimār*, i.e. the peony?, or chrysanthemum?, see Dozy, *Suppl.*, s.v. *ward*). Al-Ṭabarī's story (ii, 1912) about the Abyssinian who insulted Marwān's forces by performing lewd actions involving an ass's penis on the walls of Ḥimṣ does not seem to be an attempt to account for the name but rather implies that it was already current.

Information on Marwān's career before his seizure of the caliphate centres on his activities in the Ādharbāydjān, Armenia and Caucasus region. Following the defeat of al-Djarrāḥ b. ʿAbd Allāh al-Ḥakamī by the Khazars in 112/730, it seems that Marwān accompanied his cousin Maslama b. ʿAbd al-Malik [*q.v.*] who had been appointed over the region by the caliph

Hishām with the task of restoring the position of the Muslims in Armenia and the southern Caucasus. Having distinguished himself in the fighting, Marwān became governor of Ādharbāydjān and Armenia for Hishām, although there is some confusion as to whether he immediately succeeded Maslama as governor in 114/732, as al-Ṭabarī (ii, 1562, 1573) implies, or whether he rather followed Saʿīd b. ʿAmr al-Ḥarashī in the office (al-Balādhurī, *Futūḥ*, 207). If the latter is the case, then the beginnings of Marwān's governorship should probably be dated to 116/734 or 117/735. As governor, he supported in Armenia the Bagratids against the rival Mamikonians, sending Gregory and David Mamikonian into exile when they refused to accept his appointment of Ashot Bagrat as Biṭrīḳ of Armenia. Faced with the continuing threat from the Khazars to the north, the Armenians cooperated with the Muslims, and Armenian forces played an important part in the expedition which Marwān led into the Caucasus in 119/737 (J. Laurent, *L'Arménie entre Byzance et l'Islam*, Paris 1919, 339-40 (2nd ed. by M. Canard, Lisbon 1980, 422); R. Grousset, *Histoire de l'Arménie*, Paris 1947, 315-19; D. M. Dunlop, *The history of the Jewish Khazars*, Princeton 1954, 80-7). It is noteworthy too that Armenian troops are later reported to have played a part in helping Marwān to establish his authority over Syria following the death of Yazīd b. al-Walīd (e.g., Dennett, *Marwān b. Muḥammad*, 240, citing the chronicle of Levond).

Two passages of al-Ṭabarī (ii, 1941, 1944) refer to Marwān's adopting the military formation known as the *kurdūs* (pl. *karādīs*) and abandoning that called the *ṣaff* (pl. *ṣufūf*). A *kurdūs* was a relative small and compact detachment of soldiers (usually cavalry), while the *ṣufūf* were the more traditional long lines in which the Arabs organised themselves for battle. It has sometimes been suggested that Marwān was the first to introduce the *kurdūs* formation into the Muslim armies and that his experience in fighting on the northern borders where Byzantine influence was strong (χορτις has been proposed as the source of the Arabic word; S. Fraenkel, *Aramäischen Fremdwörter*, 239) led him to do so. However, whether Marwān was really the first to use this formation among the Muslims is doubtful (R. Levy, *The social structure of Islam*, Cambridge 1957, 430) and it is notable that al-Ṭabarī's reports do not, in any case, relate to the period of Marwān's fighting on the northern frontier but to the later fighting against Khāridjites in Mesopotamia after he had seized the caliphate.

It seems that Marwān had already contemplated marching south into Syria and taking a hand in affairs when Walīd II was overthrown and killed and Yazīd III became caliph in Djumāda II 126/April 744, but had been foiled by the dissent of the Kalbīs in his army led by Thābit b. Nuʿaym. During the short caliphate of Yazīd III, Marwān then acted as governor of Mesopotamia, basing himself in the Ḳaysī centre of Ḥarrān. With the death of Yazīd III in Dhu 'l-Ḥidjdja 126/September 744, he refused to accept the authority of the nominated successor, Ibrāhīm brother of Yazīd III, and crossed the Euphrates with his army. At this stage, it seems that he did not put himself forward as a candidate for the caliphate but merely as the champion of the two sons of the murdered Walīd II, who were imprisoned in Damascus. With the support of the Ḳaysī contingent of Ḳinnasrīn, he established control over Ḥimṣ and northern Syria and then defeated a Kalbī force led by Sulaymān b. Hishām at ʿAyn al-Djarr on the road from Damascus to Baalbek. In the aftermath of this battle the two sons of Walīd II were murdered in Damascus, Ibrāhīm and Sulaymān b. Hishām fled to the Kalbī centre of Palmyra, and Marwān was able to enter Damascus. There, it is said on the initiative of Abū Muḥammad of the Sufyānid branch of the Umayyad family, who claimed that the two sons of Walīd II had named Marwān as their successor, he was recognised as caliph and given the *bayʿa* in Ṣafar 127/December 744. Subsequently, Ibrāhīm and Sulaymān b. Hishām accepted his authority and were granted *amān*. Marwān did not, however, choose to remain in Syria but moved back to Harrān in Mesopotamia where, presumably, he felt more secure. For the first time an Umayyad caliph attempted to rule from outside Syria.

Faced, however, with a rebellion in Syria he soon had to return there. The rebellion started among the Kalb of Palestine led by Thābit b. Nuʿaym and quickly spread to the north where Ḥimṣ came out in opposition to Marwān. In Shawwāl 127/July 745 Marwān in person obtained the resubmission of Ḥimṣ and then sent a force south to relieve Damascus, under attack from Yazīd b. Khālid al-Ḳasrī. Yazīd was defeated and killed, and Marwān's army went on to capture Thābit b. Nuʿaym who was attacking Tiberias. Thābit was executed and the Kalbī settlement of al-Mizza near Damascus put to fire. Finally, al-Abrash al-Kalbī in Palmyra agreed to surrender to Marwān, and it seemed that his rule over Syria was again secure. At this point he called the Umayyad family together and had the *bayʿa* given to his two sons as his successors. But the opposition to Marwān in Syria was not yet over. When he raised a Syrian contingent to join the Mesopotamian army under Yazīd Ibn Hubayra [see IBN HUBAYRA], which was attempting to establish Marwān's authority in ʿIrāḳ, it deserted as it passed by al-Ruṣāfa where Sulaymān b. Hishām lived, and the Syrians recognised Sulaymān in opposition to Marwān. Sulaymān took possession of Ḳinnasrīn and attracted support from the rest of Syria. Withdrawing most of his Mesopotamian troops from Ibn Hubayra's force, Marwān attacked and defeated Sulaymān near Ḳinnasrīn and the vanquished Umayyad fled with the remnants of his army to Ḥimṣ and thence, leaving his forces there under the command of his brother, to Kūfa via Palmyra. Marwān now besieged Ḥimṣ for the second time, and when the town finally submitted after several months he had its walls rased together with those of several other major Syrian towns. By the summer of 128/746 Marwān had finally established his control over Syria.

The extension of his authority over ʿIrāḳ and all of Mesopotamia took even longer. Initially, he had attempted to weaken the governor of ʿIrāḳ appointed by Yazīd III, ʿAbd Allāh b. ʿUmar b. ʿAbd al-ʿAzīz, and to replace him with the Ḳaysī al-Naḍr b. Saʿīd al-Ḥarashī. Both rival governors were then overwhelmed, in 127/745, by the Khāridjite movement which had begun in Mesopotamia among the tribe of Shaybān and which is associated with the leadership of al-Ḍaḥḥāk b. Ḳays al-Shaybānī. The latter established himself in Kūfa but in the spring of 128/746 returned north and occupied Mawṣil, seeking to take advantage of Marwān's difficulties in Syria. Marwān's son ʿAbd Allāh, however, was able to hold the Khāridjites in check until Marwān had completed his subjugation of Ḥimṣ and could divert his forces to the east to deal with the threat. In the late summer Marwān defeated and killed al-Ḍaḥḥāk, under whom Sulaymān b. Hishām now fought, and the Khāridjites had to abandon Mawṣil. In the following year they were finally driven out of Mesopotamia and their danger ended when Marwān was able to withdraw men from ʿIrāḳ to deploy against them and their new leader Abū Dulaf. That Marwān was able to withdraw men from ʿIrāḳ was a consequence of the victories there in late 129/spring 747 of his general Yazīd Ibn Hubayra, who had defeated both the Khāridjite governor of Kūfa and the ʿAlid ʿAbd Allāh b. Muʿāwiya [*q.v.*], until then holding sway over large areas of western and south-western Iran.

The domination which Marwān had established by the end of 129/summer of 747 was to be ended two years later by the rising of the Hāshimiyya which had already begun in Khurāsān in Ramaḍān 129/June 747. By Rabīʿ II 132/November 749 the armies of the Hāshimiyya had destroyed Umayyad rule in Persia and ʿIrāḳ and the ʿAbbāsid caliphate had been proclaimed in Kūfa. In Djumādā II 132/January 750 Marwān himself led his forces in a last attempt to defeat the insurgents at the battle of the Greater Zab, and the destruction of his army there signalled the end of Umayyad power. Marwān himself escaped with a small band of supporters and fled through Syria to Egypt pursued by an ʿAbbāsid force. They finally caught him in Dhu 'l-Ḳaʿda 132/June 750 at Būṣīr in the province of Ushmūnayn in Upper Egypt, and there the last Umayyad caliph fell after a short struggle.

Marwān's career illustrates some of the weaknesses affecting the later Umayyad caliphate. He had obtained power as a result of his close links with the predominantly Ḳaysī army of the north Mesopotamian frontier in opposition to the Kalbī-based régime of Yazīd III. This close identification of the caliph with a particular faction clearly diminished the religious and moral claims of the Umayyad caliphate. Furthermore, his attempt to move the centre of the caliphate to Mesopotamia reflects the way in which Syria, hitherto the base of Umayyad rule, had itself been engulfed by the factionalism among the Arabs. It may seem that Marwān was unfortunate in that, having finally consolidated his authority over the central provinces, he was so soon overthrown by a movement which originated outside his control. In reality, however, the Umayyad state had been so weakened by its fundamental inability to satisfy the demands of Islam and by the factionalism among the Arab soldiers that it is doubtful whether even Marwān's forceful and energetic personality could have significantly prolonged it.

Bibliography: In addition to the indices to the more important Arabic works of *taʾrīkh* and *adab*, such as Ṭabarī, Yaʿḳūbī, Balādhurī, *Futūḥ*, Masʿūdī, *Murūdj*, and Ibn ʿAbd Rabbihi, *ʿIḳd* (for which the *Analytical indices*, to the Cairo 1321 edition, prepared by M. Shāfiʿ, Calcutta 1935, are useful), see the entries on Marwān II in Balādhurī, *Ansāb al-ashrāf*, and Ibn ʿAsākir, *Taʾrīkh madīnat Dimashḳ*, the relevant parts of which are still in ms.; for a summary of the latter, see the article on Marwān in Ṣalāḥ al-Dīn al-Munadjdjid, *Muʿdjam Banī Umayya*, Beirut 1970; for the references to Marwān in the *K. al-Aghānī*, the compiler of which, Abu 'l-Faradj al-Iṣfahānī, is claimed as a descendant of his, see Aghānī, *Tables alphabétiques*. Furthermore, the Syriac, Armenian and Georgian sources listed in the secondary literature cited in the second paragraph above are important for specific aspects of Marwān's career from a non-Muslim viewpoint. Among modern works see J. Wellhausen, *Das arabische Reich und sein Sturz*, Berlin 1902 (Eng. tr., *The Arab kingdom and its fall*, Calcutta

1927); D. C. Dennett, *Marwan Ibn Muhammad: the passing of the Umayyad caliphate*, unpubl. Ph.D. thesis, Harvard 1939; Abū Djayb al-Saᶜdī, *Marwān b. Muḥammad wa-asbāb sukūṭ al-dawla al-umawiyya*, Beirut 1972; P. Crone, *Slaves on horses*, Cambridge 1980; Hannelore Schönig, *Das Sendschreiben des ᶜAbdalḥamīd b. Yaḥyā (gest. 132/750) und den Kronprinzen ᶜAbdallāh b. Marwān II*, Stuttgart 1985.

(G. R. Hawting)

MARWĀN al-Akbar b. **ABĪ ḤAFṢA** and **MARWĀN** al-Aṣghar b. **ABI 'l-DJANŪB**, the most famous members of a family which included several poets; al-Thaᶜālibī characterises it as the most poetic of families in Islam, with six poets amongst its members.

The origins of the family's ancestor Abū Ḥafṣa Yazīd are obscure. He was a *mawlā* of the Umayyad Marwān b. al-Ḥakam, whom he aided on various historical occasions during the caliphate of ᶜUthmān and under ᶜAlī. It is impossible to decide exactly whether he was of Persian or Jewish origin. Freed by Marwān, he was entrusted with certain posts, including the collecting of the taxation from Medina. He married a girl from B. ᶜAmīr of the Yamāma, and his descendents were always to have close relations with that region of Arabia. One of them, Marwān al-Aṣghar, claimed that this woman was the grand-daughter of al-Nābigha al-Djaᶜdī, which would explain the poetic talent of the family. The ancestor Yazīd wrote verses (the *Fihrist* however, describes him as *mukill*). His son Yaḥyā was held in esteem by ᶜAbd al-Malik b. Marwān and had relations with Djarīr. The *Fihrist* attributes to him a *dīwān* of 20 leaves, of which only a small part has come down to us. The eulogy which he addressed to al-Walīd b. ᶜAbd al-Malik on the occasion of his accession to the caliphate is especially prosaic and conventional.

It is his grandson, Abu 'l-Simṭ Marwān b. Sulaymān, who can be considered as the first important poet of the family. He left the Yamāma for Baghdād, thus confirming the fact that it was impossible to attain literary fame when living remote from the capital. With a personality which was moreover strange, sordidly avaricious, clumsy and unscrupulous, he would arrive at the palace clad in rags, despite the enormous sums which the caliphs gave him for his poems. He seems to have steered his career forward with intelligence and prudence, and attached himself to the great personality of Abu 'l-Walīd Maᶜn b. Zāʾida [*q.v.*], to whom he came to owe his fame. He wrote for him numerous eulogies and a famous elegy in *-lā* considered as a model of its kind, and so fine that both al-Manṣūr and al-Mahdī took offence at a piece of praise which they considered excessive. Each of them is reputed to have excluded him from their *madjlis* for a whole year for this reason. But he was always recalled and found fresh favour with the ruler. This is attributable to the fact that he showed himself as a fierce opponent of the ᶜAlids and on every occasion proclaimed forth the legitimacy of the ᶜAbbāsids. He was one of that group of poets who, like e.g. Manṣūr al-Namarī, based their existence on their fidelity to the ruling power. He was accordingly rewarded with a prodigality which all the historians of literature stress. He was assassinated and died in *ca.* 181/797 in obscure circumstances.

Marwān b. Abī Ḥafṣa must be considered as a great classical poet. His supple and lexically straightforward vocabulary, and his clear syntax, contributed to his aim as a panegyrist who carefully sought formulae which would appear striking to his audience's minds. He was a master of the well-turned utterance; his poetry is expansive, strongly rhythmical, and his phrases follow each other in a continuous movement which gives his *ḳaṣīda* the strength of an oratorical period. He was thus, at the end of the 2nd/8th century, one of the best representatives of *shiᶜr minbarī*. Moreover, he worked over his poems with great care, as e.g. Zuhayr and al-Ḥuṭayʾa had done before him. He would read them over to grammarians in order to get their advice on his language, which does not seem to have been of the purest. It is said that Bashshār corrected his verses. Al-Aṣmaᶜī, a severe judge if ever there was one, considered him as a *muwallad* who never mastered the language. In the *ḥalḳa* of the philologist Yūnus, which he frequented in company with Khalaf al-Aḥmar, he was caught out over the explanation of a word used by Zuhayr. Yet Ibn al-Aᶜrābī considered him to be the last of the great poets. In fact, these verdicts are not contradictory, but simply show an evolution. The poets of the 2nd/8th century no longer mastered all the Arabic lexicon, and scholars could thus catch them out. Marwān represents indeed the type of these utterers of set pieces who, illustrating the academic tradition of poetry, were to serve in the 3rd/9th century as the definition of the aesthetic of that kind of beauty described as poetic.

The *Fihrist* attributes 100 leaves to Idrīs, Marwān's brother, but it is the name of his grandson Abu 'l-Simṭ Marwān b. Abi 'l-Djanūb which found a niche in posterity as the last good poet of this family. It is correct that this particular person knew how to take up a central position on the scene. He was even more a professional eulogist than his grandfather, and was successively brought into the circles of al-Maʾmūn, al-Muᶜtaṣim and then al-Wāthiḳ. The latter reproached him for being excessively close to his brother al-Mutawakkil and exiled him. Al-Mutawakkil's succession signalled his return to grace, and he went on to become one of the liveliest elements of the caliphal circles of literature. As well as the considerable sums which he got for his poems, he was awarded the governorship of the Yamāma and Baḥrayn. Al-Muntaṣir ordered him to return to the Yamāma, where all trace of him is lost.

Marwān b. Abi 'l-Djanūb kept up the anti-ᶜAlid tradition characteristic of the whole family since the time of its founder. The most shining part of his fame came from his remarkable gift as a satirist. Recovering once more the verse of the swashbucklers of the 1st/7th century, he directed his shafts against several members of the court circle, in particular, ᶜAlī b. al-Djahm, his favourite target, and ᶜAlī b. Yaḥyā b. al-Munadjdjim. He was savage and coarse, and quick to discover chinks in people's armour; he used any weapon to hand, and did nor scruple to use mendacity when he was short of arguments, all of which gave great joy to the caliph, who took a keen pleasure in following these kinds of clashes.

Marwān al-Aṣghar seems to us inferior as a poet to his grandfather. He was most at ease in attacking people, and his eulogies, even if they contain some fine verses, use above all the conventional material of this type of poetry. Caught between Abū Tammām on one side, and al-Buḥturī and Ibn al-Rūmī on the other, it was hard for him to aspire to the top positions. Moreover, he lacked the inspiration of Diᶜbil and the nobility of tone of ᶜAlī b. al-Djahm. After him, talent left the family. His son Muḥammad and his grandson Futūḥ, to whom the *Fihrist* attributes 50 and 100 leaves respectively, were merely hack versifiers.

Bibliography: *Aghānī*, x, 74, xii, 71, xxiii, 96;

Ṣūlī, *Akhbār al-Buḥturī*, index; *Fihrist*, Cairo edn., 234-5; Ibn Abī Ṭayfūr, *Kitāb Baghdād*, 126, 156; Shābushtī, *Kitāb al-Diyārāt*, 8 and n. 24; Ibn Ḳutayba, *Shiʿr*, 649, 739; Marzubānī, *Muʿdjam*, 137, 321-2; idem, *Muwashshaḥ*, 390 ff, 462 ff.; Ibn al-Muʿtazz, *Ṭabaḳāt al-shuʿarāʾ*, 392-3; Khaṭīb Baghdādī, *Taʾrīkh Baghdād*, xiii, 142, 153-5; Ṭabarī, index; Ibn Rashīḳ, *ʿUmda*, index; Thaʿālibī, *Laṭāʾif al-maʿārif*, Cairo 1960, 70-4, tr. Bosworth, *The book of curious and entertaining information*, Edinburgh 1968, 75-8; Ibn Khallikān, *Wafayāt*, v, 189, no. 716, 244, no. 732 (notice on Maʿn b. Zāʾida); Ibn al-Djarrāḥ, *Waraḳa*, 44-6; J. E. Bencheikh, *Le cénacle poétique du calife al-Mutawakkil (m. 247), contribution à l'analyse des instances de légitimation socio-littéraires*, in *Mélanges H. Laoust. I, BEO*, xxix (1977), 33-52; Muneerah al-Rasheed, *The Abū Ḥafṣah family of poets, together with a critical edition of the poetry of the principal members of the family*, unpubl. Manchester Ph.D. thesis 1980.

(J.E. Bencheikh)

MARWĀNIDS, the branch of the Umayyad dynasty of Arab caliphs in early Islam, who formed the second, and most long-lasting line of this dynasty, the first line being that of Sufyānids, that of Muʿāwiya I b. Abī Sufyān b. Ḥarb [*q.v.*], his son and his grandson (41-64/661-83). With the death of the child Muʿāwiya II b. Yazīd [*q.v.*], the caliphate passed to Muʿāwiya I's second cousin Marwān b. al-Ḥakam b. Abi 'l-ʿĀṣ, of the parallel branch of the Aʿyāṣ [*q.v.* in Suppl.]. Marwān and his descendants now formed the Marwānid line of the Umayyads (64-132/684-750), his son and successor ʿAbd al-Malik [*q.v.*] being the progenitor of all the subsequent caliphs with the exceptions of ʿUmar II [*q.v.*], son of ʿAbd al-Malik's brother ʿAbd al-ʿAzīz, and the last caliph Marwān b. Muḥammad b. al-Ḥakam.

For the general history of the dynasty, see umayyads, and also the articles on individual rulers.

(Ed.)

MARWĀNIDS, a dynasty of Kurdish origin who, having ousted the Ḥamdānids [*q.v.*], ruled Diyār Bakr from 380/990-1 to 478/1085. The founder of the dynasty, a Kurdish chief named Bādh, seized the city of Mayyāfāriḳīn [*q.v.*] after the death of the Būyid ruler ʿAḍud al-Dawla (373/983), and then took Āmid, Naṣībīn and Akhlāṭ (Ibn al-Athīr, ix, 25; Ibn al-Azraḳ, 49-52). Badh successfully fended off attacks both from a Būyid army sent against him and from the Hamdānids, but was killed by a coalition of Ḥamdānid and ʿUḳaylid forces after his unsuccessful attempt to take Mawṣil (380/990).

The dynasty itself, however, takes its name not from Bādh but from Marwān, a miller who had married Bādh's sister. It was their son Abū ʿAlī al-Ḥasan b. Marwān who, having withdrawn after Bādh's death in 380/990 to Ḥiṣn Kayfā, married his uncle's widow, routed the Ḥamdānids on two occasions and took possession of Mayyāfāriḳīn and Āmid (Ibn al-Azraḳ, 59-60; Ibn al-Athīr, ix, 50). After his murder at Āmid in 387/997, his brother Mumahhid al-Dawla Saʿīd ruled until 401/1011. These two precarious reigns paved the way for the accession of a third brother, Naṣr al-Dawla Aḥmad [*q.v.*], whose rule marks the apogee of Marwānid power.

Naṣr al-Dawla was recognised as ruler of Diyār Bakr by the Būyid *amīr* Sulṭān al-Dawla, by the Fāṭimid caliph al-Ḥākim, and by the Byzantine emperor, all of whom soon sent envoys and congratulatory messages to him (Ibn al-Azraḳ. 103). Indeed, Naṣr al-Dawla in his long reign (401-83/1011-61) was to practise a skilful policy of accommodation and self-preservation with all three powers. He also had to contend with Bedouin Arab dynasties such as the ʿUḳaylids and the Mirdāsids [*q.vv.*], who wielded power in Northern Syria and al-Djazīra, and to whom he was forced to cede Naṣībīn and Edessa respectively.

The 6th/12th century chronicler of al-Djazīra, Ibn al-Azraḳ al-Fāriḳī, gives in his chronicle a very full account of Marwānid rule. Naṣr al-Dawla was fortunate to have the services of two capable viziers, Abu 'l-Ḳāsim al-Ḥusayn al-Maghribī, who died in office (428/1037), and whose biography is given by Ibn Khallikān [see al-maghribī, banū] and the even more famous Fakhr al-Dawla Ibn Djahīr [see djahīr, banū]. Under Naṣr al-Dawla, Diyār Bakr enjoyed a high level of stability and commercial and cultural prosperity. The Marwānid court at Mayyāfāriḳīn was frequented by prominent *ʿulamāʾ* and poets, such as the Shāfiʿī *ʿālim* ʿAbd Allāh al-Kāzarūnī (d. 455/1063) (Ibn al-Athīr, ix, 52) and the poet al-Tihāmī (d. 416/1025-6) (Ibn al-Azraḳ, 82). Nāṣir-i Khusraw visited Mayyāfāriḳīn in 438/1046 and was much impressed by it (*Safar-nāma*, ed. Muḥammad Dabīr-Siyāḳī, Tehran 1335/1956, 8-11).

Naṣr al-Dawla emerges as a flamboyant ruler with political acumen and extravagant tastes. His religious stance appears to have been a pragmatic one, suitable for the ruler of a vulnerable buffer state surrounded by greater powers of the most divergent confessional loyalties. It seems likely that he ruled a predominantly Christian population in the towns of Diyār Bakr and that he enjoyed a good relationship with Byzantium. Indeed, the emperor Constantine X asked him for help in procuring the release of the Georgian prince Liparit from the Saldjūḳ sultan Ṭoghrīl (Ibn al-Athīr, ix, 372-3). It is probable that Naṣr al-Dawla was persuaded for a short while from 430/1038-9 to give the *khuṭba* in favour of the Fāṭimid al-Mustanṣir (Ibn Khaldūn, *ʿIbar*, iv, 318), but it is also noteworthy that in that same reign, ʿAbd Allāh al-Kāzarūnī went to Mayyāfāriḳīn and spread the Shāfiʿī *madhhab* throughout Diyār Bakr (Ibn al-Athīr, ix, 52).

In traditional fashion, Naṣr al-Dawla is praised for strengthening the frontiers and for building bridges and citadels, and these laudatory statements of Ibn al-Azraḳ are confirmed by the evidence of Marwānid inscriptions found on the walls of Āmid. Indeed, according to the evidence of an inscription dated 445/1053-4 on a marble slab in the Bāb Ḥiṭṭa in Jerusalem, Naṣr al-Dawla was also responsible for establishing two houses for the use of pilgrims there (Burgoyne, 118-21). The sources comment on the immense wealth accumulated by Naṣr al-Dawla. He is also said to have possessed 360 concubines who did not, however, prevent him from meticulous observance of the morning prayer. He was interested in gastronomical pleasures, too, and sent his cooks to Egypt to learn to culinary arts of that country (Ibn al-Athīr, x, 11).

When the Saldjūḳ sultan Ṭoghrīl advanced into Diyār Bakr (448/1056-7), he did not aim at abolishing the Marwānid state, so Naṣr al-Dawla recognised his suzerainty and kept his lands. Ṭoghrīl wrote to him confirming his role as a frontier lord fighting the infidels and exhorting him to continue in this task (Ibn al-Athīr, ix, 275).

On the death of Naṣr al-Dawla (453/1061), the power and prestige of the dynasty declined markedly His son Niẓām al-Dīn Naṣr succeeded him, at first only in Mayyāfāriḳīn and then two years later (having overcome his brother Saʿīd) in Āmid too. On the death of Niẓām al-Dīn (472/1079) his son Nāṣir al

Dawla Manṣūr, the last Marwānid ruler, came to power. The vizier Ibn Djahīr, who had left Diyār Bakr for Baghdād, used his influence with Malik-Shāh and Niẓām al-Mulk to persuade them to bring the Marwānid dynasty to an end and to seize their treasures. In 478/1085 Diyār Bakr fell to Ibn Djahīr and direct Saldjūḳ control was imposed (Ibn al-Athīr, x, 93-4). Ibn Djahīr took their treasury for himself and the last Marwānid ruler Manṣūr was given Djazīrat Ibn ᶜUmar, where he lived on until 489/1096.

Bibliography: 1. Primary sources: Ibn al-Azraḳ al-Fāriḳī, *Taʾrīkh Mayyāfāriḳīn wa-Āmid*, ed. B. A. L. Awad, Cairo 1959, *passim*; Ibn al-Athīr, ix, 25, 49-52, 272-6, 372-3, 416, x, 11, 86, 93, 151, 174; Ibn Khallikān, tr. de Slane; Ibn Khaldūn, Cairo 1847, iv, 315-21. 2. Secondary sources: H. F. Amedroz, *The Marwānid dynasty at Mayyāfāriqīn in the tenth and eleventh centuries A.D.*, in *JRAS* (1903), 123-54; M. van Berchem and J. Strzygowski, *Amida*, Heidelberg and Paris, 1910, 22-37; A. Gabriel, *Voyages archéologiques dans la Turquie orientale*, Paris 1940; C. E. Bosworth, in *Camb. hist. of Iran*, v, 24, 97-8; M. H. Burgoyne, *A recently discovered Marwānid inscription in Jerusalem*, in *Levant*, xiv (1982), 118-21; Zambaur, *Manuel*, 135. See also *EI*[1] MARWĀNIDS, NAṢR AL-DAWLA; and *EI*[2] DIYĀR BAKR. (CAROLE HILLENBRAND)

MARWĀNIYYA, a branch of the Khalwatiyya Ṣūfī order [*q.v.*] in Egypt, named after Marwān b. ᶜĀbid al-Mutaᶜāl (d. 1329/1911). His father, ᶜĀbid al-Mutaᶜāl b. ᶜAbd al-Mutaᶜāl (d. 1299/1881-2), had been initiated into the Khalwatiyya order by Ḥusayn al-Muṣaylihī (cf. Mubārak, *Khiṭaṭ*, xv, 45), a *khalīfa* [*q.v.*] of Muḥammad al-Ḥifnī's disciple Muḥammad b. ᶜAbd Allāh al-Shintināwī. ᶜĀbid al-Mutaᶜāl later obtained *al-khilāfa* and acted as a *shaykh* of his own Khalwatiyya order, which had not yet differentiated itself, either in name or in practice, from Muṣṭafā Kamāl al-Dīn al-Bakrī's version of the Khalwatiyya, as transmitted by al-Bakrī's *khalīfa* al-Ḥifnī. From early 1912 onwards, under ᶜĀbid al-Mutaᶜāl's son, Marwān, the order was presented under a name of its own, al-Marwāniyya. The original *silsila* [*q.v.*] going back to al-Bakrī was dropped and replaced by another *silsila* which was identical with ᶜĀbid's genealogy (cf. ᶜAbd al-Mutaᶜāl al-Ḥamzāwī al-Marwānī, *Tahdhīb al-isᶜāfāt al-rabbāniyya bi 'l-awrād al-Marwāniyya*, Cairo 1330/1912, 61-4). In addition, the order's link with the Khalwatiyya tradition, which had been cultivated and propagated by Muṣṭafā Kamāl al-Dīn al-Bakrī, was cut when the reading of Yaḥyā al-Shirwānī al-Bākūbī's *Wird al-sattār*—which according to al-Bakrī, is the pivot of Khalwatiyya ritual—was abandoned and when, at the same time, private and communal reading (in the *ḥadras* [*q.v.*]) of al-Bakrī's *aḥzāb* [see ḤIZB]) was replaced by the reading of *ṣalawāt* and other liturgical texts attributed to ᶜĀbid's ancestor Marwān al-Khalfāwī (d. 730/1329-30).

A discussion of the various factors which account for the introduction of these alterations and for the concomitant rise of the Marwāniyya, in conjunction with additional details and references, is to be found in F. de Jong, *The Ṣūfī orders in post-Ottoman Egypt, 911-1981* (in preparation), ch. 3. The Marwāniyya is one of the officially recognised Ṣūfī orders in Egypt (cf. Mashyakhat ᶜUmūm al-Ṭuruḳ al-Ṣūfiyya, *Ḳānūn raḳm 118 li-sana 1976 m. bi-shaʾn Niẓām al-Ṭuruḳ al-Ṣūfiyya....*, Cairo n.d., 29).

Bibliography: Given in the article. (F. DE JONG)

MĀRWĀŔ [see DJŌDHPŪR]

AL-**MARWAZĪ**, ABŪ BAKR AḤMAD B. MUḤAMMAD B. AL-ḤADJDJĀDJ B. ᶜABD AL-ᶜAZĪZ, the preferred disciple of Aḥmad b. Ḥanbal [*q.v.*], who, it is said, appreciated al-Marwazī's piety and virtues. His mother was originally from Marw al-Rūdh, whence his *nisba*, whilst his father was a Khᵂārazmian. Hardly any of the events of his life are known, in as much as he seems to have lived within his master's shadow, although he is depicted as once setting out on an expedition in the midst of a crowd of admirers.

The biographical notices devoted to him stress Abū Bakr al-Marwazī's role in the transmission of *ḥadīths* gathered by Ibn Ḥanbal, as well as in the formation of quite a number of Ḥanbalīs, amongst whom al-Barbahārī [*q.v.*] is especially cited. They also contain *responsa* of the Imām in reply to various questions concerning, for example, outside the sphere of *fiḳh* properly defined, the rules of conduct which a Muslim should observe in society.

He was so close to his master that it was he who closed his eyes at the latter's death, and on his own death, on 7 Djumādā I 275/17 September 888, he was buried at his feet in the Cemetery of Martyrs (*maḳābir al-shuhadāʾ*) in Baghdād.

Bibliography: Khaṭīb Baghdādī, *Taʾrīkh Baghdād*, iv, 123-5; Abū Yaᶜlā al-Farrāʾ, *Ṭabaḳāt al-Ḥanābila*, Cairo 1371/1952, 56-63; Nābulusī, *Ikhtiṣār Ṭabaḳāt al-Ḥanābila*, Damascus 1350/1931-2, 32-4; H. Laoust, *La profession de foi d'Ibn Baṭṭa*, Damascus 1958, index; idem, *Le Hanbalisme sous le califat de Bagdad*, in *REI*, xxvii (1959), 76. (ED.)

AL-**MARWAZĪ**, ABU 'L-FAḌL AḤMAD B. MUḤAMMAD AL-SUKKARĪ, Arabic poet of Marw, *floruit* later 4th/10th or early 5th/11th century. Al-Thaᶜālibī quotes specimens of his light-hearted and witty poetry, and also of an interesting *muzdawadja* in which he turned Persian proverbs into Arabic *radjaz* couplets, a conceit said to be one of his favourite activities.

Bibliography: Thaᶜālibī, *Yatīma*, Damascus 1304/1886-7, iv, 22-5, Cairo 1375-7/1956-8, iv, 87-90; C. Barbier de Meynard, *Tableau littéraire du Khorassan et de la Transoxiane au IVᵉ siècle de l'hégire*, in *JA*, Ser. 5, i (1853), 205-7. (ED.)

AL-**MARWAZĪ**, ABŪ ṬĀLIB ᶜAZĪZ AL-DĪN ISMĀᶜĪL B. AL-ḤUSAYN B. MUḤAMMAD... b. ᶜAlī b. al-Ḥusayn b. ᶜAlī b. Abī Ṭālib, a Ḥusaynī who seems to have devoted himself to the study of genealogies, although he is also credited with knowledge of astronomy and, like so many others, he was a composer of verse. His ancestors had left Medina and settled first in Baghdād, then in Ḳum(m) and finally in Marw, where he was born on 22 Djumādā 572/26 December 1176. He embarked on traditional studies in his native city, then, when 22 years old, he followed the pilgrims as far as Baghdād but refrained from completing the pilgrimage; he concluded his education as a pupil of eminent teachers of the period, in the capital of the caliphate, at Nīshāpūr, Rayy, Shīrāz, Tustar, Harāt and Yazd. In 614/1217, when Yāḳūt met him in Marw, he already had to his credit a series of works dealing especially with genealogies, but consisting in some cases of presenting in the form of ancestral trees (*tashdjīr*) the information contained in earlier works. Among his original writings figures a *Kitāb al-Fakhrī* on the genealogies of the Ṭālibīs which was commissioned from him by Fakhr al-Dīn al-Rāzī (543-606/1149-1209 [*q.v.*]) when the latter passed through Marw; it is not inconceivable that this explains the attribution to al-Marwazī of the *Fakhrī* of Ibn al-Ṭiḳṭaḳā (7th-8th/13th-14th century [*q.v.*]), which was dedicated to Fakhr al-Dīn ʿIsā b. Ibrahim al-Mawṣil (see the edition of the *Fakhrī* by H. Derenbourg, Paris 1895, 14, no. 2, 16).

The information available on Abū Ṭālib al-Marwazī (see for example al-Suyūṭī, *Bughya*, 194; F. Bustānī, *Dāʾirat al-maʿārif*, iv, 401-2) is derived exclusively from the article which Yāḳūt (d. 626/1229) devoted to him (in *Udabāʾ*, vi, 142-50) during his lifetime; this explains the fact that the date of his death is nowhere mentioned.

Bibliography: Given in the article.

(CH. PELLAT)

AL-**MARWAZĪ**, SHARAF AL-ZAMĀN ṬĀHIR, presumably a native of Marw [see MARW AL-SHĀHIDJĀN] or a descendant of such a native, physician and writer on geography, anthropology and the natural sciences, died after 514/1120. He acted as physician to the Saldjūḳ sultan Malik-Shāh [*q.v.*] and possibly to his successors down to the time of Sandjar [*q.v.*]; little else is known of his life. His main fame comes from his book the *Ṭabāʾiʿ al-ḥayawān*, which is essentially zoological in subject, but also with valuable sections on human geography, i.e. the various races of the world, extant in an India Office ms., Delhi, Arab 1949. Sections of this, in which the author reveals borrowings from *inter alia* the lost *Kitāb al-Masālik wa 'l-mamālik* of Abū ʿAbd Allāh Muḥammad b. Aḥmad al-Djayhānī and his family [see AL-DJAYHĀNĪ in Suppl.], have been edited and translated by Minorsky as *Sharaf al-Zamān Ṭāhir Marvazī on China, the Turks and India*, London 1942.

Bibliography: Minorsky, *op. cit.*; Brockelmann, S I, 903. (C. E. BOSWORTH)

MARY [see MARYAM].

MĀRYĀ or **MAREA**, a Tigre-speaking tribe some 40,000 strong in the upland region on the left bank of the river ʿAnsabā, north-west of Keren in western Eritrea [*q.v.*] They claim descent from a Saho warrior of the same name, who is said to have settled in the region with seventeen soldiers during the 14th century. This data seems to be confirmed by the *Gadla Ewosṭāṭēwos* (Turaiev, *Acta S. Eustathii*, 37-8), where the Ethiopian saint Ewosṭāṭēwos is said to have visited "the two Māryā" on his way to Jerusalem in *ca.* 1337 (cf. C. Conti Rossini, in *RSO*, ix, 452-5; Bermudez, *Breve relaçao*, 117). Until today, the tribe is indeed split into two sections of nobles, the *Māryā Ḳayiḥ* or "Red Māryā" and the *Māryā Ṣallīm* or "Black Māryā", who are by far the most numerous. The distinction must represent two migrations, for the "Black" are traditionally regarded as "the first born" and in a higher position than the "Red", which is contrary to the meaning of *ḳayiḥ* (*ḳayy*) in Amharic. On several occasion, such as the death of the chief of the "Black", the "Red" had to give presents to the other group. The tribe consists further of families who are vassals to the nobles. The descendants of the warrior Māryā became very numerous and subjugated the local tribes. Called *tigre* because of their origin—the term means "serf caste" in this context—these vassal tribes were in fact Ethiopians and Bedja [*q.v.*], whose language was taken over by the ruling class. The latter's Saho language has been long since forgotten.

The distinction between "Black" and "Red" is now entirely a territorial one, the two groups living in strictly defined plateaux, divided by deep ravines. The "Black" occupy the lower regions with abundant water, keeping camels and vast numbers of goats. The "Red" live in more elevated regions with little water, do not keep camels but have many sheep. The land around the semi-permanent encampments is cultivated by the *tigre*, who also care for the animals. They have to supply the nobles with milk, butter and grain, make special offerings of animals at the marriages and deaths of the ruling class, and help them to pay off blood money, which with the Māryā is very high amounting to 800 head of cattle.

Until the beginning of the 19th century, the Māryā were Ethiopian Christians. Ruins of churches are scattered about their land, e.g. at Erota. Somewhere between 1820 and 1835 (Münzinger, *Ostafrikanische Studien*, 228), the Māryā and the Bayt Asgedē were among the first of the Tigre-speaking tribes to join Islam under the influence of Muslim traders, the revival of missionary activities caused by Wahhābism and the preaching of Sayyid Aḥmad b. Idrīs al-Fāsī (1760-1837), a Maghribī *shaykh* settled in Mecca, the serf caste having already adopted Islam earlier. Foremost among the Islamic missionaries were the ʿĀd Shaykh, descendants of Shaykh al-Amīn (generally corrupted to Lamīn) b. Ḥamad, who gained a great reputation through his miracles and whose tomb became the centre of a special cult. Although some of the clans still bear Christian names, like the ʿĀd Te-Mikāʾēl, a section of the "Red", the Māryā and their vassals are all Muslims. In many respects, Islamic law has considerably, and positively, influenced the life of the tribe. The right of the first-born son to inherit his father's estate to the exclusion of the daughters has been modified, while the old custom of enslaving the vassals who were unable to pay the nobles has been weakened. Differences in the penal code between punishments for crimes committed by nobles or by vassals have been disappearing. Under Italian rule, the more onerous duties of the vassals were considerably lightened. The rigid noble-serf relationship was, however, still very strong until recently.

Bibliography: E. Cerulli, art. MĀRYĀ in EI^1; B. Turaiev, *Acta S. Eustathii*, Ethiopic text in *Monumenta Aethiopiae hagiologica*, iii, St. Petersburg 1905, Latin text tr. in *CSCO, Script. Aeth.*, ser. altera, xxi (1906), 1-97; J. S. Trimingham, *Islam in Ethiopia*, Oxford 1952; S. F. Nadel, *Races and tribes in Eritrea*. British Military Administration, Asmara 1943; W. Münzinger, *Ostafrikanische Studien*, Schaffhausen 1864; C. Conti Rossini, *Principi di diritto consuetudinario dell'Eritrea*, Rome 1916; E. Littmann, *Publications of the Princeton expedition to Abyssinia*, iv,... 1913-15; G. K. N. Trevaskis, *Eritrea, a colony in transition, 1914-1952*, London-New York 1960.

(E. CERULLI - [E. VAN DONZEL])

MARYAM, Mary, the mother of Jesus. The Arabic form of the name is identical with ܡܪܝܡ and μαριάμ which are used in the Syriac and the Greek Bible, in the New as well as in the Old Testament. In the latter it corresponds to the Hebrew מִרְיָם. Al-Bayḍāwī considers the name to be Hebrew; but the vowelling would seem to indicate a Christian source, according to A. Jeffery, *Foreign vocabulary of the Qurʾān*, Baroda 1938, s.v. The name Maryam, like others with the same suffix, such as ʿAmram, Bilʿam, points to the region between Palestine and Northwestern Arabia as its home. According to Muslim interpretation, the name means "the pious" (*al-ʿābida*; cf. the commentaries on sūra III,31). It occurs frequently in the Ḳurʾān in the combination [ʿĪsā] Ibn Maryam "[Jesus] the son of Mary" (sūra II,82, 254; III, 31-2; IV, 156, 169; V, 19, 50, 76, 82, 109, 112, 114, 116; IX, 31; XIX, 35; XXIII, 52; XXXIII,7; XLIII, 57; LVII, 27; LXI, 6, 14), no father being mentioned, because, according to Muslim tradition also, ʿĪsā had no earthly father. In the majority of these passages ʿĪsā is clearly regarded as the higher of the two. Yet Maryam's place is important [see ʿĪSĀ and the Bibl. there listed].

Maryam is mentioned in the Ḳurʾān, from the earliest to the later Medinan sūras.

(a) Maryam's special privileges; the annunciation.

To the first Meccan period belongs sūra XXIII, 52: "And we made the son of Maryam and his mother a sign; and we made them abide in an elevated place, full of quiet and watered with springs". Here some have seen the first allusion in the Ḳurʾān to the virgin birth. This idea is accentuated in sūra XIX,20, where Maryam says to the spirit (i.e. the angel) who announces to her the birth of a male child: "How should I have a male child, no human man having touched me?" In sūra LXVI, 12, the conception is ascribed to this divine spirit (cf. Luke, i, 34-5: "And Mary said to the angel, How can this be, since I have no husband? And the angel said to her, The Holy Spirit will come upon you, and the power of the Most High will overshadow you").

The virgin birth is also mentioned in sūra LXVI, 12 (Medinan): "And Maryam bint ʿImrān who kept her body pure. Then we breathed into it from our spirit. She acknowledged the truth of the words of her Lord and of his book and she belonged to the obedient".

A third mention of the annunciation and the virgin birth is in sūra III, 37-8: "When the angels said, O Maryam, verily Allah has elected thee and purified thee and elected thee above the women of all created beings. O Maryam, be obedient unto thy Lord and prostrate thyself and bow down with those who bow down" (cf. Luke, i, 28). The commentators remark on these verbs: *iṣṭafā* (chosen: twice) and *ṭahara*: Maryam was miraculously preserved from all bodily impurity and from spiritual failings. There is discussion too as to whether Maryam is the best of all women without exception, bearing in mind the veneration accorded to Fāṭima. Al-Rāzī, followed by al-Ḳurṭubī, takes it in an absolute sense, while most say "of that time" (R. Arnaldez, *Jésus fils de Marie prophète de l'Islam*, Paris 1980, 77). Maryam is generally held, in Muslim tradition, to be one of the four best women that ever existed, together with Āsiya [*q.v.*], K͟hadīd͟ja [*q.v.*] and Fāṭima [*q.v.*] (Aḥmad b. Ḥanbal, *Musnad*, iii, 135), and the chief of the women of Paradise (Ibn Ḥanbal, iii, 64, 80). For a comparison of Mary with Fāṭima, based on Sunnī and S͟hīʿī interpretations of verses in sūra III and XIX, see J.D. McAuliffe, *Chosen of all women: Mary and Fatima in Qur'ānic exegesis*, in *Islamochristiana*, vii (1981), 19-28.

According to tradition, the annunciation took place in the following way: D͟jibrīl appeared to Maryam in the shape of a beardless youth with a shining face and curling hair, announcing to her the birth of a male child. She expressed her amazement, but, on the angel's reassuring answer, she complied with the will of God.

Thereupon the angel blew his breath into the fold of her shirt, which she had put off. When the angel had withdrawn, she put on the shirt and became pregnant. The annunciation took place in the cavern of the well of Silwān, whither Maryam had gone, as usual, to fill her pitcher; she was then 10 or 13 years of age; and it was the longest day of the year. In Christian tradition also, the voice of the angel was heard by Mary for the first time when she had gone to fill her pitcher. According to a different tradition, ʿĪsā's spirit entered Maryam through her mouth (al-Ṭabarī, *Tafsīr*, vi, 22).

(b) Maryam's religious importance.

It has been pointed out that the Ḳurʾān seems to refer to a belief that Maryam was considered as a third deity, or a divine person; and that she and her son were venerated together as gods. Such may be reflected in sūra V, 79: "Al-Masīḥ, the son of Maryam, is an Apostle only, who was preceded by other Apostles, and his mother was an upright woman; and both were wont to take food". This verse would appear to refute any veneration of ʿĪsā and his mother as divine persons, elevated above human needs. With it may be compared sūra IV, 169: "O people of the book, beware of exaggeration in your religion and say of Allāh nothing but the truth. ʿĪsā b. Maryam is only the Apostle of Allāh and his word, which he conveyed unto Maryam and a spirit that came forth from him. Believe, therefore on Allāh and his Apostles and say not 'three'. Beware of this, this will be better for you. Allāh is but one God", etc. Clearer is sūra V, 116: "And when Allāh said, O ʿĪsā b. Maryam, hast thou said to the people, Take me and my mother as two Gods besides Allāh? He answered: Far be it, that I should say to what I am not entitled. If I should have said it, thou wouldst know it", etc.

The commentaries also describe the Trinity as consisting of Allāh, ʿĪsā and Maryam. Al-Bayḍāwī, however, admits that in sūra IV, 169, there could be an allusion to the Christian doctrine of one God in three hypostases: Father, Son and Holy Spirit.

The question has often been asked why the Ḳurʾān sees fit to refute an apparent belief in Maryam as one of the persons of the Trinity. It seems likely that what is here reflected is a background of folk-religion, and the veneration accorded to Mary within the Church, rather than any specific beliefs. Christian sects giving undue importance to Mary were not very significant. The Trinity is a notoriously difficult concept: and in an expression quoted by al-Ṭabarī, vi, 171, Father, Son, *wa-zawd͟j mutabbiʿat*[un] *minhumā, zawd͟j* is probably a misreading of the same consonantal outline, *rūḥ* (cf. J. Abd el-Jalil, *Marie et l'Islam*, Paris 1950, 66).

Attempts, however, have been made to trace the background of the Ḳurʾān's statements. Maracci has made a reference to Epiphanius, *Adv. Haereses*, Haeres. lxxviii, § 23, where this author speaks of women in Arabia who venerated Mary as God, and offered her cakes, from which the heresy is often called that of the Collyridians. Sale, in his *Preliminary discourse*, 45, mentions the Mariamites, who worshipped a Trinity consisting of God, Christ and Mary, referring to a passage in the work of al-Makīn. There could have been an identification of ʿĪsā with the Holy Spirit (cf. sūra IV, 169, as translated above) thus leaving a vacant place in the Trinity. A different explanation is attempted by Sayous, *op. cit.*, in *Bibl.*, 61.

The Story of Maryam and ʿĪsā.

Many of the features narrated in the Ḳurʾān agree, partly or wholly, with narratives in the apocryphal gospels. Sūra XXIII, 52 (see above), mentions the elevated place that was prepared for ʿĪsā and his mother. It is not clear which tradition might be here alluded to. According to Luke, i, 39, Mary went to mountains to visit Elisabeth. In the *Protoevangelium Jacobi* (ch. xxii; Syriac text, 20) it is Elisabeth who flees together with John to a mountain, which opens to protect them against their presecutors. The Muslim commentators mention Jerusalem, Damascus, Ramla and Egypt as being possibly meant by the "elevated place". Maracci thinks of Paradise.

In two passages of the Ḳurʾān there is a fuller narrative of ʿĪsā's birth and what is connected with it: sūra XIX (named *Maryam*), 1-35, and in sūra III, 31-

42 (for a very detailed analysis of relevant passages, cf. Schedl, *op. cit.*, in *Bibl.*, 189-99, 402-10).

Sūra XIX opens with the story of Zakariyyāʾ and Yaḥyā (1-15); then follows the story of Maryam and ʿĪsā (16-34). Sūra III, 31-42, contains: (a) the birth of Maryam; (b) the annunciation of Yaḥyā (33-6); and (c) the annunciation of ʿĪsā (37-41). The comparison of sūra XIX with sūra III makes it probable that Muḥammad became acquainted with the story of the birth of Maryam later than with those of Yaḥyā and ʿĪsā.

(a) The birth of Maryam. This story is found in a Christian tradition corresponding closely with that which is contained in the *Protoevangelium Jacobi* and *De nativitate Mariae*. Mary's father is called ʿImrān in the Ḳurʾān, Joachim in Christian tradition; Ibn Khaldūn (*ʿIbar*, ii, 144) is also acquainted with the name Ioachim. Maryam is called a sister of Hārūn (sūra XIX, 29), and the use of these three names ʿImrān, Hārūn and Maryam, has led to the supposition that the Ḳurʾān does not clearly distinguish between the two Maryams, of the Old and New Testament. The Ḳurʾān names two families as being especially chosen: those of Ibrāhīm and of ʿImrān (sūra III, 32). It is the family of ʿImrān, important because of Moses and Aaron, to which Maryam belongs. It is not necessary to assume that these kinship links are to be interpreted in modern terms. The words "sister" and "daughter", like their male counterparts, in Arabic usage can indicate extended kinship, descendance or spiritual affinity. This second ʿImrān, together with Hārūn, can be taken as purely Ḳurʾānic. M. Hamidullah's literal rendering of *ukht Hārūn* in a marginal note of his translation of the Ḳurʾān (p. 289) as "Sœur Aaronide" would indicate this (Arnaldez, 33-4). M. Hamidullah also refers to Maryam as "membre par adoption de la famille de ʿImrān" (*Le Prophète de l'Islam*, Paris 1959, i, 415). Muslim tradition is clear that there are eighteen centuries between the Biblical ʿAmram and the father of Maryam.

ʿImrān's wife, ʿĪsā's grandmother, is not mentioned by name in the Kurʾān. In Christian as well as in Muslim tradition, she is called Ḥanna. It is only in Muslim tradition that her genealogy is worked out. She is a daughter of Fāḳūdh and a sister of Ishbāʿ, the Biblical Elisabeth.

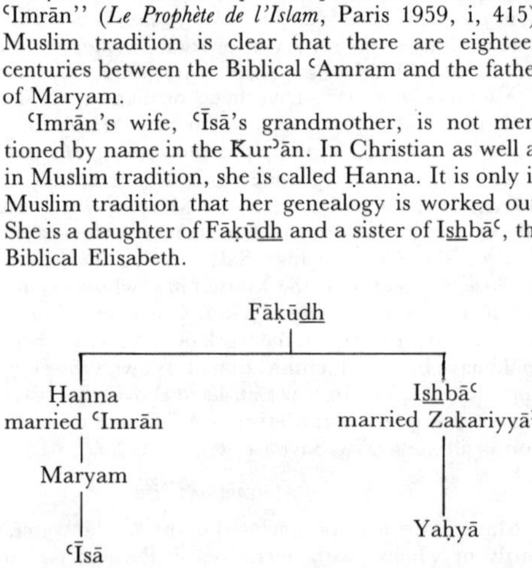

According to a different genealogy, Ishbāʿ and Maryam were sisters, daughters of ʿImrān and Ḥanna (al-Masʿūdī, *Murūdj*, i, 120-1 = §§ 117-18; al-Ṭabarī, *Tafsīr*, iii, 144).

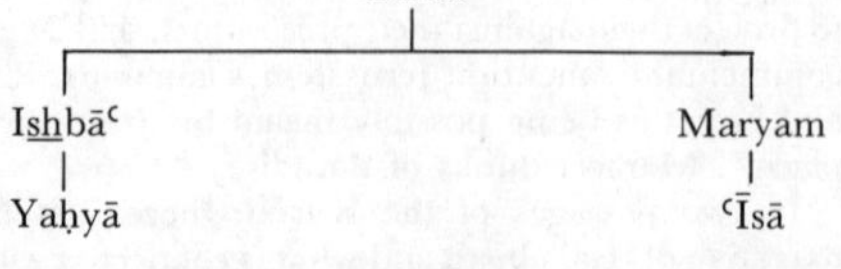

For further discussion, cf. A.M. Charfi, *Christianity in the Qur'ān commentary of Ṭabarī* (English translation), in *Islamochristiana*, vi (1980, 110; and A. Ferré, *La vie de Jésus dans Ṭabarī*, in *Islamochristiana*, v (1979), 11.

ʿImrān and Ḥanna were old and childless. One day the sight of a bird in a tree, which was feeding her young, aroused Ḥanna's desire for a child. She prays God to fulfil her desire, and vows, if her prayer should be heard, to dedicate the child to the temple. She had, however, forgotten that, according to Jewish law, this would be impossible if she should give birth to a female child (cf. *Protev. Jacobi*, chs. iii, iv; Syriac text, 4). Compare with this sūra III, 31: "How the wife of ʿImrān said, O my Lord, I have vowed to thee what is in my womb. Now accept [this vow] from me, thou art the hearing, the knowing. And when she had given birth to the child, she said, O my lord, I have given birth to a female child... and I have called her Maryam".

Then the Ḳurʾān relates how she invoked on behalf of Maryam and her posterity Allāh's protection from Satan. On this verse is based the well-known *ḥadīth* "Every child that is born, is touched (or stung) by Satan and this touch makes it cry, except Maryam and her son" (al-Bukhārī, *Anbiyāʾ*, *bāb* 44; *Tafsīr*, sūra III, 31; Muslim, *Faḍāʾil*, trad. 146, 147; Aḥmad b. Ḥanbal, *Musnad*, ii, 233, 274-5, 288, 292, 319, 368, 523). This tradition is used in support of the impeccability (*ʿiṣma*) of ʿĪsā, Maryam and the Prophets in general (cf. al-Nawawī, *ad* Muslim, *loc. cit.*, and al-Bayḍāwī, *ad* sūra III, 31).

A modern commentator, Muḥammad ʿAbduh, insists that their privilege of preservation from Satan does not set them on a higher plane than Muḥammad; all three share the quality of *ʿiṣma* (*Tafsīr al-Manār*, Cairo 1367/1947, iii, 291-2). It has also been suggested that this idea of unique privilege could come from a Christian source (Arnaldez, 46-7).

The Ḳurʾān further relates (vs. 32) that the child grows up in a chamber in the temple (*miḥrāb*; cf. the κοιτῶν in *Protoev. Jacobi*, vi; Syriac text 5-6) under the divine grace and under Zakāriyyāʾ's care. According to Muslim tradition, ʿImrān had died before the birth of Maryam, and Zakāriyyāʾ claimed authority over her on account of his being her uncle; the rabbis did not recognise his claim; his right was proved by an ordeal, consisting in the parties throwing their pens or arrows (*aḳlām*) in a river; the only one that floated was that of Zakāriyyāʾ (cf. sūra III, 39). Christian tradition knows of an ordeal only in the case of Joseph, who, because a dove comes forth from his staff, is recognised as Maryam's guardian.

As often as Zakāriyyāʾ enters Maryam's *miḥrāb*, he finds her provided with food in a miraculous way (vs. 32). This feature also belongs to Christian tradition (*Protoev. Jacobi*, ch. viii; Syriac text. 7). The person of Joseph is not mentioned in the Ḳurʾān. In Muslim tradition, he takes care of Maryam, his cousin, because Zakāriyyāʾ is no longer able to do so, on account of old age.

Muslim tradition speaks of one Djuraydj a carpenter who is betrothed to Maryam; he is the first to notice her pregnancy and to be convinced by her of its miraculous nature, as brought about directly by the power of God. (A. Charfi, 115-16; Abd al-Jalil; L. Cheikho, *Mawlid Maryam al-ʿadhrāʾ fī taḳlīd al-Islām*, in *Machriq*, xxiv [1926], 682-6).

The undoubted parallels between the Kurʾānic account and material found in the apocryphal gospels do not, however, indicate direct dependence, but are more indicative of the folklore aspect of religion, much fuller than would be implied by the canonical text of the Gospels, itself the product of careful selection. Possibly apocryphal gospels and the Ḳurʾānic stories reveal a common folklore tradition. For such stories, cf. J. Robson, *Muhammadan teaching about Jesus*, in *MW*, xxi (1939), 37-54, and idem, *Stories of Jesus and Mary*, in *MW*, xl (1950), 236-43.

(b) The annunciation of Yaḥyā. See this art. and also ZAKĀRIYYĀʾ.

(c) The annunciation and birth of ʿĪsā. The more detailed narrative is that of sūra XIX, 16-17. Maryam retires to "a place situated eastward", where she hides herself behind a curtain. The commentaries do not know whether a place to the east of Jerusalem is meant, or the eastern part of her house, to which she retired every month. It is said that this is the origin of the *ḳibla* of the Christians.

In 17-21 the story of the annunciation is given (cf. above), followed by that of ʿĪsā's birth, which, according to some Muslim traditions, followed the conception either immediately or very soon. The pains of childbirth came upon Maryam when she was near the trunk of a palm. "She said, would to God I had died before this, and had become a thing forgotten, and lost in oblivion. And he who was beneath her [i.e. the child, or Djibrīl, or the palm] called to her, saying, Be not grieved; God has provided a rivulet under thee; and shake the trunk of the palm and it shall let fall ripe dates upon thee, ready gathered. And eat and drink and calm thy mind". This story may, perhaps, be considered as a parallel to the Christian tradition in which it is related that, during the flight to Egypt, the babe Jesus ordered a palm in the desert to bow down in order to refresh Mary by its dates; whereupon the palm obeyed and stayed with its head at Mary's feet, until the child ordered it to stand upright again and to open a vein between its roots in order to quench the thirst of the holy family (Apocryphal Gospel of Matthew, ch. xx). The Ḳurʾān goes on (v. 26): "And when thou seest any man, say, I have vowed a fast unto the Merciful; so I may not speak to any man today". The commentaries say this was meant to avoid importunate questions. This feature is not in Christian tradition; yet in the *Protoev. Jacobi* it is said (ch. xii; Syriac text, 11) that Mary, who was then 16 years of age, hid herself from the Israelites. According to Muslim tradition, she stayed in a cavern during forty days. The Ḳurʾān continues (XIX, 28): "Then she brought him to her people, carrying him. They said, O Maryam, now thou hast done a strange thing. O sister of Hārūn, thy father was not a bad man, neither was thy mother a harlot. Then she pointed to the child". Then the child begins to speak, one of the well-known miracles ascribed to ʿĪsā. The "very shameful calumny" which the Israelites brought forth against Maryam is also mentioned in sūra IV, 155.

As to the words "O sister of Hārūn" (cf. above), it may be added that, according to the commentaries, this Hārūn was not Moses' brother, but one of Maryam's contemporaries, who was either a wicked man, with whom she is compared in this respect, or her pious brother.

A legend about loaves of bread which Maryam gave to the Magi is mentioned by al-Masʿūdī, iv, 79-80 = § 1405.

The flight to Egypt is not mentioned in the Ḳurʾān, unless the "elevated place" (sūra XXIII, 52; cf. above) should be an allusion to it. According to Muslim tradition, which is acquainted with it, the abode lasted 12 years. After the death of Herod the family returned to Nāṣira.

After his alleged death (according to Muslim teaching: see ʿĪSĀ), he consoled his mother from heaven. According to others it was Mary Magdalene. The stories of the *Transitus Mariae* have not obtained a place in Muslim tradition. Instead of these, there is a narrative of how Maryam went to Rome in order to preach before Mārūt (Nero), accompanied by John (the disciple) and Shimʿūn the coppersmith. When Shimʿūn (Simon Peter?) and Tadāwus (Thaddaeus?) were crucified with their heads downward, Maryam fled with John. When they were persecuted the earth opened and withdrew them from their persecutors. This miracle was the cause of Mārūt's conversion.

Maryam in popular Muslim devotion.

Maryam is much venerated in Muslim folk tradition, often along with Fāṭima (see above). Muslim women have taken her as an example and as a recourse in time of trouble, often visiting Christian shrines. Christian and Muslim traditions both honour her memory at Maṭariyya near Cairo, and in Jerusalem. In Jerusalem is Ḥammām Sittī Maryam (the bath of Maryam), near St. Stephen's Gate, where it was believed Maryam once bathed; the place would be visited by women seeking a cure for barrenness (R. Kriss and H. Kriss-Heinrich, *Volksglaube im Bereich des Islam. I. Wallfahrtswesen und Heiligenverehrung*, Wiesbaden 1960, 169; T. Canaan, *Mohammedan saints and sanctuaries in Palestine*, in *Jnal. of the Palestine Oriental Soc.*, iv/1-2 [1924], 1-84).

Some plants have been nemed after Maryam; (a) *Maryamiyya* or *mêramiyeh*, *Salvia triloba, Labiatae*, said to have acquired its sweet scent when Mary wiped her forehead with its leaves (T. Canaan, *Plant-lore in Palestinian superstition*, in *JPOS*, viii/3 [1928], 129-68). G.M. Crowfoot and L. Baldensperger, *From cedar to hyssop. A study of the folklore of plants in Palestine*, London 1932, describe the Miriamiya or "Sage of Vertue", and mention references to it by earlier travellers in Palestine (79-81). (b) *Kaff al-ʿAdhrāʾ*, *Anastatica hierochuntia, Cruciferae*, the dried seed-heads of which can last for years and are blown around the desert, the seeds germinating when water is available. The seed-head is thought to resemble a fist, hence the name; the *kaff* or "hand" is well-known as a protection against the evil eye [see KHAMSA]; it can be seen painted or carved, or worn as an amulet, generally known in Muslim circles as *kaff Fāṭima*. This plant, however, has in time past been used not to avert the evil eye—though this concept may also have been present—but as a birth charm, soaked in water when a woman was in labour, and the water sometimes given to her to drink. Known as *kaff Fāima bint al-Nabī* or *kaff Maryam*, it was sold in Egypt (Crowfoot and Baldensperger, *op. cit.*, 196; idem, *The Rose of Jericho*, in *JPOS*, xi/l [1931], 7-14); Violet Dickson, *Wild flowers of Kuwait and Bahrain*, London 1955, 16, remarks on its frequency in Central Arabia. Cf. Dalman, *Arbeit und Sitte in Palästina*, Gütersloh 1935, i, 54, for its location in Palestine. The plant can still be found, but its folk usage seems to have died out.

Bibliography: Ibn Hishām, 407; Ṭabarī, i, 711-12; idem, *Tafsīr*, iii, 144-5; vi, 21, 179; vii, 82; xvi, 28-9; xviii, 17; Yaʿḳūbī, *Taʾrīkh*, i, 74-5; Masʿūdī, *Murūdj*, i, 120-1, ii, 145, iv, 79-80; Kisāʾī, *Ḳiṣaṣ al-anbiyāʾ*, ed. Eisenberg; Ibn al-Athīr, i, 211; Thaʿlabī, *ʿArāʾis al-madjālis*, Cairo 1290, 326-7; the commentaries on the Ḳurʾān; Maracci, *Prodomi*, Padua 1698, iv, 85-7, 104-5, 178-9 and the notes to his translation of the Ḳurʾān; C. F. Gerock, *Versuch einer Darstellung der Christologie des Korans*, Hamburg und Gotha 1839, 22-3, 72-3; G. Weil, *Biblische Legenden der Musulmänner*, Frankfurt 1845, 280-1; E. Sayous, *Jésus-Christ d'après Mahomet*, Paris-Leipzig 1880; G. Smit, *Bijbel en legende bij den arab. schrijver Jaqubi*, Leiden 1907, 86-7; J. Horovitz, *Koranische Untersuchungen*, Berlin and Leipzig 1926, 138-9; A. Pieters, *Circumstantial evidence of the Virgin Birth*, in *MW*, x (1929), 350 ff.; *Evangelia apocrypha*, rec. C. de Tischendorf, 2nd ed., Leipzig 1876; *Apocrypha syriaca*, 2nd ed., Leipzig 1876; *Apocrypha syriaca, the Protevangelium Jacobi and Transitus Mariae....*, ed. and tr. A. Smith Lewis, *Studia Sinaitica*, xi, London 1902; E. de Strycker, *La forme la plus ancienne du Protoévangile de Jacques*, Brussels 1961; *Protoevangelium of James*, Eng. tr. in E. Hennecke, *New Testament apocrypha*, ed. W. Schneemelcker, Eng. tr. ed. R. McL. Wilson, London 1963, i, 370-88; J.M. Abd al-Jalil, *Marie et l'Islam*, Paris 1950; V. Courtois, *Mary in Islam*, Oriental Institute, Calcutta 1954; M. Hayek, *Le Christ de l'Islam*, Paris 1959; H. Michaud, *Jésus selon le Coran*, Cahiers Théologiques, Neuchâtel-Paris 1960; G. Parrinder, *Jesus in the Qur'an*, London 1965; O. Schumann, *Der Christus der Muslime. Christologische Aspekte in der arabischen-islamischen Literatur*, Gütersloh 1975; D. Wismer, *The Islamic Jesus: an annotated bibliography of sources in English and French*, London-New York 1977; G. Schedl, *Muḥammad und Jesus: die christologische relevanten Texte des Koran, neu übersetzt und erklärt*, Vienna 1978; R, Arnaldez, *Jésus fils de Marie prophète de l'Islam*, Paris 1980.

(A. J. Wensinck - [Penelope Johnstone])

MARZBĀN-NĀMA (also known in the Arabicised form *Marzubān-nāma*), a work in Persian prose containing a variety of short stories used as moral examples and bound together by one major and several minor framework stories. It is essentially extant in two versions written in elegant Persian with many verses and phrases in Arabic. They were made from a lost original in the Ṭabarī dialect independently of each other in the early 13th century. The oldest version, entitled *Rawḍat al-ʿuḳūl*, was completed in 598/1202 by Muḥammad b. Ghāzī al-Malaṭyawī (or Malaṭī) and was dedicated to the Saldjūḳ sultan of Rūm, Rukn al-Dīn Sulaymān Shāh. Manuscripts are preserved in Leiden (described in detail by M. Th. Houtsma, *Eine unbekannte Bearbeitung des Marzbān-nāmeh*, in *ZDMG*, lii [1898], 395-92) and Paris (cf. E. Blochet, *Catalogue des manuscrits persans*, iv, Paris 1934, 18-21; extracts are contained in the introduction to Ḳazwīnī's edition of the *Marzbān-nāma*; the first chapter was edited and translated into French by Henri Massé, *Le Jardin des Esprits, 1re partie*, in *Publications de la Société des études iraniennes*, 14, Paris 1938). Much better known is the second version by Saʿd al-Dīn al-Warāwīnī who presented his work to Abu 'l-Ḳāsim Rabīb al-Dīn, vizier to the Ildeñizid Atabeg of Ādharbydjān, Özbek b. Muḥammad (607-22/1210-25) [see ILDEÑIZIDS]. It bears the title of the original and still exists in many copies. This version was published by Mīrzā Muḥammad Ḳazwīnī in the Gibb Memorial Series (London-Leiden 1908; repr. Tehran 1352/1973 with additional notes).

According to Malaṭyawī, the author of the *Marzbān-nāma* was a descendant of the Ziyārid Ḳābūs b. Wushmagīr (reigned 366-71/977-81 [*q.v.*]), but Warāwīnī mentions Marzbān b. Sharwīn as the "originator of the book" (*wāḍiʿ-i kitāb*). He belonged to the Bāwandids, a dynasty of Ṭabaristān claiming descent from the Sāsānid prince Kāwūs who was a brother of Khusraw Anūshirwān. He was the father of Kay-Kāwūs's grandmother and is named al-Marzubān b. Rustam b. Sharwīn in the *Ḳābūs-nāma* (ed. Tehran 1345/1967, 5). This form of the name corresponds to that given by Ibn Isfandiyār in *Taʾrīkh-i Ṭabaristān*, written in 613/1216-17, where it is specified that he ruled as an *iṣfahbad* of Pirīm, or Firīm [see FIRRĪM in Suppl.], the stronghold of the Bāwandids which is also called Shahriyārkūh (cf. *An abridged translation of the history of Ṭabaristan*, by E.G. Browne, Leiden 1905, 86). It is most likely that he should be identified with al-Marzubān b. Sharwīn whose name occurs on coins dated 371/981 and 374/984-5 (cf. W. Madelung in *Cambridge history of Iran*, iv, Cambridge 1975, 217; see also the discussion in Ḳazwīnī's introduction). The language used in the ancient *Marzbān-nāma* was, in the words of Warāwīnī, "the language of Ṭabaristan and old, original Persian (*fārsī-yi ḳadīm-i bāstān*)". He refers probably to an archaic form of Persian, perhaps not unlike the *pahlawī* in which the source of Gurgānī's *Wīs u Rāmīn* is said to have been written, with an admixture of the local dialect. During the 4th/10th century a language of this kind was used in Māzandarān for literary purposes, but only a few lines of poetry have survived. Ibn Isfandiyār ascribes to Marzbān a *dīwān* in Ṭabarī verse called the *Nīkī-nāma*.

The *Marzbān-nāma* is mainly a collection of moralistic fables like the book of *Kalīla wa-Dimna*, to which it is often compared. It also contains, however, tales in which animals play no part and anecdotes about ancient kings and philosophers. The major framework is provided by the story of a prince who, after the succession of his brother to the throne, wants to withdraw to a life of seclusion. At the request of the grandees of the state he agrees to compose a book containing "wise counsels and useful directions for the conduct of life in this world". Through this book the new king should be made aware of the wicked character of his vizier. In the course of a disputation with the king and the vizier concerning his intentions, the prince starts to tell a long series of stories.

The versions in classical Persian were both made by members of the caste of secretaries serving in the chancelleries of mediaeval Islamic states. Their principal aim was to transform a comparatively simple text into a model of the style which was current in official correspondence. Warāwīnī mentions in his preface several works which are stylistically akin to his own work. Among these are the *Maḳāmāt* of Ḥamīdī, historical texts, *inshāʾ* collections as well as other collections of tales.

The differences between the two versions are considerable. Warāwīnī states that the original *Marzbān-nāma* had nine chapters. In the *Rawḍat al-ʿuḳūl*, an additional chapter contains moral teachings of an Islamic nature which contrast with the rest of the book. The latter version has also many stories which are not present in the work of Warāwīnī, who declares that he made a selection from the contents of the original. Houtsma suggested that the two adapters may have had access to different versions of the ancient text. The principal story is only in Warāwīnī's case a true framework story, as Gabrieli noted, but it is impossible to make out whether this is conformable to the original design or not.

The *Marzbān-nāma* of Warāwīnī was rendered into Turkish by Ṣadr al-Dīn Sheykhoghlu in the second half of the 8th/14th century. The latter work was translated again into Arabic by Ibn ʿArabshāh [*q.v.*] in 852/1448 under the title *Fākihat al-khulafāʾ wa-mufākahat al-ẓurafāʾ*. Another Turkish translation, also based on Warāwīnī, is the *Djewāhir ül-ḥikem* by Urfalî Nüzhet ʿÜmer Efendi (d. 1191/1778).

Bibliography: Ch. Schefer, *Notice sur le Merzban Namèh*, in *Chrestomathie persane*, ii, Paris 1885, 194-211; Fr. Gabrieli, *Il settimo capitolo del Marzbān-*

Nāmeh (*Introduzione, versione et note*), in *RSO*, xix (1941), 125-60; Muḥammad Taḳī Bahār Malik al-Shuʿarāʾ, *Sabkshināsī*, Tehran 1321/1942, iii, 14-20; A.J. Arberry, *Classical Persian literature*, London 1958, 179-85; *The Tales of Marzuban*, tr. Reuben Levy, London 1959; A. Bausani, *Letteratura neopersiana*, Milan 1960, 811-4; Dh. Ṣafā, *Taʾrīkh-i adabiyyāt dar Īrān*, ii, Tehran 1339/1960³, 1003-8; idem, *Gandjīna-yi sukhan*, iii, Tehran 1348/1969, 117-22, 201-9; Sigrid Kleinmichel, *Das Marzubān-nāme*, in *Wissenschaftliche Zeitschrift der Humboldt-Universität zu Berlin. Gesellschafts- und Sprachwissenschaftliche Reihe*, xviii/3 (1969), 519-34 (the Sheykhoghlu version in transcription); Aḥmad Munzawī, *Fihrist-i nuskhahā-yi khaṭṭī-yi fārsī*, v, Tehran 1349/1970, 3626-8; Ṣadru'd-dīn Şeyhoğlu, *Marzubān-nāme tercümesi. Inceleme-metin sözlük tıpkıbasım*, ed. Zeynep Korkmaz, Ankara 1973; E. W. Davis, *The tales of Marzbān-nāmah*, diss., Univ. of Michigan 1977, unpubl.

(J. H. KRAMERS - [J. T. P. DE BRUIJN])

MARZPĀN, Arabised form MARZUBĀN, "warden of the march", "markgrave", from Av. *marəza* and M. Parth. *mrz* "frontier", plus *pat* "protector". The MP form *marzpān* suggests a north Iranian origin. It began to be used as the title of a military governor of a frontier province in the Sāsānid empire in the 4th or 5th centuries A.D. when *marz, marzpan*, and *marzpanutʿin* (marzpānate) appear as loan words in Armenian, and *marzbanā* as a loan word in Syriac. The NP form *marzbān, marzvān* or *marzabān* was Arabised as *marzubān* (pl. *marāziba, marāzib*), possibly as early as the 6th century A.D. Arabic also formed a verb *marzaba* ("to appoint someone as *marzubān*"), the noun *marzaba* ("marzubānate") and the adjective *marzubānī*. The later Syriac forms *marzubanā* and *marzuwanā*, and the later Armenian form *marzavan*, probably came from the Arabic or NP.

A *marzpān* of Bēth Aramāyē is attested from the time of Shāpūr II (309-79) until the early 6th century, while the marzpānate of Fīrūz Shāpūr (Anbār) and that of the land irrigated by the Euphrates are also said to have been established by Shāpūr II. In the 5th and 6th centuries, Naṣībīn was under a *marzpān* who commanded at least 7,000 men in 504, and a *marzpān* was in command of Āmid during the Byzantine siege of 504-5. After the reorganisation of the Sāsānid empire into four quarters under Khusraw I Anūshirwān (531-79), the *marzpān* became a high-ranking military and administrative official in the new system. According to al-Yaʿḳūbī, the *marzpān* was a provincial governor (*raʾīs al-balad*) after the *iṣpabadh* [*q.v.*]) and *pātkōspān* and above the district governor or *shahrīdj*. But in a description of this system anachronously ascribed to Ardashīr I (226-41), al-Masʿūdī claims that the *marzpān* was the deputy of the *iṣpabadh*, and under Hurmizd IV (579-90) and Khusraw II Parwīz (591-628), military officials of the imperial quarters are sometimes called *marzpān*. In fact, al-Masʿūdī also says that a *marzpān* was the lord of a quarter of the empire, a general, a *wazīr* or the governor of an administrative district. Such military officials were not supposed to assist each other without royal permission.

There seems to have been a category of great *marzpāns* in the late Sāsānid period who were haughty grandees (*nakhāwira*), brave horsemen, officers in charge of people just below the king, who lived at the capital and were employed as royal envoys and generals. Abū Muḥammad al-ʿAbdī described Khusraw II Parwīz as surrounded by noble *marāziba*, and the land of the *marāziba* of Kisrā was confiscated by the Muslims in the Sawād, along with that of the royal family. The great nobleman al-Hurmuzān is sometimes called a *marzubān*. However, in the early 7th century *marzpān* was still used for the military governor of the frontier districts of al-Ḥīra, Hadjar and the Djazīra, as well as for the governors of Bābil and Khuṭarniyya and of Balad.

Arabic accounts of the Muslim conquest of Sāsānid territories use *marzubān* for local leaders who organised the defence or concluded treaties at Anbār, al-Madhār/Maysān, Dast-i Maysān, Sūs, Iṣfahān, Rayy, Ardabīl/Ādharbāydjān, Fārs, Kirmān, Zarang/Sidjistān, Nīshāpūr, Ṭūs, Sarakhs and Marw. This may be due to the military nature of their activity or because some of them, such as al-Hurmuzān, were great nobles, and it need not be taken as a title in every case. *Marzubān* appears to have been used in a generic sense for the *shahrīdj* of Fārs (just as Pāpak is called the *marzpān* and *shahridār* of Pārs in the *Kār-nāmak*), for the *padhghōsbān* of Iṣfahān, for the *iṣpahbādh* of Sidjistān and for the *kanārang* of Khurāsān. The Hephthalite ruler of Harāt, Bādghīs and Pūshang is also called a *marzubān*. At Marw and Marw al-Rūd, *marzubān* survived as the title of local Iranian officials under Muslim rule, and in 105/723 Muslim b. Saʿīd al-Kilābī appointed Bahrām Sīs as *marzubān* at Marw to collect taxes from the Zoroastrians or Madjūs [*q.v.*]. *Marzubān* was also used for the local notables and the *iṣpahbadh* of Ṭabaristān from the 1st/7th until the 3rd/9th century.

Meanwhile, Marzubān or Marzabān came to be used as a proper name, at first for powerful officers such as the second Persian governor of al-Yaman, al-Marzubān b. Wahrīz. It is also said to have been the name of Dhu 'l-Ḳarnayn, of a sword belonging to the Banū ʿĀʾidh of Makhzūm and of a district north of Samarḳand. Marzubāna was used as a woman's name, and al-Marzubānī was used as a *nisba* for someone who had an ancestor named al-Marzubān. *Marzubān* was also used metaphorically in poetry for a ruler or master, or for a leader of the Madjūs; *marāziba* were compared to lions, and a lion was called "the *marzubān* of roaring" and *marzubānī*.

Bibliography: For lexical matters, see Asadī Ṭūsī, *Lughāt-i Furs*, Tehran 1336/1957, 144; Djawālīḳī, *al-Muʿarrab min al-kalām al-aʿdjamī*, Cairo 1969, 365-7; Ibn Manẓūr, *Lisān al-ʿarab*, Beirut 1956, xii, 406; Ibn Khalaf, *Burhān-i ḳāṭiʿ*, Tehran 1330-42/1951-63, iv, 1987; P. Horn, *Grundriss der neupersischen Etymologie*, Strassburg 1893, 218; H. Hübschmann, *Armenische Grammatik*, Leipzig 1897, repr. Hildesheim 1962, i, 193; J. Payne-Smith, *Syriac dictionary*, Oxford 1903, 300; A. Shīr, *Kitāb al-alfāẓ al-fārisiyya al-muʿarraba*, Beirut 1908, 145; A. Siddiqi, *Studien über die persischen Fremdwörter im klassischen Arabisch*, Göttingen 1919, 82-3; W. Lentz, *Die nord-iranische Elemente in der neupersischen Literatursprache bei Firdosi*, in *ZII*, iv (1926), 255, 295; S. Iṣfahānī, *Vāzha-nāma-yi fārsī*, Tehran 1337/1958, 345-46; M, Kamil, *Persian words in ancient Arabic*, in *Bull. of the Fac. of Arts, Cairo*, xix (1957), 63; W. Eilers, *Iranisches Lehngut im arabischen Lexikon*, in *IIJ*, v (1962), 215-16, 219; M. Shūshtarī, *Farhang vāzhahā-yi fārsī dar zabān-i ʿarabī*, Tehran 1347/1969, 631-2; H. Nyberg, *A manual of Pahlavi*, Wiesbaden 1974, ii, 127.

For Bēth Aramāyē, see G. Hoffmann, *Auszüge aus syrischen Akten persischer Märtyrer*, Leipzig 1880, 38, 485, 496; O. Braun, *Ausgewählte Akten persischer Märtyrer*, Munich 1915, 146; J.B. Chabot, *Synodicon orientale*, Paris 1902, 532-3; A. Scher, *Histoire nestorienne*, ii/l, in *PO*, vii, 1905, 129, 154. For Fīrūz

Shāpūr and the Euphrates, see Dīnawarī, *al-Akhbār al-ṭiwāl*, 51; Ṭabarī, i, 839; Thaᶜālibī, *Ghurar*, ed. Zotenberg, 529; Yāḳūt, *Buldān*, i, 367-8, iii, 929. For Naṣībīn and Āmid, see Chabot, 526-9, 523-7; W. Wright, *The Chronicle of Joshua the Stylite*, Cambridge 1882, 61-2; Scher, ii/l, 176, ii/2, in *PO*, xiii, 1919. For the *marzpān* as a late Sāsānid military official, see Yaᶜḳūbī, *Taʾrīkh*, i, 203; Ṭabarī, i, 2037; Masᶜūdī, *Murūdj*, ed. Dāghir, i, 269, 287, 319 = §§ 545, 581, 647 and index; Thaᶜālibi, *Ghurar*, 643, 701; R. N. Frye, *The golden age of Persia*, London and New York 1975, 9.

For the great *marzpāns*, see Abū Yūsuf, *Kharādj*, Paris 1921, 57; al-Mubarrad, *al-Kāmil*, 118; Dīnawarī, 83, 94, 112, 133; Ṭabarī i, 2053, 2555; Ibn al-Faḳīh, *Mukhtaṣar Kitāb al-buldān*, 216; Scher, ii/1, 178; Ibn al-Djawālīkī, 364, 367; *LA*, xiii, 406; Ibn Khallikān, *Wafayāt*, Beirut 1968, iii, 281.

For the *marzpān* as the governor of a local or frontier district in the early 7th century, see Markwart, *Catalogue of the provincial capitals of Ērānshahr*, Rome 1931, 14, 21; Balādhurī, 78, 85, 242-43; Dīnawarī, 115; Ṭabarī, i, 2019, 2037-9, 2184, 2191, 2202; Ḥamza al-Iṣfahānī, *Taʾrīkh sinī mulūk al-arḍ wa 'l-anbiyāʾ*, Beirut 1961, 96; Agapius of Manbidj, *Kitāb al-ᶜUnwān* in *PO*, viii, 1912, 459; Scher, ii/2, 546, 549, 554.

For the use of *marzubān* in Arabic accounts of the conquest, see Nyberg, i, l; Ibn Saᶜd, vii/l, 3; Balādhurī, 310, 312, 313, 315, 325-6, 342, 386, 393, 404, 405-6, 408-9; Yaᶜḳūbī, *Buldān*, tr. *Les pays*, Cairo 1937, 166; Dīnawarī, 121-4, 140; Ṭabarī, i, 2385, 2386, 2638-9, 2887-90, ii, 1462, 1688; Ibn Isfandiyār, *Tārīkh-i Ṭabaristān*, Tehran 1912, i, 158; E.G. Browne, *History of Ṭabaristán*, abridged tr. Leiden and London 1905, 86, 101, 108, 113, 149; Yāḳūt, iv, 468; C. E. Bosworth, *Sīstān under the Arabs*, Rome 1968, 13, 15, 16-17; Frye, *op. cit.*, 97.

For Marzubān as a proper name, see Ibn Hishām, ed. Wüstenfeld, Göttingen 1858, 46, 197, 457; Balādhurī, 105-6; Ibn Ḳutayba, *ᶜUyūn al-akhbār*, Cairo 1964, i, 179; Dīnawarī, 402; Iṣṭakhrī, 292, 323; Ibn Ḥawḳal, ed. Leiden 1938-9, 468, 497, 499-500; Muḳaddasī, 279; Ibn Miskawayh, *Tadjārib al-umam*, ed. Margoliouth and Amedroz, London 1921, ii, 133; Ibn al-Athīr, v, 291; Ibn Khallikān, iii, 281, iv, 354-6; F. Justi, *Iranisches Namenbuch*, Marburg 1895, 197-8. For its use in poetry, see Djawālīḳī, 366-7; Ibn Khalaf, iv, 1987; Saᶜdī, *Bustān*, Vienna 1858, 73; Shīr, 145; Shūshtarī, 631-2.

(J.H. KRAMERS - [M. MORONY])

MARZUBĀN B. **RUSTAM** [see MARZBĀN-NĀMA].

AL-**MARZUBĀNĪ** ABŪ ᶜUBAYD ALLĀH MUḤAMMAD B. ᶜIMRĀN B. MŪSĀ B. SAᶜĪD B. ᶜUBAYD ALLĀH AL-KHURĀSĀNĪ AL-BAGHDĀDĪ AL-KĀTIB, was one of the most versatile and prolific of Arab scholars in the vast field of *adab* during the 4th/10th century.

1. Life. His wealthy and influential family resided in Khurāsān, and his father was deputy to the *ṣāḥib Khurāsān* at the caliphal court in Baghdād, where al-Marzubānī was born in Djumādā II 297/February-March 910 or in the year before. Here he devoted himself to the study of *ḥadīth* under the guidance of well-known traditionists such as Abū Bakr ᶜAbd Allāh b. Abī Dāwūd al-Sidjistānī and ᶜAbd Allāh b. Muḥammad b. ᶜAbd al-ᶜAzīz al-Baghawī. He studied *lugha* and *akhbār* with the most renowned scholars of his time, such as Ibn Durayd, Ibn al-Anbārī, Nifṭawayh and Abū Bakr al-Ṣūlī. His house was situated in the ᶜAmr al-Rūmī road in the eastern half of the city, not far from the Tigris, set in the midst of gardens, and was a centre for Baghdād's scholarly and literary circles. His *madjālis* frequently lasted several days and were accompanied by food and drink, and whoever felt inclined towards staying found accommodation in al-Marzubānī's hospitable house. According to his own report, he could accommodate up to fifty people. Echoes of these assemblies are found in literature, e.g. in the so-called *Amālī* of al-Sharīf al-Murtaḍā (d. 436/1044) i.e. the *Ghurar al-fawāʾid wa-durar al-ḳalāʾid*, Cairo 1373/1954, index. The personality of this distinguished and generous man, who, as his works show, stood above the constant quarrels of the religio-political parties and trends, must have been extremely impressive. The powerful Būyid *amīr* ᶜAḍūd al-Dawla (d. 372/983 in Baghdād) thought very highly of him. Whenever he was in town and riding past al-Marzubānī's residence, he would wait at the gate until the honoured *shaykh* had shown himself, so that the *amīr al-umarāʾ* was convinced of his well-being. Al-Marzubānī died at about 85 years old, according to our calendar, on Friday, 2 Shawwāl 384/9 November 994. At his burial on his estate, Abū Bakr al-Khʷārazmī (d. 403/1012), the *shaykh al-Ḥanafiyya*, led the funeral prayers.

It is striking that only a few of his pupils are named in the biographical literature, in particular, two Ḥanafī *ḳāḍīs*, a Rāfiḍī from Ḳum [*q.v.*] and a relater of *akhbār*. Al-Khaṭīb al-Baghdādī (d. 463/1071 [*q.v.*]) refers to them in his *Taʾrīkh Baghdād*, iii, 135 f., as well as to his own teacher al-Azharī (x, 385), a narrow-minded traditionalist. The latter accused the unorthodox and active scholar of being a drunkard, a Muᶜtazilī, an untrustworthy relater and—according to others—a liar. The last accusation is corrected by al-Khaṭīb with the remark that he was not a liar, but that it was the *madhhab* and *riwāya* which he followed. Both seemed ambiguous to the average intellect. Someone who published the *akhbār* of Abū Ḥanīfa alongside the *akhbār* of the Muᶜtazila, or who collected the Shīᶜī *ashᶜār* alongside the *shiᶜr* of Yazīd b. Muᶜāwiya, or who mingled the principle of *idjāza* with that of *samāᶜ*, could not possibly pass the rigid criteria of form accepted by the guardians of tradition. Once these accusations, against a man who frequently moved in Shīᶜī circles, had been taken up by the eloquent and influential Ibn al-Djawzī (d. 597/1200 [*q.v.*]) (*Muntaẓam*, vii, 177) in Baghdād—at that time under the influence of Ḥanbalism—then a like judgement, more or less founded on prejudice, was decisive and emphatic. The reputation of the *ṣāḥib akhbār wa-riwāya li 'l-ādāb*, as al-Khaṭīb spoke of him, was thereby marred. The fact that al-Marzubānī's contemporaries valued his works more than those of al-Djāḥiẓ [*q.v.*] or that his colleague in Baghdād, the well-known philologist Abū ᶜAlī al-Fārisī (d. 377/987 [*q.v.*]) counted him, the younger of the two, amongst the *maḥāsin al-dunyā*, could not improve his impaired reputation. His admirable—and admired—monumental work was soon neglected and, later on, became almost completely obscured. This must have happened because it was not in agreement with the criteria of the customary forms of tradition and because people were prejudiced about the author.

Al-Marzubānī's contemporary and admirer, the renowned bookseller in Baghdād, Ibn al-Nadīm (d. 380/990 [*q.v.*]), has listed more than fifty titles, along with the number of folios and often with a short summary of the contents in his *Fihrist*, 132 ff. (tr. Dodge, 289-95) of the year 377/987. The later bio-bibliographers like Yāḳūt, *Udabāʾ*, vii, 50 ff., Ibn al-Ḳifṭī, *Inbāh*, iii, 182 ff., and al-Ṣafadī, *Wāfī*, iv,

236 f., more or less took over this bibliography, counting altogether more than 45,000 folios. Only remnants of this tremendous work survive and these—with only one exception—are not even the original versions, but excerpts and adaptations. For this, the fault may well lie not only with the already-mentioned prejudices but also with the terrible floods which befell Bag͟hdād a few years before the Mongol conquest of the city (656/1258).

2. Works. We know concerning al-Marzubānī's 18-volume collection of biographies of scholars, the *K. al-Muḳtabas fī ak͟hbār al-nuḥāt wa 'l-udabāʾ wa 'l-s͟huʿarāʾ wa 'l-ʿulamāʾ*, that the autograph, consisting of over 3,000 folios, was kept in the library of the Niẓāmiyya Madrasa, situated on the east bank of the Tigris. During the opening years of the 7th/13th century, two excerpts were made of this single manuscript, namely a *muntak͟hab* in four volumes and a *muk͟htār* in at least two volumes. In the middle of the same century, the *Muntak͟hab* was extracted into one volume, which has been preserved and bears the title *Nūr al-ḳabas al-muk͟htaṣar min al-Muḳtabas* (= *Die Gelehrtenbiographien des Abū ʿUbaidallāh al-Marzubānī in der Rezension des Ḥāfiẓ al-Yaǵmūrī*, ed. R. Sellheim, Teil I. Text, Wiesbaden-Beirut 1964 [Bibliotheca Islamica, 23a]). It contains 125—of about 150 in all—biographies, hence approximatively one-seventeenth of the original version. The other excerpt, the *Muk͟htār*, of which only the first part has survived, has not as yet been published. The traditions in this volume which, as a rule, begin with an *isnād*, only partially correspond to those in the *Nūr al-ḳabas*. The compiler diverges considerably, in the sequence of the 33 biographies as well as in the transmission within the individual biographies, from those of the *Nūr al-ḳabas*.

(2) His *K. al-Muwas͟hs͟haḥ fī maʾāk͟hid͟h al-ʿulamāʾ ʿalā 'l-s͟huʿarāʾ* consisted of 300 folios according to the bibliography of Ibn al-Nadīm. It exists in its complete form and in two editions: Cairo 1343/1924 and ed. ʿAlī Muḥammad al-Bid͟jāwī, Cairo 1965. In this delightful piece of *adab* writing, an anthology compiled under the aspect of erudite critical standards, the author refers to numerous oral and written sources. For details, see Munīr Sulṭān, *al-Marzubānī wa 'l-Muwas͟hs͟haḥ*, Alexandria 1978, and Muḥammad ʿAlawī Muḳaddam in *Mad͟jalla-yi Dānis͟hkada-yi Adabiyyāt wa-ʿulūm-i insānī*, Mas͟hhad, xiii/1 = fasc. 49 (1356/1978), 1-34.

(3) His *K. al-Muʿd͟jam fī asmāʾ al-s͟huʿarāʾ* originally consisted of 1,000 folios with the famous verses of about 5,000 poets, arranged in alphabetical order. Only the second half has been preserved, and that moreover with numerous omissions and lacunae. It exists in two editions: ed. F. Krenkow, Cairo 1354/1935, repr. Beirut 1402/1982 and ed. ʿAbd al-Sattār Aḥmed Farād͟j, Cairo 1379/1960; cf. Ibrāhīm al-Samarrāʾī, *Min al-ḍāʾiʿ min Muʿd͟jam al-s͟huʿarāʾ li 'l-Marzubānī*, Beirut 1404/1984.

(4) His *K. As͟hʿār al-nisāʾ* is supposed to have included 500 or 600 folios. ʿAbd al-Ḳādir al-Bag͟hdādī (d. 1093/1682 [*q.v.*]) still quoted from it in his *K͟hizānat al-adab*, i, 10, and iv, 565. In an old manuscript, 59 folios of the third part are preserved and contain *ak͟hbār* and verses by almost 60 women, members of sixteen different ancient Arabian tribes. The fragment was published by Sāmī Makī al-ʿĀnī and Hilāl Nād͟jī, Bag͟hdād 1396/1976.

(5) The *Ak͟hbār al-Sayyid al-Ḥimyarī* (d. 179/795?; Sezgin, ii, 458 ff.) is not listed in al-Marzubānī's bibliography. This booklet, published in Nad͟jaf by Muḥammad Hādī al-Amīnī in 1385/1965, was probably just a fragment of al-Marzubānī's 6,000 or even 10,000-folio anthology, bearing the title *al-Mustanīr*, with accounts of the recent poets ranging from Bas͟hs͟hār b. Burd up to Ibn al-Muʿtazz [*q.vv.*]. Also, it could possibly be from his anthology of 5,000 folios called *al-Mufīd*, containing works of the lesser known poets of the D͟jāhiliyya and of Islam. The *K. al-Mufīd* was subdivided into several sections, e.g. sections on the one-eyed, the blind, etc., poets, and on S͟hīʿī, K͟hārid͟jī, Jewish, Christian, etc. poets. It also had a section on Sayyid al-Ḥimyarī (see *Fihrist*, 132, tr. Dodge, 289 f.). Of course, al-Marzubānī also dealt with the above-named poet in his *Muʿd͟jam* (see above no. 3), but only briefly (the passage has not been preserved); furthermore, he is quoted with verses by al-Ḥimyarī by the S͟harīf al-Murtaḍā (see above) in his *Ṭayf al-k͟hayāl*, Cairo 1381/1962, 104-7.

(6) *Ak͟hbār s͟huʿarāʾ al-S͟hīʿa* is a short *talk͟hīṣ* made by Sayyid Muḥsin al-Amīn al-ʿĀmilī (d. 1371/1951), ed. Muḥammad Hādī al-Amīnī, Nad͟jaf 1388/1968. It contains *ak͟hbār* and verses by 27 S͟hīʿī poets, without however one single *isnād*. If this piece really does go back to al-Marzubānī, whose name is only on the title page, then it could be a fragmentary piece from al-Marzubānī's *al-Mufīd* (see no. 5).

(7) His *K. al-Riyāḍ* (or *al-Mutayyamīn*), consisting of 3,000 folios, is also about poets, viz. those enslaved by love. Quotations, though sparse, can be found in the genre of amatory literature, see L.A. Giffen, *Theory of profane love among the Arabs: the development of the genre*, New York 1971, 18 ff., and S. Leder, *Ibn al-Ǧauzī und seine Kompilation wider die Leidenschaft*, diss. Frankfurt/Main 1982, Beirut 1983, index.

(8) His *K. S͟hiʿr Yazīd b. Muʿāwiya*, which Ibn K͟hallikān (tr. de Slane, iii, 67), impressed by the poetry, himself memorised, comprises three sheets, hence approximately 30 folios; cf. *S͟hiʿr Yazīd b. Muʿāwiya b. Abī Sufyān*, collected and edited by Ṣalāḥ al-Dīn al-Munad͟jd͟jid, Beirut 1982.

Bibliography (in addition to the works mentioned in the article): Brockelmann, S I, 190 f. S III, 1217; F. Krenkow, in *Islamica*, iv (1930), 272-82; O. Rescher, *Abriss der arabischen Litteraturgeschichte*, Stuttgart 1933, ii, 264; Ziriklī, *Aʿlām*, vii, 210; Kaḥḥāla, xi, 97 f. (R. SELLHEIM)

AL-**MARZŪḲĪ**, ABŪ ʿALĪ AḤMAD B. MUḤAMMAD B. AL-ḤASAN, philologist who acted as a tutor to certain of the Būyids of Iṣfahān and who died in D͟hu 'l-Ḥid͟jd͟ja 421/December 1030. The vizier the Ṣāḥib Ibn ʿAbbād [*q.v.*], whom he had antagonised by neglecting to rise on his entry, nevertheless recognised al-Marzūḳī's value, at the same time dubbing him (in Yāḳūt, *Udabāʾ*, xviii, 215) a weaver (*ḥāʾik*), probably without any pejorative intention, since it is possible that he worked at this trade in his youth. Apart from this, we have hardly any details about his life, and it is merely known that he studied the *Kitāb* of Sībawayh under the direction of al-Fārisī (d. 377/987 [*q.v.*]) and himself became a master to whom al-Suyūṭī (*Bug͟hya*, 159) gives the unexpected title of *imām*.

The Arab authors who devote a brief notice to him, Yāḳūt (*Udabāʾ*, v, 34-5) and al-Suyūṭī (*loc. cit.*), and also Brockelmann (S I, 502), enumerate a series of philological works (*Amālī*, *G͟harīb al-Ḳurʾān*, *Alfāẓ al-s͟humūl wa 'l-ʿumūm*) and commentaries concerned mainly with such poetical anthologies as the *Mufaḍḍaliyyāt*, the *Dīwān al-Hud͟haliyyīn* and above all the *Ḥamāsa* of Abū Tammām whose introduction taken from ms. Köprülü 1308 has been commented upon by al-Ṭāhir Ibn ʿĀs͟hūr, Tunis 1377/1958.

However, the sole work of al-Marzūḳī to have been published is his *Kitāb al-Azmina wa 'l-amākin*, printed at Hyderabad in 1332/1914. This is a work on the *anwāʾ* [*q.v.*] and is characterised by the fact that the author adds to the traditional ideas gathered by the *ruwāt* in the Arabian peninsula and put in order by philologists of the Ibn Ḳutayba type, more general concepts and ideas in which outside pieces of information, which are used to make instructive comparisons, are also taken into account.

Bibliography: Given in the article.

(CH. PELLAT)

MASʿĀ [see SAʿY].

MASĀʾIL WA-ADJWIBA (A.), "questions and answers", a technique of argumentation in mediaeval Islam. The pattern of question (*suʾāl*, pl. *suʾālāt*, *asʾila*) and answer (*djawāb*, pl. *djawābāt*, *adjwiba*) has strongly influenced, both in form and content, numerous Arabic writings in virtually all fields of knowledge. Unsolved problems, or questions and objections propounded by a third person, are followed by answers, or explanations and refutations. Sometimes the author, at the request of a third person, composed a monograph on a group of themes, and even dedicated it to him. Besides, the pattern of questions and answers often became a literary topos: as a justification for his work, the author, in his introduction, advances the plea that he composed it because of solicitations and requests of another person (Freimark, 36 ff.). Finally, the pattern also turned into a technique of scientific research or presentation, without any dialogue between teacher and pupil or between two opponents. Ancient and Patristic-Byzantine literatures show parallels with these structures: cf. ἐρωτήσεις, ἀπορίαι, ζητηματα-ἀποχρίσεις, λύσεις, προβλήματα and the Byzantine ἐρωταποχρίσεις, in evidence since the 12th century A.D. The mediaeval *quaestiones et responsiones* also belong to this genre. Since the pattern may have sprung from motives which are inherent in the matter, external influence from similarly-structured works of Christian origin or from Aristotelian-Peripatetic methodology (cf. Aristoteles, *Metaphysics*, iii, 1; *Prior and posterior analytics*, *Topics*) can only be proved after study of each individual case.

The oldest Islamic questions-and-answer literature endeavours to solve philological and textual problems of the Ḳurʾān text. Mention may here be made of the answers given by ʿUmar to questions about *ḳirāʾāt*, *iʿrāb*, *tanzīl* and meanings (*maʿānī*) of the Ḳurʾān (Abbott, 110), and of the *Masāʾil* (*suʾālāt*) of the Khāridjī leader Nāfiʿ b. al-Azraḳ (d. 65/685) on 200 difficult words in the Ḳurʾān, to which ʿAbd Allāh b. ʿAbbās answered with references to ancient Arabic poetry. This philological interest, especially present in the oldest Ḳurʾān exegesis, increasingly made way for textual interpretation as a source of Islamic law and as a starting-point of Islamic theology. Thus there have come down to us *masāʾil* collections of Mālik b. Anas and Aḥmad b. Ḥanbal [*q.vv.*] containing answers to legal, dogmatic and ethical questions, transmitted and partly edited by their pupils. Probably the most important *masāʾil* collection of Aḥmad b. Ḥanbal comes from al-Khallāl (d. 311/923) and is called *Kitāb al-Djāmiʿ li-ʿulūm* (or *al-Musnad min masāʾil) Aḥmad b. Ḥanbal.* Its aim to give answers on legal questions culminates in the development of the Islamic institution of the *futyā*, the act of giving a *fatwā* [*q.v.*]. This institution can be compared with Roman *jus respondendi*; as Goldziher has shown, it has influenced Jewish circles.

On the basis of Ḳurʾānic texts, an apologetic literature was developed which tried to prove the superiority of Islam by means of the question-answer pattern. An example is the *Kitāb al-Masāʾil* attributed to ʿAbd Allāh b. Salām (d. 43/663-4), a Jew from Medina, and probably composed by a Jewish renegade. It consists of a collection of questions put before the Prophet, at whose answers Ibn Salām is said to have been converted to Islam. The work is based on a scholastic principle which appears in an already developed stage in the disputation of Leontius of Byzantium (d. *ca.* 543) with the heretics. Reaching back to Aristotelian dialectics, this Aristotelian, influenced by Neo-Platonism, was familiar with the scholastic technique of question and refuting answer (cf. Grabmann, i, 104 ff., 107 f.). It is conceivable that Leontius' contest with the Nestorians, which was to be continued and which, more than 200 years later, reached a climax in John of Damascus and, after him, in Theodorus Abū Ḳurra (cf. Griffith, *Controversial theology*, 33 ff.), favoured in Syrian circles the development of a similar scholastic technique. Through disputations and polemics between Christians and converts to Islam, this technique may have become known to Islamic circles and have been accepted as a stimulating example in the practice of Islamic disputation (cf. Cook, *Origins*). The pattern of question (in the form of a conditional clause) and refuting answer or argument (*ḥudjdja*) (often presented in the form of a main clause expressing an irrealis) is already found in al-Ḥasan b. Muḥammad b. al-Ḥanafiyya (d. *ca.* 100/718), *al-Risāla fi 'l-radd ʿala 'l-Ḳadariyya* (ed. Van Ess, *Anfänge*). Further examples from the early Islamic period are the discussion between the caliph al-Mahdī and the patriarch Timothy I, which took place between 170/786-7 and 178/794-5 (see Putman, 191, etc.), and the *Kitāb al-Masāʾil wa 'l-adjwiba* (ed. Hayek; cf. Griffith, *ʿAmmār*, 149 ff.), a defence of Christian doctrine against the Muʿtazila by the Christian apologist ʿAmmār al-Baṣrī (first half of the 3rd/9th century). The principle of thesis and antithesis used here follows the tradition of the Christian Aristotelians, and marked the apologetic literature of Christian converts to Islam. One may compare al-Ḥasan b. Ayyūb (4th/10th century) in Ibn Taymiyya (*al-Djawāb*, ii, 318,6, 319 *in fine*, etc.). Moreover, the question-answer pattern is also found in the dogmatic literature of Islam, as well as in its learned literature in general.

At an early stage, debates with opponents from their own circles took the place of disputes with non-Islamic doctrines. One may quote the above-mentioned refutation of the Ḳadariyya by al-Ḥasan b. Muḥammad b. al-Ḥanafiyya; the debate on knowledge (*maʿrifa*) inside the Muʿtazila as related by al-Djāḥiẓ (d. 255/868-9) in his *al-Masāʾil wa 'l-djawābāt fi 'l-maʿrifa*; the discussion on the theodicy problem between al-Naẓẓām, ʿAlī al-Aswārī, Abu 'l-Hudhayl, Bishr b. al-Muʿtamir, al-Murdār, al-Ashadjdj, al-Iskāfī) and Djaʿfar b. Ḥarb (see Daiber, *Muʿammar*, 260 f.), noted down in a protocol by ʿAbd al-Ḳāhir b. Ṭāhir al-Baghdādī (*al-Farḳ*, 198,15-200,17; shorter version in *al-Milal*, 136,11-138,3); and also the protocol of a discussion on the Ḳurʾan between the Ḥanbalī Ibn Ḳudāma al-Maḳdisī and an Ashʿarī opponent from Damascus (ms. Leiden Or. 2523), which took place between 589/1193 and 595/1199. This protocol, rewritten as an independent theological treatise (ms. Manisa 6584-5), clearly shows the traces of the traditional technique of debating by way of question and answer, as well as the *reductio ad absurdum*. An example from the fields of philosophy and cosmology is the collection of question and answers of al-Ghazālī, inspired by his *Maḳāṣid al-falāsifa* and preserved in Hebrew (ed. Malter). The disputes (*munāẓarāt*), held and afterwards written down by Fakhr al-Dīn al-Rāzī, have a theological-philosophical and juridical character. For an example of the discussion on grammar in the 5th/11th century, see Samir.

The Islamic technique of disputation is directly linked to the questions discussed (cf. Van Ess, *Beginnings*) and in particular cases, Christian peripatetical examples of perhaps Syriac origin may have been followed (cf. Cook, *Origins*). Like Judaeo-Christian Hellenism (see Van Ess, *Disputationspraxis*, 54 ff.), Islam in the sphere of disputation developed a technique which became more and more the pattern of scientific treatises. In Ibāḍī circles [see IBĀḌIYYA] in the Maghrib, there was even compiled a handbook of theological disputation, the *Kitāb al-Djahālāt*, whose actual form (*terminus ante quem* 5th/11th century) certainly contains older material (Van Ess, *Untersuchungen*, 43 ff.). The question-answer pattern has become here a didactic principle, used to prepare future missionaries for their task. Later, this technique was elaborated in the so-called *djadal* literature, developed under the influence of the *Organon* of Aristotle, and intended to teach Islamic theologians as well as jurists the art of dialectic discussion. One may compare the Ḥanbalīs Ibn ʿAḳīl (see G. Makdisi, *Scholastic method*, 650 ff.; idem, *Dialectic*) or Ibn Surūr al-Maḳdisī, whose *Kitāb al-Djadal* (composed *ca.* 630/1232) has survived in manuscript (ms. Berlin 5319, fols. 17a-32). Makdisi has drawn attention to the resemblance between Ibn ʿAḳīl and the *sic et non* method used by Peter Abelard (*Scholastic method*, 648 f., 657 ff.; revised in *Rise*, 253 ff.). It remains to be proved in detail whether the method of Abelard (see for this, Grabmann, ii, 200 ff.) and his predecessors offers more than "mere parallels", and whether its origin is due to Arabic models (Makdisi).

In medical literature, the question-answer pattern served an exclusively didactic purpose, namely the transmission of specific knowledge. The *al-Masāʾil al-ṭibbiyya*, or *al-Masāʾil fi 'l-ṭibb*, of Ḥunayn b. Isḥāḳ [*q.v.*], preserved also in Syriac and Latin, which summarises in catechetical form the most important medical knowledge (see Ullmann, *Medizin*, 117 f.; idem, *Natur- und Geheimwissenschaften*, 458), became widely spread. Medical works of Galen and Hippocrates were summarised in the same way by Ḥunayn (see Ullmann, *Medizin*, 117, 206). For other medical handbooks in the question-answer pattern, see *ibid.*, 110, 166, 209, etc. From the fields of philosophy, physics and logic, mention may be made of the *Masāʾil mutafarriḳa* of al-Fārābī, and of the anonymous Syriac collection of definitions (ed. Furlani). From such didactical question-answer books it is only one step to the *ḥudūd* (definition) literature [*q.v.*] which could fall back on classical models (see Fuhrmann, part ii). Examples are al-Kindī's *Kitāb Ḥudūd al-ashyāʾ wa-rusūmihā*, and Ibn Sīnā's *Kitāb al-Ḥudūd*. Like in Syriac (cf. Baumstark, 131 ff.; Daiber, *Bar Zoʿbī*), traditions of Greco-Hellenistic dihairesis literature may have been of influence here.

To the list of the above-mentioned works, which might be divided into question-answer literature of "dialectical" and "didactical" character, should certainly be added the Greco-Arabic tradition of the *Problemata physica* (*al-Masāʾil al-ṭabīʿiyya*). The *Problemata physica* study the reasons and causes (διὰ τί) of phenomena in nature, and often use the following paradox: "Why does phenomenon X have the effect Y, but does phenomenon Xa not have the effect Ya"? The very complex history of the tradition of the Greek texts (see Flashar, 297 ff.) is reflected in the Arabic material (see, for the time being, Ullmann, *Medizin*, 92-6; idem, *Natur- und Geheimwissenschaften*, 458; Daiber, in *Gnomon*, xlii [1970], 545 f.; Sezgin, iii, 50; vii, 216; on further mss., see Daiber, *Graeco-Arabica and Philosophica in Indian libraries*, forthcoming). Numerous Arabic collections of the *Problemata*, ascribed to Aristotle, are closely related to the *Problemata inedita*, ascribed to Alexander of Aphrodisias, while others appear to be extracts from the *Problemata physica*, ascribed to Aristotle (cf. e.g. Book x in ms. 2234 of Tehran University, and see for this R. Kruk). The only, almost complete, manuscript of Ḥunayn b. Isḥāḳ's Arabic translation in 17 *maḳālāt* (mentioned also by Ibn Abī Uṣaybiʿa [*q.v.*] in his *History of physicians*), is ms. Manisa 1790/3; an edition of the Arabic text, with its translation in Hebrew, is in preparation. The Arabic text goes back to a Greek original, which was definitely more complete than the Greek text known so far. Moreover, Syriac (Job of Edessa, 769-835 A.D.) and Arabic (Balīnās, at the turn of the 8th century A.D.) traditions seem to have utilised collections of the *Problemata* of Greek origin, which have not been preserved (cf. Weisser, 55 ff., 210, 215). For other collections of the *Problemata*, which have not been identified so far, and which, in the Arabic texts, are ascribed to Theophrastus, Proclus and Galen, see Ullmann, *op. cit.* The *Problemata physica* are often quoted and commented upon in Arabic: Rhazes, Ḳusṭā b. Lūḳā, ʿAbd al-Laṭīf al-Baghdādī (*Maḳālatāni fi 'l-ḥawāss wa 'l-masāʾil al-ṭabīʿiyya*, Kuwait 1972), Ibn al-Haytham, Fakhr al-Dīn al-Rāzī and ʿĪsā b. Māssa. To this can be added the adaptations of two different collections of *Problemata* by Abu 'l-Faradj b. al-Ṭayyib in ms. Nuruosmaniye 3610 (new number 3095), written before 1076/1665: fols. 1b-21b (Alexander of Aphrodisias) and fols. 22a-33b (Aristotle). Moreover, there is the short extract (starting with Aristotle. *Problemata physica*, ii, 3) in ms. Princeton 2988 by Sulaymān b. Aḥmad, not further known.

Not related to the *Problemata physica* is the *Risāla fi 'l-asʾila al-ṭabīʿiyya* (ms. Washington, Army Medical Library A 82), a question-answer discussion, possibly fictitious, between al-Ḥārith b. Kalada [*q.v.* in Suppl.] (an older contemporary of the Prophet) and the Sāsānid ruler Kisrā Anūshirwān on practical questions of human health. This *Risāla* has become known (Sezgin, iii, 203) and published (by al-ʿAzzāwī) under the title *al-Muḥāwarāt fi 'l-ṭibb baynahu wa-bayna Nūshirwān*. The text is one of the numerous examples in which the question-answer pattern serves only to transmit knowledge, and thus has a didactic purpose. The master, the scholar, answers questions of a pupil, someone who tries to find information, but whose name is often not mentioned. This transmission of knowledge occasionally takes the form of learned correspondence. Thus the Christian Yaḥyā b. ʿAdī (d. 974 A.D.) answers fourteen questions on logic, physics and metaphysics asked by Ibn Abī Saʿīd b. ʿUthmān b. Saʿīd al-Mawṣilī (see Endress, 97 f.); the Būyid vizier Abu 'l-Faḍl Ibn al-ʿAmīd (d. 360/970) informs ʿAḍud al-Dawla [*q.v.*], at the latter's request, on all sorts of questions on natural science in letters, preserved in manuscript (ʿIrāḳ Museum, Baghdād 594; a different text in ms. Leiden Or. 184) (see Daiber, *Briefe*); Ibn Yaʿīsh (d. 643/1245) answers grammatical questions put before him by a group of scholars from Damascus (ed. R. Sellheim). A famous example is the change of ideas between Frederick II of Hohenstaufen and the Orient. In his *Adjwiba ʿan al-asʾila al-ṣaḳaliyya* (cf. Kattoura 42 f.; al-Taftāzānī, 108 ff., 178 ff.), the Spanish mystic and philosopher Ibn Sabʿīn, between 1237 and 1242 A.D., informs Frederick II about the problems of the eternity of the world, the essence of theology (ed. Yaltkaya, 24-26;

tr. M. Grignaschi), and the categories, the soul and the difference, in this subject, between Aristotle and his commentator Alexander of Aphrodisias. In his *Kitāb al-Istibṣār fī-mā tudrikuhu al-abṣār*, preserved in manuscript (Brockelmann, i, 385), the Egyptian scholar al-Ḳarāfī reports on physico-astronomical and physiological-optical questions which Frederick II put before the Arab scientist Kamāl al-Dīn b. Yūnus (tr. Wiedemann). The texts mentioned show the extent of the scientific relations of Frederick II with the Orient (see also Suter).

Occasionally, reciprocal criticism went hand in hand with the exchange of ideas between scholars. We may mention the *Asʾila wa'l-adjwiba* between al-Bīrūnī, Ibn Sīnā and the latter's pupil Abū Saʿīd al-Maʿṣūmī on questions about Aristotle's *De caelo* and about physics, or the answers of Ibn Sīnā to al-Bīrūnī's questions on metaphysics (ed. Ülken, *Ibn Sina risaleleri*, ii, 2-9; ed. M. Türker, in *Beyruni'ye armağan*, Ankara 1974, 103-12). Other correspondents of Ibn Sīnā (ed. Ülken, *op. cit.*, and ed. al-Kurdī, *Djāmiʿ al-badāʾiʿ*, 152 ff.) were Abu 'l-Faradj b. al-Ṭayyib, Abū Saʿīd b. Abī 'l-Khayr, Abū ʿUbayd al-Djūzdjānī, ʿAlāʾ 'l-Dawla b. Kākawayh, Abū Ṭāhir b. Ḥassūl, Miskawayh (*Masāʾil ʿan aḥwāl al-rūḥ*; cf. Michot) and Abu 'l-Ḥusayn al-Sahlī; also Ibn Zaylā [*q.v.*] and his *Madjālis al-sabʿa bayn al-shaykh wa 'l-ʿĀmirī*, preserved in manuscript (Rağip Paşa 1461, fols. 150a-162b).

Finally, from the fields of metaphysics and mysticism we may mention the correspondence between ʿUmar Khayyām and Ibn Sīnā's pupil Abū Naṣr Muḥammad b. ʿAbd al-Raḥīm al-Nasawī (ed. Nadwī, 375 ff. = ed. al-Kurdī, 165 ff.), and the exchange of letters between ʿAbd al-Razzāḳ al-Ḳāshānī (al-Kāshī) and Simnānī (8th/14th century) on the unity of being (see Landolt). In some cases there were also personal attacks during the learned arguments, as is clear from a polemic altercation in the 5th/11th century between Ibn Buṭlān and Ibn Riḍwān on medical and philosophical questions.

The examples given above and taken from Arabic literature show the overall importance of the dialogue. In the search for truth and its causes, the striving for knowledge (*ʿilm*) found expression in the question-answer literature, in which the didactic element often appears consciously linked to the dialectic one which tried to persuade and refute. The technique of the *reductio ad absurdum* was developed and afterwards refined under the influence of the methods of Aristotelian logic. The result was often a quasi-logical reasoning, consisting in an attempt to show the incompatibility of certain theses by proving the untenability of their conclusions (cf. Perelman/Olbrechts-Tyteca, § 45 ff., 48). This type of reasoning became a standard pattern of learned Arabic literature. In this connection, it is important to note that dialogue and discussion in different cultures have led to similar techniques. This does not however, exclude the possibility that questioning and answering in Islam were stimulated by Hellenism and by Christian, and to a lesser extent Jewish, converts and opponents.

Bibliography: 1. Texts. Brockelmann, Sezgin and Ullman (see below), index s.v. *masʾala, masāʾil, suʾālāt, asʾila; ǧawāb, ǧawābāt, aǧwiba; munāẓara, radd*, etc. ʿAbd al-Ḳāhir b. Ṭāhir al-Baghdādī, *al-Farḳ bayn al-firaḳ*, ed. Muḥammad Muḥyī al-Dīn ʿAbd al-Ḥamīd, Cairo 1964; idem, *al-Milal wa 'l-niḥal*, ed. A. N. Nader, Beirut 1970; ʿAmmār al-Baṣrī, *Apologie et controverses*, ed. Michel Hayek, Beirut 1977 (Rech. ILO, nouv. sér. B, V); al-Bīrūnī and Ibn Sīnā, *al-Asʾilah wa 'l-Ajwibah. Questions and answers, including the further answers of al-Bīrūnī and al-Maʿṣūmī's defense of Ibn Sīnā*, ed. with English and Persian introductions by Seyyed Hossein Nasr and Mahdi Mohaghegh, Tehran 1973; al-Djāḥiẓ, *al-Masāʾil wa 'l-djawābāt*, ed. Ch. Pellat, in *al-Machriq*, xxiii (1969), 316-26 = ed. ʿAbd al-Salām Hārūn, *Rasāʾil al-Djāḥiẓ*, iv, Cairo 1399/1979, 47-65 = partial tr. by Ch. Pellat, *Arabische Geisteswelt* (German tr. from French by W. W. Müller), Zürich-Stuttgart 1967, 54-62; *Djāmiʿ al-badāʾiʿ*, ed. Muḥyī al-Dīn Ṣabrī al-Kurdī, Cairo 1335/1917; Fakhr al-Dīn al-Rāzī, *Kitāb al-Munāẓarāt*, ed. and tr. Fathallah Kholeif, *A study on Fakhr al-Dīn al-Rāzī and his controversies in Transoxania*, Beirut 1966 (Rech. ILO, I, t. 31); al-Fārābī, *Masāʾil mutafarikka suʾila ʿanhā*, ed. Fr. Dieterici, *Alfārābī's philosophische Abhandlungen*, Leiden 1890, 84-103; al-Ghazālī, see below s.v. Malter; al-Ḥārith b. Kalada (Ps.?), *al-Muḥāwarāt fi l-ṭibb baynahū wa-bayna Nūshirwān*, ed. S. M. al-ʿAzzāwī, in *al-Mawrid*, vi/4 (1977), 217-21; Ḥunayn b. Isḥāk, *al-Masāʾil al-ṭibbiyya*, ed. Muḥammad ʿAlī Abū Rayyān, Mursī Muḥammad ʿAzab and Djalāl Muḥammad Mūsā, Cairo 1978 (Eng. tr. P. Ghalioungi, Cairo 1980); Ibn Buṭlān and Ibn Riḍwān, *The medico-philosophical controversy between Ibn Butlān and Ibn Riḍwān of Cairo*, Cairo 1937 (= The Egyptian University. The Faculty of Arts publics., 13); Ibn Ḳutayba, *al-Masāʾil wa 'l-adjwiba fi 'l-ḥadīth wa 'l-lugha*, Cairo 1349/1930, and ed. Shākir al-ʿĀshūr in *al-Mawrid*, iii/4 (1974), 233-552; Ibn Sabʿīn, *Correspondance philosophique avec l'empereur Frédéric II de Hohenstaufen*, Texte arabe publie par Şerefettin Yaltkaya. Avant propos par Henry Corbin, Paris 1941 (= Etudes orientales publiées par l'Institut Français d'Archéologie de Stamboul, VIII) = partial tr. M. Grignaschi, *Trattato sulle domande siciliance, domanda II*, Palermo 1956 (= Estratto del' archivo storico siciliano, serie 3, vol. vii); *Ibn Sina risaleleri*, ed. H. Z. Ölken, i-ii, Ankara-Istanbul 1953 (= Istanbul Universitesi Edebiyat Fakültesi Yayınlarından, 552); idem, *Livres des définitions*, ed., tr. and comm. A.-M. Goichon, Cairo 1963 (= *Mémorial Avicenne*, vi); Ibn Taymiyya, *al-Djawāb al-ṣaḥīḥ li-man baddala dīn al-Masīḥ*, ed. ʿAlī al-Sayyid Ṣubḥ al-Madanī, i-iv, Cairo (repr. *ca.* 1979); Ibn Yaʿīsh, see below s.v. Sellheim; al-Khallāl, *Kitāb al-Djāmiʿ li-ʿulūm Aḥmad b. Ḥanbal*, ed. Ziauddin Ahmed, Dacca 1975; partial ed. ʿAbd al-Ḳādir Aḥmad ʿAṭāʾ, *al-Amr bi 'l-maʿrūf wa 'l-nahy ʿan al-munkar min masāʾil Aḥmad b. Ḥanbal*, Cairo 1395/1975; al-Kindī, *Kitāb Ḥudūd al-ashyāʾ wa-rusūmihā*, ed. F. Klein-Franke, *Al-Kindī's "On definitions and descriptions of things"*, in *Le Muséon*, xcv (1982), 191-216; first ed. Abū Rīda, *Rasāʾil al-Kindī al-falsafiyya*, i, Cairo 1950, 163-79 (rev. ed. Cairo 1978, 109-30); also ed. with tr. and comm. D. Gimaret, in *Al-Kindī, Cinq épîtres*, Paris 1976, 7-69; Nāfiʿ b. al-Azraḳ, *Suʾālāt Nāfiʿ b. al-Azraḳ ilā ʿAbd Allāh b. ʿAbbās*, ed. Sulaymān al-Sāmarrāʾī, Baghdād 1968 (also under the title *Masāʾil Ibn al-Azraḳ*, Cairo 1950); Zayn al-Dīn al-Rāzī (end of 7th/14th century), *Masāʾil al-Rāzī wa-adjwibatuhā min gharāʾib āy al-tanzīl*, ed. Ibrāhīm ʿAṭwa ʿIwaḍ, Cairo 1961; ʿUmar Khayyām, *Works*, ed. Sulaymān Nadwī, ʿAẓamgaṛh 1933, 375 ff. = *Djāmiʿ al-badāʾiʿ*, 165 ff.

2. Studies. Nabia Abbott, *Studies in Arabic literary papyri*, ii, Chicago 1967 (= The Univ. of Chicago Oriental Inst. Publics., lxxv); M. Allard, *Le problème des attributs divins*, Beirut 1965 (= Rech.

ILO, xxviii); G. Bardy, *La littérature patristique des "quaestiones et responsiones" sur l'écriture sainte*, in *Revue biblique*, xli (1932), 210-36; xlii (1933), 211-29, 328-52; A. Baumstark, *Syrisch-arabische Biographien — Syrische Commentare zur Εισαγωγη des Porphyrios*, Leipzig 1900 (²1975) = Aristoteles bei den Syrern in V.-VIII. Jahrh. Syrische Texte, I; M. Cook, *The origins of Kalām*, in *BSOAS*, xliii (1980), 32-43; H. Daiber, *Briefe des Abū l-Faḍl Ibn al-ʿAmīd an ʿAḍudaddaula*, in *Isl.*, lvi (1979), 106-16; idem, art. *Dialog (arab. Prosa)*, in *Lexikon des Mittelalters*, iii; idem, *The Qurʾān as a matter of dispute. New material on the history of the Ḥanbalite-Ashʿarite controversy in the 12/13th century A.D.*, in *The 31st Intern. Congr. of Human Sciences in Asia and North Africa (CISHAN)*, Tokyo and Kyoto, Japan (31.8-7.9.1983), *Proceedings*; idem, *Das theol.-philos. System des Muʿammar Ibn ʿAbbād as-Sulamī (gest. 830 n. Chr.)*, Beirut 1975 (= Beiruter Texte u. Studien, 19); idem, *Ein vergessener syrischer Text: Bar Zoʿbī über die Teile der Philosophie*, in *Oriens Christianus* (forthcoming); H. Dörrie, art. *Erotapokriseis*, in *Reallexikon für Antike und Christentum*, vi, Stuttgart 1966, 342-70; 342-70; G. Endress, *The works of Yaḥyā Ibn ʿAdī*, Wiesbaden 1977; J. van Ess, *Anfänge muslimischer Theologie*, Beirut 1977 (= Beir. Texte u. Studien, 14); idem, *The beginnings of Islamic theology*, in *The cultural context of medieval learning*, ed. J. E. Murdoch and E. D. Sylla, Dordrecht-Boston 1973, 87-111; idem, *Disputationspraxis in der islamischen Theologie*, in *REI*, xliv (1976), 23-60, esp. 52 ff.; idem, *Untersuchungen zu einigen ibāḍitischen Handschriften*, in *ZDMG*, cxxvi (1976), 25-63; H. Flashar (tr.), *Aristoteles: Problemata physica*, 3rd ed., Darmstadt 1983; P. Freimark, *Das Vorwort als literarische Form in der arabischen Literatur*, thesis, Münster 1967; M. Fuhrmann, *Das systematische Lehrbuch*, Göttingen 1960; G. Furlani, *Un recueil d'énigmes philosophiques en langue syriaque*, in *ROC*, 3. seri, i (xxi) (1918-19), 113-36; I. Goldziher, *Über eine Formel in der jüdischen Responsenlitteratur und in den muhammedanischen Fetwās*, in *Ges. Schriften*, iv, Hildesheim 1970, 224-31; M. Grabmann, *Die Geschichte der scholastischen Methode*, Darmstadt 1956, i, 102 ff.; ii, 128 ff.; S. H. Griffith, *ʿAmmār al-Baṣrī's Kitāb al-Burhān: Christian Kalām in the first Abbasid century*, in *Le Muséon*, xcvi (1983), 145-81; idem, *The controversial theology of Theodore Abu Qurrah (c.750-c. 820 A.D.)*, unpubl. thesis, Washington 1978; G. Kattoura, *Das mystische und philosophie System des Ibn Sabʿīn*, unpubl. thesis, Tübingen 1977; R. Kruk, *Pseudo-Aristotle: an Arabic version of Problemata physica X*, in *Isis*, vi, no. 23 (1976), 252-6; H. Landolt, *Der Briefwechsel zwischen Kāšānī und Simnānī über Waḥdat al-wuǧūd*, in *Isl.*, 1 (1973), 29-81; G. Makdisi, *Dialectic and disputation*, in *Mélanges d'Islamologie, vol. dédié à la mémoire de A. Abel*, ed. P. Salmon, Leiden 1974, 201-6; idem, *The rise of colleges*, Edinburgh 1981, 253 ff.; idem, *The scholastic method in medieval education*, in *Speculum*, xlix (1974), 640-61; H. Malter, *Die Abhandlung des Abū Ḥāmid al-Ġazzālī. Antworten auf Fragen, die an ihn gerichtet wurden*, Frankfurt 1896; J. Michot, *Qui est l'auteur des questions sur les états de l'esprit?*, in *Bulletin de philosophie médiévale*, xxiv (1982), 44-53; Ch. Perelman, L. Olbrechts-Tyteca, *The new rhetoric. A treatise on argumentation*, Notre Dame-London 1971 (French orig. *La nouvelle rhétorique. Traité de l'argumentation²*, Brussels 1970); H. Putman, *L'église et l'Islam sous Timothée I (780-823)*, Beirut 1975 (= Rech. ILO, Nouv. sér., B, III); Khalil Samir, *Deux cultures qui s'affrontent. Une controverse sur l'iʿrāb au XIᵉ siècle entre Elie de Nisibe et le vizir Abū l-Qāsim*, in *MFOB*, xlix (1975-6), 617-49; R. Sellheim, *Die Antwort des Ibn Yaʿīš al-Ḥalabī auf einige grammatische Fragen aus Damaskus*, in *MFOB*, xlviii (1973-4), 303-19; F. Sezgin, *GAS*, i ff., Leiden 1967 ff.; H. Suter, *Beiträge zur Geschichte der Mathematik bei den Griechen und Arabern*, Hrsg. v. J. Frank, Erlangen 1922 (= Abh. zur Gesch. d. Naturwiss. u.d. Medizin, IV), 1-8; Abu 'l-Wafāʾ al-Ghunaymī al-Taftāzānī, *Ibn Sabʿīn wa-falsafatuhu 'l-ṣūfiyya*, Beirut 1973; M. Ullman, *Die Medizin im Islam*, Leiden-Cologne 1970 (= *Handbuch d. Orientalistik*, I, Erg. bd. VI/1); idem, *Die Natur- und Geheimwissenschaften im Islam*, Leiden 1972 (= *H.d.O.*, I, Erg. bd. VI/2); B. R. Voss, *Der Dialog in der frühchristlichen Literatur*, Munich 1970 (= Studia et testimonia antiqua, IX); U. Weisser, *Das "Buch über das Geheimniss der Schöpfung" von Pseudo-Apollonios von Tyana*, Berlin-New York 1980 (= Ars medica, III/2); E. Wiedemann, *Fragen aus dem Gebiete der Naturwissenschaften, gestellt von Friedrich II, dem Hohenstaufen*, in *Archiv für Kulturgeschichte*, xi, Leipzig-Berlin 1914, 483-5.

(H. DAIBER)

AL-**MASĀLIK WA 'L-MAMĀLIK** (A.) "routes and kingdoms", name given by R. Blachère (*Extraits des principaux géographes arabes du Moyen Age*, Beirut-Algiers 1934, 110-200; 2nd corrected printing by H. Darmaun, Paris 1957) to what he considered as a particular genre of Arabic geographical literature, because several works, which bear the title of *Kitāb al-Masālik wa 'l-mamālik*, present common characteristics. Nevertheless, not all those which, in his eyes, constitute this genre were given the title which has been retained, and furthermore, the *K. al-Masālik wa 'l-mamālik* which is perhaps the oldest, that of Ibn Khurradādhbih (d. between 272 and 300/885 and 912), does not form part of the genre, for we may see it simply as a manual for the use of the secretaries of the administration. Blachère thus places under this rubric the *K. al-Buldān* of al-Yaʿḳūbī (d. after 278/891), then as a group, the *K. Ṣuwar al-arḍ* of al-Balkhī (d. 322/934), the *K. al-Masālik wa 'l-mamālik* of al-Iṣṭakhrī (d. after 340/951) and the *K. Ṣūrat al-arḍ* of Ibn Ḥawḳal (d. after 367/977), the *K. Aḥsan al-taḳāsīm* of al-Muḳaddasī (d. after 378/988), the *K. al-Masālik wa 'l-mamālik* of al-Bakrī (d. 487/1094) and finally the *Nuzhat al-mushtāḳ* of al-Idrīsī (d. 560/1166), an expanded version of which, the *Rawḍ al-uns* or *K. al-Masālik [wa 'l-mamālik]*, does not seem to have come to light. A. Miquel, who often cites the *masālik wa 'l-masālik* (in *La géographie humaine du monde musulman*, i, Paris 1967, 2nd ed. 1973, index), devotes to this genre a fairly long chapter (267-330) which he entitles the "advent of genuine human geography" and in which he studies separately the works of al-Iṣṭakhrī and Ibn Ḥawḳal, adds to Blachère's list the *K. al-Masālik wa 'l-mamālik* of al-Muhallabī (d. 380/990) and simply mentions al-Bakrī and al-Idrīsī who (269, n. 1) "hardly do anything more than complete the data of the *masālik* works for Spain and the Maghrib".

Leaving aside the two latter ones cited, all the authors illustrative of the genre isolated by Blachère are easterners living at the end of the 3rd/9th century or in the 4th/10th one, i.e. in a period when the Shīʿī movement began to enjoy some remarkable successes. As against the geographers who preceded them, they were for the most part travellers who, to the data already taken traditionally by their predecessors from treatises of cosmography and geography based directly or indirectly on Greek science and particularly on Ptolemy [see BAṬLAMIYŪS], and to the information relating to the routes, distant lands and peoples who inhabit them that they could derive from various written or oral sources, now added first-hand documentation gathered in the regions that they describe. In this regard, a passage of the *K. Ṣūrat al-arḍ* of Ibn Ḥawḳal is very revealing, for it presents a totally characteristic lay-out (see Blachère, *Extraits*, 110-1; Ar. text in the 2nd ed. of the *Ṣūrat al-arḍ*, 329, and Fr. tr. Kramers-Wiet, almost identical to that of Blachère, i, pp. IX-X and ii, 321-2).

Regarding the form given to these works, these authors (with the exception of al-Idrīsī) do not follow the division of the world into climates [see IḲLĪM], but distinguish large regions, roughly corresponding to the *mamālik* [see MAMLAKA], within which they describe the routes that they traverse, their localities and the men who live there. "The authors of whom we are about to speak", writes Blachère (*Extraits*, 115), "are concerned purely with description. All their attention is directed to the recording of the general features of a country, assessing how the details relating to each place, in the past, bear on their present life. All this is no doubt written down in a generally monotonous style". However, this genre assumes a literary aspect which contrasts with the dryness of the administrative manuals, without giving as important a place to *adab* as do a Djāḥiẓ or an Ibn al-Faḳīh, just as it avoids the fables and marvellous accounts of certain other travellers who had the opportunity to go beyond the borders of the Islamic empire. Nevertheless, the eastern authors of the group do not know the Christian world and even have a poor acquaintance with the Muslim West, with the exception of Ibn Ḥawḳal whose work constitutes, on certain points, a unique historical source, for his chapters on the Maghrib, Spain and Sicily can be regarded as original. Generally, history in these works occupies a place which is not negligible, but it is doubtless the sedentary al-Bakrī who supplies in this regard the most information, while al-Idrīsī, who questioned, at the court of the Normans of Sicily, some travellers and Christian pilgrims, is quite well-informed on the routes, towns and states of Europe, not to mention the fact that he himself navigated the length of the coasts.

It was with a purely didactic purpose that Blachère marked out from the rest of the geographical literature the genre of the *masālik wa 'l-mamālik*, whose limits are far from being settled. In fact, even if the adoption of the title in question by a certain number of Arab authors of the Middle Ages has not failed to be noted by the historians of literature, other classifications can be proposed. For example, in his article DJUGHRĀFIYĀ of the Suppl. of the *EI*[1], although dating from 1936, J. H. Kramers puts into the same "literary group" Ibn Khurradādhbih, al-Sarakhsī, al-Yaᶜḳūbī, Ibn al-Faḳīh, Ibn Rusta, Ḳudāma, al-Djāḥiẓ and al-Djayhānī, and treats separately the school of al-Balkhī. As for S. Maqbul Ahmad, who was entrusted with the same article DJUGHRĀFIYĀ in the *EI*[2], he also alludes (ii, 579a) to the works which have received "the generic title of *al-Masālik wa 'l-Mamālik*", but he divides the geographical literature of the 3rd and 4th/9th-10th centuries into two large categories, comprising firstly (described as the ᶜIrāḳī school) Ibn Khurradādhbih, al-Yaᶜḳūbī, Ibn al-Faḳīh, Ḳudāma, Ibn Rusta, al-Masᶜūdī and al-Djayhānī, and secondly (the school of al-Balkhī) al-Iṣṭakhrī, Ibn Ḥawḳal and al-Muḳaddasī. Despite a certain convergence, the classifications, as we see, are appreciably different and invite us to proceed with some caution in handling the concept of *masālik wa 'l-mamālik*.

Bibliography: Apart from the works cited in the article, see the articles of the *EI* regarding the geographers concerned. (CH. PELLAT)

MASĀMIᶜA, members of a Baṣran family of the tribe of Shaybān of the confederacy of Bakr b. Wāʾil, prominent in the Umayyad period. They traced their ancestry to Djaḥdar b. Ḍubayᶜa, a participant in the war of Basūs [*q.v.*] (Ibn al-Kalbī-Caskel, *Ǧamharat an-nasab*, i, table 155; *Ḥamāsa*, ed. Freytag, i, 252 ff.; *Aghānī*[3], v, 43 f., 48 ff, 55). But apart from the report that Mismaᶜ b. Shihāb died as an apostate from Islam in eastern Arabia (according to the poetry cited by al-Balādhūrī, *Futūḥ*, 84; differently al-Ṭabarī, i, 1971), little is heard of them until they settled in Baṣra in the wake of the conquests. Here they joined the ranks of the tribal chiefs (*ashrāf, ruʾūs al-ḳabāʾil*) around whom Sufyānid politics revolved. They were one of the four families on which the Baṣrans prided themselves (see Ibn al-Faḳīh, *Buldān*, 170, tr. H. Massé, Damascus 1973, 207-8; Pellat, *Milieu*, 33 and index).

Mālik b. Mismaᶜ, the most famous member of the family, fought for ᶜĀʾisha at the battle of the Camel (allegedly already then as commander of the Bakr b. Wāʾil) and threw in his lot with the Umayyads thereafter (al-Ṭabarī, i, 3179, 3220 f.; ii, 765 f.). In the civil war which broke out at the death of Yazīd b. Muᶜāwiya, he negotiated the alliance (*ḥilf* [*q.v.*]) between the Bakr b. Wāʾil and Azd in Baṣra and played a major role in the subsequent feud between these two tribes and the Tamīm (64/683-4), emerging as the undisputed leader of the Bakr b. Wāʾil, whom he later conducted in battle against al-Mukhtār in 67/686-7 (al-Ṭabarī, i, 448 ff., 720, 726; al-Balādhurī, *Ansāb*, ivb, 105 ff.; v, 253, 259). Having joined the pro-Umayyad Djufriyya, a group of Baṣrans who unsuccessfully tried to oust Muṣᶜab from Baṣra in 69/688-9 or 70/689-90 (not 71/690-1, as stated by Caskel, *Ǧamhara*, ii, s.v. "Mālik b. Mismaᶜ" and Crone, *Slaves on horses*, Cambridge 1980 117; cf. Wellhausen, *Arab kingdom*, 190; al-Masᶜūdī, ed. Pellat, Arabic index, s.v.), he fled to the Yamāma, but returned on ᶜAbd al-Mālik's reconquest of ᶜIrāḳ in 72/691. He died shortly thereafter (al-Ṭabarī, ii, 799 ff.; al-Balādhurī, *Ansāb*, ivb, 156 ff., 160 ff., 165; Pellat, *Milieu*, 270)). His brothers Muḳātil b. Mismaᶜ and ᶜĀmir b. Mismaᶜ were also men of some prominence (for references, see Crone, *loc. cit.*).

Under the Marwānids, the family retained its leadership of the Bakr b. Wāʾil and, on the whole, its Umayyad sympathies. Thus Nūḥ b. Shaybān b. Mālik b. Mismaᶜ commanded the *khums* of Bakr b. Wāʾil against the Muhallabids in Baṣra in 101/720 (al-Ṭabarī, ii, 1380), while other members of the family were at various times governors of Fasā and Darābdjird, Sīstān and Sind (Crone, *op. cit.*, 117 f.). But they played no role in the third civil war or the ᶜAbbāsid revolution.

In the caliphate of al-Mahdī, ᶜAbd al-Mālik b. Shihāb al-Mismaᶜī commanded a naval expedition to Sind and acted as deputy governor there for a short while (al-Ṭabarī, iii, 460 f., 476 f., 491). Yet, unlike the Muhallabids or the Ḳutaybids, also Baṣran families of major importance in the Umayyad period, the Masāmiᶜa failed to effect a political comeback under the ᶜAbbāsids.

Bibliography: Practically all chronicles dealing with the Umayyad period have something to say about the Masāmiᶜa. The most important references are given in the article, to which however should be added Ibn Ḥazm, *Djamhara*, ed. Hārūn, 320-1. (P. CRONE)

MAṢĀMIDA [see MAṢMŪDA].

MĀSARDJAWAYH (in Persian Māsargōye), sometimes called Māsardjīs, is one of the few physi-

CORRIGENDA

VOLUME III
P. 1007b ʿĪD, l. 1, *instead of* sunset *read* sunrise

VOLUME VI
Fascicules 103-104, inside front cover, list of contributors, *instead of* J. Sadan, Hebrew University, Jerusalem. 360. *read* J. Sadan, Tel-Aviv University. 360.

ISBN 90 04 09082 7

PRINTED IN THE NETHERLANDS

Islamic Philosophy and Theology

Studies and Texts

edited by
H. DAIBER

ISSN 0169-8729

In Islam philosophy and theology have interacted intimately almost from the beginning. The two have played an important part in the intellectual history of Islam, notably in the classical period. For the historian of science and for the student of philosophy the rich literature of Islamic philosophy and theology has preserved much unique material from Antiquity. Above all, the field acquaints the student with new models of thought, which inspired mediaeval man and still fascinate the modern mind.

A growing interest in this field of study is noticeable among scholars both in the West and in the Muslim world. This series aims to provide an outlet for the results of research on these subjects and on the history of ideas in early Islam. It is intended to present both editions of important texts and studies for the use of the experts and for all those others interested in the cultural heritage of Islam.

1. **Ibn Rushd**'s Metaphysics. A translation with introduction of Ibn Rushd's commentary on Aristotle's Metaphysics, Book Lām, by Ch. Genequand. Photomech. repr. 1986. (vii, 219 p.)
ISBN 90 04 08093 7 *cloth* **Gld. 75.—/US$ 37.50**
2. **Daiber, H.** Wāṣil ibn ʿAṭaʾ als Prediger und Theologe. Ein neuer Text aus dem 8. Jahrhundert n. Chr. Herausgegeben mit Übersetzung und Kommentar. 1988. (x, 106 p., 4 pl.)
ISBN 90 04 08369 3 *cloth* **Gld. 40.—/US$ 20.—**
3. **Bello, I. A.** The medieval Islamic controversy between philosophy and orthodoxy. Ijmāʿ and taʾwil in the conflict between al-Ghazali and Ibn Rushd. Spring 1989. (*ca.* 184 p.)
ISBN 90 04 08092 9 *cloth ca.* **Gld. 64.—/US$ 32.—**
4. **Gutas, D.** Avicenna and the Aristotelian tradition. Introduction to reading Avicenna's philosophical works. 1988. (xii, 342 p.)
ISBN 90 04 08500 9 *cloth* **Gld. 120.—/US$ 60.—**
5. **al-Ḳāsim ibn Ibrāhīm.** Kitāb al-Dalīl al-Kabīr. Edited with introduction and annotated translation by B. Abrahamov. Summer 1989. (*ca.* 208 p.)
ISBN 90 04 08985 3 *cloth ca.* **Gld. 72.—/US$ 36.—**
6. **Maróth, M.** Ibn Sīnā und die peripatetische ,,Aussagenlogik''. Tr. from the Hungarian by J. Till. Autumn 1989. (*ca.* 224 p.)
ISBN 90 04 08487 8 *cloth ca.* **Gld. 64.—/US$ 32.—**

Prices are subject to change without prior notice. US$ prices are valid for U.S. and Canadian customers only.

Verkrijgbaar bij de erkende boekhandel — Prijzen zijn excl. BTW

E. J. Brill — P.O.B. 9000 — 2300 PA Leiden — The Netherlands

THE ENCYCLOPAEDIA OF ISLAM

NEW EDITION

PREPARED BY A NUMBER OF
LEADING ORIENTALISTS

EDITED BY

C. E. BOSWORTH, E. VAN DONZEL, W. P. HEINRICHS AND CH. PELLAT
ASSISTED BY F. TH. DIJKEMA AND MME S. NURIT

UNDER THE PATRONAGE OF
THE INTERNATIONAL UNION OF ACADEMIES

VOLUME VI

FASCICULES 109-110

MĀSARDJAWAYH — MASRAḤ

TUTA SUB AEGIDE PALLAS · EJB ·

LEIDEN
E. J. BRILL
1989

All correspondence on editorial matters should be addressed to the Editorial Secretaries, whose addresses are:

For the English Edition

Dept. of Near Eastern Studies,
The University of Manchester,
Manchester,
England M13 9PL.

For the French Edition

Centre Universitaire
94, avenue des Grésillons
92600 Asnières
France

AUTHORS OF ARTICLES IN THESE FASCICULES

Metin And, University of Ankara. 761.
P. A. Andrews, University of Cologne. 700.
A. Ayalon, Tel-Aviv University. 726.
Doris Behrens-Abouseif, Universities of Bamberg and Munich. 719.
R. Bencheneb, Paris. 757.
C. E. Bosworth, University of Manchester. 713, 726, 729.
J. T. P. de Bruijn, University of Leiden. 764.
R. M. Burrell, University of London. 730.
J. Burton-Page, Church Knowle, Dorset. 690.
A. H. Christie, University of London. 702.
[G. S. Colin, Paris]. 744.
F. Dachraoui, University of Tunis. 728.
A. Dietrich, Göttingen. 641, 727.
E. van Donzel, Netherlands Institute for the Near East, Leiden. 644.
N. Elisséeff, University of Lyons. 734.
J. Fontaine, Tunis. 712.
A. D. W. Forbes, University of London. 703.
G. S. P. Freeman-Grenville, University of York. 704.
F. Müge Göçek, Princeton University. 746.
O. Grabar, Harvard University, Cambridge, Mass. 708.
R. Hillenbrand, University of Edinburgh. 688.
G. H. A. Juynboll, The Hague. 717.
M. Khadduri, Johns Hopkins University School of Advanced International Studies, Washington. 740.
J. M. Landau, Hebrew University, Jerusalem. 750.
B. Lewis, Princeton University. 725.
D. MacEoin, University of London. 720.
[V. Minorsky, London]. 717, 745.
A. Miquel, Collège de France. 720.
R. Orazi, Rome. 720.
[J. Pedersen, Copenhagen]. 677.
Ch. Pellat, University of Paris. 709, 710, 738.
G. F. Pijper, Amsterdam. 701.
G. Rotter, University of Hamburg. 740.
J. Sadan, University of Tel-Aviv. 723.
A. Samb, University of Dakar. 707.
J. Samsó, University of Barcelona. 712.
O. Schumann, University of Hamburg. 733.
[M. Streck, Jena]. 716.
M. Talbi, University of Tunis. 713.
[A. J. Wensinck, Leiden]. 709, 726.
J. C. Wilkinson, University of Oxford. 736.

Names in square brackets are those of authors of articles reprinted or revised from the first edition of this Encyclopaedia.

cians from the Umayyad period who are known by name, and probably the first to translate a medical book into Arabic.

So far, endeavours to identify and date him have been unsuccessful. He is said to have been of Judaeo-Persian origin and to have lived in Baṣra. Occasionally he is indicated as a Syrian (*suryānī*), which is probably to be explained by the translation which he allegedly made from Syriac into Arabic of the *Kunnā<u>sh</u>* (τανδέχτης) of Ahrun [*q.v.* in Suppl.], translated into Syriac by a certain Gōsiōs. According to Ibn D̲j̲uld̲j̲ul [*q.v.*], this was done under the caliphs Marwān (64-5/684-5) or ᶜUmar b. ᶜAbd al-ᶜAzīz b. Marwān (99-101/717-20). The latter is said to have drawn the *Kunnā<u>sh</u>* out of the oblivion of his library and to have taken care that the translation became widely known. According to other authors, Māsard̲j̲awayh met Abū Nuwās, and so must have lived at the end of the 2nd/8th or the beginning of the 3rd/9th centuries. Totally mistaken are two places in Abū Sulaymān al-Sid̲j̲istānī, mentioned here only for completeness's sake. This author dates him back to Greek Antiquity, see *The Muntak<u>h</u>ab Ṣiwān al-ḥikmah of ... as-Sijistānī*, ed. D. M. Dunlop, The Hague, etc. 1979; on p. 20, l. 341, Māsard̲j̲awayh appears amidst the pupils of Hippocrates; and on p. 88, ll. 1860-3, he is ranged after Aesopus and Theophrastes and before the sophist Mūrūn (?) and Brasidas.

Two of the works ascribed to Māsard̲j̲awayh have not come down to us: one about the benefit and harm of the potency of food-stuffs (*Kitāb Ḳuwā 'l-aṭᶜima wa-manāfiᶜihā wa-maḍārrihā*), the other about the benefit and harm of the potency of medicinal drugs (*Kitāb Ḳuwā 'l-ᶜaḳāḳīr wa-manāfiᶜihā wa-maḍārrihā*). On the other hand, a treatise on substitute drugs has been preserved: *Fī Abdāl al-adwiya wa-mā yaḳūm maḳām <u>gh</u>ayrihi minhā*, see H. Ritter and R. Walzer in *SB Pr. Ak. W.*, Phil.-Hist. Kl. (1934), 831; Eng. tr. M. Levey, *Substitute drugs in early Arabic medicine, with special reference to the texts of Māsarjawaih, al-Rāzī, and Pythagoras*, Stuttgart 1971, 35-45. This short treatise has great similarity with the corresponding works of Galen and Paulus Aiginetes. It shows also that, during this early stage of translating activity, botanical nomenclature was already highly developed. In medical literature, Māsard̲j̲awayh is often quoted, especially in al-Rāzī's *Ḥāwī*, who calls him either Māsard̲j̲awayh or, more often, al-Yahūdī. The quotations have been put together by Ullmann, *Medizin*, 24, to which may be added Ibn al-ᶜAwwām, *Filāḥa*, tr. Clément-Mullet, ii/1, 88; the two quotations from Ibn Ḳutayba, *ᶜUyūn*, Cairo 1343-9/1925-30, ii, 102,4-103,3 and 108,3-5, have been translated by E. Wiedemann, *Aufsätze zur arabischen Wissenschaftsgeschichte*, Hildesheim-New York 1970, ii, 168 f. and 172 (the last quotation contains a remarkable observation about the beneficial effect of green colour on the eyes). These fragments still need careful analysis in order to answer the question whether the term "the Jew" indeed always indicates Māsard̲j̲awayh. For Ibn Abī Uṣaybiᶜa, i, 163, 24 f. this question is settled in the affirmative.

A son of Māsard̲j̲awayh, ᶜĪsā b. Māsard̲j̲īs, who, according to his name, was probably converted to Christianity, also followed the medical profession, and is said to have composed writings on colours (*K. al-Alwān*), smells and tastes (*K. al-Rawāʾiḥ wa 'l-ṭuᶜūm*), see Ibn al-Nadīm, *Fihrist*, 297, 17-8; Ibn al-Ḳifṭī, 247, 4-6; Ibn Abī Uṣaybiᶜa, i, 204, 9-10.

Bibliography: Ibn al-Nadīm, *Fihrist*, ed. Flügel, 297, ll. 6-8; Ibn D̲j̲uld̲j̲ul, *Ṭabaḳāt al-aṭibbāʾ wa 'l-ḥukamāʾ*, ed. F. Sayyid, 61; Ṣāᶜid al-Andalusī, *Ṭabaḳāt al-umam*, tr. R. Blachère, Paris 1935, 157; Ibn al-Ḳifṭī, *Ḥukamāʾ*, ed. J. Lippert, 324-6; Ibn Abī Usaybiᶜa, *ᶜUyūn al-anbāʾ*, ed. A. Müller, i. 163-4 and 204, 22. 7-8; Ibn al-ᶜIbrī (Barhebraeus), *Taʾrī<u>kh</u> mu<u>kh</u>taṣar al-duwal*, ed. Ṣāliḥānī, 192-3; L. Leclerc, *Histoire de la médecine arabe*, Paris 1876, i, 79-81; M. Steinschneider, *Masardjaweih, ein jüdischer Arzt des VII. Jahrhunderts*, in *ZDMG*, liii (1899), 428-34; idem, *Die arabische Literatur der Juden*, Frankfurt 1902, 13-15; Brockelmann, S I, 417; M. Ullman, *Die Medizin im Islam*, Leiden-Cologne 1970, 23 f., 293; Sezgin, *GAS*, iii, 206 f. (A. Dietrich)

MAṢAWWAᶜ Ar. form, also Muṣawwaᶜ; in Ethiopic, Meṣwāᶜ, Meṭwāᶜ, in Tigre and Tigriñña, Bāṣeᶜ, in Bed̲j̲a, Bāḍeᶜ = Ar. Bāṣiᶜ/Bāḍiᶜ (see al-Masᶜūdī, *Murūd̲j̲*, ed. Pellat, vi, 184 *s.v.*, but also S. Tedeschi (*Bibl.*), an island and port in Eritrea [*q.v.*] on the Red Sea, at 15° 38' N. and 39° 28' E., opposite the Dahlak [*q.v.*] archipelago. The islands of Masawwaᶜ, the site of the deep-water harbour, and Tawlūd are linked to each other and to Arkiko on the mainland (for this name, see Basset, *Histoire*, i, 128-9; Crawford, *The Fung kingdom*, 127) by causeways. From the north, the roadsteads are protected by the D̲j̲arār and ᶜAbd al-Ḳādir peninsulas. With a recorded annual average temperature of 31° C., the port is among the world's hottest places, the annual rainfall being only 7 inches.

According to popular etymology, the name is derived from Ethiopic *mĕṣuwāᶜ* "cry, loud call". A fisherman from Dahlak, driven by a storm to the then inhabited island, is said to have related that its size was such that a man, shouting in a high voice (*ṣawᶜ*), could make himself heard from one end to the other (Conti Rossini, *Il Gadla Filpos*, 162). According to another version (Conti Rossini, *Documenti*, 16; cf. Esteves Pereira, *Historia de Minas*, 62), Ethiopian caravan leaders, arriving at D̲j̲arār, had to cry aloud for the barks of the island to come and fetch them. The island is in fact one km. long and *ca.* 250 m. wide.

The Masawwaᶜ region, known as Samhar, may have been visited as early as the third millennium B.C. when Egyptian ships sailed down the Red Sea. It became better known in history when the Greek Ptolemies developed a series of stations along the African coast [see badw, i, 887a]. The region, but not the actual port, is mentioned in the famous inscription carved in the port of Adulis about 240 B.C. at the time of Ptolemy III Energetes (246-221 B.C.), and copied by Cosmas Indicopleustes who visited the area about 525 A.D. (Mc Crindle, *The Christian topography*, 57). Artemidoros of Ephesus (*ca.* 100 B.C.), whose work is known through extracts by Strabo (*ca.* 20 B.C.), mentions on this coast the port of Sabā, identified with D̲j̲arār by Conti Rossini (*Storia*, 60, 103; *Comenti e notizie*, 17). In connection with Adulis, now Zula, the region is also mentioned in the well-known *Periplus of the Erythrean Sea* (tr. Schoff, 22-3, cf. 60). This Aksumite port in the gulf of the same name must have ceased to function somewhere about the middle of the first millennium A.D. (Kammerer, *Essai*, ch. 5), and its rôle may then have been taken over gradually by Masawwaᶜ, lying about 30 miles to the north.

In early Islam, Maṣawwaᶜ is mentioned as a place of exile and thus considered by Conti Rossini (*Storia*, 212) as being in Muslim hands. Because of his love of wine, the Arab poet Abū Miḥd̲j̲ān [*q.v.*] was banished by ᶜUmar to Bāṣiᶜ in 14/634 (Caetani, *Annali*, v, 224 ff.; Brockelmann, I, 40, S I, 701; Conti Rossini, *Storia*, 212). At the death of Marwān, the last Umayyad caliph, his son ᶜAbd Allāh, on his flight to D̲j̲udda, arrived at Bāḍiᶜ (al-Masᶜūdī, *Tanbīh*, 330).

According to al-Masʿūdī, who wrote in the 4th/10th century, the coastal plains, and consequently Maṣawwaʿ, were tributary to Ethiopia, and Bāḍiʿ lay on the littoral of *al-maʿādin*, "the mines", the territory of the Bed̲j̲a [*q.v.*]. If by this term the hinterland of Masawwaʿ is meant (Bāḍiʿ is not to be identified with Badi or Airi island lying further north, see Crowfoot, *Some Red Sea ports*), al-Masʿūdī indicates that the Bed̲j̲a were working the Eritrean gold mines (Conti Rossini, *Storia*, 278) and that the port played a rôle in the gold traffic.

During the 6th-8th/12th-14th centuries, Maṣawwaʿ was under the sovereignty of the *amīr* of Dahlak, who called himself *sulṭān*. The Ethiopians, however, as in the time when the *amīr* depended on Aksum, continued to indicate him as *sĕyuma baḥr* "prefect of the sea", in opposition to the *baḥr nagāš* "ruler of the sea [-province]", who resided at Debārwā (Debaroa). Relations between Ethiopia and the *nāʾib* of the *amīr* at Maṣawwaʿ must have been uneasy, at least occasionally, as may be concluded from the capture of the port by Isaac, son of Negus Dawit I (1381- *ca.* 1410). In the 10th/16th century still, the sovereignty of Maṣawwaʿ was linked to that of Dahlak (de Barros, *Decada*, ii, 1. viii, ch. 1; Basset, *Inscriptions*; Esteves Pereira, *Os Portugueses*) The *(Is) di mas(ua)* on Fra Mauro's map is perhaps identical with Maṣawwaʿ (Kammerer, *La Mer Rouge*, iii/3, 20). An impression of the commercial activity in this and other ports on both sides of the Red Sea in the early 16th century can be gained from Ludovico di Varthema (*Travels*, 31, 37-8). Andrea Corsali (*Historiale description*, 32-3), Tomé Pires (*Suma oriental*, 43) and Duarte Barbosa (*The Book*, 16). According to the author of the *Cartas das novas* (Thomas, *Discovery of Abyssinia*, 67), there was a large number of boats at anchor at Maṣawwaʿ, including two from Gud̲j̲arāt, when he arrived there in 1521. Soon, however, foreign trade in the Horn of Africa was to suffer severely from the Portuguese interference with local commerce. The discovery and development of the trade route round Cape of Good Hope, Aḥmad Grāñ's invasion of the highlands [see ḤABAS̲H̲, ḤABAS̲H̲A] and the emergence of Turkish influence in the Red Sea caused the decline of Maṣawwaʿ, which remained however the main port of Ethiopia.

When a Portuguese exploratory mission landed in Maṣawwaʿ in 1520, the town was completely Muslim. According to Alvarez (Beckingham-Huntingford, *The Prester John*, i, 58), the Portuguese transformed the mosque into a church, but did not occupy the port, although the Ethiopian king Lebna Dengel strongly wished them to build a fortress there (*ibid.*, ii, 479 ff.). The information of the "Zorzi Itineraries" (Crawford, *Ethiopian itineraries*, 90, 159), according to which king David (= Lebna Dengel) gave the port to the Portuguese, may refer to the mission of 1520, to some earlier expedition, to negotiations, or to mere rumour.

With the disembarkation of Cristovão da Gama in 1541 [see ḤABAS̲H̲], Maṣawwaʿ began its rôle as entrance-gate into Ethiopia for Western missionaries and travellers, even after Özdemir Pas̲h̲a [*q.v.*] had conquered the port and Arkiko in 1557, which then became one of the *sand̲j̲aks* of the Ottoman province of Ḥabes̲h̲ ([*q.v.*], and also Orhonlu, *Habeş eyaleti*, 33 ff.). The difficulties between Turks and Western missionaries, both Catholic and Protestant, are described in the former's correspondence (Beccari, *Rerum*; Lobo, *A voyage*, 140 ff.; Aren, *Evangelical pioneers*; M. Kropp, in *Oriens Christianus*, lxvi [1982], 247). Turkish relations with Ethiopia, hostile at first, remained uneasy later on. After the combined forces of the Ottomans and *baḥr nagāš* Yisḥāk had been defeated in 1578 by the Ethiopian king Sarṣa Dengel (Conti Rossini, *La guerra*), Maṣawwaʿ and Arkiko remained in Turkish hands, but Turkish power declined rapidly. A pas̲h̲a was first established in Dahlak, and later in Maṣawwaʿ, but actual power was soon left to a local Balaw chieftain from a Bed̲j̲a family of the Samhar region, who acted as *nāʾib* (see Bombaci, *Notizie*, 79-86; idem, *Il viaggio*, 259-75) or deputy of the Turkish pas̲h̲a, who had taken up residence in Suʾākin [*q.v.*]. After the expulsion of the Roman Catholic missionaires from Ethiopia in 1633, King Fāsiladas made an agreement with the pas̲h̲a that the latter should execute all priests who might try to enter Ethiopia. The situation at Maṣawwaʿ in 1634 is described by Barradas (Beccari, *Rerum*, i, 295-302). The Turkish presence in the port, and especially the extortions by the *nāʾib*, remained a source of irritation to the Ethiopian kings (al-Ḥaymī, *Sīrat al-Ḥabas̲h̲a*; Van Donzel, *Foreign relations*, index *s.vv.* Turks, Massawa), the more so because imports and exports were not unimportant (Van Donzel, *op. cit.*, Appendix iv; Bruce, *Travels*, iii, 54; Beccari, *Rerum*, index *s.v.* Maçua). In 1693 the *nāʾib* Mūsā b. ʿUmar b. ʿĀmir b. Kunnu tried to use extortion against the Armenian merchant K̲h̲ōd̲j̲a Murād, who had returned from the Dutch East Indies with gifts for the Ethiopian king. When Murād refused to pay, his goods were confiscated. King Iyāsu I ordered the delivery of foodstuffs to Maṣawwaʿ to be suspended, and started preparations to attack the *nāʾib*, who then submitted (Van Donzel, *op. cit.*, 83). According to the French traveller Charles Jacques Poncet (*ca.* 1700, see Foster, *The Red Sea*, 154), the fortress in Maṣawwaʿ was not very strong, and the arrival of an English vessel "cast terror into the whole island". On learning of the arrival of this ship at Maṣawwaʿ, the Ethiopian monks made a disturbance before the palace in Gondar, probably fearing a punitive expedition from what they thought to be Portuguese. Poncet also relates that the Pas̲h̲a received him with great civility, at the recommendation of the emperor of Ethiopia, who was greatly afraid because he could easily starve the port or refuse to furnish it with water. The inhabitants of the island were obliged to fetch it from Arkiko on the mainland (Foster, *op. et loc. cit.* On the cisterns on the island, according to local tradition built by the "Furs", see Conti Rossini, *Storia*, 295-6; Puglisi, *Alcuni vestigi*, 35-47). Although claiming power over the port, the Ethiopian kings were never in fact master over it, as is also clear from the *Annals* of King Iyāsu II (1730-55) (see Guidi, *Annales Iyāsu II*, 127-30, 143-7, 155). Power remained in the hand of the *nāʾib*. When Bruce arrived in Maṣawwaʿ in 1768, the Porte had annexed the government of the port to the pas̲h̲a of D̲j̲udda, but the *nāʾib* did not pay tribute either to him or to the Ethiopian king (Bruce, *Travels*, iii, 5-6). The number of Banians or Indian merchants, in whose hands trade had formerly been (Van Donzel, *Foreign relations*, index *s.v.*), was reduced to six, who made but a poor livelihood (Bruce, *Travels*, iii, 55).

In the first decades of the 19th century, the *nāʾib* still exercised some power. According to Salt (*A voyage*, 138, 147), the *nāʾib* Idrīs tried to prevent the English from opening a communication with Ethiopia, but came then under pressure from both the S̲h̲arīf of Mecca on the one side and from Ras Wolde Sellāsie of Tigre on the other. Salt was told by the Ras that the road by Bure, south of Amphila Bay (see the map in Salt, *A voyage*, opp. p. 137), was preferable to the route by Maṣawwaʿ, but Nathaniel Pearce wrote to him that the only road into Ethiopia was by

Maṣawwaᶜ (*ibid.*, 152). He added that the *nāʾib* would not allow guns to pass through his country. In 1844, almost three centuries after their first attempt, the Turks tried again to get a foothold on the mainland by occupying Arkiko. But again they were forced back on to Maṣawwaᶜ, which in 1846 was leased to Muḥammad ᶜAlī [*q.v.*], and now became an important element in Egyptian, British, Italian and Ethiopian policies. The lease, having expired at the death of Muḥammad ᶜAlī in 1849, was renewed in 1865 in favour of Ismāᶜīl Pasha [*q.v.*]. Egyptian rule was welcomed by the local nomads who, during the anarchy of the last years of king Tēwodros of Ethiopia, had been suffering from the hill tribes. Soon some of the latter too began to seek Egyptian protection. In 1872 the Swiss Werner Münzinger, consul of France in Maṣawwaᶜ since 1865, resigned from his post and entered the service of the Egyptians. Having allegedly paid £ 1,000,000 to the Porte, Ismāᶜīl Pasha created the so-called Eastern Sudan, i.e. Taka, Suʾākin and Maṣawwaᶜ, and appointed Münzinger as governor in 1873. Münzinger initiated a plan to link Maṣawwaᶜ with the Egyptian possessions in the north-east, and constructed the causeways to the mainland. On each of them was a gate, watched by a guard who collected a toll from every passer-by (Rohlfs, *Meine Mission*, 31 ff.; Conti Rossini, *Documenti*, 16). He also fortified the port, made himself "protector" of the Bilen tribes and occupied the Keren region. The Turkish practice of having a *nāʾib* of Balaw origin was continued, and a member of his family was appointed *sirdār* [*q.v.*] of the troops in Maṣawwaᶜ. When the European powers left Egypt with a free hand with regard to Ethiopia, Ismāᶜīl Pasha appointed the Dane Søren Adolph Arendrup as commander of the Egyptian troops in Maṣawwaᶜ, and three Egyptian expeditions set out against Ethiopia [see ḤABASH. i]. After the Egyptian *débâcle* near Gura in 1876, rumours spread in Maṣawwaᶜ that the Ethiopian King Yohannes was going to attack the port. But the king wanted peace with Egypt, insisting however that Maṣawwaᶜ should be restored to his kingdom. The peace treaty, arranged by C. G. Gordon, left Egypt still in control of the Keren region and the port, where the anti-Ethiopian policy was continued by Mukhtār Bey, the Egyptian governor of Maṣawwaᶜ. He gave asylum to Fitawrāri Debbeb, an Ethiopian rebel and cousin of King Yohannes, who sold his loot openly in the markets of Arkiko and Maṣawwaᶜ and who had brought trade with the coast to a standstill. After Mukhtār Bey had been replaced by Mason Bey, an American who had been in the service of the Egyptian government, a treaty between Great Britain, Egypt and Ethiopia was signed at Adowa in 1884 by king Yohannes and Rear-Admiral Sir William Hewett. The actual control of Egypt, and consequently of the ports on the Red Sea coast which had been occupied by the Egyptians, lay indeed in the hands of Great Britain after the revolt of ᶜUrābī Pasha [*q.v.*]. Under British protection, free transit through Maṣawwaᶜ was given for all goods, including arms and ammunition, to and from Ethiopia. A general reservation with respect to the lawful claims of the Porte, explicitly mentioned in Lord Granville's instruction to Admiral Hewett, was ignored in the Treaty. Nor did the Treaty contain any concrete agreement about the possession of Maṣawwaᶜ. In a letter to Queen Victoria, King Yohannes, aware that the removal of the Egyptian garrison would leave the port open to him, expressed the hope that "the gates of heaven would open for her as she had opened Maṣawwaᶜ for him". In her answer, the Queen regretted being unable to accede to the King's wish regarding the port (Zewde Gabre-Sellasie, *Yohannes IV*, 152). Indeed, by now another European power had appeared on the scene.

Wary of the French expansion in the Red Sea [see DJIBŪTĪ], and in view of financial difficulties in Egypt, Great Britain had been seeking an alliance with Italy. Already in 1881, an Egyptian appeal to use force against Italy after the establishment of an Italian colony in Assab [*q.v.*], had been rejected by the British government. In 1882 Italy had even been invited to participate in restoring order in Egypt. In the years 1881-3 expenditure had exceeded revenue in the port of Maṣawwaᶜ (Zewde Gabre-Sellasie, *op. cit.*, 160); hence retaining possession of the port was not considered to be "in the true interests of Egypt" (*ibid.*, 161). Having thus been given a free hand in the Red Sea, Italy landed a military expedition in Maṣawwaᶜ, where on 5 February 1885, the Italian flag was flying side-by-side with the Egyptian one over the palace and the forts. King Yohannes was outraged, while Menelik, who was building up his own power in Shoa and had signed a secret treaty of friendship and trade with the Italians in 1883, acted as mediator between the Ethiopian king and Italy. The Italians quickly occupied Arafale and Arkiko, and when the Egyptian garrisons were gradually withdrawn, almost all major places between Assab and Maṣawwaᶜ came into their power. Notwithstanding the Treaty of Adowa, the Italians did not allow free transit of ammunition and arms to King Yohannes, nor in the quantities which he desired. They also rejected any form of Egyptian authority, although this was recognised at first. Tension between the Ethiopians and the Italians led to an armed encounter at Dogali (1887), where the latter suffered defeat. Menelik offered mediation, which was accepted by Yohannes but refused by the Italians, who concluded another treaty with the future Negus. Yohannes, meanwhile convinced that Great Britain and Italy were acting in accord, and considering Sir Gerald Portal's mission to him as a feint, marched against Maṣawwaᶜ in 1887. However, before reaching it he turned his attention again to the Mahdist forces. After his death in the battle of Ḳallabat (Metemma), the Italians signed the Treaty of Ucciali (Wuchali) with Menelik in 1889. Italian possession of Maṣawwaᶜ was confirmed, but Menelik was permitted to import arms duty-free through the port (see the text of the famous Treaty in Zaghi, *Crispi*, 152; cf. Marcus, *Menelik II*, index s.v. Treaties). After their defeat at Adowa in 1896, the Italians were able to retain Eritrea and the port of Maṣawwaᶜ, which played an important rôle during the Italo-Ethiopian war. Conquered by British forces in 1941, Maṣawwaᶜ remained under British administration until the federation of Eritrea with Ethiopia in 1950.

In 1931 the population was estimated at 9,300 and in 1970 at 18,490. Imports consist mainly of industrial goods, while exports comprise oilseeds, nuts, hides, coffee, salt, fish and pearl. Local industries include a salt works, fish and meat processing enterprises, a cement plant and an ice factory. A thermal power plant serves outlying areas where manganese ore is mined. The volcanic deposits of the Danakil Plains contain sulphur, sodium and potassium, gypsum, rock salt and potash.

During their brief occupation of Eritrea, the coastal settlements on the Red Sea and the Harar region, the Egyptians introduced their Ḥanafī legal code, which was kept on by the Italians. Thus the Ḥanafī *madhhab* is predominant in the coastal towns of Maṣawwaᶜ, Arkiko, Zula, Assab, etc. Of the Ṣūfī orders in Islam, the Ḳādiriyya are well represented in Masawwaᶜ. Its founder, ʿAbd al-Ḳādir al-Dj̲īlānī [*q.v.*], is said to have died at the place of the mosque dedicated in his name. His anniversary (*ziyārat al-Dj̲īlānī*) is celebrated by a pilgrimage and the accompanying ceremonies on 11 Rabīʿ al-Awwal of each year.

Bibliography: R. Basset, *Histoire de la conquête de l'Abyssinie (XIVe siècle) par Chihab eddin Ahmed ben Abd el Qâder surnommé Arab-Faqih.* 2 vols. Paris 1897-1901; O. G. S. Crawford, *The Fung kingdom of Sennar*, Gloucester 1951; C. Conti Rossini, *Il Gadla Filpos e il Gadla Yohannes di Dabra Bizan*, in *Atti della R. Accademia dei Lincei*, anno CCXVII (1900), Ser. Vª, classe di Sc. mor., vol. viii, Parta 1ª, Rome 1903; idem, *Storia d'Ethiopia*, Bergamo 1928; idem, *Comenti e notizie di geographi classici sovra il Sudan Egiziano e l'Etiopia*, in *Aegyptus*, vi (1925); idem, *Documenti per lo studio della lingua tigre*, in *Giornale della Società Asiatica Italiana*, xvi (1903); F. M. Esteves Pereira, *Historia de Minás, Ademas Saged, rei de Ethiopia*, in *Boletin de Sociedade de Geographia de Lisboa*, 7ª ser. xii, (1887-8); J. W. McCrindle, *The Christian topography of Cosmas, an Egyptian monk*, London 1897; A. Kammerer, *Essais sur l'histoire antique d'Abyssinie*, Paris 1926; idem, *La Mer Rouge, l'Abyssinie et l'Arabie aux XVIe et XVIIe siècles et la cartographie des portolans du Monde oriental*, iii/3, Cairo 1952; *Periplus of the Erythrean Sea*, tr. W. Schoff, New York 1912; L. Caetani, *Annali*; J. W. Crowfoot, *Some Red Sea ports in the Anglo-Egyptian Sudan*, in *GJ* (May 1911), 523-50; João de Barros, *Decadas da Asia*, Lisbon 1777; on the name Masawwaʿ, see I. Guidi, *Le canzoni geʿez-amariñña in onore di Re Abissini*, in *RRAL*, ser. ii, vol. v (1889), 57; S. Tedeschi, *La questione di Bāḍiʿ*, in *RSO* lxiii (1984), 179-99; J. Peruchon, *Histoire d'Eskender, de ʿAmda Seyon II et de Nāʾod*, in *JA* (1894), 22; R. Basset, *Études sur l'histoire d'Ethiopie*, in *JA* (1881), 1, 24; idem, *Les inscriptions de l'île de Dahlak*, in *JA* (1893); F. M. Esteves Pereira, *Os Portugueses em Maçua*, in *Revista das sciencias militares* (1889); G. P. Badger, *The travels of Ludovico di Varthema*, London 1863; A. Corsali, *Historiale description de l'Ethiopie*, Antwerp 1558; M. L. Dames, *The Book of Duarte Barbosa*, 2 vols. London 1918-21; C. F. Beckingham-G. W. B. Huntingford, *The Prester John of the Indies, a true relation of the lands of the Prester John...*, 2 vols., Cambridge 1961; O. G. S. Crawford, *Ethiopian itineraries circa 1400-1524*, Cambridge 1958; H. Thomas, *The discovery of Abyssinia by the Portuguese in 1520*, London 1938; C. Orhonlu, *Osmanlı imparatorluğu'nun güney siyaseti: Habeş eyaleti*, Istanbul 1974; R. Pankhurst, *History of the Ethiopian towns from the Middle Ages to the early nineteenth century*, Äthiopistische Forschungen, 8, Wiesbaden 1982, index s.v.; C. Beccari, *Rerum Aethiopicarum scriptores occidentales inediti a saeculo XVI ad XIX*, 15 vols., Rome 1903-13; G. Arén, *Evangelical pioneers in Ethiopia*, Uppsala 1978; C. Conti Rossini, *La Guerra turco-abissina del 1578*, in *OM*, i (1921-2), 634-6, 684-91, ii (1923), 48-57; A. Bombaci, *Notizie sull'Abissinia in fonti turche*, in *Rassegna di Studi Etiopici*, iii, (1943), 79-86; idem, *Il viaggio in Abissina di Evliya Celebi*, in *AIUON*, n.s. ii (1943), 259-75; al-Ḥaymī, *Sīrat al-Ḥabas̲h̲a*, ed. E. van Donzel, *A Yemenite embassy to Ethiopia 1647-1649*, Äthiopische Forschungen, 21, Stuttgart 1986; idem, *Foreign relations of Ethiopia 1642-1700*, Leiden 1979; J. Bruce, *Travels to discover the Source of the Nile, in the years 1768-73*, 5 vols., Edinburgh 1790; W. Foster, *The Red Sea and adjacent countries at the close of the seventeenth century*, London 1949; G. Puglisi, *Alcuni vestigi dell'isola di Dahlac Chebir e la leggenda dei Furs*, in *Procs. of the Third International Conference of Ethiopian Studies*, Addis Ababa 1966, i, 35-47; I. Guidi, *Annales Regum Iyastu II et Iyoas*, CSCO lxi (1910), lxvi (1912), repr. Louvain 1954; H. Salt, *A Voyage to Abyssinia, and Travels into the interior of that Country*, London 1814, repr. 1967; W. Münzinger, *Ostafrikanische Studien*, Schaffhausen 1864, 114 ff.; G. Rohlfs, *Meine Mission nach Abessinien*, Leipzig 1883; Zewde Gabre-Sellasie, *Yohannes IV of Ethiopia, a political biography*, Oxford 1975; C. Zaghi, *Crispi e Menelich nel Diario inedito del conte Augusto Salimbeni*, Turin 1956; H. G. Marcus, *The life and times of Menelik II, Ethiopia 1844-1913*, Oxford 1975. (E. van Donzel)

MASCARA [see al-muʿaskar].

MASCULINE [see mud̲h̲akkar].

MASDJID (a.), mosque, the noun of place from *sadjada* "to prostrate oneself, hence "place where one prostrates oneself [in worship]". The modern Western European words (Eng. *mosque*, Fr. *mosquée*, Ger. *Moschee*, Ital. *moschea*) come ultimately from the Arabic via Spanish *mezquita*.

I. In the central Islamic lands
- A. The origins of the mosque up to the Prophet's death
- B. The origin of mosques after the time of the Prophet
- C. The mosque as the centre for divine worship
- D. The component parts and furnishings of the mosque
- E. The mosque as a state institution
- F. The administration of the mosques
- G. The personnel of the mosque
- H. The architecture of the mosque

II. in muslim india
- A. Typology
- B. The actual monuments

III. In Java

IV. In the rest of South-East Asia

V. In China

VI. In East Africa

VII. In West Africa

I. In the central Islamic lands

A. The origins of the mosque up to the Prophet's death.

The word *msgdʾ* is found in Aramaic as early as the Jewish Elephantine Papyri (5th century B.C.), and appears likewise in Nabataean inscriptions with the meaning "place of worship", but possibly, originally "stele, sacred pillar". The Syriac form *msgdʾ* and Amharic *masged* are late loans from Arabic, though Geʿez *mes̲h̲gād* "temple, church" may be a genuine formation from the verbal root *s - g- d* (itself certainly borrowed from Aramaic). The form *ms¹gd* "oratory, place of prayer" occurs also in Epigraphic South Arabian (A. F. L. Beeston *et alii*, *Sabaic dictionary*, Louvain-Beirut 1982, 125). The Arabic *masdjid* may thus have been taken over directly from Aramaic or formed from the borrowed verb (see A. Jeffery, *The foreign vocabulary of the Qur'ān*, Baroda 1938, 263-4).

1. The Meccan period. The word is used in the Ḳurʾān especially of the Meccan sanctuary (*al-Masdjid al-ḥarām*, sūra II, 139, 144, 145, 187, 192, 214; V, 3; VIII, 34; IX, 7, 19, 28; XVII, 1; XXII, 25; XLVIII, 25, 27); according to later sources, this was already the usage in the Meccan period (*ca.* al-Yaʿḳūbī, *Taʾrīkh*. i. 285, 12). According to tradition, the term *al-Masdjid al-aḳṣā* (sūra XVII, 1) means the Jerusalem sanctuary (according to B. Schrieke, in *Isl.*, vi [1915-16], 1; cf. Horovitz, in *ibid.*, ix [1919], 159 ff., the reference is rather to a place of prayer in heaven); and in the legend of the Seven Sleepers,

masdjid means a tomb-sanctuary, probably Christian, certainly pre-Islamic (sūra XVIII, 20). The word is also applied to pre-Islamic sanctuaries, which belong to God and where God is invoked, although Muḥammad was not always able to recognise the particular cult associated with them. It is undoubtedly with this general meaning that the word is used in this verse of the Ḳurʾān: "If God had not taken men under his protection, then monasteries, churches and places of prayer (*ṣalawāt*) and *masādjid* would have been destroyed" (sūra XXII, 41). The word is also used in a *hadīth* of an Abyssinian church (al-Buḵẖārī, *Ṣalāt, bāb* 48, 54; Muslim, *Masādjid*, tr. 3) and in another of Jewish and Christian tomb-sanctuaries (al-Buḵẖārī, *Ṣalāt, bāb* 55; Muslim, *Masādjid*, tr. 3). Even Ibn Ḵẖaldūn can still use the word in the general meaning of a temple or place of worship of any religion (*Muḳaddima, faṣl* 4, 6 at the end). There is therefore no question of a word of specifically Muslim creation. This is in entire agreement with Muḥammad's original attitude to earlier religions. Just as Abraham was a Muslim, so David had a *masdjid* (al-Ṭabarī, *Taʾrīkh*, i, 2408, 7 ff.).

To the Prophet, the Meccan sanctuary always remained the principal mosque, known as *Bayt Allāh* even before the time of the Prophet. It was a grave charge brought against the Ḳuraysh in the Meccan period that they drove the believers out of *al-Masdjid al-ḥarām* (sūra II, 214; V, 3; VIII, 34; XXII, 25; XLVIII, 25), which was considered all the more unjust as they worshipped the true lord of the sanctuary. To the true God belonged *al-masādjid* (sūra LXXII, 18, Meccan); it was therefore an absurdity for the godless to prevent the worship of God in "God's own mosques" (sūra II, 108). The result was that it was revealed in the year 9/630-1: "It is not right for polytheists to frequent the mosques of God" (sūra IX, 17 f.) and the opponents of the new religion were therefore excluded from the sanctuary. The *Sīra* agrees with the Ḳurʾān, that the sanctity of *al-Masdjid al-ḥarām* to which Muḥammad had been used from childhood was always regarded by him as indisputable. Like other Meccans, he and his followers regularly made the *ṭawāf* around the Kaʿba and kissed the Black Stone (e.g. Ibn Hiṣẖām, 183, 12 ff.; 239, 8; 251, 15); it is frequently stated that he used to sit in the *masdjid* like his fellow-citizens, alone or with a follower or disputing with an opponent (Ibn Hiṣẖām, 233, 16; 251, 15; 252, 14; 259; 260; 294; 18 f.). It is related that he used to perform the *ṣalāt* between the Yaman corner and the Black Stone, apparently from the narrator's context, very frequently (Ibn Hiṣẖām, 190, 9 ff.). After his conversion, ʿUmar is said to have arranged that believers performed the *ṣalāt* unmolested beside the Kaʿba (Ibn Hiṣẖām, 224, 13 f., 17 f.). How strongly Muḥammad felt himself attached to the Arab sanctuary is evident from the fact that he took part in the traditional rites there before the *hidjra* (sūra CVIII, 2); in the year 1/622-3, one of his followers, Saʿd b. Muʿādh, took part in the pilgrimage ceremonies, and in the year 2/623-4 he himself sacrificed on 10 Ḏẖu 'l-Ḥidjdja on the *muṣallā* of the Banū Salima. He therefore, here as elsewhere, retained ancient customs where his new teaching did not directly exclude them. But when an independent religion developed out of his preaching, a new type of worship had to be evolved.

In Mecca, the original Muslim community had no special place of worship. The Prophet used to perform the *ṣalāt* in secret in the narrow alleys of Mecca with his first male follower ʿAlī and with the other earliest Companions also (Ibn Hiṣẖām, 159, 166, 13 ff.). The references are usually to the solitary *ṣalāt* of the Prophet, sometimes beside the Kaʿba (Ibn Hiṣẖām, 190, 9 ff.), sometimes in his own house (Ibn Hiṣẖām, 203, 6 f.). That the believers often prayed together may be taken for granted; they would do so in a house (cf. Ibn Hiṣẖām, 202). Occasionally also ʿUmar is said to have conducted the ritual prayer with others beside the Kaʿba (Ibn Hiṣẖām, 224) because ʿUmar was able to defy the Ḳuraysh. When the Prophet recited in the mosque the revelation, later abrogated, recognising Allāt, al-ʿUzzā and Manāt, according to the story, not only the believers but also the polytheists present took part in the *sudjūd* (al-Ṭabarī, i, 1192 f.). Abū Bakr is said to have had a private place of prayer (*masdjid*) in Mecca in his courtyard beside the gate; the Ḳuraysh, we are told, objected to this because women and children could see it and might be led astray by the emotion aroused (Ibn Hiṣẖām, 246; al-Buḵẖārī, *Ṣalāt, bāb* 86; *Kafāla, bāb* 14 etc.; *Maẓālim, bāb* 22).

In the dogma taught by Muḥammad, a sanctuary was not a fundamental necessity. Every place was the same to God, and humility in the presence of God, of which the ritual prayer was the expression, could be shown anywhere; hence the saying of the Prophet that he had been given the whole world as a *masdjid*, while earlier prophets could only pray in churches and synagogues (al-Wāḳidī, tr. Wellhausen, 403; *Corpus iuris di Zaid b. ʿAlī*, ed. Griffini, 50 and p. clxxix; al-Buḵẖārī, *Ṣalāt, bāb* 56; *Tayammum, bāb* 1; Muslim, *Masādjid*, tr. 1), and also the saying: "Wherever the hour of prayer overtakes thee, thou shalt perform the *ṣalāt* and that is a *masdjid*" (Muslim, *Masādjid*, tr. 1). That he nevertheless remained firmly attached to the traditional sanctuary of the Kaʿba, produced a confusion of thought which is very marked in sūra II, 136 ff. When in Medina he was able to do as he pleased, it must have been natural for him to create a place where he could be undisturbed with his followers and where they could perform the ritual *ṣalāt* together.

2. The foundation of the Mosque in Medina. According to one tradition, the Prophet came riding into Medina on his camel with Abū Bakr as *ridf* surrounded by the Banū Nadjdjār. The camel stopped on Abū Ayyūb's *finā*ʾ. Here (according to Anas) the Prophet performed the *ṣalāt*, and immediately afterwards ordered the mosque to be built and purchased the piece of land from two orphans, Sahl and Suhayl, who were under the guardianship of Muʿādh b. ʿAfrāʾ, for 10 *dīnārs*, after declining to accept it as a gift; he lived with Abū Ayyūb until the mosque and his houses were completed. During this period he performed the *ṣalāt* in courtyards or other open spaces (al-Buḵẖārī, *Ṣalāt, bāb* 48; Muslim, *Masādjid*, tr. 1; Aḥmad b. Ḥanbal, *Musnad*, iii, 212 above; Ibn Hiṣẖām, 336; al-Ṭabarī, i, 1258 f.; al-Masʿūdī, *Murūdj*, iv, 140-1 = § 1469). According to this tradition, the building of the mosque was intended by the Prophet from the first and the choice of the site was left to the whim of his mount. According to another tradition, the Prophet took up his abode with Abū Ayyūb, but during the first period of his stay in Medina he conducted the *ṣalāt* in the house of Abū Umāma Asʿad, who had a private *masdjid*, in which he used to conduct *ṣalāt*s with his neighbours. The Prophet later expressed the desire to purchase the adjoining piece of ground, and he bought it from the two orphans, who according to this tradition, were wards of Asʿad (al-Balādhurī, *Futūḥ al-buldān*, 6; cf. Wüstenfeld, *Gesch. d. Stadt Medina*, 60). The site was covered with graves, ruins (*khirab*; also

ḥarth, al-Ṭabarī, i, 1259, 17; 1260, 1; cf. Aḥmad b. Ḥanbal, *Musnad*, iii, 212, 7, perhaps due to an old misreading) and palm-trees and was used as a place for keeping camels (and smaller domestic animals, al-Bukhārī, *Wuḍūʾ*, *bāb* 66). The site was cleared, the palms cut down and the walls built. The building material was bricks baked in the sun (*labin*) (Ibn Hishām, 337; al-Bukhārī, *Ṣalāt*, *bāb*s 62, 65; according to one tradition they were baked at the well of Fāṭima, Wüstenfeld, *Stadt Medina*, 31); in plan it was a courtyard surrounded by a brick wall on a stone foundation with three entrances; the gateposts were of stone. On the *ḳibla* side (i.e. the north wall), at first left open, the stems of the palm trees which had been cut down were soon set up as columns and a roof was put over them of palm-leaves and clay. On the east side two huts of similar materials were built for the Prophet's wives Sawdāʾ and ʿĀʾisha; their entrances opened on to the court and were covered with carpets; they were later increased so that there were nine little houses for the Prophet's wives. When the *ḳibla* was moved to the south, the arbour at the north wall remained; under this arbour called *ṣuffa* or *ẓulla* the homeless Companions (*Ahl al-Ṣuffa* [*q.v.*]) found shelter (al-Bukhārī, *Ṣalāt*, *bāb*s 48, 62; Wüstenfeld, *Medina*, 60 f., 66; al-Diyārbakrī, *Taʾrīkh al-Khamīs*, Cairo 1302, i, 387 ff.; on the *ṣuffa*, 387 in the middle; 391 after the middle; cf. L. Caetani, *Annali dell' Islām*, i, 377 f.). In seven months, the work was completed (Wüstenfeld, *Medina*, 59), according to others in the month of Ṣafar of the year 2 (Ibn Hishām, 339, 18 f.). The mosque was very simple. It was really only a courtyard with a wall round it; the *ṣuffa* already mentioned supplied a shelter on the north side, while on the south side, later the *ḳibla* side, an arbour was probably built also, for the Prophet used to preach leaning against a palm-trunk and this must have been on the *ḳibla* side. How large the arbours were cannot be ascertained. The mosque was the courtyard of the Prophet's houses and at the same time the meeting-place for the believers and the place for common prayer.

According to the sources, it was the Prophet's intention from the very first to build a mosque at once in Medina; according to a later tradition, Gabriel commanded him in the name of God to build a house for God (al-Diyārbakrī, i, 387 below); but this story is coloured by later conditions. It has been made quite clear, notably by L. Caetani (*Annali dell' Islām*, i, 432, 437 ff.) and later by H. Lammens (*Moʿâwia*, 8, 5, 62; idem, *Ziād*, 30 ff., 93 ff.) that the earliest *masdjid* had nothing of the character of a sacred edifice. Much can be quoted for this view from *Ḥadīth* and *Sīra* (cf. *Annali dell' Islām*, i, 440). The unconverted Thaḳafīs were received by the Prophet in the mosque to conduct negotiations and he even put up three tents for them in the courtyard (Ibn Hishām, 916; al-Wāḳidī-Wellhausen, 382); envoys from Tamīm also went freely about in the mosque and called for the Prophet, who dealt with them after he had finished prayers (Ibn Hishām, 933 f.; al-Wāḳidī-Wellhausen, 386). Ibn Unays brought to the *masdjid* the head of the Hudhalī Sufyān, threw it down before the Prophet and gave his report (Ibn Hishām, 981; al-Wāḳidī-Wellhausen, 225). After the battle of Uḥud, the Medina chiefs spent the night in the mosque (al-Wāḳidī-Wellhausen, 149). The Awsīs tended their wounded here (*ibid.*, 215 f.; al-Ṭabarī, i, 1491 f.); a prisoner of war was tied to one of the pillars of the mosque (al-Bukhārī, *Ṣalāt*, *bāb* 76, 82; cf. 75). Many poor people used to live in the *ṣuffa* (al-Bukhārī, *Ṣalāt*, *bāb* 58); tents and huts were put up in the mosque, one for example by converted and liberated prisoners, another by the Banū Ghifār, in whose tent Saʿd b. Muʿādh died of his wounds (*ibid.*, *bāb* 77; Ibn al-Athīr, *Usd al-ghāba*, ii, 297). People sat as they pleased in the mosque or took their ease lying on their backs (al-Bukhārī, *ʿIlm*, *bāb* 6; *Ṣalāt*, *bāb* 85; Ibn Saʿd, i, 124, 14); even so late as the reign of ʿUmar, it is recorded that he found strangers sleeping in a corner of the mosque (al-Mubarrad, *Kāmil*, 118, 15 ff.); the Prophet received gifts and distributed them among the Companions (Bukhārī, *Ṣalāt*, *bāb* 42); disputes took place over business (*ibid.*, *bāb*s 71, 83) and in general, people conducted themselves as they pleased. Indeed, on one occasion some Sudanese or Abyssinians with the approval of the Prophet gave a display with shield and lance on the occasion of a festival (*ibid.*, *Ṣalāt*, *bāb* 69; *ʿĪdayn*, *bāb* 2, 25; *Djihād*, *bāb* 81); and on another a stranger seeking the Prophet, rode into the mosque on his camel (*ibid.*, *ʿIlm*, *bāb* 6). So little "consecrated" was this, the oldest mosque, that one of the *Munāfiḳūn* or "Hypocrites", ejected for scoffing at the believers, could call to Abū Ayyūb "Are you throwing me out of the *Mirbad Banī Thaʿlaba?*" (Ibn Hishām, 362, 10 f.).

All this gives one the impression of the headquarters of an army, rather than of a sacred edifice. On the other hand, the mosque was used from the very first for the general divine worship and thus became something more than the Prophet's private courtyard. Whatever the Prophet's intentions had been from the first, the *masdjid*, with the increasing importance of Islam, was bound to become very soon the political and religious centre of the new community. The two points of view cannot be distinguished in Islam, especially in the earlier period. The mosque was the place where believers assembled for prayer around the Prophet, where he delivered his addresses, which contained not only appeals for obedience to God but regulations affecting the social life of the community (cf. al-Bukhārī, *Ṣalāt*, *bāb*s 70, 71); from here he controlled the religious and political community of Islam. Even at the real old sanctuaries of Arabia, there were no restrictions on what one could do; what distinguished the mosque from the Christian church or the Meccan temple was that in it there was no specially dedicated ritual object. At the Kaʿba also, people used to gather to discuss every day affairs and also for important assemblies, if we may believe the *Sīra* (Ibn Hishām, 183 f., 185, 1, 229, 8, 248, 257, 19). Here also the Prophet used to sit; strangers came to visit him; he talked and they disputed with him; people even came to blows and fought there (Ibn Hishām, 183-4, 185-6, 187-8, 202, 19, 257, 259; *Chron. d. Stadt Mekka*, ed. Wüstenfeld, i, 223, 11). Beside the Kaʿba was the *Dār al-Nadwa*, where important matters were discussed and justice administered (*ibid.*, see index). From the Medina mosque was developed the general type of the Muslim mosque. It depended on circumstances whether the aspect of the mosque as a social centre or as a place of prayer was more or less emphasised.

3. Other mosques in the time of the Prophet. The mosque of the Prophet in Medina was not the only one founded by Muslims in his lifetime, and according to tradition not even the first, which is said to have been the mosque of Ḳubāʾ. In this village, which belonged to the territory of Medina (see Wüstenfeld, *Geschichte der Stadt Medina*, 126), the Prophet on his *hidjra* stopped with the family of ʿAmr b. ʿAwf; the length of his stay is variously given as 3, 5, 8, 14 or 22 days. According to one tradition, he found a mosque there on his arrival, which had been built by the first emigrants and the Anṣār, and he per-

formed the *ṣalāt* there with them (see Wüstenfeld, *op. cit.*, 56; al-Balādhurī, *Futūḥ al-buldān*, 1; al-Diyārbakrī, i, 380-1). According to another tradition, the Prophet himself founded the mosque on a site, which belonged to his host Kulthūm and was used as a *mirbad* for drying dates or, according to others, to a woman named Labba, who tethered her ass there (Wüstenfeld, *Medina*, 131; Ibn Hishām, 335; al-Ṭabarī, i, 1260, 6; Ibn Saʿd, i/1, 6; Masʿūdī, *Murūdj*, iv, 139; al-Diyārbakrī, 1, 381; *al-Sīra al-Ḥalabiyya*, Cairo 1320, ii, 58-9). Out of this tradition arose a legend based on the story of the foundation of the principal mosque in Medina. The Prophet makes (first Abū Bakr and ʿUmar without success, then) ʿAlī mount a camel, and at the place to which it goes builds the mosque with stone brought from the Ḥarra; he himself laid the first stone, and Abū Bakr, ʿUmar and ʿUthmān the next ones (al-Diyārbakrī, i, 381). The Prophet is said to have henceforth visited the mosque of Ḳubāʾ every Saturday, either riding or walking, and the pillar is still shown beside which he conducted the service (al-Bukhārī, *Faḍl al-ṣalāt fī Masdjid Makka wa 'l-Madīna*, *bāb* 2, 4; Muslim, *Ḥadjdj*, tr. 94; al-Diyārbakrī, i, 382; al-Balādhurī, 5). We are occasionally told that he performed his *ṣalāt* on the Sabbath in the mosque at Ḳubāʾ when he went to the Banū 'l-Naḍīr in Rabīʿ I of the year 4/625 (al-Wāḳidī-Wellhausen, 161).

It is obvious that the customs and ideas of the later community have shaped the legend of this mosque. The only question is whether the old tradition that the mosque was founded either by the Prophet himself or even before his arrival by his followers is also a later invention. We thus come to the question whether the Prophet founded or recognised any other mosques at all than that of Medīna. Caetani, in keeping with his view of the origin of the mosque, was inclined to deny it, pointing to the fact that there was later an obvious tendency to connect mosques everywhere with the Prophet and that sūra IX, 108, strongly condemns the erection of an "opposition mosque" (*Masdjid al-Ḍirār*). The Ḳurʾān passage is as follows: "Those who have built themselves a *masdjid* for opposition (*ḍirār*) and unbelief and division among the believers and for a refuge for him who in the past fought against God and his Prophet; and they swear: We intended only good! God is witness that they are liars! Thou shalt not stand up in it, for verily a *masdjid* which is founded on piety from the first day of its existence has more right that thou shouldest stand in it; in it are men who desire to purify themselves" (sūra IX, 108-9). According to tradition, this was revealed in the year 9/630-1; when the Prophet was on the march to Tabūk, the Banū Sālim said to him that they had built a mosque to make it easier for their feeble and elderly people, and they begged the Prophet to perform his *ṣalāt* in it and thus give it his approval. The Prophet postponed it till his return, but then his revelation was announced, because the mosque had been founded by *Munāfiḳūn* at the instigation of Abū ʿĀmir al-Rāhib, who fought against the Prophet. According to one tradition (so Ibn ʿUmar, Zayd) the "mosque founded on piety" was that of Medina, from which the people wished to emancipate themselves; according to another (Ibn ʿAbbās), the reference was to that of Ḳubāʾ; Abū ʿĀmir and his followers were not comfortable among the Banū ʿAmr b. ʿAwf and therefore built a new mosque. According to some traditions, it was in Dhū Awān. The Prophet however had it burned down (al-Ṭabarī, i, 1704-5; Ibn Hishām, 357-8, 906-7; Ibn Saʿd, i/1, 6; al-Wāḳidī-Wellhausen, 410-11; al-Ṭabarī, *Tafsīr*, xi, 17 ff.; Wüstenfeld, *Medina*, 131; *al-Sīra al-Ḥalabiyya*, ii, 60; al-Balādhūrī, 1-2; Muslim, *Ḥadjdj*, *bāb* 93). If the connection with the Tabūk campaign is correct, the *Masdjid al-Ḍirār* is to be sought north of Medina; the "mosque founded on piety" would then be the mosque of Medina rather than that of Ḳubāʾ which lies to the south of it. There is in itself nothing impossible about the rejection in principle of any mosque other than that of Medina. We should then have to discard the whole tradition, for, according to it, the Prophet was at first not unfavourably disposed to the new mosque, and his wrath, according to the tradition, arose from the fact that it had been founded by a refractory party. But as a matter of fact, there are indications that a number of mosques already existed in the time of the Prophet; for example, the verse in the Ḳurʾān, "in houses, which God hath permitted to be built that His name might be praised in them, in them men praise Him morning and evening, whom neither business nor trade restrain from praising God and performing the *ṣalāt* and the giving of alms", etc. (sūra XXIV, 36-7). If this revelation, like the rest of the sūra, is of the Medinan period, it is difficult to refer it to Jews and Christians, and this utterance is quite clear: "Observe a complete fast until the night and touch thou them (i.e. women) not while ye are in the mosques" (sūra II, 183). This shows that there were already in the time of the Prophet several Muslim mosques which had a markedly religious character and were recognised by the Prophet.

That there were really public places of prayer of the separate tribes at a very early date is evident from the tradition that the Prophet in the year 2 offered his sacrifice on 10 Dhu 'l-Ḥidjdja/3 June 624 on the *muṣallā* of the Banū Salima. In addition, there are constant references to private *masādjid* where a few believers, like Abū Bakr in Mecca, made a place for prayer in their houses and where others sometimes assembled (al-Bukhāri, *Ṣalāt*, *bābs* 46, 87; *Tahadjdjud*, *bāb* 30; cf. also *Adhān*, *bāb* 50).

B. The origin of mosques after the time of the Prophet.

1. Chief mosques. What importance the Medina mosque had attained as the centre of administration and worship of the Muslims is best seen from the fact that the first thought of the Muslim generals after their conquests was to found a mosque as a centre around which to gather.

Conditions differed somewhat according as it was a new foundation or an already existing town. Important examples of the first kind are al-Baṣra, al-Kūfa and al-Fusṭāt. Baṣra was founded by ʿUtba b. Ghazwān as winter-quarters for the army in the year 14/635 (or 16/637 or 638). The mosque was placed in the centre with the *Dār al-Imāra*, the dwelling of the commander-in-chief with a prison and *Dīwān* in front of it. Prayer was at first offered on the open space, which was fenced round; later, the whole was built of reeds and when the men went off to war the reeds were pulled up and laid away. Abū Mūsā al-Ashʿarī [*q.v.*], who later became ʿUmar's *wālī*, built the edifice of clay and bricks baked in the sun (*labin*) and used grass for the roof (al-Balādhurī, 346-7, 350; Ibn al-Faḳīh, 187-8; Yāḳūt, *Buldān*, i, 642, 6-9; cf. al-Ṭabarī, i, 2377, 14 ff.). It was similar in Kūfa, which was founded in 17/638 by Saʿd b. Abī Waḳḳās. In the centre was the mosque, and beside it the *Dār al-Imāra* was laid out. The mosque at first was simply an open quadrangle, *ṣaḥn*, marked off by a trench round it. The space was large enough for 40,000 persons. It seems that reeds were also used for building the walls here and later Saʿd used *labin*. On the south side (and only here) there was an arbour, *ẓulla*, built (cf. al-Balādhūrī, 348, i: *ṣuffa*). The *Dār al-Imāra* beside the mosque was later by ʿUmar's orders combined with the mosque (al-Ṭabarī, i, 2481, 12 ff., 2485, 16, 2487 ff., 2494, 14; Yāḳūt, *Muʿdjam*, iv, 323, 10 ff.; al-Balādhuri, 275 ff., cf. *Annali dell' Islām*, iii, 846 ff.). The plan was therefore an exact reproduction of that of the mosque in Medina (as is expressly emphasised in al-Ṭabarī, i, 2489, 4 ff.); the importance of the mosque was also expressed in its position, and the commander lived close beside it. There was no difference in al-Fusṭāṭ, which, although there was already an older town here, was laid out as an entirely new camp. In the year 21/642, after the conquest of Alexandria, the mosque was laid out in a garden where ʿAmr had planted his standard. It was 50 *dhirāʿ*s long and 30 broad. Eighty men fixed its *ḳibla*, which, however, was turned too far to the east, and was therefore altered later by Ḳurra b. Sharīk [*q.v.*]. The court was quite simple, surrounded by a wall and had trees growing on it; a simple roof is mentioned; it must be identical with the above-mentioned *ẓulla* or *ṣuffa*. ʿAmr b. al-ʿĀṣ lived just beside the mosque and around it the *Ahl al-Rāya*. Like the house of the Prophet, the general's house lay on the east side with only a road between them. There were two doors in each wall except the southern one (Yāḳūt, *Buldān*, iii, 898-9; al-Maḳrīzī, *Khiṭaṭ*, iv, 4 ff.; Ibn Duḳmāḳ, *K. al-Intiṣār*, Cairo 1893, 59 ff.; al-Suyūṭī, *Ḥusn al-muḥāḍara*, i, 63-4; ii, 135-6; cf. *Annali dell' Islām*, iv, 554, 557, 563 ff.). We find similar arrangements made in al-Mawṣil in 20/641 (al-Balādhūrī, 331-2).

In other cases, the Muslims established themselves in old towns either conquered or surrendered by treaty; by the treaty, they received a site for their mosque (e.g. al-Balādhūrī, 116, 14, 147, 2). But the distinction between towns which were conquered and those which were surrendered soon disappeared, and the position is as a rule not clear. Examples of old towns in which the Muslims established themselves are al-Madāʾin, Damascus and Jerusalem.—In Madāʾin, Saʿd b. Abī Waḳḳās after the conquest in 16/637 distributed the houses among the Muslims, and Kisrā's *Īwān* was made into a mosque, after Saʿd had conducted the *ṣalāt al-fatḥ* in it (al-Ṭabarī, i, 2443, 15 f.; 2451, 7 ff.). In Damascus, which was occupied in 14/635 or 15/636 by capitulation, according to tradition, the Church of St. John was divided so that the eastern half became Muslim, from which Muslim tradition created the legend that the city was taken partly by conquest and partly by agreement (al-Balādhūrī, 125; Yāḳūt, *Buldān*, ii, 591; Ibn Djubayr, *Riḥla*, 262; *JA*, ser. 9, vii, 376, 381, 404). As a matter of fact, however, the Muslims seem to have laid out their own mosque here just beside the church [see DIMASHḲ]; and close beside it again was the *Khaḍrāʾ*, the commander-in-chief's palace, from which a direct entrance to the *maḳṣūra* was later made (al-Muḳaddasī, 159, 4). Conditions here were therefore once more the same as in Medina. But the possibility of an arrangement such as is recorded by tradition cannot be rejected, for there is good evidence of it elsewhere; in Ḥimṣ, for example, the Muslims and Christians shared a building in common as a mosque and church, and it is evident from al-Iṣṭakhrī and Ibn Ḥawḳal that this was still the case in the time of their common authority, al-Balkhī (309/921) (al-Iṣṭakhrī[1], 61, 7 f.; Ibn Ḥawḳal[1], 117, 5; al-Muḳaddasī, 156, 15), and a similar arrangement is recorded for Dabīl in Armenia (al-Iṣṭakhrī[1], 188, 3 f.; Ibn Ḥawḳal[1], 244, 21; cf. al-Muḳaddasī, 377, 3 f.).

There were special conditions in Jerusalem. The Muslims recognised the sanctuary there, as is evident from the earlier *ḳibla* and from sūra XVII, 1 (in the traditional interpretation). It must therefore have been natural for the conquerors, when the town capitulated, to seek out the recognised holy place. Indeed, we are told that ʿUmar in the year 17/638 built a mosque in Jerusalem on the site of the temple of Solomon (F. Baethgen, *Fragmente syr. u. arab. Hist.*, 17, 110, following Īshōʿdᵉnaḥ, metropolitan of Baṣra after 700 A.D.; cf. for the 2nd/8th century Theophanes, quoted by Le Strange, *Palestine under the Moslems*, London 1890, 91 n.). That the *Ḳubbat al-Ṣakhra* [*q.v.*], which the Mosque of ʿUmar replaced, stands on the old site of the Temple is undoubted. How he found the site is variously recorded [see AL-ḲUDS]. The building was, like other mosques of the time of ʿUmar, very simple. Arculf, who visited Jerusalem about 670, says "The Saracens attend a quadrangular house of prayer (*domus orationis*, i.e. *masdjid*) which they have built with little art with boards and large beams on the remains of some ruins, on the famous site where the Temple was once built in all its splendour" (*Itinera Hierosolymitana*, ed. P. Geyer, 1898, 226-7, tr. P. Mickley, in *Das Land der Bibel*, ii/2, 1917, 19-20). It is of interest to note that this simple mosque, like the others, was in the form of a rectangle; in spite of its simple character it could hold 3,000 people, according to Arculf.

As late as the reign of Muʿāwiya, we find a new town, al-Ḳayrawān, being laid out on the old plan as a military camp with a mosque and *Dār al-Imāra* in the centre (Yāḳūt, *Muʿdjam*, iv, 213, 10 ff.). As al-Balādhūrī, for example, shows, the Muslim conquerors even at a later date always built a mosque in the centre of a newly-conquered town, at first a simple one in each town, and it was a direct reproduction of the simple mosque of the Prophet in Medina. It was the exception to adapt already existing buildings in towns. But soon many additional mosques were added.

2. Tribal mosques and sectarian mosques. There were mosques not only in the towns. When the tribes pledged themselves to the Prophet to adopt Islam, they had also to perform the *ṣalāt*. It is not clear how far they took part in Muslim worship, but if they concerned themselves with Islam at all, they must have had a Muslim place of meeting. Probably even before Islam they had, like the Meccans, their *madjlis* or *nādī* or *dār shūrā*, where they discussed matters of general importance (cf. Lammens, *Moʿâwia*, 205; *Ziād b. Abīhi*, 30 ff., 90-1; *Le Berceau de l'Islam*, 222 ff.). As the mosque was only distinguished from such places by the fact that it was also used for the common *ṣalāt*, it was natural for tribal mosques to come into existence. Thus we are told that as early as the year 5/626-7 the tribe of Saʿd b. Bakr founded mosques and used an *adhān* (Ibn Saʿd, i/2, 44, 7, not mentioned in Ibn Hishām, 943-4; al-Ṭabarī, i, 1722); it is also recorded of the Banū Djadhīma, who lived near Mecca, that they built mosques in the year 8/629-30 and introduced the *adhān* (al-Wāḳidī-Wellhausen, 351). How far one can rely on such stories in a particular case is however uncertain. A later writer like al-Diyārbakrī says of the Banu 'l-Muṣṭaliḳ that they *aslamū wa-banaw masādjida* (*Taʾrīkh al-Khamīs*, ii, 132, 20; cf. *Annali dell' Islām*, ii, 221); in the early sources, this is not found. Nor is the story told by Ibn Saʿd at all probable, that envoys from the Banū Ḥanīfa received orders to destroy their churches, sprinkle the ground with water and build a mosque (Ibn Saʿd, i/2, 56, 11 ff., while Ibn Hishām, 945-6, al-Ṭabarī, i, 1737 ff., and al-Balādhūrī, 86-7, say nothing about

it). But that there were tribal mosques at a very early date is nevertheless quite certain. The mosque at Ḳubāʾ was the mosque of the tribe of ʿAmr b. ʿAwf (Ibn Saʿd, i/1, 6, 6 and cf. above) and according to one tradition, the Banū Ghanm b. ʿAwf were jealous of it and built an opposition mosque (al-Balādhurī, 3; al-Ṭabarī, *Tafsīr*, i, 21). A Companion who had taken part in the battle of Badr, ʿItbān b. Malik, complained to the Prophet that he could not reach the *masdjid* of his tribe in the rainy season and wanted to build a mosque for himself (al-Bukhārī, *Ṣalāt*, *bāb* 46; Muslim, *Masādjid*, *bāb* 47). The Prophet himself is said to have visited the *masdjid* of the Banū Zurayḳ (al-Bukhārī, *Djihād*, *bābs* 56-8) and in the *masdjid* of the Banū Salima during the prayer, there was revealed to him sūra II, 139, which ordered the new *ḳibla*, wherefore it was called *Masdjid al-Ḳiblatayn* (Wüstenfeld, *Medina*, 62).

The tribal mosque was a sign that the independence of the tribe was still retained under Islam. Indeed, we hear everywhere of tribal mosques, for example, around Medina that of the Banū Ḳurayẓa, of the Banū Ḥāritha, of the Banū Ẓafar, of the Banū Wāʾil, of the Banū Ḥarām, of the Banū Zurayḳ (said to have been the first in which the Ḳurʾān was publicly read), that of the Banū Salima, etc. (see Wüstenfeld, *Gesch. d. Stadt Medina*, 29, 37 ff., 44, 50, 57, 136 ff.); the "mosque of the two *ḳiblas*" belonged to the Banū Sawād b, Ghanm b. Kaʿb b. Salima (Wüstenfeld, *Medina*, 41). This then was the position in Medina: the tribes usually had their own mosques, and one mosque was the chief mosque. This was probably the position within the Prophet's lifetime, for in the earliest campaigns of conquest, mosques were built on this principle. ʿUmar is said to have written to Abū Mūsā in Baṣra telling him to build a mosque *li 'l-djamāʿa* and mosques for the tribes, and on Fridays the people were to come to the chief mosque. Similarly, he wrote to Saʿd b. Abī Waḳḳāṣ in Kūfa and to ʿAmr b. al-ʿĀṣ in Miṣr. On the other hand in Syria, where they had settled in old towns, they were not to build tribal mosques (al-Maḳrīzī, *Khiṭaṭ*, iv, 4 below). It is actually recorded that the tribes in each *khiṭṭa* had their own mosques around the mosque of ʿAmr in Fusṭāṭ (cf. Ibn Duḳmāḳ, 62 below -67), and even much later, a tribal mosque like that of the Rāshida was still in existence (al-Maḳrīzī, *Khiṭaṭ*, 64, 4 ff.). Even in the chief mosque, the tribes had their own places (*ibid.*, 9, 12-10). We have similar evidence from ʿIrāḳ. In Baṣra, for example, there was a Masdjid Banī ʿUbād (al-Balādhurī, 356, 2), one of the Banū Rifāʿa (Ibn Rusta, 201, 16), one of the Banū ʿAdī (Ibn al-Faḳīh, 191, 4) and one of the Anṣār (cf. Goldziher, *Muhammedanische Studien*, i, 77, n. 5); in Kūfa we find quite a number, such as that of the Anṣār (al-Ṭabarī, ii, 284, 13 f.), of the ʿAbd al-Ḳays (*ibid.*, ii, 657, 2, 9), of the Banū Duhmān (*ibid.*, 670, 4), of the Banū Makhzūm (*ibid.*, 734, 19), of the Banū Hilāl (*ibid.*, 1687, 8), of the Banū ʿAdī (*ibid.*, 1703, 4), of the Banū Dhuhl and Banū Ḥudjr (*ibid.*, 532, 8 f.), of the Djuhayna (*ibid.*, 533, 8), of the Banū Ḥarām (*ibid.*, iii, 2509, 10), and the ʿAbsīs even had several *masādjid* (al-Balādhurī, 278, 12 f., see also 285, and Goldziher, *loc. cit.*).

During the wars, these tribal mosques were the natural rallying points for the various tribes, the mosque was a *madjlis*, where councils were held (al-Ṭabarī, ii, 532, 6 ff.) and the people were taught from its *minbar* (*ibid.*, 284); battles often centred for this reason round these mosques (e.g. al-Ṭabarī, ii, 130, 148, 6, 960). "The people of your mosque" *ahl masdjidikum* (*ibid.*, 532, 19) became identical with "your party". Gradually, as new sects arose, they naturally had mosques of their own, just as Musaylima before them is said to have had his own mosque (al-Balādhurī, 90, 4 from below; Ibn Ḥanbal, *Musnad*, i, 404 below). Thus we read later of the mosques of the Ḥanbalīs in Baghdād, in which there was continual riot and confusion (Hilāl al-Ṣābī, *Kitāb al-Wuzarāʾ*, ed. Amedroz, 335). It sometimes happened that different parties in a town shared the chief mosque (al-Muḳaddasī, 102, 5), but as a rule it was otherwise. In particular, the Sunnīs and Shīʿīs as a rule had separate mosques (cf. Mez, *Die Renaissance des Islâms*, 63). It sometimes even happened that Ḥanafīs and Shāfiʿīs had separate mosques (Yāḳūt, *Buldān*, iv, 509, 9; al-Muḳaddasī, 323, 11). These special mosques were a great source of disruption in Islam, and we can understand that a time came when the learned discussed whether such mosques should be permitted at all. But the question whether one might talk of the *Masdjid Banī Fulān* was answered by saying that in the time of the Prophet, the *Masdjid Banī Zurayḳ* was recognised (al-Bukhārī, *Ṣalāt*, *bāb* 41; cf. *Djihād*, *bābs* 56-8, and al-Ṭabarī, *Tafsīr*, xi, 20, after the middle of the page).

3. Adaptation to Islam of older sanctuaries; memorial mosques. According to the early historians, the towns which made treaties with the Muslims received permission to retain their churches (al-Baladhūrī, 121, in the middle; al-Ṭabarī, i, 2405, 2407), while in the conquered towns the churches fell to the Muslims without any preamble (cf. al-Balādhurī, 120 below). Sometimes also it is recorded that a certain number of churches were received from the Christians, e.g. fifteen in Damascus according to one tradition (*ibid.*, 124, 8, otherwise on 121; cf. *JA*, Ser. 9, vii, 403). It is rather doubtful whether the process was such a regular one; in any case, the Muslims in course of time appropriated many churches to themselves. With the mass conversions to Islam, this was a natural result. The churches taken over by the Muslims were occasionally used as dwellings (cf. al-Ṭabarī, i, 2405, 2407); at a later date, it also happened that they were used as government offices, as in Egypt in 146/763 (al-Maḳrīzī, iv, 35; cf. for Kūfa, al-Balādhurī, 286). The obvious thing, however, was to transform the churches taken into mosques. It is related of ʿAmr b. al-ʿĀṣ that he performed the *ṣalāt* in a church (al-Maḳrīzī, iv, 6) and Zayd b. ʿAlī says regarding churches and synagogues, "Perform thy *ṣalāt* in them; it will not harm thee" (*Corpus iuris di Zaid b. ʿAlī*, ed. Griffini, no. 364). It is not clear whether the reference in these cases is to conquered sanctuaries; it is evident, in any case, that the saying is intended to remove any misgivings about the use of captured churches and synagogues as mosques. The most important example of this kind was in Damascus, where al-Walīd b. ʿAbd al-Malik in 86/705 took the church of St. John from the Christians and had it rebuilt; he is said to have offered the Christians another church in its stead (see the references above, in I. B. 1; and also *JA*, 9 Ser., vii, 369 ff.; Quatremère, *Hist. Sult. Maml.*, ii/1, 262 ff. and art. DIMASHḲ). He is said to have transformed into mosques a total of ten churches in Damascus. It must have been particularly in the villages, with the gradual conversion of the people to Islam, that the churches were turned into mosques. In the Egyptian villages there were no mosques in the earlier generations of Islam (al-Maḳrīzī, iv, 28-9, 30). But when al-Maʾmūn was fighting the Copts, many churches were turned into mosques in (*ibid.*, 30). It is also recorded of mosques in Cairo that they were converted churches. Accord-

ing to one tradition, the Rās͟hida mosque was an unfinished Jacobite church, which was surrounded by Jewish and Christian graves (al-Maḳrīzī, iv, 63, 64), and in the immediate vicinity al-Ḥākim turned a Jacobite and a Nestorian Church into mosques (*ibid.*, 65). When D̲j̲awhar built a palace in al-Ḳāhira, a *dayr* or monastery was taken in and transformed into a mosque (*ibid.*, 269); similar changes took place at later dates (*ibid.*, 240) and synagogues also were transformed in this way (Masd̲j̲id Ibn al-Bannāʾ, *ibid.*, 265). The chief mosque in Palermo was previously a church (Yāḳūt, *Buldān*, i, 719). After the Crusades, several churches were turned into mosques in Palestine (Sauvaire, *Hist. de Jérus. et d'Hébron*, 1876, 7; Quatremère, *Hist. Sult. Maml.*, i/2, 40).

Other sanctuaries than those of the "people of the scripture" were turned into mosques. For example a Masd̲j̲id al-S̲h̲ams between al-Ḥilla and Karbalāʾ was the successor of an old temple of S̲h̲amas̲h̲ (see Goldziher, *Muh. Stud.*, ii, 331). Not far from Iṣṭak̲h̲r was a Masd̲j̲id Sulaymān which was an old fire-temple, the pictures on the walls of which could still be seen in the time of al-Masʿūdī and al-Muḳaddasī (4th/10th century) (al-Masʿūdī, *Murūd̲j̲*, iv, 77 = § 1403; al-Muḳaddasī, 444). In Iṣṭak̲h̲r itself there was a *d̲j̲āmiʿ*, which was a converted fire temple (*ibid.*, 436). In Maṣṣīṣa, the ancient Mopsuestia, al-Manṣūr in 140/797-8 built a mosque on the site of an ancient temple (al-Balād̲h̲urī, 165-6) and the chief mosque in Dihlī was originally a temple (Ibn Baṭṭūṭa, iii, 151); as to Ṭāʾif, cf. Abū Dāwūd, *Ṣalāt*, *bāb* 10. Thus in Islam also, the old rule holds that sacred places survive changes of religion. It was especially easy in cases where Christian sanctuaries were associated with Biblical personalities who were also recognised by Islam: e.g., the Church of St. John in Damascus and many holy places in Palestine. One example is the mosque of Job in S̲h̲ayk̲h̲ Saʿd, associated with sūra XXI, 83, XXXVIII, 40; here in Silvia's time (4th century) there was a church of Job (al-Masʿūdī, i, 91 = § 84; Baedeker, *Paläst. u. Syrien*[7], 1910, 147).

But Islam itself had created historical associations which were bound soon to lead to the building of new mosques. Even in the lifetime of the Prophet, the Banū Sālim are said to have asked him to perform the *ṣalāt* in their *masd̲j̲id* to give it his authority (see above, in I. A. 3). At the request of ʿItbān b. Malik, the Prophet performed the *ṣalāt* along with Abū Bakr in his house and thereby consecrated it as a *muṣallā*, because he could not reach the tribal mosque in the rainy season (al-Buk̲h̲ārī, *Ṣalāt*, *bāb* 47; *Tahad̲j̲d̲j̲ud*, *bāb* 36; Muslim, *Masād̲j̲id*, tr. 46; a similar story in al-Buk̲h̲ārī, *Ad̲h̲ān*, *bāb* 47, *Tahad̲j̲d̲j̲ud*, *bāb* 33, is perhaps identical in origin). After the death of the Prophet, his memory became so precious that the places where he had prayed obtained a special importance and his followers, who liked to imitate him in everything, preferred to perform their *ṣalāt* in such places. But this tendency was only an intensification of what had existed in his lifetime; and so it is not easy to decide how far the above stories reflect later conditions. Mosques very quickly arose on the road between Mecca and Medina at places where, according to the testimony of his Companions, the Prophet had prayed (al-Buk̲h̲ārī, *Ṣalāt*, *bāb* 89; al-Wāḳidī-Wellhausen, 421 ff.); the same was the case with the road which the Prophet had taken to Tabūk in the year 9/630-1 (Ibn His̲h̲ām, 907; al-Wāḳidī-Wellhausen, 394; there were 19 in all, which are listed in *Annali dell' Islām*, ii-246-7). Indeed, wherever he had taken the field, mosques were built; for example, on the road to Badr, where according to tradition Abū Bakr had built a mosque (al-Wāḳidī-Wellhausen, 39, also Wüstenfeld, *Medina*, 135). The mosque of al-Faḍīk̲h̲ was built on the spot where the Prophet had prayed in a leather tent during the war with the Banu 'l-Naḍīr in the year 4/625-6 (al-Wāḳidī-Wellhausen, 163; Wüstenfeld, *Medina*, 132). He is said to have himself built a little mosque in K̲h̲aybar during the campaign of the year 7/628-9 (al-Diyārbakrī, ii, 49-50; cf. *Annali dell' Islām*, ii, 19). Outside Ṭāʾif, a mosque was built on a hillock, because the Prophet had performed the *ṣalāt* there during the siege in the year 8/629-30, between the tents of his two wives, Umm Salama and Zaynab (Ibn His̲h̲ām, 872-3; al-Wāḳidī-Wellhausen, 369); in Liyya, the Prophet is said to have himself built a mosque while on the campaign against Ṭāʾif (Ibn His̲h̲ām, 872; al-Wāḳidī-Wellhausen, 368-9). Mosques arose in and around Medina, "because Muḥammad prayed here" (Wüstenfeld, *Gesch. d. Stadt Medina*, 31, 38, 132 ff.). It is obvious that in most of these cases, later conditions are put back to the time of the Prophet; in connection with the "Campaign of the Trench" we are told that "he prayed everywhere where mosques now stand" (al-Wāḳidī-Wellhausen, 208). Since, for example, the Masd̲j̲id al-Faḍīk̲h̲ is also called Masd̲j̲id al-S̲h̲ams (Wüstenfeld, *Medīna*, 132), we have perhaps here actually an ancient sanctuary.

Mosques became associated with the Prophet in many ways. In Medina, for example, there was the Masd̲j̲id al-Bag̲h̲la where footprints of the Prophet's mule were shown in a stone, the Masd̲j̲id al-Id̲j̲āba where the Prophet's appeal was answered, the Masd̲j̲id al-Fatḥ which recalls the victory over the Meccans, etc. (see Wüstenfeld, *Medina*, 136 ff.). In Mecca, there was naturally a large number of places sacred through associations with the Prophet and therefore used as places of prayer. The most honoured site, next to the chief mosque, is said to have been the house of K̲h̲adīd̲j̲a, also called Mawlid al-Sayyida Fāṭima, because the daughter of the Prophet was born there. This house, in which the Prophet lived till the *hid̲j̲ra*, was taken over by ʿAḳīl, ʿAlī's brother, and bought by him through Muʿāwiya and turned into a mosque (*Chroniken d. Stadt Mekka*, ed. Wüstenfeld, i, 423; iii , 438, 440). Next comes the house in which the Prophet held his first secret meetings. This was bought by al-K̲h̲ayzurān [*q.v.*], mother of Hārūn al-Ras̲h̲īd, on her pilgrimage in 171/788 and turned into a mosque (*Chron. Mekka*, iii, 112, 440). She also purchased the Prophet's birthplace, *Mawlid al-Nabī*, and made it into a mosque (*ibid.*, i, 422; iii, 439). If Muʿāwiya really bought the Prophet's house from his cousin, it was probably the right one; but the demand for places associated with the Prophet became stronger and stronger, and we therefore find more and more places referred not only to the Prophet, but also to his Companions. Such are the birthplaces of Ḥamza, ʿUmar and ʿAlī (*Chron. Mekka*, iii, 445), and the house of Māriya, the mother of the Prophet's son, Ibrāhīm (*ibid.*, i, 447, 466), who also had a mosque at Medina (Wüstenfeld, *Medina*, 133). There were also a Masd̲j̲id K̲h̲adīd̲j̲a (*ibid.*, i, 324) and a Masd̲j̲id ʿĀʾis̲h̲a (*ibid.*, iii, 454), a Masd̲j̲id of the "granted appeal" in a narrow valley near Mecca, where the Prophet performed the *ṣalāt* (*ibid.*, 453), a Masd̲j̲id al-D̲j̲inn, where the D̲j̲inn overheard his preaching (*ibid.*, i, 424; iii, 453), a Masd̲j̲id al-Raʾya, where he planted his standard at the conquest (*ibid.*, ii, 68 below and 71 above; iii, 13, 453), a Masd̲j̲id al-Bayʿa where the first homage of the Medinans was received (*ibid.*, i, 428; iii, 441). In the Masd̲j̲id al-K̲h̲ayf in Minā is shown the mark of the

Prophet's head in a stone into which visitors also put their heads (*ibid.*, iii, 438). Persons in the Bible are also connected with mosques, Adam, Abraham and Ismāʿīl with the Kaʿba, beside which the *Maḳām Ibrāhim* is shown, and in ʿArafa there is still a Masdjid Ibrāhīm (*ibid.*, i, 415, 425) and another in al-Zāhir near Mecca (Ibn Djubayr, *Riḥla*, Leiden-London 1907, 112). To these memorial mosques others were later added, e.g. the Masdjid Abī Bakr, Masdjid Bilāl, the Mosque of the Splitting of the Moon (by the Prophet), etc. (see Ibn Djubayr, *Riḥla*, 114 ff.; al-Muḳaddasī, 102-3; Snouck Hurgronje, *Mekka*, ii, 27; al-Batanūnī, *al-Riḥla al-Ḥidjāziyya*², Cairo 1329/1911, 52 ff.).

In al-Ḥidjāz, the Muslims thus acquired a series of mosques which became important from their association with the Prophet, his family and his Companions, and made Muslim history live. On the other hand, in lands formerly Christian, they took over sanctuaries which were associated with the Biblical history which they had assimilated (see Le Strange, *Palestine*, passim). Other mosques soon became associated with Biblical and Muslim story. The mosque founded by ʿUmar on the site of the Temple in Jerusalem was, as already pointed out, identified as *al-Masdjid al-Aḳṣā* mentioned in sūra XVII, 1, and therefore connected with the Prophet's night journey and the journey to Paradise. The rock is said to have greeted the Prophet on this occasion, and marks in a stone covering a hole are explained as Muḥammad's footprints (sometimes also as those of Idrīs; cf. Le Strange, *Palestine*, 136; al-Batanūnī, *Riḥla*, 165; Baedeker, *Palästina*, 1910, 52-3; cf. al-Yaʿḳūbī, *Taʾrīkh*, ii, 311). The name *al-Masdjid al-Aḳṣā* was used throughout the early period for the whole Ḥarām area in Jerusalem, later partly for it, and partly for the building in its southern part (Ibn al-Faḳīh, 100; Sauvaire, *Hist. Jérus. et Hébron*, 95, 121; cf. Le Strange, *Palestine*, 96-7). Then there were the mosques which had specifically Muslim associations, like the Masdjid of ʿUmar on the Mount of Olives where he encamped at the conquest (al-Muḳaddasī, 172).

In Egypt not only was an old Christian sanctuary called Maʿbad Mūsā (al-Maḳrīzī, iv, 269), but we are also told, for example, that the Mosque of Ibn Ṭūlūn was built where Mūsā talked with his Lord (al-Maḳrīzī, iv, 36); according to al-Ḳurdāʿī, there were in Egypt four Masdjids of Mūsā (Ibn Duḳmāḳ, ed. Vollers, 92); there was a Masdjid Yaʿḳūb wa-Yūsuf (al-Muḳaddasī, 200) and a Joseph's prison, certainly dating from the Christian period (al-Maḳrīzī, iv, 315). There was also a Mosque of Abraham in Munyat Ibn al-Khaṣīb (Ibn Djubayr, 58). The chief mosque of Ṣanʿāʾ was built by Shem, son of Noah (Ibn Rusta, 110). The old temple near Iṣṭakhr mentioned above was connected with Sulaymān (al-Masʿūdī, *Murūdj*, iv, 76-7 = § 1403; Yāḳūt, i, 299). In the mosque of Kūfa, not only Ibrāhīm but one thousand other prophets and one thousand saints, described as *waṣī*, are said to have offered their prayers; here was the tree Yaḳṭīn (sūra XXXVII, 146); here died Yaghūth and Yaʿūḳ, etc. (Yāḳūt, iv, 325; also Ibn Djubayr, 211-12), and in this mosque there was a chapel of Abraham, Noah and Idrīs (Ibn Djubayr, 212); a large number of mosques were associated with Companions of the Prophet. What emphasis was laid on such an association is seen, for example, from the story according to which ʿUmar declined to perform the *ṣalāt* in the Church of the Resurrection in Jerusalem, lest the Church should afterwards be claimed as a mosque.

4. Tomb-mosques. A special class of memorial mosques consisted of those which were associated with a tomb. The graves of ancestors and of saints had been sanctuaries from ancient times and they were gradually adopted into Islam. In addition, there were the saints of Islam itself. The general tendency to distinguish places associated with the founders of Islam naturally concentrated itself round the graves in which they rested. In the Ḳurʾān, a tomb-*masdjid* is mentioned in connection with the Seven Sleepers (sūra XVIII, 20) but it is not clear if it was recognised. As early as the year 6/627-8 the companions of Abū Baṣīr are said to have built a mosque at the place where he died and was buried (al-Wāḳidī-Wellhausen, 262). The Prophet is also said to have visited regularly at al-Baḳīʿ in Medina the tombs of martyrs who fell at Uḥud and paid reverence to them (*ibid.*, 143). Whatever the exact amount of truth in the story, there is no doubt that the story of the tomb-mosque of Abū Baṣīr is antedated. The accounts of the death of the Prophet and of the period immediately following reveal no special interest in his tomb. But very soon the general trend of development stimulated an interest in graves, which led to the erection of sanctuaries at them. The progress of this tendency is more marked in al-Wāḳidī, who died in 207/823, than in Ibn Isḥāḳ, who died in 151/768.

The collections of *Ḥadīth* made in the 3rd/9th century contain discussions on this fact which show that the problem was whether the tombs could be used as places of worship and in this connection whether mosques could be built over the tombs. The *ḥadīth*s answer both questions in the negative, which certainly was in the spirit of the Prophet. It is said that "*Ṣalāt* at the graves (*fi 'l-maḳābir*) is *makrūh*" (al-Bukhārī, *Ṣalāt*, *bāb* 52); "sit not upon graves and perform not *ṣalāt* towards them" (Muslim, *Djanāʾiz*, tr. 33); "hold the *ṣalāt* in your houses, but do not use them as tombs" (Muslim, *Ṣalāt al-musāfirīn*, tr. 28). On the other hand, it is acknowledged that Anas performed the *ṣalāt* at the cemetery (al-Bukhārī, *Ṣalāt*, *bāb* 48). We are also told that tombs cannot be used as *masādjid* (al-Bukhārī, *Ṣalāt*, *bāb* 48; *Djanāʾiz*, *bāb* 62). On his deathbed the Prophet is said to have cursed the Jews and the Christians because they used the tombs of their prophets as *masādjid*. *Ḥadīth* explains this by saying that the tomb of the Prophet was not at first accessible (al-Bukhārī, *Ṣalāt*, *bāb* 48, 55; *Djanāʾiz*, *bāb* 62; *Anbiyāʾ*, *bāb* 50; Muslim, *Masādjid*, tr. 3); as a matter of fact, its precise location was not exactly known (*Djanāʾiz*, *bāb* 96). The attacks in *Ḥadīth* insist that tomb-mosques are a reprehensible Jewish practice: "When a pious man dies, they built a *masdjid* on his tomb", etc. (al-Bukhārī, *Ṣalāt*, *bāb* 48, 54; Muslim, *Djanāʾiz*, *bāb* 71). Although this view of tomb-mosques is still held in certain limited circles (cf. Ibn Taymiyya and the Wahhābis), the old pre-Islamic custom soon also became a Muslim one. The expositors of *Ḥadīth* like al-Nawawī (on Muslim, *Masādjid*, tr. 3, lith. Dihlī 1319, i, 201) and al-ʿAsḳalānī, (Cairo 1329, i, 354) explain the above passages to mean that only an exaggerated *taʿẓīm* of the dead is forbidden so that tombs should not be used as a *ḳibla*; otherwise, it is quite commendable to spend time in a mosque in proximity to a devout man.

The name given to a tomb-mosque is often *ḳubba* [*q.v.*] a word which is used of a tent (al-Bukhārī, *Djanāʾiz*, *bāb* 62; *Ḥadjdj*, *bāb* 64; *Farḍ al-khums*, *bāb* 19; *al-Djizya*, *bāb* 15; Ṭarafa, *Dīwān*, vii, 1), but later came to mean the dome which usually covers tombs and thus became the general name for the sanctuary of a saint (cf. Ibn Djubayr, *Riḥla*, 114, 115; cf. Dozy, *Supplément*, s.v.). *Maḳām* also means a little chapel and a saint's tomb (van Berchem, *CIA*, i, no. 72, etc.; cf. index). The custom of making a *ḳubba* at the tomb of a saint was firmly rooted in Byzantine territory, where sepulchral churches always had a dome (Herzog-Hauch, *Realenzyclopädie*³, x, 784). The usual name however for a tomb-sanctuary was *mas̲h̲had*; this is applied to places where saints are worshipped, among Muslim tombs particularly to those of the friends and relations of the Prophet (van Berchem, *CIA*, i, nos. 32, 63, 417, 544; al-Maḳrīzī, iv, 265, 309 ff.), but also to tombs of other recognised saints, e.g. Mas̲h̲had D̲j̲ird̲j̲is in Mawṣil (Ibn D̲j̲ubayr, *Riḥla*, 236), etc.

The transformation of the tombs of the Prophet and his near relatives into sanctuaries seems to have been a gradual process. Muḥammad, Abū Bakr and ʿUmar are said to have been buried in the house of ʿĀʾis̲h̲a; Fāṭima and ʿAlī lived beside it. ʿĀʾis̲h̲a had a wall built between her room and the tombs to prevent visitors carrying off earth from the tomb of the Prophet. The houses of the Prophet's wives remained as they were until al-Walīd rebuilt them. He thought it scandalous that Ḥasan b. ʿAlī should live in Fāṭima's house and ʿUmar's family close beside ʿĀʾis̲h̲a's home in the house of Ḥafṣa. He acquired the houses, had all the houses of the Prophet's wives torn down and erected new buildings. The tombs were enclosed by a pentagonal wall; the whole area was called *al-Rawḍa* "the garden"; it was not till later that a dome was built over it (Wüstenfeld, *Medina*, 66 ff., 72-3, 78 ff., 89). In the cemetery of Medina, al-Baḳīʿ [see BAḲĪʿ AL-G̲H̲ARḲAD], a whole series of *mas̲h̲āhid* came to be built where tombs of the family and of the Companions of the Prophet were located (*ibid.*, 140 ff.; Ibn D̲j̲ubayr, *Riḥla*, 195 ff.). It is often disputed whether a tomb belonged to one or the other (e.g. al-Ṭabarī, iii, 2436, 2). Such tomb-mosques were sacred (*muḳaddas*; Ibn D̲j̲ubayr, *Riḥla*, 114, 13, 17), and they were visited *li 'l-baraka*. The name *al-Rawḍa* of the Prophet's tomb became later applied to other sanctuaries (*ibid.*, 46, 16; 52, 11). Separate limbs were revered in some mosques, like the head of al-Ḥusayn in Cairo, which was brought there in 491/1098 from ʿAsḳalān (ʿAlī Pās̲h̲a Mubārak, *al-K̲h̲iṭaṭ al-d̲j̲adīda*, iv, 91 ff.; cf. Sauvaire, *Hist. Jérus. et Hébr.*, 16); his head was also revered for some time in the *Mas̲h̲had al-Raʾs* in Damascus (according to Ibn S̲h̲ākir, *JA*, ser. 9, vii, 385).

Gradually, a vast number of Muslim tombs of saints came into existence; and to these were added all the pre-Islamic sanctuaries which were adopted by Islam. No distinction can therefore be drawn between tomb-mosques and other memorial mosques. It was often impossible to prove that the tomb in question ever really existed. In the Mas̲h̲had ʿAlī, for example, ʿAlī's tomb is honoured, but Ibn D̲j̲ubayr leaves it in doubt whether he is really buried there (*Riḥla*, 212) and many located his grave in the mosque at Kūfa and elsewhere (al-Masʿūdī, *Murūd̲j̲*, iv, 289, v, 68 = §§ 1612, 1825; Ibn Ḥawḳal¹, 163). In ʿAyn al-Baḳar near ʿAkkā there was also a Mas̲h̲had ʿAlī (Yāḳūt, iii, 759) and also in the Mosque of the Umayyads (Ibn D̲j̲ubayr, 267); on this question, cf. al-Muḳaddasī, 46. Names frequently become confused and transferred. In Mecca, between Ṣafā and Marwa there was a *ḳubba*, which was associated with ʿUmar b. al-K̲h̲aṭṭāb; but Ibn D̲j̲ubayr says that it should be connected with ʿUmar b. ʿAbd al-ʿAzīz (*Riḥla*, 115, 11 ff.). In D̲j̲īza there was a Mas̲h̲had Abī Hurayra, where the memory of this Companion of the Prophet was honoured; it is said to have been originally the grave of another Abū Hurayra (Maḳrīzī, i, 335, 19). Wherever S̲h̲īʿīs ruled, there arose numerous tomb-mosques of the *Ahl al-Bayt*. In Egypt, Ibn D̲j̲ubayr gives a list of 14 men and five women of the Prophet's family, who were honoured there (*Riḥla*, 46-7). Islam was always creating new tombs of saints who had been distinguished for learning or asceticism or miracle-working, e.g. the tomb of al-S̲h̲āfiʿī in Cairo and Aḥmad al-Badawī in Ṭanṭa. There were mosques, chiefly old-established sanctuaries, of Biblical and semi-Biblical personages like Rūbīl (Reuben) and Āsiya the wife of Pharaoh (*ibid.*, 46). In and around Damascus were a number of mosques, which were built on the tombs of prophets and unnamed saints (Ibn D̲j̲ubayr, *Riḥla*, 273 ff.). In Palestine could be seen a vast number of tombs of Biblical personages (cf. Le Strange, *Palestine under the Moslems*, index, and Conder, in *Palestine Explor. Fund, Quarterly Statement*, 1871, 89 ff.), usually mosques with a *ḳubba*.

After the sanctuaries of persons mentioned in the Bible came those of people mentioned in the Ḳurʾān. For example, outside the *D̲j̲āmiʿ* in ʿAkkā was shown the tomb-mosque of the prophet Ṣāliḥ (Nāṣir-i K̲h̲usraw, *Safar-nāma*, ed. Schefer, 15, 1, tr. 49), and in Syria that of his son (Ibn D̲j̲ubayr, 46); that of Hūd was also shown near ʿAkkā (Nāṣir-i K̲h̲usraw, 16, 5, tr. 52), farther east, that of S̲h̲uʿayb and of his daughter (*ibid.*, 16, 12, tr. 53); the tomb of Hūd was also pointed out in Damascus and in Ḥadramawt (Yāḳūt ii, 596, 16); then we have peculiarly Muslim saints like D̲h̲u 'l-Kifl, the son of Job (Nāṣir-i K̲h̲usraw, 16, 4, tr. 52). Then there are the sanctuaries of saints who are only superficially Muslim but really have their origins in old popular superstitions, like al-K̲h̲aḍir, who had a *mas̲h̲had* in Damascus (Yāḳūt, ii, 596, 9), or a saint like ʿAkk, founder of the town of ʿAkkā, whose tomb Nāṣir-i K̲h̲usraw visited outside the town (15, 6 from below, tr. 51). Such tombs were much visited by pious travellers and are therefore frequently mentioned in literature (on *mas̲h̲āhid* of the kinds mentioned here in ʿIrāḳ, see al-Muḳaddasī, 130; for Mawṣil, etc., *ibid.*, 146). In this way, ancient sanctuaries were turned into mosques, and it is often quite a matter of chance under what names they are adopted by Islam (cf. Goldziher, *Muh. Studien*, ii, 325 ff.). It therefore sometimes happens that the same saint is honoured in several mosques. Abū Hurayra, who is buried in Medina, is honoured not only in the above-mentioned tomb-mosque in D̲j̲īza but also at various places in Palestine, in al-Ramla and in Yubnā south of Ṭabariyya (K̲h̲alīl ed-Ḍāhiry, *Zoubdat Kachf el-Mamâlik* ed. P. Ravaisse, 42, 1 from below; Nāṣir-i K̲h̲usraw, 17, 1 from below, no. 59; Yāḳūt, iii, 512, 20; iv, 1007, 12; cf. *Symbolae Osloenses Fasc. Supplet.*, ii [1928], 31). The tomb of the Prophet Jonah is revered not only in the ancient Niniveh but also in Palestine.

Just as the *ḳubba* under which the saint lay and the mosque adjoining it were sanctified by him, so vice-versa a *ḳubba* and a mosque could cause a deceased person to become considered a saint. It was therefore the custom for the mighty not only to give this distinction to their fathers but also to prepare such buildings for themselves even in their own lifetime. This was particularly the custom of the Mamlūk sultans, perhaps stimulated by the fact that they did not found dynasties in which power passed from father to son. Such buildings are called *ḳubba* (van Berchem, *CIA*, i, nos. 82, 95, 96, 126, 138, etc.), exceptionally *zāwiya* (*ibid.*, no. 98), frequently *turba* (*ibid.*, no. 58, 66, 88, 106, 107, 116, etc.); the formula is also found: "this *ḳubba* is a *turba*" (no. 67); the latter word acquired the same meaning as *masd̲j̲id*, *mas̲h̲had*, partly saint's grave and partly sacred site (cf. Ibn Djubayr, *Riḥla*, 114, 196); but this word does not seem to be used of ordinary tomb-mosques, although the distinction between these and mosques in honour of saints often disappeared. In these *ḳubba*s, the regular recitation of the Ḳur'ān was often arranged and the tomb was provided with a *kiswa*. The mausoleum might be built in connection with a great mosque and be separated from it by a grille (Yāḳūt, iv, 509, 6 ff.).

5. Mosques deliberately founded. In the early period, the building of mosques was a social obligation of the ruler as representative of the community and the tribes. Very soon a number of mosques came into existence, provided by individuals. In addition to tribal mosques, as already mentioned, there were also sectarian mosques, and prominent leaders built mosques which were the centres of their activity, for example the Masdjid ʿAdī b. Ḥātim (al-Ṭabarī, ii, 130), the Masdjid Simāk in Kūfa (*ibid.*, i, 2653), the Masdjid al-Ashʿath, etc. As old sanctuaries became Islamised, the mosque received more of the character of a sanctuary and the building of a mosque became a pious work; there arose a *ḥadīth*, according to which the Prophet said: "for him who builds a mosque, God will build a home in Paradise"; some add "if he desire to see the face of God" (*Corpus iuris di Zaid b. ʿAlī*, ed. Griffini, no. 276; al-Bukhārī, *Salāt*, *bāb* 65; Muslim, *Masādjid*, tr. 4; *Zuhd*, tr. 3; al-Maḳrīzī, iv, 36). Like other sanctuaries, mosques were sometimes built as a result of a revelation in a dream. A story of this kind of the year 557/1162 is given by al-Samhūdī for Medina (Wüstenfeld, *Medina*, 91); and a similar one of a mosque in Damascus (*JA*, ser. 9, vii, 384); a mosque was also built out of gratitude for seeing the Prophet (*al-Madrasa al-Sharīfiyya*, al-Makrīzī, iv, 209). It was of course particularly an obligation on the mighty to build mosques. Even in the earliest period, the governors took care that new mosques were built to keep pace with the spread of Islam (cf. al-Balādhurī, 178-9). About the year 390/1000 the governor of Djibāl, Badr b. Ḥasanawayh, is said to have built 3,000 mosques and hostels (Mez, *Die Renaissance des Islâms*, 24, Eng. tr. 27). The collections of inscriptions, as well as the geographical and topographical works, reveal how the number of mosques increased in this way.

In Egypt, al-Ḥākim in the year 403/1012-13 had a census taken of the mosques of Cairo, and these were found to amount to 800 (al-Maḳrīzī, iv, 264); al-Ḳuḍāʿī (d. 454/1062) also counted the mosques, and his figure is put at 30,000 or 36,000 (Yāḳūt, iii, 901; Ibn Duḳmāḳ, ed. Vollers, 92; al-Maḳrīzī, iv, 264), which seems a quite fantastic figure (there is probably a *wa*-lacking before *alf*, i.e. 1,036). Ibn al-Mutawwadj (d. 730/1330) according to al-Maḳrīzī counted 480, and Ibn Duḳmaḳ (about 800/1398) gives in addition to the incomplete list of *djāmiʿ*s a list of 472 mosques, not including *madāris*, *khānaḳāhs*, etc.; the figure given by al-Maḳrīzī is smaller. The fantastic figure of 30,000 for Baghdād is found as early as al-Yaʿḳūbī (*Buldān*, 250). It is also an exaggeration when Ibn Djubayr was told in Alexandria that there were 12,000 or 8,000 mosques there (43). In Baṣra, where Ziyād built 7 mosques (Ibn al-Faḳīh, 191), the number also increased rapidly, but here again an exaggerated figure (7,000) is given (al-Yaʿḳūbī, *op. cit.*, 361). In Damascus, Ibn ʿAsākir (d. 571/1176) counted 241 within and 148 outside the city (*JA*, ser. 9, vii, 383). In Palermo, Ibn Ḥawḳal counted over 300, and in a village above it 200 mosques. In some streets there were as many as 20 mosques within a bowshot of one another; this multiplicity is condemned: everyone wanted to build a mosque for himself (Yāḳūt, i, 719; iii, 409, 410). As a matter of fact, one can almost say that things tended this way; al-Yaʿḳūbī mentions in Baghdād a mosque for the Anbārī officials of the tax-office (*Buldān*, 245), and several distinguished scholars practically had their own mosques. It occasionally happened that devout private individuals founded mosques. In 672/1273-4 Tādj al-Dīn built a mosque and a separate chamber in which he performed the *ṣalāt* alone and meditated (al-Maḳrīzī, iv, 90). The mosques thus founded were very often called after their founders, and memorial and tomb-mosques after the person to be commemorated. Sometimes a mosque is called after some devout man who lived in it (al-Maḳrīzī, iv, 97, 265 ff.) and a *madrasa* might be called after its head or a teacher (*ibid.*, iv, 235; Yāḳūt, *Udabā'*, vii, 82). Lastly, a mosque might take its name from its situation or from some feature of the building.

6. Al-Muṣallā. In addition to the mosques proper, al-Maḳrīzī mentions for Cairo eight places for prayer (*muṣallā*) mainly at the cemetery (iv, 334-5). The word *muṣallā* may mean any place of prayer, therefore also mosque (cf. sūra II, 119; cf. al-Maḳrīzī *Khiṭāṭ*, iv, 25, 16; idem, *Ittiʿāẓ*, ed. Bunz. 91, 17; Yāḳūt, *Buldān*, iv, 326, 3-5) or a particular place of prayer within a mosque (al-Ṭabarī, i, 2408, 16; al-Bukhārī, *Ghusl*, *bāb* 17; *Ṣalāt*, *bāb* 91). In Palestine, there were many open places of prayer, provided only with a *miḥrāb* and marked off, but quite in the open (cf. for Tiberias, Nāṣir-i Khusraw, ed. Schefer, 36). It is recorded of the Prophet that he used to go out at the two festivals (*al-Fiṭr* and *al-Aḍḥā*) to the place of prayer (*al-muṣallā*) of the Banū Sālima. A lance which the Negus of Ethiopia had presented to al-Zubayr was carried in front of him and planted before the Prophet as *sutra*. Standing in front of it, he conducted the *ṣalāt*, and then preached a *khuṭba* without a *minbar* to the rows in front of him (al-Ṭabarī, i, 1281, 14 ff.; al-Bukhārī, *Ḥayḍ*, *bāb* 6; *Ṣalāt*, *bāb* 90; *ʿĪdayn*, *bāb* 6). He also went out to the *muṣallā* for the *ṣalāt al-istisḳā'* (Muslim, *Istisḳā'*, tr. 1). This *muṣallā* was an open space, and Muḥammad is even said to have forbidden a building on it (Wüstenfeld, *Medina*, 127 ff.). This custom of performing the *ṣalāt* on a *muṣallā* outside the town on the two festivals became *sunna*. There is evidence of the custom for several towns. In Medina, however, a mosque was later built on the *muṣallā* (*ibid.*, 128) which also happened in other places. An early innovation was the introduction of a *minbar* by Marwān (*ibid.*, 128; al-Bukhārī, *ʿĪdayn*, *bāb* 6). When Saʿd b. Abī Waḳḳāṣ built a mosque in Kisrā's *Īwān* in al-Madā'in, at the festival in the year 16/637, it was expressly stated that it was *sunna* to go out to it; Saʿd, however, thought it was a matter of indifference (al-Ṭabarī, i, 2451). Shortly after 300/912-13 a *muṣallā* outside of Hamadhān is mentioned (al-Masʿūdī, *Murūdj*, ix, 23 = § 3595). There was al-Muṣallā al-ʿAtīḳ in Baghdād; here a *dakka* was erected for the execution of the Ḳarmaṭian prisoners (al-Ṭabarī, iii, 2244-5; cf. 1659, 18); in Kūfa, several are mentioned (*ibid.*, ii, 628, 16; 1704, 8; iii, 367, 8-368) two in Marw (*ibid.*, ii, 1931, 2; 1964, 19; cf. Nāṣir-i Khusraw, tr. 274), one in Farghāna (Ibn Ḥawḳal[1], 393, 11). In Tirmidh, the *muṣallā* was within the walls (Ibn Ḥawḳal[1], 349, 18) which also happened elsewhere (*ibid.*, 378, 6-377). In Cairo, the two festivals were celebrated on the Muṣallā Khawlān (a Yemeni tribe) with the *khaṭīb* of the Mosque of ʿAmr as leader: according to al-Ḳuḍāʿī, the festivals were to be celebrated on a *muṣallā* opposite the hill Yaḥmūm,

then on al-Muṣallā al-Ḳadīm where Aḥmad b. Ṭūlūn erected a building in 256/870. The site was several times changed (al-Maḳrīzī, iv, 334-5; cf. al-Muḳaddasī, 200, 14-20). In 302, 306 and 308 the *ṣalāt al-ʿīd* was performed for the first time in the Mosque of ʿAmr (al-Maḳrīzī, iv, 20, 8 ff.; al-Suyūṭī, *Ḥusn al-muḥāḍara*, ii, 137 below; Ibn Tag͟hrībirdī, ii, 194, 9 ff.). Ibn Baṭṭūṭa notes the custom in Spain (i, 20) and Tunis (i, 22) and also in India (iii, 154). Ibn al-Ḥād͟jd͟j (d. 737/1336-7) says that in his time the ceremonies still took place on the *muṣallā* but condemns the *bidaʿ* associated with them (*K. al-Madk͟hal*, Cairo 1320, ii, 82). It is also laid down in Muslim law, although not always definitely (see Juynboll, *Handbuch d. Islām. Ges.*, 1910, 127; I. Guidi, *Il Muḫtaṣar*, i, 1919, 136). The custom seems in time to have become generally abandoned. In the 9th/15th century the Masd͟jid Āḳsunḳur was expressly built for the *k͟huṭba* at the Friday services and at festivals (al-Maḳrīzī, iv, 107, 17).

C. The mosque as the centre for divine worship.

1. Sanctity of the mosque. The history of the mosques in the early centuries of Islam shows an increase in its sanctity, which was intensified by the adoption of the traditions of the church and especially by the permeation of the cult of saints. The sanctity already associated with tombs taken over by Islam was naturally very soon transferred to the larger and more imposing mosques. The expression *Bayt Allāh* "house of God", which at first was only used of the Kaʿba came now be applied to any mosque (see *Corpus iuris di Zaid b. ʿAlī*, no. 48, cf. 156, 983; *Chron. Mekka*, ed. Wüstenfeld, iv, 164; van Berchem, *CIA*, i, no. 10, 1. 18; Ibn al-Ḥād͟jd͟j, *K. al-Madk͟hal*, i, 20, 23; ii, 64, 68; cf. *Bayt Rabbihi*, *ibid.*, i, 23, 73; ii, 56). The alteration in the original conception is illustrated by the fact that the Mamlūk al-Malik al-Ẓāhir Baybars declined to build a mosque on a place for tethering camels because it was unseemly, while the mosque of the Prophet had actually been built on such a place (al-Maḳrīzī, iv, 91; Abū Dāwūd, *Ṣalāt*, *bāb* 22).

In the house of God, the *miḥrāb* and the *minbar* enjoyed particular sanctity, as did the tomb, especially in Medina (al-Buk͟hārī, *Faḍl al-ṣalāt fī masd͟jid Makka wa 'l-Madīna*, *bāb* 5). The visitors sought *baraka*, partly by touching the tomb or the railing round it, partly by praying in its vicinity; at such places "prayer is heard" (*Chron. Mekka*, iii, 441, 442). In the Masd͟jid al-K͟hayf in Minā, the visitor laid his head on the print of the Prophet's head and thus obtained *baraka* (*ibid.*, iii, 438). A mosque could be built on a site, the sanctity of which had been shown by the finding of hidden treasure (al-Maḳrīzī, iv, 75). There were often places of particular sanctity in mosques. In the mosques at Ḳubāʾ and Medina, the spots where the Prophet used to stand at prayer were held to be particularly blessed (al-Balād͟hurī, 5; al-Buk͟hārī, *Ṣalāt*, *bāb* 91; Wüstenfeld, *Medina*, 65, cf. 82, 109). In other mosques, places where a saint had sat or where a divine phenomenon had taken place, e.g. in the Mosque of ʿAmr and in the Azhar Mosque (al-Maḳrīzī, iii, 19, 52) or the Mosque in Jerusalem (al-Muḳaddasī, 170), were specially visited. Pious visitors made *ṭawāf* [see ḤAD͟JD͟J] between such places in the mosque (al-Maḳrīzī, iv, 20). Just as in other religions, we find parents dedicating their children to the service of a sanctuary, so we find a Muslim woman vowing her child or child yet unborn to the mosque (al-Buk͟hārī, *Ṣalāt*, *bāb* 74; al-Maḳrīzī, iv, 20). The fact that mosques, like other sanctuaries, were sometimes founded after a revelation received in a dream has already been mentioned (see 1. B. 5).

This increase in sanctity had as a natural result that one could no longer enter a mosque at random as had been the case in the time of the Prophet. In the early Umayyad period, Christians were still allowed to enter the mosque without molestation (cf. Lammens, *Moʿâwia*, 13-14; Goldziher, in *WZKM*, vi [1892], 100-1). Muʿāwiya used to sit with his Christian physician, Ibn Ut͟hāl, in the mosque of Damascus (Ibn Abī Uṣaybiʿa, i, 117). According to Aḥmad b. Ḥanbal, the *Ahl al-Kitāb* (or *Ahl al-ʿAhd*) and their servants, but not polytheists, were allowed to enter the mosque of Medina (*Musnad*, iii, 339, 392). At a later date, entrance was forbidden to Christians and this regulation is credited to ʿUmar (Lammens, *op. cit.*, 13, n. 6). A strict teacher of morality like Ibn al-Ḥād͟jd͟j thought it unseemly that the monks who wove the mats for the mosques should be allowed to lay them in the mosque (*Madk͟hal*, ii, 57). Conditions were not always the same. In Hebron, Jews and Christians were admitted on payment to the sanctuary of Abraham until in 664/1265 Baybars forbade it (Quatremère, *Hist. Sult. Maml.*, i/2, 27).

According to some traditions, a person in a state of ritual impurity could not enter the mosque (Abū Dāwūd, *Ṭahāra*, *bāb* 92; Ibn Mād͟ja, *Ṭahāra*, *bāb* 123). In any case, only the pure could acquire merit by visiting the mosque (Muslim, *Masād͟jid*, tr. 49; *Corpus iuris di Zaid b. ʿAlī*, no. 48), and in a later period it is specially mentioned that the *wuḍūʾ* cannot be undertaken in the mosque itself (*Madk͟hal*, ii, 47 below) nor could shaving (*ibid.*, 58-9).

It is always necessary to be careful not to spit in a mosque, although some traditions which are obviously closer to the old state of affairs say, "not in the direction of the *ḳibla*, only to the left!" (al-Buk͟hārī, *Ṣalāt*, *bāb*s 33-4). The custom of taking off one's sandals in the mosque is found as early as the time of Abū ʿUbayd (2nd/8th century) (Yāḳūt, *Udabāʾ*, v, 272, 13-237) and according to Ibn al-Ḥād͟jd͟j's *Madk͟hal* (see below) is also mentioned by Abū Dāwūd. Al-Ṭabarī puts the custom back to the time of ʿUmar (i, 2408). That it is based on an old custom observed in sanctuaries is obvious (cf. on the history of the custom, F. Cumont, *Fouilles de Doura-Europos*, 1926, 60-1). The custom, however, seems not to have been always observed. In the 2nd/8th century in the Mosque of the Umayyads, the shoes were taken off only in the *maḳṣūra*, because the floor was covered with mats; but in 212/827 an Egyptian superintendent ordered that the mosque should only be entered with bare feet (*JA*, ser. 9, vii, 211, 217). The visitor on entering should place his right foot first and utter certain prayers with blessings on the Prophet and his family (which Muḥammad is said to have done!) and when he is inside perform two *rakʿa*s (al-Bukhārī, *Ṣalāt*, *bāb* 47; *Tahad͟jd͟jud*, *bāb* 25; Muslim, *Ṣalāt al-musāfirīn*, trs. 12-13; al-Ṭabarī, iii, 2464, 2532). Certain regulations for decent conduct came into being, the object of which was to preserve the dignity of the house of divine service. Public announcements about strayed animals were not to be made, as the Bedouins did in their houses of assembly, and one should not call out aloud and thereby disturb the meditations of the worshippers (al-Buk͟hārī, *Ṣalāt*, *bāb* 83; Muslim, *Masād͟jid*, tr. 18; more fully in *Madk͟hal*, i, 19 ff.). One should put on fine clothes for the Friday service, rub oneself with oil and perfume oneself (al-Buk͟hārī *D͟jumʿa*, *bāb*s 3, 6, 7, 19) as was also done with *ṭīb* for the *Ḥad͟jd͟j* (al-Buk͟hārī, *Ḥad͟jd͟j*, *bāb* 143).

A question which interested the teachers of morality was that of the admission of women to the mosques. That many did not desire their presence is evident from the *ḥadīt͟h* that one cannot prevent them as there is no *fitna* connected with it, but they must not be perfumed (Muslim, *Ṣalāt, bāb* 29; al-Bukhārī, *Djumᶜa, bāb* 13; cf. *Chron. Mekka*, iv, 168). Other *ḥadīth*s say they should leave the mosques before the men (al-Nasāʾī, *Sahw, bāb* 77; cf. Abū Dāwūd, *Ṣalāt, bābs* 14, 48). Sometimes a special part of the mosque was railed off for them; for example, the governor of Mecca in 256/870 had ropes tied between the columns to make a separate place for women (*Chron. Mekka*, ii, 197 below). According to some, women must not enter the mosque during their menstruation (Abū Dāwūd, *Ṭahāra, bābs* 92, 103; Ibn Mādja, *Ṭahāra, bābs* 117, 123). In Medina at the present day, a wooden grille shuts off a place for women (al-Batanūnī, *al-Riḥla al-Ḥidjāziyya*, 240). At one time, the women stood at the back of the mosque here (Yāḳūt, *Udabāʾ*, vi, 400). In Jerusalem there were special *maḳṣūra*s for them (Ibn al-Faḳih, 100). Ibn al-Ḥādjdj would prefer to exclude them altogether and gives ᶜĀʾisha as his authority for this.

Although the mosque became sacred, it could not quite cast off its old character as a place of public assembly, and in consequence, the mosque was visited for many other purposes than that of divine worship. Not only in the time of the Umayyads was considerable business done in the mosques (al-Ṭabarī, ii, 1118; cf. Lammens, *Ziād*, 98) which is quite in keeping with the *ḥadīth* (al-Bukhārī, *Ṣalāt, bābs* 70-1) which actually found it necessary to forbid the sale of wine in the mosque (*ibid.*, *bāb* 73), but Ibn al-Ḥādjdj records with disapproval that business was done in the mosques: women sit in the mosques and sell thread, in Mecca hawkers even call their wares in the mosques. The list given by this author gives one the impression of a regular market-place (*Madkhal*, ii, 54). Strangers could always sit down in a mosque and talk with one another (see al-Muḳaddasī, 205); they had the right to spend the night in the mosque; according to some, however, only if there was no other shelter available (*Madkhal*, ii, 43 below, 49 above; see below I.D.1b). It naturally came about that people also ate in the mosque; this was quite common, and regular banquets were even given in them (e.g. al-Maḳrīzī, iv, 67, 121-2; cf. in *Ḥadīth*: Ibn Mādja, *Aṭᶜima, bābs* 24, 29; Aḥmad b. Ḥanbal, ii, 106, 10 from below). Ibn al-Ḥādjdj laments that in the Masdjid al-Aḳṣā people even threw the remains of their repast down in the mosque; animals were brought in, and beggars and water-carriers called aloud in them, etc. (*Madkhal*, ii, 53 ff.). It is even mentioned as a sign of the special piety of al-Shīrāzī (d. 476/1083) that he often brought food into the mosque and consumed it there with his pupils (Wüstenfeld, *Der Imâm Schâfiᶜī*, iii, 298). Gradually, the mosques acquired greater numbers of residents (see below, I.D. 2b). In the Azhar Mosque, it was the custom with many to spend the summer nights there because it was cool and pleasant (al-Maḳrīzī, iv, 54). This was the state of affairs about 800/1398. Similar conditions still prevail in the mosques.

2. The mosque as a place of prayer. Friday mosques. As places for divine worship, the mosques are primarily "houses of which God has permitted that they be erected and that His name be mentioned in them" (sūra XXIV, 36), i.e. for His service demanded by the law, for ceremonies of worship (*manāsik*), for assemblies for prayer (*djamāᶜat*) and other religious duties (cf. *Chron. Mekka*, iv, 164). The mosques were *maᶜābid* (al-Maḳrīzī, iv, 117, 140). In Medina after a journey, the Prophet went at once to the mosque and performed two *rakᶜa*s, a custom which was imitated by others and became the rule (al-Bukhārī, *Ṣalāt, bābs* 59-60; Muslim, *Ṣalāt al-musāfirīn*, tr. 11; al-Wāḳidī-Wellhausen, 412, 436). In this respect, the mosque played a part in public worship similar to that of the Kaᶜba in Mecca at an earlier date and the Rabba sanctuary in Ṭāʾif. The daily *ṣalāt*s, which in themselves could be performed anywhere, became especially meritorious when they were performed in mosques, because they expressed adherence to the community. A *ṣalāt al-djamāᶜa*, we are told, is twenty or twenty-five times as meritorious as the *ṣalāt* of an individual at home or in his shop (Muslim, *Masādjid*, tr. 42; Bukhārī, *Ṣalāt, bāb* 87; *Buyūᶜ*, *bāb* 49). There are even *ḥadīth*s which condemn private *ṣalāt*s: "Those who perform the *ṣalāt* in their houses abandon the *sunna* of their Prophet" (Muslim, *Masādjid*, tr. 44; but cf. 48 and al-Bukhārī, *Ṣalāt, bāb* 52). If much rain falls, the believers may, however, worship in their houses (al-Bukhārī, *Djumᶜa, bāb* 14). In this connection, a blind man was given a special *rukhṣa*; it is particularly bad to leave the mosque after the *adhān* (Muslim, *Masādjid*, tr. 45). It is therefore very meritorious to go to the mosque; for every step a man advances into the mosque, he receives forgiveness of sins, God protects him at the last judgment and the angels also assist him (Muslim, *Masādjid, bābs* 49-51; al-Bukhārī, *Ṣalāt, bāb* 87; *Adhān, bābs* 36, 37; *Djumᶜa, bābs* 4, 18, 31; *Corpus iuris di Zaid b. ᶜAlī*, nos. 48, 156, 983).

This holds especially of the Friday *ṣalāt* (*ṣalāt al-djumᶜa*), which can only be performed in the mosque and is obligatory upon every free male Muslim who has reached years of discretion (cf. Juynboll, *Handbuch*, 86; Guidi, *Sommario del diritto Malechita*, i, 125-6. According to Ibn Hishām (290), this *ṣalāt*, which is distinguished by the *khuṭba*, was observed in Medina even before the *hidjra*. This is hardly probable and besides is not in agreement with other *ḥadīth*s (see al-Bukhārī, *Djumᶜa, bāb* 11) but the origin of this divine worship, referred to in sūra LXII, 9, is obscure. The assemblies of the Jews and Christians on a particular day must have formed the model (cf. al-Bukhārī, *Djumᶜa, bāb* 1). Its importance in the earlier period lay in the fact that all elements of the Muslim camp, who usually went to the tribal and particular mosques, assembled for it in the chief mosque under the leadership of the general. The chief mosque, which for this reason was particularly large, was given a significant name. They talk of *al-masdjid al-aᶜẓam* (al-Ṭabarī, i, 2494; ii. 734, 1701, 1702, Kūfa; al-Balādhurī, 5; al-Ṭabarī, *Tafsīr*, xi, 21, centre; *ibid.* also *al-masdjid al-akbar*, Medina; cf. *al-masdjid al-kabīr*, al-Yaᶜḳūbī, *Buldān*, 245) or *masdjid al-djamāᶜa* (Yaḳūt, iii, 896, Fusṭāt; also al-Ṭabarī, ii, 1119; Ibn Ḳutayba, *Maᶜārif*, ed. Wüstenfeld, 106). *masdjid li 'l-djumāᶜa* (al-Maḳrīzī, iv, 4); *masdjid djāmiᶜ* (al-Balādhurī, 289, Madāʾ in; Yāḳūt, i, 643, 647, Baṣra); then *masdjid al-djamiᶜ* (Yāḳūt, iii, 899; iv, 885; Ibn Ḥawḳal[1], 298, 315, 387; al-Yaᶜḳūbī, 110, etc.). As an abbreviation we find also *al-djamāᶜa* (Yāḳūt, i, 400; Ibn Baṭṭūṭa, iv, 343; cf. *masdjid al-djamāᶜa*, al-Balādhurī, 348) and especially *djāmiᶜ*. As the *khuṭba* was the distinguishing feature, we also find *masdjid al-khuṭba* (al-Maḳrīzī, iv, 44, 64, 87), *djāmiᶜ al-khuṭba* (*ibid.*, iv. 55) or *masdjid al-minbar*, al-Muḳaddasī, 316, for *djāmiᶜ*, 1. 8).

Linguistic usage varied somewhat in course of time with conditions. In the time of ᶜUmar there was properly in every town only one *masdjid djāmiᶜ* for the Friday service. But when the community became no longer a military camp and Islam replaced the previous religion of the people, a need for a number of mosques for the Friday service was bound to arise. This demanded mosques for the Friday service in the country, in the villages on the one hand and several Friday mosques in the town on the other. This meant in both cases an innovation, compared with old conditions, and thus there arose some degree of uncertainty. The Friday service had to be conducted by the ruler of the community, but there was only one governor in each province; on the other hand, the demands of the time could hardly be resisted and, besides, the Christian converts to Islam had been used to a solemn weekly service.

As to the villages (*al-ḳurā*), ʿAmr b. al-ʿĀṣ in Egypt forbade their inhabitants to celebrate the Friday service for the reason just mentioned (al-Maḳrīzī, iv, 7). At a later period, then, the *khuṭba* was delivered exceptionally, without *minbar* and only with staff, until Marwān b. Muḥammad in 132/749-50 introduced the *minbar* into the Egyptian *ḳurā* also (*ibid.*, 8). Of a mosque in which a *minbar* had been placed, we are told *djuʿila masdjid^an li 'l-aʿyān* (al-Ṭabarī, i, 2451) and a village with a *minbar* is called *ḳarya djāmiʿa* (al-Bukhārī, *Djumʿa, bāb* 15; cf. *madīna djāmiʿa*, Ibn Ḥawḳal[1], 321), an idea which was regarded by al-Bukhārī (d. 256/870) as quite obvious. In introducing the *minbars* into the Egyptian villages, Marwān was apparently following the example of other regions. In the 4th/10th century, Ibn Ḥawḳal mentions a number of *manābir* in the district of Iṣṭakhr (1st edn., 182 ff.) and a few in the vicinity of Marw (*ibid.*, 316) and in Transoxania (*ibid.*, 378; cf. 384), and al-Muḳaddasī does the same for other districts of Persia (309, 317) and he definitely says that the *ḳurā* of Palestine are *dhāt manābir* (*ibid.*, 176; cf. al-Iṣṭakhrī[1], 58); al-Balādhurī (331) also uses the name *minbar* for a village mosque built in 239/853-4; in general, when speaking of the *ḳurā*, one talks of *manābir* and not of *djawāmiʿ* (cf. al-Iṣṭakhrī[1], 63). Later, however, the term *masdjid djāmiʿ* is used for a Friday mosque (Ibn Djubayr, 217). The conditions of primitive Islam are reflected in the teaching of the Ḥanafīs, who only permit the Friday service in large towns (cf. al-Māwardī, *al-Aḥkām al-sulṭāniyya*, ed. Enger, 177).

As to the towns, the Shāfiʿīs on the other hand have retained the original conditions, since they permit the Friday service in only one mosque in each town (see DJUMʿA and *op. cit.*, 178-8), but with the reservation that the mosque is able to hold the community. The distinction between the two rites was of importance in Egypt. When in 569/1173-4 Ṣalāḥ al-Dīn became supreme in Egypt, he appointed a Shāfiʿī chief *ḳāḍī* and the Friday service was therefore held only in the al-Ḥākim mosque, as the largest; but in 665/1266, al-Malik al-Ẓāhir Baybars gave the Ḥanafīs preference, and many mosques were therefore used as Friday mosques (al-Maḳrīzī, iv, 52 ff.; al-Suyūṭī, *Ḥusn al-muḥāḍara*, ii, 140; Quatremère, *Hist. Sult. Maml.* i/2, 39 ff). During the Umayyad period, the number of *djawāmiʿ* in the towns were still very small. The geographers of the 3rd/9th and 4th/10th centuries in their descriptions of towns as a rule mention only "the *djāmiʿ*". Ibn al-Faḳīh, *ca.* 290/903, sometimes says *masdjid djāmiʿ wa-minbar* (304-6, also *minbar* simply, 305). In keeping with the oldest scheme of town planning, it was very often in the middle of the town surrounded by the business quarters (Ibn Ḥawḳal[1], 298, 325; al-Muḳaddasī, 274-5, 278, 298, 314, 316, 375, 376, 413, 426, 427, etc.; Nāṣir-i Khusraw, ed. Schefer, 35, 41, 56) and the *dār al-imāra* was still frequently in the immediate vicinity of the chief mosque (Ibn Ḥawḳal[1], 298, 314; al-Muḳaddasī, 426).

Al-Iṣṭakhrī mentions as an innovation in Islam that al-Ḥadjdjādj built a *djāmiʿ* in al-Wāsiṭ on the west bank, although there was already one on the east bank (al-Iṣṭakhrī,[1] 82-3; cf. al-Yaʿḳubī, *Buldān*, 322). Ibn Djubayr (*Riḥla*, 211) mentions only one *djāmiʿ* in Kūfa, called *Masdjid al-Kūfa* by Ibn al-Faḳīh, although he also mentions other mosques (173; cf. 174, 183 and al-Muḳaddasī, 116). In Baṣra, where al-Yaʿḳūbī (278/891) already mentions 7,000 mosques (*Buldān*, 361), al-Muḳaddasī (375/985) gives 3 *djawāmiʿ* (117). In Sāmarrāʾ, among many mosques, there was one *djāmiʿ* (al-Yaʿḳūbī, *Buldān*, 258, 259), which was later replaced by another (*ibid.*, 260-1); al-Mutawakkil also built one outside the original town (*ibid.*, 265; see also P. Schwarz, *Die ʿAbbāsiden-Residenz Sāmarrā*, 1909, 32). In Baghdād, al-Yaʿḳūbī mentions only one *djāmiʿ* for the eastern town and for the western (*Buldān*, 240, 245, 251, 253; the almost contemporary Ibn Rusta just mentions the old western town and its *djāmiʿ*, 109) although he gives the fantastic figures of 15,000 mosques in the east town (*ibid.*, 254) and 30,000 in the west (or in the whole town?, *ibid.*, 250). After 280/893-4 there was added the *djāmiʿ* of the eastern palace of the caliph (Mez, *Renaissance*, 388, Eng. tr. 410, quoting al-Khaṭīb al-Baghdādī, *Taʾrīkh Baghdād*; a private *djāmiʿ* of Hārūn al-Rashīd in the *Bustān Umm Mūsā* is mentioned by Ibn al-Ḳifṭī, *Taʾrīkh al-Ḥukamāʾ*, ed. Lippert, 433 below). These three *djawāmiʿ* are mentioned about 340/951 by al-Iṣṭakhrī (84), who also mentions one in the suburb of Kalwādhā. Ibn Ḥawḳal in 367/977 mentions the latter and also the Djāmiʿ al-Barāthā (164-5, of 329/940-1; Mez, *loc. cit.*), a fifth was added in 379/989, a sixth in 383/993 (Mez, 389, Eng. tr. 410-11); thus al-Khaṭīb al-Baghdādī in 460 (1058 gives 4 for West Baghdād, 2 for the east town (cf. Le Strange, *Baghdad*, 324). Ibn Djubayr in 581/1185 gives in the east town 3, and 11 *djawāmiʿ* (*Riḥla*, 228-9) for the whole of Baghdād. For Cairo, al-Iṣṭakhrī gives two *djāmiʿ*s: the ʿAmr and Ṭūlūn Mosques (49) besides that in al-Ḳarāfa, which was regarded as a separate town (cf. Ibn Rusta [*ca.* 290/903], 116-17). Al-Muḳaddasī, who wrote (375/985) shortly after the Fāṭimid conquest, mentions the ʿAmr mosque (al-Azhar), also one in al-Djazīra, in Djīza and in al-Ḳarāfa (198-200, 209; the *djāmiʿ* in al-Djazīra, also Djāmiʿ Miḳyās [cf. al-Maḳrīzī, iv, 75] is mentioned in an inscription of the year 485/1092; see van Berchem, *CIA*, i, no. 39). As these places were all originally separate towns, the principle was not abandoned that each town had only one *djāmiʿ*. The Fāṭimids, however, extended the use of Friday mosques and, in addition to those already mentioned, used the Djāmiʿ al-Ḥākim, al-Maḳs and Rāshida (al-Maḳrīzī, iv, 2-3). Nāṣir-i Khusraw in 439/1047 mentions in one passage the *djawāmiʿ* of Cairo, in another seven for Miṣr and fifteen in all (ed. Schefer, 134-5, 147). This was altered in 569/1173-4 by Ṣalāḥ al-Dīn (see above), but the quarters, being still regarded as separate towns, retained their own Friday mosques (cf. for the year 607/1210-11 in al-Ḳarāfa, al-Maḳrīzī, iv, 86).

After the Friday worship in Egypt and Syria was freed from restriction, the number of *djawāmiʿ* increased very much. Ibn Duḳmāḳ (*ca.* 800/1397-8) gives a list of only eight *djawāmiʿ* in Cairo (ed. Vollers, 59-78), but this list is apparently only a fragment (in all, he mentions something over twenty in the part of his book that has survived); al-Maḳrīzī (d. 845/1442) gives 130 *djawāmiʿ* (iv, 2 ff.). In Damascus, where Ibn Djubayr still spoke of "the *djāmiʿ*", al-Nuʿaymī (d. 927/1521) gives twenty *djawāmiʿ* (*JA*, ser. 9, vii, 231 ff.), and according to Ibn Baṭṭūṭa, there were in all the villages in the region of Damascus *masādjid djāmiʿa* (i, 236). The word *djāmiʿ* in al-Maḳrīzī always means a mosque in which the Friday worship was held (vi, 76, 115 ff.), but by his time this meant any mosque of some size. He himself criticises the fact that since 799/1396-7 the *ṣalāt al-djumʿa* was performed in al-Aḳmar, although another *djāmiʿ* stood close beside it (iv, 76; cf. also 86).

The great spread of Friday mosques was reflected in the language. While inscriptions of the 8th/14th century still call quite large mosques *masdjid*, in the 9th/15th most of them are called *djāmiʿ* (cf. on the whole question, van Berchem, *CIA*, i, 173-4); and while now the *madrasa* [*q.v.*] begins to predominate and is occasionally also called *djāmiʿ*, the use of the word *masdjid* becomes limited. While, generally speaking, it can mean any mosque (e.g. al-Maḳrīzī, iv, 137, of the Muʾayyad mosque), it is more especially used of the smaller unimportant mosques. While Ibn Duḳmāḳ gives 472 *masādjid* in addition to the *djawāmiʿ*, *madāris*, etc., al-Maḳrīzī only gives nineteen, not counting al-Ḳarāfa, which probably only means that they were of little interest to him. *Djāmiʿ* is now on the way to become the regular name for a mosque of any size, as is now the usage, in Egypt and Turkey at least. In Ibn al-Ḥādjdj (d. 737/1336-7), *al-djawāmiʿ* is occasionally used in this general meaning in place of *al-masādjid* (*Madkhal*, ii, 50). Among the many Friday mosques, one was usually distinguished as the chief mosque; we therefore find the expression *al-djāmiʿ al-aʿẓam* (Ibn Baṭṭūṭa, ii, 54, 94; cf. the older expression *al-masdjid al-aʿẓam*, in *ibid.*, ii, 53). The principal *djāmiʿ* decided on such questions as the beginning and ending of the fast of Ramaḍān (*Madkhal*, ii, 68).

3. Other religious activities in the mosque. "The mentioning of the name of God" in the mosques, was not confined only in the official ritual ceremonies. Even in the time of the Prophet, we are told that he lodged Thaḳafī delegates in the mosque so that they could see the rows of worshippers and hear the nightly recitation (al-Wāḳidī-Wellhausen, 382). Although this story (which is not given in Ibn Hishām, 916) may simply be a reflection of later conditions, the recitation of the Ḳurʾān must have come to be considered an edifying and pious work at quite an early date. In the time of al-Muḳaddasī, the *ḳurrāʾ* of Naysābūr used to assemble on Fridays in the *djāmiʿ* in the early morning and recite till the *ḍuḥā*, (328), and the same author tells us that in the Mosque of ʿAmr in Egypt the *aʾimmat al-ḳurrāʾ* sat in circles every evening and recited (205). In the time of Ibn Djubayr, there were recitations of the Ḳurʾān in the Umayyad mosque after the *ṣalāt al-ṣubḥ* and every afternoon after the *ṣalāt al-ʿaṣr* (*Riḥla*, 271-2). Besides the recitation of the Ḳurʾān, there were praises of God, etc., all that which is classed as *dhikr*, and which was particularly cultivated by Ṣūfism. This form of worship also took place in the mosque. The *ahl al-tawḥīd wa 'l-maʿrifa* formed *madjālis al-dhikr*, and assembled in the mosques (al-Makkī, *Ḳūt al-ḳulūb*, i, 152). In the Mosque of the Umayyads and other mosques of Damascus, *dhikr* was held during the morning on Friday (al-Maḳrīzī, iv, 49). In the Masdjid al-Aḳṣā the Ḥanafīs held *dhikr*, and recited at the same time from a book (al-Muḳaddasī, 182). In Egypt, Aḥmad b. Ṭūlūn and Khumārawayh allowed twelve men quarters in a chamber near the minaret in order to praise God, and during the night, four of them took turns to praise God with recitations of the Ḳurʾān and with pious *ḳaṣīdas*. From the time of Ṣalāḥ al-Dīn, an orthodox *ʿaḳīda* was recited by the *muʾadhdhins* in the night (al-Maḳrīzī, iv, 48). Ibn al-Ḥādjdj demands that the recitation of the Ḳurʾān aloud should take place in a mosque for the special purpose (*masdjid madjhūr*), as otherwise pious visitors are disturbed (*Madkhal*, ii, 53, 67). Mosques and, in particular, mausoleums, had as a rule regularly-appointed reciters of the Ḳurʾān. In addition there was, e.g. in Hebron and in a mosque in Damascus, a *shaykh* who had to read al-Bukhārī (or also Muslim) for three months (Sauvaire, *Hist. Jérus. et Hébr.*, 17; *JA*, ser. 9, iii. 261). In Tunis, al-Bukhārī was read daily in a hospital (al-Zarkashī, tr. Fagnan, *Rec. Soc. Arch. Constantine* [1894], 188).

Sermons were not only delivered at the *ṣalāt al-djumʿa*. In ʿIrāḳ, even in al-Muḳaddasī's time, one was preached every morning, according to the *sunna* of Ibn ʿAbbās (130), it was said. Ibn Djubayr, in the Niẓāmiyya in Baghdād, heard the Shāfiʿī *raʾīs* preach from the *minbar* on Friday after the *ʿaṣr*. His sermon was accompanied by the skilled recitations of the *ḳurrāʾ* who sat on chairs; these were over twenty in number (Ibn Djubayr, 219-22). In the same way, the calls of the *muʾadhdhins* to prayer to the Friday *khuṭba* were delivered to a musical accompaniment (see below, I. H. 4). The unofficial sermons, which moreover were not delivered in mosques alone, were usually delivered by a special class, the *ḳuṣṣāṣ* (pl. of *ḳāṣṣ*) (on these, cf. Goldziher, *Muh. Stud.*, ii, 161 ff.; Mez, *Die Renaissance des Islâms*, 314 ff.; and ḲĀṢṢ). The *ḳuṣṣāṣ*, who delivered edifying addresses and told popular stories, were early admitted to the mosques.

Tamīm al-Dārī is said to have been the first of these; in Medina in the caliphate of ʿUmar before the latter's decease, he used to deliver his orations at the Friday *ṣalāt*, and under ʿUmar he was allowed to talk twice a week in the mosque; in the reign of ʿAlī and of Muʿāwiya the *ḳuṣṣāṣ* were employed to curse the other side (al-Maḳrīzī, iv, 16-7). In the Mosque of ʿAmr in Cairo, by the year 38/658-9 or 39/659-60 a *ḳāṣṣ* was appointed, named Sulaym b. ʿItr al-Tudjībī, who was also *ḳāḍī* (*ibid.*, iv, 17, wrongly: Sulaymān; al-Kindī, *Governors and judges*, ed. Guest, 303-4). There are other occurrences of the combination of the two offices (Ibn Ḥudjayra [d. 83/702], al-Kindī, 317; Khayr b. Nuʿaym in the year 120/738, *ibid.*, 348; cf. al-Suyūṭī, *Ḥusn al-muḥāḍara*, i, 131, Djabr, according to Thawba b. Nimr, *Ḥusn*, i, 130 below; Ibrāhīm b. Isḥāḳ al-Ḳārī [d. 204], Kindī, 427; see also al-Maḳrīzī, iv, 18), which shows that the office of *ḳāṣṣ* was quite an official one. There is also evidence of the employment of *ḳuṣṣāṣ* in the mosques of ʿIrāḳ in the ʿAbbāsid period (Yāḳūt, *Udabāʾ*, iv, 268, v, 446). The *ḳāṣṣ* read from the Ḳurʾān standing and then delivered an explanatory and edifying discourse, the object of which was to instil the fear of God into the people (al-Maḳrīzī, iv, 18). Under the Fāṭimids also, the *ḳuṣṣāṣ* were appointed to the mosques; for example in 403/1012-13 the *imām* undertook the office in the Mosque of ʿAmr (al-Maḳrīzī, iv, 18, below) and the rulers had also a *ḳāṣṣ* in the palace. The *ḳuṣṣāṣ* were called *aṣḥāb al-karāsī*, because they delivered their discourses on the *kursī* (al-Makkī, *Ḳūt al-ḳulūb*, i, 152; Ibn al-Ḥādjdj, *Madkhal*, i, 159; cf. al-Maḳrīzī, iv, 121). Their discourse was called *dhikr* or *waʿẓ* or *mawʿiẓa*, whence the *ḳāṣṣ* was also called *mudhakkir* (al-Muḳaddasī, 205) or *wāʿiẓ*. Specimens of their discourses are given by Ibn ʿAbd Rabbihi (*al-ʿIḳd al-farīd*, Cairo 1321/1903, i, 294 ff.). It was not only the appointed officials who delivered such discourses in the mosque. Ascetics made public appearances in various mosques and collected interested hearers around them (cf. e.g. al-Maḳrīzī, iv, 135). In the Djāmiʿ al-Ḳarāfa, a whole society, the Banū Djawharī, delivered *waʿẓ* discourses from a *kursī* for three months on end; their servant collected money in a begging-bowl during the discourse, and the *shaykh* distributed some of it among the poor (*ibid.*, iv, 121).

The *ḳaṣaṣ* was completely taken over by popular Ṣūfism and later writers would hardly reckon, as al-Makkī does, the "story-tellers" among the *mutakallimūn* (*Ḳūt al-ḳulūb*, i, 152). The whole system degenerated to trickery and charlatanry of all kinds, as may be seen in the *Maḳāma* [*q.v.*] literature (cf. thereon Yāḳūt, *Udabāʾ*, vi, 167-8, and see also Mez and Goldziher, *op. cit.*). Al-Maḳrīzī therefore distinguishes between *al-ḳaṣaṣ al-khāṣṣa*, the regular and seemly edifying discourse in the mosque, and *al-ḳaṣaṣ al-ʿāmma*, which consisted in the people gathering round all kinds of speakers, which is *makrūh* (iv, 17). Others also have recorded their objections to the *ḳuṣṣāṣ*. Ibn al-Ḥādjdj utters a warning against them and wants to forbid their activities in the mosque completely, because they deliver "weak" narratives (*Madkhal*, i, 158-9; ii, 13-14, 50). He says that Ibn ʿUmar, Mālik and Abū Dāwūd rejected them and ʿAlī ejected them from the *masdjid* of Baṣra. It is of little significance that al-Muʿtaḍid in 284/897 forbade people to gather round them, for he issued a similar interdict against the *fuḳahāʾ* and the reasons were evidently political (al-Ṭabarī, iii, 2165); it was for political reasons also, but with a very different motive, that ʿAḍud al-Dawla forbade their appearing publicly in Baghdād because they increased the tension between Sunnīs and Shīʿis (Mez, *op. cit.*, 319). As late as 580/1184, the *wuʿʿāẓ* still flourished in the mosques of Baghdād, as is evident from the *Riḥla* of Ibn Djubayr (219 ff., 224), and in the 9th/15th century there was in the Azhar mosque a *madjlis al-waʿẓ* as well as a *ḥalaḳ al-dhikr* (al-Maḳrizī, iv, 54).

When Ibn al-Ḥādjdj denounces speaking aloud in the mosque, it is in the interest of the pious visitors who are engaged in religious works and meditation. *Iʿtikāf* [*q.v.*], retirement to a mosque for a period, was adopted into Islām from the older religions.

The word *ʿakf* means in the Ḳurʾān the ceremonial worship of the object of the cult (sūra VII, 134; XX, 93, 97; XXI, 53; XXVI, 71; cf. al-Kumayt, *Hāshimiyyāt*, ed. Horovitz, 86, 15) and also the ritual stay in the sanctuary, which was done for example in the Meccan temple (sūra II, 119; XXII, 25). In this connection, it is laid down in the Ḳurʾān that in the month of Ramaḍān believers must not touch their wives "while ye pass the time in the mosques" (*ʿākifūn fi 'l-masādjid*, sūra II, 183), an expression which shows, firstly, that there were already a number of mosques in the lifetime of the Prophet, and secondly, that these had already to some extent taken over the character of the temple. The connection with the early period is evident from a *ḥadīth*, according to which the Prophet decides that ʿUmar must carry out a vow of *iʿtikāf* for one night in the Masdjid al-Ḥarām made in the Djāhiliyya (al-Bukhārī, *Iʿtikāf*, *bāb* 5, 15-16; *Farḍ al-khums*, *bāb* 19; *Maghāzī*, *bāb* 54; *Aymān wa 'l-nudhūr*, *bāb* 29). It is completely in keeping with this that the Prophet, according to the *ḥadīth*, used to spend ten days of the month of Ramaḍān in *iʿtikāf* in the mosque of Medina (al-Bukhārī, *Iʿtikāf*, *bābʿ*; *Faḍl Laylat al-ḳadar*, *bāb* 3), and in the year in which he died, as many as twenty days (*ibid.*, *Iʿtikāf*, *bāb* 17). During this period, the mosque was full of booths of palm branches and leaves in which the *ʿākifūn* lived (*ibid.*, *bāb* 13; cf. 6, 7). The Prophet only went to his house for some very special reason (*ibid.*, *bāb* 3). This custom was associated with the ascetism of the monks. The faithful were vexed, when on one occasion he received Ṣafiyya in his booth and chatted for an hour with her (al-Bukhārī, *Farḍ al-khums*, *bāb* 4; *Iʿtikāf*, *bāb* 8, 11, 12). According to another tradition, his *iʿtikāf* was broken on another occasion by his wives putting up their tents beside him, and he postponed his *iʿtikāf* till Shawwāl (al-Bukhārī, *Iʿtikāf*, *bāb*s 6, 7, 14, 18). According to Zayd b. ʿAlī, the *iʿtikāf* can only be observed in a chief mosque (*djāmiʿ*) (*Corpus iuris di Zaid b. ʿAlī*, no. 447). During the early period, it was one of the initiatory rites for new converts. In the year 14/1635 ʿUmar ordered the retreat (*al-ḳiyām*) in the mosques during the month of Ramaḍān for the people of Medina and the provinces (al-Ṭabarī, i, 2377). The custom persisted and has always been an important one among ascetics. "The man who retires for a time to the mosque devotes himself in turn to *ṣalāt*, recitation of the Ḳurʾān, meditation, *dhikr*, etc." says Ibn al-Ḥādjdj (*Madkhal*, ii, 50). There were pious people who spent their whole time in a mosque (*aḳāmū fīhi*; al-Maḳrīzī, iv, 87, 97); of one we were told that he spent his time in the *manāra* of the Mosque of ʿAmr (*iʿtakafa*, *ibid.*, 44). Al-Samhūdī says that during the month of Ramaḍān, he spent day and night in the mosque (Wüstenfeld, *Medina*, 95). Saʿd al-Dīn (d. 644/1246-7) spent the month of Ramaḍān in the Mosque of the Umayyads without speaking (Ibn Abī Uṣaybiʿa, ii, 192). Nocturnal vigils in the mosque very early became an established practice in Islam. According to *Ḥadīth*, the Prophet frequently held nocturnal *ṣalāt*s in the mosque with the believers (al-Bukhārī, *Djumʿa*, *bāb* 29), and by his orders ʿAbd Allāh b. Unays al-Anṣārī came from the desert for twenty-three successive nights to pass the night in his mosque in rites of worship (Ibn Ḳutayba, *Maʿārif*, ed. Wüstenfeld, 142-3). Out of this developed the *tahadjdjud* [*q.v.*] *ṣalāt*, particularly recommended in the law and notably the *tarāwīḥ ṣalāts* [*q.v.*]. In Dihlī on these occasions, women singers actually took part (Ibn Baṭṭūṭa, iii, 155).

During the nights of the month of Ramaḍān, there were festivals in the mosques, and on other occasions also, such as the New Year, sometimes at the new moon, and in the middle of the month. The mosque on these occasions was illuminated: there was eating and drinking; incense was burned and *dhikr* and *ḳirāʾa* performed.

The Friday *ṣalāt* was particularly solemn in Ramaḍān, and in the Fāṭimid period, the caliph himself delivered the *khuṭba* (see al-Maḳrīzī, ii, 345 ff.; Ibn Taghrībirdī, ii/1, ed. Juynboll, 482-6, ii/2, ed. Popper, 331-3). The mosques associated with a saint had and still have their special festivals on his *mawlid* [*q.v.*]; they also are celebrated with *dhikr*, *ḳirāʾa*, etc. (cf. Lane, *Manners and customs*, chs. xxiv ff.). The saint's festivals are usually local and there are generally differences in the local customs. In the Maghrib, for example, in certain places the month of Ramaḍān is opened with a blast of trumpets from the *manābir* (*Madkhal*, ii, 69).

The mosque thus on the whole took over the role of the temple. The rulers from ʿUmar onwards dedicated gifts to the Kaʿba (Ibn al-Faḳīh, 20-1, and *BGA*, iv, *Indices*, *glossarium*, s.v. *shamsa*), and, as in other sanctuaries, we find women vowing children to the service of the mosque (al-Bukhārī, *Ṣalāt*, *bāb* 74; al-Maḳrīzī, iv, 20). *Ṭawāf* was performed, as at the Kaʿba, in mosques with saints' tombs as is still done, e.g. in Hebron; Mudjīr al-Dīn sees a pre-Islamic custom in this (Sauvaire, *Hist. Jérus. et Hébron*, 5). Especially important business was done here. In times of trouble, the people go to the mosque to pray for help, for example during drought, for which there is a special *ṣalāt* (which however usually takes place on the *muṣallā*) [see ISTISḲĀʾ], in misfortunes of all kinds (e.g. Wüstenfeld, *Medina*, 19-20; al-Maḳrīzī, iv, 57); in time of plague and pestilence, processions, weeping and praying with Ḳurʾāns uplifted, were held in the mosques or on the *muṣallā*, in which even Jews and Christians sometimes took part (Ibn Tag̲h̲rībirdī, ii/2, ed. Popper, 67; Ibn Baṭṭūṭa, i, 243-4, cf. Quatremère, *Hist. Sult. Maml.*, ii/1, 35, 40; ii/2, 199) or for a period a sacred book like al-Buk̲h̲ārī's *Ṣaḥīḥ* was recited (Quatremère, *op. cit.* ii/2, 35; al-D̲j̲abartī, *Merveilles biographiques*, French tr., vi, 13). In the courtyards of the mosques in Jerusalem and Damascus in the time of Ibn Baṭṭūṭa, solemn penance was done on the day of ʿArafa (i, 243-4), an ancient custom which had already been introduced into Egypt in the year 27/647-8 by ʿAbd al-ʿAzīz b. Marwān (*ḳuʿūd* after the *ʿaṣr*; cf. al-Kindī, *Wulāt*, 50). Certain mosques were visited by barren women (Wüstenfeld, *Medina*, 133). An oath is particularly binding if it is taken in a mosque (cf. J. Pedersen, *Der Eid bei den Semiten*, 144); this is particularly true of the Kaʿba, where written covenants were also drawn up to make them more binding (*ibid.*, 143-4, *Chron. Mekka*, i, 160-1). It is in keeping with this idea of an oath that Jews who had adopted Islam in Cairo had to take oaths in a synagogue which had become a mosque (al-Maḳrīzī, iv, 265). The contract of matrimony (*ʿaḳd al-nikāḥ*) also is often concluded in a mosque (Santillana, *Il Muḫtaṣar*, ii, 548; *Madk̲h̲al*, ii, 72 below; Snouck Hurgronje, *Mekka*, ii, 163-4), and the particular form of divorce which is completed by the *liʿān* [*q.v.*] takes place in the mosque (al-Buk̲h̲ārī, *Ṣalāt*, *bāb* 44; cf. Pedersen, *Der Eid*, 114).

It is disputed whether a corpse may be brought into the mosque and the *ṣalāt al-d̲j̲ināza* performed there. According to one *ḥadīt̲h̲*, the bier of Saʿd b. Abī Waḳḳāṣ was taken into the mosque at the request of the Prophet's widow and the *ṣalāt* held there. Many disapproved of this, but ʿĀʾis̲h̲a pointed out that the Prophet had done this with the body of Suhayl b. Bayḍāʾ (Muslim, *D̲j̲anāʾiz*, tr. 34; cf. also Ibn Saʿd, i/1, 14-15). The discussion on this point is not unconnected with the discussions regarding the worship of tombs. In theory, this is permitted by al-S̲h̲āfiʿī, while the others forbid it (see Juynboll, *Handbuch*, 170; I. Guidi, *Il Muḫtaṣar*, i, 151). The matter does not seem to be quite clear, for Ḳuṭb al-Dīn says that only Abū Ḥanīfa forbids it, but he himself thought that it might be allowable on the authority of a statement by Abū Yūsuf (*Chron. Mekka*, iii, 208-10). In any case, it was a very general practice to allow it, as Ḳuṭb al-Dīn also points out. ʿUmar conducted the funeral *ṣalāt* for Abū Bakr in the Mosque of the Prophet and ʿUmar's own dead body was brought there; later it became a general custom to perform the ceremony in Medina close to the Prophet's tomb and in Mecca at the door of the Kaʿba; some even made a sevenfold *ṭawāf* with the corpse around the Kaʿba. This was for a time forbidden by Marwān b. al-Ḥakam and later by ʿUmar b. ʿAbd al-Azīz (Ḳuṭb al-Dīn, *loc. cit.*, Wüstenfeld, *Medina*, 77). The custom was very early introduced into the Mosque of ʿAmr (al-Maḳrīzī, iv, 7, 1 ff.). That later scholars often went wrong about the prohibition is not at all remarkable; for it is not at all in keeping with the ever-increasing tendency to found mosques at tombs. Even Ibn al-Ḥād̲j̲d̲j̲, who was anxious to maintain the prohibition, is not quite sure and really only forbids the loud calling of the *ḳurrāʾ*, *d̲h̲ākirūn*, *mukabbirūn* and *murīdūn* on such occasions (*Madk̲h̲al*, ii, 50-1, 64, 81). When a son of Sultan al-Muʾayyad died and was buried in the eastern *ḳubba* of the Muʾayyad mosque, the *k̲h̲aṭīb* delivered a *k̲h̲uṭba* and conducted the *ṣalāt* thereafter and the *ḳurrāʾ* recited for a week at the grave, while the *amīrs* paid their visits to the grave (al-Maḳrīzī, iv, 240, 2 ff.). In Persia, it was the custom for the family of the deceased to sit in the mosque for three days after the death and receive visits of condolence (al-Muḳaddasī, 440 below).

4. Mosques as objects of pilgrimage. As soon as the mosque became a regular sanctuary, it became the object of pious visits. This holds especially true of the memorial mosques associated with the Prophet and other saints. Among them, three soon became special objects of pilgrimage. In a *ḥadīt̲h̲* the Prophet says "One should only mount into the saddle to visit three mosques: al-Masd̲j̲id al-Ḥarām, the Mosque of the Prophet and al-Masd̲j̲id al-Aḳṣā" (al-Buk̲h̲ārī, *Faḍl al-ṣalāt fī masd̲j̲id Makka wa 'l-Madīna*, *bāb* 16; *D̲j̲azāʾ al-ṣayd*, *bāb* 26; *Ṣawm*, *bāb* 67; Muslim, *Ḥad̲j̲d̲j̲*, tr. 93; *Chron. Mekka*, i, 303). This *ḥadīt̲h̲* reflects a practice which only became established at the end of the ʿUmayyad period. The pilgrimage to Mecca had been made a duty by the prescription of the *ḥad̲j̲d̲j̲* in the Ḳurʾān. The pilgrimage to Jerusalem was a Christian custom which could very easily be continued, on account of the significance of *al-Masd̲j̲id al-Aḳṣā* in the Ḳurʾān. This custom became particularly important when ʿAbd al-Malik made it a substitute for the pilgrimage to Mecca (al-Yaʿḳūbī, *Taʾrīk̲h̲*, ii, 311). Although this competition did not last long, the significance of Jerusalem was thereby greatly increased. Pilgrimage to Medina developed out of the increasing veneration for the Prophet. In the year 140/757-8, Abū D̲j̲aʿfar al-Manṣūr on his *ḥad̲j̲d̲j̲* visited the three sanctuaries (al-Ṭabarī, iii, 129) and this became a very usual custom. Mecca and Medina, however, still held the preference. Although those of Mecca and Jerusalem were recognised as the two oldest (the one is said to be 40 years older than the other; Muslim, *Masād̲j̲id*, tr. 1; *Chron. Mekka*, i, 301), the Prophet is however reputed to have said "A *ṣalāt* in this mosque is more meritorious than 1,000 *ṣalāts* in others, even in *al-Masd̲j̲id al-Ḥarām*" (al-Buk̲h̲ārī, *Faḍl al-ṣalāt fī masd̲j̲id Makka wa 'l-Madīna*, *bāb* 1; Muslim, Ḥad̲j̲d̲j̲, tr. 89; *Chron. Mekka*, i, 303). The *ḥadīt̲h̲* is aimed directly against Jerusalem and therefore probably dates from the Umayyad period. According to some, it was pronounced because someone had commended performing the *ṣalāt* in Jerusalem, which the Prophet was against (Muslim, *loc. cit.*; al-Wāḳidī-Wellhausen, 349). The three mosques, however, retained their pride of place (Ibn K̲h̲aldūn, *Muḳaddima*, *faṣl*s 4, 6; Ibn al-Ḥād̲j̲d̲j̲, *Madk̲h̲al*, ii, 55), and as late as 662/1264 we find Baybars founding *awḳāf* for pilgrims who wished to go on foot to Jerusalem (Quatremère, *Hist. Sult. Maml.*, i/1, 248).

Although these three mosques officially hold a special position, others also are highly recommended, e.g. the mosque in Ḳubāʾ [see AL-MADĪNA]. A *ṣalāt* in this mosque is said to be as valuable as an *ʿumra* or two visits to the mosque in Jerusalem (al-Diyarbakrī, *K̲h̲amīs*, i, 381-2). Attempts were also made to raise the mosque of Kūfa to the level of the three. ʿAlī is said to have told someone who wanted to make a pilgrimage from Kūfa to Jerusalem that he should stick by the mosque of his native town, it was "one of the four mosques" and two *rakʿas* in it were equal to ten in others (Ibn al-Faḳīh, 173-4; Yāḳūt, *Muʿd̲j̲am*, iv, 325); in another tradition, *ṣalāts* in the provincial mosques are said to be generally worth as much as the pilgrimage (al-Maḳrīzī, iv, 4), and traditions arose about the special blessings associated at definite times with different holy places of Islam (al-Muḳaddasī, 183) and especially about their superior merits (Ibn al-Faḳīh, 174). The Meccan sanctuary, however, always retained first place, which was marked by the *ḥadjdj*. It was imitated by al-Mutawakkil in Sāmarrā˒: he built a Kaᶜba as well as a Minā and an ᶜArafa there and made his *amīr*s perform their *ḥadjdj* there (al-Muḳaddasī, 122).

D. The component parts and furnishings of the mosque.

1. The development of the edifice. Except in the case of Mecca the earliest mosques as described above (B. 1) were at first simply open spaces marked off by a *ẓulla*. The space was sometimes, as in al-Fusṭāṭ, planted with trees and usually covered with pebbles, e.g. in Medina (Muslim, *Ḥadjdj*, tr. 95; al-Balādhurī, 6) and Fusṭāṭ (al-Maḳrīzī, iv, 8; Ibn Duḳmāḳ, iv, 62; Ibn Taghrībirdī, i, 77), which was later introduced in Baṣra and Kūfa, the courtyards of which were otherwise dusty (al-Balādhurī, 277, 348). These conditions could only last so long as the Arabs retained their ancient customs as a closed group in their simple camps. The utilisation of churches was the first sign of a change and was rapidly followed by a mingling with the rest of the population and the resulting assimilation with older cultures.

ᶜUmar made alterations in the mosques in Medina and in Mecca also. He extended the Mosque of the Prophet by taking in the house of ᶜAbbās; but like the Prophet, he still built with *labin*, palm trunks and leaves and extended the booths (al-Bukhārī, *Ṣalāt*, *bāb* 62; al-Balādhurī, 6). In Mecca also, his work was confined to extending the area occupied by the mosque. He bought the surrounding houses and took them down and then surrounded the area with a wall to the height of a man; the Kaᶜba was thus given its *finā˒* like the mosque in Medina (al-Balādhurī, 46; *Chron. Mekka*, i, 306; Wüstenfeld, *Medina*, 68). ᶜUthmān also extended these two mosques, but introduced an important innovation in using hewn stone and plaster (*djaṣṣ*) for the walls and pillars. For the roof he used teak (*sādj*). The booths, which had been extended by ᶜUmar, were replaced by him by pillared halls (*arwiḳa*, sing. *riwāḳ*) and the walls were covered with plaster (al-Bukhārī, *Ṣalāt*, *bāb* 62; al-Balādhurī, 46; Wüstenfeld, *Medina*, 70). Saᶜd b. Abī Waḳḳāṣ is said to have already taken similar steps to relieve the old simplicity of the barely-equipped mosque in Kūfa. The *ẓulla* consisted of pillars of marble adorned in the style of Byzantine churches (al-Ṭabarī, i, 2489; Yāḳūṭ, iv, 324).

This was little in keeping with the simple architecture of the original town, for Baṣra and Kūfa had originally been built of reeds and only after several great fires were they built of *labin* (see above, I. B. 1; cf. Ibn Ḳutayba, *Maᶜārif*, ed. Wüstenfeld, 279). As to Ḳūfa, Saᶜd by ᶜUmar's orders extended the mosque so that it became joined up with the *Dār al-Imāra*. A Persian named Rūzbih b. Buzurdjmihr was the architect for this. He used fired bricks (*ādjurr*) for the building, which he brought from Persian buildings, and in the mosque he used pillars which had been taken from churches in the region of Ḥīra belonging to the Persian kings; these columns were not erected at the sides but only against the *ḳibla* wall. The original plan of the mosque was therefore still retained, although the pillared hall, which is identical with the *ẓulla* already mentioned (200 *dhirā*ᶜs broad), replaced the simple booth, and the materials were better in every way (al-Ṭabarī, i, 2491-2, 2494). Already under the early caliphs we can therefore note the beginnings of the adoption of a more advanced architecture.

These tendencies were very much developed under the Umayyads. Even as early as the reign of Muᶜāwiya, the mosque of Kūfa was rebuilt by his governor Ziyād. He commissioned a pagan architect, who had worked for Kisrā, to do the work. The latter had pillars brought from al-Ahwāz, bound them together with lead and iron clamps to a height of 30 *dhirā*ᶜs and put a roof on them. Similar halls, built of columns (here like the old booth in Medina called *ṣuffa*: al-Ṭabarī, i, 2492, 14; but also *ẓulla*, plur. *ẓilāl*: al-Ṭabarī, ii, 259-60) were added by him on the north, east and western wall. Each pillar cost him 18,000 *dirhams*. The mosque could now hold 60,000 instead of 40,000 (idem, i, 2492, 6 ff., cf. 2494, 7; Yāḳūt, iv, 324, 1 ff.; al-Balādhurī, 276). Al-Ḥadjdjādj also added to the mosque (Yāḳūt, iv, 325-6). Ziyād did similar work in Baṣra. Here also he extended the mosque and built it of stone (or brick) and plaster and with pillars from al-Ahwāz, which were roofed with teak. We are told that he made *al-ṣuffa al-muḳaddima*, i.e. the *ḳibla* hall, with 5 columns. This seems to show that the other sides also—as in Kūfa—had pillared halls. He erected the *Dār al-Imāra* close to the *ḳibla* side. This was taken down by al-Ḥadjdjādj, rebuilt by others, and finally taken into the mosque by Hārūn al-Rashīd (al-Balādhurī, 347, 348 above, 349; Yāḳūt, i, 642, 643). In Mecca also in the same period similar buildings were erected. Ibn al-Zubayr and al-Ḥadjdjādj both extended the mosque, and Ibn al-Zubayr was the first to put a roof on the walls; the columns were gilded by ᶜAbd al-Malik and he made a roof of teak (*Chron. Mekka*, i, 307, 309). The Mosque of ᶜAmr was extended in 53/673 with Muᶜāwiya's permission by his governor Maslama b. Mukhallad to the east and north; the walls were covered with plaster (*nūra*) and the roofs decorated; it is evident from this that here also the original booth of the south side was altered to a covered hall during the early Umayyad period. A further extension was made in 79/698 in the reign of ᶜAbd al-Malik (al-Maḳrīzī, iv, 7, 8; Ibn Duḳmāḳ, iv, 62). Thus we find that during the early Umayyad period, and in part even earlier, the original simple and primitive mosques were in some cases extended, in other cases altered. The alteration consisted in the old simple booth of the Mosque of the Prophet being gradually enlarged and transformed into a pillared hall with the assistance of the arts of countries possessing a higher degree of civilisation. In this way, what had originally been an open place of assembly developed imperceptibly into a court, surrounded by pillared halls. Very soon a fountain was put in the centre of the court, and we now have the usual type of mosque. The same plan is found in the peristyle of the houses and in the *aithrion* of a basilica like that of Tyre (Herzog-Hauch, *Realencyclopädie*[3], x, 780).

The great builders of the Umayyads, ᶜAbd al-Malik and his son al-Walīd I, made even more radical progress. The former entirely removed the original mosque in Jerusalem, and his Byzantine architects erected the Dome of the Rock as a Byzantine building (cf. Sauvaire, *Jérus. et Hébron*, 48 ff.). Al-Walīd likewise paid equally little attention to the oldest form of mosque, when, in Damascus, he had the church of St. John transformed by Byzantine architects into the Mosque of the Umayyads. As al-Muḳaddasī distinctly states, they wanted to rival the splendours of the Christian churches (159). The new mosques, which were founded in this period, were therefore not only no longer simple, but they were built with the help of Christians and other trained craftsmen with the use of material already existing in older buildings. Al-Ḥadjdjādj, for example, used materials from the surrounding towns when building his foundation of Wāsiṭ (al-Ṭabarī, iii, 321; al-Balā<u>dh</u>urī, 290). Columns from churches were now used quite regularly (e.g. in Damascus: al-Masᶜūdī, *Murū<u>dj</u>*, iii, 408 = § 1292; Ramla: al-Muḳaddasī, 165; cf. al-Balā<u>dh</u>urī, 143 ff.; for Egypt, see al-Maḳrīzī, iv, 36, 124-5). Sometimes, remains of the older style remained alongside the new. In Īrān<u>sh</u>ahr, al-Muḳaddasī found in the chief mosque wooden columns of the time of Abū Muslim along with round columns of brick of the time of ᶜAmr b. al-Lay<u>th</u> (316). The building activities of al-Walīd extended to Fusṭāṭ, Mecca and Medina (cf. Ibn al-Faḳīh, 106-7) where no fundamental alterations were made, but complete renovations were carried out. With these rulers, the building of mosques reaches the level of older architecture and gains a place in the history of art. There is also literary evidence for the transfer of a style from one region to another. In Iṣṭa<u>kh</u>r, for example, there was a *<u>dj</u>āmiᶜ* in the style of the Syrian mosques with round columns, on which was a *baḳara* (al-Muḳaddasī, iii, 436-7; cf. for <u>Sh</u>īrāz, 430). Al-Walīd also rebuilt the Mosque of the Prophet, in part in the Damascus style (*ibid.*, 80; al-Ḳazwīnī, ed. Wüstenfeld, ii, 71).

This revolution naturally did not take place without opposition, any more than the other innovations, which Islam adopted in the countries with a higher culture which it conquered. After the Mosque of the Prophet had been beautified by Christian architects with marble, mosaics, shells, gold, etc. and al-Walīd in 93/712 was inspecting the work, an old man said: "We used to build in the style of mosques; you build in the style of churches" (Wüstenfeld, *Medina*, 74). The disccusions on this point are reflected in *ḥadī<u>th</u>*s. When ᶜUmar enlarged the Mosque of the Prophet, he is reported to have said: "Give the people shelter from the rain, but take care not to make them red or yellow lest you lead the people astray", while Ibn ᶜAbbās said: "You shall adorn them with gold as the Jews and Christians do" (al-Bu<u>kh</u>ārī, *Ṣalāt*, *bāb* 62). Ibn ᶜAbbās here takes up the Umayyad attitude and ᶜUmar that of old-fashioned people, according to whom any extension or improvement of the *ẓulla* was only permissible for strictly practical reasons. The conservative point of view is predominant in *Ḥadī<u>th</u>*. It is said that extravagant adornment of the mosques is a sign of the end of the world; the works of al-Walīd were only tolerated from fear of the *fitna* (Ibn Ḥanbal, *Musnad*, iii, 134, 145, 152, 230, 283; al-Nasāʾī, *Masā<u>dj</u>id*, *bāb* 2; Ibn Mā<u>dj</u>a, *Masā<u>dj</u>id*, *bāb* 2). The lack of confidence of pious conservatives in the great mosques finds expression in a *ḥadī<u>th</u>*, according to which the Prophet (according to Anas) said: "A time will come over my *umma* when they will vie with one another in the beauty of their mosques; then they will visit them but little" (al-ᶜAsḳalānī, *Fatḥ al-Bārī*, i, 362). In *fiḳh*, we even find divergence from the oldest quadrangular form of the mosque condemned (Guidi, *Il Muḫtaṣar*, i, 71). Among the types which arose later was the "suspended" (*muᶜallaḳ*), i.e. a mosque situated in an upper storey (e.g. in Damascus, *JA*, ser. 9, vol. v, 409, 415, 422, 424, 427, 430).

2. Details of the component parts and equipment of the mosque. — a. The Minaret [see on this, MANĀRA]. — b. The Chambers. The old mosque consisted of the courtyard and the open halls running along the walls: these were called *al-mu<u>gh</u>aṭṭā* (al-Muḳaddasī, 82, 158, 165, 182) because they were roofed over. When we are told that in Palestine, except in Jericho, towers were placed between the *mu<u>gh</u>aṭṭā* and the courtyard (*ibid.*, 182), this seems to suggest that the halls were closed, which would be quite in keeping with the winter climate of this region. The halls were particularly extensive on the *ḳibla* side, because assemblies were held here. The space between two rows of pillars was called *riwāḳ*, pl. *arwiḳa* or *riwāḳāt* (*ibid.*, 158, 159; al-Maḳrīzī, iv, 10, 11, 12, 49). Extension often took the form of increasing the number of the *arwiḳa*. In some districts, a sail-cloth was spread over the open space as a protection from the sun at the time of the worship (al-Muḳaddasī, 205, 430).

The courtyard was called *ṣaḥn*. The open space around the Kaᶜba is called *Fināʾ al-Kaᶜba* (*Chron. Mekka*, i, 307; Ibn Hi<u>sh</u>ām, 822; cf. *Fināʾ Zamzam*: Yāḳūt, *Udabāʾ*, vi, 376). *Fināʾ* is also the name given to the open space around the mosque (al-Maḳrīzī, iv, 6). Trees were often planted in the courtyard: e.g. in the mosque of ᶜAmr (see above, I. B. 1; when we read in al-Maḳrīzī, iv, 6, that it had no *ṣaḥn*, this probably means that this space, planted with trees, between the covered halls was very narrow). In Medina, at the present day, there are still trees in the *Rawḍa* (al-Batanūnī, *Riḥla*, 249); in Ibn <u>Dj</u>ubayr's time there were 15 palms there (*Riḥla*, 194). Other mosques in Cairo had trees growing in them (al-Maḳrīzī, iv, 54, 64, 65, 120; in al-Mas<u>dj</u>id al-Kāfūrī, there were as many as 516 trees: *ibid.*, 266), as is still the case today. In other cases the court was covered with pebbles (see above, I. D. 1); but this was altered with a more refined style of architecture. Al-Muḳaddasī mentions that this was only found in Tiberias, out of all the mosques in Palestine (182). Frequently, as in Ramla, the halls were covered with marble and the courtyard with flat stone (*ibid.*, 165). In the halls also, the ground was originally bare or covered with little stones; for example in the mosques of ᶜAmr until Maslama b. Mu<u>kh</u>allad covered it with mats (see below). The floor of the Mosque of ᶜAmr was entirely covered with marble in the Mamlūk period (al-Maḳrīzī, iv, 13-14, cf. in <u>Sh</u>īrāz, Ibn Baṭṭūṭa, ii, 53). But in the mosque of Mecca, the *ṣaḥn* is still covered with little stones (al-Batanūnī, *Riḥla*, 99 below); 400 *dīnār*s used to be spent annually on this (*Chron. Mekka*, ii, 10-11). In Medina also, little pebbles were used (Ibn <u>Dj</u>ubayr, *Riḥla*, 190; Ibn Baṭṭūṭa, i, 263).

There were not at first enclosed chambers in the halls. A change in this respect came with the introduction of the *maḳṣūra* (on this word, cf. Quatremère, *Hist. Sult. Maml.*, i/1, 164, n. 46). This was a box or compartment for the ruler built near the *miḥrāb*. Al-Samhūdī gives the history of the *maḳsūra* in Medina (Wüstenfeld, *Medīna*, 71-2, 89). The traditions all agree that the *maḳṣūra* was introduced to protect the ruler from hostile attacks. According to some authorities, ᶜU<u>th</u>mān built a *maḳṣūra* of *labin* with windows, so that the people could see the *imām* of the community (*ibid.*, and al-Maḳrīzī, iv, 7). According to another tradition, Marwān b. al-Ḥakam, governor of Medina after an attempt had been made on him by a Yamanī in the year 44/664, was the first to build a *maḳsūra* of dressed stone with a window (al-Balā<u>dh</u>urī, 6 below; al-Ṭabarī, ii, 70). Muᶜāwiya is then said to have followed his example. Others, again, say that Muᶜāwiya was the first to introduce this innovation. He is said to have introduced the *maḳṣūrāt* with the accompanying guard as early as the year 40/660-1 or not till 44/664-5 after the <u>Kh</u>āri<u>dj</u>ī attempt (al-Ṭabarī, i, 3465, 9; Ibn al-Faḳīh, 109, 3; al-Maḳrīzī, iv, 12, 11 ff.); according to one story because had had seen a dog on the *minbar* (al-Bayhaḳī, ed. Schwally, 393 below; cf. on the whole question, H. Lammens, *Moᶜâwiya*, 202 ff.). This much seems to be certain, that the *maḳṣūra* was at any rate introduced at the beginning of the Umayyad period, and it was an arrangement so much in keeping with the increasing dignity of the ruler that, as Ibn Khaldūn says, it spread throughout all the lands of Islam (*Muḳaddima*, Cairo 1322/1904-5, 212-13, *faṣl* 37). The governors built themselves compartments in the principal mosques of the provinces, e.g. Ziyād in Kūfa and Baṣra (al-Balādhurī, 277, 348) and probably Ḳurra b. Sharīk in Fusṭāṭ (al-Maḳrīzī, iv, 12). In Medina, we are told that ʿUmar b. ʿAbd al-ʿAzīz as governor (86-93/705-12) raised the *maḳṣūra* and built it of teak, but al-Mahdī had it taken down in 160/777 and a new one built on the level of the ground (*ibid.*, 7; Wüstenfeld, *op. cit.*; al-Balādhurī, 7 centre). We are further told that in 161/778, al-Mahdī prohibited the *maḳāṣīr* of the provinces, and al-Maʾmūn even wanted to clear all the boxes out of the *masādjid djāmiʿa*, because their use was a *sunna* introduced by Muʿāwiya (al-Maḳrīzī, iv, 12; al-Yaʿḳūbī, *Taʾrīkh*, ii, 571). But this attempt did not succeed. On the contrary, their numbers rapidly increased. In Cairo, for example, the Djāmiʿ al-ʿAskar built in 169/785-6 had a *maḳṣūra* (al-Maḳrīzī, iv, 33 ff.) and the mosque of Ibn Ṭūlūn had a *maḳṣūra* beside the *miḥrāb* which was accessible from the *Dār al-Imāra* (*ibid.*, 36, 37, 42; Ibn Taghrībirdī, ii, 8, 14). The *maḳṣūra* was found in the larger mosques. In the Djāmiʿ al-Ḳalʿa, Muḥammad b. Ḳalāwūn in 718/1318 built a *maḳṣūra* of iron for the sultan's *ṣalāt* (al-Maḳrīzī, iv, 132). According to Ibn Khaldūn, the *maḳṣūra* was an innovation peculiar to the Islamic world. The question must however be left open, whether in its introduction and development there may not be some connection with the boxes of the Byzantine court, at least, for example, when the Turks in the Yeshil Djāmiʿ in Bursa put the sultan's box over the door (R. Hartmann, *Im neuen Anatolien*, 27).

Although the *maḳṣūra* was introduced with the object of segregating the ruler and was therefore condemned by the strict as contrary to the spirit of Islam (e.g. *Madkhal*, ii, 43-4), *maḳāṣīr* were probably introduced for other purposes. Ibn Djubayr mentions three in the Mosque of the Umayyads: the old one built by Muʿāwiya in the eastern part of the mosque, one in the centre, which contained the *minbar*, and one in the west where the Ḥanafīs taught and performed the *ṣalāt*. There were also other small rooms shut off by wooden lattices, which could be sometimes called *maḳṣūra* and sometimes *zāwiya*. As a rule, there were quite a number of *zāwiyas* connected with the mosque which were used by students (*Riḥla*, 265-6). We find the same state of affairs in other mosques.

While the groups of the *ḳurrāʾ*, the students, the lawyers, etc. had originally to sit together in a common room, gradually the attempt was made to introduce separate rooms for some of them. Small compartments were either cut off in the main chamber or new rooms were built in subsidiary buildings. In the former case, we get the already mentioned *maḳāṣīr* or *zawāyā*. Ibn al-Ḥādjdj says that a *madrasa* was often made by the simple process of cutting off a part of the mosque by a balustrade (*darbazīn*) (*Madkhal*, ii, 44). Thus in the halls of the Mosque of ʿAmr there were several compartments for teaching, which were called *maḳṣūra* and *zāwiya*, in which studies were prosecuted (al-Maḳrīzī, iv, 20, 16, 25). In the Azhar Mosque, a *maḳṣūrat Fāṭima* was made in the time of the Fāṭimids, where she had appeared, and the *amīrs* in the following period made a large number of such *maḳāṣīr* (*ibid.*, 52, 53). In the Aḳṣā Mosque about 300/912-13, there were three *maḳṣūras* for women (Ibn al-Faḳīh, 100). These divisions might be a nuisance at the great Friday assemblies, and this is why al-Mahdī wanted to remove them in 161/778 from the *masādjid al-djamāʿāt* (al-Ṭabarī, iii, 486), and Ibn al-Ḥādjdj condemned them as works of the *mulk* and numbers them like other embellishments with the *ashrāṭ al-sāʿa* (*Madkhal*, ii, 43-4).

The *muʾadhdhins* not only lived in the minarets, where, at any rate in the Ṭūlūnid period, they held vigils (al-Maḳrīzī, iv, 48). They had rooms (*ghuraf*, sing. *ghurfa*) on the roof and these rooms in time came to be numerous (*ibid.*, 13, 14). All kinds of rooms were put in subsidiary buildings, for the *khaṭīb* (*ibid.*, 13), for judges, for studies, etc. In addition, there were dwelling-houses, not only for the staff but also for others. As already mentioned, devout men used to take up their residence in the mosque for a considerable period for *iʿtikāf* and any one at any time could take up his quarters in the mosque; he could sleep there and make himself at home. It therefore came quite natural to the devout to reside permanently in the mosque. Ascetics often lived in the minaret (see above), a *zāhid* lived on the roof of the Azhar mosque, others made themselves cells in the mosque, as a *shaykh* in Naṣībīn did (Ibn Djubayr, *Riḥla*, 240; cf. in Ḥarrān, 245) and as happened in Ṣalāḥ al-Dīn's time in the Mosque of the Umayyads (Ibn Abī Uṣaybiʿa, ii, 182). It was, however, very usual for them to live in the side rooms of the mosque, as was the case for example, in the Mosque of the Umayyads (Ibn Djubayr, 269; Ibn Baṭṭūṭa, i, 206). In particularly holy mosques like that in Hebron, houses for *al-muʿtakifūn* were built around the sacred place (Sauvaire, *Hist. Jérus. et Hébron*, 11-12) and also beside the Masdjid Yūnis at the ancient Niniveh (al-Muḳaddasī, 146). Kitchens were therefore erected with the necessary mills and ovens and cooked food (*djashīsha*) and 14-15,000 loaves (*raghīf*) were daily distributed to those who stayed there and to visitors (Sauvaire, 20; cf. Quatremère, *Hist. Sult. Maml.*, i/1, 231). Bread was also baked in the mosque of Ibn Ṭūlūn (Quatremère, *op. cit.*, i/1, 233) and kitchens were often found in the mosques (for al-Azhar, see al-Djabartī, *Merveilles*, iii, 238-9; Sulaymān Raṣad, *Kanz al-djawhar fī taʾrīkh al-Azhar*, 71 ff., 107 ff.). Those who lived in and beside the mosque were called *mudjāwirūn* (cf. al-Muḳaddasī, 146; for Jerusalem, Nāṣir-i Khusraw, 82, 91; for Mecca, Ibn Djubayr, 149; for Medina, Ibn Baṭṭūṭa, i, 279, where we learn that they were organised under a *ḳadīm*, like the North Africans under an *amīn* in Damascus; Ibn Djubayr, 277-8). They were pious ascetics, students and sometimes travellers. The students generally found accommodation in the *madāris*, but large mosques like that of the Umayyads or al-Azhar had always many students, who lived in them. The name of the halls, *riwāḳ*, was later used for these students' lodgings (cf. van Berchem, *CIA*, i, 43, n. 1; perhaps al-Maḳrīzī, iv, 54, 23). Strangers always found accommodation in the mosques (cf. above, I. C. 1). In smaller towns, it was the natural thing for the traveller to spend the night in the mosque and to get food there (Yāḳūt, iii, 385; al-Ḳifṭī, *Taʾrīkh al-Ḥukamāʾ*, ed. Lippert, 252). Travellers like Nāṣir-i Khusraw, Ibn Djubayr, Ibn Baṭṭūṭa and al-ʿAbdarī (*JA*, ser. 5, iv [1854], 174) were able to travel throughout the whole Muslim world from one mosque (or *madrasa* or *ribāṭ*) to the other. The traveller could even leave his money for safe keeping in a mosque (*Safar-nāma*, 51). Large endowments were bequeathed for those who lived in the mosques (Ibn Djubayr, *op. cit.*; Ibn Taghrībirdī, ii/2, 105 f.).

In later times, the rulers often built a lodge or pavilion (*manẓara*) in or near the mosque (al-Maḳrīzī, ii, 345; iv, 13; cf. on the word, Quatremère, *Hist. Sult. Maml.*, ii/2, 15).

There was often a special room with a clock in the mosques; this also is probably an inheritance from the church, for Ibn Rusta talks of similar arrangements in Constantinople (126 above). Ibn Djubayr (270) describes very fully the clock in the Mosque of the Umayyads (cf. *JA*, ser. 9, vii, 205-6). It was made in the reign of Nūr al-Dīn by Fakhr al-Dīn b. al-Sāʿātī (Ibn Abī Uṣaybiʿa, ii, 183-4; an expert was kept to look after it, *ibid.*, 191). There was a clock in the Mustanṣiriyya in Baghdād (Sarre and Herzfeld, *Arch. Reise*, ii, 170), and the Mosque of ʿAmr also a *ghurfat al-sāʿāt* (al-Maḳrīzī, iv, 13, 15). In the Mosque of Ibn Ṭūlūn is still kept a sundial of the year 696/1296-7; cf. van Berchem, *CIA*, i, no. 415), but the clocks were usually mechanical (see also Dozy, *Supplément*, s.v. *mindjāna*, and on the clock generally, E. Wiedemann, in *Nova Acta der K. Leop. Carol. Akad.*, c [Halle 1915]). In the Maghrib also we find mosqueclocks, e.g. in the Bū ʿInāniyya (*JA*, ser. 11, xii, 357 ff.).

The very varied uses to which the mosques were put resulted in their becoming storehouses for all sorts of things. In 668/1269-70, the Mosque of the Umayyads was cleared of all such things; in the courtyard there were, for example, stores for machines of war, and the *zāwiya* of Zayn al-ʿĀbidīn was a regular *khān* (*JA*, ser. 9, vii, 225-6).

c. The prayer-niche or *Miḥrāb* [see for this, MIḤRĀB].

d. The pulpit or *Minbar* [see for this, MINBAR].

e. The platform or *Dakka*. In the larger mosques, there is usually found near the *minbar* a platform to which a staircase leads up. This platform (*dakka*, popularly often *dikka*) is used as a seat for the *muʾadhdhins* when pronouncing the call to prayer in the mosque at the Friday service. This part of the equipment of a mosque is connected with the development of the service (cf. below, under I. H. 4, and C. H. Becker, *Zur Geschichte des islamischen Kultus*, in *Isl.*, iii [1912], 374-99 = *Islamstudien*, i, 472-500; E. Mittwoch, *Zur Entstehungsgeschichte des islamischen Gebets und Kultus*, in *Abh. Pr. Ak. W.* [1913], Phil.-Hist. Cl., no. 2). The first *adhān* call is pronounced from the minaret, the second (when the *khaṭīb* mounts the *minbar*) and the third (before the *ṣalāt*, *iḳāma*) in the mosque itself. These calls were at first pronounced by the *muʾadhdhin* standing in the mosque. At a later date, raised seats were made for him.

Al-Ḥalabī records that Maslama, Muʿāwiya's governor in Egypt, was the first to build platforms (here called *manābir*) for the calls to prayer in the mosques (*Sīra Ḥalabiyya*, ii, 111 below). This story, however, given without any reference to older authorities, is not at all reliable. It seems that a uniform practice did not come into existence at once. In Mecca, the *muʾadhdhins* for a time uttered the second call (when the preacher mounted the *minbar*) from the roof. As the sun in summer was too strong for them, the *amīr* of Mecca, in the reign of Hārūn al-Rashīd, made a little hut (*ẓulla*) for them on the roof. This was enlarged and more strongly built by al-Mutawakkil in 240/854-5, as his contemporary al-Azraḳī relates (*Chron. Mekka*, i, 332-3). The position in the mosque of ʿAmr in Cairo was similar. Here also the *adhān* was uttered in a chamber (*ghurfa*) on the roof, and in 336/947-8 there is a reference to its enlargement (al-Maḳrīzī, iv, 11). As late as the time of Baybars, when the many chambers were removed from the roof of the Mosque of ʿAmr,. the old *ghurfa* of the *muʾadhdhin* was left intact (*ibid.*, 14; cf. al-Kindī, *Wulāt*, ed. Guest, 469, n. 2). In the Mosque of Ibn Ṭūlūn, the *adhān* was pronounced from the cupola in the centre of the *ṣaḥn* (al-Maḳrīzī, iv, 40). Al-Muḳaddasī records in the 4th/10th century as a notable thing about Khurāsān that the *muʾadhdhins* there pronounced the *adhān* on a *sarīr* placed in front of the *minbar* (327). The *dukkān* "platform" in front of the *minbar* in the mosques of Shahrastān must have had the same purpose (*ibid.*, 357).

In the 8th/14th century, Ibn al-Ḥādjdj mentions the *dakka* as a *bidʿa* in general use, which should be condemned as it unnecessarily prevents freedom of movement within the mosque (*Madkhal*, ii, 45 above). In the year 827/1424 a *dakka* in the mosque of al-Ḥākim is mentioned (al-Maḳrīzī, iv, 61); the *dakka*s mentioned in inscriptions from Cairo all date from the period before and after 900/1495. Ibn al-Ḥādjdj mentions that, in addition to the large *dakka* used for the Friday worship, there was sometimes a lower one for ordinary *ṣalāts* (*Madkhal*, ii, 46-7) and says that in the larger mosques there were several *dakka*s on which *muʾadhdhins* pronounced the *adhān* in succession so that the whole community could hear it (*tablīgh*; *ibid.*, 45-6). Lane also mentions several *muballigh*s in the Azhar Mosque (*Manners and customs*, Everyman's Library edn., 87, 2).

f. The reading-stand or *Kursī*; Ḳurʾāns and relics. In the mosques there is usually a *kursī* [*q.v.*], that is, a wooden stand with a seat and a desk. The desk is for the Ḳurʾān, the seat for the *ḳāṣṣ*, or reader, *ḳāriʾ*. Ibn Djubayr attended the worship in Baghdād at which a celebrated preacher spoke from the *minbar*, but only after the *ḳurrāʾ*, sitting on *karāsī* had recited portions of the Ḳurʾān (*Riḥla*, 219, 222). The *wāʿiẓ*, often identical with the *ḳāṣṣ*, sat on a *kursī* made of teak (Ibn Djubayr, 200. Yāḳūt, *Udabāʾ*, ii, 319; al-Maḳrīzī, iv, 121); sometimes he spoke from the *minbar* to which the *wāʿiẓ* often had access (cf. Ibn Djubayr; see Mez, *Renaissance des Islâms*, 320, Eng. tr. 332). The *ḳuṣṣāṣ* are called by al-Makkī *aṣḥāb al-karāsī*, which is in keeping with this (*Ḳūt al-ḳulūb*, i, 152, quoting *K. al-Madkhal*, i, 159). Several *karāsī* are often mentioned in one mosque (cf. for the Mosque of ʿAmr, al-Maḳrīzī, iv, 19). Whether the *karāsī* mentioned for the earlier period always had a desk cannot be definitely ascertained. The *karāsī* with dated inscriptions given by van Berchem in his *Corpus* all belong to the 9th/15th century (nos. 264, 302, 338, 359bis, 491). According to Lane, at the Friday service, while the people are assembling, a *ḳāriʾ* on the *kursī* recites sūra XVIII up to the *adhān* (*Manners and customs*, 86). The same custom is recorded by Ibn al-Ḥādjdj and condemned because it has a disturbing effect (*Madkhal*, ii, 44, middle).

The Ḳurʾān very soon received its definite place in the mosque, like the Bible in the church (cf. al-Bukhārī, *Ṣalāt*, *bāb* 91: they prayed at a pillar beside *al-muṣḥaf*). According to one tradition, ʿUthmān had several copies of his Ḳurʾān sent to the provinces (e.g. Nöldeke-Schwally, *Gesch. d. Qor.*, ii, 112-13); al-Ḥadjdjādj, a little later, is said to have done the same thing (al-Maḳrīzī, iv, 17). The mosques had many other copies beside the one kept on the *kursī*. Al-Ḥākim put 814 *maṣāḥif* in the Mosque of Ibn Ṭūlūn, where the founder had already put boxes of Ḳurʾāns (al-Maḳrīzī, iv, 36, 40; cf. al-Suyūṭī, *Ḥusn al-muḥāḍara*, ii, 138) and in 403/1012-13, he presented 1,289 copies to the Mosque of ʿAmr, some of which were written in letters of gold (al-Maḳrīzī, iv, 12; al-Suyūṭī, ii, 136). Even earlier than this there were so many that the *ḳāḍī* al-Ḥārith b. Miskīn (237-45/851-9) appointed a special *amīn* to look after them (al-Kindī, *Wulāt*, 469); there are still a very large number in the Mosque of the Prophet (see al-Batanūnī, *Riḥla*, 241 above). Of particular value was the *muṣḥaf Asmā'*, belonging to the Mosque of ʿAmr, prepared by ʿAbd al-ʿAzīz b. Marwān, later bought by his son and afterwards by his daughter Asmā'; her brother left it in 128/746 to the mosque and it was used for public readings (see its whole history in al-Maḳrīzī, iv, 17-18). Besides it, another copy was for some time also used for reading, which was said to have lain beside ʿUthmān, when he was killed and to have been stained with his blood, but this one was removed by the Fāṭimids (*ibid.*, 19). In the time of Ibn Baṭṭūṭa, a Ḳur'ān for which the same claims were made was kept in Baṣra (ii, 10). On New Year's Day, when the Fāṭimid caliphs used to go in procession through the town, the caliph at the entrance to the Mosque of ʿAmr took up in his hands a *muṣḥaf* said to have been written by ʿAlī and kissed it (Ibn Taghrībirdī, ii/1, 472 middle); it was perhaps the *muṣḥaf Asmā'*. In Syria, Egypt, and the Ḥidjāz, in the 4th/10th century, there were Ḳur'āns which were traced back to ʿUthmān (al-Muḳaddasī, 143; cf. Ibn Ḥawḳal[1], 117). One of the Ḳur'āns made for ʿUthmān was shown in the Mosque of the Umayyads in Damascus in the time of Ibn Djubayr. It was produced after the daily *ṣalāt*s and the people touched and kissed it (*Riḥla*, 268). It was brought there in the year 507/1113-14 from Tiberias (al-Dhahabī, *Ta'rīkh*, Ḥaydarābād, 1337, ii, 25). Other Ḳur'āns of ʿUthmān were shown in Baghdād and Cordova (see Mez, *Renaissance des Islâms*, 327, Eng. tr., 338-9) and Ibn Djubayr saw another in the Mosque of the Prophet; it lay in a desk on a large stand, here called *miḥmal* (*Riḥla*, 193; cf. thereon Dozy, *Supplément*, s.v.). The Fāḍiliyya *madrasa* also had a *muṣḥaf ʿUthmān*, bought by the Ḳāḍī al-Fāḍil for 30,000 *dīnār*s (al-Maḳrīzī, iv, 197) and there is one in Fās (*Archives Marocaines*, xviii [1922], 361). Valuable Ḳur'āns like these had the character of relics and belonged to the *khizāna* of the mosque. They were often kept in a chest (*ṣandūḳ*) (Ibn Djubayr, *op. cit.*; for *al-muṣḥaf*, al-Bukhārī, *Ṣalāt*, *bāb* 95, Muslim has *al-ṣandūḳ*; see al-ʿAsḳalānī, *Fatḥ al-Bārī*, i, 385), also called *tābūt* (Ibn Djubayr, 104). In the Kaʿba, Ibn Djubayr saw two chests with Ḳur'āns (84, 3). Ibn al-Faḳīh mentions 16 chests with Ḳur'āns in the Jerusalem mosque (100). In the mosques there were also *ṣanādīḳ* for other things, such as lamps (al-Maḳrīzī, iv, 53; Wüstenfeld, *Medina*, 82 = Ibn Djubayr, 194), a *tābūt* for alms *Madkhal*, ii, 44, below), for the *bayt al-māl* or the property of the mosque (see below). There were also chests for rose-wreaths (*Madkhal*, ii, 50) which were in charge of a special officer. In the Mosque of ʿAmr there was a whole series of *tawābīt* (al-Maḳrīzī, iv, 9).

The Ḳur'āns were not the only relics to be kept in the mosques. Bodies or parts of the bodies of saints (cf. above, B. 4, C. 1) and other *āthār* were kept and revered in mosques: the rod of Moses (in Kūfa, Yāḳūt, iv, 325, previously in Mecca, see Goldziher, *Muh. Stud.*, ii, 361), the Prophet's sandals (in Hebron, Ibn al-Faḳīh, 101, also in Damascus, where the Madrasa Ashrafiyya had his left and the Dammāghiyya his right sandal; *JA*, ser. 9, iii, 271-2, 402), his cloak (in Adhruḥ, al-Muḳaddasī, 178), hair from his beard (in Jerusalem among other places, al-Batanūnī, *Riḥla*, 165) and many other things (see Goldziher, *Muh. Stud.*, ii, 358 ff.; Mez, *Renaissance des Islâms*, 325-6, Eng. tr., 337-9). These relics were often kept in valuable reliquaries. The head of Ḥusayn was buried in a *tābūt* in his mosque in Cairo (Ibn Djubayr, 45). There was a black stone like that in the Kaʿba in a mosque in Shahrastān (al-Muḳaddasī, 433).

On the other hand, pictures and images were excluded from the mosques, in deliberate contrast to the crucifixes and images of saints in churches, as is evident from *Ḥadīth* (al-Bukhārī, *Ṣalāt*, *bābs* 48, 54; *Djanā'iz*, *bāb* 71; Muslim, *Masādjid*, tr. 3; cf. on the question, Becker, *Christliche Polemik und islamische Dogmenbildung*, in *ZA*, xxvi [1911] = *Islamstudien*, i, 445 ff.). It is of interest to note that in the earliest period, Saʿd b. Abī Waḳḳāṣ had no scruples about leaving the wall-paintings in the *Īwān* of Kisrā at Madā'in standing, when it was turned into a mosque (al-Ṭabarī, i, 2443, 2451). The case was somewhat different, when, before the chief mosque in Dihlī, which had been a Hindu temple, two old copper idols formed a kind of threshold (Ibn Baṭṭūṭa, iii, 151), although even this is remarkable (cf. Snouck Hurgronje, *Verspreide Geschriften*, ii, 451 ff. = *ZDMG*, lxi [1907], 186 ff.). In some circles the opposition to pictures extended to other relics also. Ibn Taymiyya condemned the reverence paid to the Prophet's footprint, which was shown, as in Jerusalem, in a Damascus mosque also (Quatremère, *Hist. Sult. Maml.*, ii/2, 246).

g. Carpets. Carpets [see on these, BISĀṬ in Suppl.] were used to improve the appearance of the mosques. The custom of performing the *ṣalāt* upon a carpet is ascribed by *Ḥadīth* to the Prophet himself. Anas b. Mālik performed the *ṣalāt* with him in his grandmother's house and the Prophet used a cloth or mat (*ḥaṣīr*), which had become black through wear; as a rule, he used a mat woven of palm leaves, *khumra* (al-Bukhārī, *Ṣalāt*, *bābs* 19, 20, 21; *Ḥayḍ*, *bāb* 30; Muslim, *Masādjid*, tr. 47; Aḥmad b. Ḥanbal, *Musnad*, iii, 145). In any case, it is clear from al-Balādhurī that the *ṣalāt* was at first performed in the mosque simply in the dust and then on pebbles (al-Balādhurī, 277, 348; cf. al-Zurḳānī, *Sharḥ ʿalā 'l-Muwaṭṭā'*, i, 283-4). Later, when the halls were extended, the ground, or the paving, was covered with matting.

The first to cover the ground in the Mosque of ʿAmr with *ḥuṣur* instead of *ḥaṣbā'* was Muʿāwiya's governor Maslama b. Mukhallad (al-Maḳrīzī, iv, 8; al-Suyūṭī, ii, 136; Ibn Taghrībirdī, i, 77). The different groups which frequented the mosque (cf. above) had their places on particular mats: when a *ḳāḍī* (middle of the 3rd/9th century) ejected the Shāfiʿīs and Ḥanafīs from the mosque, he had their *ḥuṣur* torn up (al-Kindī, *Wulāt*, 469). Ibn Ṭūlūn covered his mosque floor with ʿAbbādānī and Sāmānī mats (al-Maḳrīzī, iv, 36, 38). For the mosque of al-Ḥākim in the year 403/1012-13, al-Ḥākim bought 1,036 *dhirāʿ*s of carpeting for 5,000 *dīnār*s (al-Maḳrīzī, iv, 56; cf. for al-Azhar, *ibid.*, 50). In the year 439/1047-8 in the Mosque of ʿAmr, there were ten layers of coloured carpets one above the other (Nāṣir-i Khusraw, ed. Schefer, text, 31, tr. 149). In the Mosque at Jerusalem, 800,000 *dhirāʿ*s of carpets were used every year (Ibn al-Faḳīh, 100). In the Mosque in Mecca they were renewed every Ramaḍān (*loc. cit.*). On ceremonial occasions, the *minbar* was also draped with a carpet (*sadjdjāda*); in Medina, the *minbar* and the sacred tomb was always covered like the Kaʿba in Mecca (Wüstenfeld, *Medina*, 83; cf. Quatremère, *Hist. Sult. Maml*, ii/1, 91) and some, especially the teachers, had their skins (*farwa*), in some cases, also a cushion to lean upon. The doors were also covered with some material (al-Maḳrīzī, iv, 56). On feast-days, the mosques were adorned with carpets in a particularly luxurious fashion (see Ibn Taghrībirdī, ii/1, 483). The puritanical rejected all this as *bidʿa* and preferred the bare ground (*Madkhal*, ii, 46, 49, 72, 74, 76), as the Wahhābīs still do.

h. Lighting. Where evening meetings and vigils were of regular occurrence, artificial lighting became necessary. Al-Azraḳī gives the history of the lighting of the Meccan Mosque. The first to illuminate the Kaᶜba was ᶜUḳba b. al-Azraḳ, whose house was next to the Mosque, just on the *maḳām*; here he placed a large lamp (*miṣbāḥ*). ᶜUmar, however, is said previously to have placed lamps upon the wall, which was the height of a man, with which he surrounded the mosque (al-Balādhurī, 46). The first to use oil and lamps (*ḳanādīl*) in the mosque itself was Muᶜāwiya (cf. Ibn al-Faḳīh, 20). In the time of ᶜAbd al-Malik, Khālid b. ᶜAbd Allāh al-Ḳasrī placed a lamp on a pillar of the Zamzam beside the Black Stone, and the lamp of the Azraḳ family disappeared. In the reign of al-Maʾmūn in 216/831, a new lamp-post was put up on the other side of the Kaᶜba, and a little later two new lanterns were put up around the Kaᶜba. Hārūn al-Rashīd placed ten large lamps around the Kaᶜba and hung two lanterns on each of the walls of the mosque (*thurayyāt*; cf. Ibn Djubayr, *Riḥla*, 149, 150, 155, 271; van Berchem, *CIA*, i, no. 506). Khālid al-Ḳasrī had the *masᶜā* also illuminated during the pilgrimage, and in 119/737 the torches called *nafāṭāt* were placed here, and ᶜUmar b. ᶜAbd al-ᶜAzīz ordered the people, who lived in the streets of Mecca, to put up lamps on 1 Muḥarram for the convenience of those visiting the Kaᶜba (*Chron. Mekka*, i, 200-2, cf. 458-9). In 253/867 Muḥammad b. Aḥmad al-Manṣūrī erected a wooden pole in the centre of the *ṣaḥn* and *ḳanādīl* on ropes were hung from it. This was, however, very soon removed (*ibid.*, ii, 196-7). About 100 years later, al-Muḳaddasī saw around the *ṭawāf* wooden poles on which hung lanterns (*ḳanādīl*), in which were placed candles for the kings of Egypt, Yemen, etc. (74). Ibn Djubayr describes the glass *ḳanādīl*, which hung from hooks in the Meccan Ḥaram (*Riḥla*, 103) and lamps (*mashāᶜil*) which were lit in iron vessels (*ibid.*, 103, cf. 143). Similar silver and gold *ḳanādīl* were seen by him in Medina (*ibid.*, 192 at the top; see also Wüstenfeld, *Medina*, 83 ff.). According to Ibn al-Faḳīh (before 300/912), 1,600 lamps were lit every evening in Jerusalem (100), and in the next century al-Muḳaddasī says that the people of Palestine always burn *ḳanādīl* in their mosques, which were hung from chains as in Mecca (182). The illumination was thus very greatly increased. In the year 60/679-80, when ᶜUbayd Allāh b. Ziyād was searching for his enemies in the mosque of Kūfa, the lamps were not sufficient, and large torches had to be used in searching the pillared halls (al-Ṭabarī, ii, 259-60). This, like what has already been said about Mecca, shows out of what modest beginnings this part of the mosque's equipment developed.

In the time of the ᶜAbbāsids, lamps and lanterns were part of the regular furniture of the mosque. Al-Maʾmūn is said to have taken a special interest in this. He ordered lamps to be put in all the mosques, partly to assist those who wanted to read and partly to prevent crime (al-Bayhaḳī, 473). For this purpose, the *ḳanādīl*, already mentioned, hung on chains were used, as at the building of the mosque of Ibn Ṭūlūn (al-Maḳrīzī, iv, 36, 38), in the Azhar Mosque and elsewhere; they were often of silver (*ibid.*, 56, 63). Golden *ḳanādīl* were also used and were of course condemned by Ibn al-Ḥādjdj (*Madkhal*, ii, 54) as ostentatious. At the same time, candles (*shamᶜ* or *shamaᶜ*) were used in large numbers, the candle-sticks (*atwār*, sing. *tawr*) often being of silver (Ibn Djubayr, *Riḥla*, 45, 151, 194; cf. Wüstenfeld, *Medina*, 95, 100). About 400/1009-10, large candelabra were made in Egypt, which from their shapes were called *tannūr*, stoves. Al-Ḥākim presented the Mosque of ᶜAmr with a *tannūr* made out of 100,000 *dirhams* of silver; the mosque doors had to be widened to admit it. He also gave it two other lamps (al-Suyūṭī, ii, 136 below; cf. Nāṣir-i Khusraw, text 51, tr. 148; Ibn Taghrībirdī, ed. Popper, ii/2, 105). In the Mosque of al-Ḥākim, in addition to lamps and candle lanterns, he also put 4 silver *tanānīr* and he made similar gifts to the Azhar and other mosques: the lamps were of gold or silver (al-Maḳrīzī, iv, 51, 56, 63; cf. Ibn Taghrībirdī, ii/2, 105). The *tanānīr* and other lanterns could also be made of copper (see van Berchem, *CIA*, i, nos. 502, 503, 506, 507, 511), as, for example, the celebrated candelabrum of the Mosque of Muʾayyad (al-Maḳrīzī, iv, 137) which was made for the mosque of Ḥasan but sold by it (*ibid.*, 118).

This great interest in the lighting of the mosque was not entirely based on practical considerations. Light had a significance in the worship and Islam here, as elsewhere, was taking over something from the Christian Church. When, in 227/842 the caliph was on his deathbed, he asked that the *ṣalāt* should be performed over him with candles and incense (*bi 'l-shamᶜ wa 'l-bukhūr*) exactly after the fashion of the Christians (Ibn Abī Uṣaybiᶜa, i, 165; cf. ii, 89). The dependence of Islam on Christianity is also seen in the story that ᶜUthmān, when he was going to the evening *ṣalāt* in Medina, had a candle carried in front of him, which his enemies condemned as *bidᶜa* (al-Yaᶜḳūbī, *Taʾrīkh*, ii, 187). The Shīᶜī bias does not affect the significance of this story. A light was used particularly in the *miḥrāb*, because it represented the holy cell, to which light belongs (cf. sūra XXIV, 35). Then, in Mecca, lamps were placed before the *imāms* in the *miḥrābs* and there were considerable endowments for such *miḥrāb* lamps (Ibn Djubayr, *Riḥla*, 103, 144). Light, as was everywhere the custom in ancient times, was necessary in mausoleums, and the documents of endowment show that a large number of oil-lamps were used in this way (cf. e.g. the document for al-Malik al-Ashraf's mausoleum, van Berchem, *CIA*, i, no. 252). But in the mosque generally the use of lights had a devotional significance and lamps might be endowed for particular individuals (cf. al-Muḳaddasī, 74, quoted above). The lamps so given by al-Ḥākim were therefore placed in the mosques with great ceremony, with blasts of trumpets and beating of drums (Ibn Taghrībirdī, ii/2, 105).

On ceremonial occasions a great illumination was therefore absolutely necessary. In the month of Ramaḍān, says Ibn Djubayr, the carpets were renewed and the candles and lamps increased in number, so that the whole mosque was a blaze of light (*Riḥla*, 143); on certain evenings, trees of light were made with vast numbers of lamps and candles and the minarets were illuminated (*ibid.*, 149-51, 154, 155). In the Mosque of the Prophet in the time of al-Samhūdī, forty wax candles burned around the sacred tomb, and three to four hundred lights in the whole mosque (Wüstenfeld, *Medina*, 100). On the *mawlid al-nabī*, says Ḳuṭb al-Dīn, a procession went from the Kaᶜba in Mecca to the birthplace of the Prophet with candles, lanterns (*fawānīs*) and lamps (*mashāᶜil*) (see *Chron. Mekka*, iii, 439). In the *ḥaram* of Jerusalem, according to Mudjīr al-Dīn, 750 lamps were lit by night and over 20,000 at festivals (Sauvaire, *Hist. Jérus. et Hébron*, 138). In the dome of the Ḳubbat al-Ṣakhra in 452/1060, a chandelier and 500 lamps fell down (*ibid.*, 69); at the taking of the town in 492/1099, the Franks carried off 42 silver lamps, each of 3,600 *dirhams*, 23 lamps of gold and a *tannūr* of 40 *raṭls* of silver (*ibid.*, 71). It was similar, and still is, in Cairo and elsewhere in the Muslim world. For the *laylat al-wuḳūd* in the Mosque of ᶜAmr, 18,000 candles were made for the Mosque of ᶜAmr, and every night eleven-and-a-half *ḳinṭārs* of good oil were used (al-Maḳrīzī, iv, 21 and more fully, ii, 345-6). The four "nights of illumination" fell in the months of Radjab and Shaᶜbān, especially *niṣf Shaᶜbān* (Quatremère, *Hist. Sult. Maml.*, ii/2, 131; cf. also Snouck-Hurgronje, *Mekka*, ii, 77). In 1908 electric light was introduced into the Mosque of the Prophet (al-Batanūnī, *Riḥla*, 245-6).

(On the question in general of illumination, see Clermont-Ganneau, *La lampe et l'olivier dans le Coran*, in *Recueil d'Archéologie Orientale*, viii [1924], 183-228; on the copper candelabra, see A. Wingham, *Report on the analysis of various examples of oriental metal-work, etc. in the South Kensington Museum*, etc., London 1892; F. R. Martin, *Ältere Kupferarbeiten aus dem Orient*, Stockholm 1902; on glass lamps, see G. Schmoranz, *Altorientalische Glass-Gefässe*, Vienna 1898; van Berchem, *CIA*, i, 678 ff.; M. Herz Bey, *La Mosquée du Sultan Hasan* (*Comité de Conservation des Monuments de l'Art Arabe*), 1899, 8 ff.; see also the Bibliography in *Isl.*, xvii [1928], 217 ff.).

i. Incense. According to some traditions, even the Prophet had incense burned in the mosque (al-Tirmidhī, i, 116; see Lammens, *Moᶜâwia*, 367, n. 8) and in the time of ᶜUmar, his client ᶜAbd Allāh is said to have perfumed the mosque by burning incense while he sat on the *minbar*. The same client is said to have carried the censer (*midjmar*: cf. Lammens, *loc. cit.*) brought by ᶜUmar from Syria before ᶜUmar when he went to the *ṣalāt* in the month of Ramaḍān (A. Fischer, *Biographie von Gewährsmännern*, etc., 55 n.). According to this tradition, the use of incense was adopted into Islam very early as a palpable imitation of the custom of the Church. In keeping with this is the tradition that, in Fusṭāṭ as early as the governorship of ᶜAmr, the *muʾadhdhin* used to burn incense in the mosque (Ibn ᶜAbd al-Ḥakam, 132; cf. *Annali dell' Islām*, iv, 565). The Ḳubbat al-Ṣakhra Mosque had incense burned in it during the consecration ceremony (Sauvaire, *Hist. Jérus. et Hébron*, 53).

Under the Umayyads, incense was one of the regular requirements of the mosque (*ṭīb al-masdjid:* al-Ṭabarī, ii, 1234, 10). Muᶜāwiya is named as the first to perfume the Kaᶜba with perfume (*khalūḳ*) and censer (*ṭayyaba:* Ibn al-Faḳīh, 20, 12). It became the custom to anoint the sacred tombs with musk and *ṭīb* (*Chron. Mekka*, i, 150, 10; Ibn Djubayr, *Riḥla*, 191, 9). Baybars washed the Kaᶜba with rose-water (al-Maḳrīzī, iv, 96, 14). Incense, as well as candles, was used at burials (cf. de Goeje, *ZDMG*, lix [1905], 403-4; Lammens, *Moᶜâwia*, 436, n. 9). Al-Muᶜtaṣim's desire to be buried with candles and incense (*bukhūr*) exactly like the Christians (Ibn Uṣaybiᶜa, i, 165, 12 f., cf. above) shows that they were aware that the custom bore much the same relation to the Christian usage as the mosque building did to the church. The consumption of incense in the mosques gradually became very large, especially at festivals (see for the Fāṭimids, Ibn Taghrībirdī, ii/1, 484, 12; ii/2, ed. Popper, 106, 3; al-Maḳrīzī, iv, 51; on vessels for holding incense, see the Bibliography in *Isl.*, xvii [1928], 217-18, and MAᶜDIN. 4. In Islamic art).

j. Water-supply. Nothing is said of a water-supply in connection with the oldest mosques. The Mosque of Mecca occupied a special position on account of the Zamzam well. In the early days of Islam, two basins (*ḥawḍ*) are said to have been supplied by it, one behind the well, i.e. just at the side of the mosque for *wuḍūʾ* and one between the well and the *rukn* for drinking purposes; the latter was moved nearer the well by Ibn al-Zubayr. In the time of Sulaymān b. ᶜAbd al-Malik, a grandson of ᶜAbd Allāh b. ᶜAbbās for the first time built a *ḳubba* in connection with Zamzam (*Chron. Mekka*, i, 299). At the same time, the governor Khālid al-Ḳasrī laid down lead piping to bring water from the well of al-Thabīr to the mosque, to a marble basin (*fisḳiyya*) with a running fountain (*fawwāra*) between Zamzam and the *rukn*, probably on the site of the earlier *ḥawḍ*. It was intended to supply drinking-water in place of the brackish water of Zamzam, but a branch was led on to a *birka* at the Bāb al-Ṣafā, which was used for ritual ablutions. The people, however, would not give up the Zamzam water and immediately after the coming to power of the ᶜAbbāsids, the provision for drinking-water was cut off, only the pipe leading to the *birka* being retained (*ibid.*, i, 339-40). In Ibn Djubayr's time, there was, in addition to Zamzam, a supply of water in vessels and a bench for performing the *wuḍūʾ* (*Riḥla*, 89). Khalid's plan, arrangements for ablutions at the entrance and a running fountain in the *ṣaḥn*, seems to have been a typically Umayyad one and to have been introduced from the north. Such fountains were usual in the north, not only in private houses, but also for example in the *aithrion* (*atrium*) surrounded by pillars, which, from Eusebius's description, formed part of the church of Tyre (see Hauch, in Herzog-Hauch, *Realenzyclop. f. prot. Theol. u. Kirche*[3], x, 782).

The usual name for the basin, *fisḳiyya* (in Egypt now *fasḳiyya*), comes from *piscina*, which in the Mishna and in Syriac takes the form *piskīn* (see Levy, *Neuhebr. u. chald. Wörterbuch*, iv, 81b; Fraenkel, *Fremdwörter*, 124; *fisḳīna*, found in al-Azraḳī, *Chron. Mekka*, i, 340 is probably due to a slip). At the same time, however, *birka* or *siḳāya* or *ṣihrīdj*, which probably comes from the Persian (cf. Fraenkel, *op. cit.*, 287), or the old Arabic *ḥawḍ*, are also used. The arrangements for ablutions were called *maṭāhir* or *mayāḍiʾ*, sing. *miʾḍaʾa* (now usually *mēḍā*), "place for *wuḍūʾ*". The accommodation in Mecca just mentioned was later extended. Ibn Djubayr mentions a building at al-Zāhir, 1 *mīl* north of Mecca which contained *maṭāhir* and *siḳāya* for those performing the minor ᶜ*umra* (*Riḥla*, 111).

In Medina, Ibn Djubayr mentions rooms for *wuḍūʾ* at the western entrance to the mosque (*Riḥla*, 197, 13 f.; cf. the plan in al-Batanūnī, *Riḥla*, facing p. 244). At the same time, Ibn Zabāla mentions seventeen receptacles for water in the *ṣaḥn* in the year 199/814-15, probably for drinking-water; later (8th/14th century) a large basin surrounded by a railing is mentioned in the centre of the court. It was intended for drinking purposes, but became used for bathing and was therefore removed. Baths and latrines were built anew by al-Nāṣir's mother (Wüstenfeld, *Medina*, 99 ff.).

In Damascus, where every house, as is still the case, was amply supplied with water, Yāḳūt (d. 626/1229) found no mosque, *madrasa* or *khānaḳāh* which did not have water flowing into a *birka* in the *ṣaḥn* (Yāḳūt, ii, 590). Ibn Djubayr describes the arrangements in the Mosque of the Umayyads. In the *ṣaḥn*, as is still the case, there were three *ḳubba*s. The centre one rested on four marble columns, and below it was a basin with a spring of drinking-water surrounded by an iron grille. This was called *ḳafaṣ al-māʾ* "water-cage". North of the *ṣaḥn* was a Masdjid al-Kallāsa, in the *ṣaḥn* of which there was again a *ṣihrīdj* of marble with a spring (Ibn Djubayr, *Riḥla*, 267). There was also running water in an adjoining *mashhad* (269), in the *khānaḳāh* and *madrasa* (271), and in a hall beside the living apartments there was again a *ḳubba* with a basin (*ḥawḍ*) and spring water (269). There were also *siḳāyāt* against the four outer walls of the mosque, whole houses fitted up with lavatories and closets (273); a century earlier, we are told that at each entrance to the mosque there was a *miʾḍaʾa* (159). The whole arrangements correspond exactly to those made by Khālid al-Ḳaṣrī in Mecca in the Umayyad period and must therefore date from the Umayyads.

It was the same in other Syrian and Mesopotamian towns. In Sāmarrāʾ, al-Mutawakkil built in his new *djāmiʿ* a *fawwāra* with constant running water (al-Yaʿkūbī, *Buldān*, 265). In Naṣībīn, the river was led through the *ṣaḥn* of the mosque into a *ṣihrīdj*; there was also a *ṣihrīdj* at the eastern entrance with two *siḳāyāt* in front of the mosque (Ibn Djubayr, *Riḥla*, 239). In Mawṣil in the mosque, which dated from the Umayyad period, there was a spring with a marble cupola over it (*ibid.*, 235). In Ḥarrān, there were in the *ṣaḥn* three marble *ḳubba*s with a *biʾr* and drinking-water (*ibid.*, 246), in Aleppo, two (*ibid.*, 253). In Kūfa, there were three *ḥawḍ*s with Euphrates water in front of the Djāmiʿ (*ibid.*, 212), but in the mosque in a *zāwiya*, a domed building with running water (Yāḳūt, iv, 325, 326, here called *tannūr*; cf. Ibn al-Faḳīh, 173, Ibn Djubayr, 89, 267). It was the same in Āmid (Nāṣir-i Khusraw, ed. Schefer, 28) and in Zarandj in Sidjistān (Ibn Ḥawḳal[1], 298-9). The principal mosques of ʿIrāḳ had *mayāḍiʾ* at the entrances, for which, according to a remarkable note by al-Muḳaddasī, rents were paid (129, read *karāsī*?; cf. *maṣṭaba*: Ibn Djubayr, 89). In Palestine also, in al-Muḳaddasī's time, there were conveniences for ablutions at the entrances to the *djawāmiʿ* (*maṭāhir*: 182; *mayāḍiʾ*: al-Iṣṭakhrī[1], and in Ṣanʿāʾ in the 4th/10th century, beside each mosque, there was water for drinking and for *wuḍūʾ* (Ibn Rusta, 111). In Persia also, it was the custom to have a *ḥawḍ* in front of the mosque (al-Muḳaddasī, 318) and there was drinking-water in the mosque itself on a bench (*kursī*) in iron jars into which ice was put on Fridays (*ibid.*, 327). Not only at the Zamzam well but also in the mosques of ʿIrāḳ, men were appointed whose duty it was to distribute drinking-water (al-Ṭabarī, iii, 2165). The regular custom, therefore, was to have at the entrance to, or in front of the mosque, conveniences for *wuḍūʾ*, and in the court of the mosque itself a fountain as the traditional ornament and for drinking water. It was the exception for the *wuḍūʾ* to take place in the mosque itself.

In Egypt, at first the Mosque of Ibn Ṭūlūn was arranged similarly to the Syrian mosques. In the centre of the *ṣaḥn* there was a gilt dome, supported by sixteen marble columns and surrounded by a railing. This upper storey was supported by nineteen marble columns and below was a marble basin (*ḳaṣʿa*) with a running fountain (*fawwāra*); the *adhān* was called from the dome (al-Maḳrīzī, iv, 37; the description is not quite clear). People complained that there were no arrangements for washing (*miʾḍaʾa*) there. Ibn Ṭūlūn replied that he had not made them because he had concluded the mosque would be polluted thereby. He therefore made a *miʾḍaʾa* with an apothecary's shop behind the mosque (*ibid.*, 38, 39; *al-Suyūṭī*, ii, 139; Ibn Taghrībirdī, ii/10). This suggests that previously in Egypt, the washing arrangements had been directly connected with the mosque. After the fire of the year 376/986-7, the *fawwāra* was renovated by al-ʿAzīz (al-Maḳrīzī, iv, 40), and again in 696/1297 by Lādjīn, whose inscription still exists (*CIA*, i, no. 16). A new *miʾḍaʾa* was built in 792/1390 beside the old one on the north, outside the mosque (al-Maḳrīzī, iv, 42).

The Mosque of ʿAmr first got a *fawwāra* in the time of al-ʿAzīz. In 378-9/998-9 his vizier Yaʿḳūb b. Killis installed one in the cupola, already in existence for the *bayt al-māl*. Marble jars were put there for the water (probably drinking-water) (al-Maḳrīzī, iv, 9, 11; cf. al-Suyūṭī, ii, 136; Yāḳut, iii, 899). A new water basin was installed by Ṣalāḥ al-Dīn beside his *manẓara* in the mosque. The water was led to the *fawwārat al-fisḳiyya* from the Nile. This was prohibited in the reign of Baybars al-Bunduḳdārī (658-76/1260-77) by the chief *ḳāḍī*, because the building was being affected by it (al-Maḳrīzī, iv, 14; al-Suyūṭī, ii, 137). The *amīr*, who restored it, brought the water for the *fisḳiyya* from a well in the street (al-Maḳrīzī, iv, 15).

Like Ibn Ṭūlūn, the Fāṭimids do not seem to have considered the *miʾḍaʾa* indispensable. For the Azhar Mosque had originally no *miʾḍaʾa*: as late as al-Ḥākim's *waḳf* document for the provision of *miʾḍaʾa*, money is given only with the provision that something of the kind should be made (al-Maḳrīzī, iv, 51, 54). At a later date we hear of two *miʾḍaʾa*'s, one at the adjoining Āḳbughāwiyya (*ibid.*, 54). On the other hand, there was already a *fisḳiyya* in the centre of the court, but whether it had existed from the first is not known. It had disappeared, when traces of it were found in 827/1424 in laying-out a new *ṣihrīdj* (*ibid.*, 54). The *fisḳiyya* of the Mosque of al-Ḥākim was not erected by the founder. Like that of the Mosque of ʿAmr, it was removed in 660/1262 by the *ḳāḍī* Tādj al-Dīn, but after the earthquake of 702/1302-3, it was again rebuilt and provided with drinking-water from the Nile (*ibid.*, 56, 57) and again renovated after 780/1378 (*ibid.*, 61). A small *miʾḍaʾa*, later replaced by another, was in the vicinity of the entrance (*ibid.*, 61). Other Fāṭimid mosques had basins in the *ṣaḥn*, which were supplied from the Nile and from the Khalīdj (*ibid.*, 76, 81, 120).

The traditional plan was retained in the period following also. For example, we know that the *amīr* Ṭughān in 815/1412 placed a *birka* in the centre of the Djamiʿ of Āḳsunḳur which was covered by a roof supported by marble pillars and supplied by the same pipe as the already existing *miʾḍaʾas* (al-Maḳrīzī, iv, 107, cf. 124, 138, 139, etc.). At the ceremonial dedication of mosques, it was the custom for the patron to fill the *birka* in the *ṣaḥn* with sugar, lemonade or other sweet things (e.g. at the Muʾayyadī, in 822/1419, al-Maḳrīzī, iv, 139; at the Madrasa of Djamāl al-Dīn in 811/1408-9, *ibid.*, 253; another in 757/1356, *ibid.*, 256).

The importance of the *birka* of the mosque, as a drinking-place, diminished as pious founders erected drinking fountains everywhere (cf. for Mecca, *Chron. Mekka*, ii, 116-18; also *BGA*, *Glossarium*, 211, s.v. *ḥubb*; 258, s.v. *sabīl*) and especially when it became the custom to build a *sabīl* with a boy's school in part of the mosque (see below, I. E. 4, end). A *ḥawḍ* for watering animals was also sometimes built in the vicinity of the mosque (al-Maḳrīzī, iv, 76). Sometimes also the *birka* of the *ṣaḥn* was used for washing. In the year 799/1397 the *amīr* Yalbughā made arrangements for this in the Aḳmar mosque so that one could get water for *wuḍūʾ* from taps from a *birka* put up in the *ṣaḥn* (al-Maḳrīzī, iv, 76). Al-Maḳrīzī condemns this addition, but only because there was already a *miʾḍaʾa* at the entrance and the *ṣaḥn* was too small for the new one (*ibid.*), and not on grounds of principle; and it was only because the wall was damaged that the *amīr*'s gift was removed in 815/1412 (*ibid.*, 77). The custom of using the water supply of the *ṣaḥn* for *wuḍūʾ* survived in many places in Egypt. The arrangements were therefore usually called *miʾḍaʾa* or rather *mēḍā* (which is not found in the inscriptions). If they had taps, they were called *ḥanafiyya*; according to Lane's suggestion, because the Ḥanafīs only permitted ablutions with running water or from a cistern 10 ells broad and deep (*Lexicon*, s.v.; cf. *Manners and customs*. Everyman's Library, 69; cf. on the question M. Herz, *Observations critiques sur les bassins dans les ṣaḥns des mosquées*, in *BIE*, iii/7 [1896], 47-51; idem, *La mosquée du Sultan Ḥasan*, 2; Herz wrongly dates the modern usage from the Turkish conquest in 923/1517). In quite recent times, the *miʾḍaʾas* have often been moved outside to special buildings. Ibn al-Ḥādjdj condemns bringing water into the mosque, because the only object is for ablutions and ablutions in the mosque are forbidden by "our learned men" (*Madkhal*, ii, 47-8, 49); like shaving, ablutions should be performed outside the mosque in keeping with the Prophet's saying *idjʿalū maṭāhirakum ʿalā abwābi masādjidikum* (*ibid.*, ii, 58). It was in keeping with this principle that in earlier times the *miʾḍaʾa* was usually put at the entrance and the barbers took up their places before the entrance (cf. the name *Bāb al-Muzayyinīn* "The Barbers' Gate" for the main entrance to the Azhar mosque). *Miʾḍaʾas* were also to be found in hospitals; thus the "lower hospital" was given two in 246/957, one of which was for washing corpses (Ibn Duḳmāḳ, 99 below).

E. The mosque as a state institution.

1. The mosque as a political centre. Its relation to the ruler. It was inherent in the character of Islam that religion and politics could not be separated. The same individual was ruler and chief administrator in the two fields, and the same building, the mosque, was the centre of gravity for both politics and religion. This relationship found expression in the fact that the mosque was placed in the centre of the camp, while the ruler's abode was built immediately adjacent to it, as in Medina (and in Fusṭāṭ, Damascus, Baṣra, Kūfa). We can trace how this *dār al-imāra* or *ḳaṣr* (so for Kūfa: al-Ṭabarī, ii, 230-1; *ḳaṣr al-imāra, ibid.*, 234) with the growth of the mosque gradually became incorporated in it at Fusṭāṭ and Damascus and was replaced by a new building. The tradition remained so strong that, in Cairo, when the new chief mosque Djāmiʿ al-ʿAskar was being planned in 169/785-6, a *Dār Umarāʾ Miṣr* was built beside it with direct access to the mosque (al-Maḳrīzī, iv, 33-4), and when Ibn Ṭūlūn built his mosque, a building called the *Dār al-Imāra* was erected on its south side, where the ruler, who now lived in another new palace, had rooms for changing his robes, etc., from which he could go straight into the *maḳṣūra* (*ibid.*, 42).

The ʿAbbāsids at the foundation of Baghdād introduced a characteristic innovation, when they made the palace the centre of the city; the case was similar with Fāṭimid Cairo; but Sulaymān b. ʿAbd al-Malik in Ramla had already built the palace in front of the mosque (al-Balādhurī, 143). Later rulers, who no longer lived just beside the mosque, had special balconies or something similar built for themselves in or beside the mosque. Ṣalāḥ al-Dīn built for himself a *manẓara* under the great minaret of the mosque of ʿAmr (al-Maḳrīzī, iv, 13; al-Suyūṭī, ii, 137) and just to the south of the Azhar mosque, the Fāṭimids had a *manẓara* from which they could overlook the mosque (al-Maḳrīzī, ii, 345).

The caliph was the appointed leader of the *ṣalāt* and the *khaṭīb* of the Muslim community. The significance of the mosque for the state is therefore embodied in the *minbar*. The installation of the caliph consisted in his seating himself upon this, the seat of the Prophet in his sovereign capacity. When homage was first paid to Abū Bakr by those who had decided the choice of the Prophet's successor, he sat on the *minbar*. ʿUmar delivered an address, the people paid homage to him and he delivered a *khuṭba*, by which he assumed the leadership (Ibn Hishām, 1017; al-Ṭabarī, i, 1828-9; al-Diyārbakrī, ii, 75; al-Yaʿḳūbī, *Taʾrīkh*, ii, 142); it was the same with ʿUmar and ʿUthmān (*ibid.*, 157, 187).

The *khuṭba*, after the glorification of God and the Prophet, contained a reference to the caliph's predecessor and a kind of formal introduction of himself by the new caliph. It was the same in the period of the Umayyads and ʿAbbāsids (see for al-Walīd, al-Ṭabarī, ii, 1177 ff.; al-Amīn, *ibid.*, iii, 764; al-Mahdī, *ibid.*, iii, 398, 451, 457; cf. on this question also al-Bukhārī, *Aḥkām*, *bāb* 43). The *minbar* and the *khuṭba* associated with it was still more important than the imāmate at the *ṣalāt*, it was *minbar al-mulk* (*Ḥamāsa*, ed. Freytag, 656, v, 4). According to a *ḥadīth*, the Prophet carried the little Ḥasan up to the *minbar* and said, "This my son is a chieftain", etc. (al-Bukhārī, *Manāḳib*, *bāb* 25). This reflects the later custom by which the ruler saw that homage was paid to his successor-designate; this also was done from the *minbar* (cf. *khuṭiba yawm al-djumʿa li 'l-Muʿtaḍid bi-wilāyat al-ʿahd*, al-Ṭabarī, iii, 2131). The Fāṭimid caliph showed honour to a distinguished officer by allowing him to sit beside him on the *minbar* (al-Suyūṭī, ii, 91); in the same way, Muʿāwiya allowed Ibn ʿAbbās to sit beside him *ʿalā sarīrihi* (Ibn Abī Uṣaybiʿa, i, 119), but whether the reference is to the *minbar* is perhaps doubtful. The *bayʿa* could also be received by another on behalf of the caliph, but it had to be accepted on the *minbar*. Thus the governor of Mecca in 196/811-12 accepted on the *minbar* homage to ʿAbd Allāh al-Maʾmūn and the deposition of Muḥammad al-Amīn (al-Ṭabarī, iii, 861-2; cf. for al-Mahdī: *ibid.*, 389). There are other cases in which the solemn deposition of a ruler took place on or beside the *minbar* (*Aghānī*², i, 12; Wüstenfeld, *Medina*, 15). Even at a much later date, when spontaneous acclamation by the populace was no longer of any importance, the ceremonial installation on the *minbar* was still of importance (al-Maḳrīzī, iv, 94). It had become only a formality but still an important one. Homage was paid to the ʿAbbāsid caliphs in Egypt in the great *īwān* of the palace or in a tent in which a *minbar* had been put up, and similarly to the sultans whose investiture was read out from the *minbar* (cf. Quatremère, *Hist. Sult. Maml.*, i/1, 117, 149 ff., 183 ff.). If one dreamt that he was sitting on the *minbar*, it meant that he would become sultan (*ibid.*, ii/2, 103). The ʿAbbāsid caliph had, however, long had his own throne after the old Persian fashion in his palace (Ps. -al-Djāḥiẓ, *al-Tādj fī akhlāk al-mulūk*, ed. Aḥmad Zakī, Cairo 1914, 7 ff.; tr. Pellat, *Le livre de la couronne*, Paris 1954, 35 ff.) and so had the Fāṭimids (Ibn Taghrībirdī, ii/1, 457) and the Mamlūks (Quatremère, *op. cit.*, i/1, 87; cf. 147). When later we find mention of the *kursī 'l-khilāfa* (van Berchem, *CIA*, i, no. 33), *sarīr al-mulk* (*Chron. Mekka*, iii, 113), *sarīr al-salṭana* (al-Maḳrīzī, ii, 157; cf. *al-sarīr*, royal throne: Ibn Ḥawḳal¹, 282, 285; *kursī* similarly: cf. Ibn ʿArabshāh, *Vita Timuri*, ed. Manger, ii, 186) or *martabat al-mulk* (Quatremère, *op. cit.*, i/2, 61), the reference is no longer to the *minbar*. This does not mean that the ruler could no longer make public appearances in the mosques: thus in 648/1250, al-Muʿizz Aybak regularly gave audiences in *al-madāris al-ṣāliḥiyya* (Quatremère, *Hist. Sult. Maml.*, 17) and memorial services for Baybars were held a year after his death in several mosques, *madāris* and *khawānik* in Cairo (677/1278; *ibid.*, i/2, 164-5).

The caliph spoke chiefly from the *minbar* of the capital, but when he made the pilgrimage he also spoke from the *manābir* in Mecca and Medina (cf. e.g. al-Ṭabarī, ii, 1234; al-Yaᶜḳūbī, ii, 341, 501; *Chron. Mekka*, i, 160). Otherwise, in the provinces, the governor stood in the same relation to the mosques as the caliph in the capital. He was appointed "over *ṣalāt* and sword" or he administered "justice among the people" and the *ṣalāt* (al-Ṭabarī, iii, 860), he had "province and *minbar*" under him (*ibid.*, ii, 611), *al-wilāyāt wa 'l-khuṭba* (al-Muḳaddasī, 337). Speaking from the *minbar* was a right which the caliph had delegated to him and it was done in the name of the caliph. ᶜAmr b. al-ᶜĀṣ therefore refused to allow people in the country to hold *djumaᶜ* except under the direction of the commander (al-Maḳrīzī, iv, 7). This point of view was never quite abandoned. The *khuṭba* was delivered "in the name of" the caliph (*ibid.*, 94) or "for" him (*lahu*, *ibid.*, 66, 74, 198; Ibn Taghrībirdī, ii/1, 85 below; al-Muḳaddasī, 485 above), and in the same way an *amīr* delivered a *khuṭba* "for" a sultan (al-Maḳrīzī, iv, 213, 214). The sultan did not have the "secular" and the caliph the "spiritual" power, but the sultan exercised as a Muslim ruler the actual power which the caliph possessed as the legitimate sovereign and had formally entrusted to him. During the struggles between the different pretenders, there was thus a confession of one's politics if one performed the *ṣalāt* with the one or the other governor (al-Ṭabarī, ii, 228, 234, 258; *Chron. Mekka*, ii, 168). The pretenders disputed as to whether the one or the other could put up his standard beside the *minbar* (al-Ṭabarī, iii, 2009).

Like the caliph, the governor also made his formal entry into office by ascending the *minbar* and delivering a *khuṭba*; this was the symbol of his authority (e.g. al-Ṭabarī, ii, 91, 238, 242; *Chron. Mekka*, ii, 173; cf. *Ḥamāsa*, 660, vv. 2-3; al-Djāḥiẓ, *Bayān*, iii, 135). After glorifying God and the Prophet, he announced his appointment or read the letter from the caliph and the remainder of his address, if there was a war going on, was exclusively political and often consisted of crude threats. The *khuṭba* was not inseparably connected with the Friday service. The commander-in-chief could at any time issue a summons to the *ṣalāt* and deliver his *khuṭba* with admonitions and orders (see al-Ṭabarī, ii, as above and 260, 297-8, 300, 863, 1179) and it was the same when he left a province (*ibid.*, 241); a governor, who could not preserve his authority with the *khuṭba* was dismissed (*ibid.*, 592). Since war was inseparably associated with early Islam, and since the mosque was the public meeting-place of ruler and people, it often became the scene of warlike incidents. While the governor in his *khuṭba* was issuing orders and admonitions relating to the fighting, cheers and counter-cheers could be uttered (*ibid.*, 238) and councils of war were held in the mosque (al-Ṭabarī, i, 3415; ii, 284; al-Balādhurī, 267). Soon after his election ᶜAbd al-Malik asked from the *minbar* who would take the field against Ibn al-Zubayr, and al-Ḥadjdjādj shouted that he was ready to go (*Chron. Mekka*, ii, 20). After the Battle of the Camel, ᶜAlī sent the booty to the mosque of Baṣra and ᶜĀʾisha looked for another mosque (al-Ṭabarī, i, 3178, 3223). Rowdy scenes occasionally took place in the mosques (al-Kindī, *Wulāt*, 18); Ziyād was stoned on the *minbar* (al-Ṭabarī, ii, 88); one could ride right into the mosque and shout to the governor sitting on the *minbar* (*ibid.*, 682); fighting often took place in and beside the mosque (*ibid.*, 960, 1701 ff.; Wüstenfeld, *Medina*, 13-14). Sometimes for this reason, the governor was surrounded by his bodyguard during the *ṣalāt* or the *minbar* or even clothed in full armour (al-Walīd: al-Ṭabarī, ii, 1234; al-Yaᶜḳūbī, ii, 341; al-Ḥadjdjādj: al-Ṭabarī, ii, 254). *Ṣalāt* and sword were thus closely associated in reality.

It thus came to be the custom for the enemies of the ruler and his party to be cursed in the mosques. This custom continued the old Arab custom of regular campaigns of objurgation between two tribes, but can also be paralleled by the Byzantine ecclesiastical anathematisation of heretics (cf. Becker, *Islamstudien*, i, 485, *Zur Gesch. d. islamischen Kultus*).

The first to introduce the official cursing of the ᶜAlids from the *minbar* of the Kaᶜba is said to have been Khālid al-Ḳasrī (*Chron. Mekka*, ii, 36). The reciprocal cursing of Umayyads and ᶜAlids became general (cf. al-Ṭabarī, ii, 12, 4; *Aghānī*[2], x, 102; Ibn Taghrībirdī, i, 248; see also Lammens, *Moᶜâwia*, 180-1). Like the blessing upon the ruler, it was uttered by the *ḳuṣṣāṣ* (al-Maḳrīzī, iv, 16); it was even recorded in inscriptions in the mosque (Ibn Taghrībirdī, ed. Popper, ii/2, 63, 64; cf. also Mez, *Renaissance*, 61, Eng. tr., 64). As late as 284/897, al-Muᶜtaḍid wanted to restore the anathematisation of Muᶜāwiya from the *minbar* but abandoned the idea (al-Ṭabarī, iii, 2164). Anathemas were also pronounced on other occasions, for example, Sulaymān had al-Ḥadjdjādj cursed (*Chron. Mekka*, ii, 37), and al-Muᶜtamid had Ibn Ṭūlūn solemnly cursed from the *manābir* (al-Ṭabarī, iii, 2048, 5 ff.); and other rulers had Muᶜtazilī heretics cursed from the pulpits (see Mez, *op. cit.*, 198, Eng. tr. 206; cf. against Ibn Taymiyya, Quatremère, *Hist. Sult. Maml.*, ii/2, 256). Ibn Baṭṭūṭa describes the tumultuous scene with thousands of armed men uttering threats in a mosque in Baghdād when a Shīᶜī *khaṭīb* was on the *minbar* (ii, 58).

In was very natural to mention with a blessing upon him the ruler in whose name the Friday *khuṭba* was delivered. Ibn ᶜAbbās, when governor of Baṣra, is said to have been the first to pronounce such a *duᶜāʾ* over ᶜAlī (Ibn Khaldūn, *Muḳaddima*, *faṣl* 37, end); it is not improbable that the custom arose out of the reciprocal objurgations of ᶜAlids and Umayyads; the *ḳuṣṣāṣ*, who had to curse the ᶜAlids in the mosques, used to pray for the Umayyads (al-Maḳrīzī, iv, 17). Under the ᶜAbbāsids, the custom became the usual form of expressing loyalty to the ruler (Ibn Taghrībirdī, ii/1, 151). After the caliph, the name of the local ruler or governor was mentioned (*ibid.*, 156, 161): even in Baghdād in 369/979-80 by order of the caliph al-Ṭāʾiᶜ, the actual ruler ᶜAḍud al-Dawla was mentioned in the *duᶜāʾ* (Ibn Miskawayh, vi, 499; ed. Cairo 1915, 396) and the Būyids, according to al-Muḳaddasī, were generally mentioned in the *khuṭba* even in the remotest parts of the kingdom (this is evident from the above-mentioned expression *khuṭiba lahū*, for which we also find *ᶜalayhi*: see Ibn Ḥawḳal[1], 20; al-Muḳaddasī, 337, 338, 400, 472, 485; cf. *Glossarium*, s.v.). There is also evidence that prayers used to be uttered for the heir-apparent (al-Maḳrīzī, iv, 37; *Kitāb al-Wuzarāʾ*, ed. Amedroz, 420). Under the Mamlūks also, the sultan's heir was mentioned (Quatremère, *Hist. Sult. Maml.*, ii/1, 101; ii/2, 3). Under the Fāṭimids, it was even the custom to call *salām* upon the ruler from the minaret after the *adhān al-fadjr* (al-Maḳrīzī, iv, 45); this also took place under the Mamlūks, e.g. in 696/1297, when Lādjīn was elected (Quatremère, *Hist. Sult. Maml.*, ii/2, 45). The prayer for the sovereign in the *khuṭba* did not find unanimous approval among the learned (see Snouck Hurgronje, *Verspreide Geschriften*, ii, 214-15).

In general, the mosque, and particularly the *minbar*,

was the place where official proclamations were made, of course as early as the time of the Prophet (al-Bukhārī, *Ṣalāt*, *bābs* 70, 71), ʿUthmān's bloodstained shirt was hung upon the *minbar* (al-Ṭabarī, i, 3255); messages from the caliph were read from it (*ibid.*, iii, 2084). Al-Walīd announced from the *minbar* the deaths of two distinguished governors (Ibn Taghrībirdī, i, 242); the results of battles were announced in *khuṭbas* (Yāḳūt, i, 647; *al-ʿIḳd al-farīd*, Cairo 1321, ii, 149-50). In the Fāṭimid and ʿAbbāsid periods also, proclamations, orders, edicts about taxation, etc., by the ruler were announced in the principal mosque (al-Ṭabarī, ii, 40; iii, 2165; Ibn Taghrībirdī, ii/2, 68; al-Maḳrīzī, *Ittiʿāẓ*, ed. Bunz, 87 above; Quatremère, *Hist. Sult. Maml.*, i/2, 89; ii/2, 44, 151); documents appointing the more important officers were also read upon the *minbar* (al-Kindī, *Wulāt*, 589, 599, 603, 604, etc., *passim*; al-Maḳrīzī, ii, 246; iv, 43, 88); frequently the people trooped into the mosque to hear an official announcement (al-Kindī, *Wulāt*, 14; cf. Dozy, *Gesch. d. Mauren in Spanien*, ii, 170).

After the position of the caliph had changed, tradition was so far retained that he still delivered the *khuṭba* in the principal mosque on special occasions, particularly at festivals. Thus the Fāṭimid al-ʿAzīz preached in the Mosque of al-Ḥākim on its completion (al-Maḳrīzī, iv, 55) and in the month of Ramaḍān he preached in the three chief mosques of Cairo, one after the other (*ibid.*, 53, cf. 61-2; Ibn Taghrībirdī, ii/1, 482 ff.; exceptionally also in al-Rāshida: al-Maḳrīzī, iv, 63). The ʿAbbāsid caliph also used to preach at festivals (e.g. al-Rāḍī: Yāḳūt, *Udabāʾ*, ii, 349-50); it was the exception when a zealot like al-Muhtadī in the year 255/869 followed the old custom and preached every Friday (al-Masʿūdī, *Murūdj*, viii, 2 = § 3110). Even the *fainéant* caliph in Egypt preached occasionally (al-Maḳrīzī, iv, 94; Quatremère, *Hist. Sult. Maml.*, ii/1, 138-9). Although the mosque lost its old political importance in its later history, it has never quite lost its character as the place of assembly on occasions of public importance. This is evident from al-Djabartī's history, and even quite recently large meetings have been held in the mosques of Egypt on questions of nationalist politics.

2. The mosque and public administration. The actual work of government was very early transferred from the mosque into a special *dīwān* or *madjlis* (see al-Ṭabarī, *Glossarium*, s.v.) and negotiations were carried on and business frequently done in the *ḳaṣr al-imāra* (cf. al-Ṭabarī, ii, 230-1). But when financial business had to be transacted at public meetings, the mosque was used; of this there is particular evidence from Egypt. Here the director of finance used to sit in the Mosque of ʿAmr and auction the farming out of the domains, with a crier and several financial officers to assist him. Later, the *Dīwān* was transferred to the *Djāmiʿ* of Aḥmad b. Ṭūlūn, but even after 300/912-13, we find Abū Bakr al-Mādharāʾī sitting on such occasions in the Mosque of ʿAmr. Under the Fāṭimids, the vizier Yaʿḳūb b. Killis used first the *dār al-imāra* of the Mosque of Ibn Ṭūlūn (see above); later his own palace and afterwards the caliph's *ḳaṣr* was used (al-Maḳrīzī, i, 131-2). In the same way, in the reign of Muʿāwiya, the Coptic churches were used and the taxation commission took up their offices in them (*Papyrus Erzherzog Rainer, Führer durch die Ausstelling*, no. 577); and Ibn Rusta (*ca.* 290/903) says that the officials in charge of the measurement of the Nile, when they noticed the rising of the river, went at once to the chief mosque and announced it at one *ḥalḳa* after another, at the same time scattering flowers on those seated there (116).

The connection with administration was also seen in the fact that the treasury-chest, the *bayt al-māl* (identical with the *tābūt*; al-Kindī, *Wulāt*, 70, 117) was kept in the mosque. In Fusṭāṭ, Usāma b. Zayd, the director of finance, in 97/715-16 and 99/717-18 built in the Mosque of ʿAmr a *ḳubba* on pillars in front of the *minbar* for the *bayt al-māl* of Egypt. A drawbridge was placed between it and the roof. In the time of Ibn Rusta, it was still possible to move about freely below the *ḳubba*, but in 378-9/988-9 al-ʿAzīz put up a running fountain below it (Ibn Rusta, 116; al-Maḳrīzī, iv, 9, 11, 13; al-Suyūṭī, ii, 136; Yāḳūt, iii, 899). Al-Kindī records an attempt to steal the chest in 145/762 (*Wulāt*, 112-13). In the disturbed period around the year 300/912, the *wālī* al-Nūsharī closed the mosque between the times of *ṣalāt* for the safety of the chest, which was also done in Ibn Rusta's time (al-Kindī, *Wulāt*, 266; Ibn Rusta, 116). New approaches to the *bayt al-māl* were made in 422/1031 from the *khizāna* of the mosque and from the *Dīwān* (al-Maḳrīzī, iv, 13).

In Kūfa, the *buyūt al-amwāl*, at least during the early period, were in the *Dār al-Imāra* (al-Ṭabarī, i, 2489, 2491-2); in the year 38/658-9, during the fighting, it was saved from Baṣra and taken with the *minbar* to the Mosque of al-Ḥuddān (*ibid.*, 3414-15). In Palestine, in the chief mosque of each town, there was a similar arrangement to that in the Mosque of ʿAmr (al-Muḳaddasī, 182). In Damascus the *bayt al-māl* was in the most western of the three *ḳubbas* in the court of the Mosque of the Umayyads; it was of lead and rested on 8 columns (*ibid.*, 157; Ibn Djubayr, 264, 267; Ibn Baṭṭūṭa, i, 200-1); it is still called *ḳubbat el-khazne* ("treasure-cupola", earlier *ḳubbat ʿĀʾisha* (cf. Baedeker, *Palästina und Syrien*). In the time of the two travellers mentioned, the *ḳubba* only contained property of the mosque. Ibn Djubayr saw a similar *ḳubba* in the chief mosque of Ḥarrān and says that it came from the Byzantines (246). In Ādharbāydjān, also by the time of al-Iṣṭakhrī, the Syrian custom had been everywhere introduced (184); in Īrānshahr, in the centre of the court, there was a building with marble colums and doors (al-Muḳaddasī, 316), which perhaps points to a similar state of affairs, and in Armenia, it is recorded that the *bayt al-māl* was kept in the *Djāmiʿ* in the time of the Umayyads as in Miṣr and elsewhere (Ibn Ḥawḳal[1], 241). The *ḳubba* was usually of lead and had an iron door. Ibn al-Ḥādjdj considers it highly illegal to shut off a *dīwān* in a mosque, since this is the same as forbidding entrance to it. This shows that the custom still survived in his time.

Ibn Djubayr's remark about Ḥarrān suggests that here again we have an inheritance from Byzantium. It was probably the building belonging to the *piscina* (cf. above) that the Muslims put to a practical use in this way. For the Byzantines had the treasury (*sakellē*) in the palace, and it is doubtful if the treasure-chambers of the church (*skenophylakion*) were built in this way (cf. F. Dölger, in *Byzantinisches Archiv*, Heft 9 [1927], 26, 34).

3. The mosque as a court of justice. That the Prophet used to settle legal questions in his mosque was natural (see al-Bukhārī, *Aḥkām*, *bābs* 19, 29, etc.; cf. *Ṣalāt*, *bāb* 71; *Khuṣūmāt*, *bāb* 4), but he could also deliver judgments in other places (*ibid.*, *passim*). In *Ḥadīth*, it is recorded that some *ḳāḍīs* of the earlier period (Shurayḥ, al-Shaʿbī, Yaḥyā b. Yaʿmar, Marwān) sat in judgment beside the *minbar*, others (al-Ḥasan, Zurāʿa b. Awfā) on the open square beside the mosque (al-Bukhārī, *Aḥkām*, *bāb* 18). The custom had all the better chance of survival, as churches were used in the same way (Joshua Stylites, ed. Wright, ch.

29; cf. Mez, *Renaissance*, 223, Eng. tr., 224). Sitting in judgment was primarily the business of the ruler, but he had to have assistants and Abū Bakr's *ḳāḍī* is mentioned as assisting ᶜUmar (al-Ṭabarī, i, 2135), and a number of judges appointed by ᶜUmar are mentioned (Ibn Rusta, 227). In the reign of ᶜUthmān, ᶜAbd Allāh b. Masᶜūd is said to have been judge and financial administrator of Kūfa (Ibn Ḳutayba, *Maᶜārif*, ed. Wüstenfeld, 128). On the other hand, we are told that ᶜAbd Allāh b. Nawfal, appointed by Marwān in 42/662, was the first *ḳāḍī* in Islam (al-Ṭabarī, iii, 2477); it is recalled that in the year 132/749-50 the *ḳāḍī* of Medina administered justice in the mosque (*ibid.*, 2505). In Baṣra, we are told that al-Aswad b. Sarīᶜ al-Tamīmī immediately after the building of the mosque (i.e. in the year 14/635) worked in it as *ḳāḍī* (al-Balādhurī, 346). In the early period, ᶜUmar wanted to choose a *ḳāḍī*, who had been already acting as a judge before Islam (al-Kindī, *Wulāt*, 301-2; al-Suyūṭī, ii, 86). Even the Christian poet al-Akhṭal was allowed to act as arbiter in the mosque of Kūfa (see Lammens, *Moᶜâwia*, 435-6).

In Fusṭāṭ, as early as 23/643 or 24/644 by command of ᶜUmar, ᶜAmr b. al-ᶜĀṣ appointed a *ḳāḍī* named Ḳays (al-Suyūṭī, ii, 86; al-Kindī, 300-1). The *ḳāḍī* held his sessions in the Mosque of ᶜAmr but not exclusively there. The *ḳāḍī* Khayr b. Nuᶜaym (120-7/738-45) held his sessions sometimes before his house, sometimes in the mosque, and for Christians on the steps leading up to the mosque (al-Kindī, 351-2). A successor of his (177-84/793-800) invited Christians who had lawsuits into the mosque to be heard (*ibid.*, 391); of another judge (205-11/820-6), it is recorded that he was not allowed to sit in the mosque (*ibid.*, 428). It seems that the *ḳāḍī* could himself choose where he would sit. A judge, officiating in the year 217/832, sat in winter in the great pillared hall, turning his back towards the *ḳibla* wall, and in summer, in the *ṣaḥn* near the western wall (*ibid.*, 443-4). During the Fāṭimid period, the subsidiary building on the north-east of the Mosque of ᶜAmr was reserved for the judge. This judge, called from the year 376/986 onwards *ḳāḍī 'l-ḳuḍāt* (cf. al-Suyūṭī, ii, 91; al-Kindī, 590), sat on Tuesday and Saturday in the mosque and laid down the law (al-Maḳrīzī, ii, 246; iv, 16, 22; cf. al-Kindī, 587, 589; cf. Nāṣir-i Khusraw, tr. Schefer, 149).

In al-Yaᶜḳūbī's time in Baghdād, the judge of the east city used to sit in its chief mosque (*Buldān*, 245), in Damascus the vice-*ḳāḍī* in the 4th/10th century had a special *riwāḳ* in the Mosque of the Umayyads (al-Muḳaddasī, 158), and the notaries (*al-shurūṭiyyūn*) also sat at the Mosque of the Umayyads at the Bāb al-Sāᶜāt (*ibid.*, 17). In Naysābūr, every Monday and Thursday, the *madjlis al-ḥukm* was held in a special mosque (*ibid.*, 328). In course of time, the judge was given a *madjlis al-ḥukm* of his own (cf. al-Suyūṭī, ii, 96), and in 279/892 al-Muᶜtaḍid wanted to forbid the *ḳāḍīs* to hold sessions in the mosques (Ibn Taghrībirdī, ii/1, 87 above; perhaps, however, we should read *ḳāṣṣ*: see Goldziher, *Muh. Stud.*, ii, 164, n. 4). Justice was also administered in the *dār al-ᶜadl* (Quatremère, *Hist. Sult. Maml.*, ii/2, 79). But the administration of justice did not at once lose all connection with the mosque. Under the Fāṭimids, the custom had been introduced that the *ḳāḍī* should hold sittings in his house, but Ibn al-ᶜAwwām, appointed just after 400/1009-10, held them either in the *Djāmiᶜ* at the *Bayt al-Māl* or in a side-room (al-Kindī, 612; cf. Ibn Taghrībirdī, ed. Popper, ii/2, 69; al-Ḳalḳashandī, *Ṣubḥ al-aᶜshā*ʾ, iii, 487: for 439/1046, see Nāsir-i Khusraw, ed. Schefer, text, 51, tr. 149). In Mecca, *the dār al-ḳāḍī* was in direct connection with the mosque (Ibn Djubayr, 104). In the 8th/14th century, Ibn Baṭṭūṭa attended a court presided over by an eminent jurist in a mosque (*madrasa*) in Shīrāz (ii, 55, 63; cf. also *Madkhal*, ii, 54 below), and in Damascus the Shāfiᶜī chief *ḳāḍī* held his sessions in the ᶜĀdiliyya Madrasa (so Ibn Khallikān, in Quatremère, *Hist. Sult. Maml.*, ii/1, 22; cf. also for Egypt: *ibid.*, 87, ii/2, 253), the vice-*ḳāḍīs* sat in the Ẓāhiriyya Madrasa (Ibn Baṭṭūṭa, i, 218). The judgment might even be put into execution in the *madrasa* (*ibid.*, 220). During the Mamlūk period in Egypt, we occasionally find a small mosque being used as a *madjlis* for judges (al-Maḳrīzī, iv, 270; Ibn Duḳmāḳ, 98 above); Ibn Khaldūn held legal sittings in the Madrasa al-Ṣāliḥiyya (*ᶜIbar*, vii, 453).

A *muftī*, especially in the large mosques, was also frequently appointed; he sat at definite times in a *ḥalḳa li 'l-fatwā*, e.g. in Cairo (al-Ḳazwīnī, in al-Suyūṭī, i, 182; Djalāl al-Dīn, *ibid.*, 187), in Tunis (al-Zarkashī, *Chronicle*, tr. Fagnan, in *Rec. Mém. Soc. Arch. Constantine*, xxi [1895], 197, 202, 218, 248). In Baghdād, Abū Bakr al-Dīnawarī (d. 405/1014-15) was the last to give *fatwās* in the Mosque of al-Manṣūr according to the *madhhab* of Sufyān al-Thawrī (Ibn Taghrībirdī, ed. Popper, ii/2, 120).

F. The administration of the mosque

1. Finances. The earliest mosques were built by the rulers of the various communities, and the members of the community did all the work necessary in connection with the primitive mosques. The later mosques as a rule were erected by rulers, *amīrs*, high officials or other rich men in their private capacity and maintained by them. The erection of the mosque of Ibn Ṭūlūn cost its builder 120,000 *dīnārs*, the Mosque of Muʾayyad 110,000 (al-Maḳrīzī, iv, 32, 137, 138). The upkeep of the mosque was provided for by estates made over as endowments (*waḳf*, *ḥabs*) (cf. thereon besides the *fiḳh* books, I. Krcsmárik, *Das Waḳfrecht*, in *ZDMG*, xlv [1891], 511-76; E. Mercier, *Le code du hobous ou ouakf selon la législation musulmane*, 1899). In the 3rd/9th century we thus hear of houses which belonged to the mosque and were let by them (*Papyrus Erzherzog Rainer, Führer*, nos. 773, 837), and Ibn Ṭūlūn handed over a large number of houses as an endowment for his mosque and hospital (al-Maḳrīzī, iv, 83). This custom was taken over from the Christians by the Muslims (see Becker, in *Isl.*, ii [1911], 404). According to al-Maḳrīzī, estates were not given as *waḳf* endowments until Muḥammad Abū Bakr al-Mādharāʾī (read thus) bequeathed Birkat al-Ḥabash and Suyūṭ as endowments (about 300/912-13; this was however cancelled by the Fāṭimids again (*ibid.*). Al-Ḥākim made large endowments not only for his own, but also for mosques previously in existence, such as the Azhar, al-Ḥākimī, Dār al-ᶜIlm and Djāmiᶜ al-Maḳs and Djāmiᶜ Rāshida; the endowments consisted of dwelling-houses, shops, mills, a *ḳaysāriyya* and *ḥawānīt*, and the document (*ibid.*, 50-1) specifies how and for what purposes the revenues are to be distributed. Baths were also given as endowments for mosques (*ibid.*, 76, for 529/1135; cf. 81 for the year 543/1148-9). Ṣalāḥ al-Dīn granted lands to his *madāris*: in 566/1170-1, for example, a *ḳaysāriyya* to the Ḳamḥiyya and a *ḍayᶜa* in al-Fayyūm, and the teachers received wheat from al-Fayyūm; in the same year he endowed the Nāṣiriyya with goldsmiths' shops and a village (*ibid.*, 193-4; cf. another document, 196-7). During the Mamlūk period also, estates were given as endowments (for documents of this period, see van Berchem, *CIA*, i, nos. 247, 252, 528; Moberg, in *MO*, xii [1918], 1 ff.; *JA*, ser. 9, iii, 264-6; ser. 11, x, 158 ff., 222 f.; xii, 195 ff., 256 ff., 363 ff.). They

were often a considerable distance apart: the mosques in Egypt often had estates in Syria (van Berchem, *CIA*, i, no. 247; al-Maḳrīzī, vi, 107, 137). Not only were mosques built and endowed, but already existing ones were given new rooms for teachers, *minbars*, stipends for Ḳurʾān reciters, teachers, etc. There were often special endowments for the salaries of the *imām* and the *muʿadhdhins*, for the support of visitors, for blankets, food, etc. (see Ibn Djubayr, 277 with reference to the Mosque of the Umayyads). The endowments, and the purpose for which they might be used, were precisely laid down in the grant and the document attested in the court of justice by the *ḳāḍī* and the witnesses (cf. al-Maḳrīzī, iv, 50, 196 below). The text was also often inscribed on the wall of the mosque (cf. *ibid.*, 76; the above-mentioned inscriptions amongst others. For documents from Tashkent, see *RMM*, xiii [1911], 278 ff.). Certain conditions might be laid down, e.g. in a *madrasa* that no Persian should be appointed there (al-Maḳrīzī, iv, 202 below), or that the teacher could not be dismissed or some such condition (van Berchem, *CIA*, i, no. 201); that no women could enter (*JA*, ser. 9, iii, 389); that no Christian, Jew or Ḥanbalī could enter the building (*ibid.*, 405); etc. Endowments were often made with stipulations for the family of the founder or other purposes. That mosques could also be burdened with expenses is evident from an inscription in Edfū of the year 797/1395 (van Berchem, *CIA*, i, no. 539). If a mosque was founded without sufficient endowment, it decayed (e.g. al-Maḳrīzī, iv, 115, 201, 203) or else the stipends were reduced (*ibid.*, 251), but in the larger mosques as a rule the rulers provided new endowments. According to al-Māwardī, there were also special "Sultan mosques" which were directly under the patronage of the caliph and their officials paid from the *bayt al-māl* (*al-Aḥkām al-sulṭāniyya*, ed. Enger, 172 above, 176 above).

Just as the *bayt al-māl* of the state was kept in the mosque, so was the mosque's own property kept in it, e.g. the *kanz* or *khizānat al-Kaʿba*, which is mentioned in ʿUmar's time and may be presumed to have existed under his predecessors (al-Balādhurī, 43 above; *Chron. Mekka*, i, 307, ii, 14). The *Bayt Māl al-Djamiʿ* in Damascus was in a *ḳubba* in the *ṣaḥn* (al-Muḳaddasī, 157; Ibn Djubayr, 267; Ibn Baṭṭūṭa, i, 201. cf. for Medina, Wüstenfeld, *Medina*, 86). Rich men also had their private treasure-chambers in the mosque (see above, I. E. 2), as used to be the case with the Temple at Jerusalem (see E. Schürer, *Gesch. d. jüd. Volkes*[4], ii, 1907, 322-8; F. Cumont, *Fouilles de Doura-Europos*, 1926, 405-6).

2. Administration. As *Imām* of the Muslim community, the caliph had the mosques under his charge. This was also the case with the sultan, governor or other ruler who represented the caliph in every respect. The administration of the mosques could not however be directly controlled by the usual government offices. By its endowment, the mosque became an object *sui generis* and was withdrawn from the usual state or private purposes. Their particular association with religion gave the *ḳāḍīs* special influence, and, on the other hand, the will of the testator continued to prevail. These three factors decided the administration of the mosque, but the relation between them was not always clear.

a. Administration of the separate mosques. The mosque was usually in charge of a *nāẓir* or *walī* who looked after its affairs. The founder was often himself the *nāẓir* or he chose another and after his death, his descendants took charge or whoever was appointed by him in the foundation charter. In the older period, the former was the rule and it is said to have applied especially in the case of chief mosques, if we may believe Nāṣir-i Khusraw, according to whom al-Ḥākim paid the descendants of Ibn Ṭūlūn 30,000 *dīnārs* for the mosque and 5,000 for the minaret, and similarly to the descendants of ʿAmr b. al-ʿĀṣ 100,000 *dīnārs* for the Mosque of ʿAmr (*Safarnāma*, ed. Schefer, text 39-40, tr. 146, 148). In 378/988 we read of an administrator (*mutawallī*) of the mosque in Jerusalem (al-Maḳrīzī, iv, 11). In the case of mosques and *madāris* founded during the Mamlūk period, it is often expressly mentioned that the administration is to remain in the hands of the descendants of the founder, e.g. in the case of a mosque founded by Baybars (al-Maḳrīzī, iv, 89), in the Djāmiʿ Maḳs when the vizier al-Maḳsī renovated it (*ibid.*, 66), the Ṣāḥibiyya (*ibid.*, 205), and the Ḳarāsunḳuriyya (*ibid.*, 232), etc.; so also in the Badriyya in Jerusalem ("to the best of the descendants", cf. van Berchem, *CIA*, ii/1, 129). Other cases are also found. Sometimes an *amīr* or official was administrator, e.g. in the Muʾayyad (al-Maḳrīzī, iv, 140), the Ṭaybarsiyya (*ibid.*, 224), the Azhar (*ibid.*, 54-5) or the Mosque of Ibn Ṭūlūn (al-Ḳalḳashandī, *Ṣubḥ*, xi, 159-62). In Djamāl al-Dīn's *madrasa*, it was always the *kātib al-sirr* (al-Maḳrīzī, iv, 256), in the *khānaḳāh* of Baybars the *khāzindār* and his successors (van Berchem, *CIA*, i, no. 252); but it was more frequently a *ḳāḍī*; for example, in the mosque of Baybars just mentioned, the Ḥanafī *ḳāḍī* was to take charge after the descendants (al-Maḳrīzī, iv, 89); in the Āḳbughawiyya, the Shāfiʿī *ḳāḍī* was appointed but his descendants were expressly excluded (*ibid.*, 225). In the Mosque of the Umayyads, during the Mamlūk period the Shāfiʿī chief *ḳāḍī* was as a rule the *nāẓir* (al-Ḳalḳashandī, iv, 191), and thus also in the Nāṣir mosque in Cairo (*ibid.*, xi, 262-4). In this city, we find during the Mamlūk period that *amīrs* and *ḳāḍīs* alternately acted as *nāẓirs* in the large mosques (e.g. the Mosque of Ibn Ṭūlūn, al-Maḳrīzī, iv, 42). Cases are also found, however, in which descendants of the founder unsuccessfully claimed the office of *nāẓir* (al-Maḳrīzī, iv, 218, 255). This was the result of the increasing power of the *ḳāḍīs* (see below). In the *madāris*, the *nāẓir* was often also the leading professor; the two offices were hereditary (*ibid.*, 204, the Ṣāḥibiyya al-Bahāʾiyya; and 238 above, the Djamāliyya). In Tustar, a descendant of Sahl as *nāẓir* and teacher conducted a *madrasa* with the help of four slaves (Ibn Baṭṭūṭa, ii, 25-6).

The *nāẓir* managed the finances and other business of the mosque. Sometimes he had a fixed salary (in Baybars' *khānaḳāh*, 500 *dirhams* a month, van Berchem, *CIA*, i, 252; in the Dulāmiyya in Damascus in 847/1443-4, only 60 *dirhams* a month, *JA*, ser. 9, iii, 261), but the revenues of the mosque were often applied to his personal use. His control of the funds of the mosque was however often limited by the central commission for endowments (see below). The *nāẓir* might also see to any necessary increase of the endowments. He appointed the staff and he fixed their pay (cf. e.g. al-Maḳrīzī, iv, 41). He could also interfere in questions not arising out of the business side of administration; for example, the *amīr* Sawdūb, the *nāẓir* of the Azhar in 818/1415-16, ejected about 750 poor people from the mosque. He was however thrown into prison for this by the sultan (*ibid.*, 54). Generally speaking, the *nāẓir*'s powers were considerable. In 784/1382 a *nāẓir* in the Azhar decided that the property of a *mudjāwir*, who had died without heirs, should be distributed among the other students (*ibid.*, 54). In Mecca, according to Ḳuṭb al-Dīn, the

Nāẓir al-Ḥarām was in charge of the great festival of the *mawlid* of the Prophet (12 Rabīᶜ I) and distributed robes of honour in the mosque on this occasion (*Chron. Mekka*, iii, 349). In the Azhar, no *nāẓir* was appointed after about 493/1100 but a learned man was appointed Shaykh al-Azhar, principal and administrator of the mosque (Sulaymān Raṣad al-Zayyātī, *Kanz al-djawhar fī taʾrīkh al-Azhar*, 123 ff.). Conditions were similar in Mecca in the late 19th century (Snouck Hurgronje, *Mekka*, ii, 235-6, 252-3).

As we have seen, *ḳāḍīs* were often *nāẓirs* of mosques. This was especially the case in the *madāris*, where the *ḳāḍīs* were often teachers (cf. al-Maḳrīzī, iv, 209, 219, 222, 238, etc.); the *ḳāḍīs* were particularly anxious to get the principal offices in the large schools (cf. al-Ḳalḳashandī, xi, 235). Their influence was however further increased by the fact that, if a *nāẓir* qualified by the terms of the founder's will no longer existed, the *ḳāḍī* of the *madhhab* in question stepped into his place (cf. *ZDMG*, xlv [1897], 552). By this rule, which often gave rise to quarrels between the different *ḳāḍīs* (e.g. al-Maḳrīzī, iv, 218, the Ẓāhiriyya), a *ḳāḍī* could accumulate a larger number of offices and "milk the endowments" (*ibid.*, iii, 364). Sometimes their management was so ruthless that the schools soon declined (e.g. the Ṣāhibiyya and the Djamāliyya, al-Maḳrīzī, iv, 204-5, 238). They also exercised influence through the committee of management of the mosque.

b. Centralisation in the management of the mosques. The large mosques occupied a special position in the Muslim lands, because the caliph had to interest himself particularly in them, especially those of Mecca and Medina, where the rulers and their governors built extensions and executed renovations (cf. *Chron. Mekka*, i, 145; iii, 83 ff.). During the ᶜAbbāsid period, the *ḳāḍī* occasionally plays a certain part in this connection; for example al-Mahdī (158-69/775-85), presented the *ḳāḍī* with the necessary money to extend and repair the Meccan mosque (*ibid.*, i, 312; ii, 43). In 263/877, al-Muwaffaḳ ordered the governor of Mecca to undertake repairs at the Kaᶜba (*ibid.*, ii, 200-1). In 271/1884-5, the governor and the *ḳāḍī* of Mecca co-operated to get money from al-Muwaffaḳ for repairs, and they saw the work through (*ibid.*, iii, 136-7). In 281/894, the *ḳāḍī* of Mecca wrote to the vizier of al-Muᶜtaḍid about the *Dār al-Nadwa* and backed up his request by sending a deputation of the staff there (*sadana*). The caliph then ordered the vizier to arrange the matter through the *ḳāḍī* of Baghdād and a man was sent to Mecca to take charge of the work (*ibid.*, iii, 144 ff.).

The importance of the *ḳāḍī* was based primarily on his special knowledge in the field of religion. A zealous *ḳāḍī* like al-Ḥārith b. Miskīn in Cairo (237-45/851-9) forbade the *ḳurrāʾ* of a mosque to recite the Ḳurʾān melodiously; he also had the *maṣāḥif* in the mosque of ᶜAmr inspected and appointed an *amīn* to take charge of them (al-Kindī, *Wulāt*, 469). After the building of the Ṭūlūnid mosque, a commission was appointed under the *ḳāḍī 'l-ḳuḍāt* to settle the *ḳibla* of the mosque (al-Maḳrīzī, iv, 21-2). But at a quite early date they also obtained a say in the management of the funds. The first *ḳāḍī* to lay his hands on the *aḥbās* was Tawba b. Namir al-Ḥaḍramī; while hitherto every endowment had been administered by itself by the children of the testator or someone appointed by him, in 118/736 Tawba brought about the centralisation of all endowments and a large *dīwān* was created for the purpose (al-Kindī, 346). How this system of centralisation worked is not clear at first, but it was carried through under the Fāṭimids.

Al-Muᶜizz created a special *dīwān al-aḥbās* and made the chief *ḳāḍī* head of it as well as of the *djawāmiᶜ wa 'l-mashāhid* (al-Maḳrīzī, iv, 83 and 75; cf. al-Kindī, 585, 587, 589, according to whom al-ᶜAzīz specially appointed the chief *ḳāḍī* over the two *djāmiᶜs*), and a special *bayt al-māl* was instituted for it in 363/974; a yearly revenue of 150,00 *dirhams* was guaranteed; anything left over went to form a capital fund. All payments were made through his office after being certified by the administration of the mosque (al-Maḳrīzī, iv, 83-4). The mosques were thus administered by the *ḳāḍīs*, directly under the caliph. The *dīwān al-birr wa 'l-ṣadaḳa* in Baghdād (Mez, *Renaissance*, 72, Eng. tr., 80) perhaps served similar purposes.

Al-Ḥākim reformed the administration of the mosques. In 403/1012-13 he had an investigation made, and when it proved that 800 (or 830) had no income (*ghalla*), he made provision for them by a payment of 9,220 *dirhams* monthly from the *Bayt al-Māl*; he also made 405 new endowments (of estates) for the officials of the mosque (al-Maḳrīzī, iv, 84, 264). Under the Fāṭimids, the *ḳāḍīs* used to inspect all the mosques and *mashāhid* in and around Cairo at the end of Ramaḍān and compare them with their inventories (*ibid.*, 84). The viziers of the Fāṭimids, who also had the title *ḳāḍī*, did much for the mosques (Djawhar, Yaᶜḳūb b. Killis, Badr al-Djamālī, cf. van Berchem, *CIA*, i, nos. 11, 576, 631).

Under the Ayyūbids, conditions were the same as under the Fāṭimids. The *dīwān al-aḥbās* was under the *ḳāḍīs* (al-Maḳrīzī, iv, 84). Ṣalāḥ al-Dīn gave a great deal to the mosques, especially the *madāris*: 20,000 *dirhams* a day is a figure given (*ibid.*, 117). When Ibn Djubayr says that the sultan paid the salaries of the officials of the mosques and schools of Alexandria, Cairo and Damascus 43, 52, 275), he must really mean the *Dīwān* already mentioned.

The same conditions continued for a time under the Mamlūks. In the time of Baybars, for example, the chief *ḳāḍī* Tādj al-Dīn was *nāẓir al-aḥbās*. He caused the Mosque of ᶜAmr to be renovated, and when the funds from the endowments were exhausted, the sultan helped him from the *Bayt al-Māl* (al-Maḳrīzī, iv, 14); after conferring with experts, the chief *ḳāḍī* forbade a water-supply brought by Ṣalāḥ al-Dīn into the mosque (*ibid.*, 14; al-Suyūṭī, ii, 137). In 687 the chief *ḳāḍī* Taḳī al-Dīn complained to Ḳalāwūn that the ᶜAmr and Azhar mosques were falling into ruins, while the *aḥbās* were much reduced. The sultan would not however permit their restoration but entrusted the repairs of the mosques to certain *amīrs*, one to each (al-Maḳrīzī, iv, 14, 15). This principle was several times applied in later times, and the *amīrs* frequently gained influence at the expense of the *ḳāḍīs*. Thus after the earthquake of 707/1303 (cf. thereon Quatremère, *Hist. Sult. Maml.*, ii/2, 214 ff.), the mosques were allotted to *amīrs*, who had to see that they were rebuilt (al-Maḳrīzī, iv, 15, 53). From the middle of the 7th/13th century, we often find *amīrs* as administrators of the chief mosques. The *ḳāḍī* had however obtained so much authority that he was conceded "a general supervision of all matters affecting the endowments of his *madhhab*" (al-ᶜUmarī, *al-Taᶜrīf bi 'l-muṣṭalaḥ al-sharīf*, 117; cf. *ZDMG*, xlv [1891], 559); according to this theory the *ḳāḍī* could intervene to stop abuses. In Syria in 660/1262 Ibn Khallikān became *ḳāḍī* over the whole area between al-ᶜArīsh and the Euphrates and superintendent of *waḳfs*, mosques, *madrasas*, etc. (Quatremère, *Hist. Sult. Maml.*, i/1, 170).

Sultan Baybars reformed these endowments and

restored the office of *nāẓir al-awḳāf* or *nāẓir al-aḥbās al-mabrūra* or *n. djihāt al-birr* (al-Ḳalḳashandī, iv, 34, 38; v, 465; ix, 256; xi, 252, 257; cf. Khalīl al-Ẓāhirī, *Zubdat kashf al-mamālik*, ed. Ravaisse, 109). According to al-Maḳrīzī, the endowments were distributed among the Mamlūks in three departments (*djihāt*): 1. *djihāt al-aḥbās*, managed by an *amīr*, the *Dawādār*: this looked after the lands of the mosques, in 740/1339-40, in all 130,000 *faddāns*; 2. *djihāt al-awḳāf al-ḥukmiyya bi-Miṣr wa 'l-Ḳāhira*, which administered dwelling-houses; it was managed by the Shāfiʿī *ḳāḍī 'l-ḳuḍāt*, with the title *Nāẓir al-Awḳāf*. This department came to an end in the time of al-Malik al-Nāṣir Faradj because an *amīr*, supported by the opinion of the Ḥanafī chief *ḳāḍī*, spent a great deal and misused the funds; 3. *djihāt al-awḳāf al-ahliyya*, comprised all the endowments which still had particular *nāẓirs*, either descendants of the testator or officials of the sultan and the *ḳāḍī*. The *amīrs* seized their lands and Barḳūḳ, before he became sultan, sought in vain to remedy the evil by appointing a commission. The endowments in general disappeared somewhat later because the ruling *amīrs* seized them (al-Maḳrīzī, iv, 83-6). In modern times, as a rule, endowments in Muslim lands have been combined under a special ministry, a *Wizārat al-Awḳāf*.

To be distinguished from the administrators of the mosque is the *nāẓir* who is only concerned with the supervision of the erection of mosques. Anyone could be entrusted with the building of a mosque (e.g. al-Maḳrīzī, iv, 92). Under the Mamlūks, there was also a clerk of works, *mutawallī shadd al-ʿamāʾir* or *nāẓir al-ʿimāra*: he was the overseer of the builders (*ibid.*, 102; see *Zubdat kashf al-mamālik*, ed. Ravaisse, 115, cf. 109; van Berchem, *CIA*, i, 742, no. 751).

The caliph or the ruler of the country was in this, as in other matters, supreme. As we have seen, he intervened in the administration and directed it as he wished. He was also able to interfere in the internal affairs of the mosque, if necessary through his usual officers. In 253/867 after the rising in the Fayyūm, the chief of police issued strict orders by which it was forbidden to say the *basmala* aloud in the mosque; the number of prayers in the month of Ramaḍān was cut down, the *adhān* from the minaret forbidden, etc. (*Papyrus Erzherzog Rainer*, *Führer*, 788). In the year 294/908, the governor ʿĪsā al-Nūsharī had the Mosque of ʿAmr closed except at the *ṣalāts*, because the *bayt al-māl* was kept in it, which however produced protests from the people (al-Maḳrīzī, iv, 11; al-Kindī, *Wulāt*, 266; Ibn Rusta, 116). Many similar examples could be mentioned, especially during periods of unrest. In 205/821 the *nāʾib*, in conjunction with the *ḳāḍīs*, revised the budget of the Mosque of the Umayyads and made financial reforms (*JA*, ser. 9, vii, 220). The *adhān* formulae were laid down in edicts by the ruler (al-Maḳrīzī, iv, 44, 45). In the year 323/935 the vizier in Baghdād had a man whipped who had recited a variant text of the Ḳurʾān in the *miḥrāb*, after he had been heard in his defence in the presence of the *ḳāḍīs* and learned men (Yāḳūt, *Udabāʾ*, vi, 300). The importance of the sovereign in connection with the mosque depended on his personality. As a rule, he recognised the authority of the regular officials. When, for example, al-Khaṭīb al-Baghdādī asked the caliph al-Ḳāʾim for authority to read *ḥadīth* in the mosque of al-Manṣūr, the latter referred the question to the *naḳīb al-nuḳabāʾ* (Yaḳūt, *Udabāʾ*, i, 246-7; cf. Wüstenfeld, *Schâfiʿi*, iii, 280).

The consecration of the mosque was attended by certain ceremonies. When, for example, the midday worship was conducted for the first time in the Djāmiʿ al-Ṣāliḥ in Cairo, a representative from Baghdād was present (al-Maḳrīzī, iv, 81). At the consecration of the Mosque of Ibn Ṭūlūn, the builder gave al-Rabīʿ b. Sulaymān, a pupil of al-Shāfiʿī, who lectured on *ḥadīth* there, a purse of 1,000 *dīnārs* (al-Suyūṭī, ii, 139). Al-Maḳrīzī describes the consecration ceremony at several mosques. In the Mosque of al-Muʾayyad the sultan was present seated on a throne surrounded by his officers; the basin of the *ṣaḥn* was filled with sugar and *ḥalwa*, the people ate and drank, lectures were given, then the *ṣalāt* was read and *khuṭba* delivered and the sultan distributed robes of honour among the officials of the mosques and Ṣūfīs (al-Maḳrīzī, iv, 139); similarly at the Ẓahiriyya in 662/1264 where poems were also recited: cf. Quatremère, *Hist. Sult. Maml.*, i/1, 228), Madrasat Djamāl al-Dīn, in 811/1408-9; al-Ṣarghitmishiyya, 757 (al-Makrīzī, iv, 217-18, 253, 256).

G. The personnel of the mosque.

1. The *Imām*. From the earliest days of Islam, the ruler was the leader of the *ṣalāt*; he was *imām* as leader in war, head of the government and leader of the common *ṣalāt*. The governors of provinces thus became leaders of the *ṣalāt* and heads of the *kharādj*, and when a special financial official took over the fiscal side, the governor was appointed *ʿalā 'l-ṣalāt wa 'l-ḥarb*. He had to conduct ritual prayer, especially the Friday *ṣalāt*, on which occasion he also delivered the *khuṭba*. If he was prevented, the chief of police, *ṣāḥib al-shurṭa*, was his *khalīfa* (cf. al-Maḳrīzī, iv, 83). ʿAmr b. al-ʿĀṣ permitted the people of the villages to celebrate the two festivals, while the Friday divine service could only take place under those qualified to conduct it (who could punish and impose duties; *ibid.*, 7). This was altered under the ʿAbbāsids. The caliph no longer regularly conducted the *ṣalāts* (after the conquest of the Persians; al-Maḳrīzī, iv, 45), and ʿAnbasa b. Isḥāḳ, the last Arab governor of Egypt (238-42/852-6), was also the last *amīr* to conduct the *ṣalāt* in the *djāmiʿ*. An *imām*, paid out of the *bayt al-māl*, was now appointed (*ibid.*, 83), but the governor still continued to be formally appointed *ʿalā 'l-ṣalāt*. Henceforth, the ruler only exceptionally conducted the service, for example, the Fāṭimids on ceremonial occasions, especially in the month of Ramaḍān (Ibn Taghrībirdī, ed. Juynboll, ii, 482 ff.; al-Ḳalḳashandī, iii, 509 ff.); in many individual mosques, probably the most prominent man conducted the service; according to the *ḥadīth*, the one with the best knowledge of the Ḳurʾān and, failing him, the eldest, should officiate (al-Bukhārī, *Adhān*, *bābs* 46, 49).

The *imām* appointed was chosen from among those learned in religious matters; he was often a Hāshimite (Mez, *Renaissance*, 147, Eng. tr., 150); he might at the same time be a *ḳāḍī* or his *nāʾib* (see al-Ḳindī, 575, 589; Ibn Baṭṭūṭa, i, 276-7). During the *ṣalāt* he stood beside the *miḥrāb*; al-Muḳaddasī mentions the anomaly that in Syria one performed one's *ṣalāt* "in front of the *imām*" (202). He could also stand on an elevated position; on one occasion Abū Hurayra conducted the *ṣalāt* in the Meccan mosque from the roof (al-Bukhārī, *Ṣalāt*, *bāb* 17). In Mecca, in Ibn Djubayr's time, each of the four recognised *madhāhib* (with the Zaydīs in addition) had an *imām*; they conducted the *ṣalāt*, one after the other each in his place, in the following order: Shāfiʿīs, Mālikīs, Ḥanafīs and Ḥanbalīs; they only performed the *ṣalāt al-maghrib* together; in Ramaḍān, they held the *tarāwīḥ* in different places in the mosque, which was also often conducted by the *ḳurrāʾ* (*Riḥla*, 101, 102, 143-4). This is still the case; very frequently one performs the *ṣalāt*, not after the *imām* of one's own *madhhab* (Snouck Hurgronje, *Mekka*, ii, 79-80). In Jerusalem, according to Mudjīr al-Dīn, the order was: Mālikīs, S̲h̲āfiʿīs, Ḥanafīs and Ḥanbalīs, who prayed each in their own part of the Ḥaram; in Hebron the order was the same (Sauvaire, Hist. Jér. et Hébron, 136-7). In Ramaḍān, extraordinary imāms were appointed (ibid., 138).

When the imām no longer represented a political office, each mosque regularly had one. He had to maintain order and was in general in charge of the divine services in the mosque. In al-Muḳaddasī's time the imām of the Mosque of ʿAmr read a djuzʾ of the Ḳurʾān every morning after the ṣalāt (205). It was his duty to conduct every ṣalāt, which is only valid fī djamāʿa. He must conform to the standards laid down in the law; but it is disputed whether the ṣalāt is invalid in the opposite case. According to some, the leader of the Friday ṣalāt should be a different man from the leader of the five daily ṣalāts (al-Māwardī, al-Aḥkām al-sulṭāniyya, ed. Enger, 171; Ibn al-Ḥādjdj, Madkhal, ii, 41, 43 ff., 50, 73 ff.; al-Subkī, Muʿīd al-niʿam, ed. Myhrman, 163-4; for ḥadīt̲h̲s, see Wensinck, Handbook, 109-10). Many misgivings against payment being made for religious services were held by certain authorities, who quoted in support of their view a saying of Abū Ḥanīfa (al-Muḳaddasī, 127).

2. The K̲h̲aṭīb or preacher [see KHAṬĪB].
3. The Ḳāṣṣ and Ḳāriʾ. On these, see above, I. C. 3. Sometimes, in later usage, wāʿiẓ is used of the official speaker, very like the khaṭīb (cf. Ibn Baṭṭūṭa, iii, 9), while al-ḳāṣṣ is only applied to the street story-teller (al-Subkī, Muʿīd al-niʿam, 161-2). The ḳurrāʾ were also frequently appointed to madrasas and particularly to mausoleums (al-Maḳrīzī, iv, 223; Yāḳūt, iv, 509; al-Subkī, 162; van Berchem, CIA, i, no. 252).

4. The Muʾad̲h̲d̲h̲in. According to most traditions, the office of muʾad̲h̲d̲h̲in was instituted in the year 1, according to others only after the isrāʾ, in the year 2, according to some weak traditions, while Muḥammad was still in Mecca. At first, the people came to the ṣalāt without being summoned. Trumpets (būḳ) were blown and rattles (nāḳūs) used, or fires lit after the custom of Jews, Christians and Mad̲j̲ūs. ʿAbd Allāh b. Zayd learned the ad̲h̲ān formula in a dream; it was approved by the Prophet and when Bilāl proclaimed it, it was found that ʿUmar had also learned the same procedure in a dream (Ibn His̲h̲ām, 357-8; al-Diyārbakrī, i, 404-5; al-Buk̲h̲ārī, Ad̲h̲ān, bāb 1; al-Zurḳānī, i, 121 ff.). There are also variants of the story, e.g. that the Prophet and ʿUmar had the vision, or Abū Bakr or seven or fourteen of the Anṣār. According to some, the Prophet learned it at the miʿrād̲j̲ from Gabriel, hence the introduction of the ad̲h̲ān is dated after the isrāʾ; among the suggestions made, the hoisting of a flag is mentioned (Sīra Ḥalabiyya, ii, 100 ff.). Noteworthy is a tradition which goes back to Ibn Saʿd, according to which at ʿUmar's suggestion, at first a munādī, Bilāl, was sent out who called in the streets: al-ṣalāta djāmiʿatan. Only later were other possibilities discussed, but the method already in use was confirmed by the dream, only with another formula, the one later used al-Diyārbakrī, i, 404; Sīra Ḥalabiyya, ii, 100-1). According to this account, the consideration of other methods would be a secondary episode, and probably the tradition in general represents a later attitude to the practices of other religions. But in Islam, other methods were certainly used. In Fās, a flag was hung out in the minarets and a lamp at night (JA, ser. 11, xii, 341). The flag is also found in the legend of the origin of the practice.

The public crier was a well-known institution among the Arabs. Among the tribes and in the towns, important proclamations and invitations to general assemblies were made by criers. This crier was called munādī or muʾad̲h̲d̲h̲in (Sīra Ḥalabiyya, ii, 170; Lammens, La Mecque, 62 ff., 146; idem, Berceau, i, 229 n.; idem, Moʿāwia, 150). Ad̲h̲ān therefore means proclamation, sūra IX, 3, and ad̲h̲d̲h̲ana, muʾad̲h̲d̲h̲in, sūra VII, 70, "to proclaim" and "crier". Munādī (al-Buk̲h̲ārī, Farḍ al-khums, bāb 15) and muʾad̲h̲d̲h̲in (ibid., Ṣawm, bāb 69; Ṣalāt, bāb 10 = Djizya, bāb 16; Sīra Ḥalabiyya, ii, 270) are names given to a crier used by the Prophet or Abū Bakr for such purposes. Official proclamations were regularly made by criers (cf. al-Ṭabarī, iii, 2131, 3). Sadjāḥ and Musaylima used a muʾad̲h̲d̲h̲in to summon the people to their prayers (al-Ṭabarī, i, 1919, 1932; cf. Annali dell' Islām, i, 410; 638-9). It was therefore a very natural thing for Muḥammad to assemble the believers to common prayer through a crier (nādā liʾl or ilā ʾl-ṣalāt, sūra V, 63; lxii, 9); the summons is called nidāʾ and ad̲h̲d̲h̲ān, the crier munādī (al-Buk̲h̲ārī, Wuḍūʾ, bāb 5; Ad̲h̲ān, bāb 7) and muʾad̲h̲d̲h̲in; the two names are used quite indiscriminately (e.g. ibid., Wuḍūʾ, bāb 5; al-Ṭabarī, ii, 297 sq.). Munādī ʾl-ṣalāt, al-Muḳaddasī, 182, 12, also ṣāʾiḥ "crier" is used (al-Ṭabarī, iii, 861; Chron. Mekka, i, 340).

In these conditions, it was very natural for the crier in the earliest period to be regarded as the assistant and servant of the ruler; he is his muʾad̲h̲d̲h̲in (Ibn Saʿd, i, 7; Muslim, Ṣalāt, tr. 4; al-Maḳrīzī, iv, 43, etc.; cf. al-Ṭabarī, ii, 1120). ʿUmar sent to Kūfa ʿAmmār b. Yāsir as amīr and ʿAbd Allāh b. Masʿūd "as muʾad̲h̲d̲h̲in and wazīr" (Ibn al-Faḳīh, 165); he is thus the right hand of the ruler. Al-Ḥusayn had his munādī with him, and the latter summoned to the ṣalāt on al-Ḥusayn's instructions (al-Ṭabarī, ii, 297, 298; cf. Ibn Ziyād, ibid., 260 and in the year 196/811-12, the ʿāmil in Mecca, ibid., iii, 861, 13; also Chron. Mekka, i, 340). During the earliest period, the muʾad̲h̲d̲h̲in probably issued his summons in the streets and the call was very short: al-ṣalāta djāmiʿatan (Ibn Saʿd, 7, 7; Chron. Mekka, i, 340; al-Ṭabarī, iii, 861; cf. also in the year 196/811-12, Sīra Ḥalabiyya, ii, 101 al-Diyārbakrī, i, 404-5). This brief summons was, according to Ibn Saʿd, also used later on irregular occasions (i, 7 ff.; cf. the passage in al-Ṭabarī). Perhaps also the summons was issued from a particular place even at a quite early date (see I. D. 2a). After the public summons, the muʾad̲h̲d̲h̲in went to the Prophet, greeted him and called him to prayer; the same procedure was later used with his successor; when he had come, the muʾad̲h̲d̲h̲in announced the beginning of the ṣalāt (aḳāma ʾl-ṣalāt: cf. al-Buk̲h̲ārī, Wuḍūʾ, bāb 5; Ad̲h̲ān, bāb 48; Sīra Ḥalabiyya, ii, 104-5; al-Maḳrīzī, iv, 45; and IḲĀMA). The activity of the muʾad̲h̲d̲h̲in thus fell into three sections: the assembling of the community, the summoning of the imām and the announcement of the beginning of the ṣalāt. In the course of time, changes were made in all three stages.

The assembling of the community by crying aloud was not yet at all regular in the older period. During the civil strife in ʿIrāḳ, ʿUbayd Allāh b. Ziyād in the year 60/680 had his munādī summon people with threats to the evening ṣalāt in the mosque, and when after an hour the mosque was full, he had the iḳāma announced (al-Ṭabarī, ii, 260). When a large number of mosques had come into existence, the public call to prayer had to be organised lest confusion result, and the custom of calling from a raised position became general after the introduction of the minaret. While previously the call to prayer had only been preparatory and the iḳāma was the final summons, the public call (ad̲h̲ān) and the iḳāma now formed two distinct phases of the call to prayer. Tradition has retained a memory of the summoning in the streets, now completely fallen into disuse, when it tells us that ʿU<u>th</u>mān introduced a third *a<u>dh</u>ān*, a call in al-Zawrāʾ, which was made before the call from the minaret: this call, however, was transferred by Hi<u>sh</u>ām b. ʿAbd al-Malik to the minaret (al-Bu<u>kh</u>ārī, *<u>Dj</u>umʿa*, *bābs* 22, 25; *Sīra Ḥalabiyya*, ii, 110; Ibn al-Ḥā<u>dj</u>dj, *Mad<u>kh</u>al*, ii, 45). This may be evidence of the gradual cessation of the custom of summoning the community by going through the streets. Ibn Baṭṭūṭa (but this is exceptional) tells us that the *muʾa<u>dh</u>dhins* in <u>Kh</u>ʷārazm still fetched the people from their houses and those who did not come were whipped (iii, 4-5), which recalls Wahhābī measures. When exactly the Sunnī and, in distinction to it, the <u>Sh</u>īʿī formula, finally developed can hardly be ascertained [see ADHĀN]. The call *ḥayya ʿalā 'l-falāḥ* is known from the time of ʿAbd al-Malik (65-85/685-705) (al-A<u>kh</u>ṭal, ed. Ṣālḥānī, 254; see Horovitz, in *Isl.*, xvi [1927], 154; on *takbīr*, see *ibid.*; on *a<u>dh</u>ān* formulae, see further *Sīra Ḥalabiyya*, ii, 105-6). At first, the call was only made at the chief mosque, as was the case in Medina and Miṣr (al-Maḳrīzī, iv, 43 below), but very quickly other mosques were also given *muʾa<u>dh</u>dhins*: their calls were sufficiently audible in the whole town. The chief mosque retained this privilege, that its *muʾa<u>dh</u>dhin* called first and the others followed together (al-Maḳrīzī, iv, 43 below, 44).

The summoning by the *imām* in Medina was therefore quite a natural thing. The custom, at first associated with the ruler's mosque, was not observed in Medina only (see for ʿU<u>th</u>mān and ʿAlī, al-Ṭabarī, i, 3059-60), but was also usual under the Umayyads. The formula was *al-salām ʿalayka ayyuhā 'l-amīr wa-raḥmatu 'llāh wa-barakātuhu, ḥayya ʿalā 'l-ṣalat, ḥayya ʿalā 'l-falāḥ al-ṣalāt, yarḥamuka 'llāh* (al-Maḳrīzī, iv, 45; *Sīra Ḥalabiyya*, ii, 105). After the alteration in the *a<u>dh</u>ān* and the greater distance of the ruler from the mosque, to summon him was no longer the natural conclusion to the assembling of the community. In the ʿAbbāsid period and under the Fāṭimids, there was a survival of the old custom, in as much as the *muʾa<u>dh</u>dhins* ended the *a<u>dh</u>ān* call before the *ṣalāt al-fa<u>dj</u>r* on the minarets with a *salām* upon the caliph. This part of the *muʾa<u>dh</u>dhin*'s work was thus associated with the first *a<u>dh</u>ān* call. When Ṣalāḥ al-Dīn came to power, he did not wish to be mentioned in the call to prayer, but instead he ordered a blessing upon the Prophet to be uttered before the *a<u>dh</u>ān* to the *ṣalāt al-fa<u>dj</u>r*, which after 761/1360 only took place before the Friday service. A *muḥtasib* ordered that after 791/1389 in Egypt and Syria at each *a<u>dh</u>ān* a *salām* was to be uttered over the Prophet (al-Maḳrīzī, iv, 46; *Sīra Ḥalabiyya*, ii, 110). Ibn <u>Dj</u>ubayr relates that in Mecca after each *ṣalāt al-ma<u>gh</u>rib*, the foremost *muʾa<u>dh</u>dhin* pronounced a *duʿāʾ* upon the ʿAbbāsid *Imām* and on Ṣalāḥ al-Dīn from the Zamzam roof, in which those present joined with enthusiasm (103), and according to al-Maḳrīzī, after each *ṣalāt* prayers for the sultan were uttered by the *muʾa<u>dh</u>dhins* (iv, 53-4). Another relic of the old custom was that the trumpet was sounded at the door of the ruler at times of prayer; this honour was also shown to ʿAḍud al-Dawla in 368/978-9 by order of the caliph (Miskawayh, vi, 499; ed. Cairo 1315, 396).

The *iḳāma* always remained the real prelude to the service and is therefore regarded as the original *a<u>dh</u>ān* (al-Bu<u>kh</u>ārī, *<u>Dj</u>umʿa*, *bāb* 24). In the earliest period, it was fixed by the arrival of the ruler and it might happen that a considerable interval elapsed between the summoning of the people and the *iḳāma* (cf. al-Ṭabarī, ii, 260, 297-8). The times were later more accurately defined; one should be able to perform one to three *ṣalāts* between the two calls (al-Bu<u>kh</u>ārī, *A<u>dh</u>ān*, *bāb* 14, 16). Some are said to have introduced the practice of the *muʾa<u>dh</u>dhin* calling *ḥayya ʿalā 'l-ṣalāt* at the door of the mosque between the two calls (*Sīra Ḥalabiyya*, ii, 105). From the nature of the case, the *iḳāma* was always called in the mosque; at the Friday service, it was done when the *imām* mounted the *minbar* (al-Bu<u>kh</u>ārī, *<u>Dj</u>umʿa*, *bāb* 22, 25; *Sīra Ḥalabiyya*, ii, 110; al-Maḳrīzī, iv, 43) while the *muʾa<u>dh</u>dhin* stood in front of him. This *muʾa<u>dh</u>dhin*, according to some, ought to be the one who called the *a<u>dh</u>ān* upon the minaret (*Sīra Ḥalabiyya*, ii, 109), while Ibn al-Ḥā<u>dj</u>dj ignoring the historical facts only permits the call from the minaret (*Mad<u>kh</u>al*, ii, 45). In Tunis, the *iḳāma* was announced by ringing a bell as in the churches (al-Zarka<u>sh</u>ī, tr. Fagnan, in *Rec. Soc. Arch. Constantine* [1894], 111-12). A similarity to the responses in the Christian service is found in the fact that the call of the *muʾa<u>dh</u>dhin*, which contains a confession of faith, is to be repeated or at least answered by every one who hears it (al-Bu<u>kh</u>ārī, *<u>Dj</u>umʿa*, *bāb* 23); this is an action which confers religious merit (Ibn Ḳuṭlūbu<u>gh</u>ā, *Ṭabaḳāt al-Ḥanafiyya*, ed. Flügel, 30). It is possible that we should recognise in this as well as in the development of the formulae the influence of Christians converted to Islam (cf. Becker, *Zur Gesch. d. islam. Kultus*, in *Isl.*, iii [1912], 374 ff., and *Islamstudien*, i, 472 ff., who sees an imitation of the Christian custom in the *iḳāma* in general; on the possibility of Jewish influence, see Mittwoch, in *Abh. Pr. A. W.* [1913], Phil.-Hist. Cl. 2).

The *muʾa<u>dh</u>dhin* thus obtained a new importance. His work was not only to summon the people to divine service, but was in itself a kind of religious service. His sphere of activity was further developed. In Egypt we are told that Maslama b. Mu<u>kh</u>allad (47-62/667-82) introduced the *tasbīḥ*. This consisted in praises of God which were uttered by the *muʾa<u>dh</u>dhins* all through the night until *fa<u>dj</u>r*. This is explained as a polemical imitation of the Christians, for the governor was troubled by the use of the *nawāḳīs* at night and forbade them during the *a<u>dh</u>ān* (al-Maḳrīzī, iv, 48). In the time of Aḥmad b. Ṭūlūn and <u>Kh</u>umārawayh, the *muʾa<u>dh</u>dhins* recited religious texts throughout the night in a special room. Ṣalāḥ al-Dīn ordered them to recite an *ʿaḳīda* in the night *a<u>dh</u>ān* and after 700/1300-1, *<u>dh</u>ikr* was performed on Friday morning on the minarets (*ibid.*, 48-9, *Sīra Ḥalabiyya*, ii, 111). In Mecca also, the *muʾa<u>dh</u>dhins* performed *<u>dh</u>ikr* throughout the night of 1 <u>Sh</u>awwāl on the roof of the *ḳubba* of the Zamzam well (Ibn <u>Dj</u>ubayr, 155, 156; cf. for Damascus, al-Maḳrīzī, iv, 49). Similar litanies are kept up in modern times, as well as a special call about an hour before dawn (*ebed*, *tarḥīm*: see Lane, *Manners and customs*, Everyman's Library, 75-6, cf. 86; Snouck Hurgronje, *Mekka* ii, 84 ff.).

The original call of the *muʾa<u>dh</u>dhin* thus developed into a melodious chant like the recitation of the Ḳurʾān. Al-Muḳaddasī tells us that in the 4th/10th century in Egypt during the last third of the night, the *a<u>dh</u>ān* was recited like a dirge (205). The solemn effect was increased by the large number of voices. In large mosques, like that of Mecca, the chief *muʾa<u>dh</u>dhin* called first from a minaret, then the others came in turn (*Chron. Mekka*, iii, 242-5); Ibn <u>Dj</u>ubayr, 145 ff.; (cf. Ibn Rusta, 111, 1 ff. and above). But in the mosque itself, the *iḳāma* was pronounced by the *muʾa<u>dh</u>dhins* in chorus on the *dakka* (see above, I. D. 2e) erected for this purpose, which is also traced to Maslama. In the 3rd/9th and 4th/10th centuries we hear of these melodious recitations (*taṭrīb*) of the *muʾa<u>dh</u>dhins* on a raised podium in widely separated parts of the Muslim world (Ṣanʿāʾ, Egypt, Khurāsān, al-Muḳaddasī, 327; Ibn Rusta, 111; the expression *al-mutalaʿʿibīn*, "the musicians", if correct, probably refers to the *muʾadhdhins*, al-Muḳaddasī, 205; cf. also al-Kindī, *Wulāt*, 469; for Fārs we are expressly told that the *muʾadhdhins* call without *taṭrīb*, al-Muḳaddasī, 439, 17). Sometimes in large mosques, they were stationed in different parts of the mosque to make the *imām*'s words clear to the community (*tablīgh*). The singing, especially in chorus, like the *tablīgh*, was regarded by many as *bidʿa* (al-Kindī, *op. cit.*; *Madkhal*, ii, 45-6, 61-2; *Sīra Ḥalabiyya*, ii, 111). In other ways also, the *muʾadhdhins* could be compared to deacons at the service. The *khaṭīb* on his progress to the *minbar* in Mecca was accompanied by *muʾadhdhins*, and the chief *muʾadhdhin* girded him with a sword on the *minbar* (Ibn Djubayr, 96-7).

The new demands made on the *muʾadhdhins* necessitated an increase in their number, especially in the large mosques. The Prophet in Medina had two *muʾadhdhins*, Bilāl b. Ribāḥ, Abū Bakr's *mawlā*, and Ibn Umm Maktūm, who worked in rotation. ʿUthmān also is said occasionally to have called the *adhān* in front of the *minbar*, i.e. the *iḳāma* (al-Maḳrīzī, iv, 43). It is therefore regarded as commendable to have two *muʾadhdhins* at a mosque (Muslim, *Ṣalāt*, tr. 4; cf. al-Subkī, *Muʿīd*, 165). Abū Maḥdhūra was also the Prophet's *muʾadhdhin* in Mecca. Under ʿUmar, Bilāl's successor as *muʾadhdhin* was Saʿd al-Ḳaraẓ, who is said to have called to prayer for the Prophet in Ḳubāʾ (al-Maḳrīzī, *op. cit.*; cf. *Sīra Ḥalabiyya*, ii, 107 ff.). In Egypt under ʿAmr, the first *muʾadhdhin* in al-Fusṭāṭ was Abū Muslim; he was soon joined by nine others. The *muʾadhdhins* of the different mosques formed an organisation, the head (*ʿarīf*) of which, after Abū Muslim, was his brother Shuraḥbīl b. ʿĀmir (d. 65/684-5); during his time, Maslama b. Mukhallad built minarets (al-Maḳrīzī, iv, 44).

The office of *muʾadhdhin* was sometimes hereditary. The descendants of Bilāl were for example *muʾadhdhins* of the Medina Mosque in al-Rawḍa (Ibn Djubayr, 194). We also find in Medina the sons of Saʿd al-Ḳaraẓ officiating (Ibn Ḳutayba, *Maʿārif*, ed. Wüstenfeld, 132, 279), in Mecca, the sons of Abū Maḥdhūra (*ibid.*, 278; *Sīra Ḥalabiyya*, ii, 106), in Baṣra, the sons of al-Mundhir b. Ḥassān al-ʿAbdī, *muʾadhdhins* of ʿUbayd Allāh b. Ziyād (Ibn Ḳutayba, 279); it is, however, possible that this was really the result of a system of guilds of *muʾadhdhins*. In the *djawāmiʿ* of the Maghrib in the 8th/14th century, each had regularly four *muʾadhdhins* who were stationed in different parts of the mosque during the *ṣalāt* (*Madkhal*, ii, 47 above); but there were often quite a large number. In the Azhar mosque in the time of al-Ḥākim, there were fifteen, each of whom was paid two *dīnārs* a month (al-Maḳrīzī, iv, 51). Ibn Baṭṭūṭa found seventy *muʾadhdhins* in the Mosque of the Umayyads (i, 204). About 1900, in Medina there were in the Mosque of the Prophet fifty *muʾadhdhins* and twenty-six assistants (al-Batanūnī, *Riḥla*, 242). Blind men were often chosen for this office; Ibn Umm Maktūm, for example, was blind (al-Bukhārī, *Adhān*, *bāb* 11; *Sīra Ḥalabiyya*, ii, 104; cf. Lane, *op. cit.*, 75). The Prophet is said to have forbidden Thaḳīf to pay a *muʾadhdhin* (al-Wāḳidī-Wellhausen, 383). ʿUthmān is said to have been the first to give payment to the *muʾadhdhins* (al-Maḳrīzī, iv, 44) and Aḥmad b. Ṭūlūn gave them large sums (*ibid.*, 48). They regularly received their share in the endowments, often by special provisions in the documents establishing the foundations.

The *muʾadhdhins* were organised under chiefs (*ruʾasāʾ*: al-Maḳrīzī, iv, 14). In Mecca, the *raʾīs al-muʾadhdhinīn* was identical with the *muʾadhdhin al-Zamzamī* who had charge of the singing in the upper story of the Zamzam building (*Chron. Mekka*, iii, 424-5; Ibn Djubayr, 145; cf. Snouck Hurgronje, *Mekka*, ii, 322). The *raʾīs* was next to the *imām* but subordinate to him; in certain districts, it was the custom for him to mount the pulpit during the sermon with the *imām* (when the latter acted as *khaṭīb*) (*Madkhal*, ii, 74). The position which they originally occupied can still be seen from the part which they play in public processions of officials, e.g. of the *Ḳāḍī ʾl-Ḳuḍāt*, when they walk in front and laud the ruler and his vizier (al-Maḳrīzī, ii, 246).

Closely associated with the *muʾadhdhin* is the *muwaḳḳit*, the astronomer, whose task it was to ascertain the *ḳibla* and the times of prayer (al-Subkī, *Muʿīd*, 165-6 and see MĪḲĀT); sometimes the chief *muʾadhdhin* did this (Snouck Hurgronje, *Mekka*, ii, 322).

5. Servants. According to Abū Hurayra, the Mosque of the Prophet was swept by a negro (al-Bukhārī, *Ṣalāt*, *bāb* 72, cf. 74). The larger mosques gradually acquired a large staff of servants (*khuddām*), notably *bawwāb*, *farrāsh*, and water-carriers (cf. e.g. van Berchem, *CIA*, i, 252). In Mecca there have always been special appointments, such as supervisor of Zamzam and guardian of the Kaʿba (*sādin*, pl. *sadana*, also used of the officials of the mosque: al-Maḳrīzī, iv, 76; cf. Ibn Djubayr, 278). In Ibn Baṭṭūṭa's time, the servants (*khuddām*) of the Mosque of the Prophet were eunuchs, particularly Abyssinian; their chief (*shaykh al-khuddām*) was like a great *amīr* and was paid by the Egyptian-Syrian government (i, 278, 348); cf. the title of an *amīr* of the year 798/1395-6, *shaykh mashāʾikh al-sāda al-khuddām bi ʾl-ḥaram al-sharīf al-nabawī* (van Berchem, *CIA*, i, no. 201). In the Mosque of Jerusalem in about 300/912-13, there were no less than 140 servants (*khādim*; Ibn al-Faḳīh, 100); others give the figure 230 (Le Strange, *Palestine*, 163) and according to Mudjīr al-Dīn, ʿAbd al-Malik appointed a guard of 300 black slaves here, while the actual menial work was done by certain Jewish and Christian families (Sauvaire, *Hist. Jér. et Hébr.*, 56-7).

In other mosques, superintendents (*ḳayyim*, pl. *ḳawama*) are mentioned, a vague title which covered a multitude of duties: thus the Madrasa al-Madjdiyya had a *ḳayyim* who looked after the cleaning, the staff, the lighting and water-supply (al-Maḳrīzī, iv, 251), the Azhar Mosque had one for the *miʾḍaʾa*, who was paid twelve *dīnārs* (*ibid.*, 51) and also 4 *ḳawama*, who were paid like *muʾadhdhins* (two *dīnārs* a month) and are mentioned between them and the *imāms*, probably supervisors of the staff (*ibid.*, 51). In other cases, a *ḳayyim al-djāmiʿ*, sometimes a *ḳāḍī*, is mentioned, who is apparently the same as the *imām*, the *khaṭīb* or some similar individual of standing (*ibid.*, 75, 121, cf. 122; cf. Ibn Djubayr, 51). A *mushrif*, inspector, is also mentioned, e.g. in the Azhar (al-Maḳrīzī, iv, 51).

Bibliography: given in the article.

(J. Pedersen)

H. The architecture of the mosque.

1. Introduction. Attemps to generalise about regional variations in mosque architecture are fraught with difficulty and have often miscarried. One solution, admittedly a compromise, is to select a few of the most celebrated mosques, to imply in more or less arbitrary fashion that they are typical, and to base the requisite generalisations on them. This approach has at least the merit of clarity, and it could indeed be argued that it is in the finest mosques of a given period and region that local peculiarities are apt to find their fullest expression. Nevertheless, such a broad-brush

approach, for all its superficial attractions, is simply not specific enough. Another approach, which might be termed typological, cuts across regional and temporal boundaries in order to isolate the significant variants of mosque design and trace their development. Yet, precisely because it ignores such boundaries, this approach tends to minimise the significance of regional schools and fashions. The categories and sub-species which it proposes tend to have a somewhat academic flavour; while technically defensible, they somehow miss the point. A third approach might be to rely on statistics and, by chronicling all known mosques of pre-modern date, to discover the types and distribution of the most popular varieties. The picture to emerge from such a study might indeed be literally accurate, but it would not distinguish between the *d̲j̲āmi*ᶜ and the *masd̲j̲id*, that is, between the major religious building of a town or city and the neighbourhood mosque (on the *d̲j̲āmi*ᶜ and its functions, see above, I. C. 2.). Since virtually all the mosques under discussion here fall into the category of *d̲j̲āmi*ᶜ, such a study would be of limited value in this context, and would assuredly blur the sharp outlines of regional peculiarities of mosque design. After all, the simplest types of mosques not only vastly outnumber the more complex ones but are also to be found throughout the Muslim world. It is such mosques, therefore, which make up the standard distribution of this building type. They dominate by sheer weight of numbers, but—by the same token—they distort the overall picture, suggesting a uniformity that actually exists only at the level of the most primitive buildings. Only when a statistical survey of this kind is relieved of the effectively dead weight of such buildings can regional and temporal distinctions stand out in their full clarity.

Such are the difficulties attendant on venturing a *tour d'horizon* of formal developments in the pre-modern mosque. What, then, is the best way of tackling this problem? The most promising line of approach is probably to identify those mosque types which are most distinctive of a given area and period, describing their constituent features but avoiding a detailed analysis of individual buildings. It should be emphasised that the over-riding aim of highlighting significant regional developments entails the suppression of much corroborative detail and, more importantly, of those periods when a given region was simply continuing to build mosques in a style already well established. Admittedly the lulls in innovation have their own part to play in the history of mosque architecture; but that part is too modest to rate any extended discussion here.

For that same reason, areas in which the pace of change was sluggish are allotted less attention in the following account than those which were consistently in the forefront of experiment. The Mag̲h̲rib, for example, receives less space than Iran, while ᶜIrāḳ and the Levant take second place to Egypt and Anatolia. These emphases, moreover, reflect the basic truth that the design of a mosque was often less liable to take on a distinctively local colouring than were its decoration, its structural techniques or even specific components of that design, such as the minaret [see MANĀRA]. The time-span covered by this article is also limited. The mosque architecture of the last two centuries, which have seen the gradual invasion of a long-established Islamic idiom by European ideas and motifs, and in which a general decline is unmistakable, is omitted from this account. One final caveat should be sounded: the ensuing generalisations deliberately exclude the peripheral areas of the Islamic world, notably Indonesia, Malaysia, China and sub-Saharan Africa, for which see sections III-VII below. Nearly all the mosques in these areas are of post-mediaeval date, and therefore lie in the shadow of developments in the Islamic heartlands. There is, moreover, a strong vernacular element in these regional traditions, for they draw very heavily on a reservoir of ideas, practices and forms which owe very little to Islam. Thus for reasons which are as much historical and cultural as geographical they do not belong in the mainstream of mosque architecture.

This survey, then, will cover the central Islamic lands from al-Andalus to Afg̲h̲ānistān. The very nature of the material, however, makes it undesirable to embark directly on a series of regional summaries: the sheer lack of surviving monuments would require each summary to start at a different date. In most areas of the Islamic world it is not until the 5th/11th century that mosques survive in sufficient quantities for the lineaments of a local style to emerge. To explain that style would in most cases entail reference to earlier mosques in other regions, with consequent repetition and overlap. The crucial decisions which dictated the subsequent formal development of the mosque were taken in the early centuries of Islam; and the buildings which embodied those decisions are themselves thinly scattered over the entire area bounded by al-Andalus and Afg̲h̲ānistān. Yet the interconnections between these buildings are such as to make light of their geographical remoteness from each other.

Accordingly, a pan-Islamic survey of the early architectural history of the mosque will preface the individual accounts of local developments. These accounts in turn will be of unequal length. Pride of place will go to the Arab mosque plan, which not only had the widest diffusion but also covers the longest chronological span. Next in length will be the survey of the Persian tradition, almost as ancient as that of the Arab plan but more restricted in geographical scope. Shortest of all will be the discussion of the Turkish mosque type, whose creative development is confined in time to the 8th-11th/14th-17th centuries and in space to Anatolia.

2. Early history of the mosque: 622-1000 A.D.

(a) The house of the Prophet. Beyond doubt, the genesis of the mosque is to be sought in a single seminal building: the house of the Prophet, erected to Muḥammad's own specifications in Medina in 1/622. It was a near-square enclosure of some 56 × 53 m. with a single entrance; a double range of palm-trunk columns thatched with palm leaves (a feature of many African mosques to this day) was added on the *ḳibla* side, with a lean-to for destitute Companions to the south-east and nine huts for Muḥammad and his wives along the western perimeter. By a curious paradox, it was not built even secondarily as a mosque. This fact cannot be over-emphasised, since to ignore it is to misinterpret the subsequent history of mosque architecture. The venerated model for all later mosques itself became a mosque only, as it were, by the way and in the course of time. How is this to be explained? The accumulated deposit of many centuries of reverence makes it difficult to disinter the full original context of the building. Yet this much is clear: it was first and foremost a house for Muḥammad and his family to live in. It was also conceived from the beginning as a gathering place for the growing band of Muslims: in fact a kind of community centre, complete with the attendant associations of welfare. At the same time it served political, military and legal functions, while its high walls and single entrance allowed it at need to act as a place of refuge for the community. To be sure, by degrees people began to pray in it; but they prayed in many other places too and there is no evidence that it was used as the regular place of worship in the earliest years of the community. The mere fact that dogs and camels were allowed free access to it effectively disposes of such a notion. In short, Muḥammad had, it seems, no intention of creating a new type of building here. It is in no sense radical. In its extreme simplicity and austerity it well reflects his own life-style at that time. Its substantial scale may seem to contradict this, but is in fact somewhat deceptive, for some 80% of the interior consists of a vast empty courtyard. Yet it was this very emptiness that gave the mosque its innate flexibility, and in subsequent centuries a large open space became a standard feature of most large mosques. It is surely *à propos* to note that the earliest Christian places of worship, the so-called *tituli*, were also ordinary houses. (For a detailed discussion of the Prophet's *masdjid* and its various functions, see above, I. A. 1.).

(b) The so-called "Arab plan". Although there was thus a large measure of accident in the adoption of Muḥammad's house as the model *par excellence* of later mosques, that form could not have enjoyed the popularity it did unless it had answered to a nicety the needs of Muslim liturgy and prayer. Its components—an enclosed square or rectangular space with a courtyard and a covered area for prayer on the *ḳibla* side—could be varied at will so as to transform the aspect of the building. Thus there evolved the so-called "Arab" or "hypostyle" mosque plan. From the first it showed itself capable of quite radical modification according to circumstances. At Kūfa in 17/638 the location of the mosque within one of the garrison cities (*amṣār*) allowed the builders to dispense with the element of security, and the perimeter—its dimensions fixed, according to al-Balādhurī, by four bowshots—is marked by ditches; elsewhere, as at Baṣra in the year 14/635, a reed fence served the same purpose. At Fusṭāṭ in the rebuilt mosque of ʿAmr (53/673), corner turrets served simultaneously to articulate the exterior, to single out the mosque from afar and to provide a place from which the call to prayer could be made: the germ of the future minaret. Multiple entrances became a feature as early as the first mosque of ʿAmr at Fusṭāṭ (22/643), admitting light to the *muṣallā* [*q.v.*, and also above, I. B. 6] and allowing maximum ease of circulation.

The sunny climate of the southern Mediterranean and the Near East allowed the courtyard to accommodate the huge numbers of extra worshippers attending the Friday service. This was when its large expanse justified itself. For the rest of the week it was largely empty, and the heat and light emitted by this expanse could cause discomfort. This was especially likely if there were no provision for shade on three of the four sides, as in the early versions of the Great Mosques of Cordova (170/787), Ḳayrawān (221/836) and Tunis (250/864). Hence there arose the practice of adding arcades along the three subsidiary sides, so that people could walk around the mosque in cool shade. In time these arcades could be doubled, tripled or even quadrupled. A change in the alignment of their vaulting from one side of the mosque to another brought welcome visual relief and excluded the danger of monotony; so too did variations in the depth or number of the arcades (the second ʿAmr mosque in Cairo). As the surface area of the covered sanctuary was increased so did new spatial refinements suggest themselves, such as the progressive unfolding of seemingly endless vistas in all direction. Rows of supports (often spolia) with fixed intercolumniations created hundreds of repetitive modular units, perhaps deliberately mirroring the long files of worshippers at prayer.

Externally, the accent was on simplicity, with regular buttresses giving the structure a warlike air. At the Great Mosque of Sāmarrā (completed 238/852) there are a dozen of these on each long side, not counting the corners, with doorways after every second buttress. At Susa the exterior dispenses with buttresses in favour of rounded corner bastions, while in the mosque of al-Ḥākim in Cairo (381/991 onwards) the minarets at the corner of the façade rise from two gigantic square salients. The emplacement of the *miḥrāb* [*q.v.*] was marked by a corresponding rectangular projection on the exterior wall. Entrances were commonly allotted a measure of extra decoration—as in the series of shallow porches along the flank of the Cordova mosque—but massive portals on the scale of those in Western cathedrals found no favour in the early mosques of Arab plan. The absolute scale of some mosques (the mosque of Sāmarrā, for instance, could have accommodated 100,000 people) encouraged the adoption of fixed proportional ratios such as 3:2, which contributed in large measure to the impression of satisfying harmony which these mosques produced. The Ḳarakhānid mosque of Samarḳand (5th/11th century) illustrates the continuing use of such ratios. Sometimes the scale of the mosque was illusionistically increased by the addition of a broad open enclosure (*ziyāda*) on three of the four sides (Mosque of Ibn Ṭūlūn, Cairo, finished 264/878, presumably copying the mosques of Sāmarrā). In comparison with later mosques of similar scale, which catered for multiple subsidiary functions by adding appropriate purpose-built structures to the central core, these early mosques maintain simple and symmetrical lines, especially for their outer walls.

The architectural vocabulary of these early mosques brought further scope for diversity. In the first half-century of Islamic architecture, the system of roofing was still primitive, and even when columns and roof-beams had replaced palm-trunks and thatching, the basic scheme remained trabeate (Baṣra; Kūfa; and Wāsiṭ, 83/702) whether the roof was flat or pitched. Thus the post-and-lintel system long familiar from Graeco-Roman buildings was perpetuated, and the pervasive classical flavour was strengthened by the lavish use of spolia. Sometimes, however, as in the bull-headed capitals of the Iṣṭakhr mosque, these were of Achaemenid origin.

By degrees, wooden roofs resting on arcades gained popularity, and this was the prelude to full-scale vaulting in durable materials (especially in Iran: Tārīkhāna mosque, Dāmghān, and Fahradj *djāmiʿ*, both perhaps 3rd/9th century; Nāʾīn *djāmiʿ*, perhaps 4th/10th century). The earliest mosques all use columns, and were thereby restricted to relatively low roofs. By the 3rd/9th century the pier had ousted the column as the principal bearing member, though it occurs as early as the mosques of Damascus, Baʿlabakk and Ḥarrān, and though the column was still used for some mosques (Ḳayrawān; al-Azhar, Cairo, 362/973). This change made it possible to raise the height of the roof, an important development given the oppressive sensation produced by a low roof extending over a large surface area. At the Cordova mosque the column shafts bore piers braced by strainer arches; but this device, for all its ingenuity, could not rival the popularity of superposed arcades in the fashion of Roman aqueducts (Damascus mosque, finished 98/716).

The apparently minor detail of whether the arcades ran parallel to the *ḳibla* or at right angles to it was sufficient to transform the visual impact of the roof. In the latter case, it focused attention on the *ḳibla*, and this was the solution that recommended itself to Maghribī architects (mosques of Cordova, Tunis and Ḳayrawān). Syrian architects, on the other hand, with only one major exception (Aḳṣā mosque, Jerusalem), preferred arcades parallel to the *ḳibla* (Damascus; Ḳaṣr al-Ḥayr East, *ca.* 109/728; Baʿlabakk, *ca.* 6th/12th century; Ḥarrān, *ca.* 133/750; and Raḳḳa, *ca.* 3rd/9th century), possibly reflecting in this the influence of the Christian basilica ubiquitous in that region, and several Egyptian mosques followed suit, including those of Ibn Ṭūlūn, al-Azhar and al-Ḥākim. It was a natural development to build mosques with arcades running in both directions (Great Mosques of Sfax and Susa, both finished 236/850), but with these exceptions the early experiments with this idea are all on a relatively modest scale which betrays some uncertainty of purpose. They comprise a small group of 9-bayed mosques with a dome over each bay and no courtyard: a type represented in Toledo, Ḳayrawān, Cairo and Balkh and dating mainly from the 4th/10th century. These buildings inaugurate the much more ambitious use of vaults in later mosques. No such solutions are to be found in the larger mosques built before the 5th/11th century. This early Islamic vaulting drew its ideas impartially from the Romano-Byzantine tradition and from Sasanian Iran, and quickly developed its own distinctive styles, in which the pointed vault soon dominated.

(c) The secular element in early mosque architecture. In some mosques, the desire to emphasise the covered sanctuary (*muṣallā*) was achieved simply by adding extra bays and thus increasing its depth. In other mosques, especially those with royal associations, the requisite emphasis was achieved by some striking visual accentuation of the *muṣallā:* a more elaborate façade, a higher and wider central aisle, a gable or a dome. Once this idea of glorifying the *muṣallā* had taken root it was enthusiastically exploited, for example by furnishing this area with several carefully placed domes (Cordova, al-Azhar). On occasion, indeed, the *muṣallā*—complete with such distinguishing features as wider central aisle, dome in front of the *miḥrāb* and transversely vaulted bays adjoining the *ḳibla*—could itself become the mosque, with no attached courtyard (al-Aḳṣā).

The effect of singling out the *muṣallā* by these various means is to emphasise that this area is more important than any other in the mosque. Since this latter notion runs counter to the widely-expressed belief that all parts of the mosque are equally sacred, and that gradations of sanctity within it run counter to the spirit of Islam, its origins are worth investigating. It should be stressed at the outset that these various articulating devices cannot all be explained as attempts to draw attention to the *ḳibla*. Some measure of emphasis for this purpose was certainly required. Hence, no doubt, the greater depth of arcades on that side and the provision of an elaborate façade for the *muṣallā* alone. Similarly, the use of a different alignment or type of vaulting for the bays immediately in front of the *ḳibla* would make sense as a means of signposting this crucial area. Yet the addition of a dome or gable, or both, along the central aisle of the *muṣallā*, and the greater width and height of that aisle, cannot be explained—as is so often the case—simply as a means of highlighting the *miḥrāb*. After all, the entire *ḳibla* wall served to mark the correct orientation for prayer, so that the *miḥrāb* was technically redundant. The relatively late appearance of the *miḥrāb* (no 1st/7th century mosque appears to have possessed one and it is described as an innovation introduced by al-Walīd I in his re-building of the Mosque of the Prophet in Medina in 84/703) further suggests that it was not devised to meet some liturgical imperative.

The evidence points rather to the desire to assert in as public a way as the dictates of religious architecture would permit, the importance of the ruler in religious ceremonies. It was the duty of the caliph or of his representative to lead his people in prayer and to pronounce the *khuṭba* [*q.v.*]. The political overtones of the latter ritual, which proclaimed allegiance to the ruler in much the same spirit as the diptychs in the contemporary Byzantine liturgy, in large part explain the physical form of the *minbar* [*q.v.*] from which the *khuṭba* was pronounced. Similarly, the *miḥrāb*, another latecomer to mosque architecture, can be interpreted in secular terms, most conveniently as a throne apse transposed into a religious setting. These royal connotations could only be intensified by the addition of a dome over the bay directly in front of the *miḥrāb*.

Underneath that same dome was the preferred location for the *maḳṣūra* (see for this, above, I. D. 2.b.), usually a square enclosure of wood or stone reserved for the ruler, and ensuring both his privacy and his physical safety. Each of these elements in the mosque—*miḥrāb*, *minbar*, *maḳṣūra*, dome—drew added power from the proximity of the others, and together they stamped a secular and princely significance on this particular area of the mosque. The earliest surviving mosque which illustrates this emphasis, the Great Mosque of Damascus, adds a further refinement: a high transverse gable with a pitched roof cuts across the lateral emphasis of the *muṣallā* and thus highlights not just the *miḥrāb* area but also the way to it. The extra height of the gable and the way it cleaves across the grain of the mosque underscore its proclamatory role. Sometimes, as in the *djāmiʿ*s of Tunis and Ḳayrawān, another dome over the central archway of the *muṣallā* façade sufficed to create an axis focused on the *miḥrāb*. As at Damascus, this axis asserted itself both inside the *muṣallā* and—by virtue of its greater width and the consequent break in the even tenor of the roofing—externally, at roof level. In later mosques, such as al-Azhar and al-Ḥākim (which possibly derive in this from al-Aḳṣā) the notion of the external gable is toned down to a broad flat strip projecting only modestly above roof level; but internally, the emphasis on the broader central nave terminating in the dome over the *miḥrāb* remains unchanged. It seems likely that these articulating devices were intended to mark out a processional way, presumably the formal route by which the ruler approached the *miḥrāb*.

So much, then, for the various elements in mosque design for which princely associations have been proposed. Yet their mere enumeration does not tell the full story. For it is above all the occurrence of these features in mosques located next to the residence of the ruler that places their political associations beyond doubt. This close juxtaposition of the secular and the religious may well have had its roots in the Prophet's house. Be that as it may, at Baṣra, Kūfa, Fusṭāṭ, Damascus, to name only a few very early examples, the principal mosque and the private residence of the ruler adjoined each other, and the viceroy Ziyād b. Abīhi [*q.v.*] said of this arrangement "it is not fitting that the *Imām* should pass through the people"—a sentiment, incidentally, not shared by many later Islamic rulers. The analogy with the palatine chapel in Byzantium and mediaeval Europe—at Constantinople and Ravenna, Aachen and Palermo—is striking. Perhaps the most public expression of the idea in the mediaeval Islamic world was in the Round City of Bag͟hdād, where the huge and largely empty space at the heart of the city held only two buildings: the palace and the mosque, next door to each other. It would be hard to find the concept of Caesaropapism expressed more explicitly, or on a more gargantuan scale, than this.

The local expression of the articulating features under discussion varied from one part of the Islamic world to another, but they had come to stay. Henceforth, the *d̲j̲āmi*ʿ of Arab plan only rarely returned to the simplicity of the 1st/7th century. Such, however, was the strength of the traditions formed at that time that the basic nature of the earliest mosques remained substantially unchanged. They were proof, for example, against immense increases in size and against a growing interest in embellishment by means of structural innovations and applied ornament. Even the conversion into mosques of pre-Islamic places of worship, as at Damascus and Ḥamā, was powerless to affect their essential nature. The component parts of the Arab mosque could be redistributed and rearranged almost at will without impairing their functional effectiveness.

In much the same way, their idiosyncrasies of structure and decoration were purely cosmetic. The range of options in these areas was gratifyingly wide. Windows and lunettes bore *ajouré* grilles in stone or plaster with geometric and vegetal designs (Damascus mosque); wooden ceilings were painted or carved and coffered (Ṣanʿāʾ mosque, 1st/7th century onwards); a wide range of capitals, at first loosely based on classical models but in time featuring designs of Central Asian origin (Sāmarrā) was developed; and piers with engaged corner colonnettes (Ibn Ṭūlūn mosque, Cairo) rang the changes on the traditional classical column. Finally, the aspect of these early mosques could be varied still further by the type of flooring employed—stamped earth, brick, stone or even marble flags—and by applied decoration in carved stone or stucco, fresco, painted glass, embossed metalwork or mosaic.

3. Later history of the "Arab plan" mosque.

The essentially simple components of the Arab plan set a limit to the degree of diversity that could be achieved within these specifications. Most of the room for manoeuvre had been exhausted within the first four centuries of Islamic architecture. Thus the subsequent history of the Arab plan cannot match the early period for variety and boldness; the later mosques, moreover, lie very much in the shadow of their predecessors, to such an extent, indeed, that it is hard to single out significant new departures in these later buildings. It can scarcely be doubted that the presence of the great Umayyad and ʿAbbāsid mosques, built at the period when the Islamic world was at the peak of its material prosperity, acted as a signal deterrent to later architects with substantially less money, men and materials at their disposal. In these early centuries the caliphal permission, not readily granted, had been required for the construction of a *d̲j̲āmi*ʿ making it therefore a major undertaking, and correspondingly hard to emulate. By the 5th/11th century, moreover, most of the major Muslim cities had their own *d̲j̲āmi*ʿ, so that the need for huge mosques had much declined.

Although mosques of Arab plan have continued to be built throughout the Islamic world until the present day, in the mediaeval period there were only two areas where they achieved dominance: in the Western Islamic lands before they fell under Ottoman rule, and in pre-Ottoman Anatolia. These areas will therefore provide the material for most of the discussion which follows. Nevertheless, sporadic references will be made to mosques elsewhere, for instance in Egypt and the Yemen.

(a) The Mag͟hrib. The Mag͟hrib rightfully takes pride of place in this account because for almost a millennium virtually no mosque that was not of Arab type was built there. Here, then, is to be found the most homogeneous and consistent development of that type. Its sources lie, like so much of Mag͟hribī art, in Syria, and specifically in the Great Mosque of Damascus. Its transverse gable becomes a leitmotif in Mag͟hribī mosques, and in some cases (such as the Ḳarawiyyīn Mosque [*q.v.*], Fez, founded 226/841 but largely of the 6th/12th century) is associated with the same proportions as the Syrian building, including the relatively shallow oblong courtyard imposed on the Damascus mosque by the classical *temenos* but copied thereafter in other mosques as a deliberate feature. In the Mosque of the Andalusians at Fez (600-4/1203-7) the Damascus schema is retained despite a jaggedly irregular perimeter and trapezoidal courtyard; and, as at the Ḳarawiyyīn mosque, the main entrance to the mosque is aligned to it, a refinement not found at Damascus. The length of the gable has also increased considerably, though its height is modest.

In later Mag͟hribī mosques especially, the emphasis shifted from the exterior elevation of the gable to its impact from within the building. It attracts unusually intricate vaulting, often of *muḳarnas* [*q.v.*] type, or may be marked by domes ranging in number from two (Tlemcen, 531/1136) to six (second Kutubiyya, Marrakesh, mid-6th/mid-12th century). The latter mosque has a further five cupolas placed three bays apart along the transverse *ḳibla* aisle. Thus by means of vaulting alone is created a T-shape which combines the secular and religious emphases of the *d̲j̲āmi*ʿ. Fewer vaults or domes, more strategically placed—for example at the *miḥrāb*, the *muṣallā* entrance and the corners of the *ḳibla* wall—could suffice to carry the T-shape into the elevation, but the form could be created at ground level alone by means of a wider central nave and by ensuring that the vaults stopped one bay short of the *ḳibla*, thus opening up dramatically the space immediately in front of it. The T-shape can indeed claim to be the principal Mag͟hribī contribution to the development of mosque form, though horseshoe arches and square minarets were equally characteristic of the style.

Three other features distinguish Mag͟hribī mosques from those found elsewhere in the Islamic world, though all have their origins in al-Andalus: the use of pierced ribbed or fluted domes, especially over the *miḥrāb*; the manipulation of arch forms to create hierarchical distinctions by means of gradual enrichment; and a readiness to alter the size, shape and location of the courtyard in response to the imperatives of a specific design. The ribbed domes (e.g. *d̲j̲āmi*ʿs of Taza, 537/1142 and 691/1292, and Algiers, *ca.* 490/1097) derive from those of the Cordova mosque, but elaborate on them by cramming them with vegetal designs in carved stucco or by increasing the number of ribs from the usual eight to twelve (Tlemcen *d̲j̲āmi*ʿ) or even sixteen (Taza *d̲j̲āmi*ʿ). This practice gives free rein to the characteristically Mag͟hribī obsession with non-structural arched forms, here used as a lace-like infill between the ribs; the overall effect is one of feathery lightness and grace. The light filtered through these domes suffuses the area of the *miḥrāb* with radiance, perhaps as a deliberate metaphor of spiritual illumination, an idea rendered still more potent when, as is often the case, that *miḥrāb* bears the popular text of sūra XXIV, 36-7, "God is the Light of the heavens and the earth; the likeness of His Light is as a niche wherein is a lamp..."

Long files of arcaded columns stretching in multiple directions and generating apparently endless vistas are a particular feature of Mag͟hribī mosques. The distinctive "forest space" thereby created finds its fullest expression in the fourth major rebuilding of the Cordova mosque, the supreme generative masterpiece of Western Islamic architecture, and the major Almoravid and Almohad mosques are best interpreted as reflections of this great original. Where the Cordova mosque, however, employed systems of intersecting arches and carefully differentiated types of capital to establish hierarchical distinctions, later Mag͟hribī *d̲j̲āmiʿ*s typically use a wide range of arch profiles to the same end. These include, besides the ubiquitous horseshoe type already noted, lobed, multifoil, interlaced cusped, trefoil, lambrequin and other varieties. They spring from piers, not columns, and this, coupled with the low roof, dim lighting and the general absence of ornament unconnected with vaulting, lends these interiors a ponderous austerity. Against this general background of parsimonious simplicity, the sudden switch from plain arch profiles for most of the sanctuary to elaborate ones for the axial nave alone constitutes a dramatic enrichment of the interior. Sometimes the transverse aisle in front of the *ḳibla* wall attests a third type of arch profile, and thus a further gradation of importance is emphasised.

In most western Islamic mosques the courtyard is something of an appendage. It is almost always very much smaller than the covered space. Custom decreed that it was isolated at the opposite end of the mosque from the *miḥrāb*, and that it should either be contiguous to the outer wall or be separated from it by no more than a single aisle. By contrast, the sanctuary tended to be of disproportionate depth and extent. This meant that the courtyard was never able to function as the heart of the mosque. Only when the sanctuary was reduced, as in the Ḳaṣba mosque in Marrakesh (581-6/1185-90), with its pronounced cruciform emphasis, was the courtyard able, both literally and figuratively, to play a more central role. In narrow rectangular plans, it can be a diminutive square box hemmed in by deep lateral aisles (Mosque of al-Manṣūra, 704-45/1304-44) or an extended shallow oblong (Mosque of Seville, *ca.* 571/1175). In oblong plans, it faithfully mirrored that emphasis on a diminutive scale (Tinmal, 548/1153; first Kutubiyya, Marrakesh, *ca.* 555/1160). Exceptional on all counts is the gigantic but unfinished mosque of Ḥasan, Rabat (*ca.* 591/1195), whose scale of 180 × 139 m. makes it the second largest mosque in the world, after the Great Mosque of Sāmarrā. Here the typical shallow oblong courtyard is supplemented by two lesser and narrow courtyards perpendicular to the *ḳibla* and along the lateral walls. These were, it seems, intended for men and women respectively, but they would also have served for ventilation and lighting, besides offering visual relief to the endless march of columns.

(b) Anatolia. For all that pre-Ottoman Anatolia was a fertile field for innovation in later mediaeval experiment with the hypostyle mosque, its contribution cannot seriously match that of the Mag͟hrib and al-Andalus, not least because of the much shorter time span, a mere three centuries; discussion of it will accordingly be brief. The earliest surviving mosques well illustrate the dependence of local builders on more developed traditions of Arab and Persian origin. The Great Mosque of Diyārbakir (484/1091) follows the transept schema of Damascus, while those of Mayyāfāriḳīn (550/1155), Dunaysir (601/1204) and Mārdīn (largely 6th/12th century) follow Iranian precedent in their emphasis on a monumental dome rearing up out of the low roofing of the sanctuary and set squarely in front of the *miḥrāb* bay. Their foreshortened courtyards, however, owe nothing to Iranian precedent and instead presage later developments. So too did the increasing tendency to use domical forms rather than modular trabeate units as the principal means of defining space.

The buildings of the 6th/12th and 7th/13th centuries sufficiently demonstrate the embryonic state of mosque design in Anatolia, for the variety of plans is bewildering and defies easy categorisation. The absence of direct copies of the classical Arab type of plan is striking, though modifications of it were legion. A common solution was to do without the courtyard altogether—perhaps a response to the severe Anatolian winter—and reduce the mosque to a wooden-roofed hall resting on a multitude of columns or pillars (ʿAlāʾ al-Dīn mosque, Konya, 530/1135 to 617/1220; Sivas, *ca.* 494/1101; Afyon, 672/1273; Beyşehir, 696/1296). Usually the minaret was outside the mosque and therefore not integrated into the layout. Sometimes a similar design was executed in multiple small vaults (Divriği, castle mosque, 576/1180; Niksar, 540/1145; Urfa, 6th/12th century), and indeed the preference for vaulted as distinct from trabeated construction is well marked even at this experimental stage. Whatever the roofing system adopted in these enclosed mosques, the scope for development in either direction was small, while poor lighting, a sense of cramped space and inadequate ventilation were virtually inevitable. Huge piers and low vaults gave many of these mosques a crypt-like appearance (ʿAlāʾ al-Dīn mosque, Niğde, 620/1223; Sivas, Ulu Cami).

The obvious way forward was to allot a more significant role to the dome, a decision made at an early stage (Great Mosque of Erzurum, 530/1135; Kayseri, 535/1140; and Divriği, 626/1229) but by no means universally accepted. In such mosques the domed bay is invariably the largest of all and is placed along the axis of the *miḥrāb*. This emphasis on the totally enclosed covered mosque was to remain the principal feature of Turkish mosque architecture, and as a natural corollary fostered a compact and integrated style. Sometimes a small courtyard is integrated into this design (Malatya, 635/1237; Kayseri, Mosque of K͟hʷānd K͟hātūn, 635/1237; Harput, 560/1165). By degrees, however, the courtyard was relegated to one of two functions: as a forecourt, akin to the atrium of Byzantine churches and thus heralding the mosque proper, instead of being co-equal to the sanctuary; and as a bay within the *muṣallā*, furnished with a skylight and a fountain as a symbolic reminder of the word outside. Sometimes these two uses coincided. The skylight bay (*s̲h̲ādirwān*) was normally placed along the axis of the *miḥrāb* and thus served as a secondary accent for it, in much the same manner as a central dome.

The 8th/14th century saw no major developments in hypostyle plans. Flat-roofed prayer halls, some with wooden-roofed porches (Merām mosque, Konya, 804-27/1402-24), others, especially in the Ḳaramān region, without them, continued to be built. So too did hypostyle mosques with vaulted domical bays (Yivli Minare mosque, Antalya, 775/1373; the type recurs both in eastern Anatolia and Ottoman territory in Bursa and Edirne). Variations in the Damascus schema, with the transept replaced by one or more domes, a raised and wider central aisle, a skylight bay, or any combination of these were frequent (ᶜĪsā Bey mosque, Selcuk, 776/1374; Ulu Cami, Birgi, 712/1312; mosque of Ak͟hī Elvān, Ankara, *ca.* 780/1378). Finally, mosques with an enlarged domed bay in front of the *miḥrāb* spread from their earlier base in south-eastern Anatolia, an area bounded to the east by the Ulu Cami in Van (791-803/1389-1400) and to the west by that of Manisa (778/1376). In the latter mosque the *ḳibla* side is dominated by the dome and takes up almost half the mosque; a large arcaded courtyard with a portico accounts for the rest. With such buildings the stage is set for Ottoman architecture and Arab prototypes are left far behind.

These Anatolian mosques depart still further from the norm of the hypostyle type in their predilection for elaborate integrated façades. While earlier mosques of Arab type frequently singled out the principal entrance by a monumental archway, often with a dome behind it, the tendency was to keep the façade relatively plain. Only in the highly built-up areas of the major cities of the Near East, such as Cairo, Jerusalem, Damascus and Aleppo, did the extreme shortage of space, and often the small scale of the mosques themselves, oblige architects to decorate mosque façades if they wished to draw attention to them, e.g. the Aḳmar mosque, Cairo, 519/1125. In Anatolia the tenacious Armenian tradition, which favoured extensive external sculpture and articulation, may well have predisposed Muslim architects in Anatolia to develop integrated decorative schemes for the main façades of their mosques. A monumental stone portal or *pīs͟htāḳ* [*q.v.*], often an *īwān* [*q.v.*] was the standard centrepiece for such designs. It could be strongly salient and tower well above the roofline (Divriği Cami). Further articulation was provided by ranges of recessed arches with decorative surrounds (Dunaysir), open or blind arcades along the upper section of the façade (Mayyāfāriḳīn and ᶜAlāʾ al-Din mosque, Konya), and windows with densely carved frames (ᶜĪsā Bey mosque, Selcuk).

(c) Egypt and Syria. It seems possible that some of the more elaborate Mamlūk mosque façades in Cairo, such as those of Baybars (660/1262) and Sulṭān Ḥasan (757/1356) may derive, if at several removes, from Anatolian prototypes of the kind discussed above. It is noteworthy, however, that in general the mosques of the Ayyūbid and Mamlūk period offer little scope for large-scale reworking of the hypostyle plan, since they were too small. The mosque of Baybars and that of al-Nāṣir Muḥammad b. Ḳalawūn in the Cairo citadel (718/1318), which is a free copy of it, provide exceptions to this rule; in both cases a monumental dome over the *miḥrāb* bay is the principal accent of an extensive covered space. The relative scarcity of major mosques in this period not only reflects the primacy of the great early *d͟jāmiᶜ*s which were still in use, and which made further such buildings redundant; it also marks a shift in patronage away from mosques towards mausolea, *madrasas*, *k͟hānḳāh*s and the like. In time, not surprisingly, joint foundations became the norm, in which the mosque was a mere oratory, a component in some larger complex. Eventually, too, the forms of mosques came to reflect those of contemporary *madrasas* more than the hypostyle plans of earlier periods. Hence the dominance of small domed mosques such as the 7th/14th century Mamlūk *d͟jāmiᶜ*s of Tripoli. Such buildings have no bearing on the history of the Arab mosque plan.

(d) The Yemen. Apart from the Mag͟hrib, it was principally in the Yemen that the large hypostyle mosque maintained its popularity throughout the mediaeval period. Inadequate publication has meant that these buildings are less well known than they deserve, and without excavation the dating of many of them will remain problematic. This is particularly regrettable because several of them were built on the site of pre-Islamic temples, churches or synagogues (e.g. al-D͟jilāʾ mosque, Ṣanᶜāʾ), and spolia from these earlier buildings—such as columns, capitals, inscriptions and even sculptures of birds—are used very widely. Persistent local tradition attributes the *d͟jāmiᶜ*s of Ṣanᶜāʾ and al-D͟janad to the time of the Prophet; both were probably rebuilt by al-Walīd I. The former has preserved much more of its original appearance: perimeter walls of finely cut stone in stepped courses enclose a roughly square shape with a central courtyard with the *muṣallā* only slightly deeper than the other sides. Al-D͟janad, on the other hand, has had its similar original layout transformed by a domed transept and numerous subsidiary buildings. This gradual transformation by the addition of prayer halls, mausolea, ablutions facilities and the like is a recurrent pattern in the Yemen (*d͟jāmiᶜ*s of Zabīd and Ibb).

Small hypostyle mosques of square form (al-ᶜAbbās, 7th/13th century), or of rectangular shape, whether broad and shallow oblongs (Tit͟hid, 7th/13th century) or narrow and deep (Tamur, 5th/11th century or earlier), are common, and a few larger mosques of this kind, still without a courtyard, are known (D͟hibin, after 648/1250). The commonest form, however, comprises a structure that is rectangular or trapezoidal (Masd͟jid al-Ṣawmaᶜa, Hūt, 7th/13th century) with a central courtyard and extensive covered *riwāḳ*s on all sides (Rawḍa *d͟jāmiᶜ*, 7th/13th century). Often this formula is enriched by a lavishly carved or painted wooden ceiling over the sanctuary area alone (S͟hibām *d͟jāmiᶜ*, 4th/10th century) or by the incorporation of mausolea (Ẓafār D͟hibin, 7th/13th century; funerary mosque of the *Imām* al-Hādī Yaḥyā, Ṣaᶜda, 4th/10th century and later) or of minarets (D͟jibla, 480/1087; D͟hū As͟hraḳ, 410/1019). Influences from the central Islamic lands explain the use of wider central aisles in the *muṣallā* (Ẓafār D͟hibin, Ibb, D͟jibla, D͟hū As͟hraḳ) and a concentration of domes along the *ḳibla* wall (enlargement of Ibb *d͟jāmiᶜ*; D͟jāmiᶜ al-Muẓaffar and As͟hrafiyya mosque, both 7th/13th century, Taᶜizz). The glory of these Yemeni mosques as a group lies in their decoration: exceptionally long bands of stucco inscriptions (mosques of D͟hamār and Rada, 7th/13th century and later), frescoes with epigraphic, floral and geometric designs (Rasūlid mosques of Taᶜizz) and a matchless series of carved and painted wooden ceilings (Ẓafār D͟hibin, al-ᶜAbbās, Sirha, D͟hibin, S͟hibām, Ṣanᶜāʾ and others).

4. The Iranian tradition.

(a) The early period. Such was the prescriptive power of the "Arab plan" that its influence permeated mosque architecture in the non-Arab lands too. It would therefore be an artificial exercise to consider the development of the Iranian mosque in isolation, the more so as many early mosques in Iran (Bīs͟hāpūr, Sīrāf, Susa, Yazd) were of Arab plan. Some also had the square minarets which were an early feature of that plan (Dāmg͟hān; Sīrāf). Rather did the Iranian mosque acquire its distinctive character by enriching the hypostyle form by two elements deeply rooted in pre-Islamic Iranian architecture: the domed chamber and the *īwān*, a vaulted open hall with a rectangular arched façade. The domed chamber derived from the mostly diminutive Sasanian fire temple with four axial arched openings, the so-called *čahār ṭāḳ*. Set in the midst of a large open space, it served to house the sacred fire. This layout obviously lent itself to Muslim prayer, and literary sources recount how such fire temples were taken over and converted into mosques (e.g. at Bu<u>kh</u>ārā) by the simple expedient of blocking up the arch nearest the *ḳibla* and replacing it with a *miḥrāb*; but conclusive archaeological evidence of this practice is still lacking, though the mosques of Yązd-i <u>Kh</u>āst and Ḳurwa may be examples of it. Such domed chambers, whether converted fire temples or purpose-built Muslim structures, may have served as self-contained mosques, with or without an attached courtyard; certainly the earliest part of many mediaeval Iranian mosques is precisely the domed chamber.

The associations of the *īwān*, by contrast, were markedly more secular than religious; its honorific and ceremonial purpose in Sasanian palaces is epitomised by the great vault at Ctesiphon, where it announced the audience chamber of the Emperor. The *īwān* form was therefore well fitted to serve as a monumental entrance to the mosque, to mark the central entrance to the *muṣallā* (Tārī<u>kh</u>āna, Dām<u>gh</u>ān; Nāʾīn) or, indeed, itself to serve as the sanctuary (as at Nīrīz perhaps 363/973 onwards?). Thus both the domed chamber and the *īwān* quickly found their way into the vocabulary of Iranian mosque architecture, and by their articulating power gave it a wider range of expression than the Arab mosque plan could command. It was in the interrelationships between the domed chamber, the *īwān* and the hypostyle hall that the future of the Iranian mosque was to lie.

(b) The Sal<u>dj</u>ūḳ period. The tentative experiments of early Iranian mosque architecture crystallised in the Sal<u>dj</u>ūḳ period, especially between *ca.* 473/1080 and *ca.* 555/1160. The major mosques built or enlarged at this time have as their major focus a monumental domed chamber enclosing the *miḥrāb* and preceded by a lofty *īwān*. This double unit is commonly flanked by arcaded and vaulted prayer halls. This arrangement represents the final transformation of the *muṣallā* in Iranian mosques, using the vocabulary of Sasanian religious and palatial architecture for new ends. The sanctuary *īwān* opens onto a courtyard with an *īwān* at the centre of each axis punctuating the regular sequence of *riwāḳ*s. These arcades attain a new importance as façade architecture by their arrangement in double tiers. Yet the focus of attention is undoubtedly the great domed chamber. The simplicity of the prototypical *čahār ṭāḳ* is scarcely to be recognised in these massive Sal<u>dj</u>ūḳ *maḳṣūra* domes with their multiple openings in the lower walls and their complex zones of transition. This concentration on the domed chamber was often achieved at the expense of the rest of the mosque (Gulpāyagān *<u>dj</u>āmiʿ*, *ca.* 510/1116). The new combination of old forms created the classical, definitive version of the already ancient 4-*iwan* courtyard plan that was to dominate Iranian architecture for centuries to come, infiltrating not only other building types such as *madrasa*s and caravansarais, but also spreading as far west as Egypt and Anatolia and eastwards to Central Asia and India. The 4-*īwān* mosque thus became in time the dominant mosque type of the eastern Islamic world.

Up to the end of the Sal<u>dj</u>ūḳ period, however, the way was still open for numerous other combinations of hypostyle hall, domed chamber and *īwān*. Ba<u>sh</u>an, for example (4th/10th century) has a square layout with courtyard, hypostyle hall, domed sanctuary and sanctuary *īwān*, but lacks any further articulation of the courtyard façade by *īwāns*. The mosques of Dandānḳān [*q.v.* in Suppl.] and Ma<u>sh</u>had-i Miṣriyān [*q.v.*] (both 5th/11th century) are typologically related. At Urmiya/Riḍāʾiyya (7th/13th century) the mosque is an extensive shallow oblong with the domed chamber at one end of a hypostyle hall, and no *īwān*. Sometimes the mosque is entirely covered by five (Mas<u>dj</u>id-i Diggaron, Hazāra, 5th/11th century) or nine domed bays (Čār Sutūn mosque, Tirmi<u>dh</u>, 5th/11th century; Mas<u>dj</u>id-i Kūča Mīr, Nātanz, 6th/12th century). In its Sal<u>dj</u>ūḳ form the mosque at Ardabīl comprised a domed chamber with an *īwān* in front of it, while at Sīn (528/1136) the sanctuary, comprising a deep *īwān* with *muḳarnas* vaulting, engulfs one side of the diminutive courtyard. The huge courtyard of the Firdaws *<u>dj</u>āmiʿ* (597/1201) is dominated by its single *īwān* which heralds a low vaulted sanctuary. The *<u>dj</u>āmiʿ*s of Faryumad (7th/13th century?) and Gūnābād (606/1210) have only two *īwān*s facing each other across a narrow courtyard, and no domed chamber. Other mosques in <u>Kh</u>urāsān are simpler still, comprising only the domed chamber itself (Sangān-i Pāʾīn, 535/1140; Birrābād and ʿAbdallāhābād, both possibly Sal<u>dj</u>ūḳ) or with insignificant bays adjoining it (Ta<u>kh</u>latan Baba, 6th/12th century). Often too, the various elements were added in an unpredictable sequence, for instance at Simnān where a probably 5th/11th century columned hall had a complete mosque "unit" comprising a domed chamber, *īwān* and courtyard tacked on to its side. Even within the classical 4-*īwān* model, considerable diversity could be attained by varying the scale of the components: from long narrow courtyards (Simnān) or small square ones of domestic scale (Zawāra, 527/1133) to huge open expanses broken up by trees (<u>Sh</u>īrāz *<u>dj</u>āmiʿ*, mainly 10th/16th century), pools or fountains.

The principal emphasis on the internal façade was, however, unchanging. The exterior, by contrast, was unadorned and unarticulated to the point of austerity. Variations in the height or breadth of *īwāns* reinforced axial or hierarchical distinctions. By common consent the sanctuary *īwān* was the largest and deepest; the opposite *īwān* was next in size, though often very shallow, while the two lateral *īwāns* were usually the smallest. Minarets at the corner of the sanctuary *īwān* underlined its importance, while the twin-minaret portal *īwān* first encountered in the Sal<u>dj</u>ūḳ period (Na<u>kh</u>čivān, *ca.* 582/1186; Ardistān, Mas<u>dj</u>id-i Imām Ḥasan, 553/1158) became increasingly monumental and elaborate in later centuries (*<u>dj</u>āmiʿ*s of A<u>sh</u>tar<u>dj</u>ān, 715/1315, and Yazd, 846/1442). *Īwān* minarets of this kind gradually replaced the freestanding cylindrical minarets so popular in the Sal<u>dj</u>ūk period.

(c) The Īl<u>kh</u>ānid period. As in Mamlūk Egypt, so too in Iran the later mediaeval history of the mosque is sometimes hard to disentangle from that of the *madrasa*-, tomb- or shrine-complex. Prayer and communal worship were, after all, integral to the operation of such "little cities of God" as the shrines of Ardabīl, Nātanz, Turbat-i <u>D</u>jām, Basṭām and Lin<u>dj</u>ān—all of them the scene of much building activity in the 8th/14th century—to say nothing of the great shrines of Ḳumm and Ma<u>sh</u>had. Such new foundations as these were simply perpetuated Sal<u>dj</u>ūḳ models (Hafs<u>h</u>ūya, early 8th/14th century), though these were subtly altered by having their proportions attenuated or otherwise modified. At Ashtardjān everything is subordinated to the principal axis announced by the double minaret façade, an emphasis which is taken up and intensified by the single great *īwān* which takes up the full width of the courtyard and leads into the domed sanctuary. At Warāmīn, too (722/1322 onwards), which is of standard 4-*īwān* type, the sense of axial progression is strong, and is made rather more effective than at Ashtardjān by the absolute length of the mosque and the extended vestibule. The *djāmi*ᶜ of ᶜAlī Shāh in Tabrīz, by contrast (*ca.* 710-20/1310-20) deliberately returned, it seems, to much earlier models, for it comprised essentially a huge cliff-like *īwān* preceded by a courtyard with a central pool and clumps of trees in the corners—perhaps a deliberate reference to the Ṭāḳ-i Kisrā itself. For smaller mosques, Saldjūḳ models were again at hand; hence, for example, the trio of domed chamber mosques with *īwāns* at Azirān, Kadj and Dashtī, all datable *ca.* 725/1325. Yet another compliment to earlier masters was the Īlkhānid tendency to add new structures to existing mosques: a *madrasa* to the Iṣfahān *djāmi*ᶜ (776-8/1374-7), an *īwān* to the mosque at Gaz (*ca.* 715/1315), and so on.

(d) The Tīmūrid period. The Tīmūrid period took up still further ideas which had been no more than latent in earlier centuries. While some mosques of traditional form were built such as the Mosque of Gawhar Shād, in Mashhad, of standard 4-*īwān* type (821/1418), attention focused particularly on the portal and *ḳibla īwāns*, which soared to new heights. Turrets at the corners magnified these proportions still further. This trend towards gigantism is exposed at its emptiest in the 4-*īwān djāmi*ᶜ of Ziyāratgāh, near Harāt (887/1482), where the absence of decoration accentuates the sheer mass of the sanctuary *īwān* looming over the courtyard. At its best, however, as in the mosque of Bībī Khānum, Samarḳand (801/1399) where these exceptional proportions are consistently carried through to virtually every part of the mosque, the effect is overwhelming. Here the 4-*īwān* plan is transformed by the use of a domed chamber behind each lateral *īwān*; by the profusion of minarets—at the exterior corners and flanking both portal and sanctuary *īwāns*—and by the four hundred-odd domes which cover the individual bays.

As in the Mongol period, however, the fashion for building *khānḳāhs*, *madrasas* and funerary monuments, all of them capable of serving as places of worship (shrine of Aḥmad Yasawī, Turkestan, begun 797/1394; the Rīgistān complex, Samarḳand, begun in its Tīmūrid form in 820/1417; Gawhar Shād complex, Harāt, 821/1418) excluded an equal emphasis on architecture. This may explain the continued popularity of so many standard mosque types—the domed hypostyle (Ziyāratgāh, Masdjid-i Čihil Sutūn *ca.* 890/1485) and the two-*īwān* type so long familiar in Khurāsān (Badjistān and Nīshāpūr *djāmi*ᶜs, both later 9th/15th century)—to say nothing of the emphasis on refurbishing earlier mosques (*djāmi*ᶜs of Iṣfahān, 880/1475 and Harāt, 903-5/1497-9), which, in accordance with the Tīmūrid predilection for innovative vaulting, often took the form of transversely vaulted halls (*djāmi*ᶜs of Abarḳūh, 808/1415; Yazd, 819/1416; Shīrāz, *ca.* 820/1417; Maribud, 867/1462; and Kāshān, 867-8/1462-3; and the mosques of Sar-i Rīg, 828/1424 and Mīr Čaḳinaḳ, 840-1/1436-7, at Yazd). There was also still ample room for surprises. The winter prayer hall added to the Iṣfahān *djāmi*ᶜ in 851/1447 has multiple aisles of huge pointed arches springing directly from the ground and lit by ochre alabaster slabs let into the vaults and diffusing a golden radiance. The hoary 4-*īwān* formula was given a new twist by the addition of twin domed chambers flanking the sanctuary *īwān* (Harāt *djāmi*ᶜ, 9th/15th century), an idea which infiltrated other plan types too (Rushkhar *djāmi*ᶜ, 859/1454). At Djādjarm (late 9th/late 15th century?) the central axis marked by the domed chamber and the courtyard is flanked on each side by a trio of vaulted bays.

Yet perhaps the most original mosque designs of the period were those which focused on the single dome and thus echoed, if only distantly, the preoccupations of contemporary Ottoman architects. This concept manifested itself in several different ways. In the Masdjid-i Gunbād, Ziyāratgāh (*ca.* 887-912/1483-1506), a square exterior encloses small corner chambers and a cruciform domed central area, a layout more reminiscent of a palace pavilion than a mosque. The core of the Masdjid-i Shāh, Mashhad (855/1451), is again a large domed chamber, but this is enclosed by a vaulted ambulatory and preceded by a long façade with corner minarets and a portal *īwān*. Most ambitious of all, however, is the Blue Mosque in Tabrīz (870/1465) in which a similar idea is given much more integrated expression by virtue of the open-plan arrangement of the central space. The dome springs from eight massive piers, but this octagon has further piers in the corners, making it a square with twelve openings, and thus offering easy access to the multidomed ambulatory. A similar openness characterises the gallery area and ensures that this mosque, though entirely covered, was airy, spacious and flooded with light. The range and subtlety of its polychrome tilework makes this mosque an apt coda for a period which exploited to an unprecedented degree the role of colour in architecture.

(e) The Ṣafavid period. The restoration and enlargement of existing mosques, a trend already noted in Tīmūrid times, continued apace in the Ṣafavid period, and involved over a score of mosques in the 10th/16th century alone. Yet not one new mosque of the first importance survives from this century, though the Masdjid-i ᶜAlī in Iṣfahān (929/1522), a classic 4-*īwān* structure, has a sanctuary whose open-plan dome on pendentives provides a bridge between the Blue Mosque in Tibrīz and the Luṭfallāh mosque in Iṣfahān (1011-28/1602-10). The latter, a private oratory for Shāh ᶜAbbās I, makes a very public break with tradition, for it is simply a huge square chamber. Its lofty dome rests on eight arches via an intermediary zone of 32 niches. The whole interior is sheathed in glittering tilework whose smooth surfaces simplify all structural subtleties. Though the mosque is correctly oriented towards Mecca, it is set at an angle to the great square (*maydān*) from which it is entered, an angle dissimulated by the portal *īwān* which instead obeys the orientation of the *maydān* towards the cardinal points of the compass. A low vaulted passage linking *īwān* and dome chamber, but invisible from either, resolves these conflicting axes. It also draws attention to a discrepancy which could easily have been avoided and is therefore deliberate.

In the nearby Masdjid-i Shāh (1021-40/1612-30), which also fronts the *maydān*, the problem of discordant axes is solved with sovereign ease, for the portal leads into a diagonal vestibule which in turn opens into a 4-*īwān* courtyard now correctly orientated. Both portal and *ḳibla īwāns* have paired minarets to assert their importance. The scale is vast, but the entire mosque is conceived in due proportion to it. As at the comparably large mosque of Bībī Khānum, dome chambers behind the lateral *īwān*s give extra space for prayer, while two *madrasa*s with courtyards flank the main courtyard to the south. Thus even at the height of its popularity, the 4-*īwān* mosque could accommodate quite major innovations without impairing its essential character. Later Ṣafavid mosques, such as the *dj̲āmi*ʿs of Sarm and Čas̲h̲um, the Masd̲j̲id-i Wazīr in Kās̲h̲ān and that of ʿAlī Ḳulī Ag̲h̲a in Iṣfahān, serve by their very modesty, however, to highlight the altogether exceptional status of the two mosques on the Iṣfahān *maydān*. Even such a spacious and handsome version of the traditional 4-*īwān* schema as the Masd̲j̲id-i Ḥakim, Iṣfahān (1067/1656) could not fail to be an anticlimax in their wake.

5. The Turkish tradition.

(a) Early domed mosques. The earliest Anatolian mosques follow Arab prototypes, and by degrees some of them take on an Iranian colouring, especially in their free use of *īwān*s for portals and for sanctuary entrances. Already by the 7th/13th century, however, an emphasis on the isolated domed chamber as a mosque type began to make itself felt. This idea too might have had Iranian origins, but it soon developed in ways that owed nothing to Iran, since the contemporary preference for entirely covered mosques with no courtyard was itself enough to encourage experiments in the articulation of interior space. The dome quickly became the most favoured device to this end. In Iran, by and large, the domed chamber behind the *ḳibla īwān* remained spatially isolated from the rest of the mosque. In Anatolia, by contrast, architects were always seeking new ways of integrating the main domed space with the area around it. A consistent emphasis on domical forms created the necessary visual unity to achieve this. Already in the Sald̲j̲ūḳ period tentative experiments in this direction may be noted, for example the ʿAlāʾ al-Dīn mosque, Niğde (620/1223), whose *ḳibla* is marked by three domed and cross-vaulted bays with further parallel aisles behind. In the Ulu Cami of Bitlis (555/1160), a single great dome replaces these smaller bays, while in the Gök mosque and *madrasa*, Amasya (665/1266), the *masd̲j̲id* comprises a series of triple-domed aisles. Experiment with domical forms was therefore deeply rooted in Anatolian architecture from the beginning. It is above all, however, the hallmark of mosques erected by the Ottomans, and can be traced to the very earliest years of that dynasty.

(b) Ottoman architecture before 857/1453. The sequence begins very modestly with a series of mosques comprising a simple domed cube with a lateral vestibule (ʿAlāʾ al-Dīn mosque, Bursa, 736/1335, a structure typical of well over a score of such Ottoman mosques built in the course of the 8th/14th century) and minor variants of this schema, such as the mosque of Orhan Gazi, Bilecik, and the Yeşil Cami, Iznik, 780/1378. Such structures have a natural affinity with larger mausolea throughout the Islamic world, and with the simplest forms of Iranian mosques. It is only with hindsight that their significance for later developments, in which the theme of the single, and (above all) central, dominant dome of ever-increasing size becomes steadily more important, can be appreciated. This, then, is the main line of evolution in Ottoman mosque architecture, and the discussion will return to it shortly.

Meanwhile, two other types of mosque, in which the dome also loomed large, deserve brief investigation, especially as they bade fair in the formative early years to oust the domed, centrally planned mosque as the favoured Ottoman type, and also because they had their own part to play in the final synthesis of the 10th/16th century. The presence of three major types of domed mosque in the same century is a reminder that the pace of change was uneven. Several mosques conceived on an altogether larger scale rejuvenated the hypostyle form by investigating the impact of multiple adjoining domes. In some cases, like the Ulu Cami, Bursa, of 797/1394, a simple square subdivided into 20 domed bays of equal width though of varying height—the choice of the dome as the agent of vaulting is a diagnostic Ottoman feature—the effect was distinctly old-fashioned. At ground level this is an Arab mosque, even if its elevation is Anatolian. Contemporary with this, but marking a very different attitude to interior space, are two mosques in Bursa, that of Yïldïrïm Bāyazīd, 794/1390, and the Yeşil Cami of 816/1413, which use the dome motif on various scales and thus far more imaginatively. They represent a second preparatory stage on the way to the mature Ottoman mosque, and their large layout is by turn cruciform, stepped or of inverted T-type. Their distinguishing feature is the use of several domes of different sizes. In the two cases under discussion, the inverted T-plan highlights the *miḥrāb* aisle by two adjoining domes along the central axis flanked by a trio of domed or vaulted bays on each side, the whole knit together laterally by a 5-domed portico. Sandwiched between these two buildings in date is the Ulu Cami of Edirne, 806/1403, where the square is subdivided into nine equal bays, eight of them domed, with a domed and vaulted portico tacked on. At the mosque of Čelebi Sulṭān Meḥemmed, Dimetoka, this arrangement is refined by an increased concentration on the central dome, which is enveloped by vaults on the main axes and diagonals, the whole preceded by a 3-domed portico. Such a combination cannot fail to recall the standard quincunx plan, complete with narthex, of mid-Byzantine churches, and it was of course these buildings which dominated the Anatolian countryside in the early centuries of Turkish occupation. Steady Byzantine influence can be seen to have affected the evolution of Ottoman architecture even before the capture of Istanbul brought Turkish architects face to face with Hagia Sophia. Yet it would be grossly mistaken to regard mature Ottoman mosques as mere derivatives of Hagia Sophia. The Üç Şerefeli mosque, Edirne, of 851/1447, with its huge central dome on a hexagonal base flanked on either side by a pair of much smaller domes and preceded by a lateral courtyard enclosed by 22 domed bays, makes excellent sense within a purely Ottoman perspective as a key stage in the evolution which terminated in the great masterpieces of Sinān. The divergence between the great dome and the lesser ones flanking it has already become acute and was to end in their total suppression.

Yet one significant element, crucial to Hagia Sophia and a cliché of Ottoman architecture after 857/1453, had not yet entered the architectural vocabulary of the Turkish mosque before that date. This was the use of two full semi-domes along the *miḥrāb* axis to buttress the main dome. The long-rooted Islamic custom of marking the *miḥrāb* bay by a great dome rendered such a feature otiose. Once the decision had been taken to make the largest dome the central feature of a much larger square, the way was open for the adoption of this Byzantine feature, and with it the transformation and enrichment of interior space was a foregone conclusion. Otherwise, most of the architectural vocabulary used in mature Ottoman mosques was already to hand by 857/1453: flying buttresses, the undulating exterior profile created by multiple domes, tall pencil-shaped minarets and a certain parsimony of exterior ornament allied to exquisite stereotomy. It has to be admitted, however, that these features had yet to find their full potential, notably in the failure to develop a suitably imposing exterior to match the spatial splendours within. That potential could be realised only when these features were used in tandem with each other by masters seeking to express a newly-won confidence and bent on creating an integrated style for that purpose. The mosque was, moreover, their chosen instrument; indeed, Ottoman architecture is, first and foremost, an architecture of mosques.

(c) Ottoman architecture after 857/1453. The capture of Constantinople in 857/1453 provided both a terminus and an impetus to a radical rethinking of mosque design. Appropriately enough, the first building to express the new mood was a victory monument, as its name indicates: the Fātiḥ Mosque (867-75/1463-70). This has a single huge semi-dome buttressing the main one but also displacing it off the main axis; clearly, the spatial, aesthetic and structural implications of such a semidome had not yet been fully grasped. Within a generation, this anomaly at least had been rectified; the mosque of Bāyazīd II (completed 913/1506) has two such semi-domes on the *miḥrāb* axis, with four lesser domes flanking this central corridor on each side. On the other hand, the projecting portico sandwiched between dome chamber and courtyard is a clumsy and lopsided expedient with little functional justification. Yet the resultant emphasis on the portico is wholly typical of a period in which this feature re-appeared under numerous guises, especially in doubled form (Mihrimah mosque, completed *ca.* 973/1565). The Şehzade mosque (955/1548) presents a much more streamlined appearance, with dome chamber and courtyard of approximately equal proportions. Within the sanctuary, the great central dome opens into semi-domes on all four sides, with small diagonal semi-domes opening off the main ones and corner domes. It is instructive thus to see Ottoman architects developing the possibilities of the centralised plan like the builders of Christian churches and martyria a millennium before, and coming to very similar conclusions. Smaller mosques with domes on hexagonal (Ahmed Paşa, completed *ca.* 970/1562) or octagonal bases (Mihrimah mosque) were scarcely less popular than domed squares. A small number of wooden-roofed mosques perpetuating earlier modes, and with their roots in the Arab tradition, survive (e.g. Ramazan Efendi in Koçamustafapaşa, 994/1585, and Tekkeci Ibrahim Ağa, 999/1590) as reminders of a very widespread type of Ottoman mosque now almost entirely eclipsed by more durable structures.

In the ferment of experiment which marks 10th/16th century Ottoman architecture, the key figure was undoubtedly Sinān, an Islamic equivalent to Sir Christopher Wren, who transformed the face of the capital city as of the provinces with some 334 buildings (mostly mosques) erected in his own lifetime, and whose pivotal role as chief court architect (effectively Master of Works) allowed him to stamp his ideas on public architecture from Algeria to ʿIrāḳ and from Thrace to Arabia in the course of a phenomenally long career which spanned virtually the entire century. The Süleymaniye mosque in Istanbul (963/1556) is by common consent the masterpiece of his middle age. It takes up and refines the model of the Bāyazīd II mosque by adding ideas taken from the Şehzade mosque, like the succession of semi-domed spaces billowing out from the main dome, though only along the principal axis. Huge arches serve to compartmentalise the spatial volumes.

All these mosques are preceded by an open courtyard whose cloister is roofed by long files of adjoining domes. This standard feature typifies the new emphasis on subsidiary structures, mausolea, *ʿimārets*, *madrasas* and the like, and the consistent attempt to integrate them visually with the sanctuary itself, for example by subordinating them to the principal axes of the design. All this implies a marked increase in scale and a new sensitivity to the landscaping of the ensemble. Hence the recurrent choice of dramatic sites for these mosques, especially in Istanbul with its built-in vistas along the Bosphorus. This awareness of topography as a feature of mosque design is evident as early as the Fātiḥ mosque; its three parallel axes are grouped around and within an enclosed open piazza measuring some 210 m. per side. The climax of mature Ottoman architecture is reached with Sinān's final masterpiece, the Selimiye at Edirne (982/1574), in which the largest of Ottoman central domes (31.28 m. in diameter, hedged externally by the loftiest quartet of Ottoman minarets (70.89 m. high) rests on eight piers pushed as close to the walls as safety will allow so as to create the largest possible open space.

While the increase in the absolute height and breadth of these great domed chambers is striking, the amount of articulation and detail crammed into these spaces is scarcely less impressive. All is subordinated to a formidable concentration of purpose—for example, the carefully considered fenestration, surely a legacy from Hagia Sophia, with its superposed groupings of eights and sixes or sevens, fives and threes. In the interests of creating the maximum untrammelled space, thrusts are concentrated onto a few huge piers with spherical pendentives between them, and thus the layout is a model of clarity and logic. Flooded with light, their volumetric subdivisions apparent at a glance, these interiors are at the opposite pole from the dim mysteries of Hagia Sophia. Frescoes reminiscent of manuscript illumination and of carpet designs vie with Iznik tiles to decorate the interior surfaces, and often (as in the case of fluted piers) to deny their sheer mass.

Externally, these mosques attest a well-nigh fugal complexity by virtue of their obsessive concentration on a very few articulating devices like windows, arches and domes. The repetition of the same forms on varying scales intensifies the sense of unity. Even the minarets which mark the outer limits of the mosque's surface area are brought into play; for example, those of the Sultan Ahmed Mosque (completed 1025/1616) have the bases of their balconies so calibrated as to coincide with the top of the main dome, its collar and the collar of the main subsidiary half-domes, while their location at the corners of the building binds it together and defines the sacred space from afar. Detailing is sparse and crisp, with a strong linear emphasis, a flawless sense of interval and a pronounced attenuation of features like wall niches and engaged columns (Süleymaniye mosque). Nothing is allowed to impair the primary aesthetic impact of cliff-like expanses of smooth grey stone. Most notable of all is a dramatic but ordered stacking of units culminating in the great dome which crowns and developes the entire ensemble. These individual units are each locked into place within a gently sloping pyramidal structure whose inevitable climax is the central dome. From this peak the subsidiary domes, semi-domes and domed buttresses cascade downwards to form a rippling but tightly interlocked silhouette. These highly articulated exteriors are a triumphant reversal of the standard Islamic preference in mosque architecture for stressing the interior at the expense of the exterior. As the viewpoint changes, so too does the profile of these mosques, from a continuous smoothly undulating line to a series of sharp angular projections formed by stepped buttresses and roof-turrets. The preference for saucer domes rather than pointed domes with a high stilt fosters the sense of immovable, rock-like stability, with the topmost dome clamped like a lid onto the mobile, agitated roof-lines beneath it.

This, then, can justly claim to be architects' architecture. It merits that term by virtue of its unbroken concentration on the single germinal idea of the domed centralised mosque. It is against that consistent unity of vision that the role of the Hagia Sophia must be assessed. Of course, Turkish architects were not blind to its many subtleties, and they freely quarried it for ideas. But it was as much a challenge that inspired them to emulation as it was a source for technical expertise. Finally, it was the Ottomans who succeeded where the Byzantines had failed: in devising for these great domed places of worship an exterior profile worthy of the splendours within. The triumphant issue of their labours to that end can be read along the Istanbul skyline to this day.

Bibliography: C. Gurlitt, *Die Baukunst Konstantinopels*, 3 vols., Berlin 1907-12; F. Sarre and E. Herzfeld, *Archäologische Reise im Euphrat- und Tigrisgebiet*, 4 vols., Berlin 1911-20; M. S. Briggs, *Muhammadan architecture in Egypt and Palestine*, Oxford 1924; A. Gabriel, *Les mosquées de Constantinople*, in *Syria*, vii (1926), 353-419; E. Diez, *Masdjid. III. Architecture*, in *EI*[1], III, 378-89; E. Pauty, *L'évolution du dispositif en T dans les mosquées à portiques*, in *Ber.Or.*, ii, (1932), 91-124; L. Y. Hautecoeur and G. Wiet, *Les Mosquées du Caire*, 2 vols., Paris 1932-4; Gabriel, *Monuments turcs d'Anatolie*, 2 vols., Paris 1934; M. B. Smith, *Material for a corpus of early Iranian Islamic architecture*. I-III., in *Ars Islamica*, ii (1935), 153-71, iv (1937), 1-40, vi (1939), 1-10; A. Godard, *Les anciennes mosquées de l'Irān*, in *Athār-é Īrān*, i/2 (1936), 187-210, continued in *Arts Asiatiques*, iii (1956), 48-63, 83-8; *idem*, *Historique du Masdjid-é Djumʿa d'Iṣfahān*, in *Athār-é Īrān*, i/2 (1936), 213-82; B. Maslow, *Les mosquées de Fès*, Paris 1937; J. Sauvaget, *Observations sur quelques mosquées seldjoukides*, in *AIEO Alger*, iv (1938), 81-120; A. U. Pope and P. Ackerman (eds.). *A survey of Persian art from prehistoric times to the present*, 6 vols., Oxford 1938-9; K. A. C. Creswell, *Early Muslim architecture. II. Early ʿAbbāsids, Umayyads of Cordova, Aghlabids, Ṭūlūnids and Samānids, A.D. 751-905*, Oxford 1940; Gabriel and Sauvaget, *Voyages archéologiques dans la Turquie Orientale*, 2 vols., Paris 1940; M. Akkush, *Contribution à une étude des origines de l'architecture musulmane. La Grande Mosquée de Médine (al-Ḥaram al-Madanī)*, in *Mélanges Maspero*, iii (1940), 377-410; Sauvaget, *La mosquée omeyyade de Médina*, Paris 1947; G. Marçais, *L'église et la mosquée*, in *L'Islam et l'Occident. Cahiers du Sud*, Marseilles 1947, 174-84; E. Kühnel, *Die Moschee. Bedeutung, Einrichtung und kunsthistorische Entwicklung der islamischen Kultstätte*, Berlin 1949; E. Lambert, *La synagogue de Dura-Europos et les origines de la mosquée*, in *Semitica*, iii (1950), 67-72; H. Stern, *Les origines de l'architecture de la mosquée omeyyade*, in *Syria*, xxviii (1951), 269-79; L. Torres Balbás, *Origen de las disposiciones arquitectónicas de las mezquitas*, in *Al-Andalus*, xvii (1952), 388-99; Creswell, *The Muslim architecture of Egypt. I. Ikhshīds and Fāṭimids, A.D. 937-1171. II. Ayyūbids and Early Baḥrite Mamlūks, A.D. 1171-1326.* Oxford 1952-60; U. Vogt-Göknil, *Türkische Moscheen*, Zürich 1953; E. Egli, *Sinan, der Baumeister osmanischer Glanzzeit*, Zürich 1954; Marçais, *L'architecture musulmane d'Occident: Tunisie, Algérie, Maroc, Espagne et Sicile*, Paris 1955; D. N. Wilber, *The architecture of Islamic Iran. The Il-Khānid Period*, Princeton 1955; Lambert, *Les origines de la mosquée et l'architecture religieuse des Omeyyades*, in *SI*, vi (1956), 5-18; Gabriel, *Une Capitale turque Brousse, Bursa*, 2 vols., Paris 1958; G. A. Pugačenkova, *Puti razvitiya arkhitekturi Yuzhnogo Turkmenistana pori rabovladeniya feodalizma*, in *Trudī Yuzhno-Turkmenistanskoi Arkheologičeskoi Ekspeditsii*, vi, Moscow 1958; L. Golvin, *La Mosquée. Ses origines. Sa morphologie. Ses diverses fonctions. Son rôle dans la vie musulmane, plus spécialement en Afrique du Nord*, Algiers 1960; M. Useinov, L. S. Bretanitski and A. Salamzade, *Istoriya arkhitekturi Azerbaidzhana*, Moscow 1963; A. Dietrich, *Die Moscheen von Gurgan zur Omaijadenzeit*, in *Isl.*, xl (1964), 1-17; Pugačenkova and L. I. Rempel', *Istoriya Iskusstva Uzbekistana*, Moscow 1965; A. Lézine, *Architecture de l'Ifriqiya*, Paris 1966; Bretanitski, *Zodčestvo Azerbaidzhana XII-XV v.v., i ego mesto v arkhitekture perednego vostoka*, Moscow 1966; A. Kuran, *The mosque in early Ottoman architecture*, Chicago and London 1968; O. Grabar, *La Grande Mosquée de Damas et les origines architecturales de la mosquée*, in *Synthronon. Art et Archéologie de la fin de l'Antiquité et du Moyen Âge. Recueil d'Études*, Paris 1968, 107-14; *idem*, *The architecture of the Middle Eastern city from past to present: the case of the mosque*, in *Middle Eastern cities*, ed. I. M. Lapidus, Berkeley and Los Angeles 1969, 26-46; Creswell, *Early Muslim architecture. Umayyads. A.D. 622-750*, 2 vols., Oxford 1969; J. Sourdel-Thomine, *La mosquée et la madrasa. Types monumentaux caractéristiques de l'art islamique médiéval*, in *Cahiers de civilisation médiévale Xᵉ-XIIᵉ siècles, Université de Poitiers, Centre d'Études Supérieures de Civilisation Médiévale*, xiii/2 (1970), 97-115; Golvin, *Essai sur l'architecture religieuse musulmane*, i-iv, Paris 1970-6; G. Goodwin, *A history of Ottoman architecture*, London 1971; O. Aslanapa, *Turkish art and architecture*, tr. A. Mill, London 1971; Kuran, *Thirteenth and fourteenth century mosques in Turkey*, in *Archaeology*, xxiv/3 (1971), 234-54; S. Ögel, *Der Kuppelraum in der türkischen Architektur*, Istanbul 1972; R. A. Jairazbhoy, *An outline of Islamic architecture*, Bombay 1972; R. Bourouiba, *L'art religieux musulman en Algérie*, Algiers 1973; Grabar, *The formation of Islamic art*, New Haven 1973; D. Kuban, *Muslim religious architecture*, 2 vols., Leiden 1974-85; R. Hillenbrand, *Saljūq dome chambers in North-west Iran*, in *Iran*, xiv (1976), 93-102; D. Hill, Golvin and Hillenbrand, *Islamic architecture in North Africa*, London 1976; J. D. Hoag, *Islamic architecture*, New York 1977; Vogt-Göknil, *Die Moschee. Grundformen sakraler Baukunst*, Zürich 1978; C. Ewert and J.-P. Wisshak, *Forschungen zur almohadischen Moschee. Lieferung 1: Vorstufen. Hierarchische Gliederungen westislamischer Betsäle des 8. bis 11. Jahrhunderts: Die Hauptmoscheen von Qairawan und Cordoba und ihr Bannkreis*, Mainz 1981; B. Finster, *Islamische Bau- und Kunstdenkmäler im Yemen*, in *Archäologische Berichte aus dem Yemen*, i (1982), 223-75; R. B. Serjeant and R. Lewcock (eds.), *Ṣanʿāʾ. An Arabian Islamic city*, London 1983; Hillenbrand, *The mosque in the medieval Islamic world*, in *Architecture in continuity. Building in the Islamic world today*, ed. S. Cantacuzino, New York 1985, 30-51.

(R. Hillenbrand)

II. In Muslim India

A. Typology.

The nature of the regional building styles and their characteristic decoration have been treated s.v. HIND.

vii. Architecture, in Vol. III above. This section deals with the essential typology of mosques in India, and excludes the simplest structures used only for occasional prayer such as the *ḳibla*-indications at some tombs and graveyards [see MAḲBARA. 5. India], and the special structures (*ʿīdgāh*) provided for the *ʿīds*; for these see MUṢALLĀ. 2.

The continuous history of the mosque begins with the M. Ḳuwwat al-Islām in Dihlī, founded immediately after the Muslim conquest in 587/1191. There are however records of mosques founded earlier, e.g. under the ʿAbbāsid caliphate in Sind [*q.v.*], by small communities of Muslim traders, especially in Gudjarāt and the Malabār coast, and by individual Ṣūfī *pīrs* who gathered a community around them. The remains of these are mostly too exiguous to be of value in a general statement. Recent explorations by M. Shokoohy, not yet published, have revealed a few structures, of a century or two before the conquest, at Bhadreshwar in Gudjarāt. These, in common with the first structures of any fresh conquest of expansion, are constructed from the remains of Hindū buildings; in the case of mosques built after a conquest there has been a deliberate pillaging of Hindū or Djayn temples, as an assertion of superiority as well as for the expediency of making use of material already quarried and of local impressed labour before the arrival of Muslim artisans. Examples of this are cited for different regions of India s.v. HIND, vii. Architecture, in Vol. III, p. 441 above. (It should be pointed out that the practice of pillaging the buildings of the conquered is known in India in the case of rival Hindū kings also.)

Where a mosque is actually constructed on the plinth of a destroyed Hindū building (e.g. M. Ḳuwwat al-Islām at Dihli; Aṭālā M. at Djawnpur) the *ḳibla* [*q.v.*] will probably not be accurately located and the original cardinal west made to serve the purpose; but in general an effort is made to observe the correct *ḳibla*, which varies between 20° north of west in the south of India to 25° south of west in the extreme north, with a conventional west used only rarely in original buildings.

Mosques which might be described as "public"—i.e. not only the *Masdjid-i djāmiʿ* of a particular locality (and of course in a conurbation there may be a separate *djāmiʿ* for each original *maḥalla*) but also the individually-founded or endowed mosques within a town—are enclosed on all sides. This has not been required of mosques within a *sarāʾī* or a *dargāh*, or when the mosque is an adjunct of a tomb, and there are countless instances of small private mosques where there seems never to have been any enclosure. The enclosure for the public mosque is particularly necessary for Islam *in partibus infidelium*, and those courtyards which are *not* enclosed are protected from the infidel gaze in some other way, e.g. by the *ṣaḥn* standing on a high plinth (examples: the Djāmiʿ M. at Shāhdjahānābād, Dihlī, Aṭālā M. at Djawnpur, where in both the courtyard is limited only by an open arcade or colonnade). The principal entrance is usually on the east, although any gate may be on occasion specified as a royal entrance; it is rare, though not unknown, for any entrance to be made in the western wall, and where this has happened it is not designed for access by the general public. The internal position of the principal *miḥrāb* [*q.v.*], sometimes of subsidiary *miḥrābs* also, is indicated on the outside of the west wall by one or more buttresses; a feature of mosques in India is the way the exterior elevation of the west wall is brought to life by decorative expedients.

The interior of the mosque admits of little variation outside two well-defined types. In one the western end (known in India as *līwān*) is a simple arrangement of columns supporting a roof, usually of at least three bays in depth but possibly of many more; the roof may be supported by beam-and-bracket or by the arch; the former arrangement being by no means confined to compilations of pillaged Hindū/Djayn material. The *līwān* openings may be connected directly with the arcades or colonnades of other sides of the *ṣaḥn*. Where Hindū material has been used it is usually necessary to superimpose one column upon another in order to gain sufficient height, for not infrequently a mezzanine gallery may be incorporated in the structure, in the *līwān* or in the side *riwāḳs*. These are frequently referred to as "women's galleries", but this is surely impossible unless they are placed to the rear of the structure so that women may not make their prayers in front of men; gallery structures in the *līwān* are more likely to be either reserved for royal (male) use or to be *čillas* for the use of a local *pīr*. In the other type, the *līwān* is physically separated from the *ṣaḥn* by a screen of arches (*maḳṣūra*), which may conceal a columnar structure to the west, as in the M. Ḳuwwat al-Islām where the *maḳṣūra* is a later addition to the original structure, or in the mosques of Gudjarāt where the arch is not used with as much freedom as in other styles. More commonly, however, the arches of the *maḳṣūra* are part of a vaulting system whereby the *līwān* is composed into one or more halls; there is always an odd number of *maḳṣūra* arches, and it is common for the bay which stands in front of the principal *miḥrāb* to be singled out for special treatment, either by being made taller than the rest, or by being specially decorated (the latter treatment common in the mosques of Bīdjāpur [*q.v.*]). (This is not invariably the central bay, as mosques are not necessarily symmetrical about the principal *miḥrāb* axis; cf. the "Stonecutters' M." in Fatḥpur Sikrī, where a *čilla* occupies two additional bays at the north end of the *līwān*, or the Afhāʾī Kangūra M. at Kāshī Banāras, where the side *riwāḳs* of the *līwān* are of unequal length.) In one mosque at Bīdjāpur (Makkā M.), the *līwān* stands within and unattached to the surrounding courtyard. A staircase is commonly provided to give access to the *līwān* roof, either separately or incorporated within the walls or the base of a minaret, as this is a favourite place from which to call the *ādhān*; a staircase may be provided within a gateway for the same purpose. The *līwān* roof may be surmounted by one or more domes. Inside the *līwān*, the principal *miḥrāb* stands within the west wall opposite the main opening; if there are other *miḥrābs*, the central one is always the most sumptuously decorated and may be set deeper within the west wall than the other. The *minbar* is usually a permanent stone structure, with an odd number of steps, only occasionally made an object of decoration (splendid examples in the older Bengal mosques and in the Mālwā sultanate). A simple *minbar* is often provided when not liturgically necessary, as in the mosque attached to a tomb. There is an exceptional case at Bīdjāpur, at the mosque building for the cenotaph of Afḍal Khān: the mosque is two-storeyed, the two halls being exactly similar except that a *minbar* is provided only in the lower one. (In another first-floor mosque at Bīdjāpur, the Aṇḍā M., there is no *minbar*; the ground floor is apparently a well-guarded *sarāʾī*, and the suggestion has been made that the whole structure was intended for *zanāna* use.) The floor of the *līwān* is often marked out into *muṣallās* of *miḥrābī* shape for each individual worshipper. Lamps may be suspended from the *līwān* ceiling.

The *līwān* façade is open to the *ṣaḥn*; i.e. there is never any portion closed off like the *zimistān* of Persian mosques.

The *ṣaḥn* is usually an open courtyard, containing a *ḥawḍ* [*q.v.*] for the *wuḍūʾ*; this is usually placed centrally, except that in some Shīʿī mosques the *ḥawḍ* may be placed to one side of the central axis. There are rare cases where the *ṣaḥn* is completely or partially covered (e.g. the Djāmiʿ M. at Gulbargā [*q.v.*] is completely covered; in two mosques of the Tughluḳid period at Dihlī, Khiŕkī M. and Sandjar (Kālī) M., additional *riwāḳ*s leave only four small open courtyards in the middle of the *ṣaḥn*). In such cases provision must be made for the *wuḍūʾ* outside the *ṣaḥn*; some major mosques may also make provision, outside the *ṣaḥn*, for the *ghuṣl*. In some Gudjarāt mosques there is a water reservoir under the floor of the *ṣaḥn*, sometimes with chambers wherein to take refuge from the heat of the sun, with some sort of kiosk standing in the *ṣaḥn* from which water may be drawn; the idea is imitated on a small scale in the floor of the Djāmiʿ M. in Fatḥpur Sikrī. In one complex (Rādjōn kī bāʾīn) south of the M. Ḳuwwat al-Islām the mosque and an associated tomb seem subordinate to an enormous step-well (*bāʾōlī* [*q.v.*]).

One or more bays of the side or end *riwāḳ*s may be closed off for a special purpose, e.g. to make a room for relics, or to serve as a room for the *ḳāḍī* or *mutawallī*; in Shīʿī mosques, sometimes to house the *ʿalams*, etc., but these are usually accommodated in the *Imāmbāŕā* or *ʿĀshūrā-khāna* where there is one. The use of part of the mosque as a *madrasa* [*q.v.*] is commonplace, and many instances could be cited at the present day where there is no special provision for such a purpose; but there are instances of a special building forming an integral appendage of the mosque designated as a *madrasa*; e.g. M. Khayr al-Manāzil, near the Purānā Ḳilʿa in Dihlī, where the northern *riwāḳ*, of two storeys, forms the *madrasa* of the foundation.

The *ṣaḥn* may be used also for graves, from the simplest tombstone to elaborate mausoleums (see MAḲBARA. 5); e.g. the Djāmiʿ M. of Fatḥpur Sikrī, where most of the northern side of the *ṣaḥn* is occupied by the tomb of Salīm Čishtī, the Zanāna Rawḍa, and the tomb of Nawwāb Islām Khān (not so designed originally, and possibly a *djamāʿat-khāna* for the saint's disciples).

A *mīnār* is by no means an invariable appendage to the Indian mosque; apart from a few occasional early instances, only in the Gudjarāt sultanate, and in Burhānpur in Khāndēsh, was a functional *mīnār* provided for the *adhān* before the Mughal period; after the 10th/16th century, the *mīnār* becomes common, but not invariable. See further MANĀRA. 2. India.

The administration of the mosque may be under the *ḳāḍī* [*q.v.*] or, in the case of larger foundations, a committee headed by a *mutawallī* [*q.v.*]. Where a mosque stands on a high plinth there may be openings in it sufficiently large to be rented off as storerooms or to traders, in which case the revenues accrue to the mosque; see also WAḲF.

Bibliography: There are no studies dealing with mosque typology alone; for works on all architectural aspects, see the Bibliographies to HIND. vii. Architecture, and Section B. below.

(J. BURTON-PAGE)

B. The monuments.

The development of the mosque in the subcontinent can be recognised as an adaptation of the Arab prototype, largely as already modified by Iranian builders, to local materials, climate, and the proclivities of a long-established tradition of architecture and ornament. The Arab elements in this fusion were those basic to the expression of the *djamāʿat*, the collective act of prayer and the simple, egalitarian liturgy: the courtyard and its protective enclosure, the *ḳibla* wall, here on the western side, the *ẓulla* or prayer hall, here known as *līwān*, along the western wall, and colonnades, *riwāḳ* or *dālān*, along the other sides, with an essential severity of outline and a spare orthogonal framework. The Iranian elements were rhythmic arcading, the prominent use of *pīshṭāḳ* [*q.v.*] or frontispiece alcoves, the voussoired dome, ultimately double, and a particular sense of proportion; minarets did not become general until relatively late, and then often as decorative rather than functional features. A gamut of Iranian decorative devices including ceramic tiles [see KĀSHĪ], cut plaster-work, *gač-barī*, plaster relief work, *munabbat-kārī*, and pietra dura inlay, *parčīn-kārī*, besides the pseudostructural pendentive-work, *ḳalūb-kārī*, or squinch-netting. The Indian elements, within the context of an elaborated stone-cutting technique, were initially a certain heaviness due to the stone itself (especially in corbelled domes), complexity in individual forms, a vibration set up by the reiteration of forms at different scales, an interest in diagonal axes, and an overwhelming fertility of imagination in carved ornament. Indian traditions of massing only influenced mosque design in a limited way, and then largely through changes in dome form and grouping. The traditions of temple building were in strong contrast, creating massive, highly ornate enclosures within which progressively more intimate cells led to individual confrontation with a deity; the vertical extension was frequently emphasised as much as the horizontal. Despite this difference, a reconciliation of these traditions led to an enlivening of the mosque outline, especially on the skyline, with a frequent play of pinnacles and pavilions, much use of receding planes, and in some cases a culminating centrality comparable with the Ottoman achievement. The underlying Arab archetype retained its simplicity of arrangement in most regions, though periodically transformed in others. Evidence for the direct transfer of skills from temple-building to mosque building, which can be deduced from the earlier forms, is provided by a Māru-Gurdjara architectural manual of the 15th century A.D., the *Vṛkṣārṇava*, in a chapter on the *Rehmāṇa-prāsāda*, or temple of Rehmāna, i.e. of Allāh, giving instructions for layout, orientation, superstructure and exclusively floral decoration, all within prescribed norms. The principal modifications attributable to the climate are a tendency to raise the courtyard level to catch wind currents and escape dust and noise, a tendency to pierce the courtyard walls to allow the currents through, and a preference for riverside sites. Specific architectural features are incorporated, notably the finaly pierced *djālī* screen to reduce glare, and the *čhadjdjā* or eaves pent to throw off monsoon water and increase shade. A general trend in the chronological development is the movement from trabeated construction towards arcuate or vaulted forms, though this is achieved with some hesitation. This is in parallel with a progression from a somewhat provincial emulation of Iranian or Central Asian types through local technique to a much more accomplished creation of local types in which influence from the *Vilāyat* can still be traced. Although the relative neglect of the *madrasa* [*q.v.*] as a building form may have been due in part to a practice of teaching within the mosque, this seems not to have produced any overall adaptation of layout, unless in the development of the undercroft.

The Arab conquest of Sind. It is recorded that the first mosque in Sind was built by Muḥammad b. Ḳāsim at Daybul [*q.v.*] after his capture of the city in 92/711, followed by another at Multān [*q.v.*], next year; he was urged to build mosques in every town, the resources seized having proved unexpectedly large. A third great mosque was built at Manṣūra [*q.v.*] either by his son *ca.* 120/738, or in the early years of Abū Dja^cfar al-Manṣūr, i.e. after 136/754, with teak columns. Little remains of these. If Daybul is correctly identified with Bhambōr, and the uncertain date of 109/727 is right, then the mosque there may be among the oldest in Islam. Its plan is certainly close to that of Kūfa [*q.v.*], as rebuilt in 50/670, with the same double rows of columns for the *riwāḳ*, but only three aisles (of twelve bays) parallel to the *ḳibla* wall in lieu of five for the prayer hall; no trace has been found of a *miḥrāb* recess, but neither has one been found at Wāsiṭ [see MIḤRĀB], as built under the same governor, al-Ḥadjdjādj b. Yūsuf. Outer bays of the *riwāḳ* were walled off to form cells, *ḥudjra*, and stone bases contain traces of timber pillars. Another inscription gives 239/853-4; one in flowered Kufic for 294/906-7 probably refers to rebuilding after the earthquake of 280/893. The building thus conforms to the early ʿIrāḳī type, even to its strip foundations; though in yellow freestone, it lacks the stone columns. Pivots for gates in front of the *līwān* suggest some kind of *maḳsūra*. At Manṣūra, the Djāmiʿ Masdjid appears to have had a six-aisled prayer hall, built on an earlier Hindu site; three smaller mosques show careful alignment and external buttressing for a *miḥrāb*. In the absence of detail, the influence of these buildings is imponderable, but Daybul and Manṣūra survived until the 7th/13th century, and Manṣūra like Multān was taken by Maḥmūd of Ghazna; they can hardly have been ignored. A further early mosque in Kač́h, at Bhadreśvar, has been identified by Shokoohy as a rebuilding with purposely-carved stone *ca.* 560/1165. This has a prayer hall of two aisles, a double *riwāḳ* colonnade at the sides, and a single one to the east. The prominent *miḥrāb* is echoed outside the east wall, which faces an open hypostyle hall, no doubt for an overflow congregation. The roof is trabeated throughout, mostly on the east-west axis.

In the period preceding the Dihlī Sultanate, the principal mosques must have been at Lāhawr [*q.v.*], the Ghaznawid centre (as Maḥmūdpūr) from 412/1021, including the Khishtī Masdjid., of which nothing remains, though brickwork is still typical of the area.

Sultanate. At Dihlī [*q.v.*] the victory of Ḳuṭb al-Dīn [*q.v.*] was proclaimed by the creation (587/1191) of the Masdjid Ḳuwwat al-Islām, "The Might of Islam", on a temple plinth, with stonework taken from 27 other temples by elephant-power. The plan, of the same ʿIrāḳī type, is here elongated on the east-west axis, and includes formally symmetrical entrances to the east, north and south. The colonnades in the prayer hall are four aisles deep, those to the east three, and those down the long sides two. The hall is now modified to include a row of five corbelled domes, above five *miḥrābs*, by adjustment of the bay spacing to carry octagonal systems of lintels; this roof was set higher than the *riwāḳ* roofs, and mezzanines were built at the four angles of the court, possibly for women. Ingenious use of the strongly articulated temple pillars, with cruciform capitals and internally tiered domes, achieved a relatively light, harmonious building, whose Hindu character was scarcely disguised. In 595/1199, however, a great frontal screen of five pointed arches was added to the hall. Its clearly-framed format, with the central arch much taller, is Iranian, and related to the Ghūrid Shāh-i Mashhad in Ghardjistān (571/1175-6), or the Ribāṭ-i Sharaf [*q.v.*] (508/1114-15), but its construction is limited to Indian techniques, with corbelled arches. The marvellously vigorous combination of sinuous Hindu carving with *ṭughrā* inscriptions makes fresh use of Indian skills for a Muslim purpose. The exaggerated height of this screen, with no direct relation to the hall behind, set a pattern for later buildings. In the same year Ḳuṭb al-Dīn began the immense Ḳuṭb Mīnār [*q.v.*] outside the southeast corner of the mosque, much like that at Khʷādja Siyāh Pūsh in Sīstān, as a symbol of the centrality of faith; minarets, if used at all in Hindustān, are usually symbolic rather than functional until Mughal times. The exception is at Adjmer. There the equally symbolic re-use of temple components as "the annihilation of idolatry" achieved more orderly expression in the Aŕhāʾī-din-kā Djhōńpŕā (595/1199), under Abū Bakr al-Hirawī, with some evidence of specially-cut masonry in the lower column-shafts and tiered domes (see Meister, *op. cit.*), and a single, exquisite, cusped marble *miḥrāb*. The court is almost square, and probably had nine domes on all four sides, though there are five aisles in the prayer hall to three elsewhere; the effect is spacious, well-lit and calm. A reeded shaft graced each external angle, and the site on a mound allowed a grand approach stair to the east. Here too a great screen wall was added, with seven arches, under Iltutmish (607-33/1211-36), two lateral arches on each side reflecting the cusped form of the *miḥrāb*; the central arch is less dominant than at Dihlī, but is surmounted by two minaret shafts (now stumps), reeded and creased like the Ḳuṭb, so emulating a Saldjūḳ [*q.v.*] *pīshṭāḳ*. Iltutmish was to extend the work at Dihlī. Accepting Aybek's plan, he enlarged the prayer hall by a further three domes to north and south, with corresponding *miḥrābs* and screen wall. Corbels on the latter suggest a double storey in each central bay, as in later work in Gudjarāt. The *riwāḳ*, built as before, now enclosed the first mosque, including the Mīnār, to which he added three storeys [see DIHLĪ for plan and details] (completed 1229). The Shāhī Djāmiʿ Masdjid at Bari Khatu is of the same period and type, set on a high plinth; it introduces an ornate domed gallery over the east entrance. At Badāʾūn [*q.v.*] the great Djāmiʿ Masdjid built by Iltutmish in 620/1223-4 adheres to the same basic layout, but has been heavily rebuilt.

ʿAlāʾ al-Dīn Khaldjī's scheme to double the Ḳuwwat al-Islām again fell victim to its own ambition, for it was abandoned at his death. Remnants show that it respected the existing alignments in prayer hall, screen wall, and north gateway, and even in the immense ʿAlāʾī Mīnār which was to rise from the centre of the new prayer court. The inherent symmetry cannot have mitigated the disruption of worship by three courts set within each other. The only complete element to survive is the southern gateway, or ʿAlāʾī Darwāza (710/1311), set as a *čārṭāḳ* on the palace approach: an elegant, accomplished building of a new order. Its vocabulary is recognisable in the Djamāʿat Khāna at the *dargāh* of Niẓām al-Dīn (dated for his death 725/1325), fully Muslim in style, and built with new stone. This has no courtyard, but only a prayer hall of three domed chambers, to each of which there is a broad archway in the eastern façade. The square central space, almost the same size as the Darwāza, has a similar system of concentric keel arches for its squinches, as in earlier Khurāsānian work (cf. Ḳïrḳ Ḳïz near Termez), here carved, framed, and supporting an octagonal cornice; above, round the base of the smooth dome, are 32 arched niches, four of them pierced to admit light. The grace of the interior is achieved by a balance between the four main arches, the squinches, and at a reduced scale the *miḥrāb* and pairs of small arches at each corner, sustaining interest at each level. Each arch, inside or out, is contained by bands of inscriptions on the extrados (derived from Čis̲h̲t?), set off by lotus buds lining the intrados, in recessed planes above the angle shafts first introduced in Iltutmis̲h̲'s screen. The now-voussoired arch construction is masked by the carving. The lateral bays have two domes each on triangular pendentives, and may have been added rather later. Externally, the lateral bays are sunk, and the central one advanced and raised as a modest frontispiece; all are joined by a string course at mid-height and a lotus-bud parapet. Each archway is latticed. A provincial variant of the same style can be seen in the Ukha Masd̲j̲id at Bayāna, erected by Ḳuṭb al-Dīn Mubārak (716-20/1316-20). The mosques of the same period at D̲j̲ālōr, Dawlatābād, Pāṭan and Bharoč are built from temple spoil, but that at Dawlatābād continues the use of tapering, fluted corner buttresses, and Bharoč, with its more conscious blending of Hindu with Muslim elements, provides a starting point for the Gud̲j̲arātī style, with latticed windows, coffered ceilings over carefully-grouped columns, and domes of two sizes over the *līwān*. The D̲j̲āmiʿ Masd̲j̲id at Khambāyat (*ca.* 1325) owes a more direct debt to Dihlī in its arches and massing, but local features are evident in the merlon parapet, pinnacles on the frontispiece, latticework set in a grid-like frame, and pillars carrying a cusped arch just inside the main archway. These examples attest to the diffusion of the style in western Hindūstān.

An altogether different treatment of the mosque was to characterise Tug̲h̲luḳ building. Most of the examples at Dihlī are undated, and have been ascribed to Fīrūz S̲h̲āh, but it has been suggested (Burton-Page, *op. cit.* in *Bibl.*, 1974, 15) that the large Begampur Masd̲j̲id is better explained as built by Muḥammad b. Tug̲h̲luḳ for his new city of D̲j̲ahānpanāh (*ca.* 725/1325). Raised on a high plinth, it is important in introducing the Iranian four-*īwān* plan to India. North and south, the *īwāns* are advanced well into the court between heavy walls, boxing entrances at the centre of each side; to the east, the projection is outwards to a flight of steps, and to the west the tall arch rises to twice the roof height between tapering octagonal stair turrets, framing a triple entrance to the prayer hall. Here the main chamber is square, under a large pointed dome completely masked by this *pīs̲h̲ṭāḳ*. The hall on either side is three-aisled, with lesser domes, and 44 more domes cover the single *riwāḳ* all round the court, above arcades, and matching arched windows (for plan see ASIAR, iv [1871-2], pl. x). Muḥammad's transfer of Dihlī's population to Dawlatābād in 729/1329 appears to have depleted the skilled labour force and led to its dispersion elsewhere, notably in the Bahmanī Sultanate; southward expansion emptied the treasury. Nevertheless, the change of attitude introduced by Fīrūz S̲h̲āh (752-90/1351-88) was primarily an ethical one, in which his religious integrity required a return to prescribed simplicity and lack of ostentation. His building programme encompassed many mosques and 120 *k̲h̲ānaḳāhs* in Dihlī and Fīrūzābād alone, under the architect Malik G̲h̲āzī S̲h̲aḥna; given his stringent financial control, a modest but durable type of construction was inevitable. The fortified appearance of these mosques probably owes more to K̲h̲urāsānian prototypes, whose tapering round towers and massive walls had met the needs of mud construction, than to the need for defence (G̲h̲iyāt̲h̲ al-Dīn, a Ḳaraʾuna Turk, may have mediated this influence). The D̲j̲āmiʿ Masd̲j̲id at Fīrūzs̲h̲āh Kōṭlā (755/1354), now ruined, was built to incorporate a *tahk̲h̲āna* or undercroft, with arcaded vaults accessible from three sides, the east fronting the river. It once had three-aisled *riwāḳs* with multiple domes, and 216 stone pillars about 16 ft. (4.87 m.) high, around a central octagonal pool with its own dome. To the north, one of the As̲h̲oka's stone pillars was re-erected on a three-storey, arcaded pyramid as a marker. The materials for this and Fīrūz S̲h̲āh's other mosques are rough rubble stonework faced with *čūnā* plaster, once whitewashed or painted, with a minimum of mouldings. The common répertoire included tall plain walls with merlons, plain lintels on plain, squared quartzite piers set in twos or fours, with elementary scrolled cross-brackets and capitals, still Hindu in type, and two-centred arches of variable width sunk in panels, sometimes concentric. Domes were of a similar, helmet-like profile, set on framed, recessed squinch arches. Externally, the mass is emphasised by long flights of steps, projecting porches, and battered towers at the angles. The device of the *tahk̲h̲āna*, which allowed the lease of shop spaces to sustain the mosque, is repeated at the Kalān Masd̲j̲id (798/1387?) which exhibits these features, and an unusual corridor around the prayer hall, besides cannon-like *guldasta* pinnacles crowning the angle-towers of the porch. The Khiṙkī Masd̲j̲id, also on a *tahk̲h̲āna*, repeats the three-aisled *riwāḳ*, but in combination with three-aisled passages which traverse the court on both axes, dividing it into four smaller square courts. This four-court plan is to be seen in a perhaps earlier form at the Sand̲j̲ar Masd̲j̲id (772/1370-1) at Niẓām al-Dīn, though there the *riwāḳ* and the passages are only one aisle deep, and the courts are rectangular. This scheme, possibly derived from D̲j̲ayn temple plans, was presumably intended to provide shade; the courts themselves were probably covered by awnings, as in palaces at the time. It intruded on the essential unity of the *ṣaḥn* and its congregation, and the experiment was not repeated. The mosque of S̲h̲āh ʿĀlam includes an early example of a mezzanine gallery in the northwest corner; the inaccessibility of such retreats leaves their purpose uncertain.

The D̲j̲āmiʿ Masd̲j̲id at Irič (815/1412), some 40 miles north of Jhansi, demonstrates the transition from the Tug̲h̲luḳ to the Sayyid manner. The plan, with single-aisled *riwāḳs*, is centred on a prayer chamber whose dome spans the full depth of the hall, with two aisles and six smaller domes on each side. The structure is wholly arcuate, on low piers carefully detailed to articulate both axes, with frequent use of recessed planes; the arches are now stilted, with marked corbelling at the impost giving a shouldered effect, and set in deep panels. The *riwāḳ* has groined vaulting. The dome is single, a little pointed inside, with ribs, and still set on concentric squinch arches. The generally ponderous effect is offset by the assured but simple proportions, and the skyline is relieved with merlons (see *Mem. ASI*, xix, Calcutta 1926, for drawings).

The Lōdī mosque (Tug̲h̲luḳid) at K̲h̲ayrpur (900/1494) incorporates similar features, while its massing shows the continuity of Tug̲h̲luḳid tradition despite Tīmūr's incursion. Attached by a walled court to the Baṙā Gumbad, it is balanced by an arched structure opposite: a significant precedent for later tombs. An arcaded basement makes up the change in level at the rear, with tapering round buttresses at each rear corner, and at each angle of the projecting bay of the central *miḥrāb*, whose tops are alternately reeded below *guldasta* pinnacles; a Hindu window is corbelled out from the middle, and from either end wall. The hall has five bays; the three in the middle are domed, but the ends have low, flat vaults. The elevation reiterates the pattern, with three broad shouldered arches, and narrow ones at the extremities. As at Irič, the central *pīshṭāḳ* is raised a little, but here it is set between narrow, niched piers, and the outer two bays are united by the line of a *čhadjdjā*. Like its dome, the central arch, thrice recessed, is a little higher than the others, and a muscular tension results from the contrast of line. The surfaces, worked outside and in with deeply cut plaster, vibrate with countless arabesques; each extrados is inscribed, and inscribed rosettes fill the spandrels. Inside, they enhance pendentive systems of oversailing lintels carved with *muḳarnas* [*q.v.*] niches. The vocabulary is further enlarged by blind merlon parapets, counterset trefoils around the octagonal dome bases (precursors of later foliation), and spreading lotus finials, *mahāpadma*. The development of this type is apparent in the Mōth kī Masdjid (*ca.* 911/1505), where the lateral domes are shifted to the end bays, in a much freer spacing. There they are supported on similar corbelled pendentives, as long used in Iran, while the central dome rests on squinch arches. The five façade arches are narrower, and a lancet window is added at each end. The *pīshṭāḳ* now encloses a lofty blind arch reacing the parapet, which frames the entrance arch below, and a window above, as anticipated in the *miḥrāb* at Khayrpur. The two corner buttresses give way to polygonal towers, arcaded in two storeys. White marble is used to set off the red sandstone, with coloured tilework, notably on *čhatrīs* at the courtyard corners, and painted carved plaster.

Despite his dissatisfaction with this style, Bābur appears to have secured little improvement at his mosques (932/1526) at Kābulī Bāgh, Pānipat and Sambhal, beyond introducing Tīmūrid squinch netting. Humāyūn, however, developed it further in the Djamālī Masdjid (943/1536) at Dihlī, in the same five-bay format. This only has one dome. The *pīshṭāḳ* is contained between engaged reeded shafts that anticipate the Mughal use of minarets. The four-centred arches on either side are separated by large superimposed niches, which help to maintain the rhythm, and their haunches are slight. Khaldjī lotus buds are re-introduced on the central intrados. The Masdjid-i Kuhna at the Purānā Ḳilᶜa (*ca.* 1535-60?) shows further refinement. Each of its five arches is contained within a taller blind one, and that in a panel. The end bays, broken forward, resemble the Djamālī *pīshṭāḳ*, but the three middle ones are set deeper, with delicate angle shafts, and are proportionately taller. The fine ashlar incorporates the first geometric marble mosaic, after Tīmūrid models, and elaborate moulding profiles. Inside, the rippling recessed arches carry squinch arches below the prominent central dome, niched pendentives on either side, and arched cross ribs with vaulting at either end, again of a Tīmūrid type.

Regional developments. Bengal.

Remains from the early Muslim annexation are very limited. At Tribeni, an inscription framing the *miḥrāb* is dated 698/1298, but the mosque has been rebuilt, as has the Sāliḳ mosque at Basīrhāt (705/1305). At Čhōṫa Pānḍuā [see PANḌUA, Čhōṫa] ruins of a large brick mosque include basalt Hindu columns supporting well-rounded, two-centred arches of a type that remained typical of Bengal, and *miḥrābs* with carved trefoil heads above ringed shafts, plainly derived from Hindu niches, though within diapered Muslim frames, and a kiosk-like *minbar* [*q.v.*]. It may have been the model for the huge Ādīna Masdjid at Ḥaḍrat Pānḍuā (776/1374-5)(154.70 x 87 m.), which has similar features. There the broad courtyard resembles that of the Great Mosque at Damascus in its proportions and the dominance of a *maḳṣūra*-like bay at the centre of the prayer hall, once vaulted over. This runs through the hall, with five arches leading to five aisles of 18 bays on either side, but the presence of a royal mezzanine in the north wing leaves its purpose in doubt. Triple-aisled *riwāḳs* surround the court behind plain, stone-faced arcades, each arch recessed once within a panel. The simple pillars support brick cross arches between which spherical pendentives of corbelled brick carry 378 identical low domes, punctuated only by the *maḳṣūra*. Outside, the ashlar wall is advanced and recessed in alternate vertical strips traversed by cornice and string course, each set off by an aedicule containing a cusped arch and lamp. Although never repeated at this scale (32 *miḥrābs*!) such treatment of detail was to inform most subsequent work. From the 9th/15th century onwards, mosques took a closed form in response to the wet climate, with the characteristically curved Bangālī eaves line, but still with the massive polygonal corner buttresses of the period. Thus the Čamkatta Masdjid at Gawṛ (*ca.* 880/1475?) has a single square chamber of brickwork surmounted by a single dome; it has single openings centred north and south, and three to the east giving on to a vaulted verandah running the full width, again with single doors to north and south, and three to the east. The piers between the arched openings carried aedicules set high, and glazed tilework. The Lattan Masdjid (880/1475-6) is similar, but with a more complete symmetry, having three openings to north and south, and three *miḥrābs* opposite the doors, three domes over the verandah, and intermediate "corner" buttresses; the central verandah dome has a roof with four curved eaves—a *čawčāla*. It was once tiled outside and in. The Gunmant Masdjid at Gawṛ (889/1484?) encloses four bays of three aisles, all domed, on either side of a central *maḳṣūra*, the stonework of whose vault is carved in relief. A further variant is illustrated by three mosques at Gawṛ. The Thāntipāra Masdjid (885/1480) is rectangular, enclosing five bays of two aisles, with a single line of four stone pillars to carry its ten domes. Fine terracotta reliefs fill the spandrels and the two registers of aedicules on the piers outside. At the Čhōṫa Sōnā Masdjid, built between 899/1493 and 925/1519, the plan is comparable, but of three aisles; its central bay is wider, and has three *čawčāla* roofs in lieu of domes. Its ashlar front is finely carved, and the dome was once gilded. The Baṛā Sōnā Masdjid (932/1526) combines eleven bays of three aisles with a verandah forming a further aisle down the front, facing an open quadrangle with arched gateways; the stone is remarkably plain. Such forms continued well into the Mughal period, as seen in the Ḳuṭb Shāhī mosque at Ḥaḍrat Pānḍuā (990/1582).

Djawnpur. A mosque begun in 778/1376 by Fīrūz Shāh Tughluḳ was completed under the independent Sharḳī sultans (811/1408); its name, Aṫāla Masdjid, apparently refers to the pylon-like *pīshṭāḳ* which was to become the dominant trait of subsequent buildings here (Sk. *aṭṭāla* = "watch tower", see Lehmann, *op. cit.*, 23), exaggerating the great screen-arch at Dihlī. The four-*īwān* plan is apparently derived from the Begampur Masdjid at

Dihlī, though the *īwān* walls are reduced to massive spurs outside the enclosure, and those to north and south have domes carried on clustered columns, leaving the three-aisled *riwāḳ* unimpeded. Only the western *īwān* still boxes in space in the prayer hall, accessible through triple doors as before, but with bi-axial symmetry, three arches on either side maintaining the continuity of the three prayer hall aisles; the frontal turrets are now resolved as square towers tapering five stories to accommodate the *pīshṭāḳ* arch, whose recessed tympanum is pierced in three registers to reveal the open air beyond. This pylon, used for giving the *adhān*, is echoed at 1/3 scale on either side in the *līwān* wings, and in the remaining *īwāns* outside the remarkable two-storey colonnade; it may have been suggested by the pierced archway of the Shaykh Bārha mosque at Ẓafarābād (711/1311), though its scale perhaps owes something to Pānduā [for further description, see DJAWNPUR]. Tapering cylindrical turrets at the angles of the rear wall attest to Tughluḳid influence. At the Lāl Darwāza Masdjid (*ca.* 852/1447), built on the same pattern, the structure behind the main *īwān* is still lighter, minimising obstruction of the prayer hall below the central dome, though mezzanines are set on either side; the absence of lateral domes, due to the smaller scale, leaves that at the centre uncluttered. The dome piers, with massive Hindu brackets, contrast oddly with the Iranic slenderness of the colonnades. In structural terms, the Djāmiʿ Masdjid (842/1438, but finished under Ḥusayn Sharḳī) is a reversion to the Begampur type, with boxed-in, domed *īwāns* on all four sides, and the same high undercroft. In the prayer chamber the colonnades are eliminated except under the mezzanines either side of the central chamber, where the pillars are paired to match its piers, for the wings are again boxed in by heavy masonry supporting the roof of a single pointed barrel vault spanning east and west, on either side. The prayer hall is thus divided into three spaces free of supports, but separated by their cross walls and the two-storey mezzanines. The same triality is seen in the façade. The simply niched towers and arcaded tympana of the earlier *pīshṭāḳs* are transmuted into a rhythmic display of framed and fretted openings. The dichotomy between high frontal screen and the dome hidden behind is nowhere more pronounced than here. Related mosques are to be found at Iṫāwā (Djāmiʿ Masdjid) and Banāras (Aṙhāʾī Kanguar).

Gudjarāt. In a sandstone architecture, drawing more than that of any other region on the Hindu and Jain traditions, two tendencies in mosque design had already emerged in the Khaldjī phase already referred to: the screening of the prayer-hall front between a series of archways, as at Khambāyat (after Niẓām al-Dīn at Dihlī), or the treatment of the hall as an open colonnade, given additional rhythm by the surge of domes above the *čhadjdja* line, as at Bharoč. In either case the domes were carried by the Hindu device of beams spanning between two columns grouped to convert each square bay to an octagon. Remaining square bays were panelled in intricately recessed layers of coffering, whose cellular carving matched that of the domes. Pillars with markedly stratified round shafts above squared, faceted pedestals, carry vigorously curved brackets never far from living movement. The proportions of the three-arched screen are carefully repeated at Dhōlkā in the mosque of Hilāl Khān Ḳāḍī (733/1333), but with bracketed, tiered pinnacles marking the *pīshṭāḳ* so prominently as to suggest the minarets which followed; the central dome, raised a storey above the roof, is surrounded by pierced screens. The same scheme, with its lower wings on either side, recurs at Aḥmadābād in Sayyid ʿĀlam's mosque (815/1412), with half-rounded, tiered and bracketed buttresses framing the central arch as bases for fully functional *mīnārs* in a comparable style. The larger domes are now true, hemispherical ones. The development reaches fruition in the Djāmiʿ Masdjid at Aḥmadābād (826/1423) where the roof at the front of the three central bays is raised for a clerestory, with mezzanine galleries between, and the central dome is raised a further storey, so that light can enter indirectly at two levels, filtered by a pierced screen set in the usual Gudjarātī gridframe of stone: the remaining domes, three deep and five in the length of the hall, surround these three at the lower level. The *mīnārs*, once four times this height, fell in 1819 (see J. Forbes' drawing of 1781 in *ASWI*, vii [1906], 30). The Masdjid of Malik ʿĀlam (1422?) combines a single arch with such minarets and an open front. Continuing interest in the open type of hall is seen, as at the mosque at Sarkhēdj (855/1451), where 140 pillars, grouped as usual to support two rows of five equal domes, are set throughout in pairs to achieve an elegantly simple unity below a continuous roof line; there is little carving but for the *miḥrābs*. The Djāmiʿ Masdjid at Čāmpānēr (Maḥmūdābād) (924/1518-9) works variations on that at Aḥmadābād. The eleven main domes are staggered, the central one being set over a single central bay rising through three roof levels, behind a *pīshṭāḳ* which now overlaps the *mīnār* on either side, and incorporates three corbelled bay windows. The hall wings (*bāzūhā*) thus maintain a single roof line, with a plain walled front pierced by two arches each side, but there are now corner turrets to match the octagonal *mīnārs*. The main dome is ribbed inside, the side ones still corbelled, and the carved panels have filigree tendril-work. As at Aḥmadābād, the *riwāḳ* is one aisle deep; three entrance pavilions outside the wall carry prominent *čhatris*, and the wall itself is strongly modelled. The mosque of Rānī Rūpawātī (*ca.* 916/1510) shows a hall of only three domes treated similarly, with bay windows playing a more conspicuous role in modulating the front and ends. The culmination of the open hall design at the mosque of Rānī Siprī (Sabarī), also at Aḥmadābād (920/1514), fronting her tomb, has two rows of three corbelled domes, with only one row of pillars down the centre, and another, paired, in front, enlivened by alternate spacing. The extreme delicacy of this small-scale scheme is most evident in the slender, but solid and purely decorative *mīnārs* now set at each end of the façade—a device already introduced at the mosque of Muḥāfiẓ Khān (897/1492) with full minarets. These two traditions were reconciled in the mosque of Shaykh Ḥasan Muḥammad Čishtī (973/1565-6), a pillared hall of three *miḥrābs* in which the front is arcaded between terminal *mīnārs*, and the central five bays are raised in an upper storey of verandahs around a single dome. Sīdī Saʿīd al-Ḥabshī's mosque (980/1572-3), still at Aḥmadābād, has five bays of three aisles with intersecting arches, supporting shallow domes over squinches, lintels and corbels, but is remarkable for its ten large tracery lunettes, of which two are unrivalled in the sinuous naturalism they bring to the interior.

Mālwā. An initial phase of redeployed temple material is distinguished by a simple grace which remained typical of the kingdom. At the Djāmiʿ Masdjid (or Laṫ Masdjid) at Dhār (807/1404-5) the proportions of a single smooth hemispherical dome impart a spaciousness to the centre of the prayer hall colonnades, complemented by a pattern of flagstones, and a peaked, cusped *miḥrāb* arch; outside, its coronet of merlons enhances the traces of a tiled merlon parapet over the open front. One domed porch is surrounded by coved vaults, and in another false arch profiles are inserted between the pillars as in Gudjarātī temples. The first mosque at Māndū, that of Dilāwar Khān (808/1405-6) is spartan, however, with its hall of elemental columns relieved only by seven *miḥrābs*. Its successor, that of Malik Mughīth (835/1432) presents a more Tughluḳid exterior, with an arcaded undercroft in front between domed turrets, and the prominent stair often used here. The open, pillared prayer hall has three low, helmet-like domes. These, though still supported by an octagon of lintels, are partly enclosed by similar false arches below, with web spandrels, well integrated with the *miḥrābs* behind. The Djāmiᶜ Masdjid (858/1454) has the same undercroft and steps, and the three main domes again span three rear aisles of the hall, but there are now two aisles in front of them, which with the triple aisles of the side *riwāḳs* are covered with ranks of small domes, one to each bay, 158 in all. The building is mature, wholly Muslim, and of a sturdy dignity. The heaviness of strongly stilted domes is balanced by the grace of matching arcades round the court; the lofty hall is intersected by arches over plain, squared pillars, and articulated with blind wall arches and a characteristic flaring squinch. Each end dome covers a mezzanine set on nine bays of cross-vaulting. The pink stone is almost plain. The Djāmiᶜ Masdjid at Čanderī is comparable, though remarkable for serpentine brackets developed from those of the *minbar* at Māndū.

Khāndēsh. A similar restraint in the Djāmiᶜ Masdjid at Burhānpur is conspicuous in its open hall front of 15 uniform arches, relieved only by a dancing alternation of large and small trefoil merlons, and the reiteration of *čhadjdjā* brackets, the arcaded court appearing larger thereby (997/1589). The interior of the hall is equally regular, with five aisles of cross vaulting sustained by plain squared pillars decorated only on their bases, and a crested *miḥrāb* to each bay, rising above the string course, with three recessed arches finely chiselled in the dark stone. A substantial octagonal *mīnār* rises from a faceted square base at each end of the hall front, topped by a square lantern and a dome. Similar tall but plain *mīnārs* appear elsewhere in the city, and most notably as a pair flanking the *pīshṭāḳ* arch of the Bībī kī Masdjid, with four *djharōkhā* windows below their domes. Their tiered form otherwise resembles that at Čāmpānēr, there is even a *djharōkhā* on either side fronting the three-domed hall, whose organisation is apparently based on Rānī Rūpawatī's mosque at Aḥmadābād (see *ASI, NIS,* ix, 1873-5).

Bahmanī Sultanate. The interpretation of the *līwān* as a simple repetition of arched bays is already present in the Shāh Bāzār Masdjid at Gulbargā (*ca.* 761/1360?), in an open-fronted hall of 15 bays of crossed arches in six aisles, all of them domed. The arches, set on tall piers, are recessed once, shouldered at the impost and stilted; the domes are low. At the Djāmiᶜ Masdjid (769/1367, thus contemporary with the Khiṙkī and Sandjar mosques at Dihlī) similar arches and squared piers are deployed quite differently to cover what would normally be the court with 63 domes on pendentives of corbelled work on angle. The *riwāḳs* are replaced by broader aisles roofed by rows of transverse pointed barrel vaults countering the thrust of these, with a large dome at each corner; these vaults rest on arches set on very low imposts, the contrasts in height adding interest to the interior, while light floods in from arcades in the outer wall. A still larger dome is set in front of the *miḥrāb*, heavily stilted, over trilobed squinches echoing the *miḥrāb* itself, and set in a square clerestory (cf. that in the mosque of Karīm al-Dīn at Bīdjāpur, 720/1320). The ensemble recalls *bāzār* architecture in Iran; it was without sequel, like the experiments at Dihlī. A variant of the arcaded open *līwān* at the Dargāh of Mudjarrad Kamāl (*ca.* 802/1400) has carved stucco archivolts and rosettes, with an extraordinary "entablature" of depressed cusped arches on sinuous brackets. The Djāmiᶜ Masdjid (Solah Khamba) in the Fort at Bīdar [*q.v.*] is another version (827/1423-4), whose long front of 19 arched bays has square piers, and the five-aisle interior round pillars, carrying small domes on squinches. Heavy piers form a *maḳṣūra* enclosing the central three bays, from which squinches on sinuous brackets carry a tall 16-sided drum lit by fine *djālīs*, and a single large dome whose outer form is close to the domes at Mūltān [*q.v.*] while its supports recall the Tughluḳid *īwān* at Begampur. The small three-bayed Langar kī Masdjid at Gulbargā (*ca.* 838/1435?) introduces a single pointed brick vault over two arched ribs.

Barīd Shāhī. At Bīdar, the use of tall arches on low imposts is resumed at the Djāmiᶜ Masdjid (*ca.* 926/1520?), recessed once, with angular matching squinches articulated with great clarity below plain domes (cf. those in southern Iran). A transition to the Bīdjāpur vocabulary can be seen in the Kālī Masdjid (1106/1694-5), where the three front arches are framed by a pair of slender, formalised *mīnārs*, and the decagonal *miḥrab* recess is housed in a square rear tower carrying a *čārṭāḳ* lantern, and a slightly bulbous dome as introduced at the Madrasa of Maḥmūd Gawan (877/1472); a domical vault roofs the central bay. A small mosque at the tomb of ᶜAlī Barīd (984/1576), handled similarly, has three domes on squinch-net pendentives, and a fretted cresting.

ᶜImād Shāhī. The Djāmiᶜ Masdjid at Gāwilgaṙh [*q.v.*], rebuilt in 893/1488, already combined a seven-arched hall façade on square piers with a square pylon at either end topped by a *čhatrī* with *djālī*-work in the sides, and *čhadjdjas* on serpentine brackets, but otherwise follows the Bahmanī pattern of a dome over every bay, and a larger one raised on a tall drum at the centre; an arcaded screen wall surrounds its court. This is repeated at a smaller scale in the Djāmiᶜ Masdjid at Rohankhed (990/1582), where four pylons with *čhatrīs* now form the hall ends, with a single central dome: the imposing south gateway has extensive carving.

Niẓām Shāhī. The Damrī Masdjid at Aḥmadnagar, small and precise, has a three-arched façade flanked by ornate pylons, which carry four graceful *mīnārs* capped by bud-like domelets. Octagonal pillars form two arched aisles supporting a flat roof. At the centre of a decorative parapet two slim minarets frame an arch profile, as in the Bādal Maḥall Darwāza at Čanderī. No superstructure remains on the corner piers of the Dilāwar Khān mosque at Khed, but the exterior is enhanced by cusped arches, with two panelled bands running all round, and lotus medallions in relief. The central dome set on a square base imitates a tomb, complete with *čhadjdjās* and corner *čhatrīs*. Inside, columns with volutes carry a coved ceiling.

ᶜĀdil Shāhī. At Rāyčūr [*q.v.*] in the disputed Dōāb, a series of *līwāns* were built with flat ceilings over black basalt Čālukyan pillars whose short, heavy profiles are compensated by a deep parapet; the Ek Mīnār kī Masdjid has a tapering, free-standing *mīnār*

20 m. high (919/1513). In Bīdjāpūr [*q.v.*] the Bīdar vocabulary was elaborated in dark stone. Thus in the Djāmiᶜ Masdjid of Yūsuf (918/1512-3) the slightly bulbous dome, set on a tall cylindrical drum, is familiar but for the foliation around its base, as is the dominance of the central arch, its form, and the articulation of line and squinch within; what is new, and characteristic, is the prominence given the dome, and the domed *čārṭāḳ* lanterns at each corner, well above the roof line. The same three-bay format is used in the Djāmiᶜ Masdjid of Ibrāhīm (*ca.* 957/1550?), where a flat, domeless roof with sturdy domed *guldasta* pinnacles at each corner is relieved by a panelled *mīnār* set over each front pier. Cusped arches surround its *miḥrāb*. The mosque of Ikhlāṣ Khān (*ca.* 968/1560?) is similar, with the addition of a lantern in two storeys above the *miḥrāb*, and a cusped central arch. All three arches are cusped, and repeatedly recessed, in the mosque of ᶜAlī Shahīd Pīr where a pointed vault (as at Gulbargā) runs parallel to the front, and a tall domed shaft rises over the *miḥrāb*. In all of these carved stucco decoration, notably rosettes, is prominent. A mosque in the fort at Naldrug (968/1560) may have one of the first double domes in India. At the Djāmiᶜ Masdjid of Bīdjāpūr, the largest in the Deccan (985/1577-8?), these elements achieve mature expression. Its prayer hall, nine bays long and five aisles deep, is articulated with a calm strength, only an alternation of squinch detail varying a uniform structure with shallow domes; four piers at the centre are omitted, and intersecting pendentive arches are inserted in a miraculous change of scale to carry the dome (as already found in the tomb of Sulṭān Kalīm Allāh at Bīdar and based on Tīmūrid antecedents. Clerestory arches with fine *djālī*s light it through a square base rising above the roof, but the dome, still of the Mūltān shape above its foliation, remains dim, as usual here. Two features are innovations. At the east end of each seven-bayed *riwāḳ* is an octagonal base for an unbuilt *mīnār*; the entire external wall is modelled with two registers of arcading, the upper a corridor, and the lower blind. Both may be derived from the Muṣallā at Harāt (841/1437-8) [*q.v.*]. A central courtyard tank anticipates Mughal practice. Stucco is partly replaced by carved stone at Malika Djahān Bēgam's mosque (*ca.* 995/1586-7), in which the dome now suggests a sphere in its collar of leaves, repeated at each stage of four corner minarets; *guldasta* lanterns, fretted cresting, and pendant stone chains compound a new elegance. The same character informs the Andā Masdjid (1017/1608) in fine ashlar, set back above a *sarāʾī*, with a gadrooned dome, and the mosque at the Mihtar-i Maḥall, domeless, with rod-like *mīnār*s, and four prolonged *čhadjdjā* brackets engaged to the piers. Its acme is the mosque at the Ibrāhīm Rawḍa (1036/1626), facing the tomb across a plinth within a walled garden; brilliant use is made of elements repeated at a miniature scale to complement the whole. Afḍal Khān's mosque (1064/1653) is on two floors, the upper probably for women, as at the Andā mosque. The style was taken as far south as Sante Bennur. Much of the extravagant ornament is discarded in the Makka Masdjid, in the latter half of the century, free-standing within a *riwāḳ* continued to the west.

Ḳuṭb Shāhī. At Golkondā [*q.v.*], the first capital, the ruins include a Djāmiᶜ Masdjid built by Sulṭān Ḳulī Ḳuṭb al-Mulk in 924/1518 near the Bālā Ḥiṣār Darwāza. The regional achievement is best represented by the mosques at Ḥaydarābād [*q.v.*], which were given a new emphasis on height, accentuated by the concentration of external detail in the fascia between the *čhadjdjā* and the skyline, and complemented by arcaded galleries around powerfully contoured *mīnār*s. The multiple *guldasta*s on fretted parapets, and foliated bulbous domes are, like the stucco, inherited from Bīdjapūr. The Djāmiᶜ Masdjid (1006/1597-8) has a spacious arched hall behind a front of seven bays divided unusually into two registers, the upper one of cusped arches being carried on struts from the pier imposts; the central arch, broader and taller than the others, is surmounted by a plain profile in the upper section. The Makka Masdjid, begun *ca.* 1026/1617, and continued until finished by Awrangzīb in 1105/1693, is set behind a square courtyard reputed to hold 10,000 worshippers, with a hall two aisles deep and five tall bays wide. In the plain ashlar façade, the central arch is slightly larger, as the only variation below the strong horizontal of a *čhadjdjā* on linked brackets, spanning between the broad galleries of the turrets at either end, each of which is crowned by a bulbous dome on a marked necking. The columns carry arched pendentives and domes, with a coved central bay. Verticality is particularly pronounced in the Tolī Masdjid (1043/1633-4), where the five narrow arches of the front are stilted above impost blocks on the tall piers, and a tall parapet of arched screens joins the *mīnār* galleries for their full height; each shaft has two further galleries above roof level. Extensive use is made of cut plaster, syncretic in style. For other developments in the south, see MAHISUR. 2. Monuments.

Kashmīr [*q.v.*]. The combination of a mountain climate and plentiful timber have resulted in a tradition of mosque building in a blockhouse technique of laid *dewdār* logs and pitched roofs with birchbark sarking topped by turf. In parallel with Dakhani mosques, the basic constructional unit had much in common with the local tomb type, a near-cubical volume set on a stone base, the corners emphasised by timber jointing, and roofed by a pyramid, sometimes tiered, with a slim spire at the centre. Frequent renewal after fires renders dating unreliable, though the type seems to have been used since the 8th/14th century. At Shrinagar in the mosque of Shāh Hamadān, the volume is modulated by large roofed balconies on each outside face, and the roof by a square arcaded *muʾadhdhin*'s gallery below the peaked spire. Four tapering octagonal columns support a painted ceiling, with small rooms ranged to north and south. Cusped round arches contrast with the rhythms of varying timber lattices and panelling. At the Djāmiᶜ Masdjid (last built 1085/1674), a variant of the four-*īwān* plan places four of these units symmetrically around a square court, joined by four-aisled *riwāḳ*s full of timber columns. Three form arched gateways, while the larger one to the west rises between walls of arched panelling over paired columns at the *riwaḳ* ends in an expansion of light and space, focussed on the simple arches of a large *miḥrāb* in a fenestrated wall. In this case the outer walls are of brick with a simple repeated window, contrasting with the four spired roofs. In Baltistān and Kuhistān simple open *līwān*s of one or two aisles are supported on wooden columns, often fluted above a waisted base, and with brackets carved in repeated waves supporting beams on the long axis; here the connection with Turkestan building is evident.

Mughal Empire. During Akbar's minority, the Tīmūrid innovations introduced under Humāyūn remained in currency, associated with the harem faction, as in the mosque and *madrasa* of Māham Anaga (Angā), the Khayr al-Manāzil (969/1561-2) whose three bays to the court are close in format to the central three at Purānā Ḳilʿa with a slightly raised *pīshṭāḳ* advanced between clustered shafts, and four-centred arches whose tympana are pierced with archways at a lower level; only the single dome has an awkward, old-fashioned stilt. The arch spandrels are inlaid. The screened upper storey of rooms enclosing the court on three sides appears to be unique for the period, while the portal is the first to use a semidomed *īwān*. At Fatḥpur Sīkrī [*q.v.*] these forms are less in evidence. Although the front of the Stonecutters' Mosque (*ca.* 973/1565) is arched, originally in five bays, the arch profile is cut from thin slabs set between thicker posts, the *čhadjdjā* is supported by long, sinuous brackets, and the internal row of pillars is Hindū. The organisation of the great Djāmiʿ Masdjid (979/1571-2) stems from Djawnpur via Bayānā, where the technique of assembling cut stone components was already well-developed a century earlier (fieldwork by Shokoohy 1981). Three domed spaces at the centre and amid either wing of the *līwān* are each contained within massive walls pierced by symmetric arches to communicate with the columned spaces between, where flat, beamed roofs are supported on Hindū brackets, all in red sandstone; the central dome set on squinch arches is painted with swirling floral patterns, and the lateral ones are ribbed, lit through the drum, and carried on corbelled pendentives. The front of the hall with its alternation of broad and narrows bays, thin spandrels, long *čhadjdjā*s, and the form of the pillars appears to be Gudjarātī in origin, as does the great tank under the courtyard. At the centre, however, is a great *pīshṭāḳ* of the Dihlī type, with a semi-dome, completely screening the stilted and lumpish dome behind. The wings are of half the height, and relieved by queues of little *čhatrī*s along the skyline, like the *riwāḳ*s with their central *īwān*s: these once served as lanterns. Although the awkward column-spacing under the lateral domes of the Aṭāla Masdjid has been resolved, and much is made of the three main spaces, their walls still interrupt the unity of the hall.

The Mosque of Maryam Zamānī (1023/1614) at Lāhawr [*q.v.*], known as the Bēgam Shāhī Masdjid, and built of brick following local practice, achieves an unencumbered prayer hall of five square, domed compartments in line, interconnected by single arches springing from heavy piers at front and rear. The central compartment is wider, with a larger dome than the others, still stilted, but housing an inner shell which, though only of plaster, was probably the first used in a mosque in the north. The new arch shape extends to the squinches, with *muḳarnas* semi-domes, and the domes are articulated with netting, the whole being elaborately painted with floral, geometric, and inscriptional designs. Outside, the *līwān* front follows the model of the Djamālī Masdjid, with blind superimposed niches on the pier faces, but the arches are now simple in profile, the front is in one plane but for the vaulted *īwān*, and there are square, domed turrets at either end. The Masdjid-i Wazīr Khān (1044/1634-5) in the same city has a *līwān* of the same kind, both outside and in, as before punctuated by a *miḥrāb* below a semidome in each bay, with pendentives rising to carry the inner dome shells in the wings, and squinches at the centre. The dome profile is lower, with minimal stilting, but still unlike the profile of the five arches. The turrets are here full-sized octagonal minars with *čhatrī*s above the galleries, and are echoed by a second pair at the east of a long court. The brickwork forms shallow panels between orthogonal fillets, containing a sumptuous variety of tile mosaic; the interior is painted.

A series of court mosques faced entirely in white marble—seen as "pure like the heart of the austere" (*Bādshāh-nāma*, ii/1, 155)—was probably initiated at Āgra [*q.v.*] with the tiny, perfectly simple Mīnā Masdjid and the larger, three-bayed Nagīna Masdjid within the Fort. The latter, in which the lower dome profile has been transformed by necking above a torus moulding into a smooth bulbous shape with a large pointed *mahāpadma* (Bīdjāpūrī influence is suggested by the crescent above), represents an attempt to eliminate the conflict between emphasis on the central bay, and that on the dome behind, by replacement of the *pīshṭāḳ* with an upward curve of the *čhadjdjā* and parapet, in the new Bangālī fashion, at the middle. This accommodates the larger central arch; the arches are engrailed, probably to reduce glare when viewed from inside. In the mosque at the Tādj Maḥall [*q.v.*], the same conflict is resolved by raising the level of the façade over the two lateral arches almost to *pīshṭāḳ* level, and including a blind arched panel above each. This scheme is repeated at Lāhawr in the mosque of Dāʾī Angā (1045/1635-6), the corner turrets containing the taller front as before; the side arches are surmounted by great cusped arch heads, and the Lāhawrī panelling is of tile mosaic inside and outside the three interpenetrating square compartments. The treatment of the Madrasa Masdjid at Paṭnā (*ca.* 1040/1630) is comparable. The Fatḥpurī Masdjid at Āgra, flanked by the same flaring turrets, has a fully bulbous dome, but a tall marble *pīshṭāḳ* in front over a deep *īwān*, and low wings; its red stone is finely worked in relief, notably in the pendentives and inner dome. Like it, the Mōtī Masdjid at Lāhawr (*ca.* 1055/1645) is fronted by cusped arches flanking a plain central one, but it offers a further solution to the problem with a barely raised *pīshṭāḳ* linked to the wings by a continuous parapet in *parčīn-kārī*. The three marble domes still have the cavetto and profile of Dāʾī Angā's mosque, now clearly visible. These smaller mosques owe much to the consonant detail of arcuate screens which separate their courts from the outside world, and a finesse that extends to *sadjdjāda* inlaid in the floor. On a larger scale, the Shāh Djahānī Masdjid at Adjmēr (1048/1638-9), with a prayer hall two aisles deep with arched piers, presents a long, unbroken façade of eleven bays, accented only by a needle-like *guldasta* over each octagonal column, to a balustrated court adjoining the *dargāh* of Muʿīn al-Dīn Čishtī; the whole is in marble.

Some of these tendencies are resolved at the Djāmiʿ Masdjid at Āgra, completed in red stone in 1058/1648. Its plan is essentially that of the five-compartment prayer hall from Lāhawr, complete with its corner turrets and another pair at the east corners of the court. Its capacity is increased by the addition of a second row of compartments in front of the first, the central one forming a deep *īwān*, whose *pīshṭāḳ* is thus spaced well forward from the domes over the main row behind; the two lateral domes are placed over the ends, for better balance, and all three are double and distinctly bulbous, with a pointed profile accentuated by inlaid chevrons of white marble (structural inner domes were from henceforward the norm). The front is of the tall type, with panels above and between the well-spaced plain arches, and two prominent shafts frame the marble *pīshṭāḳ*. *Čhatrī*s enliven the whole skyline. The interior is a smooth progression of netted pendentives and plain arches with a broad extrados, at a noble scale. Its equivalent at Dihlī (1066/1656), also raised on a high podium, and approached by three great pyramids of steps on the axes, is the largest enclosed mosque in northern India. Gateway *īwān*s on these axes regain their prominence, and the *riwāḳ*s are open to the external air on all three sides. A collision between these and the *līwān*, a weakness at Āgra, is avoided by returning them along the west, and then advancing the hall forward between full-size minarets at the corners. The *līwān* plan fuses those of Āgra and Fatḥpur Sīkrī, with alternating main compartments, and slimmer piers at the front; cusped arches are used throughout. The domes, now on tall drums are, like the *mīnār*s and the *īwān*, striped with marble inlay, and the entire front is panelled in marble, with plain merlons above. Such detail, and especially the marble calyces topping the angle shafts, introduce a mannered deviation from the former simplicity. The scale is such that the *īwān* itself forms a *miḥrāb* to the courtyard.

The Mōtī Masdjid at Āgra Fort (1063/1653), the largest of the marble series, complete with *riwāḳ* and axial gateways, combines a restraint of outline and of plan with an extravagance in the intersecting, cusped arch profiles. Eighteen identical piers in three aisles carry plain coved ceilings alternating with three domes on smooth pendentives, that rise bulbous among the *čhatrī*s outside. That in the Dihlī Fort (1074/1663-4) shows the full extent of the stylistic change at a small scale, with a Bangālī curve in the *čhadjdjā* over the central bay, set off by Bangālī vaults within, reticulated coving, clustered *guldasta*s with calyces, and floral relief playing on many surfaces; the domes, rebuilt after the Mutiny, were originally lower, and gilded.

The last of the great congregational mosques, the Bādshāhī Masdjid at Lāhawr (1084/1673-4) derives its plan almost entirely from the great mosque at Dihlī, the principal differences being that the three-storey octagonal *mīnār*s are now set at the four corners of the court, and the *līwān* itself reverts to the local scheme with a domed octagonal turret at each corner. The *riwāḳ*s, too, are subdivided into an alternating series of *hudjra*s for teaching, accessible only through doorways, and though raised as before, the court is thus closed in. The *līwān*, of brick faced with red stone, is rather taller than at Dihlī, and panelled in the local manner, but the surfaces swarm with relief carving; the marble domes formerly had dark drums to relate them to the wings. Internally the squinched dome chambers alternate with Bangālī vaults, and the walls, arch soffits and domes are panelled or worked in net-patterns, *islīm-i khaṭāʾī*, of plaster relief, or else painted. The mosque is claimed as the largest in the world. The gateways of such structures served to house the *imām* and other staff. The Sonahrī Masdjid at Dihlī (1164/1751) repeats the Motī Masdjid at the Fort in fawn sandstone. In subsequent work in Awadh the curvilinear and vegetal elements were to become dominant [see LAKHNAW], and were still vigorous in the Djāmiʿ Masdjid of *ca.* 1840 in the capital.

Provincial developments within the Mughal empire predictably show an adaptation of the court style to local practice. In Bengal, the mosque of the Lālbāgh Fort at Ḍhākā (1089/1678) has the closed appearance and panelled front typical of the area, but the height of the prayer hall, its three cusped and netted front *īwān*s, its three low domes and the four octagonal turrets at its corners all refer to the experience of Lāhawr. The interior of the lateral bays is remarkable for semidomes set below the apical dome, with two sets of pendentives. Other mosques at Ḍhākā follow the same format, as in that of Khān Muḥammad Mirdha (1118/1706), with tall minars at the *līwān* corners, or the Sātgunbadh mosque with octagonal corner towers.

The brick architecture of Sind is extensively clad in fine glazed tilework, owing much to Iranian influence, and apparently that of Harāt [*q.v.*] in particular. This is already apparent in the Dābgīr Masdjid at Ṭhaṭṭā (997/1588-9), of which the *līwān* remains in a ruined state, containing a square central compartment flanked by a rectangular one at each side, with arches connecting them between massive piers, and three deep *īwān*s, set in slightly raised *pīshṭāḳ*s. The central dome, like the *īwān* below it, is notably larger than those either side, but all three are set on double octagonal drums of an Iranian type. The walls of the central compartment each house one well-shaped arch within another; at the west the interval contains an arched window set on either side of the buff carved sandstone *miḥrāb*. The tilework, floral, geometric and calligraphic, in cobalt and azure on a white ground, filled arch spandrels and soffits. The Djāmiʿ Masdjid of Shāhdjahān (1057/1647) in the same city is unusual in plan, with repeated heavy piers forming the two aisles of the broad *riwāḳ*s, and the three of the prayer hall, around a very deep court, focussed on a great *pīshṭāḳ*, with small subsidiary courts on each side of an east entry passing under two domes in series (cf. the Masdjid-i Djāmiʿ at Kirmān). The multiple bays are roofed by 80 small domes, with larger single ones over the central *īwān*s, backed to the west by a single shell dome replacing four bays in front of the *miḥrāb*; this rises from intersecting pendentive work over a zone of 16 arches, pierced for a clerestory at the angles, and tiled throughout in mosaic (more than 100 pieces per sq. ft.) in ranks of wheeling stars. The smallest sound at the *miḥrāb* can be heard throughout the mosque, perhaps by virtue of its domes. In both these mosques the red brick is defined by white pointing which accents the arches. Further excellent tilework at the Djāmiʿ Masdjid of Khudābād has been badly damaged. The treatment of its façade shows stronger Lāhawrī influence in proportions and panelling; the external walls, however, are noteworthy for three superimposed registers of repeated blind arches, a few being pierced at the lower levels.

At Aḥmadābād, the mosque of Nawwāb Sardār Khān (*ca.* 1070/1660?) combines a relatively orthodox Gudjarātī treatment of a three-bayed *līwān*, having three plain arches between narrow piers, a *djharōkhā* bay on each end wall, and balconied *mīnār*s framing the front, with features that seem to bridge the styles of Bīdjāpūr and Āgra. The three closely-spaced domes are bulbous, above torus mouldings, with steep *mahāpadma*s as in the Nagīna and Mōtī Masdjids. The *mīnār*s, however, carry long foliations, lotus buds and the elongated, bulbed finial of the later ʿĀdil Shāhī style, close to those at the similar and contemporary Mosque of Afḍal Khān in the Dargāh of Gīsū Darāz at Gulbargā. The mosque, unlike its counterparts, is of brick and stucco. The mosque of Nawwāb Shadjāʿat Khān (1107/1695-6) has a five-arched front, with Gudjarātī merlons, and *mīnār*s placed to contain the central three bays, but the piers are panelled with rows of little niches, and a line of cartouches runs overhead, with three low domes of the Dāʾī Angā type; the *mīnār*s once more have foliations, but have lost their tops. In its ceiling, the domes alternate with coved bays, as in the Mōtī Masdjid at Āgra, and it is finished with marble and polished plaster.

In general, it may be seen that whereas the enclosure of the court only achieves full architectural expression in cathedral mosques, or the later court mosques, the prayer hall is the subject of consistent architectural development. The particular structural means adopted in each region for enclosing the space become the vocabulary for a series of variations which in most cases go far beyond the immediate needs of the liturgy or of mere shelter, and can be recognised as successive resolutions of the need for balance, harmony, and unity at the chosen scale.

Bibliography: For general works, see HIND. vii. Architecture. To these may be added Z. Desai, *Indo-Islamic architecture*. N. Delhi 1970; J. D. Hoag, *Islamic architecture*, New York 1977, 280-307, 364-88; R. A. Jairazbhoy, *An outline of Islamic architecture*, Bombay etc. 1972; B. Gray, ed., *The arts of India*, Oxford 1981. Works on mosques in general include E. La Roche, *Indische Baukunst, II. Teil: Moscheen und Grabmäler*, Munich 1921; Z. Desai, *The mosques of India*, N. Delhi 1971; and Y. K. Bukhari, *The mosque architecture of the Mughals*, in *Indo-Iranica* ix/2 (1956), 67-75. For the early Arab mosques, see H. Cousens, *The antiquities of Sind*, Calcutta 1929, repr. Karachi 1975, 48 ff., and S. M. Ashfaque, *The grand mosque of Banbhore*, in *Pakistan Archaeology*, vi/1 (1969), 182-209. The Ḳuwwat al-Islām is still best described by J. A. Page in *A guide to the Quṭb, Delhi*, Delhi 1938, but see also M. C. Joshi, *Some Nagari inscriptions on the Qutb Minar*, in *Medieval India—a miscellany*, ii, Aligarh Muslim University 1972, 3-7, and S. K. Bannerji, *The Qutb Minar: its architecture and history*, in *Jnal. of the United Provinces Historical Soc.*, x/1 (1937), 38-58. The Aṛhāʾī-din-kā Dj̲hōṅpṛā is described by M. Meister, *The two-and-a-half-day mosque*, in *Oriental Art*, xviii (1972), 57-63, and plan in *ASIAR*, ii, 1864-5; and see R. Hillenbrand, *Political symbolism in early Indo-Islamic mosque architecture: the case of Ajmīr*, in *Iran, JBIPS*, xxvi (1988), 105-18. For the mosque at Badāʾūn, see J. F. Blakiston, *The Jami Masjid at Badaun and other buildings in the United Provinces*, *MASI*, xix, Calcutta 1926, and A. Cunningham, *ASI*, xi, 1880. The Dj̲amāʿat K̲h̲āna is given a brief description by M. Zafar Hasan in *A guide to Niẓāmu-d Dīn*, *MASI*, x, 1922, 14-6. The early mosques at Pāṭan are described by J. Burgess and H. Cousens in *Architectural antiquities of northern Gujarat*, *ASI*, NIS, xxxii, London 1903, and those of Bharoč and Khambayāt in Burgess's *On the Muhammadan architecture of Bharoch, Cambay, Dholka, Champanir and Mahmudabad in Gujarat*, *ASI*, NIS, xxiii, London 1896 (these two vols. being *ASWI*, ix and vi). The mosque at Fīrūzs̲h̲āh Kōṭlā is treated somewhat inadequately by Page in *A memoir on Kotla Firoz Shah, Delhi* (= *MASI*, lii) Delhi 1937; a few details and a plan of the Sand̲j̲ar Mosque are in M. Zafar Hasan, *op. cit.*, 35-6. See J. Burton-Page, *Indo-Islamic architecture: a commentary on some false assumptions*, in *AARP*, vi (Dec. 1974), 15, for the Begampur Masd̲j̲id. The mosque at Irič is well illustrated in Blakiston, *op. cit.* pls. xxii-v, but without description. For the identification of the K̲h̲ayrpur mosque, see S. Digby, *The tomb of Buhlūl Lōdī, in BSOAS*, xxxviii (1975), 550-61. Sultanate work in general is admirably illustrated with measured drawings in T. Yamamoto, M. Ara, and T. Tsukinowa, *Architectural remains of the Delhi Sultanate period* (text in Japanese), 3 vols. Tokyo 1967. For Bengal, refer to A. H. Dani, *Muslim architecture in Bengal*, Dacca 1961; S. M. Hasan, *Muslim monuments of Bangladesh*, Dacca 1980; idem, *Mosque architecture of pre-Mughal Bengal*, Dacca 1979, and his unpublished Ph.D. thesis *Development of mosque architecture with special reference to pre-Mughal Bengal*, 2 vols., University of London 1965; some useful photographs and plans in *Marg*, xxviii/2 (March 1972). Dj̲awnpur: A. Führer and E. Smith's *The Sharqi architecture of Jaunpur*, *ASI* NIS, i, Calcutta 1889, is still unsurpassed; also F. Lehmann, *The name and origin of the Aṭāla Masjid*, Jaunpur, in *IC*, lii/1 (1978), 19-27; Cunningham, ASI, xi. Gud̲j̲arāt: besides the volumes by Burgess and Cousens given above, see Burgess, *The Muhammadan architecture of Ahmadabad*, 2 vols., *ASI*, NIS, xxiv, xxiii (= ASWI, viii and vii), London 1905, 1906, with excellent drawings and photographs. Mālwā: E. Barnes, *Mandu and Dhar*, *ARASI*, 1903-4, Calcutta 1906; G. Yazdani, *Mandū, the city of joy*, Oxford 1929; D. R. Patil, *Mandu*, N. Delhi (*ASI*) 1975, the current official guidebook; M. B. Garde, *Guide to Chanderi*, Gwalior 1928. K̲h̲āndēs̲h̲: no adequate sources other than general works, and Cunningham, *ASI*, ix, *Central Provinces*, 1873-5. Dakhanī architecture is reviewed by E. S. Merklinger, *Indian Islamic architecture, the Deccan, 1347-1686*, Warminster 1981, with a chronological catalogue and useful thematic treatment. For Bahmanī buildings, see G. Yazdani, *The Great Mosque of Gulbarga*, in *IC*, ii (1928), 14-21, and idem, *Bidar, its history and monuments*, Oxford 1948, with full descriptions and good plans. Barīd S̲h̲āhī: *ibid.* ʿImād S̲h̲āhī: see bibl. to GĀWILGAṚH. Niẓām S̲h̲āhī: see bibl. s.v. ʿĀdil S̲h̲āhī: excellent coverage in Cousens, *Bījāpūr and its architectural remains*, *ASI*, NIS, xxxvii, Bombay 1916. Ḳuṭb S̲h̲āhī: for Golkonḍa, *s.v.*; for Ḥaydarābād, see the *Annual reports of the Archaeological Department, Hyderabad* for 1916-17, 3 ff. and pls. ii-iii; for 1924-5, 2-4 and pls. iii-vi; for 1936-7, 2 ff. Kashmir: W. H. Nicholls, *Muhammadan architecture* in Kashmir, in *ARASI*, 1906-7, 164-70. Mug̲h̲al: for the K̲h̲ayr al-Manāzil, see *ASI*, NIS, xxii, 6 and pl. i, *ARASI*, 1903-4, 25-6 and pl. x-xi; for Fatḥpur Sīkrī, E. W. Smith's superb *Mughal architecture of Fatḥpūr-Sīkrī*, *ASI*, NIS, xviii, Allāhābād 1894-7, now augmented by the intelligent discussion in S. A. A. Rizvi and V. J. A. Flynn, *Fatḥpur-Sīkrī*, Bombay 1975 (but beware error in description of domes, p. 74a). For Lāhawr, see Ahmad Nabi Khan, *Maryam Zamani Mosque*, Lahore-Karachi 1972, and M. A. Chaghatai, *The Wazir Khan Mosque, Lahore*, Lahore 1975, with good plans, sections, and photographs; also J. Burton-Page, *Wazir Khan's mosque*, in *Splendours of the East*, ed. Mortimer Wheeler, London etc. 1965, 94-101. For Āgra, see Nūr Bak̲h̲s̲h̲, *The Agra Fort and its buildings*, in *ARASI*, 1903-4, 185, and M. A. Husain, *Agra Fort*, N. Delhi 1956, 22 and 27; also R. Nath, *Agra and its monumental glory*, Bombay 1977, 35-8, and idem, *The immortal Taj Mahal*, Bombay 1972; The Fatḥpurī Masd̲j̲id is illustrated in *ARASI*, 1902-3, pl. xii. For the Dāʾī Angā mosque, see W. H. Nicholls, in *ARASI*, 1904-5, 20-22 and pl. iv; and for the Mōtī Masd̲j̲id, idem in *ARASI*, 1903-4, 26-7 and pl. xii-xiii, and M. Z. Hasan, *Moti Masjid or the Pearl Mosque in the Lahore Fort*, in *Proceedings of the Pakistan History Conference, 2nd session, Lahore 1952*, 8-16. For the Mōtī Masd̲j̲id at Āgra, see Nūr Bak̲h̲s̲h̲, *op. cit.*, 181-4, and Nath, *op. cit.* (1977), 39-42; for that at Dihlī, see G. Sanderson, *A guide to the buildings, Delhi Fort*, Delhi 1937, 55-7, and idem in *ARASI*, 1911-12, 13. Chaghatai gives comprehensive treatment to *The Badshahi Masjid, history and architecture*, Lahore 1972, with useful comparative plans of the *d̲j̲āmiʿ masd̲j̲ids* at Āgra and Dihlī. The later mosques in Sind are reviewed in Cousens, *The antiquities of Sind, ed. cit.*, though not in full detail, and by M. A. Ghafur in *Muslim architecture in Sind area*, Karachi 1961; for those in Aḥmadābād, see

Burgess, *op. cit.* (ASWI, viii, 1905). Epigraphy is mainly available in *EIM*; a useful index is provided by V. S. Bendrey, *A study of Muslim inscriptions*, Bombay 1942, for 1907-38, supplementing J. Horowitz, *A list of the published Mohammedan inscriptions of India* in *EIM*, 1909-10, 30-144. Much material relating to mosques in Pakistan is set out by S. Mahmood in *Islamic inscriptions in Pakistani architecture to 1707*, unpubl. Ph.D. thesis, Edinburgh University 1981. Some of the principal mosque inscriptions are also quoted at length by R. Nath in *Calligraphic art in Mughal architecture*, Calcutta 1979. (P. A. Andrews)

III. In Java.

In Java, the Arabic form *masdjid* is practically limited to religious circles. The Indonesian languages have developed the derivatives *mesigit* (Javanese, in Central- and East Java), *masigit* (Sundanese, in West Java) and *masèghit* (Madurese, on the island of Madura and in part of East Java). In general, these terms are used only for the mosques in which on the Friday *ṣalāt al-djumʿa* is held. Smaller mosques serving for the daily cult and religious instruction alone, are called *langgar* (Javanese), *tadjug* (Sundanese) and *balé* (in Bantĕn).

Indonesian Islam has produced its own type of mosque, clearly to be distinguished from that of other Islamic countries. Since this type was probably first developed in Java, it can be termed the Javanese type of mosque. Its standard characteristics are the following: (1) The ground plan is a square one. (2) The massive foundations are raised. The Friday mosque is not built on piles, as is the case with the classical Indonesian houses and the smaller mosques mentioned above. (3) The roof is tapering, and consists of two to five storeys narrowing towards the top (4) An extension on the western or north-western side serves as *miḥrāb* [*q.v.*]. (5) At the front—sometimes also at the two lateral sides—is an open or closed veranda. (6). The courtyard around the mosque is surrounded with a stone wall with one or more gates. Another characteristic is that in Java the mosque stands on the west side of the *alun-alun*, the grass-covered square which is found in virtually all chief towns of regencies and districts. In Tjeribon, Indramayn, Madjalèngka and Tjiamis—all regions in West Java—even each *dèsa* has an *alun-alun* with a mosque at its west side.

In Java, the direction of the *ḳibla* [*q.v.*], is, however, not west but north-west, and so, in order to indicate the exact *ḳibla*, the *miḥrāb* or niche is sometimes built obliquely against the back wall. There are, however, also regions, like the Priangan, where the exact *ḳibla* is taken into consideration at the time of construction of the mosque.

The gate at the front which gives access to the courtyard surrounding the mosque is sometimes covered. The mosques of Central and East Java are characterised by their monumental entrance gates.

The veranda (Javanese: *surambi*, *sĕrambi*, *srambi*; Sundanese: *tĕpas masdjid*, *tĕpas masigit*) is not considered as belonging to the mosque itself, as is evident from the various purposes which it serves. It is the place where, at night, after the mosque has been closed, the *ṣalāt* is performed; where travellers and other people who have no home pass the night; where marriages are concluded; where in former times (see Raffles, *The history of Java*) religious courts were functioning; where sometimes religious instruction is given and where *riyalat* (Javanese; in Arabic *riyāḍa* = ascetic abstinence from sleep, food and sexual intercourse) is practised. It is also the place for religious meals (*walīma*) on feast days like *Mawlid al-nabī* and *Miʿrādj* [*q.vv.*].

The walls of the mosque itself are rather low, but the roof tapers and ends in a sphere, on top of which is an ornament, called *mastaka* or *mustaka* in those regions where Javanese is spoken. It later times, this ornament was crowned by a crescent as the decisive symbol of Islam. This type of roof, in fact a piling-up of ever-smaller roofs, dates from pre-Islamic times and recalls the *mĕru* on Bali. In the present century, the cupola-shaped roof (Ar. *ḳubba* [*q.v.*]), an imitation of the mosques in other Islamic countries, and in particular India, is competing with the traditional piled-up roof of ancient Indonesia. Already before its restoration in 1935, the *Masdjid Kemayoran* in Surabaya diverged from the usual architectural pattern in that its base was not square but octagonal. In that year, two *ḳubba*s were constructed to the left and the right of the veranda. Another *ḳubba* was added to the monumental minaret, which is said to be an imitation of the Ḳuṭb Minār in Dihlī [*q.v.*]. At the same period, the *ḳubba* was also introduced into West Java. The use of the cupola-shaped roof became firmly established after Indonesia's independence in 1949. Impressive, huge mosques, all with *ḳubba*s, have been constructed since that time. The *Masdjid al-Shuhadāʾ* in Yogyakarta and the *Masdjid Istiḳlāl* in Jakarta can be considered as examples of a new type of architecture applied to the mosque.

The interior of a mosque built in the ancient Indonesian style can be described as a closed hall, sometimes provided with pillars, of a sober character, reflecting the simplicity which is the characteristic of the *masdjid*s in Java. There are no pictures of man or animal on the walls, only sacred Arabic names and some religious texts like the *shahāda* [*q.v.*] and the *ḥadīth* in which the builder of a mosque is praised: "Allāh has built a house in Paradise for whoever has built a mosque for Allāh". Since the floor of the mosque has to be clean, it consists of cement, tiles or marble. The grey colour of cement is occasionally alternated with rows of red tiles, indicating the rows (Arabic *ṣaff*) of the faithful when performing the *ṣalāt*. Mats are usually spread on the floor. In mosques which have not been constructed in the exact direction of the *ḳibla*, these mats are laid out in the right direction. Regular mosque-goers have their own small mat or rug (Ar. *sadjdjāda*), preferably one brought back by pilgrims to Mecca.

The *miḥrāb* at the rear side of the mosque is usually rather narrow, consisting of a small gate with a round arch. Sometimes the niche, or rather the extension, is large enough to contain the *minbar* on the right side. There are, however, also mosques with two or even three niches next to each other, each provided with a small gate. Occasionally, the *miḥrāb* is built out into a large pentagon with the *minbar* in the centre and the place of the *imām* to the left, the front side being fenced off by a wooden fencing with green and yellow sheets of glass and decorated with religious texts. Sometimes the *miḥrāb* is built out into a large, square place with the *minbar* in the centre, the place of the *imām* for the daily *ṣalāt* to the left, and to the right a small movable construction with an open front, this being the place of the regent of the region. The *minbar* (Javanese and Sundanese: *mimbar*, Javanese and Sundanese of Bantĕn: *imbar*) is always found to the right of the *miḥrāb*. Unlike other Islamic countries where the *minbar* is reached by a high flight of stairs, the *minbar* in Java is rather low. The height may vary from one to five steps, three steps being the average. Some *minbar*s are very simple, but many others are conspicuous for their woodcarving. As Islam permits, decorations consist of plants and flowers which sometimes look like pictures of men and animals. On closer inspection, however, they prove to be representations of flowers and leaves of the lotus, arranged as wings and birds. Sometimes the *naga* (serpent) motive can be recognised on the arms of the *minbar*, as is the case in the holy mosque of Demak in Central Java and in the ancient, holy mosque of Kuṭa Deḍé in the same region.

Each mosque in Java possesses a drum, called *bĕḍug*, stretched with buffalo-skin. Before the *adhān* [*q.v.*] (Javanese and Sundanese: *adan*) this drum is beaten vigorously at least five times a day. The *adhān* itself is made either from the minaret (Javanese: *mĕnara*, Sundanese: *munara*) or, more often, in the mosque itself since not every mosque has its minaret. The *muʾadhdhin*, called *modin* or *bilal*, stands at the entrance of the mosque or on its roof.

The highest official of the mosque is the *panghulu* (thus in Sundanese; Javanese: *pangulu*; Madurese: *pangòlò*, *pangòlòh*; Malay, *penghulu*), often a learned man (Ar. *ʿālim*) who has studied theology and is a pupil of the *pĕsantrèn*, the Indonesian religious school, or of the more modern *madrasa*; he may even have studied in Mecca. Traditionally, the *panghulus* are highly-considered in Indonesian society. Sometimes the function is hereditary. One of his tasks is to supervise and coordinate the functions of the lower officials of the mosque: the *imām*, the *khaṭīb*, the *muʾadhdhin* [*q.v.*] and the *marbūṭ*, the official who is responsible for maintenance. According to the linguistic area, these officials are called *imām*, *kĕtib* or *ketip*, *modin* or *bilal*, and *mĕrbot*, *mĕrĕbot* or occasionally *marbot*.

In Java the mosque is also used for *iʿtikāf* [*q.v.*], especially during the last ten days of Ramaḍān.

Bibliography: H. Aboebakar, *Sedjarah Mysdjid, dan amal ibadah dalamnja*, 1955 [in Indonesian]; P. A. Hoessein Djajadiningrat, *Islam in Indonesia*, in *Islam, the straight path, Islam interpreted by Muslims*, ed. W. Morgan, 1958; G. F. Pijper, *De Moskeeën van Java*, and *De Panghulu's van Java*, both in *Studiën over de geschiedenis van de Islam in Indonesia 1900-1950*, Leiden 1977; idem, *The minaret in Java*, in *India Antiqua, a volume of oriental studies presented to Jean Philippe Vogel*, Leiden 1947. (G. F. Pijper)

IV. In the rest of South-East Asia.

That the traditional South-East Asian mosque originated in Indonesia and that it is formally *sui generis* cannot be disputed. Whether, as has been claimed, it developed in Java is less certain. Indeed, the history of Islam in Indonesia would suggest another possibility. The building in question was of wooden construction. It consisted of a simple structure on a square groundplan, erected on a substantial base. This distinguished it from the classic Indonesian house on stilts. The existence of internal pillars probably depended on its size. It had openings in the walls, probably closed with shutters, and an entrance in the east side, opposite the later *miḥrāb*. It is not known how the *ḳibla* was originally indicated, but some mark on the west wall seems likely. Above this groundfloor hall, which had relatively low walls, there were a number of upper storeys of decreasing area, up to a total of four: each individual storey, including the main hall, had its own roof, usually in palm thatch, with widespreading eaves. The upper stories contained loft-like rooms which were functional. The whole building was topped by a finial which, in later times, seems to have been crowned by a crescent. The whole building was enclosed within a wall which had a more or less elaborate gateway in the east side. Occasionally there was more than one gate. There is some evidence to suggest that the main structure was surrounded by an irregular moat which may have formed part of a stream which traversed the enclosure. There was no *manāra*; the *adhān* was given either from the doorway of the mosque or from its top storey. This was probably preceded by the vigorous beating of a large skincovered drum, as is generally the practice today. A more simple structure, essentially a traditional Indonesian dwelling on stilts, serves as the model for a prayer hall which does not have the status of the mosque. It is still to be found in communities which cannot muster the requisite forty souls to constitute a congregation or, on occasions, as a supplementary building in a compound where it serves as a meeting place, a rest-house for visitors, an administrative centre as well as for *ṣalāt* when the mosque proper is closed.

This Indonesian prototype did not have the verandah, Javanese *serambi*, which is such a distinctive feature of the Central Javanese mosque. There is no evidence that this formed an original part of the mosque, from which it is, in fact, separated, both architecturally and dogmatically: shoes may be worn there. It seems to have derived from a royal building in pre-Islamic Central Java. Neither it, nor the externalised *miḥrāb*, belong to the original square mosque.

Various origins have been proposed for the basic Indonesian mosque. It has been derived from: (1) the *čaṅḍi*, a temple of either Hindu or Buddhist intention, ultimately of Indian origin but modified by Indonesian religious concepts; (2) the traditional bamboo and thatch cockpit used in Bali for the quasi-ritual cockfighting; (3) the multi-tiered sacred mountain which is of widespread significance in Indonesian religions (the Balinese temple with multi-tiered thatched roofs known as a *meru*, after the Indian sacred mountain, is an architectural example of this). The objection to (1) is that, quite apart from its possible unacceptability to Muslim teachers, the *čaṅḍi* does not occur in those parts of Indonesia where conversions to Islam first took place. The cockpit hypothesis appears to suffer from inherent implausibility. There is, however, good reason for holding the concept of the sacred mountain as one component in the undoubtedly complex origin of the Indonesian mosque. It differs so profoundly from mosques elsewhere in the Islamic world, not least in Cambay [see KHAMBĀYAT] and other parts of Gudjarāt [*q.v.*] from which the main impetus towards conversion seems to have come.

South-East Asia lies across the sea route from the Middle East and the Indian sub-continent to China and beyond. The Malay Peninsula and Sumatra mark the area where the monsoon system of the Indian Ocean meets that of the Pacific, and constitute a natural interchange point. For two millennia or more merchants have travelled and traded through this region. After the coming of Islam many of these travellers were Muslims, but, although there were without doubt Muslim communities in the ports and harbours of the region, some of whose members may have traded in the interior, there is no evidence at all for conversion to Islam among the local peoples. (Nor, incidentally, is there any evidence for mosques to serve the needs of such Muslim traders.) The first instances of such conversion comes at the end of the 7th/13th century. A hint in a Chinese source dated 683/1281 receives striking confirmation from Marco Polo who spent several months in Sumatra, on his way home from China ten years later. Of Ferlec (Perlak) he noted "the people were all idolaters, but, on account of the Saracen traders who frequent the kingdom with their ships, they have been converted to the Law of Mahomet'', adding that this was only the townspeople, those of the mountains being like wild beasts. The ruler of Samudra (Pasai), where Polo spent some months waiting for the wind to change, and who died in 699/1297, certainly died a Muslim for his tombstone, which was imported from Cambay, gives his name as Malik al-Ṣāliḥ. It was from this remote, in Javanese terms, area of Aceh that Islam spread to the Malay Peninsula, above all to Malacca, [*q.v.*], to the north coast of Java and thence to other parts of Sumatra, to the coasts of Borneo and to the sources for the much sought-after spices, by way of the ports of Sulawesi and Maluku. Over a period of some three centuries, Islam followed the trade routes and with it there went the Indonesian *masdjid*, with its tiered, overhanging roofs. More than a dozen have been identified, notably by De Graaf. What is noticeable is that it was precisely in areas which had not been strongly influenced by Indo-Javanese architecture of Hindu or Buddhist tradition that the mosque of this type developed. Its origins have to be sought in the socio-religious structures of northern Sumatra in the communal house which, as elsewhere in Indonesia, once constituted the men's house. Now without windows or its original interior divisions, in Aceh it has become the *meunasah* which serves as a prayer house, a meeting place, and an administrative centre as well as a Ḳurʾānic school. It had the advantage that it had never housed idols, but this does not explain how the teachers from Gudjarāt and elsewhere were persuaded to permit the adoption of such an aberrant form of mosque.

Bibliography: Illustrations of many of the mosques are in François Valentijn, *Oud en Nieuw Oost Indien*, 5 vols., Dordrecht-Amsterdam 1724-6. See also H. J. de Graaf, *De oorsprong der javaanse moskee*, in *Indonesie*, I, 289-305; B. Schrieke, *The shifts in political and economic power in the Indonesian Archipelago in the sixteenth and seventeenth centuries*, in *Indonesian Sociological Studies*, i. The Hague 1955, 1-82, W. F. Stutterheim, *De Islam en zijn komst in de Archipel*, Groningen 1952. (A. H. CHRISTIE)

V. IN CHINA.

The Chinese term is *Ch'ing-chen ssu*, lit. ''Pure and True temple''. *Ch'ing-chen chiao* (''Pure and True Religion'') being a Chinese synonym for Islam. The first Muslim settlements in China, dating from the early centuries of Islam, were established either by the sea route along the southern and eastern coasts (Canton and Hainan Island in Kwantung Province; Chuan-chou in Fukien Province, Hang-chou in Chekiang Province, Yang-chou on the lower Yangtze in Kiangsu Province); or by the overland ''Silk Road'' route at the ancient city of Ch'ang-an (some miles south of present-day Sian, Shensi Province), T'ang dynastic capital between 618-906 (corresponding approximately to the first three centuries *Hidjrī*).

Chinese Muslim tradition holds that numbers of mosques were established in these and several other cities by Saʿd b. Abī Waḳḳāṣ and various Companions of the Prophet or itinerant holy men during the first century, quite probably during the Rāshidūn caliphs' period. Pending further archaeological excavation, however, most of these oral traditions must be treated with caution, and according to Leslie (*op. cit.*, in *Bibl.*, 40), but few sites ''merit serious consideration'', the most important of which are:

1. Canton (the *Huai-sheng* mosque and *Kuang-t'a* minaret). This mosque, claimed by Muslim tradition as the first and oldest in China, may well date back to T'ang times, but the earliest extant reference dates from *ca.* 603/1206, whilst the earliest mosque inscription (in Chinese and Arabic) records the re-building of the *Huai-sheng ssu* in 751/1350 after its destruction by fire seven years before. The presence of a mosque in Canton in 755/1354 is attested by Ibn Baṭṭūṭa.

2. Chuan-chou (the *Sheng-yu* mosque), also sometimes claimed as the earliest mosque in China, though Leslie considers this to be ''*a priori*, less convincing'' than the claim of the *Huai-sheng ssu*. The mosque inscription of 710/1310-11 (in Arabic) dates the first building of the mosque to 400/1009-10, commemorating a restoration which took place over three centuries later. It claims that the *Sheng-yu ssu* was the first mosque ''in this land'', and calls it ''The Mosque of the Companions'' (*al-Aṣḥāb*).

3. Hang-chou (the *Chen-chiao* or Feng-huang mosque), ascribed by late Ming (11th/17th century) inscriptions to T'ang times, though Leslie rejects these unsubstantiated claims in favour of a Sung Dynasty establishment, Hang-chou being the capital of the Southern Sung (*ca.* 521-678/1127-1279), and by Yuan times ''the greatest city in the world'' (according to Marco Polo), with a substantial Muslim population living in its own ward (Ibn Baṭṭūṭa, Odoric).

4. Ch'ang-an (the *Ch'ing-chiao* or *Ch'ing-ching* mosque), which differs from those other mosques listed so far in that its foundation is ascribed to the arrival of Muslim soldiers travelling overland, rather than sailors coming by sea. Undated epigraphic evidence and long-established tradition date this mosque to the early T'ang (late Umayyad) period, but this remains inconclusive, and Leslie suggests that ''until further evidence is forthcoming its is better to reject a T'ang date and query a Sung one, whilst taking for granted a Yuan [Mongol] presence''.

Leslie continues by providing ''Desultory Notes'' for numerous other cities in Eastern. Central and Northern China (49-53), before concluding that many thousands (or even tens of thousands) of Muslims, mostly of Persian and Arab origin, were resident in China during T'ang Dynasty times, though little definitive evidence exists for the number of mosques which had been established during this early period of Chinese Islam. It is clear, however, that most of these *Hsi-yu jen* or ''Westerners'' were semi-permanent or permanent residents, many of whom would have intermarried freely with the indigenous Chinese population, thereby giving rise to a nascent Chinese-speaking, increasingly Sinicised Muslim population which would, by Ming times, develop into the Hui Chinese Muslim community. Certainly by T'ang times, the distinction was already being made between ''foreigners'' and ''native-born foreigners''. *Sharīʿa* law requires the establishment of congregational mosques wherever communities of more than forty adult male Muslims are gathered together; the presence of many small mosques along the Chinese coast and (to a lesser extent) in the interior may, therefore, be taken for granted by late T'ang/Sung times. Doubtless, except in the more important coastal towns such as Canton (Khanfu) and Chuan-chou (Zaitun) these mosques would have been fairly insubstantial buildings, long since altered beyond recognition or destroyed; thus, definitive proof of the extent of mosque-building in China during this early period will depend upon future archaeological excavations.

The Yüan period (*ca.* 678-770/1279-1368) was characterised by a substantial expansion of Islam in the central and western parts of China, most particularly in Yunnan, where Sayyid Adjall Shams al-Dīn Bukhārī (who conquered and subsequently administered the former Nan-ch'ao area for the Mongols) is credited with establishing two mosques in the region. Sayyid Adjall and his family may be seen as the archetypical example of Muslims in service under the Mongols—by whom they were employed as soldiers, administrators and financial middlemen—and from Yüan times the central focus of Islam in China moved definitively away from the southern coastal ports towards the north and west. Certainly, the oldest mosques in Yunnan and the north-west are likely to have been established during this period, a trend which was continued under the Ming Dynasty (*ca.* 771-1054/1368-1644) which is also known as a period of Sinicisation for the Chinese Muslim community—indeed, it may be that the Chinese-speaking Hui Muslim community emerged as a separate and distinct entity (paralleling, for example, the Swahili [*q.v.*] in East Africa and the Mappila [*q.v.*] of southern India) during this period.

It is probable that the mosques of the Hui (Chinese-speaking) Muslims, which are scattered throughout China but are particularly numerous in the provinces of Kansu, Ningsia, Tsinghai and Yunnan, evolved in their characteristic form during this period. Certainly under the Ming, the nascent Hui community expanded greatly as a result of intermarriage, overt (and, perhaps more frequently, covert) missionary work, and their success in the fields of military and commercial venture. Wherever Hui settled in any numbers, *halāl* establishments (caravanserais, restaurants, inns), mosques and attendant *madrasas* soon followed. As Israeli notes (*op.cit.* in *Bibl.*, 29), many mosques constructed during the Ming period were built in a style reminiscent of indigenous Chinese temple architecture, either eliminating the minaret altogether, or eschewing the distinctive styles associated with the mosques of Central Asia, South Asia and the Middle East in favour of Chinese-style pagodas. As a result of this architectural development, the muezzin could no longer call the faithful to prayer in the usual way, but stood inside the mosque instead, calling the *adhān* behind the main mosque entrance. "And when one entered the mosque, one was struck by the traditional Muslim flavour; cleanliness and austerity. Except for the Emperor's tablets that were mandatory in any house of prayer, there was no sign of Chinese characters or Chinese characteristics. On the walls there were Arabic inscriptions of verses from the Qur'an and the west end (*qibla*) was adorned with arabesques. Once the believers were inside, they put on white caps, shoes were taken off, elaborate ablutions were ritually performed, and the prayers began in Arabic, with heart and mind centred on Mecca. When prostrating themselves before the Emperor's tablets, as required, the Muslims would avoid bringing their heads into contact with the floor... and thus did they satisfy their consciences in avoiding the true significance of the rite—this prohibited worship was invalid because it was imperfectly performed" (Israeli, *op.cit.*, 29).

Israeli defines this combination of external Sinicisation of mosque building and internal Islamic orthodoxy as a manifestation of the dichotomy of Chinese Islam. Certainly, the functions of the mosque remained immediately recognisable in their Islamic purpose. Thus, besides the area set aside for prayer, the interior of larger Chinese mosques is generally divided between lecture hall, dormitory, conference rooms, community leaders' offices, and the "dead man's room" for washing and otherwise preparing deceased Muslims for burial. Amongst the best-known and most beautifully decorated of these traditional Chinese mosques are the *Niu-chieh ssu* (Ox Street mosque) in Peking, and the *Hua-chueh ssu* in Sian.

By contrast with the Sinicised Hui Chinese mosques scattered throughout "China Proper", the mosques of the periphery are often very different. Thus the mosque architecture of Sinkiang conforms closely to that of neighbouring Western Turkestan, whilst in the far north-east (Heilungkiang Province), an area formerly much influenced by Russian culture, mosque may sometimes outwardly resemble Orthodox churches. In this context, an informative trilingual study illustrating many of the best-known mosques in China and clearly depicting the different architectural forms has recently been published by the China Islamic Association (*op.cit.* in *Bibl.*, 1981).

Bibliography: K. Himly, *Die Denkmäler der Kantoner Moschee*, in *ZDMG* xli (1887), 141-74; G. Phillips, *Two mediaeval Fuh-Kien trading ports: Chuan-Chow and Chang-Chow*, in *T'oung Pao*, vii (1896), 223-40; G. Arnaiz and M. van Berchem, *Mémoire sur les antiquités musulmanes de Ts'iuan-tcheou*, in *TP*, xii (1901), 677-727; Cl. Huart, *Le texte turc-oriental de la stèle de la mosquée de Péking*, in *ZDMG*, lvi (1902), 210-22; W. Bang, *Über die Mandschu Version der Viersprachigen Inschrift in der Moschee zu Peking*, in *Keleti Szemle*, iii (1902), 94-103; H. Saladin, *Monuments musulmans de Chine et d'Extrême-Orient*, in *Manuel d'art musulman*, Paris 1907, 579-83; "N.", *Les Mosquées de Pekin*, in *RMM*, ii (1907), 570-73; E. Blochet and A. Vissière, *Épigraphie musulmane chinoise*, in *ibid.*, v (1908), 289-93; R. Ristelhuber, L. Bouvat, F. Farjenel, *Études chinoises*, in *ibid.*, iv (1908), 512-30; anon., *Liste des mosquées de Pékin*, in *ibid.*, vi (1908), 699; M. Broomhall, *Islam in China: a neglected problem*, London 1910, 83-120, 183-90; Le Commandant D'Ollone, A. Vissière, E. Blochet, *et alii*, *Recherches sur les Musulmans chinois*, Paris 1911, *passim*; G. Cordier and Vissière, *Études sino-mahométanes: deuxième série. Renseignements envoyés par M. G. Cordier sur la chambre funéraire et le temple commémoratif du Seyyid Edjell à Yun-nan-fou*, in *RMM*, xv (1911), 60-9; eidem, (*Note on two photographs of the Mosque of Seyyid Edjell Omar*), in *ibid.*, xxv (1913), 306; Vissière, *Études sino-mahométanes: deuxième série. VII. L'Islamisme à Hang-tcheou*, in *ibid.*, xxii (1913), 1-84; Cordier, *Études sino-mahométanes: troisième série. Les Mosquées de Yun-nan-fou*, in *ibid.*, xxvii (1914), 141-61; Vissière, *Inscriptions sino-mahométanes de Fou-tcheou*, in *ibid.*, xxvii (1914), 162-73; A. Von le Coq, *Buried treasures of Chinese Turkestan*, London 1928 (photographs); Ito Chuta, *Shina kenchiku soshoku* ("Chinese architectural decoration"), Tokyo 1941, i, 107-9; ii, plates 42-8; A. Hutt, *The Central Asian origin of the Eastern Minaret form*, in *Asian Affairs*, viii 3 (June 1977), 157-62 (with reference to Sinkiang); R. Israeli, *Muslims in China*; *a study in cultural confrontation*, London 1980; China Islamic Association, *The religious life of Chinese Muslims*, Peking 1981; D. D. Leslie, *Islam in traditional China*, Canberra 1986, esp. 40-68 (plus extensive Chinese language bibliography, glossary, etc.; a uniquely competent and useful reference work).

(A. D. W. Forbes)

VI. In East Africa.

In East Africa the mosque is commonly spoken of in Swahili as *msikiti*, pl. *misikiti*, but *msihiri*, *misihire* in the Comoro Islands; and cf. Swahili *sijida*, the act of adoration, and verb *sujudu* "to prostrate oneself", from Ar. *sadjada*. Nineteenth-century traditional histories claim the setting up of Muslim cities on the eastern African coast in the 7th and 8th centuries

A.D. Of this there is no earlier literary evidence, but a mosque is mentioned in the Arabic *History of Kilwa* named *Kibala* (possibly a Bantu form from *ḳibla*) as existing on that island *ca.* 950 A.D. In spite of recent excavations at Kilwa [*q.v.*] by H. N. Chittick, there has so far been no positive identification of a mosque of this period. The first reliable evidence is from inscriptions. Cerulli reports one in the Friday Mosque at Barāwa, Somalia, dated 498/1104-5, while on Zanzibar Island there is the well-known Friday Mosque at Kizimkazi [*q.v.*] which has an inscription dating its foundation to 500/1107. The inscription is certainly of Sīrāfī provenance, which does not argue that Zanzibar was much Islamicised at this period. The 4th/10th century *Kitāb ʿAdjāʾib al-Hind* of Buzurg b. Shahriyār of Rāmhurmuz contains, however, the tale of the conversion of an eastern African king of a place of which no identification is given; he was followed by his people. In the same century al-Masʿūdī, who visited eastern Africa, speaks of the people and their sovereigns as pagan. By the 6th/12th century al-Idrīsī says that "the people, although mixed, are actually mostly Muslims", which would accord with the epigraphical evidence.

Between 1962 and March 1964 the greater number of known mosques, from mediaeval times to the 18th century, both standing and ruined, were planned and photographed by P. S. Garlake. He omitted, however, an important series of foundation inscriptions of mosques at Lamu [*q.v.*], some twenty in all, and ranging from the 14th to the 19th century. He rightly says that "the most sensitive indicator of change and development in style and decoration is bound to be the mosque mihrab": he distinguishes a clear and unbroken development of style and technique from the early classic *miḥrāb* with a plain architrave of the 14th and 15th centuries; a developed classic *miḥrāb* in which the plain surfaces of the architrave are broken by decoration; a neo-classic *miḥrāb* of greater elaboration, both this and the foregoing in the 16th century; a simplified classic *miḥrāb* restricted to northern Kenya, and a derived classic *miḥrāb* on the Tanzanian coast in the 18th century, in which, however, there were new developments that led to multifoliate arches of an elaborate character. The dating of some of these *miḥrāb*s derives from inscriptions, but is based to a great extent upon the evidence of imported pottery and Chinese porcelain, the latter coming to be used as a decoration by insetting it into the architrave of the *miḥrāb*.

All the 19th century Swahili settlements in eastern Africa are on the edge of the shore: Gedi, two miles from the Mida creek, is the sole exception. Some earlier mosques, however, are found on cliffs or headlands, where they may have been placed to serve as mariners' marks. Some of them are still of special veneration for seafarers. The population in these places was on the whole small, and only at Kilwa [*q.v.*] and at Mogadishū [see MAḲDISHŪ] was the need felt for mosques of more than modest size. Throughout the coast from Somalia to Mozambique, the only available building material of a permanent character was coralline limestone, obtained either from old raised beaches or directly from coral reefs. Mouldings, arches, and all features wherever precision was required, were of finely dressed coral blocks. A fine concrete, whose aggregate was coral rubble, was used for circular and barrel vaults. The method of burning it has survived to this day. From it also was made the plaster which in the 18th century was used to decorate not only the *miḥrāb* but also elaborately decorated tombs. There was a limited répertoire of mouldings, used also on tombs, and—more sparingly—in domestic architecture. The planning of all buildings, religious and domestic, was restricted by the span of the timber rafters, always of mangrove wood, which never exceeds 2,80 metres or approximately 9 feet. Even the vaulted buildings conform to this as to a fixed and unalterable convention. Thus even in the Great Mosque of Kilwa, with its five aisles and six bays, there is a sense of constriction rather than of spaciousness. Walls may be built of dressed coral limestone but quite commonly of coral rubble plastered over. Piers occur in mosques in Kenya and Pemba during the 14th to 16th centuries, but not in the south. After the 13th century in Tanzania, columns alone are found, some square and some octagonal. Generally, these were of dressed coral, but occasionally, as at Kaole (southern mosque) and in the northern *muṣallā* of the Great Mosque of Kilwa, wooden columns fitted into coral sockets were used. Because of the difficulty imposed by the length of the rafters, the master-builders—for only rarely can architects have been employed, and perhaps only for the Fakhr al-Dīn Mosque at Mogadishu—in seeking to erect a building of a particular breadth, frequently encumbered the perspective of the *miḥrāb* by constructing a central arcade of pillars. This clumsy feature (which occurs quite unconnectedly in certain mediaeval European churches) appears not only in two-aisled mosques such as those of Tongoni and Gedi but also in the four-aisled Friday Mosque of Gedi and the original North Mosque which forms part of the Great Mosque of Kilwa.

Minarets [see MANĀRA. 3. In East Africa] are very rare, and *minbars* [*q.v.*] have certain idiosyncratic features. In all, the mosques of the eastern African coast have a distinct regional character of their own, deriving in earlier times from the common use of ogival or returned-horseshoe arches, and in later times from the elaborate plaster decoration of the *miḥrāb* and its architrave.

Bibliography: H. N. Chittick, *Kilwa*, 1975, describes the Kilwa mosques, bringing up to date P. S. Garlake, *The early Islamic architecture of the East African coast*, Nairobi 1966, with its numerous plates and plans and exhaustive bibliography up to that date; G. S. P. Freeman-Grenville, *Some preliminary observations of medieval mosques near Dar es Salaam*, in *Tanganyika Notes and Records*, no. 36 (1954), is wholly superseded by the finding of better evidence for date; see also J. S. Kirkman, *Men and monuments of the East African coast*, London 1964, and *Fort Jesus*, Oxford 1974; and, for inscriptions, G. S. P. Freeman-Grenville and B. G. Martin, *A preliminary handlist of the Arabic inscriptions of the eastern African coast*, in *JRAS* (1973).

(G. S. P. FREEMAN-GRENVILLE)

VII. IN WEST AFRICA.

In Muslim West Africa, the smallest hamlet has its mosque, and the quarters of an individual town compete with one another in the construction of cultic sites. In most villages, the mosque is situated in the middle of the public square, near the tree which is the traditional place for bargaining and discussion ("palaver"); it is generally constructed in the style of a large shed, roofed with zinc plates and bamboo partitions or with banco or with moulded clay, and has the appearance, in the majority of cases, of the most attractive building in the locality, often surrounded by bushy trees. The mosque is regarded with pious respect, and is kept clean. Volunteers, often women of a certain age, accept responsibility for maintenance, cleaning and the supply of drinkable water for the faithful.

In towns, the mosque is a more substantial building

and it dominates the neighbourhood with its minaret or minarets. Sometimes, as in the case of the Great Mosque of Dakar, it has only one, while that of Touba, the most important centre of the religious brotherhood of the Murids, has three, of which the tallest, known as the "Lamp" (*Fall*) measures 83 m. In fact, it is the modern mosques which possess minarets; the most ancient have none, but still dominate their surroundings with cubic pillars. In small villages, the floor of the mosque is covered with matting or with fine sand which is sifted every day. In the urban setting, oriental carpets cover the floor. A palisade of bamboo or zinc plates or even a cement wall forms an enclosure within which a spacious courtyard is set out, to enable those worshippers who cannot pray at the times when the mosque is crowded to perform their religious duties. On the left side of the larger mosques, the place reserved for women is separated from that where the men pray by a metal grill.

The *imām* leads the prayer standing in a niche (*minbar*) in the *ḳibla wall*. The Great Mosque is furnished with a throne, a kind of raised dais where the *imām* takes his place to preach his sermon and to harangue the faithful, first in Arabic and then in the local language.

All the other facilities, including lavatories and taps for ablutions, are located on the exterior. In a corner of the courtyard there is a hut for the washing of corpses.

Each *imām* is served by a *nāʾib* or deputy who officiates in his absence. Two or more muezzins make the call to prayer from the tops of the minarets. In the larger mosques loud-speakers have been installed, to relay either the call to prayer or the sermon of the *imām*. The majority of *imām*s receive no monthly salary. The *imām* of the Great Mosque of the Senegalese capital is one of the few who receives regular payment and occupies an official residence; more often, the *imām* and his family are accommodated in the mosque.

The architectural style reproduces especially that of the Maghrib. It is thus that the Great Mosque of Dakar, inaugurated by King Ḥasan II, was built under the supervision of a Moroccan architect, as was the Islamic Institute which adjoins it. However the ancient mosques of northern Senegal, including those of Halwâr, Ndioum, Guédé and Dialmath, are in the Sudanese style of the mosque-institutes of the towns of Mali (Djenné, Mopti, Timbuktu, etc.) and of the land of the Sahel (cf. J. Boulègue, *Les Mosquées de style soudanais au Fuuta-Tooro (Sénégal)*, in *Notes africaines*, 136 (Oct. 1972), 117-19). This is a style characterised by its massive buttresses exceeding the height of the roof, in a rounded, conical form, with a small cubic minaret; the whole is constructed in brick made from dried earth and covered with a facing of the same material and ochre or beige in colour. The walls are very thick. An elaborate system of ventilation maintains a freshness similar to that provided by air-conditioning.

Religious function. In West Africa, the principal function of the mosque is still religious; each quarter possesses several, and in this context a genuine rivalry prevails between quarters or between members of different brotherhoods. It is thus that the mosque of the Tidjānīs is found alongside those of the Murīds [see MURĪD], of the Ḳādirīs [see ḲĀDIRIYYA] or of the Hamallites [see ḤAMĀLIYYA]. The faithful fill the mosques without regard for their particular affiliation. The Tidjānīs organise gatherings in the mosque after morning and evening prayers to recite, in chorus, the litanies (*dhikr*) peculiar to their religious order. This ritual is performed around a carpet and in darkness. But on Fridays or at times of canonical festivals, great crowds of Muslims are seen streaming towards the mosques clad in their splendid boubous or flowing robes.

Special prayers for the dead are also offered in the mosque. In this case, the bier is placed before the faithful, who pray upright without bowing or sitting. After these funeral rites, the parents of the deceased arrange a ceremony of recitation of the Ḳurʾān "for the repose of his soul".

The veneration of which the mosque is the object inspired Cheikh El-Hadji Malik Sy (1853-1922), founder of the *zāwiyya tidjāniyya* of Tivaouane, to compose a poem in Arabic consisting of forty verses in *radjaz* style and revealing the details of a whole system of etiquette. Cheikh Aliou Faye, the chief marabout of the Gambia, revised and embellished his master's poem, entitling his version *Tabshīrat al-murīd* or "The way of success for the disciple". The following are a few of the verses:

Whosoever wishes to enter Paradise without punishment and without the need to give an exact account of his actions at the Resurrection, should build a mosque for God the Merciful, and he will be granted one hundred and thirty palaces in Paradise.

Every believer who enters this mosque to pray will obtain a pleasant dwelling in Paradise.

A mosque may be built in any place, even in the square of a church or a or a synagogue.

There it is forbidden to grow crops, to dig wells, to sew and to compose [profane] poetry.

There it is forbidden to eat garlic, leek, onion, to shave, to cause an injury to a human being, to cut the nails, to cast lice or fleas and to kill them.

To tie animals, confine the mentally ill, to allow a criminal to enter and be seated.

All mosques are of equal worth, with three exceptions: those of Mecca, Medina and Jerusalem, which are the best mosques.

Social function. Besides this predominant religious role, the mosque also performs a very important social function. It is there, in fact, that, under the patronage of the *imām*, marriages are contracted between the parents of the betrothed parties. The father or guardian of the prospective bride gives her hand to the father or guardian of the suitor and receives the dowry. This function is so important that when information is sought regarding the marital status of a female person, the question is asked: "Have the men gone to the mosque for her?" (in Wolof: *Ndax demnañu jaka ja?*). As a form of pleasantry and to tell a girl that she is nubile, the remark is made: "I shall go to see the *imām* about it." Parents or guardians may be accompanied to the mosque by other parents and friends who act as witnesses. The relatives of the suitor bring the dowry which they entrust to the *imām*; the latter gives it to the father or guardian of the prospective bride and recites the sacramental formula. In the presence of all, the *imām* blesses the couple. Cola, non-alcoholic drinks or delicacies are distributed.

Even though, since the promulgation of a "Family Code" in Senegal, for example, some ten years ago, marriages must be contracted before the mayor or the representative of the public authorities, it is considered that, without the mosque playing a part, the matrimonial union is not valid. Thus the *imām* in fact represents the municipal magistrate.

Often the elders of the village hold meetings not under the traditional tree, but inside or in the courtyard of the mosque at any hour of day or night to discuss public matters; finance for the sinking of wells, construction of a market, division of the produce of common land, preparations for the reception of distinguished guests, etc. In this case, the mosque represents a kind of national assembly where all the affairs of the village community are the object of wide and democratic debate.

Sometimes the mosque performs the role of a tribunal where disputes between members of the village are laid public and closely examined. Solutions are always formed on the basis of the *Sharīʿa*, or of local custom, or of both. These may be disputes between spouses, between two dignitaries, between two families, between herdsmen and stock-breeders, between a representative of the state and local landowners, between traditional chiefs and religious leaders. Sometimes the division of bequests is performed in the mosque under the supervision of the *imām*.

Some mosques provide places of lodging for strangers. It is in this way that travelling Muslims are accommodated. Furthermore, any person who is regarded as having lived a pious life and who has contributed to the building of the mosque, is buried there after his death. Such is the case of Cheikh Ahmadou Bamba Mbacke, Cheikh El-Hadji Malik Sy, Cheikh Ibrahima Niasse, Cheikh Ahmadou Anta Samb, and Bouh Kounta respectively at Touba, Tivaouane, Kaolack, Kébémer and Ndiassance (Senegal).

Many other men renowned for their piety or for their work in the service of Islam are entombed within or in close proximity to the mosque.

Economic function. The economic function of the mosque is explained by the fact that the temporal is always closely linked with the spiritual. Thus, for example, the sums raised from legal alms (*zakāt*) are in most cases entrusted to the *imām* of the mosque who, as an expert in the matter, ensures that they are distributed to those entitled to them. Sometimes cattle are led to the mosque to be slaughtered by the *imām*, who distributes the meat to the needy. Every Friday, a whole army of beggars is seen flocking to the mosques, attracted by the prospect of receiving charity from the wealthier believers. The same spectacle is witnessed during the major Islamic feasts of *Tabaski* and *Korite*.

The *imām* received a gratuity for his services when marriage is celebrated. Even though the sum is by no means considerable, it is important for the *imām* who is not salaried. In the course of one Sunday afternoon he may preside over several marriage ceremonies. Furthermore, numerous mosques receive requests for readings of the Ḳurʾān in exchange for a certain sum, the amount being left to the discretion of the customer.

Mosques which incorporate tombs receive a profitable income as a result of daily, weekly, monthly and annual pilgrimages or on the occasion of major Islamic feasts. This applies in the case of the mosque of Touba during the well-known feast of *Magal*, which commemorates the departure into exile (in 1895) of Cheikh Ahmadou Bamba Mbacke, founder of the brotherhood of the Murīds, and that of Tivaouane at the time of the *Mawlūd* [see MAWLID].

Cultural function. Although the mosque in West Africa fulfils a considerable economic role, its function in the cultural sphere is more striking. In the majority of cases, the courtyard of the mosque is the setting for a Ḳurʾānic school. Sometimes dozens of young children, boys and girls, are seen squatting in a half-circle before their master, who sits either on the ground, on a sheepskin rug or reclining on a couch, holding a cane. Each pupil places on his knees a tablet on which the lesson to be learned is inscribed in ink made from soot from cooking-pots. In the evening, after twilight and before the meal, a large fire is lit and the verses to be learned are read by the light of the flames. By this educational method, in the shadow of the mosque, many scholars arrive at the point where they can recite the entire Holy Book by heart.

The mosque also serves as a high school and university when, having memorised the Ḳurʾān, the pupils become students and learn the other Islamic sciences: exegesis, *ḥadīth*, theology, mysticism, Muslim law and even literature, history, logic, astronomy, rhetoric, etc.

It is also in the mosque that lectures are held on various subjects relating to religion, as well as educational lectures given by scholars or distinguished guests from other Muslim countries. In the mosque, throughout the month of Ramaḍān, marabout exegetes expound and comment on the Ḳurʾān before an audience, either to recall the teaching of the Holy Book or to instruct the faithful. On the "Night of Destiny" nobody sleeps, and reverent vigil is held in the mosque. Also in the mosque, particularly at Tivaouane, the sanctuary of Tidjānism in Senegal, the head *khalīfa* of the disciples of the brotherhood founded by Aḥmad al-Tidjānī (1737-1815 [*q.v.*]) expounds and comments on the *Burda* of al-Buṣīrī (608-*ca.* 695/1212-*ca.* 1295 [*q.v.* in Suppl.]).

Political function. Finally, the mosque performs in West Africa a political function which is far from insignificant, because the region contains a very substantial percentage of Muslims. This figure is increasing as a result of large-scale conversion to Islam of followers of other religions (Christianity and animism). Islam has enjoyed a revival of activity under pressure exerted both from the interior of this zone and, to a lesser extent, from the exterior. In Senegal, for example, the quite recent appointment of M. Abdou Diouf to the post of chief magistrate has had a considerable influence in this domain, to such an extent that, unlike his predecessor, the head of state, accompanied by the presidents of the National Assembly and the Economic and Social Council, participates behind the senior *imām* in the prayers conducted on the occasion of major festivals. In his *khuṭba*, the latter invariably affirms his loyalty to the authorities and invites the believers present to pray, with him, for the President of the Republic and the members of his government, whom he mentions by name, appealing to God to "perpetuate their rule and assist them, giving peace, health and long life to them, to their families and to Senegal".

This account of the activity of the present President of the Republic of Senegal applies to the other Muslim Heads of State of West Africa.

The *imām* often uses the occasion of the Friday Prayer to draw attention in his *khuṭba* to themes of concern to the government such as the misappropriation of public funds, corruption, juvenile delinquency, drugs, prostitution, the degradation of morals, the urgent need to combat bush-fires and desertification.

After this survey of the functions of the mosque in West Africa, it may be affirmed that it performs a multifarious role in this region by virtue of its status as the supreme place of prayer.

Bibliography : J. M. Cuoq, *Les Musulmans en Afrique*, Paris 1975, 103-271, gives information and bibliographies concerning religious life in West Africa; see also, in particular, J. Schacht, *Sur la diffusion des formes d'architecture religieuse musulmane à travers le Sahara*, in *Travaux de l'Inst. de Rech. Sahariennes*, xi (1954), 11-27. (A. SAMB)

AL-**MASDJID** AL-**AKṢĀ**, literally, "the remotest sanctuary." There are three meanings to these words.

1. The words occur in Ḳur'ān, XVII,1: "Praise Him who made His servant journey in the night (*asrā*) from the sacred sanctuary (*al-masdjid al-ḥarām*) to the remotest sanctuary (*al-masdjid al-aḳṣā*), which we have surrounded with blessings to show him of our signs." This verse, usually considered to have been revealed during the Prophet's last year in Mecca before the Hidjra, is very difficult to explain within the context of the time. There is no doubt that *al-masdjid al-ḥarām* is the then pagan sanctuary of Mecca. But whether the event itself was a physical one and then connected with a small locality near Mecca which had two mosques, a nearer one and a farther one (A. Guillaume, *Where was al-Masjid al-Aqṣā?*, in *Al-Andalus*, xviii [1953]), or a spiritual and mystical night-journey (*isrā'*) and ascension (*mi'radj* [*q.v.*]) to a celestial sanctuary; a consensus was established very early (perhaps as early as the year 15 A.H., cf. J. Horovitz, *Koranische Untersuchungen*, Berlin 1926, 140) that *al-masdjid al-aḳṣā* meant Jerusalem. By the time of Ibn Hishām's *Sīra*, nearly all the elements of what was to grow into one of the richest mystical themes in Islam were in place. Their study and the diverse and at times contradictory interpretations found in early commentaries of the Ḳur'ān derive from a complex body of religious sources (references in R. Blachère, *Le Coran*, Paris 1949, ii, 374) which have not yet been completely unravelled.

2. The words were occasionally used in early Islamic times for Jerusalem, and, during many centuries, more specifically for the Ḥaram al-Sharīf [*q.v.*], the former Herodian Temple area transformed by early Islam into a restricted Muslim space.

3. The most common use of the words is for the large building located on the south side of the Ḥaram platform and, next to the Dome of the Rock (Ḳubbat al-Ṣakhra [*q.v.*]), the most celebrated Islamic building in Jerusalem. Its archaeological history has been superbly established by R. W. Hamilton, *The structural history of the Aqṣā Mosque*, and his conclusions were entirely accepted by K. A. C. Creswell and incorporated in his *Early Islamic architecture*, Oxford 1969, 373-80. Such points of debate as do exist (H. Stern, *Recherches sur la Mosquée al-Aqṣā et ses mosaïques*, in *Ars Orientalis*, v [1963]) deal only with the precise dating of the archaeologically-determined sequences of building, not with their character. From the 4th/10th century onward, precious descriptions by al-Muḳaddasī, Nāṣir-i Khusraw and, much later, Mudjīr al-Dīn's chronicle of Jerusalem, provide a unique written documentation which has been made accessible in several books, of which the more important ones are G. Le Strange, *Palestine under the Moslems*, London 1890, and M. S. Marmardji, *Textes géographiques arabes sur la Palestine*, Paris 1951, 210-60. An easily accessible survey of drawings and plans is found in Eli Silad, *Mesgid el-Aksa*, Jerusalem 1978. For inscriptions, one should consult M. van Berchem, *CIA, Jérusalem*, Cairo 1927, ii/2, and S.A.S. Husseini, *Inscription of the Khalif El-Mustansir*, in *QDAP*, ix (1942); A. G. Walls and A. Abul-Hajj, *Arabic inscriptions in Jerusalem*, London 1980, 24-5, for a checklist. Finally, it is possible that a unique picture of Zion in the celebrated 9th century A.D. Byzantine manuscript known as the Chludoff Psalter is a representation of the Aḳṣā Mosque *ca.* 850 A.D.; cf. O. Grabar, *A note on the Chludoff Psalter*, in *Harvard Ukrainian Studies*, vii (1983) (= a volume in honour of Professor Ihor Ševčenko). The recent excavations carried out south of the Ḥaram have brought a lot of contextual information pertinent to the uses of the Aḳṣā mosque, but, at least to the writer's knowledge, nothing immediately pertinent to its forms or history.

The latter can be summarised in the following manner: (a) There was an Umayyad hypostyle mosque consisting of several aisles (their exact number cannot be ascertained) perpendicular to the *ḳibla*, with a central, wider, aisle on the same axis as the Dome of the Rock. This mosque, like many Umayyad ones, reused a lot of materials of construction from earlier buildings and was either built from scratch or completed under the caliph al-Walīd I. The only item of contention is whether it already contained a large dome in front of the *miḥrāb* which would have been decorated with mosaics (Hamilton and Creswell argue that it did not, Stern that it did; the argument of the latter has historical logic on his side, as al-Walīd was lavish in his imperial buildings, but the archaeological arguments against it are weighty indeed). Many decorative remains of painted and carved woodwork (kept in various Jerusalem museums) which have been preserved probably date from the Umayyad period, but they, as well as numerous fragments of mosaics, marble, etc., whose records remain in the archives of the Palestine Archaeological Museum (the so-called Rockefeller Museum), still await a full investigation. This first Aḳṣā mosque was the congregational mosque of the city of Jerusalem, but it was also seen as the covered part (*mughaṭṭā*) of the whole Ḥaram conceived as the mosque of the city.

(b) A series of major reconstructions took place in early 'Abbāsid times, possibly because of a destructive earthquake in 746. But the extent of the reconstructions carried out under al-Manṣūr, al-Mahdī and 'Abd Allāh b. Ṭāhir between 771 and 844 suggests more than a simple restoration. It was certainly a major attempt to assert 'Abbāsid sponsorship of holy places. It is essentially this 'Abbāsid building which is described by al-Muḳaddasī (*ca.* 985). It consisted of fifteen naves perpendicular to the *ḳibla*, of a fancy porch with gates inscribed with the names of caliphs, and of a high and brilliantly decorated dome. Its greatest pecularity is that it was open to the north, towards the Dome of the Rock and the rest of the Ḥaram *and* to the east. The latter is unusual and is probably to be explained by the ways in which the Muslim population, mostly settled to the south of the Ḥaram, ascended the holy place. We know that the main accesses to the Ḥaram were through underground passages, and the eastern entrances of the Aḳṣā may indicate that the Triple Gate and the so-called Stables of Solomon in the southeastern corner of the Ḥaram played a much greater rôle in the life of the city than has been believed.

(c) The earthquake of 1033 was a devastating one, leading, among other causes, to a major reorganisation of the whole city [see AL-ḲUDS]. The Aḳṣā was rebuilt under al-Ẓāhir between 1034 and 1036 and the work completed under al-Mustanṣir in 1065. Except for the latter, it is the mosque described by Nāṣir-i Khusraw in 1047, and most of the central part of the present mosque dates from that time. Shrunk to seven aisles only, probably without side doors, it was a very classical mosque adapted to the peculiar circumstances of Jerusalem, whose major characteristic was the brilliance of its mosaic decoration. The triumphal arch with its huge vegetal designs surmounted by a royal inscription in gold mosaics, the gold pendentives with their huge shield of "peacock's eyes," and the drum with its brilliant panels of an idealised garden with Umayyad and possibly Antique reminiscences, transformed the mosque into a true masterpiece of imperial art and exemplified the political ambitions of the Fāṭimids in Jerusalem.

(d) The Crusaders used the mosque as a palace and as living areas for the Knights Templar, and much of the present eastern and western façades date from this occupation. In 1187, when the mosque was reconsecrated to Islam, Ṣalāḥ al-Dīn re-did the decoration of the whole *ḳibla* wall, including the beautiful *miḥrāb* and the long inscription along the *ḳibla* wall. He also brought in the *minbar* made in 1169 by order of Nūr al-Dīn for the reconquered Holy City, but this great masterpiece of Syrian woodwork was destroyed by an arsonist in 1969 before it had been possible to study it fully. The northern porch was restored in 1217 and the eastern and western vaults re-done in 1345 and 1350. Under the later Ottomans, numerous repairs, often of dubious quality, and plasterings or repaintings altered considerably the expressiveness of what was essentially a Fāṭimid building with major Crusader, Ayyūbid and Mamlūk details. It was only in the nineteen-twenties and especially between 1937 and 1942 that a major and carefully supervised programme of restoration took place.

In spite of scholarly debates which will continue to grow about this or that detail, and this or that date for some aspect of the building, the history of the monument is reasonably set. What is far more difficult to define and to explain is its function, and on that issue the debate has barely begun. As a work of art, should it be considered as a finite monument to be explained entirely in its own architectural terms? Or should it always be understood as physically and visually part of a broader vision, whether even completed or not, of the Ḥaram as a unit? Socially and culturally, was it always, as it has become today, the city's mosque, different from its other sanctuaries, or was it, at times, simply the covered part of a single sanctuary? In all likelihood, the answers to these questions will differ according to the periods of the city's history. But beyond the fascinating vagaries of meaning of an extraordinary building in a unique setting, the problem is still unresolved of when it became known as the Masdjid al-Akṣā. The Ḳur'ānic quotation XCII,1, appears for the first time in the 5th/11th century official Fāṭimid inscription on the mosque's triumphal arch, and it is possibly at that time that it acquired its name. But in the early 10th/16th century, Mudjīr al-Dīn still calls it a *djāmiᶜ*, while acknowledging that it is popularly known as the Akṣā.

These confusions are all part of the complexities of Jerusalem's meaning in the Muslim world. Yet it should be noted that the spiritual and onomastic impact of the mosque extended much beyond its location, since in the Javanese city of Ḳudus the main mosque is also called the Masdjid al-Akṣā.

Bibliography: Given in the article.

(O. GRABAR)

AL-**MASDJID** AL-**ḤARĀM**, the name of the Mosque of Mecca. The name is already found in the pre-Islamic period (Horovitz, *Koranische Studien*, 140-1) in Ḳays b. al-Khaṭīm, ed. Kowalski, v. 14: "By Allāh, the Lord of the Holy Masdjid and of that which is covered with Yemen stuffs, which are embroidered with hempen thread" (?). It would be very improbable if a Medinan poet meant by these references anything other than the Meccan sanctuary. The expression is also fairly frequent in the Ḳur'ān after the second Meccan period (Horovitz, *op. cit.*) and in various connections; it is a grave sin on the part of the polytheists that they prohibit access to the Masdjid Ḥarām to the "people" (sūra II, 217, cf. V,2; VIII, 34; XXII, 25; XLVIII, 25); the Masdjid Ḥarām is the pole of the new *ḳibla* (sūra, II, 134, 149); contracts are sealed at it (sūra IX, 7).

In these passages, *masdjid ḥarām* does not as in later times mean a building, but simply Mecca as a holy place, just as in sūra XVII, 1, al-Masdjid al-Akṣā [*q.v.*] "the remotest sanctuary" does not mean a particular building.

According to tradition, a *ṣalāt* performed in the Masdjid al-Ḥarām is particularly meritorious (al-Bukhārī, *al-Ṣalāt fī masdjid Makka*, *bāb* 1). This *masdjid* is the oldest, being forty years older than that of Jerusalem (al-Bukhārī, *Anbiyā'*, *bāb* 10, 40).

This Meccan sanctuary included the Kaᶜba [*q.v.*], the well of Zamzam [*q.v.*] and the Maḳām Ibrāhīm [*q.v.*], all three on a small open space. In the year 8, Muḥammad made this place a mosque for worship. Soon however it became too small, and under ᶜUmar and ᶜUthmān, adjoining houses were taken down and a wall built. Under ᶜAbd Allāh b. al-Zubayr, the Umayyad and Ābbāsid caliphs, successive enlargements and embellishments were made. Ibn al-Zubayr put a simple roof above the wall. Al-Mahdī had colonnades built around, which were covered by a roof of teak. The number of minarets in time rose to seven. Little columns were put up around the Kaᶜba for lighting purposes. The mosque was also given a feature which we only find paralleled in a few isolated instances: this was the putting up of small wooden buildings, or rather shelters for use during the *ṣalāt* by the *imām*, one for each of the four orthodox rites. The fact that one of these *maḳāms* might be more or less elaborate than another occasionally gave rise to jealousies between the Ḥanafīs and the Shāfiᶜīs. Ultimately, the ground under the colonnades, originally covered with gravel, was paved with marble slabs, also in the *maṭāf* around the Kaᶜba as well as on the different paths approaching the *maṭāf*.

The mosque was given its final form in the years 1572-7, in the reign of the Sultan Selīm II, who, in addition to making a number of minor improvements in the building, had the flat roof replaced by a number of small, whitewashed, cone-shaped domes.

A person entering the mosque from the *masᶜā* or the eastern quarters of the town has to descend a few steps. The site of the mosque, as far as possible, was always left unaltered, while the level of the ground around—as usual in oriental towns and especially in Mecca on account of the dangers of sudden floods (*suyūl*)—gradually rose automatically in course of centuries (cf. Snouck Hurgronje, *Mekka*, i, 18-20).

The dimensions of the Ḥarām (interior) are given as follows (al-Batanūnī, *Riḥla*, 96): N.W. side 545, S.E. side 553 feet, N.E. side 360, S.W. side 364 feet; the corners are not right angles, so that the whole roughly represents a parallelogram.

Entering the *maṭāf* from the eastern side, one enters first the Bāb Banī Shayba, which marks an old boundary of the *masdjid*. Entering through the door, the Maḳām Ibrāhīm is on the right, which is also the Maḳām al-Shāfiᶜī, and to the right of it is the *minbar*. On the left is the Zamzam building. As late as the beginning of the 19th century, there stood in front of the latter, in the direction of the north-east of the mosque, two domed buildings (*al-ḳubbatayn*) which were used as store-houses (*Chron. der Stadt Mekka*, ii, 337-8). These *ḳubbas* were cleared away (cf. already, Burckhardt, i, 265); they are not given in recent plans.

Around the Kaᶜba are the *maḳāms* for the *imāms* of

the *madhhabs*, between the Kaᶜba and the south-east of the mosque, the *maḳām* (or *muṣallā*) *al-Ḥanbalī*, to the south-west the *maḳām al-Mālikī* and to the north-west the *maḳām al-Ḥanafī*. The latter has two stories; the upper one was used by the *muʾadhdhin* and the *muballigh*, the lower by the *imām* and his assistants. Since Wahhābī rule has been established, the Ḥanbalī *imām* has been given the place of honour; it is also reported that the *ṣalāt* is conducted by turns by the *imāms* of the four rites (*OM*, vii, 25). The *maḳām al-Ḥanafī* stands on the site of the old Meccan council-chamber (*dār al-nadwa*) which in the course of centuries was several times rebuilt and used for different purposes. The *maṭāf* is marked by a row of thin brass columns connected by a wire. The lamps for lighting are fixed to this wire and in the colonnades. In the 1930s, the mosque was provided with an installation for electric light (*OM*, xvi, 34; xviii, 39).

The mosque has for centuries been the centre of the intellectual life of the metropolis of Islām. This fact has resulted in the building of *madrasas* and *riwāks* for students in or near the mosque, for example, the *madrasa* of Ḳāʾit Bey on the left as one enters through the Bāb al-Salām. Many of these *wakfs* have however in course of time become devoted to other purposes (Burckhardt, i, 282; Snouck Hurgronje, *Mekka*, i, 17). For the staff of the mosque, cf. SHAYBA, BANŪ; Burckhardt, i, 287-91.

Bibliography: F. Wüstenfeld, *Die Chroniken der Stadt Mekka*, ii, 10-11, 13-16, 337 ff.; i, 301-33, 339-45; iii, 73 ff; iv, 121, 139, 159, 165, 190, 203, 205, 227-8, 268-9, 313-14; Ibn Djubayr, *Riḥla*, in *GMS*, v, 81 ff.; Ibn Baṭṭūṭa, ed. and tr. Defrémery and Sanguinetti, i, 305 ff.; Yāḳūt, *Muᶜdjam*, iv, 525-6; Iṣṭakhrī, *BGA*, i, 15-16; Ibn al-Faḳīh, v, 18-21; index to vols. vii and viii, s.v.; Ibn ᶜAbd Rabbihi, tr. Muḥ. Shafīᶜ, in *ᶜAjab-námah, a volume of oriental studies presented to E. G. Browne*, Cambridge 1922; 423 ff; Muḥammad Labīb al-Batanūnī, *al-Riḥla al-ḥidjāziyya*, Cairo 1329, 94 ff.; *Travels of Ali Bey*, London 1816, ii, 74-93 and pls. liii, liv; J. L. Burckhardt, *Travels in Arabia*, London 1829, 243-95; R. F. Burton, *Personal narrative of a Pilgrimage to Mecca and Medina*, London 1855-6, iii, 1-37; C. Snouck Hurgronje, *Mekka*, The Hague 1888-9, i, ch. i; ii, 230 ff.; *Bilderatlas*, nos, i, ii, iii; ibid., *Bilder aus Mekka*, Leiden 1889, nos. 1 and 3; P. F. Keane, *Six months in Mecca*, London 1881, 24 ff.; Eldon Rutter, *The Holy Cities of Arabia*, London 1928; E. Esin, *Mecca the blessed, Madinah the radiant*, London 1963; G. Michell (ed.), *Architecture of the Islamic world, its history and social meaning*, London 1978, 17, 209-10. (A. J. WENSINCK)

MASDJIDĪ (A.), pl. *masdjidiyyūn*, an adjective formed from *masdjid*, but specifically concerning the Friday mosque of Baṣra and used to designate groups (see al-Djāḥiẓ, *Ḥayawān*, iii, 360) of adults or young people who were accustomed to meet together in that building, near the gate of the Banū Sulaym, as well as of poets, popular story-tellers (*ḳuṣṣāṣ* [see ḲĀṢṢ]), and transmitters of religious, historical and literary traditions, in particular, those regarding poetic verses. The information which we possess on the *masdjidiyyūn* in general comes from al-Djāḥiẓ, who seems clearly to have acquired from them, in his youth, part of his cultural formation and perhaps also some of the traits of his character. He was especially interested in a group which was probably composed of Baṣran bourgeois or, at all events, of idlers who exchanged ideas and held conversations on subjects which were probably more varied (see e.g. *Bayān*, i, 243) than those for which he puts forward some examples in his *K. al-Bukhalāʾ* (ed. Ḥādjirī, 24-8; tr. Pellat, 41-8); the conversations thus reproduced are concerned essentially with how to spend as little money as possible, and allow us to classify the persons taking part in these conversations as part of the class of misers.

Nevertheless, al-Djāḥiẓ frequented other *masdjidiyyūn*: not only poets—al-Āmidī (*Muwāzana*, 116) could not appreciate their verses, and al-Marzubānī (*Muᶜdjam*, 379) states that Abū ᶜImrān Mūsā b. Muḥammad, e.g., was a *masdjidī*—but also traditionists who themselves wrote books, since, in regard to two *ḥadīths*, he states that he did not gather them directly from the mouth of some scholar but that he had read them in some book of *masdjidiyyūn* (*Bayān*, iii, 57-8). He mentions however (*ibid.*, iii, 220) that one *shaykh* of the mosque only wanted to frequent persons amongst whom were included traditionists handing on *ḥadīths* on the authority of al-Ḥasan (sc. al-Baṣrī [*q.v.*]) and *ruwāt* [see RĀWĪ] who were reciting the verses of al-Farazdaḳ [*q.v.*]. It should be noted that it is concerning the transmiters of classical poetry installed at the Mirbad [*q.v.*], the *mirbadiyyūn*, or in the Friday mosque, that al-Djāḥiẓ observes the changes of taste among lovers of poetry which were discernable precisely in these *ruwāt*'s audience (*Bayān*, iv, 23).

Bibliography: Given in the article. See also Pellat, *Le milieu baṣrien et la formation de Ǧāḥiẓ*, 244-5. (CH. PELLAT)

AL-**MASḤ ᶜALĀ 'L-KHUFFAYN** (A.), literally: "act of passing the hand over the boots", designates the right whereby Sunnī Muslims may, in certain circumstances, pass the hand over their shoes instead of washing their feet as a means of preparing themselves for the saying of the ritual prayer. Al-Djurdjānī (*Taᶜrīfāt*, ed. Tunis 1971, 112) proposes a definition of the *masḥ*: "passing the moistened hand without making (water) flow" (*imrār al-yad al-mubtalla bi-lā tasyīl*), which justifies the translation by "wetting of the shoes" which is adopted by L. Bercher and G. H. Bousquet (see below), but the term in question nevertheless remains ambiguous. In fact, if in the verses IV, 46/43, and V, 8-9/6, of the Ḳurʾān, the verb *masaḥa* refers to ablutions which necessarily entail the use of a certain quantity of water and consequently has the sense of "to wash", as is suggested by the *Lisān*, it is also employed in the same verses in reference to ritual purification with sand or soil (*tayammum* [*q.v.*]) and therefore no longer has the same meaning. In his translation of the Ḳurʾān (iii, 1115), R. Blachère points out moreover that it is quite inaccurate to render this verb by "to wipe" or "to rub", since it properly signifies, in these contexts, "to pass the hand over".

Unlike the *tayammum*, the *masḥ ᶜalā 'l-khuffayn* is not envisaged by the Holy Book, and it is probable that the practice in question, although ancient, was only tolerated at a relatively late date, to take into account difficulties which could face armies in the field, and after provoking debate in the very bosom of the Medinan school. Ultimately it constituted, along with, especially, *mutᶜa* [*q.v.*], one of the most manifest signs of the rift between Sunnīs and Shīᶜīs, for the latter, like the Khāridjīs, do not recognise it. The different Sunnī schools now base their doctrine, in this context, on a half-dozen *ḥadīths* whose authenticity is accepted by al-Bukhārī and Muslim, and on a number of other more liberal, but nevertheless for that reason more suspect traditions.

From "authentic" *ḥadīths* it emerges that the Prophet was observed to practise the *masḥ ᶜalā 'l-*

khuffayn. However, Djarīr b. ʿAbd Allāh al-Badjalī, who was converted after the revelation of the Medinan sūra *al-Māʾida* (V), which contains instructions relating to ablutions and to the *tayammum* (see above), claimed that he himself had seen Muḥammad passing the hand over his shoes; but his colleagues contested the validity of his statements and declared that the revelation of the verses in question had *ipso facto* put an end to the legality of this practice. This testimony, which has not been retained by al-Bukharī, does not seem to have shaken the conviction of later *fukahāʾ*, any more than another more or less controversial tradition which official doctrine has retained, no doubt because it provides an additional benefit: according to Khuzayma b. Thābit and Abū Bakra, the Prophet was reported to have permitted the Muslim to observe the *masḥ ʿalā 'l-khuffayn* for a day and a night when he is in fixed residence (*muḳīm*), and for three days and three nights when he is travelling.

According to another "authentic" *ḥadīth*, al-Mughīra b. Shuʿba, who travelled in the company of Muḥammad, bent down to take off his shoes in order to perform his ablutions, but the Prophet said to him: "Leave them, for I put them (= the feet) into [my boots], when they were in a state of ritual purity (*ṭāhiratānⁱ*)", and he passed his hand over his shoes. From this *ḥadīth*, the *fuḳahāʾ* have retained the obligation, for the believer who wishes to cleanse himself of a minor defilement (*ḥadath* [*q.v.*]) by means of this indulgence, to wash his feet and polish his shoes before putting them on, and not to take them off in the meantime.

Regarding the legal manner of performing the *masḥ*, Ibn Abī Zayd al-Ḳayrawanī, of the Mālikī school, describes it clearly in his *Risāla* (ed. and tr. L. Bercher, Algiers, 1949, 50/51): "The believer will place the right hand on the upper part of the shoe [for the right foot], beginning with the extremity of the toes. He will place his left hand underneath and thus make the hands glide as far as and including the pegs. He will do the same for the shoe of the left foot, putting his left hand above and his right hand underneath. But he will not let his hand touch the ground which may be under his shoe, or touch the dung of a beast of burden. He must previously raise his foot when rubbing or washing." The author adds that, according to another opinion, "the believer must wet the underside of the shoes, beginning with the pegs and ending with the extremities of the toes."

The classical manual of Western Mālikism, the *Mukhtaṣar* of Khalīl b. Isḥāḳ (tr. G. H. Bousquet, Algiers 1956, i, 34-5) presents an even more detailed account of the *masḥ ʿalā 'l-khuffayn*. It envisages in fact the use of a kind of slipper (*djawrab*) inside the boot proper, and prescribes that the *masḥ* should be performed on both pieces of leather; it forbids the use of a slipper which is too large or torn, because it must be firmly fixed to the foot, cover it completely and not let water penetrate through any crevice. This author also considers cases where the *masḥ* is invalidated, for example if the *ghusl* [*q.v.*] is obligatory, if the individual has forgotten to pass his hand over the upper part of the shoe, etc.

Bibliography: All the *ḥadīth*s concerning the *masḥ* have been conveniently assembled by Ibn al-Djārūd al-Naysābūrī (d. 307/919-20) in his *Kitāb al-Muntaḳā min al-sunan al-musnada ʿan Rasūl Allāh*, ed. Cairo 1382/1963 by ʿAbd Allāh Hāshim al-Yamanī al-Madanī, who has taken care to indicate in his notes (37-9) the more or less important collections in which they figure; the same editor has proceeded in the same fashion with the *Djamʿ al-fawāʾid min djāmiʿ al-uṣūl* (Medina 1381/1971, i, 104-7) of the Moroccan Muḥammad b. Muḥammad b. Sulaymān (1039-94/1630-83). See also R. Strothmann, *Kultus der Zaiditen*, Strasburg 1912, 21 ff.; A. J. Wensinck, *The Muslim creed*, Cambridge 1932, index, s.v. *shoes*; J. Schlacht, *The origins of Muhammadan jurisprudence*, Oxford 1950, 263-4.

(CH. PELLAT)

MĀSHĀʾ ALLĀH (A.), a phrase occurring in the Ḳurʾan (VI, 128; VII, 188; X, 50; XVIII, 37; LXXXVII, 7; cf. XI, 109-10, LXXII, 8) and widely used in the Islamic lands of the Middle East with the general meaning of "what God does, is well done". The formula denotes that things happen according to God's will and should therefore be accepted with humility and resignation. In a cognate signification, the phrase is often used to indicate a vague, generally a great or considerable, but some times a small, number or quantity of time (Lane, *Lexicon*, *s.v.*, who refers to S. de Sacy, *Relation de l'Egypte*, 246, 394). One might compare *ilā mā shāʾa Allāhu* "forever and ever" (Wehr, *Dictionary of modern written Arabic*, s.v.). The phrase is also the equivalent of the English "God knows what", and, as signifying "what God has willed", expresses admiration or surprise.

According to *TA*, in Lane, *Lexicon*, s.v., a Jew addressed the Prophet, objecting to his people's saying *mā shāʾa Allāhu wa-shiʾtu* "what God has willed and I have willed", as implying the association of another being with God. The Prophet then ordered them to say *mā shāʾa Allāhu thumma shiʾtu* "what God has willed and then I have willed".

In Konya, blue hemispheres are found, representing half an eyeball, covered with silver-thread textile with which the phrase is embroidered. Because of the decorative character of the Arabic script, the hemispheres are also worn as ornaments (R. Kriss and H. Kriss-Heinrich, *Volksglaube im Bereich des Islam*, ii, 12, 65 and pl. 7). As a charm to protect from the effect of the evil eye, the phrase is found on *zār* [*q.v.*] amulets and on amulets worn by children and domestic animals (*ibid.*, ii, 43, 66, 67, 153, and pl. 76; F. Th. Dijkema, *The Ottoman historical monumental inscriptions in Edirne*, Leiden 1977, 137; the amulet collection of the Ethnographical Museum, Cairo; Lane, *Manners and customs*, ch. xi). According to L. Einnsler, *Das böse Auge*, in *ZDPV*, xii (1889), 200 ff., there were silver amulets in Jerusalem with the formula on the obverse, the reverse bearing the invocations *yā kāfī*, *yā shāfī*, *yā ḥāfiẓ*, *yā amīn*. In Turkey, the phrase is often found on the fronts of trucks and cars.

Bibliography: In the article, and see also M. Piamenta, *Islam in everyday Arabic speech*, Leiden 1979; idem, *The Muslim conception of God and human welfare as reflected in everyday Arabic speech*, Leiden 1983.

(ED.)

MĀSHĀʾ ALLĀH B. ATHARĪ OR B. SĀRIYA, Jewish astrologer of Basra (although the frequent confusion between Baṣrī and Miṣrī has sometimes led to him being considered an Egyptian). His Hebrew name was perhaps Manasseh (the *Fihrist*, 273-4, and Ibn al-Ḳifṭī, 327, call him Mīshā) and in Persian he was known as Yazdānkhʷāst which, like Māshaʾallāh, signifies "that which God wills".

According to the *Fihrist*, the period of his activity extended from the reign of al-Manṣūr (135-58/754-75) to that of al-Maʾmūn (198-218/813-33), but the last date to be placed definitely within his lifetime is 193/809 (in *Fī ḳiyām al-khulafāʾ*, he shows in fact that he knew that of the death of al-Rashīd). With Nawbakht, ʿUmar b. Farrukhān al-Ṭabarī and al-Fazārī, he drew the horoscope favourable to the foundation of Baghdād (3 Djumādā I 145/30 July 762); this horoscope, which has been preserved (see al-Bīrūnī, *al-Āthār al-bāķiya*, ed. Sachau, Leipzig 1923, 270-1), had probably been calculated on the basis of the Pahlavi original text of the *Zīdj al-Shāh*. On the evidence of his *Kitāb al-Ķirānāt*, he seems to have been of pro-Iranian and anti-ʿAbbāsid sentiment; he hoped in fact that the caliphate would be overthrown in 200/815 and that power would pass to the Persians.

In the *Fihrist*, Ibn al-Nadīm mentions 19 works of Māshāʾ allāh, and al-Ķifṭī reproduces this list in his *Taʾrīkh al-Ḥukamāʾ*. The generally most complete and most recent studies which mention the titles of these works and the mss. in which they are preserved are those of D. Pingree, *Māshāʾallāh*, in *Dict. of scientific biography*, New York 1974, 159-62, and F. Sezgin, *GAS*, vi, 127-9, viii, 102-8.

Of the corpus of known works, discussion here will be limited to the following:

— *Fi 'l-ķirānāt wa 'l-adyān wa 'l-milal* ("On conjunctions, religions and communities"), an astrological history of mankind, and of Islam in particular, which is known to us by means of a summary by Ibn Hibintā. E. S. Kennedy and D. Pingree (*The astrological history of Māshāʾallāh*, Cambridge, Mass. 1971, 1-25) have published a facsimile of the ms., with a translation and a study of the summary of this work, which is based on an amalgam of the Sāsānid theory which explains the major changes which have taken place in human history by reference to conjunctions of Jupiter and Saturn, and of the Zoroastrian theory of millennia which attributes a thousand years to each planet from the time of the creation of the world (-8291), the cycle being repeated up until the figure of 12 millennia which will be reached in the year 3709 A.D. Ibn Hibintā's summary also contains 16 horoscopes, probably those of Māshāʾallāh himself and calculated on the basis of the *Zidj al-Shāh*: Kennedy and Pingree have made use of the numerical figuring in these horoscopies, combined with the sparse information supplied by other sources (essentially al-Bīrūnī) to reconstruct the principal parameters employed in the Persian tables mentioned above (see also J. J. Burckhardt and B. L. van der Waerden, *Das astronomischen System der persischen Tafeln I*, in *Centaurus*, xiii [1968], 1-28).

— *Fī ķiyām al-khulafāʾ wa-maʿrifat ķiyām kull malik* ("On the accession of caliphs and knowledge of the accession of each king"), of which the original Arabic, preserved, has been translated and studied by Kennedy and Pingree, in *The astr. history*, 129-43. After a general theoretical survey, the work contains horoscopes of the spring equinoxes at which the Prophet and 18 caliphs (from Abū Bakr to Hārūn al-Rashīd) acceded to power. To calculate these, Māshāʾallāh also made use of the *Zidj al-Shāh*.

— *Kitāb al-Mawālīd* ("Book of genethliac themes"), known only through some quotations made by a disciple of the author, Abū ʿAlī al-Khayyāṭ, and through a Latin translation edited and studied by Pingree (*The astr. history*, 145-74). It contains 12 natal horoscopes dating from between 36 and 542 A.D.; three of them derive from the *Pentateuch* of Dorotheus of Sidon (50-75 A.D.), and the other nine from an unknown Greek astrological work dating from the 6th century. He interprets the horoscopes according to the doctrine of Dorotheus, whose work he probably knew through the Pahlavi translation. The influence of this writer is also perceptible in the *Super significationibus planetarum in nativitate* of Māshāʾallāh, which survives only in Latin translation.

— *De receptione*, preserved in Latin translation (ed. J. Heller, Norirbergae 1549), comprises 6 horoscopes dating between 791 and 794. One of them figures in the Peterhouse ms. 75.1, which contains the treatise of Chaucer (*ca.* 1340-*ca.* 1400) on the equator (E. S. Kennedy, *A horoscope of Messehalla in the Chaucer Equatorium manuscript*, in *Speculum*, xxxiv [1959], 629-30; repr. in E. S. Kennedy (ed.), *Studies in the Islamic exact sciences*, Beirut 1983, 336-7; cf. Kennedy-Pingree, *The astr. history*, 175-8).

— *De scientis motus orbis* or *De elementis et orbitus coelestibus* or *De sphaera mota*, preserved in Latin translation, contains a study of the *Physics* of Aristotle (chs. 1-7), as well as an introduction to astronomy (chs. 8-24), both of these based on Syriac sources. The astronomical source mentions Ptolemy and Theo of Alexandria, but the planetary models described are pre-Ptolemaic Greek (they do not, in fact, employ the equant and introduce no specific apparatus for the moon and Mercury) and similar to those found in Sanskrit texts since the end of the 5th century (cf. D. Pingree, *Mashaʾallah: some Sasanian and Syrian sources*, in G. F. Hourani (ed.), *Essays on Islamic philosophy and science*, Albany 1975, 5-14).

— *Kitāb al-Amṭār wa 'l-riyāḥ* ("Book of the rains and the winds"), ed. and tr. by G. Levi Della Vida (*Un opusculo astrologico di Māšʾāllāh*, in *RSO*, xiv [1933-4], 270-81), concerns the astrological procedure for predicting rain. A Latin version also exists.

— *Epistola de rebus eclipsium*, *De ratione circuli et stellarum*, *Liber Messehalla in radicis revolutionum* or *Epistola Messallach de planetarum efficacis* (cf. J. M. Millás Vallicrosa, *Las tables astronómicas del rey don Pedro el Ceremonioso*, Madrid-Barcelona 1962, 87), preserved in Latin translation (by John of Seville, ed. Basle 1551) and Hebrew translation (by Abraham b. ʿEzra). The latter, which is entitled *Sefer li-Mashaʾallāh bi-ķadrūt ha-levanah we ha-shemesh*, has been translated by B. R. Goldstein (*The Book on eclipses by Mashaʾallah*, in *Physis*, vi [1964], 205-13). It is divided into 12 chapters, of which the first contains a curious reference to magnetism in a cosmological context: the ascending node, the stars and the planets exert an influence on the earth in the same manner that magnetic stone attracts iron. It is appropriate also to mention the use, in this text, of a classification of planetary conjunctions distinct from that which figures in *Fi 'l-ķirānāt*.

— Ibn al-Nadīm attributes to Māshāʾallāh a *Kitāb Ṣanʿat al-asṭurlābāt wa 'l-ʿamal bi-hā* ("Construction and use of astrolabes"), often identified with the treatise on the astrolabe in Latin, which has been edited, notably by R. T. Gunther (*Early science in Oxford*, v, Oxford 1929, 195-231). A second treatise on the astrolabe in a Latin version, likewise attributed to Māshāʾallah, has been edited by Millás Vallicrosa (in *Las traducctiones orientales en los manuscritos de la Biblioteca Catedral de Toledo*, Madrid 1942, 322-7). P. Kunitzch has rejected the attribution of the two texts to Māshāʾallāh (see *Typen von Sternverzeichnissen in astronomischen Handschriften des zehnten bis vierzehnten Jahrhunderts*, Wiesbaden 1966, 313-21; idem, *On the authenticity of the treatise on the composition and use of the astrolabe ascribed to Messahallah*, in *AIHS*, xxxi [1981], 42-62). A part at least of the text edited by Gunther appears to be linked to the school of Maslama al-Madjrīṭī (d. *ca.* 398/1007-8; cf. R. Martí and M. Viladrich, in J. Vernet (ed.), *Textos y estudios sobre astronomía española en el siglo XIII*, Barcelona 1981, 79-99, and in idem (ed.), *Neuvos estudios sobre astronomía española en el siglo de Alfonso X*, Barcelona 1983, 9-74; M. Viladrich, *On the sources of the Alphonsine treatise dealing with the construction of the plane astrolabe*, in *JHAS*, vi [1982], 167-71).

The work of Māshāʾallah is that of a writer who has

little interest in astronomy, but has cultivated all the branches of astrology which he has widely promulgated and popularised; nevertheless, it has considerable interest from the astronomical point of view on account of the sources used (Persian, Syriac and, directly or indirectly, Greek), which throw light on a very early period in the history of Arab-Islamic astronomy.

Bibliography : Given in the article. See also L. Thorndike, *The Latin translations of the astrological works by Messahala*, in *Osiris*, xii (1956), 49-72; F. J. Carmody, *Arabic astronomical and astrological sciences in Latin translation*, Berkeley-Los Angeles 1956, 23-38; E. S. Kennedy, *The Sasanian astronomical handbook Zīj-i Shāh and the astrological doctrine of "transit"* (mamarr), in *JAOS*, lxxviii (1958), 246-62 (re-ed. in Kennedy and others, *Studies*, 319-35); Kennedy, D. Pingree and F. I. Haddad, *The Book of the reasons behind astronomical tables by ʿAlī ibn Sulaymān al-Hāshimī*, New York 1981, 183, 186-7, 191, 264, 284, 321-3. (J. Samsó)

MAṢḤAF [see muṣḥaf]

MAS̲H̲ĀḲA, Mīk̲h̲āʾil, a person of secondary importance of the *Nahḍa* [*q.v.*] (b. Ras̲h̲maya 20 March 1800, d. Damascus 6 July 1888). Born in the Greek Melkite rite, he began his studies in Egypt in astronomy, mathematics and the natural sciences. As a silk weaver, he studied music (*Risāla fī fann al-mūsīkī*, ed. Ronzevalle, in *al-Machriq* [1899], pp. 146). As an official, a representative of S̲h̲ihāb and vice-consul for the United States, and then merchant, he took up medicine (doctor of medicine at Cairo, 1845). In 1848 at Damascus he joined the Protestant faith. The ensuing polemics can be found in *al-Dalīl ilā ṭāʿat al-Ind̲j̲īl*², Beirut 1860, pp. 332, and in *K. al-Barāhīn al-ind̲j̲īliyya ḍidd al-abāṭīl al-bābawiyya*, Beirut 1864, pp. 187. As the Arabic translator of Voltaire, a close connection of the al-S̲h̲idyāḳ family and of Buṭrus al-Bustānī, he reacted, through his attitude and his writings, against confessionalism, and opened the way, through his advocacy of reason, to scientific attitudes. His chronicle of Syria (1783-1841) remains in manuscript; the autograph is in the AUB Library, ms. 956, 9 M 39a.

Bibliography : Ḳasāṭilī, in *al-Muḳtaṭaf*, xii (August 1888), 703-5; Zaydān, *Tarād̲j̲im mas̲h̲āhīr al-s̲h̲arḳ*, ii, 156-9; S̲h̲aykh̲ū, in *al-Ḳarn al-tāsiʿ ʿas̲h̲ar*, ii, 140-1; Kurd ʿAlī, *K̲h̲iṭaṭ al-S̲h̲ām*, xxiv, 71; Sarkīs, 1747-8; Brockelmann, II, 496 S II, 779-80; Graf, *GCAL*, iv, 297-9; Bag̲h̲dādī, *Īḍāḥ*, i, 175, 178, 221, 565; Kaḥḥāla, xiii, 57-8; Ziriklī, viii, 295-6; *Muntak̲h̲abāt min al-d̲j̲awāb ʿalā iḳtirāḥ al-aḥbāb*, ed. Asʿad Rustum and Ṣubḥī Abū S̲h̲akrā, Beirut 1955, pp. 180; *Ruwwād ind̲j̲īliyyūn*, in *al-Mas̲h̲ʿal* (1962), 24-42; A. Hourani, *Arabic thought in the liberal age*, 58; *Travaux et jours*, xl (July-Sept. 1971), 57-67; Dāg̲h̲ir, iii/2, 1212-14. (J. Fontaine)

MAS̲H̲ĀRIḲA (a.), the Arabs and Arabised peoples of the East (*Mas̲h̲riḳ*) in contrast to those of the West (*Mag̲h̲rib*) called *Mag̲h̲āriba* [*q.v.*]. The history of the Mas̲h̲āriḳa in the East, a history which is inseparable from the region itself, will not be treated here. The concern here is rather with the Mas̲h̲āriḳa who were perceived as such in the West by the Mag̲h̲āriba. The distinction between the two great groups, with a certain specificness proper to Muslim Spain, becomes perceptible less than half-a-century after the expansion of the Arabs in the West, i.e. around 122/740 [see mag̲h̲āriba].

It is impossible to determine, even with an approximative exactness, the number of Mas̲h̲āriḳa who, in successive waves and during periods stretching from the middle of the 1st century to the middle of the 5th one/last quarter of the 7th to the middle of the 11th, established themselves in the West and especially in Ifrīḳiya, where their settlement was the densest and most enduring. As the newcomers became "Mag̲h̲ribised", i.e. at the latest from the second generation onwards, they thereby ceased to be perceived as Mas̲h̲āriḳa. The first waves of them, up to the last quarter of the 2nd century/beginning of the 9th one, were made up of sedentaries who founded new towns or who settled in already existing towns. Their number cannot have exceeded a quarter of a million: fighters for the faith, often coming with wives and children; officials; men of religion; merchants; and all kinds of persons attracted by the prospect of profits offered by a new land (see M. Talbi, *L'émirat aghlabide*, Paris 1966, 21-2, and art. al-ʿarab, v, at 542-3). The towns where they settled formed at one and the same time centres for religious Islamisation and cultural Arabisation, i.e., for the orientalisation of the Mag̲h̲rib. A certain number of the Ṣaḥāba, the Companions of the Prophet, are said to have died in the Mag̲h̲rib (see Abu 'l-ʿArab, *Ṭabaḳāt*, ed. Ben Cheneb, Paris 1915, 16-18; and al-Mālikī, *Riyāḍ*, ed. B. al-Bakkūs̲h̲ and M. A. al-Miṭwī, Beirut 1981, i, 60-98, where, in the notes, the editors refer in a virtually exhaustive fashion to the other sources), and certain towns have retained the memory of them till this day, embodied in sanctuaries and tombs, as features of great glory. Thus at al-Ḳayrawān, the presumed tomb of Abū Zamʿa al-Balawī, transformed into the centre of a sanctuary—the Zāwiya Sīdī al-Ṣāḥib—enjoys a particular prestige (see B. Roy and P. Poinssot, *Inscriptions arabes de Kairouan*, Paris 1950, ii/1, 65-76). Nevertheless, the sources attach a particular importance to ten Successors or Tābiʿūn who were sent by the caliph ʿUmar b. ʿAbd al-ʿAzīz (99-101/717-20) into Ifrīḳiya in order to spread Islam in the Mag̲h̲rib (al-Mālikī, *Riyāḍ*, i, 99-118, with reference to other sources). One should however note that there was no figure of the first rank among these Mas̲h̲āriḳa.

Politically, the most outstanding of the eastern dynasties who reigned in the Islamic West were the Ag̲h̲labids of al-Ḳayrawān, the Idrīsids of Fez, the Umayyads of Cordova and the Fāṭimids [*q.vv.*], the founders of al-Mahdiyya [*q.v.*] on the Tunisian coast. The last Mas̲h̲āriḳa who infiltrated into the Mag̲h̲rib and then Spain in large numbers—several hundred thousands?—were the nomadic Banū Hilāl [*q.v.*], who were victorious in 443/1052 at Ḥaydarān [*q.v.*] and were backed up by the Banū Sulaym. Views on the extent of his "catastrophe" of the Hilālian invasions vary considerably (see Talbi, *Droit et économie en Ifrīḳiya...*, in *Etudes d'histoire ifrīḳiyenne*, Tunis 1982, 205 and n. 4, Eng. tr. in *The Islamic Middle East*, ed. A. L. Udovitch, Princeton 1981, 222-3 and n. 77). But the Hilāl and Sulaym were not perceived in the Muslim West as Mas̲h̲āriḳa *stricto sensu*.

This term too, together with those of *ʿIrāḳī* and *Kūfī*, denoted fairly frequently in the Muslim West, though not inevitably and constrainedly, the geographical connection with a socio-cultural area, but equally, the belonging to a religious school. In particular, the S̲h̲īʿīs are often described in Ifrīḳiya, after the coming of the Fāṭimids, as being *mas̲h̲riḳīs*, even when the persons in question were authentic Mag̲h̲ribīs. Thus Ibn Ghāzī was a pious Sunnī of al-Ḳayrawān and a zealous frequenter of *ribāṭs*. "When ʿUbayd Allāh made his entry [into al-Ḳayrawān], he embraced S̲h̲īʿism (*tas̲h̲arraḳa*)" (Talbi, *Biographies aghlabides*, Tunis 1968, 284). Another similar person was "a *mas̲h̲riḳī* who had abandoned Islam" (al-

Mālikī, *Riyāḍ*, ii, 502) in order to convert to the Shīʿī heresy. An assembly at al-Ḳayrawān brought together "Sunnīs and *mashāriḳa*" (*ibid.*, ii, 338), i.e. Shīʿīs. See other examples in *ibid.*, ii, 425, 427, and in Talbi, *op. cit.*, 369, 383, 394.

The terms *ʿIrāḳī* (or *ahl al-ʿIrāḳ*) and *Kūfī* were, on the other hand, more often reserved for Ifrīḳiyan Ḥanafīs (al-Mālikī, *Riyāḍ*, i, 181, 256, 263, 264, 266, 277, 374, 375, 451, 452, 463, 500, ii, 29, 73, 207, 339; and Talbi, *op. cit.*, index s.v. *ʿIrāḳiyyūn*). These last, in contradistinction from the Mālikīs who made up the spear-head of opposition to the Fāṭimids, showed themselves as much more receptive to Shīʿī propaganda, which may be a contributory cause to their disappearance from the North African scene, after having formed the majority there (Talbi, *L'émirat aghlabide*, 233), once Shīʿism was finally extirpated.

Above all, it was in a dual role, religious and cultural, that the Mashāriḳa played an outstanding part in the Muslim West. Certainly, none of their outstanding stars went beyond the Nile valley. The Maghrib was to some extent a land of exile where only persons relatively in the second rank sought their fortune, which does not however mean that their role was any the less decisive. Let us mention, for example, that ʿIyāḍ [*q.v.*] had among his masters two Mashāriḳa who had visited Ceuta, Abu 'l-Ḥasan al-Rabʿī al-Maḳdisī (d. at al-Nāṣiriyya in 531/1137, ʿIyāḍ, *Ghunya*, no. 81) and the Shāfiʿī Sahl b. ʿUthmān al-Nīsābūrī (no. 89; al-Maḳḳarī, *Nafḥ*, ed. Iḥsān ʿAbbās, Beirut 1968, iii, 67). Naturally, one cannot give here an exhaustive survey. Such a survey, which has not yet been done, would however show itself as very suggestive and open up many directions for research. The sources at our disposal at present have not, in any case, kept note of everything. Al-Maḳḳarī, who devotes 86 biographical notices to the Mashāriḳa who resided in al-Andalus (*Nafḥ*, iii, 5-149), remarks that "one cannot give an exhaustive list of them, even when limiting oneself to the most outstanding ones (*ibid.*, iii, 5). For his part, Ibn Bashkuwāl provides us with over 50 names of Mashāriḳa established in Muslim Spain (*al-Ṣila*, classified in an approximately alphabetical order at the end of each section, under the rubric *wa-min al-ghurabāʾ* ...).

Among the top figures, three are especially representative of the role played by the Mashāriḳa in the Muslim West, comprising two philologist *adībs* and a musician. Abū ʿAlī al-Ḳālī (288-356/901-67 [*q.v.*]) arrived in Cordova in 330/942 and was received with great pomp (al-Maḳḳarī, iii, 71-2). Drawing on his rich library, and also on his memory, he spread eastern culture over a wide range, and he thus occupies the position of "the key figure in the ʿIrāḳī tradition in the West" (R. Sellheim, *EI²* art. s.v.). The figure of Ṣāʿid al-Baghdādī (d. ?417/1026 [*q.v.*]) is in a sense even more representative and of heightened relief (see R. Blachère, *Un pionnier de la culture arabe orientale en Espagne au Xᵉ siècle: Ṣâʿid de Bagdad*, in *Analecta*, Damascus 1975, 443-65). This was that of "a fairly picturesque Bohemian" (*op. cit.*, 445), certainly, enough of a flamboyant figure to shine at court. Having been compelled to "give up the idea of making a name for himself in Iraq", he took the road for Cordova, where he became "something like the type of the pioneer of oriental literary culture in Spain during the second half of the 10th century" (465). Ziryāb (173-243/789-857 [*q.v.*]) was a black musician who had first of all gravitated into the orbit of the ʿAbbāsid court in Baghdād. Having aroused jealousies there, he also had to renounce making an impression in ʿIrāḳ, and, after a brief stay in al-Ḳayrawān, went to seek his fortune at Cordova, arriving there in 207/822. His enormous influence was not just in the muscial sphere. "Under the unchallenged arbitration of Ziryāb, the court and the town altered their dress, their furnishings [and] their cuisine" (E. Lévi-Provençal, *Hist. Esp. mus.*, Paris 1950, i, 272).

Bibliography: There is no specific bibliography for this topic. In addition to references given in the text, information can be gleaned from all the historical works, from the *adab* literature and, above all, from the *ṭabaḳāt*. (M. Talbi)

MASHHAD (A.), noun of place from the verb *shahida* "to witness, be present at" > "be a martyr, *shahīd*" (a post-Ḳurʾānic semantic development which Goldziher thought was influenced by Eastern Christian Syriac parallel usage; see *Muh. Studien*, ii, 387-9, Eng. tr. ii, 350-2). In post-Ḳurʾānic times also, the noun *mashhad* developed from its designating any sacred place, not necessarily having a construction associated with it, but often in fact a tomb in general, the burial place of an earlier prophet, saint or forerunner of Muḥammad or of any Muslim who had had pronounced over him the *shahāda* or profession of faith. Later, it might mean a martyrium specifically or be used for any small building with obvious religious features like a *miḥrāb* [*q.v.*] (see O. Grabar, *The earliest Islamic commemorative structures, notes and documents*, in *Ars Orientalis*, vi [1966], 9-12). Literary sources, e.g. the early geographers, mention *mashhads* of what are clearly highly varying natures (see e.g. al-Muḳaddasī, tr. A. Miquel, *La meilleure répartition*, Damascus 1963, 6 n. 15), but an early epigraphic instance of the term's usage is on the frieze of the Mīl-i Rādkān, the tomb tower in Gurgān erected by the Bāwandid local ruler, the Ispahbadh Muḥammad b. Wandarīn, in 407-11/1016-21, where this edifice is described as a *mashhad* (see M. Van Berchem, *Die Inschriften der Grabtürme*, 1, in E. Diez, *Churasanische Baudenkmäler*, i, Berlin 1918, 87-90; *RCEA*, vi, nos. 2312-13; KITĀBĀT. 9. Iran and Transoxiana and Pl. XIX no. 22).

For the tomb of the caliph and First Imām of the Shīʿīs, ʿAlī, the Mashhad ʿAlī, see AL-NADJAF; for that of the Third Imām, al-Ḥusayn, the Mashhad (al-) Ḥusayn, see KARBALĀ; and for that of the Eighth Imām, ʿAlī al-Riḍā, the Mashhad in Khurāsān, see the next article.

Bibliography: (in addition to references given in the article): See M. Hartmann, in *ZDPV*, xxiv (1901), 65-6 and 65 n. 2; Van Berchem, *Opera minora*, ed. A Louca and Ch. Genequand, Geneva 1978, index s.v.; and the arts. BUḲʿA in Suppl., ḲUBBA, MASDJID. I. B. 4 Tomb-mosques, and TURBA. (C. E. Bosworth)

MASHHAD, a city of northeastern Persia, the capital of the present province of Khurāsān [*q.v.*] and the location since medieval times of one of the most important shrines of the Shīʿī world built round the tomb of the Eighth Imam ʿAlī al-Riḍā [*q.v.*].

1. Geography, history and topography to 1914. Mashhad lies 3,000 feet above sea level in 59° 35′ E. long. and 16° 17′ N. lat. in the valley from 10 to 25 miles broad of the Kashaf-Rūd, also called Āb-i Mashhad, which joins the Harī Rūd [*q.v.*] about 100 miles S.E. of Mashhad on the Russo-Persian frontier. Mashhad lies about 4 miles south of the bank of the Kashaf-Rūd. The hills which run along the valley rise to 8,000 or 9,000 feet near Mashhad. In consequence of its high situation and proximity to the mountains,

the climate of Mas̲h̲had is in the winter rather severe, in the summer, however, often tropically hot; it is regarded as healthy.

Mas̲h̲had may in a way be regarded as the successor of the older pre-Islamic Ṭūs [*q.v.*], and it has not infrequently been erroneously confounded with it.

The fact that Ṭūs is the name of both a town and a district, together with the fact that two places are always mentioned as the principal towns of this district, has given rise among the later Arab geographers to the erroneous opinion that the capital Ṭūs is a double town consisting of Ṭābarān and Nūḳān; e.g. Yāḳūt, iii, 560, 5 (correct at iv, 824, 23) and in the *Lubāb* of Ibn al-At̲h̲īr quoted by Abu 'l-Fidāʾ (*Taḳwīm*, 453). Al-Ḳazwīnī (*Āt̲h̲ār al-bilād*, 275, 21) next made the two towns thought to be joined together into two quarters (*maḥalla*). This quite erroneous idea of a double town Ṭūs found its way into European literature generally. Sykes (*JRAS* [1910], 1115-16) and following him, E. Diez (*Churasanische Baudenkmäler*, Berlin 1918, i, 53-4) have rightly challenged this untenable idea. The older Arab geographers quite correctly distinguish between Ṭābarān and Nūḳān as two quite separate towns. Nūḳān, according to the express testimony of the Arabic sources, was only ¼ parasang (*farsak̲h̲*) or one Arabic mile from the tomb of Hārūn al-Ras̲h̲īd and ʿAlī al-Riḍā (see below) and must therefore have been very close to the modern Mas̲h̲had. The ruins of Ṭābarān-Ṭūs and Mas̲h̲had are about 15 miles apart.

In Nūḳān, or in the village of Sanābād̲h̲ belonging to it, two distinguished figures in Islamic history were buried within one decade: the caliph Hārūn al-Ras̲h̲īd and the ʿAlid ʿAlī al-Riḍā b. Mūsā [*q.vv.*].

When Hārūn al-Ras̲h̲īd was preparing to take the field in K̲h̲urāsān, he was stricken mortally ill in a country house at Sanābād̲h̲ where he had stopped, and died in a few days (193/809). The caliph, we are told (al-Ṭabarī, iii, 737, 13-17), realising he was about to die, had his grave dug in the garden of this country mansion and consecrated by Ḳurʾān readers.

About 10 years after the death of Ḥārūn, the caliph al-Maʾmūn on his way from Marw spent a few days in this palace. Along with him was his son-in-law ʿAlī al-Riḍā b. Mūsā, the caliph designate, the eighth *imām* of the Twelvers. The latter died suddenly here in 203/818; the actual day in uncertain (cf. Strothmann, *Die Zwölfer-S̲h̲īʿa*, Leipzig 1926, 171).

It was not the tomb of the caliph but that of a highly venerated *imām* which made Sanābād̲h̲ (Nūḳān) celebrated throughout the S̲h̲īʿa world, and the great town which grew up in course of time out of the little village actually became called *al-Mas̲h̲had* (Mas̲h̲had) which means "sepulchral shrine" (primarily of a martyr belonging to the family of the Prophet). Cf. on the conception of *mas̲h̲had*, MASD̲J̲ID. I. B. 4; the previous article; and M. van Berchem in Diez, *op. cit.*, i (Berlin 1918), 89-90. Ibn Ḥawḳal (313) calls our sanctuary simply Mas̲h̲had, Yāḳūt (iii, 153) more accurately al-Mas̲h̲had al-Riḍāwī = the tomb-shrine of al-Riḍā; we also find the Persian name *Mas̲h̲had-i muḳaddas* = "the sanctified shrine" (e.g. in Ḥamd Allāh al-Mustawfī, 157). As a place-name, Mas̲h̲had first appears in al-Muḳaddasī (352), i.e. in the last third of the 4th/10th century. About the middle of the 8th/14th century the traveller Ibn Baṭṭūṭa (iii, 77) uses the expression "town of Mas̲h̲had al-Riḍā". Towards the end of the Middle Ages, the name Nūḳān, which is still found on coins in the first half of the 8th/14th century under the Īlk̲h̲āns (cf. Codrington, *A manual of Musalman numismatics*, London 1904, 189), seems to have been gradually ousted by al-Mas̲h̲had or Mas̲h̲had. At the present day, Mas̲h̲had is often more precisely known as Mas̲h̲had-i Riḍā, Mas̲h̲had-i muḳaddas, Mas̲h̲had-i Ṭūs (so already in Ibn Baṭṭūṭa, iii, 66). Not infrequently in literature, especially in poetry, we find only Ṭūs mentioned, i.e. New Ṭūs in contrast to Old Ṭūs or the proper town of this name; cf. e.g. Muḥammad Mahdī al-ʿAlawī, *Taʾrīk̲h̲ Ṭūs aw al-Mas̲h̲had al-Riḍawī*, Bag̲h̲dād 1927, 3.

The history of Mas̲h̲had is very fully dealt with in the work of Muḥammad Ḥasan K̲h̲ān Ṣanīʿ al-Dawla entitled *Maṭlaʿ al-s̲h̲ams* (3 vols., Tehran 1301-3 A.H.). The second volume is exclusively devoted to the history and topography of Mas̲h̲had; for the period from 428/1036-7 to 1302/1885 he gives valuable historical material. On this work, cf. C. E. Yate, *Khurasan and Sistan*, 313-14, and E. G. Browne, *LHP*, iv, 455-6. The *Maṭlaʿ al-s̲h̲ams* forms the chief source for the sketch of the history of the town in Yate, 314-26. Cf. also the chronological notes in Muḥammad Mahdī al-ʿAlawī, *op. cit.*, 13-16.

The importance of Sanābād̲h̲-Mas̲h̲had continually increased with the growing fame of its sanctuary and the decline of Ṭūs. Ṭūs received its death blow in 791/1389 from Mīrāns̲h̲āh, a son of Tīmūr. When the Mongol noble who governed the place rebelled and attempted to make himself independent, Mīrāns̲h̲āh was sent against him by his father. Ṭūs was stormed after a siege of several months, sacked and left a heap of ruins; 10,000 inhabitants were massacred (see Yate, 316; Sir Percy Sykes, in *JRAS* [1910], 1118 and Browne, *op.cit.*, iii, 190). Those who escaped the holocaust settled in the shelter of the ʿAlid sanctuary. Ṭūs was henceforth abandoned and Mas̲h̲had took its place as the capital of the district.

As to the political history of Mas̲h̲had, it coincides in its main lines with that of the province of K̲h̲urāsān [*q.v.*]. Here we shall only briefly mention a few of the more important events in the past of the town. Like all the larger towns of Persia, Mas̲h̲had frequently saw risings and the horrors of war within its walls. To protect the mausoleum of ʿAlī al-Riḍā in the reign of the G̲h̲aznawid Masʿūd [*q.v.*], the then G̲h̲aznawid governor of K̲h̲urāsān erected defences in 428/1037. In 515/1121 a wall was built round the whole town which afforded protection from attack for some time. In 556/1161 however, the G̲h̲uzz [*q.v.*] succeeded in taking the place, but they spared the sacred area in their pillaging. We hear of a further visitation by Mongol hordes in 695/1296 in the time of Sultan G̲h̲āzān [*q.v.*]. Probably the greatest benefactors of the town and especially of its sanctuary were the first Tīmūrid S̲h̲āh Ruk̲h̲ (809-50/1406-46 [*q.v.*]) and his pious wife D̲j̲awhar-S̲h̲ād̲h̲.

With the rise of the Ṣafawid dynasty [*q.v.*], a new era of prosperity began for Mas̲h̲had. The very first S̲h̲āh of this family, Ismāʿīl I (907-30/1501-24 [*q.v.*]), established S̲h̲īʿism as the state religion and, in keeping with this, care for the sacred cities within the Persian frontier, especially Mas̲h̲had and Ḳumm, became an important feature in his programme as in those of his successors. Pilgrimage to the holy tombs at these places experienced a considerable revival. In Mas̲h̲had, the royal court displayed a great deal of building activity. In this respect Ṭahmāsp I, Ismāʿīl I's successor (930-84/1524-76 [*q.v.*]), and the great S̲h̲āh ʿAbbās I (995-1037/1587-1627 [*q.v.*]) were especially distinguished.

In the 10th/16th century the town suffered considerably from the repeated raids of the Özbegs (Uzbeks). In 913/1507 it was taken by the troops of the S̲h̲aybānī K̲h̲ān [see S̲H̲AYBĀNIDS]; it was not till

934/1528 that Shāh Ṭahmāsp I succeeded in repelling the enemy from the town again. Stronger walls and bastions were then built and another attack by the same Özbeg chief was foiled by them in 941/1535. But in 951/1544 the Özbegs again succeeded in entering the town and plundering and murdering there. The year 997/1589 was a disastrous one for Mashhad. The Shaybānid ʿAbd al-Muʾmin after a four months' siege forced the town to surrender. The streets of the town ran with blood, and the thoroughness of the pillaging did not stop at the gates of the sacred area. Shāh ʿAbbās I, who lived in Mashhad from 993/1585 till his official ascent of the throne in Ḳazwīn in 995/1587, was not able to retake Mashhad from the Özbegs till 1006/1598.

At the beginning of the reign of Ṭahmāsp II in 1135/1722, the Afghān tribe of Abdālī [*q.v.*] invaded Khurāsān. Mashhad fell before them, but in 1138/1726 the Persians succeeded in retaking it after a two months' siege. Nādir Shāh (1148-60/1736-47 [*q.v.*]) had a mausoleum built for himself in Mashhad.

After the death of Nādir Shāh, civil war broke out among the claimants to the throne, in the course of which the unity of the Persian empire was broken. The whole eastern part of the kingdom of Nādir Shāh, particularly Khurāsān (except the district of Nīshāpūr), passed in this period of Persian impotence under the rule of the vigorous Afghān Shāh Aḥmad Durrānī [*q.v.*]. An attempt by Karīm Khān Zand [*q.v.*] to reunite Khurāsān to the rest of Persia failed. Aḥmad defeated the Persians and took Mashhad after an eight months' siege in 1167/1753. Aḥmad Shāh and his successor Tīmūr Shāh left Shāh Rukh in possession of Khurāsān as their vassal, making Khurāsān a kind of buffer state between them and Persia. As the real rulers, however, both these Afghān rulers struck coins in Mashhad.

Otherwise, the reign of the blind Shāh Rukh, which with repeated short interruptions lasted for nearly half a century, passed without any events of special note. It was only after the death of Tīmūr-Shāh (1207/1792) that Agha Muḥammad Khān, the founder of the Ḳādjār [*q.v.*] dynasty, succeeded in taking Shāh Rukh's domains and putting him to death in 1210/1795, thus ending the separation of Khurāsān from the rest of Persia. The death soon afterwards of Agha Muḥammad (1211/1796) enabled Nādir Mīrzā b. Shāh Rukh, who had escaped to Harāt, to return to Mashhad and take up the reins of government again. A siege of his capital by a Ḳādjār army remained without success; but in 1803 Fatḥ ʿAlī Shāh was able to take it after a siege of several months when Nādir's funds were exhausted.

From 1825 Khurāsān suffered greatly from the raids of Turkoman hordes and the continual feuds of the tribal leaders (cf. Conolly, *Journey*, i, 288 and Yate, 53). To restore order, the crown prince ʿAbbās Mīrzā entered Khurāsān with an army and made Mashhad his headquarters. He died there in 1833.

The most important political event of the 19th century for Mashhad was the rebellion of Ḥasan Khān Sālār, the prince-governor of Khurāsān, a cousin of the reigning Shāh Muḥammad-i ʿAbbās. For two years (1847-9) he held out against the government troops sent against him. At the time of the accession of Nāṣir al-Dīn (1848), Khurāsān was actually independent. It was only when the people of Mashhad, under pressure of famine, rebelled against Sālār that Ḥusām al-Salṭana's army succeeded in taking the town.

In 1911 a certain Yūsuf Khān of Harāt declared himself independent in Mashhad under the name of Muḥammad ʿAlī Shāh, and for a period disturbed Khurāsān considerably with the help of a body of reactionaries who gathered round him. This gave the Russians a pretext for armed intervention, and on 29 March 1912, they bombarded Mashhad in gross violaton of Persia's suzerain rights and many innocent people, citizens and pilgrims, were slain. This bombardment of the national sanctuary of Persia made a most painful impression in the whole Muslim world. Yūsuf Khān was later captured by the Persians and put to death (cf. Browne, *The press and poets of modern Persia*, Cambridge, 1914, 124, 127, 136; Sykes, *History of Persia*, London 1927, ii, 426-7).

Mashhad is now the centre of eastern Persia, the capital of the province of Khurāsān which, since its eastern part was taken by the Afghāns in the 18th century, is barely half its former size (cf. Le Strange, *Lands*, 383-4; *Isl.*, xi, 108-9). In the middle ages it was not Ṭūs, Mashhad's predecessor, but Naysābūr (modern Persian Nīshāpūr) that was the capital of this extensive and important province. A royal prince has usually been governor since the fall of the Nādirids. Since 1845, the lucrative and influential post of Mutawallī-Bāshī, the controller or treasurer of the sanctuary of the Imām, has usually been combined with the governorship (cf. Yate, 322).

Like most pre-modern Persian towns, Mashhad was enclosed by a great girdle of walls. The lines built to stiffen the defences, namely a small moat with escarpment before the main wall and a broad ditch around outside, were by the early 20th century in ruins and in places had completely disappeared.

The citadel (*ark*) in the southwest part of the town was directly connected with the system of defences. It was in the form of a rectangle with four great towers at the corners and smaller bastions. The palace begun by ʿAbbās Mīrzā but finished only in 1876, with its extensive gardens, was connected with the fortress proper, by the end of the 19th century fallen into disrepair (cf. Yate, 327). It was used as the governor's residence. The whole quarter of government buildings which, according to MacGregor, occupied an area of 1,200 yards, was separated from the town by an open space, the Maydān-i Tōp (Cannon Place) which was used for military parades.

There were six gates in the city walls.

The town was divided into six great and ten smaller quarters (*maḥalla*) (see Yate, 328). The six larger bore the names of their gates; see al-Mahdī al-ʿAlawī, *op. cit.*

The principal street which divides the whole town into two roughly equal halves, the Khiyābān, is a creation of Shāh ʿAbbās I, who did a great deal for Mashhad (see Yate, 319; cf. the pictures in Sykes, *The glory of the Shia world*, 231). This street, a fine promenade, is, being the main thoroughfare, filled all day with a throng of all classes and nationalities, including numerous pilgrims, and caravans of camels and asses; the bustle is tremendous, especially in the middle of the day.

The canal, which flowed through the Khiyābān in a bed about 9 feet broad and 5 feet deep, was fed, not from the Kashaf Rūd (see above) which runs quite close to Mashhad, for it has too little water, but from the Česhme-yi Gīlās, where the river rises, and which used to provide Ṭūs with water. When this town had been almost completely abandoned, Shīr ʿAlī, the vizier of Sultan Ḥusayn b. Manṣūr b. Bāyḳarā (1468-1506 [see ḤUSAYN MĪRZĀ]), at the beginning of the 10th/16th century had the water brought from this source to Mashhad by a canal 45 miles long, thus sealing the ruin of Ṭūs; cf. Yate, 315; al-Mahdī al-ʿAlawī, 13.

The making of this canal (see Yate, 315; Mahdī al-

ʿAlawī, 13) contributed essentially to the rise of Mas͟hhad; for the greater part of its inhabitants relied on it for water, although after entering the town, the canal became muddy and marshy (which was often a subject of satire; cf. ʿAbd al-Karīm, *Voyage*, 74), and used it for drinking, washing and religious ablutions without hesitation. There were also large and deep reservoirs before the main gates. The water was saline and sulphurous and therefore had an unpleasant taste (cf. Conolly, i, 333 4; Khanikoff, 105; Curzon, i, 153).

The *Ḥaram-i S͟harīf* or sacred area, often called the *Bast* [*q.v.*], literally "place of refuge, asylum", straddles the lower part of the main street; for a detailed consideration of the shrine, see 3. below.

Bibliography: In addition to references already given: *BGA*, i, 257; ii, 313; iii, 25, 50, 319, 333; vi, 24; vii, 171, 278; *Ḥudūd al-ʿālam*, tr. Minorsky, 55, 103, 185, 326; Yāḳūt, *Muʿd͟jam*, iii, 113, 486, 560-1; iv, 824; Ḳazwīnī, *Āt͟hār al-bilād* 262, 275; Abu 'l-Fidāʾ, *Taḳwīm al-buldān*, 450, 452; Ḥamd Allāh Mustawfī, *Nuzhat al-ḳulūb*, 150-1; Ibn Baṭṭūṭa ii, 79; ʿAbd al-Karīm (1741), *Bayān-i wāḳiʿa*, French tr., *Voyage de l'Inde à la Mekke par Abdoul-Kérym* by Langlès, Paris 1797, 69-74; Nāṣir al-Dīn S͟hāh's *Reise nach Khorāsan* (1866), Pers. text, Tehran 1286/1869, 180-225; Ibrāhīm Beg, *Siyāḥet-nāme*, ed. Istanbul, tr. W. Schultz, *Zustände des heutigen Persiens, wie sie das Reisetagebuch Ibrahim Beys enthüllt*, Leipzig 1903, 40-9; Sāmī Bey Frās͟herī, *Ḳāmūs al-aʿlām*, Istanbul, 1316, vi, 4290-1; Muḥammad Mahdī al-ʿAlawī, *Taʾrīk͟h Ṭūs aw al-Mas͟hhad al-Riḍawī*, Bag͟hdād 1346/1927. Cf. also the manuscript diary of a pilgrimage to Mas͟hhad in 1819-20 by Ḥusayn K͟hān b. D͟jaʿfar al-Mūsawī in the Berlin State Library, see Pertsch, *Verzeichniss der persisch. Hdschr... zu Berlin*, Berlin 1888, 378-9, no. 360. On the *Maṭlaʿ al-s͟hams* of Ṣanīʿ al-Dawla, see above.

As to descriptions of Mas͟hhad by Europeans, we owe the first full description to Fraser (1822); Conolly (i, 260) and Burnes (ii, 78) both say it is thoroughly reliable. Valuable notes on the town are given by Conolly, Ferrier, Khanikoff, Eastwick, MacGregor, Bassett, O'Donovan, Curzon, Massy, E. Diez, and especially by C. E. Yate and P. M. Sykes, each of whom spent several years (1893-7 and 1905-12 resp.) in Mas͟hhad as British Consul-General for K͟hurāsān.—Ruy Gonzales de Clavijo (1404), *Embassy to the court of Timur*, ed. C. R. Markham London 1859, 109-10; Truilhier (1807), in *Bulletin de la Société de Géogr.*, ix, Paris 1838, 272-82; J. B. Fraser (1822), *Narrative of a journey into Khorasan in the years 1821-1822*, London 1825, 436-548; A. Conolly (1830), *Journey to the North of India*, London 1834, i, 255-89, 296-368; A. Burnes (1832), *Travels into Bokhara*, London 1834, ii, 76-87; J. B. Fraser (1833), *A winter's journey from Constantinople to Teheran*, London 1838, i, 213-55; J. Wolff, *Narrative of a mission to Bokhara in the years 1843-1845*³, London 1846, 177-96, 386-408; J. P. Ferrier (1845), *Caravan journeys and wanderings in Persia*², London 1857, 111-33; J. J. Benjamin, *8 Jahre in Asien und Europa*², Hanover 1858, 189-90; N. de Khanikoff (1858), *Mémoire sur la partie méridionale de l'Asie centrale*, Paris 1861, 95-111; idem, *Méched, la ville sainte et son territoire*, in *Le Tour du Monde*, Paris 1861, nos. 95-6; Eastwick (1862), *Journal of a diplomat's three years residence in Persia*, London 1864, ii, 190-4; H. Vámbéry (1863), *Reise in Mittelasien*², Leipzig 1865 (1873), 248-58; identical with H. Vámbéry, *Meine Wanderungen und Erlebnisse in Persien*, Pesth 1867, 313-27; H. W. Bellew (1872), *From the Indus to the Tigris*, London 1874, 358-68; F. J. Goldsmid (and Evan Smith, 1872), *Eastern Persia*, London 1876, i, 356-66; H. C. Marsh (1872), *A ride through Islam*, etc., London 1877, 96-112; V. Baker (1873), *Clouds in the East*, London 1876, 177-94; C. M. MacGregor (1875), *Narrative of a journey through the province of Khorasan*, London 1879, i, 277-309; ii, 4; J. Bassett (1878), *Persia, the land of the Imams*, London 1887, 219-47; E. O'Donovan (1880), *The Merw Oasis*, London 1882, i. 478-502; ii, 1-14; A. C. Yate (1885, brother of C. E. Yate), *Travels with the Afghan Boundary Commission*, Edinburgh 1889, 367-84; G. Radde (1886), *Transkaspien und Nordchorasan*, in *Petermanns Geogr. Mitteil.*, Erg.-H. 126, 174-8; G. N. Curzon (1889), *Persia and the Persian Question*, London 1892, i, 148-76; H. St. Massy (1893), *An Englishman in the shrine of Imam Reza in Mashad*, in *The Nineteenth Century and after*, London 1913, lxxiii/2, 990-1007; C. E. Yate (1885, 1893-7), *Khurasan and Sistan*, Edinburgh 1900, 40-50, 53, 140-9, 249-346, 406, 418-21 (with pictures); P. Sykes (1893, 1902, 1905-12), *Ten Thousand Miles in Persia*, London 1902, 24-6, 256, 301, 367, 385, 401; idem, *Historical notes on Khurasan*, in *JRAS* 1910, 1114-48, 1152-4;. idem, (and K͟hān Bahādur Aḥmad Dīn K͟hān), *The glory of the Shia world*, London 1910, 227-69 (with pictures); Ella C. Sykes, *Persia and its people*, London 1910, 88-105; H. R. Allemagne (1907), *Du Khorassan au pays des Bakhtiaris*, Paris 1911, iii, 75-114 (with very fine illustrations); A. V. W. Jackson (1907), *From Constantinople to the home of Omar Khayyam*, New York 1911, 263-77; H. H. Graf von Schweinitz (1908), *Orientalische Wanderungen in Turkestan und im nordöstl. Persien*, Berlin 1910, 15-28; E. Diez (1913), *Churasanische Baudenkmäler*, i, Berlin 1918, 52-61, 66-9, 76-8, 85-6, with index; ii, 19-20, 23-9, 36,2; 32, 38; idem, *Persien*: *Islamische Baukunst in Churāsān*, Hagen i. W. 1923, 43-79, 91, 154; O. von Niedermayer (1913, 1915-16), *Unter der Glutsonne Irans*, Dachau 1925, 207; A. Gabriel, *Die Erforschung Persiens*, Vienna 1952, index s.v. *Meschhed*; L. Lockhart, *Persian cities*, London 1960, 32-41; W. Barthold, *An historical geography of Iran*, tr. S. Soucek, ed. C. E. Bosworth, Princeton 1984.—In the general works of K. Ritter, *Erdkunde*, viii (1838), 11, 127, 238-308, 310; ix (1840), 904, and G. Le Strange, *The lands of the Eastern Caliphate*, Cambridge 1905, 388-91, 431. Ṭūs and Mas͟hhad are not satisfactorily distinguished.

(M. Streck)

2. History and topography from 1914 to the present day [see Suppl.]

3. The shrine, and Mas͟hhad as a centre of S͟hīʿī learning and piety [see Suppl.]

MAS͟HHAD ʿALĪ [see al-nad͟jaf].

MAS͟HHAD ḤUSAYN [see karbalāʾ].

MAS͟HHAD-I MIṢRIYĀN, a ruined site in Transcaspia (the modern Türkmenistan SSR) north-west of the confluence of the Atrak and its right bank tributary the Sumbar, or more exactly, on the road which runs from Čat at right angles to the road connecting Čikis͟hler with the railway station of Aydîn.

The ruins are surrounded by a wall of brick and a ditch and have an area of 320 acres. The old town, situated in the steppes which are now peopled by Turkomans, received its water from a canal led from the Atrak about 40 miles above Čat. Near the latter place, the canal diverged northwards from the river, crossed the Sumbar by a bridge and finally followed an embankment 6 feet high on which the bed of the canal was 12 feet broad.

The ruins of a fine mosque can still be seen, the gateway of which, decorated with faience, has an inscription according to which this *ṭāḳ* was built by ʿAlāʾ al-Dunyā wa 'l-Dīn Ghiyāth al-Islām wa 'l-Muslimīn Ẓill Allāh fī 'l-ʿĀlamīn Sulṭān Muḥammad b. Sulṭān Takish Burhān Amīr al-Muʾminīn. The Khwārazmshāh Muḥammad in question reigned 596-617/1200-20 [see KHWĀRAZM-SHĀHS]. On one of the two towers (minarets?) is written: *bismillāh* ... *barakat*^{un} *min Allāh*^{i}, *mimmā amara bihi Abū Djaʿfar Aḥmad b. Abi 'l-Aʿazz* (?) *ṣāḥib al-ribāṭ, aʿazzahu 'llāh*^{u}. *ʿAmal ʿAlī R* .... (?). The identity of this Aḥmad is unknown but the title "lord of the *ribāṭ*" which he gives himself, confirms the fact that Mashhad-i Miṣriyān was a frontier fortress (*ribāṭ*). Near the east gate stood another white mosque.

Tradition (Conolly) ascribes the destruction of Miṣriyān to the "Ḳalmuḳ Tatars". The appearance of the Ḳalmuḳs in these regions may be dated about 1600.

The name Mashhad-i Miṣriyān (variants: Mestorian, Mest-Debran, Mest-Dovran, Mastān) is obscure, unless Mestorian is to be explained as * Nestoriyān i.e. "Nestorian Christians"; it may be recalled that during his campaign in the Čōl (*صول), to the east of the Caspian, Yazdagird II persecuted the Christians (Hoffmann, 50; J. Labourt, *Le christianisme dans l'Empire Perse*, Paris 1904, 26).

The site of the ruins (to the north of Djurdjān) is given the name Dihistān in Muslim sources; for the town of this name, and the promontory of Dihistānān-Sur, as the *Ḥudūd al-ʿālam* calls it, see DIHISTĀN. 2.

The ruins of Mashhad-i Miṣriyān (as the inscription on the mosque suggests !) must correspond to the *ribāṭ* of Dihistān which al-Muḳaddasī, 358 (cf. also 312, 367, 372), mentions as distinct from Akhūr. This *ribāṭ*, situated on the borders of the steppes, had fine mosques and rich markets. Relying on Yāḳūt, i, 39, Barthold thought that in the 6th/12th century the *ribāṭ* (and not Akhūr to the east of the Djurdjān-*ribāṭ* road) was the capital of the district of Dihistān.

Bibliography: The Muslim sources as given in the text; *Ḥudūd al-ʿālam*, tr. Minorsky, 60, 133-4, 385-6; A. Conolly, *Journey to the North of India*, London 1838, i, 76-7; A. Vambéry, *Reise in Mittelasien*[2], Leipzig 1873, 85 (fantastic statements on the Greek origin of the ruins); Lomakin, *Razvalinī dvukh drevnikh gorodov Mesteriyan i Meshkheda v Turkmenskoi stepi*, in *Izv. Kavk. Otd. Russ. Geogr. Obshč.*, iv/1, 15-17; A. Kohn, *Die Ruinen d. alten Städte Mesched und* (sic!) *Mesterian*, in *Globus* (1876), no. 71; Blaramberg, *Die Ruinen d. Stadt Mestorian*, in *Pet. Mitt.* (1876), xxii/1; Hoffmann, *Auszüge aus syrischen Akten*, Leipzig 1880, 277-81 (lucid analysis of the Arabic statements); Marquart, *Ērānšahr*, 51, 73, 310; Barthold, *Istor.-geogr. obzor Irana*, St. Petersburg 1903, 82, Eng.tr., *An historical geography of Iran*, Princeton 1984, 118-19; A. A. Semënov, *Nadpisi na portale mečeti v Meshkhedi-Misriyane*, in *ZVORAO*, xviii/4 (1908), 0154-0157; Barthold, *K istorii orosheniya Turkestana*, St. Petersburg 1914, 31-7; S. Flury, *Notes on the miḥrāb of Mashhad-i Miṣriyān*, in *Survey of Persian art*, iii, 2721-4; L. I. Rempel', *Arkhitekturnī ornament yuzhnogo Turkmenistana x.-načala xiii. v.v. u problema "Sel'dzhukskogo Stilya"*, in *Trudī Yu TAKE*, xii (Ashkhabad 1963), 249-308. (V. MINORSKY)

MASHHŪR (A.), technical term used in the science of *ḥadīth* [*q.v.*] for a well-known tradition transmitted via a minimum of three different *isnāds* [*q.v.*].

Bibliography: Nūr al-Dīn ʿItr, *Muʿdjam al-muṣṭalaḥāt al-ḥadīthiyya*, Damascus 1976, 98, and the literature quoted there. (G. H. A. JUYNBOLL)

MASHRABIYYA (A.) designates a technique of turned wood used to produce lattice-like panels, like those which were used in the past to adorn the windows in traditional domestic architecture.

1. In Egypt. The term derives from Arabic *shariba* "to drink". The connection between the turned wood technique and drinking was established last century by E. W. Lane, who describes the *mashraba* as a niche attached to such lattice wooden

1. (Top third) *al-ṣalīb al-malyān*, "filled cross"; (lower two-thirds) *kanāʾisī ḳibṭī* "Coptic church style".

2. *Nudjūmī* "star-shaped".

windows and used to keep the water jars cool and fresh for drinking. This interpretation is confirmed by *waḳf* [*q.v.*] documents, which since the 10th/16th century refer to such niches as *mashraba* and also to the turned wood technique as *mashrabiyya.* Muḥammad ʿAlī [*q.v.*] is said to have prohibited the use of *mashrabiyya* windows, in order to replace traditional by European architecture. The *mashrabiyya* technique is a speciality of Cairo, where it was used with a multitude of patterns and combinations, as the collection of the Islamic Museum in Cairo shows, as well as the remains of some old houses of the Ottoman period. Each type of *mashrabiyya* has its own name, such as *nudjūmī* "star-like", *sāḳiya* "like a water-wheel", *muthallath* "triangular", *ṣalībī fāḍī* "cross-shaped and empty", *ṣalībī malyān* "cross-shaped and filled in", *kanāʾisī ḳibṭī* "Coptic church type", *kanāʾisī fāḍī* "church type and empty", *ʿayn al-katkūt* "chick's eye, *maymūnī mudawwar* "circular *maymūnī*", *maymūnī nudjūmī* "star-like *maymūnī*" and *maʿkūs* "reversed".

Mashrabiyya panels are composed of small pieces of wood which are turned in various forms and are fixed together without glue or nails, but simply by being inserted into each other, thus giving the panel more resistance towards the flexibility of the wood with the change of temperature. Geometric patterns of great complexity and diversity can be obtained with the combination of the wooden pieces. The result is a transparent screen which is very decorative due to the variation of patterns and density, according to which the pieces, of various shapes, can be fixed together. The panel filters the light and the sun rays in a pleasant manner; at the same time, it allows a view to the exterior without exposing the interior to outside view. This device had an important impact on the fenestration system, since it allowed large surfaces, like a whole wall in a room, to be made in turned wood and thus offered a panorama to the inhabitants at the same time as the introduction of fresh air. This could be combined with the use of glass panels or curtains for additional protection. *Mashrabiyya* windows could be made of painted wood in various colours, or could simply show the natural colour of the wood. Hence Cairo's façades in the 19th century as seen by orientalist painters and in early photographs, were characterised by the multitude of projecting *mashrabiyya* windows that almost touched each other on both sides of the narrow streets.

Historically, the technique of turned wood in Cairo seems to have been used first on other architectural objects before it was applied to windows. Mamlūk *waḳf* deeds, which include detailed descriptions of buildings, refer to turned wood, though not usually in connection with windows. Only in the very late Mamlūk *waḳf* deeds in the early 10th/16th century do we find, and then only sparsely, references to turned wood used on windows. It is referred to as *khashab kharṭ* or sometimes as *shughl al-kharrāṭ*, i.e. "made by the turner", to distinguish it from *shughl al-nadjdjār*, which means "made by the carpenter".

Whereas Lane reports that in his time, the houses of the rich differed from those of the poor by their larger display of *mashrabiyya* panels, in the Mamlūk period the windows of the rich had iron or bronze grills that were gilded like those of the royal palaces at the Citadel, whereas the more common ones were made of wood. Al-Maḳrīzī, deploring the ruins of the palace of Tashtimur, writes that its marble was replaced by stone, and its iron windows by wooden ones. Mamlūk *waḳf* deeds describe the windows of residences of the period as having the same system of fenestration used in the mosque architecture: the lower windows were rectangular, large and adorned with iron or bronze grills, whilst above them were

3. *Nudjūmī maymūnī "star-shaped maymūnī* style".

arched windows with stucco grills filled with coloured glass. The more common house type, or the less visible windows in a residence, were made of wood, in general without turned wood panels, according to the *wakf* descriptions. Whenever this technique is mentioned in Mamlūk *wakf* descriptions, it usually refers to balustrades, like that which adorns the *makʿad*, i.e. loggia, or the wooden lantern which surmounts the central part of a *ḳāʿa* or reception hall, also found in late Mamlūk mosques. *Khashab kharṭ* is also mentioned in connection with *maghānī*, also called *aghānī*, which are a pair of loggias that flank a *ḳāʿa* on both sides and which, as the name indicates, were intended for the singers and musicians, who traditionally performed behind curtains or screens.

There are three mediaeval mosques in Cairo that display magnificent examples of *mashrabiyya* technique. The mosque of al-Ṣāliḥ Ṭalāʾiʿ, built in the Fāṭimid period (555/1160) and restored more than once under the Mamlūks, has a screen of turned wood, today at the portico but originally inside the mosque. The present one is a modern copy made after a 19th century illustration. The mausoleum of Sultan Ḳalāwūn (built 683-4/1284-5) also has a turned wood screen around the cenotaph, restored at the beginning of this century. Further, the mosque of al-Māridānī (739-40/1340) has its sanctuary screened by a *mashrabiyya* wall from the courtyard.

Regular reference to turned wood *mashrabiyya* in connection with windows in domestic architecture, starts after the Ottoman conquest of Egypt (923/1517) and is found in *wakf* descriptions. Although windows of turned wood are a characteristic feature of the domestic type of architecture, there is one Ottoman mosque in Cairo that has a large *mashrabiyya* window, the mosque of Yūsuf Agha al-Ḥīn (1035/1625), which was erected along the shore of the Canal of Cairo. The *mashrabiyya* window must have been intended to allow the worshippers to enjoy the view of the water and the greenery.

Nowadays, after modern European architecture was definitely adopted in Cairo from the first half of the 19th century under the initiative of Muḥammad ʿAlī Pasha, *mashrabiyya* windows have disappeared from Cairo's façades. In the second half of that century, European architects introduced a kind of orientalist style in architecture and decoration which revived some traditional crafts, and turned wood became again fashionable, this time, however, with purely decorative functions. It was no more used in its original architectural context, but as decoration for European-style furniture and on small objects. With time, the *mashrabiyya* technique became a touristic craft only practiced in the bazaar, and the term *mashrabiyya* itself became equivalent to local traditional handicraft.

Bibliography: Maḳrīzī *Khiṭaṭ*, Būlāḳ 1270, ii, 68, 71; Lane, *Manners and customs of the modern Egyptians*, introd.: *wakf* documents of the Mamlūk and Ottoman periods in Cairo, at the Ministry of Waḳf (Daftarkhāna) and at the Dār al-Wathāʾiḳ al-Ḳawmiyya, Citadel (Ḥudjadj al-Mulūk wa 'l-Umarāʾ).

(Doris Behrens-Abouseif)

2. In Iran. As in many other Islamic countries, so too in Iran the use of *mashrabiyya* serves both practical and aesthetic functions. The former includes the protection of the private environment from indiscreet glances, the ability to see without being seen, and the requirements of ventilation. The latter operates in the context of an architecture which lacks deep voids and which strives for an effect of large surfaces over which decoration can extend.

The type most frequently encountered consists of rectangular grilles, grilles with ogee arches and grilles of larger dimensions containing three or more panels with a vertical and stepped movement (*urūsī*). The material most frequently used is wood, and in particular, plane (*čınār* or *platanus orientalis*) which, since it could secure optimum durability, and, since it had a high and straight trunk, also came to be used for columnar porticoes (*tālār*). Sometimes grilles of plaster or of coloured glass were employed (e.g. the specimen removed from the Darb-i Imām at Iṣfahān), as were grilles of stone or plaster and tile mosaic (e.g. the Masjid-i Shaykh Luṭf Allāh and the Masdjid-i Djumʿa, both *in situ* in Iṣfahān).

The main decorative themes comprise vegetal, figural and animal motifs (cf. the above-mentioned grille of the Darb-i Imām); inscriptions (e.g. the large *urūsī* of the Haftdah Tan at Shahr-i Kurd); and, above all, geometric motifs.

In all the types recorded to date—rectangular, ogival, and stepped—the wooden grille is always subdivided for decorative purposes into two main parts, sc. an outer border and an inner field. The first of these, namely the border, always comprising a series of square "modules", is obtained by the repetition of a single decorative motif all along the edge of the grille. This establishes an exact correspondence between the width and height of a single grille. By contrast, the second—namely the inner field—constitutes the principal motif of the whole composition and is therefore subject to certain regulatory "laws".

Such laws are illustrated above all by the use of rotations around precisely located axes; or of rotations of a single basic motif; or of various renderings of a given decorative theme—unless, indeed, a single part of the design is isolated. This makes it possible to obtain, with minimum artifice, a most varied range of compositions.

The geometric schemes highlighted in these various compositions consist in the main of equilateral or isosceles triangles or of squares often rotated at an angle of 45°, and, more rarely, of rectangles. The geometrical figures are above all regular polygons such as hexagons, octagons, decagons and dodecagons, which, with their numerous symmetrical axes, allow the creation of complex ensembles. The decorative motifs employed have very ancient origins and go back to the first centuries of Islamic art and even to the period of Near Eastern late antiquity.

This répertoire was used and elaborated for centuries, with the result that today it is possible to find identical decorative motifs in periods far removed from each other in time. With the Ṣafawids, the decorative motif, initially simple and with a wide mesh, tends to thicken and to become more complicated with the creation of complex stellar figures or those with polygonal matrices. There is an increasing use of coloured glass, mirrors and perforated elements with a progressively increasing use of curvilinear motifs.

With the advent of the Ḳādjārs, this love of curvilinear motifs increases apace and the decorative design changes totally. The mesh widens yet again, the geometric motifs disappear almost entirely while curvilinear motifs prevail. These include floral themes, in which large areas of coloured glass occur; their colour scheme is dominated by blue, red and green.

Bibliography: B. Deniké, *Quelques monuments de bois sculpté au Turkestān occidental*, in *Ars Islamica*, ii (1935), 69-83; M. S. Dimand, *Dated Persian doors of the fifteenth century*, in *Bull. of the Metropolitan Museum of Art*, xxxi (1936), 79-80; L. Bronstein, *Decorative woodwork of the Islamic period*, in Pope, *Survey of Persian art*, London 1939, iii, 2607-27 and pls. 1434, 1460-77; Amy Briggs, *Timurid carpets. I. Geometric carpets*, in *Ars Islamica*, vii (1940), 20-54; R. Orazi, *Wooden gratings in Safavid architecture*, Rome 1976. (R. Orazi)

MAS̲H̲RIḲ (a.), the East, linked with and opposed to the West (Mag̲h̲rib [*q.v.*]), either in general or from the strictly geographical point of view; for the Arab world, the Mag̲h̲rib embraces all the lands to the west of Egypt, and the Mas̲h̲riḳ all those to the east. Nevertheless, the parallelism is not absolute; whilst the term Mag̲h̲rib is particularly applied either to the grouping North-Africa-Tripolitania or to North Africa properly so-called or to its most western part, Morocco (Mag̲h̲rib, al-Mag̲h̲rib al-Aḳṣā [*q.v.*]), the word Mas̲h̲riḳ seems to cover the Orient in general, without reference to any one country or another (the name of one of the *mik̲h̲lāfs* of Yemen, cited in Yāḳūt, *Buldān*, s.v., but not in al-Hamdānī, can only be understood, from all the evidence, in a local context).

An interesting attempt was, however, made in the 4th/10th century to take to its logical conclusion a rigorous parallelism between the two geographical groupings. It emanated from the Arabic geographer al-Muḳaddasī, whose originality of thought and conceptions is well-known. For him, the land of Islam (*mamlakat al-Islām*), going beyond its fourteen provinces, embraces several binary oppositions. Just as there exist two seas (those of Rūm and Ṣīn) and two deserts (the *bādiyat al-ʿArab* and the *mafāza* of Iran), there likewise exist two particular provinces (*iḳlīm*), hence binary also (a third province, Arabia, further has, like the two preceding ones, two capitals, Mecca and Zabīd, for the two lands of the North and the South, and this last, Yemen, is also described to us as having two lands, one of seacoast and one of the mountains (*Aḥsan al-taḳāsīm*, 56, 69-70, 260-1); but the parallelism with the other two great provinces is not pushed any further). To the Mag̲h̲rib, made up of two *d̲j̲ānibs* (al-Andalus and the Mag̲h̲rib properly speaking) and with two metropolises (*miṣr*) of Cordova and al-Ḳayrawān, there corresponds the Mas̲h̲riḳ, defined as the assemblage of lands more or less strictly under the aegis of the Sāmānids, including Sid̲j̲istān, K̲h̲urāsān and Transoxania (*mā warāʾ al-nahr*), this assemblage being divided into two *d̲j̲ānibs* separated by the D̲j̲ayḥūn river (sc. the Oxus); to the south, K̲h̲urāsān and its *miṣr*, Naysābūr and to the north, Hayṭal and its *miṣr*, Samarḳand. It should be noted that al-Muḳaddasī, in the introduction to his work, adds to the distinction Mag̲h̲rib/Mas̲h̲riḳ a further parallelism between G̲h̲arb and S̲h̲arḳ, one which does not however seem to be operative in the rest of the book; for the author, G̲h̲arb embraces the ensemble Mag̲h̲rib-Egypt-S̲h̲ām (sc. Syria-Palestine) and S̲h̲arḳ the ensemble Mas̲h̲riḳ-Fārs-Kirmān-Sind.

Bibliography: In addition to the references given in the text, see Muḳaddasī, 7, 47, 57, 260 ff. and *passim*. (A. Miquel)

MAS̲H̲RIḲ al-AD̲H̲KĀR, a term used in the Bahāʾī movement for four related concepts: 1. In Iran (loosely) to describe early morning gatherings for reading of prayers and sacred writings. 2. Generally of any house erected for the purpose of prayer. 3. Most widely, to refer to Bahāʾī temples (*maʿbad*) or "houses of worship", of which six have been built on a continental basis. The earliest was constructed in As̲h̲kābād, Russian Central Asia by the expatriate Iranian Bahāʾī community there (begun 1902; completed 1920; damaged by earthquake 1948; demolished 1963). The others are: Wilmette, Illinois (begun 1912; dedicated 1953); Kampala, Uganda (1961); Sydney, Australia (1961); Frankfurt, W. Germany (1964); Panama City, Panama (1972). Temples are under construction in India and Western Samoa, while land has been acquired for over 100 national buildings. Architecturally, temples differ widely, but conform to minimum requirements of a nine-sided circular construction. Internal ornamentation is sparse, with prohibition on images and use of a *minbar*; seating is provided for congregations on the Western church pattern, facing the Bahāʾī *ḳibla* (Bahd̲j̲ī, near Acre, Israel). In the absence of formalised clergy, worship takes the simple pattern of reading from Bahāʾī or other scriptures; sermons, instrumental music, and communal prayer are forbidden, although chanting (*tilāwa*), unaccompanied singing, and a capella choral singing are permitted. "Elaborate and ostentatious ceremony" is proscribed, and set forms of service are not laid down; private *ṣalāt* may be performed (communal *ṣalāt* is forbidden in Bahāʾī law). Temples are open to non-adherents for private worship. 4. In its widest application, to refer to a central temple in conjunction with various dependencies regarded as intrinsic to the overall institution. These include a school for orphans, hospital and dispensary for the poor, home for the aged, home for the infirm, college of higher education, and traveller's hospice. With the exception of a home for the aged in Wilmette, no dependencies have as yet been established. Temples may be erected on a national or local basis; administrative buildings (*ḥaẓīrat al-ḳuds*) are kept separate from the *mas̲h̲riḳ al-adhkār*.

Bibliography: ʿAbd al-Ḥamīd *Is̲h̲rāḳ K̲h̲āvarī* (ed.), *Gand̲j̲īna-yi ḥudūd wa aḥkām*, Tehran 1961, 188-9, 230-40; *The Bahāʾī World*, xiii (Haifa 1970), 699-748; xiv (1974), 475-95; xv (1976), 629-49; Mīrzā Asad Allāh Fāḍil Māzandarānī, *Amr wa k̲h̲alḳ*, iv (Tehran 1970), 147-53. (D. MacEoin)

MAS̲H̲RŪBĀT (ar.), drinks.

I. *Problems of identification and of permissibility.*

The problem of the distinction between "permitted" and "forbidden" in relation to drinks is a subject of great interest to Islamic religious literature, on account of the prohibition, in the Ḳurʾān, of the consumption of wine [see k̲h̲amr]. By extension, everything alcoholic is forbidden, and doctors of law devote entire chapters, and even independent works, to the subject of drinks (*as̲h̲riba*; for example: *Kitāb al-As̲h̲riba* by Aḥmad b. Ḥanbal, numerous editions). The use of certain receptacles is forbidden to Muslims, because of the ease with which they may be employed for the fermentation of liquids (see for example, *dubbāʾ*, *ḥantam*, *naḳīr*, in the *Concordance de la tradition musulmane*; the epistle of al-D̲j̲āḥiẓ, *al-S̲h̲ārib wa 'l-mas̲h̲rūb*; the art. k̲h̲amr; and especially the legal and literary sources quoted in Sadan, *Vin—fait de civilisation*, in *Studies in memory of Gaston Wiet*, 129-60; one of the best later sources (somewhat polemical) is *Ikrām man yaʿīs̲h̲ bi-aḥkām al-k̲h̲amr wa 'l-ḥas̲h̲īs̲h̲* by al-Aḳfahsī, B.L. ms. 9646, fols. 1b-7a, which makes a distinction, from a judicial point of view, between all kinds of musts, beers, etc.; drinks composed of fruits (dates, etc.) mixed in water are called *fadīk̲h̲*, *naḳīʿ* (cf. *ʿIlm al-tilmīd̲h̲ bi-aḥkām al-nabīd̲h̲*, Princeton, Yahuda 2090, ms. 5084, fols. 15a-20a). Liquids which tend to ferment are produced on the basis of fruits, various berries, cereals or honey (mead is called *bitʿ*, *nabīd̲h̲ al-ʿasal*); from syrup or from preserves of fruit there derives the *dūs̲h̲āb* which is sometimes non-alcoholic, but which al-Djāḥiẓ and other authors mention in the context of drinks (*dūshāb*, *dādhī*, etc.) which can ferment and become alcoholic (see the references cited above, as well as Abū Hilāl al-ʿAskarī, *Dīwān al-maʿānī*, i, 331: *nabīdh al-dibs*—identical to *dūshāb*; M. Ahsan, *Social life under the ʿAbbasids*, 111). Certain jurists of the Ḥanafī and Muʿtazilī schools had a tendency to permit the consumption of some of these drinks, under certain conditions, excluding only wine made from grapes. A more limited group of the Muʿtazilīs (to which al-Djāḥiẓ did not belong) even tried to legalise wine made from grapes, and it is for this reason that Ibn Ḳutayba, *al-Ashriba*, ed. M. Kurd ʿAlī, calls them "theologians of debauchery" (*mudjdjān ahl al-kalām*) (for other details, see Sadan, *op. cit.*, and for *dādhī*, see also al-Balawī, *al-Alif bāʾ*, ii, 80, and S. D. Goitein, *A Mediterranean society*, iv, 1983, 260).

Now these tendencies count for nothing in Islamic jurisprudence at present (even among the Ḥanafīs), and these numerous and rich testimonies from mediaeval texts are cited only to show the difficulty, in a given historical context, of distinguishing between the "permitted" and the "forbidden", the "soft" and the alcoholic, and above all, to underline the rich variety of fermented drinks, soft or relatively so, musts and beers. The term *nabīdh* [*q.v.*], for example, most often denotes a true wine made from dates (very potent according to pre-Islamic poetry; see Sadan, *op. cit.*), or from various berries, but—with reference to the *nabīdh* consumed by the Prophet—the religious texts stress the non-alcoholic nature of this drink, which was lightly fermented (or, rather, exposed to the sun for only a few hours, according to the definitions of the texts themselves), in order to prevent any other interpretation of this term in the context of the biography of the Prophet (see Ibn Ḥayyān, *Akhlāḳ al-nabī*, Cairo 1959, 225-8; Ibn al-Djawzī, *al-Wafāʾ*, Cairo 1966, 617; cf. al-Bādjūrī, [Commentary on] *al-Shamāʾil* by al-Tirmidhī, Cairo 1301).

II. *Beers.*

In fact, beers were well-known in the civilisation of that time. For example: 1. *Mizr*, see *Concordance*, s.v.; Dozy, *Suppl.*, under *mizr*, *mazr*, *mizār*; S. D. Goitein, *op. cit.*, iv, 261 (under "beer") and cf. al-Ḥalabī, *Nuzhat al-udabāʾ*, Camb. ms. or. 1256(8), fol. 218b, where the Egyptian author describes *mizr* as the favourite drink of the Negroes living in Egypt. See also al-Aḳfahsī, *op. cit.*, fol. 5a, who calls *mizr* by the name of *nabīdh al-dhura*, "beer" of maize or of sorghum, while "beer" of wheat is called in Egypt, *apud* al-Aḳfahsī, *ḥatīʿā*; as for barley beer, *māʾ shaʿīr*, see below under the heading *fuḳḳāʿ*. On *mazzār* = "brewer", see Ibn Mawlāhum, *Maḳāma fī khamsīn marʾa*, B.L. ms. Add. 19, 411, fol. 94a: *mazzāra* (= "brewer" in the fem.) and her implements, her receptacles and the preparation of the drink. 2. *Djāʿa*, see, for example, Ibn Ḥadjar, *Fatḥ al-Bārī*, x, 258-9; on the revived use of this term in this century, in place of the more widespread borrowing *bīra* (= modern beer), see *Machriq*, xii, 401-7. 3. *Māʾ shaʿīr* and *aḳsimā*, see below. 4. *Boza*, see towards the end of the article. 5. *Fuḳḳāʿ*, see Ibn Ḳutayba, *ʿUyūn*, iii, 280; Kushādjim, *Dīwān*, 1313, 84; al-Sarī al-Raffāʾ, *Dīwān*, Baghdād 1981, ii, 180: *fuḳḳāʿ* = sparkling drink; al-Ḥuṣrī, *Zahr*, ed. al-Bidjāwī, i, 116: *faḳḳāʿ* = producer and vendor of this drink; al-Rāghib al-Iṣfahānī, *Muḥāḍarāt al-udabāʾ*, Beirut 1961, ii (4), 379; P. Kahle, in *ZDMG* (1935), 344; Darrāg, *L'acte de waqf de Barsbay*, Cairo 1963, 52; Sadan, in *REI* (1977), 50, 56, n. 18; Goitein, *loc. cit.* The long and narrow vessels which, among their others functions, were used for the preparation or storage of this "beer", were the *kīzān* (sing. *kūz*, see above). The *kūz*, often fitted with a handle (see al-Ghuzūlī, *Maṭāliʿ al-budūr*, Cairo 1299-1300, ii, 72) is frequently mentioned and described in Arabic literature. However, Goitein, *op. cit.*, iv, 146, translates *kīzān* as "bowls", a sense which the word possesses in certain dialects. With reference to the producer/vendor of this drink (*faḳḳāʿ*), see also the popular *Story of the Caliph Hārūn al-Rashīd and the fuḳḳāʿī* (= *faḳḳāʿ*), B.N. Ar. ms. 3658 fols. 26b-34a. On the *faḳḳāʿ*/*fuḳḳāʿī* = brewer, see also al-Nawādjī, *Marātiʿ al-ghizlān*, B.N. ar. ms. 3402, fol. 36a; al-Ṣarīḥī, *Nuzhat al-afrāḥ*, Oxford ms. Marsh 2, fol. 46a; al-Khafādjī, *Ṭirāz al-madjālis*, Cairo 1284, 71-3; S. de Sacy, *Exposé de la religion des Druzes*, i, pp. cccxxxii-iii.

There existed numerous kinds of *fuḳḳāʿ*: they are mentioned in culinary literature, among sauces and drinks (see the mss. mentioned below and M. Rodinson, in *REI* [1949], 131, whose material is based on *al-Wuṣla* (see below); art. GHIDHĀʾ and Ḥ. Zayyāt, in *Machriq*, xli, 25). The sense of "beer" is clearly evident when the text describes the fermentation (*yakhmar*, *yathūr*) of this drink. In addition to the references given above concerning the *fuḳḳāʿ*, see anon., *Kanz al-fawāʾid*, Camb. ms. Qq. 196, fols. 108a-b, 109a: *fuḳḳāʿ* sweetened and flavoured with fruit (the mediaeval equivalent of "shandy" or almost so; it may thus be with justification that Ahsan, *loc. cit.*, attempts to conclude from a very partial reference of *adab* that this drink was invariably soft or even non-alcoholic; however, *apud* al-Ghuzūlī, *op. cit.*, who accurately reflects life in mediaeval Egypt, various kinds of *fuḳḳāʿ* were sweetened to a considerable extent), 108b, 109a-b: *māʾ shaʿīr*, literally "barley water", when fermented becomes "barley beer", of which a special variety exists for the nights of the month of Ramaḍān (according to this text and according to anon., *K. al-Ṭabīkh*, Chester Beatty ms. 4018, fol. 48a), 107a, 110a, 111a: *aḳsimā* = liquid, syrup, but, since one of these recipes mentions the presence of yeast among the ingredients of this drink, it must presumably be a variety of sweetened beer and not a simple syrup as it is usually translated (for the Egyptians, according to al-Ghuzūlī, *loc. cit.*, both the term and the recipe of *aḳsimā* often replace those of *fuḳḳāʿ*, 180a-b, 111b, 112a: *shīsh*, a drink or sauce which Rodinson, *loc. cit.*, reads as *šašš*, defining it as an unidentified liquid (without examining the recipes for it in the *Kanz*), but a humorous treatise in B.L. ms. Add. 19.411, fol. 15a, supplied the plural *ashyāsh* (which would seem to justify the reading accepted here, *shīsh*; the suggestion that it derives from the Turkish *shīshe* "bottle", cf. Lane, *Manners and customs*, 331, does not seem plausible). See also al-Warrāḳ, *K. al-Ṭabkh*, ms. Oxford, Hunt. 187, which contains recipes of *fuḳḳāʿ*, fols. 148b, 151b, and cf. Zayyāt, *loc. cit.*; anon. *al-Wuṣla*, B.L. ms. 6388, fol. 27a-b: *aḳsimā* and *fuḳḳāʿ*, 28b-29a: *aḳsimā* prepared with yeast, and various kinds of *fuḳḳāʿ*; cf. Rodinson, *loc. cit.* Certain physicians are inclined to define *fuḳḳāʿ*, made of barley or rice, as a relatively soft drink, when compared to real intoxicants (al-Rāzī, *Manāfiʿ al-aghdhiya*, Beirut 1982, 91; who notes, on the other hand, that the *fuḳḳāʿ* "goes to the head"), but for the jurists, the mediaeval experts in Islamic law, this drink brings up some difficult legal questions (see al-Ṭūsī, *Masʾala fī taḥrīm al-fuḳḳāʿ*, Bodl. MS.Arab.f.64, fols. 94v-97v).

III. *Milk.*

The same works of culinary art also provide a wide range of recipes of which the primary ingredient is milk, but it may be assumed, judging by the method of preparation, that in the majority of cases the references are to sauces accompanying food rather than to drinks as such (cf. also Ahsan, *op. cit.*, 97-8, and the references given below). In fact, without refrigeration, it was not easy to preserve milk, except with the addition of preservative elements, e.g. salt, or allowing it to curdle. In fact, ever since the pre-Islamic period the Arabs were well aware of the importance of milk as a nutritive element, with numerous terms denoting its varieties and properties and verbs and adjectives used to identify the stages of curdling (*rā'ib* = clotting, for example), and it is thus that numerous pages are devoted to milk in the lexical literature (specialised works, including *Kitāb al-Laban wa 'l-liba'* by Abū Zayd al-Anṣārī, ed. Haffner-Cheikho, in *Dix traités*, as well as entire chapters in longer works; see also the references in Sadan, *op. cit.*). The pre-Islamic Arabs were great breeders of camels and dromedaries, and it is often to their milk that these terms apply. Muslim civilisation was familiar with the milk of all kinds of beasts (see for example the work attributed to al-Suyūṭī [Sidi-Siouti], *Livre de la miséricorde*, Paris 1856, 19-21) and geographical literature refers to it at times (see e.g. Ibn Ḥawḳal, tr. Kramers and Wiet, ii, 364). Ibn Ḳutayba (*al-Ashriba*) knew that it was possible to ferment these milks, e.g. that of the camel, although it was the milk of the mare which was more popularly used for fermentation a few centuries later (koumiss [see KUMĪS] was often produced from fermented mare's milk, as was *kefir*, generally less potent; some varieties still exist today which are even given to children to drink). This came about through the influence of the peoples of Central Asia and those from the native lands of the Mamlūks; the latter also drank koumiss, in spite of the hot climate of Egypt [see KHAMR].

As has already been mentioned, curdling, or even salting, were effective means of preserving lactic drinks, in a period when refrigeration was still unknown, and in relatively hot regions. It is thus that a land may be renowned beyond its geographical borders for the quality of its lactic products (the Syro-Palestinian region, for example, is praised for its yoghourts, etc., in a humorous work on the gastronomic art which does not however include recipes: untitled B.L. ms., Add. 19.411, fols. 4b-5a). Moreover, it is thus that certain of these drinks are still known today, for example *laban* (originally *laban* means nothing more than "milk", but in certain dialects the distinction has arisen of *ḥalīb* = milk, *laban* = fully or partially curdled milk), *ayran*, among the Turks, and there is an Iranian equivalent, *dūgh*, sometimes a little more salted. Some ancient texts describe yoghourts (*yoghurt*) and give the recipes: *Kanz*, the above-mentioned Cambridge ms., fol. 132a, with instructions on how to dilute it with water, producing a drink which would resemble the above-mentioned *ayran*; al-Warrāḳ, *op. cit.*, fols. 54b-56a (see also fols. 28b-30a): types of milk and their treatment; the untitled ms. mentioned above, B.L. Add. 19.411, fol. 4b; curdled milk and various yoghourts, including that made from the milk of the buffalo. Ibn Rāzin al-Tīdjānī, ed. Ibn Shaḳrūn, *Faḍālat al-khiwān (La cuisine andalou marocaine au XIIIième siècle)*, Rabat 1981, 147: *rā'ib* (explained above).

In the course of the last two centuries, Egyptian scholars and physicians have developed a genre of polemical debate in favour of and against milk and its products: Alī al-Dabbāgh al-Ḥalabī, *Radʿ al-djāhil ʿan dhamm al-kishk wa 'l-ma'ākil*, ms. Taymūriyya, Adab 370 (replying to a treatise against certain lactic products); and Aḥmad al-Tābiʿī, *Fayḍ al-minan*, Cairo 1315 (replying to a treatise, *al-Wadjh al-ḥasan*, in favour of fish and against milk).

IV. *Literary and semiotic questions.*

In works of a moral and religious nature, milk is also a literary symbol (even a semiotic value) of the purity of Islam: it was chosen by the Prophet at the time of his nocturnal travels through the heavens (*isrā'* and *miʿrādj*), when he was offered water, wine, milk, etc. (on this and other symbolic senses attributed to milk, see Sadan, *op. cit.*; and, regarding the importance of milk in the eyes of the Prophet, see also Ibn Ḳayyim al-Djawziyya, *al-Ṭibb al-nabawī*, Beirut 1957, 299 ff.). For certain *mādjin* poets, wine characterises the sedentary life of Muslim society, especially that of ʿAbbāsid society (the relatively more affluent circles), while milk, of less worth in their eyes, characterises the pre-Islamic Arabs. This is not a case of true contradiction, but of two semiotic and literary levels. After all, this is not an objective notion (in fact, the ancient Arabs were not unaware of the existence of wine, but they did not drink it very very often) but one that arises from a variety of literary elements, showing, among other topics, the different roles that the pair "milk" and "wine" play as symbols in the various genres (see Sadan, *op. cit.*).

V. *Water as a drink.*

In spite of the afore-mentioned preference for milk over other drinks on the part of the Prophet, he is also credited with such remarks as "Water is the mother of all drinks", or "the master of all drinks" (on the importance of water in Muslim legal tradition, see also al-Kulīnī, *al-Kāfī*, vi, 380-1; Ibn Ḳayyim al-Djawziyya, *op. cit.*, 302 ff.; al-Urmawī, *Siyāsa*, ms. Köprülü 1200, fol. 164a; al-Madjlisī, *Biḥār*, xiv, 752-5).

Water was an element of prime importance in the life of the ancient Arabs, especially those who lived in desert regions (see E. Bräunlich, in *Islamica*, i, 41-76, 288-343, 454-528). The literature of medical traditions speaks of the importance of this element as a drink, and gives detailed accounts of its properties and different varieties (see e.g. Sidi-Siouti, *op. cit.*, 38). In fact, geographical and topographical conditions made it necessary for each region to be content with a given, and often unalterable, quality of water: water from wells (*ābār*), from canals, rivers, etc. [see MĀ'], a subject of frequent interest to Arab geographers (in particular the so-called "classical" ones of the 4th/10th century; al-Muḳaddasī, in his *Aḥsan al-taḳāsim*, often adds at the end of each description of a region a sub-chapter entitled *djumal shu'ūn hādhā 'l-iḳlīm* which contains, among other things, information concerning the different waters of the region, their qualities, etc.). Similarly, culinary literature (fols. 13a ff. of the *Kanz*, Cambridge ms., and cf. al-Ghuzūlī, *op. cit.*, ii, 74-7) also devotes special chapters to water, in its capacity as a drink. Well-organised systems of provision of water were rare, but not unknown in the mediaeval period (see e.g. R. B. Parker and R. Sabin, *A practical guide to Islamic monuments in Cairo*, 91). The water of certain rivers was often neither pure nor clean (al-Djāḥiẓ, *al-Bukhalā'*, ed. al-Ḥādjirī, 113, describes how sewage was dumped in one of the channels of the Tigris; see also E. Lévi-Provençal, *Trois traités hispaniques de ḥisba*, 33; idem, *Séville musulmane*, 70). The quality of drinking water often depended on the social condition of the consumer, in particular the money available to him to pay the water-bearer (*saḳḳā'*; see Lane, *op. cit.*, 327-31), but there were also receptacles, or even special constructions (*sabīl*, pl. *subul*, testifying to the generosity of the benefactors who built them) designed for the use of the general public. By such means, water was distributed to travellers or to the visitors of markets.

VI. *Water mixed with snow.*

The wealthy were not satisfied with ordinary water; they were not only prepared to pay more highly for water of good quality but they sought also to refrigerate it. In addition to porous jugs (which had the effect of lowering the temperature of water by a few degrees), it was possible, even at the height of summer (al-Sarī al-Raffāʾ, *op. cit.*, ii, 23) to buy snow, which was one of the most expensive products. The caliph al-Mahdī even ordered a supply of snow to be brought to him at the time of his pilgrimage (al-Ṭabarī, iii/1, 484). The vendors of snow (*thallādjūn*), in Baghdād for example, had their own storehouses which were filled with snow (often brought from afar: al-Shābushī, *al-Diyārāt*, Baghdād 1966, 88, in winter; al-Ḳalḳashandī, *Ṣubḥ*, *maḳāla* 10, ch. 3; al-Hānī, *al-Thaldj wa 'l-thallādjūn*, in *Ṣuwar ʿabbāsiyya*, Sidon-Beirut, n.d., 89-130; in his edition of al-Ṣābī, *Rusūm dār al-khilāfa*, M. ʿAwwād mentions (24, n. 7) that he has published two articles on this subject in *Ahl al-naft* (Beirut), xxxviii and xxxix [1954]; it may be—added that the afore-mentioned Oxford ms. of the *K. al-Ṭabkh* contains a chapter devoted to "water with snow", fol. 147b; cf. fol. 148b: water cooled simply by air; cf. Ḥ. Zayyāt, in *Machriq*, xli, 25). Water mixed with a small quantity of snow (*māʾ muthalladj*) was such a "rarity" that it was preferred to lemonade (A. Mez, *Renaissance*, 408). One of the doctors of law even went so far as to write a short treatise on the question of whether it was permitted occasionally to distribute water mixed with snow to less affluent people and to the poor (al-ʿAynī, *Aḥkām al-ʿināya*, Chester Beatty ms. 4400 (8), fols. 92a-95b). It is thus that social stratification and its problems are reflected in the domain of *mashrūbāt*. See the series *Le voyage en Égypte*, I.F.A.O., Cairo, *passim* (e.g. volume for 1587-8, tr. and annot. by U. Castel and N. and S. Sauneron, n.d., 257).

VII. *Fruit-flavoured water, juices and other fresh drinks.*

Typical examples of the great variety of drinks based on fruits (or pure juice, or mixtures of juice with spices and other ingredients) emerge clearly from books of culinary recipes, including, for example, the afore-mentioned Cambridge ms., fol. 107a (lemonades and a drink made from ginger). The afore-mentioned London ms., fol. 30a (lemonade, orangeade, drinks flavoured with sumac); see A. Huici Miranda, *Kitāb al-Ṭabīkh*, in *RIEIM*, vi (1961-2), 235-48 (and now B.N. ms. 7009, fols. 76a-81a; a variety of soft drinks, sugared and flavoured with fruits, flowers, vegetables, spices etc., e.g. jujubes, apples, lemons, tamarinds, pomegranates and violets); the afore-mentioned ms., fols. 152a-154a (one ch. on vegetal-based drinks, and another on fruit-based drinks). A luxury drink was often a combination of one of these kinds of mineral waters with, in addition, *fuḳḳaʿ* (see above) and a little snow (see above and al-Ghuzūlī, *op. cit.*, ii, 88-9). This may be compared with Mez, *loc. cit.*, and especially idem, *Abulkâsim*, Heidelberg 1902, 38, 39, mentioning the same drinks as early as the 4th/10th century (for example *māʾ laymūn* = lemonade, probably made from green lemons/limes; *māʾ ḥiṣrim* = verjuice drink which is described in a more detailed manner, with two recipes in the mss. mentioned above).

Since certain of these drinks were considered to be medicines or tonics, some of them may be encountered in medical literature, often in a chapter entitled *ashriba* "drinks" and there even exist independent medical treatises on this subject (see e.g. Sezgin, *GAS*, iii, index, s.v. *K. al-Ashriba*), but this topic is beyond the scope of the present article. However, some literary works show a fairly profound knowledge of the secrets of medicine (or of popular medicine), including for example al-Djāḥiẓ in his epistle concerning drinks; in another mediaeval literary work, written in colloquial or quasi-colloquial Arabic, a drink made from jujubes is found in the shop of a popular perfumer-pharmacist (Sadan, in *St. Isl.* [1982], 46); this may be compared with al-Saḳaṭī, ed. G. S. Colin and E. Lévi-Provençal, *Un manuel hispanique de ḥisba*, 46: *Sharāb al-ʿunnāb* (= drink made from jujubes sold in the streets in marketplaces). There is a certain continuity with a whole range of mediaeval drinks, extending into the contemporary period, where fresh or cold drinks are still sold in the streets, often by itinerant traders (see Lane, *op. cit.*, 154-5, 331), such as, e.g., tamarind drink (*tamr hindī*, see above, and al-Saḳaṭī, *loc. cit.*) and liquorice drink (*sūs*), which are very popular; the drink made from dried grapes (*zebeeb* according to Lane, *loc. cit.*, *zabīb* or *zbīb* in colloquial speech), *djallāb* (which was known to the mediaeval world, see the above-mentioned Cambridge ms., fol. 133; al-Ghuzūlī, *loc. cit.*; Huici Miranda, *loc. cit.*). These recipes are not always based on dried grapes and the drink is most often non-alcoholic, but, even today, some devout Muslims abstain from consuming this drink made from dried grapes when it is prepared by non-Muslims, since it is feared that over-long soaking of the fruit produces alcohol. Also worthy of mention here is the *boza* of the Ottomans (whence *būza* in the Egyptian dialect, see Spiro, *Dictionary*, defining it as *bière*; but it is necessary to distinguish this term from *boza*, *būza* "ice cream" in some dialects of colloquial Arabic, which must rather be derived from Turkish *buz* "ice"). This may contain alcohol (see, the series *Le voyage en Égypte*, I.F.A.O., Cairo, *passim* (e.g. vol. for 1634-6, tr. and annot. by V. Volkoff, n.d., 255 and n. 157; *bouso*). But soft varieties of *boza/būza* are known (see E. G. Gobert, *Usages et rites alimentaires des Tunisiens*, in *Archives de l'Institut Pasteur de Tunis* [1904], 64; see also 43, 72, on other drinks such as *bsīsa*, for which see Beaussier, s.v. *bsīsa* and the other terms). The last-mentioned drinks recall the problem of the "permitted" and the "forbidden" explored in detail at the beginning of the present article (e.g. the *naḳīʿ*, mentioned above).

In this context of continuity, we may also compare the *sūbiyya* of the ancient texts (afore-mentioned Cambridge ms., fols. 112a-113a, and afore-mentioned London ms. *al-Wuṣla*, fol. 26b, although the references here are to a fairly thick liquid) with the *soobiya* described by Lane, *op. cit.*, in the 19th century (a similar drink, prepared from the pips of melons, is also described by R. Khawam, *La cuisine arabe*, 172: *boûzoûrate*).

VIII. *Hot drinks.*

As regards hot drinks, see the arts. ḲAHWA "coffee" (see also on this, R. J. Hattox, *Coffee and Coffeehouses*, Washington D.C. 1985) and SHĀY "tea", but besides these two drinks, the lands of the Near East are familiar with a wide variety of infusions of flowers, leaves, etc.

Bibliography: In addition to the references given in the article: F. A. ʿUkkāz, *al-Khamr fi 'l-fiḳh al-islāmī*, Djudda 1982; Faradj Zahrān, *al-Muskirāt, aḍrāruhā wa-aḥkāmuhā*, Cairo 1983; Aḥmad ʿA. Ṭ. Rayyān, *al-Muskirāt, āthāruhā wa-ʿilādjuhā*, Cairo 1984; Ṣāliḥ Āl Manṣūr, *Mawḳif al-islām min al-khamr*, Cairo 1985; ʿIzzat Ḥasanayn, *al-Muskirāt al-mukhaddirāt*, Cairo 1986. (J. SADAN)

MASHRŪṬIYYA [see DUSTŪR].

MASHWARA (A.) or MASHŪRA, a common term for consultation, in particular by the ruler of his advisers, the latter being various defined. The term sometimes also appears to mean some kind of deliberative gathering or assembly.

The practice of consultative decision was known in pre-Islamic Arabia [see MADJLIS, and MALAʾ in Suppl). Two passages in the Ḳurʾān (III, 153/159, *wa-shāwirhum fī 'l-amr* and XLII, 36/38, *wa-amruhum shūrā baynahum*) are commonly cited as imposing a duty of consultation on rulers. The merits of consultation (*mushāwara* and *mashwara*) and the corresponding defects of arbitrary personal rule (*istibdād*) are supported by a considerable body of material both in *ḥadīth* and *adab* (on *ḥadīth*, see Wensinck, *Concordance*, iii, 212; for examples of *adab*, see Ibn Ḳutayba, *ʿUyūn*, i, 27-36; Ibn ʿAbd Rabbihi, *ʿIḳd*, Cairo 1953, i, 46-8). Similar recommendations are made by the Ḳurʾān commentators (e.g. al-Zamakhsharī, *Kashshāf*, Cairo 1373/1953, i. 322-3, iv, 179; i, 226; al-Rāzī, *Mafātīḥ al-ghayb*, iii, 120). The desirability of consultation by rulers becomes a commonplace in Islamic political literature. It is urged by representatives of the scribal and bureaucratic tradition (see for examples ʿAbd al-Ḥamīd, *Risāla ... fī naṣīḥat walī al-ʿahd*, in Muḥammad Kurd ʿAlī, ed., *Rasāʾil al-bulaghāʾ*, Cairo 1374/1953, 185; Ibn al-Muḳaffaʿ, *Ḥikam*, in *ibid.*, 155; Niẓām al-Mulk, *Siyāsat-nāma*, ch. 18, "On having consultation with learned and experienced men", ed. Ch. Schefer, Paris 1891, 84-5; French tr. idem, Paris 1893, 124-6; Eng. tr. H. Darke, London 1960, 195-6; etc.).

In general, bureaucrats urge the need to consult bureaucrats, while *ʿulamāʾ* lay greater stress on the importance of consulting the *ʿulamāʾ*. Ibn Taymiyya (*Minhādj al-sunna*, Būlāḳ 1321, ii, 86; idem, *al-Siyāsa al-sharʿiyya*, Cairo 1961, 161-4, French tr. H. Laoust, *Le traité de droit public d'Ibn Taimīya*, Beirut 1948, 168-9) goes further than most of his colleagues. Citing Ḳurʾān and *ḥadīth*, he insists that the ruler must consult not only with the *ʿulāmāʾ* and with his political and military officials, but also with spokesmen of the general population.

In the early Islamic centuries there seems to have been no formal procedure of consultation. As Gibb remarks: "There is, in fact, nothing in the texts to justify the suggestion that ʿUmar's consultation was more than informal, or that there was at Medina any recognized consultative committee, still less a cabinet" (H. A. R. Gibb, in *Law in the Middle East*, ed. Majid Khadduri and H. J. Liebesny, Washington D.C. 1955, 16). The nearest approach to a consultative body was the famous committee appointed by the caliph ʿUmar on his deathbed, with the function of choosing one of their own number as his successor [see SHŪRĀ]. The Umayyad caliphs, at least the earlier ones, do however seem to have continued the old Arabian practice of consultation with the elders of the tribes [see WUFŪD]. The increasingly authoritarian character of government after the accession of the ʿAbbāsids is vividly expressed in a passage quoted by many authors. Sudayf, a *mawlā* of the Hāshimīs, is quoted as complaining of the changes resulting from the ʿAbbāsid accession: "By God, our booty, which was shared, has become a perquisite of the rich; our leadership, which was consultative (*mashwara*), has become arbitrary; our succession, which was by the choice of the community, is now by inheritance ..." (Ibn Ḳutayba, *ʿUyūn*, ii, 115; Eng. tr. in Lewis, *Islam*, ii, 54-55; cf. *ʿIḳd*, iii, 32; *Aghānī*, xiv, 162; Ibn ʿAsākir, vi, 68; Ibn Ḳutayba, *Shiʿr*, 419; etc.).

The mediaeval literary tradition, though generally in favour of consultation, is not uniformly so. Some texts indeed, without formally condemning consultation, indicate that in excess it may lead to anarchy and destruction. Thus the traveller Ibn Faḍlān, describing the system of government of the Volga Bulgars whom he visited in 309/921, remarks that their form of government was consultative (quoting the Ḳurʾānic verse *wa-amruhum shūrā baynahum*) and goes on to remark that whenever they agree among themselves to do anything, their decision is nullified by the meanest and lowest among them (Ibn Faḍlān, *Riḥla*, ed. Sāmī Dahhān, Damascus 1379/1959, 91-2, French tr. M. Canard, *AIEO*, xvi [1958], 68). An equally harsh judgment on democracy in action is given by al-Ḳalḳashandī, *Ṣubḥ*, viii, 30, who, in speaking of the city of Sīs in Asia Minor, notes that "authority became consultative, the populace became anarchic, the fortifications fell into disrepair" and the city thus fell prey to Christian conquest. Consultation as usually interpreted meant that the ruler before reaching a decision should discuss matters with competent and experienced persons and not act in an arbitrary fashion on his own. It did not mean that he should set up any consultative body, still less share authority with it.

The existence of such bodies is first attested in the period following the Mongol conquest, and may be a reflection of Mongol practice in east Asia. The Ilkhāns in Iran seem to have adopted the practice of covening a great council of high dignitaries (*Dīwān-i Buzurg*), presided over by the Vizier. Regular meetings of a council are attested under the Ṣafawid Shahs, by both Persian and western sources [see DĪWĀN. iv]. The name Djānḳī, applied to this council, indicates a Mongol origin (see V. Minorsky, *Tadhkira*, 44, 53, 113 n. 5, 120; G. Doerfer, *Türkische und Mongolische Elemente im Neupersischen*, i, Wiesbaden 1963, 280-2; H. H. Zarinezade, *Fars dillinde Azerbaydjan sözleri*, Baku 1962, 248-50).

The Ottoman historian, Kemālpashazāde, in discussing the eastern campaigns of the Ottoman sultan Meḥemmed II, describes the holding of such a council in Persia. When the Persian monarch received a spy's report that the Ottoman sultan was moving eastward, he convened a meeting of "the dignitaries of his state and the notables of his realm and consulted with them (*erkān-i dewletini we aʿyān-i memleketini bir yere dirüb onlarīnla meshweret etdi*)", Ibn Kemāl, *Tewārīkh-i āl-i ʿOthmān*, vii, *Defter*, ed. Ş. Turan, Ankara 1957, 544).

In Egypt, under the Baḥrī Mamlūks there appears to have existed a supreme council of high ranking *amīrs*. The members of this council were variously known as *Amīr Mashwara* and *Mushīr al-Dawla*. Its head was called *Raʾīs al-Mashwara*. References to appointments to this council and to its meetings are of frequent occurrence in the Mamlūk chronicles for the Baḥrī period (see D. Ayalon, *Studies on the structure of the Mamluk army. III*, in *BSOAS*, xv [1954], 69; E. Tyan, *Institutions de droit public musulman*, ii, Paris-Beirut 1956, 171-81; Björkman, *Beiträge*, 153; al-Ḳalḳashandī, *Ṣubḥ*, vi, 28, xi, 153-6; al-Maḳrīzī, *Sulūk*, ii, 64, 85-6, 182, 485, 551, 626, 634, 645, 746, 890, with an editorial note; idem, *Khiṭaṭ*, ed. Bulāḳ, ii, 64; Abu 'l-Maḥāsin, *Nudjūm*, ed. Cairo, x, 190; see further MUSHĪR). Under the Circassian Mamlūks, references to this council become extremely rare.

According to an Ottoman historical tradition, the very foundation of the Ottoman dynasty and state was due to a deliberative act. According to this version, the Beys and Ketkhudās of that region met together and held a *mashwara*. After much discussion they came to ʿOthmān Bey and asked him to become their chief

(Luṭfī, *Taʾrīk͟h*, 21; Yazīd͟jīog͟hlu ʿAlī, *Seld͟jūḳ-nāme*, cited in Agah Sırrı Levend, *Turk dilinde gelişme ve sadeleşme safhaları*, Ankara 1949, 34). Ottoman authors, like other Islamic authors, urged the importance of consultation by the ruler, and in the Ottoman empire such was indeed the practice. The high council (*dīwān-i hümāyūn* [*q.v.*]) was an important part of the Ottoman governmental system. Presided over in earlier times by the Sultan, in later times by the Grand Vizier, it had a prescribed membership and prescribed times of meeting. The term *mas͟hwara* (Ottoman *mes͟hweret*) is used commonly by the Ottoman historians to denote ad hoc meetings and councils of military and other dignitaries to consider problems as they arose. Such *mes͟hwerets* were already held in the course of the wars in Europe in the 15th century (see for example Kemālpas͟hazāde, 127). References to such meetings are common in the Ottoman chronicles in the 16th, 17th and 18th centuries. Naʿīmā offers many accounts of military *mes͟hwerets* held in the field by the commanders as well as of civilian gatherings held in Istanbul by official dignitaries. The Sultan was not normally present at such gatherings (see for example Naʿīmā, i, 131, 146, 155, 180, 273, 413, ii, 354, 360, iii, 54, iv, 298, 413, v, 60, 203, 281-3). Towards the end of the 18th century such gatherings become more frequent, particularly in the periods of crisis associated with the Russian and other wars, and were sometimes held in the presence of the Sultan (examples in Wāṣif, i, 316-18, 221, 222, 274; D͟jewdet, ii, 276 ff., iv, 289). A new phase began with the accession of Sultan Selīm III who, at the start of his reign, on 20 S͟haʿbān 1203/16 May 1789, convened a consultative asembly (*mes͟hweret*) of leading officials to discuss the problems of the Empire and the way to remedy them. Such gatherings were often held under Selīm III and his successors. The early 19th century historian S͟hānīzāde [*q.v.*] makes frequent reference to such gatherings and ascribes to them a representative character and significance not mentioned by previous authors (S͟hānīzāde, i, 66, 73-5, 199-201, 365, iv, 2-5, 201, 37 ff., 155-8, etc.). For a full treatment of these informal consultative assemblies, see MAD͟JLIS AL-S͟HŪRĀ.

S͟hānīzāde's account marks the transition from a purely traditional Islamic interpretation of *mas͟hwara* to a new approach influenced by the practice of European states, to which indeed he alludes under the polite euphemism *düwel-i muntaẓame* "well-organised states". He may have been thinking of the British parliament, a description of which, by the young Ottoman diplomatist Maḥmūd Raʾīf was available to him in Istanbul. S͟hānīzāde notes that the holding of such *mes͟hwerets* was common in these states, where they served a useful purpose. At the same time, he was naturally concerned to justify the holding of such meetings with both Islamic and Ottoman precedents [see further ḤURRIYYA. ii].

Perhaps the earliest use of the term in a clearly western context occurs in the Turkish translation of the first volume of Carlo Botta's *History of Italy from 1789 to 1814*, first printed in Cairo as *Bonapart taʾrīk͟hi* in 1249/1833. This speaks of the *parlamento mes͟hwereti* established by the liberals in that country.

In the course of the 19th century, the term *mas͟hwara* or *mes͟hweret* was much used by Turkish and Arabic authors, first to describe European representative institutions, and then to justify their introduction into the Islamic lands. Thus the Egyptian *s͟hayk͟h* Rifāʿa Rāfiʿ al-Ṭahṭāwī, discussing the functioning of French parliamentary institutions, makes common use of the term *mas͟hwara* to describe the various consultative bodies (*Tak͟hlīṣ al-ibrīz fī talk͟hīṣ Bārīz*, ed. Mahdī ʿAllām *et alii*, Cairo n.d., ch. 3, 138-43). This important book was published in a Turkish translation as well as in the original Arabic and provided the first detailed and documented description, in these languages, of constitutional and representative government. The term was adopted by the young Ottoman liberal patriots of the mid-century [see YEÑI ʿOT͟HMĀNLİLAR] and was much used in their writings. By 1876 it was sufficiently well-accepted in Ottoman usage to figure in the Sultan's speech from the throne at the opening of the first Ottoman parliament (*Ḳāʿide-yi Mes͟hweret*, in *Ḍabīṭlar D͟jerīdesi*, 10), and in 1909 the speech from the throne even speaks of constitutional and consultative government (*Mes͟hrūṭiyyet we-mes͟hweret*), "as prescribed by the holy law as well as by both reason and tradition" (*Taṣwīr-i efkār* of 15 November 1909).

Bibliography: Given in the text. In general, see L. Gardet, *La cité musulmane*, Paris 1954, 172-5; H. Laoust, *Essai sur les doctrines sociales et politiques de Taḳī-d-dīn Aḥmad b. Taimīya*, Cairo 1939, 301-2; Muḥammad Ḍiyāʾ al-Dīn al-Rayyis, *al-Naẓariyyāt al-siyāsiyya al-islāmiyya*, Cairo 1952, 224-8. See also MAD͟JLIS. 4. A. In the Middle East and North Africa, sections i-ii, and MAD͟JLIS AL-S͟HŪRĀ, the latter with full bibliography. (B. LEWIS)

MAS͟HYAK͟HA or *mas͟hīk͟ha*, one of several plural forms of A. *s͟hayk͟h*, literally "an elder, i.e. a distinguished person usually of an advanced age [*q.v.*]. In its classical usage, *mas͟hyak͟ha* also served as an abstract noun denoting a *s͟hayk͟h*'s position or authority (e.g. in *mas͟hyak͟hat al-Islām*, the authority of the *s͟hayk͟h al-Islām* [*q.v.*]).

In the Muslim West *mas͟hyak͟ha* was used to designate the collectivity of urban elders and notables often wielding considerable political influence in the cities. Such groups of dignitaries sometimes acted as virtual advisory councils of local rulers, hence *mas͟hyak͟ha* also carried the sense of "a municipal council". This was so in Muslim Spain (D. Wasserstein, *The rise and fall of the Party-Kings*, Princeton 1985, 142-45) and, according to clues offered by Ibn K͟haldūn, in North Africa as well (ref. in Dozy, *Suppl.*, s.v. *s͟hayk͟h*; *Muḳaddima*, ed. Quatremère, ii, 269; tr. Rosenthal, ii, 305).

During Bonaparte's Egyptian expedition, the word acquired a new meaning. Seeking an Arabic expression for "republic", Bonaparte's orientalist experts came to use *mas͟hyak͟ha*. This was apparently an intended allusion to the Directoire of five who were governing France at the time; endeavouring to simplify an idea novel to their audience, the translators chose to refer to the persons making up the governing body ("the elders") rather than to the abstract principle underlying it. The French administration employed the term extensively in its proclamations to the Egyptians—issued "on behalf of al-*mas͟hyak͟ha al-faransawiyya*"—using it interchangeably with *d͟jumhūr*, the common Ottoman word for the notion [see D͟JUMHŪRIYYA]. *Mas͟hyak͟ha* then became a popular name for "republic" in Arabic writings as well, in which it was considerably more common during the first half of the 19th century than either *d͟jumhūr* or *d͟jumhūriyya*; the latter term was introduced by al-Ṭahṭāwī [*q.v.*] in the 1830s.

The choice of a word with established connotations to express a new idea was bound to produce some confusion. Certain writers of Arabic thus understood "republic" to mean "government by elders", erroneously identifying the foreign notion with a more familiar concept (e.g. Niḳūlā Turk, *Mud͟hakkirāt*.

Cairo 1950, 3, 97, 98; Rifāʿa Rāfiʿ al-Ṭahṭāwī. *Ḳalāʾid al-mafākhir*, Būlāḳ 1833, i, 52, ii, 104). In addition, the simultaneous application of the word, by similar logic, to other notions—such as *al-mashyakha al-baladiyya* ("city council"), *mashyakhat al-bilād* ("the country's government"), *mashyadhat Bārīz* ("the Paris Commune") etc.—further attested to the vagueness of the term and, perhaps, of some of the concepts it was chosen to express.

In the second half of the 19th century, *mashyakha* in the sense of republic gradually gave ground to *djumhūriyya*, although some writers continued to vindicate the older usage until the 1870s. Thereafter, *mashyakha* lost this meaning, retaining only the loose import of an institution of elders at large or a sheikhdom.

Bibliography: For the classical usage, see Lane, *Lexicon*, s.v.; Ḳalḳashandī, *Ṣubḥ al-aʿshā*, s.v. in index (ed. Muḥammad Ḳandīl al-Baḳlī), 425. For its use in French proclamations, see examples in Aḥmad Ḥusayn al-Ṣāwī, *Fadjr al-ṣiḥāfa fī Miṣr*, Cairo 1975, pls. 43, 48, 49, 70, 79, 87A, 90-7. See further A. Ayalon, *Language and change in the Arab Middle East*, Oxford 1987, ch. vii.

(A. AYALON)

AL-**MASĪḤ**, the Messiah; in Arabic (where the root *m-s-ḥ* has the meanings of "to measure" and "to wipe, stroke") it is a loanword from the Aramaic, where *meshīḥā* was used as a name of the Redeemer.

Horovitz (*Koranische Untersuchungen*, 129) considers the possibility that it was taken over from the Ethiopic (*masīḥ*). Muḥammad of course got the word from the Christian Arabs, amongst whom the personal name ʿAbd al-Masīḥ was known in pre-Islamic times, but it is doubtful whether he knew the true meaning of the term (see K. Ahrens, *Christliches im Qoran, eine Nachlese*, in *ZDMG*, lxxxiv [1930], 24-5; A. Jeffery, *The foreign vocabulary of the Qur'ān*, Baroda 1938, 265-6). In Arab writers we find the view mentioned that the word is a loanword from Hebrew or Syriac. Al-Ṭabarī (*Tafsīr* on sūra III, 40 = iii, 169) gives only purely Arabic etymologies, either with the meaning "purified" (from sins) or "filled with blessing". Horovitz, *op. cit.*, calls attention to the occurrence of the word in inscriptions, proper names and in the old poetry.

In the Ḳurʾān, the word is first found in the Mecca sūras: (a) alone: sūra, IV, 170, IX, 30; (b) with Ibn Maryam; sūra, V, 19, 76, 79; IX, 31; (c) with ʿĪsā b. Maryam: sūra III, 40; IV, 156. None of these passages make it clear what Muḥammad understood by the word. From sūra III, 40: "O Maryam, see, Allah promises thee a word from Him, whose name is al-Masīḥ ʿĪsā b. Maryam", one might suppose that al-Masīḥ was here to be taken as a proper name. Against this view, however, is the fact the the article is not found with non-Arabic proper names in the Ḳurʾān. One can assume with reasonable certainty that al-Masīḥ is a title of Jesus in the Ḳurʾān, but not a messianic one; clearly, no eschatological interpretation of Christ's mission could have been known in Arabia (see J. S. Trimingham, *Christianity among the Arabs in pre-Islamic times*, London 1979, 267).

In canonical Ḥadīth al-Masīḥ is found in three main connections: (a) in Muḥammad's dream, in which he relates how he saw at the Kaʿba a very handsome brown-complexioned man with beautiful locks, dripping with water, who walked supported by two men; to his question who this was, the reply was given, "al-Masīḥ b. Maryam" (al-Bukhārī, *Libās*, *bāb* 68; *Taʿbīr*, *bāb* 11; Muslim, *Īmān*, trad. 302); (b) in the descriptions of the return of ʿĪsā [*q.v.*]; (c) at the Last Judgment, the Christians will be told; "What have you worshipped?". They will reply, "We have worshipped al-Masīḥ, the Son of God". For this they shall wallow in Hell (al-Bukhārī, *Tafsīr*, sūra IV, *bāb* 8; *Tawḥīd*, *bāb* 24; Muslim, *Īmām*, trad. 302).

In Ḥadīth also, we frequently find references to al-Masīḥ al-Kadhdjāl; see AL-DADJDJĀL.

Bibliography: In addition to references given in the article, see T. P. Hughes, *A dictionary of Islam*, 328; O. H. Schumann, *Der Christus der Muslime: Christologische Aspekte in der arabisch-islamischen Literatur*, Gütersloh 1975; D. Wismer, *The Islamic Jesus: an annotated bibliography of sources in English and French*, New York 1977; G. Schedl, *Muhammad und Jesus, die christologische relevante Texte des Koran, neu übersetzt und erklärt*, Vienna 1978; R. Arnaldez, *Jésus fils de Marie, prophète de l'Islam.* Paris 1980; Abdelmajid Charfi, *Christianity in the Qur'an commentary of Tabari*, in *Islamochristiana*, vi (1980), 105-48; and the *Bibls.* to ʿĪSĀ and MARYAM.

(A. J. WENSINCK - [C. E. BOSWORTH])

AL-**MASĪḤĪ** AL-DJURDJĀNĪ, ʿĪsā b. Yaḥyā Abū Sahl, Christian physician born in Djurdjān, and one of the teachers of Ibn Sīnā, who dedicated some of his works to him.

He studied in Baghdād, and then taught in Khurāsān and later in Khʷārazm. He had no social intercourse with his coreligionists, but performed religious worship alone in his house (al-Bayhaḳī, *Taʾrīkh*, 95). In 401/1010, together with a number of other scholars who had settled in Khʷārazm—among them al-Bīrūnī—, he was summoned by al-Maḥmūd of Ghazna [*q.v.*] to this city under the suspicion of heresy. In the company of Ibn Sīnā he succeeded in fleeing to Māzandarān, but met his death in a sandstorm. So far, none of his works, in large part preserved, has been edited. The most important, existing in numerous manuscripts, is the *K. al-Miʾa* ("hundred [treatises]"), a comprehensive medical encyclopaedia, arranged in a hundred sections, probably the oldest work of its kind and perhaps the model for Ibn Sīnā's *Ḳānūn*. An edition of this work is most desirable. A very much smaller work, the *K. al-Ṭibb al-kullī*, gives in 39 chapters an introduction to the general fundamentals of medicine. The third work to be mentioned here is the *K. Iẓhār ḥikmat Allāh taʿālā fī khalḳ al-insān*, dealing with the physiology of the human organs and their meaning and purpose as intended by God. Ibn Abī Uṣaybiʿa (i, 328,2) says explicitly that this work is based on Galen's [see DJĀLĪNŪS] *K. fī manāfiʿ al-aʿḍāʾ* περὶ χρείας μορίων, see G. Bergsträsser, *Ḥunain ibn Isḥāq über die syrischen und arabischen Galen-Übersetzungen* (AKM, xvii/2), no. 49. Already the title of al-Masīḥī work reflects Galen's teleological way of thinking: in the latter's work just mentioned, the single chapters deal with "God's wisdom with regard to the perfect creation of the hands" and of the other organs (see Bergsträsser, *loc. cit.*). Al-Masīḥī indeed was "a philosopher for whom medicine was dominant" (*ḥakīm istawlā ʿalayhi 'l-ṭibb*, al-Bayhaḳī, 95); with some exaggeration, Niẓāmī ʿArūḍī even calls him, together with Ibn Sīnā, "successor of Aristotle in philosophy, which includes all sciences" (*Čahār maḳāla*, 118, 8-9). His special investigations, which are smaller in extent, deal with smallpox, the pulse, and also with matters of geometry, psychology and the interpretation of dreams, and contain also an extract from the *K. al-Midjisṭī*. A work on the plague he dedicated to his patron, the Khʷārazmshāh Abu 'l-ʿAbbās Maʾmūn b. Maʾmūn.

Al-Masīḥī's knowledge of theoretical and practical

medicine, his lucid terminology and the clear composition of his writings are generally praised. The *K. al-Miʾa*, in particular, has been commented upon and recommended to posterity by prominent experts like Amīn al-Dawla Ibn al-Tilmīḏh. Only one single voice—but then a powerful one—is of an opposite opinion: al-Madjūsī gave a harsh verdict on the *K. al-Miʾa*, and in particular denounced the arrangement of the book, unsystematical in his eyes (al-Madjūsī, *Kāmil al-ṣināʿa al-ṭibbiyya*, Būlāḳ 1294/1877, i, 4, 29-33).

Bibliography: Niẓāmī ʿArūḍī, *Čahār maḳāla*, ed. M. Ḳazwīnī and M. Muʿīn, Tehran 1955-7, 118,11-121,1, and the *Taʿlīḳāt*, 415-17, 423-5 (with a divergent version on al-Masīḥī's death); Bayhaḳī, *Taʾrīkh ḥukamāʾ al-Islām*, ed. M. Kurd ʿAlī, Damascus 1365/1946, 95-7; Ibn al-Ḳifṭī, *Ḥukamāʾ*, ed. J. Lippert, 408-16-409,2; Ibn Abī Uṣaybiʿa, *ʿUyūn al-anbāʾ*, ed. A. Müller, i, 327,30-328,29; Ibn al-ʿIbrī (Barhebraeus), *Taʾrīkh mukhtaṣar al-duwal*, ed. Ṣāliḥānī, 330,9-11; L. Leclerc, *Histoire de la médecine arabe*, Paris 1876, i, 356 f.; Brockelmann, *GAL*², I, 273 f., S I 423 f.; Graf, *GCAL*, ii, 257 f.; A. Dietrich, *Medicinalia Arabica*, Göttingen 1966, 69-73; M. Ullmann, *Die Medizin im Islam*, Leiden-Cologne 1970, 151; idem, *Die Natur- und Geheimwissenschaften im Islam*, Leiden 1972, 26; Sezgin, *GAS*, iii, 326 f., v, 336 f.; Ghada al-Karmī, *A mediaeval compendium of Arabic medicine: Abū Sahl al-Masīḥī's "Book of the hundred"*, in *Jnal. Hist. Arabic Science*, ii (Aleppo 1978), 270-90 (detailed summary).

(A. Dietrich)

MASĪLA (current orthography M'sila), a town in Algeria founded by the Fāṭimids in 315/927 on the northern edge of the depression of Ḥodna as an outpost of their rule in the Zāb. This remote province of their domain was in fact to play, from the foundation of their caliphate, the role of a military frontier to the west of Ifrīḳiya. As with his predecessors, the Aghlabid *amīrs*, the primary task of the first Fāṭimid sovereign, al-Mahdī ʿUbayd Allāh [*q.v.*], in ensuring the defence of the western side of the realm consisted in raising a powerful barrier on the desert route leading towards al-Ḳayrawān: this entailed the blocking of the natural course of penetration which followed, at the southern limit of Numidia, the defile of al-Ḳanṭara known as "mouth of the Sahara" (*fam al-Ṣaḥrāʾ*) and proceeded to the north-east by way of Wadi Miskyana and Wadi Mellegue, thus offering to the desert tribes access to the wealthy provinces of Ifrīḳiya.

As early as the ancient period, in Roman and subsequently Byzantine Africa, a line of fortresses (*limes*), including the powerful stronghold of Lambesus (Lambaesis), sealed this gateway to the Sahara at the western limit of the Zāb, where the renowned Third Augustan Legion was stationed on desert guard for a considerable period of time.

Intended as a military base, Masīla was founded not far from the ancient Zabi, to the west of Lambaesis, inheriting from the latter the rôle of giving protection against the Berber tribes always eager to pillage the prosperous Ifrīḳiyan regions, sc. the Birzāl, Muzāta, Kamlān and other Huwwāra clans. The threat that they posed became still more serious since the Ifrīḳiyan realm had come just under the control of the Shīʿī ʿAlids, who were just as accursed, from the point of view of the Khāridjī doctrines which the tribes professed, as were the Sunnī Aghlabids. Furthermore, the "auxiliaries" of these new masters of the coveted land of Ifrīḳiya were none other than the Kutāma, long-standing enemies of the Zanāta clan of which they had taken advantage.

It was thus with the object of holding these hostile tribes in check that the presumptive heir of al-Mahdī, Abu 'l-Ḳāsim Muḥammad, the future al-Ḳāʾim bi-Amr Allāh [*q.v.*], took the decision to found Masīla at the time of the expedition which he conducted in the Zāb and then in the region of Tāhart in 315/927-8, on territory occupied by the most troublesome tribe, that of the Kamlān. He entrusted the task to his officer ʿAlī b. Ḥamdūn, ordering him to station himself there with his troops, ʿAdjīsa elements and slaves, and instructing the Kamlān to join with his army before going to establish themselves in the region of al-Mahdiyya on the route leading to al-Ḳayrawān. Called Muḥammadiyya after its founder, the new town was soon to bear the name of Masīla on account of its position on the edge of a water-course, the Wādī Ṣahr, currently the Wādī Ksob.

It soon supplanted Ṭobna as regional capital of the Zāb and became, under the rule of Ibn Ḥamdūn, in addition to its importance as a military base, a prosperous city and the seat of a powerful principality within the Fāṭimid realm. The father of ʿAlī, Ḥamdūn, also known as Abū ʿAbd Allāh al-Andalusī, scion of a Djudhāmī family of Yemen, had counted among the most valued Arab "auxiliaries" (*awliyāʾ*) of the Fāṭimid cause, those who had been loyal from the outset. Sent to the canton of Elvira in Muslim Spain and then to the region of Bougie, he had been one of the disciples of al-Ḥulwānī, the first Shīʿī missionary in Ifrīḳiya, before becoming a loyal companion of Abū ʿAbd Allāh al-Shīʿī [*q.v.*] at Ikdjān where he died, apparently before the fall of the Aghlabids. As for ʿAlī, he joined al-Mahdī at Sidjilmāssa before entering his service at Raḳḳāda in 297/910, barely a year after the conquest of Ifrīḳiya by Abū ʿAbd Allāh. He rapidly distinguished himself in the entourage of the sovereign, along with other Yemenis, notably the Kalbīs, acting as a counterweight to rebellious Kutāmī elements and to certain elements of the Muḍarī Arab aristocracy who had remained loyal to the Aghlabids.

But it was with the foundation of Masīla that he reinforced his rôle in supporting the cause of his Fāṭimid masters. Surrounded by a fortified wall, the new town was soon to be endowed with a second perimeter wall and its defences were strengthened by a canal dug between the two walls and fed by the river, in such a way as to provide water for the needs of the population and for irrigation. This permitted the development of extensive plantations of fruit, as well as fertile ground for the growth of cereals and a prosperous stock-breeding sector. These agricultural resources were supplemented by the produce of flourishing trade favoured by the town's position at the crossroads of the mercantile routes linking Ifrīḳiya to western Barbary. Varied victuals and provisions supplied vast reserves for the purpose of feeding troops in the course of punitive expeditions against the rebel tribes.

Thus during the revolt of Abū Yazīd [*q.v.*], Masīla played its rôle of a base for operations effectively. When the Khāridjī rebel arrived at the gates of al-Mahdiyya, ʿAlī b. Ḥamdūn attempted to take the enemy from the rear and to unite his forces with those of Ibn al-Kalbī who had left Tunis to come to the aid of besieged Mahdiyya. But he was defeated by the son of Abū Yazid, Ayyūb, on the banks of the Medjerda and perished in Rabīʿ I-II 334/November 945. His son Djaʿfar, brought up at the court of Mahdiyya with his brother Yaḥyā, and foster-brother of the *amīr* Maʿadd, the future al-Muʿizz li-Dīn Allāh, succeeded him in command at Masīla. Subsequently, when, defeated before al-Ḳayrawān, Abū Yazīd was obliged to fall back towards Ḥoḍna and to entrench himself in the mountains of Koyāna, it was from Masīla that the Fāṭimid Ismāʿīl al-Manṣūr [*q.v.*] conducted the campaign against the rebels and ultimately crushed them in Muḥarram 336/August 947.

Henceforward, Masīla became, in addition to its strategic rôle, one of the most important provincial capitals of the realm and underwent rapid development, while, in the mountain range of Titteri, the *amīr* of the powerful neighbouring Ṣanhādja, Zīrī b. Manād, founded Ashīr, an impregnable fortress intended to reinforce Fāṭimid control over the troublesome Zanāta. Masīla inspired its foundation and assisted its development.

Bordered, on the one hand, by Zanāta hostile to the Fāṭimids, on the other, by Ṣanhādja, who had recently become supporters of the ʿAlid cause on the side of the Kutāma, Djaʿfar began to rule, within the limits of his prerogative, as a veritable suzerain, thus acting in rivalry to Zīrī, and to raise Masīla to the status of a principality. Endowing it with castles and palaces and lavishing there large sums of money, he succeeded in making himself a conspicuous personality and even maintained a literary court frequented by numerous poets and scholars. The eminent Ibn Hānī [*q.v.*], who spent some time there and sang the praises of Djaʿfar and his family, did not hesitate, in lauding the Zāb, to compare it to ʿIrāḳ. Moreover, the administrative status accorded to Masīla by the Fāṭimid monarch, which endowed Djaʿfar with almost unlimited authority over his territory, was that of *istikfāʾ*, which conferred upon the governor of a province the right to exercise, like a viceroy, full powers and thus to maintain a high degree of military, judicial, financial and religious control. Djaʿfar was enabled to administer his territory "with trustworthiness" (*bi 'l-amāna*) without first being obliged to pay a fixed sum to the State Treasury (*ḍamān*). The process of autonomous administration then being developed in the provincial organisation of the realm thus authorised him to deduct from the annual revenues of the Zāb, which were considerable, all his public expenses before paying only the surplus as tax. Such a favourable status did not fail to arouse jealousy in the Fāṭimid court against the all-powerful suzerain of Masīla. In addition, his disagreements with the chieftain of the Ṣanhādja, Buluggīn b. Zīrī, and his good-neighbourly relations with the Zanāta who were the implacable enemies of the Kutāma and of his sovereign, caused severe irritation to al-Muʿizz. The presence at the court of Masīla of Umayyad agents, and the sentiments of allegiance to the Andalusian monarchy flaunted by the Zanāta with the blessing of Djaʿfar, gravely worsened his relations with his sovereign. Not hesitating to defy his anger, Djaʿfar espoused the cause of the Zanāta in their contentions with his rival, the *amīr* of the Ṣanhādja, then embarked upon open rebellion against al-Muʿizz. Subsequently, he proclaimed his allegiance to the Umayyad al-Ḥakam II and made haste to abandon Masīla with his family, arriving at Cordova in 360/971.

With the defection of the Banū Ḥamdūn, Masīla began to lose its importance to the advantage of Ashīr, already its rival. The predominance of Ashīr was confirmed with the designation of Buluggīn as viceroy of al-Muʿizz in Barbary, when the latter finally left the region for Egypt, to which the seat of the caliphate was transferred.

Under the first Ṣanhādja dynasties, supremacy over the Zāb and its regional capital Masīla became the object of the struggle in which they were continually embroiled with one of the components of the Zanāta clan, the powerful tribe of the Maghrāwa commanded by Zīrī b. ʿAṭiyya. In the course of this struggle during the reign of Bādīs, distinction was achieved by his uncle Ḥammād who conceived the idea of founding, a score of kilometres to the northeast of Masīla, a new town, al-Ḳalʿa [see ḲALʿAT BANĪ ḤAMMĀD], destined to supplant the former in its role of provincial capital and military base capable of controlling the Zanāta tribes.

There then began for Masīla a long period of decline. Abandoned, to the advantage of its neighbour during the first half of the 5th/11th century, it conceded to it its status as the major city of the Zāb, where the Ḳalʿa became in its turn the seat of a principality founded by the powerful branch of the Ṣanhādja, the Banū Ḥammād. Then with the Hilālian invasion, the regions of the Zāb and of Ḥoḍna were, like Ifrīḳiya, devastated by nomadic Arab tribes, the Athbadj, Riyāḥ, Zughba and other elements of Sulaym. Masīla was ravaged, as was the Ḳalʿa. However, it outlived both the latter and Ashīr, which was laid to ruin under the empire of the Almohads, to the advantage of a new provincial capital, Bougie [see BIDJĀYA]. Then, despite the destruction caused by the Banū Ghāniya in revolt against the Almohads, it regained during the 6th/12th century a little of its lost glory in the wake of Bougie, with the renown of scholars such as Abū ʿAlī al-Masīlī or Aḥmad b. Ḥarb. But Masīla was to suffer again under the Ḥafṣids as a result of their struggles with the ʿAbd al-Wādids [*q.vv.*]. The Dāwūdiyya attempted in the meantime to assert their domination over the region. It regained for the last time some political importance and reputation with scholars such as Aḥmad al-Masīlī, a disciple of Ibn ʿArafa, and especially as a result of the rôle played there in the mid-8th/14th century by the renowned Ibn Khaldūn and his brother Yaḥyā in the service of the ʿAbd al-Wādid sultan Abū Ḥammū. Finally, with the ascendancy of nomadic Arab tribes over the Zāb and Ḥoḍna, during the 9th/15th century Masīla definitely lost its status as a major city, becoming nothing more than an undistinguished locality eking out a meagre existence through manufacturing and agriculture.

Bibliography: Besides the information supplied by the chroniclers and the writings of Arab geographers, especially those of Ibn Ḥawḳal and Bakrī used by G. Marçais in, notably, *Les Arabes en Berbérie du XIe au XIVe siècle*, Constantine-Paris 1913, see the accurate Fāṭimid documentation used by M. Canard, in *Une famille de partisans, puis d'adversaires des Fāṭimides en Afrique du Nord*, in *Mélanges G. Marçais*, ii, 33-49, and *Vie de l'ustadh Jawdhar*, Algiers 1958 (tr. of the *Sīra* of Djawdhar, ed. M. K. Ḥusayn and M. ʿAbd H. Shaʿira). See also F. Dachraoui, *Le califat fatimide au Maghreb*, Tunis 1981, and IBN HĀNĪ in *EI*²; M. Yalaoui, *Un poète chiʿite d'Occident au IVe/Xe siècle, Ibn Hâni al-Andalusî*, Tunis 1976. Also to be consulted is a general work, exhaustive but uneven, by P. Massiera, *M'Sila du Xe au XVe siècle*, reprinted in *CT*, xxii/85-6 (1974). (F. DACHRAOUI)

MAʾṢIR, a technical term of fiscal practice in the hydraulic civilisation of early Islamic ʿIrāḳ, doubtless going back to earlier periods there. It is defined by al-Khwārazmī in his *Mafātīḥ al-ʿulūm*, 70, as "a chain or cable which is fastened right across a river and which prevents boats from getting past", and more specifically by Ibn Rusta, 185, tr. Wiet, 213, as a barrier across the Tigris at Ḥawānīt near Dayr al-ʿĀḳūl [*q.v.*] consisting of a cable stretched between two ships at each side of the river, preventing ships passing by night (and thus evading the tolls levied by the official traffic and toll house regulators, *aṣḥāb al-sayyāra wa 'l-maʾāṣir*). The term has no obvious Arabic etymology from the root ʾ-ṣ-r, but may be connected with Akkadian *maṣāru* "to delimit, set a boundary", *muṣṣuru* "to fix a borderline", *maṣṣartu* "watchman, guard, watch house" (Von Soden, *Akkadisches Handwörterbuch*, ii, 619-21, 659; *Chicago Assyrian dictionary. Letter M*, x/1, 333 ff., x/2, 245).

From being a barrier across the river to halt shipping, it soon acquired the meaning of "customs house where tolls are collected" (for such tolls, see MAKS and MAʿŪNA), and then the actual tolls themselves. In the caliphate of al-Muʿtaḍid (279-89/892-902) one hears of a body of officials attached to the *shurṭa* [*q.v.*] or police guard of Baghdād, called *maʾāṣiriyyūn*, who collected tolls from river traffic on the Tigris.

Bibliography: Le Strange, *Lands*, 36; M. ʿAwwād, *al-Maʾāṣir fī bilād al-Rūm wa 'l-Islām*, Baghdād 1948; A. S. Ehrenkreutz, *Al-Būzajānī (A.D. 939-997) on the "Māʾṣīr"*, in *JESHO*, viii (1965), 90-2; C. E. Bosworth, *Abū ʿAbdallāh al-Khwārazmī on the secretary's art* ... in *JESHO*, xii (1969), 155. (C. E. BOSWORTH)

MAṢĪRA, an island to the north of a gulf of the same name, lying parallel to the eastern coast of Arabia, some 150 miles south-west of Raʾs al-Ḥadd. It is part of the Sultanate of Oman (ʿUmān). The irregular oblong island, which is composed almost entirely of igneous rocks, is some 40 miles in length and has a maximum breadth of nearly ten miles. Its total area is approximately 200 square miles, and Maṣīra is therefore the largest island in the Arabian Sea after Socotra (Sukuṭrā). A low mountain ridge traverses the island reaching a maximum height of 740 feet at Djabal Madhrūb (lat. 20° 34' N, long. 58° 53' E) in the north. The shallow channel which separates Maṣīra from the mainland of Arabia is from 8 to 12 miles wide, but the existence of a large number of shoals and coral outcrops makes it hazardous for all except local craft. From mid-December until March, the northeast monsoon adds to the dangers of navigation in this Strait.

The landscape of the island is largely barren and vegetation is scant, consisting of a few stunted trees, some shrubs and scattered tufts of grass. In the past this lack of grazing has greatly restricted the number of domesticated animals kept by the local people. In 1845 an Indian Navy survey party put the total number of inhabitants at about 1,000—the overwhelming majority of whom belonged to the Djanaba tribe [*q.v.*], while a smaller number were said to be Ḥikmān. Water supplies were then reported to be adequate. In 1957 de Gaury estimated the population to be just under 2,000. The climate is generally good; in May—the hottest month—the average maximum is 96° F., while in January—the coolest—the average minimum is 66° F.

The islanders have long derived their livelihood from the sea. Large numbers of turtles provided both food and tortoise shell for export; dried fish and shark fins were also traded for rice and dates from the mainland. The presence of sperm whales off the east coast of the island meant that lumps of valuable ambergris were sometimes washed ashore, and these too were exported. Lead and copper ores are known to exist on the island. Some apparently ancient smelting sites have been located, and it has been suggested that these may constitute evidence of an early Persian presence on Maṣīra.

The history of the island is, however, obscure, for clear and reliable documentary sources are few, and archaeological evidence is slight. Sprenger suggests that the classical geographers may have had some knowledge of the island under several different names. The author of the *Periplus of the Erythraean Sea* refers to it as the Island of Sarapis (Σαράπιδος νῆσοι); he also notes that the inhabitants ate fish and exported tortoise shell. The former fact was also observed by Ibn Baṭṭūta, who anchored off Maṣīra but did not land there. According to de Gaury, there are some vestigial ruins from the Portuguese period at Sūr Maṣīra in the west of the island.

Several foreign vessels are known to have foundered in the dangerous coastal waters, and some of the local tribes, who were extremely reluctant to acknowledge any external authority, indulged in wrecking and plundering as recently as the early years of the 20th century. (When the tribesmen did recognise such suzerainty, it was apparently that of the Shaykh of Ṣūr in ʿUmān). On 2 August 1904 a British vessel, the *Baron Inverdale*, went aground on the island of Djubayla in the Khūryān-Mūryān [*q.v.*] (Kuria-Muria) group. Some of the passengers and crew took to two boats, one of which was lost at sea. The other, carrying 17 people, landed on the northern shore of Maṣīra in mid-August. Those survivors were robbed and murdered by local inhabitants. After an abortive investigative visit in mid-September, the Sultan of Maskaṭ, Fayṣal b. Turkī Āl Bū Saʿīd, returned to the island at the end of that month and arrested several tribesmen who were taken to the capital for trial. Those found guilty were then returned to the island, and shot at the scene of their crime. A monument recording the execution of the murderers was erected nearby, and so too was a memorial slab in honour of the victims of the outrage. These events were very important in helping to establish the control of the Sultan of Maskaṭ over Maṣīra.

The inauguration of air routes across the Middle East in the 1930s began to give the island a new significance. During the Second World War, the British Royal Air Force and the United States' Air Force made use of the staging-post airfield, which was constructed at the northern tip of the island, in moving men and supplies to and from India and the Far East. A new agreement was reached in July 1958 between the Sultan of Maskaṭ and the British government which permitted the Royal Air Force to continue its use of that base. In 1962 a 9,000 feet hard-surface runway was added to the two shorter natural-surface landing strips which were already in operation. New fuel storage tanks and better communications equipment were also installed at this time. The Royal Air Force withdrew from Maṣīra in 1977, and control of the facilities then passed to the government of Oman. The Britsh Broadcasting Corporation maintains a radio-relay station on the island. A severe and prolonged hurricane struck Maṣīra in June 1977, causing considerable loss of life and destroying most of the buildings there.

Bibliography: References to Maṣīra are scattered and often fragmentary. There is also a degree of repetition involved in some of the works cited here. Admiralty (Great Britain) Hydrographic Department, *Red Sea and Gulf of Aden pilot*, London 1955 and later; H. J. Carter, *A geographical description of certain parts of the southeast coast of Arabia, to which is appended a short essay on the comparative geography of the whole of this coast*, in *JBBRAS*, iii/2 (1841), 224-317; J. R. Povah, *Gazetteer of Arabia*, Calcutta 1887; J. G. Lorimer, *Gazetteer of the Persian*

Gulf, ʾOmān and Central Arabia, Calcutta 1908-15; Admiralty (Great Britain) Intelligence Divison, *A handbook of Arabia*, i, London 1916; S. B. Miles, *Countries and tribes of the Persian Gulf*, ii, London 1919; Arabian American Oil Company (Research division) *Oman and the southern shore of the Persian Gulf*, Cairo 1952; H. J. Carter, *Reports accompanying copper ore from the Island of Maseera and on lithographic limestone from the southern coast of Arabia*, in *JBBRAS*, ii (1847), 400-3; G. de Gaury, *A note on Masira Island*, in *Geogr. Jnal.*, cxxiii (1957), 499-502; A. Sprenger, *Die alter Geographie Arabiens*, Berne 1875; *The Periplus of the Erythraean Sea*, tr. and ed. G. W. B. Huntingford, Hakluyt Society 2nd series, cli, London 1980; *Ibn Baṭṭūṭa*, ii, 219-20, tr. H. A. R. Gibb, ii, 394; C. F. Beckingham, *Some notes on the Portuguese in Oman*, in *Jnal. of Oman Studies*, vi/1 (1983), 13-19; D. Lee, *Flight from the Middle East*, London 1980; D. Watts, *Severe cyclone in the Arabian Gulf*, in *Weather*, xxxiii/3 (1978), 95-97.

(R. M. Burrell)

MASJUMI (*Madjelis Sjuro Indonesia*, "Consultative Council of Indonesian Muslims"), the name of two different Indonesian Islamic organisations: (a) during the Japanese occupation of Indonesia 1942-5, and (b) in independent Indonesia.

(a) During the Japanese occupation. The Japanese Military Government, during the first stage of its occupation of Indonesia after 1 March 1942, tried to mobilise the Islamic groups for its anti-Western political and military aims. Most of the Islamic leaders had, in different degrees, opposed actively Dutch rule and a number of Islamic nationalist organisations had been established in pre-war Indonesia, with the *Madjelis Islam A'la Indonesia* (*MIAI*, "Supreme Indonesian Islamic Council") in 1937 as their co-ordinating organ.

In November 1943, Masjumi was founded more or less as the successor of *MIAI*. Membership was open only to those organisations which had been granted legal status by the Japanese authorities. These were, at that time, the traditionalist-oriented *Nahdatul Ulama* (*NU*, "Renaissance of the Scholars"), and the modernist social organisation *Muhammadiyah*, joined later by two smaller organisations. In addition, personal membership could be granted to those *ʿulamāʾ* and *kiyai* (religious leaders) who had obtained the consent of the Office for Religious Affairs (*Shūmubu*), established by the Japanese in March 1942 and since 1 October 1943 under Indonesian leadership. The aim and purpose of Masjumi was defined as sponsoring and coordinating the relations between the different Islamic associations in Java and Madura, guiding and guarding the activities of these associations in order to improve cultural life and thus enable the Muslim community to help and contribute their efforts for establishing the Commonwealth of Greater Asia under the leadership of *Dai Nippon*, "in accordance with God's commandments" (cf. van Nieuwenhuijze, 155; Soebagijo, 67). Masjumi's pro-Japanese stand resulted in a certain estrangement with the more radical Islamic organisations which were still waiting for their legalisation, with the associations of Arab Muslims, and with the religiously "neutral" nationalists whose activities were severely restricted.

Masjumi was not a merger, but "constituted a working agreement between Muhammadiyah and Nahdatul Ulama" (Benda, 152). It may be presumed that the interest of the Japanese authorities originated in the personal influence and respect which most leaders of *Muhammadiyah* and *NU* exercised on the populace, mainly in the villages, as religious teachers. Winning their support would mean for the Japanese a guarantee for a certain degree of quiescence and stability among the people. As a consequence of this policy, the traditional power balance in the Muslim society shifted from the jurisdictional and administrative representatives, the *penghulu*, who had obtained some support from the Dutch administration, to the Muslim teachers and scholars. On 1 August 1944, the *Shūmubu* was reorganised, its new leading personnel taken mostly from Masjumi. Thus Masjumi functioned practically as part of the government and was linked to its goals more than before. As go-betweens, the religious leaders had to explain the Japanese policy to the people, endeavouring to gain their support in spite of all kinds of increasing shortages and suffering; at the same time, they were responsible to the military administration, especially in cases of turmoil or revolt.

On 7 September 1944, the Japanese government had announced its plan to prepare Indonesia for independence. Now, Masjumi's political agitation received new momentum. During a rally sponsored by Masjumi and held in Jakarta on 12-14 October, a statement was adopted which stressed the task to prepare the Indonesian Muslim community so as "to be ready and able to receive freedom for Indonesia, and freedom for the religion of Islam" (cf. also W. Hasjim, 341). Independence was understood as an opportunity to establish the nation on Islamic principles, without restrictions imposed by a foreign or non-Islamic power.

The growing militancy in the country finally led to the formation of a military branch of Masjumi, the *Barisan Hizbullah* ("The Front of God's Party"), in December 1944. Already in September 1943, Masjumi had urged the Japanese, although in vain, to establish a Muslim volunteer corps, after the "secular" nationalists had made a similar plea and were allowed to form Peta (*Pembela Tanah Air*, "Defenders of the Home Country"). Hizbullah's aim was defined as to realise the solidarity of the Indonesian Muslim community, to stand and fight together with Japan, in the path of God (*fī sabīl Allāh*), and to realise Indonesian independence, all in accordance with the commandments of Islam (van Nieuwenhuijze, 159; van Dijk, 73). Japanese officers were in charge of the military training, whereas religious instruction was given by Indonesian Islamic teachers, preferably members of Masjumi.

After January 1945, Masjumi broadened its field of activity and started to infiltrate into the "Neighbourhood Associations", a "grass roots control apparatus to the *Djawa Hōkōkai*" ("People's Service Association in Java"), which was under direct Japanese control and staffed with *priyai*. This move, although apparently profitable for Masjumi, indicated that it had passed its climax as the favourite of the Japanese. These felt that Masjumi's agitation against the "infidel" (Western) imperialists became more and more ambiguous and could include the Japanese occupiers as well. The Japanese, therefore, began to deal with the different nationalist groups on more equal terms. This encouraged non-Masjumi Muslims to appeal for a larger basis of the Islamic movement. Finally, Masjumi lost its political monopoly among the Muslims, although its leaders remained the most eminent spokesmen of the Muslim community.

With the re-emergence of the "secular" nationalists, a fierce contest for ideological leadership in the national movement was inaugurated. This contest dominated the discussions in the "Study Committee for the Efforts to Prepare Independence" (*Badan*

Penyelidikan Usaha Persiapan Kemerdekaan), established by the Japanese on 1 March 1945, of whose 62 members only six were from Masjumi. After Soekarno, as a representative of the "secular" nationalists, had presented his concept of *Panca Sila* ("Five Pillars") on 1 June, in which not Islam but more generally the belief in One Divinity (*ketuhanan*) should be the religious element in the state ideology, the Masjumi members led by Wahid Hasjim agreed to this principle on 22 June, after it was amended with the "seven words": *dengan kewajiban menjalankan Syari'at Islam bagi pemelukpemeluknya* ("with the obligation for its adherents to practice the Islamic Law"), and some other Islamic provisions. This "compromise", later known as the "Jakarta Charter", stimulated the acceptance of other religions considered to be monotheistic in the state, but it made it also obligatory for the state to force Muslims into obedience to the *sharīʿa*.

In the last weeks before Indonesia's independence, Masjumi as a political force speedily declined. Its aim to maintain the identification of nationalist and Islamic goals proved to be unrealistic. Opposition against the "Jakarta Charter" and its "seven words" were not only voiced by non-Muslims but also by Muslims, especially those coming from the Outer Islands. Some considered the *sharīʿa* as a foreign juridical concept with only particular applicability, and they therefore favoured traditional or *adat* law as an inclusive Indonesian basis for legislation and ideology. Thus, when after the Proclamation of Independence issued by the "secularists", and not Masjumi, on 17 August 1945, the draft of the Constitution was discussed, their repeated efforts to maintain, or include, Islamic preceptions, were finally refuted, and even the "seven words" of the "Jakarta Charter" were dropped. Masjumi as an organisation vanished together with its former protectors.

(b) In independent Indonesia. After the proclamation of Independence, Soekarno aimed at establishing only one party, a *Partai Nasional Indonesia*, in which all frictions in society would be overcome through consultation followed by unanimous decisions. The government was headed by the President, and power lay in his hands. There was, however, growing opposition against Soekarno's understanding of "unity" and leadership, and a desire to form political parties increased. On 7 November 1945, the Muslim leaders from various groups and orientations who had gathered at Yogyakarta in a national congress, transformed the old Masjumi into "the only political Islamic party in Indonesia". In contrast to the old Masjumi, the new party seems to have laid more stress on individual membership than on membership of organisations. There were granted extraordinary membership only, and were considered as mere "social organisations" not questioning Masjumi's political monopoly. The leadership mainly originated from *NU*, *Partai Serikat Islam Indonesia* (*PSII*, the oldest nationalist Islamic party founded in 1911), and Muhammadiyah.

Masjumi's pretensions to represent all Muslims in Indonesia presented an alternative, and challenging, conception of "unity" against the all-inclusive one of Soekarno. In the field of doctrine, this meant that differences about the role of the *madhhabs* and other questions of *khilāfiyyāt* were considered to belong to the *furūʿ*, not the *uṣūl al-fikh*. In actual policy-making, this call for Islamic unity actually urged co-operation between a number of Islamic leaders who had been bitterly opposed against each other before the war, and new controversies about *Pancasila* and its meaning for the Muslims added to the difficulties of this task.

Under the leadership of Masjumi, a women's organisation was founded to promote knowledge and political as well as religious awareness, and to strengthen their feeling of responsibility at home and in society. Besides this women's organisation, Masjumi established also an Islamic Youth Movement, an Islamic Labour Union, an Islamic Farmers' Union, and it was closely related to the Islamic Students Organisation *HMI* (*Himpunan Mahasiswa Indonesia*), established in 1947.

Although the original Islamic goals were not achieved in the Republic proclaimed in August 1945, the leaders of Masjumi called for a general mobilisation of the Muslims to defend it against the returning Allies. Internally, it intensified its strife for controlling the state. There has been much discussion whether the aim of Masjumi at this time was to erect the Islamic State (*Negara Islam*), or whether its intention was to develop an Islamic society in the state which implemented the Islamic law, without changing formally the constitution or abrogating Pancasila. Both tendencies had their protagonists. Social responsibility, sometimes even expressed in socialist terms, was a constant factor in Masjumi's working programs. In some areas with a strong feudal system, Masjumi presented itself as a forerunner of social renewal, or even social or Islamic revolution (H. Feith and L. Castles, *Indonesian political thinking 1945-1965*, Ithaca and London 1970, 55 ff.).

After 1946, Masjumi became more and more dominated by intellectuals who had received a modernist or western education. Some of them had been expelled by *PSII* before the war and were, more or less, affiliated with organisations like Muhammadiyah, Persatuan Islam, and others. This led to internal conflict which finally caused the exodus of former adherents of *PSII* and the re-foundation of this party in 1947. A similar exodus, although less spectacular, had already taken place in 1946 when the traditionalist "Movement for Islamic Education" (*Pergerakan Tarbiyah Islamiyah Perti*) of Central Sumatra, declared itself as a political party.

After the secession of *PSII*, there were three main groups within Masjumi (Ward, 10). The first one may be styled as "religious socialist", and indeed, they were occasionally political partners of Sutan Sjahrir's Socialist Party. Its members were mainly the above-mentioned intellectuals like Dr. Soekiman, Moh. Natsir, Mohammed Roem, Sjafruddin Prawiranegara, Jusuf Wibisono and others. After 1948 especially, they sometimes took over leading positions in government activities, including the negotiations with the Dutch which finally led to the recognition of Indonesia's sovereignty in 1949.

Another group left in Masjumi after 1947 were the traditionalist *ʿulamāʾ* related to *NU* under the leadership of K. H. Wahid Hasjim. Their participation in the government was usually focussed on the Ministry of Religious Affairs, founded in January 1946.

The third group of Masjumi members, and the smallest one, was that of the "radical fundamentalists". They represented the militant wing of the modernist movement, being more illiberal and anti-Western than the moderates of the first group. Isa Anshary, chairman of Masjumi's branch in West Java, became their spokesman. They became the most outspoken advocates of an "Islamic state".

A serious blow to the integrity of Masjumi was launched in 1948. S. H. Kartosoewirjo, a Masjumi leader in West Java, renounced the Renville Agreement of January 1948 between the Indonesians and the Dutch, which called for a withdrawal of Republican troops from West Java. He let himself be declared as the *Imām* (Head of State) of the provisional "Islamic State of Indonesia" proclaimed in West Java as an alternative to the Indonesian Republic. His rebellion, known as the *Darul Islam* movement, lasted until 1962, when he was captured and executed. The leaders of Masjumi, although disagreeing with the measures which he had taken, were eager to avoid a definite break, but in 1951 they had to accept the demand of the army leaders and approve military actions against the rebels.

In the meantime, a new crisis developed in Masjumi. The *NU*-oriented *ʿulamāʾ* felt a growing decrease of their influence. In both the Natsir and Soekiman cabinets of 1950 and 1951, only the portfolio of Religious Affairs was entrusted to a representative of *NU*. When in the Wilopo cabinet of 1952, Faqih Usman from Muhammadiyah was appointed as Minister of Religious Affairs, the time had come for *NU* to separate from Masjumi and establish itself as a political party on its own (H. Feith, *Decline of constitutional democracy*, 233-7).

With two great rival Islamic parties, the political atmosphere in Indonesia changed considerably. The cabinet presided over by Ali Sastroamidjojo (*PNI*) from July 1953 to July 1955 was supported by *NU*, whereas Masjumi opposed it as being too much compromised with the Communists.

The uncompromising attitude against the Communists had been a characteristic of Masjumi since its very beginning. This led to conflicts with Soekarno, for whom Communism was one of the most powerful and therefore indispensable anti-imperialist ideological forces. In combining it with his understanding of nationalism, he outlined the ideology of his *Partai Nasional Indonesia* (*PNI*). A compromising attitude among some of Masjumi's leaders with the *PNI* had, however, already been apparent before the secession of NU, when Soekiman succeeded Natsir as Prime Minister, leading a Masjumi-*PNI* cabinet. Soekiman, being a Javanese, tried to counteract a *PNI-PKI* co-operation by strengthening ties with *NU*. On the other side, Natsir was more linked to the "radical fundamentalists" in his own party, and to the Socialist Party which was also strictly anti-Communist and opposing *PNI*.

After Soekarno's speech in Amuntai in January 1953 in which he attacked the concept of a Negara Islam and praised *Pancasila* as a guarantee for freedom of religious practice and civil rights of every single Indonesian, the different basic convictions of Masjumi leaders and their cultural and ideological roots became more apparent. Isa Anshary and his team stressed that their conception was based on divine revelation and therefore not open to compromise like the human-made concepts of Christians, secularists and others. He questioned the religious sincerity of Soekarno and those Muslims who were in favour of *Pancasila* as understood by the "religious neutral" nationalists, and he accused them of being hypocrites or unbelievers.

Natsir, like Soekiman, took a much more moderate position in this matter. He felt that the voters would reveal their aspirations in the coming elections and stressed that the people should be well prepared to cast their votes for the "right" party. Therefore he urged the start of new efforts in the fields of Islamic education and self-awareness.

During the election campaign in 1954-5, the voices heard from Masjumi and launched through its party organ *Suara Masjumi*, the daily newspaper *Abadi* and other media, became more and more adapted to the language of the radical fundamentalists. This was partly due to other Islamic revolts, besides the *Darul Islam* in West Java, which were shaking Aceh and South Sulawesi since 1953. Both provinces had a strong Islamic, and generally pro-Masjumi, population. They justified their revolt by pointing to, among other grievances, the neglect by the central government of the development of their provinces, and the growing influence of atheistic Communism in the state. If Masjumi wanted to obtain the votes of these groups, it had to show clearly its opposition to the incriminating trends and its struggle for Islamic goals.

The other Islamic parties taking part in the campaign had formed an Islamic anti-Masjumi bloc. Thus Masjumi became isolated; it was denounced as being extremist and even in sympathy with the Darul Islam, and therefore disturbing the national brotherhood based on the *Pancasila* which had even been accepted by the *PKI* in 1954.

In the Parliamentary elections on 29 September 1955, Masjumi gained 20.9% of the votes. It was thus the second largest party, after *PNI* with 22.3%. Next were *NU* with 18.4% and *PKI* with 16.4%. There were no major differences in the elections to the Konstituante (cf. H. Feith, *Elections*, 57 ff.). All Islamic parties together gained 43.7% of the valid votes. During the years after the elections, Masjumi remained in opposition to the governments, after a short initial period of co-operation. But in the debates in the Konstituante which started working on 10 November 1956 in Bandung and which had to draft the final Indonesian Constitution replacing those from 1945, 1949 and 1950, Masjumi was joined by *NU* and the other Islamic parties in its struggle for a constitution which would base state and society on the principles of Islam. Against this Islamic bloc, a *Pancasila* bloc formed itself from the other parties. Regarding the basic question, *Pancasila* or Islam, none was strong enough to reach the two-thirds majority needed for any decision. This deadlock encouraged Soekarno finally to dissolve the Konstituante on 5 July 1959 and to decree a return to the 1945 Constitution, together with the proclamation of Guided Democracy.

In these years after the elections, Masjumi experienced its political decline. This was partly due to its futile position, in that it still claimed to defend the interests of the Muslims or 90% of the Indonesian population and thus refrained from defining its role as constructive partner in the midst of Indonesia's pluralism of ideologies and religions. But more decisive for its decline than these failures was the involvement of some of its leaders like Moh. Natsir and Sjafruddin Prawiranegara in new regional uprisings which had broken out in North Sulawesi and in West Sumatra in 1957.

This again led to serious clashes in Masjumi between the "regionalists" and the "Javanese" wing led by Soekiman, who was in favour of Soekarno's centralisation policy. Others like Moh. Roem feared that another split in Masjumi could only serve the Communists and their growing influence on Soekarno, and thus endanger Masjumi's political role. He therefore urged the maintenance of the unity of the *umma*. But finally, some leaders like Soekiman left Masjumi in early 1960 and joined *PSII*. Muhammadiya, too, terminated its affiliation as a "special member". Thus the remaining faithful had to bear the consequences of Masjumi's image as "a party of separation and rebellion" (A. Samson, quoted by Ward, 14). They were viewed, moreover, with suspicion by the military leaders who, although outspoken anti-Communist themselves, had to fight the rebels. On 17 August 1960, Soekarno announced his decree that Masjumi, together with Sjahrir's Socialist Party (*PSI*), were to be dissolved because both parties refused to condemn their party members who were active in the regional rebellions.

Bibliography: H. E. Saifuddin Anshary, *The Jakarta Charter of June 1945*, M. A. thesis, Kuala Lumpur 1979, Indonesian tr. Bandung 1981; H. Benda, *The Crescent and the Rising Sun*, The Hague - Bandung 1958; B. J. Boland, *The struggle of Islam in modern Indonesia*, The Hague 1971 (= VKI, 59); B. Dahm, *Soekarnos Kampf um Indonesiens Unabhängigkeit*, Frankfurt/M and Berlin 1966 (= Schriften des Instituts für Asienkunde Hamburg, 18); C. van Dijk, *Rebellion under the banner of Islam. The Darul Islam in Indonesia*, The Hague 1981 (= VKI, 94); H. Feith, *The Indonesian elections of 1955*, Ithaca 1957 (Cornell Interim Report Series); idem, *The decline of constitutional democracy in Indonesia*, Ithaca 1962; Wahid Hasjim, *Serajah Hidup K. H. A. Wahid Hasjim dan karangan tersiar*, Djakarta 1957; Oey Hong Lee, *Indonesian government and press during Guided Democracy*, Zug 1981 (= Hull Monographs on South-East Asia, 4); D. Lev, *Political parties in Indonesia*, in *Jnal. of South East Asian History*, viii/1 (1967); M. P. M. Muskens, *Indonesië. Een strijd om nationale identiteit*, Bussum 1969; Moh. Natsir, *Capita selecta*, i, Bandung and The Hague 1955, ii, Djakarta 1957; idem, *Islam sebagai Dasar Negara*, Bandung 1957; C. A. O. van Nieuwenhuijze, *Aspects of Islam in postcolonial Indonesia*, The Hague and Bandung 1958; Deliar Noer, *Masjumi. Its organization, ideology, and political role in Indonesia*, unpubl. M. A. thesis, Ithaca 1960; D. Noer, *The Modernist Muslim movement in Indonesia*, Singapore and Kuala Lumpur 1973 (Indonesian tr., with extensive introd., Jakarta 1980); idem, *Contemporary political dimensions of Islam*, in M. B. Hooker (ed.), *Islam in South East Asia*, Leiden 1983, 183-215); Soebagijo I. N., *K. H. Mas Mansur. Pembaharu Islam di Indonesia*, Jakarta 1972; K. E. Ward, *The foundation of the Partai Muslimin in Indonesia*, Ithaca 1970 (Cornell Interim Report Series); W. Wawer, *Muslime und Christen in der Republik Indonesia*, Wiesbaden 1974. (O. Schumann)

MASKANA, Greek Μασχάνη, from the Syriac Maškenē (cf. Pauly-Wissowa, xiv/1, col. 2963), a small town, now a village, in the northern part of Syria. The name is mentioned by Stephanus of Byzantium in regard to the war of Septimius Severus against the Parthians in 224 A.D. The Arabic geographers and chroniclers of the Middle Ages only mention Bālis [*q.v.*] in this region, situated 4 km./2½ miles to the south-east of Maskana.

The place is situated in long. 38° 05' N. and 36° lat. E. at about 100 km./63 miles to the east of Ḥalab [*q.v.*] or Aleppo on a Pleistocene terrace which forces the Euphrates (al-Furāt [*q.v.*]) to turn eastwards after having flowed from northwards to southwards on leaving the Taurus, like its two left-bank affluents the Balīkh and Khābūr [*q.v.*]. Being on the 25 mm. isohyet, at the southern limit of the cultivable steppe land and the desert zone, Maskana is on the line of contact between the sedentary, peasant world and that of the nomadic pastoralist. The region has been populated since the Bronze Age, as is attested by numerous ancient sites, the most notable being Tell Muraybat, above the left bank.

Having developed down-stream from Ḳalᶜat Nadjm [*q.v.*] and at a distance of 5 km./3 miles to the north-north-west of Bālis at a spot where the route coming from Ḥalab rejoins the route which follows the right bank of the Euphrates towards Baghdād, Maskana has since Antiquity experienced the vicissitudes of warfare, for it lies on a bend of the river in a region where there are fords. It should be noted that the Euphrates has in the course of the centuries several times changed its bed in the region of Maskana, a fact which may perhaps explain the variations in distance given in the written sources between the river bank and the actual course of the river. It is at this point that the Euphrates becomes navigable, and flat-bottomed barges (*shakhtūra*, pl. *shakhātīr*) constructed from wood are used for river navigation.

In pre-Islamic times, the tribe of the Ḥadīdīn pastured their sheep in the region of the middle Euphrates, and one of the tombs attributed to their mythical ancestor Shaykh Ḥadīd lay in the neighbourhood of Maskana. In the second half of the 6th century, members of the ᶜAnaza [*q.v.*] and Bakr moved into the region and installed themselves there definitively. Over a thousand years later, there took place a new migration of the ᶜAnaza towards this middle Euphrates region, and then a further one *ca.* 1800. In the 20th century, the Shammar and the ᶜAnaza are the main sheep-rearing tribes of the region.

During mediaeval times, the history of Maskana is intertwined with that of Bālis, and it passed under the rule of the master of Ḥalab like all the region to the west of the Euphrates between Ḳalᶜat Nadjm and al-Raḳḳa [*q.v.*]. At the beginning of the 6th/12th century, the Atabegs of Mawṣil disputed with the rulers of Ḥalab for this region which, at Nūr al-Dīn's death (569/1174) suffered successive blows from the rivalries of his successors and then those of the heirs of Ṣalāḥ al-Dīn. From the second half of the 7th/13th century onwards until the end of the 8th/14th century, the invasions of the Mongols were to provoke damage in this region, which always remained the inevitable route for anyone heading from Baghdād towards Ḥalab via the Euphrates valley.

At the time of Mamlūk control in Syria (8th-9th/14th-15th centuries), Maskana does not seem to have been a place worthy of mention. In Ottoman times, the population of the region was made up of turbulent nomads. When ᶜAbd al-Ḥamīd II [*q.v.*] became sultan in 1876, he confiscated the fertile lands of the *wilāyet* of Ḥalab in order to bring them into his own personal domains administered by a special organisation (*čiftlik* [*q.v.*]). In 1908, ᶜAbd al-Ḥamīd accepted the integration of his personal domains into those of the state, so that the *čiftlik* lands became *mīrī* ones, i.e. lands of the empire. The measures taken in 1326/1908 and in the following year were still regulating land ownership in the district of Maskana in 1923. Until the mid-20th century, this region remained almost exclusively one of traditional large ownership.

In May 1915, Alois Musil mentioned at Maskana a barracks for gendarmes, a large *khān* and the residence of the head of the telegraph service (*Palmyrena*, 89). At this time, camels browsed below the settled part. There was in the valley an ancient canal whose branches received, when the waters were high, water from the Euphrates for irrigating the cultivated lands.

Under the French mandate, the *ḳaḍāʾ* of Maskana, the second in the region of the province of Aleppo in 1923, was made up of 80% lands administered by the office of domain lands (*al-amlāk al-mudawwara*), following the system of tenant farming; 15% lands with the system of métayage; and 5% small landowners. In this *ḳaḍāʾ*, situated on the periphery of the province, and only linked with Aleppo in 1922 by a single track impracticable for cars which went along the telegraph line, hence lacking any means for transport or commincations, the price of land was markedly less than that in other ḳaḍāʾs. There were two classes of lands in this region. Those alongside the Euphrates, called *hawī*, with a covering of alluvium left by the river at periods of high water, were irrigated for both summer and winter crops. Yields were 15 to 30 for one measure for corn and barley, whilst maizc and sorghum gave 100 for one measure (Parvie, 104). The lands in the second category were to be found on the old slopes of the river some 10-15 m./33-50 feet above the distant river level, at the beginning of the 20th century, a distance of one to 5 km. These were less good, and corn, barley, cats and lentils were grown there.

Until a recent date, the construction material of this region was mud brick made from earth and chopped straw dried in moulds by the sun. In times farther back, there was also used clay from the Euphrates baked in kilns. In the opening years of the 20th century, Maskana became in spring time one of the centres for producing milk from cows for Aleppo, and this milk was used to make butter for exporting. In May could also be found dromedaries put out to pasture. Like Ḳalʿat Nadjm and al-Raḳḳa, it was one of the points where flocks of sheep coming from Mawṣil and heading for Aleppo crossed the Euphrates. Transhumance was practised on the pastures of Maskana.

In 1945 the village had 430 inhabitants. At the present time, the modern road network allows in this region, thanks to road bridges at al-Raḳḳa, Dayr al-Zōr [*q.v.*] and Mayyadīn, the transporting of sheep in two-level lorries to Aleppo without any need to halt at Maskana.

Bibliography: F. Chesney, *Expedition for the survey of Rivers Euphrates and Tigris*, London 1850, i, 48, 415-16; V. Chapot, *Frontières de l'Euphrate de Pompée à la conquête arabe*, Paris 1907, 283 n. 1; G. Bell, *Amurath to Amurath*, London 1911, 24; K. Baedeker, *Palestine et Syrie*, 4th Fr. ed., Leipzig 1912, 428; Ch. Pavie, *Etat d'Alep, Renseignements agricoles*, Aleppo 1924, 5, 55, 67, 73, 91, 103-4, 118, 125-30, 170-1; R. Dussaud, *Topographie historique de la Syrie*, Paris 1927, 453, 462 n. 7; A. Musil, *The Middle Euphrates*, New York 1927, 320; idem, *Palmyrena*, New York 1928, 189, 219; Guide Bleu, *Syrie-Palestine*, Paris 1932, 219; R. Grousset, *Histoire des Croisades*, Paris 1934, i, 501; A. Latron, *La vie rurale en Syrie et au Liban*, Beirut 1936, 78, 119; R. Mouterde, A. Poidebard, *Le Limes de Chalcis*, Paris 1945, 127 ff. *Syrie, Répertoire alphabétique des noms de lieux habités*, 3rd. ed., Beirut 1945, 124; J. Weulersse, *Paysans de Syrie*, Paris 1946, 50, 253; R. Dussaud, *La pénétration des Arabes en Syrie avant l'Islam*, Paris 1955, 19; L. Dillemann, *Haute Mésopotamie*, Paris 1962, 35; N. Elisséeff, *Nūr ad-Dīn*, Damascus 1967, i, 99, 148, 170, ii, 303, 323, 488, iii, 776, 782; E. Wirth, *Syrien*, Darmstadt 1971, 71, 92, 145, 156, 172, 268, 350.

MASKANA is also the name of a village of Syria situated in a zone of cultivated land on the road linking Aleppo with Damascus, near al-Ḳarā and in the ḳaḍāʾ of Ḥimṣ; in 1945 it had 900 inhabitants.

Bibliography: A. Musil, *Palmyrena*, 819; *Syrie, répertoire alphabétique*, F. F. L. Beirut, 3rd ed. 1945, 125. (N. Elisséeff)

MASKAṬ (lat. 23° 28' N., long. 58° 36' E.), Eng. Muscat, Fr. Mascate, a port on the Gulf of Oman and since the end of the 18th century notionally the capital of what came to be called the Sultanate of Muscat and Oman, since 1970 the Sultanate of Oman. ʿUmānī sources often write the name as Maskad, and even as Maska/Muska with *tāʾ marbūṭa*, the former in accordance with local dialectal pronunciation.

1. Geographical situation and demography.

The site of the town is a constricted one, in a cove where the mountains come almost down to the sea, with the Portuguese Fort Mīrānī at the western end of the cove and a second Portuguese fortress, that of Djalālī, on one of the two off-shore islets. The town itself is on a gravel plain, but until modern times, access to Maskaṭ by land has always been difficult, and communication with it has more often been by sea. In effect, it is the cul-de-sac of the Bāṭina coastal plain, and the nearby port of Maṭraḥ [*q.v.*] is in many ways the more favoured centre. But the natural mountain defences plus a line of fortifications have given Maskaṭ a strategic significance, despite the limited space for settlement and the unattractive climate, with its high temperature and humidity.

The 19th century travellers and visitors commented unfavourably on the town's squalor and its narrow streets. Lorimer, in his *Gazetteer*, estimated the town's permanent population at 8,000, of which 3,000 lived within the town and the rest in the suburbs, whereas he estimated that of Maṭraḥ at 14,000, reflecting the latter's superior commerical role. After a period of steep decline, the population of Maskaṭ has been reliably estimated in 1970 at 6,000, mainly detribalised ʿUmānī Arabs or foreigners, including Baḥraynīs, Balūč, Persians and Ḥaḍārim (southern Arabian tribesmen) and a lowest stratum of the *bayāsira*, slaves and ex-slaves from Africa. In the 19th century there was also a small Jewish population. But the most significant element was that of the Banians, Hindu merchants and middlemen, who had certainly been there since Portuguese times; see C. H. Allen, *op. cit.* in *Bibl.* Their quarter was in the east of the town, where they have had their temples, traditionally since the 17th century.

2. History.

Maskaṭ's real rise to prominence goes back to the Hurmuzī period of the late 15th century, just before the arrival of the Portuguese; up to the 12th century, the main emporium of the ʿUmānī coast has been Ṣuḥār [*q.v.*], and the town of Maskaṭ's main importance was as the last watering place on the Arabian coast for ships trading with India (see the mediaeval Arabic sources, notably al-Muḳaddasī, 93; Ibn al-Faḳīh, 11; Yāḳūt, iv, 529; Ibn al-Mudjāwir, ed. Löfgren, ii, 284; ?the merchant Sulaymān, *Akhbār al-Ṣīn wa 'l-Hind*, ed. and tr. J. Sauvaget, Paris 1948, §§ 13-14). Now, in the later 15th century, Maskaṭ grew at the expense of Ḳalhāt [*q.v.*], apparently under the patronage of the Hurmuzī ruling family, and Ibn Mādjid [*q.v.*] stresses that his home port had become the main centre of the ʿUmānī coast for trade with India (see G. R. Tibbetts, in *Arabian studies*, i, 87-101), the export trade in horses, bred in eastern Arabia as far away as al-Ḥasā, being especially important (see S. Digby, *War horse and elephant in the Delhi Sultanate*, Oxford 1971; Serjeant, *op. cit.* in *Bibl.*, 27; J. Aubin, in *Mare Luso-Indicum*, ii, 112).

On 2 September 1507 Afonso d'Alboquerque arrived at Maskaṭ after subduing Ḳalhāt and destroying Ḳurayyāt, seizing and sacking the town and massacring its population, perhaps amounting to 7,000 at that time, three days later. The Portuguese soon realised Maskaṭ's strategic value, and it came to play an important part in their control of the Gulf, above all after their loss of Hurmuz in 1622; previous to that, the Portuguese operated as nominal vassals of the ruler of Hurmuz, whilst nevertheless requiring an annual tribute from him, by 1523, of 60,000 *as͟hrafīs*. In the middle years of the 16th century, the Portuguese faced threats from the Ottoman occupation of al-Baṣra 61546) and of al-Ḳaṭīf (1550), but above all from the Ottoman fleet operating in the Indian Ocean from its base at Suez; in 1552 the Ottoman admiral Pīrī Reʾīs [*q.v.*] temporarily captured Maskaṭ, but was subsequently defeated by D. Fernando de Menezes in a naval battle off the ʿUmānī coast. Maskaṭ now became integrated into the Portuguese trading empire, and although the Portuguese creamed off the main profit, seems to have benefited also, whereas Ḳalhāt declined *pari passu* with Maskaṭ's rise. In the later 16th century new threats appeared from the Dutch and English, but the two main fortresses, still surviving today, San João or D͟jalālī and Fort Capital (now known as Mīrānī, ? < *almirante*), were built in 1587-8 as a reply to Turkish corsair raids. When the Portuguese were dislodged from Hurmuz, Maskaṭ received most of Hurmuz's Portuguese garrison and was built up against the Ṣafawids and the native ʿUmānīs, now uniting under the Yaʿrabid *Imām* Naṣr b. Murs͟hid. Further defences were constructed, and the town had two churches according to Pietro della Valle, who visited it in 1625 (*Travels*, London 1665, 223-36), and soon afterwards, a Carmelite staging-house, at some later period erected into a "cathedral"; used under the Āl Bū Saʿīd as a stable, remains of it were visible till the 1890s.

The Yaʿāriba [see YAʿRABIDS] first attacked Maskaṭ in the 1630s, forcing the Portuguese to seek peace and possibly to pay tribute or protection money; by 1643 the Yaʿrabids had taken Ṣuḥār and now had independent access to the sea which enable the *Imāms* to bypass the Portuguese export licensing system. In 1649 Sulṭān b. Sayf al-Yaʿrabī finally stormed Maskaṭ and took it from the Portuguese, and though the war continued at sea, with the Portuguese blockading and harassing the port, by 1697 they had to give up all hope of retaking it. The *Imāms* now built up Maskaṭ's trade with India, South Arabia and East Africa for themselves, skilfully using the Dutch and English to further their own interests, though no foreign power, then or later, was allowed to establish a factory in ʿUmān. ʿUmānī aggression and buccaneering in the Gulf of Oman, in effect taking over the role of the old European powers, led to tension with Persia. With the decline of the Yaʿāriba and increased disorder within ʿUmān, involving the Hināwī-G͟hāfirī civil war, there arose possibilities for Persian intervention. Persian military help was summoned by Sayf b. Sulṭān in 1737, and for a while in 1738 Maskaṭ was occupied by a force under Muḥammad Taḳī K͟hān, *Beglerbeg* of Fārs.

Eventually during these years of anarchy in ʿUmān, Aḥmad b. Saʿīd was recognised as *Imām ca.* 1167/1743-4 [see BŪ SAʿĪD], and Maskaṭ now began to develop again in importance during this period when Ottoman and Persia power in the Gulf was weak and when there were no foreign rivals for the trade there, until the Ḳawāsim and the ʿUtub [*q.vv.*], who captured Baḥrayn island in 1783, emerged as maritime rivals. Maskaṭ's main trade was at this time directed at South India, and close relations developed between Maskaṭ and Tīpū Sulṭān (1782-99 [*q.v.*]) of Mysore, who established a trade mission there (the Nawwāb's house was still in existence in the mid-19th century); fear that Maskaṭ might follow Tīpū Sulṭān into the camp of the French was one of the reasons for the first agreement (*ḳawl-nāma*) with the British in 1798.

A further factor operative at this time in ʿUmānī affairs was internal division within the country, although it was not until after 1913 that the split between Sultan and *Imām*, coastal ʿUmān and the interior, became a significant factor; before that, ʿUmānīs from the interior had been as strongly involved as any others in maritime expansion and trade until German and Belgian expansion in Central Africa excluded them from Africa and British intervention along the ʿUmānī coast excluded them from Maskaṭ. Now, after the arbitration of the Canning Award in 1861, the two separate Bū Saʿīdī rulers of ʿUmān and Zanzibar became in effect British puppet rulers [see BŪ SAʿĪD and ZANZIBAR].

Under the Bū Saʿīdīs, Maskaṭ flourished as the naval and commercial centre of ʿUmān until in the 19th century, Zanzibar became the main centre for the dynasty's political control of overseas commerce. The rule of Sulṭān b. Aḥmad (1792-1804) saw the apogee of Maskaṭ's florescence as the basis for ʿUmānī control of Gulf trade, with 15 ships of 400-500 tons each based there; fine houses were constructed there, including a residence for the ruler, the Bayt Grayza, by the site of the old Portuguese *igrezia* ("church") complex. After his death, however, pressure on ʿUmān from the Ḳawāsim, the Wahhābī-Suʿūdī state and the ʿUtub increased. Protection increasingly came from the British, and when the Ḳawāsim were quelled in 1819, the ruler Saʿīd b. Sulṭān, after attempts to assert the old ʿUmānī control in the Gulf ended in disaster at Baḥrayn in 1829, eventually turned ʿUmānī interest away from the Gulf-Indian trade axis in order to concentrate on the South Arabian-East African one. Also, during this first half of the 19th century, Banian (Hindu) and other Indian merchants were encouraged to settle in Maskaṭ and then Zanzibar, and they built up a dominating position in the increasingly monetarised ʿUmānī-East African-Indian commercial system, especially as customs-tax farmers, in which role they were protected by the British. One effect of this was that the Indians came to own most of the property in Maskaṭ and Maṭraḥ. In the decades 1880-1910 Maskaṭ was for a while incorporated into a wider pattern of world trade, as a port of call and coaling station; port facilities were therefore extended, a new palace built and foreign consulates set up. But already before World War I, decline was setting in. Attacks on Maskaṭ from the interior were resumed, till in 1920, (Sir) Ronald Wingate arranged terms which effectively divided ʿUmān into two, with the sultanate of Taymūr b. Fayṣal based on Maskaṭ and the coastlands only. Maskaṭ became a commercial backwater, whilst Maṭraḥ grew in trade and in population at its expense. Taymūr's son Saʿīd (1932-70) effectively moved his capital to Salāla in Ẓafār [*q.v.*] and after 1954 ceased to visit Maskaṭ. With this increased isolation, Maskaṭ had no foreign representives beyond those of Great Britain and India, one bank and one mission hospital. When Saʿīd's son Ḳābūs succeeded after the coup of 1970, the latter had never seen Maskaṭ, let alone the rest of ʿUmān.

At the present time, Maskaṭ continues to be a backwater, within the capital area extending outwards beyond al-Sīb (ancient Damā). The problem of road access has been solved by the construction of a corniche round the rocky Raʾs Kalbuh, but the whole question of communication along a narrowly-constricted area of settlement has led to major developments now occurring at the southern end of the Bāṭina plain. Various facilities have grown up at nearby points, such as the oil port of Mīnā al-Faḥl and at the commercial centre of Maṭraḥ, with its modernised port of Mīnā Ḳābūs. Since the Sultan's real capital is Salāla, Masḳaṭ proper remains only a notional capital, devoid of almost all functions and in effect a museum piece.

Bibliography : The *Bibl.* of A. Grohman in his *EI¹* art. contains detailed references to the classical and mediaeval Arabic geographical and historical sources on Masḳaṭ; see also that to ʿUMĀN.

For basic geographical information, J. G. Lorimer, *Gazetteer of the Persian Gulf, ʾOmān and Central Arabia*, Calcutta 1908-15, repr. 1970, is probably the most useful source and may be supplemented by various British Admiralty handbooks and charts, notably the *Persian Gulf Pilot* 1942. For details of the Arab population of the area, al-Siyābī (Sālim b. Ḥumūd) *Is ʿāf al-aʿyān fī ansāb ahl ʿUmān*, Beirut 1965 (esp. 163-4) is useful, whilst C. H. Allen, *The Indian merchant community of Masqat*, in *BSOAS*, xliv (1981), 39-53, provides further details about the Banians.

Travellers' accounts are useful adjuncts, and D. G. Hogarth, *The penetration of Arabia*, New York 1904, still contains useful material. A valuable summary of their descriptions can be found in R. Bidwell, *Bibliographical notes on European accounts of Muscat 1500-1900*, in *Arabian Studies*, iv, 123-59. To his list of references may be added the account and drawings of E. Kaempfer discussed in G. Weisgerber, *Muscat in 1688: Engelbert Kaempfer's report and engravings*, in *J. Oman Studies*, v (1979), 95-101; and C. G. Miles, *The countries and tribes of the Persian Gulf*, London 1919, where descriptions of Masḳaṭ (1966 repr., 462-9) really describe the period when he was living there (1872-86). Collections of photographs also provide interesting details, notably the Fuad Dabbas Collection in Harvard University Semitic Museum, and W. D. Peyton, *Old Oman*, London 1983. This last contains a map which seems to derive from the unpublished *Muscat City planning survey* of 1972, a useful source for the state of the town before the impact of modern development; a description of that period may also be found in I. Skeet, *Muscat and Oman: the end of an era*, London 1974.

For the history of Masḳaṭ, the following sources contain material which is particularly useful. J. Aubin, *Cojeatar et Albuquerque*, in *Mare Luso-Indicum*, i (1971), 99-134, and *Le Royaume d'Ormuz au début du XVIᵉ siècle*, in *ibid.*, ii (1972, publ. 1973), 77-179, provides a detailed study of the Gulf in the late Hurmuzī and early Portuguese period with extensive critiques on the sources, notably de Barros, Correia and Albuquerque. In *Ottoman Turks and the Portuguese in the Persian Gulf, 1534-1581*, in *Jnal. of Asian History*, vi (1972), 45-87, Salih Özbaran uses both Portuguese and Ottoman sources; whilst R. D. Bathurst's unpubl. D. Phil. thesis, Oxford 1967, entitled *The Ya ʿrubī dynasty of Oman*, completes the Portuguese period. See further R. B. Serjeant, *The Portuguese off the South Arabian coast*, Oxford 1963, and N. Steensgaard, *Carracks, caravans and companies. The structural crisis in the European-Asian trade in the early seventeenth century*, Copenhagen 1972. A vast number of Portuguese engravings and charts have been collected in the *Portugaliae monumenta cartografica*, but the *Livro das cidades e fortelezas da India* in its various original forms repays further study. Additionally, some useful notes on Mīrānī have been compiled in the mimeographed notes (nos. 2 and 3) of the Oman Historical Association.

For the post-Portuguese period down to the rise

of the Āl Bū Saʿīd, Bathurst, *op. cit.*, remains the main study until the end of the Yaʿāriba period, while Anne Kroell, *Louis XIV, la Perse et Mascate*, Paris 1977, adds material from French sources. Then comes a lacuna, for which A. A. Amin, *British interests in the Persian Gulf*, London 1967, provides some background to the end of the 18th century and for which Mrs P. Risso's forthcoming thesis (Toronto University) should help fill the gap (*non vidi*).

From the 19th century to the early 20th century, there is no shortage of studies. The most useful summary of material in the India Office archives is in Lorimer's *Gazetteer*, whilst J. B. Kelly, *Britain and the Persian Gulf 1795-1880*, Oxford 1968, is a massive study based on British records. See also C. H. Allen, *The State of Masqat in the Gulf and East Africa*, in *IJMES*, xiv (1982), 117-27 and his full thesis, *Sayyids, Shaykhs and Sultans: politics and trade in Masqat under the Al Bu Sa'id 1785-1914*, University of Washington 1978, unpubl.; R. G. Landen, *Oman since 1856*, Princeton 1967; and J. E. Peterson, *Oman in the twentieth century*, London 1978.

The two great ʿUmānī sources for Masḳaṭī history are (down to 1856) Ibn Ruzayḳ (Ḥumayd b. Muḥammad), tr. G. P. Badger as *History of the Imâms and Seyyids of Oman*, Hakluyt Society, London 1971, and al-Sālimī (ʿAbd Allāh b. Ḥumayd, d. 1914) *Tuḥfat al-aʿyān bi sīrat ahl ʿUmān* (ed. Aṭfayyis̱h, many printings). Further details of ʿUmānī sources can be found in Bathurst, *op. cit.*, and J. C. Wilkinson, in *AS*, iii, iv. The latter's *Water and tribal settlement in South-East Arabia*, Oxford 1977, and his forthcoming *The Imamate of Oman* provide further information on the Masḳaṭ setting.

(J. C. Wilkinson)

MASḴH (A.) "metamorphosis", that is, according to *LA*, s.v., "transformation of an exterior form (*ṣūra*) into a more ugly form"; the product of the metamorphosis is itself called *masḵh/misḵh* or *masīḵh/mamsūḵh*.

Belief in the fact that, as a result of supernatural intervention—divine punishment in the majority of cases—humans have been transformed into animals, statutes or even into stars was as widespread, before Islam, among the Arabs as among the peoples of Antiquity whose mythologies are known to us. The growth of the concept of punishment inflicted by God has led to the survival of this belief under Islam, not only among a populace conscious of ancestral tradition, but also in religious doctrine, since numerous Ḳurʾānic verses justify it: "You know of those among you who have broken the Sabbath; We have said to them: 'Be abject monkeys'" (II, 61/65; cf. VII, 166); "Those whom Allah has cursed, those on whom His wrath has fallen, those whom He has turned to the monkeys and the pigs" (V, 65/60); "If We wished, We would have transformed them where they stood" (XXXVI, 67). The verb *masaḵha* occurs only in the last-mentioned verse, which concerns deviants in general, whereas the others are applied to the Banū Isrāʾīl. Al-Dj̱āḥiẓ (*Ḥayawān*, iv, 39) explains that God has chosen monkeys and pigs because they are uglier and more antipathetic than other animals, and adds (iv, 39) that if monkeys only are mentioned in II, 61/65 and VII, 166, it is because the punishment in question is more severe.

Jews are also the subject of the principal ḥadīth relating to *masḵh* (*apud* al-Damīrī, *Ḥayāt al-ḥayawān*, i, 573, s.v. *ḍabb*; cf. ii, 182, s.v. *ḳird*; see also al-Ḳurṭubī, *al-Dj̱āmiʿ li-aḥkām al-Ḳurʾān*, i, 439-40). Seeing somebody eating the flesh of the lizard, the Prophet said, "A nation of the Banū Isrā'īl has been transformed, and I fear lest this creature is a part of it; I do not eat this meat, but I do not forbid it". This text is absolutely characteristic because, while testifying to the growth of traditions concerning punishments inflicted on the impious (cf. al-Damīrī, i, 386, s.v. *khinzīr*, where God changes to swine some Jews who have molested Jesus), it relates to an animal which is never mentioned in the Ḳur'ān and is corroborated by various anecdotes. In particular, al-Djāḥiẓ (*Ḥayawān*, vi, 77) describes how a *faḳīh*, also seeing a person eating the flesh of the lizard, says to him: "Know that you have eaten a *shaykh* of the Banū Isrā'īl". The popular belief is in fact that two Israelite tribes have been transformed, one into lizards which have remained on dry land, the other into eels (*djirrī*) which have gone to live in the sea; the reason for this transformation is not indicated, and it is simply stated that it is likely because the foot of the lizard resembles a man's hand. Ibn Ḳutayba (*Mukhtalif*, 10, 362-3, tr. G. Lecomte, §§ 15, 300 c) refutes the interpretation of the proverb *aʿaḳḳ min ḍabb* "more irreverent than a lizard", according to which a Jew showing disrespect towards his parents had been transformed (al-Maydānī, *Madjmaʿ al-amthāl*, i, 509-10, proposes a different explanation). According to another ancient legend, all dishonest tax collectors were transformed (al-Djāḥiẓ, *Ḥayawān*, vi, 80), and there is reference to one of them who changed into a lizard (*Ḥayawān*, vi, 81, 155); of two others, one became a hyena and the other a wolf (*Ḥayawān*, vi, 80, 148), while Canopus (Suhayl, *Ḥayawān*, iv, 69, vi, 81, 155; *Tarbīʿ*, § 41; Ibn Ḳutayba, *Mukhtalif*, 10, tr. Lecomte, § 15) is none other than the fourth metamorphosed tax-collector. As for Venus (al-Zuhara), she was a prostitute who ascended into the sky by virtue of her knowledge of the greatest name of God (*bi-smi llāh al-aʿẓam*) which Hārūt [*q.v.*] and Mārūt had communicated to her (al-Samarḳandī, *Bustān al-ʿārifīn*, Ḳāzān 1298/1880, 131) and was transformed into a comet (*Ḥayawān*, iv, 69; *Tarbīʿ*, § 41 and index; Ibn Ḳutayba, *Mukhtalif*, 10 = § 15).

The story of Isāf [*q.v.*] and Nā'ila, turned to stone in the Kaʿba, is well known, but it will be noted that the Ḳur'ān (XI, 83/81) does not say that the wife of Lot "became a pillar of salt" (Genesis, xix, 26); al-Djāḥiẓ (*Ḥayawān*, vi, 70) makes the comment in this context that the Ahl al-Kitāb refer to no case of the metamorphosis of an human being into a pig or a monkey and simply state that this guilty woman was changed into a pillar of stone (*sic*). There are also encountered in the pre-Islamic period some individual instances of transformation into animals, but, after Islam, divine punishment does not seem frequently to take this form. There are however Shīʿī legends according to which ʿUmar b. al-Khaṭṭāb wanders in the guise of an owl, and the murderer of Ḥusayn b. ʿAlī, Shimr, "runs about incessantly in search of water, transformed into a dog with four eyes; he observes at least one spring which he never reaches, because at Karbalā' he forbade the family of Ḥusayn to approach the water" (H. Massé *Croyances et coutumes persanes*, Paris 1938, 185). On the other hand, the Iranians attribute to post-Islamic metamorphoses the origin of several species of animal: the bear, the elephant, the tortoise, the vulture, the crow, the owl, the hoopoe, the hornet, in addition to the monkey, the pig, the dog and the lizard (*op. laud.*, 185-6).

To these latter attributions relating to Iran, should be added some cases of collective metamorphosis mentioned in the ancient Arab world. For example, it is stated, without undue emphasis, that the mouse (*fa'r* [*q.v.* in Suppl.]) has for its ancestor a miller's wife (*Ḥayawān*, i, 297) and that the shrimp (or the lobster, *irbiyāna*) was a dressmaker who stole thread: this is why the creature has threads, to remind her of the crime that she committed (*Ḥayawān*, i, 297; Ibn Ḳutayba, *Mukhtalif*, 364 = § 300 c); the snake (*ḥayya*) had the form of a camel but, as a punishment (*Ḥayawān*, i, 297), God compelled it to crawl on the ground. According to popular belief, the dog is also the result of a metamorphosis (*Ḥayawān*, i, 222, 292, 297, 308, vi, 79), but in i, 297-8, al-Djāḥiẓ conjectures that the wolf would be the more likely case! Ibn ʿAbbās (*apud* Ibn Ḳutayba, *Mukhtalif*, 167 = § 172 a) comes close to believing in this metamorphosis; he has elsewhere handed down a tradition according to which the elephant, the hare, the spider, the eel and, naturally, the mouse, the monkey and the pig, are humans transformed (*Ḥayawān*, i, 309).

Obliged by the Ḳur'ān to accept the reality of *maskh*, jurists and theologians ponder the real meaning of such transformation and pose the question as to whether it is effected gradually or at a single stroke, whether it has led to the creation of new animal species and, consequently, whether the animals that are the result of it have survived and become numerous, in other words, whether the monkeys, pigs and lizards that we see today are their descendants and theirs alone. Al-Djāḥiẓ (*Tarbīʿ*, § 44) adds this secondary question, which he refrains from answering: "Do they recognise one another and do they know what has brought about their origin?".

To the first question, the author of *K. al-Ḥayawān* (iv, 70), one of whose most original ideas is the influence exerted by the soil and the climate on the somatic and psychological characters of living beings, replies by conveying, without however associating himself with it explicitly, the opinion of certain of the Dahriyya [*q.v.*] who accept the concept of gradual modifications capable of leading ultimately to a total transformation; conversely, there are others who do not deny the existence of collective divine punishments such as *khasf* or engulfment (of Sodom and Gomorrah in particular), poisonous wind and flood, but do not recognise *maskh*. On the part of the Muʿtazilīs, al-Naẓẓām accepts the phenomenon and considers that it falls within the category of divine miracles, while Abū Bakr al-Aṣamm and Hishām b. al-Ḥakam reject it and accept only *ḳalb*, modification (*apud Ḥayawān*, iv, 73). According to al-Bayḍawī (on II, 61/65; cf. al-Damīrī, ii, 183, s.v. *ḳird*), Mudjāhid [*q.v.*] interpreted in a limited fashion the verse relating to the *maskh* of the Banū Isrā'īl, stating that they were not metamorphosed, but that their heart was transformed and their spirit rendered similar to that of monkeys; he was, however, the only one to hold this opinion.

As to the question of whether the monkeys and pigs of which the Ḳur'ān speaks and the above-mentioned animals in general derive exclusively from metamorphosis and were thus, originally, humans, or whether such species existed before the event in question, the answers are by no means unanimous, since points of view vary perceptibly, even though in II, 61/65, the words *ḳirada* and *khanāzīr* are defined by the article, which would seem to allow no freedom of interpretation. For some (*Ḥayawān*, iv, 68), the Ḳur'ān refers only to individual cases designed simply to impress minds and teach a lesson. For others, on the contrary, the lizards, pigs and monkeys, as well as the eels, dogs, etc., which are alive today are the descendants of those who have been transformed. It is thus that, for example, Ibn Ḳutayba, in referring to verse V,

65/60, accepts (*Mukhtalif*, 326 = § 284 a) that monkeys are indeed the product of a transformation and that this product has increased and multiplied (cf. 167, 37 = §§ 172 a, 280 h). According to al-Ḳurtubī (*loc. cit.*) the *ḳāḍī* Abū Bakr Ibn al-ʿArabī (468-543/1076-1148 [see IBN AL-ʿARABĪ] professed the same opinion, on the basis of a *ḥadīth* handed down by Abū Hurayra, according to which the Prophet said: "A nation of the Banū Isrāʾīl has disappeared and nobody knows what has become of it. I consider this the origin of the mouse. Do you not agree that when mice are offered the milk of the camel, they do not drink it, but if it is the milk of the ewe, they drink it". Al-Djāḥiẓ himself, at the end of the *Tarbīʿ* (§ 206), complains that God has radically transformed for the worse (*masakha*) this temporal world, as He has changed certain polytheists into monkeys and certain nations into pigs, with the difference however that in the world at large nothing survives of the previous situation, whereas the animals in question have retained some characteristics of their former humanity (cf. what has been said above concerning the foot of the lizard); this author thus implies that they were not previously created, although he does not believe in the reality of the phenomenon and in this passage has simply allowed himself to be carried away by his pen.

However, according to the prevailing opinion, the metamorphosed animals have died without leaving descendants, since, as objects of the anger and chastisement of God, they would be incapable of surviving. Al-Ḳurtubī (*loc. cit.*, cf. al-Damīrī, ii, 182, s.v. *ḳird*) states that, for Ibn ʿAbbās, they survived no longer than three days, during which they neither ate, drank nor copulated; these details are attributed to the Prophet, who affirmed elsewhere (see al-Damīrī, ii, 183) that monkeys and pigs existed previously; having related the *ḥadīth* concerning the lizard which is quoted at the beginning of the present article, al-Damiri adds the curious comment: "It is probable that the Prophet said this before he knew that metamorphoses do not reproduce themselves (*anna 'l-mansūkh la yuʿḳib*)".

The same of course does not apply to the animals that have undergone a simple modification. Such is the case of the gecko (*wazagha*) struck deaf and leprous for having stirred up the fire that was to burn Abraham (*Ḥayawān*, iv, 68, cf. iv, 289-91; Ibn Ḳutayba, *Mukhtalif*, 10 = § 15; al-Damīrī, ii, 379, s.v. *wazagha*); the geckos that are seen today are indeed the descendants of the one that was modified and, although they are innocent, it is permitted, even recommended, to kill them. H. Massé (*op. laud.*, 187), also cites the case of the mule, rendered sterile for having, unlike the other beasts of burden, caused weariness to ʿAlī at the time of the assault on Khaybar, and the camel, whose organ of generation was made to point backwards so that the rider, Abraham, would not be soiled by the animal's urination; this last-mentioned case is clearly different from all the others.

All the excamples mentioned, including the Ḳurʾānic verses, belong ultimately to folklore, and there is no cause for surprise in that al-Djāḥiẓ treats them with irony in various passages of the *K. al-Ḥayawān* (in particular, i, 297). Also to be noted in this context is the belief according to which, "when an angel disobeys God in Heaven, he is sent to the earth in the form and with the nature of a man" (*Ḥayawān*, i, 187); this applies in the case of the father of Djurhum (see *Tarbīʿ*, § 40 and index) and also of Hārūt and Mārūt.

The notion of metamorphosis as a magical process was a natural source of inspiration for the writers of fabulous tales. In the *Thousand and one nights* (see N. Elisséeff, *Thèmes et motifs des Mille et Une Nuits*, Beirut 1949, 127, 141-4), it is generally by means of sprinkling with water that humans are changed into animals (cow, calf, gazelle, dog, mule, monkey, bird, ass, bear) or that metamorphosed beings are returned to their initial form. Culprits are sometimes petrified (*ibid.*, 151), like Isāf and Nāʾila, and rocks which present a vaguely human appearance are invariably considered to represent men who have suffered divine punishment (as, for example, the rocks of Ḥammām Maskhūṭīn in eastern Algeria).

It may be noted finally that the metamorphoses of insects, well-known to the authors of zoological works, are not designated by the term *maskh* (a detailed example is to be found in al-Damīrī, s.v. *dūd*).

Bibliography: Given in the article.

(CH. PELLAT)

MAṢLAḤA, the concept in Islam of the public interest or welfare.

Maṣlaḥa (pl. *maṣāliḥ*) is the abstract noun of the verb *ṣalaḥa* (or *ṣaluḥa*), "to repair or improve". Strictly speaking, *maṣlaḥa*, like *manfaʿa*, means "utility" and its antonyms are *maḍarra* and *mafsada* ("injury"); but generally speaking, *maṣlaḥa* denotes "welfare" and is used by jurists to mean "general good" or "public interest". Anything which helps to avert *mafsada* or *ḍarar* and furthers human welfare is equated with *maṣlaḥa*. As a legal concept, *maṣlaḥa* must be distinguished from *istiṣlāḥ*, a method of legal reasoning through which *maṣlaḥa* is considered a basis for legal decisions [see ISTIḤSĀN and ISTIṢLĀḤ]. In this article, *maṣlaḥa* will be dealt with as a concept and a legal principle.

The first important case in which the notion of public welfare (*al-khayr* and *nafʿ*) was invoked as a basis for legal decision was the land of southern ʿIrāḳ (al-Sawād), which the caliph ʿUmar decreed should become state-land and a land tax (*al-kharādj*) was imposed on it. Earlier, the practice of the Prophet in such a situation varied from dividing the land among the participants in *djihād*, as in the case of the land taken from the Banū Ḳurayẓa, to turning it into state-land as in the case of Khaybar (Abū Yūsuf, *Kitāb al-Kharādj*, 51). Some of the Companions, like al-Zubayr and Bilāl, urged ʿUmar to divide the Sawād among the warriors, but others, like ʿUthmān, ʿAlī and Ṭalḥa, suggested that it should become state-land. After consultation with several other Companions, the caliph came to the conclusion that the interests of the community as a whole would be better served if the Sawād were brought under state control rather than divided. "If it were divided among the warriors", the caliph ʿUmar asked, "what would be the position of the believers as a whole and their descendants?" Retention of the land under state control would, he argued, bring about greater welfare and utility for the believers (*al-khayr li-djamīʿ al-Muslimīn* ... [and] *ʿumūm al-nafʿ li-djamāʿatihim* (Abū Yūsuf, 27). Though ʿUmar did not use the word *maṣlaḥa* per se, its notion was clearly implied in the words *khayr* ("welfare") and *ʿumūm al-nafʿ* ("public utility"). Supported by the opinion of leading Companions, he issued instructions to immobilise the land of al-Sawād and required its people to pay the *kharādj* (Abū Yūsuf, 23-7; Yaḥyā b. Adam, *Kitab al-Kharādj*, 17-21; M. Khadduri, *War and peace in the law of Islam*, 181-3). ʿUmar's decision on the basis of public interest may be said to have influenced other caliphs to make similar decisions, e.g. concerning the compilation of the Ḳurʾān. But these cases, though often cited as precedents, did not establish *maṣlaḥa* as a principle or source of law. It was indirectly used through the derivative sources of *ḳiyās* and *istiḥsān* (al-Shāṭibī, *al-Iʿtiṣām*, ii, 287-8).

Mālik b. Anas (d. 179/795) is reputed to have been the first jurist to make decisions directly on the basis of *maṣlaḥa* through the use of *istiṣlāḥ* or *al-maṣlaḥa al-mursala*. Although no reference to *maṣlaḥa* or *istiṣlāḥ* is to be found in Mālik's writings, his disciples cited cases in which *maṣlaḥa* as a concept of law had been used by him. Both al-Shāfiʿī in the *Risāla* and Saḥnūn in *al-Mudawwana* cite the *ʿariyya* sale (the sale of fresh for dried dates, contrary to the rule that fresh fruit cannot be sold for dried) as a case in point in which *maṣlaḥa* was the basis of Mālik's rulings (al-Shāfiʿī, *Risāla*, 331-5, tr. M. Khadduri, *Islamic jurisprudence*, 235-6; and Saḥnūn, *al-Mudawwana*, x, 93-4). As a method of legal reasoning, however, *istiṣlāḥ* was developed later and used by jurists who claimed that Mālik was the first to initiate the use of it (al-Shāṭibī, *al-Iʿtiṣām*, ii, 281-316). No clear evidence, however, has yet come to light indicating that Mālik had used *maṣlaḥa* as a concept of law. Djuwaynī (d. 478/1085) is mentioned as the first to call attention to it (al-Shāṭibī, *op. cit.*, 282), and other jurists must have made their contribution before it suddenly appeared as a mature concept in the writings of Abū Ḥāmid al-Ghazālī (d. 505/1111).

Al-Ghazālī states that in the narrow sense, *maṣlaḥa* may be defined as the furthering of the *manfaʿa* and the averting of *maḍarra*, but in a broad sense it is the ultimate purpose of the *Sharīʿa*, consisting of the maintenance of religion, life, offspring, reason and property. "Anything which furthers these aims," he adds, "is *maṣlaḥa*, and anything which runs contrary to them is *mafsada*" (*al-Mustaṣfā*, i, 139-40). Considering *istiḥsān* and *istiṣlāḥ* as imaginary (i.e. subjective) legal methods, he confirms the use of *ḳiyās* as a positive method of legal reasoning on the grounds that the achievement of *maṣlaḥa* is a necessity (*fī rutbat al-ḍarūrāt*) and develops the doctrine of necessity (*ḍarūra*) as a means by which to realise the ultimate purpose of the *Sharīʿa*. *Al-maṣlaḥa*, he maintains, consists of three categories: *al-ḍarūrāt* ("necessities"), *al-ḥādjiyyāt* ("needs") and *al-taḥsīnāt* ("improvements"). In order to make a decision on the basis of the second and third categories, the jurists must find a textual reference by means of *ḳiyās*; but the first category — the *ḍarūrāt*— constitutes by itself a basis for legal decision without resort to *ḳiyās* or any other method, on the grounds that the *maṣlaḥa* of that description is the ultimate purpose of the *Sharīʿa*. Thus by al-Ghazālī's time, *maṣlaḥa* had become a definite concept of law on the basis of which jurists could make legal decisions. Other jurists called legal reasoning *istiṣlāḥ*, but al-Ghazālī rejected *istiṣlāḥ*. If such a method is needed, *ḳiyās* can adequately provide it. In the case of *ḍarūrāt*, he argued, no dependence on a textual reference is needed. Thus *maṣlaḥa* of the highest rank itself becomes a source of the *Sharīʿa*. Al-Ghazālī cites as an example the case of unbelievers who shield themselves with a group of Muslim captives. He maintains that the killing of innocent Muslims, though not allowed by the Sharīʿa, would allow the unbelievers to gain mastery over the *dār al-Islām* and kill both the Muslims and the prisoners. Since minimising killing and the preservation of the community as a whole is closer to the purpose of the *Sharīʿa*, a decision to strike at the enemy shielded with Muslims can be justified on the strength of *maṣlaḥa*, since its protection is a *ḍarūra* (i.e. a necessity) and an implied purpose of the *Sharīʿa* (*op. cit.*, i, 141). But al-Ghazālī warns against the use of cases other than *ḍarūrāt*, such as if a few men in a ship, afraid of sinking or starvation, should kill one of them to save the rest.

It was, however, not a Mālikī or Shāfiʿī jurist who went further in the use of *maṣlaḥa*, but the Ḥanbalī jurist Nadjm al-Dīn al-Ṭawfī (d. 716/1316). In principle, he agreed with al-Ghazālī on the use of *maṣlaḥa* as a basis for legal decisions irrespective of others sources. He also argued that the other sources of the *Sharīʿa* recognised *maṣlaḥa* as the ultimate purpose of the Divine Legislator. Al-Ghazālī restricted its use to only the vital necessities (*ḍarūrāt*). So far, al-Ṭawfī seems to have said nothing innovative save that he universalised the principle to all cases of public interest. But then he went further by holding that, even if the principle of *maṣlaḥa* contradicts a primary source, it should override on the grounds that the *Sharīʿa* itself was laid down to protect *maṣlaḥa* as the ultimate purpose of the Divine Legislator (for the text of al-Ṭawfī's treatise on *maṣlaḥa*, see the appendix in Muṣṭafā Zayd, *al-Maṣlaḥa fi 'l-tashrīʿ al-Islāmī*, 7-48). Although he cites textual references from the Ḳurʾān and Tradition in support of his argument, the principal textual evidence is the tradition *lā ḍarar wa-lā ḍirār* ("no injury should be imposed nor an injury to be inflicted as a penalty for another injury"). From this and other citations, he asserted that the principle of *riʿāyat al-maṣlaḥa* must be overriding in all legal aspects of human relationships (*muʿāmalāt*), though not in matters relating to *ʿibādāt* (devotional duties), because these are relating to worship of God and are fundamentally different from *maṣlaḥa*.

The principle of *riʿāyat al-maṣlaḥa*, though ably defended by some of its adherents, like the Mālikī jurist Abū Isḥāḳ al-Shāṭibī (d. 790/1388) and others, found no great supporters in an age in which *idjtihād* was discouraged and *taḳlīd* prevailed, mainly because it stressed dependence on evidence that cannot be clearly identified by *ḳiyās* or other derivative sources. In the modern age, however, under the impact of Western legal thought, the concept of *maṣlaḥa* has become the subject of an increasing interest among jurists who have sought legal reforms in order to meet the needs of the modern conditions of Islamic society. Muḥammad ʿAbduh (d. 1905) equated the *Sharīʿa* with natural law (M. H. Kerr, *Islamic reform*, 103 ff.) and opened the door for modern jurists to use reason as a basis for legal interpretation. Pursuing this line of thought, Rashīd Riḍā (d. 1935) might be regarded as the most effective protagonist of the use of *maṣlaḥa* as a source for legal and political reform. In his treatise *al-Khilāfa wa 'l-imāma al-ʿuẓmā* (1923) ("The caliphate, or the supreme authority"; tr. H. Laoust, *Le Califat dans la doctrine de Rašīd Riḍā*), Riḍā tried to re-interpret the *Sharīʿa* on the basis of *maṣlaḥa* and *ḍarūra* as the expression of public interest. Like al-Ṭawfī, he made a distinction between *muʿāmalāt* and *ʿibādāt*, and sought to reform the *Sharīʿa* by an elected assembly in which the *ʿulamāʾ* would be represented on the basis of the principles of *maṣlaḥa* and *ḍarūra*, presumably by the method of *idjtihād*, guided by reason, which Muḥammad ʿAbduh had eloquently explained. This approach to legal reform, partly on the basis of *maṣlaḥa* (often expressed by the modern usage of "national interest") and other legal devices, encouraged modern jurists such as ʿAbd al-Razzāḳ al-Sanhūrī (d. 1968) and others to provide modern civil codes based partly on the *Sharīʿa*, but mainly on Western law.

Bibliography: Abū Yūsuf, *Kitāb al-Kharādj*, Cairo 1352, tr. Ben Shemesh, *Taxation in Islam*, Leiden 1958-69; al-Ghazālī, *al-Mustaṣfā*, Cairo 1356; Abū Isḥāḳ al-Shāṭibī, *al-Iʿtiṣām*, Cairo 1331; Nadjm al-Dīn al-Ṭawfī, *Risāla fi 'l-maṣāliḥ al-*

mursala, in *Madjmū^c rasā'il fī uṣūl al-fiḳh*, Beirut 1324, 37-70; a more critical edition of Ṭawfī's *Risāla* is in Muṣṭafā Zayd, *al-Maṣlaḥa fī 'l-Sharī^ca al-Islāmiyya*, Cairo 1954; Rashīd Riḍā, *al-Khilāfa, aw al-imāma al-^cuẓmā*, Cairo 1341; M. H. Kerr, *Islamic reform*, Berkeley 1966. (MADJID KHADDURI)

MASLAMA B. **^cABD** AL-**MALIK** B. **MARWĀN**, son of the caliph ^cAbd al-Malik and one of the most imposing Umayyad generals, whose siege of Constantinople 98-9/716-18 earned him lasting fame. Like his uncle Muḥammad b. Marwān [*q.v.*], whom he succeeded in Asia Minor in many respects, he was, as the son of a slave-girl, excluded from the succession to the caliphate. His date of birth is unknown. He died on Muḥarram 121/24 December 738.

Starting in 86/705, the last year of his father's reign, Maslama led the regular summer campaigns (*ṣawā'if*), sometimes prolonged over the winter, into the Byzantine territories of Asia Minor, often accompanied by al-^cAbbās b. al-Walīd [*q.v.*] and/or other sons of his half-brother, the caliph al-Walīd. The range of these campaigns stretched from the region of Malatya in the east to Amasya in the north and to Pergamon in the west. Among his early conquests, those of Ṭuwāna (Tyana) and ^cAmmūriyya (Amorium) in 88/707 and 89/708 are best known. In 91/710 he succeded Muḥammad b. Marwān in the governorship of al-Djazīra, Armenia and Ādharbāydjān after having already served as governor of Ḳinnasrīn. In this capacity, he advanced as far as Bāb al-Abwāb (Darband) [*q.v.*] on the Caspian Sea, an operation which he repeated in 95/714 and in the course of which he conquered and destroyed the town. After Sulaymān had succeeded al-Walīd in the caliphate during the following year, Maslama was given chief command of the expedition against Constantinople which was carried out by land and sea [see ḲUSṬANṬĪNIYYA]. The siege proper started in the beginning of 99/mid-August 717 and ended exactly one year later without success. The fiasco was caused mainly by supply difficulties, the plague and the use of the Greek fire by the Byzantines against the Arab fleet. The loss did not injure Maslama's military reputation, but marked an interruption of his activities in Asia Minor for some years. Legend actually transformed the failure into a victory. Already in 100-1/719 he was ordered by ^cUmar II again to lead the *ṣā'ifa*, but he had to use this army in ^cIrāḳ, first against the Khāridjites and then, under the caliphate of Yazīd II, against the rebellious Yazīd b. al-Muhallab [*q.v.*], whom he defeated completely in Ṣafar 102/August 720 at ^cAḳr in the vicinity of Wāsiṭ. Together with this expedition, he was entrusted with the governorship of both ^cIrāḳs at the beginning of 102/July 720, but lost his office a year later because he apparently had not delivered the surplus taxes to Syria. This and his interference in the question of succession in favour of his half-brother Hishām and against Yazīd's son al-Walīd adversely affected his relations with the caliph, so that he did not exercise any military or administrative functions in the remaining years of Yazīd's caliphate. Hishām, however, reverted to the experienced general soon after his assumption of power, and conferred upon him the governorship of Armenia and Ādharbāydjān from 107/725 until 111/729 and again from 112/730 until 114/732. Maslama began this last phase of his military activities with a *ṣā'ifa* in the summer of 108/726 which resulted in the conquest of Caesarea in Cappadocia. His main attention, however, was turned further to the east against the Khazars [*q.v.*], who in these years threatened Ādharbāydjān and Armenia. The culminating point of these activities was his new expedition to Bāb al-Abwāb in 112-13/730-1, during which he reconstructed and fortified the town and stationed a permanent Syrian garrison in it, whereby he became the founder of Islamic Darband. In 114/732 he retired from the political stage, and seems to have passed the remaining years of his life in northern Syria, where he possessed large estates, especially in the region between Ḥarrān and Raḳḳa.

Bibliography: See the general histories of Khalīfa b. Khayyāṭ, Balādhurī (*Futūḥ* as well as *Ansāb*), Ya^cḳūbī, Ṭabarī, Ibn al-Athīr, etc.; *Aghānī*, index; Ibn ^cAsākir, *Ta'rīkh Dimashḳ*, Ẓāhiriyya 3380, vol. xvi, fols. 222a-226b; J. Wellhausen, *Die Kämpfe der Araber mit den Romäern in der Zeit der Umaijaden*, in *NGW Gött.*, phil.-hist. Klasse (1901), Heft 4; F. Gabrieli, *Il califfato di Hishâm. Studi di storia omayyade*, Alexandria 1935 (Mémoires de la Société Royale d'Archéologie d'Alexandrie, vii/2); idem, *L'eroe omayyade Maslamah Ibn ^cAbd al-Malik*, in *Rend. Lin.* (1950), serie VIII, vol. v, 22-39; R. Guilland, *L'expédition de Maslama contre Constantinople (717-718)*, in *Al-Machriq* (1955), 89-112 (= *Études Byzantines*, Paris 1959, 109-33). (G. ROTTER)

MASLAMA B. **MUKHALLAD** B. AL-ṢĀMIT AL-ANṢĀRĪ, ABŪ MA^cN or SA^cĪD or ^cUMAR), Companion of the Prophet who took part in the conquest of Egypt and remained in the country with the Muslim occupying forces. Subsequently, loyal to the memory of ^cUthmān b. ^cAffān and hostile to ^cAlī b. Abī Ṭālib, whose accession to the caliphate he had not recognised (see al-Ṭabarī, i, 3070), he opposed, with Mu^cāwiya b. Ḥudaydj [*q.v.*], the arrival of Muḥammad b. Abī Bakr [*q.v.*] who, having had a hand in the murder of the third caliph, had been appointed governor of Egypt, and it is probable that he was involved in the campaigns which took place in 38/658 and ended with the death of the son of Abu Bakr. He faithfully served ^cAmr b. al-^cĀṣ [*q.v.*], who governed the country until his death (43/663), and lived unobtrusively under his two successors, ^cUtba b. ^cAbī Sufyān and ^cUḳba b. ^cĀmir. Al-Ṭabarī (ii/1, 84, 93) says that in 47/667-8 Mu^cāwiya b. Ḥudaydj was appointed governor of Egypt and performed this function until 50/670, but other sources claim that Maslama governed Egypt from 47 onward; he was retained in his official responsibilities by Yazīd b. Mu^cāwiya, from 60/680 until his death on 25 Radjab 62/9 April 682 aged 62 or 66 years, since he was 10 or 14 years old on the death of the Prophet. During his period of office, he conducted regular operations against the Byzantines and rebuilt the mosque of ^cAmr which he endowed with minarets [see MANĀRA]. Some authors state that, from the time of his nomination, he had responsibility for the Maghrib and Ifrīḳiya, and Ibn ^cAbd al-Ḥakam for example (partial ed. and tr. A. Gateau, 66-7) specifies that it was he who, in 51/671, replaced ^cUḳba b. Nāfi^c [*q.v.*] with Abu 'l-Muhādjir Dīnār al-Anṣarī; but the chronology is not easily established and Ibn ^cIdhārī (i, 17) dates in the year 55/675 the decision on the part of Mu^cāwiya to join Ifrīḳiya to Egypt and the subsequent appointment of Abu 'l-Muhādjir.

Bibliography: Besides the references in the text, see Djāḥiz, *^cUthmāniyya*, 174; Ibn ^cAbd al-Barr, *Istī^cāb*, commentary on the *Iṣāba*, iii, 463; Ibn al-Kalbī-Caskel, *Djamhara*, Tab. 187; Ibn Sa^cd, v, 195; Ibn ^cAbd al-Ḥakam, *Futūḥ Miṣr*, partial ed.-tr. A. Gateau, Algiers[2] 1947, 67, 69, 71; Ibn al-Athīr, *sub annis*; ^cAsḳalānī. *Iṣāba*, no. 7989; Ibn al-^cImād, *Shadharāt*, i, 70; Ibn Taghribardī, *Nudjūm*, i, 132-57 *passim*; see also AL-ḲAYRAWĀN. (ED.)

MASLAMA AL-**MADJRĪṬĪ** [see AL-MADJRĪṬĪ].

MAṢMŪDA (the broken plural *Maṣāmida* is also found), one of the principal Berber ethnic groups forming a branch of the Barānis.

If we set aside the Maṣmūda elements mentioned by al-Bakrī in the neighbourhood of Bône, the post-Islamic Maṣmūda seem to have lived exclusively in the western extremity of the Maghrib; and as far back as one goes in the history of the interior of Morocco, we find them forming with the Ṣanhādja [*q.v.*], another group of Barānis Berbers, the main stock of the Berber population of this country. Indeed, from the first Arab conquest in the 1st/7th century to the importation of the Hilālīs by the Almohad sultan Yaᶜḳūb al-Manṣūr in 586/1190, it was the Maṣmūda who inhabited the great region of plains, plateaux and mountains, which stretches from the Mediterranean to the Anti-Atlas to the west of a line from north-east to south-west passing through Miknāsa (Meknès) and Damnāt; the only parts of this territory which were not occupied by them were three small Ṣanhādja enclaves: the Ṣanhādja of Tangier, of the valley of the Wargha and of Azammūr. To the north and to the west, the land of the Maṣmūda was bounded by the Mediterranean and the Atlantic. To the east and south it was bounded by the land of the Ṣanhādja. To the north were the Ṣanhādja of the region of Tāzā and those of Wargha; in the centre, the Zanāga or Ṣanhādja of the Central Atlas, to which should be added the Zanāta of Fāzāz; to the south, the Haskūra, the Lamṭa [*q.v.*] and the Gazūla [see DJAZŪLA].

It was from the presence of this Maṣmūda block, extending continuously from Sūs to the Mediterranean, that eastern Morocco generally must have received the name of Sūs, a name found for example in Yāḳūt (s.v. Sūs) who distinguishes a Hither Sūs (capital Tangier) and a Farther Sūs (capital Ṭarḳala?) separated from the other by two months' journey. It is also to this racial unity that are due the legends according to which all the northwestern corner of Morocco was once inhabited by the people of Sūs (*ahl Sūs*).

Before the coming of the Hilālī Arabs, the Maṣmūda peoples were divided into three groups:

1. In the north, from the Mediterranean to the Sabū and Wargha, the Ghumāra [*q.v.*].
2. In the centre from the Sabū to the Wādī Umm Rabīᶜ, the Baraghwāṭa [see BARGHAWĀṬA].
3. In the south, from the Wādī Umm Rabīᶜ to the Anti-Atlas, the Maṣmūda in the strict sense of the word.

Like the majority of the Barānis, who in this respect are a contrast to the Butr, who are inclined to be nomads, the Maṣmūda were all settled; for if, in one passage, Ibn Khaldūn mentions two nomad tribes, the Lakha and the Zaggan, as forming part of the Maṣmūda confederation of the Ḥāḥa, he also points out that they were tribes of the Lamṭa, i.e. of the nomadic Ṣanhādja, who finally became incorporated in the Dhawū Ḥassān, Maᶜḳilī Arab nomads [see MAᶜḲIL] of Sūs. Ibn Khaldūn further makes special mention of the fortresses and fortified villages (*maᶜāḳil wa-ḥuṣūn*) of the Maṣmūda who lived in the mountains of Daran or the Great Atlas. Other Arab historians and geographers mention the many little towns (*ḳarya*) in the plains occupied by the Dukkāla or the Baraghwāṭa, a pastoral and agricultural people; but these were gradually ruined and destroyed in the course of the fighting which went on without interruption in their country from the establishment of the Zanāta principalities of Shālla, Tādlā and Aghmāt: the Almoravid and Almohad conquests, repeated campaigns against the heretical Baraghwāṭa, the Hilālī occupation, the struggle between the Almohads and the Marīnids, the rivalry between the Marīnid kingdom of Fās and that of Marrākush and lastly the wars with the Portuguese. Exterminated as heretics, dispossessed of their lands and driven from them by the Arab or Zanāta nomads brought into their territory, transported to a distance (region of Fās) by the Waṭṭāsid sultans, for whose taste they showed too little hostility to the Portuguese, the central Maṣmūda, the original inhabitants of the Azghār, of Tāmasnā and of the land of the Dukkāla, finally disappeared; their place was taken by nomads, Hilālī Arabs (in the north, in Habṭ and Azghār, the Riyāḥ; in the south, the Djusham, Sufyān, Khulṭ and Banū Djābir) and the Berbers (Zanāta Hawwāra); in the 10th/16th century the coming to power of the Saᶜdid dynasty brought about the immigration of Maᶜḳil Arab tribes to the same region: ᶜAbda, Aḥmar, Raḥāmina, Barābīsh, Udāya, Awlād Dulaym, Zuᶜayr, etc.

From the 10th/16th century onwards, as a result of the occupation of their central plains by the Arabs, Hilālī then Maᶜḳilī, the Maṣmūda only survived in the mountainous regions which formed the northern and southern extremes of their old domains.

The Maṣmūda of the north (or *Maṣmūdat al-Sāḥil*: "M. of the shore" of *al-Bayān*) were chiefly represented by the Ghumāra group. But, alongside of them, we find two small groups having the same racial origin:

a. The Maṣmūda of the Straits, settled between the district of Ceuta, which belonged to the Ghumāra and that of Tangier, a Ṣanhādja country. It was they who gave their name to the fortified port of Ḳaṣr Maṣmūda, also called Ḳaṣr al-Madjāz, the modern al-Ḳaṣr al-Ṣaghīr. Their presence here is attested in the 4th/10th century, for it was while fighting here against them that Ḥā-Mīm, the prophet of the Ghumāra, was slain; al-Bakrī (5th/11th century) knew them in the same area corresponding to that of the modern Andjra.

b. Al-Bakrī mentions another group of Maṣmūda (tribe of the Aṣṣāda) settled in the land lying between al-Ḳaṣr al-Kabīr and Wazzān; there is still a small Maṣmūda tribe between these two towns.

The Maṣmūda of the south, who inhabited the lands between the Wādī Umm Rabīᶜ and the Anti-Atlas, were divided into two groups: those of the plain and those of the mountain.

2. The Southern Maṣmūda of the plain lived to the north of the Great Atlas. The chief tribes were the Dukkāla; the Banū Māgir (around Safi); the Hazmīra; the Ragrāga and the Hāḥa (to the south of the lower course of the Tansift). The chief town in this region was Safi [see ASFĪ], for the town of Azammūr [*q.v.*] and the *ribāṭ* of Tīṭ [*q.v.*] were in the enclave of Ṣanhādja; beside the port of Safi, we must also mention that of Ḳūz (the *Agoz* of the Portuguese) at the mouth of the Tansift, which gave Aghmāt access to the sea and had a *ribāṭ*, and that of Amagdūl (the *Mogador* of the Portuguese) which served the district of Sūs. Besides these three centres, there were, as in Tāmasnā, a large number of fortified little towns (*ḳarya*) many of which survived down to the 10th/16th century; the Portuguese chroniclers, Leo Africanus and Marmol have preserved for us many names of these places which have now disappeared, their very memory being lost; the local hagiographic collections, and notably the *Kitāb al-Tashawwuf* of al-Tādilī (7th/13th century), have preserved a good deal of valuable information on this subject. At the present day, all the country to the north of the Atlas is arabicised and if the old Berber element has not com-

pletely disappeared, it is at least overwhelmed by Arabs, of whom the majority seem to be of Maʿḳilī origin. The Ḥāḥa alone, between Mogador and Agadir, have remained almost intact and have retained the use of the Berber language.

b. The Southern Maṣmūda of the mountains occupied the Great Atlas (*Djabal Daran*), the massif of Sīrwā (anc. Sīrwān) and the Anti-Atlas or mountains of the Nagīsa (Berber, I n Gist).

In the Great Atlas, the Maṣmūda extended to the east as far as the upper course of the Tansift (a pass called Tizi-Telwet). From east to west, the following were the chief groups: the Glāwa; the Haylāna (or Aylāna), the Warīka and the Hazradja, near Aghmāt; the Aṣṣādan, including the Maṣfīwa, the Māghūs and the Dughāgha or Banū Daghūgh; the Hintāta, including the Ghayghāya; the people of Tin-Mallal, on the upper course of the river of Naffīs; the Ṣawda or Zawda, in the lower valley of the Asif al-Māl; the Gadmīwa and lastly in the west, the Ganfīsa, the chief tribe of which was the Saksāwa or Saksīwa.

The massif of Sirwā and the high valley of the Wādī Sūs were inhabited by the Banū Wāwazgīt and the Saktāna. The northeastern part of the Anti-Atlas was occupied by the Hargha.

Farther to the south, the Sūs, properly so-called, was inhabited by heterogeneous elements of Maṣmūda origin (al-Idrīsī, *akhlāṭ min al-Barbar al-Maṣāmida*). Describing the road leading from Tarūdant to Aghmāt, al-Idrīsī mentions between Tarūdant and the land of the Hargha, four tribes the names of which, corrupted by the copyists, are unfortunately hardly identifiable.

Besides these highlanders, who were strictly Maṣmūda, we must mention the Haskūra (or Hasākira). These were highlanders of Ṣanhādja origin, brethren of the Lamṭa and Gazūla, who led a nomadic existence to the south of the Great Atlas and the Anti-Atlas. The Haskūra were settled in the high valley of Tansift and the Wādī al-ʿAbīd, on the two slopes of the mountain range which links the Great Atlas, the home of the Maṣmūda, with the Central Atlas, the home of the Zanāga (= Ṣanhādja) of Tādla; their chief tribes were the Zamrāwa, the Mughrāna, the Garnāna, the Ghudjdāma, the Faṭwāka, the Maṣṭāwa, the Hultāna, and the Hantīfa, who, according as they lived on one slope or the other, belonged to the Haskurāt al-Ḳibla (H. of the south) or to the Haskurāt al-Ḍill (Ḥ. of the north [< *ẓill*]). Ibn Khaldūn, who calls attention to the Ṣanhādja origin of the Haskūra, adds that, as a result of their taking up the Almohad cause, it became customary to associate them with the Maṣmūda tribes, but that they never enjoyed the same privileges as these latter.

History. In 62/682, ʿUḳba b. Nāfiʿ [*q.v.*] marched against the Maṣmūda of the Atlas with whom he fought several battles. On one occasion, he was surrounded in the mountains and owed his safety solely to the help given him by a body of Zanāta. In the same year, he attacked and took the town of Naffīs which was occupied by "Rūm" and Berbers professing Christianity. Thence he went to Igli, a town of Sūs which he also took. Legend adds that he even thrust his way to the Atlantic where he rode his horse into the water, calling God to witness that there were no more lands for him to conquer.

This first submission of the Maṣmūda does not however seem to have lasted after the departure of ʿUḳba. In 88/707, Mūsā b. Nuṣayr had to reconquer Morocco; he in person took Darʿa and Tāfīlālt and sent his son to the conquest of Sūs and the land of the Maṣmūda.

In 114/732 ʿUbayd Allāh b. al-Ḥabḥāb was appointed governor of the Maghrib; he appointed his son Ismāʿīl as assistant to the governor of Morocco and gave him particular charge of the district of Sūs.

In 117/735, the same ʿUbayd Allāh sent Ḥabīb, grandson of ʿUḳba, to make an expedition into Sūs against the Maṣmūda and the Ṣanhādja (Massūfa). Later the latter's son ʿAbd al-Raḥmān al-Fihrī (d. 127/745) becoming semi-independent governor of the Maghrib occupied Igli and built a camp there, the remains of which could still be seen in al-Bakrī's time. It is to the same governor that is attributed the making of the wells which supply the road from Tāmdalt to Awdaghost [*q.v.*] via Waddān, through the modern Mauritania.

The land of the Maṣmūda then disappears from history till the 3rd/9th century. The conquests of Idrīs I did not extend in the south beyond Tāmasnā and Tādlā. But in 213/812 Idrīs II made an expedition against the town of Naffīs; on his death in 213/828, his son ʿAbd (or ʿUbayd) Allāh obtained as his share of the kingdom, Aghmāt, Naffīs, the lands of the Maṣmūda and of the Lamṭa as well as Sūs. Al-Bakrī records that some of his descendants ruled as lords of Naffīs and among the Banū Lamās, not far from Igli. Other Idrīsids, descendants of Yaḥyā b. Idrīs, were at this time lords of Darʿa.

With the decline of Idrīsid power in the 4th/10th century, the Maṣmūda again became independent and were ruled by elected chiefs or *imgharen* (sing. *amghar* [*q.v.*], Arabic *shuyūkh*); al-Bakrī tells us that those of Aghmāt were appointed by the people for a term of one year. When at the end of the 4th/10th century, Zanāta principalities became established in Morocco (at Fās, Shālla and Tādlā), Maghrāwa established themselves at Aghmāt; but all we know of them is that they were attacked by the Almoravids. In 449/1057, after receiving the submission of Sūs and of the Maṣmūda (Zawda, Shafshāwa, Gadmīwa, Ragrāga and Ḥāha), the Almoravid chief ʿAbd Allāh b. Yā-Sīn took Aghmāt, the last Maghrāwa ruler of which, Lagūṭ b. ʿAlī, fled to Tādlā. His wife, the famous Zaynab, who was one of the Nafzāwa, finally became the wife of Yūsuf b. Tāshfīn, whom she initiated into the fine art of diplomacy.

From 449/1057, Aghmāt was the capital of the Almoravids till 454/1062, when Yūsuf b. Tāshfīn founded Marrākush [*q.v.*]. In 466/1074 the same ruler, having divided his empire among several governors, gave his son Tamīm the governorship of Marrākush, Aghmāt, of the Maṣmūda and of Sūs, then of Tādlā and Tāmasnā.

The Maṣmūda seem to have remained subject to the Almoravids till the rebellion in 515/1121 provoked by the *mahdī* Ibn Tūmart [*q.v.*] of the tribe of Hargha, who, supported by ʿUmar Īntī, *shaykh* of the Hintāta, and by ʿAbd al-Muʾmin [*q.v.*], brought about the foundation of the Almohad dynasty. The history of the Maṣmūda is henceforth involved with that of the dynasty which they brought to power and which was to last till 1269. The Maṣmūda, together with the Almohad dynasty, thus contributed to the rise of the Ḥafsids [*q.v.*], who ruled over Ifrīḳiya from 625/1228 to 982/1574, through the descendants of Abū Ḥafṣ ʿUmar Īntī, *shaykh* of the Hintāta.

During the first half of the 7th/13th century, the power of the Almohads, routed by the Christians of Spain at the battle of Ḥiṣn al-ʿUḳāb (Las Navas de Tolosa) in 609/1212 and vigorously attacked in Morocco by the Banū Marīn, soon began to decline. The Maṣmūda of the Atlas, indifferent to the fate of the dynasty, took advantage of its plight to regain their independence. It was the tribes of the Hintāta and the Haskūra, which in 621/1224 at the proclamation of al-ʿĀdil assumed the leadership in the movement; frequently allied with the Hilālī Arabs of the plains, Sufyān and Khulṭ, we find them fighting in all the civil wars and supporting various pretenders to the throne.

When in 667/1269, the Marīnids had definitely crushed the Almohads, the Maṣmūda retained a certain amount of independence and lived more or less in submission to the central power, ruled by chiefs chosen from the great local families: Awlād Yūnus among the Hintāta; Awlād Saʿd Allāh among the Gadmiwa; among the Saksāwa, ʿUmar b. Ḥaddū was an independent chief who went so far as to claim the Berber title *agellid* (= king). In Sūs, the Banū Yaddar (Idder) founded an independent principality which lasted from 652/1254 till about 740/1340. As to the Haskūra, the power among them was exercised by the Banū Khaṭṭāb.

Down to the 9th/15th century, except during the first half of the reign of the Almohad dynasty of which they had been the principal supporters, the Maṣmūda of the Atlas were hardly ever under the direct rule of the Moroccan government; only the tribes of the plains, Dukkāla and Ḥāḥa, in a position of inferiority as a result of their geographical situation, were able to offer less resistance and had to submit. The later dynasties, Saʿdid and ʿAlawī, were no better able to subdue the Maṣmūda of the highlands; but instead of gathering round local chiefs with temporal power, the latter now placed themselves under the leadership of holy men with religious prestige.

In the beginning of the 10th/16th century, the land of the Maṣmūda was in a state of anarchy. Some *ashyākh* of the tribe of the Hintāta held the lands of Marrākush; the most famous was Abū Shantūf; to the south of Tansift, the 8th/14th century saw the rise of the warlike group of the Ragrāga; in the 9th/15th century, the power of the mystic al-Djazūlī [*q.v.*] spread among the Ḥāḥa. In the adjoining country of Darʿa, the Saʿdid dynasty was rising, which, after occupying Sūs, imposed its domination on the whole of Morocco. But it did not, however, succeed in subjecting completely the highlanders of the Atlas. The powerful Aḥmad al-Manṣūr himself had to fight against a pretender who had proclaimed himself king of the Saksāwa. After the death of al-Manṣūr, the Atlas and Sūs were all under the authority of local religious leaders of whom the most important were to be found among the Ḥāḥa and in Tāzarwālt (family of Aḥmad u-Mūsā).

It was the ʿAlawid Sultan Mawlāy Rashīd who restored Sūs and the Atlas to the Moroccan empire. The only episode to note is the constitution in Tāzarwālt, by a marabout Sayyidī (Sīdī) Hishām of a kind of independent kingdom, the capital of which was Ilīgh and which lasted from the end of the 18th century till 1886.

Henceforth, the Maṣmūda disappear from history. The Atlas remained more or less independent, according to the degree of power of the ruling sovereigns, but all the important events in the region took place among the Ḥāḥa or in Sūs [*q.v.*]. The French occupation found the old Maṣmūda grouped, since the death of the ʿAlawid Sultan Mawlāy al-Ḥasan, into three bodies each under the authority of a local family: the Glāwa in the east, the Gunḍāfa in the centre, ad the Mtugga in the west.

The name Maṣmūda, still preserved in the north of Morocco in the name of a little tribe of al-Ḳaṣr al-Kabīr, seems to have completely disappeared in the south, where the former Maṣmūda peoples, continuing to talk Berber, bear the name of *Shulūḥ* (French *Chleuhs* [*q.v.*]. It may even be asked if the name Maṣmūda, which is found so often in the Arab historians and geographers, was ever in regular use among the peoples to whom they apply it; it is, indeed, suggestive that it is not found in the long lists of ethnics given in the *Kitāb al-Ansāb*, published in the *Documents inédits d'histoire almohade.*

Social structure. The Maṣmūda of the Atlas lead a settled life, living by a little agriculture and breeding a poor type of cattle; they live in villages or hamlets of stone houses with clay roofs. Ibn Khaldūn notes the existence among them of numerous little strongholds and fortified villages (*maʿāḳil wa-ḥuṣūn*), the ancestors of the modern *tighremts* and *agadirs* [*q.v.*]. There were no towns among the mountains; Tīn Mallal, famous for the mosque where Ibn Tūmart was buried, was never a town. Before the Almoravid ruler Yūsuf b. Tāshfīn founded Marrākush in 454/1062, built moreover in the plains out of reach of the highlanders, whom it was to control, the only urban centres in the district were situated at the foot of the Atlas on its lowest slopes. The principal towns were in the north, the double town of Aghmāt [*q.v.*] and that of Naffīs on the river of the same name; in the south, in Sūs, Igli and Tarūdant; as places of less importance we may mention in the north, Shafshāwa (mod. Shīshāwa), Afīfan and Tamarurt; in the east, among the Ḥāḥa and in the borders of Sūs, Tadnast. The great trade-routes which traversed the region started from Aghmāt for the port of Ḳūz (at the north of the Tansift), Fās (via Tādlā), Sidjilmāssa (through the land of the Hazradja and the Haskūra), and Sūs (via Naffīs, the land of the Banū Māghūs and Igli; no doubt using the pass now called Tizi n-Test). Al-Bakrī particularly mentions the industry and application and the thirst for gain, characteristic of the Maṣmūda of the Atlas of Sūs. The principal products of the country were fruits (nuts and almonds), honey and oil of *argan* [*q.v.*], a tree peculiar to the country, of which there were regular forests among the Ḥāḥa. The Maṣmūda could cast and work iron and also copper, which they exported in the form of ingots or "loaves" (*tangult*); they also worked and chased silver jewellery. In Sūs also the cultivation of the sugar-cane enabled sugar to be made.

From the intellectual point of view, the Maṣmūda seem to occupy a place of first rank among the Berbers. Each of their three principal groups has produced a "reforming prophet", the author of sacred works in the Berber language: Ḥā-Mīm of the Ghumāra; Ṣāliḥ b. Ṭarīf of the Baraghwāṭa; Ibn Tūmart of the Maṣmūda of the Atlas. It may also be noted that Sūs is one of those few districts in which books were written in Berber down to a quite recent date (cf. H. Basset, *Essai sur la littérature des Berbères*, 73-81).

Religious life. The Maṣmūda were converted to Islam in the 1st/7th century by ʿUḳba b. Nāfiʿ, who left his comrade Shākir among them to teach the new religion. The latter died among them and was buried on the banks of the Tansift where his tomb is still venerated. The place is now called Ribāṭ Sayyidī Shikar near the confluence with the river of the Shīshāwa. The Mosque of the town of Aghmāt of the Haylāna was founded at the beginning of the 2nd/8th century in 85/704.

Ibn Khaldūn describes the Maṣmūda of the Atlas as being attached to Islam from the first conquest, in which they differed from their brethren of the north, the Baraghwāṭa and the Ghumāra, who remained faithful to their heretical beliefs. At the beginning of the 2nd/8th century, several of them accompanied Ṭāriḳ on his conquest of Spain; the best known of these was Kuthayyir b. Waslās b. Shamlāl, of the tribe of the Aṣṣāda, who settled in Spain and was the grandfather of Yaḥyā b. Yaḥyā, one of the *ruwāt* of the *Muwaṭṭa*ʾ; many others also settled in Spain and their descendants played important parts under the Umayyads.

In the 5th/11th century, however, al-Bakrī notes Rāfiḍī heretics among the Maṣmūda; these were the Banū Lamās settled to the north of the Hargha and the town of Igli. In this district he also mentions the existence of idolators who worshipped a ram; perhaps we have here a relic of the cult of the god Ammon among the ancient Berbers. The towns, however, formed important centres of Muslim culture, the influence of which was felt not only by the Maṣmūda of the district but also by the Ṣanhādja of the adjoining deserts, Lamṭa and Gazūla. We know that it was in the town of Naffīs, with Uggʷag b. Zallū, a learned jurist of Lamṭa origin and a pupil of Abū ʿImrān al-Fāsī [*q.v.* in Suppl.] of al-Ḳayrawān, that in 430/1039 Yaḥyā b. Ibrāhīm al-Gudālī recruited ʿAbd Allāh b. Yā-Sīn al-Gazūlī who was the promoter of the Almoravid movement. For the Almohad period, al-Tādilī's hagiographic collection, entitled *Kitāb al-Tashawwuf*, shows us the land of the Maṣmūda of the south full of wonder-working saints. Later, the tribe of the Ragrāga, settled on the lands now occupied by the Shayāḍima, was the cradle of a movement at once religious and warlike, the details of which are little-known but the memory still alive. In the first half of the 11th/17th century, religious activity seems to be concentrated in the south of Sūs, in Tāzarwālt where the descendants of the saint Sīdī Aḥmad u-Mūsā carved themselves out an independent marabout principality.

Bibliography: See the indices to the geographers, especially Bakrī and Idrīsī; Tādilī, *K. al-Tashawwuf ilā (maʿrifat) ridjāl al-taṣawwuf*, ed. A. Faure, Rabat 1958; Leo Africanus, ed. Schefer, i, 181-231; Ibn Khaldūn, *K. al-ʿIbar*, chapters devoted to the Maṣāmida; E. Lévi-Provençal, *Documents inédits d'histoire almohade*, Paris 1928, principally 55-67; R. Montagne, *Les Berbères et le Makhzen dans le Sud du Maroc*, Paris 1930; H. Basset and H. Terrasse, *Timmel*, in *Hespéris* (1924), 9-91.

(G. S. Colin)

MAṢMUGHAN, ("great one of the Magians") a Zoroastrian dynasty which the Arabs found in the region of Dunbāwand (Damāwand [*q.v.*]) to the north of Ray.

The origins of the Maṣmughāns. The dynasty seems to have been an old, though not particularly celebrated, one, as is shown by the legends recorded by Ibn al-Faḳīh, 275-7, and in al-Bīrūnī, *Āthār*, 227. The title of *maṣmughān* is said to have been conferred by Farīdūn upon Armāʾīl, Bēwarāsp's former cook (Zohāk), who had been able to save half the young men destined to perish as food for the tyrant's serpents. Armāʾīl (according to Yāḳūt, ii, 606, a Nabataean, a native of the Zāb) showed to Farīdūn in the mountains of Daylam and Shirriz, a whole nation of these refugees, which caused Farīdūn to exclaim *was mānā kata āzād kardī*, which is explained to mean: "What a large number of people of the house (*ahl bayt*ⁱⁿ) thou hast saved' ".

The first historical reference to a *maṣmughān* is found in al-Ṭabarī's (i, 2656) account of the taking of Ray by Nuʿaym b. Muḳarrin in the time of the caliph ʿUmar (according to Ibn al-Athīr in the years 18, 21 or 22; Marquart, however, puts these events as late as 98/716-17). The King of Ray, Siyāwakhsh b. Mihrān b. Bahrām-Čubīn, had received reinforcements from the people of Dunbāwand, but when he was defeated, the *maṣmughān* of Dunbāwand made peace at once with the Arabs and received honorable terms (*ʿalā ghayrⁱ naṣrⁱⁿ wa lā maʿūnatⁱⁿ*) promising an annual payment of 200,000 *dīnārs*. The charter given by Nuʿaym was addressed "to the *maṣmughān* of Dunbāwand, Mardān-shāh, to the people of Dunbāwand, of Khʷār, of Lāriz (Lāridjān) and of Shirriz". This gives us an idea of the extent of the sway of the *maṣmughān*. His possessions included the country round Mount Damāwand and stretched down the plains as far as the east of Ray. The district of Dunbāwand (* Dubā-wand, [the land occupied by] the * Dubān clan?) did not form part of Ṭabaristān. The Arabs mention it along with Ray (al-Ṭabarī, i, 2653-6; al-Muḳaddasī, 209; Ibn al-Faḳīh, 275-7); but as we have seen, at the time of the conquest, Ray and Dunbāwand were under different dynasties. The old capital of Dunbāwand may have been at Mandān, where, according to Ibn al-Faḳīh, Armāʾīl had built a wonderful house of teak and ebony, which in the reign of Hārūn al-Rashīd was taken to pieces and transported to Baghdād. In the Arab period there were two towns in Dunbāwand, sc. Wīmā and Shalanba (the latter is marked on Stahl's map to the south of the modern town of Damāwand, which lies on the slopes of Mount Damāwand). According to Yāḳūt, the *maṣmughān*'s principal stronghold was called Ustūnāwand or Djarhud. This should be sought above the village of Rayna, which must correspond to the old Ḳaryat al-Ḥaddādīn. (Ibn al-Faḳīh's story of the shops (*ḥawānīt*) in which worked the smiths, the noise of whose hammers exorcised the enchained Bēwarāsp, must refer to the chambers carved out of the rock near Rayna; cf. E. Crawshay-Williams, *Rock-dwellings at Reinah*, in *JRAS* [1904], 551; [1906], 217.)

An attempt made by Abū Muslim in 131/748-9 to conquer the *maṣmughān* was a disastrous failure: his general Mūsā b. Kaʿb was attacked by the *maṣmughān*'s men and on account of the difficult nature of the country (*li-ḍīkⁱ bilādihi*) was forced to return to Ray (Ibn al-Athīr, v, 304; cf. Ḥāfiẓ-i Abrū, in Dorn, *Auszüge*, 441).

The principality was not conquered until 141/758-9. In this period, there were dissensions in the family of the *maṣmughān*. Abarwīz b. al-Maṣmughān quarrelled with his brother and went over to the caliph al-Manṣūr, who gave him a pension (al-Ṭabarī, iii, 130). The *Kitāb al-ʿUyūn wa 'l-ḥadāʾiḳ*, 228, testifies to his bravery in the rising of the Rāwandiyya and calls him "al-Maṣmughān Mālik b. Dīnār, *malik* of Dunbāwand". This Abarwīz (or Mālik) had enjoyed considerable influence, for, according to Ibn al-Faḳīh, the appointment of ʿUmar b. ʿAlāʾ as commander of the army sent against Ṭabaristān was made on the advice of Abarwīz, who had known him since the trouble with Sunbādh (on the partisans of this "Khurramī" in Ṭabaristān, cf. al-Masʿūdī, *Murūdj*, vi, 188 = § 2400) and with the Rāwandiyya.

In the year 141/748-9, the brother of Abarwīz who occupied the throne of Dunbāwand was at war with his father-in-law, the *ispahbad* Khurshīd of Ṭabaristān; but when he heard that the forces sent by al-Manṣūr were on their way to Ṭabaristān, he hastened to effect a reconciliation with his adversary (al-Ṭabarī, iii, 136; Ibn al-Athīr, v, 386).

The stories of the campaign against Ṭabaristān directed by al-Mahdī by order of his father al-Manṣūr are very contradictory, as is shown by their very detailed analysis in Vasmer, *op. cit.*, in *Bibl.* After the defeat of the *ispahbad*, the Arabs conquered the *maṣmughān* and captured him and his daughters Bakh-tariyya (?) and Ṣmyr (? or Shakla). Of these princesses, one became the wife of al-Mahdī b. al-Manṣūr and the other the *umm walad* of ᶜAlī b. Rayṭa. According to a story in Ibn al-Faḳīh, 314, Khālid b. Barmak (Vasmer, *op. cit.*, 100, thinks that his expedition was sent especially against the lord of Dunbā-wand) sent the *maṣmughān* and his wife and his two daughters to Baghdād, but in another passage, 275, the same writer says that the *maṣmughān* obtained *amān* from al-Mahdī and came down from the mountain of al-ᶜAyrayn (?). He was taken to Ray, and there al-Mahdī ordered him to be beheaded.

After the death of the *maṣmughān*, the people of these mountain regions lapsed into barbarism (*ḥawziyya*) and became like wild beasts (al-Ṭabarī, iii, 136). According to Ibn al-Faḳīh (276), however, the descendants of the *maṣmughān* (= Armāʾīl?) were still well-known.

Spiegel's and Marquart's hypotheses. Yāḳūt, i, 244, interprets *maṣmughān* as *kabīr al-madjūs* "the great one of the magi" (*mas* "great", N.W. Iranian form). Spiegel thought of connecting this dynasty with the prince-priests of Ray, whose existence is known from a well-known passage in the Avesta (*Yasna*, ix, 18, tr. Darmesteter, i, 170; cf. Jackson, *Zoroaster*, 202-5). In spite of Marquart's criticisms, who says it is impossible to quote the authority of Avestan traditions which relate to much earlier state of affairs, Spiegel's suggestion is still of interest. We have certainly to deal with vague memories and not with actual facts. In the time of the Arab conquest, the descendants of Bahrām Čubīn were ruling in Ray, but the Arabs (al-Ṭabarī, i, 2653-6) installed there a certain al-Zaynabī, son of Ḳūla and father of al-Farrukhān. It remains to be seen if this family of Zaynbadī "whom the Arabs call al-Zaynabī" (al-Balādhurī, 317) is connected with Dunbāwand. Their stronghold in Ray was called ᶜĀrīn (?), which resembles the name of the mountain al-ᶜAyrayn from which the last *maṣmughān* came down (cf. the note by de Goeje in Ibn al-Faḳīh, 275). Marquart wanted to connect the *maṣmughāns* of the Bāwandid dynasty, the eponymous ancestor of which Bāw, a descendant of Kāwūs, brother of Khusraw I, is said to have lived in the time of the later Sāsānids [see BĀWAND]. This Bāw was a man of piety, and after the fall of Yazdagird III had retired to his father's fire-temple. Marquart regards him as a "magus" and identifies him with the father of the Christian martyr Anastasius, who bore this name (βαῦ) and was a "master of Magian lore". Lastly, he quotes the fact that the Bāwandids appeared in 167/783-4 only after the disappearance of the *maṣmughāns* (after 141), as if to continue their line. Unfortunately, several details of the ingenious argument are not accurate: our sources (Ibn Isfandiyār; Ẓahīr al-Dīn, 204-5) give not the slightest suggestion that Bāw belonged to the priestly caste. According to Ibn Isfandiyār (tr. Browne, 98), his grandfather's temple was at Kūsān, which Rabino, *Mázandarán and Astarábad*, 160, locates a little distance west of Ashraf i.e. quite remote from Dunbāwand. The passage in al-Ṭabarī, iii, 1294, which Marquart quotes to prove the occurrence of the name Maṣmughān among the Bāwandids refers to the cousin of Māzyār of the Ḳārinid dynasty [*q.v.*], which is quite different from the Bāwandids (cf. below).

The Ḳārinid *maṣmughāns*. It is curious that neither Ibn Isfandiyār nor Ẓahīr al-Dīn speaks of the dynasty of the *maṣmughān* of Dunbāwand, perhaps because they do not include this region in Ṭabaristān proper. On the other hand, they mention a *maṣmughān* (*maḍmughān* > * *mazmughān*) Walāsh, who was the *marzubān* [*q.v.*] of Miyān-du-rūd (Ẓahīr al-Dīn, 42, says that this canton was near the Sārī between the rivers Kalārud and Mihribān and that on the east it adjoined Ḳaratughān; Miyān-du-rūd is thus quite close to where Rabino puts Kūsān !). This *maṣmughān* Walāsh (Ibn Isfandiyār, 101; Ẓahīr al-Dīn, 42) lived in the time of Djamāspid Farrukhān the Great (709-22?) and belonged to the elder branch of the Ḳārinids descended from Zarmihr b. Sūkhā. (it is unclear why Justi, *Iranische Namenbuch*, 430, takes this Walāsh to be the son of the last *maṣmughān* of Dunbāwand). The Ḳārinid Wandād Hurmuzd (of the younger line, descended from Ḳārin, brother of Zarmihr) in his rising against the caliph (al-Mahdī, 158-69/775-85) had combined with the *ispahbad* Sharwīn (772-97) and the *maṣmughān* Walāsh of Miyān-du-rūd. This latter (Ibn Isfandiyār, 126; Ẓahīr al-Dīn, 155) seems to have been one of the successors of the *maṣmughān* Walāsh mentioned above.

Under 224/838 al-Ṭabarī (iii, 1294) mentions a cousin of the Ḳārinid Māzyār, who was called Shāhriyār b. al-Maṣmughān. According to this, al-Maṣmughān would be identical with Wandād Ummīd, uncle of Māzyār (cf. Justi, 430). On the other hand, under the year 250/864, al-Ṭabarī, iii, 1529, mentions a Māṣmughān (*sic*) among the allies of the ᶜAlid Ḥasan b. Zayd. Ibn Isfandiyār, 165, calls him Maṣmughān b. Wandā-Ummīd. One must either suppose there is an error in al-Ṭabarī's genealogy or admit that the title of *maṣmughān* was borne both by Wandā-Ummīd and his son, but the form of the designation of the latter (ماصمغان without the article) would rather show that the title had become a simple proper name (Browne was thus wrong in translating "*the* Maṣmughān").

To sum up then. Alongside of the *maṣmughāns* of Dunbāwand, we have the *maṣmughāns* of Miyān-du-rūd. These *marzubāns*, if we may rely on Ẓahīr al-Dīn, belonged to the Zarmihrid branch of the dynasty of Sūkhrā (Sāsānid governor of Ṭabaristān descended from Ḳārin, son of the famous smith Kāwa [see KĀWAN]). Later we find the title (or proper name!) of *maṣmughān* recurring in the younger branch of the line of Sūkhrā (the Ḳārinid branch), which occupied a position in Ṭabaristān subordinate to the Bāwandid *ispahbads* (Ẓahīr al-Dīn, 154, 14).

Bibliography: Ṭabarī, i, 2656; iii, 130, 136 (1294, 1529); Bīrūnī, *al-Āthār al-bāḳiya*, 101, tr. 109, 227, 213; *Kitāb al-ᶜUyūn wa 'l-ḥadāʾiḳ*, ed. de Goeje and de Jong, 228; Ibn al-Athīr, iii, 18; v, 304, 386-7; Ibn Isfandiyār, index; Yāḳūt, i, 243-4 (Ustūnāwand); ii, 606-10 (Dunbāwand); Ẓahīr al-Dīn, index; F. Spiegel, *Eranische Alterthumskunde*, 1871, iii, 563; idem, *Über d. Vaterland d. Avesta*, in *ZDMG*, xxxv (1881), 629-45; F. Justi, *Iranische Namenbuch*, 199 and 430 (tables); J. Marquart, *Beiträge*, in *ZDMG*, xlix (1895), 661; idem, *Ērānšahr*, 127; R. Vasmer, *Die Eroberung Tabaristans ... zur Zeit des Chalifen al-Manṣūr*, in *Islamica*, iii (1927), 86-150; see also ḲĀRINIDS. (V. MINORSKY)

MAṢRAF DEFTERI, the household account book of high-level Ottoman administrators such as viziers or governors, or of palace personnel such as waterbearers. The account book covered, for time periods of a month up to several years, detailed monthly inventories of household economic transactions. These inventories are often organised under subject headings such as kitchen, clothing, or food expenses, purchases of household goods from merchants and artisans, salaries of household members, or gifts given and received during religious holidays. Each entry of the inventory usually contains a description of the transaction, the price, quantity and the names of the people involved in the transaction. No systematic study of these books, hundreds of which are to be found in the Topkapı and Ottoman State archives, has yet been undertaken. (F. MÜGE GÖÇEK)

MASRAḤ (A.), "scene", increasingly employed as "theatre" (in the same sense as "Bühne" in German); frequently synonymous with *tiyātrō* (from the Italian).

1. In the Arab East.

Primarily an artistic and literary phenomenon of the last two centuries, the Arab theatre has its roots in local performances of passion plays [see TAʿZIYA], marionette and shadow plays [see ḲARAGÖZ], mimicry and other popular farces, and was affected by the then contemporary (rather than the classical) foreign theatre as well. Although some popular open-air plays in Arabic have occasionally been presented publicly since the 12th/18th century, if not earlier, an Arabic theatre in the modern sense of this term has been in existence only since the mid-19th century. It was in 1847-53 that Mārūn al-Naḳḳāsh [*q.v.*], under the impact of the Italian theatre, wrote and produced several plays, chiefly adapted from Molière, before select audiences in Beirut. His plays arabicised the locale, the names of the *dramatis personae* and certain elements of the plot, in order to increase the appeal; with the same intent, the language combined the literary with the vernacular, and both vocal and instrumental music was added. To moderate possible opposition from religious circles, men and boys acted the female parts (later on, non-Muslim—and afterwards, Muslim—women joined theatre troupes). These features, which remained characteristic for some time, were introduced into Egypt by Syrian-Lebanese immigrant actors, who soon rendered Egypt (and, most particularly, Cairo) the centre of Arab theatrical activity. Performances continued in Syria as well, and gradually spread to other Arab lands in the Middle East and North Africa. Most troupes were made up of amateurs, e.g. students, or at most, of semi-professionals; gradually, however, the number of the professional actors increased, although they had to await the establishment of semi-independent states, following World War I, in order to benefit from the public funds which were vital for their unhampered activity.

These developments were parallelled by playwriting. At first, most plays were written by people of other professions. Mārūn al-Naḳḳāsh was a clerk and merchant; his successors were journalists or, even more often, troupe directors, stage managers or actors. Only much later did the writing of plays become a full-time profession. Adaptations, mostly from the French, came first, as al-Naḳḳāsh's literary output indicates. An even more prolific writer was Muḥammad ʿUthmān Djalāl (1829-98) of Egypt, who adapted into Arabic French tragedies and comedies, introducing appropriate changes, chiefly in the latter; in general, the former were performed in literary Arabic, the latter in the vernacular. Increased education and changes in taste led to more literal translations (although adaptations did not disappear for some time). One typical translator was the Beirut-born Nadjīb al-Ḥaddād (1867-99), who wrote in Egypt. Although he changed the names of the plays and some of the characters and added music, al-Ḥaddād usually remained faithful to the originals (mostly translated from the French); his works served as a model for the strictly literal translators which soon followed. These generally translated from French or English and, to a lesser extent, from Italian and other languages. There followed an impressive number of original playwrights, whose output continued simultaneously with active translation work (and, initially at least, adaptations). These cover the entire gamut of dramatic writing, contributing to the répertoire of farces, historical plays, melodramas, dramas, tragedies, comedies, political and symbolic plays, as well as works pertaining to the theatre of the absurd. One of the most deservedly-famous of these playwrights, who successfully tried his hand at several of these genres, is Tawfīḳ al-Ḥakīm (born in ?1902), one of Egypt's prominent 20th century men-of-letters.

There was evident interaction between dramatic output and the further development of the troupes. While the musical theatre continued to attract crowds, the acting, the stage-directing and theatrical criticism achieved gradual professionalisation: the number of theatre halls increased, and troupes performed an increasing variety of plays to a steadily growing public of diverse interests and tastes. Of all the troupe directors and actors in Egypt after World War I, perhaps the ones with the most impact were Djūrdj Abyaḍ [*q.v.* in Suppl.] who, having studied acting in the Paris Conservatoire, promoted an Arabic classical theatre in the grand style; Yūsuf Wahbī (1899-1981), promoter of the often tear-jerking melodrama with social background; and Nadjīb al-Rīḥānī (1891-1949), nicknamed "The Oriental Molière", whose comedies amused the crowds while criticising the social mores of his time. Numerous other troupes have joined these during the Inter-War period and since World War II, particularly in Egypt, Lebanon, Syria and ʿIrāḳ, less so in Jordan, and hardly at all in the Arabian Peninsula. Most are ephemeral unless supported by public funds, while usually means government allocations. Obviously, schools for the dramatic arts and theatre halls are dependent on such funds. All this has, again, led to a certain politicisation of the Arab theatre, differing from one country to the other. This process has been evident from the early days of the Arab theatre, e.g. in the plays of Yaʿḳūb Ṣanūʿ Abū Naḍḍāra [*q.v.*] in the Egypt of the 1870s; since World War II, however, it has acquired an obvious social content, often fully committed and starkly realistic. Theatrical criticism, too, has become increasingly outspoken, with critics generally vying among each other in their caustic remarks on play-writing, acting and stage-directing. They readily find an outlet not only in journals specially devoted to theatrical criticism (see *Bibl.*, below, for examples), but in many Arabic dailies and periodicals as well. All this is yet another indication of the great interest in the theatre throughout much of the Arab East.

Bibliography: Few bibliographies are devoted exclusively to the Arab theatre, e.g. Ṣalāḥ Djawād al-Ṭuʿma, *Bibliyūghrafiyyat al-adab al-ʿArabī al-masraḥī al-ḥadīth, 1945-1965*, Baghdād 1969; or *al-Nuṣūṣ al-masraḥiyya al-maḥfūẓa fī masāriḥ al-Ḳāhira mundhu nashʾatihā ḥattā al-ān*, in *al-Kātib al-ʿArabī*, xlv (April 1969), 60-83. For a list of plays in Arabic (both original and translated), see Dār al-Kutub, *Ḳāʾima ʿan al-tamthīliyyāt al-ʿArabiyya wa 'l-muʿarraba*, Cairo 1960. Bibliographies concerning the Arab countries or modern Arabic literature are relevant, in part, as are some bibliographies of the theatre, like N.B. East (ed.), *African theatre: a checklist of critical materials*, New York 1970, 15-19 (for Egypt and the Maghrib). Several of the books mentioned below also comprise useful bibliographical lists. Source materials, as well as memoirs (but excluding plays) include Salīm al-Naḳḳās̲h̲, *Fawāʾid al-riwāyāt aw al-tiyātrāt*, in *al-D̲j̲inān* (Beirut), vi (1875), 521; *al-Tamt̲h̲īl al-ʿArabī*, in *al-Hilāl* (Cairo), xiv (1 Dec. 1905), 141-9; xv (1 Nov. 1906), 117-18; *al-Tamt̲h̲īl al-ʿArabī: māḍīhī wa-mustaḳbaluhu, ibid.*, xxxii (1924), 481-4, 638-41, 751-3 (a referendum); *al-Masraḥ aw al-marzaḥ*, in *al-Muḳtaṭaf* (Cairo), lxix (1 Aug. 1926), 223-4; Fāṭima al-Yūsuf, *D̲h̲ikrayāt*, Cairo 1953; Nad̲j̲īb al-Rīḥānī, *Mud̲h̲akkirāt*, Cairo 1959; Fāṭima Rus̲h̲dī, *Fāṭima Rus̲h̲dī bayn al-ḥubb wa 'l-fann*, Cairo 1971; eadem, *Kifāḥī fi 'l-masraḥ wa 'l-sīnimā*, Cairo 1971; Futūḥ Nas̲h̲āṭī, *K̲h̲amsūn ʿām*[an] *fī k̲h̲idmat al-masraḥ*, i-ii, Cairo 1973-4; Nāzik Bāsīlā (ed.), *Mud̲h̲akkirāt Badīʿa Maṣābnī*, Beirut n.d.; Muḥammad Rifʿat (ed.), *Mud̲h̲akkirāt ʿAbd al-Ḥalīm Ḥāfiẓ*, Beirut, n.d.; idem (ed.), *Mud̲h̲akkirāt ʿAbd al-Wahhāb*, Beirut n.d.; idem, *Mud̲h̲akkirāt ʿamīd al-masraḥ al-ʿArabī Yūsuf Wahbī*, Beirut n.d.; idem (ed.), *Mud̲h̲akkirāt Badīʿ K̲h̲ayrī: 45 sana taḥt aḍwāʾ al-masraḥ*, Beirut n.d.; idem (ed.), *Mud̲h̲akkirāt Fāṭima Rus̲h̲dī, Sarah Bernhardt al-s̲h̲arḳ wa-mumat̲h̲t̲h̲ilat al-masraḥ al-ʿArabī*, Beirut n.d.; idem (ed.), *Mud̲h̲akkirāt Fātin Ḥamāma wa-ʿUmar al-S̲h̲arīf*, Beirut n.d.; idem (ed.), *Mud̲h̲akkirāt Umm Kult̲h̲ūm*, Beirut n.d. In addition, several Arabic periodicals dealing with the threatre might be profitably consulted, of which one of the most important is *al-Masraḥ*, edited in Cairo until his death (in 1981) by Ṣalāḥ ʿAbd al-Ṣabbūr. See also E. W. Lane, *An account of the manners and customs of the modern Egyptians*, London 1846, ii, 113 ff.; D. Urquhart, *The Lebanon (Mount Syria): a history and a diary*, London 1860, ii, 178-81; H. Brugsch, *Das morgenländische Theater*, in *Deutsche Revue* (Breslau), xii/3 (1887), 25-34; K. Vollers, *Der neuarabische Tartuffe*, in *ZDMG*, xlv (1891), 36-96; M. Sobernheim, *Zur Metrik einiger in's Arabische übersetzter Dramen Molière*, in *MSOS* (1898), part 2, 185-7; Nad̲j̲īb Ḥubayka, *Fann al-tamt̲h̲īl*, in *al-Mas̲h̲riḳ* (Beirut), ii (1899), 20-3, 71-4, 156-60, 250-7, 341-5, 501-7; *al-Tamt̲h̲īl al-ʿArabī: nahḍatuhu al-ak̲h̲īra ʿalā yad al-d̲j̲anāb al-ʿālī*, in *al-Hilāl*, xviii (1 May 1910), 464-72; in *ibid.* (1 June 1910), 545-7; C. Prüfer, *Drama (Arabic)*, in *Encyclopaedia of Religion and Ethics*, iv (1911), 872-8; *D̲j̲awḳ Abyaḍ*, in *al-Hilāl*, xxi (1 Nov. 1912), 125-6; *al-Tamt̲h̲īl fī Miṣr: D̲j̲awḳ Abyaḍ*, in *ibid.*, xx (1 April 1912), 436-8; Sulaymān Ḥasan al-Ḳabbānī, *Bug̲h̲yat al-mumat̲h̲t̲h̲ilīn*, Alexandria n.d. [1912-14]; D̲j̲ūrd̲j̲ Ṭannūs, *al-S̲h̲ayk̲h̲ Salāma Ḥid̲j̲āzī*, in *al-Hilāl*, xxvi (1 Nov. 1917), 186-9; W. H. Worrell, *Kishkish: Arabic vaudeville in Cairo*, in *MW*, x/2 (Apr. 1920), 134-7; K̲h̲alīl Muṭrān, *al-Tamt̲h̲īl al-ʿArabī wa-nahḍatuh al-d̲j̲adīda*, in *al-Hilāl*, xxix (1 Feb. 1921), 465-72; Ahmed Abdul Wahhab, *A thesis on the drama in the Arabic literature*, n.p. (Dacca ?) 1922; *D̲h̲ikrā Mulyīr wa-riwāyātih fi 'l-lug̲h̲a al-ʿArabiyya*, in *al-Hilāl*, xxx (1 Mar. 1922), 555-8; F. J. Bonjean, *Une renaissance égyptienne*, in *Europe* (Paris), i (June-July 1923), 83-95, 199-217; *al-Tamt̲h̲īl fī Miṣr: nahḍatuhu al-d̲j̲adīda*, in al-*Hilāl*, xxxiii (1 Nov. 1924), 185-6; A. and L. Lewisohn, *Little theatre in Egypt*, in *Atlantic Monthly* (Boston), cxxxiv (July 1924), 93-103; Muhammad Aḥmad, *Fann al-tamt̲h̲īl*, Cairo 1925; Tawfīḳ Ḥabīb, *S̲h̲iksbīr fī Miṣr*, in *al-Hilāl*, xxxvi (1 Dec. 1927), 201-4; *al-Masraḥ wa-mustaḳbaluhu wa-mā ḥazzunā minhu*, in *ibid.*, 175-6; Maḥmūd Kāmil al-Muḥāmī, *al-Masraḥ al-d̲j̲adīd*, Cairo 1932 (Arabic summaries of foreign plays); I. Kratschkowsky, art. *Arabia. Modern Arabic literature, II. c. Drama*, in *EI*[1], Suppl.; Edwār Ḥunayn, *S̲h̲awḳī ʿalā 'l-masraḥ*, in *al-Mas̲h̲riḳ*, xxxii (1934), 563-80; xxxiii (1935), 68-92, 273-88, 394-427 (reprinted as a booklet, Beirut 1936); N. Barbour, *The Arabic theatre in Egypt*, in *BSOS*, viii (1935-7), 173-87, 991-1012; Saʿīd ʿAḳl, *al-Ittid̲j̲āhāt al-d̲j̲adīda fi 'l-adab al-ʿArabī: al-masraḥ*, in *al-Mas̲h̲riḳ*, xxxv (1937), 41-52; E. Fabré, *Le théâtre arabe*, in *L'illustration* (Paris), cxcvii (15 May 1937), 71; Bis̲h̲r Fāris, *Fī 'l-taʾlīf al-masraḥī*, in *al-T̲h̲aḳāfa* (Cairo), 7 March 1939, 44-5; Skandar Fahmy, *La renaissance du théâtre égyptien moderne*, in *Revue du Caire*, iv (1940), 107-12; Brockelmann, S III, 264-81 and index; U. Rizzitano, *Il teatro arabo in Egitto: opere teatrali di Taufīq al-Ḥakīm*, in *OM*, xxiii/6 (June 1943), 247-66; Zakī Ṭulaymāt, *al-Riwāya al-tamt̲h̲īliyya wa-lī-mā-d̲h̲ā al-ʿArab*, in *al-Kitāb* (Cairo) (Nov. 1945), 101-8; idem, *Kayfa dak̲h̲ala al-tamt̲h̲īl bilād al-s̲h̲arḳ*, in *ibid.* (Feb. 1946), 581-7; idem, *al-Masraḥ al-miṣrī fī ʿām*, in *ibid.* (July 1946), 481-8; idem, *Drama in Egypt*, in M. L. Roy Choudhury (ed.), *Egypt in 1945*, Calcutta 1946, 207-17; C. Alexander, *Theatre in Egypt*, in *Theatre Arts* (New York), xxx (June 1946), 367; Rus̲h̲dī Kāmil, *S̲h̲ahriyyat al-masraḥ*, in *al-Kātib al-Miṣrī* (Cairo), i (June 1946), 139-40; ʿAbd al-Raḥmān Ṣidḳī *S̲h̲ahriyyat al-masraḥ*, in *ibid.*, xv (Dec. 1946), 540-4; J. M. Landau, *ʿAl ha-teyʾaṭrōn etsel ha-ʿAravīm* (Hebrew, *About the theatre of the Arabs*), in *Bamah* (Tel-Aviv), xlvii (Jan. 1946), 48-53; xlviii (June 1946), 65-75; xlix (Sep. 1946), 48-60; 1 (Jan. 1947), 107-15; idem, *ha-Teyʾaṭrōn ha-ʿAravī bĕ-Erets-Israʾel ba-s̲h̲anah ha-aḥarōna* (Hebrew, *The Arab theatre in Palestine during the past year*), in *ibid.*, lii (Dec. 1947), 43; Ṣalāḥ D̲h̲uhnī, *al-Firḳa al-miṣriyya fī ʿām*, in *al-Kitāb* (July 1947), 1418-22; M. Jacobs, *Neguib el-Rihani*, in *The Bulletin (of the Egyptian Educational Bureau*, London), xii (Nov. 1947), 16-18; idem, *Egyptian stage actresses*, in *ibid.*, xxii (March 1948), 15-17; Maḥmūd Ḥāmid S̲h̲awkat, *al-Masraḥiyya fī s̲h̲iʿr S̲h̲awḳī*, n.p. 1947; Landau, *Shadow plays in the Near East*, Jerusalem 1948; Habib Moutran, *La troupe nationale égyptienne et Khalil Bey Moutran*, in *Le Semaine Egyptienne*, xxii/23-4 (1948), 25-6; G. R. Orvieto, *La genesi del teatro arabo in Egitto*, unpubl. Ph.D. diss., Rome Univ. 1948; Yūsuf Asʿad Dāg̲h̲ir, *Fann al-tamt̲h̲īl fī k̲h̲ilāl ḳarn*, in *Machriq*, xlii (1948), 434-60; xliii (1949), 118-39, 271-96; ʿUt̲h̲mān al-ʿAntablī, *Nad̲j̲īb al-Rīḥānī*, Cairo 1949; M. Jacobs, *The Cairo opera house*, in *The Bulletin...*, xxxiii (March 1949), 17-18; Jeanette Tagher, *Les débuts du théâtre moderne en Egypte*, in *Cahiers d'Histoire Egyptienne* (Cairo), série I, 1-2 (1949), 192-207; Aḥmad Haykal, *al-Adab al-ḳasaṣī wa 'l-masraḥ fī Miṣr min aʿḳāb t̲h̲awrat 1919 ilā ḳiyām al-ḥarb al-kubrā al-t̲h̲āniya*, Cairo 1951; Abdel M. Ramadan, *Egypt's theatre is international*, in *United Nations' World* (Vienna), v (March 1951), 61-2; Landau, *Li-s̲h̲ĕʾelat res̲h̲ītō s̲h̲el ha-teyʾaṭrōn bĕ-Mitsrayim* (Hebrew, *The problem of the beginnings of the theatre in Egypt*), in *Hamizraḥ Heḥadas̲h̲* (Jerusalem), ii/4 (July 1951), 389-91; Jabbour Abdel Nour, *La contribution des Libanais à la renaissance littéraire arabe au XIX*[e] *siècle*, unpubl. diss., Univ. of Paris 1952, esp. 172-6; G. A. Astre, *Le théâtre philosophique de Tewfiq el Hakim*, in *Critique* (Paris), lxvi (1952), 934-45; ʿAbd al-Fattāḥ al-Bārūdī, *al-Mawsim al-masraḥī*, in *al-Kitāb*, vii (June 1952), 753-5; idem, *al-Mawsim al-ṣayfī*, in *ibid.*, vii (Oct. 1952), 1003-5; Ch. Pellat, *Langue et littérature arabes*, Paris 1952, 208-13; ʿAbd al-Raḥmān Ṣidḳī, *Mawāsim al-tamt̲h̲īl al-miṣriyya wa 'l-ad̲j̲nabiyya*, in *al-Kitāb*, vii (Jan. 1952), 94-8; Landau, *Abū Naḍḍāra: an Egyptian Jewish nationalist*, in

Jnal. of Jewish Studies (Cambridge), iii/1 (1952), 30-44; idem, *The Arab theatre*, in *MEA*, iv/3 (March 1953), 77-86; idem, *Dramaṭūrgiyya mitsrīt: A. Shawḳī* (Hebrew, *Egyptian playwriting: A. Shawḳī*), in *Bamōt* (Jerusalem), i (1953), 305-9; Ibrāhīm ʿAbduh, *Abū Naḏḏāra*, Cairo 1953; Abdel Rahman Sidky, *Le théâtre*, in *Revue du Caire*, xxxi (Feb. 1953), 161-206; F. Ga. (= Gabrieli) and U. Ri. (= Rizzitano), *Arabo, teatro*, in *Enciclopedia dello Spettacolo* (Rome), i (1954), cols. 769-74; Yaḥyā Ḥaḳḳī, *Masraḥ al-Rīḥānī*, in *al-Adīb* (Beirut), xiii/4 (April 1954), 14-18; Landau, *Aziz Domet, d'origine araba, scrittore di romanzi e opere drammatiche di soggetto orientale in lingua tedesca (1890-1943)*, in *OM*, xxv/6 (June 1955), 277-89; Muḥammad Yūsuf Naḏjm, *Aḥmad Abū Khalīl al-Ḳabbānī*, in *al-Adīb*, xiv/1 (Jan. 1955), 19-22; xiv/2 (Feb. 1955), 17-21; idem, *Madrasat Mārūn al-Naḳḳāsh*, in *ibid.*, xiv/3 (March 1955), 24-6; *Tournée officielle de la nouvelle troupe égyptienne sous la direction de Youssef Wahbi*, n.p. n.d. [1955]; Yūsuf Asʿad Dāghir, *Maṣādir al-dirāsa al-adabiyya*, ii-iii/2, Beirut 1955-72, indexes; A. Papadopoulo, *La saison théâtrale au Caire*, in *Revue du Caire*, xix (April 1956), 325-38; M. Perlmann, *Memoirs of Rose Fatima al-Yusuf*, in *MEA*, vii/1 (Jan. 1956), 20-7; *Maḥmūd Taymūr, Mushkilat al-lugha al-ʿArabiyya*, Cairo 1956, partial Engl. tr. Landau, in Landau (ed.), *Man, state and society in the contemporary Middle East*, New York 1972, 332-40; O. Kapeliuk, *The Theater in Egypt*, in *New Outlook* (Tel-Aviv), i/4 (Oct. 1957), 32-8; ʿUmar al-Dassūḳī, *al-Masraḥiyya: nashʾatuhā wa-taʾrīkhuhā wa-uṣūluhā²*, n.p. n.d. [1958]; J. Stetkewycz, *Reflexiones sobre el teatro árabe moderno*, in *Revista del Instituto de Estudios Islámicos* (Madrid), vi (1958), 109-20; Landau, *Studies in the Arab theater and cinema*, Philadelphia 1958 (Fr. tr. *Études sur le théâtre et le cinéma arabes*, Paris 1965; Arabic tr. *al-Masraḥ wa 'l-sīnimā ʿind al-ʿArab*, Cairo 1972); Muḥammad Mandūr, *al-Masraḥ al-nathrī*, Cairo n.d. [1959]; L. ʿAwaḍ, *Dirāsāt fī adabinā al-ḥadīth*, Cairo 1960, 1-150; Muḥammad Kāmil Ḥusayn, *Fī 'l-adab al-masraḥī*, Beirut 1960; Akram Midani, *New forms in Arab literature and drama*, in *Arab World* (New York) vii/10 (Nov. 1960), 12-13; Fuʾād Rashīd, *Taʾrīkh al-masraḥ al-ʿArabī*, Cairo 1960; *Revival of the theatre*, in *Asiatic Review* (Woking, Surrey), i/8 (Nov. 1960), 24-8; Muḥammad Zakī al-ʿAshmāwī, *Dirāsāt fī 'l-adab wa 'l-masraḥ*, Cairo 1961; I. L. Genzier, *James Sanua and Egyptian nationalism*, in *MEJ*, xv/1 (Winter 1961), 16-28; Rashad Rushdy, *The impact of the revolution on literature; the drama*, in *Asiatic Review*, ii/19 (Nov. 1961), 56-8); *Our theatre ... old and new*, in *ibid.*, ii/23 (April 1962), 25-33; U. Rizzitano, *Reactions to Western political influences: ʿAlī Aḥmad Bākathīr's drama*, in B. Lewis and P. M. Holt (eds.), *Historians of the Middle East*, London 1962, 442-8; Fuʾād Dawwāra, *Fī 'l-naḳd al-masraḥī*, Cairo 1963; Khalīl Hindāwī et alii, *al-Thaḳāfa al-masraḥiyya*, Damascus 1383/1963; Muḥammad Mandūr, *al-Masraḥ²*, Cairo 1963, 14-122; Maḥmud Ḥāmid Shawkat, *al-Fann al-masraḥī fi 'l-adab al-ʿArabī al-ḥadīth*, Cairo 1963; Maḥmūd Taymūr, *Ṭulūʿ al-masraḥ al-ʿArabī*, Cairo 1963; V. Sol. (= V.I. Solovʾyev), *Yegipyetskiy tyeatr i dramaturgiya*, in *Tyeatral'naya Entsiklopyediya*, Moscow 1963, ii, cols. 628-33; S. A. Abulnaga, *Theatre revival in the U.A.R.*, in *New Africa* (London), vi (1964), 13; I. Brown, *The effervescent Egyptian theatre*, in *Theatre Annual* (Cleveland), xxi (1964), 57-68; Muḥammad ʿAbd al-Raḥīm ʿAnbar, *al-Masraḥiyya bayn al-naẓariyya wa 'l-taṭbīḳ*, Cairo 1966, 209 ff. (list of Arabic theatrical terms and English equivalents:

243-71); Fikrī Buṭrus, *Min aʿlām al-masraḥ al-ghināʾī*, Cairo 1966; A. Faraḏj, *Dalīl al-mutafarriḏj al-dhakī ilā 'l-masraḥ*, Cairo 1966; Gendzier, *The practical visions of Yaʿḳub Sanuʿ*, Cambridge, Mass. 1966, 31-40; *al-Masraḥ* (Cairo), xxxi (July 1966) (special issue on the Egyptian theatre, 1952-66); Zakī Ṭulaymāt, *al-Tamthīl, al-tamthīliyya, fann al-tamthīl al-ʿArabī*, Kuwayt n.d. [1966]; G. Wiet, *Introduction à la littérature arabe*, Paris 1966, 281-307 and index; ʿAṭiyya ʿĀmir, *Lughat al-masraḥ al-ʿArabī*, Stockholm 1967; J. Berque (ed.), *Les arts du spectacle dans le monde arabe depuis cent ans*, Paris 1967 (mimeographed); Ali El Rai, *The spirit of the Arab theatre from the early beginnings to the present day*, in *ibid.*, 1-13; Nabil Selame, *Le théâtre en République Arabe Unie et en Irak*, in *ibid.*, 23 ff.; P. Cachia, *The use of the colloquial in modern Arabic literature*, in *JAOS*, lxxxvii/1 (1967), 12-22; Abdel Monem Ismail, *Drama and society in contemporary Egypt*, Cairo 1967; Yusuf Mustafa, *Antecedents of modern Arabic drama*, unpubl. Ph.D. diss. Cambridge Univ. 1967, 57-68; Rushdī Ṣāliḥ, *al-Masraḥiyyāt: ʿarḍ li-funūn al-masraḥ fī sab ʿat mawāsim*, n.p. [Cairo] n.d. [1964]; *Colloquium on the modern Arab theatre*, in *World Theatre* (Brussels-Paris), xiv/2 (March-April 1965), 187-91; Tewfiq al-Hakim, *A reply*, in *ibid.*, 134-5; L. F. Gad, *The Puppet theatre in Cairo*, in *ibid.*, xiv/5 (Sept.-Oct. 1965), 452-3; *A glance at the origins of the Arab theatre*, in *ibid.*, xiv/6 (Dec. 1965), 607-10; Muḥammad Ghanīmī Hilāl, *Fi 'l-naḳd al-masraḥī*, Cairo 1965; al-Sayyid Ḥasan ʿĪd, *Taṭawwur al-naḳd al-masraḥī fī Miṣr*, Cairo 1965; Abdal Ghaffar Mikkawy, *Neue Wege ägyptischen Theaters*, in *Orient*, vi/1 (April 1965), 15-19; Abdel-Fattah I. El Mously, *The contemporary theatre and its application to a national theatre center in Cairo, Egypt, UAR*, Washington. D.C. 1965, 79 ff.; Raḏjāʾ al-Naḳḳāsh, *Fī aḍwāʾ al-masraḥ*. Cairo 1965; B. Sabry, *Shakespeare's reputation in Egypt 1900-50*, unpubl. Ph.D. diss., Exter Univ., 1965-6; Muḥammad Yūsuf Naḏjm, *al-Masraḥiyya fi 'l-adab al-ʿArabī al-ḥadīth, 1847-1914²*, Beirut 1967, index (1st edition, Beirut 1956); Raḏjāʾ al-Naḳḳāsh, *al-Zawba ʿa wa 'l-masraḥ al-ḏjadīd*, in Maḥmūd Diyāb, *Masraḥiyyāt ḥadītha: al-Zawba ʿa, al-Gharīb*, n.p. [Cairo] n.d. [1957 ?], 3-33; *The precursors of the Arab theatre*, in *World Theatre*, xvi/2 (1967), 188-93; ʿAli al-Zubaydī, *al-Masraḥiyya al-ʿArabiyya fi 'l-ʿIrāḳ: muḥāḍarāt*, n.p. [Cairo] 1967; Laila Nessim Abou-Saif, *The theatre of Naguib al-Rihani: The development of comedy in modern Egypt*, unpubl. Ph.D. diss., Univ. of Illinois 1968; H. Aboul Hussein, *Les mille et une nuits dans le théâtre égyptien*, unpubl. Ph.D. diss., Univ. of Paris 1968; Leila Gad, *Documentary theatre in Egypt*, in *World Theatre*, xvii/5-6 (1968), 415-17; Ibrahim Muhammad Hamada, *Treatments of Sophocles' "Oedipus the King" in contemporary French and Egyptian drama*, unpubl. Ph.D. diss., Indiana Univ., Bloomington 1968; Aḥmad Haykal, *al-Adab al-ḳaṣaṣī wa 'l-masraḥī fī Miṣr min a ʿkāb thawrat sanat 1919 ila ḳiyām al-ḥarb al-kubrā al-thāniya*, Cairo 1968; ʿAlī al-Rā ʿī *al-Kūmīdiya al-murtaḏjala fi 'l-masraḥ al-Miṣrī*, Cairo 1968; Muṣṭafā ʿAlī ʿUmar, *Wāḳi ʿiyya fi 'l-masraḥ al-Miṣrī*, Cairo 1968; Mohammad ʿAbd al-Hamid Ambar, *Le théâtre en République Arabe Unie*, Cairo 1969; Rashid Bencheneb, *Les grands thèmes du théâtre arabe contemporain*, in *Revue de l'Occident Musulman et de la Méditerranée* (Aix-en-Provence), vii (1969), 7-14; idem, *Les sources françaises du théâtre égyptien*, in *ibid.*, viii (1970), 9-23. Hamadi Ben Halima, *Les principaux thèmes du théâtre arabe contemporain de 1914 à 1960*, Tunis 1969; Berque, *Les arts du spectacle dans le monde arabe depuis cent* ans, in Nada Tomiche (ed.), *Le théâtre arabe*, Paris 1969, 15-38; Ali al-Rai, *Le génie du théâtre arabe des origines à nos jours*, in *ibid.*, 81-97; Tomiche, *Niveaux de langue dans le théâtre égyptien*, in *ibid.*, 117-32; Chérif Khaznadar, *Le théâtre en Syrie et au Liban au cours des dix dernières années*, in *ibid.*, 141-51; Nabil Maleh, *Radio, télévision, cinéma et théâtre en Arabie saoudite*, in *ibid.*, esp. 169-72; Nâsser al-Dîn al-Assad, *Le théâtre en Jordanie*, in *ibid.*, 173; Muḥammad Kamāl al-Dīn, *Djurdj Abyaḍ wa 'l-tamthīl al-trādjīdī*, in *al-Masraḥ* (Cairo), lxvi (Oct. 1969), 46-9; C. W. R. Long, *Taufīq al-Ḥakīm and the Arabic theatre*, in *MES*, v/1 (Jan. 1969), 69-74; Paul Nodet, *Théâtre et cinéma dans les pays arabes et asiatiques*, in *Travaux et Jours* (Beirut), xxxiii (Oct.-Dec. 1969), 45-52; Rizzitano, *Letterature araba*, Milan 1969, 212-29; Kh.I. Semaan, *T. S. Eliot's influence on Arabic poetry and theater*, in *Comparative Literature Studies* (Urbana, Ill.), vi (1969), 472-89; Ḥilmī ʿAbd al-Djawād al-Sibāʿī, *al-Masraḥ al-ʿArabī, ruwwāduhu wa-nudjūmuhu*, Cairo 1969; Nadjīb Surūr, *Ḥiwār fi 'l-masraḥ*, Cairo 1969, 1-212; Suʿād Abyaḍ, *Djūrdj Abyaḍ, al-Masraḥ al-Miṣrī fī miʾat ʿām*, Cairo 1970; Mohamed Aziza, *Regards sur le théâtre arabe contemporain*, Tunis 1970, 13 ff.; A. M. Elmessiri, *Arab drama*, in J. Gassner and E. Quinn (eds.), *The reader's encyclopedia of world drama*, London 1970, 21-5; ʿAdnān Ibn Dhurayl, *Fi 'l-shiʿr al-masraḥī*, Damascus 1970; Muḥammad Kamāl al-Dīn, *Ruwwād al-masraḥ al-Miṣrī*, n.p. [Cairo] 1970; Maḥmūd Ḥāmid Shawkat, *al-Fann al-masraḥī fi 'l-adab al-ʿArabī al-ḥadīth*^{3}, Cairo 1970; Maḥmūd ʿAwaḍ, *Muḥammad ʿAbd al-Wahhāb*, Cairo 1971; Mohamed Aziza, *Molière et le théâtre arabe*, in *Etudes Philosophiques et Littéraires* (Temara, Morocco), v (1971), 129-32; Nahman Bar Nissim, *An approach to Tawfiq al-Hakim the dramatist*, unpubl. Ph.D. diss., Univ. of Pennsylvania, Philadelphia 1971; Cachia, *Themes related to Christianity and Judaism in modern Egyptian drama and fiction*, in *JAL*, ii (1971), 178-94; Nadia Raouf Farag, *Yussef Idris and modern Egyptian drama*, unpubl. Ph.D. diss., Columbia Univ., New York 1971; Ibrāhīm Ḥamāda, *Muʿdjam al-muṣṭalaḥāt al-drāmiyya wa 'l-masraḥiyya*, Cairo 1971; Maḥmūd Kāmil, *Muḥammad al-Ḳaṣṣābdjī ḥayātuhu wa-aʿmāluhu*, n.p. [Cairo] 1391/1971, 35 ff.; A. Ye. Krimskiy, *Istoriya novoy Arabskoy lityeraturi XIX-načalo XX vyeka*, Moscow 1971, index; Muḥammad Mandūr, *Fi 'l-masraḥ al-Miṣrī al-muʿāṣir*, Cairo 1971; Radjāʾ al-Naḳḳash, *Maḳʿad ṣaghīr amām al-sitār*, n.p. [Cairo] 1971; ʿAli al-Rāʿī, *al-Kūmīdiyā min khayāl al-ẓill ilā Nadjīb al-Rīḥānī*, Cairo 1971; Djalāl al-Sharḳāwī, *al-Masraḥ abu 'l-funūn: fi 'l-naḳd al-taṭbīḳī*, Cairo 1971; ʿUmar al-Ṭālib, *al-Masraḥiyya al-ʿArabiyya fi 'l-ʿIrāk*, i-ii, n.p. 1971; Zakī Ṭulaymāt, *Fann al-mumaththil al-ʿArabī: dirāsāt wa-taʾammulāt fi māḍīhi wa-ḥāḍirihi*, Cairo 1971; El Sayed Attia Abul Naga, *Le théâtre arabe et ses origines*, in *Journal of World History* (Boudry, Switzerland), xiv/4 (1972), 880-98; idem, *Les sources françaises du théâtre égyptien (1870-1939)*, Algiers 1972; Laylā Nasīm Abu 'l-Sayf, *Nadjīb al-Rīḥānī wa-taṭawwur al-kūmīdiyā fī Miṣr*, Cairo 1972; *Arab drama*, in M. Matlaw (ed.), *Modern world drama: an encyclopedia*, London 1972, 34-5; Ramsīs ʿAwaḍ, *al-Taʾrīkh al-sirrī li 'l-masraḥ ḳabla thawrat 1919*, Cairo 1972; ʿAbd al-ʿAziz Ḥammūda, *Masraḥ Rashād Rushdī: dirāsa taḥlīliyya ʿan Nūr wa-Ẓalām*, n.p. 1972, 7 ff.; A.S.A. Hassan, *La société orientale à travers le théâtre arabe en vers, 1876-1966*, unpubl. Ph.D. diss., Univ. of Paris 1972; Sāmī Khashaba, *Ḳaḍāyā muʿāṣira fi 'l-masraḥ*, Baghdad 1972; Matti Moosa, *Naqqāsh and the rise of the native Arab theatre in Syria*, in *JAL*, iii (1972), 106-17; L. Abou Saif, *Najīb al-Rīḥānī: from buffoonery to social comedy*, in *ibid.*, iv (1973), 1-17; Atia Abul Naga, *Recherches sur les termes du théâtre et leur traduction en arabe moderne*, Algiers 1973; S.A. A.N. (= Abul Naga), *Le théâtre dans le monde arabe*, in *Encyclopaedia Universalis*, Paris 1973, xv, 1058-60; Maḥmūd Amīn al-ʿĀlim, *al-Wadjh wa 'l-ḳināʿ fī masraḥinā al-ʿArabī al-muʿāṣir*, Beirut 1973; Fatḥī al-ʿAsharī, *Diḳḳāt al-masraḥ*, Cairo 1973; ʿAdnān Ibn Dhurayl, *al-Shakhṣiyya wa 'l-ṣirāʿ al-maʾsāwī: dirāsa nafsiyya fī ṭalāʾiʿ al-masraḥ al-shiʿrī al-ʿArabī*, Damascus 1973; Saʿd al-Dīn Ḥasan Dughmān, *al-Uṣūl al-taʾrīkhiyya li-nashʾat al-drāmā fi 'l-adab al-ʿArabī*, Beirut 1973; ʿAlī al-Rāʿī, *Masraḥ al-dam wa 'l-dumūʿ*, Cairo 1973; Farouk Abdul-Wahab, *Modern Egyptian drama: an anthology*, Minneapolis and Chicago 1974, esp. 9-40; Badr Eddin Aroudky, *Theatre in Syria*, in *Lotus: Afro-Asian Writings* (Cairo), xix (Jan. 1974), 74-93; Rachid Bencheneb, *Les dramaturges arabes et le récit-cadre des Mille et Une Nuits*, in *ROMM*, xviii (1974), 7-18; Sami Hanna and R. Salti, *Ahmad Shauqi: a pioneer of modern Arabic drama*, in *American Journal of Arabic Studies* (Leiden), i (1973), 81-117; J. M. L. [= Landau], *Islamic dance and theatre*, in *The New Encyclopaedia Britannica* (Micropaedia part), ix (1974), 976-82; Matti Moosa, *Yaʿqûb Ṣanûʿ and the rise of Arab drama in Egypt*, in *IJMES*, v/4 (1974), 401-33; Ghassan Salamé, *Le théâtre politique au Liban (1968-73)*, Beirut 1974 (= Hommes et Sociétés du Proche Orient, 7); Ahmad al-Haggagi, *European theatrical companies and the origin of the Egyptian theater (1870-1923)*, in *AJAS*, iii (1975), 83-91; idem, *al-ʿArab wa-fann al-masraḥ*, Cairo 1975; idem, *al-Usṭūra fi 'l-masraḥ al-Miṣrī al-muʿāṣir, 1933-1970*; Cairo 1975; Ibrahim Hamada, *Le théâtre au Koweït*, unpubl. Ph.D. diss., Univ. of Paris 1975; Muḥammad Ghanīmī Hılāl, *Fi 'l-naḳd al-masraḥī*, Beirut 1975; Muhammad Kamāl al-Dīn, *al-ʿArab wa 'l-masraḥ*, Cairo 1975; S. Moreh, *The Arabic theatre in Egypt in the eighteenth and nineteenth century*, in *Actes du 29e Congrès des Orientalistes, Paris 1973*, section II, vol. iii, Paris 1975, 109-13; S. Somekh, *Two versions of dialogue in Maḥmūd Taymūr's drama*, Princeton 1975 (= Princeton Near East Papers, 21); Stetkevich, *Classical Arabic on stage*, in R. C. Ostle (ed.), *Studies in Arabic literature*, London 1975, 152-66; ʿAlī al-Rāʿī, *Some aspects of modern Arabic drama*, *ibid.*, 167-78; L. ʿAwad, *Problems of the Egyptian theatre*, in *ibid.*, 179-93; ʿAlāʾ al-Dīn Waḥīd, *Masraḥ Muḥammad Taymūr*, Cairo 1975; N. K. Kotsaryev, *Pisatyeli Yegipta XX vyek: materiali k biobibliografii*, Moscow 1976; index; Edwār Sāmī Ṣabānikh al-Yāfī, *Nadjīb al-Ḥaddād al-mutardjim al-masraḥī*, Cairo 1976; Naṣr al-Dīn al-Baḥra, *Aḥādīth wa-tadjārib masraḥiyya*, Damascus 1977; ʿAdnān Ibn Dhurayl, *al-Adab al-masraḥi fī Sūriya*, Damascus n.d. [1977], index; Mahmoud Menzalaoui (ed.), *Arabic writing today: drama*, Cairo 1977; T. A. Putintsyeva, *Tisyača i odin god Arabskogo tyeatra*, Moscow 1977, index; P. Starkey, *Philosophical themes in Tawfiq al-Ḥakīm's drama*, in *JAL*, viii (1977), 136-52; ʿĀdil Abū Shanab, *Bawākīr al-taʾlīf al-masraḥī fī Sūriya*, Damascus 1978; Yūsuf Asʿad Dāghir, *Muʿdjam al-masraḥiyyāt al-ʿArabiyya wa 'l-muʿarraba, 1848-1975*, Baghdād 1978; Ḥayāt Jāsim Muḥammad al-Jābir, *Experimental drama in Egypt 1960-1970, with reference to Western influence*, unpubl. Ph.D. diss., Indiana Univ. 1978; Chakib El-Khouri, *Le théâtre arabe de l'absurde*, Paris 1978, 63-143; Amel Amin Zaki, *Shakespeare in Arabic*, unpubl. Ph.D. diss., Indiana Univ. 1978; Sāmī Munīr Ḥusayn, *al-Masraḥ al-*

Miṣrī baʿd al-ḥarb al-ʿālamiyya al-thāniya bayn al-fann wa 'l-naḳd al-siyāsī wa 'l-idjtimāʿī, 1945-70, i-ii, Alexandria 1978-9; Salah Abolsaud, *Theaterproduktion und gesellschaftliche Realität in Ägypten (1952-1970)*, unpubl. Ph.D. diss., Cologne Univ. 1979; R. Allen, *Egyptian drama after the revolution*, in *Edebiyat* (New York) iv/1 (1979), 97-134; Ramsīs ʿAwaḍ, *Ittidjāhāt siyāsiyya fi 'l-masraḥ ḳabl thawrat 1919*, Cairo 1979; Abdel-Aziz Hammouda, *Modern Egyptian theatre: three major dramatists*, in *World Literature Today* (Norman, Okla.), liii/4 (Autumn 1979), 601-5; ʿIzz al-Dīn Ismāʿīl, *Ḳaḍāyā al-insān fi 'l-adab al-Miṣrī al-muʿāṣir*, n.p. 1980; R. Karachouli, *Nationale Problematik und internazionaler Bezug des modernen Theaters in den arabischen Ländern*, in *Weimarer Beiträge* (East Berlin), ix (1980), 94-103; ʿAlī al-Rāʿi, *al-Masraḥ fi 'l-waṭan al-ʿArabī*, Kuwait 1980; Rotraud Wielandt, *Das Bild der Europäer in der modernen arabischen Erzähl- und Theaterliteratur*, Beirut 1980; Halim El-Dabh, *The state of the arts in Egypt today*, in *MEJ*, xxxv/1 (Winter 1981), 15-24; Hind Ḳawwāṣ, *al-Madkhal ilā al-masraḥ al-ʿArabī*, Beirut 1981; Cachia, *The theatrical movement of the Arabs*, in *MESA Bulletin*, xvi/1 (July 1982), 11-23; L. ʿAwaḍ, *al-Masraḥ al-Miṣrī*, Cairo n.d.; M. Aziza, *Le théâtre et l'Islam*, Algiers n.d.; ʿAbd al-Ḥalīm al-Bayūmī, *Nadjīb al-Rīḥānī wa 'l-kūmīdiyā al-Miṣriyya*, Cairo n.d.; Fawzī Shāhīn, *al-Tamthīliyya al-idhāʿiyya*, Cairo n.d.; Maḥmūd Taymūr, *Dirāsāt fi 'l-ḳiṣṣa wa 'l-masraḥ*, Cairo n.d.; idem, *Ṭalāʾiʿ al-masraḥ al-ʿArabī*, Cairo n.d.; Mohammed A. al-Khozai, *The development of early Arabic drama 1847-1900*, London 1984; P. Chelkowski, *Islam in modern drama and theatre*, in *WI*, xxxiii-xxxiv (1984), 45-69; Aḥmad Samīr Baybars, *al-Masrah al-ʿArabī fi 'l-karn al-tāsiʿ ʿashar*, Heliopolis 1985; Chelkowski, *Western Asian and North African performance: general introduction*, in: B. Fleshman, ed. *Theatrical movement: a bibliographical anthology*, Metuchen, N.J. and London 1986, 480-560; Landau, *Popular Arabic plays, 1909*, in *JAL* xvii (1986), 120-5.

(J. M. Landau)

2. In North Africa.

Tunisia. — The first attempt at introducing theatre into Tunisa dates back to the early years of the 20th century. It owed much to the initiative of a fine actor of Syrian origin, Sulaymān al-Ḳardāḥī, who, in the course of his long career, travelled along the Nile Valley between Cairo and Asyūṭ, mounting performances of an extremely varied nature (tragedy, drama, melodrama and comedy), featuring music and dance and with themes borrowed almost entirely from the *Thousand and one nights* and from the European répertoire (Shakespeare, Racine, Molière and Voltaire). Al-Ḳardāḥī's influence was consolidated by the fact that his troupe included talented performers such as the comedienne Ḥanīna, the singer Layla and, in particular, the singer Salāma al-Ḥidjāzī.

When he arrived in Tunis in 1907, al-Ḳardāḥī found support on the part of the Bey Muḥammad al-Nāṣir, and he obtained a municipal subsidy towards the realisation of his objectives. He was to devote the last two years of his life to training young comic actors, founding the first Tunisian drama company and performing various items from his vast répertoire in partnership with his best pupils, of whom the most gifted seem to have been Brāhīm Lakudī and Muḥammad Bourguiba. It was the latter who, on the death of the master, continued in his footsteps. In 1909, he formed his own troupe, with which that of ʿAlī al-Khaznī was soon to be a serious competitor.

In the period following the First World War, groups of amateur performers proliferated in all the major towns. They toured the country, playing Egyptian tragedies and dramas in literary Arabic, as well as comedy and farce in colloquial language. But it was the popular entertainments which appealed most to the public. Nevertheless, the Egyptian influence remained apparent, especially in the more serious genre as a result of the tours which the major troupes of Cairo made periodically in the Maghrib, visiting Tunis in particular: Djūrdj Abyaḍ in 1921, Yūsuf Wahbī in 1927, Fāṭima Rushdī in 1932 and Nadjīb al-Rīḥānī in 1935.

In a theatre quite openly dependent on foreign material, a play such as *al-Sudd* ("The Dam") by Maḥmūd al-Masʿadī takes on the nature of an original experiment. This transparently symbolic drama evokes the failure of a person engaged in an enterprise which is beyond him and which ultimately testifies in favour of the man and of his destiny. The action is stark, the scene set at the foot of a mountain. Two persons arrive, Ghaylān and Maymūna, leading a heavily-laden mule. The man decides to construct a dam, but he encounters enormous difficulties. Barely begun, the work is stopped, the scaffolding soon abandoned. To add to his misfortune, the man is swept away by a storm with his work unfinished, while his consort rushes headlong towards the plain exclaiming: "The Land, it is the Land that I discover!". Written *ca.* 1940 in a very pure prose style, intended to be read rather than performed, *al-Sudd*, on its publication in 1955, came to be regarded as a kind of masterpiece by Tunisian and Egyptian scholars and French Arabists.

However, dramatic production after 1940 seldom strayed from the beaten tracks. Authors were not concerned with presenting scenes that were new, true and pertinent to the human condition. Whether engaged in serious or in comic vein, they made strenuous efforts to achieve pathos or, on the other hand, contented themselves with facile gaiety. Innovations were rare, and performances of mediocre quality. For their part, the majority of actors were young amateurs whose enthusiasm did not compensate for their lack of training. Moreover, the absence of producers and technicians meant poor preparation and clumsy performance. Ultimately, the achievements gained by each troupe were all the more precarious in that the public was heterogeneous and fickle. The theatre thus underwent a crisis which found an echo in the local Arabic and French language press, where considerable space was devoted to exposing the problems with which it was faced: too few writers, insufficient training of actors, poor standards of performance-venues, diversity and unreliability of the public, etc. At this stage, Tunisian theatre seemed doomed to failure. It was certainly in a state of stagnation.

It was not until the years following Independence that significant efforts were made at various levels with a view to reviving the theatre. Writers, mostly of dual Arab and French culture, generally occupying posts in public administration which guaranteed their material security, set about laying the ground-work for a new dramatic movement. The example set by the foreign plays which were frequently produced in Tunis encouraged them to give freer rein to the imagination. In this process of renovation, producers, hitherto an unknown breed, played a rôle of the highest importance. The greatest of them was undoubtedly the Egyptian Zakī Ṭulaymāt, a man of expertise and experience, who for a long time enjoyed a well-deserved reputation in artistic circles of the Near East and the Maghrib.

When he arrived in Tunis in 1956, eight competing

companies of amateur comic actors shared between them the patronage of a sparse and eclectic public. Actors variously performed Egyptian plays in literary Arabic, adaptations of European works, comedies and farces in the colloquial style of the locality, normally concluding the show with singing, dance and music. There were among them some talented individuals, whom Ṭulaymāt chose in order to form a company of quality. He strove to make the scenery more authentic, the performance of actors more natural; he required his casts to rehearse thoroughly, to work in a spirit of team collaboration, to present well-constructed, living productions in which the element of convention is mingled with fantasy. The training which he gave bore fruit. In fact, when Zakī Ṭulaymāt left Tunisia in 1961, the theatre experienced a new era of prosperity through the efforts of some of his young successors, including ʿAlī Ben ʿAyād.

The latter was then director of the Municipal Theatre of Tunis. Both a man of grand aspiration and a man of the people, he was active in all spheres of artistic pursuit, with imagination and zeal as well as with realism. He adopted a dramatic technique which consisted in transposing the themes of works borrowed from the foreign répertoire to ancient or contemporary Arab-Islamic society, with the appropriate beliefs, costumes and conventions. Thus for example, his *Caligula* (1961) is set in the Middle Ages, at the court of a Maghribī sultan surrounded by his viziers, *amīr*s and Arab retainers. There is nothing in common with the historical character nor with the protagonist of Camus' play, whom the Tunisian dramatist takes as the symbol of a sovereign ruling in bloody tyranny over his people. Ben ʿAyād applied similar treatment to a series of foreign works which he presented in Tunis and at the international cultural centre of Hammamet before performing them before the heterogeneous audiences of provincial towns and rural villages: *Measure for Measure* and *Othello* by Shakespeare, *L'Ecole des femmes* und *L'Avare* by Moliere, *En attendant Godot* (1965), *La Derniere bande* and *Oh les beaux jours!* (1966) by Samuel Beckett, etc. In a few years, he became acquainted with a vast comic and tragic répertoire. The success of his productions earned him renown both in Tunisia and abroad, especially in Paris, at the Théâtre des Nations.

At the same time, other young dramatists who favoured strong characters, violent emotions and local colour, attempted to find new sources of inspiration in drawing their themes from Arab-Islamic history. They preferred the ages of glamour, retaining the facts but moulding them according to their imagination, developing the classical ideals of love, faith, honour and valour. The heroes, princes, military chieftains or simple waariors are obliged to risk their lives for the glory of Islam and the love of the homeland. Thus for example, Ahmad Khayr al-Dīn dramatised the epic of the Berber queen al-Kāhina who, at the end of the 1st/7th century offered fierce resistance to the Arab army of Ḥasan b. al-Nuʿmān before finally collapsing under his onslaught (*al-Kāhina*). For his part, Fattāḥ Wālī devoted his *Pearl of Sicily* (*Djawhar al-Ṣiḳillī*) to the exploits of the Muslims who, embarking from Sousse in 210/827 under the command of Asad b. al-Furāt, flung themselves into the conquest of Christian Sicily. Nor is romance absent from these pseudo-historical tableaux. ʿAbd al-Razzāḳ Karabaka brings alive on the stage the famous couple Ibn Zaydūn and Wallāda, with a nostalgic evocation of the Cordova of the 5th/11th century (*Wallāda wa-Ibn Zaydūn*). In this category of plays of heroic or historical pretensions, *Murād III* (1966) by Ḥabīb Boulares (Bu 'l-ʿArīs) is reminiscent of *Caligula* by ʿAlī Ben ʿAyād rather than of Shakespeare's *Richard III* which the Tunisian playwright seems to claim as his inspiration. The net result is that these dramas borrow the methods of melodrama, compounded by inferior dialogue and action filled with sensation and interludes of pathos. Written by young authors, they show the exuberance of youth. On the other hand, the wealth of invention, the intensity of colour and the epic grandeur of the subjects create an atmosphere of heroic legend capable of capturing the imagination of the spectators. Ultimately, the characters are of quite elementary simplicity, entirely good or totally evil, clad in their symbolic guises.

Alongside this serious theatre, the comic genre has made a worthy contribution. In the relaxed atmosphere of the period 1960-70, numerous humorists provided comedies, farces or simple entertainments of circumstance, introducing hilarious, pathetic or cynical characters. It was during this time that Aḥmad Khayr al-Dīn enjoyed his greatest popular success with the creation of the character of Ḥādj Klūf, distant cousin of the Egyptian Kish Kish Bey. All such plays, a little simplistic but well-constructed, have delighted popular audiences.

It may be added that the efforts made over the past twenty-five years to interest all classes of society in theatre in its most diverse forms have succeeded well. In the context of decentralisation, provincial drama companies have evolved, so that today every town boasts its own troupe of comic actors, whose active members contribute both to improvement in standards of production and to the opening up of the theatre to new audiences. On the other hand, theatre has made its presence felt in the school, the academy and the university, and every years competitions are organised to reward the best young dramatists. Thus a new spirit is alive in theatrical life. Attendance at dramatic performances, formerly the preserve of a narrow circle of intellectuals, has become within a few years a social event shared by the scholar, the artisan and the peasant. It is beyond doubt this fact which, more than the number and quality of works, best characterises the rebirth of theatre in Tunisia.

Algeria. — It was only in the years following the First World War that Arab theatre appeared for the first time in Algeria. In 1921, the Egyptian troupe led by Djūrdj Abyaḍ, after performing in Tunis, presented in Algiers two historical dramas by Nadjīb al-Ḥaddād written in classical Arabic: *Ṣalāḥ al-Dīn al-Ayyūbī* ("Saladin the Ayyūbid") and *Thārāt al-ʿArab* ("Vengeance of the Arabs"). Although encountering only limited success before a public generally ignorant of the literary language, these performances made the Algerian élite aware of the existence of a militant and didactic Arabic theatre. Drawing on this experience a few months later, a handful of young intellectuals, for the most part former *madrasa* students, formed a cultural association, *al-Muʾaddiba* ("The Educating [Society]") one of whose leaders, Ṭāhir ʿAlī Sharīf, organised the performance in the capital of three plays in literary Arabic which had the purpose of awakening the national sentiment of his compatriots and educating them concerning the horrendous consequences of social scourges such as alcoholism: *al-Shifāʾ baʿd al-ʿanāʾ* ("Recovery after the trial", 1921), *Khadīʿat al-gharām* ("Perfidy of Love," 1923) and *Badīʿ* (1924). Another company, that of *al-Tamthīl al-ʿarabī* ("The Arab Theatre"), founded in 1921, had as its leading personality a former student of Arabic literature, Muḥammad al-Mānṣālī. This company performed in Algiers two plays in literary Arabic borrowed from the Egyptian répertoire: *Fī sabīl al-waṭan* ("For the homeland", 1922) and *Futūḥ al-Andalus* ("The conquest of Andalusia," 1923). This attempt at the introduction of dramatic art was hindered by two apparently unsurmountable obstacles: on the one hand, it encountered the incomprehension of a public barely familiar with Arabic literature; on the other hand, it incurred the disapproval of the bourgeois élite, which had little taste for performances whose themes seemed incompatible with the principles of Arab-Islamic ethics.

Taught by this experience, some young enthusiasts performed during the same period plays which would be universally accessible, drawing their themes from contemporary life and from popular tradition. They shared their predecessors' concern with moral and social, even political issues, and their simplistic philosophy, but they were at pains to express them in the daily patois of their fellow-citizens. During the inter-war period, three names are pre-eminent: ʿAllālū, Ksentini and Bachtarzi. With quite dissimilar gifts, all three gained reputations in comedy and in song, perpetuating in the theatre the tradition of popular poetry whose rhythms lend themselves particularly to music and dance. They embody, in varying degrees, the tastes and the spirit of their time.

In many respects, ʿAllālū is a pioneering figure. Born in Algiers in 1902, he first participated as a singer in public concerts which a musical society, *al-Muṭribiyya*, organised during the evenings of Ramaḍān. Later he began performing in local cinemas, at Bab el Oued in particular, short sketches in the style of farces dramatising domestic situations. Enriched by this experience and confident of his methods, he formed in 1925 his own drama company, the Zahia troupe, and composed satirical, romantic comedies and comic ballets, written entirely in dialect, which he presented successfully in Algiers and the surrounding region, between 1926 and 1931: "Djeha" (*Djḥā*, 1926)," The marriage of Bou-Akline" (*Abū ʿAḳlīn*, 1926), "Abou-Hassan or the sleeper awakened" (*Abu 'l-Ḥasan*, 1927), "The Fisherman and the Genie" (1928), "Antar el-Hachaîchi" (*ʿAntar al-Ḥashāyishī*, 1930), *El-Khalifa oues-Sayyad* (*al-Khalīfa wa 'l-ṣayyād*, "The Caliph and the Fisherman," 1931) and *Hallaq Guernata* (*Ḥallāḳ Gharnāṭa*," The Barber of Granada," 1931). However, his company, the beneficiary of neither public nor private aid, was not a commercial success and ʿAllālū soon found himself beset by serious financial difficulties. As writer, actor and director of the troupe, he led an exhausting life and consequently his health suffered. Disillusioned, in 1932 he decided to renounce all his theatrical activities.

ʿAllālū had no pretentions to originality, and little interest in novelty. Three of his productions were adaptations of very well known stories from the *Thousand and one mights*: *Abou-Hassan or the sleeper awakened*, *The Fisherman and the genie* and *El-Khalifa oues-Sayyad.* His *Djeha* does indeed contain numerous humorous episodes traditionally attributed to the popular character of the same name, but the general theme is borrowed, via *Le Médecin malgré lui*, from a mediaeval fable, *Le vilain mire*, which depicts the triumph of a cunning woman. In *The Marriage of Bou-Akline* there are numerous echoes both of Arab folklore and of the French theatre. However, ʿAllālū does not venture to follow Molière in the direction of comedy of character. His figures confine themselves to stereotyped theatrical roles; they never become authentic human beings. Nevertheless, he excels in devising plots and situations which automatically arouse laughter: in *Djeha*, the hero is soundly beaten by the emissaries of the sultan before admitting that he is indeed the famous physician capable of curing the son of the sovereign. Similarly, the wife of Bou-Akline, finding the door closed on returning from an assignation with her lover, simulates suicide by throwing a great stone into the garden well; later, when everyone believes her dead, she appears before her husband who, terrified, imagines himself confronted by the ghost of his wife. Thus, the plays of ʿAllālū appear to be a compromise between farce and comedy of intrigue. Invariably, the audience is held in suspense by theatrical sensations or amused by the disguises: Abu 'l-Ḥasan, a nonentity dressed as a caliph and flaunting the trappings of his temporary authority; Hārūn al-Rashīd and his vizier Djaʿfar disguised as merchants; etc.

Furthermore, ʿAllālū is a skillful writer, deploying many witticisms, puns, amusing expressions: he gives to the hero of his first play, *Djeha*, the name of a popular character in the Arab world and to his wife that of *Ḥīla* ("Stratagem, trick"); the aged retainer of Bou-Akline, Mekidech (*Mḳīdash*) is the homonym of another fictitious character whose adventures have for a long time been a feature of Algerian popular tradition. Furthermore, the choice of names often reveals the parodic intention of the author: Hārūn al-Rashīd becomes *Ḳarūn al-rāshī* ("Ḳārūn the Corrupt"), his vizier *Djʿfar al-markhī* ("Djaʿfar the soft-witted") and his sword-bearer Masrūr is named *Maṣrūʿ* ("The Sot"). Following the same procedure, a wretched cobbler is made to appear ridiculous by bearing the prestigious name of ʿAntar, the chivalrous hero so much admired by Arabs past and present. All such pitiful dupes he places in the gallery of legendary characters who inhabit the popular imagination and still influence minds.

In addition, he endows them with a popular, vivid, colourful style of language. As well as their demeanour and their gestures, their speeches provoke laughter. Their verbal comedy is constituted partly by aphorisms, maxims and proverbs in current Algerian usage, partly by the repetition of exclamations habitually employed by the people to express joy, surprise or sadness (*wilī wilī*, "Alas for me"; *yā saʿdī*, "Just my luck!"). The borrowings from the spoken language and the verbal novelties are evidently designed to make the audience share the gaiety of the actors. In sum, there is no profundity, but the revelation, through laughter, of a good humour free from vulgarity, a joyous, irrepressible, infectious enthusiasm. This cheerful mood makes everything acceptable: Djeha and his wife Ḥīla are arrant rogues, Bou-Akline is not entirely honest, and no more so is Abu 'l-Haṣan. It would be folly to object and to attach any importance to their actions or their concerns. ʿAllālū has succeeded in the gamble of turning quasi-serious issues into the material of farce, without any pretension of displaying to the audience the illusion of reality. His principal achievement has been the definitive establishment in Algeria of a theatre of essentially popular inspiration and expression, adapted to the taste of his contemporaries.

The second actor-writer who has contributed significantly to the growth of the theatre in Algeria during the 1930s is incontestably Rashīd Ksentini, but in this instance the reader is referred to the lengthy article devoted to him, s.v. al-ḲUSANṬĪNĪ.

The third motive force of Algerian theatre between the two World Wars is Bachtarzi (Muḥyī 'l-Dīn Bāsh

Ṭarzī), who was born and died in Algiers (1896-1985). When he came to prominence in the 1930s, he was already a veteran of the stage where he had acquired a fine reputation as a singer and an actor. Initially, he confined himself to repeating the principal successes of his predecessors in a slightly amended version. His players merged with those of ʿAllālū and Ksentini, and the company thus formed comprised Algerian actors (al-Mānṣālī, Bās̲h̲ D̲j̲arrāḥ, Daḥmūn and Hāmel) and French ones (Louis Chaprot, Georges Baudry and Georges Hertz), who were joined by comic actresses such as Kalt̲h̲ūm and Marie Soussan, the last named being Jewish. On the other hand, Bachtarzi created a répertoire: to the comedies, farces and sketches of his predecessors he added his own works, the first composed in collaboration with Ksentini, Chaprot and Hāmel, and some seventy plays in all, all written in colloquial speech and several containing scenes where the actors express themselves in French. Among those which delighted the Algerian audience are the following: *Faqo* (*Fāḳū*, "That's no good!", 1934); *El Bouzerii fel Askaria* (*al-Būzrīʿī fi 'l-ʿaskariyya*, "The Bouzarian at the barracks," 1934); *Alennif* (*ʿAlā 'l-nīf*, "From self-respect", 1934); *Beni oui-oui* (1935); *Syndicat des chomeurs* (1935); *Le Mariage par téléphone* (1936); *El-Kheddaine* (*al-K̲h̲addāʿīn*, "The Traitors", 1937); *El Keddabine* (*al-Kaddābīn*," The Liars" 1938); *El Mechehah* (*al-Mas̲h̲ḥāḥ*, "The Miser," 1940); and *Sliman Ellouk* (*Slīmān al-lukk*, "Sliman wax," (1942), the two last-named being adaptations of, respectively, *L'Avare* and *Le Malade imaginaire* by Molière.

Bachtarzi was indeed a performer, but he was above all an impresario of performances. He was also a writer conscious of the rôle which the theatre had to play in the evolution of Algerian society. Eager to encourage the broadest public to discover new horizons, he organised tours throughout Algeria and in Morocco, France and Belgium, playing to the significant Algerian communities present in these countries. However, his situation was precarious, as may be judged from the account in his *Mémoires*: in 1934, his troupe gave 61 performances in 44 localities; the following year it appeared in 55 urban centres; in 1936 and in 1937, the number of towns visited was respectively 59 and 89. Audiences varied between 150 in small towns and 2,000 in Algiers, Constantine, Oran and Tlemcen. Successes were inconsistent and receipts poor.

Such signs are a clue to understanding the difficulties faced by the new guiding spirit of Algerian theatre encountering a society which remained backward and an admininistration uneasy about the intentions of a potentially subversive movement. In fact, Bachtarzi did not content himself, like his predecessors, with exploiting the public taste for entertaining spectacles. He saw it as his mission to inform and educate his Muslim fellow-citizens regarding the various issues then exciting public opinion. In his plays and dramatic tirades, he denounces the danger posed to the Algerian community by the relaxation of morals, the adoption of a poorly understood modernism and the revival of social evils: unemployment, alcoholism, prostitution and usury. With the same zeal, he condemns the disunity of his compatriots, the compromises of elected administrators, religious busybodies and hypocrites. In this mood, he readily employs terms of ideological connotation (*ḥuḳūḳ*, "political rights;" *ittiḥād*, "union; "*ittifāḳ*, "accord; "*waṭan*, "homeland;" *umma*, "nation"), henceforward to become part of the normal vocabulary of every Algerian of any degree of education, and evidence of a willingness to take political and cultural initiatives in accordance with the social ferment dominating the country from the year 1930 onward. Inevitably, the irreverent style of Bachtarzi aroused serious hostility. His plays were banned or subjected to censorship. His career declined and he was only able to ensure the survival of his company by compromising with the authorities. However, he was appointed during the Second World War to entertain the Muslim soldiers receiving treatment in military hospitals.

The year 1947 marked the revival of Algerian theatre with the formation at the Algiers Opera of an Arab troupe and the appointment of Bachtarzi as its director. This initiative created conditions of a degree of professionalism and of greater stability. In fact, the players henceforward had facilities for rehearsing at leisure before every performance; they were guaranteed at least one performance per week; and finally they received a regular income as a result of a municipal subsidy. This company initially comprised about a score of actors, actresses, singers and musicians, most of them quite young: Mustapha Kateb, Muḥammad Tourī, Muḥammad Ḥaṭṭāb, D̲j̲alāl Sissānī, Riḍā Falakī, ʿAyād Rouiched, Kalt̲h̲ūm, Dalīlā and Laylā Ḥākim. Most often, they played comedy in the colloquial language, but they also on occasion performed serious plays such as *Hannibal*, a historical drama by Tawfīḳ al-Madanī (1952). They remained active until the dissolution of the troupe in 1956.

Meanwhile, numerous troupes of players made their appearance in Algeria. Four of them were based in Algiers: *Les fervents du théâtre arabe algérien*, which was managed by Muḥammad Ṭāhir Fuḍalā; *Firḳat al-fann al-tamt̲h̲īlī* ("The Company of Dramatic Art") whose main guiding spirit was Mustapha Grībī; *al-Masraḥ al-d̲j̲azāʾirī* ("The Algerian Theatre") of Mustapha Kateb and *Masraḥ al-g̲h̲aḍ* ("Theatre of Tomorrow") of Riḍā Falakī, the two last-named being former members of Bachtarzi's team. Other dramatic activists made their appearance in the provinces: Aḥmad Riḍā Ḥūḥū at Constantine, Ḥasan Derdour at Bone, Mūsā K̲h̲addāwī at Blida, etc. While Falakī specialised in producing children's programmes for Radio Algeria, the others composed comedies, farces, entertainments, romances, plays full of enthusiasm and fantasy, mostly written in dialect, but with a rapidly increasing number in classical Arabic. It seems that the impression made by Egyptian productions performed by the major companies of Cairo in the course of their tours of Algeria encouraged the activists of the Algerian theatre to give more scope to the literary language.

In the same period, companies of actors were formed in the major cities with the encouragement of organisers of the association of reformist *ʿulamāʾ* and of the M.T.L.D. (*Mouvement pour le triomphe des libertés démocratiques*). The former presented, on the occasion of the celebration of religious feasts or of the annual distribution of prizes in private Arab schools, small dramas of cultural instruction intended to glorify Islam and the Arabic language. The latter were clearly oriented towards political and social action. For example, the play *Aimak and Rouibah*, performed in Algiers in the 1950s, dramatises the career of a young Algerian who "joins the party of the struggle for liberty" and evokes "the most noble cause". Such a committed theatre naturally had recourse to history with the object of exalting national sentiment: Hannibal, al-Kāhina, Barbarossa and Ṣalāḥ Bey, each of these characters being seen as a champion of patriotism. On the other hand, in numerous plays a conspiracy is forged against the sovereign to put an end to "the servitude of the people" and to "deliver" the country from tyranny. These transparent allusions enable the audience to make straightforward comparisons and offer as a desirable prospect "the punishment of the despot" and "the revenge of the oppressed". The performance normally ends with the singing of patriotic anthems (*anāshīd waṭaniyya*). It need hardly be stressed that all these performances took place in private places, before a limited audience of militants and sympathisers. After the rebellion of 1954, the Arab theatre virtually ceased to exist in Algeria. Some of its guiding spirits, members of the F.L.N., took refuge in Tunisia where they occasionally performed propaganda pieces.

The years following 1962 saw considerable changes taking effect in the theatre. At the Algiers Opera, renamed the Algerian National Theatre, there were efforts, under the guidance of Mustapha Kateb, to renew theatrical presentation and communication with the public by introducing aesthetic and ideological preoccupations. In this spirit numerous national companies were invited to perform, from Black Africa, Eastern Bloc countries, Asia and Central America. The actors performed in their own languages and boasted of the benefits accruing to the people as a result of revolution in their countries. On the other hand, there were dialectal adaptations of foreign works such as those of Bertold Brecht and Sean O'Casey, but it must be admitted that neither the satire on rural and clerical society of the latter, nor the parables employed by the former to illustrate his communist principles, genuinely interested the public, which was thoroughly bored by these spectacles and found in them none of the entertainment for which it had come to the theatre. Other producers including Kākī, Raïs, Rouiched, Safīrī, dramatised episodes from the war (*Les Enfants de la Casbah* and *Hassan Terro*) or popular tales borrowed from oral tradition (*El-Ghoula* and *Dīwān al-Garagouz*).

After 1965, Algiers no longer held a monopoly over theatrical life. While, in the context of cultural decentralisation, five regional theatres were progressively established in Constantine, Oran, Sidi Bel Abbas, ᶜAnnaba and Bejaia, groups of amateurs proliferated in the provinces. In 1970, seventy such groups were counted as regularly attending the annual festival of Mostaganem. Their members gave dramatic treatment to topics of contemporary interest: agrarian reform, socialist development of commerce, emigration, education of the young and the position of women in Algerian society. This last problem formed the subject of lengthy public debates at the conclusion of plays devoted to it which the troupe *Théâtre et culture* performed in Algiers in 1970. Similarly, *Le groupe théâtral de l'action culturelle des travailleurs* scored a major success both in Algeria and among expatriate communities in France with the performance in 1972 and 1973 of a dual Arabic and dialect version of *Mohammed, pick up your case*! by Kateb Yacine, in which the protagonist, a modern follower of Djḥā, condemns the activity of all those who shamelessly exploit workers. Agrarian reform gave numerous dramatists the opportunity to reveal their attitude to the subject, notably in *El-Meida* (*al-Mayda*, "The Table"), and *Beni Kelboun* by Kākī, *El Khobza* (*al-Khubza*, "Bread") by Abdelkader ᶜAllūla and *El Agra* (*al-ᶜĀgra*, "The Sterile") by Zāhir Bouzrar (1972-4).

The intentions of other authors are not displayed so overtly, but they are discernible. Such for example is the case of Slīmān Benaissa who, in *Boualem zid el-goudem* (*Būᶜlām zīd al-guddām*, "Boualem, come forward!") and *Youm el djemaa* (*Yūm al-djamᶜa*, "Friday," 1979) deals in a Marxist perspective with the relationships of politics, culture and religion and the social conflicts provoked by their confrontation. Furthermore his work, like that of his colleagues who have read Ionesco and Beckett, breaks with traditional technique and approaches anti-theatre. Scenery is almost non-existent: a deserted island in *Babour eghraq* (*Bābūr ghrak*, "A ship has foundered," 1982); the action is reduced to a few gestures, barely-scripted dialogues between two or three characters without substance who behave like puppets. Similar experiments have been undertaken to reform the presentation and the language of the theatre. But already, since the first seminar of young writers held at Saida in 1973, discussions have given rise to the following concepts: the man of the theatre needs the cooperation of all those who, in various ways, contribute to the staging of the play. Dramatic work is thus a collective creation. It is, furthermore, based on a close collaboration between actors and audience. In order to achieve this objective, it must be performed in the language common to both. It is to this trend of popular expression that the majority of Algerian dramatists adhere today.

Born out of private initiative, Algerian theatre has long suffered from poor material and financial resources. It has neither hierarchy nor organisation. Combination of style is the norm: drama, melodrama, comedy in each of its different elements. Plays rarely display a unity of tone. Written in dialectal prose—the use of literary Arabic is exceptional—they reflect familiar modes of conversation. This is nevertheless a good style of theatre, and it would be a mistake to attribute to it a literary quality which it does not have and which it does not claim. The concepts of authors evidently vary according to their temperament, but all are in agreement on one point: the primary objective is to please and to move the audience. ᶜAllālū, Ksentini and Bachtarzi understood this well. Of the three, it is without doubt the second who, both as a man of the theatre and as a man of the people, best interprets the taste and the nature of his contemporaries with the composition of comedies and lively, jovial farces, often leavened with rational contemplation. His successor, Bachtarzi, aware of the educactive role of the theatre, is mainly concerned with familiarising his audience with the issues of concern to Muslim opinion during the inter-war period. In his view, the man of the theatre is a creator and the spectacle that he presents consists only in dramatising serious or comic situations: it is a kind of celebration of novelty and hope.

Like other cultural activities, since 1962 the theatre has been brought under state control. Many national companies are invited to perform, most of them from self-styled socialist and Third World countries, and their performances are aimed essentially at exhibiting communist and anti-imperialist doctrines. At the same time, youth has leapt to the forefront of the stage. Scores of regular and amateur companies, established in the towns, tour the provinces, performing plays in dialect with themes generally borrowed from contemporary life. Their promoters are obsessed with conceptual debates, seeking only to promote the principles dear to them. The public follows such ideological debates with passionate interest, but by excessively stereotyping characters they make for poor theatre. The best dramatists among the contemporaries are those who, avoiding extreme didacticism, are capable of going beyond narrative or pictorial analysis and taking the measure of the human condition.

Morocco.—As in Algeria, it was not until after the First World War that theatre made its appearance in Morocco. In 1923, an Egyptian troupe led by ʿIzz al-Dīn al-Maṣrī made a tour of the country during which its most notable production was *Ṣalāḥ al-Dīn al-Ayyūbī*, a historical drama in literary Arabic by Nadjīb al-Ḥaddād, which Djūrdj Abyaḍ had performed two years earlier before Muslim audiences in Algiers. This event inspired several young intellectuals of Fez to present similar spectacles to their compatriots. They formed a company whose principal organisers were Muḥammad al-Durrī, Mahdī al-Mniaï and Ibn Shaykh. The first wrote about a dozen plays on themes dealing with the political and social scene: he denounced the protectorate régime, extolled national sentiment and stressed the poverty and ignorance which were the lot of the popular masses. Soon arrested, he died prematurely. His successors, who shared the same ideas, embraced political theatre with increased vigour. In 1929, there were enough of them to justify the holding at Fez of a contest to find the best dramatic actor. The winner was a student of the university of al-Ḳarawiyyīn who celebrated in literary Arabic the virtues of education in the cause of progress and of the struggle for the liberation of the country.

From 1934 onward, the theatre reflected the demands of the *Comité d'action marocaine* of ʿAllāl al-Fāsī which, in particular, sought the reform of Arab education, freedom of the press and the repeal of the dahir of 16 May 1930 codifying traditional Berber law. In the wake of violent public demonstrations at Fez and Meknès in 1934 and 1937, public meetings were forbidden. This measure had a severe impact on the theatre which took refuge in semi-secrecy. Henceforward, groups of players performed only in private sessions on the occasion of family celebrations. Short, humorous and sometimes satirical plays were shown, featuring known characters or current events, and these were much enjoyed by the audience. The state of limbo to which this theatre of controversy was reduced, banned or legalised according to changing circumstances, persisted until Independence.

The years following 1956 were marked by an intense intellectual ferment, to which the theatre contributed a major part. In the chief cities of the country, numerous amateur companies mounted spectacles combining all elements: evocations of the recent past and of ancient history, borrowings from Arab folklore or from foreign literature. To this scintillating period belong several remarkable works, including *Les Fourberies de Joha* by Atawakīl, adapted from Molière's *Les Fourberies de Scapin*, which achieved a huge success both in Morocco and in France, where it was awarded a prize at the Paris Festival of the Nations in 1956.

The public authorities encouraged initiatives aimed at popularising the theatre and took various measures with the purpose of putting its activities on a sound footing. It was thus that there was established in 1959 a centre for drama studies designed to train actors and theatre technicians. At the same time, a national company was founded, bringing together the best actors of the time: al-Ṭayyib al-Ṣiddīḳī, Aḥmad al-Ṭayyib al-ʿAldj, ʿAbd al-Ṣamad Dinyā and Bashīr Skīradj. Finally, financial support was henceforward offered to groups of amateurs who were invited to participate in the annual festival of dramatic art. This official attempt at imposing structure on the theatre was a failure. It encountered difficulties which twenty years later were still not fully surmounted and which had as much to do with the conflicting ambitions of men of the theatre, their personal concepts of dramatic art and the use of the means laid at their disposal, as with the refusal of some of them to join in a process which would integrate them in a bureaucratic system. The combination of these various factors soon put an end to an experiment which had barely begun. In 1962, the centre for drama studies closed its doors. Soon afterwards, the national company broke up and fragmented into several competing groups, while amateur actors were as destitute of support as they had been in the past.

The theatre born immediately after Morocco's accession to independence produced diverse works of very inconsistent quality. The different comic genres continued to enjoy popular approval: sketches, farces, comedies based on mime and gesture, humorous and satirical playlets featuring traditional types such as the naïve and miserly Berber, the cunning and selfish Marrākshī, the greedy Jew, etc. On the other hand, adaptations of foreign works abounded: a characteristic example is supplied by *The Inquisitive ones* by Aḥmad al-Ṭayyib al-ʿAldj, after Molière's *Les Femmes savantes*. Finally, serious theatre was enriched by historical dramas which, written by young authors, sometimes display the exuberance of youth. In this spirit ʿAzīz Saghrūshnī describes, in *The Battle*, the heroic attitude of the inhabitants of al-Djadīda (formerly Mazagan) in their opposition to the occupation of their town by the Portugese at the beginning of the 16th century. Similarly, ʿAbd Allāh Shaḳrūn devotes numerous plays to the past of his country and develops the theme of resistance to foreign occupation, especially in *al-Wāḳiʿa* ("The Battle").

Around the year 1965, changes took place in the world of the theatre. The majority of those who, for ten years, had contributed to the development of dramatic art, abandoned the stage to enter public administration. Among the pioneers, only one remained at the forefront: al-Ṭayyib al-Ṣiddīḳī.

Born at Mogador in 1938, his father a teacher of Arabic and his mother of rural origin, al-Ṣiddīḳī spent his childhood in his native town. After studying at the High School of Casablanca and a brief period of working in postal administration, he began his stage career at eighteen years old, in an Arabic adaptation of *Les Fourberies de Scapin* which, as indicated above, enjoyed major success in Morocco and in France. Al-Ṣiddīḳī then spent two years in Paris, where he learned techniques of production from Hubert Ginioux at the Comédie de l'Ouest before acting for a season at the Théâtre National Populaire, under the direction of Jean Vilar. Returning to Morocco in 1958, he devoted himself entirely to the theatre. Under the auspices of the *Union marocaine du travail*, he established the *Théâtre travailliste*, setting up his stages on the Casablanca waterfront and mounting productions adapted from plays by Aristophanes and Gogol. This experiment lasted no longer than two years, after which he formed his own company, consisting of a dozen players who followed him to the Municipal Theatre of Casablanca when in 1964, at twenty-six years old, he took over its direction. Simultaneously actor, producer, director and administrator, al-Ṣiddīḳī exerted himself unstintingly in efforts to draw the masses of his fellow-citizens to the theatre.

In ten years, he wrote, translated, adapted, presented—almost invariably in dialect—about fifty plays with widely varied themes. First, productions, or more precisely, large-scale exhibitions dramatising events of the past or of the present: *Maroc I*, *La Bataille d'Oued Meghezem*, *Maroc 1973*, or huge pseudo-historical tableaux performed in the open air on the occasion of the annual festival of the *tolba.* Next came pieces inspired either by classical Arabic literature, such as the *maḳāmāt* of al-Hamadhānī, or by the oral tradition as expressed, for example, in the rhymes of al-Madjdhūb [*q.v.*] which are still today recited on many occasions in the Maghrib. Finally, al-Ṣiddīḳī adapted some forty foreign plays, from *Jeu de l'amour et du hasard* by Marivaux to *Amédée* by Eugene Ionesco and *En attendant Godot* by Samuel Beckett. In sum, we have burgeoning répertoire continually enriched.

In fact, al-Ṣiddīḳī sought to provide himself with a lasting supply of material by vigorously seizing everything suited to his purposes, as much in the living popular culture as in foreign works. This versatility corresponded, in his personality, to a threefold concern: to try to interest the largest possible public by offering it numerous and varied productions; to make it aware of the problems faced by contemporary man in the political as well as the social and cultural domain; and to engage it in debate by establishing a dialogue between actors and audience. These parties could not communicate except by using the language of daily conversation. Al-Ṣiddīḳī knew that he was risking the disapproval of the partisans of literary Arabic, but he believed that this was a price worth paying for the development of the theatre in his country.

The prestige of al-Ṣiddīkī should not obscure the efforts of writers and actors of lesser importance who for the most part have shared his motivations. There are several scores of them contributing to theatrical life in the main cities of the kingdom, Rabat, Fez, and especially Tangiers. Radio and television regularly devote broadcasts to the theatre, both in literary Arabic and in dialect. Studies of the traditional methods of performance (*bisāṭ*, *ḥalḳa* and *sirr*) are followed at centres of popular arts. As in Algiers and Tunisia, annual competitions are formed to reward the best dramatists. In short, significant efforts are being made in Morocco to promote and to popularise the theatre.

In the three countires of North Africa, there is periodic talk of crisis in the theatre, expressed in various terms of which the most often heard related to the paucity of writers, poor standards of performance-venues, public apathy, meagre patronage and the excessive cost of seats. In fact, it is perhaps in the very prosperity of the theatre that the true reasons for the crisis should be sought. Dramatic art in the Maghrib is suffering from inflation. There, as elsewhere, many are called and few chosen. The quite considerable number of mediocre works, hastily mounted productions, insufficiently trained actors, the excessive publicity applied to performances or performers of average quality, the constant confusion between original works and those which only pretend to be such, the urge to educate at any price—all these factors are liable to hinder the progress of the theatre without, however, truly threatening its existence. On the contrary, one is constantly surprised by its vitality, the constant innovation on the part of the young people who devote their daily energies to it—writers, producers, designers and actors—even if the co-ordination necessary between these elements is not always evident and the style of the particular period is not accurately invoked. What is clear, in any case, is that theatrical people are not doomed, as were their predecessors, to work in isolation. The problem of the relationship that they must establish with the public—one involving all classes of society—has been better addressed than ever before. In conclusion, the basis of hope for the future is founded as much on the development of communication between actors and audience as on the success of an art form.

Bibliography: I.—Tunisia. Muḥ. al-Ḥabīb, *La marche du théâtre tunisien*, in *al-Nahḍa al-adabiyya*, no. 6 (Tunis March 1944); H. Ben Halima, *Un demi-siècle de théâtre arabe en Tunisie (de 1907 à 1957)*, thèse complém. (Sorbonne) 1968, unpubl.; Bū Snīna, *La crise du théâtre tunisien*, in *al-Thurayyā*, no. 11 (Tunis, Nov. 1945); R. Darmon, *Le théâtre à Tunis de 1850 à 1914*, lecture of *L'Essor. Revue de la vie tunisienne*, no. 12 (Tunis, Dec. 1945); ʿUthmān al-Kaʿāk, *Histoire du théâtre tunisien*, in *al-Mabāḥith*. nos. 15-22 (Tunis, June 1945-January 1946, and no. 33 (Dec. 1946); J. L. Maurve, *Situation du théâtre tunisien*, dipl. d'études supér., Paris, d.s.; Abū Zakariyyā Murābiṭ, *Evolution nouvelle du public de théâtre à Tunis*, in *al-Nahḍa al-adabiyya*, no. 6 (Tunis, March 1944); L.V., *Le théâtre arabe à Tunis (14932-1933)*, in *REI*, vi (1932), 537-44; X., *Le théâtre tunisien*, in *al-Saʿāda*, Rabat, Dec. 1946; X., *La Société théâtrale "El Aghalibah" de Kairouan*, in *al-Salām*, no. 5 (Algiers, Nov. 1946); *Le Renouveau du théâtre tunisien*, in *ibid.*, no. 8 (Febr. 1947); Hasan Emerlī, *Echec du théâtre à Tunis*, in *Al-Nahḍa al-adabiyya*, 8 (March 1944); idem, *Le théâtre encore et toujours: causes de l'insuccès du théâtre*, in *ibid.*, no. 9 (March 1944); idem, *Comment nous "renaissons" par le théâtre*, in *ibid.*, no. 10 (April 1944).

II. Algeria. Allalou, *L'aurore du théâtre algérien (1926-1932)*, in *Cahiers du C.D.S.H.*, no. 9 (Oran 1982); Abdelkader El Arabi, *Théâtre et musique arabes. Une soirée à Alger*, in *Afrique*, no. 51 (Algiers, June 1929); M. Bachetarzi (*sic*), *Mémoires (1919-1939)*, i, Algiers 1968, ii (*1939-1951*), Algiers 1984; R. Bencheneb, *Rachid Ksentini (1887-1944), le père du théâtre arabe en Algérie*, in *Documents Algériens*, no. 16 (Algiers 1946); idem, *Aspects du théâtre arabe en Algérie*, in *L'Islam et l'Occident*, *Cahiers du Sud*, 1947, 271-6; idem, *Littérature et arts arabes en Algérie*, in *Le Monde Illustré*, no. 4412 (Paris May 1947); idem, *Les Mémoires de Mahieddine Bachtarzi ou vingt ans de théâtre algérien*, *ROMM*, no. 9 (1971), 15-20; idem, *Une adaptation algérienne de L'Avare*, in *ibid.*, nos. 13-14 (1973), 87-95; idem, *ʿAllālū et les origines du théâtre algérien*, in *ibid.*, no. 24 (1977), 29-37; S. Bencheneb, *Le théâtre arabe à Alger*, in *R. Afr.*, lxxvii (1935), 72-85; idem, *La littérature populaire (en Algérie)*, in *Initiation à l'Algérie*, Paris 1957, 307; M. Blanchet, *L'art dramatique en Algérie*, in *Le Journal d'Alger*, 24 Aug. and 2 Sept. 1961; H. Cordeaux, *Théâtre et publics algériens*, in *La Revue théâtrale*, no. 31, Paris 1955, 44-9; J. Déjeux, *La littérature algérienne contemporaine*, Paris 1975, 119-20; El Boudali Safir, *Théâtre arabe en Algérie*, in *Simoun*, Oran 1953; P. Enckell, *Le théâtre populaire selon Slimane Benaissa*, in *Les Temps Modernes*, nos. 432-3 (July-Aug. 1982), 341-7; *Hunā al-Djazāʾir—Ici-Alger* (*Revue mensuelle des émissions en langue arabe et kabyle de Radio-Algérie*), Algiers, no. 12 (April 1953), 8-9 and 23, no. 15 (July 1953), 10-11, 16-17, no. 16 (Aug. 1953), 6-9; Mustapha Kateb, *Théâtre d'expression arabe*, in *Consciences Algériennes*, no. 1 (Algiers, Dec. 1950), 74-6; idem, *Théâtre d'expression arabe: langue et répertoire*, in *ibid.*, no. 2 (Feb.-March. 1951), 73; A. Roth, *Le théâtre algérien de langue dialecale, 1926-1954*, Paris 1976; N. Tomiche-Dagher, *Représentations parisiennes du jeune théâtre algérien*, in *BE* (1952); X., *Le théâtre musulman algérien*, in *al-Salām*, Algiers, no. 10 (Feb. 1947); X., *Théâtre: "Rentrée" des professionnels*, *El-Moudjahid*, Algiers, 8-9 Aug. 1986; N. Zand, *Kateb, le premier des beurs*, in *Le Monde*, 26 Dec. 1986.

III. Morocco. Hassen El Mniaï, *Du côté des*

amateurs, in *Le Monde*, 21-2 Nov. 1976, 14; J. P. Péroncel-Hugoz, *Profil d'un intellectuel arabe: Tayyeb le Véridique*, in *ibid.*, 4-5 Feb. 1973; Abdallah Stouky, *Où va le théâtre au Maroc?* in *Souffles*, no. 3 (1966); X., *Deux pièces de théâtre en arabe jouées par une troupe marocaine*, in *al-Saʿāda*, no. 6692 (Rabat, May 1946); X., *Le théâtre musulman en Algérie et au Maroc*, in *al-Salām*, no. 9 (Feb. 1947); *Le théâtre au Maroc*, in *ibid.*, no. 1 (April 1947); A. Bennani-Mechita, *Le théâtre de Taïeb Saddiki*, unpubl. diss., Université de Provence 1985; A. Lhachimi, *Le théâtre amateur marocain contemporain*, unpubl. diss., Univ. de Provence 1986. (R. Bencheneb)

3. In Turkey.

The art of theatre in Turkey developed from the same religious, moral and educational urge to imitate human actions that accompanied its growth in ancient Greece. There are four main traditions of theatre in Turkey: folk theatre, popular theatre, court theatre and Western theatre. Improvised theatre developed in two complete different social environments: as part of the popular theatre tradition in big cities, such as Istanbul, and as part of folk-literature. Although the two traditions seem poles apart, they are essentially not so different in spirit as external characteristics might suggest. Both are extempore and non-literary. In both theatres, the action gains naturalism and vividness by spontaneity, and in both the language is simple, direct and strong. Performances were held at ground level in an arena, thereby lending flexibility to the acting and helping to create intimacy with the audience. Although highly different in presentation, techniques and conventions, both theatres have approximately the same genres: puppetry, story-telling (acted out), dramatic dancing and rudimentary play by actors.

Unlike most Asiatic countries, Turkey had no greatly individualised and distinctive court theatre tradition. Until the period of Westernisation, court theatre simply imitated popular theatre. The courts of mediaeval rulers all over Anatolia attracted dancers, actors, story-tellers, clowns, puppet masters and conjurors. They performed only for the aristocracy of the palace, and hence they were more refined and literary. But the court also supported theatrical entertainment outside the palace. The birth of a prince or his circumcision, a court marriage, the accession of a new ruler, triumph in war, departure for a new conquest or the arrival of a welcome foreign ambassador or guest, were occasions for public festivities, sometimes lasting as long as forty days and nights. These served the double purpose of amusing the courtiers and the people and impressing the world at large with a display of magnificence. The festivities included not only processions, illuminations, fireworks, equestrian games and hunting, but also dancing, music, poetry recitations, and performances by jugglers, mountebanks, and buffoons. Beginning in the 19th century, in reaction to Western influence, sultans started building theatres in their palaces. ʿAbd al-Me<u>dj</u>īd constructed a theatre near the Dolma Ba<u>gh</u>če Palace in 1858, and the theatre that ʿAbd al-Ḥamīd II built in his Yi̊ldi̊z Palace in 1889 has survived. In these theatres, dramatic and operatic performances were given by both professional and amateur players.

The development of the Turkish Western theatre tradition is fairly recent, and can be conveniently divided into three periods, which are determined not only by theatrical developments but also by political and constitutional changes. The first period, from 1839 to 1908, is subdivided into the *Tanẓīmāt* and *Istibdād* periods—that is, the periods of "reorganisation" and "despotism"; the second major period, from 1908 to 1923, is that of the Revolution of 1908; and the third from 1923 to the present can be called the Republican period.

Four public playhouses were built in the first year of the *Tanẓīmāt* period: a Western theatre, a playhouse for performances of traditional Turkish theatre, and two large amphitheatres for circus-like spectacles. (Before this date, however, there were probably several temporary theatres. For instance, documents have established that in 1830 a theatre was under construction in Izmir.) This theatre construction was important to the development of Western theatre in Turkey. As the *Tanẓīmāt* intelligentsia pointed out, what distinguished Turkish traditional theatre from Western theatre was the latter's reliance on playhouses and written texts. With the opening of four theatre buildings in 1839, the first major distinction had been breached. The second, the development of written text, was to follow.

To go ahead in time, 1908 saw the restoration of the constitution of 1876, and what is commonly called the "Declaration of Freedom" (*Ḥürriyyetiñ iʿlānı̊*). The political change brought a reawakening of the nation's creative theatre life, and the years that followed have been identified by drama historians as the theatre of the constitutional period. A new theatrical period can be said to have begun with the declaration of the Republic on 23 October 1923, first of all because the Republican period finally saw the removal of an obstacle which had been blocking the development of Turkish theatre: the ban against the appearance of Turkish Muslim women on the stage. Though some courageous Turkish women had previously attempted to break this ban, legal proceedings and police persecution had discouraged them. In July 1923, however, Atatürk attended a performance in Izmir, given by a group of actors from the Istanbul Municipal Theatre. He assured them that from then onwards, Turkish women would be free to appear on the stage and that the theatre arts would be supported by the government. In that same year, Turkish women appeared in a musical comedy called *The fugitives from the ballroom (Bala ḳačaḳları̊)*, and the picture of the leading actress Sedād Naẓīre <u>Kh</u>ānîm, was featured on the cover of a women's magazine. The following year two women appeared in a performance of Shakespeare's *Othello*, Badʿiyya Muwaḥḥid as Desdemona and Neyyire Neyyir as Emilia. With this general view in mind, the development of Western-style theatre in Turkey can be analysed in detail.

In 1839 the Royal Decree of Gülhane inaugurated the *Tanẓīmāt* period, important as a period when an audience for theatre was created, professional personnel developed and playwrights emerged to write hundreds of plays. Among the factors which helped facilitate the establishment of European theatre in Turkey, the following are important:

The sultan and his environment. Three reformist sultans were especially important to this development: Selīm III and Maḥmūd II, both prior to 1839, and ʿAbd al-Ma<u>dj</u>īd. In 1836 Maḥmūd II's library contained 500 plays, of which 40 were tragedies, 40 were dramas, 30 were comedies, and the rest farces and vaudevilles. The sultans sometimes attended public performance, and were a kind of insurance against opposition from fanatical orthodox quarters. When the latter attacked the notion of theatre, intellectuals could use the sultan's support as a defence: "Would you know better than His Majesty, not only our Sovereign but the Caliph of all Muslims, who is building a theatre in his own palace, and rewarding foreign and native actors? He himself honours performances on many occasions." ʿAbd al-ʿAzīz was not so keen on the theatre as his predecessors, but it was during his rule that Turkish theatre had its golden age. During the thirty-three year reign of his successor, ʿAbd al-Ḥamīd II, despotism and rigid censorship halted positive developments in the theatre, and public theatre almost ceased. Nevertheless, he himself had two theatres built in his palace, where he maintained two permanent, salaried theatrical companies, one foreign and the other native.

Turkish statesmen and ambassadors also contributed to the development of Western-style theatre. Early in 1870, the Grand Vizier ʿAlī Pas̲h̲a unsuccessfully tried to establish a national theatre, but later that year he achieved his objectives by granting Güllü Agop, director of the Ottoman Theatre Company, a ten-year monopoly.

The press was another important factor in promoting Western-style theatre. Newspapers appeared in Turkey at just about the same time as the theatre, and many journalists began to write plays. Naturally, newspaper reports and reviews of theatre activities helped stimulate and guide public opinion. Foreign embassies, especially the French and Italian ones, played an important role, since many of these embassies had their own theatres, to which Turks were often invited to private performances. The embassies were also instrumental in bringing theatre and opera troupes to Turkey from their own countries. Non-Muslim minorities contributed greatly to the development of Western theatre in Turkey, most importantly, the Armenian community. An important role was also played by the cultural centres of other minorities of residents: the German one with their Teutonia, the French with their Alliance Française and the British and Italians through various theatre organisations.

Western theatre was perhaps most strongly promoted by visiting foreign troupes, many of which stayed as long as a whole season and gave regular performances. Some of these companies included the leading actors and artists of their times, and Turkish actors often learned their profession by watching these performances. Some seasons were so rich that the several foreign companies gave parallel performances, as for example on 11 September 1896, when there were three different performances of Verdi's *Aida* in Istanbul. Some of the operas of Verdi, Donizetti and Bellini were performed in Turkey before they were seen in Paris or other European capitals. Because of the influx of foreign companies, many more theatres were built. Often when these companies returned home, some of their members remained in Turkey, and it was from these actors, directors, set designers and conductors that Turkish theatre people learned their skills.

As has been pointed out, for the intelligentsia of the *Tanẓīmāt* period, the establishment of a Western theatrical tradition in Turkey was dependent on the building of theatres and the availability of written texts. The first modern Turkish play dates from 1859. Called *The poet's marriage* (*Bir s̲h̲āʿir evlenmesi*), this satire on prearranged marriages by the poet Ibrāhīm S̲h̲ināsī had been commissioned for the newly-completed court theatre of the Dolma Bag̲h̲če Palace. Though it was the first Turkish play written by a Turk in Turkey, it was not the first Turkish play. The first theatre texts in Turkish are those of the Azerbaijani playwright Mīrzā Fatḥ ʿAlī Ak̲h̲undov (1812-78), who wrote six comedies between the years 1850 and 1855. His popular plays were translated into Russian and later into the various languages of the present-day Soviet Union, as well as into Persian, French, English and German. Though Ak̲h̲undov preceded Ibrāhīm S̲h̲ināsī and enjoyed wide popularity outside his own country, S̲h̲ināsī's short play demonstrates greater skill.

Mention should also be made of a Turkish manuscript found in Viennese archives by Professor Fahir Iz, *The strange and curious tale of Ahmet the Cobbler* (*Waḳāyiʿ-i ʿad̲j̲ībe we ḥawādit̲h̲-i g̲h̲arībe-yi kefs̲h̲er Aḥmed*). Dated 1809, the manuscript, contains translations of the play in Italian, German and French; the name Iskerleč on it is probably that of the copyist. Two more plays were subsequently found: one, *Godefroi de Bouillon*, dealing with the First Crusade; the other, in both Turkish and French, was by a foreigner, Thomas Chabert, and its long title can be shortened to *Ḥād̲j̲d̲j̲ī Bektās̲h̲ or the founding of the Janissaries.* The source of these texts was the Paris Ecole des Langues Orientales, which trained translators for the European embassies in the Middle East countries. Some of these plays were actually produced in the school. Years later, the catalogue of Turkish and Persian manuscripts in Poznan listed another version of *Aḥmed the cobbler* and another work entitled *Nasreddin Hoca's appointment to an official post (Naṣreddīn K̲h̲ōd̲j̲a'niñ manṣibi).* The manuscript, translated into German, Italian and French was like the earlier-found version of *Aḥmed the cobbler* dated 1809, but the Poznan copy of *Aḥmed the cobbler* bore the signature Dombay, instead of Iskerleč, and the *Naṣreddīn K̲h̲ōd̲j̲a* play was signed Johann Lippa. The evidence suggests that in the School of Oriental Languages, Turkish was taught by members of the Turkish embassy staff. Though they no doubt wrote these plays, they chose as professional diplomats to remain anonymous. They probably dictated them as exercises to students, who in turn translated them into the three major languages of the Austrian Empire. Written from dictation, the manuscripts contain spelling errors, but since the authors were Turks, there are not many mistakes in syntax.

Other plays in Turkish that pre-date S̲h̲ināsī's were only translations, some of which were performed but never published. For instance, ʿAbd al-Med̲j̲īd's chamberlain, Ṣaffet Bey, translated Molière's plays for performance by the young Turkish musicians of the imperial band, and in 1845 the sultan invited three of his doctors to be present at the Turkish performance of two of Molière's plays, one of which ridiculed the medical profession.

Many foreign plays were translated into Turkish and performed by the Armenian theatre companies prior to the foundation of the Ottoman Theatre. Some copies of the translations that predate S̲h̲ināsī's play are in Armenian characters. The earliest, published in 1813, is a translation of Molière's *Le médecin malgré lui.* Four plays by Metastasio were translated into Turkish and published in Armenian in 1831. Since the source of these latter plays was the Bible, it seems likely that they were used to propagate the Christian faith. Unlike contemporary Turkish texts, they do not contain Persian or Arabic words. Lithographed translated texts of opera libretti for Tukish audiences are very rare, but there are some in the Topkapı Museum and in private collections. An Italian opera on Turkish subject, *The siege of Silistria*, written in Turkey and performed there, has libretti in both Italian and Turkish.

Some students of Turkish theatre consider the first Turkish play to be K̲h̲ayr Allāh Efendi's *Ḥikāye-yi Ibrāhīm Pas̲h̲a*, a 19th century version of a 16th century story about Ibrāhīm Pas̲h̲a of Sulaymān the Magnificent's time. The manuscript of this play by the father of the well-known Turkish poet and playwright ʿAbd al-Ḥaḳḳ was discovered by Ismail Hami Danişment in 1939. Written in 1844, fifteen years before S̲h̲ināsī's play, when K̲h̲ayr Allāh was a student in medical school, it is little more than a rough draft by an amateur, probably never meant to be seen by others.

The Armenians and Levantines of Istanbul gave Turkey its first Western theatre in the Turkish language, generally adapted to local theatre tastes and conditions. Before the Armenians became active in theatre, the private residences of foreign embassy personnel were the only places in which Turks could see Western theatre and opera companies in their own languages. By the third quarter of the 19th century, however, the Istanbul Armenians had established two companies that sought a wider Turkish audience. First, a company called S̲h̲arḳ ("The Orient") and, later, one called Vaspuragan, came into existence, both of which translated, adapted, and performed European plays in both Armenian and Turkish.

The most important effort in this Armeno-Turkish development was that of the Ottoman Theatre Company at the Gedikpas̲h̲a Theatre in Istanbul. Headed by an Armenian Agop Vartovian (Güllü Agop), the company prepared the way for a genuinely national Turkish theatre by introducing Turkish actors in original Turkish plays. Sometimes given minor roles, the Turkish actors helped correct the pronunciation of Armenian performers, and Turkish writers were employed to make sure that the translations were idiomatically correct. The proceedings inevitably aroused the enthusiasm and support of university students.

But the guiding spirit remained Güllü Agop, who completed this Armeno-Turkish integration by eventually becoming a Muslim. In 1868 he committed his company to performances of plays in Turkish, and in April of that year he offered Istanbul its Turkish-language modern theatre production, a translation of a French play entitled *César Borgia.* This production was received somewhat unenthusiastically, and Güllü Agop immediately followed it with a tragedy based on the Turkish romance *Laylā and Medjnūn* by Muṣṭafā Efendi. The following year saw a marked increase in original Turkish plays.

As noted earlier, in 1870 the Grand Vizier ʿAlī Pas̲h̲a granted Güllü Agop a ten-year monopoly of the production of dramas in the Turkish language. This patent, however, required him to open new theatres in various parts of Istanbul within a given time. Other would-be-producers barred from producing plays in Istanbul by Güllü Agop's monopoly, were encouraged, occasionally by prominent statesmen, to open theatres in the provinces. One such man, Ḍiyāʾ Pas̲h̲a (1825-80), brought a company from Istanbul, and another theatre was opened in Trabzon by the governor ʿAlī Bey, who was a playwright. In Bursa, the governor Aḥmed Wefīḳ Pas̲h̲a adapted nearly all of Molière's plays into Turkish and personally ran his own theatre, training and directing his actors and inspiring talented Turkish authors to write plays.

In Istanbul, Güllü Agop's monopoly was soon challenged, first by an open company which claimed that his patent did not apply to musical performances on stage, and then by *ortaoyunu* [*q.v.*] actors, who used every subterfuge to put on plays indoors as well as outdoors. They charged Güllü Agop with having failed to build the new theatres called for in his patent, and that in any case their performances were improvised, without text or employment of a prompter, and therefore not covered by the monopoly. Thus the seed was sown for a new theatre that could perhaps better nourish itself in the native tradition than the borrowed theatre translated from European literatures or directly imitative of them. With their *ṭulūʿat* (improvisatory) theatre, which filled the outline of a vague plot with local events, incidents picked up from the newspapers, or from street gossip, the *ortaoyunu* players gave their generation a kind of *commedia dell'arte* which stands midway between the traditional Turkish theatre and the imported Western theatre. However, after the Ottoman Theatre Company, was abruptly abolished by an order of the sultan in 1884, theatre activity in Turkey generally suffered an eclipse.

The second phase of the Western theatre tradition in Turkey is considered to have begun in 1908, the year of the constitutional revolution and to have ended in 1923, the year of the proclamation of the Republic. It was an important transitional period, a time of political turmoil. It also marked the restoration of theatre and some attempts to develop in new directions. The early months of 1908 were full of tension and excitement, as the new régime was being greeted with understandable delight. The theatres shared this enthusiasm, and put on productions suited to special occasions. Many new theatres sprang up under the stimulus of the events of this year, and during the next fifteen years they changed names and administration in rapid succession, some managing to survive only briefly. Too often, dramatic offerings were supplanted by political speeches and demonstrations meant to fire audiences with liberal enthusiasm. Plays previously banned by ʿAbd al-Ḥamīd's censorship were revived to stir up the populace against the former régime. The dominant genre of theatre was the *pièce de circonstance.* These works were set in contemporary Turkey, and their protagonists were the Young Turks, the leaders of the Union and Progress Party, who were shown as patriots, while the supporters and followers of ʿAbd al-Ḥamīd were portrayed as opportunistic villains. Playwrights of the time saw theatre as a vehicle for the abasement of the former régime on the one hand and for enthusiastic praise of the constitutional reforms on the other. Thus the deluge of bad plays continued.

The theatre was also an ideal instrument for the strengthening of civilian and military morale. Wars followed in dizzy succession during that period, among them the Turco-Italian War of 1911, the Balkan War of 1912, World War I, and finally the Turkish War of Independence. A long series of Turkish plays were loosely constructed from topical scenes derived from some recent ware, glorifying the struggle of the Turkish people against their enemies. Other plays dealt with Ottoman history, lauding Turkish heroes of the past. The emphasis was always on solidarity and preparedness for war. Needless to say, most of these plays were extremely ephemeral.

Nevertheless, this period saw a number of significant developments in the theatre. Religious and official attitudes militating against the appearance of Turkish Muslim women on stage began to give way in 1919, when for the first time an actress—her name was ʿAfīfe—appeared in a play on the Turkish stage. Though her career was not without difficulties, her example was soon followerd by others.

The same period also saw the establishment of a school of drama and music in Istanbul. It was organised in 1914 by André Antoine (1859-1943), founder of Paris's Théâtre Libre, who had come to Turkey at the invitation of the mayor of Istanbul. In

1916, it started giving public performances, gradually becoming more of a theatre than a school and leading to the establishment of the present Istanbul Municipal Theatre.

It was also during this period that many native playwrights and theatre men of distinction started their careers. Until the Constitution of 1908 and the dethroning of ʿAbd al-Ḥamīd, government censorship discouraged the development of playwrights. After the reforms, however, there appeared dramatists who treated a variety of previously forbidden subjects.

Several professional, semi-professional, and amateur companies were active in this period. Among these were the Ṣaḥne-yi Hewes (formed by amateurs, among whom there were playwrights), and the short-lived Ṣanāyiʿ-i Nefīse. Amateurs later formed other troupes, such as Mürebbī Ḥiṣṣiyyāt, which was housed in the ʿOthmān Agha Theatre. Burhān al-Dīn Tepsi, a pupil of Silvain, studied drama in Paris and subsequently formed a company which gave regular performances. It was followed by another company called Dār al-Tamthīl-i ʿOthmānī, formed by the actor Hüseyn Kāmī Bey. Certain playwrights, intellectuals and actors unsuccessfully planned to found a national theatre. Other attempts in this direction were the ʿOthmānlî Tiyatro Kulübü (Ottoman Theatre Club), the Istanbul Ḳumpanyasî, and the Ertughrul Tiyatrosu. To raise money for the purchase of warships, the ʿOthmānlî Donanma Djemʿiyyeti was formed. Other important companies included Minakian's Ottoman Theatre and the Binemedjiyan Company.

The present period of Turkish drama dates from the proclamation of the Republic. This and the reforms of 1925-8 opened a new era and quickly brought about official approbation and government support of culture and drama in Turkey. The Turkish language was revivified, and there was increased interest in bringing to audiences works based on national history and folklore. Because the state considered drama to be an essential element in the modernisation of Turkey, it assumed full responsibility for the actor's professional career. The state conservatory established in 1936 in Anakara for training actors, acresses, opera singers and ballet dancers has since then greatly advanced the development of Turkish dramatic arts. When the course at that school has been completed, the student is taken on as a member of the leading State Theatre Company, which is founded by the government and functions under the Ministry of Culture. Additional funds are obtained from the sale of low-priced tickets. Providing security and opportunities for work in the theatrical profession, the State Theatre now operates with ten or eleven stages. In recent years it has produced excellent productions of foreign playwrights, from Sophocles to Edward Albee, and has introduced new Turkish dramatists. Along with several private theatres, it has been sending companies on one or two-month tours throughout the country.

The Halk evleri (People's houses) [see KHALḲ EVI] were established in 1931 and furthered cultural emancipation through a concerted programme of literary, artistic and mainly drama projects. Despite its success, this movement was disbanded on political grounds. The present trend is toward the establishment of regional theatre companies.

Theatre activity in Turkey is still mostly confined to the two largest cities, Ankara and Istanbul. The latter has about 25 private theatres, as well as 5 owned by the municipality. Privately-owned and managed theatres do not receive government subsidies or tax relief. In addition to the 4 theatres of the State Theatre Company, Ankara has several private companies, although the number varies from season to season. Owing to the competition of television, most theatres are almost invariably half-empty; therefore, while there appears to be a highly active theatre life in Turkey, this is now only superficially so.

From the point of view of the development of Turkish drama, the Republican period can be subdivided into two main sub-periods: from 1923 to 1960, and from 1960 to the present day. Though rooted in a relatively short tradition, recent Turkish drama has shown considerable promise.

Until 1960, the works seen on the Turkish stage reflected few of the changes which had overtaken the country. Some were poor copies of Western plays, in which an effort was made to assimilate the latter's surface qualities. The pre-1960 dramatists tended toward pseudo-symbolism or psychological realism, in which characters worked out their fate in an almost societyless vacuum. Highly popular were the traditional lightweight comedies that amused the audiences without ruffling their composure: plays focusing on unusual or off-beat characters: plays hammering on the theme that money is the root of all evil; plays on the inevitability of fate; plays involving dreams and psychoanalytic themes; plays on the eternal triangle; plays on the vicissitudes of married life; plays contrasting big city and provincial life; plays in verse which failed to be poetic; and sentimental plays on themes of love, altruism and self-sacrifice. Dramatists most often provided only a sketchy treatment of these themes.

After the Army junta overthrew the Menderes government in 1960 and promulgated a new constitution in the following year, the theatre turned to a more outspoken treatment of contemporary problems. Though theatre was excluded from preliminary censorship, a long list of moral and political taboos remained in effect. Nevertheless, the new values imposed by the 1961 constitution lie behind every problem play of the period. Turkish dramatists were working toward some moment of release from constrictions, both self- and externally-imposed. Not only did new dramatists emerge, but many playwrights writing before 1960 suddenly seemed to find new energy and new forms of expression. This lasted until the 1970s. During those memorable ten years, Turkish theatre enjoyed a vitality that enabled it to deal with problems of current social and political importance. In 1969 serious social, economic, and political unrest descended upon Turkey. Rural inhabitants were flocking to the big cities in search of work and student violence was erupting in the streets. Severe new codes were enacted which subjected the big cities to martial law. People naturally prefered to spend their evenings at home watching television, then quite a recent innovation in Turkey.

Between 1960 and the 1970s, private theatre had mushroomed in Istanbul and Ankara, but many now closed their doors, leaving others that are still struggling to survive. Two theatres deserve special mention: Dostlar Tiyatrosu (Friends' Theatre) in Istanbul, and Ankara Sanat Tiyatrosu (Ankara Arts Theatre). Both are private theatres, and are socially and politically committed to the left. Thanks to their loyal audiences and staffs, they have been able to resist the tide.

A new generation of aspiring playwrights began to appear in the 1960s, and a changing society provided them with ever-new material. For convenience, the considerable dramatic output of the Republican period can best be broken down by its main focus and theme. Contemporary man's sense of isolation, alienation, and loss of identity are dealt with in various plays. Plays about individuals caught in the cultural conflict between traditional values and modern Westernised ideas and manners are the subject of a number of plays. Peasants flooding into the big cities and being forced to live in slums are another topic. Many plays involve lower-middle class or working-class families in the grip of financial difficulties, and show the family as a microcosm of world problems as they fight against disintegration. Since 1960s there have been plays highlighting and revealing the role, the problems, and the social position of modern Turkish women. Some plays can best be described as village or peasant plays offering authentic pictures of village life in out-of-the way places. They deal with such problems as corrupt landlords and local administrators, marriage customs, jealousy intolerance, superstitions and family feuds. Some playwrights take their inspiration from mythology, old legends, local history and the history of previous civilisations. Plotless plays presenting glimpses of assorted characters and their everyday lives are often introduced by a narrator and depend largely on their atmospheric quality. Often they contrast an "inner" and an "outer" world. Many plays highlight political and social revolutionary ideals, the conflict between capital and labour, business ethics, and the fight against Fascism. Idealists whose zeal alienates them from contemporary Turkish reality are dealt with in a number of plays. Of a more general nature are those symbolic dramas concerned with such themes as man's place in the universe, analyses of social organisation and criticism of contemporary mores. In recent years, Turkish dramatists and theatre groups have been experimenting with new forms and unconventional structures. Western culture is now seen not as an ideal model but as a contrasting tradition. Playwrights have also become aware that "modern" theatrical trends in Europe have their counterparts in Turkish traditional theatre, and this has facilitated their absorption into contemporary Turkish theatre. For example, the tradition of Karagöz [*q.v.*] or shadow theatre has been supplied with new scripts designed for performance by live actors. The contribution of traditional Turkish theatre far transcends mere borrowing or superficial treatment. It stems from the very essence of traditional theatre: a sense of anti-illusionistic rapport between the actors and the audience, an open or flexible form, the attempt to give the impression of improvisation and total theatre in performance, and the use of music, dance and songs as adjuncts to drama.

Bibliography: Metin And, *A history of theatre and popular entertainment in Turkey*, Ankara 1963-4; C.-Ü. Spuler, *Das Türkische Drama der Gegenwart*, in *WI*, xi (1968), 1-229; Ö. Nutku, *Darülbedavi'nin elli yılı*, Ankara 1969; M. And, *Meşrutiyet döneminde türk tiyatrosu (1908-1923)*, Ankara 1971; idem, *Tanzimat ve Istibdat döneminde türk tiyatrosu (1839-1908)*, Ankara 1972; idem, *Cumhüriyet döneminde türk tiyatrosu*, Ankara 1983; idem *Osmanlı tiyatrosu. Kurulusu-gelişimi-katkısı*, Ankara 1976; Sevda Şener, *Çağdaş türk tiyatrosunda ahlâk. Ekonomi, kültür sorunları (1923-1970)*, Ankara 1971; eadem, *Çağdaş türk tiyatrosunda insan*, Ankara 1972; B. Robson, *The drum beats nightly. The development of the Turkish drama as a vehicle for social and political comment in the post-revolutionary period 1924 to the present*, Tokyo 1975; T. S. Halman, *Modern Turkish drama. An anthology of plays in translation*, Minneapolis and Chicago 1976.

(METİN AND)

4. In Iran.

The history of the theatrical arts in Iran is obscured by the fact that they have only recently acquired a place among the manifestations of Iranian culture considered to be serious. Written drama as a branch of polite literature emerged under the influence of the West in the second half of the past century, and the development of a theatrical tradition with formal institutions started at an even younger data. This does not mean, however, that before that time no indigenous types of drama were in existence. References to performances of various kinds are known from pre-Islamic times onwards, although they do not become numerous enough to allow us to describe their origin and development in detail until the last few centuries. Iran even made a unique contribution to Islamic civilisation by creating a form of religious drama [see TAʿZIYA]. A common feature of these types of drama is that they are based almost entirely on improvisation so that they only rarely have left traces of their past existence in the form of written plays. They belong essentially to popular culture, even if they were adopted by the courts and by members of the educated class as forms of entertainment.

Religious objections to the impersonation of living beings, and to frivolous entertainment in general, being as they were prevalent during the Islamic period, have undoubtedly been an impediment to the development of serious drama. Already before Islam, however, dramatics did not play a prominent part in Iranian culture, at least not in that section of it about which we possess any knowledge. The Greek theatres which existed in some places after the invasion of Alexander remained a foreign element and soon disappeared without having exerted a noticeable influence.

The Sāsānid kings amused themselves with the performances of minstrels, singers and musicians, as well as with many other kinds of entertainment. Descriptions of these court traditions can be found in the Pahlawi book *Khusraw and his page* and in many Islamic sources (cf. M. Boyce, in *JRAS* [1957], 10-45). They provided a model for the amusements of polite society in later times. This tradition continued without fundamental changes till it came under the attack of modern types of entertainment. It remained close to the popular tradition of performances, called *maʿrika*, *hangāma* or *tamā<u>sh</u>ā*, which mostly took place in public squares. The performer (*maʿrika-gīr*) could be a storyteller (*ḳiṣṣagū*), a rope-dancer, an acrobat, a magician or a leader of dancing animals. Literary sources seldom pay attention to these types of folk art, but a remarkable exception is the *Futuwwat-nāma-yi sulṭānī* by Kā<u>sh</u>ifī (*q.v.*; see also Galunov, *Iran*, iii, 94). The earliest observations of such performances made by European travellers date from the 17th century (cf. e.g. J. B. Tavernier, *Les six voyages... en Turquie, en Perse et aux Indes*, Amsterdam 1678, i, 442-3 (performances at the *maydān* of Tabrīz); J. Chardin, *Voyages en Perse*, ed. L. Langlès, Paris 1811, iii, 326 f. (variety at Tabrīz), 180 ff. (wrestlers, sword fighters and fighting animals at Iṣfahān), 436-64 ("Exercices et jeux des Persans")). At the social occasions held at the courts or in private mansions, singing, playing and dancing were among the principal amusements. Central figures were the minstrel (*<u>kh</u>unyāgar*; cf. the description of his craft in ch. 36 of the *Ḳābūs-nāma* by Kay Kāwūs [*q.v.*], ed. Tehran 1345/1967, 193-7), and the singer-musician (*muṭrib*), who appears frequently in Persian poetry. A picture of the entertainment at a local court about the end of the 5th/11th century is presented in a short *ma<u>th</u>nawī* poem by Masʿūd Saʿd-i

Salmān [*q.v.*] (*Dīwān*, ed. Tehran 1339/1960, 562-79), which makes mention of musicians playing various instruments, singers and dancers.

The art of the narrator (*naḳḳāl*), who accompanied his recitation with musical and gesticular means of expression, may rightly be regarded as a branch of indigenous dramatics. The relationship with polite literature, which often exists, puts this performer in a special category. Until the beginning of this century, the narrator was a man of some education whose performances were appreciated at all levels of society. His rôle as a transmitter of epics in prose or in poetry must have been considerable throughout the history of Persian literature, although he usually remained in the shadow of the writers and the poets. He also provided the latter with much of raw material, consisting of stories of all kinds, for their prose works and *mat͟hnāwī* poems. Several terms were in use to differentiate between specialisations within the profession of narrator. In more recent times, the best-known religious narrator is the *rawḍa-k͟hʷān* [*q.v.*]. The national epic provided the subject matter to the *s͟hāh-nāma-k͟hʷān*, who narrated fragments from Firdawsī's poem. His popularity at the court of the Ṣafawids has been recorded by the historians of the period, together with the names of the most celebrated narrators of this type (for further details, see Bayḍāʾī, *Namāyis͟h*, 60-81).

To the common people, the *naḳḳāl*, performed in particular at the coffee- or teahouses which are known to have existed in Iran since the 17th century [see ČAY-K͟HĀNA in Suppl.]. Sitting on a platform (*tak͟ht*), he chanted his text using only a small stick (*miṭrāḳ*, *čūbdastī*) to accentuate his gesticulations. Sometimes his recitation was accompanied by one or two musicians. Pictures on the walls representing scenes from the *S͟hāh-nāma* or from the tales about the *Imāms* called *s͟hamāyil*, often helped him to make his audience visualise his narrative. Story-telling with the help of pictures was also practiced outdoors by people named *pardazān* or *s͟hamāyil-gardān* who mainly dealt with religious subjects. Subsequent scenes were usually combined on one canvas covered by a curtain which was gradually uncovered as the narration proceeded. A remarkable tool, described by Galunov as it could be seen at Iṣfahān in the twenties of of this century, was the *s͟hahr-i firang* (a name referring probably to its European origin), a metal case inside which a roll (*ṭūmār*) could rotate to show pictures one by one through an opening at the front of the case (*Narodniy teatr Irana*, 67 ff.).

Puppet-shows were known in Iran already during the Middle Ages, as is witnessed by many references in the works of classical poets to puppets (*k͟hiyāl*, *luʿbat*) as well as to certain props of the puppet-player, e.g. the curtain (*parda*), the cloth (*naʿt*) on which the plays were enacted, and the box (*ṣandūḳ*) into which the puppets were put away after the show had ended. Mention is also made sometimes of a magic lanterm (*fānūs-i k͟hiyāl*), but it is uncertain whether any of the known references may be interpreted as evidence of the existence of shadow play in mediaeval Iran (see P. N. Boratav, art. ḲARAGÖZ). Whenever mention is made of puppet-shows in these sources, the intention is to use them as symbols pointing to the thought that the existence of this world and its inhabitants is dependent entirely on God's will. In the *Us͟htur-nāma*, a mystical *mat͟hnawī* poem attributed by tradition to ʿAṭṭār [*q.v.*], a Turkish puppet-player is presented as an emblem of the divine rule over human destiny. This is also the proper meaning of the puppet-play according to the description in the *Futuwwat-nāma* of Kās͟hifī (see Galunov, *Iran*, ii, 72-4).

The most important types of puppet-play which until quite recently were current in Iran belong to the kind in which the puppets are shown directly to the public. The shadow-play never gained in Iran the prominence which it had in the folklore of other peoples of the Middle East [see K͟HAYĀL AL-ẒILL] and disappeared already quite early without leaving many traces. A variety making use of glove puppets was called *pahlawān kačal* ("the bald hero") after its leading character who also appears however in other forms of popular theatre. It was sometimes called *pand͟j* because five figures were required to play the stock parts of the show. Much more elaborate was the *k͟hayma-s͟hab-bāzī*, a marionette theatre operating, as the name implies, at night and enacted, at least originally, in a tent. The performers were itinerant artists who were reckoned among the *lūṭīs* [*q.v.*] or the gypsies. In the present century, the *k͟hayma-s͟hab-bāzī* was also played at a fixed locality such as the *kafa-yi s͟hahrdārī* at Tehran between 1941 and about 1950 (Bayḍāʾī, *Namāyis͟h*, 110 f.). The puppet-player (*ustād*) and his assistant (*s͟hāgird*) manipulated the figures from behind a screen and let them speak. They used a small whistle (*sutsutak*) to imitate high-pitched voices. In front of the scene, the leader (*murs͟hid*) introduced the performance and argued occasionally with the characters of the play. Musical accompaniment was played on the *ḍarb*, the *tār* or the *kamanča*.

The variety shows performed by live actors originated from the acts of individual performers of different types. There is perhaps a historical connection with folk traditions, such as the installation of a mock king at the time of the New Year festival, which was practised in parts of Iran until quite recently (cf. M. Ḳazwīnī, *Mīr-i Nawrūzī*, in *Yādgār*, i/3, 13-6, who described an instance of the custom witnessed at Bud͟jnūrd in 1923). Wandering groups of actors used to perform humorous sketches during this holiday. One of the stock figures was known as Ḥād͟jd͟jī Fīrūz, a clown with a blackened face. Jesters, called *dalḳak* (originally *ṭalḳak*) or *mask͟hara*, have been common in Iran since ancient times. They were present in the private *mad͟jlis* [*q.v.*], as well as in the public square. Miniatures of the 10th/16th century depict groups of itinerant performers wearing high, pointed hats or animal masks and goatskins. Their comic dances were accompanied by tambourines. Comparable representations can be recognised already in the decoration of objects dating from the Muslim Middle Ages (cf. R. Ettinghausen, *The dance with zoomorphic masks*, in G. Makdisi, ed., *Arabic and Islamic studies in honour of H. A. R. Gibb*, Leiden 1965, 211-24). A bald clown by the name of Kal ʿInāyat was, according to Chardin (*op. cit.*, viii, 124-30), an entertainer at the court of S͟hah ʿAbbās I. Mimic dancing combined with singing, which constituted a kind of bawdy "opera", is mentioned in the same travel account (iv, 61) as the amusement of an aristocratic audience.

According to Bayḍāʾī (168), the popular theatre gradually expanded from the middle of the Ṣafavid period onwards. This began with the appearance of itinerant groups of musicians and dancers, who performed at private houses, usually during the night. Their répertoire consisted of ballets featuring local dances as well as some element of mime, e.g. in a piece called *ḳahr u ās͟htī* ("quarrel and reconciliation"). The curtain raisers (*pīs͟h-parda*) introducing such performances gave rise to more elaborate farces, called *muḍḥika*. In addition to *tamās͟hā*, the term *taḳlīd* became a general designation for secular theatre, although it refers more in particular to mime, which was a prominent element in most plays (see for an example of a farce performed about 1838, A. Chodzko, *Théâtre persan*, Paris 1878, pp. x-xiv).

A special type of popular theatre was known as *baḳḳāl-bāzī* because the play's main character was a rich grocer who claimed to be a *ḥādjdjī* and was made fun of by his insolent servant. The latter was often represented as a negro, and plays in which he appeared in a major role were also called *siyāh-bāzī*. A variety show including various kinds of entertainment is the *rū-ḥawḍī* or *takht-i ḥawḍī*, which derives its name from the stage where it was commonly performed: a platform on a pond in the courtyard of a house. Occasions when the artists could be summoned, such as weddings and circumcisions, were especially important days in the life of a family. Popular theatre also attracted the attention of the court, where performances are on record from the time of the Zand dynasty onwards. Under Nāṣir al-Dīn Shāh, the favourite court-jester Karīm Shīraʾī led a group who performed *baḳḳāl-bāzīs*. Plays were also enacted in teahouses and, in the present century, in small theatres, notably at Tehran.

In spite of its great popularity, popular drama was always under attack from the side of the religiously minded. In the thirties of this century, the government, suspicious of the satire of the popular performers, tried to censure it by demanding that scripts should be made and submitted to the authorites beforehand. Perhaps its most formidable opponent, however, presented itself in the form of modern entertainment as offered by cinema and television. Yet the oral tradition of drama somehow managed to survive long enough to make its impact on the development of modern drama.

The theatrical arts were an element of such prominence in Western civilisation during the 19th century that they could not fail to impress Iranians who travelled to the West, including Nāṣir al-Dīn Shāh himself. In comparison with other countries in the Middle East, however, the introduction of Western-style drama to Iran proceeded at a very slow pace. The only instance of a theatre fitted up to stage modern plays before the end of the century was an auditorium in the building of the Dār al-Funūn at Tehran. It was used merely for private performances attended by the Shah and his retinue, and even these were discontinued after some time. Plays by Molière were the first to be translated, or rather adapted to a Persian audience: *Guzārish-i mardumgurīz* (*Le Misanthrope*) was published at Istanbul 1286/1869-70 (cf. Browne, *LHP, iv, 459-62); other early translations were Ṭabīb-i idjbārī* (*Le Médecin malgré lui*) and *Gīdj* (*L'Étourdi*).

A separate development was the use of drama as a medium for criticism about social conditions and the spread of modern ideas. The anonymous *Baḳḳāl-bāzī dar ḥuḍūr*, which contains comments on the administrative reforms introduced by Mīrzā Ḥusayn Khān Sipahsālār (1871-3) and has been preserved in a written form, shows how drama of the traditional type could be used in this manner. Much more important was the example set by Mīrzā Fatḥ-ʿAlī Ākhundzāda [*q.v.*] who between 1850 and 1855 wrote six comedies in the Turkish of Ādharbāydjān. In Tiflis he was in close contact with the Russian tradition of drama, which contained an influential strain of critical comedy, its most famous product being Gogol's *The Inspector* (1834). The plays of Ākhundzāda were translated into Persian by Mīrzā Djaʿfar Ḳarādjadāghī, who in his preface stressed their educational intent. The translations appeared first at Tehran (1291/1874) and were subsequently edited as well as translated in Europe by several scholars (cf. Browne, iv, 462; see also H. W. Brands, *Azerbaidschanisches Volksleben und modernistische Tendenz in den Schauspielen Mīrzā Feth-ʿAlī Ahundzāde's (1812-1878)*, 's-Gravenhage-Wiesbaden 1958). The foreign interest in Ḳarādjadāghi's translations was roused in particular by his use of colloquial Persian. Most Western editions are for that reason accompanied by vocabularies.

For a long time, Malkum Khān [*q.v.*] was regarded as the author of three original Persian plays, the publication of which began in the newspaper *Ittiḥād* (Tabrīz 1326/1908) but was left unfinished (cf. E. G. Browne, *The press and poetry of modern Persia*, Cambridge 1914, 34); a complete edition based on a ms. then owned by Fr. von Rosen appeared at Berlin, Kāviyānī Press, 1340/1921-2. The discovery of a letter by Ākhundzāda preserved in the Akhundov Archive at Baku has made it more than likely that the recipient of this letter was the real author. He was Mīrzā Āḳā Tabrīzī, a Persian secretary at the French embassy in Tehran. The plays must have been written already about 1870 (cf. A. E. Ibrahimov and H. Mémédzadé, *Trudī Instituta Yazīka i Literaturī imeni Nizami*, ix, Baku 1956; Guseyni Abul'Fas, in *Narodov Azii i Afriki* [1965-6], 142-5; see also H. Evans, in *Central Asian Review*, xv [1967], 21-5; G. Scarcia, in *OM*, xlvii/2-3 [1967], 248-66). The plays satirise the political conditions in Ḳādjār Iran, especially the oppression exerted by local governors and their corruption. Tabrīzī gave them lengthy titles, which in an abbreviated form run as follows: (1) *Sargudhasht-i Ashraf-Khān ḥākim-i ʿArabistān dar ayyām-i tawaḳḳuf-i ū dar Ṭihrān...*; (2) *Ṭarīḳa-yi ḥukūmat-i Zamān Khān-i Burūdjirdī...* (3) *Ḥikayat-i Karbalā raftan-i Shāh-ḳulī Mīrzā...wa tawaḳḳuf-i čand rūza dar Kirmanshāhān...* (the plays were recently published by Ḥ. Ṣadīḳ, together with two others by the same author, Tehran 2536/1977; they were translated into French by A. Bricteux, *Les comédies de Malkom Khān*, Liège 1933, and into Italian by G. Scarcia, *Tre commedie*, Rome 1967). They are closet dramas written without much concern for the requirements of theatrical performance.

The beginning of theatricals performed in public cannot be dated earlier than the first decade of this century. Tabrīz seems to have preceded other cities. The Russian consul B. Nikitine saw performances at Rasht in 1912. They included at least one original Persian play, on the problem of alcoholism. The female parts were played by men (*Īrānī ki man shinākhta am*, Tehran 1329/1951, 127-8). In the capital, theatrical activities started about the same time. Among the first companies which gave regular performances were *Kūmīdī-yi Īrān* (1915), led by Sayyid ʿAlī Naṣr, and the drama section of *Īrān-i djawān* (1921), an organisation of progressive intellectuals. The *Kūmīdī-yi mūzīkāl* (1919) brought musical shows on the stage which were modelled on shows performed in Caucasian Russia. Non-Muslims were at this stage very prominent in the Iranian theatre. From their midst came especially the female actors, as the religious objections to the appearance of Muslim women on the stage were still very strong.

Although translated plays continued to hold their important place in the répertoire of the Iranian companies, original plays were also produced. The biweekly magazine *Tiʾātr* published already in 1908 dialogues which criticised the government. A playwright of the earliest period was Aḥmad Maḥmūdī, also known as Kamāl al-Wizāra (1875-1930). In his *Ḥādjdjī Riyāʾī Khān* he presented a Persian Tartuffe, and in *Ustād Nawrūz-i pambadūz* a type similar to the *baḳḳāl* of the popular farce. Ḥasan Muḳaddam (1898-1925) published, under the name ʿAlī Nawrūz, his *Djaʿfar-Khān az Firang āmada*. This successful comedy ridicules the type of the westernising Iranian (cf. I. Djamshīdī, *Ḥasan Muḳaddam wa Djaʿfar Khān az Firang āmada*, Tehran 1357/1978 repr. Oakland 1984, with a French translation by the author himself). Its first performance at the Grand Hotel, Tehran, on 23 March 1922, was an important event in the history of the modern theatre in Iran. The drama was used as a literary genre by the poet Muḥammad Riḍā Mīrzāda ʿIshḳī (1894-1924) for works like *Īdiʾāl*, *Kafan-i siyāh* and the "opera" *Rastākhīz*. Ṣādiḳ Hidāyat [*q.v.*] and many others wrote plays on episodes from the History of Iran. Notable as a playwright was also Dhabīḥ Bihrūz (1891-1971).

Under the Pahlawī régime, the theatre was subjected to censorship, but it also received for the first time official recognition as an important section of modern Iranian culture. In 1939 a college for the training of actors, the *Hunaristān-i hunarmandān*, was founded. The leading personality of the theatre in Iran during the Riḍā Shāh period was the actor and playwright Sayyid ʿAlī Naṣr (d. 1961). A similar rôle was later played by ʿAbd al-Ḥusayn Nūshīn (1905-70) who was active as a director and a translator of foreign drama, and wrote the handbook *Hunar-i tiʾātr* (1952).

The rise of the cinema and afterwards of television in Iran broadened the scope of the dramatic arts. Together with the theatre, they benefited from the remarkable flourishing of these arts, which took off in the 1960s and continued until the revolutionary turmoil began about a decade later. The promotion of indigenous theatre became a matter of official concern. A special department (*Idāra-yi tiʾatr*), which became a part of the Ministry of Culture and Arts, was created for this purpose. Dramatic education at an academic level was introduced in Tehran and the production of original Persian plays was encouraged. Shāhīn Sarkīsiyyān, ʿAlī Nāṣiriyyān, ʿAbbās Djawānmard and Bīzhan Mufīd were prominent stage directors and theatrical leaders. They also write a number of new plays based either on modern Persian literature (e.g. the short stories of Ṣādiḳ Hidāyat) or popular theatre, from which the type of the black clown (*siyāh*) was borrowed. Mufīd's *Shahr-i ḳiṣṣa* (1968) is a social satire based on children's stories, and put on stage with the use of animal masks. Active in all fields of drama were Bahrām Bayḍāʾī and Ghulām-Ḥusayn Ṣādighī (1935-85), a distinguished writer of short stories who under the name *Gawhar Murād* wrote many plays and film scripts.

The facilities for dramatic productions were enlarged through the opening of new auditoriums at Tehran and Iṣfahān. Of particular importance was the Festival of Arts (*Djashn-i Hunar*) of Shīrāz (1967-76), organised at the initiative of the National Iranian Television. It brought leading foreign directors to Iran, where they received the opportunity to stage experimental theatre of the most advanced kind. At the same time, special symposia on national drama were held featuring the epic tradition, the passion play and popular traditions. Another offshoot of the Festival was a theatre workshop (*Kārgāh-i namāyish*). The Iranian film attracted a great amount of attention at international festivals during the 1970s.

The Islamic revolution of 1979 changed the course of these developments considerably, but did not bring the dramatic activities in Iran to a standstill. They have also been continued outside the country by emigrants, especially in the United States.

Bibliography: The best survey of indigenous drama is Bahrām Bayḍāʾī, *Namāyish dar Īrān*, Tehran 1344/1965 (a new and revised edition has been announced). See further: Y. N. Marr, *Koečto o Péhlévan kéčele i drugikh vidakh narodnogo teatra v Persii*, in *Iran*, ii (1928), 75-88; R. A. Galunov, *Pakhlavān Kačal' - persidskiy petrushki*, in *Iran*, ii (1928), 25-74; idem, *Khéymé shab bāzī - persidskiy teatr marionetok*, in *Iran*, iii (1929), 1-50; idem, *Ma'riké gīrī*, in *Iran*, iii (1929), 91-106; idem, *Narodnïy teatr Irana*, in *Sovetskaya Etnografiya*, 1936/4-5, 55-83; M. Rezvani, *Le théâtre et la danse en Iran*, Paris 1962 (repr. 1981); J. Cejpek, *Dramatic folk-literature in Iran*, in J. Rypka *et alii*, *History of Iranian Literature*, Dordrecht 1968, 682-93; U. Gehrke and H. Mehner, *Iran. Natur-Bevölkerung-Geschichte-Kultur-Staat-Wirtschaft*, Tübingen-Basel 1975, 101-4; Y. Āryanpūr, *Az Ṣabā tā Nīmā*, Tehran 2535/1976, i, 325-66, ii, 288-315; M. Istiʿlāmī, *Barrasī-yi adabiyyāt-i imrūz-i Īrān*, Tehran 2535/1976, 155-70; M. H. Farahnakianpoor, *A survey of dramatic activity in Iran from 1850 to 1950*, Brigham Young University 1977 (diss.; ed. University Microfilms International, Ann Arbor 1979); W. O. Beeman, *A full arena: the development and meaning of popular performance traditions in Iran*, in M. E. Bonine and N. R. Keddie, eds., *Modern Iran. The dialectics of continuity and change*, Albany 1981, 361-81; idem, *Why do they laugh?*, in *Journal of American Folklore*, xliv (1981), 506-26; idem, *Culture, performance and communication in Iran*, Tokyo 1982; F. Gaffary, *Evolution of rituals and theatre in Iran*, in *Iranian Studies*, xvii/4 (1984), 361-89; idem, *Secular theatre*, in L. P. Elwell-Sutton, ed., *Bibliographical guide to Iran*, Brighton 1983, 343-4. *Abstracta Iranica* has had a special section on music and theatrical arts since vol. v (1982).

(J. T. P. de Bruijn)

5. *In Central Asia and Afghānistān.*

Islamic Central Asia—Western Turkistan including Kazakstan, Eastern Turkistan (Shinjiang) encompassing the area of the present Uyghur Autonomous Province, Afghānistān and contiguous territory where Islam was or is professed and Central Asian Iranian or Turkic languages are spoken—has known three main types of theatre. Oral folk art probably pervaded the region long before the advent of Islam, although documentation is as yet unavailable to prove it. Muslim religious drama, known especially to Shīʿīs [see taʿziya], received performance as late as the end of the 19th century in certain areas. Modern indigenous drama and theatre using written scripts, fixed stages and enclosed auditoria began activity within the region no earlier than the second decade of the 20th century.

Historical precedents for organised, formal theatrical presentations long existed in the region. A great, 35-tier, semi-circular outdoor Greek theatre was built and ruins survive at Ay Khanum, a fortified capital city located on the left bank of the Oxus River (Āmū Daryā) at the confluence of the Kokča River under the Greco-Bactrian Kingdom in the 3rd-2nd centuries B.C. Additional archaeological finds from the vicinity of Termez (Tirmidh) and Bukhārā—in the form of Hellenic carvings, dishes, frescoes and sculptures dating from the 1st to 8th centuries A.D.—have depicted the head of Dionysus, the youthful god, patron of drama and wine, as well as musicians playing harps, drums and local stringed instruments. A ceramic ossuary dated to the early centuries A.D. unearthed at Afrāsiyāb, near Samarḳand, shows the clear depiction of several actors holding tragic masks. A comic figure originated from the same sites. More direct evidence for theatrical life in that period is difficult to come upon. No clear evidence has been reported conclusively linking that ancient legacy with the development of indigenous Central Asian theatre art in the Islamic epoch, beginning there no earlier than the 1st/7th century in western Central Asia. It has been surmised that the obligatory attributes of recent folk performers from K͟hʷārazm known to follow the oldest traditions of *mäsk͟häräbäz* (clown) art in Central Asia—such as the goatskin mask and two-horned, cone-shaped or simply dishevelled cap of goat's wool—refer to the ancient Dionysian cult, and particularly to the 5th-6th centuries A.D. in K͟hʷārazm. (L. A. Avdeeva, in *Uzbekskii sovetskiii teatr*, Tas͟hkent, Izdatel'stvo "Nauka" Uzbekskoy SSR, 1966, 22, 18; Annaya F. Korsakova, *Uzbekskii opernyi teatr*, Tas͟hkent, Gosudarstvennoe. Izdatel'stvo K͟hudoz͟hestvennoy Literaturï, 1961, figure facing p. 24, 33).

Oral folk art. Undoubtedly the oldest continuous forms of Central Asia theatre still existing late in the 20th century belonged to the folk tradition. At their most uncomplicated level came performances by bear trainers, jugglers, stilt walkers, wrestlers and acrobats, horsemen, slight-of-hand artists, balancing artists, animal imitators and dancers. The last two categories often differed from the other entertainers by representing imagined actions to an audience rather than merely executing certain practiced skills. From at least the 9th/15th century onwards in Harāt and Samarkand, the existence of the *māddaḥ* [see MEDDĀḤ] is recorded. He was a professional story teller who, with gesture and facial expression, added action to words with an extensive repertory of saint's lives, legends and tales told in public. Several storytellers continued actively to render their dramatic oral narratives as late as the reign of the Amīr ʿAbd al-Aḥad of Buk͟hara (1885-1910) in towns such as Mazār-i S͟harīf, Afg͟hānistān (Muhsin H. Ḳadiraw, *Ozbek k͟hälḳ tamas͟hä ṣänʿäti*, Tas͟hkent, "Oḳituwči", 1981, 8).

Puppeteers went even further in the direction of dramatisation. One of the two best-known varieties of puppet theatre seen in Central Asia was *čadirk͟häyal*, a marionette show with full-bodied miniature *ḳog͟hirčaḳlär* (marionettes) suspended and activated from above on strings. The second sort of puppet, usually a half-torso figure, was manipulated from below by the hand of the *ḳol ḳog͟hirčaḳbaz* (puppeteer). Both kinds of shows presented in confined space the interactions of lively figures whose sounds or words came from behind the scene, uttered by the puppet master, who sometimes talked through a tube or thin disk in order to alter his voice for different puppets. Musicians habitually accompanied both puppet shows. Rather elaborate playlets could be offered by accomplished puppeteers. Well-known to Western Turkistanis were the hand-puppet characters, long-nosed (and therefore un-Central Asian and "ridiculous") Palwan Kačal, also to be found in Iran, and his wife, Pučukk͟han-ayim or Biče K͟hanim-ayim, with their marital squabbles. One marionette play, called *Särkärdälär* ("The mighty ones"), has a certain Karparman acting as master of ceremonies at a royal gathering. He requires the chieftains, who enter the scene one after another in order of increasingly high rank, to announce themselves. The chief figure is the Yasawul, a Cossack officer embodying the Tsarist Russian administration, and there is a drunk who also shows Christians in a repulsive condition (T. Menzel, *Meddāḥ, Schattentheater und Orta Ojunu*, Prague 1941, 37-41; Avdeeva, 66-8). Then begins a spectacle within the shows, as the powerful men observe monkey trainers, various sensuous dancers in costume, and a military parade. At the end, a devil sometimes abruptly rushes these high-ranking sinners off to Hades in punishment for watching idle, profane theatricals. Puppet theatre came rather late to the Afg͟hānistān of ʿAbd al-Raḥmān K͟hān (1880-1901) [*q.v.*] from Buk͟hārā and Samarḳand, whence a court storyteller brought it and called it *butley bawz* ("puppet play"), from the Urdu. For this show, the storyteller invented the long-popular females, Onion Lady and Lady Sweet (S. Heuisler, *Two years and two months of involvement with theatre in Afghanistan*, Mimeographed Essay, Kabul, 18 Jan. 1975, 4). This emphasis upon movement and brusque gesture to entertain viewers was carried over to a notable degree into skits and farces by human actors in folk theatricals. Among Central Asians a form of *tämas͟ha* ("show") could be seen that edged much closer than other folk art to modern comedy.

Typical was the short play, *Raʾis* ("The Keeper of morals"), in which a governor's beadle, the main figure, enforces the injunctions of religion and keeps order as well as verifying the correctness of weights and measures in the marketplace. The keeper of morals suddenly appears in a bazaar, creating consternation among shopkeepers and tradesmen, who must submit their scales and measuring rods to his men for inspection. Violators bribe the officials flagrantly. In both Tajik and Uzbek versions of *The keeper of morals*, the traits of a semi-amateur folk performance are well exemplified. Flexible, unstable dialogue typifies the improvisation in the absence of any written script. Audience volunteers and other, less-experienced performers are openly coached during a show by the master of the troupe. The comic vein is almost invariably ribald, and the subject of the skit confined to everyday activity in town or countryside. No specific site or stage was used or needed for the presentation. This brief comedy placed emphasis, like the puppet shows, upon slapstick, pantomime, and stock characters. The skit depended for its effect largely upon minimal, repeated variants of one action. In *The Keeper of morals*, peddler after peddler encounters the same treatment at the hands of inspectors. The action moves forward through reiteration and rough jokes made at the expense of offenders publicly humiliated and by the surprisingly varied sorts of bribes offered to ward off extortion. The second part of the same farce portrays the keeper of morals similarly cross-examining hapless Muslims concerning their religious duties and the obligatory rituals, and meting out harsh discipline for infractions (Nizam Nurdzhanov, *Tadz͟hikskii narodnyi teatr*, Moscow: Izdatel'stvo Akademii Nauk SSSR, 1956, 145-50, 309-14; Muhsin Ḳadiraw, *Ozbek k͟hälḳ ag͟hzäki drämäsi*, Tas͟hkent, Uzbekistan SSR Fänlär Äkädemiyäsi, Näs͟hriyati, 1963, 57-63).

The many playlets extant differed greatly in size of cast. *The Keeper of morals* used as many as 50 performers, but some required only one or two. Many received command performances at the Central Asian courts, and most diverted townspeople or villagers as late as the early 20th century. A sizeable troupe of *ḳiziḳčis* (buffoons) at the Ḳoḳan (K͟hoḳand) court of ʿUmar K͟hān (1809-22) was led by a star, Bedas͟him. Succeeding generations of buffoons consider him to be their patron and founding father. (*Uzbekii sovetskii teatr*, i, 1966, 47). Troupes of buffoons were maintained also at the K͟hīvan and Buk͟hāran courts, except during the reign of an *amīr* or *k͟hān* whose piety prompted a ban on public theatricals. In Kās͟hg͟har, under Yaʿḳūb Beg (1865-77) [*q.v.*], the *raʾīs* and his *muḥtasibs* strictly enforced the *S͟hariʿat*. They actively prevented mimes, storytellers and actors from diverting bazaar-goers. Before Yaʿḳūb Beg's day. Chinese administrators had allowed all sorts of amusements there (D. Boulger, *Central Asian questions*, London 1878, 6). Popular folk plays included *Uylänis͟h* ("The wedding"), humorously revealing a bridegeroom's reluctance to start life with an unknown woman, especially when it is discovered at the unveiling that she is not the promised bride. Another favourite skit, *Zärkakil* ("Golden tresses"), portrays forbidden dances and rituals engaged in by a group of men and women. They make their bacchanal so alluring that even the keeper of morals sent to censure them joins in the festivities. In *Mudärris* ("The seminary teacher"), the vices of a Marg͟hīlān schoolman become the subject of the farce. *Mazar* ("The tomb") turns on the interaction between a venal custodian of a sacred shrine and women and men who bring offerings to the saint buried there.

Plays in this genre depended for their appeal not only upon the familiar themes but upon theatrical style and verve of the performers, as well as on special effects utilising such devices as flashes of gunpowder, fire, the antics of animals imitated by human performers, and stylised, rudimentary costuming. Most of these playlets would not have required more than 20 minutes to perform unless the characteristic repetitions were greatly multiplied. Their bawdy nature and irreverence offended the strict religious leaders of the capitals and repelled the urban literati with their crudity. Thus although folk theatre prepared the way for new developments in Central Asian stage activity by whetting an appetite among the public for more plays, it also created obstacles and provoked prohibitions which affected what was to follow.

Muslim religious drama. Strictly speaking, Muslim miracle plays also constituted a part of folk theatre, but their content and tone made a significant difference between the two genres and set religious drama far apart from the folk comedy found in Central Asia. Performances of mystery plays associated with the S͟hīʿī holy festival during the first ten days of al-Muḥarram have been reported in Central Asia relatively seldom. This is because the region has remained almost entirely Sunnī beginning from around the 4th/11th century. The earliest presentations of Muslim mystery plays anywhere are conventionally dated to the mid-18th century in Iran (P. J. Chelkowski, *Taʿziyeh: indigenous avant-garde theatre of Iran*, in *Taʿziyeh. Ritual and drama in Iran*, ed. idem, New York University Press and Soroush Press, n.p. 1979, 4). None seems to be attested in Central Asia before the late 1200s/1800s. But in at least three zones—in Turkmenistan along the Iranian frontier; in the Farg͟hāna valley; and in the city of Buk͟hārā and its environs—S͟hīʿī ritual ceremonies connected with *ʿĀs͟hūrā* received much attention in the 13th-14th/19th-20th centuries. Descendants of over 30,000 Persians had been transferred to the Uzbek-Tajik state of Buk͟hārā after S͟hāh Murād (1785-1800) captured and devastated Merv (Marw) in 1790. They augmented an existing core of mainly enslaved S͟hīʿī population already there. As late as January 1910, bloody riots erupted in the city of Buk͟hārā when S͟hīʿī processions, usually confined to the Persian quarter, moved by permission of a S͟hīʿī *Ḳus͟hbegi* (Prime minister) through Sunnī sections of the city during *ʿĀs͟hūrā*. They very likely performed mystery plays on that occasion as well. Not far from Buk͟hārā city was a well-known Persian garden called *ʿĀs͟hūrāk͟hāni*, whose name meant that it was a place connected with rites linked to the martyrdom of Ḥusayn, grandson of the Prophet Muhammad (Sadriddin Aini, *Vospominaniya*, Moscow-Leningrad: Izdatel'stvo Akademii Nauk SSSR, 1960, 1021; G. Tsvilling, *Buk͟harskaya smuta*, in *Srednyaya Aziya*, no. 2 [Feb. 1910], 79-95; O. A. Suk͟hareva, *Islam v Uzbekistane*, Tashkent: Izdatel'stvo Akademii Nauk Uzbekskoy SSR, 1960, 27-8). In the Farg͟hāna valley among Sunnī Muslims, performances consisted mostly of readings, recitations, and ritual feasting, but *atins* (women mourners), especially, were famed for their eloquence during *ʿĀs͟hūrā* in dramatically rendering poetry devoted to Ḥasan and Ḥusayn. Certainly, the people of southwestern Tekke Turkmen villages such as Muḥammadābād or Derguez in the holy days followed extended daily presentations of the mystery plays. Known as *s͟habih* ("imitation"), among them, and as *taʿziya* in Iran and India, the episodes attracted fascinated attention of all villagers. These performances, with lines chanted in Turkmen—one source who observed the plays between 1878-81 says that they were in Čag͟hatay—were offered by professional players who travelled from town to town during al-Muḥarram (E. O'Donovan, *The Merv Oasis*, London 1882, ii, 40-50).

The main segments of this cycle portray the suffering of Ḥasan, Ḥusayn, adolescent Ḳāsim the bridegroom, and other members of the Muslim Holy Family and their offspring and retinue. The martyrdom of Ḥusayn, in particular, the bereavement of their women, and the death of some children in the unequal battle on the field at Karbalāʾ in 60/680, comprise the central theme of the drama. Besides the sacred religious power of these episodes, tremendously effective theatrical use is made in them of physical suffering, acute thirst and hunger, personal sacrifice and loss, heroism, and inevitable human destruction. European witnesses have declared that these village presentations offered the most realistic acting the outsiders had ever seen (O'Donovan, ii, 42). Nevertheless, the producers and performers firmly rejected the notion that the *s͟habih* qualified as drama and theatre at all. If universal participation of those off-stage in such ritualistic performances deprives these presentations of a separated audience to watch without acting, and if that lack thus removes the requirement obligatory for theatre, the Central Asians may be justified in distinguishing such celebrations from what they otherwise call "theatre". No serious person denies that the Islamic mystery or miracle play, as it is designated in Western literature, exerts dramatic force and theatrical effect upon both Muslim and non-Muslim. Notwithstanding this fact, no vestige of this precedent, except possibly in historical tragedy, seems to have carried over into the new drama and stage that overlapped chronologically with it in Central Asia.

Modern drama and theatre. Nearly all forms of theatre known actively to the region began to coexist in the civilisation of Central Asia once the modern genre appeared. That innovation occurred separately in the three main sectors of the region only after the first decade of the 20th century. Two factors delayed adoption of the new theatre by Central Asians long after visiting troupes began touring in Tashkent and other cities of the Tsarist Russian sector. Racy folk skits had given "theatre" in Central Asia a bad name in polite society. In addition, the Armenian or Russian troupes that acted there after the Russian conquest in 1865 were not merely Christian but included women who showed their faces openly. Only after

Azerbaijani and Tatar troupes brought their all-male, Muslim casts and plays to Western Turkistan's cities were educated Central Asians able to accept European-style drama and theatre as their own institution. Central Asian women initially performed on stage in Tashkent and Samarḳand, when several actresses were recruited as trainees for the Model Uzbek Troupe established in December 1920. Women could not act publicly in Kābul theatres until 1959, much later than they went on stage in Kāshghar and Urumči in Eastern Turkistan, where, following Societ Central Asian models, they freely played roles beginning around the mid-1930s.

Modern indigenous drama and theatre of the region drew its initial audience in Samarḳand, Russian Turkistan, in January 1914. *Padarkush yakhud oḳumagan balaning hali* ("The patricide, or the plight of an uneducated boy"), written by the Samarḳand author Maḥmūd Khōdja Behbudiy (1874-1919) in 1911, provided the premier performance of a play by a local dramatist. Thereafter, the short tragedy quickly went on tour throughout the Tsarist Russian sector among Uzbeks, Tajiks, Uyghurs and others. Behbudiy's theme—the crying need for education—became a standard subject for Central Asian playwrights. Like some folk plays, these Djadīd (Reformist) dramas invariably focused upon some social problem or abuse, though the Djadīdīs would not have acknowledged any link with folk theatre. *The patricide* influenced the entire theatrical development for years to come by inspiring many young poets to begin writing for the theatre. They as a rule created didactic works meant to edify or reform the public and its behaviour, and usually avoided politics or outright comedy. Kölbay Toghïs ulï (b. and d. unknown) wrote the first Kazak-language drama, *Nadandïḳ ḳūrbandarï* ("Victims of ignorance"), which was printed at Ufa in 1914 and performed at Orenburg in 1916, both towns being located in the Tatar-Bashkir sphere at or beyond the northern fringe of Kazak territory. The play explored serious difficulties arising among the nomads from the practice of polygamy, again blaming abuses upon a lack of enlightenment in the society. Another theme, the curse of pederasty, also persisted in early Reformist drama and literature, reflecting public concern over the prevalence of that practice in the sexually segregated urban life of Central Asia. Abdurrauf Shahidi (Shashudilin) (b. and d. unknown), a Tatar schoolteacher living in Ḳoḳan, wrote the play first published (1912) in the Turki (later, "Uzbek") language of southern Central Asia. The plot of *Māḥrāmlār* ("Forbidden to marry") dramatised the destructive effect upon young Turkistan boys of the organised homosexual circles in which many were kept by older men of means.

An acknowledged follower of what was termed *Behbudiy aḳimi* (the Behbudiy tendency), Abdullah Ḳadiriy (1894-1939), chose the second most common serious plot, after backwardness, for his drama, *Bäkhtsiz kuyaw* ("The unfortunate bridegroom"), published in 1915 and staged the same year. In it, Ḳadiriy explored the practice and often unhappy consequences of arranged or forced marriage in Central Asian life. That theme emerged, as well, in one of the earliest original plays presented in Kābul, Afghānistān, in the 1920s, in *Izdewādje idjbārī* ("A girl's forced marriage"). Similar social themes animated the modern Uyghur theatre in Kāshghar during its first period, starting after 1933. Drug addiction, polygamy, bribery, stupid pretension and forced or arranged marriage led the list of subjects in the Chinese sector of the region. Exposure to modern theatre in capitals of the Near and Middle East strengthened the conviction of reform-minded Central Asians that the theatre offered a compelling medium with which to educate and indoctrinate the woefully illiterate population (96.8% of the total, on average, in 1920) of Central Asians (E. Allworth, *Central Asian publishing and the rise of nationalism*, New York 1965, 22). In 1913, for example, the disgruntled, socially alienated Ḳoḳan poet, Hämzä Häkimzadä Niyaziy (1889-1929), visited Egypt, Syria, Turkey and Russian Azerbayjan, each of which had enjoyed lively indigenous modern stage activity beginning in the 1850s to the 1870s (Mamadzh Rakhmanov, *Khamza i uzbekskii teatr*, Tashkent: Gosudarstvennoye Izdatel'stvo Khudozhestkvennoy Literaturï UzSSr, 1960, 58, 70, 81). He returned to write several plays, similarly focused upon social abuses, during 1915-16. His works, unlike the better-known Djadīd drama, aimed not so much toward constructive persuasion and change as at exacerbating social tension and increasing civil strife. For this reason, Niyaziy remained little staged and outside the mainstream of new Central Asian dramaturgy in the initial period. But the same antagonistic quality was to earn this pro-Russian writer an ideological approval from Communist leaders in the 1920s that persisted long after his death. Niyaziy's first play, the four-act *Zähärli ḥäyat yakhud ʿishk ḳurbanläri* ("A poisoned life, or, victims of love"), written 1915, published by the author in 1916 at Tashkent, dramatises the anguishing forced marriage already portrayed in Central Asian poetry, fiction and drama. His version blames religion for permitting the practice. The playwright staged, directed, publicised and organised a company to act in this tragedy in Ḳoḳan's military assembly building at the end of 1915. Religious controversy closed the show and he disbanded his troupe after two performances (Mämäjan Rähmanaw, *Ozbek teätri tärikhi*, Tashkent, Uzbekistan SSR "Fän" Näshriyati, 1968, 313-16).

Plays that avoided treating contemporary life, usually historical dramas, in the beginning mainly served patriotic purposes, and often ended tragically. They started appearing about 1918, initially in the Russian-controlled sector of the region, notably in works written by another protégé of Behbudiy, the prolific Bukhārā author Abdurauf Abdurahim-oghli Fiṭrat (1886-1937) [*q.v.*]. He employed actual historic figures from early to late mediaeval times for many stage portraits. Fiṭrat composed *Begijan* in 1917, *Abu Muslim* in 1918, *Timurning saghanasi* ("Timur's mausoleum") in 1919, *Oghuzkhan* in 1919, *Abul Fayz Khan* in 1924, *ʿIṣyan-i Vose* ("Vose's uprising") in 1927, and others, either in Turki or Farsi. Like many educated authors or poets of that period, Fiṭrat was bilingual in Turkic and Iranian languages. Among his historical dramas, only the final two, the first in Turki, the second in Farsi, came out in print, though troupes staged all of them in various towns of Central Asia (V. Ya., art. *Fitrat, Abdul Rauf*, in *BSE*[1], lvii, 656; M. Rakh., art. *Fitrat*, in *Teatral'naya Entsiklopediya*'', 1967, col. 475). Historical drama rapidly spread to other parts of Central Asia. Among the first modern plays staged, starting in the 1920s in Afghānistān, was *Fatḥ-i Andluz* ("The conquest of Andalus"), translated from Arabic and dealing with the Moorish invasion of southern Spain in 92/711, the very year in which Arab forces firmly planted Islam in Bukhārā. Another treatment, seen in the Russian sector of Central Asia, was *Andalis songgiläri* ("The last days of Andalus"). *The conquest of Andalus*, along with *Shahawn-i Afghān* ("The Afghān kings") were among the very first modern dramas staged, like most Afg͟hān plays, in the Darī language. King Amān Allāh (1919-29) [*q.v.* in Suppl.] took another step towards westernising Afg͟hānistān in 1926 when he caused a theatre building to be constructed in the Pag͟hman suburb of Kābul (Heuisler, *loc. cit.*). Historical themes likewise attracted Afg͟hān dramatists in later decades, despite the risk entailed in writing about kings unflatteringly in a monarchy. Abdur G͟hafur Bres͟hna (1907-74) wrote his *Haji Mirwais K͟han* about an 8th-century clan leader and k͟hān who leads intrigues and battles for possession of the fortress of Ḳandahār (Bres͟hna, *Haji Mirwais K͟han. A historical play in 3 scenes and 17 acts*, in *Afg͟hanistan: Historical and Cultural Quarterly*, xiii/2 [Summer 1349/1970], 59-81).

In the Russian sector, the earliest historical plays served supra-ethnic patriotic, but not nationalistic, purposes. They represented Islam at the height of expansion against Christianity or made allegories for the Central Asian situation under foreign rule. After the *coup d'état* in November 1917, and the increasing Russian Communist domination of cultural development in the sector, historical drama became explicitly civil- (i.e. class-) war-minded and anti-patriotic. Such plays were meant to depict rulers and most other past leaders as "class enemies", a procedure that persisted into following decades. An exception was made in works devoted to a few approved potentates who were usually also poets or scholars. Thus Uzbek drama furnishes an example; the Tīmūrids Ulug͟h-Beg (1394-1449), Mīr ʿAlī S͟hīr Nawāʾī (1441-1501), and Ẓahīr al-Dīn Muḥammad Bābur Pādis͟hāh (1493-1530), or ʿUmar K͟hān's talented wife Nādira K͟hānim (1792-1842) has each furnished the subject for at least one full-length stage work in Uzbekistan alone. Selected historical figures served similar ends elsewhere in Central Asia.

Most active among the first prominent local Uyg͟hur playwrights of Eastern Turkistan became the poet Abdurähim Tiläs͟h Ötkür (1922-), from Komul district. He wrote his initial play, "A million flowers from one drop of blood" (*Tamča ḳandin miliyon čičeklär*) (1943) in a patriotic vein. With the poet Lutpulla Mutällip (1922-45)—author of several other, ideological plays—Ötkür wrote "The Steadfast peony" (*Čing modangül*) (1943), soon staged in Urumči. And, when Ötkür served as Editor-in-Chief of *S͟hinjiang gazeti*, the principal East Turkistan newspaper, he published his drama, *Niyazḳiz* (1948) (Yusup K͟hojayef, *Čaḳmaḳ käbi hayat*, in *Bizning wätän*, no. 2 (Jan. 1983), 3; personal interview, Istanbul 1956, with Mr Polat Ḳadir, former Managing Editor, *S͟hinjiang gazeti*).

At Urumči and Turpan in Chinese Turkistan in 1982, Uyg͟hur troupes staged a new historical drama, *Ḳanliḳ yillar* ("Bloody years") that had been published in the revived, modified Arabic script in 1981. The Uyg͟hur author Tursun Yunus (b. and d. unknown), issued it in the unusual Uyg͟hur language journal, *S͟hinjian sänʾiti* ("Art of S͟hinjiang") from Urumči. Sidiḳ Zälili, an 18th-century Uyg͟hur poet and hero of this six-act play, affirms the identity of his country within the world of Islam when he prays for an end to religious conflict, rhetorically asking in his final speech: "When will the sectarian slaughter of the world of Islam (*Islamiyät dunyasi*) come to an end?" Commenting to Chinese critics upon his reason for creating this long historical drama, Yunus once remarked that he meant it to oppose the old Muslim sect of Īs͟hāns which had "raised its head again in recent years in some parts of southern S͟hinjiang". (Tursun Yunus, *Ḳanliḳ yillar*, in *S͟hinjiang, sänʾiti*, no. 1 [July 1981], 24-93; Z͟horhilimizning muk͟hbiri, *Tarik͟hiy dirama "ḳanliḳ yillar" sohbät yig͟hinining k͟hatirisi*, in *S͟hinjiang säʾniti*, no. 4 [1982], 123).

Alongside historical plays there came staged versions of legendary tales, heroic epics and popular romances. Muk͟htar Auez ulī (1897-1961) not only gave Kazak audiences such a rendition of legendary motifs based upon oral epic and entitled his four-act work *Englik Kebek* (1922), but directed the first performance in Semey (Semıpalatinsk) himself that same year (*Ḳazaḳ teatrīnīng tarikhī*, Alma Ata: Ḳazaḳ SSR-nīng "G͟hīlīm" Baspasī; 1975, 353). Numerous selections of instrumental and vocal music often entered into these productions. The musician S͟harahim S͟haumar adapted well-loved motifs from the classical Central Asian cycle S͟häs͟hmäḳam to the text of the Turki-language scenarios written by S͟hämsiddin S͟häräfiddinaw K͟hurs͟hid (1892-1960) for *Färhäd wä Shirin* and *Läyla wä Mäjnun* (1922) (*K͟hurs͟hid. Tänlängän. äsärlär*, Taskent: Uzbekistan SSR "Fän" Näs͟hriyati, 1967, 10-11). Music added great feeling and appeal to the stage presentation of these tragic, mystical romances and made them increasingly popular throughout the region. Complete opera started relatively late. Conventionally, it is said to have begun in the Russian sector of Central Asia with *Boran* (1937, staged 1939), by Kamil Nuʿmanaw Yäs͟hin (1909-). The work speaks about the tragic love and death of young D͟jorä and his beloved Nargul during the Central Asian uprising against Russian colonists in 1916. Music, based upon genuine Uzbek melodies, was arranged by the Uzbek composer M. Ashrafi and the Slavic musicologist, S. N. Vasilenko. In the Chinese sector, indigenous opera began at Kās͟hg͟har with *Rabiʿä Saʿdin* (1948), in five acts, by the Uyg͟hur author, Ahmad Ziyaʾi (b. unknown). It, too used a traditional eastern Romeo and Juliet theme to the accompaniment of indigenous music. According to an eye-witness, audiences jammed the theatre's opera performances (A. Korsakova, *Uzbekskii opernyi teatr...*, 142-7; Ziya'i Ahmad, *Rabiʿä Saʿdin*, in *Tozomas čičeklar*, Kās͟hg͟har: S͟hinjiang Gazitä Idarasidä Basildi, 13 February 1948, 73-169; Ghulamettin Pahta, personal memoir, 30 January 1983).

More pleasant to audience taste in the region than opera were musical comedy and a form of serious theatre termed "musical drama" which combines spoken and sung parts for the personages. This type of theatre became institutionalised first in the Soviet Russian sector, then appeared in Afg͟hānistān as well as S͟hinjiang. G͟hulam Zafariy (1889-1944) wrote one of the earliest regional musical dramas, the four-act *Hälima*, 1918-19. A Tas͟hkent cast with a woman in the lead role staged it in 1919-20. Uyg͟hur theatre in Ḳazakstan saw its first formal Uyg͟hur musical drama, *Änärk͟han*, by D͟j. Asim and A. Sadīr, and based again upon popular folk songs, staged in 1934 at D͟jarkent, now Panfilov, located just eleven miles from the S͟hinjiang frontier near Ḳuld͟ja [*q.v.*]. Like the reformist plays of two decades earlier in Samarkand and Ḳoḳan, *Änärk͟han* elaborates the unhappy consequences of a forced marriage between a young bride and an unloved older and wealthy man. In Kazakstan, among the small Uyg͟hur population of 109,000 recorded for the USSR in 1926, a succession of Uzbek theatrical directors, producers and actors from Uzbekistan helped with the first staging of *Änärk͟han*. Männan Uyg͟hur (1897-1955) and ʿAli Ardobus Ibrahim (1900-59) infused those initial Soviet Uyg͟hur endeavours with the brief Uzbek experience in drama. Ibrahim had also worked earlier in Stalinabad

ISBN 90 04 09084 3

PRINTED IN THE NETHERLANDS

THE ENCYCLOPAEDIA OF ISLAM

NEW EDITION

PREPARED BY A NUMBER OF
LEADING ORIENTALISTS

EDITED BY

C. E. BOSWORTH, E. VAN DONZEL, W. P. HEINRICHS AND CH. PELLAT
ASSISTED BY F. TH. DIJKEMA AND MME S. NURIT

UNDER THE PATRONAGE OF
THE INTERNATIONAL UNION OF ACADEMIES

VOLUME VI

FASCICULES 111-112

MASRAḤ — MAWLID

LEIDEN
E.J. BRILL
1989

EXECUTIVE COMMITTEE:

All correspondence on editorial matters should be addressed to the Editorial Secretaries, whose addresses are:

For the English Edition

Dept. of Near Eastern Studies,
The University of Manchester,
Manchester,
England M13 9PL.

For the French Edition

Centre Universitaire
94, avenue des Grésillons
92600 Asnières
France

AUTHORS OF ARTICLES IN THESE FASCICULES

C. H. Allen, Jr., School of the Ozarks, Point Lookout, Miss. 843.
E. Allworth, Columbia University, New York. 772.
[P. Berthier, Rabat]. 891.
A. Bjørkelo, University of Bergen. 794.
P. N. Boratav, Centre National de la Recherche Scientifique, Paris. 827.
C. E. Bosworth, University of Manchester. 780, 782, 783, 872.
[C. Brockelmann, Halle]. 869.
J. T. P. de Bruijn, University of Leiden. 835.
J. Burton-Page, Church Knowle, Dorset. 815, 839, 867.
P. Cachia, Columbia University, New York. 868.
P. Chalmeta, University of Madrid. 852.
J. W. Clinton, Princeton University. 783.
[G. S. Colin, Paris]. 774, 815.
[C. Collin Davies]. 780.
[A. Cour, Constantine]. 893.
Patricia Crone, University of Oxford. 848, 882.
Anne-Marie Delcambre, Paris. 870.
S. Digby, Rozel, Jersey. 784.
N. Elisséef, University of Lyon. 792, 871.
G. Endress, University of Bochum. 846.
Barbara Flemming, University of Leiden. 837.
W. Floor, Bethesda, Maryland. 804.
A. D. W. Forbes, University of London. 849.
G. S. P. Freeman-Grenville, University of York. 774.
J. A. Haywood, Lewes, East Sussex. 773, 827.
[E. Honigmann, Brussels]. 779, 792.
R. S. Humphreys, University of Wisconsin, Madison. 782.
H. İnalcik, University of Chicago. 813.
F. de Jong, University of Utrecht. 888.
D. A. King, University of Frankfort. 794, 840.
J. Knappert, Barnet, Herts. 828.
Günay Alpay Kut, Boğaziçi Üniversitesi, Istanbul. 803.
Ann K. S. Lambton, Kirknewton, Northumberland. 858.
T. Lewicki, Cracow. 842.
W. Madelung, University of Oxford. 847, 848.
[D. S. Margoliouth, Oxford]. 883.
Ö. Nutku, University of Izmir. 865.
Ch. Pellat, University of Paris. 789, 829, 843, 895.
Munibur Rahman, Oakland University, Rochester, Mich. 839.
Chr. Robin, Centre National de la Recherche Scientifique, Paris. 832.
F. C. R. Robinson, Royal Holloway College, Egham, Surrey. 874.
Paula Sanders, Harvard University, Cambridge, Mass. 851.
R. Sellheim, University of Frankfort. 825.
G. W. Shaw, British Library, London. 806, 807.
D. Waines, University of Lancaster. 809.
[A. J. Wensinck, Leiden]. 843, 874.
G. M. Wickens, University of Toronto. 826.
T. Yazici, Istanbul. 887.
H. G. Yurdaydin, University of Ankara. 844.

Names in square brackets are those of authors of articles reprinted or revised from the first edition of this Encyclopaedia.

(Dus͟hanbe) with the fledgling modern Tajik theatre. This government-sponsored cooperation between nationalities imitated the frequent collaboration and borrowing in stage work initiated earlier by Central Asians themselves. For directing his first staging of *The patricide*, Behbudiy had brought in an Azerbayjanian, ᶜAli Askar Askar-oghli (b. and d. unknown). The first decade and a half of modern Uyg͟hur drama and theatre, including its répertoire, starting *ca.* 1933 in S͟hinjiang, also came to life under direct influence of the Soviet Central Asian theatre. In the folk tradition, when 19th-century puppetry came to Afg͟hānistān from the Russian sector, it became more than simple borrowing. A puppeteers' troupe immediately formed around it and acquired the name *Mad͟kharawi-yi Sayin* ("Clowns of Sayin", i.e. sugar) from the leading puppeteer, Sayin Ḳanad (Heuisler, *op. cit.*, 4).

Organised troupes, amateur or professional, coalesced wherever traditional or modern theatre was performed. The Ḳoḳan K͟hanate's next-to-the-last indigenous ruler, K͟hudāyār K͟hān (1854-8, 1862-3, 1866-75) [see KHOḲAND], maintained a well-known folk troupe at court. Itinerant troupes of performers often presented Muslim religious drama in the villages. Neither folk nor religious drama troupes could effectively adapt themselves to the modern stage when it appeared. The first Reformist dramas necessitated creation of entirely new theatre groups to perform them. At Samarḳand in 1913, Behbudiy acknowledged his difficulty in forming the initial indigenous troupe of amateurs because of lack of interest and experience. His group soon turned semi-professional through rehearsals and exposure during active road tours outside Samarḳand, playing also in Buk͟hārā, Ḳoḳan, Andid͟jan and other towns until it disbanded in 1916 (Mämäjan Rähmanaw, 281-2). The future playwright, Abdullah Awlaniy (1878-1934) established one of the earliest of these troupes, the semi-professional "Turkistan" group, basing itself on Tas͟hkent, in 1914. Like the first Samarḳand group, "Turkistan" began assembling a répertoire around Behbudiy's *The patricide*, presenting various additional Central Asian plays and some translations from Turkish, Azerbayjani, and the like. Numbers of other private theatre groups came into being, mirroring the custom in folk theatricals. Traditionally, ensembles of clowns, buffoons, puppeteers, conjurors, stilt walkers, equilibrists, horn players, bellringers and related performers had been combined in one *käsäbä-yi sazändä* or *mihtärliḳ* (guild of musicians) rather than separated into guilds for each special art. As late as the early 20th century, this guild still possessed its own *risalä* (statute or treatise), giving a legendary history of the art's origins, naming saintly protectors, and setting forth religious duties and prayers linked to each phase of the vocational activity. In 1926, political authorities in the Soviet sector incorporated these folk performers into a "Union of Art Workers" and continued their performances under government auspices (A. Samoilovič, *Turkestanskii ustav-risolya tsek͟ha artistov*, in *Materialy po etnografii*, Leningrad: Izdanie Gosudarstvennogo Russkogo Muzeya 1927, 54-6). Thus sponsorship by provincial governors, added to some patronage of the *k͟hāns* and *āmirs*, along with guild structure and tradition, gave performers in folk theatre systematic recognition and status comparable to the position enjoyed by many artisans of the region in different vocations.

In the initial modern period, amateur troupes attempting new productions regularly drew to them in various centres as actors persons who were already accomplished teachers, poets or playwrights. A Tatar author, Abdullah Badriy (b. and d. unknown), later a playwright, originally acted to acclaim the women's roles offered by Behbudiy's Samarḳand troupe. As "Bay", Abdullah Awlaniy had the lead in the first Tas͟hkent presentation of *The patricide* on 27 February 1914. Hämzä Häkim Zadä Niyaziy acted in his drama *A poisoned life* in Ḳoḳan on 22 October 1915. Männan Uyg͟hur and Awlaniy performed in the "Turkistan" troupe when it put on Abdullah Ḳadiriy's *The unfortunate bridgeroom* in Tashkent, November 4, 1915. Ubaydullah K͟hod͟ja's troupe toured all over the Farg͟hāna valley. Following the March and November 1917 changes in Russian governments, some private theatricals had continued in Central Asia. Except for folk art shows, most of their activity was soon curtailed by political authorities. All theatre houses and properties became government-owned after 2 October 1918. By 1922, in the Russian sector among the Central Asians, only state theatre groups received approval or support, and political censorship was again firmly established. Uzbekistan's comprehensive law code in this field became a model for all Soviet Central Asia. It controlled répertoires as well as productions. The decree, enacted by the Turkistan Autonomous SSR on 16 April 1923 and codified by the successor Uzbekistan SSR on 8 February 1927, provided for Union republic censors in publishing houses and press and at all levels of local political hierarchy down to the county (*okrug*) (*Uzbekistan Id͟jtimaᶜi S͟horalar D͟joralar D͟jomhoriyäti Is͟hči wä Dihḳan Ḥokomätining Ḳanon wä Boyroḳlarining Yig͟hindisi*, no. 9 [7nči Mart 1927inči yil], 199-202).

Nevertheless, the legacy of theatres, troupes and faithful audiences had already created the environment needed for enlarging modern drama performances on a regular basis. A network of new troupes and theatres quickly grew up in the Russian sector, though there were setbacks. The "Karl Marx Drama Troupe" organised there in October 1918 was led in 1921 to Buk͟hārā, which was at the time still semi-independent from Soviet Russia, by Männan Uyg͟hur, to propagandise for the new régime's ideology. During a performance of Fiṭrat's *Abu Muslim* in 1922, opponents burned down the theatre and dispersed the troupe, leaving Buk͟hārā again without a professional theatre group for years. At Alma Ata in Kazakstan, in order to lay a stable foundation for guided theatrical growth in its area, the Kazakstan Autonomous S.S.R. Ministry of Education ordered the establishment of a Kazak Theatre Studio to accommodate 40 students from January 1933 onwards. This followed by almost a decade the founding of a studio for Uzbek theatre trainees in Moskow. The 24 young people sent to Moscow from Uzbekistan had included several who contributed greatly, as authors, directors, actors or translators, to the development of Central Asian theatre. They included the mature ᶜAbdulhämid Suläyman Čolpan (1896-1938), a promising 14-year old actress Sarä Is͟hanturayewa (1911-), Männan Uyg͟hur, and Äbrar Hidayätaw (1900-57). The latter subsequently achieved fame in the role of Hamlet during 21 consecutive Uzbek performances after the première in 1935. Cultural leaders dispatched another group of 17 from Uzbekistan to Baku in Azerbayjan for a theatrical apprenticeship (*Ḳazaḳ teatrïnïng tarik͟hï*, Alma Ata: Ḳazaḳ SSRnïng "G͟hïlïm Baspasï, 1975, 201-2; *Uzbekskii sovetskii teatr*, i, Tas͟hkent: Izdatel'stvo "Nauka" Uzbekskoy SSR, 1966, 246-8). In 1937, there were 24 theatres, including both Russian and Uyg͟hur ones, functioning in Kazakstan.

By 1934, the quantity of regularly performing local-language theatres in all Uzbekistan had reached its peak of 32, after which the numbers gradually subsided to a fairly constant 22 to 28. This did not include provincial Uzbek houses operated in the Kirgiz SSR at Osh and Tajik SSR at Now (Nau). The quantity of Tajikistan's theatres working in various languages rose from four in 1934 to 24 by 1941. (Mämäjan Rähmanaw, 413-5; N. L'vov, *Kirgizkii teatr. Očerk istorii*, Moscow: Gosudarstvennoe Izdatel'stvo "Iskusstvo", 1953, 127; Yakov Mosheev, *My recollections of Now Raion: the status of a peripheral theater in Soviet Tajikistan*, in *Central Asian Survey*, nos. 2-3 [1982-3], 108-22; Nizam Khabiblullayewič Nurdjänaw, *Istoriya tadzhikskogo sovetskogo teatra (1917-1941 gg.)*, Dushanbe: Izdatel'stvo "Donish", 1967, 401). Thus the quantity of theatres in all Central Asia multiplied strikingly from 1913 onwards, reaching an estimated 150 official houses, government sponsored and supported, in the three sectors, during the 1950s and thereafter. The capital cities saw a division of labour among serious drama theatres, musical drama houses, opera, and comedy or children's playhouses, as well as between the major languages and traditions. In 1983, Tashkent possessed nine of Uzbekistan's 28 active theatres. Leading administrators in the three principal theatrical organisations of Uzbekistan in 1983 were the drama critics and historians, Professor Häfiz Sh. Äbdusämätaw (1925-), former Editor of *Shärḳ yulduzi*, the principal Uzbek journal publishing drama, and Director of the Hämza Institute for the Arts of the Ministry of Culture, Uzbekistan SSR; Professor Mämädjan R. Rähmanaw (1914-), Rector of the Ostrovsky Tashkent Theatre Arts Institute, the main training centre for theatre arts; Sara Ishanturayeva, Bähriddin Näsriddinaw and other officers of the sole membership organisation for stage, the Uzbekistan Theatre Society (*Djämiyäat*). The vigour of the theatrical institution implied a constant need for an attractive repertory, and, especially, for many original indigenous plays. The numbers of original Central Asian stage works written had risen from about 20 altogether by the end of 1916 to many hundreds by the 1980s. New Uzbek scripts of varying quality were being received at the rate of some 25 annually in the early 1980s. Yet critics and historians spoke soberly at the same time about a decline in drama, attributed generally to the emergence of radio, television and new popular music. Most keenly missed were good serious plays about contemporary subjects. Even before the strong growth of mass media in broadcasting, Central Asian theatre had endured slumps in attendance to a marked degree. Many auditoria remained nearly empty night after night in the 1920s and 1930s owing to public indifference to the offerings being brought to the stage, especially to those heavily ideological in content.

From the beginning, modern Central Asian drama bore three distinct traits: it was socially or politically didactic; purely entertaining and comic; or the plays were historical and patriotic, sometimes legendary. Newer drama combined some of these characteristics, remaining resolutely instructive in the Russian and Chinese sectors, but more balanced in spirit and aims in Afghānistān until the late 1970s. The theatre of all three sectors began to explore contemporary life seriously, in particular, after an opening period that was notably tendentious. Since the coming of Communist régimes to the three sectors, the nature of drama has shifted remarkably in the direction of propagandising political-social directives from the central authorities. In each case, the acknowledged ideological base is a kind of official Marxism. As a result, plays written and staged in the period following that political change in each sector have become at first outspokenly rhetorical and sloganeering. Themes announced by political authorities for each period can be found reflected in the dramaturgy and repertories. In addition, plays have persistently enunciated such principles as atheism, espoused by Communist régimes. Many Central Asian stage works originating in the Russian sector, far more than in the others, have openly and specifically opposed the religion of Islam. This paralleled the intensification of political and social tensions in the USSR in the 1930s, when Central Asian plays, too, mirrored the times. Zinnat Fathullin (1903-) wrote a drama typical of the period in 1932 entitled *Niḳab yirtildi* ("The mask torn away"), one which is engrossed with a search for "enemies" ostensibly hidden inside Central Asian society. A related obsession with "external enemies" and "traitors" coloured political plays such as *Ḳanli särab* ("Bloody mirage") (1961-4) in two acts and ten scenes, by Sarwar Äzimaw (1923-), a political activist and diplomat.

In the 1960s, dramas with a more human content began to appear increasingly. It was indicative of this evolution that Bähram Rähmanaw (1915-61) turned to themes such as *Yuräk sirläri* ("Secrets of the heart") (1953), a play that ignored political topics and simply concentrated upon the private lives of its people. Rähmanaw, a Communist Party member, headed the Administration for Art Affairs in Uzbekistan from 1953-5; thereafter, he became Director of the Scientific Research Institute for Studies of the Arts, and finally, in 1958, took the post of First Secretary of the powerful government-controlled Union of Writers of Uzbekistan. Another influential intellectual, Izzat Sultan (1910-), in his play *Iman* addressed the ethical dilemma put before a family that finds a dishonest scholar in its midst. The senior Uzbek poet and playwright, Rähmätullä Atäḳoziyew Uyghun (1905-), soon made audiences face the crucial test of social and political ethics in Soviet Central Asia. He looked, in his play *Dostlär* ("Friends") (1961), at the havoc raised among farmers by the Stalinist terror and false denunciations that had resulted in unlawful treatment to the extremes of execution and exile. For Central Asian theatre this was a pointed theme, for many of the important earlier playwrights and other theatre people, including the Kazaks Mir Djaḳib Duwlat-ulï (1885-1937) and Säken Sadvaḳas Seyfullah-ulï (1894-1937) and the Uzbeks Čolpan, Fiṭrat, Ḳadiriy, Ziya Said (1901-38) and Zafariy, had lost their lives in the political repression.

The Kirgiz dramatist and novelist, Čingiz Äytmätaw (1928-) and the Kazak author, Kaltay Muḥammadjanaw (1928-), joined in examining that very controversial ethical subject. They translated their Kazak language drama, *Köktöbedegï kezdesu* ("Mountain top encounter") (1972) based upon a story by Äytmätaw, into Russian as *Voskhozhdenie na Fudziyamu* ("The ascent of Mount Fuji") and gave it its première in Moscow in 1973. They recreated the tension in society over collective indifference and guilt toward innocent victims of political repression and social discrimination. But the writers in the end concern themselves more forcefully with basic problems of individual honesty and responsibility for personal actions and outlook.

After those ethical dramas during the 1970s-1980s in the Soviet sector, historical tragedy and domestic comedy seemed to predominate, leaving assertively political and ideological plays less in the forefront that they had been previously. Yā<u>sh</u>in returned to the story of climactic events in early 20th-century Central Asian history with a three-act musical drama he called *Inḳilab tangi (Bu<u>kh</u>ara)* ("Dawn of the Revolution: Bu<u>kh</u>ārā"), published in 1973. Its *dramatis personae* included the Bolshevik dictator Vladimir I. Lenin, the Young Bu<u>kh</u>aran politician Fazil <u>Kh</u>od<u>j</u>äyew, the last Amīr of Bu<u>kh</u>ārā Saʿīd ʿĀlim<u>kh</u>ān and other historical figures, portrayed on stage with a cinematic flashback technique. Yā<u>sh</u>in represents the prominent old-time and doctrinaire Central Asian dramatists educated almost entirely in the Soviet period. Like Rāhmanaw, he held key positions in the administration of the theatrical arts and served as Secretary of the Government's Union of Writers in Uzbekistan. The contribution of these playwrights hardly lay in the comic genre.

Comedy originally defined Central Asian theatre, for it was the essence of folk skits and acts long before and well after religious or modern drama appeared on the scene. In the early decades of the 20th century, both the <u>D</u>jadīds and the very first Communist Soviet playwrights, as well as Af<u>gh</u>ān writers, initially for the most part rejected light comedy. They believed their message to be paramount and serious. In the first decade, the official bulletin, *I<u>sh</u>tirakiyun*, published by the Central Committee of the Turkistan Autonomous S.S.R. at Ta<u>sh</u>kent, demanded that theatre cease to be "a place of amusement and love intrigues", and it specifically criticised attempts to present "diverting comedy" (*I<u>sh</u>tirakiyun*, 11 December 1919, 12 October 1920). Consequently, from the 1920s to the 1950s in Soviet Central Asian theatre, most stage comedy spoke with a heavy satirical voice. Hämid <u>Gh</u>ulam (1919-) wrote *Ta<u>sh</u>baltä ʿa<u>sh</u>iḳ* ("Ta<u>sh</u>baltä in love") (1962), a musical sharply attacking religion and the practice of Islam in Central Asia. Folk humour incorporated in modern plays from the 1920s onward repeatedly conformed to the vision of comedy preferred by cultural managers. The Uy<u>gh</u>ur dramatist Yusufbek Muhlisi (1920-), who emigrated from the Chinese sector to Soviet Central Asia at about the same time as other writers, sc. around 1964, provided Uy<u>gh</u>ur performers in Kazakstan and Uzbekistan with a later specimen of this genre. Muhlisi's *Näsriddin Äpändim* (1966), a musical staged in 1967 at Alma Ata, adapted several anecdotes from the widely popular Nasriddin tradition to fashion, in the Uy<u>gh</u>ur idiom, what critics called an anti-Islamic satirical comedy. (A<u>kh</u>me<u>dzh</u>an Kadyrov, *Godî stanovleniya (Iz istorii uygurskogo teatra muzîkal'noy komedii)* Alma Ata: Izdatel'stvo "Zhalyn", 1978, 62-3).

Subtler, often lighter, humour characterised more of the works written later in the 1960s by younger dramatists. The new generation of playwrights interests itself directly in personal feelings, contemporary values and ways of life. Most notable in Uzbekistan in the 1970s-80s became Olmäs Umärbekaw (1934-) and Äbduḳähhar Ibrähimaw (1939-), both natives of Ta<u>sh</u>kent. Ibrähimaw's initial play, *Birinči bosä* ("First kiss") (1969), which the author calls "a lyric drama", ran for 500 performances between 1971-5 on the "Young Guard Theatre" stage in Ta<u>sh</u>kent. The comedy focuses exclusively upon the personal motives, lives and loves of several teenagers, shown as growing into young adulthood by the end of the second and final act. Ibrähimaw's unideological but bitter comedy, the two-act *Ärrä* ("The saw"), 1970, staged in the Far<u>gh</u>ana Oblast Theatre, is about the Mänsuraw family. It dramatises the character and ideals of Murad, the head of the family. He is an influential medical administrator and professor who is the cutting "saw" of the play Mänsuraw is convinced that everyone acts only out of selfishness or, out of what is closely related, a sense of obligation rooted in the principle of *quid pro quo.* He disallows the elements of affection, generosity, spontaneity and similar affirmative forces in human relationships. Ibrähimaw's two-act play *Meni äytdi demäng* ("Not a word about me") satirises a hearty but impervious country town borough politician and educator, Häshim-äkä. His callousness, like that of Professor Mänsuraw in *The saw*, permits any positive human urge to wither and die. This is symbolised in *Not a word...* by the corruption and demoralisation of the borough's best, most generous part-time gardener, a roofer, Ali, whose small courtyard plot has decorated, pleased and fed the whole neighbourhood well up until he acquires false values from a chain of irresponsible bureaucrats, including Häshimäkä, and allows the lush garden to dry up. Ibrähimaw's later play, *Tusmal* ("Supposition"), ran at the Samarḳand Alim<u>dj</u>an Uzbek Drama Theatre in 1983, and another one, *Čakana säwda* ("Retail trade"), was published in 1984. Six of Ibrähimaw's plays, including *First kiss, The saw* and *Not a word about me*, came out in Russian translation in 1982. (Äbdukähhar Ibrähimaw, *Birinči bosä. Ärrä. P'esälär*, Ta<u>sh</u>kent: <u>Gh</u>äfur <u>Gh</u>ulam namidägi Ädäbiyat wä Sänʿät Nä<u>sh</u>riyati, 1978; Abduka<u>khkh</u>ar Ibragimov, *Obo mne ni slova. P'esy*, translated from the Uzbek, Moscow: Sovetskii Pisatel', 1982; *Čakana säwda*, in *<u>Shärḳ</u> yulduzi*, no. 8 [Aug. 1984], 73-99; Äbduḳahhar Ibrähinaw, *Tusmal. P'esälär*, Ta<u>sh</u>kent: <u>Gh</u>äfur <u>Gh</u>ulam namidägi Äbdäbiyat wä Sänʾat Nä<u>sh</u>riyati, 1985). Crimean Tatars, Tajiks and Turkmens also contributed new plays.

After the earliest days of modern Central Asian theatre, translations and borrowings from plays written outside the region were frequently published in Central Asian languages and included in the repertory. Although Tsarist Central Asians originated their own earliest dramas, the relatively few local productions soon required supplementing by adaptations from playwrights of Azerbayjan, Tatarstan and Turkey in order to make an adequate répertoire available. Into Af<u>gh</u>ānistān, modern stage plays first came from the Arabic, English or Turkish. To <u>Sh</u>injiang in the 1930s, the active theatre of Soviet Central Asia supplied numbers of its plays, easily adapted to the linguistic needs of Uy<u>gh</u>ur and Kazak actors and audiences. Throughout the region, the range of dramaturgy widened further with renditions of European and Russian dramas. Molière's comedies, especially *L'Avare, Le Médecin malgré lui, Georges Dandin* and *Les fourberies de Scapin* became perhaps the most popular in Soviet Central Asia and Af<u>gh</u>ānistān, as they had been in Egypt and Turkey. Shakespeare, most often represented by *Hamlet, The merchant of Venice* and *Othello*, appeared nearly everywhere. Čolpan made the first published Uzbek translation of *Hamlet* in 1934. It was staged, along with *Othello*, in Ta<u>sh</u>kent in the mid-30s. By the 1960s and 1970s, Af<u>gh</u>ānistān's city theatres were staging recent American plays by Eugene O'Neill (*Desire under the elms*), Tennessee Williams (*The glass menagerie*), Edward Albee (*The zoo story*) and others. Translations of standard Russian plays seen in Soviet Central Asia included Gogol's comedy, *The Inspector-General*, Ostrovsky's melodrama, *Thunderstorm*, Gorky's ideological *Yegor Buličev and others*, and many dozens of works from Soviet Russian dramatists concerning selected political and historical themes. The importance of foreign sources for the Central Asian repertory is emphasised in the fact that translations supplied around one-half of the 130 to 140 plays staged each year in Uzbekistan as late as the early 1980s (*Ozbekistan ädäbiyati wä sänᶜäti*, no. 8 [19 February 1982] 4, 7).

Bibliography: A critical bibliography of Central Asian theatre and drama has not been published. Selected bibliographies are found in E. Allworth, *Drama and theater of the Russian East: Transcaucasus, Tatarstan, Central Asia*, in *Middle East Studies Association Bulletin*, xvii/2 (December 1983), 151-60; a short version of the same survey appears in R. Fleshman (ed.), *Theatrical movement: a bibliographical anthology*, New Orleans 1986; in Soviet Central Asia some lists for subdivisions of the region are in print: *Uzbekskoy iskusstvo (Teatr, muzyka, kino na stranitsakh pečati). Bibliografičeskii ukazatel'*, Tashkent 1936 [in Uzbek]; E. Baybulov *et alii*, *Saken Seyfuliin. (Ukazatel' literatury k 70-letiyu so dnia rozhdeniya)*, Alma Ata 1965; editions of plays: Mahmud Khōdja Behbudiy, *The patricide or the plight of an uneducated boy*, in *Ural-Altaic Yearbook*, lviii (1986), 65-96; Čingiz Äitmatov and Kaltai Mukhamedzhanov, *The ascent of Mount Fuji*, New York 1975; Abdulla Kakhar, *Silk Suzanei*, in *Soviet Literature*, no. 8 (1958), 43-98; writings about drama and theatre: L. Hughes, *The Soviet theatre in Central Asia*, in *Asia*, xxxix/10 (October 1934), 590-3; Nabi Ganiev, *Fifteen years of the Khamza Uzbek Academic Dramatic Theater*, in *Sovietland*, no. 3 (1935), 25-7, 42; *Drama in the Central Asian Republics and centralization of art*, in *Bull. of the Inst. for the Study of the History and Culture of the USSR*, i/3 (June 1954), 37-40; K. Stolz, *Le théâtre afghan*, in *Afghanistan* (Kābul), ix/3 (1954) 34-44; O. Spies, *Türkisches Puppentheater. Versuch einer Geschichte des Puppentheaters im Morgenland*, Emsdetten 1959, 41-4; A. Bombaci, *On ancient Turkish dramatic performances*, in *Uralic and Altaic Series*, xxiii (1963), 81-117; H. Wilfrid Brands, *"Askiya", ein wenig bekanntes Genre des usbekischen Volksdichtung*, in *Ural-Altaische Jahrbücher*, xliii (1971), 100-6; M. N. Kadyrov, *Women's Folk Theatre in Uzbekistan*, in *Trudï VII Meždunarodnyi kongress antropologičeskikh i etnografičeskikh nauk*, vi (Moscow 1969), 94-9; N. Kh. Nurdzhanov, *Old Tadjik pantomimes*, in *ibid.*, vi, 87-93; Allworth, *The beginnings of the modern Turkestanian theater*, in *Slavic Review*, xxiii/4 (December 1964), 676-87; idem, *Drama and the theater*, in *Uzbek Literary Politics*, 1964, 215-35; idem, *Reform and revolution in early Uzbek drama*, in *Central Asian Review*, xii/2 (1964), 86-96; idem, *A document about the cultural life of Soviet Uzbeks outside their SSR*, in *Central Asian Survey*, i/2-3 (1982-3), 103-25; idem, *Mahmud Khoja Behbudiy*, in *Encycl. of World Literature in the Twentieth Century*, i, 1981, 219; idem, *Abdalrauf Fitrat*, in *ibid.*, ii, 1982, 143-4; idem, *Murder as metaphor in the first Central Asian drama*, in *UAYb*, lviii (1986), 65-97; Imin Äkhmidi *et alii*, *Möljär tagh boranliri*, Urumči 1985; Säypidin Äzizi, *Amannisakhan (Tarikhiy diramma)*, Beijing 1983; Äkhmätjan Ķadiraw (compiler), *P'esilar (Uyghur dramaturgliri p'esilirining toplimi)*, Alma Ata 1978. (E. Allworth)

6. In Muslim India and Pakistan.

The classical Sanskrit drama in India had reached its apogee two centuries before the first Muslim penetration. Its gradual decline—often blamed partly on the religious objections of the new Muslim rulers—was probably due as much to linguistic developments, through the mediaeval local Prākrits to the modern regional languages. But whilst Sanskrit drama, which was essentially court theatre, died out, popular vernacular drama prospered. Strolling players went from village to village performing various types of plays, pageants, monologues or other entertainment (Haywood, 294-6), often on familiar Hindu themes such as Krishna and Rādhā, with singing, dancing and, at times, coarse humour. Among the actors were Muslims: female parts were performed by men or boys.

Some efforts were made in the 17th and 18th centuries to write plays in various languages such as Hindi, Bengali, Assamese and Gujarati of literary, and not merely of entertainment value. But there is no doubt that it was the influence of European—especially British—drama which provided the main impetus for the growth of a new interest in the theatre, though the heritage, both classical and popular, played part. Towards the end of the 19th century, English plays were performed in Calcutta, and two were performed in Bengali translation (Guha Thakurta, 40 ff.). Lord Macaulay's Minute of 1833 led to the spread of English higher education in India. This in its turn led to the study, then the translation or adaptation of English plays, and especially of Shakespeare. R. K. Yajnik, 270-8, lists 200 versions of 29 Shakespeare plays in nine languages between 1864 and 1919. These languages are Urdu-Hindustani, Hindi, Panjabi, Gujarati, Marathi, Bengali, Tamil, Telegu and Kanarese. In this period, the Indian government regarded Hindustani as a lingua franca and official language which could be written in either Persian or Devanagari script, depending largely on whether one was a Muslim or Hindu. People spoke of High Urdu and High Hindi, but the distinction was one of vocabulary, style and script rather than grammar. The entry of Muslims into playwriting led to the development of Urdu or Hindustani drama. Very occasionally, they used other scripts such as Devanagari or Gujarati. However, it is fair to say that practically all their plays—certainly all plays of note—were written and published in the Persian script, and may fairly be described as Urdu drama.

The form of popular drama which appealed to Muslims was called Rahas (cf. Sanskrit *rāsa* "sentiment", a technical term of the Classical dramaturgy), which was on Hindu themes and included singing and dancing and formed a sort of operetta. This became popular in Lucknow, thanks to the patronage of the last Nawwāb of Awadh (Oudh.), Wādjid ᶜAlī Shāh, who himself wrote a number of them. It was there that what is considered as the first real Urdu drama, Amānat's *Indar Sabhā*, was performed in 1853. So successful was it that it was translated into several languages and performed all over the subcontinent. The scene is Indar (Indra)'s court, and the play recounts how a peri falls in love with a mortal, and finally wins Indar's approval. Songs predominate in this play, which is almost entirely in verse. The curtain is lowered and then raised again whenever a new character comes on stage, and characters announce their identity, as in English Miracle plays.

In some strange way, this play heralded the development of modern drama in several Indian languages. The commercial instincts of the Parsis led to the establishing of a number of theatrical companies in Bombay, but they soon opted for Urdu, rather than Gujarati, Marathi or Hindi, as the language medium. This new drama thrived until the first quarter of the 20th century, and not only did companies tour outside Bombay, but new companies were formed in distant cities such as Dihlī and Benares. Drama prospered rather as it did in

Elizabethan England. Each company had a resident playwright, most of them Muslims. Plots were often taken from Islamic Persian or Indian folk-lore or history, but contemporary social themes gradually emerged. The leading dramatist was Āg͟hā Ḥas͟har Kās͟hmīrī [*q.v.* in Suppl.]. Plays were largely in verse, but rhymed prose, and increasingly prose, were also used. Plays by Shakespeare were adapted. There were sub-plots and many short scenes, and the general tone tended to be melodramatic.

This Urdu drama was certainly lively, but it was decried by purists on both moral and literary grounds. Its influence on drama in other languages, such as Hindi and Gujarati, has often been deplored (Tindal, 180-1, and Munshi, 304-5).

The theatre declined after the First World War, due to the emergence of the cinema, and especially of the talkies. Āg͟hā Ḥas͟har became a film-star in Calcutta, and then founded his own film company in Lahore. On the other hand, radio, and even more, television, have given a new impetus to drama. Thus in Urdu, Mīrzā Adīb (b. 1914), who has specialised in one-act plays on social themes, has worked for Radio Pakistan. Imtiyāz ʿAlī Tād͟j, (1900-70), who wrote for radio and films, excelled in comedy. His *chef d'oeuvre* is *Anārkalī*. On the other hand, ʿIs͟hrat Raḥmānī, who is best-known as a critic and editor of dramas, has continued the tradition of translation of Western plays, with *Hansī hansī meṅ* (Brandon Thomas's farce, *Charlie's Aunt*) and *Ēk ḥamām māṅ* (Booth Tarkington's *Clarence*).

The limited scope of this article precludes reference to some leading dramatists with no Islamic connections, particularly in Bengali, Marathi and Hindi. Information on them will be found in the works listed in the *Bibl.* There has not yet been sufficient theatrical activity to warrant reference to regional languages of Pakistan such as Sindhi and Pashto.

Panjabi, however, spoken in adjacent provinces of India and Pakistan, is a special case. The Gurmukhi script, a variety of Devanagari, is used by Sikhs, most of whom live in India; whilst the Arabic-Persian script has long been used by Muslims, and has been encouraged by the Pakistan Government. Plays have been written and published in both scripts. They are not numerous, but Mohan Singh, 87-8, lists 6 prose plays, 6 translations or adaptations from Shakespeare, and 3 from Sanskrit.

Bibliography: The following should be supplemented by reference to the art. ĀG͟HĀ ḤAS͟HAR KĀS͟HMĪRĪ, and the footnotes in J. A. Ḥaywood, *Urdu drama—origins and early development*, in *Iran and Islam. In memory of Vladimir Minorsky*, ed. C. E. Bosworth, Edinburgh 1971, 293-302.

General works include R. K. Yajnik, *The Indian theatre*, London 1933, which has much to say about Western influence, especially of Shakespeare. Hemendra Nath Das Gupta, The *Indian Stage*, 4 vols., Calcutta 1934-44, despite its title, deals mostly with Bengali drama, though there are useful chapters on other languages and on the English theatre in Calcutta. For classical Sanskrit drama, see Biswanath Bhattacharya, *Sanskrit drama and dramaturgy*, Varanasi [Benares] 1974; and, for a more popular account, E. P. Horrowitz, *The Indian theatre, a brief survey of the Sanskrit drama*, Glasgow 1912, repr. New York 1967, which aims to convey the spirit and atmosphere rather than factual details. For drama in various languages, the following may be consulted: K. B. Jindal, *A history of Hindi literature*, 1955, 271-88; Kanayalal M. Munshi, *Gujarat and its literature*, London, Calcutta, etc., 1935, 248-9, 304-5, 373; P. Guha Thakurta, *The Bengali drama, its origin and development*, London 1930. For Urdu drama. Ram Babu Saksena, *A history of Urdu literature.* Allahabad 1927, 346-67, lists many plays by Āg͟hā Ḥas͟har Kās͟hmīrī and his contemporaries. Collections of the works of many of them have been published by Mad͟jlis-i-Taraḳḳī-yi-Urdū in Lahore. Of more recent dramatists, Mīrzā Adīb's *Lahū awr ḳālīn—čand khēl*[2], Lahore 1959, contains 13 one-act plays. Of ʿIs͟hrat Raḥmānī's translations, *Hansi hansi māṅ* was published in Lahore 1964, and *Ēk ḥamām mēṅ*, in Lahore n.d. For Panjabi drama, see Mohan Singh, *A history of Panjabi literature*[2], Amritsar 1956.

(J. A. HAYWOOD)

MĀSSA (Berber Masst), the name of a small Berber tribe of the Sūs of Morocco, from which comes the name of the place where it is settled, some 30 miles south of Agadir at the mouth of the Wādī Māssa; the latter is probably the *flumen Masatat* mentioned by Pliny the Elder (v. 9) to the north of the *flumen Darat*, the modern Wādī Darʿa, and the *Masata* of the geographer would correspond to the modern *ahl Māssa*.

The name Māssa is associated with the first Arab conquest of Morocco: according to legend, it was on the shore there that, after conquering the Sūs, ʿUḳba b. Nāfiʿ drove his steed into the waves of the Atlantic, calling God to witness that there were no more lands to conquer on the west. In any case, Māssa appears very early as an important religious and commercial centre. Al-Yaʿḳūbī (*Buldān*, 360, tr. Wiet, 226) notes that the harbour was a busy one, where ships built at al-Ubulla and "sewn" (i.e. not nailed) anchored, and mentions a *ribāṭ* already renowned, that of Bahlūl. Al-Bakrī (*Descr. de l'Afrique septentrionale*, 306) and al-Idrīsī (*Opus geographicum*, 240) mention the harbour of Māssṭ; al-Bakrī emphasizes the fame of the *ribāṭ* and the importance of the fairs held there. Ibn K͟haldūn devotes several passages (*Hist. des Berbères*, ii, 181, 279) to the *ribāṭ* of Māssa, where according to popular belief the expected Mahdī [*q.v.*] will appear; this belief induced many devout people to go and settle in this *ribāṭ* and also sent many adventures there to raise rebellions.

Towards the middle of the 15th century A.D., the Portuguese began to become interested in Māssa, where they very soon acquired a privileged position (see R. Ricard, *Études sur l'histoire des Portugais au Maroc*, Coimbra 1953, 133, 136) and, at the opening of the 16th century, the Genoese came there to purchase gold, wax, cow and goat hides, lac and indigo.

Towards the end of the 15th century, the religious movement begun by al-D͟jazūlī [*q.v.*] made Māssa one of the great *zāwiya*s of Sūs, a remarkable centre for culture and piety (see M. Hajji, *L'activité intellectuelle au Maroc à l'époque Saʿdide*, Rabat 1976-7, ii, 626-8 and index). In the middle of the 9th/16th century, Leo Africanus (tr. Épaulard, 87-9) describes Māssa as a group of three little towns surrounded by a drystone wall in the middle of a forest of palmtrees; the inhabitants were agriculturists and turned the rising of the waters of the Wādī to their advantage. Outside the town on the seashore was a highly venerated "temple", from which the Mahdī was to come; a peculiar feature of it was that the little bays in it were formed of ribs of whalebone. The sea actually throws up many cetaceans on this coast and ambergris was collected here; local legend moreover says that it was on the shore of Māssa that Jonah was cast up by the whale.

After the fall of the Saʿdīds, the development of the

Marabout principality of Tazerwalt again made Māssa a commercial centre. The port was frequented by Europeans, but it was soon supplanted by that of Agadir. The rapid decline of the principality of Tazerwalt and the steadily increasing influence of the central Moroccan power finally destroyed almost completely any religious and economic importance of Māssa.

Bibliography: In addition to references in the article, see Ibn Khaldūn, *Muḳaddima*, tr. de Slane, ii, 201-202; R. Basset, *Relation de Sidi Brahim de Massat*, Paris 1883; E. Fagnan, *Extraits inedits relatifs au Maghreb*, Algiers 1924, index; R. Montagne, *Une tribu berbère du Sud Marocain: Massat*, in *Hespéris*, iv (1924), 357-403; D. Jacques-Meunié, *Le Maroc saharien des origines à 1670*, Paris 1982, index.

(G. S. COLIN*)

MASSALAJEM, the name given to two Islamic settlements in North-West Madagascar: Old Massalajem, otherwise Langani, is also known as Nossi Manja, and the daughter settlement of New Massalajem, also known as Boeny (Swa. correctly Bweni). The original town is reputed to have been founded from Kilwa [*q.v.*], and to have had regular trade relations with it and with Malindi and Pate, until its destruction by the Sakalava at the end of the 18th century. Sherds found there do not antedate the 14th century. New Massalajem served the Sakalava first as their northern capital, until they moved to Majunga, also a town of Islamic origin.

Bibliography: H. Deschamps, *Histoire de Madagascar*², Paris 1961; M. C. Poirier, *A propos de quelques ruines arabes et persanes*, in *Bulletin de l'Académie Malgache*, Tananarive, n.s. xxv (1942-3); P. M. Vérin, *Les recherches archéologiques à Madagascar*, in *Azania*, i (Nairobi 1966); idem, *Histoire ancienne du Nord-Ouest de Madagascar*, numéro spécial, *Taloha* 5, *Revue du Musée d'Art et d'Archéologie*, University of Madagascar, Tananarive 1972.

(G. S. P. FREEMAN-GRENVILLE)

AL-**MAṢṢĪṢA,** the Arabic form of the classical Mopsuestis, Byzantine Greek form Μαμίστρα, Syriac Maṣīṣtā, Armenian Msis, Ottoman Tkish. Miṣṣīṣ. or Missīs, modern Tkish. Misis, a town of Cilicia on the western or right bank of the Djayḥān [*q.v.*], 18 miles/27 km. to the east of Adana [*q.v.*] and now in the modern *vilayet* of Adana.

In antiquity it was called Μόψου ἑστία, a name, which (like that of Μόψου κρήνη in the Cilician passes) is derived from the cult of the legendary seer Mopsos (cf. Meyer, *Gesch. d. Altert.*, i/2², § 483). In ancient times, the town was chiefly famous for its bishop Theodorus (d. 428), the teacher of Nestorius and friend of the suffragan bishop and inventor of the Armenian alphabet, Mashtʿocʿ.

The emperor Heraclius is said to have removed the inhabitants and laid waste the district between Antioch and Mopsuestia on the advance of the Arabs, in order to create a desert zone between them (al-Ṭabarī, i, 2396; al-Balādhurī, *Futūḥ* 163: between al-Iskandarūn and Ṭarsūs), and under the Umayyads all the towns taken by the Arabs from al-Maṣṣīṣa to the fourth Armenia (Malatya) are said to have been left unfortified and uninhabited as a result of the inroads of the Mardaites (Theophanus, ed. de Boor, i, 363, 17). According to Abu 'l-Khaṭṭāb al-Azdī (in al-Balādhurī, 164), the Arabs conquered al-Maṣṣīṣa and Ṭarsūs under Abū ʿUbayda, according to others under Maysara b. Masrūḳ, who was sent by him and who thereafter advanced as far as Zanda (in 16/637: Caetani, *Annali dell' Islām*, iii, 805, § 311). Muʿāwiya, on his campaign against ʿAmmūriyya in 25/645-6, found all the fortresses abandoned between Anṭakiya and Ṭarsūs (see above). According to the *Maghāzī Muʿāwiya*, he himself destroyed all the Byzantine fortresses up to Anṭākiya in 31/651-2 on his return from Darawliyya (Δορύλαιον in Phrygia) (al-Balādhurī, 164-5). After the Syrian rebellion against ʿAbd al-Malik, the emperor Constantine IV Pogonatos in 65/684-5 advanced against the town and regained it (al-Yaʿḳūbī, ii, 321). Yaḥyā b. al-Ḥakam in 77/696 marched against Mardj al-Shaḥm between Malaṭya and al-Maṣṣīṣa (al-Yaʿḳūbī, ii, 337). It was only in 84/703 that ʿAbd al-Malik's son ʿAbd Allāh retook the town and had the citadel rebuilt on its old foundations (al-Balādhurī, 165; al-Yaʿḳubī, ii, 466; al-Wāḳidī, in al-Ṭabarī, ii, 127; Ibn al-Athīr, iv, 398; Theophanus, *Chron.*, ed. de Boor, 372, 4; Michael Syrus, tr. Chabot, ii, 477; Elias Nisiben, *Opus chronolog.*, ed. Brooks, 156, tr. 75; *Script. Syri, chronica minora*, ed. Guidi, 232. tr., 176, under 1015 Sel. year; Weil, *Gesch. d. Chalifen*, i, 472). In the following year, he installed a garrison in the fortress, including 300 specially picked soldiers, and built a mosque on the citadel hill (Tall al-Ḥiṣn); a Christian church was turned into a granary (*huryun, huryā* = *horreum, horrea*; al-Balādhurī, 165; Ibn al-Shiḥna, ed. Beirut, 179). To the same event no doubt refers the wrongly-dated reference in the *Chronicle* of the Armenian Samuel of Ani of the year 692 A.D. to the fortification with strong walls of the town of "Mamestia, i.e. Msis" by the Muslims under ʿAbd al-Malik (*Ratio temporum usque and suam aetatem presbyteri Samuelis Aniensis*, in Euseb. Pamphil., *Chron.*, ed. A. Mai and I. Zohrab, Mediolani 1818, App. 57; Alishan, *Sissouan*, 286). Every year, from 1,500 to 2,000 men of the advance troops (*ṭawāliʿ*) of Anṭākiya used to winter in the town. According to Michael Syrus (tr. Chabot, iii, 478), ʿAbd al-Malik died in 1017 Sel. (705 A.D.) in al-Maṣṣīṣa.

ʿUmar II is said to have intended to destroy the town and all the fortifications between it and Antioch and to have been either prevented by his own death (al-Balādhurī, 167) or dissuaded by his advisers; according to this version, he then had a large mosque built in the suburb of Kafarbayya in which there was a cistern with his inscription. It was called the "Citadel Mosque" and kept up till the time of al-Muʿtaṣim (al-Balādhurī, 165; but Kafarbayya was probably not really built till the time of al-Mahdī or Hārūn al-Rashīd, see below). Yazīd b. Djubayr ('Αζιδος ὁ τον χοννεί (in 85/704 attacked Sīs (τὸ Σίσιον κάρτρον, in al-Ṭabarī and Ibn al-Athīr: Sūsana in the *nāḥiya* of al-Maṣṣīṣa) but was driven off by Heraclius, the emperor's brother (Theophanus, ed. de Boor, 372, 23: A. M. 6196; according to al-Ṭabarī, ii, 1185, and Ibn al-Athīr, iv, 419, wrongly not till 87 A.H.). Hishām built the suburb (*al-rabaḍ*), Marwān II the quarter of al-Khuṣūṣ east of the Djayḥān, which he surrounded with a wall with a wooden door and a ditch. The bridge of Djisr al-Walīd between al-Maṣṣīṣa and Adhana, 9 *mīls* from the former, was built in 125/742-3 and restored in 225/840 by al-Muʿtaṣim (al-Balādhurī, 168; Yāḳūt, *Muʿdjam*, ii, 82; Ṣafī al-Dīn, *Marāṣid*, ed. Juynboll, i, 255). In the first half of the 2nd/8th century the caliphs al-Walīd II and Yazīd III brought the gipsy tribe of the Zuṭṭ [*q.v.*], who had been deported to Baṣra by Muʿāwiya in 50/670, and settled them with great herds of buffalo in the region of al-Maṣṣīṣa in order to fight the plague of lions in the district of the Djabal al-Lukkām (al-Balādhurī, 168; De Goeje, *Bijdrage tot de Geschiedenis der Zigeuners*, Leiden 1875, 17-22).

The first ᶜAbbāsid, Abu 'l-ᶜAbbās al-Saffāḥ, on his accession strengthened the garrison by 400 men, to whom he gave lands; the same estates were later allotted to them by al-Manṣūr. The latter in 139/756-7 restored the wall, which had been damaged by an earthquake in the preceding year, and increased with 8,000 settlers the much diminished population of the town, which he called al-Maᶜmūra (al-Balād͟hurī, 166; Ibn al-At͟hīr, v, 382; Yāḳūt, iv, 579, s.v. al-Maᶜmūriyya; Ibn S͟hiḥna, 179). On the site of a heathen temple, he built a large mosque which far surpassed the mosque of ᶜUmar in size. When ᶜAbd Allāh b. Ṭāhir was governor of the West (i.e. in 211/826), it was enlarged by al-Maʾmūn. Al-Manṣūr increased the garrison to 1,000 men and settled in the town the inhabitants of al-K͟huṣūṣ, Persians, Slavs and Christian Arabs (Nabataeans), whom Marwān had transplanted thither (see above), and gave them allotments of land. It is probably to the same event that the story refers that Ṣāliḥ b. ᶜAlī, when in the ᶜAbbāsid period the inhabitants of al-Maṣṣīṣa, harassed by the Byzantines, resolved to migrate, sent D͟jibrīl b. Yaḥyā al-Bad͟jalī al-K͟hurāsānī in 140/757-8 to rebuild the town and settle it with Muslim inhabitants (al-Balād͟hurī, 166; according to al-Ṭabarī, ii, 135 in the year 141). Under al-Mahdī, the garrison was increased to 2,000; in addition, there was the Anṭākiya corps of almost the same size which wintered here regularly until Sālim of Burullus became their *wālī* and increased the garrison by 500 men instead. There is a brief reference in the Syriac inscription of ᶜEnes͟h to a raid by al-Mahdī to the D͟jayḥan (Syr. Giḥōn) in 780 A.D. (1091 Sel; Chabot, in *JA*, ser. 9, xvi [1900], 287; Pognon, *Inscr. semit. de la Syrie et de la Mésop.*, 148-50, no. 84). Hārūn al-Ras͟hīd built Kafarbayya or, according to another story, altered the plans for this suburb prepared by al-Mahdī and fortified it with a ditch; he also built walls which were only completed after his death by al-Muᶜtaṣim. In 187/803 an earthquake laid waste the town (al-Ṭabarī, iii, 688). In the following year, the Byzantines invaded and pillaged the region of al-Maṣṣīṣa and ᶜAyn Zarba and carried off the inhabitants of Ṭarsūs into captivity, whereupon Hārūn al-Ras͟hīd attacked and defeated them (Michael Syrus, iii, 16). According to al-Ṭabarī (iii, 709) and Ibn al-At͟hīr (vi, 135), the Byzantines in 190/806 invaded ᶜAyn Zarba and Kanīsat al-Sawdāʾ and took prisoners there; but the people of al-Maṣṣīṣa regained all their loot from them. If, as it seems, the curious story in the Byzantine chroniclers (Theophanes, *Chron.*, ed. de Boor, 446, 18; Georg. Kedren, Bonn, Corpus, ii, 17) that in 771-2 (A. M. 6264) Ἀλφαδὰλ Βαδινάρ, i.e. al-Faḍl b. Dīnār, who had 500 Byzantine prisoners with him, lost 1,000 men and all his booty through a sortie of the Μομφουερτεῖς, refers to the same events, the latter would appear to be wrongly reported and wrongly dated.

On 13 Ḥazīran 1122 Sel. (811 A.D.), the walls and many houses in the town and three adjoining villages fell in a great earthquake; near al-Maṣṣīṣa the course of the D͟jayḥān was dammed for a week so that the boats lay on the dry bed (Michael Syrus, iii, 17). In 198/813-14 T͟hābit b. Naṣr al-K͟huzāᶜī was fighting in the Syrian marches of al-Maṣṣīṣa and Ad͟hana (al-Yaᶜḳūbī, ii, 541). On his campaign into Bilād al-Rūm, al-Maʾmūn passed through al-Maṣṣīṣa and Ṭarsūs in Muḥarram 215/March 830 (al-Ṭabarī, iii, 1103; Ibn al-At͟hīr, vi, 294; Abu 'l-Fidāʾ, *Annales Moslem.*, ed. Reiske, ii, 152; Weil, *Gesch. d. Chal.*, ii, 239). In revenge, the emperor Theophilus in 216/831 raided the lands around these two towns and slew or took prisoner 2,000 men (al-Ṭabarī, iii, 1104; Ibn al-At͟hīr, vi, 295).

After the emperor's campaign against Zibaṭra (837 A.D.) in which he also defeated the Μομφουεστῖται (Const. Porophyrog., *De caeremoniis*, ed. Bonn, 503; Vasilev, *Vizantiya i Arabi*, in *Zapiski ist.-filol. fak. imp. S.-Ptbg. Univ.*, *čast* lvi [1900], 88-9, n. 4), al-Muᶜtaṣim in the following year attacked ᶜAmmūriyya; his general Bas͟hīr commanded a part of the army which included the Maṣṣīṣa contingents (Michael Syrus, iii, 96). In 245/859, the town was again visited by an earthquake which destroyed many places in Syria, Mesopotamia and Cilicia (al-Yaᶜḳūbī, iii, 1440). The caliph al-Muᶜtaḍid after restoring order in the T͟hug͟hūr al-S͟hāmiyya (287/900) returned from al-Maṣṣīṣa via Funduḳ al-Ḥusayn, al-Iskandariyya and Bag͟hrās to Anṭākiya, Ḥalab and al-Raḳḳa (al-Ṭabarī, iii, 2198-2200; al-Funduḳ, a place in the *t͟hug͟hūr* near al-Maṣṣīṣa: Yāḳut, iii, 918; Ṣafī al-Dīn, *Marāṣid*, ii, 365).

When in 292/904-5 the Byzantine Andronicus invaded the district of Marᶜas͟h, the people of al-Maṣṣīṣa and Ṭarsūs met him, but were defeated and lost their leader Abu 'l-Rid͟jāl b. Abī Bakkār (al-Ṭabarī, iii, 2251; Ibn al-At͟hir. vii, 371; Vasilev, *Zap. ist.-fil. fak. imp. S.-Ptbg. Univ.*, *čast* lvxi [1902], 154, 2).

In 344/955-6, the Ḥamdānid Sayf al-Dawla was visited by horsemen from the frontier towns of Ṭarsūs, Adana and al-Maṣṣīṣa and with them an envoy from the Greek king, who concluded a truce with him (al-Nuwayrī and Kamāl al-Dīn, in Freytag, *ZDMG*, xi, 192); Ibn Ẓāfir al-Azdī. *Kitāb al-Duwal al-munḳatiᶜa*, tr. Vasilev, *op. cit.*, Priložen., 86). Defeated by Leo Phocas in 349/960 in the pass of al-Küčük, Sayf al-Dawla spent the night in al-Ḥawānīt and returned to Ḥalab via al-Maṣṣīṣa (Kamāl al-Dīn, in Freytag, *op. cit.*, 196; Yaḥyā b. Saᶜīd, *Taʾrīk͟h*, ed. Kračkovskiy-Vasilev, in *Patrol. Orient.*, xiii, 1924, 782).

In 352/963, the emperor Nicephorus took Adana, the inhabitants of which fled to al-Maṣṣīṣa, and sent the Domesticus John Tzimisces (Yānīs b. al-S͟himis͟hīḳ al-Dumistiḳ) against this town. The latter besieged it for several days but had to withdraw as his supplies were running short, and after laying waste the country round burned the adjoining al-Mallūn (Μαλλός) at the mouth of the D͟jayḥān (Yaḥyā b. Saᶜīd, 793-4). The emperor himself came again in D͟hu 'l-Ḳaᶜda 353/Nov. 964 to the marches (*al-t͟hag͟hr*) and besieged al-Maṣṣīṣa for over 50 days, but had again to abandon the siege owing to shortage of supplies and retired to winter in Ḳaysariyya. Finally, the town was stormed by John Tzimisces (Arm. Kuiř Žan) on Thursday 11 Rad͟jab 354/13 July 965. The inhabitants set it on fire and fled to Kafarbayya. After a desperate struggle on the bridge between the two towns, the Greeks took this suburb also and carried off all the inhabitants into captivity (Yaḥyā b. Saᶜīd, 795; Ibn al-At͟hīr, viii, 408-11; Abu 'l-Fidāʾ, *Ann. Mosl.*, ed. Reiske, ii, 482-3; Michael Syrus, iii, 128; Elias Nisiben., ed. Brooks, 218, tr. 106; Georg., Cedren., ed. Bonn, ii, 362; Leon Diakon., ed. Bonn, 52-3; Mattᶜeos Uřhayecᶜi, ed. Dulaurier in *Rec. hist. crois.*, *Doc. arm.*, i, 5; Stepᶜan Asołik of Taron, *Armen. Gesch.*, tr. H. Gelzer and A. Burckhardt, Leipzig 1907, 134, 24). They were, to the number of 200,000, it is said, led past the gates of Ṭarsūs, which at that time was being besieged by the emperor's brother Leo, to terrify the people of the town (Ibn S͟hiḥna, *Rawḍat al-manāẓir*, in Freytag, *ZDMG*, xi; Elias Nisiben., *op. cit.*). The gates of Ṭarsūs and of al-Maṣṣīṣa were gilded and taken as trophies to Constantinople, where one set was put in the citadel and the others on the wall of the Golden Gate (Georg. Cedren., ii, 363).

The town remained for over a century in the hands of the Byzantines; the Emperor Basil II Bolgaroctonus stayed for six months in the region of al-Maṣṣīṣa and Ṭarsūs before going to Armenia, after the death (31 March 1000 A.D.) of the Kuropalates Davitʿ of Taykʿ, to take possession of his lands by inheritance (Yaḥyā b. Saʿīd, *Taʾrīkh*, ed. Rosen, 39, in *Zap. Imp. Akad. Nauk*, xliv, St. Petersburg 1883). In 1042 the Armenian prince Aplg̲h̲arib, son of Ḥasan and grandson of K̲h̲ačʿik of the house of the Artsrunians, was sent by the emperor Constantine Monomachos as governor to Cilicia (St. Martin, *Mém. sur l'Arm.*, i, 199). In 1085 Philaretos Brachomios, who was appointed in Constantinople perhaps as Sebastos (Michael Syrus, iii, 173) or at least Kuropalates (Mich. Attal., Bonn ed., 301) and whose ephemeral kingdom comprised the land from Ṭarsūs to Malaṭya, Urfa and Anṭākiya, held al-Maṣṣīṣa (Michael Syrus, *loc. cit.*; Laurent, *Byzance et Antioche sous le curopalate Philarète*, in *Rev. des Et. Arm.*, ix [1929], 61-72). Shortly before the arrival of the Crusaders, the Sald̲j̲ūḳ Turks took Ṭarsūs, al-Maṣṣīṣa, ʿAyn Zarba and the other towns of Cilicia (Michael Syrus, iii, 179). About the end of September 1097, the Franks under Tancred, who had been invited thither from Lambron by Ōs̲h̲in III, took the town, which was stormed after a day's siege: the inhabitants were slain and rich booty fell into the hands of the victor (Albert. Aquens., iii, 15-16, in Migne, *Patrol. Lat.*, clxvi, col. 446-7; Radulf. Cadom., *Gesta Tancredi*, ch. 39-49). William of Tyre describes al-Maṣṣīṣa on this occasion (iii, 21, in Migne, *Patrol. Lat.*, cci, col. 295): *Erat autem Mamistra una de nobilioribus eiusdem provinciae civitatibus, muro et multorum incolatu insignis, sedet optimo agro et gleba ubere et amoenitate praecipua commendabilis.* Count Baldwin, who had quarrelled with Tancred, followed him along with the admiral Winimer of Boulogne and encamped in a meadow near the D̲j̲ayḥān bridge; Winimer left him there and went with his fleet to al-Lād̲h̲iḳiyya, while the two rivals had a desperate fight, after which Baldwin withdrew to the east (Albert. Aquens., iii, chs. 15, 59, in Migne, *op. cit.*, cols. 446, 472). Tancred followed him, after he had imposed on the city *plus paternas quam principis leges* (Radulf. Cadom., ch. 44). The Byzantine general Tatikios, who had joined the Crusaders to take over their conquests in name of the Emperor, left them in the lurch in the beginning of February 1098 at the siege of Anṭākiya and ceded to Bohemund the town of Tursol (Ṭarsūs), Mamistra and Addena (Adana) (Raymond of Agiles, in Bongars, *Gesta Dei per Francos*, Hanover 1611, 146, 5). Bohemund only took possession of the towns of Ṭarsūs, ʿAyn Zarba and al-Maṣṣīṣa in August (William of Tyre, vii, 2). After the town had again fallen to the Greeks for a period, Tancred again took it in 1101 (Rad. Cad., ch. 143), but had to hand it over with Ṭarsūs, Adana and ʿAyn Zarba to Bohemund on his return from captivity in 1103 (William of Tyre, vii, 2, in Migne, *op. cit.*, col. 379). In the following year, however, Longinias, Ṭarsūs, Adana and Μάμιρτα were regained for Byzantium by the campaign of the general Monastras (Anna Comnena, *Alexaid*, ed. Reifferscheid, ii, 140, 5, who apparently did not recognise the identity of Μάμιρτα with Μόφου ἑρτίαι, which she mentions several times). In the treaty between Bohemund and the emperor Alexius of September 1108, the town was promised to the former (Anna Comnena, *op. cit.*, ii, 218), Tancred having taken it in the preceding year with 10,000 men from

the Byzantine general, the Armenian Aspietes (*ibid.*, ii, 147). At this time, of the quarters of the town one (probably Kafarbayya) was in ruins (*ibid.*). Baldwin of Burg and Joscelin of Courtenay, who allied themselves against Tancred with Ko̲g̲h̲ Vasil of Kaysūm, were supported by the latter with a detachment of 800 men and a body of Pečenegs, who were stationed in al-Maṣṣīṣa as Greek mercenaries (Mattʿeōs Uṙhayecʿi, tr. Dulaurier, 266-7 = *RHC, Doc. arm.*, i, 86). The great earthquake of 1114 destroyed the town, like many others in Cilicia and Syria (Smbat, in *Doc. arm.*, i, 614).

Under the Frankish patriarchate of Antioch, Mopsuestia-Mamistra was separated from the ecclesiastical province of Anazarbos and made an autocephalous metropolis (Michael Syrus, iii, 191; recensions of the *Notitia Antiochena* of the Crusading period). The ἐνορία Μοφουεστίας stretched (according to *Notitia Antiohena* on the boundaries of the Antiochene dioceses, ed. Papadopoulo-Keramevs, 67) from Seleuceia in Syria and Adana ἀπο τοῦ μεγάλου Ξηροποταμοῦ (now Ozerlü or Rabaṭča?) "ἑως τοῦ μεγάλου ποταμοῦ φυρῶν. The latter is undoubtedly identical with αὐτὸς ὁ μέγας ποταμὸς 'Αδανας, the Sayḥān.

In 1132-13 the Rupēnid Levon I (Λεβούνης), son of Constantine, took the town (Arm. Msis, Mises, Mamestia or Mamuestia) from the Greeks (Cinnamos, i, 7; iii, 14; Smbat Sparapet, *Chronicle*, in *Doc. arm.*, i, 615). The brother of the emperor John II Comnenus went to him, and Levon gave his sons his daughters as wives with the towns of al-Maṣṣīṣa and Adana as dowries. But when they quarrelled he took back from the Greeks all that he had given them, and Isaac had to flee with his sons to sultan Masʿūd (Michael Syrus), ii, 230). Levon, falling through treachery into the hands of Raymond of Poitiers, had to cede (1136-7) al-Maṣṣīṣa, Adana and Sarvantikʿar (now Sawuran Ḳalʿe?), but regained his liberty in a couple of months; he very soon retook these towns (*Doc. arm.*, i, 152-3 = *Chron. de Matthieu d'Édesse*, tr. Dulaurier, 457; Smbat, *op. cit.*, 616). The emperor John in 1137 (1448 Sel.) had his revenge on Levon. He invaded Cilicia, took Ṭarsūs, Adana and al-Maṣṣīṣa, seized Levon himself with his wife and children and took them to Constantinople, where Levon subsequently died (Ibn al-At̲h̲īr, xi, 35; Michael Syrus, ii, 245; Gregor. presbyt., *Forts. d. Chronik des Mattʿeōs*, tr. Dulaurier, 323; cf. *Docum. arm.*, i, p. xxxii, 1 and 153, 4; William of Tyre, xiv, 24; Röhricht, *Gesch. d. Kgr. Jerusalem*, 211). John installed Coloman (*Calamanus*), son of Boris and grandson of Cilicia (William of Tyre, xiv, 24, xix, 9, in Migne, *Patr. Lat.*, cci, cols. 603, 756; a *Dux Ciliciae* mentioned in *Regum et principum epistolae*, no. 24, in Bongars, *Gesta Dei per Franc.*, 1182, 1. 46 and *passim*). When the emperor John died at Mard̲j̲ al-Dībād̲j̲ on 8 April 1143 (William of Tyre, xv, 22; Röhricht, *Gesch. d. Kgr. Jerus.*, 228, 4), his successor Manuel I Comnenos had his body brought by boat from Mopsuestia down the Pyramos to the sea and taken by sea to the capital (Niketas Choniat., *Man. Komn.*, i, Bonn ed., 67).

Thoros II, the son of Levon, who had escaped home from his confinement in Constantinople, was again able to cast off the Byzantine yoke. When in 1151 he took Msis and Tʿil (Tall Ḥamdun) from the Byzantines (Smbat, in *Doc. arm.*, i, 619) and made their general Thomas prisoner, the emperor Manuel in the following year sent against him with 12,000 cavalry Andronicus Comnenus, whom he had appointed governor of Ṭarsūs and al-Maṣṣīṣa (Gregor. presbyt., in *Doc. arm.*, i, 167 = Matthew of Edessa, tr. Dulaurier, 334; Smbat, *Chron.*, in *Doc. arm.*, i, 619). Andronicus, who did not recognise Thoros as ruler of Asia Minor, advanced against al-Maṣṣīṣa, but was surprised by the Armenians and put to an ignominious flight with his 12,000 men. Thus not only the town, which was very well supplied with provisions and military material of all kinds, fell into his hands, but also a great part of Cilicia (Gregor. presbyt., tr. Dulaurier, 334-6 = *Doc. arm.*, i, 167 ff.; Smbat, *op. cit.*). The emperor, himself too weak to avenge the insult, twice induced by gifts the sultan Ḳilīdj Arslān II (Gregor. wrongly: Masᶜūd) of Ḳonya to attack Thoros. The sultan, who on the first occasion (548/1153) was content with the defeat of the Armenian and the return of the lands taken from the Greeks, again attacked al-Maṣṣīṣa, ᶜAyn Zarba and Tall Ḥamdūn (Arm. Tᶜiln Hamtunoy) in 1156, but could do nothing against them and had finally to retire after heavy losses (Gregor., *op. cit.*, 338 = *Doc. arm.*, i, 171).

The emperor Manuel himself passed through Cilicia in 1159 with a large army to the assistance of the Crusaders. Thoros had already retired to Vahka in the desolate mountains (*Armen. Rhymea Chron.*, in *Doc. Arm.*, i, 505) when the emperor entered al-Maṣṣīṣa at the beginning of November, but he did no injury to any one there (Gregor., tr. Dulaurier, 353-4 = *Doc. arm.*, i, 187). The Frankish kings led by Baldwin came to pay homage to him in the town or on the adjoining *pratum palliorum* (as William of Tyre, xiii, 27, translates Mardj al-Dībādj) where his court was held in camp for seven months (Gregor., tr. Dulaurier, 358; Röhricht, *Gesch. d. Kgr. Jerusal.*, 298). Thoros was also able with great tact to become reconciled with him, and on acknowledging Byzantine suzerainty and ceding several towns in Cilicia, was recognised as *Sebastos* of Msis, Anazarbos and Vahga (*Doc. arm.*, i, 186; Smbat, *ibid.*, 622). His brother Mleh, who attempted his life while out hunting between al-Maṣṣīṣa and Adana, was banished by Thoros and given by Nur al-Dīn the town of Ḳūrus (Kyrrhos; Smbat, *loc. cit.*). After the death of Thoros of Msis (1168-9; Smbat, 623), Mleh (Arab. Malīḥ b. Liwun al-Armanī) succeeded him and at first ruled only over the district of the passes (*Bilād al-Durūb*). In 1171 he surprised Count Stephen of Blois at Mamistra and plundered him (William of Tyre, xx, 25-8). In 568/1172-3, supported by troops of his ally Nūr al-Dīn, he took from the Greek Adana, al-Maṣṣīṣa and Ṭarsūs (Ibn al-Athīr, xi, 255; Kamāl al-Dīn, tr. in Röhricht, in *Beiträge z. Gesch. d. Kreuzzüge*, i, Berlin 1874, 336).

When Mleh's successor Rupēn III fell through treachery into the hands of Bohemund of Antioch, his brother Łevon (II) obtained his release in 1184 by ceding al-Maṣṣīṣa, Adana and Tall Ḥamdūn (Tᶜiln) and paying 3,000 *dīnārs*; immediately afterwards, Rupēn retook these strongholds from the Franks (Michael Syrus, iii, 397; *Doc. arm.*, i, 394).

Hetᶜum, the nephew of the Catholicos Grigor IV and son of Čᶜortvanēl of Ṭarōn, who came to Cilicia in 1189 with his brother Shahinshah, received from Łevon II (1185-1219) his niece Alice, daughter of Rupēn III, in marriage and the town of Msis, but died in the same year (Smbat, in *Doc. arm.*, i, 629; Marquart, *Südarmenien und die Tigrisquellen*, Vienna 1930, 481-2). The Emperor Frederick Barbarossa in 586/1190 was about to go to Syria via Ṭarsūs and al-Maṣṣīṣa when he met his tragic end in the Kalykadnos (alleged[?] letter of the Armenian Catholicos in Ibn Shaddād, in *Rec. Hist. Orient. des Crois.*, iii, 162); a portion of his army thereupon went to Antioch via Ṭarsūs, *Mamistria* and *Thegio* (Ḥiṣn al-Muthakkab; not *Portella*, the Syrian passes, with which Röhricht, *Gesch. d. Kgr. Jerus.*, 530, 4, identifies it).

Wilbrand of Oldenburg, who visited the East in the train of Duke Leopold VII of Austria and Styria and the Teutonic Grand Master Hermann von Salza, came in the beginning of 1212 to *Mamistere* which he describes as follows: (Wilbr., ch. 18, ed. Laurent, *Peregrinatores*, Leipzig 1864, 175): *Haec est civitas bona, super flumen sita, satis amoena, murum habens circa se turritum, sed antiquitate corrosum, paucos in quodam respectu habens inhabitatores, quibus omnibus rex illius terrae imperat et dominatur.* In the vicinity lay *quoddam castrum quod erat de patrimonio beati Pauli .... sed nunc temporis possidetur a Graecis. In hac civitate* [Mamistere] *habetur sepulchrum beati Pantaleonis. Ipsa vero distat a Canamella* (cf. Tomaschek, *SB Ak. Wien* [1891], app. viii, p. 71) *magnam dictam.* Łevon II granted the republics of Genoa and Venice the privilege of having their own trading centres in al-Maṣṣīṣa, which could be reached by ship from the sea before the mouth of the Djayḥān became silted up (Alishan, *Sissouan ou l'Arméno-Cilicie*, 287). The attempt of Raymund Rupēn of Antioch to seize the throne of Armenia after Łevon's death in 1219 failed; he was, it is true, able to take Ṭarsūs and attack al-Maṣṣīṣa but he was taken prisoner by Constantine of Baržberd and died in prison in 1222 (*Doc. arm.*, i, 514; Röhricht, *Gesch. d. Kgr. Jerus.*, 741-2).

For a century the Rupēnids ruled almost undisturbed in the town. Their glory reached its height under the splendour-loving Hetᶜum I (1219-70). Here were held the annual festivals of the Church at which numerous princes and nobles used to gather down to the last and difficult years of the king. Here was held the brilliant ceremony at which his 20-year old son Łevon was dubbed knight. Hither the king brought the seat of government after the destruction of Sīs (Alishan, *Sissouan*, 287-8).

Baybars sent a punitive expedition against Hetᶜum in 664/1266 under al-Malik al-Manṣūr of Ḥamā, who advanced as far as Ḳalᶜat al-ᶜAmūdayn and into the district of Sīs, while Sayf al-Dīn Ḳalāwūn took al-Maṣṣīṣa, Adana, Ayās and Ṭarsūs (al-Maḳrīzi, *Hist. d. Sult. Maml.*, tr. Quatremère, i/2, 34-5; Abu 'l-Fidāᵓ. *Annal. Mosl.*, ed. Reiske, v, 18; al-Nuwayrī, in Weil, *Gesch. d. Chal.*, iv, 56). Three years later (1269), the district of al-Maṣṣīṣa was visited by an earthquake (al-Suyūṭī, in *Doc. arm.*, ii, 1906, 772, n. f.). Baybars (Arm. *Pntukhtar* = Arab. *Bundukdār*) himself in 673/spring of 1275 took the field against Łevon III, son of Hetᶜum, laid waste the whole of Cilicia as far as Koricos and stormed al-Maṣṣīṣa and Sīs, the former on 26 March. The inhabitants were massacred, almost all the houses burned and the great bridge destroyed (Arm. Kandarayn Msisay, i.e. Ḳanṭarat al-Maṣṣīṣa; cf. al-Maḳrīzī, i/2, 123-4, with n. 154; Mufaḍḍal b. Abi 'l-Faḍāᵓil, *Gesch. d. Mamlūkensultane*, ed. Blochet, in *Patrol. Orient.*, xiv, 389; Barhebraeus, *Chron. syr.*, ed. Bedjan, 531, 6; Smbat, *Chronik*, in *Doc. arm.*, i, 653; Röhricht, *Gesch. d. Kgr. Jerusalem*, 967; van Berchem, *CIA*, i, 688, n. 2). When in 697/1297-8 an army under the *amīrs* Sayf al-Dīn Kīpčāḳ, the *Nāᵓib* of Dimashk, Fāris al-Dīn Ilbekī al-Sāḳī al-Ẓāhiri, the *Nāᵓib* of Ṣafad, Sayf al-Dīn Bizlār al-Manṣūrī and Sayf al-Dīn ᶜAzāz al-Ṣāliḥī invaded the land of Sīs, al-Maṣṣīṣa is not specially emphasised among the unimportant places taken like Tall Ḥamdūn, Ḥammūṣ (Ḥumaymis), Kaᶜlāt Nadjīma, al-Maṣṣīṣa, Sirfandikār, Ḥadjar, Shughlān, al-Nuḳayr and Zandjfara (al-Maḳrīzī, ii/2, 60-5; Mufaḍḍal, *op. cit.*, 602; al-Nuwayrī, in Blochet, *ibid.*). In 722/1322, the Egyptians crossed the Djayḥān by a bridge of boats, got behind the Armenians who had retired to Msis and inflicted a severe defeat upon them; among those who fell are mentioned the barons Hetᶜum of Djlnocᶜ, his brother Constantine, Wahram Lotik, Ōshin, the son of the marshal, along with 21 knights and many men (Smbat's Continuator, in *Doc. arm.*, i, 688). This authority also mentions a raid by an Egyptian force against al-Maṣṣīṣa (Mamuestia), Adana, al-Mallūn (Mlun) and Ṭarsūs in 735/1334-5 (*Doc. arm.*, i, 6/1; Tomaschek, in *SB Ak. Wien* [1891], part viii, 68). The last Egyptian invasion took place in 775/1373-4. Among the towns destroyed were Sīs, Adana, al-Maṣṣīṣa and ᶜAyn Zarba, and Łevon IV had to surrender in 1375 after a siege of nine months in Ghaban (*Doc. arm.*, i, 686, n. 3). The town thus passed nominally into the *Futūḥāt al-Djahāniyya* of the Mamlūk empire; it had, it is true, by now sunk into insignificance and it is not mentioned, for example, among the towns taken by Shahsuwār in 871/1467 (Alishan, *Sissouan*, 290).

Armenian sources mention eight archbishops of the town from 1175 to 1370 (1175-1206 David, 1215 Johannes, 1266 Sion, 1306 Constantine, 1316 John, 1332 Stephen, 1342 Basil, 1362-1370 unnamed; cf. Alishan, *op. cit.*, p. 290). Michael Syrus knows only Job of about 800 A.D. (*Chron.*, tr. Chabot, iii, 23-4, 451, no. 27), and the Frankish writers from 1100 onwards Bartholomaeus, before 1234 Radulphus and in the years from 1162-1238 three or four more unnamed bishops (Albert. Aquens., ix, 16; William of Tyre, xiv, 10; Le Quien, in *Oriens Christianus*, iii, 1198-1200; Röhricht, *Gesch. d. Kgr. Jerusal.*, 42, 202). On account of the many Egyptian invasions, the Latin archbishopric was removed to Ayās by Pope John XXII in 1320 (Alishan, *Sissouan*, 290).

After the fall of the kingdom of Little Armenia, the power of the Ramaḍān-Oghlu [*q.v.*] and Dhu 'l-Ḳadr-Oghlu [see DHU 'L-ḲADR] gradually spread in Cilicia. Selīm I on his campaign against Egypt in 922/1516 and on his return also preferred to keep to the east of their land (Taeschner, *Anatol. Wegenetz*, ii, 32). Al-Maṣṣīṣa has been Turkish-controlled since that year, in which the decisive battle was fought on Mardj al-Dābiḳ [*q.v.*].

In Kafarbayya, a *khān* was built for caravans passing through in 949/1542 and restored in 1830 by Ḥasan Pasha. The Djayḥān bridge became useless in 1736 when the central arch collapsed; in 1766 this was repaired but was blown up in 1832 on the retreat of the Turkish troops from the fighting at Baylān in order to hold up the advance of Ibrāhīm Pasha's pursuing army. As late as the middle of the 19th century, it could only be crossed by an improvised wooden footbridge.

In modern times, al-Maṣṣīṣa is mentioned mainly by western pilgrims and travellers, who as a rule only spent a short time there. Thus it was visited in 1432 by the Burgundian Bertrandon de la Brocquière ("*Misse-sur-Jehan*"), in the 16th century by P. Belon, 1682 the Mecca-bound pilgrim Meḥmed Edīb, 1695 the Armenian Patriarch of Antiochia Makarios, 1704 Paul Lucas, 1736 Chevalier Otter, 1766 the Dane Carsten Niebuhr, 1813 Macd. Kinneir, 1834 Aucher Eloy, 1836 Colonel Chesney, 1840 Ainsworth and 1853 Victor Langlois, whose reports were exhaustively used by Carl Ritter (*Erdkunde*, xix, 66-115). The "Merges Galles" visited by Ludwig von Rauter on 8 July 1568, is not (as in Röhricht-Meisner, *Deutsche Pilgerreisen nach dem hl. Lande*, 1880, 434, n. 43) al-Maṣṣīṣa, but Merkez Ḳalᶜesi on the Bāb Iskandarūn (Cilic.-Syr. passes). Somewhat fuller descriptions of the recent Miṣṣīṣ and its ancient and mediaeval ruins were given in the 19th century by Langlois, Alishan and at the beginning of the 20th one by Cousin (see *Bibl.*).

The stretch of the Baghdād railway from Dorak south of the Taurus via Adana and Miṣṣīs to Maᶜmūra at the foot of the Amanos was opened on 27 April 1912. As a station on the railway (the station is actually 1½ miles north-west of the place) the town gained a certain strategic importance in the Cilician campaign of the French in 1919-20 (1919: settlement of about 1,200-1,500 Armenians; 27-8 May 1920: futile Turkish blockade of the garrison there, about a company strong; end of July: withdrawal of the troops to Adana; cf. E. Brémond, *La Cicilie en 1919-1920*, in *Rev. Étud., Arm.* [1920], i, 311, 360, 363, 365). After the Turkish occupation, the newly-settled Armenians were probably exterminated in the usual way. The importance of the town has now passed to the neighbouring Ceyhan.

According to the Arab geographers, al-Maṣṣīṣa lay on the Djayḥān (Πύραμος, sometimes confused by the Byzantine authors with the Σάρος, Arabic. Sayḥān, with which it seems to have had at one time a common mouth: George Cedren, ii, 362; Anna Comn., ii, 147), 1-2 days' journey from Bayyas and one from ᶜAyn Zarba and Adhana, 12 *mīls* from the Mediterranean coast. The sea could be seen from the Friday mosque in the town; in front of the town lay a beautiful fertile plain (the ancient Ἀλήιον πεδίον). Al-Maṣṣīṣa lying on the right bank was connected with Kafarbayya by an ancient stone bridge built by Constantius and restored by Justinian. The country round was rich in gardens and cornfields, watered by the Djayḥān. According to Yāḳūt, the town originally had a wall with 5 gates, and Kafarbayya, one with 4 gates. A speciality of the town was the valuable fur-cloaks exported all over the world. Ten miles from al-Maṣṣīṣa, which is somewhat inaccurately placed by Ibn Khurradādhbih, Yāḳūt and others on the Djabal al-Lukkām (Amanus), was the plain of Mardj al-Dībādj, which is often mentioned in the records of the fighting between the Mamlūks and Little Armenia (probably the *ager Mopsuestiae* on which Cicero encamped: *Ad fam.*, iii, 8). In it, to the north-east of the town on the road to Sīs, was the fort of al-ᶜAmūdayn (al-Maḳrīzī, ed. Quatremère, ii/2, 61; cf. Ḳalᶜat al-ᶜAmudayn in Abu 'l-Fidā', *Ann. Mosl.*, ed. Reiske, v, 18; located by Alishān, *Sissouan*, 225-6 too far east in "Hémétié-Kaléssi"). A field of Mardj al-Aṭrākhūn is also mentioned near al-Maṣṣīṣa (Yāḳūt, iv, 487; Ṣafī al-Dīn, *Marāṣid*, iii, 74). Tall Ḥāmid, a strong fortress of the Thughūr al-Maṣṣīṣa, corresponds to the recent Ottoman Ḥāmidiyye, now called Ceyhan (*ZDMG*, xi, 191, 200; Yāḳūt, i, 866; Ṣafī al-Dīn, *Marāṣid*, i, 211; Ibn al-Shiḥna, 339). There also was Tall Ḥūm (Yāḳūt, i, 867; *Marāṣid*, i, 211; Ibn al-Shiḥna, *ibid.*; exact site unknown). Al-ᶜAyn at the foot of the Djabal al-Lukkām, over which the Darb al-ᶜAyn pass went, was also one of the forts of al-Maṣṣīṣa (Yāḳūt, iii, 756; *Marāṣid*, ii, 293); on the frontier against Ḥalab lay Būḳa [*q.v.*; cf. van Berchem, *Voyage en Syrie*, i, 257, 8]. Hiṣn Sinān (al-Balādhurī, 165; Yāḳūt, iii, 155) is probably also to be sought near al-Maṣṣīṣa. A pass called Thaniyyat al-ᶜUḳāb, to be distinguished from that of the same name near Damascus, was in the region of al-Maṣṣīṣa (Yāḳūt, i, 936; *Marāṣid*, i, 230). Even the remote fortress of Samālū (on its site cf. Tomaschek, in *Festschrift f. H. Kiepert*, 144) was sometimes reckoned in the Syrian *thughūr* and located near al-Maṣṣīṣa and al-Ṭarsūs (al-Balādhurī, 170: Dhamālū; Yāḳūt, iii, 416;

Marāṣid, ii, 167; Byzantine τό κάστρον Σημαλοῦος), al-Ṣafṣāf on the present Sügüdlī-ṣū (*ZDMG*, xi, 180; Reiske on Abu 'l-Fidā', *Annal.*, ii, 649, n. 76, according to Ḥadjdjī Khalīfa: "Hiṣn Ṣafṣāf, that is Sögüd") is also reckoned by Yāḳūt (iii, 401) to the marches of al-Maṣṣīṣa. Not far from the town was a Syrian monastery, Gawīkāth (mentioned in *ca.* 1200 A.D.: Barhebr., *Chron. eccles.*, ed. Abbeloos-Lamy, i, 624; in Alishan, *Sissouan*, 295: Djokhath, probably identical with *Joacheth*). The neighbouring fortress of Adamodana (now Tumlu-Ḳalʿe) and Cumbetefort (*in territorio Meloni*, i.e. of Mlun, Ar.: al-Mallūn) were, according to Wilbrand of Oldenburg (*op. cit.*), in *ca.* 1212 in the possession of the Teutonic Order (*Allemani*). The Venetians had a church in al-Maṣṣīṣa (*Gestes des Chiprois*, in *Doc. arm.*, ii, 831). Armenian authors mention there the churches of St. Sarkis, Thoros and Stephan (Alishan, 288-9).

The present Misis is a large village or small town whose population was, according to the 1950 census, 1,177. A stone bridge with nine arches (in Baedeker, *Konstantinopel und Kleinasien*, 1914, 303, wrongly: "five-arched"), the foundations of which are in part ancient (picture in Alishan, *Sissouan*, 289; Lohmann, *Im Kloster zu Sis*, 15), leads to the left bank of the Djayḥān where pieces of walls and inscriptions still mark the site of the ancient Mopsuestia. Here lay the mediaeval Kafarbayya; while this form is the one in general use in Arabic texts and in modern authors, Ḥādjdjī Khalīfa (*Djihān-numā*, Constantinople 1145/1732, 602) has Kafarbinā (Taeschner, *op. cit.*, 145, 1), as Langlois (*Voyage*, 462) and others apparently heard it on the spot. The name is unknown there now (Heberdey-Wilhelm, *Denkschr. Ak. Wien*, xliv, part vi, 11-12; the Turkish General Staff map in the German version of July 1918, Adana Sheet, calls the two halves of the town "Misis Nahijesi" and "Huranije"). According to Ibn al-Shiḥna, 179, Kafarbayya was also called "Little Baghdād".

Misis lies where the river emerges from a gorge with walls of yellow loess at which the last foothills of the highlands between the Sayḥān and Djayḥān in the north-west and the Djabal Nūr (Nur Dagh, 2,200 feet; picture in Alishān, 284), a part of the Djabal Miṣṣīṣ (*Stadiasm. mar. magn.*: Πάριον ὄρος), in the south-east meet. This ridge, which takes its name from the town, lying in the centre of the Cilician plain on the left bank of the lower Djayḥān and linked up with the Amanus in the east, is celebrated, particularly in the Djabal Nūr, for its rich flora, which was studied by the Austrian Theodor Kotschy on 24-6 April 1859. On account of its medicinal herbs, Ibn al-Rūmiyya in his commentary on the book of Dioscurides says that many writers took al-Maṣṣīṣa to be the city of the wise Hippocrates (Ibuḳrāt) who, however, according to others, belonged to Ḥimṣ (Mufaḍḍal b. Abi 'l-Faḍā'il, in *Patrol. Orient.*, xiv, 393; Ibn al-Shiḥna, 180).

Near the mouth of the Djayḥān, which at one time was navigable for small ships up to al-Maṣṣīṣa, lay al-Mallūn, the site of which is not known (Μαλλός; now rather Bebeli than Ḳaraṭash; cf. R. Kiepert, *Form. orb. antiqu.*, viii, text, 19a). The Frankish writers also speak of a *portus de Mamistra* (Raimundus de Aigulers, *Historia Francor. qui ceperunt Iherusalem*, c, xi; cf. *Doc. arm.*, i, p. xlvi, n. 1), probably on the *fauces fluminis Malmistrae*, where al-Idrīsī mentions the place al-Buṣā (*ZDPV*, viii, 141; Tomaschek, *SB Ak. Wien*, cxxiv [1891], fig. viii, 69, writes al-Būṣā).

Bibliography: Khwārazmī, *Kitāb Ṣūrat al-arḍ*, ed. von Mžik, in *Bibl. arab. Histor. u. Geogr.*, iii, Leipzig 1926, no. 275; Battānī, *al-Zīdj*, ed. Nallino, ii, 173; iii, 237, no. 121; Iṣṭakhrī, 63; Ibn Ḥawḳal, 122; Muḳaddasī, 22, 35; Ibn al-Faḳīh, 7, 25, 112, 113, 116, 118, 123, 295, 300; Ibn Khurradādhbih, 99, 108, 170, 173, 177; Ḳudāma, 229, 253, 258; Ibn Rusta, 83, 91, 97, 107; Yaʿḳūbī, *Buldān*, 238, 362; Masʿūdī, *Tanbīh*, 58, 152; idem, *Murūdj*, viii, 295 = § 3449; Hamdānī, *Ṣifat Djazīrat al-ʿArab*, ed. Müller, i, 2; Idrīsī, ed. Gildemeister, in *ZDPV*, viii, 24; Dimashḳī, ed. Mehren, 214; Abu 'l-Fidā', ed. Reinaud, 251; Balādhūrī, *Futūḥ*, 165-6. 168; Ibn al-Athīr, *Kāmil*, indices, ii, 809; Ṭabarī, indices, 778; Yaʿḳūbī, *Ta'rīkh*, ii, 321, 337, 466, 541; Yāḳūt, *Muʿdjam*, ii, 82, iv, 287, 558, 579; Safī al-Dīn, *Maraṣid al-iṭṭilāʿ*, ed. Juynboll, i, 255, ii, 502, iii, 112, 124; Ḥamd Allāh al-Mustawfī, *Nuzhat al-ḳulub*, ed. Le Strange, 209, tr. 201; al-Maḳrīzī, *Hist. d. Sult. Mamlouks de l'Égypte*, ed. Quatremère, i/2, Paris 1840, 123, 124, 154; ii/1, Paris 1842, 260; Ḳalḳashandī, *Ṣubḥ al-aʿshā'*, iii, 237, iv, 77, 82, 134, tr. in Gaudefroy-Demombynes, *La Syrie à l'époque des Mamelouks*, Paris 1923, p. cvi, 9, 19, 100; Ibn al-Shiḥna, *al-Durr al-muntakhab fī ta'rīkh Ḥalab*, ed. Sarkīs, Beirut 1909, 178-81, cf. index, 292; Le Strange, *Palestine under the Moslems*, 26-7, 37-8, 62-3, 78, 82, 505; idem, *Lands*, 128, 130-2, 141; *RHC*, *Doc. armén.*, i, index, 824; K. Ritter, *Erdkunde*, xix, Berlin 1859, 95-115 (the older travellers are given there); Saint Martin, *Mémoir hist. et géorgr. sur l'Armén.*, i, Paris 1818, 199 (according to P. Čʿamčʿian, *Armen. Gesch.*, ii, 995, iii, 50, 157, 335); W. M. Leake, *Journal of a tour in Asia Minor*, London 1824, 217; W. B. Barker, *Lares and Penates*, London 1853, 34, n. 2, 111; J. von Hammer, *Gesch. der Ilchane*, i, Darmstadt 1842, 291; V. Langlois, *Voyage en Cilicie*, *Mopsueste*, in *Rev. Arch.* xii (1855), 410-20; F. X. Schaffer, *Cilicia*, in *Peterm. Mitteil.*, Erg.-Heft, cxli, 40; C. Favre and B. Mandrot, in *Bulletin de la Société de Géographie* (Jan.-Feb. 1878), and in *Globus*, xxxiv (1878), 236; W. R. Ramsay, *Histor. geogr. of Asia Minor*, London 1890, 385 and index, 483; W. Tomaschek, in *SB Ak. Wien* (1891), part viii, 68-71, 76; V. Cuinet, *La Turquie d'Asie*, ii, Paris 1891, 42-3; Heberdey-Wilhelm, in *Denkschr. Ak. Wien*, xliv (1896), part vi, 11-12; Łevond Alishan, *Sissouan ou l'Arméno-Cilicie*, Venice 1899; E. Lohmann, *Im Kloster zu Sis*, Striegau 1901, 3, 15, 31; A. Janke, *Auf Alexanders d. Gr. Pfaden*, Berlin 1904, 76; G. Cousin, *Kyros le Jeune en Asie Mineure*, Nancy 1904, 277-8, 436-8; G. L. Bell, in *Rev. Arch.*, Serie IV, vol. vii (1906), 386; F. Taeschner, *Das anatolische Wetenetz nach osmanischen Quellen*, i (Türk. Bibliothek, xxii), 1924, 102, 145, 151, ii (*ibid.*, xxiii), 1926, 30; idem, *al-ʿUmarī's Bericht über Anatolien in seinem Werke Masālik al-abṣār fī mamālik al-amṣār*, i, Leipzig 1929, 66; E. Honigmann, *Die Ostgrenze des byzantinischen Reiches von 363 bis 1071*, Brussels 1935, index s.v. *Mopsuhesia*.

(E. HONIGMANN)

MASTŪDJ, village, fort, and district in the upper Yārkhūn valley formerly included in the Dīr, Swāt and Čitrāl Political Agency of the North-West Frontier Province of British India and now in Pakistan. It apparently formed part of the ancient territory of Syāmāka (Sylvain Lévi, in *JA*, ser. 11, vol. v, 76; and H. Lüders, *Weitere Beiträge zur Geschichte und Geographie von Ostturkestan*, 1930, 29 ff.). Stein identifies Mastūdj with the territory of Čü-wei or Shang-mi which was visited by the Chinese pilgrim Wu-k'ung in the 8th century A.D. (*Ancient Khotan*, Oxford 1907, i, 15-16, *Serindia*, i, 18). An inscription discovered at Barenis points to the fact that Mastūdj was included in the dominions of the Hindū<u>sh</u>āhiyya dynasty of Wayhind [see HINDŪ-<u>SH</u>ĀHĪS]. The village of Mastū<u>dj</u> lies at an altitude of 7,800 feet, and is 71 miles north-east of Čitrāl town and to the west of Gilgit [*q.v.* in Suppl.].

The history of Mastū<u>dj</u> is closely connected with that of Čitrāl [*q.v.*]. British relations with these two states arose as a result of their relations with Ka<u>sh</u>mīr, which state recognised British suzerainty in the year 1846. During the viceroyalty of Lord Lytton, it was deemed expedient, in view of Russian military activities in Central Asia, to obtain a more effective control over the passes of the Hindū Kū<u>sh</u>. With this objects in view, the Māharā<u>dj</u>a of Ka<u>sh</u>mīr was encouraged to extend his authority by means of peaceful penetration over Čitrāl, Mastū<u>dj</u> and Yāsīn. (The fullest account of early British relations with these states is to be found in Foreign Office mss. no. 65, 1062.) After the introduction of Lord Curzon's tribal militia scheme, Mastū<u>dj</u> became the headquarters of the Čitrālī irregulars.

Bibliography: J. Biddulph, *Tribes of the Hindoo Koosh*, Calcutta 1880; *Public Record Office*, London, Foreign Office mss. no. 65, 1062; Sir Aurel Stein, *Serindia*, Oxford 1921, i, and iii, appendix C; C. Collin Davies, *The problem of the North-West Frontier 1890-1908*², London 1975, 80, 103; D. Dichter, *The North-West Frontier of Pakistan, a study in regional geography*, Oxford 1967, 28-9, 42.

(C. COLLIN DAVIES*)

MASᶜŪD B. MAḤMŪD, ABŪ SAᶜĪD, <u>SH</u>IHĀB AL-DAWLA, <u>DJ</u>AMĀL AL-MILLA, etc., sultan of the <u>Gh</u>aznawid [*q.v.*] dynasty, reigned 421-32/1030-40.

The eldest son of the great Maḥmūd b. Sebüktigin [*q.v.*], he was born in 388/998. In 406/1015-16, as *walī ᶜahd* or heir apparent, he was made governor of Harāt and in 411/1020 led an expedition into the still-pagan enclave of <u>Gh</u>ūr [*q.v.*] in central Af<u>gh</u>ānistān. When in 420/1029 Maḥmūd annexed the northern Būyid amirate of Ray and <u>Dj</u>ibāl and attacked the Kākūyids [*q.v.*] of Iṣfahān and Hama<u>dh</u>ān, Masᶜūd was placed in charge of these operations in western Persia.

Shortly before his death, Maḥmūd had changed his mind and made another son, Abū Aḥmad Muḥammad, his heir, despite the latter's lack of experience as compared with Masᶜūd. When Maḥmūd died in Rabīᶜ II 421/April 1030, Muḥammad accordingly succeeded in <u>Gh</u>azna, but was unable to retain support there when Masᶜūd marched eastwards with his army, and later that summer, Muḥammad was deposed, sent into captivity and succeeded by Masᶜūd as sultan in <u>Gh</u>azna (<u>Sh</u>awwāl 421/October 1030), receiving caliphal confirmation and a grant of fresh *alḳāb* or honorific titles from Ba<u>gh</u>dād.

Masᶜūd's aim was doubtless to carry on his father's tradition of military conquest, but he was in fact less able than Maḥmūd and faced problems which demanded qualities of skill and foresight which he did not possess. Masᶜūd in 422/1031 successfully intervened in a succession dispute in the client state of Makrān [*q.v.*], and in 426/1035 asserted his authority in Gurgān and Ṭabaristān, where the local ruler Abū Kālī<u>dj</u>ār was two years in arrears with tribute. In India, raids were made into Ka<u>sh</u>mīr (424/1032-3), but policy regarding India in the middle years of his reign was taken up with lengthy operations against the rebellious commander of the army of India at Lahore, the Turkish officer Aḥmad Inaltigin, against whom Masᶜūd appointed as his commander the Hindu Tilak (424-6/1033-5). When order was restored in the Pan<u>dj</u>āb, the sultan in 427/1036 led a successful expedition against Hānsī, leaving his son Ma<u>dj</u>dūd as governor in the Pan<u>dj</u>āb.

This concentration on India meant that Masᶜūd could not give adequate attention to the western parts of the empire, where the situation grew increasingly menacing. On the death in 423/1032 of the <u>Gh</u>aznawid governor in <u>Kh</u>ʷārazm, the <u>Kh</u>ʷārazm-<u>Sh</u>āh Altunta<u>sh</u> [*q.v.*], that distant province, which had been annexed by Maḥmūd less than twenty years before, fell away from <u>Gh</u>aznawid control under less amenable governors there. The loss of this outpost, guarding approaches from the steppes to northeastern Persia, hampered Masᶜūd in dealing with the incursions of the Turkmens led by the Sal<u>dj</u>ūḳ family, who had been repulsed from Harāt and Farāwa early in the reign but who were by 425/1033-4 making systematic raids into <u>Kh</u>urāsān. Although the <u>Gh</u>aznawid armies were better armed, they lacked the mobility of the Turkmen cavalrymen, who were able to defeat a <u>Gh</u>aznawid army under the Ḥā<u>dj</u>ib Begto<u>gh</u>dī in 426/1035, and then temporarily to occupy Bal<u>kh</u> and Ni<u>sh</u>āpūr whilst Masᶜūd was involved in India (429-31/1038-9). The sultan mounted a final effort against the Sal<u>dj</u>ūḳs, but in the desert, en route for Marw, was decisively defeated at Dandānḳān [*q.v.* in Suppl.] (Ramaḍān 431/May 1040).

Masᶜūd's prestige and military reputation were now shattered. Fearing that even eastern Af<u>gh</u>ānistān and <u>Gh</u>azna might fall to the Sal<u>dj</u>ūḳs, he resolved to leave for India, but after crossing the Indus his army rebelled at the *ribāṭ* of Mārīkala, deposed him and soon afterwards killed him, having set up his brother Muḥammad again for a brief second reign (Rabīᶜ II 432/December 1040), before Masūd's son Mawdūd [*q.v.*] was able to avenge his father.

The verdict of contemporaries such as the official Abu 'l-Faḍl Bayhaḳī [*q.v.*] was that Masᶜūd was inferior in capability and determination to his father; his advisers complained of this capriciousness and lack of sound judgement. But in retrospect, one may well conclude that the <u>Gh</u>aznawid empire had reached a high point by the end of Maḥmūd's reign which no successor of his, however competent, could have sustained.

Bibliography: The primary sources are copious; they include Gardīzī, Bayhaḳī, Ibn Bābā al-Ḳā<u>sh</u>ānī, Ibn al-A<u>th</u>īr, <u>Dj</u>ūz<u>dj</u>ānī and Sayf al-Dīn Faḍlī ᶜUḳaylī's *Ā<u>th</u>ār al-wuzarāʾ*. Of secondary sources, see W. Barthold, *Turkestan down to the Mongol invasion*, London 1928, 293-303; M. Nāẓim, *The life and times of Sulṭān Maḥmūd of <u>Gh</u>azna*, Cambridge 1931, index s.v.; R. Gelpke, *Sulṭān Masᶜūd I. von Gazna. Die drei ersten Jahre seiner Herrschaft (421/1030-424/1033)*, Munich 1957; C. E. Bosworth, *The Ghaznavids, their empire in Afghanistan and eastern Iran 994-1040*, Edinburgh 1963, index s.v.; idem, *The later Ghaznavids, splendour and decay. The dynasty in Afghanistan and northern India 1040-1186*, Edinburgh 1977, 6-20; idem, arts. on the Ghaznavids in *The medieval history of Iran, Afghanistan and Central Asia*, London 1977, index s.v.

(C. E. BOSWORTH)

MASᶜŪD B. MAWDŪD B. ZANGĪ, ᶜIZZ AL-DĪN, fifth Zangid Atābak of al-Mawṣil (Mosul) (576-89/1180-93).

Masᶜūd's public career was entangled from beginning to end with that of his great adversary Ṣalāḥ al-Dīn, and it is easy to regard him as no more than a troublesome shadow in the latter's path. But Masᶜūd had a positive policy of his own—to maintain, under his leadership, the legacy of Zangī and Nūr al-Dīn in

North Syria and the Djazīra. Though he had neither the material resources nor the political imagination to block Ṣalāḥ al-Dīn's ambitions altogether, he nevertheless proved a tenacious opponent, and in the end was able to retain in the hands of his family al-Mawṣil and the core districts of Diyār Rabīᶜa. We should also note that he seems to have enjoyed the active support of his subjects, whose energy and stubbornness were decisive factors in the defence of al-Mawṣil in 581/1185.

Like every other Syro-Djazīran prince of the 6th/12th century, Masᶜūd operated within the framework of a family confederation. Once he came to the throne of al-Mawṣil, he was the senior member of a group of Zangid princes, but he had little capacity to intervene in the affairs of their appanages or to compel them to accept his leadership. At the time of his accession in 576/1180, Ḥalab (Aleppo) was held by his cousin al-Ṣāliḥ Ismāᶜīl b. Nūr al-Dīn Maḥmūd; Djazīrat Ibn ᶜUmar by his nephew Muᶜizz al-Dīn Sandjar Shāh b. Sayf al-Dīn Ghāzī II; and Sindjār by his younger brother ᶜImād al-Dīn Zangī II. But with Ṣalāḥ al-Dīn's occupation of Aleppo (Ṣafar 579/June 1183), Zangid rule was restricted to the principalities of al-Mawṣil (always the principal one), Sindjār and Djazīrat Ibn ᶜUmar. These three towns remained in fact the main elements of the Zangid conferation down to its end in the early 7th/13th century. As always in such political formations, the princes were seldom united among themselves, and Ṣalāḥ al-Dīn played with great skill on the petty ambitions of Sandjar Shāh and ᶜImād al-Dīn Zangī II. On the other side, Masᶜūd hoped to establish a close supervision over his relatives, but Ṣalāḥ al-Dīn's presence prevented that.

Masᶜūd began his career in the service of his older brother, Sayf al-Dīn Ghāzī II (565-76/1170-80). He was commander of al-Mawṣil's contingent at the disastrous battle of Ḳurūn Ḥamāt (Ramaḍān 570/April 1175), which marked Ṣalāḥ al-Dīn's first great military triumph in Syria, and was likewise present at the equally unfortunate Tall al-Sulṭān the following year, though on this occasion his brother Ghāzī was in command.

After this we hear nothing of Masᶜūd until the death of Ghāzī (Ṣafar 576/June 1180). Ghāzī had intended to name his twelve-year-old son Sandjar Shāh to succeed him, but was persuaded by the *amīr* Mudjāhid al-Dīn Ḳāymāz—the éminence grise of Zangid politics throughout this period—to assign al-Mawṣil to his brother Masūd and to compensate Sandjar Shāh with Djazīrat Ibn ᶜUmar. In spite of these beginnings, Masᶜūd's succession went without incident and was never seriously challenged throughout his reign.

Masᶜūd now had the primary responsibility for checking Ṣalāḥ al-Dīn's evident ambitions, and the first six years of his reign were almost entirely taken up with this problem. The first crisis came with the death of al-Ṣāliḥ Ismāᶜīl of Aleppo (Radjab 577/December 1181). Ismāᶜīl bequeathed Aleppo to his cousin Masᶜūd as the only Zangid prince with sufficient resources to hold the city. Masūd in fact did occupy Aleppo during the winter of 577/1182. But he soon negotiated an exchange of Aleppo for Sindjār with his younger brother ᶜImād al-Dīn Zangī II. Ibn al-Athīr states that the reason was Zangī's threat to turn Sindjār over to Ṣalāḥ al-Dīn; equally a factor, no doubt, was Masᶜūd's desire to consolidate his territories around al-Mawṣil. The exchange was consummated in Muḥarram 578/May 1182, and at once provoked Ṣalāḥ al-Dīn's great Syro-Djazīran campaign of the same year. Al-Mawṣil was subjected to a short siege in the autumn of 578/1182, but far more important was Ṣalāḥ al-Dīn's capture of a string of major Djazīran towns, including Sindjār itself. Masᶜūd's effort to assemble a defensive alliance (including Ḳuṭb al-Dīn Il-Ghāzī of Mārdīn and the Shāh-Arman of Khilāṭ) failed, and in the spring of 579/1183 Ṣalāḥ al-Dīn captured Āmid and Aleppo. The latter city was taken through negotiations with Zangī, and this prince was compensated with the restoration of his old seat of Sindjār together with several other towns. Masᶜūd's strategy had thus utterly failed; he was now isolated, while Ṣalāḥ al-Dīn had gained a powerful new client in ᶜImād al-Dīn Zangī II. Worse, a moment of turbulence in the palace politics of al-Mawṣil caused Masᶜūd to lose control of a traditional client-state in Irbil, whose ruler also went over to Ṣalāḥ al-Dīn.

At this juncture, Masᶜūd sought the support of the powerful Atābak of al-Djibāl and Ādharbāydjān, Pahlawān Muḥammad b. Eldigüz [see ILDEÑIZIDS]. Pahlawān never really intervened effectively in the region, but the possibility that he might seems to have induced a certain caution in Ṣalāḥ al-Dīn's policy until his death early in 582/1186.

In the spring of 581/1185, Ṣalāḥ al-Dīn launched his last offensive in the Djazīra; among his allies this time was Sandjar Shāh of Djazīrat Ibn ᶜUmar. He was hoping for an easy victory over a presumably demoralised Masᶜūd, but it did not happen. The garrison and townspeople of al-Mawṣil put up a spirited defence, and the caliph's envoys made it quite clear that Ṣalāḥ al-Dīn's venture did not enjoy the support of Baghdād. Finally, a grave illness forced Ṣalāḥ al-Dīn to withdraw to Ḥarrān in late autumn, and negotiations throughout the winter at length led to a treaty in Dhu 'l-Ḥidjdja 581/March 1186. Masᶜūd would retain al-Mawṣil and would have full autonomy in internal affairs, but he would recognise Ṣalāḥ al-Dīn's supremacy in the *khuṭba* and *sikka* and would supply him with military aid as demanded. These terms did in fact govern relations between the two princes for the rest of their lives. Masᶜūd's support to Ṣalāḥ al-Dīn during the reconquest and the Third Crusdade even earned for him permission to attack his troublesome nephew Sandjar Shāh in Djazīrat Ibn ᶜUmar in 587/1191. He did not succeed in taking the city, but did compel Sandjar Shāh to concede him half his lands.

With Ṣalāḥ al-Dīn's death (Ṣafar 589/March 1193), Masᶜūd hoped to recoup the fortunes of his house. Joining forces with Zangī of Sindjār, he moved to occupy as much of the Djazīra as possible. But before any major results could be achieved, Masᶜūd fell ill and returned to al-Mawṣil. Meantime, Ayyūbid forces under al-ᶜĀdil were able to compel the hapless Zangids to make a quick peace before they suffered irreparable territorial losses. After an illness of some two months, Masᶜūd died on 29 Shaᶜbān 589/30 August 1193. He left al-Mawṣil to his son Nūr al-Dīn Arslān Shāh (d. 607/1211), who would be the last effective ruler among the Zangid Atābaks of al-Mawṣil.

Bibliography: The Arabic sources for ᶜIzz al-Dīn Masᶜūd are essentially those for Ṣalāḥ al-Dīn. Of particular importance are Ibn al-Athīr, *Atabegs*, ed. Ṭulaymāt, Cairo 1963, and with a French translation by Barbier de Meynard in *RHC*, *historiens orientaux*, ii, 1876; *idem*, *al-Kāmil*, xi-xii, *passim*; Ibn Khallikān, *Wayfayāt al-aᶜyān*, ed. I. ᶜAbbās, Beirut 1972, nos. 236, 521, 721 (Ibn Khallikān follows Ibn al-Athīr closely but adds some fresh details). Modern works: the Zangid background is given in N. Elisséeff, *Nūr al-dīn*, 3 vols., Damascus 1967; of the many works on Ṣalāḥ al-Dīn, the most useful are A. Ehrenkreutz, *Saladin*, Albany, N.Y. 1972, and M. C. Lyons and D. E. P. Jackson, *Saladin*, Cambridge 1982. On the later Zangids, see R. S. Humphreys, *From Saladin to the Mongols*, Albany 1977, *passim*. There are no specialised monographs or articles on Masᶜūd.

(R. Stephen Humphreys)

MASᶜŪD b. MUḤAMMAD b. MALIK-SHAH, Abu 'l-Fatḥ Ghiyāth al-Dunyā wa 'l-Din, Saldjūḳ sultan in ᶜIrāḳ and western Persia 529-47/1134-52.

Like the other sons of Muḥammad b. Malik-Shah [*q.v.*], Masᶜūd was entrusted as a child to the tutelage of Turkish Atabegs [see atabak], latterly with Ay-Aba Djuyūsh Beg acting thus, and given the appanage of Ādharbāydjān and al-Djazīra; at Djuyūsh Beg's prompting, Masᶜūd unsuccessfully rebelled in 514/1120 at the age of 12 against his elder brother Sultan Maḥmūd b. Malik-Shāh [*q.v.*], but was pardoned.

When Maḥmūd died in 525/1131, a period of confusion ensued, during which various Saldjūḳ princes contended for power: Maḥmūd's son Dāwūd, and his brothers Masᶜūd (with a power base in ᶜIrāḳ), Saldjūḳ-Shāh (in Fārs and Khūzistān) and Ṭoghrïl (the preferred candidate of the ruler in the east, Sandjar [*q.v.*]). After complex military operations and several changes of fortune, Ṭoghrïl secured the throne, but died in 529/1134 after a reign of only two years, and Masᶜūd was then proclaimed sultan by the *amīrs* of ᶜIrāḳ.

Masᶜūd now began a reign of 20 years, the longest of any sultan since Malik-Shāh's day, relying for his vizier first of all on Anūshirwān b. Khālid [*q.v.*], then on ᶜImād al-Dīn Darguzīnī and then on the former treasurer Kamāl al-Dīn Muḥammad. Masᶜūd's effective power was confined to central ᶜIrāḳ and Djibāl, and for many years, his nephew Dāwūd, installed in Ādharbāydjān, remained a potential rival. Then after Dāwūd's death in 538/1143-4, northwestern Persia was in the hands of powerful and ambitious Turkish *amīrs*, by the end of Masᶜūd's reign, in those of Eldigüz or Ildeñiz [*q.v.*] of Arrān and most of Ādharbāydjān, Atabeg of Arslan b. Ṭoghrïl (the later sultan), and Aḳ Sunḳur Aḥmadīlī of Marāgha, both of whom were to found Atabeg lines in the region [see aḥmadilīs and ildeñizids]. Fārs was under the control of Masᶜūd's enemy, the *amīr* Boz-aba, until the sultan defeated and killed him in 542/1147-8, having before his death espoused the cause of Maḥmūd b. Muḥammad's two sons Muḥammad [*q.v.*] and Malik-Shāh [see malik-shāh. 3].

Within ᶜIrāḳ, Masᶜūd asserted his authority at the outset by deposing the ᶜAbbāsid caliph al-Rāshid [*q.v.*] in 530/1130 after disputes over the caliph's non-payment of tribute due to the Saldjūḳ. This marked the apogee of the sultan's influence in ᶜIrāḳ, for the new caliph al-Muḳtafī [*q.v.*] gradually proved to be a much more powerful and effective force in Baghdād. Masᶜūd, meanwhile, had over the next years to deal with various hostile coalitions involving at times the caliph, the sons of the Mazyadid of Ḥilla Dubays, the Turkish *amīr* of Mawṣil Zangī b. Aḳ Sunḳur, and his own brothers and their Atabeg backers. Despite some successes, the combined strength of the Turkish *amīrs* restricted his freedom of action. They compelled him in 533/1139 to dismiss his vizier Kamāl al-Dīn Muḥammad. In the latter part of his reign, he fell more and more under their control, with much of the land in his dominions appropriated by the *amīrs* as *iḳṭāᶜ*s, thus reducing the sphere of his direct control and consequently his financial resources. He was now increasingly forced to accept nominees of the *amīrs* for the vizierate and other high offices of state. Masᶜūd defeated a coalition of discontented *amīrs* in 542/1147 and killed a major thorn in his flesh, Boz-aba; but jealousy of the sultan's favourite, the *amīr* Khāṣṣ Beg Arslan, provoked further warfare in the next year, with the rebel group endeavouring, unsuccessfully, to place Malik-Shāh b. Maḥmūd on the throne in Baghdād. Masᶜūd later gave him one of his daughters in marriage and made him his heir, and when Masᶜūd died at Hamadhān on 11 Djumādā 547/13 September 1152, Malik-Shāh succeeded briefly to power as the protégé of Khāṣṣ Beg. Ibn al-Athīr regards the fortunes of the Saldjūḳ dynasty as going into steep decline on Masᶜūd's death.

Bibliography: 1. Sources: See the general chronicles, Ibn al-Athīr, Ibn al-Djawzī and Sibṭ Ibn al-Djawzī *sub annis*; and of the specifically Saldjūḳ sources, Bundārī, *Zubdat al-nuṣra*, 163-6, 172-227; Rāwandī, *Rāḥat al-ṣudūr*, 234-49; Ṣadr al-dīn Ḥusaynī, *Akhbār al-dawla al-saldjūḳiyya*, 106-27, Eng. tr. Qibla Ayaz, *An unexploited source for the history of the Saljūqs...*, Edinburgh Univ. Ph.D. thesis, 1985, unpubl., 290-319; Ẓahīr al-Dīn Nīshāpūrī, *Saldjūḳ-nāma*, 55-65; Yazdī, *ᶜUrāḍa*, 117-28; a brief biography in Ibn Khallikān, ed. Iḥsān ᶜAbbās, v, 200-2, no. 720, tr. de Slane, iii, 355-6.

2. Studies. See M. A. Köymen, *Büyük Selçuklu imparatorluğu tarihi. ii. İkinci imparatorluk devri*, Ankara 1954, 250-305; Bosworth, in *Cambridge hist. of Iran*, v, 124-34; C. L. Klausner, *The Seljuk vezirate*, Cambridge, Mass. 1973, index.

(C. E. Bosworth)

MASᶜŪD BEG, minister in Central Asia of the Mongol *Khāns* in the 13th century A.D.

Soon after 1238, in the reign of the Great Khān Ögedey (1227-41), parts of Transoxania and Mogholistān [*q.v.*] (the region of the steppes to the north of Transoxania) were ceded to Čaghatay as an *indjü* or appanage [see čaghatay khān and mā warā' al-nahr. 2. History]. Masᶜūd Beg's father Maḥmūd Yalawač [*q.v.*] was transferred from his governorship of the sedentary population of Transoxania and Mogholistān to China, and the son then appointed to succeed him there. Indeed, according to Rashīd al-Dīn, tr. J. A. Boyle, *The successors of Genghis Khan*, New York and London 1972, 94, cf. 183, 218, Masᶜūd Beg administered the affairs of the entire sedentary population, sc. all but the nomadic Turks and Mongols, throughout Inner Asia from Khʷārazm to Kāshgharia and Uyghuria, Muslims and non-Muslims alike. Djuwaynī praises him for his just rule over the Muslims of Transoxania. His benefactions included such buildings as the Khāniyya *madrasa* (built by him with money given by the Christian Queen Sorḳotani, widow of Toluy and mother of Möngke Khān and Hülegu) and the Masᶜūdiyya *madrasa*, both situated near the Rīgistān of Bukhārā, and also, it seems, the Masᶜūdiyya *madrasa* in Kāshghar (Djuwaynī-Boyle, i, 108).

Masᶜūd Beg remained governor of Inner Asia under Möngke and Batu, during the civil strife of Alghu and Berke and after the victory of Ḳaydu over his rivals in 1269, showing remarkable powers of survival. He died in 1289 and was buried in the rebuilt Bukhārā Masᶜūdiyya. He was succeeded in turn as minister to the Khāns by his three sons, the first two under Ḳaydu till the latter's death in 1301, and the third in Kā<u>sh</u><u>gh</u>ar under Ḳaydu's son and successor Čapar.

Bibliography (in addition to references already given): <u>D</u>juwaynī-Boyle, index s.v.; W. Barthold, *Turkestan down to the Mongol invasion*³, London 1968, 469-93 *et passim*; V. Minorsky, *Four studies on the history of Central Asia*, i, Leiden 1962, 46-8, 50.

(C. E. Bosworth)

MASᶜŪD-I SAᶜD-I SALMĀN, eminent Persian poet of the 5th/11th century (*ca.* 440/1046 to *ca.* 515/1121-2) who early and late in his life enjoyed position and fame at the <u>Gh</u>aznawid court, but spent some eighteen years of his maturity in onerous imprisonment. As a poet, he is most famous for the powerful and eloquent laments he wrote from his various places of incarceration [see ḤABSIYYA in Suppl.].

Masᶜūd-i Saᶜd was born in Lahore to a family of means and education. The family's original home was Hamadān, but had been settled in the region long enough for his father to have become a responsible official at court. About Masᶜūd-i Saᶜd's early life no reliable information survives. He makes his first dateable appearance in 460/1076-7 as a panegyrist in the retinue of prince Sayf al-Dawla Maḥmūd, son of the ruling sultan (Ẓahīr al-Dawla Ibrāhīm [see <u>GH</u>AZNAWIDS]), who was appointed governor-general of India in that year. The *ḳaṣīda-yi madīḥa* which Masᶜūd-i Saᶜd composed on that occasion is the work of a mature and accomplished poet. By his own assertion in other poems from about this period, he was also a brave warrior, and a responsible and highly-regarded member of the prince's court. In about his fortieth year, Masᶜūd-i Saᶜd went to <u>Gh</u>azna to reclaim land that had been seized from him by persons unspecified in the sources. While there, he fell under suspicion, and possibly more because of the suspected disloyalty of his patron than of his own, he was imprisoned. This period of imprisonment, which he spent in the fortresses of Sū, Dahak and Nāy, lasted some ten years despite the repeated entreaties of a number of officials friendly to the poet, and the supplications of Masᶜūd-i Saᶜd himself.

He was released early in his reign by sultan Ibrāhīm's successor, ᶜAlāʾ al-Dawla Masᶜūd (III) who also made the poet curator of the royal library. Masᶜūd-i Saᶜd also enjoyed the patronage of Abū Naṣr-i Fārsī, deputy to the current governor of India, ᶜAḍud al-Dawla Shīrzād, and was appointed by him to the governorship of <u>D</u>jālandhar/Čalandhar, a dependency of Lahore. When shortly thereafter Abū Naṣr-i Fārsī was disgraced and fell from favour, his protégé suffered a like fate and was again imprisoned, this time in the Indian fortress of Maran<u>dj</u>, and for a period of eight or more years.

Masᶜūd-i Saᶜd was released from his second and final period of incarceration in *ca.* 500/1106-7, shortly after the opening of the reign of Sultan Masᶜūd's successor, Kamāl al-Dawla <u>Sh</u>īrzād, but he remained in obscurity throughout both his reign and that of his successor, Sulṭān al-Dawla Arslān <u>Sh</u>āh. Only toward the close of his life, with the beginning of the reign of Yamīn al-Dawla Bahrām <u>Sh</u>āh, a notable patron of literature, did the now aged poet once again enjoy the recognition that his poetic talents merited.

Masᶜūd-i Saᶜd was a skilful court panegyrist who continued the style of his eminent predecessors, ᶜUnṣurī, Farru<u>kh</u>ī and Manūčihrī [*q.vv.*]. His work does not reflect either the shift toward mystical subjects nor the more complex metaphorical structure that can be seen in the poetry of his contemporaries Sanāʾī and Azraḳī. His panegyrics have a special interest for the historian because they contain a measure of historical data about a period for which other sources are rare. However, his most enduring contribution as a poet has been his prison poems (*ḥabsiyyāt*), in which, through the skilful deployment of conventional language, he conveys with originality and power the wretchedness of his days. One hears in these poems that intensely personal voice whose lack is so frequently decried in studies of Persian poetry.

Bibliography: The notices of Masᶜūd-i Saᶜd-i salmān in mediaeval *Ta<u>dh</u>kiras* are not to be trusted, and the only reliable source for his biography is his *Dīwān*, which has been capably edited by Ra<u>sh</u>īd Yāsimī, Tehran 1338/1939, and frequently reprinted. Although he boasted of his knowledge of Arabic, no Arabic poetry by him has survived. The best study of his life and work remains that of Mīrzā Muḥammad b. ᶜAbd al-Wahhāb Ḳazwīnī, *Masᶜúd-i Saᶜd-i Salmán. Translated by E. G. Browne*, in *JRAS* (1905), 693-740, and (1906), 11-15. C. E. Bosworth makes a number of comments on the life of Masᶜūd-i Saᶜd and the general literary situation at the <u>Gh</u>aznawid court in his *The Later Ghaznavids, splendour and decay: the dynasty in Afghanistan and northern India 1040-1186*, Edinburgh 1977. There is a lengthy chapter on his imagery in M. <u>Sh</u>afīᶜī-Kadkanī, *Ṣuwar-i <u>kh</u>iyāl dar <u>sh</u>iᶜr-i Fārsī*, Tehran 1350/1971.

(J. W. Clinton)

MASᶜŪD, Sayyid Sālār, called <u>Gh</u>āzī Miyān, a legendary hero and martyr of the original Muslim expansion into the Gangetic plain of India.

He is alleged to have been the son of a sister of Sultan Maḥmūd of <u>Gh</u>azna [*q.v.*], to have been born at A<u>dj</u>mēr [*q.v.*] in 405/1014, and to have been killed in battle against Hindu idolaters, aged 19, in 424/1033. His tomb is on a pre-Muslim sacred site in Bahraič, in the sub-Himalayan plain of northern Uttar Pradesh, and is the centre of a widespread cult. The hero-cult was well-established by the beginning of the 8th/14th century, and is succinctly described by Ibn Baṭṭūṭa. The Sultans Muḥammad b. Tu<u>gh</u>luḳ and Fīrūz <u>Sh</u>āh Tu<u>gh</u>luḳ visited the tomb. The procession of the hero's *nēza* ("lance", a tall tufted pole) was prohibited by Sultan Sikandar Lodī (d. 923/1517) but remains a highlight of the annual festival (cf. similar poles of Lāl Beg of the Čuhṛās, and of <u>Sh</u>āhbāz Ḳalandar at Sehwan). The myth of Sālār Masᶜūd was elaborated in Persian in the early 11th/17th century in the *Mirʾāt-i Masᶜūdī*, a heroic romance which owes something to the *Dāstān-i Amīr Ḥamza* though it strives for a greater air of historical authenticity. <u>Gh</u>āzī Miyān's cult extends to Bengal and the Pan<u>dj</u>ab, probably sometimes conflated with the cult of other local Muslim <u>*sh*</u>*ahīds*. The main *ᶜurs* or death anniversary is celebrated on the first Sunday of the solar month of <u>D</u>jyes<u>h</u>t'ha/<u>D</u>jet'h, between 14 and 21 May, but an *ᶜurs* is also mentioned on the significant date of 11 Muḥarram. The martyr-cult is combined with a fertility-cult (cf. the secondary sexual symbolism of the pole, and the "mystic-marriage" implication of *ᶜurs*). Legends and songs of the marriage of <u>Gh</u>āzī Miyān before his last battle are widely distributed and were sung at Muslim weddings. At an extreme popular level a conflation may occur (e.g. in west Nepal), with the celebration of the martyrdom of Ḥusayn at Karbalā, with the bridegroom figure of Ḳāsim b. Ḥasan, lamented in Indian *mar<u>th</u>iyas*. The *ᶜurs* of <u>Gh</u>āzī Miyān is celebrated by lower-class Hindus as well as Muslims. Mendicant followers of <u>Gh</u>āzī Miyān carry a *daff* (tambourine) and are known as *dafāli faḳīrs*.

Bibliography: Amīr <u>Kh</u>usraw Dihlavī, *Iᶜ<u>dj</u>āz-i <u>Kh</u>usravī*, Lucknow 1872, i, 155; Ibn Baṭṭūṭa,

Riḥla, iii, 155, tr. M. Husain, Baroda 1953, 110; Baranī, *Ta'rīkh-i Fīrūzshāhī*, Calcutta 1862, 491; ᶜAfīf, *Ta'rīkh-i Fīrūzshāhī*, Calcutta 1891, 372; ᶜAbd Allāh, *Ta'rīkh-i Dāw'ūdī*, Aligarh 1954, 38; ᶜAbd al-Raḥmān Čishtī, *Mir'āt-i Masᶜūdī*, Storey no. 1329(7), extracts tr. in Elliot and Dowson, *History of India*, ii, 513-49; Djaᶜfar Sharīf, tr. G. A. Herklots, ed. W. Crooke, *Islam in India*, London 1921, 67, 141; R. C. Temple, *Legends of the Panjâb*, Bombay-London (1884), i, 98-120; J. A. Subhan, *Sufism: its saints and shrines*, Lucknow 1969, 123-6; M. Gaborieau, *Légende et culte du saint musulman Ghâzi' Miyā au Népal occidental et en Inde du nord*, in *Objets et Mondes*, xv/3 (Autumn 1975) 289-318, with further bibl. (S. Digby)

al-**MASᶜŪDĪ**, Abu 'l-Ḥasan ᶜAlī b. al-Ḥusayn, Arab writer whose activity, in the words of Brockelmann (in *EI*[1], s.v.) "has been undertaken outside the well-trodden paths of professional scholarship", with the result that he has been rather neglected by biographers and copyists and that a normally well-informed writer like Ibn al-Nadīm, who has obviously not read his works, takes him (*Fihrist*, 154) for a Maghribī and devotes to him only a short, moreover probably truncated, article. In fact, the only reliable account which is available concerning the biography of this eminent individual must be drawn from his two surviving works, the *Murūdj al-dhahab* (abbreviated here as *M*, refering to Pellat's edition-translation) and the *Tanbīh* (ed. De Goeje = *T*).

Al-Masᶜūdī was born in Baghdād (*M*, 987; *T*, 19, 42) into a Kūfan family which traced back its generalogy and connected its *nisba* to the Companion Ibn Masᶜūd [*q.v.*]. He himself does not record his ancestry in entirety, but it could well be as follows (see Ibn Ḥazm, *Djamharat ansāb al-ᶜArab*, ed. Cairo 1962, 197; Ibn Khaldūn, *ᶜIbar*, ii, 319): ᶜAlī b. al-Ḥusayn b. ᶜAlī b. ᶜAbd Allāh (*M*, § 522) b. Zayd b. ᶜUtba b. ᶜAbd al-Raḥmān b. ᶜAbd Allāh b. Masᶜūd (for the rest of the genealogy, see Ibn al-Kalbī-Caskel, *Djamhara*, Tab. 58: Hudhayl, who does not however allot to ᶜAbd al-Raḥmān a son named ᶜUtba). The date of his birth is unknown; however, if we are to take literally the expression (*ḥaddatha-nā*) preceding the reference (*T*, 254) to Ibrāhīm b. ᶜAbd Allāh al-Kashshī (d. 292/904) or that (*shāhadnā*) which is used (*T*, 396) to introduce a series of authorities which includes al-Nāshi' (d. 293/906 [*q.v.*]), he must have been born no later than some years before 280/893, and not *ca.* 283/896, as is suggested by A. Shboul (*Al-Masᶜūdī and his world*, London 1979, p. xv).

His youth was spent in Baghdād, but he gives no information regarding the development of his studies. From a reading of the *M.* and *T.*, it may however be deduced that he had the opportunity, during the period of his religious, judicial and literary education, to attend classes given by a number of eminent teachers who died in the early years of the 4th century, notably (*T.*, 296) Wakīᶜ (d. 306/918 [*q.v.*]), (*M*, § 2242) al-Faḍl b. al-Ḥubāb (d. 305/917 [*q.v.* in Suppl.]), (*M*, §§ 159, 2282) al-Nawbakhtī (d. at the beginning of the 4th century [*q.v.*]), (*T*, 396) Abū ᶜAlī al-Djubbā'ī (d. 303/915, see al-djubbā'ī), (*M*, § 3382) al-Anbārī (d. 304/916 [*q.v.*]); he may also have been acquainted at this time with: (*T*, 267) al-Ṭabarī (d. 310/923 [*q.v.*]), (*M*, *passim*) al-Zadjdjādj (d. 311/924 [*q.v.*]), (*T*, 396) Abu 'l-Ḳāsim al-Balkhī (d. 319/931, see al-balkhī), (*M*, § 764) Ibn Durayd (d. 321/934 [*q.v.*]), (*T*, 396) al-Ashᶜarī (d. 324/935 [*q.v.*]), (*M*, *passim*) Niftawayh (d. 323/934 [*q.v.*]), and others besides; it is also known that in 306/918 (al-Subkī, *Ṭabaḳāt al-Shāfiᶜiyya*, ii, 307) he was present at the death bed of Ibn Suraydj [*q.v.*]. It would be tedious to list the personalities with whom he associated in the course of his career, but a further exception is to be made in the case of (*M*, § 3382) Djaᶜfar b. Muḥammad b. Ḥamdān al-Mawṣilī (d. 323/934; see Sezgin, *GAS*, ii, 625) and of (*M*, *passim*) Abū Bakr al-Ṣūlī (d. 336/946, see al-ṣūlī), who seem to have played a particularly important role in his life. The scholars and men of letters cited above represent, at the highest level, the principal disciplines cultivated in this period (see, in this context, A. Shboul, *op. laud.*, 29-44; T. Khalidi, *Islamic historiography*, Albany 1975, 148-50; in the encyclopaedic index which follows the new edition of the *Murūdj*, brief biographies of the contemporary personalities mentioned in this work are to be found).

Whatever may have been the interest and the value of the knowledge thus acquired through direct transmission, an echo of which is also to be found in his work, al-Masᶜūdī would never have attained his eminence had he not been endowed with an extraordinary intellectual curiosity which impelled him, on the one hand, to educate himself with books, and, on the other, to enrich his human experience by undertaking long journeys both within and outside the Muslim world. For the composition of his principal surviving work, the *Murūdj*, he had recourse to no fewer than one hundred and sixty-five written sources, including, in addition to Arabic texts, translations of Plato, Aristotle and Ptolemy, as well as Arabic versions of monuments of Pahlavi literature. In one paragraph of the *Tanbīh* (154), he mentions Christian authors with whom he was in the majority of cases personally acquainted, and passes judgment on their works; he seems to have had them make translations of or to explain passages which provided documentation for chapters of his own works (e.g. *M*, §§ 523 ff.), and the transcription into Greek characters of the name Helen (*M*, § 735) is proof of his breath of interest and his curiosity.

The latter are also exhibited in the accounts, unfortunately dispersed, of his travels, a topic which raises the question of his profession, which he does not reveal, and thereby of the resources which enabled him not only to live but furthermore to undertake expensive foreign expeditions. By all appearances, he had no connection with regular commerce and he was neither an official representative nor a religious authority who could depend on hospitality from Muslim communities visited. The hypothesis of A. Miquel (*Géographie humaine*, i, 205-6) according to which he could have been an emissary of the Ismāᶜīlis seems hard to sustain, and ultimately it has to be assumed that this traveller possessed a personal fortune out of which he met the costs of his travels and that he perhaps drew some profits from the occasional commercial venture.

In 300/912, al-Masᶜūdī was still in Baghdād (*M*, § 2161); three years later (303/915), he is found visiting Persia (*T*, 106, 224), then India (*M*, §§ 269, 417-8; *T*, 224); it is hardly probable that he travelled as far as Ceylon and China (*M*, §§ 175, 342) since, when he speaks of these lands, he copies from Abū Zayd or the *Akhbār al-Ṣīn wa 'l-Hind* [*q.v.* in Suppl.]. In 304/916, he returned to his own country by way of ᶜUmān and the island of Ḳanbalū (*M*, § 246). From 306 to 316/918-26 he was travelling around ᶜIrāḳ and Syria (*M*, § 3326) and it was perhaps during this time that he made his way to Arabia (cf. Shboul, *op. laud.*, 8, 12-13). In 320/932 or a little later he visited the provinces of the Caspian and Armenia (*M*, § 494), then, from 330/941 or 331 onward, he resided in Egypt, where, in 332/943, he composed the *Murūdj* (*M*, § 874 and *passim*), also returning to Syria in the same year (*M*, § 220) and visiting Damascus (*T*, 194) and Antioch (*M*, §§ 704-5) in 334/946. Naturally he visited Alexandria (*M*, §§ 679, 841) and Upper Egypt (*M*, §§ 811-18, 822, 893 ff.). It is in Fusṭāṭ that he seems to have spent his last years, reviewing his works and writing some new ones, in particular the *Tanbīh*, completed in 345/956 (*T*, 401), shortly before his death, which came about in Djumādā II 345/September 956. On his travels, see especially Maqbul Ahmad, *Travels of... al-Masʿūdī*, in *IC*, xxviii (1954), 509-21; A. Shboul, *op. laud.*, 1-28.

It is not known exactly at what period al-Masʿūdī began the composition of his work and committed himself fully to his vocation as a writer, but the titles that he quotes in the *Murūdj* suggest that he began with relatively short treatises before embarking on his major works and before turning to account the notes which he must have accumulated in the course of his travels. The first point that commands attention is the care which he devoted to the correction and enrichment of the original versions of his writings, in particular the *Murūdj*, of which the first "edition" dates from 332/943 and the last, from 345/956 (*T*, 154). The second point is the fact that this abundant and diverse corpus of work has, in total, been curiously neglected by posterity, with the exceptions, specifically, of the *Murūdj*, the success of which has never ceased but of which only the "edition" of 332, revised in 336, has been preserved, and of the *Tanbīh*, which, owing to its conciseness, responds to the Muslim taste for abstracts; a third text that has been attributed to him, the *Ithbāt al-waṣiyya*, has survived for obvious reasons (see below) but it is of doubtful authenticity.

The content of the surviving works, which are presented in a historico-geographical framework, shows that this prolific writer has a close interest in various disciplines which are not to be arbitrarily classified as history or geography; since he displays in addition an active sympathy for the *Ahl al-Bayt* and Twelver Imāmī Shīʿism, it is, to say the least, surprising that the Imāmīs, who mention al-Masʿūdī as one of their partisans, but are principally familiar with the *Murūdj* (and subordinately with the *Ithbāt al-waṣiyya*), have not devoted their efforts to the preservation of his works, beginning with the most "committed"; in fact, even if it can be understood that his major work, the *Akhbār al-zamān*, might not have tempted the copyists on account of its volume, it is hard to see the reason for a general indifference with regard to the majority of his other writings which ought to have been interesting and more easily manageable. While IBn al-Nadīm and later biographers have conscientiously enumerated the works, now lost, of so many less prestigious writers, not one of them has apparently entertained the idea of going through the *Murūdj* and the *Tanbīh*, in which thirty-four titles are mentioned, enabling us to establish thirty-six as the total number of al-Masʿūdī's writings. It must be supposed that the article in the *Fihrist* has been truncated by a few lines, because it contains only five titles, whereas Yāḳūt, who revised it and therefore must have known it well, refers to eleven (*Udabāʾ*, xiii, 90-4) and the same number recurs in the work of al-Kutubī (*Fawāt*, ii, 94-5); the Shīʿī al-Nadjāshī (*Ridjāl*, 178) increases the number to fourteen, and Ḥādjdjī Khalīfa (*passim*) to sixteen. Ibn Ḥadjar al-ʿAskalānī (*Lisān al-Mīzān*, iv, 224-5) confirms the general impression when he asserts that with the exception of the *Murūdj*, copies of the work of al-Masʿūdī are rare. In the West, a number of authors have attempted to compile inventories of his work: De Goeje in the Introduction to his edition of the *Tanbīh* (vi-vii), Carra de Vaux in his translation of the latter (569-70), Sarton in his *Introduction to the history of science* (Baltimore 1927, i, 637-9), Brockelmann (I, 150-2, S I, 220-1), Sezgin (*GAS*, i, 333-4), but more recently, Khalidi (*op. laud.*, 154-64) and Shboul (*op. laud.*, 55-77) have made strenuous efforts, working on the basis of the titles mentioned in *M* and *T* and especially of such references to their content as are available, to identify the subjects of the lost works. When the researcher is confronted by such a discursive writer as al-Masʿūdī, this method is often dangerous, but there is no reason why it should not be used in order to gain an impression of at least some of the questions examined and to establish an approximative classification.

I. A first category comprises works of general culture set in a framework of geography and history or of the latter alone:

1.—*K. Akhbār al-zamān wa-man abādahu 'l-ḥidthān min al-umam al-māḍiya wa 'l-adjyāl al-khāliya wa 'l-mamālik al-dāthira* (before 332/943); the author draws attention in *M* (§§ 1-2) to its general content and refers to it frequently in *M* and *T*, thus giving the impression that it contained a great deal more detail than the two surviving works; history was presented here in the form of annals (*M*, §§ 1498, 3240). The *K. Akhbār al-zamān* published in Cairo, in 1938, by Ṣāwī, has nothing in common with that of al-Masʿūdī; it had been translated as early as 1898, under the title *Abrégé des merveilles*, by Carra de Vaux, who considered it a popular work (*JA*, 9th series, vii [1896], 133-44; cf. D. M. Dunlop, *Arab civilization to AD 1500*, London-Beirut 1971, 110 ff.).

2.—*K. Rāḥat al-arwāḥ* (before 332/943); despite the title, it is a supplement to the above-mentioned work and it concerns expeditions and wars (especially those of the mythical kings of Egypt) which did not figure in the preceding (*M*, § 819).

3.—*al-Kitāb al-awsaṭ* (before 332/943); this "Middle book" must have followed the same format as the *Akhbār al-zamān*, since it was both an abridgement and a supplement on points of detail. The Oxford and Istanbul mss. mentioned by Brockelmann (in *EI*[1], s.v. AL-MASʿŪDĪ) and Sezgin (*GAS*, i, 334) do not correspond with *al-Kitāb al-awsaṭ* (see Shboul, *op. laud.*, 89, n. 127, who has examined them).

4.—*K. Murūdj al-dhahab wa-maʿādin al-djawhar* (*fī tuḥaf al-ashrāf min al-mulūk wa-ahl al-dirāyāt*, *T*, 1): it is to this work, written in 332/943, revised in 336/947, again in 345/956 (*T*, 97, 110-1, 155-6, 175-6) that al-Masʿūdī owes his reputation. The text of 332-6, the only version that has survived, was published at Būlāḳ in 1283 and in Cairo in 1313, in the margins of the *Nafḥ al-ṭīb* of al-Maḳḳarī in Cairo in 1302 and of the *Kāmil* of Ibn al-Athīr at Būlāḳ in 1303; Muḥyī 'l-Dīn ʿAbd al-Ḥāmīd has made from it an annotated edition which has enjoyed a degree of success (2nd ed. Cairo 1368/1948, 3rd ed. 1377/1958, further ed. by Yūsuf Dāghir, Beirut 1973). As early as 1841, the first volume of an English translation, the work of A. Sprenger, appeared in London, and later Barbier de Meynard and Pavet de Courteille edited and translated the entire text into French (Paris 1861-77, 2nd ed. 1913-30); this work has been extensively exploited by orientalists, notably by Marquart (*Streifzüge*, Leipzig 1903) and A. Seippel (*Rerum normannicarum fontes arabici*, Oslo 1896-1928), who amended it on points of detail; finally. Ch. Pellat has revised the edition-translation by Barbier de Meynard and Pavet de Courteille (5 vols. of text, Beirut 1966-74 and 2 vols. of index in Arabic, Beirut 1979; 3 vols. of translation, Paris 1962-71, have so far appeared, but the last two and the French index have been complete for some years); this revision has been based on secondary sources rather than on new mss. (which are listed in Brockelmann, I, 151, S I, 220 and Sezgin, i, 334).

Brockelmann (in *EI*[1], s.v.) and other authors have accepted without reservation the interpretation by Gildemeister, who (in *WZKM*, v [1894], 202) asserted that *Murūdj al-dhahab* should be rendered as "gold-washings" rather than "meadows" of gold; taking as a basis the fact that the earth "makes gold to grow" (*tunbit al-dhahab*: *M*, § 796); the author of the present article regards this suggestion as nonsensical, and in this respect is followed by Khalidi (*op. laud.*, 2, n. 2) and Shboul (*op. laud.*, 71).

The *Murūdj* comprise two essential parts. The firs (§§ 34-663) contains "sacred" history up to the time of the Prophet, a survey of India, geographical data concerning seas and rivers, China, the tribes of Turkey, a list of the kings of ancient Mesopotamia, Persia, Greece, Rome, Byzantium, Egypt, and chapters on Negroes, Slavs, Gaul and Galicia. Next come the ancient history of Arabia and articles on the beliefs, the various calendars, the religious monuments of India, of Persia, of the Sabaeans, etc., and a summary of universal chronology. In this first part, which takes up roughly two-fifths of the work, al-Masᶜūdī has set down, so as not to have to return to them, generalities regarding the universe and information of a historical nature on non-Muslim peoples (including the pre-Islamic Arabs), In the second part (§§ 664-3661), by contrast, there are only exceptional references to the peoples of countries outside the Islamic world, and it is the history of Islam, from the Prophet up to the caliphate of al-Muṭīᶜ, which is recounted; the *khulafāʾ rāshidūn*, the Umayyad "kings" (only ᶜUmar b. ᶜAbd al-ᶜAzīz has a right to the title of caliph, while al-Ḥadjdjādj enjoys special treatment) and the ᶜAbbāsid caliphs each form the subject of a chapter in which a brief biographical article is followed by accounts (*akhbār*), anecdotes and digressions on various subjects. In view of the fact that the author declares (§ 3) that this work contains a summary of studies which had been more fully developed in the *Akhbār al-zamān* and *al-Kitāb al-awsaṭ*, as well as supplementary notices on certain points, the table of contents of the *Murūdj* allows an impression to be formed of the general format of these two works, where the points are perhaps presented with greater rigour.

5.—The *K. Waṣl al-madjālis bi-djawāmiᶜ al-akhbār wa-mukhtaliṭ/mukhallaṭ al-ādāb/al-āthār*, foreshadowed in *M* (§§ 3014, 3428, 3608) and mentioned in *T* (333), was a collection of various traditions, especially concerning al-Andalus (the history of which is neglected in the *Murūdj*); it was probably composed in an unsystematic way and would certainly have appeared in a form closer to *adab* than to methodical history.

6.—The *K. al-Akhbār al-masᶜūdiyyāt*, also composed after *M*, dealt (*T*, 259, 333) with the history of pre-Islamic Arabia and of al-Andalus.

7.—The *K. Maḳātil fursān al-ᶜAdjam* (332/943) was no doubt a collection of traditions concerning Persian heroes, which was some sort of a counterpart of the *K. Maḳātil fursān al-ᶜArab* by Abū ᶜUbayda (*T*, 102).

8.—The *K. Funūn al-maᶜārif wa-mā djarā fi 'l-duhūr al-sawālif* (after 332/943), which is mentioned several times in *T* (121, 144, 151, 153, 158, 160, 174, 182, 261), seems to have dealt especially with the Greeks, the Byzantines and North Africa and to have filled in the gaps left in preceding works.

9.—The *K. Dhakhāʾir al-ᶜulūm wa-mā kāna fī sālif al-duhūr* (after 332/943) seems to have been more detailed than the *Tanbīh* (*T*, 97, 175, 400) on certain questions, particularly on the history of Byzantium.

10.—The *K. al-Istidhkār li-mā djarā fī sālif al-aᶜṣār*, mentioned in *T* (1, 53-4, 102, 137, 144, 176, 271, 279, 401) was perhaps a kind of aide-mémoire.

11.—The *K. Taḳallub al-duwal wa-taghayyur al-ārāʾ wa 'l-milal* (*T*, 334) must have been a reflecting upon history with regard to the events which culminated in the seizure of power by the Fāṭimids in North Africa. This suggestive title makes one regret the loss of a work which Ibn Khaldūn, who had a high regard for al-Masᶜūdī (see below), probably did not have the leisure to consult.

12.—Finally, the *K. al-Tanbīh wa 'l-ishrāf*, composed in 344-5/955-6, is probably the last work of al-Masᶜūdī. It is not exactly an abridgement of the major historico-geographical works which came before it, although it does return to and express, with greater rigour and precision, their essential points of information concerning astronomical and meteorological phenomena, the divisions of the earth, the seas, ancient nations, universal chronology, and then the history of Islam until the caliphate of al-Muṭīᶜ. As its title indicates, it is basically a combination of overall review and a setting in temporal perspective. The *Tanbīh* has been edited by De Goeje, in the *BGA*, viii, 1893-4, and by Ṣāwī, in Cairo, in 1357/1938; Carra de Vaux has translated it under the title *Le Livre de l'avertissement et de la révision*, Paris 1897.

II. A second category is also of historical nature, but it is devoted especially to ᶜAlī b. Abī Ṭālib, the *Ahl al-Bayt* and the Twelver *Imāms*.

13.—The *K. al-Zāhī* (before 332/943) concerned ᶜAlī and the controversies to which he gave rise (*M*, § 1463).

14.—The *K. Ḥadāʾiḳ al-adhhān fī akhbār Ahl/Āl Bayt al-Nabī wa-tafarruḳi-him fi 'l-buldān* (before 332/943) was apparently the history of the twelve *Imāms* and of the partisans of ᶜAlī (*M*, §§ 1013, 1943, 2506, 2742, 3023).

15.—The *K. Mazāhir al-akhbār wa-ṭarāʾif al-āthār fī akhbār Āl al-Nabī* [*al-akhyār?*], also prior to *M*, must have been, like the preceding, a history, or, doubtless, a "sacred history" of ᶜAlī and of his partisans (*M*, §§ 1677, 1755, 3032).

16.—The *Risālat al-Bayān fī asmāʾ al-aʾimmā al-ḳiṭṭiᶜiyya min al-Shīᶜa*, written before 332/943, contained (*M*, §§ 2532, 2798; *T*, 297) detailed biographies of the Twelve *Imāms* who, unlike the Wāḳifiyya, maintained that Mūsā al-Kāẓim [*q.v.*] was dead and had designated as his successor their eighth *Imām*, ᶜAlī al-Riḍā [*q.v.*].

III. His Imāmī Shīᶜī beliefs inspired al-Masᶜūdī to write two works on the question of the Imāmate from the point of view of different sects and schools, as well as on other points of doctrine, such as temporary marriage, the religion of the ancestors of Muḥammad, the beliefs of ᶜAlī before his conversion, etc.:

17.—*K. al-Istibṣār fī waṣf aḳāwīl al-nās fi 'l-imāma* (*M*, §§ 6, 1138, 1463, 1952, 2190), and

18.—*K. al-Ṣafwa fi 'l-imāma* (*M*, §§ 6, 1138, 1463, 1952).

IV. These writings border upon heresiography and comparativism, subjects to which the author devoted numerous articles of a more or less polemical nature:

19.—The *K. al-Maḳālāt fī uṣūl al-diyānāt*, prior to 332/943, was a survey, probably polemical, of the beliefs of Islamic sects and schools (Shīᶜīs, Khāridjīs, Muᶜtazilīs, Khurramīs, etc.) and of non-Islamic religions (Sabaism, Mazdaism, Judaism and Christianity). Judging by the number of passages where it is cited (*M*, §§ 783, 1138, 1205, 1715, 1945, 1994, 2078, 2225, 2291, 2359, 2420, 2741, 2800, 3156; *T*, 154, 161-2), this work must have been regarded as quite important by its author.

20.—The *K. al-Ibāna ʿan uṣūl al-diyāna*, also prior to 332/943, dealt with the differences between Imāmism and Muʿtazilism (from which al-Masʿūdī admits having borrowed some doctrines, *M*, § 2256) and attacked Mazdaism, Manichaeism, Dayṣānism, etc. (*M*, §§ 212, 2256; *T*, 354).

21.—The *K. al-Intiṣār* was a refutation of Khāridjism (*M*, § 2190); this must be the text which Yāḳūt (*Udabāʾ*, xiii, 94) mentions under the title *Akhbār al-Khawāridj*.

22.—The *K. al-Istirdjāʿ fi ʾl-kalām* must also have been a refutation, but of certain beliefs of the Mazdaeans, the Manichaeans, the Christians, etc. (*M*, § 1223).

23.—The *K. al-Daʿāwī/al-Daʿāwā al-shanīʿa*, mentioned only once (*M*, § 1195, where the translation needs correction) was directed against "abominable" beliefs such as the transmigration of souls.

24.—The *K. Khazāʾin al-dīn wa-sirr al-ʿālamīn*, written after 332/943, dealt with the opinion of various sects, especially the Carmathians, and revealed the differences between Manichaeism, Mazdaism and Mazdakism (*T*, 101, 161-3, 385).

V. Various passages of the *Murūdj* show that al-Masʿūdī was interested in general philosophy, to which he devoted a number of treatises, and that he was by no means indifferent to political philosophy. Since the question of the transmigration of souls has been raised in no. 23 above, the first to be cited is:

25.—The *K. Sirr al-ḥayāt*, which took up the same subject, but dealt more generally with the soul and also touched on themes such as the Trinity, the *ghayba*, the *mahdī*, etc. (*M*, §§ 533, 988, 1195, 1248, 2800, 3156; *T*, 155, 353).

26.—The *K. al-Zulaf* also dealt with the soul, but a number of other subjects were also discussed: the qualities of sovereigns, cosmology, diseases, music, animals, etc. (*M*, §§ 533, 630, 743, 928, 1325, 1335).

27.—The *K. Ṭibb al-nufūs* was also devoted to the soul (*M*, §§ 988, 1247), as was:

28.—The *K. al-Nuhā wa ʾl-kamāl* (*M*, § 1247).

29.—The *K. al-Ruʾūs al-sabʿiyya* (?) *min al-siyāsa al-mulūkiyya/al-madaniyya wa-ʿilali-hā wa-milali-hā al-ṭabīʿiyya* seems to have been a treatise of political philosophy (*M*, §§ 928, 1222-3, 1232, 1336), as was

30.—The *K. Naẓm al-djawāhir fī tadbīr al-mamālik wa ʾl-ʿasākir*, which is mentioned only in *T* (400-1), whereas the preceding were prior to the *Murūdj*.

VI. Two major works of scientific nature may legitimately be classed separately:

31.—The *K. al-Mabādiʾ wa ʾl-tarākīb*, where there is a discussion of the influence of the two luminaries (*M* § 1325) and

32.—The *K. al-Ḳaḍāyā wa ʾl-tadjārib*, in which al-Masʿūdī gives an account of observations made in the course of his travels of various phenomena, the three domains of Nature, etc. (*M*, §§ 369, 705, 815, 817, 846, 1208, 2247).

VII. Finally, although he can hardly be described a priori as a *faḳīh*, he did take an interest in the Sharīʿa and its principles, as is shown by four treatises:

33.—The *K. al-Wādjib fi ʾl-furūḍ al-lawāzim*, on points of *fiḳh* on which Sunnīs and Shīʿīs were in disagreement (*M*, § 1952) and

34.—The *K. Naẓm al-adilla fī uṣūl al-milla*, both of them prior to 332/943 (*M*, § 5; *T*, 4);

35.—The *K. Naẓm al-aʿlām fī uṣūl al-aḥkām*, mentioned only in *T* (4), but probably composed much earlier; it is not impossible, in fact, that this text was known to al-Subkī, who had in his possession (*Ṭabaḳāt al-Shāfiʿiyya*, ii, 307) a treatise by al-Masʿūdī completing the notes that he had taken in 306/918 when Ibn Suraydj recited his *Risālat al-Bayān ʿan uṣūl al-aḥkām*; this was a survey of the principles of the law according to al-Shāfiʿī, Mālik, Sufyān al-Thawrī, Abū Ḥanīfa and Dāwūd al-Iṣfahānī. Lastly,

36.—The *K. al-Masāʾil wa ʾl-ʿilal fi ʾl-madhāhib wa ʾl-milal*, mentioned in *T* (4, 155).

It will be noted that, in the introduction to the *Tanbīh*, al-Masʿūdī lists in chronological order nos, 1, 3, 4, 8, 9, 10, then the three last (nos. 34, 35, 36) and considers the *Tanbīh* to be the seventh of the first series.

It is appropriate to note in addition that the *Fihrist* (154) and Yāḳūt (*Udabāʾ*, xiii, 94) mention a *K. al-Rasāʾil*, while al-Kutubī (*Fawāt*, ii, 94) refers to a *K. al-Rasāʾil wa ʾl-istidhkār bi-mā marra fī sālif al-aʿṣār* (cf. above, no. 10). Similarly, the *K. al-Taʾrīkh fī akhbār al-umam min al-ʿArab wa ʾl-ʿAdjam (Fihrist, Udabāʾ, Fawāt)* must be the *K. Akhbār al-zamān*. Finally, Ibn Abī Uṣaybiʿa (*ʿUyun al-anbāʾ*, i, 56, 82) credits al-Masʿūdī, as a result of a confusion, with a *K. al-Masālik wa ʾl-mamālik*.

However, there remains one little book, the *K. Ithbāt al-waṣiyya li ʾl-Imām ʿAlī b. Abī Ṭālib*, published at Nadjaf (n.d.; *ca.* 1955 for the 1st ed.), which poses a problem difficult to solve. Omissions excepted, this title is not mentioned by any Sunnī author, although the Shīʿīs unreservedly attribute it to al-Masʿūdī, and the anonymous editor identifies it with the *Bayān fī asmāʾ al-aʾimma* (no. 16 above). In spite of elements which militate in favour of this identification, it is doubtful whether the *Ithbāt al-waṣiyya* comes from the pen of the author of the *Murūdj*; but the question remains open, and is unlikely ever to be settled definitively (see Ch. Pellat, *Masʿūdī et l'Imāmisme*, in *Le Shîʿisme imâmite*, Paris 1970, 69-80).

Even if it is decided that this "anti-history" or this "sacred history" of the twelve *Imāms* is apocryphal, and speculation on the titles of the works catalogued above under the nos. 13-18 is abandoned, it is impossible to deny the Shīʿism or, more accurately the Imāmism, of al-Masʿūdī. Shīʿī authors are unanimous in considering him one of their number, and a reading of the *Murūdj* largely confirms this opinion. Among the Sunnīs it is quite curious that al-Subkī (*loc. cit.*) and Ibn Taghrībardī (*Nudjūm*, iii, 315-6) follow al-Dhahabī in seeing him only as a Muʿtazilī, while Ibn Taymiyya (*Minhādj al-sunna*, ii, 129-31) is one of the few who recognises his Shīʿism, and Ibn Ḥadjar al-ʿAsḳalānī reconciles all points of view in pointing out, quite rightly (*Lisān al-Mīzān*, iv, 224-5), that his writings "abound with signs showing that he was Shīʿī and Muʿtazilī". Al-Masʿūdī in fact acknowledges this dual allegiance when he declares 6*M*, § 2256) that he has chosen some Muʿtazilī doctrines for his own use (cf. above, no. 20), and such an eclecticism was by no means astonishing in the 4th/10th century. As for his *madhhab*, it would seem to be largely Shāfiʿī, but nothing can be definitely asserted and it is possible that, in his treatises of *fiḳh*, he confined himself to dealing with comparative law.

Although J. D. Pearson, in his *Index islamicus*, reserves for al-Masʿūdī a special mention under the rubric "Muslim geographers", it is in the ranks of the historians that he is normally counted, because he is characterised and classified on the basis of the *Murūdj* and the *Tanbīh* and because the opinion of the Arab authors who qualify him as *muṣannif li-kutub al-tawārīkh wa-akhbar al-mulūk* (Ibn al-Nadīm), *muʾarrikh kabīr* (al-Kutubī), *imām* (= model) *li'l-muʾarrikhīn* (Ibn Khaldūn, *Muḳaddima*, i, 52; tr. Slane, i, 67; tr. Rosenthal, i, 64) is accepted. The esteem in which he was held by Ibn Khaldūn (who mentions him frequently but does not hesitate to criticise him) seems to have been inspired by his historical method, his interest in nations foreign to Islam, whether ancient or contemporary, and in the religions practised there, by his open-mindedness and his universal vision of history (on the links between the two authors, see in particular M. Mahdi, *Ibn Khaldun's philosophy of history*, London 1957, 152-3, 164 ff., 255 ff.; W. J. Fischel, *Ibn Khaldūn and al-Masʿūdī*, in *al-Masʿūdī Millenary commemoration volume*, Aligarh 1960, 51-9).

To be sure, the *Tanbīh* is presented in the form of a universal history from Adam to al-Muṭīʿ, preceded by a survey of general geography; to be sure also, the table of contents of the *Murūdj* given the same impression. But this voluminous work does not contain only history and geography; in addition, it has been observed that, in the list of works of al-Masʿūdī, at least twenty are generally of a heresiographical, doctrinal, philosophical or legal nature. Even if it is considered that disciplines thus cultivated belong to global history, the qualification of "historian" in the normal sense of the term is only partially appropriate to this polygraph. A. Shboul has not hesitated to describe him, in the subtitle of his treatise, as *A Muslim humanist*, and A. Miquel (*Géographie humaine*, i, 202) confers on him the title of "*imām* of encyclopaedism", thus justifying the quality of *adīb* of the Djāḥiẓian type which the author of these present lines has been led to acknowledge in him (in *Jnal of the Pakistan Historical Soc.*, ix [1961], 231-4). Eager to acquire all available types of knowledge, of whatever origin, and anxious to present them in a form responding to the exigencies of *adab* which seeks to instruct without burdening the reader, al-Masʿūdī writes for a public which seeks to educate itself, to escape from the narrow confines of traditional instruction and to extend the field of Arab-Islamic culture, while not regarding as negligible everything that happens outside the Muslim world. On the subject of Gaul, B. Lewis recalls (in *Mas. Mill. commem. vol.*, 10) that, from the first millenium of Islam, there have survived only three works dealing with the "history" of Western Europe, and that the oldest of these is by al-Masʿūdī, the *Murūdj*. This author established no school, and in this there is no cause for surprise, in the sense that the last-named work was in itself adequate to satisfy the curiosity of readers for many years, to say nothing of the encyclopaedists of later times who continued to exploit it without reservation (e.g. al-Ḳalḳashandī cites him forty-two times in the *Ṣubḥ*, the editor of which finds no other reference to the Persian calendar (ii, 385) than that contained in the *Murūdj*); these authors give the impression that nothing of equal substance has been written in the course of the intervening centuries on questions which nevertheless appear to have been broadly set forth.

In a period when rhymed prose was beginning to invade literature, it is remarkable that al-Masʿūdī did not seek to elaborate his style, and only a few rhymed sentences are to be found in his writings. It will be observed, however, that he himself gave rhymed titles to around fifteen of his works, and that in only three of them is the first unit artificial. To the extent that it is possible to verify his quotations, he has sometimes introduced modifications in them, but he seldom voluntarily embellishes the form. The general arrangement of his works is not exempt from defects, and attention should be drawn to his numerous digressions, without however reproaching him for them, since they constitute one of the characteristics of *adab*. On his style, see Khalidi, *op. laud.*, 19-23.

Finally, even if it may be reckoned that the *Akhbār al-zamān* and *al-Kitāb al-awsaṭ*, in spite of their documentary worth, were too voluminous to be preserved, the fact remains that the loss of thirty-four works out of thirty-six is hard to explain, especially considering the enduring success of the *Murūdj*. Essentially, it is perhaps this very success which has contributed most to the casting of a shadow over the major historico-geographical works and has driven the Shīʿīs to take no further interest in the other writings of an Imāmi author who was sufficiently independent to play into the hands of the Sunnīs by giving pride of place, not to the *Imāms* (as in the *Ithbāt al-waṣiyya*) but to the caliphs, and by preferring, as he emphasises on numerous occasion, objective accounts (*khabar*) to speculation (*naẓar*). It can easily be understood how the Sunnīs, for their part, should have concentrated their attention on the *Murūdj*, and it may be supposed that al-Masʿūdī has been a victim of the suspicion which was attached to both the Shīʿīs and the Muʿtazilīs, since he was regarded as belonging to this school.

Bibliography: The Arabic biographical sources are not particularly detailed: see Ibn al-Nadīm, *Fihrist*, 154 (ed. Cairo, 219-20); Nadjāshī, *Ridjāl*, Bombay 1317, 178; Yāḳūt, *Udabāʾ*, xiii, 90-4; Kutubī, *Fawāt*, Cairo 1951, ii, 94-5; Subkī, *Ṭabaḳāt al-Shāfiʿiyya*, ii, 307; Ibn Ḥadjar, *Lisān al-Mīzān*, iv, 224-5; Ibn Taghrībirdī, *Nudjūm*, iii, 315-6; Ḥādjdjī Khalīfa, *Kashf al-ẓunūn*, index; Ibn al-ʿImād, *Shadharāt*, ii, 371; Khʷānsārī, *Rawḍāt al-djannāt*, 379-82; Nūrī, *Mustadrak*, iii, 310; ʿĀmilī, *Aʿyān al-Shīʿa*, xli, 198-213; Ziriklī, v, 87; Kaḥḥāla, vii, 80.

Studies: The many orientalists who have exploited the *Murūdj* and, to a lesser extent, the *Tanbīh*, have been led to review certain passages and, where appropriate, to amend them; this is especially the case with V. Minorsky, in the commentary on the *Ḥudūd al-ʿālam*, London 1937. Different aspects of the work of al-Masʿūdī have been the object of independent studies: particularly worthy of mention are: the writings of T. Lewicki (in Polish) on the Slavs and other peoples; A. Czapkiewics, *Al-Masʿūdī on balneology and balneotherapeutics*, in *Fol. Or.*, iii (1962), 271-5; Ch. Pellat, *La España musulmana en las obras de al-Masʿūdī*, in *Actas del primer congreso de estudios árabes e islámicos*, Madrid 1964, 257-64; and especially, S. Maqbul Ahmad and A. Rahman (eds.), *al-Masʿūdī Millenary commemoration volume*, Aligarh 1960, which contains some twenty contributions on particular subjects. J. de Guignes appears to have been the first to draw attention to the *Murūdj*, in *Notices et extraits*, i, 1787, 27, but the earliest monograph is the work of E. Quatremère, *Notice sur la vie et les ouvrages de Masoudi*, in *JA*, 3rd series, vii (1839), 1-31; see also are Wüstenfeld, *Geschichtsschreiber der Araber*, no. 119; Marquart, *Streifzüge*, Leipzig 1903, pp. xxxiv-xxxv; Brockelmann, I, 141-3, S I, 220-1, I², 150-2; Sezgin, *GAS*, i, 332-6; F. Rosenthal, *Muslim historiography*, index. The works of S. Maqbul Ahmad, *Al-Masʿūdī's contribution to medieval Arab geography*, in *IC*, xxvii (1953), 61-77, xxviii (1954), 275-86, and *The travels*, in *ibid.*, xxviii, 509-25, in fact mark the beginning of a resurgence of interest in the author of the *Murūdj*, illustrated by A. Miquel, *Le géographie humaine du monde musulman jusqu'au milieu du IIe siècle*, Paris, i, 1967, 202-12, and index, ii, 1975, index; then by two successive works based on dissertations: T. Khalidi, *Islamic historiography. The histories of Masʿūdī*, Albany 1975 (an important study of the historical method of this author) and A. Shboul, *Al-Masʿūdī and his world. A. Muslim humanist and his interest in non-Muslims*, London 1979 (fundamental monograph, with comprehensive bibliography). (CH. PELLAT)

MĀSŪNIYYA [see FARĀMUSH-KHĀNA and FARMĀSŪNIYYA in Suppl.].

MAṢYAD, a town of central Syria on the eastern side of the Djabal al-Nuṣayriyya situated at 33 miles/54 km to the east of Bāniyās [*q.v.*] and 28 miles/45 km to the east of Ḥamāt [*q.v.*], in long. 36° 35' E. and lat. 35° N., in the massif of the Djabal Anṣāriyya at the foot of the eastern slopes of the Djabal Baḥrāʾ, at an altitude of 1,591ft./485 m. and to the west of the great trench of the fault of the Ghāb [*q.v.*]. The pronunciation and orthography of the name varies between the forms *Maṣyād*, *Maṣyāf* (in official documents and on the inscriptions mentioned below of the years 646 and 870 A.H.), *Maṣyāt* and *Maṣyāth* (on the interchange of *f* and *th*, see O. Rescher, in *ZDMG*, lxxiv, 465; Praetorius, in *ibid.*, lxxv, 292; Dussaud, *Topographie hist. de la Syrie*, 143, n. 4, 209, 395, n. 3). The variants *Maṣyāb* (Yāḳūt, *Muʿdjam*, iv, 556), *Maṣyāh* (Khalīl al-Ẓāhirī, *Zubda*, ed. Ravaisse, 49), *Messiat* in tr. Venture, 73 and *Maṣyāt* (al-Nābulusī, in Von Kremer, in *SB Ak. Wien*, 1850, ii, 331) are no doubt due to mistakes in copying (Van Berchem, in *JA*, Ser. 9, ix [1897], 457, n. 2). At a later period, the pronunciation *Miṣyāf*, *Miṣyād*, became usual (al-Dimashḳī, ed. Mehren, 208; al-Ḳalḳashandī, *Ṣubḥ al-aʿshā*ʾ, iv, 113; Ibn al-Shiḥna, ed. Beirut, 265; cf. *Meṣyāf* on von Oppenheim's map in *Petermans Mitteilungen*, lvii [1911], ii, Taf. 11). The name is perhaps a corruption of a Greek Μαρσύα (= Μασσύα) or Μαρσου χώμη, which presumably lay on the *Marsyas amnis*, the boundary river of the Nazerini (ancestors of the Nuṣayrīs? Pliny, *Nat. hist.*, v. 81) (cf. Pauly-Wissowa-Kroll, *Realenzyklopädie*, xiv, cols. 1985-6, s.v. *Marsyas*, no. 3).

Maṣyād is an important settlement which has developed under the protection of a powerful citadel whose traces are visible on a limestone outcrop. The region gets an average of 31.5 inches/800 mm of rain, and the climate is good. Various small watercourses have allowed not only the cultivation in the region of barley and wheat but also the existence of gardens and orchards (*basātīn*). In her travel account, Gertrude L. Bell noted the abundance of flowers—anemones, iris, narcissus, and white and red orchids (*Syria: the desert and the sown*, 217).

The main communication routes between northern and southern Syria do not pass through the Orontes valley, but more to the east on the fringes of the desert steppes. In order to travel from Maṣyād to northern Syria, one has to reach the Orontes valley by a road passing through Laḳba and Dayr al-Shamīl, where a road coming from Ḥamāt is crossed, leaving to the west, on the mountain flank, the fortresses of Kharība and Abū Ḳubays [*q.v.*]. The Ghāb is descended into, and then the Orontes is crossed at the bridge of ʿAsharna, a bridge from the Roman period 8 miles/15 km below Shayzar [*q.v.*]. Beyond the bridge, the route passes by Ḳalʿat al-Muḍīk and then reaches the plateau and goes through Afāmiya [*q.v.*] to reach Anṭākiya [*q.v.*] in northern Syria. There also exists a route linking Maṣyād with Shayzar via Tell al-Salhab. Finally, at the beginning of the 20th century the traces of the paved way (*raṣīf*) of a Roman road which linked Ḥamāt with the Mediterranean (Bell, *op.cit.*, 232) could still be seen; it then crossed the Nahr Sarūt by a bridge before passing through the settlement of Maṣyād in the direction of the sea. The coast could also be reached after Maṣyād by going through Rafāniyya, where there was a bifurcation of the ways either towards Ḳalʿat Yaḥmūr in the direction of Ṭarṭūs [*q.v.*] or towards Tell Kalakh if the journey to Ṭarābulus [*q.v.*] or Tripoli was intended. At the present day, asphalted roads allow access to Maṣyād without any difficulty.

Maṣyād is not mentioned in the early Middle Ages; the first mention of the fortress is probably in a Frankish account of the advance of the Crusaders in 1099: *pervenimus gaudentes hospitari ad quoddam Arabum castrum (Anonymi gesta Francorum et aliorum Hierosolymitanorum*, ed. Hagenmeyer, 1890, 418 with n. 29; Dussaud, *Histoire et religion des Noṣairîs*, Paris 1900, 21 n. 4). In the course of the campaign which he conducted in Syria during the autumn of 389/99 to regain Antioch, threatened by the Fāṭimids, the Byzantine Emperor Basil II occupied the Djabal Baḥrāʾ, at the limits of his empire, and dismantled the defences of Ḥiṣn Maṣyād and Rafāniyya, which at this time formed part of the province (*djund*) of Ḳinnasrīn [*q.v.*]. When, after the capture of Tripoli on 11 Dhu 'l-Ḥidjdja 502/12 July 1109, the Franks advanced on Rafāniyya, Ṭughtakīn set out to relieve it; by the terms of the peace concluded between them, the Franks bound themselves to abandon all designs on Maṣyāth and Ḥiṣn al-Akrād and in compensation, these two places and Ḥiṣn Ṭūfān were to pay them tribute (Sibṭ Ibn al-Djawzī, *Mirʾāt al-zamān*, in *Rec. hist. or. crois.*, iii, 537). This agreement did not last long. Around this time, the frontiers between the Latin states began to be precisely delimited; on the other hand, one may note the presence of Ismāʿīlīs, who profited from the anarchy of the years following the arrival of the First Crusade and tried to find places of refuge in the mountainous region to the west of the middle Orontes.

Before 521/1127 the fortress was in possession of a branch of the Mirdāsids [*q.v.*], who sold it to the Banū Munḳidh [*q.v.*]. The Ismāʿīlīs, having in 524/1130 ceded to the Franks the stronghold of Bāniyās in the Wādī al-Tayim, which the Būrid Ṭughtakīn had given to them, now tried to establish themselves in the Djabal Baḥrā' around Maṣyād. In 527/1132-3, Sayf al-Mulk Ibn ʿAmrūn, the lord of al-Kahf, sold to them Ḳadmūs, seized from the Franks in the previous year, after which they soon occupied al-Kahf and Kharība. In Ramaḍān 535/April-May 1141, they also seized the fortress of Maṣyāf by outwitting the commandant Sunḳur, a *mamlūk* in the service of the Banū Munḳidh of Shayzar, who was surprised and slain (Abu 'l-Fidā, *Mukhtaṣar fī akhbār al-bashar*, in *Rec. hist. or. crois.*, i, 25; Ibn al-Athīr, *Kāmil*, in *ibid.*, i, 438; al-Nuwayrī, Cod. Leiden 2m, fol. 222b, in Van Berchem, *JA* [1897], 464, n. 1). Maṣyād now became the residence of the Syrian "Master" of the sect, as we may call him, with Van Berchem, to distinguish him from the Grand Master in Alamūt [*q.v.*], known as *Shaykh al-Djabal.* The Ismāʿīlīs now proceeded to make themselves independent there for a century-and-a-half. In 543/1148, after the check to the Second Crusade, the Ismāʿīlīs of Maṣyād made common cause with the Franks against Nūr al-Dīn, but in 552/1157 these same Ismāʿīlīs joined in the defence of the fortress of Shayzar, besieged by the Crusaders. Whilst the Ismāʿīlīs had just been regrouped in the mountainous region of Ḳadmūs by the Master (*muḳaddam*) Abū Muḥammad, there appeared in Syria around

557/1162 Ras͟hīd al-Dīn Sinān b. Salmān b. Muḥammad al-Baṣrī [*q.v.*] as envoy of the Grand Master of Alamūt, the head of the Nizārī Ismāʿīlīs, sometimes known as the Assassins [see NIZĀRĪS, ḤAS͟HĪS͟HIYYA]. He soon took over the direction of them in this region, and until his death in 588/1192, showed an extraordinary talent for organisation, making the sect a formidable military force which sowed terror amongst both the Crusaders and the Syrian Muslims. Ṣalāḥ al-Dīn, who wanted to punish them for two attempts on his life, invaded the land of the Ismāʿīlīs in Muḥarram 572/July-August 1176, laid it waste and laid siege to Sinān in Ḳalʿat Maṣyād. Whilst besieging Maṣyād, Ṣalāḥ al-Dīn learnt that the Crusaders had attacked in the Biḳāʿ [*q.v.*]. Since the siege became a lengthy one, he decided to negotiate through the mediation of his uncle S͟hihāb al-Dīn Maḥmūd b. Takas͟h al-Ḥārimī, the master of Ḥamāt, and at the beginning of Ṣafar/August, he retired with his army in the direction of Ḥamāt (Abu 'l-Fidā and Ibn al-Athīr, in *Rec. hist. or. crois.*, i, 47, 626). The exact terms of the agreement are not now known, but it is certain that Ṣalāḥ al-Dīn never again attacked the Ismāʿīlīs and that the latter ceased to plot against him. Shortly before he raised the siege of Maṣyād (about 1 Ṣafar), he received from Usāma b. Munḳid͟h, who was in Damascus, a letter containing a panegyric of his great patron (Derenbourg, *Vie d'Ousâma*, Paris 1893, 400-1). Rās͟hid al-Dīn died in 588/September 1192. The Syrian Masters, as the official epithet *al-Dunyā wa 'l-Dīn* henceforth regularly borne by them shows, were raised by him to a position with power and privileges equal to those of sovereign rulers (Van Berchem, *op. cit.*, 470). While Sinān had completely emancipated himself from the suzerainty of the headquarters of the sect in Alamūt, in 608/1211-12 we find the old conditions completely restored (Abū S͟hāma, *al-D͟hayl fi 'l-rawḍatayn*, in Van Berchem, *op.cit.*, 475ff., n. 1).

The fortress of Maṣyād lies to the northeast of the settlement, at the foot of the D͟jabal Baḥrāʾ and within the town wall, a few traces of which are still today visible. The fortress is perched on a rocky limestone block and has a situation running from north to south; the eastern edge of this bluff rises vertically for some ten metres and gives the appearance of a cliff. Like S͟hayzar, Maṣyād is an Arab citadel antedating the Crusades and having no connection with them; in its dimensions and size, it cannot be compared with such great mediaeval fortresses of Syria as Ḥiṣn al-Akrād, Marḳab [*q.vv.*] or Ṣahyūn. For Van Berchem and Fatio (*Voyage en Syrie*, 115, 172), this fortress resembles in silhouette those of al-Musayliḥa and S͟humaymis. It is one of the best-preserved of the Ismāʿīlīs castles of Syria (Dussaud, *Topographie*, 138-48). It is made up of a curtain wall of only modest appearance with numerous rectangular salients. A donjon or keep, also rectangular, is built in the centre and dominates the ensemble. According to P. Deschamps (*Tripoli*, 39), the Ismāʿīlīs are said to have repaired in the 7th/13th century, with good-quality materials, a Byzantine building of minor importance, of which a certain number of columns and capitals embedded in the doorways of the fortress (partially reproduced in Gertrude Bell, *op. cit.*, 217-19) are still visible witnesses. The castle is entered by a grand gateway on the north side reached by several steps; the entrance is vaulted like that of Ḥiṣn al-Akrād; and the fitting-out of the interior is the work of the Ismāʿīlīs. The keep is in poor condition, and later accretions over the course of the centuries of shacks and constructions have disfigured this piece of military architecture, which merits study and publication of the results. A certain number of Arabic inscriptions mention the various building works made in the castle. The oldest, dating from the middle of the 6th/12th century, is the signature of a master of works, the *mamlūk* Ḳuṣta (*RCEA*, viii, 3197); another inscription from 560/1165 bears the signature of a certain Ibn Mubārak (*RCEA*, ix, 3264). According to two inscriptions on a doorway inside the castle (*RCEA*, x, 3890-1), the building was put into a state of repair by the Syrian Master Kamāl al-Dunyā wa 'l-Dīn al-Ḥasan b. Masʿūd under the suzerainty of the Grand Master of Alamūt ʿAlāʾ al-Dīn Muḥammad III (618-53/1221-55). The reference is probably to the al-Kamāl, who, according to al-Nasawī (*Hist. du Sultan Djelal al-Din Mankobirti*, ed. Houdas, 132), was for a period before 624/1227 governor in Syria for the Grand Master of the Ismāʿīlīs. It is uncertain whether the commandant (*mutawallī*) Mad͟jd al-Dīn, who received in 624/1227 the ambassadors of Frederick II (al-Ḥamawī, in Amari, *Bibl. arabico-sicula*, App. ii, 30) was one of the Masters (Van Berchem, in *JA* [1897], 501, n. 1). About 625-6/1228-9 and still in 635/1237-8, Sirād͟j al-Dīn Muẓaffar b. al-Ḥusayn was Syrian Master (Nasawī, *op. cit.*, 168; inscription of al-Kahf, in *RCEA*, x, 4143). In the village, there remain the traces of a mediaeval rampart provided with gateways and three inscriptions recording the repairs and works carried out.

A Persian from Alamūt, Tād͟j al-Dīn, was in 637/1239-40 *muḳaddam* of the Syrian Ismāʿīlīs (Ibn Wāṣil, *Mufarrid͟j al-kurūb*, Paris, ms. ar. 1702, fol. 333b, in Van Berchem, 466, n. 2). As Tād͟j al-Dīn Abu 'l-Futūḥ he appears in an inscription in Maṣyād of D͟hu 'l-Ḳaʿda 646/February-March 1249, according to which he had built the city wall of Maṣyāf and its south gate. The commander of the fortress under him was ʿAbd Allāh b. Abi 'l-Faḍl b. ʿAbd Allāh (inscriptions A and B in Van Berchem, *JA* [1897], 456 = Van Berchem-von Oppenheim, *Beitr. z. Assyr.*, vii, no. 19). Probably it was Tād͟j al-Dīn to whom the Dominican monk Yvo the Breton, a member of an embassy sent by Louis IX to the "Old Man of the Mountains" in May 1250, sent a naive and fruitless appeal for his conversion (Jean de Joinville, *Hist. de St. Louis*, ed. Wailly, 246; Van Berchem, in *JA* [1897], 478-80).

After having got possession of Alamūt in 654/1256 and having sacked Bag͟hdād two years later, the troops of Hülegu or Hūlākū [*q.v.*] invaded northern Syria in 658/1260 and temporarily occupied Maṣyād. In this year, in the time of the Master Riḍā al-Dīn Abu 'l-Maʿālī, the Mongols seized and held the fortress for a time, but after the victory of the Egyptian Sultan Ḳuṭuz at ʿAyn D͟jālūt [*q.v.*], they abandoned it. About two years later, Baybars began to interfere in the affairs of the Ismāʿīlīs and to demand tribute from them. He very soon deposed the Master Nad͟jm al-Dīn Ismāʿīl and appointed his son-in-law Ṣārim al-Dīn Mubārak in his place and took Maṣyād from him. When the latter returned there, Baybars had him seized and brought to Cairo, where he was thrown into prison. Nad͟jm al-Dīn was again recognised as Master for a brief period and then his son S͟hams al-Dīn, on payment of an annual tribute before the sultan definitely incorporated Maṣyād in his kingdom in Rad͟jab 668/1270 (Abu 'l-Fidā, in *Rec. hist. or. crois.*, i, 153; Mufaḍḍal b. Abi 'l-Faḍāʾil, *Gesch. d. Mamlūkensultane*, ed. Blochet, in *Patrol. Orient.*, xiv, 445; Van Berchem, in *JA* [1897], 465, n. 2). Having now become a Sunnī Muslim possession, Maṣyād presumably at first belonged to the "royal province of fortunate conquests" the capital of which was Ḥiṣn al-

Akrād, then to Ṭarābulus (after its capture in 688/1289).

Within the scheme of administrative reorganisation within the Mamlūk empire, a route was established in the 7th/13th century for the *barīd* [*q.v.*] or postal service between Ḥimṣ [*q.v.*] and Maṣyād, which was at the time an important strategic point under the authority of a commander responsible directly to the sultan because of the fortress's rôle in the defence of the *dār al-Islām* [*q.v.*] just like Ḥiṣn al-Akrād and Raḥba [*q.v.*].

Abu 'l-Fidā˒ (about 720/1320) describes Maṣyād as an important town, with beautiful gardens through which streams flowed; it had a strong citadel and lay at the eastern base of the D̲jabal al-Lukkām (more accurately D̲jabal al-Sikkīn) about a *farsak̲h̲* north of Bārīn and a day's journey west of Ḥamā (not Ḥimṣ, as Le Strange, *Palestine*, 507 erroneously says; Abu 'l-Fidā˒, *Geogr.*, ed. Reinaud, 229 ff.). As a result of its high situation, it has a more temperate climate than the low ground on the Nahr al-ʿĀṣī; the young Usāma in 516/1122-3 brought to Maṣyād the wife and children of the *amīr* of S̲h̲ayzar, his uncle ʿIzz al-Dīn Abu 'l-ʿAsākir Sulṭān, from the heat of S̲h̲ayzar which was causing the *amīr* anxiety about their health (Derenbourg, *Vie d'Ousâma*, 43).

Ibn Baṭṭūṭa, who visited Maṣyād in 756/1355, mentions (*Riḥla*, i, 166-7, tr. Gibb, i, 106) as lying near this stronghold the Ismāʿīlī fortresses of Ḳadmūs, al-Manayḳa, ʿUllayḳa and al-Kahf. These five places, the *ḳilāʿ al-daʿwa* "fortresses of the [Ismāʿīlī] mission", formed, with the castle of al-Ruṣāfa, the *niyāba* of Maṣyād which, in the 8th/14th century, was a dependency of Ṭarābulus. Later, it was separated from this province and attached to the *niyāba* of Damascus, to which it still belonged in the time of al-Ḳalḳas̲h̲andī (*Ṣubḥ*, iv, 113, 202, 235), *ca.* 814/1412. Its *nā˒ib* was nominated from Cairo and was at various times an *amīr* of *ṭabalk̲h̲āna* or an *amīr* of ten, and it had a garrison of Mamlūks. In 826/1423, under Barsbay [*q.v.*] there was no longer a *barīd* service, but there was a road which allowed one to travel from Ṭarābulus to Maṣyād and then to reach, via al-Ruṣāfa and K̲h̲awalī, Ḳadmūs, where it passed through al-Kahf and then ʿUllayḳa to end up at Balāṭunus [*q.v.*]. In the middle of the 9th/15th century, K̲h̲alīl al-Ẓāhirī, in his *Zubda* (ed. Ravaisse, 49, tr. Venture, 73), tells us that around 850/1446 "the town of Maṣyād is still within this province (sc. Ḥamāwiyya); it is a pleasant town with an extensive surrounding countryside". An inscription of Maṣyād of Ramaḍān 870/April-May 1466 contains a decree about taxes of the Sultan al-Malik al-Ẓāhir K̲h̲us̲h̲ḳadam (Van Berchem-von Oppenheim, *Beitr. z. Assyr.*, vii, 20, no. 23: no. 22 is perhaps of the same al-Malik al-Ẓāhir).

Under Egyptian rule, the position of the lands of the Ismāʿīlīs with Maṣyād as capital was to some extent exceptional (Gaudefroy-Demombynes, *La Syrie à l'époque des Mamelouks*, Paris 1923, 182, no. 3).

In the 10th/16th century, after the Ottoman conquest of Syria, Maṣyād is mentioned in the cadastral survey amongst the *ḳilāʿ al-daʿwa* situated to the west of Ḥamāt; these villages of the Ismāʿīlīs paid a special tax. Maṣyād formed part of the *liwā* of Ḥimṣ; there was situated there a *k̲h̲ān* [*q.v.*] on which the Ottomans levied tolls which were abolished in the middle of the 10th/16th century (Mantran and Sauvaget, *Règlements fiscaux*, 92). In 1105/1693-4 ʿAbd al-G̲h̲ānī al-Nābulusī [*q.v.*] passed through Maṣyād and mentions a certain Sulaymān, from the tribe of Tanūk̲h̲, as governor of the town at that time. In 1697 d'Herbelot cited the place in his *Bibliothèque orientale* as "Massiat". In the middle of the 12th/18th century, Maṣyād continued to be the residence of Ismāʿīlī *amīrs*. On the map drawn up by the Sieur d'Anville in 1750, the place is called "Masiat". Of more recent date are two inscriptions of an *amīr* Muṣṭafā b. Idrīs: one from the year 1203/1788-9 relating to the building of a fountain (*sabīl*) (Van Berchem-Von Oppenheim, *op. cit.*, 21, no. 24), and the other to the building of the house of the Ismāʿīlī *amīrs* (*ibid.*, no. 25).

The Ismāʿīlīs lived constantly in open or secret enmity with the Nuṣayrīs, although various tribes of the latter had offered their services to the Ismāʿīlī Masters, for example, as early as 724/1324 to Rās̲h̲id al-Dīn (S. Guyard, *Un grand maître des Assassins au temps de Saladin*, in *JA* [1877], 165; R. Dussaud, *Histoire et religion des Noṣairîs*, 80). A number of Nuṣayrīs of the tribe of Raslān, whom the *amīr* of Maṣyād had allowed to settle in the town under their S̲h̲ayk̲h̲ Maḥmūd, in 1808 murdered the *amīr*, his son and about 300 Ismāʿīlīs, and seized the town. The other inhabitants, who had sought refuge in flight, applied for protection to Yūsuf Pās̲h̲ā, the governor of Damascus. He sent a punitive expedition of 4-5,000 men against the Nuṣayrīs; Maṣyād had to be surrendered by the Banū Raslān after three month's stubborn resistance, and the fugitive Ismāʿīlīs returned to Maṣyād in 1810 (Dussaud, *op. cit.*, 32; Burckhardt, *Reisen in Syrien*, 258). In 1812 Burckhardt estimated the population of Maṣyād at 250 Ismāʿīlī and 30 Christian families. The population since then seems to have diminished still further. Burckhardt and Lammens found many houses in the town in ruins and large gardens within its walls. According to Burckhardt, the land east of the town was a desert heath, while in the north at the foot of the hills the citadel stands on a high steep rock; on the west side is a valley, in which the inhabitants grow wheat and oats. The town, which lies on the slope of a hill, is about half an hour's walk in circumference. Three older gates have been incorporated in the present more modern walls. The mosque is in ruins. The old citadel is for the most part destroyed; only a few buildings have been roughly restored and in parts were still inhabited at the beginning of the 20th century.

From the 19th century onwards, the "Assassins" of Maṣyād, the generations of whom had lived since the 7th/12th century under the authority of delegates from the Nizārīs of Alamūt before becoming subjects of first the Mamlūks and then the Ottomans, were exposed to repeated attacks by the Nuṣayrīs. In February 1919 the region between Maṣyād and Tartūs [*q.v.*] was shaken by the revolt of S̲h̲ayk̲h̲ Ṣāliḥ against the French, whose troops were held in check on the road from S̲h̲ayk̲h̲ Badr to Maṣyād. According to Latron, *Vie rurale*, 208, the Government of Lād̲h̲iḳiyya compelled some of the large landowners of Ḥamāt to hand over to it in 1929 their villages in the *ḳaḍā˒* of Maṣyād: Bayāḍiyya, Miryamīn, ʿAkākir and Ruṣāfa, whose cultivated lands have been distributed amongst the peasants working them. In this way, the ʿAlawī part of the *ḳaḍā˒* of Maṣyād, including the fortress of Abū Ḳubays, was taken away from the *sand̲j̲aḳ* of Ḥamāt for attachment to the new State of the ʿAlawites.

In the mountain regions to the west of Maṣyād there exist deposits of iron known since Antiquity and still capable of exploitation. In order to provide a legal framework for disputes over the division of water, a list of the sharers and their entitlements was set down in writing and registered officially (Latron, *op. cit.*, 160).

Until 1938, the *minṭaḳa* of Maṣyād was part of the province of Ḥamāt, but in 1939 the *ḳaḍā*ᵓ of Maṣyād was integrated *in toto* into the *muḥāfaẓa* of the ᶜAlawites, the *ḳaḍā*ᵓ then having a population of 4,059 people.

In 1945, according to Robin Fedden, the road linking Ḥamāt and Maṣyād climbed westwards up a small valley whose watercourse is an affluent of the Orontes. At the approach to the village one met, among the orchards, pathways lined with pomegranate trees. The village, with its stone houses, was formerly enclosed by a wall, and formed a compact unit of Ismāᶜīlī cultivators. In our own time, Maṣyād still preserves an aspect different from that of the plains villages. The region situated beyond and to the south of the region of the G͟hāb does not benefit directly from the investment in the "G͟hāb Project". Nevertheless, the plans for this region and the settlement of nomads have favoured a perceptible development of the *minṭaḳa* which has, according to the 1970 census, 75,437 inhabitants, 37,922 men and 37,515 women. Since 1965, the Syrian government has set up at Maṣyād a centre for carpet weaving, with workshops having an essentially female working force. Production amounted to 740 m^2 of carpets in 1979 but only 410 m^2 in 1980.

At present, Maṣyād is linked with the new autoroute which travels along the eastern bank of the Orontes northwards. There is a loop 7 km to the east of Maṣyād running northwards from the asphalt road linking Ḥamāt with Bāniyās via Maṣyād. An oil pipeline connecting Ḥimṣ with the Mediterranean coast passes just to the south of Maṣyād and then follows the road across the mountain as far as the sea.

Bibliography: Yāḳūt, iv, 556, ed. Beirut, v, 144 (the article *Ṣafad*, Yāḳūt, iii, 399, ed. Beirut, iii, 412, according to Dussaud, in *Syria*, iv, 332ᵇ, is based on a misspelling of *Maṣyād*); Ṣafī al-Dīn, *Marāṣid al-iṭṭilāᶜ*, ed. Juynboll, iii, 111; Usāma b. Munḳid͟h, *K. al-Iᶜtibār*, tr. A. Miquel, Paris 1983, 321, 323; Ibn al-At͟hīr, xi, 52; Abu 'l-Fidā, *Taḳwīm al-buldān*, ed. Reinaud, 229 ff.; Dimas͟hḳī, ed. Mehren, 208; Ibn Baṭṭūṭa, i, 166; Ibn Muyassar, *Ak͟hbār Miṣr*, ed. H. Massé, *Annales d'Égypte*, Cairo 1919, 65, 96-7; K͟halīl al-Ẓāhirī, *Zubdat kas͟hf al-mamālik*, ed. Ravaisse, 49, tr. Venture de Paradis, ed. J. Gaulmier, Beirut 1950, 73; Ibn al-S͟hiḥna, *al-Durr al-muntak͟hab fī taᵓrīk͟h mamlakat Ḥalab*, Beirut 1909, 265; ᶜUmarī, *Taᶜrīf*, Cairo 1312, 182, tr. R. Hartmann, in *ZDMG*, lxx (1916), 36 with n. 11; Ḳalḳas͟handī, *Ṣubḥ al-aᶜs͟hā*ᵓ, iv, 113 (where in l. 13 the words *Ḥamā wa-* should be deleted, cf. l. 14); Nābulusī, tr. A. von Kremer, in *SB Ak. Wien* (1850), ii, 331; G. Le Strange, *Palestine under the Moslems*, 81, 352, 507; M. Gaudefroy-Demombynes, *La Syrie à l'époque des Mamelouks*, Paris 1923, 77, 108, 116, 143, 182-227, 246, 249; J. L. Burckhardt, *Travels in Syria and the Holy Land*, London 1822, 150 ff., German tr. by Gesenius, 254; E. Quatremère, in *Fundgruben des Orients*, iv, 340, n. *c*; Ritter, *Erdkunde*, xvii, 822, 918, 922, 935, 967-8, 972-3; E. G. Rey, *Rapport sur une mission scientifique dans le Nord de la Syrie (1864-1865)*, in *Archives des missions scient. et litt.*, ser. ii, iii, Paris 1866, 344; idem, *Études sur les monuments de l'architecture militaire des Croisés en Syrie*, Paris 1871, 6, 42; R. Röhricht, *Regesta regni Hierosolymitani*, 191, no. 715 (1193 A.D.); H. Derenbourg, *Vie d'Ousâma*, Paris 1893, 8, 43, 281, 399-400; M. Van Berchem, *Epigraphie des Assassins de Syrie*, in *JA*, Ser. 9, ix (1897), 453-501; R. Dussaud, in *Rev. Archéol.* (1897), i, 349; idem, *Histoire et religion des Noṣairîs* (= *Bibl. de l'école des hautes études*, fasc. cxxix), Paris 1900, 21, n. 4, 23, 32, 80; idem, *Topographie historique de la Syrie antique et médiévale*, Paris 1927, 142-3, 153, 187, 209, 395; H. Lammens, *Au pays des Noṣaïris*, in *ROC*, v (1900), 423-7; G. L. Bell, *Syria: the desert and the sown*, London 1907, 217-18, German tr. *Durch die Wüsten u. Kulturstätten Syriens*, Leipzig 1908, ²1910, 211-12; M. von Oppenheim, in *ZG Erdk. Berl.*, xxxvi (1901), 74; Van Berchem, *Inschriften aus Syrien, Mesopot.*, *Kleinasien*, 1913 (= *Beiträge z. Assyriol.*, vii/1), 17-22; Van Berchem and E. Fatio, *Voyage en Syrie*, MIFAO, Cairo 1914, 113-16, 172; Dussaud, P. Deschamps and H. Seyrig, *La Syrie antique et médiévale illustrée*, Paris 1931, pl. 128; Guide Bleu, *Syrie-Palestine*, Paris 1932, 256-9; E. Honigmann, *Die Ostgrenze des byzantinischen Reiches von 363 bis 1071*, Brussels 1935, 107, 109; A. Latron, *La vie rurale en Syrie et au Liban*, Paris 1936, 160, 208; J. Weulersse, *Le pays des Alaouites*, Tours 1940, index s.v., and Album, pl. XCVIII figs. 219-20; Cl. Cahen, *La Syrie du nord*, Paris 1940, 170, 174-6, 255, 354; J. Sauvaget, *La poste aux chevaux dans l'empire des Mamelouks*, Paris 1941, 26 n. 114, 27 n. 116; R. Fedden, *Syria, an historical appreciation*, London 1946, 192-5; M. Canard, *Histoire de la dynastie des H'amdânides*, i, Algiers 1951, 206; R. Mantran and Sauvaget, *Règlements fiscaux ottomans. Les provinces syriennes*, Beirut 1951, 92; S. Runciman, *A history of the Crusades*, Cambridge 1951², i, 269, ii, 410; N. N. Lewis, *The Ismāᶜīlīs of Syria today*, in *JRCAS*, xxxix (1952), 69-77; R. Le Tourneau, *Damas de 1075 à 1154*, Damascus 1962, 89, 260; M. Dunand, *De l'Amanus au Sinai*, Beirut 1953, photo at p. 65; M. G. S. Hodgson, *The order of Assassins*, The Hague 1955, 105, 107, 133-4; B. Lewis, *The Ismāᶜīlites and the Assassins*, in K. M. Setton and M. W. Baldwin, eds., *A history of the Crusades*, Philadelphia 1955, i, 99, 132, see also index s.v. *Maṣyaf*, and ii, 789; Guide Bleu, *Moyen-Orient*, Paris 1956, 355-8; Deschamps, *Terre Sainte Romane*, Paris 1964, 139; N. Elisséeff, *Nūr al-Dīn*, Damascus 1967, 224-5, 351, 427, 521, 687; B. Lewis, *The Assassins*, London 1967, index s.v.; Deschamps, *Châteaux des Croisés*. iii. *Comté de Tripoli et Principauté d'Antioche*, Paris 1973, index s.v., and Album, pl. XCIIa; A. Raymond, ed., *La Syrie d'aujourd'hui*. Paris 1980, 18, 108, 419.

(E. HONIGMAN - [N. ELISSÉEFF])

MAṢYĀF [see MAṢYĀD].

AL-**MAṬĀLIᶜ** (A, pl. of *maṭlaᶜ*), ascensions, an important concept in mediaeval spherical astronomy and astronomical timekeeping [see MĪḲĀT]. Ascensions represent a measure of the amount of apparent rotation of the celestial sphere, and are usually measured from the eastern horizon, hence the name ascensions. Two kinds were used: (1) right ascensions, or ascensions in *sphaera recta*; and (2) oblique ascensions, or ascensions in *sphaera obliqua* [see also FALAK and MAṬLAᶜ].

(1) Right ascensions refer to the risings of arcs of the ecliptic over the horizon of a locality with latitude zero, and were called in mediaeval scientific Arabic *al-maṭāliᶜ fi 'l-falak al-mustaḳīm*. In Fig. 1, which displays the horizon of such a locality and the celestial equator (perpendicular to the horizon) as well as an instantaneous position of the ecliptic, an arc λ of the ecliptic (measured from the vernal equinox γ) rises in the same period of time as the arc α of the celestial equator. The function $\alpha(\lambda)$ called the right ascensions measures the rising time of the ecliptic arc λ. Such ascensions were called *maṭāliᶜ min awwal al-ḥamal*, since they were measured from the first point of Aries, that is, the vernal equinox γ.

The function $\alpha(\lambda)$ was often tabulated in the

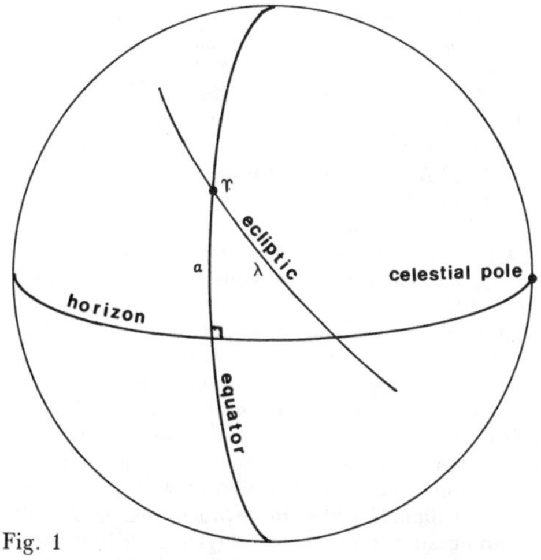

Fig. 1

astronomical handbooks known as *zīdjs* [see zīdj] for each degree of λ to two or three sexagesimal digits. The underlying formula expressed in modern notation is:

$$\alpha(\lambda) = \text{arc sin } (\tan \delta(\lambda) \cot \varepsilon),$$

where ε is the obliquity of the ecliptic and δ is the declination [see mayl]. The function $\rho(\lambda) = \tan \delta(\lambda)$ (multiplied by an appropriate constant related to the bases used for the various trigonometric functions) was also tabulated separately to facilitate computation of $\alpha(\lambda)$—it was called *al-maṭāliʿ li-kull al-arḍ*, "ascensions for all the earth". More commonly, however, the quantity $\alpha' = \alpha + 90°$, called *al-maṭāliʿ min awwal al-djady*, that is, ascensions measured from the first point of Capricorn, was tabulated. The use of this function, now referred to as "normed ascensions", is explained below.

The ascensions of celestial bodies not on the ecliptic, such as stars, were also called *maṭāliʿ*. Fig. 2 shows a star with equatorial coordinates α for ascensions and

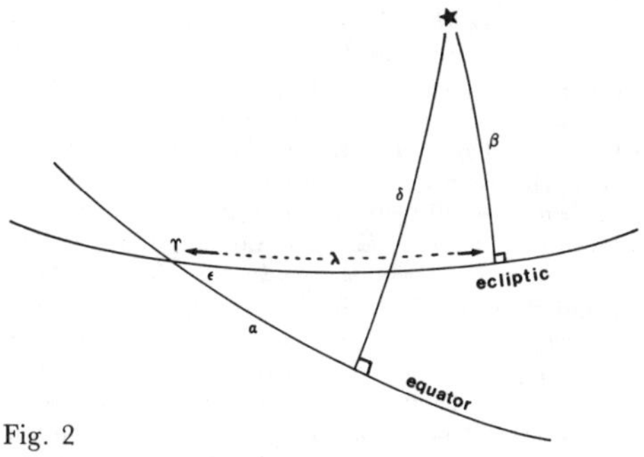

Fig. 2

δ for declination. Islamic star tables displayed either ecliptic longitudes and latitudes (λ and β) or equatorial ascensions (regular or normed) and declinations (α and δ) for a specific epoch. Since stellar longitudes increase steadily with time and stellar latitudes are constant, star tables could be modified for a different epoch by simply adding the amount of longitude increase (known as precession). Tables of equatorial coordinates could be prepared either by direct observation or by calculation from tables of ecliptic coordinates; in mediaeval times they could not be prepared from earlier tables of coordinates of the same kind because both stellar right ascension and declination are not linear functions of time. Formulae for the conversion of ecliptic to equatorial coordinates and *vice versa*, that is $(\lambda, \beta) \leftrightarrow (\alpha, \delta)$ were available to Muslim astronomers from Ptolemy's *Almagest*, and were simplified by them. The universal astrolabe [see shakkāziyya] was particularly useful for performing transformations of ecliptic and equatorial coordinates.

(2) Oblique ascensions, associated with a specific latitude, were called *maṭāliʿ al-balad* or *al-maṭāliʿ al-baladiyya*. In Fig. 3, the arc λ of the ecliptic rises in the same time as arc α_φ of the equator over the horizon of a locality with latitude ρ. Muslim astronomers tabulated $\alpha_\varphi(\lambda)$ for specific latitudes. From *ca.* 400/1010 onwards, they often tabulated it for each degree of terrestrial latitude, usually for each degree of λ. The oblique ascensions, $\alpha_\varphi(\lambda)$, are related to the right ascension, $\alpha(\lambda)$, by the identity:

$$\alpha_\varphi(\lambda) = \alpha(\lambda) - d(\varphi, \lambda)$$

where $d(\varphi, \lambda)$ is half the excess of daylight over 180°, called in Arabic the *niṣf faḍl al-nahār*. In Fig. 3, ♈H =

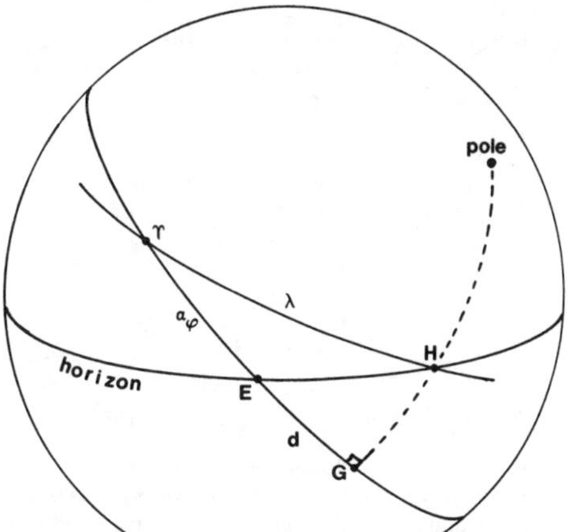

Fig. 3

λ, ♈E = α_φ, and EG = *d*. The formula for $d(\varphi, \lambda)$ used by mediaeval astronomers was equivalent to the modern formula:

$$\delta(\varphi, \lambda = \text{arc sin } (\tan \delta(\lambda) \tan \varphi.$$

Again, the function $e(\lambda) = \tan \delta(\lambda)$ was used to generate values of $d(\varphi, \lambda)$ and, hence, tables of $\alpha_\varphi(\lambda)$ for different latitudes.

Oblique ascensions are of singular importance in timekeeping and in mathematical astrology. In both disciplines, the point of the ecliptic instantaneously rising over the horizon, which is known as the horoscopus [see ṭāliʿ], is of interest. In Fig. 4, it is labelled H. Clearly, from the geometry of the sphere, the oblique ascensions of the horoscopus (with ecliptic longitude λ_H) are given by the relation:

$$\alpha_\varphi(\lambda_H) = \alpha_\varphi(\lambda_\odot) + T$$

where $\lambda_\odot$ is the longitude of the sun and *T* is the time in equatorial degrees since sunrise. In order to measure the time of day, it is thus sufficient to control the oblique ascensions of the horoscopus and the solar longitude. Similar procedures hold for timekeeping by the stars at night. Muslim astronomers, following a tradition started in Ptolemy's *Handy tables*, generally preferred to use the normed ascensions $\alpha' = \alpha + 90°$ because of the relation

$$\alpha_\varphi(\lambda_H) = \alpha(\lambda_M) + 90° = \alpha'(\lambda_M),$$

where λ_M is the longitude of upper mid-heaven, the

point of the ecliptic culminating on the meridian. If a star whose ecliptic longitude is known is observed to be culminating, then the longitude of the horoscopus can be found immediately from tables of $\alpha_\varphi(\lambda)$ and $\alpha'(\lambda)$. Once the latter is found, the astrological houses can be determined using tables of ascensions. Ascensions, then, were important in both timekeeping and astrology. In all *zīdjs* and treatises on astronomical timekeeping they figure prominently.

Ascensions were also important in determinations of lunar crescent visibility [see RUʾYAT AL-HILĀL]. Since one of the most popular conditions for crescent visibility was that the difference in setting times of the sun and moon be twelve equatorial degrees (= 48 minutes of time), the problem could easily be expressed in terms of ascensions. The situation is shown in Fig. 4. Note that the "descensions" (*maghārib*) of an ecliptic arc λ are $\alpha_\varphi\ (\lambda + 180°)$. Thus if $\lambda_\odot$ and $\lambda_m = \lambda_\odot + \Delta\lambda$ represent the longitudes of the sun and moon, the condition may be expressed as:

$$\alpha_\varphi\ (180° + \lambda_m) - \alpha_\varphi\ (180° + \lambda_\odot) = 12°$$

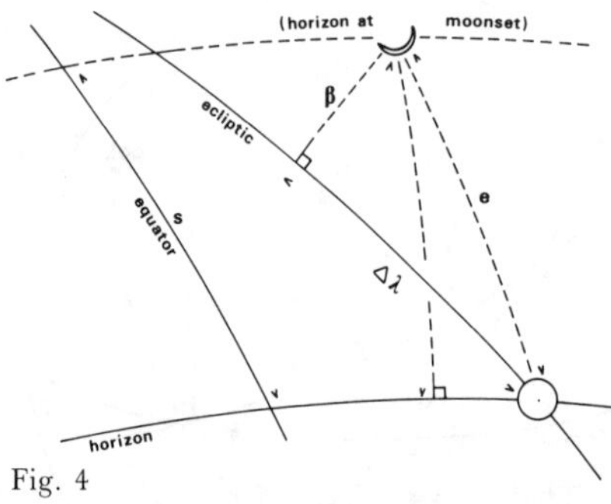

Fig. 4

Using tables of $\alpha_\varphi\ (\lambda)$ for a specific latitude, as well as linear interpolation (*al-taʿdīl bayn al-saṭrayn*), it is possible to calculate values of $\Delta\lambda$ satisfying this condition for each range of $\lambda_\odot$. Tables of such values, for each zodiacal sign of solar longitude, were compiled already in the 3rd/9th century for the latitude of Baghdād. Certain later Islamic lunar visibility tables display such information for several latitudes.

Bibliography: E. S. Kennedy, *A survey of Islamic astronomical tables*, in *Trans. American Philosophical Soc.*, N.S., xlvi/2 (1956), 140, 170; D. A. King, *Spherical astronomy in medieval Islam: the Ḥākimī Zīj of Ibn Yūnus*, forthcoming, sections II.4-5 and III.13-15; J. Hamadanizadeh, *A medieval interpolation scheme for oblique ascensions*, in **Centaurus*, ix (1963), 257-65; Y. Id, *An analemma construction for right and oblique ascensions*, in **The Mathematics Teacher*, lxii (1969), 669-72; King, *Studies in astronomical timekeeping in medieval Islam* (forthcoming), part I, section 7 (on auxiliary tables for computing ascensions).

On a highly sophisticated method for converting ecliptic and equatorial coordinates, see idem, *Al-Khalīlī's auxiliary tables for solving problems of spherical astronomy*, in *Jnal. for the History of Astronomy*, iv (1973), 99-110, esp. 105-7. On the use of ascensions in astrology, see, for example, Kennedy and H. Krikorian-Preisler, *The astrological doctrine of projecting the rays*, in **al-Abḥāth*, xxv (1972), 3-15.

On the use of ascensions in lunar crescent visibility determinations, see Kennedy and M. Janjanian, *The crescent visibility table in al-Khwārizmī's Zīj*, in **Centaurus*, xi (1965), 73-8, and King, *Some early Islamic tables for determining lunar crescent visibility*, in King and G. Saliba (eds.), *From Deferent to Equant: Studies in the History of Science in the Near East in Honor of E. S. Kennedy, Annals of the New York Academy of Sciences* d(= 500) (1987), pp. 185-225.

* Articles marked with an asterisk are reprinted in E. S. Kennedy *et alii*, *Studies in the Islamic exact sciences*, Beirut 1983.

(D. A. KING)

AL-MAṬĀMĪR [see MAṬMŪRA].

AL-MATAMMA, a town in the Democratic Republic of the Sudan, located in Shandī District, western bank of the Nile, opposite Shandī town [*q.v.*]. The number of households there in 1973 was 1,108.

Its origins are unknown, but its development was closely connected with caravan traffic that crossed the Nile there, and its status as a sister-town of Shandī is indicated by the fact that it was also known as Shandī al-Gharb. At the end of the 18th century it became involved in the upheavals of the Fundj kingdom [*q.v.*]; and around 1801 a rival faction of the Saʿdāb royal family of Shandī settled in al-Matamma, eventually becoming an ally of the Shāʾiḳiyya in their struggle against Fundj domination. By the time of the Egyptian invasion (1820-1), the population of al-Matamma numbered about 6,000, being ruled by King Musāʿid who was subordinate to his cousin Nimr, king of Shandī. Subjected to foreign rule, the rival kings united in a plot to kill the Egyptian commander Ismāʿīl Pasha [*q.v.*] (1822). After the subsequent reprisals in 1823, which hit Shandī more severely than al-Matamma, the latter grew into the most important tribal and commercial centre of the Djaʿaliyyūn [*q.v.*], with a large merchant class, and served as a transit point for caravans as in former times. By the middle of the century it was celebrated throughout the Sudan for the manufacture of coarse cotton scarfs. During the Mahdiyya [*q.v.*], on the eve of the British invasion in 1897, the people of al-Matamma refused to evacuate the town in order to make it a stronghold, and instead established contact with the invaders. A battle ensued in which the Mahdist forces killed most of the rebels (30 Muḥarram 1315/1 July 1897). During the present century, al-Matamma has gradually recovered but has not regained its commercial role.

Bibliography: Early references to al-Matamma are mostly found in the travel literature: G. B. English, *A narrative of an expedition to Dongola and Sennaar*, London 1822, 133-5; F. Caillaud, *Voyage à Méroé*, Paris 1826, ii, 180; E. Rüppel, *Reisen in Nubien, Kordofan und dem peträischen Arabien*, Frankfurt-am-Main 1829, 110-11; G. A. Hoskins, *Travels in Ethiopia*, London 1835, 123-4; J. Petherick, *Egypt, the Soudan and Central Africa*, London 1861, 177-8; R. Hill (ed.), *On the frontiers of Islam. Two manuscripts concerning the Sudan under Turco-Egyptian rule, 1822-1845*, Oxford 1970, 165. Sudanese tribal traditions: H. A. MacMichael, *A history of the Arabs in the Sudan*, London 1967, i, 233, ii, 376-7. Valuable secondary sources: O. G. S. Crawford, *The Fung kingdom of Sennar, with geographical account of the middle Nile region*, Gloucester 1951, 61-4; P. M. Holt, *The Mahdist state in the Sudan*, Oxford 1966, 213-18; idem, *A modern history of the Sudan*, London 1974, 40, 46, 72, 106; R. S. O'Fahey and J. L. Spaulding, *Kingdoms of the Sudan*, London 1974, 96-7, 102-3.

(A. BJØRKELO)

MAṬBAʿA (A.), printing.

1. IN THE ARAB WORLD

The Arabic verb *ṭabaʿa*, in the sense of printing a book, is a neologism probably inspired by the Italian or the French. This meaning is already attested in the

Dictionnaire français-arabe of Bocthor (1829): "printing", "the art of printing" is *ṭibāʿa* or *ṣināʿāt al-ṭabʿ*, while "printing-house", "printing-press" is *maṭbaʿa* or *dār al-ṭibāʿa*. It is the art of printing, in the context of the three technical processes that it comprises, xylography or wood-block printing (the discovery of which dates back to remote antiquity), printing by means of moving type (developed during the second half of the 15th century), and lithography (invented by G. A. Senefelder in 1796), which is the subject of this article.

Of the three processes, it seems that the Arabs, and the Muslims in particular, preferred lithography, especially during the 19th century. According to Demeerseman (see below, Tunisia) there are numerous reasons for this preference. The first reason is technical: lithography is more versatile than printing, and offers a greater range of possibilities in the production of designs and of maps. The second is artistic: it is an art which lends itself remarkably well to the reproduction of writing. As a corollary, there is the cultural reason: lithography causes no problem to the reader who is accustomed only to the manuscript style adopted for the writing-tablets of the Ḳurʾān school. Finally, there are social and economic reasons. In the East, the profession of copyist was highly developed, giving prestige and prosperity to a large section of the urban working class. According to the Bolognese scholar Luigi Ferdinando Marsigli (1658-1730), the number of Turkish copyists in Constantinople, when he visited the city, was as high as 80,000. The creation of printing-presses would therefore have caused devasting unemployment among the educated population. Further reasons are moral, doctrinal and political, and these may easily be imagined.

Regarding the relatively late date of the introduction of printing in the Arab countries (except in Lebanon and Syria, the practice did not emerge until the beginning of the 19th century) two other factors, besides those already mentioned, played an important role. In the first place, the majority of the Arab countries had been under the Ottoman domination since the beginning of the 16th century. Before establishing its own official press in 1726, the Sublime Porte had hitherto forbidden (edicts of Bāyezīd II in 1485 and of Selīm I in 1515) the Muslims to print texts in Arabic characters (although it permitted the Jews to print texts in Hebrew). The second factor is the economic problem which would have faced the innovators. To found presses of even modest size required the investment of substantial capital sums, which the book market, revolutionised by the availability of large-scale mechanical production, remained incapable of repaying properly. It should not be forgotten that the Medici Press in Rome was virtually bankrupt in 1610, because its proprietor-director, Raimondi, lacked the expertise to distribute the books that he printed. And such must have been the fate, undeserved, of many other presses, whose record is confined to the production of a single work! A copyist, on the other hand, worked to a contract, and his only capital outlay was the purchase of paper.

A. Xylography

Xylography, or printing by means of plates or characters engraved on wood, was used by the Arabs, judging by the specimens which have been noted in the collections of manuscripts and papyri possessed by certain libraries in Europe (Vienna, Heidelberg, Berlin and the British Library). America (Museum of the University of Pennsylvania), or the Arab countries (National Library of Cairo and the ʿAbd al-Wahhāb Collection in Tunis). There is no precise indication of the dates of these specimens, of which the majority are amulets. According to Moritz, six printing-plates in the collection of the ancient Khedival Library of Cairo date from the Fāṭimid period. A study of xylographed Arabic texts would be a worthwhile undertaking, rendering it possible to observe whether the Arabs confined themselves to plates or whether whole books were composed according to this process. See G. Levi Della Vida, *An Arabic block print*, in *The Scientific Monthly*, lix (December 1944), 473-4; F. Bonola Bey, *Note sur l'origine de l'imprimerie arabe en Europe*, in *BIE*, 5th series, iii (1909), 75; A. Demeerseman, *L'imprimerie en Orient et au Maghreb*, in *IBLA*, xvii (1954), 21-3; R. W. Bulliet, *Medieval Arabic* ṭarsh: *a forgotten chapter in the history of printing*, in *JAOS*, cvii (1987), 427-38.

B. Printing and lithography

1. *In Europe*.

Arabic printing with mobile characters originated and developed, through a curious combination of circumstances which have yet to be fully explained, in Europe in the 16th century. It was in fact with the purpose of publishing Christian religious texts in Eastern languages and in Arabic in particular, that the Cardinal Ferdinando de' Medici, on the advice of Pope Gregory XIII, in 1585 entrusted to the orientalist Giovan Battista Raimondi the task of establishing and administering the *Typographia Medicea linguarum externarum*. Until the death of Raimondi in 1614, this press was to print a whole series of Arabic works including the translation of the Bible and of the Four Gospels, the *Canon Medicinae* of Avicenna, and the anonymously-edited text of the *Kitāb Nuzhat al-mushtāḳ* by al-Idrīsī [*q.v.*].

There exist, however, numerous works printed well before the *Typographia Medicea* began to operate, such that printing in Arabic characters must be deemed to have emerged at the beginning of the 16th century, or even in the final year of the 15th. The first book in Arabic characters seems in fact to have been a Ḳurʾān printed in Venice by Paganino de' Paganini (the dates given vary between 1499 and 1530); many authors speak of this work but no specimen of it survives, all copies having been destroyed by fire (see Maria Nallino, *Una cinquecentesca edizione del Corano stampata a Venezia*, in *Atti dell'Istituto Veneto di Scienze, Lettere ed Arti*, cxxiv, Classe di scienze morali, lettere ed arti [Venice 1965], 1-12).

The earliest Arabic text that has reached us is a book of Christian prayers, the *Kitāb Ṣalāt al-sawāʿī* (or *Horologium breve*). It was produced at Fano, in the region of the Marches which constituted part of the States of the Church, in 1514, by the master printer Gregorio de' Gregori (or de' Gregoris). Two years later, in Genoa, the typographer Pier Paolo Porro printed the trilingual *Psalterium* (Greek, Hebrew and Arabic), or else the Book of Psalms (*Kitāb al-Mazāmīr*) with an Arabic preface. In 1556, in Rome, the press of the Collegium Societatis Jesu produced an anonymous religious treatise in Arabic (probably to be attributed to the Jesuit Giambattista Eliano or Romano) with the Latin title *Fidei orthodoxae brevis et explicata confessio* and the Arabic title *Iʿtiḳād al-amāna*, which was to be reprinted many times during the same century and in the following century.

The first work of a non-religious nature was printed, again in Rome, by the Venetian master printer Domenico Basa at his Roman printing-press in 1585, the book in question being the *Kitāb al-Bustān fī ʿadjāʾib al-arḍ wa 'l-buldān*, a work of descriptive geography by an author of whom nothing is known but his name, Salāmish b. Kundukdjī al-Ṣāliḥī.

Outside Italy, worthy of note is an Arabic grammar

by Guillaume Postel, printed in Paris, probably in 1538, of which the Arabic characters are unfortunately almost illegible. At Neustadt in 1582, with characters engraved on wood, there was published an *Alphabetum arabicum* by Jacob Christmann, professor of Arabic at Heidelberg. The same characters were used in Heidelberg, the following year, for the printing of a translation by Ruthger Spey of the *Epistle to the Galatians* of St. Paul.

Again at Rome, in 1627, there began the intensive typographical activity of the press of the Sacra Congregatio de Propaganda Fide, responsible for the printing of two particularly monumental works. The first is the Arabic translation of an abridged version of the *Annales ecclesiastici*, or history of the Church edited in twelve volumes by Cardinal Cesare Baronio, published between 1653 and 1671, and the second, the *Biblia arabica ad usum Ecclesiarum orientalium*, in four folio volumes.

At least three other presses, active in the 17th century, are worthy of mention. The first is that of the Collegio Ambrosiano of Milan where, in 1632, there was printed the Latin translation of the well-known *Ḳāmūs* of al-Fīrūzābādī, made by Antonio Giggei under the title of *Thesaurus linguae arabicae* in four large folio volumes.

The second is that of the Seminary of Padua, in the state of Venice, which ceased to operate in 1698 after printing, in two large volumes, the Arabic text of the Ḳurʾān, with Latin translation, an introduction and a commentary (drawn from as yet unedited Arabic works) by Ludovico Marracci, confessor to Pope Innocent XI, at the latter's request.

The third is the Reale Stamperia of Palermo, in Sicily, which published the first collection of accounts relating to the Arab occupation of Sicily intitled *Rerum arabicarum, quae ad historiam Siculam spectant, ampla collectio,* the *Libro del Consiglio d'Egitto*, or *Kitāb Diwān Miṣr*, by the notorious forger, the Abbé Giuseppe Vella, and finally the first Italian edition of the *Grammatica arabica* of Erpenius.

It is extremely difficult to establish even a rudimentary list of the Arab presses of Europe (nevertheless, see J. Balagua, *L'imprimerie arabe en Occident. (XVIe, XVIIe et XVIIIe-siècle)*, Paris 1984). Documentation is often fragmentary, sometimes non-existent. Certain presses are known only because they are mentioned in the works that have survived from them and available for study. Four editions of the Ḳurʾān, published in Europe between the end of the 17th and the first half of the 19th century, indicate the existence of other Arabic presses in Germany and in Russia. The first is that of Hinckelmann, produced in the Free City of Hamburg in 1694. Two Russian editions represent the first two Ḳurʾāns published by Muslims: the first in 1787 in Saint Petersburg, the then capital of the Tsarist Russian Empire; and the second in 1803 in Kazan, in the region of the Volga, today the capital of the Tatar Republic. Finally, in 1834, at Leipzig in Saxony, the centre of the book trade, Gustav Flügel published the first edition of his Ḳurʾānic text, later to be used by several generations of orientalists.

See Olga Pinto, *La tipografia araba in Italia dal XVI al-XIX secolo*, in *Levante*, 1-2 (1964), 8-16; Angelo Piemontese, *I fondi dei manoscritti arabi, persiani e turchi in Italia*, in *Gli Arabi in Italia*, Milan (privately printed edition by Credito Italiano-Libri Scheiwiller) 1979, 661-88; idem, *Les fonds de manuscrits persans conservées dans les Bibliothèques d'Italie*, in *JA*, cclxx/3-4 (1982), 273-93.

In Eastern Europe, it should be noted that towards the end of the 17th century, at the request of the Melkite patriarch of Aleppo, Athanasius Dabbās, the Voivode of Wallachia (a tributary of the Ottoman sultanate in the kingdom of Rumania) Constantin Bassaraba Brancoveanul, installed at Sinagovo an Arabic press which edited numerous liturgical books in Arabic. This press seems to have ceased production in 1704, when Athanasius returned to Syria (see below, Syria) and took the initiative of installing a printing-press in the city of Aleppo, his patriarchal seat. See J. Nasrallah, *Les imprimeries Melkites jusqu'à la fin du 18e siècle*, in *al-Maçarrat*, 34th year (1948), 438-40.

2. *In the Near East.*

a. Lebanon. The Lebanese claim the honour of having printed the first book in an Arab country. The work in question is a Psalter printed in 1610 at the Convent of Saint Antony of Quzḥaya (Dayr Mār Anṭuniyūs or Dayr Qizḥayya ?). The pages are divided into two columns, that on the right being for the text in Syriac, and that on the left for the Arabic text in *kar<u>sh</u>ūnī* script [*q.v.*]. According to a note appended to the work, the printing was done under the supervision of the master (*muʿallim*) Pasquale Eli, a native of Camerino in central Italy. This edition marked a short-lived enterprise. More than a century was to elapse, and numerous unsuccessful attempts were to be made, before the *<u>Sh</u>ammās* ʿAbd Allāh Zā<u>kh</u>ir, with his second experiment in typography (the first having been in Aleppo) established a press at the Convent of Mār Yūḥannā al-Ṣābig<u>h</u> in 1734. Subsequently, other presses were founded, invariably among religious communities.

The American Press and the Imprimerie Catholique deserve special mention, particularly for their editing activities. The Protestant Mission of the American Board of Commissioners for Foreign Missions had installed an Arabic press in Malta, where it functioned from 1822 to 1842. When the Mission transferred its headquarters to Beirut, on 10 July 1823, the decision was taken to move the Arabic press to the Lebanese capital. This was accomplished on 8 May 1834.

The Imprimerie Catholique was founded to some extent with the object of countering the activity of Protestant missionaries. Its operations commenced in 1848, but the press soon developed into one of the best-equipped publishing houses of the Near East. See J. Joseph Nasrallah, *L'imprimerie au Liban*, Beirut 1949, 160.

b. Syria. In Syria, it was the same Melkite Patriarch, Athanasius Dabbās, who, on his return from Europe, undertook to install a press in the city that was his patriarchal seat, Aleppo, and with the aid of the *<u>Sh</u>ammās* ʿAbd Allāh Zā<u>kh</u>ir the press operated from 1706 to 1711. More than a century was to pass before a Sardinian printer, Belfante (?), came, in 1841, to establish a lithographic press at Aleppo. Curiously, the first book printed under his supervision was the *Dīwān* of Ibn al-Fāriḍ. See <u>Kh</u>. Ṣābāt, *Taʾrī<u>kh</u> al-Ṭibāʿa*, ch. iv, 96-128, and Wahid Gdoura, *Le début de l'imprimerie arabe à Istanbul et en Syrie*, Tunis 1985.

c. Palestine. Palestine—and Jerusalem in particular—has throughout history been a centre of interest for all the revealed religions. As early as 1830, a Jew, Nessim Bāḳ (?) had opened a press in Jerusalem for the printing of religious texts in Hebrew. (The Jews were the first Ottoman subjects to use printing for this purpose; in Constantinople their typographical activity dates back to 1490 !) In 1848, it was the turn of the Franciscans, encouraged by the young Emperor of Austria, Franz Josef, through the intermediary of a monk of Austrian origin, Frotchner, to establish the Tipografia dei Padri Francescani di Gerusalemme. Again in 1848, a printing press was founded, called the London Press, by Protestant missionaries whose aim was the propagation of the Gospel among the Jews. Within a short time, the city of Jerusalem was full of presses producing works in Arabic and other oriental languages including Russian, Armenian, Greek and Turkish, invariably operated by religious organisations or on their behalf. See Ṣābāt, *op. cit.*, ch. vii, 319-24.

d. Jordan. Jordan did not become an independent Arab state in the form of an emirate until after the First World War, in 1921 (even though it was subject to British Mandate until 1946). It was in fact in 1922 that a printing-press belonging to the typographer K͟halīl Naṣr, who had founded it in Haifa in 1909, was transferred to Amman. It was used for printing the journal *al-Urdunn.* Three years later, the Government Press was established. See Ṣābāt, *op. cit.*, ch. vii, 325-6.

e. ʿIrāḳ. Historians do not agree as to the date at which printing was introduced to ʿIrāḳ. According to Razūḳ ʿĪsā, the first ʿIrāḳī lithographic works was founded at al-Kāẓimiyya and the first and only work printed was *Dawḥat al-wuzarāʾ fī taʾrīk͟h waḳāʾiʿ al-Zawrāʾ* by the *S͟hayk͟h* Rasūl Efendi al-Kirkūkī, in 1237/1821 or, according to others, in 1246/1830.

Rufaʾīl Buṭī (?), states that Dāwūd Pas͟ha al-Kurd͟jī, the last independent Mamlūk, published in Bag͟hdād in 1816, by means of lithography, an official bilingual Turkish-Arabic journal intitled *D͟jurnāl al-ʿIrāḳ.* Although no copy has survived, Buṭī claims that the existence of the journal was mentioned by foreign travellers who visited ʿIrāḳ in this period.

After the creation of another lithographical press, this time in Karbalāʾ, the first press using mobile characters was established by the Dominican Fathers in Mawṣil in 1859. One year later, it received sets of Arabic, Syriac and Latin types offered by the Imprimerie Nationale of Paris. The latter was the only establishment which possessed machinery for the casting of type.

The first official press was founded by Midḥat Pas͟ha, who used it for the publication of a bilingual Turkish-Arabic journal, *al-Zawrāʾ* (15 June 1869). See Ṣābāt, *op. cit.*, ch. vi, 293-313; K͟hālid Ḥabīb al-Rāwī, *Min taʾrīk͟h al-ṣaḥāfa al-ʿirāḳiyya*, Bag͟hdād 1978.

3. *In the Arabian Peninsula.*

a. Saudi Arabia. The first printing-press introduced in the country was that of the Ottoman *wilāyet* of the Ḥid͟jāz in the year 1300/1882. It was used to print the official journal entitled *al-Ḥid͟jāz.* Two years later, a lithographical press was also introduced. With the creation of the Kingdom of the Ḥid͟jāz, the new king, the *S͟harīf* Ḥusayn, installed a small printing-press at Mecca. This was in 1919, and the press was used to print the official journal *al-Ḳibla.* According to some, the *S͟harīf* personally performed the roles of writer, publisher and printer. See Ṣābāt, *op. cit.*, ch. vii, 331-6.

b. North Yemen. In 1877, the Ottoman Sultan ʿAbd al-Ḥamīd II ordered the establishment of a press at Ṣanʿāʾ, capital of the Yemen, for the publication of an offical Turkish-Arabic weekly paper intitled *Ṣanʿāʾ* after the name of the city. The same press was put to use by the Imām Yaḥyā after the recognition of the independence of his country in 1923. See Ṣābāt, *op. cit.*, ch. vii, 327-30.

c. Baḥrayn. It was a poet known by the name of *S͟hāʿir al-K͟halīd͟j* ("The Poet of the Gulf"), ʿAbd Allāh ʿAlī al-Zāʾid, who in 1938 purchased a printing press in England and called it *Maṭbaʿat al-Baḥrayn.* The press was used for the printing of material required by local administration and trading-houses, as well as for textbooks. In 1939 it began printing the journal *al-Baḥrayn*, published by its proprietor. See Ṣābāt, *op. cit.*, ch. viii, 339-42.

d. Kuwait. Before 1947, Kuwait imported all its printed materials from abroad. The *al-Maʿārif* Press was founded with the importation of a small press and a set of characters bought second-hand in ʿIrāḳ. Three years later, it was repurchased by the *Dāʾirat al-Maʿārif* (a kind of local education authority). In 1954, the Kuwaiti government decided to set up an official organisation for printing and publishing (*Dāʾirat al-maṭbūʿāt wa ʾl-nas͟hr*) equipped with modern machinery. See Ṣābāt, *op. cit.*, ch. viii, 343-6.

e. Ḳaṭar. In spite of its small size, the emirate of Ḳaṭar has, since 1956, possessed a typographical establishment known as *Maṭābiʿ al-ʿurūba.* Since 1961, this has printed *al-D͟jarīda al-rasmiyya* ("The Official Journal") and a monthly information sheet in Arabic intitled *al-Mas͟hʿal*, organ of the Qatar General Petroleum Corporation. See Ṣābāt, *op. cit.*, ch. viii, 347-8.

4. *In the Nile Valley.*

a. Egypt. It was with the expedition of Bonaparte that printing was introduced to Egypt in 1798. The Arabic characters used were those of the official Press of the French Republic, in addition to those of the Arabic Press of the Propaganda of Rome. The latter also supplied a number of its staff, to serve as overseers, typographers and printers. The first French and Arabic printed works were produced on board the flagship *Orient*, the headquarters of Bonaparte and his staff, and bear the mention "printed on board the *Orient* by the naval military press". After disembarkation at Alexandria, a press was installed there and given the name of the "Imprimerie Orientale et Française". A second press was established in Ezbekieh Square in Cairo, and this was known as the Imprimerie Nationale. Alongside the latter, there existed for some time a private press belonging to Joseph Marc Emmanuel Aurel, a printer and bookseller from Valence (France) and a friend of Bonaparte. His press was entrusted with the printing of the *Courrier d'Egypte*, a journal of local information, and of the *Décade Egyptienne*, a literary journal reporting the activities of the Institut des Sciences et des Arts d'Égypte. When the National Press began to operate at full capacity, this put an end to the activity of Marc Aurel, who sold his press and returned to France in 1800.

It should be noted that, among the administrative or political texts published, the orientalist Jean Joseph Marcel, who was responsible for the supervision of these presses, published the Arabic text of the Fables of Luḳmān, accompanied by a French translation. The activities of the expedition's presses ceased in 1801 with the evacuation of the French troops.

Official typographical activity was revived some twenty years later, on the instructions of Muḥammad ʿAlī Pas͟ha, with the establishment of a press at Būlāḳ. This began to function *ca.* 1822. The staff consisted partly of Egyptians, including a certain Nicolas Masabki (Masābikī) who had been sent for training to Milan, Italy, and partly of Europeans, among them some Italian typographers who had worked in the presses of the French expedition and remained in the country.

The significance of this event is immense; the inauguration of this "Press of the Pas̲h̲a" in fact marks the beginning of the movement towards the renaissance of the Arab world which has characterised these past two centuries.

Alongside the Būlāḳ Press, which was later to be known by the name of *al-Maṭbaʿa al-amīriyya*, a number of private presses, large and small, were established, usually combined with a publishing house, managed by Egyptians or by Europeans. The history of these presses has yet to be written, but with their publications they contributed in a significant manner to establishing the primacy of Egypt in the great process of evolution which the *Nahḍa* was to be.

See A. Geiss, *Histoire de l'imprimerie en Egypte*, in *Bulletin de l'Institut Egyptien*, 5th series, i, (1907), 133-57. 2nd part, in *ibid.*, ii (1908), 195-220; on the publications of the expedition's presses, see R. G. Canivet, *L'Imprimerie de l'expédition d'Egypte. Les journaux et les procès-verbaux de l'Institut (1798-1801)*, in *ibid.*, iii (1909), 1-22; on the first publications of the Būlāḳ press, see T. X. Bianchi, *Catalogue général des livres arabes, persans et turcs imprimés à Boulac, en Egypt, depuis l'introduction de l'imprimerie dans ce pays*, in *JA*, 4th series, ii (1843), 24-63; on the private presses, see O. Pinto, *Mose Castelli, tipografo italiano al Cairo*, in Univ. di Roma—Studi Orientali pubblicati a cura della Scuola orientale, v. A *Francesco Gabrieli. Studi orientalistici offerti nel sessantesimo compleanno dai suoi colleghi e discepoli*, Rome 1964, 217-23.

b. Sudan. It was during the Turkish-Egyptian occupation of this country (1820-85), at a date which cannot be fixed precisely, that a lithographic work was introduced with the object of responding to the needs of the administration. It is known that it was used by Gordon Pas̲h̲a, when he was appointed Governor of Sudan, to print paper money as a replacement for the metal coinage which gave out during the siege of Khartoum, between the end of 1884 and January 1885. After the capture of the town, the press fell into the hands of the Mahdists [see AL-MAHDIYYA], who used it to print the *k̲h̲iṭābāt al-daʿwa* (messages for religious dissemination) of the Mahdī and other books of a religious nature. See Muḥammad Ibrāhīm Abū Salīm, *al-Ḥaraka al-fikriyya fi 'l-Mahdiyya*, Khartoum 1970, 58-62; idem, *Taʾrīk̲h̲ al-K̲h̲arṭūm*, Khartoum 1971, 212.

5. *In the Mag̲h̲rib.*

a. Libya. The first press was the official one introduced by the governor of the *wilāyet* of Tripoli in 1866. Installed in the fortress of the town, it possessed lithographical and typographical facilities. It was here that the first issue of *Ṭarābulus G̲h̲arb*, the official Turkish-Arabic journal of the local Ottoman administration, was printed. According to R. L. Playfair, *The bibliography of the Barbary States, Pt. I., Tripoli and the Cyrenaica*, London-Royal Geographic Society Suppl. Papers, ii, 1889, 557-614, in 1827, a journal entitled *L'Investigateur Africain* was published in Tripoli. However, researches, especially by E. Rossi, have shown that the work involved was in fact a manuscript journal, a sort of *ante litteram* newsletter, composed by the Swedish Consul, Gråberg de Hemsö, with the collaboration of his European colleagues resident in Tripoli. See also M. Scaparro, *La stampa di Tripoli turca (1866-1911)*, in *Tripolitania*, iii/3-4 (1933), 10-20; idem, *La stampa di Tripoli (1866-1933)*, in *ibid.* iii/7-8, 13-21.

b. Tunisia. Tunisia is one of those instances where printing was not introduced at the official level. Under Aḥmad Bey (1837-55), the Abbé François Bourgade, with the aid of a refugee from Leghorn, Pompeo Sulema, opened in Tunis, in the first months of 1845, the St. Louis College, to which a small lithographical press was attached. It was here that there appeared, in 1849, the first Arabic text printed in Tunisia, a translation into Arabic by Sulaymān al-Ḥarāʾirī, Arab secretary to the French Consulate, of a text by the Abbé Bourgade, of which the French title is *Soirées de Carthage ou dialogue d'un prêtre catholique, un mufti et un cadi.* The subsequent history of this press is not known in detail, but it is known that it was closed by the Ottoman authorities in the wake of a scandal involving forged banknotes.

The official lithographical press was founded in 1857. The first text was, according to Demeerseman, the *ʿAhd al-amān* (see *Dustūr*. i. Tunisia) solemnly promulgated at the Palace of the Bardo by Muḥammad Bey on 9 September 1857.

On 7 November 1859, a decree of the Bey authorised an English merchant, Richard Holt, to establish a press and to publish a gazette in Arabic and Italian which would provide "commercial news, statistical information and extracts from other publications, with the exception of anything of a political nature". Following difficulties raised especially by foreign representatives, Sadok Bey decided on 18 July 1860 to establish an official press. This was to print *al-Rāʾid al-tunisī* (a title rendered in French by *L'indicateur tunisien*), the first issue appearing in fact on 23 July of the same year. See A. Demeerseman, *Une étape importante de la culture islamique. Une parente méconnue de l'imprimerie arabe et tunisienne: la lithographie*, in *IBLA*, xvi/64 (1953), 347-89; idem, *Une étape décisive de la culture et de la psychologie sociale islamique. Les données de la controverse autour du problème de l'imprimerie*, in *ibid.*, xvii (1954), 1-48, 113-40.

c. Algeria. The first journal printed in Algeria was the *Estafette d'Alger*, which first appeared at Sidi Ferruch on 14 June 1830, produced by French troops who had landed in this small bay to the west of Algiers and who used a field printing-press. Apparently the same press was used to print the *Moniteur Algérien*, a bilingual French-Arabic journal, two years later. It is interesting to note that the Arabic text was lithographed. Almost a hundred years were to elapse before, in 1925, the founder of the Islamic orthodox reformist movement in Algeria, Ibn Bādīs, was able to establish an Algerian press in Constantine, *al-Maṭbaʿa al-islāmiyya al-d̲j̲azāʾiriyya*, subsequently known as *Maṭbaʿat al-S̲h̲ihāb*, after the name of the monthly magazine which it published until 1939. See Christiane Souriant-Hoebrechts, *La presse maghrébine*, Paris 1975; ʿAbd al-Malik Murtāḍ, *Maʿālim al-adab al-ʿarabī al-ḥadīt̲h̲ fi 'l-D̲j̲azāʾir*, in *al-Aḳlām*, xiv/11 (1979), 44-51 (*Ins̲h̲āʾ al-maṭābiʿ al-ʿarabiyya fi 'l-D̲j̲azāʾir*, 45).

d. Morocco. The first press in Morocco was a state foundation, founded on the instructions of the Filālī *S̲h̲arīf* Muḥammad b. ʿAbd al-Raḥmān (1859-73). This was a lithographical press (*maṭbaʿat ḥad̲j̲ar*) supervised by an Egyptian master printer, Muḥammad al-Ḳabbānī, which operated from January to August 1865 at Meknès, and was subsequently transferred to Fās. The first book printed seems to have been *al-S̲h̲amāʾil al-Muḥammadiyya* (according to Ayache, "The portrait of the Prophet") by the author, compiler of one of the six canonical *sunan*, died at the end of the 3rd/9th century, Muḥammad b. ʿĪsā al-Tirmid̲h̲ī. See. G. Ayache, *L'apparition de l'imprimerie au Maroc*, in *Hespéris-Tamuda*, v (1964), 143-61; M. Ben Cheneb and E. Lévi-Provençal, *Essai de répertoire chronologique des éditions de Fès*, Algiers 1922.

General bibliography: There exists no general work covering all the Arab countries. The most important works concerning the various regions are mentioned at the end of each section. On printing with movable characters, the most complete survey remains that of K̲h̲alīl Ṣābāt, *Taʾrīk̲h̲ al-ṭibāʿa fi ʾl-s̲h̲ark̲ al-ʿarabī*, Cairo 1966, 378 ff., with an ample bibliography of works in numerous languages; the Mag̲h̲rib is however completely excluded. Other countries, including Oman, the United Arab Emirates and South Yemen, also pass without mention in this work.

On the question of the slow pace of the diffusion of printing in the Arab countries, see, besides Demeerseman (cited in the bibliography relating to Tunisia), T. F. Carter, *Islam as a barrier to printing*, ch. xv of *The invention of printing in China*, in *MW*, xxxiii (1943), 213-16.

Finally, on the Arabic works published in Europe, reference may be made to the bibliographical works of C. F. de Schnurrer, *Bibliotheca arabica*, Halle-a.-S. 1811, covering the period from 1505 to 1810, and V. Chauvin, *Bibliographie des ouvrages relatifs aux Arabes publiés dans l'Europe chrétienne de 1810 à 1885*, Liège 1892. (G. OMAN)

2. IN TURKEY

Books in Turkish, primarily grammars and dictionaries and phrase-books, were printed in Western European countries within a century or so from the beginning there of printing in Arabic characters by means of movable type, whilst the Christian (Greek Orthodox and Armenian) and Jewish communities of the Ottoman empire also at an early date took the new invention for the production in their own languages and scripts.

The printing of books in Arabic characters from Italian presses (see section 1 above) soon began to acquire an additional motive to that of the interests of Arabic and Italian scholarship in the West, sc. the hope of finding export markets for the new books in the Islamic East itself, and in particular, in the Ottoman Empire, In Dhu ʾl-Kaʿda 996/September-October 1588, two merchants, Branton and Orazio Bandini, acquired a *firmān* from Sultan Murād III (982-1003/1574-95) for the import of printed books (this is reproduced at the end of the Arabic text of the mathematical text of Euclid, *K. Taḥrīr uṣūl li-Uḳlīdis*, produced at the Medici Press in Rome in 1594 from typeface made by Robert Granjon), indicating that official opinion in Istanbul, at this time at least, was not implacably opposed to the new invention (see Bonola Bey, 74-6; Gerçek, 23-4).

The French ambassador to the Porte, François Savary de Brèves (ambassador 1591-1605), had Arabic type cast in Istanbul intended for future use in his own printing house, and these were improved when he returned to Paris by the engraver Guillaume Le Bé the Elder (Bernard, 4; Brun, 170). Then when he was stationed in Rome, he printed at his own house, *Ex Typographia Savariana*, an Arabic version of the Book of Psalms (*al-Mazāmīr*), together with a Latin translation (*Liber Psalmorum Davidi Regis et Prophetae*), but the origins of the type used for printing this Psalter are uncertain (see Vaccari, 37-43). It was Savary de Brèves' diplomatic skill which brought about the agreement on trade, involving a grant of capitulations [see IMTIYĀZĀT], between Sultan Aḥmed I and Henry IV of France, signed on 20 May 1604, and in 1615 Savary de Brèves printed the text of this agreement with the help of the printer Etienne Paulin in Paris, with the Turkish and French versions on alternate pages and with the Turkish title of *Fransa*

pādis̲h̲āhi ile āl-i̊ ʿOt̲h̲mān pādis̲h̲āhi beyninde munʿaḳid olan ʿaḳidnāmedir ki d̲h̲ikr olunur. After Savary de Brèves' death in 1627, the famous printer Antoine Vitré bought his typefaces from his heirs in the name of King Louis XIII (Bernard, 5-6, 8 ff.).

It should be noted that the first work on Turkish grammar printed in the west, at Leipzig in 1612 by Hieronymus Megiser, in Latin with Turkish examples in the Arabic script, *Institutionum linguae turcicae libri quattuor*, dates from this time also.

J e w i s h   p r e s s e s. The first Jewish press in Istanbul was established by David and Samuel Nahmias, immigrants who had moved into the Ottoman lands from the West, but there are disputes over the date of the first book produced from this press. The date on this book, in letters rather than in numbers, is Friday, 4 Tebet 5254/13 December 1493, but it has been argued (cf. Steinschneider, 17) that this date cannot be right, because (a) it would have been difficult for immigrants from Spain to have established and been able to print books only a year after their arrival in 1492, and (b) there is an otherwise inexplicable gap between this date and that of the printing of the second book at this press, a *Torah* (Nisan 5265/April 1505) (Yaary, 17-18); but the earlier date still has wide acceptance. In any case, it is certain that this first book, whatever its date, the *Arbaʿah Turim* of Rabbi Jacob ben Asher, was the earliest to appear from this press (Posner, 91, no. 126).

A r m e n i a n   p r e s s e s. In 1562 the future Catholicos of Etchmiadzin, Michael I of Sivas (Catholicos 1567-76), sent a mission led by Abgar Tibir of Tokat to Pope Pius IV in Rome to discuss certain religious issues. Whilst nothing concrete was in fact achieved by this mission, Abgar Tibir stayed on and subsequently received permission from the Pope and the Doge to visit Venice, with the aim of learning the art of printing in order to produce Armenian books (Zarpanelyan, 43). In 1565, whilst still in Venice, he printed with the aid of his son Sultan Shah (who later took the name of Marc Antonio) the single-paged *Harnapuntur dumari* (perpetual calendar) and the *Sagmos* (Psalter) (Anasyan, 6, nos. 8, 10). In their second book produced, they included an engraving of the Pope with some of his cardinals (Teotik, 41). But Abgar Tibir became estranged from the Pope and found the censorship prevailing in Italy oppressive, hence returned to Istanbul in 1567. He probably set up his printing press in the Church of Surp Nigogos (the present Kefeli Mescid), which was used jointly by the Armenians and the Latin Dominicans, and using the founts brought from Venice and with the help of a monk named Hotor, printed six books between 1567 and 1569 (Ishkhanyan, 212). The first book printed, in 1567, was *Pokir keraganutyan gam ayppenaran* ("Elementary Armenian alphabet") (Anasyan, 6, no. 11). The first Turkish language book printed in the Armenian alphabet came much later, this being Mekhitar of Sivas's (1676-1749) *Turun keraganutyan ashkharapar levzin hayotz* ..., a grammar written in Turkish and teaching spoken Armenian, printed in Italy, at Antionio Bortoli's press in Venice in 1727 with the proviso that the Papal imprimatur, *Con Licenza de' Superiori e Privilegio*, was to be printed on the book's cover (Anasyan, 91, no. 354). However, the first Turkish language book printed in the Armenian alphabet in Istanbul was Bagdasar Tibir's *Bu kitāb oldur ki Krisdoneyag̲h̲an ḥayātîmîza iḳtiḍālî* ("This is a book containing what is necessary for our Christian life") of 1742 (Anasyan, 115-16, no. 465).

G r e e k   p r e s s e s. Nicodemus Metaxas of Cephalonia, who graduated from Balliol College,

Oxford, in 1622, started a business in London for printing religious books and with the financial backing of his merchant brother. These books were probably printed under Metaxas's supervision by William Jones or at the Elliot's Court press, and it may be that the first book published by Metaxas in Istanbul was printed in London at the latter press (Roberts, 19-24; Layton, 155). The Oecumenical Patriarch Cyril Lucaris (1572-1638), who held views similar to those of Calvinism, invited Metaxas to Istanbul in order to use his press against Jesuit Roman Catholic propaganda, to educate the Orthodox and to reform his Church (Roberts, 13). Arriving in 1627 on a Levant Company ship, he brought with him his Greek fount, the books he had printed in London and two skilled Dutch printers (Layton, 145). His printing house began in rented premises near to the English and French embassies, and the first book produced there in 1627 was a treatise against the Jews (Legrand, no. 166); but Jesuit intrigue aroused the Janissaries against the innovation of the press, and the latter destroyed it in January 1628 (Hadjiantoniou, 80-3).

The first Turkish text printed in the Greek alphabet (originally written by the Patriarch in Greek and then translated into the Turkish dialect of Ḳaramān, *Ḳaramānlid̲j̲a*), was the profession of faith of the first post-Ottoman conquest Orthodox Patriarch, Gennadios Scolarios, addressed to Sultan Meḥemmed II Fātiḥ, the *Iʿtiḳād-nāme*; the Sultan requested that it be translated into Turkish and it was also printed by Martin Crusius in *Turco-Graeciae libri octo*, Basel 1584, 109-20. Another religious work in *Ḳaramānlid̲j̲a* is the *Gülzār-i īmān-i Mesīḥī*; no press or place of printing is mentioned in it, but it may have been produced at the Armenian press in Istanbul by Panoggiotis Kyriakides (Salaville and Dalleggio, 3-4).

In all these cases, the presses of these minority faiths had to be imported from outside, and none of them were able to construct them within the Ottoman borders.

One inevitably wonders why no Turkish press existed at this time, when printed books imported from Europe were sold in Turkey and when the non-Muslim communities were printing books. A section on printing in Pečewī's *Taʾrīk̲h̲*, Istanbul 1283/1866, i, 107, argues that the printing press was no longer an alien thing and that Turkish society was slowly accepting it, because of the great speed with which a large number of books can be produced once the tedious work of type-setting has been done; clearly, this historian approved of printing; yet it was to be 78 years after Pečewī's death before the first Turkish Muslim press was to be established. The reason for the Muslims' aversion from printing doubtless included motives of religious conservatism but also the vested social and economic interests of the professions of calligraphers (*k̲h̲aṭṭāṭ*) [see K̲H̲AṬṬ], book illustrators, binders, etc.; and when printing eventually was established in the 18th century, only small numbers of books were produced and demand remained at a low level.

Ibrāhīm Müteferriḳa and his press. Some eight years before the establishment of his press in 1140/1727, Ibrāhīm Müteferriḳa had in 1132/1719-20 printed a map of the Sea of Marmara, probably dedicated to the Vizier Dāmād Ibrāhīm Pas̲h̲a and presented to him, since a note on the map's bottom right-hand corner reads "If Your Excellency my master so commands, larger ones can be produced. [Dated] year 1132". It seems therefore that attempts at setting up a printing press antedated 1132 by some years (see Kortoğlu, 14-15). A second map, of the Black Sea, followed in 1137/1724-5, and a third one, *Memālik-i Īrān*, in 1142/1729-30. A fourth map, *Iḳlīm-i Miṣr*, was known to have existed (Ersoy, 37), but remained lost until it surfaced recently for sale (see Brill's *Turcica catalogue no. 484*, June 1976, 16).

Concerning Ibrāhīm Müteferriḳa's Transylvanian origins, his conversion to Islam, his career in the Ottoman service as a diplomat and as an author, see the article IBRĀHĪM MÜTEFERRIḲA. Here is mentioned too his written proposal, the *Wesīlet al-ṭibāʿa*, to the Grand Vizier Dāmād Ibrāhīm Pas̲h̲a of 1139/1726-7 on the benefits of printing: the benefits for the masses needing instruction and for the ruling classes alike, the perpetuation of books by printing when manuscripts could and had been destroyed by war (as in the Christian Reconquista of al-Andalus and in the Mongol invasions) and the general usefulness of the new technique for Islam (this opuscule was printed as the first five pages of the first book which he printed, Wānḳulī's Turkish version of al-D̲j̲awharī's famous dictionary, the *Ṣiḥāḥ*). He feared religious opposition, and made a formal approach to the Vizier, requested a *fatwā* from the S̲h̲ayk̲h̲ al-Islām on the licitness of printing and asked Sultan Aḥmed III for a *firmān* authorising him to print books, promising that the first work undertaken would be Wānḳulī's dictionary, enclosing a few specimen pages of this already printed, explaining the process of proof-reading, setting forth how he had been working towards the project for eight years with the patronage and financial assistance of the high official Saʿīd Efendi and promising that at the end of each book printed the sale price would be given (see the specimens from this application at the end of Gerçek, and also Sungu).

With the help of Saʿīd Efendi, the Grand Vizier Dāmād Ibrāhīm Pas̲h̲a and the S̲h̲ayk̲h̲ al-Islām ʿAbd Allāh Efendi's *fatwā*, Aḥmed III was persuaded to issue a *firmān* to Saʿīd and Ibrāhīm Müteferriḳa in D̲h̲u 'l-Ḳaʿda 1139/1727 authorising the opening of a printing-works and enjoining the printing of books not on such subjects as *fiḳh*, *ḥadīt̲h̲*, *tafsīr*, *kalām*, but on practical subjects like medicine, crafts, geographical guides, etc., based on the authority of the *fatwā*s of the former *ḳāḍī*s of Istanbul, Salonica and G̲h̲alaṭa and of the S̲h̲ayk̲h̲ al-Islām (whose names were recorded in the written petition to the sultan); these last are to take charge of the proofreading, for which great care is to be exercised.

With this security behind them, Saʿīd and Ibrāhīm went ahead with the setting-up of the *dār al-ṭibāʿa* (popularly known as the *basma-k̲h̲āne*) in Ibrāhīm's own house in the Sultan Selīm neighbourhood of the Fātiḥ quarter. Documents dated 29 Rabīʿ II 1140/14 December 1727 and 2 D̲j̲umādā I 1140/16 December 1727 show that the press had begun work on Wānḳulī's dictionary, and this was completed and the book ready by 1 Rad̲j̲ab 1141/31 January 1729. In the 16 years up to Ibrāhīm's illness of 1156/1743, only 17 books were produced, explicable partly by his own carefulness but also by an apparent lack of enthusiasm for printed books in Ottoman society. The Patrona K̲h̲alīl revolt of 1143/1730 which led to the Sultan's abdication [see AḤMAD III] did not affect the progress of Ibrāhīm's work, but the idea of printing does not seem to have made a deep impression on society. In this same year, that of the new Sultan Maḥmūd I's [*q.v.*] accession, a pamphlet on military organisation, *Uṣūl al-ḥikam fī niẓām al-umam*, was printed, and on 11-20 S̲h̲aʿbān 1144-1145/early February 1732, Maḥmūd renewed the *firmān* originally granted to Saʿīd and Ibrāhīm by Aḥmed III, but this time to Ibrāhīm only. Ibrāhīm's 13th book, the *History* of Naʿīmā [*q.v.*], was printed in two volumes in 1147/1734-5. Then followed five years of inactivity, till between 1153/1740-1 and 1156/1743 four more books were produced, bringing the total to 17. In this last year, Ibrāhīm fell ill and died in 1158/1745.

The books printed between 1141/1729 and 1156/1743 are as follows:

1. *Kitāb-î lughat-i Wānḳulī*—1 Radjab 1141/31 January 1729
2. *Tuḥfat al-kibār fī asfār al-biḥār*—1 Dhu 'l-Ḳaʿda 1141/29 May 1729
3. *Taʾrīkh-i sayyāḥ dar bayān-i ẓuhūr-i Aghwāniyān wa sabab-i inhidām-i bināʾ-i dawlat-i shāhān-i Ṣafawiyān*—1 Ṣafar 1142/26 August 1729
4. *Taʾrīkh al-Hind al-Gharbī al-musammā bi-ḥadīth-i naw*—middle third of Ramaḍān 1142/beginning of April 1730 (illustrated)
5. *Taʾrikh-i Tīmūr-i Gurkhān*— 1 Dhu 'l-Ḳaʿda 1142/18 May 1730
6. *Taʾrīkh-i Miṣr al-Djadīd, Taʾrīkh-i Miṣr al-Ḳadīm*—1 Dhu 'l-Ḥidjdja 1142/17 June 1730
7. *Gülshan-i khulafāʾ*—1 Ṣafar 1143/16 August 1730
8. *Grammaire turque*—1730
9. *Uṣūl al-ḥikam fī niẓām al-umam*—middle third of Shaʿbān 1144/beginning of February 1732
10. *Fuyūḍāt-i miḳnāṭisiyya*—1 Ramaḍān 1144/27 February 1732
11. *Djihān-nümā*—10 Muḥarram 1145/3 July 1732
12. *Taḳwīm al-tawārīkh*—1 Muḥarram 1146/14 June 1733
13. *Taʾrīkh-i Naʿīmā*—vol. i, middle third of Muḥarram 1147/middle-late June 1734, vol. ii, Djumādā I 1147/middle October 1734
14. *Taʾrīkh-i Rāshid Efendi*—1 Dhu 'l-Ḥidjdja 1153/17 February 1741
15. *Taʾrikh-i Čelebi-zāde Efendi*—1 Dhu 'l-Ḥidjdja 1153/17 February 1741
16. *Aḥwāl-i ghazawāt dar diyār-i Bosna*—1 Muḥarram 1154/19 March 1741
17. *Farhang-i Shuʿūrī*—1 Shaʿbān 1155/1 October 1742

With the exception of no. 8, Holdermann's *Grammaire turque*, the size of the editions of these books printed at the *dār-i ṭibāʿa-yi ʿāmira* is given at the end of the second volume of Naʿīmā's *History:* 1,000 each for nos. 1 and 2; 1,200 for no. 3; and 500 each for the rest.

After Ibrāhīm's death, his foreman Ḳāḍī Ibrāhīm Efendi (who is thought to have been his son-in-law also) and Ḳāḍī Aḥmed Efendi got a *firmān* from Maḥmūd I, but for unknown reasons were unable to start printing (Gerçek, 92). At the beginning of Rabīʿ II 1168/1755 they got a new *firmān* from ʿOthmān III and started printing, their first publication being a second edition of Wānḳulī's dictionary, but soon after this, Ḳāḍī Ibrāhīm Efendi died and the press was abandoned. Subsequently, two secretaries of the Sublime Porte, the *Waḳʿa-nüwīs* Rāshid Meḥmed Efendi and the *Waḳʿa-nüwīs* Wāṣīf Efendi, bought the press from Ibrāhīm Müteferriḳa's heirs, obtained a *firmān* from Sultan ʿAbd al-Medjīd I and in 1198/1783-4 printed the histories of Sāmī, Ṣubḥī and Shākir in one volume; in the following year they printed the history of ʿIzzī, a sequel to the preceding three ones. After the grammatical work *Iʿrāb al-Kāfiyya* of the next year, no book was printed, and then between 1207/1792-3 and 1209/1794-5 three books on military topics were produced. Rāshid Meḥmed Efendi died in 1212/1796-7 and the press was closed down. It had hardly been a shining success in its 64 years of existence; for only 18 of these had it been actually operated, and it had printed just 24 books (including the second edition of Wānḳulī).

The books printed between 1169/1755-6 and 1209/1794-5 are as follows:

1. *Kitāb-î lughāt-î Wānḳulī*, 2 vols., the first in 1169/1755-6 and the second in 1170/1756-7
2. *Tawārīkh-i Sāmī wa Ṣubḥī wa Shākir* — 1198/1783-4
3. *Taʾrīkh-i ʿIzzī* — 1199/1784-5
4. *Iʿrāb al-Kāfiyya* — 1200/1785-6
5. *Fann-i ḥarb* — 1207/1792-3
6. *Fann-i laghīm* — 1208/1793-4
7. *Fann-i muḥāṣara* — 1209/1794-5.

In the meantime, another press has been established in the French Embassy in Istanbul, founded by the ambassador, Choiseul-Gouffier, which printed three books, two on military topics and one on Turkish grammar. These books are as follows:

1. *Uṣūl al-maʿārif fī tartīb al-ordū* — 1201/1787
2. *Uṣūl al-maʿārif fī wadjh taṣnīf safāʾin-i donanma* ... — 1202/1787-8
3. *Elemens de la langue turque* — March 1790

A second Turkish printing-works was opened in the School of Engineering and Artillery (*Mühendiskhāne*) at Hasköy in 1210/1795-6. The state purchased the equipment for this and the books which were in the possession of Rāshid Efendi, and appointed ʿAbd al-Raḥmān Efendi, a teacher in the School, as director of the press. The first book produced was Aḥmed ʿĀṣim Efendi's translation of the Persian dictionary, the *Burhān-i ḳāṭiʿ*, entitled *Kitāb-î tibyān-î nāfiʿ*, published on 23 Rabīʿ I 1214/25 August 1799 under the supervision of ʿAbd al-Raḥmān Efendi and at the *dār al-ṭibaʿa al-maʿmūra.* The first foreign-language book to appear from it was a French manual of the Turkish language for foreigners written by *Reʾīs al-Küttāb* Maḥmūd Rāʾif Efendi, *Tableau des nouveaux règlemens de l'Empire Ottomane*, illustrated, published in 1798 (see Sungu, 9-12).

A third press was opened in 1217/1802-3, again under the supervision of ʿAbd al-Raḥmān Efendi but whilst the Mühendis-khāne press was itself still active, at Üsküdār and in the Boyadjî Khān built by Sultan Selīm III at the head of the slope running up from the Harem pier. The first volume of the third edition of Wānḳulī was printed in 1217/1802 at the Mühendis-khāne press, described as the *dār al-ṭibāʿa*, but the second volume, printed at the Üsküdār one in 1218/1803-4, records this as the *dār al-ṭibāʿa al-djadīda.* The newer press expanded and was used for general printing, whilst the Mühendis-khāne press, after a period of inactivity, was used to print school books, and continued in use till the First World War. The Üsküdār press continued in its original premises till 1247/1831-2, issuing books on language, history and medicine, when Maḥmūd II transferred it to the building known as the Bath of Ḳapudan Ibrāhīm Pasha, which stood where the Central Library of Istanbul University now stands. The house next to this building was also bought, and a fourth press started here under the name of the *Taḳwīm-khāne-yi ʿāmire* to print the official newspaper *Taḳwīm-i waḳāʾiʿ* (1 November 1831).

The Būlāḳ press. During this same period, the governor of Egypt Muḥammad ʿAlī Pasha [*q.v.*] set up the press at Būlāḳ in direct competition with the Istanbul presses, and which was known as the *maṭbaʿa-yi dār al-ṭibāʿa* or *maṭbaʿat ṣāḥib al-saʿāda* or *al-maṭbaʿa al-amīriyya* or simply *maṭbaʿat Būlāḳ*. It issued as its first book Don Rafael's *Dizionario italiano e arabo*, printed in 1822 (Heyworth-Dunne, 333). This press had the responsibility of printing the official newspaper *al-Waḳāʾiʿ al-Miṣriyya*, starting on 25 Djumādā I 1244/3 December 1828 (al-Futūḥ, 263), as well as the texts of laws, calendars and general books. It printed books in

Turkish, Arabic and Persian, the majority however being in Turkish (Heyworth-Dunne, 334-5).

Cayol's lithographic press. Lithographic printing, invented in 1798 by Alois Senefelder of Munich (1771-1834) and further developed after Senefelder in 1818 published his technical manual on the process, was in use in Istanbul not much more than 30 years after its invention. Henri Cayol (1805-65) of Marseille and his cousin Jacques Cayol came to Istanbul and under the patronage of Khüsrew Pasha set up a lithographic press in the grounds of the Ministry of War, at a location whose exact spot cannot be traced today (Gerçek, 13), with machinery ordered from Paris. Fifty soldiers were assigned to the Cayols to work with them and learn the trade, and for five years books on military subjects, including drill, were produced, the first book printed by lithography being Meḥmed Khüsrew Pasha's *Nukhbat al-taʿlīm* in 1247/1831-2 and with 79 illustrations.

On Khüsrew Pasha's removal from office, the Cayols moved in 1836 to Kuleḳapî and opened a press there on the basis of a *firmān* from Sultan Maḥmūd II (Zellich, 47). On 27 Rabīʿ II 1267/1 March 1851 Henri Cayol applied to the *Medjlis-i Wālā* Presidency and received permission to print books in any language, as well as printing the Armenian monthly journal *Panacer* ("The Philologist") (Khayr al-Dīn Nedīm, 73-4). In January 1852 he printed the only issue of the *Journal Asiatique de Constantinople* (Bianchi, 248-9), but in mid-1852 the printing-works were burnt down during type-casting. It re-opened on 1 November 1855 in Beyoğlu at the corner of the street leading to the French Embassy (Zellich, 52). Henri Cayol died of cholera on 18 August 1856, and after his death, his family worked the press in his name but under the management of Antoine Zellich.

In 1840 the Djerīd-khāne press was opened to print the official newspaper *Djerīde-yi ḥawādith*; and in 1299/1881-2 the Ebu 'l-Ḍiyāʾ (Ebüzziyā) press, which was to have a special place in the history of Turkish printing, was opened by Ebu 'l-Ḍiyāʾ Meḥmed Tewfīḳ Bey in Ghalaṭa in the Maḥkeme Street. In 1864 the *Dār al-Ṭibāʿa* and the *Taḳwīm-khāne* had been combined and moved to a building within the grounds of the Topḳapî Palace, at first called the *Dār al-Ṭibāʿa al-ʿĀmira*, then up to Republican times as the *Maṭbaʿa-yi ʿĀmire*, and later, the *Millī Maṭbaʿa* and *Dewlet Maṭbaʿasî*; in 1939 it was given over to the Ministry of Education.

With the "alphabet revolution" of 1928 introduced by Kemal Atatürk [*q.v.*] as part of his westernising reforms, and the consequent change from the Arabic to a Latin system for the writing of Turkish, Turkish printing henceforth became divorced, typographically speaking, from the history and development of printing in Arabic characters.

Bibliography: 1. General. P. K. Hitti, *The first book printed in Arabic*, in *The Princeton University Library Chronicle*, iv/1 (Nov. 1942), 5-9; F. Bonola Bey, *Note sur l'origine de l'imprimerie arabe en Europe*, in *Bulletin de l'Institut Egyptien*. 5e Série, Vol. iii (1909), 74-84; A. Bernard, *Antoine Vitré et les caractères orientaux*, Paris 1857; R. Brun, *Le livre français*, Paris 1948; A. Vaccari, *I caratteri arabi della Typographia Savariana*, in *RSO*, x (1923-5), 37-47; Yasin H. Safadi, *Arabic printing and book production*, in Diana Grimwood-Jones *et alii* (eds.), *Arab Islamic bibliography, the Middle East Library Committee guide*, Hassocks, Sussex 1977, 221-34.

2. Jewish printing. M. Steinschneider, *Jüdische Typographie*, Jerusalem 1938; Abraham Yaary, *Ha-Defus ha-ʿivri be-Konstantinopl* ("Hebrew printing at Constantinople, its history and bibliography"), Supplement to *Kirjath Sepher*, xlii, Jerusalem 1967 [in Hebrew]; Israel Mehlman, *Genuzot sefarim* ("Bibliographical essays"), Jerusalem 1975 [in Hebrew]; Raphael Posner and Israel Ta-Shema (eds.), *The Hebrew book, an historical survey*, New York 1975; see also A. M. Habermann, *The history of the Hebrew book*, Jerusalem 1968 [in Hebrew]; A. Freimann, *A gazetteer of Hebrew printing*, Jerusalem 1946 [in Hebrew]; Ch. B. Friedberg, *History of Hebrew typography in Italy, Spain-Portugal and Turkey*, 2nd, enlarged edn., Tel Aviv 1956 [in Hebrew].

3. Armenian printing. Karekin Zarpanelyan, *Badmutyun Haygagan Dıbakrutyan* ("The history of Armenian printing"), Venice 1895 [in Armenian]. Hagop Anasyan (ed.), *Hay Hınadib Kırki Madenakidagan Tzutzak 1512-1800*, ("Bibliography of the old Armenian printed books"), Erivan 1963 [in Armenian]; Teotik (Lapcinciyan), *Dip u Dar* ("Armenian printing and characters"), Istanbul 1913 [in Armenian]; Raphael Ishkhanyan, *Hay Kırki Batmudyun* ("History of the Armenian book"), Erivan 1977 [in Armenian]; see also anon., *Les Arméniens et l'imprimerie*, Istanbul 1920; Kınarik Gorgodyan, *Hay Dibakir Kırki Gosdantnubolsun 1567-1850* ("Armenian books printed in Istanbul"), Erivan 1964 [in Armenian].

4. Greek printing. R. J. Roberts, *The Greek press at Constantinople in 1627 and its antecedents*, in *The Library*, Ser. 5, vol. xxli (1967), 13-43; E. Layton, *Nikodemos Metaxas, the first Greek printer in the Eastern world*, in *Harvard Library Bulletin*, xv/2 (April 1967), 140-168; E. Legrand, *Bibliographie Hellénique*, i, Paris 1894; G. Hadjiantoniou, *Protestant Patriarch. The life of Cyril Loucaris 1572-1638, Patriarch of Constantinople*, Richmond, Va. 1961; Sévérien Salaville and Eugène Dalleggio, *Karamanlidika. Bibliographie analytique*, i, Athens 1958; see also Nikos E. Skiadas, *Hroniko tis Ellinikis tipografias. Sklavia-Diafotismos Epanastasii I. 1476-1828*, Athens 1976.

5. Muslim Turkish printing. Feyzi (Kurtoğlu), *Türkiyede matbaacılık nasıl başladığını gösteren bir vesika*, in *Resimi Şark*, sayı 42 (Haziran 1934), 14-15; Osman Ersoy, *Türkiye'ye matbanın girişi ve ilk basılan eserler*, Ankara 1959; Niyazi Berkes, *İlk Türk matbaası kurucusunun dinî ve fikrî kimliği*, in *Belleten*, sayi 104 (Ekim 1962), 715-37; Iḥsān (Sungu), *İlk Türk maṭbaʿasîna dāʾir yeñi wethīḳalar*, in *Ḥayāt*, sayî 73 (1928), 409-15; Selim Nüzhet Gerçek, *Türk matbaacılığı. I.* Istanbul 1939; Iḥsān (Sungu), *Maḥmūd Rāʾif Efendi ve etherleri*, in *Ḥayāt*, sayî 16 (1927), 9-12; see also G. B. Toderini, *De la littérature des Turcs*. Paris 1789; F. Babinger, *Stambuler Buchwesen im 18. Jahrhundert*, Leipzig 1919; Server İskit, *Türkiyede neşriyat hareketleri tarihine bir baskış*, Istanbul 1939; W. J. Watson, *İbrahim Müteferrika and Turkish incunabula*, in *JAOS*, lxxxviii (1968), 435-41; Jale Baysal, *Müteferrika'dan birinci meşrutiyete kadar Osmanlı Türklerinin bastıkları kitaplar*, Istanbul 1968.

6. The Būlāḳ Press. Aḥmad Riḍwān al-Futūḥ, *Taʾrīkh Maṭbaʿat Būlāḳ*, Cairo 1953; J. Heyworth-Dunne, *Printing and translation under Muhammad Ali of Egypt*, in *JRAS* (1940), 325-49; A. Geiss, *Histoire de l'imprimerie en Égypte*, in *Bull. de l'Institut Égyptien*, Ser. 5, vol. i (1907), 133-57; R. N. Verdery, *The publications of the Būlāq Press under Muḥammad ʿAlī of Egypt*, in *JAOS*, xci (1971), 129-32.

7. The Cayol Lithographic Press. G. Zellich, *Notice historique sur la lithographie et sur les origines de son introduction en Turquie*, Constantinople

1895; Selim Nüzhet Gerçek, *Türk taş basmacılığı*, Istanbul 1939; Khayr al-Dīn Nedīm, *Wethāʾiḳ-i taʾrīkhiyye we siyāsiyye*, Istanbul 1326/1908; X. Bianchi, *Bibliographie*, in *JA*, Ser. 4, vol. xx (1852), 248-9. (GÜNAY ALPAY KUT)

3. IN PERSIA

1. Under the Mongols.

Wood-block printing was introduced into Persia in 693/1294. In that year Gaykhatu Khān ordered the printing of paper money (*čaʾo*; Persianised as *čaw*) in imitation of Chinese practice. The paper money was printed in Tabrīz and circulated for the first time on 19 Shawwāl 693/12 September 1294. The paper money was probably printed with wooden blocks, which were manufactured by Chinese artisans living in Tabrīz. Despite the threat of capital punishment in case of refusal to accept paper money, the populations's reaction was one of outright rejection. Gaykhatu Khān was forced to abandon his experiment in Dhu 'l-Ḥidjdja 693/November 1294, as a result of which the art of printing was momentarily lost to Persia (see Jahn, *Paper currency*, 125-35).

2. Under the Ṣafawids.

Although the Torah was printed in Persian (with Hebrew characters) in Istanbul in 1594, it was not until 1629 that printing was reintroduced to Persia, this time in the form of typography. For in January 1629, Carmelite friars received a printing press from Rome. It had matrices of 349 Arabic letter types and two instruments to set up type. It is not known whether the press produced any actual books. The Carmelites certainly tried, but "because of the dryness of the country" they failed, according to Fr. Angelus (Gazophylacium). Their printing (*basma*, *ṭibāʿa*) experiments took place between 1629 and 1642, when Fr. Bernard of St. Theresia handed the printing press over to the Vicar-General of the Carmelites in Iṣfahān. From 1648 till 1669 the press was kept in storage by the Dutch East Indies Company, which in 1669 handed the press over to Fr. Raphael Du Mans. In 1676 Fr. Angelus reports that the Carmelites still had the press, but from the context it is clear that it had not been used for a long time (Floor, *The first printing press*).

About the same time that the Arabic-Persian printing press was introduced in Persia, an Armenian press also was established in Djulfā [*q.v.* in Suppl.], the Armenian suburb of Iṣfahān. This was done at the initiative of Bishop Khacʿatur Kesaracʿi in 1637. After 17 months of trial and error he succeeded in printing the Psalms in 1638. The Bishop's main problem was how to produce good quality paper and ink. Moreover, his type was not made out of lead, but of wood, copper and iron. He preserved and printed another two religious books, one in 1641 and the other in 1642. Both the letter types and the books can be seen in the Armenian museum at Djulfā (see Richard, *Un témoignage*...).

Despite his success, Bishop Kasaracʿi was troubled by technical problems. He therefore sent one of his pupils, Hovhannes, to Europe to obtain the required technical expertise. In 1644 Hovhannes printed a book in Armenian in Leghorn. He returned to Persia in 1646 to continue the work of Bishop Kesaracʿi, who had died in that year. To that end, Hovhannes brought lead types and a printing press with him. It was his intention to print the Bible, but "not having the way of making good Ink, and to avoid the ill consequences of the Invention, he was forc'd to break the press. For on one side the Children refus'd to learn to write, pretending they wrote the Bible themselves, only to get it sooner by heart: on the other side many persons were undone by it, that got their living by writing", according to Tavernier. The latter argument also had constrained the introduction of the art of printing in, for example, the Ottoman empire (see section 2, above). Tavernier was wrong in believing that the Armenian press had been broken, for in 1687 it was used again and this time nine books were printed. For unknown reasons, it fell into disuse again. It was only in 1771 that an Armenian printing press was established in Etchmiadzin, in 1786 in Nakhčewān and in 1796 in Astrakhān (Rāʾīn, *Armanīhā*).

3. Under the Ḳādjārs.

The art of printing was thus lost for a second time. Although the printing of the Armenian language was resumed fairly quickly, printing in Persian took somewhat longer. Persian language books were regularly printed since 1639, when in Leiden the first books in both the Persian language and characters were printed. After that date, both in Europe and towards the end of the 18th century also in India, many books in Persian were printed. The generally accepted date for the first book printed in Ḳādjār Persia is 1233/1817, when in Tabrīz the *Djihādiyya* by Mīrzā ʿĪsā Ḳāʾim-Maḳām was printed on a typographic press. Because there is no thorough analytical study on Persian incunabula, it is impossible to settle the question of the earliest printing date. The author of the *Maʾāthir al-mamālik* ascribes the introduction of the art of printing (*ʿamal al-ṭibāʿa* or *basma*) to ʿAbbās Mīrzā, the heir-apparent and governor-general of Ādharbāydjān. Iʿtimād al-Salṭana (*al-Maʾāthir wa 'l-athar*, 100), mistakenly, ascribes this initiative to Manūčihr Khān Muʿtamid al-Dawla, an influential Tehran courtier. The early books were printed by Mullā Muḥammad Bāḳir Tabrīzī, who in 1241/1825 also printed ʿAbd al-Razzāḳ Dunbulī's *Maʾāthir al-sulṭāniyya*. In 1825 another printer in Tabrīz, ʿAlī son of Ḥādjdjī Muḥammad Ḥusayn, printed the *Nasab al-ṣibyān* a well-known school text by Abū Naṣr Farāhī. By 1825, Tabrīz therefore boasted already of at least two typographic printing presses (*čāp-i surbī*).

In that same year, Muʿtamid al-Dawla established a typographic press in Tehran, which was operated by Mīrzā Zayn al-ʿĀbidīn Tabrīzī. With the support of Muʿtamid al-Dawla, who is said to have financed the printing of 8,000 copies, he printed many books, mainly religious, which were known as "Muʿtamadīs". In 1815 ʿAbbās Mīrzā had sent seven students to Great Britain to learn modern techniques. One of these students was Mīrzā Ṣāliḥ Shīrāzī, who apprenticed himself in London to a master printer (*čāp-sāz*) who specialised "in printing (*čāp zadan*) the Bible in Persian, Hindi, and Arabic and other languages". Mīrzā Ṣāliḥ returned to Persia in 1234/1819, where he established himself as a printer in Tabrīz. He shortly thereafter (1829) was sent to Russia as member of an embassy, from which he returned with a printing press. He was later engaged in printing in both Tabrīz and Tehran.

Mīrzā Ṣāliḥ in his turn sent a certain Mīrzā Asad Allāh to Russia to learn the printing trade. On his return to Persia in 1835, Mīrzā Asad Allāh stayed in Tabrīz and, together with Āḳā Riḍā, operated the first lithographic press (*čāp-i sangī*) in Iran. In that same year, Fatḥ ʿAlī Shāh summoned Mīrzā Asad Allāh to Tehran to start working there.

Because "printing in types is not relished by Persians, the characters being necessarily stiff and uncouth, and very displeasing to an eye accustomed to the flowing written hand" (Binning, i, 312), lithography became very popular in Iran. Especially, the fact that lithography permitted Iranian artists to practice both calligraphy and illustrations in their normal way was an important advantage. Moreover, illustrated printed books became very popular, of which an increasing number, after the first items printed in 1259/1843, were produced in this way.

By 1850 there were five lithographic presses in Tehran (Sheil, 201) and in 1845 not less than 15 in Tabrīz (Schwarz, 85). However, books also continued to be published "both in types and lithograph; but the execution is rather coarse; in the latter style in particular", Binning observed in 1851 (i, 312, ii, 217). In 1256/March 1840, American missionaries in Urmiya printed the first text in Syriac; moreover, this press could also print Persian and English (Perkins, 456). Other presses followed in S̲h̲īrāz, Iṣfahān, Bushire, Mas̲h̲had, Enzelī, Ras̲h̲t, Ardabīl, Hamadān, K̲h̲ōy, Yazd, Ḳazwīn, Kirmāns̲h̲āh, Garrūs and Kās̲h̲ān (Maḥbūbī Ardakānī, i, 217).

The list of early prints shows that a great variety of books were printed. Apart from religious texts, there were historical texts, popular works such as the *Thousand and one nights*, *Iskandar-nāma*, and a comic text such as *Duzd wa Ḳāḍī*. With the establishment of the *Dār al-Funūn* [*q.v.*] in 1852, a great number of scientific texts were printed on the school's own printing press. The publications were in the field of engineering, chemistry, physics, mathematics, biology, medicine, geography, military science and music. With the establishment of the government press (*dār al-ṭibāʿa*) and the state translation institute (*dār al-tard̲j̲uma*), hundreds of translations were made from European authors. Further, Persian and Arab classics were printed, while contemporary official chronicles were solicited and published, such as the *Rawḍat al-ṣafā-yi Nāṣirī* and the *Nāsik̲h̲ al-tawārīk̲h̲*. Under the direction of Iʿtimād al-Salṭana, who was in charge of the state press, translation, and censor's bureau, many of these books were published. He himself also published a great many useful official chronicles, such as the *Mirʾāt al-buldān* (3 vols.), the *Muntaẓam-i Nāṣirī* (3 vol.), and the *Maṭlaʿ al-s̲h̲ams* (3 vols.).

A separate development was the publication of newspapers (*kāg̲h̲ad̲h̲-i ak̲h̲bār*), of which the first lithographed issue was printed by Mīrzā Ṣāliḥ in Tehran on 25 Muḥarram 1253/1 March 1837. This paper had no special time, but only a long general heading, a shortened rendering of which is "Current news from Tehran" (*Ak̲h̲bār-i Waḳāyiʿ*). The paper, which lasted three years, offered foreign and local news, the latter focussing on the reforms initiating and progress promoted by Muḥammad S̲h̲āh (1834-48). In 1267/February 1851 the second newspaper to appear in Persia was published at the initiative of Mīrzā Taḳī K̲h̲ān Amīr Kabīr [*q.v.* in Suppl.]. This paper was edited by Edward Burgess and published under the name of *Rūz-nāma-yi Waḳāyiʿ-i Ittifāḳiyya*. Burgess also printed an uncensored newspaper for the eyes of Nāṣir al-Din S̲h̲āh (1848-96) and the Amīr Kabīr. In 1868 Nāṣir al-Dīn S̲h̲āh ordered the establishment of four newspapers, viz. an official gazette, both with and without illustrations, a semi-official newspaper and a scientific newspaper. Towards the end of the 19th century, many semi-official and private periodicals were published in increasing numbers. In 1874 one issue of a French newspaper, *La Patrie*, was published, which, because of its outspokenness, was immediately forbidden by the S̲h̲āh. It was soon followed by other French newspapers, one of which, *Le Journal de Perse*, was published by Iʿtimād al-Salṭana.

Since the press was mainly an instrument of the government, the latter in the 1850s established a Censor's Bureau (*Idāra-yi Sansūr*). All books and newspapers had to be approved by the censor before these could be printed or imported. Despite this censorship, these newspapers were carriers of some new ideas. Because all government officials were obliged to subscribe to the official papers, new ideas reached all parts of the kingdom. However, in general these "semi-official" newspapers were dull, mainly offering repetitious court activities. More effective in disseminating new political ideas were Persian newspapers printed outside Persia such as *Ḳānūn* (London), *Ak̲h̲tar* (Istanbul), *Ḥabl al-Matīn* (Calcutta) and *T̲h̲urayyā* (Cairo), which often had to be smuggled into Persia because of their unsettling contents. It was only with the advent of the constitutional movement in 1906 that newspapers started to play a very important role in political and cultural life of Persia.

Bibliography: Angelus a S. Joseph, *Gazophylacium lingua Persarum*, Amsterdam 1684 (see *Stamparia*); R. A. Binning, *Two years' travel*, 2 vols., London 1857; E. G. Browne, *The press and poetry in Persia*, London 1914; Mīrzā Ḥasan K̲h̲ān, Iʿtimād al-Salṭana, *Kitāb al-Maʾāt̲h̲ir wa 'l-at̲h̲ar*, Tehran 1306/1889; H. Farmanfarmayan, *The forces of modernization in nineteenth century Iran*, in W. Polk and R. Chambers, eds., *The beginning of modernization in the Middle East*, Chicago 1968, 119-151; W. M. Floor, *The first printing-press in Iran*, in *ZDMG*, cxxx (1980), 369-71; K. Jahn, *Paper currency in Iran*, in *Journal of Asian History*, iv (1970), 101-35; Ḥusayn Maḥbūbī Ardakānī, *Tārīk̲h̲-i Muʾassasat-i tamaddunī-yi d̲j̲adīd dar Īrān*, Tehran 1352/1972, i, 211-20; J. Perkins, *A residence of eight years in Persia*, Andover 1845; *Čāp-i surb wa sangī*, in *Rahnamā-yi Kitāb*, xix (2535/1976), 208-16; Ismāʿīl Rāʾīn, *Armanīhā*, Tehran 1352/1971 (chapter *Nak̲h̲ustīn čāpk̲h̲āna dar Īrān*); Fr. Richards, *Un témoignage sur les débuts de l'imprimerie à Nor Jula*, in *Revue des Études Armeniennes*, n.s., xiv (1980), 483-84; *Safar-nāma-yi Mīrzā S̲h̲īrāzī*, ed. Ismāʿīl Rāʾīn, Tehran 1347/1968; Muḥammad Ṣadr Hās̲h̲imī, *Tārīk̲h̲-i D̲j̲arāʾid wa mad̲j̲allāt-i Īrān*, 4 vols., Iṣfahān 1338/1959; B. Schwartz, *Letters from Persia written by Charles and Edward Burgess*, New York 1942; J. B. Tavernier, *The six voyages in Turkey, Persia and the Indies*, 6 vols., London 1677, v, 229.

(W. Floor)

4. In Muslim India

South Asia below the Himalayas remained beyond the diffusion of xylography from the Far East. Printing reached the subcontinent as European movable type technology introduced by Portuguese Jesuits who set up the first press in the College of St. Paul at Goa in 1556. In 1580 the Mug̲h̲al emperor Akbar was presented with a copy of the Royal Polyglot Bible printed by Plantin at Antwerp, one of the finest products of the 16th-century European press, but the Mug̲h̲al court did not adopt printing technology, being well served by its studio of calligraphers and artists. From the 1570s to the 1670s vernacular printing by the Portuguese in India to aid conversion was confined to Tamil, Konkani and Syriac, and that of the German and Dutch missionaries in the 18th century to Tamil and Sinhalese. Until the early 19th century, Christian literature in Arabic, Persian or Urdu was imported from Europe, such as Benjamin Schultze's Urdu New Testament printed at Halle in 1758.

The earliest known specimen of Arabic printing i

India is a small woodcut New Testament quotation on the title-page of *Dialogus inter Moslimum et Christianum*, a Tamil polemic against Islam printed at the Tranquebar Mission Press in 1727. But Arabic, Persian and Urdu printing in India really began in Calcutta under the East India Company from the 1780s onwards. Of the three languages, Persian was paramount to the Company's interests and the medium of the law-courts and the land-revenue system inherited from Mug͟hal Bengal. In the late 1770s the Governor-General Warren Hastings engaged Charles Wilkins, a Company servant with a gift for oriental languages, to manufacture Bengali and Nastaʿlīḳ types. With the Nastaʿlīḳ, Wilkins in 1780 printed Francis Gladwin's *A compendious vocabulary, English and Persian* at Malda in north Bengal. In 1781 he became first superintendent of the Honorable Company's Press in Calcutta which issued a plethora of Persian translations of the regulations, notices and blank-forms required for the administration of Bengal. The first of these was a selection of Dīwānī ʿAdālat regulations translated by William Chambers in 1781. From 1793 until 1837, when Persian ceased to be the language of the courts, Persian translations of Company regulations were reprinted in annual volumes. At Madras also Persian translations of local Company regulations were printed from 1802 onwards. Persian historical works valuable as sources on the Mug͟hal system of government were printed at Calcutta, such as William Davy's edition of *Tūzūkāt-i Tīmūrī* (1785), Muḥammad Sāḳī's *Muntak͟habāt-i ʿĀlamgīr-nāma* prepared by Henry Vansittart (1785) and Amīr Ḥaydar Bilgrāmī's *Risāla*, a treatise on land-revenue and tenure with Gladwin's translation (1796). A Siyāḳat fount (the earliest such?) was specially cast for printing Gladwin's *A compendious system of Bengal revenue accounts* (1790 and 1796). Some linguistic works were printed to help Company servants master Persian, Gladwin again preeminent with *A vocabulary, English and Persian* (1791, 1800), *The Persian moonshee* (1795, 1799, 1800) and *The Persian guide* (1800). As the classical literary language of Muslim India, Persian was studied by the British orientalists forming the nucleus of the Asiatic Society of Bengal (founded 1784). The first work of Persian literature printed was *Ins͟hā-yi Harkaran* edited by Francis Balfour (1781). Other important texts printed were Gladwin's edition of Saʿdī's *Pand-nāma* (1788) followed by *Kulliyyāt-i Saʿdī* prepared by J. H. Harington (1791-5), Sir William Jones' edition of Hātifī's *Laylī Mad͟jnūn* (1788), the *Dīwān* of Ḥāfiẓ (1791) and Nak͟hs͟habī's *Ṭūṭī-nāma* with Gladwin's translation (1792). Arabic printing was far less extensive, but one important text printed before 1800 was al-Sad͟jāwandī's *al-Sirād͟jiyya* (1792), published as part of Jones' digest of Hindu and Muslim law. A concordance to the Ḳurʾān was printed at Calcutta in 1811, but the Arabic text (together with ʿAbd al-Ḳādir's Urdu translation) was not printed till 1829. The most famous translation of the Ḳurʾān printed in the subcontinent was S͟hāh Walī Allāh's Persian rendering (Dihlī 1866, etc.). The leading scholar of Urdu in 18th-century Calcutta was John B. Gilchrist, who published *A dictionary, English and Hindoostanee* (1786-7 to 1790), *A grammar of the Hindoostanee language* (1796) and *The Oriental linguist* (1798). In 1789 *The new Asiatick miscellany* contained the first Urdu literary text to be printed, a *rek͟hta* of Walī Dakhanī. In the same year, W. H. Bird's *The oriental miscellany* also printed the words and music of several Urdu songs. From 1793 onwards, Urdu translations of Company regulations in Bengal were required to be printed as well as Persian. At Madras in 1790 the physician Henry Harris published *A dictionary, English and Hindostany*, but his grammar was never printed.

Fort William College, founded at Calcutta in 1800, provided a further stimulus for the printing of Arabic, Persian and particularly Urdu texts needed to instruct Company servants in those languages. Gladwin presented Nastaʿlīḳ types to the College, and these Gilchrist used as Professor of Urdu to equip the Hindoostanee Press, which issued many celebrated Urdu works: Mīr Ammān's version of "The Four Dervishes", *Bāg͟h-o-bahār* (1802); Mīr Shīr ʿAlī Afsūs' translation of Saʿdī's *Gulistān*, *Bāg͟h-i Urdū* (1802); Mīr Ḥasan's *Naṣr-i bī-naẓīr* (1803); Ḥaydar Bak͟hs͟h Ḥaydarī's *Totākahānī* based on the *Ṭūṭī-nāma* (1804); etc. The largest book issued by this press was *Kulliyyāt-i Mīr Taḳī* with 1,085 pages (1811). Besides some forty Urdu works, by 1820 about twenty Arabic and another twenty Persian texts were also printed for the College's use at various Calcutta presses: John Baillie's *Arabic syntax* (1801); Joseph Barretto's edition of the *S͟hams al-lughāt* (1806); Walī al-Dīn's *Mis͟hkāt al-maṣābīḥ* (1809); Matthew Lumsden's *A grammar of the Arabic language* (1813) and the *Dīwān al-Mutanabbī* (1814); *Anwār-i Suhaylī* (1805); Lumsden's *A grammar of the Persian language* (1810); Niẓāmī's *Sikandar-nāma* (1812); Mīrzā Abū Ṭālib K͟hān's European travelogue *Masīr-i Ṭālibī* (1812); etc. At Madras, the equivalent College of Fort St. George also stimulated the printing of texts, such as the *Anwār-i Suhaylī* issued by the College Press in 1826.

The *muns͟hī*s of Fort William College and the Rev. Henry Martyn were equally important in early missionary printing in Islamic languages in India. Mīrzā Muḥammad Fiṭrat's translation of St. Matthew into Persian and of the Gospels into Urdu (edited by William Hunter) were both printed at Calcutta in 1805. In 1809 the Persian St. Matthew prepared by Nathaniel Sabat under Martyn's direction was printed at Serampore, the complete New Testament at Calcutta in 1816, and the Old Testament in parts (1828-38) by the Calcutta Auxiliary Bible Society. Sabat's Arabic New Testament was printed at Calcutta in 1816. Martyn's own translation of the New Testament into Urdu (the basis for all subsequent editions) was printed in 1814 at Serampore, where the Sindhi St. Matthew was issued in 1825. The mass of early 19th-century evangelical literature in Urdu, Persian, Panjabi, Sindhi, etc., was mainly printed by the various Christian tract and book societies formed (those of Calcutta, Benares, Āgra, North India, Punjab, Madras (for Dakhanī), Bombay, etc.).

The East India Company introduced lithography to India in the early 1820s, which rapidly displaced typography for Islamic printing as presses were established right across Northern India: Patna 1828; Kānpur 1830, Dihlī and Meerut 1834, Āgra 1835, Lūdhiāna 1836, Mīrzāpūr and Allāhābād 1839, Benares 1844, etc. The earliest Urdu works lithographed were medical treatises by Peter Breton, the first being *Bayān zaharōn kā* on poisons (Calcutta 1826), and in Persian editions of Saʿdī's *Gulistān* and *Būstān* (Calcutta 1827, 1828). The development of Lakhnaw as a major centre of Urdu and Persian printing exemplifies the transition to lithography. Nawwāb G͟hāzī al-Dīn Ḥaydar set up the royal press about 1817, its most famous product being the typeset Persian dictionary *Haft ḳulzum* (1820-2). His successor Nāṣir al-Dīn Ḥaydar brought Edward Archer's Asiatic Lithographic Press from nearby Kānpur to Lakhnaw in 1830, and the Arabic dictionary *Tād͟j al-lug͟hāt* begun by typography was then completed (vols.

iv-viii) lithographically. Under Wāḏjid ʿAlī S̲h̲āh, all lithographic presses in Lak̲h̲naw were closed because the Nawwāb disliked a history of his family lithographed by one Kamāl al-Dīn Ḥaydar. Some presses moved to Kānpur, while others continued surreptitiously and books were often issued without details of printer, etc., so that many early Lak̲h̲naw and Kānpur imprints are indistinguishable. The single most important Lak̲h̲naw press was that of Muns̲h̲ī Nawal Kis̲h̲ōr founded in 1858. By his death in 1895 he had issued about 500 titles, mainly religious, historical and poetical texts, particularly Urdu translations from Arabic, Persian and Sanskrit, subsidised by his newspaper and his printing for government. Sikandar Ḏjāh, Niẓām of Ḥaydarābād (Deccan), acquired a press as a curiosity of western technology during Lord Minto's vice-royalty (1807-13), but did not apparently use it.

Bombay was not important for Persian printing until the introduction of lithography, although the Dasātīr of 1818 printed with Nas̲k̲h̲ types deserves mention. Among the earliest works lithographed there were the Anwār-i Suhaylī and the Dīwān of Ḥāfiẓ, both in 1828. Bombay and Karāčī were the twin centres of early Sindhi printing, one of the first Sindhi books lithographed being Sadāsukh Lālā's drawing manual Citra jī pār (Karāčī 1852). Karāčī had been the first city in what is modern Pakistan to acquire printing in the mid-1840s. The American Presbyterian Mission Press, Lūdhiāna, printed extensively in Panjabi (as well as Persian and Urdu) from the 1840s, but the main centres of Muslim Panjabi printing were Lāhawr and Siyālkūt, from the 1860s issuing kiṣṣas and other popular literature. The first press in modern Bangladesh was at Ḍhākā in the 1850s, but printing became widespread in East Bengal by the 1870s at Sylhet, Rajshahi, Barisal, Jessore, etc., and Calcutta also remained an important centre of Muslim Bengali printing. A number of Pas̲h̲to works were printed in Dihlī, Pes̲h̲āwar and Lāhawr in the 1870s.

Bibliography: For the history of printing in the subcontinent generally, see A. K. Priolkar, *The printing press in India*, Bombay 1958. N. Ahmad, *Oriental presses in the world*, Lāhawr 1985, contains much useful information on Islamic printing in South Asia. On early Persian, Arabic and Urdu printing in the 18th century, see G. Shaw, *Printing in Calcutta to 1800*, London 1981; C. A. Storey, *The beginnings of Persian printing in India*, in J. D. Cursetji Pavry (ed.), *Oriental studies in honour of Cursetji Erachji Pavry*, London 1933; and (on Gilchrist) N. Ahmad, *A Scottish orientalist and his works*, in *Libri*, xxviii (1978), 196-204. On Fort William College, see S. K. Das, *Sahibs and munshis*, New Delhi 1978; and on early missionary printing, see J. Murdoch, *Catalogue of the Christian vernacular literature of India*, Madras 1870; H. U. Weitbrecht, *A descriptive catalogue of Urdu Christian literature*, London 1886; and The British and Foreign Bible Society, *Scriptures of the Indian subcontinent*, London 1977. On Lak̲h̲naw printing, see K. S. Diehl, *Lucknow printers 1820-1850*, in N. N. Gidwani (ed.), *Comparative librarianship*, Dihlī 1973; and S. J. Haider, *Munshi Nawal Kishore (1836-1895): mirror of Urdu printing in British India*, in *Libri*, xxxi (1981), 227-37. On Sindhi printing, see A. R. Butt, *Origin and development of printing press in Sind*, in *Pakistan library bulletin*, xii/3-4 (1981), 1-10.   (G. W. SHAW)

5. IN AFG̲H̲ANISTĀN

The printing-press was only introduced to Afg̲h̲ānistān, geographically remote and beyond sustained British control, towards the end of the 19th century and then only for printing in Persian, the language of the court and of literature. The national language Pas̲h̲to was therefore first printed, whether from scholarly, evangelical or military and administrative motives, in Europe and, more extensively, in India. With British expansion north-westwards in the subcontinent, printing spread into the regions bordering Afg̲h̲ānistān itself. The first Afg̲h̲ān of note to encounter printing at first hand was the exiled king S̲h̲udjāʿ al-Mulk, who visited the American Presbyterian Mission Press at Lūdhiāna (Pandjāb) in the mid 1830s.

The pioneer of Pas̲h̲to studies in Europe was Bernhard Dorn of the Russian Imperial Academy of Sciences, whose *Chrestomathy of the Pushtu or Afghan language* (St. Petersburg 1847) included selections from poets such as ʿAbd al-Raḥmān, Mīrzā K̲h̲ān Anṣārī and ʿUbayd Allāh. Other notable early scholars were Ernest Trumpp, whose grammar of Pas̲h̲to was published at London (1873), and James Darmesteter, whose monumental collection of *Chants populaires des Afghans* was issued at Paris (1888-90). Selections from both Pas̲h̲to prose and poetry compiled by H. G. Raverty appeared as *Guls̲h̲an-i roh* (London 1860), adopted by the Government of India as the text-book for its Pas̲h̲to examination from 1866 onwards. This work included verses by the national poet K̲h̲us̲h̲ḥāl K̲h̲ān K̲h̲aṭak [q.v.], whose complete dīwān was lithographed at the Jail Press, Pes̲h̲āwar, in 1869 under the superintendence of H. W. Bellew.

The earliest Pas̲h̲to printing in India was at the Serampore Mission Press in Bengal: the New Testament in 1818 followed by the Pentateuch 1820 and Historical Books (incomplete) about 1832. British occupation of land between the Indus river and the Tak̲h̲t-i Sulaymān mountains in 1849 renewed missionary interest in Pas̲h̲to and in 1856 revision of the Serampore editions began under Isidor Loewenthal of the American Presbyterian Mission. The resulting New Testament was published at Hertford (1863) by the British and Foreign Bible Society. From 1859 onwards Pas̲h̲to tracts were lithographed at the press of the Pes̲h̲āwar Church Mission founded specifically for the conversion of the Afg̲h̲āns, as well as primers such as T. Tuting's *Kitāb al-Durr*. In 1883 a Pas̲h̲to Revision Committee was formed under T. J. L. Mayer of the Church Missionary Society and the translation of the complete Old Testament was published at London (1889-95).

Most early Pas̲h̲to linguistic works were compiled by officers of Pathān troops in India. Lt. Robert Leech, Bombay Engineers, who had accompanied a mission to Kābul, published *A grammar of the Pashtoo or Afghanee language* (Calcutta 1839), describing the Ḳandahārī dialect and including a specimen of verse by ʿAbd al-Raḥmān. Capt. John Vaughan, who had commanded the 5th Punjab Infantry at Derā G̲h̲āzī K̲h̲ān, compiled *A grammar and vocabulary of the Pooshtoo language* (Calcutta 1854). Most successful of all was Major H. G. Raverty, Bombay Native Infantry, who first studied Pas̲h̲to while stationed at Pes̲h̲āwar 1849-50. His Pas̲h̲to grammar went into three editions (Calcutta 1855; London 1860 and 1867) and he also published a dictionary (London 1867) and *The Pushto manual* (London 1880). All these works were printed using Nas̲k̲h̲ types with extra sorts specially cut for the letters peculiar to Pas̲h̲to. As lithographic presses spread across north-western India, more Pas̲h̲to works began to be printed, e.g. *Ḳānūn al-ḳirāʾa*, rules for Ḳurʾān recitation (Dihlī 1865), *Kalīd-i Afg̲h̲ānī*, verse and prose selections (Pes̲h̲āwar 1872), *Sayr al-sālikīn*, *Pilgrim's progress* (Amritsar 1877), *Ḳiṣṣa-yi ḥirnī*,

Muḥammad and the deer (Abbottābād 1883) and T. C. Plowden's *Idiomatic colloquial sentences*, *English-Pakkhto* (Jail Press, Derā Ghāzī Khān 1884).

According to ʿAbd al-Raḥmān Khān's autobiography, there was no printing-press in Afghānistān before he became Amīr in 1880. But the first lithographic press (Maṭbaʿa-yi Muṣṭafawī) was set up under his predecessor Amīr Shīr ʿAlī Khān whose Persian polemic against the Wahhābīs, *Risāla-yi shihāb-i thāḳib*, was printed at Kābul in 1288/1871, followed by ʿAbd al-Ḳādir Khān's religious tract *Tuḥfat al-ʿulamāʾ* in 1292/1875. ʿAbd al-Raḥmān attributed the introduction of printing to Munshī ʿAbd al-Razzāḳ of Dihlī who trained many Kābulī lithographers before dying of fever. Several of the Amīr's own works in Persian were printed, including *Naṣāʾiḥ-nāmča*, advice on Afghānistān's relations with Russia (1303/1886), and *Mirʾāt al-ʿuḳūl*, on human intelligence (1311/1894). Most famous of all was his tract advocating *djihād*, *Kalimāt Amīr al-bilād fi 'l-targhīb ila 'l-djihād* (1304/1887), printed at the Humāyūn Press which also issued an almanac in the same year. The press was also used to promulgate laws, e.g. *Ḳānūn-i kār-gudhārī* relating to crimes and their punishments (1309/1892) and *Ḳawāʿid-i sirādj al-milla* relating to foreign imports and issued by ʿAbd al-Raḥmān's son, Amīr Ḥabīb Allāh Khān [*q.v.*], in 1321/1904. ʿAbd al-Raḥmān's desire to modernise his army is reflected in several military tracts printed, e.g. *Mīzak-i ṭūpkhāna* on gunnery manoeuvres (1303/1885) and *Ḳawāʿid-i risāla* on cavalry drill (1304/1887).

Bibliography: Given in the article.

(G. W. Shaw)

MAṬBAKH (A), kitchen, cookhouse, a noun of place, defined by lexicographers as "the cook's house" (*bayt al-ṭabbākh*) from the verbal root meaning "the cooking of flesh meat". The root *ṭ-b-kh* is common to the Semitic family. Already in Akkadian, OT Hebrew, Syriac, Ethiopic and post-Biblical Hebrew we find the further, related connotation of "slaughtering" in addition to that of "cooking". Undoubtedly, the mediaeval domestic *maṭbakh* combined both these functions. By extension of the root meaning, the *maṭbakh* was the place where every conceivable kind of food, including fleshmeat, was transformed from its raw state for consumption at the table.

1. In the mediaeval caliphate.

The kitchen has been described as the "birthplace" (Forbes) and the "foster home" (Needham) of innumerable terms, operations and apparatuses in the early stage of man's development of technology. Laboratory operations employed by the ancient pharmacist and cosmetician reveal their origin in the preparation of food; so too do the techniques of crushing or disintegration (pressing, grinding, impaction), the technology of fermentation, the methods for the preservation of perishable organic material and, the oven. The chemistry and technology of cooking were thus realms of practical knowledge which the Islamic world inherited from the ancient centres of Middle Eastern civilisation. This inheritance was not, however, shared equally by all the population. Techniques which had perhaps originated or else been refined in the kitchens of the ancient temple and the palace were appropriated by the mediaeval urban cook, whereas the rural and nomadic populations retained the more primitive methods of food preparation. The technological gap between the urban and rural domains can be explained as a function of the distribution of power in the economic sphere and ultimately of social stratification and its ramifications in the political sphere.

Data relating to the kitchen in the classical period (*ca.* 200-800 A.H.) are found most abundantly in the specialist culinary treatises. Few of these, unfortunately, are extant. The social milieu reflected by the cookbook is clearly that of prosperous urban households, although it would be safe to assume that both palace and domestic kitchens shared a culinary lore and a range and type of utensils in common. Apart from this we know little of the operations and personnel of the palace kitchens in particular, except that they were of a far greater scale than those in the domestic sphere. For example, Hilāl al-Ṣābī reports that in the time of al-Muʿtaḍid (d. 289/902) the imperial "cook houses" (*maṭābikh*) were separate from the bakeries (*makhābiz*) and the caliph was served from his own private kitchen while the public's needs were catered to from a different one. (*Tuḥfat al-umarāʾ fī taʾrīkh al-wuzarāʾ*, ed. ʿAbd al-Sattār Faradj, Cairo 1958, 20-2). Domestic households of a comfortable standard would have had their bread baked and food cooked in the same complex.

The concept and design of the kitchen in a traditional open courtyard house has probably remained unchanged from mediaeval times to the last surviving examples in modern-day Baghdad. Indeed, the essential characteristics of the mediaeval open courtyard house in ʿIrāḳ are said to be the Mesopotamian in origin and inspiration (see Ṣubḥī al-ʿAzzāwī, *A descriptive, analytical and comparative study of traditional courtyard houses and modern courtyard houses in Baghdad*, Bartlett School of Architecture and Planning, University of London Ph.D. thesis, unpubl.). The kitchen (the contemporary expression *bayt al-maṭbakh* being equivalent to the lexicographers' *bayt al-ṭabbākh* and *maṭbakh*) in multi-courtyard dwellings was a whole complex comprising the kitchen proper, opening on to its own courtyard with adjoining ancilliary areas such as store rooms, latrine and bathroom, well and possibly a cook's room. The upper part of the courtyard, level with the first floor of the house, was surrounded by blank walls and open to the sky. The kitchen of a single courtyard house faced directly on to the courtyard itself and had either fewer or no ancilliary areas attached to it. Larger multi-courtyard houses might have a second kitchen adjacent to the rooms where guests were entertained. Palaces of the caliph and the ʿAbbāsid princes were doubtless fashioned on a much larger scale but along essentially similar lines. Contrast this special function kitchen complex with Lane's description of a peasant's house in Lower Egypt in the 19th century, in which one room generally had an oven (Eg. *furn*) "at the end farthest from the entrance and occupying the whole width of the chamber. It resembles a wide bench or seat and is about breast high: it is constructed of brick and mud, the roof arched within and flat on top." During the cold months, the inhabitants would sleep either on top of a warmed oven or on the floor of the same room (*Manners and customs of the modern Egyptians*, London 1837, i, 30). Along the social spectrum, therefore, food preparation was performed in areas ranging from greater to lesser specialisation: from the separate public and private kitchens and bakehouses of the palaces to the shared kitchen-habitable area of the peasant's dwelling.

The well-equipped kitchen in an urban household generally contained two major appliances. One was the baking oven, the *tannūr*, of Mesopotamian origin (Akkadian *tinûrû*; see A. Salonen, *Die Öfen der alten Mesopotamier*, in *Baghdader Mitteilungen*, iii [1964], 100-24). Cylindrical and bee-hive shaped, it gave the appearance of a large, inverted pot, from which it probably evolved. Fuel, preferably good charcoal, was inserted through a side opening, ignited, and when the oven was sufficiently hot, baking could commence. The oven's temperature could be adjusted to some extent by closing its open top, the so-called "eye" *ᶜayn*, or "mouth" *fam*, and its other apertures, *at͟hk̲āb* (see Fawzi Rasūl, *al-Tannūr wa-ṣināᶜatuhu fi 'l-Kāẓimiyya*, in *al-Turāt͟h al-S͟haᶜbī*, iii/12 [1972], 95-116). The earliest extant culinary manuscript, of late 4th/10th century ᶜIrāḳī provenance, provides a list of implements specifically used in baking bread in a *tannūr* (see *Kitāb al-Ṭabīk͟h wa-iṣlāḥ al-ag͟hd͟hiya al-maʾkūlāt wa-ṭatyīb al-aṭᶜima al-maṣnūᶜāt*, by Abū Muḥammad al-Muẓaffar b. Naṣr b. Sayyār al-Warrāḳ, Oxford, Bodleian, ms. Hunt. 187; now ed. K. Öhrnberg and S. Mroueh, Helsinki 1987). These include a dough board (*lawḥ*); a small rolling pin (*s͟hawbaḳ*) for the ordinary loaf (*rag͟hīf*) and a large one for the thin *riḳāḳ*; a feather for coating the dough in certain preparations; a wooden bowl (*d̲jafna* or *miᶜd̲jan*) in which the dough was mixed and a metal scraper (*miḥakk*) for cleaning it afterwards. Yeast was kept in a wooden container called a *miḥlab*. A cloth (*mandīl*) was used to wipe a loaf clean before baking and another was used for wiping down the oven to remove unwanted moisture or condensation. A poker (*ṣinnāra*) was used to remove the loaf from the oven if it fell upon the floor inside, and a metal instrument (*miḥrak*) was used for raking out the embers and ash from the oven when baking was finished.

The *tannūr* was not used exclusively for baking bread. A recipe for a kind of chicken pie made in a pan (*miḳlā*) is described as being lowered into the oven to cook and another dish, a meat, rice and vegetable casserole made in a pot (*ḳidr*) was placed in the oven to finish cooking. Both these dishes were called *tannūriyya*, or oven-dish, which were often left to stew gently overnight in a slowly cooling oven and served the following day (al-Warrāḳ, *bāb* 87).

The second major cooking contrivance found in the kitchen was known simply as the "fire-place", *mustawḳad*. This was designed to accommodate several cooking pots and/or pans side-by-side at the same time. It was erected to about half-a-person's height, giving easy access to the cooking food and was provided with vents allowing for an intake of air over the coals and for the expulsion of smoke. It is evident that many dishes required more than one pot in their preparation, hence several "elements" might be used in the preparation of a single meal. Another, apparently independent, type of *mustawḳad* was recommended for the preparation of sweetmeats. Its single element accommodated a *miḳlā* or *tand̲jīr*, the vessels in which sweetmeats were commonly made. These dishes required long cooking over a low heat accompanied by vigorous stirring of the pan's contents. The shape and position of this *mustawḳad* would have made it easier to hold the pan and to control the heat (al-Warrāḳ, fol. 13a).

Al-Warrāḳ's depiction of the mediaeval *batterie de cuisine* continues with a list of utensils employed in the preparation of the innumerable main dishes. Cooking pots (*ḳudūr*, sing. *ḳidr*) made of stone, earthenware, copper or lead came in various sizes. The largest pots were reported to hold the carcasses of four goats (al-Masᶜūdī, *Murūd̲j*, viii, 54 = §3173). Such cauldrons, however, were more apt to be found in the palace kitchens or an army field mess than in a domestic kitchen; contemporary recipes do not suggest such crude bulk of ingredients. Judging from certain archaeological evidence, kiln pottery vessels of the "cooking pot" and "casserole" types appear more modest in size. Remains from a Byzantine pottery factory in Cyprus reveal that the largest restored cooking pot item was 0.27 m high and 0.31 m at its greatest diameter; the smallest was 0.135 m high and 0.21 at its greatest diameter. Casseroles with lip-edge type rims which were probably provided with lids were smaller still, the largest restored item being 0.11 m high and 0.27 m in diameter (H. W. Catlong, *An early Byzantine pottery factory at Dhiorios in Cyprus*, in *Levant*, iv [1972], 1-82). These vessel sizes seem appropriate to the needs of even large domestic households.

Pans (sing. *miḳlā* or *miḳlāt*) generally used for frying fish and the like were made of iron. A stone-made *miḳlā* was used for other purposes, although the distinction between it and the former is unclear. Other utensils found in the kitchen were roasting skewers (sing. *saffūd*); a copper basin (*nuḳra*) for washing smaller containers and vessels in hot water; a large copper rod-like instrument (*miḥas͟hs͟h*) for stuffing intestines; a large knife for jointing meat and smaller ones for cutting up vegetables; several kinds of strainer (*miṣfāt*) made of wood or metal; a ladle (*mig͟hrafa*) and a mallet (*miḍrab*). Spices were crushed or powdered in a mortar (*hāwun*) and kept in glass vessels. A similar but larger stone mortar (*d̲jāwun*) was used for pounding meat or crushing vegetables; while meat was cut up on a wooden table or large wooden surface (*k͟hiwān*).

As with bread-making operations, al-Warrāḳ lists separately implements for making sweetmeats (*ḥalwā*). Frequently these dishes were served shaped in the form of a fish or bird fashioned thus by means of a mould (*ḳālab*, pl. *ḳawālib*). In other cases sweetmeats were presented at a table decorated in a manner appropriate for the occasion. The thick syrupy substance which was the base of many kinds of *ḥalwā* was stirred slowly in a pan over the fire with utensils called an *iṣṭām* and a *ḳasba fārisiyya*. Some preparations were rolled out after cooking on a marble slab (*ruk͟hāma*) before being cut into individual pieces. (The above data may be compared with Athenian household utensils in the classical period in B. A. Sparkes, *The Greek kitchen*, in *J. of Hellenic Studies*, lxxxii [1962], 121-37.)

The separate lists of utensils for different tasks mentioned in al-Warrāḳ's work suggests that at least in the larger, prosperous households both a baker and possibly a sweetmaker might have been retained in addition to a cook and other assistants. It may indeed be the case too, as Pellat has proposed, that the baker's (*k͟habbāz*) initial function evolved into that of a chief kitchen steward or even household majordomo (al-D̲jāḥiẓ, *Buk͟halāʾ*. tr. Ch. Pellat, *Le livre des avares*, 213, 258). The sweetmaker, on the other hand, may have been more often a market-based specialist commissioned to make his wares in people's kitchens when the need or occasion demanded. By and large, therefore, a household's status was marked socially, in part, by its degree of independence from the commercial cooked food establishments of the market which catered more to the needs of other sections of the population. Despite allusions in the *Thousand and One Nights* to "sending out" for food cooked in the market, the *ḥisba* manuals convey the impression that such fare was to be regarded with some suspicion. This impression is underlined by the existence of one market institution which must have served many urban households. Dishes initially prepared in the kitchen could be taken to the communal oven (*furn*), cooked there and returned to the kitchen to be garnished with chopped vegetable leaves and additional spices. Preparation of such a dish in the kitchen ensured a control over its quality; for its part, the *furn* served the needs of households which possessed neither adequate kitchen space, equipment or labour for meal preparation or else catered for a household's special festive occasions. In any event, the very affluent establishments would seldom, if ever, require the services of a communal oven manager.

Although we do not possess data on the day-to-day details of kitchen management, food preparation was a time-consuming and labour-intensive process. So too were the efforts to keep the cooking pots and pans clean in order to prevent the food becoming spoiled. Al-Bag͟hdādī's instructions in his mid-7th/13th century cookbook run briefly as follows: "The utmost care must be taken when washing the utensils used in cooking and the pans; let them be rubbed with brick dust, then with powdered dry potash and saffron and finally with the fresh leaf of citron" (*A Baghdad cookery book*, tr. A. J. Arberry, in *IC*, xiii [1939], 33). The opening chapter of al-Warrāḳ's work deals with many of the causes of spoiled food and how to avoid such results. Meat must be thoroughly cleaned of any blood and washed in pure cold (not hot) water in a clean bowl; a knife used to cut up vegetables should not be used at the same time to cut up meat; spices which are old, have lost their essential flavour and have become "bitter", should not be used lest they "corrupt the pot". Likewise, salt and oil should be tasted before adding them to the cooking food so as to ensure they are still in good condition; attention must be paid to see that the liquid of stews or bits of onion and the like has not dried on the inside of pots and so might spoil the food when next they were used; and only fuel which does not give off acrid smoke should be used, as the smoke could alter the taste of the food.

Finally, the kitchen or kitchen complex of the single or multi-courtyard house (*bayt maftūḥ*) allowed a sheep or goat and several fowl to occupy the yard awaiting slaughter and the cooking pot; thus meat could be kept and cooked fresh. Fruits, herbs and certain vegetables were also dried and then stored in the kitchen's ancilliary area along with food prepared by pickling and special condiments such as *murrī*. Home-made beer and wine could be stored there as well. The wide range of activities associated with the transformation of food from its "raw to cooked" state (clearly reflected in the treasury of contemporary recipes) indicates the central importance of the kitchen and its management not only to the smooth running of day-to-day family life but also to the broader social and political aspects of food preparation and consumption which existed within the enclosed world of the domestic compound.

Bibliography: In addition to works cited in the article, the following items have been selected which contain data more closely related to kitchen technology than to cooking as such: R. J. Forbes, *Food and drink*, in *A history of technology*, ed. C. Singer *et alii*, Oxford 1957, ii, 103-45; idem, *Chemical, culinary and cosmetic arts*, in *ibid.*, i, 270-85; J. Needham, *Science and civilisation in China*, Cambridge 1980, v/4, 1-210; M. M. Ahsan, *Social life under the Abbasids*, London 1979, 76-164; Margaret Arnott (ed.), *Gastronomy: the anthropology of food and food habits*, The Hague 1975; D. Waines, *Prolegomena to the study of cooking in Abbasid times*, in *School of Abbasid Studies, Occasional Papers*, no. 1, St. Andrews University 1986, 30-9.

(D. Waines)

2. In Ottoman Turkey.

In Ottoman society, *maṭbak͟h*, in vernacular Turkish *mutfak*, the kitchen, had a central importance not only because the members of the ruling élite had to feed their large retinues but also because, as a social institution, it served to establish and symbolise patrimonial bonds in society. Feeding people gave rise to a variety of elaborate organisations related to the Sultan's palace, to the élite and to the charitable institutions. By fulfilling charitable duties as prescribed by Islam and by leading to the accumulation and redistribution of wealth, these organisations played a crucial role in Ottoman social life and in the economy in general.

a. Special feasts and foods. Feeding people or giving public feasts had an important ritualistic-ceremonial and political function among the pastoral nomads of Eurasia. In the Kök-Türk inscriptions dated 732-5 A.D. (ed. H. N. Orkun, IC 10, ID 16, 17), the primary task and accomplishment of a Kag͟han was described as "the feeding and clothing of his people". In the *Ḳutadgu bilig*, a royal advice book written in 1070 in Turkish, being generous and "entertaining people with food and drink" are counted among the chief virtues of a prince (tr. R. Dankoff, 107; İnalcık, *Kutadgu Bilig'de...*, 270).

Later references to this custom indicate that "feeding his people" was institutionalised within the state organisation. To give a public feast was a privilege and a duty of the ruler. The institution was known as *toy* in Turkish (in Mongol *toyilan*: *Mang͟hol-un Niuča Tobča'an*, tr. A. Temir, 53), *s͟hölen* (in Mongol, *s͟hulen*: Temir, 202) or *as͟h*. It was originally associated with the institution of a potlatch (Abdülkadir İnan, "*Han-i yagma*" *deyiminin kökeni*, in *Türk Dili*, vi, 543-6). Ögedey ordered that one sheep from each herd was to be taken annually and given to the poor. This institution was called *s͟hülen* (A. Temir, *ibid.*). Following his election to the khanate, Čingiz K͟hān had set up a kitchen as part of the state organisation (Temir, 58; cf. ch. on the qualifications of a chief cook in the *Kutadgu bilig*, 133). In the public feast given by the Kag͟han at the meeting of the tribal chiefs, the customarily-determined seat (*orun*) and share of mutton served (*ülüs͟h*) to each chief was scrupulously regulated, for this was considered a ceremonial recognition of his rank (see İnan, *Orun ve ülüş meselesi*, in *THIM*, i, 121-33; cf. A. Z. V. Togan, *Oğuz destanı*, Istanbul 1972, 47-48; Abu 'l-G͟hāzī Bahādur K͟hān, *S͟hedjere-yi Terākime*, ed. R. Nur, Istanbul 1925, 31). Arbitrary change in the order and hierarchy might lead to a rebellion. At such *toy*s or *s͟hülen*s, important issues concerning the khanate were discussed and decisions taken. The practice was apparently introduced into the Islamic world by the Saldjūḳs. Niẓām al-Mulk (*Siyāsat-nāma*, ed. Darke, 162) speaks of it as a custom, scrupulously observed by the Saldjūḳs; Ṭog͟hrïl Beg held an open eating table in his palace every morning. Because it was interpreted as a proof of the ruler's care for his subject, he was personally interested in the quality of the food served. The Ḳarak͟hānids, says Niẓām al-Mulk (*ibid.*), considered *toy* an important state affair. Early Ottoman traditions (see ʿĀs͟hïḳ-Pas͟ha-zāde, ed. N. Atsız, 98), tell us that in the Ottoman palace it was the custom for a band to play every afternoon to invite people to come and eat. At any rate, it was a carefully observed custom to offer, in the second court of the Ottoman palace, food to anyone who came to submit a case to the imperial council (see S. Cantacassin, 75).

The Ottomans also followed the Islamicised forms of the ancient Iranian rituals of *Mihragān* [*q.v.*] and *Nawrūz* [*q.v.*] which became occasions for public festivities. The offering of *pīs͟hkas͟h* or presents by high officials and governors to the Sultan at such times was an occasion for the renewal of bonds of loyalty, as had been the case in ancient Iran (D̲h̲abīḥ Allāh Ṣafā, *Gāh-s̲h̲umārī wa d̲j̲as̲h̲nhā-yi Īrāniyān*, n.d., n.p., 43-5, 47-51, 55, 81-102; İ. H. Uzunçarşılı, *Saray*, 366, 371, 507). The 21st (in the old calendar, 9th) of March was accepted by the Ottomans as *nevrūz* (*nawrūz*) or the beginning of the new year (for different dates, see Ṣafā, *ibid.*). On that day, it was a widespread custom to eat and offer a special paste, *maʿd̲j̲ūn*, called *nevrūziyye* (M. Celâl, *Eski İstanbul*, 99; Uzunçarşılı, *Saray*, 366). *Nawrūz* was also the beginning of the fiscal year in the Ottoman financial calendar.

Festivals of Iranian origin were, in the course of time, identified with the memorable events of Islam. For Bektās̲h̲īs, *nawrūz* is the most important festival, celebrated with a special feast, since 9 March is believed to be the birthday of ʿAlī. It is a religiously meritorious act to celebrate nights of special importance in the history of Islam. The night of the Prophet's birth, 12 Rabīʿ I, as well as those of *rag̲h̲āʾib*, 3 Rad̲j̲ab; of the prophet's *miʿrād̲j̲* [*q.v.*], 27 Rad̲j̲ab; of *barāʾa* or *barāt*, 15 S̲h̲aʿbān; and the *laylat al-ḳadr*, 3 Ramaḍān, are celebrated with special prayers. After prayers, special dishes or sweets (*ḥelvā*) are offered which are an important part of the ritual: special *waḳf*s [*q.v.*] called *taʿāmiyye* were established specifically for the distribution of food in the *zāwiye*s and *ʿimāret*s on these days (examples of Ayverdi and Barkan, *İstanbul vakıfları*, nos. 1788, 1790). The day of *ʿās̲h̲ūrā* [*q.v.*], 10 Muḥarram, had special meaning for the *ṭarīḳa*s of S̲h̲īʿī tinge. It was the occasion of a ritual at the dervish convents, the elements of which were reminiscent of the ancient Iranian *nawrūz* ritual (cf. Ṣafā, 88, 101). The preparation of a special food for the day called *as̲h̲ūre* (*ʿās̲h̲ūrā*) at the convents had its own elaborate ritual (see Grace M. Smith, *ʿAshure and, in particular, the ʿAshure of Muharrem*, in *Jnal. of Turkish Studies*, viii, 229-31; *eadem*, *Food customs at the Kadirihane Dergâh*, in *JTS*, vii, 403). The day of *ʿās̲h̲ūrā* was observed commonly by all classes of society, including the Sultan's palace.

During the month of Ramaḍān, it was a custom for the Sultan and the principal dignitaries to invite their subordinates to the *ifṭār* meals in the evening, which were occasions for the renewal of the *nisba* or patrimonial relations among the élite (see M. Celâl, 93-5; B. Felek, *Yaşadığım Ramazanlar*, in the newspaper *Hürriyet*, June 1985). Special dishes were expected at the *ifṭār* meals. The introduction of a Western menu in the 19th century drew criticism regarding this. On the *ʿĪd al-aḍḥā*, Turkish *Ḳurbān bayrami̊*, thousands of sheep were slaughtered and distributed to the poor by the Sultan and well-to-do citizens. Offering sweets was customary at the *ʿĪd al-fiṭr* (Ali Riza, *Bir zamanlar İstanbul*, 120-81; M. Celâl, 89-100).

Also on special occasions, such as the Sultan's accession to the throne, a major victory on the battlefield, weddings or burials, elaborate public feasts were given which in their size and character resembled old Turkish *toy*s (for the *Sūr-nāme*s which contain full description of the feasts, A. S. Levend, *Türk edebiyatı tarihi*, 641; Edirne, 265-96; Ö. Nutku, *IV. Mehmed'in Edirne şenligi*; on the *toy* given by Meḥemmed II after the conquest of Constantinople, Ewliyā Čelebī, i, 60-2; the *k̲h̲ʷān-i yag̲h̲mā* given to the Crimean troops was a typical *toy*, described by Fi̊ndi̊ḳli̊li̊ Meḥmed, *Silāḥdār taʾrīk̲h̲i*, ii, 27).

The festival of K̲h̲iḍr-Ilyās, in vernacular Turkish *Hidrellez* [see K̲H̲IḌR and ILYĀS], celebrated universally in the Ottoman lands, was also an occasion for a communal ritual feast usually called *tafarrud̲j̲*. Like *nawrūz*, it was associated with a cult celebrating the beginning of spring with the difference that *Hidrellez* was celebrated on 6 May (or 23 April, O.S.). It is to be noted that the Christian festival of St. George, who was identified with K̲h̲iḍr, was held on the same day (Hasluck, i, 48, 319-26).

The *ḥalwā* (Turkish *ḥelvā*) gathering, celebrated on 1 May, is a ritual related rather to the *futuwwa* [*q.v.*] tradition of the craft guilds and the *ṭarīḳa*s [*q.v.*] (I. Mélikoff, *Le ritual du Helva*; A. Y. Ocak, *Islâm-Türk inanclarında Hızır*). Ritual foods, *tuz-ekmek* (Ş. Elçin, *Tuz-ekmek hakkı deyimi üzerine*), *s̲h̲erbet*, *loḳma*, *ḥelvā*, were all prepared and served ritually along with suitable prayers (see Grace Smith, *ibid.*).

In general, ritual food signified submission and mystical union in the *ṭarīḳa* ceremonies (see *Hacı Bektaş vilâyetnâmesi*, ed. A. Gölpınarlı, 17-18, 27).

The Janissary [see YENIČERI] corps was symbolically organised on the model of a kitchen. The explanation may lie in the *futuwwa* and Bektās̲h̲ī connections of the corps, or in the old Turkish custom of *toy* (see above). The *ḳazān-i s̲h̲arīf*, or sacred cauldron of *čorba* (soup), attributed to Ḥād̲j̲d̲j̲ī Bektās̲h̲ [*q.v.*] was the emblem of the whole Janissary corps. The Janissary headgear was ornamented with a spoon. High officers were called *čorbad̲j̲i̊*. Also, each *orta*, or division, had its own *ḳazān*, and the head cook of the *orta* kitchen was the most influential officer in the division. The kitchen was also used as a detention place. Important meetings were held around the *ḳazān-i s̲h̲arīf*. Overturning it meant rejecting the Sultan's food, i.e. rebellion, whilst to accept one's food meant submission in general (see Ş. Elçin, *Tuz-ekmek hakkı...*).

b. The *Maṭbak̲h̲-i ʿĀmira* or Palace Kitchen. In addition to visitors, there was in the Sultan's palace a large body of palace servants who had to be fed every day. In 933/1527 servants in the *Bīrūn*, Outer Service, alone, numbered 5,457 (*IFM*, xvii, 300). The annual account books of the New Palace (the Ṭopḳapi̊ Palace) (in *Belgeler*, ix, 72-81, 108-49) list separately the following kitchens: the *Maṭbak̲h̲-i ʿĀmira*, or Imperial Kitchen; the *Ḥelwā-k̲h̲āne* (formerly *s̲h̲erbet-k̲h̲āne*, confectioner's kitchen); and the two bake-houses for *simid* and *fodula*. Within the *Maṭbak̲h̲-i ʿĀmira* itself, reference is made to particular kitchens: *Maṭbak̲h̲-i Āg̲h̲ā-yi Saray* (K. for the Chief Eunuch of the Palace), the *Maṭbak̲h̲-i Āg̲h̲āyān* (K. for the Chief Eunuchs), and the *Maṭbak̲h̲-i G̲h̲ulāmān-i Enderūn* (K. for the Palace pages). A special kitchen called *ḳus̲h̲k̲h̲āne* (not to be confused with the Palace aviary) was reserved exclusively for the Sultan himself. The entire southern part of the Second Court in the Palace was occupied by kitchens, storerooms, apartment for the Kitchen personnel and offices (see Plan I, in B. Miller, *Beyond the Sublime Porte*, 8). After a destructive fire, ten kitchens were rebuilt under Süleymān I by the architect Sinān [*q.v.*], who created a grandiose construction with domes and chimneys. Each of the ten kitchens served a special group.

There were two storehouses, *kilār* or *kiler*, one in the *Bīrūn*, the other in the *Enderūn (Andarūn)* where provisions for the Palace were stored. The more valuable items such as sugar and spices mainly provided from Egypt (*Mi̊ṣi̊r irsāliyyesi*) were preserved in the inner *kiler* under the direct supervision of the *kilerd̲j̲i-bas̲h̲i̊*. The bulkier goods were stored in the outer *kiler* under the supervision of the *Maṭbak̲h̲ kilerd̲j̲isi*. Other palaces in Istanbul, such as the Sarāy-i ʿAtīḳ, Üsküdār Sarāyi̊ and G̲h̲alaṭa Sarāyi̊, and the palaces in Edirne and Bursa, had their own kitchen organisations similar to those of the Ṭopḳapi̊ Palace.

During the classical period (1400-1600), all the

work involved in the procurement of provisions and the preparation and distribution of food within the Palace was under the responsibility of the *kilerdji-bashi*, also known as *sar-kilārī-i khāṣṣa*, or the Head of the Imperial Larder. He was the chief of the third of the Imperial Chambers which were in direct contact with the Sultan. The staff under the *kilerdji-bashi* grew considerably over the course of time, from 20 in the early 16th century to 134 in 1090/1679 (Uzunçarşılı, 315). The number of cooks in the ten Imperial Kitchens also increased considerably, as follows:

Table I
Cooks of the Imperial Palace (Ṭopḳapi)

Date	*Number*	*Salary*	*Source*
916/1510	260 (50 of the *usta*)	—	S. Cantacassin, 74
933/1526	277	654,900	*IFM*, xv, 308-12
978/1570	1570 (includes staff of storerooms and ovens)	2,536,056	*IFM*, xvii, 333-5
ca. 1060/1650	1370	2,500,000	Eyyūbī Efendi

tasnifi, *Maṭbakh-i ʿĀmira muḥāsebe defterleri*; for Ottoman cookery in the mid-17th century, see Seyyid Meḥmed, *Ṣoḥbet-nāme*, Topkapı Sarayı Library, Hazine K. 1425 and 1418).

Provisions were to be supplied regularly to the imperial kitchens under the supervision of a *maṭbakh emīni*, who organised their delivery. Also responsible for book keeping and accounts, he was assisted by a *katkhudā*, two *kātibs* (scribes) and a larder attendant (*kilerdji*). A bureaucrat of the rank of *khʷādje*, the *emīn* was nevertheless a dependent of the *kilerdji-bashi* (for

The cooks, *āshdjis* or *ṭabbākhs*, were organised in an *odjaḳ* (corps), which was divided into *bölüks*, in the same way as other military corps at the Porte. The corps was headed by the *sar-ṭabbākhīn-i khāṣṣa*, also known as *bash-āshdji-bashi* with the rank of *āghā*. As in other corps, the *āghā* was assisted by a *katkhudā* (lieutenant) and a *kātib*, secretary. As professionals, the cooks were subjected to a hierarchy as in any craft, which consisted of *usta* or *ustād*, *ḳalfa* or *khalīfa*, and *shāgird* (master, foreman and novice). As a rule, a *shāgird* joined the corps from the corps of *ʿadjemī-oghlans* [see ḲAPĪ-ḲULU]. He learned the profession while working under an *usta* or *āshdji-bashi*, later becoming an *āshdji*, then being promoted to *āshdji-bashi*.

Servants under the *kilerdji-bashi* in the storerooms in the *Bīrūn* formed a separate corps in ten *bölüks*. Under him were the following: *khabbāzān* (bakers), *ḳaṣṣābān* (butchers), *ḥalwādjiyān* (*ḥelvā*-makers), *yoghurtdjiyān* (yoghurt-makers), *sebzedjiyān* (keepers of vegetables), *simiddjiyān* (makers of ring bread), *buzdjiyān* and *ḳardjiyān* (keepers of ice and snow), *ʿashshābān* (keepers of herbs), *tavuḳdjiyān* (keepers of poultry), *ḳalaydjiyān* (tinners of the copper ustensils), *mūmdjiyān* (makers of candles), *saḳḳāyān* (water-carriers), *gandum-kūbān* (wheat-pounders). *Čashnīgīrān* (waiters), made a completely independent group under a *čashnīgīr-bashi* in the *Bīrūn* section. The Sultan was served by the *kilerdji-bashi* and his staff in the *Enderūn*.

Table II
Čashnīgīrs

Date	*Number*	*Source*
900/1494	9	*IFM*, xv, 308
916/1510	31	Cantacassin, 70
ca. 920/1514	24	*IFM*, xv, 313
1018/1609	117	ʿAynī ʿAlī, 97
1079/1668	21	*IFM*, xvii, 228

The Sultan's cooks competed to please the Sultan by preparing special dishes of their own cooking. The Sultan showed his pleasure by giving a reward (*inʿām*) (records in *Belgeler*, ix, 300, 305). Thus the Ottoman palace was considered as a centre where Ottoman Turkish cooking excelled and where creative chefs were trained (see A. Muhtar, *Aş-evi*). Detailed records on the ingredients used are to be found in the kitchen expenditure books (see the registers called *Muḥāsebe-yi ikhrādjāt-i khāṣṣa* published by Ö. L. Barkan, *Belgeler*, ix; and the Başvekâlet Archives, Istanbul, K. Kepeci

the functions of the *emīn*, see, e.g. *Muḥāsebe defteri*, BA, K. Kepeci no. 7291). Provisions were bought either from the market or as *irsāliyye* or *odjaḳlïḳ* [see MUḲĀṬAʿA] procured regularly from the resources under the control of the finance department.

The tremendous amount of meat consumed at the imperial palaces give rise to a vast organisation under a *ḳaṣṣāb-bashi*, who was financially dependent on the *maṭbakh emīni*. For the kitchens of the Topkapı Palace alone, the annual consumption of lamb was about 1,270 tons, costing 12 million *aḳčas*. The other three palaces consumed 458 tons annually (*IFM*, xvii, 295-8).

The kitchen expenditures of the temporary embassies were met by the Porte. In 1079/1669, e.g., the Russians received provisions worth 347,000 *aḳčes*.

Table III
The total annual expenditure for the provisions of the Palace Kitchens

	Million aḳčes	*In gold pieces*
Under Süleymān I	4.8	80,000
,, Selīm II	6.3	105,000
,, Murād III	21	175,000
In 1072/1661	44.3	369,000
In 1164/1750	900,000 *ghurush*	328,000

The organisation of the kitchen in the houses of the élite was a miniature replica of the Sultan's one. It included two separate kitchens, one for the lord and the other for the servants. Both had master cooks (*usta*) and apprentices or assistants (*shāgird*). In 1082/1671 a vizier-governor, ʿUmar (ʿÖmer) Pasha's kitchen personnel (see M. Kunt, 15-22) consisted of one *maṭbakh emīni*, also known as *wakīl-khardj*, six cooks, six pantrymen (*kilārī*), two shopping boys and one butler. Expenditure for provisions through the *wakīl-khardj* amounted to about 8,600 gold pieces or 16.7% of the Pasha's total expenditure. Members of the élite spent an unusual amount of money for kitchen expenses, not only because they had large retinues to feed (in ʿUmar Pasha's case, 220 persons) but also because they were expected "to keep the house open" to visitors.

In the houses of the élite and well-to-do, the *maṭbakh* and the *furūn* (oven) were to be found often as separate constructions in the courtyard.

c. The *ʿImāret* and *Zāwiye*. The *ʿimārets* functioned as an extensive network of social aid in Ottoman society, particularly in the cities. Numerous

*ʿimāret*s provided food for thousands of people who did not have an independent source of income. Charity, materialised through the institution of *ʿimāret*, was accepted as an integral part of the Islamic *waḳf* system, but considered extensively, the *ʿimāret* system might also be related to pre-Islamic Turkish traditions.

Through this system, the immense wealth, which was accumulated in the hands of the ruling élite, was redistributed among the unprivileged and dependent people. Built within a religious complex, an *ʿimāret* compound usually included a *maṭbakh*, a *taʿām-khāne* or *dār al-ḍiyāfa* (eating hall), *ḥudjras* (rooms for visitors), an *anbār* or *kilār* (larder), a *furūn* (oven), an *isṭabl* (stable) and a *maḥṭab* or *odunluḳ* (store for firewood). The entire *ʿimāret* compound was put under a *shaykh-i ʿimāret*, while each section came under the responsibility of an employee specialising in that service. The *Maṭbakh* personnel of a large *ʿimāret* (see *Belgeler*, i, 235-377; *Kara Ahmed Paşa vakfiyyesi*, in *Vakıflar Dergisi*, ii, 83-97) included first a *wakīl-khardj* (steward), *kilārī* (larder attendant), *anbārī* (keeper of the storeroom for bulky provisions), *naḳībs* (distributors and supervisors), *ṭabbākh*s (cooks), a head cook, and *khabbāz*s (bakers); in the second category came a *gandum-kūb* (wheat-pounder), a *kāse-shūy* (bowl-washer), *ḥammāl*s (porters) and *bostānī*s (gardeners). There were also *ḳapīdjī*s (gate-keepers), *teberdār*s (halberdiers), *ākhūrī* (stable boy), *čirāghdjī* (candle-lighter), *kāse-keskh* (waiter), *ferrāsh* (sweeper) and *mezbele-kesh* (carrier of garbage). At smaller *ʿimāret*s or *zāwiye*s, there were to be found only a *shaykh*, cooks, bakers and a store-keeper. At the derwish *zāwiye*s, the main services were assumed by the *baba*s and others by dervishes, in a hierarchical order. According to the Ṣūfī interpretation, each service represented a station in the training of a disciple. In the Bektāshī order, the *ekmekdji-baba* and *āshdjī-baba* came second and third after the *pust-nishīn* in the hierarchy, which corresponded to the *ekmek-evi* and *āsh-evi* in the *tekke* (J. K. Birge, *The Bektashi order*, 175, 250; S. Faroqhi, *Der Bektaschi-Orden*, 105; eadem, *Seyyid Gazi*, in *Turcica*, xiii, 94, 103; A. Gölpınarlı, *Mevlânadan sonra mevlevîlik*, Istanbul 1953, 391). The administrators comprised a *mutawallī* (trustee and administrator), a *nāẓir* (supervising trustee), a *kātib* (secretary) and *djābī*s (collectors of revenues). All this gives an idea of how an *ʿimāret* or *zāwiye* was organised and functioned.

The word *ʿimāret* is sometimes used synonymously with *khānaḳāh* or *zāwiye*; but in all categories, the running of a *maṭbakh* and cooking and distributing food for the needy constituted the most important function.

*Imāret*s founded by the sultans in large cities were the most developed form of public soup kitchen. The *ʿimāret* of Fātiḥ, part of the charitable complex established by Meḥemmed II [*q.v.*], had an annual income of about 20,000 gold ducats. This income was derived from 57 *waḳf* villages and the *djizya* tax of the non-Muslims (8,677 taxpayers) of Istanbul. At least 1,117 persons received food from this *ʿimāret*. The figure included 957 students, employees and servants of the *ʿimāret* and 160 travellers (*IFM*, xxiii, 306-41). For better service, a *tawzīʿ-nāma*, or regulation for distribution (ed. A. S. Ünver, *Fâtih aşhânesi tevzi' nâmesi*, Istanbul 1953) was drawn in 952/1545. The food, when left over, was further distributed among the poor in the neighbourhood, with widows and orphans getting priority. Those benefiting from an *ʿimāret* are listed, in order, as the *fuḳarāʾ* (destitute) coming first, and then *masākīn* (those unable to make a livelihood) and *musāfirīn* (travellers). Sometimes poor orphans (*yatīm*) and school children are also mentioned in the *waḳf* deeds among the beneficiaries. Dervish *zāwiye*s are included in the category of establishments which offer food and shelter to travellers and the needy. In the documents granting arable land as *mulk*/*waḳf* to the *shaykh* of a *zāwiye*, it is always stipulated that his primary duty is to provide food and shelter to travellers (see *Vakıflar Dergisi*, ii, 304-53). In the countryside, the *zāwiye* was thought indispensable for people travelling and a factor promoting settlement and prosperity. Anyway, helping travellers was included among the *zakāt* [*q.v.*] duties and the performance of this duty in the name of the Sultan was given to the care of a dervish community, as an old Islamic tradition. The *zāwiye*s of the *akhī*s [*q.v.*] were particularly active during the first period of Ottoman expansion and settlement, when hundreds of *zāwiye*s and similar institutions were established throughout the empire; in 936/1530 there were 626 *zāwiye*s and *khānaḳāh*s, 45 *ʿimāret*s, 1 *ḳalender-khāne* and 1 *mevlevī-khāne* in the province of Anatolia (western Asia Minor).

As a rule, a *zāwiye* encompassed two sections, a *tekke* (convent), where the dervishes performed their religious rites, and a *maṭbakh* or *āsh-evi*, where food was prepared and distributed to the dervishes, to travellers and to the needy. The *maṭbakh* was considered so important that usually it dominated the whole *zāwiye* structure, and took up by far the largest share of the *zāwiye*'s revenue (see Faroqhi, *Der Bektashi-Orden*, 48-75). In the urban *zāwiye*s, the residents of the quarter where the *zāwiye* was built set up additional *waḳf*s to supplement the salaries of the servants or to pay for the preparation and distribution of food on holy days (*ḳandīl*s). Thus the *zāwiye*, like the mosque of the quarter, constituted a common religious centre as well as a charitable institution (see *İstanbul vakıfları*, ed. Ayverdi and Barkan) in the *maḥalla* [*q.v.*].

Bibliography: Başvekâlet Archives, Istanbul: *Sarāy-i Hümāyūn Maṭbakh-i ʿāmire ve Kiler defterleri*, K. Kepeci Tasnifi, nos. 7270-7388; Maliyeden Müdevver Defterler, nos. 214, 15907; Ö. L. Barkan, *İstanbul saraylarına ait muhasebe defterleri*, in *Belgeler*, xi (1979), 1-380; idem, *Osmanlı imperatorluğu bütcelerine dair notlar*, in *İst. Üniversitesi İktisat Fakültesi Mecmuası* (abbrev. *IFM*), xv, 304, 308, 311-13; xvii, 228, 233, 253, 286, 295-98, 308, 311-13, 334-35; idem, *Saray mutfağının 894-895 (1489-1490) yılına ait muhasebe bilânçosu*, in *IFM*, xxiii, 380-98; idem, *Fâtih camii ve imâreti tesislerinin 1489-1490 yıllarina ait muhasebe bilançoları*, in *ibid.*, 296-341; idem, *Edirne ve cıvarındaki bazı imâret tesislerinin yıllık muhasebe bilançoları*, in *Belgeler*, i, 235-377; *Istanbul vakıfları tahrir defteri*, eds. E. H. Ayverdi and Ö. L. Barkan, Istanbul 1970; O. Nuri (Ergin), *Medjelle-yi umūr-i belediyye*, Istanbul 1922, 393-878. Food cults and rituals of the Turks: Abdülkadir İnan, *Orun ve ülüş meselesi*, in *Makaleler ve incelemeler*, Ankara, TTK 1968, 241-54; idem, *Kazak ve Kırgızlarda "Yeçenlik hakkı" ve konuk aşı meseleleri*, in *ibid.*, 281-91; idem, *Han-ı Yagma deyiminin kökeni*, in *ibid.*, 645-48; B. Ögel, *Türk kültür tarihine giriş*, iv, Istanbul 1978; idem, *Türkiye halkının kültür kökenleri*, in *Beslenme teknikleri*, Istanbul 1976; idem, *Kurut, eski bir türk azığı*, in *Folklor Araştırmaları Kurumu yıllığı*, Ankara 1975; M. A. Köymen, *Alp Arslan zamanı Türk beslenme sistemi*, in *Selçuklu araştırmaları dergisi*, iii (1971), 15-50; Mahmūd el-Kaşgarī, *Divanü Lugāt-it-Türk*, ed. and tr. R. Dankoff and J. Kelly, ii, Cambridge, Mass. 1985, 253-60. For the food preparation of the Altay Turks, see W. Radloff, *Aus Siberien*, i, Turkish tr. A. Temir, Istanbul 1954, 306-9. See also Dhabīḥallāh Ṣafā, *Gāhshumārī wa-djashnhā-yi millī-i Irāniyān*, n.p., n.d.,; Djāḥiẓ, *Kitāb al-Tādj*, tr. Ch. Pellat, Paris 1954, 39-48; M. Rodinson, *Recherches sur les documents arabes relatifs à la cuisine*, in *REI* (1945), 95-165; A. J. Arberry, *A Baghdad cookery book*, in *IC*, xiii/1 (1939), 30-47, 189-214. For Islam's prescriptions on food and eating see arts. DHABĪḤA, GHIDHĀ᾽, ḤARĀM, ḤADJDJ, ṢAWM, ṢAYD, SHARĀB. On food rituals in the *ṭarīḳas*, see A. Gölpınarlı, *Fütüvvet-nāme-i Sulṭānī...*, in *IFM*, xvii, 150; J. K. Birge, *The Bektashi order of dervishes*, London 1937, 169, 175-6; M. T. Oytan, *Bektaşiliğin iç yüzü*, Ankara 1960, 59; S. Faroqhi, *Der Bektaschi-Orden in Anatolien*, Vienna 1981, 48-75, 105; eadem, *Wakf administration in sixteenth-century Konya, the zaviye of Sadreddīn-i Konevī*, in *JESHO*, xv, I/2, 45-72; eadem, *Agricultural activities in a Bektashi center: the Tekke of Kızıl Deli 1750-1830*, in *Südost-Forschungen*, xxxv, 69-96; eadem, *Seyyid Gazi revisited...*, in *Turcica*, xiii, 90-122; I. Mélikoff, *Le rituel du Ḥelvā*, in *Isl.*, xxxix (1964), 38-9, 180-91; *Vilâyet-nâme-i Hünkâr Hacı Bektaş Veli*, ed. A. Gölpınarlı, Istanbul 1958, 21, 24, 35; F. W. Hasluck, *Christianity and Islam under the Sultans*, repr. London 1973, i, 148-9, 244, and index, s.v. food; J.-P. Roux, *Les traditions des nomades de la Turquie méridionale*, 311-17, and index, s.v. repas communiels; Grace Smith, *Food customs at the Kadirihane Dergah in Istanbul*, in *JTS*, vii (1982); B. Noyan, *Bektaşi ve Alevilerde Muharrem âyini, aşure ve matem erkâni*, in *Halk Kültürü*, 1984/1, 81-102; K. Wulzinger, *Drei Bektaschi-Klöster Phrygiens*, in *Beiträge zur Bauwissenschaft*, Berlin 1910; S. Eyice, *Zaviyeler ve zaviyeli camiler*, in *IFM*, xxiii, 1-80; idem, *Çorumun mecidözü'nde Âşik Paşa-oğlu Elvan Çelebi zâviyesi*, in *TM*, xv, 46; H. Zubeyir (Koşay), *Hacı Bektaş türbesi*, in *TM*, ii, 365-82; A. Y. Ocak, *Islam-Türk inançlarında Hızır yahut Hızır-Iliyas kültü*, Ankara 1985. For the festivities and festivals, see M. F. Köprülü, in *THIM*, i, 270-2; S. Zorlutuna, *Şâhâne sünnet ve evlenme dügünleri*, in *Edirne*, Ankara 1965, 265-96. Ö. Nutku, *IV. Mehmed'in Edirne şenliği*, Ankara 1972. On *sur-nāmes*, see A. S. Levend, *Türk edebiyatı tarihi*, Ankara 1973, 159-60; Musahipzâde Celâl, *Eski Istanbul yaşayışı*, Istanbul 1946, 89-104; Ahmet Rasim, *Ramazan sohbetleri*, Istanbul n.d.; Ali Riza, *Bir zamanlar İstanbul*, in *Tercüman 1001 Temel Eser*, no. 11, n.d.; *Ramazanname*, ed. A. Çelebioğlu, in *ibid.*; A. R. Balaman, *Gelenekler, töre ve törenler*, Izmir 1983; Burhan Oğuz, *Türkiye halkının kültür kökenleri*, i, Istanbul 1976, 315-854. For folk *destāns* on food, see *Halk kültürü*, i (1984), 59-63; Seyyid Meḥmed, *Ṣoḥbet-nāme*, Topkapı S. K. Hazine, nos. 1425 and 1418. For an analysis of it, see O. Ş. Gökyay, *Sohbetnâme*, in *Tarih ve toplum*, no. 14 (1985), 129-37; *Türk mutfağı senpozyumu*, Ankara 1982; R. Genc, *Eski Türk ziyafetleri ve diş kirası âdeti*, in *II. Milletlerarası Türk Folklor Kongresi Bildirileri*, iv, Ankara 1982, 175-82; H. Karpuz, *Eski Türk evlerinin bölmeleri*, in *Türk folklor araştırmaları*, ii (Ankara 1982), 37-48. For coffee houses, see A. Galland, *De l'origine et du progrès du Caffé*, Caen 1669; Pečuyī, *Ta᾽rīkh*, i, Istanbul 1283/1866, 363-65; M. D'Ohsson, *Tableau général de l'empire ottoman*, ii, Paris 1790, 123-6; R. Hattox, *Coffee and coffeehouses*, Seattle and London 1985. For the *Maṭbakh-i ʿĀmire* or imperial kitchens, in addition to the documents mentioned above, see Idrīs-i Bidlīsī, *Hasht bihisht*, Topkapı P. Lib. H. no. 1655, p. 651; Th. Spandouyn Cantacassin, *Petit traicté de l'origine des Turcqz*, ed. C. Schefer, Paris 1892, 71-4; İ. H. Uzunçarşılı *Saray teşkilâtı*, Ankara 1945, 313-15, 379-84, 455-60; B. Miller, *Beyond the Sublime Porte*, New York 1931, 185-200; Koči Bey, *Risāle*, ed. A. K. Aksüt, Istanbul 1939, 81-2, 114-15; Ḥāfiẓ Khiḍīr Ilyās, *Ta᾽rīkh-i Enderūn*, Istanbul 1276/1859, 384-85. For eating and table manners, see Kay Kāwūs b. Iskandar, *Ḳābūs-nāma*, tr. R. Levy, London 1951, 55-60; Mustafā ʿAlī, *Mawāʿid al-nafā᾽is fī ḳawāʿid al-madjālis*, ed. C. Baysun, Istanbul 1951, 87, 117-20. For Turkish cuisine, see a Turkish tr., with additions, of Muḥammad b. al-Ḥasan al-Kātib al-Baghdādī, *Kitāb al-Ṭabīkh* (on this work see above, Arberry, and Günay Kut, *13. yüzyıla ait bir yemek kitabı*, in *Kaynakalar*, iii [Istanbul 1984], 50-7); Meḥmed Kāmil, *Maldja᾽ al-ṭabbākhīn*, ms. in Topkapı S. K. Hazine 1186, Istanbul 1275/1859; N. Sefercioğlu, *Türk yemekleri*, Ankara 1985; Aḥmed Mukhtār, *Āsh-evi*, Istanbul 1319/1901; Hādiyye Fakhriyye, *Yemek kitabi*, Istanbul 1340/1924; eadem, *Tatlīdjī bashī*, Istanbul 1342/1926; Süheyl Ünver, *Fâtih devri yemekleri*, Istanbul 1952; idem, *Tarihte 50 Türk yemeği*, Istanbul 1948; idem, *Fâtih aşhânesi tevzi'-nâmesi*, Istanbul 1953; H. Z. Koşay and A. Ülkücan, *Anadolu yemekleri ve Türk mutfaği*, Ankara 1961; E. Z. Oral, *Selçuk devri yemekleri ve ekmekleri*, in *Türk etnografya dergisi*, i, ii; M. K. Özergin, *Bolvadin yemekleri*, in *Türk folklor araştırmaları*, no. 227 (1968); S. Yüce, *Bucak'ta sofra ve yemek gelenekleri*, in *ibid.*, no. 210 (1967); N. Gözaydın, *Bazı Anadolu yemekleri*, in *ibid.*, 223 (1968); A. Turgut Kut, *Açıklamalı yemek kitapları bibliyografyası*, Ankara 1985.

(HALIL INALCIK)

3. In Persia [see Suppl.].

4. In Mughal India.

It is not easy to determine to what extent the Mughal commissariat perpetuated earlier Indian models: consistent information comes only from the times of Akbar and his successors, and although there are copious references to banquets from earlier reigns, and some allusions to favourite articles of food, there is almost nothing recorded about kitchen organisation.

Under Akbar, the Imperial kitchen, *maṭbakh* (called in Humāyūn's time *bāwarčī-khāna*), including its dependent branches of *ābdār-khāna* (the court water-supply), *mēwa-khāna* (supply of fruits both fresh and dried) and *rikāb-khāna* (pantry, specially where bread is prepared), was one division of the imperial household under the control of the Khān-i Sāmān. The kitchen itself was controlled by a *mīr bakāwal*, on whose staff were several assistant *bakāwals*, a treasurer and his assistants—for the kitchen estimates and accounts were kept separately—clerks, marketers, a large retinue of cooks "from all countries", food-tasters, table spreaders and servers, and perhaps most important, a large number of storekeepers, for the Imperial Kitchen had to be ready to move a day in advance of the Emperor when he went on tour.

The *mīr bakāwal* was required, according to the *Ā᾽īn-i Akbarī*, to prepare both annual and monthly estimates for his department, to determine the rates of materials required, and to make the necesary purchases, entering all these in a day-book; he had also to pay the monthly wages of the staff. Provisions such as rice from various sources, other grains, *ghī* (clarified butter), live goats and sheep, ducks and fowls, etc., were collected at the beginning of each season (doubtless to take advantage of seasonal fluctuations in prices); the livestock would be fattened under the care of the cooks; a kitchen-garden was also established to provide a continual supply of fresh vegetables. Livestock was slaughtered outside the city or camp by a river or tank, and the meat washed and sent to the kitchen in sealed sacks; within the kitchen it would again be washed in selected water taken from sealed vessels before being cooked. During the cooking processes, in which every dish would be under the supervision of one of the sub-*bakāwal*s, awnings would be spread and lookers-on carefully kept away; the finished dishes, after being tasted by the cooks and the *bakāwal*s, would be served in utensils of gold or silver, tinned copper or earthenware, tasted by the *mīr bakāwal*, tied up in cloths and sealed, with a note of their contents, before being sent to the table; as an additional precaution a storekeeper would send also a list of the vessels used, so that none of the dishes might be substituted by an unauthorised one, and the used vessels had to be checked against the list when they were returned. As the food was carried from the kitchen by the *bakāwal*s, cooks and others, guarded by mace bearers, a similar procession would be sent from the bakery, the *ābdār-khāna*, and the *mēwa-khāna*, all dishes again sealed by a *bakāwal*. Some dishes from the Imperial table might be sent, as a mark of special favour, to the queens and princes; but of course the kitchen was kept busy the whole time, apart from the meals required for the emperor's table, in providing meals for the *zanāna*.

As remarked above, s.v. GANGĀ, the water of the Ganges had a special reputation for purity, and here perhaps pre-Mughal usage is perpetuated in that Muḥammad b. Tughluḳ is known to have used special couriers to bring Ganges water to his court; Akbar while at Āgra or Fatḥpur Sikrī is said to have obtained Ganges water from Sōrōn (miscalled Sarun in Blochmann's tr. of *Āʾīn-i Akbarī*, *āʾīn* 22), a town of some antiquity now no longer on the main channel of the Ganges, and while in Lāhawr from Hardwār. His practice was followed by later Mughal rulers. This was used for drinking water; but even water for cooking purposes had a small amount of Ganges water mixed with it. Trustworthy persons drew the water and despatched it to court in sealed jars. Drinking water was at first cooled in sealed containers stirred in a vessel containing a solution of saltpetre, although after the court moved to the Pandjāb, ice was regularly used, brought from the Pandjāb hills by land or water. For all these arrangements the *ābdār-khāna* was responsible, and also for the provision of *sharbat* when required; indeed, in the reign of Djahāngīr [*q.v.*] the *ābdār-khāna* was known as the *sharbat-khāna*. On the march or in camp, drinking water was cooled by being carried in a tinned flask covered with a cloth wrapping which was kept constantly moist, so that the contents were cooled by evaporation from the surface, as in the modern army water-bottle (the evidence of Mughal paintings shows a simpler method, still in use: the water is kept in a large earthenware vessel (*surāhī*), only lightly glazed or unglazed, mounted on a simple stand and placed so as to catch any breeze).

The *mēwa-khāna* received much attention from the Mughal emperors. Bābur, in a touching passage in the *Tūzuk*, recalls the delights of the grapes and melons of his homeland and regrets their absence from India; but such luxuries were later regularly imported after the conquest of Kābul, Ḳandahār and Kashmīr, and Akbar settled horticulturists from "Īrān and Tūrān" for the cultivation of fruit trees in India. Abu 'l-Faḍl, *Āʾīn-i Akbarī*, *āʾīn* 28, gives a list of some two dozen imported fruits and nuts, three dozen native Indian sweet fruits, and a score of sour and sub-acid fruits. A special "fruit" described in this section is the *pān*, a heart-shaped green leaf smeared with lime and catechu, to which is added slices or granules of betel-nut with aromatic spices, sometimes camphor, musk, or costly perfumes, and rolled into a *bīṛā*, which may then be finished with silver or even gold leaf. A *pān* was often presented to a courtier as a mark of royal favour, and Mughal brass *pāndān*s, with compartments to hold the leaves, nuts and other requisites, were also presented as gifts.

Abu 'l-Faḍl's account shows further what kinds of dishes were prepared for the Imperial table, and he gives thirty specimen receipts—or rather lists of ingredients, since there is no information about the cooking processes involved. These are divided into three categories: *bē-gōsht* (meatless), "commonly called *ṣūfiyāna*"; *gōsht bā-birandj*, meat with rice; and *abāzīr*, spiced dishes. The categories, however, do not seem to be mutually exclusive. There is already ample evidence for the Indianisation of the Mughal fare, in both the ingredients (including cardamoms, cinnamon, saffron, ample fresh ginger root, asafoetida, turmeric and others among the spices; chillis are conspicuously absent, and *summāḳ*, a favourite Persian condiment, appears only once) and the nomenclature (*dāl*, lentils; *sāg*, a spinach dish; *čapātī* among the breads; *khičrī* among the rice dishes). Abu 'l-Faḍl's list of current market prices for common commodities (*āʾīn* 27) refers to many by Indian names (e.g. *mūng* and *mōṭh* among the lentils) and includes such Indian favourites as mangoes-in-oil and lemons-in-oil, among the pickles.

The large number of meatless dishes calls for comment. Akbar declared a number of *ṣūfiyāna* days in which he ate no meat, including Fridays, Sundays (because, according to Djahāngīr, it was the day of his birth), the first day of each solar month, and throughout the month of Ābān and at least part of Farwardīn, and on many other days detailed by Abu 'l-Faḍl; he increased the number of *ṣūfiyāna* days each year, and on these days no animals were permitted to be slaughtered. Djahāngīr, whose *Tūzuk* shows him to have been a connoisseur of good food, ate *ṣūfiyāna* meals on Sundays in his father's memory, and on Thursdays to commemorate his own accession.

The kitchen department had also obviously to provide for the wine and other intoxicants used in the court, for although the official chroniclers are understandably reticent on the subject it is inconceivable that similar precautions to those taken for foodstuffs and water should not be applied also to wine. Khwāndamīr records (*Ḳānūn-i Humāyūnī*, 49) that a *sūčī khāna* issuing wines existed apart from the *ābdār-khāna*. Besides wine from the grape, *ʿaraḳ*, such drugs as opium, *bhāng* (hemp, *Cannabis sativa*) and the electuary *maʿdjūn*, of variable components, were freely used by many of the Mughal rulers and the nobles (too freely, to judge by the fate of Akbar's sons Murād and Dāniyāl, and many others!).

A subordinate kitchen department, not part of the household, existed to provide food in the *langar-khāna*, soup-kitchen, established as a charity around many of the royal courts to provide simple food for the poor.

Bibliography: The most complete information is to be found in Abu 'l-Faḍl ʿAllāmī, *Āʾīn-i Akbarī*, i, *āʾīns* 22-8. Sporadic information in *Tūzuk-i Bāburī*; Gulbadan Begam, *Humāyūn-nāma*; Khwāndamīr, *Ḳānūn-i Humāyūnī*; *Tūzuk-i Djahāngīrī*. Occasional light is thrown by the accounts of European travellers, especially Manucci, *Storia do Mogor*; Monserrate, *Mongolicae legationis commentarius*, Eng. tr. J. S. Hoyland, 1922, 199; Bernier; Tavernier; Peter Mundy; and Sir Thomas Roe, *Embassy ... to the court of the Great Moghul*, ed. Hakluyt Soc., 1926. M. Azher Ansari, *The diet of the great Mughals*, and *The Abdar Khanah of Mughals*, in *IC*, xxxiii (1959), 219-27 and 151-60 respectively.

(J. Burton-Page)

MATERIALISTS [see dahriyya, māddiyya].

MAṬG͟HARA, the name of a Berber tribe belonging to the great family of the Butr [*q.v.*]; they were related to the Zanāta and brethren of the Maṭmāṭa, Kūmiya, Lamāya, Ṣaddīna, Madyūna, Mag͟hīla, etc., with whom they form the racial group of the Banū Fātin. Like the other tribes belonging to this group, the Maṭg͟hara originally came from Tripolitania; the most eastern members of the Maṭg͟hara, however, known to al-Bakrī and Ibn K͟haldūn were those who lived in the mountainous regions along the Mediterranean from Milyāna and Ténès to the north of Oujda (port of Tābaḥrīt); those of the western part of this zone were allied with the Kūmiya; their mountains rose not far from Nadrūma and the fortress of Tāwunt was in their territory.

Three sections had reached the western Mag͟hrib as early as the 2nd/8th century and formed there an important bloc. These were:

1. The Maṭg͟hara of Fās and the corridor of Taza; al-Bakrī observes that the source of the Wādī Fās was on their territory, in the region where Leo Africanus still mentions the *Sūḳ al-k͟hamīs* of the Maṭg͟hara "fifteen miles west of Fās".

2. The Maṭg͟hara of the Middle Atlas in the D̲j̲abal Maṭg͟hara, which Ibn K͟haldūn locates to the south-east (*ḳiblī*) of Fās and which Leo Africanus says is five miles from Taza (to the south?). The reference then is to the mountain region now occupied by the Ayt Warayn; an important section of the latter, the Ayt D̲j̲ellidasen, represents the Banū Gallidāsan whom al-Bakrī gives as a section of the Maṭg͟hara, settled near Ténès in Algeria. We still find among the Ayt Warayn several sections of the Img͟hilen who represent the Mag͟hīla, brethren of the old Maṭg͟hara. The name of Mṭāg͟hra is today applied to all the eastern splinters of the G͟hayyāt͟ha tribe; Taza is situated in their territory. In al-Bakrī's time (5th/11th century) these two sections of the Maṭg͟hara had as neighbours in the west the Zawāg͟ha of Fāzāz and of Taza.

3. The Maṭg͟hara of the oases of the Sahara settled in the region of the Sid̲j̲ilmāssa and in the town itself, in which they constitute the main element of the population, in the region of Fīgīg, in Tuwāt, Tamanṭit and as far away as Wallen (Ouallen).

At the beginning of the Arab conquest, the Maṭg͟hara are represented by Ibn K͟haldūn as settled and living in huts built of branches of trees (*k͟haṣāṣ*); those of the Sahara lived in fortified villages (*ḳuṣūr*) and devoted themselves to growing dates. In the time of Leo Africanus, the Maṭg͟hara of the Central Atlas occupied about fifty large villages.

Like other peoples belonging to the group of the Banū Fātin, the Maṭg͟hara took an active part in the events at the beginning of the Arab conquest and weakened themselves considerably in the fighting. As soon as they had become converted to Islam, a number of groups of Maṭg͟hara went over to Spain and settled there. Later, like their brethren, the Maṭmāṭa [*q.v.*], they adopted the principles of the Ṣufriyya [*q.v.*]; one of their chiefs, Maysara, provoked the famous schismatic rising of 122/740, which was the beginning in Morocco of the Barag͟hwāṭa heresy [see barg͟hawāṭa]. In a list of the tribes which adopted this heretical teaching, we find the Maṭmāṭa and Maṭg͟hara of the Central Atlas, as well as the Banū Abī Naṣr, the modern Ayt Bū-Nṣar, the eastern section of the Ayt Warayn.

With the rise of Idrīs, the chief of the Maṭg͟hara, Bahlūl, declared himself at first a supporter of the caliph of Bag͟hdād, Hārūn al-Ras͟hīd, then rallied to the new dynasty. Later and down to the 11th/17th century, the Maṭg͟hara of the Central Atlas do not seem to have played any part in politics; but they nevertheless retained their independence. From the 11th/17th century, they seem to have been supplanted on their territory by invaders from the south. As to the Maṭg͟hara of the shore, settled in the region of Nadrūma, their alliance with the Kūmiya gained them considerable political importance, when the latter became supporters of the Almohads. It was at this period that they built the fortress of Tāwunt. They then rallied to the Marīnids [*q.v.*] but this brought upon them the wrath of the ruler of Tlemcen, the celebrated Yag͟hmurāsen, who finally crushed them.

Ibn Ḥazm, *D̲j̲amharat ansāb al-ʿArab*, ed. Lévi-Provençal, 496, and Ibn K͟haldūn use the form *Maḍg͟hara* instead of *Maṭg͟hara*; in Moroccan texts of late date we also find *Madg͟hara*.

Bibliography: Bakrī and Idrīsī, indices; Ibn K͟haldūn, *Kitāb al-ʿIbar*, tr. de Slane, i, 237-41; Leo Africanus, *Description de l'Afrique*, tr. Épaulard, 303-4, 353 and index.

(G. S. Colin)

MAT͟HAL (a., pl. *amt͟hāl*) proverb, popular saying, derives—similarly to Aram. *mat͟hlā*, Hebr. *mās͟hāl* and Ethiop. *mesl*, *mesālē*—from the common Semitic root for "sameness, equality, likeness, equivalent" (cf. Akkad. *mas͟hālum* "equality", *mis͟hlum* "half"). In Arabic, to create a proverb is *fa-arsala(t)hā*, or *d̲j̲aʿala(t)hu mat͟hal^{an}*, *fa-ḍaraba(t) bihi 'l-mat͟hal^{a}*; to become proverbial is *ḍuriba bihi 'l-mat͟hal^{u}*, *mat͟hal^{un} yuḍrabu fa-d͟hahaba(t)*, or *d̲j̲arā/d̲j̲arat mat͟hal^{an}*, or, simply, *fa-ṣāra mat͟hal^{an}*.

1. In Arabic

i. Definition
ii. Arabic proverbs
 (1) Earliest layer
  (a) fables
  (b) stories
  (c) inscriptions, verse
  (d) *ḥikma*
 (2) Second layer
  (a) ʿAlī
  (b) turns of speech
  (c) Islamic forms
 (3) Third layer
  (a) mouthes of people
  (b) parallels
 (4) *afʿal^{u} min*
 (5) *muwallada*
 (6) NT and OT, etc.
 (7) stories
 (8) only locally current
 (9) quoted verses
 (10) Ḳurʾān and *ḥadīt͟h*
  (a) "wisdom"
iii. Arabic collections
 (1) Abū ʿUbayd
  (a) al-Mufaḍḍal
  (b) Muʾarrid̲j̲
 (2) Muḥammad b. Ḥabīb
 ....
 (18) Ibn ʿĀṣim
iv. Modern collections
 (1) European
 (2) Oriental
Bibliography

i. Definition.

The Arabic philologists have since Abū ʿUbayd (d.224/838) repeatedly defined the concept of *mat͟hal*.

They have discerned and set forth its three essential characteristics: comparison, sc. the metaphorical way of expression (*ta<u>sh</u>bīh*); brevity (*īdjāz al-lafẓ*); and familiarity (*sāʾir*). They have established (a) that *am<u>th</u>āl* are based on experience and therefore contain practical commonsense (*ḥikma*); (b) that by their use facts can be stated pointedly and intelligibly in an indirect way (*kināya*); and (c) that by making use of *am<u>th</u>āl* it becomes possible to communicate matters that it would be difficult to communicate in a more straightforward way. This quality of the *ma<u>th</u>al* is owing to the fact that it can be used individually to represent all, even only remotely, analogous cases and can always remain unchanged in the process, even though the origin of the *ma<u>th</u>al* may long be forgotten. Abū ʿUbayd stresses the fact that the *ma<u>th</u>al* "accompanies" the discourse; in doing so he exactly defines the etymological meaning of proverb, παροιμία in Greek (cf. also the more recent παραβολή) and in the Latin *adagio*, *adagium* as well as in the later *proverbium*. Al-Zamak<u>hsh</u>arī (d. 538/1144) correctly remarks, that—corresponding to its true etymological meaning—*naẓīr* should be considered to be the basic meaning of *ma<u>th</u>al*; cf. R. Sellheim, *Die klassisch-arabischen Sprichwörtersammlungen, insbesondere die des Abū ʿUbaid*, Ph.D. thesis, Univ. of Frankfurt am Main 1953, The Hague 1954, 8-20; idem, Arabic, revised and enlarged edition, *al-Am<u>th</u>āl al-ʿarabiyya al-ḳadīma*, tr. Ramaḍān ʿAbd al-Tawwāb, Beirut 1391/1971 (repr. 1402/1982 and 1404/1984), ²21-35; W. Heinrichs, *The hand of the north wind*, Wiesbaden 1977, 7.

The totality of these characteristics and qualities do not apply to each and every *ma<u>th</u>al*. Many *am<u>th</u>āl* can only lay claim to two of them. This shows that by *ma<u>th</u>al* we have to understand something wider than our (1) proverb; *ma<u>th</u>al* includes, in addition, the (2) proverbial saying, also comprising the extensive group of comparisons involving a comparative in the form *afʿal^u min*, (3) adages (gnomes, dicta), that is, *ḥikam* and *aḳwāl* which, like many a proverb, can also be found among the *aḥādī<u>th</u>* as maxims and saws, including mottoes, personal maxims, apophthegms and aphorisms, (4) set turns of speech, that is *kalimāt* and *muḥāwarāt* (characteristic modes of expression) as used in optative and maledictive exclamation, in address and salutation, in prayer, and in speech generally, and, at some time or other, (5) parable, fable, just as in the Ancient Orient; cf. O. Eissfeldt, *Der Maschal im Alten Testament*, Giessen 1913; K.-M. Beyse, in *Theologisches Wörterbuch zum AT*, v (1984), 69ff., E.I. Gordon, in *BiOr*, xvii (1960), 130; O. E. Moll, *Über die ältesten Sprichwörtersammlungen*, in *Proverbium*, vi (1966), 114ff.; ʿAbd al-Hādī al-Fuʾādī, *Baḥth fi 'l-am<u>th</u>āl al-ʿirāḳiyya, dirāsa muḳārana li-am<u>th</u>āl al-mudjtamaʿ al-ʿirāḳī al-ḳadīm wa 'l-muʿāṣir*, in *Sumer*, xxix (1973), 83-106, xxx (1974), 27-46; J. M. Sasson (ed.), *Oriental wisdom, six essays of the sapiental traditions of Eastern Civilisations*, Worcester, Mass. 1981 (= *JAOS*, ci/1 [1981], 1-131).

ii. Arabic proverbs.

The *Kitāb al-Am<u>th</u>āl* of Abū ʿUbayd (d. 224/838) is the oldest collection of *am<u>th</u>āl* in the form of a genuine book compiled by the author. It contains a little less than 1,400 *am<u>th</u>āl* in systematic order, arranged in 19 chapters with, in all, 259 sub-chapters and 11 more in an appendix. This material can be classed as belonging in three layers: (1) *am<u>th</u>āl* from pre-Islamic times, (2) *am<u>th</u>āl* from the early times of Islam and its religious-political centres, and (3) *am<u>th</u>āl* dating back to the emergence of the Islamic centralised state, chiefly under the first ʿAbbāsid caliphs.

(1) The *am<u>th</u>āl* of the earliest layer in their majority are derived from the narrative tradition of the 2nd/8th century. In the context of a recall of the glorious Arabic past, favoured by early anti-<u>Sh</u>uʿūbiyya tendencies, stories (*a<u>kh</u>bār*), poems (*a<u>sh</u>ʿār*) and other relics (*ā<u>th</u>ār*) of the pre-Islamic times were very much alive in the centres of urban civilisation and much in demand at court and in various offices. Whatever in them ran counter to Islamic notions, laws and bans, was excused as having happened in the Djāhiliyya and as being worth preserving. In the struggle for survival under desert conditions, solidarity at any price among tribesmen is insisted upon: *unṣur a<u>kh</u>āka ẓālim^{an} aw maẓlūm^{an}* "assist thy brother whether he is right or wrong" (Abū ʿUbayd [see below, iii, 1], no. 397: 519, further references here, as for all the following quotations); the father sets an example for the son: *man a<u>sh</u>baha abāhu fa-mā ẓalama* "who does as his father does, cannot be wrong—whatever be the merits of the deed" (*ibid.*, no. 408; 833), and the daughter admires him and his exploits unreservedly: *kull^u fatātⁱⁿ bi-abīhā muʿdjabat^{un}* (*ibid.*, no. 402). In the permanent search for new pastures for his never-satisfied livestock, the Bedouin must necessarily be irked when he stumbles on pasturages without having his camel with him: *ʿu<u>sh</u>b^{un} wa-lā baʿīr^{un}* "fresh herbage and no camel" (*ibid.*, no. 581); of course, he knows how to appreciate the quality of the fodder, so he measures a normal pasture with the *saʿdān* plant, which is optimal for camels: *marʿan wa-lā ka 'l-saʿdānⁱ* (*ibid.*, no. 370), Figurative and metaphoric speech has with great tenacity held its ground among the Semites and especially among the Arabs, and plays an important part even in the higher forms of literature. To the Bedouin, illustrations taken from the animal world around him most easily come to mind. He knows the habits and the reactions of wild animals from his own lifelong experience and observation: *mā yadjmaʿu bayna 'l-arwā wa 'l-naʿāmⁱ* "what could bring a mountain goat and an ostrich together?" (*ibid.*, no. 898), if two things are incompatible, for the goat lives among the rocks and the ostrich on the desert plain! Allusions to human beings are expressly added: *innahu la-a<u>kh</u>daʿ^u min ḍabbⁱⁿ ḥara<u>sh</u>tahu* "he is trickier than a hunted lizard" (*ibid.*, no. 1229; cf. no. 597), or *laysa ḳaṭan mi<u>th</u>l^a ḳuṭayyⁱⁿ* "a *ḳaṭā*-hen is not like a *ḳaṭā*-chicken (*ibid.*, no. 953), or *al-<u>dh</u>iʾb^u yaʿdū li'l-<u>gh</u>azālⁱ* "the wolf waylays the gazelle" (*ibid.*, no. 180), or, expressed in the earthy Bedouin style: *la-ḳad <u>dh</u>alla man bālat ʿalayhi 'l-<u>th</u>aʿālib^u* "contemptible is he who is pissed on by foxes" (*ibid.*, no. 319), the comparison involving a comparative (cf. below, ii, 4) as a figure of speech is widely used (*afʿal^u min*): *anwam^u min fahdⁱⁿ* "sleepier than a cheetah" (*ibid.*, no. 1215 [see FAHD]), or *innahu la-aḥ<u>dh</u>ar^u, azhā, abṣar^u min <u>gh</u>urābⁱⁿ* "more watchful, or shining, or sharp-sighted than a raven" (*ibid.*, no. 1210ff.); cf. T. Fahd, *Psychologie animale et comportement humain dans les proverbes arabes*, in *Revue de Synthèse*, iii série, lxi-lxii (1971), 5-43; lxv-lxvi (1972), 43-63; lxxv-lxxvi (1974), 233-56; xcii (1978), 307-56.

(a) Some such *am<u>th</u>āl* about animals occur in connection with a fable. In these, different kinds of animals customarily are assigned well-defined parts: the hyena (*ḍabuʿ*), e.g., appears as stupid (*ibid.*, nos. 77-80), and the lizard (*ḍabb*) as clever (*ibid.*, nos. 296, 597, 1229); cf. C. Brockelmann, *Fabel und Tiermärchen in der älteren arabischen Literatur*, in *Islamica*, ii (1926), 96-128 (cf. below, iii, 1, b); Gholam-Ali Karimi, *Le conte animalier dans la littérature arabe avant la traduction de Kalila wa Dimna*, in *BÉT. Or.*, xxviii (1975), 51-6; M. Ullmann, *Das Gespräch mit dem Wolf*, Munich 1981 (= *SB Bayer. Ak.*, 1981, 2).

(b) Much more numerous than these fables with animals for characters are the stories of the type of the *akhbār* of the *ayyām al-ʿArab*, which are rendered with preference according to al-Mufaḍḍal al-Ḍabbī or Ibn al-Kalbī; cf. the lists of *ayyām al-ʿArab* in *al-Fākhir* (see below, iii, 4), no. 442 (360), and al-Maydānī (see below, iii, 12), ch. xxix. The "heroes" in these stories are sometimes known from tradition or genealogy, as e.g. al-Basūs [*q.v.*], whose she-camel triggered a forty years' war between the Banū Bakr b. Wāʾil [*q.v.*] and their kinsmen, the Banū Taghlib b. Wāʾil (*ibid.*, no. 1280), or al-Mundhir, or al-Nuʿmān b. al-Mundhir, the prince of the Lakhmids, who had the innocent poet ʿAbīd b. al-Abraṣ [*q.v.*] killed in order not to break an oath (*ibid.*, nos. 1048, 1130), or the nameless poor butter dealer, who was violated by a ruffian after he had caused her to close tightly the necks of two butter-filled skins with both her hands at the same time (*ibid.*, no. 1278). Many of these mostly short stories may have originated in an actual happening. Time and place however remain, as a rule, undefined. Their etiological character is obvious: the storyteller is interested in the question of who used the saying first, or of how it came to be coined at all, that is, in the *awāʾil* [*q.v.*] problem. The information which they contain can be exploited to answer questions concerning names and genealogies, but they are not historical, at the most anecdotal; cf. esp. the *Kitāb al-Amthāl* of al-Mufaḍḍal al-Ḍabbī (see below, iii, 1, a; Sellheim, *op. cit.*, 47f., ^{2}73ff., and 27-39, ^{2}50-63). Many of them are overgrown with myths, legends, and fairy tales; internationally disseminated themes have thus found their way into them, most likely by way of the Lakhhmid court at al-Ḥīra as an intermediary: the letter of Uriah (*ṣaḥīfat al-Mutalammis* [*q.v.*]), the legend of Zenobia, the reward of Sinimmār [see AL-KHAWARNAḲ], "bailment" (Bürgschaft), Gothamites of Arabia, etc.; cf. I. Lichtenstaedter, in *Folk-Lore* (London), li (1940), 195-203 (cf. below, ii, 4 and 7). It is striking that at times these *amthāl* are linked up with the ʿAmālīḳ [*q.v.*]; one of these is, e.g., ʿUrḳūb in Yathrib who makes "empty promises" to his brother, *mawāʿīd*^{u} *ʿUrḳūb*^{in} (Abū ʿUbayd, no. 195)—could this be a reminiscence of the Jacob-Esau story according to Genesis, xxvii (cf. Escorial [Derenbourg], no. 651)? There were Jews in Yathrib! Often stories and explanations about a *mathal* widely or completely diverge from one another, because its origin and its original meaning had long been forgotten, when the paroemiographers collected the material, e.g. in the case of "the gatherer of acacia shoots of the tribe of ʿAnaza" (*ibid.*, no. 1142; al-Bayhaḳī [see below, iii, 14], no. 71), or in that about "the shoes of Ḥunayn" (*ibid.*, no. 779; *al-Fākhir*, no. 159; al-Bayhaḳī, pp. 87ff.), or in that about "the naked warner" (*al-Fākhir*, no. 146; al-Bayhaḳī, no. 261), or in that about "the repentance of al-Kusaʿī" (*ibid.*, no. 155), or in that about the poor Ḳuʿays of whom we know no more than that his aunt once gave him as a surety and never redeemed him (*ibid.*, no. 61), a story called in question by the transmitter. Not infrequently, stories may have been spun out of a *mathal*. Thus the saying *ḥidā ḥidā warāʾaki bunduḳa* (*ibid.*, no. 93) probably only means "O kite, O kite, a pellet (projected from a bow) is behind thee", which Abū ʿUbayda refers to a children's game; Ibn al-Kalbī and al-Sharḳī b. al-Ḳuṭāmī however take *Ḥidā* and *Bunduḳa* as names of South Arabian tribes who had fought with one another. Al-Aṣmaʿī rightly takes the proverb *tarakahu djawf*^{a} *ḥimār*^{in} (*ibid.*, no. 18) at its face value: "he left him like the belly of an ass", i.e. like a useless thing, while again the two genealogists identify *Ḥimār* with an Amalekite or Azdite and *djawf* with *wādī* in the Syrian dialect (cf. Ibn Durayd, *Ishtiḳāḳ*, 287, ^{2}490).

(c) Beyond any doubt, the proverbs which demonstrably occur in Thamudic inscriptions date back to pre-Islamic times, as e.g. *man ʿazza bazza* "he who overcomes takes the spoil" (Abū ʿUbayd, no. 285). But also *amthāl* in the verse of pre-Islamic poets—assuming they are genuine—can be assigned to this oldest level (cf. below, ii, 9). The question whether the poet created them, or whether—already in current use as *mathal*—they were only adopted by him, as a rule, remains undecided, so e.g. *wa-ḥasbuka min ghinan shibaʿ*^{un} *wa-riyy*^{u} (*ibid.*, no. 479) in a *wāfir* verse of Imruʾ al-Ḳays, or *ayy*^{u} *'l-ridjāl*^{i} *'l-muhadhdhab*^{u} (*ibid.*, no. 67) in a *ṭawīl* verse of al-Nābigha al-Dhubyānī, or *mā ashbaha 'l-laylat*^{a} *bi 'l-bāriḥa*^{h} (*ibid.*, no. 423) in a *sarīʿ* verse of Ṭarafa, or *al-dhiʾb*^{u} *yuknā Abā Djaʿda* (*ibid.*, no. 198) in a *mutaḳārib* verse of ʿAbīd b. al-Abraṣ, or *innamā yadjzi 'l-fatā laysa 'l-djamal* (*ibid.*, no. 380) in a *ramal* verse of Labīd. In verses of this time, internationally-known proverbs (cf. below, ii, 3, bff.) can also be shown to exist (cf. Sellheim, *op. cit.*, 40, ^{2}65f.), e.g. the much discussed one of the goat (sheep, bull) who digs up his own slaughtering knife out of the ground with his hooves, in Greek: αἲξ τὴν μάχαιραν. Abū ʿUbayd gives four different versions: *lā takun ka 'l-ʿanz*^{i} *tabḥathu ʿan*^{i} *'l-mudyat*^{i} (Abū ʿUbayd, nos. 1088, 797, 1086f.). Furthermore, *ka-ṭālib*^{i} *'l-ḳarn*^{i} *fa-djudiʿat udhunuhu* "like the one (ostrich) who wanted horns and ended up with cut-off ears" (*ibid.*, no. 796; cf. no. 527 and al-ʿAskarī [see below, iii, 7], no. 47), a *mathal* which has equivalents in Greek (camel): ἡ κάμηλος ἐπιθυμήσασα κεράτων καὶ τὰ ὦτα προσαπώλεσεν, in the Talmud (Sanhedrin, 106a) and in the different versions of *Kalīla wa-Dimna* (ch. x, 2: ass for camel). Zuhayr b. Abī Sulmā was wont to insert *amthāl* into his verse, and Kaʿb b. Saʿd al-Ghanawī, who already extends into early Islam, was for the same reason called Kaʿb al-Amthāl. In their majority, these *amthāl* belong to the category of gnomic sayings, as e.g. the *ṭawīl* verse of Zuhayr: ... *wa-man lā yaẓlim*^{i} *'l-nas*^{a} *yuẓlam*^{i} "and whoever does not wrong his fellow-men, will be wronged [by them]" (Abū ʿUbayd, in no. 282); cf. A. Bloch, *Zur altarabischen Spruchdichtung*, in *Westöstliche Abhandlungen (Festschrift R. Tschudi)*, ed. F. Meier, Wiesbaden 1954, 181-224.

(d) *Amthāl* of this kind are likely to have been written down already in ancient times as *ḥikma* on, e.g., small scrolls of leather or parchment (*madjalla*), papyrus, or palm-leaves (*ṣaḥīfa*), bone, wood-tablets, or on stones (see below, iii). In the Ḳurʾān, these dicta of ethic content usually are ascribed to the legendary Luḳmān [*q.v.*] (cf. Sūra XVIII [Luḳmān], 18), and all the more in later literature (cf. Solomon's *Book of Proverbs* in the Old Testament!). The paroemiographers have joined to him the no less legendary umpire of the ancient Arabs Aktham b. Ṣayfī [*q.v.*] (cf. *al-Mawrid*, x/3-4 [1402/1981], 161-8); small collections of his *amthāl* can be found in books on *adab*, e.g. in the *Kitāb al-Muʿammarīn* of Abū Ḥātim al-Sidjistānī (ed. I. Goldziher, Leiden 1899, 9-18), or, together with *amthāl* of the equally legendary Sāsānid *wazīr* Buzurdjmihr [*q.v.*, see DJĀWĪDHĀN KHIRAD in Suppl.] in the *Kitāb al-ʿIḳd al-farīd* of Ibn ʿAbd Rabbih (ed. A. Amīn *et alii*, Cairo 1372/1952, iii, 76-80; cf. E. García Gómez, in *al-And.*, xxxvii [1972], 249-323). It ought to be stressed that among the sayings of Aktham can be found Matt. vii, 16, *innaka lā tadjnī min*^{a} *'l-shawk*^{i} *'l-ʿinab*^{a} "you cannot pluck grapes from thorns" (Abū ʿUbayd, nos. 849, 870; cf. Ibn Hishām, 124f.). This and related material, e.g., the parable of the "beam in thine own eye" (Matt. vii, 3) quoted by

Abū ʿUbayd (no. 152; cf. below, ii, 6), seems to have been in circulation as *amthāl al-ḥukamāʾ*. In the same direction points, too, the parable of the "camel and the eye of a needle" (Matt. xix, 24; Mark x, 25; Luke xviii, 25; cf. G. Aichler, *Kamel und Nadelöhr*, Münster 1908) in the Ḳurʾān (VII, 40; cf. M. B. Schub, in *Arabica*, xxiii/3 [1976], 311ff.; S. Khalil, in *ibid.*, xxv/1 [1978], 89-94; A. Rippin, *ibid.*, xxvii/2 [1980], 107-13). Concerning the Arabic-Hebrew-Aramaic-correspondences, e.g., *man nahashathu 'l-ḥayyatu hadhira 'l-rasana*, "he who has been bitten by a snake is afraid of a rope" (Abū ʿUbayd, no. 686), cf. S. D. Goitein, *The present-day Arabic proverb as a testimony to the social history of the Middle East*, in his *Studies in Islamic History and Institutions*, Leiden 1966, ²1968, 361-79, esp. 375; M. Grünbaum, *Neue Beiträge zur semitischen Sagenkunde*, Leiden 1893, 40-9, esp. 42; O. E. Moll, *op. cit.*, 113-20; S. P. Brock, *A piece of wisdom literature in Syriac*, in *JSS*, xiii (1968), 212-17; Anīs Furayḥa (Frayha), *Aḥiḳār ḥakīm min al-shark al-adnā al-ḳadīm*, Beirut 1962; G. E. Bryce, *A legacy of wisdom, the Egyptian contribution to the wisdom of Israel*, Lewisburg-London 1979; esp. D. Gutas, *Classical Arabic wisdom literature: nature and scope*, in *JAOS*, ci (1981), 49-86 (= J. M. Sasson [ed.], *op. cit.*).

(2) The formation of the young Islamic community into a new society was an effect of the word. This process is also reflected in the *amthāl* of the second layer. Here pagan lore was adapted and integrated, old concepts were filled with new meaning, supplemented, changed, or formulated in a different way. The *akh* of the Djāhiliyya, for instance, became a brother in the faith, a brother in Islām. If the formula up to that time was *akhūka man ṣadaḳaka* "your brother is he who gives you a frank piece of advice", the Prophet now says *al-muʾminu mirʾātu akhīhi* "the believer is the mirror of his brother" (Abū ʿUbayd, no. 530), i.e., he tells him openly what he sees, or, to put it more directly, *raḥima 'llāhu radjulan ahdā ilayya ʿuyūbī* "God be merciful on the man who shows me my faults!" (*ibid.*, no. 531). The ancient Arabic solidarity in right or wrong (cf. above ii, 1) causes was—supposedly by the Prophet, too (cf. al-Bukhārī, *al-Ṣaḥīḥ*, *Kitāb* 46 [*al-Maẓālim*], *bāb* 4)—interpreted to the effect that the brother helps his brother when he is in the right but restrains him from doing wrong (*ibid.*, no. 519; cf. e.g. Ḳurʾān, XLII, 39ff. Caetani, *Annali*, x, 45). As this method had thus been authorised by the Prophet, ancient *ḥikma* which he liked (Ibn Hishām, 285 = al-Ṭabarī, i, 1208), could live on to be elaborated by himself, his Companions and his Successors. He knew the power of words: *inna mina 'l-bayāni la-siḥran* "verily there is a kind of eloquence that is enchantment" (*ibid.*, no. 13), also in the negative sense, for instance if the word of a poet hurts or tempts (cf. Ḳurʾān, XXVI, 224; I. Shahid, in *JAL*, xiv [1983], 1-21; below, ii, 10); the great ʿUmar is said to have pronounced the words *walli ḥārrahā man tawallā ḳārrahā* "appoint over what is evil one who has been appointed over what is good" (*ibid.*, nos. 702, 920; cf. Lane and *Dict. arabe-français-anglais*, s.v. *ḥ-r-r*).

(a) The number of *amthāl* like this—mostly maxims and aphorisms—attributed to ʿAlī, is, as is known, great. Most widely spread is a quite recent collection of 100 dicta, also in Persian and Turkish translation; cf. the collection in *al-Tuḥfa al-bahiyya*, Constantinople 1302/1884, 107-114, etc., the latest up to date being A. Zajączkowski, *Sto sentencyj i apoftegmatów arabskich kalifa ʿAlī'ego w parafrazie mamelucko-tureckiej*, Warsaw 1968; al-Ḳuḍāʿī, *Dustūr maʿālim al-ḥikam wa-maʾthūr makārim al-shiyam min kalām amīr al-muʾminīn ʿAlī b. Abī Ṭālib*, Beirut 1401/1981; al-Sharīf al-Raḍī or his brother al-Murtaḍā, *Nahdj al-balāgha*, i-ii, ed. Muḥammad Abu 'l-Faḍl Ibrāhīm, Cairo 1383/1963. Al-Maydānī (d. 518/1124), *Madjmaʿ al-amthāl*, chap. xxx (see below, iii, 12) has compiled dicta (*kalām*) by the Prophet, by the first four caliphs, by Ibn ʿAbbās, Ibn Masʿūd, and others. Cf. *Oriens*, xxxi (1988), 354-7.

(b) Down to this level in time extend, too, the roots of those numerous *amthāl*—in this case turns of speech in the more restricted sense of the word—which not infrequently contain the name of the Lord, and which in the collections of *amthāl* are usually introduced with the words *min duʿāʾihim*, e.g. *balagha 'llāhu bika aklaʾa 'l-ʿumuri*, "may God grant you an extremely long life" (*ibid.*, no. 132; cf. *WKAS* s.v. *k-l-ʾ*), or, negatively *djadaʿa 'llāhu masāmiʿahu* "may God cut off his organs of hearing" (*ibid.*, no. 166).

(c) The ancient *mathal*: *andjaza ḥurrun mā waʿada* "an ingenuous man fulfils what he promises" (*ibid.*, no. 145), could naturally be maintained in Islām as well as the negative statement *āfatu 'l-murūʾati khulfu 'l-mawʿidi* (*ibid.*, no. 144), but in common speech only as the Islamic form of the same thought: *al-wafāʾu mina 'llāhi bi-makānin* "with God, fulfilling a promise has its worth" (*ibid.*, no. 146; cf. Ḳurʾān, XIX, 54; *WKAS*, s.v. *k-w-n*). Whereas up to then you said *laysa ʿabdun bi-akhin laka* "a slave is not your brother" (*ibid.*, no. 522), that is, treat him as you like!, the Muslim now said, because a believer could happen to be a slave: *ʿabdu ghayrika ḥurrun mithluka* "the slave who is not your slave is a free man like your" (*ibid.*, no. 377), or, similarly, *sāwāka ʿabdu ghayrika* (*ibid.*, no. 376), meaning, do not be arrogant, someone else can easily perform this or that! Success and victories won against the infidels made the faithful self-confident: *lā yulsaʿu 'l-muʾminu min djuḥrin marratayni* "the believer is not bitten twice out of the same nest (of snakes)" (*ibid.*, no. 683), a *mathal* that is traced back to the Prophet himself (cf. Ibn Hishām, 591). The more the young community had to face the tasks of political routine, the more often it was forced to make use of its ways and means: *innā la-nakshiru fī wudjūhi aḳwāmin wa-inna ḳulūbanā la-taḳlīhim* "we outwardly smile at people, while inwardly we hate them (*ibid.*, no. 451; *WKAS*, s.v. *k-sh-r*), a statement which the companion of the Prophet Abu 'l-Dardāʾ [*q.v.*] is said to have uttered.

(3) The Arabisation of the ancient civilised areas of the Near East, conquered under the first caliphs, has greatly enriched the treasures of *amthāl*; on the one hand, by new creations, on the other by loans and by newly-developed ones by way of analogies taken from the languages of the aborigines. These *amthāl* form the third layer. Its level extends into the lifetime of Abū ʿUbayd, that is, into the time of the early ʿAbbāsids. Setting apart the popular wisdom expressed in sayings, which are more or less correctly ascribed to currently known personalities of the political or religious sphere, as e.g. Muʿāwiya (d. 60/680), al-Ḥadjdjādj b. Yūsuf (d. 95/714), ʿUmar II (d. 101/720) and al-Ḥasan al-Baṣrī (d. 110/728), they are, first of all, proverbs, the "place in life" ("Sitz im Leben") of which is to be looked for in the towns and in the country.

(a) Abū ʿUbayd has heard many of them from the mouth of people engaged in conversation; occasionally he notes *min amthāl al-ʿawāmm* (e.g. no. 779) or *al-ʿāmma* (no. 1141), *ibtadhalathu 'l-ʿawāmm* (no. 1269) or *al-ʿāmma* (no. 81), *mubtadhal fī 'l-ʿāmma* (no. 919) or *al-nās* (no. 524), etc. (nos. 42, 65, 146, 560, 636, 954, 1058, 1068). Some examples: *asmaʿu djaʿdjaʿatan wa-lā arā ṭiḥnan* "I hear a sound of the mill, but I see no flour'' (Abū ʿUbayd, no. 1057), in English ''much talk and little wool'', or *inna 'l-bulag͟hāth^a bi-arḍinā yastansiru* ''verily in our land the small bird (e.g. the sparrow) becomes/plays an eagle'' (*ibid.*, no. 212), or *biʿtu d͟jārī wa-lam abiʿ dārī* ''I sold my neighbour, but not my house'' (*ibid.*, no. 894), or *akl^an wa-d͟hamm^an* ''eating and (afterwards) dispraising (the benefactor)'' (*ibid.*, no. 861), or *al-nās^u s͟had͟jarat^u bag͟hy^in* ''people are the tree on which all evil grows'' (*ibid.*, no. 891).

(b) If it can be said in a very general way that parallels to the Arabic proverbs in other languages and related cultures can be shown the more frequently to occur the younger these are, the question whether any particular *mat͟hal* has in fact been newly coined, or borrowed, or modelled on an existing proverb must be left unanswered in most cases; for, as concerns the social surroundings against the background of which the *amt͟hāl* must be observed, there are scarcely any differences any more (cf. above, ii, 1, c). In the case of similes and comparisons which spontaneously offer themselves to the mind, foreign models must not always be sought, much as they may obtrude on our attention, e.g. *man ḥafara mug͟hawwāt^an waḳaʿa fīhā* (*ibid.*, no. 872; al-Ṭabarī, ii, 1142), in English ''hoist with one's own petard'', a proverb which can already be found in Ps. vii, 16 and lvii, 7, as well in Prov. xxvi, 27. In the case of rare metaphors, however, an appropriation of foreign material can be assumed with a greater degree of probability, e.g. *in kunta rīḥ^an fa-ḳad lāḳayta iʿṣār^an* (*ibid.*, no. 225), a proverb—albeit with a slightly different meaning—that can likewise be shown to occur in the Old Testament, Hosea viii, 7: ''for they have sown the wind, and they shall reap the whirlwind'', and which probably has an echo in the New Testament, Galatians vi, 7 (cf. below ii, 6). There is a high degree of likelihood that the well-known Latin saying *res ad triarios redit, rediit*, or *venit*, that is, in order to arrange a completely bungled affair, is at the bottom of the *mat͟hal*: *ṣāra 'l-amr^u ila 'l-nazaʿat^i* (*ibid.*, no. 438). The question is more difficult to answer in the case of a *mat͟hal* like the following one: *man^i starʿa 'l-d͟hiʾb^a ẓalama* ''he who makes the wolf a shepherd, is in the wrong'' (*ibid.*, no. 959), a saying familiar to the Greeks as of old: λύκος ποιμήν. The Romans know the simile of the hawk who is entrusted with pigeons: *accipitri columbas credere*; in English it is ''to give a wolf the wether to keep'', similarly in French ''donner la brébis (sheep) à garder au loup'', while in German, as in Greek, it is the wolf who becomes a shepherd, or, in a parallel phrase, the ram a gardener. In all these cases we cannot advance much beyond a simple registration of parallels (cf. E. Moll, *op.cit.*, 114f.; Ch. Speroni, ''*The beauties of a woman*'', in *Proverbium*, vi [1966], 139ff. and ix [1967], 216; below, ii, 5).

The Arabic paroemiographers of the succeeding three centuries augmented Abū ʿUbayd's *amt͟hāl* materials from all three layers and beyond these to five times the original number, i.e. to approximately 7,000 *amt͟hāl*. Among these there are more than 1,200 *amt͟hāl* in the form of a comparison involving the (4) comparative, *afʿal^u min* (cf. above, ii, 1), and more than 1,500 which are called (5) ''new ones'', *al-amt͟hāl al-muwallada*. Those of the first group have come to light in their majority in the 3rd/9th century, and those of the second one in the two subsequent centuries. The amount of ''wandering'' international motifs among them is remarkable.

(4) *Amt͟hāl* in the form of *afʿal^u min*. Reminiscences of Penelope come to the surface in *ak͟hraḳ^u min nākit͟hat^in g͟hazlahā* ''stupider than a woman who continually undoes her spinning (weaving)'' (Ḥamza [see below iii, 6], no. 204), a simile that certainly has its source in Ḳurʾān, XVI, 92, or of Sisyphus, *aṭmaʿ^u min ḳālib^i 'l-ṣak͟hrat^i* ''more covetous than the one who turns over the rock'' (Ḥamza, no. 431). As a matter of course, both persons, female and male, from the pre-Islamic past are designated by their names and genealogies! How much or how little account can be taken of this so-called ''historical'' tradition becomes still more evident in the following instance: *amḥal^u min ḥadīt͟h^i K͟hurāfat^a* ''fuller of artifices than the stories of K͟hurāfa'' (Ḥamza, no. 641). Here *k͟hurāfa*, ''fairy tale'' (actually ''nonsense'', cf. *EI²*, iii, 369 b, s.v. ḤIKĀYA), is personified, as happens, too, in the proverbs and sayings of other peoples (cf. Sellheim, *op.cit.*, 35-8, ²59-62). Even the Prophet is reported to have told his wives the story of K͟hurāfa (*al-Fāk͟hir*, no. 280: typical fairy tales)! This group of *amt͟hāl* of the *afʿal^u min* type, in which—like in Greek—attributes from ''intelligent'' to ''stupid'', from ''clearsighted'' to ''trusty'', etc., and names—among them that of the Owlglass character D͟juḥā [*q.v.*] (Ḥamza, no. 125)—pseudo-names, animals, plants, etc. can be exchanged indiscriminately, has proliferated into our own times.

(5) *Amt͟hāl muwallada*. The widely spread Latin saying *lupus in fabula*, that is, ''if you talk of the wolf, he is not far off'', is probably present in the ''new'' saying *id͟hā d͟hakarta 'l-d͟hiʾb^a fa 'ltafit* (al-Maydānī [see below, iii, 12], i, 57u/Freytag, ch. i, no. 436), which already Abū ʿUbayd knows in its abstract form *ud͟hkur^i 'l-g͟hāʾib^a yaḳtarib*, or *ud͟hkur g͟hāʾib^an tarahu* (Abū ʿUbayd, nos. 140f.), in English ''speak of an angel, and you hear his wings''. Of internationally-known sayings we may list *inna li 'l-ḥīṭān^i ād͟hān^an* (al-Maydānī, i, 57, 21/ ch. i. no. 427), just as, e.g., in the Midrash, in Persian (cf. M. Grünbaum, *op.cit.*, 43) and in English ''walls have ears''; or *id͟hā kunta sindān^an fa 'ṣbir wa-id͟hā kunta miṭraḳat^an fa-awd͟jiʿ* (*ibid.*, i, 58, 18/ch. i, no. 465), in English ''hammer and anvil''; or *farra min^a 'l-maṭar^i wa-ḳaʿada taḥta 'l-mīzāb^i* ''fleeing the rain he is sitting under the drippings (from the roof)'' (*ibid.*, ii, 25, 9/ch. xx, no. 112; just as in German; cf. R. Jente, *German proverbs from the Orient*, in *Publs. of the Modern Lang. Assoc. [of America]*, xlviii [1933], 17-37), in English ''he jumps out of the frying-pan into the fire''; or *al-ḥarakat^u barakat^un* (*ibid.*, i, 155, 20/ch. vi, no. 244), in English ''bliss is in action'' (Pope) or ''action gives satisfaction'' (modern). To this category belong, even if not expressly identified as *amt͟hāl muwallada*, e.g. *in kunta kad͟hūb^an fa-kun d͟hakūr^an* (*ibid.*, i, 49, 13/ch. i, no. 366), in English ''a liar must have a good memory'' (just as in Latin); or *ka 'l-sāḳiṭ^i bayna 'l-firās͟hayn^i* (*ibid.*, ii, 64, 7/ch. xxii, no. 89), in English ''between two stools one sits on the ground'' (just as in Latin); or *ka-annahu ḳāʿid^un ʿala 'l-radf^i* (*ibid.*, ii, 74, 18/ch. xxii, no. 197), in English ''to be on tenterhooks'' (cf. above, ii, 1, c; 3, b; 4).

(6) In al-Maydānī's collection of *amt͟hāl* can be found anonymous sayings from the New Testament; mainly taken from the Sermon on the Mount, partly they are very close, corresponding almost literally to the New Testament text, partly they only render its meaning, e.g. Matt. vii, 3; Luke vi, 41, *kayfa tubṣiru 'l-ḳad͟hā fī ʿayn^i ad͟hīka watadaʿu 'l-d͟jid͟hʿa 'l-muʿtarid^a fī ʿaynika* (*ibid.*, ii, 67, 26/ch. xxii, no. 115 = Abū ʿUbayd, cf. above, ii, 1, d), or *yaʿuddu (yaʿkidu) fiyy^a mit͟hl^a 'l-ṣuʾābi wa-fī ʿaynayhi mit͟hl^u 'l-d͟jarrat^i ('l-d͟ja/izzat^i)* ''he counts things (e.g. faults) with regard to me like nits, whilst there is in his own eyes something like a jar'' (*ibid.*, ii, 254, 17/ch. xxviii, no. 78),

with a verse that renders the NT text word by word; cf. I. Goldziher, in *ZDMG*, xxxi (1877), 765ff.; idem, *Muh. Stud.*, ii, 391; further, A. Müller, in *ZDMG*, xxxi (1877), 513, 519-20, 524. There is Matt. vii, 15, with its generally-known simile of "the wolf in sheep's clothing", in *dhiʾbun fī maski sakhlatin* (*ibid.*, i, 192, 23/ch. ix, no. 70). There are several versions of Matt. vii, 16, the parable of "the grapes picked from thorns", an older one (*ibid.*, i, 34, 8/ch. i, no. 210 = Abū ʿUbayd, cf. above; *ibid.*, ii, 120, 8/ch. xxiii, no. 358), and a younger one (*ibid.*, i, 336, 31/ch. xviii, no. 255, according to Ḥamza [no. 498], with further variants, one of them in verse = *ibid.*, ii, 182, 4/ch. xxiv, no. 367). Matt. xix, 24, with its well-known parable of the "camel and the ear of a needle" (*ibid.*, ii, 113, 23/ch. xxiii, no. 316) was known already to Muḥammad (Ḳurʾān, VII, 40; cf. above). Matt. xxiii, 24—the parable of the "straining at gnats and swallowing camels"—is known in a slightly changed form as a *mathal*: *yaʾkulu ʾl-fīla wa-yaghtaṣṣu bi ʾl-baḳḳati* "he eats an elephant, but a gnat obstructs his throat" (*ibid.*, ii, 259, 16/ch. xxviii, no. 157). Galatians vi, 7, is there in a literal translation: *kamā tazraʿu taḥṣudu* (ibid., ii, 73, 2/ch. xxii, no. 185; cf. Ibn Hishām, 124f.; cf. above, ii, 3, b). As for wise sayings that can be shown to have parallels in the Old Testament, see above (= al-Maydānī, ii, 168, 11/ch. xxiv, no. 256; i, 20, 14/ch. i, no. 113); there are also reminiscences of Noah's Ark and his raven (*ibid.*, i, 79, 14/ch. ii, no. 168; ii, 9, 29/ch. xix, no. 66; cf. ii, 210, 20/ch. xxv, no. 154), as well as echoes of sayings in Deut. xxxii, 15 (*ibid.*, i, 228, 20/ch. xii, no. 50), and in Ecclesiastes and Proverbs; cf. J. Barth, *Arabische Parallelen zu den Proverbien*, in *Festschrift D. Hoffmann*, Berlin 1914, 38-45; Müller, *op.cit.*, 520, 524.—The Mandaean creator Fiṭaḥl owes his inclusion into a *mathal* probably to two verses of the widely known Radjaz poet Ruʾba (*Dīwān*, ed. W. Ahlwardt, xlvi, 14 = al-Maydānī, i, 334, 26/ch. xviii, no. 246 [= Ḥamza, no. 486]; cf. ii, 169, 25/ch. xxiv, no. 264).

(7) The historical yield of the many stories which the later paroemiographers know how to tell about several *amthāl* is as poor as that of the earlier story-tellers (cf. above, ii, 1, b); for, as a rule, these stories also belong to the realm of worldly or pious legend, fairy-tale, fable, droll tale, and anecdote. Quite frequently they can be traced back—as concerns their central idea—to a "wandering" international motif. On the following occasion we might be reminded of the legend of the Seven Sleepers (*al-Fākhir*, no. 239; al-Ḳālī, *al-Amālī*, Cairo 1344/1926, i, 61) which is already mentioned in the Ḳurʾān (XVIII, 9-12: *aṣḥāb al-kahf* [*q.v.*]; cf. R. Gramlich, in *Asiatische Studien*, xxxiii [1979], 99-152), or of the martyrdom of Djurdjus (*al-Fākhir*, no. 517). Each of the following reminiscences is attached to a historical personage or occurrence; there is an allusion to Muʿāwiya's delighted shout when he hears of the poisoning of al-Ashtar (Abū ʿUbayd, no. 555; Ibn Ḳutayba, *ʿUyūn al-akhbār*, Cairo 1343/1925, i, 201; see AL-ASHTAR); or to his remark when his ambassador is returning from the Byzantine court (Abū ʿUbayd, no. 1052; Ibn Ḳutayba, *op.cit.*, i, 198; Ibn al-Athīr, *al-Nihāya*, s.v. *ḥ-ṣ-ṣ*); or to the fine voices of the beloved girl-singers of the caliph Yazīd II (Ḥamza, no. 624; see YAZĪD B. ʿABD AL-MALIK), or to the defeat and death of the Khāḳān of the Khazars [*q.v.*] at the hands of Hishām's governor Saʿīd b. ʿAmr al-Ḥarashī (*al-Fākhir*, no. 160; al-Ṭabarī, iii, 1531; Zambaur, index); or to the assassination of al-Mahdī's governor ʿUḳba b. Salm (*al-Fākhir*, no. 158; al-Ṭabarī, iii, 367f., 520). The realistic account of a devastating nightly storm, which frightened the Baghdādīs out of their wits and provoked the caliph al-Mahdī and his retinue to do such penance (al-Maydānī, i, 176/ch. vii, no. 140), is not reported in other collections. It is a striking fact that the paroemiographers do not record any stories that deal with events after al-Mahdī, except for occasional references to the fact that a certain person used a certain *mathal*; the most recent of these personalities referred to in connection with a *mathal muwallad* (*ibid.*, i, 80, 7/ch. ii, no. 189) is Ibn al-Muʿtazz (d. 296/908). In this respect, a pupil of al-Maydānī, Abu ʾl-Ḥasan al-Bayhaḳī, proves a great exception (see below, iii, 14).

(8) At times the paroemiographers make note of the fact that a certain *mathal* is current locally, e.g., in Syria (Abū ʿUbayd, no. 1070), or in ʿUmān (Ḥamza, no. 443), or in Medina (Ḥamza, nos. 56, 224, 340, 397), or in Mecca (Ḥamza, no. 115), or in al-Baṣra (al-Maydānī, i, 145, 16/ch. vi, no. 149; cf. Abū ʿUbayd, no. 1144; below, iii, 8). It is interesting to learn by way that in Syria in the 3rd/9th century the Greek φησίν "says he" was much used by the Arabs (*al-Fākhir*, no. 137), a fashionable expression then, similar to to day's American "O.K." of worldwide acceptance. Already Abū ʿUbayd (no. 1349) has recorded: *ayyu ʾl-barnasā*—or *ʾl-baransāʾi*—*huwa* (cf. al-Djawālīḳī, *al-Muʿarrab*, Cairo 1361/1942, 45), in other words, the Aramaic *bar nāshā* "Son of Man" or the obscure *tālaʾmūr* "any one, anything" (Abū ʿUbayd, nos. 1344f.; J. Barth, *Nominalbildung*, Leipzig ²1894, 300; Th. Nöldeke, *Belegwörterbuch*, Berlin 1952, 40b). Actually, at times the collectors admit that the meaning of some *mathal* or other has remained dark to them (*ibid.*, no. 185), or that people in the streets use it but do not correctly understand (*ibid.*, no. 919), or that they had altered an ancient (*ḳadīm*) *mathal* for just this reason. As an example, one may cite *tadjūʿu ʾl-ḥurratu wa-lā taʾkulu bi-thadyayhā* "a free woman starves herself rather than eats for the price [she is paid for] her breasts" (*ibid.*, no. 569), i.e., she prefers starving to hiring herself out as a wet-nurse, which becomes distorted into the quite meaningless *lā taʾkulu thadyayhā* "and does not eat her breasts". From a misunderstanding of a verse of al-Farazdaḳ in which the way to al-ʿUnṣulayn (*ibid.*, no. 1127; Yāḳūt and Lane, s.v.) is mentioned, this expression became typical of taking the wrong way (cf. *al-Fākhir*, no. 496; Ḥamza, no. 423).

(9) The few examples adduced here show that for the majority of the *amthāl* a certain formative process can be shown at work, and that includes the inner form—the shaping of the thoughts—and an outer form which exists in the shape of linguistic, stylistic, and metrical peculiarities. Both these phenomena cannot be pursued here (cf. al-Dhubaib, *Study* [cf. below, iii, 12]; Ch. Pellat, *Sur la formation de quelques expressions proverbiales en arabe*, in *Arabica*, xxiii [1976], 1-12). Well-known, appreciated and much-quoted verses, so-called *abyāt sāʾira*, were compiled in special collections, e.g. Ḥamza al-Iṣfahānī's *Kitāb al-Amthāl al-ṣādira ʿan buyūt al-shiʿr* (Brockelmann, I, 152; Sezgin, viii, 200f.; a Cairo edition is under way). Poets like Ṣāliḥ b. ʿAbd al-Ḳuddūs or Abu ʾl-ʿAtāhiya have also made use of many *amthāl* in their verse (cf. above, ii, 1, c); the figurative sayings which can be found in al-Mutanabbī's *dīwān*, were, e.g., already extracted and arranged in the poet's own century by al-Ṭālaḳānī (d. 385/995). Such *abyāt sāʾira* and countless *amthāl* are spread far and wide across the whole body of Arab literature (cf. Sellheim, *op.cit.*, 21-2, ²39ff.); one finds it richly represented especially in the *adab* literature from al-Djāḥiẓ to al-Ābī (cf. Maḥmūd Ghanāyim, in

al-Karmil, Haifa, vi [1985], 165-87; U. Marzolph, in *OC*, lxix [1985], 81-125) and al-Tha^c^ālibī (regarding his *K. al-Amthāl*, cf. Sezgin, viii, 235, 276; further, A.U.B. Library, ms. no. 398, 9 T.35, cf. *al-Mashrik*, xlvi [1952], 407), from the poets of the *makāmāt* to the encyclopaedists of the post-Mongol times like al-Nuwayrī or al-Suyūṭī and Bahā᾽ al-Dīn al-ʿĀmilī. The *amthāl* presented here would be especially numerous, exceptionally so in the case of *al-amthāl al-muwallada* (cf. above, ii, 5), with parallels in other languages, e.g. *ʿuṣfūr^un^ fi 'l-kaffi khayr^un^ min kurkiyy^in^ fi 'l-djawwi* "a sparrow in the fist is better than a crane in the air" (al-Hamadhānī, *Rasā᾽il*, Constantinople 1298/1881, 44; al-Thaʿālibī, *al-Tamthīl*, Cairo 1381/1961, 372; Burckhardt [see below, iv, 1], no. 3 etc.), in English, "a bird in the hand is worth two in a bush".

(10) In the case of *amthāl* contained in the Ḳur᾽ān and in the tradition (*ḥadīth*)—specifically named *al-amthāl al-nabawiyya*—they were treated in books of their own (cf. R. Sellheim, *op.cit.*, 20f., ²36ff.), e.g. (most recent publications), al-Ḥakīm al-Tirmidhī (3rd/9th century), *al-Amthāl min al-Kitāb wa 'l-Sunna*, ed. ʿAlī M. al-Bidjāwī, Cairo (1395/1975); Abū Muḥammad al-Rāmhurmuzī (d. *ca.* 360/970), *Kitāb al-Amthāl*, ed. Amatulkarim Qureshi, Ph.D. thesis, University of Bonn 1959, Hyderabad-Pakistan 1388/1968; Abu 'l-Shaykh (d. 369/979), *Kitāb al-Amthāl*, ed. Ibrāhīm Yūsuf ʿIrsān, M.A. thesis, University of Riyāḍ 1403/1983; Ibn Ḳayyim al-Djawziyya (d. 751/1350), *al-Amthāl fi 'l-Ḳur᾽ān al-karīm*, ed. Saʿīd M. Nimr al-Khaṭīb, Beirut 1401/1981; ʿAbd al-Madjīd Maḥmūd, *Amthāl al-ḥadīth*, Cairo 1395/1975; Muḥammad al-Gharawī, *al-Amthāl al-nabawiyya*, i-ii, Beirut 1401/1981; L. Pouzet, *Une herméneutique de la tradition islamique: le commentaire des Arbaʿūn al-Nawawīya de Muḥyī al-Dīn Yaḥyā al-Nawawī (m. 676/1277)*, introduction, texte arabe, traduction, notes et index du vocabulaire, Beirut 1982.

(a) For "wisdom" from classical sources, one should refer to the most recent publications: D. Gutas, *op.cit.*, in *JAOS*, ci (1981), 49-86; idem, *Greek wisdom literature in Arabic translation, a study of the Graeco-Arabic gnomologia,* New Haven, Conn. 1975; idem, *The life, works, and sayings of Theophrastus in the Arabic tradition*, in W. W. Fortenbaugh, *Theophrastus of Eresus*, New Brunswick-Oxford 1985, 63-102; I. Alon, *Isocrates' Sayings in Arabic*, in *IOS*, vi (1976), 224-8; J. K. Walsh, *Versiones peninsulares del "Kitab ādāb al-falāsifa" de Ḥunayn ibn Isḥāq, hacia una reconstrucción del "Libro de los buenos proverbios"*, in *al-And.*, xli (1976), 355-84; Ḥunayn b. Isḥāḳ, *Ādāb al-falāsifa*, ikhtaṣarahu Muḥammad b. ʿAlī al-Anṣārī (d. before 594/1198), ed. ʿAbd al-Raḥmān Badawī, Kuwait, 1406/1985. For Islamic wise sayings (*ḥikma* [*q.v.*]), consult al-Māwardī (d. 450/1058), *al-Amthāl wa 'l-ḥikam*, ed. Fu᾽ād ʿAbd al-Munʿim Aḥmad, Ḳaṭar 1403/1983; P. Nwyia, *Ibn ʿAṭā᾽ Allāh (m. 709/1309) et la naissance de la confrérie šādilite*, édition critique et traduction des *Ḥikam*, Beirut (1972); V. Danner, *Ibn ʿAṭā᾽illāh's Ṣūfī aphorisms (Kitāb al-Ḥikam)*, translated with an introduction and notes, Leiden 1973, etc.; for personal observations, cf. furthermore the biographical literature from Ibn Saʿd (d. 230/845) to al-Sulamī (d. 412/1021), from Abū Nuʿaym (d. 430/1038) to al-Shaʿrānī (d. 973/1565).

iii. Arabic collections.

In no other branch of classical Arabic Literature can beginning, development and termination be demonstrated as clearly as in its *amthāl* branch. The results up to now will be summed up as follows (cf. Sellheim, *op.cit.*, 45-153, ²71-225; idem, *al-Qālī* [cf. below, iii, 5, a]; idem, *al-Baihaqī* [cf. below iii, 1]; R. Blachère, *Contribution à l'étude de la littérature proverbiale des Arabes à l'époque archaïque*, in *Arabica*, i [1954], 53-83).

The first setting down of *amthāl* and *amthāl* stories in writing occurred at the instigation of the caliph al-Mahdī (158-69/775-85) in Baghdād by the hand of his tutor al-Mufaḍḍal al-Ḍabbī [*q.v.*] (al-Ṭabarī, iii, 536). He had already compiled for him an anthology of 30 ancient Arabic poems, which later on became widely known under the title of *al-Mufaḍḍaliyyāt* [*q.v.*]. Both these works have not been preserved in their original form, but only in late versions, in parts, widely differing from each other. The text of the *amthāl* that has come down to us goes back to al-Ṭūsī, a pupil of Ibn al-Aʿrābī (d. 231/845), the stepson and pupil of the author (d. *ca.* 170/786). This proves that al-Mufaḍḍal left behind him and others no definite edition. Rather, his *amthāl* in conjunction with the stories were handed on by word of mouth in different forms and put down in writing only by pupils or the pupils of pupils, because the booklet, composed for the use at court, was not at the disposal of the transmitters any more than the anthology. Similar was the fate of the *Kitāb al-Amthāl* ascribed to Mu᾽arridj (d. 204/819?). We have it in a version dictated by his pupil Abū ʿAlī al-Yazīdī from the year 263/876. These written notes taken down during lectures cannot be said to conform at all with the Mu᾽arridj quotations in the *amthāl* literature from Abū ʿUbayd to al-Maydānī. These two examples—as well as others from other branches of literature—cause us to look at later assertions, as e.g. in the *Fihrist* of Ibn al-Nadīm (d. 380/990), that well-known early philologists, as for instance Abū ʿAmr b. al-ʿAlā᾽, Yūnus b. Ḥabīb, Abū Zayd al-Anṣārī or al-Aṣmaʿī also wrote books of *amthāl*, with a wary eye. Information of this kind is all the more doubtful, as also later authorities on the matter, as, e.g., al-ʿIrāḳī (Pseudo-al-Wāḳidī; see below, iii, 11), expressly spreak of a book "ascribed" (*al-mansūb*) to him in the case of the *Kitāb al-Amthāl* of al-Aṣmaʿī (see below, iii, 1, b; 2; 5, a). *Amthāl* become available in book form—and moreover in the original draft of their author himself—only in the *Kitāb al-Amthāl* of Abū ʿUbayd (d. 224/838). He is indebted for his plentiful materials—in so far as he has not gathered them himself (cf. above, ii, 3, a)—to the tradition, chiefly according to his teachers, among others, to the above-named philologists. This clearly results from instances where he writes "I do not know from whom I have heard the *mathal* (nos. 349, 1088), or "I have heard it from somebody other than Abū ʿUbayda, I think, from Ibn al-Kalbī" (no. 59), or similarly (nos. 1228 and 134, 253, 492, 744). His quotations in the name of al-Mufaḍḍal which he uses to introduce in an impersonal way, e.g. *ḥukiya ʿan ..., ruwiya ʿan ..., mā balaghanī ʿanhu ...*, or correspondingly, can only partly be found in the *Kitāb al-Amthāl* of the author in the version of al-Ṭūsī (see above); of his quotations in the name of Mu᾽arridj, whom he always introduces with *ḳāla*—as he also does with the other philologists (see above)—none at all can be exemplified in the *Kitāb al-Amthāl* of that authority in the version of al-Yazīdī (see above). The *kutub al-ḥikma* quoted by Abū ʿUbayd once (no. 663; cf. nos. 152, 250 and 48, 250, 271, 658; above, ii, 1, d) probably stand for nothing but loose leaves (*kitāb* [*q.v.*]) on which wise sayings were written, for the purpose, e.g., of being stuck up on the wall of a room. His contemporary al-Djāḥiẓ [*q.v.*] knows a collection like that with sayings of the caliph al-Manṣūr which was familiar to the scribes of Baghdād (*al-Bayān*, Cairo 1368/1949, iii, 367). Ibn al-

Muᶜtazz's collection exists in the form of his *Kitāb al-Ādāb*, ed. I. Kratchkovsky, in *Le Monde Oriental*, xviii (1924), 56-121. Wise sayings of this kind were also called *al-āthār*, not only by Abū ᶜUbayd (nos. 153, 704).

After the death of Abū ᶜUbayd in Mecca, one of his pupils, ᶜAlī b. ᶜAbd al-ᶜAzīz al-Baghawī, who survived his master there for 60 years, had his text glossed by authorities on the Arabic and Islamic past, as, e.g., by al-Zubayr b. Bakkār (d. 256/870), or Salama b. ᶜĀṣim, a pupil of al-Farrāʾ. This annotated text he would read and explain to pilgrims in his circles (*ḥalaḳāt*). In consequence, Abū ᶜUbayd's collection of proverbs—in conjunction with these and further glosses—was spread far and wide, in the West as far as al-Andalus, and in the East as far as Khurāsān. His collection has not only been supplemented and commented on six times, but has become, more or less, a point of departure for all subsequent collections. Its materials were adopted, while this fact was frequently not signalised specifically, as well as the glosses, which again and again were added to these copies in their entirety, in selections, or with further additions; in Cordova they were standardised in the form of "editions" in the 4th/10th century by Ḳāsim b. Saᶜdān or integrated into al-Bakrī's commentary in the 5th/11th century. One such "edition" of Ḳāsim's existed in Naysābūr in the 6th/12th century, where al-Maydānī compiled his *Madjmaᶜ al-amthāl*, the most comprehensive of all collections of Arabic proverbs.

At the present moment, the following collections exist in print or are in the press or in preparation:

(1) Abū ᶜUbayd al-Ḳāsim b. Sallām (d. 224/838), *Kitāb al-Amthāl*, ed. ᶜAbd al-Madjīd al-Ḳaṭāmish, Damascus 1400/1980 (here quoted according to nos.), as to its systematics, see above, ii; parts in print since J. Scaliger and Th. Erpenius, Leiden 1614; etc.; *Libri proverbiorum Abi ᶜObaid elQasimi filii Salami elChuzzami lectiones duae, octava et septima decima* ...., ed. E. Bertheau, Ph.D. thesis, Univ. of Göttingen 1836; ed. G. W. Freytag, in *Arabum proverbia* (see below, iii, 12), iii; arranged alphabetically according to the first letter (ms. Esat 3542?), in *al-Tuḥfa al-bahiyya wa 'l-ṭurfa al-shahiyya*, Constantinople 1302/1884, 2-16 (repr. Beirut 1401/1981). Abū ᶜUbayd al-Bakrī (d. 487/1094) has shortened the text and commented on it on the strength of glosses (see above, and below, iii, 1, b) under the heading of *Faṣl al-maḳāl fī sharḥ Kitāb al-Amthāl*, ed. ᶜAbd al-Madjīd ᶜĀbidīn and Iḥsān ᶜAbbās, Khartoum 1378/1958 (cf. *Oriens*, xiii-xiv [1960-1], 469ff.), new edn. Beirut 1391/1971.

(a) Abu 'l-Ḥasan al-Ṭūsī, a pupil of Abū ᶜUbayd, who put down in writing a *Kitāb al-Amthāl* of al-Mufaḍḍal [I] b. Muḥammad al-Ḍabbī (d. *ca.* 170/786) which is lacking any discernible structure, in doing that following al-Mufaḍḍal's stepson and pupil Ibn al-Aᶜrābī (d. 231/845), printed (ms. Esat 3598?) Constantinople 1300/1882 = Cairo 1327/1909; new edition, considerably enlarged and emendated by Iḥsān ᶜAbbās, Beirut 1401/1981. The more than 200 *amthāl* have been ensconced within 88 *akhbār al-ᶜArab* (cf. above, ii, 1, b).

(b) Abū ᶜAlī al-Yazīdī, who dictated more than 100 *amthāl* in the name of his teacher Abū Fayd Muʾarridj al-Sadūsī (d. 204/819?) in the course of a lecture (*madjlis*) in the year 263/876 thus recording in written form a *Kitāb al-Amthāl* by Muʾarridj; ed. Aḥmad Muḥammad al-Ḍubayb, in *Madjallat Kulliyyat al-Ādāb*, Riyad, i (1390/1970), 231-345 (cf. *MMLᶜA*, Damascus, xlvi [1391/1971], 786f.); ed. Ramaḍān ᶜAbd al-Tawwāb, Cairo 1391/1971. Also, this text with its stories, among them fables (cf. above, ii, 1, a), and philological explanations, together with verses commenting on the *amthāl* in the stricter sense of the word *muḥāwarāt*, conveys in its loose, unsystematic form the atmosphere of spontaneous lecturing and conservation. In the *madjālis* of this generation, the roots of the pseudepigraphic collections of the time of the Umayyads must be looked for, sc. ᶜAbīd b. Sharya al-Djurhumī, ᶜIlāḳa b. Kurshum (Karīm) al-Kilābī, Ṣuḥār b. al-ᶜAbbās (al-ᶜAyyāsh) al-ᶜAbdī and the somewhat younger al-Sharḳī b. al-Ḳuṭāmī; cf. *Oriens*, ix (1956), 135; below, iii, 12 and 14; to the early philologists, above, iii (rectify Sezgin, i, 260ff. and viii, 7, etc.).

(2) A small fragment containing 7 *amthāl* of the *afᶜal^u min* type, allegedly by Muḥammad b. Ḥabīb (d. 245/860) of whom—as the literature about proverbs and biographical literature maintains—a *Kitāb al-Amthāl ᶜalā afᶜal min* said to be containing 390 *amthāl*, is known; ed. Muḥammad Ḥamīdallāh, in *MMᶜIᶜI*, Baghdād, iv (1956), 44 f. (cf. R. Şeşen, *Nawādir al-makhṭūṭāt*, Beirut 1975, i, 68, no. 63). According to Ḥamza (see iii, 6), he owes his materials chiefly to the collection of Abū ᶜUbayd and to the "books" (notes taken down in lectures, cf. iii, 5, a) of al-Aṣmaᶜī and al-Liḥyānī. For two further "quotations", see Abu 'l-ᶜAlāʾ al-Maᶜarrī, *al-Fuṣūl wa 'l-ghāyāt*, Cairo 1356/1938, 61, and al-Khafādjī, *Shifāʾ al-ghalīl*, Cairo 1325/1907, 173.

(3) Abū ᶜIkrima ᶜĀmir b. ᶜImrān al-Ḍabbī (d. 250/864), *Kitāb al-Amthāl*, ed. Ramaḍān ᶜAbd al-Tawwāb, Damascus (1394/1974). 111 *amthāl*, chiefly *muḥāwarāt*, with many verses of reference, no system; quotations in the name of al-Mufaḍḍal in only one instance in the text of al-Ṭūsī; judging from the introduction, the booklet was conceived as such and not dictated.

(4) al-Mufaḍḍal [II] b. Salama v. ᶜĀṣim al-Ḍabbī (d. after 290/903), *al-Fākhir*, ed. C. A. Storey, Leiden 1915 (here quoted according to nos.; repr. Cairo 1402/1982); ed. ᶜAbd al-Raḥmān b. al-Nūrī b. al-Ḥasan, Tunis 1353/1934 (?); ed. ᶜAbd al-ᶜAlīm al-Ṭaḥāwī and Muḥammad ᶜAlī al-Nadjdjār, Cairo 1380/1960 (nos. identical, exception Storey 442 = Nadjdjār 360; 361-441 = 361-442; 443 = 443; etc.); printed in part, nos. 1-123; *Ghāyat al-arab fī maᶜānī mā yadjrī ᶜalā alsun al-ᶜāmma fī amthālihim wa-muḥāwarātihim min kalām al-ᶜArab*, in *Khams rasāʾil*, Constantinople 1301/1884, 232-63. A total of 521 *amthāl*, partly *muḥāwarāt*, mostly circumstantial *amthāl* stories (cf. above, ii, 1, b); quotations in the name of al-Mufaḍḍal can, as a rule, be demonstrated in the text of al-Ṭūsī (cf. no. 123!), likewise, the only quotation in the name of Muʾarridj in the lecture-notes of 263/876. The author was the son of that Salama who glossed the *amthāl* of Abū ᶜUbayd (see above).

(5) Abū Bakr Ibn al-Anbārī (d. 328/940), *al-Zāhir fī maᶜānī kalimāt al-nās*, ed. Ḥātim Ṣāliḥ al-Ḍāmin, i-ii, Baghdād-Beirut 1399/1979. A total of 896 *amthāl*, similar to iii, 3; authorities are mentioned; the cited materials can, in part, be found in their works, e.g., in Abū ᶜUbayd's *Gharīb al-ḥadīth* and *al-Gharīb al-muṣannaf*, and in part they are derived from the oral *madjālis*-tradition, e.g., the quotations from Abū ᶜIkrima. Cf. furthermore Ḥusām Saᶜīd al-Nuᶜaymī, in *MMᶜIᶜI*, xxxi/3 (1400/1980), 383-97.

(a) The so-called *Kitāb Afᶜal min kadhā* of Abū ᶜAlī al-Ḳālī (d. 356/967) represents an example of the oral *madjālis* tradition, ed. Muḥammad al-Fāḍil Ibn ᶜĀshūr, Tunis 1392/1972. A total of 363 *amthāl ᶜalā afᶜal min* contained in notes taken in lectures (cf. above), no systematics; quotations, for instance in the name of Muḥammad b. Ḥabīb (see iii, 2), diverge widely, in parts completely from the parallel tradition (cf. iii, 6 and 12). This fact shows that the oral handing-on of *am<u>th</u>āl* materials, too, was common practice still in the 4th/10th century, and that it was very variable and loose into the bargain; about particular ones, cf. Sellheim, *Abū ʿAlī al-Qālī*, in *Studien zur Geschichte und Kultur des Vorderen Orients, Festschrift für Bertold Spuler*, Leiden 1981, 362-74.

(6) Ḥamza al-Iṣfahānī (d. between 350/961 and 360/970) [*q.v.*], *Kitāb al-Am<u>th</u>āl ʿalā afʿal min*, or *al-Durra al-fā<u>kh</u>ira fī 'l-am<u>th</u>āl al-sāʾira*, (i-ii), ed. ʿAbd al-Ma<u>dj</u>īd Ḳaṭāmī<u>sh</u>, Cairo 1391-2/1971-2; supplements in al-<u>Th</u>aʿālibī *<u>Kh</u>āṣṣ al-<u>kh</u>āṣṣ*, ch. 3, Cairo 1326/1908, 29-37. The author has enlarged the collection of Muḥammad b. Ḥabīb to more than 1,800 *am<u>th</u>āl* of the *afʿalᵘ min*-type, among them more than 500 *muwallada*, arranged alphabetically according to the first letter, augmented by 500 more linguistically special features (*nawādir*: compounds containing *abū*, *umm*, *ibn* etc., and dual forms); partly circumstantial *am<u>th</u>āl* stories; he distinguishes, occasionally, between *al-ma<u>th</u>al al-ḳadīm*, *al-islāmī* and *al-muwallad*.

(7) Abū Hilāl al-ʿAskarī (d. after 395/1005), *<u>Dj</u>amharat al-am<u>th</u>āl*, Bombay 1307/1889; idem, i-ii (printed in the margin of the text of al-Maydānī [see iii, 12]), Cairo 1310/1893; idem, i-ii, ed. Muḥammad Abu 'l-Faḍl Ibrāhīm and ʿAbd al-Ma<u>dj</u>īd Ḳaṭāmī<u>sh</u>, Cairo 1384/1964 [1389/1969] (quoted here). Barely 2,000 *am<u>th</u>āl*, including approximately 800 *am<u>th</u>āl ʿalā afʿal min*, arranged alphabetically according to the first letter. The author proceeds from Ḥamza's work whom he, being a purist, reproaches with having included too many "new ones" (*muwallada*), and accumulates the materials transmitted from his teachers, and their authorities, in the *ma<u>dj</u>ālis*; the only quotation in the name of Abū ʿIkrima (i, 266) is missing in latter book (see iii, 3); he takes pain to tighten the innumerable philological and "historical" annotations, rejects *am<u>th</u>āl* which are linguistically incorrect and now and then distinguishes between *al-ma<u>th</u>al al-ḳadīm* and *al-muwallad* or *al-muḥda<u>th</u>*. The *am<u>th</u>āl* of his collection are largely "literary" ones and have not too much in common any more with everyday life in the streets.

(8) Abu 'l-Ḥasan ʿAlī b. al-Faḍl al-Muʾayyadī al-Ṭāl(a)ḳānī, *Risālat al-Am<u>th</u>āl al-ba<u>gh</u>dādiyya*, ed. L. Massignon, Cairo 1331/1913. The most ancient local collection with more than 600 *am<u>th</u>āl (muwallada)*, in contrast to iii, 7, topical and not literary, arranged alphabetically according to the first letter, as a rule accompanied by short explanations, in many cases for the proper application of the *ma<u>th</u>al* in question; forerunner of later collections containing *am<u>th</u>āl* in dialect; compiled by the author and read during lectures in Bal<u>kh</u> in 421/1030; cf. too ʿAbd al-Raḥmān ʿAbd al-<u>Dj</u>abbār Ṭālib, in *Sumer*, xxxii (1396/1976), 237-338; al-Ābī, above, ii, 9.

(9) Abu 'l-Faḍl al-Mīkālī (d. 436/1044) [see MĪKĀLĪS], *Nuba<u>dh</u> min am<u>th</u>āl al-amīr al-Mīkālī*, edition in preparation. Small collection (*ca.* 250 nos.), arranged alphabetically, divided up into sub-chapters, each one beginning with one or more sayings from the Ḳurʾān and *ḥadī<u>th</u>* (cf. *Oriens*, xxxi [1988], 353 and xxxii).

(10) Anonymous (5th/11th cent.), *Kitāb al-Am<u>th</u>āl*, Hyderabad 1351/1932. Just under 1,400 *am<u>th</u>āl*; a "medium-sized al-ʿAskarī" (see iii, 7). For no obvious reason, the catalogue of the Dairatu'l-Maʿarifil-Osmania, and consequently Brockelmann, I, 237, ascribe the book to Zayd b. Rifāʿa (d. *ca.* 400/1010), while Brockelmann, S III, 1195, lists it among the writings of Ibn al-Sikkīt (d. 243/857).

(11) Pseudo-al-Wāḥidī (see iii, 15), *al-Wasīṭ fī 'l-am<u>th</u>āl*, ed. ʿAfīf Muḥammad ʿAbd al-Raḥmān, Kuwait 1395/1975; cf. Muḥ. Aḥmad al-Dālī, in *MMMʿA* Kuwait, xxix/2 (1405/1985), 781-99.

(12) Abu 'l-Faḍl al-Maydānī (d. 518/1124), *Ma<u>dj</u>maʿ al-am<u>th</u>āl*, i-ii, Būlāḳ 1284/1867; idem, Tehran 1290/1873 (re-arranged in more or less strict alphabetical order by al-Ḥusayn b. Abī Bakr al-Na<u>dj</u>m al-Kirmānī); idem, i-ii, Cairo 1310/1893 (quoted here); idem, i-ii, Cairo 1352-3/1933-4; idem, i-ii, ed. Muḥyi 'l-Dīn ʿAbd al-Ḥamīd, Cairo 1374/1955 (repr.), ²1378-9/1959 (revised) and ³1393/1972(!) (= ²1 + ¹2!); idem, i-ii, Beirut 1382/1962; idem, i-iv, ed. Muḥammad Abu 'l-Faḍl Ibrāhīm, Cairo 1397-9/1977-9 (more or less identical with Muḥyi 'l-Dīn's first edition, including numbering of the *am<u>th</u>āl*; poor index); parts in print since J. Scaliger and Th. Erpenius, Leiden 1614; E. Pocock, Cambridge 1671; etc.: G. W. Freytag, *Arabum proverbia*, i-iii, Bonn 1838-43 (i-ii: the complete proverbs according to al-Maydānī in Arabic with Latin translation, shortened and revised commentary in Latin; iii: 3,321 proverbs according to Abū ʿUbayd and others, according to al-Maydānī *ayyām al-ʿArab*, dicta of the Prophet, the first four caliphs, etc., Arabic with Latin translations, alphabetically, useful indices [repr. Osnabrück 1968]); Ibrāhīm al-Aḥdab (d. 1308/1891), *Farāʾid al-laʾāl fī Ma<u>dj</u>maʿ al-am<u>th</u>āl*, i-ii, Beirut 1312/1894 (versification with commentary). The author has, so he maintains in his preface, perused and excerpted more than 50 works containing *am<u>th</u>āl*, among them some pseudepigrapha (cf. iii, 1, b and 14). He has compiled in all just about 6,200 *am<u>th</u>āl* in alphabetical sequence according to the first letter, including about 900 of the *afʿalᵘ min* type according to Ḥamza (see iii, 6), about 1,000 "new ones" (*muwallada*), more than 200 *ayyām al-ʿArab* and more than 200 sayings of the Prophet and others (cf. ii, 1, b; 2, a). His *Ma<u>dj</u>maʿ* was the most comprehensive and therefore most widely spread collection and has remained so to this day, witness the numerous manuscripts, of which the oldest dates from the year 533/1138 (Paris [de Slane] 3958?; cf. Hilāl Nā<u>dj</u>ī, *ʿAla 'l-hāmi<u>sh</u>*, Ba<u>gh</u>dād 1395/1975, 79, no. 16), the abridgements, comments and printings [see AL-MAYDĀNĪ]. A critical edition is still overdue; as to the sources, compare now also ʿAbd al-Raḥmān al-Tikrītī, *Maṣādir al-Maydānī fī kitābihi "Ma<u>dj</u>maʿ al-am<u>th</u>āl"*, in *al-Mawrid*, iii/2 and 3 (1394/1974), 11-32 and 99-122 (uncritical compilation); Ahmad M. al-Dhubaib, *A critical and comparative study of the ancient Arabic proverbs contained in al-Maidani's collection*, unpubl. Ph.D. thesis, Univ. of Leeds 1968; Samīr Kāẓim <u>Kh</u>alīl, *Ma<u>dj</u>maʿ al-am<u>th</u>āl*, in *al-Mawrid*, xii/3 (1403/1983), 161-78. Cf. Oriens, xxxi (1988), 359.

(13) Abu 'l-Ḳāsim al-Zama<u>khsh</u>arī (d. 538/1144), *al-Mustaḳṣā fī am<u>th</u>āl al-ʿArab*, i-ii, Hyderabad 1381/1962. Nearly 3,500 *am<u>th</u>āl* with good philological and concise "historical" annotations, in strict alphabetical order; in spite of these merits, the work of the great scholar could not emerge from the shadow of the more comprehensive collection—along with favourite "new ones" (*muwallada*)—of his senior colleague al-Maydānī, which overshadowed it from the first. A second work of his is known to us only by its title *Sawāʾir al-am<u>th</u>āl*. His major collection of *adab*, including sayings, *Rabīʿ al-abrār wa-nuṣūṣ al-a<u>kh</u>bār*, a source of al-Ib<u>sh</u>īhī's (d. after 850/1446) *al-Mustaṭraf*, has been printed repeatedly in an abridgement, newly complete edited by Salīm al-Nuʿaymī, i-iv, Ba<u>gh</u>dād 1396-1402/1976-82, His minor collections of sayings—with added translations—appeared in print in

Europe already in the 18th and 19th centuries [see AL-ZAMAKHSHARĪ].

(14) Abu 'l-Ḥasan al-Bayhaḳī (d. 565/1169), *Ghurar al-amthāl wa-durar al-aḳwāl*, ed. in part Hussam El-Saghir, Ph.D. thesis, Univ. of Frankfurt/Main 1984 (complete edition in preparation). About 2,900 *amthāl*, including the "new ones" (*muwallada*), in alphabetical order according to the first letter. Al-Maydānī's pupil has retained a high degree of independence in regard to his teacher, clear grouping: *mathal, lugha, iʿrāb, maʿnā, sabab, ḍarb, ḥall, ḥikāya*; good philological comments; many of the *amthāl* are inserted into the context of "world", local and family history and personal experience by lively stories and reports; a revealing document of its time, esp. as regards Khurāsān; at some time or other the author quoted pseudepigrapha (cf. El-Saghir, *op.cit.*, 88-9, 97-8, 116-17; iii, 1, b, and 12) and, like Ḥamza and al-ʿAskarī (see iii, 6 and 7), Persian proverbs. A second work containing *amthāl* in four volumes and two collections of sayings (?), which he itemises in his autobiography (Yāḳūt, *Udabā*ʾ, v, 212) have not apparently survived; cf. Sellheim, *Eine unbekannte Sprichwörtersammlung*, in *Isl.*, xxxix (1964), 226-32.

(15) Raḍī al-Dīn Abū Saʿīd (Abū ʿAbd Allāh) Muḥammad b. ʿAlī al-ʿIrāḳī (d. 561/1166), *Nuzhat al-anfus wa-rauḍat al-madjlis*, a collection— disregarded up to now—containing about 900 *amthāl*, partly *muḥāwarāt*, and old, frequently rather long-winded stories dealing with the *awāʾil*-problem (*awwal*[u] *man ḳālahu*) (cf. above, ii, 1, b). It is arranged alphabetically in 29 chapters. The author, a pupil of the well-known philologist Abū Zakariyyāʾ al-Tibrīzī [*q.v.*], draws from the ʿIrāḳī *madjālis* tradition. Only one manuscript, damaged at the beginning, is known to exist (Gotha [Pertsch], no. 1250, cf. Brockelmann, I, 333); an edition is being prepared. Al-ʿIrāḳī's *Kitāb al-Wasīṭ fi 'l-amthāl* is mainly only an abridgment of the *Nuzha*, comprising about a quarter of its volume. Its editor (cf. iii, 11) has erroneously ascribed this "median" collection to Abu 'l-Ḥasan al-Wāḥidī (d. 468/1076), the teacher of al-Maydānī, following in this (?) the defective unicum in a Maghribī hand (Rabat, al-Khizāna al-ʿāmma, no. 102). In al-ʿIrāḳī's preface to his *Kitāb al-Wasīṭ*, we read that, besides the *Nuzha*, which he repeatedly quotes, he has written two more collections of *amthāl*, to wit, a "large one", *Kitāb al-Basīṭ*, and a "small one", *Kitāb al-Wadjīz*. Of both these works, as far as is known, no manuscripts have come down to us. For details, see Sellheim, in *Oriens*, xxxi (1988), 82-94.

(16) Abu 'l-Maḥāsin al-Shaybī (d. 837/1433), *Timthāl al-amthāl*, i-ii, ed. Asʿad Dhubyān, Ph.D. thesis, Lebanese University, Beirut 1402/1982; printed in part as *First half of the book Timthāl al-amthāl of Jamāl al-Dīn al-Shaibī*, ed. Muḥammad Bahāʾ al-Ḥaqq Rānā, unpubl. Ph.D. thesis, Punjab Univ. Lahore 1961. The majority of the 441 *amthāl* in alphabetical order were extracted by the author from the two collections of al-Maydānī and al-Zamakhsharī; the remainder he owes to literature as, for instance, to the *Kitāb al-Aghānī*, or to the verses of poets; only in a few cases is the source not mentioned; not infrequently, he reproduces stories at length.

Of other collections of this time and of later times (cf. the list in Ahlwardt [Berlin], no. 8729) little can be expected to be forthcoming in regard to the classical *amthāl*—witness the work of al-Shaybī, or Muṣṭafā b. Ibrāhīm's *Zubdat al-amthāl* of 999/1591 (Brockelmann, II, 557, S II, 631; Flügel [Vienna], no. 339), and Ibrāhīm Sarkīs' (d. 1302/1885) *al-Durra al-yatīma fi 'l-amthāl al-ḳadīma*, Beirut 1288/1871. In any case, the *Madjmaʿ al-aḳwāl fī maʿāni 'l-amthāl* of Muḥammad b. ʿAbd al-Raḥmān b. Abi 'l-Baḳāʾ, hence the grandson of the noted Baghdadian philologist Abu 'l-Baḳāʾ al-ʿUkbarī (d. 616/1219), deserves the attention of the researcher. Of his work in six volumes, parts are preserved in the author's autograph of the year 665/1267; he makes use of 30 sources which are conscientiously identified by characters the meaning of which is given in the preface; cf. A. J. Arberry, in *JAL*, i (1970), 109-12, and in reference to that, Sellheim, in *Isl.*, l (1973), 341ff.

New and revealing are the collections of *amthāl* in dialect form which date from the 7th/13th century onwards:

(17) Abū Yaḥyā al-Zadjdjālī (d. 694/1294), *Amthāl al-ʿawāmm fi 'l-Andalus*, i-ii, ed. Muḥammad b. Sharīfa (M. Bencherifa), Ph.D. thesis, Cairo Univ. 1969, Fās 1391-5/1971-5 (containing further literature on the subject). A total of 2,157 *amthāl* without illustrations, but with extensive explanations, etc. by the editor.

(18) Abū Bakr Ibn ʿĀṣim (d. 829/1426), *Ḥadāʾiḳ al-azhār*, ed. ʿAbd al-ʿAzīz al-Ahwānī (who was the teacher of Bencherifa), in *Ilā Ṭāhā Ḥusayn* (*Mélanges T.H.*), Cairo 1382/1962, 235-367, text 295-364. A total of 851 *amthāl* without illustrations.

iv. Modern collections.

In Europe the interest in Arabic proverbs was aroused towards the end of the 16th century (cf. Sellheim, *op.cit.*, 1-7, [2]13-20). These literary *amthāl* survived for generations into the 19th century in readers and exercise-books, especially for the supplementation of Hebrew studies. E. Pocock's plan of 1671, to edit the whole of al-Maydānī's collection, was only realised by G. W. Freytag in the years 1838-43 (cf. above, iii, 12). Since that time, European learned travellers and linguists have recorded and published Arabic proverbs—mostly in dialect form—in great numbers. They have been succeeded by Oriental collectors, especially after the end of the Second World War. The following deserve to be quoted:

(1) J. L. Burckhardt, *Arabic proverbs or the manners and customs of the modern Egyptians* [Cairo 1817], London 1830, [2]1875 (repr. London 1972, paperback ed. 1984), in German, Weimar 1834; A. Socin, *Arabische Sprichwörter und Redensarten*, Tübingen 1878 (repr. Wiesbaden 1967); C. de Landberg, *Proverbes et dictons de la province de Syrie, section de Ṣaydâ*, Leiden-Paris 1883; C. Snouck Hurgronje, *Mekkanische Sprichwörter und Redensarten*, The Hague 1886; K. L. Tallqvist, *Arabische Sprichwörter und Spiele*, Helsingfors 1897; M. Ben Cheneb, *Proverbes arabes de l'Algérie et du Maghreb*, i-iii, Paris 1905-7; E. Westermack, *Wit and wisdom in Morocco, a study of native proverbs*, London 1930, New York 1931; E. Littmann, *Arabic proverbs*, collected by Mrs. A. P. Singer, Cairo 1913; idem, *Kairiner Sprichwörter und Rätsel*, Leipzig 1937 (repr. Nendeln 1966); S. D. F. Goitein, *Jemenica: Sprichwörter und Redensarten aus Zentral-Jemen*, Leipzig 1934 (repr. Leiden 1970); Saʿīd ʿAbbūd, G. Kampffmeyer, M. Thilo, *5000 arabische Sprichwörter aus Palästina*, i-iii, Berlin 1933-7; M. Feghali, *Proverbes et dictons Syro-Libanais*, Paris 1938; A. Frayha, *Modern Lebanese proverbs*, i-ii, Beirut 1953 = *A dictionary of modern Lebanese proverbs (Muʿdjam al-amthāl al-lubnāniyya al-ḥadītha)*, i-ii, Beirut 1394/1974; Fatma M. Mahgoub, *A linguistic study of Cairene proverbs*, Bloomington-The Hague 1968 (cf. *Oriens*, xxiii-iv [1974], 551ff.); Omar al Sasi, *Sprichwörter und andere volkskundliche Texte aus Mekka*, Ph.D. Thesis, Univ. of Münster 1972; R. Y. Ebied and M. J. L. Young, *A collection of Arabic proverbs from Mosul*, in *AIUON*, xxxvi (1976), 317-50; E. García

Gómez, *Hacia un "Refranero" arábigo-andaluz*, I-II, in *al-Andalus*, xxxv (1970), 1-68, 241-314; III: xxxvi (1971), 255-328; IV-V: xxxvii (1972), 1-75, 249-323; cf. xlii (1977), 375-90, 391-408; F.-J. Abela, *Proverbes populaires du Liban Sud, Saïda et ses environs*, i-ii, Paris 1981-5 (3,694 proverbs; bibliography).

(2) Na^cc^ūm S̲h̲uḳayr, *Amt̲h̲āl al-^cawāmm fī Miṣr wa 'l-Sūdān wa 'l-S̲h̲ām*, Cairo 1302/1894; Maḥmūd Ef. ^cUmar al-Bād̲j̲ūrī, *Amt̲h̲āl al-mutakallimīn min ^cawāmm al-miṣriyyīn*, Cairo 1311/1893; Aḥmad Taymūr, *al-Amt̲h̲āl al-^cāmmiyya*, Cairo 1368/1949, ²1375/1956, ³1390/1970; idem, *al-Kināyāt al-^cāmmiyya*, ³Cairo 1970 (cf. *ZDMG*, cxxiii [1973], 403ff.); Fā'iḳa H. R. Rafīḳ, *Ḥadā'iḳ al-amt̲h̲āl al-^cāmmiyya*, i-ii, Cairo 1358-62/1939-43; Ibrāhīm A. S̲h̲a^clān, *al-S̲h̲a^cb al-miṣrī fī amt̲h̲ālihi al-^cāmmiyya*, Cairo 1391/1972; al-Ṭāhir al-K̲h̲umayrī (Khmiri), *Muntak̲h̲abāt min al-amt̲h̲āl al-^cāmmiyya al-tūnisiyya*, Tunis 1387/1967; Ismā^cīl b. ^cAlī al-Akwa^c, *al-Amt̲h̲āl al-yamaniyya*, i-ii, ²Beirut 1405/1984; ^cAbd al-Karīm al-D̲j̲uhaymān, *al-Amt̲h̲āl al-s̲h̲a^cbiyya fī ḳalb D̲j̲azīrat al-^cArab*, i-iii, Beirut 1383/1963, ²i-vi, Riyad 1399-1400/1979-80; Aḥmad al-Sibā^cī, *al-Amt̲h̲āl al-s̲h̲a^cbiyya fī mudun al-Ḥid̲j̲āz*, Jeddah 1401/1981; Hānī al-^cAmad, *al-Amt̲h̲āl al-s̲h̲a^cbiyya al-urdunniyya*, Amman 1398/1978; Nitār Abāẓa, *al-Amt̲h̲āl al-s̲h̲a^cbiyya al-s̲h̲āmiyya*, Beirut (in print); ^cAbd al-K̲h̲āliḳ al-Dabbāg̲h̲, *Mu^cd̲j̲am amt̲h̲āl al-Mawṣil al-^cāmmiyya*, i-ii, Mosul 1375/1956; D̲j̲alāl al-Ḥanafī, *al-Amt̲h̲āl al-bag̲h̲dādiyya*, i-ii, Bag̲h̲dād 1382-4/1962-4; ^cAbd al-Raḥmān al-Tikrītī, *al-Amt̲h̲āl al-bag̲h̲dādiyya l-muḳārana*, i-iv, Bag̲h̲dād 1386-9/1966-9 (containing further literature to the subject); Muḥammad Ṣādiḳ Zalzala, *Mad̲j̲ma^c al-amt̲h̲āl al-^cāmmiyya al-bag̲h̲dādiyya wa-ḳiṣaṣuhā*, Kuwait 1396/1976; Aḥmad al-Bis̲h̲r ar-Rūmī and Ṣafwat Kamāl, *al-Amt̲h̲āl al-kuwaytiyya al-muḳārana*, i-ii, Kuwait 1398-1400/1978-80; etc. A thesaurus of Arabic proverbs is being prepared by ^cAfīf ^cAbd al-Raḥmān (Irbid); until now he has published: *Mu^cd̲j̲am al-amt̲h̲āl al-^carabiyya al-ḳadīma*, i-ii, Riyad 1405/1985; another one by Riyāḍ ^cAbd al-Ḥamīd Murād (Damascus), 4 vols., is under way.

Bibliography: In addition to the works mentioned in the article, see W. Bonser and T. A. Stephens, *Proverb literature, a bibliography of works relating to proverbs*, London 1930, 355-68, 394-8 (repr. Norwood, Pa. 1977); A. Fischer, in *MSOS As.*, i (1898), 197-201; Ch. A. Ferguson and J. M. Echols, *Critical bibliography of spoken Arabic proverb literature*, in *Journal of American Folklore*, lxv, no. 255 (1952), 67-84; O. E. Moll. *Sprichwörter-Bibliographie*, Frankfurt/Main 1958, 489-502, 573; W. Mieder, *International proverb scholarship, an annotatea bibliography*, New York—London 1982, index s.v. Arabic; ^cAfīf ^cAbd al-Raḥmān, in *al-Mawrid*, ix/3 (1400/1980), 248-52, 260; Pearson, ch. vii, d; E. Rehatsek, *Some parallel proverbs in English, Arabic, and Persian*, in *JBBRAS*, xiv (1878-80), 86-116; C. Brockelmann, *Alttürkestanische Volksweisheit*, in *Ostasiatische Zeitschrift*, viii (1920), 50-73 (with Arabic and other parallels); S. L. Khazradji, *A paroemiological experiment (comparison of Russian proverbs and sayings with Arabian, Tadjiko-Persian and English)*, in *Narody Azii i Afriki*, xx/1 (1974), 147-51 (in Russian); W. P. Zenner, *Ethnic stereotyping in Arabic proverbs*, in *Journal of American Folklore*, lxxxiii (1970), 419-29; R. A. Barakat, *A contextual study of Arabic proverbs*, Helsinki 1980; Anonymi, *al-Ḥikam wa 'l-amt̲h̲āl* (preface by Ḥannā al-Fāk̲h̲ūrī), Cairo (*ca.* 1956) (Funūn al-adab al-^carabī, al-fann al-ta^clīmī, 3); ^cAbd al-Mad̲j̲īd ^cĀbidīn, *al-Amt̲h̲āl fi 'l-nat̲h̲r al-^carabī al-ḳadīm*, Ph.D. thesis, Univ. of Cairo 1375/1956; Muḥammad Abū Ṣūfa, *al-Amt̲h̲āl al-^carabiyya wa-maṣādiruhā fi 'l-turāt̲h̲*, Amman 1402/1982; Yūsuf ^cIzz al-Dīn, *al-Ta^cbīr ^can al-nafs fi 'l-amt̲h̲āl al-^carabiyya*, in *MM^cI^cI*, xxxi/1 (1400/1980), 149-67; Ṣalāḥ al-Dīn al-Munad̲j̲d̲j̲id, *Amt̲h̲āl al-mar'a ^cind al-^cArab*, Beirut 1401/1981; Muḥammad Kāmil ^cAbd al-Ṣamad, *al-Amt̲h̲āl al-s̲h̲a^cbiyya allatī tuk̲h̲ālifu mā d̲j̲ā'a fī nuṣūṣ al-Islām wa 'l-rūḥihi*, Cairo 1405/1985; R. C. Trench, *Proverbs and their lessons*, ed. A. Smythe Palmer, London-New York 1905; A. Taylor, *The proverb*, Cambridge, Mass. 1931; idem, *An index to "The proverb"*, Helsinki 1934 (repr. of both, Hatboro, Pa.-Copenhagen 1962); P. Grzybek (ed.), *Semiotische Studien zum Sprichwort, simple forms reconsidered I*, Tübingen-Philadelphia-Amsterdam 1985 (*Kodika/Code, Ars semeiotica*, vii/3-4 [1984]). On a fragment of Abū Zayd al-Anṣārī's (d. 215/830) alleged *Kitāb al-Amt̲h̲āl*, cf. Sellheim, in *Festschrift J. Blau*, Jerusalem 1989, and on al-Yūsī's (d. 1102/1691) collection, cf. *Oriens*, xxxi (1988), 357-9.

(R. Sellheim)

2. In Persian

Persian, despite its elegant literary uses, has always remained a true speech of "the folk", the language (until very modern times) of an essentially simple, unlettered society based on agriculture and pastoralism, crafts and trading. It is therefore hardly surprising that it should be extremely rich in idioms and proverbial expressions. Most of these are brief and pithy, but some are fairly elaborate in both concept and construction. The high-culture literature itself—particularly ethical works and such edifying-entertaining writing as Sa^cdī's *Gulistān*—abounds in proverbial material; and (as, for example, with Shakespeare) it is often virtually impossible to determine if the author himself invented a proverbial story or coined an aphorism which subsequently gained general currency, or whether he merely appropriated anecdotes and saws already in common use. Even such ostensibly remote literature as the *g̲h̲azal*s of Ḥāfiẓ lend themselves, by their often atomistic, line-by-line structure, to easy sententious quotation or divinatory employment.

Overall, at least until affected by a marked modern tendency towards updating, the corpus contains obviously archaic features of vocabulary, grammar and style, most of which are undoubtedly genuine, though some may have been more or less consciously manufactured in an urge to offer authenticity of the "ye olde" type. Part of the material seems to have been rendered from Arabic (probably in the early centuries of Islam); other items have parallels or equivalents in Turkish, and the traffic may not always have been from Persian to the latter language. A considerably body of proverbs is dialectal, with the most generally attractive and appropriate instances being also rendered into more or less standard Persian at some point. Given all these varied factors, as well as the rapid transformation of Iranian society and the decline of traditional education over the last 50 years, the same tendency has arisen as in Western culture for many proverbs no longer to be perfectly understood, accurately cited, or rightly applied. Fortunately, individual scholarly (and even amateur) initiatives have assured their survival, at least in libraries both in Iran and around the world.

While there must inevitably be a certain common humanity to all proverbial literature, generally considered, it is rarely true that any given adage in Persian will exactly match an item in almost unvaried use across the broad spectrum of Western languages. A good sampling of the uniquely Persian flavour and idiosyncratic reference-frame can be gained from the following works, where it is possible to compare translations, parallels, and originals: R. Levy, *Persia viewed through its proverbs and apologues*, in *BSOAS*, xiv/3 (1952), 540-9; L. P. Elwell-Sutton, *Persian proverbs*, London 1954; L. Bonelli, *Detti proverbiali persiani*, Rome 1941; S. Haïm, *Amthāl-i Fārsī-Ingilīsī*, Tehran 1334 *sh*/1955. As usual, stupidity, incompetence and dishonesty are deprecated, but the terms used extend to such items as donkeys. Islamic religious functionaries, minarets and water-melons; resignation to modest station is enjoined by the consideration that a grand house demands hard work to clear its vast, flat roof of the winter snows that fall on the Iranian high plateau; everything should be in season, like a sheepskin cloak worn for the month of Day (December-January), and not at the sudden arrival of the Persian spring; and so on. As in other cultures, many of the proverbs contradict each other if taken too literally.

Bibliography: (in addition to the works mentioned in the text): The major Iranian study is still ʿAlī Akbar Dihkhudā, *Amthāl u ḥikam*, Tehran 1338 *sh*/1959-60 (4 vols.); also Abu 'l-Ḳāsim Andjawī Shīrāzī, *Tamthīl u mathal*, vol. i only, Tehran 1352 *sh*/1973 and again 1357 *sh*/1978; Yūsuf Djamshīdīpūr, *Farhang-i amthāl-i fārsī*, Tehran 1347*sh*/1968; Amīr Ḳulī Amīnī, *Farhang-i ʿawāmm*, n.d., n.p., (but probably Tehran in the 1960s); Kamāl al-Dīn Murtaḍawīyān (Fārsānī), *Dāstānhā-yi amthāl*, Iṣfahān 1340*sh*/1961 (purports to give plausible anecdotal background to many proverbs). For proverbs of dialectal provenance: Maḥmūd Pāyanda, *Mathalhā u iṣṭilāḥāt-i Gīl u Daylam*, Tehran 1352*sh*/1973; ʿAlī Naḳī Bihrūzī, *Wāzhahā u mathalhā-yi Shīrāzī u Kāzirūnī*, Shīrāz 1348*sh*/1969. Additional minor or peripheral items can be found at the head of the article by Levy cited above.

(G. M. Wickens)

3. In Turkish

In Turkish, *Mathal*/Modern Turkish *mesel* is often used in the phrase *ḍarb-ï methel* (pl. *ḍurūb-ï emthāl*); this pedantic form which may be translated as "stated by an example", has also passed into the spoken language.

The terms *mesel* and its variants *metel, matal, metal* are also used to designate a riddle, and *masal* is a story. Other terms attested in the written sources, in oral tradition and in learned terminology to denote a proverb are: *sav* (Ḳarakhānid Turkish), *atalarsözü* (plural *atasözleri*, old Osmanli, Azerbaijani, Turkmen and Ḳaraḳalpaḳ as well as in the modern terminology of Turkey), *šin-söz* (dialect of Chinese Turkestan), *ülgär-sös* (Altay), *ülgür-söz* (Nogay), *temsil, makal* (Ḳaraḳalpaḳ), *zarpumesele* (Karayïm of the Crimea), *nakïl* (Turkmen), *ḥikmet* (plural *ḥikäm*, Iranian Azerbaijani) and *deyişet* (dialect of Içel in Turkey).

The proverb being the concise and stereotyped enunciation of a rule of conduct, an axiom or a statement and the fruit of long experience, is used as a means of giving speech a greater persuasive force; this being the case, it has no independent existence, but is integrated into speech. Besides its frequent usage in day-to-day conversation, it constitutes a corroborative and ornamental element of literary, scholarly or popular creation. In the epic tradition, for example, a series of linked proverbs, often alliterated or rhymed together and in the metre adopted for the epic narration, serve as a kind of preamble to the story proper. Through this functional characteristic, the proverb is distinguished from the other genres of oral literature. It has been noted, however, that among the Karayïm of the Crimea and in the popular tradition of Içel in Turkey, the proverb is used independently as the essential element of a verbal game. This is in the context of a competition in the course of which two teams (or two persons) confront one another; each in turn utters a proverb beginning with the same letter of the alphabet; the winning team—or person—is the one who succeeds in reciting the greatest number of proverbs.

Classified according to their themes, a first category of proverbs contains those which pronounce a simple judgement; among them, some imply a moral or suggest a rule of conduct. In a second category, are those which make a statement, on daily life, on human nature, on natural phenomena, or on "works and days", sometimes implying criticism or practical advice. Finally, a third category, of exclusively local or regional origin and usage, consists of the opinions regarding one another held by various communities—ethnic, religious, etc.

In the formal and stylistic context, there are four categories to be distinguished: (1) Proverbs stated in simple prose; (2) Proverbs containing prosodic elements. In this category the texts are of various types: in one type, the proverb is stated in the form of a verse or a distich in traditional metre (the two lines are rhymed in the latter case); in a second type, the text is composed with alliterations or internal rhymes between the various component parts. Finally, a third type is that where several proverbs of different themes, rhymed or alliterated together, are joined in sequence, such as are encountered in the epic texts, e.g. in the Oghuz *Kitāb-ï Dede Ḳorḳut* and in the Ḳïrgïz *Manas* [*q.v.*]; (3) Proverbs and proverbial statements which have an anecdotal structure. Sometimes, this is a "miniature narrative" without direct speech; elsewhere, the narrative is reduced to a minimum, or disappears completely, and the text takes the form of a dialogue. (4) The proverbs of this third group are to be distinguished from those which have an anecdotal "origin". The latter allude to a historical event, or to an anecdotal character; such are the proverbs and proverbial sayings which refer to one or another of the facetious stories of Nasreddin Hoca.

From the 2nd/8th century, some proverbs are attested in the Kök Türk inscriptions. Later, after the 4th/10th century, a greater number of examples is found in the Uyghur texts. As many as 290 proverbs, of which a large number have survived into the present day, are contained in the dictionary of Maḥmūd Kāshgharī [*q.v.*] (5th/11th century). The two most ancient Ottoman Turkish collections, both the work of anonymous compilers, are the *Risāle min kelimāt-ï Oghuznāme el-meshhūr bi-atalarsözi*, undated, probably from the 9th/15th century; and the *Kitāb-ï Atalar*, compiled in 885/1480-1. The *Pend-nāme*, by the Ottoman poet Güwāhī (10th/16th century), is a collection of proverbs from oral tradition cast in the form of classical prosody. (For collections of more recent date, still in manuscript, see the bibl. in Aksoy, 1977, 1267-70.)

Numerous poets of the Ottoman era, including Thābit (15th/17th century) and Ḥïfẓï (12th/18th century), have a reputation for embellishing their poetry with proverbs. (For a more complete list of the proverbs used in literary works, see Eyüboğlu, 1973-5.) Others, including Rūḥī of Baghdād (10th/16th century), Nābī (11th/17th century), Rāghïb Pasha and Ḳānī (12th/18th century) Ḍiyāʾ Pasha and Seyrānī (13th/19th century), are, on the contrary, admired for their verses and couplets which, with the passage of time, have acquired the status and usage of proverbs.

It was in the second half of the 19th century that westernised Turkish intellectuals began to show an interest in the collection and comparative study of proverbs. The first anthology of this type is the *Durūb-i emthāl-i ʿOthmāniyye* (1863) of Shināsī; in the second edition (1870), the number of proverbs and proverbial sayings amounts to 2,500; in the third, edited by Abu 'l-Ḍiyāʾ (Ebüzziya) Tawfīḳ in 1885, 4,000. The collection of Aḥmed Wefīḳ Pas̲h̲a, intitled *Muntak̲h̲abāt-i ḍurūb-i emthāl-i türkiyye* (1871) contains 4,300 proverbs. (On later collections and studies, see the bibliography of the present article and that of Aksoy, 1977, 1271-1328, which included 716 titles.)

Bibliography: Ömer Asım Aksoy, *Atasözleri ve deyimler*, Ankara 1965; idem, *Bölge agizlarinda atasözleri ve deyimler*, Ankara 1971; idem, *Atasözleri ve deyimler sözlüğü*, i. *Atasözleri sözlüğü*, Ankara 1971; ii. *Deyimler sözlüğü*, Ankara 1976; iii. *Dizin ve kaynakça*, Ankara 1977; İlhan Başgöz and A. Tietze, *Bilmece. A corpus of Turkish riddles*, Berkeley-Los Angeles-London 1973; Ferit Birtek, *Dîvân-î luğât-it Türkten derlemeler*. i. *En eski Türk savları*, Ankara 1944; P. N. Boratav, *Quatre vingt quatorze proverbes turcs du XVᵉᵐᵉ siècle restés inédits*, in *Oriens*, vii/2 (1954), 223-49; idem, *Le «Tekerleme»*. *Contribution à l'étude typologique et stylistique du conte populaire turc*, Paris 1964 (Cahiers de la Société Asiatique, xvii); idem, *Les proverbes*, in *PhTF*, ii, Wiesbaden 1964, 67-77; idem, *100 soruda Türk halk edebiyati⁴*, Istanbul 1982, 118-25; C. Brockelmann, *Alttürkestanische Volksweisheit*, in *Ostasiatische Zeitschrift*, viii (1911-20), 49-73; Ahmet Caferoğlu, *Orhon âbidelerinde atalarsözü*, in *Halk Bilgisi Haberleri*, i/3 (1930), 43-6; H. F. von Diez, *Denkwürdigkeiten von Asien*, i-ii, Berlin 1811; Kemal Eyüboğlu, *On üçüncü yüzyıldan günümüze kadar şiirde ve halk dilinde atasözleri ve deyimler*, i-ii, Istanbul 1973, 1975; A. von Gabain, *Die alttürkische Literatur*, in *PhTF*, ii, Wiesbaden 1964, 213-14; Avram Galanti, *Eski sawlarîn eskilig̲h̲i*, in *Edebiyyāt Fakültesi Medjmūʿasî*, ii/6 (1923); Orhan Şaik Gökyay, *Dedem Korkudun kitabı*, Istanbul 1973, pp. cxxix ff., ccxlvii; Velet Izbudak, *Atalarsözü*, Istanbul 1936; Nedjīb ʿĀṣim, *Eski sawlar*, in *Edebiyyāt Fakültesi Medjmūʿasî*, ii/2, 4, 5, 6 (1922); idem, *Dīwān-î Lug̲h̲āt-it Türkden meʾk̲h̲ūdh eski sawlar*, Istanbul 1924; W. Radloff, *Proben der Volksliteratur der türkischen Stämme*, St. Petersburg, i-vii, 1866-96, in viii, 1899 (texts collected by I. Kunos), ix, 1907 (texts collected by N. F. Katanov), x, 1904 (texts collected by V. Mos̲h̲kov). (P. N. BORATAV)

4. IN URDU

In Urdu, proverbs are variously called *mathal* (*masal*), *ḍarb al-mathal* (*zarb ul-masal*) or *kahāwat*, and they are often associated with *muḥāwarāt* (idioms—proverbial figures of speech). The language is rich in them, and they are used not only in conversation but in official and formal language, and in literature, especially poetry. Yet little has been written about them, and few collections have been published. The pioneer work is by an Englishman, S.W. Fallon, *A dictionary of Hindustani proverbs*, Benares-London 1886. It was published after Fallon's death, edited and revised by Capt. R. C. Temple, with free English translations. About 12,500 proverbs in Romanised Urdu are arranged alphabetically according to their first words, and there is no subject index. Important as it is, it would probably have contained much more information had the author lived to complete it. Many of the proverbs are better set-out in Fallon's earlier

New Hindustani-English dictionary, Benares-London 1879; and his example has been followed by Urdu-speaking lexicographers in their monolingual Urdu dictionaries, which contain numerous references to proverbs. The best in this respect is K̲h̲ʷādja ʿAbd al-Madjīd's *Djāmiʿ al-lug̲h̲āt* (4 vols., Lucknow 1933-5). There is also a section on proverbs in the Introduction (16), while the Bibl. (17-18) gives the titles of several Urdu-Hindi works on proverbs. Unfortunately, neither authors nor publication details are given. But one, *Darb al-amthāl*, may refer to a little book, *Urdu proverbs and idioms*, published in Dihlī, undated and with no author's name, for the benefit of "junior and senior boys, teachers and professors". It contains 1,122 *Urdū ḍarb al-amthāl* and 325 *Urdū muḥāwarāt*. There are English equivalent proverbs and expression—not in any sense translations—on alternate pairs of pages. Other collections of Urdu proverbs include Subḥān Bak̲h̲sh, *Muḥāwarāt-i-Hind*, Dihlī 1913, and Sayfī Nawgānwī, *Ḍarb al-amthāl wa muḥāwarāt*, Karachi 1982.

Bibliography: In addition to that *Djāmiʿ al-lug̲h̲āt* mentioned in the text, proverbs are found in the following general Urdu dictionaries: K̲h̲ān Ṣāhib Mawlawī Sayyid Aḥmad Dihlawī, *Farhang-i-Āṣafiyya*, 4 vols., Dihlī 1896, repr. 1974; Mawlawī Nūr al-Ḥasan Nayyir Kākōrawī, *Nūr al-lug̲h̲āt*, 4 vols., Lucknow 1924-5, repr. Karachi 1957; Sayfī Prōmī, *Kahāwat awr kahānī*, Dihlī 1977, contains 110 proverbs and proverbial idioms each amplified by a short story. For an example of a poet (Sawdāʾ) quoting a proverb, see MAZ̲HAR, MĪRZĀ DJĀNDJĀNĀN.

(J. A. HAYWOOD)

5. IN SWAHILI

In Swahili, the majority of known proverbs have been collected from oral sources, i.e. from the memory of the elders among the people. The most important collection is still W. Taylor's *African aphorisms* of 1891. The written sources will, when tapped, yield an even richer harvest. Most of the written literature in Swahili is poetry, and poets love weaving proverbs into their poems, both religious and secular, both lyrical and epic. Even the political poetry in contemporary Kenya and Tanzania is full of proverbs, behind which the poets conceal their true opinions of the political situation; these are to be guessed only by their close associates and by Swahili scholars who can follow all the allusions. Even love songs and other lyrical songs are full of proverbs; a special type of short (36 syllables) song exists which may be called "proverb song", in which the proverbs actually contain the message of the song to the beloved, concealed from the ears of those whose wrath is to be feared. This type of political poetry composed with proverbs is at least 300 years old, as witness certain allusions to it in the chronicles. If one considers that there are numerous expressions, set phrases, idioms and conventional metaphors in the Swahili language which are to a high degree the building bricks, as it were, of the proverbs, one realises that these same expressions permit the Swahili speakers, and, *a fortiori* the poets, to refer to these proverbs without even mentioning them (e.g. "hen" may refer to a good wife; "kite" to an adulterous visitor; compare the English expression "crocodile's tears" for hypocrisy), showing how Swahili proverbs are enmeshed in the very thoughts of the people. The proverbs from the purely written tradition may include quotations from Islamic sources, often couched in strongly Arabicised Swahili. The two main sources are the Ḳurʾān and the Ḥadīth. Scholars will quote the Ḳurʾān in Arabic, then interpret its contents for the people in Swahili. Every quotation from the Ḳurʾān is accepted as an (often ill-understood) proverb. Especially popular are the "forty *ḥadīth*s", of which there is more than one Swahili translation in print.

Bibliography: The classical work on the subject is W. E. Taylor, *African aphorisms. Saws from Swahililand*, London 1891. Most of these proverbs are in the Mombasa dialect, but a few are in the Nyika dialect of the hinterland. For a classification of Swahili proverbs, see J. Knappert, *On Swahili proverbs*, in *African Language Studies*, xvi (1975), 117-46; idem, *Rhyming Swahili proverbs*, in *Afrika und Uebersee*, xlix (1965), 59-68; idem, *Swahili proverb songs*, in *ibid.*, lix (1976), 105-12. A. Scheven, *Swahili proverbs*, is the most important publication to date on the subject; it has a full bibl. including S. S. Farsy's work on proverbs from Zanzibar. The only work that, it seems, escaped Scheven's net, is C. K. Omari, E. Kezilahabi and W. D. Kamera, *Misemo na methali toka Tanzania*, Dar es Salaam 1975-6.

Proverbs of the prophets are very popular; there are various editions of the *Hadithi arobaini* ("Forty *ḥadīth*s") in Swahili. The largest collection is one of 130 *Hadithi* compiled by the famous Mombasa scholar Al Amin Bin Aly El-Mazrui and his cousin M. Kasim Mazrui, published in Zanzibar in 1356/1937-8 in Swahili and Arabic; the Arabic title is *al-Aḥādīth al-mukhtāra al-djāmiʿa al-miʾa wa-thalāthīn ḥadīth^an nabawiyy^an fi 'l-ḥikma wa' 'l-ādāb wa 'l-akhlāḳ al-marḍiyya.* Many of the sayings of the Prophet Muḥammad and of other prophets (Yūsuf, Yūnus, Mūsā, ʿĪsā, Zakariyyāʾ) have been woven into the Swahili epics, see Knappert, *Traditional Swahili poetry*, Leiden 1967. (J. KNAPPERT)

MATHALIB (A.), pl. of *mathla/uba*, from the root *th.l.b.*, which means "to criticise, to blame, to slander, to point out faults with the intention of being hurtful". Although it is not a Ḳurʾānic term, it is attested from ancient times and has been used continuously until to-day to mean "faults, vices, defects, disgrace, etc." (see further, Wehr).

In earliest times and in the first centuries of Islam, it had a specialised usage, for it was broadly applied to what were regarded as subjects of shame for the tribes, the ethnic groups or even clans, rather than separate individuals. Later, it appeared in the titles of a number of works usually written by genealogists and collectors of historical traditions, but the origin of which the *Kitāb al-Aghānī* (ed. Beirut xx, 21) attributes to Ziyād b. Abīh, who indeed is said to have written a *Kitāb al-Mathālib*. The word *mathālib* can be contrasted in meaning with *mafākhir* or *maʾāthir*, "exploits, feats, glorious titles" as well as with *manāḳib* [*q.v.*] in its original meaning (see, for example, al-Djāḥiẓ, in the *Risāla fī manāḳib al-Atrāk*, ed. Hārūn, *Rasāʾil*, i, 22: *lanā al-taʿāyur bi 'l-mathālib wa 'l-tafākhur bi 'l-manāḳib* "we reproach each other for our *faults* and we vie in praising ourselves for our *virtues*"; see also i, 36, 70). It is used in connection with themes in *hidjāʾ* [*q.v.*] or satire to denigrate an enemy (see for example, *Naḳāʾiḍ*, ed. Bevan, 907-8: *mā yuhdjā bihi*; al-Djāḥiẓ, *Bukhalāʾ*, ed. Ḥādjirī, 184). it is well known that the pre-Islamic poets never failed to recall the disgrace of the other side (see R. Blachère, *HLA*, index, s.v. *mafâḫir wa-maṯâlib*). Since *hidjāʾ* tried to make much of the dishonourable aspects of the group that was under attack, it is possible that *mathālib* is a word indicating an amalgam of these features and that it was used a little indiscriminately, with no special emphasis on one particular shameful matter. This much can be deducted from the examples given of the use of *mathālib* and from many other also.

However, I. Goldziher (*Muh. Studien*, i, 43; Eng. tr. i, 48) stated that the *mathālib* were intended to discredit the enemy, and in particular his ancestors, and that they aimed at casting doubt on the authenticity of his genealogy. The nobility of one's ancestry (*nasab*) was a basic requirement of honour (see B. Farès, *L'honneur chez les Arabes avant l'Islam*, Paris 1932, 84ff.), and it was normal for genealogies to be closely examined, and any weak point would be exploited by the enemy. Furthermore, even if *mathālib* were not exclusively concerned with *ansāb*, it is not surprising that some relatively objective genealogists should be eager to take up the faults mentioned in them and make them more widely known, at the risk of attracting dangerous hostility (see, e.g., the case of ʿAḳīl b. Abī Ṭālib, who was keenly disposed to take note of *mathālib*; al-Djāḥiẓ, *Bayān*, ii, 323-4). Those who specialised in such descriptions were accused of nourishing deep hatred, and this became something of a proverbial expression (*daghīnat ḥuffāẓ al-mathālib*, in al-Djāḥiz, *Risāla fi 'l-djidd wa 'l-hazl*, ed. Kraus and Ḥādjirī, 65; ed. Hārūn, *Rasāʾil*, i, 236).

Goldziher again refers to the relationship between *mathālib* and genealogies when discussing the famous Daghfal (see al-Masʿūdī, *Murūdj*, index, s.v.). Among the authors of works which contain this term in their titles, he mentions Hishām Ibn al-Kalbī and al-Haytham b. ʿAdī; these last remarks appear in the chapter on the Shuʿūbiyya and its different manifestations in *Muh. Studien*, i, 191, Eng. tr. i, 176-7. Although accusations are made against him (see Goldziher, *op.cit.*, i, 187, Eng.tr. i, 173), it would probably be wrong to count as an opponent of the Arabs and a supporter of the ʿAdjam the famous writer Ibn al-Kalbī (d. 204/819 [*q.v.*], the author of a *Kitāb Mathālib al-ʿArab* (*Fihrist*, ed., Cairo 141; Yāḳūt, *Udabāʾ*, xii, 191, where it is stated that ʿAllān (see below) used the same classification of the tribes; Brockelmann, S I, 212; Sezgin, *GAS*, i, 270, ii, 61). However, it should be noted that Ibn al-Kalbī had already used the same term as this of a work containing a severe criticism of the three first caliphs, the *Kitāb Mathālib al-Ṣaḥāba.* This pro-ʿAlid manifesto caused "a great stir" and was used by al-Ḥillī (d. 726/1325 [*q.v.*]) to defend Shīʿism (see H. Laoust, *Les schismes dans l'islam*, 78). His contemporary, al-Haytham b. ʿAdī (d. *ca.* 206/821) [*q.v.*], who had an extremely poor reputation, produced for his part another *Kitāb Mathālib al-ʿArab* (Brockelmann, S I, 213; Sezgin, *GAS*, i, 272) in two versions (one longer, the other shorter, according to Ibn al-Nadīm (*Fihrist*, Cairo, 145), as well as the *Mathālib Rabīʿa*, the Arabs from the North.

Abū ʿUbayda (d. *ca.* 209/824) [*q.v.*]) was vigorously criticised for having provided the Shuʿūbiyya with arguments for their cause, just as all the other writers of *mathālib* were criticised, and even accused of Shuʿūbī doctrines. However, he does seem to have shown some objective judgement when he wrote not only a *Kitāb Maʾāthir al-ʿArab* and a *Kitāb Maʾāthir Ghaṭafān*, but also the *Manāḳib Bāhila* in opposition to his *Mathālib Bāhila* (*Fihrist*, Cairo, 80; Sezgin, *GAS*, ii, 61, 321). Al-Masʿūdī (*Murudj*, vii, 80 = § 2765) refers to his *Kitāb al-Mathālib* (cf. Brockelmann, S I, 162), and shows that recording the Arab genealogies with all the vices that were embodied in them naturally led him to make certain serious accusations which, by their very nature, must have displeased a considerable number of individuals and families. In addition, al-Masʿūdī (*Murūdj*, v, 480-1 = § 2235) mentions a work attributed to Abū ʿUbayda, "or to another Shuʿūbī", though the exact title of this work cannot be established. It must presumably have contained the *manāḳib* and the *mat̲h̲ālib* of the Arabs as well as the entitlements to glory and shameful deeds of the various tribes of the north and south of Arabia, as presented by their supporters and by their detractors in the meeting-room of His̲h̲ām b. ʿAbd al-Malik, who apparently inaugurated discussions on these questions in the manner of those which made up the genre of *al-maḥāsin wa 'l-masāwī* [*q.v.*].

A few decades earlier, Ziyād b. Abīhi [*q.v.*] could have dedicated his efforts to such an activity; he is credited with having written a book of *mat̲h̲ālib*, which was used by some of the authors already mentioned (see Sezgin, *GAS*, i, 261, as well as 249, 257, 265, ii, 24, 60). According to Ḥammād ʿAd̲j̲rad [*q.v.*], the *zindīḳ* named Yūnus b. [Abī] Farwa sent a book (or a letter, *kitāb*) to the Emperor of Byzantium about the *mat̲h̲ālib* of the Arabs and the vices (*ʿuyūb*) of Islam (al-D̲j̲āḥiẓ, *Ḥayawān*, iv, 448; cf. al-D̲j̲ahs̲h̲iyārī, 125; al-Ḥuṣrī, *D̲j̲amʿ al-d̲j̲awāhir*, 256; al-Murtaḍā, *Amālī*, i, 90; Ibn Ḥad̲j̲ar, *Lisan al-mīzān*, vi, 334; Brockelmann, S I, 109). This appears to be the one real case of treason which has been recorded; since the Persian ʿAllān al-Warrāḳ al-S̲h̲uʿūbī, who maintained relations with the Barmakids as well as doing the job of copyist at the Bayt al-Ḥikma [*q.v.*] for al-Ras̲h̲īd, and subsequently for al-Maʾmūn, cannot really be blamed for his work; he is indeed the author of a *Kitāb al-Maydān* which collects together, tribe by tribe, all the *mat̲h̲ālib* of the Arabs, from Ḳurays̲h̲ to the Yemenis. The list of tribes and clans which have their shameful matters recorded occupies a whole page of the *Fihrist* (Cairo, 154), where it is stated that the classification adopted there is the same as that of Ibn al-Kalbī. ʿAllān himself also seems to have been objective in his judgement, for he wrote other works, among which may be mentioned a *Kitāb Faḍāʾil Kināna* and a *Kitāb Faḍāʾil Rabīʿa* (see Yāḳūt, *Udabāʾ*, xii, 191-6, with a passage borrowed from al-D̲j̲ahs̲h̲iyārī, which does not appear in the *Kitāb al-Wuzarāʾ*, but which has been reproduced by M. ʿAwwād in *Nuṣūṣ dāʾiʿa min Kitāb al-Wuzarā*, Beirut 1384/1964, 49; Sezgin, *GAS*, i, 271, ii, 61). Sezgin (i, 603) also mentions a *Kitāb al-Mat̲h̲ālib* of Ibn Bis̲h̲r al-As̲h̲ʿarī (d. 260/874), and (ii, 62) the *Mat̲h̲ālib T̲h̲aḳīf wa-sāʾir al-ʿArab* by someone named al-Daymartī.

Although it is possible, it is not likely that later authors continued to use the word *mat̲h̲ālib* in the titles of polemical works against some tribes, for the general situation hardly encouraged this kind of literature to survive. It must have come to an end quite quickly. We have seen that *mathālib* are to be contrasted with *maʾāt̲h̲ir*, *mafāk̲h̲ir* and *manāḳib* (see above); even so, it proved impossible for a parallel to be maintained between works devoted to the praise of groups of people and individuals and those which aimed at discrediting an enemy. The short list that has been given here and what we know of comparable works suggest that Goldziher was correct, for over the centuries the divisions between the tribes weakened so that a growing feeling of fellow-citizenship could develop. Moreover, writers seem to have heeded the *ḥadīt̲h̲* which condemns *al-ṭaʿn fi 'l-ansāb wa 'l-niyāḥa wa 'l-anwāʾ*, and consequently they avoided the temptation of attacking genealogies. On the other hand, as a result of an understandable semantic evolution the term *mat̲h̲ālib* has been used in a meaning close to that of *hid̲j̲āʾ* and has been applied to individuals; see e.g. the *Kitāb Mat̲h̲ālib Abī Nuwās* by Aḥmad b. ʿUbayd Allāh al-T̲h̲aḳafī (d. 314/926; see Yāḳūt, *Udabāʾ*, iii, 240) and the famous *Mat̲h̲ālib al-wazīrayn* by Abū Ḥayyān al-Tawḥīdī (d. 414/1023 [*q.v.*]).

Bibliography: Given in the article. See also J. Sadan, *Pérennité et écarts conceptuels Ǧāhiliyya-Islam à travers les belles-lettres et les recueils de* Mat̲h̲ālib, in *From Jahiliyya to Islam*, Jerusalem 1987.

(Ch. Pellat)

al-**MAT̲H̲ĀMINA,** the name given by the Yemenite historians to eight noble families of South Arabia who, before Islam, enjoyed important political privileges, either in the kingdom of Ḥimyar (from the end of the 3rd century AD to 520 [or 525]), or under the Abyssinian and Persian régimes which followed. Mat̲h̲āmina is a plural noun whose singular, which is not attested, could be *Mut̲h̲amman or *Mut̲h̲man (since these participles mean "repeated eight times", "to the number eight"). It is certainly from the Arabic number *t̲h̲amāniya* "eight", and not from the concept of price or value also contained in the root, that the name of these eight families is derived, since they could also be called al-T̲h̲amāniya ("the Eight"), as in al-Hamdānī, *al-Dāmig̲h̲a*, 64.

Mention of the Mat̲h̲āmina is to be found in the works of only three authors, all Yemenite. The oldest is al-Ḥasan al-Hamdānī (280-after 360/893-after 971) [*q.v.*]. Next comes Nas̲h̲wān al-Ḥimyarī, who died in D̲h̲u 'l-Ḥid̲j̲d̲j̲a 573/June 1178 (on this author see al-Akwaʿ, *Naschwān*). The third is the Rasūlid ruler al-Malik al-As̲h̲raf ʿUmar b. Yūsuf b. Rasūl, who reigned from 694 to 696/1295-7 (Sayyid, *Sources*, 396). It is to be noted that the non-Yemenite Arab historians, notably His̲h̲ām Ibn al-Kalbī [*q.v.*] appear to ignore these Mat̲h̲āmina.

The definitions of the historians. These three authors give somewhat divergent definitions of the Mat̲h̲āmina. Dealing with the descent of D̲h̲ū D̲j̲adan, al-Hamdānī (*al-Iklīl*, ii, 283 ff.) mentions incidentally that four of the sons of S̲h̲uraḥbīl b. al-Ḥārit̲h̲ belonged to the Mat̲h̲āmina "eight lineages (*abyāt*) between whom power was shared after the death of D̲h̲ū Nuwās" (a phrase follows whose meaning is obscure). This scholar, like the other Yemenite historians knew that D̲h̲ū Nuwās [*q.v.*] was the nickname of a Ḥimyarite king called Yūsuf (for al-Hamdānī, see for example *al-Dāmig̲h̲a*, 63-4, and *al-Iklīl*, x, 22; for Nas̲h̲wān, we may refer to *Mulūk*, 147-8). The full name and exact title of this ruler are known thanks to a South Arabian inscription engraved by the commanders of one of his armies and dated *d̲-md̲rʾn* 633 of the Ḥimyarite era (July 518 or July 523 AD, since there is some question as to whether the Ḥimyarite era begins in 115 or 110 before the Christian era): "Yūsuf Asʾar Yat̲h̲ʾar, king of all the tribes" (*Yws*^{1}*f ʾs*^{1}*r Yt̲ʾr mlk kl ʾs*^{2c}*b*^{n}, in Ja 1028, line 1) (the name of the king should thus be corrected in the article dhū nuwās).

The dates of the reign of Yūsuf, a ruler especially known for having persecuted the Christians of Nad̲j̲rān, which led to an Abyssinian intervention that challenged him and drove him to suicide, are not established with certainty. He came to power between June 516 (or 521) and June 517 (or 522) (according to the evidence of Ry 510 and Ja 1028/8-9) and was overthrown by the Abyssinians shortly after Pentecost 520 (or 525) (Beeston, *Judaism*, 272 ff.; Huxley, *Martyrium*, 51). After the death of Yūsuf, the kingdom of Ḥimyar passed under the tutelage of Abyssinia for fifty years; then, in the year 570, it was conquered by the Sāsānids and remained under Persian domination until it was won over to Islam during the lifetime of Muḥammad. For al-Hamdānī, the Mat̲h̲āmina were thus the noble lineages who dominated Yemen after the fall of the Ḥimyarite dynasty, that is, during the Abyssinian occupation and perhaps after that. This scholar in the meantime neglects to mention that the Ḥimyarite throne did not remain vacant; the Abyssinians placed on it a Ḥimyarite Christian, Samyafaʿ (*S*^{1}*myfʿ*), then one of their own people, Abraha [*q.v.*].

The definition of the Mathāmina that Nashwān gives differs somewhat from that of al-Hamdānī. In *Mulūk*, 157, he states that "these eight kings and their descendants are eight lines called the Mathāmina of Ḥimyar; in order for the royal dignity of a king of Ḥimyar to be effective, these eight had to establish him and if they agreed on his removal, they deposed him". In *Shams al-ʿulūm*, 16, under the root ThMN, he adds: "*Thamāniya*: rulers (*amlāk*) descended from Ḥimyar the Younger b. Sabaʾ the Younger, called the Mathāmina; this is made into a proper noun for them so as to distinguish it from the number eight without the article". For Nashwān, the Mathāmina were thus great barons who exercised strict control over the Ḥimyarite ruler, since they confirmed him in office and could also remove him. The reference to such a ruler probably implies an earlier date for the Abyssinian invasion; the Mathāmina were thus an institution dating from the splendour of the Ḥimyarite kingdom.

A modern Yemenite scholar, Muḥammad Bāfaḳīh, has linked this definition of Nashwān with a passage of al-Hamdānī (*al-Iklīl*, ii, 114), where it is noted that the Ḥimyarite king was enthroned by a college of 80 *ḳayl*s [*q.v.*], supposing that this number 80 should be corrected to eight (which should be another mention of the Thamāniya/Mathāmina) (Bāfaḳīh, *al-Hamdānī*, 106). This possible correction is not imperative, for it is not necessary for a good understanding of the text, especially as the pre-Islamic inscriptions acquaint us with a number of *ḳayl*s, far more than eight.

As for the Rasūlid ruler al-Malik al-Ashraf, he gives two different definitions of the Mathāmina several pages apart (*Ṭurfat al-aṣḥāb*, 73, 77); it is clear that he copied two divergent sources without investigating or succeeding in harmonising them. He states firstly (73): "among (the *ḳayl*s), (are counted) the Mathāmina: these are eight men who belonged to Ḥimyar and who were kings of their people; they were subordinate to the kings of Ḥimyar, and their descendants are the tribes of Ḥimyar; they are called the Mathāmina; their powers included the fact that a king of Ḥimyar could not reign without their goodwill and, if they agreed on his removal, they deposed him". This text, like the list of the Mathāmina which follows (see below), is a simple paraphrase of Nashwān's text, *Mulūk*, 157-8.

Several pages later (77), al-Malik al-Ashraf returns to the subject: "the Mathāmina — of the Ḥimyarites — are eight *ḳayl*s who arose after Sayf b. Dhī Yazan and to whom the Yemenites gave power". Here is a new evaluation; these Mathāmina are seen as reigning after the arrival of the Persians, called to Yemen by Sayf b. Dhī Yazan to chase out the Abyssininans (in the year 570).

Variants in the list of the Mathāmina. The list of the Mathāmina was already disputed in the time of al-Hamdānī, who gives two different versions of it with two of the eight names varying; other variants were defended by later authors. We can sum up these diverse opinions in the following table:

	H1	H2	N1	N2	N3	M1	M2
Dhū Saḥar	x	xx	xxx		x	(x)	
Dhū Thaʿlabān	x	xx	xxx	x	x	x	x
Dhū Khalīl	x	xx	xxx	x	x		x
Dhū ʿUthkulān	x	xx	xxx	x	x	x	x
Dhū Djadan	x	xx	xxx	x	x	x	x
Dhū Manākh	x						x
Dhū Ṣirwāḥ	x		xxx	x	x	x	
Dhū Maḳār	(x)	xx	xxx	x		x	x
Dhū Ḥazfar		xx	xxx	x	x	x	
Dhū Ḳayfān		xx					
Dhū Murāthid				x			
Dhū Yazan				x			x
Dhū Maʿāfir							x

(the crosses indicate the number of occurrences of the list in the work of the author considered)

H1 = al-Hamdānī, list no. 1: see *al-Iklīl*, ii, 294. It is this which the present author takes into account. In the only available edition of *al-Iklīl*, ii, by M. al-Akwaʿ, it is necessary to correct Dhū ʿUshkulān to Dhū ʿUthkulān; besides, the list only consists of seven names (in place of the eight announced in the text), without our knowing whether it is a case of an error by the editor or a deficiency in the unique manuscript. In fact, it is necessary to add Dhū Maḳār, as is proved by the five verses attributed to ʿAlḳama b. Dhī Djadan, which al-Hamdānī cites to justify this list and which he takes from Muḥammad b. Ibrāhīm b. al-Maḥābī al-Kalāʿī. In this fragment of ʿAlḳama (a great Yemenite poet who was a contemporary of the Prophet Muḥammad: *al-Iklīl*, ii, 300-1; on this poet, see also Löfgren, *ʿAlqama*), the Mathāmina are treated as if they already belonged to past times. Unfortunately, we cannot conclude anything from this, for the authenticity of these verses seems doubtful; al-Hamdānī himself did not find any trace of them in the work of ʿAlḳama.

H2 = al-Hamdānī, list no. 2: see *al-Iklīl*, ii, 294-5. It is given in two pieces of verse. The first is that which serves as a justification for H1, but with some variants, notably the replacement of Dhū Manākh and Dhū Ṣirwāḥ by Dhū Ḥazfar and Dhū Ḳayfān; al-Hamdānī takes it from an Arab of Ṣanʿāʾ who attributes it, not to ʿAlḳama, but to a Ḥimyarite. The second piece, which numbers six verses, is "the famous saying of ʿAlḳama b. Dhī Djadan on the Mathāmina in his poem"; it gives the same names as the preceding.

N1 = Nashwān, list no. 1: see *Mulūk*,156-7. It is provided by the *Ḳaṣīda ḥimyariyya*, a nostalgic poem that Nashwān devoted to the annals of the Ḥimyarite Empire. It is a compromise between the H1 and H2 versions: of the two innovations in H2, it retains only the replacement of Dhū Manākh by Dhū Ḥazfar. The author justifies his list by citing, in the commentary on his poem, ʿAlḳama's verses already encountered with the support of H1 (but attributed in H2's statement to a Ḥimyarite), with new variants. The same list is found in a piece of three verses, without the author's name, that Nashwān cites in the encyclopaedic dictionary that he composed entitled *Shams al-ʿulūm*, under the root SḤR, 48.

N2 = Nashwān, list no. 2: see *Shams al-ʿulūm*, under the root ThMN, 16. It follows N1, but replaces Dhū Saḥar with Āl Murāthid. This list is provided by a poem attributed to an Arab from the North (from the tribe of ʿAtīk b. Aslam b. Yadhkur b. ʿAnaza b. Asd b. Rabīʿa b. Nizār). It is a variant without real significance, seeing that Dhū Murāthid is, according to the genealogists, the "son" of Dhū Saḥar (see notably Nashwān, *Mulūk*, 158, and al-Hamdānī, *al-*

Iklīl, ii, 317-18). Al-Hamdānī himself (*al-Iklīl*, viii, 159) considers D̲h̲ū Murāt̲h̲id as one of the Mat̲h̲āmina, although this lineage does not appear in his own lists. The preference shown for D̲h̲ū Murāt̲h̲id in this text of Nas̲h̲wān may have a personal motive; this author claimed descent from Ḥassān D̲h̲ū Murāt̲h̲id b. D̲h̲ī Saḥar (*S̲h̲ams al-ʿulūm*, under the root RT̲h̲D, 40).

N3 = Nas̲h̲wān, list no. 3: see *S̲h̲ams al-ʿulūm*, on the word *d̲h̲ū*, 39. It differs from N1 in one name, D̲h̲ū Yazan, who takes the place of D̲h̲ū Maḳār. It may be a slip by the author for, in his works, he never puts D̲h̲ū Yazan among the Mat̲h̲āmina, not even in the article devoted to this line in the same work (116). All the other names on the list, by contrast, are explicitly described as Mat̲h̲āmina, when Nas̲h̲wān discusses them. Moreover, it will be noted that this list is not supported by any poetic reference.

M1 = al-Malik al-As̲h̲raf, list no. 1: see *Ṭurfat al-aṣḥāb*, 73. The list of the Mat̲h̲āmina comprised, following the manuscripts used by Zetterstéen: Yazīd, Ṣak̲h̲ar, T̲h̲aʿlabān the Elder, Murra D̲h̲ū ʿUt̲h̲kulān, Maḳār b. Mālik, D̲h̲ū Ḥazfar b. Aslam, ʿAlḳama D̲h̲ū D̲j̲adan and D̲h̲ū Ṣirwāḥ. This passage is actually a rather corrupt citation and taken from the commentary of the *Ḳaṣīda ḥimyariyya* of Nas̲h̲wān (*Mulūk*, 157-8). Also, the two first names ("Yazīd wa-Ṣak̲h̲ar") may be a corruption of the double name Barīl D̲h̲ū Saḥar. When the correct reading is established, the list, a simple repetition of N1, only consists of seven persons. But al-Malik al-As̲h̲raf intended to give eight names, and not seven. So it is probable that the copying error already existed in the source that he used.

M2 = al-Malik al-As̲h̲raf, list no. 2: see *Ṭurfat al-aṣḥāb*, 77. It takes the name D̲h̲ū Yazan, already given in N3, and provides an entirely new name, D̲h̲ū Maʿāfir. If comparison is made with H1, these two names take the place of D̲h̲ū Saḥar and D̲h̲ū Ṣirwāḥ.

The Mat̲h̲āmina in the pre-Islamic inscriptions and in tradition. Almost all the lines of Mat̲h̲āmina cited by the traditionists are confirmed in the South Arabian inscriptions. This allows us to determine their origin, which has been totally obscured by tradition. It is established that they were:
— Sabaeans from Maʾrib: D̲h̲ū Saḥar, D̲h̲ū K̲h̲alīl, D̲h̲ū ʿUt̲h̲kulān, D̲h̲ū D̲j̲adan, D̲h̲ū Maḳar, D̲h̲ū Ḥazfar.
— Sabaean from a region adjoining Maʾrib: D̲h̲ū Ṣirwāḥ, hypothetically since this line has not been attested before Islam with this name; but D̲h̲ū Ṣirwāḥ clearly refers to the important ancient site of Ṣirwāḥ, at least 40 km. west of Maʾrib.
— Sabaean from the Highlands (to the north of Ṣanʿāʾ): D̲h̲ū Murāt̲h̲id
— Ḥimyarites: D̲h̲ū Manāk̲h̲ and D̲h̲ū Maʿāfir
— Ḥaḍramite: D̲h̲ū Yazan
— Nad̲j̲rānites: D̲h̲ū T̲h̲aʿlabān and possibly D̲h̲ū Ḳayfān.

If we discard from the lists of Mat̲h̲āmina the most doubtful names, D̲h̲ū Murāt̲h̲id (a doublet of D̲h̲ū Saḥar), D̲h̲ū Ḳayfān (mentioned in only one list and furthermore a descendant, in the genealogies, of D̲h̲ū D̲j̲adan), D̲h̲ū Yazan and D̲h̲ū Maʿāfir (who only appear at a late date), of the 9 remaining names, 6 are of Sabaean lineages of Maʾrib, plus a seventh (D̲h̲ū Ṣirwāḥ) who can be assimilated with them. The preponderance of lines originating from the Sabaean capital is overwhelming. On the other hand, it is curious to find so few lines drawn from Ḥimyar and any of the Sabaean tribes of the highlands, whereas the traditionists have preserved the memory of a number from among them. The Mat̲h̲āmina are thus essentially the old Sabaean nobility of Maʾrib. This observation reminds us that al-Hamdānī mainly invokes the authority of the poet ʿAlḳama b. D̲h̲ī D̲j̲adan, himself originating from one of these old lines of Maʾrib: it is probable that it is he, and he alone, who is at the origin of this tradition.

It is further to be noted that, in the genealogy of Ḥimyar composed by al-Hamdānī, the great majority of the lines of Mat̲h̲āmina, and notably all those of Sabaean origin, are grouped in the same branch (see *al-Iklīl*, ii), parallel to that in which are grouped the Ḥimyarite kings (on this, see Bāfaḳīh, *al-Ḥārit̲h̲*). It would seem that the traditionists had integrated in the same branch of this genealogy two bodies of traditions, on one hand that of the tribe of Ḥimyar in the strict sense, on the other that of the Sabaeans of Maʾrib. Finally, we will observe that in Yemen in the 9th-12th centuries AD, numerous clans, lines and even villages were claiming descent from the Mat̲h̲āmina; an eloquent picture is supplied by the works of al-Hamdānī, notably in the genealogies of Ḥimyar.

The later vogue of the Mat̲h̲āmina. The tradition of the Mat̲h̲āmina is certainly ancient: it is based on some fragments of reputed archaic poetry, whose antiquity can be confirmed by the mention of D̲h̲ū ʿUt̲h̲kulān, an authentic pre-Islamic Sabaean line which is known to the historians only from these fragments. We may assume that it dates back to the Ḥimyarite period (end of the 3rd century AD - beginning of the 6th), after Ḥimyar had annexed Sabaʾ around 275 and at a time when the ancient noble Sabaean lines had to defend an authority that was being increasingly threatened.

Meanwhile, this tradition seems to have been neglected by the earliest of the great traditionists, whose work established the genealogical outline of the Arab tribes, notably His̲h̲ām Ibn al-Kalbī (around 120-204 or 206/around 737-819 or 821) and Ibn Durayd al-Azdī (223-321/837-933) [*q.v.*]. Ibn al-Kalbī knew, however, 7 of the 13 lines of Mat̲h̲āmina recorded above (Caskel, *Ǧamhara*, index): D̲h̲ū S̲h̲ahar (*sic*), D̲h̲ū K̲h̲alīl, D̲h̲ū D̲j̲adan, D̲h̲ū Manāk̲h̲, D̲h̲ū Ṣirwāḥ, D̲h̲ū Ḳayfān and D̲h̲ū Yazan, to whom we may add the two tribe names, T̲h̲aʿlabān and al-Maʿāfir (without *d̲h̲ū*).

So it is at a late date that the tradition of the Mat̲h̲āmina enjoyed a certain vogue, when the Yemenite scholars, beginning with al-Hamdānī, raised it from oblivion. It is probable that they only had at their disposal in order to do this some allusions from archaic poetry, which would explain the notable differences of definition from one author to another.

The interest that the Yemenites showed in these Mat̲h̲āmina from the 9th-10th centuries onwards probably has a political cause. The dissolution of the ʿAbbāsid empire left the field open to many ambitions, particularly in Yemen where the struggles for power became fierce. In this context, prestigious Ḥimyarite ancestors gave an incontestable historical legitimacy, even if the religious authorities saw in it a manoeuvre against Islam. It was probably impossible to claim a royal ascendancy, whether it was owing to public knowledge that the rulers of Ḥimyar had had no posterity or because their engagement in favour of Judaism had disqualified them. But there were the Mat̲h̲āmina, mentioned in archaic poetry, and they resorted to this idea which had fallen into oblivion. It is probable that the D̲j̲aʿfarids who appealed to D̲h̲ū Manāk̲h̲ for their authority and the Yuʿfirids (and perhaps the Zawāḥids) who claimed descent from D̲h̲ū

Maḳār owed their success, among others, to the prestige of these ancestors. The addition of Dhū Maʿāfir in list no. 2 of al-Malik al-Ashraf could be explained in the same way; would the Rasūlids not have needed a prestigious local ancestry in order to establish their power better? Many other lines, even modest ones, attempted to ennoble themselves in the same way, by claiming to have one of the Mathāmina for an ancestor.

To supply arguments for certain princes seeking historical legitimacy and roots, it is probable that some scholars did not hesitate to replace one name with another in the poetical fragments and in the list, to such an extent that the number of variants increased. We know the bad reputation that the genealogists had; was not al-Hamdānī himself accused of falsification for payment (Bāfaḳīh, *al-Ḥārith*, 428)?

Finally, one should mention that the name Mathāmina was also borne by a branch of the ʿAlids of Yemen (see al-Malik al-Ashraf, *Ṭurfat al-aṣḥāb*, 116).

Bibliography: Ismāʿīl b. ʿAlī al-Akwaʿ, *Naschwān Ibn Saʿīd al-Ḥimyarī und die geistigen, religiösen und politischen Auseinandersetzungen seiner Epoche*, in Werner Daum (ed.), *Jemen*, Innsbruck-Frankfurt/Main 1987, 205-16; Muḥammad ʿAbd al-Ḳādir Bāfaḳīh, *al-Hamdānī wa 'l-Mathāmina*, in Yusuf Mohammad Abdallah (ed.), *al-Hamdānī, a great Yemeni scholar, Studies on the occasion of his millenial anniversary*, Ṣanʿāʾ 1407/1986 (Arabic title: *al-Hamdānī, Lisān al-Yaman*), 99-110; idem, *al-Ḥārith al-Rāʾish "wa-nasabu-hu al-mukhtalaf fīhi"*, in Chr. Robin, *Mélanges linguistiques offerts à Maxime Rodinson, C.R. du G.L.E.C.S.*, xii, Paris 1985, 411-34 (Fr. summary, 411); A. F. L. Beeston, *Judaism and Christianity in Pre-Islamic Yemen*, in J. Chelhod (ed.), *L'Arabie du Sud, histoire et civilisation*, i, Paris 1984, 271-8; al-Hamdani, *Kitāb Ḳaṣīdat al-Dāmigha*, ed. al-Akwaʿ al-Ḥiwālī, Cairo 1978; idem, *Kitāb al-Iklīl*, ii, ed. al-Akwaʿ, Cairo 1386/1967, viii, ed. N. A. Faris, Princeton 1940 (repr. Ṣanʿāʾ-Beirut n.d. [1978]), x, ed. Muḥibb al-Dīn al-Khaṭīb, Cairo 1368[/1948-9]; idem, *al-Maḳāla al-ʿāshira min sarāʾir al-ḥikma*, ed. al-Akwaʿ, n.p. n.d. [1981]; G. L. Huxley, *On the Greek Martyrium of the Negranites*, in *Proc. R. Ir. Acad.*, 80c (1980), 41-55; Ja 1028 = A. Jamme, *Sabaean and Ḥasaean Inscriptions from Saudi Arabia*, Studi semitici, 23, Rome 1966, 39 ff.; O. Löfgren, *ʿAlqama Ibn ḏī Ǧadan und seine Dichtung nach der Iklîl-Auswahl in der Bibliotheca Ambrosiana*, in *al-Hudhud, Festschrift Maria Höfner*, ed. Roswitha G. Stiegner, Graz 1981, 199-209; al-Malik al-Ashraf, *Ṭurfat al-aṣḥāb fī maʿrifat al-ansāb*, ed. K. V. Zetterstéen, Damascus 1949 (repr. Ṣanʿāʾ 1406/1985); Nashwān b. Saʿīd al-Ḥimyarī, *Mulūk Ḥimyar wa-akyāl al-Yaman, ḳaṣīdat Nashwān...*, ed. ʿAlī b. Ismāʿīl al-Muʾayyad and Ismāʿīl Aḥmad al-Djirāfī, Cairo 1378[/1958-9]; idem, *Die auf Südarabien bezüglichen Angaben Našwān's im Šams al-ʿulūm*, ed. ʿAẓīmuddīn Aḥmad, Leiden-London 1916; Ry 510 = G. Ryckmans, *Inscriptions sud-arabes. Dixième série*, in *Le Muséon*, lxvi (1953), 307 ff.; Ayman Fuʾād Sayyid, *Sources de l'histoire du Yémen à l'époque musulmane*, Cairo 1974 (in Arabic).

(Chr. Robin)

AL-MATHĀNĪ [see AL-ḲURʾĀN].

MATHEMATICS [see DJABR, HANDASA, ḤISĀB].

MATHNAWĪ (A.), the name of a poem written in rhyming couplets.

1. In Arabic literature, see MUZDAWIDJ.

2. In Persian.

According to the prosodist Shams-i-Ḳays (7th/13th century), the name refers to "a poem based on independent, internally rhyming lines (*abyāt-i mustaḳill-i muṣarraʿ*). The Persians call it *mathnawī* because each line requires two rhyming letters.... This kind (*nawʿ*) is used in extensive narratives and long stories which cannot easily be treated of in poems with one specific rhyming letter" (*al-Muʿdjam*, ed. Tehran 1338/1959, 418f.). The first part of this definition mentions the single characteristic which separates the *mathnawī* from all other classical verse forms, namely its rhyme scheme *aa bb cc*, etc. Otherwise, the name is given to poems differing greatly in genre as well as in length.

Etymologically, it is often explained as a *nisba* adjective to the Arabic word *mathnā*, "two by two"; but *mathnāt*[un] (according to al-Djawharī, the equivalent of the Persian *du-baytī*, "which is a song") is mentioned as another possibility in the *Tādj al-ʿarūs* (cf. Lane, *s.v.*). It is reasonable to think that the term was coined by the Persians in spite of its Arabic derivation. The Arabs used the term *muzdawidj* [*q.v.*] instead. By this they designated poems with rhyming couplets, usually written in the trimeter of the *radjaz* which has either eleven or twelve syllables. Such poems were composed at least since the beginning of the 8th century A.D., but the verse form remained of little importance in Arabic literature (cf. G. E. von Grunebaum, *On the origin and early development of Arabic* muzdawij *poetry*, in *JNES*, iii [1944], 9-13, repr. in *Islam and medieval Hellenism*, London 1976).

The much more successful Persian *mathnawī* is first known from the Sāmānid period (4th/10th century). Although it made its appearance at a much later date than the *muzdawidj*, the *mathnawī* is regarded by nearly all modern scholars as a continuation of an Iranian verse form and not of its Arabic counterpart. Yet this theory meets with a few thorny problems pertaining to the history of prosody in Iran. Prior to the Islamic period, rhyme—the most prominent feature of a *mathnawī*—was apparently not in use as a characteristic of a verse form. The metrical system of pre-Islamic Iranian poetry is still very imperfectly understood. The early opinion of modern scholarship was that it must have been governed by the principle of syllable counting. On the basis of this assumption, an Iranian origin of some Persian metres, which were frequently used in early *mathnawīs*, was held to be likely (cf. G. E. von Grunebaum, *Islam. Essays in the nature and growth of a cultural tradition*, London 1955, 177-80).

The syllabic principle was rejected by W. B. Henning and M. Boyce in favour of the theory that the pre-Islamic metres were accentual and allowed a variable number of syllables within certain limits. It has been shown more recently that a rather great irregularity in the length of verse lines was permitted, probably under the influence of the accompanying music (see S. Shaked, *Specimens of Middle Persian verse*, in *W. B. Henning memorial volume*, London 1970, 395-405, with further references). L. P. Elwell-Sutton, on the other hand, arguing in support of his thesis that the metres of classical poetry continue the system used in pre-Islamic Iran, opted for the principle of syllabic quantity (*Persian metres*, 168ff.). It has often been observed that the Persian *mathnawīs* are written in a restricted number of metres. These metres always have eleven or, more rarely, ten syllables. A verse form marked by such inflexible rules for its rhyme and the number of its syllables can only have developed in the early Islamic period. It is most likely, therefore, that the *mathnawī* came into being through a process of adaptation of pre-Islamic verse forms to the prosody of the Islamic period which was dominated by the metric principles of Arabic poetry. The stages of this process can no longer be traced from the scant remains of pre-classical Persian poetry which have been preserved (cf. e.g. Chr. Rempis, *Die ältesten Dichtungen in Neupersisch* in *ZDMG*, ci [1951], 235-8; Fr. Meier, *Die schöne Mahsatī*, Wiesbaden 1963, 9ff.; G. Lazard, *Les premiers poètes persans*, Paris 1964, 10ff.).

In the view of the classical poets, the *mat͟hnawī* was undoubtedly on a par with other forms of poetry. To Gurgānī [*q.v.*], the treatment in a *mat͟hnawī* of the story about Vīs and Rāmīn, known up to his days only in an unadorned "Pahlawī" form, amounted to bringing it to the level of poetic expression (*Vīs-u Rāmīn*, ed. Tehran 1337/1959, 20). The poems of Niẓāmī [*q.v.*] show which heights of stylistic art could be reached in this form. In some respects, however, it was also akin to prose. The narrative and didactic contents of many poems could equally be dealt with in prose works. In principle, there were no limits to the length of a *mat͟hnawī*. A few works of exceptionable size like the *S͟hāh-nāma*, some of the later heroic poems, and the *Mat͟hnawī-yi maʿnawī* left aside, most of the better-known poems fall within a range of 2,000 to 9,000 *bayts*, but the form was also used for texts of a much lesser extent. Fragments of no more than a few lines with the rhyme scheme of the *mat͟hnawī* can be found as inserted lines in prose works, for example in the *Gulistān* of Saʿdī [*q.v.*], who sometimes wrote an entire story on this scheme in 10 or 12 *bayts*.

Other poems were occasionally inserted into a *mat͟hnawī* text, either with or without the use of their specific rhyme scheme. The first poet to do the former was, to our knowledge, ʿAyyūḳī (*fl.* in the early 5th/11th century), who put short poems in monorhyme into the mouths of the protagonists in his *Warḳa u Guls͟hāh* (ed. by D͟h. Ṣafā, Tehran 1343/1964). This insertion of *g͟hazal*s was also a characteristic of the *Dah-nāma* genre and occurs sometimes in versions of the legend of Mad͟jnūn Laylā [*q.v.*], notably in the poem of Maktabī (9th/15th century). Lyric poems adjusted to the pattern of the *mat͟hnawī* can be found frequently in the works of Firdawsī [*q.v.*], Gurgānī, Niẓāmī and others.

Prose and poetry were in some cases used alternatively, e.g. in the *Walad-nāma* of Sulṭān Walad [*q.v.*]. The *Tuḥfat al-ʿIrāḳayn* of K͟hāḳānī [*q.v.*] is in most copies introduced by a prologue in ornate prose; a similar prologue belongs to one of the early versions of the *Ḥadīḳat al-ḥaḳīḳa* of Sanāʾī [*q.v.*], but was certainly not written by the poet himself. D͟jalāl al-Dīn Rūmī [*q.v.*] added a composition of this kind to each of the six books into which his *Mat͟hnawī* is divided.

The composition of *mat͟hnawī*s shows the same variety as most of their other features. Yet certain conventions can be recognised in a number of poems and can be used therefore as the basis of a classification. A common type is exemplified in *mat͟hnawī*s with a clear distinction between introductory sections and the proper text of the poem concerned. The former (which are often collectively designated as the *dībāča*, a term also applied to prologues in prose) deal with a series of topics, some of which can be regarded as obligatory whereas others were added at the pleasure of the poet. To the first category belonged praise of the One God and prayers (*tawḥīd*, *munād͟jāt*), a eulogy of the Prophet (*naʿt*), which usually included the praise of his Family and his Companions, a dedication to the poet's patron, and digressions on the occasion for writing the poem, its subject matter, etc. Reflections of the value of poetry, usually referred to as *suk͟han*, meaning both "speech" and "logos" (see e.g. J. Chr. Bürgel, *Niẓāmī über Sprache und Dichtung*, in *Festschrift für Fr. Meier*, Wiesbaden 1974, 9-28), and other sections of a moralising nature have frequently been added. A *dībāča* of this kind can already be found in the *S͟hāh-nāma* together with a series of sections on the origin of the world which form a prelude to the subject-matter of Firdawsī's epic. The obligatory part of the scheme was further enlarged by Niẓāmī, who added it to the treatment of the *miʿrād͟j* [*q.v.*] of Muḥammad following upon the *naʿt*. Ṣūfī poets like Amīr K͟husraw and D͟jāmī [*q.vv.*] inserted the praise of their spiritual guides. In some poems, a few sections of the *dībāča* were placed at the end by way of an epilogue.

Less frequently found is a type of poem introduced by the description of one particular object treated as an emblem from which symbolic meanings relevant to the following poem are derived. This device may have been borrowed from the *nasīb*s of *ḳaṣīda*s. Such emblems were: the wind in Sanāʾī's *Kār-nāma* and *Sayr al-ʿibād ilā 'l-maʿād*, the sun in *Tuḥfat al-ʿIrāḳayn*, the flute in the *Mat͟hnawī-yi maʿnawī*, and the *rabāb* in Sulṭān Walad's *Rabāb-nāma*.

A distinction between an introduction and the poem itself cannot always be recognised. This is especially not possible in many of the shorter *mat͟hnawī*s and in some didactic works like the *Ḥadīḳat al-ḥaḳīḳa*.

Several devices could serve to articulate the contents of poems. Firdawsī inserted passages of various kinds into the *S͟hāh-nāma* to introduce the major stories contained in the text. The night scene describing how the poet was inspired by a "beloved idol", who brought him a lamp, and the theme of the tale of Bīz͟han and Manīz͟ha, is the best known example. The genre of nature poetry provided Niẓāmī with the means to mark transitions in the structure of his romances; reflective intermezzi could fulfil the same purpose. More systematic was his use of short addresses to the cupbearer (*sāḳī*) and the singer (*mug͟hannī*) respectively in the two parts of the *Iskandar-nāma* as introductions to each section of the narrative. Didactic poems were often, like treatises in prose, divided into chapters styled *bāb*, *maḳāla* or otherwise.

The genres cultivated in *mat͟hnawī*s are not restricted to the heroic [see ḤAMĀSA], the romantic and the didactic, the three usually associated with this verse form. Panegyrics and satire, topical events, love and wine, and many others subjects could also be dealt with in a *mat͟hnawī*. The larger poems nearly always contain passages of other genres than the one they are mainly concerned with. Sections dealing with ethical, philosophical or religious themes are hardly ever missing in narrative poems. The didactic poet, on the other hand, used both long and short tales to exemplify the ideas propounded in his works. They can be found already in one of the oldest specimens of the didactic genre, the *Āfarīn-nāma* of Abū S͟hakūr Balk͟hī [*q.v.* in Suppl.].

The *mat͟hnawī* was also a useful tool to present factual information on account of its memotechnic advantage. An early example of this is Ḥakīm Maysarī's *Dānis͟h-nāma*, the oldest integral text in rhyming couplets which has been preserved. It was completed in 370/980-1 and treats of medical matters (partial edition and translation by G. Lazard, *Les premiers poètes persans*, Tehran-Paris 1964, ii, 178-94; i, 163-80, see also 36-40). A wide range of subjects pertaining to the religious and the natural sciences, astrology, occultism and the arts were treated in the same fashion.

The choice of a metre for a *mat͟hnawī* was determined by convention and not by some intrinsic quality of the metre concerned. A clear example is provided by the metre *mutaḳārib-i muthamman-i maḥdhūf* which, because of its occurrence in the *Shāh-nāma*, was chosen by most poets who subsequently wrote heroic *mathnawīs*. Already in the time of Firdawsī, however, it was used also in a didactic poem by Abū Shakūr and in a love story by ʿAyyūḳī. Similar divergences of use can be noticed in the case of other metres. A decisive factor was the tendency towards the imitation of authoritative models according to their most important characteristics of form and content. The classical poets tried to bring their originality to bear through the emulation of predecessors. This consisted both of repetition and of change. The former made it clear that they were following the example of a great master; the latter that they were clever enough to find new variations on one aspect or the other of their model. The long series of imitations based on the *khamsa* [*q.v.*] of Niẓāmī provides the best-known instance of the workings of this artistic principle. The metre was usually among the features which were retained in an imitating poem. The metre of a genuine work was also carefully maintained in pseudepigraphical forgeries as they were based, e.g., on the works of Sanāʾī and ʿAṭṭār [*q.v.*]. On the other hand, a change of the metre could also serve to demonstrate a poet's independence with regard to a model followed in other respects, e.g. in the case of Niẓāmī's replacing the *khafīf* of Sanāʾī's *Ḥadīḳat al-ḥaḳīḳa* for the *sarīʿ* of his own *Makhzan al-asrār* (cf. E. É. Bertel's, *Nizami i Fuzuli*, Moscow 1962, 183).

Sometimes the imitation of one particular element of a poem gave rise to an independent genre of *mathnawīs*. The exchange of ten letters between Wīs and Rāmīn in Gurgānī's poem became the source of the *Dah-nāmas*, short works in *mathnawī* and *ghazals*, which were written from the beginning of the 8th/14th century onwards (cf. T. Gandjeï, *The Genesis and definition of a literary composition: the Dah-nāma ("Ten love-letters")*, in *Isl.*, xlvii [1971], 59-66). Another example is the even longer sequence of *Sāḳī-nāmas* which had its origin in the call of the cup-bearer used by Niẓāmī in the first book of his *Iskandar-nāma*. It was a genre of anacreontic verse written in the *mutaḳārib* metre of its original. The authors of *Sāḳī-nāmas* were numerous enough to become the subject of a special *tadhkira*, the *Maykhāna* of ʿAbd al-Nabī Fakhr al-Zamānī, completed in 1028/1619 (Storey, i/2, 813; ed. by A. Gulčīn-i Maʿānī, Tehran 1340/1961).

During the later Middle Ages, new subjects were added to the répertoire of the narrative *mathnawī* by poets like Khwādjū Kirmānī [*q.v.*], ʿImād al-Dīn Faḳīh-i Kirmānī [*q.v.* in Suppl.] and Djāmī. At the same time, mystical poems continuing the examples set by Sanāʾī, ʿAṭṭār and Djalāl al-Dīn Rūmī proliferated. The didactic genre includes several masterworks of Persian poetry, such as Saʿdī's *Būstān*, the often-imitated *Makhzan al-asrār* and the didactic poems of Djāmī's *Haft awrang*. Among the many writers of short Ṣūfī *mathnawīs*, Maḥmūd Shabistarī [*q.v.*] and Ḥusaynī Sādāt Amīr [*q.v.*] should be mentioned. The Indo-Persian poet Bīdil [*q.v.*] was the most versatile author of mystical *mathnawīs* in later centuries. The narrative and the didactic strains were intertwined in allegoric poems, for which Fattāḥī [*q.v.*] provided influential models. The great variety of subjects dealt with in shorter poems cannot be completely described here. Mention should be made, however, of a few genres which were fashionable in the 10th-11th/16th-17th century: *shāhrāshub* or *shahrangīz*, poems dealing with the playful description of young craftsmen and artisans which also exist in the form of series of quatrains (cf. A. Gulčīn-i Maʿānī, *Shahrāshūb dar shiʿr-i fārsī*, Tehran 1346/1967); *sarāpāy*, devoted to the description of an ideal human body "from top to toe"; *sūz-u gudāz*, the description of painful experiences (see for a specimen, Ṭālib-i Āmulī, *Kulliyyāt-i ashʿār*, ed. Tehran 1346/1967-8, 193-208); and *ḳaḍāʾ u ḳadar*, stories about the workings of fate (cf. *Armaghān*, viii [1306/1927], 120-3; x [1308/1929], 458-64, 554-60: specimens by Ruknā Masīḥ-i Kāshānī and Muḥammad-Ḳulī Salīm). Biblical themes were taken as the subject of *mathnawīs* in Judaeo-Persian literature [*q.v.*].

In modern literature, the *mathnawī* proved still to be a useful medium for the Persian poets as long as they were mainly interested in a renewal of contents. Imitations of the *Shāh-nāma* with a nationalist tendency were the *Nāma-yi bāstān* or *Sālār-nāma* (1313/1895-6) by Āḳā Khān Kirmānī [*q.v.* in Suppl.], the *Ḳayṣar-nāma* by Adīb Pīshāwarī [*q.v.* in Suppl.] and the *Pahlawī-nāma*, an unfinished history of Islamic Iran in heroic verses by Nawbakht, published in 1926-8. Social and political criticism was voiced in *mathnawīs* by Amīrī [*q.v.* in Suppl.] and Parwīn [*q.v.*]. Īradj Mīrzā (1874-1924) used the form for satire in his *ʿĀrif-nāma* and for a modern love story in *Zuhrā wa Manučihr*. The Indo-Persian poet Muḥammad Iḳbāl [*q.v.*] adopted it for some of his most famous works, like the *Djawīd-nāma* and *Gulshan-i rāz-i djadīd*, an imitation of the short mystical poem of Maḥmūd Shabistarī. The last major *mathnawī* to be written by a Persian poet was the *Kār-nāma-yi zindān* by Malik al-Shuʿarā Bahār [*q.v.*]. It contains the account of the poet's imprisonment and exile during the 1930s in the style of the great didactic poets of the past (*Dīwān-i ashʿār*, ed. Tehran 1345/1966, ii, 2-126).

Other prosodic forms—stanzaic poems and even *ḳaṣīdas*—were however increasingly used for epic poetry, even by poets who remained faithful to the classical canons. The experiment with a *mathnawī-yi mustazād* made by Bahār (*op. cit.*, ii, 234-8) was not pursued. Under the influence of the theories of Nīmā Yūshīdj [*q.v.*], the *shiʿr-i naw* poets of the period after the Second World War abandoned the *mathnawī*, mainly because the rigid isochronism of its verse was considered to be an impediment to the expressive use of metre (see e.g. Mahdī Akhawān-Thālith (M. Umīd), *Bidāʿathā wa badāyiʿ-i Nīmā Yūshīdj*, Tehran 1357/1978, 70 ff.).

Persian literary theory had little to add to the brief definition of the *mathnawī* given by Shams-i Ḳays. A few remarks on the subject by later writers were assembled by H. Blochmann, *The prosody of the Persians*, Calcutta 1872, 87-90. Works on *inshāʾ* [*q.v.*] sometimes pay attention to the corrections of the *dībāča* of a *mathnawī* (one of such works is quoted by Aḥmad ʿAlī, *Haft Ásmán or History of the Masnaví of the Persians*, ed. Blochmann, Calcuta 1873, 41-2; ʿAlī's book contains the introduction to an unfinished work on *mathnawī* poets).

Bibliography: M. ʿA. Tarbiyat, *Mathnawī wa mathnawī-gūyān-i Īrān*, in *Mihr*, v (1316-7/1937-9), 225-31 and continuations; A. Bausani, *Il Masnavī*, in A. Pagliaro and A. Bausani, *Storia della letteratura persiana*, Milan 1960, 579-777; M. Dj. Maḥdjūb, *Mathnawīsarāʾī dar zabān-i fārsī tā pāyān-i ḳarn-i pandjum-i hidjrī*, in *Nashriyya-yi Dānishkada-yi adabiyyāt-i Tabrīz*, xv (1342/1963), 183-213, 261-85; Fr. Machalski, *La littérature de l'Iran contemporain*, i-ii, Wroclaw 1965-7, *passim*; J. Rypka et alii, *History of Iranian literature*, Dordrecht 1968, passim; A. Munzawī, *Fihrist-i nuskhahā-yi khaṭṭī-yi fārsī*, iv,

Tehran 1349/1970 (with an alphabetical list of the opening lines of all the *mat͟hnawīs* mentioned in this catalogus catalogorum); L. P. Elwell-Sutton, *The Persian metres*, Cambridge 1976, 243-5; F. Thiesen, *A manual of classical Persian prosody*, Wiesbaden 1982, *passim*; J. T. P. de Bruijn, *Of piety and poetry*, Leiden 1983, 185ff. (J. T. P. DE BRUIJN)

3. In Turkish.

The Turkish *mat͟hnawī* developed late under the influence of that of Persia and alongside it. The oldest monument of Muslim Turkish literature that has chanced to be preserved, the *Ḳutadg͟hu bilig* [*q.v.*], is a long didactic *mat͟hnawī* (R. Dankoff, *Yūsuf Khāṣṣ Ḥājib. Wisdom of Royal Glory (Kutadgu Bilig). A Turko-Islamic Mirror for Princes*, Chicago 1983). Turkish and Persian *mat͟hnawīs* shared a great stock of authoritative models, ranging from the themes themselves to the choice of the appropriate metres (*mutaḳārib* for the heroic genres [see ḤAMĀSA], *ramal* for the religio-didactic type and *hazad͟j* for the romance). Up to now, this division into three genres has served as the main principle of organisation. But more attention needs to be paid to the social and cultural context in which these works were written, and to the way in which the three genres overlap. Turkish *mat͟hnawīs* had the same architectural framework as their Persian counterparts [section 2 above]. The authors' possibilities lay in the "internal" significance of the details rather than in the "external" aspects of plot and metre, the choice of the formal means being largely determined by the theme, for which terms as *ḳiṣṣa* [*q.v.*], *dāstān*, or *ḥikāya* [see ḤIKĀYA. iii] were used.

The chief element of the narrative *mat͟hnawī* was the plot, turning on love between two chief characters, male and female, who gave it its title. Opening chapters dealt with the reason for writing and its true purpose, incidentally drawing the patron's attention to his skills as a poet. Structure and contents of the framework could be modelled on that of the *ḳaṣīda* [*q.v.*], without the tautness of that form. Changing metres could be used as structural boundaries dividing parts of the prologue. In his religious exordium, an author could combine the praise of the One God with a meditation on the works of creation. The eulogy of the prophet Muḥammad and his heavenly journey [see MIʿRĀD͟J] have been treated in all Islamic poetry, whereas the praise of the four first caliphs would only be found in the *mat͟hnawī* of a Sunnī author. In the dedicatory passage, a local patron could be praised next to the ruler. If there was no response, the dedication might be removed and replaced with a complaint to Fate. Since it was the poets' desire to prove their own superiority, they hardly ever felt the need to mention their immediate predecessors. An attitude of reverence for the great classical models was present in the poets' reflections on the value and essence of poetry. A favoured way of expression was that of mystically-coloured love poetry, depicting the author in a dialogue with the "speaker of the heart", the cupbearer, *sāḳī*, or the pen, *ḳalem*. In the epilogue, the date and the author's name could be transmitted. The author would seek to disarm adverse criticism, justifying his adaptation of a foreign classic or an old "native" story in the Turkish of his own time and environment. Disavowal of the vernacular in general need not prevent a poet from praising his own elegant idiom which he had substituted for the obsolete language of the original.

As for his narrative, the themes being familiar and speaking for themselves, a mediaeval author could trust his audience to appreciate the significance of his particular treatment. In this way, the *mat͟hnawī* could combine religious teachings, offer historical truth, serve as tool of learning or simply offer entertainment. Chapter headings divided the more voluminous texts. Short lyrical insertions belonging to *g͟hazal* [*q.v.*, iii. In Ottoman Turkish literature, in Suppl.] poetry acted as breathing spaces. Without shifting his point of view, the author presented the inmost thoughts of his protagonists, using lyrical monologues, dialogues of the lovers or the old technique of inserting letters; he could also express his own feelings in signed *g͟hazals*, using mystical images (R. Dankoff, *The lyric in the romance*, in *JNES*, xliii [1984], 9-25). Much research is needed into the great mass of Turkish *mat͟hnawīs* in order to relate them to the social and cultural contexts which define their significance. Most of the old poems did not appear in print before the Republic. Only a fragment of this material has been translated into a modern language.

Mystic-didactic *mat͟hnawīs* were introduced into Anatolia by D͟jalāl al-Dīn Rūmī [*q.v.*] and his son Sulṭān Walad [*q.v.*]. The short *Čark͟h-nāme* seems to have been overvalued as compared with Gülş͟hehrī's [*q.v.*] *Manṭiḳ al-ṭayr* and ʿĀs͟hıḳ Pas͟ha's [*q.v.*] *G͟harīb-nāme*. Süleymān Čelebi's *Wesīlet el-ned͟jāt (Mewlid)* on the birth and miracles of the Prophet, completed in 1812/1409, has remained immensely popular (N. Pekolcay, art. *Süleyman Çelebi*, in *İA*). *K͟husraw and S͟hīrīn* [see FARHĀD WA-S͟HIRĪN], *Mad͟jnūn and Laylā* [*q.v.*] and *Yūsuf and Zulayk͟hā* were loved as moving romances; such compositions were often religious in their purport, even though the actions and emotions they displayed did not always accord with an orthodox ethical code.

In Čag͟hatay, Azeri and Ottoman literatures, great poets like Mīr ʿAlī S͟hīr Nawāʾī [*q.v.*] and Fuḍūlī [*q.v.*] deployed all the resources of Persian and Turkish literature in the perfection of this form. From the 8th/14th century onwards, Turkish poets supplied inventive translations and adaptations of Persian originals. The anonymous author of the *ʿIs͟hḳ-nāme* (S. Yüksel, *Mehmed. Işk-Nâme. İnceleme metin*, Ankara 1965) already made satirical use of the stock formulas of the epic with its exciting adventures in strange lands. Ḍarīr [*q.v.*] composed early versions of the Yūsuf-Zulayk͟hā theme, to which the great *muftī* Kemālpas͟hazāde [*q.v.*] later was to contribute a *mat͟hnawī*; Ḳuṭb and Fak͟hrī (both 8th/14th century). must now be looked upon as pioneers in the Turkish K͟husraw-S͟hīrīn versions. Weighted with a heavily Persianised vocabulary, S͟heyk͟hī's version (F. K. Timurtaş, *Şeyhi'nin Husrev ü Şirin'i*, Istanbul 1963), in which Fak͟hrī's verses can be traced, had a great influence on later poets. Under the Ottomans, new subjects were added to the répertoire. Dāʿī [*q.v.*] contributed an allegorical *Čeng-nāme*; Lāmiʿī [*q.v.*] dealt with comparatively new (Salāmān and Absāl) or nearly forgotten themes, such as Vīs and Rāmīn [see GURGĀNĪ], and Wāmiḳ and ʿAd͟hrā. It is doubtful whether he ever saw a complete copy of the latter poem in the version of ʿUnṣurī [*q.v.*], who ultimately drew from a Greek source (see M. Nazif Şahinoğlu, art. *Unsurî*, in *İA*; art. *Vâmik u Azrâ*, in *İA*; B. Utas, in *Orientalia Suecana*, xxxiii-xxxv [1984-6]). Lāmiʿī and D͟hātī [*q.v.*] both composed a *S͟hemʿ u Perwāne*; Faḍlī [*q.v.*] introduced the *Gül we Bülbül* theme. D͟jaʿfar Čelebi [*q.v.*] wrote an original *Heves-nāme*; to Mesīḥī (d. 918/1512 [*q.v.*]) the first Ottoman *s͟hehr-engīz* is attributed, a genre later to be elaborated as a social satire by Faḳīrī [*q.v.*]. Indeed, as in the *ḳaṣīda*, praise could turn into satire and invective; Aḥmadī [*q.v.*] in his medical *Tarwīḥ el-erwāḥ* flung abuse at the people of Bursa who had obstructed his work; the *K͟har-nāme* by Sheykhī [*q.v.*] contains a vigorous satire on the bad luck of a poet who is robbed of his *tīmār* (F. Timurtaş, *Şeyhî'nin Harnâmesi*, Istanbul 1971). In 933/1526 Güwāhī completely rewrote ʿAṭṭār's [*q.v.*] popular moral *Pand-nāma*, using colloquial expressions and a whole collection of Turkish proverbs (P. N. Boratev, in *Oriens*, vii) and fables (R. Anhegger, in *TM*, ix). Aḥmadī appended the first versified chronicle of the Ottomans to his *Iskender-nāme.* The term *ghazāwāt-nāme* is used with reference to narrative poems celebrating the military triumphs of the Ottomans. Epics to honour contemporary sultans in Persian and Turkish in the *shāh-nāme* style, sumptuously produced in the 10th/16th century (see LUḲMĀN; H. Sohrweide, in *Isl.*, xlvi), were already criticised by contemporaries for their lack of literary or historical merit. *Sūr-nāmes* celebrated royal festivities in the capital. Prognostics deduced from meteorological phenomena of the solar year had been the subject of an old *mathnawī* entitled *Shemsiyye* by Yazīdjī Ṣalāḥ al-Dīn; the poet-calligrapher Djevrī reworked them in his *Melḥeme* (Gibb, *HOP*, iii, 298; Levend, *Ümmet Çağı Türk edebiyatı*, Ankara 1962, 46-7), Apocalyptic aspects of history [see DJAFR] dominated Mewlānā ʿĪsā's rhymed chronicle *Djāmiʿ el-meknūnāt*, which predicted the advent of the Mahdī after Sultan Süleymān (B. Flemming, in *Studien zur Geschichte und Kultur des Vorderen Orients* [= *Festschrift Spuler*], ed. H. H. Roemer and A. Noth, Leiden 1981, 79-92).

Not every poet had the time and concentration to work with this epic form; sultans and princes wrote *ghazals*. But an author who had composed one *mathnawī* from hundreds or thousands of *beyts* could go further and compose a set of five [see KHAMSA]; Bihishtī, Ḥamdī, ʿAṭāʾī [*q.vv.*] and others performed this feat. Dukaginzāde Yaḥyā Beg (d. 990/1582), who turned his back on "the dead Persians", brought homoerotic love to the traditionally heterosexual romance by giving the (Persian) theme of the King and the Beggar, *Shāh u Gedā*, an Ottoman background and including it in his *Khamsa* (*İstanbul kütüphaneleri Türkçe Hamseler kataloğu*, Istanbul 1961). By the end of the 10th/16th century, the straightforward versified adventure story seems to have lost its appeal, while allegorical, didactic and descriptive *mathnawīs* remained in demand. Nābī's long didactic *Khayriyye*, addressed to his son in plain Turkish, and his *Khayrābād*, "out-Persianising" the Persians, are typical for the late 11th/17th and early 12th/18th centuries (*HOP*, iii, 370-74), Sheykh Ghālib [*q.v.*] Dede's allegorical subject is the mystic devotion of Beauty and Love. Fāḍil-i Enderūnī [*q.v.*] described the attractions of young men and women. Subtlety remained the stock-in-trade of the inevitable *Sāḳī-nāme.* But as more people learned to read for themselves, there was a great increase in the quantity of Turkish prose works of all sorts; standard ingredients of the rhymed romances of action found their way into prose; ʿAlī ʿAzīz [*q.v.*] stands out with his famous collection. He is a forerunner of literary westernisation, which led to the introduction of the novel and the drama. In the 19th century, the *mathnawī* form was cultivated for some last *Ẓafer-nāmes* "Books of victory" on the wars with Russia and on uprisings of the Greeks and Serbians. ʿIzzet Mollā [*q.v.*] revived the narrative *mathnawī* for his great autobiographical elegy *Miḥnet-keshān*, completed in 1825. As late as 1874. Ḍiyāʾ (Żiyā) Pasha [*q.v.*] prefaced his *Kharābāt*, a three-volume anthology of classical poetry, with a long and elaborate *mathnawī* in the old manner (*HOP*, v, 78-83); Nāmıḳ Kemāl [see KEMĀL, NĀMIḲ] responded in prose. The vitality of the *mathnawī* was sustained right to the end of Ottoman literature; the Islamist poet Meḥmed ʿĀkif [*q.v.*] Ersoy brought a new ease to it, using it for conversational verses as well as rhetorical passages in his written sermons on religious and moral subjects.

Bibliography: Given largely in the article, but see further M. Fuad Köprülü, art. *Arûz (Türk)*, in *İA*; A. S. Levend, *Ġazavāt-nāmeler ve Mihaloğlu Ali Bey in Ġazavāt-nāmesi*, Ankara 1956; A. Ateş, art. *Mesnevî* in *İA*; *PTF*, ii; A. Bombaci, *La letteratura turca*, Milan 1969; N. Çetin, art. *Şiir*, in *İA*; T. Gandjeï, *The Dah-nāma*, in *Isl.*, xlvii (1971); a full list of Turkish *mathnawīs* has been compiled by A. S. Levend, *Türk edebiyatı tarihi. I. cilt. Giriş*, Ankara 1973, 103-13; A. Çelebioğlu, *XIII-XV yüzyıl mesnevilerinde Mevlana tesiri*, *Mevlana ve yaşama sevinci*, Konya 1978, 99-126; H. Ayan, *XIV. yüzyıl Türk edebiyatında büyük mesnevi*, in *1. Millî Türkoloji Kongresi*, Proceedings, Istanbul 1980, 83-9; H. Tolasa, *15 yy. edebiyatı Anadolu sahası mesnevileri*, in *Türk Dili ve Edebiyatı Araştırmaları Dergisi*, i (1982), 1-13.

Printed editions of *mathnawīs* in Anatolian Turkish: J. H. Mordtmann, *Suheil und Nevbehâr*, Hanover 1925; N. H. Onan, *Fuzuli. Leylâ ile Mecnun*, Istanbul 1956; A. Zajączkowski, *Najstarsza wersja Ḫusräv i Šīrīn Qutba*, Warsaw 1958-61; F. İz, *Eski Türk edebiyatında nazım. I. Divan şiiri*, Istanbul 1967; N. Hacıeminoğlu, *Kutb'un Husrev ü Şirin'i*, Istanbul 1968; G. Alpay, *Ahmed-i Da'i ve Çengnamesi. Eski Osmanlıca bir mesnevi*, Cambridge, Mass. 1973; B. Flemming, *Faḫrīs Ḫusrev u Šīrīn. Eine türkische Dichtung von 1367*, Wiesbaden 1974; T. Karacan, *Nev'i-zāde Atayi: Heft-hvan mesnevisi. İnceleme, metin*, Ankara 1974; M. Akalın, *Ahmedî. Cemşid ü Hurşid. İnceleme-metin*, Erzurum-Ankara 1975; G. M. Smith, *Varqa ve Gülşāh. A fourteenth-century Turkish Mesnevī*, Leiden 1976; H. Ayan, *Şeyhoğlu Mustafa. Ḫurşid-nâme (Ḫurşid u Ferahşâd)*, Erzurum 1979; M. Çavuşoğlu, *Yahyâ Bey. Yûsuf ve Zelîhâ*, Istanbul 1979; İ. Olgun and İ. Parmaksızoğlu, *Firdevsî-i Rumî. Kutb-nâme*, Ankara 1980; T. Gandjeï, *The Baḥr-i dürer: an early Turkish treatise on prosody*, in *Studia turcologica memoriae Alexii Bombaci dicata*, Naples 1982, 237-49; K. Yavuz, *Muini. Mesnevi-i Muradiye*, Ankara 1982; M. Hengirmen, *Güvâhî. Pend-nâme*, Ankara 1983; M. Demirel, *Kemal Paşazade. Yusuf u Züleyha*, Ankara 1983. I. Ünver, *Ahmedi. Iskender-name. İnceleme-tıpkıbasım*, Ankara 1983; A. Gallotta, *Il "Gazavat-i Hayreddin Paşa" di Seyyid Murad*, Naples 1983.

Individual *mathnawis* have been studied by T. Gandjeï, *Zur Metrik des Yūsuf u Zulaiḫā von Šayyād Ḥamza*, in *UAJb*, xxvii (1959); A. Bombaci, in D. Huri, *Leylā and Mejnūn*, London 1970; Gandjeï, *Notes on the attribution and date of the "Čarḫnāme"*, in *Studi preottomani e ottomani*, Naples 1976, 101-4; H. Sohrweide, *Neues zum "ʿIšqnāme"*, in *ibid.*, 213-18; Flemming, *Die Hamburger Handschrift von Yūsuf Meddāhs Varka vü Gülşāh*, in *Hungaro-Turcica. Studies in honour of Julius Németh*, Budapest 1976, 267-73; A. Karahan, *Un nouveau mathnawī de la littérature turque ottomane: Le Mevlid Hatīcetül-Kubrā, ou la description du mariage de Khadīja avec le Prophète*, in *VII. Kongress für Arabistik und Islamwissenschaft*, Proceedings, Göttingen 1976, 230-5; I. Ünver, *Ahmedi'nin İskender-nâmesindeki Mevlid bölümü*, in *Türk Dili Araştırmaları Yıllığı Belleten 1977* (1978), 355-411; C. Dilçin, *XIII. yüzyıl metinlerinden yeni bir yapıt: Ahval-i kıyamet*, in *Ömer Asim Aksoy armağanı*, Ankara 1978, 49-86; N. Tezcan, *Lâmiʿînin Gûy u Çevgân mesnevisi*, in *ibid.*, 201-25; A. Uğur, *Şükrü-i Bitlisî ve Selimnamesi*, in *İlâhiyat Fakültesi Dergisi*, xxv (1981), 325-47; M. A. Çatıkkaş, *Türk Firdevsi'si ve Süleymanname-i kebir*, in *Türk Dünyası Araştırmalari*, xxv (1983), 169-78. M. Anbarcıoğlu, *Türk ve Iran edebiyatlarında Mihr u Mah ve Mihr u Müşteri mesnevileri*, in *Belleten*, xlvii (1985), 1151-89. İ. E. Erünsal, *The life and works of Tâcî-zâde Caʿfer Çelebi, with a critical edition of his Dîvân*, Istanbul 1983; M. N. Onur, *Ak-Şemseddin-zâde Hamdullah Hamdî'nin Yûsuf ve Züleyhâ mesnevisindeki önemli motifler*, in *Türk Kültürü*, xxii (1984), 651-58; M. Köhbach, *Die Parabel vom gefundenen Dirhem in der frühen anatolischen Versepik*, in *Türk Edebiyatı Dergisi*, xii (1981-2), 499-506; S. Aktaş, *Roman olarak Hüsn u Aşk*, in *Türk Dünyası Araştırmaları*, xxvii (1983), 94-108.

(B. Flemming)

4. In Urdu.

The development of the Urdu *mat͟hnawī* falls broadly into three periods: early, middle and modern. The early period is associated mainly with the Dakkanī phase of Urdu literature. In Dakkanī verse, the *mat͟hnawī* constitutes the most popular form, and is represented by a large output of both religious and secular poems. Many of these are long pieces comprising several thousand couplets. Often they are translated or adapted from Persian sources, but not a few of them are works of an original character.

The growth of the early *mat͟hnawī* reached its most productive stage in the 10th/16th and 11th/17th centuries with the emergence of Bīd͟jāpūr and Golkonḍa as the main centres of Dakkanī literature. Hitherto, the *mat͟hnawī*s were more concerned with religious subjects, but subsequently stories of love and heroism began to find increasing prominence in their content. In Bīd͟jāpūr, under the enlightened patronage of the ʿĀdil S͟hāhī dynasty (895-1097/1490-1686 [*q.v.*]), there flourished many important poets who are known exclusively for their *mat͟hnawī*s. One of them was Mīrzā Muḥammad Muḳīmī (d. *ca.* 1075/1665), author of *Čandarbadan u Mahyār*, which was the first *mat͟hnawī* with a purely literary motif. Its subject deals with a contemporary incident involving the tragic love of a Muslim merchant, Mahyār, for Čandarbadan, daughter of a Hindu rajah. Another poet living at the same time was Kamāl K͟hān Rustamī, who composed in 1059/1649 the first artistic work of epic poetry in Urdu, the *mat͟hnawī K͟hāwar-nāma* ("The book of the East"). This poem, written in imitation of Ibn Ḥusām's Persian epic of the same name, follows the model of *Dāstān-i Amīr Ḥamza*, and also borrows some topics from Firdawsī's *S͟hāh-nāma*. At the court of ʿAlī ʿĀdil S͟hāh II (1068-83/1656-73) was the poet laureate Muḥammad Nuṣrat Nuṣratī (d. 1095/1684), who has left behind several *mat͟hnawī*s, the most famous being the *Gul͟shan-i ʿis͟hḳ* ("The rose-garden of love"). This poem, written in 1067/1657, is a fairy tale describing the love between prince Manohar and princess Madhumāltī. His other notable *mat͟hnawī* is the long historical epic *ʿAlī-nāma* ("The book of ʿAlī"), which contains a narrative of the wars fought by ʿAlī ʿĀdil S͟hāh with the Mug͟hals and the Marāṭhās. He also composed the historical *mat͟hnawī Taʾrīk͟h-i Iskandarī* ("The history of Iskandar"), a poem dealing with events during the reign of ʿAlī ʿĀdil S͟hāh's son and successor, Sikandar (1083-97/1673-86). Other commonly known *mat͟hnawī*s produced by ʿĀdil S͟hāhî poets include *Bahrām u Bāno Ḥusn*, a love poem begun in about 1029/1620 by Amīn and completed in 1049/1639 by Dawlat; *Ḳiṣṣa-yi bēnaẓīr* ("The incomparable story"), written by Ṣanʿatī in 1054/1644 to describe the exploits attributed to Abū Tamīm Anṣārī, a companion of the Prophet Muḥammad; the poetical adaptation of Amīr K͟husraw's *mat͟hnawī Has͟ht bihis͟ht*, executed by Malik K͟hus͟hnūd in about 1056/1646; and *Yūsuf u Zulayk͟hā*, composed in 1098/1687 by the last major poet of the ʿĀdil S͟hāhī era, Sayyid Mīrān Hās͟himī (d. 1108/1697).

Rivalling Bīd͟jāpūr in the patronage of literature and literary men was the Ḳuṭb S͟hāhī dynasty (918-1098/1512-1687 [*q.v.*]) of Golkonḍa. Several of its rulers were poets themselves, and their generous support of literary activities provided encouragement to the development of Dakkanī verse. Many outstanding *mat͟hnawī*s were written during this time. In 1018/1609 Mullā Wad͟jhī, poet laureate of Muḥammad Ḳulī Ḳuṭb S͟hāh (988-1020/1580-1611), composed a *mat͟hnawī* entitled *Ḳuṭb u Mus͟htarī* ("Polar Star and Jupiter"), which allegedly describes the love affair of his patron with a famous courtesan of the day. In 1034/1625 the most outstanding poet of ʿAbd Allāh Ḳuṭb S͟hāh's reign (1034-83/1625-72), G͟hawwāṣī, composed for the ruler the *mat͟hnawī Sayf al-Mulūk wa Badīʿ al-D͟jamāl*, which took its theme from a story of the *Arabian Nights*. Another *mat͟hnawī*, the *Ṭūṭī-nāma* ("The book of the parrot"), which he wrote in 1050/1640, was a poetical rendering of Ḍiyāʾ al-Dīn Nak͟hs͟habī's earlier Persian adaptation of the same name. G͟hawwāṣī's contemporary, Maẓhar al-Dīn Ibn Nis͟hāṭī, was the author of the *mat͟hnawī Phūlban* ("The flower garden"), which he completed in 1065/1655 and dedicated to ʿAbd Allāh Ḳuṭb S͟hāh. Adapted freely from a lost Persian work, *Basātīn* ("Gardens"), written under Muḥammad S͟hāh II Tug͟hluḳ (725-52/1325-51), Ibn Nis͟hāṭī's *mat͟hnawī* provides a picture of the life in Deccan in the late 11th/17th century, and is interesting both from a literary as well as historical point of view. During the reign of Abu 'l-Ḥasan Tānā S͟hāh (1085-98/1674-87), who was the last ruler of the Ḳuṭb S͟hāhī dynasty, two important *mat͟hnawī*s were written. The first was *Bahrām u Gulandām*, composed in 1081/1670 by Ṭabʿī in imitation of Niẓāmī's *Haft Paykar*, and the second was *Riḍwān S͟hāh u Rūḥafzā*, a romance by Fāʾiz written in 1094/1683 and based upon a Persian prose tale describing the love between the Chinese prince Riḍwān and the princess of the d͟jinns.

The middle period of the Urdu *mat͟hnawī* may be said to begin from the early 12th/18th century, when the language of Urdu poetry acquired an idiom distinct from the Dakkanī. This period, known also for the impetus received in it by the *g͟hazal* [*q.v.*], witnessed the appearance of some excellent *mat͟hnawī*s which have left their mark on Urdu literature. Heroic *mat͟hnawī*s lost favour during this period, but romantic *mat͟hnawī*s continued to prosper and gained a richness in their diction and approach. Of particular significance was the growth of *mat͟hnawī*s dealing with love themes based upon personal experience.

The poem *Būstān-i k͟hayāl* ("The garden of imagination") must be regarded as the first important *mat͟hnawī* of the middle period. Written in 1160/1747 by Sirād͟j al-Dīn (1126-76/1714-63) of Awrangābād, it describes a love episode in the life of the poet. The chief distinction of the poem lies in its intimate note and, especially, in its refined language which almost verges on the modern idiom. Personal love found an outspoken exponent in Mīr At͟har (d. 1208/1794), best known for his *mat͟hnawī K͟hʷāb u k͟hayāl* ("Dream and imagination"), which represents a plaint by the poet suffering the loss of his mistress. The famous poet Muḥammad Taḳī Mīr (1136-1225/1724-1810 [*q.v.*]), who excelled in the *g͟hazal*, is equally noted for his *mat͟hnawī*s, some of which express the disappointment of love, and are regarded as autobiographical by the critics. The *mathnawīs* of Muḥammad Muʾmin Khān Muʾmin (1215-67/1800-51), like those of Mīr, provide a record of the poet's emotional involvements, whether real or imaginary, and have won recognition from literary authorities.

In the poetic creations of Nawwāb Mīrzā Shawḳ (1197-1288/1783-1871), whose real name was Taṣadduḳ Ḥusayn, the Urdu romantic *mathnawī* with a personal motif reached its maturity. Shawḳ, who devoted his talents almost exclusively to the writing of *mathnawīs*, is the author of three works in that genre, namely *Farīb-i ʿishḳ* ("The deception of love"), *Bahār-i ʿishḳ* ("The spring of love") and *Zahr-i ʿishḳ* ("The poison of love"). The last-named poem, written probably in about 1860, is Shawḳ's masterpiece, and indeed stands out as one of the great narrative pieces of Urdu literature. Both in diction as well as theme it displays a level of realism seldom attained by any other Urdu *mathnawī*.

Among the writers of non-personal romantic *mathnawīs*, Mīr Ghulām Ḥasan (d. 1200/1786), generally known as Mīr Ḥasan, holds a distinguished position. He is the author of one dozen known *mathnawīs* of varying length. His reputation rests chiefly on his long *mathnawī Siḥr al-bayān* ("The magic of eloquence"), which was finished in 1199/1784-5, and comprises approximately 2,500 couplets. It is a fairy tale of the conventional type containing a description of the love between prince Bēnaẓīr and princess Badr-i Munīr. Besides its literary qualities, such as simple and elegant language, faithful interpretation of emotions, effective portrayal of nature and convincing characterisation, it also provides details regarding such contemporary topics as people's dress, social etiquette, customs and ceremonies.

Sharing honours with Mīr Ḥasan's *Siḥr al-bayān* is the poem *Gulzār-i Nasīm* ("The rose-garden of Nasīm") written in 1838 by Paṇḍit Dayā Shankar Nasīm (1811-43). This work has left a marked impact on contemporary and later poets, as seen from the *mathnawīs* composed after its example. Its central plot revolves around the adventures of prince Tādj al-Mulūk, whose search takes him into a fairyland where he expects to find the magical flower needed to cure his father's blindness. The poem has been praised for its terse description, its flights of fancy, and its choice of similes, words and idioms.

The Urdu *mathnawī* in its modern phase dates from the latter part of the 19th century, and its origin is linked with the campaign initiated at that time to achieve literary reforms. The reformers, dissatisfied with the *ghazal*, advocated the adoption of the *naẓm* or "thematic poem" patterned after Western models. The *mathnawī*, with its tradition of continuous themes and a comparatively less inhibiting rhyme scheme, provided a ready-made form for the *naẓm*, and it came to be employed by the reformers as an effective literary instrument to popularise the new trends in Urdu poetry.

The predominant theme of the modern Urdu *mathnawī* is social. As such, it differs from the earlier *mathnawī* which was identified with romantic subjects. In other respects also, it evokes differences from older models. Lengthy *mathnawīs* like those composed in the past are now extremely rare, and the restriction imposed by custom on the type of metres to be employed by the *mathnawī* is no longer observed.

It was the poet Alṭāf Ḥusayn Ḥālī (1837-1914 [*q.v.*]) who critically examined the role of the *mathnawī* in Urdu poetry and laid the foundation for its future development. He pointed out that the *mathnawī* provided a medium best suited for expressing continuous themes. The *mathnawīs* he wrote reflect his social and reformist leanings. Conspicuous among them are *Ḥubb-i waṭan* ("Patriotism"), *Taʿaṣṣub u inṣāf* ("Bigotry and justice") and *Munādjāt-i bēwa* ("The widow's prayer"), which appeared respectively in 1874, 1882 and 1884.

Following the pioneering efforts of Ḥālī, the *mathnawī* acquired a new dimension. It was used by Muḥammad Ismāʿīl Mēraṭhī (1844-1917) for his short, descriptive poems which, written in a simple language and dealing with everyday subjects, represent the first successful attempts in Urdu to compose children's poetry. Aḥmad ʿAlī Shawḳ Ḳidwāʾī (1853-1925) gave special attention to *mathnawīs*, his most famous work being the *ʿĀlam-i khayāl* ("The world of imagination"), a sentimental poem expressing the feelings of a lonely woman whose husband has gone on a journey. Shawḳ's contemporary Sayyid ʿAlī Muḥammad Shād ʿAẓīmābādī (1846-1927) was an avid *mathnawī* writer displaying a maturity of style. The greatest Urdu poet of the 20th century, Muḥammad Iḳbāl (1877-1938 [*q.v.*]) adopted the *mathnawī* for many of his poems, of which the *Sāḳī-nāma* ("The book of the cup-bearer") is undoubtedly one of the great masterpieces of Urdu literature. Mention must also be made of Ḥafīẓ Djalandharī's (1903-82) *mathnawī*-style narrative *Shāh-nāma-yi Islām*, which appeared in four volumes from 1929 to 1947, and represents a lengthy attempt to record the history of Islam in a versified form.

Bibliography: I. Works on literary history and criticism: Alṭāf Ḥusayn Ḥālī, *Muḳaddama-yi shiʿr u shāʿirī*, ed. Waḥīd Ḳurayshī, Lahore 1953; Muḥammad Ḥusayn Āzād, *Āb-i ḥayāt*, repr. Lahore 1967; Garcin de Tassy, *Histoire de la littérature Hindoue et Hindoustani*, 3 vols., Paris 1870-1; R. B. Saksena, *A history of Urdu literature*, repr. Lahore 1975; T. G. Bailey, *A history of Urdu literature*, Calcutta 1932; ʿAbd al-Salām Nadwī, *Shiʿr al-Hind*, 2 vols., Aʿẓamgaṛh 1939; A. Bausani, *Storia della letteratura de Pakistan*, Milan 1958; Muhammad Sadiq, *A history of Urdu literature*, London 1964; Annemarie Schimmel, *Classical Urdu literature from the beginning to Iqbāl*, Wiesbaden 1975; Naṣīr al-Dīn Hāshimī, *Dakkan mēṇ Urdū*, repr. Lakhnaw 1963; Muḥyī al-Dīn Ḳādirī Zor, *Dakkanī adab kī taʾrīkh*, repr. Karachi 1960; ʿAbd al-Ḳādir Sarwarī, *Urdū mathnawī kā irtiḳā*, repr. Karachi 1966; S. M. ʿAḳīl, *Urdū mathnawī kā irtiḳā*, Allahabad 1965; Giyān Čand Djayn, *Urdū mathnawī shimālī Hind mēṇ*, ʿAlīgaṛh 1969; Farmān Fatḥpūrī, *Urdū kī manẓūm dāstānēṇ*, Karachi 1971; Khushḥāl Zaydī, *Urdū mathnawī kā khāka*, Dihlī 1978.

II. Poetical works: *Ḳiṣṣa-yi Čandarbadan wa Mahyār*, ed. Muḥammad Akbar al-Dīn Ṣiddīḳī, Hyderabad 1956; Rustamī, *Khāwar-nāma*, Karachi 1968; Nuṣratī, *Gulshan-i ʿishḳ*, ed. ʿAbd al-Ḥaḳḳ, Karachi 1952; idem, *Dīwān-i Nuṣratī*, ed. Djamīl Djālibī, Lahore 1972; idem, *ʿAlī-nāma*, IO ms. P. 834; Ṣanʿatī, *Ḳiṣṣa-yi Bēnaẓīr*, ed. ʿAbd al-Ḳādir Sarwarī, Hyderabad 1938; Wadjhī, *Ḳuṭb u Mushtarī*, ed. ʿAbd al-Ḥaḳḳ, Karachi 1953; Ghawwāṣī, *Sayf al-Mulūk wa Badīʿ al-Djamāl*, ed. Mīr Saʿādat ʿAlī Riḍwī, Hyderabad 1938; idem, *Ṭūṭī-nāma*, ed Mīr Saʿādat ʿAlī Riḍwī, Hyderabad 1939; Ibn Nishāṭī, *Phūlban*, ed. ʿAbd al-Ḳādir Sarwarī, Hyderabad 1938; Fāʾiz, *Riḍwān Shāh u Rūḥafzā*, ed. Sayyid Muḥammad, Hyderabad 1956; Sirādj al-Dīn Awrangābādī, *Būstān-i khayāl*, ed. ʿAbd al-Ḳādir Sarwarī, repr. Hyderabad 1969; Mīr Athar, *Khʷāb u khayāl*, ed. ʿAbd al-Ḥaḳḳ,

Karachi 1950; Muḥammad Taḳī Mīr, *Kulliyyāt-i Mīr*, ii, ed. Masīḥ al-Zamān, Allahabad 1972; Muḥammad Muʾmin Khān Muʾmin, *Kulliyyāt-i Muʾmin*, ii, Lahore 1964; *Kulliyyāt-i Nawwāb Mirzā Shawḳ Lakhnawī*, ed. Shāh ʿAbd al-Salām, Lakhnaw 1978; Mīr Ḥasan Dihlawī, *Mathnawiyāt-i Ḥasan*, i, ed. Waḥīd Ḳurayshī, Lahore 1966; idem, *Mathnawī siḥr al-bayān*, ed. Waḥīd Ḳurayshī, Lahore 1966; Dayā Shankar Nasīm, *Mathnawī gulzār-i Nasīm*, ed. Amīr Ḥasan Nūrānī, Dihlī 1965; Alṭāf Ḥusayn Ḥālī, *Kulliyyāt-i naẓm-i Ḥālī*, 2 vols., ed. Iftikhār Aḥmad Ṣiddīḳī, Lahore 1968-70; Shawḳ Ḳidwāʾī, *ʿĀlam-i khayāl*, Lakhnaw 1918; Sayfī Prēmī (Khalīl al-Raḥmān), *Ḥayāt-i Ismāʿīl*, Dihlī 1976; *Shād ʿAẓīmābādī kī mathnawiyāṅ*, ed. Naḳī Aḥmad Irshād, Dihlī 1971; Muḥammad Iḳbāl, *Kulliyyāt-i Iḳbāl* (Urdū), Lahore 1973; Ḥafīẓ Djalandharī, *Shāh-nāma-yi Islām*, 4 vols., Djalandhar 1929-47.

(Munibur Rahman)

MATHURĀ (earlier English spelling, now discarded, "Muttra"), an Indian city lying between Dihlī and Āgrā, of considerable antiquity and of high reputation in India as a place of high religious sanctity for Hindūs and, formerly, for Djayns and Buddhists also; it was already a place of some renown when it became the eastern of the two Kushāna capitals.

It is, surprisingly, not mentioned in the *Ḥudūd al-ʿālam*, and only incidentally by al-Bīrūnī, although for Ptolemy it had been Μόδουρα τῶν Θηῶν. Its great reputation led to its being plundered by Maḥmūd of Ghazna in 408/1018 and by many later Muslim rulers, more in an excess of iconoclastic zeal than in a settlement of the district; notably by Sikandar Lōdī *ca.* 905/1500, who is reported to have destroyed many idols and to have prohibited head-shaving and ritual bathing. Some temples were allowed to be built in the tolerant reign of Akbar (the temple of Govind Dēva at Brindāban in the Mathurā district, built by Mān Singh [*q.v.*], even shows architectural borrowings from north Indian Muslim art); but Shāhdjahān in 1046/1636-7 appointed a governor to "extirpate idolatry", Awrangzīb some thirty years later destroyed its finest temple and built a mosque on top of it, and Aḥmad Shāh Durrānī in 1170/1757 not only plundered the temples but butchered a large group of pilgrims. Otherwise, it saw little of Islam, the Mēwātīs, in whose territories it lay [see MEWĀT] not being renowned for their orthodoxy. A Djāmiʿ mosque, built in 1071/1660-1 (inscr. chronogram) by ʿAbd al-Nabī, a governor under Awrangzīb, is an excellent building for its period, with fine inlay in encaustic tilework, four tall *mīnārs*, and two side pavilions with the curved-cornice "Bengali" roof flanking the courtyard which stands 4 m. above road level; Awrangzīb's own mosque is rather effete.

Bibliography: F. S. Growse, *Mathura: a district memoir*, Benares 1874 and many subsequent reprints, is highly praised but barely acknowledges the presence of Muslims. The mosque has not been adequately published. (R. F. Chisholm's account of "Tiroomal Naik's palace, Madura", listed in Creswell, *Bibliography*, s.v. Mathura, is not at Mathura at all but at Madurai, the former capital of the Madura sultanate = Maʿbar [*q.v.*].)

(J. Burton-Page)

AL-**MAṬLAʿ** (A.), the rising point of a celestial body, usually a star, on the local horizon. This concept was important in Islamic folk astronomy [see ANWĀʾ and MANĀZIL on some aspects of this tradition], as distinct from mathematical astronomy [see ʿILM AL-HAYʾA], because it was by the risings and settings of the sun and stars that the *ḳibla* [*q.v.*] or direction of Mecca was usually determined in popular practice. The terms used for the rising and setting points of the sun were usually *mashriḳ* and *maghrib*, *maṭlaʿ* being generally reserved for stars. The directions of sunrise at the equinoxes and solstices were usually associated with the corresponding zodiacal signs [see MINṬAḲA] or seasons, thus e.g. *mashriḳ al-djady* and *mashriḳ al-shitāʾ* both refer to winter sunrise, since the sun enters the sign of Capricorn at midwinter.

In pre-Islamic Arabian folklore, the directions of the winds (see RĪḤ) were defined in terms of astronomical risings and settings (see Fig. 1) and one such wind scheme is associated with the Kaʿba itself (see Fig. 2). These wind schemes are recorded in later Arabic treatises on lexicography, folk astronomy, cosmography, as well as in encyclopaedias and various legal treatises on the *ḳibla*. The major axis of the rectangular base of the Kaʿba points towards *maṭlaʿ Suhayl*, the rising point of Canopus, and the minor axis roughly towards *mashriḳ al-ṣayf*, the rising point of the sun at midsummer. The later Islamic attempts to define the *ḳibla* for different localities in terms of astronomical risings and settings stem from the fact that these localities were associated with specific segments of the perimeter of the Kaʿba, and the *ḳibla*s adopted were the same as the astronomical directions which one would be facing when standing directly in front of the appropriate part of the Kaʿba [see MAKKA iv].

The term *maṭlaʿ* was also used to denote the "time of rising" in the expression *maṭlaʿ al-fadjr*, daybreak or the beginning of morning twilight.

Bibliography: That given in the article ḲIBLA is to be supplemented with the information con-

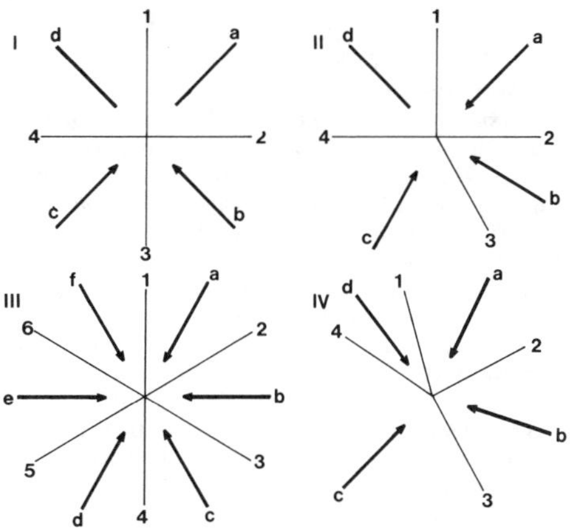

Fig. 1. Four early Arabian wind schemes defined in terms of astronomical risings and settings and attributed to early Muslim authorities.

I Khālid b. Ṣafwān. Limits of winds: 1-4 cardinal directions (defined in terms of the Pole Star and sunrise and sunset at the equinoxes); names of the winds: a *ṣabā*, b *djanūb*, c *dabūr*, d *shamāl*.

II ʿAlī b. Abī Ṭālib. Limits: 1, 2, 4 cardinal directions; names: as in I.

III Ibn Djandab. Limits: 1 north, 2 summer sunrise, 3 winter sunrise, 4 south, 5 winter sunset, 6 summer sunset; names: a *nakhbāʾ*, b *ṣabā* or *ḳabūl*, c *maḥwa*, d *djanūb*, e *dabūr*, f *shamāl*.

IV Ibn al-Aʿrābī. Limits: 1 setting (or rising ?) of the Banāt Naʿsh, 2 rising of the Pleiades, 3 rising of Canopus, 4 setting of Vega; names: as in I.

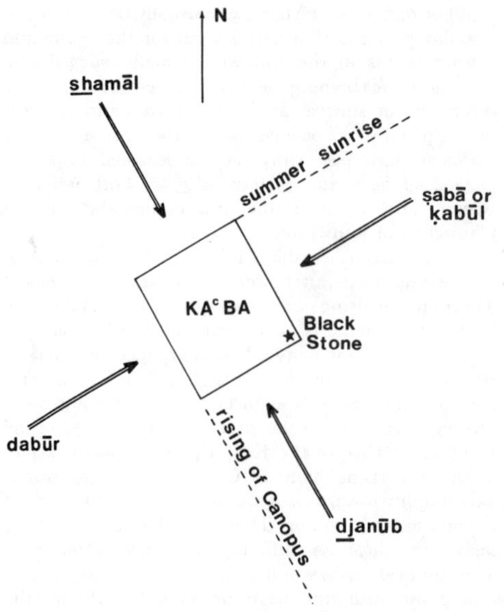

Fig. 2. The most popular early Arabian wind scheme, in which the four winds strike the walls of the Kaᶜba head-on. The rectangular base of the Kaᶜba points in astronomically significant directions, and so the limits of the four winds are likewise astronomically defined. The rising of Canopus and the solstitial risings and settings of the sun were widely used for finding the *ḳibla* in popular practice, in order to ensure that one would be "facing" a particular wall of the Kaᶜba, that is, standing in a direction "parallel" to the appropriate axis of the Kaᶜba.

tained in D. A. King, *Astronomical alignments in medieval religious architecture*, in *Annals of the New York Academy of Sciences*, ccclxxxv (1982), 303-12, and *The sacred geography of Islam*, in *Islamic Art*, iii (to appear); G. S. Hawkins and King, *On the orientation of the Kaᶜba*, in *Jnal. for the History of Astronomy*, xiii (1982), 102-9. For a survey of the whole problem, see King, *The world about the Kaᶜba: a study of the sacred direction in Islam* (forthcoming); summaries are given in *Proceedings of the Second International Qurʾān Conference, New Delhi, 1982* and *Interdisciplinary Science Reviews*, ix (1984), pp. 315-328. See also MAṬĀLIᶜ. (D. A. KING)

MAṬMĀṬA, name of a large Berber people mentioned as early as the middle of the 3rd/9th century in the geographical work of Ibn K̲h̲urradād̲h̲bih as being among the thirty most important Berber tribes of this period. According to the majority of Berber genealogists cited by Ibn K̲h̲aldūn (including Sābiḳ al-Maṭmāṭī), the Maṭmāṭa, who were brothers of the Maṭg̲h̲ara, Ṣadīna, Malzūza, Madyūna and Lamāya, belonged to the great Berber family of the Butr; they constituted, with the above-mentioned tribes, the family of Fāṭin, son of Tamzīt. However, some other genealogists mentioned by Ibn K̲h̲aldūn hold that the Maṭmāṭa belonged, along with the Barg̲h̲awāṭa and Azdād̲j̲a, to the Berber stock of Barānis (Brānes). There is also another genealogy of the Maṭmāṭa, according to which this tribe is regarded as belonging, along with the Barg̲h̲awāṭa and Azdād̲j̲a, to the great Berber family of the Zanāta, being descended from D̲j̲ānā, ancestor of the Zanāta.

1. Tunisia. It seems that the original homeland of the Maṭmāṭa, a people who were early converts to Islam and who adopted, around the middle of the 2nd/8th century the beliefs of the Ibāḍī sect, was the land situated in the south-east of Tunisia and more exactly to the west and south of the town of Gabès, ancient Tacapae, Ḳābis of the mediaeval Arab geographers. They were called by this name by around 196/811, at the time when the Ibāḍī *imām* of Tāhart ᶜAbd al-Wahhāb b. ᶜAbd al-Raḥmān b. Rustam sent, on the occasion of his siege of the town of Tripoli, the Ibāḍī general Ḳaṭᶜān b. Salma al-Zawāg̲h̲ī to Ḳābis with orders to besiege it. We owe this information to the Ibāḍī historian Abu 'l-ᶜAbbās al-S̲h̲ammāk̲h̲ī (928/1522), who used in his work several much older sources. In speaking of Ḳaṭᶜān b. Salma (in another passage of al-S̲h̲ammāk̲h̲ī's work this person is called Salma b. Ḳaṭfa), who was appointed governor of Ḳābis in this period by the *imām* ᶜAbd al-Wahhāb, the Ibāḍī historian in question adds that under this governor's régime, the Berber tribes of the Maṭmāṭa, Zanzafa, Dammar, Zawāg̲h̲a and others were still living outside Gabès. It seems that the Maṭmāṭa in this period were already occupying the mountainous country called D̲j̲abal Maṭmāṭa, situated about 30 or 40 km. south of Gabès. This country was also at one time called D̲j̲abal Lawāta, owing to the Lawātī population which lived there with the Maṭmāṭa. The survivors of the Maṭmāṭa and Lawāta still live there today. Apart from this area, the Maṭmāṭa also inhabited, in times gone by, the town of al-Ḥāmma (ancient Aquae Tacapitanae), situated 23 km. to the west of Gabès. According to Ibn K̲h̲aldūn's *Histoire des Berbères*, al-Ḥāmma was founded by the Maṭmāṭa. According to the *Kitāb al-Istibṣār* of *ca.* 587/1191, al-Ḥāmma was a very ancient town inhabited by the Maṭmāṭa. The Tunisian scholar of the 7th-8th/13th-14th century al-Tid̲j̲ānī mentions, in his account of a journey from Tunis to Tripoli, this place by the name of Ḥāmmat Maṭmāṭa, although in the view of this scholar, the Maṭmāṭa may already have left, ceding the place to the Zanāta who were divided into three groups: the Banū Tūd̲j̲īn, Banū Wartad̲j̲īn and Awlād Yūsuf.

The later history of the Tunisian Maṭmāṭa (who, apparently having adopted in the 4th/10th century the beliefs of the Ibāḍī sub-sect of the Nukkāriyya [*q.v.*], as had their neighbours the Banū Dammar, established in the south of the area occupied by the Maṭmāṭa in the D̲j̲abal Dammar) is little known. It seems that the Maṭmāṭa living in the D̲j̲abal of this name recognised the authority of the last representative of the Almoravid family of the Banū G̲h̲āniya, Yaḥyā, who, having his seat and base of operations in the Bilād al-D̲j̲arīd, extended his power, around 1200 A.D., over the whole of Ifrīḳiya. In any case, the *sayyid* Abū Isḥāḳ who pursued, in 603/1207, in the name of his brother the Almohad caliph al-Nāṣir, the Almoravid rebels in Ifrīḳiya, subdued the country situated behind Tripoli and chastised, according to Ibn K̲h̲aldūn, "the Banū Dammar, the Maṭmāṭa and the Nafūsa", the inhabitants at that time of the vast mountainous crescent which stretches from Gabès to ancient Leptis Magna, on the edge of the plain of D̲j̲efāra (D̲j̲effāra). Under the domination of the Turks, the inhabitants of the D̲j̲abal Maṭmāṭa and the D̲j̲abal Dammar who, until this period, had remained practically independent and had not recognised the authority of the sovereigns of Ifrīḳiya, refused to pay taxes. The Turkish bey of Tunisia, Muḥammad Bey (1631-63 A.D.), had a fort built in the Maṭmāṭa Mts. in order to contain the rebels. We owe this information to the Tunisian historian Ibn Abī Dīnār, who dealt with this event in *al-Muʾnis fī ak̲h̲bār Ifrīḳiya wa-*

Tūnis, probably written in 1092/1681 or 1100/1698. In the 18th and the first part of the 19th century, in the reign of the Ḥusaynid dynasty (from 1705), there took place various rebellions by Berber and Arab tribes in south-east Tunisia, whose instigators sought refuge in the Maṭmāṭa Mts.

The survivors of the Maṭmāṭa, partially Arabised, still live in their old homeland in south-east Tunisia.

2. Algeria. It seems that at an unknown period, probably in the 2nd/8th century, or perhaps even before this date, one or several important clans of the Maṭmāṭa detached themselves from the main body of this people inhabiting south-east Tunisia and may have come to settle in western Algeria and Morocco. If it is a case of some Maṭmāṭa elements being settled in western Algeria, it is necessary to mention firstly a clan which was settled on the plateaux of Sersū to the north-east of Mindās and to the north of the town of Tāhart and in the Ouarsénis Mts. According to Ibn Khaldūn, these Maṭmāṭa adopted the beliefs of the Ibāḍīs at a time when the Khāridjī doctrine was widespread among the Berbers, i.e. around the middle of the 2nd/8th century. Besides, it is not impossible that the Maṭmāṭa of the Tāhart district may have been settled in this area in the time of Abu 'l-Khaṭṭāb, Ibāḍī *imām* of Tripoli (from 140/757-8), who also seized al-Ḳayrawān and the whole of Ifrīḳiya. This man entrusted the government of al-Ḳayrawān to ᶜAbd al-Raḥmān b. Rustam. After the defeat of the Ibāḍi Berber army of Abu 'l-Khaṭṭāb by the ᶜAbbāsid general Muḥammad b. al-Ashᶜath al-Khuzāᶜī in 144/761-2, ᶜAbd al-Raḥmān b. Rustam then hastened, if we are to believe Ibn Khaldūn, to evacuate al-Ḳayrawān and to take his sons and household to the Ibāḍī Berbers of the central Maghrib. Having reached his old friends and allies the Lamāya, he rallied them to his side and decided to found the town of Tāhart, future capital of the Rustamid imāmate. It is not impossible that a party of the Maṭmāṭa who were neighbours of the Lamāya in south-east Tunisia, original homeland of the first of these peoples, may already have been in the vicinity of the future Tāhart around 144/761-2. In any case, the Maṭmāṭa belonged by the reign of the Rustamid *imām* Aflaḥ b. ᶜAbd al-Wahhāb b. ᶜAbd al-Raḥmān b. Rustam (*ca.* 308-58/823-71) to the rich and powerful Ibāḍī Berber tribes of the Tāhart district. We owe this information to Ibn Ṣaghīr, historian of this town and of the Rustamid dynasty, who wrote his chronicle *ca.* 290/902-3. After the fall of the Rustamid imāmate, the Maṭmāṭa of the Tāhart district were forced (*ca.* 298/910) to abandon, in the words of Ibn Khaldūn, "for ever" Ibāḍī beliefs and to embrace Shīᶜī doctrines. To judge by the Arabic sources, the Maṭmāṭa later rejected Shīᶜī doctrines and became Sunnīs.

Some groups of the Maṭmāṭa, having come to settle in the central Maghrib, occupied the plateaux of Sersū in the neighbourhood of Tāhart, in the north-east of the Mindās area, which was inhabited in the first place by a clan of the large Berber tribe of the Hawwāra. Later, these Maṭmāṭa came to settle in the Mindās area, having driven out the Hawwāra in question. Then the Maṭmāṭa were expelled from the plateaux of Sersū by the Zanāta tribe of Banū Tūdjin, and were forced to seek refuge in the mountainous massif of Wānsharīs (present day Ouarsénis), where al-Bakrī mentions them in the 5th/11th century, al-Idrīsī in the 6th/12th century and Ibn Khaldūn in the 8th/14th century.

We know also, thanks to al-Yaᶜḳūbī, the name of another clan of Maṭmāṭa living, around the end of the 3rd/9th and beginning of the 4th/10th century, in the central Maghrib. One should mention here a clan of this tribe living to the west of Ouarsénis and Sersū and to the west of the town of Yalal (Hilil of our maps) under the domination of the dynasty descended from Muḥammad b. Sulaymān b. ᶜAbd Allāh b. al-Ḥasan b. al-Ḥasan, related to the Idrīsids of Morocco, who ruled in this period in Tlemcen and the district around it. This clan of the Maṭmāṭa had nothing in common with the Maṭmāṭa of Ouarsénis, who were Ibāḍīs and who recognised the suzerainty of the Rustamid *imāms* of Tāhart. One of the clans of the Maṭmāṭa of Tlemcen was in control of the town of Ayzradj (?) situated near the western fringes of Tlemcen, probably in the area of the modern Algero-Moroccan frontier.

The history of the Maṭmāṭa of the Tāhart district, after the fall of the Rustamid imāmate and the forced conversion of this clan to Shīᶜī beliefs at the beginning of the 4th/10th century, is little known to us. We know, however, that they took an active part in the war which broke out between the Zīrid princes Ḥammād b. Buluggīn (405-19/1015-28) and Bādīs b. al-Manṣūr (396-406/996-1016), Ibn Khaldūn even mentions a famous *amīr* of the Maṭmāṭa of the Tāhart district; he was called Zīrī and lived towards the end of the 4th/10th century and beginning of the 5th/11th; defeated by the Ṣanhādja Zīrids, he was forced to go to Spain.

The survivors of the powerful Maṭmāṭī clan of the Tāhart district were still living in this area in the 19th century. They were living to the north of the plateau of Sersū, in Thaza (Tāza) and the surrounding district.

3. Morocco. Some advanced groups of the Maṭmāṭa pressed on, probably a little before the 4th/10th century, as far as Morocco. A group of this people settled in the territory of Nukūr, in the eastern Rīf, where they are mentioned by al-Bakrī in the 5th/11th century. Al-Yaᶜḳūbī (3rd/9th century) mentions also the clans of Maṭmāṭa settled in the town of Fālūsen (?) situated to the east of the town of Nukūr. Another clan of the Maṭmāṭa lived on the upper course of Wadi Moulouya, in an area called Maṭmāṭa Amaskūr, to the south of Fās. It is mentioned by al-Bakrī and by Ibn Khaldūn. The latter author also speaks of a mountain called Maṭmāṭa situated between Fās and Sefrou (Ṣufrūy). One should add that there were also some Maṭmāṭa between Fās and Tāza; furthermore, a place in this area still bears the name Maṭmāṭa.

Finally, there was also a group of Maṭmāṭa settled in the far west of Morocco, in the region called Tāmasnā, where there existed in the Middle Ages a kingdom founded by the anti-Muslim Berber tribe of Barghawāṭa [*q.v.*]. The Maṭmāṭa of Tāmasnā formed part of the confederation of Barghawāṭa and professed the faith of this tribe. We know of it through the account of Zammūr, sent by the Barghawāṭa to the caliph of Cordova in 352/963, which is cited in the *Kitāb al-Masālik wa 'l-mamālik* of al-Bakrī. Zammūr gives in this account two lists of Berber tribes of Tāmasnā under the suzerainty of the Barghawāṭa empire, that is, those who profess the Barghawāṭī faith and the Muslims. The Maṭmāṭa of Tāmasnā are mentioned in the first of these lists. The history of this clan of the Maṭmāṭa is entirely unknown to us; however, we know, thanks to al-Idrīsī, that it still existed in the 6th/12th century.

4. Spain. There were also some Maṭmāṭa groups among the Berber tribes who went across to Spain at different periods. We know this from Ibn Khaldūn, who gives us some details in his *Histoire des Berbères*. We have already mentioned a famous Maṭmāṭi *amīr* of

the central Maghrib called Zīrī, who lived towards the end of the 4th/10th century and beginning of the 5th/11th century; this *amīr* was originally chief of the Maṭmāṭa of the Wānsharīsh (Ouarsénis) plateaux, as well as of Ghazūl, a mountain dominating the country around Tāhart. Defeated by the Ṣanhādja, he crossed into Spain, where he went to see the powerful Umayyad *wazīr* al-Manṣūr b. Abī ʿĀmir [*q.v.*], who received him with alacrity and enrolled him among the Berber *amīrs* admitted to his service. It is very likely that Zīrī was accompanied, on his journey to Spain, by members of his household and perhaps by several Maṭmāṭī warriors; he soon became one of the most distinguished officers in al-Manṣūr's Berber corps. After the latter's death in 392/1002, his sons al-Muẓaffar (d. in 398/1008) and ʿAbd al-Raḥmān continued to treat Zīrī with the same favour as their father. However, from the time of the revolt of the Umayyad Muḥammad II b. Hishām b. ʿAbd al-Djabbār (399-400/1008-10), Zīrī and all the other Berber *amīrs* and officers, recognising the lack of ability in their chiefs, went over to the side of Muḥammad b. Hishām b. ʿAbd al-Djabbār, who had become caliph with the title of al-Mahdī. The end of Zīrī is unknown to us. According to Ibn Khaldūn, he stayed in the service of al-Mahdī until the great revolt of the Berbers in Spain. The year of his death is unknown.

Another great Maṭmāṭī figure, probably originally from Wānsharīsh and Ghazūl and who crossed into Spain, is Kahlān b. Abī Lawā, one of the most famous Berber genealogists. He made his way to al-Nāṣir, first ruler of the Banū Ḥammūd dynasty (is this the Muḥammad, lord of Algeciras who reigned in 428-40/1036-48, or the Ḥammūdid prince ʿAlī, lord of Malaga in 1001-21 and 1022-25?).

Finally, one should add that the greatest Berber genealogist, Sābiḳ b. Sulaymān b. Harāth b. Mūlāt. Ibn Dūnās, who is one of Ibn Khaldūn's sources, belonged to the Maṭmāṭa tribe.

Bibliography: Yaʿḳūbī, *Buldān*, 356, 357; Ibn Khurradādhbih, 90, Fr. tr. 65; *Chronique d'Ibn Ṣaghir sur les imams rostémides de Tahert*, ed.-Fr. tr. A. de C. Motylinski, in *Actes du xive Congrès International des Orientalistes*, Algiers 1905, Part 3, Paris 1908, Ar. text 27, Fr. tr. 86-7; Bakrī, *Description*, text 66, 67, 75, 90, 140-1, 152 (Fr. tr. de Slane, Algiers 1913, 137, 139, 154, 180-1, 270, 281, 290); Idrīsī, *Description de l'Afrique et de l'Espagne*, ed.-Fr. tr. Dozy and De Goeje, Leiden 1866, Ar. text, 85, Fr. tr. 98; *Kitāb al-Istibṣār*, Alexandria 1958, 193, 200; Tidjānī, *Riḥla*, ed. Ḥ. Ḥ. ʿAbd al-Wahhāb, Tunis 1377/1958, 134; Ibn Khaldūn, *Berbères*², i, 169, 172, 236, 239, 241-8, ii, 287, iii, 154-55, 187, 188, 301-4, iv, 515; Shammākhī, *Kitāb al-Siyar*, Cairo 1301/1883-4, 161, 203, 596 (appendix); Ibn Abī Dīnār, *Kitāb al-Muʾnis*, Fr. tr. in Pélissier and Rémusat, *Histoire de l'Afrique*, 1845, 391; R. Brunschvig, *Ḥafṣides*, i, 314; H. Fournel, *Les Berbères*, i-ii, Paris 1875-81, *passim*; H. R. Idris, *Zīrīdes*, ii, 464; J. Lelainville, *Les Troglodytes du Matmata*, in *Bull. Soc. Normande de Géographie*, 1909, 119-42; T. Lewicki, *Les Ibāḍites en Tunisie au moyen âge*, Accademia Polacca di Scienze e Lettere, Biblioteca di Roma, Conferenze, Fasc. 6, Rome 1959, 5-7; A. Louis, *Aux Matmata et dans les ksars du Sud, l'olivier et les hommes*, iii, 1970, 44-5; *Tunisie du Sud*, Paris 1975, 17, 20, 27-30; Piesse, *Itinéraire de l'Algérie*, 1882-3, 139.

(T. Lewicki)

MAṬMŪRA (A), from *ṭamara*, which signifies in particular "to hide", denotes a natural or man-made cavity used for the concealment of victuals (*ṭaʿām*) or of riches (*māl*); such is the definition adopted by the *LA* (s.v.), which specifies that it is the plural *maṭāmīr* which should be applied to underground silos where grain is stored. In fact, the singular currently denotes a silo, and the plural, a group of silos garded by a *ṭammār* and called *mərs* in Morocco (*rətba* in Takrūna, where the guardian is known as *rattāb*; W. Marçais, *Glossaire de Takroûna*, v, 2408-9, with discussion of the figurative expressions drawn from the root).

In the Maghrib, in addition to the communal granaries [see agadir], silos were the most usual method of storing cereals. The authorities sometimes dug out such silos, which reached vast sizes. Thus the ʿAlawid sultan Muḥammad b. ʿAbd Allāh [*q.v.*] caused to be built at Marrakesh, between 1173 and 1181/1760-8, two enormous silos on top of which was an inclined plane from which the grain, brought thither by beasts of burden, was despatched down chutes to the different parts of the subterranean storehouse, which was not visible from the outside (G. Höst, *Nachrichten von Marokos und Fes*, Copenhagen 1781, 75-7; cf. J. Delarozières, *Habs Zebbala à Fès Djedid*, in *IVe Congrès des Soc. savantes*, ii, Algiers 1929; G. Deverdun, *Marrakech*, i, 495). In Algeria, as early as 1848, an officer had presented a project for setting up reserve silos (or "matmores") and this was actually done some years later (see Capasset, *Mémoires sur la colonisation* ..., Algiers 1848). The CNRS has recently organised in Paris a series of conferences on *Les techniques de conservation des grains à long terme*, vol. iii of whose proceedings was published in 1985.

The technique for the excavation of silos differs little from one region to another. In general, the opening is narrow in such a way that it may be hermetically sealed, and the cavity is enlarged lower down, although attaining no great depth. If the nature of the soil requires it, the interior walls are lined with the object of protecting the cereals stored from humidity. But the latter must also be shielded from some subtle dangers, so that ensilage, entry into a silo and the withdrawal of a quantity of grain, are surrounded by precautions of a magical nature which, as regards Berber Morocco, have been fully documented by E. Laoust, *Mots et choses berbères*, Paris 1920, 403-5.

The plural *maṭāmīr* (or *maṭāmir*, from *maṭmar*, which also has the sense of "pit") is a toponym which may be quite frequently encountered (see Le Strange, *Lands*, 138). It is in any case the name of a locality in ʿIrāḳ close to Ḥulwān (see al-Masʿūdī, *Murūdj*, § 3597; Ibn Ḥawḳal², 358, tr. Kramers-Wiet, 350; Yāḳūt, iv, 562), while Dhāt al-Maṭāmīr, or simply Maṭāmīr, was the name for homes of cave-dwellers situated in the "Syrian March" (see A. A. Vasiliev, *Byzance et les Arabes*, ii/1, Brussels 1968, 82; M. Canard, *H'amdanides*, 730; cf. Ibn Ḥawḳal, 200, tr. 194-5; al-Masʿūdī, *Tanbīh*, ed. Ṣāwī, 151, which seems to give to *maṭmūra* the sense of "village of cave-dwellers"). It should be noted that the (subterranean?) cells of monks are called *maṭāmir* by al-Djāḥiẓ, *Ḥayawān*, iv, 458-9.

Besides the character from the Spanish comedy (*Matamoros*) whose (masculine) name in French is *Matamore*, the traveller Jean Mocquet has noted in his *Voyages en Afrique*, etc., 1617, 166, a feminine *matamore* denoting a large and deep pit, and C. P. Richelet (*Dictionnaire français*, ed. of 1693) supplies the following definition of the same term: "It is a prison where slaves are confined underground every night ... The matamore is very uncomfortable and cruel, and it seems that it was invented solely with the purpose of tormenting the slaves. A flight of 20 or 30 steps leads down to it. Air and light are supplied only through a small aperture. The slaves there are horribly over-crowded ... A. Gallard, *Histoire d'une esclave''* (F. Nasser, *Emprunts lexicologiques du français à l'arabe*, Beirut 1966, 472). It is a fact that, among the meanings of *maṭmūra* recounted by Dozy (*Suppl.*, s.v.), there figures the sense of "a cave, large or small and very deep, in which prisoners or Christian slaves are confined; in these subterranean prisons, which are beneath fortresses or in the country, the only contact with the world outside is through very narrow ventilators'' (see also R. Brunschvig, *Ḥafṣides*, i, 449-50 about a *maṭmūra* in Tripoli). Dozy's account applies to Muslim Spain, where *maṭmūra* has given rise to the Spanish word *mazmorra* (see J. Corominas, *Diccionario crítico etimológico de la lengua castellana*, Berne 1954-7, iii, 306-9), which denotes, like the Portuguese *masmorra* or *matamorra*, a subterranean prison (on those which have been discovered at Granada, see L. Torres Balbás, *Las mazmorras de la Alhambra*, in *al-And.*, ix/1 (1944), 198-218; see also R. Arié, *L'Espagne musulmane au temps des Naṣrides*, Paris 1973, 322).

Bibliography: Given in the article.

(CH. PELLAT)

MATN (A.), a term with various meanings, of which that of t e x t o f a *ḥadīth* [*q.v.*] is to be noted.

Matn already appears with the sense of "text" in pre-Islamic poetry, and has been used thus in Arabic literature up to the present day. It denotes especially the text of a book as distinguished from its oral explanation or its written or printed commentary.

In connection with traditions, *matn* denotes the content or text itself, in distinction from the chain of traditionists who have handed it down (*isnād* [*q.v.*]). The choice of this term to designate the body of a *ḥadīth* led Goldziher to put forward the view that the traditions were put into writing at an early date, but he recognised that he was unable to determine the first occurrence of this. However, it should be remarked that the *matn* has rarely been the subject of textual criticism on the part of the *fuḳahāʾ* and, as G. H. A. Juynboll observes (*The authenticity of the tradition literature*, Leiden 1969, 139), if the criteria which modern authors enumerate had been applied, there would have been very little left of the "authentic" collections.

Bibliography: Goldziher, *Muhammedanische Studien*, ii, 6ff., Eng. tr. *Muslim studies*, ii, 20ff.

(A. J. WENSINCK*)

MAṬRAḤ (lat. 23° 38 N., long. 58° 34 E.) the largest city and major port of the Sultanate of ʿUmān. Maṭraḥ was only a small fishing village in September 1507 when Afonso d'Albuquerque anchored his fleet there in preparation for the sacking of Masḳaṭ [*q.v.*]. The Portuguese later fortified Maṭraḥ with one fort on the waterfront and a second on a hill at the southwest corner of the town. The Yaʿāriba *imām* Sulṭān b. Sayf expelled the Portuguese from Maṭraḥ in 1651. During the ʿUmānī civil war of the early 18th century, the city was occupied by Persian troops, who were driven out by Aḥmad b. Saʿīd of the Āl Bū Saʿīd [*q.v.*] in 1741. Since the establishment of the Āl Bū Saʿīd dynasty, Maṭraḥ has been subjected to attacks by opponents of the régime on several occasions.

Maṭraḥ's rise to commercial prominence began during the period of Portuguese occupation. Masḳaṭ was the entrepot for Portugal's trade, but that city was made inaccessible to the rest of ʿUmān by the mountains surrounding it. Maṭraḥ, with its excellent harbour and ease of access to both Masḳaṭ, only 4 km. distant by water, and to the population centres of interior ʿUmān via Wādī Samāʾil, came to dominate the domestic trade. In addition, Maṭraḥ had important weaving and ship-building industries. With Masḳaṭ's decline as an entrepôt during the 19th century, Maṭraḥ's commercial importance increased, and the construction of Mīnā Ḳābūs in the early 1970s has insured the city's dominant position.

Because of its commercial activity, Maṭraḥ historically has had a cosmopolitan population, with Arabs, especially Banū D̲j̲ābir and Banū Ḥasan tribes, Balūc̲īs, Africans, Persians and Indians all residing there. Among the Indians, the Liwātiyya from Sind are distinctive. The Liwātiyya (sing. Lūtī), who were originally K̲h̲ōd̲j̲a Ismāʿīlīs but converted to Ithnā ʿAs̲h̲arī S̲h̲īʿism in the 1860s, have been in Maṭraḥ for more than 100 years. Although very active in business, the Liwātiyya were, until recent times, socially isolated in a walled portion, probably the original Portuguese fort, of Maṭraḥ known as Sūr Liwātiyya, from which all outsiders were excluded. During the 19th century, many Hindu Banyans began leaving Masḳaṭ and settling in Maṭraḥ to take advantage of the better business opportunities. ʿUmān's recent economic development has served to increase Maṭraḥ's international flavour.

Bibliography: The best description of Maṭraḥ during the Portuguese period is Pedro Barretto de Resendes, *Livro do Estado da India Oriental*, 1646, mss. B.L., Sloane 197, Sch. no. 11690, fols. 124-7. The principal Arabic sources are: to 1728, Sirḥān b. Saʿīd al-Azkawī, *Kas̲h̲f al-g̲h̲umma*, and a continuation to the 1780s by al-Maʿwalī, *Ḳiṣaṣ wa-ak̲h̲bār*, ed. ʿAbd al-Mad̲j̲īd Ḥasīb al-Ḳaysī, *Taʾrīk̲h̲ ʿUmān* [Beirut 1976], 101-2, 140, 142, 157; two works by Ibn Ruzayḳ (Ḥumayd b. Muḥammad), *al-S̲h̲uʿāʿ al-s̲h̲āʾiʿ* [Cairo] 1398/1978, 206, 215, 234-5, 297, 312, 337-8, 340, 343-5, 347, and *al-Fatḥ al-mubīn*, Masḳaṭ 1397/1977, 275, 284-90, 345-9,. 356, 364, 374-5, 396, 412-3, 516, tr. G. P. Badger, *History of the Imâms and Seyyids of ʾOmân ...*, London 1871, see index, concluded in 1856; and ʿAbd Allah b. Ḥumayd al-Sālimī, *Tuḥfat al-aʿyān⁵*, Kuwayt 1394/1974, ii, 10, 64-7, 153-8, 242-4, 298, concludes with 1910. Modern descriptions of Maṭraḥ are to be found in J. R. Wellsted, *Travels in Arabia*, London 1837, i, 31-3; W. S. W. Ruschenberger, *Narrative of a voyage round the world*, London 1838, i, 120-5; G. B. Brucks, *Memoir descriptive of the navigation of the Gulf of Persia*, in *Selections from the records of the Bombay Government*, n.s. xxiv, Bombay 1856, 629; J. G. Lorimer, *Gazetteer of the Persian Gulf*, ii, Calcutta 1908, 1197-1200; I. Skeet, *Muscat and Oman*, London 1974, 53-9. Important secondary works include: S. B. Miles, *Countries and tribes of the Persian Gulf*, London 1919; R. G. Landen, *Oman since 1856*, Princeton 1967; J. Peterson, *Oman in the twentieth century*, London 1978; and C. H. Allen, Jr., *The Indian merchant community of Masqat*, in *BSOAS*, xliv (1981), 48-52, which discusses the Liwātiyya.

(C. H. ALLEN, JR.)

MAṬRĀK̲C̲Ī, NAṢŪḤ AL-SILĀḤĪ AL-MAṬRĀḲĪ, or Naṣūḥ b. Ḳaragöz b. ʿAbd Allah al-Bōsnawī (?-971/ ?1564), outstanding k n i g h t, i n v e n t o r of some new forms of the game of *maṭrāḳ* (a contest with a stick, cudgel or rapier for training and knight-errantry), m a t h e m a t i c i a n, h i s t o r i a n, calli-g r a p h e r and p a i n t e r of the period of Süleymān the Magnificent (926-74/1520-66).

He was a student in the Palace School during the reign of the Bāyezīd II (886-918/1481-1512). His first book *D̲j̲amāl al-kuttāb wa-kamāl al-ḥussāb* on mathematics was written in 923/1517 and dedicated to Selīm I (918-26/1512-20). He had started by this time also to distinguish himself as a knight. He began his career as an historian to translate al-Ṭabarī's famous history from Arabic into Turkish in 926/1520. The title of his translation was *Madjmaʿ al-tawārīkh*, and the manuscripts of this translation constitute three huge volumes. He wrote also a Turkish supplement to his translation as the fourth volume of his work, which includes the history of the Ottomans from the beginning to the year of 958/1551. But we have manuscripts from this period dealing only with the time of Bāyezīd II, Selīm I and Süleymān I, such as *Taʾrīkh-i Sulṭān Bāyezīd wa-Sulṭān Selīm*, the illuminated *Taʾrīkh-i Sulṭān Selīm*, the illuminated *Taʾrīkh Sulṭān Bāyezīd*, the illuminated *Beyān-ĭ menāzil-i sefer-i ʿIrāḳeyn* (944/1537), *Süleymān-nāme* (926-44/1520-37), *Fetḥ-nāme-i Ḳaraboghdān* (945/1538), the illuminated *Taʾrīkh-i Fetḥ-i Shiklos* (950/1543), and the second part of the *Süleymān-nāme* (950-8/1543-51).

He was also the painter, with a group of other artists, of his illuminated historical works indicated above. He participated in different expeditions and sketched at least the outlines of his documentary paintings of townscapes in their own localities. Meanwhile, a letter of 936/1529 of Sultan Süleymān praises him as the master knight of his time, incomparable in the whole Ottoman Empire. He completed his *Tuḥfat al-ghuzāt* on the art of using various weapons in 939/1532, and his *ʿUmdat al-ḥisāb* in 940/1533. Finally, he produced a second version of al-Ṭabarī's history, the *Djāmiʿ al-tawārīkh*, by abridging its original with the encouragement of Rüstem Pasha, the famous Grand Vizier of Süleymān, in 957/1550. The part of the *Djāmiʿ al-tawārīkh* which concerns Ottoman history, in one large volume containing the events of the reign of Süleymān until 968/1561, is attributed to Rüstem Pasha himself. When he died on 16 Ramaḍān 971/28 April 1564, he was the head of the office of the *ketkhüdā-yi bārgīr (ketkhüdā-yi iṣṭabl-i ʿāmire).*

Bibliography: ʿĀshiḳ Čelebi, *Meshāʿir al-shuʿarāʾ*, B. L. Or. 6434, fol. 153a; Djelāl-zāde Muṣṭafā, *Ṭabaḳāt al-memālik ve deredjāt al-mesālik*, Vienna, Nat. Bibl., H. O. 41, fol. 136a; ʿĀlī, *Künh al-akhbār*, B.L. Or. 7892, fol. 34a; idem, *Menāḳib-ĭ hünerverān*, ed. Ibnü 'l-Emīn M. Kemāl (Inal), Istanbul 1926, 61; Ḥādjdjī Khalīfa, *Kashf al-ẓunūn*, i, 594, ii, 1166, 1520; Ismāʿīl Pasha al-Baghdādī, *Hadiyyat al-ʿārifīn, asmāʾ al-muʾallifīn wa-āthār al-muṣannifīn*, ii, 494; Evliyā Čelebi, *Seyāḥat-nāme*, Istanbul 1314, i, 257; Mustaḳīm-zāde, *Tuḥfe-yi khaṭṭāṭīn*, Istanbul 1928, 568; Ḥabīb, *Khaṭṭ ve khaṭṭāṭān*, Constantinople 1305, 159; C. Rieu, *Catalogue of the Turkish manuscripts in the British Museum*, London 1888, 22; Bursalĭ Meḥmed Ṭāhir, *ʿOthmānlĭ* müʾellifleri, Istanbul 1343, iii, 150, 305; F. Babinger, *GOW*, 67; A. Gabriel, *Les étapes d'une campagne dans les deux Irak d'après un manuscrit turc du XVIe siècle*, in *Syria*, ix (1928), 328-45; E. Blochet, *Catalogue des manuscrits turcs*, Paris 1932-3, 21; H. S. Selen, *XVI. asırda yapılmış Anadolu atlası: Naṣūḥ Silāḥīʾnin Menāzil'i*, in *II. Türk Tarih Kongresi Tebliğleri, Istanbul 20-25 Eylül 1937*, Istanbul 1943, 813-17; A. Decei, *Un "Fetiḥ-nāme-i Karaboğdān" (1538) de Naṣūḥ Maṭrāḳčī*, in *Fuad Köprülü armağanı*, Istanbul 1953, 113-24; F. Taeschner, *The itinerary of the first Persian campaign of Sultan Suleyman, 1534-1536, according to Naṣūḥ al-Maṭrāḳī*, in *Imago Mundi*, xii (1956), 53-5; H. G. Yurdaydın, *Maṭrāḳčī Naṣūḥ'un Süleymān-nāmesi*, in *V. Türk Tarih Kongresi, Ankara 12-17 Nisan 1956, Kongreye sunulan tebliğler*, Ankara 1960, 374-8; F. Taeschner, *Das Itinerar der ersten Persienfeldzuges des Sultans Suleyman Kanuni 1934-35 nach Maṭrāḳčī Naṣūḥ*, in *ZDMG*, cxii (1962), 62-93; Yurdaydın, *Matrakçı Nasûh*, Ankara 1963; idem, *Two new illuminative works of Matrakcı Nasûh*, in *Il Congresso internazionale di Arte Turca, Venezia 26-29 Septembre 1963*, 133-6; idem, *Maṭrāḳčī Naṣūḥ'un minyatürlü iki yeni eseri*, in *Belleten*, xxviii, no. 110 (1964), 229-33; idem, *Matrakçı Nasûh'un hayatı ve eserleri ile ilgili yeni bilgiler*, in *Belleten*, xxix, no. 114 (1965), 329-54; Taeschner, *Maṭraḳçı*, in *Isl.*, xl (1965), 200-6; W. B. Denny, *A sixteenth-century architectural plan of Istanbul*, in *Ars Orientalis*, viii (1970), 49-63; N. J. Johnston, *The urban world of Matraki manuscript*, in *JNES* (1971), xxx, 159-76; M. K. Özergin, *Sultan Kanuni Süleyman Han çağına ait tarih kayıtları*, Erzurum 1971, 28; Yurdaydın, *An Ottoman historian of the XVIth century: Naṣūḥ al-Maṭrāḳī and his Beyān-i Menāzil-i Sefer-i ʿIrāḳeyn and its importance for some Iraki cities*, in *Turcica*, vii (1975), 179-87; Naṣūhu's-Silāḥī (Maṭraḳcī), *Beyān-i menāzil-i sefer-i ʿIrāḳeyn-i Sulṭān Süleymān Ḫān*, ed. Yurdaydın, Ankara 1976; idem, *Maṭrāḳčī Naṣūḥ'a göre Istanbul-Budapeşte arası menzilleri*, in *VIII. Türk Tarih Kongresi, Ankara 11-15 Kasım 1976, Kongrese sunulan bildiriler, II*, Ankara 1981, 1247-56. (HÜSEYİN G. YURDAYDIN)

MAṬRĀN, KHALĪL [see MUṬRĀN].

MATRŪK, a technical term of Ottoman Turkish law concerning a category of land, See MARʿĀ. 3. Turkey.

MATTĀ B. **YŪNUS** (YŪNĀN) AL-ḲUNNĀʾĪ, ABŪ BISHR, translator of and commentator on Aristotle, was one of the principal initiators of the reception of Peripatetic philosophy through Arabic translations from Syriac in its final phase in the 4th/10th century. He was a Nestorian Christian who studied and taught at Dayr Ḳunnā [*q.v.*] (see also J. M. Fiey, *Assyrie chrétienne*, iii, Beirut 1968, 187-93) in the *schola* of the convent of Mār Mārī before he came to Baghdād during the caliphate of al-Rāḍī (i.e., after 322/934). He died on Saturday, 11 Ramaḍān 328/20 June 940.

Among his teachers were some of the Syrian Christians who brought the tradition of the Alexandrian school, which had been continued in Antioch and Ḥarrān, to Baghdād, as reported by al-Fārābī and al-Masʿūdī (see Meyerhof, *Von Alexandrien nach Bagdad*, 19-21, 27-8; Zimmermann, *Al-Farabi's commentary*, pp. cv-cviii): Abū Yaḥyā al-Marwazī, a doctor who taught logic in Syriac (with him Mattā read Aristotle's *Analytica posteriora*; Ibn al-Nadīm, *Fihrist*, 249_{14}, 263_{16}; Walzer, *Greek into Arabic*, 100f.), and Abū Isḥāḳ Ibrāhīm Ḳuwayrā (*sic*, i.e. Kyros), who commented on the *Organon* (*Fihrist*, 262; his commentary on the *Sophistici elenchi*, I, 1-11, mentioned in Badawī [ed.], *Manṭiḳ Arisṭū*, 951); also the Muslim Abū Aḥmad al-Ḥusayn b. Isḥāḳ Ibn Karnīb, a *mutakallim* interested in natural philosophy (*Fihrist*, 263).

His own translations—which were all made from Syriac versions of the 8th and 9th centuries—go far beyond the Aristotle reading (confined to elementary logic) of both the Nestorian *scholae*, where the Alexandrian curriculum of Ammonius and his disciples had been all but forgotten, and the medical schools which, for logic, preferred Galen's *De demonstratione* (cf. Zimmermann, *Al-Farabi's commentary*, pp. lxxvi, ciii-cviii). They represent a revival of Aristotelian studies which, relying on the available commentaries of Alexander of Aphrodisias and Themistius, recovered an Aristotle more complete and more authentic than had been known heretofore to Arabic readers. The works of Aristotle known to Ibn al-Nadīm in Mattā's translation (*Fihrist*, 249-51, 263-4) comprise the *Analytica posteriora*, including the commentary of Alexander and Themistius's paraphrase, the *Sophistici elenchi* (revision of an older version, cf. Badawī (ed.), *Manṭiḳ Arisṭū*, 785 n. 2, 1018), the *Poetica*, *De caelo* ("part of book I") and its paraphrase by Themistus, *De generatione et corruptione* with the commentaries of Alexander and Olympiodorus, the *Meteorologica* with Olympiodorus's commentary, and book *Lambda* of the *Metaphysica* with Alexander's commentary as well as Themistius's paraphase. Only three of these have survived:

(a) The Paris ms. of the Arabic *Organon* (Bibl. nat., ar. 2346) contains the *Analytica posteriora* in Mattā's version as copied from the exemplar of his pupil Yaḥyā b. ʿAdī (ed. ʿAbd al-Raḥmān Badawī, *Manṭiḳ Arisṭū*, Cairo 1948-52, 309-465); for the revised version of Book I read by Ibn Rus̲h̲d and translated into Latin by Gerard of Cremona, see H. Gätje and G. Schoeler, *Averroes' Schriften zur Logik. Der arabische Text der zweiten Analytiken im Grossen Kommentar des Averroes*, in *ZDMG*, cxxx (1980), 556-85, esp. 564-83.

(b) His version of Alexander's commentary on *Metaph.* Λ, 1-7 (1069 a 18-1072 b 16), including the lemmata of Aristotle's text, served Ibn Rus̲h̲d as the basis of his *Tafsīr* (ed. M. Bouyges, *Averroès. Tafsîr Mâ baʿd aṭ-ṭabîʿat*, Beirut 1938-52; cf. Notice, pp. cxxx f.); see also the quotations from a commentary of Mattā on *Metaph.* α, B, and Θ in Ps.-Mad̲j̲rīṭī, *Picatrix. Das Ziel des Weisen*, ed. H. Ritter, Leipzig-Berlin 1933, 282-3 = tr. H. Ritter and M. Plessner, London 1962, 290, 292.

(c) Mattā's translation of the *Ars poetica* (edd. D.S. Margoliouth, London 1887; J. Tkatsch, Vienna 1928-32; ʿAbd al-Raḥmān Badawī, Cairo 1953; S̲h̲ukrī ʿAyyād, Cairo 1967) has become notorious for its inadequacies rather than for its merits [cf. BALĀG̲H̲A, ḤAMĀSA, ḤIKĀYA, HID̲J̲Āʾ, ISTIʿĀRA], but it must be kept in mind that the *Poetics*, as well as the *Rhetoric*—both regarded as part of the *Organon* in the Alexandrian curriculum (Walzer, *Greek into Arabic*, 129-36)—were read for the study of certain types of "logical" argument, but not with regard to a literary tradition which had become extinct already in late Hellenism.

The commentaries of Mattā and his school, if we may judge from the little that is preserved, were in the form of more or less extensive notes, marginal or annexed to lemmata of the texts (*taʿālīḳ*) and in some cases combined with those of other teachers in the style of the late Patristic *catenae* on the Bible. An important number of such notes is to be found in the Paris *Organon*, referring to *An.pr.* (see Walzer, *Greek into Arabic*, 78), *An. post.* (see *ibid.*, 102), the *Topica* (ed. Badawī, *Manṭiḳ Arisṭū* 630 n. 3), and Porphyry's *Isagoge* (*ibid.*, 1046 n. 1, 1048, n.l. 3, 1053, n. 2, 1054 n. 1), in a 10th-century *catena* commentary on the *Categories* (see M. [Küyel-] Türker, *El-ʿĀmirî ve Kategoriler'in şerhleriyle ilgili parçalar*, in *Araştırma*, iii [1965], 65-122), and on the margins of Alexander's treatise on the *differentia specifica* (*M. fi 'l-Fuṣūl*, ed. Badawī, *Arisṭū ʿind al-ʿArab*, 295-308, cf. J. van Ess, *Über einige neue Fragmente des Alexander*, etc., in *Isl.*, xlii [1966], 146-68, esp. 154-8); others are quoted by his pupil Yaḥyā b. ʿAdī (Endress, *The works of Yaḥyā ibn ʿAdī*, 52, 93) and by Ibn al-Muṭrān (d. 587/1191, see M. Riḍā al-S̲h̲abībī, *Bustān al-aṭibbāʾ wa-rawḍat al-alibbāʾ*, in *MMIA*, iii [1923], 2-8 [p. 7, nos. 9, 19, 20]: notes on *Isag.*, *Cat.*, *De int.*); still others were available to Ibn al-Nadīm (who also mentions two introductory treatises on the *Analytica*, *Fihrist*, 264) and ʿAbd al-Laṭīf al-Bag̲h̲dādī (*R. fī Mud̲j̲ādalat al-ḥakīmayn al-kīmiyāʾī wa'l-naẓarī*, ms. Bursa, Hüseyin Çelebi 823, fol. 113b 5-7, see S. M. Stern, *A collection of treatises by ʿAbd al-Laṭīf al-Baghdādī*, in *Islamic Studies*, i [Karachi 1962], 55, 66).—Fairly extensive commentaries of his on the *Physica*, books II, 3-III,4, have survived in ms. Leiden, Or. 1433 (containing Isḥāḳ b. Ḥunayn's Arabic translation and a course on the *Physics* edited in 395/1004 by Abu 'l-Ḥusayn al-Baṣrī from the lectures of Abū ʿAlī Ibn al-Samḥ, ed. Badawī, *Arisṭūṭālīs. al-Ṭabīʿa*, Cairo 1965-6). His view of Nature as an immanent creative being (*al-ṭabīʿa al-faʿʿāla*, ed. Badawī 151, cf. Ioh. Philoponus, *In Phys.*, ed. Vitelli, 317_{18}) was explicitly attacked by Ibn Sīnā (H.V.B. Brown, *Avicenna and the Christian philosophers in Baghdad*, in *Islamic philosophy and the classical tradition*, Oxford 1972, 35-47, esp. 43-5).

Among his Christian and Muslim contemporaries of the *falāsifa*, he was recognised unanimously as the scholarch of logic in his time (*Fihrist*, 263_{25}; al-Masʿūdī, *Tanbīh*, 122). With him, al-Fārābī [*q.v.*] studied the *Organon*, and the Jacobite Yaḥyā b. ʿAdī [*q.v.*] transmitted his teaching to the subsequent generation of Muslim and Christian philosophers in Bag̲h̲dād, notably ʿĪsā b. Zurʿa, al-Ḥasan b. Suwār, and the Muslim Abū Sulaymān al-Sid̲j̲istānī [*q.v.*]. On the other side, a vehement polemic, surging since the traditionalist reaction of the mid-9th century, was directed by the religious establishment of the *ʿulūm al-s̲h̲arʿiyya* against the claim of Greek logic and philosophy to universal truth, and more especially against the influence of logic apparent in the *uṣūl al-naḥw* of contemporaries like Ibn al-Sarrād̲j̲ [*q.v.*] and his pupil al-Rummānī [*q.v.*] (cf. *Fihrist*, 62; Ibn al-Anbārī, *Nuzha*, ed. Amer, 189). The attack led by Abū Saʿīd al-Sīrāfī against Mattā in the *mad̲j̲lis* of the vizier Abu 'l-Fatḥ Ibn al-Furāt in 326/937-8, as reported by al-Rummānī to Abū Ḥayyān al-Tawḥīdī (*al-Imtāʿ wa 'l-muʾānasa*, i, 107-28), is an impressive illustration. The leader of the logicians (depicted by al-Tawḥīdī's informants as a covetous drunkard who sells his learning for profit) is shown, not without malicious tricks, to be unable to defend the philosophers' claim that logic is a tool necessary "to know truth from falsehood, veracity from lying, good from bad", and to dispute his opponent's argument that the only way to "logical speech" (*nuṭḳ*) is through the grammar of a particular conventional language. But if Mattā had no more to say to his unsympathetic audience than the report credits him with, his pupils al-Fārābī (cf. Zimmermann, *Al-Farabi's commentary*, pp. cxxvi ff.) and Yaḥyā b. ʿAdī (cf. Endress, *The works of Y. b. ʿA.*, 45f.), defending logic as universal grammar while assigning to grammar the rules peculiar to the utterances (*alfāẓ*) of a particular language, made up for his silence.

Bibliography: 1. Texts. Ibn al-Nadīm, *Fihrist*, 248-51, 263-4; Abū Ḥayyān al-Tawḥīdī, *al-Imtāʿ wa 'l-muʾānasa*, ed. A. Amīn and A. al-Zayn, i, 107ff.; al-Masʿūdī, *al-Tanbīh wa 'l-ishrāf*, ed. de Goeje, 122; al-Bayhaḳī, *Tatimmat Ṣiwān al-ḥikma*, no. 14; al-Ḳifṭī, *Taʾrīk̲h̲ al-ḥukamāʾ*, 323; Ibn Abī Uṣaybiʿa, *ʿUyūn al-anbāʾ fī ṭabaḳāt al-aṭibbāʾ*, ed. Müller, i, 235; Ibn K̲h̲allikān, *Wafayāt*, ed. ʿAbbās, v, 153-4; Ibn al-ʿIbrī, *Taʾrīk̲h̲*, 285, 296 = ²164, 170. 2. Studies. Brockelmann, I, 228, S I, 370; Graf, *GCAL*, ii, 153-4; G. Endress, *The works of Yaḥyā ibn ʿAdī*, Wiesbaden 1977, 5-6, 52, index; idem, *Grammatik und Logik*, in *Sprachphilosophie in Antike und Mittelalter*, ed. B. Mojsisch, Amsterdam 1984, §6; W. Heinrichs, *Arabische Dichtung und griechische Poetik*, Beirut-Wiesbaden 1969, 118-23; M. Mahdi, *Language and logic in classical Islam*, in *Logic in classical Islamic culture*, Wiesbaden 1970, 51-83; D. S. Margoliouth, *The discussion between Abū Bishr Mattā and Abū Saʿīd al-Sīrāfī on the merits of logic and grammar*, in *JRAS* (1905), 79-129; M. Meyerhof, *Von Alexandrien nach Bagdad*, Berlin 1930, 29; N. Rescher, *The development of Arabic Logic*, Pittsburgh 1964, 119-22; J. Tkatsch, *Die arabische Übersetzung der Poetik des Aristoteles*, Vienna and Leipzig 1928-32, i, 126-8; R. Walzer, *Greek into Arabic*, Oxford 1962, 66, 77f., 99f., 102; F. W. Zimmermann, *Al-Farabi's commentary and short treatise on Aristotle's De interpretatione*, London 1918, pp. ciii-cviii, cxxii-xccix. (G. ENDRESS)

MATTER [see HAYŪLĀ].

AL-**MĀTURĪDĪ**, ABŪ MANṢŪR MUḤAMMAD B. MUḤAMMAD B. MAḤMŪD AL-SAMARḲANDĪ, Ḥanafī theologian, jurist, and Ḳurʾān commentator, founder of a doctrinal school which later came to be considered one of the two orthodox Sunnī schools of *kalām* [see MĀTURĪDIYYA].

His *nisba* refers to Māturīd (or Māturīt), a locality in Samarḳand. On the basis of a misunderstood reference of al-Samʿānī (fol. 498b) to his son-in-law, some late sources consider him of distinguished Medinan descent and call him al-Anṣārī. His main teacher, Abū Naṣr Aḥmad b. al-ʿAbbās al-ʿIyāḍī, was killed between 261/874 and 279/892, probably closer to the latter date. Al-Māturīdī thus must have been born before 260/873, especially since he is described as having been highly esteemed by his teacher, who would not engage in scholarly debate except in his presence. According to some late authors, al-Māturīdī also studied under al-ʿIyāḍīʾs teachers Abū Sulaymān al-Djūzdjānī, Nuṣayr b. Yaḥyā al-Balkhī (d. 268/881-2) and Muḥammad b. Muḳātil al-Rāzī (d. 226/841). The latter cannot have been his teacher, and the report is most likely unreliable also in respect of the other two. Not much else is known about his career. He is described as leading an ascetic life and as occasioning miracles (*karāmāt*). The death date given by the later sources, 333/944, may be approximately correct, though the earliest biographer, Abu 'l-Muʿīn al-Nasafī (d. 508/1114), did not know it. Alternate dates mentioned in two late sources are 336/947 and 332/943. Al-Māturīdī's tomb in the cemetery of Djākardīza in Samarḳand was still known in the 9th/15th century. Among his students were Abū Aḥmad al-ʿIyāḍī, son of his teacher Abū Naṣr, Abu 'l-Ḥasan al-Rustughfanī, and ʿAbd al-Karīm b. Mūsā al-Bazdawī (al-Pazdawī), great-grandfather of Abu 'l-Yusr al-Bazdawī.

Of al-Māturīdī's works, the published text of the *Kitāb al-Tawḥīd* (ed. F. Kholeif, Beirut 1970) is definitely authentic. The book, however, seems to have existed in different versions since some quotations from it in Abu 'l-Muʿīn al-Nasafī's *Tabṣirat al-adilla* are missing in the edited text (see D. Gimaret, *Théories de l'Acte humain et théologie musulmane*, Paris 1980, 175-8). Al-Māturīdī's extensive Ḳurʾān commentary *K. Taʾwīlāt al-Ḳurʾān* (vol. i, ed. Ibrāhīm ʿAwaḍayn and al-Sayyid ʿAwaḍayn, Cairo 1391/1971) was, according to its commentator ʿAlāʾ al-Dīn Abū Bakr Muḥammad b. Aḥmad al-Samarḳandī (d. *ca.* 540/1145), assembled by his pupils and therefore less obscure than his other works which were written by himself. Also attributed to al-Māturīdī are three short published texts, a *Risāla fī 'l-ʿaḳāʾid*, a *K. al-Tawḥīd* (both ed. Y. Z. Yörükan, *Islam akaidine dair eski metinler*, Istanbul 1953), and a *sharḥ* on Abū Ḥanīfa's *al-Fiḳh al-akbar*. These works appear to have been composed by later representatives of the school on the basis of his doctrine. Abu 'l-Muʿīn al-Nasafī does not list them among his works. He mentions, on the other hand, the following, apparently lost, books: *K. al-Maḳālāt*; *K. Bayān wahm al-Muʿtazila*; refutations of three books of the Muʿtazilī Abu 'l-Ḳāsim al-Balkhī al-Kaʿbī (d. 319/932), his *K. Awāʾil al-adilla*, *K. Tahdhīb al-djadal*, and his *K. fī waʿīd al-fussāḳ*; a refutation of *al-Uṣūl al-khamsa* by the Muʿtazilī Abū ʿUmar al-Bāhilī, a close companion of Abū ʿAlī al-Djubbāʾī; a refutation of a *K. al-Imāma* by an Imāmī Shīʿī author; two refutations of the Ismāʿīlīs (Ḳarāmiṭa); and two books on legal methodology (*Uṣūl al-fiḳh*), *K. Maʾkhadh al-sharāʾiʿ* and *K. al-djadal*.

In contrast to al-Ashʿarī, the founder of the other Sunnī *kalām* school, who espoused the doctrines of Ḥanbalī traditionalism, al-Māturīdī adhered to the doctrine of Abū Ḥanīfa as transmitted and elaborated by the Ḥanafī scholars of Balkh and Transoxania. He developed previous eastern Ḥanafī teaching systematically in arguing against the positions of the Muʿtazila, in particular, their chief representative in the east Abu 'l-Ḳāsim al-Balkhī; of the Karrāmiyya, Sunnī traditionalists (Ḥashwiyya); of the Imāmī Shīʿa; and of the Ismāʿīlīs, represented in Transoxania by Muḥammad b. Aḥmad al-Nasafī (d. 332/943). Of other religions, he refuted the views of Christians, Jews, Zoroastrians, Manichaeans, Bardesanites and Marcionites (see G. Vajda, *Le témoignage d'al-Māturīdī sur la doctrine des Manichéens, des Daysanites et des Marcionites*, in *Arabica*, xii [1966], 1-38, 113-28). His doctrine was in substance generally more rationalist and, with the exception of his Murdjiʾī definition of faith (*īmān*), closer to Muʿtazilism than al-Ashʿarī's. In his concepts and technical terminology he was, however, less influenced by the Muʿtazila than al-Ashʿarī, who had been a trained Muʿtazilī before his break with them.

In substantial agreement with the Muʿtazilī position, al-Māturīdī held that man is able and obliged to gain knowledge of God and his obligation to thank Him through reason independent of prophetic revelation. In respect of the attributes of God, he, like the Muʿtazila, allowed and practised metaphorical interpretation of anthropomorphic expressions in the Ḳurʾān, though he rejected some specifically Muʿtazilī interpretations. In other instances he relied on the traditionalist *bilā kayf* formula, insisting on unquestioning acceptance of the revealed text. Against the Muʿtazila, he considered divine attributes like knowledge and power as real and eternally subsisting in his essence (*ḳāʾima bi 'l-dhāt*). Although he accepted the terminological distinction between attributes of essence and attributes of act, he maintained, against the Muʿtazila and al-Ashʿarī, that the attributes of act are equally eternal and subsistent in the divine essence. Thus he insisted that the expressions "God is eternally the Creator" and "God has been creating from eternity (*lam yazal khāliḳan*)" are equally valid, even though the created world is temporal. In particular, his doctrine that the *takwīn*, bringing into existence, was eternal and distinct from the *mukawwan*, the existing things, became a famous point of controversy with the Ashʿarīs. Al-Māturīdī affirmed the vision (*ruʾya*) of God by the faithful in the hereafter, but consistently rejected the possibility of *idrāk*, which he understood as grasping, of God by the eyes. He held speech (*kalām*) to be an eternal attribute of God which could, however, not be heard. Like the Muʿtazila, he thus affirmed, in respect to Ḳurʾān, IV, 165, *wa-kallama llāhu Mūsā taklīman*, that God created a voice which He made Moses hear.

In regard to predestination and human free will, al-Māturīdī's position was intermediate between the Muʿtazila and al-Ashʿarī. He affirmed that the acts of man are created by God, subject to His will and decree. While they are thus acts of God in one respect (*djiha*), they are in another respect really, and not metaphorically, man's acts and his free choice (*ikhtiyār*). Al-Māturīdī insisted that God will lead astray (*aḍalla*) only those who, He knows, will choose the wrong way and will guide only those who, He knows, will choose the straight path. The initial choice is man's, not God's as for al-Ashʿarī. Al-Māturīdī thus also rejected the predestinarian interpretation of the primordial covenant (*mīthāḳ*, according to Ḳurʾān, VII, 137), according to which God separated the chosen from the condemned before creation and the latter confessed belief in His Lordship falsely under duress. Man's power (*ḳudra*), given by God, is valid for opposite acts. Capability (*istiṭāʿa*) is of two kinds, one preceding the act, the other simultaneous with it. The imposition by God of something beyond man's capacity (*taklīf mā lā yuṭāḳ*) is in principle inadmissible.

Faith (*īmān*) was defined by al-Māturīdī essentially as *taṣdīḳ bi 'l-ḳalb*, inner assent, expressed by verbal confession (*iḳrār bi 'l-lisān*). Works (*aʿmāl*) are not part of faith. Faith cannot decrease nor increase in substance, though it may be said to increase through renewal and repetition. Al-Māturīdī condemned *istithnāʾ*, adding the formula "if God will" to the affirmation "I am a believer". The faithful sinner may be punished by God but will eventually enter Paradise. The traditionalist tenet backed by al-Ashʿarī that faith is uncreated was rejected by al-Māturīdī.

Bibliography: Bazdawī, *Uṣūl al-dīn*, ed. H. P. Linss, Cairo 1383/1963, index s.v.; Abu 'l-Muʿīn al-Nasafī, *Tabṣirat al-adilla*, quoted in Muḥammad b. Tāwīt al-Ṭāndjī, *Abū Manṣūr al-Māturīdī*, in *IFD*, iv/1-2 (1955), 1-12; Ibn Abi 'l-Wafāʾ, *al-Djawāhir al-muḍīʾa*, Ḥaydarābād 1332/1914, ii, 130-1; Bayāḍī, *Ishārāt al-marām*, ed. Yūsuf ʿAbd al-Razzāḳ, Cairo 1368/1949, 23; Zabīdī, *Itḥāf al-sāda*, Cairo n.d., ii, 5; Laknawī, *al-Fawāʾid al-bahiyya*, Cairo 1924, 195; M. Allard, *Le problème des attributs divins dans la doctrine d'al-Ašʿarī*, Beirut 1965, 419-27; M. Götz, *Māturīdī und sein Kitāb Taʾwīlāt al-Qurʾān*, in *Isl.*, xli (1965), 27-70; H. Daiber, *Zur Erstausgabe von al-Māturīdī, Kitāb al-Tauḥīd*, in *Isl.*, lii (1975), 299-313; Sezgin, *GAS*, i, 604-6. Further relevant literature is given under the article on AL-MĀTURĪDIYYA.

(W. MADELUNG)

MĀTURĪDIYYA, a theological school named after its founder Abū Manṣūr al-Māturīdī [*q.v.*] which in the Mamlūk age came to be widely recognised as the second orthodox Sunnī *kalām* school besides the Ashʿariyya. The name Māturīdiyya does not appear to have been current before al-Taftazānī (d. 792/1390), who used it evidently to establish the role of al-Māturīdī as the co-founder of Sunnī *kalām* together with his contemporary al-Ashʿarī. In view of the late appearance of the name, the reality of a theological school founded by al-Māturīdī has been questioned. In earlier times, the school was commonly called that of the scholars of Samarḳand or of Transoxania. It claimed to represent the doctrine of Abū Ḥanīfa and sometimes identified itself as the *ahl al-sunna wa 'l-djamāʿa* and "the great mass", *al-sawād al-aʿẓam*. The dominant influence of al-Māturīdī's thought and works on the later representatives of the school is, however, evident, and the latter did not deviate more substantially from his doctrine than did the later Ashʿarīs from the doctrine of al-Ashʿarī. The latter was more readily recognised as the founder of a new school both because he was originally a Muʿtazilī and because he was repudiated by the Ḥanbalī traditionalists whose doctrine he claimed to defend, while al-Māturīdī was considered fully representative of traditional Transoxanian Ḥanafism whose theology he elaborated.

The theological doctrine of the Ḥanafī scholars of Samarḳand spread in the 4th/10th and 5th/11th centuries throughout Transoxania, eastern Khurāsān, Balkh and among the newly converted Turks in the Ḳarakhānid territories of Central Asia. In the 4th/10th century there were some differences on a few theological questions with the Ḥanafī scholars of Bukhārā, who were more strongly influenced by traditionalist, anti-rationalist tendencies. These were mostly harmonised by later Māturīdī scholars with compromise solutions. Māturīdī teaching remained virtually unknown west of Khurāsān, where the Ḥanafīs adhered to other theological schools, many of them to Muʿtazilism. Only the Saldjūḳ expansion into the central Islamic world since the middle of the 5th/11th century brought a radical change. Ashʿarī authors now took note of Māturīdī doctrine concerning the divine attributes, characteristically describing it as an innovation propounded only after the year 400/1009. The militant support of the Turks for eastern Ḥanafism including its theological doctrine led to a major clash with the Shāfiʿīs, now identified with Ashʿarī theology. This is the background of the official cursing of al-Ashʿarī from the pulpits in Khurāsān ordered by the Saldjūḳ Ṭoghrïl Beg in 445/1053 and of the persecution of Ashʿarīs and the extensive factional warfare between Ḥanafīs and Shāfiʿīs in the major towns of Iran in the later Saldjūḳ age. Māturīdī works of this period are highly critical of Ashʿarism, excluding the Ashʿariyya from the *ahl al-sunna wa 'l-djamāʿa* and describing some Ashʿarī doctrines as *kufr*. As a result of the Turkish expansion, eastern Ḥanafism and Māturīdī theological doctrine were spread throughout western Persia, ʿIrāḳ, Anatolia, Syria and Egypt. Numerous Transoxanian and other eastern Ḥanafī scholars migrated to these regions and taught there from the late 5th/11th to the 8th/14th century. Māturīdī doctrine thus gradually came to prevail among the Ḥanafī communities everywhere. In Damascus and Syria it was first propagated by Burhān al-Dīn ʿAlī b. al-Ḥasan al-Sikilkandī al-Balkhī (d. 548/1153), to whom the Ḥanafī scholars of Samarḳand send a copy of Abū Ḥafṣ al-Nasafī's *ʿAḳāʾid* with their explanations, describing it as the creed of the *ahl al-sunna wa 'l-djamāʿa* on which they had agreed.

As the antagonism between the Ḥanafīs and Shāfiʿīs subsided in the Mamlūk age, the Ashʿarī Shāfiʿī Tādj al-Dīn al-Subkī (d. 771/1370) composed a *nūniyya* poem about the points of difference between al-Ashʿarī and "Abū Ḥanīfa", meaning Māturīdī doctrine. He listed thirteen such points, defining seven of them as merely terminological (*lafẓiyya*) and six as objective (*maʿnawiyya*). The latter were in his view so minor that they could not justify mutual charges of infidelity or heresy (*tabdīʿ*). A commentary on the *Nūniyya* was composed by al-Subkī's student Nūr al-Dīn Muḥammad b. Abi 'l-Ṭayyib al-Shīrāzī. This commentary with al-Subkī's thirteen points of difference was largely copied by Abū ʿUdhba, writing *ca.* 1125/1713, in his well-known *K. al-Rawḍa al-bahiyya fī mā bayn al-Ashāʿira wa 'l-Māturīdiyya* (a summary of the thirteen points is given by A. S. Tritton, *Muslim theology*, London 1947, 174-6).

Notable representatives of the school of al-Māturīdī in the later 5th/11th century were Abū Shakūr al-Sālimī al-Kishshī, author of a *K. al-Tamhīd fī bayān al-tawḥīd*, and Abu 'l-Yusr al-Bazdawī (d. 593/1099), *ḳāḍī* of Samarḳand and author of the *K. Uṣūl al-dīn*. Most influential in expounding and elaborating the doctrine of al-Māturīdī was, however, Abu 'l-Muʿīn al-Nasafī al-Makḥūlī (d. 508/1114), who wrote the largest comprehensive work of Māturīdī theology entitled *K. Tabṣirat al-adilla*, a shorter *K. Baḥr al-kalām* and a *K. al-Tamhīd li-ḳawāʿid al-tawḥīd*.

Most important in the dissemination of Māturīdī dogma was the creed (*ʿAḳāʾid*) of Nadjm al-Dīn Abū Ḥafs al-Nasafī (d. 537/1142) which closely followed Abu ʾl-Muʿīn's formulations in his *Tabṣirat al-adilla*. It received many commentaries and glosses for scholastic teaching and was repeatedly versified. Another popular Māturīdī creed in verses, known as *al-Lāmiyya fi ʾl-tawḥīd* or *Badʾ al-amālī*, was composed by ʿAlī b. ʿUthmān al-Ūshī (d. 569/1173) and was later explained in numerous commentaries, some in Persian and Turkish. Also in the 6th/12th century, there wrote Nūr al-Dīn al-Ṣābūnī al-Bukhārī (d. 580/1184), whose *K. al-Bidāya min al-kifāya*, extracted from his larger *K. al-Kifāya fi ʾl-hidāya*, has been published.

Among the later Māturīdī authors, Abu ʾl-Barakāt al-Nasafī (d. 710/1310) composed a popular brief treatise *ʿUmdat al-ʿaḳīda li-ahl al-sunna* with his own commentary entitled *K. al-Iʿtimād fi ʾl-iʿtiḳad*, both strongly influenced by Abu ʾl-Muʿīn al-Nasafī's *Tabṣirat al-adilla*. A theologian with a more personal profile was ʿUbayd Allāh b. Masʿūd al-Maḥbūbī (d. 747/1346), who dealt with theological questions in the context of both his *K. Taʿdīl al-ʿulūm* and his *K. al-Tawḍīḥ*, a work on legal methodology (*uṣūl al-fiḳh*). Saʿd al-Dīn al-Taftazānī (d. 792/1310) wrote the best-known commentary on Abū Ḥafṣ al-Nasafī's *ʿAḳāʾid*. A student of ʿAḍud al-Dīn al-Īdjī, representative of the philosophical *kalām* of late Ashʿarism, he himself seems to have progressively moved towards Ashʿarī positions. This is apparent in his later *K. al-Maḳāṣid* and his own commentary on it, which were patterned after al-Īdjī's *K. al-Mawāḳif*, and its commentary by the Sharīf al-Djurdjānī. The Egyptian Ḥanafī theologian Kamāl al-Dīn Ibn al-Humān (d. 861/1457), author of a *K. al-Musāyara fi ʾl-ʿaḳāʾid al-mundjiya fi ʾl-ākhira*, fully accepted the now prevailing view of the equal orthodoxy of Ashʿarism and Māturīdism, but showed a degree of independence in regard to both schools. In contrast, the Ottoman Ḥanafī Kamāl al-Dīn al-Bayāḍī (d. 1078/1687) in his *K. Ishārāt al-marām min ʿibārāt al-imām* emphasised the independence and priority of Māturīdī *kalām*, founded on the teaching of Abū Ḥanīfa, in relation to Ashʿarism.

Unlike Muʿtazilism and Ashʿarism, Māturīdī theology always remained associated with only a single legal school, that of Abū Ḥanīfa. It also generally lagged behind the other two *kalām* schools in methodical sophistication and systematisation, especially in the questions of natural science treated by them, and was less subject to the pervasive influence of the terminology and concepts of *falsafa* on later Ashʿarism and later, particularly Imāmī Shīʿī, Muʿtazilism. While the conflict of the Māturīdiyya with the Muʿtazila was obviously most fundamental, the differences with the Ashʿariyya were more substantial than the later harmonising theologians would admit. They involved mainly Māturīdī doctrine affirming the eternity of God's attributes of act subsisting in His essence, the rational basis of good and evil, the reality of free choice (*ikhtiyār*) of man in his acts, and the Murdjiʾī definition of faith as assent and confession excluding works (*aʿmāl*). However, other, less significant points of difference dominated at times the controversy between the two schools.

Bibliography: In addition to the works cited in AL-MĀTURĪDI, see L. Gardet, *De quelques questions posées par l'étude du ʿIlm al-kalām*, in *SI*, xxxii (1970), 135-9; W. Madelung, *The spread of Māturīdism and the Turks*, in *Actas do IV Congresso de Estudos Árabes e Islâmicos Coimbra-Lisboa 1968*, Leiden 1971, 109-68; W. M. Watt, *The formative period of Islamic thought*, Edinburgh 1973, 312-16; idem, *The problem of al-Māturīdī*, in *Mélanges d'Islamologie. Volume dédié à ... Armand Abel*, Leiden 1974, 264-9; idem, *The beginnings of the Islamic theological schools*, in *Islam et Occident au Moyen Âge: l'enseignement en Islam et en Occident au Moyen Âge*, Paris 1976, 19-20; D. Gimaret, *Théories de l'Acte humain en théologie musulmane*, Paris 1980, 171-234; J. M. Pessagno, *The uses of evil in Māturīdian thought*, in *SI*, lx (1984), 59-82.

(W. MADELUNG)

MAʿŪNA (A., pl. *maʿūnāt*, *maʿāwin*), "assistance", an administrative term of early Islamic history with several meanings.

In texts relating to the pre-ʿAbbāsid period, it refers to allocations comparable with, but distinct from, stipends (*ʿaṭāʾ* [*q.v.*]) and rations (*rizḳ* [*q.v.*]). *Maʿūna* was sometimes a gratuity paid to those who were not in receipt of stipends (al-Ṭabarī, i, 3410; ii, 1794), sometimes a bonus supplementary to stipends (al-Ṭabarī, ii, 407; al-Balādhurī, *Futūḥ*, 187-8; cf. idem, *Ansāb*, ivb, 33), and sometimes a regular (more precisely annual) payment made to those in receipt of stipends and rations alike (al-Ṭabarī, i, 2486, 2524; ii, 755; Ibn Saʿd, v, 277); *maʿūnāt* is even used as a global term for private income from public funds (al-Ṭabarī, i, 3026). One would assume the *ʿāmil* or *ṣāḥib al-maʿūna* of this period to have been a fiscal officer, especially as he was often appointed to the *kharādj* [*q.v.*] as well, or to the civil administration in general (al-Ṭabarī, ii, 822, 929, 1069; cf. iii, 863); but it is possible that he was an officer charged with the maintenance of law and order (al-Ṭabarī, ii, 1470f. could be read in support of either view).

From the 3rd/9th century onwards, there is at any rate no doubt that the leader of the *maʿūna* was charged with police duties. He might be identical with the leader of the *shurṭa* (later *shiḥna*) [*q.vv.*] or with the military governor (al-Ṭabarī, iii, 1816, 1822, 1875). In so far as he was not, he performed functions such as bringing accused persons to court, executing verdicts and collecting fines (Hilāl al-Ṣābī, *Rusūm dār al-khilāfa*, ed. M. ʿAwwād, Baghdād 1964, 9 and n. 3 thereto; A. A. Duri, *Governmental institutions*, in R. B. Serjeant (ed.), *The Islamic city*, Paris 1980, 61; R. Levy, *The social structure of Islam*, Cambridge 1969, 332, 381; see also E. Tyan, *Histoire de l'organisation judiciaire en pays d'Islam*, Paris 1938-43, ii, 69, 365-6; and ʿĀMIL). The actual police building was called *maʿūna* too, at least by the time of the Geniza documents (S. D. Goitein, *A Mediterranean society*, ii, Berkeley and Los Angeles 1971, 368, cf. also Tyan, *op.cit.*, ii, 401, 432.

Bibliography: Given in the article.

(P. CRONE)

MAURITANIA [see MŪRĪTĀNIYĀ].

MAURITIUS, an island of the south-western Indian Ocean, one of the three Mascarene Islands (together with Réunion and Rodrigues), located some 2,300 miles (3,680 km) north-west of Cape Town, a similar distance south south-east of Aden, and 2,000 miles (3,200 km) south-west of Colombo.

Although probably known to Arab navigators from as early as the 12th century A.D., none of the Mascarene Islands (or of the more northerly Seychelles) were ever colonised by Muslim—or any other—peoples before their discovery by Europeans in the early 16th century A.D.

During subsequent centuries, the Island of

Mauritius (named by the Dutch, after the *Stadthouder* Maurice of Nassau in 1598) passed successively under Dutch, French and British suzerainty, falling to the latter power during the Napoleonic Wars on 3 December 1810. Whilst the Portuguese discoverers of Mauritius in the early 16th century made no attempt to settle or develop the Mascarenes, Dutch settlers began the colonisation of Mauritius in 1638 when numbers of European convicts, together with slaves from Indonesia and Madagascar, were landed on the island. It is probable that most of the Indonesians, and certainly some of the Madagascans, were Muslims. By 1710, however, Dutch attempts at settling Mauritius ended in failure, and during the subsequent French administration of the island slave labour was imported almost exclusively from Madagascar and the Swahili Coast. Few of these enforced settlers are likely to have been of Muslim origin, however, for the African Muslims of the Swahili Coast tended to be the controllers, rather than the victims, of the Arabian Sea slave traffic.

Muslims, therefore, came to Mauritius in large numbers only after the British seizure of power in 1810 and, more particularly, after the abolition of slavery in 1835 and the introduction of large-scale indentured labour from the Indian subcontinent, for work in the sugar plantations, at about the same time. Indian migrants to Mauritius during the mid-19th century tended to be drawn mainly from the poor labouring classes of Bihar, the United Provinces (Uttar Pradesh), Orissa and Bengal (migrating via Bombay and Calcutta), or from similar social groups in Tamil Nadu and southern India (migrating via Madras). In this way, nearly 450,000 Indians entered Mauritius between about 1835 and 1907, with a few additional South Asians entering the colony in 1922-3. The indentured labourers who made up the great majority of Indian migrants were generally engaged on five-year contracts, but during the whole period of immigration only 160,000 were returned to India, the great majority remaining beyond the end of their contracts to swell the population of Mauritius. In addition to these poorer, indentured classes, comparatively well-to-do Indians, particularly Muslim traders from Gudjarāt (erroneously known as "Arabs" in contemporaneous Mauritian circles) and *Chettiars* from South India also began to settle in the island, where they soon became to dominate the trade of Port Louis and the outlying provincial centres.

Thus in 1835 Indo-Mauritians numbered a minute and demographically insignificant portion of the Mauritian population, whilst by 1845 their numbers had grown to *ca.* 33%, and by 1861 fully 64% of the total population. The process of Indian migration to Mauritius was officially halted in 1909, but by this time the ethnic composition of the island had been radically transformed, with Indo-Mauritians comprising the overwhelming majority of the population, a situation which continues today; other important sections of the Mauritian population include Creoles, Chinese, and an influential French community.

Among Indo-Mauritians, approximately 25% (or 16% of the total population) are of Muslim faith. They live scattered throughout the island, with about 43% of their number located in urban communities (especially in Port Louis, the capital), and 57% located in smaller rural communities. Within Port Louis, the Gudjarātī Muslims are chiefly engaged in trade, whilst those descended from poorer indentured labourers form an urban labour force.

The great majority of Muslim Mauritians are Sunnīs, especially of the Ḥanafī *madhhab* (83%); Sunnī Shāfiʿīs are also well represented (*ca.* 7%), whilst smaller identifiable groups include the Shīʿa (0.8%), the Bohrās [*q.v.*] (0.3%) and (counted as Muslim for census purposes) a flourishing Aḥmadiyya [*q.v.*] community (*ca.* 9%). According to Benedict (1965), in general terms Muslim Mauritians are more highly organised on a religious basis than the Hindu Indo-Mauritians. This is related to their minority status, to the appearance early in Mauritian history of wealthy Muslims who supported their religion through *wakf* endowments, and "most of all to the nature of Islam itself, which lays down tenets for a religious community". In 1965, there were 65 mosques on the island, governance of each being in the hands of a *mutawali* or manager, usually elected by the congregation. All but one of these mosques have been constituted as a *wakf* endowment for purposes of support. The mosque is the focal point of Mauritian Muslim society, around which are formed *jammats* or religious associations. In 1952 the total Muslim population of Mauritius was listed as 77,014; by 1962 this had reportedly risen to 110,332.

Bibliography: R. N. Gassita, *L'Islam à l'Île Maurice*, in *RMM*, xxi (1912), 291-313; B. Benedict, *Mauritius: the problems of a plural society*, London 1965; Moomtaz Emrith, *The Muslims in Mauritius*, Port Louis 1967; A. Tousaint, *History of Mauritius*, London, 1977; L. Riviere, *Historical dictionary of Mauritius*, Metuchen, N.J. 1982, esp. arts. "Indian immigration" (58-9), "Indo-Mauritians" (59-60) and "Muslims" (86-7).

(A. D. W. Forbes)

MAWĀKIB (A., sing. *mawkib*), processions.

1. Under the ʿAbbāsids and Fāṭimids

The basic meaning of procession (mounted or unmounted), cortège, is found in *ḥadīth* (al-Bukhārī, *Badʾ al-khalḳ*, 6; Ibn Ḥanbal, iii, 213; al-Dārimī, 2695). This is the precise sense given in the dictionaries, and that used by the Umayyads, ʿAbbāsids and Fāṭimids, often to describe the cortège of an *amīr*, *wazīr*, or other official (see, e.g., al-Ṭabarī, ii, 1731; Hilāl al-Ṣābī, *Rusūm dār al-khilāfa*, 9-10, 12, 14ff.).

By the 4th/10th century, it had acquired the broader meaning of audience as well as procession. Examples of this usage of *mawkib* abound in the literature. In addition to the references for the ʿAbbāsids in Sourdel, *Vizirat*, ii, 452, 653, 684, 685, see also *Tadjārib al-umam*, 195 (*yawm mawkib wa-dawla djadīda*), and al-Ṣābī, *Rusūm*, 71-2 (under rules for *hidjāba*), 78, 90; for the Fāṭimids, al-Ḳalḳashandī, *Ṣubḥ*, iii, 481, 494 (*djulūs al-khalīfa fī 'l-mawākib*). The phrase most often designating an audience is *ayyām al-mawākib*. In both ʿAbbāsid and Fāṭimid sources, this seems to refer specifically to the general audiences held on Mondays and Thursdays (Hilāl al-Ṣābī, *Historical remains* ..., ed. Amedroz, Leiden 1904, 242, 244 (Thursday); *Tadjārib*, 195, refers to a Monday; al-Ḳalḳashandī, *Ṣubḥ*, iii, 494, 496, 518, 523). For details on audiences, see marāsim).

There was a strict protocol to be observed when accompanying the ruler (*al-musāyara*) in procession. The most important and oft-repeated exhortation was to be vigilant in keeping to one's assigned place (*yalzam al-mawḍiʿ alladhī fīhi rutbatuhu*), reflecting the emphasis on *tartīb*, arrangement of the *mawkib* according to rank. The rider must know the position of the caliph, without, however, turning too often to see him. He must maintain a silent and dignified bearing, speaking only in response to the caliph's questions. He should not ride where the caliph will get wind of his horse or where dust will be kicked up into his face.

He should not enter the caliph's shadow; but he must ride on the sunny side of the *mawkib* to shade the caliph from the sun.

If a person was chosen to accompany the caliph, he was cautioned not to consider this as a permanent position but rather as a privilege granted each time the caliph invited him. If the caliph decided to walk, all had to follow suit. If he were to dismount because of a call of nature, everyone had to dismount because they may not be mounted while he stands on the ground. If he dismounts to prayer, they should pray with him. And if he drinks something, they should avert their glance (further elaboration in al-Ṣābī, *Rusūm*, 86-9; al-Ḳāḍī al-Nuʿmān, *Kitāb al-Himma*, 116-19; al-Djāḥiẓ, *K. al-Tādj*, 72, 77-83).

There are precious little data on the processions of the ʿAbbāsids, almost certainly a reflection of the static and non-processional character of ʿAbbāsid ceremonial. Neither of the two *mawākib* about which we have significant details (al-Ṣābī, *Rusūm*, 9-10, the *mawkib* of Nāzūk; 12-14, Byzantine embassies) describes a caliphal procession.

The Fāṭimids had, perhaps, the most elaborate processions of any of their contemporaries. This has been attributed to the influence of Byzantium (see M. Canard, *Le cérémonial fāṭimide et le cérémonial byzantin: essai de comparaison*, in *Byzantion*, xxi [1951], 408ff.). Where there is a dearth of information for the ʿAbbāsids, there is an abundance for the Fāṭimids. This is probably due largely to the fact that most of the sources for the Fāṭimids were transmitted by Mamlūk authors, reflecting the Mamlūk predilection for elaborate public processions.

The Fāṭimids staged grand processions on the New Year, the first of Ramaḍān, the last three Fridays of Ramaḍān, the Two Festivals and the inundation of the Nile. The most complete descriptions are those of Ibn al-Ṭuwayr, the late Fāṭimid-early Ayyūbid historian. Both Ibn Taghrībirdī and al-Ḳalḳashandī rely almost exclusively (albeit without attribution) on his undated descriptions. Only al-Maḳrīzī, in the monumental *Khiṭaṭ* and his history of the Fāṭimids, *Ittiʿāẓ al-ḥunafāʾ* (published in 3 volumes, Cairo 1967-72), relies on the dated accounts of Ibn Zūlāḳ, al-Musabbiḥī and Ibn al-Maʾmūn al-Baṭāʾiḥī, in addition to Ibn al-Ṭuwayr. These dated accounts reveal considerable changes in processions over the course of time, although many general features remained constant.

Al-Ḳalḳashandī enumerates the insignia of sovereignty (*al-ālāt al-mulūkiyya*) used in processions (*Ṣubḥ*, iii, 468-71; cf. Ibn Khaldūn, *Muḳaddima*, tr. Rosenthal, ii, 48-73, and Canard, *Cérémonial fâtimite*, 388-93): crown (*tādj*—not a crown *per se*, but an elaborate turban wound in a particular fashion); sceptre (*ḳaḍīb al-mulk*), held by the caliph during the procession; sword (*al-sayf al-khāṣṣ*); inkstand (*dawāt*); lance (*rumḥ*); shield (*daraḳa*); *ḥāfir*, "horseshoe", a crescent-shaped ruby affixed to a piece of silk and attached to the top of the *tādj*; parasol (*miẓalla*, carried over the head of the caliph); flags (*aʿlām*); fly-swatters (*midhabba*); arms (*silāḥ*); drums (*naḳḳārāt*); and tents (*al-khiyām wa 'l-fasāṭīṭ*).

Not all of these insignia appeared in every procession. For example, on the processions for the *ʿīd al-naḥr* and the anointment of the Nilometer during the time of Ibn al-Maʾmūn, the caliph carried no *ḳaḍīb* (al-Maḳrīzī, *Khiṭaṭ*, i, 436, 473). Ibn al-Ṭuwayr notes that the caliph did not have a *miẓalla* on the procession to the anointment (*ibid.*, i, 476). The *miẓalla* was not carried in the palace. When the caliph rode in a procession in which the *miẓalla* was carried, it was customary for him to visit the tomb of his ancestors (*al-turba al-muʿizziyya*) upon his return to the palace (*ibid.*, i, 407). The costumes of the caliph and his retinue, and of the *wazīr*, produced in the *dār al-kiswa* (see *ibid.*, i, 409-13) were different in each procession; the caliph sometimes changed costume for the return to the palace (*ibid.*, i, 436, 471).

The *rukūb* on the New Year (*awwal al-ʿām*) is considered as the prototype for Fāṭimid processions by Ibn al-Ṭuwayr, a claim not made by other historians of the Fāṭimid period, and perhaps representing later practice (see al-Maḳrīzī, *Khiṭaṭ*, i, 446-50; Ibn Taghrībirdī, *Nudjūm*, iv, 79-94; al-Ḳalḳashandī, *Ṣubḥ*, iii, 499-505; and Canard's translation of al-Maḳrīzī's text, *La procession du nouvel an chez les Fatimides*, in *AIEO Alger*, x [1952], 364-98, with copious annotation, based on Inostrantsev, *La sortie solennelle des Califes Fatimides*, St. Petersburg 1905 [in Russian]).

The preparations for the New Year procession began in the last ten days of Dhu 'l-Ḥidjdja, when the arms, swords, saddles, shields, spears, flags, banners, mounts and costumes were brought out of their respective treasuries for inspection. On the 29th, the caliph sat in the *shubbāk* (grilled loge) to review the horses and costumes chosen for the procession.

On Muharram, the caliph's *mawkib* was arranged in *bayn al-ḳaṣrayn*, the parade ground between the two palaces. When the caliph appeared at the gate of the palace, wearing a *mandīl* with the *yatīma*, girded with the *maghribī* sword and holding the sceptre, the drums were struck and trumpets sounded. The *miẓalla*, which matched the costume of the caliph, was unfurled. The caliph's entourage mounted up, and the whole cortège began to move.

The prefect of Cairo (*wālī al-Ḳāhira*) and the *isfahsalār* rode up and down the length of the procession, keeping the route clear and maintaining order. The caliph was surrounded by his *ṣibyān*, who were followed by the *wazīr* and his entourage. Then came the bearer of the lance, detachments of soldiers, standard bearers, and squadrons of the cavalry. The mounted soldiers numbered more than 3,000.

The *mawkib* departed from Bāb al-Naṣr and re-entered through Bāb al-Futūḥ (sometimes vice-versa), returning to *bayn al-ḳaṣrayn*. The procession dispersed, and coins struck for the New Year were distributed.

A procession inaugurated the month of Ramaḍān. The sources provide almost no details other than the fact that the procession was modelled exactly on the *rukūb* of the New Year (al-Maḳrīzī, *Khiṭaṭ*, i, 491; al-Ḳalḳashandī, *Ṣubḥ*, iii, 509). Only two accounts are imbedded in a historical narrative. Al-Musabbiḥī describes the procession of the caliph al-Ẓāhir and his troops on 1 Ramaḍān 415/6 November 1024 with a *miẓalla* and *rumḥ* (al-Maḳrīzī, *Ittiʿāẓ*, ii, 158-9; al-Musabbiḥī, *Akhbār Miṣr*, ed. Ayman Fuʾād Sayyid and Thierry Bianquis, *IFAO*, 1978, 61). Ibn al-Maʾmūn provides a very brief account of the procession of al-Āmir in 517/23 October 1123 (*Ittiʿāẓ*, iii, 102).

The caliph rode in procession to lead the prayer on three Fridays during Ramaḍān. The locations of the prayers varied somewhat. Ibn al-Ṭuwayr reports Friday prayers at the Anwar, Azhar and ʿAtīḳ mosques. Under al-Ḥākim, the Rāshida mosque was also the site of Friday prayer (see *Ṣubḥ*, iii, 509-12; Ibn Taghrībirdī, *Nudjūm*, iv, 102-4; *Khiṭaṭ*, ii, 280-2; *Ittiʿāẓ*, ii, 20, 58, 96-7, 104, 109, 118-19, 160).

The mosque was furnished and carpeted with tapestries and rugs by the *ṣāḥib bayt al-māl* (director of the public treasury). On each side of the *minbar*, curtains embroidered in red silk, containing the *basmala*, *fātiḥa*, and Sūra LXII on one and Sūra LXIII on the other, were hung. The caliph delivered the *khuṭba* under a perfumed *ḳubba*, which was fastened to conceal him from view (mentioned as early as 388/998 and 415/1024, al-Maḳrīzī, *Ittiʿāẓ*, ii, 20, 161). Then the caliph descended to the *miḥrāb* and led the prayer from inside the *maḳṣūra* [see MASDJID].

On the *ʿīd al-fiṭr* and *ʿīd al-aḍḥā* (or *al-naḥr*), the caliph rode in procession to the *muṣallā* outside of Bāb al-Futūḥ. Muezzins, sitting upon *maṣṭabas* from Bāb al-ʿĪd to the *muṣallā*, pronounced the *takbīr* continuously while the caliph was en route. The caliph wore his full costume with the *miẓalla* and the *yatīma*. Like prayer during Ramaḍān, the *miḥrāb* was hung with two curtains, the one on the right with the *basmala* and Sūra LXXXVII, on the left with Sūra LXXXVIII (*Khiṭaṭ*, i, 451-7; *Ittiʿāẓ*, i, 137-8; ii, 5, 58, 79, 82, 87, 97, 109, 160-1; iii, 60, 83-168-9).

Upon returning from the *muṣallā*, a banquet was held in the *īwān* (in some periods, in the *ḳāʿat al-dhahab*), when the silver *māʾida* called *al-mudawwara* was set up, covered with magnificent foods, including sugar castles made in the *dār al-fiṭra*. There were two banquets on *ʿīd al-fiṭr*, one before and one after prayer. People were encouraged to carry food away from the banquet and redistribute it (on banquets, see *Khiṭaṭ*, i, 387-8).

On the *ʿīd al-naḥr*, the caliph sacrificed animals either in the *muṣallā* or the *manḥar*, which were then distributed to notables of the state (see *Khiṭaṭ*, i, 436-8; *Ṣubḥ*, iii, 523-4; *Nudjūm*, iv, 97-8). Ibn al-Maʾmūn describes in detail the inventory of sacrifices and distributions for the years 515 and 516 (*Khiṭaṭ*, i, 437, and *Ittiʿāẓ*, iii, 95-6). Ibn al-Ṭuwayr reports three consecutive *rukūbs*: on the first day to the *muṣallā*; on the second and third to the *manḥar* next to Bāb al-Rīḥ (cf. Ibn al-Ṭuwayr's description of the way the caliph slaughters, with the general rules as described in art. DHABĪḤA]. These rich details about the distribution of portions constitute important data for the as-yet unwritten social history of ritual (for individual years, see *Ittiʿāẓ*, i, 141-2; ii, 7, 37, 41, 59, 79, 83, 88, 91, 104, 110, 124).

Two processions took place at the time of the inundation of the Nile (*wafāʾ al-Nīl*): one to anoint the Nilometer (*takhlīḳ al-miḳyās*) and the other to cut the canal (*kaṣr al-khalīdj, fatḥ al-khalīdj*). When the water reached sixteen cubits, the *ḳayyās*, Ibn Abi 'l-Raddād (always called thus), sent a formal announcement to the caliph. The height of the rising water was measured every day, but a policy established under al-Muʿizz prohibited public announcement until it was only a few marks short of sixteen (*Khiṭaṭ*, i, 61; *Ittiʿāẓ*, i, 138-9).

The preparations for the anointment of the Nilometer began as soon as the caliph received word that the water was close to inundation. The *ḳurrāʾ* spent the night in the Nilometer, reciting the Ḳurʾān continuously. The next day, the caliph went in an *ʿushārī* (Nile boat) to the Nilometer (without a *miẓalla*, Ibn al-Ṭuwayr, *Khiṭaṭ*, i, 476, 1. 16). He entered along with the *wazīr* and the *muḥannak ustādhs*. The caliph and the *wazīr* each prayed two *rakʿas*. Then the director of the public treasury brought out saffron and musk, which the caliph mixed in a vessel and then handed over to Ibn Abi 'l-Raddād. The *ḳayyās* threw himself into the *fisḳiyya*, took hold of the pillar with his feet and left hand, and anointed it with his right hand, while the *ḳurrāʾ* recited.

The next day, Ibn Abi 'l-Raddād received a robe of honour (*khilʿa* [*q.v.*]; see an early reference in *Ittiʿāẓ*, ii, 150). On the third or fourth day following the anointment, the caliph went out in procession to the banks of the Nile, passing through Fusṭāṭ (decorated by its residents) and crossing to the west bank, where grand tents had been erected for the occasion. The magnificent *khayma* known as *al-Ḳātūl* (so-called because someone was invariably killed when it was set up) was put up (*Khiṭaṭ*, i, 471; *Ittiʿāẓ*, iii, 72-3). The canal was cut and the *ʿushārīs* sailed in it. The caliphs used to take up residence in one of two pleasures-houses (*manẓaras*) during the days of these festivities (for complete descriptions, see *Khiṭaṭ*, i, 470-9; *Ṣubḥ*, iii, 518ff.; *Nudjūm*, iv, 99-100; Schefer, *Relation du voyage de Nasiri Khosrau en Syrie, en Palestine, en Egypte, en Arabie*, Paris 1881, 136-7; particular years, in Ibn Muyassar, *Akhbār Miṣr*, 44; *Ittiʿāẓ*, i, 319, ii, 59, 148-50, iii, 72-3, 81, 108, 129).

These major processions were announced to the provinces in letters from the *dīwān al-inshāʾ*. A number of these literary specimens remain, most from the pen of the celebrated *kātib* Ibn al-Ṣayrafī (*ʿĪd al-fiṭr*; *Khiṭaṭ*, i, 456-7 (536/1141-2); *al-Sidjillāt al-mustansiriyya*, ed. ʿAbd al-Munʿim Mādjid, Cairo 1954, no. 1 (451/1059), no. 13 (445/1053); *Ṣubḥ*, viii, 320-4. *ʿĪd al-naḥr*: *Khiṭaṭ*, i, 437-8; *Ṣubḥ*, viii, 324-8; *Sidjillāt*, no. 64 (476/1083). New Year: *Ṣubḥ*, viii, 314-15. Ramaḍān and Friday prayer: *Ṣubḥ*, viii, 316-19. Nile: *Khiṭaṭ*, i, 479; *Ṣubḥ*, viii, 328-9. An unidentified procession is described in *Rasāʾil al-ʿĀmidī*, ms. 4059 [Cat. 4365], fols. 24-5, in the Garrett Collection, Princeton University Library).

There were several minor processions, called "abbreviated" (*al-mawākib al-mukhtaṣara*) between the New Year and Ramaḍān, but there are almost no details on them except that they took place on Tuesday and Saturday, four or five times. They were much less elaborate than the major processions (see *Ṣubḥ*, iii, 521-2).

The only Shīʿī holiday marked by a procession was the *ʿĪd al-ghadīr* on 18 Dhu 'l-Ḥidjdja, commemorating the *waṣiyya* to ʿAlī by the Prophet [see GHADĪR KHUMM]. In the early part of the Fāṭimid period, it was essentially a popular celebration of the Shīʿī population. During the time of Ibn al-Maʾmūn, it had become a court ceremony modelled on the rituals of *ʿīd al-naḥr*, with a procession to the *manḥar*. At the end of the Fāṭimid period, it had acquired a much different and complex character. Now an internal palace procession, attended only by professed Ismāʿīlīs, it took place at the Shrine of Ḥusayn and the *īwān*. The caliph delivered a *khuṭba*, but rode without insignia or *miẓalla*. Upon returning to the *īwān*, the text of the *naṣṣ* of ʿAlī was read to the assembly. This late procession was, in fact, a ceremonial polemic against the Ṭayyibīs (on the history of the celebration, see al-Maḳrīzī, *Ittiʿāẓ*, i, 273, 276, 280, 284, ii, 24, 67, 74, 91, 168, iii, 96; *Khiṭaṭ*, i, 388-90, 436, 492-3; al-Musabbiḥī, *Akhbār Miṣr*, 84-5; on the late Fāṭimids, see S. M. Stern, *The succession to the Fāṭimid Imām al-Āmir, the claims of the later Fāṭimids to the Imamate, and the rise of Ṭayyibī Ismailism*, in *Oriens*, iv [1951], 193-255).

Bibliography: In addition to the citations in the text, see the bibliography at the end of MARĀSIM. 1. (P. SANDERS)

2. IN MUSLIM SPAIN

The sovereign power of the *amīrs* and caliphs of al-Andalus showed itself in the etiquette [see MARĀSIM] of public audiences and during their official movements when, surrounded by their processional retinue (*mawkib*), they went into or came out of their residence. This was generally at the departure for a military campaign, to review the troops or to travel from one residence to another.

According to Ibn Khaldūn's *Muḳaddima*, "the

insignia of sovereignty are the displaying of flags, the beating of drums and the sounding of trumpets and horns'', but as it happens, the historical sources for Muslim Spain have not preserved any traces of this use of wind instruments. Already under Hishām I (172-80/788-96), ''the hubbub and din of the procession (*ladjab al-mawkib*) prevented the complaint of a petitioner being heard'' (*Akhbār*, 121). This was the occasion for the people to see the *amīr* ʿAbd Allāh; the latter was surrounded by cavalrymen at the moment when the future al-Nāṣir's mule bolted; before the battle of Polei, the *amīr* had his canopy (*maẓall*) raised; that of the prince Abān was carried off by a gust of wind at the same time as the *ḳāʾid*'s *ḳubba* (Ibn Ḥayyān, *Muḳtabas*, iii, 36, 40, 95, 120). These processions were festivals, in the words of Ibn ʿAbd Rabbihi (*Crónica anónima*, 40).

The first riding forth of al-Nāṣir was in order to go hunting. In 322/934, it seems, at the time of his departure for the Osma campaign, ''dressed in a coat of mail, with his sword at his side, mounted on a chestnut-coloured charger and surrounded by his generals and his troops'', this was the first time that ''the eagle standard was unfurled''. In 326/938, Muḥammad b. Hāshim al-Tudjībī had the honour of accompanying him on horseback from the caliphal palace to the residence at al-Ramla. For the attack on Osma and on Ega, the caliph had his *maẓall* raised. It would thus appear that we have here a tent or a fixed canopy and that the *maẓall* is synonymous with the *ḳubba.* But there was also a mobile ''parasol'' or sunshade, for at the time of the attack on Calatayud, al-Nāṣir rode along until the evening in full exposure to the sun (*ghayr muẓallal*). The caliph used to travel along surrounded by guards, who on one occasion killed a madman who threw himself at his mount's head. The caliphal procession was regarded as something of a serious occasion, and imitating or parodying it was considered to be a ''crime'' on the part of al-Nāṣir ''when he set astride a mount his female buffoon Rasīs, rigged out in a *ḳalansuwa* and a sword'' (*Muḳtabas*, v, 22-3, 34, 109, 124, 225, 269, 287). Kettledrums were known and must have formed an element of the procession since al-Nāṣir sent some of them to the rallied Maghribīs (*ibid.*, 239, 290, 312).

In 361/972, the street of the Furn Burriel proved too narrow for the procession of al-Ḥakam II; it was after one of these march-pasts that he ordered the burning of the Berber saddle of one of his *ghulāms*. Surrounded by his chief *fatās*, his approach was regulated by the *aṣḥāb al-madīna* of Cordova and al-Zahrāʾ, and the people kissed the ground and greeted and blessed the caliph before making known their petitions. The route was always ''lined with the troops''. To march past was a signal honour which was given to the emigrés Djaʿfar and Yaḥyā b. ʿAlī, who marched along preceded by the heads of the fallen Zīrids and by flags and escorted by the troops, Abu 'l-ʿAysh, the *fatā* Fāʾiḳ and Ghālib, returned victorious from his campaigns in the Maghrib. The *maẓall* continued to be an attribute of the sovereign which he delegated for the expedition against the Madjūs [*q.v.*] in 361/972 or else to the Dhu 'l-Sayfayn Ghālib (*Muḳtabas*, vi, 45, 67, 79, 115, 152, 173, 190, 195-6, 212).

In 387/997, after having thwarted the plot of Ṣubḥ, al-Manṣūr [*q.v.*] decided to show to the people the caliph Hishām II ''clothed in a *ḳalansuwa* wound round with a white turban, whose ends were flowing free, and with a sceptre in his hand'' (*muʿammam^an^ ʿalā 'l-ṭawīla sādil^an^ li 'l-dhuʾāba wa 'l-ḳaḍīb fī yadihi*); to his left rode forward al-Manṣūr, preceded by the *ḥādjib* ʿAbd al-Malik who went on foot, followed by the army, *djund*, *ghilmān* and *fityān*, ''in front of an enormous crowd'' (Ibn Bassām, *Dhakhīra*, vii, 73; *Dhikr*, 156). In 393/1003, al-Muẓaffar went forth ''armed from top to toe in a new coat of mail, with a new golden helmet on his head, surrounded by generals, freedmen, etc.'' (*Bayān*, iii, 5). The assassination of ʿAlī b. Ḥammūd in his bath was discovered because ''the army was waiting for the order to march forth, with its standards unfurled and the kettledrums ready'' (*Dhikr*, 170). If Ibn ʿAmmār [*q.v.*] entered Silves at the head of ''a splendid procession, followed by black slaves and guards'', al-Muʿtamid [*q.v.*] mockingly made him enter Cordova ''in the most shameful manner, mounted on a mule, between two sacks of straw, bare-headed and loaded with fetters, and having ordered everybody, nobles and plebs, to come out and see the spectacle'' (al-Marrākushī, *Muʿdjib*, 80, 86). When the *ḳāḍī* Ibn Djaḥḥāf [*q.v.*] of Valencia got rid of al-Ḳādir b. Dhi 'l-Nūn [*q.v.*], ''he behaved like a sovereign ruler, surrounded by royal pomp ... he only mounted his horse when preceded by black soldiers and guards, escorted by troops, whilst his creatures decorated the streets, shouting out blessings and praises'' (Ibn ʿIdhārī, *Nuevos fragmentos* ..., 69-70).

The processions of the Almohads or Muwaḥḥidūn [*q.v.*] were rich and complex. The caliph rode forth surrounded by the great leaders of the Almohads, preceded by a richly-caparisoned camel bearing the Ḳurʾān of ʿUthmān and followed by another with that of the Mahdī. The caliph was accompanied by his sons, standard-bearers and a hundred kettledrummers, and followed by the high dignitaries of state. The caliph would mount at the entrance of his tent or his residence, whilst the vizier walked at the side of his stirrup. The order of precedence was immutable and fixed by custom (*ʿāda*) (Ibn Ṣāḥib al-Ṣalāt, *al-Mann bi 'l-imāma*; al-Marrākushī, *Muʿdjib*; Ibn ʿIdhārī, *Bayān*, ed. Huici Miranda, Tetouan 1963). Certain items of clothing were special to the caliph. In 582/1186, during his campaign of Gafsa, ''al-Manṣūr inspected his retinue and observed that the majority of his brothers and uncles had distinguished themselves by wearing violet-coloured mantles and musk-coloured burnouses (*libās al-ghafāʾir al-zabībiyya wa 'l-barānis al-miskiyya*). He reproached them for this, since these adornments formed part of the caliph's prerogatives of state, whether he were mounted on horseback or seated in his audience chamber ... he reminded them of the usages of royal power which they should respect and should refrain from imitating the royal privileges and using the royal colours''. In 568/1172, during the siege of Huete, Abū Yaʿḳūb was ''surrounded by his guard, accompanied by the sons of the *djamāʿa* and by those of the Fifty, by the *ahl al-bayt* and by the slaves; behind him came his brother, the Sayyid Abū Ḥafṣ and his other brothers, followed by standards and by a hundred kettledrums playing'' (*Mann*, 493). When in 578/1182 his remains were brought from Santarem to Seville, the great men of state, in order to conceal his death, ''began to walk, in accordance with the customary procedure, at the side of the animals bearing his litter, then they mounted their horses and the litter was covered with a green flag'' (*Muʿdjib*, 192).

We do not possess any exact information about the processions of the Naṣrids [*q.v.*]; one can only suppose that they were very simple, in view of the exiguousness of their territories. Ibn Khaldūn seems to confirm this, mentioning that ''the Banu 'l-Aḥmar used only seven musical instruments in their processions''.

Bibliography: Given in the article.

(P. Chalmeta)

3. In Iran

From ancient times, processions were connected with court ceremonial. Religious and triumphal processions are illustrated on ancient monuments. In Islamic times, the purpose of processions was mainly to emphasise the glory and power of the ruler. Only those concerned with the ruler and his entourage will be considered in this article. (For the Muḥarram processions see TAʿZIYA.) On the whole, processions do not appear to have been highly organised, but often to have consisted of a great concourse of men, mainly mounted but also on foot. Only in the immediate vicinity of the ruler was there a certain order and discipline. It was customary for the ruler to ride in procession from time to time to the Friday mosque for the performance of the Friday prayers and also to the *muṣallā*, the place outside the town where prayers were held to celebrate the breaking of the fast at the end of Ramaḍān (*ʿīd al-fiṭr*) and on the *ʿīd-i ḳurbān* (*ʿīd al-aḍḥā*). On such occasions, he would be accompanied by a cortège formed by his officials, officers and followers, and standard-bearers would bear his standards before him (*liwāʾ*, *ʿalam* [*q.v.*]; see also Spuler, *Iran*, 349). Sometimes a parasol (*čatr*, see MIẒALLA) would be held over his head.

Whereas the mule was customarily the mount of the caliph and religious dignitaries, the horse was the mount of him who held temporal power. The point at which a visiting ruler or envoy dismounted was a frequent cause of contention and the privilege of remaining mounted when entering the presence of another ruler was eagerly contested (see further Spuler, *Iran*, 343). ʿAḍud al-Dawla, the Būyid, sent a message to the caliph al-Ṭāʾiʿ in 367/977-8 asking permission to enter the court (*ṣaḥn*) of the caliph's palace (*dār al-khilāfa*) mounted (Faḳīhī, *Shāhinshahī-i ʿAḍud al-Dawla*, Tehran, AHS 1347/1969, 59; Hilāl al-Ṣābī, 80).

The custom of having a saddled horse (*asb-i nawbatī*, *faras al-nawba*) at the palace gate on which the ruler could mount in an emergency or on other occasions apparently existed from the 2nd century A.H. The practice appears to have been started by Abū Muslim. According to Djūzdjānī, a saddled horse was always kept ready at the gate of the palace which had been built for him in Marw-i Shāh-Djahān until the Mongol invasion in 617/1220-1 (*Ṭabaḳāt-i Nāṣirī*, ed. ʿAbd al-Ḥayy Ḥabībī, Kābul 1964, i, 107; see also Muḥammad Taḳī Dānishpazhūh, *Asp-i nawbatī bar dar-i kākh-i Abū Muslim*, in *Rāhnamā-yi kitāb*, xii [AHS 1348/1967-8], 225-8). The anonymous author of the *Mudjmal al-tawārīkh* states that the ʿAbbāsid caliph al-Manṣūr mounted the *asb-i nawbatī* during operations against the Rāwandīs (ed. Malik al-Shuʿarāʾ Bahār, Tehran AHS 1318/1939-40, 329). The Sāmānid rulers Aḥmad b. Ismāʿīl (295-301/907-14) and Naṣr II (301-31/914-43) always had a saddled horse ready at the gate of the palace (Spuler, *Iran*, 352; see also Browne, *LHP*, i, 317). The Saldjūḳs of Kirmān also appear to have kept a saddled horse ready. Afḍal al-Dīn Kirmānī relates an occasion when Muḥammad b. Arslānshāh (537-51/1142-56) gave the *asb-i nawbatī*—an Arab horse with *maghribī* harness—to one of his intimates, Mukhtaṣṣ al-Dīn ʿUthmān (*Badāyiʿ al-azmān wa waḳāyiʿ Kirmān*, reconstructed text by Mihdī Bayānī, Tehran AHS 1326/1947-8, 26; Muḥammad b. Ibrāhīm, *Tārīkh-i Saldjūḳiyān-i Kirmān*, ed. Th. Houtsma, Leiden 1886, 31).

Whether the *asb-i nawbatī* was used for processions or not, saddled horses, magnificently caparisoned, were an important part of royal pageantry. They were also often given by rulers, together with *khilʿas* [*q.v.*] to high officials, visiting envoys and others [see MARĀSIM. 3]. The Ghaznawids kept many elephants, and Masʿūd probably more often rode an elephant than a horse on ceremonial occasions. Bayhaḳī states that when Masʿūd went from Ghazna on 5 Shawwāl 422/29 July 1031 to the Dasht-i Shābahār to hold a *maẓālim* court, he was mounted on an elephant. It was an occasion of great pomp and splendour. Three hundred *ghulāms*, magnificently apparelled, and many elephants and led horses, including 30 caparisoned with jewel-encrusted harness and 50 with golden harness, were in his train. The *ghulāms* of the palace, equipped with bows and arrows and golden and silver staffs went on foot in front with armour-bearers from Marw and 3,000 footmen of various origins and other soldiers and the notables and the "pillars of the state" (Abu 'l-Faḍl Bayhaḳī, *Tārīkh-i Masʿūdī*, ed. ʿAlī Akbar Fayyāḍ, Mashhad AHS 1350/1971, 372-3).

When the ruler rode out to a garden or to summer quarters, or made a progress through his domains, he would be accompanied by his retinue. Royal marriages and betrothals, the sending of the marriage portion of the bride (*mahr*, *ṣadāḳ*), and funerals were other occasions for processions. When the daughter of the Ḳarā Khānid Ḳadir Khān Yūsuf of Turkistān, who had been betrothed to Masʿūd b. Maḥmūd, was brought to Ghazna in Shawwāl 425/August-September 1034, the *martabadārān* (for the meaning of this term, see MARĀSIM. 3), the head of the royal guard (*wālī-yi ḥaras*) and the officials charged with the reception of envoys (*rasūldārān*) went out with led horses to meet the envoys of Ḳadir Khān, who had come with the bride, and to bring them to Ghazna. The city was decorated from end to end and when the envoys arrived coins were cast at their feet. Then, at the time of the afternoon prayer, the women of the great men of Masʿūd's court, accompanied by eunuchs, set out to greet the bride with a cortège "such as no one could remember" (Bayhaḳī, 548-9).

Processions took place when envoys and others came to the ruler's court. When the caliph's envoy arrived at the court of Masʿūd b. Maḥmūd in Balkh at the end of 422/1032 to announce the death of the caliph al-Ḳādir and the accession of al-Ḳāʾim, he was brought with great ceremony into the presence of Masʿūd on 1 Muḥarram 423/19 December 1031. Four thousand palace *ghulāms*, magnificently attired, were drawn up at the palace in several lines; half of them held silver maces and half were armed with swords and carried bows and three wooden arrows. Three hundred *ghulāms* of the royal bodyguard with golden maces stood near the throne. The great men of the court, provincial governors and chamberlains in their court dresses were also there. The *martabadārān* stood outside the palace. There were also large numbers of elephants [see FĪL. 2. As beasts of war]; soldiers with their arms and standards were drawn up in two lines, between which the envoy was to pass. The *rasūldār* with led horses and a great crowd went to fetch him from his lodging, mounted him on one of these horses and, amid the sound of drums and trumpets, brought him to the palace where Masʿūd was awaiting him (*ibid.*, 382). On the following Friday, Masʿūd went to the Friday mosque for the pronouncement of the *khuṭba* in the name of the new caliph. The scene was again one of great splendour. The procession was led by 4,000 splendidly dressed foot *ghulāms*, followed by the Ghaznawid general Beg Toghdī and the royal *ghulāms* with the ruler's banner, the *martabadārān* and chamberlains. After them Masʿūd, preceded by the chief chamberlain, set out along the road from the palace to the mosque, which had been decorated on his orders by the notables of the city. Behind him came his chief minister, more chamberlains and the notables of the court. They were followed by the *ra*ʾ*īs*, Khʷādja ʿAlī Mīkālī [see MĪKĀLĪS], with the caliph's envoy on his right, the *ḳāḍīs*, *fuḳahā*ʾ and *ʿulamā*ʾ and the headman (*zaʿīm*) of Balkh. As the procession slowly approached the mosque, "no sound was heard except the sound of the whips and the shouts of the *martabadārān* to clear the way" (*ibid.*, 384-5).

The following year when an envoy from al-Ḳāʾim reached Rayy on his way to Masʿūd's court, with a diploma from the caliph, Masʿūd ordered a reception (*istiḳbāl*) to be prepared for him. An escort was sent with him from Rayy and when he reached Nīshāpūr on 8 Rabīʿ I 424/11 February 1033, the *fuḳahā*ʾ, *ḳāḍīs* and notables of the city went out to meet him. On the following day, the *martabadārān* and *rasūldārān* also went to welcome him. The road from the Rayy gate to the Friday mosque was decorated, as also was the bazaar. *Dirhams* and *dīnārs* and valuable objects were scattered before him. A week later, after the envoy had rested from his journey, he was brought to Masʿūd's presence with great ceremony. Crowds assembled along the road from the residence of the envoy to the gate of the garden in Shādyākh, where Masʿūd was to receive him. The soldiers, notables and army leaders were mounted and held standards in their hands. Heavily-armed foot soldiers stood in front of the mounted soldiers. The *martabadārān* were drawn up in two rows. Army leaders (*sālārān*) and chamberlains were also present. A chamberlain, together with several attendants, led horses and a mule, was taken early in the morning by the *rasūldār* with twenty *khilʿas* to the envoy's residence to bring him to Masʿūd, who was to receive him sitting on his throne on a platform (*ṣuffa*). The *rasūldār* caused the envoy and the eunuch (*khādim*), who accompanied him, to mount and had the *khilʿas* which the caliph had sent with them put in boxes on mules. The cortège set out amid the sound of drums and trumpets preceded by treasury officials (*shāgirdān-i khazīna*) and eight horses with golden saddles and harness led by their bridles. Then came the envoy, preceded by the royal chamberlains and *martabadārān*, followed by the envoy and behind him two horsemen, one carrying a standard and the other the diploma and letter of the caliph rolled up in black brocade (*ibid.*, 471-2; see also MARĀSIM. 3).

A new feature of royal ceremonial was introduced by the Saldjūḳs, namely the *ghāshiya* [*q.v.*]. This was a kind of saddle-cover, probably covered with precious stones, which was carried before the sultan in processions. This custom appears to have died out in Persia after the Saldjūḳs, but was found later in Egypt (see GHĀSHIYA, and also Ibn Baṭṭūṭa, *Travels*, tr. H.A.R. Gibb, Cambridge 1956-71, iii, 664). When Ṭoghril Beg brought the ʿAbbāsid caliph al-Ḳāʾim back to Baghdād after he had left the city on the attack of al-Basāsīrī in 450/1059, he dismounted at the gate of Baghdād but was told by the caliph to remount (Rāwandī, *Rāḥat al-ṣudūr*, ed. Muḥammad Iḳbāl, London 1921, 110, and see Spuler, *op.cit.*, 343). On entering Baghdād, it appears that Ṭoghril Beg again dismounted and carried the *ghāshiya* in front of the caliph until they came near to the caliph's palace, when Ṭoghril took the bridle of the caliph's mule and walked beside him until they entered the Bāb al-Ḥudjra (the Privy Chamber Gate) (Ṣadr al-Dīn al-Ḥusaynī, *Akhbār al-dawla al-Saldjūḳiyya*, ed. Muḥammad Iḳbāl, Lahore 1933, 21).

On an earlier occasion, when Ṭoghril Beg was to have an audience with the caliph in 449/1057-8, the caliph's boat was sent to bring him down the Tigris to the caliph's palace. He was accompanied by his intimates (*khawāṣṣ*), some in boats and some mounted on elephants. Alighting from the boat, Ṭoghril mounted one of the caliph's horses which had been sent to meet him and entered the caliph's palace, preceded by the sons of Abū Kālīdjār b. Būya and Ḳutlumush, army leaders and Daylamīs and nearly 500 unarmed Turkish and Gīlānī *ghulāms*. When he reached the gateway of the passage (*dihlīz*) leading to the audience hall, he was kept waiting for a long time on his horse until the gate was opened for him and then he entered on foot (Sibṭ Ibn al-Djawzī, *Mirʾāt al-zamān*, ed. Ali Sevim, Ankara 1968, 25). On a subsequent occasion in Muḥarram 455/January 1063 when Ṭoghril came to Baghdād, the caliph excused himself from going to meet him and sent instead his *wazīr* Ibn Djahīr, who took with him two horses and other presents. On the following day, Ṭoghril entered the Dār al-Mamlaka in a boat sent by the caliph (*ibid.*, 97).

In 480/1087, when the caliph invited Malikshāh to the Dār al-Khilāfa, he sent a boat for him. Disembarking at the Bāb al-Ghurabāʾ, Malikshāh mounted a richly caparisoned horse sent for him by the caliph, which carried him to the gate of the caliph's audience chamber (*ibid.*, 244-5). In Muḥarram of that year, when Malikshāh sent the marriage portion (*djahāz*) of his daughter to the caliph, to whom she had been betrothed, it was carried by 130 camels (a second instalment being apparently carried by 74 mules on the following day), preceded by 30 led horses, all splendidly caparisoned. The cortège was led by Saʿd al-Dawla Gōhar-Āʾīn, the *shiḥna* of Baghdād, and the *amīr* Bursuḳ. The city was decorated for the occasion and as the cortège went through the Nahr Muʿallā quarter the people cast *dīnārs* and precious stuffs before it. The sultan had meanwhile left Baghdād on a hunting trip, and so the caliph sent his *wazīr* Abū Shudjāʿ to Terken Khātūn, Malikshāh's chief wife and mother of the bride, with some 300 men bearing lanterns with a litter to bring the princess to the caliph's palace. She set out by night riding in the litter, surrounded by 200 Turkish slave girls on splendid mounts, preceded by the women of the *amīrs* and others, led by Niẓām al-Mulk, the *mustawfī* Abū Saʿd and the *amīrs*, all bearing lanterns (*ibid.*, 245-6; Ibn al-Athīr, *sub anno* 480; Ibn al-Djawzī, *al-Muntaẓam*, Hyderabad 1359/1940-1, ix, 36-7).

Processions do not appear to have been a special feature of Ilkhānid or Tīmūrīd ceremony. Women of the royal house took part from time to time in public ceremonies. Clavijo describes the cortège which accompanied Tīmūr's chief wife on the occasion of a public audience which he gave in the Great Pavilion in Samarḳand. She was attended by some 300 women and eunuchs. "Over the head of the princess was borne a parasol, a man holding it, and the stick was a pole the size of a lance. This parasol was of white silk, dome-shaped and round like the top of a tent, with wooden ribs that kept the stuff extended: it was very carefully held over her head as she walked to keep the sun off her face. In front preceding her and the ladies of her suite marched many eunuchs ... Thus the procession advanced entering the Pavilion where Timur was already seated. The Great Khanum now took her place beside his Highness but slightly behind on a low dais" (*Embassy to Tamerlane 1403-1406*, tr. from the Spanish by G. Le Strange, London 1928, 259-60). Others of the Tīmūrid princesses in succession then came into the pavilion with similar processions (*ibid.*, 260-1). Clavijo also mentions the presence of elephants at Tīmūr's court. They appear to have been used to entertain visitors (*ibid.*, 257).

Information on processions and court ceremonial in Ṣafawid times is fuller than for earlier periods; and it would seem that both became more elaborate. Much importance was attached to the procedure for welcoming the shah when he returned to his capital after some expedition or when he entered some city, and similarly for welcoming honoured guests. This ceremony was known by the term *istiḳbāl*. When S͟hāh ʿAbbās returned to Ḳazwīn in 1007/1598 after crushing the Özbegs in K͟hurāsān, Sir Antony Sherley and his party, which included, among others, Abel Pinçon, had already been some three weeks in Ḳazwīn awaiting the return of the shah. When the shah approached within five miles of the city, he encamped. He ordered Sherley and his party to come out two miles outside the gates of the city to meet him. Abel Pinçon describes the shah's triumphal entry in the following words. "When our company had approached to within five or six steps of the King, the steward made a sign to Monsieur Sherley, his brother and myself to dismount in order to kiss His Majesty's feet ..... He was five or six steps ahead of a large squadron of cavalry, and while he stretched out his leg he pretended the whole time to look in another direction. After we had kissed his boot he spurred his horse sharply and, guiding it dexterously, dashed across the camp after the manner of the country .... In his hand he carried a battle-axe, playing with it, carrying it now high, now low, and now and then placing it on his shoulder with rather strange movements.

"In his triumphal entry he caused to be carried on the end of strong and heavy spears twenty thousand heads of Tartars whom he had defeated in Usbeg, which appeared to me a hideous spectacle. After those who carried the heads came young men dressed like women richly decked, who danced in a manner and with movements which we had never seen elsewhere, throwing their arms about and extending them above their heads even more than they raised their legs from the ground, to the sound of *atabales* (sc. drums), flutes and certain instruments which are provided with strings, and to the sound of a song composed on the victory which they had gained, this being sung by four older women. In the midst of these young men were two grown men who carried while dancing, two lanterns like those of the largest galleys at the end of a stick which was attached to their girdle. On these lanterns were painted flowers, crowns, laurel-leaves, and birds, and along the stick hung mirrors and other glittering things. Among all this crowd was a large troop of courtesans, riding astride in disorder, and shouting and crying in every direction as if they had lost their senses, and frequently they approached the person of the King to embrace him. Behind the noble squadron there came on foot a number of pages who carried good bottles and flasks of wine and cups, which they presented very frequently to the King and his nobles. On either flank followed the cavalry, and in the first ranks there were four trumpeters who played on certain trumpets and sackbuts of extraordinary dimensions, which gave a bitter and broken sound very alarming to hear. The cavalry numbered two thousand five hundred horse; the first and those which were near the King were in good condition, covered with large cloths of brocade on which were represented angels and horses and other animals of all kinds, after the manner in which they decorate their materials in this country. All the inhabitants of Casbin and of the neighbourhood were come to receive their King two miles outside the gates of the city. They were separated into two groups between which the King was to pass with his triumphal retinue. And so the King on entering the town would go straight to the Midan (sc. the *maydan*), which is the public square, in which they have horse-races and training and shooting with the bow and other exercises" (*Sir Antony Sherley and his Persian adventure, including some contemporary narratives relating thereto*, ed. E. Denison Ross, London 1933, 153-5. See also the accounts of William Parry, in *ibid.*, 116-7, and George Manwaring, in *ibid.*, 204-6).

Chardin, describing S͟hāh Sulaymān's coronation in Iṣfahān in 1077/1677, states that after the ceremony he sat until 10 o'clock in the Tālār-i Ṭawīla to receive the homage of the grandees of Iṣfahān who came to kiss the ground before him, and then "rising from his Seat took Horse; and that was the first time that ever he rode out of the Place where he was born [having been immured in the *ḥaram*]. And according to the Custom of the *Persians*, he made a Cavalcade round his Palace very leisurely, and with little attendance, riding in the middle of the distance of twenty Paces from them that marched before, and those that followed after, only twelve Footmen went on each side before and behind his Horse; and all this to the end he might be the better seen by the People" (*The coronation of Solyman III. The present king of Persia*, published with *The Travels of Sir John Chardin into Persia and the East Indies*, London 1691, 56). Normally, however, when the shah rode abroad he was accompanied by a large retinue. Kaempfer describes the procedure under S͟hāh Ṣafī (by which name S͟hāh Sulaymān was known after his second coronation). In the case of his daily ride, when he came out of the *ḥaram* and prepared to proceed along the Čahār Bāg͟h, the master of the horse would lead out three horses, one of which the ruler would choose. Two groups of the bodyguard, on foot and armed, would set out in front, followed by the *is͟hiḳaḳasi-bas͟hi* on horseback and the *ḳurči-bas͟hi*, and behind them some twenty mounted troops with their leader, all wearing red twelve-sided head-dresses, adorned in the case of some by a magnificent plume of feathers. They rode without discipline, but watched over the safety of the shah. The shah followed, surrounded by twelve *s͟hāṭirs* (runners); behind him rode the grand *wazīr* or some other high dignitary. The presence of the shah was indicated by his *čatr* carried by a standard-bearer. Among the retinue, not in any special order, there would also be some twenty eunuchs, some white, some black, who carried the weapons, water-pipe and other paraphernalia of the shah. Then came those courtiers whom the shah had bidden to his table and the sons of the great men, for whom it was considered an honour to be allowed to accompany the shah. When possible, there was also a physician and an astrologer present. Officials armed with axes would be sent in front of the procession to remove any obstacles in the way of the shah's progress (*Am Hofe des persischen Grosskönigs 1684-1685*, tr. W. Hinz, Tübingen-Basle 1977, 237-8. Cf. also Du Mans, *Estat de la Perse en 1660*, ed. Schefer, Paris 1890, repr. 1969, 33).

On certain special occasions, the shah also rode out. Kaempfer describes the celebration of the *ʿĪd-i ḳurbān* in 1095/1684 in the Hazār D͟jarīb district of Iṣfahān. A large and fine camel was prepared for the sacrifice. For ten days preceding the *ʿīd* on 10 D͟hu 'l-Ḥid͟jd͟ja, it was paraded through the different quarters of the town. On the day of the sacrifice it stood in the appointed place, with its feet tied, surrounded by thousands of people, waiting for the arrival of the shah. As soon as he arrived, he dismounted and was given a lance with which he struck the camel. After its throat had been slit and its head cut off, its corpse was divided into twelve parts, one for each quarter of the city. The shah then remounted and rode back as he had come, while the people of the city assembled round their banners and accompanied their portion of the camel, which was laid on a horse and went before them to their several quarters to the sound of trumpets and drums (*op.cit.*, 239-40; see also Du Mans, *op.cit.*, 74-5; *The Travels of Monsieur de Thevenôt into the Levant*, London 1687, 107 (*bis*)-108(*bis*)).

Exceptionally, the shah rode out himself to welcome distinguished guests. In the case of a guest of royal blood, he would go half-a-mile, having sent his representative with a company of *ḳurčis* one *farsakh* (or one hour's ride) in advance. The townspeople, in festal dress, would line the streets and spread precious stuffs in front of the horses of the royal guest. Such was the procedure when the Özbeg khān ᶜAbd al-ᶜAzīz came back after performing the *ḥadjdj* in 1670 and when Akbar the son of Awrangzīb came to Persia in 1099/1688 (Kaempfer, *op.cit.*, 242).

If the shah went out hunting and took his women with him, he was accompanied by a large cavalcade, and when he moved to summer quarters in Māzandarān an enormous train accompanied him. Men would be sent in front to choose a suitable place for the camp. When they came back with their report, if the shah approved, some 7,000 camels with tents, carpets and household equipment would be sent in advance. Some days later the *ḳuruḳčis* would follow to clear all males from the neighbourhood of the road along which the royal cavalcade would travel. The shah's women, or those of them whom he decided to take with him, travelling in litters and accompanied by eunuchs, would follow. After them would come the shah with his retinue. In front would be the master of the horse with his subordinates and five or six led horses richly caparisoned, with sixty or so of the bodyguard, also mounted. Then would come the standard-bearers followed by the *ishiḳaḳasi-bashi*, the *ḳurči-bashi*, and the master of the hunt (*mīr-shikār*), accompanied by falconers with falcons on their wrists, and the chief kennelman with hunting-dogs led by attendants on foot. Then would come the shah with twelve personal attendants. Immediately behind the shah came the great men of the court, and finally numerous mounted slaves, among them the water-pipe carriers and those in charge of boxes of ice, sugar and other condiments carried on mules, and carpet-spreaders with carpets, mats and cushions for use on the way and light tents, and lastly water-bearers with water-pipes on camels or mules for the use of men and animals. Twelve dancing girls of great beauty, who were always present when the shah went on a journey, followed several hours behind (*ibid.*, 242-5). The *Dastūr al-mulūk* mentions an official called the *ḳurčı-yi rikāb*, who was always in attendance on the shah. When the latter went riding, it was the duty of the *kurči-yi rikāb* to hold the bridle of the horse which the shah was to mount with one hand and to help him mount with the other. In the royal assembly, the *ḳurči-yi rikāb* sat below the *muḥtasib al-mamālik* (ed. Muḥammad Taḳī Dānishpazhūh, in *Rev. de la Faculté des lettres et des sciences humaines*, Tehran, xvi/3 [1968], 318).

Hanway describes the procession of the Afghān Maḥmūd on his entry to Iṣfahān after Shāh Sulṭān Ḥusayn had resigned his throne to him on 29 Dhu 'l-Ḥidjdja 1134/11 October 1722): "The procession was opened by ten officers on horseback, and about two thousand cavalry, among whom were several lords of the PERSIAN court. Next came his master of the horse, at the head of fifteen led horses magnificently caparisoned: this officer was followed by some musketeers on foot, and these by a thousand common infantry. Immediately after came the grand master of the ceremonies, in the midst of three hundred negroes dressed in scarlet cloth: these negroes had been chosen from among the slaves of ISFAHAN to compose the conqueror's guard. Forty paces from thence was MAGHMUD, mounted on a horse, of which the VALI of ARABIA had made him a present, on the day of the abdication. The unfortunate HUSSEIN rode on his left. The princes were followed by about three hundred pages on horseback" (*The Revolution of Persia*,[3] London 1762, ii, 182). Maḥmūd's chief officials followed, and behind them came the principal officials of the dethroned monarch. The procession was closed by a hundred camels carrying arquebuses, preceded by a great band of musicians and followed by nearly six thousand horse. Having crossed the Shīrāz bridge, Shāh Sulṭān Ḥusayn was sent to his place of confinement, and Maḥmūd continued alone. Arriving at the gates of the town the inhabitants laid rich stuffs under his horse's feet and filled their air with perfumes. The guns on the camel's backs were often fired as they marched along; "and in the intervals, the ten AFGHANS who walked at the head of the procession, pronounced loud imprecations against the followers of ALI" (*ibid.*).

The practice of *ḳuruḳ*, i.e. the prohibition of men and boys from any place where the king's wives were to pass, though probably not new, was rigorously enforced under the Ṣafawids and caused great inconvenience to the population. Olearius states that when the shah went hunting, taking his *ḥaram* with him, runners were sent in advance through the streets so that the population remained in their houses and the streets were empty (*Vermehrte Newe Beschreibung der Muscowitischen und Persischen Reyse*, Schleswig, 1656, ed. Dieter Lohmeier, repr. Tübingen 1971, 529). Chardin claims that Shāh Ṣafī commanded no less than 62 *ḳuruḳs* as he went abroad with his wives visiting places around Iṣfahān during the five months from his coronation till the year 1078/1667 (*Coronation, op.cit.*, 77. Cf, also Jean-Baptiste Tavernier, *Voyages en Perse*, Geneva 1970, 186-7, 188). The custom continued under later rulers. According to Hanway, the consequences to those who failed to get out of the way when notice of Nādir Shāh's approach was given were sometimes fatal (*op.cit.*, i, 169).

Under the Ḳādjārs, processions took place very much on the same sort of occasions as under earlier rulers. Special importance was attached to the ceremony of *istiḳbāl*. This was *de rigueur* when the shah or one of the princes visited some town or village or when he returned to his seat of government after absence on some expedition or other. On these occasions, civil and military officials and local notables would take part in the *istiḳbāl*, while wrestlers, jugglers, tumblers and other would display their skills; the slaughter of oxen, cows and sheep and the breaking of vessels containing sugar candy in the way of the prince was also customary. Morier states that when Fatḥ ᶜAlī approached Tehran on his return after an expedition to Khurāsān in 1815, rows of well-dressed men were drawn up at some distance from the road and made low bows as he passed, while members of the religious classes were drawn up nearer the city. Oxen and sheep in great numbers were sacrified as he passed and their heads thrown under his horse's feet. Glass vases, filled with sugar, were broken before him and their contents strewed on his road. Dervishes made loud exclamations for his prosperity, while wrestlers and dancers twirled their clubs and performed all sorts of antics to the sound of drums. "Amongst the crowd", Morier continues, "I perceived the whole of the Armenians headed by their clergy bearing crosses, painted banners, the Gospels, and long candles. They all began to chant Psalms as His Majesty drew near; and their zeal was only surpassed by that of the Jews, who also had collected themselves into a body, conducted by their rabbis, who raised on high a carved representation of wood of the tabernacle.... In all the bustle I perceived the King constantly looking at the watch carried by Shatir Bashi, anxious that he should enter the gates exactly at a time prescribed by his astrologers" (*A second journey through Persia, Armenia, and Asia Minor to Constantinople 1810-16*, London 1818. 387-8).

Fraser, describing the return of Fatḥ ʿAlī to Tehran in April 1833 after a visit to Ḳumm, states that half the town went out to welcome him, while the other half lined the bazaars to make a show upon his entrance. "A confused assemblage of horsemen of all ranks and distinctions, from whom were continually issuing individual pairs to skirmish and show off, were followed by those of more respectability ... gholaum-peishkhidmats, nassakchees, and personal attendants on his majesty; then a number of shatirs, or running footmen; and then after a long vacant space came Futeh Alee Shah himself, mounted on a horse ... Behind, at a due distance, came a group of princes and nobles ... a dense crowd of horsemen, gholaums, jeloodars, peishkhidmats, and servants of all sorts, brought up the rear, crossing the road and country in a line at right angles to the line of march; from these it was that most of the skirmishers issued ... tearing across the plain, and firing guns at each other or nothing at all, and showing off some very fine horses with great spirit and address (*A winter's journey (Tatar) from Constantinople to Tehran*, London 1838, ii, 76ff.).

It was the custom of Fatḥ ʿAlī to march out of his capital on the Naw Rūz, attended by his ministers and as many of the army as could be assembled [see MARĀSIM. 3]. He would be mounted sometimes on a horse, sometimes on an elephant (cf. Morier, *A journey through Persia*, 210). Among the amusements were horse-racing (Malcolm, *History of Persia*, London 1829, ii, 405). Naw-Rūz audiences were also held in the capital. Ker Porter describes the royal procession as it came into the audience hall on one such occasion. First, the elder sons of the shah entered, ʿAbbās Mīrzā went to the right side of the throne, followed by his brothers; his younger brothers then took up their places opposite. They were all superbly dressed. Near the front of the palace, mullas and astrologers were drawn up. Fatḥ ʿAlī's entry into the gate of the citadel was announced by a volley fired by the camel corps and the clang of trumpets and "the appalling roar of two huge elephants" (*Travels in Georgia, Persia, Armenia, ancient Babylon*, London 1921, i, 320ff.

The Naw-Rūz races were a state occasion under Nāṣir al-Dīn S̲h̲āh, who would attend them either on horseback or in a carriage drawn by eight horses (Muʿayyir al-Mamālik, *Yāddās̲h̲thā-ī az zindagānī-i k̲h̲uṣūṣī-i Nāṣir al-Dīn S̲h̲āh*, Tehran n.d., 120-1). When the shah mounted his carriage at the races, or his horse to go to his special stand, the camel corps would fire a volley. Muʿayyir al-Mamālik describes the scene in the following words. "Runners (*s̲h̲āṭirs*) on either side and the camels bearing the ruler's kettle-drums would set off in front followed by the shah in his carriage. Covered in jewels and wearing the aigrette (*d̲j̲īg̲h̲a*) on his headdress, with a red parasol with diamond tassels held over him, he would look out benevolently on the people who hurried forward to welcome him. Thus, surrounded by this pomp and magnificence, he would drive up to the special stand from which he would watch the races, where the great men and ministers would be awaiting the arrival of the royal cortège" (*ibid.*, 121-2).

The reception of foreign envoys was also the occasion for processions and cavalcades. Morier states that at every place through which the Harford Jones' mission passed in 1808 on its way to Tehran, the local people came out to welcome him. They were frequently armed with pikes, matchlocks, swords and shields, and would often fire a volley as a salute (*A Journey into Persia*, 76). At Kāzirūn, "a bottle, which contained sugar candy, was broken under the feet of the Envoy's horse, a ceremony never practiced in Persia to any but royal personages" (*ibid.*, 84-5). Displays of wrestlers, jugglers and tumblers, as in the case of receptions welcoming the shah, often formed part of the *istiḳbāl*. Lady Sheil describes the welcome given to her husband in Tabrīz on his way to Tehran as envoy to the court of Persia in 1849 in the following words: "There were princes and priests, and merchants, and mollas, and mountebanks, and dervishes, and beggars; there were Koordish and Toork horsemen of the tribes, and soldiers, and Ghoolams... The cavalcade began four miles from the town, and each step brought a fresh reinforcement to the procession" (*Glimpses of life and manners in Persia*, London 1856, 86). Writing of the procedure for her husband's *istiḳbāl* in Tehran, she states: "The village we were residing in was three miles distant from Tehran, and etiquette requires the ceremony to commence four miles from the city ... A tent was pitched at the requisite distance; and my husband was accordingly obliged to return a mile towards Tabreez, to receive the congratulations of the Shah's representatives" (*ibid.*, 120-1).

The shah or one of the royal princes used to take part in the procession on the *ʿīd-i ḳurbān*. Fraser, describing the celebration in Tehran on 20 April 1833, states: "It was customary for the king himself, or, in his default, for one of the elder princes, with a grand cortège of the rest, and their followers, to superintend the ceremony, which consists of a procession to a particular appointed place, where a camel is provided for the sacrifice. The king or elder prince, taking a knife, draws it across the animal's throat, which is then despatched and cut up on the spot .... On the present occasion not one of the princes attended, except Saheb-keran Meerza (aged about ten) ..... nor was he accompanied by a single person of distinction.

"The first part of the show which issued from the gate was a parcel of ragamuffin musicians with kettle-drums, and horrid screeching pipes, who preceded a number of mules and horses, strangely caparisoned and painted, having tawdry trappings on, and gold and silver tinsel, with ostrich feathers on their heads, and along with these came sundry flags of silk, red, green, and scarlet, and some striped like shawls; and the animals were mounted and ridden to and fro at speed by the fellows who brought them. These, as I understood, were intended to carry away pieces of the unhappy camel when he should be cut up: they were attended also by a number of dervishes, in their caps and patched robes. Next came six of the King's *kernechees*, or trumpeters, in their scarlet coats, with spears and horns; then came three or four led horses; than a couple of hundred *topechees*, or artillerymen, in two lines, forming a street, through which rushed thirty or forty furoshes with sticks, and gholaums with shields. After these came the little prince, gallantly dressed in a scarlet coat, well bedizened with embroidery of pearls and diamonds, his sword-belt to match, and having handsome diamond ornaments on his cap and on his breast, and a pretty little sabre depending from his side. He was mounted on a fine horse .... Behind the prince at due distance, came a rabble of horsemen, tofungchees, etc...... Before the gates of the Nigaristan ..... the poor camel lay bound and ready" (*A Winter's journey*, ii, 73-5; see also Muᶜayyir al-Mamālik, *op.cit.*, 93-5; and for a description of the procession in Iṣfahān, see Mīrzā Ḥusayn Khān b. Muḥammad Ibrāhīm Khān Taḥwīldār, *Djughrāfiyā-yi Iṣfahān*. ed. Manučihr Sotoodeh, Tehran AHS 1342/1963, 88-90).

Towards the end of the 19th century the tendency was for royal processions to become less elaborate. Curzon writes that formerly the Shah's court ceremonial was a blaze of splendour but that "he now affects a simplicity of costume in striking contrast to his predecessors. The bediamonded sword and the flashing aigrette, which was so familiar on his first visit to England in 1873, had disappeared in 1889; and in Tehran I have seen him walking in the streets in a braid frock coat with prodigious skirts ... holding a walking stick in his hand. Upon other occasions he either appears on horseback, or, more commonly, is driven through the streets of the town in a sort of coach with glass panels drawn by six or eight white horses with henna-dyed tails. In front and behind ride a small detachment of the royal bodyguard or gholams, whose full number stands at 2,000, or two corps of 1,000 apiece, who are recognizable by their gold-braided tunics and by the muskets, wrapped up in red cases, which they wear slung across their shoulders. A number of the liveried harlequins, or royal runners ..... are also in attendance to clear a way, while the less ornamental ferashes, with their long switches, keep back the crowd" (*Persia*, London 1892, i, 396). The royal runners or *shāṭirs* (whose dress was a faithful representation of that worn by the *shāṭirs* of the Ṣafawid kings) preceded the shah whenever he went out riding or in his carriage (*ibid.*, i, 332).

Bibliography: Given in the article.

(A. K. S. Lambton)

4. In the Ottoman empire

Ottoman processions (Tk. *ālāy*) were frequently assembled on festive and solemn occasions. The Ottoman court celebrated the birth and circumcision of a prince, or the marriage of a princess, a victory of the army, a new campaign of a sultan, or his succession to the throne, the arrival of a royal guest, or an important foreign ambassador, with imperial festivities, which sometimes lasted 50 days and nights (like that of the circumcision festival of Prince Meḥmed, later Meḥemmed III, in 990/1582) or more (the festival of 853/1449, under Murād II, to celebrate the wedding of his son, Prince Meḥmed—later Meḥemmed II, the conqueror of Constantinople in 857/1453—and Sitt Khātūn, which continued for three months). Sometimes an occasion for a public rejoicing was created after an unsuccessful campaign or a defeat of the Ottoman army, with the intention of turning the attention of Sultan's subjects elsewhere and to falsify the result of a battle (the best examples of such festivities are in 862/1457, after Meḥemmed II was compelled to draw back from Baghdād; and in 937/1530, when Süleymān the Magnificent had to retreat from the siege of Vienna; and also in 990/1582, after the failure of Murād III in the war against the Persians). The wedding and circumcision ceremonies very often and deliberately coincided with *ḳurbān bayramî* [see ᶜĪd]. There were also court festivities, which were organised merely to solemnise the pilgrimage of the Prophet (among others, a recent one was in 1866, under Sultan ᶜAbd al-ᶜAzīz). All these festivals were enriched by spectacular and colourful processions, which consisted *inter alia*, of architectural displays, festival palms, sugar work in figures and of artificial flower gardens; these are considered below. One should note as a preliminary the following three definitions, before proceeding to examine the different types of processions: 1. *Ālāy-ı Hümāyūn*, Imperial procession. A customary procession organised when the Sultan or the Grand-Vizier started for or returned from a campaign, on a route between the palace and the barracks at Dāwūd Pasha (a district in Old Istanbul). 2. *Ālāy Ḳānūnu*, Code for processions: the Ottoman code pertaining to the rules for the arrangement, order and the costuming of the viziers, scholars, high officials, staff and the military personnel, who were prescribed by the government to participate in the imperial processions. 3. *Ālāy Köshkü*, Kiosk for spectacles: a kiosk built especially for the Sultan and his harem, from where they watched the processions, celebrations and the festivities. This kiosk was generally used by the Sultanas and the ladies of the court. The Sultan had a special room with attendants.

Bibliography: A detailed description of such processions is to be found in Djelāl-zāde, (Muṣṭafā b. Djelāl), *Ṭabaḳāt al-memālik ve deredjāt el-mesālik*, ms. Nationalbibliothek, Vienna, H.O. 41; and in Teshrīfātīzādē Meḥmed b. Aḥmed's *Defter-i teshrifāt*, ms. Nationalbibliothek, Handschriften-Sammlung, Mxt. 301; the processions in the festival of 1086/1675, in Edirne, under the reign of Meḥemmed IV, are given by Ḥüseyin Hezār-fenn, *Telkhīṣ al-beyān fī ḳawānīn-i Āl-i ᶜOthmān*, ms. B.N., Fonds Turc, 40; ᶜAbdī, *Sūr-i pūr sūrūr-i hümāyūn*, ms. Millet Kütüphanesi, Istanbul, Ali Emirī Kit. 343; John Covel, *Diary*, ms. B.L., Add. 22,912; vivid sketches of the processions in the 18th century may be seen in *Sūr-nāme*, ms. Nationalbibliothek, Vienna H.O. 95, written for the festival of 1724, under the reign of Aḥmed III, and also in ᶜĀkif Bey's *Teshrīfāt-nāme*, Süleymaniye Kit. Esᶜad Ef. no. 2108, written for the birth of a prince, during the reign of Muṣṭafā III, modern Tkish. tr., *Beşik Alayı*, by Şevket Rado, in *Tarih Mecmuası*, x (Nov. 1972), 4-5; for the etymology of *alay*, see Fuat Köprülü, *Bizans müesseselerinin Osmanli müesseselerine te'siri*, in *Türk hukuku tarihine dair tetkikler*, Istanbul 1931, 277, in which the author indicates that the Byzantine Greek word *alagion* is the source of the Ottoman word *alay*. In the beginning, *alagion* meant a ceremonial detachment of troops in an emperor's suite and later, in the 13th century, it meant a regiment. E. Stern, *Untersuchungen zur Verfassung und Wissenschaftsgeschichte*, in *MOG*, ii/1-2, 49, supports Köprülü's statement; an illuminating book about the processions is İ. H. Uzunçarşılı's *Osmanlı devletinin saray teşkilâtı*, Ankara 1945, 168-71; also see Özdemir Nutku, *IV. Mehmet'in Edirne şenliği*, Ankara 1972, 57-60, 62-76; the basic books on the *Ālāy Köshkü* are by İbrahim Hakkı Konyalı, *Istanbul sarayları*, Istanbul 1942; Oktay Aslanapa, *Edirne'de Osmanlı devri abideleri*, Istanbul 1949; and Rifat Osman, *Edirne sarayı*, ed. Süheyl Ünver, Ankara 1957.

The different types of procession.

1. BAYRAM ĀLĀYĬ, "Holiday procession", traditionally organised to accompany the Sultan to the mosque and back to the palace, on the first days of two religious holidays, *Ḳurbān Bayramĭ* (festival of sacrifices) and *Sheker Bayramĭ* (the feast during the first three days after the Ramaḍān fast). The respective order of the participants in this procession was generally as follows:

— the *khōdjas* of the imperial palace, on foot;
— the Chief White Eunuchs, on foot;
— the Director of the Registry of landed property, on horseback;
— the second and third Accountants, on horseback;
— the Finance Minister, on horseback;
— the Master of Orders, on horseback;
— the Steward to the Grand Vizier, on horseback;
— the Grand Vizier and the viziers, on horseback, on both sides the Janissaries, on foot;
— the Steward to the chief white eunuchs, carrying a silver sceptre in his right hand, and wearing a short fur-coat, a *selīmī* turban, Tatar baggy trousers of violet velvet and a pair of Circassian shoes, on foot;
— the first and the second Masters of the horse, on foot;
— the Sultan, on horseback: on each side walked the bodyguards with their red and light brown conical hats and five-edged sceptres in their hands; lackeys and messengers; the clothing masters, wearing large wadded headgears with bejewelled crests;
— the Chief Lifeguard of the Janissaries and the Chief Clothing Master, both wearing bejewelled knitted caps with tassels, loose robes embroidered with gold threads, over it valuable robes of honour, girdles made of pearls and bejewelled daggers;
— the Head of the Black Eunuchs, wearing a *selīmī* turban, an embroidered robe with a bejewelled girdle and a four-sleeved sable skin coat;
— the Masters of the Porte, with *selīmī* turbans;
— the Chief Treasurer and the officials of the palace, wearing headgear, bejewelled daggers and knives and with bracelets of solid gold.

Bibliography: For designs and colours of the costumes, see Johannes Lewenklaw, *Bilder türkischen Herrscher, Soldaten, Hofleute, Städte*, Vienna 1586; anon., *Bilder aus dem türkischen Volksleben*, Vienna 1586; anon., *Türkische Trachten*, Vienna (17th century); anon., *Türkische Trachten*, 3 volumes, Italy (18th century); the most reliable source for the Bayram procession is Ṭayyār-zāde ʿAṭā, *Enderūn taʾrīkhi*, i, Istanbul 1293; a short section in Paul Rycaut's *The present state of the Ottoman Empire*, London 1668, 162-4; a description of such a procession may be seen in Hezār-fenn, *Telkhīṣ*, fols. 32b-33a; a detailed description, with a personal view of an English lady, of Maḥmūd II, may be found in Julie Pardoe, *The City of the Sultan*, London 1837, ch. vi; for further information, see R. E. Koçu, *Osmanlı sarayında Bayram tebriki ve Bayram Alayı*, in *TM*, xii (Jan. 1972), 6-11; for an extensive article, see *Das Fest des Kurban-Beiram in Konstantinopel*, in *Globus*, xiii (1866), 148-52.

2. BESHIK ĀLĀYĬ, "Cradle procession", customarily organised to conduct the cradle of a new-born prince or a princess through the streets to the birth place of the baby. There were two specific processions for such an occasion: one was the procession disposed by the Sultana-Mother, and the other was arranged by the orders of the Grand-Vizier. The procession of the Sultana-Mother took place subsequent to the birth of the baby. The cradle, the bejewelled quilt and the

valuable blanket were all taken from the old Saray and brought to the Ṭopkapĭ Palace. This procession consisted respectively of the following participants:

— the guide, in uniform;
— the officers of the Harem, two in a row;
— all the stewards of the lady who gave birth to the child, with their ceremonial girdles, equipments and headgears;
— numerous itinerant vendors, carrying trays of fruits, candies, flowers and cakes;
— the master vendors of sweetmeats, carrying the silver cradle;
— numerous coaches with lattice-windows, and two eunuchs at the sides of each coach: in these coaches were the visiting ladies;
— the Messenger to the Chief of the Flag, and the Head of Musicians;
— the musicians.

The procession walked most of the way to the accompaniment of rhythmical beats of a kettledrum. When the procession was over, various presents were given to the participants.

The procession disposed by the Grand Vizier was much more spectacular and crowded. It was a custom to put on this display six days after the birth of the child. The Grand Vizier, immediately after the imperial baby was born, ordered a cradle, a quilt and a blanket, embroidered with pearls, diamonds, emeralds and with other precious stones. The procession comprised the following participants in respective order:

— the guide, together with the attendants of the imperial house;
— the officers of the Grand Vizier's Harem;
— the Clerk of the Attendants and the Superintendent to the Attendants;
— the adjutants and the messengers of the court;
— the Steward to the Chief White Eunuchs of the Grand Vizier, and the Superintendent to the Grand Vizier;
— the vendors, carrying trays of fruits and flowers;
— the *telkhīṣī* (an official charged with making summaries and reports);
— the bodyguards;
— the Assistant of Ceremonies, and the Treasurer of Ceremonies;
— the Master of Ceremonies;
— the stewards to Sultanas;
— the Head of Musicians, carrying the blanket, and the footmen holding the blanket from its four corners;
— the Second Clothing Master, carrying the quilt;
— the First Clothing Master, carrying the cradle;
— the Steward to the Grand Vizier;
— the military band.

When the procession was completed, presents were given to all the participants, according to their ranks. The procession looked like a huge flower garden. The coloured turbans, caps and headgears, various furcoats, yellow, red, green shoes, light boots, top-boots, etc., the artificial flower gardens, and hundreds of sugar boxes in different colours gave the atmosphere of a spectacular celebration.

Bibliography: The principal source is ʿĀḳif Bey's *Teshrīfāt-nāme*; the author was the master of ceremonies of the court during the reign of Muṣṭafā III (second half of the 18th century), tr. Rado, 4-5; for the festivities of 1189/1775, to celebrate the birth of Khadīdje Sulṭān, the daughter of ʿAbd al-Ḥamīd I, on 20 Dhu 'l-Ḳaʿda 1189/14 February 1775, see Ṭopkapı Archive E. no. 1562; for an illuminating example of a letter of congratulation, see the letter of the Grand Vizier written for the birth of Khayriyye Sulṭān, the daughter of Maḥmūd II, on 8 Shawwāl 1246/21 March 1830, Topkapı Archive, E. no. 5932, for the celebrations of the birth of Ṣāliḥa Sulṭān, the daughter of Maḥmūd II, see Uzunçarşılı, *op.cit.*, Çağatay Uluçay, *Harem*, ii, Ankara 1971, 78-9.

3. DJĀʾIZ ĀLĀYĪ, "Procession of the trousseau" arranged to transport the trousseau of an imperial bride to the house of the bridegroom. Before the procession started, the festal palms (*nakhīls*) were brought to the palace very early in the morning, and were included in the procession as symbols of fecundity of the bride; for this reason, the festal palms prepared for a bride should be made of fruits, candies and flowers. The procession started after the prayer for the newly-wedded was completed. The respective order of the participants in this procession was generally as follows:

— the Commander-in-Chief of the Janissaries, with ceremonial dress;
— the Steward to the Commander-in-Chief, with crest;
— the chiefs of various Janissary corps, with crests;
— the Chief of Cavalry and the Chief Lifeguard of Janissaries, with their men;
— the Chief Reciter of the Ḳurʾān, accompanied by his assistants;
— the Chief of Police, accompanied by the policemen;
— the Police Superintendent, with his men;
— the court messengers;
— the court adjutants;
— the court assayers;
— the *khōdjas* and the scholars of the court;
— the Chief of the White Eunuchs;
— the Steward to the Sultana-Mother, and the Steward to the favourite wife of the Sultan;
— the Chief Architect, and the Steward of the Dockyards;
— two artifical sugar gardens with figures made of sugar, and numerous festal palms of gold and silver, adorned with fruits, candies and flowers;
— the vendors and attendants, carrying the boxes containing the trousseau: mosquito-nets with gold lanterns; bejewelled clogs, slippers, boots, shoes; crowns full of diamonds, emeralds, rubies, turquoises, jades; necklaces, bracelets, earrings set with pearls, emeralds and brilliants; trays of precious stones; bejewelled cases for reed pens and ink; hundreds of embroidered cushions. At both sides of the vendors and the attendants, walked the guards to watch over;
— the Chief of Messengers;
— the Minister of Foreign Affairs and the two Chief Military Judges;
— the viziers;
— the Grand Vizier and the *Shaykh al-Islām*;
— the Captain of the festal palms;
— artificial fruit gardens;
— the imperial military band;
— pure-bred rams guarded by the black eunuchs, one at each side;
— the concubines of the trousseau, and the Chief of Palace Guards, accompanied by his men. The furniture and the big pieces were carried by mules, adorned with precious clothes, such as brocade, satin and silk.

When the procession arrived at its destination, the participants were rewarded according to their ranks, with gold coins fur coats and silk robes.

Bibliography: For information on how the payments were realised for transporting a trousseau, see Topkapı Archive, E. no. 7004; for a detailed description of the *djāʾiz ālāyī* in the festival of 1086/1675, Hezār-fenn, fols. 174b, 176a, 177b; Covel, *Diary*, fols. 200a, 217b; for such processions in the 18th century, *Sūr-nāme*, ms. Nationalbibliothek, Vienna, cod. H.0.95; there were three different processions of the trousseau in the festivities of 1137/1724, during the reign of Aḥmed III, for princesses Ümm Külthūm, see 7a-10b, Khadīdje, 19a-b, ʿĀtiḳa, 20a-21b; see Topkapı Archive E. no. 7029 for the imperial mandate of ʿAbd al-Ḥamīd I, stating the obligatory trousseau, whatever the economic situation of the bridegroom was; for further information on the obligatory trousseau, Topkapı Archive E. nos. 361, 692, 962; for the gifts given by this same Sultan to the high officials of the state, during the wedding festivities of 1202/1787, Topkapı Archive E. no. 247; for a recent procession of the trousseau, see von Moltke, *Türkiye'deki durum ve olaylar üzerine mektuplar*, Tkish. tr. Hayrullah Örs, Ankara 1960, 46-7; a detailed description of the same procession in 1252/1836, Julie Pardoe, *op.cit.*, ch. xi; another example is the procession of Fāṭima Sulṭān's trousseau, the daughter of ʿAbd al-Medjīd, in 1271/1854, see Topkapı Archive E. no. 8270; Ç. Uluçay, *Fatma ve Safiye Sultanların düğünleri*, in *Istanbul Enstitüsü Mecmuası*, iv (Istanbul 1958); idem, *Harem*, ii, 104; Nutku, *op.cit.*, 63-4.

4. EṢNĀF ĀLĀYĪ, "Procession of the guilds or corporations", held in the presence of the Sultan, where each guild displayed its own profession, as well as acted scenes mostly concerning the special field with which the guild was occupied. Some of the guilds, however, had clowns, rope dancers, illusionists, equilibrists, some others, mimics and actors; and the bigger corporations possessed all of these.

It was a custom in the imperial festivals that the procession of the guilds should take place always in the afternoons, and that they should appear in alphabetical order. Only four or five guilds were allowed each day to have a procession; for example, the processions of 181 guilds in the festival of 990/1582 first started on 11 June and ended on 6 July. Before the procession was over, each guild had to give to the Sultan its gifts, which were determined long before by the treasurer of the court. The representatives of the guilds, after presenting their gifts, would pray for the Sultan. After the ceremony, all members of these guilds would take their seats at dinner tables prepared for them as guests at the feast given by the Sultan.

All the guilds and the corporations had their own pennants; for example, the guild of lady's slipper-makers had a pennant with golden and silver threads and tassels, the cord-makers had a red and a white pennant, and the sword-makers had a red and green one. The weavers had two different pennants: one, red, and the other red, yellow and green. Sometimes these guilds included wild animals in the procession, just for the sake of attracting the interest of the spectators. Some guilds, which preserved the tradition of having warriors, namely swordsmen and archers, would include them into the procession as symbols of traditional combatants; these men walked with their traditional uniforms and demonstrated their skill when the time came.

The representative scenes of each guild, showing the profession, were exhibited on carts, pulled by horses or oxen. The bakers, for instance, while passing ceremonially, displayed their profession on two successive carts: on the first, the millers ground wheat with an all-functioning miniature mill, while on the next the bakers baked bread in a burning furnace; and the products were presented to the Sultan and given to the spectators. The guild of tailors, in the festival of 990/1582, sewed an interesting and valuable dress, which could be worn on both sides; one side of this dress was red and yellow, the other white and blue.

Another kind of demonstration was either to show skills or to perform farces of mythological stories, in which the actors and clowns generally had stylised phalluses in their hands and wore costumes of cloth, paper and grass.

Most of the guilds presented gifts related to their profession: for example, the weavers presented the cloth they had been weaving during the procession. A few of the guilds presented things other than their profession: the haberdashers, for instance, presented to the Sultan, in the festival of 1086/1675, the following items: 2 silver decanters, 2 silver trays, 4 ornamented silver candlesticks, 8 silver candlesticks, 1 *okka (ūḳiyye*, equivalent to 1283 gr.) of rose-water, 2 plates with a case, 3 plates full of cloves, 4 plates full of walnuts, 3 plates full of coconuts, 2 plates full of cinnamon, 1 tray full of musk-soap, 4 jars of sugar candy, 18 bottles of incense water, 60 bottles of flower-water, 3 trays full of dates, 6 plates full of sugar, 15 plates of candy, 4 plates full of sugar candy (of a different sort) and 7 Kaᶜba glasses.

In every festival, the procession of the guilds were the centre of attraction, with presentations of products, displays of professional occupations, demonstrations of skills and performances of plays.

Bibliography: For the display of professional occupations, see Georges Lebelski, *La Description des yeux et magnifiques representez a Constantinople...*, 1584, 63-4; Nicholas von Haunolt, *Particular Verzeichnuss mit das Ceremonien Gepraeng und Pracht das Fest der Beschneidung...*, in Lewenklaw, *Neuewe Chronica Turkischer Nation...*, Franckfurt am Mayn 1595, 481-509; Hezār-fenn, fols. 154a-172b; Covel, *Diary*, fol. 216a; for the costumes of the furriers, Pétis de la Croix, *Mémoires*, ii, Paris 1684, 119; Seyyid Hüseyin Wehbī, *Sūr-nāme*, ms. Nationalbibliothek, Vienna, cod. 94, and BL no. Or. 7218: Meḥmed Khazīn, *Sūr-nāme-i Khazīn*, ms. Beyazıt Kit., Nurettin Pasha, 10267, fols. 73b-120a; for a detailed description of clowns, ᶜAbdī, fols. 3a, 5b, 7b, 9a; Nabī, *Waḳāyiᶜ-i khitān-i Shehzādegān-i Ḥaḍret-i Sulṭān Meḥemmed-i Ghāzī li-Nabī Efendi*, ed. A. S. Levend, Istanbul 1944, 48, 51; for the farces, see Mary Wortley Montagu, *Letters of Milady Montagu*, London 1764, 64; a summary description of the procession of guilds may be seen in Tietz, *Ceremonien und Festlichkeiten bei der feierlichen Beschneidung eines türkischen Prinzen von Geblüt in Konstantinopel*, in *Ausland* (22 May 1836), 572-84; G. F. Abbot, *Under the Turk in Constantinople: a record of Sir John Finch's embassy, 1674-1681*, London 1920; for the rules of ceremony, Fīndīḳlīlī Meḥmed Agha, *Silaḥtār taʾrīkhī*, ii, Istanbul 1928, 645; further reference to the procession of the guilds is to be found in Nutku, *op.cit.*, 73-6; and in Metin And, *Osmanlı şenliklerinde Türk sanatları*, Ankara 1982, 227-48.

5. GELIN ĀLĀYĪ. "the Procession for the bride", to chaperone the bride to the house of the bridegroom. Up till the 18th century it was deemed lucky to have the bridal procession on Thursdays. This solemnity surpassed the pomp of the procession organised for the transportation of the trousseau. Almost all the viziers, the scholars and the high officials of the state took their places in this ceremony. The respective order of the train was generally as follows:

— the Chief of Police;
— the messengers of the palace;
— the holders of the fief;
— the *khōdjas*, the scholars of the court, and the Chief of Artillery, the Chief Armourer and the Steward to the Commander-in-Chief;
— the Master of Janissaries and a commanding officer of a division;
— the chiefs of various Janissary corps, cavalry and the Chief Lifeguard;
— the Chief White Eunuch;
— the Minister of Finance, Master of Orders and the Commander-in-Chief;
— the Chief of Messengers and the memoranda officials;
— the *Sherīf* of Mecca and the *Ḳāḍī* of Istanbul;
— the Chief Military Judges;
— the pashas, who act as intimates of the bridegroom;
— the Grand Vizier and the *Shaykh al-Islām*;
— the Inspector and the Accountant of the Prophet's Tomb at Medina;
— the Revenue-collector and the Senior official of Mecca and Medina;
— the Stewards to the Sultana-Mother and to the bridegroom;
— the Steward to the bride;
— two big festival palms carried by the dockyard stewards, the stewards walking at each side, and the white eunuchs in the middle;
— the Steward to the palace guards and the Secretary to the Chief Black Eunuch of the Sultan's Harem;
— two smaller festal palms of silver carried by the dockyard stewards;
— the guards of the old serail;
— two other silver festal palms, followed by the secretary of the guards of the old serail, on horseback, holding a Ḳurʾān with a bejewelled cover and case;
— the Chief Saddler to the Chief Black Eunuch, leading thoroughbred horses, which were richly equipped;
— the Chief Black Eunuch; the guards of the old serail at each side, and in front of the Chief, the men carrying purses and throwing gold pieces to the spectators;
— the bride in a silver or a bejewelled coach;
— numerous carriages of accompaniment, with the ladies of the court;
— the military band;
— numerous coaches carrying the ladies of the Harem.

The horses of the coaches were generally covered with expensive cloths, such as brocade, silk and satin. All the coaches were surrounded by the black eunuchs on horseback. The stewards, who carried the silver palms were richly dressed. This procession was so long that it usually took one hour or more from the beginning to the end.

Bibliography: A detailed description of the bridal procession of the eldest daughter of Murād III may be seen in von Haunolt, *Verzeichnuss des Hochzeitlichen Fest...*, in *op.cit.*, 532-5; the bridal procession in the festival of 1086/1675, ᶜAbdī, fol. 17a; Hezār-fenn, fols. 177a-178b; Covel, *Diary*, fol. 216a; and also Thomas Coke, *A True Narrative of the Great Solemnity of the circumcision of Mustapha, Prince of Turkie, eldest son of Sultan Mahomed present Emperor of the Turks*, London 1676; *Sūr-i Hümayūn*, Nationalbibliothek, Vienna, cod. H.O. 88; *Sūr-nāme*,

Nationalbibliothek, Vienna, cod. H.O. 95, fols. 10a-14b; a brief section on the wedding of Ṣāliḥa Sulṭān, the daughter of Aḥmed III, may be seen in Topkapı Archive, E. no. 277; Ḥas̲h̲met, *Velādet-nāme-yi Hibetallāh Sulṭān*, ms. Süleymaniye Kit. Esʿad Efendi, no. 2511/2, İstanbul Üniv. Kit. T. 1940 and Topkapı Sarayı Kit. no. 1603; Pardoe, *op.cit.*, ch. xii, describes in detail the procession of Mihrimāh Sulṭān; for the bridal processions during the reign of ʿAbd al-Ḥamīd II, Archive of the Prime Ministry, Cevdet tas. Saray no. 6212, ms., Ankara; Marquis de Nointel, *L'Odyssée d'un ambassadeur, les voyages du Marquis de Nointel 1670-1680*, ed. A. Vandal, Paris 1900; Topkapı Sarayı, ms., new. no. 151; R. Lubenau, *Beschreibung der Reisen des Reinhold Lubenau,* ii, ed. W. Sahm, Königsberg 1914, 276-82; for further information, Uzunçarşılı, *op.cit.*; Uluçay, *op.cit.*, ii, 105-7; Nutku, *op.cit.*, 63.

6. ḲADÎR ĀLĀYÎ, "Procession for the 'Night of Power'", sc. of Ramaḍān, (*Ḳadîr Ged̲j̲esi*), because it is the night when the Ḳurʾān was revealed, and it was the custom to organise a procession. One of the squares of the city, where a big mosque existed, was illuminated by lamps and lanterns. The sultanas and the women in the Harem would go to the square with coaches to watch the procession. The black eunuchs offered them light food, fruits, ice cream and coffee on silver trays. In front of each coach two attendants waited, with silver-framed lanterns of camel skin in their hands. The Sultan came to the mosque with a train, resembling that escort of the *Bayram Ālāyî*, with *k̲h̲ōd̲j̲a*s of the imperial palace, the Chief White Eunuchs, the Minister of Finance, the Master of Orders, the Grand Vizier, the *S̲h̲ayk̲h̲ al-Islām*, the viziers, the Head of the Black Eunuchs, the Master of the Porte, etc., guarded by Janissaries and the cavalry. When the Sultan entered the mosque, *pide* (a kind of bread baked in thin flat strips), candy and *s̲h̲erbet* were distributed to the soldiers. While the procession was on its way back to the palace, fireworks would begin illuminating the sky with various kinds of rockets.

Bibliography: This is only very limited for this procession; see, however, Halit Ziya Uşaklıgil, *Saray ve ötesi*, ii, Istanbul 1941, 129-34; Leyla Saz, *Saray ve harem hatıraları*, in *Yeni Tarih Dergisi*, ii, Istanbul 1958, 539; Ayşe Osmanoğlu, *Babam Abdülhamid*, Istanbul 1960, 88; Safiye Ünüvar, *Saray hatıralarım*, Istanbul 1964, 110; Uluçay, *op.cit.*, ii, 163.

7. ḲILIČ ĀLĀYÎ, "The Procession to gird on the sword". The Sultan, as Caliph of all Muslims, had to take the oath of allegiance when he succeeded to the throne. The procession would usually take place two weeks later. The place of this ceremony was the tomb of Abū Ayyūb al-Anṣārī in Eyüp (a district named after this tomb). The Sultan, with a long train of high officials and soldiers would go to Eyüp either by boat or on horseback. If he went to Eyüp via the sea, then he would return via the land, or vice-versa.

The procession was generally composed of the following persons: the Grand Vizier, the *S̲h̲ayk̲h̲ al-Islām*, the Chief Military judges, the *S̲h̲erīf* of Mecca, the Viziers, and certain number of high officials.

The ceremony was usually directed by the *S̲h̲ayk̲h̲ al-Islām* and sometimes by the *S̲h̲erīf* of Mecca. After the ceremony, the Sultan visited the tombs of his ancestors, and returned to the palace in processional order.

This tradition was started by Selīm I. It was a custom that every Sultan issued money, sacrificed sheep and distributed these to the poor. It was the task of the Steward to the Chief White Eunuch and the First Master of the Horse to take the petitions of the subjects while the procession was on its way to the palace.

Bibliography: Tes̲h̲rifātī-zāde Meḥmed b. Aḥmed, *Defter-i tes̲h̲rīfāt*, ms., Nationalbibliothek, Vienna, cod. mixt. 301; *İA*, i, 293; *Meydan-Larousse*, vii, Istanbul 1972, 234-5.

8. MEKTEB (ĀMĪN) ĀLĀYÎ, "School (or Amen) procession", to celebrate the first school day of a prince. In this ceremony, the *S̲h̲ayk̲h̲ al-Islām* and the *k̲h̲ōd̲j̲a*s of the court would stand on the right side of the throne, and on the left were the Grand Vizier, viziers, chief military judges and the captains of the sea. The prince would come, with his escort, towards the throne and would kiss the skirt of his father, the Sultan. He would then sit on a sofa placed between the throne and the *S̲h̲ayk̲h̲ al-Islām*. After the prayer, the prince was delivered to the *k̲h̲ōd̲j̲a*s for his education. One such a celebration was ordered by Maḥmūd II for his elder son ʿAbd al-Med̲j̲īd in 1248/1832, when the Prince was nine years of age.

The procession took place both on the Marmara Sea with war-galleys and on land with the army. The Sultan and the Prince had an escort of high officials and soldiers amounting to 24,000 men. The escort included the infantry, the cavalry and the artillery.

Bibliography: For a vivid description of the procession in 1832, see *Ein Volksfest in Konstantinopel*, in *Magazin für Literatur des Auslands*, Berlin 1833, 531; also Uluçay, *Haremden mektuplar*, Istanbul 1956; Ayşe Osmanoğlu, *op.cit.*, 106; Safiye Ünüvar, *op.cit.*, 27, 88; Uluçay, *Harem*, ii, 87.

9. MEWLID ĀLĀYÎ, "The imperial procession organised to celebrate the birthday of the Prophet", on 12 Rabīʿ al-Awwal, for which the Sultan went to the mosque for the ceremony and returned to his palace. The high officials of the state gathered in the mosque, which was, until the second half of the 18th century, the Blue Mosque (sc. of Sultan Aḥmed), and waited for the Sultan to come. The *S̲h̲ayk̲h̲ al-Islām*, the Chief Military Judges of Rumeli and Anadolu, all provincial *ḳāḍī*s, who were at that time in Istanbul, the scholars and the *k̲h̲ōd̲j̲a*s, had to take their places on the left side of the pulpit (*minber*) according to their ranks. The viziers had to sit on the prayer rugs on the left side of the niche (*miḥrāb*). Next to them were the Commander-in-Chief of the Janissaries, the Minister of Finance, the First Adjutant, the Minister of Foreign Affairs, the Steward to the Commander, the second and third accountant, the Chief of the Flag, the Chief of Messengers, the Chief Lifeguard, the First Master of the Horse, the commanding officers of Cavalry, the Chief Armourer, the Chief of Artillery and other high officials in their places. If the Commander-in-Chief were not present, because of a war or of any reason, the senior commanding officer had to represent him in the mosque.

The high officials of the palace, namely, the commanding officers of various regiments, were arranged standing in a line from the door of the pulpit to the desk, and the Janissaries would form a square arranged in rows between the centre columns of the mosque.

The Grand Vizier (wearing his ceremonial *kallāwī* turban) was accompanied by the palace guards to the mosque, where he was to be before the Sultan arrived. The Chief White Eunuch (wearing the ceremonial *selīmī* turban) would go to the palace, in order to escort the Sultan to the mosque, together with the palace guards. This procession was not as spectacular as the others, but was nevertheless effective and colourful.

On entering the mosque, the Sultan was met by the Commander-in-Chief and the Trustee of the Pious Foundations. It was the duty of the Commander-in-Chief to take off the boots of the Sultan and offer him slippers. It was an honour given to him by the Sultan. If it was the first time that the Commander was doing this, he was rewarded with a dagger with diamonds on the handle. After this welcome, Sultan was escorted to his private pew by the Commander and the Chief Lifeguard. On leaving the mosque, the boots of the Sultan were put on again by the Commander.

In the procession back to the palace, the Commander walked in front of the Sultan's horse and the Trustees, carrying censers at each side, until they were dismissed by the Sultan.

Bibliography: For such a procession, see Hezār-fenn, fols. 170b-171b; Česhmī-zāde Muṣṭafā Reshīd, *Česhmī-zāde taʾrīkhi* (1180-2/1766-8), ed. Bekir Kütükoğlu, Istanbul 1959, 47; a vivid description may be seen in Ayşe Osmanoğlu's autobiography, 59-61; and in Safiye Ünüvar's one, 103; also see, Midhat Sertoğlu, *Osmanlı imparatorluğu devrinde mevlid alayı*, in *TM*, iv (April 1976), 45-9; also *op.cit.*, ii, 160.

10. NISHĀN ĀLĀYÎ. "Procession of engagement", held on the engagement of a sultan or a princess. In this procession, the gifts of the bridegroom were taken to the bride's house with an escort, which was generally composed of the following persons:
— the guide;
— the Chief Saddler of the palace;
— the Steward to the Chief White Eunuch;
— the Superintendent to the Grand Vizier;
— the Steward to the Grand Vizier;
— the Steward to the bride;
— the vendors and attendants carrying the gifts;
— twenty festal palms, each carried by two Janissaries;
— thirty large, ornamented trays full of confectionery;
— two artificial gardens made of sugar;
— one silver festal palm, at each side of which silver boxes of jewelry, carried by the attendants;
— bejewelled girdles, diamond rings, earrings with emeralds and diamonds, mirrors covered with precious stones, bejewelled clogs, shoes, light boots, slippers, all carried by the white eunuchs and guarded by palace watchmen;
— the Stewards to the bridegroom;
— the pashas, who act as intimates of the bridegroom;
— the Captain of the Sea, with his men;
— the Janissaries;
— the military band.

The gifts were delivered to the Chief Black Eunuch, who showed them to the Sultan, and upon the Sultan's approval sent them to the Harem with the black eunuchs.

Bibliography: *Sūr-nāme*, Nationalbibliothek, Vienna, cod. H.O. 95, fols. 2b-4a; N. M. Penzer, *The Harem*, London 1936; for the values of the gifts, Uluçay, *op.cit.*, 100-1.

11. SÜNNET ĀLĀYÎ, "Procession of circumcision". This escorted the prince, who was going to be circumcised, from his residence to the field where the festivities took place. The respective order of the train was generally as follows:
— the Janissary corps;
— the adjutants, the messengers, and the white eunuchs of the court;
— forty small festal palms, twenty at each side, each carried by three Janissaries;
— the Chief Architect and the Steward to the Dockyards;
— two giant festal palms, "as high as pine trees", each carried by 160 to 200 dockyard slaves, who according to the custom, were released for this occasion. These palms were balanced by the captains of the sea, holding ropes tied to the top of the palms; on each rope hung three different kinds of expensive cloth, each adequate in size for one dress;
— artificial gardens made of sugar: these gardens were full of trees, flowers, birds, domestic and wild animals; and in these gardens were jets of water running from the fountains, with nightingales singing;
— the viziers;
— the Grand Vizier and the *Shaykh-al-Islām*;
— the Master of the Horse, followed by thoroughbred horses, the harnesses of which were adorned with jewels;
— the Prince on horseback, with the private bodyguards on each side of him;
— the Chief Black Eunuch, followed by black eunuchs;
— the gentlemen-in-waiting, and the Chief White Eunuch;
— the Chief Ushers;
— the military band;
— the Chief Lifeguard, followed by the guards;
— the Chief of Cavalry, followed by the cavalry corps;
— the Chief of Artillery, with artillerymen;
— the Chief Armourer, with armourers.

When the procession was over, some of the festal palms would be set up in front of the imperial tent, and the others would be stuck up before the kiosk where the prince was going to be circumcised, as symbols of power and virility.

Bibliography: For the order of this procession, Georges Lebelskı, *A True Description of the Magnificall Tryumphes and Pastimes, represented at Constantinople, at the solemnizing of the Circumcision of the Soldan Maumet, the sonne of Amurath, the thyrd of that name, in the year of our Lorde God 1582, in the Monathes of Maie and June*, in François de Billerberg, *Most Rare and Strange Discourses of Amurathe, the Turkish Emperor that now is*, London 1585 (no page number); Haunolt, *Particular Verzeichnis....*, in *op.cit.*, 468-9, 472-3; Jean Palerne, *Peregrinations du S. Jean Palerne, Foresien Secretaire de François de Valois Duc d'Anjou et d'Alencon. Ensemble un Bref discours des Triomphes et Magnificences faictes a Constantinople en la solennite de la circoncision de Mahomet fils de Sultan Amurath III de ce nom Empereur des Turcs*, Lyons 1606, 465-70; *Sūr-nāme-i Hümāyūn*, ms., Nationalbibliothek, Vienna, cod. H.0.70; Hezār-fenn, fols. 166a-b; Covel, *Diary*, fol. 198a; and also ʿAbdī, fols. 10a-b; for the day of circumcision, apart from the afore-mentioned sources, Thomas Coke, *A True Narrative of the Great Solemnity of the circumcision of Mustapha, Prince of Turkie, eldest son of Sultan Mahomed present Emperor of the Turks. Together with an account of the Marriage of his Daughter to his favorite Mussaip at Adrianople*, London 1676; Pétis de la Croix, *Mémoires*, ii, Paris 1684; Wehbī, *Sūr-nāme*, British Museum, ms., cod.Or 7218 and Nationalbibliothek, Vienna, ms., cod. H.O. 94; Khazīn, *Sūr-nāme*, Beyazıt Kit. ms., Nurettin Paşa, no. 10267; Lebīb, *Sūrnāme-yi Lebīb*, ms., İst. Üniv. Kit. T. no. 6197; *Sūr-nāme-yi Khiḍīr*, İst. Üniv. Kit. T. ms., no. 6122; Nointel, *L'Odysse d'un Ambas-*

sadeur, 195-6, 197; Lubenau, *op.cit.*, ii, 55-7; Roger North, *The lives of Francis North, Dudley North and John North*, London 1826, 213 (gifts submitted to the Sultan); for the practice of the circumcision, see *Silaḥtār taʾrīkhī*, 645; Nabī, *Sūr-nāme*, ed. A. S. Levend, Istanbul 1944, 39-40; Salih Zorlutuna, *XVII. yüzyılın ikinci yarısında Edirne'nin sahne olduğu şahane sünnet ve evlenme düğünleri*, in *Edirne'nin 600. fethi yildönümü armağan kitabı*, Ankara 1965, 279-80; Nutku, *op.cit.*, 42-62.

12. ṢURRE ĀLĀYI̊, "Procession of the Purse", organised when the donation was sent by the Sultan, as the Caliph of Islam, to the people of Mecca and Medina. This procession took place at the courtyard of the palace. The camel carrying the gift made tours, together with a small group of participants, in the presence of the Sultan and his suite. The procession was directed by the Chief White Eunuch. Before the group set forth on its journey, the Ḳurʾān was recited. After leaving the palace, the crowd waiting for the procession hailed and blessed the small caravan as far as the city limits.

Bibliography: Penzer, *op.cit.*; Česhmī-zāde, *Taʾrīkh*, 10; Ayşe Osmanoğlu, *op.cit.*; Uluçay, *op.cit.*, ii, 161; *Meydan Larousse*, xi, Istanbul 1973, 628.

13. WĀLIDE ĀLĀYI̊, "Procession of the Sultana-Mother". This had become a custom since the enthronement of Aḥmed I (1012/1603), and with it the Sultana-Mother was brought to the palace. When a Sultan succeeded to the throne, he would invite his mother to the palace; and for this occasion a cortège was organised, the order for it being given a few days before his accession to the throne. It was generally composed of the following officials:

— the messengers of the court;
— the hunters of the court;
— the Chief White Eunuch;
— the trustees of the Sultan's Pious Foundations;
— the high officials of the pious foundations of Mecca and Medina;
— the black eunuchs;
— the palace guards;
— the Chief Black Eunuch;
— the Steward to the Sultana-Mother;
— the Sultana-Mother, formerly on a closed palanquin, and later in a coach with lattice windows;
— the attendants, scattering silver and gold pieces to the crowd;
— the ladies of the court, in 80 to 100 carriages;
— the military band.

Bibliography: For a detailed description of the procession, Waṣīf Efendi, *Waṣīf taʾrīkhi*, Maṭbaʿa-yi ʿĀmire, Istanbul 1219/1804, 42, 44; further, Uzunçarşılı, *op.cit.*, 155-6; and Uluçay, *op.cit.*, ii, 62-3.

Adjuncts of the processions included:

1. NAKHI̊L, "Festal palm". This phallophoric symbol sometimes took the form of a wreath or a fir branch, but generally it was made in the form of a cypress. In earlier periods it was in the shape of a date palm decorated with different kinds of ornaments, mouldings, fruits and emblems. We observe such emblems in Anatolia as far back as the Hittites and Phrygians (terracotta panels with reliefs decorated in coloured glaze from the Phrygian city of Pazarlı, near Ankara, show such palms as fertility symbols). The excavations at Altıntepe, situated on the plain of Erzincan (eastern central Anatolia), have revealed panels decorated with palmettes belonging to the period of Urartu in Anatolia; also, the sculptures of the main gallery in Yazılıkaya (east of Ankara) show the Hittite phallophoric symbols. In the region of Afyon and Konya (central Anatolia), during the reign of the Phrygian kings, the symbols headed ritualistic processions, mostly in spring.

In the Ottoman processions, these *nakhi̊ls* had an important place not only in the weddings, but also in the circumcision ceremonies. For the weddings, they were prepared by the bride's family, and in the circumcisions by the parents of the boy. In these ceremonies, the palms were carried in front of the procession, and if it was an imperial celebration, the Grand Vizier, the viziers and the high officials walked behind them. If the *nakhi̊ls* were in various sizes, the biggest would generally be carried first, and it would be followed by other smaller ones, together with gardens of sugar work, sweets in gold, silver and bronze trays, gold and silver decanters of *sherbet* (a sweet, cold drink, made of various fruit juices), bundles of the bride's trousseau, coloured purses full of silver coins, and caskets full of precious stones. Of course, the arrangement of *nakhi̊ls* differed according to the taste of the superintendent of the procession.

There were special craftsmen who constructed these festal palms. Ewliyā described them in his travel journal as *eṣnāf-i̊ nakhi̊ldjiyān-i̊ sūr-i hümayūn* ("guild of *nakhi̊l*-makers for imperial festivities"). According to him, the guild had four workshops in Istanbul, with 55 skilled members in the 17th century. The founder of this guild was Meyser Ezherī. These craftsmen, Ewliyā writes, "constructed *nakhi̊ls* in wax as tall as the minaret of the Süleymāniyye Mosque, with coloured ribbons, silver and golden threads, which could also be illuminated". The iron-structured gigantic *nakhi̊ls* "were carried by hundreds of galley-slaves supervised by guards, who gave with whistles such orders as: 'pull it to the right, to the left,' etc." A similar scene is described in detail by an English priest, Dr. John Covel, who had the occasion to see the festivities of Sultan Meḥmmed IV, in the summer of 1086/1675 in Edirne. He witnessed these guards—generally dockyard stewards—with whistles, directing each group, carrying gigantic *nakhi̊ls*, approximately 25 metres high. The lower end (approximately 4.50 to 5.50 metres in diameter) had eight or ten long parallel bars, and the slaves carried the *nakhi̊ls*, holding these bars. There was someone who directed them: he commanded the slaves to rest or to carry on at the sound of the whistle.

The gigantic *nakhi̊ls* were so big that in order to carry them through the narrow streets of old Istanbul, very often, the projecting parts of the houses, such as eaves and balconies, were pulled down and afterwards rebuilt. Although the rebuilding of the houses required a great deal of money, the value of the *nakhi̊ls* were almost twice the expenses thus incurred. The most important fertility symbols were each a work of art and very expensive. Some of them were entirely in silver and some were adorned with jewelry. At the wedding in 931/1524 of Khadīdje Sulṭān, sister of Süleymān the Magnificent, one of the *nakhi̊ls* consisted of 40,000 and another of 60,000 pieces of handwork; and they were skilfully ornamented with beautiful, precious stones, in the shape of legendary birds.

In sum, the *nakhi̊ls* represented the virility of men and the fecundity of women, as well as the economic power and marks of supremacy in society.

Bibliography: *Sūr-nāme-i hümayūn*, Nationalbibliothek, Vienna, cod. H.O.70; Lebelski, *A True Description*...; Palerne, *op.cit.*, 442-88; von Haunolt, *Verzeichnuss des hochzeitlichen Fest*...., in *op.cit.*, 532,

534; idem, *Particular Verzeichnuss...*, 469, 473; Melchior Besolt, *Dess Wolgeborenen Herrn Heinrichs Herrn von Lichtenstein von Nicolspurg u. Röm. Keys. Maiest. Abgesandten Reyss auff Constinopel im 1584*, in Lewenklaw, 515-31; Salomon Schweigger, *Ein newe Reisbeschreibung aus Deutschland nach Constantinopel und Jerusalem*, Nürnberg 1608; Stephan Gerlach (d. Aeltere), *Tagebuch...*, Franckfurt am Mayn 1674, 265; Hezār-fenn, *op.cit.*, fol. 178a; ʿAbdī, fol. 8a-b; Nāʿīmā writes that, in the festival of 1056/1646 to celebrate the wedding of Fāṭima Sulṭān, the daughter of Sultan Ibrāhīm, who was then four years of age, since the two minarethigh *nakhīls* were too tall and too wide to pass through the streets of Istanbul, terraces, balconies and the eaves of various houses had to be pulled down, and the streets to be widened, see his *Taʾrīkh*, Maṭbaʿa-yi ʿĀmire, Istanbul 1280/1863; the case was the same in the festival of 1086/1675. Dr. Covel witnessed the demolishing process in Edirne: some of the houses were completely pulled down, see his *Diary*, fol. 200a; Wehbī states that in the festival of 1133/1720, the money for the reconstruction was granted to the owners of the houses while the process of demolishing was under way, see his *Sūr-nāme-yi Sulṭān Aḥmed*, Nationalbibliothek, Vienna, H.O. 94; Keshfī, *Sūr-nāme*, Nat. bibl. Vienna, H.O.95, fols. 3b, 13a-b; also Haunolt, *Verzeichnuss des Hochzeitlichen Fest...*, 432; he describes some of the expensive *nakhīls* constructed for the wedding of ʿĀʾishe Sulṭān, one of the daughters of Murad III, in 1586, which were decorated with gilded balls, big pieces of turquoise and hundreds of pearls. One such palm cost forty or fifty thousand golden ducats; J. von Hammer, *GOR*, iv, Vienna 1829, 451 (von Hammer is the first Ottoman historian to have drawn attention to the symbolical significance of the *nakhīls*). According to him, the size of these palms implied the power of virility of the bridegroom, and the fruits on their branches alluded to the fecundity of the bride. He indicates that while the *nakhīls* represented the phallophores, the red tulle on the wedding palanquin suggests the flammeum and the torches the flambeau of Cupid and Hymen; here the fescennium and corybantes are replaced by sensual songs and orgiastic dances in unison with the pulsating beats of drums and castanets; he shows 24 kinds of festal palm, see *ibid.*, iv, 312; Ewliyā, *Seyāḥāt-nāme*, i, Istanbul 1314/1896, 612; Lubenau, *Beschreibung der Reisen...*, i, 277, ii, 50; Konyalı, *İstanbul sarayları*, Istanbul 1942, 137-8: here the author describes how the Arabic word *nakhl* later became *nahil*, *nakıl* or *nakil* in common Turkish usage; İ. H. Danişmend, *İstanbul sarayları*, Istanbul 1943, ii, 104; Nabī, *Sūr-nāme*, 57-8; Uzunçarşılı, *op.cit.*, 162; M. And, *Osmanlı dügünlerinde nahıllar*, in *TM*, xii (January 1969), 16; Ö. Nutku, *The* Nahıl: *a symbol of fertility in Ottoman festivities*, in *Annales de l'Université d'Ankara*, xii (Ankara 1972), 63-71; And, *Osmanlı şenliklerinde Türk sanatı*, 210-24.

2. SHEKER TAṢWĪRLER, "Sugar figures". The confectionery displayed in various processions was one of the most attractive spectacles in this event. The sugar figures made by skilled confectioners had always been a colourful public attraction. These figures, together with artificial gardens, were almost indispensable parts of the festal palms; and that is why they had always been considered all together. If the festal palms were necessary, so were the sugar figures and the artificial gardens, all being meaningful in the matrimonial and circumcisional processions as symbols of fertility and fecundity.

The confectionery played an important role in the Ottoman celebrations from the beginning. The figures of lions, birds, fishes, peacocks, camels, elephants, gazelles, horses and a variety of monsters made of sugar in different colours and flavours, were generally between 75 cm. and 1.35 m. in size. These and the figures of mermaids, lanterns, ewers, pots, fruits, flowers, festal palms and jugs filled with water were all made by the skilled confectioners. Yet the most astonishing works in sugar were the ones in bigger sizes, such as models of a mosque, a castle, a town, a kiosk, a garden or a fountain with running water.

Apart from these models and the figures, there were also large circular trays or large boxes of confectionery, carried by two attendants and sometimes by three or four. In the festivities of 1086/1675, for instance, there were 200 coffers of confectionery, all distributed to the spectators.

Bibliography: An illuminating description of sugar figures may be seen in Gerlach's *Tagebuch...*, 97, 265; for the confectionery and the confectioner, Haunolt, *Particular Verzeichnuss...*, 472, 476, 489-90; and idem, *Verzeichnuss des Hochzeitlichen Fest...*, 528, 534; ʿAbdī, *Sūr-nāme*, fol. 8b; Covel, *Diary*, fol. 215a; Hezār-fenn, fols. 168a, 174b; *Sūr-nāme* of 1137/1724, ms., Nat. bibl. Vienna, H.O.95, fols. 3b, 7a; for Nointel's letter to his friend Pomponne, de Nointel, *L'Odyssée d'un ambassadeur*, 197; a later description of confectionery may be seen in Lebīb's *Sūr-nāme*, ms. Ist. Üniv. Kit. T. no. 6197, fols. 13b, 89a-90b; for the skill of confectioners, *Beschreibung der Reisen*, ii, 50; a detailed description may be found in Dursun Bey's *Taʾrīkh-i Ebu 'l-Fetḥ*, Istanbul 1330/1911, 80; Nabī, *Sūr-nāme*, 62; for recent information, Nutku, *IV. Mehmet'in Edirne şenliği*, 72; and And, *Osmanlı şenliklerinde Türk sanatları*, 209-24.

3. YAPMA BAGHČE, "Artificial garden". In the processions organised for weddings, and circumcision celebrations, the artificial gardens were one of the exhibits, which interested the spectators, together with the festal palms and the sugar figures. These models were approximately 2.70 m² or 3.60 m² in size, with fruit trees, flowers, kiosks and fountains. There were nightingales singing on the trees, and water running from the hill tops. If the model was going to be presented to the Sultan, it was decorated with precious stones, mostly turquoise and mother-of-pearls. These artificial gardens moved on four, six or sometimes eight wheels, and each garden were pulled by four or six dockyard slaves, who were later liberated by the Sulṭan. In some cases, there were also real musicians on these models, playing for the public. In short, the artificial gardens were pieces of artistic composition.

Bibliography: For the miniatures showing the artificial gardens, *Sūr-nāme-i Hümāyūn*, Nat. bibl. Vienna, cod. H.O./70; and Wehbī, *Sūr-nāme*, Nat. bibl. Vienna, H.O. 94; ʿAbdī, *Sūr-nāme*, Millet Kit. no. 277, fol. 10a; Covel, *Diary*, fols. 15b, 215a, 217a; Hezār-fenn, fols. 165a, 166b, 177a; de Nointel, *op.cit.*, 199; Hüseyin Yurdaydın, *Matrakçı Nasuh*, Ankara 1963, 12-5, and for the pictures of the models, see 86; Nutku, *op.cit.*, 73; And, *op.cit.*, 220. (Ö. NUTKU)

5. IN MUSLIM INDIA

Many of the terms used here have already been defined in the account of court ceremonial above, for which see MARĀSIM, 5.

Processions in India are of great popular appeal, from the panache of the simple wedding ceremonies to the pomp of royal ceremonial; and even these extremes have something in common.

The wedding (for full details see NIKĀḤ) involves a procession to escort the first contractual presents from bridegroom to bride, the preliminary exchange of presents (*sāčaḳ*) between bride and groom, the bride's night procession (*mēhndī*) to anoint the bridegroom with henna, and the bridegroom's procession in which he comes to carry away his bride; even in the simplest forms the bridegroom is mounted on a decorated horse, or the bride carried in a palanquin (*pālkī*) or on a litter (*ḍōlī*) [see NAḲL] accompanied by friends on foot and by a musical escort. The essentials of Muslim weddings in India (which incorporate many details derived from Hindū customs) are described, especially for the Deccan, in Dja^cfar Sharīf, ch. viii; but the difference is only one of degree from such an elaborate wedding ceremonial as that of the (Anglo-Muslim) granddaughter of Col. W. L. Gardner at Kāsgandj in 1835 to a grandson of Shāh ʿĀlam II, sultan of Dihlī, described in Fanny Parks, *Wanderings of a pilgrim in search of the picturesque*, London 1850 (repr. Karachi 1975), i, 420-50, and similar in its lavish ostentation to the processions, for various purposes, of the royal court: the escort for the bride's dress in *ʿamārīs* on elephants and in covered bullock-carts (*ratha*) and palanquins with 100 trays of presents carried on men's heads; a similar procession to escort the bridegroom's dress; the *sāčaḳ* procession, with fully caparisoned elephants and horses, *nālkīs*, palanquins and *rathas* [see NAḲL], 200 earthen pots, covered with leaf silver, containing sweetmeats and carried on men's heads, "a number of men dressed up as horses ... playing antics", and ten travelling platforms (*takht-i rawān*), each supporting two dancing-girls and a musician, also carried on men's heads and accompanied by kettle-drums; the *mēhndī* procession, the grandest of all, when the road was enclosed with bamboo screens and had triumphal arches at intervals, all lighted with thousands of small lamps, fireworks were let off all along the route, and the usual elephants, horses, *nālkīs*, palanquins, *rathas*, and the portable stages, were lit up by men carrying 5,000 torches; and the bridegroom's procession to carry away his bride (described as an old Tatar, or Tīmūrid, custom; but Ibn Baṭṭūṭa, iii, 275, tr. Gibb, iii, 687, writes of a similar ceremony at the marriage of the sister of Muḥammad b. Tughluḳ), similarly accompanied by many musical bands and innumerable flags, with the young prince at the head on a horse with an ornamental armour made of flowers, flanked by an *āftābgīr* and followed by a gold-embroidered *čhatr*; besides the usual train of elephants and horses, etc., carrying the escort, and the portable stages, there were added a great number of led horses, and a small forest of artificial trees of wax and paper, decorated with gold and silver foil and mica. Not mentioned in the above account, but known from other sources, are the distribution of small copper coins from one of the elephants to the bystanders lining the route, and the liberation of caged birds at frequent intervals.

Descriptions of royal processions are less frequent than notices of other ceremonial observances. Ibn Baṭṭūṭa does, however, describe, sketchily, certain processions in the time of Muḥammad b. Tughluḳ: on his return to his palace from a journey, wooden pavilions were set up at intervals on the road from city gate to palace gate, several storeys high with well-dressed singers and dancing girls on each storey; the street walls were hung with silk cloths, and silk cloths carpeted the space between the pavilions for the sultan's horse to walk on. He was preceded by several thousand of his own slaves on foot, sixteen brocaded and jewelled elephants bearing sixteen parasols, and the *ghāshiya*, and followed by mounted troops; three or four small catapults set up on elephants might scatter silver coin among the populace (iii, 237-8, tr. Gibb, iii, 668; another ceremonial entry is described at iii, 395-6, tr. Gibb, iii, 744). At the reception of a person of rank (e.g. the *amīr* Ghiyāth al-Dīn Muḥammad, descendant of the ʿAbbāsid caliph al-Mustanṣir bi'llah) the sultan sent envoys to a distance to meet him, and himself rode out ten miles to greet him personally, dismounting to pay homage and offer a *khilʿa* before both mounted for the journey to the palace shaded by the one royal umbrella (*ibid.*, iii, 260, tr. Gibb, iii, 680). When the sultan rode out to the great festival of the *ʿīd al-aḍḥā* [*q.v.*] the procession was headed by the *ḳāḍīs* and by *muʾadhdhins*, calling out *allāhu akbar*, mounted on elephants; then came the slaves and *mamlūks* on foot and some 300 *nāḳibs*, all wearing gold caps and girdles; then the sixteen royal elephants with their sixteen parasols, one of them bearing the sultan himself, preceded by his *ghāshiya*. Foreign dignitaries later in the procession were also mounted on elephants. Behind the sultan were his "honours" [see MARĀTIB] and all the members of his personal entourage, and then his half-brother, his father's adopted son, his nephew Fīrūz b. Radjab, the *wazīr*, and some half-dozen "great *amīrs* who are never separated from his company", all mounted and followed by their *marātib* and troops; other *amīrs* rode without "honours"; those riding in the procession wore armour, both on themselves and on their horses. At the gate of the *ʿīdgāh*, the procession halted and the judges, the principal *amīrs* and the "chiefs of the foreigners" (envoys from other courts?) entered before the sultan; after the prayers and the address by the *imām*, the sultan protected his dress by a silk overall and himself stabbed the sacrificial camel in the throat with a spear before returning to his palace. Ibn Baṭṭūṭa also describes (iii, 109ff., tr. Gibb, iii, 600-2) a river-journey with the governor of Lāharī in Sind: the governor rode in a central raised cabin in an *ahawra* (possibly connected with the Hindī *hōlā*, a cargo boat of some 35-55 tonnes; here evidently a state barge) rowed by 40 men; of the fifteen vessels which made up his baggage-train, four flanked the *ahawra*, two carrying his *marātib* and two carrying singers. Singers and the instruments of the *marātib* performed alternately until the midday meal, when the ships closed up and gangways were set between them; at dusk the parties disembarked and set up camp on the river bank. When the procession moved to land, six horsemen rode ahead with drums and reed pipes, followed by the governor's *ḥādjibs*, flanked by singers, and his personal troops, and the governor himself.

There is little difference on the composition of royal processions over the years, as far as can be determined from the limited evidence available; certain practices mentioned later, such as water-carriers walking ahead of the procession to lay the dust, may in fact not be innovations. When the Mughal ruler moved out of his palace he was accompanied almost always by the bearer of the flywhisk, and invariably by the *ḳur*, as described above s.v. MARĀSIM. 5; the ruler's person would be further guarded by mace-bearers (*gurz-bardār*), who obviously inherited the functions of the *dūrbāsh* [*q.v.*] as described by Amīr Khusraw and Baranī. Processions are the subject of frequent illustration in Mughal painting; the use of the *ghāshiya* seems by now to have been discontinued. There is evidence of some rulers taking part in processions on foot on grounds of piety; Akbar so covered part of the journey to the shrine of Muʿīn al-Dīn Čishtī at Adjmēr, and Djahāngīr visited Akbar's tomb on foot in 1017/1608; in 1028/1619, however, he rode to the tomb in full procession, as shown by a superb miniature painting in the Chester Beatty collection. The height of ostentation and opulence is perhaps best expressed in the royal participation in the *ʿīd al-aḍḥā* celebrations at Lucknow [see LAKHNAʾŪ] in the first quarter of the 19th century, as described by Mrs. Meer Hassan Ali, *Observations on the Mussulmanns of India...*, [1832], ed. Crooke, London 1917, 142-4; here the procession started with 50 camels carrying swivelguns, each with two gunners and driver, then a body of artillery, two troops of armed cavalry, and a regiment of militia, all in new uniforms of different colours; the horses were caparisoned with embroidered horsecloths, silver ornaments and necklaces, with tails and manes dyed red with henna. These were followed by the mounted kettledrums, these with horse and rider ornamented with the royal fish emblem (representing the *māhī-marātib*; see under MARĀTIB. 5. Fanny Parks remarks, *op.cit.*, i, 178, that the royal pleasure-boat on the river Gōmatī was "made in the shape of a fish, and the golden scales glittered in the sun"). The ruler followed in an open silver carriage drawn by four elephants with costly caparisons, flanked by chowry-bearers and the *āftābgīr* and guarded by cavalry, and followed by the king's horses, led by grooms; other elephant-carriages, with two elephants apiece, conveyed the British Resident, the *wazīr*, and other favoured nobles. The golden *nālkī* followed, with a golden palanquin and a state carriage drawn by eight horses with a European coachman. Some fifty ridden elephants followed, wtih the Europeans of the King's court and the *umarāʾ* and the great officers of state, and the regiments, both horse and foot, marching with their colours unfurled, and their bands "playing English pieces". After the sacrifice at the *ʿīdgāh*, the procession returned to the royal palace in the same order, where the king held court firstly to receive *nadhrs* [*q.v.*], then to garland his favoured guests and to award distinctions and present *khilʿa*s; a feast followed, with animal fights, music and dancing, and fireworks. "This magnificent style of celebrating ... is perhaps unequalled by any other Native Court now existing in Hindoostaun."

The royal hunt—highly esteemed in India since it kept the army ready and exercised—involved the sultan and his retinue and troops marching out in battle array; Baranī (*Taʾrīkh-i Fīrūz-Shāhī*, Bibl. Ind. ed., 55) estimates that the sultan might be accompanied by 500-600 courtiers, 1,000 mounted troops and 1,000 foot-soldiers (the beaters, perhaps 3,000 in number, were probably engaged locally); the trainers of the hunting-leopards [see FAHD], dogs and hawks [see BAYZARA] would also have marched out with the sultan from the *kārkhāna*s specialising in breeding and training these animals (Shams-i Sirādj ʿAfīf, *Taʾrīkh-i Fīrūz-Shāhī*, Bibl. Ind. ed., 317-18). When Ibn Baṭṭūṭa accompanied Muḥammad b. Tughluḳ (iii, 414-15, tr. Gibb, iii, 752-3) the royal procession was similar to those described above, and each traveller of importance had to provide his own camping enclosure (*sarāča*) and tent to be erected within it, carpets, cooking utensils, litter (*ḍōlā*), and camels and men to carry everything, grass-cutters for fodder for the animals, and torch-bearers for night travel. The sultan selected each camping site, and his own red *sarāča* was erected before any other *sarāča*s (white trimmed with blue) were allowed to be set up. (A story is told of Akbar by Manucci, *Storia do Mogor*, i, 87, Eng. tr. W. Irvine, i, 133, who while graciously dismissing a Hindū prince demanded the surrender of his scarlet tents, reserving this colour for himself and for princes of the blood royal.) It is notable that in depictions of the hunt in Mughal painting, the *ḳur* is almost always present, close to the royal person, no matter how attenuated the retinue has become during the chase. (For the royal hunt, see ṢAYD; for the camp, see URDŪ.)

The processions at the Muḥarram are described s.v. TAʿZIYA; certain features of them must however be noticed here. The Muḥarram procession at Lucknow, as described by Mrs. Meer Hassan Ali, *op.cit.*, 42ff., is scarcely less elaborate than the royal procession described above, except that the ruler himself does not take part; but the royal umbrella is carried over the head of the Duldul, a mule representing that which the Prophet gave to ʿAlī. There is also much distribution of food to the poor as the cavalcade passes along; and the kettledrums are muffled. There are many extraneous events, however, in the Muḥarram processions as celebrated in the Deccan; besides the orthodox *faḳīrs* there are many who personate the *faḳīrs*, and others, such as those intended to represent paddy-birds (the heron *Ardeola grayii*) and the hawk who catches them; the Crow King, who carries a cage of crows and makes jokes; the *ḥādjdjī bī-wuḳūf*, the sham *ḥakīm*, the *sharābī*, the *ḳāḍī bī-dīn*, whose irreverent names reveal their functions, join with men dressed as tigers or camels, or personating Hindū shopkeepers or Djayn moneylenders, in coarse buffoonery all along the procession, rather like the men "dressed as horses and playing antics" mentioned earlier. There are many similar by-plays, nothing at all to do with, or in keeping with, the solemnity of the occasion. (Djaʿfar Sharīf, *Ḳānūn-i Islām*, ed. as *Herklots' Islam in India* by W. Crooke, Oxford 1921, 168-82). The author has observed quarter-staff fights, doubtless derived from the *idea* of the battle of Karbalāʾ, enacted in the Muḥarram procession at Udaypur [*q.v.*] by obviously non-Muslim Rādjpūts, showing the Indian love of turning any procession into a *tamāsha*.

Bibliography: In addition to references in the article, see *Bibl.* to MARĀSIM. 5. Muslim India.

(J. BURTON-PAGE)

MAWĀLĪ [see MAWLĀ].

MAWĀLIYĀ (A., pl. *mawāliyāt*) or *mawāliyyā*, also reportedly *mawālī* and *muwālayāt*, a non-classical Arabic verse form. Together with the cognate *mawwāl*, this is best considered in three contexts.

1. In written sources.

Among the "seven arts" *al-funūn al-sabʿa* [see KĀN WA-KĀN])—non-classical verse forms are always made to number seven, although the lists are not identical—the *mawāliyā* is given pride of place next to the *muwashshaḥ* and the *zadjal*, on the ground that its metre is classical and its language either classical or colloquial.

Two traditions place its beginnings in ʿIrāḳ in early ʿAbbāsid times. One is that non-Arab (*mawālī*) labourers in the orchards of Wāsiṭ sang it, using the words *yā mawāliyā* ("O, my master!") as a refrain. The other is that a slave-girl of the Barmakīs, herself called Mawāliyā, created the form to circumvent Hārūn al-Rashīd's ban on poetry praising her disgraced masters, the contention being that since the language was uninflected, the composition could not be said to be *shiʿr*. Both accounts are suspect as they occur only in late sources and appear to have been fabricated to account for the otherwise unexplained appellation.

The form was, however, well-established by the

6th/12th century, when it always occurs as four hemistichs of *basīṭ*, all with the same rhyme. Later, perhaps from the 11th/17th century onward, it was elaborated into a variety of multi-rhyme compositions (see section 2, below).

The composer of *mawāliyā*s was sometimes called a *mawwāl*.

2. In folk-verse.

The form is a favourite in Arab lands, extending all the way from ʿIrāḳ to North Africa. Variations are almost innumerable, and the observations that follow relate to prevalent practice in Egypt alone.

The terminology is often vague and inconsistent. The word *mawāliyā* itself is still used, especially in writing, but in common parlance the composition itself is almost always called a *mawwāl*, and a master of the art is known as *rayyis il-mawwāl*.

The metre is seldom as regular as the pundits would have it, but if the composition can be scanned at all it is recognisably in the *basīṭ*, with two variations added to those allowed by the classical prosodists: the *fāʿilun* foot is often reduced to two long syllables even in the body of the line, and the *mustafʿilun* foot is occasionally changed to *mutafāʿilun*. It may therefore be scanned:

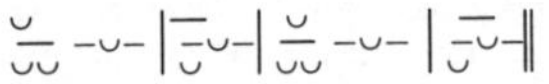

What in classical prosody is a hemistich is here clearly the basic metrical unit, for it is always rhymed, occurs more often in odd than in even numbers, and is never enjambé. In this entry, it will be referred to as a line.

The most marked development has been in rhyme schemes. The monorhyme quatrain (*aaaa*), called *rubāʿī* or *mirabbaʿ*, is now comparatively rare. Variations appear to have been created mostly by insertions between the third line and the last. The first three lines are then called the *ʿataba* ("doorstep")—although the term is also sometimes applied to each of the three lines—or the *farsha* ("spread, mat"), and the last line is then the *ghaṭā* ("cover") or, in longer compositions, the *ṭāḳiyya* ("skull-cap").

The simplest elaboration consists of the addition of an unrhymed line in fourth place: *aaaxa*. This line is said to be *ʿardjā* ("lame"), and the *mawwāl* itself is *aʿradj*.

Another augmented form has the rhyme scheme *aaa zzz a*. The composition is then called *sabʿānī* or *misabbaʿ* ("sevener"), *nuʿmānī*, or *baghdādī*.

Yet another elaboration is brought about by adding a number of lines, usually six, with alternating rhymes after the *farsha*—*aaa bcbcbc zzz a*—the last line also having an internal *z* rhyme. The sestet of alternating rhymes is called *shadjara* ("tree") or *ridfa* ("alternate"), or else each of the two rhymes is called a *ridfa*, and they are distinguished from each other as *dakar* and *intāya* ("male" and "female"). The *mawwāl* is then said to be *mardūf* or *Ṣaʿīdī* ("Upper Egyptian").

By multiplying the number of sestets, or by using any variety of the *mawwāl* as a stanza, the composition can be extended indefinitely, particularly for narrative purposes.

A somewhat rare further refinement is the addition of internal rhymes to some of the lines; these are then called *misaḳḳaf* ("clapping or roofed").

Another feature strongly associated with the folk *mawwāl* but not exclusive to it is the expansion of the rhymes into polysyllabic paronomasias, achieved by deliberate distortion of the normal pronunciation. The art is called *zahr* ("flower'). A *mawwāl* devoid of it is described as *abyaḍ* ("white, blank"); if so ornamented, it is either *aḥmar* ("red") or *akhḍar* ("green"), the distinction most often made—but not consistently applied—between these two being that the first deals with sad themes and the second with joyful ones.

The following illustrates the rhyme scheme, metrical variations, and the *zahr*, with the normal pronunciation of the punning rhymes added between square brackets:

yā dākhil il-karm(i) khud bālak min illī fīh
You who enter the vineyard, beware of what is in it;
wi giss(i) nabḍ il-ʿinab w iḥras min illifīh [līfuh]
Feel the pulse of the grapes, be watchful of its fibres,
w ittabbaʿ il-ʾaṣl(i) law titʿab min illifīh [il-laffa]
And trace back the root, though you weary of the winding trail.
il-ḥilw(i) fōḳ ish-shawāshī w il-wiḥish ʿa l-ʾarḍ
What is good is high on the trellises; what is bad is on the ground.
iʿlam bi ʾinn il-hawā li l-ḥukm(i) ʾawʿādī ['awʿad]
Take note that passion is a threat to wisdom.
il-ward(i) lammā zuhī ḳaṭafu l-gabān ʿal-ʾarḍ [ʿalā riḍā]
Roses when deluded consent to being plucked by the unworthy;
khallāni tayhān m aʿraf ʾahli ʾawʿādī [ʾaw ʾaʿādiyya]
They so befuddle me, I make out neither my kinsmen nor my foes.
shuft il-ghazāl māl min ḥubb il-fulūs ʿal-ʾarḍ [ʿalā l-ḳird]
I have seen the gazelle, for love of money, lean towards the monkey.
ya ma ḳult(i) li l-ḳalb(i) buṣṣ(i) w shūf ʾaʿwādī [ʾiwʿa di]
How often have I told my heart: Look! Consider! Guard against this!
bēn il-milīḥ wi l-ḳabīḥ farḳ(i) b-dalīl wisabāt [wi ʾisbāt]
The fair and the ugly differ—for this there is evidence and proof.
wi ṭ-ṭabʿ(i) wi r-rūḥ fi l-gasad is-salīm wisabāt [wasabāt]
In a healthy body, one's nature and spirit leap up.
il-ḥurr(i) ʿanduh shahāmah fi l-karam wi sabāt
The freeborn man is resolute and staunch in his nobility,
wi n-nadl(i) law māt ma ytubshī ʿan illifīh [il-ʾāfa]
Whereas the vile one—though he die—never turns away from shame.

3. In folk music.

The word *mawwāl* stands for an interpretative freesong, with no set tune. The words sung may fall within the norms detailed above, but more often than not metrical regularity and even rhyme are sacrificed to dramatic effect.

Bibliography: For earlier works, see the *Bibl.* to *EI*[1] art. *Mawālīyā* (Moh. Bencheneb). Of more recent ones, see Ṣafiyy ad-Dīn al-Ḥillī, *Die vulgärabische Poetik—al-Kitāb al-ʿAṭil al-Ḥālī wal-Muraḫḫaṣ al-Ġālī*, ed. W. Hoenerbach, Wiesbaden 1956; ʿAbd al-Karīm al-ʿAllāf, *al-Mawwāl al-Baghdādī*, Baghdād 1964; Aḥmad Mursī, *al-Ughniya al-shaʿbiyya*, Cairo 1970; P. Cachia, *The Egyptian Mawwāl*, in *JAL*, viii (1977), 77-103; Serafin Fanjul, *El Mawwāl Egipcio*, Madrid, Instituto Hispano-Árabe de Cultura 1976; Tiberiu Alexandru, *The folk music of Egypt* (booklet and two discs), Cairo, Ministry of Culture n.d. [*ca.* 1970].

(P. Cachia)

At the end of his article in *EI*[1] Mawāliyā, Mawwāl, M. Bencheneb adds numerous bibliographical references, amongst which should be given here the following in particular: Ibn Khaldūn, *Muḳaddima*, tr.

de Slane, iii, 451 ff., tr. Rosenthal, iii, 475 ff.; Sayyid Amīn, *Bulbul al-afrāh ... fi 'l-mawāwīl al-khudr wa 'l-humr*, Cairo 1316/1898-9; J. David, *Les Maouals*, Caen 1864. To these may be added Muḥammad b. Abī Shanab, *Tuḥfat al-adab*², Paris 1954, 129-31.

(Ed.)

al-**MĀWARDĪ**, Abu 'l-Ḥasan ʿAlī b. Muḥammad b. Ḥabīb, Shāfiʿi *faḳīh*, was born in Baṣra in 364/974 and died in Baghdād on 30 Rabīʿ I 450/27 May 1058, aged 86 years.

After completing his studies in Baṣra and in Baghdād, he became a teacher. The renown which he acquired, owing to the extent and the variety of his knowledge, drew to him the attention of the authorities; he was appointed *ḳāḍī* and fulfilled the responsibilities of this post in various towns, in particular at Ustuwā, near Nishāpūr, before being entrusted with the role in Baghdād itself. In 429/1038, he was awarded the honorific surname (*laḳab*) of *aḳḍā 'l-ḳuḍāt* or supreme *ḳāḍī* in spite of the opinions of eminent jurists, including al-Ṭabarī, who denied the legality of this title. In addition, he was on four occasions chosen by the caliph al-Ḳāʾim (422-67/1031-74) to perform diplomatic missions in 422/1031, 428/1037, 434/1042-3 and 435/1043-4. Anecdotes confirm that his rank and his vast learning did not in any way detract from his modesty and that he was an enthusiastic and eloquent speaker. He was furthermore highly regarded by the preceding caliph al-Ḳādir (381-422/991-1031), who employed him not only in the conduct of his negotiations with the Būyids who were then the rulers of ʿIrāḳ (al-Māwardī was thus the contemporary of two caliphs known for their pro-Sunnī policy), but also for the purpose of restoring Sunnism, this accounting for the composition of manuals propounding the doctrines of each of the four orthodox schools.

Other details regarding the biography of al-Māwardī are supplied by Arab writers. From the account given by the Shāfiʿī al-Khaṭīb al-Baghdādī (d. 463/1072), in his *Taʾrīkh Baghdād*, i, 53-4, ix, 358, it is known that his father was a manufacturer and seller of rose-water and that our *faḳīh* was buried in Baghdād. Ibn Kathīr (d. 774/1373) in *al-Bidāya wa 'l-nihāya* (xi, 80, xii, 79) says of him that he was gentle, dignified and polite, qualities which had been attributed to him even earlier by the Ḥanbalī Ibn al-Djawzī (d. 597/1200) in the *Muntaẓam* (viii, 199-200). Al-Dhahabī (d. 748/1348) in the *Mīzān al-iʿtidāl fī naḳd al-ridjāl* (no. 342) and Ibn Ḥadjar al-ʿAsḳalānī (d. 852/1449) in the *Lisān al-Mīzān* (iv, 260) give examples of the perfect rectitude of al-Māwardī even when confronted by the powerful. The most striking example is that of the *fatwā* declared in 429/1037-8 against the Būyid Djalāl al-Dawla, who was demanding from al-Ḳāʾim the right to bear the title of *shāhanshāh*. However, al-Māwardī did not escape the suspicions of the orthodox, and the great Shāfiʿī jurist al-Subkī (d. 756/1355) speaks of Muʿtazilī views for which he was criticised (*Ṭabaḳāt al-Shāfiʿiyya*, iii, 303, v, 12).

As regards the works of al-Māwardī, the classification followed is that of Muṣṭafā al-Saḳḳāʾ, in the introduction to the *Adab al-dunyā wa 'l-dīn*:

1. Religious works: *Tafsīr al-Ḳurʾān*, also known as *al-Nukat wa 'l-ʿuyūn* (still in manuscript); *Kitāb al-Ḥāwī al-kabīr fi 'l-furūʿ*, on the legal system of the Imām al-Shāfiʿī, of which the various portions (more than thirty) are scattered throughout the East and the West; *Kitāb al-Iḳnāʿ*, a summary in 40 pages of the preceding, which numbered 4,000 pages, mentioned by Ibn al-Djawzī in *al-Muntaẓam* (viii, 199); *Kitāb Aʿlām al-nubuwwa* (ed. Cairo 1319, 330); *Kitāb Adab al-dunyā wa 'l-dīn* (ed. in the margins of the *Kashkūl* of al-ʿĀmilī, Cairo 1316/1898-9; ed. M. al-Saḳḳāʾ, Cairo 1955).

2. Works of a political and social nature: *Kitāb al-Aḥkām al-sulṭāniyya*, translated notably by Fagnan (Algiers 1915; new edition, Paris 1982) under the title of *Traité des statuts gouvernementaux* or *Constitutiones politicae*; this is the work which made al-Māwardī known in the West, and it is considered a classic work of public law; *Kitāb Ḳawānīn al-wizāra wa-siyāsat al-mulk*, on the *adab* of the vizier (ms. in Vienna); *Kitāb Tashīl al-naẓar wa-taʿdjīl al-ẓafar*, on politics and different forms of government (ms. in Gotha); *Kitāb Naṣīḥat al-mulūk* (ms. in Paris).

3. Studies of language and of *adab*: *Kitāb fi 'l-naḥw*, on grammar (lost); *Kitāb al-Amthāl wa 'l-ḥikam*, collection of 300 traditions, 300 proverbs and 300 verses (ms. Univ. of Leiden); *Kitāb Ādāb al-takallum* (selection from works of al-Māwardī chosen by Muḥammad b. ʿĀli al-Zuhra; ms. Univ. of Leiden, Or. 989-9); *Kitāb Adab al-ḳāḍī*, which in fact represents two of the thirty sections of the *Ḥāwī* (ed. Baghdād 1971); *Kitāb Maʿrifat al-faḍāʾil, Tractatus paroeneticus de virtutibus moralibus*, attributed to al-Māwardī (ms. Escurial).

Bibliography: Besides the sources mentioned, see Ibn Khallikān, *Wafayāt al-aʿyān*, ed. Cairo 1299, i, 410, ed. Iḥsān ʿAbbās, Beirut 1968-72, iii, 382-4; Yāḳūt, *Udabāʾ*, xv, 52-5; Brockelmann, I, 386, S I, 668 for the mss.; H. A. R. Gibb, *Al-Mawardī's theory of the Khilafah*, in *IC*, xi (1937), 291-302, repr. in *Studies on the civilization of Islam*, Boston 1962, 151-65; E. I. J. Rosenthal, *Political thought in medieval Islam*, Cambridge 1958, 27-37; H. Laoust, *La pensée et l'action politique d'al-Māwardī*, in *REI* xxxvi (1968), 11-92. See also maẓālim.

(C. Brockelmann)

MAWĀT (a.), juridical term designating dead lands.

Fiḳh makes the practical distinction between dead land (*arḍ mawāt*) and living land. According to Abū Ḥanīfa, dead land is that which is not well cultivated and is without water; for al-Shāfiʿī, it is all that is neither cultivated nor dependent on a cultivated place. Dead land is of two kinds: that which, from time immemorial, has always been in this state, of a kind that bears no mark of cultivation and concerning which no property right has been established; whereas dead land of the second category is that which, once cultivated, has then been neglected, become dead and allowed to lie fallow.

But dead land can be brought to life. Revivification (*iḥyāʾ*) is a task performed on the land and intended to make it usable. Both near neighbours and those at a greater distance have the right of revivification. For Mālik, however, the nearest neighbours are the most qualified to undertake the work of revivification. Giving value to the land allows the one who has carried out the task of revivification to become a man of property. A piece of dead land that has been revivified becomes the property (*milk*) of the revivifier. According to the Ḥanafīs, revivification of the land is only allowed with the caliph's authorisation, but, according to al-Shāfiʿī, the one who revivifies dead pieces of land becomes the owner with or without the caliph's permission.

On the nature of what constitutes giving value to land so as to create a property right, the different juridical schools are not in agreement: according to the Mālikīs, it is not enough to enclose the land, to sink a well in it or to pasture a flock on it. One must, for example, find a spring and then exploit the spring by means of water channels, or else clear the land in such a way as to make it usable, or even build; in short, giving value to it must consist of useful and productive work. The Mālikīs, however, appear less demanding than the other juridical schools on the subject of the conditions required to acquire the soil by revivification.

The land surrounding the revivified land (*ḥarīm*) also becomes revivified land, but on this the four juridical schools are not in agreement on the extent of these neighbouring lands which satisfy the juridical condition of revivified land. As for that which has channels dug in it to revivify the dead lands, it becomes the property of those who have them dug, and no-one else has the right to draw water there or to make a side channel leading off from them. It should be noted that the channel or water-pipe, is regarded simply as a hidden water-course.

Dead lands can be made into reserves and charges levied on them. To reserve dead lands is to protect them from revivification and private ownership, so that they may remain accessible to all and so that cattle can be put out to pasture on them. They can also be granted as a concession. A piece of dead land that has been reserved can lose its character as a "reserve", under certain conditions, if someone comes to revivify it. In the same way, if dead land granted as a concession is revivified by an individual who takes possession of it to the detriment of the one who has been granted the concession, the right of the revivifier does not prevail over that of the concessionary; in any case, where dead lands are granted as concessions, the beneficiaries of the concessions do not really become the owners before having revivified them. According to *fiḳh*, this is explained by the Prophet's saying "To the one who quickens a dead piece of land, that land belongs." In practice, one can understand all the importance that could be attached to making an ownerless and abandoned land usable and productive, a fiscal importance especially, since quickening involved the payment to the public treasury of the tax for the land, tithe or *kharādj*, in accordance with regional conditions.

Bibliography: Khalīl, 183 = Fr. tr. Perron, 11, tr. Seignette, 384; Māwardī, *Les statuts gouvernementaux*, Fr. tr. and notes E. Fagnan, ch. xv, Ger. tr. of this ch. by Kremer, in *SBAk. Wien*, iv (1850), 267-81; Abū Yūsuf, *Kitāb al-Kharādj*, 36, 37, 54; V. Chauvin, *Le régime légal des eaux chez les Arabes*, Liège 1899; G. H. Bousquet, *Le droit musulman*, Paris 1963, 139.

(A.-M. DELCAMBRE)

MAWĀZĪN [see MAKĀYĪL].

MAWDŪD B. ᶜIMĀD AL-DĪN ZANKĪ, KUṬB AL-DĪN, Atabeg [see ATABAK] of al-Mawṣil.

ᶜImād al-Dīn Zankī, on his death on 6 Rabīᶜ II 541/15 September 1146, left four heirs: of these Mawdūd b. ᶜImād al-Dīn Zankī, Ḳuṭb al-Dīn al-Aᶜradj, the youngest of his sons, was only sixteen years old. The eldest, Sayf al-Dīn Ghāzī represented his father at al-Mawsīl of which Zankī [*q.v.*] held only the usufruct; the second son, Nūr al-Dīn Maḥmūd [*q.v.*], twenty-nine years old, accompanied his father in his campaigns; the third, Nuṣrat al-Dīn Amīr-Amīrān was named as heir presumptive when the former was ill, in Ramaḍān 552/October 1157, and later sent to Ḥarrān as governor. Mawdūd also had a sister who married the *amīr* Nāṣir al-Dīn al-Ṣūrī. The task of appointing Zankī's successor was in the hands of two trusted counsellors: the vizier Djamāl al-Dīn Muḥammad b. ᶜAlī al-Djawād al-Isfahānī, and the chamberlain (*ḥādjib*) Ṣalāḥ al-Dīn Muḥammad al-Yāghīsiyānī, titulary *amīr* of Ḥamāt.

At the time of his illness, Sayf al-Dīn Ghāzī I transferred power to his youngest brother Ḳuṭb al-Dīn Mawdūd at the request of his loyal counsellors Djamāl al-Dīn and Zayn al-Dīn Küčük, who had previously served Zankī. The young prince was placed under the supervision of the vizier and the Begteginid [*q.v.*] *amīr*. Some weeks later, in Djumādā II 544/October 1149, Sayf al-Dīn died at about forty years old, leaving a son of tender years. Mawdūd, on his succession, maintained in office the two loyal retainers of his father and of his eldest brother. The council was completed with the appointment of the *amīr* ᶜIzz al-Dīn Abū Bakr al-Dubaysī. Also associated with this triumvirate was another loyal supporter of Zankī, a jurist, the *ḳāḍī* Kamāl al-Dīn Abu 'l-Faḍl Muḥammad al-Shahrazūrī. On his assumption of power, Ḳuṭb al-Dīn Mawdūd, succeeding to the eldest of the family, took up residence in the governor's palace and ordered the imprisonment of his elder brother Nuṣrat al-Dīn Amīr-Amīrān who had sought to establish a faction of *amīrs*. Nūr al-Dīn, for his part, had favoured the installation of Mawdūd at al-Mawṣil. Recognised by the army and the population as sovereign of the entire Djazīra, his position was confirmed by the investiture of the Saldjūḳ sultan Masᶜūd b. Muḥammad [*q.v.*] and that of the caliph al-Muḳtafī [*q.v.*]. Shortly after his accession to power, Ḳuṭb al-Dīn Mawdūd married the princess Zumurrud Khātūn, daughter of Tīmurtāsh, the Artuḳid prince of Mardīn [*q.v.*] who had previously offered her to Sayf al-Dīn as a means of sealing an alliance with the Zankids.

A crisis soon erupted in 544/1149 between Ḳuṭb al-Dīn and his elder brother Nūr al-Dīn regarding the town of Sindjār [*q.v.*], where a third of the treasure of Zankī was stored in the citadel. The *amīr* ᶜAbd al-Malik, governor of Sindjār, receiving no reply from Aleppo to the overtures that he had made to Nūr al-Dīn, made his way to al-Mawsīl to pledge allegiance to Mawdūd. Meanwhile, his son Shams al-Dīn had offered Sindjār to Nūr al-Dīn on condition that he himself should retain the treasure. On Monday 10 Radjab 544/13 November 1149, Nūr al-Dīn occupied Sindjār and succeeded in winning over to his side the *amīr* Fakhr al-Dīn Ḳara Arslān b. Dāwūd of Ḥiṣn Kayfā, a rival of Tīmurtāsh of Mārdīn, the father-in-law of Ḳuṭb al-Dīn. Learning of the forthcoming alliance of the Aleppo and the Artuḳid troops, Mawdūd returned to Sindjār. Accused of improperly appropriating the treasure. Nūr al-Dīn was able to argue his right of superior age in his defence; he expressed his wish to discuss with Mawdūd the problems raised by the succession to Sayf al-Dīn, and drew his attention to the considerable number of *amīrs* who had rallied to his cause. Mawdūd's counsellors feared desertions to the side of Nūr al-Dīn and considered that if the ruler of Aleppo were to emerge the victor in the confrontation, the sultan would come to attack al-Mawṣil which, enfeebled, would be incapable of resisting him. On the other hand, if Nūr al-Dīn were to be defeated, the most reliable bastion against the Crusaders would collapse and the Franks would then be able to extend still further. With the threat from common adversaries, the Saldjuḳ sultan to the East and the Crusaders to the West, the only solution was to make peace between the members of the Zankid family. The negotiations, skilfully conducted by Djamāl al-Dīn al-Djawād, led to an agreement between the two brothers. Nūr al-Dīn returned Sindjār in exchange for Ḥimṣ which had been given to his brother Sayf al-Dīn to reward him for his support against the second Crusade. Nūr al-Dīn also received al-Raḥba and al-Raḳḳa on the Euphrates as well as Edessa or al-Ruhā [*q.v.*]. The portion of the treasure of Zankī stored at Sindjar was to be used to finance the djihād of Nūr al-Dīn.

In 553/1158, when ill, Nūr al-Dīn named his brother Ḳuṭb al-Dīn Mawdūd as eventual successor and made his own *amīrs* promise to obey him. Mawdūd, crossing the Euphrates between Ṣiffīn [*q.v.*] and al-Raḳḳa, made his way towards Damascus to visit his brother. Meanwhile, having recovered, Nūr al-Dīn had returned to northern Syria; the two Zankid princes set out to take Ḥarrān, which they entrusted to the *isfahsālār* Zayn al-Dīn ʿAlī Küčük.

In the following year, Mawdūd arrived with powerful reinforcements to assist Nūr al-Dīn, who was threatened at Aleppo by the advance of a Frankish-Byzantine coalition. In Dhu 'l-Ḥidjdja 554/December 1159-January 1160, news came of the death of the Saldjūḳ sultan Muḥammad b. Maḥmūd [*q.v.*] at Hamadhān. This event was of importance to Mawdūd, who was holding prisoner at al-Mawṣil Sulaymān Shāh, one of the candidates for the succession. After long negotiations, Mawdūd agreed to release his prisoner on condition that he be appointed Atabeg of the new sultan and that the latter take Djamāl al-Dīn al-Djawād as vizier and ʿAlī Küčük as commander of the sultan's armies. Escorted by troops from al-Mawṣil, Sulaymān Shāh set out for Hamadhān, but, the victim of a conspiracy, he was poisoned and died on the way. Mawdūd's troops turned back, and there were no further links between al-Mawṣil and Khurāsān. In Ramaḍān 559/August 1164, Mawdūd received an appeal yet again from Nūr al-Dīn, who wanted the assistance of his allies in causing a diversion in northern Syria with the aim of averting an invasion of Egypt by the Franks. Mawdūd responded by sending considerable contingents which laid siege to Ḥarīm [*q.v.*], but on hearing of the presence in the region of the Byzantine troops of the Emperor Manuel, the army of al-Mawṣil withdrew, linked up with the contingents of Nūr al-Dīn and contributed to the victory of ʿImm which enabled the Zankid princes to take Ḥarīm.

During the second campaign of the *amīr* Shīrkūh in Egypt, Mawdūd sent, at the request of Nūr al-Dīn, reinforcements to take part in operations against the Count of Tripoli.

At the end of summer 562/1167 he returned to al-Mawṣil with troops exhausted by the campaign and by the fast of Ramaḍān. In token of gratitude to his brother, Nūr al-Dīn ceded al-Raḳḳa to him. Having learned that after the death on 27 Ramaḍān/17 July of Ḳara Arslān, the prince of Ḥiṣn Kayfā and of Diyār Bakr, his succession reverted to his son and designated heir, Nūr al-Dīn Muḥammad (562-81/1167-85), Mawdūd wanted to attack the territories of the young Artuḳid prince; but Nūr al-Dīn Maḥmūd ordered his brother to abstain from any hostile action. In 563/1168, the Begteginid *amīr* Zayn al-Dīn ʿAlī Küčük, who had served Zankī and then Mawdūd, asked leave to go into retirement; he then returned to his master all the places that he had received in *iḳṭāʿ* in order to cover the expenses incurred by his professional duties. The *amīr* Ṭāhir, the lieutenant of Zayn al-Dīn at Takrīt [*q.v.*], refused to concede his charge to the representatives of Mawdūd, but promised his continuing loyalty to him. In order to avoid any intervention on the part of the caliph, the Zankid princes accepted the *status quo* at Takrīt. As a replacement for the retired *amīr*, Mawdūd appointed as vizier at al-Mawṣil one of his own *mamlūks*, the eunuch Fakhr al-Dīn ʿAbd al-Masīḥ. When Mawdūd's illness worsened, he decided to name as his successor his eldest son ʿImād al-Dīn Zankī, who had married one of his cousins, the daughter of Nūr al-Dīn Maḥmūd. Fakhr al-Dīn, who conducted affairs of state at al-Mawṣil, did not approve of this decision, since he wanted to withdraw from the tutelage of the ruler of Aleppo, who did not like him. He decided to engineer the downfall of ʿImād al-Dīn, and allied himself with one of the wives of Mawdūd, the daughter of the Artuḳid Ḥusām al-Dīn Tīmurtāsh b. Īlghāzī and mother of Sayf al-Dīn Ghāzī. The vizier succeeded in making his master revoke his decision. Mawdūd, being close to death, summoned his *amīrs* together and made them pledge allegiance to his youngest son. It was thus that the young Sayf al-Dīn Ghāzī acceded to the throne as legitimate heir when his father died following his illness on 22 Dhu 'l-Ḥidjdja 565/6 September 1170. Fakhr al-Dīn ʿAbd al-Masīḥ continued to administer all the business of al-Mawṣil, while Nūr al-Dīn lost the control which he had exercised over the city during the lifetime of his youngest brother.

One of the daughters of Mawdūd, ʿAzīzat al-Dīn Akhshāwrā Khātūn, wife of al-Malik al-Muʿaẓẓam, constructed in 610/1213, on the banks of the river Ṭawra, at Ṣāliḥiyya, the Ḥanafī funerary *madrasa* of al-Māridāniyya. One of his grand-daughters, Tarkan Khātūn, daughter of ʿIzz al-Dīn Masʿūd b. Ḳuṭb al-Dīn Mawdūd, wife of al-Malik al-Ashraf Mūsā, who died in 640/1242, constructed at Ḳāsiyūn [*q.v.*] in the same suburb of Damascus the Shāfiʿī funerary *madrasa* of al-Atābakiyya.

In the writings of western chroniclers of the Crusades the name of Mawdūd is transcribed in such renderings as Malducus, Maldutus or Manduit.

Bibliography: 1. Arabic texts. Ibn al-Ḳalānisī, tr. H. A. R. Gibb, *Damascus chronicle of the Crusades*, 295, 296, 307, 350-3; Usāma b. Munḳidh, *Kitāb al-Iʿtibār*, ed. H. Derenbourg, i, 298, 301-3, 350-3; Ibn al-Djawzī, *K. al-Muntaẓam*, ed. Hyderabad 1359/1940, x, 119, 121, 138; ʿImād al-Dīn al-Iṣfahānī, *al-Fatḥ al-ḳussī*, Fr. tr. H. Massé, Paris 1972, 205; Ibn al-Athīr, *Atabegs*, *RHOrC*, ii/2, Paris 1876, 171, 175-6, 221, 224, 264-5; Ibn al-Athīr, *Kāmil*, ed. Cairo 1348/1929, ix, 23, 24, 49, 69, 86, 97, 109; Ibn al-ʿAdīm, *Zubdat al-Ḥalab*, ed. S. Dahhān, Damascus 1954, ii, 296-8, 310-11, 318, 331; Abū Shāma, *K. al-Rawḍatayn*, ed. Hilmy M. Ahmad and Mustafa Ziyada, Cairo 1962, i/2, 339-40, 348, 368, 374, 375, 384, 471-5; Ibn Khallikān, tr. de Slane, ii, 441, 535, iii, 295, 458; Ibn Wāṣil, *Mufarridj al-kurūb*, ed. Cairo 1953, i, 143-4, 152, 159, 188-9; Ibn Kathīr, *Bidāya*, ed. Cairo 1929, xii, 225-6, 233, 236, 261; *RHOrC*, see Index.

2. Non-Arabic text. Michael the Syrian, *Syriac chronicle*, reimpr. Paris 1962, iii, 339-42.

3. Studies. S. Lane-Poole, *The Mohammadan dynasties*, London 1893, 163; H. Sauvaire, *Description de Damas*, 1894-6, iii, 386-7, iv, 282-3; Zambaur, *Manuel*, 226-7; J. Sauvaget, *Les Monuments historiques de Damas*, Beirut 1932, 100, nos. 96, 98; R. Grousset, *Croisades*, Paris 1935, ii, 464-5, 557; Cl. Cahen, *Syrie du Nord*, Paris 1940, 398-9, 409-10; S. Runciman, *History of the Crusades*, Cambridge 1952, ii, 244, 336, 385, 390, 412; K. M. Setton (ed.), *History of the Crusades*, Philadelphia 1955, ch. XVI (H. A. R. Gibb), 516, 522-6; N. Elisséeff, *Nūr al-Dīn*, Damascus 1967, 438-42 and index.

(N. Elisséeff)

MAWDŪD B. MASʿŪD, Abu 'l-Fatḥ, Shihāb al-Dīn wa 'l-Dawla, Ḳuṭb al-Millā, sultan of the Ghaznawid [*q.v.*] dynasty, reigned 432-40/1041-winter of 1048-9.

He was probably born in 401/1010-11 or 402/1011-12 as the eldest son of Masʿūd b. Maḥmūd [*q.v.*], and during his father's reign was closely associated with the sultan on various military expeditions. When Masʿūd was deposed and then killed in Djumādā I 432/January 1041, Mawdūd made himself the avenger against the rebellious commanders and their puppet, his uncle Muḥammad b. Maḥmūd. He marched from Balkh, secured the capital Ghazna, and met Muḥammad's army coming from India near Djalālābād, at a place subsequently named Fatḥābād, for Mawdūd completely defeated the rebels in Radjab 432/March 1041. Muḥammad and all but one of his sons were executed, and a threat from Mawdūd's younger brother Madjdūd, governor of Multān, scotched by the latter's mysterious death, so that Mawdūd became unchallenged ruler now in Ghazna.

He faced formidable problems in combatting the Saldjūḳs in eastern Khurāsān and Sīstān. He attempted an alliance with the Saldjūḳ's Ḳarakhānid enemies in Transoxania [see ILEK-KHĀNS], and in 435/1043-4 invaded Ṭukharistān, but was repulsed by Čaghrī Beg's son Alp Arslan. Northern Afghānistān now passed definitively to the Saldjūḳs, and a further endeavour by Mawdūd to organise a grand coalition of anti-Saldjūḳ princes in Transoxania and Persia was cut short by his own death. Early in his reign, Mawdūd sent forces into Sīstān in order to retain Ghaznawid overlordship over the Ṣaffārids there and to exclude Saldjūḳ influence, but the local *amīr* Abu 'l-Faḍl Naṣr b. Aḥmad had to pursue a policy of balance between his two powerful neighbours. The concerns of India had latterly much occupied Masʿūd, but his violent end provided an opportunity for the reassertion of independence by various Indian tributary rulers. A coalition of *rādjā*s recaptured Hānsī, Thānesar, etc., but was however driven back from Lahore in 435/1043-4.

Mawdūd died of an internal complaint just at the beginning of his new attempt at a revanche against the Saldjūḳs, probably in Djumādā II 440/December 1048, although the sources diverge on this. He was clearly a skilful commander and able ruler who managed to pull the empire together after the cataclysms which had come upon it and who withstood the eastwards pressure of the Saldjūḳs; but even had he been granted a long reign, it is doubtful whether he would have been able to recover the lost western provinces.

Bibliography: The main primary sources are Gardīzī, Djūzdjānī, Ibn al-Athīr, Ibn Bābā and Fakhr-i Mudabbir; these are used in C. E. Bosworth, *The later Ghaznavids, splendour and decay. The dynasty in Afghanistan and Northern India 1040-1186*, Edinburgh 1977, 20-37. (C. E. Bosworth)

MAWDŪDĪ, SAYYID ABU 'L-AʿLĀ (commonly anglicised to Maudoodi), journalist, fundamentalist theologian, major influence in the politics of Pakistan and one of the leading interpreters of Islam in the twentieth century. He was born on 3 Radjab 1321/25 September 1903 at Aurangabad in India's Hyderabad State. His family claimed direct descent from Khwādja Ḳuṭb al-Dīn Mawdūd Čishtī (d. 577/1181-2); his ancestors migrated to the subcontinent in the later 9th/15th century and produced many spiritual leaders. His father, a lawyer, came from Dihlī and was associated with Sayyid Aḥmad Khān [*q.v.*], but preferred to live in Hyderabad, which was the last significant centre of the Mughal tradition. When young, Mawdūdī was carefully insulated from western culture and the English language; educated at home, and briefly in one of Hyderabad's *madrasas*, he experienced neither the typical schooling of the *ʿālim* nor that of the British Indian government. After Mawdūdī's father died when he was sixteen, he supported himself for a decade as a journalist, most notably as editor of *al-Djamʿiyyat* from 1924 to 1927, the organ of the *Djamʿiyyat-i ʿUlamā'-i Hind.* During this decade he was involved in the *Khilāfat* movement [see KHILĀFA], came to know many *ʿulamā'* and became thoroughly versed in Arabic. He also learned English, went clean-shaven and wore western dress.

In the mid-1920s, Mawdūdī's activities gained a significant new focus. Stung by Hindu accusations that Islam was spread by the sword, after a Muslim assassinated the Arya Samaj leader, Swami Shraddhanand, he embarked on an exhaustive study of the doctrine of *djihād* [*q.v.*]. This work, which was first serialised in *al-Djamʿiyyat* and then published under the title *al-Djihād fi 'l-Islām*, heralded most elements of his later thought. The effort of composition greatly intensified his understanding of his faith, and in 1928 he retired to Hyderabad to do further research and writing. In 1932 he undertook the editorship of the monthly journal *Tardjumān al-Ḳur'ān*, which was to be the main vehicle of his ideas for the rest of his life. He knew now what he had to do: "The plan of action I had in mind was that I should first break the hold which Western culture and ideas had come to acquire over the Muslim intelligentsia, and to instil in them the fact that Islam has a code of life of its own, its own culture, its own political and economic systems and a philosophy and an educational system which are all superior to anything that Western civilisation could offer. I wanted to rid them of the wrong notion that they needed to borrow from others in the matter of culture and civilisation." (Sayyid Abul Ala Maudoodi, *Twenty-nine years of the Jamaat-e-Islami*, in *The Criterion*, v/6, 45). The intensity of this feeling runs through the pages of his *Risāla-yi Dīniyyāt* of 1932; the fear of the corrupting influence of western civilisation is manifest in his articles on *pardah* first published in 1935.

The last decade of British rule brought new fears: that independence would bring the absorption of the Muslim identity into a secular Hindu-dominated nation-state, and that the Muslim response of aiming to found a separate Muslim nation-state of Pakistan was not the right one. Mawdūdī now intervened in politics. In a series of articles, later published under the title *Musalmān awr mawdjūda siyāsī kashmakash*, he reminded Muslims that they were a separate nation in the Indian environment, while at the same time emphasising that they were not one in any European sense, as the All-India Muslim League was suggesting. Muslims were in danger of forgetting that they had a message for all humanity. The way to carry this message forward was to establish not a nation state of Muslims but an Islamic state in which every constituent part would reveal Islam in ideal and practice. In August 1941 Mawdūdī founded the *Djamāʿat-i Islāmī*, a carefully-selected righteous élite of which he was the leader, to put these ideas into effect.

The emergence of Pakistan in 1947 gave Mawdūdī a forum in which he could act. From 1948 to 1956 his writings and deeds, supported by the *Djamāʿat-i Islāmī*, played the key role in directing Pakistan away from developing the form of the secular state which its founders had in mind towards the goal of an Islamic state. His pressure was primarily responsible for the Islamic content of the "Objectives Resolution" of the Constituent Assembly (March 1949) which laid down the main principles on which Pakistan's constitution was to be based. His leadership brought the representatives of all groups of *ʿulamāʾ* to agree in January 1951 on twenty-two principles of an Islamic state, which were to remain for all concerned in constitution-making the benchmark of the "conservative" position. His authority brought him to the fore in the agitation of 1952-3 against the Aḥmadiyya community of Pakistan, which helped to keep these twenty-two principles alive in the constitution-making process. It was in large part his achievement that the first constitution, which was promulgated in 1956, looked towards reconstructing "Muslim society on a truly Islamic basis and revising all existing laws in the light of the Qurʾan and Sunna". In 1953 Mawdūdī was for a period condemned to death; he was imprisoned during the years 1948-50 and 1953-5.

From 1956 the discussion of the role of Islam in the constitution died down and Mawdūdī, until restricted by ill-health in 1969, travelled widely outside Pakistan. He was a particularly frequent visitor to Saudi Arabia, where he took part in both the establishment and the running of Medina's Islamic university and the World Muslim League. Whenever an Islamic issue arose in Pakistan, like the Muslim Family Laws Ordinance of 1961 or the Aḥmadiyya question in 1974, he was prominent. Throughout he opposed the régimes governing Pakistan and, although he resigned from the headship of the *D̲j̲amāʿat-i Islāmī* in 1972, he was behind its involvement in the movement to overthrow Z. A. Bhutto in 1977. General Ḍiyāʾ (Ziyā) al-Ḥaḳḳ's régime, with its promise of Islamisation, was the first that he felt able to support. When Mawdūdī died on 22 September 1979, he did so knowing that Pakistan was at last ruled by a government that was trying to realise a version of his Islamic order.

Mawdūdī's academic output was voluminous: tradition, law, philosophy, history, politics, economics, sociology and theology being amongst the subjects covered. Many of his works have been translated, some into over a dozen languages. His masterwork is his Ḳurʾān commentary, *Tafhīm al-Ḳurʾān*, which took him thirty years to finish. His Islamic vision, nevertheless, is scattered through many different publications, many of which were written to meet problems of the moment. Good points of access are a series of radio talks he gave in 1948, *Islām kā niẓām-i ḥayāt*, and the collection of his writings on the Islamic state *The Islamic law and constitution.*

Central to Mawdūdī's vision is the belief that God alone is sovereign; man has gone astray because he has accepted sovereigns other than God, for instance, kings, nation states or custom. All the guidance which man needs can be found in the *S̲h̲arīʿa*, which offers a complete scheme of life where nothing is superfluous and nothing lacking. Political power is essential to put this divinely-ordained pattern into effect; the Islamic state has a missionary purpose. Moreover, because God's guidance extends to all human activity, this state must be universal and all-embracing, and because the state's purpose is to establish Islamic ideology it must be run by those who believe in it and comprehend its spirit—those who do not may just live withing the confines of the state as non-Muslim citizens (*d̲h̲immīs*). Naturally, this state recognises that God not man is the source of all law. The state is merely God's vicegerent (*k̲h̲alīfa*) on earth. It is a vicegerency, however, which is shared by all Muslim citizens of the state with whom, in consequence, the ruler must consult in the process of government. So Mawdūdī describes his policy as a "theo-democracy" in which the whole community of Muslims interpret the law of God within the framework supplied by the *S̲h̲arīʿa*. The ruler (*amīr*) is to be elected by whatever means are appropriate, providing that they ensure that the man who enjoys the greatest mesure of national confidence is chosen. His legislature (*mad̲j̲lis-i s̲h̲ūrā*) is also to be elected by whatever means are appropriate, provided that they ensure the choice of men with the confidence of the people. Legislation itself takes place in four ways: by interpretation, by analogy, by inference, and, in that area of human affairs about which the *S̲h̲arīʿa* is silent, by independent judgement.

The major feature of Mawdūdī's thought is to have transformed Islam into an ideology, an integrated and all-embracing system. He aimed to set out the ideal order of the time of the Rightly-Guided Caliphs. The outcome is the most comprehensive statement of the nature of the Islamic state in modern times, and one which, while conjuring an ideal from the past, has been shaped by contemporary concerns and modes of thought. His exposition, as might be expected from a man who was primarily a theologian, is strong on general principles but weak on detail.

Mawdūdī is amongst the most influential of those Muslims who have felt, as the 20th century has progressed, that the answer to western domination need not be formulated in terms of nationalism and secularism but in terms of Islam. Himself inspired by Ibn K̲h̲aldūn, S̲h̲āh Walī Allāh, Muḥammad Iḳbāl and Ḥasan al-Bannāʾ [*q.vv.*], he has influenced in his turn men ranging from the leaders of Islamic movements in Egypt, Syria and Iran to many ordinary Muslims throughout the Islamic world.

Bibliography: A list of Mawdūdī's 138 works, with the details of English translations, and an indication of translations into other languages, plus a list of writings about Mawdūdī, can be found in Khurshid Ahmad and Zafar Ishaq Ansari (eds.), *Islamic perspectives: studies in honour of Mawlana Sayyid Abul Aʿla Mawdudi*, Leicester 1979, 3-14. Among Mawdūdī's more important publications the following should be noted: *Dīn-i ḥaḳḳ*, Lahore 1952, Eng. tr. *The religion of truth*, Lahore 1967; *Insān kā maʿās̲h̲ī masʾala awr us kā islāmī ḥall*, Lahore 1941, Eng. tr. *Economic problem of man and its Islamic solution*, Lahore 1947; *Islām kā ak̲h̲lāḳī nuḳṭa-yi naẓar*, Lahore 1955, Eng. tr. *Ethical viewpoint of Islam*, Lahore 1966; *Islām kā naẓariyya-yi siyāsī*, Lahore 1939, Eng. tr. *Political theory of Islam*, Delhi 1964; *Islām kā niẓām-i ḥayāt*, Lahore 1948, Eng. tr. *Islamic way of life*, Lahore 1950; *The Islamic law and constitution*, ed. and tr. Khurshid Ahmad, Lahore 1955; *al-D̲j̲ihād fi 'l-Islām*, Aʿẓamgaṛh 1930; *K̲h̲uṭbāt*, Lahore 1957, Eng. tr. *Fundamentals of Islam*, Lahore 1975; *Musalmān awr mawd̲j̲ūda siyāsī kas̲h̲makas̲h̲*, 3 vols., Lahore 1937-9; *Pardah*, Lahore 1939, Eng. tr. *Purdah and the status of women in Islam*, Lahore 1972; *Ḳādiyānī masʾala*, Karachi 1953, Eng. tr. *The Qadiani problem*, Karachi 1953; *Risāla-yi dīniyyāt*, Hyderabad, Deccan 1932, Eng. tr. *Towards understanding Islam*, Lahore 1940; *Tafhīm al-Ḳurʾān*, 6 vols., Lahore 1949-72, Eng. tr. *The meaning of the Qurʾān* (incomplete), Lahore 1967-

The following writings about Mawdūdī should be noted: Freeland K. Abbot, *Maulana Maududi and Quranic interpretation*, in *MW*, xlviii/1 (1958), 6-19, and *Islam and Pakistan*, Ithaca 1968, 171-228; Charles J. Adams, *The ideology of Mawlana Mawdudi*, in D. E. Smith (ed.), *South Asian politics and religion*, Princeton 1966, 371-97, and *Mawdudi and the Islamic state*, in J. L. Esposito (ed.), *Voices of resurgent Islam*, New York 1983, 99-133; Aziz Ahmad, *Islamic modernism in India and Pakistan, 1857-1964*, London

1967, 208-23; Sayed Riaz Ahmad, *Maulana Maududi and the Islamic state*, Lahore 1976; Kalim Bahadur, *The Jamaᶜat-i-Islami of Pakistan; political thought and political action*, New Delhi 1977; L. Binder, *Religion and politics in Pakistan*, Berkeley 1961; Maryam Jameelah, *Who is Maudoodi?*, Lahore 1973; Khalid bin Sayeed, *The Jamaat-i-Islami movement in Pakistan*, in *Pacific Affairs*, xxx/1 (March 1957), 59-68; Cheila McDonough, *Muslim ethics and modernity: a comparative study of the ethical thought of Sayyid Ahmad Khan and Mawlana Mawdudi*, Waterloo, Ont. 1984; H. Mintjes, *Mawlana Mawdudi's last years and the resurgence of fundamentalist Islam*, in *al-Mushir*, xxii/2 (1980), 46-73; E. I. J. Rosenthal, *Islam in the modern national state*, Cambridge 1965, 137-53, 221-72.

(F. C. R. Robinson)

MAWḲIF (a.), nomen loci from *w-ḳ-f* "to stand" hence "place of standing". Of the technical meanings of the term, three may be mentioned here:

(a) The place where the *wuḳūf* [*q.v.*] is held during the pilgrimage, viz. ᶜArafāt [*q.v.*] and Muzdalifa [*q.v.*] or D̲jamᶜ. In well-known traditions, Muḥammad declares that all ᶜArafāt and all Muzdalifa is *mawḳif* (Muslim, *Ḥad̲j̲d̲j̲*, trad. 149; Abū Dāwūd, *Manāsik*, bāb 56, 64, etc.; cf. Wensinck, *Handbook of early Muhammadan tradition*, s.v. ᶜArafa). Snouck Hurgronje (*Het mekkaansche feest*, 150 = *Verspreide Geschriften*, i, 99) has conjectured that these traditions were intended to deprive the hills of ᶜArafāt and Muzdalifa of their sacred character, which they doubtless possessed in pre-Islamic times.

(b) The place where, on the day of resurrection, several scenes of the last judgment will take place; cf. al-G̲h̲azālī, *al-Durra al-fāk̲h̲ira*, ed. Gautier, 577, 683,12, 813; cf. *Kitāb Aḥwāl al-ḳiyāma*, ed. M. Wolff, 65ff.

(c) In pre-Islamic times, *mawḳif* was one of the terms (together with *mas̲h̲ᶜar*, *nuṣub*, *mansak*, etc.) used to designate the religious shrines, usually in the form of stones, to be found along tracks and at camping sites, of the nomadic Arabs; cf. Wellhausen, *Reste*², 101ff., and T. Fahd, *Le panthéon de l'Arabie centrale à la veille de l'hégire*, Paris 1968, 238ff.

Bibliography: Given in the article; see also ḥad̲j̲d̲j̲ and ḳiyāma. (A. J. Wensinck)

MAWLĀ (a.), pl. *mawālī*, a term of theological, historical and legal usage which had varying meanings in different periods and in different social contexts. Linguistically, it is the noun of place of the verb *waliya*, with the basic meaning of "to be close to, to be connected with someone or something" (see *LA*, xx, 287ff.; *TA*, x, 398-401), whence acquiring the sense "to be close to power, authority" > "to hold power, govern, be in charge of some office" (see Lane, s.v.) and yielding such administrative terms as *wālī* "governor", and *wilāya* [*q.v.*] "the function of governor" or, in a legal context, "sphere of jurisdiction, competence".

I. In the Ḳurʾān and Tradition

Here we find *mawlā* used in two meanings.

(a) Tutor, trustee, helper. In this sense, the word is used in the Ḳurʾān, XLVII, 12: "God is the *mawlā* of the faithful, the unbelievers have no *mawlā* (cf. III, 143; VI, 62; VII, 41; IX, 51; XXII, 78; LXVI, 2). In the same sense, *mawlā* is used in the S̲h̲īᶜī tradition, in which Muhammad calls ᶜAlī the *mawlā* of those whose *mawlā* he is himself. According to the author of the *Lisān*, *mawlā* has the sense of *walī* in this tradition, which is connected with G̲h̲adīr K̲h̲umm (*q.v.*; cf. C. van Arendonk, *De opkomst van het Zaidietische imamaat*, 18, 19). It may be observed that it occurs also in the *Musnad* of Aḥmad b. Ḥanbal (i, 84, 118, 119, 152, 330-1; iv, 281, etc.).

(b) Lord. In the Ḳurʾānit it is in this sense (which is synonymous with that of *sayyid*) applied to Allāh (II,286; cf. VI,62; X,31), who is often called *Mawlānā* "our Lord" in Arabic literature. Precisely for this reason, in Tradition the slave is prohibited from calling his lord *mawlā* (al-Buk̲h̲ārī, *D̲j̲ihād*, *bāb* 165; Muslīm, *Alfāẓ*, trad. 15, 16).

It is not in contradiction to this prohibition that Tradition frequently uses *mawlā* in the sense of "lord of a slave", e.g. in the well-known *ḥadīt̲h̲* "Three categories of people will receive a two-fold reward ... and the slave who fulfils his duty in regard to Allāh as well as to his lords" (al-Buk̲h̲ārī, *ᶜIlm*, *bāb* 31; Muslim, *Aymān*, trad. 45).

Composition of *mawlā* and suffixes are frequently used as titles in several parts of the Muslim world, e.g. *mawlāy(a) (mulay)*, "my lord (especially in North Africa and in connection with saints); *mawlawī* (*mullā* [*q.v.*]), "lordship" (especially in India and in connection with scholars or saints).

The term *mawlā* is also applied to the former lord (patron) in his relation to his freedman, e.g. in the tradition "Who clings to a [new] patron without the permission of his [legal] *mawlā*, on him rests the curse of Allāh" (al-Buk̲h̲ārī, *D̲j̲izya*, *bāb 17;* Muslim, *ᶜItḳ*, trad. 18, 19).

Bibliography: Given in the article. See also Wensinck, *A handbook of early Muhammadan tradition*, Leiden 1927, 148. (A. J. Wensinck*)

II. In Historical and Legal Usage

Here the meaning of *mawlā*, a person linked by *walāʾ* ("proximity") to another person, similarly known as *mawlā*, varies according to the context in which it is found. In pre-Islamic poetry, it usually designates a party to an egalitarian relationship of mutual help, that is, a kinsman (*ibn ᶜamm*), confederate (*ḥalīf*), ally or friend, a meaning also attested in the Ḳurʾān (IV, 37; XIX, 5; XLIV, 41) and some later literature (P. Crone, *Slaves on horses*, Cambridge 1980, appendix VI). In later literature, however, it more commonly designates a party to an unequal relationship of assistance, that is a master, manumitter, benefactor or patron on the one hand, and a freedman, protégé or client on the other. This sense too is attested in the Ḳurʾān, where the typical *mawlā* is God (VIII, 41; XXII,78, and *passim*; cf. XXXIII,5, where it means protégé). Applied to the inferior party in an Islamic context, *mawlā* almost always means a client of the type recognised in early Islamic law, though its use in the opposite sense was more flexible. The Islamic world has of course known many other types of client, but not by this name.

The client recognised in early law was a non-Arab freedman, convert or other newcomer in Muslim society. Since non-Arabs could only enter this society as clients, *mawlā* came to be synonymous with "non-Arab Muslim", and the secondary literature usually employs the word in this sense (though the lexicographers fail to list it, cf. *LA* and *TA*, s.v. *w-l-y*). It is also with non-Arab Muslims that this article will be concerned.

1. Pre-Islamic Arabia.

The Islamic institution of *walāʾ* is generally assumed to be of Arabian origin (cf. Goldziher, *Muh. Stud.*, i, ch. 3; J. Juda, *Die sozialen und wirtschaftlichen Aspekte der Mawālī in frühislamischer Zeit*, Tübingen 1983), but this is scarcely correct. Leaving aside foreign merchants and colonists under imperial protection, the non-Arab population of pre-Islamic Arabia consisted of Jews, slaves and freedmen of African and Middle Eastern extraction, half-bred descendants of colonists, and presumably also ethnic and occupational pariah groups of the type attested in modern times (Ḳawāwila, Bayādīr, Ṣulubbīs, etc.). There is no reason to doubt that all were known as *mawālī* in the sense of "kinsmen", in so far as they were free and came under Arab protection (cf. the modern use of the word *a<u>kh</u>* "brother"), but the question is, what this implied. Are we to take it that all non-Arabs were individually assigned to Arab patrons and acquired partial membership of Arab tribes through them, having no social organisation of their own? Or did they form social groups of their own, so that they were collectively placed under the protection of Arab tribes in which they acquired no membership at all, merely becoming their satellites? The first solution is that enshrined in Islamic *walāʾ*, but it is the second which is attested for Arabia.

Thus it is well known that the Jews of Arabia formed tribal groups of their own. In fact, Jewish tribes were sometimes strong enough to escape Arab protection altogether (and thus also the status of *mawālī*). But this was hardly the common pattern. The Jews of Fadak, for example, paid protection money to Kalb (M. J. Kister, *On the wife of the goldsmith from Fadak and her progeny*, in *Muséon*, xcii [1979], 321); the Jews of Wādī 'l-Ḳurā similarly paid what would nowadays be known as *<u>kh</u>uwwa* to Arab overlords (al-Bakrī, *Muʿ<u>dj</u>am mā istaʿ<u>dj</u>am*, ed. F. Wüstenfeld, Göttingen 1876-7, i, 30); and those of Ya<u>th</u>rib were reduced to client status by the Aws and <u>Kh</u>azra<u>dj</u> [*q.vv.*] some time before the rise of Islam (J. Wellhausen, *Skizzen und Vorarbeiten*, iv, Berlin 1889, 7ff.). Naturally, client status weakened the tribal organisation of the Jews; the same is true of modern pariah groups. But the Jewish tribes were not dissolved, nor were the Jews assigned to individual patrons: clientage was a relationship between groups. Similarly, the Arabised descendants of the Persian workmen and prostitutes of Ha<u>dj</u>ar clearly formed a quasi-tribal group of their own under ʿAbdī protection, for all that they adopted the *nisba* of their protectors (al-Ṭabarī, i, 986).

The question is thus, whether freedmen were treated differently? On this point, the evidence is less conclusive. Continuing relations between manumitter and freedman were clearly common, and there is evidence that the pre-Islamic Arabs practised manumission with what the Greeks called *paramonē*, a clause requiring the freedman to stay with the manumitter for a specified number of years or until the latter died (P. Crone, *Roman, provincial and Islamic law*, Princeton 1987). But continuing relations between manumitter and freedman in no way imply that the latter was incorporated in the manumitter's kin; the paramonar freedman only became a member of his household, and then only for a specified time; and one would in general have thought the pre-Islamic Arabs as reluctant to contaminate their agnatic kin with non-Arab freedmen as were their descendants in more recent times. The freedmen (and indeed slaves) of modern Arabia formed lineages of their own, and it was through them, not through their manumitters, that they acquired their rights and duties in respect of marriage, succession and vengeance; and it was to the manumitters' tribe as a political entity that they stood in a relationship of dependence, paying it military assistance and/or *<u>kh</u>uwwa* (J. L. Burckhardt, *Notes on the Bedouins and the Wahábys*, London 1830, i, 181f.; A. Jaussen, *Coutumes des Arabes au pays de Moab*², Paris 1948, 125f.; cf. A. Musil, *The manners and customs of the Rwala Bedouins*, New York 1928, 276).

It should be noted that non-Arabs were not generally affiliated as confederates. *Ḥilf* [*q.v.*] was a mechanism for the partial or total incorporation of foreigners, individually or as groups, and it is frequently regarded as ancestral to Islamic *walāʾ*. But *ḥilf* was used only for *Arab* foreigners, or more precisely for foreigners with full tribal status. The Jews thus qualified on occasion, as did others such as the Abnāʾ [*q.v.*] but only to the extent that they escaped client status (though there are admittedly ambivalent cases); non-Arab freedmen never qualified (cf. Goldziher, *Muh. Stud.*, i, 106). The *ḥalīf* is thus irrelevant to the question. By the same token, so is most of pre-Islamic poetry. The vast majority of *mawālī* mentioned in this poetry (where the word is exceedingly common) are Arabs from whom help of one sort or another could be expected: real, fictitious or metaphorical kinsmen (cf. *ibid.*, 105 n.; many more examples are given in Crone, *Roman, provincial and Islamic law*). Confederates are occasionally singled out as *mawālī 'l-yamīn*, "kinsmen by oath", as opposed to *mawālī 'l-wilāda* or *ḳarāba*, "kinsmen by birth/kinship" (G. W. Freytag, *Hamasae carmina*, Bonn 1828, 187; C. Lyall, ed. and tr., *The Mufaḍḍalīyāt*, Oxford 1918-21, no. 12:3; Ibn Hi<u>sh</u>ām, 467; Nābi<u>gh</u>a al-<u>Dj</u>aʿdī, *Dīwān*, ed. and tr. M. Nallino, Rome 1953, no. 12:41). But the distinction is usually quite neutral, and though confederates could obviously find themselves in a subservient position so that the dividing line between them and client groups was blurred (as it is in Nābi<u>gh</u>a; cf. Juda, *Aspekte*, 14-15) they were followers of a type quite different from that of non-Arab clients. It is only when the poets distinguish between *ṣamīm* (or *ṣarīḥ*) and *mawālī* that the latter would seem regularly to encompass servile and non-Arab elements, and the same is perhaps true when they speak of "tails" and "fins" of tribes (cf. Goldziher, *Muh. Stud.*, i, 105-6); but these passages are perfectly compatible with the proposition that freedmen and other non-Arabs should be seen as members of satellite groups rather than as persons "assimilated to the tribe by affiliation" (Goldziher).

2. The Rā<u>sh</u>idūn caliphs and the Umayyads.

With the conquests, the Arabs found themselves in charge of a huge non-Arab population. Given that it was non-Muslim, this population could be awarded a status similar to that of clients in Arabia, retaining its own organisation under Arab control in return for the payment of taxes [see <u>Dh</u>imma]. But converts posed a novel problem in that, on the one hand they had to be incorporated, not merely accommodated, within Arab society; and on the other hand, they had "forgotten their genealogies", suffered defeat and frequently also enslavement, so that they did not make acceptable *ḥalīf*s; the only non-Arabs to be affiliated as such were the Ḥamrāʾ and Asāwira, Persian soldiers who deserted to the Arabs during the wars of conquest in return for privileged status (al-Balā<u>dh</u>urī, *Futūḥ*, 280, 373). It was in response to this novel problem that Islamic *walāʾ* was evolved, presumably by the authorities and at an early stage, though nothing can be said with certainty about its emergence.

(a) Early Islamic *walāʾ*. What follows is based on a collation of information in classical law (below, section 5), *ḥadī<u>th</u>* and historical sources. All non-Arabs who aspired to membership of Arab society had to procure a patron (an "upper" *mawlā* in the terminology of the lawyers). Freedmen automatically acquired a patron in their manumitter, unless the latter renounced the tie. Free persons and those freed without *walāʾ* had to acquire one by agreement. Contractual clientage was known as *walāʾ* of *muwālāt* ("inclination", "attachment", the term generally used in Ḥanafī literature), *tibāʿa* ("following", al-Ṭabarī, ii, 1853), *khidma* ("service", *Aghānī*, xii, 48) or *islām*, conversion: whoever converted "at the hands of" another became a client of the other according to a famous *ḥadīth* (*man aslama ʿalā yad ghayrih fa-huwa mawlāhu*). *Walāʾ* was a solution to the problem of affiliating non-tribesmen to a tribal society, and though most such non-tribesmen were clearly converts, conversion was not necessary for the legal validity of the tie. A fair number of non-Muslim clients, both freeborn and freed, are attested (Crone, *Slaves*, n. 358; al-Ṭabarī, i, 3185).

From the point of view of the authorities, the main role of the patron was to provide the client with an *ʿāḳila* [*q.v.*]. The patron and his agnates were required to pay compensation (*ʿaḳl, diya* [*q.v.*]) for bodily harm inflicted by the client, to the extent that the latter had no agnates of his own. Refusal to pay seems to have been a common problem (al-Kindī, *The governors and judges of Egypt*, ed. R. Guest, Leiden and London 1912, 333f., 335f.). Conversely, if the client was killed they were entitled to blood-money in compensation for him (cf. al-Kindī, *op.cit.*, 333f.). In return for his obligations, the patron acquired a title to the client's estate, though not an indefeasible one. The classical rules of exclusion are not, on the whole, favourable to the patron, but it is not known whether they applied in pre-classical law. The role of the client, on the other hand, was purely passive. He did not contribute to blood-money payable for damage inflicted by the patron, nor did he share in the receipt of blood-money if the patron was killed or acquire a title to his estate. He was not formally obliged to render *obsequium*. The patron by manumission could make over the patronate to a third party by sale, gift or bequest, and the parties to the contractual relationship could terminate theirs (in which case the client would need a new patron). If not, it would pass to the descendants of the two parties in perpetuity, though it would lose legal (but not necessarily social) importance as the client acquired agnates in Islam, Muslim clients could and frequently did have clients of their own.

From the point of view of the client, the main role of the patron was to provide him with access to a privileged society, and in practice the patron's rewards were far greater than those provided by the authorities. For one thing, the patron might qualify his grant of freedom with stipulations requiring the freedmen to pay regular sums, gifts or labour services to himself or a third party for a specified period, or reserving part or all of the freedman's estate for himself regardless of the presence of heirs (practices condemned in early *ḥadīth*; cf. Crone, *Roman, provincial and Islamic law*). For another thing, freedmen were notoriously loyal. They would stay by their manumitters in danger (al-Ṭabarī, i, 3001f., ii, 1959; cf. Ch. Pellat (tr.), *The life and works of Jāḥiẓ*, London 1969, 215, 260), share their sorrows (cf. al-Ṭabarī, ii, 384), assist them in need (though for one who refused, see *Aghānī*³, xvi, 107), attend to them in death (al-Ṭabarī, i, 3046, ii, 1751) and seek to avenge them (*ibid.*, ii, 1049; al-Balādhurī, *Ansāb*, v, 338). Concerning the services provided by contractual clients, we are less well informed. Like freedmen, they clearly went to swell their patrons' retinues, both military and civilian (M. J. Kister, *The Battle of the Ḥarra*, in *Studies in memory of Gaston Wiet*, Jerusalem 1977, 44; Crone, *Slaves*, 53f.), and they must have performed other types of *khidma* too. But patrons preferred freedmen to *mawālī tibāʿa* (al-Ṭabarī, ii, 1852f.).

(b) The *mawālī* in Umayyad society. No formal disabilities seem to have attached to the status of client in public law. In principle, clients were in a dependent position only vis-à-vis their patrons, enjoying the same rights and duties as other Muslims in society at large (*lahum mā lanā wa-ʿalayhim mā ʿalaynā*). In practice, of course, there was massive prejudice against them. The Arabs generally equated them with slaves, partly because they were unwarlike agriculturalists (Ḥassān b. Thābit, *Dīwān*, ed. and tr. H. Hirschfeld, Leiden and London 1910, no. 189:8; cf. Dhu 'l-Rumma, *Dīwān*, ed. C. H. H. Macartney, Cambridge 1919, no. 29:48), partly because they had suffered spectacular military defeat ("O men, do you not see how Persia has been ruined and its inhabitants humiliated? They have become slaves who pasture your sheep, as if their kingdom was a dream", Nābigha al-Djaʿdī, no. 8:12f.), and, finally, because the majority of clients were freedmen. Christian and Muslim sources are agreed that the Arabs took enormous numbers of prisoners-of-war during the wars of conquest. "He killed and took prisoners" is the standard expression for the activities of a conqueror in the Muslim ones (Khalīfa b. Khayyāṭ, *Taʾrīkh*, ed. S. Zakkār, Damascus 1967-8, i, 127, 163, 168, 171, 178, 237, 242; Sebeos, *Histoire d'Héraclius*, tr. F. Macler, Paris 1904, 100f., 110, 146; Bar Penkaye in A. Mingana, ed. and tr., *Sources syriaques*, Leipzig [1907], *147 = *175; Michael the Syrian, *Chronique*, ed. and tr. J.-B. Chabot, Paris 1899-1910, iv, 417 = ii, 422); and the usual fate of prisoners-of-war was enslavement. Moreover, many localities were required by treaty to supply a specified number of slaves to the Arabs, such as 30,000 or 100,000 once and for all or a smaller number annually (al-Ṭabarī, ii, 1238, 1245, 1246, 1321, 1329, 1667; al-Balādhurī, *Futūḥ*, 208; C. E. Bosworth, *Sīstān under the Arabs*, Rome 1968, 17; M. Hinds and H. Sakkout, *A letter from the governor of Egypt to the King of Nubia and Muqurra concerning Egyptian-Nubian relations in 141/758*, in *Studia Arabica et Islamica I. ʿAbbās*, ed. W. al-Qāḍī, Beirut 1981; Juda, *Aspekte*, 64-5). Victims of war and their descendants thus outnumbered freeborn clients, and "slaves" was the standard term of abuse for a client of any kind (al-Ṭabarī, ii, 1120, 1431; al-Balādhurī, *Ansāb*, iva, 247, v, 356; *Aghānī*³, xvi, 107). Naturally, such men were subject to numerous disabilities in the society of their conquerors. Slaves and clients were "vile" (*TA*, s.v. *h-w-y*), and clients of clients were "the most miserable persons to walk on earth" (al-Balādhurī, *Ansāb*, ivb, 10; cf. al-Farazdak in *LA* and *TA*, s.v. *w-l-y*). Thus a *mawlā* who married an Arab woman risked both penalties and the dissolution of his marriage (*Aghānī*³, xvi, 106f.; cf. also Goldziher, *Muh. Stud.*, i, 128ff.), though such marriages are unlikely to have been officially prohibited (below, (d)). A *mawlā*'s life was felt to be worth less than that of an Arab, so that an Arab should not be killed in retaliation for a client (al-Balādhurī, *Ansāb*, iva, 220), while conversely, retaliation inflicted upon a client failed to compensate for harm suffered by an Arab (al-Ṭabarī, ii, 1849). A *mawlā* was not worth avenging (though Ḳutayba b. Muslim [*q.v.*] invoked a moral obligation to do so in an unusual situation where the client was a Transoxanian prince, al-Ṭabarī, ii, 1249); it was by way of insult to their victim that Arab avengers would claim to have killed so-and-so for a mere *mawlā* or slave (al-

Azdī, *Taʾrīkh al-Mawṣil*, ed. ʿA. Ḥabība, Cairo 1967, 62; al-Dīnawarī, *al-Akhbār al-ṭiwāl*, ed. V. Guirgass, Leiden 1888, 350; al-Ṭabarī, i, 3276, ii, 710). Above all, *mawālī* were felt to be unsuitable for positions of authority, such as that of prayer-leader, judge or governor (Goldziher, *Muh. Stud.*, i, 109 n., 116; Ṣ. A. al-ʿAlī, *al-Tanẓīmāt al-idjtimāʿiyya wa 'l-iḳtiṣādiyya fi 'l-Baṣra*[2], Beirut 1969, 96f.; Ibn Ḳudāma, *al-Mughnī*, ed. T. M. al-Zaynī and others, Cairo 1968-70, vii, 33; Juda, *Aspekte*, 182-4); as late as 133/750-1 the inhabitants of Mawṣil objected to the appointment of a *mawlā* as governor (al-Azdī, *Mawṣil*, 146). Confronted with this prejudice, non-Arab Muslims initially made their careers mainly in the service of their patrons, and the tie between patron and client remained important throughout the Umayyad period; but their education, skills and sheer number was such that they rapidly achieved positions of influence in their own right.

Civilian careers. Many non-Arabs had worked as labourers, craftsmen, traders and shopkeepers while still slaves, and many continued in such occupations on their manumission (cf. Juda, *Aspekte*, 109ff.) But we hear more about those who remained members of their patrons' households, especially those of governors, who would employ them as messengers, spies, executioners and other agents of various kinds (al-Ṭabarī, i, 2138, ii, 40, 246f., 268, 1276, 1649). Governors and caliphs alike also employed their own freedmen as *ḥādjibs* [*q.v.*], see the information at the end of each reign in Khalīfa, *Taʾrīkh*, and al-Masʿūdī, *Tanbīh*, 284ff.; al-Balādhurī, *Ansāb*, v, 172; al-Ṭabarī, ii, 1650). But *mawālī* played a more important role as administrators. Some administered their patron's estate (al-Balādhurī, *Futūḥ*, 8; al-Ṭabarī, ii, 1734; Juda, *Aspekte*, 119-20); a great many administered the empire. Thus a secretary (*kātib* [*q.v.*]) was usually a non-Arab, sometimes a non-Muslim (al-Masʿūdī, *Tanbīh*, 302, 307, 312; al-Balādhurī, *Ansāb*, xi (= *Anonyme arabische Chronik*, ed. W. Ahlwardt, Greifswald 1883, 343), but more commonly a convert (cf. al-Djahshiyārī, *Kitāb al-wuzarāʾ wa 'l-kuttāb*, ed. M. al-Saḳḳāʾ and others, Cairo 1938, 61) or a freedman; being appreciated for their skills rather than their personal loyalties, such men were employed not only by their own patrons (e.g. al-Djahshiyārī, 54, 64; al-Ṭabarī, ii, 837ff.) but also by others (e.g. al-Masʿūdī, *Tanbīh*, 302, 312, 316, 317, etc.; al-Ṭabarī, *loc.cit.*; al-Djahshiyārī, 66).

The various sections of the *dīwān* [*q.v.*] in a particular province, or indeed the entire *dīwān*, were commonly headed by *mawālī* (al-Ṭabarī, ii, 837ff., 1649, 1650; al-Djahshiyārī, 42, 69; al-Balādhurī, *Ansāb*, ivb, 83, 123). Moreover, *mawālī* soon came to be appointed as fiscal governors, sometimes on behalf of top Arab governors, but frequently in their own right. We hear of such appointments in Mecca and Medina (Ibn Ḥabīb, *al-Muḥabbar*, ed. I. Lichtenstädter, Hyderabad 1942, 379). Transoxania (al-Ṭabarī, ii, 1253, 1421, 1509), and ʿIrāḳ, where non-Arab fiscal governors played a major role in Arab politics (*ibid.*, 1282f., 1648; al-Djahshiyārī, 42f., 49, 63; Ibn ʿIdhārī, i, 39; al-Balādhurī, *Ansāb*, ivb, 123), as well as in Egypt, where three non-Arabs rose to the position of effective governor thanks to their control of the taxes, that is Usāma b. Zayd al-Salīḥī, a *mawlā* of Muʿāwiya (al-Djahshiyārī, 51) under Sulaymān, ʿUbayd (or ʿAbd) Allāh b. al-Ḥabḥāb [*q.v.*], a *mawlā* of Salūl under Hishām, and ʿAbd al-Malik b. Marwān b. Mūsā b. Nuṣayr, a *mawlā* of Lakhm (or the Umayyads) under Marwān II (al-Kindī, *Governors*, 93). Lesser administrative jobs were also in the hands of *mawālī* (al-Ṭabarī, ii, 1845; in general, see also Juda, *Aspekte*, 119-20).

Outside the administration, non-Arab Muslims rapidly came to dominate the world of scholarship. *Mawālī*, mainly descendants of captives, played a crucial role in the formation of the Islamic faith [see AL-ḤASAN AL-BAṢRĪ], Islamic law [see ABŪ ḤANĪFA, AL-AWZĀʿĪ, ṬĀWŪS], Ḳurʾānic studies [see ABŪ ʿUBAYDA] and the Prophet's biography [see IBN ISḤĀḲ], as well as in the collection of pre-Islamic poetry [see ḤAMMĀD AL-RĀWIYA]. They also produced some notable poets [see BASHSHĀR B. BURD]. Contemporaries were well aware of the preponderance of *mawālī* in scholarship (Goldziher, *Muh. Stud.*, i, 114f.), and in the second half of the Umayyad period it was usually *mawālī* who were accorded the role of tutor to the caliph's children (Ibn Ḥabīb, *Muḥabbar*, 476ff.; al-Ṭabarī, ii, 1741). In the same period they also began to receive appointment as judges (al-ʿAlī, *Tanẓīmāt*, 96 n).

Careers in the army. Leaving aside the Persian soldiers enrolled during the wars of conquest, non-Arabs initially entered the army only as private servants of their patrons. Every soldier had a number of slaves and freedmen registered under him in the *dīwān*; some governors acquired sizeable bodyguards of slaves and freedmen; and towards the end of the period it was common for governors and generals to have semi-private retinues of freedmen, contractual clients and other protégés (Crone, *Slaves*, 38, 53, 198f.). The *ḥaras*, or palace-guard, of the caliphs and their governors also seems usually to have been composed of and headed by *mawālī*, though not necessarily *mawālī* of the employer (cf. Khalīfa, *Taʾrīkh*, at the end of each reign; al-Ṭabarī, ii, 1384, 1499, 1569, 1650; al-Balādhurī, *Ansāb*, v, 172f.). But already Muʿāwiya placed a *mawlā* in command of troops in an expedition against Byzantium (Khalīfa, *Taʾrīkh*, i, 198, cf. 102), an example followed by ʿAbd al-Malik (al-Ṭabarī, ii, 1487; al-Balādhurī, *Futūḥ*, 160f.); and the Second Civil War decisively undermined the Arab monopoly of military power. Non-Arabs being available, everybody made use of them: thus Mukhtār [*q.v.*]; adherents of Ibn al-Zubayr (Kister, *Battle of the Ḥarra*, 44f.); and the Umayyads themselves (Crone, *Slaves*, 198; Khalīfa, *Taʾrīkh*, i, 335; al-Balādhurī, *Ansāb*, v, 356ff.), with the result that a *mawlā* became military governor of Medina for ʿAbd al-Malik (al-Ṭabarī, ii, 834, 852, 854). Thereafter, non-Arabs were regularly admitted as soldiers in their own right (cf. the rich documentation in Juda, *Aspekte*, 120ff.). Some were placed in special corps for *mawālī* with native skills of their own, such as the Berber *Waḍḍāḥiyya* or the Indian *Ḳīḳāniyya*. Others joined the ordinary army, *mawlā* divisions being set up for their reception. According to a *Kitāb Mawālī ahl Miṣr* cited by Yāḳūt (i, 734), there were *mawlā* divisions in the Egyptian army already at the end of the First Civil War, when a freedman from Balhīb was made *ʿarīf* [*q.v.*] of the *mawālī* of Tudjīb. But the *ʿarīf* in question belongs to the end of the Second Civil War (cf. al-Kindī, *Governors*, 51), and it is only after the Second Civil War that such divisions are regularly mentioned, be it in Egypt, Khurāsān or elsewhere (Crone, *Slaves*, 38). There were *mawālī* in the Syrian army too, for all that *mawlā* divisions are not mentioned here after ʿAbd al-Malik (cf. *ibid.*, 274); we are incidentally given to understand that the Syrian troops in Egypt in 125/742-3 included *mawālī ahl Ḥimṣ* (al-Kindī, *Governors*, 83), and that those brought to Spain by Baldj b. Bishr [*q.v.*] included *mawālī* of the Umayyads, clearly among others (Lévi-Provençal, *Hist. Esp.* mus., i 98;

cf. also Juda, *Aspekte*, 84-5). *Mawālī* also participated in the revolt against al-Walīd II, but whether as regular soldiers or private retainers is not clear (al-Ṭabarī, ii, 1800, 1806f., 1809).

The proportion of non-Arabs to Arabs in the late Umayyad armies cannot be estimated. In 96/714-15 the *mawālī* of Khurāsān were numerically on a par with Bakr b. Wāʾil [*q.v.*], numbering 7,000 out of a total of 54,000 (al-Ṭabarī, ii, 1290f.). They must have become more numerous thereafter. Contrary to what is often stated, the Umayyads did not try to keep non-Arabs out of the army (cf. below); and the attempt to show that their numbers decreased after 96, at least in Khurāsān, rests on a misreading of the sources (M. A. Shaban, *The ʿAbbāsid revolution*, Cambridge 1970, 113, 115 and *passim*: the figure of 1,600 given for the rearguard in the Battle of the Pass scarcely refers to *mawālī*, and at all events, not to their total number; we are explicitly told that the governor had dispersed his troops before the battle and that two *mawlā* commanders, one in charge of 10,000, were among those who had gone elsewhere, cf. al-Ṭabarī, ii, 1532f., 1538, 1549, 1551). In fact, *mawālī* must have been particularly numerous in Khurāsān, where they are constantly mentioned and their participation in all military activities is taken for granted, be it in campaigns (*ibid.*, 1023, 1080, 1225, 1447, 1478, 1485, 1516, 1518, 1538, 1630f., cf. 1184f.) feuds (*ibid.*, 1856), or revolts and their suppression (*ibid.*, 1582, 1589, 1605, 1920f., 1926, 1933, cf. 1163, 1867, 1918f., 1922).

Once admitted to the army, *mawālī* began to receive both military *and* fiscal governorship. Thus the governor and general of Ḳinnasrīn in 75/694-5 was a *mawlā* of ʿAbd al-Malik (al-Balādhurī, *Futūḥ*, 188), and we incidentally learn that the governor of Baʿlabakk in 126/743-4 was also a client of the Umayyads (al-Ṭabarī, ii, 1790). The Djazīra received its first non-Arab governor under ʿUmar II and/or Yazīd II in Maymūn b. Mihrān, a *mawlā* of B. Naṣr (or Azd) who had been tutor to ʿUmar II's children and who was later to command the Syrian army against Byzantium (al-Azdī, *Mawṣil*, 37; Ibn Ḥabīb, *Muḥabbar*, 478; al-Ṭabarī, ii, 1487). *Mawālī* appear as sub-governors in Transoxania from the time of Ḳutayba onwards (al-Ṭabarī, ii, 1206, 1448, 1694f.), and they regularly ruled North Africa. Abu 'l-Muhādjir, who administered North Africa for ten years under Muʿāwiya, was appointed by his own patron, the governor of Egypt (al-Ṭabarī, ii, 94; al-Balādhurī, *Futūḥ*, 228). Similarly, Mūsā b. Nuṣayr [*q.v.*], a *mawlā* of disputed origin who enjoyed the protection of ʿAbd al-ʿAzīz b. Marwān [*q.v.*], ʿAbd al-Malik's governor of Egypt, was appointed by his protector. He in turn appointed a *mawlā* of his own, Ṭāriḳ b. Ziyād [*q.v.*] as commander in the conquest of Spain (al-Balādhurī, *Futūḥ*, 230f.; Ibn ʿIdhārī, i, 39f., 43). Thereafter, a succession of *mawālī* were appointed by the caliphs themselves. Sulaymān chose Muḥammad (or ʿAbd Allāh) b. Yazīd, a *mawlā* of the Umayyads (Ibn ʿIdhārī, i, 47). ʿUmar II appointed Ismāʿīl b. ʿAbd Allāh b. Abi 'l-Muhādjir, a *mawlā* of Makhzūm who had worked as tutor to his children (al-Balādhurī, *Futūḥ*, 231; Ibn Ḥabīb, *Muḥabbar*, 476). Ismāʿīl was followed by Yazīd b. Abī Muslim, a freeborn *mawlā* of al-Ḥadjdjādj's [*q.v.*] appointed by Yazīd II (al-Djahshiyārī, 42; al-Balādhurī, *Futūḥ*, 231); and when he in turn was murdered for his harsh policies, a *mawlā* of the Anṣār by the name of Muḥammad b. Yazīd was elevated from the troops by popular choice and, subsequently, caliphal appointment (al-Ṭabarī, ii, 1435; al-Djahshiyārī, 57; according to al-Ṭabarī, he was identical with the previous governor of that name). Hishām appointed ʿUbayd Allāh b. al-Ḥabḥāb, *mawlā* of Salūl, to Egypt, North Africa and Spain, and ʿUbayd Allāh neatly reversed the pattern by appointing his own patron to Spain (Ibn ʿIdhārī, i, 51ff.; al-Balādhurī, *Futūḥ*, 231).

Local influence. From the Second Civil War onwards, *mawālī* begin to appear in Muslim society and politics as men of local importance. Thus Ḥumrān b. Abān, a captive from ʿAyn al-Tamr [*q.v.*] and former secretary of ʿUthmān's, joined the pro-Umayyad Djufriyya in Baṣra in the Second Civil War and briefly achieved the position of governor there (Ch. Pellat, *Le milieu baṣrien et la formation de Ǧāḥiẓ*, Paris 1953, 270, 278; cf. 268, probably a doublet). Similarly, the wealthy family of ʿAbd Allāh b. Hurmuz, *mawālī* of the Umayyads and directors of the Baṣran *dīwān al-djund* from the time of al-Ḥadjdjādj onwards, are said to have been very influential in this city (al-Balādhurī, *Ansāb*, ivb, 123). In Khurāsān, the B. Ṣuhayb, *mawālī* of the B. Djaḥdar, enjoyed a position of eminence among the Rabīʿa and intervened in the local feuds during the Second Civil War (al-Ṭabarī, ii, 491ff.). In the Third Civil War, a certain Muḥārib b. Mūsā, *mawlā* of the B. Yashkur, emerged as *ʿaẓīm al-ḳadr* in Fārs, where he took to expelling Umayyad governors (*ibid.*, 1976f.). And of Ḥarīsh, a *mawlā* of Khuzāʿa who joined the ʿAbbāsid revolution, we are told that he was *ʿaẓīm ahl Nasā* (al-Dīnawarī, *Akhbār*, 341).

All in all, the *mawālī* must thus be said to have penetrated Arab society extremely fast. They played a predominant role in most activities outside the world of politics, controlled the civil administration almost from the start and made their presence felt in military politics within a generation of the conquests. Certainly, the Arabs retained their control of military politics until the end of the Umayyad period, most governorship and other politically influential posts being allocated to them; but the popular image of *mawālī* as an excluded people passively exposed to Arab whim and prejudice is quite wrong. Given the cultural and numerical discrepancy between the conquerors and their subjects, it is not really surprising that the latter acquired influence so fast: the conquerors simply could not govern without non-Arab help, as later Shuʿūbīs were to point out; indeed, they needed their advice even in matters of food and drink (al-Ṣūlī, *Adab al-kuttāb*, ed. M. B. al-Atharī, Cairo 1341, 193). What is surprising is that the Arab integument of Muslim society withstood the pressure.

(c) Fiscal status. The secondary literature generally associates *mawālī* with fiscal disabilities. Thus all the Umayyads other than ʿUmar II are said wrongfully to have collected poll tax (*djizya* [*q.v.*]) from converts and to have refused them registration in the army, being assisted in this by the leaders of the non-Muslim communities who had an interest in penalising conversion (J. Wellhausen, *The Arab kingdom and its fall*, Calcutta 1927, ch. 5; D. C. Dennett, *Conversion and poll-tax in early Islam*, Cambridge Mass. 1950; H. A. R. Gibb, *The fiscal rescript of ʿUmar II*, in *Arabica* ii/1 [1955], 1-16). But this view is in need of modification. On the one hand, the vast majority of *mawālī* were freedmen and descendants of freedmen who had never paid any poll-tax at all; and free converts who acquired a respectable patron also escaped fiscal disabilities (Crone, *Slaves*, 52). The conventional picture applies only to a special type of convert, the fugitive peasant. On the other hand, the Umayyad treatment of such *mawālī* should not be seen as a violation of the law; the law on this question was what the

Umayyads themselves decreed. The fact that the classical rules of taxation have been attributed to ʿUmar I does not mean that they in fact existed so early (cf. K. Morimoto, *The fiscal administration of Egypt in the early Islamic period*, Kyoto 1981); and they would not have helped the Umayyads even if they had. Thus the classical rules lay down that the convert should be freed of his poll-tax, but not of his land-tax (*kharādj* [*q.v.*]). In the Umayyad period, however, no villager converted without leaving his villages and thus also such land as he might possess: the distinction between a *dhimmī* poll-tax and a religiously neutral land-tax was quite irrelevant. Converts invariably left their land because the attraction of conversion lay in its promise of access to the ranks of the conquerors: converting without joining these ranks would have been pointless and, locally, extremely unpleasant. To convert was thus to make a *hidjra* [*q.v.*] from the land of unbelief to the land of Islam, that is, the garrison cities, as ʿUmar II explained (Ibn ʿAbd al-Ḥakam, *Sīrat ʿUmar b. ʿAbd al-ʿAzīz*, ed. A. ʿUbayd, Beirut 1967, 93f.); and the problem confronting the Umayyads was not whether converts should be freed of this or that part of their fiscal burden, but whether they should be allowed to make their *hidjra* and thus escape their fiscal burden altogether. Naturally, Umayyad policies varied. ʿUmar II accepted such converts (his problem was thus the fate of their land, cf. *ibid.*). But most Umayyads adopted a harsh policy vis-à-vis fugitives regardless of whether they claimed conversion or not (cf. Morimoto, *Fiscal administration*, 120ff.; Crone, *Slaves*, 52), resettling them in their villages or at best allowing them to stay where they were in return for continuing fiscal liability. Three points follow from this. First, the fugitives in question were required to pay all their customary taxes, whatever these might be, not merely a religiously neutral land-tax: having been denied access to the conquest society, they were not Muslims at all in the eyes of the authorities; and all their taxes, not merely the poll-tax, were regarded as *dhimmī* taxes at this stage. Secondly, such converts were not eligible for membership of the army. Naturally, when ʿUmar II decided to admit them to Muslim society, he admitted them to the army as well; but the fact that others refused them entry to the army does not mean that *mawālī* as such were kept out of the *dīwān*. The numerous *mawālī* who fought in the army without pay were runaway peasants who were still being held to their fiscal obligations and who fought as volunteers in the hope of being picked up by a patron, as is clear from the story of Yūnus b. ʿAbd Rabbih, who acquired a patron in Nasr b. Sayyār (Crone, *Slaves*, 52f.). Thirdly, it was such converts, not converts in general, who were open to penalisation by the leaders of the Christian, Jewish and Zoroastrian communities; had their *hidjra* been accepted, they would of course have been placed under Muslim administration (cf. al-Ṭabarī, ii, 1688; Dennett, *Conversion*, 124ff.).

It should be clear that the entire problem of the fiscal treatment of converts was a problem for *dhimmī*s, not for *mawālī*. It was *dhimmī*s who were frustrated by the closure of "the gate of the *hidjra*" (cf. Ibn ʿAbd al-Ḥakam, *Sīra*, 94); a *mawlā*, by contrast, was somebody already admitted. It was accordingly also *dhimmī*s, not *mawālī*, who would enrol in the service of anyone who promised them tax-relief. "Whoever converts is freed from *kharādj*" is a slogan on a par with that addressed to slaves, "whoever joins us is free" (cf. Crone, *Slaves*, nn. 399-400, 647). Both are addressed, usually by rebels, to malcontents *outside* free Muslim society, not to oppressed elements within in; it was only on responding to such slogans that the non-Muslims and slaves in question acquired client status.

(d) The issue of assimilation. The Umayyads are generally credited with an active policy of discrimination against non-Arab Muslims (cf. most recently, M. A. Shaban, *Islamic history*, i, Cambridge 1971). This impression arises largely from their treatment of fugitive peasants. But though they discouraged flight from the land and no doubt shared the common prejudice against non-Arabs, they do not seem to have had an actual policy of discrimination against accredited members of Muslim society. Practically every Umayyad caliph is known to have appointed a *mawlā* governor. Al-Ḥadjdjādj, a man notorious for his harsh treatment of runaway peasants, appointed the first non-Arab judges in ʿIrāḳ (al-ʿAlī, *Tanẓīmat*, 96 ṇ); he also appointed a *mawlā* to his *shurṭa* (al-Yaʿḳūbī, ii, 328), an unusual step (for a later example, see al-Kindī, *Governors*, 70). ʿUmar II, a caliph famous for his encouragement of conversion, is said to have disapproved of intermarriage between Arabs and *mawālī* (al-ʿAlī, *Tanẓīmāt*, 96 ṇ). But no prohibition of such unions has been recorded, and *mawālī* are known to have married female relatives of other Umayyads (al-Balādhurī, *Ansāb*, iva, 247; al-Ṭabarī, ii, 1420); the right to repudiate or endorse such unions presumably rested with the guardians of the bride (cf. also Juda, *Aspekte*, 178ff.). The fact that *mawālī* formed quasi-tribal groups of their own in the army reflects the tribal organisation of this army, not a policy of segregation; and it was the Umayyads themselves, not Abū Muslim, who abolished this organisation in Khurāsān (Crone, *Slaves*, 38). The belief that *mawālī* were relegated to the infantry rests on a failure to distinguish *mawālī* inside Muslim society from runaway peasants trying to enter it: governors and generals such as Ṭāriḳ b. ʿAmr, Dīnār b. Dīnār, Mūsā b. Nuṣayr, Ṭāriḳ b. Ziyād or Ibrāhīm b. Bassām were scarcely disqualified from riding horses. (See also al-Ṭabarī, ii, 1118f., 1599; Lévi-Provençal, *Hist. Esp. mus.*, i, 98.) Conversely, the enemies of the Umayyads do not seem to have regarded assimilation as an issue of political opposition. No rebel of the Umayyad period mentioned the treatment of non-Arab Muslims in his proclamations, and the belief that the ʿAbbāsids [*q.v.*] regarded assimilation as their prime objective is gratuitous. Obviously, assimilation accelerated on the fall of the conquest society, but scarcely as a result of official encouragement. The legitimacy of favouring Arabs over non-Arab Muslims in matters of appointment, vengeance and marriage clearly did become an object of debate in the Umayyad period, as did the refusal to accept runaway converts as Muslims, and in principle the question could have been taken up by politicans. In practice, however, the debate remained divorced from politics, and it continued long after the Umayyads had fallen.

(e) *Mawlā* grievances. As the prominence of non-Arab Muslims in Muslim society increased, so did their contribution to revolts. It is customary to interpret their participation in rebellious and/or heterodox movements as an expression of protest against a social inequality which ultimately led to the fall of the Umayyad dynasty. But for one thing, it is by no means clear that *mawālī* were disproportionately represented in movements of protest. For another, they scarcely clamoured for social equality. Not one revolt of the Umayyad period was conducted exclusively by *mawālī* in the name of concerns exclusive to them; and the only two revolts in which such concerns came to the forefront, revealed somewhat different aims. The first is that of Mukhtār, an Arab opportunist whose non-Arab followers are described as slaves and freedmen (*ʿabīd wa-mawālī*) in the Muslim sources, and as prisoners-of-war in the contemporary Christian work of Bar Penkaye (Mingana, *Sources syriaques*, *156ff. = *183ff.). They were thus captives trying to escape their Arab masters, not converts seeking equality with them (indeed, the extent to which they were Muslims is disputable); and though Mukhtār was of course forced to extend Arab privileges to them in order to gain their co-operation, neither he nor they would seem to have had any views on the position of non-Arab Muslims in general. The second is that of the Berbers, recruited into Khāridjism [see KHĀRIDJITES] by Baṣran missionaries; and Berber Khāridjism did not of course express a desire for social equality, but rather for political independence in Islam. Once more, the conventional picture rests on a failure to distinguish between *dhimmī*s denied recognition as Muslims on the one hand and *mawālī* within Muslim society on the other. The former did indeed clamour for Arab privileges, such privileges being denied them altogether; but the latter clamoured for such privileges (social, cultural or political) as were appropriate to the social group in which they happened to find themselves. The fact that all non-Arabs were exposed to insult and prejudice does not mean that they responded by forming a trade-union. A non-Arab peasant in search of a patron such as Yūnus b. ʿAbd Rabbih had little in common with non-Arabs who had long been members of Muslim society; and of these, a general such as Ibrāhīm b. Bassām had little in common with *mawālī* working as secretaries, scholars or businessmen, let alone as domestic servants. To attribute the fall of the Umayyads to "*mawlā* discontent" is accordingly meaningless; what grievances did Ḥammād al-Rāwiya, an ʿIrāḳī collector of Arabic poetry at home at the Umayyad court, share with an uncouth Berber general such as Ṭāriḳ b. Ziyād, and what sympathy did either feel for the miserable peasants rounded up by Umayyad governors (Arab *and* non-Arab) throughout the caliphate? Non-Arab Muslims simply did not form a single social group. The fact that numerous *mawālī* participated in the ʿAbbāsid revolution is accordingly also meaningless unless it is specified what kind of *mawālī* they were. In fact, they were of three quite different kinds: long-standing members of Muslim society such as the family of the above-mentioned Ibrāhīm b. Bassām (al-Ṭabarī, ii, 1996-7, iii, 17f., 21, 37, 48, 75ff.; for their origin, see al-Balādhurī, *Futūḥ*, 393); freedmen and other clients who automatically followed their (Arab or non-Arab) patrons (e.g. al-Ṭabarī, ii, 1954); and *dhimmī* villagers for whom joining the rebel armies constituted both conversion and admission to Muslim society, as it did for Sunbādh [*q.v.*] and other recruits of Abū Muslim's who were later to opt out of this society as followers of prophets of their own. The causes of the revolution are clearly to be sought in the first type of *mawlā* and his Arab counterpart (from whom he is frequently indistinguishable), the long-standing member of Khurāsānī society. Such men were subject neither to fiscal disabilities nor to exclusion from the army, the cavalry, high office or general respect. The identification of their aims depends on whether one regards them as coming from inside or outside the local army, the evidence suggesting the former (on this question see Shaban, *ʿAbbāsid revolution*; M. Sharon, *Black banners from the East*, Jerusalem 1983; cf. also E. L. Daniel, *The political and social history of Khurasan under Abbasid rule*, Minneapolis and Chicago 1979).

3. The ʿAbbāsids.

The ʿAbbāsid revolution deprived the Arabs of such social and political privileges as they retained. Access to political office, influence and wealth now rested overwhelmingly on membership of an army recruited mainly in Khurāsān and a bureaucracy recruited mainly in ʿIrāḳ, as well as of the ruler's household. Non-Arab Muslims reached top positions through all three institutions (Crone, *Slaves*, appendix 5; cf. BARĀMIKA), while at the same time the majority of Arabs and *mawālī* found equality as ordinary subjects. Since Muslim society was no longer constituted by Arab privilege, non-Arab Muslims ceased to require a patron for membership of it. Freedmen continued to become clients of their manumitters, but most of the classical schools rejected the patronate over converts as offensive (below, section V), and the careers of free converts and the descendants of freedman ceased to be shaped by *walāʾ*. Yet Arab superiority on the one hand and the institution of *walāʾ* on the other were still to be of major importance in other ways.

(a) The Shuʿūbiyya. In cultural and religious terms, the Arabs continued to be regarded as a superior people, a fact which underlay the so-called Shuʿūbī movement, the "movement of the gentiles". Shuʿūbī sentiments had undoubtedly been common already in the Umayyad period, but it was only in the early ʿAbbāsid period that they came into the open, clearly because the *mawālī* were now in a position to get a hearing for their case: the exponents of Shuʿūbism were drawn primarily from among members of the caliphal bureaucracy and court. Purely literary in manifestation (cf. Goldziher, *Muh. Stud.*, i, chs. 4-5), the movement campaigned for cultural rather than social or political objectives, its ultimate aim being to break the nexus between Islam and Arabism, partly because this nexus stood in the way of non-Arab self-esteem and more particularly because it obstructed the reception of non-Arab culture. Ultimately, the issue behind the controversy was the cultural orientation of Islam (cf. H. A. R. Gibb, *Studies on the civilization of Islam*, Princeton 1962, ch. 4). The controversy only petered out in the 6th/12th century (cf. R. P. Mottahedeh, *The Shuʿûbîyah controversy and the social history of early Islamic Iran*, in *IJMES*, vii [1976]), and the issue was never properly resolved, though in practice the Shuʿūbīs lost (cf. P. Crone and M. Cook, *Hagarism*, Cambridge 1977, 102 f.). For further details, see SHUʿŪBIYYA.

(b) *Walāʾ*. Having lost its social importance, the institution of *walāʾ* acquired a new political significance. Unlike the Umayyads, the ʿAbbasids trusted their freedmen and other private servants better than the public servants of the state. Thus al-Manṣūr [*q.v.*] is said to have esteemed *mawālī* (in the sense of clients, not non-Arab Muslims) for their loyalty and to have accumulated more of them than any caliph before him, recommending them to his son (al-Ṭabarī, iii, 414, 444, 448). Clients of the caliphal household appear as a separate group at court soon after the revolution, and both al-Manṣūr and al-Mahdī [*q.v.*] selected a fair number of governors from their ranks (al-Ṭabarī, iii, 429, 545, 1027; Crone, *Slaves*, appendix Vb). Al-Mahdī, who similarly expressed a preference for *mawālī* (al-Ṭabarī, iii, 531), turned them into an army of their own (*ibid.*, 459). *Mawālī* of domestic origin continued to form troops of their own side by side with Turks and others far into the ʿAbbāsid period, as well as in Ṭūlūnid Egypt (*ibid.*, 1400, 1501; al-Yaʿḳūbī, ii, 606, 624; cf. *Aghānī*, xii, 52). Already al-Manṣūr, however, recruited non-Muslims for military use, attaching them to the ʿAbbāsid house by contractual *walāʾ*, and this example was followed by Hārūn [*q.v.*] (Crone, *Slaves*, 74). And from the time of al-Muʿtaṣim [*q.v.*] onwards, the core of the caliph's armies typically consisted of men who were both slaves and non-Muslims by origin [(cf. DJAYSH and GHULĀM]; D. Ayalon, *Preliminary remarks on the Mamluk military institution in Islam*, in V. J. Parry and M. E. Yapp, eds., *War, technology and society in the Middle East*, Oxford 1975; D. Pipes, *Slave soldiers and Islam*, New Haven 1981; Crone, *Slaves*, ch. 10).

As political power came to rest on private ties with the caliph, the title *mawlā amīr al-muʾminīn* became a common honorific. First attested under al-Manṣūr, it was bestowed on governors and other dignitaries of non-Arab origin regardless of whether they were clients of the caliph in a legal sense. From the time of al-Muʿtaṣim onwards, it was regularly granted to Turkish generals and other favourites. It was also the title usually held by non-Arab rulers of successor states (Crone, *Slaves*, 75, appendix Vb, note 610; al-Balādhurī, *Futūḥ*, 134, 330; al-Yaʿḳūbī, ii, 597; Hilāl al-Ṣābiʾ, *Rusūm dār al-khilāfa*, ed. M. ʿAwwād, Baghdād 1964, 122 f.).

4. Muslim Spain.

The relationship between Arab and non-Arab Muslims in Spain differed from that of the east in three major respects. First, *walāʾ* played virtually no role in it. On the one hand, many of the conquerors were Berbers, and such ties of *walāʾ* as they had with Arab patrons lost all significance when they acquired the status of conquerors themselves. On the other hand, the conquerors settled all over the land, not merely in garrison cities. Muslim Spain thus lacked not only the purely Arab conquest élite characteristic of the east, but also the privileged *amṣār* which elsewhere attracted *dhimmī* immigrants and caused the Muslims to exclude from their ranks all converts without a patron. Conversion in Spain did not normally involve either *hidjra* or *walāʾ*, the converts adopting Islam wherever they happened to be. Indeed, they were not normally known as *mawālī* at all, but rather, in the first generation, as *musālima* and thereafter as *muwalladūn* (originally meaning home-born slaves; Lévi-Provençal, *Hist. Esp. mus.*, i, 75). Having adopted Islam in their own homes, the non-Arab Muslims of Spain failed to penetrate Arab society. Naturally Spain had its freedmen who, here as elsewhere, entered Arab society as clients. But whereas freedmen of the most diverse origin were exceedingly numerous in the cosmopolitan East, they were relatively few in Spain. Spanish society thus came to be characterised by the coexistence of three quite distinct ethnic groups, Arabs, Berbers and *muwallads*, rather than by relationship of dependence between Arabs and ethnically heterogeneous clients. Furthermore, since Spain escaped Khurāsānī conquest, these groups were able to retain political importance right down to ʿAbd al-Raḥmān III [*q.v.*].

Secondly, Spain saw armed conflicts between Arabs and indigenous Muslims. Throughout most of the Umayyad period, the *mawālī* of the East were ethnically too diverse and socially too dispersed in Arab society to rebel as *mawālī* against Arabs, while at the same time non-Arabs who had stayed together had also failed to adopt Islam. Only shortly before and after the ʿAbbāsid revolution, when on the one hand whole localities adopted Islam together, while on the other hand government was still identified as Arab, did non-Arab Muslims rebel against Arab rule. They did not, however, rebel as *mawālī*, but rather as heretics (as in North Africa) or even non-Muslims, rejecting the Arabs and Islam together (as in both North Africa and Iran). In Spain, where Arabs and *muwallads* coexisted as distinct groups, such revolts could in principle have erupted any time. In practice, they only came in the 3rd/9th century, perhaps provoked by the growth of the Umayyad state (Arab and Berber leaders also rebelled, and the upshot was the centralised state of ʿAbd al-Raḥmān III); and here for once the rebels took action as *mawālī*, explicitly invoking the cause of the non-Arab Muslims (*daʿwat al-muwalladīn wa 'l-ʿadjam*, Ibn Ḥayyān, *al-Muḳtabis*, ed. M. M. Antuña, Paris 1937, 24) under the leadership of men such as ʿUmar b. Ḥafṣūn [*q.v.*]. Being short of traditions of their own, partly because they were natives of provincial Spain and partly because they were Muslims of long standing, they had no alternative to Cordovan Islam. Accordingly, they did not deny the legitimacy of the Cordovan state as heretics; and though Ibn Ḥafṣūn did in the end reject Islam for Christianity, few *muwallads* followed suit (cf. Lévi-Provençal, *Hist. Esp. mus.*, i, 295 ff.).

Thirdly, there were practically no Shuʿūbīs in Spain. The fact that the *muwallads* did not have much of a cultural legacy to vindicate would hardly in itself have prevented them from adopting Shuʿūbī arguments in response to Arab prejudice: the one Shuʿūbī author attested for Spain, a Slav secretary equally lacking in cultural traditions of his own, simply adopted the arguments of eastern writers (cf. J. T. Monroe, *The Shuʿūbiyya in al-Andalus*, Berkeley and Los Angeles 1970). But having avoided enslavement and migration, the *muwallads* had also failed to acquire culture and positions of influence in the society of their conquerors. Where eastern *mawālī* had spokesmen among bureaucrats and courtiers, the leaders of the *muwallads* were country squires more noted for their *virtù* than for their polish; indeed, the smarts and insults suffered by such rural lords at the court of Cordova played a role in the outbreak of several *muwallad* revolts. The *muwallads* thus lacked both the education and the influence required for a literary onslaught on Arab superiority. Instead, however, they were in a position to take up arms in their castles, as they did until ʿAbd al-Raḥmān III reduced both them and their opponents to docile subjects.

In political terms, however, the institution of *walāʾ* played much the same role in Spain as it did in the ʿAbbāsid East. Thus ʿAbd al-Raḥmān I [*q.v.*], who relied considerably on freedmen and clients of the Umayyads for the conquest of Spain, is said by some to have recruited an army among non-Arab Muslims; al-Ḥakam I [*q.v.*] expanded this army and created the palatial guard of *khurs* ("mute ones"), i.e. foreign slaves and freedmen as well as local Christians (Lévi-Provençal, *Hist. Esp. mus.*, i, 129 f., iii, 71 ff.). The *djund* [*q.v.*], however, survived much longer in Spain than it did elsewhere, being abolished only by Ibn Abī ʿĀmir [see AL-MANṢŪR]; and thanks to the geopolitical position of Spain, it was Berber mercenaries rather than Turkish slaves and freedmen who replaced it.

5. *Walāʾ* in classical law.

(a) Sources of *walāʾ*. All schools accept manumission as a source of *walāʾ*. Only the Ḥanafīs, Imāmīs and Ḳāsimī Zaydīs, however, accept contractual agreement as such, and then in different ways. According to the Ḥanafīs and Imāmīs, contractual clientage (*walāʾ al-muwālāt* or, in the terminology of the Imāmīs, *al-taḍammun bi 'l-djarīra*) arises from a contractual agreement distinct from the act of conversion at the hands of another; conversion does not in itself give rise to the tie. But according to the Ḳāsimīs, it arises from conversion at the hands of another; mere agreements cannot create *walāʾ*.

(b) *Walāʾ al-ʿitḳ*. All the schools are agreed that *walāʾ* arises automatically on manumission, but they disagree about the invariability with which it does so. According to the Imāmīs, it only arises when the manumission is gratuitous, i.e. not expiatory, not made in fulfilment of a vow or other legal requirement, and not made by *kitāba* [see ʿABD]; and both the Imāmīs and other schools enable the manumitter to exempt himself from *walāʾ* by declaring the freedmen *sāʾiba*, though the Sunnīs disapprove of the practice. In Ḥanafī and Shāfiʿī law, however, manumission invariably gives rise to *walāʾ*, whatever the circumstances or the inclinations of the manumitter. If the freedman is a non-Muslim, the tie is deprived of most of its legal effects.

The manumitter acquires responsibility for the payment of *diya* on behalf of the freedman and qualifies for the role of marriage guardian to his freedwoman or freedman's daughter. In return, he is granted a title to the freedman's estate in all schools except that of the Ibāḍīs (not that of the Ẓāhirīs, as stated in ʿABD). In Sunnī and Ḳāsimī Zaydī law, he inherits as the remotest agnate of the freedman; he is thus excluded by the freedman's own agnates (e.g. a son), but inherits together with Ḳurʾānic heirs (e.g. a daughter) and himself excludes remoter relatives (*dhawu 'l-arḥām*, e.g. a sister's son). In Imāmī, Ismāʿīlī and Nāṣirī Zaydī law he is excluded by any blood relation of the freedman, though he inherits together with the spouse.

The freedman does not, on the whole, acquire any corresponding rights and duties. Only the Ismāʿīlīs call him to succession, and only in default of all other heirs. The Mālikīs do hold him responsible for the payment of *diya* on behalf of the manumitter if the latter has no agnates, *ahl al-dīwān* or patrons of his own; but a similar opinion transmitted from al-Shāfiʿī failed to become school doctrine, and all other schools exempt him. The possibility that he might act as marriage guardian is not considered.

The relationship survives the death of both parties, passing to their heirs in perpetuity, though it loses practical importance as the client acquires agnates of his own. It also extends to the freedmen of the freedman and their freedmen in perpetuity, again with decreasing practical significance.

(c) *Walāʾ al-muwālāt*. The prospective patron must be a free, male and adult Muslim. The prospective client, according to the Ḥanafīs and Imāmīs, must be a free and adult non-Muslim of either sex who has no agnates or patrons in Islam, that is a *dhimmī*, convert, foundling or (in Imāmī law) a freedman without *walāʾ*; the Ḳāsimīs, however, require him to be a *ḥarbī* convert: conversion of a *dhimmī* does not give rise to *walāʾ*. The patron agrees to pay bloodmoney on behalf of the client in return for a title to the latter's estate; the parties may stipulate mutual succession. Either way, the heir by contractual *walāʾ* is excluded by any blood-relation of the deceased. Whether the contractual patron may act as marriage guardian is disputed. Unlike *walāʾ al-ʿitḳ*, the contractual relationship may be terminated as long as the patron has not had occasion to pay, but it becomes permanent thereafter.

(d) The nature of *walāʾ*. Practically every lawbook states that *walāʾ* should be regarded as a fictitious kinship tie (*al-walāʾ luḥma ka-luḥmat al-nasab*, as a famous maxim has it), and this view underlies a number of subsidiary rules generally accepted by Sunnīs and non-Sunnīs alike. Thus *walāʾ* cannot be alienated by sale, gift or bequest in classical law, though such transactions were permitted in pre-classical law; one cannot sell or give away *nasab*, as various authorities point out in *ḥadīth*. Equally, *walāʾ* cannot be inherited in the strict sense of the word; the devolution of the rights and duties vested in the tie follows special rules ensuring that the relationship functions like an agnatic tie (cf. R. Brunschvig, *Un système peu connu de succession agnatique dans le droit musulman*, in his *Etudes d'Islamologie*, Paris 1976). *Pace* Brunschvig, however, this view of *walāʾ* is not an archaic survival, but on the contrary a juristic interpretation of the late Umayyad and early ʿAbbāsid periods. It was adopted with particular forcefulness and consistency by the Sunnīs, to whom the essence of *walāʾ* lies in *taʿṣīb*, "agnatisation".

In fact, however, the legal nature of *walāʾ* is quite different from that of an agnatic tie even in classical law. For one thing, it is only in Sunnī law that the patron inherits as an agnate, and then only if he is a manumitter, not a contractual patron. For another thing, the relationship lacks reciprocity. The client is a purely passive member of the patron's agnatic kin. Indeed, for some purposes he is not a member of it at all. Thus Sunnī lawyers do not usually consider clients of Ḳuraysh [*q.v.*] eligible for the caliphate; and the question whether clients of the Hāshimites were excluded from receipt of *zakāt* [*q.v.*] on a par with their patrons remained controversial; as Ibn al-Athīr pointed out, the maxim *mawlā 'l-ḳawm minhum* (which originated in this very context) could be interpreted in a purely metaphorical vein (al-*Nihāya*, Cairo 1963, v, 228). In legal terms, *walāʾ* is a tie of dependence which derives its efficacy from the fact that the client is detached from his natal group without acquiring full membership of another. The tie undoubtedly owes its existence primarily to administrative convenience, though the administrators may well have been influenced by the legal institutions of the pre-conquest Near East (see further Crone, *Roman provincial and Islamic law*, with full references).

(e) *Mawālī* and *kafāʾa* [*q.v.*]. Classical law does not in general attach any legal significance to servile and/or non-Arab origin outside the private relationship between patron and client, but there is one major exception. Non-Arabs and freedmen cannot marry Arab women, according to the Ḥanafīs and the Shāfiʿīs. The same view prevails among the Ḥanbalīs, while contradictory views are found in the Zaydī schools. The Mālikīs, who see no harm in such unions, nonetheless allow an Arab woman to have her marriage dissolved if she marries a freedman in the belief that he is an Arab (as opposed to merely freeborn (Khalīl b. Isḥāḳ, *Mukhtaṣar*, tr. I. Guidi and D. Santillana, Milan 1919, ii, 37). Only the Ibāḍīs, the Imāmīs and, following them, the Ismāʿīlīs, consistently refuse to distinguish between Arab and non-Arab, freeborn and freed for purposes of marriage [cf. NIKĀḤ]. The complete assimilation of Arab and non-Arab Muslims allegedly brought about by the ʿAbbāsids cannot be said ever to have been achieved.

Bibliography: Given in the article.

(P. CRONE)

MAWLĀNĀ KHŪNKĀR, a title of the head of the Mawlawī order of dervishes [see MAWLAWIYYA]. The second word is the Turkish form of the Persian *khudāwandigār*, the equivalent of *mawlā*, which according to Aflākī (*Saints des derviches tourneurs*, i, 59) was bestowed on Djalāl al-Dīn by his father (the derivation from *Khūn-kār*, Persian "blood-shedder", must depend on popular etymology). Sāmī in his *Ķāmūs al-aʿlām* states that the word, besides used for "Sultan", "King", is applied to certain saintly personages, in such combinations as *pīr khūnkār* or *mullā khūnkār*. The underlying idea of such a title is probably that the saint has had committed to him the government of the world, if he choose to undertake it, an idea elaborated by Ibn ʿArabī (*Futūḥāt Makkiyya*, i, 262, ii, 407), who regards such a saint as the true *khalīfa*. The title *čelebi* is more generally recognised as that belonging to the head of the Mawlawī order (Sāmī, *op.cit.*, 510a).

Bibliography: Given in the article.

(D. S. Margoliouth*)

MAWLAWĪ, Mullā ʿAbd al-Raḥīm Taydjawzī, a Kurdish poet who composed an *ʿAķīda-nāma* and a celebrated *dīwān* in the Hawrāmī dialect of Gūrānī. He was born *ca.* 1222/1807 at Tāwagōz in Djawānrūd and died at Sarshāta, on the river Sīrwān near Ḥalabdja, *ca.* 1300/1883.

Bibliography: V. Minorsky, *The Gūrān*, in *BSOAS*, xi (1943-5), 94; Pīramērd, *Dīwān-i Mawlawī*, 2 vols., Sulaymānīya, 1938-40; ʿAlāʾ al-Dīn Sadjdjādī, *Mēzhū-y adab-ī kurdī*, Baghdād 1952.

(Ed.)

MAWLAWIYYA, a Ṣūfī order or *ṭarīķa*, in Turkish Mewlewiyye, modern Mevlevî, which takes its name from the Mawlānā ("Our Master"), the sobriquet of Djalal al-Dīn Rūmī [*q.v.*]. Although not called by this name, it appears that such a *ṭarīķa* was formed already in the Mawlānā's time, and this view is reinforced by the existence of a group of disciples around the Mawlānā, by his concern for their education and by his appointment of deputies to carry out this task during his absences. However, like many *ṭuruķ* (e.g. the Khalwatiyya [*q.v.*]), this *ṭarīķa* acquired its name at a later stage. There is no definite information that the Mawlānā's followers were called Mawlawiyya in his own time, but it is known that already at that time, the epithet Mawlānā had replaced the name Djalāl al-Dīn (see Aflākī, *Manāķib al-ʿārifīn*, ed. T. Yazıcı, Ankara 1959-61, ii, 597), and it is therefore probable that his followers were even then called Mawlawiyya.

1. Origins and ritual of the order.

An attempt will be made here to demonstrate to what extent the subsequent and relatively developed form of the order is connected with that of the Mawlānā's era. Such a demonstration shows that a great part of the contemporary customs and rules of the order also existed in the time of the Mawlānā (see Yazıcı, *Mevlânâ devrinde semâ'*, in *Şarkiyat Mecmuası*, v [1964], 135-59). In particular, it appears that certain elements of the *samāʿ* [*q.v.*] or musical ceremony, which occupies an important place in the customs and rules of the *ṭarīķa*, were found in the *samāʿ* gatherings of the Mawlānā's era (Yazıcı, *loc. cit.*). It is known that there was found a special meeting-room which formed the nucleus of the *samāʿ-khāna* of later Mawlawī *tekke*s. It is also known that there was a *djamāʿat-khāna* among the rooms constructed alongside the Mawlānā's *madrasa* by the Saldjūķ statesman Tādj al-Dīn Muʿtazz, and that the Mawlānā there listened to conversation, men of letters and the playing of the *rabāb*, and in all probability also conducted *samāʿ* (see Aflākī, i, 97, 125, 138, 252, 255). In the same fashion, the *madrasa* at which the Mawlānā taught served at that time as the *ṭarīķa*'s *tekke*, or as subsequently named, *dargāh*. It is highly probable that the *djamāʿat-khāna* adjacent to the *madrasa* was used during the Mawlānā's lifetime and after his death as a place to train novices or *murīd*s, and that a *shaykh* was found there. The first of these *shaykh*s was Ṣalāḥ al-Dīn Zarkūb, who was followed by Ḥusām al-Dīn Čelebi, Karīm al-Dīn Bektemur and Sulṭān Walad. Aflākī (i, 232) records that while the Mawlānā was alive he had two *khalīfa*s outside Konya, one at Luʾluwe Maʿdeni, the other called Madjd al-Dīn Walad-ī Čagha in the lands of Rūm, and that he gave to them the spiritual genealogy or *shadjara* of the *ṭarīķa* which he had written. However, the fact that, until Sulṭān Walad, none of these appointees came from the Mawlānā's family suggests that the Mawlānā may not have intended to found an order. For, as frequently occurs in many orders, the successor of the founder of a *ṭarīķa* is generally a member of his family. Had he had such an intention, there was no reason why he should not have appointed as his successor his son Sulṭān Walad, who possessed all the requisite qualities of a *shaykh* of a *ṭarīķa*.

There is a great probability that the chief principles of the Mawlawiyya, such as *samāʿ*, were already established in the Mawlānā's era, and that after some further development they took the form they bear today.

After Sulṭān Walad's succession, a new centre for the *ṭarīķa* was formed with the building of the *türbe*, which survives today, by ʿAlam al-Dīn Ķayṣar. At this centre—as in a *tekke*—the Ķurʾān and *Mathnawī* of the Mawlānā were read, prayers were recited and the *samāʿ* was conducted. At this period, as in the Mawlānā's time, *samāʿ* was performed individually and collectively (Aflākī, i, 356, 104, ii, 759 ff.). Such gestures as that of salutation, which occur in today's *samāʿ* ceremony, were also encountered in the Mawlānā's *samāʿ* (*ibid.*, i, 412). This type of element continued under Sulṭān Walad and Ulu ʿĀrif Čelebi (*ibid.*, ii, 613, 795, 892, 966).

However, none of the Mawlawī sources prior to 754/1353 refers to the *naʿt*, *dawr-i waladī*, *pust duʿāsī* and the organised salutation which feature in the *samāʿ* ceremonies of later eras. In sum, at that period there was no *samāʿ* taught in advance. Rather, music or some event bringing a person to ecstasy was the occasion for *samāʿ*. As is apparent from its name, the *dawr-i waladī* was linked to Sulṭān Walad. However, it appears that the reading of the Ķurʾān and of *ghazal*s [*q.v.*] before the *samāʿ* was established in the time of Ulu ʿĀrif Čelebi (Aflākī, ii, 846 ff.). It is most likely that the *samāʿ* took its final form, known as *muķābala*, in the time of Pīr ʿĀdil Čelebi (d. 864/1460).

In the hope of showing all the characteristics of the Mawlawiyya, an account will be given of its customs and rules, beginning with entry or initiation to the *ṭarīķa*.

Entry to the Mawlawiyya. Initial entry is as a *muḥibb*, and for this, application is made to a Mawlawī *shaykh*. Having indicated to the candidate that he will be admitted to the *ṭarīķa*, the *shaykh* instructs him to bathe and appear on an appointed day. The *muḥibb*, that is, the candidate *murīd*, appears on the appointed day with a *sikke* (a type of conical cap). He kisses the *shaykh*'s hand and then sits on his left. With the faces of both turned towards the *ķibla*, the *shaykh* informs him that they will read together a prayer of repentance (see A. Gölpınarlı, *Mevlevî âdâb ve erkânı*, 133). After the prayer is read, the *shaykh* takes in both hands the *sikke* brought by the candidate *murīd*, and three times—to the right, left and front of the *sikke*—reads the sūra *Ikhlāṣ* (CXII) and blows upon the *sikke*. Then he settles the candidate *murīd*, with his face to the *ķibla*, down upon his left knee and holds the *sikke* towards the *ķibla*, and having stated that he is acting on behalf of the Mawlānā, he kisses the *sikke* from the right, left and front and places it upon the candidate. With his hands upon the *sikke* he pronounces the *takbīr*, and the *sikke* is thus said to be *tekbirlenmish*. The *shaykh* then caresses the back of the candidate, whose head is resting upon his knee, raises him to his feet, and with their right hands held together they kiss. Thus the person whose *sikke* has received the *takbīr* acquires the name of *muḥibb*. The *shaykh* takes the *muḥibb* to the *dede* in the *maṭbakh* or kitchen, who will educate him. The *dede* is a person resident in one of the cells (*ḥüdjre*) of the *dargāh* or *zāwiya*, who has fulfilled his *čile* (period of trial) and been elevated to the rank of *derwīsh*.

The *muḥibb*, who is also known as *naw-niyāz*, is informed of the difficulty of the path. The *muḥibb* undertakes to devote himself completely to this path, and is then set for three days in the *maṭbakh* upon a skin known as the *saḳḳā pustu* which is believed to remove the thirst of those who thirst for the *ṭarīḳa*. The *muḥibb*, seated upon this skin upon his knees with his head bent, observes the services performed by other *murīds* who are named *djān* (literally "soul"), does not speak without need and when required to urinate, he takes over his shoulders the *khirḳa* or gown with sleeves of one of the *djāns* and goes to the latrine. When the three days are up, he is taken to the *ḳazandjī dede* (the person responsible for the *murīds*' discipline) and if he declares himself resolved to remain in the *ṭarīḳa*, he runs errands for eighteen days in the clothes in which he has come, that is to say, he carries and fetches at the double for the persons of the *tekke*. When this period ends, the position is explained to the *ashčī dede*. Upon his request, the clothes of the *muḥibb* are removed and he is dressed in the *maṭmaᶜ tennūresi*, and over this *tennūre* (or long, sleeveless gown) there is bound a belt called the *elif-i nemed*. Thus the *muḥibb* intending to enter the Mawlawiyya order (*soyunan*, "changing his garments for work") is delivered to the *ḳazandjī*, who explains to him the services which he will perform (errands, floor-sweeping etc.). While these services continue, the *muḥibb* is also taught to perform the *samāᶜ*. The *muḥibb* may not wear the *sikke* until successful in *samāᶜ*. Once his success in this matter has been demonstrated, he is given a temporary *sikke* and only after participating in the *mübtedī muḳābelesi* (a *samāᶜ* ceremony for beginners) does he join in the true ceremony. While participating in the real ceremony, he removes the *tennūre* worn for service (*ḥizmet tennūresi*) and wears instead the *samāᶜ tennūresi*, with a narrow shirt (*deste-gül*) over it and a *khirḳa* upon his back.

Upon completing the service of errand-runner, the *muḥibb* leaves his service and undertakes the functions of *pazardjīlīḳ*, that is to say, he does the *tekke*'s daily shopping. While performing this service he wears a towel on his back, a chain upon his waist and tongs upon his belt (*elif-i nemed*). At prayer times, he goes to the *masdjid* of the *dargāh* or *zāwiya*, and in the mornings joins the circle where the *ism-i djalāl* ("glorious name [of God]") is repeated. He carries out the shopping, sets and clears the table, does internal housework and other services. Thus the *muḥibb* completes 1,001 days of service. The *meydāndjī dede* informs him when he has completed his trial (*čile*), and explains that one week later a *samāᶜ* will be performed for this occasion, that *sharbat* will be drunk at this ceremony and gives the name of the *murīd* (*djān*) who will distribute the *sharbat*.

One week later, having completed his trial (*čile*), the *derwīsh* goes to the *ḥammām* and bathes, and coming to the kitchen, he removes his *tennūre* and puts on the *shalwār* or trousers, while on his upper part he puts on the *derwīsh* costume of *mintan* and *khirḳa* and again sits upon the *saḳḳā pustu* in the kitchen. That night a candlestick of 35 or 70 branches is lit. After all but the *derwīsh* performing the trial (*čile*) have eaten, the *sharbatčī* serves the prepared *sharbat* to those present. The *čilekesh* (performer of *čile*) converses with the *ṭarīḳatčī*, the *ashčī dede* or the *dedes*, and proceeds to the middle and performs a salutation (*niyāz*). The *ṭarīḳatčī* or the *ashčī dede* recites the *gülbang* (a prepared prayer) for him (for the text of the *gülbang*, see Gölpınarlı, *Mevlânâ'dan sonra mevlevîlik*, Istanbul 1953, 393). After all have departed from this ceremony, the *meydāndjī* takes him first to the *türbedār* and then to the kitchen and gives him *sharbat* to drink and food to eat. Then a white skin called *Sulṭān Walad pustu* is spread. The *meydāndjī* seats the *ashčī dede* upon the skin, and brings the *derwīsh* who has completed his trial to him. After praying that he may continue upon the path (reading the *gülbang*), the *ashčī dede* goes to his cell. The new *derwīsh* too is taken to the cell set aside for him. The *dedes* come there to congratulate him, each bringing with him a different present. He does not leave his cell for three days, and his meals are brought to his cell. After this period he is taken by the *meydāndjī dede* to the *shaykh* of the *tekke* and the ceremony of *bayᶜat* is performed (for details, see *ibid.*, 394). The *shaykh* cuts some hairs from the middle of the eyebrow and from the moustache of the *derwīsh* and pronouncing the *takbīr*, he dresses him in the *khirḳa* of the *derwīsh*. He then tells him to perform the trial of the cell (*ḥüdjre čilesi*). This trial consists of not leaving the cell for 18 days. When this period, too, has ended he is dressed by the *shaykh* in the *sikke*. With this, he acquires the title of *derwīsh* or simply of *dede* (Gölpınarlı, *Mevlevî âdâb ve erkânı*, 135). Thereafter, he begins to teach the knowledge and arts (music, etc.) which he has acquired to date to the *muḥibbs* who come after him. A *dede*, depending upon his ability, may become a *shaykh* and *khalīfa* [see KHALIFA. 3. In Islamic mysticism]. The *shaykhs* represent the Mawlawiyya order. If *shaykhs* are not *sayyids*, they wear white turbans; if they are *sayyids*, they wear turbans of a smoky colour close to purple.

Shaykhs dwell in places called *āstāna*, *dargāh* or *zāwiya*. A Mawlawī *dargāh* is composed of a *ḥaram*, *salāmlīḳ*, *samāᶜ-khāna*, *türbe*, *masdjid*, *maydān*, *maṭbakh* and *derwīsh* cells. In addition, a room called *maydān-i sharīf* is located close to the *maṭbakh*. *Muḥibbs* may not enter here; the others enter one by one after the morning prayer, the last to do so in Konya being the *ṭarīḳatčī* and elsewhere the *ashčī dede*, and having kissed the ground they sit. The *dede* called the *ṭīshārī meydāndjī* gives to each of those seated a small piece of bread from a tray. After these have been eaten, coffee is drunk and then the *murāḳaba* ("vigil") is begun. Later, the *ṭarīḳatčī* or the *ashčī bashī dede* reads sura CX of the Ḳurʾān and recites the *fātiḥa*. After the *fātiḥa* has been read together, all withdraw.

The Mawlawiyya are distinguished from all other orders by the importance which they give to *samāᶜ*. *Samāᶜ* is performed in a circular room called *samāᶜ-khāna*. Its furnishings are covered with unnailed walnut planks, and these planks appear as if polished as a result of the periodic *samāᶜ*. The room is entered through the external main door. The *samāᶜ-khāna* comprises the following sections: the space in which *samāᶜ* is conducted, the side sections reserved for male and female visitors, the *muṭrib-khāna* for the musicians, above the door opposite the *shaykh* and approached by steps, or else the section where the musicians and the tombs of the former *shaykhs* are located. This last section is separated from the *samāᶜ-khāna* by a grille which reaches to the roof. At times when the *samāᶜ* is to be performed, the *shaykh*'s skin (sc. hide or rug) is spread opposite the *miḥrāb* [*q.v.*]; it is assumed that a line stretches from the edge of this skin to the middle of the *khaṭṭ-i istiwāʾ*. This line must in no way be stepped upon.

The *samāʿ* ceremony—also known as *muḳābele* (see Anḳarāwī, *Minhādj al-fuḳarāʾ*, 68)—is performed after prayers. Beforehand, the *meydāndjī* who supervises the affairs of the *dargāh* or *meydān* goes to the *samāʿ-khāna* on the day or night when *samāʿ* will be performed, and takes the *shaykh*'s skin which is there to his apartment. With the approval of the *shaykh*, the *meydāndjī dede* stands facing the *ḳibla* opposite the location of the cells, and summons the *derwīsh*s to perform their ablutions and don the *tennūre*. Afterwards he goes to the *samāʿ-khāna* and spreads the skin of the *shaykh*. He emerges to tell the *muʾadhdhin* to call the *adhān* [*q.v.*]. After this person has called the *adhān*, the *dede*s and the *muḥibb*s perform their ablutions, don their *tennūre* and with their *khirḳa* on their backs they proceed to the *samāʿ-khāna*. After the performance of prayer, the *shaykh* sits upon his skin, and those who are to perform the *samāʿ* also sit together with him. After all have taken their places, the band of musicians takes its place. The *Mathnawīkhwān* reads an extract from the *Mathnawī*, while the *shaykh* reads his *pust duʿāsī*. They then listen to the *naʿt* performed by the musicians, and afterwards the *shaykh* and the *samāʿ-zan*s or participants all rise, striking their hands to the ground. The *shaykh*, in harmony with the music of the musicians, walks very slowly to the right, and once he has taken three steps from the skin, the person behind him takes up a position near the skin and, bowing his head in salutation, passes in front of the skin to the other side without stepping upon the *khaṭṭ-i istiwāʾ* and stands with his face towards the skin. The one who follows him also passes before the skin. These two participants, standing opposite one another, look at one another face to face. They then salute one another, drawing the right hand from above the left from within the *khirḳa* to the heart, and the left hand to the right side. Next, one turns and follows the other who goes in front. All the *djān*s act in this way before the skin. Then they walk in harmony with the tempo. When the *shaykh* comes before the skin, he stops and finds the most senior *naw-niyāz* before him. They exchange mutual salutations. Thus the first *dawra* or sequence is completed. Second and third *dawra*s follow in the same fashion. When the third *dawra* is finished, the *shaykh* goes towards his skin and at this moment a *nay* or flute improvisation begins and continues until the *shaykh* sits upon his skin: once he has done, so the ceremony begins. The *shaykh* and the *samāʿ-zans* salute. The *samāʿ-zans* remove their *khirḳa*s and place them on the ground. Then, passing the right arm over the left they link arms in a diagonal fashion, with the right hand holding the left shoulder and the left hand holding the right shoulder. The *shaykh* walks in front of the skin, salutes, and the others perform the same movement. Next the *samāʿ-zans*, setting off on the right foot, approach the *shaykh* one by one, salute him and kiss his hand. They then open their arms, the left hand being a little higher, take three short steps and begin to turn. The *samāʿ-zan bashī* or leader of the participants has charge of the *samāʿ*. The first to turn is followed in identical fashion by the others. When the *salām* is to be given, the *shaykh*, who is beside the skin, advances and makes salutation. The *samāʿ-zans* come together in twos and threes, touching each other's shoulders diagonally, and form groups. The second *dawra* is then begun; this resembles the first. This time, the *samāʿ-zans* perform a salutation before the *shaykh* and kiss his hand. The third and fourth *dawra*s follow in the same fashion.

According to a tradition among the Mawlawiyya, until the reign of Selīm III (1789-1807 [*q.v.*]) the custom of the Mawlānā's era was maintained and *samāʿ* was performed only at moments of ecstasy; nonetheless, it appears that before this date *samāʿ* was performed on specific days. D'Ohsson (*Tableau général de l'empire Othoman*, Paris 1789, ii, 304) records that Tuesdays and Fridays were chosen for *samāʿ* ceremonies. There is a strong probability that Selīm III's frequent visits to *mawlawī-khāna*s and the need to perform *samāʿ* in his honour led to the ending of this custom, and *samāʿ* began to be performed every day. However, the difficulty of performing *samāʿ* daily in any single *samāʿ-khāna* was recognised, and it became the practice to perform it in a different *mawlawī-khāna* on each day of the week. Yet in cities outside Istanbul, the *samāʿ* ceremony was performed only on Fridays, after Friday prayers. Nowadays, for reasons which are touristic rather than religious, the *samāʿ* ceremony is performed for one week annually in Konya between 11 and 17 December (see H. Ritter, *Die Mevlanafeier in Konya vom 11-17 Dezember 1960*, in *Oriens*, xv, 249-70; cf. Gölpınarlı, *Mevlânâ'dan sonra mevlevîlik*, 371-80, and *Mevlevî âdâb ve erkânı*, 77-89).

The Mawlawiyya have a further *samāʿ* ceremony, called *ʿayn-i djemʿ* (*ʿayn al-djamʿ*). It is used in the sense of uniting or gathering. This was often performed at night, when the Mawlawī brothers gathered in ecstasy and love in the consciousness of unity with God. This ceremony was performed either to fulfil a condition set by a donator of a *waḳf* [*q.v.*] to the *tekke*, or for the sake of someone who had made a vow, or upon the personal request of an *ʿāshiḳ* or devotee of the Mawlānā. This *samāʿ* was not performed in the *samāʿ-khāna* but in a rectangular room. If the *samāʿ* took place at night, it was performed after the eating of a meal and the performance of the evening prayer (details in Gölpınarlı, *op. cit.*, 101). This ceremony was also performed on the anniversary of the Mawlānā's death (6 Djumādā II 672/17 December 1273). For according to the Mawlawiyya, this day marks the Mawlānā's birth into eternity. As this date changes annually in accordance with the *hidjrī* calendar, when the anniversary occurred in summer or spring rush mats and rugs would be spread on the *türbe*-facing side of the pond which lies outside the *maydān odasī* of the *dargāh* in Konya, and the *ʿayn-i djemʿ* would be performed in the open air.

The Mawlawiyya have striven to give meanings to the *samāʿ-khāna* and to the gestures made by the *samāʿ-zans* during *samāʿ*. Thus the right-hand arc of the circular *samāʿ-khāna* represents the apparent world, while the left-hand arc represents the unseen world of meaning within the apparent world. Similarly, the right arc represents the descent from absolute being to humanity, the left, spiritual ascent, maturity and the path to God (*sulūk*). The starting-point of the *khaṭṭ-i istiwāʾ* (i.e. the place of the *shaykh*) is a sign of the world of absolute being, while the point directly opposite is a sign of the rank of humanity.

The *derwīsh* who performs the *samāʿ* is called *samāʿ-zan*. During the *samāʿ*, the *samāʿ-zan*'s hand raised to heaven is a sign of taking from God, while his downward-pointing left hand is a sign that what is taken from God with the right hand is given to the people. The *samāʿ-zan* believes that what has thus been taken from God is given to the people, that he himself exists only in appearance and in reality does not exist, and that he is nothing but an intermediary between God and the people. In this position, his arms resemble a *lām-alif* (لا), while the body between the two arms is like an *alif*, thus giving the form of *Lā ilāha illā 'llāh*.

The first *dawra* of the *samā*ᶜ ceremony shows the manifestation of God, in whom all names and qualities are found. At the end of this *dawra*, God is manifested with the name "*salām*". Thus the *sālik*'s knowledge of God's unity reaches the degree of *ᶜilm al-yaḳīn*, i.e. his knowledge of God's unity has the degree of certain knowledge. In the second *dawra*, this knowledge reaches the degree of vision (*ᶜayn al-yaḳīn*). In the third *dawra* he becomes what he sees, i.e. his knowledge becomes *ḥaḳḳ al-yaḳīn*. The fourth *dawra* represents God's existence and being (Gölpınarlı, *ibid.*, 107 ff.).

Another characteristic which distinguishes the Mawlawiyya from other orders is *čile* (trial). The Mawlawī *čile* does not, as in other orders, consist of the endurance of such hardships as eating and drinking little, remaining without sleep and the performance of an extreme degree of *dhikr*, all generally in a closed place; instead, it consists of 1,001 days of service, the equivalent in *abdjad* enumeration of the word *riḍā*, particularly in the kitchen of the *tekke*. The *muḥibb* or *naw-niyāz* fulfils his *čile* by assisting those who direct the "eighteen service" and accomplishing the tasks they order (for the services, see Gölpınarlı, *Mevlânâ'dan sonra mevlevîlik*, 397 ff., and *Mevlevî âdâb ve erkanı*, 45 ff.). Those who principally accomplish this "eighteen service" are the *ḳazandjî dede*, who takes care of the discipline of the *naw-niyāz*, the *khalīfa dede* who instructs them in the customs of the *ṭarīḳa*, the *čamashîrdjî dede* who washes or has washed the linen of the *dede*s and the *naw-niyāz*, the *ābrīzdjî dede* who cleans the latrines, the *bulashîḳčî* (washer-up), the *süpürüdjü* (sweeper), the *pazardjî dede* who does the shopping in the mornings, the *somatčî dede* who lays and clears the table, etc.

The Mawlawiyya have developed in two forms: the Shems ḳolu or branch which takes love and ecstasy as its basis and acts like the Ḳalenderiyya, and the Sulṭān Walad ḳolu which strives to remain attached to the *Sharīᶜa*. The Shems ḳolu has accepted as a principle the Malāmatiyya [*q.v.*]; there is thus a close resemblance between this branch and the Bektashīs [*q.v.*]. This resemblance derives from the fact that both spring from a Ḳalender source. The 10th/16th century Ottoman author Wāḥidī ranks the Shemsī, Bektashī and the Ḳalenderiyya together both on account of their attire and on account of their beliefs (*Manāḳib-i Khʷādja-yi djihān ve natīdja-yi djān*, fols. 65b-75b; cf. Khaṭīb-i Fārsī, *Manāḳib-i Djamāl al-Dīn-i Sāwī*, preface, p. xxi).

The Sulṭān Walad ḳolu has been more influential upon orders which conform to the *Sharīᶜa*. Amongst these the Gülshaniyya, a branch of the Khalwatiyya, have been considerably influenced by this branch of the Mawlawiyya. The customs of the Gülshaniyya openly reveal this influence (cf., Shemelī-zāde Aḥmed Efendi, *Shīve-yi ṭarīḳat-i Gülshaniyye* (with the *Manāḳib-i Ibrāhīm-i Gülshanī*), 509-44).

In general, the Mawlawiyya show extreme respect and love for all that may be of use to man, whether animate or inanimate, and in this connection they have created a new language. For example, in place of *öpmek* ("to kiss") they use *görüshmek* ("to converse"), in place of *ḳapamaḳ* ("to close") they use *ṣîrlamaḳ*, in place of "to eat or drink something" they use *djünbüshlenmek*, in place of *murīd* they use *djān* or *naw-niyāz*; these aside, they employ as technical terms *ayaḳ mühürlemek* for "to place the big toe of the right foot on top of the big toe of the left foot", *direk* for "the *samā*ᶜ*-zan* not to turn with the left foot revolving on its axis", *čivi tutmaḳ* for "to put one's foot down on the spot and turn to make *samā*ᶜ", etc. (see Gölpınarlı, *Mevlevî âdâb ve erkânı*, 5-47).

As a result of the efforts of the members of this order, which has enjoyed close links with literature from its inception, a Mawlawī literature has been formed. This has not been confined simply to themselves, but has also left its imprint upon a number of famous poets of the Ottoman *Dīwān* literature. Amongst the poets of this literature, Nefᶜī, Nabī and Shaykh Ghālib [*q.vv.*] were Mawlawīs.

From the Mawlānā's era to most recent times, music has always occupied an important place among the members of this *ṭarīḳa*. To the musical instruments which initially consisted solely of the *nay* and the *rabāb*, there were subsequently added the *ᶜūd*, *kaman*, *ḳānūn*, *santūr*, *ṭanbūr*, *kemenče* and *girift*, and most recently the piano and the violincello. The first piano brought to Istanbul was played in the *mawlawīkhāna* at Ḳumḳapîsî. However, the piano and violincello have not won much favour. It is most probable that the musical compositions recited in the Mawlānā's time were anonymous, but later, especially during *samā*ᶜ, the recitations were selected from the poems of the Mawlānā, Sulṭān Walad and Ulu ᶜĀrif Čelebi. The Mawlawis produced a number of composers (see Gölpınarlı, *Mevlana'dan sonra mevlevilik*, 456 ff.).

In conclusion, this order took its basic principles from the Mawlānā. These principles, which rest upon a limitless love of humanity and a moderate permissiveness, secured the *ṭarīḳa*'s popularity within a short period. To these principles should be added the importance given to music and dance, which were not well-viewed in religious circles, but which human beings cannot do without. The considerable interest which was shown by outsiders (*čevre*) for these reasons further developed the order. Just as the customs and rules of the *ṭarīḳa* were from time to time re-ordered on this pretext, so also new ones were added to them. Further, the Mawlawī *tekke*s partook of the nature of schools, in order first to understand the thoughts of the Mawlānā, which are the basis of the order, and also to be of service to society. This ensured that the *ṭarīḳa*'s members were in general literate, and were qualified in one of the fine arts like literature, music and calligraphy. For this reason, this order was popular in intellectual circles.

Bibliography: Aflākī, *Manāḳib al-ᶜārifīn*, ed. T. Yazıcı, Ankara 1959, 1961, 2 vols.; Farīdūn b. Aḥmed Sipahsālār, *Risāla-yi Aḥwāl-i Mawlānā Djalāl al-Dīn Mawlawī*, ed. Saᶜīd Nafīsī, Tehran 1325/1946; Thaḳib Dede, *Safīna-yi nafīsa-yi Mawlawiyyān*, Cairo 1283/1867; Fayḍ Allāh, *Ishārāt al-maᶜnawīya fi āyīn al-Mawlawiyya*, Istanbul 1283/1866-7; anon., *Āstāna-yi ᶜaliyya ve bilād-i thalātha'de kā'in olan mewdjūd ve muḥtariḳ tekkelerin isim ve shöhretleri ve muḳābala-yi sharīfa günleri*, Istanbul 1256/1840; Rusūkhī Ismāᶜīl Anḳarawī, *Minhādj al-fuḳarā'*, Istanbul 1256/1840; idem, *Risāla-yi mukhtaṣara ve mufīda-yi uṣūl-i ṭarīḳat-i nāzanīn we bey'at az dast-i yaḳīn-i djanāb-i Mawlawī*, Süleymaniye Kütüphanesi, Halet Ef. no. 351; Meḥmed Ḍiyā (Iḥtifāldjî), *Yeñiḳapî mewlewī-khānesi*, Istanbul 1329/1911; idem, *Istanbul ve Boghazîdjî*, Istanbul 1336/1918, 2 vols.; *Mevlevî âyinleri* (Istanbul Konservatuarı neşriyatı), Istanbul 1934-9; S. N. Ergun, *Türk musikisi antolojisi*, Istanbul 1942; Şehabeddin Uzluk, *Mevlânâ'nın türbesi*, Konya 1946; Badīᶜ al-Zaman Furūzānfar, *Risāla dar taḥḳīḳ-i zindagānī-i Mawlānā Djalāl al-Dīn Muḥammad* ..., Tehran 1354/1975; A. Gölpınarlı, *Mevlânâ Celaleddin*, Istanbul 1952; idem, *Mevlânâ'dan sonra mevlevîlik*, Istanbul 1953; idem, *Mevlevî âdâb ve erkâni*, Istanbul 1963; Rıfkı Melûl Meriç, *Hicrî 1131 tarihinde Enderunlu şairler, hattatlar ve musiki san'atkârları*, in *Istanbul Enstitüsü Dergisi*, ii (Istanbul

1956); Fāḍīl Meḥmed Pas̲h̲a Bosnalî, *S̲h̲arḥ al-awrād al-musammā bi-ḥaḳāʾiḳ ad̲h̲kār Mawlānā*, Istanbul 1283/1866-7; *Awrād-î mawlawiyya*, Istanbul 1282/1865-6; ʿAbd al-G̲h̲anī al-Nābulusī, *al-ʿUḳūd al-luʾluʾiyya fī ṭarīḳat al-sāda al-mawlawiyya*, Istanbul Üniversitesi Kütüphanesi, no. AY 3511, Tkish. tr., no. TY 2128; Esrār Meḥmed Dede, *Defter-i derwīs̲h̲ān*, nr. TY 6765; Fāḳîrî, *Taʿrīfāt*, TY 3051; Meḥmed Čelebi (Dīwāne), *Manẓūm risāle* (explanation of the Mawlawī *muḳābele*), Konya Müze kütüphanesi, no. 109/49.4.17; ʿAlī Nuṭḳî, *Defter-i derwīs̲h̲ān*, Süleymaniye kütüphanesi, Nafiz no. 1194; Aḥmed Dede (Köseč), *al-Tuḥfa al-bahiyya fī ṭarīkat al-Mawlawiyya*, Istanbul Üniv. Kütüphanesi, no. AY 3905; K̲h̲alīl Ibrāhīm (As̲h̲čî Dede), *As̲h̲čî Dede'nin k̲h̲āṭîratî*, no. TY 78-80, 3 vols.; Wāḥidi, *Manāḳib-i K̲h̲ʷad̲j̲a-yi d̲j̲ihān va natīd̲j̲a-yi d̲j̲ān*, Atıf Efendi Kûtüphanesi, no. 242 (very interesting 10th/16th century survey of ten orders in the Ottoman empire; edition prepared by T. Yazıcı in the press).

For accounts of the Mawlawī ritual and organisation by western travellers and observers, see J. P. Brown, *The dervishes*, Istanbul 1868, 196-206, new ed. by H. A. Rose, London 1927, 250-8; Cl. Huart, *Konia, la ville des derviches tourneurs*, Paris 1897 (who also translated Aflākī's *Manāḳib al-ʿārifīn* into French as *Les saints des derviches tourneurs*, Paris 1918-22); V. Cuinet, *La Turquie d'Asie*, Paris 1890, 832; M. Hartmann, *Der islamische Orient*, 1910, iii, 12; Lucy M. Garnett, *Mysticism and magic in modern Turkey*, London 1912; H. C. Lukach, *The city of dancing dervishes*, London 1914; S. Anderson, *The whirling and howling dervishes*, in *MW*, xiii (1923), 181-92. (T. Yazıcı)

2. Relations with other orders.

Although the earlier mystics, such as al-D̲j̲unayd, Bisṭāmī and al-Ḥallād̲j̲ are mentioned in Aflākīs' *Manāḳib* with profound reverence, the treatment of founders of orders who came near D̲j̲alāl al-Dīn's time is very different. ʿAbd al-Ḳādir al-D̲j̲īlānī is ignored, Ibn ʿArabī mentioned with contempt, and al-Rifāʿī with severe condemnation. Ḥād̲j̲d̲j̲ī Bekṭās̲h̲ is represented as having sent a messenger to inquire into the proceedings of D̲j̲alāl al-Dīn and to have acknowledged the supremacy of the latter. At a later period, the rivalry of the Mawlawī with the Bekṭās̲h̲ī order became acute.

It has been shown by F. W. Hasluck (*Christianity and Islam under the Sultans*, Oxford 1929, ii, 370 ff.) that the environment wherein the Mawlawī order originated was favourable to Christians, and that throughout its history it showed itself tolerant and inclined to regard all religions as reconcilable on a philosophic basis. He suggests that the veneration of the Muslims of Konya for the supposed burial-place of Plato (in a mosque which was once the church of St. Amphilochius) may have been intentionally favoured by the Mawlawī dervishes, or possibly their founder, as providing a cult which Muslim and Christian might share on equal terms. In three other sanctuaries of Konya, one of them the mausoleum of D̲j̲alāl al-Dīn himself, he found evidence of a desire to provide an object of veneration to the adherents of both systems. It is not, however, easy to accept his inference that some sort of religious compromise on a philosophic basis was devised between the Sald̲j̲ūḳ Sultan ʿAlāʾ al-Dīn, D̲j̲alāl al-Dīn, and the local Christian clergy. It appears from Aflākī that the order was frequently exposed to persecution from the *fuḳahāʾ* in consequence of the music and dancing; and they found an analogy in Christian services to the employment of the former. They were credited in recent times with having restrained the massacres of Armenians.

3. Spread of the order.

Aflākī attributes its propagation outside Konya to D̲j̲alāl al-Dīn's son and second successor, Sulṭān Bahāʾ al-Dīn Walad who "filled Asia Minor with his lieutenants" (tr. Huart, ii, 262). It would appear, however, from Ibn Baṭṭūṭa's narrative (*Riḥla*, ii, 282-4, Eng. tr. Gibb, ii, 430-1) that the order's following was not at that time extensive outside Konya and was largely confined to Anatolia, although it does seem that in the time of Ulu ʿĀrif Čelebī (d. 720/1320) a Mawlawī *dargāh* existed in the Il-K̲h̲ānid centre of Sulṭāniyya in Ād̲h̲arbāyd̲j̲ān (see Aflākī, ii, 896). At this period, *zāwiya*s or *tekke*s were set up in such Anatolian towns as Toḳat, Lāranda and Kütahya, and thanks to the efforts of Dīwāna Maḥmūd Čelebi (d. in the first half of the 10th/16th century), others were founded in Istanbul, Rumelia and other Anatolian towns, and in the Arab lands, at Lād̲h̲aḳiyya and Aleppo and in Egypt and Algiers.

The story told after Saʿd al-Dīn by Von Hammer (*GOR*, i, 147) and others, that as early as 759/1357, Sulaymān son of Ork̲h̲ān received a cap from a Mawlawī dervish at Bulayr, has been shown by Hasluck (ii, 613) to be a fiction. The historians make no allusion to any importance attaching to the Mawlawī chief when Murād I took Konya in 788/1386; but when the city was taken by Murād II in 838/1435, peace was negotiated, according to Saʿd al-Dīn (i, 358) by Mawlānā Ḥamza, but according to Nes̲h̲rī (quoted in *ibid.*) by the descendant of Mawlānā D̲j̲alāl al-Dīn al-Rūmī, ʿĀrif Čelebi, "who united all the glories of worth and pedigree, and possessed mystic attainments"; the rebellious vassal supposed that a holy man of the family of the Mawlānā would inspire more confidence. The same person performed a similar service in 846/1442 (Saʿd al-Dīn, i, 371). According to V. Cuinet (*La Turquie d'Asie*, i, 829) Selīm I when passing through Konya in 922/1516 in pursuit of the Persians (?) ordered the destruction of the *Mawlawī-k̲h̲āna*, at the instance of the *S̲h̲ayk̲h̲ al-Islām*; and though this command was repealed, the moral and religious authority of the head of the order was gravely compromised. That the saints of Konya were highly reverenced in the Ottoman Empire later in the 10th/16th century appears from the list of graves visited by Sayyid ʿAlī Ḳapūdān in 961/1554, which commences with those of D̲j̲alāl al-Dīn, his father and his son (Pečewī, *Taʾrīk̲h̲*, Istanbul 1283/1866-7, i, 371). In 1043/1634 Murād IV assigned the *k̲h̲arād̲j̲* of Konya to the Čelebi. Yet the first reference to "dancing dervishes" in Istanbul which Hasluck produces is from the time of Sultan Ibrāhīm (1049-58/1640-8).

Mawlawī *tekke*s were divided into two classes, the *āstāna* and the *zāwiya*, the former being considered as more prestigious, with the *čile* (see section 1. above) being performed there. During the high Ottoman period, there were *āstāna*s, apart from the *āstāna-yi ʿaliyya* called Ḥuḍūr-i Pīr at Konya itself, at Bursa, Kütahya, Ḳaraḥiṣār, Manisa, Eskis̲h̲ehir, Ḳasṭamonu and Gelibolu in Anatolia, at Yeñis̲h̲ehir in Rumelia, and at Aleppo and in Egypt, plus the *āstāna* which served as the fourth of the Mawlawī *tekke*s in Istanbul. During this period, there were 76 Mawlawī *zāwiya*s in towns alone (details in A. Gölpınarlı, *Mevlânâ'dan sonra mevlevîlik*, 335). Of European authors writing towards the end or just after the Ottoman era, Cuinet mentions three *Mawlawī-k̲h̲āna*s of the first rank and one *tekke* of the second in Istanbul and the neighbourhood; he gives the names of the saints whose tombs they contain, without dates. He mentions seven other *Mawlawī-khānas* of the first rank, at Konya, Manisa, Ḳaraḥiṣār, Baḥariyya, Egypt (Cairo?) Gallipoli and Bursa; and as the more celebrated of the second rank, that of Shams-i Tabrīzī at Konya, and those in Medina, Damascus and Jerusalem. To these, Hasluck adds *tekke*s at Canea (Crete), founded about 1880, Ḳaramān, Ramla, Tatar (in Thessaly), and possibly Tempe (for one in Izmir, see Anderson, in *MW*, xiii [1922], 161; for one in Salonica, see the work of Garnett, and for one in Cyprus, that of Lukach cited in the *Bibl.* to section 1. above).

In the aftermath of the Kurdish revolt in eastern Anatolia against the new Republican Turkish government in February-April 1925, which had been led by the Naḳshbandī Shaykh Saʿīd of Palu, Kemāl Atatürk decided upon the suppression of all the dervish orders in Turkey. Hence by the decree of 4 September 1925, all the dervish *tekke*s were closed, and the library of the *Mawlawī-khāna* of Konya was transferred to the Museum of that town (see *OM* [1925], 455, [1926], 584).

4. Political importance of the order.

Reference may be made to Hasluck's *Christianity and Islam under the Sultans*, ii, 604-5, for refutation of the stories uncritically reproduced by Cuinet and some less authoritative writers. In these "the Shaykh of the Mawlawī becomes first the legitimate successor by blood of the Saldjūḳ dynasty, and finally the real caliph!" Hasluck supposes these tales to be based on the supposed "traditional right" of the Mawlawī Shaykh to gird the new sultan with a sword. This right cannot be traced earlier than 1058/1648, and appears to have obtained recognition in the 19th century. It would seem that reforming sultans used the Mawlawī order as a makeweight against the Bekṭāshīs, who supported the Janissaries, and then against the ʿulamāʾ, who supported the treatment of the Muslim community as a privileged community against the *dhimmī*s. In later Ottoman times, Sultans ʿAbd al-ʿAzīz and Meḥemmed Reshād were members of the order. (D. S. Margoliouth*)

5. The last vestiges of the order in the Arab world and the Balkans.

Following the suppression of the Ṣūfī orders in Turkey, the last Čelebi (Muḥammad Bākir) took up residence in the *āsitāna* of the Mawlawiyya in Aleppo (L. Massignon, *Annuaire du monde musulman 1954*, Paris 1955, 201). Ritual gatherings were held regularly till the early 1950s, when the last active *shaykh* of this *āsitāna* (Muḥammad Shāhū) died. In the *takiyya* of the Mawlawiyya in Ḥimṣ (last *shaykh*, Nūr ʿUthmān), ritual gatherings were held into the 1940s, and in the *takiyya* in Latakia (last *shaykh*, Bākir Efendi) gatherings continued into the 1950s.

The small but active Mawlawiyya community in Damascus, where the *āsitāna* dates back to the late 10th/16th century (Muḥammad Kurd ʿAlī, *Khiṭaṭ al-Shām*, Beirut 1972, vi, 139), disappeared in the 1960s. The last *shaykh* of the order in Damascus, *shaykh* Fāʾiḳ b. Muḥammad Saʿīd al-Mawlawī, died in 1965 (F. de Jong, *Les confréries mystiques musulmanes au Machreq arabe: centres de gravité, signes de déclin et de renaissance*, in A. Popovic and G. Veinstein, *Les ordres mystiques dans l'Islam. Cheminements et situation actuelle*, Paris 1986, 214). His son, Muḥammad Djalāl, published a new edition of the *awrād (Awrād al-sāda al-Mawlawiyya*, Damascus 1395/1975) and tried to revive the order without much success. In Damascus, the Mawlawiyya played a prominent role in the religious celebrations in which the Ṣūfī orders used to participate (cf. Muḥammad Djawād Mashkūr and Ḥasan Ghurawī Iṣfahānī, *Ṣufiyān-i Mawlawī dar Dimashk*, in *Honar va Mardom*, Tehran [April 1976], 2-6, and Munīr Kayyāl, *Ramaḍān wa taḳālīduhu al-Dimashḳiyya*, Damascus n.d., 108, 117). The gathering in the Mawlawiyya *āsitāna* on the night of 27 Ramaḍān used to draw large crowds (Kayyāl, 116).

In Lebanon, the Mawlawiyya had *takiyya*s in Tripoli and in Beirut. The *takiyya* in Tripoli still functioned in the 1960s. It fell into a state of dilapidation after the death of its last *shaykh*, Anwar al-Ṭarābulusī. In the early 1970s, the *takiyya* was restored (ʿAbd al-Salām Tadmurī, *Taʾrīkh wa-āthār masādjid wa-madāris madīnat Ṭarāblus fī ʿaṣr al-Mamālīk*, Tripoli 1974, 52-4). In Beirut in the 1960s and 1970s, members of the order gathered in the *takiyya* twice weekly to recite the *awrād* and to study mystical texts; the *samāʿ* was not performed any more. The last *shaykh* of the Mawlawiyya in Beirut, *shaykh* Aḥmad ʿUshshāḳ, lost his life in the Israeli bombardment of the city in May 1982. The *takiyya* in Jerusalem ceased to function at the end of the 19th century (De Jong, *The Sufi orders in nineteenth- and twentieth-century Palestine*, in *SI*, lviii [1983], 171).

In Cairo, the *samāʿ* performed in the *takiyya* (*āsitāna*) of the Mawlawiyya after the Friday worship was a tourist attraction at the end of the 19th and in the early 20th century (cf. De Jong, *Ṭuruq and Ṭuruq-linked institutions in nineteenth-century Egypt*, Leiden 1978, 170). In 1903, the *takiyya* was placed under the jurisdiction of the *Dīwān al-Awḳāf*, which had the right to appoint the *shaykh* of the *takiyya* and administered its *awḳāf* (De Jong, 137). The *takiyya* was closed in December 1954, as were all the *takāyā* in Egypt which fell under the jurisdiction of the Ministry of *Awḳāf* (*al-Ahrām*, 13 Dec. 1954). Subsequently, the Ministry also suspended the regular payments from the revenues of the *awḳāf* established in favour of the Mawlawiyya to the resident dervishes, who then left the *takiyya* and dispersed. Thereafter, the *takiyya* was used as a primary school.

In the Balkans, the Mawlawiyya survived into the post-Ottoman era in Greece and in Yugoslavia only. In Greece, the *tekke* in Thessaloniki seems to have functioned till the exchange of the Orthodox and Muslim populations between Greece and Turkey in 1923-4 (Cf. B. Δημητριάδη, *Τοπογραφία τῆς Θεσσαλονίκης κατὰ τὴν ἐποχὴν τῆς Τουρκοκρατίας*, Thessaloniki 1983, 386 f.). In Yugoslavia, the *tekke* of Sarajevo, known as Tekija na Bendbaši, still functioned in the early 1920s. It was demolished in 1959 (cf. Dž. Ćehajić, *Dželalludin Rumi i Mevlevizam u Bosni i Hercegovini*, in *Prilozi za orijentalnu filologiju*, xxiv [1974], 100 ff.). In 1925, *tekke*s still existed in the towns of Štip, Bitola, Veles, Peć and Skopje. Cf. D. Gadžanov, *Mohamedani pravoslavni i mohamedani sektanti v Makedonija*, in *Makedonski pregled*, i/4 (sofia 1925), 63; and N. Hafiz, *Yugoslavya'da Mevlevi tekkeleri*, in Fevzi Halici (ed.), *Mevlâna ve yaşama sevinci*, Ankara 1978, 175 ff. (also published in *Çevren*, vi [Priştine 1978], no. 20, 37-43). The *tekke* in Peć ceased to function in 1941, and the *tekke* in Skopje in 1945 (Hafiz, 40).

Bibliography: Given in the article.

(F. de Jong)

MAWLĀY (a.), "my lord", an honorific title borne by the Moroccan sultans of the Sharīfian dynasties (Saʿdids and ʿAlawids) who were descended from al-Ḥasan b. ʿAlī [see ḤASANĪ], with the exception of those who were called Muḥammad and whose title was therefore Sayyidī/Sīdī (but the form Maḥammad freely altered does not exclude the usage of Mawlāy in front of the monarch's name). The articles devoted to the two dynasties considered [see ʿALAWĪS and SAʿDIDS] contain or will contain in general sufficient information on the constituent sultans, but some of these have been or will be the subjects of articles in the alphabetical place of their name (i.e. without Mawlāy or Sayyidī). These include among the Saʿdids: ʿAbd Allāh al-G̲h̲ālib bi-llāh and Aḥmad al-Manṣūr; and among the ʿAlawids: al-Ras̲h̲īd, ʿAbd Allah b. Ismāʿīl, Muḥammad b. ʿAbd Allāh, Sulaymān, ʿAbd al-Raḥmān b. His̲h̲ām, Muḥammad b. ʿAbd al-Raḥmān, ʿAbd al-ʿAzīz, ʿAbd al-Ḥafīẓ [s.v. AL-ḤAFĪẒ], Yūsuf and Muḥammad V. As the result of an error of classification, the biographies of four other sultans will have to appear later.   (ED.)

MAWLĀY IDRĪS, Zāwiyat Mawlāy Idrīs, town in Morocco, an urban settlement of some 10,000 inhabitants situated on the west bank of D̲j̲abal Zarḥūn and attached to the slopes of the Farṭ al-Bīr. It is a mountain city, in contrast to the ancient Roman city of Volubilis (Walīlā/Walīlī) which stands nearby, in the plain on the north-western side. In spite of this contrast between the two towns, their histories are linked and neither can be studied in isolation.

First of all, it is necessary to dismiss the belief according to which Mawlāy Idrīs was founded by Idrīs I when he came to take refuge in the area accompanied by his freedman Ras̲h̲id, fleeing from the Orient where he had drawn upon himself the wrath of the great ʿAbbāsid caliph Hārūn al-Ras̲h̲īd. This is, indeed, the version which is given by local guides to visiting tourists, but it is of no relevance for the historian.

For a proper concept of the origin of the Zāwiya, it is to Volubilis that the researchers must turn. In the view of many people, the latter is an essentially and solely Roman town which apparently fell into ruins with the departure of its first inhabitants. The truth is quite otherwise: in fact, Volubilis survived not only the departure of the Romans (early 4th century A.D.) but also the advent of Islam, and was still in existence at the time when Fās was founded jointly by Idrīs I and Idrīs II (cf. Lévi-Provençal, *La fondation de Fès*, in *AIEO Alger*, iv (1938), 23-52; art. repr. in *Islam d'Occident*, Paris 1948, 3-41). The evidence for the survival of Volubilis beyond the Roman period is, in fact, substantial and may appropriately be considered here.

The first indications of the survival of this town are of an archaeological nature. In his work *Essai sur l'histoire du massif de Mawlāy Idrīs* (Rabat 1938), P. Berthier has published 12 photographs which illustrate very clearly, above the Roman stratum, strata of an early period where Roman materials have been re-used for construction purposes; these materials include shafts of columns, counter-weights of oil-presses and even ornamental cornices which have obviously been detached from their original location. Furthermore, it is possible to observe between the Roman stratum and the later strata a considerable difference in base level, amounting in places to 1 m or 1.20 m.

These indications of a prolonged existence after the Roman period are confirmed by more precise evidence: for the first period, between the Imperial reforms of Diocletian and the advent of Islam (early 4th century A.D. to end of 7th century, approximately four centuries), we possess three Christian funeral inscriptions dating from the years 595, 649 and 655 A.D. (see J. Carcopino and R. Thouvenot, in *Hespéris*, 1928/2, 135-45, 1935/3-4, 131-9). It is to be noted that one of these inscriptions has been used for a second time in a later context.

Walīlī, no longer known as Volubilis, continued throughout this long lapse of time to lead an independent existence. This period, corresponding in the general history of Africa to the ascendancy of the Vandals and Byzantium, is one of almost total obscurity with regard to Morocco. All that can be stated with certainty is that this land had facing it, in the Iberian peninsula, the kingdom of the Visigoths, and was inhabited by Christians, Jews (N. Slousch, *Hébréo-Phéniciens et Judéo-Berbères*, in *AM*, xiv [1908], 1-473), and no doubt also by animists and idolators.

This strange gap in our knowledge is one of the most perplexing features of the history of Morocco, in view of the fact that we are relatively well informed as to the history of other North African countries and, in particular, of Tunisia and eastern Numidia.

With the arrival of Islam, according to the Arabic texts, ʿUḳba b. Nāfiʿ presented himself before Walīlī and there routed a Berber army (cf. Ibn ʿId̲h̲ārī, tr. Lévi-Provençal, in *Arabica*, i/1 [1954], 38), but he does not seem to have entered the town, which from this time onward began to serve as a magnet for numerous Muslim arrivals.

It seems that the two Idrīs [*q.vv.*] were not the first Muslims to establish themselves on the site of the former Roman settlement, since Muslim coinage of a time prior to the arrival of the former has been discovered. The tribe of the Awraba, also fugitives from the East, apparently preceded him there. In his *Rawḍ al-ḳirṭās* (tr. Beaumier, 24, 29), Ibn Abī Zarʿ indicates also that a mosque, of which no trace has been discovered, existed at Walīlī, and it was there, he says, that Ras̲h̲id presented Idrīs, son of Idrīs, to the people in order to have him recognised as sovereign of the Mag̲h̲rib.

Evidence that all these events did indeed take place on the former site of the Roman town exists in the form of the many coins of the Muslim period which have been discovered there: these discoveries in fact include not only Muslim coins originating in the East, sometimes in the form of treasure, but also products of other Moroccan mints such as Ṭudg̲h̲a as well as Walīlī itself, which possessed a mint of its own (see P. Berthier, *Essai*, 59; G. S. Colin, *Monnaies de la période idrisside trouvées à Volubilis*, in *Hespéris*, 1936/2, 113-25; D. Eustache, *Monnaies musulmanes trouvées à Volubilis*, in *ibid.*, 1956/1-2, 133-97; idem, *Monnaies musulmanes trouvées dans la maison au compas*, in *Bulletin d'Archéologie marocaine*, vi [1966], 349-64; on the entire question of coinages, idem, *Corpus des dirhams idrissites et contemporains*, Rabat 1970-1, is extremely informative, in particular with regard to Walīlī, 162-9).

Volubilis was still in existence at the time of the foundation of Fās by the two Idrīs since it is known, thanks to the famous article of Lévi-Provençal quoted above, that the two Idrīs participated in the foundation of this capital. To find the demise of the old Roman town, it is apparently necessary to look to the Almohads who, throughout North Africa, brought extinction to towns which had, hitherto, sheltered Christians. According to some historians, this behaviour of the Almohads was a consequence of the tension between Islam and Christianity caused by the Crusades (on the massacres perpetrated by the Almohads, see D. Jacques-Meunié, *Le Maroc saharien des origines à 1670*, Paris 1982, i, 260-1).

There is thus no doubt that the Roman town of Volubilis was the scene upon which the first stage of the Idrīsid drama was performed. It is now necessary to attempt to discover how the events of history have been transferred, no doubt gradually, towards the site of the mountain known today by the name of Mawlāy

Idrīs. First, it should be noted that all the Arabic texts prior to the 9th/15th century declare that both Idrīs died at Walīlī and were buried there, not however within the town but *extra muros:* Ibn Abī Zarᶜ, in the *Rawḍ al-ḳirṭās*, says simply "near Walīlī"; al-D̲j̲aznāʾī specifies "outside the gate of Walīlī"; Ibn al-Ḳāḍī, "in a guard-tower opposite Walīlī"; and al-Ḥalābī, "in the courtyard of the guard-tower situated at the gate of Walīlī" (see M. Ben Talha, *Mawlāy-Idrīs du Zarhūn*, *passim*).

It would be inappropriate to give an exhaustive account of the detailed information provided by these authors. The only fact which needs to be stressed is that the burial of the two Idrīs did not take place at Walīlī but in the immediate proximity. It is therefore logical to suppose that it took place, specifically, on the site where the Zāwiya is currently located, i.e. in that fold of land (*al-ḥufra*) between the two heights of K̲h̲aybar and Tazg̲h̲a, upon which the two main quarters of the new town were to be erected. All those who have visited Volubilis know, in fact, that Mawlāy Idrīs is very clearly visible beyond the ruins of the Roman town. This is, furthermore, the conclusion offered by D. Eustache in his *Corpus* (165 n. 5). The names of K̲h̲aybar and Tazg̲h̲a appear for the first time in the writings of Ibn G̲h̲āzī, author in the 9th-10th/15th-16th century of *al-Rawḍ al-hatūn*, though it is impossible to tell whether these are simple place names or the quarters of a town in the process of construction.

The 16th century texts of Leo Africanus and of Marmol are confusing. These two authors describe, in fact, two different sites: Gualili and the Palace of Pharaoh in one case, Tiulit and Caçar Faraon in the other. But none of these descriptions corresponds exactly either to Volubilis or to Mawlāy Idrīs. It is hard to understand, in fact, how these authors were able to speak of towns situated on the "summit of the mountain", a description applying neither to Volubilis nor Mawlāy Idrīs. A further complication is introduced by the existence of the Ḳaṣbat al-Naṣrānī which seems to have been known to these authors and which is also situated "on the summit of the mountain." Possibly the Ḳaṣbat al-Naṣrānī should be located across the Pietra Rossa or Dār al-Ḥamrāʾ, terms employed by Leo Africanus and Marmol.

Amid all this confusion, which seems to prove that these authors had a very poor knowledge of the region or described it on the basis of hearsay, there nevertheless emerges from a comparison of the two texts a glimmer of light which could provide the key to the mystery that surrounds the origin of the new city. It may be observed that the former, the work of Leo Africanus, mentions only two or three houses around the tomb of the two Idrīs, while the latter, the work of Marmol, who wrote a half-century after him, mentions fifteen to twenty. Circumstantial evidence points to this as the origin of Mawlāy Idrīs, a town which must have begun to develop around a venerated tomb during the 10th/16th century, the period of the great maraboutic movement in Morocco.

This, then, is the time at which the town under discussion began to develop. Obviously, there is a long gap between the 10th/16th century and the end of the 2nd/8th or the beginning of the 3rd/9th. The factor which enables us to fill the space framed between these two dates would be the cult of Idrīs, since Leo Africanus tells us that his grave, at that time separate from any urban settlement, "is venerated and visited by almost all the tribes of Mauritania" (tr. Épaulard, 245).

It is thus from the 10th/16th century onward that the Zāwiya developed. There is nothing surprising in this, since it may be observed that Bū-D̲j̲aᶜd was founded at the end of the same century, Wazzān at the beginning and Mogador or al-Sawīra towards the end of the 18th century.

However, the accelerating impulse seems to have been given during the 12th/18th century by Mawlāy Ismāᶜīl, who ordered the destruction of an ancient mausoleum and replaced it with the one that still exists today; this, according to the *Kitāb al-Istiḳṣāʾ*, in 1132-4/1720-2. There is nothing surprising in this initiative on the part of the great ᶜAlawid sultan. In fact, it conforms perfectly with his repugnance for the independent and irreverent town of Fās and his preference for Miknās, which he was to make his capital and where he was to erect sumptuous palaces. The Zarhūn, to some extent, must have benefited from the prosperity of Miknās.

It was with Mawlāy Ismāᶜīl that the Zāwiya of Zarhūn attained its full dimensions and made, so to speak, its début in history. The best evidence attesting to this relatively recent appearance of the urban settlement which bears this name today, consists in the complete silence of Arab or European historians and geographers prior to the 17th century. Here may be added the text of Mouëtte (beginning of the 17th century) declaring that at this time there were, in the Zarhūn, only small villages forming a dispersed habitat "here and there", but "no town" (Mouëtte, *Histoire des conquestes de Mouley Archy*, in *Sources inédites de l'histoire du Maroc*, 2nd series, *France*, ii, 1924, 182-3). On the other hand, with the start of the ᶜAlawid dynasty, the town entered a phase of lively prosperity.

A curious text contained in the *Kitāb al-Istiḳṣāʾ* places it, at this early stage, alongside the most eminent Muslim sanctuaries: the Kaᶜba, Jerusalem, the Mausoleum of Sīdī ᶜAlī S̲h̲arīf at Tafilalt and that of Mawlāy Idrīs II at Fās. Its sanctified nature led to the following consequences: (1) all non-Muslims, whether Jews or Christians, were excluded from its territory; (2) this territory, and especially the Zāwiya, became an inviolable place of sanctuary for any political criminal or fugitive from common law; and (3) its prestige, or what might be termed its *baraka*, extended over the entire range of the Zarhūn.

Currently, the exclusion of Jews and Christians is still sanctioned by the law which prohibits them from acquiring property there. The protection of criminals has never been other than relative, even in the most prestigious times of the sanctuary. Some have found there an effective refuge, for others it has proved less advantageous. As for access to the locality for Europeans, although it was rigorously controlled before the Protectorate, as certain travellers discovered to their cost, all restrictions have now ceased to exist, and a visit to Mawlāy Idrīs is recommended to tourists visiting Morocco.

In history, the piety of the sultans is attested not only through pious visits but also through the care shown for the maintenance and embellishment of the sanctuary and the mosques (details may be found in Berthier's *Essai*). These visits sometimes take on a political nature, as to a place of symbolic meetings, where alliances are sealed and treaties or truces concluded. A visit to Mawlāy Idrīs is obligatory for every newly-installed sovereign. In the course of his campaign against Muḥammad V, in 1953, El-Glāwī did not fail to comply with this tradition, and Muḥammad V did likewise on his return from Madagascar. Such evidence shows that the cult of Mawlāy Idrīs has today lost none of its prestige, and it may legitimately be supposed that it could play a similar role in the future.

In the cultural sphere, it is known that distinguished scholars have taught at the Zāwiya. A *madrasa* of some repute exists in the locality, and this has been endowed, quite recently, with a cylindrical minaret, a form most unusual in the Muslim architecture of Morocco. Its decorative frieze, made of green pottery, is inscribed with verses from the Ḳurʾān in a very stylised Kufic script (cf. *Guide bleu, Maroc*, 1975, 206; A. Paccard, *Le Maroc et l'artisanat traditionnel*, i, 315).

Although Idrīs al-Akbar has numerous saintly rivals in the massif of the Zarhūn, such as Sīdī ʿAlī Ibn Ḥamdūsh, Sīdī Aḥmad Dghūghī and Sīdī ʿAbd Allāh al-Khayyāṭ of Talaghza, in the urban settlement itself his cult is challenged only by that of his barber, Sīdī ʿAbd Allāh al-Ḥadjdjām, to whom a mosque is dedicated.

The population of the small town consists of a teeming mass of Idrīsid Shurfā and ʿAlawids subdivided into a multitude of branches which the author of this article will not attempt to enumerate.

It is necessary, however, to stress the importance not of the moussem (*mawsim* [*q.v.*]) of Mawlāy Idrīs but of the moussems which are conducted there almost daily at certain times of the year. The present writer was able, in 1934, to witness a moussem of the Sūs people, a crowd of two or three thousand, climbing towards the sanctuary and chanting a curious recitative which has been described by A. Chottin (see his *Tableau de la musique marocaine*, Paris 1938).

Naturally enough, there is a vast number of brotherhoods, ranging from the most aristocratic to the most coarse and primitive. The disciples of Sīdī ʿAlī Ibn Ḥamdūsh and of Sīdī Aḥmad Dghūghī honour their founders not only on the southern slope of the mountain where their sanctuaries are located, but also in the town of Mawlāy Idrīs itself, and this seven days after the mouloud (*mawlid* [*q.v.*]). In his *Essai* (134-5), the present writer has hesitated to assess the influence from the Roman period which could have stimulated the appearance in Morocco of extravagant rites on the part of certain religious brotherhoods. In his recent article *Le Temple B. de Volubilis*, H. Morestin has prompted the present writer to revive this hypothesis. At the conclusion of his excellent archaeological study, Morestin indicates, in fact, that the sanctity and the mysticisms of the Zarhūn could have preceded Islam. Was Temple B. a temple of Saturn or was it not? Prudently, Morestin refrains from making this identification, which does not prevent him from declaring, in the last sentence of his book, that "indirectly the spiritual heritage of Temple B. could have played a role, at the dawn of the history of Muslim Morocco".

Bibliography: All questions concerning the Zarhūn, the Muslim phase of the history of Volubilis, the mystery surrounding the name of Walīlī (from a Berber word signifying rose-laurel), the history of the Zāwiya, etc., have been examined by the author of this article in his *Essai sur l'histoire du massif de Mawlāy Idrīs*, Rabat 1938; the remarkable preface contributed by H. Terrasse would be sufficient, in its own right, to convey an impression of all these issues. It concentrates, however, on the Zarhūn as a whole rather than on the town of Mawlāy Idrīs in particular. For Terrasse, the Zarhūn represents irrefutable evidence of pre-Hilālian Morocco; in this, he is in agreement with X. de Planhol in his *Fondements géographiques de l'histoire de l'Islam*, 148. More recently, a work by N. Ben Talha, former director of the Museum of Dār Djāmaʿ at Miknās, *Mawlāy Idrīs du Zarhūn*, 1965, has provided a very thorough study of daily life in the Holy City; it is to be noted that the closed and unique nature of the milieu examined contributes considerably to the interest of this work. Some useful material is to be found in the works of L. Chatelain and R. Thouvenot on *Le Maroc des Romains*, *Volubilis* and *Banassa*, also in the publications of the Service des Antiquités Marocaines (P.S.A.M.) in the time of the Protectorate, superseded since independence by the *Bulletin d'Archéologie Marocaine.* On the Zarhūn in general, recourse may be had to the doctoral thesis of M. Belarabi, *Etude de géographie rurale*, Bordeaux 1980, which merits only too well the title which the author has given to it.

(P. BERTHIER)

MAWLĀY ISMĀʿĪL B. AL-SHARĪF, ABU 'L-NAṢR, the second ruler of the Moroccan dynasty of the ʿAlawids [see ʿALAWĪS and ḤASANĪ].

On the death of sultan Mawlāy al-Rashīd, the empire of Morocco was divided. Mawlāy Ismāʿīl, governor of Meknès [see MIKNĀS] and brother of the deceased sultan, was proclaimed sultan in this town. He advanced at once on the capital Fās, which had declared against him and seized it. He was proclaimed there on 11 Dhu 'l-Ḥidjdja 1082/14 April 1672), being then 26 years of age.

But three rivals, his brother Mawlāy al-Ḥarrānī in Tāfīlālt, his nephew Aḥmad b. Muḥriz, proclaimed in Marrakesh and in Sūs, and thirdly the guerilla chief al-Khiḍr Ghaylān in the north-west, took the field against him. They were supported by the Turks of the Regency of Algiers, who feared the establishment of a solid power in the west of the Maghrib and endeavoured to make trouble there. Muḥriz Ismāʿīl at first drove his nephew Aḥmad b. Muḥriz out of the town of Marrakesh, defeated Ghaylān to the north of Fās and had him put to death. But Aḥmad b. Muḥriz once more raised the lands of the south and the Atlas. To obtain peace, Ismāʿīl had to recognise his nephew as *amīr* of the lands south of the Atlas and his brother al-Ḥarrānī as *amīr* of Tāfīlālt.

These civil wars, which had lasted five years, had hardly terminated when a descendant of the Marabouts of Dilāʾ [*q.v.* in Suppl.], Aḥmad b. ʿAbd Allāh (d. 1091/1680), also supported by the Turks of Algiers, fomented a terrible rebellion in the country of Tādla and the provinces of western Morocco. But his Berber troops could not withstand Māwlay Ismāʿīl's disciplined troops, especially his artillery. Marrakesh fell in Rabīʿ II 1088/June 1677. The victorious Ismāʿīl terrorised the people to keep them quiet; more than 10,000 were beheaded; thousands of prisoners of war along with Christian slaves had to help to build the palace of Meknès, which the sultan made his military capital. At the same time, the plague carried off thousands of victims (1090/1679) in the regions of the Gharb and the Rīf.

The vigorous repression of the Berber revolts and the epidemic afforded Mawlāy Ismāʿīl a certain respite. He took advantage of it to raise a professional army. He enlisted former negro slaves, gave them wives, allotted estates to them, trained them in the use of arms, and made of them the famous Black Guard of the ʿAbīd al-Bukhārī (so-called because they took their oath on a copy of the *Ṣaḥīḥ*) which was to assure him supremacy over all Morocco.

At the same time, allegedly to favour the intransigent religious party, but in reality to watch the dealings of the Turks and Europeans in the seaports, and to counteract the influence of the corsairs, he organised the corps of the *Mudjtahidūn* or "volunteers of the faith". The latter corps, the cadre of which was formed by several hundred carefully selected ʿAbīd, waged an unceasing irregular warfare against the European possessions. They took La Mamora (al-Maʿmūra), the modern al-Mahdiyya, by surprise from the Spaniards, and Mawlāy Ismāʿīl collected over 100 pieces of artillery there (15 Rabīʿ II 1092/4 May 1681). They harassed the English at Tangiers and the latter evacuated the town after blowing up the mole and the fortifications (1 Djumādā I 1095/15 April 1684) (cf. Davis, *The history of the Second Queen's Royal Regiment*, i, London 1883, 118 ff.). Larache (al-ʿArāʾish) also was forced to succumb to the blows of the "volunteers of the faith" in 1689, and Aṣīla in 1691. But all attempts against Melilla and Ceuta failed. It was in vain that Mawlāy Ismāʿīl endeavoured to get Louis XIV to aid him against Spain. French commerce had to suffer for some time as a result.

But the Peace of Ryswick in 1697 raised Louis XIV's prestige considerably above his enemies. Mawlāy Ismāʿīl then sought his alliance against the Turks of Algiers, who were mixed up in all the plots hatched in the Atlas against the *sharīf*s of Fās. An entente between France, the Bey of Tunis and the sultan of Fās was then concluded. The latter even tried to cement it by a matrimonial alliance and demanded the hand of the Princess de Conti (cf. Plantet, *Mouley Ismaïl et la Princesse de Conti*, Paris 1893). In spite of the failure of the latter plan, the entente secured to France great commercial benefits at Salé, Tetouan and Safi. Frenchmen superintended the building of the palaces, roads, and forts of the sultan and sometimes (like Pillet) accompanied his artillery. On his part, Mawlāy Ismāʿīl organised several expeditions against the Turks with the help of France, whose merchants supplied him with arms and munitions. But the slowness of the Moroccan armies did not enable Ismāʿīl to reap the advantages expected. He even allowed his ally, the Bey of Tunis, to be defeated near Constantine, which enabled the Turks of Algiers to come to fight the Moroccans in the west in full strength in 1701 and to drive them back.

The expeditions of Mawlāy Ismāʿīl against the Turks, in spite of their relative lack of success, enabled him to pacify his frontiers where he built or renovated the fortifications. He built the fort of Reggāda in the mountain of the Banū Yaʿlā commanding the high valley of the Wēd Shāref and the lands of the Arab tribes of the High Plateaux. He built the fort of ʿUyūn Sīdī Mallūk in the plain of Angād and that of Salwān in the land of the Ṭrīfa. He thus closed the exits on his north-east frontier. Forts built in the lands of each tribe kept the country quiet, especially the marabouts, the natural allies of the Turks, whose privileges were tending to pass into the hands of the *sharīf*s. The latter gradually took over the direction of the religious elements, which were organised into brotherhoods. Ismāʿīl completed his system of domination by the creation of military zones. Tāza, notably, had its walls rebuilt. This town became the headquarters of the eastern march. A garrison of 2,500 ʿAbīd secured the passage from western to eastern Morocco by the pass of Tāza. It also had to keep in control the Berbers of the Rīf in the north of this ravine and the Berbers of the middle Atlas in the south.

Apart from his constructions of a military nature, Mawlāy Ismāʿīl was very active as a builder in the various towns of Morocco, and especially at Meknès, where thousands or European slaves worked on the erection of palaces, mosques and *madrasas*. In order to raise the resources for all the expenses of the army's upkeep and his building enterprises, he derived money from taxes raised brutally and regardlessly by his agents, from continual raids on the tribes, from custom duties, from the sixth levied on the spoils of the corsairs, from the ransoms of captives and from the presents, often sumptuous, given by foreign ambassadors. The monopoly of trade, by supplying the treasury, prevented moreover the illicit sale of horses and arms.

Mawlāy Ismāʿīl was a man of vigorous character, of adroitness and of an uncommon agility and bravery, but these positive qualities were accompanied by an unparalleled cruelty and sadism, many examples of which are given by the chroniclers and writers of memoirs. On the other hand, he gave the appearance of being interested in the intellectual activities of his subjects and showed himself respectful of the external aspects of the Islamic cult; he even went as far as engaging in proselytisation and tried to convert Louis XIV.

In regard to foreign policy, he enjoyed fairly good relations with Britain and France, shown by the despatch of embassies which were more or less successful. The French were thus left with a free hand in the Mediterranean, but he did not utilise profitably this diversion of their energies in order to combat victoriously the Turks of Algiers, the aim of his North African policy. Nevertheless, he was able to reduce considerably the foreign occupation of Moroccan ports. In regard to internal policy, much of his reign was filled with the suppression of tribal revolts, which the army was not always able to contain within bounds, whilst his main effort was involved in consolidating the *makhzan* [*q.v.*], upholding it against the turbulent Berbers through the use of Arab and Negro troops.

He had thus succeeded, as much by the reign of terror which he evoked as by his own skilfulness, in imposing peace on the internal regions of his possessions, when he died, after a reign of 55 years, on 27 Radjab 1139/20 March 1727 at the age of 80. Amongst the several hundred children which his innumerable wives had given him, it was Mawlāy Aḥmad al-Dhahabī who succeeded him.

Bibliography: Ḳādirī, *Nashr al-mathānī*, Fās 1309, *passim*; Wafrānī, *Nuzhat al-ḥādī*, ed. Houdas, Paris 1888-9, text 308-9, tr. 504 ff.; Ziyānī, *al-Tardjumān*, ed. Houdas, 24-55; Salāwī, *Kitāb al-Istiḳṣāʾ*, Cairo 1312, iv, 31-50; Mouëtte, *Histoire des Conquestes de Mouley Archy et de Mouley Ismail son frère*, Paris 1683; idem, *Relation de la captivité du sieur Mouëtte...*, Paris 1683, 2nd edn. 1702, partial re-edn. Tours 1863, 1927; F. de Meneçes, *Historia de Tangere*, Lisbon 1732, 277 ff.; [Seran de la Tour,] *Hist. de Mouley Mahomet, fils de M. Ismael*, Geneva 1794; Pidoux de Saint Olon, *Estat de l'empire de Maroc*, Paris 1695, 60-74 and *passim*; Abū Rās, *Voyages extraordinaires*, tr. Arnaud, Algiers 1885, 119 f., 124 ff.; Chénier, *Recherches historiques sur les Maures*, Paris 1787, iii, 362-422; Godart, *Description et histoire du Maroc*, Paris 1860, 510 ff.; P. Busnot, *Histoire du règne de Moulay Ismaïl*, Rouen 1714; Mercier, *Hist. de l'Afrique Septentrionale*, iii, 273; H. de Castries, *Moulay Ismaïl et Jacques II*, Paris 1903; A. Cour, *Etablissement des dynasties de Chérifs*, Paris 1904, 193-218; E. M. G. Routh, *Tangier, England's lost Atlantic outpost, 1661-1684*, London 1912; E. Lévi-Provençal, *Les historiens des Chorfa*, Paris 1922, *passim* (esp. p. 403, the names of Mawlāy Ismāʿīl's viziers, secretaries, etc.); Ch. Penz, *Les captifs français du Maroc au XVIIe siècle (1577-1699)*, PIHEM, xli, Rabat 1944; idem, *Les émerveillements parisiens d'un ambassadeur de Moulay Ismaïl (janvier-février*

1682), Casablanca 1949; W. Blunt, *Black sunrise. The life and times of Mulai Ismail, Emperor of Morocco (1646-1727)*, London 1951; J. Berque, *Al-Yousi. Problèmes de la culture marocaine au XVIIe siècle*, Paris 1958; G. Deverdun, *Marrakech des origines à 1912*, Rabat 1959-66, index; M. Lakhdar, *La vie littéraire au Maroc sous la dynastie ʿalawide*, Rabat 1971; Ch. de la Véronne, *Vie de Moulay Isma'il, roi de Fès et de Maroc d'après Joseph de Léon (1708-1728)*, Paris 1974. See also the general histories of Morocco, esp. that of H. Terrasse, Casablanca 1949-50, ii, 252-78, as well as the *Sources inédites de l'histoire du Maroc*, 2nd series. (A. Cour*)

MAWLĀY MAḤAMMAD AL-SHAYKH, name of three Moroccan sultans belonging to the dynasty of the Saʿdids [*q.v.*].

I. The first, Abū ʿAbd Allāh, who also bore the title of al-Mahdī and is sometimes known as al-Imām, is generally counted second or third in the list of members of the dynasty, but he may to a certain extent be considered its true founder, since it was he who put an end to that of the Marīnids [*q.v.*]. Born probably at Tagmaddart (a district of the Darʿa) in 896/1490-1, he was the younger son of Muḥammad b. ʿAbd al-Raḥmān al-Ḳāʾim bi-amr Allāh, who was proclaimed sultan in 916/1510 and died in 923/1517. According to legend, the great destiny to which he was called was predicted to him in his infancy when, at the Ḳurʾānic school which he attended, a cock came and perched on his head, as well as on that of his elder brother, Aḥmad al-Aʿradj. The two young boys received a quite extensive religious and literary education and were sent on the Pilgrimage to Mecca in *ca.* 911/1506. The lack of precision and the contradictions in the chronology of events found in the sources make any attempt at biography particularly difficult, but it seems clear that al-Aʿradj was appointed by his father governor of the Sus, where he too received the *bayʿa* [*q.v.*] in the same year (916/1510). With his younger brother as his subordinate, he waged without much success a holy war against the Christians established in the region, especially at Santa Cruz, the coastal outlet of the Sus which was to become Agadir [*q.v.*]. The two *sharīfs* also profited at this time from the aid of the Waṭṭāsid ruler [*q.v.*] of Marrakesh, who supplied them with arms. Maḥammad al-Shaykh was not slow, however, to free himself from the tutelage of this elder brother and to take into his own hands the administration of the plain and of the southern flank of the High Atlas, over which his authority extended at the time that Leo Africanus [*q.v.*] visited the region (919/1513). Moreover, the entire province came under his control on the death of al-Ḳāʾim. Aḥmad was then in power to the north of the Atlas.

Making his capital at Tarudant [*q.v.*] which he fortified and renamed Maḥammadiyya and where he built the citadel, the great mosque, the *madrasa* and sugar refineries, he was obliged to solve problems of an economic and political, even religious nature, since he needed to trade with the Christians in order to obtain arms and munitions, but resented the fact that Santa Cruz was occupied by the Portuguese, who in addition exercised a monopoly over the export of sugar. As a result of treaties concluded with the Portuguese rulers of Safi and Azemmour in 930/1524, and then renewed in the two following years, and after ill-fated expeditions against Santa Cruz, relative peace reigned in the south of Morocco. On the one hand, Mawlāy Maḥammad remained on good terms with the influential marabout of the locality where his family had resided, Tidsī, and even married his daughter; on the other, he attracted Christian merchants to the Sus in order to develop trade in the leather, wax and sugar produced in the region.

In Dhu 'l-Ḥidjdja 930/October 1524, Aḥmad al-Aʿradj had taken Marrakesh from the Waṭṭāsids, and the two brothers had made further attacks on the last sovereigns of this dynasty who ruled at Fās; they had also taken a large quantity of artillery with which they were able once more to undertake an expedition against the port of Funti [see AGADIR], which was besieged and captured on 13 Dhu 'l-Ḳaʿda 947/11 March 1541. The Christian captives were taken to Tarudant, while the arms and munitions seized from the enemy enabled Mawlāy Maḥammad to subdue the Berbers of the region, always an unruly element.

Until this point the two brothers had, apparently, made common cause, but a quarrel broke out between them, the specific grounds of the rift being a dispute over the sharing of the booty. A few months after the capture of Funti, al-Aʿradj attacked and defeated Maḥammad, who was determined to avenge himself and succeeded, in 951/1544, in taking possession of Marrakesh, capturing his elder brother and exiling him to Tafilalt with all his followers. Although theoretically a vassal of his brother for a few months more, Mawlāy Maḥammad al-Shaykh, henceforward sole master of the territory controlled by the Saʿdids, was able to contemplate putting an end to the power of the Waṭṭāsids and unifying Morocco to his own advantage. The outcome of the first encounter, which took place on the Umm al-Rabīʿ, was favourable to him. The treaty concluded on that occasion was, however, soon to be broken, and the Saʿdid called upon his adversary to submit; when the latter refused, Fās was attacked in 952/1545, and the ruler of the town, Aḥmad al-Waṭṭāsī, captured and then released. While his son took possession of numerous towns of the Atlantic coast, Mawlāy Maḥammad, who had lost Fās in the meantime, was obliged to put the place under a prolonged siege, capturing it on 2 Muḥarram 956/31 January 1549. It may be reckoned that this considerable event marks the beginning of the dynasty.

The following year, around the month of Djumādā I 957/June 1550, al-Shaykh sent two of his sons, al-Ḥarrān, governor of the Sus, and ʿAbd al-Ḳādir, to conquer Tlemcen; but this enterprise was unsuccessful and al-Ḥarrān fell sick and was forced to return to Fās where he died a few months later.

Meanwhile, an uncle of the defeated Waṭṭāsid, Abū Ḥassān, attempted to revive hostilities; he even went so far as to appeal for aid to the Emperor Charles V (20 Shaʿbān 957/3 September 1550) and, after various vicissitudes, finally obtained from the Janissaries of Algiers an army with which he returned to attack Mawlāy Maḥammad al-Shaykh and to defeat him on a tributary of the Sebou, the Innawen, in Ṣafar 961/January 1554. Forced to leave Fās and to abandon all his property, al-Shaykh rapidly returned to the fray, recaptured the capital which had been pillaged by the Turks and, on 24 Shawwāl 961/22 September 1554, executed Abū Ḥassān, whose head was sent to Marrakesh. He stayed until the end of Ramaḍān 962/beginning of August 1555 at Fās, where he left his heir presumptive, ʿAbd Allāh al-Ghālib bi 'llāh [*q.v.*] and entrusted the administration of Meknès to another of his numerous sons, ʿAbd al-Muʾmin, before setting out once more for the Sus.

In 959/1552, the Ottoman sultan Sulaymān Ḳānūnī [*q.v.*] (926-74/1520-66) had written to Mawlāy Maḥammad al-Shaykh on the subject of the eastern frontiers of Morocco, but the messenger had been very badly received by the new sultan, who thus condemned himself to death. Resolved to settle definitively at Marrakesh, he left Fās, but a dozen hired assassins, sent from Algiers to execute him, mingled easily with his entourage which consisted almost wholly of Turks; they performed the deed on 29 D̲h̲u 'l-Ḥid̲j̲d̲j̲a 964/23 October 1557 and bore his head, so it is said, to Istanbul. His body lies in Marrakesh, among the members of his dynasty, in the hall known as Lālla Masᶜūda which contains the famous "Saᶜdian tombs", where his epitaph may be seen as well as a long commemorative plaque dedicated to him (see G. Deverdun, *Inscriptions*, nos. 123 and 85, pp. 125, and 82-6); another marble plaque bearing a fairly long inscription (*ibid.*, nos. 127-8, pp. 131-4) extols the merits of the sultan's Berber wife, Masᶜūda, who gave birth to Aḥmad al-Manṣūr [*q.v.*] and her name to the hall.

Diego de Torres has left a portrait of Mawlāy Maḥammad al-S̲h̲ayk̲h̲ from which it emerges that he had a round and pale face, large and vivid eyes, a long grey beard, curly hair and two teeth of great size; of modest stature, but robust, he was unscrupulous by nature, but a bold and valiant fighter (*Histoire des Cherifs*, *apud* Marmol, iii, 212). He was also, according to the least sympathetic Arab sources, a man of piety. He was furthermore a scholar, knowing by heart the *Dīwān* of al-Mutanabbī, and it was he who founded the library of the great mosque of Tarudant and expanded the faculties of *ḥadīt̲h̲* and of *fiḳh* (teaching the *Ṣaḥīḥ* of al-Buk̲h̲ārī, the *Risāla* of al-Ḳayrawānī and the *Mukhtaṣar* of K̲h̲alīl b. Isḥāḳ).

When he was in Fās, he attended certain courses himself, but he did not refrain from inflicting cruel punishment on those *fuḳahā*ᵓ whose only crime was to have served the preceding dynasty, such as al-Wans̲h̲arīsī [*q.v.*], put to death in D̲h̲u 'l-Ḥid̲j̲d̲j̲a 955/January 1549, al-Zaḳḳāḳ and Sīdī ᶜAlī Ḥarzūz.

From his life in the south, he had retained simple manners, and many sources recall, not without irony, that a former vizier of the Marīnids, Ḳāsim al-Zarhūnī, and the matron of the harem (*ᶜarīfa*) of Fās, were engaged in educating the numerous members of the court in refinement and instructing them on such topics as etiquette, dress, cuisine and even administration.

From an economic and financial point of view, Mawlāy Maḥammad al-S̲h̲ayk̲h̲ caused some problems as a result of the weight of taxation that he levied, but he was at pains to increase the wealth of the country and to develop both the cultivation of cane and the manufacture of sugar, constructing seven refineries at Tarudant in 951/1544. In addition, he had ambitions to take possession of the salt mine of Tag̲h̲āzā situated approximately midway between the estuary of the Niger and the bend of the Drāᶜ (Darᶜa); he called upon the ruler of Gao to surrender it to him, but the latter sent 2,000 Touaregs to seize the possessions of the Saᶜdid as a gesture of defiance. In the year of the sultan's death, his troops killed the governor of Tag̲h̲āzā and pillaged a caravan of salt, and he himself undertook an expedition to the Sudan, but he was forced to turn back and it fell to his grandson, Aḥmad al-Manṣūr al-D̲h̲ahabī [*q.v.*], to conquer the land of gold.

Bibliography: The earliest sources are Diego de Torres, *Histoire des Chérifs*, vol. iii of *L'Afrique* by Luis de Marmol Carvajal, and vols. i and ii of this latter work (the whole, composed in Spanish, was first published in French translation by N. Perrot d'Ablancourt, Paris 1667). As regards the Arabic sources, see Fis̲h̲tālī, *Manāhil al-ṣafā fī ak̲h̲bār al-mulūk al-s̲h̲urafā*ᵓ, ed. ᶜA. D̲j̲annūn, Tetouan 1384/1964; Ibn ᶜAskar, *Dawḥat al-nās̲h̲ir*, ed. M. Ḥad̲j̲d̲j̲ī, Rabat 1396/1976; Ifrānī (Oufrani), *Nuzhat al-ḥādī*, ed. and tr. O. Houdas, Paris 1888-9; Saᶜdī, *Ta*ᵓ*rīk̲h̲ al-Sūdān*, ed. and tr. O. Houdas, Paris 1913-14, 2nd ed. 1964; *Chronique anonyme de la dynastie saᶜdienne*, ed. G. S. Colin, Rabat 1934; Leo Africanus, *Description de l'Afrique*, tr. A. Épaulard, Paris 1956; Nāṣirī, *K. al-Istiḳṣā*ᵓ, tr. Naciri, in *AM*, 1936; A. Cour, *L'établissement des dynasties de chérifs au Maroc*, Paris 1904; E. Lévi-Provençal, *Les historiens des chorfa*, Paris 1922; E. Fagnan, *Extraits inédits relatifs au Maghrib*, Algiers 1924; *Sources inédits de l'histoire du Maroc*, Paris, 1st series: *Angleterre*, 1918, 1925, 1936, *Espagne*, 1921, 1956, 1961, *France*, 1905-26, *Pays-Bas*, 1906-23, and *Portugal*, 1934-53; R. Ricard, *L'occupation portugaise d'Agadir*, in *Hesperis*, 1946/1-2; P. Berthier, *Les anciennes sucreries du Maroc et leurs réseaux hydrauliques*, Rabat 1966; M. Hajji, *L'activité intellectuelle au Maroc a l'époque saᶜdide*, Rabat 1976-7; D. Jacques-Meunié, *Le Maroc saharien des origines à 1670*, Paris 1982 (detailed study, extensive bibliography).

II. The second, who bore the regal title of al-Maᵓmūn, was the grandson of the preceding and the son of Aḥmad al-Manṣūr [*q.v.*] and a negro woman named K̲h̲ayzurān. After the battle of Wādī 'l-Mak̲h̲āzin (or Battle of the Three Kings) which took place on 30 D̲j̲umādā I 986/4 August 1578, and the proclamation of Aḥmad al-Manṣūr as sultan, Maḥammad al-S̲h̲ayk̲h̲ II was declared heir presumptive by his father who appointed him governor of Fas. But he abandoned himself to debauchery, neglected his religious duties and antagonised the population, to such an extent that the sultan sent him to Sid̲j̲ilmāsa, whence he was impatient to return. After the death of his father (1012/1603), he was obliged to compete with his brothers who disputed his claim to the throne, raised an army which, under the command of his son ᶜAbd Allāh, marched on Marrakesh and captured the town, and he was finally proclaimed sultan at Fās in 1015/1606. The concession of Larache (al-ᶜArāᵓish [*q.v.*]) to the Spanish on 4 Ramaḍān 1019/20 November 1610 incited the rebel Abū Maḥallī [*q.v.* in Suppl.] to launch an appeal to holy war, and three years later (1022/1613), Maḥammad al-S̲h̲ayk̲h̲ II was assassinated near Tetouan.

Bibliography: To the Arab historians of the 11th/17th century and to the comprehensive works cited in the preceding article, the following should be added: R. Le Tourneau, *La décadence saᶜdienne et l'anarchie marocaine au XVIIe siècle*, in *Annales de la Faculté des Lettres d'Aix*, xxxii (1960), 187-225. J. M. Gandin, in *Hommes et destins* (Publ. of Acad. des Sciences d'Outre-Mer), Paris-Aix-en-Provence, vii (1986), 369-71, with Bibl. See also the *Bibl.* of the article ABŪ MAḤALLĪ.

III. The third was the nephew of the preceding and the son of Mawlāy Zaydān and of a Spanish woman. He had been imprisoned by his brother al-Walīd, sultan of Marrakesh, who was assassinated on 14 Ramaḍān 1045/21 February 1636; immediately released, he was proclaimed sultan with the title of al-Ṣag̲h̲īr or al-Aṣg̲h̲ar = the Young. Shortly after this, the holy man of Tazerwalt named Sīdī ᶜAlī, who already occupied the Sus, Tafilalt and Tag̲h̲āzā, took possession of Agadir, with the result that the territory of the Saᶜdid barely extended beyond the suburbs of Marrakesh. In 1048/1638, Mawlāy Maḥammad al-S̲h̲ayk̲h̲ III concluded a treaty with King Charles I of England, by which the king's subjects were forbidden to trade with the sultan's enemies, but he does not seem to have derived any great profit from it.

Meanwhile, the *zāwiya* of al-Dilāᵓ [*q.v.* in Suppl.],

which had not recognised the sultan of Marrakesh, had become a temporal power to be reckoned with, at a time when, in addition, the emergence of the s͟harīfs of Tafilalt began to be a troublesome influence. An important event in the reign of this sultan was the defeat inflicted on him by the army of al-Dilāʾ on the Wādī ʾl-ʿAbīd, on 17 D̲j̲umādā II 1048/26 October 1638. In spite of this reverse, he succeeded in reigning for some twenty years and died on 22 Rabīʿ I 1065/30 January 1655 (date indicated, according to an official document, by the *Taʾrīk͟h al-Sūdān*, which contains effusive eulogies on the conduct of this sultan).

Bibliography: See that of the preceding article. (CH. PELLAT)

MAWLID (A.), or **MAWLŪD** (pl. *mawālid*), is the term for (1) the time, place or celebration of the birth of a person, especially that of the Prophet Muḥammad or of a saint [see WALĪ], and (2) a panegyric poem in honour of the Prophet.

1. Typology of the *mawlid* and its diffusion through the Islamic world.

From the moment when Islam began to bring the personality of Muḥammad within the sphere of the supernatural, the scenes among which his earthly life had been passed naturally began to assume a higher sanctity in the eyes of his followers. Among these, the house in which he was born, the *Mawlid al-Nabī*, in the modern Sūḳ al-Layl in Mecca, the history of which is preserved principally in the chronicles of the town (*Chroniken der Stadt Mekka*, ed. Wüstenfeld, i, 422), does not seem at first to have played a part of any note. It was al-K͟hayzurān (d. 173/789 [*q.v.*]), the mother of Hārūn al-Ras͟hīd, who first transformed it from a humble dwelling-house to a place of prayer. Just as the pious made pilgrimages to the tomb of the Prophet in Medina, so they now visited the site of his birth to show their reverence for it and to receive a share of its blessings (*li ʾl-tabarruk*). In time, the reverence in which the house was held also found expresssion in its development in a fitting architectural fashion (Ibn D̲j̲ubayr, *Riḥla*, 114, 163; and see for a description of the house in the late 19th century, Snouck Hurgronje, *Mekka*, i, 106, ii, 27).

Records of the observation of the birthday of the Prophet as a holy day only begin at a late date; according to the generally accepted view, the day was Monday, 12 Rabīʿ I. The earliest mention of a special public celebration on the occasion of the Prophet's birthday is found in Ibn D̲j̲ubayr, 113. In his time (late 6th/12th century), a special celebration, as distinct from private observance, was arranged in Mecca. The essential feature of the celebration was however only an increase in the number of visitors to the *mawlid* house, which was open the whole day, as an exception, for this purpose. This visit and the ceremonies associated with it (*masḥ*, etc.) were carried through entirely in forms which are characteristic of the older Muslim cult of saints. But just as the later cult of the Prophet had to be raised above the reverence shown to other holy men, so new and special forms developed for his birthday celebrations, which in spite of minor differences in time and place show the same general features everywhere and are comprised under the name *laylat al-mawlid, mawlid al-nabī*, or *mawlid al-nabawī*.

In Fāṭimid Cairo, the *mawlid* of the Prophet was celebrated by the court, as were the *mawlid*s of ʿAlī, Fāṭima and the reigning *k͟halīfa* [*q.v.*]. Essential elements of these celebrations were the procession of the dignitaries to the palace of the *k͟halīfa* followed by three sermons, each by one of the three *k͟huṭabāʾ* [see K͟HAṬĪB] of Cairo (al-Maḳrīzī, *K͟hiṭaṭ*, i, 433 ff.; cf. i, 466, for the temporary suspension of the *mawlid* celebrations). These occasions were not festivals of the common people, however, but mainly of the S͟hīʿī ruling class. This no doubt explains why—except in al-Maḳrīzī and al-Ḳalḳas͟handī, the great historians of Fāṭimid Cairo—there is hardly any reference to these celebrations in the literature emanating from Sunnī circles.

The memory of these Fāṭimid *mawālid* seems to have almost completely disappeared before the festivals in which Muslim authors unanimously find the origin of the *mawlid*: the *mawlid* which we find first celebrated in Irbil in 604/1207-8 by al-Mālik Muẓaffar al-Dīn Gökburi, a brother-in-law of Ṣalāḥ al-Dīn [see BEGTEGINIDS]. The fullest account is given by the great historian Ibn K͟hallikān (d. 681/1282), himself a native of Irbil. Later writers base their statements upon his description of the *mawlid* (Ibn K͟hallikān, Būlāḳ 1299, ii, 550 ff.; see G. E. von Grunebaum, *Muhammadan festivals*, New York 1951, 73-6, for an English translation of the account).

In Cairo, the large-scale participation of the common people and the Ṣūfī orders dates from at least the 7th/13th century. In a comparatively short time thereafter, the observance of the festival spread all through the Muslim World. We have many descriptions of the festival from various parts of the Muslim World in different periods (see *Bibl.*).

In 996/1588 the Ottoman Sultan Murād III introduced the *mawlid* (Tk. *mevlid, mevlūd*) celebration at his court (cf. M. D'Ohsson, *Tableau général*, Paris 1787, i, 255 ff.; Von Hammer, *GOR*, viii, 441). From 1910, it was celebrated as a national festival in the Ottoman Empire. Today, the festival comprises one or more official holidays in the Arab states and in most of the countries where Islam predominates. In many of these countries, an official celebration attended by the head of government or his representatives is held in one of the main mosques in their capitals.

In West Africa, the anniversary of the Prophet's birthday is sometimes associated with pre- or non-Islamic festivals, e.g. among the Nupe in Nigeria, where it is identified with the *gani* age-grade ceremonies (F. Nadel, *Nupe religion*, London 1954, 217), and among the Kotocoli in Northern Togo, where it is associated with "the festival of the knives" (R. Delval, *Les musulmans au Togo*, Paris 1980, 151-3). For some Ṣūfī orders in this area, notably for the Tīd̲j̲ānī branches in Senegal (in Tivaouane, Dakar and Kaolack), the occasion has become the principal yearly gathering for the members of these orders. Poems exist in Hausa, classed technically as *madīḥ* and *sīra*, which are used as *mawlid*s (see M. Hiskett, *A history of Hausa Islamic verse*, London 1975, ch. 5), and in Fulani (Fulfulde), are to be found several panegyrics of the Prophet with phraseology very similar to that of the *mawlid*s (see J. Haafkens, *Chants musulmans en Peul*, Leiden 1983, 173-216). In Chad, the Sudan, North-East and East Africa (see below), the feast is regularly celebrated, and indications exist that the occasion is becoming more widely observed throughout West Africa. The celebrations staged on this occasion are more or less identical to the ones known in the Arab lands.

Central to these celebrations is the recitation of a *mawlid*, i.e. of a panegyrical poem of a legendary character. These poems normally follow a standard sequence of introductory praises to God, an invocation, a description of the creation of *al-nūr al-muḥammadī* [*q.v.*], then proceed through various stages and digressions (e.g. on the Prophet's ancestry) to the actual physical birth, which is preceded by an account of a miraculous announcement to his mother Amina [*q.v.*] that she is bearing the Prophet. In the Arab world, *mawlid* recitation became a common feature of the celebrations in the course of the 9th/15th century and had become universal at the end of the 12th/18th.

The origins of these recitals may be found in the religious addresses in Fāṭimid Cairo and in Irbil. The *K. al-Tanwīr fī mawlid al-sirādj*, which Ibn Diḥya composed during his stay in Irbil at the suggestion of Gökburi, was already famous as a *mawlid* at this period (Brockelmann, *GAL*[1], II, 310). It was not till later times, however, that *mawlids* became a predominant element in the celebration, along with torchlight processions, feasting and the fairs in the street, ever increasing in size. The number of the poems used at *mawlids* is quite considerable. Beside the famous *Bānat Suʿād* of Kaʿb b. Zuhayr of the older period, the *Burda* and the *Hamziyya* of al-Būṣīrī and their numerous imitations, there is a whole series of poems regularly employed here, some of which are intended to instruct like that of Ibn Ḥadjar al-Haytamī, while others are merely eulogistic.

One of the most widely recited *mawlids* in Arabic at present is one composed by Djaʿfar b. Ḥasan al-Barzandjī (d. 1179/1765). It is also known under the title *ʿIḳd al-djawāhir* and has been published many times (cf. *GAL*[1], II, 384 and see J. Knappert, *Swahili Islamic poetry*, Leiden 1971, 48-60, for a slightly abridged English tr.). The most popular of the *mawlids* in Turkish was composed by Süleymān Čelebi (d. 825/1421). It is still recited in mosques throughout Turkey and in mosques of the Turkish-speaking Sunnī community in West and South-Eastern Europe as part of the celebrations for the birthday of the Prophet. This *mawlid* was recited during the official Ottoman court celebrations (for a full translation, see F. Lyman MacCallum, *The Mevlidi Sherif*, London 1943; and E. J. W. Gibb, *A history of Ottoman poetry*, London 1900, i, 232-48, for a translation of extracts and data on the author). Similar *mawlids* have been composed in Persian, Bengali, Sindhi and other languages of the Indo-Pakistani subcontinent (cf. A. Schimmel, *Die Verehrung des Propheten in der islamischen Frömmigkeit*, Düsseldorf-Cologne 1981, 136), and also in Serbian (cf. S. M. Zwemer, *Islam in South Eastern Europe*, in *MW* xvii [1927], 353), Albanian (Hafëz Ali, *Mevludi*, Grosvenor Dale, Conn. 1332/1916, 2nd edition. Waterbury, Conn. 1370/1950) and Swahili (cf. Knappert, *op.cit.*, 276-341).

A *mawlid* of the Imām ʿAlī by Sulaymān Djalāl al-Dīn, *Mawlūd-i Djanāb-i ʿAlī*, Istanbul 1308/1890-1, seems to have had some popularity in ʿAlevī circles in the Ottoman Empire in the last decades of the 19th century.

Apart from the occasion of the Prophet's birthday, a *mawlid* recital is sometimes held as part of the ceremonial of the rites of passage. Occasionally, the recitation of a *mawlid* takes place in fulfilment of a religious vow (T. Canaan, in *Jnal. Pal. Or. Soc.*, vi [1926], 55). When a *mawlid* is recited on any of these occasions, it is normally followed by a *dhikr* [*q.v.*] session. In some Ṣūfī orders (e.g. in the Mīrghaniyya and some branches of the Ḳādiriyya) a *mawlid* is recited as part of the standard liturgical ritual [see ḤAḌRA].

The *mawlid* celebration as an expression of reverence for Muḥammad has found almost general recognition in Islam, partly in consequence of the strength of the Sūfī movement. At all times, however, there has also been vigorous opposition to it by those who considered it to be a *bidʿa* [*q.v.*].

It is significant of the character of the opposition that its opponents object to those very forms which show the influence of Islamic mysticism (dancing, *samāʿ*, ecstatic phenomena, etc.) or of Christianity (processions with lamps, etc.). An interesting document concerning this feud is a kind of *fatwā* by al-Suyūṭī (d. 911/1505, Brockelmann, II[1], 157, *Ḥusn al-maḳṣid fī ʿamal al-mawlid*) which gives a brief survey of the history of the festival, then discusses the pros and cons very fully and concludes that the festival deserves approval as *bidʿa ḥasana*, provided that all abuses are avoided. Ibn Ḥadjar al-Haytamī in his *Mawlid*, and Ḳuṭb al-Dīn (*Chroniken der Stadt Mekka*, iii, 439 ff.), take the same view, while Ibn al-Ḥādjdj (d. 737/1336-7), as a more strict Mālikī, condemns it most vehemently (*K. al-Madkhal*, i, 153 ff.).

Although the height of this struggle was apparently reached in the 8th-9th/14th-15th centuries, it did not really die down in later years. Indeed, it received new life with the coming of Wahhābism [see WAHHĀBIYYA]. This movement, while deriving its arguments for their opposition to the *mawlid* celebrations mainly from Ibn Taymiyya, inspired the growth of non- or anti-mystical Islam throughout the Islamic world and of the opposition to reference to the Prophet, including the celebration of his birthday, in consequence. Wahhābī teaching is equally directed against the veneration of saints (*awliyāʾ* [see WALĪ]) and against the *mawlids* held in many parts of the Islamic world in their honour. These *mawlids* normally follow the Islamic calendar, but there are exceptions. Accounts of such *mawlid* celebrations exist from many parts of the Islamic world.

The term *mawlid* (colloquial, *mūlid*) to denote a feast held in honour of a saint is used in Egypt and the Sudan in particular. Elsewhere, different terms are used, e.g. *mawsim* [*q.v.*] (coll. *mūsem*) in the Maghrib and parts of the Middle East, *ḥawliyya* (coll. *ḥōliyya*) in the Sudan and the horn of Africa, *ʿurs* in the Indo-Pakistan sub-continent and *ḥol* in Malaysia. Everywhere, the characteristics of such celebrations are more or less the same: crowds gather for one or more days, a fair of varying size and importance accompanies the religious celebrations, *dhikr* and/or Ḳurʾān reading sessions take place inside and/or outside the sanctuary of the saint concerned, one or more processions are held in which the keeper of the sanctuary (often the saint's descendant) and (frequently) Ṣūfī orders participate, and the cloth (*kiswa*) covering the saint's shrine is replaced by a new one in the course of the celebrations. Frequently, communal meals are staged and a centrally organised distribution of alms takes place.

In some parts of the Sunnī world, like Afghānistān, no *mawlids* are celebrated, notwithstanding the widespread cult of saints in these areas; in the Shīʿī world no *mawlids* of the type described here seem to be known.

In Egypt, the celebration of the numerous *mawlids* (about 300 *mawlids* of varying size were celebrated yearly with official permission in the 1970s) is centrally co-ordinated and supervised (by the *mashyakhat al-ṭuruḳ al-ṣūfiyya*, in consultation with the Ministry of Awḳāf), so as to prevent these celebrations from overlapping and to guarantee public order. Some of these *mawlids* were or still are known for special rituals or customs observed as part of the celebrations [see DAWSA]. During most of the *mawlids*, special sugar dolls (*ʿarāʾis*, sing. *ʿarūsa*) are sold (cf. ʿAbd al-Ghanī al-Nabawī al-Shāl, *ʿArūsat al-mawlid*, Cairo 1977). In Egypt, the celebration of *mawlids* is not limited to Islamic saints but extends to Coptic Christian ones as well.

The predominance of *mawlid* celebrations in Egypt

ADDENDA AND CORRIGENDA

VOLUME I

P. 436b, AL-ʿĀMILĪ, Muḥammad b. Ḥusayn Bahāʾ al-Dīn, *add* to Bibl.: A. Newman, *Towards a reconsideration of the "Isfahān school of philosophy": Shaykh Bahāʾī and the role of the Safawid 'ulamā*, in *Studia Iranica*, xv (1986), 165-98; C. E. Bosworth, *Bahāʾ al-Dīn ʿĀmilī and his literary anthologies*, Manchester 1989.

VOLUME IV

P. 759a, **KĀTIB**, l. 23 from below, *instead of* Amīr Khusraw *read* Amīr Ḥasan

VOLUME V

P. 39, **KHOTAN**, *add*:

The language of ancient Khotan was a Middle Iranian language, closely related to Soghdian. It is now commonly called Khotanese, though, since it was the descendant of one of the languages of the numerous, but ill-definable, pre-historic "Saka" tribes of Central Asia, it is sometimes called "Khotan Saka" (see e.g. H. W. Bailey, *Dictionary of Khotan Saka*, Cambridge, etc. 1979). E. Leumann, one of the earliest decipherers of the language, thought that it was a separate branch of Indo-Iranian and therefore called it "Nordarisch", but this theory was shown to be untenable by scholars such as S. Konow and Bailey. See Bailey, *Indo-Scythian studies, being Khotanese texts volume IV. Saka texts from Khotan in the Hedin collection*, Cambridge 1963, introd. 1-18; R. E. Emmerick, *Saka grammatical studies*, London 1968; idem, *A guide to the literature of Khotan*, Studia Philologica Buddhica. Occasional Papers Series III, Tokyo 1979; idem, *Khotanese*, in *Compendium linguarum iranicarum*, ed. R. Schmitt, Wiesbaden 1989.

The following kings of Khotan are known from the Khotanese documents: Viśya Vikrraṃ, Viśaʾ (Viśya) Sī(m)hya, Viśaʾ Dharma, Viśaʾ Kīrtti and Viśaʾ Vāhaṃ (all probably 8th century A.D.); Viśaʾ Saṃgrāma (? 9th century); Viśaʾ Sa(ṃ)bhava/Saṃbhata (regn. 912-66), Viśaʾ Śūra (regn. 967-at least 971), Viśaʾ D(h)arma (regn. 978-at least 988). See for useful surveys, J. Hamilton, *Les règnes khotanais entre 851 et 1001*, in M. Soymié (ed.), *Contributions aux études sur Touen-Houang*, Centre de recherches d'histoire et de philologie de la IVe section de l'EPHE II, Hautes études orientales 10, Geneva and Paris 1979, 49-54; idem, *Sur la chronologie khotanaise au IXe-Xe siècle*, in Soymié (ed.), *Contributions aux études de Touen-Houang III*, Publs. de L'Ecole française d'Extrême-Orient, cxxxv, Paris 1984, 47-8; and see further, H. Kumamoto, *Some problems of the Khotanese documents*, in *Studia grammatica iranica*, ed. R. Schmitt and P. O. Skjaervø, Munich 1986, 227-44, and Skjaervø, *Kings of Khotan in the 8th-10th centuries...*, in *Acts of the colloquium on "Histoire et cultes de l'Asie Centrale préislamique: sources écrites et documents archéologiques", Paris 22-8 November 1988*, CNRS Paris (forthcoming).

The islamisation of Khotan apparently took place already around 1006, at any rate before 1008, since the Chinese annals for the year 1009 report the arrival of a *huei-hu* (= Turk) sent by the *hei-han* (= Khaghan) of Yu-t'ien (= Khotan) with tribute to the Imperial Chinese court; the envoy had been travelling for a year (see M Abel-Rémusat, *Histoire de la ville de Khotan tirée des annales de la Chine et traduite du chinois*, Paris 1820, 86-7). The Muslim ruler at this time was the Ḳarakhānid Yūsuf Ḳadīr Khān of Kāshghar (on whom see O. Pritsak, *Die Karachaniden*, in *Isl.*, xxxi [1953-4], 30-3, repr. in *Studies in medieval Eurasian history*, London 1981, xvi, and ILEK-KHĀNS).

The conflict between Khotan and Kāshghar must have started earlier, however, for in a letter written in Khotanese by King Viśaʾ Śūra in 970, the ruler refers to "Our evil enemy the Tazhīk (Khot. Ttaśīʾkä) Tcūṃ-hyai:nä [Ts'ung hsien?], who [is] there among the Tazhīkṣ", and in a letter in Chinese from the ruler of Sha-chou (Tun Huang) to the king of Khotan, in the Pelliot collection, from around 975 we read that "the prince of the west is leading Tadjik (Ta-shih) troops to attack [your] great kingdom" (see Bailey, *Saka documents, text vol.*, Corpus inscr. iranicarum, ii, V, London 1968, 58-61, ll. 50-1; Hamilton, *Sur la chronologie*, 48-9). Hamilton has suggested that the "evil enemy" may be Viśaʾ Śūra's brother, another son of Viśaʾ Saṃbhava (in Chinese, Li Sheng-t'ien), two of whom are known to have borne the name Tcūṃ/Ts'ung. Kumamoto, *op. cit.*, 231, suggests

ISBN 90 04 09239 0

PRINTED IN THE NETHERLANDS

that his mother may have been a Ḳara<u>kh</u>ānid. The last known king of <u>Kh</u>otan was Viśaʾ D(h)arma (still ruling in 988), whose name shows that he was not a Muslim. The definitive struggle over <u>Kh</u>otan must therefore have taken place during the ensuing two decades. See also M. A. Stein, *Ancient Khotan*, 2. vols., Oxford 1907, repr. New York 1975, i, 180-1; W. Samolin, *East Turkistan to the twelfth century*, The Hague, etc. 1964, 80-2.

VOLUME VI

P. 459[a], **MAPPILA**, l. 37, *instead of* 1948 *read* 1498

P. 460[a], l. 10, *instead of* ist *read* its
l. 30, *instead of* or *read* of

P. 461[a], l. 13 from below, *instead of* wiser *read* wider

P. 462[b], l. 17, *instead of* nor *read* not

P. 463[b], ll. 29-30 from below, *instead of* remaining *read* remains

P. 464[a], l. 16 from below, *instead of* wisely *read* widely

Pp. 511 and 517, **MARʿA<u>SH</u>ĪS**. Owing to an unfortunate oversight Table A has been included twice.

P. 641[a], **MĀSAR<u>DJ</u>AWAYH**, l. 10, *instead of* πανōέχτης *read* Πανδέκτης
l. 24-25, *instead of* p. 20, 1. 341 *read* p. 20, l. 341
l. 26, *instead of* p. 88, 11. 1860-3 *read* p. 88, ll. 1860-3

P. 764[b], **MASRAḤ**, *add at the end of the Bibliography*: *Modern Persian drama. Anthology*, tr. G. Kapuscinski, Lanham 1987; G. Kapuscinski, *Modern Persian drama*, in *Persian literature*, ed. E. Yarshater, Albany 1988, 381-402.

SUPPLEMENT

P. 395[a] **IBN NĀẒIR AL-<u>DJ</u>AY<u>SH</u>**, *add* to Bibl.: The *Ta<u>th</u>ḳīf* is now available in the edition of R. Veselý, IFAO, Cairo 1987; see also on the author, D. S. Richards, *The Tathqīf of Ibn Nāẓir al-Jaish*: *the identity of the author and the manuscripts*, in *Cahiers d'onomasticon arabe*, iv (1985-7), 97-101.

THE ENCYCLOPAEDIA OF ISLAM

NEW EDITION

PREPARED BY A NUMBER OF
LEADING ORIENTALISTS

EDITED BY

C. E. BOSWORTH, E. VAN DONZEL, W. P. HEINRICHS AND CH. PELLAT

ASSISTED BY F. TH. DIJKEMA AND MME S. NURIT

UNDER THE PATRONAGE OF
THE INTERNATIONAL UNION OF ACADEMIES

VOLUME VI

FASCICULES 113-114

MAWLID — MESĪḤ MEḤMED PASHA

LEIDEN
E. J. BRILL
1990

EXECUTIVE COMMITTEE:

All correspondence on editorial matters should be addressed to the Editorial Secretaries, whose addresses are:

For the English Edition

Dept. of Near Eastern Studies,
The University of Manchester,
Manchester,
England M13 9PL.

For the French Edition

Centre Universitaire
94, avenue des Grésillons
92600 Asnières
France

AUTHORS OF ARTICLES IN THESE FASCICULES

M. Abdesselem, University of Tunis. 911.
Z. Abrahamowicz, Cracow. 986.
M. Aktepe, University of Istanbul. 1004.
Edith G. Ambros, University of Vienna. 967, 969.
[F. Babinger, Munich]. 1000, 1023, 1024.
J.-L. Bacqué-Grammont, French Institute of Anatolian Studies, Istanbul. 993.
[W. Barthold, Leningrad]. 942.
N. Berkes, Hythe, Kent. 969.
E. Birnbaum, University of Toronto. 1020.
[W. Björkman, Uppsala]. 1007.
J. R. Blackburn, University of Toronto. 912.
the late J. Bosch Vilá, Grenade. 899, 927.
C. E. Bosworth, University of Manchester. 901, 903, 912, 914, 915, 916, 918, 942, 966, 1024.
[F. Buhl, Copenhagen]. 918.
J. Burton-Page, Church-Knowle, Dorset. 970, 1019.
Cl. Cahen, University of Paris. 1017.
G. E. Carretto, University of Rome. 1024.
[G. S. Colin, Paris]. 1009.
F. M. Donner, University of Chicago. 917.
E. van Donzel, Netherlands Institute for the Near East, Leiden. 910, 933.
H. Eisenstein, University of Vienna. 1003.
T. Fahd, University of Strasbourg. 923.
W. Feldman, University of Pennsylvania, Philadelphia. 1008.
C. V. Findley, Ohio State University, Columbus. 972.
A. D. W. Forbes, University of Aberdeen. 1022.
G. S. P. Freeman-Grenville, Sheriff Mutton, Yorkshire. 965, 1023.
Y. Friedmann, Hebrew University, Jerusalem. 968.
F. Müge Göçek, University of Michigan, Ann Arbor. 1017.
A. H. de Groot, University of Leiden. 992, 993, 994, 995, 996, 997, 998, 999, 1000, 1001, 1002, 1003.
[M. Guidi, Rome]. 952.
J. A. Haywood, Lewes, E. Sussex. 953.
C. J. Heywood, University of London. 972.
Carole Hillenbrand, University of Edinburgh. 932.
[E. Honigmann, Brussels]. 901.
H. İnalcik, University of Chicago. 961, 978, 981.
F. İz, Boğaziçi Üniversitesi. 986, 989, 1003, 1016.
Barbara Kellner-Heinkele, University of Frankfort. 989, 1016.
M. Kiel, Bonn. 1015.
D. A. King, University of Frankfort. 915.
J. Knappert, Barnet, Herts. 897.
M. Köhbach, University of Vienna. 989.
[J. H. Kramers, Leiden]. 983.
E. Kuran, Hacettepe Üniversitesi, Ankara. 1004.
B. Kütükoğlu, University of Istanbul. 971, 990, 991.
[H. Lammens, Beirut]. 924.
J. M. Landau, Hebrew University, Jerusalem. 1013.
O. N. H. Leaman, Liverpool Polytechnic. 903.
[G. Levi Della Vida, Rome]. 954.
[E. Lévi-Provençal, Paris]. 923, 969.
T. Lewicki, Cracow. 948, 949.
D. MacEoin, Newcastle-upon-Tyne. 953.
W. Madelung, Oxford University. 917.
A. J. Mango, London. 984, 985.
E. Merçil, University of Istanbul. 1018, 1019.
[V. Minorsky, Cambridge]. 929.
S. Moreh, Hebrew University, Jerusalem. 928.
M. Morony, University of California, Los Angeles. 923, 952.
[M. Nāẓim]. 916.
J. S. Nielsen, University of Birmingham. 935.
Ch. Pellat, University of Paris. 907, 916, 933, 943.
I. Poonawala, University of California, Los Angeles. 1010.
W. Röllig, University of Tübingen. 1023.
K. S. Salibi, American University, Beirut. 918.
A. Salmi, Rabat. 898.
Biancamaria Scarcia Amoretti, University of Rome. 959.
[J. Schacht, New York]. 926.
R. Sellheim, University of Frankfort. 914, 955.
S. J. Shaw, University of California, Los Angeles. 973.
D. Shulman, Hebrew University, Jerusalem. 968.
the late Susan A. Skilliter, Cambridge. 982.
P. Sluglett, University of Durham. 902.
S. Soucek, New York Public Library. 1011, 1016, 1022.
[M. Streck, Jena]. 923.
[R. Vasmer, Leningrad]. 942.
G. Veinstein, École des Hautes Études en Sciences Sociales, Paris. 1006.
Ž. Vesel, Centre National de la Recherche Scientifique, Paris. 908.
Ch. Vial, University of the Provence, Aix-en-Provence. 958.
F. Viré, Centre National de la Recherche Scientifique, Paris. 913.
[A. J. Wensinck, Leiden]. 903.

Names in square brackets are those of authors of articles reprinted or revised from the first edition of this Encyclopaedia.

would seem to explain why it is in this country above all that the most abundant polemical literature concerning the religious status of *mawlid* celebrations was produced. Those critical of such celebrations range in their demands from minor reforms of ritual, such as the prohibition of musical instruments in processions and the staging of profane forms of amusement in the *mawlid* grounds, to total abolition. Most of those who have declared against the celebration of *mawlids* in their traditional form seem to have been of Wahhābī inspiration. Some of the most vocal and well-known 20th century critics who deserve mention were Muḥammad Rashīd Riḍā, Maḥmūd Khaṭṭāb al-Subkī and Muḥammad Ḥāmid al-Fiḳī. Elsewhere in the Islamic world, similarly inspired groups and individuals have opposed or are still actively opposing veneration of saints.

Bibliography: In addition to the works mentioned in the article, see Ḥasan al-Sandūbī, *Taʾrīkh al-Iḥtifāl bi ʾl-mawlid al-nabawī*, Cairo 1948 (mainly on the history of the *mawlid* in Cairo, with short excursions on the celebrations in Istanbul, Morocco and Tunisia in different eras; based upon published sources). For descriptions of *mawlid al-nabī* celebrations in different parts of the Islamic world and in various periods, see e.g. Wüstenfeld (ed.), *Chroniken*, iii, 438 ff.; Ibn Ḥadjar al-Haytamī, *Mawlid* (see Brockelmann, *GAL*[1], II, 389); Snouck Hurgronje, *Mekka*, ii, 57 ff., 147 (for Mecca); idem, *The Achenese*, i, 210, 212; idem, *Verspreide Geschriften*, iii, 8 ff., 83-5; and R. A. Kern, *De Islam in Indonesië*, The Hague 1947 (for Indonesia); J. S. Trimingham, *Islam in the Sudan*, Oxford 1949, 146 f. (for Omdurman), and also von Grunebaum, *Muhammadan festivals*, (a general discussion mainly derived from the article *Mawlid* in *EI*[1]).

Works containing descriptions and/or other information concerning the *mawlid al-nabī* and other *mawlids* are e.g. T. Canaan, *Mohammedan saints and sanctuaries in Palestine*, London 1927, 193 ff.; Muṣṭafā Yūsuf Salām al-Shādhilī, *Djawāhir al-iṭlāʿ*, Cairo 1350/1931-2, 241; J. Hornel, *Boat-processions in Egypt*, in *Man*, xxxviii (Sept. 1938), 145-6; J. W. McPherson, *The Moulids of Egypt*, Cairo 1941; Aḥmad Amīn, *Ḳāmūs al-ʿādāt wa ʾl-taḳālīd wa ʾl-taʿābīr al-miṣriyya*, Cairo 1953, 387-8; R. Kriss and H. Kriss-Heinrich, *Volksglaube im Berich des Islams. Band I. Wallfahrtswesen und Heiligenverehrung*, Wiesbaden 1960, *passim*; M. Berger, *Islam in Egypt today*, Cambridge 1970, 81-3; M. Gilsenan, *Saint and Sufi in Modern Egypt. An essay in the sociology of religion*, Oxford 1973, 48-64; P. Rabinow, *Symbolic domination. Cultural form and historical change in Morocco*, Chicago 1975, 89-94; D. F. Eickelman, *Moroccan Islam. Tradition and society in a pilgrimage center*, Austin-London 1976, 171-8; P. Shinar, *Traditional and reformist maulid celebrations in the Maghrib*, in M. Rosen-Ayalon (ed.), *Studies in memory of Gaston Wiet*, Jerusalem 1977, 371-413; F. de Jong, *Ṭuruq and Ṭuruq-linked institutions in nineteenth century Egypt. A historical study in organizational dimensions of Islamic mysticism*, Leiden 1978, 61-4 and *passim*; Fārūḳ Aḥmad Muṣṭafā, *al-Mawālid*, Alexandria 1981[2]; de Jong, *The Ṣūfī orders in post-Ottoman Egypt, 1911-1981* (forthcoming), chs. 3, 7, for a discussion of the conservative versus the reformist orientations and objections concerning the *mawlids* with references to the relevant polemical literature. In addition, see ʿAlī Mubārak, *al-Khiṭaṭ al-Tawfīḳiyya*, i, 90-2 (an enumeration of *mawlids* in Cairo at the end of the 19th century), I. Goldziher, *Le culte des saints chez les Musulmans*, in *Revue de l'Histoire des Religions*, ii (1891), 257-351 (for a still valuable general discussion); and E. Sidaway, *Les manifestations religieuses de l'Egypte moderne*, in *Anthropos*, xviii-xix (1923-4), 278-96 (on Coptic *mawlids*). There is no study devoted to the *mawlid* as a literary genre. (H. Fuchs - [F. de Jong])

2. In East Africa.

In a region of the Islamic periphery, such as East Africa, the desire to preserve the communal rituals and devotional ceremonies—of which the *mawlid* is the most popular celebration—is often stronger than in the heartlands of Islam (see Annemarie Schimmel, *Mystical dimensions of Islam*, Chapel Hill, N. C. 1975, 216-17; J. Knappert, *Traditional Swahili poetry*, Leiden 1967, ch. 5). For the masses of people in the fringes, Muḥammad is the personage behind whose banner the faithful will enter Paradise. Numerous popular tales and poems about him raise him almost to a superhuman level of deification, and these form the basis for much *mawlid* material; also, the Prophet's life forms the closing section of the voluminous popular cycle on the lives of the 24 prophets who preceded him (see idem, *Swahili Islamic poetry*, Leiden 1971, i, ch. 3; idem, *Islamic legends*, Leiden 1985, i, 56-184; and cf. Th. G. Pigeaud, *The literature of Java*, The Hague 1967, 132).

In East Africa, proper *mawlid* poems contain at least some of the successive episodes of Muḥammad's life, culminating in his death—the date of this being popularly regarded as the same date as his birth—and the *wafāt al-nabī* may comprise an entire book, in prose or verse (see Hemedi bin Abdallah bin Saidi el Buhriy, *Utenzi wa kutawafu nabii*, tr. R. Allen, ed. J. W. T. Allen, Kampala 1956; similar examples can be quoted in Malaysia and Indonesia). Of these *mawlid* texts proper, by far the most popular in Kenya, Tanzania and Somalia (as also in Malaysia and Indonesia) is al-Barzandjī's one (see section 1. above), contained in a book—first printed *ca.* 1885 and noted as a red-bound book by Snouck Hurgronje in Atjèh [*q.v.*] and by Becker in Dar es Salaam—called the *Madjmaʿ mawlid sharaf al-anām*, the best-known single prayer book in the Islamic world. It comprises prose and poetic versions (*nathr* and *naẓm*) of al-Barzandjī's *mawlid* (both also translated into Swahili), the *Burda* of al-Būṣīrī and several other prayers. In Somalia, al-Barzandjī's *mawlid* composition is widely recited during the *mawlid* celebrations in Arabic form, although a Somali poetic version exists. In *The library of Muḥammad b. ʿAlī b. ʿAbd al-Shakūr, Sulṭān of Harar, 1272-92/1856-75*, in *Arabian and Islamic studies ... presented to R. B. Serjeant*, ed. R. L. Bidwell and G. R. Smith, London 1983, 68-79, A. J. Drewes has mentioned three *mawlids*, including apparently Abu 'l-Ḥasan Nūr al-Dīn's *ʿUnwān al-sharīf*. After al-Barzandjī's, the most popular *mawlid* in Kenya and Somalia is the *Mawlid al-sharīf* of Shaykh ʿAbd al-Raḥmān b. ʿAlī al-Dībaʿī al-Zabīdī; the printed editions of this, from Cairo and Aden-Singapore respectively, contain at the end a *fatwā* by the *muftī* of Mecca permitting the use of drums at the *mawlid* festival. But the *mawlid* is often performed at other times too, e.g. 14 days after the birth of a child in Tanzania (see C. Velten, *Sitten und Gebräuche der Suaheli*, Göttingen 1903, ch. 2).

Bibliography: Given in the article.

(J. Knappert)

MAWLIDIYYA (A.) (or *milādiyya*; dial. *mulūdiyya*), pl. *-āt*, a poem composed in honour of the Prophet on the occasion of the anniversary of his birth [see mawlid] and recited as a rule before the sovereign and court after ceremonies marking the *laylat al-mawlid.*

A relatively large number of *mawlidiyyāt* are extant, drawing their inspiration from the famous *Bānat Suᶜād* of Kaᶜb b. Zuhayr [*q.v.*] so often imitated by versifiers, of whom the best known is certainly al-Būṣīrī (608-94/1212-97) [*q.v.* in Suppl.], whose poems enjoy a renown which has never diminished, especially the *Burda* [*q.v.*] and, to a lesser extent, the *Hamziyya*, which is recited in mosques and *zāwiya*s during the month of Rabīᶜ I, between the *maghrib* and *ᶜishāʾ* prayers. Among the mediaeval authors who have left poems classifiable within the category of *mawlidiyyāt* may be cited al-Barᶜī (5th/11th century), al-Ṣarṣarī (d. 556/1160), Ibn al-Djawzī (510-97/1116-1200 [*q.v.*]), Ibn Ḥadjar al-Haytamī (909-74/1504-67 [*q.v.*]) and al-Barzandjī (1040-1103/1530-91). Furthermore, it is possible to gain an overall idea of this production thanks to the four-volume collection made at the beginning of the century by Yūsuf b. Ismāᶜīl al-Nabhānī and published in Beirut in 1320/1902.

In the Islamic West, *mawlidiyyāt* were mainly the work of court poets, but also of administrative officials and viziers for whom the composition of poems of this type constituted a part of their professional education; some well-known personalities figure among them, such as Ibn Marzūḳ (710-81/1310-79 [*q.v.*]), Ibn al-Khaṭīb (713-76/1313-75 [*q.v.*]), and above all, Ibn Zamrak (733-95/1333-93 [*q.v.*]). Due to the occasional nature of this poetry, it is understandable that a large number of poems have not been preserved; the majority of those that survive, thanks, in particular, to al-Maḳḳarī (d. 1041/1632 [*q.v.*]) and to al-Ifrānī (d. 1157/1745 [*q.v.*]), belong to a relatively short period from 761 to 768/1360-7, corresponding to the reigns of the Marīnid Abū Sālim Ibrāhīm (d. 762/1361) in Fās and of the Naṣrid Muḥammad V (d. 793/1391) in Granada; to be sure, al-Fishtālī (956-1031/1549-1633), himself the author of at least one *mawlidiyya*, reproduced in his *Nuzha* (ed. and Fr. tr. Houdas, 149-57), these poems being composed in the reign of Aḥmad al-Manṣūr in 999/1590.

Generally, the framework of the *ḳaṣīda* is respected, but adapted to suit the fundamental purpose of the poet in the sense that, while the apology of the Prophet is preceded by a *nasīb* and a *raḥīl*, it is followed in the West by a eulogy of the sovereign which is explicable by the circumstances in which these poems were recited.

The *nasīb* contains the traditional recollection of the remains of an encampment, but the author must avoid any allusion to a woman and show the decency appropriate to the situation. He expresses on the contrary the violent passion which he feels for the Prophet, leaving some doubt as to this love, whose true mystical nature is not at all clear. The abandoned encampment is situated on the route that the poet must follow to visit the Holy Places, but, as he is very far distant from them, he calls upon a caravan guide or some pilgrims in order to ask them to bear his greetings to the Prophet and describe to him the ardour of his passion.

This sentimental and moving prologue is followed by a brief lyrical expansion on the theme, or, more frequently, a narrative full of details borrowed from the traditional *raḥīl*, of an imaginary journey across deserts as far as Medina. It goes without saying that this general theme undergoes numerous variants ranging from an account of the pilgrimage to Mecca to the insertion of paranetic verses or commonplaces on the flight of time, white hair, etc. The Spanish *mawlidiyyāt* are always distinguished by a large number of descriptions.

The recollection of the Holy Places introduces the eulogy of the Prophet, which must theoretically be based on reality and never drift into hyperbole. The principal themes concern the birth, foretold by earlier prophets, the signs of prophecy visible from infancy, his mission, etc.; next, the epithets of Muḥammad are enumerated; then come his physical and moral portraits; and finally, the description of the miracles that he performed. In this central part of the *mawlidiyya*, the elements of the panegyric, expressed by means of a profusion of superlatives, are drawn from the Ḳurʾān and *ḥadīth* as well as popular beliefs which have embellished the life of the Prophet with legendary details. It may be remarked further that the poets, idealising his image, adopt some characteristics taken from the Gospels so as to invest the founder of Islam with an aura of sanctity which makes him vie with Jesus.

After the account of the miracles, the versifiers generally express a wish to be able to visit the Holy Places, offer supplications to their "saviour" and invoke God's blessing on him and his Companions.

This invocation, followed by a similar invocation on behalf of the sovereign and mention of the *laylat al-mawlid*, marks the transition to the third part of the *mawlidiyya* which is often as developed as the second and consists of the panegyric of the reigning prince. This part offers nothing really new corresponding to the classical *madīḥ* [*q.v.*]. The author attributes all the virtues to the *mamdūḥ*, who is the restorer of the kingdom and whose arms are always victorious; but his cardinal virtue is naturally generosity, which is appealed to more or less discreetly. After the sovereign come the turns of the heir presumptive and the royal family. To conclude, the poet wishes that the prince's prosperity may endure.

One can hardly expect to find much originality in these compositions crammed with rhetorical flourishes and adorned with clichés which savour of affectation and artificiality. However, the choice of images, the variety of stylistic devices, the subtle play on vocabulary and the constant appeal to the religious or literary culture of the listener, retain a certain attraction.

As well as some poems in classical Arabic, there are many *mūlūdiyyāt* in dialect which generally contain only the eulogy of the Prophet; among those which have been preserved—or those which are still composed today—some follow the classical tradition and contain moreover the *nasīb* and the *raḥīl*, but the eulogy of the sovereign does not figure at all in them [see MALḤŪN].

Bibliography: A. Salmi, *Le genre des poèmes de nativité (mawlūdiyya-s) dans le royaume de Grenade et au Maroc du XIIIᵉ au XVIIᵉ siècle*, in *Hespéris*, 1956/3-4, 335-435.

(A. SALMI)

MAWRŪR, name given to the *kūra* of Morón, currently Morón de la Frontera, in the province of Seville, to the south-east of the latter and of Carmona and to the south-west of Cordova. The Arabo-Islamic conquest of the territory occupied today by Morón and its dependencies must have taken place in 92/714 shortly after that of Shadūna [*q.v.*] by Ṭāriḳ b. Ziyād [*q.v.*].

Mawrūr is also the name of a *ḥiṣn* of the province of Málaga (see J. Valvé, *De nuevo sobre Bobastro*, in *al-And.*, xxx [1965], 142, no. 11) and of one (known by the name of el-Mauror) of the hills at the foot of which Granada is situated [see GHARNĀṬA].

The population of the *kūra* was constituted of Butr Berbers, or Arabs of the tribe of Djudhām, of neo-Muslims and, to a lesser degree, of Mozarabs, The region combined all the advantages of plain and mountain. Cereals, olives and fruit-trees were cultivated there, according to al-Rāzī and other writers, who add that the area possessed good wells and substantial fortresses, in particular that of Carpio, which is not easily located today but which some have identified with the Ḳalb which, according to Ibn G͟hālib, al-Ḥimyarī and perhaps other writers, was the regional capital (*ḳāʿida*) of the *kūra* and the seat of the *wālī* and which possessed a Great Mosque and a very busy market.

Under the amīrate, Mawrūr seems to have been nothing more than an agricultural region of which the neighbouring territories were subjected to a raid on the part of the Mad͟jūs [*q.v.*], if reliance is to be placed on the *Ak͟hbār mad͟jmūʿa* (text, 64; tr. 51). Mawrūr is also mentioned in connection with events occurring at Seville in the period of Ibrahīm b. al-Ḥad͟jd͟jād͟j (al-ʿUd͟hrī, 103), and with an invasion mounted by Muṭarrif, son of the *amīr* ʿAbd Allāh (*ibid.*, 104). In the time of the *amīr* al-Ḥakam [*q.v.*], the total sum of taxation contributed by the *kūra* of Mawrūr rose to 21,000 *dīnārs* (al-Ḥimyarī, *Rawḍ*, text, 186, tr. 227) and the number of horsemen that it supplied for the summer campaigns against the Christians commanded by ʿAbd al-Raḥmān b. Muḥammad, stood at 1403 (Ibn Ḥayyān, *Muḳtabis*, ed. Makkī, text 272). The fortress of Mawrūr was also affected by the consequences of the rebellion of ʿUmar b. Ḥafṣūn [*q.v.*], to such an extent that it became necessary to send several expeditions against these territories, which were ultimately subjected to the authority of Cordova in 311/923-4 (Ibn Ḥayyān, *op.cit.*, text 115, 167; tr. 139, 192). During the *fitna*, Mawrūr became the seat of the Berber *ṭāʾifa* of the Banū Dammar or Banū Nūḥ, until the time when, under the third king of the dynasty, Manād b. Muḥammad b. Nūḥ (449-58/1057-66), it was incorporated into the ʿAbbādid kingdom of Seville [see ʿABBĀDIDS and ISHBĪLIYYA] and experienced the same fate as the latter when it was conquered by the Almoravids.

Judging by the silence of the sources, it may be stated with confidence that no event of note took place at Mawrūr and on its territory under the Almoravids and the Almohads. Cordova fell in 1236, and in 1240 in the reign of Fernando III, king of Castile, the *kūra* passed under the domination of the Christians, at the same time as Luque, Aguilar, Ecija, Estepa, Lucena, Marchena and Osuna, and became part of the territory known as Banda Morisca, to the south of the Campiña and to the west of the Nasrid kingdom of Granada. For a period of 529 years, Mawrūr had belonged to the *dār al-Islām*.

Bibliography: Besides the references cited in the article, see ʿUmarī, *Masālik al-abṣār*, tr. Gaudefroy-Demombynes, Paris 1927, 228, no. 3; E. Fagnan, *Extraits*, 210, 211, 213; Ibn al-K͟haṭīb, *Aʿmāl*, 23, 32, 119; Ibn ʿId͟hārī, *Bayān*, iii, 113, 214, 220; Ibn Saʿīd, *Mug͟hrib*, i, 232, 312, 422.

(J. BOSCH VILÁ)

AL-MAWṢIL, in European sources usually rendered as Mosul, a city of northern Mesopotamia or ʿIrāḳ, on the west bank of the Tigris and opposite to the ancient Nineveh. In early Islamic times it was the capital of Diyār Rabīʿa [*q.v.*], forming the eastern part of the province of al-D͟jazīra [*q.v.*]. At the present time, it is the third largest city of the Republic of ʿIrāḳ.

1. History up to 1900.

Al-Mawṣil takes its name from the fact that a number of arms of the river there combine (Arabic, *waṣala*) to form a single stream. The town lies close beside the Tigris on a spur of the western steppe-plateau which juts out into the alluvial plain of the river. Close beside its walls are quarries in which the plaster for the buildings and for the mortar is obtained. The site of the town, almost 3 km^2 in area and enclosed by the already-mentioned wall and the Tigris, slopes from the old fortress gradually to the south. To the south-east there stretch, as in the Middle Ages, the suburbs surrounded by fertile plants. A little above the spot where the wall joins the river on the south-east is the bridge of boats. All the old buildings and even the court of the Great Mosque lie, according to E. Herzfeld's investigations, below the level of the streets in which the accumulation of mounds of débris from houses is a result of a thousand years of continuous occupation.

Whether the town already existed in antiquity is unknown. E. Herzfeld (*Archäol. Reise*, ii, 207, 259) has suggested that Xenophon's Μέσπιλα, reproduces its old name and that we should read *Μέπσιλα (= *Mawṣil*); but against this view we have the simple fact that this town lay on the east bank of the Tigris (F. H. Weissbach, in Pauly-Wissowa, xv, col. 1164).

The Muslims placed the foundations of the town in mythical antiquity and ascribed it to Rēwand b. Bēwarāsp Ad͟jdahāk. According to another tradition, its earlier name was K͟hawlān. The Persian satrap of al-Mawṣil bore the title Būd͟h-Ardas͟hīrāns͟hāh, so that the official name of the town was Būd͟h-Ardas͟hīr (Le Strange, *Lands*, 87; Herzfeld, *op.cit.*, 208). Lastly, Bar Bahlūl says that an old Persian king gave it the name Bih-Hormiz-Ḳawād͟h (G. Hoffmann, *Auszüge aus syr. Akten pers. Märtyren*, 178).

As the metropolis of the diocese of Āt͟hūr, al-Mawṣil took the place of Nineveh, whither Christianity had penetrated by the beginning of the 2nd century A.D. Rabban Īs͟hōʿ-yahb͟h, called Bar Ḳūsrā, about 570 A.D. founded on the west bank of the Tigris opposite Niniveh a monastery (still called Mār Īs͟haʿyā) around which K͟husraw II built many buildings. This settlement is probably the fortress mentioned in the Syriac chronicle edited by Guidi as Ḥesnā ʿEb͟hrāyā (according to Herzfeld, "citadel on the opposite bank") (Nöldeke, in *SB. Ak. Wien*, cxxviii, fasc. 9 [1893], 20; Sachau, *Chronik von Arbela*, ch. iv, 48,1; Herzfeld, *op.cit.*, 208) which later was developed into a town by the Arabs (*Chronicle of Seʿert*, at the end).

Nineveh is attested as a separate Nestorian bishopric from 554 till the early 3rd/9th century, when it was merged with the see of al-Mawṣil, and for roughly the same period, Monophysite bishops are recorded for the monastery of Mar Mattā and Nineveh (later al-Mawṣil) (see J.-M. Fiey, *Assyrie chrétienne*, Beirut 1968, ii, 344 ff.). The area just to the north of al-Mawṣil was known at this time as Bēt͟h Nūhād͟hrā, and that to the south-west as Adiabene, in early Islamic parlance, Arḍ Ḥazza (from the village, Syriac Ḥ^{e}zā, which seems to have been the main centre, towards the end of the Sāsānid period, for the administrative division of Nōd͟h-Ardas͟hīrakan (see M. G. Morony, *Continuity and change in the administrative geography of late Sasanian and early Islamic al-ʿIrāq*, in *Iran*, *JBIPS*, xx [1982], 10 ff.).

After the taking of Nineveh by ʿUtba b. Farḳad (20/641) in the reign of ʿUmar b. al-K͟haṭṭāb, the Arabs crossed the Tigris, whereupon the garrison of the fortress on the west bank surrendered on promising to pay the poll-tax and obtained permission to go where they pleased. Under the same caliph, ʿUtba was dismissed from his post as commander of al-Mawṣil, and Hart͟hama b. ʿArfad͟ja al-Bāriḳī succeeded him. The latter settled Arabs in houses of their own, then allotted them lands and made al-Mawṣil a camp city (*miṣr*) in which he also built a Friday Mosque (al-Balādhurī, 332). According to al-Wāḳidī, ʿAbd al-Malik (65-86/685-705) appointed his son Saʿīd as governor of al-Mawṣil, while he put his brother Muḥammad over Armīniya and al-Djazīra. According to al-Muʿāfā b. Ṭāwūs on the other hand, Muḥammad was also governor of ʿĀdharbāydjān and al-Mawṣil, and his chief of police Ibn Talīd paved the town and built a wall round it (al-Balādhurī, *op.cit.*). His son Marwān II is also described as a builder and extender of the town; he is said to have organised its administration and built roads, walls and a bridge of boats over the Tigris (Ibn Faḳīh, 128; Yāḳūt, *Muʿdjam*, iv, 682-4). The foundation of a Friday Mosque was also ascribed to him. Al-Mawṣil became under him the capital of the province of al-Djazīra.

After al-Mutawakkil's death, the Khāridjī Musāwir seized a part of the territory of al-Mawṣil and made al-Ḥadītha [*q.v.*] his headquarters. The then governor of al-Mawṣil, the Khuzāʿī ʿAḳaba b. Muḥammad, was deposed by the Taghlibī Ayyūb b. Aḥmad, who put his own son Ḥasan in his place. Soon afterwards, in 254/868, the ʿAzdī Allāh b. Sulaymān became the governor of al-Mawṣil. The Kharidjīs took the town from him and Musāwir entered into possession of it. Al-Muʿtamid appointed the Turkish general Asātigin governor of the town, but in Djumādā I 259/March 873 the latter sent his son Azkūtigīn there as his deputy. The latter was soon driven out by the citizens of the town, who chose Yaḥyā b. Sulaymān as their ruler.

Haytham b. ʿAbd Allāh, whom Asātigīn then sent to al-Mawṣil, had to return after achieving nothing. The Taghlibī Isḥāḳ b. Ayyūb, whom Asātigīn sent with 20,000 men against the city, among whom was Ḥamdān b. Ḥamdūn, entered it after winning a battle, but was soon driven out again.

In 261/874-5 the Taghlibī Khiḍr b. Aḥmad and in 267/880-1 Isḥāḳ b. Kundādj were appointed governors of al-Mawṣil by al-Muʿtamid. A year after Isḥāḳ's death, his son Muḥammad sent Hārūn b. Sulaymān to al-Mawṣil (279/892); when he was driven out by the inhabitants, he asked the Banū Shaybān for assistance, and they besieged the town with him. The inhabitants, led by Hārūn b. ʿAbd Allāh and Ḥamdān b. Ḥamdūn, after an initial victory were surprised and defeated by the Shaybānīs; shortly afterward, Muḥammad b. Isḥāḳ was deposed by the Kurd ʿAlī b. Dāwūd.

When al-Muʿtaḍid became caliph in 279/892, Ḥamdān (the grandfather of Sayf al-Dawla) managed to make himself very popular with him at first, but in 282/895 he rebelled in al-Mawṣil. When an army was sent by the caliph against him under Waṣīf and Naṣr, he escaped while his son Ḥusayn surrendered. The citadel was stormed and destroyed, and Ḥamdān soon afterwards was captured and thrown into prison. Naṣr was then ordered to collect tribute in the city and thus came into conflict with the followers of the Khāridjī Hārūn; Hārūn was defeated and fled into the desert. In place of Tuktamīr, who was imprisoned, the caliph appointed Ḥasan b. ʿAlī as governor of al-Mawṣil and sent against Hārūn, the main cause of the strife, the Ḥamdānid Ḥusayn, who took him prisoner in 283/896. The family thus regained the caliph's favour.

When after the subjection of the Khāridjīs, raiding Kurds began to disturb the country round al-Mawṣil, al-Muktafī again gave a Ḥamdānid, namely Ḥusayn's brother Abu 'l-Haydjāʾ ʿAbd Allāh, the task of bringing them to book, as the latter could rely on the assistance of the Taghlibīs settled around the city to whom the Ḥamdānids belonged. Abu 'l-Haydjāʾ came to al-Mawṣil in the beginning of Muḥarram 293/October 906 and in the following year subdued the Kurds, whose leader Muḥammad b. Bilāl submitted and came to live in the city.

From this time, the Ḥamdānids [*q.v.*] ruled there, first as governors for the caliph, then from 317/929 (Nāṣir al-Dawla Ḥasan) as sovereign rulers.

The ʿUḳaylids who followed them (386-498/996-1096) belonged to the tribe of the Banū Kaʿb. Their kingdom, founded by Ḥusām al-Dawla al-Muḳallad, whose independence was recognised by the Būyids, extended as far as Tāʾūḳ (Daḳūḳā), al-Madāʾin and Kūfa. In 489/1095-6, al-Mawṣil passed to the Saldjūḳs.

The town developed considerably under the Atābeg ʿImād al-Dīn Zangī, who put an end to Saldjūḳ rule in 521/1127-8. The city which was for the most part in ruins, was given splendid buildings by him; the fortifications were restored and flourishing gardens surrounded the town. Under one of his successors, ʿIzz al-Dīn Masʿūd I, it was twice unsuccessfully besieged by the Ayyūbid Ṣalāḥ al-Dīn (1182 and 1185 A.D.); after the conclusion of peace, ʿIzz al-Dīn, however, found himself forced to recognise Ṣalāḥ al-Dīn as his suzerain.

The town was at this time defended by a strong citadel and a double wall, the towers of which were washed on the east side by the Tigris. To the south lay a great suburb, laid out by the vizier Mudjāhid al-Dīn Ḳāʾimāz (d. 595/1199). From 607/1210-11 his son Badr al-Dīn Luʾluʾ [*q.v.*] ruled over al-Mawṣil first as vizier of the last Zangids and from 631/1234 as an independent ruler. In 642/1244-5 he submitted to Hūlāgū and accompanied him on his campaigns, so that al-Mawṣil was spared the usual sacking. When however his son al-Malik al-Ṣāliḥ Ismāʿīl joined Baybars against the Mongols, the town was plundered in 660/1261-2; the ruler himself fell in battle (van Berchem, in *Festschrift für Th. Nöldeke*, Giessen 1906, 197 ff.).

The Arab geographers compare its plan to a headcloth (*ṭaylasān*), i.e. to an elongated rectangle. Ibn Ḥawḳal, who visited al-Mawṣil in 358/968-9, describes it as a beautiful town with fertile surroundings. The population in his time consisted mainly of Kurds. According to al-Muḳaddasī (*ca.* 375/985-6, the town was very beautifully built. Its plan was in the form of a semi-circle. The citadel was called *al-Murabbaʿa* and stood where the Nahr Zubayda canal joined the Tigris (now Ič-ḳalʿa or Bāsh Ṭābiya?; cf. Herzfeld, *op.cit.*, 209). Within its walls were a Wednesday market (*Sūḳ al-Arbaʿāʾ*), after which it was sometimes called. The Friday Mosque built by Marwān stood on an eminence not far from the Tigris to which steps led up. The streets in the market were for the most part roofed over. The same geographer (136) gives the eight main streets of the town (discussed in Herzfeld, *op.cit.*, 209). The castle of the caliph (*Ḳaṣr al-Khalīfa*) stood on the east bank, half a mile from the town, and commanded Nineveh; in the time of al-Muḳaddasī it was already in ruins, through which the Nahr al-Khawṣar flowed.

Ibn Djubayr visited al-Mawṣil on 22-6 Ṣafar 580/4-8 June 1184. Shortly before, Nūr al-Dīn had built a new Friday Mosque on the market place. At the highest point in the town was the citadel (now Bāsh Ṭābiya); it was known as *al-Ḥadbāʾ* "the hunchbacked", and perhaps as the synonymous *al-Dafaʾā* (G. Hoffmann, *Auszüge aus syr. Akten pers. Märtyren*, 178-9; Herzfeld, *op.cit.*, 210), and according to al-Ḳazwīnī was surrounded by a deep ditch and high walls. The city walls, which had strong towers, ran down to the river and along its bank. A broad highway (*shāriʿ*) connected the upper and lower towns (the north-south road called *Darb Dayr al-Aʿlā*). In front of the walls suburbs stretched into the distance with many smaller mosques, inns and baths. The hospital (*māristān*) and the great covered market (*ḳaysariyya*) were celebrated.

Most houses in al-Mawṣil were built of tufa or marble (from the Djabal Maḳlūb east of the town) and had domed roofs (Yāḳūt, *op.cit.*). Later, it was given a third Friday Mosque which commanded the Tigris and was perhaps the building admired by Ḥamd Allāh al-Mustawfī (*ca.* 740/1339-40).

The site of the ancient Nineveh (Arabic *Nīnawāy*) was in al-Muḳadasī's time called Tall al-Tawba and was said to be the place where the prophet Yūnus stayed when he wished to convert the people of Nineveh. There was a mosque there around which the Ḥamdānid Nāṣir al-Dawla built hostels for pilgrims. Half a mile away was the healing spring of ʿAyn Yūnus with a mosque beside it, perhaps also the Shadjarat al-Yaḳṭīn, said to have been planted by the Prophet himself. The tomb of Nabī Djirdjīs [*q.v.*], who according to Muslim legend had suffered martyrdom in al-Mawṣil, was in the east town, as was also that of Nabī Shīth (Seth; cf. Herzfeld, *op.cit.*, 206-7).

The textiles of al-Mawṣil were especially famed, and from the city's name came Eng. *muslin* and Fr. *mousseline*, although it appears from Marco Polo's mention of *mosolino* cloth as made with gold and silver threads that these luxury cloths differed from the present-day thin and delicate cottons (see Sir Henry Yule, *The book of Ser Marco Polo the Venetian*, London 1871, i, 57-9; R. B. Serjeant, *Islamic textiles, material for a history up to the Mongol conquest*, Beirut 1972, 38-9).

The Mongol dynasty of the Djalāʾirids succeeded the Īlkhāns in Baghdād, and Sultan Shaykh Uways in 766/1364-5 incorporated al-Mawṣil in his kingdom. The world-conqueror Tīmūr not only spared the city but gave rich endowments to the tombs of Nabī Yūnus and Nabī Djirdjīs, to which he made a pilgrimage, and restored the bridge of boats between al-Mawṣil and these holy places.

The Turkoman dynasty of the Aḳ Ḳoyūnlū, whose founder Bahāʾ al-Dīn Ḳarā ʿUthmān had been appointed governor of Diyārbakr by Tīmūr, was followed by the Ṣafawids, who took over al-Mawṣil after their conquest of Baghdād in 914/late 1508, but lost it again to Sulaymān the Magnificent in 941/1535, who appointed Sayyid Aḥmad of Djazīrat Ibn ʿUmar as its governor. From the year 1000/1592 onwards, we have lists of the Ottoman *pashas* of the *sandjaḳ* of al-Mawṣil (for long attached to the *eyālet* of Diyārbakr), whose tenure of power was usually short-lived; thus from 1048/1638 to 1111/1699-1700 there were 48 *pashas*. Nādir Shāh besieged it in 1156/1743, but the governor Ḥusayn Djalīlī refortified the city and heroically defended it. It was at this time and thereafter that the *pashalïḳ* of al-Mawṣil was fairly continuously in the hands of the local family, originally Christians, of ʿAbd al-Djalīl; Ḥusayn b. Ismāʿīl held this office on eight separate occasions, and the hold of the Djalīlīs was only broken in 1834, when Sultan Maḥmūd II extended his centralising power over the *derebeys* and other previously largely autonomous local potentates and removed Yaḥyā b. Nuʿmān al-Djalīlī.

European travellers frequently passed through al-Mawṣil and mention it in their travel narratives; they often comment unfavourably on the unclean streets and on the sectarian strife there amongst both Muslims and the rival Christian churches. After 1879, the *sandjaḳ* of al-Mawṣil, after being attached to Vān, Hakkārī and then Baghdād, became a separate *wilāyet.* There was a long tradition of French missionary and educational work in the city, by e.g. Carmelites and Dominicans, largely among the indigenous Eastern Christian churches. In the later 19th century, travellers describe al-Mawṣil's mud brick walls, with their seven gates, as largely ruinous, and record the dominant form of domestic architecture as stone-built houses with *sardābs*; the population then was around 40,000, including 7,000 Christians and 1,500 Jews.

Bibliography (in addition to references given in the text): al-Muḳaddasī, 136-8; Ibn Khurradādhbih, 17; Yāḳūt, *Muʿdjam*, iv, 682-4; Ṣafī al-Dīn, *Marāṣid al-iṭṭilāʿ*, ed. Juynboll, i, 84; Ibn al-Athīr, *Taʾrīkh al-Dawla al-Atābakiyya Mulūk al-Mawṣil*, in *Recueil des Historiens des Croisades*, ii/2, Paris 1876, 1-394; A. Socin, *Mosul and Mārdīn*, in *ZDMG*, xxxvi (1882), 1-53, 238-77; xxxvii (1883), 188-222; Le Strange, *The lands of the eastern caliphate*, Cambridge 1905, 87-9; M. van Berchem, *Arabische Inschriften von Mosul*, in F. Sarre-E. Herzfeld, *Archäologische Reise im Euphrat- und Tigrisgebiet*, i, Berlin 1911, 16-30; Herzfeld, *ibid.*, ii, 1920, 203-304 (ch. vii); iii, tables v-ix, lxxxviii-cx; Sir Charles Wilson, *Murray's handbook for travellers in Asia Minor, Transcaucasia, Persia, etc.*, London 1895, 293-4; S. H. Longrigg, *Four centuries of modern Iraq*, Oxford 1925, 35-7, 95-7, 149-52, 158, 253, 284; A. Birken, *Die Provinzen des Osmanischen Reiches*, Wiesbaden 1976, 179, 192, 203, 222. For the 10th/16th century Ottoman *mufaṣṣal ṭapu defters* for the Mawṣil *liwāʾ*, see B. Lewis, *The Ottoman archives as a source for the history of the Arab lands*, in *JRAS* (1951), 149.

(E. HONIGMANN -[C. E. BOSWORTH])

2. Since 1900.

By the beginning of the 20th century, the prosperity and political importance of al-Mawṣil were evidently waning, largely because the opening of the Suez Canal in 1869 had occasioned an immediate reduction in the overland trade between the city and its traditional commercial partners, Aleppo and Damascus. Furthermore, the development of the port of Baṣra and of steam navigation on the Tigris gradually had the effect of subordinating the economy of al-Mawṣil to that of Baghdād, which became the entrepot for all the former city's imports and exports.

The effects of the *Tanẓīmāt* were even more lightly felt in the province of al-Mawṣil than in the rest of ʿIrāḳ, and there is no sign that the various administrative changes had any particular effect in curbing the powers of the local notables and tribal leaders. As noted above, in 1879 the city itself became the headquarters of a *wilāyet* of the same name, comprising the *ḳaḍāʾs* of al-Mawṣil, Kirkūk, Arbīl and Sulaymāniyya, but for the rest of the period of Ottoman rule, the state's control over most of what is now ʿIrāḳī Kurdistān was purely nominal, and between 1895 and 1911, one man, Muṣṭafā Čalabi Ṣābūndjī, was virtual dictator of al-Mawṣil town, far more powerful than any of the numerous *wālīs* sent from Istanbul (see Hanna Batatu, *The old social classes and the revolutionary movements of Iraq: a study of Iraq's old landed and commercial classes, and of its Communists, Ba'thists and Free Officers*, Princeton 1978, 289-92). Using Ottoman sources, J. McCarthy (*The population of Ottoman Syria and Iraq, 1878-1914*, in *AAS*, xv [1981], 3-44) has calculated that the population of al-Mawṣil *wilāyet* in 1330/1911-12 was about 828,000, which is considerably higher than earlier estimates (e.g., see S. H. Longrigg, *Iraq 1900 to 1950*, London

1953, 7). It is even more difficult to establish an accurate figure for al-Mawṣil town alone; McCarthy (*op.cit.*, 41) suggests 36,500 adult males, which accords with the estimated total of 70,000 inhabitants given in *al-ᶜIrāq Yearbook* for 1922 (Batatu, *op.cit.*, 35).

For most of the First World War, the fighting on the ᶜIrāḳī front took place in the Baṣra and Ba<u>gh</u>dād *wilāyet*s, with the result that al-Mawṣil town itself was relatively little affected, and was in fact only occupied by British troops some days after the Armistice of Mudros (30 October 1918; see A. T. Wilson, *Mesopotamia 1917-1920: a clash of loyalties*, London 1931, 11). The area had been assigned to France in the Sykes-Picot Agreement of 1916, but Clemenceau immediately acquiesced in Lloyd George's request in December 1918 that it should be attached to ᶜIrāḳ, and thus to the British sphere of influence, provided that France would be assured of equality in the exploitation of Mesopotamian oil (see J. Nevakivi, *Britain, France and the Arab Middle East 1914-1920*, London 1969, 91-2). Although the mandate for ᶜIrāḳ was assigned to Britain under the Treaty of San Remo (April 1920 [see MANDATES]), the Turkish Republican government continued to contest the new ᶜIrāḳī state's right to al-Mawṣil and the *wilāyet* was only finally awarded to ᶜIrāḳ in 1925 after an enquiry carried out by the League of Nations (for details, see C. J. Edmonds, *Kurds, Turks and Arabs: politics, travel and research in North-eastern Iraq 1919-1925*, London 1957). Oil was struck in commercial quantities near Kirkūk in 1927, and these northern oilfields, exploited until nationalisation in 1973 by the Iraq Petroleum Company, an Anglo-French-Dutch-American consortium, form one of the country's most valuable economic assets.

Under the mandate and monarchy (1920-32; 1932-58) the status of al-Mawṣil continued to decline, partly because the inauguration of the new state and the establishment of Ba<u>gh</u>dād as its capital inevitably deprived it of its importance as an independent provincial centre, and partly because al-Mawṣil *wilāyet* itself was further sub-divided into four provinces (al-Mawṣil, Sulaymāniyya, Kirkūk and Arbīl). The city maintained its somewhat conservative reputation throughout the period, and in comparison with Ba<u>gh</u>dād and Baṣra seems to have been relatively little affected by the independence struggles of the 1940s and 1950s. During this period, members of the city's prominent families, notably the <u>Sh</u>ammar *<u>sh</u>ay<u>kh</u>s* and members of the Ka<u>sh</u>mūla, <u>Kh</u>udayr and <u>Sh</u>allāl families, gradually came to acquire legal ownership of much of the land in the surrounding countryside. Such individuals naturally felt threatened by the avowedly revolutionary aims of the government of ᶜAbd al-Karīm Ḳāsim [*q.v.*], which came to power on 14 July 1958, and in particular by its immediate introduction of an agrarian reform law.

In March 1959, some of the landowners and their followers joined together with local Arab nationalists and a number of Ḳāsim's former supporters in the armed forces in an attempt to overthrow his régime, with assistance promised (but not ultimately forthcoming) from Cairo and Damascus. Four days of fighting broke out in the city between the supporters and opponents of Ḳāsim, in which some 200 people were killed. The attempted coup was unsuccessful, but the incident was to be used many times in the future as a rallying cry for revenge on the part of Baᶜthists and nationalists against Ḳāsim and his left-wing supporters (see Batatu, *op.cit.*, 58-61, 866-89).

Al-Mawṣil was finally connected with the rest of the ᶜIrāḳī railway system in 1939, and served by Iraqi Airways after 1946; the existing tertiary colleges in the city were amalgamated into a university in 1967, which has since been expanded considerably. In the course of a provincial reorganisation in 1969, al-Mawṣil province was divided into two new units, Nineveh (Nīnawā) and Duhūk. In the 1977 census, al-Mawṣil emerged as the third largest city in ᶜIrāḳ with a population of 430,000, preceded by Baṣra (450,000) and Ba<u>gh</u>dād (2.86 million). In spite of attempts on the part of the central government to promote regional economic development, al-Mawṣil is inevitably at a disadvantage through being some distance from the country's main industrial concentrations, 75% of which are located around Ba<u>gh</u>dād and Baṣra. Its principal industries are agriculturally-based, including food-processing, and leather working, but textiles and cement are also produced, and an oil refinery was opened in 1976. The city retains much of its traditional ethnic and religious heterogeneity, and its mediaeval core still remains clearly distinct, despite the intrusion of various unattractive manifestations of modern town planning.

Bibliography: In addition to the works mentioned in the text (especially Batatu, which is indispensable): M. Kyriakos, *Fiançailles et mariages à Mossoul*, in *Anthropos*, vi (1911), 744-84; W. Heinrichs, *Eine Karawanenreise von Mosul nach Aleppo vom 9 März bis 25 April 1911*, in *PGM*, lx (1914), 189-93, 257-59; H. C. Luke, *Mosul and its minorities*, London 1925; A. Giannini, *La contesa anglo-turca per Mossul*, in *OM*, iv (1924), 409-29; S. H. Longrigg, *Four centuries of modern Iraq*, London 1925 (repr. Farnborough 1969); idem, *Oil in the Middle East: its discovery and development*, London 1954; H. E. Wilkie Young, *Mosul in 1909*, in *MES*, vii (1971), 229-35; P. Sluglett, *Britain in Iraq 1914-1932*, London 1976, esp. 103-40; K. McLachlan, *Iraq: problems of regional development*, in A. Kelidar (ed.), *The integration of modern Iraq*, London 1979, 135-49; P. J. Beck, *"A tedious and perilous controversy"; Britain and the settlement of the Mosul question 1918-1926*, in *MES*, xvii (1981), 256-76; R. Owen, *The Middle East in the world economy 1800-1914*, London 1981, esp. 180-8, 273-86; Government of Iraq, *Annual abstract of statistics*. (P. SLUGLETT)

AL-**MAWṢILĪ** [see IBRĀHĪM and ISḤĀḲ B. IBRĀHĪM AL-MAWṢILĪ].

AL-**MAWṢILĪ,** BAKR B. AL-ḲĀSIM B. ABĪ <u>TH</u>AWR, philosophical writer, is known only as the author of an epistolary philosophical work entitled *Fī 'l-nafs* ("Concerning the soul"). It was written between 278/900 and 328/950 and sent to the distinguished translator and doctor Abū ᶜU<u>th</u>mān Saᶜīd b. Yaᶜḳūb al-Dima<u>sh</u>ḳī. The author seems to have lived in the Mawṣil region, and is not to be confused with another philosopher from that area, Ibn Abī Saᶜīd al-Mawṣilī. The text deals not with the soul as such, but only with a part of it, the rational soul (*nafs nāṭiḳa*) or intellect (*ᶜaḳl*). His technique is explicitly that of <u>Th</u>ābit b. Ḳurra and Plato in analysing the characteristics of the definition of the intellect in order to draw out its essence. The intellect impresses a form upon our sense-data, and what we know can either be acquired (*mustafād*) from outside of ourselves or not. As Aristotle put it, it is a question of whether the intellect which forms all things is part of the soul or rather something outside the soul—the latter being the normal Islamic religious interpretation. Al-Mawṣilī argues that the intellect does not acquire knowledge by means of contact with a transcendent being, but rather by reflection of the intellect upon itself. We can indeed make mistakes (e.g. be misled by imagination), but not if we reflect rationally upon the first principles (*al-awāʾil*) of logical thought, since they are the grounds upon which the truth or falsity of everything else depends. These universals (*al-umūr al-kulliyya*) are true, real in themselves and their own objects, and are not equivalent to the body, but constitute a substance not susceptible to decay. Thereby al-Mawṣilī elegantly tackles an Aristotelian problem (without mentioning Aristotle) in a Platonic manner, actually referring to the *Phaedo* and its doctrine of reminiscence as the route to genuine knowledge.

Bibliography: Plato, *Phaedo*; Aristotle, *De Anima*, 3.4.429a, 21-22, 429b, 6. 5.430a, 10-15; Bakr al-Mawṣilī, *Fi 'l-nafs*, ms. British Museum, Add. 7473, 6a-12a; S. Pinès, *La doctrine de l'intellect selon Bakr al-Mawṣilī*, in *Studi Orientalistici in onore di Giorgio Levi della Vida*, Rome 1956, ii, 350-64; H. Davidson, *Alfarabi and Avicenna on the active intellect*, in *Viator*, iii (1972), 109-78.

(O. N. H. LEAMAN)

MAWSIM (A., from the root *w-s-m* "to mark, imprint"), market, festival. In this sense the term is used in *ḥadīth*, especially in connection with the markets of early Arabia, such as those which were held in ʿUkāẓ, Madjanna, Dhu 'l-Madjāz, ʿArafa, etc. (al-Bukhārī, *Ḥadjdj*, *bāb* 150; *Tafsīr*, sūra II, *bāb* 34). At these markets, the worst elements of Arabia gathered (*al-mawsim yadjmaʿ raʿāʿ al-nās*, al-Bukhārī, *Ḥudūd*, *bāb* 31). Advantage was also taken of these assemblies to make public proclamations and inquiries, e.g. in order to regulate the affairs of deceased persons (al-Bukhārī, *Khums*, *bāb* 13; *Manāḳib al-Anṣār*, *bāb* 27). As the pilgrimage was at the same time one of the chief markets of early Arabia, the term *mawāsim* is often combined with it (*mawāsim al-ḥadjdj*, al-Bukhārī, *Ḥadjdj*, *bāb* 150; *Buyūʿ*, *bāb* 1; Abū Dāwūd, *Manāsik*, *bāb* 6). Upon this basis, the term *mawsim* has developed chiefly in two directions.

First, it has acquired the meaning of a festival, generally with a religious basis. When such a festival signifies the birthday of a prophet or local saint, the term more generally used is *mawlid* (dialectically, *mūlid*, etc.) [*q.v.*], but often some other event in a holy man's life, or even his death, may be celebrated, often at a date which shows continuity with some ancient nature festival or other rite. Cf. the *mawsim* of Nabī Mūsā, held between the centres of Jerusalem and the shrine near Jericho from the Friday preceding Good Friday till Maundy Thursday; see G. E. Von Grunebaum, *Muhammadan festivals*, repr. London 1976, 80 ff. A *mawsim* might, however, be a secular occasion, at least in its developed form, such as the festival traditionally held in Cairo during August to celebrate the rising of the Nile waters, the *mawsim al-khalīdj* or *yawm wafāʾ al-Nīl/yawm djabr al-baḥr*; see Lane, *The Manners and customs of the modern Egyptians*, ch. xxvi "Periodical public festivals".

Second, it has come to mean season. Thus in Lebanon, *mawsim* denotes the season of the preparation of silk (al-Bustānī, *Muḥīṭ*, s.v.), whilst in India and in European terminology referring to these parts of the world, it has acquired the meaning of "season" in connection with the weatherconditions special to those regions, such as the regularly returning winds and rain periods. *Monsoon*, *mousson*, *moesson* and other corruptions of the term are found in this literature.

Bibliography: In addition to the works mentioned in the art. cf. *LA*, xvi, 123 ff.; Wellhausen, *Reste arabischen Heidentums*,[2] Berlin 1897, 84 ff., 246; Yule and Burnell, *Hobson-Jobson*, ed. W. Crooke, London 1903, s.v. *monsoon*.

(A. J. WENSINCK -[C. E. BOSWORTH])

MAWSŪʿA (A.), "encyclopaedia".

1. In Arabic.

In the sense of "a work dealing with all the sciences and arts", the idea of an encyclopaedia was not expressed in Classical Arabic, and it was not until the 19th century that the expression *dāʾirat al-maʿārif* "circle of items of knowledge" was coined, corresponding approximately to the etymological meaning of the word current in Western languages, and not until the 20th that a neologism, *mawsūʿa*, emerged, which contains an idea of breadth, of wide coverage, etc. Nevertheless, the absence of a perfectly adequate descriptive term—although we may cite for example *ādāb* or *maʿārif*—does not necessarily imply the non-existence of a tendency to encyclopaedic writing, translated into practice by the composition of general works due to some scholars applying themselves to the acquisition and diffusion of knowledge belonging to a wide range of intellectual and technical disciplines. Indeed, secular *maʿārif* [*q.v.*], as opposed to *ʿulūm* [see ʿILM] of a religious nature, nourished the literary genre designated *adab* [*q.v.*] (pl. *ādāb*), which branched out and became conducive to the moral, cultural and professional formation of the Muslims and consequently presupposed the bringing together of a mass of different notions. The definition of *adab*, which consists of "taking a little of everything" (*al-akhdh min kulli shayʾin bi-ṭaraf*), may mean that, in the traditional and speculative sciences (*ʿulūm naḳliyya wa-ʿaḳliyya*) developed since the beginnings of Islam, one proceeded to a choice which assumed, by force of circumstances, an encyclopaedic aspect and was given shape in works which bear witness to the level of the average culture and the tastes of the public to whom they were addressed. The latter consisted of those who were particularly desirous of being well-informed, but also of the bureaucracy, the *kuttāb* [see KĀTIB], who needed to possess extensive and varied knowledge, within the limits which precisely by their nature were to define the variable content of encyclopaedic works.

In the 3rd/9th and the 4th/10th centuries, "the Arabo-Islamic world, under the thrust of the cultural primacy of ʿIrāḳ, showed its capacity to combine the creation of humanism with that of encyclopaedic activity" (R. Blachère, *Réflexions*, 521) and began to be exposed to beneficial foreign influences which led the most open spirits to inquire into the universe, while respecting as far as possible Ḳurʾānic teachings. At the beginning of the 3rd/9th century, a similar attitude found expression in al-Djāḥiẓ (d. 255/868-9 [*q.v.*]), who dominated *adab* in the broad sense. He restrains himself from adopting a static viewpoint while abstaining from explaining the point of the information, but displays an astonishing dynamism in indicating some directions for investigation and proposing a method of acquisition and enrichment of knowledge by observation, experimentation, reflection, in a huge output covering *de omni re scribili*; this collection, in which the *Kitāb al-Ḥayawān* stands out, finally assumed an encyclopaedic character clearly illustrated furthermore by the *Kitāb al-Tarbīʿ wa 'l-tadwīr* and evidenced in our own times not only by the indices of the works concerned, but further, notably, by such works as *al-Mawrūth al-shaʿbī fī āthār al-Djāḥiẓ* (anonymous, Baghdād 1396/1976) with regard to folklore, and the *Muʿdjam al-Djāḥiẓ* of Ibrāhīm al-Sāmarrāʾī (Baghdād 1982).

Given that the temperament of this author hardly enables him to follow a methodical order, the *Kitāb al-Ḥayawān* is far from being a zoological dictionary, and one must refer to the excellent index which accompanies it in order to locate the details relating to the various animals presented in the body of the text. It is quite different in the *ʿAdjāʾib al-makhlūḳāt* of al-Ḳazwīnī (600-82/1203-83 [*q.v.*]), which contains an alphabetical series of notices concerning animals in its section on the description of the universe dealing with terrestrial matters. But the efforts deployed in this field reach their culmination in the *Ḥayāt al-ḥayawān al-kubrā* of al-Damīrī (742-808/1341-1405 [*q.v.*]), a true zoological encyclopaedia whose great merit is the alphabetical classification adopted by the author and the division of the entries into philological remarks, description of the animal concerned, mentions which are made of it in the Ḳurʾān and Sunna, whether the consumption of its flesh is allowed or forbidden, proverbs concerning it, medicinal qualities and interpretation of dreams in which it appears. The above details show the spirit in which this compilation was conceived: a useful one, but deprived of originality due to a writer of traditional training who had been able to draw on works already founded on the mass of texts written initially in Arabic or translated into that language that the public did not always have the leisure or the taste to procure. In any case, al-Damīrī lived in an age when intellectual curiosity had waned considerably and had largely lost the openness which had marked the century of al-Djāḥiẓ and the Muʿtazila. All the same, shortly after the death of this latter author, the religious policy of the caliphate brought to the forefront Muslims disturbed by the turn taken by the rather anarchic quest for knowledge and by the danger to the integrity of Islam that they perceived to be posed by a curiosity which appeared reprehensible. This resulted in according primacy to the Islamic and Arab sciences, to the detriment of foreign ideas already partly acclimatised. Among those who are noted for their conservative attitude, the most characteristic is certainly Ibn Ḳutayba (d. 276/889 [*q.v.*]), who opposed the liberalism and eclecticism of al-Djāḥiẓ with a programme limited to the needs of various social categories. To the secretaries of the administration, who began to be the real preservers of culture, he proposed a vade-mecum, the *Adab al-kātib*, in which he adopts the following classification of necessary knowledge: philological disciplines, applied sciences, techniques of public works, principles of jurisprudence, history and ethics. When he is concerned with the training of religious scholars, he adds to philology and ethics the Ḳurʾān and Sunna, plus some rudiments of *falsafa* [*q.v.*] by way of documentation and in order to be in a position to refute it. So much for the *kātib* and the *faḳīh*. There remains the *adīb*, for whom are intended the *Kitāb al-Maʿārif*, an encyclopaedia of historical knowledge useful to the cultured Muslim, and, especially, the *ʿUyūn al-akhbār*, in which most of the ideas which should be mastered are grouped under ten headings: the ruler, war, greatness in this world, qualities and faults, rhetoric, oratorical art, piety, how to choose one's friends, how to achieve one's ends, table manners and women (see G. Lecomte, *Ibn Qutayba*, Damascus 1965, 145). The programme recommended by Ibn Ḳutayba appeared not to allow any improvement or amplification.

On this point, some progress was nevertheless achieved by his successor, the Cordovan Ibn ʿAbd Rabbih (246-328/860-940 [*q.v.*]), who remarks that each generation leaves its gift of new knowledge and that consequently, one should summarise and complete periodically the elements of the common patrimony that have been accumulated. In his practical encyclopaedia, the *ʿIḳd*, which is richer and more subtle than the *ʿUyūn al-akhbār*, the subject matter is divided into 25 chapters, each bearing the name of one of the precious stones of which the "necklace" (*ʿiḳd*) is made up. The list is as follows: the ruler, war, generosity, delegations (to the Prophet), addressing kings, *ʿilm* and *adab*, proverbs, moral exhortations, elegies, virtues of the Arabs, language of the Arabs, retorts, speeches, epistles, the caliphs, Ziyād b. Abīhi, the pre-Islamic battles, poetry, metrics, song, false prophets, madmen, misers, human temperaments, food and drink and pleasantries. The coverage of this encyclopaedia, whose popular character is evident, hardly allows us to glimpse the country where it was compiled, Spain, for everything, or almost everything, is borrowed from the Eastern tradition.

After the *ʿIḳd*, the encyclopaedic tendency appears in a more diffuse manner, in the sense that the same writer, when he possesses wide erudition, multiplies the specialised treatises and abstains from proceeding to a synthesis. It is only in the 9th/15th century that the series represented by the *ʿUyūn al-akhbār* and the *ʿIḳd* is resumed by a new popular encyclopaedia, the *Mustaṭraf* of the Egyptian al-Ibshīhī (d. after 850/1446 [*q.v.*]), who, claiming to be inspired by Ibn ʿAbd Rabbih, nevertheless shows a concern for edification and manages to combine, in a manual written on a relatively limited scale, all that a good Muslim ought to know. It is of some value to enumerate the 84 chapters of this work: the edifice of Islam; reason; the Ḳurʾān; religious and secular knowledge; good manners; proverbs; rhetoric; retorts; oratorical art and poetry; trust in God; advice; moral exhortations; modesty, the sovereign; courtiers; ministers; escaping observation; magistrature; justice; injustice; the way of treating the people; the happiness of the people; qualities and faults; social life; concord; simplicity; pride; boastfulness; nobility; saints; miracles; rogues; generosity; avarice; table manners; magnanimity; promises kept; discretion; perfidy; courage; heroes; praises and gratitude; satires; sincerity and falsehood; filial piety; physical beauty; ornaments and care for the body; youth and health; names; journeys; wealth; kinship, the manner of begging; presents; work; acceptance of one's lot; changes of fortune; slavery; early Arabs; soothsaying; tricks; animals; wonders of creation; the djinn; wonders of the waters; wonders of the earth; mines and precious stones; music and song; singers and musicians; singing girls; love; specimens of songs; women; wine; pleasantries; anecdotes; invocations; fate; return to God; illnesses; death; patience; the lower world; prayers upon Muḥammad. It would not be impossible to discover in this sequence of chapters an ordering concept, an effort at logical classification which the apparent disorder of the arrangement belies. Besides, the *adab* which underpins al-Ibshīhī's work is less secular and more ethical. For this author, the best answer for those minds who are profoundly disturbed by the situation of the Arabo-Islamic world is a return to the sources, a recollection of the records of the classical period, which represents a perfect ideal for the average Muslim.

The authors that we are about to cite are not at all concerned with what is happening beyond the frontiers of *dār al-Islām*, and the *Kitāb al-Maʿārif* of Ibn Ḳutayba is, in this respect, characteristic, for it limits the historical ideas that a good Sunnī ought to have: a sacred history from Adam to Jesus followed up by means of traditions relating to the personalities of the "Interval" [see FATRA], genealogies of the Arabs, a somewhat anecdotal history of the caliphs and some celebrities, the religion of the ancient Arabs, sects of

Islam, and finally the kings of Yemen, Syria, al-Ḥīra and Persia. To put it another way, this historian is exclusively concerned—but only in a partial manner—with the Islamised countries.

On the other hand, after the eclipse of Muʿtazilism, openness was the feature of Shīʿīs. If one excludes the work of al-Barḳī [*q.v.* in Suppl.] whose *Kitāb al-Maḥāsin* is too mutilated to be assessed, the first author to cite is al-Yaʿḳūbī (d. 284/897 [*q.v.*]), who, in his *Taʾrīkh*, does not fail to devote some chapters not only to the same subjects as Ibn Ḳutayba, but also to the ancient rulers of India, Greece, Rome, Byzantium, Persia and even China. After this attempt at a historical encyclopaedia comes the *Taʾrīkh* of al-Ṭabarī (225-310/839-934 [*q.v.*]), which has some of the same character as a universal history, much more developed, but the real successor of al-Yaʿḳūbī is the polygraph al-Masʿūdī (d. 345/956 [*q.v.*]) who was led by an extraordinary intellectual curiosity to acquire a truly encyclopaedic knowledge which was able to nourish a series of general works in a historico-geographical framework, of which only some résumés have survived, such as the *Tanbīh* and especially the *Murūdj*. Here, before embarking on his discussion of the history of Muslim rulers also in an anecdotal fashion (this being one of the features of *adab*), al-Masʿūdī presents essential information on the outstanding characters of the world and reproduces lists of kings of peoples foreign to Islam, and notably those of France since Clovis. The encyclopaedic nature of the *Murūdj* is evident from the index in two volumes which the present author has added to his edition of the Arabic text; it is also illustrated by the citations to be found mainly in later encyclopaedists.

The summaries which we have reproduced above reveal a concern for exhaustiveness which is not, however, accompanied by a logical classification, and it is only among the *falāsifa* [*q.v.*], heirs of Greek thought, that one can discover the first attempts if not to establish a hierarchy of the sciences, at least to classify them. Among them, al-Farābī (d. 339/950 [*q.v.*]) covers human knowledge in a rich and diverse work which lies outside Islam and suggests a classification of the sciences well-known in the Western Middle Ages, thanks to the translation made by Gerard of Cremona (*De scientiis*): (i) Linguistic sciences (morphology; lexicography; syntax; art of writing; art of reading well; poetry and metre). (ii) Logic. (iii) Mathematics (arithmetic; geometry; optics; astronomy; music; metrology; mechanics). (iv) Physics and metaphysics. (v) Political science, jurisprudence and theology.

Whereas the concessions of al-Farābī to Arabism and Islam consist merely of expressing in Arabic terms the linguistic sciences and in Islamic terms jurisprudence (*fiḳh*) and theology (*kalām*), al-Khwārazmī (wrote *ca.* 366/976 [*q.v.*]) divides the branches of knowledge into two main categories in his *Mafātīḥ al-ʿulūm*: sciences of the Islamic law (*sharīʿa*) and subjects connected with it (*fiḳh*; *kalām*; grammar; artistic composition; poetry and prosody; history), and foreign sciences (philosophy; logic; medicine; arithmetic; geometry; astronomy and astrology; music; mechanics; alchemy).

Later, the respective parts of the "Arab" sciences and the "foreign" sciences were to distinguish various classifications, which could be illustrated by more developed encyclopaedias than that of al-Farabī (on the classifications of the sciences, see L. Gardet and M.-M. Anawati, *Introduction à la théologie musulmane*, Paris 1948, 101 ff.; also Abū Ḥayyān al-Tawḥīdī, *Risāla fi 'l-ʿulūm*, by M. Bergé, in *BEO Damas*, xviii [1963-4], 240-98; Ibn Ḥazm, *Marātib al-ʿulūm*. For his part, Ibn Khaldūn (732-808/1332-1406 [*q.v.*]) distinguishes two main categories of sciences, the religious and the philosophical, but confines himself to a theoretical discussion without encyclopaedic elaboration).

It is only right that we should regard as an encyclopaedia the collective work of the Ikhwān al-Ṣafāʾ [*q.v.*] who discuss in 52 treatises or epistles (*risāla* [*q.v.*], pl. *rasāʾil*) all the accessible knowledge of their time (second half of the 4th/10th century). Rationalists and heirs of the Greek philosophers, the Muʿtazilīs and al-Djāḥiẓ, they accept all that can contribute to enrich the cultural patrimony. Their treatises (arranged as follows: 1 to 14: mathematics, logic and ethics; 15 to 30: natural sciences (including philosophy), 31 to 42: metaphysics; and 43 to 52: religion, mysticism, astrology, magic, do not correspond to their own classification which figures in the seventh *risāla*: I. Sciences of *ādāb* (writing and reading; lexicography and grammar; arithmetic and commercial transactions; poetry and prosody; divination, magic; alchemy and mechanics; arts and crafts; commerce, agriculture; animal husbandry; biography and history). II. Positive sciences of the *Sharīʿa* (revelation; interpretation of scriptures; Tradition of the Prophet; jurisprudence; judgments; moral exhortations; preaching; asceticism; Ṣūfism; interpretation of dreams). III. Truly philosophical sciences: mathematics (arithmetic; geometry; astronomy; music); logical sciences (poetics; rhetoric; *topoi*; apodeictic demonstration; sophistry); natural sciences (basic principles, heaven and earth; generation and decay; meteorology; mineralogy; botany; zoology; medicine; veterinary skill; dressage; agriculture; animal husbandry; crafts); divine sciences (knowledge of the Creator; angelology; psychology; politics; eschatology).

This encyclopaedia, written by Shīʿīs, is far from having a disinterested goal, for its authors uphold some kind of a thesis; they advocate indeed a radical reform of Islam in order to establish an extremist Shīʿism combining the *Sharīʿa* and Greek philosophy as well as the wisdom of the Indians and Persians and ancient paganisms. It corresponds to the modern definition of the encyclopaedia in the breadth of its coverage and the collaboration of a number of authors, mainly anonymous.

All the same, it was only favourably received in limited circles of philosophers and Shīʿīs, and provoked in the following century a remarkable reaction from al-Ghazālī (450-505/1058-1111 [*q.v.*]) who, in his *Iḥyāʾ ʿulūm al-dīn* seeks to defend orthodoxy. For him, there are two kinds of sciences: religious, which are obligatory, and non-religious, which are optional, when they are not harmful. The first comprise the *uṣūl al-dīn* (Ḳurʾān; Tradition; *consensus omnium*; traditions of the Companions) and the *furūʿ* (jurisprudence; sciences of the soul), the propaedeutic sciences (language; grammar; writing) and advanced ones (on the Ḳurʾān, Tradition, etc.); theology and philosophy (geometry and arithmetic; logic; natural theology; sciences of nature) are set in order. The second are sometimes commendable (medicine and calculation for example), sometimes blameworthy (notably magic and talismans; conjuring; spells), sometimes simply allowed (poetry and history for example). This classification appears in the first quarter of the *Iḥyāʾ* on practices of the Islamic cult; it is followed by social customs, causes of perdition and how to ensure one's salvation. It is in respecting an Islamic ethic developed in this large work that the Muslim can prepare his salvation in the Hereafter.

The collections that we have cited are distinguished by a subjectivity which is opposed to the relative objectivity of the bibliographical catalogues, which are in effect encyclopaedic guides. The earliest, the *Fihrist*, was composed in 377/987-8, hence in the period of the Ikhwān al-Ṣafāʾ, by the Baghdādī librarian Ibn al-Nadīm [*q.v.*], according to a logical plan corresponding to a personal classification of knowledge; generalities on known languages and scripts, materials for writing; revealed books; the Ḳurʾān and Ḳurʾānic sciences; grammar; lexicography; history; poetry and poets; theology according to the various schools and sects, Ṣūfism, Ismāʿīlism; jurisconsults of different schools; ancient and modern philosophers; mathematics; music; medicine; folklore; various anecdotes; conjuring; magic; equitation; engines of war; games; moral exhortations, maxims; interpretation of dreams; cookery; enchantments; religions other than Islam (notably Manichaeism, on which the *Fihrist* is one of the principal sources, and the religions of India and China); and alchemy. After Ibn al-Nadīm, a number of specialised bibliographies were produced, notably the *Fihrist* of Muḥammad b. al-Ḥasan al-Ṭūsī (385-460/995-1067 [*q.v.*]) who reviewed the works written by Shīʿīs, up to the compiling of the famous *Kashf al-ẓunūn* of Ḥādjdjī Khalīfa (1017-67/1608-57 [*q.v.*]), which marks the last stage before the modern catalogues of libraries.

Previously, the biographical genre had undergone considerable development, at first in order to meet the need for knowing the life of the transmitters of traditions in order to know whether the chains of guarantors had any gaps in continuity. The logical division of biographies by generation had finally given way to an alphabetical classification and resulted in dictionaries such as the *Muʿdjam al-udabāʾ* (to which the *Muʿdjam al-buldān* was added) of Yāḳūt (d. 626/1229 [*q.v.*]), the *Wafayāt al-aʿyān* of Ibn Khallikān (608-81/1211-82 [*q.v.*], the works of Ibn al-Ḳifṭī (568-646/1172-1248 [*q.v.*]), and many histories of towns and countries presented in the form of biographies of personalities who were famous in them.

All these works and many others besides, even if it is difficult to regard them as encyclopaedias since they only contain one specific section of information, were to become the instruments of a new form of encyclopaedia born of the vicissitudes of history, particularly of the fear of seeing the disappearance of the vast mass of knowledge accumulated over the centuries and of the concern to salvage at least a part from the irreparable catastrophe represented by the Mongol invasions and the fall of Baghdād in 656/1258. The latter events certainly provoked serious disquiet which was translated into the composition of enormous encyclopaedias intended to some extent to preserve the acquisitions of preceding generations at the moment when the Arabo-Islamic world could be seen as despairing of achieving new progress and felt itself threatened by the worst calamities. In the following centuries, the Black Death (749/1348) was further to aggravate this feeling of insecurity.

Ibn Manẓūr (630-711/1232-1311 [*q.v.*]), who left the most highly-developed dictionary of the Arabic language, already clearly expresses this disquiet and the wish to salvage whatever could be rescued from total destruction, when he writes in the preface of the *Lisān al-ʿArab:* "My sole purpose is to preserve the elements of this language of the Prophet... . I assert indeed that, in our days, the use of the Arabic language is regarded as a vice. The letter writers are better in foreign languages and rival one another in the eloquence in idioms other than Arabic. I have composed the present work in an age in which men boast of [using] a language different from that which I have recorded and *I have built it like Noah built the ark*, enduring the sarcasm of his own people".

What applies to the language also applies to the other cultural elements and, setting aside the stylistic clause about sarcasm, Ibn Manẓūr's enterprise has parallels in other fields. During the "Alexandrine" period (F. Gabrieli, *Storia della litteratura araba*, Milan 1951, 259), the decline of Arabic culture, under the blows of the events which seriously affected ʿIrāḳ, at that point incited the Egyptians, who benefited from the transfer of the caliphate to Cairo, to launch a new encyclopaedic movement whose principal actors were the high-ranking *kuttāb*.

The earliest is al-Nuwayrī (677-732/1279-1332 [*q.v.*]), whose *Nihāyat al-arab fī funūn al-adab* contains all the knowledge that would be necessary for a *kātib* assuming important responsibilities: cosmography, zoology, botany, ethics, history. The materials gathered were summarised and methodically arranged according to an Islamic conception of the world, but in a form that was both literary and practical. Then comes Ibn Faḍl Allāh al-ʿUmarī (700-49/1301-49 [*q.v.*], author of the *Masālik al-abṣār*, which seems to be intended on the whole for men of culture and constitutes a geographico-historical encyclopaedia containing a cosmography and information of a religious, juridical, political and administrative character. In spite of evident differences, it is tempting to liken the *Masālik* to the *ʿAdjāʾib al-makhlūḳāt* of al-Ḳazwīnī (see above), who describes the celestial and earthly worlds by borrowing extensively, like al-ʿUmarī, from his predecessors. The last encyclopaedist to be mentioned is al-Ḳalḳashandī (d. 821/1418 [*q.v.*]), whose huge *Ṣubḥ al-aʿshā* really places at the disposal of its users all that a good secretary could need to know in order to be able to acquit himself perfectly in his profession as writer in the chancellery (*ṣināʿat al-inshāʾ*). In his highly suggestive article on *Les classiques du scribe égyptien* (in *SI*, xviii [1963], 41-80), G. Wiet reproduces the classification of the sciences adopted by al-Ḳalḳashandī: I. Belles lettres (lexicography; morphology; grammar; style; rhetoric; the science of tropes; metrics; rhyme; calligraphy; Ḳurʾān reading). II. Sciences of the law (Ḳurʾān; Sunna; law, etc.). III. Physical sciences (medicine; veterinary skill; falconry; physiognomy; oneiromancy; astrology; magic; talismans; conjuring; alchemy; agriculture; geomancy). IV. Geometry (construction methods; optics; mirrors; centre of gravity; surveying; water-catchment; mechanisms for hoisting objects; water-clocks; engines of war; pneumatic machines). V. Astronomy (astronomical tables; projection of the sphere on a flat surface; sundials). IV. Arithmetic (arithmetic properly so-called; algebra, abacuses, etc.). VII. Practical sciences (politics; ethics; domestic economy). Although these notions did not all undergo considerable development, al-Ḳalḳashandī's encyclopaedia proves that in spite of the reversals experienced by the Islamic world, Arabic culture had lost nothing of its richness in books, but it had exhausted itself since the already distant age of its great prosperity and it was scarcely able to make any more obvious progress. The information gathered scarcely bears, in relation to the preceding centuries, any new features, owing much more to the march of history than to a calculated concern for enrichment.

Thus we have to pass over those authors whose total

work has an encyclopaedic aspect, as for example, al-Suyūṭī (849-911/1445-1505 [*q.v.*]), in order to arrive at the Turk Ṭāshköprüzāde (901-68/1495-1561 [*q.v.*]) who, through his encyclopaedia of arts and letters written in Arabic and then translated into Turkish, aimed to put at the disposal of his compatriots a summary of the knowledge possessed by the Arabic-speakers.

Then we have to wait until the second half of the 19th century in order to encounter the first attempt made in the Near East to offer the educated public a working instrument and reference work meeting modern scientific criteria, the *Dāʾirat al-maʿārif* published in Beirut from 1876 by Buṭrus al-Bustānī and continued by other members of his family [see AL-BUSTĀNĪ in Suppl.]. This encyclopaedia was resumed on a larger scale, from 1956, by F. E. al-Bustānī, who enlisted the collaboration of specialists from all disciplines; the new *Dāʾirat al-maʿārif* is only distinguishable from Western encyclopaedias by language and the place legitimately occupied by the Arabs.

Finally, we should remark that the word *mawsūʿa* has been used correctly to describe dictionaries of a technical nature, such as *al-Mawsūʿa fī ʿulūm al-ṭabīʿa* of E. Ghaleb (Beirut 1965), and also some collections in which each fascicule is devoted to a particular subject, such as *al-Mawsūʿa al-ṣaghīra* published in Baghdād, which is a "cultural, bi-monthly series dealing with sciences, arts and letters". For example, it contains some studies on "philosophical thought among the Arabs", as well as on "the petrochemical industries and the future of Arab oil".

Bibliography: Apart from the *EI* notices relating to the authors cited, see A. Zaki, *Études bibliographiques sur les encyclopédies arabes*, Būlāḳ 1308 (not seen); Ch. Pellat, *Les encyclopédies dans le monde arabe*, in *Cahiers d'histoire mondiale/Journal of World History/Cuadernos de historia mundial*, UNESCO, ix/3 (1966), 631-58; R. Blachère, *Quelques réflexions sur les formes de l'encyclopédisme en Égypte et en Syrie du VIIIe/XIVe siècle à la fin du IXe/XVe siècle*, in *BEO Damas*, xxiii (1970), 7-19, repr. in R. Blachère, *Analecta*, Damascus 1975, 521-40. For a comparison with the composition of encyclopaedias in Antiquity and the Middle Ages as well as in India and China, see the issue of *Cahiers d'histoire mondiale* cited above.

(CH. PELLAT)

2. In Persian.

Persian writings of an encyclopaedic character begin to appear about a century after the constituting of Persian as a language of culture. From then onwards they were to enjoy an important florescence until a late date, as much in India as in Persia. According to their contents, they can be divided into different groups. Here, only the major works will be mentioned; for an exhaustive examination of this genre, including the old translations into Persian, see the Persian manuscript catalogues (A. Munzawī, *Fihrist-i nuskha-hā-yi khaṭṭī-yi fārsī*, i, Tehran 1348/1969, ch. 9; idem, *Fihrist-i nuskha-hā-yi khaṭṭī-yi kitābkhāna-yi Gandjbakhsh*, i, Islāmābād 1979, ch. 10; Storey, ii, section F; etc.). One should also consult Ž. Vesel, *Les encyclopédies persanes. Essai de typologie et de classification des sciences*, Paris 1986.

The first Persian encyclopaedia of philosophy is Ibn Sīnā's *Dānish-nāma-yi ʿAlāʾī*, composed between 414-28/1023-37 for the Kākūyid ruler of Iṣfahān ʿAlāʾ al-Dawla Muḥammad b. Dushmanziyār. This is a compendium of the Aristotelian speculative sciences laid out here in an order different from that of the *Shifāʾ* and the *Nadjāt*: logic, metaphysics, physics and mathematics. The final section, which includes geometry, astronomy, arithmetic and music, was put together on the basis of the Arabic works of Ibn Sīnā and after his death, by his disciple and biographer al-Djuzdjānī. The *Dānish-nāma*, in which Ibn Sīnā sets forth the hierarchy of the Aristotelian sciences and for the first time elaborates in Persian a vocabulary of philosophical concepts, exercised a great influence on Persian authors (partial edn., *Abū ʿAlī Sīnā, Dānish-nāma-yi ʿAlāʾī (manṭiḳ, ilāhiyyāt, ṭabīʿiyyāt)*, ed. M. Mishkat and M. Muʿīn, 3 vols.², Tehran 1353/1974; a tr. of the whole text by M. Achena and H. Massé, *Avicenne, Le livre de science,* Paris 1986, 2nd. edn. revised and corrected by M. Achena). Another encyclopaedia of philosophy of great importance is the *Durrat al-tādj li-ghurrat al-Dībādj* of Ḳuṭb al-Dīn Shīrāzī [*q.v.*], written between 693-705/1294-1306 for the prince of Gīlān Dībādj b. Filshāh (ed. Mishkat, 2 vols., Tehran 1317-209/1938-41). In this, the author deals successively with logic, with the first philosophy (*al-falsafa al-ūlā*), with physics, with mathematics (the *quadrivium*) and with metaphysics. In an epilogue, he starts on Islamic theology, practical philosophy (*ḥikmat-i ʿamalī*) and Ṣūfism. The author was a philosopher, mathematician and astronomer who had worked, between 658-63/1259-64, at the Marāgha observatory under the direction of Naṣīr al-Dīn Ṭūsī [*q.v.*], and he devoted a large part of his encyclopaedia to the mathematical sciences. Both these encyclopaedias represent a compilation of the Arabic sources for the use of Persian, non-Arabic speaking rulers (for the relationship of the *Dānish-nāma* and Ibn Sīnā's Arabic works, see *EIr* art. *Avicenna*. xi, by Achena; and for a survey of the Arabic sources of the *Durra*, see Mishkat's introd., i, pp. xl-xliii).

The Persian encyclopaedias of the religious sciences are relatively numerous. In these, the Islamic religious sciences, including Ṣūfism, have the outstanding role. Following the répertoire of the traditional sciences, the Arabic literary and linguistic sciences and history might be joined with them, and occasionally, the philosophical and such strictly speaking scientific topics like medicine and calculation, as well as the occult sciences, might also figure there. There is frequent allusion to the works of al-Ghazālī and Fakhr al-Dīn al-Rāzī. Some authors tackle on a wider scale all the subjects capable of guiding the believer. As a result of this, one often finds chapters on moral and ethical topics drawn from the Persian cultural heritage. Two anonymous works of the 6th/12th century, the *Yawāḳīt al-ʿulūm wa-darārī 'l-nudjūm* (ed. M. T. Dānish-Pazhūh, Tehran 1345/1956) and the *Baḥr al-fawāʾid* (ed. idem, Tehran 1345/1956), give a conspectus of the varied contents of this type of encyclopaedia in the Persia of the pre-Mongol period.

The encyclopaedias of the natural sciences are extremely varied. In general, it is a question of popular compositions put together with a didactic aim, for amusement or to provide a "book of recipes". The authors may treat of Aristotelian physics in the wide sense, beginning with a description of the heavens and ending with the three kingdoms of nature. According to the classification of the sciences in use in the mediaeval Persian world, physics subsumes moreover a great number of subordinate sciences (*furūʿ*). Ḥamd Allāh Mustawfī Ḳazwīnī's *Nuzhat al-ḳulūb* (cf. Munzawī, *Fihrist ... fārsī*, 689-91; Storey, ii, section D, 129-31) and Ghiyāth al-Dīn Iṣfahānī (cf. *ibid.*, 357-8) fall into this category. The "books of marvels", such as Muḥammad Ṭūsī's

ʿAdjāʾib al-makhlūkāt (see B. Radtke, in *Isl.*, lxiv [1987], 278-88), written in the second half of the 6th/12th century (ed. M. Sutūda, Tehran 1345/1956), similarly adopted this structure broadly speaking. However, sometimes only the three realms of nature are treated, especially when it is a question of the "special properties of things" (*khawāṣṣ al-ashyāʾ*) used in popular medicine and in occult practices. One example is the *Farrukh-nāma-yi Djamālī* of Abū Bakr Djamālī Yazdī (ed. I. Afshār, Tehran 1346/1957), put together in 580/1185 with the aim of "completing" the *Nuzhat-nāma* (see below). On the other hand, one may have encyclopaedias concerned with divers scientific subjects with a high proportion of subject-matter belonging to physics in the widest sense. A typical example is the *Nuzhat-nāma-yi ʿAlāʾī* of Shahmardān b. Abi 'l-Khayr al-Rāzī (ed. F. Djahānpur, Tehran 1362/1973), written between 506-13/1113-20 for the Kākūyid ruler of Yazd ʿAlā' al-Dawla Bā Kālīdjār Garshāsp with the aim of amusing. Another work of this type is the *Nawādir al-tabādur li-tuḥfat al-Bahādur* of Shams al-Dīn Dunaysirī (ed. Afshār and Dānish-Pazhūh, Tehran 1350/1971), composed in 699/1299-1300 for an unknown dedicatee. The encyclopaedias of the natural sciences are very revelatory of the spread of scientific knowledge in mediaeval Persia and are an important source for our knowledge of occult practices and technological questions.

The first Persian encyclopaedia in the narrow sense of the term was that of the Ashʿarī theologian Fakhr al-Dīn Rāzī (d. 606/1210 [*q.v.*]). His *Djāmiʿ al-ʿulūm*, also known as the *Ḥadāʾiḳ al-anwār* or *Kitāb-i Sittīnī* and containing sixty sciences (for the different versions, see Munzawī, *op. cit.*, 656-7; Storey, ii, 351-2), was written in 574-5/1179 for the ruler of Khʷārazm ʿAlā' al-Dīn Tekesh (facs. edn. of 1906 Bombay lith. by M. Tasbīḥī, Tehran 1346/1967). Rāzī says explicitly in his introduction that he has gathered together there all the sciences of his age in order to establish a répertoire for scholars at the court to use. He begins his work by an exposition of the traditional sciences (*ʿulūm-i naḳlī*) in the following order: Islamic religious sciences, Arabic literary and linguistic sciences, and history. He links this up with an exposition of the Aristotelian rational sciences (*ʿulūm-i ʿaḳlī*); logic, physics, mathematics and metaphysics. A large number of subordinate sciences figure in the framework of physics and mathematics: the medical sciences, the occult ones, technological questions, etc. Then comes an exposition of practical philosophy (ethics, politics, domestic economy). The work's conclusion is devoted to the religious practices, the conduct of rulers (*ādāb al-mulūk*) and to a description of the game of chess.

Comparable to the *Djāmiʿ al-ʿulūm*, but more important in its greater size, is the *Nafāʾis al-funūn fī ʿarāʾis al-ʿuyūn* of Shams al-Dīn Āmulī (ed. A. Ḥ. Shaʿrānī, Tehran 1377 AH, 3 vols.). The author was a *mudarris* in Sulṭāniyya under Öldjeytü. His encyclopaedia covers 160 sciences and was put together for the Indjūʾid prince of Shīrāz Abū Isḥāḳ, representing a real climax to the genre by the elegance of its form and the exhaustiveness of its content. Āmulī adopts the same principle for his exposition as Rāzī, dealing first of all with the traditional sciences "originating in Islam" (*ʿulūm-i awākhir*) and then with the philosophical sciences "coming into existence before Islam" (*ʿulūm-i awāʾil*; cf. *Nafāʾis*, i, 16). It does, however, contain some innovations in regard to Rāzī. The internal order of the two main sections is put together differently; a chapter on Ṣūfism appears among the traditional sciences; and the range of the subordinate sciences of physics and mathematics is richer than that of the *Djāmiʿ al-ʿulūm*. Both these encyclopaedias enjoyed wide popularity, and two Persian encyclopaedists tried later to imitate them: Ḥusayn ʿAḳīlī Rustamdārī in his *Riyāḍ al-abrār*, written in 979/1571 (cf. Munzawī, *op. cit.*, 669; Storey, ii, 359), and Muḥammad Fāḍil Samarḳandī in his *Djawāhir al-ʿulūm-i humāyūnī* written in *ca.* 962/1555 (cf. Storey, ii, 358-9). An interesting example of the evolution of the Persian encyclopaedia is provided by Wādjid ʿAlī Khān's *Maṭlaʿ al-ʿulūm wa-madjmaʿ al-funūn*, written in 1261-2/1845-6 (cf. Storey, ii, 366-7).

For other types of encyclopaedic writing in Persian, whether of a specialised nature or from the sphere of *adab* works, see the catalogues of Munzawī, Storey, etc. But regarding the question of the originality of this literature in relation to the Arabic models by which it was largely inspired, this work of evaluation still remains to be done for the majority of the texts.

Bibliography: Given in the text.

(Ž. Vesel)

3. In Turkish. (see Supplement].

4. The Encyclopaedia of Islam, First edition.

The *Encyclopaedia of Islam* owes its existence to the renewed interest in Islam and the Islamic peoples which manifested itself in Europe at the turn of the twentieth century. The idea of such an enterprise, however, dates from a much earlier period. Already in 1697 the French Orientalist Barthélemi d'Herbelot had published in Paris the *Bibliothèque Orientale ou dictionnaire universel contenant généralement tout ce qui regarde la connoissance des Peuples de l'Orient* (see H. Laurens, *Aux sources de l'Orientalisme, la* Bibliothèque Orientale *de Barthélemi d'Herbelot.* Publications du Département d'Islamologie de l'Université de Paris-Sorbonne (Paris IV), vi, Paris 1978). It was to be followed by other classics like the *Dāʾirat al-maʿārif* (1876-98) of the Bustānī family [*q.v.* in Suppl.], T. P. Hughes, *Dictionary of Islam* (London 1885, 2nd ed. 1896), and W. Beale, *An oriental biographical dictionary* (Calcutta 1881, 2nd ed. by H. G. Keene, 1894). But these publications, notwithstanding their merits, could no longer satisfy the European general public interested in things Islamic, let alone the European scholars.

Around 1890, Messrs. Trübner in Strassburg envisaged a series of monographs on Semitic philology, in the same way as they had done for Iranian and Indian philology. However, the plan could not be carried out because of the untimely death in 1892 of A. Müller, to whom the work had been confided (see *ZDMG*, xlvi [1892], 778).

In the same year 1892, at the International Congress of Orientalists in London (see *Transactions of the IXth International Congress of Orientalists*, i, p. xxxviii), W. Robertson Smith proposed the idea of an *Encyclopaedia of Islam.* The initiative of the man who may be considered as the *auctor intellectualis* of the enterprise was accepted by the members attending the Congress, and an international committee of twelve members was established.

At the International Congress of Orientalists held in Geneva in 1894, it was clear that no progress had been made, the more so because Robertson Smith had meanwhile died. I. Goldziher then proposed to put the direction of the enterprise in the hands of M. J. de Goeje. When the latter declined, the Hungarian orientalist found himself charged with the organisation of *the Encyclopaedia of Islam* (see *Transactions of the IXth International Congress of Orientalists*, 1st part, 105, 1305). However, to the dismay of all those who considered him as the man able to realise the idea, Goldziher handed in his resignation at the International Congress of Orientalists held in Paris in 1897 (see *Transactions*, 1897, Bulletin no. 11; *ZDMG*, li [1897], 766).

One of the reasons brought forward by Goldziher for his resignation was the decision, taken meanwhile, to have the work printed in Leiden. Consequently, he opined, the editor should reside in Holland. The scientific advisor of Messrs. Brill, Dr. P. Herzsohn, had already started assembling a certain number of entries. A specimen was published in 1897 under the title *Erste Sammlung von Stichwoertern für eine Encyclopaedia des Islâms. Mit orientierenden Bemerkungen. Gedruckt als Manuscript, mit Vorbehalt einer hier und da noch auszuführenden genaueren Verification*, pp. 63, 8°.

At De Goeje's request, Professor Houtsma, notwithstanding a certain scepticism, accepted to replace Goldziher "because I knew to what trouble De Goeje was going to realise the *Encyclopaedia of Islam*".

In 1897 a new international committee had been appointed in Paris, consisting of A. C. Barbier de Meynard (Paris), E. G. Browne (Cambridge), I. Goldziher (Budapest), M. J. de Goeje (Leiden), I. Guidi (Rome), J. Karabacek (Vienna), C. Landberg (Tübzing), V. von Rosen (St. Petersburg), A. Socin (Leipzig) and F. de Stoppelaar (Leiden).

In order to get some idea of the readiness of his colleagues to collaborate, Houtsma asked several of them what kind of articles they were ready to write, and invited them to send one or more articles in order to have them printed at Brill's and to submit them to the opinion of the experts. The answers were positive, and in 1899 Houtsma was able to publish a *Specimen of a Muslim Encyclopaedia by a number of Orientalists.* It consisted of several monographs, arranged alphabetically and written in English, French and German by sixteen future collaborators. In the Preface, Houtsma remarks that no agreement had as yet been reached about the language in which the *Encyclopaedia* was to be published. In the same year 1899, Goldziher presented this *Specimen* to the members of the Committee present at the xiii^th^ International Congress of Orientalists in Rome (see *Acta*, i, pp. clxxix ff.), who accepted it favourably. While waiting for the resolution of the financial problems, Houtsma and Herzsohn were correcting and completing the list of entries.

At the first session of the recently-founded International Association of Academies (Paris 1901), a proposition of the Academies of Leipzig, Munich and Vienna for the publication of an *Encyclopaedia of Islam* was admitted into the working plan, after approval by the literary section. Under the presidency of De Goeje, a Committee was appointed in order to study the project of the enterprise, and Houtsma was charged with the editorship. The Committee consisted of Goldziher, Browne, Barbier de Meynard, Von Rosen, Guidi, Karabacek (all already appointed at the Paris Congress of 1897), and Chauvin (Brussels Academy), Buhl (Copenhagen Academy) and Fischer (Leipzig Academy, Socin having died in 1899).

A smaller Committee, consisting of De Goeje, Goldziher and Karabacek, was charged with drafting by-laws, which were completed in 1902. The costs were calculated at 140,000-150,000 marks for ten years. Financial support was promised by the Academies of Amsterdam, Budapest, Christiania, Copenhagen, Lisbon, Madrid, Munich, St. Petersburg, Vienna, the Academy of Saxony, the Académie des Inscriptions et Belles Lettres, the Reale Accademia dei Lincei, the Gouvernement Général de l'Algérie, the British Academy, the Dutch Colonial Government, the Italian Government, the Dutch Company of Commerce in Amsterdam, the Deutsche Morgenländische Gesellschaft, the Deutsche Kolonialgesellschaft, the Senate and municipal council of Hamburg, the Egyptian Government, the Johns Hopkins University of Baltimore, the Theological Seminary of Hartford, Mr. C. R. Crane in Chicago, the Ministère Français de l'Éducation, the American Oriental Society, the American Committee for Lectures on the History of Religions, and the Résidence Générale de France au Maroc. In general, subventions were promised for several years, but in some cases a single gift was granted. The amount of the subventions and gifts was very unequal, and not all subventions were granted immediately; some were only allowed for 1906, 1908 or 1909, others for 1910, 1911 or 1912.

Before the actual printing could start, two other questions had to be solved, that of orthography and that of the language. As for the orthography of Arabic, Persian, Turkish and other Oriental terms, it was decided to follow broadly the one which the Geneva Congress had deemed admissible. The question in which language the articles should be published was more difficult to solve. In the *Specimen*, the articles had appeared in English, French and German, but it seemed undesirable to let the *Encyclopaedia* have such a polyglot appearance. On the other hand, certain subventions had been granted under the express condition that the *EI* should be published in the language of the giver. One of the direct consequences of the decision to publish the *Encyclopaedia of Islam* in English, French and German was that the articles had to appear under headings in oriental languages, generally in Arabic. Furthermore, three separate editions would very probably triple the costs, because the project thus was going to take much more time than the foreseen ten years. Finally, it was necessary to assign an English, French and German editor to assist Houtsma, the editor-in-chief.

In 1906, M. Seligsohn and A. Schaade, who had been meanwhile appointed, arrived in Leiden. The first fascicule, published in 1908, was severely criticised in England, France and also in Leiden because of the rather low standard of Seligsohn's translations of German articles. Nor was the American orthography acceptable on the other side of the North Sea. After the death of De Goeje in 1909, Seligsohn resigned, followed by Schaade a year later. For the latter, R. Hartmann was appointed, but the post of Seligsohn remained vacant: it was practically impossible to find a qualified Orientalist who was able to deal satisfactorily with the three languages. Only after T. W. Arnold of London and R. Basset of Algiers had assumed the editorship of the English and French editions (without remuneration), did the enterprise make good progress. In 1913 the first volume, comprising the letters A-D, was completed. Hartmann, who resigned in the same year, was replaced by H. Bauer. As president of the Executive Committee, De Goeje had been succeeded by Chr. Snouck Hurgronje, who had been able to redress the financial position.

As for the editorial work, Houtsma may be quoted. "Apart from a few exceptions, my collaborators are all Christians, and belong to quite different peoples. It is the Editor's task to maintain the scientific and neutral character of the work on a high and impartial level, and to be very careful not to entrust articles to incompetent hands. On the other hand, a scholar whose scientific qualities are above all suspicion, cannot be refused the right to publish in all liberty the results of his research, even if occasionally they are provocative. That is "why", remarks Houtsma in a note, "the articles of H. Lammens have been accepted, although personally I can in no way agree with their spirit and tendency. Therefore, from the very beginning, every article of a certain importance has been signed by the author, in order not to extend the responsibility of the Editors beyond what can be reasonably expected".

Houtsma also remarks that he took upon himself the editing of articles which he considered less important but which, on the other hand, could not be left out. He published them without signature, considering that the *Encyclopaedia of Islam* is not primarily a collection of basic monographs on a particular subject, but should be a mirror of the progress of research, in such a way that the Orientalist scholar finds rather an impulse there to further research.

In 1922, Bauer handed in his resignation, and Schaade resumed his activities for the *EI*. At the death of R. Basset in 1924, his son H. Basset was found ready to continue temporarily the work of his father. In 1924, following a decision of the Royal Academy of the Netherlands, Professor A. J. Wensinck became editor-in-chief. The publication of the last volume S-Z was started, while work on the letter K was continued. At the death of H. Basset in 1926, his task was taken over by E. Lévi-Provençal and when, in the same year, Schaade handed in his resignation, he was replaced by W. Heffening.

After the death of Arnold in 1929, the editing of the English edition was ensured by Professor H. A. R. Gibb, and afterwards the Editorial Committee remained unchanged until the completion of the *EI* and its Supplements in 1939. As has been said above, from 1924 onwards two volumes were being prepared at the same time. Volume II (E-K) was published in 1927, volume IV (S-Z) in 1934, and volume III (L-R) in 1936.

After 1934, the Editors also envisaged an Index which should contain all names of persons, tribes, clans, the geographical names, etc., which appear in one way or another in the articles. With the help of a few collaborators, Heffening compiled a card index, based on the first three volumes. Unfortunately, the 1939 War put an end to his work.

A final point of the history of the first edition of the *Encyclopaedia of Islam* is the *Handwörterbuch des Islam*, begun by Wensinck in 1937. This compendium of articles from the *Encyclopaedia* was to consist of one volume only, containing articles which treat Islam as a religion. However, in many cases it was necessary to complete the bibliography. Besides, some new articles were added while others, considered obsolete, were replaced. After the death of Wensinck in 1939, Professor J. H. Kramers was charged with the work of editing. Because of the financial position, it was decided to finish the German text first, and to shorten some articles, without however reducing their value. Thus in 1941, the *Handwörterbuch des Islam* was published. The change of the title was justified by the fact that quotation from two editions whose titles would practically be identical, might lead to confusion. A German index was added, and the differences with the complete Encyclopaedia indicated.

Bibliography: A. J. Wensinck, *De Encyclopedie van den Islam*, in Oostersch Instituut—Leiden, *Jaarverslag 1927-1928*, Leiden 1929, 15-7; M. Th. Houtsma—J. H. Kramers, *De wordingsgeschiedenis van de Encyclopaedie van den Islam*, in *ibid.*, *Jaarverslag 1941*, Leiden 1942, 9-20. What are sometimes quite personal details are to be found in P. Sj. van Koningsveld, *Orientalism and Islam. The letters of C. Snouck Hurgronje to Th. Nöldeke from the Tübingen University Library. Abdoel-Ghaffaar. Sources for the history of Islamic studies in the Western world*, i, Leiden 1985, esp. 143-5, 163-4, 212-6; idem, *Scholarship and friendship in early Islamwissenschaft. The letters of C. Snouck Hurgronje to I. Goldziher. From the Oriental Collection of the Library of the Hungarian Academy of Sciences, Budapest. Abdoel-Ghaffaar. Sources, etc.* ii, Leiden 1985, esp. 149-51, 180-1, 280-339, 387-92, 403-4, 407-9.

(E. van Donzel)

MAWT (A.) is the term employed in Arabic to express the actual notion of death, while synonyms such as *maniyya* and its variant *manūn*, *radā*, *halāk*, *ḥimām*, *ḥayn* and *bilā* convey particular connotations and are less frequently used and regarded as more literary. The term for death *wafāt*, more exactly "accomplishment, fulfilment", i.e. of a man's term of life, is in origin Ḳurʾānic, and stems from the use in the early Medinan period of the verb *tawaffā* for describing how God brings to its close a man's foreordained period of life and gathers the man to Himself; hence the use of the passive form of this verb *tuwuffiya* "his term was brought to an end [by God]" = "he died". The idea behind the use of this verb is closely connected with the use in the Ḳurʾān of other verbs like *ḳaddara* and *ḳaḍā* which carry the sense of God's predetermining a man's lifespan or executing His decree concerning a man's term of life (see T. O'Shaughnessy, *Muhammad's thoughts on death*, Leiden 1969, 37 ff.). In modern Arabic, *wafāt* has a more delicate and euphemistic sense than the stark word *mawt*, something like Eng. "demise, decease" and Fr. "décès", with *al-mutawaffā* therefore meaning "the deceased". The same distinction is made in Turkish between the bald *ölüm* "death" and *wafāt*, modern Turkish *vefat*, and in Persian between *marg* and *wafāt* and such terms as *fawt* (A., literally "passing away, disappearing").

The conception of death held by the Arabs prior to the advent of Islam was deeply rooted in the animist beliefs inherited from their distant past. Taken to be a manifestation of disruptive action on the part of *dahr* [*q.v.*] "time-destiny", death was considered the specific destiny of the animate world, a concept uniting humans and animals as opposed to the physical world, inanimate and therefore imperishable. It was defined, in these terms, as the extinction of the vital spirit which animates beings endowed with life, as the separation of the body and the organic soul. As it is known that the residences most frequently attributed to a man's "double" are the blood and the breath, it may be understood how the Arabs could believe that in the case of violent death, the double (*ḳarīna*) is released through the flowing of the blood and that, in the case of "natural" death, it escapes through the nose; hence the expression *māta ḥatfa anfihi*.

Furthermore, while it is accepted, as stressed by the Ḳurʾān, that the ancient Arabs had no conception either of the resurrection of the dead or of life in the Beyond, they seem nevertheless to have believed in the survival of the dead. Two terms which evoke wandering and thirst, *hāma* and *ṣadā*, denote these spirits of the dead. But, unlike other Semitic peoples, such as the Hebrews for example (cf. A. Lods, *La croyance à la vie future et le culte des morts dans l'antiquité israélite*, Paris 1906), the ancient Arabs did not entertain the idea of a special world of the dead, a world of shadows and of gloom. In addition, for them it was inconceivable that their dead might be disgraced.

Only the spirits of the dead deprived of burial and those whose blood had not been avenged were left to wander, thirsting, in desert lands. To abandon its dead to such a destiny was considered the worst ignominy that could befall a tribe. By vengeance in cases of murder and by the scrupulous observance of funeral rites and of burial in particular, the Arabs preserved their dead from such a fate and their society from such a disgrace. Their essential preoccupation was to re-affirm with respect to their dead the validity and permanence of tribal solidarity. But, while doing this, did they not also seek to assure themselves of the protection of these dead?

The existence of a cult of the dead among the ancient Arabs is a much debated question (see in particular: I. Goldziher, *Le culte des ancêtres et le culte des morts chez les Arabes*, Fr. tr., Paris 1885; Lods, *op.cit.*; H. Lammens, *L'Arabie occidentale avant l'hégire*, Beirut 1928, 151 f.). In spite of differing opinions and the scarcity of reference documents, it seems probable that the Arabs did, at one point in their history, practise the cult of the dead. But this cult, which belongs, as Lods emphasises, to "an inferior stage of religion", seems, in the period immediately before Islam, to have completely disappeared under the combined impact of the sedentarisation of the tribes and the emergence of polytheism. Only the rites rendered to the deceased immediately after death (washing of corpses, mourning and interment) were perpetuated. The other rites, such as sacrifice or offering, were reserved for the gods. (On the funeral rites and their significance, see M. Abdesselem, *Le thème de la mort dans la poésie arabe, des origines à la fin du III/IX siècle*, Tunis 1977, ch. ii).

But this ancient cult of the dead has, by extending beyond death the fulfilment of the duty of tribal solidarity, contributed to the sanctification of blood lineage, thus giving solid foundations to the social system of the Arabs and perpetuating, over the generations, the same moral ideal (cf. B. Farès, *L'honneur chez les Arabes avant l'Islam*, Paris, and ʿIRḌ). This ideal enables the Arab to contemplate death without fear and to place the preservation of his honour and the honour of his group above the preservation of his life. This is clearly shown in the themes developed in pre-Islamic poetry and especially in the eulogistic nature of the dirges [see MARTHIYA. 1].

Islam was to appeal to the Arabs to adopt a radically different conception of death. This conception results from a new definition of the soul and of life. According to the Ḳurʾān, man is moved by two distinct principles, one thinking and the other vital: *nafs* and *rūḥ* (see R. Blachère, *Note sur le substantif "nafs"*, in *Semitica*, i [1948], 71). *Nafs* has the sense of "self" in its most conscious and permanent state. *Rūḥ* is the principle of life which proceeds from God and is enlivened and given substance by Him.

Birth and death are divine decrees. Parents do not give life. Events are not the cause of death. These are only the intermediaries through which the will of God is realised.

This new definition of life revolutionised the metaphysical and moral conceptions of the Arabs. Life being no longer immanent, the opposition between the animate and inanimate world loses all foundation and gives way to a new conception whereby God, the creator, source of life, is opposed to everything that is not Him and which, therefore, is the creation, including the physical world whose permanence is only an illusory appearance.

On the other hand, by affirming that life proceeds from God and not from the group and that "the loins of fathers and the womb of mothers are [only] receptacles" (Ḳurʾān, VI, 98), Islam confers on the life of the individual a new significance and on his action a new perspective. First, the life of the individual becomes sacred. "Except with justice, do not kill your fellow-man whom God has declared sacred" (Ḳurʾān, XVII, 33). This is a new precept for the Arabs. Hitherto, only the blood of the group could not be spilled. Henceforward, only those who refuse to recognise the authority of God or seriously contravene His commandments may legitimately be killed. By substituting the notion of the community of faith for that of the community of blood, Islam led the Arabs to liberate themselves from the ascendancy of the clan and to take cognisance of their existence as free and responsible persons. Even though the believers are declared brothers, they are individually responsible for their actions before their judges in this world as well as before God on the final day of judgment.

The echoes of the debates which have brought into prominence these notions and the place occupied by the evocation of the afterlife and the final day of judgement in the Ḳurʾān, show to what an extent such a message would overturn the beliefs of the Arabs. Death is no longer the end of life. It is only the appointed time (*adjal*), decreed by God to conclude the period of man's testing in this world. The *post-mortem* fate of man is no longer dependent on the solidarity of the group, but on the action of the individual and the mercy of God. Eternal happiness or damnation is now the question that each person is required to ask himself and to which none can reply with certainty. This lack of certainty led the Arabs to experience a sentiment which had until then been unknown to them, anguish. This was quite clearly reflected in a new poetic genre, the *zuhdiyyāt* [*q.v.*].

Thus it was not only the beliefs of the Arabs which were revolutionised by the Ḳurʾānic message, but also their attitudes and their behaviour. It may be noted, in this context, that the funeral ceremony, the *djanāza* [*q.v.*], also underwent profound modifications. Certainly, Islam has retained some ancient practices such as the washing of the dead, the shroud and interment; but is has forbidden certain pagan rites such as lamentations or offerings and, above all, it has introduced a new obligation, the prayer for the dead which confers upon the entire funeral ceremony a radically different significance. This is no longer a glorification of the dead but an appeal for divine mercy. For an ethic of exaltation Islam has substituted a morality of humility.

Bibliography: Given in the article.

(M. ABDESSELEM)

MAWWĀL [see MAWĀLIYĀ].

AL-**MAWZAʿĪ**, SHAMS AL-DĪN ʿABD AL-ṢAMAD B. ISMĀʿĪL B. ʿABD AL-ṢAMAD (d. after 1031/1621), the author of an important independent chronicle of early Ottoman Yemen to 1031/1621-2, particularly of the south and of the city of Taʿizz. As his *nisba*, al-Mawzaʿī (mistakenly given as al-Manzilī in Brockelmann, S II, 550), indicates, the family originated in the Tihāma town of Mawzaʿ, south of Zabīd; but his residence was at Taʿizz, where, like his father before him, he served as a Shāfiʿī magistrate and teacher. Being a prominent member of the town's Sunnī *ʿulamāʾ*, and closely connected with the region's Ottoman officials, it is not surprising that his chronicle, *al-Iḥsān fī dukhūl mamlakat al-Yaman taḥt ẓill ʿadālat āl ʿUthmān*, which for the later period is rich in precise details, is sympathetic in tone to the Turks and hostile to the Zaydī *imāms*. It is difficult to determine how much, if any, of the work's content was contributed by the author's father who, it is disclosed, planned a similar chronicle before his death.

Bibliography : As al-Mawzaʿī's name appears in none of the known biographical and other source books for the area and era, we have to rely on what he reveals about himself in his chronicle, and this has been summarised by Muṣṭafā Sālim, *al-Muʾarriḵẖūn al-Yamaniyyūn*, Cairo 1971, 55-63. For the mss. of *al-Iḥsān* (in particular Paris 5973), consult A. F. Sayyid, *Maṣādir taʾrīkẖ al-Yaman*, Cairo 1974, 225-6. See also F. Babinger, *GOW*, 150-1.

(J. R. Blackburn)

MAWZŪNA [see sikka].

MAYBUD, a small town in the *shahrastān* of Ardakān [*q.v.*] in the modern Persian *ustān* or province of Yazd, situated 32 miles/48 km. to the northwest of Yazd. The mediaeval geographers (e.g. Ibn Ḥawḳal², 263, 287, tr. Kramers and Wiet, 260, 281; *Ḥudūd al-ʿālam*, tr. Minorsky, 29, § 29.45; Le Strange, *Lands*, 285) describe it as being on the Iṣfahān-Yazd road, 10 *farsakẖ*s from Yazd. Lying as it does on the southern fringe of the Great Desert, its irrigation comes from *ḳanāt*s [*q.v.*] (see Lambton, *Landlord and peasant in Persia*¹, 219). Its population in *ca.* 1950 was 3,798.

Bibliography : In addition to references given in the article, see *Farhang-i djughrāfiyā-yi Īrān*, x, 190.

(C. E. Bosworth)

AL-MAYBUDĪ, the *nisba* of two scholars from the small town of Maybud [*q.v.*] near Yazd in Persia and also of a vizier of the Great Saldjūḳs.

1. RASHĪD AL-DĪN ABU 'L-FAḌL AḤMAD B. MUḤAMMAD, author of an extensive Ḳurʾān commentary in Persian, begun in 520/1126, the *Kashf al-asrār wa-ʿuddat al-abrār*, extant in several mss.

Bibliography : Storey, i, 1190-1; Storey-Bregel, i, 110-11; and on the *nisba* in general, al-Samʿānī, *Ansāb*, f. 547b.

2. MĪR ḤUSAYN B. MUʿĪN AL-DĪN AL-MANṬIḲĪ, pupil of Djalāl al-Dīn al-Dawānī [*q.v.*], *ḳāḍī* and philosopher, author of several works on philosophy and logic, including a *Mukẖtaṣar maḳāṣid ḥikmat falāsifat al-ʿArab* and a popular textbook on philosophy, the *Hidāya*, executed by the militant Shīʿī Shāh Ismāʿīl I [*q.v.*] for his strongly-held Sunnī views in 909/1503-4 (Ḥasan-i Rūmlū, *Aḥsan al-tawārikẖ*, ed. C. N. Seddon, i, Baroda 1931, 82), *pace* the date of *ca.* 904/1498 in Brockelmann, S II, 294.

Bibliography : Browne, *Lit. hist. of Persia*, iv, 57; Brockelmann, II², 272, S II, 294.

3. KHAṬĪR AL-MULK ABŪ MANṢŪR MUḤAMMAD B. ḤUSAYN, first mentioned as vizier to the Saldjūḳ sultan Berk-yaruḳ in 495/1101; then as *mustawfī* to Muḥammad b. Malik-Shāh in 500/1106-7 and as vizier in 504/1110-1; and finally as *tughrāʾī* to Maḥmūd b. Muḥammad b. Malik-Shāh in 512/1118-19, till he was demoted to the post of a provincial vizier in Fārs to the prince Saldjūḳ-Shāh b. Muḥammad b. Malik-Shāh. Khaṭīr al-Mulk seems to have been a mediocre public servant. Anūshīrwān b. Khālid [*q.v.*] was deputy vizier under him during Muḥammad's reign; his relations with him became bad, and he comments unfavourably on Khaṭīr al-Mulk's woeful ignorance of the Ḳurʾān and of the Arabic language, he being a Persian (Bundārī, 104).

Bibliography : Bundārī, *Zubdat al-nuṣra*; Zambauer, *Manuel*, 224; ʿAbbās Iḳbāl, *Wizārat dar ʿahd-i salāṭīn-i buzurg-i saldjūḳī*, Tehran 1338/1959, 150-4; C. L. Klausner, *The Seljuk vezirate, a study of civil administration 1055-1194*, Cambridge, Mass. 1973, index.

(C. E. Bosworth)

MAYDĀN (A., pl. *mayādīn*), masculine noun denoting a large, open, demarcated area, flat and generally rectangular, designed for all kinds of equestrian activity. Arab philologists and lexicographers have differing opinions regarding the root to which *maydān* should be attributed. For al-Zamakẖshari, this term is derived from the root *w-d-n* since, as he explains (*Asās al-balāgha*), the horses "are flogged there severely" (*tūdan bi-hi*). For others, this is the paradigm *faʿlān* from the root *m-y-d* with the sense of urging and manoeuvring of horses. For others, finally, the same paradigm *faʿlān* is allegedly drawn from the root *m-d-y* with metathesis of the last two consonants, *maydān* taking the place of *madyān* with the sense of "pushing to the limit", since the horses perform there to the limits of their strength. Of these three propositions, it seems the attribution of *maydān* to the root *m-y-d* is the most plausible.

According to the sporting activities which took place there, the *maydān* represented the hippodrome or race course (*ḥalba*) when used for horse races (*sibāḳ*), the ring or display ground for equestrian manoeuvres and exercises, the arena or lists for mock-battles, jousts and symbolic armed tournaments between the mounted groups, and the pitch for the ancient and traditional games of polo and "lacrosse", *ṣawladjān*, *čawgān* [*q.v.*] and *djerīd* [*q.v.*] or *burdjās/birdjās*. In his *Khiṭaṭ*, al-Maḳrīzī relates, with regard to the ancient site of Santaria in the Oasis district of Egypt, that its founder, the Coptic king Minaḳiyūsh, also founder of the town of Akhmīm [*q.v.*], was the first to construct *maydān*s for the equestrian training of his courtiers; in its use as a drill-ground, the *maydān* soon became indispensable for the training of cavalry, a military element which grew considerably in importance with the rise of Islam.

When not engaged in military campaigns, the Muslim trooper (*djundī*) spent much of his time on the *maydān*, perfecting his skills in mounted archery, shooting either at a target (*burdjās*) placed at the top of a lance or at "gourd-shooting" (*ḳabaḳ*) suspended from the end of a long spar; this latter exercise, introduced by the Turks, became the object of keen competitions. Shooting of the style known as *ulkī* (Turkish *ülkü*) at a large target (*hadaf tamām*) placed at long distance (*maydān ṭawīl*), and with arrows of a specified pattern called *maydānī*, required archers capable of a range of 200 metres and more. Short-range precision shooting (*ulkī ḳaṣīr*) was aimed at a small target at a distance of no more than 70 metres. Pure long-distance shooting without a target (*niḍāl*) was practised only at a fairly late stage by the sultans. To the north of Istanbul there still exists the Ok Meydanı "field of the arrow" founded by sultan Meḥemmed II (855-86/1451-81), at the end of which stand some twenty commemorative plaques marking the record distances achieved since this period; thus it is known that in 1213/1798 sultan Selīm III shot an arrow to a distance of almost 900 metres. It was also at a late stage that there was practised, on the *maydān*, shooting with the crossbow, at a target, with bolts and quarrels.

All these sporting activities had, in fact, no object other than military training, and every town with a Muslim garrison of any importance had one or more *maydān*s; al-Fīrūzābādī mentions in this context (*al-Ḳāmūs al-muḥīṭ*, s.v.) those of Nīshāpūr, Iṣfahān, Khʷārazm and Baghdād. In the last-named, the first *maydān*, according to al-Yaʿḳubī, *Buldān*, tr. Wiet, 37, 41), extended along the left bank of the Tigris, near the palace of the vizier al-Faḍl b. al-Rabīʿ [*q.v.*].

Under the Mamlūk sultans, the construction of a *maydān* constituted a large-scale project and mobilised a considerable labour-force; it was necessary, in effect, to level a surface of sufficient size to accommodate the manoeuvring of several hundred horsemen. Enclosures, water-conduits, shelters, stables, studs, personnel quarters, pavilions, baths and other amenities represented enormous expense, and every sultan was eager to establish his own *maydān*, neglecting those already in existence, which rapidly fell into ruin. Thus, in Cairo, during the period of the Baḥrī Mamlūks [*q.v.*], the apotheosis of "chivalry" (*furūsiyya* [*q.v.*]), there were as many as seven *maydāns*, all built between the 7th and 8th/13th-14th centuries. An eighth and last was inaugurated there by the Circassian Ḳānṣawh al-Ghawrī in 909/1503, but it was quickly abandoned, *furūsiyya* then being in decline as a result of the development of firearms. Sometimes, former *maydāns* were transformed into public squares or fair-grounds.

By metonymy, the term *maydān* (sometimes with the plural *mayādīn*) was applied to the exercises of mounted formations, and works devoted to *furūsiyya* present diagrams of these exercises which were performed by numerous groups of horsemen according to a well-established pattern (*tartīb al-mayādīn*). The major western riding schools, even today, give an accurate impression in public performances of the likely nature of these complex and interwoven movements of squads of troopers with their colourful banners.

In figurative usage, *maydān* evokes the confrontation of two parties, in the expressions *maydān al-ḥarb* ("field of battle"), *ṭalaba li 'l-maydān* ("challenge to combat"), *nahār al-maydān* (the day of battle). Among the Marazig of southern Tunisia, *mādān* (pl. *mwādīn*) denotes "battle", "fray" (see G. Boris, *Lexique*..., Paris 1958, s.v.).

Alongside this limited sense, *maydān* is, like the French "champ", the English "field" and the German "Feld", extended to the broad sense of "domain of activity", physical, intellectual or spiritual.

Finally, al-Maydān is the name of a locality of Fārs [*q.v.*] in the *kūra* of Sābūr, mentioned by Ibn al-Faḳīh al-Hamadhānī (*Abrégé du Livre des Pays*, tr. H. Massé, Damascus 1973, 246).

Bibliography: Besides the references mentioned in the text, see D. Ayalon, *Notes on the Furūsiyya exercises and games in the Mamluk sultanate*, in *Scripta Hierosolymitana*, ix (Jerusalem 1961), 31-62; J. D. Latham and W. F. Paterson, *Saracen archery*, London 1970; L. Mercier, *La chasse et les sports chez les Arabes*, Paris 1927; Ibn Hudhayl al-Andalusī-L. Mercier, *La parure des cavaliers et l'insigne des preux*, Paris 1924. (F. VIRÉ)

AL-**MAYDĀNĪ**, ABU 'L-FAḌL AḤMAD B. MUḤAMMAD B. AḤMAD B. IBRĀHĪM AL-NAYSĀBŪRĪ, Arab philologist, domiciled in Naysābūr in the upper part of the Maydān (square) of Ziyād b. ʿAbd al-Raḥmān. In the cemetery of this quarter (al-Maydān) he was buried after his death on Wednesday, 25 Ramaḍān 518/5 November 1124. In his home town, his teachers were the philologists and Ḳurʾān scholars Abu 'l-Ḥasan al-Wāḥidī (d. 468/1076), Yaʿḳūb b. Aḥmad al-Kurdī (d. 470/1078), and ʿAlī al-Mudjāshiʿī al-Farazdaḳī (d. 479/1086), who had seen much of the world. Like them, al-Maydānī was less of an original and perspicacious scholar—comparable to his famous contemporary Abu 'l-Ḳāsim al-Zamakhsharī [see MATHAL. 1. In Arabic, iii, 13]—than a knowledgeable *adīb* who knew how to condense traditional lore and to arrange it in a practical and pleasing way.

Among the works of his which have been preserved or are known by their titles, his great collection of proverbs, (1) *Madjmaʿ al-amthāl*, is outstanding. It was created subsequent to a *madjlis* of the *kātib* Muntadjab al-Mulk Abū ʿAlī Muḥammad b. Arslān (d. 534/1139), one of the most influential men at the court of Sultan Sandjar [*q.v.*] in Marw, at about the same time as the collection of al-Zamakhsharī (499/1106). The *Madjmaʿ* has remained the most comprehensive and most popular collection of classical Arabic proverbs up to our days (Ibn Khallikān, tr. de Slane, i, 131; Ziriklī, *Aʿlām*, i, 208). This is proved by the great number of mss. and the numerous prints; the *Madjmaʿ* is also the only collection that has been translated into a European language, to wit, into Latin by G. W. Freytag (Bonn 1838-43; see MATHAL. 1. In Arabic, iii, 12; R. Sellheim, *Die klassisch-arabischen Sprichwörtersammlungen*, The Hague 1954, 145-51, Arabic enlarged edition Beirut 1391/1971, 209-18; further ancient mss.: Paris [de Slane] no. 3958 [533/1138!]; Chester Beatty [Arberry], no. 3017 [586/1190]; Paris [Blochet], no. 6511 [587/1191], cf. no. 6702; Istanbul, Türk İslam Eserleri Müzesi, no. 2005 [6th/12th century]; Damat İbrahim, no. 957 [601/1204]; Munich [Aumer], no. 643 [603/1206]; Tashkent, no. 1781 [628/1230]; Brit. Mus., Suppl. [Rieu], no. 997 and Berlin [Ahlwardt], no. 8671, 2 [631/1234]; in addition, see N. M. Çetin, in *İA*, viii, 178; R. Şeşen, *Nawādir al-makhṭūṭāt al-ʿarabiyya*, Beirut 1400/1980, ii, 458; etc.). In 532/1137, his pupil Yūsuf b. Ṭāhir al-Khuwayyī (Khūwī) arranged an abridged edition under the title of *Farāʾid al-kharāʾid fi 'l-amthāl wa 'l-ḥikam* (Sellheim, *op. cit.*, 145, [2]209), and in 1037/1627, from this an anonymous scholar published an extract with annotations in Turkish, entitled *ʿUḳūd al-ʿuḳūl* (Vienna [Flügel], no. 343; cf. Cairo[1] [Turk. mss.], 136); a third abridgement, entitled *Muntakhab Madjmaʿ al-amthāl* (Cairo[2], iii, 389), originates from a certain al-Mawlā Āḳ Shams al-Dīn (10th/16th century?), and a fourth from Ḳāsim b. Muḥammad b. ʿAlī al-Ḥalabī al-Bakradjī (d. 1169/1756), entitled *al-Durr al-muntakhab min amthāl al-ʿArab* (Berlin [Ahlwardt], no. 8672; Cairo[2], iii, 97; cf. Cairo[1] [Turk. mss.], 136). In 1079/1668, an anonymous Ottoman writer turned the *Madjmaʿ* into verse under the title *Naẓm al-amthāl* (Laleli, no. 1953; a fragment at Gotha [Pertsch], in no. 1250), and two hundred years later, the Lebanese Ibrāhīm al-Aḥdab (d. 1308/1891), did this also, under the title *Farāʾid al-laʾāl fī Madjmaʿ al-amthāl* (Beirut 1312/1894). A Turkish translation by al-Sayyid al-Ḥāfiẓ Muḥammad Shākir b. al-Ḥādjdj Ibrāhīm Ḥilmī al-ʿAyntābī of 1294/1877 has survived in the autograph (Istanbul, Üniversite Kütüphanesi, TY, no. 167-70). Al-Maydānī's pupil Abu 'l-Ḥasan al-Bayhaḳī (d. 565/1169) is the author of an original collection of proverbs which in its explanations and comments is independent of that of his teacher (see MATHAL. 1. In Arabic, iii, 14).

(2) *Sharḥ al-Mufaḍḍaliyyāt* (mentioned, e.g., by Yāḳūt, *Udabāʾ*, ii, 108). (3) *Sharḥ Ḳaṣīdat al-Nābigha* (Paris [Blochet], no. 6022). (4) *Sharḥ Ḳāfiyyat Ruʾba* (Sezgin, ii, 369). (5) *Munyat al-rāḍī bi-rasāʾil al-ḳāḍī*, a collection of *rasāʾil* by the *ḳāḍī* of Harāt, Manṣūr b. Muḥammad al-Azdī al-Harawī (d. 440/1048; Brockelmann, S I, 154 f.). (6) *Maʾwa 'l-gharīb wa-marʿā 'l-adīb* (mentioned by Ḥādjdjī Khalīfa, s.t.).

(7) *al-Sāmī fi 'l-asāmī*, an Arabic-Persian dictionary of common terms and words, finished in 497/1104, classified in four categories: (a) *sharʿiyyāt* (technical terms of *fiḳh*), (b) *ḥayawānāt* (animate things), (c) *ʿulwiyyāt* (celestial) and (d) *sufliyyāt* (terrestrial things). They are divided up into numerous chapters, and these, in their turn, into further not expressly

characterised sub-chapters, arranged, as a rule, according to the subjects that are treated, and not alphabetically; said to have been lithographed at Tehran 1265/1849, 1267/1851, 1272/1856, 1273 and 1274/1857, 1275/1859, 1294/1877, n.d.; Tabriz n.d.; India 1284/1867; numerous mss. (e.g. Bursa, Haraççızade/oğlu, lugat, no. 15 [565/1169; cf. H. Ritter, in *Oriens*, ii (1949), 239]; Berlin [Ahlwardt], no. 7040 [*ca.* 600/1203]; Chester Beatty [Arberry], no. 3028 [631/1233]; Topkapı Sarayı [Karatay], no. 7556 [633/1235]; Çetin, in *İA*, viii, 178 f.; Şeşen, *op. cit.*, ii, 458; Tehran, Dānishgāh [Dānish Pazhūh], no. 1338,3 [682/1283]; Storey, iii, 81f.). For this, the author composed a commentary, entitled *al-Ibāna fī sharḥ al-Sāmī fi 'l-asāmī* (mss.: Tehran, *op. cit.*, no. 1338,2 [12th/18th century]; Leiden [de Goeje-Houtsma], no. 107 [692/1293]), another one was written by Asʿad b. Masʿūd b. Khalaf al-ʿIdjlī (d. 600/1203), entitled *Sharḥ al-kalimāt al-mushkila fī kitāb al-S.* (mss.: Topkapı Sarayı[Karatay], no. 7557 [7th/13th century]; Leiden [de Goeje-Houtsma], no. 106 [692/1293]). A synopsis prepared by the author's son, Abū Saʿd Saʿīd (d. 539/1145; al-Samʿānī, *al-Taḥbīr*, Baghdād 1395/1975, i, 302-3; al-Ṣafadī, *Wāfī*, vii, 327; al-Suyūṭī, *Bughya*, 254, ²i, 582; cf. al-Samʿānī, fol. 548a), in the order of al-Djawharī's (d. 398/1008) *al-Ṣiḥāḥ*, entitled *al-Asmāʾ fi 'l-asmāʾ* is preserved perhaps in Leiden (de Goeje-Houtsma), no. 108 (725/1325).

(8) *Ḳayd al-awābid min al-fawāʾid*, a criticism of al-Djawharī's well-known dictionary *al-Ṣiḥāḥ*, mainly based on al-Azharī's (d. 370/980) *Tahdhīb al-lugha* (ms.: Berlin [Ahlwardt], no. 6942). (9) *Kitāb al-Maṣādir*, a treatise on infinitives (mentioned, e.g., by Ibn al-Ḳifṭī, *Inbāh*, i, 124); on this work, his pupil, Abū Djaʿfar al-Bayhaḳī (d. 544/1167) has, perhaps, based his *Kitāb Tādj al-maṣādir* (Brockelmann, I, 350, S I, 513; Topkapı Sarayı [Karatay], no. 7565; *RIMA*, xvii [1971], 191). The *Kitāb Gharīb*, or *Gharāʾib al-lugha*, ascribed to him by the author of the *Hadiyya*, i, 82, is likely to be a work of his son Saʿīd of the same title (cf. al-Ṣafadī, *Wāfī*, xv, 199).

(10) *al-Hādī li 'l-shādī*, a syntax with Persian notes in three parts (nouns, verbs, particles), compiled after his *Kitāb al-Sāmī* (see above, no. 7); printed at Tehran 1374/1954; mss.: see e.g. Çetin, in *İA*, viii, 179; Şeşen, *op. cit.*, ii, 459 with commentary on the verses by the author (= Leiden [de Goeje-Houtsma], no. 162 [692/1293]); Storey, iii, 148. (11) *Nuzhat al-ṭarf fi 'l-ʿilm al-ṣarf*, a treatise on grammatical forms; prints: Constantinople 1299/1882; Tehran 1322/1904; Cairo 1402/1982; mss.: see e.g. Şeşen, *op. cit.*, ii, 458 f. (12) *al-Unmūdhadj fi 'l-naḥw*, and (13) *al-Naḥw al-maydānī*, two grammatical books (mentioned, e.g., by Ibn al-Ḳifṭī, *Inbāh*, i, 124). A minor grammatical treatise on (14) *ṣarf* (Paris [de Slane], no. 4000 [cf. Vajda, 599]), and another on (15) *djumūʿ* and *ḥurūf* (Leiden [de Goeje-Houtsma], no. 163; cf. Berlin [Ahlwardt], no. 7040, fol. 3a; Ibn al-Ḳifṭī, *op. cit.*, i, 122: *al-Hādī fi 'l-ḥurūf wa 'l-adawāt*; above, nos. 7 and 10).

Bibliography: In addition to the works mentioned in the text, see Brockelmann, I, 344 f., S I, 506 f., 964 (the reference to a *Kitāb Tafṣīl al-nashʾatayn*, Carullah, no. 2078, 42v-77v, should be applied to al-Rāghib al-Iṣfahānī, cf. Brockelmann, S I, 505-6, 9, no. 5; H. Ritter, in *Isl.*, xxv [1939], 61); Kaḥḥāla, *Muʿdjam al-muʾallifīn*, ii, 63 f.; E. Quatremère, *Mémoires sur la vie et les ouvrages de Meïdani*, in *JA*, 2. série, i (1828), 177-233; idem, *Proverbes arabes de Meïdani*, in *JA*, 3. série, iv (1837), 497-543, v (1838), 5-44, 209-58; see MATHAL. 1. In Arabic, iii, 12; his poor biography according to ʿAbd al-Ghāfir al-Fārisī's (d. 529/1134) lost *Kitāb al-Siyāḳ li-taʾrīkh Naysābūr* is preserved in Istanbul, Üniversite Kütüphanesi, FY, no. 695, fol. 128b.

(R. SELLHEIM)

MAYHANA, MĪHANA, a small town of mediaeval Khurāsān, now in the USSR, situated to the east of the Kūh-i Hazār Masdjid range and on the edge of the "Marw desert", the later Ḳara Ḳum [*q.v.*], 40 miles/62 km. to the east-north-east of Ḳalʿat-i Nādirī and 60 miles/93 km. south-east of Mashhad [*q.vv.*]. In mediaeval times, it was the chief settlement of the district of Khāwarān or Khābarān which lay between Abīward and Sarakhs [*q.vv.*]; by Yāḳūt's time, Mayhana itself had largely decayed, though Mustawfī describes Khāwarān as a whole as flourishing, with good crops and cereals and fruit (*Ḥudūd al-ʿālam*, tr. Minorsky, 103, § 23.12; Mustawfī, *Nuzha*, 157-8, tr. 155; Le Strange, *Lands*, 394).

Its main historical fame is as the birthplace in 357/967 of the Ṣūfī saint and thaumaturge Abū Saʿid Faḍl Allāh b. Abi 'l-Khayr, who alternated between residence there and in Nīshāpūr for most of his life till his death at Mayhana in 440/1049 [see ABŪ SAʿID B. ABI 'L-KHAYR; to the references there add F. Meier, *Abū Saʿīd-i Abū l-Ḫayr (357-440/967-1049), Wirklichkeit und Legende*, Tehran-Liège 1976]. Mustawfī quotes verses praising the *Shaykh* and other great men from Khāwarān, including the minister of the Saldjūḳ Ṭoghrïl Beg, Abū ʿAlī Shādhān, and the poet Anwarī [*q.v.*].

Mayhana is now a town situated some 14 miles/20 km. within the Turkmenistan SSR and appears on modern maps as Meana.

Bibliography (in addition to references given in the article): H. Halm, *Die Ausbreitung der šāfiʿitischen Rechtsschule von den Anfangen bis zum 8./14. Jahrhundert*, Wiesbaden 1974, 83; Meier, *op. cit.*, 39 ff.

(C. E. BOSWORTH)

AL-**MAYL** (A.), declination, an important notion in spherical astronomy.

Declination is a measure of the distance of a celestial body from the celestial equator. Muslim astronomers tabulated either the declination and right ascensions of stars or their ecliptic coordinates [see MAṬĀLIʿ]. Also of concern to them was the solar declination, *mayl al-shams*. They distinguished two kinds of solar declination, *al-mayl al-awwal*, the distance δ_1 of the sun from the ecliptic measured perpendicular to the celestial equator, and *al-mayl al-thānī*, the distance δ_2 of the sun from the ecliptic measured perpendicular to the ecliptic; see Fig. 1.

Fig. 1.

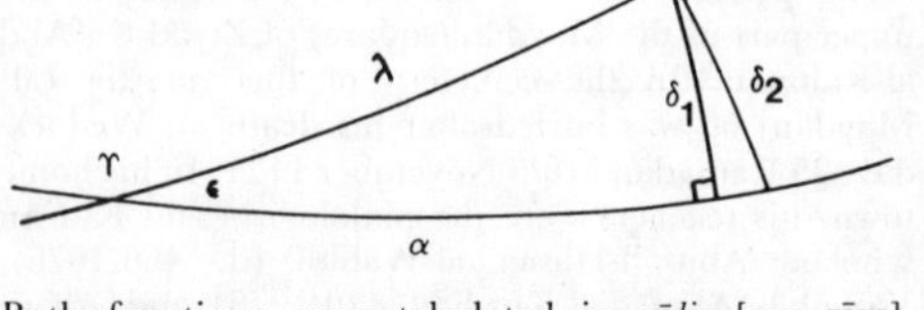

Both functions were tabulated in *zīdjs* [see ZĪDJ], usually for each degree of ecliptic longitude λ. The underlying formulae in modern notation are

$$\delta_1(\lambda) = \text{arc sin } (\sin \lambda \sin \varepsilon)$$

and

$$\delta_2(\lambda) = \text{arc tan } (\sin \lambda \tan \varepsilon),$$

were ε is the obliquity of the ecliptic, called in Arabic *al-mayl al-aʿẓam* or *al-mayl al-kullī*.

The obliquity of the ecliptic is the basic parameter of spherical astronomy. Since it varies with time,

Muslim astronomers over the centuries conducted observations to derive the current value. Most of them did this by means of meridian observations of the sun at the solstices. If h_{min} and h_{max} are the solar meridian altitudes at the winter and summer solstices at a locality with latitude φ, then

$$h_{min} = 90° - \varphi - \varepsilon \text{ and } h_{max} = 90° - \varphi + \varepsilon$$

see Fig. 2. Clearly, from such observations ε may be found using

$$\varepsilon = \tfrac{1}{2}(h_{max} - h_{min}).$$

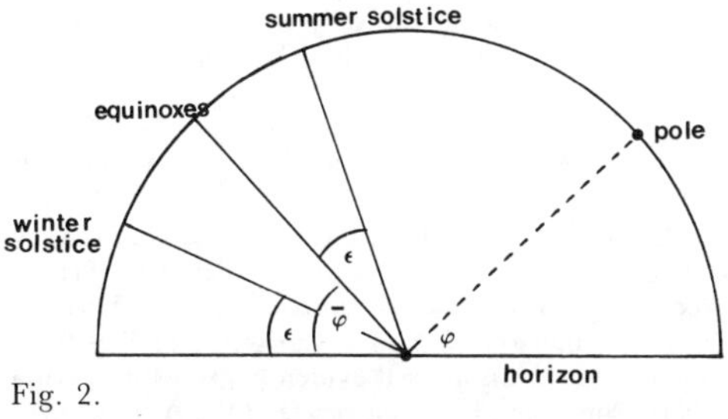

Fig. 2.

Likewise, the local latitude φ can be determined from the same observational data. The most complete discussions of the subject were by Ibn Yūnus and, more especially, al-Bīrūnī [*q.v.*].

Bibliography: E. S. Kennedy, *A survey of Islamic astronomical tables*, in *Trans. American Philosophical Society*, xlvi/2 (1956), 123-77, esp. 140; D. A. King, *Spherical astronomy in medieval Islam: the Ḥākimī Zīj of Ibn Yūnus*, forthcoming, Part II, Sections 11-12; Kennedy, *A commentary upon al-Bīrūnī's Taḥdīd al-amākin*, Beirut 1973, esp. 16-90. A valuable study which needs updating is O. Schirmer, *Studien zur Astronomie der Araber: Arabische Bestimmungen der Schiefe der Ekliptik*, in *SBPMS Erl.*, lviii (1926), 43-79. (D. A. KING)

MAYMANA, a town of northwestern Afghānistān (lat. 35° 55' N., long. 64° 67' E.), lying at an altitude of 2,854 feet/870 m. on the upper reaches of the Āb-i Maymana, one of the constituent streams of the Āb-i Ḳayṣar which peters out in the desert beyond Andkhūy [*q.v.*] and the sands of the Ḳîzîl Ḳum [*q.v.*].

The site of the settlement seems to be ancient. The *Vendidad* speaks of Nisāya, and the ?8th century Armenian geography of Iran records Nsai-mianak = MP * Nisāk-i Miyānak "the Middle Nisā", possibly identical with Ptolemy's Νισαία in Margiana (Marquart, *Ērānšahr*, 78-9). This seems to have been where lay the town known in early Islamic times as al-Yahūdiyya (*Ḥudūd al-ʿālam*, tr. Minorsky, 107, § 23.53, cf. comm. 335: Djahūdhān), indicating a sizeable community of Jews there. Al-Yaʿḳūbī, *Buldān*, 287, tr. Wiet, 99, al-Iṣṭakhrī, 270, Ibn Ḥawḳal, ed. Kramers, 442-3, tr. idem and Wiet, 427-9, al-Muḳaddasī, 427-9, describe the town as a flourishing one, with a Friday mosque, and as the seat of the ruler of Faryāb of the principality of Gūzgān, which remained independent till incorporated into the Ghaznawid empire by Sulṭān Maḥmūd [see DJŪZDJĀN and FARĪGHŪNIDS]. Yāḳūt, *Buldān*, ed. Beirut, ii, 194, calls it Djahūdhān al-Kubrā, presumably to distinguish it from the Yahūdiyya of Iṣfahān.

The actual name Maymana "the auspicious, fortunate town" does not occur in the 3rd-4th/9th-10th century texts. It is possible that a form Maymand existed by the 7th/13th century, since it apparently occurs in some manuscripts of Djūzdjānī's *Ṭabaḳāt-i Nāṣirī* (though the latest editor, ʿAbd al-Ḥayy Ḥabībī, adopts the reading Maymana for his text, 2nd ed. Kābul 1342-3/1963-4, i, 358, 374, whereas the manuscript(s) which Raverty used for his translation, London 1881-99, ostensibly had Maymand, cf. i, 378, 391, 399); but the Maymand which was the family origin of the great Ghaznawid vizier Aḥmad b. Ḥasan Maymandī [*q.v.*] was almost certainly one in Zābulistān, the region around Ghazna. It is certainly the form Maymana which is henceforth used for the town in Afghān Turkistān.

Towards modern times, Maymana was under Uzbek control, being one of the petty, semi-independent khānates (together with Sar-i Pul, Shibarghān and Andkhūy) known as the Čahār Wilāyat, and oriented essentially towards the Bukhārā Khānate. The Hungarian traveller Vambéry visited it in 1863 and describes the town as possessing 1,500 mud-brick houses and a dilapidated bazaar. The Afghān *amīr* of Kābul Dūst Muḥammad [*q.v.*] disputed possession of Maymana with Bukhārā in 1855, and only with the Anglo-Russian agreement of 1873 did the four khānates come definitely within the orbit of Kābul; not till 1844 did the *amīr* ʿAbd al-Raḥmān Khān [*q.v.*] secure the submission of the *wālī* of Maymana.

At present, Maymana, lying as it does within a fertile agricultural area, and being on the Harāt to Mazār-i Sharīf road, is a flourishing town, the administrative centre of a *wilāyat* or province (since 1964, called that of Faryāb), and with a population (mainly Uzbek, but with some Tādjīks and Pushtūns) estimated by Humlum at 30,000. It has an airfield and is important for the weaving of fine carpets and for wool and camels'-hair textiles.

Bibliography (in addition to sources mentioned in the article): H. Vambéry, *Travels in Central Asia*, London 1864, 244; C. E. Yates, *Northern Afghanistan or letters from the Afghan Boundary Commission*, Edinburgh and London 1888, 233; Barthold, *Istoriko-geografičeskii obzor Irana*, St. Petersburg 1903 = *Sočineniya*, vi, 57-8, Eng. tr. Princeton 1984, 32-4; Le Strange, *The lands of the eastern caliphate*, 424-5; Sir Thomas Holdich, *The gates of India*, London 1910, 249; J. Humlum *et alii*, *La géographie de l'Afghanistan, étude d'un pays aride*, Copenhagen 1959, 132, 148-9; L. Duprée, *Afghanistan*, Princeton 1973, index; J. Lee, *The history of Maimana in northwestern Afghanistan 1731-1893*, in *Iran, Jnal. of the BIPS*, xxv (1987), 107-24. (C. E. BOSWORTH)

MAYMANDĪ, ABU 'L-ḲĀSIM AḤMAD B. ḤASAN, called Shams al-Kufāt "sun of the capable ones", vizier of sultans Maḥmūd and Masʿūd of Ghazna [*q.vv.*]. He was a foster-brother of Maḥmūd, and had been brought up and educated with him. His father had been *ʿāmil* of Bust under Sebüktigin, and apparently stemmed from Maymand in Zābulistān; but on a charge of misappropriation of the revenue, he was put to death. In 384/994, when the Amīr Nūḥ b. Manṣūr the Sāmānid conferred on Maḥmūd the command of the troops of Khurāsān, Maḥmūd put Aḥmad at the head of his correspondence department. After this, Aḥmad rapidly rose in the service of his master, and occupied in succession, the posts of *Mustawfī-i Mamlakat* (Accountant General), *Ṣāḥib-i Dīwān-i ʿArḍ* (Head of the War Department), and *ʿāmil* of the provinces of Bust and Rukhkhadj. In 404/1013, Sultan Maḥmūd appointed him *wazīr* in place of Abu 'l-ʿAbbās al-Faḍl b. Aḥmad Isfarāʾinī. For twelve years, Aḥmad managed the affairs of the growing empire of Sultan Maḥmūd with great tact and diplomacy. Aḥmad was very strict and exacting, and did not tolerate any evasion of duty or departure from the usual official procedure, with the result that many of the dignitaries of the Empire became his enemies and worked to bring about his ruin. He was disgraced and dismissed in 415/1024, and sent as a prisoner to the fort of Kālin<u>dj</u>ar, in the southern Ka<u>sh</u>mīr hills.

After his accession to the throne in 421/1030, the new sultan Mas^cūd b. Maḥmūd, whose cause Aḥmad had always favoured, wished to re-appoint him vizier in 422/1031 in place of the disgraced Ḥasanak [*q.v.*]; ostensibly on account of his age, Aḥmad was reluctant to accept, and before doing so, insisted on a *muwāḍa^ca* [*q.v.*] or contract defining his own duties and rights *vis-à-vis* the sultan and other ministers. He died in Muḥarram 424/December 1032, much mourned, according to Bayhaḳī, by other members of the bureaucracy.

From both his competence and learning, Aḥmad subsequently enjoyed a great reputation as a vizier and stylist; ^cUtbī expressly praises him for his restoration of Arabic as the official language of the *dīwāns*, whereas Isfarā[>]inī had—no doubt, more realistically—introduced the use of Persian, so that "the bazaar of eloquence had suffered loss, the traffic in fine expressions and beautiful language had perished, and there was no differentiation between incapacity and capability".

Bibliography: ^cUtbī-Manīnī, *Yamīnī*, Cairo 1286/1869, ii, 166-72, Lahore 1300/1883, 266-74; Bayhaḳī, *Ta[>]rī<u>kh</u>-i Mas^cūdī*, passim; Gardīzī, *Zayn al-a<u>kh</u>bār*, ed. Nāẓim, Berlin 1928, 96, 98-9; Sayf al-Dīn Faḍlī ^cUḳaylī, *Ā<u>th</u>ār al-wuzarā[>]*, I.O. ms. 1569 fols. 89b-111a, ed. <u>Dj</u>alāl al-Dīn Urmawī, Tehran 1337/1959, 152-86; Naṣīr al-Dīn Kirmānī, *Nasā[>]im al-asḥār*, ed. Urmawī, Tehran 1338/1959, 40-3; Barthold, *Turkestan*, 291; Nāẓim, *The life and times of Sulṭān Maḥmūd of <u>Gh</u>azna*, 130-1, 135-6.

(M. NĀẒIM-[C. E. BOSWORTH])

AL-**MAYMANĪ** AL-**RĀ<u>DJ</u>(A)KŪTĪ**, ^cABD AL-^cAZĪZ, Indo-Muslim Arabic scholar, known by the name MEMON. His family probably came originally from Maymana [*q.v.*], but he was born at Rā<u>dj</u>(a)kūt (Kāfhiyāwāṙ) in 1888 and died at Karachi on 27 October 1978.

The major part of his teaching career was undertaken at the Muslim University of ^cAlīgaṙh, where he was Reader from 1924 to 1942, then Professor until his retirement in 1950; previously, having graduated in Arabic and Persian in 1909, he was Lecturer in Arabic, from 1913 onward, at the Edward College of Pe<u>sh</u>āwar, before transferring to the Oriental College of Lāhawr. A few years after the creation of Pakistan, he made his way to Karachi where, from 1955 to 1958, he resumed teaching duties at the newly-inaugurated University, and also directed, until 1960, the Central Institute of Islamic Research. At various times he resided in different Arabic-speaking countries and, a pious Muslim, he made the Pilgrimage to Mecca on several occasions.

Primarily a philologist, al-Maymanī possessed a perfect mastery of classical Arabic which enabled him to edit preserved or partially reconstructed *dīwāns* (Ibn ^cUnayn, Ḥumayd b. <u>Th</u>awr al-Hilālī, Suḥaym ^cAbd Bani 'l-Ḥasḥās), works of philology such as the *<u>Th</u>alā<u>th</u> rasā[>]il* (by Ibn Fāris, al-Kisā[>]ī and Ibn ^cArabī), *al-Manḳūṣ wa 'l-mamdūd* by al-Farrā[>] or *Kitāb mā ttafaḳa lafẓuh* by al-Mubarrad, historical texts (*Nasab Ḳaḥṭān wa-^cAdnān* by al-Mubarrad) or literary texts (*Risālat al-malā[>]ika* by al-Ma^carrī; *al-Fāḍil* by al-Mubarrad). It should be noted that he took an interest in the literature of the Muslim West and that, in addition to *al-Nutaf min <u>sh</u>i^cray Ibn Ra<u>sh</u>īḳ wa-zamīlih Ibn <u>Sh</u>araf* (Cairo 1343/1925), he wrote a work entitled *Ibn Ra<u>sh</u>īḳ... wa-tar<u>dj</u>amat Ibn <u>Sh</u>araf* (likewise Cairo 1343/1925) and left a highly-esteemed commentary on al-Ḳālī [*q.v.*], *Simṭ al-la[>]ālī fī <u>sh</u>arḥ Amālī 'l-Ḳālī*, Cairo 1354/1936, 3 vols.

A member of the Arabic Academy of Damascus, al-Maymanī contributed actively to the *MMIA*, and it is typical of him that in his capacity as a corresponding member (being of Pakistani nationality) of the recently-created Indian Academy of the Arabic Language, he contributed the first article to the first issue of the *Ma<u>dj</u>allat al-Ma<u>dj</u>ma^c al-^cIlmī al-Hindī* (i, 1386/1976, 1-19), on the subject of Abū ^cUmar al-Zāhid, better known as <u>Gh</u>ulām <u>Th</u>a^clab [*q.v.*], whose *Kitāb al-Mudā<u>kh</u>alāt* he had published.

Bibliography: Obituary notice, by A. S. Bazmee Ansari, in *Hamdard Islamicus*, ii/2 (1979), 113-15.

(CH. PELLAT)

MAYMŪN B. **MIHRĀN**, ABŪ AYYŪB, early Islamic *faḳīh* and Umayyad administrator. According to traditional sources he was born in 40/660-1, the son of *mawālī* who were captives from Iṣṭa<u>kh</u>r. Maymūn himself evidently grew up in Kūfa where, some say, he was a *mawlā* of the Arab tribe of Hawāzin or Azd; others say that he was the slave of a woman of the Azd, who later manumitted him. After winning his freedom, he remained in Kūfa until the turbulence of the Dayr al-<u>Dj</u>amā<u>dj</u>im [*q.v.*] episode (82/701), which pitted the ^cIrāḳīs against the Umayyad authorities; presumably because of his neutral or pro-Umayyad sympathies, Maymūn moved at this time to the <u>Dj</u>azīra, where he became the leading figure among the local men of religion at Raḳḳa. A few accounts describe him as having made the pilgrimage to Mecca and as having visited Baṣra, where he had an interview with the famous saint al-Ḥasan al-Baṣrī; but travelling does not seem to have been his main activity, and most sources describe him simply as the sage of Raḳḳa.

Maymūn is remembered in numerous accounts for his religious and ethical maxims. Most of these emphasise such themes as the dangers of wealth and gluttony or the importance of God-fearing piety and of good works, but they also include some which can be considered as at least mildly anti-<u>Sh</u>ī^cī, while others suggest an effort to strike a politically non-committal pose: "Do not speak about four things: ^cAlī, ^cU<u>th</u>mān, *ḳadar*, and the stars". Although he served as a source of religious and ethical guidance, however, he does not seem to have been much concerned with the transmission of *ḥadī<u>th</u>*s, which were just beginning to be circulated widely in his day. As a transmitter of *ḥadī<u>th</u>*s he is generally adjudged reliable (*<u>th</u>iḳa*); but among his maxims is one that stresses the primacy of the Ḳur[>]ān over the "*ḥadī<u>th</u>*s of men" as a source of guidance, and only about two dozen *ḥadī<u>th</u>*s on his authority (mostly via Ibn ^cAbbās or ^cAbd Allāh b. ^cUmar) are extant. A good number of these *ḥadī<u>th</u>*s deal with ritual law; a few deal with sectarian or political issues, some of which are clearly *mawḍū^c* (e.g. Abū Nu^caym, *Ḥilya*, iv, 95 on the Rāfiḍīs), and which generally are slightly anti-^cAlid in tone. Some of these "*ḥadī<u>th</u>*s" are doubtless sayings of Maymūn himself or of his informants, which his pupils "raised" to the status of prophetic utterances. Accounts going back to Maymūn also convey considerable information about several central figures among the Companions of the Prophet and their successors, e.g. ^cU<u>th</u>mān, ^cAlī, Mu^cāwiya, Ibn ^cAbbās, ^cAbd Allāh b. ^cUmar, Ibn Sīrīn, al-Ḥasan al-Baṣrī and Sa^cīd b. al-Musayyab—including several significant *awā[>]il* (e.g. Mu^cāwiya was the first who sat between the two *<u>kh</u>uṭbas*; ^c*Iḳd al-farīd*, v, 105).

Maymūn's close ties to the Umayyads are reflected both by the fact that he held office for some of them and by his many accounts of the activities of ʿUmar b. ʿAbd al-ʿAzīz (ruled 99-101/717-20) and some other members of the dynasty. He is first said to have administered the treasury in Ḥarrān for ʿAbd al-Malik's brother, Muḥammad b. Marwān, who served that caliph and his successor al-Walīd as governor of the Djazīra. Maymūn was then appointed by ʿUmar b. ʿAbd al-ʿAzīz over the *ḳaḍāʾ* and *kharādj* (judgeship and tax-collection) of the Djazīra—offices he apparently held only with some moral reservations—while his son ʿAmr ran ʿUmar's *dīwān* (Ibn Saʿd, vii/1, 178). After ʿUmar's death he was retained in his post for a time by Yazīd b. ʿAbd al-Malik. He was still evidently part of the official establishment in Ḥarrān under Hishām (al-Balādhurī, *Ansāb*, Beirut iii, 100), and is also said to have commanded the army of Syria that went to Cyprus in 106/724-5 for Hishām (al-Ṭabarī, ii, 1487). Maymūn appears to have been one of ʿUmar b. ʿAbd al-ʿAzīz's close confidants, and the two were evidently bound by mutual admiration, to judge from the many extant accounts in which one relates anecdotes emphasising the piety and wisdom of the other.

Maymūn died, according to most authorities, in the Djazīra in 117/735-6. He does not seem to have left behind any written works—further evidence, perhaps, that he was primarily a *faḳīh* known for his piety and good judgement in religious matters rather than a *muḥaddith*—but he did bring to Raḳḳa a tradition of religiosity that lived on in his pupils bearing the *nisba* "al-Maymūnī", among them Djaʿfar b. Burḳān, Abu 'l-Malīḥ, and his own son ʿAmr b. Maymūn. The esteem in which he was held by later authorities is aptly summed up in a statement ascribed to Sulaymān b. Mūsā (d. 115/733-4 or 119/737): "If knowledge (*ʿilm*) came to us from the Ḥidjāz on the authority of al-Zuhrī, or from Syria on the authority of Makḥūl, or from ʿIrāḳ on the authority of al-Ḥasan [al-Baṣrī], or from the Djazīra on the authority of Maymūn [b. Mihrān], we accepted it" (Abū Zurʿa, *Taʾrīkh*, 315 [no. 588]).

Bibliography: Abū Zurʿa al-Dimashḳī, *Taʾrīkh*, Damascus 1980, index; Ibn Saʿīd, iv/1, 121-2; v, 271-7, 280, 291-2, 296; vii/2, 177-9; viii, 95-6; Ṭabarī, index; Azdī, *Taʾrīkh al-Mawṣil*, Cairo 1967, 37; Balādhurī, *Ansāb al-ashrāf*, Beirut 1978-9, iii, 100; iv/1, 566; *ibid.*, Jerusalem 1936-7, iv/l, 54, 130-1; v, 75; Muḥammad b. Ḥabīb, *Kitāb al-Muḥabbar*, Hyderabad-Deccan 1942, 347, 478; Ibn Ḳutayba, *Maʿārif*, Cairo 1969, 448-551, 577; Ibn ʿAbd al-Ḥakam, *Sīrat ʿUmar b. ʿAbd al-ʿAzīz*, Cairo 1346/1927, 127-8; Djahshiyārī, *Kitāb al-wuzarāʾ wa 'l-kuttāb*, Cairo 1938, 53-4; Ibn ʿAbd Rabbihi, *ʿIḳd al-farīd*, ed. Muḥammad Saʿīd al-ʿIryān, n.p. 1953, ii, 241; v, 13, 105, 170-1, 283; Muḥammad b. Saʿīd b. ʿAbd al-Raḥmān al-Ḳushayrī, *Taʾrīkh al-Raḳḳa*, Ḥamā 1957, esp. 21-38; Ibn ʿAsākir, *Taʾrīkh madīnat Dimashḳ*, ms. Ẓāhiriyya Library, Damascus xviii, fols. 329b-335a; Abū Nuʿaym Aḥmad al-Iṣbahānī, *Ḥilyat al-awliyāʾ*, Cairo 1351-7/1932-8, iv, 92-7, gives one of the most complete collections of *ḥadīths* related on Maymūn's authority; Ibn al-ʿImād, *Shadharāt*, *sub anno* 117; Ibn al-Athīr, *al-Nihāya fī gharīb al-ḥadīth*, Cairo 1383/1963, i, 164, ii, 198; iii, 100; Wakīʿ, *Akhbār al-ḳuḍāt*, Cairo 1366-9/1947-50, ii, 66-7; Ibn Ḥadjar al-ʿAsḳalānī, *Tahdhīb al-tahdhīb*, Hyderabad 1325-7/1907-10, x, 390-2; Dhahabī, *al-Kāshif fī maʿrifat man lahu riwāya fī 'l-kutub al-sitta*, Cairo 1972, iii, 193 (no. 5861).

(F. M. DONNER)

MAYMŪN B. AL-ASWAD AL-**ḲADDĀḤ**, obscure Meccan transmitter from the *Imāms* Muḥammad al-Bāḳir and Djaʿfar al-Ṣādiḳ who, two centuries after his death, gained notoriety as the father of the alleged founder of Ismāʿīlism and ancestor of the Fāṭimid caliphs, ʿAbd Allāh b. Maymūn [*q.v.*]. According to the Imāmī sources, he was a client of Makhzūm and a shaper of arrow shafts (*yabrī al-ḳidāḥ*). He became a personal servant of al-Bāḳir and al-Ṣādiḳ in Mecca. A few traditions of the two *Imāms* related on his authority are contained in the canonical collections of Imāmī *ḥadīth*. Al-Ṭūsī counts him also among the companions of *Imām* ʿAlī Zayn al-ʿĀbidin (d. 95/713-14) (*Ridjāl al-Ṭūsī*, ed. Muḥammad Ṣādiḳ Āl Baḥr al-ʿUlūm, Nadjaf 1381/1961, 101, 135, 317). He died probably during the imāmate of al-Ṣādiḳ (d. 148/765). W. Ivanow's suggestion that he had, besides ʿAbd Allāh, another son called Abān (*The alleged founder of Ismailism*, 68) rests on a faulty *isnād* in some copies of al-Kulaynī's *K. al-Kāfī* (see Muḥammad b. ʿAlī al-Ardabīlī al-Ḥāʾirī, *Djāmiʿ al-ruwāt*, Ḳumm 1403, ii, 287).

Neither Imāmī nor Sunnī biographical dictionaries and heresiographies of the 3rd/9th century suggest that Maymūn al-Ḳaddāḥ or his son inclined to Shīʿī extremism or was involved in the sect backing Ismāʿīl b. Djaʿfar. The earliest mention of him as a heresiarch is by the Sunnī polemicist Ibn Rizām (writing *ca.* 340/951) who describes him as a Dayṣānī dualist and founder of a sect called the Maymūniyya which backed the heretic Abu 'l-Khaṭṭāb [*q.v.*], teaching the divinity of ʿAlī. Later anti-Ismāʿīlī authors greatly elaborated Ibn Rizām's story and added to the catalogue of his heresies. Akhū Muḥsin (writing *ca.* 373/985) calls him Maymūn b. Dayṣān, making him a son of Bardesanes. Ibn Shaddād (d. *ca.* 509/1115) gives him the *kunya* Abū Shākir, evidently identifying him with a Dayṣānī of the time of al-Ṣādiḳ notorious in Imāmī tradition. Muḥammad b. al-Ḥasan al-Daylamī (writing in 707/1307) calls him Maymūn b. Dayṣān al-Ḳaddāḥ al-Ahwāzī al-Fārisī and asserts that he appeared in Kūfa in 176/792 after having been nominally converted to Islam by al-Ṣādiḳ. All these accounts are obviously pure fiction.

Ibn Rizām's story is based, however, on information from Ḳarmaṭī Ismāʿīlī sources. There is clear evidence of a wide-spread belief among Ismāʿīlīs in the pre-Fāṭimid and early Fāṭimid age that the leadership after the disappearance of Muḥammad b. Ismāʿīl b. Djaʿfar had been transferred to one ʿAbd Allāh b. Maymūn al-Ḳaddāḥ, who was not of ʿAlid descent. He and his successors were not *Imāms*, but lieutenants (*khulafāʾ*) of the absent *Imām* pending his return as the Mahdī. Against this, Fāṭimid Ismāʿīlī tradition maintained that the name Maymūn had been used in the missionary activity for the *Imām* to conceal his identity and that the ancestors of the Fāṭimids, though claiming merely the rank of *ḥudjdjas*, were in fact the *Imāms*.

Bibliography: In addition to the works quoted in the article on ʿAbd Allāh b. Maymūn, see now S. M. Stern, *Heterodox Ismāʿīlism at the time of al-Muʿizz*, in *BSOAS*, xvii (1955), 10-33; H. F. al-Hamdani, *On the genealogy of the Fatimid Caliphs*, Cairo 1958; W. Madelung, *Das Imamat in der frühen ismailitischen Lehre*, in *Isl.*, xxxvii (1961), esp. 73-80; A. Hamdani and F. de Blois, *A re-examination of al-Mahdī's letter to the Yemenites on the genealogy of the Fatimid Caliphs*, in *JRAS* (1983), 173-207.

(W. MADELUNG)

MAYMŪN-DIZ, a castle of the Ismāʿīlīs [see ISMĀʿĪLIYYA] in the Alburz Mountains in north-western Iran, the mediaeval region of Daylam [*q.v.*].

Rashīd al-Dīn states that it was built in 490/1097 by the Grand Master of the Assassins Ḥasan-i Sabbāḥ or by his successor Kiyā Buzurg-Ummīd in the early 6th/12th century. Djuwaynī, tr. Boyle, II, 621-36, cf. M. G. S. Hodgson, *The order of the Assassins*, The Hague 1955, 265 ff., has a detailed account of the fortress's reduction by the Il-Khān Hülegü in Shawwāl 654/November 1256. The Mongols besieged it briefly till it was surrendered by the last Grand Master Rukn al-Dīn Khūr-Shāh, who had latterly resided there with his treasury instead of at Alamūt [*q.v.*]; they then went on to capture the latter fortress.

In expeditions of 1959-61, Willey identified the site as an easily-defensible plateau some 1,500 ft./480 m. by 300 ft./95 m., with extensive caverns and standing buildings, just north of the village of Shams-Kilāya in the valley of a right-bank affluent of the Alamūt-Rūd, itself running into the Shāh-Rūd/Safīd-Rūd river system (*contra* Ivanow's tentative identification of Maymūn-Diz with the modern place Nawīzār-Shāh).

Bibliography (in addition to references given in the article): W. Ivanow, *Alamut and Lamasar, two mediaeval Ismaili strongholds in Iran. An archaeological study*, Tehran 1960, 75-81; P. J. E. Willey, *The castles of the Assassins*, London 1963, 158-92 (with plan and photographs); B. Lewis, *The Assassins, a radical sect in Islam*, London 1967, index. See also LANBASAR. (C. E. Bosworth)

MAYMŪNA BINT AL-ḤĀRITH, the last wife that Muḥammad married. She stemmed from the Hawāzin tribe of ʿĀmir b. Ṣaʿṣaʿa and was a sister-in-law of al-ʿAbbās. After she had divorced her first husband, a Thaḳafī, and her second, the Kurashī Abū Rukm, had died, she lived as a widow in Mecca where the Prophet wooed her, primarily no doubt for political reasons, on the *ʿumra* allowed to him in the year 7/629. His wish to marry her in Mecca was refused by the Meccans, in order not to prolong his stay there; the marriage therefore took place in Sarif, a village north of Mecca. Her brother-in-law al-ʿAbbās acted as her *walī* or guardian at the ceremony. The question whether the Prophet on this occasion was still in the *iḥrām* or not is a much-disputed and variously-answered question. The bridal gift is said to have been 500 *dirhams*. Married at the age of 27, Maymūna survived the other wives of the Prophet and died in 61/681 in Sarif, where she is said to have been buried on the spot where she was married.

Bibliography: Ibn Hishām, 790-1; Ibn Saʿd, ed. Sachau, viii, 94-100; Ṭabarī, i, 1595-6; Bakrī, ed. Wüstenfeld, 772-3; Caetani, *Annali dell' Islām*, ii, 66-7; W. M. Watt, *Muhammad at Medina*, Oxford 1956, 397; cf. M. Hamidullah, *Le Prophète de l'Islam*, Paris 1959, 111, 458-9. (Fr. Buhl)

MAYSALŪN, a pass in the Anti-Lebanon Mountains where, on 24 July 1920, the French forces under the command of General Henri Gouraud, recently appointed High Commissioner in Beirut, defeated the forces of King Fayṣal of Syria and proceeded to occupy Damascus and establish the French mandatory authority there.

A son of Sharīf Ḥusayn of Mecca who, prompted by Britain, had revolted against the Turks and proclaimed himself king of the Arab countries in the Ḥidjaz in 1916, Fayṣal had been allowed by the British to occupy Damascus on 1 October 1918 and establish an Arab régime there as a representative of his father. On 8 March 1920, Fayṣal was proclaimed King of Syria, shortly before the San Remo conference convened in April to assign the territory of Syria and Lebanon as a mandate to France. The French mandatory authority was forthwith established in the Lebanese territory, which had been under French occupation since 1918, and Fayṣal was anxious to negotiate an agreement with Gouraud which would save his Arab régime in Damascus. The French, however, were of a different mind, and as the negotiations between the two sides faltered, Gouraud sent an ultimatum to Damascus, while his forces advanced against the city. Fayṣal's small army, led by his War Minister Yūsuf al-ʿAẓm, a Damascene notable, tried to stop the advance at the Maysalūn pass, but was easily defeated, and al-ʿAẓm was killed in the battle. Thereupon Fayṣal and his government fled Damascus, which was occupied by the French. The British later made him king of ʿIrāḳ.

Modern Arabs regard the battle of Maysalūn as the event that first awakened them to the harsh realities of imperial power politics. The event forms the central theme of a book by Sāṭiʿ al-Ḥuṣarī, a man who served as a minister under Fayṣal in Damascus, called *Yawm Maysalūn* ("The Day of Maysalūn", first published in Beirut in 1947). The village of Maysalūn stands today on the border between Lebanon and Syria, and a monument marks the grave of Yūsuf al-ʿAẓma there. Apart from its modern fame as a battlefield, Maysalūn was known in earlier Islamic times as a horse-post relay station along the Beirut-Damascus highway.

Bibliography: R. de Gontant-Biron, *Comment la France s'est installée en Syrie*, Paris 1922; S. H. Longrigg, *Syria and Lebanon under French Mandate*, London 1958; E. Kedourie, *England and the Middle East: the reconstruction of the Ottoman Empire, 1914-1921*, London 1956; Muḥammad Kurd ʿAlī, *Khiṭaṭ al-Shām*, Beirut 1970; Sāṭiʿ al-Ḥuṣarī, *Yawm Maysalūn*, Beirut 1947; G. Antonius, *The Arab awakening*, London 1938; see also FAYṢAL I. (Kamal S. Salibi)

MAYSĀN, the region along the lower Tigris River in southeastern al-ʿIrāḳ. This region is called Μεσήνη by Strabo, Mēshan in the Babylonian Talmud, Mayshan in Syriac. Mēshān in Middle Persian, Mēshun in Armenian, Maysān in Arabic, and T'iao-tche (Chaldaea) in the Han sources. The earliest references from the first century A.D. indicate that Μεσήνη was an ethnic toponym, the land of the people called Μεσηνός who lived along the Arabian side of the coast at the head of the Persian Gulf (Μαισανιτης κολπος in Ptolemy). Whether or not these people were Arabian themselves, some of them lived at Gerrha, and their land was regarded as lying along the ethnic border with Arabs. Arabic has the *nisbas* Maysānī and Maysanānī, the latter from the Persian plural for people.

Ancient Mesene lay between two branches of the lower Tigris, but its exact extent was subject to change and is therefore difficult to determine. Pliny explicitly states that Mesene extended 125 miles up the Tigris above Babylonian Seleucia to the town of Apamea where overflow water from the Euphrates reached the Tigris, that it adjoined Chalonitis (Ḥulwān), and that the branch of the Tigris along its northeastern border traversed the plains of Cauchae (Djukhā, the Diyāla plains). Whether or not this description was meant to reflect a brief extension of the Characene kingdom, which was known to include Apamea, Pliny seems to indicate that Mesene could be defined hydrographically as the territory irrigated by the combined waters of the Tigris and Euphrates. The Apamea in question, however, tends to be identified with Fam al-Ṣilḥ where the Tigris and Sillas divided. Ammianus Marcellinus, in the 4th century A.D., says that Apamea had been called Mesene formerly, but traces of a more extensive Maysān survive in the Arabic-writing geographers. Ibn Rustah calls Djabbul, at the Tigris end of two large canals coming from Sūrā, one of the cities of Maysān. Yāḳūt describes the district of Kaskar [*q.v.*] as overlapping Maysān and extending from the lower end of the Nahrawān canal to the sea. To the extent that ancient Mesene was identified with Chaldaea, it bordered on Babylonia in the west and the Chaldaean Lakes in the southwest. To the north it overlapped Djukhū [*q.v.*], which normally lay along the left bank of the Tigris, probably as a result of changes in the course of the river. It extended to Elymais (Khūzistān [*q.v.*]) in the east, but this border was also subject to change. The town of Ḥuwayza (modern Ḥawīza [*q.v.*]) was once part of Maysān, but by the 8th/14th century belonged to Khūzistān.

Politically, ancient Mesene was identical with the Hellenistic kingdom of Characene (*ca.* 129 B.C.—*ca.* 224 A.D.). The region between Babylonia and the Gulf coast had formed an administrative division (but not an eparchy) of the Seleucid state in the 3rd century B.C. called the territory of the Erythraean Sea. Alexander the Great had settled Macedonian veterans at a city called Alexandria which he founded above the confluence of a former course of the lower Karkeh River with the Tigris, 1¼ miles from the coast. After this city was destroyed by floods, Antiochus IV (175-164 B.C.) restored it by 166-165 B.C., called it Antiochia, and put Hyspaosines son of Sagdodonacus, king of the neighbouring Arabs, in charge of it and its territory. The latter became independent between 141 and 139 B.C., and in 129 B.C. built new embankments to protect the flood-damaged city, renaming it Charax Spasinou ("the palisade of Hyspaosines") as the capital of Characene. In 127 B.C. he defeated the Arsacid governor of Babylon and occupied Babylon and Seleucia briefly, but was defeated by Mithradates II in 121 B.C., after which he and his successors continued as rulers of Characene subject to the Parthians.

Charax is transcribed as Karak Āspasinā (KRK ʾSPSNʾ) and identified as Karkā dē Mēshan (KRKʾ DY MYŠN) in Palmyrene inscriptions of the 1st and 2nd centuries. It was called Karkhā dhᵉ Mayshan in Syriac and Karkh Maysān in Arabic. Its site, formerly sought in the vicinity of Muḥammara, has been convincingly identified by Hansman with modern Djabal Khayābir near the left bank of the Shaṭṭ al-ʿArab. By Pliny's time, Charax was 193 km. from the coast although the tide went upstream far beyond it. The left bank of the lower Tigris was inhabited by Chaldaeans, the right bank by Arabian brigands called Attali beyond whom were nomadic Scenitae. T'iao-Tche is described in Han sources as a hot, low, densly populated, rice-growing region with lions, rhinoceroses, zebu, peacocks, ostriches, and clever jugglers. Strabo adds the production of barley, sesame oil, and dates. By the 1st century B.C., Charax was a major commercial centre where Indian ships met caravans from Petra and Palmyra. In the 1st century A.D., caravans from Petra arrived at the town of Forat 11 or 12 miles downstream from Charax. Its site was either near the modern town of al-Tanūma on the left bank of the Shaṭṭ al-ʿArab, or, according to Hansman, at Maghlūb, 17.4 km. (10.8 miles) southeast of Djabal Khayābir. Apologos (al-Ubulla) also appears as an emporium on the right bank of the Shaṭṭ al-ʿArab opposite Forat at ʿAshshār, the modern port of al-Baṣra, in the 1st century. Copper, sandalwood, teak, ebony, spices and gems were imported from Barygaza in Gudjarāt through Apologos, while Characene merchants exported pearls, clothing, wine, purple, dates, gold and slaves. In the winter of 115-16, Trajan occupied Characene briefly, collecting tribute from Attembelos V, after which it returned to Arsacid rule.

In *ca.* 224 Characene fell to Ardashīr I (*ca.* 226-41), the founder of the Sāsānid dynasty, who killed the king of Characene and made his own son, Mihrshāh, ruler of Maysān. Although it is claimed in Arabic literature that Ardashīr refounded Karkh Maysān as Astarābādh Ardashīr, this name has not been found in Sāsānid inscriptions. Under Shāpūr I (*ca.* 241-73), his eldest son, Shāpūr, and the latter's wife, Dēnak, were king and queen of Māshān. A certain Ātrofarnabag is called Mēshān Shāh in Narseh's inscription at Paikuli, and the Babylonian Talmud mentions a governor (*ōstāndār*) of Meshān. However, Shāpūr I is said to have formed a separate district called Shādh Sābūr in northwestern Maysān around the city of Kaskar which had its own *ōstāndār*.

By the 3rd century, the formerly pagan population of Maysān was mixed with Jews, Magians, gnostics and possibly Christians. The priest Kartīr claimed to have established Magians and sacred fires there, and the title of *magōpat* of Mēshān inscribed on a gem indicates the establishment of the priestly hierarchy. Jews of mixed descent were scattered throughout Maysān, and the gnostic, baptist sect called al-Mughtasila located there was joined by Mānī's father. Mānī [see MĀNĪ B. FĀTTIK] grew up in this sect, and Mihrshāh, the governor, was one of his earliest converts and supporters. Whether or not Christianity was carried to Maysān in the 1st century by the apostle Mārī, as legend claims, by the year 310 Pᵉrāth dᵉ Mayshan (al-Furāt) was the see of the metropolitan bishop of Mayshan. By 410 there were suffragan bishoprics at Karkhā dhᵉ Mayshan, Rīmā and Nahrgūr.

Ammianus Marcellinus describes huge groves of date palms extending from Babylon to Mesene and the sea in the 4th century, and reports that Mesene was included in the province of "Assyria" that embraced all of lower Mesopotamia in the middle Sāsānid period. In the 3rd and 4th centuries, Mēshān remained a centre for the import of spices, drugs and gems from India as well as silk and cotton cloth and steel. Kushān coins found in Mēshān also testify to trade with northern India.

Conditions in Maysān were transformed when the lower Tigris began to shift from its former course below Fam al-Ṣilḥ, which had gone via Bādhibīn and ʿAbdasī to al-Madhār. During floods in the reigns of Bahrām V Gūr (420-38), Ḳubādh b. Fīrūz (488-96, 498/9-531), and under Khusraw II in 7/628, the lower Tigris burst its banks and changed its main course to the Dudjayla/Shaṭṭ al-Akhādhar channel (not the Nahr Gharrāf/Shaṭṭ al-Hayy as formerly thought) which went via Kaskar into the swamps (*al-Baṭāʾiḥ* [*q.v.*]). Western Maysān was turned into swamps, northern Maysān and south-eastern Djukhā into desert, and Maysān was reduced to the territory along the former course of the Tigris below al-Madhār called the Blind or One-Eyed Tigris (Didjlat al-ʿAwrāʾ). What remained of Maysān formed the district of Shādh Bahman and was put in the Quarter of the South when the Sāsānid empire was reorganised in the 6th century. Al-Furāt, said to have been refounded as Bahman Ardashīr I, may have become the capital. By extension, Yāḳūt identifies Bahman Ardashīr, Arabicised as Bahmanshīr, also called Furāt al-Baṣra, as the entire district (*kūra*). The Tigris estuary from al-Maftaḥ and al-Ubulla to ʿAbbādān was also called Bahmanshīr by the Persians, according to al-Masʿūdī, similar to Bamishīr for a branch of the lower Kārūn [*q.v.*]. Vahman Ardashīr is first attested in 544 as the see of the Nestorian metropolitan bishop of Mayshan. The bishoprics of Rīmā and Karkhā dhᵉ Mayshan are last attested in 605, Nᵉhargūr (as Nᵉhargūl) in *ca.* 23-5/644-6, although Fiey has argued for the survival of the latter two under other names. None of the late Sāsānid mint-marks ascribed to al-Furat, Karkh Maysān or Maysān is conclusive. The subdivisions of this district at the time of the Muslim conquest were Bahman Ardashīr around al-Furāt, Maysān, Dast-i Maysān and Abarḳubādh.

In Ṣafar 12/633, Khālid b. al-Walīd took al-Ubulla, invaded Maysān and defeated Persian forces at al-Madhār. After his victory at Buwayb about two years later, al-Muthannā b. Ḥāritha also sent forces to Maysān and Dast-i Maysān. The actual conquest was undertaken by ʿUtba b. Ghazwān in 14/635 and the spring of 15/636. ʿUtba defeated and captured the ruler (*ṣāḥib*) of al-Furāt, took al-Ubulla and al-Furāt, conquered Maysān, defeating and killing the *marzubān* [*q.v.*] at al-Madhār; Abarḳubādh; and Dast-i Maysān, defeating its *marzubān*. After ʿUtba withdrew to al-Baṣra, al-Mughīra b. Shuʿba [*q.v.*] pacified Maysān and Abarḳubādh again, killing the *marzubān* or *dihḳān*. The captives taken in Maysān included Yasār, the father of al-Ḥasan al-Baṣrī [*q.v.*], who was taken to the Ḥidjāz, and Arṭabān, the grandfather of ʿAbd Allāh b. ʿAwn b. Arṭabān, who lived at al-Baṣra. Some captives from Maysān were released at ʿUmar's order. In 18/639 al-Hurmuzān raided Dast-i Maysān and Maysān from Khūzistān, taking captive Abraham, Nestorian bishop of Pᵉrāth, but was driven out by Abū Mūsā al-Ashʿarī, the governor of al-Baṣra.

Abū Mūsā is also credited with establishing the Tigris districts (*Kuwar* or *Kūra* Didjla) along the Didjlat al-ʿAwrāʾ in Shādh Bahman/*arḍ* Maysān in 16/637-8, ordering a cadastral survey there and levying taxes according to the degree of productivity. Al-Nuʿman b. ʿAdi collected taxes in the *Kuwar* Didjla for ʿUmar I, who refused to let him take his wife there. Ḥuṣayn b. Abi 'l-Ḥurr is also said to have been ʿUmar's *ʿāmil* over Maysān until the time of al-Ḥadjdjādj [*q.v.*]. The *kharādj* of the *Kuwar* Didjla is given as ten million *dirhams* under Muʿāwiya, and as 900 *kurr* of wheat, 4,000 *kurr* of barley and 430,000 *dirhams* by Ḳudāma in 260/874. All four subdistricts (*ṭasāsīdj*) of Bahman Ardashīr, Maysan, Dast-i Maysān and Abarḳubādh lay east of the Tigris, although the entire district is said to have extended to al-Marūmat towards Wāsiṭ and to Dayr Mābanat towards Khūzistān. Under ʿUmar I, al-Ḥadjdjādj b. ʿAtīk al-Thaḳafī collected the taxes of al-Furāt/Bahman Ardashīr, and, in 75/695, Kurāz b. Mālik al-Sulamī held combined authority over al-Ubulla and al-Furāt for al-Ḥadjdjādj b. Yūsuf. Although there was clearly a subdistrict (*nāḥiya*) called Maysān in *arḍ* Maysān, the city of Karkh Maysān appears to have been replaced by al-Madhār as the most important place by the time of the conquest, and it is often difficult to tell whether unspecified references to Maysān in Islamic times are to this subdistrict, to geographical Maysān, to Karkh Maysān or even to Furāt Maysān. In 38/658-9, the Nādjī Khawāridj halted at al-Madhār; the Khawāridj under al-Mustawrid b. ʿUllafa fought Kūfan forces there in 43/663-4; and Muṣʿab b. al-Zubayr defeated al-Mukhtār's army under Aḥmad b. Sumayt al-Nakhlī there in 67/686. Abarḳubādh (also Abazḳubādh, Īzadhḳubādh, Bazḳubādh and Azḳubādh) with the town of Fasā lay near al-Madhār, although it is easily confused with Barḳubādh/Arradjān. Dast-i Maysān was the plain (Persian *dasht*) north and northeast of Maysān. Its capital was Basāmatā (possibly also Basāmī and Bāsāmiyya); it included ʿAbdasī on the old course of the Tigris, eight stages (*sikkas*, 51.5 to 64.4 km.) above al-Madhār and it stretched eastwards to Khuzistān. In 20/641 ʿUmar I instructed Djazʾ b. Muʿāwiya, governor of Dast-i Maysān and Manādhir (on the border with Khūzistān) combined, to kill every magician (*sāḥir*) and sorceress, to separate Magians who were married to close relatives (*dhū muḥram*), and to forbid Magians to practice ritual murmuring (*zamzama*). Three sorcerers were killed and Djazʾ had begun to break up families of Magians and to force them to eat without *zamzama* when ʿUmar wrote telling him to collect *djizya* [*q.v.*] from them instead. ʿĀṣim b. Ḳays al-Sulamī also collected taxes in Manādhir under ʿUmar I. The *DShT* mint-mark on Arab-Sāsānid coins from 52/672 until 67/686 may stand for Dasht-i Maysān. Post-reform *dirhams* were struck at al-Furāt from 81/700-1 to 97/715-6, in Maysān from 79/698-9 to 97/715-6, Abarḳubādh in 83/702 and 96/714-5 and in Dasht-i Maysān in 80/699-700, followed by Manādhir from 81/700 until 96/714-15. By the 3rd/9th century, al-Ubulla was the administrative centre for the *Kūra* Didjlat, which may be why Ibn Khurradādhbih and Yāḳūt identify Dast-i Maysān with al-Ubulla. The Nestorian metropolitanate of Pᵉrāth dᵉ Mayshan survived well into the Islamic period, and is first identified as the metropolitanate of al-Baṣra in 174/790. The bishopric of ʿAbdasī, attested in 174/790 and *ca.* 215/830, however, was in the patriarchal see of Baghdād.

Some natives of Maysān, such as ʿAnbasa b. Maʿdān, settled in al-Baṣra shortly after its foundation. They were generally called Banu 'l-ʿAmm and settled with the Banū Tamīm. Maysānī origin (accurate only in the broadest sense) was attributed to the family of Ziyād b. Abīhi [*q.v.*] in a derogatory way by the poets al-Farazdaḳ and Ibn Mufarrigh. Al-Akhṭal used attribution to Aẓkubādh as an insult. However, Sahl b. Hārūn [*q.v.*], a native of Maysān who settled at al-Baṣra and was a secretary for al-Maʾmūn (197-218/813-33), praised the people of Maysān in a kind of feeling of regional *shuʿūbiyya* [*q.v.*]. The Muslim belief that God exiled Iblīs to Maysān after the temptation of Ādam and Ḥawwāʾ (Eve) may have been related to these attitudes.

Early Islamic land reclamation and development around al-Baṣra extended into Maysān. Ziyād granted an estate on the Gulf coast north of the estuary to Ḥumrān b. Abān, who subsequently gave the western part of it to ʿAbbād b. Ḥusayn al-Ḥibatī, after whom the entire estate and the town that grew there came to be called ʿAbbādān, considered as the southeastern limit of Maysān. Under Sulaymān (96-8/715-17), Yazīd b. al-Muhallab reclaimed land from the *Baṭāʾiḥ* in Kaskar and the *Kūra* Didjlat with imported Indian labour (Zuṭṭ [*q.v.*]) and at least 4,000 water buffaloes (*djawāmīs*). Under al-Rashīd (170-93/786-809), the villagers of al-Shuʿaybiyya in the subdistrict of al-Furāt turned their property, which then became tithe land, over to the caliph's son ʿAlī, and became sharecroppers paying a lower rate than before. A slave of al-Rashīd called Ghasīb is also said to have built a fort (*ḥiṣn*) just west of ʿAbbādān at Brīm (modern Brēm ʿAbbādān or ʿAbbādān al-Ḥadītha). East African slaves (Zandj [*q.v.*]) were also imported as labour by the late 1st/7th century. In 70/689-90 and 75/695 they gathered at al-Furāt, and, joined by people from the river harbour, devastated the countryside. During the great Zandj revolt in the 3rd/9th century, they were again supported or joined by the people of al-Furāt and the villages of Djubbā and Djaᶜfariyya. In 254/868 the Zandj invaded Maysān from Khūzistān, took Djaᶜfariyya and Ḳaryat al-Yahūd, and attacked al-Madhār unsuccessfully before turning south-east to ᶜAbbādān. In 267/880-1 al-Muwaffaḳ, the brother of the caliph al-Muᶜtamid (256-79/870-92), established the city of al-Muwaffaḳiyya on the north bank of the Shaṭṭ al-ᶜArab facing the Zandj stronghold of al-Mukhtāra, as a military base to pursue the war with them. Al-Muwaffaḳiyya had a treasury, a *masdjid al-djāmiᶜ*, and markets, and *dirhams* and *dīnārs* were struck there. A *dīnār* of 270/883 is attested, but al-Muwaffaḳiyya appears to have been abandoned after the fall of al-Mukhtāra in that year. In 287/900 the Ḳarāmiṭa [*q.v.*] ravaged the subdistricts of Maysān.

In spite of such conflicts, in the 4th/10th century ᶜAbbādān and al-Madhār were small cities and palm groves extended continuously for over 20 *farāsikh* (241 km.) from ᶜAbbādān to ᶜAbdasī. A low-grade silk brocade was produced in Maysān; dyed cloth and cushions were exported, and Maysānī clothing was produced at Djabbul. After flowing into the *Baṭāʾiḥ*, Tigris water emptied into the Didjlat al-ᶜAwrāʾ via branching channels such as the Nahr Abi 'l-Asad, the Nahr al-Marʾa (possibly the Bathḳ Shīrīn) in the vicinity of al-Madhār, and the Nahr al-Yahūd. The tide came upstream as far as al-Madhār. Nahr Djūr lay on the old course of the Tigris between ᶜAbdasī and Darmakān and may have extended eastwards towards Khūzistān. The Mughtasila (now called Ṣābat al-Baṭāʾiḥ) were still numerous in the swamps and may be the same as the Ṣābian sect [*q.v.*] called al-Kīmāriyyūn that al-Masᶜūdī says lived in or near the swamps between Wāsiṭ and al-Baṣra. The Mandaean sect, reputedly formed in Maysān in late Sāsānid or early Islamic times, grew out of this milieu.

Al-Madhār remained locally important. In 329/941 the *amīr* Badjkam [*q.v.*] sent Tūzūn there with an army, where he defeated the forces of Abū ᶜAbd Allāh al-Barīdī, while Badjkam himself drove the Kurds from Nahr Djūr. In 331/943 Sayf al-Dawla [*q.v.*] sent Khadjkhadj against the Barīdiyya there. In 409/1018 the Būyid Sulṭān al-Dawla set out from there in pursuit of al-Ḥasan b. Dubays al-Asadī, and when Djalāl al-Dawla's army defeated his rival, Abū Kālīdjār [*q.v.*], there in 421/1030, his partisans took over the town. In about 443/1051, Nāṣir-i Khusraw [*q.v.*] noted that ᶜAḳr Maysān (possibly Karkh Maysān) and Mashān were subdistricts of al-Baṣra. Mashān was just above al-Baṣra and was also known as the birthplace, in 446/1054, of the author of the *Maḳāmāt*, al-Ḥarīrī [*q.v.*], who is said to have died at al-Madhār. A noted family of *ḥadīth* transmitters, Abu 'l-Ḥasan ᶜAlī b. Muḥammad b. Aḥmad b. al-Ḥusayn b. ᶜUthmān al-Madhārī (516-85/1122-89), a native of Baghdād, and his two brothers, was identified with al-Madhār in the 6th/12th century. In 591/1195 Maysān is called a subdistrict of Khūzistān ruled by Ḳutlugh Īnāndj b. al-Bahlawān.

According to Yāḳūt in the 7th/13th century, the Tigris divided into five main channels below Wāsiṭ: the Nahr Sāsī (possibly an orthographic error for Basāmī), Nahr Gharrāf, Nahr Djaᶜfar, Nahr Daḳla and Nahr Maysān (possibly the Nahr Ṭuhyathā according to El-ᶜAlī). They reunited near the village of Maṭāra, one day's journey from al-Baṣra, where the Euphrates joined them. Yāḳūt defined the Didjlat al-ᶜAwrāʾ as the combined stream from Maṭāra to the Gulf. He describes Maysān as "an extensive district with numerous villages and palm groves between al-Baṣra and Wāsiṭ." Its main town (*madīna*) was Maysān, and its capital (*ḳaṣaba*) was al-Madhār, four days' journey from al-Baṣra. Al-Haṭra, across the river from al-Madhār, was a well-watered village on solid ground with many date palms, fruit trees, and chickens. Below al-Madhār, on the Nahr Maysān, was the small town (*bulayda*) of al-Bazzāz; al-Furāt lay in ruins. The people of al-Madhār were all *ghulāt* Shīᶜīs, and a splendid shrine (*mashhad*) there, where ᶜAbd Allāh b. ᶜAlī b. Abī Ṭālib was buried, was the object of endowments (*wuḳūf*) and votive gifts (*nudhūr*). This shrine is located on a slight rise east of the Tigris, within a river bend, just below modern Ḳalᶜat Ṣāliḥ near the ruins of al-Madhār about 48 km. directly north of modern Ḳurna. In March 1927 Streck found a domed tomb there, visible at a great distance, standing in the southern end of an oblong courtyard that was entered through a door in the north wall. A descendant of the *Imām* Mūsā al-Kāẓim [*q.v.*] is also said to be buried at ᶜAlī al-Gharbī, on the west bank of the Tigris 100 km. above al-ᶜAmāra, and a descendant of al-Ḥusayn b. ᶜAlī at ᶜAlī al-Sharḳī, about 38 km. away on the east bank. At an undetermined time, most of the people of ᶜAbbādān, having been Shāfiᶜī, became Shīᶜī. According to al-Ḳazwīnī, the people of Maysān district were fanatical (*ṭughāt*) Shīᶜīs. Yāḳūt also describes the tomb of Ezra (al-ᶜUzayr) which he visited at the village of Nahr Samura (popularly called Simmara) in *arḍ* Maysān as tended by Jews and as the object of endowments and votive gifts. Modern al-ᶜUzayr is a large village on the west bank of the Tigris about 33 km. south of Ḳalᶜat Ṣāliḥ.

Abu 'l-Fidāʾ calls Maysān a small town (*bulayda*) in the lower part of *arḍ* al-Baṣra, but after the 8th/14th century this name passed out of use. Al-ᶜAmāra [*q.v.*] was founded in 1277/1860 at a place called al-Awradī from the 10th/16th century onwards. *Ḳanūn* no. 48, in 1969, changed the name of the ᶜAmāra Liwāʾ to Maysān.

Bibliography: For the land and people of Maysān, see Strabo, *Geographica*, ii. 1. 31; xvi. 1. 8; xvi. 3. 3; Ptolemy, *Geographica*, v. 19. 1; Pliny, *Natural History*, vi. 31; Yāḳūt, *Buldān*, iv, 714; H. Schaeder, *Ḥasan al-Baṣrī*, in *Isl.*, xiv (1925), 11-37; Weissbach, *Mesene* in Pauly-Wissowa, xv, cols. 1082, 1087, 1094; S. N. Nodelman, *A preliminary history of Characene*, in *Berytus*, xiii (1960), 106.

On its ancient extent, see Pliny, vi, 31-32; Ammianus Marcellinus, *Rerum gestarum libri qui supersunt*, Cambridge, Mass. 1935-9, xxiii. 6. 23; Ibn Rustah, 187; Yāḳūt, iv, 274-5; Mustawfī, *Nuzhat al-ḳulūb*, Tehran 1336/1958, 132; Weissbach, cols. 1082-3, 1086-7, 1090; Nodelman, 104.

On Charax and Characene, see Polybius, *The Histories*, London, 1923, v. 46. 7; 48. 13; 54. 12; Pliny, vi. 30-2; A.-J. de Saint-Martin, *Recherches sur l'histoire et la géographie de la Mésène et de la Characène*, Paris 1838; Reinaud, *Mém. sur le commencement et la fin du royaume de la Mésène et de la Characène*, in *JA*, xviii (1861), 161-262; E. Drouin, *Notice historique et géograph. sur la Characène*, Paris 1890, repr. in *Muséon*, ix, 148 ff.; E. Newell, *Mithradates of Parthia and Hyspaosines of Charax*, in *NNM*, xxvi (1925); ᶜA. al-Ḥasanī, *Riḥla fi 'l-ᶜIrāḳ*, Baghdād 1925, 118; H. al-Saᶜdī, *Djughrāfiyat al-ᶜIrāḳ (al-ḥadītha)*, Baghdād 1927, 156; Andreas, *Alexandreia*, in Pauly-Wissowa, i, cols. 1390-5; Weissbach, *Charax Spasinu*, in *ibid.*, iii, 2122; idem,

Mesene, cols. 1085, 1093-4; J. Starcky, *Inventaire des inscriptions de Palmyre*, x, Damascus 1949, 13-14, 52, 57, 65, 67; F. W. Walbank, *A historical commentary on Polybius*, Oxford 1957, i, 578; G. Le Rider, *Monnaies de Characène*, in *Syria*, xxxvi (1959), 230-1; Nodelman, 102, 106, 114; J. Hansman, *Charax and the Karkeh*, in *Iranica Antiqua*, vii (1967), 21-58; *Cambridge History of Iran*, iii, Cambridge 1983, 40, 90, 310-4, 487, 755, 757; R. Frye, *The history of ancient Iran*, Munich 1983, 275-8. The Han sources are quoted by W. Schoff (ed.), Isidore of Charax, *Parthian stations*, Philadelphia 1914, 41, from F. Hirth, *China and the Roman Orient*, Leipzig and Munich 1885.

For the early Sāsānid period, see Ammianus Marcellinus, xxiv. 3. 12; *Bab. Tal.*, B. Kidd. 72b; E. Herzfeld, *Paikuli*, Berlin 1924, i, 81, 103, 107, pl. 140, no. 9; J. Obermeyer, *Landschaft Babylonien*, Frankfurt a. M. 1929, 91; Nodelman, 102; L. Dillemann, *Ammien Marcellin et les pays de l'Euphrate et du Tigre*, in *Syria*, xxviii (1961), 139-41; Hansman, 26; B. Dodge (tr.), *The Fihrist of al-Nadīm*, New York 1970, ii, 774; *CHI*, iii, 126, 594, 707-8, 731, 756-7, 965-6. For Astarābā<u>dh</u>/ Kar<u>kh</u> Maysān see Dīnawarī, *K. al-A<u>kh</u>bār al-ṭiwāl*, Leiden 1912, 45; Ṭabarī, i, 820; Ibn al-Faḳīh, 198; Ḥamza al-Iṣfahānī, *Taʾrī<u>kh</u> Sinī mulūk al-arḍ*, Beirut 1961, 43; <u>Th</u>aʿālibī, *<u>Gh</u>urar a<u>kh</u>bār mulūk al-Furs wa-siyaruhum*, Paris 1900, 486; Yāḳūt, iv, 257; T. Nöldeke, *Gesch. der Perser und Araber zur Zeit der Sāsāniden*, Leiden 1879, 14, 19-20. For <u>Sh</u>ā<u>dh</u> Sābūr/Kaskar, see *Bab. Tal.*, B. Gittin 80b; Ibn <u>Kh</u>urradā<u>dh</u>bih, 7; Ḥamza, 45; <u>Th</u>aʿālibī, 494; Ṭabarī, i, 830; Yāḳūt, iii, 227. On the Jews, see *Bab. Tal.*, B. Yebamoth 17a; A. Neubauer, *La géographie du Talmud*, Paris 1868, 352; H. Graetz, *Das Königreich von Mesene und seine jüdische Bevölkerung*, Breslau 1879; A. Berliner, *Beiträge zur Geographie und Ethnogr. Babyloniens im Talmud und Midrasch*, Berlin 1883, 17; Obermeyer, 201; J. Newman, *The agricultural life of the Jews in Babylonia*, London 1932, 170; J. Neusner, *A history of the Jews in Babylonia*, Leiden 1970, v, pp. xix, 276. On Christians, see J.-B. Chabot, *Synodicon orientale*, Paris 1902, 34, 272; J. Labourt, *Le Christianisme dans l'Empire perse*, Paris 1904, 9-17; J. M. Fiey, *Assyrie chrétienne*, Beirut 1968, iii, 263-4.

For the late Sāsānid Tigris, see Balā<u>dh</u>urī, *Futūḥ*, 292-3; Masʿūdī, *Murū<u>dj</u>*, i, 223 = § 235; idem, *Tanbīh*, Beirut 1965, 53-4; Ibn Rustah, 94-5; Yāḳūt, i, 669; F. Safar, *Wāsiṭ*, Cairo 1945, 6-7; Ṣ. al-ʿAlī, *Minṭaḳat Wasiṭ*, (2), in *Sumer*, xxvii (1971), 165-6, 169, 171, 175. For <u>Sh</u>ā<u>dh</u> Bahman and Bahman Arda<u>sh</u>īr, see Ibn <u>Kh</u>urradā<u>dh</u>bih, 7; Ḳudāma, *<u>Kh</u>arā<u>dj</u>*, 235; Masʿūdī, *Tanbīh*, 52; Ibn al-Faḳīh, 198; Ḥamza, 43; Yāḳūt, i, 770; iii, 227, 861-2; J. Marquart, *Ērānšahr nach der Geographie der Ps. Moses Xorenacʿi*, in *AKGWG*, Ser. 2, iii, 2 (1899-1901), 8, 16, 40; Chabot, 34, 71, 272, 321; M. Morony, *Continuity and change in the administrative geography of late Sasanian and early Islamic al-ʿIrāq*, in *Iran*, xx (1982), 34-9. On Nestorian bishoprics, see Chabot, 213, 214, 478; I. Guidi, *Chronica Minora I*, in *CSCO*, I, *Scr. Syri*, i, 34, *CSCO*, II, *Scr. Syri*, ii, 28, Louvain 1955; Y. Sarkis, *Madīnat Bay<u>th</u> Raymā*, in *Mabāhi<u>th</u> ʿIrāḳiyya*, ii, Ba<u>gh</u>dād 1955, 103-13; Fiey, 255-7, 272, 274, 277-82. For Sāsānid mint-marks, see F. Paruck, *Sāsānian coins*, Bombay 1924, 157, 159-63; idem, *Mint-marks on Sasanian and Arab-Sasanian coins*, in *Jnal of the Numismatic Soc. of India*, vi (1944), 118; R. Göbl, in F. Altheim and R. Stiehl, *Ein Asiatischer Staat*, Wiesbaden 1954, 87-8; idem, *Sasanidische Numismatik*, Brunswick 1968, 84; A. Bivar, *A Sasanian hoard from Hilla*, in *NC* (1963), 167-8.

For the Muslim conquest, see Guidi, i, 36; ii, 30; Ibn Saʿd, vii/1, 3; Balā<u>dh</u>ūrī, 341-4; Yaʿḳūbī, *Taʾrī<u>kh</u>*, ii, 163, 166; Dīnawarī, 123-4; Ṭabarī, i, 2021-8, 2030, 2202, 2379, 2384-6, 2534; Yāḳūt, iii, 861-2; iv, 468; Ibn al-A<u>th</u>īr. ii, 445, 454, 542. For the captives, see Ibn Saʿd, vii/1, 88, 92, 114; Balā<u>dh</u>ūrī, 344; Ṭabarī, i, 2029, 2387; Ibn al-A<u>th</u>īr, ii, 488; Ibn <u>Kh</u>allikān, *Wafayāt*, Beirut 1968, ii, 72. For the *Kuwar* Di<u>dj</u>la, see Ibn Saʿd, vii/1, 91; Ḳudāma, 235, 239; Ibn <u>Kh</u>urradā<u>dh</u>bih, 7, 12; Balā<u>dh</u>urī, *Ansāb*, x, Greifswald 1883, 305; idem, *Futūḥ*, 344-5, 385; Yaʿḳūbī, *Taʾrī<u>kh</u>*, ii, 181, 277; Ṭabarī, iii, 1752, 2097; Ibn Rustah, 95; <u>Th</u>aʿālibī, 486; Yāḳūt, iii, 227; iv, 319, 714-15; Ḳazwīnī, *Ā<u>th</u>ār*, 311; Ṣ. al-ʿAlī, *Minṭaḳat Wāsiṭ* (1), in *Sumer*, xxvi (1970), 241, 243-4; idem, *Minṭaḳat Wasiṭ* (2), 169-70. For Abarḳubā<u>dh</u>, see Yaʿḳūbī, *Buldān*, 322-3; Ḥamza, 57; Ibn al-Faḳīh, 199; Yāḳūt, i, 605; *Marāṣid al-iṭṭilāʿ*, Leiden 1862, i, 14; J. Markwart, *Südarmenien und die Tigrisquellen*, Vienna 1930, 199-200. On Dast-i Maysān and Mana<u>dh</u>ir, see Ibn <u>Kh</u>urradā<u>dh</u>bih, 7; Ḳudāma, 126; Balā<u>dh</u>urī, *Futūḥ*, 385; Ṭabarī, iii, 1958; Muḳaddasī, 114; Ibn Rustah, 94; Yāḳūt, i, 574; ii, 227, 605; iv, 644; *Marāṣid*, i, 402; v, 468; Ibn <u>Kh</u>allikān, i, 247-50. For <u>Dj</u>azʾ b. Muʿāwiya, see Abū Yūsuf, *<u>Kh</u>arā<u>dj</u>*, Bulāḳ, 1302, 129; Ibn Saʿd, vii/1, 94; Ibn Sallām, *K. al-Amwāl*, Cairo 1969, 44; Bu<u>kh</u>ārī, *Ṣaḥīḥ*, Gu<u>dj</u>ranwalla 1971, iv, 252-3. On Islamic coins, see J. Walker, *A catalogue of the Arab-Sasanian coins*, London 1941, pp. xlv, xlviii, lvi, cxvii-cxviii, cxl-cxli, 69-70, 104; idem, *A catalogue of the Arab-Byzantine and post-Reform Umaiyad coins*, London 1956, 168, 185; G. C. Miles, *Abarqubā<u>dh</u>, a new Umayyad mint*, in *ANS Museum Notes*, iv (1950), 115, 117; idem, *Rare Islamic coins*, in *ANS Numismatic Notes and Monographs*, no. 118, New York 1950, 24-5, 27; H. Gaube, *Arabosasanidische Numismatik*, Brunswick 1973, 94. For Nestorian bishoprics under Islam, see Chabot, *Synodicon*, 602, 607; idem, *Le livre de la chasteté*, in *Mélanges d'archéologie et d'histoire*, xvi, 228; Fiey, 257. On events at al-Ma<u>dh</u>ār in the 1st/7th century, see Dīnawarī, 312; Ṭabarī, ii, 44-6; Yāḳūt, iv, 468-9; Ibn al-A<u>th</u>īr, iii, 365, 431; iv, 268, 277.

For settlement in al-Baṣra and Maysān's reputation, see Farazdaḳ, *Dīwān*, Paris 1870, 48-9; Ṭabarī, i, 121, 2538; ii, 160; Iṣfahānī, *A<u>gh</u>ānī*, Bulāḳ 1285/1868-9, xvii, 65; xviii, 67; xix, 28, 32; *Fihrist*, tr. Dodge, i, 90-1; Yāḳūt, i, 233; iv, 715; Ibn al-A<u>th</u>īr, Beirut 1965, i, 37; Leiden, iii, 494; Mustawfī, *Nuzhat al-ḳulūb*, Tehran 1336/1958, 30, tr. Le Strange, *Description of Persia and Mesopotamia in 1340*, London 1915-19, 46; al-Ḥuṣrī, *Zahr al-ādāb*, Cairo 1372/1953, 577; Kaḥḥāla, *Muʿ<u>dj</u>am ḳabāʾil al-ʿArab*, Beirut 1967, i, 820-1; I. Goldziher, *Muslim Studies*, tr. Stern, London 1967, i, 149.

On early Muslim development, see Balā<u>dh</u>urī, *Futūḥ*, 167-8, 368-9, 371; *Lu<u>gh</u>at al-ʿArab*, i (1911), 126. On the Zan<u>dj</u>, see Balā<u>dh</u>urī, *Ansāb*, xi, 303-6; Wakīʿ, *A<u>kh</u>bār al-ḳuḍāt*, Cairo 1366/1945, ii, 57; Ibn al-A<u>th</u>īr, iv, 388; Pellat, *Milieu*, index; A. Popovic, *La révolte des esclaves*, Paris 1976; H. Halm, *Die Traditionen über den Aufstand Ali ibn Muhammad des "Herrn der Zanj"*, Bonn 1967, 59-62, 70, 79. On al-Muwaffaḳiyya, see Ṭabari, iii, 1989; Ibn al-A<u>th</u>īr, vii, 245-6; İ, Artuk, *Abbasi ve Anadolu Selçuklerine ait iki eşsiz dinar*, in *İstanbul*

Arkeoloji Müzeleri, viii (1958), 44-5; Halm, 110. For the Ḳarāmiṭa, see Ibn al-Athīr, vii, 500. On conditions in the 3rd-4th/9th-10th centuries, see Khwārazmī, *K. Ṣūrat al-arḍ*, Leipzig 1926, 130; Ḳudāma, 233; Balādhurī, *Futūḥ*, 292; Ps.-Djāḥiẓ, *al-Tabaṣṣur bi 'l-tidjāra*, Cairo 1354/1935, 21, 32; Yaᶜḳūbī, *Buldān*, 322; Ṭabarī, iii, 1980; Iṣṭakhrī, 81; Ibn Ḥawḳal, *K. Ṣurat al-arḍ*, Leiden 1938-9, 159; Ibn Rustah, 94-5, 187; Masᶜūdī, *Murūdj*, i, 263; idem, *Tanbīh*, 48, 161; Dodge, *Fihrist*, ii, 811; Yāḳūt, iv, 838; H. Pognon, *Inscriptions mandaïtes des coupes de Khouabir*, Paris 1898, 6, 154, 224-5; M. Streck, *Die alte Landschaft Babylonien nach der arabischen Geographen*, Leiden 1900-1, 41-2; al-ᶜAlī, *Minṭaḳat Wāsiṭ (1)*, 260-1; idem, *Minṭaḳat Wāsiṭ (2)* 166, 169.

For the 4th-6th/10th-12th centuries, see Nāṣir-i Khusraw, *Safar-nāma*, Tehran 1354/1975, 160; Ibn al-Athīr, viii, 371, 396; ix, 306, 403, 624; xii, 111; Yāḳūt, iv, 469. For Mashān and al-Ḥarīrī, see Yāḳūt, iv, 536; idem, *Irshād*, vi, 167; Ḳazwīnī, *Āthār*, 308; Abu 'l-Fidāᵓ, *Taḳwīm al-buldān*, Paris 1840, 296; ᶜA. al-Ḥasanī, *al-ᶜIrāḳ ḳadīm^an^ wa-ḥadīth^an^*, Ṣaydā 1956, 194.

For the 7th-8th/13th-14th centuries, see Yāḳūt, i, 603, 770; ii, 553; iii, 11, 745; iv, 468, 714, 830, 840, 947; v, 838; Ḳazwīnī, 310-11; Abu 'l-Fidāᵓ, 296; Mustawfī, ed. Le Strange, 46, 207; Streck, 40; *Lughat al-ᶜArab*, i, 126-7; iv, 377-8, 536; J. Ghanīma, *Nuzhat al-mushtāḳ fī taᵓrīkh Yahūd al-ᶜIrāḳ*, Baghdād 1924, 189; al-Ḥasanī, *ᶜIrāḳ*, 192-4; al-ᶜAlī, *Minṭaḳat Wāsiṭ* (1), 260-1.

On more recent matters, see ᶜA. al-ᶜAzzāwī, *Taᵓrīkh al-ᶜIrāḳ bayn al-iḥtilālayn*, Baghdād 1937-57, iv, 74, 823; vii, 129, 130-1, 136-7, 139, 168, 194; viii, 52, 266, 268, 270; *The Middle East and North Africa, 1982-83*, London 1982, 450, 456.

(M. Streck-[M. Morony])

MAYSARA, a Berber chief of the Maghrib, who rebelled against Arab authority in 122/739-40. He belonged to the tribe of the Maṭghāra/Madghāra and the historians give him the surname of al-Ḥaḳīr "the low-born" because he was of humble origin and had been before his rebellion a water-seller in the market of al-Ḳayrawān.

After the recall of Mūsā b. Nuṣayr [*q.v.*] at the end of the 1st/opening of the 8th century in North Africa, under the influence of Khāridjite propaganda, incited by the Arabs' financial exactions, ᶜUmar b. ᶜAbd Allāh al-Murādī, governor of Tangier, and a grandson of ᶜUḳba b. Nāfiᶜ [*q.v.*], Ḥabīb b. Abī ᶜUbayda, governor of Sūs, had received orders from the caliphal representative in Egypt and Ifrīḳiya, ᶜUbayd Allāh b. al-Ḥabḥāb [*q.v.*], and were inflicting grievous wrongs on the Berbers by treating them, as regards taxation, as a conquered people not converted to Islam, and by taking the fairest of their women to send as slaves to Damascus. The general Ḥabīb having been sent from Sūs with his troops to the conquest of Sicily, his departure was the signal for insurrection. For the first time in Morocco, a movement on a large scale broke out; at its head the Berbers put Maysara al-Maṭgharī, who assumed the title of caliph. With the related tribes of the Miknāsa and Barghawāṭa [*q.v.*], Maysara advanced on Tangier and seized it, killing the governor ᶜUmar b. ᶜAbd Allāh. The Arabs tried in vain to withstand him; the governor of Spain, ᶜUkba b. al-Ḥadjdjādj, received the order to go and relieve the town, and after the defeat of the contingent which he sent, crossed the straits himself; he massacred the Berbers of the region, but was unable to retake Tangier, where Maysara left ᶜAbd al-Aᶜlā b. Ḥudaydj al-Ifrīḳī and went on to seize the Sūs, whose governor Ismāᶜīl b. ᶜUbayd Allāh he killed.

However, it was not long before Maysara was deposed from the leadership and killed by his followers. His successor, Khālid b. Ḥamīd/Ḥumayd al-Zanātī, inflicted on the Arabs a bloody defeat on the banks of the Wādī Shalīf (Oued Chélif), a battle which took place at the beginning of 123/740 and was known as "the battle of the noble ones" (*ghazwat al-ashrāf*). It required a great expeditionary force to be prepared in the East to put an end, not however without considerable losses, to this general revolt [see BALDJ and KULTHŪM B. ᶜIYĀḌ], which had grave repercussions in Spain, where the Berbers in turn rebelled, and in North Africa, where it provoked an intense movement towards Islamisation.

Bibliography: Ibn al-Ḳūṭiyya, *Taᵓrīkh Iftitāḥ al-Andalus*, Madrid 1926, 14-15, text, 10-11; Ibn ᶜIdhārī, *al-Bayān al-mughrib*, ed. Dozy, i, 39-40, tr. Fagnan, i, 50-3; Ibn ᶜAbd al-Ḥakam, ed. and tr. A. Gateau, *Conquête de l'Afrique du Nord et de l'Espagne*², Algiers 1947, index; Ibn al-Athīr, *Kāmil*, v, 142 = *Annales du Maghreb et de l'Espagne*, 63-5; al-Nuwayrī, *Histoire d'Afrique*, ed. Gaspar Remiro, 34-5; Ibn Khaldūn, *ᶜIbar*, *Histoire des Berbères*, ed. and tr. de Slane, text, i, 137, 151, tr. i, 216-17, 237-8; *Mafākhir al-Barbar*, 47; Fournel, *Les Berbers*, Paris 1875, i, 286-9; R. Dozy, *Hist. des Musulmans d'Espagne*, 241-3; E. F. Gautier, *Les siècles obscurs du Maghreb*, 260 ff.; G. Marçais, *La Berbérie et l'Orient*, 43 ff.; F. Gabrieli, *Il califfato di Hishâm*, Alexandria 1935, 92-103, 113-14; E. Lévi-Provençal, *L'Espagne musulmane au Xe siècle*, Paris 1932, 10-14; idem, *Hist. Esp. mus.*, i, 41 ff.; H. Muᵓnis, *Thawrat al-Barbar fī Ifrīḳiya wa 'l-Andalus bayn sanatay 102-136 (721-755)*, in *Madjallat Kulliyyat al-Ādāb*, x/1 (Cairo 1948).

(E. Lévi-Provençal)

AL-**MAYSIR** (A.), a noun derived from *y-s-r* "to be easy, simple", a root from which derives, by antiphrasis, a qualificative of the left hand, *al-yusrā*, with which the *ḥurḍa* (cf. Hebrew *ḥ-r-ṣ* and Akkadian *ḫarāšu* "decide, fix, determine"), the equivalent of the *sādin* of the *istiḳsām* [*q.v.*], shot arrows one by one. Hence the term *maysir* could be rendered by "the game of the left-handed", although its present morphological state is inexplicable.

The game consisted of dividing a slaughtered beast into ten parts, for which the game was played: these being the thighs and shins of both fore and rear legs, plus two shoulders. The head and the feet were given back to the butcher and the remaining inferior pieces were added proportionally to the ten parts. The best pieces were called *abdāᵓ* or *budūᵓ* and the least esteemed were the thighs of the two fore legs, on account of the large number of veins which they contain. The process of the game often required the slaughtering of numerous beasts, generally camels (*djuzur*). In view of the sum total of parts represented by the seven arrows (28), every time that the arrows were drawn, the ten parts were soon exhausted.

Two kinds of arrows were used in this game of chance:

(1) Seven winning arrows (*anṣibāᵓ*), each bearing a name and with notches (*farḍ* or *ḥazz*), by which they were identified; and

(2) Three or four white arrows (*ghufl*, *aghfāl*), neither winning nor losing.

The winning arrows were named:

(1) *al-Fadhdh*, "the single (arrow)", bearing one notch and winning or losing a single part (= 1/28).

(2) *al-Tawᵓam*, "the twin (arrow)", bearing two notches and winning or losing two parts (= 2/28).

(3) *al-Raḳīb*, also called *al-Ḍarīb*, "the (arrow of the) supervisor" of the game or of the "thrower" of the lots, bearing three notches and winning or losing three parts (= 3/28).
(4) *al-Ḥils* or *al-Ḥalis*, "the dressed" or "equipped" or even "strong (arrow)" (cf. Hebrew *ḥ-l-ṣ* and *ḥemeṣ*), bearing four notches and winning or losing four parts (= 4/28).
(5) *al-Nāfis*, "the precious" or "coveted (arrow)" (name sometimes given to the fourth arrow), bearing five notches and winning or losing five parts (= 5/28).
(6) *al-Mufsaḥ*, "the long and flat (arrow)", also called *al-Musbil*, "the elongated (arrow)", bearing six notches and winning or losing six parts (= 6/28).
(7) *al-Muʿallā*, "the superior (arrow)", also called *al-Mig̲h̲laḳ*, "the (arrow) that closes", a name also given to every winning arrow, bearing seven notches and winning or losing seven parts.

The white arrows bore no notches and their purpose consisted in slowing (*yut̲h̲aḳḳil*) the game and making it more difficult. They are, in fact, "rivets"; every time that one of them was drawn, it was immediately replaced in the quiver; thus chances for the successive drawing of notched arrows steadily diminished. These were three in number, called:
(1) *al-Safīḥ*, "the profitless (arrow)" (name given to the fourth by al-Liḥyānī, who puts *al-Muṣaddar* in the first place). Considering the root, it seems that the shooter would receive the blood of the victim.
(2) *al-Manīḥ*, "the generous (arrow)", considered to be of good omen; its repeated return to the quiver was a portent of success. The shooter could receive the hide of the victim (cf. *TA*, ii, 234, 11. 21 f.).
(3) *al-Wag̲h̲d*, "the scoundrel" or "(arrow of) the miser", particularly he who does not take part in the game, afraid of losing; it has the synonym *al-baram*.
(4) Some place a fourth arrow after the first (*TA*) or after the second (al-Liḥyānī, al-Nuwayrī), called *al-Muḍaʿʿaf* "the double (arrow)."

The players could not be more than seven in number; when they were fewer than seven, they needed to buy the remaining parts in order for the game to take place. The player who bought these parts was called *al-Tamīm* "he who completes". When he won twice in succession he was called *mutammim*, generously donating his winnings to his entourage, whence the laudatory title of *mut̲h̲annā 'l-ayādī* applied to him, as well as to the one who purchased the parts which had not been won to give them to the poor. It is to this charitable act that certain commentators attribute the term *manāfiʿ* "advantages", which the Ḳurʾān uses in speaking of *maysir* and of wine (II, 219).

The players of *maysir* were called *al-aysār* (sing. *yasar*), and those who presided over the division of the parts *al-yāsirūn*. The archer, called *al-ḥurḍa*, had his right hand wrapped in a piece of leather or fabric in order to prevent him identifying the arrows by touch. A piece of white fabric, called *al-mid̲j̲wāl*, was held above his hands and a *raḳīb* or "supervisor" stood close beside him, passing him the quiver containing the arrows when the face of the *ḥurḍa* was averted. Having taken it, the latter inserted his left hand (*al-yusrā*) under the *mid̲j̲wāl*, shook (*yunakkir*) the arrows, revealed them to view (*nahada*) one after the other and handed them to the *raḳīb* (for references, see *Bibl.*).

This is the essence of what is known concerning the practice of *maysir*, the details of which had been forgotten by the Bedouins questioned in the first half of the 3rd/9th century by Abū ʿUbayd al-Ḳāsim b. Sallām al-Harawī (d. 223/837) (cf. T. Fahd, *Divination*, 208, n. 2). The reason for this forgetting lies in its prohibition by the Ḳurʾān, which, in two instances (II, 219 and V, 90) forbids it together with wine, while acknowledging in both certain "advantages" (*manāfiʿ*). They are seen, primarily, as a diversion from prayer and, subsequently, a factor of divisiveness and a cause of hostility among the faithful (v, 91). But, being condemned along with *anṣāb* (idols) and *azlām* (divining arrows), they are considered "impure" practices (*rid̲j̲s*) belonging to pagan cults (v, 90), and thus it may be supposed that the victims divided up for drawing by lot were originally blood-sacrifices offered to deities.

Bibliography: The present article is an abbreviated form of the analysis of *maysir* presented in T. Fahd, *La divination arabe. Études religieuses, sociologiques et folkloriques sur le milieu natif de l'Islam*, Leiden 1966, 204-13, where the reader will find complete references to the numerous sources and studies used, among which the following are especially worthy of mention: Ibn Ḳutayba, *K. al-maysir wa 'l-ḳidāḥ*, ed. Muḥibb al-Dīn al-K̲h̲aṭīb, Cairo 1342/1923; Nuwayrī, *Nihāyat al-arab*, iii, 114-15 (German tr. and comm. by A. Huber, *Über das "Meisir" genannte Spiel der heidnischen Araber*; Arabic text with Latin translation by Rasmussen, *Additamentum*, 67/61); Zabīdī (author of *TA*), *Nas̲h̲wat al-irtiyāḥ fī bayān ḥaḳīḳat al-maysir wa 'l-ḳidāḥ*, ed. Landberg, in *Primeurs arabes*, i, 29-38; see also *Divination*, 212, n. 6; Freitag, *Einleitung in das Studium der arabischen Sprache*, Bonn 1861, 170-83; G. Jacob, *Ramaḍān*, Greifswald 1895, 110-13.

(T. Fahd)

MAYSŪN, daughter of the Kalbī chief Baḥdal b. Unayf [*q.v.*], mother of the caliph Yazīd I. We do not know if after her marriage with Muʿāwiya she retained the Christian religion which had been that of her family and of her tribe. A few verses are attributed to her in which she sighs for the desert and shows very slight attachment for her husband (see Nöldeke, *Delectus*, 25). But the attribution to Maysūn of this fragment of poetry, which is in any case old, has been rightly disputed. She took a great interest in the education of her son Yazīd and accompanied him to the desert of the Kalb where the prince passed a part of his youth; this temporary separation from her husband gave rise to the legend of her repudiation by Muʿāwiya. She must have died before Yazīd became caliph.

Bibliography: Given in Lammens. *Études sur le règne du calife omaiyade Moʿāwia I*, in *MFOB*, iii (1906-8), 286-7, 305, 312-14. (H. Lammens)

MAYSŪR [see MAHISUR].

MAYTA (A.), feminine of *mayt*, dead (used of irrational beings); as a substantive it means an animal that has died in any way other than by slaughter. In later terminology, the word means firstly an animal that has not been slain in the ritually prescribed fashion, the flesh of which therefore cannot be eaten, and secondly all parts of animals whose flesh cannot be eaten, whether because not properly slaughtered or as a result of a general prohibition against eating them.

In addition to sūra XXXVI, 33, where *mayta* appears as an adjective, the word occurs in the following passages in the Ḳurʾān in the first of these meanings: XXI, 116: "He has forbidden you *mayta*, blood, pork and that over which another than Allāh has been invoked; if however anyone is forced [to eat these] without wishing to transgress or sin, Allāh is merciful and indulgent" (from the third Meccan period, since VI, 119 may refer to this context and the appearance of the same exception for cases of coercion in VI, 146 (cf. below) is then only easily explained in view of the whole trend of the passage, if there were an earlier passage, namely XVI, 116, in which it was given full justification; cf. Nöldeke-Schwally, *Geschichte des Qorāns*, i, 146-7; Grimme, *Mohammed*, ii, 26, transfers the whole sūra to the later Meccan period); VI,140, 146: "They have said: 'What is in the womb of this cattle belongs to the males, and is forbidden to our females'; but if it is *mayta* (stillborn), all have a share in it ... Say: I find in what is revealed to me nothing forbidden, which must not be eaten, except it be *mayta* or congealed blood or pork—for this is filth—or a slaughter at which another than Allāh is invoked, but if anyone is forced [to eat it] without wishing to commit a transgression or sin, thy heart is merciful and indulgent" (of the third Meccan period; cf. Nöldeke-Schwally, i, 161; Grimme, ii, 26); II, 168: "He has forbidden you *mayta*, blood, pork and that over which another than Allāh is invoked but if anyone is forced [to eat it] without wishing to commit a sin or transgression, it is not reckoned as a sin against him; Allāh is merciful and indulgent" (from the year 2 of the *hidjra*, before the battle of Badr; cf. Nöldeke-Schwally, i, 178; Grimme, ii, 27): vv. 4-5: "Forbidden to you is *mayta*, blood, pork, that over which another than Allāh is invoked, and that which has been strangled, killed by a blow or a fall, or by the horns [of another beast], that which has been eaten by wild beasts—with the exception of what is made pure—and that which has been sacrified to idols ... But if anyone in [his] hunger is forced to eat of them without wishing to commit a sin, Allāh is merciful and indulgent" (in all probability revealed after the valedictory pilgrimage of the year 10; cf. Nöldeke-Schwally, i, 227-8; Grimme, ii, 28, dates the sūra to the year 7).

It is quite evident from sūra, XI, 140, that the *mayta* was of some significance for the Meccans in the many laws about food with which Arab paganism was acquainted (cf. Wellhausen, *Reste arabischen Heidentums*[2], 168 ff.). Although it is no longer possible to define exactly the part it played (even the statements recorded by al-Ṭabarī from the earliest interpreters of this passage, which moreover only refers to a detail, reveal the complete disappearance of any reliable tradition), it may be assumed without misgiving that the Ḳurʾānic prohibition contained a corresponding pre-Islamic prohibition, although it perhaps modified it. Both go back to the religious reluctance to consume the blood of animals, and indeed in all the Ḳurʾān passages quoted, blood is mentioned alongside of *mayta.* It is unnecessary to assume that Muḥammad was influenced by Judaism on this point, and the suggestion may be rejected especially as the prohibition in its stereotyped form occurs again in sūra II, 168, just at the time of vigorous reaction against Judaism, and in sūra VI, 147 (Medinan, a late insertion) which contrasts the prohibition of *mayta*, etc., with the Jewish laws relating to food. The meaning of *mayta* is explained in the latest passage dealing with it, v. 4: in the second half of the verse the principal kinds of *mayta* are given (with the exception of the animal that dies of disease), which had already been mentioned in general terms; the commentators were thus able to interpret the single cases given as examples wrongly as being different from the *mayta* proper. The purification (in the Ḳurʾān only mentioned in this passage) must mean ritual slaughter, by which, even if done at the last moment, the animal does not become *mayta* but can be eaten.

These prescriptions of the Ḳurʾān are further developed in the traditions. According to the latter, it is forbidden to trade in *mayta* or, more accurately, its edible parts; some traditions (mainly on the authority of Aḥmad b. Ḥanbal) even forbid any use being made of all that comes from *mayta*; others again expressly permit the use of hides of *mayta.* An exception from the prohibition of *mayta* is made in the cases of fish and locusts; these are in general considered as the two kinds of *mayta* that are permitted, i.e. no ritual slaughter is demanded in their case (because they have no "blood", cf. above). While some traditions, extending this permission by the earliest *ḳiyās*, say that all creatures of the sea, not only fishes, can be eaten without ritual slaughter, including even seafowl (in this case it is said that "the sea has performed the ritual slaughter"), others limit the permission to those animals and fishes which the sea casts up on the land or the tide leaves behind, in contrast to those which swim about on the water. But there is also quoted a saying of Abū Bakr expressly declaring what swims on the surface to be permitted. In this connection, we have the story of a monster cast up by the sea (sometimes described as a fish) which fed a Muslim army under the leadership of Abū ʿUbayda when they were in dire straits; but in this tradition and in the interpretation that has been given it (that they only ate of it out of hunger i.e. took advantage of the Ḳurʾānic permission for cases of need) is clearly reflected the uncertainty that prevailed about such questions which were on the border line. In the traditions, we find it first laid down that portions cut out of living animals are also considered *mayta.* The way is at least paved for the declaration that all forbidden animal-dishes are *mayta.* The regulations found in the Ḳurʾān appear again here, e.g. the permission to eat *mayta* in case of need and to slay properly dying animals at the moment to prevent them becoming *mayta.*

Some traditions handed down through Ḥammād from Ibrāhīm al-Na<u>kh</u>aʿī bring us to a somewhat late period (in the *Kitāb al-Ā<u>th</u>ār*): one says that of the creatures of the sea, only fishes can be eaten; another, which is found in two versions, limits the permission to what is thrown up by the sea or left behind by the tide; ritual slaughter is not demanded in this case. The question whether the embryo of a slaughtered dam requires a special purification, i.e. ritual slaughter, is raised in one tradition and decided in the affirmative.

The most important regulations of Muslim law about *mayta*, which express the last stage of development, are as follows. It is unanimously agreed that *mayta* in the legal sense is impure and "forbidden" (*ḥarām*), i.e. cannot be eaten, and also that fish are exceptions to this; the Mālikīs and Ḥanbalīs also except the majority of creatures of the sea, and according to the more correct <u>Sh</u>āfiʿī view, this applies to all marine creatures (the Ḥanbalīs here hold the opinion of Ibrāhīm al-Na<u>kh</u>aʿī, except that the two ideas of "thrown up" and "swimming on the surface" are later overlaid and destroyed by the to some extent synonymous phrase "slain by another cause", "died of itself"). The edible parts of *mayta* are also *mayta*, as are the bones, hair etc. among the <u>Sh</u>āfiʿīs, but not the Ḥanafīs, and among the Mālikīs only the bones; the hide, when tanned, is considered pure and may be used. Emergency slaughter (*<u>dh</u>akāt* or *ta<u>dh</u>kiya*; ritual slaughter in general is *<u>dh</u>abḥ* or *naḥr*) is, according to the Ḥanafīs and the better-known view of the <u>Sh</u>āfiʿīs (also according to al-Zuhrī), permitted, even if the animal will certainly die, provided it still shows signs of life at the moment of slaughter. According to the view predominant among the Mālikīs, such slaughter is not valid and the animal becomes *mayta* (in contrast to Mālik's own view). The question of the embryo (cf. above) is answered in the affirmative by the Ḥanafīs, following Ibrāhīm al-Nakhaʿī and Abū Ḥanīfa (al-Shaybānī himself held the Mālikī view, to be mentioned immediately below) but in the negative by the Mālikīs and Shāfiʿīs (in this case, it is said that "the ritual slaughter of the dam is also the ritual slaughter of the embryo"), except that the Mālikīs made it a condition that the embryo should be fully developed (Mālik himself also demanded its slaughter "to draw the blood from it" in the case where the embryo had been dropped). That anyone who is forced to eat *mayta* may do so, is the unanimous opinion; only on the questions whether one is bound to eat *mayta* to save his life, whether he should satisfy his hunger completely, or only eat the minimum to keep life alive, etc., is there a difference of opinion. The Shāfiʿīs and Ḥanbalīs further demand that one should not have been brought to these straits through illegal action (a different interpretation of the Ḳurʾānic regulations).

A clear definition of *mayta* and its distinction from other kinds of forbidden animal foods was never reached. Sometimes it is separated on the authority of the Ḳurʾānic passage itself from its own four subdivions given in sūra V. Sometimes its validity is extended over extensive allied fields. As is evident from the *fiḳh* books, this terminological uncertainty has not infrequently caused still further confusion in the discussion of differences of opinion.

Bibliography: Lane, *Lexicon*, s.v.; the books of *ḥadīth* and *fiḳh*; Wensinck, *Handbook of early Muhammadan tradition*, s.v.; Juynboll, *Handleiding tot de kennis van de Mohammedaansche Wet*³, 169-70; E. Gräf, *Schlachttier und Jagdbeute im islamischen Recht*, Bonn 1959; J. Schacht, *An introduction to Islamic law*, Oxford 1964, 134. (J. Schacht)

MAYŪRḲA, Majorca or Mallorca, name of the largest (*umm*) of the Balearic islands (or eastern islands of al-Andalus: *al-djazāʾir al-sharḳiyya*), the others being Minūrḳa (Minorca or Menorca) and Yābisa (Ibiza). Its name figures as early as the *Crónica del Moro Rasis*, ed. D. Catalán, 13. At approximately the same distance from Ibiza to the west and from Minorca to the east, it is situated four days' sailing time from Sardinia (Sardāniya) according to al-Idrīsī (*Maghrib*, text 214, tr. 266) and lies opposite Bougie (al-Ḥimyarī, *al-Rawḍ al-miʿṭār*, text 188-91, tr. 228-31). Al-Ḥimyarī, Ibn Saʿīd (*Mughrib*, ii, 466) and al-Zuhrī (*K. al-Djaʿrāfiya*, 177-9) differ as to the terrain of the island. According to the testimony of this last-named author in particular, and according to the data supplied by Christian sources following the Catalan-Aragonese conquest of the 13th century, the island, which enjoyed a fine climate, was fertile and possessed abundant resources, especially cereals, fruits, trees, pack-animals, sheep and cattle, horses and mules, a few goats, and also, for hunting, hares, rabbits and foxes. Cotton and flax were cultivated there, but silk was an imported commodity (Ibn Saʿīd, in E. Fagnan, *Extraits inédits*, 23, 24). Curiously there is no mention of the olive and the raisin, but their existence cannot be doubted, nor that of the fig; cultivation of these products, of little significance during the Islamic occupation, was developed subsequently. A Flemish document of the 13th century mentions rice as one of the principal commodities exported from Majorca to Flanders, but there is no evidence for the cultivation of this product in the Islamic period. From the work of al-Zuhrī (178) and from other sources, it appears that the town and the island were endowed with a good defensive system and substantial buildings.

Nothing is known of the situation of Majorca and its dependencies at the time of the first Arab incursions into the western Mediterranean. It may reasonably be assumed that it comprised a population which was at first Romanised, later Christianised, of Hispano-Roman descent, and possibly some Jews. In the *K. al-Imāma wa 'l-siyāsa* (ed. Ṭ.M. al-Zaynī, n. p., n.d., i, 73), in the *Annales* of Ibn al-Athīr (33), the *Mughrib* of Ibn Saʿīd (ii, 466) and the *Analectes* of al-Maḳḳarī (i, 177), there is mention of a first incursion carried out in 89/707-8, from the direction of Ifrīḳiya, by the son of Mūsā b. Nuṣayr, ʿAbd Allāh, who—according to one of these sources—was the *fātiḥ Mayūrḳa*, who captured its king (*malik*) and who took possession of a rich store of booty. Other sources, including Ibn ʿIdhārī (*Bayān*, ii, text 89, tr. 145), who speaks of a state of revolt and of a refusal to pay the levies due for the years 234 and 235/846-50, give the impression that, subjected to a treaty and required to pay the *djizya* and possibly other contributions, the Majorcans refused on more than one occasion and lived for a considerable period of time in a state of more or less nominal independence until the conquest of the island in the time of the *amīr* Muḥammad I (al-Zuhrī, 178) or until the arrival, in 290/902-3, of ʿIṣām al-Khawlānī who contributed to the Islamisation of the island by constructing hostelries, baths and mosques (Ibn Khaldūn, *ʿIbar*, iv, 164), all this after the island had suffered, in 255/869, the devastating effects of a Norman invasion. Majorca was a constant source of difficulties for the Cordovan administration, to such an extent that in 336/947-8 al-Nāṣir was obliged to send his *kātib* Djaʿfar b. ʿUthmān al-Muṣḥafī to restore order there (*Bayān*, ii, text 215, tr. 356). In the 5th/11th century, there begins a new period in the history of Majorca. Annexed to the kingdom of Mudjāhid [*q.v.*] of Denia (see Clelia Sarnelli Cerqua, *Mudjāhid al-ʿĀmirī ḳāʾid al-usṭūl al-ʿarabī fī gharbī al-baḥr al-mutawassiṭ*, Cairo 1961), the islands became the centre of intense piratical activity. After the disappearance of ʿAlī b. Mudjāhid and the incorporation of Denia, in 468/1076, into the kingdom of the Banū Hūd [*q.v.*] of Saragossa (Afif Turk, *El reino de Zaragoza en el siglo XI de Cristo* (*V de la Hégira*), Madrid 1978, 109-14), there followed, from 480 to 508/1087-1115, some obscure years of independence during which the islands, having undergone a devastating attack on the part of the Pisans and the Catalans, were occupied by the Almoravids. The rule of the latter, continued, after their collapse and their disappearance from the Iberian peninsula and North Africa, with the dynasty of the Banū Ghāniya [*q.v.*] until the occupation of the island by the Almohads in 599/1202-3 (see especially al-Ḥimyarī, *al-Rawḍ al-miʿṭār*, text 189-91, tr. 228-31). The reign of the Almohads represents a period of obscurity which lasted until the year 627/1229 when James I of Aragon put an end to Islamic domination; the last centre of resistance were crushed in Rabīʿ I 628/January-February 1231.

Majorca was Islamised and Arabised from the 4th to the 6th century/10th to the 12th, and under the Almoravids and the Almohads its ethnic composition became increasingly Berberised, a factor which has left visible traces in the toponomy of the Baleares (M. Barcelo, *De toponimia tribal i clànica berber a les illes orientals d'al-Andalus*, Societat Onomàstica, Buttletí interior, vii Colloqui Mallorca, April 1982, 426; A. Poveda Sánchez, *Introductión al estudio de la toponimia árabe-musulmana de Mayūrqa, según la documentación de los archivos de la ciutat de Mallorca (1232-1276)*, in *Awrāq*, iii [1980], 76-100). Majorca displayed, especially from the 5th to the 7th/11th-13th centuries, an intensive cultural activity (D. Urvoy, *La vie intellectuelle et spirituelle dans les Baléares musulmanes*, in *And.*, xxxvii [1972], 87-132). The other islands were also conquered by the Catalan-Aragonese: Ibiza in 632/1235 and Minorca in 686/1287.

Bibliography: Besides the works mentioned, see Guillem Roselló Bordoy, *L'Islam a les Illes Balears*, Palma, Majorca 1968, which contains fuller references to the Arabic sources and puts into context the information supplied by the classic work of Alvaro Campaner y Fuertes, *Bosquejo histórico de la dominación islamita en las Islas Baleares*, Palma 1888. Also see the works of Miquel Barcelo (extensive bibliography), A. Poveda Sánchez and Richard Soto, author *inter alia* of *Quan Mallorca era Mayúrqa*, in *L'Avenç*, xvi (May 1979), 25-33 and of *Mesquites urbanes i mesquites rurales a Mayūrqa*, in *Butlletì de la Soc. arqueològica Luliana*, any xcv (1979), no. xxxvii, 114-35. On the subject of Minorca, E. Molina López, *El gobierno independiente de Menorca y sus relaciones con al-Andalus e Ifrīqīya*, in *Revista de Menorca*, Mahón 1982, 5-88. Also recommended is M. de Epalza, *Orígenes de la invasión cordobesa de Mallorca en 902*, in *Estudis de Prehistòria, d'Història de Mayūrqa i d'Història de Mallorca dedicats a Guillem Roselló i Bordoy*, Majorca 1982, 113-129 (these *Estudis* also contain other interesting articles).

(J. Bosch Vilá)

AL-**MAYURḲĪ**, the *nisba* of several persons originally from Majorca (Mayurḳa [*q.v.*]) or residents of the island. In his *Muʿdjam al-buldān*, iv, 720-3, s.v. Mayurḳa, Yāḳūt mentions a certain number.

In addition to al-Ḥumaydī [*q.v.*], the best-known person with this last *nisba*, one should mention the name of Abu 'l-Ḥasan ʿAlī b. Aḥmad b. ʿAbd al-ʿAzīz b. Ṭunayz, who seems to have led quite a lively existence. According to Yāḳūt, iv, 722-3, he was a good grammarian (cf. al-Suyūṭī, *Bughya*, 327) who was also concerned with the Ḳurʾān readings; he naturally collected *ḥadīth*s at Damascus, Baṣra and elsewhere. He is said to have gone to ʿUmān and the land of the Zandj, where he stayed for some time before returning to die at Kāẓimayn, near Baghdād (rather than at Baṣra, in Yāḳut's second version) in *ca.* 475/1082. Two verses by him are cited by Yāḳūt and al-Suyūṭī, but others are preserved in the Escurial ms. 467/2 (Derenbourg). See Brockelmann, S I, 479.

Another Mayurḳī worthy of notice is a Christian convert to Islam, Fray Anselmo Turmeda, better known under the name of ʿAbd Allāh al-Tardjumān [see AL-TARDJUMĀN]. (Ed.)

MAYY ZIYĀDA, pen name of Mārī Ilyās Ziyāda, pioneer writer of poetry in prose, essayist, orator and journalist in Arabic, French and English; translator from several European languages; and a zealous feminist who defended the case of Arab women's education and freedom.

Born in Nazareth on 11 February 1886 to a Lebanese Christian father who worked as a teacher and journalist, and a Galilee mother from a village near Nazareth, Mayy received a French education at St. Joseph's School in Nazareth (1892-9), in ʿAyntūra in Lebanon (1900-4), and at the Lazarist Nuns in Beirut (1904-8). In 1908 her parents emigrated to Cairo, where her father was appointed as the editor of the journal *al-Maḥrūsa*. Her first literary work was a booklet of a collection of romantic poems and poems in prose in French, influenced by Lamartine and dedicated to him, entitled *Fleurs de rêve* (Cairo 1911). It was published under the pseudonym of Isis Copia. Djamīl Djabr translated it into Arabic as *Azāhir ḥulm* (Beirut 1952).

In Egypt she studied various European languages and European romantic poets and writers, and became interested in European feminist activities. She also came under the influence of Arabic Islamic culture, especially through Lutfī al-Sayyid [*q.v.*]. She published in *al-Maḥrūsa* novels by European writers which she translated into Arabic, and later these were published in book form. Some of these were from the French: Brada's novel *Le retour du flot*, which she entitled *Rudjūʿ al-mawdja* (1925); a novel by Sir Arthur Conan Doyle, *The Refugees*, which she entitled *al-Ḥubb fi 'l-ʿadhāb* (1925) and from German the novel *Deutsche Liebe* by F. Max Müller under the title *Ibtisāmāt wa-dumūʿ* (Cairo 1911).

In 1916 she joined the Egyptian University (*al-Djāmiʿa al-Miṣriyya*), where she studied literature and philosophy. She also collected her social essays which were published in *al-Mahrūsa* and other Arabic journals under the title *Sawāniḥ fatāt* (Cairo 1922). She took an active part in the social and cultural life in Lebanon and Egypt by lecturing at mixed meetings of men and women in various clubs and societies such as Fatāt Miṣr, where she lectured on *Ghāyat al-ḥayāt* (Cairo 1921). She published articles in various journals—in Arabic, *al-Maḥrūsa*, *al-Muḳtaṭaf*, *al-Hilāl*, *al-Ahrām*, and *al-Siyāsa al-Usbūʿiyya*; in French, *Sphynx*, *Le Progrès Égyptien*; and in English, *The Egyptian Mail*—on various cultural subjects such as Arabic language and literature, Arab and Eastern women and the awakening of the Eastern nations such as the Turkish and the Japanese. She defended the "spiritualism of the East" as opposed to the materialism of the West, but condemned the poverty, illiteracy and illness which prevailed in the East. Her lectures were collected in her book *Kalimāt wa-ishārāt*, (Cairo 1922). Her articles on French and Arab personalities she collected in her book *al-Ṣaḥāʾif* (Cairo 1924), and on Arabic language and literature in *Bayn al-djazr wa 'l-madd* (Cairo 1924). Her collection of romantic and lyrical poetry-in-prose (*shiʿr manthūr*) influenced by Khalīl Djabrān [*q.v.*] she published in her book *Ẓulumāt wa-ashiʿʿa* (Cairo 1923) in which she expressed her pantheism.

In her essays she called for brotherhood, justice, mercy and secular humanism. Yet Mayy did not believe in equality in society. She expressed her ideas on aristocracy, slavery, passive and revolutionary socialism, democracy, anarchism and nihilism in her book *al-Musāwāt* (Cairo 1922), where she ended her discussion with a play emphasising that equality in society is impossible.

In various works, Mayy extolled the literary achievements of her contemporary Arab pioneer poetesses and writers such as in *Bāḥithat al-Bādiya* (pseudonym of Malak Ḥifnī Nāṣif [*q.v.*]) (Cairo 1920), *Warda al-Yāzidjī* (Cairo 1924), and *ʿĀʾisha al-Taymūriyya*, published in serial form in *al-Muḳtaṭaf* (1923-5) and in book form in 1956.

French literary and cultural life made a great impression on Mayy. She styled her weekly salon according to Mme de Rambouillet. Her circle, which exercised deep influence on Egyptian literary and cultural life, included eminent Egyptian and Syro-Lebanese men and women of the pen such as Malak Ḥifnī Nāṣif and Hudā Shaʿrāwī, the poets Ismāʿīl Ṣabrī, Aḥmad Shawḳī, Ḥāfiẓ Ibrāhīm, Muṣṭafā Ṣādiḳ al-Rāfiʿī, Walī al-Dīn Yagan and Khalīl Muṭrān, and writers such as Luṭfī al-Sayyid, Shiblī Shumayyil, Muṣṭafā ʿAbd al-Rāziḳ, Salīm Sarkīs, Salāma Mūsā, Yaʿḳūb Ṣarrūf, Ṭāhā Ḥusayn and ʿAbbās Maḥmūd al-ʿAḳḳād. In her salon, literary and cultural questions, and philosophical and scientific trends, were discussed and poems were read. Many writers said that some of these personalities were in love with Mayy; yet it is agreed that her great love was D̲j̲abrān whom, though she corresponded with him, she never met in person.

Mme de Sévigné was her example for literary correspondence. Beside D̲j̲abrān and the attendants of her salon, she corresponded also with Salmā Ṣāyig̲h̲ and Amīn al-Rīḥānī. Some of these letters were collected and published by the Lebanese D̲j̲amīl D̲j̲abr in his book *Mayy wa-D̲j̲abrān* (Beirut 1950), *Rasāʾil Mayy* (2nd ed. Beirut 1954) and by Ṭāhir al-Ṭunnāḥī in *Aṭyāf min ḥayāt Mayy* (Cairo 1974). A common fault among Arab writers is that they have looked at *Rasāʾil Mayy* (1948) by Madeleine Arḳas̲h̲ as a collection of Mayy Ziyāda's genuine letters while, in fact, these are imaginary letters giving advice to women on problems of life.

Mayy's style is influenced by Christian Arabic liturgical literature and the French Romantics. She treats her subjects emotionally and metaphorically, loading them with allusions to French and Arabic history and culture.

The deaths of her father in 1930, of D̲j̲abrān in 1931 and of her mother in 1932 made her feel lonely and deserted. Her journeys to France and England in 1932 and then to Rome did not release her from her melancholy. In 1935 her relatives suspected her of neurasthenia and hysteria; they lured her back to Lebanon and she was put into a mental hospital for nine months. The Lebanese journal *al-Maks̲h̲ūf* defended her case with the help of her friends Amīn al-Rīḥānī, Charles Mālik and Ḳusṭanṭīn Zurayḳ and Prince ʿAbd al-Ḳādir al-D̲j̲azāʾirī, and she was released from hospital. Two years later she returned to Cairo, where she died on 19 October 1941. In 1975 Muʾassasat Nawfal in Beirut published all Mayy's works and translations, twelve in number.

Bibliography (in addition to the works mentioned in the text): Y. A. Dāg̲h̲ir, *Maṣādir al-dirāsa al-adabiyya*, Beirut 1956, ii, 435-41; Muhammad ʿAbd al-G̲h̲anī Ḥasan, *Ḥayāt Mayy*, Cairo 1942; Amal Dāʿūḳ Saʿd, *Fann al-murāsala ʿinda Mayy Ziyāda*, Beirut 1982; D̲j̲amīl D̲j̲abr, *Mayy fī ḥayātihā al-muḍṭariba*, Beirut 1953; and *Mayy Ziyāda fī ḥayātihā wa-adabihā*, Beirut 1960; ʿAbd al-Latīf S̲h̲arāra, *Mayy Ziyāda*, Beirut 1965; Manṣūr Fahmī, *Mayy Ziyāda wa-rāʾidāt al-adab al-ʿarabī al-ḥadīt̲h̲* Cairo 1954; T. Khemiri, *Leaders in contemporary Arabic literature. Pt. 1*, in *WI*, ix/2-4 (1930), 24-7; I. Kratchkovsky, *Proben der neu-arabischen Literatur (1880-1925)*, in *MSOS*, xxxi/2 (1928), 196-7; E. Rossi, *Una scrittrice araba cattolica Mayy (Marie Ziyādah)*, in *OM*, v, no. 11 (Nov. 1925), 604-13; Brockelmann, S III, 259-62; N. K. Kots̲a̲rev, *Pisateli Egipta, XX vek*, Moscow 1975, 136-7.

(S. Moreh)

MAYYĀFĀRIḲĪN, a town in the northeast of Diyār Bakr [*q.v.*]. The other Islamic forms of the name are Māfārḳīn, Mafārḳīn, Fārḳīn (whence the name of origin al-Fāriḳī), etc. The town is called in Greek Martyropolis, in Syriac Mīpherḳēt, in Armenian Nphkert (later Muharkin, Muphargin). According to Yāḳūt, iv, 702, the old name of the town was Madūr-ṣālā (read *ḳāla* < **matur-khalakh* in Armenian, "town of the martyrs"). On the identification of Tigranocerta with Mayyāfāriḳīn, see below.

1. *Topography and early history.*

Geography. The town lies to the south of the little range of the Ḥazrō which rises like the first tier of the amphitheatre of the mountains, the higher parts of which consist of the summits (Darkōs̲h̲, Antok) rising to the south of Mūs̲h̲ and separating the course of the eastern Euphrates (Murād čay) from those of the Tigris and its left-bank tributaries.

Mayyāfāriḳīn lies 25 miles north of the Tigris and 12 west of the Baṭmān-Ṣū. It is watered by a little river (now called the Fārḳīn-Ṣū) which flows into the Baṭmān-Ṣū 12 miles to the southeast, an important left-bank tributary of the Tigris which drains the wild and mountainous country south of Mūs̲h̲ (the cantons of Ḳulp and Sāṣūn). The old names of the Baṭmān-Ṣū are Nicephorius (Roman period), Nymphios (Byzantine period), Syriac Kallat̲h̲, Arabic Sātīdamā (a word of Aramaic origin transcribed S̲h̲ithithma in Armenian and explained as "drinker of blood"; Armenian *Geography* of the 7th century = Marquart, *Ērānšahr*, 161), Armenian Khalirt and perhaps Mamus̲h̲el (Faustus of Byzantium). Some of these identifications, as we shall see, are still uncertain.

Mayyāfāriḳīn is the meeting-place of a number of roads from the north following the different streams which go to form the Baṭmān-Ṣū: 1. Čabak̲h̲d̲j̲ūr (on the Murād čay) — D̲h̲u 'l-Ḳarnayn — Līd̲j̲e — Bos̲h̲āt — Mayyāfāriḳīn; 2. Mūs̲h̲ — Ḳulp — Pāsūr — Mayyāfāriḳīn; 3. Mūs̲h̲ — K̲h̲oyt — Tingirt (= Ṣāsūn) — Mayyāfāriḳīn. Routes 3 and 4 passing Ṣāṣūn are still little known. The distance between Diyārbakr and Mayyāfāriḳīn is about 45 miles. The old road Diyārbakr — Bitlīs, which used to run through Mayyāfāriḳīn, now runs farther south and crosses the Baṭmān-Ṣū south of Almadīn (Diyārbakr — Sinān — Zok — Weisiḳaranī — Bitlīs).

Mayyāfāriḳīn has thus lost the advantage of being a stage on the road between Armenia and upper Mesopotamia. Since 1260 it has no longer been a political centre around which gravitated the interests of the surrounding country. It retains only its importance as a market for the produce of the mountainous and pastoral country drained by the Baṭmān-Ṣū.

Ancient history. The mountains to the north of Mayyāfāriḳīn have long sheltered the remnants of ancient aboriginal peoples. About 600 A.D., Georgius Cyprius (ed. Gelzer, 48), mentions the Χοθαῖται and Σανασουνῖται there who gave their names to the districts of K̲h̲oyt and Ṣāṣūn. Marquart (1916) supposes there are elements of the aboriginal language in names like *M-īpher-ḳēt and *Ma-mus̲h̲el(i) which are, he says, formed with Caucasian ("südkaukasisch"?) prefixes. According to tradition (Yāḳūt, iv, 703), the founder of Martyropolis, Marūt̲h̲ā b. Layūṭā, was the son of a woman on the mountains, and Marquart sees in Layūṭā a mutilated form of the name of the people Urṭā(n) < Urarṭu (*Handes Amsorya* [1915], 96; [1916], 126). The Marwānid Abū Naṣr (see section 2. below) was married to the daughter of Sank̲h̲arīb, lord of the Sanāsuna; cf. Amedroz, in *JRAS* (1903).

Lehmann-Haupt thought that he could recognise at Mayyāfāriḳīn traces of an ancient Assyrian settlement, "eine von Haus aus assyrische Anlage" (*Armenien*, i, 396, 398).

Tigranocerta = Mayyāfāriḳīn (?). As early as 1838, von Moltke had suggested that Mayyāfāriḳīn was the ancient Tigranocerta, i.e. the new capital founded by Tigranes II about 80 B.C., which was taken by Lucullus after the victory won on the banks of the Nicephorius (6 Oct. 69 B.C.) and again in the reign of Nero by the legate Corbulo (*ca.* 63 A.D.); it is regularly mentioned down to the middle of the 4th century A.D. Other scholars had sought Tigranocerta at Siʿirt (d'Anville), Arzan (H. Kiepert, 1873), near Kefr-D̲j̲ōz (Kiepert 1875), at Tell-Armen west of

Niṣībīn (E. Sachau; cf. DUNAYSĪR), etc. Late Armenian tradition gives the name Tigranocerta to Diyārbakr. Moltke's idea was taken up vigorously by Lehmann-Haupt and W. Belck after their expedition to Armenia in 1898-9.

On the north wall of Mayyāfāriķīn is a multilated Greek inscription. It was deciphered and published by Lehmann-Haupt, who attributes it to the Armenian King Pap (369-74), which is quite in keeping with the known facts of the reign of this monarch. In spite of his criticism of the details of Lehmann-Haupt's hypothesis, Marquart (1916) has rather corroborated him by bringing forward new considerations.

In view of the many contradictions found in the classical sources regarding Tigranocerta, the question comes to be, if Mayyāfāriķīn is not Tigranocerta, what other unknown town existed here in the time of Pap, unless the stones on which the inscription is engraved and which are now hopelessly dissarranged ("in heilloser Verwirrung") were brought from another place when Martyropolis was being built?

The main objection to the identification of Tigranocerta with Mayyāfāriķīn is that, according to Eutropius, vi, 9, 1 and Faustus, v, 24, Tigranocerta was in Arzanene (Ałdznikh); on the other hand, the river Mamus͟heł seems to have formed in the 4th century the western frontier of this latter province. From this fact (Hübschmann, *Die altarmen. Ortsnamen*, *Indogerm. Forsch.*, Leipzig 1904, 473-5), it seems that Tigranocerta ought to be placed east of the Baṭmān-Ṣū if this river is identical with the Mamus͟heł. This last name was connected by Marquart with the name al-Musūliyāt, which al-Muķaddasī, 144, gives to one of the tributaries of the Tigris (on the left bank) and apparently corresponding to the Baṭmān-Ṣū. (A district of Musūliya (?) still exists farther east on the upper course of the Bidlīs čay, in the area of the ancient possessions of the Baṭrīķ Mus͟hālīķ; cf. Kisrawī, in Yāķūt, ii, 551-2.)

To reconcile the statements of Faustus, iv, 24, 27, with the position of Mayyāfāriķīn (12 miles west of the Baṭmān-Ṣū), Marquart proposes to identify the Mamus͟heł = Nicephorius with the Fārķīn-Ṣū, while the Musūliyāt would be applied to the whole system of the Baṭmān-Ṣū (Nymphios, Sātīdamā, etc.). The insignificance of the Fārķīn-Ṣū, which rises in the hills about 3 miles north of Mayyāfāriķīn (Ibn al-Azraķ calls its source Ra'ˀs al-ʿAyn; the *D̲jihān-numā*, 437, ʿAyn al-Ḥawḍ) and does not suit the description of the hermitage of Mambrē, which, according to Faustus, must have been on the right bank, makes Marquart's hypothesis less attractive. If finally we consider the position of Mayyāfāriķīn from the point of view of the interests of Tigranes, one is forced to admit that against an enemy coming from the west (Lucullus!) Tigranocerta = Mayyāfāriķīn was devoid of natural defences, while in the event of an enemy coming from the east it ran the risk of being easily cut off from Armenia on the main road from Bitlīs (the ancient Κλεισοῦρα Βαλαλείσων, cf. Tomaschek, *Sasun* in *SBAW Wien* [Vienna 1895], 8). On the other hand, Mayyāfāriķīn from its position later played an important part in the defensive system of the Byzantine empire.

In these circumstances and before a more detailed study has been made on the spot, it is a mistake to think that all the difficulties in the identification of Tigranocerta have been cleared up.

Mayyāfāriķīn = Martyropolis. The identity of these two towns is quite certain. The Christian sources (Syriac, Armenian and Greek) referring to the foundation of Martyropolis are numerous. A Syriac "history" (*tas͟hʿīt͟hā*) kept in the Jacobite church of Mayyāfāriķīn was translated for the historian of the town Ibn al-Azraķ and is given in a synopsis in Yāķūt, iv, 703-7 and al-Ķazwīnī, ii, 379-80 (tr. with notes by Marquart, in *Handes Amsorya* [1916], 125-35).

The town is said to have been founded on the site of a "large village" (*ķarya ʿaẓīma*) by the bishop Marūt͟hā) (Mār Marūt͟hā) who had obtained the authority of Yazdigird I of Persia to do so. This ecclesiastic flourished between *ca.* 383 and 420 (on the sources for his biography, cf. Marquart, *op. cit.*, 91-2, 125). The town of Martyropolis to which Marūt͟hā brought the remains of the Christian martyrs of Persia is mentioned for the first time in 410. The etymology of the Syriac name Mīpherķēṭ is uncertain (cf. above). In Amenian, the town is mentioned for the first time in the *Geography* of the 7th century as Nphrkert (once Nphṛet).

By the peace of 297 with Diocletian, the province of Sophanene, within which Martyropolis lay, had become part of the Roman empire. Even after the disastrous peace made by Jovian in 363, Sophanene remained to the Emperor. Under Theodosius II (401-50), the new town, situated quite near the frontier, acquired considerable importance and became the capital of Sophanene (= Great Tsopkh). The town was still insufficiently fortified, and in 502 the Sāsānian Kawād͟h b. Pērōz seized it and carried the inhabitants off to K͟hūzistān, where he founded for them the town of Abaz-Ķubād͟h (Yāķūt, iv, 707) Weh-Āmid͟h-Kawād͟h = Arrad͟jān; cf. Marquart, *Ērānšahr*, 41, 307). Anastasius began the fortification of Martyropolis but Justinian, after his accession in 527, was the first to reorganise completely the eastern frontier between Dārā and Trebizond. Martyropolis, the headquarters of a commander under the *strategos* of Theodosiopolis (Erzerūm), became one of the most important military centres. Procopius, *De aedificiis*, iii, gives a complete description of the walls of the town, the height and thickness of which were doubled and a full account of the system of defences (outer walls, advanced forts etc.); cf. Adontz, *op.cit.*, 10-12, 140-2. In 589 the town fell into the hands of the Sāsānids, but in 591 came back to the Byzantines in return for the support given by the Emperor Maurice to K͟husraw II. Heraclius held it still the year 18/639 (Yāķūt, *loc. cit.*). (The date is not given in Muralt, *Chronogr. byz.*, i).

The vicissitudes of Martyropolis probably explain the fact that in the Armenian *Geography* of the 7th century (ed. Patkanov, tr. 45; Marquart, *Ērānšahr*, 18, 161) the Persian province of Ałdznikh (Arzanene) is separated from Tsophkh (Sophanene) by the line of the Khałirt (= Baṭmān-Ṣū) while in the description of parts of Armenia Nphret (= Nphrjert) figures as one of the 10 cantons of Arzanene.

Christian legend as preserved by Ibn al-Azraķ and Yāķūt gives very full details of the building of the town in the time of Mār Mārūt͟hā: the arches (*ṭīķān*) of the walls in which the remains of the martyrs were placed, the eight gates of the town, the names of which are carefully recorded, the convent of SS. Peter and Paul, the buildings erected by the three ministers of the Byzantine emperor, each of whom built a tower and a church. There is still to be seen in Mayyāfāriķīn the ruins of a magnificent basilica and of the Church of the Virgin (al-ʿAd͟hrā). Gertrude Bell dated the basilica "not much later than the beginning of the fifth century", and suggested that the Church of the Virgin was one of the two built by K͟husraw II in recognition of the assistance lent by Maurice; cf. Abu 'l-Farad͟j, *Muk͟htaṣar*, ed. Pococke, 98.

(V. MINORSKY)

2. *The Islamic period.*

The conquest and caliphal rule. In the wake of the conquest of the D̲jazīra by ʿIyāḍ b. G̲h̲anm, Mayyāfāriḳīn fell to him peacefully. The caliph ʿUmar b. al-K̲h̲aṭṭāb had made him governor of the D̲jazīra in 18/639 (al-Balādhurī, *Futūḥ*, 179). From that time until the early ʿAbbāsid period, the city was ruled as part of the D̲jazīra, sometimes jointly with al-S̲h̲ām and on other occasions with Armenia and Ād̲h̲arbāyd̲jān. The names of individual governors of Mayyāfāriḳīn for this period are listed by the town chronicler Ibn al-Azraḳ al-Fāriḳī and copied by ʿIzz al-Dīn Ibn S̲h̲addād, the 7th/13th century geographer of the D̲jazīra.

During the reign of the ʿAbbāsid caliph al-Muhtadī (255-6/869-70), Mayyāfāriḳīn and Āmid [*q.v.*] were seized by the S̲h̲aybānid ʿĪsā b. al-S̲h̲ayk̲h̲ [*q.v.*] (Ibn S̲h̲addād, ms. Oxford, Marsh 333, fol. 10a). The S̲h̲aybānids continued to govern the area until its reconquest by the caliph al-Muʿtaḍid in 286/ 899. The grandson of ʿĪsā b. al-S̲h̲ayk̲h̲, Muḥammad, built the minaret of the Friday mosque in Mayyāfāriḳīn in 270/883-4 or 273/886-7. His name was inscribed on it (*ibid.*, fol. 69a).

Ḥamdānid and Būyid involvement in Mayyāfāriḳīn. Mayyāfāriḳīn fell under the sway of the Tag̲h̲libī Arab family, the Ḥamdānids [*q.v.*], after the appointment of Nāṣir al-Dawla al-Ḥasan as governor of Mawṣil in 324/935. His brother, Sayf al-Dawla ʿAlī (d. 356/967), ruled Aleppo and Diyār Bakr and showed a particular liking for Mayyāfāriḳīn. Sayf al-Dawla repaired its walls and rebuilt the old citadel, where he stayed when visiting the city. He also provided Mayyāfāriḳīn with a proper water supply. The entourage of Sayf al-Dawla at Mayyāfāriḳīn included the famous preacher Ibn Nubāta [*q.v.*], and al-Mutanabbī. The latter recited an elegy over ʿAbd Allāh b. Sayf al-Dawla, who died in the town in 338/949 (Ibn al-Azraḳ, B.L. Or. 5803, fol. 113b; Ibn Shaddād, fols. 77a-78a).

During the rule of Sayf al-Dawla, the D̲jazīra was under frequent attack from the Byzantines, whose territorial possessions extended at times almost as far as Āmid. The future Byzantine emperor John Tzimisces besieged Mayyāfāriḳīn in 348/959, and it was on this occasion that Ibn Nubāta began to deliver sermons exhorting the citizens to engage in *d̲jihād* (al-Anṭākī, 774-7; Ibn al-Azraḳ, Or. 5803, fol. 114b). Thereafter Sayf al-Dawla began to strengthen the fortifications of the city (Ibn Shaddād, fol. 78b).

When Sayf al-Dawla died in 367/967, he was buried in the Ḥamdānid family *turba* at Mayyāfāriḳīn (Ibn al-Azraḳ, Or. 5803, fol. 117a; Ibn Shaddād, fol. 78a), a detail which reveals the high esteem in which the city was held by his line. Moreover, Mayyāfāriḳīn was the residence of his wife and children (al-Anṭākī, 807). After the death of Sayf al-Dawla, Mayyāfāriḳīn—along with the rest of Diyār Bakr—fell to the Ḥamdānid ruler of Mawṣil, Abū Tag̲h̲lib al-G̲h̲aḍanfar. The sister of Sayf al-Dawla stayed on in Mayyāfāriḳīn and in 362/972-3 completed the task of improving the defences of the city. This was probably occasioned by another siege of Mayyāfāriḳīn conducted by John Tzimisces, now elevated to the purple, in 361/972 (Ibn al-Azraḳ, Or. 5803, fol. 118b).

In 368/978-9 Abu 'l-Wafāʾ, the general of the Būyid ruler ʿAḍud al-Dawla, took Mayyāfāriḳīn on his behalf (Ibn Miskawayh, ii, 388-90). The name of ʿAḍud al-Dawla was recorded on the city walls (Ibn Shaddād, fol. 69b).

The Marwānid dynasty, 372-478/983-1085. After the death of ʿAḍud al-Dawla in 372/983, Bādh, the founder of the Kurdish dynasty of the Marwānids [*q.v.*], seized Mayyāfāriḳīn (Ibn al-At̲h̲īr, ix, 25; Ibn al-Azraḳ, ed. ʿAwaḍ, 49-52). Bād̲h̲'s successors were able to hold on to the city, making it their capital for over a century. The Marwānid period witnessed another cultural flowering in Islamic Mayyāfāriḳīn. The second Marwānid ruler, Mumahhid al-Dawla, repaired the city walls and inscribed his name on them in many places (*ibid.*, 86, 163; Ibn S̲h̲addād, fol. 70a). An inscription of his is illustrated by Lehmann-Haupt (*Armenien*, 424).

The greatest of the Marwānid rulers, Naṣr al-Dawla (ruled 401-53/1011-61), was responsible for much building activity in the city, including a new citadel with gilded walls and ceilings which was completed in D̲h̲u 'l-Ḥid̲jd̲ja 403/June-July 1013 and which stood on a hill, the site of the Church of the Virgin. The Christian relics were transferred to the Melkite church (Ibn al-Azraḳ, ed. ʿAwaḍ, 107-8). Naṣr al-Dawla also restored the old observatory (*manẓara*), put a clock (*bankām*) in the Friday mosque, constructed and endowed a hospital (*bīmāristān*), planted the citadel garden and built bridges, public baths and a mosque in the suburb of al-Muḥaddat̲h̲a (*ibid.*, 123, 138, 141, 143, 145, 163-4, 168). The Marwānid capital attracted prominent religious and literary figures (*ibid.*, 82, 144, 166); from it, for example, ʿAbd Allāh al-Kāzarūnī spread the Shāfiʿī *mad̲h̲hab* in Diyār Bakr (Ibn al-At̲h̲īr, ix, 52). S̲h̲ayk̲h̲ Abū Naṣr al-Manāzī, a high official at the time of Naṣr al-Dawla, collected books and established *waḳfs* for libraries in the mosques of Mayyāfāriḳīn and Āmid (Ibn al-Azraḳ, ed. ʿAwaḍ, 131). Naṣr al-Dawla died in 453/1061 and was buried in the *turba* of the Banū Marwān at Mayyāfāriḳīn (*ibid.*, 177).

After this, the Marwānids held on to Mayyāfāriḳīn until the town and the rest of Diyār Bakr were taken by the Sald̲j̲ūḳs in 478/1085 during the campaign conducted by Ibn D̲j̲ahīr [*q.v.*], the erstwhile vizier of the Marwānids. Ibn D̲j̲ahīr had persuaded the Sald̲j̲ūḳ sultan Malik-S̲h̲āh [*q.v.*] to authorise him to besiege Mayyāfāriḳīn, and the vizier was able to carry off vast treasures belonging to the Marwānids (Ibn al-At̲h̲īr, x, 86-8, 93-4; Ibn al-Azraḳ, ed. ʿAwaḍ, 208-12).

In the brief quarter-century following the death of Malik-S̲h̲āh in 485/1092, Mayyāfāriḳīn changed hands many times and was ruled by a succession of Sald̲j̲ūḳ princes and other local rulers, including Tutus̲h̲, Duḳāḳ, Ḳilid̲j̲ Arslān and Suḳmān al-Ḳuṭbī of Ak̲h̲lāṭ.

The Artuḳids. After the death of the Sald̲j̲ūḳ sultan Muḥammad b. Malik-S̲h̲āh [*q.v.*] in 512/1118, Mayyāfāriḳīn fell under the sway of the Turcoman Artuḳids [*q.v.*]. According to its chronicler Ibn al-Azraḳ, the town was seized in 512/1118-19 by the Artuḳid Nad̲j̲m al-Dīn Il-G̲h̲āzī, who had already taken Mārdīn around 502/1108-9 (ms. B.L., Or. 5803, fol. 161a). Ibn al-At̲h̲īr puts the Artuḳid capture of Mayyāfāriḳīn three years later, in 515/1121-2 (x, 418), but this is one instance where the dating of the local historian is more likely to be accurate.

After Il-Ghāzī's death in 516/1122, his son Temürtas̲h̲ was able to hold on to Mārdīn and Mayyāfāriḳīn for thirty years and to withstand Zangī's attempts to extend his sphere of influence in Diyār Bakr (Ibn al-Azraḳ, Or. 5803, fols. 169a, 171a; Ibn al-ʿAdīm, 271; Ibn al-At̲h̲īr, *Atabegs*, 79). Temürtas̲h̲'s most ambitious project was the building of the Ḳaramān bridge over the Satidāmā river (the Baṭmān-Ṣū) five miles east of Mayyāfāriḳīn. The work was begun in 541/1146-7 and was completed by his son Nad̲j̲m al-Dīn Alpī in 548/1153-4. The stone arch of the bridge measured more than sixty spans and was "one of the marvels of the age" (Ibn al-Azraķ, Or. 5803, fols. 171b, 179b). The bridge is described fully by Gabriel (*Voyages*, 236), who notes that Sauvaget read the name Temürtash and the year 542/1147-8 on the bridge (*ibid.*, 345). A copper mine was discovered in the time of Temürtash in the area north of Mayyāfāriķīn (Ibn al-Athīr, x, 215) and it is noteworthy that Temürtash is known to have minted copper coins (Ibn al-Azraķ, Or. 5803, fol. 172b).

The Artuķids held on to Mayyāfāriķīn after the death of Temürtash in 548/1152; but, unlike the Ḥamdānids and Marwānids, they preferred generally to live at Mārdīn. Continuity in the administration of Mayyāfāriķīn was provided by the Nubāta family, who are often mentioned as holding the office of *ķāḍī* (*ibid.*, fols. 161a, 162b, 169b). The third Artuķid ruler of Mayyāfāriķīn, Nadjm al-Dīn Alpī, was responsible for a major reconstruction of the Friday mosque. The *minbar* and arcades of the mosque had collapsed in 547/1152-3, the last year of the reign of his father, Temürtash (*ibid.*, fol. 175a). According to Ibn Shaddād, Nadjm al-Dīn Alpī pulled down the rest of the building (fol. 104b) and it was rebuilt with substantial changes by the year 552/1157-8 (Ibn al-Azraķ, Or. 5803, fol. 175b). There is an inscription in the name of Nadjm al-Dīn Alpī at the base of the dome (Gabriel, *Voyages*, 227).

The Ayyūbids. After its conquest by Ṣalāḥ al-Dīn in 581/1185, the city walls were decorated with a fine commemorative inscription. This was discovered by Gertrude Bell and analysed by Van Berchem (in Diez, *Baudenkmäler*, 108) and by Flury (*Schriftbänder*, 44-8). It is apparently the only Kūfic inscription in the name of Ṣalāḥ al-Dīn. Minorsky (*EI*[1], art. *Mayyāfāriķīn*) stated on the authority of Gertrude Bell that this ruler built a mosque at Mayyāfāriķīn for which the columns of the Byzantine basilica were used. There would appear to be no evidence in the sources for this. Possibly the mosque in question was the one outside the walls, of which only the Ayyūbid minaret remains (Gabriel, *Voyages*, 210, 228).

Ṣalāḥ al-Dīn entrusted Mayyāfāriķīn to his brother Sayf al-Dīn in 591/1195 and the city was ruled by this branch of the Ayyūbid family until the Mongols conquered the city in 658/1260. In addition to the literary record, there is architectural, epigraphic and numismatic evidence of this short-lived Ayyūbid dynasty at Mayyāfāriķīn. Awḥad Nadjm al-Dīn Ayyūb (596-607/1200-10) left an inscription dated Ramaḍān 599/May-June 1203 on a tower of the eastern inner wall (illustrated and described by Lehmann-Haupt, *Armenien*, 425-6) and the name of his successor, Ashraf Mūsā (607-12/1210-20), is inscribed on a tower to the north (*ibid*). Mūsā's brother, Muẓaffar Shihāb al-Dīn Ghāzī (617-42/1220-44) built a fine mosque of red baked brick with an inscription dated 624/1227 which was seen and analysed by Taylor (*ibid.*, 428). The inscription on the *miḥrāb* is given by Gabriel (*Voyages*, inscription no. 124). The coins struck by the Ayyūbids of Mayyāfāriķīn have aroused a certain interest amongst scholars (Grabar, 167-78; Lane-Poole, iv, 122-30; Lowick, 164-5). A series of them minted between 582/1186-7 and 612/1215-6 represent crowned human figures. Some have long locks of hair; others are wearing caps with tassels; sometimes these figures are enthroned (*ibid.*).

The Mongols devastated the area around Mayyāfāriķīn as early as 628-9/1231. In 638/1240-1 a Mongol embassy reached the town and demanded that it should surrender and that its fortifications be destroyed. On this occasion, Muẓaffar Shihāb al-Dīn Ghāzī succeeded in deflecting the attentions of the embassy elsewhere. His son, Kāmil Muḥammad (642-58/1244-60), defied the Mongols in a brave stand at Mayyāfāriķīn, but the city fell in 658/1260 to the Mongol army of Hülegü under the command of Yashmūṭ and it was then that this last Ayyūbid ruler was killed (Rashīd al-Dīn, 77-81; Ibn Shaddād, fol. 120a).

Descriptions of Mayyāfāriķīn in the Muslim geographers. There is some disagreement in the classical Muslim geographical works on the placing of Mayyāfāriķīn. Al-Muķaddasī (137) puts it in Diyār Bakr, al-Iṣṭakhrī (188) considers it to be part of Armīniyya, whilst Ibn al-Faķīh (133) places it in Diyār Rabīʿa. Ibn Shaddād lists Mayyāfāriķīn as one of the four *amṣār* of Diyār Bakr, the other three being Āmid, Arzan and Mārdīn (fol. 65a).

Al-Iṣṭakhrī (76, n. *k*) describes Mayyāfāriķīn as having an encircling wall and an abundant water supply, but he comments on the town's unhealthy climate. Al-Muķaddasī (140) mentions the fortifications, including battlements, an encircling wall and ditch; he also notes that the water there is muddy in winter. According to Ķudāma (246), the combined revenue of Arzan and Mayyāfāriķīn in ʿAbbāsid times was 4,100,000 *dirhams*. Nāṣir-i Khusraw visited the town in 438/1046-7. He was impressed by the excellent condition of its walls, which seemed as if they had only just been completed (tr. Schefer, 24-5).

Yāķūt (d. 626/1229) praised the city, especially its surrounding wall of white stone and its prosperous suburb (*rabaḍ*) (*Muʿdjam*, iv, 703-7). When Ibn Shaddād visited Mayyāfāriķīn in the 7th/13th century, he found thriving *khāns* and markets, as well as two *madrasas*, one Ḥanbalī, the other Shāfiʿī (fol. 71a). Both Ibn Shaddād and Yāķūt mention eight city gates at Mayyāfāriķīn, seven of which probably corresponded to those of Byzantine Martyropolis (Gabriel, *Voyages*, 218).

The 8th-9th/14th-15th centuries. In the Ilkhānid period (654-754/1256-1353), Mayyāfāriķīn shared the fate of the rest of Diyār Bakr and was ruled by Mongol *amīrs*. After the collapse of the Ilkhānid state, after 736/1336, Diyār Bakr fell into disarray and became the arena for power struggles between rival Turcoman (the Aķ Ķoyunlu and Ķara Ķoyunlu confederations), Kurdish and Arab groups, before falling victim to the depredations of Tīmūr who attacked the area (but not, apparently, Mayyāfāriķīn) in 796/1394 and 803/1400-1 (Ibn ʿArabshāh, 65-6, 164-5). Thereafter, Mayyāfāriķīn was in the hands of one branch of the mostly nomadic Sulaymānī Kurds [see KURDS] until it was taken in 827/1427 by the Aķ Ķoyunlu leader Ķara ʿUthmān (d. 839/1435), who appointed his son Bāyazīd governor of the town and other citadels in the area (Tihrānī, 95).

The Ṣafawid and Ottoman periods. The Ṣafawid Shāh Ismāʿīl I occupied the whole of Diyār Bakr in his campaign against the last Aķ Ķoyunlu ruler Murād in 913/1507-8. He then allotted Diyār Bakr to Khān Muḥammad Ustādjlū (Iskandar Beg Munshī, *ʿĀlam-ārā*, i, 32-3). After Ismāʿīl's defeat at Čāldirān [*q.v.*] in 920/1514, Mayyāfāriķīn was seized by the Kurdish chief Sayyid Aḥmad Beg Rūzakī. The city fell under Ottoman control in 921/1515 after the battle of Kosh Ḥiṣār, when the Ṣafawids were forced to cede Diyār Bakr to the Ottomans. In his history of the Kurds, the 10th/16th century writer Sharaf al-Dīn Khān Bidlīsī lists the governors of Mayyāfāriķīn in his own time (*Sharaf-nāma*, 270-2).

Information on Mayyāfāriķīn in the Ottoman

period is scanty. The Portuguese traveller Tenreyro went there in 936-7/1529 and found it "almost deserted" (*Itinerario*, 406). Ewliyā Čelebī (d. *ca.* 1095/1684) visited the town (*Seyāḥat-nāma*, iv, 76-8) and gave a long laudatory description of the Satidāmā bridge. Von Moltke, who passed through the city in the 19th century, while noting the well-preserved state of its walls and towers, commented on the ruined condition of the rest of the city which he said had been caused by Ottoman-Kurdish struggles in the area (Lehmann-Haupt, 394, 419). Indeed, the city was to remain *de facto* in Kurdish hands until the beginning of this century.

Christianity in Mayyāfāriķīn during the Islamic period. The Arabic sources record little of the transition from Christianity to Islam within Mayyāfāriķīn, a major centre of Oriental Christianity. Isolated references indicate, however, that Christianity continued to prosper after the Muslim conquest until recent times. This evidence is of course corroborated and expanded by surviving Christian architecture in the area. Al-Muķaddasī (146) records without comment that in the monastery of Thomas (*dayr Tūmā*) one *farsakh* from Mayyāfāriķīn there was a mummified corpse; it was allegedly that of one of the disciples [of Jesus]. Ibn al-Azraķ mentions the existence of a Melkite church in the Marwānid period and that Christians held office in the Marwānid government (ed. ʿAwaḍ, 149, 164). The Jacobites had a bishopric in Mayyāfāriķīn by the 5th/11th century (Vryonis, 53), although this is not mentioned in the detailed chronicle of Ibn al-Azraķ. Ibn Shaddād does, however, mention an incident in which a Saldjūķ governor, Ķiwām or Ķawām al-Mulk Abū ʿAlī al-Balkhī, became exasperated by the *nāķūs* from a monastery in Mayyāfāriķīn and, refusing a large sum of money offered him by the Christians if he would leave the building intact, destroyed it (fol. 70b). The same author records that in his own time (the 7th/13th century) there were monasteries on a hill to the north of Mayyāfāriķīn (*ibid.*). In 936-7/1529 Tenreyro describes "beautiful monasteries and churches without roofs, containing sumptuous monuments with inscriptions in Greek letters. On the walls were pictures of apostles and other saints, painted in very fine colours and gold". He remarks that the town had only a small number of inhabitants who were Jacobite Christians and spoke Arabic (*Itinerario*, 376).

Mayyāfāriķīn in recent times. In 1891 the population of the town was 7,000, divided about equally between Muslims and Christians (Cuinet, ii, 470-2). During its occupation by the Sulaymānī Kurds, the name Mayyāfāriķīn had been eclipsed by Silvan (cf. *EI*[1], art. *Maiyāfāriķīn*, and Minorsky's etymology there of Silwān). According to the 1945 census, the population was 2,155. The most recent information indicates that according to the 1980 census, the population of the administrative unit (*idari birim*) of Silvan was 43,624 (*Türkiye istatistik yıllığı*, 39).

Bibliography (for earlier bibliography, see *EI*[1] art. *Maiyāfāriķīn*): 1. Primary sources. Abū Bakr Tihrānī-Iṣfahānī, *Kitāb-i Diyārbakriyya*, ed. N. Lugal and F. Sümer, Ankara 1962-4; Balādhurī, *Futūḥ*; Ewliyā Čelebī, *Seyāḥat-nāma*, Istanbul 1314-8; Ibn al-ʿAdīm, *Zubdat al-ḥalab min taʾrīkh Ḥalab*, ed. S. Dahan, Damascus 1954; Ibn ʿArabshāh, *ʿAdjāʾib al-maķdūr fī nawāʾib Tīmūr*, tr. J. H. Sanders, London 1936; Ibn al-Athīr, *Kāmil*; idem, *Taʾrīkh al-dawla al-atābakiyya*, ed. A. Ṭulayma, Cairo 1963; Ibn al-Azraķ al-Fāriķī, *Taʾrīkh Mayyāfāriķīn wa-Āmid*, ed. B. A. L. ʿAwaḍ, Cairo 1959 (Marwānid section); B. L. ms. Or. 5803 (covers the early Islamic period up to 572/1176-7); Ibn al-Faķīh; Ibn Ḥawķal, ed. Kramers; Ibn Khallikān, tr. de Slane; Ibn Miskawayh, *Tadjārib al-umam*, ed. and tr. Margoliouth and Amedroz, Oxford 1920-1; Ibn Rusta; Ibn Shaddād, *al-Aʿlāķ al-khaṭīra fī dhikr umarāʾ al-Shām wa 'l-Djazīra*, Oxford, Bodleian ms. Marsh 333; Iskandar Beg Munshī, *Taʾrīkh-i ʿālam-ārā-yi ʿAbbāsī*, tr. R. M. Savory, Boulder, Colorado 1978; Iṣṭakhrī; Ķudāma; Muķaddasī; Nāṣir-i Khusraw, *Safar-nāma*, ed. and tr. Ch. Schefer, Paris 1881; Rashīd al-Dīn. *Djāmiʿ al-tawārīkh*, iii, ed. A. A. ʿAlīzāda, Bākū 1957; Sharaf al-Dīn Khān Bidlīsī, *Sharaf-nāma*, Arabic tr. M. J. B. Ruzhbiyānī, Baghdād 1953; Yaḥyā b. Saʿīd al-Anṭāķī, *Annales*, in *Patrologia Orientalis*, xviii, Paris 1924; Yāķūt, *Muʿdjam al-buldān*. 2. Secondary sources. A. Altun, *Anadolu'da Artuklu devri Türk mimarisi'nin gelişmesi*, Istanbul 1978; H. F. Amedroz, *Three Arabic manuscripts on the history of the city of Mayyāfāriķīn*, in *JRAS* (1901), 785-812; Gertrude L. Bell, *The churches and monasteries of the Tur ʿAbdīn and neighbouring districts*, articles reprinted with an introduction by M. Mango, London 1982; C. Cahen, *La Djazira au milieu du treizième siècle d'après ʿIzz ad-Din Ibn Chaddad*, in *REI*, viii (1934), 109-28; idem, *Le Diyār Bakr au temps des premiers Urtuķides*, in *JA*, ccxxvii (1935), 219-76; M. Canard, *Histoire de la dynastie des H'amdânides*, i, Paris 1953; idem, *La date des expéditions mésopotamiennes de Jean Tzimisces*, in *Mélanges Henri Grégoire*, ii, *Annuaire de l'Institut de Philologie et d'Histoire orientales et slaves*, x (1950), 99 ff.; V. Cuinet, *La Turquie d'Asie*, Paris 1891-4; E. Diez, *Churasanische Baudenkmäler*, Berlin 1918; A. M. Eddé-Terrasse, *ʿIzz al-Dīn Ibn Shaddād. Description de la Syrie du Nord*, Damascus 1984; S. Flury, *Islamische Schriftbänder*, Basel 1920; A. Gabriel, *Voyages archéologiques dans la Turquie orientale*, Paris 1940; O. Grabar, *On two coins of Muẓaffar Ghāzī, ruler of Maiyāfāriqīn*, in *Amer. Num. Soc.*, *Museum Notes* 5 (1952), 167-78; R. Hartmann, *Zu Ewlija Tschelebi's Reisen im oberen Euphrat- und Tigrisgebiet*, in *Isl.*, ix (1919), 184-244; C. Hillenbrand, *The history of the Jazīra 1100-1150; the contribution of Ibn al-Azraq al-Fāriqī*, Ph. D. thesis, Univ. of Edinburgh 1979; unpubl.; S. Lane-Poole, *Catalogue of oriental coins in the British Museum*, London 1879-89; C. F. Lehmann-Haupt, *Armenien einst und jetzt*, Berlin 1910; N. Lowick, *The religious, the royal and the popular in the figural coinage of the Jazīra*, in *The art of Syria and the Jazīra 1100-1250*, ed. J. Raby, Oxford 1985, 159-74; J. Markwart, *Südarmenien und die Tigrisquellen nach griechischen und arabischen Geographen*, Vienna 1930; T. Sinclair, *Early Artuqid mosque architecture*, in *The art of Syria and the Jazīra 1100-1250*, 49-68; A. Tenreyro, *Itinerario de Antonio Tenreyro*, Coimbra 1725; *Türkiye istatistik yıllığı 1985*, Ankara 1985; S. Vryonis Jr., *The decline of Medieval Hellenism in Asia Minor and the process of Islamization from the eleventh through the fifteenth century*, Berkeley, Los Angeles and London 1971; H. von Moltke, *Briefe über Zustände und Begebenheiten in der Türkei aus den Jahren 1835 bis 1839*, Berlin 1917; J. E. Woods, *The Aqquyunlu: clan, confederation, empire*, Minneapolis and Chicago 1976.

(Carole Hillenbrand)

MAYYĀRA, Abū ʿAbd Allāh Maḥammad b. Aḥmad, Moroccan scholar and teacher, born 15 Ramaḍān 999/7 July 1591 at Fās, where he studied and taught law and *ḥadīth* until his death in the same town on 3 Djumādā II 1071/24 January 1662.

He was the author of several commentaries,

notably on the *Tuḥfa* of Ibn ʿĀṣim [*q.v.*], of which a manuscript exists in the Bibl. Générale, Rabat (D 873), and on the theological poem called *al-Murs̲h̲id al-muʿīn* of his master Ibn ʿĀs̲h̲ir (d. 1040/1631) completed in 1044/1634-5 and called *al-Durr al-t̲h̲amīn wa 'l-mawrid al-maʿīn fī s̲h̲arḥ al-Murs̲h̲id al-muʿīn ʿalā 'l-ḍarūrī min ʿulūm al-dīn* (lith. Fās, printed Tunis 1293, Cairo 1305, 1306). In 1048, he made an abridgement of it, *Ik̲h̲tiṣār al-Durr al-t̲h̲amīn*, which was lithographed at Fās in 1292 and printed at Cairo in 1301, 1303, 1305 and 1348; it should be noted that in his commentary, he took account of criticisms raised concerning his lack of objectivity and its lacunae (ii, 339-41; cf. Hajji, *Activité intellectuelle*, 202-3). Amongst other works of his extant, as well as the *Naẓm al-laʾālī wa 'l-durar* (mss. Rabat 855 and 3702 Z) which contains a *fahrasa* [*q.v.*] and consequently, autobiographical details, one might mention the *Tuḥfat al-aṣḥāb wa 'l-rufḳa bi-baʿḍ masāʾil al-ṣafḳa* (ms. Rabat 989 D; cf. O. Pesle, *Le contrat de safqa au Maroc*, Rabat 1932, *passim*), and particularly, the *Naṣīḥat al-mug̲h̲tarrīn wa-kifāyat al-muḍtarrīn fī 'l-tafrīḳ bayn al-Muslimīn* (ms. Bibl. Royale, Rabat 7248), composed in 1051/1641 in defence of those Muslims of Jewish ancestry who were once more, after the death of sultan al-Manṣūr al-D̲h̲ahabī (1603) the victims of a certain ostracism by traders and scholars in Fās. After the publication of this book, a cabal was formed against Mayyāra, who was the object of violent attacks, but who nevertheless benefited from the protection of Muḥammad al-Ṭayyib al-Dilāʾī, who wrote a *Taḳrīẓ Naṣīḥat al-mug̲h̲tarrīn* (mss. Bibl. Gén., Rabat 923 K, 125-8), and from a defence by al-ʿAwfī, also the author of a *Taḳrīẓ* (in the text of the *Naṣīḥa*, 126-7). Like Mayyāra's other works, the *Naṣīḥa* contains interesting pieces of historical information which would justify its publication. On account of his Jewish ancestry, this scholar, like al-Mand̲j̲ūr [*q.v.*], was not allowed to fill any official post of a religious nature, although often described as *imām*, and it is said that he had to make a living by hiring out dresses and ornaments for ladies on the occasion of marriage (see al-Ifrānī, *Ṣafwat man intas̲h̲ar*, lith. Fās n.d., 140; Hajji, *op.cit.*, 147).

The epithet of "the Elder" (*al-Akbar*) is sometimes appended to his name in order to distinguish him from his grandson, Maḥammad b. Muḥammad (or Aḥmad) al-Ḥafīd or al-Aṣg̲h̲ar, also considered as *imām* of Fās (d. 15 Muḥarram 1144/20 July 1731; see al-Ḳādirī, *Nas̲h̲r al-mat̲h̲ānī*, ii, 235; al-Kattānī, *Ṣalwat al-anfās*, i, 167; Lévi-Provençal, *Chorfa*, 318-19; M. Lakhdar, *Vie littéraire*, index).

Bibliography: Ḳādirī, *Nas̲h̲r al-mat̲h̲ānī*, i, 235; Kattānī, *Ṣalwat al-anfās*, i, 165; Ḥudayd̲j̲ī, *Ṭabaḳāt*, Casablanca 1357/1938, ii, 64-5; Muḥammad Mak̲h̲lūf, *S̲h̲ad̲j̲arat al-nūr*, Cairo 1349/1930, 309; E. Lévi-Provençal, *Chorfa*, 258-9; Brockelmann, II, 461, S II, 299; M. Hajji, *L'activité intellectuelle à l'époque saʿdide*, Rabat 1976-7, index; Ibn Sūda, *Dalīl*, i, 111. See also *Ḥawliyyāt al-D̲j̲āmiʿa al-Tūnusiyya*, vii (1970), ʿAbd al-Wahhāb's mss. nos 241, 336, etc. (comm. on Mayyāra). (CH. PELLAT)

MAYYŪN, volcanic island of *ca.* 14 km² and 400 inhabitants in the Straits of the Bāb al-Mandab [*q.v.*], off the coast of the People's Democratic Republic of Yemen (the former Aden Protectorate). Known in classical times as Διοδαρος it became known in the West as Perim, probably from the other Arabic term used for the island *barīm* "rope", possibly connected with the story of the chain at al-S̲h̲ayk̲h̲ Saʿīd [see BĀB AL-MANDAB]. Perhaps visited by the French Crusader Reynaud de Chatillon, whose vessels were destroyed by Ṣalāḥ al-Dīn, the island was explored by Albuquerque in 1513, who called it Meyo (after Mayyūn), but found it waterless and unsuitable for a fortress. Occupied for a short time by the French in 1738, the British landed there in 1799, but left because of the lack of water. They returned in 1857 from Bombay and established a coaling station, called Brown Bay, which was abandoned however in 1936. In 1915, Turkish troops made an unsuccessful attempt to land on the island. Incorporated into the British Crown Colony of Aden in 1937, Mayyūn became part of the People's Democratic Republic of Yemen in 1967. With the coastal strip, running up the Red Sea as far as the frontier with Yemen (Ṣanʿāʾ), the islands of Kamarān and Socotra (Suḳuṭrā) [*q.vv.*], Mayyūn forms the so-called first governorate.

Bibliography: *The Periplus of the Erythraean Sea*, tr. W. H. Schoff, ²New Delhi 1974, 23, 31, 114; A. Sprenger, *Die alte Geographie Arabiens*, p. vii, 73, 76; J. Rijckmans, *La persécution des chrétiens himyarites au sixième siècle*, Leiden-Istanbul 1956, 14; Ibn al-Mud̲j̲āwir, *Taʾrīk̲h̲ al-Mustabṣir, Descriptio Arabiae meridionalis*, ed. O. Löfgren, Leiden 1951, i, 96; B. Doe, *Südarabien. Antike Reiche am Indischen Ozean.* Bergisch Gladbach 1970, 126; idem, *Southern Arabia*, London, 1970; British Admiralty, *Western Arabia and the Red Sea*, London 1946 (with view from the air and map); U.S. Hydrographic Office, *Sailing Directions for the Red Sea and Gulf of Aden*³, Washington 1943. (E. VAN DONZEL)

MAʿZ [see G̲H̲ANAM].

MAZAGAN [see AL-D̲J̲ADĪDA].

MAẒĀLIM (A.), a word whose sing. *maẓlima* denotes an unjust or oppressive action. Closely related to *ẓulm*, it is an antonym to *ʿadl* [*q.v.*] and thus signifies basically something "not in its right place" (*LA*). At an early stage in the development of Islamic institutions of government, *maẓālim* came to denote the structure through which the temporal authorities took direct responsibility for dispensing justice.

Precedents for the institution of *maẓālim* can be found in Byzantium and, more particularly, in the Sāsānid bureaucratic office which functioned as a jurisdiction parallel to the ordinary judiciary headed by the *mōbed̲h̲-mōbed̲h̲ān* [*q.v.*] (A. Christensen, *L'Iran sous les Sassanides*², Copenhagen 1944, 301 f.). It is also suggested that the ideal of open access to tribal leaders in pre-Islamic Arabia was carried over into the early Islamic experience.

The establishment in Medina of the rudiments of an Islamic polity did little to change the situation. Muḥammad combined in himself the rôles both of the traditional tribal chief and of the *ḥakam* [*q.v.*]. The early caliphs and provincial governors inherited this position, where judicial functions were not distinguished from other functions of government. Only in relation to the *d̲h̲immī*s [*q.v.*] did caliph or governor function as an alternative judicial authority (E. Tyan, *Histoire*, 87-98).

The growth in size and complexity of the Muslim community soon obliged caliphs and governors to appoint *ḳāḍī*s [*q.v.*] to whom their judicial functions were delegated. The development of the *s̲h̲arīʿa* [*q.v.*] as a distinct system of law during the 2nd/8th and 3rd/9th centuries, its identification with the office of *ḳāḍī*, and its increasing importance as a test of Islamic legitimacy, combined to form a context in which it becomes possible to identify a discrete *maẓālim* system. Al-Māwardī's suggestion (*Aḥkām*, 65) that the Umayyad caliph ʿAbd al-Malik b. Marwān [*q.v.*] was the first to arrange for the regular hearing of *maẓālim* petititions seems to be premature.

The ʿAbbāsid period. More certainty surrounds reports that the caliphs al-Mahdī and al-Hādī [*q.vv.*] ensured the regular holding of *maẓālim* sessions. The practice for the first several decades was usually for the *wazīr* [*q.v.*] to take charge (Sourdel, *Vizirat*, 640-8), and there are indications that the *maẓālim* jurisdiction was regarded both by them and by the *ḳāḍīs* and *ʿulamāʾ* as a rival to the *s̲h̲arīʿa* jurisdiction. Although Abū Yūsuf [*q.v.*] suggested to Hārūn al-Ras̲h̲īd [*q.v.*] that the caliph should personally take charge (*K. al-K̲h̲arād̲j̲*, Cairo 1352, 111 f.), this seldom happened. In the longer term, *maẓālim* remained a disputed institution. Following the fall of the Barmakids [see BARĀMIKA], more influence was given to the *ḳāḍīs*, culminating when a series of Muʿtazilī chief *ḳāḍīs* also held responsibility for *maẓālim*.

The end of Muʿtazilī influence under al-Mutawakkil [*q.v.*] returned *maẓālim* to the control of the *wazīrs*, where it remained, until the Būyid *amīr al-umarāʾ* [*q.v.*] downgraded the *wazīr* and handed control of *maẓālim* to the It̲h̲nā ʿAs̲h̲arī S̲h̲īʿī *naḳīb al-as̲h̲rāf* [*q.v.*] (H. Busse, *Chalif und Grosskönig*, Wiesbaden 1969, 286-9).

From a comparatively early date, it became usual for the *wazīr* or *ḳāḍī* in charge to appoint a deputy to take responsibility for the routine management of the institution. On occasions, this official, variously known as *ṣāḥib* or *nāẓir al-maẓālim*, might also be appointed directly by the caliph.

The jurisdiction of *maẓālim* tended to be very wide. Receiving and processing petitions against official and unofficial abuse of power was an important part of its activity, but it also on occasion functioned as a court of appeal against the decisions of *ḳāḍīs*. Additionally, it is evident that, for an early stage, *maẓālim* was often the office through which military and civilian officials and dignitaries applied for the allocation of *iḳṭāʿ*s and through which such grants might also be confiscated and their holders fined.

Theory. Before the work of al-Māwardī [*q.v.*], little theoretical consideration of *maẓālim* is to be found. Statements in general terms of principle were not developed in detail. Al-Fārābī's view that the head of the just city should "favour justice and the just, hate tyranny and injustice, and give them both their just deserts" (*al-Madīna al-fāḍila*, ed. Dieterici, repr. Leiden 1964, 60), is typical.

Working in the service of the caliphs al-Ḳādir and al-Ḳāʾim, al-Māwardī's object was to restore the authority of the caliphate in preparation for the approaching Sald̲j̲ūḳs. His work *al-Aḥkām al-sulṭāniyya* therefore included an extensive chapter on the structure, procedure and jurisdiction of *maẓālim*, which is paralleled with minor differences in Abū Yaʿlā b. al-Farrāʾ's work of the same title (cf. *Bibl.*).

Supervision of *maẓālim* is the responsibility of the caliph, his viziers and governors, or their appointed deputies, who must have personal qualities combining honesty, power and judiciousness. The *maẓālim* session is duly constituted when the official in charge is assisted by guards, *ḳāḍīs*, *faḳīhs*, secretaries and notaries (*s̲h̲uhūd*). Ten classes of cases are detailed as coming within the jurisdiction of *maẓālim*, falling into two main categories, namely abuse of official powers and enforcement of *ḳāḍīs*' decisions.

The major difference from the *ḳaḍāʾ*, according to al-Māwardī, lies in the area of procedure. The *ṣāḥib al-maẓālim* has a wide scope for active direction and participation in the proceedings, including powers of coercion, admitting evidence below the standards required by *ḳāḍīs*' courts, subpoena of witnesses and postponement of hearings to allow judicial investigation. Al-Māwardī presents his discussion in terms of a relaxation of the rules of the *s̲h̲arīʿa*, with the purpose of controlling powerful officials who otherwise might subvert the normal judicial process. Later writers link *maẓālim* with the concept of *siyāsa s̲h̲arʿiyya*. In fact, the theory of *maẓālim*—as also later Ḥanbalī theory of *siyāsa s̲h̲arʿiyya*—actually represents an attempt to bring the current practice closer into line with the requirement of the *s̲h̲arīʿa*.

Later theory reverts to the common pattern of more general statements of principle, in terms of "helping the weak against the strong", a phrase often appearing in the obituaries of sultans and governors. Expositions in detail are rare and, when they do occur, as in al-Maḳrīzī (*K̲h̲iṭaṭ*, Cairo 1270, ii, 207 f.) and al-Nuwayrī (*Nihāyat al-arab*, Cairo 1923-55, vi, 265-90), are based on al-Māwardī.

The mediaeval period. In the event, the hopes of al-Māwardī and his patrons did not materialise, and *maẓālim* continued to develop with little reference to theory. The main feature during this later period is an increased bureaucratisation, a process which took place simultaneously under the Sald̲j̲ūḳs, under the K̲h̲ʷārazm-S̲h̲āhs in Persia and Central Asia, and under the Fāṭimids in Egypt. The various parts of this development came together under the Ayyūbids and continued with little change through much of the Mamlūk period.

The first step in opening a case was to present a petition (*ruḳʿa* or *ḳiṣṣa*) drawn up according to detailed formulae (described in al-Ḳalḳas̲h̲andī, *Ṣubḥ al-aʿs̲h̲ā*, Cairo 1913-19, vi, 202 f.). While the ideal remained the personal presentation of the *ḳiṣṣa* in public session, the vast majority were dealt with administratively. Al-Ḳalḳas̲h̲andī (vi, 206-10) describes six different channels through which the *ḳiṣṣa* could be dealt with, and these procedures are confirmed by other sources. Several different officials are to be found taking decisions, including the sultan, his deputies and provincial governors (*nuwwāb*), and high-ranking military officials (most commonly the *atābak*, *dawādār* and *ḥād̲j̲ib*). Common to all channels of petition was the central role of the chancery (*dīwān al-ins̲h̲āʾ*), headed by the *wazīr* or *ṣāḥib dīwān al-ins̲h̲āʾ*, and from the late 7th/13th century by the *kātib al-sirr*. Oversight of the routine clerical work was handled by a secretary explicitly appointed to deal with *maẓālim* work, called *ṣāḥib* (or *muwaḳḳiʿ*) *al-ḳalam al-daḳīḳ* under the Fāṭimids and *kātib* (or *muwaḳḳiʿ*) *al-dast* under the Mamlūks. From the early Fāṭimid period, elaborate rules also determined the form of the decree (*tawḳīʿ* or *marsūm*) containing the final decision in a case (*Ṣubḥ*, xi, 127-33). Such decrees would normally be signed by the sultan or a high officer of state, regardless of where in the administrative process the decision had been taken.

The site of the public session (*mad̲j̲lis*) was normally the place where the presiding official conducted his general duties. A departure from this took place when Nūr al-Dīn Zankī established a house of justice (*dār al-ʿadl*) in Damascus soon after 549/1154, with the specific purpose of providing a setting for *maẓālim*. Situated outside the citadel by the Bāb al-Naṣr [see DIMAS̲H̲Ḳ], it became more commonly known as *dār al-saʿāda* when it was turned into the seat of provincial government in 634/1236. By this time, other provincial capitals in the Ayyūbid state had also acquired a *dār al-ʿadl*. In Cairo, *maẓālim* sessions were usually held in a S̲h̲āfiʿī *madrasa*. Held twice a week on Mondays and Thursdays, these sessions were associated with an increasing amoung of official ceremonial, as the sultan and his officials went to the *dār al-ʿadl* in public procession (*mawkib*) [see MAWĀKIB]. To the *mawkib* and *madjlis* was soon added an official banquet (*simāṭ*), and the whole ceremony was known as *khidma*.

The *khidma* reached its most elaborate form under the early Mamlūks. Baybars I [*q.v.*] transferred the hearing of *maẓālim* petitions to a new *dār al-ʿadl* in Cairo in 662/1264, just below the Citadel, and this also became the site for the *khidma*. The *mawkib* now included a growing number of military officers of state, and the *madjlis* widened its functions to include most official public ceremonial, such as the reception of foreign emissaries, the publication of government decisions, the granting of royal favours, etc. Hearing *maẓālim* cases soon became a minor formality, symbolised by the continuing presence of *ḳāḍīs* and *kātib al-sirr* and the new office of *muftī dār al-ʿadl* in the official seating order (cf. *Ṣubḥ*, iv, 44 f.). Sultan Ḳalāwūn's move of the *khidma* to his new *īwān kabīr* and the demolition of Baybars's *dār al-ʿadl* a few decades later confirmed the position of *maẓālim* as a function of the bureaucracy.

Throughout the early Mamlūk period, the identity of *maẓālim* as a bureaucratic process meant that there was little definition of its jurisdiction. Al-Maḳrīzī's claim (*Khiṭaṭ*, ii, 220 f.) that it was the forum for the implementation of the Mongol Yāsa can be discounted (cf. D. Ayalon, in *SI*, xxxiii [1971], 97-140). The sources report petitions dealing with every conceivable aspect of government activity, including requests for offices or *iḳṭāʿ*s, the suppression of particular *ʿulamāʾ* and their teachings, the implementation of law and order, as well as appeals for justice and the application of *ḳāḍīs*' decisions. This situation prevailed in all the provinces of the Mamlūk state.

The confusion of *maẓālim* and the general apparatus of government was common in other parts of the pre-Ottoman Arab world, but there were exceptions, such as Ḥafṣid Tunisia (R. Brunschvig, in *SI*, xxiii [1965], 27 ff.), where *maẓālim* remained a more distinct jurisdiction. Towards the end of the 8th/14th century, measures were also taken by the Mamlūks to clarify the situation. In 789/1387, Sultan Barḳūḳ detached *maẓālim* from the *khidma* and moved it to the Royal Equerry (*iṣṭabl al-sulṭān*) [see AL-ḲĀHIRA]. The term *dār al-ʿadl*, however, remained synonymous with the *khidma* in the *īwān*. The jurisdiction of *maẓālim* was likewise clarified, and in the 9th/15th century a distinction is made between petitions for justice in the face of injustice and oppression and petitions requesting *iḳṭāʿ*s or official posts (*al-Ṣāliḥī*, Copenhagen Royal Library ms. 147, fols. 32b-33a).

Bibliography (additional to references given above): Māwardī, *al-Aḥkām al-sulṭāniyya*, Cairo 1298, 64-82, and Abū Yaʿlā b. al-Farrāʾ, *al-Aḥkām al-sulṭāniyya*, Cairo 1966, 58-74. H. F. Amedroz, in *JRAS* (1911), 635-74, provides an extensive paraphrase and commentary to al-Māwardī's text. E. Tyan, *Histoire de l'organisation judiciaire en pays d'Islam*², Leiden 1960, 433-520, surveys the history of *maẓālim* with an emphasis on juridical theory. S. M. Stern deals in great detail with the bureaucratic processes in *Oriens*, xv (1962), 172-209, and in *BSOAS*, xxvii (1964), 1-32, xxix (1966), 233-76. The Mamlūk period and the role of *dār al-ʿadl* are discussed by J. S. Nielsen, *Secular justice in an Islamic state: Maẓālim under the Baḥrī Mamlūks*, Istanbul 1985. H. Ernst, *Die mamlukischen Sultansurkunden*, Wiesbaden 1960, has published some of the petitions and drecrees preserved at St. Catherine's, Mount Sinai, and a basic source for Mamlūk bureaucratic procedure is Aḥmad b. Faḍl Allāh al-ʿUmarī, *Masālik al-abṣār*, Ayasofya ms. 3416, fols. 138a-142a. On *maẓālim* in Persia, see MAḤKAMA. 3.

(J. S. NIELSEN)

MĀZANDARĀN, a province to the south of the Caspian Sea bounded on the west by Gīlān [*q.v.*] and on the east by what was in Ḳadjār times the province of Astarābād [*q.v.*, formerly Gurgān); Māzandarān and Gurgān now form the modern *ustān* or province of Māzandarān.

1. The name. If Gurgān to the Iranians was the "land of the wolves" (*vəhrkāna*, the region to its west was peopled by "Māzaynian dēws" (Bartholomae, *Altir. Wörterbuch*, col. 1169, under *māzainya daēva*). Darmesteter, *Le Zend-Avesta*, ii, 373, n. 32, thought that Māzandarān was a "comparative of direction" (**Mazana-tara*; cf. Shūsh and Shushtar) but Nöldeke's hypothesis is the more probable (*Grundr. d. iran. Phil.*, ii, 178), who thought that Māzan-dar = "the gate of Māzan" was a particular place, distinct from the part of the country known as Tapuristān. (A village of Mesderan (?) is marked on Stahl's map 12 km. south of Fīrūzkūh!). In any case, the name Māzandarān seems to have no connection with Τοῦ Μασωράνου ὄρος which, according to Ptolemy, vi, ch. v., was situated between Parthia and Areia (Hārī-rūd) and was connected by Olshausen (*Mazdoran und Mazandaran*, in *Monatsberichte Ak. Berlin* [1877], 777-83) with Mazdūrān, a station 12 *farsakh*s west of Sarakhs; cf. Ibn Khurradādhbih, 24; al-Muḳaddasī, 351 (cf. however the late source of 881/1476 quoted by Dorn, in *Mélanges asiat.*, vii, 42).

The Avestan and Pahlavi quotations given by Darmesteter, *loc. cit.*, show to what degree the people of Mazandarān were regarded by the Persians as a foreign group and little assimilated. According to the *Bundahishn*, xv, 28, tr. West, 58, the "Māzandarān" were descended from a different pair of ancestors to those of the Iranians and Arabs. The *Shāh-nāma* reflects similar ideas (cf. the episode of Kay Kāwūs's war in Māzandarān, and esp. Vullers ed., i, 332, v, 290: the war is waged against Ahriman; 364, vv. 792-3: Mazandarān is contrasted with Iran; 574, v. 925: the bestial appearance of the king of Māzandarān).

Among historical peoples in Māzandarān are the Tapyres (Τάπυροι), who must have occupied the mountains (north of Simnān), and the Amardes (Ἄμαρδοι), who according to Andreas and Marquart, have given their name to the town of Āmul (although the change of *rd* to *l* is rather strange in the north of Persia). These two peoples were defeated by Alexander the Great. The Parthian king Phraates I (in 176 B.C.) transplanted the Mardes (Amardes) to the region of χάραξ (Khʷār to the east of Warāmin) and their place was taken by the Tapyres, whose name came to be applied to the whole province.

The Arabs only knew the region as Ṭabaristān (<Tapurstān, on the Pahlavi coins). The name Māzandarān only reappears in the Saldjūḳ period. Ibn al-Athīr, x, 34, in speaking of the distribution of fiefs by Alp Arslān in 458/1065, says that Māzandarān was given to the *amīr* Inandj Bīghū. Ibn Isfandiyār, 14, and Yāḳūt, iii, 502, 9, think that Māzandarān as a name for Ṭabaristān is only of fairly modern origin (in Arabic?), but according to Zakariyyāʾ Ḳazwīnī, 270, "the Persians call Ṭabaristān Māzandarān". Ḥamd Allāh Mustawfī distinguishes between Māzandarān and Ṭabaristān. In his time (1340), the 7 *tūmān*s of the "*wilāyat* of Māzandarān" were Djurdjān, Mūrūstāḳ (?), Astarābād, Āmul and Rustamdār, Dihistān, Rūghad and Siyāh-rustaḳ (?); on the other hand, the *diyār-i Ḳūmis wa-Ṭabaristān* included Simnān, Dāmghān, Fīrūzkūh, a town of

Damāwand, Firrīm, etc. We find a similar distinction in Khwāndamīr, ed. Dorn, 83.

2. Geography: The actual extent of Māzandarān (Rabino) is 300 miles from east to west and 46 to 70 miles from north to south. Except for the strip along the coast—broader in the east than the west—Māzandarān is a very mountainous country. The main range of the Elburz forms barriers parallel to the south of the Caspian, while the ridges running down to the sea cut the country up into a multitude of valleys open on the north only. The principal of the latter ridges is the Mazārčūb, which separates Ṭabaristān from Tunakābun. The latter is bordered on the south by the chain of the Elburz in the strict sense, which separates it from the valley of the Shāhrūd (formed by the waters of the Alamūt and Talaḳān and flowing westward into the Safīd-rūd).

To the east of Mazār-čub, a number of ranges run out of the central massif of the Elburz: 1. to the east, the chain of Nūr, which cuts through the Hārāz-pay; and 2. to the south-east, the southern barrier which forms the watershed between the Caspian and the central plateau. Between the two rises in isolation the great volcanic cone of Damāwand [*q.v.*] (5,604 m./18,386 ft.).

To the east of Damāwand, the southern barrier rejoins the continuation of the Nūr and the new line of the watershed of eastern Māzandarān is marked by the ranges of Bänd-i-pay, Sawād-kūh, Shāh-mīrzād (to the south of Simnān), of Hazārdjarīb (to the south of Dāmghān), of Shāh-kūh (to the south of Shāhrūd), etc.

The rivers of Māzandarān are of two kinds. A hundred short streams run straight down into the sea from the outer mountains of Māzandarān. Much more important are the rivers which rise in the interior and after draining many valleys form a single great river when they break through the last barrier. Such are (from west to east); the Sard-ābrūd; the Čālūs; the Harāz-pay, which drains the region of mount Damāwand and then runs past Āmul; the Bābul (the river of Bārfurūsh); the Tālār (river of ʿAlīābād); the Tīdjin (river of Sārī) and the Nīkā (or Äspayzä) which flows from east to west; its valley forms a corner between the southern chain (cf. above) and the mountains which surround the Gulf of Astarābād on the north.

Bibliography of travels: Pietro della Valle (1618), *Viaggi*, part ii, letter iv, Brighton 1843, 578-702; Isfāhān-Siyāhkūh (to the east of modern Lake of Ḳum)—Fīrūzkūh-Shīrgāh-Sārī-Faraḥābād-Ashraf-Sārī-Fīrūzkūh-Gilyārd-Tehrān; Sir Thomas Herbert, *Some years' travels*, London 1627, and Fr. ed., *Relation du voyage*, Paris 1663, 265-311: Isfāhān-Siyāhkūh-Fīrūzkūh-ʿAlīābād-Ashraf-Āmul-Tehrān; Hanway, *A historical account*, London 1754, ch. xxvii, i, 139-49: Astarābād-Bārfurūsh, ch. xlii, i, 192-8: Langarūd-Āmul-Bārfurūsh-Ashraf; S. G. Gmelin, *Reise d. Russland*, iii. (*Reise d.d. Nördliche Persien*, 1770-2), St. Petersburg 1774, 446-72 (Āmul-Bārfurūsh-ʿAlīābād-Sārī-Ashraf); G. Forster, *A journey from Bengal to England* (1784), London 1798, ii, 179-210 (Bistām-Dehi-mullā-Čālūs-Sārī-Barfurūsh); J. Morier, *Second journey*, London 1818, ch. xxiii. (Tehrān - Būmihin - Damāwand - Bāgh-i Shāh - Fīrūzkūh - Asarān - Fūlād-maḥalla - Čashme - ʿAlī-Sāwar-Astarābād); Macdonald Kinneir, *Geogr. Memoir.*, London 1813, 161-7; W. Ouseley, *Travels*, London 1819, iii. (Fīrūzkūh - Surkh-rabāt - Zīrāb-Shīrgāh - ʿAlīābād - Sārī - Ashraf - Faraḥābād - Āmul - Miyānkala-Damāwand); Trézel, *Notice sur le Ghilan et Māzenderan*, in Jaubert, *Voyage en Arménie et en Perse*, ii, 417-63; J. B. Fraser, *Travels and adventures... on the southern banks of the Caspian Sea*, London 1826, chs. ii-viii, 12-125; Ashraf-Sārī-Bārfurūsh-Āmul - Izideh - ʿAlīābād - Towar - Ābgarm - Lāhīdjān; Eichwald, *Reise auf d. Kasp. Meere* (1825-6), Stuttgart 1834, i, ch. xi. (Māzandarān), 330-58 (Mashhadisar Bārfurūsh); Conolly, *Journey to the North of India overland*, London 1834, i, 20-7 (Tehrān-Fīrūzkūh-Sārī-Ashraf); A. Burns, *Travels into Bokhara*, 1835, iii, 103-22 (Astarābād-Ashraf-ʿAlīābād-Fīrūzkūh-Tehrān); Stuart, *Journal of a residence in Northern Persia* (1835), London 1854, 247-89 (town of Damāwand - Fīrūzkūh - Zīrāb - Sārī - Āmul-Tehrān); d'Arcy Todd, *Memoranda to accompany a sketch of part of Mazandarān*, in *JRGS*, viii (1838), 101-8, map (Tehrān - Āmul - Bārfurūsh - Shīrgāh - Surkh - rabāt - Fīrūzkūh - Tehrān - Damāwand - Fīrūzkūh-sources of the Tālār - Dīw-safīd - Shīrgāh - ʿAlīābad - Sārī - Bārfurūsh - Āmul - Tehrān; Fīrūzkūh-Fūlād-maḥalla); C. Ritter, *Erdkunde*, vi/1 = part viii/3, Berlin 1838, 471-514 (routes through the Elburz), 514-50 (coast region of Māzandarān), 550-95 (Damāwand); Fraser, *A winter's journey*, 1838, ii, 131-45 (Fīrūzkūh-Shamīrzāde-Shāhrūd); ii, 416-82 (Tehrān - Lār - Kalārastaḳ - Parasp - Āmul - Bārfurūsh - Mashhadisar - Izideh - Sakhtasar); Wilbraham, *Travels in the Trans-caucasian provinces* (1837), London 1839, 423-77 (Tehrān - Fīrūzkūh - Zirāb - Sārī - Ashraf - Āmul); Holmes, *Sketch of the shores of the Caspian*, London 1845, ch. x. (Kalārastaḳ - Nūr - Āmul - Faraḥābād - Astarābād), ch. xvii. (Sāwar-Shāhkūh-Shamshīrbur-Čashme-ʿAlī-Samnān); Voskoboinikov, *Puteshestviye po severnoi Persii (1843-1844)*, in *Gornïi Žurnal* (St. Petersburg 1846), v, 171-220, map, German tr. in *Ermans Russ. Archiv.*, v, Heft 4, 674-708 (geology: Shāh-kūh; Sārī-Fīrūzkūh; Kudjūr-Tehrān): Buhse, Bergreise von Gīlān nach Astarābād, in *Baer & Helmersens Beiträge z. Kenntniss des russ. Reiches*, 1847, xiii, 217-36 (Läspūh - Kalārdasht - Kudjūr - Ask - Fīrūzkūh - Fūlād-maḥalla); Hommaire de Hell, *Voyage en Turquie et en Perse*, Paris 1855, iii, 214-336 (Tehrān-Lār - Āmul - Ashraf - Astarābād - Rādkān - Kurd-maḥalla - ʿAlī - čashma - Simnān); iv, 285-306 (itineraries; atlas, plates 74-82, by Laurens); de Bode, *Očerki turkmen. zemli i yugovostoč. pribrež. Kaspiiskago moria*, in *Otečest. Zapiski*, 1856, no. 7, pp. 123-50 (Tehrān - Sarbandān - Fīrūzkūh - Čahārdeh - Hazārdjarīb - Astarābād), no. 8, pp. 459-72 (Sāwar - Rādkān); F. Mackenzie, *Report on the Persian Caspian Provinces*, Rasht 1859-60 (manuscript quoted by Rabino); Gasteiger-Rawenstein-Kobach, *Rundreise durch die nördl. Prov. Persiens*, in *Z.f. allgem. Erd.*, xii (1862), 341-56 (Tehrān - Fīrūzkūh - "Sabbat-kuh" [Sawād-kūh]-Sārī-Ashraf-Astarābād); B. Dorn, *Bericht über eine wissensch. Reise in den Kaukasus*, etc., in *Mél. Asiat.*, iv (1863), 429-500 (Ashur-ada - Ashraf - Bārfurūsh - Mashhadisar); Dorn, *Reise nach Masanderan im J. 1860*, section 1 (St. Petersburg-Aschref), St. Petersburg 1895 (with an atlas); Melgunov, *O yužnom beregě Kaspiiskago moria*, appendix to vol. iii. of *Zapiski Akadem. Nauk*, St. Petersburg 1863, 95-195, German tr. Zenker, *Das südliche Ufer d. Kasp. Meeres*, Leipzig 1868 (with some mistakes in the transcriptions); Eastwick, *Three years' residence*, London 1864, ch. iii, ii, 50-101 (Astarābād - Ashraf - Sārī - ʿAlīabād - Shīrgāh - Zīrāb - Surkh-rabāt-Fīrūzkūh-Sarbandān-Būmihin); Seidlitz, *Handel und Wandel an d. Kaspischen Südküste* (from *Russkii věstnik*), in *Pet. Mitt.* (1869) 98-103, 255-68 (Safīd-rūd - Mashhadisar - Bandargaz; Ashraf; Ṣafīābād); G. C. Napier, *Extracts from a diary of a tour in Khorasan*, in *JRGS*, xlvi (1876), 62-171 (good map: Gulhak - Gilyārd - Fīrūzkūh - Gūrsafīd - Khing Rūdbār-Čashma-ʿAlī-Čārdih-Shamshīrbur-Aspinezia - Shārūd); V. Baker, *Clouds in the east*, London 1876 (62-89: Ashraf-Sārī-Shīrgāh-Zīrāb-Fīrūz-kūh - Sarbandān - Būmigin - Tehrān; 87-142: Lār-Ask-Khaloe (?)-ʿAlīābād-Zīrāb-Casaleone (?)-ʿAlīābād - Attené (?) - Surkada - Čashme - ʿAlī - Dihmullā - Dāmghān); E. Stack, *Six months in Persia*, chs. vii and viii, London 1882, ii, 170-202 (Tehrān-Mount Damāwand - Mashhadisar); Beresford Lovett, *Itinerary notes of route surveys in Northern Persia*, in *Procs. RGS*, v (Feb. 1883), 57-84 (Tehrān - Čālūs - Nūr - Balada - Lār - Ask - Fīrūzkūh - Fūlād-maḥalla-Čārdeh-Ziyārat-Astarābād); G. N. Curzon, *Persia and the Persian question*, London 1892, i, 354-89, ch. xii (Māzandarān and Gīlān) with a sketch; Sven Hedin, *Genom Khorasan*, Stockholm 1892, i, 57-69 (Dāmghān - Čārdih - Djahān-numā - Astarābād); E. G. Browne, *A year amongst the Persians*, London 1893, 557-68 (Tehrān - Mashhadisar); J. de Morgan, *Missions scientifiques, Études géographiques*, i, 1894, 113-208 (numerous illustrations); A. F. Stahl, *Reisen in Nord- und Zentral-Persian*, in *Pet. Mitt.*, Ergänzungsheft no. 118 (1896), 7-18 (Tehrān-Kelārestaḳ-Nūr-Lār-Damāwand; Tehrān-Āmul; Fīrūzkūh-ʿAlīābād; Āmul-Astarābād-Tāsh-Čahārdih - Simnān) (with a detailed map); H. L. Wells, *Across the Alburz mountains*, in *The Scottish Geogr. Magazine*, xiv (1898), 1-9 (supplement to Lovett: Afča-Varasun-Kudjūr-Nawrūdbār-Mullā-ḳalʿa); Sarre, *Reise in Mazanderan*, in *Z. Gesell. Erdkunde* (1902), 99-111 (Damāwand-Āmul-Ashrāf-Bandargaz); Stahl, *Reisen in Nord- und Westpersien*, in *Pet. Mitt.* (1907), Heft vi, 121-31 (with a map: Bārfurūsh-Fīrūzkūh); O. Niedermayer, *Die Persien-Expedition*, in *Mitt. d. Geogr. Gesell. in München*, viii (1913), 177-88 (Fīrūzkūh-Turud-Pelwār-Sārī; Nīka - Sefīddje); H. L. Rabino, *A journey in Māzandarān*, in *JRGS* (Nov. 1913), 435-54 (Rasht-Sārī); Golubiatnikov, *Petrol in Northern Persia* [in Russian], in *Neftiyanoye i slantsevoye khoziaystvo*, Moscow (Sept.-Oct. 1921), 78-91; Noel, *A reconnaissance in the Caspian provinces of Persia*, in *JRGS* (June 1921), 401-18 (Tehrān - Āmul - Faraḥabād - Nūr - Kudjūr - Tunakābun); Herzfeld, *Reisebericht*, in *ZDMG* (1926), 278-9 (Bistām - Rādkān - Shamshīrbur - Dāmghān); Stahl, *Die orographischen und hydrographischen Verhältnisse des Elburgs-Gebirges in Persien*, in *Pet. Mitt.* (1927), Heft 7-8, 211-15 (with a map); Rabino, *Māzandarān and Astarābād*, GMS, London 1928 (itineraries on the coast, administrative divisions with lists of villages, Muslim inscriptions); cf. p. xx, complete list of previous works. G. M. Bell, *Geological Notes on part of Mazandaran*, in *Geol. Transactions*, series ii, vol. v, 577.

3. Ethnology. N. Khanykov, *Mémoire sur l'ethnographie de la Perse*, Paris 1866, 116-17; C. Inostrantsev, *The customs of the inhabitants of the Caspian provinces in the tenth century* [in Russian], in *Živaya Starina* (1909), part ii-iii, 125-52.

4. Language. Cf. Geiger, *Die Kaspischen Dialecte*, in *Grundriss d. iran. Phil.*, i/2, 344-80, where the literature of the subject is given (esp. Dorn's works).

5. Historical geography. This is still full of difficulties, although Vasmer's very full study has considerably reduced their number. The matter is complicated by the fact that certain well-known names are used in different periods for more or less identical districts.

The eastern frontier of Māzandarān (Ṭabaristān) in the strict sense, with Astarābād (Djurdjān) seems to have always run near Kulbād (on the river Kirrind; cf. Ptolemy's Χρίνδοι), where there used to be a wall (*djar-i Kulbād*) which barred the narrow strip of lowland between the Gulf of Astarābād and the mountains; cf. Ibn Rusta, 149, who speaks of the brick wall (*ādjurr*) and of the Gate of Ṭamīs through which travellers had to pass (cf. Ibn al-Faḳīh, 303). To the west, the town of Shālūs (Čālūs) was situated on the frontier of Daylam (Ibn Rusta, 150: *fī naḥw al-ʿaduww*) but later the valley of the Sard-āb-rūd (Kalār-dasht) seems to have been annexed to Ṭabaristān. Farther west, the coast of Tunakābun was governed sometimes with Māzandarān and sometimes with Gīlān.

The Arab geographers distinguished between the plain (*al-sahliyya*) and the mountains (*al-djabaliyya*) of Ṭabaristān (al-Iṣṭakhrī, 211, 271). The important towns of Ṭabaristān were in the lowlands: Āmul, Nātil, Shālūs (Čālūs), Kalā (Kalār), Mīla, Tardjī (Tūdjī, Bardjī?), ʿAyn al-Humm, Māmṭīr (= Bārfurūsh), Sārī, Ṭamīsha (cf. al-Iṣṭakhrī. 207; cf. al-Muḳaddasī, 353). The principal town (*madīna*) of Ṭabaristān in the time of al-Yaʿḳūbī, 276, was still Sāriyya [*q.v.*], but in the time of al-Masʿūdī, *Tanbīh*, 179, Al-Iṣṭakhrī, 211, and Ibn Ḥawḳal, 271, the principal town (*ḳaṣaba*) and the most flourishing one in Ṭabaristān was Āmul (larger than Ḳazwīn).

The mountain area was quite distinct, and its connection with the plain is not very clear in the Arabic texts; cf. the confused summary in al-Iṣṭakhrī, 204. Al-Ṭabarī, iii, 1295, under the year 224/838, distinguishes three mountains in Ṭabaristān: 1. the mountain of Wandā-Hurmuz in the centre (*wasaṭ*); 2. that of his brother Wandāsandjān (*sic*) b. Alandād b. Ḳārin; and 3. that of Sharwīn b. Surkhāb b. Bāb. Now according to Ibn Rusta, 151, [the Ḳārinid] Wandā-Hurmuz lived near Dunbāwand. On the other hand, the same writer, 149, says that during the rule of Ṭabaristān by Djarīr b. Yazīd, Wandā-Hurmuz had bought 1,000 *djarībs* of domain lands (*ṣawāfī*) outside the town of Sārī. These *alf djarīb* seem to correspond to the region round the sources of the rivers Tīdjin and Nīkā, which in Persian is called Hazār-djarīb. Later, the lands of Wandā-Hurmuz included the greater part of eastern Māzandaran. *Wandāspdjān seems to have ruled over the greater part of Māzandarān, for his capital Muzn was the rallying point from which expeditions set out against Daylam. Finally, the mountain of Sharwīn comprised the south-eastern part of Māzandarān, for according to Ibn al-Faḳīh, 305, it was close to Ḳūmis.

In the time of al-Iṣṭakhrī, the three divisions of the mountains specified are: the mountains of Rūbandj, of Fādūsbān and of Ḳārin. "They are high mountains (*djibāl*) and each of them (*djabal*) has a chief".

Rūbandj, according to Ibn Ḥawḳal, lay between Rayy and Ṭabaristān. Barthold, *Očerk*, 155, emends the name to *Rūyandj and identifies it with Rūyān. Ibn Rusta, 149, says that Rūyān, near the lands of Rayy, did not form part of Ṭabaristān but formed a special *kūra* with the capital Kadjdja, which was the headquarters of the *wālī* (cf. Kačarustāḳ in the *bulūk* of Kudjūr). According to this, *Rūyand = Rūyān is to be located in the south-western part of Māzandarān (north of Tehrān). In the Mongol period, Ḥamd Allāh Ḳazwīnī, 160, is the first to mention Rustamdār (on the Shāh-rūd). As Vasmer, *op.cit.*, 122-5, has shown, Rustamdār later included all western Māzandarān between Sakhtasar (Gīlān) and Āmul. Rustamdar therefore included Rūyān, without the two terms being completely synonymous.

Djibāl Ḳarīn had only one town, Shahmār, a day's journey from Sāriyya. The local chiefs of the dynasty of Ḳārin lived in the stronghold of Firrīm [*q.v.* in Suppl.] which must have stood on the western branch of the river Tīdjin, which later flows past Sārī. The modern *bulūk* of Firrīm is in the Hazār-Djarīb (more accurately in its western half which is called Dudānga). According to Ibn Isfandiyār, 95, the possessions of the Ḳārinids included the mountains of Wandā-ummīd (*ibid.*, 25; the water supply of the mosque of Āmul came from this mountain), Āmul, Lafūr (on the eastern source of the river Bābul which runs to Bārfurūsh) and Firrīm, "which is called Kūh-i Ḳārin". According to Yāḳūt, iii, 283, the lands of the Ḳārinids included Djibāl Sharwīn (cf. above) which Iʿtimād al-Salṭana, *Kitāb al-Tadwīn*, 42, identifies with Sawād-kūh i.e. the sources of the Tālār (river of ʿAlīābād between Āmul and Bārfurūsh); the pass leading to Sawādkūh is still called Shalfīn <Sharwīn.

The Djibāl Pādūspān lay a day's journey from Sārī. The district had no Friday mosque; the chief lived in the village of Uram (Ibn Ḥawḳal, 268, 17: Uram-khāst, Ārum). As Vasmer has shown, 127-30, this must be sought on the middle course of the rivers of Bārfurūsh and ʿAlīābād (to the north of Lafūr and near Shīrgāh).

Bibliography: *BGA*, s.v. Daylam, Ṭabaristān, Āmul, Sāriyya, etc. Ibn al-Faḳīh, 301-14, in particular, gives very detailed information about Ṭabaristān. Masʿūdī, *Murūdj al-dhahab*, index; Idrīsī, tr. Jaubert, ii, 169, 179-80, 333, 337-8 (of little originality); Zakariyyāʾ Ḳazwīnī, *Athār al-buldān* (clime iv.): Āmul, 190; Bilād al-Daylam, 221; Rūyān, 260; Ṭabaristān; Yāḳūt, cf. Dorn, *Auszüge*, 1858, 2-45, where are collected all the articles relating to Ṭabaristān (but the text of Wüstenfeld's edition is preferable); Ḥamd Allāh Ḳazwīnī, *Nuzhat al-ḳulūb*, GMS, 159, 161; Dorn, *Auszüge aus 14 morgenl. Schriftstellern betreffend d. Kaspische Meer*, in *Mélanges Asiatiques*, vi, 658, vii, 19-44, 52-92; cf. also the *Bibl.* to section on History below. European works: Spiegel, *Eran. Altertumskunde*, 1871, i, 64-74; Dorn, *Caspia*, 1875 (a mass of rather undigested information); Geiger, *Ostiranische Kultur*, 1882, index; Brunnhofer, *Von Pontus bis zum Indus*, Leipzig 1890, 73-93: Alburs and Mazanderan (the author seeks to explain Iranian geography from Sanskrit texts); Barthold, *Istor.-geogr. obzor Irana*, St. Petersburg 1903, 158-161, Pers. tr., Tehrān 1930, 289-95, Eng. tr. Princeton 1984, 115-20; Le Strange, *The Lands of the eastern caliphate*, 368-76; Vasmer, *Die Eroberung, etc.*

6. History. The local dynasties of Māzandarān fall into three classes: 1. local families of pre-Islamic origin, 2. the ʿAlid *sayyids*, and 3. local families of secondary importance.

I. At the coming of the Sāsānid dynasty, the king of Ṭabaristān and of Padashwārgar (Marquart, *Ērānšahr*, 130: "the district opposite the region of Khᵂār"; Farshuwādgar is a misreading of the name, which is also found in the *Bundahishn*, xii, 17) was Gushnasp, whose ancestors had reigned since the time of Alexander. In 529-36 Ṭabaristān was ruled by the Sāsānid prince Kāwūs son of Kawādh. Anūshirwān put in his place Zarmihr, who traced his descent from the famous smith Kāwa [see KĀWAH]. His dynasty ruled till 645 when Gīl Gawbara (a descendant of the Sāsānid Djamāsp, son of Pērōz) annexed Ṭabaristān to Gīlān. These families, on whom their coins might throw some light (cf. below), had descendants ruling in the Muslim period.

The Bāwandids [see BĀWAND] who claimed descent from Kāwūs) provided three lines: the first 45-397/665-1007 was overthrown on the conquest of Ṭabaristān by the Ziyārid Ḳābūs b. Wushmagīr [*q.v.*]; the second reigned from 466/1073 to 606/1210 when Māzandarān was conquered by ʿAlāʾ al-Dīn Muḥammad Khᵂārazmshāh; the third ruled from 635/1237 to 750/1349 as vassals of the Mongols. The last representative of the Bāwandids was slain by Afrāsiyāb Čulāwī.

The Ḳārinids [*q.v.*] (in the Kūh-i Ḳārin) claimed descent from Ḳārin, brother of Zarmihr (cf. above). Their last representative Māzyār [see ḲĀRINIDS] was put to death in 224/839.

The Pādūspānids or Bādusbānids [*q.v.*] (Rūyān and Rustamdār) claimed descent from the Dābūyids of Gīlān (their eponym was the son of Gīl Gawbāra; cf. above). They came to the front about 40/660 and during the rule of the ʿAlids were their vassals. Later, they were vassals of the Būyids and Bāwandids, who deposed them in 586/1190. The dynasty, restored in 606/1209-10, survived till the time of Tīmūr; one of its branches (that of Kāwūs b. Kayūmarth) reigned till 975/1567 and the other (that of Iskandar b. Kayūmarth) till 984/1574.

II. Alongside of these native dynasties, the ʿAlids were able to establish themselves, principally in Ṭabaristān. In 250/864 the people of Rūyān, rebelling against the governor, sent to Rayy for the Zaydī Sayyid Ḥasan b. Zayd, a descendant of the caliph ʿAlī in the sixth generation. This (Ḥasanid) branch ruled in Ṭabaristān till 316/928. The Ḥusaynid branch ruled from 304/916-17 to 337/948-9 (?). Another dynasty of Marʿashī Sayyids [*q.v.*] ruled in Māzandarān between 760/1358 and 880/1475. The founder of this dynasty was Ḳiwām al-Dīn, a descendant of ʿAlī in the twelfth generation. A third family of Murtaḍāʾī Sayyids is known in Hazār-Djarīb between 760/1359 and 1005/1596-7.

III. The noble families who enjoyed considerable influence, mainly in their fiefs, are very numerous. Rabino mentions the Kiyā of Čulāw (at Āmul, Ṭalaḳān and Rustamdār) between 795/1393 and 909/1503-4; the Kiyā Djalālī of Sārī in 750-63/1349-61; the house of Rūzafzūn of Sawādkūh, 897-923/1492-1517; the Dīw in the period of Shāh Tahmāsp in certain parts of Māzandarān; the Banū Kāwūs 857-957/1453-1550; the Banū Iskandār 857-1006/1453-1598 and the different princes of Tamīsha, of Miyāndūrūd, of Lāridjān, of Māmṭīr, of Lafūr, etc.

Besides this confusion of feudal dynasties, a series of conquerors from outside has ruled in Māzandarān: the Arabs beginning in 22/644, the Ṭāhirids, the Ṣaffārids, the Sāmānids, the Ziyārids, the Ghaznawids, the Saldjūḳs the Khᵂārazmshāhs, the Mongols, the Sarbadārs, Tīmūr and the Ṣafawids. For the detailed consideration of the period of domination by outside powers from the Arab conquest to the suzerainty of the Saldjūḳs, during which Māzandarān appears in the historical sources as Ṭabaristān, see ṬABARISTĀN.

It is in the Saldjūḳ period, as already noted, that the name Māzandarān reappears in historical literature. Towards the end of the period of Great Saldjūḳ rule in eastern Persia, Māzandarān was ruled by the ambitious and expansionist Bāwandid prince Shāh Ghāzī Rustam I (534-58/1140-63) (see Bosworth, in *Camb. hist. of Iran*, v, 28-9, 156, 185-6). It then passed briefly, after the murder in 606/1209-10 of Shāh Ghāzī Rustam II, into the control of the Khᵂārazmshāhs, but in 617/1220 was devastated by Mongol incursions under either Djebe or Sübetey (both commanders being mentioned by Djuwaynī as leading the Mongol forces). It was, of course, on an island off the coast of Māzandarān that the fugitive Khwārazmian ruler ʿAlāʾ al-Dawla Muḥammad died in this same year [see KHWĀRAZM-SHĀHS]. Māzandarān in the Mongol and Il-Khānid periods was frequently a corridor through which Mongol armies passed, but it and Gīlān do not seem ever to have been directly governed by the Mongols, presumably because of their relative inaccessibility and their uncongenial climate. Māzandarān, however, often played a rôle as the winter camping-ground [see ḲĪSHLAḲ] of such Khāns as Abaḳa, Ghazan and Öldjeytü, in conjunction with Khurāsān, which was favoured as a summer pasture ground for the Mongol hordes and their flocks. In the later 8th/14th and the 9th/15th centuries we hear of governors appointed over Māzandarān by the Sarbadārids and then the Tīmūrids, but in practice, the local princes seem largely to have been undisturbed. Also in the period of the Mongols and their successors, we know that trade was carried on across the Caspian Sea to South Russia and the lands of the Golden Horde from the port of Nīm Murdān off the coast from Astarābād (Mustawfī, *Nuzha*, 160, tr. 156).

Shāh Ismāʿīl Ṣafawī had failed to take over Māzandarān in 909/1503-4 from the local Shīʿī prince Ḥusayn Kiyā Čulawī, who had sheltered fugitive troops of Ismāʿīl's Aḳ Ḳoyunlu opponents. He also sent an expedition into Māzandarān in 923/1517, but it remained substantially independent under its native princes (a Ṣafawid governor ruled part of it 977-84/1569-76) until Shāh ʿAbbās I's definitive annexation in 1005-6/1596-7; he claimed hereditary rights in Māzandarān through his family's connections with the Marʿashī Sayyid Ḳiwām al-Dīn (see Iskandar Beg Munshī, *Taʾrīkh-i ʿĀlam-ārā-yi ʿAbbāsī*, Tehran 1350/1971, i, 518-22, 534-7, 542-3, 579-86, tr. R. M. Savory, Boulder, Colorado 1978, ii, 693-8, 713-17, 722-3, 765-73). ʿAbbās's mother Mahd-i ʿUlyā was the daughter of a local Māzandarān chief who claimed descent from the Fourth Shīʿī Imām Zayn al-ʿĀbidīn, and the Shāh showed a particular liking for the province, constructing there two winter palaces, which formed a kind of northern Iṣfahān for him. Faraḥābād was founded in 1020/1611 or 1021/1612, and Ashraf in 1021/1612; they were visited and described by European travellers like Pietro della Valle (1618) and Sir Thomas Herbert (1627), and it was at Faraḥābād that the Shāh died in 1038/1629 (cf. Savory, *Iran under the Safavids*, Cambridge 1980, 96-100). It was Shāh ʿAbbās who implanted in Māzandarān 30,000 Georgian and Armenian Christian families, many of whom proved unable to survive the unhealthy climate there.

Māzandarān was originally one of the *mamālik*, i.e. *dīwānī* or state land provinces, but under Shāh ʿAbbās II (1052-77/1642-66), Māzandarān and Gīlān became *khāṣṣa* or royal domains. It suffered in 1668 from the attack of Stenka Razin and his Cossacks, and in the early decades of the 18th century Māzandarān and Gīlān were coveted by Peter the Great; this was of course the period when the Ṣafawid state was falling into dissension and anarchy under pressure from the Afghāns in the east. Hence the two provinces were in 1723 in principle ceded to the Tsar by the fainéant Ṭahmāsp II (1135-45/1722-32) in return for the promise of help against his rival Ashraf. The plan was cut short by Peter's death in 1725, and the Empress Catherine I offered to abandon the Russian claim on the south Caspian provinces in return for recognition of Russian annexations in Dāghistān and Shirwān. Ṣafawid control over Māzandarān was however established by Ṭahmāsp with the aid of the chief of the Ḳizilbāsh [*q.v.*] Turkmen chief of the Ḳādjār tribe there, Fatḥ ʿAlī Khān. The Ḳādjārs now began to consolidate their power in the region, despite Ṭahmāsp's enforced grant of Māzandarān, Khurāsān, Sīstān and Kirmān to Nādir Shāh Afshār after the latter's expulsion of the Afghāns from Persia, and in 1744 the Ḳādjārs of Māzandarān in fact rebelled against Nādir.

Under the Ḳādjār Shahs, Māzandarān and Gurgān continued to be of strategic importance against Turkmen incursions, and were royal governorates. The local economy seems to have flourished, with its staples of rice, cotton, sugar, timber and the fisheries of the Caspian, the latter however leased in the latter part of the 19th century to Russia in return for an annual rent. Curzon noted that the revenue of Māzandarān in 1888-9 was 139,350 *tūmāns* in cash, with government expenditure on public buildings, expenses of collection, etc., amounting to a mere 4,590 *tūmāns* (*Persia and the Persian question*, i, 354 ff.). The ancient town of Sārī declined in the 19th century, whilst Āmul and above all Bārfurūsh [*q.v.*] expanded commercially; much of the trade with Russia went from the port of Bārfurūsh at Mashad-i Sar (later Bābul-i Sar) at the mouth of the Bābul river, and there was a Russian consul for trade in the town. In the middle years of the century, this district was a centre of Bābism, one of whose leaders was Mullā Muḥammad ʿAlī Bārfurūshī [*q.v.*]. The convention of Badasht took place in Mazandarān, and a fortified site near Bārfurūsh called Shaykh Ṭabarsī was the centre of the Bābī rising of 1848-9, barbarously suppressed by government forces [see BĀBĪS]. The father of Mīrzā Ḥusayn ʿAlī, the later Bahāʾ Allāh [*q.v.*], was a native of Nūr in Māzandarān. In 1889-90 there was a pioneer attempt at railway-building in Persia when a short line was built by Belgian engineers from Āmul to the Caspian coast; a road over the Elburz Mountains from Āmul to Tehran, 120 miles/190 km. long, had already been constructed by Nāṣir al-Dīn Shāh in 1877-8.

In the present century, with the confusion after the First World War, Māzandarān was, with Gīlān, involved in the Bolshevik rising of 1920-1 in the Caspian provinces under Kūčak Khān [*q.v.*] and Amīr Muʾayyad, in the ending of which the commander of the Cossack Brigade Riḍā Khān, later Shāh, achieved prominence; he was himself a native of Māzandarān, having been born at Elasht in the Elburz mountains (see L. P. Elwell-Sutton, in *Iran under the Pahlavis*, ed. G. Lenczkowski, Stanford 1978, 4-6). After he was made Shāh (December 1925), much of Māzandarān became crown land (*khāliṣa* [*q.v.*]), actually in the form of personal estates (*amlāk-i shāhī*) of the Shāh himself; but these were returned to their original owners in 1941 and subsequently distributed to small proprietors under the land reform policy of Riḍā Shāh's son Muḥammad Riḍā Shāh (see A. K. S. Lambton, *The Persian land reform 1962-1966*, Oxford 1979, 11-12, 120-2, 218-21).

Bibliography: On the campaigns of Alexander the Great and Antiochus III (in 209 B.C.; cf. Polybius, x, 28-31), cf. Dorn, *Caspia*, s.v. Alexander; idem, *Reise*, 156-61; Marquart, *Alexander's Marsch von Persepolis nach Herāt*, in *Untersuch. z. Gesch. von Eran*, ii, 1905, 45-63; Stahl, *Notes on the march of Alexander the Great from Ecbatana to Hyrcania*, in *JRGS* (Oct. 1924), 312-19. On the Arsacid and Sāsānid period: Darmester, *Lettre de Tansar à Jasnasf, roi de Tabaristan*, in *JA* (Jan.-March 1894), 185-250, 502-55 (Tansar [Tūsar?], the priest of the Sāsānid Ardashīr I, exhorts Djushnasf to submit;

the document translated from Pahlavi into Arabic by Ibn al-Muḳaffaʿ is given in Persian in Ibn Isfandiyār); Justi, *Iranisches Namenbuch*, Marburg 1895, 430-5 (tables); idem, in *Grund. d. iran. Phil.*, ii, 547; Marquart, *Ērānšahr*, 129-36. For the Muslim period: Balādhurī, 334-40; Ṭabarī, index; Yaʿḳūbī, *Historiae*, ii, 329-30, 355, 447, 465, 479, 514, 582; *Kitāb al-ʿUyūn*, ed. Jong and de Goeje, 399-405, 502-16, 520-3; Ibn al-Fāḳīh; Ibn al-Athīr, index; as well as the local histories given below (an asterisk marks the works which seem to be lost): Abu 'l-Ḥasan ʿAlī b. Muḥammad al-Madāʾinī (d. 225/890), **Kitāb Futūḥ Djibāl al-Ṭabaristān*; **Bāwand-nāma* (written for Shahriyār b. Ḳārin who reigned 466-503/1072-1109); ʿAbd al-Ḥasan Muḥammad Yazdādī, **ʿUḳūd al-siḥr wa-ḳalāʾid al-durar*; Muḥammad b. al-Ḥasan b. Isfandiyār, *Taʾrīkh-i Ṭabaristān* (written in 613/1216) abbr. tr. E. G. Browne, GMS, Leiden-London 1905; the manuscript mentioned by Dorn has been continued to 842/1488; Badr al-Maʿālī Awliyāʾ Allāh Āmulī, **Taʾrīkh-i Ṭabaristān* (written for Fakhr al-Dawla Shāh Ghāzī, 761-80/1359-78); ʿAlī b. Djamāl al-Dīn b. ʿAlī Maḥmūd al-Nadjībī Rūyānī, **Taʾrīkh-i Ṭabaristān* (written for the Kārkiyā Mīrzā ʿAlī before 881/1476, used by Ẓahīr al-Dīn); Sayyid Ẓahīr al-Dīn (born in 815/1412) b. Sayyid Nāṣir al-Dīn al-Marʿashī, *Taʾrīkh-i Ṭabaristān wa-Rūyān wa-Māzandarān*, completed in 881/1476, ed. Dorn, St. Petersburg 1266/1850; Dorn's German tr. was printed in 1885, but only a few copies are known; Ibn Abī Musallim, **Taʾrīkh-i Māzandarān* (date unknown); *Kitāb-i Gīlān wa-Māzandarān wa-Astarābād wa-Simnān wa-Damghān wa-ghayrih* (Pers. ms. of 1275/1859, cf. Dorn, *Bericht*); Muḥammad Ḥasan Khān Iʿtimād al-Salṭana, *Kitāb al-Tadwīn fī aḥwāl Djibāl Sharwīn*, Tehran 1311 (geography and history of Sawād-kūh, lists of the Bāwandids, Pādūspānids, etc.). Cf. also the local histories of Gīlān: Ẓahīr al-Dīn Marʿashī, *Taʾrīkh-i Gīlān wa-Daylamistān* (to 1489), ed. Rabino, Rasht 1330/1912 (Annex 476-98: correspondence of Khān Aḥmad Gīlānī); ʿAlī b. Shams al-Dīn, *Taʾrīkh-i Khānī* (880-920/1475-1514), ed. Dorn, 1858; ʿAbd al-Fattāḥ Fūmanī, *Taʾrīkh-i Gīlān* (923-1038/1517-1629), ed. Dorn, 1858; and the local histories of Djurdjān: Abū Saʿīd al-Raḥmān b. Muḥammad al-Idrīsī (d. 405/1014), **Taʾrīkh-i Astarābād*, continued by Ibn al-Ḳāsim Ḥamza b. Yūsuf al-Sahmī al-Durdjānī (d. 427/1036) who is the author of a *Taʾrīkh Djurdjān* or *Kitāb Maʿrifat ʿulamāʾ ahl Djurdjān*, Hyderabad 1369/1950; ʿAlī b. Aḥmad al-Djurdjānī al-Idrīsī, *Taʾrīkh-i Djurdjān* (date unknown). A large number of Islamic sources relating to Māzandarān have been collected by Dorn, *Die Geschichte Tabaristans und der Serbedare nach Chondemir*, in *Mém. de l'Acad. de St. Pétersbourg*, 1850, viii; and *Auszüge aus Muham. Schriftstellern betreffend d. Gesch. und Geographie*, St. Petersburg 1858 (extracts from 22 works). For Tīmūr's campaigns: *Ẓafar-nāma*, i, 348, 358, 379, 570, ii, 577; Münedjdjim-bashî (1040-1114/1630-1702), *Ṣaḥāʾif al-akhbār*, Istanbul 1285/1868 (dynasties of Māzandarān; cf. Sachau's translation, *Ein Verzeichniss d. muhamm. Dynastien*, Berlin 1923: *Die Kaspischen Fürstentümer*, 3-13). Cf. further, Storey, i, 359-63, 1298; Storey-Bregel, 1070-7. European works: d'Ohsson, *Hist. des Mongols*, 1835, iii, 2, 10, 44, 48, 106-9 (Čintimur as governor in Māzandarān), 120-2, 193, 414-18 (Abaḳa), iv, 4, 42, 44-5 (Māzandarān an apanage of Ghāzān), 106, 124, 155, 159, 600 (Abū Saʿīd in M.), 613, 622 (revolt of Yasawur), 685 (Ḥasan b. Čobān in M.), 726, 730 (Ṭughā Tīmūr), 739 (the Sarbadārs [*q.v.*]); Melgunov, *op. cit.* (lists of the dynasties and governors of Māzandarān); Rehatsek, *The Bāw and Gaobārah sepahbuds*, in *JBBRAS*, xii (1876), 410-45 (according to Ẓahīr al-Dīn, Mīrkhʷand and the *Muntakhab al-tawārīkh*); Howorth, *History of the Mongols*, index (publ. in 1927); Horn, in *Grundr. d. iran. Phil.*, ii, 563 (ʿAlids); Lane-Poole, *The Muhamm. dynasties*, cf. the additions by Barthold in the Russ. tr., 1899, 290-3; Casanova, *Les Ispehbeds de Firim*, in *A Volume... presented to E. G. Browne*, Cambridge 1922, 117-26 (the identification of Firīm with Fīrūzkūh is wrong); Huart, *Les Ziyārides*, in *Mém. de l'Acad. des Inscr.*, xlii (Paris 1922), index; Barthold, *The place of the Caspian provinces in the history of the Muslim world* (Russ.), Baku 1925, 90-100 (Tīmūr in Māzandarān); Rabino, *Les dynasties alaouides du Mazandaran*, in *JA*, ccx (1927), 253-77 (lists without references); Zambaur, *Manuel*, ch. ix. and tables C and P; Vasmer, *Die Eroberung Ṭabaristāns durch die Araber zur Zeit des Chalifen al-Manṣūr*, in *Islamica*, iii (1927), 86-150 (very important analysis of the Islamic sources); Rabino, *Māzandarān and Astarābād*, 133-149 (lists of dynasties and governors: detailed, but without references; idem, *Les dynasties du Māzandaran... d'après les chroniques locales*, in *JA*, ccxxviii (1936), 397-474; idem, *Les préfets du califat au Tabaristan...*, in *JA*, ccxxxi (1939), 237-74; idem, *L'histoire du Mâzandarân*, in *JA*, ccxxxiv (1947-5), 211-43. On the Russian expeditions to Māzandarān, see Dorn, *Caspia*; Kostomarov, *Bunt Stenki Razina (1668-1669)*, in *Sobraniye sočinenii*, St. Petersburg 1903, Kniga I, vol. ii, 407-505 (Persian sources call the Cossack chief Stenka Razin "Istīn Gurāzī"); Butkov, *Concerning the events which took place in 1781 at the time of a Russian establishment on the Gulf of Astarabad* (Russ.), in *Žurn. Min. Vnutr. del.* (1839), xxxiii, 9; idem, *Materiali dlia novoi istorii Kavkaza*, St. Petersburg 1869, index (in the Persian sources the leader of the Russian expedition of 1781 Count Voinovič is called "Käräfs [= Graf]-khān"). Archaeology. Bode, *On a recently opened tumulus in the neighbourhood of Astarabad*, in *Archaeologia* (London 1844), xxx, 248-55 (on the circumstances of the find made at Tūräng-täpä cf. idem, in *Otečestvennyia Zapiski* [1865], no. 7, 152-60); Rostovtsev, *The Sumerian treasure of Astarabad*, in *Journ. of Egyptian Archaeol.*, vi (1920), 4-27; Minorsky, *Transcaucasica*, in *JA* (1930); De Morgan, *Mission scientifique, Recherches archéologiques*, part i, Paris 1899, 1-3 (prehistoric sites of Māzandarān); Crawshay-Williams, *Rock-dwellings in Raineh*, in *JRAS* (1904), 551-2; (1906), 217; Hommaire de Hell, cf. above (atlas); Häntzsche, *Paläste Schah Abbas I in Mazanderan*, in *ZDMG*, xv (1862), xx (1866), 186; Sarre, *Denkmäler persischer Baukunst*, Berlin 1901-10, *Textband*, 95-116: Die Bauwerke d. Landschaft Tabaristan (Grabtürme von Mazandaran; Amul; Sari; die Palastanlage von Aschref; Safi-abad; Farah-abad); Diez, *Churasanische Baudenkmäler*, Berlin 1918, 88, inscription of Rādkān of the Ispahbad Abū Djaʿfar Muḥammad b. Wandarīn Bāwand of 407/1016, see Pope, *Survey of Persian art*, ii, 1022-3, 1721-3. See also MARʿASHĪ SAYYIDS. (V. MINORSKY - [C. E. BOSWORTH])

7. The coins of Māzandarān. The question whether the Sāsānids struck coins in Māzandarān is still an open one and can only be settled when the groups of letters that mark the mints on Sāsānid coins have been properly explained. According to the so far insufficient attempts to explain them, the letters *AM*

found from the time of Fīrūz onwards are an abbreviation for Āmul, but this explanation is quite without proof.

The Dābwayhids and the earlier Arab governors of Ṭabaristān struck in the 2nd/8th century coins of the type of the Sāsānid *dirhams* of Khusraw II; on the obverse, with the bust of the ruler, his name is given in Pahlavi characters and on the reverse is the fire-altar with its two guardians and on the right the mint *Tpurstan* and on the left the year in the Ṭabaristān era (began on 11 June 652). These silver coins average in weight 1.90 gr. = 29.3 grains and are hemidrachms. Of the Dābwayhid rulers, Ferkhwān, Dātbūrdjmatūn and Khūrshīd are mentioned upon them. The coins of the first bear the years 60-77 (711-28), of the second 86-7 (737-8) and of the third 89-115 (740-66); these dates enable us to correct the chronology given by the historians. On some coins with the name Khūrshīd, earlier students read the dates 60-3, but this is to be explained by the similarity of *shast* and *dehsat* in the Pahlavi script and these coins are really of the years 110 and following. The assumption of a Khūrshīd I, who reigned in the sixties of the Ṭabaristān era (Mordtmann), is thus quite unfounded. As Khūrshīd died in 144 A.H. = 110 Ṭabaristān era, and there are coins with the names of Arab governors earlier than the year 116 Ṭab. era, it must be assumed that the Arabs continued to strike coins in the name of the earlier ruler of the land for a period after the conquest of Māzandarān, just as they did after the conquest of Persia under the caliph ʿUmar.

It was not till after Khūrshīd's death in 144/761 that ʿAbbāsid control was established over Ṭabaristān, and after a series of posthumous coins in Khūrshīd's name 110-14 Ṭab. era = 144-8 A.H./761-5 A.D., we get the first coins of the Arab governors, Khālid b. Barmak (coins from 150/767, Pahlavi legend *Halit*), and then ʿUmar b. al-ʿAlāʾ (coins from 155/772, Pahlavi legend *Aumr*). Kūfic legends appear in 122 Ṭab. era = 157/774 under ʿUmar b. al-ʿAlāʾ, and thereafter, governors' names are exclusively in this script (for Saʿīd b. Daʿladj, Yaḥyā b. Mikhnāḳ, etc.). See J. Walker, *A catalogue of the Muhammadan coins in the British Museum, i. Arab-Sassanian coins*, London 1941, pp. lxix-lxxx (list of ʿAbbasid governors and their coins at pp. lxxiv-lxxv), 130-61. The issue of these coins with Sāsānid types ended in the year 143 Ṭabaristān era (794, anonymous) but we have a coin of 161/812 on the obverse of which in place of the king's head—as earlier on the coins of the governor Sulaymān (136-7)—there is a rhombus with the puzzling Arabic letters *bḥ* and on the margin al-Faḍl b. Sahl Dhu 'l-Riyāsatayn (in Arabic) is named; on the reverse, instead of the altar with its guardians are three parallel designs like fir branches, between them an inscription in four lines giving the Muslim creed in Kūfic and the date and mint in Pahlavi (Tiesenhausen, in *ZVOAO*, ix, 224).

The mint name of these Arab-Sāsānid coins of the Arab governors of Ṭabaristān appears in Pahlavi script as *Tpurstan*, and the name of the actual town is not given. Presumably, it was mostly Āmul, but may have been at times other places, e.g. Sārī/Sāriyya, which was on occasion the capital of the province; only on one coin of the period, a *fals* of 168/784-5, is Āmul mentioned specifically. It should be noted, however, that odd Umayyad and ʿAbbāsid *dirhams* of conventional type are known from 102/720-1 onwards with the Arabicised name of the mint *Ṭabaristān*.

In the 3rd/9th century, in addition to the coins of the caliphal governors, we begin to find coins of the ʿAlid *dāʿīs*, beginning with al-Ḥasan b. Zayd b. Muḥammad, al-Dāʿī al-Kabīr [*q.v.*], from 253/867 onwards, and al-Ḥasan b. ʿAlī al-Uṭrūsh al-Nāṣir li 'l-Ḥaḳḳ [*q.v.*] and his successor al-Ḥasan b. Ḳāsim al-Dāʿī ilā 'l-Ḥaḳḳ [*q.v.* in Suppl.], who controlled Āmul at times. From 395/966 onwards, we possess coins of the Zaydī *imām* Abu 'l-Faḍl Djaʿfar b. Muḥammad, al-Thāʾir fi 'llāh [*q.v.*] and his son al-Mahdī, minted at Hawsam or Rūd-i Sar on the borders of Gīlān and Daylam (see S. M. Stern, *The coins of Āmul*, in *Num. Chron.*, 7th ser., vii [1967], 210 ff., 269-77, and HAWSAM in Suppl.). Interspersed with these coins bearing Shīʿī-type legends are found those of Sunnī type acknowledging the ʿAbbāsid caliphs, e.g. those minted by the Sāmānids, who held Āmul from 289/902, and then by the Ziyārid Wushmagīr b. Ziyār, who held it from 323/935, generally as a Sāmānid vassal. With the capture of Rayy in 334/945-6 by the Būyid Rukn al-Dawla, there began a long period of rivalry between the Būyids, the Sāmānids and the Ziyārids over possession of Gurgān and Ṭabaristān, reflected in coin issues of all three powers, sometimes with coins with more than one of them from the same year, e.g. 341/952-3 (Sāmānids, and unknown ? ʿAlid prince and Būyids) and 356/967 and 357/968 (Sāmānids and Ziyārids). Also in this period begins the series of coins (353-mid-6th century/964-mid-12th century) of the Bāwandid *ispahbadhs* or local rulers of Firrīm in the highlands of Ṭabaristān [see BĀWAND, and FIRRĪM in Suppl.], minted at first in Firrīm but latterly at Sārī, which bear Shīʿī-type legends which nevertheless acknowledge other suzerains like the Būyids, the ʿAbbāsid caliphs and the Saldjūḳs, see G. C. Miles, *The coinage of the Bāwandids of Ṭabaristān*, in *Iran and Islam, a volume in memory of Vladimir Minorsky*, ed. C. E. Bosworth, Edinburgh 1971, 443-60. No coins are extant of the Ziyārid *amīr* Ḳābūs b. Wushmagīr [*q.v.*] and his descendants (cf. Bosworth, in *Isl.*, xl [1964], 25-6), and coins of the Saldjūḳ sultans who replaced them only appear under Berk-yaruḳ from 481/1095 onwards.

After the Mongol invasions, we find issues of Māzandarān by the Il-Khānids, Sarbardārids, Tīmūrids, Ṣafawids, Afshārids and Ḳādjārs. In Āmul, anonymous copper coins were struck from the 10th/16th century onwards. On several pieces of this period the mint Ṭabaristān occurs. As these are all very rare, the issue must have been an occasional one. The dates are not preserved on any specimens. More common are copper pieces of the value of 4 *ḳāzbekī* (18-22 grammes = 280-340 grains) with the lion and sun and mint Māzandarān, which belong to the 12th/18th century. During the Russian occupation of Gīlān in 1723-32, to meet the shortage of currency provoked by the financial crisis in Russia at this time, Persian copper coins were overstruck with a Russian die (double-eagle) and circulated in the occupied provinces in place of Russian money. These coins are often called Māzandarān pieces, but this is not correct, as only Gīlān and not Māzandarān was occupied.

Bibliography: Olshausen, *Die Pehlevi-Legenden auf den Münzen der letzten Sasaniden*, Copenhagen 1843; Krafft, *Wiener Jahrbücher*, cvi, *Anzeigeblat*, 1844; Mordtmann, in *ZDMG*, viii, xii, xix, xxxiii; idem, in *SB Bayr. Ak.* (1871); Dorn, *Mélanges Asiatiques*, i-iii, vi, viii; Thomas, in *JRAS*, 1849, 1852, 1871. For the later period, see the coin catalogues by S. Lane-Poole and R. Stuart Poole; Markov, *Inventarnyi Katalog*; E. von Zambaur, in *Numism. Ztschr.*, xlvii, 136; R. Vasmer, in *Sbornik Ermitaža*, iii, 119-32 (Russ.); J. M. Unvala, *Numismatique du Tabaristan et quelques monnaies sassanides provenant de*

Suse, Paris 1938; idem, *Supplementary notes on the coins of Tabaristan*, in *Jnal. Num. Soc. of India*, vi (1944), 37-45; Zambaur, *Die Münzprägungen des Islams, zeitlich und örtlich geordnet*, i, Wiesbaden 1968, 34-5 (Āmul), 136 (Sārī/Sāriyya), 170 (Ṭabaristān), 185 (Firrīm), 221 (Māzandarān); A. H. Morton, *Dinars from western Māzandarān of some vassals of the Saljūq sultan Muḥammad b. Malik-Shāh*, in *Iran, JBIPS*, xxv (1987), 77-90.

(R. Vasmer - [C. E. Bosworth])

MĀZAR [see ṢIḲILIYYA].

MAZĀR [see MAḲBARA, ZIYĀRA].

MAZĀR-I SHARĪF, a town in northern Afghānistān, situated in lat. 36° 42' N. and long. 67° 06' E., at an altitude of 1,235 feet/380 m. in the foothills of the northern outliers of the Hindū-Kush [*q.v.*].

The great classical and mediaeval Islamic town of Balkh [*q.v.*], modern Wazīrābād, lay some 14 miles/20 km. to the west of Mazār-i Sharīf, and until the Tīmūrid period was the most important urban centre of the region. Previously to that time, the later Mazār-i Sharīf was marked by the village of Khayr, later called Khōdja Khayrān. On two different occasions, in the 6th/12th century after 530/1135-6 in the time of Sultan Sandjar [*q.v.*], and in 885/1480-1, in the reign of the Tīmūrid Sultan Ḥusayn, the tomb of the caliph ʿAlī was "discovered" here and its genuineness declared to have been proved. A place of pilgrimage (*mazār*) at once arose around the tomb with a considerable market; the second tomb which is still standing (the first is said to have been destroyed by Čingiz-Khān), was built in 886/1481-2. The *mazār* does not seem to have been of any particular importance during the time of the Özbegs and is hardly mentioned, although several Özbeg sultans were buried there. In the first half of the 19th century, the place is usually simply called *mazār* by travellers, the name *Mazār-i Sharīf* seems only to have arisen within the last hundred years. ʿAbd al-Karīm Bukhārī (ed. Schefer, 4) does not mention Mazār at all among the towns of Afghānistān; in 1832 when Alexander Burnes passed through it, it was a little town with about 800 houses. In 1866, the Afghān governor Naʾib ʿĀlim Khān, a Shīʿī, chose Mazār-i Sharīf as his residence; since then Mazār-i Sharīf has been the capital of Afghān Turkistān. In 1878 it was described by the Russian general Marveyev as one of the best towns in Northern Afghānistān with about 30,000 inhabitants (L. F. Kostenko, *Turkestanskiy kray*, St. Petersburg 1880, ii, 157).

It was the selection of Mazār-i Sharīf as the administrative capital of northern Afghānistān which caused the town's fortunes to rise, so that in recent times, it has become a centre for local government as well as continuing to fulfill its old commercial role arising from its position on a route from Kābul to the ferry-point of Pata Kesar on the Oxus [see ĀMŪ-DARYĀ], by means of which goods have for long been exported to Russian Central Asia. In particular, it is a centre for the trade in karakol fur [see ḲARĀ-KÖL]. The visits of pilgrims seeking healing and blessing at the shrine are still important, as are the religious festivals there of the Nawrūz "raising of the standard" and that of its lowering 40 days or so later. Mazār-i Sharīf now has civil and military airfields, a power station and a fertiliser plant. It is the chef-lieu of the province (*wilāyat*) of Balkh; in *ca.* 1959, Humlum estimated its population at 75,000.

Bibliography: On the first discovery of the tomb of ʿAlī, see Abū Ḥāmid al-Andalusī al-Gharnāṭī, *Tuḥfat al-albāb*, ed. G. Ferrand, in *JA*, ccvii (1925), 145-8, and on the second discovery, Khwāndamīr, *Ḥabīb al-siyar*, lith. Tehran 1271/1855, iii, 260-1. For the town in recent times, see C. E. Yate, *Northern Afghanistan or letters from the Afghan Boundary Commission*, Edinburgh and London 1888, 279 ff.; J. Humlum *et alii*, *La géographie de l'Afghanistan, étude d'un pays aride*, Copenhagen 1959, 132, 153-4, 327; L. Duprée, *Afghanistan*, Princeton 1973, 105-6, 631; L. Golombek, *Mazār-i Sharīf—a case of mistaken identity ?*, in M. Rosen-Ayalon (ed.), *Studies in memory of Gaston Wiet*, Jerusalem 1977, 335-43; L. Adamec, *Historical and political gazetteer of Afghanistan. iv. Mazar-i Sharif and north-central Afghanistan*, Graz 1979, 411-14.

(W. Barthold - [C. E. Bosworth])

AL-**MĀZARĪ**, Abū ʿAbd Allāh Muḥammad b. ʿAlī b. ʿUmar, jurist of Ifrīḳiya who was surnamed "al-Imām" on account of his learning and his renown. His *nisba* refers to the Sicilian town of Mazzara (*Māzar* in Arabic), the native place of his family, but it is not known whether the latter had emigrated to Ifrīḳiya before his birth, which may be dated at 453/1061 since he died in Rabīʿ I 536/October 1141, at al-Mahdiyya [*q.v.*], at the age of 83 lunar years. It was in this last-named town that he settled after completing his traditional studies at Sfax as a pupil of al-Lakhmī (d. 478/1085), and at Sousse, under the guidance of Ibn al-Ṣāʾigh. These two masters, who had left Kairouan (al-Ḳayrawān) after the Hilālian invasion, transferred to the Mediterranean coast the Ifrīḳiyan Mālikī tradition, which was linked to the founder of the *madhhab* by a continuous chain; notable figures belonging to this chain include Saḥnūn, Ibn Abī Zayd, Abū ʿImrān al-Fāsī, etc. (see the table in M. M. Ould Bah, *La littérature juridique et l'évolution du Mālikisme en Mauritanie*, Tunis 1981, 25). Al-Māzarī perpetuated this tradition by establishing it at al-Mahdiyya, where he became head of the local judicial school, while representing a link in the chain which came to its end with Khalīl b. Isḥāḳ [*q.v.*], the supreme authority of Maghribī Mālikism.

Although sympathetic to the doctrine of the Shāfiʿīs, as well as to the opinions of the Ashʿarīs in *kalām*, since he is said to have passed on to posterity the *Tamhīd* of al-Bāḳillānī (d. 403/1013 [*q.v.*]), he founded his numerous and henceforward renowned *fatwās* on strictly Mālikī doctrine, without feeling himself completely bound by the interpretations of his predecessors; in general, he opted for what was *mashhūr*, applied the principle according to which "of two evils, the lesser must be chosen", and, in a sense, tended towards a moderate practice of *idjtihād*. Al-Māzarī attracted a considerable number of disciples and had dealings with other individuals who were to become famous, including Ibn Tūmart (d. 534/1130 [*q.v.*]), whose life he saved when the latter was being chased by the governor of al-Mahdiyya after having broken jars of wine at a market in the town. Ibn al-Abbār (in the *Takmilat al-Ṣila*, ed. Codera, Madrid 1887-9) mentions prominent Andalusians who attended his lectures or corresponded with him, in particular, Ibn al-ʿArabī (Abū Bakr, d. 543/1148 [*q.v.*]); the *ḳāḍī* ʿIyāḍ (d. 544/1149 [*q.v.*]), who nevertheless gives no biography of him in the *Madārik*; Ibn Khayr al-Ishbīlī (d. 575/1179 [*q.v.*]; and Ibn Rushd (d. 595/1198 [*q.v.*]).

This jurist seems to have cultivated the humanities and poetry, and to have studied mathematics and medicine, but he does not appear to have excelled in these disciplines, even if the *Kitāb fi 'l-ṭibb* which is attributed to him is indeed his own work. In fact, his name remains linked specifically to the *fatwās* which may be found in the various mss. of the *Djāmiʿ masāʾil al-aḥkām* by al-Burzulī (d. *ca.* 841/1438 [*q.v.*]), as well as in the *Miʿyār* of al-Wans̲h̲arīs̲h̲ī (d. 914/1508 [*q.v.*]), lith. Fās 1314-15 (e.g. ii, 192-4, 206-7, 321, iii, 230-1, 234-6, 241-2, 244-7, 249-51, 280, vi, 212, 214, 217, 219, 226-7, vii, 154, viii, 114-5, 130-1, 205, 220, 271, 285, ix, 52-3, 417, 421, 454, x, 245, 291, xii, 233, 243-7). His works numbered about a dozen, but only three of them have survived and not one has been published; they consist after all of commentaries which nevertheless may be regarded as holding a certain interest, since they contain a wealth of documentation and tackle various important questions; this is especially so in the case of *al-Muʿlim bi-fawāʾid Kitāb Muslim*, which appears to be the earliest commentary on the *Ṣaḥīḥ* of Muslim (see the judgment of Ibn K̲h̲aldūn in the *Muḳadimma*, ii, 403; tr. de Slane, ii, 475-6; tr. Rosenthal, ii, 459; on the mss. and the sequel attributed to the *ḳāḍī* ʿIyāḍ, the *Ikmāl al-Muʿlim*, see Brockelmann, S I, 265): the other works preserved are the *Kitāb Īḍāḥ al-maḥṣūl min Burhān al-uṣūl*, on the *Burhān* of al-D̲j̲uwaynī (d. 478/1085 [*q.v.*]) and the *S̲h̲arḥ ʿalā Talḳīn ʿAbd al-Wahhāb* [*al-T̲h̲aʿlabī*] (d. 422/1031; see Brockelmann, S I, 660).

Bibliography: Two monographs have been devoted to this jurist, one in Arabic, by Ḥ. Ḥ. ʿAbd al-Wahhāb, *al-Imām al-Māzarī*, Tunis 1955, and the other, in French, by H. R. Idris, *L'école mālikite de Mahdia: l'imām al-Māzarī (m. 536/1141)*, in *Etudes d'orientalisme ... Lévi-Provençal*, i, Paris 1962, 153-63; see also idem, *Essai sur la diffusion de l'asʿarisme en Ifrîqiya*, in *CT*, ii (1953), 12-13; *idem*, *La Berbérie orientale sous les Zīrīdes*, Paris 1959, index; see also M. Amari, *Bibliotheca arabo-sicula*, Leipzig 1857, i, 125, 133, 522, 629, ii, 65-8; idem, *Storia dei Musulmani di Sicilia*, 2nd ed., revised by C. A. Nallino, Catania 1937-9, ii, 544-9; *Centenario della nascita di Michele Amari*, Palermo 1910, i, 384-9, 390-402, ii, 92-4, 217-23, 224-44, 492-3; A. M. Turki, *Consultation juridique d'al-Imām al-Māzarī...*, in *MUSJ* l/2 (1984), 691-704. Arabic sources: Ibn Farḥūn, *Dībād̲j̲*, 279-81; Ibn Ḳunfud̲h̲, *K. al-Wafayāt*, Algiers 1939, 42; Ibn ʿId̲h̲ārī, *Bayān*, tr. Fagnan, i, 469; Ibn al-ʿImād, *S̲h̲ad̲h̲arāt*, iv, 114; Mak̲h̲lūf, *S̲h̲ad̲h̲arāt al-nūr al-zakiyya fī ṭabaḳāt al-Mālikiyya*, Cairo 1350, i, 127-8.

Two colleagues of this jurist, bearing the same *kunya*, the same *ism* and the same *nisba* are often confused with him, especially since they are practically contemporaries:

The first, ABŪ ʿABD ALLĀH MUḤAMMAD B. ABI 'L-FARAD̲J̲ AL-MĀZARĪ, surnamed al-Zakī (d. 512/1118), who was also a native of Mazzara and an As̲h̲ʿarī, resided at the Ḳalʿa of the Banū Ḥammād [*q.v.*], then was taught by numerous masters of Kairouan before going to settle in the East. He is the author of a work on Ḳurʾānic readings, of a treatise on physical contacts effected through error, the *Kas̲h̲f al-g̲h̲iṭāʾ ʿan lams al-k̲h̲aṭāʾ*, and of an appraisal of certain *ḥadīt̲h̲s* quoted by al-G̲h̲azālī (d. 505/1111 [*q.v.*]), in the *Iḥyaʾ, al-Kas̲h̲f wa 'l-inbāʾ ʿalā 'l-mutard̲j̲am bi 'l-Iḥyāʾ*.

Bibliography: Ibn Nād̲j̲ī, *Maʿālim al-īmān*, iii, 250-2; Amari, *Storia*², ii, 561-2; M. Asín Palacios, *Un faqīh siciliano contradictor de al-Gazzālī*, in *Centenario ... Amari*, i, 380-2, 548, n. 3, ii, 216; H. R. Idris, *Essai sur la diffusion de l'asʿarisme en Ifrîqiya*, in *CT*, ii (1953), 12; idem, *Le crépuscule de l'école mālikite kairouanaise*, in *ibid.*, iv (1956), 505-7; idem, *Quelques juristes ifrîqiyens de la fin du Xᵉ siècle*, in *RAfr.*, c (1956), 361; idem, *Zīrīdes*, ii, 731-2.

The second, ABŪ ʿABD ALLĀH MUḤAMMAD B. MUSLIM B. MUḤAMMAD AL-MĀZARĪ AL-ḲURAS̲H̲Ī AL-ISKANDARĀNĪ (d. 530/1135), who lived in Alexandria, was also an As̲h̲ʿarī, but more of a theologian (*mutakallim*) than a jurist as such, judging from the *Kitāb al-Mihād*, a commentary on the *K. al-Irs̲h̲ād ilā tabyīn ḳawāʿid al-iʿtiḳād* of al-D̲j̲uwaynī (d. 478/1085 [*q.v.*]).

Bibliography: Ibn Farḥūn, *Dībād̲j̲*, 280; M. Asín Palacios, *op.cit.*, ii, 216; Amari, *Storia*², ii, 546, 548; H. R. Idris, *A propos d'un extrait du "Kitâb al-Mihâd" d'al-Mâzarî al-Iskandarânî*, in *CT*, ii (1953), 155. (CH. PELLAT)

MAZĀTA, the name of an ancient and powerful Berber people which belonged to the great tribal family of the Lawāta [*q.v.*]. According to Ibn K̲h̲aldūn, who makes brief mention of the Mazāta in his *Histoire des Berbères*, they constituted an important branch descended from Zayr, son of Lawā, ancestor of the Lawāta. According to Ibn Ḥawḳal (4th/10th century), the Mazāta and the Lawāta belonged to the major Berber tribal group of the Zanāta. Yet another historian of the Berbers, Ibn Ḥazm (d. 456/1064), considers the Mazāta and the Lawāta as belonging to the Coptic, i.e. the Egyptian, race. This conception is to be understood as meaning that the ancestors of the Mazāta (who were, in the opinion of the present writer, the people known to the ancient Egyptians as the Mas̲h̲awas̲h̲a) as well as those of the other Libyan tribes (called Lebū or Libū in the hieroglyphic sources) became intermingled, in antiquity, with the true Egyptians. This process of fusion probably took place predominantly in the western part of the Delta.

In considering the name of the tribe of the Mas̲h̲awas̲h̲a and its identification with that of the Mazāta, it must be stated that the form of this nomenclature as found in the ancient hieroglyphic sources is a collective noun composed of the singular noun *Mas̲h̲a(wa)*—which is the name of the eponymous founder of the tribe—and the suffix *-s̲h̲a*, the designation of a collective in Libyan and Old Berber. It appears furthermore that the Libyco-Berber suffix *-s̲h̲a* (or *-sa*) derives from another language which the linguists call Aegean and which was spoken by certain small tribes belonging, in the 13th and 12th centuries B.C., to the "Peoples of the Sea". It is read, for example, in the Egyptian inscriptions dating from this period that one of the tribes in question, the Achaeans, bore the name of *Aḳaywas̲h̲a* and that the tribe of the Siculi which was later to inhabit Sicily was called *S̲h̲akalas̲h̲a* (or *Sakalasa*). The same ethnic suffix was also used in Old Berber. Thus, e.g. it is discovered from the writings of Ibn K̲h̲aldūn that the descendants of a certain Ḍarī formed the tribe which bore the name of Ḍarīsa, a collective nomenclature with the collective suffix *-sa*. Returning to the question of the Mas̲h̲awas̲h̲a (or Masawasa, i.e. Mazāta), it is to be believed that these two tribes were identical, or rather that the Mazāta were distant descendants of the ancient Mas̲h̲awas̲h̲a. In fact, the termination *-āta*, which concludes certain Berber ethnic names (e.g. that of the Law-āta) is composed of two suffixes, of which the first, *-āt-*, which is Berber, added to the eponymous name, makes it a collective noun, and the second, the final *-a* (as in the names of the Lawāt-a and the Mazāt-a) has been added by mediaeval Arab authors to give this noun an Arabic plural (Lawāta, Mazāta). In this manner, the Berber suffix *-āt-* has the same function as the Libyco-Berber suffix *-s̲h̲a* or *-sa*.

Initially, the Mas̲h̲awas̲h̲a inhabited western Libya, in other words Tripolitania and what is now Tunisia. At about the time of the end of the New

Empire, they took the decision to conquer Cyrenaica and Marmarica, lands which had been occupied by other Libyan tribes. The population of these lands offered fierce resistance, but the Ma<u>sh</u>awa<u>sh</u>a massacred them and subjugated them by force. Since the conquerors brought with them their families and their livestock, this constituted a veritable *Völkerwanderung*. After the conquest of Cyrenaica and Marmarica, the Ma<u>sh</u>awa<u>sh</u>a resolved to attack Egypt. Their first attempts at conquest took place during the reigns of the Pharaohs Sethi I and Rameses II in the 13th century B.C., and ended in failure. It was only during the reign of the Pharaoh Mineptah that the chieftain of the Ma<u>sh</u>awa<u>sh</u>a named Meriaï, son of Didi, achieved a degree of success. This chieftain was assured of the support of the "Peoples of the Sea", a federation of tribes originating from southern Europe and western Asia who sowed terror throughout the Near East. With the aid of these peoples the Ma<u>sh</u>awa<u>sh</u>a succeded, in 1227 B.C., in seizing the oases situated on the Egypt-Libya frontier, as well as part of the western Delta. Later however, the Egyptians struck a terrible blow against the Ma<u>sh</u>awa<u>sh</u>a and their allies in a major battle which took place at Per-Ir, to the north-west of Memphis. The soldiers of the Pharaoh, riding in chariots, pursued and massacred the fugitives. Among those slain on the battlefield were thousands of Ma<u>sh</u>awa<u>sh</u>a, of eastern Libyans and of Aḳaywa<u>sh</u>a, and hundreds of *Tursa* (*Tur<u>sh</u>a*), of *Sakalasa*, of *Sardana* (<u>Sh</u>ardana) and of Lycians. In spite of this defeat the Ma<u>sh</u>awa<u>sh</u>a, aided by the eastern Libyans, mounted a fresh invasion in 1194 B.C. during the reign of Rameses III. The war was keenly contested, but the Ma<u>sh</u>awa<u>sh</u>a were eventually defeated and forced to evacuate the western Delta. In the year 1188 B.C., during the reign of the same Pharaoh Rameses III, there was yet a third attempt at the conquest of Egypt on the part of the Ma<u>sh</u>awa<u>sh</u>a, aided by their Libyan allies, and this too ended with victory going to the Egyptians. But on this occasion the Pharaoh understood that it would be impossible to subdue the Ma<u>sh</u>awa<u>sh</u>a and the eastern Libyans, who had been driven to despair by the catastrophic state of their country which was becoming an arid wilderness. He therefore permitted the Ma<u>sh</u>awa<u>sh</u>a and the eastern Libyans to settle in the Delta, in exchange for an undertaking on their part to supply mercenaries to the Egyptian army. In this manner, the military conflict between the Ma<u>sh</u>awa<u>sh</u>a and the eastern Libyans on the one hand and the Egyptians on the other was concluded in a kind of amicable arrangement. There thus began in the Delta a vigorous process of intermingling between the native Egyptians and the Ma<u>sh</u>awa<u>sh</u>a and Libyan settlers, facilitated by mixed marriages which became commonplace not only among the lower strata of society, but also among the upper classes, where the Ma<u>sh</u>awa<u>sh</u>a achieved posts of seniority in the sacerdotal and military hierarchy. In the 11th century B.C. one of these dignitaries, named Sheshonq, married an Egyptian princess of the royal family, and his great-grandson, also named Sheshonq, who was commander of the Egyptian army and bore the title of "Grand Chieftain of the Ma<u>sh</u>awa<u>sh</u>a", took over supreme power in the country in the year 950 B.C. and, after the death of the Pharaoh Psousennes II, founded the XXII Egyptian dynasty. The Ma<u>sh</u>awa<u>sh</u>a and the Libyans of the Delta and of Libya recognised the authority of Sheshonq. It should be added that until this moment, these two ethnic groups had lived in complete autonomy.

Towards the end of the XXII dynasty, a prince of this dynasty named Pedoubastis founded the XXIII dynasty. It is interesting to note that for a period of time the Libyan Pharaohs of these two dynasties reigned simultaneously, and also maintained the best of mutual relations. Thus there began the partition of the Delta, where in 747-30 B.C. three princes claimed the title of Pharaoh. Ultimately, a Libyan prince of Sais, probably himself a descendant of Sheshonq I, displaced the last Pharaohs of the two rival dynasties and founded the XXIV dynasty, known as the Saite. The Libyan period lasted two centuries, during which Egypt remained under the domination of the minority composed of Ma<u>sh</u>awa<u>sh</u>a and of other Libyan tribes.

The Ma<u>sh</u>awa<u>sh</u>a and the Egyptianised Libyans were still in evidence in the 2nd century A.D. These are without doubt the Libu-Aegyptii who, according to Ptolemy, constitute the population of Mareotis, territory situated in the western Delta around Lake Mariout.

With regard to the non-Egyptianised Ma<u>sh</u>awa<u>sh</u>a, outside Egypt, they may be identified, in all probability, with the nomads of Libya known as Mazues and mentioned by Stephanus of Byzantium following Hecateus (6th century B.C.), and are to be distinguished from the Maxues who were established, according to Herodotus (5th century B.C.) in the coastal region of the lesser Syrte. It should be added that the Mazues were nomads while the Maxues were cultivators. Hecateus does not specify which part of Libya they inhabited. It is very likely that they are the ancestors of the Mazāta of Cyrenaica and eastern Tripolitania. As for the name of this tribe, it is composed of the root *Maz-* (singular noun, of which Mazāta is the Berber collective form) with the Greek termination *-ues* (*-yes*).

It also seems necessary to identify with the ancient Ma<u>sh</u>awa<u>sh</u>a (*Ma<u>sh</u>a(wa)-<u>sh</u>a*) known from the hieroglyphic inscriptions and the mediaeval Mazāta of the Arab authors, the Libyan tribe of the Mastites (*Mas-t-itae*) located by Ptolemy in the province of Mareotis, in the region of Lake Mariout, on the western frontiers of the Delta. In this ethnonym, the termination *-itae* may probably be of Greek origin, and the suffix *-t-* (in place of *-āt*) the sign of the collective in Libyan.

The Arab historians and geographers knew of the Mazāta at a very early date. In fact, when the renowned general ᶜUḳba b. Nāfiᶜ set out for the Ma<u>gh</u>rib in 46/666-7, passing through Ma<u>gh</u>madā<u>sh</u> (formerly Macomades Selorum, currently Marsa Zafran or Medinet es-Soltan), through Waddan (currently the oasis of Djofra) and through the Fazzān as far as the territory of Kawār, he made his return journey through the town of Zawīla, one of the capitals of the Fazzān, whence he made his way towards the territory of the tribe of the Mazāta in eastern Tripolitania. This tribe was, in the 7th century A.D., quite powerful and it possessed a number of fortresses (Ar. *ḳuṣūr*) which ᶜUḳba b. Nāfiᶜ captured. This account, which is known to us through the intermediary of Ibn ᶜAbd al-Ḥakam (d. 257/871), is the earliest information available concerning the Mazāta emanating from Arabic sources, being based on the accounts of numerous early informants, the earliest of whom, Yazīd b. Abī Ḥabīb, died in 128/746, only eighty years after the expedition of ᶜUkba b. Nafiᶜ. The other Arabic references to the Mazāta are of much later date and derive from the period of the 3rd-8th/9th-14th centuries.

According to mediaeval Arab authors, the Mazāta were a very numerous and prosperous people, simultaneously nomadic (or semi-nomadic) stockbreeders and cultivators, whose centres of population and pastures were dispersed throughout North Africa, from the province of al-Buḥayra (between Alexandria and Old Cairo) to the east as far as the neighbourhood of Tāhart (Tiaret) to the west. They adopted orthodox Islam at a very early stage, but at the time of the Khāridjī revolution which affected all the Berbers of North Africa at about the middle of the 8th century A.D., they went over to Khāridjism. It is not impossible that they initially adopted Ṣufrī doctrines, as did the majority of the Berber tribes. However, some twenty or thirty years later, they were already professing Ibāḍism, sometimes following the very moderate doctrines of the Wahbī branch, sometimes the very extremist doctrines of the Nukkarī branch, which became very popular among the Berbers from the period of Abū Yazīd [*q.v.*], the "Man on the Donkey", who rebelled in the first half of the 4th/10th century against the Fāṭimid caliphate. It was only at a fairly late date, probably about the 7th/13th century, that the Mazāta began, little by little, to reject Ibāḍī beliefs, turning to Sunnism. The written sources supply little information on this subject. It may be added, furthermore, that according to Ibn Ḥawḳal (4th/10th century), a section of the Mazāta of Ifrīḳiya professed Muʿtazilī doctrines.

The Mazāta were divided into numerous more or less powerful sub-tribes (Ar. *ḳabīla*, *fakhdh*) and many of their names are indicated by Ibn Ḥawḳal, Ibn Khaldūn, an anonymous list from the 7th/13th century of eminent Ibāḍī personalities classified by tribe, and finally the *Kitāb al-Siyar* of Abu 'l-ʿAbbās al-Shammākhī, an Ibāḍī historian of the 10th/16th century. Among these texts, that of Ibn Ḥawḳal gives a list of the sub-tribes of the Mazāta mingled with those of the Lawāta, in such a way that it is impossible to separate these peoples. The list of the Mazāta sub-tribes presented by Ibn Khaldūn is very incomplete (it includes the names of only six of these segments). As for al-Shammākhī, he supplies the names of the sub-tribes of the Mazāta and the *nisba*s on these names, and they are found dispersed among the biographies of renowned personalities mentioned in his *Kitāb al-Siyar.* It should be added that some sub-tribes of Mazāta are also mentioned in other Ibāḍī works, including the *Kitāb al-Sīra* of Abū Zakariyyāʾ al-Wardjalānī (6th/12th century) or the *Kitāb Ṭabaḳāt al-mashāyikh* of Abu 'l-ʿAbbās al-Dardjīnī (7th/13th century).

The names of these Mazāta sub-tribes are as follows: — 1. Banū Maṭkūd; 2. Banū Wīslū; 3. Banū Madūna; 4. Zamrata (this name is known only from the *nisba* al-Zamratī; the Berber form of it is Izəmratən and the reading given by Ibn Ḥawḳal is to be thus corrected); 5. Banū Zimmarīn; 6. Banū Ardjān; 7. Banū Dadjma or Dadjama (read Dagma, Dagama); 8. Banū Masāra; 9. Banū Īlayan (in Ibn Khaldūn's work, the incorrect orthography of this name is found: B. Layān); 10. Banū Faṭnāsa; 11. Banū Kazīna; 12. Banū Ḳarna; 13. Banū Madjīdja; 14. Banū Ḥamza (thus according to Ibn Ḥawḳal; Ibn Khaldūn incorrectly writes it as Ḥamra); 15. Awmāsht (also Ūmāsht); this last ethnonym seems to be composed of the prefix *Aw-* (*Ū-*) which signifies "son" in Berber, and of the eponymous name *-mash-*, to which has been added the Berber sign of the collective *-t*; it closely resembles one of the ancient names of the Mazāta, this being *Mas-t-itae*, which has been considered above.

1. *Egypt.* The most easterly settlements of the Mazāta embraced, in the Middle Ages, the Egyptian province called al-Buḥayra [*q.v.*] situated on the western borders of the Delta, between Alexandria and Old Cairo, i.e. the same region previously inhabited by the ancestors of the Mazāta, the Mashawasha of the hieroglyphic sources and the Mastitae of the ancient sources. According to Ibn Khaldūn, there were to be found in the Buḥayra numerous nomadic (or rather semi-nomadic) peoples who belonged to the Berber tribes of the Mazāta, Hawwāra and Zanāta. According to him, these tribes tarried in the Buḥayra to sow their crops but, at the approach of winter, moved to the neighbourhood of al-ʿAḳaba and Barḳa. He adds that the above-mentioned tribes paid a tax (Ar. *kharādj*) to the sultan of Egypt. It is not known which al-ʿAḳaba is in question here, since there are two places with this toponym, al-Aḳaba al-Ṣaghīra ("the small slope, pass", Catabathmus parvus of the ancient sources), forty leagues from Alexandria to the west, and al-ʿAḳaba al-Kabīra ("the great slope, pass", Catabathmus magnus of the ancient sources), forty leagues to the west of the former. Al-Bakrī (5th/11th century) mentions the settlements (or rather the winter habitat) of these Mazāta "at the foot of the slope of al-ʿAḳaba", without specifying whether this is Catabathmus magnus or parvus. It is on this side of Egypt, to the east of al-ʿAḳaba al-Ṣaghīra, that the place known as Rammāda is to be located, a site which according to al-Yaʿḳūbī was inhabited by the Mazāta and other Berber tribes.

2. *Cyrenaica* (Barḳa). If Ibn Khaldūn is to be believed, the regular haunts of these Mazāta who possessed agricultural land in Egypt, in the province of al-Buḥayra, on the Western borders of the Delta, were located in part in Cyrenaica (Barḳa), where this people invariably spent the winter. Arabic sources of information regarding the Mazāta of Cyrenaica are few in number and relatively late. The earliest reference to the Mazāta of Cyrenaica is owed to Ibn Khaldūn. According to this historian, they participated in the Umayyad revolt which took place in Cyrenaica *ca.* 395/1004-5. Al-Idrīsī (6th/12th century) claims that in his time the Mazāta of Barḳa were already Arabised. These courageous horsemen inhabited the regions of Cyrenaica situated between the town of Ṭulmaytha (the ancient Ptolemais) and Laḳḳa (Cape Locco or Luca on modern maps, not far from Tobruk). Two centuries later, Muḥammad b. Ibrāhīm al-Kutubī (Waṭwāṭ, d. 718/1318) locates the settlements of the Mazāta of Barḳa on a mountain (Djabal al-Akhḍar) situated to the west of the town of Barḳa. An analogous reference is also found in the *Cosmography* of al-Dimashḳī (d. 727/1327).

3. *Tripolitania.* A very significant portion of the Mazāta inhabited the eastern part of what is now Tripolitania, as neighbours of the Lawāta of Barḳa to the east and the Hawwāra of central Tripolitania to the west. The eastern limit of their domain was constituted, at about the end of the 3rd/9th century, by a point situated at one day's journey to the west of Adjdābiya. The western limit of the territory of the Tripolitanian Mazāta passed near Tawargha (Taouordga or Taourga), to the south of Misurata. In the south, the habitat of this tribe extended beyond the Djebel es-Soda, towards the frontier of the Fazzān, the population of which remained, in the 3rd/9th century, in a state of war with the Tripolitanian Mazāta. The Mazāta formerly constituted the majority of the inhabitants of Waddān, ancient provincial capital of the oasis of Djofra, where nevertheless there are also to be noted, in this period, the presence of two Arab tribal groups. The desert town of Tādjrift, situated between Waddān and the town of Surt (currently Medinet es-Soltan) on the coast, three

days' journey from the first-named place, which may be identified with what is now Tagrift (Tagrefet), was populated in the 4th/10th century by inhabitants of Waddān, in other words by Mazāta mingled with Arabs. The oasis of Zalhā (Sella or Zella on modern maps) also formed, in the 4th-5th/10th-11th centuries, part of the territory of the Mazāta, as is revealed by a passage from the writings of al-Bakrī (Muḥammad b. Yūsuf, Ibn al-Warrāḳ). Finally, in this period there belonged to the people of Waddān an unnamed *manzil* ("station") situated midway between Tamassā (Tmassa on modern maps, to the northeast of Mourzouk) and Zalhā, and apparently to be identified with what is now el-Fugha or Fogha, a pleasant oasis and a village with ruins probably of Garamantian origin.

In the early Middle Ages, the land of the Mazāta embraced two different districts, these being Surt and Waddān. The district of Surt corresponded to the coastal zone of what is now eastern Tripolitania, and that of Waddān occupied the whole interior of this land. The former of these districts was known, from the year 46/666-7, by the name of Surt or *arḍ Surt* ("land of Surt"). Later, the localities belonging to this territory received the name of Ḳuṣūr Surt ("Castles of Surt"). As for Waddān, which appears for the first time in the same year of 46/666-7 as a country having its own king, it was still considered in the 6th/12th century as an administrative district (A. *ʿamal*, also *arḍ*, "country") apart. It was, furthermore, closely linked to the land of Surt. The district of Waddān embraced, no doubt, all the places in the interior of eastern Tripolitania which were inhabited by Mazāta and by people of Waddān, these being Zalhā (Sella), Ta<u>dj</u>rift (Tagrift) and el-Fugha.

The Mazāta of eastern Tripolitania who had probably inhabited this land since earliest times (it is likely that this land was the cradle of the ancient Ma<u>sh</u>awa<u>sh</u>a, distant ancestors of the Mazāta) rallied at an early stage to the cause of Ibāḍism. The district of Surt constituted a province of the ephemeral Ibāḍī state of the *imām* Abu 'l-<u>Kh</u>aṭṭāb ʿAbd al-Aʿlā b. al-Samḥ al-Maʿāfirī (140-4/757-61). Numerous individuals, probably members of the branch of the Mazāta which inhabited eastern Tripolitania, played a significant role in the army of this *imām*. It was also in the territory of Surt, at Ma<u>gh</u>madās (in ancient times Macomades Syrtis or Macomades Selorum), that there took place in 141/759 a battle between the army of Abu 'l-<u>Kh</u>aṭṭāb and that of the ʿAbbāsid general Abu 'l-Aḥwaṣ ʿUmar b. al-Aḥwaṣ al-ʿI<u>dj</u>lī. After the defeat and death of Abu 'l-<u>Kh</u>aṭṭāb in 144/761, the victorious Arab general Ibn al-A<u>sh</u>ʿa<u>th</u> took control of the district of Surt and sent troops, in 145/762-3, to conquer the land of Waddān. The capital of this region was taken and its Ibāḍī population put to the sword.

In spite of the defeat of Abu 'l-<u>Kh</u>aṭṭāb, Ibāḍism survived for a long period of time in eastern Tripolitania. In fact, the land of Surt appears in the time of the Ibāḍī *imām* ʿAbd al-Wahhāb b. ʿAbd al-Raḥmān b. Rustum (168-208/784-823) to be a province of the Rustumid state of Tāhart. The Mazāta of eastern Tripolitania continued to profess Ibāḍī doctrines. In fact, at about the end of the 3rd/9th century, the Mazāta were still independent and governed by an indigenous chieftain, apparently an Ibāḍī. At a later date, al-Dar<u>dj</u>īnī (7th/13th century) notes the presence of encampments of Mazāta in the neighbourhood of Tripoli, in the first half of the 5th/11th century, but he considers that the people in question are not the Mazāta of eastern Tripolitania, but the branch of this tribe occupying the region of Ḳābis (Gabès) in south-eastern Tunisia, which will be considered below. Similarly, nothing definite is known regarding the origin of Dūnās b. al-<u>Kh</u>ayr al-Mazātī who was the chieftain (Ar. *raʾīs*) of the Ibāḍīs of Tripolitania under the dynasty of the Banū <u>Kh</u>azrūn (493-540/1100-45). The sources of the 8th/14th and 9th/15th century are almost entirely silent regarding the inhabitants, evidently Mazāta and Ibāḍīs, of eastern Tripolitania. It is known however that the people of Sokna, in the oasis of el-Djofra, recall having formerly been Ibāḍīs, which proves that Ibāḍism has survived in these regions until a relatively recent period.

Remnants of the Mazāta also lived in the <u>Dj</u>abal Nafūsa, in the hinterland of western Tripolitania. Thus it is known, from Ibāḍī chronicles, that people originally of the Mazāta tribe of Da<u>dj</u>ma (Dagma, Dagama) lived at Di<u>dj</u>ī (currently Deggui) in the western part of the <u>Dj</u>abal Nafūsa. It is also interesting to note that the name of the important village of Ar<u>dj</u>ān or Arkān (currently Kherbet Ardjan, not far from Mezzou, to the north of <u>Dj</u>ādū in the eastern part of the <u>Dj</u>abal Nafūsa) recalls that of the Banū Ar<u>dj</u>ān, a sub-tribe of the Mazāta which has been mentioned above.

4. *Tunisia*. A segment of the Mazāta also lived in the mountains of south-eastern Tunisia, alongside tribes of the Lawāta, the Lamāya and the Zanzafa, and not far from the major Berber population of Banū Dammar (Demmer). The Mazāta, the Lawāta, the Lamāya and the Zanzafa lived in the vicinity of a place called Tāmūlast, of which the exact location is not known. It was this place which produced the great Ibāḍī historian, theologian and lawyer Abu 'l-Rabīʿ Sulaymān b. Ya<u>kh</u>laf al-Mazātī (d. 471/1078-9 [*q.v.*], and see below). It was the regional centre of a district called <u>Dj</u>abal Tāmūlast, situated "below" the <u>Dj</u>abal Dammar.

Another branch of the tribe of the Mazāta resided in the vicinity of the town of Ḳābis (Gabès), alongside other Berber peoples, such as the Lawāta, the Lamāya, the Nafūsa, the Zawā<u>gh</u>a and the Zawāra. This is known from a passage of the *Kitāb al-Masālik wa 'l-mamālik* of al-Bakrī (5th/11th century). It is interesting to recall that Ibn Ḥawḳal (4th/10th century) mentions the Berber populations living in the neighbourhood of Gabès as tillers of the soil. According to this author, they were heretics, i.e. Ibāḍīs. The chroniclers call this people Mazātat Ḳābis. There were also Ibāḍī Mazāta at Zarīḳ (Zerig el-Barraniya on modern maps), a locality situated close to Kettana, to the south-east of Gabès. Among the residents of this place was the Ibāḍī <u>*shaykh*</u> ʿAbbūd b. Manār al-Mazātī, the maternal uncle of Abu 'l-Rabīʿ Sulaymān b. Ya<u>kh</u>laf al-Mazātī.

Ibn Ḥawḳal also speaks of the large tribe of the Mazāta living in the region of Ḳasṭīliya (Tozeur?), of Ḳafṣa (Gafsa), of Nafzāwa, of al-Ḥammā, of Sumāṭa and of Bi<u>sh</u>rī (Bechri on modern maps). It is probably among this segment of the Mazāta that there were recruited the *fityān* and the *talāmi<u>dh</u>a* of Mazāta origin who lived, at about the 5th/11th century, if al-<u>Sh</u>ammā<u>kh</u>ī (10th/16th century) is to believed, in the Ḳasṭīliya (here = Bilād al-<u>Dj</u>arīd). In the canton of Nafzāwa (Nefzaoua on modern maps) there lived a segment of the Mazātian sub-tribe of the Banū Izəmratən (or Izmərtən) which professed the Ibāḍī-Wahbī faith; according to Ibn <u>Kh</u>aldūn this group belonged not to the Mazāta, as stated by Ibāḍī sources, but to the great Berber family of the Zanāta. The town of Faṭnāsa (Fetnassa on modern maps) also owes its name to the homonymous Berber sub-tribe, a branch of the Mazāta. Between Tawzar (Tozeur) and al-Ḥāmma lived the Mazāta sub-tribe of the Kazīna.

Further to the north-east of the Bilād al-Djarīd and of Ḳafṣa (Gafsa), there were numerous Ibāḍī-Wahbī Mazāta on the plain of Kayrawān (called Faḥṣ al-Ḳayrawān in the Ibāḍī chronicles). It is curious to note that, in spite of their Khāridjī faith, these Mazāta were loyal servants of the Zīrid kings of Ifrīḳiya. A renowned Zīrid general had his origin in this segment of the Mazāta which bore, in the chronicles of this seat, the name of Mazātat al-Ḳayrawān.

In all probability, there were formerly also Ibāḍī Mazāta in the Djebel Ousselet, the Djabal Wasalāt of the Arab geographers, a canton situated to the west of the town of Ḳayrawān. It is no doubt with this name that there should be associated the ethnic al-Wasalātī, applied to numerous Ibāḍī individuals of the 4th/10th and 5th/11th centuries, members of the tribe of the Mazāta, including for example of the *shaykh* ʿAbd al-Ghanī al-Wasalātī al-Mazātī, and the *shaykh* Fatūḥ b. Abī Ḥadjdjī al-Wasalātī al-Mazātī. According to the anonymous list of Ibāḍī *shaykhs* of the 7th/13th century, ʿAbd al-Ghanī belonged to the Mazāta branch of Awmāsht.

According to the Ibāḍī historian Abu ʾl-ʿAbbās al-Dardjīnī, the Mazāta of Ifrīḳiya were very rich (in particular, they possessed a large number of horses) and very warlike.

5. *Algeria.* An important branch of the Mazāta lived in what is now Algeria, in particular in the Zāb and the Hodna, as well as in the region north of Aurès, the Djabal Awrās of the Arabic sources. The mediaeval Arab authors mention there, among others, a segment of the Mazāta in the vicinity of Baghāya (Baghaï on modern maps), in a plain intersected by streams. In speaking of the Berber inhabitants of this region, al-Bakrī (5th/11th century) says that they belonged to the Berber tribes of the Mazāta and the Ḍarīsa and that they professed the doctrines of the Ibāḍī sect. According to this geographer, they were semi-nomads; they spent the winter in desert regions where they bred camels. When the Ibāḍī-Wahbī *shaykh* Abū Khazar al-Wisyānī rebelled, in the middle of the 4th/10th century, against the Fāṭimid government, the Mazāta of Baghāya, of the Zāb and of the Hodna, who were very numerous and then numbered "12,000 horsemen and an incalculable multitude of foot-soldiers", were among the most fervent supporters of this chieftain. Furthermore, the same Mazāta also supported, some years earlier, the Ibāḍī-Nukkārī *imām* Abū Yazīd ("the Man on the Donkey"). These two items of information are owed to the Ibāḍī historian Abū Zakariyyāʾ al-Wardjalānī (beginning of the 6th/12 century). When Buluggīn b. Zīrī, chief of the Ṣanhādja and loyal supporter of the Fāṭimid caliphs, took the field to conquer the central Maghrib (in 360/971), according to the Arab historians he exterminated the Mazāta and other Berbers living in the district of Baghāya.

Another group of Mazāta lived further towards the west, in the vicinity of what is now the town of Batna, in a stronghold which al-Bakrī calls Billizma li-Mazāta ("Billizma of the Mazāta"), on territory known today by the name of Djebel Bellezma. Nothing else is known with any certainty concerning this segment of the Mazāta, who were apparently tillers of the soil.

A sizeable Berber population composed of Mazāta, of Zanāta and of Hawwāra, lived, in the mediaeval period, in the town of al-Masīla [*q.v.*] (Msila on modern maps), formerly capital of the canton of the Hodna, as well as in brushwood shacks situated in the suburbs of this town. These Berbers were also massacred by the warriors of Buluggīn b. Zīrī in 360/971. However, the Mazāta of these regions later regained their strength, since the Arab geographer of the 6th/12th century, al-Idrīsī, refers to this tribe as still inhabiting the territory of al-Masīla, which it shared with the Banū Birzāl, the Zandādj, the Hawwāra and the Ṣadrāta. The Berber tribes in question, according to Ibn Ḥawḳal and al-Idrīsī, were engaged in the raising of livestock and in agriculture. Undoubtedly, it is the same segment of the Mazāta of which Ibn Ḥawḳal speaks, locating it between Tifāsh (the ancient Tipasa) and al-Masīla, alongside a branch of the tribe of the Kutāma. Ibn Ḥawḳal also mentions a village named Dakma (Dagma), situated close to al-Masīla, which in the time of this geographer was inhabited by the Kutāma, but the name of which is associated with that of one of the sub-tribes of the Mazāta, this being Dadjma (read Dagma). The same facts were repeated at a later date by al-Idrīsī.

As for the Zāb, the Mazāta of this land lived, being semi-nomadic, in brushwood shacks in the vicinity of the towns of Ṭubna (the ancient Tubunae) and of Biskra. In 360/971, they were massacred by Buluggīn b. Zīrī, but subsequently they regained their strength. Al-Shammākhī (10th/16th century) refers to the Mazāta in question, describing various features of their history during the 5th/11th and 6th/12th centuries. They lived in encampments (Ar. *aḥyāʾ*) and professed the Ibāḍī-Wahbī faith, with a certain tendency towards Nukkārī Ibāḍism. They were, among others, military supporters of the renowned Nukkārī chief Abū Yazīd, mentioned above.

The names of the Mazāta sub-tribes which inhabited the Zāb are not known. It is very likely that it is to these groups that the Madūna belonged, and perhaps also the Awmāsht (Ūmāsht). In fact, the name of this latter people is found in that of the locality, Oumach on modern maps, which is situated midway between Tehouda (the ancient Thabudeos) and Mlili (the ancient Gemellae).

The Mazāta of the Zāb and of the Hodna belonged to very rich tribes which did not use their wealth to support the Rustamid imāmate of Tāhart. The Ibāḍī historians state in this context, quoting the words of one of the Rustamid *imāms*, that the Ibāḍī-Wahbī religion "exists through the swords of the Nafūsa and the possessions of the Mazāta", also alluding to the religious zeal of the former of these tribes. Ibn Ṣaghīr, author of a chronicle of Tāhart composed at the beginning of the 4th/10th century, says of the Mazāta, the Sadrāta and other tribes inhabiting the Zāb and the Hodna, that they "were in the habit, in the season of spring, of leaving the temporary lands that they occupied in the Maghrib or other regions to come to Tāhart or its surrounding areas on account of the pastures that they found there and other advantages which the land offered them... When the nomads arrived to install their encampments, their dignitaries and leaders of groups presented themselves in the town where they were received with kindness and respect (by the *imāms*). Then they returned to their encampments where they remained until the time of their departure".

Bibliography: A. de C. Motylinski, *Chronique d'Ibn Ṣaghir sur les imams rostémides de Tahert*, in *Actes du XVIe Congrès International des Orientalistes. Alger 1905. Troisième partie*, Paris 1908, Ar. text, 17, Fr. tr. 74; Ibn ʿAbd al-Ḥakam, *Futūḥ Ifrīḳiya wa-l-Andalus. Conquête de l'Afrique et de l'Espagne*, ed. A.

Gateau, Algiers 1947, 60-7, 144, 145; Yaʿḳūbī, *Buldān*, 1892, 344-6; Ibn Ḥawḳal, ed. Kramers, i, 68, 70, 86, 87, 96; Bakrī, *Description de l'Afrique septentrionale*, Ar. text ed. de Slane, Algiers 1911, 8, 12, 13, 14, 17-18, 50, 144-5; Fr. tr. de Slane, Algiers 1913, 13, 23-4, 29, 30, 31, 32, 33, 35, 42, 107, 277; E. Masqueray, *Chronique d'Abou Zakaria*, Algiers 1878, 194-5, 230-6, 288-98; Idrīsī, *Description de l'Afrique et de l'Espagne*, ed.-tr. R. Dozy and de Goeje, Leiden 1866, Ar. text 57, 85-6, 120, 132-3, Fr. tr. 66, 95., 141, 158, 159; Dardjīnī, *Kitāb Ṭabaḳāt al-mashāyikh*, ed. Ṭallāʾī, Blida 1394/1974, i, 87, 100, 111-12, 124, 128; Dimashḳī, *Cosmographie*, ed. Mehren, Leipzig 1923, 234; idem, *Manuel*, tr. Mehren, Copenhagen 1874, 329; Ibn Khaldūn, *Berbères*, i, 8, n. 2, 9, 40, 1/1, 232, 311, ii, iii, 186; Shammākhī, *Kitāb al-Siyar*, Cairo 1301/1883-4, 130, 142, 143, 161, 203, 205, 260-2, 271, 290, 298, 348-9, 364, 371, 392-3, 409, 419, 427; E. Fagnan, *Extraits inédits relatif au Maghreb*, Algiers 1924, 43; J. Despois, *Djebel Nefousa*, Paris 1935, 137, n. 1; T. Gostynski, *La Libye antique et ses relations avec l'Égypte*, in *BIFAN*, xxxvii (1975), 472-588; H. R. Idris, *La Berbérie orientale sous les Zīrīdes, Xᵉ-XIIᵉ siècles*, Paris 1962, i, 36, ii, 430, 458, 462, 464, 476, 477, 478, 485; T. Lewicki, *Études ibāḍites nord-africaines*, Warsaw 1955, 98, 122-3; idem, *Les Ibāḍites en Tunisie au moyen âge*, in *Accademia Polacca di Scienze e Lettere. Biblioteca di Roma.* Conferenze, Fasc. 6, Rome 1959, 7, n. 18, 8, 11, 13, 15; idem, *La Répartition géographique des groupements ibāḍites*, in *RO*, xxi (1957), 317-19, 333, 335.

(T. Lewicki)

al-**MAZĀTĪ**, Abu 'l-Rabīʿ Sulaymān b. Yakhlaf, famous Ibāḍī historian, theologian and jurisconsult. He was a member, as his *nisba* indicates, of the Berber tribe of Mazāta [*q.v.*], probably from the branch who lived in the mountains of south-east Tunisia beside the tribes of the Lawāta and Zanzafa. All these tribes were living around a district which was called Tāmūlast but whose exact location eludes us and which was, in all probability, the place from which Abu 'l-Rabīʿ originated. It is, indeed, in this locality that there lived his paternal uncle Iṣlītan (Yaṣlītan) and it is not far from this place, at a point in the neighbouring desert, called Asarkīm, that his family and herds lived for some time. His maternal uncle, ʿAbbūd b. Manār al-Mazātī, lived not far from there, in Zarīḳ, to the south-east of the town of Gabès. One should add that Abu 'l-Rabīʿ had a brother called ʿAlī.

The date of his birth is uncertain. We know, however, that, as a young man, in the first decade of the 5th/11th century, he studied under the famous Ibāḍī *shaykh* Abū ʿAbd Allāh Muḥammad b. Bakr in Tīn Yaṣlī (Tīn Īṣlī) in the Oued Righ. He learned from him the fundamental principles of the law. Then, he went to study the law in Djarba [*q.v.*] with several famous *shaykh*s of that island, which was in this period one of the cultural centres of the Ibāḍīs of North Africa.

After having finished his studies in Djarba, Abu 'l-Rabīʿ returned to Tāmūlast, where he was soon surrounded by a wide circle of students whom he taught, among other subjects, *al-āthār*, i.e. the history of the Ibāḍī sect and the biographies of distinguished Ibāḍīs. He was already there at the time of the death of his old master Abū ʿAbd Allāh Muḥammad b. Bakr in 440/1048-9. From Tāmūlast, Abu 'l-Rabīʿ set out, before 449/1057-8, for Ḳalʿat ʿAlī (also Ḳalʿat Banī ʿAlī), a place situated in the Djabal Zanzafa, near Tāmūlast; he lived there with his students until 462/1069-70. He felt safer in this place than in Tāmūlast, through which passed the route of some Arab tribes (notably the Banū Hilāl) going from Tripolitania to Ifrīḳiya and returning to Tripolitania. In the same year, Abu 'l-Rabīʿ returned to Tāmūlast, where he stayed for some time, always surrounded by his students. Towards the end of his life, he went to settle in Tūnīn, a desert place situated in the mountains near Tāmūlast, where a *ḥalḳa* or circle of students soon gathered around him. His students were recruited from among the peoples of the Sūf (Oued Souf), Arīgh (Oued Righ), Wārdjlān (Ouargla), Zāb and Ḳasṭīliya. Among those who were specially interested in Ibāḍī history and *siyar*, one should mention principally the famous future historian Abū Zakariyyāʾ Yaḥyā b. Abī Bakr al-Wardjalānī.

According to the old Ibāḍī chronicles, Abu 'l-Rabīʿ died in 471/1070-9 in Tūnīn. However, the Ibāḍī tradition of Ouargla places the tomb and mosque of Shaykh Abu 'l-Rabīʿ Sulaymān al-Mazātī, who is doubtless none other than Abu 'l-Rabīʿ Sulaymān b. Yakhlaf al-Mazātī, in this latter town.

Abu 'l-Rabīʿ travelled extensively. We have already seen that he had passed his youth in the Oued Righ and on the island of Djarba in order to study there. From the Oued Righ, he went at least twice to Ouargla, once in the company of his master Abū ʿAbd Allāh Muḥammad b. Bakr. In 459-60/1057-60 he visited, accompanied by his students, most of the Wahbī Ibāḍī groups of Tunisia and Algeria, passing by Ḳasṭāliya (Ḳasṭīliya), Nafzāwa (Nefzaoua), Asūf (Oued Souf), Waghlāna (Ourlana), Tamāsīn (Temacin) and Ouargla, from where he returned to the Djabal Zanzafa and Tāmūlast.

Abu 'l-Rabīʿ Sulaymān b. Yakhlaf al-Mazātī is the author of three works, of which one is of particular interest for the history of the Ibāḍīs of North Africa; this is the *Kitāb al-Siyar*, a collection of biographies of distinguished Ibāḍīs of the Maghrib. We do not know the date of composition of this work, which appears to have been written after the year 450/1078-9. We know of the existence of two manuscript copies of the *Kitāb al-Siyar*, of which one, apparently complete, is in Mzāb in Beni Isguène, in a library known as *al-Maktaba al-ghannāʾ*, while the other, incomplete, was formerly part of the collection of Ibāḍī manuscripts gathered by Z. Smogorzewski at Lwów (Poland). This work was lithographed in Tunis in 1321/1903-4 in a collection beginning with the *al-Radd ʿalā 'l-ʿUḳbī* of Shaykh Aṭfiyyash. It seems that numerous citations of Abu 'l-Rabīʿ which appear in some later Ibāḍī historical and biographical works in the 5th/11th century come from the *Kitāb al-Siyar*, while it is not impossible that a part of these citations come directly from the mouth of this historian and were noted by his students. This applies especially to the citations of Abu 'l-Rabīʿ inserted in the historical work of Abū Zakariyyāʾ Yaḥyā b. Abī Bakr al-Wardjalānī (6th/12th century) who, as we know, was one, of the students of Abu 'l-Rabīʿ. One also finds several citations of Abu 'l-Rabīʿ in al-Shammākhī's work.

It is curious that the *Kitāb al-Siyar* of Abu 'l-Rabīʿ should not have been cited in the catalogue of Ibāḍī books composed in the 8th/14th century by al-Barrādī, an Ibāḍī scholar who was moreover originally from the same region of Tunisia as Abu 'l-Rabīʿ. Al-Barrādī knows only two other works of this historian which dealt with theology and law.

Bibliography: Abū Zakariyyāʾ Yaḥyā b. Abī Bakr al-Wardjalānī, *Kitāb al-Sīra*, unnumbered ms. from the collection of Z. Smogorzewski, *passim* (about 30 citations); E. Masqueray, *Chronique d'Abou Zakaria*, Algiers 1878, 40, 250, 287, 299, 309, 311; Dardjīnī, *Ṭabaḳāt al-mashāyikh*, ed. Ṭallāʾī, Blida 1394/1974, *passim*; Shammākhī, *Kitāb al-Siyar*, Cairo 1301/1883-4, 212, 348, 353, 394-5, 397, 398, 411, 412, 415, 418-19, 433, 440, 491; T. Lewicki, *Les historiens biographes et traditionnistes ibāḍites-wahbites de l'Afrique du Nord du VIIIe au XVIe siècle*, in *Folia Orientalia*, iii (1961), 72-5; J. Schacht, *Bibliothèques et manuscrits ibadites*, in *RAfr.*, c/445-9 (1956), 397, no. 139. (T. Lewicki)

MAZDAK (also Mazdaḳ, Mazhdak), the leader of a revolutionary religious movement in Sāsānid Iran, during the reign of Ḳubādh, son of Fīrūz (Kavād, son of Pērōz) 488-96, 498-9 to 531). Klima regarded the name of Mazdak as a conflation of an Iranian name, Mazdak, Mizdak, or Muzhdak ("the justifier"), with a Semitic name, Mazdeḳ, from the root *zdḳ* ("righteous"). Klima also suggested that *mazdak* may have been what the leaders of this movement were called rather than a proper name, or even what its members were called (al-Mazdaḳān, al-Mazādiḳa in Arabic sources as well as al-Mazdaḳiyya).

Almost everything known about this movement comes from hostile sources. The earliest and only contemporary account is in the Syriac *Chronicle* of Pseudo-Joshua the Stylite (ed. and tr. W. Wright, Cambridge 1882, paras. ix, xx, xxi-xxiv). Subsequent, sixth-century, Greek accounts are given by Procopius (*Persian Wars*, i. v-xi, ii. ix), Agathias (*Histories*, tr. J. D. Frendo, Berlin-New York 1975, iv, chaps. 27-30, pp. 130-4), and Malalas of Antioch (*Chronographia*, in J. P. Migne (ed.), *Patrologia Cursus Completus*, Series Graeca, xcviii, Paris 1860, cols. 465, 633, 653). Theophanes (Migne, *op. cit.*, cviii, Paris 1863, col. 396) merely repeats Malalas. There are scattered allusions to Mazdak in Mazdaean Middle Persian literature. Klima suggested that references to Mazdak were deliberately omitted from the original Middle Persian text of the Sāsānid royal chronicle, the *Khwadāy-nāmag*, and credited Ibn al-Muḳaffaʿ (d. 143/760 [*q.v.*]) with inserting an account about Mazdak into his Arabic translation of the *Khwadāy-nāmag*. References to the main Arabic and Persian accounts of Mazdak based on this and other translations are given by Yarshater. Ibn al-Muḳaffaʿ also translated a Middle Persian work of fiction called the *Mazdak-nāmag* into Arabic. This work was also translated into Arabic poetry by Abān b. al-Ḥamīd al-Lāḥiḳī (d. 200/815-16 [*q.v.*]). According to Yarshater, who identifies the main fictional themes, this work was the basis for the Niẓām al-Mulk's account in the *Siyāsat-nāma* and of the poetic version in Dārāb Hormazdyār's *Rivāyāt*. It was also used by al-Bīrūnī (*Āthār*), Ibn al-Balkhī (*Fārs-nāma*), the *Mudjmal al-tawārīkh*, and Ibn al-Athīr (*Kāmil*). The most important source for Mazdakī doctrine is Abū ʿĪsā Muḥammad b. Hārūn al-Warrāḳ (d. 247/861), a Manichaean or Mazdaean convert to Islam who seems to have used some authentic Mazdakī work for his religious history (*Kitāb al-Maḳālāt*). His account is al-Shahrastānī's (468-548/1076-1153) source for Mazdakī doctrine in his *Kitāb al-milal wa 'l-niḥal*. The Mazdakī book called the *Dēsnād* cited in Mūbadh Shāh's 11th/17th-century *Dabistān-i madhāhib* [*q.v.*] is generally considered to be a fabrication because everything cited from it can also be found in al-Shahrastānī or other works, although it could be argued on the same basis that this might have been the name of the work used by al-Warrāḳ. Some of the information in the *Fihrist* of Ibn al-Nadīm [*q.v.*] appears to be independent and rather neutral.

The Mazdakī movement is said to have been founded by a certain Zarādusht (or Zardusht), son of Khurragān, *mōbadh* or chief *mōbadh* of Fasā in Fārs, after whom its members were called Zarādushtaḳān, Christensen identified this Zarādusht with a Manichaean called Bundos who, according to Malalas, appeared at Rome in the time of Diocletian (245-313), held doctrines opposed to the majority of Manichaeans, and left for Persia where he spread his doctrine. His sect was called "those of the right religion" (τῶν Δαρισθενῶν) from MP *darist-dēnān*), and Malalas says that Ḳubādh himself was a *Dərist-dēn* (ὁ Δαράσθενος for ὁ Δαρίσθενος). Christensen took Bundos to be an honorific title of Zarādusht, from MP *bwyndk* ("the venerable"), and regarded Mazdakism as a reforming Manichaean sect. However, Klima regarded Zarādusht and Bundos as separate persons, and Yarshater puts Zarādusht in the 5th century A.D. According to Arrigoni, Bundos is a mistake for Budos, therefore a fictive re-personalisation of Buddha. Yarshater suggests that the founding of Zarādusht's movement may have coincided with the end of the millennium of Zoroaster, which some calculations would put at the end of the 4th or the beginning of the 5th century A.D. It might also have been the doctrine combatted by Adurbād Māraspandān, who underwent an ordeal by fire to refute it in the time of Shāpūr II. The movement seems to have been Zoroastrian rather than Manichaean in origin, although it acquired gnostic features that gave it an affinity to Manichaeism. It may have begun as an attempt to popularise Mazdaism and to spread it in a non-élitist form that would transcend class barriers and appeal to the general population. Textual support for the egalitarian sharing of wealth, women, and wisdom exists in the extant Avesta, such as *Vendidād* iv. 44: "If fellow-believers (*hāmōdaēna*), brothers or friends, come to ask for money, wife, or wisdom, he who asks for money should be given money; he who asks for a wife should be given a wife to marry; he who asks for wisdom should be taught the holy word." Ibn al-Nadīm describes the early Khurramiyya (Mazdakīs) as a Zoroastrian sect founded by a certain Mazdak the Older (*al-Ḳadīm*), who enjoined his followers to enjoy life's pleasures, to satisfy their desire to eat and drink in a spirit of equality, to avoid dominating each other, to share women and family, to try to do good deeds, to avoid shedding blood and harming others and to be hospitable.

In the time of Ḳubādh, the movement of Zarādusht was revived under Mazdak, son of Bāmdādh ("the Sunrise"), called Mazdak the Younger by Ibn al-Nadīm. According to al-Ṭabarī, he was a native of المدريه which tends to be identified with al-Madharayya, near modern Kūt al-ʿAmāra [*q.v.*], although von Wesendonk located it in Khuzistān. Iṣṭakhr and Tabrīz are also given as Mazdak's birthplace. He is said to have been a *mōbadh* and is identified by Christensen with the Manichaean bishop Indarazar, whom Malalas says was killed by the Persian king *ca.* 527. Indarazar (Indazaros in Theophanes) is explained as *andarzgar* ("teacher") by Nöldeke; Klima suggested that the proper name Vindārāzār lies behind it and speculated that if *mazdak* were an epithet, then that might have been his real name.

A series of disasters in the late 5th century increased distress and raised apocalyptic expectations. Iran suffered a seven-year long drought and famine during the reign of Fīrūz. Defeat by the Hephthalites in 484 put the Sāsānids under the burden of paying tribute to them. The Hephthalite and dynastic civil wars also decimated the military nobility, undermining their ability to preserve their privileged position. The common interest of the monarch and the people in curbing the power of the great nobles may haved led Ḳubādh to identify himself with the Zarādushtaḳān. He may have seen this movement as a potential base of mass support against the nobles, and its programme as a means of restoring by transforming his kingdom. Nöldeke represented Ḳubādh as a forceful, capable ruler, who, for purely secular motives, favoured Mazdakism as an expedient to reduce the power of the nobles and priests. Christensen argued that Ḳubādh was a sincere convert and humanitarian ruler, motivated by religious belief and a desire for the welfare of his subjects. Pigulevskaya saw Ḳubādh as a sincere Mazdakī rather than a shrewd and subtle politician. Klima rejected Christensen's "humanitarian" characterisation of Ḳubādh based on his behaviour in his wars, although an Arabic source with a hostile bias says that, as a *zandīḳ*, Ḳubādh feared to shed blood. Although there is no way to be certain, Ḳubādh is most likely to have been motivated by a combination of political interests and religious belief.

To the extent that doctrines ascribed to Mazdak himself can be reconstructed from later sources, he seems to have advocated the enjoyment of material things in moderation and a peaceful, egalitarian and non-competitive social and economic order. Miskawayh says that the Mazdakiyya were called "the adherents of justice" (*al-ʿAdliyya*), and they are sometimes compared to the egalitarian, gnostic sect of Carpocratians that also stood for social justice. According to al-Thaʿālibī, Mazdak taught that God had put provisions for livelihood (*arzāḳ*) on earth for people to divide equally among themselves, with no one having more than his share. But people had wronged each other and sought to dominate; the strong had defeated the weak and monopolised the means of livelihood and property. It was necessary to take from the rich and give to the poor for everyone to become equal in wealth. Whoever had a surplus of property, women, or goods had no more right to it than anyone else. In Firdawsī, Mazdak is said to have taught that wealth and women must be shared in order to overcome the five demons of envy, wrath, vengeance, need and greed that turn men from righteousness. This appears to be reflected in the refutation of a sectarian who represents sharing women and property as a remedy for passions in *Dēnkart*, iii. 5.

If authentic, such a positive, anti-élitist attitude toward material possessions could hardly have been Manichaean in origin. Christensen accepted the Manichaean origin of the Mazdakiyya because they are called Manichaeans in the Greek sources. They may have been accused of Manichaeism by their enemies in Iran, and Malalas may simply have repeated the slander or have used the only name for an Iranian sect that he knew. Klima's argument that Mazdak had to use Mazdaean terminology as a vehicle for the mass communication of his propaganda because he was in Iran is based on the assumption that Mazdaism was spread uniformly, socially and geographically, in 5th-century Iran. But it is questionable that the lower classes were already Mazdaean in the 5th century; Mazdakism seems rather to have been a vehicle to spread Mazdaean doctrine among them. Puech regards Mazdakism as an optimistic reform of Manichaeism, but, as Yarshater points out, most sources describe Mazdakism as a reform of Zoroastrianism. What is known about Mazdak's doctrine is dualist and generally gnostic in character rather than specifically Manichaean. The gnostic elements that are claimed as the basis for affinity between Mazdakism and Manichaeism include pacifism, asceticism, fatalism, esoteric interpretation and the antinomian rejection of ritual. The prohibition of bloodshed appears in the context of social concord and is not necessarily either pacifist or vegetarian. The only other basis for claiming an ascetic element in Mazdakism is a hostile gloss to *Vendīdad*, iv. 49 saying that Mazdak, son of Bāmdād, ate fully himself but subjected others to hunger and death. This is just as likely to refer to the consequence for the rich of redistributing property as to refer to Mazdak's regulations for his own followers without additional corroboration. The alleged contrast between ascetic and hedonistic tendencies in Mazdakism is explained by Yarshater, by comparison with gnostic movements, in terms of a self-denying élite and wordly lay members. But this is the reverse of what the gloss suggests, and there is no other evidence for such élitism among the Mazdakiyya. According to al-Shahrastānī, Mazdak's doctrine resembled Mani's except that Darkness did not act of its own will and out of choice (*bi 'l-ḳaṣd wa 'l-ikhtiyār*), but blindly and by chance (*bi 'l-khabṭ wa 'l-ittifāḳ*), and that the mixture of Light with Darkness was produced in this way as will be their separation. Al-Shahrastānī also reports that some Manichaeans believed that mixture was produced *bi 'l-khabṭ wa 'l-ittifāḳ*, in opposition to the others. According to al-Muṭahhar b. Ṭāhir al-Maḳdisī, the Ṣābians [*q.v.*] also believed in mixture *bi 'l-khabṭ wa 'l-ittifāḳ*. Although Ṣābians are sometimes mistaken for Manichaeans, belief in a blind fate is central to Zurvanism and thus available in a Zoroastrian context. Regarding esoteric interpretation, al-Masʿūdī says that Mazdak was the first to interpret the Avesta according to its hidden meanings (*bāṭin*). Although this may have been a matter of adjusting Mazdaean doctrine for the masses, it made the Mazdakiyya into *Zindīḳs* [*q.v.*] along with the Manichaeans. According to the 3rd/9th century al-Mutawakkilī, Mazdak is also said to have persuaded Ḳubādh to have all but the three original fires extinguished. Rather than being an attack on cult observance as such, Yarshater interprets this to mean that Mazdak sought to reduce the power of the Mazdaean priesthood and deprive them of property held by fire-temples. There may have been an attempt to found alternative institutions, since the Nestorian *Chronicle of Siʿirt* reports that Ḳubādh ordered temples (*hayākil*) and hospices (*fanādiḳ*) to be built throughout his kingdom where men and women would congregate for adultery.

Beginning with the earliest sources, the Mazdakī ideal of sharing women has been represented in terms of sexual promiscuity with the resulting confusion of paternity. According to Pseudo-Joshua, the Zarādushtaḳān believed that women should be shared and that every man should have intercourse with whom he pleased. This text also reports that Ḳubādh allowed the wives of the nobles to commit adultery, while Procopius relates that Ḳubādh issued a law that Persians should have intercourse with women in common νόμον ἔγραφεν ἐπὶ κοινὰ ταῖς γυναιξὶ μίγνυσθαι Πέρσας). Although such reports received lurid embellishments in later literature, it is more likely, according to Klima and Yarshater, that the Mazdakiyya advocated the right of each man to have a wife and the abolition of social barriers to marriage between nobles and commoners. They may also have encouraged the marriage of women outside of their immediate families. Klima suggests that famine and the decimation of the nobility in recent warfare had caused a demographic crisis in Iran, and that Ḳubā<u>dh</u> released the wives of nobles and allowed them to marry commoners in order to repopulate the country. How this may have been related to changes in the legal status of women in 5th and 6th century Iran remains unresolved, but the Mazdakiyya apparently regarded women as a form of possession to be shared.

Land was also redistributed to new individual owners, perhaps to help restore agriculture after the famine. Modern Soviet scholars interpret the sharing of property as the restoration of ancient village communes, but there is no direct evidence for this. Whether the sharing of women and property was intended to undermine the position of noble families or whether matters simply got out of control, disorders broke out and granaries were plundered at unspecified places in 494-5. In 496 the Persian nobles deposed and imprisoned Ḳubā<u>dh</u> because of his policy toward women and enthroned his brother <u>Dj</u>āmāsp. Christensen put the worst of the Mazdakī risings during the reign of <u>Dj</u>āmāsp and described them imaginatively as veritable *jacqueries*. Ḳubā<u>dh</u> escaped to the Hephthalites, who helped restore him to the throne *ca.* 498-9.

The situation seems to have been stabilised with the Mazdakiyya in control after Ḳubā<u>dh</u>'s return. The Mazdakī period is generally understood in terms of class conflict and the overturning of the social order. Soviet scholars see the movement as one of peasant protest and identify Mazdak's followers as poor farmers, although Pigulevskay<u>a</u> notes that the sources are not specific in this respect. Al-Ṭabarī calls his followers commoners (*ʿāmma*, while al-Thaʿālibī simply calls them the poor (*fuḳarāʾ*, *masākīn*) or the rabble (*al-<u>gh</u>aw<u>gh</u>āʾ*). However, some nobles were Mazdakī, such as Siyāvu<u>sh</u>, who commanded Ḳubā<u>dh</u>'s army after his restoration, and Ḳubā<u>dh</u>'s eldest son, Kāwūs, who governed Ṭabaristān as the Pa<u>dh</u>a<u>shkh</u>ʷār <u>Sh</u>āh. Ḳubā<u>dh</u> seems to have favoured the conversion of non-Zoroastrians in order to increase religious conformity. He tried to force the Armenians to convert before he was deposed, and after he was restored, he required the Arab ruler of al-Ḥīra, al-Mun<u>dh</u>ir III (*ca.* 505-54 [see LA<u>KH</u>MIDS]) to adopt Mazdakī doctrines. When al-Mun<u>dh</u>ir refused, Ḳubā<u>dh</u> got the ruler of the Kinda, al-Ḥāri<u>th</u> b. ʿAmr, to agree to impose Mazdakism on the Arabs of the Na<u>dj</u>d and the Ḥi<u>dj</u>āz. Some Arabs in Mecca are said to have adopted Mazdakism (*tazandaḳa*) at that time, and some *zanādiḳa* are said to have still been there in the time of Muḥammad. Efforts to spread some form of Zoroastrianism lie behind the forced conversion of Jewish children that began under Fīrūz in 474, according to <u>Sh</u>erīra, or in 477 according to Ibn Dāwūd. Graetz and others have seen the revolt of the exilarch, Mar Zuṭrā, who is said to have made himself briefly independent at Maḥoza near Ctesiphon in the early 6th century, as a reaction to the Mazdakiyya, although Neusner considers the entire episode implausible.

Since the Mazdakiyya supported the succession of Kāwūs, his younger brother, <u>Kh</u>usraw, allied himself with the Mazdaean priests, challenged Mazdak's influence over Ḳubā<u>dh</u>, arranged for the Mazdakiyya to assemble at the capital for a religious disputation or for the proclamation of Kāwūs as successor, convinced his father that Mazdak's doctrines were false, and had him executed with thousands of his followers in 528 or early 529. When <u>Kh</u>usraw succeeded his father in 531, there may have been a second persecution of Mazdakites; the sect was suppressed and its books destroyed. In reaction to thirty years of Mazdakī ascendancy, the distinction between nobles and commoners was restored. Some indication of what had happened can be seen in the reforms of <u>Kh</u>usraw I, who confiscated the property of Mazdakī leaders and gave it to the poor. He executed those who had taken property by force and returned it to its former owners. Those who had damaged property were ordered to pay for it. A child of disputed descent was to belong to the family with which it lived. A man who had seized a woman was to give her a marriage portion that satisfied her family; she could then decide to stay with him or marry someone else, but should return to her former husband if she had one. <u>Kh</u>usraw took personal charge of children from noble families without anyone to care for them; he gave the girls dowries and found noble husbands for them, and found noble wives for the youths.

Any Mazdakiyya who survived did so in secret or escaped beyond the Sāsānid borders to Central Asia. There may have been an early centre near Rayy. By the early Islamic period, Neo-Mazdakī groups were scattered throughout Iran; they were called Mazdakiyya around Rayy and Hamadān, "wearers of red" (*Muḥammira*) in <u>Dj</u>ur<u>dj</u>ān, and "wearers of white" (*Sapīd-<u>dj</u>āmagān/Asbī<u>dh</u>-<u>dj</u>āmakiyya* or *Mubayyiḍa*) in Central Asia. During the 2nd/8th and 3rd/9th centuries, they broke up into numerous subsects named after some leader. According to al-Warrāḳ, as cited by al-<u>Sh</u>āhrastānī, in the 3rd/9th century, Mazdakī doctrine was based on a dualism of Light and Darkness; Light, having knowledge and sensation, acted intentionally, while Darkness, being ignorant and blind, acted randomly. Both their mixtures and separation were accidental. The mingling of the three elements of Water, Fire, and Earth produced two demiurge-like Managers of Good and of Evil. Their object of worship (*maʿbaduhu*) was enthroned in the upper world as the supreme monarch (*<u>kh</u>usraw*) was in the lower world. Four spiritual powers (*ḳuwā*) called Discernment (*tamyīz*), Understanding (*fahm*), Preservation (*ḥifẓ*), and Joy (*surūr*) stand before His throne corresponding to the chief judge (*mōba<u>dh</u>ān mōba<u>dh</u>*), religious teacher (*hērba<u>dh</u>ān hērba<u>dh</u>*), army commander (*sipāhbad*), and entertainment master (*rāmi<u>sh</u>gar*) who stood before the earthly king. The world was directed by the four powers with the aid of seven *wazīrs* and twelve spiritual forces. Anyone in whom the four, the seven, and the twelve were combined became godly (*rabbānī*) and freed from religious duties. Those who knew the sum of the letters that amounted to the most supreme Name (*al-ism al-aʿẓam*) also knew the greatest secret (*al-sirr al-akbar*). Those who did not know it remained blind and ignorant. The doctrine of correspondence seems to reflect late Sāsānid conditions, but it is difficult to tell whether the rest went back to Mazdak himself or whether it was the result of continuing doctrinal development. The Mazdakiyya tend to be credited with introducing number and letter mysticism, and may have contributed it to the Kaysāniyya [*q.v.*] <u>Sh</u>īʿī groups with which they associated in the 2nd/8th century. The Neo-Mazdakī groups that emerged from this association such as the Abū Muslimiyya, Sunbā<u>dh</u>iyya, Muḳannaʿiyya and, above all, the <u>Kh</u>urramiyya [*q.v.*] or <u>Kh</u>urramdīniyya and its subsect of Kū<u>dh</u>akiyya, seem to have acquired additional gnostic content from *<u>gh</u>ulāt* <u>Sh</u>īʿī groups as a semi-Islamic disguise. However, both al-<u>Sh</u>āfiʿī and al-Maḳdisī regarded the <u>Kh</u>urramiyya as a category of Ma<u>dj</u>ūs [*q.v.*]. Mazdakiyya survived in Central Asia as late as the early 6th/12th century living at Ki<u>sh</u>,

Na<u>kh</u>s<u>h</u>ab and villages near Bu<u>kh</u>ārā according to Nar<u>sh</u>a<u>kh</u>ī. According to Yāḳūt, they inhabited the village of Dargazīn between Hamadān and Zan<u>dj</u>ān. The last references to Mazdakiyya occur in the Īl<u>kh</u>ānid period, although the Mazdakiyān are listed as the fourteenth Zoroastrian sect in the *Dabistān*, and a Mazdakī community called Marā<u>gh</u>iyya reported by Mustawfī as living in the Rūdbar of Ḳazwīn in the 8th/14th century still survived in seven villages there in the 20th century.

Bibliography: Th. Nöldeke, *Geschichte der Perser und Araber*, 455-67; idem, *Orientalischer Socialismus*, in *Deutsche Rundschau*, xviii (Berlin 1879), 284-91; H. Graetz, *History of the Jews*, Philadelphia 1894, 1941, iii, 3-5; O. G. von Wesendonk, *Die Mazdakiten: Ein kommunistisch-religiöse Bewegung im Sassanidenreich*, in *Der Neue Orient*, vi (Berlin 1919), 35-41; A. Christensen, *Le règne du roi Kawādh I. et le communisme mazdakite*, Copenhagen 1925; Browne, *LHP*, i; G. Olinder, *The Kings of Kinda of the family of Ākil al-Murār*, Lund 1927, 63-4; N. Pigulevskaya, *Mazdakitskoye dviženiye*, in *Izvestiya Akademii nauk SSSR*, Seriya istorii i filosofii (1944), i, 171-81; idem, *Goroda Irana v rannem sredievekov'e*, Moscow-Leningrad 1956, tr. *Les villes de l'État iranien aux époques parthe et sassanide*, Paris 1963, 195-230; F. Altheim and R. Stiehl, *Mazdak und Porphyrios*, in *La Nouvelle Clio*, v (Brussels 1953), 356-76, repr. in their *Geschichte der Hunnen*, Berlin 1961, iii, 61-84; O. Klima, *Mazdak, Geschichte einer sozialen Bewegung im Sassanidischen Persien*, Prague 1957; idem, *Beiträge zur Geschichte des Mazdakismus*, Prague 1977; Abraham Ibn Daud, *The Book of Tradition (Sefer Ha-Qabbalah)*, ed. and tr. G. Cohen. Philadelphia 1967, 42; M. Kister, *Al-Ḥīra, Some notes on its relations with Arabia*, in *Arabica*, xv (1968), 144-5; J. Neusner, *A history of the Jews in Babylonia*, Leiden 1970, v, 97, 104-5; P. Carratelli, *Genesi ed aspetti des Mazdakismo*, in *La Parola del Passato*, xxvii (1972), 66-88; D. Goodblatt, *Rabbinic instruction in Sasanian Babylonia*, Leiden 1975, 26; E. Arrigoni, *Manicheismo, Mazdakismo e sconfessione dell'eresiarca Romano-Persiano Bundos*, Milan 1982; E. Yarshater, ch. *Mazdakism*, in *Camb. hist. of Iran*, iii, Cambridge 1983, 991-1024.

(M. Guidi - [M. Morony])

MAẒHAR (a.), pl. *maẓāhir*, literally "place of outward appearance", hence "manifestation, theophany", a technical term used in a wide variety of contexts in aiʿism, Ṣūfism, Bābism, and, in particular, Bahāʾism, where it is of central theological importance. At its broadest, the term may be applied to any visible appearance or expression of an invisible reality, reflecting the popular contrast between *ẓāhir* and *bāṭin*. In its more limited application, however, it refers to a type of theophany in which the divinity or its attributes are made visible in human form. The term is, therefore, of particular value in those forms of Islam in which the tension between a wholly transcendent and an incarnate God is most keenly felt.

In esoteric <u>Sh</u>īʿism, the term is applied to the Prophet and the *imāms* in a variety of applications. Thus, prophets in general and the *imāms* in particular are the *maẓāhir* in which the pre-existent Reality of Muḥammad (*al-ḥaḳīḳa al-Muḥammadiyya*) appears; the human soul is the *maẓhar* of the universal Forms in the next world; the Perfect Man (*al-insān al-kāmil*) or the *ḥaḳīḳa Muḥammadiyya* is the *maẓhar* of the divine names and attributes; and the individual *imāms* are the *maẓāhir* of the "eternal *imām*" and of the divine attributes. (For these and other uses, see Corbin, *En Islam iranien*, index, s.vv. "*maẓhar*", "théophanie", "théophanies", "théophanique", and "théophanismes".)

It is the *imāms* in particular who function as loci for the visible appearance of the divinity. In a tradition attributed to the fourth *imām*, ʿAlī b. al-Ḥusayn, it is claimed that the *imāms* are God's "meanings" and his external presence within creation (*naḥnu maʿānīhi wa ẓāhiruhu fīkum*, quoted in al-Aḥsāʾī, <u>Sh</u>*arḥ al-ziyāra*, iv, 269). Similarly, ʿAlī is reported to have said: "My external appearance is that of the imāmate (*al-wilāya*), but inwardly I am that which is unseen and incomprehensible" (quoted in *ibid.*, ii, 135).

In the work of Ibn al-ʿArabī [*q.v.*] the term is closely linked to that of *ta<u>dj</u>allī* or divine self-revelation; the *maẓāhir* provide the external loci for the appearance of the *ta<u>dj</u>alliyāt* emanating from the Absolute. In this context, the word *maẓhar* is a synonym for *ma<u>dj</u>lā*, used of an external attribute manifesting a divine name. In his theory of the Perfect Man who acts as a mirror in which the Absolute may see itself manifested, Ibn al-ʿArabī parallels the <u>Sh</u>īʿī notion of the *imām*: man is the place of manifestation of the divinity, *huwa ma<u>dj</u>lā al-ḥaḳḳ*. In this sense, the Perfect Man is the Isthmus or *barza<u>kh</u>* joining the worlds of the Absolute and Creation (See Ibn al-ʿArabī, *Fuṣūṣ al-ḥikam.*)

The Bāb [*q.v.*] developed a complex theory of theophanies in his later works, notably the *Bayān-i Fārsī* and the *Kitāb-i pan<u>dj</u> <u>sh</u>aʾn*. The term *ẓuhūr* applies to the self-revelation of God to his creation and to the period in which he is thus manifest, as contrasted with *buṭūn*, the state and period of his concealment. This revelation takes place in the *maẓhar*, a created being in whom the Divinity manifests himself to other created beings: "the hidden reality of the divine unity (*<u>gh</u>ayb al-tawḥīd*) is only affirmed through that which is revealed in the outward aspect (*ẓāhir*) of the messenger" (the Bāb, *Pan<u>dj</u> <u>sh</u>aʾn*. 40); and "God... makes Himself known to his creation in the place of manifestation (*maẓhar*) of his own self, for whenever men have recognised God, their Lord, their recognition of him has only been attained through what their prophet has caused them to know" (*ibid.*, 125).

It is not, strictly speaking, the divine essence but the Primal Will that is manifested to men: "That command (i.e. the *maẓhar*) is not the eternal and hidden essence, but is a Will that was created through and for himself out of nothing" (*ibid.*, 31); and "From the beginning that has no beginning to the end that has no end, there has ever been but a single Will which has shone forth in every age in a manifestation (*ẓuhūr*) (idem, *Bayān-i Fārsī*. 4:6, 120-1).

This *maẓhar* (referred to variously as a "throne" (*ʿar<u>sh</u>*), "seat (*kursī*), "temple" (*haykal*), or "mirror" (*mirʾāt*), or as the "tree of reality" (*<u>sh</u>a<u>dj</u>arat al-ḥaḳīḳa*) and "primal point" (*nuḳta-yi ūlā*) is an ambivalent creature. He is outwardly mortal ("what your eyes behold of the outward form of the thrones is but a handful of clay", *Pan<u>dj</u> <u>sh</u>aʾn*, 242), but inwardly divine: "Look within them, for God has manifested Himself (*ta<u>dj</u>allā*) to them and through them" (*ibid.*). The historical *maẓāhir* are ontologically a single being, often compared to a single sun appearing in different mirrors; their number is incalculable. They are particularly identified with the chief prophetic figures of the past and with the <u>Sh</u>īʿī *imāms*.

In the final phase of his career (*ca.* 1848-50), the Bāb himself claimed to be the latest *maẓhar* of the Primal Will, initiating a new religious dispensation and *<u>sh</u>arīʿa*. Beyond this, he attributed to many of his followers the status of partial or general manifestations of the divinity (see MacEoin, *Hierarchy*, 109 ff.). His chief follower, Mīrzā Muḥammad ʿAlī Ḳuddūs, is referred to in one source quite simply as *maẓhar-i khudā* (*ibid.*, 110). In theological terms, this is explained by the concept of an infinite progression of mirrors reflecting the Divine Will and forming a complex descending hierarchy of *maẓāhir*. These secondary, tertiary, and subsequent mirrors appear, not only during the lifetime of the primary mirror, but throughout the period of *buṭūn*, when he is in a state of concealment (*ibid.*, 117-19).

Bahāʾī doctrine follows that of Bābism very closely, but tends to be more restrictive in its attribution of the status of *maẓhariyya*, which is generally limited to the founders of the major religions. The full technical term for such figures is *maẓhar ilāhī* (in English Bahāʾī usage, "Manifestation of God"). At the same time, a broader definition of religious truth allows Bahāʾīs to include among the *maẓāhir* figures such as Buddha and Krishna (whom they regard as the "founder" of Hinduism). Bahāʾ Allāh [*q.v.*] is the latest *maẓhar* and will not be followed by another for at least one thousand years. Not only is he accorded a high status with regard to previous and future *maẓāhir* (who have either prepared the way for him or will function under his shadow), but he himself often speaks in terms that are close to those of incarnationism. Thus he is "the creator of all things", in whom "the essence of the pre-existent has appeared"; in one place, he claims that "he has been born who begets not nor is begotten" (see MacEoin, *Charismatic authority*, 168). Modern Bahāʾī doctrine, however, explicitly rejects an incarnationist interpretation of the status of the *maẓāhir*.

Bibliography: Shaykh Aḥmad al-Aḥsāʾī, *Sharḥ al-Ziyāra al-djāmiʿa al-kabīra*[4], 4 vols., Kirmān 1355 sh./1976-7; H. Corbin, *En Islam iranien*, Paris 1971-2; J. W. Morris (tr.), *The Wisdom of the Throne. An introduction to the philosophy of Mulla Sadra*, Princeton 1981 (see index, s.v. *maẓhar*); Muḥyī 'l-Dīn Ibn al-ʿArabī, *Fuṣūṣ al-ḥikam*, ed. Abu 'l-ʿAlāʾ ʿAfīfī, Cairo 1946 (repr. Beirut, n.d.); idem, *The Bezels of Wisdom*, tr. R. W. J. Austin, London 1980; T. Izutsu, *Sufism and Taoism, A comparative study of key philosophical concepts*, rev. ed., Berkeley-Los Angeles-London 1984; Sayyid ʿAlī Muḥammad Shīrāzī, the Bāb, *Bayān-i Fārsī*, n.p. [Tehran] n.d.; idem, *Kitāb-i pandj shaʾn*, n.p. [Tehran] n.d.; D. MacEoin, *Hierarchy, authority and eschatology in early Babi thought*, in P. Smith (ed.), *In Iran. Studies in Bābī and Bahāʾī history*, iii, Los Angeles, 1986, 95-155; idem, *Changes in charismatic authority in Qajar Shiʿism*, in E. Bosworth and C. Hillenbrand (eds.), *Qajar Iran. Political, social and cultural change, 1800-1925*, Edinburgh 1984, 148-76; Mīrzā Ḥusayn ʿAlī Nūrī Bahāʾ Allāh, *Kitāb-i īḳān*, Cairo 1352/1933; J. R. Cole, *The concept of manifestation in the Bahāʾī writings*, in *Bahāʾī Studies*, ix (Ottawa 1982).

(D. MacEoin)

MAẒHAR, Mīrzā Djāndjānān (1111-95/1700-81), an Urdu poet and eminent Ṣūfī, was born in Tālābāgh, Mālwā. He was received into the Naḳshabandī order by Sayyid Mīr Muḥammad Badāʾūnī, and into the Ḳādirī order by Muḥammad ʿĀbid Sumāmī. He was shot in Dilhī by a Shīʿī fanatic in revenge for his critical remarks about the Muḥarram celebrations, but though he survived three days, he refused to identify his assailant to the Emperor. He was—and remains—a famous religious leader. He had many disciples and was even credited with miracles. As a writer, however, his position is not so clear-cut. His letters, in Persian, have been published together with letters addressed to him: but they shed little, if any, light on his poetry, being mostly concerned with religious and social affairs. In Persian poetry, his *dīwān* is his own selection of 1,000 from 20,000 verses. The same fastidious self-criticism may perhaps explain why so little of his Urdu poetry is extant: what remains is found scattered in *tadhkiras*, anthologies and other books. Yet he has been recognised as one of the four pillars of 18th century Urdu poetry, alongside Sawdāʾ [*q.v.*], Mīr Taḳī Mīr [*q.v.*] and Dard. Sawlā complained that Maẓhar's poetic language was neither Persian nor Rēkkhta (Urdu), likening it to the proverbial "*dhobi*'s dog, neither of the house nor the river-side". This remark is unjust, to judge by such of his poetry as remains, which makes us wish there were more.

Bibliography: For short accounts of Maẓhar, see Muhammad Sadiq, *A history of Urdu literature*, London-Karachi, etc. 1964, 81-2 (Sawdāʾ's remarks will be found in Urdu verse and English translation at pp. 74-5); Ram Babu Saksena, *A history of Urdu literature*, Allahabad 1927, 49-51; Muḥammad Ḥusayn Āzād, *Āb-i-ḥayāt*, 7th ed. Lahore 1917, 137-41, contains interesting anecdotes but gave offence by its account of the poet's relationship with a handsome young poet, Tābān. Published collections of his correspondence include *Maḳāmāt Maẓharī or Laṭāʾif khamsa*, ed. Muḥammad Bēg b. Raḥīm Bēg, Dihlī 1309/1892; *Lawāyiḥ khānḳāh-i Maẓhariyya*, ed. Ghulām Muṣṭafā Khān, Hyderabad-Sind 1392/1972. Most of the *tadhkiras* include short examples of his poetry, including Shēfta, *Gulshan bēkhār* and Ḳudrat ʿAlī Shawḳ, *Ṭabaḳāt al-shuʿarāʾ*, Lahore 1968, 61-4. See also Karīm al-Dīn, *Taʾrīkh-i shuʿarāʾ-i Urdū*, Dihlī 1848, 105-7; Sprenger, *Oude catalogue*, 488; Rieu, *Cat. Persian mss. British Museum*, i, 363a.

(J. A. Haywood)

MĀZIN, the name of several Arab tribes who are represented in all the great ethnic groupings of the Peninsula; this finds typical expression in the anecdote recorded in *Aghānī*, viii, 141 (= Yāḳūt, *Irshād*, ii, 382-3), according to which the caliph al-Wāthiḳ asked the grammarian Abū ʿUthmān al-Māzinī [*q.v.*], who had come to his court, to which Māzin he belonged: whether to the Māzin of the Tamīm, to those of the Ḳays, to those of the Rabīʿa or to those of the Yemen?

The first are the Māzin b. Mālik b. ʿAmr b. Tamīm (Wüstenfeld, *Geneal. Tabellen*, L. 12; Ibn al-Kalbi, Tab. 82); the second, the Māzin b. Manṣūr (D. 10; Ibn al-Kalbī, Tab. 92) or the Māzin b. Fazāra (H. 13; Ibn Ḳutayba, *Maʿārif*, ed. Okasha, 83); the third, the Māzin b. Shaybān b. Dhuhl (C. 19; Ibn al-Kalbī, Tab. 192); the last, the Māzin b. al-Nadjdjār a clan of the Khazradj Anṣār (19, 24). But alongside of these, many other tribes and clans bore this name. The *Djamharat al-nasab* of Ibn al-Kalbī gives no less than seventy, of whom the best known are the: Māzin b. ʿAbd Manāt b. Bakr b. Saʿd b. Ḍabba (Tab. 89); Māzin b. Ṣaʿṣaʿa b. Muʿāwiya b. Bakr b. Hawāzin (Tab. 92); Māzin b. Rayth b. Ghaṭafān (Tab. 92); Māzin b. Rabīʿa b. Zubayd or Māzin Madhḥidj (Tab. 270); Māzin b. al-Azd (Tab. 1761-9). The large number of tribes named Māzin and their distribution over the whole of Arabia makes the hypothesis that we have here a single tribe that had been broken up into small sections impossible and we are led to suppose that the name Māzin is a descriptive rather than a proper name; since the verb *mazana* means to "go away", one might suppose that

Māzin originally meant "the emigrants" and was used in a general way of any ethnic group which became separated from its own tribe and was incorporated in a strange tribe. This etymology, like almost all those of the names of Arab tribes, is of course only a hypothesis.

The sources give a certain number of geographical and historical references to different tribes called Māzin; but they are generally very scanty, none of these tribes having attained sufficient importance to make it independent of the larger body to which it was attached. We have a few details about the Māzin b. al-Nadjdjār (not cited by Ibn al-Kalbī), a fairly important group of Medinan Khazradj (on the part played by them at the beginning of Islam, see Caetani, *Annali*, index to vols. i-ii), as well as about the Māzin b. Fazāra who took part as members of the tribe of Dhubyān, in the war of Dāḥis and al-Ghabrā᾽ [*q.v.* in Suppl., and see *Aghānī*, xvi, 27]. Ibn Mayyāda, himself a Dhubyānī, directed a violent satire against them at the end of the 1st century A.H. (*Aghānī*, ii, 90, 102). As to the Māzin b. Shaybān b. Dhuhl, to whom the grammarian Abū ᶜUthmān belonged, we know from the anecdote above quoted that in their dialect, *m* (initial?) was pronounced like *b* (*ba᾽smuka* for *ma᾽smuka*, what is your name?), a peculiarity which does not seem to be recorded of the dialect of other Rabīᶜa. Lastly the Māzin b. al-Azd, whom tradition makes migrate to the north, changed their name to Ghassān [*q.v.*], under which they became celebrated.

It is only of the Māzin b. Mālik b. ᶜAmr b. Tamīm (Ibn al-Kalbī, Tab. 82) that we have fairly full information. Legend, which has developed with unusual detail around the sons of Tamīm [*q.v.*], gives Māzin a part in the story of his uncle ᶜAbd Shams b. Saᶜd b. Zayd Manāt b. Tamīm's fight against al-ᶜAnbar b. ᶜAmr b. Tamīm (cf. al-Mufaḍḍal b. Salama, *al-Fākhir*, ed. Storey, 233, and the references given in the note), This tribe of Māzin never left the great group of the ᶜAmr b. Tamīm to which it belonged and dwelled with them in the lands in the extreme north-west of Nadjd; their headquarters were around the well of Safāri near Dhū Ḳār (*Naḳā᾽iḍ*, ed. Bevan, 48, n. to 1. 17; Yāḳūt, iii, 95; Bakrī, 724, 1. 1; 787-8); their principal subdivisions were the Banū Ḥurḳūṣ, Khuzāᶜī, Rizām, Anmār, Zabīna, Uthātha and Ra᾽lān. In the Djāhiliyya, the Māzin followed their parent tribe and we find them sharing in the wars of the latter; in rotation with the other Tamīmī tribes, they held the office of *ḥākim* at the fair of ᶜUkāẓ (*Naḳā᾽iḍ*, 438). At the coming of Islam, their chief was Mukhāriḳ b. Shihāb, also known as a poet (cf. especially al-Djāḥiẓ, *Bayān*, ed. Hārūn, IV, 41-3; al-Ḳālī, *Amālī*, iii, 50; Ibn Ḥadjar, *Iṣāba*, Cairo 1325, vi, 156). Without being particularly zealous partisans of the new religion, they did not take part in the *Ridda* with the other Tamīmī tribes (11 A.H.) and they even drove away the messengers sent them by the prophetess Sadjāḥ [*q.v.*] and made one of them prisoner, the Taghlibī al-Hudhayl b. ᶜImrān; the latter waited for his revenge till the troubled period that followed the murder of the Caliph ᶜUthmān (35/656), of which he took advantage to ravage the district of Safāri; but the Māzin met him and slew him and threw him into the well (al-Ṭabarī, i, 1911, 1915; cf. *Aghānī*, xix, 145-6, tr. in Caetani, *Annali*, x, 552-3; in the last passage, the expedition against the people of Safāri appears to be independent of the events of the *Ridda*).

At a later date, the Māzin settled in large numbers, like the rest of the Tamīm, in Khurāsān and took part in the conquest of Central Asia; among the Māzinīs who distinguished themselves there were Shihāb b. Mukhāriḳ, son of the chief already mentioned (al-Ṭabarī, i, 2569, 2707); Hilāl b. al-Aḥwaz, who in 102/720 slew the members of the family of Yazīd b. al-Muhallab after the defeat of the latter (al-Ṭabarī, ii, 1912-13); ᶜUmayr b. Sinān, who killed the Persian chief Rutbīl (Ibn al-Kalbī, *Nasab al-khayl*, 30, n. to 11. 3-4). We also find many of the Banū Māzin among the *ḳuwwād* of the ᶜAbbāsid army in the time of the rising against the Umayyads. But a no less number went to swell the ranks of the Khāridjīs; the celebrated chief of the Azraḳīs, Ḳaṭarī b. al-Fudjā᾽a [*q.v.*], belonged to the Māzinī clan of Kābiya b. Ḥurḳūs.

Very few of the remarkable number of poets produced by the Tamīm belonged to the Māzin. We may note however Hilāl b. Asᶜar of the Umayyad period (*Aghānī*, ii, 186); Mālik b. al-Rayb, poet and brigand, contemporary of al-Ḥadjdjādj (*Aghānī*, xix, 162-9; Ibn Ḳutayba, *al-Shiᶜr wa 'l-shuᶜarā᾽*, ed. de Goeje, 205-7, etc.); Zuhayr b. ᶜUrwa al-Sakb (*Aghānī*, xix, 156; the few verses that we have by him, often quoted, are also attributed to his father, ᶜUrwa b. Djalham, and even to ᶜAbd al-Raḥmān b. Ḥassān b. Thābit: cf. *Mufaḍḍaliyyat*, ed. Lyall, 249, n. *y*). Lastly, it may be mentioned that the Māzin have given to Arab philology two of its most illustrious masters: Abū ᶜAmr b. al-ᶜAlā᾽ [*q.v.*], d. 154/771, and al-Naḍr b. Shumayl, whose genealogies are given in Wüstenfeld, *Tabellen* (L).

Bibliography: Wüstenfeld, *Register z.d. geneal. Tabellen*, 291; Ibn Ḳutayba, *K. al-Maᶜārif*, ed. Wüstenfeld, 36-42, ed. Okasha, 87-115, *et passim*; Ibn Durayd, *K. al-Ishtiḳāḳ*, ed. Wüstenfeld, 124-6, 171, 211, 258; Ibn al-Kalbī-Caskel, *Djamharat al-nasab*, Register, ii, 405a-406b.

(G. Levi Della Vida)

AL-MĀZINĪ, Abū ᶜUthmān Bakr b. Muḥammad. Arab philologist and Ḳur᾽ān reader from al-Baṣra.

Information about his life and works is scarce and partly contradictory. Already discutable is the name of his grandfather and his supposed lineal descent from the Banū Māzin [*q.v.*]; the tradition that he was only a *mawlā* of the Banū Māzin is more likely to be correct. Al-Māzinī uses materials taken from Abū Zayd al-Anṣārī, Abu 'l-Ḥasan al-Akhfash al-Awsaṭ, al-Aṣmaᶜī and Abū ᶜUbayda [*q.vv.*]. Among his disciples, al-Mubarrad (d. 286/900 [*q.v.*]) is to be mentioned in the first place. The stories—some of which refer to his arrival in Baghdād during the caliphate of al-Muᶜtaṣim (218-27/833-42) and connect him with the court of his successors al-Wāthiḳ and al-Mutawakkil in Sāmarrā—are not to be distinguished by their anecdotal character and pointed narration from the numerous comparable *akhbār* of the *adab* and *ṭabaḳāt* literature. Within these traditions, judgements and opinions about al-Māzinī's learning and *madhhab* are interspersed. Al-Mubarrad considered him, next to Sībawayh, as one of the most learned of grammarians; others suggested that he was an adherent of the Imāmiyya or Murdji᾽a, or else of the Ḳadariyya or Muᶜtazila. Even the information about the date of his death in his home town is varying. The dates differ by up to 19 years. Preference is to be given to the note that he died in the same year as the caliph al-Mutawakkil (232-47/847-61) or—as often quoted—a little later in the year 249/863.

Nothing is preserved of al-Māzinī's supposed works on grammar, lexicography and metrics, of his explanations concerning Sībawayh's *Kitāb* and the Ḳur᾽ān, books which have been enumerated, e.g. by Yāḳūt, *Udabā᾽*, ii, 388. Only one text, the *Kitāb al-*

Taṣrīf, a very significant treatise on morphology, has been transmitted in a *riwāya*, that is to say, lecture notes. The teacher is addressing the student directly; he starts with the question which letters can enlarge an *aṣl*—the basic radicals of a word—and finishes his essay treating the form *iftaʿala* and some of its derivations. Repeatedly he interposes *fa-ʿrifhā, wa-ʿlam, sa-uk̲h̲biruka, sa-ubayyinu, katabtu, fassartu, d̲h̲akartu* or *bayyantu laka* (cf. Ibn D̲j̲innī's *Sirr ṣināʿat al-i ʿrāb*). Occasionally he quotes his own teachers (see above) or else he refers to the authority of al-K̲h̲alīl [*q.v.*]. This treatise, which is subdivided into 18 chapters, was studied and worked on by Ibn D̲j̲innī under the guidance of his teacher al-Fārisī (d. 377/987 [*q.v.*]) in Aleppo. Moreover, he wrote a comprehensive commentary on it called *al-Munṣif* and enlarged it with two appendices (see his preface, i, 1; ii, 208, 261). The first appendix comprises additional lexicographical explanations, including verses of reference to the previous chapters. It is entitled *Tafsīr al-lug̲h̲a min kitāb Abī ʿUt̲h̲mān bi-s̲h̲awāhidihi wa-ḥudjadjihi wa-innamā d̲h̲ālika fī 'l-g̲h̲arīb minhā*. The second appendix, is called *Masāʾil min ʿawīṣ al-Taṣrīf*, deals with 15 specific questions. Ibn D̲j̲innī derives his entire material from the *madjlis* traditions, referring mainly to his teacher al-Fārisī. Besides speculative topics, he inserts numerous observations concerning the use of language, not infrequently embedded in *ak̲h̲bār* of learned men. These works have been edited under the title *al-Munṣif, s̲h̲arḥ Abi 'l-Fatḥ ʿUt̲h̲mān b. D̲j̲innī li-Kitāb al-Taṣrīf li-Abī ʿUt̲h̲mān al-Māzinī*, by Ibrāhīm Muṣṭafā and ʿAbd Allāh Amīn, 3 vols., Cairo 1373-9/1954-60.

Bibliography: Of studies, see G. Flügel, *Die grammatischen Schulen der Araber*, Leipzig 1862, repr. Nendeln 1966, 83 f.; O. Rescher, *Abriss der arabischen Literaturgeschichte*, Stuttgart 1933, repr. Osnabrück 1983, ii, 145 ff.; Brockelmann, I, 108, S I, 168; Sezgin, viii, 92, ix, 75 f.; J. R. Guillaume, *Le statut des représentations sous-jacentes en morphophonologie d'après Ibn G̲inni*, in *Arabica*, xxviii (1981), 222-41; S̲h̲. Ḍayf, *al-Madāris al-naḥwiyya*, Cairo 1968, 115-22; Ras̲h̲īd ʿA. al-ʿUbaydī, *Abū ʿUt̲h̲mān al-Māzinī*, Bag̲h̲dād 1969; Kh. Ziriklī, *al-Aʿlām*, Cairo 1955, ii, 44; ʿU. R. Kaḥḥāla, *Muʿdjam al-muʾallifīn*, Damascus 1959, iii, 71; al-ʿĀmilī, *Aʿyān al-S̲h̲īʿa*, Beirut 1383/1961, ²xiv, 87-90,. no. 2674; M. ʿA. Mudarris, *Rayḥānat al-adab*, ²Tabrīz n.d. (*ca.* 1347/1969), v, 149 ff. The main sources are Zadjdjādjī, *Madjālis al-ʿulamāʾ*, Kuwait 1962, index; idem, *Amālī al-Z.*, Cairo 1382/1962, index; Abu 'l-Ṭayyib al-Lug̲h̲awī, *Marātib al-naḥwiyyīn*, Cairo 1955, 77-80, 2nd ed. Cairo 1974, 126-9; Marzubānī, *al-Muḳtabas*, Beirut-Wiesbaden 1964, 220-3; Sīrāfī, *Ak̲h̲bār al-naḥwiyyīn al-baṣriyyīn*, Beirut-Paris 1936; Zubaydī, *Ṭabaḳāt al-naḥwiyyīn wa 'l-lug̲h̲awiyyīn*, Cairo 1373/1954, 2nd ed. Cairo 1973, 87-93; *Fihrist*, 57; Tanūk̲h̲ī, *Taʾrīk̲h̲ al-ʿulamāʾ al-naḥwiyyīn*, Riyadh 1401/1981, 65-71; Nadjās̲h̲ī, *Kitāb al-ridjāl*, n.d., n.p. [Tehran 1337/1959], 85; al-K̲h̲aṭīb al-Bag̲h̲dādī, *Taʾrīk̲h̲ Bag̲h̲dād*, vii, 93 f.; Samʿānī, facs. ed. fol. 500b, ed. Hyderabad 1401/1981, xii, 26; Ibn al-Anbārī, *Nuzhat al-alibbāʾ*, Cairo 1967, 182-7; Yāḳūt, *Udabāʾ*, ii, 380-90; Ḳifṭī, *Inbāh al-ruwāt ʿalā anbāh al-nuḥāt*, Cairo 1369/1950, i, 246-56; Ibn K̲h̲allikān, tr. de Slane, i, 264-67; Ṣafadī, *Wāfī*, x, 211-16; Ibn al-D̲j̲azarī, *G̲h̲āyat al-nihāya fī ṭabaḳāt al-ḳurrāʾ*, Cairo-Leipzig 1932, i, 179; Suyūṭī, *Bug̲h̲ya*, 202 f. (Cairo 1384/1964, i, 463-6); idem, *Muzhir*, Cairo 1378/1958, index.

(R. SELLHEIM)

AL-MĀZINĪ, IBRĀHĪM ʿABD AL-ḲĀDIR, Egyptian writer, translator, poet and journalist (1890-1949). He was the son of an ʿālim of al-Azhar who became a judge at the s̲h̲arʿī tribunal of Cairo; his maternal grandmother came originally from Mecca.

On the completion of his secondary studies, he entered the Teachers' Training College, since his family was not sufficiently wealthy to enable him to pursue any other career. Licensed as a secondary school teacher in 1909, he was appointed teacher of English at the Madrasa Saʿīdiyya where he remained for some ten years. His appointment to the same post at Dār al-ʿUlūm could be considered a promotion, but he himself well knew that he was suffering a penalty. In fact, the Minister of Education had decided to transfer al-Māzinī as a way of punishing him for having published in the press an article severely critical of the poet Ḥāfiẓ Ibrāhīm, who was a friend of the Minister. Al-Māzinī resigned his post and abandoned public education in order to teach in private schools. In 1918, his friend, the eminent writer al-ʿAḳḳād [*q.v.* in Suppl.], who was then an editor at *al-Ahālī* of Alexandria, helped him to obtain work as a translator and editor with the review *Wādī 'l-Nīl*.

This was not in fact al-Māzinī's first contact with the press. Since 1907, he had published some poems in *al-Sufūr*, a review then edited by Farīd Wadjdī; subsequently—from 1911 to 1914—also some articles in *al-D̲j̲arīda* of Aḥmad Luṭfī al-Sayyid and in the *Bayān* of ʿAbd al-Raḥmān al-Barḳūḳī. It was in the latter monthly that he published in 1913 a series of articles on the ʿAbbāsid poet Ibn al-Rūmī. The library of the review was one of the meeting places for Egyptian intellectuals; al-Māzinī there renewed his acquaintance with al-ʿAḳḳād, whom he had known then for three years, and it was there that he introduced to him the poet S̲h̲ukrī, who had been his fellow-student at the Teachers' Training College.

But from 1918 onwards, al-Māzinī became a full-time journalist. He collaborated, successively, in the editing of various daily papers (*al-Ak̲h̲bār*, *al-Balāg̲h̲* and *al-Ittiḥād*, which lasted for only a few issues) or weekly publications. In 1926, he even founded a new review, *al-Usbūʿ*. The most recent and most serious study of al-Māzinī reveals that he is credited with more than two thousand titles "of articles, meditations and studies", some of which have never been assembled in book form (Ḥ. al-Sakkūt and J. M. Jones, *Ibrāhīm ʿAbd al-Ḳādir al-Māzinī*, Cairo-Beirut 1979). Since he did not confine himself to literary questions but was also concerned with politics, and since, on the other hand, he was a man of frank speech and caustic wit, as a result, he became the object of criticism and even lost his job.

Translation constituted his other major activity. By the end of his life he had translated, from English, eight books as well as five literary texts published in reviews. It is appropriate to mention here that he also worked as an interpreter, both as a press correspondent at the Military Tribunal where the proceedings were conducted in English, and on behalf of various societies.

It is no doubt the press article (*maḳāl* or *maḳāla* [*q.v.*]) which represents the literary genre in which al-Māzinī particularly excelled. But his activity extended over various domains, in all of which he made an impression with his strong personality.

Poetry. He has a place, with al-ʿAḳḳād, at the head of the Egyptian poetic revival, of which the true initiator was however ʿAbd al-Raḥmān S̲h̲ukrī, who acquainted them with English literature and in particular its romantic poets and its literary critics. At the

Teachers' Training College, al-Māzinī had benefited from his readings in English which enabled him to discover Byron, Shelley, the "Lake Poets" Wordsworth and Coleridge, and Browning. Since that time al-Māzinī, captivated by romantic sensibility, felt the need to express melancholy, sadness and the pain of living, the result of which was his *Dīwān* (first section 1913; second 1917; third, posthumously, 1960; published in entirety in 1961).

However, this convinced modernist hardly sanctioned a revolution in poetical forms; his greatest audacity consisted in abandoning the single rhyme in favour of the alternate rhyme. This is no doubt explained by the fact that his discovery of foreign poetry was accompanied by a deepening of his Arabic culture. At this time, the publication of the Arabic classics was in progress, and al-Māzinī thus read the poets al-Sharīf al-Raḍī, Ibn al-Rūmī and al-Maᶜarrī, being also drawn to the prose-writer al-Djāḥiẓ, whose spirit and style left their mark on him. Not all of these published editions were perfect, and it is said that he often went to Dār al-Kutub to consult the manuscript of *al-Aghānī*; it also seems that Shukrī and he spent hours there recopying the manuscript of the *Dīwān* of Ibn al-Rūmī. He was 55 years old when, in an article appearing in *al-Mashriḳ* of December 1944, he announced that he had undertaken a reasoned and systematic study of Arab literature, applying the method which he had acquired from the school of the English writers.

But he quite soon gave up composing poetry. In explaining this decision, he said that he had never been entirely satisfied with his production in this field, even regretting that he had not had the courage to destroy his compositions. On the other hand, his role as a literary critic continued to command respect.

Criticism. In an article appearing in *al-Mustamiᶜ al-ᶜarabī* of 1949, Ṭaha Ḥusayn expressed the opinion that for some twenty years, the Egyptian writer had ceased to limit his horizon to his own country and had begun to take an interest in the outside World. There were in fact two schools of modernists: a French school where, following Aḥmad Luṭfī al-Sayyid, the most distinguished figures were Ṭāhā Ḥusayn and Muḥammad Ḥusayn Haykal; and an English school where, following ᶜAbd al-Raḥmān Shukrī, the two leaders were al-ᶜAḳḳad and al-Māzinī. This "school" published its manifesto, *al-Dīwān*, in 1921. To be more exact, this was the beginning of an uncompleted critical work. The two writers al-ᶜAḳḳad and al-Māzinī declared their intention to write ten fascicles in which they would show, successively, in what ways the literary celebrations of the time were overrated and what should be the new characteristics of Arabic poetry. Only the first two fascicles appeared, and what is known as the *Dīwān* is thus limited to violent criticism of the contemporary idols, the poet Aḥmad Shawḳī and the prose-writer al-Manfalūṭī. To these two targets, the two iconoclasts added a completely unexpected third, ᶜAbd al-Raḥmān Shukrī! It is even in reference to him that al-Māzinī—to whom it fell to analyse him—uses the term "idol". It is impossible not to be astonished at this sudden reversal when it is known what close friends the two men were, a friendship which rested in particular on perfect similarity of views in questions of poetry.

Some years before the publication of the *Dīwān*, al-Māzinī had, for the first time, propounded entirely new principles for the criticism of Arabic poetry, principles which he had drawn from his reading of Hazlitt, Arnold and Macaulay. In a small monograph which appeared in 1915 (*al-Shiᶜr, ghāyātuhu wa-wasāʾiṭuh*), he demands of the poet that he should be sincere and that he should not produce work in a mechanical fashion but compose a personal poetry. The same year, under the title *Shiᶜr Ḥāfiẓ*, he reprinted articles which he had devoted to the eminent Egyptian poet and had published in the review *ᶜUkāẓ* in 1913. According to him, Ḥāfiẓ is a charlatan who is capable of composing poetry on subjects which do not genuinely affect him, which are supplied to him by the circumstances of actuality; he is a criminal who perverts the taste of readers, accustoms them to lie and damns them! In order the better to pursue this vulgar versifier (*nāẓim bi 'l-ṣanᶜa*) he compares him with a true poet, a poet of innate talent (*maṭbūᶜ*) ... Shukrī in fact. His method consists in comparing, theme by theme, the verses of each of the two men in order to demonstrate the accuracy of his judgment. But since certain partisans of Ḥāfiẓ reproach him for concentrating on only the worst verses of the poet, he adduces proof to show that his best compositions, for their part, are only plagiarism of the ancients. It may be noted in passing that the modernist al-Māzinī falls into step with the most traditional of Arabic criticism, since he practises parallelism (*muwāzana*) and is concerned to uncover plagiarisms (*sariḳāt*). However, the harmonious relationship between al-Māzinī and Shukrī did not survive an article by the latter published in the *Muḳtaṭaf*, in which he revealed that his colleague had borrowed many of the themes of his *Dīwān*—if not entire verses—from Palgrave's *Golden treasury*, an anthology of English lyric poetry after Shakespeare. Nothing more is needed to explain the sudden antipathy of al-Māzinī with regard to Shukrī in his two fascicles of the *Dīwān*, even though, subsequently, he felt obliged to retract his strictures and to acknowledge, in an article in *al-Siyāsa* of 5 April 1930, that it was to him that he owed his discovery of the essence of poetry.

With regard to ancient Arabic poetry, he is interested particularly in al-Mutanabbī and Ibn al-Rūmī, whom he studies as a priority, as does his companion and model al-ᶜAḳḳād. He seeks to reconsider the question of the scale of traditionally fixed values. Ibn al-Rūmī seems to him to have been unfairly treated, no doubt because he was of Byzantine ancestry (*rūmī*). He considers that this should be in itself a sufficient reason for placing him above other poets. He states: "We do not try to mock the Arabs or to discredit their poetry. We mean only to say that the Arabs are not the most poetic people". According to him, all the human qualities are to be found in Western poetry, and he concludes by declaring himself a fanatical partisan of the West, eulogising the "Aryan peoples". Western theoreticians assist him to make progress in the evaluation of the resources of poetry: the German Lessing enables him to verify, in the work of Ibn al-Rūmī, again, that descriptive poetry, unlike painting on canvas, creates the illusion of movement; the Englishman Locke uncovers for him the possibilities offered by figurative sense (*madjāz*) and symbol (*ramz*). Through contact with European works, he poses in new terms the problem of the imagination. He tends to see here only the faculty of establishing a new combination of given elements from which innovation emerges. If he seems to ignore creative imagination, this is because of his rejection of the implausibilities which sometimes mar classical Arabic poetry. Like al-ᶜAḳḳād, he does not accept gratuitous extravagance, the senseless hyperbole which Arabic poetry shamelessly displays, under the guise of poetic genius.

Al-Māzinī is renowned as being a man of hard judgment, but while he has a grasp of concise formulae, he also possesses an immoderate taste for digression, and it is the middle course, commonplace assessment of the subject under discussion, which is lacking in him, with the result that tangible elements in his critical works are somewhat limited. It is unusual to see him take a precise example, as in the *Dīwān* where he shows that a story of al-Manfalūṭī (*al-Yatīm*) displays well the characteristics which he denounces: hollow and oratorical style, peevish and effeminate writing, coincidences and implausibilities. Most often, he speaks of everything except the book which he is supposed to be examining. His "criticisms" of works by Ṭaha Ḥusayn, Mayy Ziyāda [*q.v.*] and even al-ʿAḳḳād are astonishing examples of this. Ironical posturing suits him better than demonstration based on analytical argument.

Narrative fiction. When the attempt is made to assess the contribution of al-Māzinī as a novelist, it is appropriate to consider him in the perspective of the time. After the first edition of *Zaynab* by Haykal—which dates from 1914—few works of note appared in the succeeding years: *Thurayyā* (1922) by ʿĪsā ʿUbayd is rather a long short story, and *Ibnat al-mamlūk* (1926) by Ibn Abī Ḥadīd is a historical novel. This being so, chronologically al-Māzinī produced the second novel which had ever appeared in Egypt when he published *Ibrāhīm al-kātib* (1931), the second edition of *Zaynab*, in 1929, having refreshed the already distant memories of the first. It is also appropriate to mention that al-Māzinī had published a version of the first five chapters from the end of 1925 in several issues of the review *Rūz al-Yūsuf*. The author was already known, was even eminent, as an innovating poet counted among the proponents of the modern school of literary criticism, and the role that he played in crossing swords with Ḥāfiẓ, Shawkī and others was not to be forgotten on account of the fact that he renewed his attacks in the columns of the press, also making a name for himself in the discussion of social and political questions in *al-Akhbār*, *al-Ittiḥād* and *al-Siyāsa*, in which his vivid style and caustic tone were widely recognised. On account of all these factors, his novel was eagerly awaited, and it did indeed, in a general sense, achieve real success, for three essential reasons. The leading character who bears the same name as the author is, in fact, his double, and nobody can doubt that they both think, act and feel in the same way; he is charming and impulsive, a sceptic if not a pessimist, considering others and himself with humour. The story related, on the other hand, does not fail to engage curiosity, since the three women with whom Ibrāhīm is romantically involved pose such fundamental questions as the importance of tradition, the role of women and the meaning of marriage. Finally, as to the tone of the novel, its unity is maintained on account of the fact that the narration is in the first person, facilitating the transfer from abstract meditation to lively and satirical description or to vivid dialogue. Al-Māzinī's first contribution to fiction would thus appear to be entirely creditable, leading one to suppose that he would not be slow to repeat this success. However, it was not until 1943 that he added to his corpus, publishing four novels in the same year: *Ibrāhīm al-thānī*, *Thalāthat ridjāl wa-mraʾa*, *ʿAwd ʿalā badʾ*, *Mīdū wa-shurakāhu*. Some have tended to attribute special significance to the first two, linking them with the novel already discussed to constitute a "trilogy" (cf. Ṭāhā Wādī, *Ṣūrat al-marʾa fi 'l-riwāya al-muʿāṣira*, Cairo 1973). This cannot be substantiated except in reference to *Ibrāhīm al-thānī*, which could indeed be taken to represent that which befalls the hero of the earlier novel some years after his marriage, when conjugal monotony begins to weigh upon him and he finds himself dangerously tempted by the young women who surround him. It is true, however, that a certain evolution is perceptible running through the three books in question as regards the role of the wife. Time has passed since *Ibrāhīm al-kātib*, but some ten years more and the equality in principle of the two spouses are not sufficient to make the life of the couple in *Ibrāhīm al-thānī* euphoric. On the other hand, the acquisition by the wife of responsibility in *Thalāthat ridjāl* makes of her a character quite unique, capable of initiatives, and the form accords with the content—it is no longer an account written in the first person.

During the five remaining years of his life, al-Māzinī was not to publish a new novel. It may be mentioned here that he published a single theatrical piece, *Ghazīrat al-marʾa aw ḥukm al-ṭāʿa* (1930), not only to indicate that, on the stage also, the question of feminine rights seems to him to require treatment—like many other intellectuals, he supported the movement for the reform of ideas initiated by Ḳāsim Amīn at the beginning of the century—but also to tackle a question which has taken on a particular importance in the eyes of Egyptian critics studying the works of al-Māzinī. The point at issue is the "borrowings" of this writer. In itself, the subject seems predominantly to concern Egypt, since it sets out to show that the kind of "compulsion to remain at home" (*ḥukm al-ṭāʿa*) which every Egyptian husband has the right to impose on his reputedly disobedient wife is a scandalous sexual privilege, a denial of justice which should not long be tolerated by the legislators. The literary critic of *al-Balāgh* revealed that, in essence, the plot and some of the scenes of the play had been taken from a novel by Galsworthy. It was in 1932 that there took place the polemic between al-Māzinī and his accuser, this being the year that Galsworthy, the famous author of *The Forsyte Saga*, received the Nobel Prize. Although he did not admit his plagiarism, our writer's protestations were far from convincing. The opinion of scholars has been quite united in this regard, just as nobody doubts that al-Māzinī padded out his novel *Ibrāhīm al-kātib* (1931) by incorporating in it five pages from a Russian novel (*Sanine* by Artzybachev) which he himself had translated in 1920 for the *Musāmarāt al-shaʿb*. When challenged on this point, the author did not deny it, contenting himself with a declaration of his good faith (he read a great deal, retained material easily and was ultimately unable to tell what genuinely was his own creation!). Such disarming naïvety is perplexing, all the more so since it is hard to understand what real benefit he could have gained from the practice. One may also ask why—again in his first novel—he is observed to repeat several pages already published some years before in a collection of his articles, *Ḳabḍ al-rīḥ* (1927). In this instance he is plagiarising himself. The answer to this question supplied by a enquirer very favourably disposed towards him is that he is consistent in his ideas which he puts into the mouth of his fictional hero (on this question, cf. Mme Niʿmāt Aḥmad Fuʾād, *Adab al-Māzinī*, Cairo 1961).

If his theatre is almost non-existent and his work as a novelist less significant than might have been hoped, al-Māzinī remains a remarkable storyteller. He is seen fulminating in the *Dīwān* against the morbid, grandiloquent and ultimately dishonest literature of al-Manfalūṭī. The first fruits of Arabic narrative writing, more credible because more in tune with society and people as they are, appear in the short stories of the Taymūr brothers, but are also to be found among the many texts published by al-Māzinī himself. In fact, alongside his analysis and assessment of works, and his literary studies, alongside his political writings, he published a quantity of stories which may be found today in eight collections, of which the most notable are *Ṣundūḳ al-dunyā* (1929) and *Khuyūṭ al-ʿankabūt* (1935). The bibliography of the work by Sakkut and Jones mentioned above refers to a further 114 "narrative works" which appeared in periodicals, of which 76 have never been reprinted. All these narratives, of variable length, approximate more or less to the living tableau or short story as such, tending rather to resemble what Anglo-Saxons call the "essay" or "sketch". Most often, the fiction is minimal, the author embroidering with humour and fantasy upon a reflection, a memory or an observation. He also enjoys making himself a central figure in the scene that is sketched out or making himself a target for his own jesting, since his small stature and the limp from which he suffered are easily evoked in a few words. Some suppose that this constant jesting is a means of exorcising a sense of shame which could have become a complex. In any event, this quasi-systematic procedure facilitates the establishment of a complicity with his reader which al-Māzinī manifestly seeks. He does not take himself seriously, and treats other writers, whoever they may be, with equal levity. Much affected by reading the Bible and in particular the Book of Job, he has a tendency to agree with the famous line "Vanity of vanities, all is vanity". It is noticeable that each chapter of his *Ibrāhīm al-kātib* bears as a heading a phrase drawn from a verse of the Old Testament and the titles of almost all his collections indicate the illusory nature of human existence and of its works; already there has been observed the illusion of writing symbolised by "the kaleidoscope" (*Ṣundūḳ al-dunyā*) and the incongruity of the "threads of the spider" (*Khuyūṭ al-ʿankabūt*), but to these may be added the mirage of a "harvest of grass" (*Ḥaṣād al-hashīm*, 1924) and the nothingness of a "handful of wind" (*Ḳabḍ al-rīḥ*, 1927). Our writer expresses himself on a very flexible canvas, since all that he hears is his fantasy. Malicious sketches, incidental remarks, paradoxes, aphorisms, follow one another for the enjoyment of the reader. To be sure, not everything is said in a jocular tone, for he has written moving pages describing his mother, whom he adored, or his daughter, who died at an early age. Nor is everything bizarre, and there are times when reality prevails over the "nonsense", in particular when he evokes his childhood, giving the reader the opportunity to imagine a Cairo home at the end of the last century and the life that was lived there. But this is a retrospective view conducted with a sense of the humorous and the unusual. Humour is always in evidence with him, even when he travels to Mecca; his *Riḥla ḥidjāziyya* (1930) contains some excellent jokes. In the attempt to decide with whom to compare this virtuoso of comic prose, this independent spirit hostile to protocol and to the conventional, the names of al-Djāḥiẓ and Mark Twain spring to mind. But al-Māzinī was most certainly both typically Egyptian and tremendously modern. Towards the end of his life, he became a member the Cairo Academy and the speech that he gave on this occasion was striking for its anti-conformism—as might indeed be expected from the man who nicknamed this venerable institution "the cemetery of the immortals".

Bibliography: Besides the references cited in the article, see Ḥāmid ʿAbduh al-Hawwāl, *al-Sukhriyya fī adab al-Māzinī*, Cairo 1972; Muḥammad Mandūr, *al-Shiʿr fī Miṣr baʿd Shawḳī*, Cairo 1944; P. Counillon, *A propos d'une nouvelle d'al-Mâzinî* in *Bull. Et. arabes*, v (January-February 1942), 3-6.

(CH. VIAL)

MAẒLŪM (A.) a technical term of Shīʿī, especially Twelver, Islam, which nevertheless retains its current *ism mafʿūl* meaning from the root *ẓalama*: someone or something "treated or used wrongfully, unjustly, injuriously, or tyrannically" (Lane, 1923). In Persian, a language in which a large part of the literature referred to here mentions it, the word means also *sitam rasīda* (*Farhang-i Ānandarādj*, vi, 4042) or "injured, oppressed, seized forcibly ..." and, consequently, "mild, gentle, modest" (Steingass, 1263).

Maẓlūm is one of the attributes which characterise the *Imāms*, and it is coupled with *shahīd* and sometimes substituted for it. This fits in with the theological and hagiographical vision in the time of the *Imāms*, a vision which claims them as martyrs, pure (*maʿṣūm*) victims because they are pure by definition, their role being to bear a witness which is expressed by means of the conscious sacrifice of their life. Thus they are *maẓlūm* because they have for their opposites those who are *ẓālim: ... man aẓlamu mimman katama shahādatan ʿindahu min Allāh...* (Ḳurʾān, II, 140/134, "Who then is more unjust than he who conceals testimony which he possesses from God?"). The testimony in the case of the *Imāms* becomes their *shahāda*, their martyrdom. The full meaning of this testimony depends, moreover, on the fact that they are, vis-à-vis humanity, the *ḥudjdjat Allāh*, the proof of God par excellence, i.e. the proof that man should recognise in order to obtain his eternal salvation.

Until now the discussion has been general, and may perhaps be further generalised, in the sense that all the *ahl al-bayt* are defined as *maẓlūm* according to a famous *ḥadīth*, for which we give here a typical reference, Kāshifī, 170: *naḥnu ḳawm maẓlūmūn, naḥnu ḳawm maṭrūdūn, naḥnu ḳawm makhūrūn*, which indicates in the genealogy of Abū Ṭālib, the "we" in question.

To belong to the "family" means to be ready for martyrdom, to undergo the violence of the *ẓālim* and be destined for exile, as the word *maṭrūd* explains; but the root *ẓalama* also indicates in its primary meaning "to put something in a place which is not its own" (*LA, s.v.*) and Shīʿī Persian literature appears moreover to refer to it when it adds to the attributes *maẓlūm* and *shahīd* that of *gharīb*.

Maẓlūm has a particular significance in the case of two *Imāms* who are the symbol of the perfect martyr, being *maʿṣūm* and *maẓlūm*, sc. al-Ḥusayn b. ʿAlī and ʿAlī al-Riḍā. The former is often defined as the *maẓlūm-i Karbalāʾ* (Djawharī, 138 ff.), but another important meaning of the word is, in some way, present. *Maẓlūm* (or rather *maẓlūma*) is the adjective for land where rain does not fall, or where it is difficult to sink a well to find water (cf. the Arabic dictionaries s.v. *ẓ-l-m*). Al-Ḥusayn is *maẓlūm* due also to the particular manner of his martyrdom, due to thirst, since his enemies here denied him water. However, in the case of ʿAlī al-Riḍā, *maẓlūm* becomes synonymous rather with *gharīb*, the victim who chooses to die far off, "in the East" and who makes of his "Eastern" exile the testimony of his mission, which, emblematically, contains all the ideas peculiar to the *Imāms*, whether in religious terms or in mythological terms (B. Scarcia Amoretti, *Un interpretazione iranistica di Cor. XXV, 38 e L, 12*, in *RSO*, xliii/ [1968], 46-52).

In present-day Shīʿī thought, the word *maẓlūm* is still in frequent use. When the martyrdom of al-Ḥusayn is put forward as the example to follow in order to be liberated in this world and to find salvation in the next, the matter is clear enough. The history of mankind finds in the life of al-Ḥusayn and in Karbalāʾ its paradigm and a daily proof (*ḥudjdja yawmiyya*). And, in this sense, *maẓlūm* is a word which also defines, in opposition to all that is *ẓālim* (law, existing order, etc.) the man who is *maʿzūl*, oppressed (Shams al-Dīn, 11 ff.), who alone can become what al-Ḥusayn is for the Shīʿī religious conscience.

Bibliography: There is no specific bibliography on the subject. The texts drawn upon for the definition of *maẓlūm* (the parts concerning the *Imām* al-Ḥusayn b. ʿAlī and the *Imām* ʿAlī al-Riḍā) are the following: Ibn Babūya al-Ḳummī, *ʿUyūn akhbār al-Riḍā*, lith. Tehran 1275/1858-9; Wāʿiẓ Kāshifī, *Rawḍat al-shuhadāʾ*, Tehran 1334/1962-3; Mīrzā Muḥammad Ibrāhīm al-Djawharī, *Ṭūfān al-bukāʾ*, lith. Tehran n.d. As far as contemporary literature is concerned, much has been written on the concept of martyrdom. One may mention in translation: ʿAlī Sharīʿatī, *Martyrdom: arise and bear witness*, Tehran 1981; Murtaḍā Muṭahharī, *The martyr*, Tehran 1980; Muḥammad Taḳī Sharīʿatī, *Why Husain took stand*, Tehran n.d. In Persian: ʿAlī Sharīʿatī, *Ḥusayn wārith Ādam*, Tehran n.d.; Maḥmūd Ṭāliḳānī, *Djihād wa shahāda*, Tehran n.d. In Arabic: Shaykh Muḥammad Mahdī Shams al-Dīn, *ʿĀshūrāʾ mawkib al-shahāda* (on the occasion of 10 Muḥarram 1403/1982 in Beirut).

(B. Scarcia Amoretti)

MAZRAʿA (a.), *mazraʿa, mezra* or *ekinlik* in Turkish, means in general arable land, a field; as used in the Ottoman survey registers, it designates a periodic settlement or a deserted village and its fields. According to a regulation, to register a piece of land as *mazraʿa* it was required that it be checked whether the place had a village site in ruins, its own water supply and a cemetery (Barkan, 53, 133, 190). Such a piece of land is occasionally called *matrūk yer*, abandoned land. In the *daftars* [*q.v.*] we often find the following note on *mazraʿas*: "previously it was a village, now its population is scattered and the fields abandoned (*khālī*)". Usually a *mazraʿa* has fixed boundaries. A *mazraʿa* might have gained over time a few families of settlers, but would still be registered as a *mazraʿa*.

Every *mazraʿa* is referred to by a specific name which often reveals its origin or first possessor. In the province of Ḳaramān, for example, many *mazraʿa* names are coupled with *ḥiṣār*, referring probably to abandoned Byzantine castles, or with *aghîl* "sheep-fold", or having reference to a nomadic group which used the site as pastureland. A great number of village names in Anatolia bearing the name *vīrān* or *ören* must originally have been *mazraʿas* which over the course of time were transformed into full villages. But when we speak of *mazraʿa* as an abandoned village we mean basically not just the site of the village itself, but rather its fields.

In western Anatolia and the Balkans, the Ottomans inherited the Byzantine rural landscape with its sub-villages and periodic settlements. The earliest reference to a *mazraʿa* appears in Sultan Orkhan's *waḳf* for the bridge he built at Alma-Pînarî. Under the Byzantines, the *mazraʿa*-type lands as dependencies of a village were known as *agridia* and *proasteia*, the former designating partly settled and the latter unsettled satellite land (Ostrogorsky, 1962, 149). As was the case under the Ottomans, when the village rented such land collectively it paid the rent collectively (*ibid.*, 114), but this special case cannot be used as an argument for the theory that in general village land was subject to collective ownership under the Byzantines.

In the survey registers, abandoned villages or *čiftliks* are shown also as *khālī*, uninhabited, or *kharāb*, in ruins, or *khirbat* (in Syria). In these registers, the deserted or periodically settled and used lands were of different sizes and were shown under different names. Theoretically, the largest one was a *mazraʿa*, sometimes with water and a cemetery, and was always considered capable of being converted into a village, so that all *mazraʿas* were carefully recorded. Other such lands of smaller size are, in order, *čiftlik* [*q.v.*], *zamīn* (in Turkish *zemīn*), *ḳiṭʿa* and *tarla* "individual field". In practice, the word *mazraʿa* was occasionally used for a *čiftlik* or a *zamīn* of a few *dönüm* (1 *dönüm* equals about 920 m^2) or any piece of land not possessed under the *tapu* system.

The abandoned land might be turned into a pasture or a vineyard and still retain the name *mazraʿa*. From the standpoint of land use, a *mazraʿa* is a field for grain production as opposed to pasture, vineyard, orchard, etc.

The hypothesis that in Anatolia the settled population chose to have their settlement sites on the hillsides in order to escape malaria and all kinds of marauders, soldiers, brigands, and passers-by, and maintained as a satellite exploitation a *mazraʿa* down on the flat land (*düzlük, ova*) (Tanoğlu, 1954, 27-8), holds true for many areas. Hütteroth (1968, 36-53) demonstrated it for central Anatolia, and Tanoğlu gives some examples for eastern Anatolia. While on the hillsides viticulture, horticulture, olive growing, and livestock breeding were preponderant, fields for grain production were located in the *mazraʿa* down on the flat land. The Syrian and Palestinian villages with vineyards, orchards and olive groves on the hillsides and *mazraʿa* down on the lowland or in the valleys also provide instances of this pattern (Hütteroth and Abdulfattah, 1977; B. Lewis and A. Cohen, 1978). This village-*mazraʿa* pattern develops into an upper village and a lower village when the satellite *mazraʿa* on the lowland is settled. Village names preceded with *zīr-* and *bālā-*, *yuḳarî-* and *ashaghî-*, or in the Balkans *dolni-/dolne-/dolnje-* and *gorni-/gorne-/gornje-* reflect the same process.

The fact that most of the *mazraʿas* were registered as dependent (*tābiʿ*) on a village as its *ekinlik*, reserved fields, can be taken as proof that the Ottoman administration generally recognised the *mazraʿa* as an indivisible part of village economy. Such *mazraʿas* secured an extra source of income for the villagers and provided land for the surplus population. Often villagers cultivated such land without the government's knowledge, arguing that it had always belonged to them. As a result, the rule was made that no abandoned land could be exploited without the Sultan's prior approval (Meḥemmed the Conqueror's *Ḳānūn-nāme*, Barkan 390, art. 16). Because the benefits of such exploitation were vital for the village economy, villagers vigorously contended against *tīmār*-holders or government agents who chose to rent such *mazraʿas* to outsiders. In opposition to such outsiders, including members of the military élite, who were particularly interested in renting *mazraʿas* in order to turn them into big *čiftliks*, villagers often rented them collectively.

Whether a *mazraʿa* was registered in the *daftar* or not determined its status. It could be registered as part of a village or of a *tīmār* or of a *waḳf* or independently in the register. A *mazraʿa*, being abandoned land, quite often escaped the surveyor. When discovered it was called "unregistered *mazraʿa* with no fixed taxes" (*khāridj az daftar bilā rüsūm olan mazraʿa*). Such *mazraʿas* were rented out and their revenue collected by government agents called *khāridj emīni*. Such lands could also be assigned to a *tīmār*-holder (*Arvanid defteri*, no. 178). This was because the government was concerned that no arable land, however small, be left uncultivated and without bringing in some sort of revenue. Under the *muḳāṭaʿa* [*q.v.*] system, such abandoned or unregistered lands as *mazraʿa, čiftlik*, or *zamīn* were offered to any bidder, military or townsfolk, Muslim or Christian, or even to a foreigner, anyone who would guarantee to the treasury a steady revenue from it. In 1545 in Bosnia, Venetians were able to rent *mazraʿas* (Gökbilgin, 1964, 208). Otherwise, in principle, the government's policy was ultimately to convert all such lands into villages or *raʿiyyet čiftliks* [see ČIFTLIK] under the *tapu* [*q.v.*] system. In other words, arable lands were basically reserved for the exploitation of the registered peasants, *raʿāyā* [*q.v.*], excluding the townsfolk and the military, and such lands, comprising the great majority of arable land in the empire, were categorised as *tapulu arāḍī*. Under the *tapu* system, the peasants were responsible for paying regular *raʿiyyet* taxes, including *čiftresmi* [*q.v.*]. In contrast, those lands not in the possession of the registered *raʿāyā* were treated fiscally as a separate category under the *muḳāṭaʿa* system, and such lands were called *muḳāṭaʿalu arāḍī* as opposed to the *tapulu arāḍī*.

Newly-conquered and abandoned land, since no previous record was available for its taxation, was also treated as a *mazraʿa* and was submitted to auction in order to achieve the highest possible revenue derivable under the circumstances (*Kanun i Kanunname*, i, 64). It was through an auction that the *muḳāṭaʿa* amount of a *mazraʿa* was determined.

The usual reference, "it is cultivated by those who come from outside" (*khāridjden ekilür*) on *mazraʿas* and *muḳāṭaʿalu čiftliks* indicates a situation in which the land was not possessed and cultivated by *yerlü*, the local *raʿāyā*, under the *tapu* system, but by those *raʿāyā* who were not registered with the land and were consequently considered "outsiders". The latter were normally *khaymānegān*, literally "people living in tents", but in practice meaning any wandering *raʿāyā* who might come and exploit the land on a temporary basis, paying rent or tithes to the "owner", *ṣāhib*, of the *muḳāṭaʿa*, the "owner" being the renter of the land. If the "outsider" settled on a *tīmār*-holder's or on *waḳf* land for three consecutive years he automatically became a *yerlü* and then the land was given to him under the *tapu*.

Thus in principle, *mazraʿas* were fiscally exploited under the *muḳāṭaʿa* system, which consisted simply of renting under a contract, *temessük* or *ḥüdjdjet*. The record of the rental in the register, which specified the possessor and the obligation, had binding force for both the state and the individual. The possessor's payment for the *mazraʿa* consisted either of tithes or of a fixed amount in cash.

When a *mazraʿa* was given in the way of *yurdluḳ* (*ber vedjh-i yurdluḳ*), it was possessed as a hereditary freehold property, usually on condition of sending a cavalryman [see ESHKINDJI] to the sultan's campaigns. In some cases, this obligation was forgiven (Konya TT40, 17).

The next question is to determine how *mazraʿas* emerged and under what conditions their number increased or decreased. The peasant populations would abandon their villages, temporarily or permanently, for various reasons. Natural and economic conditions conducive to mass flight included exhaustion of the land, desertification, and epidemics. Social and political conditions were no less important. First and foremost, peasants left their villages en masse to avoid being despoiled by passing troops, brigand bands, or caravans. A particularly important cause of flight was to avoid registration for taxes [see TAḤRĪR] and tax collection. The peasant's most effective means of getting a tax reduced or abolished was the threat of being scattered abroad (*perākende ve perīshān olmak*). Assuming the character of a mass protest, scattering became in effect a peasant strike and was frequently resorted to. What made it more frequent was that peasants did not own the land they cultivated under the *tapu* system, and there were always other lands available. The growing number of villages in the forests is largely due to this situation. On the other hand, the big landowners, and particularly *waḳf* lands, promised better conditions in order to attract the registered *raʿāyā* of the *tapu* lands. Thus the rural population in the Ottoman Empire, especially in Anatolia and the Balkans, became quite a mobile population, which accounts for the unusually large number of deserted villages in the Empire.

The increase or decrease in the number of *mazraʿas* can be taken as an indication of demographic and economic decline or development in a particular region; and the relative number of villages and *mazraʿa* can be determined for most of the provinces through the survey books (see TAḤRĪR, and maps in Tanoğlu, 1954; Hütteroth and Abdülfattah, 1977). In 1597 in some districts in Palestine (Hütteroth and Abdülfattah, 23, 24, and maps nos. 3, 10, and 13) the number of *mazraʿas* was two or three times greater than the number of villages (in the *sandjaḳ* of Ṣafad there were 610 *mazraʿas* as against 282 villages), whereas in the *sandjaḳ* of Aleppo both the villages and the *mazraʿas* numbered about one thousand (Venzke). Hütteroth (1986, 25) estimates that at the turn of the 18th century, about half of the Anatolian population depended on the various types of periodic settlements, and he finds it one of the most important features of the Middle Eastern cultural area.

In the formation of *mazraʿas* conditions other than peasant flight have also to be considered. Sometimes the peasants used nearby marginal land for cultivation, or reclamations were made on wasteland (*mawāt* [*q.v.*]) in the forests or swamps, or pasturelands in the *yayla* were used for cultivation; *mazraʿas* formed in these ways are frequently referred to in the survey registers. Also, conversion of the *tapulu* lands into livestock ranches gave rise to *mazraʿa*-type formations. When the central bureaucracy's control weakened during protracted wars, struggles for succession to the throne, uprisings, etc., the military's acquisition of abandoned lands became widespread. Those who acquired such lands under *muḳāṭaʿa* were called *aṣḥāb-i muḳāṭaʿa*, owners of the *muḳāṭaʿalu* land.

Since the abandoned *mazraʿas* could be given to anybody paying the rent, *muḳāṭaʿa*, including the military, the latter used this loophole in the Ottoman land system to enter into possession of the *mīrī* [*q.v.*] or state-owned lands, and to run the land as an estate. As such *mazraʿas* needed a labour force for their cultivation, the military offered favourable conditions to attract registered *raʿāyā* and thus caused disruption in the *mīrī*-based settlements. At other times, because of the labour shortage, they converted their *mazraʿas* into livestock ranches.

When *mazraʿa* owners were able to attract *raʿāyā* to their lands, they usually had recourse to the method of sharecropping (*ortaḳdjīlīḳ*). They furnished land and often seed, oxen, and domiciles to the sharecroppers.

In Anatolia, large areas of arable land abandoned by villagers were converted into ranches, partly because of the high price of meat in general and partly because of the military's difficulty in finding sufficient labour for cultivation. In any case, the Ottoman military class, unlike western landlords, was not capable, for various reasons, of owning land and organising it as big estates. In the period 1596-1610, the Djelālī [see DJALĀLĪ in Suppl.] depredations and insecurity in the countryside caused a tremendous increase of *mazraʿas* and *mazraʿa*-type land use throughout Asia Minor, resulting in a great diminution of agricultural land and grain production. A similar usurpation of the small plots of peasant families by "the powerful" in the provinces occurred in Byzantine Asia during the 10th century, and the emperors were forced to take radical measures against this development.

The second method used by the military to provide agricultural labour was the settlement of war prisoners on the land. As early survey registers demonstrate, the first Ottoman sultans as well as the members of the military class, the frontier begs in particular, employed this practice quite extensively.

The sub-village periodic settlements and exploitations could increase or decrease, and thus a pasture (*čayïr, yayla, ḳïshla*, or *oba*) could become a *mazraʿa* over the course of time by being converted into fields, or vice-versa. The state took the initiative in promoting settlement and cultivation and in restoring abandoned villages. The grant of land as freehold, *tamlīk* [see MILK] is one method.

In Serbia, abandoned villages were brought back to cultivation by the settlement of the Vlachs in the same way that nomads or wandering peasants (*khaymānegān*) were encouraged to settle *mazraʿas* in Anatolia. The state also encouraged *tīmār*-holders to assemble dispersed peasants to restore a village, promising them promotion.

Ottoman survey registers show that, besides belonging to villages, a great number of "vacant", *khālī, čiftliks* and *mazraʿas* were registered as "dependent", *tābiʿ*, on towns within the boundaries of the central district, *nāḥiye(t)* (Faroqhi, 1984, 191-266). This situation reflects the economic dependence of the towns on such agricultural reserve land, without which the towns could not survive. Given the exhorbitant transportation costs of the time, towns had to rely on this hinterland for an important part of the foodstuffs, fuel for their populations and raw materials such as cotton, wood, and hides for their handicrafts. The social and economic dynamics of such villages and sub-village settlements appear to be vivid and complex compared to that of "independent" rural settlements. The villages near towns were transformed into *mazraʿas* or *čiftliks* probably because the village population, attracted by better opportunities in town, migrated there, and once deserted, the village land was acquired under *muḳāṭaʿa* by well-to-do town residents and turned into a kind of estate-*čiftlik* (Faroqhi, 1980, 87-99).

As far as present-day Anatolia is concerned, human geographers (A. Tanoğlu, 1954; Hütteroth, 1968, 24-52; Tunçdelik, 1971, 17-55; Hütteroth and Abdülfattah, 1977, 29-32) study *mazraʿas* among the periodic settlements or small rural settlements on the way to becoming villages—rural *maḥalle, yayla(ḳ), ḳïshla(ḳ), ḳom, oba,* and *dīwān*. Throughout eastern Anatolia today, a great number of villages with a small settlement and having no formal village institutions such as *mukhtārlïḳ* come under the name *mezra, mezre,* or *mezri*. Settlement of marginal lands as a result of rural overpopulation is considered to be the underlying reason for such settlements. In the survey books, no mention is made of *ḳom* or rural *maḥalle,* which may be local names for *mazraʿa* (cf. Tunçdelik, 1971, 43).

Ḳom is to be found in eastern Anatolia; it differs from a *mazraʿa* by being a kind of ranch for animal breeding and is usually owned by an absentee landlord. It surrounds sheepfolds and shepherd huts. *Oba* is the grazing area of a nomadic household and should be studied rather within the *yayla* structure (Tunçdelik, 1971, 44). When settled by the nomad households which shift to agriculture as their main occupation, the *oba* assumes rather the character of a *mazraʿa*. The process is attested from early Ottoman history. At the present time, all *obas* are of this developed type. *Dīvān* was apparently a tribal superstructure over the *obas* (Tunçdelik, 47-8; Barkan, *Kanunlar*, 28-32), which disappeared as settlement progressed. Some isolated *čiftliks*, settled by one or a few families devoted to agriculture and livestock breeding, are considered, like the *mazraʿa*, as a kind of settlement liable to develop into a village (Tunçdilek, 43). In Palestine, Transjordan, and Syria (Hütteroth and Abdülfattah, 1977, 29-32), *mazraʿas* were "small agricultural areas, dispersed amongst the hills, lying within the village area but apart from the main fields belonging to the village, as is still the case today". According to the regulations and survey registers (*ibid.*, 31), the size of a *mazraʿa* varies widely. It may consist of only one or two *čiftliks* or have the size of a village, judging from its estimated revenue. However, as was made explicit in some *ḳānūn-nāmes* [*q.v.*], the typical *mazraʿa* is a deserted village which always has a large area of arable land, a water source and a cemetery.

Bibliography: *Konya tapu tahrir defteri*, Başvekâlet Arşivi, Istanbul, no. 40; Ö. L. Barkan, *XV ve XVI-ıncı asırlarda Osmanlı imparatorluğunda ziraî ekonominin hukukí ve malí esasları*: *kanunkar*, Istanbul 1943; W.-D. Hütteroth, *Ländliche Siedlungen im südlichen Inneranatolien in den letzten vierhundert Jahren*, Göttingen 1968; Hütteroth and Kamal Abdulfattah, *Historical geography of Palestine and Transjordan and Southern Syria in the late 16th century*, Erlangen 1977; Ali Tanoğlu, *Iskân coğrafyası, esas fikirler, problemler ve metod*, in *TM*, xl (1954); B. Djurdjev *et al.* (eds.), *Kanun i Kanunname*, Sarajevo, Orientalni Institut 1957; N. Tunçdilek, *Types of rural settlement and their characteristics*, in Benedict *et al.* (eds.), *Turkey, geographic and social perspectives*, Leiden 1974; *Şûret-i defter-i Sancak-i Arvanid*, ed. H. Inalcık, Ankara 1954; idem, *ʿAdâletnameler*, in *Belgeler*, ii (1967), 49-105; T. Gökbilgin, *Venedik devlet arşivindeki vesikalar*, in *Belgeler*, i/2 (1965), 119-225; G. Ostrogorsky, *Commune rurale byzantine*, in *Byzantion*, xxxii (1962), 139-66; S. Faroqhi, *Towns and townsmen of Ottoman Anatolia*, Cambridge 1984; M. L. Venzke, *The sixteenth century Ottoman sanjak of Aleppo*, Ph.D. diss., Columbia Univ. 1981, unpubl.; A. Cohen and B. Lewis, *Population and revenue in the towns of Palestine in the sixteenth century*, Princeton 1978.

(H. İNALCIK)

MAZRŪʿĪ (Ar. pl. Mazāriʿ, Swa. Wamazrui), an Arab tribe found in the Gulf States and in East Africa, where for two centuries they have intermarried with the local population. In the Gulf States they are found in Abu Dhabi, where they are regarded as a section of the Banī Yās. Outside Abu Dhabi, it is uncertain whether they are regarded as a section of the Banī Yās. Some are found in Dubai, in Sharjah, and in various districts and villages of ʿUmān, their centre being the walled town of al-Alāya, where the *shaykh* recognised as head of the family resides. In East Africa, in Kenya and on the island of Pemba (in the present Republic of Tanzania), fourteen lineages are recorded, descended from three lineages which migrated from ʿUmān between *ca.* 1698 and *ca.* 1800. Of these, the most celebrated provided an almost uninterrupted succession of rulers of Mombasa from 1698 until 1837, when twenty-five of the principal males were banished to Bandar ʿAbbās by Sayyid Saʿīd of ʿUmān and Zanzibar, many of them dying unaccountably on the voyage and the remainder in prison. Other Mazrūʿī lineages and the main one also provided subordinate rulers at Takaungu and Gazi, and of Pemba Island, generally with the Swahili title *liwali*, corrupted from Ar. *al-wālī*. In addition, the family produced a remarkable number of men of high ability and personal distinction, *ḳāḍī*s and junior magistrates, lawyers, administrators, historians, genealogists, scholars, poets, merchants and landowners, military commanders, a steamship captain and a harbourmaster, as well as men of religion. The history of the family from 1698 to 1835 is recounted in Shaykh al-Amīn b. ʿAlī al-Mazrūʿī, *History of the Mazrūʿī dynasty of Mombasa*, a unique Arabic manuscript written in lead pencil on foolscap. The author was Chief *Ḳāḍī* of Kenya 1937-47, a distinguished Islamic scholar, jurist and journalist. Very much other material exists bearing upon the history of the family, in official archives in London, Paris and Zanzibar, in printed primary sources and also in secondary sources, of which the most useful summary is in C. S. Nicholls, *The Swahili coast: politics, diplomacy and trade on the East African littoral, 1798-1856*, London 1971, 390-400. Shaykh al-Amīn's work is notably impartial, and based upon documents in family possession and some European printed works. Nevertheless, it is restricted by his lack of access to much other material, by an understandable leniency in judging his forebears, and also by chronological errors that sometimes lead to confusion. Two of these arise from misreadings of epitaphs in the Mazrūʿī cemetery beside Fort Jesus, Mombasa, in which he appears to have perpetuated the errors of European writers who were using interpreters.

The following table shows the *Liwali*s of Mombasa in order of their succession, with their regnal years.

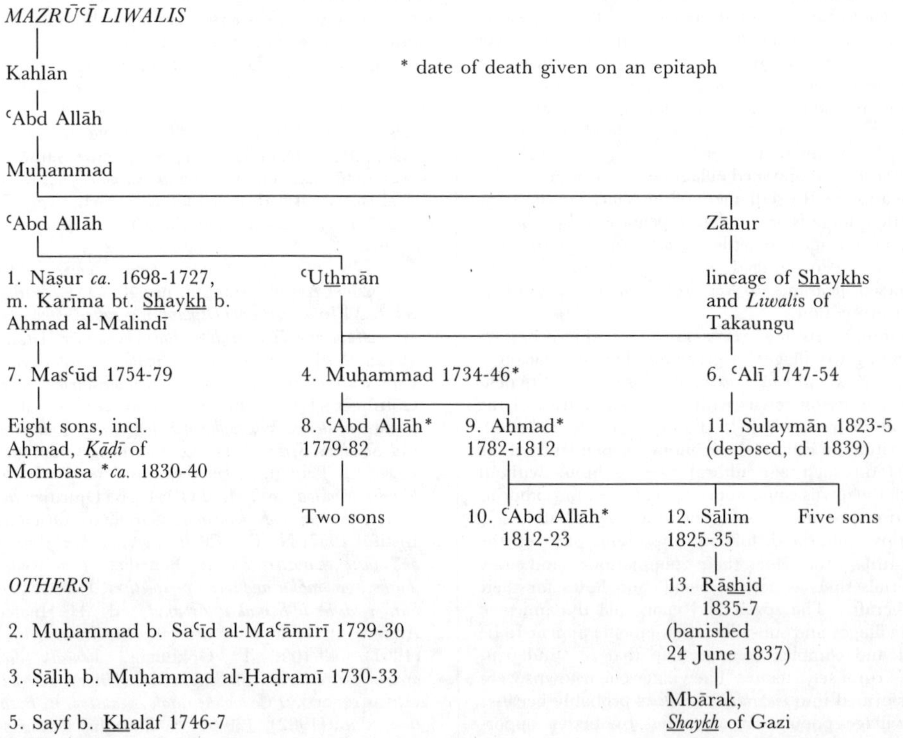
MAZRŪʿĪ LIWALIS
Kahlān
* date of death given on an epitaph
ʿAbd Allāh
Muḥammad
ʿAbd Allāh
Zāhur
1. Nāṣur ca. 1698-1727, m. Karīma bt. Shaykh b. Aḥmad al-Malindī
ʿUthmān
lineage of Shaykhs and Liwalis of Takaungu
7. Masʿūd 1754-79
4. Muḥammad 1734-46*
6. ʿAlī 1747-54
Eight sons, incl. Aḥmad, Ḳāḍī of Mombasa *ca. 1830-40
8. ʿAbd Allāh* 1779-82
9. Aḥmad* 1782-1812
11. Sulaymān 1823-5 (deposed, d. 1839)
Two sons
10. ʿAbd Allāh* 1812-23
12. Sālim 1825-35
Five sons
OTHERS
13. Rāshid 1835-7 (banished 24 June 1837)
2. Muḥammad b. Saʿīd al-Maʿāmirī 1729-30
3. Ṣāliḥ b. Muḥammad al-Ḥaḍramī 1730-33
5. Sayf b. Khalaf 1746-7
Mbārak, Shaykh of Gazi

According to Shaykh al-Amīn, the first of the family to come to East Africa, Nāṣur b. ʿAbd Allāh, was appointed *Liwali* of Mombasa at the same time that Mbārak b. Gharīb was appointed commander of the ʿUmānī forces at the siege of Fort Jesus, Mombasa [see MOMBASA], in 1696-8. The actual date of appointment is not known. His remit was as "overseer of all the ʿUmānī possessions in East Africa", an area defined by Shaykh al-Amīn as from Ras Ngomeni, north of Malindi, to the town of Pangani, on the River Ruvu, and including several subordinate rulers of towns and settlements. At the successful conclusion of the siege in December 1696, Nāṣur's appointment was by no means uncontested. The Swahili had, as they saw it, called the ʿUmānīs in as allies; and an important faction, lead by an individual with the strange name of Sese Rumbe, rebelled against the ʿUmānī determination to stay as conquerors. After some fighting, a composition was reached by which Nāṣur was recognised in office and married either a sister or a daughter of a certain Shaykh b. Aḥmad al-Malindī, a member of the former royal family of Malindi [*q.v.*], which the Portuguese had installed as sultans of Mombasa in 1592, when the Shīrāzī dynasty of Mombasa failed for want of heirs. (The word Shaykh is used as a given name quite commonly in East Africa.) This was a political move of profound local significance, with precedents at Kilwa and at Pate [*q.vv.*] at the foundation of both dynasties. Thereafter, apart from Portuguese raids, Nāṣur's term of office appears to have been peaceable. He died on a visit to ʿUmān.

No concept of a hereditary succession of governors is apparent at this point. Nāṣur had recommended the succession of his nephew Muḥammad b. ʿUthmān, but two other *Liwalis* followed in rapid succession who were not members of the family. It is not known why Muḥammad b. Saʿīd al-Maʿāmīrī was relieved after only a year, but Ṣāliḥ b. Muḥammad al-Ḥaḍramī was so harsh in his dealings with the people that he was removed from office when civil war broke out. Muḥammad b. ʿUthmān was now proclaimed *Liwali*, and his succession welcomed in Mombasa. He had ruled for ten years when the Yaʿrubī dynasty was deposed in ʿUmān by Aḥmad b. Saʿīd al-Bū Saʿīdī. This was no clear-cut transition [see ʿUMĀN], for chaos ensued for several years, and ʿUthmān ceased to remit taxes to Masḳaṭ. That he said "The Imām has usurped ʿUmān, and I have usurped Mombasa" is a most unlikely use of language that several writers have placed in his mouth. Nevertheless, it reflects local sentiment, in the same way that the Swahili *History of Pate* speaks of Aḥmad b. Saʿīd al-Bū Saʿīdī as a shopkeeper, with every assumption of an air of aristocratic disdain. Shopkeeper or not, Aḥmad knew how to consolidate power, and he had Muḥammad b. ʿUthmān assassinated, by assassins sent from ʿUmān, but with the support of the faction that had earlier opposed Nāṣur. One of the assassins, Sayf b. Khalaf, was now appointed *Liwali*. Shaykh al-Amīn's account at this point is by no means clear, and by mischance there is no reliable account in any European source. Muḥammad b. ʿUthmān's brother ʿAlī was imprisoned by Sayf b. Khalaf, and several accounts exist of his exciting escape from the fort with the connivance of Balūčī soldiers of Aḥmad b. Saʿīd's that, nevertheless, were loyal to the Mazrūʿī. Then, at the critical moment, a European arrived with an armed vessel, which by agreement with ʿAlī, bombarded the fort. Sayf b. Khalaf was taken prisoner and killed, and ʿAlī acclaimed as *Liwali* by those who had supported his brother and uncle. An attempt by Aḥmad b. Saʿīd to install one ʿAbd Allāh b. Djaʿīd al-Bū Saʿīdī as *Liwali* was frustrated, and ʿAlī now ruled with confidence.

It is a mark of that confidence that was now felt in Mombasa that in 1754 ʿAlī assembled a fleet and an army to take Zanzibar from the Bū Saʿīdī. It is claimed that he went with 80 ships, but we do not know their size or complements. Certainly, they were enough for success to be immediate. At this juncture, however, ʿAlī's nephew Khalaf ran amok and stabbed him in the back. Various reasons have been suggested, that he was mad, that he was possessed by magical powers, or that he had a genuine ambition to seize power from his uncle. Occurrences such as this are paralleled in plenty in the annals of the Gulf States. A son of Nāṣur, Masʿūd, now took power, and led a demoralised army back to Mombasa. There is some argument whether or not a second attack on Zanzibar was to take place, but nothing happened.

By all accounts, Masʿūd was an astute politician, adroit in seeking conciliation. It is in his reign that Mombasa's involvement in the affairs of the sultanate of Pate begins, with a garrison sent to Pate to assist the sultan in keeping out the Bū Saʿīdī. In 1776 the Kilifi faction that had opposed the preceding Mazrūʿī *Liwalis* encouraged certain persons in Pate to attack Mombasa. It was not countenanced by the Sultan of Pate, and amounted to no more than a raid that was easily scotched. A rebellion now took place in Pate against Sultan Bwana Mkuu b. Shehe, and in the mêlée of his assassination the Khalaf who had murdered ʿAlī b. ʿUthmān was himself murdered while attempting to defend the sultan. Then in 1779 Masʿūd died. Shaykh al-Amīn praises him for his cunning—should we not say diplomacy? His days, he says, were days of prosperity, ease and peace, in which he was much engaged in trade. This, perhaps, was the halcyon period of Mazrūʿī rule.

On his death, eleven sons of previous *Liwalis* contested the succession "violently", but within the day they settled upon ʿAbd Allāh b. Muḥammad. Shaykh al-Amīn is silent about his short reign of two years only: "like his predecessor, he was of good character, and far from making war". His next brother, Aḥmad, succeeded him and now ruled for twenty years. Shortly after his accession he had to deal with a rebellion in Tanga. At the end of his reign, war arose between Mombasa and Pate on the one hand, and Lamu on the other [see PATE], with the result that the Mombasa forces were severely defeated at Shela. Very shortly after, Aḥmad died: his epitaph in the Mazrūʿī cemetery describes him as *malik*, the only *liwali* so to describe himself or be so described on an epitaph. It is a reflection, perhaps, of the weakness in East Africa of the earlier part of the reign of Sayyid Saʿīd that a *liwali* should be able to use so uncompromising a title of royalty with impunity.

Aḥmad's son ʿAbd Allāh, the former commander of the Lamu garrison, now succeeded him, without any opposition, as the man with the most experience and competence. His first action was to reorganise the army and the administration, appointing several new subordinate *liwalis*. One of these, Saʿīd b. ʿAbd Allāh al-Buhrī, was murdered by the Digo tribe on his way to take up his post as *Liwali* at Mtang'ata. (His great-grandson, ʿAlī b. Ḥumayd b. ʿAbd Allāh, of Tanga, was said by the late J. Schacht to be the most learned authority on Islamic law that he had ever encountered.) The murderer was none other than the chief and spiritual head of the Digo, but he was forgiven on payment of the blood price. ʿAbd Allāh now turned his attention to Lamu, and to Sayyid Saʿīd, to whom he sent, as a gesture to show his independence, a coat of mail, a horn for measuring powder, a small quantity of powder and some musket balls, intimating that Saʿīd could come and fight. Here indeed was provocation, and on the monsoon of 1238/1822 Saʿīd's uncle Ḥamad b. Aḥmad al-Bū Saʿīdī came with 4,000 men and thirty ships. At Lamu, he defeated ʿAbd Allāh's son Mbārak, and got possession of Pate as well. He then proceeded to Pemba, which he took after several days' battle. The loss broke ʿAbd Allāh's heart, and he died.

His uncle Sulaymān b. ʿAlī was now elected as a compromise candidate. Shaykh al-Amīn describes him as "an intelligent man, decisive and a lover of peace"; a British official document describes him as "aged and feeble", while Captain W. F. W. Owen, who met him personally, described him as "an old dotard who had outlived every passion except avarice". Fearing to lose Mombasa to Sayyid Saʿīd, a delegation was sent to Bombay to ask for the protection of the British Government. Before a reply could arrive, a letter came to request that the British be permitted to survey Mombasa Island and to purchase cattle. No one could read it. The Mazrūʿī and the people took it as an affirmative answer, and hoisted the Union Flag. On 3 December 1823, H. M. S. *Barracouta*, under the command of Lieutenant Boteler, arrived at Mombasa, as part of Captain Vidal's command engaged in surveying the Indian Ocean. Boteler, joined shortly by Vidal, knew of no reason to acquire for Britain an unimportant city on the African coast that had no commercial or strategic advantages. They fended the Mazrūʿī off as best they could. But on 7 February, Captain W. F. W. Owen arrived on H. M. S. *Leven*, at the very moment that a fleet sent by Sayyid Saʿīd was bombarding the Mazrūʿī into submission. Owen was a passionate crusader against the slave trade, and believing that Mombasa could be used as a centre from which to destroy it, he acceded to the request for a Protectorate. A treaty was drawn up, of which Shaykh al-Amīn's version differs somewhat, but only in detail, from British sources. It was that:

(1) Great Britain would cause to return to the *Liwali* all the territories he had ruled formerly;

(2) The Chief of the Mazrūʿī should administer the sultanate which would be hereditary in his descendants;

(3) A Commissioner of the Protecting Power would reside with the *Liwali*;

(4) Customs duties would be divided between the contracting powers;

(5) British subjects would have permission to trade in the interior;

(6) An end would be put to the slave trade in Mombasa.

Shaykh al-Amīn claims that ʿAbd Allah b. Sulaym, the commander of Sayyid Saʿīd's forces, was delighted with the treaty, a view wholly contrary to that evidenced in British official documents. Saʿīd, indeed, awaited the reaction of Bombay, which, with Whitehall, took the view that neither Mombasa nor its use, as yet unexplored, to end the slave trade could counterbalance the advantages of good relations with Sayyid Saʿīd in the Gulf. Accordingly, in October 1826, the British were instructed to withdraw. Before this had been done, *Liwali* Sulaymān had been deposed by the sons of *Liwali* Aḥmad b. Muḥammad, chosing instead one of their number, Sālim. Shaykh al-Amīn quotes in full a laudatory *ḳaṣīda* written by Shaykh Muḥyī al-Dīn b. al-Shaykh al-Ḳaḥṭānī al-Barāwī, later Shāfiʿī *ḳāḍī* of Zanzibar, whose knowledge and learning in Arabic letters was later to be praised by Sir Richard Burton.

Saʿīd himself lost no time. A fleet was assembled immediately in Masḳaṭ, with a substantial army, and he advanced on Mombasa. Nevertheless, he preferred diplomacy, and a judicious bribe led to a treaty of conciliation. It was agreed that:

(1) Fort Jesus was to be surrendered to Sayyid Saʿīd; he would install a garrison limited to fifty, and of a tribe agreeable to the Mazrūʿī;

(2) the *Liwali* would live in the fort with his family as heretofore;

(3) sovereignty should belong to Sayyid Saʿīd, but Sālim would be *Liwali* for life, and his descendants after his death;

(4) customs duties would be divided equally between the contracting powers, and the *Liwali* would have the right to appoint customs officials.

The fort was now garrisoned with Arabs and Balūčīs, and Nāṣur b. Sulaymān al-Ismāʿīlī, formerly *Liwali* of Pemba, put in command. His harshness and insulting behaviour alienated the Mazrūʿī, and led to friction. Sālim determined to refer the matter to ʿUmān, whereon Nāṣur demanded the surrender of the town to him, under pain of war. Sālim then besieged him in the fort, and starved him out, an occasion for yet another lengthy *ḳaṣīda* from the pen of Shaykh Muḥyī al-Dīn. Sālim returned to the fort. Nevertheless Saʿīd was not satisfied with the Mazrūʿī account of the affair, and came in force on the monsoon of 1245/1829. A six-day battle ensued, in which Saʿīd's forces were soundly defeated. Sālim then fortified Mombasa with a wall, and by 1248/1832 felt strong enough to attempt to regain Pemba. His force was insufficient, and returned defeated. Next year, civil war broke out between Siyu and Pate following a succession dispute in Pate, in the course of which Salim angered Saʿīd by allying with the side opposed to him. On his way to Zanzibar, Saʿīd bombarded Mombasa, but without doing any more than set some houses on fire. For the rest of his reign, Sālim was left in peace. Sālim is the only *Liwali* known to have minted coins, which, Guillain reports, were struck from a bronze cannon on account of a shortage of small currency during his struggle with Sayyid Saʿīd. They bear no date, and only the Arabic words for *O.* "struck" / *R.* "in Mombasa". They were known in Swahili as *buruzuku*, which apparently derives from Portuguese *bazaruco*, small change, a word already currently used in Goa in a different form when the Portuguese occupied it in the 16th century. An almost identical issue was made in Lamu, Lamu being substituted for Mombasa, but so far nothing has been discovered about either of these issues.

In 1835 Sālim was succeeded on his death by his son Rāshid, but he had gained the fort with the support of the townsfolk while the family were still quarrelling about the succession. Returning to Zanzibar in 1837 from ʿUmān, Saʿīd first won over the opponents within the Mazrūʿī family by bribery, and then, changing sides, supported Rāshid on condition that the fort should be surrendered to Zanzibar. Rāshid was left with no choice. Saʿīd then arrested twenty-five of the family by inviting them to Zanzibar, but instead the ship sailed to Bandar ʿAbbās, at this time an ʿUmānī possession; and there those who had not died unaccountably on the voyage died in prison. It was the end of the independence of Mombasa, and the completion of Sayyid Saʿīd's assertion of his suzerainty over the East African coast.

Saʿīd did not, however, destroy the whole family. Mbārak, who had led the siege of the fort, is not to be confused with a younger son of Rāshid b. Sālim, also Mbārak. From Gazi, where he resided, in 1850 he attacked Takaungu, and expelled Rāshid b. Khāmis al-Mazrūʿī, a member of another branch of the family who had just been appointed *Liwali* of Takaungu, a position held by many other members of his lineage. Saʿīd sent troops to aid his nominee, and Mbārak returned to Gazi. Later he was forgiven, and in 1860 appointed *Liwali* of Gazi.

Fort Jesus, where so many of the events described here took place, is now a Museum. From 1895 to 1958 the British Colonial administration used it as a prison, choking the interior with cells and other buildings. These had superseded its use between 1837 and 1895 as the barracks of the ʿUmānī garrison, when it was filled with "mean huts" seen by Guillain, Owen and others. All this was cleared and restored by J. S. Kirkman, F. S. A., with a subvention from the Calouste Gulbenkian Foundation, between 1958 and 1970. The Portuguese Captain's House, which had been occupied later by the Mazrūʿī *Liwali*s, was now rid of later excrescences. Of their period there survived what is known as the Audience Hall of the Mazrūʿī, in fact a *madjlis* (or *selāmlik*) normal in Arab houses. It is decorated with inscriptions, Ḳurʾān verses and poems, and painted decorations surrounding them on the wooden beams. The Pilgrimage to Mecca of the fifth *Liwali*, Aḥmad b. Muḥammad, in 1208/1793, is commemorated by an inscription that states that none of the *Liwali*s before him had made the Pilgrimage. The ornamental decorated roof is mentioned by Owen, together with the stone benches that still remain, and it was here that the negotiations for the British Protectorate Treaty of 1824 took place. Sadly, when the fort was in use as a prison, the madjlis was used as a gaol for women, and the nearby gun platform for lunatics.

Biographical details are lacking for members of the family other than Shaykh al-Amīn b. ʿAlī al-Mazrūʿī, author of the *History* already cited. Born in 1891, he was brought up in the house of Shaykh Sulaymān b. ʿAlī b. Khāmis al-Mazrūʿī, Chief *Ḳāḍī* of Kenya. He studied under him and with *ʿulamāʾ* in Zanzibar, and then himself acquired a reputation as a teacher of Islamic law. Among others, he taught *ʿulamāʾ* from Lamu, Tanga and Zanzibar, among them the famous Shaykh ʿAlī b. Ḥumayd al-Buhrī, the former *ḳāḍī* of Tanga already mentioned. Shaykh al-Amīn was active in starting libraries and Ḳurʾānic schools, and writing religious textbooks, including textbooks for the instruction of children. He was the first to write religious textbooks in Swahili. In 1930 he instituted a Swahili newspaper, dealing with political, social and religious questions; and in 1932 an Arabic and Swahili weekly *al-Iṣlāḥ* ("Reform"). Although he never visited Egypt, he was immersed in the writings of Djamāl al-Dīn al-Afghānī, Shaykh Muḥammad ʿAbduh and Rashīd Riḍā, and gave instruction in the Mazrūʿī Mosque in Arabic and other subjects. More conservative persons in Mombasa were highly critical of his attitude, especially towards women, finding his ideas "revolutionary". He was appointed *ḳāḍī* of Mombasa in 1932, and Chief *Ḳāḍī* of Kenya in 1937, dying in office in 1947.

Bibliography: Shaykh al-Amīn b. ʿAlī al-Mazrūʿī, *History of the Mazrūʿī dynasty of Mombasa*, ms. *ca.* 1944, ed. and tr. in preparation by B. G. Martin, and ms. tr. and notes by J. M. Ritchie; G.S.P. Freeman-Grenville, *East African coin finds and their historical significance*, in *Jnal. of African History*, i/1 (1960), 40; idem, *The East African Coast: select documents*, London 1962, 1977; idem, *The French at Kilwa Island*, Oxford 1965; idem, *The Mombasa rising against the Portuguese*, London 1980; idem, with B. G. Martin, *A preliminary handlist of the Arabic inscriptions of the Eastern African coast*, in *JRAS* (1973); Sir J. M. Gray, *The British in Mombasa, 1824-1826*, London 1957; C. Guillain, *Documents sur l'histoire, la géographie et le commerce de l'Afrique orientale*, 3 vols., Paris 1856, with *Album*, 1857, showing views of Mombasa and Fort Jesus; J. B. Kelly, *Britain and the Persian Gulf, 1795-1880*, Oxford 1968; J. S. Kirkman, *Fort Jesus: a Portuguese fortress on the East African coast*, Oxford 1974; J. L. Lorimer, *Gazetteer of the Persian Gulf, ʾOman and Central Arabia*, 2 vols., Calcutta 1908-15; C. S. Nicholls, *The Swahili coast: politics, diplomacy and trade on the East African littoral, 1798-1856*, London 1971; R. Oliver and G. Mathew, *History of East Africa*, i, Oxford 1963; A. I. Salim, *Swahili-speaking peoples of Kenya's coast, 1895-1965*, Nairobi 1973; idem, *Sheikh al Amin bin Ali al-Mazrui: un réformiste moderne au Kenya*, in F. Constantin (ed.), *Les voies de l'Islam en Afrique Orientale*, Paris 1987, 59-71. W. H. Valentine, *Modern copper coins of the Muhammadan dynasties*, London 1911, 83, illustrates the Lama and Mombasa issues. (G. S. P. Freeman-Grenville)

MAZYAD, Banū, or Mazyadids, an Arab dynasty of central ʿIrāḳ, which stemmed originally from the clan of Nāshira of the Banū Asad [*q.v.*] established in the area between al-Kūfa and Hīt, and which flourished in the 4th-6th/10th-12th centuries.

The origins of the Mazyadids, as established by G. Makdisi (see *Bibl.*) *pace* the older view (expressed e.g. in *EI*[1] Mazyadīds) that the family did not appear in history till the early years of the 5th/11th century, go back to the period soon after the establishment of Būyid domination in ʿIrāḳ. Ibn al-Djawzī relates that the Būyid *amīr* Muʿizz al-Dawla's vizier Abū Muḥammad al-Ḥasan al-Muhallabī (in office 345-52/956-63) entrusted to Mazyad (read rather, Ibn Mazyad or ʿAlī b. Mazyad) the protectorate (*ḥimāya* [*q.v.*]) over Sūrā and its vicinity. Sanāʾ al-Dawla Abu 'l-Ḥasan ʿAlī's amīrate must have been a lengthy one. The same source mentions that he led a punitive expedition on the Būyids' behalf against the Banū Khafādja [*q.v.*]; that in 393/1003 his jurisdiction over unspecified territories was confirmed by the Buyid governor in ʿIrāḳ, the ʿAmīd al-Djuyūsh al-Ḥasan b. Ustādh Hurmuz; but also that he established a pattern of subsequent Mazyadid attitudes towards their suzerains of alternate submissiveness and defiance according to the degree of control exercised by the squabbling Būyid princes. Indeed, the continuance of the Mazyadids' authority in central ʿIrāḳ was always to depend on a readiness to shift alliances with various contending powers in ʿIrāḳ, aiming at the preservation of a balance of power there between the ʿAbbāsid caliphs and the latter's would-be protectors, whether Būyid or Saldjūḳ, and thereby ensuring that one element did not achieve total political domination, an attitude complicated at times by the fact that the Mazyadids, like so many of the Arab tribes of the Syrian desert fringes, were Shīʿīs, with their rule from al-Ḥilla extending over what became the heartland of ʿIrāḳī Shīʿism and what already contained the two great shrines of al-Nadjaf and Karbalāʾ [*q.vv.*].

The dynasty comes more clearly into the light of history with the accession, apparently, at the age of 14 years and with the prospect before him of a long reign like his father's, of Nūr al-Dawla Abu 'l-Aʿazz Dubays (I) b. ʿAlī in 408/1017-8. Shortly before then, in 397/1006-7, ʿAlī had acquired by grant from the Būyid *amīr* Bahāʾ al-Dawla [*q.v.* in Suppl.], after its previous tenure by the ʿUḳaylids [*q.v.*] of al-Mawṣil, the town of al-Djāmiʿayn on the Euphrates. During ʿAlī's amirate, mention of al-Djāmiʿayn gradually drops out of the sources by the mid-5th/11th century, and what had apparently been only a temporary encampment (*ḥilla*), either within or adjacent to al-Djāmiʿayn, became more permanent and evolved into an enduring town, increasing in prosperity as the political influence of the Mazyadids grew, and being fortified by a wall and embellished by the greatest ruler of the dynasty, Ṣadaḳa (I) b. Manṣūr (see G. Makdisi, *Notes on Ḥilla and the Mazyadids in medieval Islam*, which should be added to the *Bibl.* for al-ḥilla).

Dubays did not continue the policy of strife with the related tribe of the Banū Dubays on the borders of ʿIrāḳ and al-Ahwāz which had occupied his father's later years. But through his brother al-Muḳallad's designs on the headship of the Mazyadid family, Dubays became embroiled with the ʿUkaylid Ḳirwāsh b. al-Muḳallad, to whom at al-Mawṣil b. ʿAlī had fled after the failure of his last bid for power, and likewise was caught up in the rivalry of the Būyid contenders for power in ʿIrāḳ, Djalāl al-Dawla b. Bahāʾ al-Dawla and his nephew Abū Kālīdjār al-Marzubān b. Sulṭān al-Dawla [*q.vv.*] in the years after 416/1025. Dubays supported Abū Kālīdjār and al-Muḳallad Djalāl al-Dawla, and in 421/1030 Dubays's lands were overrun by his enemies, compelling him to submit and to pay a substantial tribute to Djalāl al-Dawla. He faced further trouble from a third brother Th̲ābit, who allied with the Turkish commander Arslān Basāsīrī [*q.v.*], and from the rival K̲h̲afādja Bedouins. During the fighting in central ʿIrāḳ which finally led to the establishment of the Saldjūḳ protectorate over Bag̲h̲dād, Dubays now supported Basāsīrī in proclaiming the cause of the S̲h̲īʿī Fāṭimids at Bag̲h̲dād, espousing what was in the end to prove the losing side, whilst his enemy the ʿUḳaylid Ḳurays̲h̲ b. Badrān at first supported Ṭog̲h̲rïl Beg. Nevertheless, after the pacification by Ṭog̲h̲rïl of ʿIrāḳ, Dubays managed to retain his position, dying in 474/1082 at the age of 80.

After the brief reign of his son Bahāʾ al-Dawla Abū Kāmil Manṣūr, the latter was succeeded in 479/1086-7 by Sayf al-Dawla Abu 'l-Ḥasan Ṣadaḳa (I) b. Manṣūr, who was recognised by the Saldjūḳ sultan Malik S̲h̲āh as lord of the central ʿIrāḳ lands to the west of the Tigris. In the subsequent struggle for power between Malik S̲h̲āh's two sons Berk-Yaruḳ and Muḥammad, Ṣadaḳa at first supported the former, but after a dispute with Berk-Yaruḳ's vizier, in 494/1100-1 switched his allegiance to Muḥammad, at first making the *k̲h̲uṭba* in al-Ḥilla for Muḥammad but soon afterwards dropping the name of both Saldjūḳs from it and acknowledging only the ʿAbbāsid caliph al-Mustaẓhir. It was Ṣadaḳa who, as noted above, launched extensive building operations in his capital. The confused situated in ʿIrāḳ further allowed him to expand Mazyadid influence over a wide sector of the country, including Hīt, Wāsiṭ (in 497/1104), al-Baṣra (499/1106) and Takrīt (500/1106). Muḥammad, by now the sole Saldjūḳ sultan in the west, became alarmed at the rising power of his subject; he set out in 501/1108 with an army from Bag̲h̲dād, defeated and killed Ṣadaḳa at al-Nuʿmāniyya and captured his son Dubays. Like others of his family, Sadaka had been commonly accorded the title of *Malik al-ʿArab* "Lord of the Arabs" (i.e. of the Bedouins along the ʿIrāḳ desert fringes), *Rex Arabum* in Latin Crusader sources, and contemporaries mourned his passing as a brave and noble figure, uniting the ideals of Bedouin chivalry and Islamic fervour, and as a generous patron of Arabic learning.

The same sort of praise is accorded to his son and successor Nūr al-Dawla Abu 'l-Aʿazz Dubays (II), whom al-Ḥarīrī [*q.v.*] refers to in his 39th *maḳāma*, that of ʿUmān, as an ideal figure for nobility and piety. He was only able to regain his seat in al-Ḥilla after Muḥammad's death in 511/1118, but soon enjoyed a new authority as a consequence of the rivalry between the two Saldjūḳ contenders for the sultanate, Muḥammad's sons Maḥmūd and Masʿūd, harassing both Maḥmūd and the ʿAbbāsid caliph al-Mustars̲h̲id, against whom the S̲h̲īʿī Dubays uttered threats of razing Bag̲h̲dād to the ground. During these years, various reverses at the hands of these rulers nevertheless sent him in temporary flight to the Frankish Crusaders in northern Syria, where in 518/1124 he allied with the King of Jerusalem Baldwin II in a fruitless attack on Aleppo; to his father-in-law the Artuḳid Il-G̲h̲āzī in Mārdīn; and, in alliance with the Saldjūḳ prince Ṭog̲h̲rïl b. Muḥammad, to the Saldjūḳ sultan in the east, Sandjar. The reviving power of the ʿAbbāsid caliphate blocked his plans for expansion in ʿIrāḳ, and he had finally to take refuge at Marāg̲h̲a [*q.v.*] in Ād̲h̲arbāydjān with the Saldjūḳ Masʿūd, who in 529/1135 treacherously killed both al-Mustars̲h̲id and Dubays.

Dubays's son Sayf al-Dawla Ṣadaḳa (II) supported Masʿūd's cause against his nephew Dāwūd b. Maḥmūd, but lost his life in the course of this warfare (532/1137-8). His brother Muḥammad was then recognised as lord of al-Ḥilla, but soon afterwards lost the town to his brother ʿAlī (II), and when the latter died in 545/1150-1, control of the town oscillated between the ʿAbbāsid caliph al-Muḳtafī and Turkish commanders of the Saldjūḳ sultan Muḥammad b. Arslān S̲h̲āh. The caliphal troops withdrew from al-Ḥilla in 551/1156-7, but in 558/1163 the caliph al-Mustandjid, whose power in ʿIrāḳ was increasing with the decline of Saldjūḳ authority, sent an army against al-Ḥilla. His troops and their allies of the Banu 'l-Muntafiḳ wrought slaughter amongst the remaining Mazyadids and their Asadī supporters, and expelled those left alive. The hold of the Asad on the town was thus permanently broken.

That the Mazyadids, coming as they did from an untutored Bedouin background, were able to survive for two centuries as a significant force in the intricate politics and changing patterns of alliances in ʿIrāḳ is a tribute to the skill and sagacity of their leaders; and it is probable that their leadership as fervent S̲h̲īʿīs furthered the expansion of S̲h̲īʿism in central and southern ʿIrāḳ.

Genealogical table of the Mazyadids

Mazyad
1. ʿAlī I
al-Muḳallad — 2. Dubays I — Th̲ābit
3. Manṣūr
4. Ṣadaḳa I
5. Dubays II — Badrān — Manṣūr
6. Ṣadaḳa II — 7. Muḥammad — 8. ʿAlī II

Bibliography: The main primary sources are those for the history of ʿIrāḳ in the Būyid and Saldjūḳ periods, including Rūd̲h̲rāwarī, Ibn al-Djawzī, Bundārī and Ibn al-At̲h̲īr (follows Ibn al-Djawzī). Ibn K̲h̲allikān has biographies of Ṣadaḳa I (ed. ʿAbbās, ii, 490-1, no. 302, tr. de Slane, i, 634-5) and of Dubays II (ii, 263-5, no. 226, tr. i, 504-7). Of secondary sources, see J. von Karabaček, *Beiträge zur Geschichte der Mazjaditen*, Leipzig-Vienna 1874; M. von Oppenheim, *Die Beduinen*, iii, Wiesbaden 1952, 455-6; G. Makdisi, *Notes on Hilla and the Mazyadids in medieval Islam*, in *JAOS*, lxxiv (1954), 249-62; ʿAbd al-Djabbār Nādjī, *al-Imāra al-Mazyadiyya*, Baṣra 1970; and scattered mentions in histories dealing with the period such as H. Busse, *Chalif und Grosskönig, die Buyiden im Iraq* (945-1055), Beirut-Wiesbaden 1969, and Bosworth, in *Cambridge history of Iran*, v. On the relations of Dubays II with the Crusaders, see R. Grousset, *Histoire des Croisades et du Royaume Franc de Jérusalem*, i, Paris 1934, 625 ff.; S. Runciman, *A history of the Crusades*, ii, Cambridge 1952, 171-3; M. W. Baldwin *et alii* (eds.), *A history of the Crusades. i. The first hundred years*, Philadelphia 1955, 423-5. For chronology, see Zambaur, *Manuel*, 137, and Bosworth, *The Islamic dynasties*, 51-2. See also *EI*¹ arts. DUBAIS, MAZYADIS, ṢADAḲA and *EI*² art. ASAD.

(C. E. BOSWORTH)

MĀZYĀR [see ḲĀRINIDS].

MBWENI, a settlement on the East African coast. It lies on the Tanzanian coast north of Dar es Salaam, and has a ruined Friday mosque of 14th or

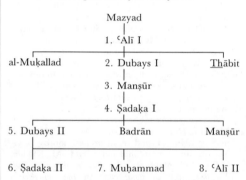

15th century date divided into two aisles by three central pillars. There is an extensive cemetery, with tombs, some highly decorated with elaborate carvings, of the past five centuries. It includes a pillar tomb [see MANĀRA. 3. In East Africa] decorated with green celadon plates, of date *ante* 1350. A small tomb has an inscription commemorating Masᶜūd b. Sulṭān Shafīᶜ ᶜAlī b. Sulṭān Muḥammad al-Barāwī, who died in 1306/1888. It is the object of a cult, and numerous pottery vessels ranging over most of the past century are to be seen beside the tomb, having held offerings of food and incense. The deceased was a member of a family celebrated for its energy in disseminating the teachings of the Uwaysī branch of the Ḳādiriyya.

Bibliography: G. S. P. Freeman-Grenville, *Medieval history of the coast of Tanganyika*, London 1962, 168; B. G. Martin, *Muslim brotherhoods in nineteenth-century Africa*, Cambridge 1976, 152, 160 ff. (G. S. P. FREEMAN-GRENVILLE)

MEʾALĪ, minor Ottoman poet of the first half of the 10th/16th century, known under this *makhlaṣ* and also as Yarḥiṣār-oghlï Köse Meʾālī (whilst his given name was Meḥmed). He is one of a considerable number of modestly gifted, as yet imperfectly known poets who share the popular Turkish taste in choice and handling of subject matter. (It is true, perhaps, that Meʾālī led a rather more libertine life than most of his peers.) He is very fond of puns and lavish in his use of idiomatic expressions. At times he has a candid tongue. His sense of humour, though never subtle (and sometimes more than crude), can show an endearing playfulness.

Meʾālī's father was Muṣṭafā b. Ewḥad al-Dīn Yarḥiṣārī, a *müderris* and later *ḳāḍī* of Istanbul; his mother Fāṭima bint Meḥmed Beg was a Fenārī. The date and place of his birth are unknown. He became a *mülāzim* [*q.v.*] of Tādjī-zāde Djaᶜfer Čelebi and of Zeyrek-zāde Rūkn al-Dīn Efendi and subsequently *ḳāḍī* of Mīkhālīdj-Kebsūd-Firṭ, of Filibe, and lastly of Gelibolu, where he died in 942/1535-6.

Meʾālī's poems are to be found in the one known (incomplete) copy of his *Dīwān* and in various *medjmūᶜas*. The bulk of his *Dīwān* consists of 270 *ghazels*; of special interest is a *destān* in *hedje* metre and a charming *murabbaᶜ* on the death of his cat.

Bibliography: Cf. the *tedhkires* of Sehī, Laṭīfī, ᶜĀshïḳ Čelebi, Ḳïnalï-zāde, Ḥasan Čelebi, ᶜĀlī, and Riyāḍī: Hammer-Purgstall, *GOD*. ii, 214-6: Tarlan, *Şiir mecmualarında XVI ve XVII. asır divan şiri*, Istanbul 1948, 33-44; Kocatürk, *Türk edebiyatı tarihi*, Ankara 1964, 323-4; Ambros, *Candid penstrokes: the lyrics of Meʾālī, an Ottoman poet of the 16th century*, Berlin 1982 (edition of the *Dīwān* with full specification of the relevant *tedhkires*).

(E.G. AMBROS)

MEASURES [see DHIRĀᶜ; MAKĀYĪL; MISĀḤA].

MECCA [see MAKKA].

MECELLE [see MEDJELLE].

MECHANICAL TECHNOLOGY [see ḤIYAL].

MĒD, a people who lived in Sind at the time of the early Arab invasions. Arab historians mention the Mēd in their brief descriptions of the battles which the Arabs waged in Sind but fail to furnish us with any substantial information concerning them. Even the form of the name is not certain: the manuscripts read either *m-y-d* or *m-n-d* (cf. al-Balādhurī, 435 n. *f*; al-Iṣṭakhrī, 176 n. *c*), and the article on this people appeared in *EI*[1] under MAND. However, some modern ethnographers report that the name is Mēd (H. Risley, *The people of India*, London 1915, 145, 328); this is valuable evidence in support of this version.

Several encounters with the Mēd are reported by al-Balādhurī. Rāshid b. ᶜAmr al-Djudaydī, appointed by Ziyād b. Abīhi to rule the area of Makrān [*q.v.*] on the Indian frontier, was killed by them during an incursion into Sind (al-Balādhurī, 433). An attack perpetrated by the "Mēd of Daybul" [*q.v.*] on a ship bringing Muslim women from "the island of rubies" (*djazīrat al-yāḳūt*; this has been frequently identified with Ceylon, but see S. Q. Fatimi, *The identification of Jazirat al-Yaqut*, in *Jnal. of the Asiatic Soc. of Pakistan*, ix [1964], 19-35, who suggested identifying it with Sumatra) is given as the reason for which al-Ḥadjdjādj decided to launch around 90-2/708-11 a major expedition to Sind (al-Balādhurī, 435-6; Gabrieli, in *East ad West*, xv [1964-5], 282-3; Friedmann, in M. Rosen-Ayalon, ed., *Studies in memory of Gaston Wiet*, Jerusalem 1977, 312 n. 19). Muḥammad b. al-Ḳāsim, who commanded this expedition, concluded an armistice with the people of Surast (?), who were "Mēd, pirates of the sea" (*yaḳṭaᶜūna fī 'l-baḥr*) (al-Balādhurī, 440); the name of this place recalls Surāshtra, i.e., Kāthiāwāŕ (B.C. Law, *Historical geography of ancient India*, Paris 1954, 297-9). In the reign of al-Muᶜtaṣim, ᶜImrān b. Mūsā attacked the Mēd, killed 3,000 of them and built a dam known as "the dam of the Mēd" (*sakr al-Mēd*), probably to disturb their irrigation (*ibid.*, 445). Then he resumed the campaign against the Mēd with the support of the Zuṭṭ [*q.v.*], whom he had subjugated; a canal (*nahr*) was dug from the sea and the lagoon (*baṭīḥa*) of the Mēd was inundated with salt water. Later on, a certain Muḥammad b. al-Faḍl b. Māhān launched a naval expedition against "the Mēd of Hind" and conquered a city of theirs (*ibid.*, 446).

Of the geographers, Ibn Khurradādhbih mentions al-Mēd both as a geographical region (56) and as a people who lived about four days' journey to the east of the Indus and were robbers (62). Al-Masᶜūdī, who went to India in 304/916-17 (Brockelmann, I, 44) says that the city of al-Manṣūra [*q.v.*] is continually at war with the Mēd (*Murūdj*, i, 378; cf. also *Tanbīh*, 55). Al-Iṣṭakhrī (176 = Ibn Ḥawḳal, 323-4) says that the infidel peoples of Sind are the Budha and the Mēd. The Mēd lived on the banks of the Indus (*shuṭūṭ Mihrān* [see MIHRAN], from Multān [*q.v.*] to the sea, and occupied pasturages in the desert which stretched between the Indus and the city of Ḳāmuhul. According to al-Idrīsī (*Opus geographicum*, Naples-Rome 1970-8, 170; tr. Jaubert, i, 163), the Mēd dwelt on the borders of the desert of Sind. They were nomads (*raḥḥāla*; Jaubert, *loc. cit.*, seems to have read *radjdjāla* and translated "un peuplade très brave"; cf. S. Maqbul Ahmad, *India and the neighbouring territories as described by ... al-Idrīsī*, Aligarh 1954, 33) and pastured their flocks up to the border of Māmahal (Ḳāmuhul?). They were numerous and owned many horses and camels; their raids extended as far as al-Rūr (cf. Elliot and Dowson, *The history of India as told by its own historians*, London 1867, i, 363) and sometimes even to Makrān.

The town of Ḳāmuhul, which marks the south-eastern limit of the area inhabited by the Mēd, was identified by Elliot and Dowson (*op. cit.*, i, 363; S. Hodīvālā, *Studies in Indo-Muslim history*, Bombay 1939, 38) with Anhalwāra, which is modern Patan in northern Baroda (cf. *EI*[2], III, 407; *Imperial gazetteer of India*[2], Oxford 1908, xx); Cunningham (*Report 1863-1864*, 290) places "Māmhal" at ᶜUmarkōt; this would place the Mēd much more firmly in Sind.

Of special interest among the Muslim sources is the anonymous *Mudjmal al-tawārīkh* (Storey, i, 67). A part of this work seems to be a résumé of the *Mahābhārata*. It begins with a chapter on the Mēd and the Zuṭṭ who lived in Sind and are said to be descendants of Ḥām, the son of Noah. The two peoples were hostile to each other and fought a number of wars. Having become tired of fighting, they resolved to approach king Daḥūs̲h̲an b. Dahrān (Duryodhana son of Dhṛtarāṣṭra) and asked him to appoint a ruler over them. Daḥūs̲h̲an gave the country to his sister Dusal (Duḥśalā), who married the powerful king D̲j̲andrat (Jayadratha). The country was then divided between the Zuṭṭ and the Mēd (J. Reinaud, *Fragments arabes et persans inédits*, Paris 1845, repr. 1974, 2-3, 25-7). The story reflects an attempt to forge a link between the history of the Mēd and the Zuṭṭ and the Indian tradition. It must be noted, however, that the Sanskrit original of the *Mahābhārata* makes no mention of peoples bearing these names in the passage dealing with Duḥśalā's marriage to Jayadratha, king of Sindhu (*Mahābhārata*, i. 108. 18). Moreover, the Indian tradition does not seem to contain anything definite about the Mēd, with the possible exception of occasional remarks in the *dharmaśāstra* literature about a low caste or, according to some, untouchable people called Meda, of unspecified geographical location or provenance (*Manusmṛti* 10.36, with Medhātithis's remarks; cf. Rai Bahadur B.A. Gupte, *The Meds of Makran*, in *Indian Antiquary*, xl [1941], 147-9).

It seems that the Mēd are not mentioned in later Muslim sources. It is noteworthy that the *Čač-nāma* [*q.v.* in Suppl.], which was written in the 7th/13th century, does not mention the Mēd in the context in which they appear in al-Balād̲h̲urī. In its description of the act of piracy which is said to have caused Muḥammad b. al-Ḳāsim's invasion of Sind, the *Čač-nāma* (ed. Daudpota, New Delhi 1939, 89) mentions a people called *N-k-a-m-r-a* instead of the Mēd. Neither are they mentioned in the *Čač-nāma* version of Rās̲h̲id b. ʿAmr al-D̲j̲udaydī's death (*ibid.*, 81-2). Despite their apparent disappearance from later Muslim sources, the Mēd are reported in existence by some modern ethnographers (Risley, *loc. cit.*, Elliot and Dowson, *op. cit.*, i, 519-31; H.T. Lambrick, *Sind. A general introduction*, Ḥaydarābād (Sind) 1964, 209-10, esp. at n. 17).

Bibliography: Given in the article; see also S. Razia Jafri, *Description of India (Hind and Sind) in the works of al-Iṣṭak̲h̲rī, Ibn Ḥauqal and al-Maqdisī*, in *Bull. of the Inst. of Islamic Studies* (Aligarh), v (1961), 60-1; al-Bīrūnī, *al-D̲j̲amāhir fī ma-ʿrifat al-d̲j̲awāhir*, Ḥaydarābād (Deccan) 1355/1936-7, 47-8.

(Y. Friedmann and D. Shulman)

MEDAL [see nis̲h̲ān, wisām].

MEDDĀḤ [see maddāḥ].

MEDEA [see al-madiyya).

MEDENIYYET (t.), "civilisation". As a term referring to a political system, *medeniyyet* seems to have been introduced into Ottoman Turkish towards the middle of the 19th century. Before it was coined on the basis of the old Arabic word *madīna*, the French term *civilisation* was used for a short while, and in its French pronunciation written in Arabic letters. In both senses, what was meant was the secular political system believed to be common in Europe. As a polity, *civilisation* or *medeniyyet* was contrasted with the traditional oriental dynastic despotism.

Muṣṭafā Res̲h̲īd Pas̲h̲a used the French word in his official writings in Ottoman Turkish in 1834. Ṣādiḳ Rifʿat Pas̲h̲a did likewise in 1837. Another writer, Muṣṭafā Sāmī, used the same French word written in Arabic letters and according to French pronunciation in his account of his observations in European capitals.

In spite of minor variations in their accounts of the civilisation, the main emphasis of such writers was on pointing out the superiority of the European polities which they named *civilisation* or *medeniyyet*. They were also in a great deal of agreement on identifying the distinguishing features of *medeniyyet*, e.g. enlightenment, rationalism, freedom of conscience, the dissemination of education and the prevalence of literacy, the accumulation of scientific knowledge and its rôle in the advancement of inventions, equality of subjects before the law and orderly application of it by government officials, and economic policies pursued to promote the interests of the people. Ṣādiḳ Rifʿat attempted to go even deeper and to discern that at the basis of these features lay a mode of thinking sharply different from the traditional views held in the East. He spoke of the natural rights of men as the sole basis of legitimacy of government in civilisation, adding that "there the governments are for the people, and not the people for governments".

In truth, similar ideas which may be taken as the sign of a degree of awareness of "the emergence of a new political phenomenon in Europe", as B. Lewis has pointed out, were not unknown to the Turkish reformers even before the outbreak of the French Revolution. Ironically, the very same revolution, with its Napoleonic aftermath, had been responsible, at least partly, for a violent reactionary uprising in 1807 which not only swept away all such new ideas but brought a period of anarchy and indecisiveness lasting until 1839, when a new era of the *Tanẓīmāt* [*q.v.*] reforms was opened. The reformers mentioned above were describing the model to be emulated and were pointing out decisively the desirability of the appropriation of the superior (*merg̲h̲ūb*) methods of civilisation.

The shortcomings of the *Tanẓīmāt* efforts of appropriating the fundamentals of *Medeniyyet* were due to a great extent to the vagueness, devoid of historical and sociological dimensions, and the naïveté displayed in the mechanistic views of these men. A small group of intellectuals (the "New Ottomans" or Yeñi ʿOt̲h̲mānlar), who lived abroad in exile, saw shortcomings in the *medeniyyet* current in Europe. In their criticisms of the *Tanẓīmāt* reforms they made implicit, and sometimes explicit, distinctions between the "material" and the "moral" parts in all civilisations. They too lavished praises on the advancements of material civilisation achieved in Europe, but they were less enthusiastic about the second part.

Thus from the late 1860s onward the word *medeniyyet* ceased to imply a political régime and one peculiar only to Europe. Later years saw the rise of much wider connotations of the term and of controversies, particularly when it was challenged by another term, *ḥart̲h̲*, coined by Ziyā (Ḍiyāʾ) Gökalp to correspond to the much older Western concept of culture.

Though the term *medeniyyet* had lost its early political meaning, it still carried a political tinge in 1920s during the War of Independence. A poem written and intended as the national anthem contained a verse cursing *medeniyyet* as "the monster with one remaining tooth"—an obvious reference to European imperialism. When Muṣṭafā Kemāl (Atatürk) glorified what he called "contemporary civilisation", he appears to have taken side with those who identified *medeniyyet* only with enlightenment and progress, but not with a political régime.

Bibliography: Ağaoğlu Ahmed, *Üç medeniyet*, Ankara 1928; Yūsuf Akčura, *ʿAṣrī Türk dewleti*, in *Türk Yurdu*, iii/13 (1341/1925), 1-16; Niyazi Berkes, *The development of secularism in Turkey*, Montreal

1964; idem, *Türkiye'de çağdaşlaşma*², Istanbul 1978; Ziya Gökalp, *Turkish nationalism and western civilization*, essays tr. and ed. N. Berkes, London 1958; Reşat Kaynar, *Reşit Paşa ve Tanzimat*, Ankara 1954; Mustafa Kemal, *Atatürk'ün söyler ve demeçleri*, ii, Ankara 1959; B. Lewis, *The impact of the French Revolution on Turkey*, in *Jnal. of World History*, i (January 1953), 105-25; idem, *On some modern Arabic political terms*, in *Orientalia Hispanica*, i, Leiden 1974, 466-71; Aḳyigitzāde Mūsā, *Awrūpā medeniyyetine bir naẓar*, Istanbul 1897; Şerif Mardin, *The genesis of Young Ottoman thought*, Princeton 1962; Ṣādiḳ Rifʿat, *Muntakhabat-i āthār*, ii, Istanbul 1844; Muṣṭafā Sāmī, *Awrūpā risālesi*, Istanbul 1840.

(NIYAZI BERKES)

MEDḤĪ, the pen name (*makhlaṣ*) used by a number of Ottoman poets whose poetry is known to date mainly through the samples found in *medjmūʿas* and *tedhkires*. Judging by these, they are all poets of secondary importance at best. Two should be singled out.

1. Maḥmūd Efendi of Gelibolu (Gallipoli), known as Ḳara Maḥmūd (or Ḳara Ḳāḍī-zāde according to Beyānī). A *mülāzim* of *Shaykh al-Islām* Abu 'l-Suʿūd Efendi [*q.v.*], he first became a *müderris*. After being dismissed from a position with a daily salary of forty *akčes*, he was appointed in 984/1576 to the Shāh Khūbān *medrese* in Istanbul (cf. Câhid Baltacı, *XV-XVI. asırlarda Osmanlı medreseleri*, Istanbul 1976, 435). In 987/1579 he became *müftī* of Kefe, in 992/1584 *ḳāḍī* of Marʿash, from 994/1585-6 until 995/1586 he was *ḳāḍī* of Kütahya, from 996/1588 until 998/1590 again *ḳāḍī* of Marʿash, from 1000/1592 until 1002/1594 and from 1003/1595 until 1004/1596 *ḳāḍī* of Gelibolu, and from 1005/1597 until 1006/1597 *ḳāḍī* of Tripoli in Syria. He died in 1006/1597-8 in Gelibolu, and is buried there in the vicinity of the Ghāzī Süleymān Pasha mosque. The *tārīkh* or chronogram *Fātiḥa Maḥmūd Efendi rūḥina* inscribed on his tombstone (as described by Bursalı Meḥmed Ṭāhir), which is by Naʿtī or according to others by Niʿmetī, confirms this. A very short passage of his *Ḳalemiyye*, a treatise in Arabic, is quoted by ʿAṭāʾī. Two mss. of his *Dīwān* are known to exist (Millet Ktp., Emirî, *manzum eserler* 399, and Hüsrev Paşa Ktp., *Mihrişah Sultan* 370).

Bibliography: Cf. the *tedhkires* of ʿAhdī, Millet Ktp., Emirî, *tarih*, 774, fol. 177a; Ḳınalı-zāde Ḥasan Čelebi, ed. İ. Kutluk, ii, Ankara 1981, 885-6; Beyānī, Millet Ktp., *Emirî, tarih*, 757, fols. 94b-95a; Riyāḍī, Nuruosmaniye Ktp., 3724, fol. 133b; Ḳāf-zāde Fāʾiḍī, Millet Ktp., *Emirî, manzum*, 1325, fol. 99a; also ʿAṭāʾī, *Dheyl-i Shaḳāyiḳ*, Istanbul 1268, 415-6; M. Thüreyyā, *Sidjill-i ʿOthmānī*, iv, Istanbul 1315, 353; Bursalı Meḥmed Ṭāhir, *ʿOthmānlı müʾellifleri*, ii, Istanbul 1333, 384-5.

2. Nūḥ-zāde Seyyid Muṣṭafā Čelebi of Bursa stands out because his name has come down to us also as a *meddāḥ* [*q.v.*]. Actually, he started a career as a *müderris* after being a *mülāzim* of *Shaykh al-Islām* Abū Saʿīd Efendi. Upon his dismissal from a position with a daily salary of forty *akčes*, he aspired to a career as *ḳāḍī*. When, however, he was promised the *ḳaḍāʾ* of Čorlu but the realisation of this promise was delayed, he became a *meddāḥ*. He died on 18 Redjeb 1091/14 August 1680, and was buried in Bursa in the vicinity of the tomb of Emīr Sulṭān.

Bibliography: *Ṣafāyī tedhkiresi*, Österr. Nationalbibl., H.O. 139, fol. 250a, Süleymaniye Ktp., *Es'ad Ef.* 2549, fol. 319a (255a); Belīgh, *Güldeste-i riyāḍ-i ʿirfān*, Bursa 1302, 531; Sheykhī, *Waḳāyiʿ al-fuḍalāʾ*. Österr. Nationalbibl., H.O. 126, fol. 355a-b, Süleymaniye Ktp., *Hamidiye* 941, fol. 361a: *Süleymān Fāʾiḳ Efendi medjmūʿasī*, İstanbul Üniv. Ktp. Ty., 3472, fol. 61b.

(E.G. AMBROS)

3. Medḥī is the *makhlaṣ* also of a certain Dervīsh Ḥasan, a prolific but obscure prose-writer, who described himself as the panegyrist (*meddāḥ*) of Murād II (982-1003/1574-95). To that sultan he dedicated a Turkish translation, entitled *Ḳiṣṣa-yi newbāwe*, of Abū Sharaf Nāṣiḥ's Persian version of al-ʿUtbī's *Taʾrīkh al-Yamīnī* (Rieu, *Cat. of Tkish. mss.*, 42-3; cf. Browne, ii, 471), and also a (completely fictional) *Ḥikāyet-i Ebū ʿAlī-yi Sīnā*, i.e. Ibn Sīnā [*q.v.*] (Rieu, 231). He served also Murād's successors, up to ʿOthmān II (1027-31/1618-22), at whose command he made a prose translation of the *Shāh-nāma* of Firdawsī [*q.v.*] (see Blochet, i, 314, with the names of other works he claimed to have written or translated; W.D. Smirnow, *Manuscrits turcs...*, St. Petersburg 1897, 82-7).

(ED.)

MEDĪḤĪ, the pen name (*makhlaṣ*) of two Ottoman poets whose poetry is known to date only as far as the samples found in *medjmūʿas* and *tedhkires* allow. On the strength of these, neither appears to be of more than minor importance.

1. Muṣṭafā (according to Ḳınalı-zāde Ḥasan Čelebi and Beyānī, whereas ʿĀshıḳ Čelebi gives his name as Muṣlī—or Muṣlu, the Turkish abbreviation of Muṣliḥ al-Dīn) Čelebi of Sīrōz (Serres), who lived during the reigns of Süleymān I (926-74/1520-66), Selīm II (974-82/1566-74) and up to the middle of that of Murād III (982-1003/1574-95). A *dānishmend* of Ḳāḍī-zāde Aḥmed Efendi (who became *ḳāḍī-ʿasker* under Selīm II), then a *mülāzim* of ʿAṭāʾ Allāh Efendi, he served as *ḳāḍī* of a number of *ḳaṣabas*, the last being Sīrōz. He came to be known in the circle of his peers for his numerous servants and attendants and his love of display.

Bibliography: The *tedhkires* of ʿĀshıḳ Čelebi, ed. G. M. Meredith-Owens, London 1971, fol. 121a-b, mss. in Süleymaniye Ktp., Pertev Paşa 440, *Hamidiye* 1064, *Âşir Ef.* 268, Ḳınalı-zāde Ḥasan Čelebi, ed. İ. Kutluk, ii, Ankara 1981, 886-7, Beyānī, Millet Ktp., *Emirî, tarih*, 757, fol. 95a.

2. Meḥmed of Istanbul was a *mülāzim*, then a *müderris* until he attained a position with a daily salary of forty *akčes*. Upon dismissal from this position, he agreed to a career as *ḳāḍī* and went to Egypt (according to the ms. Österr. Nationalbibl., H.O. 139, of Ṣafāyī's *tedhkire*, he was appointed as *ḳāḍī* to the *ḳaḍāʾ* of Burullus), where he became renowned for his ability for story-telling and his indulgence in the pleasures of life. He died in 1083/1672-3.

Bibliography: *Ṣafāyī tedhkiresi*, Österr. Nationalbibl., H.O. 139. fol. 248a-b, Millet Ktp., *Emirî, tarih*, 771, 367-8; Sheykhī, *Waḳāyiʿ al-fuḍalāʾ*, Österr. Nationalbibl., H.O. 126, fol. 355b, Süleymaniye Ktp., *Hamidiye*, 941, fol. 361a.

(E.G. AMBROS)

MEDICINE [see ṬIBB].

MEDINA, from Arabic *madīna* "town", is used in French (*médina*) to designate, above all in the Maghrib, the ancient part of the great Islamic cities, beyond which have been constructed the modern quarters of the city. Moreover, Medina has survived in Spain in a certain number of toponyms. The main ones of these are: Medina de las Torres, in the province of Badajoz; Medina del Campo and Medina de Rioseco, in that of Valladolid; Medina de Pomar, in that of Burgos; and also, Medinaceli [see MADINĀT SALĪM] and Medina-Sidonia [see SHADHŪNA].

(E. LÉVI-PROVENÇAL)

MEDINA, town in Saudi Arabia [see AL-MADĪNA].

MEDINACELI [see MADĪNAT SĀLIM].

MĒDINĪ RĀʾĪ, a leader, as Rāʾī Čand Pūrbīya, of the Pūrbīya (= "eastern") Rādjpūts, with tribal possessions in the Čāndērī [*q.v.*] district and hence feudatories of the sultans of Mālwā [*q.v.*], who became prominent in Mālwā-Gudjarāt-Mēwār-Dihlī politics early in the 10th/16th century.

The Mālwā succession had been fiercely contested after the death of Nāṣir al-Dīn Shāh Khaldjī in 916/1510, who had designated his third son, Aʿẓam Humāyūn, as his heir. He duly succeeded, as Maḥmūd Shāh Khaldjī II [*q.v.*], with his elder brothers Shihāb al-Dīn and Ṣāḥib Khān as active contenders for the throne in a situation exacerbated by rival factions of Muslim nobles at court; one faction had already compassed the assassination of the strong and competent (Hindū) *wazīr* and the banishment of a second Hindū minister. The perpetrators remained unpunished by Maḥmūd, and their power increased until the leader of the second faction, Muḥāfiẓ Khān, turned the sultan against them. They escaped to Khāndēsh [*q.v.*] to join Shihāb al-Dīn, but the latter died suddenly before any action could be taken. In the meantime, Muḥāfiẓ Khān, now appointed *wazīr*, had become too powerful, and confined Maḥmūd to his palace, proclaiming Ṣāḥib Khan sultan as Muḥammad Shāh in the capital Māndū [*q.v.*]. Maḥmūd managed to escape, chased by his brother, to Čāndērī, where he received no support from the governor Bahdjat Khan, on the pretence that he obeyed only the ruler of Māndū. At this point, Rāʾī Čand Pūrbīya brought his Rādjpūt troops to Maḥmūd's assistance, and, becoming Maḥmūd's adviser, was given the title of Mēdinī Rāʾī. He pursued Ṣāḥib Khān and expelled him from Māndū (917/1512); Ṣāḥib Khān fled to Gudjarāt, accompanied by Muḥāfiẓ Khān.

Mēdinī Rāʾī, appointed *wazīr* at Māndū, strengthened the administration and appointed his own Rādjpūts to some important posts; but there was some opposition from Muslim nobles, increased when Ṣāḥib Khān returned from Gudjarāt without, however, having secured any assistance from its sultan. In 918/1512 the governors of both Satwās (Nēmāwar) and Čāndērī rebelled; Mēdinī Rāʾī quelled the disturbances at Satwās and then, with Maḥmūd, marched on Čāndērī, where Bahdjat Khān (*not* obeying the ruler of Māndū!) had not only proclaimed Ṣāḥib Khān as sultan but also sought help from the Dihlī sultan Sikandar Lōdī, promising to read the *khuṭba* in his name. Sikandar did temporarily annex Čāndērī, but finally Mēdinī Rāʾī and his Rādjpūts recaptured the place in 920/1514. After this, Maḥmūd relied increasingly on Mēdinī, who gradually built up his own position until all administrative power was in his hands, and the sultan virtually a puppet. Maḥmūd tried unsuccessfully to have Mēdinī assassinated, provoking a Pūrbīya Rādjpūt revolt; eventually, Maḥmūd left Māndū secretly in 923/1517 to obtain the assistance of Muẓaffar Shāh II of Gudjarāt. The latter led an attack on, and later a siege of, Māndū, whereupon Mēdinī left the defence of the fort to his troops and sought help from Rānā Sanga of Mēwār at Čitawŕ. Māndū fell to Muẓaffar (924/1518), who expelled the Rādjpūt troops, reinstated Maḥmūd on the Mālwa throne, and left a Gudjarātī body of troops for his protection. Maḥmūd then marched on Mēdinī Rāʾī, then holding Gagrāʾūn, but Rānā Sanga came to Mēdinī's assistance, defeated Maḥmūd's army, and took him prisoner, wounded, to Čitawŕ; Rānā Sanga released him and restored him to his throne after his wounds were healed (926/1520). Maḥmūd, resenting the Gudjarātī bodyguard and the continuing Gudjarātī influence, requested Muẓaffar to recall it; but after this was done, Malwā lost much of its territories to Rānā Sanga or those under his protection, including Mēdinī Rāʾī, who was established in the now independent Čāndērī. He fought with Rānā Sanga against Bābur in the battle of Khānuʾā in 933/1527, and shortly afterwards was killed in Bābur's assault on Čānderī. He was the most able of the minor Rādjpūt chieftains, as skilful in warfare as in administration; he never abandoned his respect for or courtesy to Maḥmūd Shāh, treating him and his family with consideration and generosity.

Bibliography: Sikandar b. Muḥammad "Mandjhū", *Mirʾāt-i Sikandarī*, ed. S.C. Misra, Baroda 1961, 174 ff.; Niẓām al-Dīn Bakhshī, *Ṭabaḳāt-i Akbarī*, Bibl. Ind. text, Calcutta 1927-35, esp. iii, 383 ff.; Ḳāniʿī, *Taʾrīkh-i Muẓaffar Shāhī*, ed. M. A. Chagtai, Poona 1947 (deals especially with Muẓaffar Shāh's Mālwā campaign in 923/1517); ʿAbd Allāh Muḥammad b. ʿUmar al-Makkī ("Ḥādjdjī al-Dabīr"), *Ẓafar al-wālih* (= *Arabic History of Gujarat*, ed. E.D. Ross, London 1921-8), 213; Kavirādja Shyāmaldās, *Vīr-vinōd*, i, 350 ff., confirms much of the Muslim historians' material from the Rādjpūt viewpoint; S.C. Misra, *Gujarat and Malwa in the first half of the 16th century*, in *Procs. Ind. Hist. Congr.*, xvi (1953), 245-8.

(J. BURTON-PAGE)

MEDJDĪ, MEḤMED ČELEBI, an Ottoman littérateur and biographer of the 10th/16th century known by the pen-name of Medjdī, d. 999/1591. He was born the son of a merchant in Edirne (ʿĀlī, *Künh al-akhbār*, Ist. Univ. Lib. TY 5959, fol. 493b). He completed his education at the Bāyezīdiyye *medrese* in Edirne and became the *dānishmend* ("advanced student") of the Bāyezīdiyye *müderris* Ḳāf Aḥmed Čelebi (Medjdī, *Ḥadāʾiḳ al-Shaḳāʾiḳ*, Istanbul 1269. 503). He served as repetiteur (*muʿīd*) to Ḳaramānī Akhaweyn Meḥmed Čelebi and thereafter entered the judicial career; according to ʿĀshīḳ Čelebi (*Meshāʿir ül-shuʿarāʾ*, ed. G.M. Meredith-Owens, London 1971, fol. 117b) and Ḳïbalï-zāde Ḥasan Čelebi (*Tezkiret uş-şuarâ*, ed. İ. Kutluk, Ankara 1981, ii, 854), Medjdī was Akhaweyn's *muʿīd* during the latter's tenure at the Bāyezīdiyye, while Newʿī-zāde ʿAṭāʾī (*Ḥadāʾiḳ al-ḥaḳāʾiḳ fī takmilat al-Shaḳāʾiḳ*, Istanbul 1268, 334) states that he became a candidate for office (*mulāzim*) under the quota of nominees allowed Akhaweyn as a *müderris* at the Ṣaḥn, where he taught before being appointed to the Bāyezīdiyye. Medjdī held a number of *ḳāḍīlïk*s in Rumeli and reached the rank of 150 aspers' daily salary; he died in Istanbul in 999/1591 while awaiting a new appointment and was buried at the *zāwiye* of Emīr Bukhārī outside the Edirne gate.

As a poet, Medjdī was particularly influenced by Emrī (also a native of Edirne) and by his teacher Akhaweyn, and his contemporaries ʿAhdī (*Gülshen-i shuʿarāʾ*, Ist. Univ. Lib. TY 2604, fols. 110 ff.), and ʿĀshīḳ Čelebi, *loc. cit.*, acknowledged him as an accomplished scholar and littérateur known for the perfection of his poetic forms, his mastery of the *ḳaṣīde* and *ghazel*, and his skill in the use of fresh imagery. Selections from his poetry are found in the *tedhkire*s of poets (ʿAhdī, ʿĀshīḳ Čelebi, Ḳïnalï-zāde, *locc. cit.*; Riyāḍī Meḥmed, *Tedhkire*, Ist. Univ. Lib. TY 761, fol. 119a; Beyānī Muṣṭafā, *Tedhkire*, Ist. Univ. Lib. TY 2568, fol. 79a; Ḳāfzāde Fāʾiḍī, *Zubdat al-ashʿār*, Ist. Univ. Lib. TY 1646, fols. 97a-98a; ʿAṭāʾī, 335-6) and in the histories of Edirne (Ḥibrī, *Enīs al-musāmirīn*, Millet Lib., Emirî, *tarih* no. 68, fol. 80b; Bādī, *Riyāḍ-ī belde-yi Edirne*, Bayezid Devlet Lib. no. 10392, ii, 545-6; O.N. Peremeci, *Edirne tarihi*, Istanbul 1940, 216), and his *ghazels* were collected in his *Dīwānče* (Millet Lib., Emîrî, *manzum* no. 398; for a description, see *İstanbul kitaplıkları türkçe yazma divanlar kataloğu*, Istanbul 1947, i, 175). Medjdī demonstrated his ability to compose good Arabic prose with two treatises, the *Sayfiyya* (Süleymaniye Lib., Esad Ef. no. 3416, fols. 28b-30b) and the *Shamᶜiyya* (quoted in part by ᶜĀlī, Ḳînalî-zāde, Beyānī and ᶜAṭāʾī, *locc. cit.*).

Medjdī displayed his scholarly and literary ability in the work for which he is justly renowned, his translation of the *Shaḳāʾiḳ al-Nuᶜmāniyya fī ᶜulamāʾ al-dawla al-ᶜOthmāniyya*. As previous translations and continuations of Tashköprü-zāde's famous biographical work (see Kātib Čelebi, *Kashf al-ẓunūn*, Istanbul 1941, ii, 1057-8; B. Gönül (Necatigil), *İstanbul kütüphânelerinde al-Şaḳâʾiḳ al-Nuᶜmânîya tercüme ve zeyilleri*, in *Türkiyat Mecmuası*, vii-viii [1945], 136 ff.) had been made, some scholars had added explanatory and supplementary notes (*ḥāshiyas* and *taᶜlīḳāt*) to the margins of the Arabic text. Medjdī, in order to make the work more widely available, undertook its translation into Turkish, which he completed and dedicated to Murād III in 995/1587. Medjdī compensated for the dry simplicity of the original with a courtly style and ornate language, adorning his translation with poetry, aphorisms, word plays and chronograms. He also used the sources at his disposal to expand and correct the work. These sources included marginal additions to the original *Shaḳāʾiḳ*, such as the notes made by ᶜArab-zāde (see Medjdī, 331, 373-4, 385, 486) and Seyrek-zāde (*ibid.*, 494); documents such as *waḳf-nāmes*, *ḥudjdjets* and *temessüks* found in the judicial (*ḳāḍīlīḳ*) archives; authors such as al-Suyūṭī, Ibn ᶜArabshāh and Ḥanbalī-zāde; early Ottoman chronicles, particularly the *Hesht bihisht*; *tedhkire* authors such as Sehī, Laṭīfī and ᶜĀshıḳ Čelebi; and such works written by the subjects of his biographies as he was able to see plus accounts transmitted by their relatives and students (for an indication of the extent of these additions, which Medjdī labels *tedhyīl*, see A. Subhi Furat's notes to his edition of the original, *eş-Şeḳāʾiḳu n-Nuᶜmānīye fī ᶜulemāi 'd-devleti l-Osmānīye*, Istanbul 1985). Thus it can be said that Medjdī's work, which he entitled *Ḥadāʾiḳ al-Shaḳāʾiḳ*, rather than being a translation represents an attempt to produce a new work based on the *Shaḳāʾiḳ*. Medjdī's *Ḥadāʾiḳ*, as a complement to the *Shaḳāʾiḳ* which was of high literary quality, became the formal and stylistic model for later continuations, and the edition published in 1269/1852 is a primary reference work for researchers.

Bibliography: Given in the article.

(Bekir Kütükoğlu)

MEDJELLE (a. madjalla). Originally meaning a book or other writing containing wisdom, or even any book or writing, the term refers in its best-known application to the civil code in force in the Ottoman Empire, and briefly in the Turkish republic, from 1285/1869 to 1926.

Known in full as the *Medjelle-yi Aḥkām-ĭ ᶜAdliyye*, this covers contracts, torts and some principles of civil procedure. It reflects Western influence mainly in its division into numbered books, sections and articles, as in European codes. Critics have found a number of flaws in the work, such as the dispersion at times of related subjects in different parts of the code. Nevertheless, the *Medjelle* was extremely important for several reasons. It represents the first attempt by an Islamic state to codify, and to enact as law of the state, part of the *sharīᶜa* (Schacht, 92). Further, the code, while derived from the Ḥanafī school of law, which enjoyed official status in the Ottoman Empire, did not always incorporate the dominant opinions of that school. Rather, of all the opinions ever advanced by Ḥanafī jurists, the code incorporated those deemed most suited to the conditions of the times, in accordance with the principle of *takhayyur*. While the justificatory memorandum (*esbāb-ĭ müdjibe maḍbaṭasĭ*) submitted to the Council of Ministers, said that the authors of the code "never went outside the Ḥanafī rite" (Liebesny, 69; Berki, 12; *Düstūr*[1], i, 27; Aristarchi, vi, 15), some of these opinions had in fact originated with non-Ḥanafī jurists (Anderson, 17, 47-8). Such eclecticism became a major feature of later efforts at reform of *sharīᶜa* law and, by nature, provided added impetus for codification (Liebesny, 137-8). Finally, since the *Medjelle* was applied in the secular *niẓāmiyya* courts set up in the period [see maḥkama, 2, ii] as well as in the *sharīᶜa* courts, it applied to non-Muslim subjects of the empire as state law (*ḳānūn*), as well as to Muslims, on whom the code's *sharᶜī* content would have been binding in any case (Aḥmed Djevdet, *Tezâkir 1-12*, 64; idem, *Maᶜrûzât*, 200; Heidborn, i, 387; cf. Schacht, 92-3).

The decision to draft the *Medjelle* grew out of a controversy over whether the Ottomans should simply translate and adopt the French civil code. The Ottoman Council of Ministers decided instead to commission a work based on *fiḳh* and entrusted this task to a commission under the chairmanship of Aḥmed Djewdet Pasha [*q.v.*], who had been the leading advocate of this course of action. The commission completed the sixteen books (*kitāb*) of the *Medjelle* over the period from 1285/1869 to 1293/1876 (*Düstūr*[1], i, 20-164; ii, 38-425; iv, 93-125; Berki, *passim*; Aristarchi, vi-vii; Young, vi). The various books were placed in force by decrees (*irāde*) of the sultan, dating from 6 Dhu 'l-Ḳaᶜda 1286/1870 (Berki, 113) to 26 Shaᶜbān 1293/1877 (*ibid.*, 422). In *sharᶜī* terms, the *Medjelle* thus acquired legal force from the power of the sultan as *imām al-muslimīn* to order which of several legal opinions should be followed in a given matter (*Düstūr*[1], i, 29; Heidborn, i, 286; Anderson, 48).

The *Medjelle* opens with two sections which define *fiḳh* and its divisions and which state its basic principles largely according to the *Ashbāh wa 'l-naẓāʾir* of Ibn Nudjaym (d. 970/1562-3). Following these sections, the sixteen books deal with sales (*buyūᶜ*); hire and lease (*idjāra*); guaranty (*kafāla*); transfer of debts (*ḥawāla*); pledge (*rahn*); deposit (*amānāt*); gift (*hiba*); usurpation and property damage (*ghaṣb wa-itlāf*); interdiction, duress, and pre-emption (*ḥadjr, ikrāh, shufᶜa*); joint ownership and partnership (*shirka*); agency (*wakāla*); amicable settlement and remission of debt (*ṣulḥ wa-ibrāʾ*); acknowledgment (*iḳrār*); lawsuits (*daᶜwā*); evidence and oaths (*bayyināt wa-taḥlīf*); courts and judgeship (*ḳaḍāʾ*) (Velidedeoğlu, 190-6). The drafting commission evidently intended to continue its work by codifying the law on the family and inheritance, but soon found itself paralysed by the suspicions of the new sultan. ᶜAbd ül-Ḥamīd II (1876-1909 [*q.v.*]) (Heidborn, i, 285; Mardin, art. *Mecelle*, 435).

Despite its bases in *fiḳh*, the *Medjelle* differs from traditional *sharīᶜa* law in several respects, including its codification and official promulgation and its implicit admission—necessary, given its intended scope of application—of non-Muslims as witnesses (Schacht, 93). The *Medjelle* also differs from European civil codes in omitting non-contractual obligations, types of real property other than freehold (*milk*), family law, and inheritance, as well as in including some *sharᶜī* procedural provisions (Liebesny, 65).

The significance of the *Medjelle* can be measured not

only from the respect that it continues to command as evidence of the possibility of achieving its original purpose, that of systematising the *sharīʿa* so as to obviate the adoption of purely secular law codes (Fazlur Rahman, 29), but in a more tangible way, the code's significance also appears from its remarkable afterlife. In the *niẓāmiyya*, though not the *sharīʿa* courts, the Ottoman government did replace the procedural provisions of the *Medjelle* with a Code of Civil Procedure, based on French law, in 1879 (Liebesny, 66; Heidborn, i, 386-7; *Düstūr*[1], iv, 257-317; Young, vii, 171-225). The Turkish republic then abrogated the *Medjelle* in 1926. Yet it remained in force in Bosnia-Herzegovina after the Austrian occupation of 1878, in Albania until 1928, and in Cyprus at least into the 1960s. In the Middle East, the *Medjelle*, though never in force in Egypt, was not replaced by new civil codes until 1932 in Lebanon, 1949 in Syria, and 1953 in ʿIrāḳ, where many elements of it survived in the new civil code of that year. The *Medjelle* has remained basic to the civil law of Israel and Jordan. It has also continued to serve as the civil law of Kuwayt (Schacht, 93; Liebesny, 93, 100, 109).

In terms of the approach to legal reform which it represented, another aspect of the *Medjelle*'s continuing influence appears in the Ottoman Law of Family Rights (*Ḥuḳūḳ-i ʿĀʾile Ḳarārnāmesi*) of 8 Muḥarram 1336/1917 (*Düstūr*[2], ix, 762-81; x, 52-57; Anderson, 39-40, 48-50; Schacht, 103). Enactment of this law completed what appears to have been the original programme of the drafters of the *Medjelle*. In addition, the new law resembled the *Medjelle* in combining codification with an eclectic approach to *sharʿī* sources, as well as in applying to both Muslim and non-Muslim subjects, a breadth achieved in this case by incorporating provisions drawn from the religious law of the various communities (Shaw and Shaw, 307). The 1917 family law further resembled the *Medjelle* in that it remained in force in various of the successor states much longer than in Ottoman territory, where it was repealed in 1337/1919 (Shaw and Shaw, 333; *Düstūr*[2], xi, 299-300). For the 1917 law "remained valid in Syria, Lebanon, Palestine, and Transjordan (as they then were), and is still part of the family law of the Muslims in Lebanon and in Israel" (Schacht, 1964, 103).

Bibliography: J.N.L. Anderson, *Law reform in the Muslim world*, London, 1976; Grégoire Aristarchi, *Législation ottomane, ou recueil des lois, réglements, ordonnances, traités, capitulations et autres documents officiels de l'empire ottoman*, 7 vols., Istanbul 1873-88; Salīm b. Rustam Bāz, *Sharḥ al-Madjalla*, 2 vols., Beirut 1888-9; Ali Himmet Berki, *Açıklamalı Mecelle* (*Mecelle-i Ahkâm-ı Adliyye*), Istanbul 1982; Aḥmed Djevdet Pasha, *Maʿrûzât*, ed. Yusuf Halaçoğlu; idem, *Tezâkir 1-40*, ed. Cavid Baysun, Ankara 1953-67; *Düstūr*, first series (*birindji tertīb*), 4 vols. plus 4 appendices (*dheyl*) and a later "completion" volume (*mütemmim*), Istanbul, 1289-1335/1872-1917, as well as 4 additional vols. published as vols. v-viii, Ankara 1937-43; *Düstūr*, second series (*ikindji tertīb*), 123 vols., Istanbul 1329/1911-27; Fazlur Rahman, *Islam and modernity: transformation of an intellectual tradition*, Chicago 1982; W. E. Grigsby, tr., *The Medjellè*, London 1895; ʿAlī Ḥaydar, *Dürer ül-Ḥükkām: Sherḥ Medjellet ül-Aḥkām, Sherḥ ül-Ḳawāʿid il-Külliyye*, 3d printing, 4 vols., Istanbul 1330/1911; A. Heidborn, *Manuel de droit public et administratif de l'Empire ottoman*, 2 vols., Vienna-Leipzig 1908-12; C.A. Hooper, *The law of Palestine and Trans-Jordan*, Jerusalem 1933-6, 2 vols.; H.J. Liesbesny, *The law of the Near and Middle East: readings, cases, and materials*, Albany 1975; Ebül'ulâ Mardin, *Medenî hukuk cephesinden Ahmed Cevdet Paşa*, Istanbul 1946; idem, art. *Mecelle*, in *İA*, vii, 433-6; Şerif Arif Mardin, *Some explanatory notes on the origins of the "Mecelle"*, in *WI*, li (1961), 189-96, 274-9; J. Schacht, *An introduction to Islamic law*, Oxford 1964; S.J. Shaw and Ezel Kural Shaw, *History of the Ottoman empire and modern Turkey. II. Reform, revolution, and republic: the rise of modern Turkey, 1808-1975*, Cambridge 1977; Sir Charles Tyser *et alii, The Mejelle translated*, Nicosia 1901; Hıfzi Veldet Velidedeoğlu, *Kanunlaştırma hareketleri ve tanzimat*, in *Tanzimat I*, Istanbul 1940, 139-209; G. Young, *Corps de droit ottoman: recueil des codes, lois, règlements, ordonnances et actes les plus importants du droit intérieur, et d'études sur le droit coutumier de l'Empire ottoman*, 7 vols., Oxford 1905-6.

(C.V. Findley)

MEDJĪDIYYE (Romanian, Medgidia), a small town in eastern Romania, situated in the central Dobrudja [*q.v.*], midway between the Danube and Constanta (Kustendje), and on the site of the earlier Ottoman settlement of Ḳaraṣu, which had served as a relay-station on the old *ṣagh ḳol*, the military road from Istanbul to the lower Danube and the Crimea. The importance of Medjīdiyye stems from its being, in its inception, a mid-19th century Ottoman planned town, founded by the local *wālī*, Saʿīd Pasha, in the course of the Crimean war, to house Ḳrîm Tatar refugees, and named in honour of the reigning sultan ʿAbd al-Medjīd. Within a few months of its foundation in 1854 it contained over one thousand completed houses, a *khān* and a bazaar. The large mosque, which still stands, and serves a population still 30% Muslim, is dated 1277/1860-1. In the reorganisation of the provincial administration of Rumeli in 1284/1864, Medjīdiyye, as a *ḳaḍāʾ* in the *sandjaḳ* of Tuldja (not Varna, as in *EI*[2], art. *Dobrudja*), formed part of the new Ṭuna *wilāyet* (*Sālnāme 1294*, 432), and its prosperity was subsequently increased by the building of the railway from Bucharest to Constanţa. By the terms of the Treaty of Berlin (art. xlvi), Medjīdiyye passed from Ottoman into Romanian possession, along with all that part of the Dobrudja north of a line drawn from Silistre to the Black Sea. At the time of the outbreak of the Russo-Turkish war of 1877-8, the population of Medjīdiyye and its surrounding *ḳaḍāʾ* was estimated at approximately 2,200 Muslim and 1,300 non-Muslim households.

Bibliography: *Sālnāme 1294*, Istanbul 1294; *Gazette autrichienne*, fév. 1855; A. Ubicini, *La Dobrodja et le delta du Danube*, in *Revue de Géographie*, iv (1879); E.H. Ayverdi, *Avrupada Osmanlı mimari eserleri*, i/1-2, Istanbul 1979, 53, 55-6; *İA* art. *Dobruca* (A. Decei); *EI*[2] art. *Dobrudja* (H. İnalcık).

(C.J. Heywood)

MEDJĪDIYYE [see sikka].

MEDJLIS-I WĀLĀ, in full, the Ottoman Medjlis-i Wālā-yî Aḥkām-î ʿAdliyye, or Supreme Council of Judicial Ordinances.

This was created in 1838 by the reformer Muṣṭafā Reshīd Pasha for the purpose of taking over the legislative duties of the old *Dīwān-î Hümāyūn* in order to originate or review proposed legislation and thereby create an "ordered and established" state by means of "beneficent reorderings" (*tanẓīmāt-î khayriyye*) of state and society, with all other legislation being turned over to a second legislative body, the *Dār-î Shūrā-yî Bāb-î ʿĀlī* (Deliberative Council of the Sublime Porte). The *Medjlis-i wālā* hardly had a chance to begin its deliberations when, following the accession of Sultan ʿAbd al-Medjīd I [*q.v.*] and promulgation of the *Khaṭṭ-î Hümāyūn* of Gülkhāne which proclaimed the *Tanẓīmāt* reform movement as the major goal of the new régime, it was expanded into the principal legislative body of state with the abolition of its sister body. Beginning its work on 8 March 1840 in a new building constructed especially for it near the office of the Grand Vizier at the Sublime Porte, it originated most of the *Tanẓīmāt* legislation, though its powers were severely limited by regulations which allowed it only to consider legislation proposed to it by the ministries or the executive. It was supplanted for reform legislation by the *Me<u>dj</u>lis-i ʿĀlī-yi Tanẓīmāt* in 1854, but it continued to originate lesser laws and regulations and also to act as supreme court of judicial appeals. Conflicts of jurisdiction between the two bodies, however, and a substantially increasing workload created such a backlog of legislation that in 1861 the two were brought back together into a new *Me<u>dj</u>lis-i Wālā-yi Aḥkām-i ʿAdliyye*, which was divided into departments for Laws and Regulations, which assumed the legislative functions of both councils, Administration and Finance, which investigated complaints against the administrative misconduct, and Judicial Cases, which assumed the old council's judicial functions, acting as a court of appeals for cases decided by the provincial councils of justice and as a court of first instance in cases involving misconduct on the part of higher officials in the central government. Regulations allowing it to originate as well as to review proposed legislation, and to question members of the executive and to try such officials for misdeeds, greatly increased its ability to act decisively in order to meet the problems of the time, with the sultans interfering only rarely to veto or change the results of its work. In 1867, however, in response to complaints about the autocratic nature of the *Tanẓīmāt* system, the *Me<u>dj</u>lis-i Wālā* was replaced by separate legislative and judicial bodies, the *<u>Sh</u>ūrā-yi Dewlet*, or Council of State, whose members were at least partially elected and representative, and the *Dīwān-i Aḥkām-i ʿAdliyye*, chaired respectively by the famous *Tanẓīmāt* leaders Midḥat Pa<u>sh</u>a and Aḥmed <u>Dj</u>ewdet Pa<u>sh</u>a.

Bibliography: S.J. Shaw, *The Central Legislative Councils in the nineteenth century Ottoman reform movement before 1876*, in *IJMES*, i (1970), 51-84; S.J. Shaw and E.K. Shaw, *History of the Ottoman empire and modern Turkey*, London and New York 1977, repr. 1985, ii, 38, 76-81; Başbakanlık Arşivi, *Irade, Meclis-i Mahsus*, 79; *Meclis-i Tanzimat*, I, 1-3, 6-10; *Teşkilat-ı Devair* I/25; Luṭfī, *Taʾrī<u>kh</u>*, fol. 29a-b; *Düstūr*, Series 1, i, 703-5. C.V. Findley, *Bureaucratic reform in the Ottoman empire: the Sublime Porte, 1789-1922*, Princeton 1980, 172-9. (S.J. SHAW)

MEERUT [see MĪRAṬH].

MEHEDAK [see AL-MAHDIYYA].

MEḤEMMED is one of the Turkish forms of the name Muḥammad which, having been borne by the Prophet of Islam, is by far the commonest used name in the Islamic world.

Independent of the modifications which it may undergo from the influence of the speech habits of allophonic groups and the phonetic structure of languages other than Arabic, this name has undergone, in spite of—and perhaps because of—the veneration which it inspires, various deliberate modifications on the part of sincere Muslims who hold fast to what exactly respects the Prophet's memory. If the Turkish form "Meḥemmed" may be explained by the vocalic structure of that language, the form "Maḥammad", widespread in North Africa and distinguished from "Muḥammad" by a *fatḥa* on the first *mīm* or the prefixing of a purely orthographical *alif* (which also serves to indicate the dialectical pronunciation "Mḥammed"), is certainly in fact due to a desire to let the persons thus named share in the *baraka* [*q.v.*] attached to the Prophet's name without risking letting it become profaned, above all by insults and abuse addressed specifically by name to these persons. On the problems posed by alterations of this kind in the sphere of Islam and those which the name of Muḥammad has undergone in the European languages, see G.S. Colin, *Muḥammad-Mahomet*, in *BSLP*, xxvi (1925), 109; J. Mouradian, *Notes sur les altérations du nom de Mohammad chez les Noirs islamisés de l'Afrique Occidentale*, in *Bull. du Comité d'études historiques et scientifiques de l'Afrique Occidentale Française*, xxi (1938), 459-62; A. Fischer, *Vergöttlichung und Tabuisierung des Namen Muḥammad's bei den Muslimen* in *Beiträge zur Arabistik, Semitistik und Islamwissenschaft*, Leipzig 1944, 307-39; F. de la Granja, *A propósito del nombre Muḥammad y sus variantes en Occidente*, in *al-And.*, xxxiii (1968), 231-40 (where Colin's note, mentioned above, is also given); see also, for an example of deliberate alteration (*Mamad*), L.P. Harvey, *Crypto-Islam in sixteenth century Spain*, in *Actas del primer congreso de estudios árabes e islámicos*, Madrid 1964, 169, no. 15, 177, l. 9.

Contemporary Byzantine and European texts indicate that in the 9th/15th century the predominant pronunciation of the name was "Mehemet": F. Babinger, commenting on the form "Memmet" in *Die Aufzeichnungen des Genuesen Iacopo de Promontorio ... um 1475*, Munich 1957, 29, n. 1 (and there, with further bibliography, proposing "Mehemmed" as the current pronunciation), adduces Angiolello's "Mehemet", and the Μεχεμέτ and similar forms which is regular in Ducas, Sphrantzes and Critoboulos (for these and the other Byzantine texts see G. Moravcsik, *Byzantinotourcica*, ii, s.v. Μουχαμέτης).

In modern Turkey, the name finally appears as "Mehmet", as a consequence of the general phonological principles (J. Deny, *Principes de grammaire turque*, Paris 1955) of the devoicing of a final voiced consonant, the predilection for front vowels in loanwords, the assimilation (progressive and regressive) of vowels, and the fall of an unstressed middle vowel in a tri-syllable.

The Editors, taking the view that to employ the spelling "Muḥammad" in the Ottoman context would be hypercorrect (and "Meḥmed", for the earlier centuries, anachronistic) have adopted the convention that all the relevant Ottoman rulers figuring in the *Encyclopaedia* shall be referred to consistently as "Meḥemmed", whilst lesser personages shall be referred to as "Meḥmed". (ED.)

MEḤEMMED I, Ottoman sultan, reigned 816-24/1413-21, also known as *Čelebi* (Turkish "of high descent", "prince") or as *Kiri<u>shdj</u>i* (from *Krytzes*, meaning in Greek "young lord"). During the period of interregnum, 804-16/1402-13, he ruled over Anatolia from Tokat, Amasya, and Bursa while his brothers Süleymān (804-13/1402-11) and Mūsā (813-16/1411-13) had control of Rūmili from Edirne. Meḥemmed brought under his rule Bursa and western Anatolia in the years 805-6/1403-4 and 813-16/1410-13, and finally achieved the unification of the two parts of the Ottoman state under his sole sovereignty in 816/1413. He was the fourth son of Bāyezīd I [*q.v.*] by a slave girl Dewlet <u>Kh</u>ātūn (Uzunçarşılı, in *İA*, viii, 496).

1. *Birth and early years.*

Born in 788/1386 or 789/1387, Meḥemmed was sent when he reached the *<u>Sh</u>arʿī* age of adolescence in

Shawwāl 801/June 1399 as governor over the province of Rūm, which included Amasya, Tokat, Sivas and Ankara, formerly the territory of the Eretna [*q.v.*] dynasty. Meḥemmed's six brothers were Ertoghrul (died 802/1400, Zachariadou, *Ertogrul*, 157), Muṣṭafā (captured by Tīmūr and taken to Samarḳand in 804/1402; *Dustūr-nāme*, 90), Süleymān (in contemporary sources also known at Muslumān or Amuslumān), ʿĪsā, Mūsā and Ḳāsim. In 804/1402, Ḳāsim, aged under 12, was in Bursa in the palace while Mūsā was captured together with his father by Tīmūr. Süleymān, ʿĪsā, Meḥemmed and Mūsā fought to get control of Bursa, still considered as the *Dār al-Salṭana*, and of Edirne, capital city of Rūmili.

2. *The status quo established by Tīmūr in Anatolia.*

During Tīmūr's siege of Izmir (from 6 Djumādā I 805/2 December 1402 until 10 Djumādā II/6 January 1403), Süleymān was given a *yarlīgh* granting him the rule "over all the territories beyond the Bosphorus" (*asra-yaḳa*, Yazdī, fol. 424b). Meḥemmed, whom Tīmūr called to come in person to Kütayha, could not or would not obey the order (for details in the *Manāḳib-nāme*, see *Bibl.*).

Meḥemmed's first deeds against the Turcoman begs in the Tokat-Amasya region, rendered in an epic style in the *Manāḳib-nāme*, appear actually to have been local clashes which evidently resulted in compromises giving recognition of Meḥemmed's overlordship in return for his confirmation of the begs' freehold possession of their lands (cf. Neshrī, ii, 480). In the future, these hereditary *mülk tīmārs* would create problems when Ottoman centralist control was re-established. These local dynasts in control of Turcoman and "Tatar" forces would provide the bulk of Meḥemmed's army (cf. divisions of Tatars and Türkmens in the battle against Mūsā in 816/1413; Neshrī, ii, 512-13).

Ḳara Dewletshāh, Ḳubād-oghlu, Mezīd Beg and the family of Tashan (on the family's origin, see *Bazm u razm*, 397) were all local dynasts who after the battle of Ankara accepted Tīmūr's overlordship and challenged Ottoman domination, showing his diplomas (Neshrī, i, 372). Meḥemmed, too, was wise enough to accept Tīmūr's suzerainty and thus legitimise his lordship in the region of Tokat-Amasya (for Meḥemmed's silver coin bearing Tīmūr's name, see *Table*, no. 3). In his fight to assert his authority against his rivals there, he appears to have been supported by *ʿulemā*ʾ and urban notables (see Hüsameddin, iii, 157-98), while local begs, with their Tatar and Türkmen followers, had neither the prestige nor the legitimacy of an Ottoman prince.

In the well-established Turkish tradition, every son of a ruler had the right to succeed his father, and his legitimacy could not be contested since there was no law which regulated succession (see Inalcik, *Verâset*). As the *Menāḳib-nāme* (see Neshrī, ii, 432, 434, 446, 456, 462, 504, 508) makes clear, people at large often told the rival princes struggling for recognition that they had first to win the fight, which was interpreted as a sign of God's favour. The principle of seniority was not decisive, although Meḥemmed at the beginning recognised his elder brother Süleymān as representing supreme authority (Anonymous chron. Paris, Bibl. Nat. 1047, fol. 29b; ed. Giese, 47).

On the struggle among the Ottoman princes, Čelebis, the account of the *Menāḳib-nāme*, which is actually a contemporary account of the events for the period 1402-13, should be followed. According to this source, in various encounters Meḥemmed defeated ʿĪsā and took Bursa, although the latter secured the alliance of the western Anatolian begs and Isfendiyār of Kastamuni (*Menāḳib-nāme*, in Neshrī, ii, 422-50; Idrīs, 263-7). Meḥemmed finally captured and killed him at Eskishehir (apparently in 806/403-4; Zachariadou, *Süleymān*, 283-91, believes that ʿĪsā was killed by Süleymān in 1403). Then, in 806 (begins 21 July 1403), Meḥemmed lost Bursa and Ankara to Süleymān (Meḥemmed minted an *aḳče* in Bursa in the same Hidjra year, see *Table*, nos. 3, 4). Meḥemmed had to retreat to his Tokat-Amasya base, and later encouraged Mūsā to go to Rūmeli (*Menāḳib-nāme*, in Neshrī, ii, 474; Idrīs, 275-6). Accepting the Wallachian Voyvode Mircea's invitation, Mūsā arrived by sea in Wallachia in 809/1406 (A. Dersca

TABLE

Ottoman coins minted during the period 805-822

Ruler and title	*Year*	*Minting place*	*Metal*
1. Amīr Sulaymān b. Bāyazīd	805	—	silver
2. Amīr Sulaymān Bāyazīd	806	—	silver
3. Muḥammad b. Bāyazīd Khān/Demür Khān Kurḳān	806	Bursa	silver
4. Ghiyāth al-Dunyā wa 'l-Dīn Muḥammad b. Bāyazīd	806	Bursa	silver
5. Ghiyāth al-Dunyā wa 'l-Dīn Muḥammad b. Bāyazīd	806	Engüriyye	silver
6. al-Sulṭān al-Aʿẓam Muḥammad b. Bāyazīd Khān	808	Amasya	silver
7. Ghiyāth al-Dunyā wa 'l-Dīn Muḥammad b. Bāyāzīd Khān	810	Amasya	silver
8. Djunayd Ghāzī/Muḥammad b. Bāyazīd	—	—	silver
9. Amīr Sulaymān b. [......]	813	Edirne	silver
10. al-Sulṭān al-Malik al-Aʿẓam Muḥammad b. Bāyazīd	813	—	copper
11. Mūsā b. Bāyazīd	813	Edirne	silver
12. Sulṭān b. Sulṭān Muḥammad [b.] Bāyazīd Khān	816	Temirhisar	copper
13. Sulṭān b. Sulṭān Muḥammad [b.] Bāyazīd Khān	—	Serez	silver
14. Amīr Sulaymān b. Bāyazīd	811	Edirne	silver
15. Sulṭān b. Sulṭān Muḥammad [b.] Bāyazīd Khān	816	Edirne, Bursa, Amasya Serez, Ayaṣoluḳ, Balat, Timurhisar, Karahisar	silver
16. Sulṭān b. Sulṭān Muḥammad [b.] Bāyazīd Khān	821	Edirne	silver
17. Muḥammad b. Bāyazīd Khān	822	Edirne, Bursa, Amasya, Serez, Ayasoluk	silver
18. Muṣṭafā b. Bāyazīd Khān	822	Edirne	silver

Bulgaru, *Les relations*, 116-17, citing Guboglu, gives the year 1406; the date is confirmed by the details in *Manāḳib-nāme*, in Neshrī, ii, 478: ʿAlī Pasha's death which occurred in 17 Radjab 809/28 December 1406; Idrīs, 278). His success in the eastern Balkans finally forced Süleymān to leave Bursa for Rūmili. At first victorious at the battle of Yanbolu (13 February 1410), Mūsā was later twice defeated (June and July 1410, A. Dersca Bulgaru, 122, 123). Finally, by a surprise attack, Mūsā captured Edirne and killed Süleymān (17 February 1411). Upon Süleymān's departure from Anatolia, Meḥemmed re-occupied Bursa (*Menāḳib-nāme*, in Neshrī, ii, 480). Not honouring his agreement with Meḥemmed, Mūsā acted independently, and espousing the frontier begs' aggressive policy, he alienated the vassal states from himself, who now sided with Meḥemmed (*Menāḳib-nāme*, in Neshrī, ii, 486-516; Idrīs, 281-8). After two unsuccessful attempts against Mūsā (*Menāḳib-nāme*, in Neshrī, ii, 490-500; Idrīs, 281-4) in 814 (begins 25 May 1411); these two clashes are confirmed by Ducas, 109-110) Meḥemmed finally overcame his rival and eliminated him, thanks to the alliance of the frontier begs and vassal states (*Menāḳib-nāme*, in Neshrī, ii, 506-16, Idrīs, 286-8; Braun, 47-55) on 5 Rabīʿ II 816/5 July 1413. According to the *Menāḳib-nāme*, in Neshrī, 88, 486, 516, 550, starting from 805/1402, Süleymān reigned 8 years, 10 months and 17 days, Mūsā 2 years, 7 months and 20 days and Meḥemmed 7 years, 11 months and a few days.

The principal Anatolian dynasties, the Djandārids, the Ḳaramānids, the rulers of Germiyān, Ṣarukhān, and Aydîn in Western Anatolia, which had all been restored to their principalities under Tīmūr's overlordship, were actively involved in the struggle between the Ottoman princes for Bursa, still considered the principal capital or *Dār al-Salṭana*. Their policies were basically determined, like those of Byzantium, Wallachia and Serbia, by their concern to maintain the status quo established after the battle of Ankara. Each Ottoman prince, for his part, tried to gain their support or neutrality by showing himself respectful of their autonomy or independence. However, Tīmūr's departure made the Anatolian dynasties realise that Ottoman power and supremacy were still a fact, and some of them, for the sake of survival, recognised the overlordship of whichever Ottoman prince had control of Bursa.

Byzantium and the vassal states in the Balkans, subjected and paying tribute under Murād I [*q.v.*] and Bāyezīd I, were now independent and even recovered some of their territories (see Jorga, *GOR*, i, 325-77; Barker, 200-385; Zachariadou, *Süleyman*; Jirecek, ii, 137-56). They played off one Ottoman prince against another, gave refuge to and used the Ottoman pretenders against any Ottoman prince whenever he became powerful enough to assert his suzerainty over them. Thus the political manœuvres of Mircea and the Byzantine Emperor Manuel II strongly influenced the struggle between the Ottoman princes. Except for Mūsā, who adopted the policy of the frontier begs of recovering lost lands and engaging in raiding, the other princes, Süleymān and Meḥemmed, involved themselves politically with the Christian rulers, often making compromises and concessions to them. All through the Ottoman interregnum, Byzantium played a central role and managed to keep the respect of rival Ottoman princes. This was actually due to the fact that, after the treaty of 1403 (Denis, *Treaty*; Zachariadou, *Süleyman*, 270-83), the Byzantines controlled the sea passage between Anatolia and Rūmeli. Ottoman public opinion (see Anonymous Paris 1047, fol. 29b). interpreted the treaty of 1403 as such. When in 806/1403 Süleymān decided to pass over to Anatolia to march against Meḥemmed in Bursa, he delivered his younger brother Ḳāsim and his sister Fāṭima as hostages to the Emperor. Later, as part of his appeasement policy, Süleymān also sent his son Orkhan as hostage to Manuel II. Against Mūsā, and after his elimination, against Meḥemmed in 1413, the Emperor tried to use Orkhan, who claimed the Ottoman throne as the legitimate successor of Süleymān.

Meḥemmed's final success depended a great deal on his conciliatory and even compliant attitude towards the Emperor, whom he called father (Ducas, iii, 114). Apparently, Mūsā's harsh personality, or rather, his centralist and autocratic policy, which the hereditary frontier begs resented, alienated them from him.

3. *Unification and the resurgence of the Ottoman supremacy*.

In 816/1413, upon his accession to the throne in Edirne as the sole ruler of the Ottoman lands, Meḥemmed I received embassies from tribute-paying vassal countries, including Byzantium, Serbia, Wallachia, Yanina, the Morean despotate and the Prince of Achaia (Athens), and sent them back with strong guarantees of peace and friendship (Ducas, iii; Setton, ii, 6, cf. Anonymous Paris 1047, fol. 33a).

Feeling secure in the Balkans, Meḥemmed made in the following two years a series of campaigns to reassert his sovereignty in Anatolia and to punish those *amīrs* who had helped Mūsā against him, In 817/1414 he made the whole of western Anatolia submit by defeating Djunayd, who, abandoning Mūsā, had returned and revived his emirate of Izmir (Ducas, 115-19). The emirate was invaded and turned into an Ottoman *sandjaḳ*. In this campaign, Germiyān, Menteshe, and the Genoese of Chios, Mytilene and Phocea and the Hospitallers of Rhodes, were allied with Meḥemmed on account of Djunayd's aggressive acts. During this campaign, Meḥemmed demolished the fortress which the Hospitallers had begun to construct again in Izmir. The ruler of Menteshe now recognised Meḥemmed as suzerain (Wittek, *Mentesche*, 97).

In 816/1413, while Meḥemmed was in Rūmili proceeding against Mūsā, the Ḳaramānid Meḥmed II laid siege to Bursa and burned down the quarters around the castle (al-Maḳrīzī, *Sulūk*, iv, 47a; Neshrī, 141-2). Upon the news of Meḥemmed's victory over Mūsā, the Ḳaramānids retreated after a 31-day siege. Meḥemmed at first proposed a campaign against Isfendiyār of Kastamuni, who however submitted in time, promising to send auxiliary forces to Meḥemmed's planned campaign against Ḳaramān. Germiyān, which had been invaded by the Ḳaramānids, was a natural ally and vassal (Neshrī, ii, 516-34). Prior to the major campaign against Ḳaramān, Meḥemmed sent an embassy with rich presents to the Sultan of Egypt, who was considered a protector of the Ḳaramānids (Ibn Ḥadjar, iii, 518; letter from Inegöl, in Ferīdūn, i, 145, dated *awāsiṭ Dhi 'l-Ḥidjdja* 817/February 1415). Meḥemmed defeated the Ḳaramānids and laid siege to Ḳonya (Muḥarrem 818/13 March-11 April 1415). The Ḥamīd-ili and Saʿīd-ili were annexed to the Ottoman state (*Takvimler*, 20, 56; al-Maḳrīzī, iv, 51a).

With the Ottoman re-unification of Anatolia and Rūmili under one ruler and that ruler's attempts at reimposing suzerainty on the former Ottoman vassal states, the Emperor increased his diplomatic activities in conjunction with the Pope and Venice, calling for a crusade against the Ottomans (Barker, 290-353; Thiriet, ii, no. 1592). Profiting from the Ottoman interregnum, Venice had succeeded in extending her control in Epirus, Albania and the Morea. Negotiation for an agreement with Meḥemmed after his final victory over his brothers dragged on unsuccessfully. During the campaign against Djunayd in 1414, the Venetian Duke of Naxos had not joined the other Aegean Latin rulers in the renewal of submission. So, in 1415, Meḥemmed released the sea *ghāzī*s of western Anatolia against Venetian possessions in the Aegean, and sent his fleet of Gallipoli (112 ships, 13 of them galleys) under Čalī Beg to strike at the Cyclades (Ducas, 119; Thiriet, ii, nos. 1569, 1573, 1584, 1588, 1597, 1598). Venice decided to strike back. A Venetian fleet under Pietro Loredano made a surprise attack and destroyed the Ottoman fleet at Gelibolu (Gallipoli) on 1 Rabīʿ II 819/29 May 1416 (Jorga, i, 372; al-Maḳrīzī, iv, 66a).

Released by the Tīmūrid Shāhrūkh, Meḥemmed's brother Muṣṭafā had arrived in Trebizond (January 1415), and his envoy began to negotiate with Venice and with the Emperor (Thiriet, ii, nos. 1563, 1564). Arriving in Ḳonya and then Ḳastamuni, Muṣṭafā went by sea to Wallachia. Djunayd, the former ruler of Izmir, who had been appointed by Meḥemmed governor of Nicopolis, joined him there. The appearance on the scene of Meḥemmed's elder brother Muṣṭafā brought back the internecine war, coupled with a terrible social-religious insurrection and a hostile attitude on the part of the vassal states in Rūmili and Anatolia. Although militarily supported by Mircea, Muṣṭafa and Djunayd failed to attract the frontier forces and had to return to Constantinople. The Emperor this time (spring 819/1416) sent them to Salonica (Jorga, *GOR*, i, 373). Meḥemmed declared war against Byzantium. Muṣṭafā and Djunayd captured Serres and hoped to obtain the support of the Ottoman frontier forces there. They failed, and Meḥemmed forced them to take refuge in Salonica again (autumn 1416, Jorga, i, 374). The Emperor finally agreed to keep them in custody as long as Meḥemmed lived and was to receive an annual compensation of 300,000 *aḳčes* (about 10,000 gold ducats) for their upkeep (Ducas, 125).

While fighting against Muṣṭafā in Rūmili, Meḥemmed had at the same time to deal with a violent Ṣūfī insurrection fomented by Shaykh Badr al-Dīn [*q.v.*] in western Anatolia and Deli-Orman (summer and autumn of 1416, Filipović, *Princ Musa*; Werner, *Ketzer*; Neshrī, ii, 542-6; Idrīs, 294). Mircea, who had given refuge to the *shaykh* and actively supported him, invaded Deli-Orman on his heels and attacked Silistre (autumn 1416, Jorga, *GOR*, i, 374). Meḥemmed captured the *shaykh* in Zagra and hanged him in Serres on 18 December 1416. While Meḥemmed was kept busy in Rūmili, the Anatolian begs had again become hostile. Meḥemmed marched first against Isfendiyār, who had aided the *shaykh* to pass over to Wallachia (early 1417). Isfendiyār obtained peace by recognising the full suzerainty of Meḥemmed I. Since the latter fell seriously ill in 820/1417, the campaign against Ḳaramān was conducted by Bāyezīd Pasha, who captured the Ḳaramānid ruler (Neshrī, ii, 530-4; Idrīs, 289-91: in the early Ottoman compilations, various campaigns against Ḳaramān are confused).

During the interregnum period, Mircea, supported by the Hungarian King Sigismund, emerged as the principal opponent of Ottoman supremacy in the Balkans. Meḥemmed's 822/1419 campaign against Mircea (for the correct date, see Ibn Ḥadjar, iii, 526; and Meḥemmed's letter to Shāhrūkh in Ferīdūn, i, 164: Shawwāl 822/21 October-18 November 1419) is connected with Sigismund's plans for the invasion of the Balkans.

Meḥemmed's Anatolian vassals, the Ḳaramānid and Djandārid rulers, sent auxiliary forces under their sons to this major campaign. The Ottomans raided Wallachia, and Meḥemmed constructed the fortress of New Giurgiu (later Rusdjuḳ) on the right bank of the Danube; he then invaded "the Hungarian territory" and took Severin (Neshrī, ii, 536; Anonymous, Paris 1047, fol. 34; there, the dates 817/1414 and 819/1416 for this campaign of Meḥemmed I must belong to the frontier beg's earlier raids, cf. Ducas, 125). According to Neshrī, the Wallachian Voyvode (Mircea or Michael I) submitted, paying tribute and sending his three sons to the sultan as hostage.

4. *Tīmūrid intervention, 1416-20.*

The successes of the Ḳara Ḳoyunlu (Woods, 56-60) in Ādharbāydjān and western Iran and the overthrow of the status quo in Anatolia by Meḥemmed presented a challenge to the Tīmūrids. Shāhrukh [*q.v.*], having established his sovereignty in the east, moved to restore Tīmūrid control in the west. First, he released Muṣṭafā from captivity in Samarḳand, an action which brought back internecine war in the Ottoman domains in 819/1416. That Muṣṭafā's release was connected with a Tīmūrid plan becomes clear in Shāhrukh's protest against Meḥemmed's elimination of his brothers (his letter to Meḥemmed, Ferīdūn, i, 150-1). In his reply, the latter tried to prove that he did not support the Ḳaraḳoyunlu Ḳara Yūsuf, and argued that the division of the Ottoman state only helped the enemies of Islam, many places including Salonica having been lost to Islam because of that division. Shāhrukh's preparations for a large-scale campaign in the west in 822/1419 caused great concern in the Ottoman capital and generated an exchange of embassies between the Ḳara Ḳoyunlu and the Ottomans (Ferīdūn, i, 150-7). Invading Ādharbāydjān, Shāhrukh warned Meḥemmed not to give aid to Iskandar, the son of Ḳara Yūsuf, who might take refuge in Ottoman territory (Dhu 'l-Ḥidjdja 823/January 1420. In his reply, Meḥemmed expressed his complete submission (*farmān-bar*). The Ottoman court was meanwhile following in great anxiety the developments on the eastern frontier (see *Takvimler*, 20, 56). Upon Iskandar's victory over the Aḳ Ḳoyunlu Ḳara ʿOthmān (Rabīʿ II 824/April 1421), Shāhrukh entered eastern Anatolia and won a crushing victory against Iskandar (Radjab 824/July 1421). All this time, Meḥemmed was maintaining friendly relations with the Mamlūks (Ferīdūn, i, 145-6, 164-7), equally threatened by Shāhrukh.

In his last years, Meḥemmed appears to have fallen ill. Now his great concern was to secure the throne for his eldest son Murād without a crisis. Although Sülaymān's son Orkhan was blinded and kept in custody, Meḥemmed's brother Muṣṭafā was a serious rival, since he had actually been recognised as sultan by some of the Ottoman leaders and could be released by the Emperor at any time. Prince Murād's supporters spread the rumour that Muṣṭafā had died and that the challenger was a false (*düzme*) Muṣṭafā. To make sure of Murād's accession, Meḥemmed showed himself most liberal toward the members of the ruling élite and made an agreement with the Emperor (Ducas, 129; for the agreement of the same nature with Stefan of Serbia, see Braun, 56-8) that Murād would succeed him in Edirne; his other son Muṣṭafā would remain in Anatolia; the two minor sons Yūsuf (aged 8) and Maḥmūd (aged 7) would be sent to Constantinople to the custody of Manuel II, who in return would not release their uncle Muṣṭafā (see Inalcik, *Murad II*, in *İA*, v, 598-9). The Emperor was to receive a yearly sum for the upkeep of the two Ottoman princes. When Meḥemmed died (5 Ra<u>dj</u>ab 825/25 June 1421) Murād [*q.v.*] succeeded him on the throne in Bursa, refusing to deliver his brothers up to the Emperor.

5. *Conclusion.*

For the reign of Meḥemmed I, the fundamental question is to ascertain how the Ottoman state re-emerged as the dominant power in Anatolia and the Balkans under the most adverse conditions after the disaster of 1402. First of all, it must be noted that, despite military dissolution after the battle of Ankara, the Ottomans continued to be the major military power in both regions. Secondly, the Ottoman dynasty was able to create an imperial tradition which was considered the only source of legitimation for the feudal lords and dynasts in this area. In 1405 and 1413, for example, Serbian princes sought the resolution of differences among themselves through the intervention of the Ottoman ruler (Braun, 27, 55). Perhaps equally important was the fact that the Ottoman military groups of *sipāhīs*, *yaya* and *müsellems*, and the *ḳapî-ḳulus*, as well as the peasantry, saw that the confirmation and legitimation of their status and rights in the land were dependent on the existence and functioning of the Ottoman sultan's centralist government, and we have to remember that the Ottoman survey [see TAḤRĪR] and *tīmār* system was fully developed and widely applied in this period (see Inalcik, *Arvanid*).

Bibliography: A book of exploits in the style of a *menāḳib-nāme* has come down to us in the compilations of Ne<u>sh</u>rī, apparently most faithfully reproduced in his revised version, ed. F.R. Unat and M.A. Köymen, *Kitâb-i Cihannümâ*, i-ii, Türk Tarih Kurumu, Ankara 1949-57, repr. 1987, i, 366-419, ii, 422-516, and Idrīs Bidlīsī, *Ha<u>sh</u>t bihi<u>sh</u>t*, ms. TKS Library, Hazine 1655; with extensive omissions in Pseudo-Rūḥī, Oxford, Bodleian ms. Marsh 313, and Staatsbibliothek, Berlin, or. quart. 821, and in Bihi<u>sh</u>tī, Babinger, *GOW*: "Sinan Čelebi"; V. Ménage, *Bihi<u>sh</u>tī*, in *EI*²; Saʿd al-Dīn, *Tā<u>dj</u> al-tawārī<u>kh</u>*, Istanbul 1279/1862, i, 191-273, follows Idrīs; also Muṣṭafā ʿĀlī, *Künh al-a<u>kh</u>bār*, iv, Istanbul 1285/1868, 144-94. Other Ottoman chronicles are brief and confused; among them ʿĀ<u>sh</u>iḳ-Pa<u>sh</u>a-zāde, *Tawārī<u>kh</u>-i āl-i ʿO<u>th</u>mān*, ed. Ç.N. Atsız, Istanbul 1949, 146-57; for the anonymous chronicles, see *Die altosmanischen Anonymen Chroniken*, ed. F. Giese, i. *Text und Variantenverzeichnis*, Breslau 1922; one good version of the latter is ms. Bibl. Nat., Paris, supp. turc. 1047; Orū<u>dj</u>, *Tawārī<u>kh</u>-i āl-i ʿO<u>th</u>mān*, ed. F. Babinger, Hanover 1925, is basically a variant of the anonymous chronicles; see Ménage, *Ne<u>sh</u>rī's History of the Ottomans: the sources and development of the text*, Oxford 1964; an independent Ottoman source is *Dustūrnāme-yi Enwerī*, ed. M.H. Yinanc, Istanbul 1928, 90-2; for Tīmūr and Meḥemmed, see <u>Sh</u>araf al-Dīn Yazdī, *Ẓafar-nāma*, ed. A. Urunbayev, Tashkent 1972, 417-31; Ibn ʿArab<u>sh</u>āh, *ʿA<u>dj</u>āʾib al-maḳdūr fī nawāʾib al-Tīmūr*, ed. A.M. ʿUmar, Cairo 1979, 203-19; for <u>Sh</u>āhru<u>kh</u>'s western policy and campaign, Ferīdun, *Mün<u>sh</u>eʾāt al-selāṭīn*, Istanbul 1274/1867, i, 150-63; *Tarihi takvimler*, ed. O. Turan, TTK, Ankara 1954; J.E. Woods, *The Aqquyunlu*, Minneapolis and Chicago 1976; M.M. Alexandrescu-Dersca, *La campagne de Timur en Anatolie*, Bucharest 1942, repr. London, Variorum editions, 1977; A.-D. Bulgaru, *Les relations du Prince de Walachie Mircea...*, in *TAD*, x-xi (1968), 113-25; R.G. de Clavijo, *Embajada a Tamerlan*, ed. F. Lopez Estrada, Madrid 1943. On Byzantium, Doukas, *Historia Turco-Byzantina*, tr. H.J. Margoulias, Detroit 1975, 96-152; J.W. Barker, *Manuel II Palaeologus (1391-1425): a study in Late Byzantine statesmanship*, Rutgers, New Brunswick 1969; E.A. Zachariadou, *Süleyman Çelebi in Rumili and the Ottoman chronicles*, in *Isl.*, lx (1983), 268-96; eadem, *Erto<u>gh</u>rul Bey, il sovrano di Teologo (Efeso)*, in *Atti della Società Ligure di storia Patria*, N.S., v (lxxix), fasc. 1, 155-61; eadem, *Marginalia on the history of Epirus and Albania (1380-1418)*, in *WZKM*, lxxviii (1988), 195-210; N. Jorga, *Une description grecque sur le sultan Mousa, 1407-1408*, in *RHSEE*, iii, 8-13; G.T. Dennis, *The Byzantine-Turkish treaty of 1403*, in *Orientalia Christiana Periodica*, xxxi (1967), 72-88; P. Schreiner, *Die byzantinischen Kleinchroniken*, i-ii, Vienna 1975-7; M. Balivet, *Un épisode méconnu de la campagne de Mehmed I...*, in *Turcica*, xviii (1986), 137-46; K.M. Setton, *The Papacy and the Levant (1205-1571)*, i, Philadelphia 1976, 370-404; ii, 1978, 1-38. On Meḥemmed and the Balkans, N. Jorga, *Geschichte des Osmanischen Reiches*, Gotha 1918, i, 325-78; *Lebensbeschreibung des Despoten Stefan Lazarević*, ed. and tr. M. Braun, Wiesbaden 1956; C. Jireček, *Geschichte der Serben*, Amsterdam 1967, 139-56; M.S. Năsturel, *Une victoire du Voévode Mircea l'Ancien sur les Turcs devant Silistra (c. 1407-1408)*, in *Studia et Acta Orientalia* (Bucharest), i (1958), 247; P.P. Panaitescu, *Mircea cel Bătrân*, Bucharest 1943, 292-354; *Hicrî 835 tarihli sûret-i Defter-i Sancak-i Arvanid*, ed. H. Inalcik, Ankara 1954; E.H. Ayverdi, *Osmanlı mimarisinde Çelebi ve II. Sultan Murad devri, 806-855 (1403-1451)*, ii, Istanbul 1972. On Western Anatolia, see P. Wittek, *Das Fürstentum Mentesche*, Istanbul 1934, repr. 1967; Zachariadou, *Trade and Crusade: Venetian Crete and the emirates of Menteshe and Aydin (1300-1415)*, Venice 1983; F. Thiriet, *Régistre des déliberations du sénat de Venise*, i, Paris-The Hague 1958. On the Mamlūks, see Şevkiye Inalcık, *Ibn Hacer'de Osmanlılara dâir haberler*, in *DTCFD*, v/3, 189-95, vi/4, 349-58, vi/5, 517-29; Ferīdūn, *Mün<u>sh</u>eʾāt al-selāṭīn*, i; H. Hüsameddin, *Amasya taʾrī<u>kh</u>i*, Istanbul 1927, iii; İ.H. Uzunçarşılı, *Çelebi Sultan Mehmed tarafından verilmiş bir Temliknâme ve Sasa Bey ailesi*, in *Belleten*, iii/11-12 (1939), 389-99; idem, *Çelebi Sultan Mehmed' in kızı Selçuk Hatun kimile evlendi*, in *Belleten*, xxi (1957), 253-60; idem, *Mehmed I*, in *İA*, viii, 496-506; Wittek, *De la défaite d'Ankara à la prise de Constantinople*, in *REI*, xii (1938), 1-34; Cüneyt Gökçer, *Yıldırım Bayezid'in oğullarîna ait akça ve mangırlar*, Istanbul 1968; N. Pere, *Osmanlılarda madenî paralar/Coins of the Ottoman Empire*, Istanbul 1968, 59-71; I. and C. Artuk, *Islami sikkeler kataloğu*, Istanbul 1974, iii, 459-64. Documents: see Wittek, *Zu einigen frühosmanischen Urkunden*, in *WZKM* liii, 300-13; liv, 240-56; lv, 122-41; lvi, 267-84; lvii, 102-17; lviii, 165-97; lix-x, 201-23. On the crisis of 1416 and the insurrection of <u>Sh</u>ay<u>kh</u> Badr al-Dīn, see N. Filipović, *Princ Musa i šeyh Bedreddin*, Sarajevo 1971; E. Werner, *Ketzer und Weltverbesserer*, Berlin 1974; K.E. Wadekin, *Der Aufstand des Bürklüdsche Mustafa*, diss., Leipzig 1950 (unpubl.); Babinger, *Scheych Bedr-ed-din*, in *Isl.*, xi (1934), 1-106; H.J. Kissling, *Das Menakybname Scheich Bedr ed-din des Sohnes des Richters von Simavna*, in *ZDMG*, c (1950), 112-76; A. Gölpınarlı, *Simavna kadısıoğlu*

Şeyh Bedreddin, Istanbul 1966; ʿAzīz Astarābādī, *Bazm u razm*, ed. Kilisli Rifʿat, Istanbul 1928; Inalcik, *Osmanlılarda saltanat verâseti usûlü...*, in *SBFD*. xiv (1959), 69-94. (H. INALCIK)

MEḤEMMED II, Ottoman sultan (reigned 848-50/1444-6 and 855-86/1451-81), called *Abu 'l-Fatḥ* or *Fātiḥ* "the Conqueror".

Considered the ultimate founder of the Ottoman Empire, he was born in Edirne on 27 Radjab 835/30 March 1432 as the fourth son of Murād II [*q.v.*] from a slave girl in the harem, and as a youth was sent to the governorship of the province of Amasya with his two *lalas* [*q.v.*] in the spring of 846/1443. In Rabīʿ II 848/July 1444, at the age of twelve, he was recalled and declared sultan by his father, who abdicated in his favour in order to ensure his succession against Orkhan, an Ottoman pretender in Constantinople. Meḥemmed's first sultanate, Rabīʿ II 848/July 1444-Djumādā II 850/August 1448, witnessed a fierce rivalry for power between the grand vizier, Čandarlî Khalīl, and the young sultan's two *lalas*, Zaghanos (Zaghanuz) and Ibrāhīm. While Čandarlî, of *ʿulamāʾ* background, favoured a foreign policy of peace and compromise, Zaghanos, who belonged to the military faction, advocated a programme of conquest — having particularly in mind the conquest of Constantinople — which would secure full authority to the young sultan and his *lala*. Because of the youth of the sultan and his inability to neutralise the rivalry among the two factions, the Ottoman state could not deal decisively with the fateful internal and external crises facing it (the *Ḥurūfī* uprising in Edirne on 8 Djumādā II 848/22 September 1444 and a Crusader army which crossed the Danube 4-8 Djumāda II 848/18-22 September 1444). Everywhere in the Balkans the vassal rulers and seigneurs set about recovering their independence and lost territories. In panic, many Turks began to emigrate to Anatolia. However, Orkhan's attempt in the summer of 848/1444 to attract the frontier begs and to seize Edirne failed. When the Crusader army came to lay siege to Varna in Radjab 848/November 1444, Čandarlî hastened to call the sultan's father with the Anatolian army to come and take command of the Ottoman forces. The Ottoman victory at Varna (28 Radjab 848/10 November 1444) created an ambiguity about who was really the sultan. Officially, Meḥemmed II was still sultan, but Čandarlî acted as if Murād had resumed the sultanate. Finally, by secretly inciting the Janissaries to rise, Čandarlî brought Murād back to the throne in actuality (9 Djumādā I 850/2 August 1446). Meḥemmed was sent to the governorship of Manisa with his *lalas* Zaghanos and Ibrāhīm. Although deposed, Meḥemmed was treated by his supporters as still having the supreme power (see Inalcik, *Fatih devri*, 102-9). Anxious to ensure his son's succession after his death, Murād II took Meḥemmed with him to his major campaigns in the Balkans — against the Hungarians at Kossova in 852/1448, and against the Albanians in the summer of 854/1450. Murād married his son to Sittī Khātūn, the daughter of the Dhu 'l-Ḳādirid [see DHU 'L-ḲADR] ruler, who was traditionally considered an Ottoman ally against the Ḳaramānids. It was only shortly thereafter that Meḥemmed received the news of the death of his father; he acceded to the Ottoman throne for the second time on 16 Muḥarram 855/18 February 1451.

In order to obtain concessions from Meḥemmed, who was seen as an inexperienced young man, the Byzantine Emperor threatened to release Orkhan, while the Ḳaramānid Ibrāhīm invaded disputed territories in Ḥamīd-ili [*q.v.*]. As a skilful diplomat and statesman, Čandarlî appeased Byzantium and Serbia by territorial concessions so that the young sultan could make his first campaign in Anatolia against the Ḳaramānid. While Meḥemmed was in Anatolia with his army, the Byzantine Emperor attempted to obtain further concessions by a second threat to release Orkhan. Meḥemmed came to an agreement with the Ḳaramānid and quickly returned to Edirne to deal with this new threat. Under the influence of Zaghanos, he decided to put an end to the truncated Byzantine empire and began to make preparations for the conquest of Constantinople, sc. by the construction of the Boghaz-Kesen castle on the Bosphorus. Already agreements with Venice (13 Shaʿbān 855/10 September 1451) and Hungary (25 Shawwāl 855/20 November 1451) secured peace in the west and the hire of Urban, a Hungarian expert, who would make for Meḥemmed the most powerful cannons ever seen in order to batter the city's legendary walls. In an extraordinary meeting in Edirne, where the decision for the siege was taken, Čandarlî drew attention to the impregnability of the walls and the danger of a crusade from the West, while the war party, principally Zaghanos and Shihāb al-Dīn, enthusiastically supporting the sultan's decision, emphasised the constant threat which Byzantium posed to the existence and unity of the Ottoman state. The outcome of the siege depended on the time factor and the efficiency of the Ottoman artillery. A long siege would give the Hungarian and Venetian forces the opportunity to come to the aid of the besieged. Thanks to the bombardment of the Ottoman heavy cannons, which tore down the walls, the whole siege took less than two months (26 Rabīʿ I 857/6 April 1453 until 20 Djumādā I 857/29 May 1453; on the siege itself, now see sources collected and edited by A. Pertusi). The most dramatic moment during the siege was the failure of the Ottoman navy to bar the entry of provision ships into the Golden Horn. At this critical point, defeatist rumours arose among the besiegers, and Čandarlî advised the lifting of the siege. Zaghanos and Aḳ Shams al-Dīn [*q.v.*], Meḥemmed's spiritual mentor, emerged as strong supporters of the young sultan, who was being blamed for lack of resolution by the soldiery. The preparations for the final general assault were made by Zaghanos. On 20 Djumādā I 857/29 May 1453, the city was taken by assault [see ISTANBUL. I] and the consequences of an *ʿanwatan* conquest were inevitable [see ḤARB]. Meḥemmed regretted the ruin of the imperial city, which he immediately declared his capital. Throughout his reign, one of his main concerns was to build and repopulate it [see ISTANBUL. I.]. The Podestà of the Genoese Pera [see GHALATA in Suppl.] surrendered *ṣulḥan* on the same day. Meḥemmed granted an *ʿahd-nāme* on 1 June 1453 which guaranteed *amān* [*q.v.*] and certain communal privileges for the indigenous non-Muslim population as *dhimmī* subjects of the Ottoman state and capitulary privileges for the Genoese merchants. Meḥemmed's first acts after the victory were the arrest of Čandarlî and the execution of Prince Orkhan, who had fought against Meḥemmed on the walls. Zaghanos was made grand vizier.

By the conquest of *Ḳusṭanṭīniyya al-ʿUẓmā* [see ḲUSṬANṬĪNIYYA], as it was designated in Islamic tradition, Meḥemmed II assumed an unprecedented charisma and claimed to be the sole "holder of the sword of the *ghazāʾ* " in the Islamic world (in his *fatḥ-nāme* to the Sultan of Egypt; Ferīdūn, i, 236). *Ghazāʾ* indeed became the legitimising principle of the Ottoman sultan even against his Islamic rivals. Muslim rulers who resisted or challenged him

(Anatolian Turcoman rulers, the Aḳ Ḳoyunlu Uzun Ḥasan [*q.v.*] and the Mamlūk sultan of Egypt) were declared to be acting against the true interests of Islam by hindering his *g̲h̲azā*ʾ activities. This assumption would lead the Ottomans to claim supremacy throughout the whole Islamic world in the 10th/16th century (see *Camb. hist. of Islam*, i, 320-3). Also, by declaring himself the *Ḳayṣar*, the sole heir to the Roman Empire, as the possessor of the imperial city, Meḥemmed believed that he could eliminate all the members of the Byzantine imperial families (Ibn Kamāl, vii, 86, 113) and lay claim to all the territories once under the eastern Roman Empire, including the Balkans, the southern coasts of the Crimea and Italy. Following Byzantine tradition, he claimed the supremacy of Constantinople over Rome, and his taking of Otranto in 885/1480 was considered a prelude to the conquest of Italy. The conquest of Rome, symbolised as *Ḳîzîl Elma*, the Golden Globe, remained as the ultimate goal for the Ottoman *g̲h̲azā*ʾ ideology. Meḥemmed's use of historical traditions and images served as legitimation of his efforts at conquest. Again, in order to legitimise his campaigns to annex the Serbian despotate, he always cited his inheritance rights through the marriage of his predecessors with Serbian princesses [see BĀYAZĪD I]. On the other hand, the revival of the first Ottoman Empire as founded under Bāyazīd ((791-804/1389-1402) definitely motivated the Conqueror in his conquests (Ibn Kamāl, vii, 288).

Although his conquering activities were determined basically by his plan to build up a centralist empire in the Balkans and Anatolia, the course of his military actions followed historical circumstances (Babinger's work, *Mehmed the Conqueror and his time*, is the latest attempt to establish a chronology of events; for a review of it, see Inalcik, *Mehmed*, in *Speculum*, xxxv [1960], 408-27; A. Pertusi, *La caduta*; Inalcik, art. *Mehmed II*, in *İA*, v, 510-12). In the last analysis, Meḥemmed's wars appear to have been motivated by his plan to establish his control of the Straits, the Black Sea and the Aegean, the Balkans north to the Danube and the principalities in the lower Danubian basin, as well as central Anatolia and the lands west of the Euphrates. His main interest was in the west. During the fourteen-year period after 1453, Meḥemmed made a series of campaigns in Europe to eliminate the Balkan dynasts: the Serbian despot (1454-9), the Greek despots and Latin seigneurs in the Morea and central Greece (1458-60), the Bosnian king (1463-4) and Iskender Beg [*q.v.*] in Albania (1465-7). He was not so successful against the Rumanian principalities beyond the Danube. While Wallachia renewed its submission (866/1462) [see EFLĀḲ], Moldavia (Ḳara-Bog̲h̲dan [see BOG̲H̲DĀN]) under Stephen the Great put up a fierce resistance (881/1476). Meḥemmed's campaigns in the Balkans brought him into confrontation with two powerful rivals, Hungary, which considered Serbia, Bosnia and Wallachia to be under its protection, and Venice, which had extensive territorial and commercial interests in the Aegean basin (where he campaigned in 861-3/1457-9), in the Morea (862/1458 and 864/1460), and in Albania (867-84/1463-79). Constantly attempting to mobilise the whole of Christendom in a crusade in cooperation with the Popes, Venice and Hungary confronted Meḥemmed in Serbia (his defeat at Belgrade, 860/1456) and in Bosnia (Hungarian capture of Jajce, 868/1463). The alliance of Venice and Hungary in 867/1463 resulted in what was known as the Long War against Venice (867-84/1463-79), and hostilities with Hungary lasted until Meḥemmed's death (see Setton, *The Papacy and the Levant*, ii, 231-363). The Venetian Long War, which cost Venice Euboea (Eğriboz [*q.v.*], 875/1470) and Is̲h̲kodra [*q.v.* in Suppl.] (Shkodër), as well as its trade with the Ottoman Empire, ended in a humiliating peace for Venice, which had to pay an annual tribute of 10,000 gold pieces (2 D̲h̲u 'l-Ḳāʿda 883/25 January 1479). Meḥemmed's complete control of the passage through the Straits, with the construction of Bog̲h̲az-Kesen (1452), Ḳalʿa-yi Sulṭāniyye and Kilīdülbaḥr (868/1463-4), and the fortification of Bozd̲j̲a Ada (Tenedos), which had already enabled him to force the Genoese, Moldavian and Greek rulers to pay tribute (858-60/1454-6), put Istanbul out of reach of Venetian seapower. Later on, taking advantage of anti-Genoese developments in the Crimea, he occupied Amasra (Amastris, 863/1459), Kaffa and Azak (880/1475), Anapa and Copa (884/1479). With the conquest of the Greek empire of Trebizond and the occupation of the Isfendiyārid principality, with Sinope and Kastamoni, in 865/1461, he turned the Black Sea into an Ottoman lake. In 879/1474 his navy consisted of 92 galleys (*ḳadirg̲h̲a*), 5 galleots (*ḳalyata*), 59 horse-transports (*at gemileri*) and a number of small boats. Besides these *mīrī* ships which were based at Gelibolu (Gallipoli) [*q.v.*] there were a number of privateers. However, Meḥemmed always felt that his navy could not challenge the Venetian sea power (Babinger, *Mehmed*, 448-50). In 885/1480 his fleet of Gallipoli attacked Rhodes, and that of Avlonya (Vlorë) attacked Otranto. The siege of Rhodes (Muḥarram-D̲j̲umādā II 885/May-August 1480) failed, but Otranto was captured (4 D̲j̲umādā II 885/11 August 1480).

Keeping Hungary and Venice neutral with peace talks over the period 873-8/1468-73, Meḥemmed focused his attention on central Anatolia, where the dynastic disputes among the Ḳaramānids had given a pretext to the rising Aḳ Ḳoyunlu (Woods, *The Aqquyunlu*, 100-14) to extend their influence in the region. The Ottoman-Aḳ Ḳoyunlu rivalry developed into an extremely dangerous crisis for Meḥemmed, since Uzun Ḥasan [*q.v.*] and Venice attempted to make a concerted attack and to bring together all the small states in the Levant into an anti-Ottoman coalition (Inalcik, art. *Mehmed II*, in *İA*, v, 523-9; Babinger, *Mehmed*, 267-327, Setton, *op. cit.*, 315-45). Meḥemmed's victory at Bas̲h̲-kent (16 Rabīʿ I 878/11 August 1473) was indeed a turning point in his whole career and confirmed the Ottoman annexation of the Ḳaramānid territory (863/1468). However, it took six years to subdue the Turcoman tribes in the Taurus range. This also led to an open rivalry between Meḥemmed and the Mamlūks, who claimed a protectorate over the Ḳaramānids and saw a challenge in Meḥemmed's alliance with and protection of the D̲h̲u'l-Ḳādirids. It was said (Ṭursun Beg, *Taʾrīk̲h̲*, text, fols. 157b-158a) that Meḥemmed's last campaign, on which he was engaged when he died (4 Rabīʿ I 886/3 May 1481), was against the Mamlūks rather than against the Hospitallers of Rhodes.

Meḥemmed II is the true founder of the classical Ottoman Empire, establishing its territorial, ideological and economic bases. Territorially, he organised under his autocratic rule the lands between the Danube and the Euphrates as a centralised domain which remained for four centuries afterwards the solid core of the Ottoman Empire. Byzantine tradition and experience taught him to endeavour to establish full control over the Danube, the Straits, the Aegean and the Euphrates as the natural borders of his empire. By fortifying the Dardanelles and the

Bosphorus, he achieved a compact empire, duly taking the title of the sultan of the two continents, Anatolia and Rumili, and the *khāḳān* of the two seas, the Black Sea and the Mediterranean. His centralist empire came into being by the suppression or reduction under central control of the local aristocratic landed families in the Balkans and Anatolia. Such families either became regular Ottoman *tīmār*-holders or were totally replaced by the sultan's *ḳuls* [*q.v.*]. His sweeping "land reform" of 883/1478, in which a great number of the freehold (*mülk*) and *waḳf* lands in the control of such hereditary landlords were turned into state lands (see Inalcik, *op. cit.*, at 533), constituted his major move in this direction. Also, by emerging as the greatest *ghāzī*, he overshadowed and reduced the autonomy of the principal frontier beg families who had thus far played a determining role in the empire's politics [see MEḤEMMED I and MURĀD II]. In brief, Meḥemmed II created in his person the typical autocratic Ottoman *Pādishāh*.

In his efforts to establish a bureaucratic machinery, the principal tool of his centralist empire, Meḥemmed employed indiscriminately experts of various origins, Persian Azerīs, Arabs, Greeks, Jews, Italians, as well as native Ottoman Turks (*rūmīs*). In this, as attested by his *ḳānūn-nāme* [*q.v.*] of state organisation and by biographies of the *nishāndjīs* [*q.v.*] and the *defterdārs* [*q.v.*] of his reign, the *ʿulamāʾ* appear to have played a major role, as before. However, such *ʿulamāʾ* only made up a part of his bureaucracy, and were unable to interfere in the sultan's autocratic and independent conduct of state affairs. Meḥemmed appears to have been the first Ottoman, perhaps the first Muslim ruler, to codify state laws based on the ruler's independent law-making power, *ʿurf* [*q.v.*], apparently inspired by a Turko-Mongol tradition. His two codes [see ḲĀNŪNNĀME] dealt with state organisation, penal law, and the relations of the state and the "military" class with the taxpaying subjects, the *raʿāyā*. The latter law code, considered as the basis of a "just rule", strictly defines the impositions upon the *raʿāyā*. Meḥemmed's law codes remained the core and basis of subsequent Ottoman laws to the 11th/17th century.

With the guidance of the great astronomer ʿAlī Ḳūshdjī [*q.v.*], Meḥemmed also organised religious teaching (*tadrīs*, *ḳaḍāʾ*) and the *ʿulamāʾ* hierarchy (*ṭarīḳ*) in the Ottoman Empire. It was his unprecedented charisma as *Abu 'l-Fatḥ* which enabled him, with the help of a host of talented leaders from East and West, to put into place a centralist bureaucratic empire perhaps never before so perfectly accomplished in Islamic history. His rationalistic and practical education under a legist, Mollā Khosrew [*q.v.*], his faith in the support of God and the inspiration of his *shaykh*, Aḳ Shams al-Dīn [*q.v.*], his espousal of a combination of Islamic and Roman imperial traditions, might explain his extraordinary accomplishments. But no less important in the foundation of the empire appears the fact that the peasant masses, exploited by the local rent-gathering landlords, military and religious, who were operating free from any control in the Balkans and Asia Minor, tacitly or openly welcomed the restoration of a strong centralist power as a guarantee of protection. The sultan's edicts always professed that the imperial power was with "the poor" (*yoḳsullar*) against "the powerful" (*ḳudretlüler*). His bureaucratic apparatus, the land surveys [see TAḤRĪR] and the law codes reveal emphatically the concern to maintain peasant families in possession of small farm exploitations, the so-called *khāne bā čift* units. Meḥemmed's "abrogation", *naskh*, measures with respect to the exploitative *waḳfs* and *mülks*, meant more than just a military reform. It also meant the extension of state ownership and a closer protection and control by the state of the peasant producer and labourer against feudal exploitation.

On the other hand, the native urban populations, Greeks and Slavs, and the Orthodox Church, do not seem to have resented the establishment of the autocratic rule of the Ottoman *pādishāh*, who was seen as, and called, *basileus* or *czar*. But Meḥemmed was only following his predecessors, or in fact the Islamic tradition, when he re-installed the Greek Orthodox Church with all its traditional privileges as an integral part of the Ottoman imperial system (Muḥarram 858/January 1454), while he banned all Latin Catholic organisations, which were under the Roman papacy, from his dominions.

Autocratic principle, which made the sultan's person the one and only source of authority and legitimation and claimed it as the foundation of both state and society (for this political theory expounded by Meḥemmed's contemporary Ṭursun Beg, see text, 2-17), found its full expression under Meḥemmed II. The urban economy and the conditions of craftsmen and merchants, too, were regulated by the sultan through his establishment of bazaars, *bedestāns* (*bazzāzistān*), *ḳapans* (*ḳabbān*), weighing stations (*ḳanṭār*), customs and market regulations, and his periodic issuance of new silver coins, *aḳča*, and prohibition of the use of the old ones, which was tantamount to taxing all cash capital in the hands of individuals, thus making a strong impact on the economy. Turning all rice-growing lands into state-owned properties and organising labour on them under close state control (Inalcik, *Rice cultivation*, 78-113) well demonstrates his autocratic handling of economic issues (for the basic source on his economic regulations, see Anhegger and Inalcik, *Ḳānunnāme*; also ISTANBUL, at IV, 531-4; Inalcik, *Türkiye'nin iktisadî vaziyeti*, 676-84), Meḥemmed fully espoused the theory that the monarch's presuming to organise society and economy as complementary to the state was based on the ruler's ultimate duties of *ghazāʾ*, making God's word, Islam, to rule over the world, and, as *imām*, to guide and take care of his subjects' well-being, conduct and salvation in this and the next world. As is repeatedly underlined in the sultan's edicts, "the *raʿāyā* were a trust (*wadīʿa*) of Allāh to the ruler." The Marxist interpretation, however, is that all these superstructural and ideological assumptions were designed to serve the exploitation of the direct producers by the Ottoman "feudal" state and classes (Moutafchieva, *Agrarian relations*; Werner, *Die Geburt*, 273-358).

Bibliography: Ibn Kamāl, *Tavârîh-i Âl-i Osman, VII. Defter*, ed. Şerafettin Turan, Ankara 1954; Tursun Beg, *Tārīkh-i Abu 'l-Fatḥ*, ed. H. Inalcik and R. Murphey, Minneapolis and Chicago 1978; Ferīdūn Beg, *Münsheʾāt al-selāṭīn*, i, Istanbul 1274/1857, 221-89; Agostino Pertusi, *La caduta di Costantinopoli. i. Le testimonianze dei contemporanei; ii. L'eco nel mondo*, Verona 1976; F. Babinger, *Mehmed the Conqueror and his time*, tr. Ralph Manheim, ed. W.C. Hickman, Princeton 1978; K.M. Setton, *The Papacy and the Levant. ii. The fifteenth century*, Philadelphia 1978, 82-381; J.E. Woods, *The Aqquyunlu: clan, confederation, empire*, Minneapolis and Chicago 1976; Vera P. Moutafchieva, *Agrarian relations in the Ottoman Empire in the fifteenth and sixteenth centuries*, Boulder, Colorado 1988; E. Werner, *Die Geburt einer Grossmacht — die Osmanen*, Weimar 1985; H. Inalcik, *Mehmed the Conqueror (1432-1481) and his time*, in *Speculum* xxxv (1960), 408-27; idem, art. *Mehmed II*, in *İA*, v, 506-35; idem, *Fâtih devri üzerinde tetkikler ve vesikalar*, Ankara 1954; idem, *Rice cultivation and the Çeltükci-reʿāyā system in the Ottoman Empire*, in *Turcica*, xiv, 69-141; idem, *Türkiye'nin iktisadî vaziyeti*, in *Belleten*, xv (1951), 629-90; idem, *The rise of the Ottoman Empire*, in *Camb. hist. of Islam*, i, Cambridge 1970, 295-323. (Halil İnalcik)

MEḤEMMED III, thirteenth Ottoman Sultan (1003-12/1595-1603). He was the son of Murād III [*q.v.*] and his Albanian *k̲h̲āṣṣekī*, Ṣafiyye [*q.v.*], born early in the first decade of D̲h̲u 'l-Ḳaʿda 973/20-29 May 1566 in the summer-camp on Bozdğ near Manisa when his father was *sand̲j̲aḳ-begi* of Ṣaruk̲h̲ān, his birth being announced to his great-grandfather Sulaymān I [*q.v.*], who named the baby, at Pazard̲j̲ik as he marched towards Hungary, on 13 D̲h̲u 'l-Ḳaʿda 973/1 June 1566 (Selānīkī, 22).

After his father's accession on 8 Ramaḍān 982/22 December 1574, he lived with his mother and sisters in the New Palace in Istanbul. In 990/1582 his circumcision, to which monarchs of East and West had been invited, was celebrated with feasting and pageants of unrivalled magnificence (splendidly recorded in Topkapı Museum, ms. Hazine 1344), lasting from 6 D̲j̲umādā I-3 Rad̲j̲ab/29 May-24 July, the operation being performed by D̲j̲errāḥ Meḥmed Pas̲h̲a on the fortieth evening. The break-up of Murād's life with Ṣafiyye culminated in the death of his mother Nūr Bānū[*q.v.*] on 22 D̲h̲u 'l-Ḳaʿda 991/7 December 1583 and the departure on 9 D̲h̲u 'l-Ḥid̲j̲d̲j̲a/24 December of Meḥemmed to Manisa, the last heir-apparent to be *sand̲j̲aḳ-begi* of Ṣaruk̲h̲ān. During his 11 years' residence there, four of his five sons were born; Selīm in 993/1585, died 3 Ramaḍān 1005/20 April 1597; Maḥmūd in *ca.* 995/1587; the future Aḥmad I [*q.v.*] on 12 D̲j̲umādā II 998/18 April 1590; the future Muṣṭafā I [*q.v.*] in 1000/1591. He had a fifth son D̲j̲ihāngīr, who died young in 1011/1602, and six daughters. Upon Murād III's death on 5 D̲j̲umādā I 1003/16 January 1595, in great secrecy Ṣafiyye sent the *Bostānd̲j̲ī-bas̲h̲ī* Ferhād Ag̲h̲a to Manisa, and Meḥemmed returned to the capital for his accession, followed by his father's funeral, in 16 D̲j̲umādā I/27 January. The next day his 19 half-brothers (names listed by Ṣolāḳ-zāde, 621) were executed and laid to rest beside their father. Meḥemmed III was the last Sultan to implement the law of fratricide promulgated by Meḥemmed II [*q.v.*] (see H. İnalcik, in *Cambridge history of Islam*, i, 303). Murād's harem, his dwarfs and jesters, were swept away, and Ṣafiyye, as Wālide Sulṭān, took absolute control over her weak and superstitious son. A donative of 660,000 gold pieces was distributed to the Janissaries.

The reign, lying within the Long War (1593-1606) with the Holy Roman Empire, was disastrous, torn by civil and military disturbances, high inflation and insecure government; there were twelve changes of Grand Vizier, of whom three, Ferhād Pas̲h̲a, K̲h̲ādīm Ḥasan Pas̲h̲a Ṣoḳollī and Yemis̲h̲d̲j̲i Ḥasan Pas̲h̲a [*q.vv.*], were executed. During 1003-4/1595 the princedom of Wallachia was occupied and made into an Ottoman voivodeship, and on 1 D̲h̲u 'l-Ḥid̲j̲d̲j̲a/7 August, Esztergom, under the Grand Vizier Ḳod̲j̲a Sinān Pas̲h̲a [*q.v.*], fell to the Imperialists. Next year, 1004/1596, Meḥemmed, influenced by his father's tutor K̲h̲od̲j̲a Saʿd al-Dīn Efendi [*q.v.*] and under pressure from the Janissaries, resolved to lead the army into Hungary, a custom abandoned since the reign of Sulaymān I. On 23 S̲h̲awwāl/20 June, with the Grand Vizier Dāmād Ibrāhīm Pas̲h̲a [*q.v.*], he set out for Eğri [*q.v.*], which fell after a siege of three weeks on 19 Ṣafar 1005/12 October 1596. On 3 Rabīʿ I/25 October a great battle was fought on the plain of Mezö-Keresztes [*q.v.*], and the following evening the Ottomans, reinforced by a Tatar army under their K̲h̲ān Fetḥ Girāy, were victorious almost at the very moment of defeat, thanks to the strategy of Čig̲h̲āle-zāde Sinān Pas̲h̲a [*q.v.*], who was promoted Grand Vizier. The English ambassador Edward Barton was present on the campaign; he, his successor Sir Henry Lello, and the French ambassador François Savary de Brèves were playing important roles in Ottoman policies. On the return march, Ibrāhīm Pas̲h̲a was reinstated as Grand Vizier at the behest of Ṣafiyye. On 2 D̲j̲umādā I/22 December the sultan entered Istanbul, with great rejoicing. However, the violence of the D̲j̲alālīs [*q.v.* in Supplement], dissatisfied elements who had gathered under Ḳarā Yazīd̲j̲ī [*q.v.*], a rebellious press-gang leader conscripting for the campaign, together with the Firārīs, Anatolian *sipāhīs* who had fled before the battle and thus had been deprived of their *tīmārs*, raged until 1603, devastating Anatolia. Peace initiatives were rejected by the Imperialists, who regained Raab on 21 S̲h̲aʿbān 1006/29 March 1598. During 1008/1599-1600 the deaths occurred of Saʿd al-Dīn and the poet Bāḳī [*q.v.*], and the murder of Ṣafiyye's Jewish Kira Esperanza Malchi on 17 Ramaḍān/1 April in the course of a rising of the *sipāhīs* against the power of the harem. A similar rising in the capital on 23 Rad̲j̲ab 1011/6 January 1603 took as victims two more Palace officials, G̲h̲aḍanfer Ag̲h̲a [see ḳapî ag̲h̲asî] and ʿOt̲h̲mān Ag̲h̲a. As the crippling war with the Empire dragged on, with the castle of Kanizsa [*q.v.*] surrendering to the Ottomans on 13 Rabīʿ II 1009/22 October 1600, in 1012/1603 the Persian S̲h̲āh ʿAbbās I [*q.v.*] launched an offensive in the east, taking Tabrīz on 19 Rabīʿ II/26 September. On 27 D̲h̲u 'l-Ḥid̲j̲d̲j̲a 1011/7 June 1603 Meḥemmed, in a fit of suspicious rage, ordered the execution of his eldest son Maḥmūd; he lies buried, with his mother, in a mausoleum beside the S̲h̲eh-zāde mosque. Consequently, the child Aḥmad was to succeed his father, who died suddenly, probably after a heart-attack, on 17 Rad̲j̲ab 1012/21 December 1603. His mausoleum is beside Aya Sofya. He composed poetry under the *mak̲h̲laṣ* ʿAdlī. During his corrupt reign, chronic inflation (the rate of 60 *aḳčes* to the ducat in 1580 had trebled by 1600) undermined society, and the decline which is evident from the latter years of Sulaymān I reached a critical stage, with the empire close to anarchy.

Bibliography: As many of the chronicles and documents of this reign are not yet published, for details of mss. see M. Tayyib Gökbilgin, in *İA* s.v. *Mehmed III*; Hammer-Purgstall, *GOR*, iv; Babinger. Selānīkī, *Taʾrīk̲h̲*, Istanbul 1281, is published only to 1001/1593; for a summary of his account of the reign, see M. Ipşirli, *Mustafa Selânikî and his history*, in *Tarih Enstitüsü Dergisi*, ix (1978), 417-72. Meḥmed b. Meḥmed, *Nuk̲h̲bat al-tawārīk̲h̲*, Istanbul 1276, 176-219; Pečewī, *Taʾrīk̲h̲*, Istanbul 1283, ii, 163-290; Ḥād̲j̲d̲j̲ī K̲h̲alīfa, *Fed̲h̲leke*, Istanbul 1286, i, 46-221; Ṣolāḳ-zāde, *Taʾrīk̲h̲*, Istanbul 1297, 620-83; Ḳara Čelebi-zāde, *Rawḍat al-abrār*, Būlāk 1248, 477-96. For the contemporary publications to the end of 1600, see C. Göllner, *Turcica*, Bucharest 1968, ii; for social analysis, extensive modern bibliography and illustrations, H. İnalcık, *The Ottoman Empire: the classical age, 1300-1600*, London 1973; contemporary European histories, L. Soranzo, *L'Ottomano*, Ferrara 1598; R. Knolles, *The generall historie of the*

Turkes, 4th ed. London 1631, 1055-1201 (with portrait). His family, birth, and early life are discussed by E. Spagni, *Una sultana veneziana*, in *Nuovo Archivio Veneto*, xix (1900), 241-348; S. A. Skilliter, *Three letters from the Ottoman "Sultana" Ṣāfiye to Queen Elizabeth I*, in *Documents from Islamic chanceries*, ed S. M. Stern, Oxford 1965, 119-57; H. G. Rosedale, *Queen Elizabeth and the Levant Company*, London 1904, with facsimiles of the report in Italian made for Edward Barton by Salamon Usque on 2 February 1595, after p. 18; portrait, 73. For the circumcision festivities, the contemporary account by N. Haunolth in H. Lewenklaw, *Neuwe Chronica Türckischer nation*, Frankfurt-am-Main 1595, 468-514: a modern assessment, M. And, *Kırk gün kırk gece*, Istanbul 1959. On the Long War, A. Randa, *Pro Republica Christiana*, Munich 1964; the revolt in Anatolia, M. Akdağ, *Celâlî isyanları*, Ankara 1963. Among the many accounts of European merchants, travellers and diplomats, W. Foster, ed., *The travels of John Sanderson in the Levant, 1584-1602*, London 1931; *The diary of Master Thomas Dallam, 1599-1600*, in T. Bent, *Early voyages and travels in the Levant*, London 1893; O. Burian, *The report of Lello*, Ankara 1952; F. Moryson, *An itinerary*, London 1617. On the Jewish Kira and her death, J. J. Mordtmann, *Die jüdischen Kira im Serai der Sultane*, in *MSOS As.*, xxxii/2 (1929), 1-38. For contemporary Turkish discussions of the decline, Ḥasan al-Kāfī, *Uṣūl al-ḥikam fī niẓām al-ʿālam*, Istanbul 1278; A. Tietze, *Muṣṭafā ʿĀlī's description of Cairo of 1599*, Vienna 1975. On the inflation, Ö. L. Barkan, *XVI asrın ikinci yarısında Türkiye'de fiyat hareketleri*, in *Belleten*, xxxiv (1970), 557-607. For the poetry of the Sultan and his reign, A. Navarian, *Les Sultans poètes*, Paris 1936, 100-3; Gibb, *Ottoman poetry*, iii, London 1904, 170-204. The events of the reign inspired two works of Meḥmed Nāmiḳ Kemāl [*q.v.*], *Djezmī*, Istanbul 1297, and *Ḳanīzhe*, Istanbul 1290.

(S. A. Skilliter)

MEḤEMMED IV, nineteenth sultan of the Ottoman dynasty in Turkey, known as awdjī "the hunter" from his excessive passion for the chase, reigned 1058-99/1648-87.

Born on 30 Ramaḍān 1051/2 January 1642, he was the son of Sultan Ibrāhīm [*q.v.*] and Khadīdja Turkhān Sulṭān. He was placed on the throne in Istanbul at the age of seven after the deposition in 18 Radjab 1058/8 August 1648 of the sensualist and possibly mentally deranged "Deli" Ibrāhīm, at a moment when Ibrāhīm was the sole surviving adult male of the house of ʿOthmān, but in fact, two others of his five or six sons survived also to attain the throne after Meḥemmed, sc. Süleymān II and Aḥmed II [*q.vv.*].

The power in the state was at that time divided between the court, where the old *wālide* Kösem [*q.v.*] and Meḥemmed's mother, the *wālide* Tarkhān, held the reins, and the rebellious soldiery of the Janissaries and the Sipāhīs. The lack of stability in the government at this time is shown by the fact, that, until the nomination of the grand vizier Köprülü Meḥmed [see KÖPRÜLÜ] in 1066/1656, there were no less than thirteen grand viziers. In 1061/1651 the old *wālide* Kösem was strangled and at the same time the resistance of the Janissaries was broken; the régime of the court party that followed under the sultan's mother did not improve the situation. The grand vizierate of Ipshir Muṣṭafā Pasha (1064-5/1654-5 [*q.v.*]), who at first seemed to be the strong man needed, was brought to an early end by his rival Murād Pasha, and in the meantime the Cretan war against Venice was exhausting the resources of the Empire. In Djumādā I 1066/March 1656 a military rebellion forced the sultan to allow the execution of several of his favourite courtiers.

The real strong man proved to be Köprülü Meḥmed Pasha (vizier 1066-72/1656-61), who eliminated immediately the influence of the harem on state affairs and became until his death the real ruler of the empire. His régime began with a Turkish maritime defeat by the Venetians at the Dardanelles, but already in the following year he obtained as *serʿasker* successes in Transylvania and succeeded at the same time in establishing firmly Turkish authority in the Danube principalities; the collaboration with the Khān of the Crimea [see ḲIRĪM] was here of great value. In 1068/1658 and 1069/1659 he was able to suppress rebellions in Anatolia, and in the Venetian war a great fleet of Venetian ships and other Christian allies did not succeed against the Turkish forces on Crete. After his death (1072/1661), he was succeeded in his office by his son Köprülü Aḥmed Pasha, who completed the work of his father by carrying through the final conquest of Crete (surrender of Ḳandiya [*q.v.*] in Rabīʿ II 1080/September 1669) followed by peace with Venice. In 1071/1661 the war with Austria had begun again, where Sultan Meḥemmed took part in several campaigns, notably that of 1073/1663 in which Újvár (Neuhäusel or Nové Zámky) was taken. In 1075/1664 took place the famous battle of St. Gotthard-am-Raab, where the Turks were beaten by an allied army, a part of which was formed by French troops; still, the peace concluded with Austria in 1075/1664 at Vasvár was favourable for Turkey. In 1083/1672 the sultan took part in the campaign against Poland, after the Ukrainian Cossacks had invoked Ottoman aid against the Polish king; the Polish war, ending in a peace treaty of 1087/1676, strengthened still further the empire's position in the north. Köprülü Aḥmed Pasha died in 1087/1676. Though the sultan, who had developed in the meantime a morose and capricious character, never showed him the same deference as to his father, Aḥmed had been easily able to maintain himself against enemies in the interior, not least by forming new troops, the *beshli* and the *gönüllü* [*q.v.*], who were far more reliable than the Janissaries and Sipāhīs. He had not been able, however, to put an end to the extravagant luxury of the court, which wasted enormous sums. The sultan had an abnormal liking for big hunts, that were organised at enormous cost in the environs of Edirne, which town he preferred as a residence to Istanbul [see further, KÖPRÜLÜ].

After Aḥmed's death the sultan did not himself take the affairs of state in hand; he appointed Ḳara Muṣṭafā Pasha Merzifonlu [*q.v.*] as his grand vizier. The latter continued in an unnecessary way the tradition of warfare; in 1088/1677 and 1089/1678 he obtained successes against the Cossacks, behind whom the Muscovite power now began to gain in importance in Turkish affairs. In 1093/1682 war broke out again with the Austrian monarchy and led to the second Turkish siege of Vienna (18 Radjab-20 Ramaḍān 1094/12 July-12 September 1683), ending in a Turkish débâcle, thanks to the intervention of the Polish king John Sobieski. This disaster cost Ḳara Muṣṭafā his office and his life, and at the same time the influence of the palace became again predominant. The grand viziers now following proved unequal to their task and in the years 1096-8/1685-7 nearly the whole of Hungary was lost to the Austrian armies (Turkish defeat at Mohács [*q.v.*] on 11 Shaʿbān 1098/22 June 1687). At the same time, the hostilities with Venice had been reopened in the Morea [*q.v.*] and in the Archipelago.

All these disasters caused a revolt of the troops in the field; they marched on the capital in Dhu 'l-Ḳaᶜda 1098/September 1687 under Siyāwush Pasha of Aleppo. This time the sultan himself fell a victim to them, and was made to bear the responsibility for the defeats. To satisfy popular demands and to forestall further rebellions, Meḥemmed was deposed on 2 Muḥarram 1099/8 November 1687 by the *ḳāʾim-maḳām* Fāḍil Muṣṭafā Pasha Köprülü, the *Shaykh al-Islām* Dabbāgh-zāde Meḥmed Efendi and other religious dignitaries. He is said to have accepted the decision gracefully, and he retired to his beloved Edirne, dying there on 28 Rabīᶜ II 1104/6 January 1693. He was buried in Istanbul by the side of his mother in the Yeñi Djāmiᶜ.

Bibliography: 1. Primary sources. These include Naᶜīmā, ii; Kātib Čelebi, *Fedhleke*; Rāshid, *Taʾrīkh* (till 1070/1660); Ewliyā Čelebi, *Seyāḥat-nāme*; Silaḥdār Meḥmed Agha, *Taʾrīkh*; ᶜAbdī Pasha, *Wekāʾiᶜ-nāme*; Ḳara Čelebi-zāde ᶜAbd al-ᶜAzīz, *Rawḍat al-abrār*; Meḥmed Khalīfe, *Taʾrīkh-i Ghilmānī*. These, some still in ms., are utilised by M. Cavid Baysun in his *İA* art. *Mehmed IV*.

2. Secondary sources. European ones include P. Rycaut, *Histoire des trois derniers empereurs des Turcs depuis 1624 jusqu'à 1677*, Paris 1683; von Hammer, *GOR*, v-vi; Zinkeisen, iv-v; Jorga, iv; A. D. Alderson, *The structure of the Ottoman dynasty*, Oxford 1956, 65-6 and Tables XXXVII and XXXVIII; S. J. and Ezel Shaw, *History of the Ottoman empire and modern Turkey*, Cambridge 1976-7, i, 203-19. Of Turkish studies, see Aḥmed Refīḳ, *Felâket seneleri (1094-1110)*, Istanbul 1332/1914; idem, *Ḳadînlar salṭanatî*, Istanbul 1332-42/1914-24; I. H. Uzunçarşılı, *Osmanlı tarihi*, iii, Ankara 1951.

(J. H. Kramers*)

MEḤEMMED V RESHĀD, thirty-fifth and penultimate Ottoman Sultan, was born on 2 November 1844, the son of Sultan ᶜAbd al-Madjīd [*q.v.*].

During the reign of his brother ᶜAbd al-Ḥamīd II [*q.v.*] he lived in seclusion: his very existence inspired ᶜAbd al-Ḥamīd with such terror that even the mention of the name Reshād had to be avoided in his presence (cf. Snouck Hurgronje, *Verspreide Geschriften*, ii, 232). He was a man of mild character, who owed his accession to the throne (27 April 1909) to the victory of the Young Turks (the Committee of Union and Progress [see ittiḥād we teraḳḳī djemᶜiyyeti]) over the mutineers who had briefly ejected them from power in "the incident of 31 March" (13 April 1909 in the Gregorian calendar), and to their subsequent decision to depose ᶜAbd al-Ḥamīd II. Meḥemmed Reshād was a pious man; he felt particular sympathy for the Mewlewī Ṣūfī order (Ali Fuat Türkgeldi, *Görüp işittiklerim*, 123); he prized politeness and good food and enjoyed simple pleasures. As the first Ottoman constitutional monarch, he spent most of his reign doing the bidding of the Unionist party, which achieved total power in January 1913. He was twice called upon to second government policy: in 1911 he undertook a tour of Ottoman possessions in the Balkans, but was unable to prevent another Albanian rising; and after the outbreak of the First World War he proclaimed the *djihād* against the Allies, but did not sway their Muslim subjects. It can be said that he exerted no influence on the course of events during his reign. His residence, the Dolmabahçe Palace on the Bosporus, was as empty of visitors as the Yîldîz Palace had been full during the reign of his predecessor (Halid Ziya Uşaklıgıl, *Saray ve ötesi*, 134-6).

At the very beginning of his reign, Turkey lost her last vestige of authority over Bosnia and Herzegovina by Austria-Hungary's annexation, and over Bulgaria by its declaration of independence (5 October 1909). The cabinets under Ḥüseyn Ḥilmī (until 18 January 1910) and Ismāᶜīl Ḥaḳḳī Pasha [*q.v.*] (until 29 September 1911) were not able to bring about a peaceful situation in the interior (revolts in Albania and Yaman). Ḥaḳḳī Pasha had to resign as a result of the declaration of war by Italy. Under the grand vizierate of Saᶜīd Pasha [*q.v.*], the Italian war led to the loss of Tripoli, confirmed by the treaty of Ouchy (15 October 1912). Saᶜīd Pasha resigned, and when Sultan Meḥemmed Reshād asked him why he had done so, given that he had won a vote of confidence in the Chamber, he replied "They had confidence in me, but I had no confidence in them" (İbnülemin Mahmud Kemal İnal, *Osmanlı devrinde son sadrıazamlar*, vii, 1089). Peace was signed under the anti-Unionist cabinet of Aḥmed Mukhtār Pasha, but in the same month the Balkan states declared war on the Ottoman Empire. As Ottoman armies suffered immediate defeats, Aḥmed Mukhtār Pasha was forced to resign, and his successor, the veteran anti-Unionist statesman Kāmil Pasha soon showed an inclination to conclude a disastrous peace through the mediation of the European powers (Conference of London). Then in January 1913, a coup d'état brought in a Unionist government under Maḥmūd Shewket Pasha [*q.v.*]. Hostilities were reopened unsuccessfully, but the defeat of Bulgaria at the hands of its former Balkan allies allowed the Ottomans to recapture Edirne or Adrianople on 22 July 1913. In the meantime, Maḥmūd Shewket had been murdered (28 June) by anti-Unionists, but this did not loosen the Unionist grip on power; his place was taken by Saᶜīd Ḥalīm Pasha, whose government signed the peace treaties with Bulgaria (29 September 1913), Greece (14 November) and Serbia (14 March 1914). The Ottoman Empire thus lost all its European possessions west of the Meriç [*q.v.*] (Maritza) river, and also the Aegean islands and Crete.

However, it was not the grand vizier, but Unionist leaders like Enwer Bey and Ṭalᶜat Bey [*q.vv.*] who came to control the destiny of the Empire. Enwer's pro-German views triumphed over the hesitations of the government, which had decided to stay neutral when the First World War broke out. A secret treaty was signed with Germany; the German battleships *Goeben* and *Breslau* were given refuge in the Straits (where they were formally handed over to the Ottomans); and finally, the Ottoman fleet under the command of the German admiral Souchon bombarded Russian harbours in the Black Sea (29 and 30 October 1914). This led to the Allied declaration of war, in which Enwer Pasha became Deputy Commander-in-Chief (deputising nominally for the Sultan), while Ṭalᶜat Pasha became grand vizier in February 1917. Initial Ottoman offensives were repelled (Sarîkamîsh operation against the Russians; Suez operation against the British), but the Turks successfully defended the Dardanelles (the Allied forces which had landed on the Gallipoli peninsula were all withdrawn by January 1916); they were at first successful in ᶜIrāḳ (surrender of General Townshend at Kūt al-ᶜAmāra [*q.v.*], April 1916), and fought also in Palestine, Macedonia and Galicia. Before the end of the war, as Ottoman armies were being gradually worn down and while the country was prey to increasing privations, Meḥemmed V died on 2 July 1918. His last official functions were to welcome the Austro-

Hungarian Emperor Charles on a state visit to Istanbul in May, and, a few days before his death, to visit the Prophet's relics at the Topkapı Palace. He was a sad and ineffective figure: "Is Edirne ours?", he asked after the city had been recaptured; and his comment on the effects of the Great War was "The Palace excelled in two things: prayers and food. Both have gone off" (*Görüp işittiklerim*, 269, 268).

Bibliography: The events of the reign are related in all standard histories, e.g. S.J. Shaw and Ezel Kural Shaw, *History of the Ottoman empire and modern Turkey*, ii, Cambridge 1977; B. Lewis, *The emergence of modern Turkey*, Oxford 1961, and there are references to Meḥemmed V Re<u>sh</u>ād in many memoirs, especially those of his two Chief Secretaries: Halid Ziya Uşaklıgıl, *Saray ve ötesi*, Istanbul 1965, and Ali Fuad Türkgeldi, *Görüp işittiklerim*, Ankara 1951, and of his Chief Chamberlain, Lütfi Simavi, *Osmanlı sarayının son günleri*, Istanbul n.d. (the edition in modern Turkish of his *Sultan Mehmet Reşad ve halefinin sarayında gördüklerim*). The Sultan's decrees appointing grand viziers, as well as biographies and evaluations of the latter, are to be found in İbnülemin Mahmud Kemal İnal, *Osmanlı devrinde son sadrıazamlar*[2], Istanbul 1966. See also P. Mansel, *Sultans in their splendour: the last years of the Ottoman world*, London 1988; *İA* art. *Mehmed Reşad* (Enver Ziya Karal). (A. J. Mango)

MEḤEMMED VI WAḤĪD al-DĪN (Waḥdeddīn), thirty-sixth and last Ottoman Sultan, was born on 14 January 1861.

He was the son of Sultan ʿAbd al-Ma<u>dj</u>īd [*q.v.*] and succeeded to the throne on 3 July 1918, after the death of his brother Meḥemmed V Re<u>sh</u>ād [*q.v.*], the former heir to the throne Yūsuf ʿIzz al-Dīn, son of Sultan ʿAbd al-ʿAzīz, having died in 1916. In November of the same year, Waḥdeddīn, as the new heir, represented the Sultan at the funeral of the Austro-Hungarian Emperor Francis Joseph. In December 1917 he paid an official visit to Germany. On both occasions he made a favourable impression on his suite (on his German visit he was accompanied by Muṣṭafā Kemāl Pa<u>sh</u>a, the future founder of the Turkish Republic [see atatürk]). Waḥdeddīn was presumed to be critical of the Unionist party, in view of his closeness with his brother-in-law Dāmād Ferīd Pa<u>sh</u>a [*q.v.*], who was a leading member of the Liberal party (*Iʾtilāf ve Ḥürriyyet*) (Lütfi Simavi, *Osmanlı sarayının son günleri*, 265). Having reappointed the Unionist grand vizier Ṭalʿat Pa<u>sh</u>a on his accession, Waḥdeddīn accepted his resignation when the collapse of the Macedonian and southern fronts forced the Ottoman empire to seek an armistice with the victorious Allies. He sought to replace him by the veteran statesman Tewfīḳ Pa<u>sh</u>a, to whom Waḥdeddīn was related by marriage and whose loyalty to the dynasty he therefore trusted. However, as Tewfīḳ Pa<u>sh</u>a was unable to form a government, the Sultan appointed Marshal Aḥmed ʿIzzet Pa<u>sh</u>a, a veteran soldier known for his opposition to the war. The new grand vizier rejected Waḥdeddīn's suggestion that Dāmād Ferīd Pa<u>sh</u>a be included in the Ottoman delegation which signed the armistice agreement at Mudros [see mondros] on 30 October 1918. As the Allies prepared to occupy the remnants of the Empire, Aḥmed ʿIzzet Pa<u>sh</u>a fell foul of the palace and resigned as a result of his refusal to dismiss Unionist sympathisers from the cabinet. He was replaced first by Tewfīḳ Pa<u>sh</u>a and then on 4 March 1919 by Dāmād Ferīd Pa<u>sh</u>a, when the former was also seen as insufficiently diligent in rooting out Unionists.

The new grand vizier encouraged the Sultan in a policy of seeking to win the confidence of the Allies by meeting their demands. However, the decision of the Allies to allow Greek forces to land in Izmir on 15 May 1919 led to the growth of a Turkish national resistance movement which opposed the policy of appeasement pursued by the Sultan and his government. Muṣṭafā Kemāl Pa<u>sh</u>a, who was appointed by the Sultan as Inspector-General of the 9th (later 3rd) Army in Anatolia, and landed in Samsun on 19 May 1919, assumed the leadership of this movement. Having disregarded the order to return to Istanbul and having resigned from the army, Muṣṭafā Kemāl succeeded in cutting off Anatolia from the capital, thus forcing the resignation of Dāmād Ferīd Pa<u>sh</u>a on 5 October 1919. This was followed on 7 November by the election of a new parliament in which the nationalists were represented. The attempts of two subsequent grand viziers, ʿAlī Riḍā Pa<u>sh</u>a and Ṣāliḥ Pa<u>sh</u>a, to reach an accommodation with Muṣṭafā Kemāl's nationalists, who moved their headquarters to Ankara on 27 December, came to an end when the Allies placed Istanbul under military occupation on 16 March, and arrested a number of nationalist sympathisers. On 5 April, Waḥdeddīn re-appointed Dāmād Ferīd Pa<u>sh</u>a as grand vizier, overruling contrary advice with the words "If I so desire, I can appoint the Greek or the Armenian patriarch, or the Chief Rabbi" (Ali Fuad Türkgeldi, *Görüp işittiklerim*, 261). On 11 April the Sultan dissolved parliament, which had itself decided to adjourn. On the same day, the <u>*Shaykh*</u> *al-Islām* ʿAbd Allāh Dürrī-zāde issued a number of *fatwās* outlawing the nationalist resistance in Anatolia (texts in Ibnülemin Mahmud Kemal İnal, *Osmanlı devrinde son sadrıazamlar*, xiii, 2054-5).

Nevertheless, a number of deputies from the dissolved parliament made their way to Ankara and, together with other nationalist representatives, met as the Grand National Assembly (*Büyük Millet Me<u>dj</u>lisi*) on 23 April, which selected its own government (*I<u>dj</u>rāʾ Wekīlleri Heyʾeti*, Committee of Executive Commissioners) from among its own members. However, the Assembly sent a petition to Waḥdeddīn in which it proclaimed its loyalty to the Sultan and Caliph (extracts in Sabahattin Selek, *Anadolu ihtilâli*, Istanbul 1963, 289). As an open clash developed between the governments in Ankara and in Istanbul, the latter trying unsuccessfully to suppress the nationalist movement by sending troops against it and fomenting risings in Anatolia, Waḥdeddīn ratified on 24 May 1920 the death sentence passed *in absentia* on Muṣṭafā Kemāl. The signature by Ottoman delegates of the peace treaty of Sèvres on 10 August 1920 was repudiated by the Grand National Assembly. After the first major nationalist victory against the Greeks at the first battle of Inönü, the GNA voted a new constitution on 29 January 1921 which was based on popular sovereignty. Allied moves to establish contact with the Ankara government led to the resignation and departure for Europe of Dāmād Ferīd Pa<u>sh</u>a, drawing from the Sultan the comment "The rascal brought the state to these straits and then left" (*Son sadrıazamlar*, xiii, 2067). Tewfīḳ Pa<u>sh</u>a, who became grand vizier for the last time (21 October 1920), deferred to the representatives of the Ankara government at the unsuccessful London conference in February-March 1921.

The final success of the nationalists, whose forces defeated the Greeks and entered Izmir on 9 September 1922, brought about the armistice of Mudanya [*q.v.*] (11 October 1922), to which the Sultan's government was not a party. A nationalist commissioner, Reʾfet Pas̲h̲a, arrived in Istanbul and warned the Sultan to confine himself to the palace and receive no visitors, advice which the Sultan disregarded (*Son sadrıazamlar*, xiv, 2097-8). Matters were brought to a head when the Allies invited the Sultan's government, along with the Ankara government, to send delegates to the peace conference in Lausanne. Rejecting any rival government, the GNA passed a law on 1 November 1922, separating the offices of sultan and caliph, and declaring the Ottoman sultanate abolished from 16 March 1920 (the date of the Allied occupation of Istanbul). Tewfīḳ Pas̲h̲a resigned accordingly on 4 November. At his last *selāmlīḳ* on 10 November, which was attended by a handful of courtiers, Waḥdeddīn was given only the title of caliph in the *k̲h̲uṭba*. Believing his life to be in danger, he asked the British commander General Sir Charles Harington to arrange his departure abroad. He was smuggled aboard HMS *Malaya* and left Turkey on 17 November 1922. The next day, the GNA divested him of the caliphate, in favour of his uncle ʿAbd al-Mad̲j̲īd, son of Sultan ʿAbd al-ʿAzīz. Having gone first to Malta, the ex-Sultan proceeded to Mecca as the guest of King Ḥusayn. From here he launched a proclamation to the Islamic world, in which he maintained that the separation of the caliphate from the sultanate was contrary to the *s̲h̲arīʿa* (text in *OM*, ii, 702-5). This appeal found hardly any response in the Islamic world. The last Ottoman Sultan left Mecca again, and went to live in San Remo, where he died on 16 May 1926. In 1924, he had even recognised King Ḥusayn's claim to the caliphate.

Waḥdeddīn has been described by his courtiers as short-tempered, pious, intelligent, but fearful, hesitant and unwise in his judgments, above all in the trust which he placed in his brother-in-law Dāmād Ferīd Pas̲h̲a. Throughout his reign he paid lip-service to the Ottoman constitution, while being inspired by a desire to secure the survival of the dynasty. He had not studied Arabic and Persian, but was credited with a knowledge of *fiḳh*. He was fond of music, and composed Turkish songs. His failure to grow a beard after his accession was considered a break with tradition.

Bibliography: See the general histories of the period, especially S. J. Shaw and Ezel Kural Shaw, *History of the Ottoman empire and modern Turkey*, Oxford 1961; also Lord Kinross, *Atatürk: the rebirth of a nation*, London 1964, and P. Mansel, *Sultans in splendour*, London 1988. Reminiscences and documents are to be found in İbnülemin Mahmud İnal, *Osmanlı devrinde son sadrıazamlar*, xi-xiv (esp. xiv, 2095-2104), Istanbul 1965, and in the memoirs of the Sultan's Chief Chamberlain (*Bas̲h̲mabeyind̲j̲i*) Lütfi Simavi, *Osmanlı sarayının son günleri*, Istanbul n.d., and his Chief Secretary, Ali Fuad Türkgeldi, *Görüp işittiklerim*, Ankara 1951. See also *İA* art. *Mehmed Vahdettin* (Enver Ziya Karal).

(A. J. Mango)

MEḤKEME [see maḥkama].

MEḤMED, MEHMET. [On the use of these Turkish forms of the name Muḥammad in this *Encyclopaedia* see meḥemmed].

MEḤMED ʿĀKIF, modern Turkish Mehmet Akif Ersoy (1873-1936), Turkish poet, patriot and proponent of Pan-Islamism.

He was born in Istanbul of a father, Meḥmed Ṭāhir, originally from Ipek in northern Albania (modern Peć in Yugoslavia) and a mother of Buk̲h̲āran origin. He was educated in the classical Islamic tongues, Turkish, Arabic and Persian, in Istanbul, graduating from the Fātiḥ *rüs̲h̲diyye* or secondary school and continuing his higher education at the School of Political Science and then the Civilian Veterinary School. He served as a veterinary surgeon in the Ministry of Agriculture for 20 years, travelling extensively in Anatolia, the Balkans and the Arab lands, whilst at the same time teaching, including lecturing on literature at Istanbul University; and after his resignation from government service in 1913, he taught in various schools and preached in the mosques of Istanbul.

He had already shown an enthusiasm for Pan-Islamism at the time of the Young Turk Revolution and during the Balkan Wars of 1912-13, hence in 1915, during the First World War, when Turkey had entered the war on the side of the General Powers, ʿĀkif was invited to visit Germany by the Kaiser's government to study and report on the state of Muslim prisoners-of-war in that country; this trip gave him his first contact with the West and its differing attitudes and conditions from those of the Islamic East. Then in 1917 he was sent by the Committee of Union and Progress [see ittiḥād we teraḳḳī d̲j̲emʿiyyeti], after the outbreak of the S̲h̲arīf Ḥusayn of Mecca's revolt, on a mission to the pro-Turkish Āl Ras̲h̲īd of Ḥāʾil in Nad̲j̲d. He further became Secretary-General of the *Dār ül-Ḥikmet ül-Islāmiyye* attached to the *S̲h̲eyk̲h̲ ül-Islām*'s office, but lost his post in 1919 when he called for resistance against the Greek forces entering Anatolia in the wake of the October 1918 Mudros Armistice. He now threw in his lot with the Nationalist cause under Muṣṭafā Kemāl (Atatürk) [*q.v.*], and joined the Grand National Assembly (GNA) in Ankara in 1920 as deputy for Burdur. In the following year, the Nationalist Minister of Education, Ḥamdullāh Ṣubḥī Tanrıöver (1886-1966), persuaded ʿĀkif to compose a stirring Independence March (*Istiḳlāl mars̲h̲ī*), which was immediately adopted as the Turkish National anthem. He was still concerned, also, with religious affairs, as a member of an Islamic research committee (*Tedḳīḳat we teʾlīfat-i islāmiyye end̲j̲ümeni*) in the Ministry of *S̲h̲arīʿa* and *Ewḳāf*. But as a devout Muslim and convinced Pan-Islamist, he became increasingly concerned about the trend of events after the Nationalist triumph, with the abolition of the caliphate in March 1924, the abolition of the office of *S̲h̲eyk̲h̲ ül-Islām*, of the Ministry of *S̲h̲arīʿa* and *Ewḳāf*, and of the *S̲h̲arīʿa* itself, and of the closing of all the *madrasa*s in the spring of 1924. Unlike the ideologist of Pan-Turkism, Ḍiyāʾ (Ziya) Gök Alp [*q.v.*], ʿĀkif was unable to adjust his ideas to the new, secularist Nationalist ideals, for he had still hoped that the new Turkey could be the focus of Pan-Islamic aspirations.

In the 1923 elections, he did not get a seat in the GNA, and at the age of 50 was jobless and virtually pensionless. Hence in October of that year, he left for Egypt to stay with an old friend, the Egyptian Prince ʿAbbās Ḥalīm (d. 1934), and in 1925 settled there, teaching Turkish in Cairo, but by now, as a disappointed man, producing little of his own literary work. He returned to Istanbul after eleven years, a sick man, and died there on 27 December 1936.

Already as a student, ʿĀkif had been a voracious reader of the Islamic classics, with a particular love for the poetry of Fuḍūlī, Ibn Fāriḍ and above all Saʿdī, and also of French Romantic literature. He published Turkish translations of the Persian classics in the *T̲h̲erwet-i Fünūn* from 1898 onwards, and his own poetry in the *Resimli Gazete* from 1896 onwards. After 1904, he seems really to have found his artistic feet, and he began to write poetry on social themes, showing a sympathy with the depressed classes of society, but was unable to publish these in the period of the Ḥamīdian censorship, until the Revolution of July 1908 opened the floodgates for publication. ʿĀkif and his friend Eshref Edīb began to publish the *Ṣirāṭ-ī Müstaḳīm*, a conservative journal concentrating on religious and social topics; this periodical soon began to have a wide circulation amongst the Turkish peoples outside the Ottoman lands, including in Russia, and later changed its name to the *Sebīl ür-Reshād*. At the same time as he put forward his ideas of Pan-Islamism, he also acquired an interest in Islamic modernism, studying the works of Muḥammad ʿAbduh and of Djamāl al-Dīn al-Afghānī [*q.vv.*]. The popularity of new ideas, such as Pan-Turkism and Pan-Turanianism, Ottomanism and Westernism, in the ferment of ideas preceding the First World War, forced him to rethink and clarify his own principles; but he never compromised his view that the unity of Islam came before separate nationalisms.

From 1911 onwards, he began publishing collections of his poetry as *Ṣafaḥāt* ("Phases"), with a total of seven volumes, the last, entitled *Gölgeler* ("Shadows") containing his work done during the years 1918-33. In these collections, he used a simple Turkish style, and often dwelt on such themes as the present state and future destiny of Islam and on contemporary events. In *Ṣafaḥāt*, v, *Khāṭiralar* ("Memories") (1335/1917), he attacked "westernisers" and "progressives" who slavishly imitated everything, good or bad, drawn from the West, and especially the poet Tewfīḳ Fikret (d. 1915), whose atheistic poem *Taʾrīkh-i ḳadīm* ("Ancient history") he regarded as corrupting Turkish youth. ʿĀkif also engaged in translating the Ḳurʾān into Turkish, and this remains a controversial episode in his life. The successor to the Ministry of *Sharīʿa*, the Directorate of Religious Affairs (*Diyānet Ishleri Riyāseti*) decided to commission a new translation of and commentary on the Ḳurʾān. ʿĀkif was persuaded, with some misgivings connected with his firm belief in the basic untranslatability of the Holy Book, to undertake the actual translation, but after spending several years of his stay in Egypt at the task, retracted what he had written, fearing that his translation might be used as part of Atatürk's Turkicisation plans in religious matters; the eventual fate of his translation remains a mystery to this day.

Meḥmed ʿĀkif was thus an enthusiastic Muslim but not a fanatic, a conservative in politics who nevertheless openly proclaimed his detestation of ʿAbd ül-Ḥamīd II and Meḥemmed VI and who joined the Nationalist cause; nor did his conservative inclinations prevent him from appreciating Western literature and even Western classical music.

Bibliography: Süleymān Naẓīf, *Meḥmed ʿĀkif*, Istanbul 1924; İbnülemin M. K. İnal, *Son asır türk şairleri*, Istanbul 1931, 91 ff.; M. C. Kuntay, *Mehmet Akif*, Istanbul 1939; Eşref Edib, *Mehmed Akif*, 2 vols., Istanbul 1938-9, 2nd edn. 1962; F. A. Tansel, *Mehmed Akif, hayatı ve eserleri*², Istanbul 1973; Fahir İz, *Meḥmed Ākif Ersoy, a biography*, in *Turkish Studies: Continuity and Change*, no. 1, Boğazıçı University, Istanbul 1987. The Introd. by Ömer Riza Doğrul (ʿĀkif's son-in-law) to the roman script edn. of the *Ṣafaḥāt* contains biographical notes of the poet left to his friend Nevzad Ayas, see 10th edn., ed. Ertuğrul Düzdağ, Istanbul 1975, pp. XI-XXII, ʿĀkif's private letters to Mahir İz, his student and friend, and Mahir İz's oral communications to the author. Eşref Edib's book contains almost complete bibliographical data on ʿĀkif's poems, articles, translations, etc. (FAHIR İZ)

MEḤMED ʿALI PASHA [see MUḤAMMAD ʿALĪ PASHA].

MEḤMED ʿĀSHİḲ [see ʿĀSHİḲ].

MEḤMED BĀGHČESARĀYĪ, surnamed THANĀʾĪ (d. after 13 Shaʿbān 1061/1 August 1651), Crimean Tatar author of the history of Khān Islām Girāy III from his arrival in Kaffa and his enthronement in Bāghčesarāyi̊ (1 and 5 Djumādā I 1054/6 and 10 July 1644 respectively) until the spring of 1651.

He had been formerly *munshī-yi dīwān-i khāḳānī* at the khān's court; the excellent Turkish of his work may be a proof that he was educated in Istanbul and was responsible for the khān's correspondence with the Ottoman court. Charged by Sefer Ghāzī Agha with the task of compiling the history of the khān's successful rule, he created a panegyric adorned with his own Turkish and Persian verses, founded in the historical part on the diaries of the three Tatar-Cossack expeditions against Poland of 1648-9 and other materials given him presumably by this vizier. It was finished on 1 August 1651, but the author did not mention even the preparations for a new Tatar expedition against Poland which ended with the khān's and his Cossack allies' defeat at Beresteczko, 28-30 June of the same year. The information about the very origins of Islām Girāy III's alliance with B. Chmielnicki of 1648 is rather unsatisfactory. The diaries of the expeditions of 1648-9 are additionally important sources of the now forgotten Turkic toponyms, as much in the Crimea as in the steppes and in the Ukraine. This work, hitherto not mentioned in the history of the Crimean Tatar literature, throws a new light on the culture of the khanate of Crimea and on Khān Islām Girāy III's political and cultural aspirations. It is preserved only in a copy from 1092/1681, now in the British Library.

Bibliography: Ch. Rieu, *Catalogue of the Turkish Manuscripts in the British Museum*, London 1888, 250-1; Babinger, *Geschichtsschreiber*, 236, no. 206 (who erroneously takes this work for a copy of the *Taʾrīkh* by Meḥmed Girāy); Hadży Mehmed Senai z Krymu, *Historia chana Islam Gereja III*. Tekst turecki wydał, przełożył i opracował Zygmunt Abrahamowicz. Uzupełniający komentarz historyczny: Olgierd Górka i Zbigniew Wójcik ["Ḥādjdjī Meḥmed Thanāʾī of Crimea, The history of Khān Islām Girāy III. Turkish text published, translated and commented by Z. Abrahamowicz. Additional historical annotations by O. Górka and Z. Wójcik"], Warsaw 1971.

(Z. ABRAHAMOWICZ)

MEḤMED BALṬADJİ [see MEḤMED PASHA BALṬADJİ].

MEḤMED ČELEBI [see GHAZĀLĪ, MEḤMED].

MEḤMED EMĪN, in modern Turkish Mehmet Emin Yurdakul (1869-1944), Turkish poet and patriot, the pioneer of modern Turkish poetry in spoken Turkish and syllabic metre. He was born in the Beshiktash district of Istanbul on 13 May 1869. The family originated from Zekeriyyā Köyü, a village near Lake Terkos, in Eastern Thrace, some 30 miles north-west of Istanbul. His grandfather Ḥalīm Agha was a trawler owner. His father Ṣāliḥ Agha, later called Ṣāliḥ Reʾīs (Captain) when he owned a large trawler rowed by several men, was an illiterate fisherman and his mother a peasant woman from a village near Edirne. They both possessed a rich store of oral folk literature which they transmitted to their son. Meḥmed Emīn attended a primary school and the military secondary school (*rüshdiyye-yi ʿaskeriyye*) in Beshiktash, then registered at a civilian *Lycée* (*ʿidādī*) which he did not finish. He continued his education, as was still possible at that time, by serving, without pay, in the chancery of the office of the grand vizierate (*Ṣadāret Ewrāḳ Ḳalemi*). In 1888 he married Müzeyyen Khānïm, from a notable family of Ḳara-Ḥiṣār-ï Sharḳī (modern Şebinkarahisar), in north-eastern Anatolia, which he visited several times, sometimes for long periods and where he enriched his observations on the plight of the Anatolian peasantry. In 1889 he registered at the School of Law (*Mekteb-i ḥuḳūḳ*) which he abandoned two years later for an opportunity of studying further in America, which did not however materialise. While still a student in the Law School, he published his first book (see below) and sent a copy to the grand vizier Djewād Pasha [*q.v.*], on whose recommendation he was appointed (1890) as a clerk of the secretariat of the Custom's office (*Rüsūmāt emāneti taḥrīrāt ḳalemi*). Two years later he became director of the archives (*ewrāḳ müdīri*) of the same office, where he remained for 15 years. In 1907, he became a member of the secret revolutionary Committee of Union and Progress (CUP [see ITTIḤĀD WE TERAḲḲĪ DJEMᶜIYYETI]). The same year, he was sent to Erzurum, in Eastern Anatolia, as superintendent of the customs (*rüsūmāt nāẓïrï*) which, under the Ḥamīdian régime, amounted to political exile. The Sultan had become suspicious of his choice of subjects in his poems, particularly his insistence on the poor (see below).

After the restoration of the Constitution in July 1908, he was transferred to Trabzon with the same office. After a short service as counsellor at the Ministry of Marine and as governor (*wālī*) of the Ḥidjāz (1909) and Sivas (1910), he resigned and joined in Istanbul the Turkist movement (see B. Lewis, *Emergence*², 343-52 and TÜRKDJÜLÜK) and was made president of the Turkish Hearth [see TÜRK ODJAGHÏ] in 1911. He soon set up another Turkist association, the *Türk Yurdu* ("Turkish Home"). As he was preparing to publish the organ of the association, with the same name, which later became famous as the organ of the Turkish Hearths [see TÜRK YURDU], he was appointed governor of Erzurum. In the meantime, he expressed, in many writings, his disappointment with the CUP and his disagreement with many arbitrary and despotic actions of the administration. He was retired from Government service in 1912. Elected deputy for Mawṣil (Mosul), he settled in Istanbul and continued his literary and patriotic activities. He witnessed the collapse of the Empire and the occupation of Istanbul by the Allies. He joined the Nationalist government of Ankara in April 1921, which sent him on a special mission to Antalya and Adana where he stayed until the end of the War of Liberation, when he went to Izmir to join Muṣṭafā Kemāl Pasha (Atatürk [*q.v.*]) with whom he returned to Ankara (September 1922). He was elected deputy for Sharḳī Ḳaraḥiṣār. Later, he continued to serve in Parliament as deputy for Urfa and Istanbul. He died in Istanbul on 14 January 1944. During the last years of his life, he had been collaborating with the Turkish Historical Society in Ankara (to which he donated all his personal archives) to prepare a revised and critical edition of his complete works (see *Bibl.*).

Meḥmed Emīn who, following the law on surnames, took in 1934 the family name of Yurdakul ("slave of the fatherland"), was known in his lifetime as *Millī shāᶜir* or *Türk shāᶜiri Meḥmed Emīn* ("Meḥmed Emīn, the national poet or Turkish poet *par excellence*"), as he consistently wrote in the spoken Turkish of ordinary people and used exclusively the syllabic metre of folk poets as opposed to the Arabo-Persian prosody (*ᶜarūḍ*) of both old and most modern poets of his day [see BÖLÜKBASHÏ, RÏḌĀ TEWFĪḲ, in Suppl.] and devoted all his literary work to his country and its people, their plight, their misfortunes and their glories, completely leaving out his own personality and private life. He published his first book (a short essay), while a law student in 1308 A.H./1891, *Faḍīlet we aṣālet* ("Virtue and nobility)", in which he claims that real virtue and nobility are not necessarily hereditary but are rather obtained by a person's talent, diligence and spiritual maturity. As was customary at the time, he sent the draft to several literary authorities, who all wrote complimentary *taḳrīẓ*s (presentation pieces) which were printed with the book. Meḥmed Emīn's first published poem *Köyde fïrtïna* ("Storm in the village") appeared in *Resimli Ghazete* of 5 October 1311 A.H./17 October 1895, which was confiscated before distribution (Aḳčuraoghlu Yūsuf, *Türk yïlï*, Istanbul 1928, 387, where the date is wrongly given as 1903); it was reprinted in *Muḳtebes*, no. 10, 1317 A.H./1900. This remarkable poem, with its social implications and which contains most of the characteristics of his later poems, with typical language, style and content, was written as the height of the famous westernist *Therwet-i Fünūn* [*q.v.*] literary movement, which was linguistically conservative to the degree of preciosity and which disdained the "finger counting" (*parmaḳ ḥisābï*) metre of the "ignorant bards". Although almost all the sources, including the poet himself, assert otherwise, it seems chronologically probable that the young poet read this particular poem to Djamāl al-Dīn al-Afghānī [*q.v.*], who recommended him to continue (see below). Several poems of the same type, published in various periodicals, including in the *Therwet-i Fünūn* itself, immediately before and during the April-September 1897 war with Greece, particularly the one called *Anadoludan bir ses yākhud djenge giderken* ("A voice from Anatolia, or Going to war") published previously but in the same year in the newspaper *ᶜAṣïr* ("Century") in Salonica, made a sensation in Turkey, among the Muslim Turks in Russia and among orientalists abroad (see *Bibl.*; for a correct text of this poem, see Nüzhet Hāshim, *Millī edebiyyata doghru*, Istanbul 1918, 6).

Although there was a long but often ignored tradition of simple, straightforward Turkish prose (see Fahir İz, *Ottoman and Turkish*, in *Essays in Islamic civilisation presented to Niyazi Berkes*, ed. D. P. Little, Leiden 1976, 118-39), a similar but occasional movement to write simple, pure, common or exclusive Turkish (*basīṭ, sāde, ḳaba, ṣïrf, yalñïz türkdje*) verse always existed also (for a detailed discussion of this subject, see Köprülü-zāde Meḥmed Fuᵓād, *Millī edebiyyāt djereyānïnïn ilk mübeshshirleri we dīwān-ï türkī-yi basīṭ*, Istanbul 1928, Roman script edition in *Edebiyat araştırmaları*, published by T.T.K., Ankara 1966, 271-315). The *Tanẓīmāt* writers claimed that simple, everyday Turkish was necessary to communicate with the public, but did not apply their principle except in a few pieces. The revolutionary and journalist ᶜAlī Suᶜāwī [*q.v.*] and the publicist and novelist Aḥmed Midḥat [*q.v.*] did write a remarkably simple language, and their associates gave occasional examples of simple Turkish verse. But as the famous lexicographer and writer Shems el-Dīn Sāmī [*q.v.*], who was the most conscious and advanced of them, admitted in an article, greeting the publication of Meḥmed Emīn's first book of poems *Türkdje shiᶜrler* ("Poems in Turkish") (see below), "...although they (the *Tanẓīmāt* writers) talked and wished to write in simple Turkish, it was Meḥmed Emīn who carried it out, and this book was the foundation stone of future Turkish literature" (*Sabah*, 1 March 1313 *Rūmī*/13 March 1899). The British orientalist E.J.W. Gibb congratulated Meḥmed Emīn warmly in a letter in Turkish of 6 June 1899, in which he said "... The Turk has found his natural voice... your predecessors imitated the Persians and the French. You expressed the feeling of your countrymen in their own language... Six centuries have been waiting for you" (the original letter is in the Meḥmed Emīn Archives, in the Turkish Historical Society, Ankara). Like the sporadic examples in the *dīwāns* of the 18th century poets Nedīm [*q.v.*] and G̲h̲ālib Dede [*q.v.*] and in most of the 19th century poets, there seems to be a latent desire to express themselves occasionally in everyday Turkish and sometimes in syllabic metre. These examples seem to multiply particularly in the works of minor poets during the last decades of the century [see TURKS. LITERATURE]. However, as S̲h̲ems el-Dīn Sāmī points out in the above-mentioned article, Meḥmed Emīn's work was not a random experiment. It was the beginning of a conscientious, systematic and lasting movement. So much so that his colleague and biographer Aḳčuraog̲h̲lu Yūsuf [see YŪSUF, AḲČURA] says that *A voice from Anatolia* can be called the manifesto of linguistic Turkism (Aḳčuraog̲h̲lu, *op. cit.*, 391). This current was enriched with the deeply felt lyricism and more inspired poems of Rīḍā Tewfīḳ (Bölükbas̲h̲ī), who, during the ensuing violent controversy between the partisans of simple Turkish and those who supported the fashionable *Mischsprache* of the leading poets and writers, became his most enthusiastic defender (see Nüzhet Hās̲h̲im, *op. cit.*, 7-10; Aḳčuraog̲h̲lu, *op. cit.*, 387-91). This "simple Turkish" movement spread to the provinces and was supported by several minor writers, including Meḥmed Nedjīb (see Tahir Alangu, *Ömer Seyfettin*, Istanbul 1968, *passim*) who had launched a similar movement independently in Izmir, culminated in April 1911, in Salonica, with the "New language" (*Yeñi lisān*) movement of ʿÖmer Seyf el-Dīn [*q.v.*] which Ḍiyāʾ (Ziya) Gökalp [*q.v.*] espoused and propagated among young poets and writers, setting up a new literary current, the "National literature" (*millī edebiyyāt djereyānī*) [see TURKS. LITERATURE]. Meḥmed Emīn candidly admits his association with Djamāl al-Dīn al-Afg̲h̲ānī and the latter's influence on the development of his ideas. The standard biographies of the S̲h̲ayk̲h̲ are usually silent on his unofficial Turkish connections (see, e.g., Nikki R. Keddie, *Sayyid Jamāl ad-Dīn "al-Afg̲h̲ānī", a political biography*, Berkeley, 1972). But this influence has been much exaggerated by later biographers and critics. In the early years of al-Afg̲h̲ānī's second sojourn in Istanbul (July 1892-March 1897), Meḥmed Emīn, then in his mid-twenties, was one of the many young intellectuals—Turks, Persians and Arabs—who flocked twice a week to the Mansion (*kös̲h̲k*) in Nis̲h̲āntas̲h̲ī, not far from the Imperial Palace, which the Sultan ʿAbd ül-Ḥamīd II assigned to him, giving also a monthly allowance. Meḥmed ʿĀkif [*q.v.*], M. S̲h̲ems el-Dīn (Günaltay) [see S̲h̲EMS EL-DĪN] and Meḥmed Emīn were among the more assiduous Turks. It is reported in most Turkish sources (see *Bibl.*) and summarised by his close friend Aḳčuraog̲h̲lu (*op. cit.*, 374 ff. and *passim*) and the noted educationist Ismāʿīl Ḥaḳḳī Balṭadjīog̲h̲lu [see ISMĀʿĪL ḤAḲḲĪ in Suppl.], who interviewed the poet six months before his death (İ. H. Baltacı-og̲h̲lu, *Mehmed Emin Yurdakul ile konuştum*, in *Yeni Adam*, no. 452 [26 August 1943], Istanbul) and repeated by many later authors including Uluğ İğdemir, F.A. Tansel and Kenan Akyüz (see *Bibl.*),

that al-Afg̲h̲ānī told his young circle of friends that the writers of the individual Muslim countries should write with the simple vernacular of their people in order to alert them against despotism, social evils and foreign domination and that he (Meḥmed Emīn), like most young men who frequented al-Afg̲h̲ānī's house, owed much to his illuminating conversation and to his constant encouragement. He adds, however, "I was mainly inspired by my own God on my own Mount Sinai and transferred my revelations to my works" (for al-Afg̲h̲ānī's second sojourn in Turkey, see Keddie, *op. cit.*, ch. "The final years 1892-1897: Istanbul"). The circumstances of the last three years of al-Afg̲h̲ānī's life (he died of cancer of the jaw, after a long illness and three operations, on 9 March 1897) make the close relationship, reported in the sources, during the period when Meḥmed Emīn wrote his most famous poems (April-September 1897), chronologically impossible. It seems that a legend, based on a confusion by the poet, has survived until the present day.

Strictly speaking, Meḥmed Emīn had no literary masters or followers. The movement which he had started, and which was sincerely defended by Rīḍā Tewfīḳ, was followed up by the latter and by the next generation, in a new style and inspiration more akin to the technique and spirit of the traditional folk (*saz*, *ʿās̲h̲īḳ*) and popular mystic (*derwīs̲h̲*) poetry. His own work is to-day appreciated more for its historico-literary importance than its intrinsic value.

Meḥmed Emīn is the author of the following major works:

1. *Türkdje s̲h̲iʿrler* ("Poems in Turkish") Istanbul 1316 A.H./1898;
2. *Türk sazî* ("Turkish *saz*"), Istanbul 1330 *rūmī*/1914, contains 191 poems written between 1898 and 1914, most of them published previously in different periodicals. Two of them are taken from the preceding. The majority of the poems dwell upon social problems. Some are inspired by the Pan-Turkist movement of the second decade of the century.

The following three works contain patriotic poems written during the First World War:

3. *Ey Türk uyan* ("Turk, wake up"), Istanbul 1330 *rūmī*/1914;
4. *Tan sesleri* ("Voices of dawn"), Istanbul 1331 *rūmī*/1915; and
5. *Ordunuñ destânî* ("The epic of the army"), Istanbul 1334 *rūmī*/1918.
6. *Tūrāna dog̲h̲ru* ("Towards Tūrān"), poems written during the last years of the First World War and inspired by Pan-Turanism.

The following two works contain his poems written during the War of Liberation (1919-22):

7. *Aydîn ḳîzlarî* ("The daughters of Aydîn"), Ankara 1921, 3rd edn. as *Mustafa Kemal*, Istanbul 1928; and
8. *Ankara*, Istanbul 1939.

Meḥmed Emīn's other poems, published in various periodicals but not included in his books, have been collected in F.A. Tansel (see *Bibl.*).

Bibliography: In addition to references given in the article, see Köprülü-zāde Meḥmed Fuʾād, *Meḥmed Emīn Beg*, in *Newsāl-i Millī*, Istanbul 1330 *rūmī*/1914, 159-61; Rūs̲h̲en Es̲h̲ref, *Diyorlarki*, Istanbul 1918, 157-67 and *passim*; Rīḍā Tewfīḳ, *Emīn Beg we Emīn Beg türkdjesi*, in *Türk Yurdu*, i/4 (1912); Uluğ İğdemir, *Mehmet Emin Yurdakul*, in *Aylık Ansiklopedi*, no. 10 (February 1945), 321-3; Ahmet İhsan, *Matbuat hatıralarım*, i, Istanbul 1930, 10 ff.; Kenan Akyüz, *Batı tesirinde Türk şiiri antolojisi*[3], Ankara

1970, 499-533; Agâh Sirri Levend, *Türk dilinde gelişme ve sadeleşme evreleri*[3] Ankara 1972, index; B. Lewis, *The emergence of modern Turkey*[2], Oxford 1968; Hilmi Ziya Ülken, *Türkiye'de çağdaş düşünce tarihi*[2], Istanbul 1979, index; Fevziye Abdullah Tansel, *Mehmed Emin Yurdakul'un eserleri. I. Şiirler*, T.T.K. Ankara 1969 (based on two files, prepared by the poet himself, in collaboration with Uluğ İğdemir of the Turkish Historical Society; contains M.E.'s collected works in verse with his own corrections and alterations. A promised second volume, which should contain a detailed biography, his prose writings and his translations, has not yet [November 1984] been published); for al-Afghānī's Turkish connections, see Osman Ergin, *Türkiye maarif tarihi*, Istanbul 1939, passim; Osman Keskioğlu, *Cemâleddin Efgânî*, in *İlâhiyat Fakültesi Dergisi*, x (1962), 91-102; Niyazi Berkes, *The development of secularism in Turkey*, Montreal 1964, index; for translations from M.E.'s works into foreign languages, see O. Spies, *Die moderne türkische Literatur*, in *Handbuch der Orientalistik*, v/1, Leiden 1963, 360 ff. (Fahir İz)

MEḤMED ESʿAD [see esʿad efendi; ghālib dede].

MEḤMED GIRĀY, Derwīsh Meḥmed Girāy b. Mübārek Girāy Čingizī, member of the Crimean Girāy [*q.v.*] dynasty, probably a brother of Khān Murād Girāy (1678-83) and historian. His chronicle, *Taʾrīkh-i Meḥmed Girāy*, preserved in the unique ms. H.O. 86, Austrian National Library, Vienna (Flügel, *Catalogue*, ii, 277-8), deals with Ottoman and Crimean history from 1094/1682 to 1115/1703, from Ḳara Muṣṭafā's unsuccessful Viennese campaign to Sultan Aḥmed III's accession to the throne, covering the reigns of the Crimean khāns from Murād Girāy to Selīm I Girāy (third reign, 1702-4); it was finished in Radjab 1115/Nov.-Dec. 1703. Written in clumsy Ottoman Turkish and being of narrow scope, it nevertheless offers an interesting view of Ottoman history in a critical phase by a Crimean prince; some passages, describing events in which the author took part, have the value of a primary source.

Bibliography: Von Hammer, *GOR*, vi, p. VI, ix, 206-7; idem, *Geschichte der Chane der Krim unter osmanischer Herrschaft*, Vienna 1856, 9; Babinger, *GOW*, 235-6; Z. Abrahamowicz, *Kara Mustafa pod Wiedniem*, Cracow 1973; M. Köhbach, *Der Tārīḫ-i Meḥemmed Giray—eine osmanische Quelle zur Belagerung Wiens durch die Türken im Jahre 1683*, in *Studia Austro-Polonica*, iii, Warsaw-Cracow 1983, 137-64. (M. Köhbach)

MEḤMED GIRĀY I, khān of the Crimea from Dhu 'l-Ḥidjdja 920/Feb. 1515 to Dhu 'l-Ḥidjdja 929/October-November 1523.

He was the eldest son, heir-apparent (*ḳalghay* [*q.v.*]), and successor of Menglī Girāy I. According to *Gülbün-i khānān*, Istanbul 1287/1870, 11, the title *ḳalghay* goes back to Menglī Girāy I, who appointed Meḥmed Girāy as his deputy. The relationship between the Crimean khānate and the Ottoman Empire was at that time still largely a corollary of the relationship between their respective rulers. Meḥmed Girāy remained khān until his death, although he was an inveterate opponent of his sovereign, Sultan Selīm I [*q.v.*], who was distracted by his wars against Persia and the Mamlūks. The rising Muscovite state under the Grand Prince Vasiliy III (1505-33) had created a new power among the heirs of the Golden Horde. Meḥmed Girāy reacted by alternately allying himself with Poland-Lithuania and Muscovy, and by interfering in the dynastic affairs of Ḳāzān and Astrakhān [*q.vv.*]. He also tried to dominate the nomadic Nogay [*q.v.*] tribes of the region. In 1521 he refused Sultan Süleymān Ḳānūnī's [*q.v.*] order to join him in a campaign against Hungary, and instead, led a great expedition against Muscovy, which so far had been on friendly terms with the Ottomans. Meḥmed Girāy's lifelong struggle for a new steppe empire remained without lasting success. He was temporarily able to impose the Crimean claim to the throne of Ḳāzān through his own brother (1521), but lost his life in a plot which he had devised to chase the Muscovite candidate from the throne of Astrakhān (1523). Abandoned by the Crimean nobility, whom he had alienated by his ruthlessness, disloyalty and dissolute life, he was massacred by his Nogay allies.

Bibliography: The main source for Meḥmed Girāy I is A. Bennigsen *et alii* (eds.), *Le Khanat de Crimée dans les Archives du Musée du Palais de Topkapı*, Paris 1978, with further references; V. D. Smirnov, *Krymskoe khanstvo pod verkhovenstvom otomanskoy portî do načala XVIII veka*, St. Petersburg 1887; S. M. Solov'ev, *Istoriya Rossii s drevneyshikh vremen*, iii, Moscow 1960, s.v. *Magmet-Girej*, based on N. M. Karamzin's history of the Russian Empire. (B. Kellner-Heinkele)

MEḤMED ḤĀKIM EFENDI, 18th century Ottoman literary personality, statesman and official court chronicler (*waḳʿa-nüwīs*).

Born in Istanbul, his father was *seyyid* Khalīl Efendi, known as "Emīr Čelebi the knife-maker (*bičaḳdjî*)". Meḥmed pursued his education under well-known scholars such as Yanyalî Esʿad Khōdja and Bursalî Ismāʿīl Ḥaḳḳī, received a certificate of competence in calligraphy from Suyoldju-zāde Nedjīb Efendi, author of the *Dewḥat al-küttāb*, spent some fifteen years in Egypt and became an adept of Sezāʾī Ḥasan Efendi, founder of the Sezāʾī branch of the Gülshenī mystical order (*ṭarīḳat*). Despite having completed a very specialised training, Meḥmed decided to forego a career in the theological field and instead filled successive positions as trainee (*khalīfe*) in the secretarial bureau of the Grand Vizierate, beginning in 1155/1742 as assistant to the chief at the Arsenal (*tersāne*), followed in quicker succession by posts such as bureau chief in the treasury department of imperial estates (*khāṣṣlar muḳāṭaʿadjîsî*) in 1164/1753, chief secretary of the regiment of the armourers (*djebedjiler kātibi*) in 1172/1759, chief secretary of the cavalry regiments (*sipāhiler kātibi*) in 1174/1761, and a second appointment as *djebedjiler kātibi* in 1176/1763.

In addition to these secretarial positions in the departments of the treasury, Ḥākim was appointed official court chronicler (*waḳʿa-nüwīs*) from 1 Redjeb 1166/4 May 1753, when this position was vacated through the incumbent ʿIzzī Süleymān Efendi's resignation prior to his performing the pilgrimage to Mecca. Ḥākim strove to record all the events from the date of his appointment in 1753 until his resignation in mid-1180/October-November 1766. Four years later, on the night of Reghāʾib 1184/25-6 October 1770, he died and was buried in the cemetery of Ayrîlîḳ Česhmesi in Ḥaydar Pasha (see B. Kütükoğlu, *Müverrih Vâsıf'ın kaynaklarından Hâkim tarihi*, in *Tarih Dergisi*, v/8 [1953], 70 ff.).

Meḥmed Ḥākim's command of both Arabic and Persian and his ability of composing poetical and other literary works was recognised by his contemporaries (see the lists of his works in Bursalî Meḥmed Ṭāhir, *ʿOthmānlî müʾellifleri*, Istanbul 1333, ii, 142, and Kütükoğlu, *op. cit.*, 74-5. See also *Rūḥī-i Baghdādī terkīb-i bendine naẓīre*, Ist. Univ. Libr. İbnülemin 3352, fols. 100b-105a; the *Nafḥat al-dhāt wa 'l-ṣifāt*, a commentary in verse on one of ʿAṭṭār's mystical works, Millet, Emîrî *manzum* 940 (the autograph copy); and the *Miʿrādjiyye*, Cambridge Or. 1268, and Süleymaniye, Hacı Mahmud Efendi 4477. For two collective works (*medjmūʿa*) containing poetical works and treatises in Ḥākim's own hand, see İbnülemin 3144 and Süleymaniye, Esad Ef. 3495); but it is nonetheless chiefly through his history writing as official court historian that Ḥākim gained his literary fame. In this, written in a very ornate style and ponderous language, Ḥākim gives special emphasis to events in the capital and the palace, in particular, to audiences with the sultan, court protocol, appointments and dismissals, natural disasters such as fires and earthquakes experienced in the capital and reconstruction efforts after these disasters; but, albeit infrequently, he also touches on developments in the provinces, news of which reached the palace, and reports the content of texts submitted by Ottoman ambassadors on their return from foreign assignments.

Portions of Ḥākim's history are preserved in the form of final revisions in the author's own hand (*tebyīḍ*) in several different locations. The events of 1166-79 are covered in the fourth revision now found in the İbnülemin collection (ms. 2472), while the fifth revision of vol. i covering the years 1166-70 is preserved in the library of the Istanbul Archaeological Museum (ms. 483). A continuation in rough draft form covering the years 1171-6 is also found in the same collection (ms. 484). A complete set of volumes covering the entire period from Muḥarrem 1166 to Djumādā I 1180/November 1752—October 1766 is found in Topkapı Sarayı, Bağdad Köşkü 231 and 233 (fols. 1a-248b; autograph copy). For a description of the Marburg ms. covering the events of 1166-70, see B. Flemming, *Türkische Handschriften*, Wiesbaden 1968, i, 150 ff., and for a description of the Uppsala ms., see C.J. Tornberg, *Codices*..., Uppsala 1849, 199.

One of Ḥākim's successors as *waḳʿa-nüvīs*, Aḥmed Wāṣif [*q.v.*], strongly criticised Meḥmed's work, accusing him of failure to concern himself with questions of historical causation and the consequences of events through limiting his coverage only to palace events; he branded his style as "careless" and overly ornate, and his historical sense as lacking in both truthfulness and reliability and precision. When Wāṣif was commissioned in 1216-17/1802 to rewrite the events of the period falling between the *waḳʿa-nüwīs* ʿIzzī and Enwerī, he considered that by reducing Ḥākim's history, whose style he found repellent, to a simple index of events, he had created a new work which could be easily utilised by everybody. However, on comparison of the works, sc. Ḥākim's chronicle and the section of Wāṣif's *Maḥāsin al-āthār* which bases itself upon it (ed. Istanbul, i, 10-280), it becomes clear that Wāṣif's abbreviated version does not provide additional clarification and a wider scope of events, and his over-hasty attempts at simplifying Ḥākim resulted in loss of useful content and at times even in inexactitude and incompleteness; as a result of this, his index of events was not entirely successful in its aim of being universally understandable. It should be further noted that some of the stylistic shortcomings in Ḥākim's history were an inescapable consequence of the limitations imposed by his position as court chronicler (see Kütükoğlu, *art. cit.* in *TD*, vi/9 [1954], 91-122, vii/10 [1954], 79-102).

Bibliography: Başbakanlık Arşivi, Kepeci Tas., Ruus defteri, no. 261-6/61; Müstaḳīmzāde Saʿd el-Dīn (Ḥākim's disciple), *Tuḥfe-yi khaṭṭāṭīn*, Istanbul 1928, 408; Ḥüseyin Rāmiz, *Ādāb-ï ẓurefāʾ*, Esad Ef. 3873, fols. 23a-24a, and Emîrî, *tarih* 762, pp. 66-7; Shemʿdānī-zāde Süleymān, *Mürʾī al-tewārīkh*, ed. M. Aktepe, i, 1976, 172, 179, iiA, 1978, 57; Silaḥdār-zāde Meḥmed Emīn, *Tedhkire*, Ist. Univ. TY 2557, fol. 11b; ʿAbd al-Fettāḥ Shefḳat, *Tedhkire*, Emîrî, *tarih* 770, p. 42; Meḥmed Esʿad, *Baghče-yi ṣafā-endūz*, Ist. Univ., TY 2095, p. 106; ʿĀrif Ḥikmet, *Tedhkire*, Emîrî, *tarih* 789, fol. 14a; Dāwūd Faṭīn, *Khātimet al-eshʿār*, Istanbul 1271, 52-3.

(BEKİR KÜTÜKOĞLU)

MEḤMED KHALĪFE B. ḤÜSEYN, Ottoman courtier and historian who flourished under the three sultans Murād IV, Ibrāhīm and Meḥemmed IV [*q.vv.*] (reigned 1032/1623 to 1099/1687).

From Bosnia, he came to Istanbul in 1043/1633-4 as *ič-oghlan* of Ḳodja Kenʿān Gurdjī Pasha and stayed with him in the Balkans until the Pasha was in 1047/1637 appointed to lead an expedition against the prince of Transylvania George Rákoczi [see ERDEL]. Returning to Istanbul, he probably entered Sultan Ibrāhīm's office for diplomatic missions as a *seferli*, and at some unknown date became a *khalīfe* at court. He was also a poet, using the *takhalluṣ* of Ülfetī; the date of his death is unknown. See Refīḳ, biographical introd. to the *Taʾrīkh-i Ghilmānī* edition cited below; Babinger, *GOW*, 209-10, no. 180.

Meḥmed Khalīfe is best known for a chronicle of his time that he called the *Taʾrīkh-i Ghilmānī* because it was written for the personnel of the Inner Palace. In its initial form the work is a disorganised and unsystematic personal memoir which does however reflect the author's own ideas and attitudes and depicts vividly scenes of life in the Ottoman Palace of the 11th/17th century. The first version is represented by an amateurishly-written manuscript that covers the events of the year 1043-70/1633-60; it lacks its final pages (Vienna, Nationalbibliothek, H.O. 82; for a description, see G. Flügel, *Die arabischen, persischen und türkischen Handschriften*, ii, 271, no. 1068; for a facsimile, see Bugra Atsız, *Das osmanische Reich um die Mitte des 17. Jahrhunderts nach den Chroniken des Vecîhî (1637-1660) und des Mehmed Halîfa (1633-1660)*, Munich 1977; on the value of this manuscript as an historical source and its comparison with the final recension, see B. Kütükoğlu, *Tarih-i Gılmânî'nin ilk redaksiyonuna dâir*, in *Tarih Dergisi* no. 27 [1973], 21-40).

The *Taʾrīkh-i Ghilmānī* was given a somewhat more elevated literary form between 1070/1659-60 and 1075/1665 as corrections and additions were made to this first recension; events were arranged in chronological order, the text was divided into sections and subsections (*bābs* and *faṣls*), and occasionally verses and chronograms were inserted. This last recension comprises events from the accession of Murād IV (1032/1623) until the Treaty of Vasvar (1075/1664). Although it does not contain the author's biography and passages that reveal some of his attitudes and concerns which are found in the first recension, this final recension includes an epilogue (*khātime*) dealing with the necessity of mildness in the behaviour of rulers, the special qualities of Sultan Meḥemmed IV and the scholars and craftsmen trained in the Enderūn who were contemporaries of the author.

Meḥmed Khalīfe's work, which presents the events he experienced from the perspective of a functionary of the inner Palace, was used by ʿAbdī Pasha and Naʿīmā (see Atsız, *op. cit.*, pp. CXXVII-CXXVIII). With its publication by Aḥmed Refīḳ (Altınay) as suppl. no. 11 to *TOEM*, nos. 78-83 = N.S. 1-6 (1340-

1/1921-2), based on a manuscript of the final recension (Türk Tarih Kurumu Lib., ms. 509) it has also become one of the sources most frequently referred to by researchers.

Finally, Bursalı̊ Meḥmed Ṭāhir, *ʿO͟thmānlı̊ müʾellifleri*, iii, 142, attributes to a Meḥmed b. Ḥüseyin of Sultan Ibrāhīm's time a translation of the Persian history of ʿAlī b. S͟hihāb al-Dīn Hamadānī, the *D͟hak͟hīrat al-mulūk*, at the command of the governor of Bag͟hdād, Derwīs͟h Meḥmed Pas͟ha [*q.v.*], in 10 *bābs*, to which he added two further *bābs* and called the whole the *Tuḥfat al-maʾmūn*. This history must nevertheless be by Muṣliḥ al-Dīn Muṣṭafā b. S͟haʿbān (d. 969/1561-2) (see Kātib Čelebi (Ḥādjdjī K͟halīfa), *Kas͟hf al-ẓunūn*, Istanbul 1941, i, 824, and from it, Bursalı̊ Meḥmed Ṭāhir, ii, 226), and this is strengthened by the fact that the *D͟hak͟hīrat al-mulūk*, as described in the above two sources, is not a history but a treatise on political ethics (see Storey, i, 946-7 n. 4).

Bibliography: In addition to sources mentioned in the article, see *İA* art. *Mehmed Halîfe* (Bekir Kütükoğlu). (BEKIR KÜTÜKOĞLU)

MEḤMED LALA PAS͟HA [see MEḤMED PAS͟HA, LALA].

MEḤMED LĀLEZĀRĪ [see LĀLEZĀRĪ].

MEḤMED PAS͟HA, BALṬADJI̊, ṬEBERDĀR (1071-1124/1660-1 to 1712), Ottoman Grand Vizier under Sultan Aḥmed III [*q.v.*].

Born in Osmancık (Merzifon), as the son of Turkish Muslim parents, he was able to enter the outside service of the Sultan's palace thanks to patronage (*intisāb*). He began his career in a secretarial function. By favour and through the patronage of Ḥabes͟hī ʿAlī Ag͟ha and other *bīrūn ag͟has*, he entered the service of the *Wālide Sulṭān* K͟hadīdje Tark͟hān, attaining the rank of *k͟halīfe* in 1099/1687. The prince Aḥmed (the later Aḥmed III) appointed Meḥmed as apprentice to the corps of the "Balṭadjı̊s of the Old Sarāy", where he became known as the "beautiful muezzin" because of the musical qualities of his voice. When in 1695 Ḥabes͟hī ʿAlī became *Dār al-Saʿāde Ag͟hası̊* to Sultan Muṣṭafā II [*q.v.*], Balṭadjı̊ Meḥmed became personal scribe to his protector and was thus admitted to the proximity of the sultan and of Prince Aḥmed. At the accession of the latter on 10 Rabīʿ II 1115/21 August 1703, Meḥmed, with 9 years' experience of confidential service and having travelled all over the empire, was promoted to the rank of *Mīr Āk͟hūr*, but his appointment as *taḥṣīldār* of Aleppo removed him from the palace service. The Grand Vizier Ḳalaylı̊ḳoz Aḥmed Pas͟ha promoted him to the rank of vizier (8 Radjab 1116/6 September 1704) with the function of *Ḳapudān Pas͟ha*. Already on 27 S͟haʿbān 1116/26 December 1704 he became Grand Vizier (1704-6/1116-18). He had to maintain his position against the rival faction led by Čorlulu ʿAlī Pas͟ha and News͟hehirli (Dāmād) Ibrāhīm Pas͟ha [*q.vv.*]. He made himself indispensable to his monarch by playing upon the latter's constant fear of revolt and deposition. The Grand Vizier managed to free himself from the supervision of financial affairs by means of an intrigue, falsely accusing the *Nis͟hāndjı̊* Ḥüseyin Pas͟ha of plotting a revolt and consequently sending him into exile at Istanköy Island (Cos). The Sultan for long tolerated his old familiar companion in spite of his marked lack of ability in financial matters.

At last, the Sulṭan decided to replace Balṭadjı̊ Meḥmed Pas͟ha by Čorlulu ʿAlī Pas͟ha (19 Muḥarram 1118/3 May 1706), his trusted intimate as well as a competent statesman. The ex-Grand Vizier was honourably exiled with the appointment as *Beglerbegi* of Erzurum. In 1119/1707 he was transferred to Chios (Ott. Saḳı̊z [*q.v.*]), from which post he went to Aleppo as *Beglerbegi*. In that city, the poet Nābī [*q.v.*] belonged to Balṭadjı̊ Meḥmed Pas͟ha's salon.

On 14 Djumādā II 1122/10 August 1710, Aḥmed III decided to appoint his old companion as Grand Vizier again. The latter actually took office in Istanbul by 3 S͟haʿbān/27 September. By this time a "war party," which aimed at a renewal of the war against Russia, had gained the upper hand. The intrigues to that end were assisted by the King of Sweden, "Iron Head" (*Demir Bas͟h*) Charles XII, who had found refuge in Ottoman territory since 1709. His Ottoman ally was the K͟hān of the Crimea Dawlat Giray II [see GIRAY] (second reign, 1120-5/1708-13) who came to Istanbul in 1122/1710 to further his aims of war against the Russian Tsar Peter. A Council was held in the Sultan's palace (*Mes͟hweret-i ʿAẓīme* of 28 Ramaḍān 1122/21 November 1710) and war was declared on Russia. The new Grand Vizier was to command the army. The so-called Pruth campaign began in the spring of 1123/1711. The Tsar's diplomacy could not curb the Ottoman initiative and the two armies marched towards each other, meeting on 12 Djumādā II/28 July 1711 in Moldavia (Ott. Bog͟hdan [*q.v.*]) near K͟hān Tepesi (= Stanilesti) on the river Pruth, downstream on the road from Jassy (Ott. Yas͟h [*q.v.*]). Nobody in the Russian army was aware that Balṭadjı̊ Meḥmed Pas͟ha was already close by. The Ottomans, reinforced by a large body of Tatars, Cossacks and Polish troops, totalling 120,000 men and 400 guns, were in perfect condition. The Russian army (40,000 infantry, 14,000 horse and 122 guns) had been suffering from lack of food and forage for three weeks. The support promised in a secret treaty concluded in view of the Russo-Turkish war by the prince of Moldavia Demetrius Cantemir (1673-1723) was not delivered, for the crops had failed as a result of drought and locusts. On 5 Djumādā II/21 July 1711, Balṭadjı̊ Meḥmed's army completely surrounded the Russians and was preparing for the general attack with an artillery barrage. The Tsar Peter, who was with his army, realised that his forces would be annihilated and decided quickly to sue for an armistice and peace. For this move, he found support not only from his Vice-Chancellor Peter S͟hafirov but also from his wife Catherine. This lady's involvement probably gave rise to the historical legend that the corrupt Ottoman Grand Vizier gave in easily to the Russian proposals, as these were accompanied by the offer of the jewelry and the charms of the Tsarina to his person. In any case, lacking insight into the true situation of the two powers, Balṭadjı̊ Meḥmed was too easily content with the Russian proposals. He was already satisfied with the retrocession of Azov (Ott. Azaḳ [*q.v.*]), the demolition of the newly-built Russian fortresses at Taganrog, Kamenny Zaton and along the Dniepr, the closing of the permanent Russian embassy at the Porte, the evacuation of Polish territory and a guarantee of non-interference in Polish affairs. All Ottoman prisoners were to be set free and the King of Sweden was to be allowed safe passage. The Russian troops were provided with food for their free retreat. A preliminary treaty of peace was hurriedly agreed upon on 6 Djumādā II 1123/23 July 1711 (O.S. 12 July), notwithstanding the protests of Dawlat Giray II K͟hān and the representative of Charles XII, the Polish general Stanislas Poniatowski. Balṭadjı̊ Meḥmed Pas͟ha seems to have been carried away by his own unexpected success. It must be realised, however, that the Janissaries had little stomach for fighting in this desolate country and that the Sipāhīs were always reluctant to face the costs of prolonged fighting. Moreover, the Grand Vizier's distrust of the political pressure group around the Swedish King at Bender may have induced him to come to terms before these could interfere on the spot.

The news of the victory and the peace was well received at Istanbul at first. The Sultan, however, became suspicious of his Grand Vizier when the latter postponed his return to the capital because of protracted negotiations with the Russians concerning the implementation of the treaty. Indeed, the absence of direct positive results of the peace caused a general dissatisfaction with the Grand Vizier's policy. The anti-Russian party, joined by the leading *ʿulamāʾ*, was able to gain the upper hand over those loving peace. After the arrival of the army at Edirne the Commander-in-Chief Balṭadjī Meḥmed was instructed to give up the seal of office. He was put under arrest in the prison of the *Bostāndjībashī*. An inventory of his possessions and money was ordered. He himself was banished to the islands of Midilli and subsequently to Limni [*q.vv.*]. During his stay there, he learned of the confiscation of all his possessions. The *Wālide Sulṭān* probably interceded to save his life, but two main assistants in office, his *kāhya* ʿOthmān Agha and his *mektūbču* ʿÖmer Efendi, were condemned to death. Balṭadjī Meḥmed Pasha died on Limni, after a short illness, in 1124/1712-13. The judgment of him in Ottoman historiography varies between the accusation of high treason against Islam and the Ottoman state and fulsome praise for a victorious Turkish commander. He seems to have been a typical product of the seraglio culture, and according to A.N. Kurat, was a man of the pen rather than a statesman, an Ottoman gentleman rather than a Turkish warrior.

Bibliography: See *İA*, art. s.v. (A.N. Kurat), with an extensive listing of sources and literature; this article forms the basis of the present one; also Kurat, *XII. Karl'in Türkiye'de kalışı ve bu sıralarda Osmanlı Imparatorluğu*, Istanbul 1943; idem, *Ekler I* (documents), Istanbul 1943; *Arşiv kılavuzu*, 1- pl. V. 10 (facs. and summary of Balṭadjī Meḥmed's memorandum to the *Wālide Sulṭān*, 18 August 1711); Silāḥdār Fındıḳlılı Meḥmed Agha, *Nuṣret-nāme*, ed. İ. Parmaksızoğlu, (2 pts.), Istanbul 1966-9, ii (index); Voltaire, *Remarques d'un seigneur polonais* [= St. Poniatowski] *sur l'histoire de Charles XII, roi de Suède*, The Hague 1741; A.N. Kurat (ed.), *The despatches of Sir Robert Sutton, Ambassador in Constantinople (1710-1714)*, London 1953 (= Camden Soc., 3rd Series, 78); ʿAṭāʾ, *Taʾrīkh-i ʿAṭā*, Istanbul 1291-3, ii, 146-9; *SʿO*, iv, 208 ff.; Aḥmed Refīḳ (Altınay), *Balṭadjī Meḥmed Pasha ve Büyük Petrū 1711-1911*, Istanbul 1327; idem, *Memālik-i ʿOthmāniyyede Demirbash Sharl*, Istanbul 1332 (= *TOEM, Külliyyatī*, i); Kurat and K. V. Zetterstéen (eds.), *Türkische Urkunden*, Uppsala-Leipzig 1938 (docs. V, VI, VII); Kurat, *Prut seferi ve Barışı 1123 (1711)*, 2 vols., Ankara 1951-3 (= Ankara Ün. Dil-Tarih ve Coğrafya Fak. Y. 8-9) (the definitive monograph on the subject); idem, *Der Pruthfeldzug und der Pruthfrieden von 1711*, in *Jahrb. f. d. Gesch. Osteuropas*, x (1962), 13-66; idem (ed.), *Hâzine-i birûn kâtibi Ahmed b. Mahmud'un 1123-1711 Prut seferine ait defteri* (= ms. Preuss. Stsb. Or. Abt. 1209), in *TED*, iv (Ankara 1966) 261-426; D. Cantemir, *The history of the growth and decay of the Othman Empire*, London 1734-5, 2 vols. in 1, ii, 442-5 n., 450-3; B.H. Sumner, *Peter the Great and the Ottoman Empire*, Oxford 1949, 37-43; W. Theyls, *Gedenkschriften betreffende het leeven van Karel de XII ... geduurende sijn verblijf in het Ottomannische gebied...*, Leiden 1721, i, 6-29 (Fr. tr., *Mémoire pour servir à l'histoire de Charles XII*, Leiden 1722); M. Münir Aktepe, *Baltacı Mehmed Paşa'nin 1711 Prut Seferi ile ilgili emirleri*, in *TED*, i (Istanbul 1970), 131-70 (with corrections of Kurat 1951-3); A. K. Anıt, *Baltacı Mehmet Paşa ve Birinci Katerina*, Istanbul 1946 (unscholarly work). (A. H. DE GROOT)

MEḤMED PASHA, BĪYĪḲLĪ, ("moustachioed") Ottoman general and administrator, d. 928/1521.

He seems to have been in the service of the Shehzād Selīm b. Bāyazīd II, at the time when the latter was governor of Trebizond. There is evidence that he held the post of Chief Equerry (*amīr-ākhōr-bashi*) from the time of the accession of Selīm I, and he fought alongside him in battles against the Shehzād Aḥmed b. Bāyazīd: near Bursa, where he commanded the vanguard and his force was routed on 7 Ṣafar 919/14 April 1513; then at the battle of Yeñishehir on 24 April. The following year, he took part in the campaign of Čāldīrān [*q.v.*] and, on his return to Tabrīz, was entrusted with the mission of storming the stronghold of Bayburd, which had been unsuccessfully besieged since Djumādā I 920/July 1514 by an Ottoman expeditionary force. The conquest of this fortress earned him the title, granted on 25 October, of *beg* of the *sandjaks* of Bayburd, Trebizond, (Shebīn) Ḳara Ḥiṣār and Djānik. In the spring of 1515 he was given the task of laying siege to Kemākh [*q.v.*], and he maintained a blockade on this Ṣafawid-held town until the arrival of the sultan, who took it by assault on 5 Rabīʿ II 921/19 May 1515. In the course of the summer, Selīm I appointed him commander-in-chief of an army of considerable size (Ottoman troops, volunteers and contingents from the Kurdish principalities) raised for the purpose of conquering western Kurdistan, which was in revolt against the Safawids and where the diplomatic activity of Idrīs Bidlīsī [*q.v.*] had ensured that the territory would affirm its loyalty to the Ottoman government. Meḥmed Pasha entered Āmid on 10 Shaʿbān 921/19 September 1515, was made *beglerbeg* of Diyār Bakr on 5 November, and completed the conquest of the country by annihilating in Rabīʿ II 922/May 1516, at Eski Ḳoč Ḥiṣār, near Mārdīn, the last Ṣafawid army still present in the region, that of Ḳara Khān Ustādjalū. When Selīm I marched against the Mamlūks, Meḥmed Pasha joined forces with him at Malaṭya, fought on the left flank at the battle of Mardj Dābiḳ [*q.v.*], then, at Aleppo, was granted authority to undertake the conquest of the fortresses of Mārdīn and Ḥiṣn Kayfa, still held by Ḳizilbash garrisons. Shortly after this he took possession of Mawṣil, Kirkūk and Tāwūḳ. Promoted to the rank of vizier, Meḥmed Pasha devoted the remainder of his period of office to the establishment of Ottoman rule in the Kurdish emirates of Diyār Bakr on the one hand, and to the monitoring of the activities of Shāh Ismāʿīl on the other. He died on 24 Muḥarram 928/24 December 1521 (of dysentery, cf. document E. 6102 of the Archives of Topkapı, and not in battle as claimed by Meḥmed Thüreyyā) and was buried at Āmid, near the Fātiḥ Pasha mosque of which he had laid the foundations.

In spite of the important role which he played and the relatively plentiful documentation concerning him, little research has been so far done on Bīyīḳlī Meḥmed Pasha. In any case, examination of the sources gives the impression that, under Selīm I, he was one of the few senior Ottoman dignitaries—if not the only one—who, entrusted with a considerable weight of responsibility, enjoyed the unlimited confidence of the sultan and, in return, served him with exemplary loyalty. This loyalty continued to be asserted under the reign of Selīm I's successor, when, as is shown by the still unpublished documents of the Topkapı Archives, Meḥmed Pas͟ha remained, against the advice of Süleymān and his advisers, the last supporter of all-out struggle against Ḳïzïlbas͟h Iran, the primary objective of the foreign policy of Selīm I.

Bibliography: Saʿd al-Dīn, *Tād͟j al-tawārīk͟h*, ii, Istanbul 1280/1863, 235, 284, 289, 308-10, 329, 333, 339, 372; the "Journal" of Ḥaydar Čelebī, in Ferīdūn Beg, *Müns͟heʾāt al-selāṭīn*, i, 1274/1858, 464/479; Idrīs Bidlīsī and Abū Faḍl Ibn Idrīs, *Selīm-nāme*, ms. Bibliothèque Nationale, A. F. persan 235; Meḥmed T͟hüreyyā, *Sid͟jill-i ʿot͟hmānī*, Istanbul 1308/1890-1, i, 445, iv, 109; M. Mehdi İlhan, *Bıyıklı Mehmed Paşa'nın doğu Anadolu'daki askeri faaliyletleri*, in *IX. Türk Tarih Kongresi bildirileri*, Ankara 1988, 807-17.

(J.-L. Bacqué-Grammont)

MEḤMED PAS͟HA, ČERKES (d. 1034/1625), Ottoman Grand Vizier.

Educated in the palace school or Enderūn [*q.v.*], he reached the rank of *silāḥdār* and left the palace with the appointment of *Beglerbegi* of Damascus. In 1621 he is mentioned as the fifth *Ḳubbe Wezīri* (Nāʿīmā, *Taʾrīk͟h*, Istanbul 1280, ii, 208). Upon the execution of the Grand Vizier Kemānkes͟h ʿAlī Pas͟ha [*q.v.*] (14 D͟jumādā II 1033/3 April 1624), Murād IV [*q.v.*] forced him to accept the appointment of himself as successor. Čerkes Meḥmed Pas͟ha thus became commander-in-chief of the army sent to suppress the revolt of Abāẓā Meḥmed Pas͟ha [see ABĀẒĀ]. and to reconquer Bag͟hdād from the Persians. Passing Konya, he failed to take Niğde from the hands of the rebels. On 21 D͟hu 'l-Ḳaʿda 1033/3 September 1624, near Kayseri, he found Abāẓā Meḥmed's troops in position at the bridge of Ḳarasu. In a bloody battle, the Grand Vizier, thanks to his field artillery, was able to defeat the rebel forces. Kātib Čelebi [*q.v.*], being among the corps of the *silāḥdārs*, witnessed this battle and gives a detailed description (cf. his *Fed͟hleke*, Istanbul 1287, ii, 54 ff.). Pursuing Abāẓā's fleeing troops, the Grand Vizier was able to capture Abāẓā Meḥmed's wife and daughter who were escorted by Abāẓā's commander from Niğde to Sivas. Having come as far as Tercan, the Grand Vizier was met by a mission from the rebellious Pas͟ha of Erzurum with the request for a pardon. Considering it as being late in the campaigning season, Čerkes Meḥmed Pas͟ha accepted this on the condition of a Janissary garrison being placed in the citadel of Erzurum. Following this, the Grand Vizier withdrew the army to Tokat for the winter (December 1624). There he fell ill and died on 17 Rabīʿ II 1034/27 January 1625. His last days are reported by the historian Pečewī Ibrāhīm Efendi, who met Čerkes Meḥmed in Tokat (cf. Pečewī, *Taʾrīk͟h*, Istanbul 1283, ii, 401). All Ottoman historians agree on the just and incorruptible character of this old vizier, described as a *pīr-i nūrānī* by Naʿīmā (*Taʾrīk͟h*, ii, 296).

Bibliography: See *İA*, art. s.v. (by M.C. Baysun, of which the present article is a summary); Von Hammer, *HEO*, ix, 42-5; *SʿO*, iv, 150; A.H. de Groot, *The Ottoman Empire and the Dutch Republic*, Leiden 1978, 76, 286. (A.H. de Groot)

MEḤMED PAS͟HA, ELMĀS (1071-1109/1662-97), Ottoman Grand Vizier.

He was born in Hoşalay (formerly Mesed, to the east of Kerempe Burnu) (Kastamonu), the son of a shipmaster. As a young man (reputedly beautiful, hence his surname *Elmas* "Diamond"), he was taken into the service of the state by a chief inspector of the Sultan's treasury (*Bas͟h Bāḳī Ḳulu*), Divrigili Meḥmed Ag͟ha, who was appointed governor of Tripoli in Syria in 1089/1677-8. From the service of the treasury, Meḥmed Pas͟ha Elmās was soon promoted to the palace service, to the *K͟hāṣṣ Oda* [*q.v.*] from where he made quick career as *Riḳābdār*, *Silāḥdār* in 1099/1687-8, *Mīr-i ʿAlem* (Standard-bearer) and *K͟hāzine Ketk͟hüdāsï*, leaving the palace service with the rank of Beglerbegi to become *Nis͟hānd͟jï* in 1101/1698-90. Soon afterwards he was made a vizier (*Ḳubbe Wezīri* [*q.v.*]). Sultan Muṣṭafā II (1106-15/1695-1703 [*q.v.*]) appointed him *Ḳāʾim-maḳām* at Istanbul on 23 D͟jumādā II 1106/9 February 1695. During the preparations for the campaign against the Emperor in Hungary, the Sultan decided to make him Grand Vizier instead of Sürmeli ʿAlī Pas͟ha [*q.v.*], who was executed (4 S͟hawwāl 1106/18 May 1695). Meḥmed Pas͟ha Elmās joined the three campaigns of Sultan Muṣṭafā II and was seen fighting at times. He distinguished himself during his second campaign when on 27 Muḥarram 1108/26 August 1696 the Ottoman army defeated the *Naʿl-Ḳirān* Frederick Augustus, Elector of Saxony, who had laid siege to Temes͟hwār [*q.v.*], in the battle near the Bega River at Cenei (Buldur Köyü Bog͟hazï). During the campaign of 1697, he was again accompanied by the Sultan. In the council of war held at Belgrade on 27 Muḥarram 1109/15 August 1697, the Grand Vizier and Commander-in-Chief followed the advice of the majority of his commanders who agreed with the Vizier Ḳod͟ja D͟jaʿfer Pas͟ha, and ordered his army to march north across the Banat instead of following ʿAmūd͟ja-zāde Ḥüseyn Köprülü Pas͟ha's [*q.v.*] suggestion to go west in the direction of Peterwardein (Waradin [*q.v.*]). While crossing the Tisza river eastwards, the Grand Vizier's army was surprised by the Imperial army commanded by Prince Eugene of Savoy, who had reached this spot by a forced march towards nightfall on 11 September. This was near Zenta [*q.v.*]. A frightful bloodbath was the result of Prince Eugene's immediate attack. The Turks lost about 20,000 killed and 10,000 drowned. The Sultan, who watched the disaster, fled. The Janissaries broke into a mutiny and killed the Grand Vizier and many officers of his staff.

Elmās Meḥmed Pas͟ha was a young and elegant man of the palace (*čelebi*), of a lively character, intelligent and with experience in financial affairs, all of which assets made Muṣṭafā II select him for the highest office. However, it seems that he did not make himself popular with the viziers and the army. He left behind a son, Muṣṭafā Bey.

Bibliography: See *İA*, art. s.v. (C. Orhonlu), with a listing *in extenso* of ms. sources and literature; Silāḥdār Fïndïḳlïlï Meḥmed Ag͟ha, *Nuṣret-nāme*, ed. İ. Parmaksızoğlu (in simplified version with defective transcriptions), Istanbul 1962-4, i, 177, 188, esp. 277-300; *Prinz Eugen von Savoyen 1663-1736. [Katalog der] Ausstellung zum 300. Geburtstag 9. Oktober bis 31 Dezember 1963*, Heeresgeschichtliches Museum, Vienna 1963, 32-7, pl. 4 (showing the Seal (*mühr-i hümayūn*) lost by Elmās Meḥmed Pas͟ha and now kept in the Vienna Museum of Military History, Inv. N1 2533); L.F. Marsigli, *L'état militaire de l'empire Ottoman*, The Hague 1782, ii, 100-3; Von Hammer, *HEO*, xii, 374-424, 538-9; Temes͟hwarlï ʿAlī, *Taʾrīk͟h-i Waḳʿa-nāme-yi D͟jaʿfer Pas͟ha*, ed. and tr. R.F. Kreutel and K. Teply, *Der Löwe von Temeschwar. Erinnerungen an Caʿfer Pascha den Älteren, aufgezeichnet von seinem Siegelbewahrer ʿAli*, Graz-Köln 1981 (= Osmanische Geschichtsschreiber, 10), esp. 161-270 (covering the years 1688-97); *İA*, art. *Zenta* (M. İlgürel).

(A. H. de Groot)

MEḤMED PASHA, GÜRDJÜ, Khādim (I) (d. 1035/1626), Ottoman Grand Vizier.

Of Georgian origin, he served among the white eunuchs of the imperial harem under Sultan Meḥemmed III [*q.v.*] (1003-12/1595-1603). He was appointed *Khāṣṣ-Oda Bas̲h̲i̊* by Sultan Aḥmed I shortly after his accession (2 Shaʿbān 1012/4 January 1604). Around Rabīʿ II 1013/September 1604, Khādim Meḥmed Agha was given the rank of Third Vizier in the *Dīwān*, but already on the 27 Rabīʿ II/22 September was appointed *beglerbegi* of Egypt. He was able to restore order in that province and punished the rebels among the Ottoman regular troops (*ḳul ṭāʾifesi*). Dismissed around Ṣafar 1014/June 1605, he left Egypt for Istanbul and was appointed *beglerbegi* of Bosnia (Ott. Bosna [*q.v.*]) as well as being put in charge of the military government (*muḥāfaẓa*) of Belgrade and the shores of the Danube. In Ṣafar 1018/May 1609, upon appointment as *serdār-i ekrem* (commander-in-chief) of the Grand Vizier Ḳuyudju Murād Pasha [*q.v.*], he was made *ḳāʾimmaḳām* while still at Belgrade. During the next year's campaign, Meḥmed Pasha Gürdjü was again left in charge as *ḳāʾim-maḳām* in the capital, in which function he continued till the return from the Persian front of the succeeding Grand Vizier Naṣūḥ Pasha [*q.v.*] (1 Shaʿbān 1021/27 September 1612). During his tenure of this office, he supported the granting of capitulations to the Dutch Republic (6 July 1612). Remaining in the rank of Third Vizier, he had enough support from the palace to be able to refuse to be removed from Istanbul by the Grand Vizier by means of an appointment in a distant province; instead, he was ordered to reside inside the Sultan's palace. On 11 Shawwāl 1022/24 November 1613, at the departure of the Sultan to Edirne, he was appointed governor of Istanbul. The next Grand Vizier, Öküz Meḥmed Pasha, made Meḥmed Pasha Gürdjü Second Vizier and *ḳāʾim-maḳām* for the duration of the campaigning season (Rabīʿ II 1024/May 1615). Later, he joined the Khotin [*q.v.*] campaign. In October 1619 he was degraded to the rank of Third Vizier, during the disgrace of Mere Ḥüseyn Pasha, till July 1620. Before the outbreak of the revolt against Sultan ʿOthmān (7 Radjab 1031/18 May 1622), he was made military governor of Edirne by that Sultan.

During Sultan Muṣṭafā I's second reign, the post of Grand Vizier was given to Meḥmed Pasha Gürdjü on 15 Dhu 'l-Ḳaʿda 1031/21 September 1622. At this time of unrest and open revolt in the capital and in the Anatolian provinces, the new Grand Vizier's main task was to restore order, in which he was moderately successful as far as Istanbul was concerned, and this in spite of the fact that the rebellious Abāẓā Meḥmed Pasha [*q.v.*] was the son-in-law of Gürdjü Meḥmed Pasha's brother Ḥüseyn Pasha. By Rabīʿ I 1032/January 1623, he had been able even to have executed some of those involved in the assassination of ʿOthmān II. The military rebels in the capital, at the instigation of Mere Ḥüseyn Pasha, sucessfully demanded the dismissal of the Grand Vizier, allegedly on account of his being an incompetent eunuch. He was exiled (to Malḳara [*q.v.*] in Thrace?) till Dhu 'l-Ḳaʿda 1032/September 1623, when after the deposition of Muṣṭafā I, the Grand Vizier Kemānkesh Ḳara ʿAlī Pasha [*q.v.*] had both Meḥmed Pasha Gürdjü and Khalīl Pasha (Ḳayṣariyyeli) [*q.v.*] arrested on the suspicion of collaborating with the rebel Abāẓā Meḥmed Pasha, since both viziers were personally linked with the latter by family, *intisāb* and *ṭarīḳat* relationships. Gürdjü Meḥmed Pasha was one of the favourite targets of the satirical verse of the poet Nefʿī [*q.v.*].

Soon the two prisoners were released again, and Meḥmed was made *ḳāʾim-maḳām* once more by the Grand Vizier Čerkes Meḥmed Pasha [*q.v.*] (April 1624). The lack of success of the seven months' siege of Baghdād by the Grand Vizier (Ṣafar-Shawwāl 1035/November 1625-July 1626) led the Janissary and Sipāhī soldiery at Istanbul to level once more their suspicions of treason or incompetence against Meḥmed Pasha Gürdjü (Dhu 'l-Ḳaʿda 1035/August 1626). This time the probably unfounded accusations led to the execution of the old statesman who, according to some sources, was 90 years old by this time.

Three water fountains (*česhme*) were piously founded by *Khādim* Gürdjü Meḥmed Pasha in the Khalīdjilar, Khirḳa-yi̊ Sherīf and Shehzāde-Bashi̊ quarters of Istanbul. His *türbe* is at Eyyūb in the second courtyard of the great mosque.

Bibliography: See *İA* art. s.v. (F.Ç. Derin), of which the present article is a summary; İ.H. Danişmend, *İzahlı Osmanlı tarihi kronolojisi*, iii², Istanbul 1972, 315, 320, 321, 329; A.H. de Groot, *The Ottoman Empire and the Dutch Republic*, Leiden-Istanbul 1978, 107, 119-24, 147, 170, 309, 313; M.O. Bayrak, *Istanbul'da gömülü meşhur adamlar (1453-1978)*, Istanbul 1979, 48 (no. 33); *İA* art. *Nefʿi* (A. Karahan).

(A.H. de Groot)

MEḤMED PASHA, GÜRDJÜ (II) (d. 1076/1666), Ottoman Grand Vizier.

Having been a slave (but not an eunuch) of Ḳodja Sinān Pasha [*q.v.*], he entered the palace service, beginning as an apprentice in the kitchen (*maṭbakh emīnliği*) department. By Djumādā II 1023/ July 1614, he reached the rank of a *djebedji bashi̊*. While on campaign with Öküz Meḥmed Pasha [*q.v.*] in the East, he was appointed *čawush bashi̊* [*q.v.*] in Dhu 'l-Ḳaʿda 1026/November 1617. In Rabīʿ I 1029/February 1620 he was made *ḳapi̊dji̊, bashi̊*, in which function he participated in Sultan ʿOthmān II's Khotin campaign of that year. His career was not affected by the political upheavals of those years, and in Radjab 1032/May 1623 he became *beglerbegi* of Rumeli, the first of a long series of provincial government posts in the Asiatic and European parts of the empire.

Meḥmed Pasha Gürdjü saw a great deal of active military service, both in the successful suppression of revolts and in the Persian wars. Having reached vizieral rank as *beglerbegi* of Damascus previously, he was made *beglerbegi* of Diyārbekr in 1035/1626 and member of the *Dīwān* in the next year, holding successive provincial appointments next to that office. He joined Sultan Murād IV [*q.v.*] during the Eriwān campaign of 1635 and the Baghdād campaign of 1638 in various governmental capacities. After 3 Dhu 'l-Ḳaʿda 1049/25 February 1640, he was a *ḳubbe vezīri* once again till he fell out with the Grand Vizier Sulṭānzāde Semīn Meḥmed Pasha [*q.v.*] (Muḥarram 1055/March 1645). At the behest of the all-powerful *Dār al-seʿāde Aghasi̊* Uzun Süleymān Agha, Sultan Meḥemmed IV [*q.v.*] appointed the old and debilitated Pasha, the oldest of all viziers at the time, Grand Vizier on 11 Shawwāl 1061/27 September 1651, in which function he lasted eight months and twenty-three days. He was unable to turn the campaign in Crete in a favourable direction, and could not dislodge the Venetian fleet from the Dardanelles. Nor were his diplomatic efforts to reach an armistice with Venice in any way effective. On the other hand, he provided posts for his brothers, son and many friends and relations. His dismissal followed on 13 Radjab 1062/20 June 1652. After a short stay in Yedi Kule prison, he was allowed to live in his private residence in the Eyyūb quarter of the capital till he managed again to secure an appointment as provincial governor successively of Temeshwār and Cyprus (Ḳubruṣ [*q.v.*]) and Buda (Budun [*q.v.*]). It was probably there that he died of old age before 1 Shawwāl 1076/6 April 1666, when the news of his death reached Istanbul, according to the historian ʿAbdī Pasha (*Weḳāyiʿ-nāme*, ms. Beyazid, *Umumi* 5154 946).

Bibliography: See *İA* art. s.v. (F.Ç. Derin), of which the present article is a summary, which gives a full indication of Ottoman sources; İ.H. Uzunçarşılı, *Osmanlı tarihi*, iii/2, Istanbul 1954, 402-4; Nāʿīmā, *Taʾrīkh*, Istanbul 1283, v, 168-76, 215-25. (A.H. de Groot)

MEḤMED PASHA, ʿIWAḌ, Ḥadjdjī (el-Ḥādjdj) (1085 or 1086-1156/1675-1743), Ottoman Grand Vizier.

He was the son of a descendant of the *Ewlād-i Fātiḥān*, one Naṣr Allāh, a *tīmār* holder at Jagodina. Educated for state service (hence *ʿiwaḍ*), he served with high-placed officials at Belgrade (1100/1689) and at Djudda (1107-8/1696), during which period he made the pilgrimage to Mecca. Having returned to Istanbul just before the Patrona Khalīl rebellion of 1730, he acted as *Gümrük Emīni*, Commissioner of the Istanbul customs house, on behalf of Yegen Meḥmed Efendi (Pasha). Later, he served as Treasury Inspector (*Bash-Bāḳī Ḳulu*). The Grand Vizier Ḥekīmoghlu ʿAlī Pasha [*q.v.*] promoted him *Čawush Bashi* [*q.v.*] (1732).

In 1735 he became a vizier and acted for a short time as *ḳāʾim-maḳām* at Istanbul, after which he was sent to govern the *sandjaḳs* of Niğbolu and Vidin. During the war, he for two years successfully defended his area against Austrian attacks. He was able to retake the fortresses of Hirsova and Fethülislam (the Yugoslavian Kladovo) as well as Semendire (the Yugoslavian Smederevo), Mehādiye (the Rumanian Mehadia) and Yeñi Palanka. Meḥmed Pasha ʿIwaḍ served as commander-in-chief (*serdār*) on that front when, at the behest of the powerful *Ḳizlar Aghasi* (*Dār al-Seʿāda Aghasi*) Ḥadjdjī Beshīr Agha, he was also appointed Grand Vizier (12 Dhu 'l-Ḥidjdja 1151/23 March 1739) to replace Yegen Meḥmed Pasha, whose policies he continued however along the same lines, on the one hand by opening diplomatic contact with the Austrians, on the other by aiming at the reconquest of Belgrade. He became famous for his splendid defeat of the Austrian army under Field-Marshal Olivier Wallis (56,000 strong plus light cavalry, artillery and irregulars). The Grand Vizier took up a defensive position to the north-west of Grocka (Ott. Ḥiṣārdjiḳ) (on 15 Rabīʿ II 1152/22 July 1739) overlooking the road from Belgrade which went through a defile. After fifteen assaults by the Janissaries, Field-Marshal Wallis retreated at nightfall, losing 3,000 killed and 7,000 wounded. Four days later, Belgrade was laid under siege by the Ottomans. Negotiations led to the conclusion of the peace treaty (1-18 September) between the Sultan, the Austrian Emperor and the Tsar at Belgrade, which meant an important restoration of Ottoman power in the Danube area.

In Rabīʿ 1153/June 1740 a local disturbance in the capital formed the pretext for Beshīr Agha and the *Wālide Sulṭān* to have Meḥmed Pasha ʿIwaḍ dismissed as Grand Vizier, relegating him to the governorship of Djudda, from which place he soon was able to transfer to Canea (Ott. Ḥanya). During the next three years, he successively served as military governor of Salonica, in Herzegovina (Ott. Hersek), Bosnia, Negroponte (Ott. Eghriboz) and in Crete again. He died while acting as military governor of Lepanto (Aynabakhti [*q.v.*]) in Djumādā I 1156/July 1743. His elder son Ibrāhīm became twice *Sheykh ül-Islām* and his younger son Khalīl became Grand Vizier in 1183/1769.

Bibliography: Meḥmed Ṣubḥī, *Taʾrīkh-i Weḳāʾiʿ*, Istanbul 1198 (*Taʾrīkh-i Sāmī we Shākir we Ṣubḥī*), fols. 72-258, esp. 135, 150, 160 ff. (eyewitness account of the battle of Grocka, 15 Rabīʿ I 1152/22 June 1739; İ.H. Uzuncarşılı, *Osmanlı tarihi*, v/1, Istanbul 1956, 260, 267, 272 f., 281-96, iv/2, Istanbul 1959[1], 350-4; *İA* art. *Belgrad* (M.C. Baysun); *Şemdâni-zâde Fındıklılı Süleyman Efendi Tarihi Mür'i 't-tevârih*, ed. M. M. Aktepe, i, Istanbul 1976, index s.v. "Ivaz Mehmed"; Von Hammer, *HEO*, xiv, 417, 419, 424, 439-70, xv, 1-11, 25 f.; D. Nicolle, *Armies of the Ottoman Turks, 1300-1774*, London 1983, 33 f.; L. Cassels, *The struggle for the Ottoman Empire 1717-1740*, London 1966, 156-96 (based on A. Vandal, *Une ambassade française en Orient. La mission du marquis de Villeneuve 1728-1741*, Paris 1887, esp. 357-91).(A.H. de Groot)

MEḤMED PASHA, ḲARAMĀNĪ, Nishāndjî, (d. 886/1481), Ottoman Grand Vizier and historian.

A descendant of Djalāl al-Dīn Rūmī [*q.v.*], he grew up in Ḳonya where he received his education as an *ʿālim* from Muṣannifak al-Ṣiddīḳī who introduced him into the patronage of Maḥmūd Pasha [*q.v.*]. Meḥmed Pasha served as a clerk in the *dīwān* of that Grand Vizier and later became *müderris* in the *medrese* founded by the same at Istanbul, being at the same time a general adviser to his patron. Thanks to the latter, he became *nishāndji* [*q.v.*] in 869/1464, which high office he kept for about 12 years. From 4 Dhu 'l-Ḳaʿda 862/13 September 1458, he already ranked as a vizier. His appointment as Grand Vizier following the dismissal of Gedik Aḥmed Pasha [*q.v.*] dates from Muḥarram 881/May 1476 (cf. Ḳiwāmī, *Fetḥ-nāme-yi Sulṭān Meḥemmed*, ed. F. Babinger, Istanbul 1955, 273). In his new position, he became the main author of Sultan Meḥemmed II's [*q.v.*] legislative policy. This statesman, with his years of experience in matters of state and administration, must be seen as the creator of the new state institutions laid down in the the *ḳanūn-nāme*s [*q.v.*] of this period (cf. the editions of *MOG*, i [1922], *TOEM* [1330/1912] and Özcan [1982]). One of his lasting innovations was the division of the judiciary among two *Ḳāḍī ʿasker*s , one for Rumeli and one for Anadolu. A great number of *waḳf* and private landed properties were converted into state property as a base of the *tīmār* system, which had to support an increasing amount of military personnel. Meḥmed Pasha's full support of the centralising policy of the Sultan caused his unpopularity among his fellow *ʿulamāʾ* and the old-established landowners of the *ghāzī* aristocracy (cf. ʿĀshiḳpashazāde, *Tewārīkh-i Āl-i ʿOthmān*, ed. Ç.N. Atsız, Istanbul 1947, 244).

When Grand Vizier, Meḥmed Pasha Ḳaramānī supported Meḥemmed II in furthering the claim to the succession of Prince Djem [*q.v.*] against Prince Bāyezīd. His personal link with the city of Ḳonya must have offered a special opportunity, since Djem Sulṭān was governor of Ḳaramān. Bāyezīd (II) [*q.v.*] counted Ḳaramānī Meḥmed amongst his enemies henceforth (cf. R.C. Repp, *The Müfti of Istanbul*, 21, 72, 144, 199-201). The Grand Vizier accompanied the Sultan at the departure for the campaign of

886/1481. Thus he assisted his monarch during his last illness in camp at Maltepe (cf. Tursun Beg, *Taʾrīkh-i Abu 'l-Fatḥ*, ed. and tr. H. İnalcık and R. Murphey, Minneapolis, etc. 1978, 64, Ay 157 b-158 a). The Grand Vizier kept the death of the Sultan (4 Rabīʿ I 886/3 May 1481) a secret, but sent the news to both Prince Bāyezīd and Prince Djem. His aim was for Djem to arrive first in Istanbul and to make his accession there a *fait accompli*. For that purpose, the mortal remains of Meḥemmed II were secretly brought back to the capital by the court physicians, and then all communication was cut between the two shores of the Bosphorus. Meḥmed Pasha moved the *ʿAdjem-oghlans* out of town and had the city gates closed, but his enemies intercepted his men and the news of the Sultan's death spread quickly. The Janissaries managed to cross the water by private means. Public order was utterly disturbed; Meḥmed Pasha could no longer halt the movements of the soldiery; he withdrew to his residence, but the insurgent Janissaries pursued him there and killed him in his private office (5 Rabīʿ I 886/4 May 1481). Meḥmed Pasha's men reached Ḳonya only on 3 May. The accession of Djem seems to have been doomed from the start, and Ḳaramānī Meḥmed Pasha thus failed to bring about his late Sultan's apparent last wishes.

Meḥmed Pasha Ḳaramānī's importance lies in his institutional and legal work, sc. in building up the state apparatus of what was becoming the Ottoman Empire. He practised his statecraft whilst also being an accomplished master of ornate prose. His *inshāʾ* writings include a famous letter addressed to the Aḳ Ḳoyunlu ruler Uzun Ḥasan [*q.v.*] (see Feridūn, *Münsheʾāt al-selāṭīn*, Istanbul 1264/1848, i, 271 ff.). He wrote poetry under the *makhlaṣ* Nishānī. In Arabic, he wrote a history of the Ottoman Empire in the form of two treatises, one dealing with the period from ʿOthmān I till Meḥemmed II's accession in 855/1451, the other covering the years 855/1451 to early 885/1480, the *Risāla fī tawārīkh al-salāṭīn al-ʿuthmāniyya* and the *Risāla fī taʾrīkh Sulṭān Muḥammad b. Murād Khān min āl ʿUthmān*. The latter includes 10 chronograms in verses describing his own deeds:

1. the building of Rumeli Ḥiṣārî (856/1453).
2. the conquest of Albania (871/1466-7).
3. the (re)construction of the *ič-ḳalʿe* on the castle hill of Ḳonya (872/1467-8).
4. the building of the "New Seraglio" (Ṭopkapî Sarāyî) at Istanbul (873/1468-9).
5. the taking of the fortress of Eghriboz [*q.v.*] (Negroponte) (874/1469-70).
6. the victory over Uzun Ḥasan (877/1472-3).
7. the death of Prince Muṣṭafā (878/1473-4).
8. the taking of Sharḳî Ḳaraḥiṣār (878/1473-4).
9. the building of the wall containing the "New Seraglio" (883/1478-9).
10. the building of the Imperial Stables (*Iṣṭabl-i ʿāmire* (883/1478-9).

These chronicles seem to be a recasting into Arabic of a simple calendar (*taḳwīm*) to which chronograms and ornate passages of *sadjʿ* have been added (cf. Ménage, *The beginnings of Ottoman historiography*). Ḳaramānī Meḥmed's text is one of a number of early historical works representing a group of sources distinct from the group of ʿĀshîḳpasha-zāde, Urudj and the anonymous *Tewārīkh*. This group contains a different tradition about the origin of the Ottomans which is based on an older source than that used by the other group of histories dating from *ca.* 1399 (cf. İnalcık, *Rise*). Minor poets such as Ḳabūlī and Ḥamīdī wrote *ḳaṣīdas* and other poetry in praise of the *nishāndjî* and Grand Vizier.

Meḥmed Pasha Ḳaramānī had two wives. The first was Muṣannifak ʿAlāʾ al-Dīn ʿAlī al-Bisṭāmī's daughter, who gave him a son Zayn al-ʿĀbidīn ʿAlī Čelebi, who in his turn had a son of some renown, "al-Mawlā Muṣṭafā b. ʿAlī b. Meḥmed al-Ḳaramānī" (d. 965/1558). His second wife from 1471 was Sittī Shāh, daughter of the ex-Bey of ʿAlāʾiyye (Alanya), Ḳîlîdj Arslan. With the money of his second wife, he was able in addition to his other pious foundations to pay for the building of the mosque he wished to leave behind as a *waḳf*, the Nishāndjî Djāmiʿi in the Ḳumḳapî quarter of Istanbul. On the *ḳibla* side of it stands the ornamental tomb of the founder, called martyr of the Islamic faith, *shehīd*, in an inscription written by the *sheykh* Abu 'l-Wefāʾ (896/1491) (cf. tr. İ.H. Konyalı, in *Osmanlı tarihleri*, i/4, esp. 330-6).

Bibliography: *Taʾrīkh-i Nishāndjî Meḥmed Pasha*, Istanbul 1279/1862-3, *Osmanlı tarihleri. I/4. Karamanlı Nişancı Mehmed Paşa, Osmanlı sultanları tarihi* (Turkish tr. with extensive introd. by İ.H. Konyalı, Istanbul n.d. [1949], 321-69); F. Babinger, *Die Chronik des Qaramānī Mehmed Pascha, eine neuerschlossene osmanische Geschichtsquelle*, in *MOG*, ii (1926), 242-7; idem, *GOW*, no. 11 (24-6); *İA* art. *Mehmed Paşa, Karamânî* (M.C.Ş. Tekindağ), on which the present article is based; H. Inalçık, *The rise of the Ottoman historiography*, in B. Lewis and P.M. Holt (eds.), *Historians of the Middle East*, London 1962, 1964^{2}, 152-67; V.L. Ménage, *The beginnings of Ottoman historiography*, in *ibid.*, 168-79; İnalcık, *İA* art. *Mehmed II*; Babinger, *Mehmed the Conqueror and his time*, Princeton 1978; U.L. Heyd, ed. V.L. Ménage, *Studies in Old Ottoman criminal law*, Oxford 1973, 10, 20; A. Özcan, *Fatih'in teşkilat Kanunnamesi ve Nizam-i Alem için kardeş katlı meselesi*, in *TD*, xxxiii (1980-1, publ. 1982) 7-56 (new ed. of text); S. Unver, *Sadrazam Karamanlı Mehmet Paşa'nın Eyüp Sultan Medresesi kütüphanesine vakfettiği iki kitaba dair*, in *Konya*, 74-7 (Konya 1945); R.C. Repp, *The Müfti of Istanbul. A. study in the development of the Ottoman learned hierarchy*, London 1986.

(A.H. de Groot)

MEḤMED PASHA, LĀLĀ, Melek-Nihād (II), Ottoman Grand Vizier, who served Sultān Meḥemmed III [*q.v.*] for ten days only and then died on 19 Rabīʿ I 1004/22 November 1595. (Ed.)

MEḤMED PASHA, LĀLĀ, Shāhīnoghlu, Bosnalî (d. 1015/1606, Ottoman Grand Vizier.

Born in Jajce as a descendant of the Bosnian Shāhinoghullarî family, he was related to Ṣoḳollu Meḥmed Pasha [*q.v.*]. Taken into Ottoman service as a *dewshirme* [*q.v.*] boy, he was educated in the so-called Palace School [see enderūn]. During those years he was probably engaged in giving lessons in fighting to one or more Ottoman princes, hence his surname of *Lālā* "tutor". Lālā Meḥmed successively held the court functions of *Peshkīr aghasî*, *Küčük Mīr Ākhūr* and *Büyük Mīr Ākhūr* and left the palace service holding the post of Agha of the Janissaries (999?/1590-1?).

It was in this command that he served far away from the court and the Sultan's person on the battlefields in Hungary during the "Long War" (1001-15/1593-1606). Notably, he saw service under the Grand Vizier Ḳodja Sinān Pasha (1001-3/1593-5) before Raab (Ott. Yanîḳ-ḳalʿe, Hung. Györ) in 1002/1594. Dismissed following the siege of Tata (3 Shawwāl 1002/23 June 1594), he was made successively *beglerbegi* of Ḳaramān of Anadolu and then acted as military governor of the region of Buda (Ott. Budin). In 1003/1595, Lālā Meḥmed Pasha took over the command of the besieged fortress town of

Esztergom [*q.v.*] which he had to surrender to the imperial Commander-in-Chief Peter Ernst, Count Mansfeld (1517-1604). The negotiations were conducted on the Ottoman side by *inter alios* Ibrāhīm Pečewī [*q.v.*], Lālā Meḥmed's trusted secretary, who served him during 15 years of his life (cf. Pečewī, *Taʾrīkh*, ii, 64-6). The next year, Lālā Meḥmed Pasha was ordered to come to the bridge near Eszék [*q.v.*] to join the Ottoman main army and Sultan Meḥemmed III [*q.v.*] in person. He was promoted to vizieral rank. He assisted at the siege of Erlau (Ott. Eğri [*q.v.*]), of which town he was made commander after its fall on 17 Ṣafar 1005/12 October 1596. Lālā Meḥmed Pasha commanded the troops of Rumeli, i.e. the right wing in the battle of Mezö-Keresztes [*q.v.*] (Ott. Hač Owasï, 3-4 Rabīʿ I 1005/25-6 October 1596). In 1597 he served again on the front in Hungary. In Dhu'l-Ḥidjdja 1006/July 1598 he was appointed *Beglerbegi* of Rumeli, a promotion by favour of the Sultan. Lālā Meḥmed Pasha was present at the unsuccessful siege of Gross Wardein (Tk. Warad, now Rumanian Oradea Mare) from 1 October to 3 November 1598. Next year, he served in the army of the new Grand Vizier and *Serdār-i ekrem*, Commander-in-Chief, Dāmād Ibrāhīm Pasha against Neuhäusel (Hung. Ersekújvār, Ott. Uywar, Czech Nové Zámky). In 1600 Lālā Meḥmed served in the army of the Grand Vizier before (Nagy) Kanisza (Ott. Kaniče). In August, he was commander of the troops of Rumeli again and military governor of Buda. He was present at the 34 days' siege of Stuhlweissenburg (Ott. Ustolni Belgrad), which fortress surrendered to the Ottomans on 17 Ṣafar 1011/6 August 1602 (cf. Pečewī, *Taʾrīkh*, ii, 242 ff.). In November of the same year, he was ordered to succour Buda with 2,000 Janissaries, *djebedjis* and artillery against an imperial army (Pečewī, ii, 250). The Ottoman Commander-in-Chief was defeated at first near Pest on 4 Ṣafar 1012/14 July 1603, but soon afterwards was victorious north of Buda and thus able to carry reinforcements into the besieged fortress. The Imperial Army, commanded by the Archduke Matthias, then withdrew. Lālā Meḥmed Pasha was rewarded with the promotion to Third Vizier and the appointment as *serdār*. As such, he organised the defences of Buda and the bridges at Eszék, putting Murād Pasha, then *Beglerbegi* of Rumeli [see MURĀD PASHA, ḲUYUDJU] and Djelālī Deli Ḥasan Pasha, *Beglerbegi* of Bosnia, in command. He then sent the Anatolian troops on leave and withdrew to Belgrade for the winter (29 Rabīʿ II 1012/6 October 1603). At the death inside Belgrade of the Grand Vizier and Commander-in-Chief of the Western front Malḳoč ʿAlī Pasha (27-8 Ṣafar 1013/25-6 July 1604), Lālā Meḥmed took his place (cf. Pečewī, ii, 296). During a short campaign, he was able to reoccupy Pest and take the fortress towns of Hatvan and Waitzen (Vác). Esztergom was laid under siege (24 Djumādā I 1013/18 October 1604). The onset of winter made an end to warfare, since the Janissaries were unwilling to fight. Crimean Tatar light horse and the *Aḳïndjïs* were left in Hungary.

Alongside the conduct of war, Lālā Meḥmed Pasha also kept up diplomatic contact with the enemy in order to seek a peaceful end to the conflict; Murād Pasha (Ḳuyudju) played an important part in these negotiations. Lālā Meḥmed Pasha left for Istanbul to meet the Sultan in his quality of Grand Vizier and returned to the front again on 3 Muḥarram 1014/21 May 1605 with instructions to end the war by means of a treaty with the Emperor. The Grand Vizier recognised Stephen Bocskai as King of Hungary and invited him to join the army. A council of war was held at Eszék. The taking of Esztergom was declared to be the principal war aim. Párkány (Czech Sturovo, Ott. Čigerdelen) was taken on 29 August and Visegrad on 8 September 1605. Esztergom surrendered on conditions on 20 Djumādā I 1014/3 October 1605 (cf. the eyewitness account of Pečewī, *Taʾrīkh*, ii, 305 f.). The taking of this famous fortress and its surrounding places was followed by the conquest of others: Veszprém and Palota, and Neuhäusel on 9 Radjab 1014/20 November 1605. The Grand Vizier ordered a razzia of Tatar and Hungarian light cavalry into the Austrian lands, Croatia and Styria under the command of his nephew "Sarhosh" Ibrāhīm Pasha, the *Beglerbegi* of Kanisza. At Rakos on 7 Djumādā II 1014/20 October 1605, Lālā Meḥmed Pasha held a coronation ceremony for Stephen Bocskai, proclaimed King of Hungary. A crown had been especially made at Istanbul for this ceremony (this is now in the Kunsthistorisches Museum of Vienna, cf. H. Fillitz, *Die Schatzkammer in Wien*, Vienna 1964, 133, 17). Leaving Murād Pasha in charge, the Grand Vizier departed for Istanbul. It was his intention to exercise the supreme command over both the western and the eastern fronts from there. The Sultan's government, however, insisted on him going in person to the war in the east in the next season. The horse-tails (*tugh* [*q.v.*], were already put out at Üsküdar when the Grand Vizier died suddenly on 15 Ṣafar (or 16 Muḥarram?) 1015/23 June (or 25 May?) 1606. Rumours were current at the time that his rival Derwīsh Meḥmed Pasha [*q.v.*] had made the Sephardic Jewish court physician administer poison. Lālā Meḥmed Pasha was buried next to the mausoleum of his kinsman Ṣoḳollu Meḥmed Pasha at Eyyūb.

Bibliography: See *İA* art. s.v. (M.C. Ş. Tekindağ), on which the present article is largely based. A main source is Pečewī's *Taʾrīkh*, whose author personally witnessed the most important years of Lālā Meḥmed Pasha's career as a trusted official: İ.H. Danişmend, *Osmanlı tarihi kronolojisi*, Istanbul 1971, iii, index; C. Ballingal Finkel, *The provisioning of the Ottoman Army during the campaigns of 1593-1606*, in *Habsburgisch-osmanische Beziehungen. CIEPO Colloque Wien, 26-30 September 1983*, ed. A. Tietze, Vienna 1985, 107-23; Von Hammer, *HEO*, vii, 271 f., viii, 84 f., 97; ʿOthmānzāde Aḥmed Tāʾib, *Ḥadīḳat ül-wüzerāʾ*, 53 f. (A.H. de Groot)

MEḤMED PASHA, MELEK, Dāmād (1131-1216/1719-1802), Ottoman Grand Vizier under Sultan Selīm III [*q.v.*].

He was the son of Bosnalï Khodja Süleymān Pasha, Vizier and *Ḳapudān-ï dervā* in 1126/1714 and 1130/1718 till his death in 1133/1721. Born in Istanbul, he followed his father's footsteps in a naval career, becoming commander (*Deryā begi*) in 1736, *Tersāne ketkhüdāsï* and *Ḳapudān-ï deryā* himself (1165-8/1752-5). Sultan Muṣṭafā III (1171-87/1757-74) appointed him *Nishāndjï*, and married him to the Princess Zeyneb ʿĀṣïma Sulṭān, a daughter of Aḥmed III (1757) (cf. A.D. Alderson, *The structure of the Ottoman dynasty*; no. 1268, Table XLI). He was then promoted Vizier and received the title of *Sandjaḳ begi* of Yanya. From 1763 onwards, he received appointments as military governor successively of Vidin and Belgrade, *Beglerbegi* of Anadolu, *Ḳāʾim-maḳām* (1765) *Beglerbegi* of Aydïn, of Rumeli and in 1767-9 *Ḳapudān-pasha* again, during which tenure he made one tour through the Archipelago. In 1769 he was made both *Muḥaṣṣil* of Morea and *Ḳāʾim-maḳām* at Istanbul, which function he held during the Russo-Ottoman War (1769-74).

After a spell out of office, he was made *Ḳapudān-*

pās͟ha a third time in 1774. From 1774 to 1776 he served as commander of K͟hotin [*q.v.*], also charged with the exchange of the Russian and Ottoman ambassadors. Governor of Belgrade 1776-9, he again became *Muḥaṣṣil* of Morea, then governor of Egriboz [*q.v.*], Egypt (1781), Belgrade, Candia (Ott. K͟handaḳ), Bender (1784) and Vidin (1786). Sultan Selīm III [*q.v.*] saved him from temporary disgrace, restored his vizier's rank and appointed him governor of Candia. On 12 Ramaḍān 1206/4 May 1792, Melek Meḥmed Pas͟ha received the imperial signet as token of his appointment as Grand Vizier. He stayed in office for two years and five months, being the senior of all viziers then living (*S͟heyk͟h ül-Wüzerāʾ*).

He did not take part in the policy-making of the reformers around Selīm III, but loyally supported the Sultan's policy with the residual influence which he still had. The reason for his dismissal must have been extreme old age, having served the state for 59 years. Meḥmed Pas͟ha was allowed to retire to his waterside villa at Ortaköy on the Bosphorus, where he died on 16 S͟hawwāl 1216/19 February 1802. His tomb is next to the *türbe* of his wife Zeyneb Sulṭān at the mosque founded by her at Soğukçeşme near the Bāb-ï ʿĀlī.

Bibliography: ʿOt͟hmānzāde Tāʾib Aḥmed, *Ḥadīḳat ül-wüzerāʾ*, continuation of Aḥmed Dj̲āwīd, Istanbul 1271, 45-7; İ.H. Danişmend, *Osmanlı tarihi kronolojisi*, Istanbul 1971, v, 68; S.J. Shaw, *Between old and new*, Cambridge, Mass. 1971, 369 f.

(A.H. de Groot)

MEḤMED PAS͟HA, MUḤSIN-ZĀDE (1116?-1188/1704?-74), Ottoman Grand Vizier.

Son of the Grand Vizier Muḥsin-zāde ʿAbd Allāh Pas͟ha (held office in 1150/1737) and born in Istanbul, he entered the Palace service as a *Ḳapïdj̲ï Bas͟hï*. In 1150/1737 he became *Ḳapïdj̲ïlar Ketk͟hudāsï* and in 1151/1738 vizier and *Beglerbegi* of Marʿas͟h. After 10 years of provincial governmental posts he was in 1160/1747 appointed to the reorganised province of Adana with special orders to hunt down the rebellious elements in Anatolia. From 1162/1749 onwards in various provincial posts in the European provinces, he became in 1171/1758 *Beglerbegi* of Aleppo. On this occasion he was married to the princess Esmāʾ Sulṭān (cf. A.D. Alderson, *The structure of the Ottoman dynasty*, Oxford 1956, no. 1244, Table XLI), a daughter of Aḥmed III. There followed quickly, one after another, the appointments as *Beglerbegi* of Diyārbekr, Anadolu (at Kütahya) and Bosnia (1760), staying one year with his wife at his palace at Ḳadïrga (Istanbul), before proceeding to his post. From 1175/1762 he occupied the governorships of Rumeli and Bosnia, twice each, before being called to the Grand Vizierate on 7 S͟hawwāl 1178/30 March 1765. During his tenure of office, revolts in Arabia, Egypt and Georgia broke out and Russian pressure increased. The Grand Vizier did not think the Empire could sustain a war with that power, but his opinion did not prevail in the *Dīwān*.

Muḥsin-zāde Meḥmed resigned on 23 Rabīʿ II 1182/6 September 1768 and was ordered to reside in Bozdj̲a-Ada (Tenedos [*q.v.*]), Gallipoli (Gelibolu [*q.v.*]) and Rhodes (Rodos [*q.v.*]). In 1182/1769 appointed military governor (*Muḥāfiẓ*) of the Morea, he was able to defeat the Russian-inspired rebellion there in a battle at Tripolitza (Ott. Tripoliče) in D͟hu l-Ḥidj̲dj̲a 1183/April 1770, after which he restored Ottoman authority in the main centres of Patras (Ott. Balya Badra [*q.v.*]), Modon (Ott. Muṭun [*q.v.*]), Navarino (Ott. Navarin [*q.v.*]). In 1185/1771 he went as commander of the Ottoman troops to the Danube front. From S͟haʿban/November 1771, Muḥsin-zāde Meḥmed was Grand Vizier again till his death on 26 Dj̲umādā I 1188/4 August 1774. During those three years, Ottoman arms were unsuccessful against the Russians. The Grand Vizier opened peace negotiation again, first with the Austrians and then with the Russians (Bucharest conference, from November 1772 to February 1773). The Russian demands, including the independence of the Khanate of the Crimea [see ḲÏRÏM] and high war indemnities were not yet acceptable to the Ottomans, and peace was not reached till the Russian army under the Field Marshall Peter A. Rumyants͟ev encircled the Grand Vizier at S͟humnu (Bulg. Shumen) and proposed negotiations again.

Muḥsin-zāde Meḥmed Pas͟ha accepted this proposal immediately. The negotiations between the two delegations, the Ottoman one led by his *Ṣadāret-Ketk͟hüdāsï* (afterwards *Nis͟hāndj̲ï*) Aḥmed Rasmī Efendi [*q.v.*] (see idem, *K͟hulāṣat ül-iʿtibār*, cf. *GOW*, 288, 309-12), were held at the Russian headquarters 17-21 July 1774 and led to the treaty of Küčük Kaynardj̲a [*q.v.*]. The Grand Vizier became ill soon afterwards and withdrew to return to Istanbul. On the way near Karnobad (Tk. Ḳarïnābād) he died on 26 Dj̲umādā I 1188/4 August 1774. On the orders of his widow Esmāʾ Sulṭān, he was buried at Eyyūb next to the gate of the great mausoleum.

Bibliography: Ahmed Vâsif Efendi, *Mehâsinu'l-âsâr ve hakâiku'l-ahbâr*, ed. M. İlgürel, Istanbul 1978, p. XXII, 92, 125, 399; *Şemdânî-zâde Fındıklılı Süleyman Efendi tarihi. Mür'i-i tevârih*, ed. M. M. Aktepe, 3 vols. in 4, Istanbul 1976-81, ii B (index), iii, 27-8; İ.H. Danişmend, *İzahlı Osmanlı tarihi kronolojisi*, Istanbul 1971, iv, 42, 48, 52-3, 59; *İA* art. *Küçük Kaynarca* (C. Tukin); ʿOt͟hmānzāde Tāʾib Aḥmed, *Ḥadīḳat ül-wüzarāʾ*, cont. by Aḥmad Dj̲awīd, *Ward-i muṭarrāʾ*, repr. ed. Freiburg i. Br. 1969, 12-16; *İA* art. *Vâsif* (M. İlgürel); Y. Nagata, *Muhsin-zade Mehmed Paşa ve ayanlik müessesi*, Tokyo 1976.

(A. H. de Groot)

MEḤMED PAS͟HA, ÖKÜZ, Dāmād, Ḳara, 964?-1029/1557?-1620) Ottoman Grand Vizier.

Born in Istanbul the son of a Muslim blacksmith, he entered the palace service in spite of the fact of his being of Muslim Turkish origin. After about 40 years service as a *silāḥdār*, he left the Palace with the rank of a Vizier and became *Beglerbegi* of Egypt (D͟hu 'l-Ḥidj̲dj̲a 1015/April 1607). Arriving there the same year in May (Muḥarram 1016), he became busy with administrative reform. He abolished the illegally-imposed levies of *ṭulba*, *kulfa* and *kus͟hūfiyya*, which formed an excessively heavy burden for the tax-paying population. He was able to suppress a resulting rebellion of the (*ḳul*) *sipāhī*, *tüfenkčis* and *gönüllüs* of the Ottoman garrison, together with the Mamlūk cavalry corps (1017/1608). This "second conquest" of Egypt gained him the epithet *Ḳul-ḳïran* "Breaker of the Slave Soldiers". Thanks to his efficient government, Öküz Meḥmed Pas͟ha was able to send a surprisingly large sum as tribute of Egypt to the Porte. This success brought him 1020/1611 favour from on high. He was made *Ḳapudān Pas͟ha* and Second Vizier instead of K͟halīl Pas͟ha Kayṣariyyeli [*q.v.*]. Sultan Aḥmed I [*q.v.*] gave him his seven-year old daughter Dj̲awhar K͟hān Sulṭān in marriage (1020/1612) (cf. A.D. Alderson, *The structure of the Ottoman dynasty*, Oxford 1956, Table XXXIV, no. 1154 "Gevherhân"). In spite of his new status, Öküz Meḥmed Pas͟ha was not successful in his opposition to the granting of an *ʿahd-nāme* involving capitulations [see IMTIYĀZĀT] to the Dutch Republic 1/10 Dj̲umādā I 1021/6 July 1612 [see K͟HALĪL PAS͟HA ḲAYṢARIYYELĪ].

In command of a squadron of 30 galleys, he went out to sea in the 1022/1613 season. His aim was to attack Maltese and Tuscan corsairs who had ravaged the southern shores of Anatolia and had raided Agha Limanī (near Silifke). His defeat, however, by the Spanish admiral in the service of the Viceroy of Naples, Ottaviano de Aragon, off Samos [see SUSAM] brought him relative disgrace.

He was made *Ḳāʾim-maḳām*, but after the execution of the Grand Vizier Naṣūḥ Pasha [*q.v.*], he succeeded to the highest office on 13 Ramaḍān 1023/17 October 1614. In this new capacity, he restored the members of his faction to office again. Öküz Meḥmed Pasha was appointed Commander-in-Chief of the army formed to counter the aggression of Shāh ʿAbbās I of Persia [*q.v.*], who had violated the treaty concluded with Naṣūḥ Pasha (26 Ramaḍān 1021/20 November 1612). In Djumādā I 1024/June 1615 the Grand Vizier left for Aleppo, too late however for action that year. The army stayed in winter quarters in Marʿash (now Kahramanmaraş), Malaṭya, Sivas and Ḳaramān. In April 1616 Öküz Meḥmed Pasha left Aleppo and marched towards Eriwān to confront the Persian Shāh. The Grand Vizier himself went to Ḳars via Göksün Yayla and Erzurum, despatching important contingents of his large army in the direction of Eriwān and Nihāwand. Having ordered the strengthening of the fortifications of Ḳars, he marched to Eriwān (Ott. Rewān), defeated the Persian forces and laid siege to that fortress. His lack of siege artillery and the strong resistance of the garrison forced him to lift the siege after 60 (or 44?) days, agreeing to a settlement based on the terms of 1021/1612 accepting a reduction by half of the Persian tribute of silk, i.e. to only 100 *yük*. The Ottoman main army then returned to Erzurum (27 Shawwāl 1025/7 November 1616). The Grand Vizier wintered at Ṣoghanlī Yayla. The accusation of neglect of duty levelled at the Grand Vizier after this meagre result of his campaign led the Sultan to dismiss his favourite son-in-law (8 Dhu l-Ḳaʿda 1025/17 November 1616), who nevertheless retained the rank of Second Vizier and was ordered to assist his successor in office, Khalīl Pasha, towards the conclusion of a definitive treaty of peace with Shāh ʿAbbās I. Peace was at last concluded on 6 Shawwāl 1027/26 September 1618 in the Ottoman camp in the plain of Sarāb (near Ardabīl), deep inside Ṣafavid territory.

Sultan ʿOthmān II [*q.v.*] appointed Öküz Meḥmed Pasha Grand Vizier again in place of Khalīl Pasha (1 Ṣafar 1028/18 January 1619). In his new quality, he sent the Ottoman ratification of the Sarāb treaty to Shāh ʿAbbās on 13 Shawwāl 1028/23 September 1619 (cf. *Ghazā-nāme-yi Khalīl Pasha*, ms. Es'ad Efendi 2139, fol. 119b; Ferīdūn, *Münsheʾāt*, Istanbul 1275, ii, 325). Later in 1029/1619, a conflict broke out between the Grand Vizier and the then favourite of the Sultan, the *Ḳapudān-pasha*, the Vizier Güzeldje Istanköylü ʿAlī Pasha [*q.v.*], Meḥmed Pasha once again, as in 1021/1612 in his conflict with Khalīl Pasha, tried to use the help of the ambassadors of Venice and France against his rival, but to no avail, since the Sultan dismissed him and made ʿAlī Pasha Grand Vizier instead (16 Muḥarram 1029/23 December 1619). Öküz Meḥmed's private property was confiscated and he himself banished from Istanbul with the appointment as *Beglerbegi* of Aleppo, and it was in that city that he died not long afterwards.

A *türbe* was built inside the *zāwiya* of Shaykh Abū Bakr (cf. Kātib Čelebi, *Fedhleke*, i, 402). *Waḳf*s founded by Öküz Meḥmed Pasha included a *külliyye* in the Ḳaragümrük quarter of Istanbul where he was born, and a complex including a great *khān* and a market at Ulukışla (in Niğde province on the road to the Cilician Gates (Gülek Boghazī, see CILICIA) (cf. A. Gabriel, *Monuments turcs d'Anatolie*, Paris 1931, i, 156, pl. LV). At Cairo, he built barracks for the Janissary and *ʿAzab* corps and a *zāwiya* with a row of shops for the benefit of the Mawlawiyya [*q.v.*] order of dervishes to which he was himself linked. Elsewhere in Egypt and Syria he erected facilities along the main routes to Mecca.

Bibliography: See *İA* art. *Mehmet Paşa Damad* (M.C.Ş. Tekindağ), with a full listing of sources and literature; also, P.M. Holt, *The pattern of Egyptian political history from 1517 to 1789*, in *idem* (ed.), *Political and social change in modern Egypt*, London 1968, 79-90; S.J. Shaw, *The financial and administrative organization and development of Ottoman Egypt 1517-1798*, Princeton 1962, 40, 89-90, 318; A.H. de Groot, *The Ottoman Empire and the Dutch Republic*, Leiden 1978, 67 ff., 120, 160, 164, 314 f.; İ.H. Danişmend, *Kronoloji*, iii, 262-4, 276; Ḥāfiẓ Ḥüseyin Aywānsarāyī, *Wefeyāt-ī selāṭīn we meshāhīr-i ridjāl*, ed. F.Ç. Derin, Istanbul 1978, 75; İ.H. Uzunçarsılı, *Osmanlı tarihi*, Istanbul 1954[1], iv/2, 367-70.

(A.H. DE GROOT)

MEḤMED PASHA RĀMĪ, Ottoman Grand Vizier and poet, was born in 1065/1655 or 1066/1656 in Eyyūb, a suburb of Istanbul, the son of a certain Ḥasan Agha. He entered the chancellery of the Reʾīs Efendi as a probationer (*shāgird*), and through the poet Yūsuf Nābī [*q.v.*] received an appointment as *maṣraf kātibi*, i.e. secretary for the expenditure of the palace. In1095/1684, through the influence of his patron, the newly appointed *Ḳapudān pasha* [*q.v.*] Muṣṭafā Pasha, he became *dīwān efendi*, i.e. chancellor of the Admiralty. He took part in his chief's journeys and campaigns (against Chios) and on his return to Istanbul became *reʾīs kesedārī*, i.e. pursebearer to the Reʾīs Efendi. In 1102/1690 he was promoted to *beylikdji*, i.e. vice-chancellor, and four years later *Reʾīs Efendi* in place of Abū Bakr, in which office he was succeeded in 1108/1697 by Küčük Meḥmed Čelebi. After the battle of Zenta (12 September 1697), he became *Reʾīs Efendi* for a second time and was one of the plenipotentiaries at the Peace of Carlowitz (Ḳarlofča [*q.v.*]), by the conclusion of which "he put an end to the ravages of the Ten Years' War but also for ever to the conquering power of the Ottomans" (J. von Hammer). As a reward for his services at the peace negotiations he was appointed *ḳubbe wezīri* with 3 horse tails (*tugh*) in 1114/1703 and 6 Ramaḍān 1114/January 24, 1703, appointed to the highest office in the kingdom in succession to the grand vizier Daltaban Muṣṭafā Pasha. In this office he devoted particular attention to the thorough reform of the civil administration, by reform of the civil administration, through the abuses in which he saw the security of the state threatened (cf. von Hammer, *GOR*, vii, 64). "By lessening the burden of fortresses on the frontiers in east and west, by raising militia against the rebel Arabs, by securing the pay of the army from the revenues of certain estates, by making aqueducts, by restoring ruined mosques, by taking measures for the safety of the pilgrim caravans and for the security of Asia Minor, by settling Turkmen tribes, by ordering the Jewish cloth manufacturers in Selānik and the Greek silk manufacturers in Bursa in future to make in their factories all the stuffs hitherto imported into Turkey from Europe" (von Hammer), he exercised a most beneficent activity, which however soon aroused envy and hatred, and since Meḥmed Pasha Rāmī was entirely a man of the pen and not of the sword, he was unpopular with the army, particularly the Janissaries, and this was bound to lead to his fall (cf. *GOR*, vii, 72). In the great rising in Istanbul which lasted four weeks, beginning with the enthronement of Sultan Muṣṭafā II and ending with his deposition (9 Rabīʿ II, 1115/22 August 1703), his career came to an end. He was disgraced, but pardoned in the same year and appointed governor, first of Cyprus, then of Egypt (October 1704). His governorship there terminated as unhappily as his grand viziership (cf. *GOR*, vii, 133, following Rās͟hid and La Motraye). In D̲jumādā I 1118/September 1706, he was dismissed and sent to the island of Rhodes, where he died in D̲h̲u 'l-Ḥid̲jd̲ja 1119/March 1707, either under torture or a result of it (cf. *GOR*, vii, 134, quoting the *internuntius* Talman). Meḥmed Pas͟ha Rāmī is regarded as a brilliant stylist, as the two collections of his offical documents (*ins͟hāʾ*) containing no less than 1,400 pieces, distinguished by their simple clear and elevated style, amply show (cf. the mss. in Vienna, Nat. Bibl. nos. 296 and 297, in G. Flügel, *Die arab., pers. u. türk. Hss.*, i, 271-2). Meḥmed Pas͟ha Rāmī also left a complete *Dīwān*, of which specimens are available in the *Ted̲h̲kire* of his son-in-law Sālim (cf. F. Babinger, *GOW*, 272-3; printed Istanbul 1315). His poetical gifts were inherited by his son ʿAbd Allāh Reʾfet (cf. Bursalí Meḥmed Ṭāhir, *ʿOt̲h̲mānlí müʾellifleri*, ii, 187).

Bibliography: J. von Hammer, *GOR*, vii, *passim*; the history of the Istanbul rising was written by Meḥmed S͟hefīḳ; *ʿOt̲h̲mānlí müʾellifleri*, ii, 186; Sālim, *Ted̲h̲kire*, 252-8; ʿOt̲h̲mānzāde Aḥmad Tāʾib, *Ḥadīḳat ül-wüzarāʾ*, Istanbul 1271, at the end; Aḥmad Resmī [*q.v.*], *K̲h̲alīfat al-ruʾasāʾ*, Istanbul 1269, 47; *Sid̲jill-i ʿot̲h̲mānī*, ii, 367; von Hammer, *Geschichte der Osmanischen Dichtkunst*, iv, 26; *İA*, art. *Meḥmed Paşa Râmî* (Bekir Sıtkı Baykal).

(F. Babinger)

MEḤMED PAS͟HA, RŪM or Rūmī (d. 883/1478), Ottoman Grand Vizier.

Being of *ḳul* status, his origins, whether Greek or Albanian, are obscure. Sultan Meḥemmed II [*q.v.*] admitted him into his intimate circle after the unsuccessful Albanian campaign of 870/1466 during which Meḥmed Pas͟ha became Second Vizier. In 1468/872 he joined the campaign against Ḳaramān [see ḳaramān-og͟hullarí], during which he manifested his rivalry with the Grand Vizier Maḥmūd Pas͟ha [*q.v.*]. Instead of him, Meḥmed Pas͟ha was charged with the deportation of selected members of the populations of the cities of Ḳaramān, Ḳonya [*q.v.*] and Laranda [*q.v.*], mainly artisans, other professionals and merchants. The older Ottoman chronicles agree in the disapproval of the Greek's harsh treatment of the Muslim people in question, giving a picture of this Pas͟ha as if he were effecting an act of revenge for the Istanbul Greek population's fate (cf. ʿĀs͟hīkpas͟ha-zāde, tr. R.F. Kreutel, *Vom Hirtenzelt zur Hohen Pforte*, Graz, etc. 1959[1], 201 f., 238, 240 f., see also *idem*, ed. ʿĀlī, Istanbul 1332, 143, 170, 191).

As a reward for his zeal in serving his master's policy of repopulating the city of Istanbul, Rūm Meḥmed Pas͟ha was appointed Grand Vizier instead of Maḥmūd Pas͟ha in 873/1468-9. The members of his faction were given important positions too; *inter alios*, Mollā Meḥmed Wildān became *Ḳāḍī-ʿasker*, whilst K̲h̲āṣṣ Murād, Gedik Aḥmed and Özgürog͟hlu ʿĪsā Bey all became viziers. His continued harsh policy towards the Muslim population of Ḳaramān, which included the wide-scale confiscation of freehold property and *waḳf*s, caused an armed resistance organised by the Ḳaramānog͟hlu princes Pīr Meḥmed and Ḳāsím, who made themselves masters of the town of Laranda. Meḥmed Pas͟ha's counter-offensive was swift. Laranda and Ereğli were destroyed in 874/1469-70. All local *waḳf* and private property was confiscated. Moving to Alanya (ʿAlāʾiyye [*q.v.*]), he was unable to conquer that fortress town. Contemporary sources tried to explain this lack of vigour as due to Meḥmed Pas͟ha's being married to a sister of Ḳílíd̲j Arslan, the last Bey of Alanya. The Grand Vizier continued his punitive expedition by persecuting the Warsak Türkmen tribe, who were able to inflict a defeat on Rūm Meḥmed's forces in the Cilician mountains. Meḥemmed II dismissed his Grand Vizier for this failure (875/1470-1). Rūm Meḥmed Pas͟ha was thereupon given a command in the expedition to conquer Negroponte (Eg͟hriboz [*q.v.*]) in D̲h̲u 'l-Ḥid̲jd̲ja 874 and Muḥarram 875/June and July 1470. The rivalry between him and Maḥmūd Pas͟ha and Ḳaramānī Meḥmed Pas͟ha [*q.v.*] must have been the cause of his downfall and execution in 877/1472-3. Some sources cite Rūm Meḥmed Pas͟ha's involvement in the repopulation of Istanbul as an example of his talent as a financial administrator. He seems to have introduced the levy of rent on houses (the so-called *muḳāṭaʿa*) from the newly-settled inhabitants of the new capital, who till then had enjoyed their new property rights free of any taxation (cf. *İA* art. *Meḥmed II* (H. İnalcık)). Rūm Meḥmed Pas͟ha seems to have been an efficient instrument of Meḥemmed II's centralising policies, especially those of turning private landholdings into state property (*mīrī*) at the expense of the old-established local population, in this way creating *tīmār* estates for the Sultan's servants.

He was the founder of *inter alia* a beautifully situated *külliyye* at Üsküdar, of which the mosque is still standing, overlooking the Bosphorus: one of the few buildings in fact left from the days of the Conqueror. Next to the mosque stands the *türbe* in which the founder lies buried, together with a grandson and his daughter.

Bibliography: *İA* art. *Meḥmed Paşa, Rūm* (M.C.Ş. Tekindağ), where sources and literature are indicated; *İA* art. *Meḥmed II* (H. İnalcik); ʿĀs͟hīkpas͟ha-zāde, *Taʾrīk̲h̲*, tr. R. F. Kreutel, *Vom Hirtenzelt zur hohen Pforte*, Graz, etc. 1959 (= Osmanische Geschichtsschreiber, 3), 201 f., 238, 240 f., F. Babinger, *Mehmed the Conqueror and his time*, ed. W.C. Hickman, tr. R. Manheim, Princeton 1978, 254, 292 f., 286 f., 299, 454; İ.H. Danişmend, *Osmanlı tarihi kronolojisi*, Istanbul 1971, i, 266-7, 306-7, 313, 315, 319, 322-3, 337, 354, 377-8 (with different chronology); N. Beldiceanu, *Recherches sur la réforme foncière de Mehmed II*, in *Acta Historica* (*Soc. Acad. Dacoromana*), iv (1965), 27-39; İ.H. Konyalı, *Üsküdar tarihi*, 2 vols., Istanbul 1976, i, 249-52; G. Goodwin, *A history of Ottoman architecture*, London1971, 114-15 (with wrong date), 283.

(A. H. de Groot)

MEḤMED PAS͟HA ṢARÎ, Defterdār, Baḳḳāl-og͟hlu [see ṣarî meḥmed pas͟ha]

MEḤMED PAS͟HA ṢOḲOLLĪ, Ṭawīl [see ṣoḳollī, ṣoḳollu]

MEḤMED PAS͟HA, SULṬĀN-ZĀDE, D̲jiwān Ḳapíd̲jí-Bas͟hí, Semīn (1010-56/1602-46), Ottoman Grand Vizier.

He was born in Istanbul as the son of ʿAbd al-Raḥmān Bey (himself a son of Semīz Aḥmed Pas͟ha, Grand Vizier 887-8/1579-80, by origin an Albanian *dews͟hirme* boy) and of Hümās͟hāh ʿĀʾis͟he K̲h̲aním Sulṭān, a daughter of Čig͟hala-zāde Sinān Pas͟ha [*q.v.*], thus being a grandson of Princess Mihr-i Māh

Sulṭān [*q.v.*], hence his surname Sulṭān-zāde (cf. A.D. Alderson, *The structure of the Ottoman dynasty*, Oxford 1956, Table XXX, no. 2128). Meḥmed Pa<u>sh</u>a was educated in the imperial harem and the *<u>Kh</u>āṣṣ Oda* [*q.v.*]. Whilst only 19 years old, he became a *Ḳapīd<u>j</u>ī-Ba<u>sh</u>ī* during the <u>Kh</u>otin campaign of Sultan ʿO<u>th</u>mān II. Already in 1040/1630-1, because of the highest patronage, he became a *ḳubbe wezīri* [*q.v.*]. In 1042/1633 Sultan Murād IV dismissed him for reasons of incompetence in the preparation of the campaign against Persia, and banished him to Rhodes. In 1047/1637-8, reinstated as Second Vizier, he went for three years to Egypt as *Beglerbegi*. Having been back in Istanbul since 1050/1640, he became *wālī* of Oczakov (Ott. Özü) with the task of retaking Azov [see AZAḲ] (4 <u>Dh</u>u 'l-Ḳaʿda 1051/4 February 1642). Thanks to the Don Cossacks having abandoned the fortress previously, Meḥmed Pa<u>sh</u>a became master of Azaḳ without any bloodshed. Upon his return to the capital, the Grand Vizier Kemānke<u>sh</u> Ḳara Muṣṭafā Pa<u>sh</u>a (1048-52/1638-43) removed him from the centre of power by making him *Beglerbegi* of Damascus (Ra<u>dj</u>ab 1053/October 1643). It was there that he received the seal of office and the appointment as Grand Vizier (21 <u>Dh</u>u 'l-Ḳaʿda 1053/31 January 1644), thanks to his collaboration with the faction of <u>Dj</u>in<u>dj</u>i <u>Kh</u>o<u>dj</u>a [see ḤUSAYN EFENDI], Sultan Ibrāhīm's [*q.v.*] favourite. On 1 Muḥarram 1053/10 March 1644, the new Grand Vizier arrived in the capital.

Next year, he was involved in the preparations of the war against Crete (1055-79/1645-69). He was highly critical of the conduct of the *Ḳapudān-ī deryā* and *serdār*, Silāḥdār Yūsuf Pa<u>sh</u>a, whose only success was the taking of Canea (Ott. Ḥanya). The Grand Vizier lost the struggle with this rival when the Sultan justified Yūsuf Pa<u>sh</u>a in all respects, and he was dismissed. In <u>Dh</u>u 'l-Ḳaʿda 1055/January 1646 he was in his turn appointed *serdār* of the Cretan campaign. Outside the Dardanelles, Meḥmed Pa<u>sh</u>a's fleet of galleys encountered the Venetian sailing squadron of Tommaso Morosini off Tenedos (Ott. Boz<u>dj</u>a Ada [*q.v.*]) and successfully passed the Venetian blockade (19 Rabīʿ II 1056/4 June). Arriving at Crete on 27 <u>Dj</u>umādā II 1056/10 August 1646, he decided to lay siege to the fortresses of Suda and Aprikorno near Canea. Already ill during the voyage thither, Meḥmed Pa<u>sh</u>a died on 28-9 <u>Dj</u>umādā II 1056/11-12 August 1646 in camp before Suda. His body was brought home to be buried next to his mother ʿĀʾi<u>sh</u>e <u>Kh</u>anīm Sulṭān in the cemetry of the *türbe* of ʿAzīz Maḥmūd Hüdāʾī at Üsküdar. A son and grandsons of his are mentioned in *SʿO*, iv, 161 ff.

Bibliography: In addition to the Ottoman and European sources mentioned in *İA* art. s.v. (by M.M. Aktepe, of which the above article is an abridgment), see İ.H. Danişmend, *İzahlı Osmanlı tarihi kronolojisi*, Istanbul 1971, iii, 389, 391-4, 401; Kātib Čelebi, *Tuhfat*, Istanbul 1329/1911, 120 ff.; H.K. Yılmaz, *Aziz Mahmud Hüdayi ve Celvetiyye tarikatı*, Istanbul n.d. (? 1980), 69 f.; E. Eickhoff, *Venedig, Wien und die Osmanen*, Münich 1970, 27 f., 40, 42, 45 f., 52 f.; M.O. Bayrak, *Istanbul'da gömülü meşhur adamlar* (*1453-1978*), Istanbul 1979, 49; Z. Tezeren, *Seyyid Aziz Mahmud Hüdayi I*, Istanbul 1984, 23, 27, 30, 120. (A.H. DE GROOT)

MEḤMED PA<u>SH</u>A, TABANĪYASSĪ (997?-1049/1589?-1639), Ottoman Grand Vizier.

Of Albanian origin, he was taken from his home at Ta<u>sh</u>līd<u>j</u>a as a *dev<u>sh</u>irme* boy and entered the palace service [see ENDERŪN]. The protection of the *Dār al-Saʿāda A<u>gh</u>asī* Ḥad<u>j</u>dj̲ī Muṣṭafā A<u>gh</u>a provided him with a quick career from *Mīr Ā<u>kh</u>ūr* to vizier and *Beglerbegi* of Egypt before becoming Grand Vizier on 28 <u>Sh</u>awwāl 1041/18 May 1632. He assisted Sultan Murād IV [*q.v.*] in suppressing opposition forces in the capital, thus making it possible for the sultan to rule in person. Meḥmed Pa<u>sh</u>a favoured a foreign policy of neutrality in the European wars, which implied discreet contacts with Swedish and Transylvanian diplomacy. While on campaign against Persia, the Grand Vizier wintered at Aleppo (1043/1633-4). At the end of the season, he stayed in Diyārbekr (1043-4/1634-5) till 18 <u>Sh</u>awwāl 1044/6 April 1635 in order to meet Murād IV at Erzurum on 17 Muḥarram 1045/3 July 1635, the two of them marching together to Eriwān. This Persian fortress surrendered on 18 Ṣafar/3 August, but was lost again next year (24 <u>Sh</u>awwāl 1045/1 April 1636). Before that date, Meḥmed Pa<u>sh</u>a had been already dismissed (24 <u>Sh</u>aʿbān 1045/2 February 1636). Later the same year, he was military governor of Oczakov (Ott. Özü). In <u>Sh</u>aʿbān 1047/January 1638 he was moved to Buda, but shortly afterwards became *Ḳāʾim-maḳām* at Istanbul. After a short time in disgrace again, Meḥmed Pa<u>sh</u>a was jailed in Yedi Kule prison and killed. His tomb is at Miskinler Tekkesi.

Bibliography: İ.H. Danişmend, *Osmanlı tarihi kronolojisi*, Istanbul 1971, iii, 354-62, 367-70, 372; M.I. Kunt, *The Sultan's servants*, New York 1983, 131-3; ʿO<u>th</u>mānzāde Tāʾib Aḥmed, *Hadīḳat ül-wüzerāʾ*, repr. Freiburg i. B. 1969; Nāʿīmā, *Taʾrī<u>kh</u>*, Istanbul 1280/1863-4, iii, 110-19; Von Hammer, *HEO*, ix, 184, 213 ff., 219 f., 260-4, 277, 286 ff., 298 f. (A.H. DE GROOT)

MEḤMED PA<u>SH</u>A, TIRYĀḲĪ, ḤAD<u>J</u>DJ̲Ī (? 1091-1164/?1680-1751), Ottoman Grand Vizier.

The son of an *Odaba<u>sh</u>ī* (Janissary Officer) born in Istanbul, he was himself enrolled in the Janissary Corps, and made a career as a "civil servant", reaching the post of Corps Secretary (*A<u>gh</u>a Ḳapīsī Yazīd<u>j</u>īsī* or *Yeničeri Efendisi*) in 1149/1736. He was removed from that position because of his misappropriations of pay money while serving with the corps on campaign. In fact, he was denounced by the "Corps Merchant", Dāwūd. Thanks to the protection of the *Ketk<u>h</u>üdā* [*q.v.*] of the Grand Vizier, he was appointed soon afterwards *Süwārī Muḳābeled<u>j</u>i* (Audit Officer of the Cavalry Corps of the Sublime Porte). This new career made Meḥmed Efendi one of the chief clerks of the Ottoman chancery (*<u>Kh</u>ʷād<u>j</u>egān-i Dīwān-ī Hümayūn* [*q.v.*]). In 1739 he became *Mewḳūfātī*, a high official in the *Defter-<u>kh</u>āne* [*q.v.*]. In this capacity, Meḥmed Efendi served at the negotiations of the Peace of Belgrade held with the Imperial Austrian and Russian plenipotentiaries. He remained in and around Belgrade till 1154/1741, serving on the mixed Ottoman-Austrian boundary commission with Ḳāḍī Ebū Sehil Nuʿmān Efendi. Later, he was twice made *Yeničeri Efendisi* again. In 1745 he became *Tersāne Emīni* [see TERSĀNE] in which capacity he directed the complete restoration and extension of the Imperial Naval Dockyard at Istanbul after its destruction by fire. He earned Sultan Maḥmūd's [*q.v.*] favour and was promoted to be "General Deputy" (*ketk<u>h</u>üdā* = *kāhya*) [*q.v.*] of the Grand Vizier on 7 <u>Dj</u>umādā II 1159/27 June 1746. A month and a half later, he succeeded his chief in office as Grand Vizier himself on 21 Ra<u>dj</u>ab 1159/10 August 1746 (cf. *Si<u>dj</u>ill-i ʿO<u>th</u>mānī*, iv, 237, with wrong date). According to contemporary sources his lifelong habit of taking drugs (*tiryāḳ*) made Meḥmed Pa<u>sh</u>a often behave in an ill-mannered and insulting way towards high officers of state and *ʿulamāʾ*. At the same time, it must be noted, he made a large number of changes in official appointments while in power (cf. Süleymān ʿIzzī, Taʾrīkh, fols. 66a-72a).

During his tenure of office, Ottoman diplomacy saw great events. Peace was made with Nādir Shāh [q.v.] on 17 Shaʿbān 1159/4 September 1746 (cf. Nāẓif Muṣṭafā Efendi, Īrān sefāretnāmesi, in F.R.Unat, Osmanlı sefirleri ve sefâretnâmeleri, Ankara 1968, 84 + ill.). In 1160/1747 Meḥmed Pasha rejected the French overtures to make an offensive alliance against Austria; the Porte had not forgotten how France refused the Ottoman offer of mediation in 1158/1745 and remained distrustful of French motives (cf. I. de Testa, Recueil des traités de la Porte Ottomane, Paris 1864, ii, 178 f.). On the contrary, Meḥmed Pasha had the peace confirmed with the new Austrian ruler, the Empress Maria Theresa, on 10 April 1747. This agreement was followed up by a treaty of friendship and commerce with Tuscany on 27 May 1747 (cf. Muʿāhedāt Medjmūʿasî, Istanbul 1297, iii, 135 ff.; ʿIzzī, op. cit., fols. 114-121).

Sultan Maḥmūd I (1143-68/1730-54)—following his personal policy of maintaining his viziers only during a limited time in office—dismissed Meḥmed Pasha himself on 18 Shaʿbān 1160/24 August 1747. As the reason for this, the imperial firmān adduced the Grand Vizier's ill-treatment of persons in high places. Meḥmed Pasha ran into conflict with the Sheykh ül-Islām Meḥmed Esʿad Efendi; so much is certain. The ex-Grand Vizier was banished to Rhodes. Soon afterwards he was given the sandjaḳ of Içel [q.v.] in arpalîk. On 7 Rabīʿ I 1161/7 March 1748, Meḥmed Pasha became Beglerbegi of Mawṣil, and eight months later Beglerbegi of Baghdād. This latter appointment was made during the interregnum between the mamlūk Aḥmed Pasha (d. 1160/1747) and his chosen successor, Süleymān Pasha, "Abū Laylā", who in 1162/1749 was to be the true founder of the Mamlūk dynasty which ruled from Baghdād till 1831. The Ottoman central government tried to reassert its authority in the province by sending thither appointees of its own, but this policy remained unsuccessful. Tiryāḳī Meḥmed Pasha was not able to establish his authority against the will of the local opposition. He was recalled and appointed Beglerbegi of the eyālet of Ḥabesh and Sheykh ül-Ḥarem of Mecca. He refused to accept this honour, fell into disgrace and lost his vizierial rank and private fortune as a consequence. He was ordered to live in the provincial backwater of Rethymno (Ott. Resmo) on Crete, where he died early in 1164/1751. This news reached Istanbul on 8 Ramaḍān 1164/34 July 1751 (hence an error in Sidjill-i ʿOthmānī, iv, 38).

The life of Tiryāḳī Meḥmed Pasha was characteristic of the age. It shows how an able Janissary-born servant of the Sultan (ḳul) could enter upon a career in the chancery of the central government, attaining the supreme office of Ṣadr-i Aʿẓam [q.v.] when he was about 66 years old. The Sultan's policy at this time seems to have been to limit the tenure of his Grand Viziers to only a year or two, so that dismissal did not automatically mean disgrace, although the conflict with the Islamic religious hierarchy must have shortened his tenure in the case of Meḥmed Pasha, and his refusal of office led in the end to his complete undoing.

Bibliography: See İA, art. s.v. (M.M. Aktepe); idem (ed.), Şemdânîzâde Fındıklılı Süleyman Efendi tarihi. Mürʾi 't-tevârih, 3 vols. in 4, Istanbul 1976-81, 1, 116, 119, 122, 124-5, 127-34, 138, 141-2, 145-6, 151-2, 156, 159; Dilâwerzâde ʿÖmer Efendi, Dheyl to ʿOthmānzāde Tāʾib Aḥmed, Ḥadīḳat ul-wüzerāʾ, Istanbul 1271/1854-5, repr. Freiburg 1969, 73-4,

s.v. el-Ḥādj M.P.; I.H. Danişmend, Osmanlı tarihi kronolojisi, Istanbul 1961, iv, 32-3, v, 59; Hâfiz Hüseyin Ayvansarâyî, Vefeyât-i selâṭîn ve meşâhîr-i ricâl, ed. F.Ç. Derin, Istanbul 1978, 75; J. Hammer-Purgstall, HEO, xv, 110-12, 124-42; Süleymān ʿIzzī, Taʾrīkh-i Weḳāyiʿ, Istanbul 1199/1784; E. Prokosch, tr., Molla und Diplomat. Der Bericht des Ebû Sehil Nuʿmân Efendi über die österreichisch-osmanische Grenzziehung nach dem Belgrader Frieden 1740/41, Graz, etc. 1972, index s.v.; İ.H. Uzunçarşılı, Osmanlı tarihi, iv/2, Ankara 1959[1], 1983[3], 363-7 (text of imp. docs.); idem, Osmanlı imperatorluğu merkez ve bahriye teşkilâtı, Ankara 1948, 347-8, 425 ff.; idem, Osmanlı imparatorluğu kapukulu ocakları, 2 vols., Ankara 1943-4, i, 408-9, 173, 180, 185; V. Aksan, Ottoman-French relations 1739-1768, in S. Kuneralp, ed., Studies on Ottoman diplomatic history, i, Istanbul 1987, 41-58.

(A.H. DE GROOT)

MEḤMED PASHA, YEGEN, GÜMRÜKČÜ (d. 1158/1745), Ottoman Grand Vizier.

Son of a sister of the then influential statesman Defterdār Kel Yūsuf Efendi (hence the surname "Nephew"), he was born in Antalya and began public life as a Mültezim in the region of his origin. He went to Istanbul to take up a career in the secretarial service, becoming a khadjegān. From 1140/1728 to 1141/1729 he was Commissioner of the Customs of Istanbul (Gümrük Emīni). Around 1144/1732 he became Ḳapu-Ketkhudāsî of the Beglerbegi of Erzurum, Topal ʿOthmān Pasha, as well. In 1145/1733 he acquired the post of Mewḳūfātčî and later again Commissioner of the Customs, leaving that position to become Ḳapu-Ketkhudāsî to Köprülü-zāde Ḥāfiẓ Aḥmed Pasha. In 1737/1150 he was appointed vizier and got the function of Ḳāʾim-maḳām (23 (26?) Shaʿbān 1150/16 (19?) December 1737), Shemdāni-zāde, Mürʾī-i tewārīkh, 67, 77-85: 29 Shaʿbān 1150/22 December 1737). Yegen Meḥmed then became Grand Vizier. Preparing for war, he desired at the same time the French ambassador Villeneuve to undertake mediation with the Emperor and with Russia. He left Istanbul as serdār on 15 Dhu 'l-Ḥidjdja 1150/5 April 1738 and moved the army via Edirne and Nish towards Ada-Ḳalʿe [q.v.]. After heavy fighting in that area, he was successful in the retaking of Mehādiye, Ada-Ḳalʿe and Semendire (26 Rabīʿ II 1151/13 August 1738). Having returned to Istanbul at the end of the campaigning season, preparations of war were mainly directed towards the reconquest of Belgrade. The Crimean Khān was his main adviser on the conduct of the war against Russia at this time. Through the influence of the powerful Dār al-Saʿāde Aghasî Beshīr Agha, Sultan Maḥmūd I [q.v.] dismissed his Grand Vizier before he could leave for the front (12 Dhu 'l-Ḥidjdja 1151/23 March 1739).

Meḥmed Pasha was now exiled to Chios (Ott. Saḳîz [q.v.]) for one-and-a-half years. On 19 Rabīʿ II 1153/14 July 1740, Yegen Meḥmed was made military governor of Candia. Afterwards he received the governorates of Negroponte (Ott. Eghriboz [q.v.]), Bosnia and (in 1157/1744) Aydîn [q.v.]. At the end of the same year, he was made Beglerbegi of Anadolu and serdār, being sent to Ḳars and the Persian front with a large army. Thanks to the initiative of the Crimean Khan Selīm Giray II (1743-8) and his Tatar troops, the Ottomans attacked the Persian army in its fortified position near Eriwān (12 Radjab 1158/10 August 1745). After a week of fighting, the Grand Vizier fell ill and could not exercise his command any more. Disorder ensued among the Ottoman Lewend [q.v.] troops, and fighting was broken off. The Grand Vizier died on 21 Radjab 1158/19 August 1745; his body was brought inside the citadel of Ḳars and buried there.

Bibliography: *İA* art. s.v. (by M.M. Aktepe), of which the present article is a summary; idem (ed.), *Şemdânîzâde Fındıklılı Süleyman Efendi tarihi. Mür'i-i tevârih*, 3 vols. in 4, Istanbul 1976-81, i, pp. XVII f., 10, 66, 69, 77-85, 87 f., 90, 96, 112 f., 115, 118, 120, 125, 377; Hâfız Hüseyin Ayvansarâyî. Vefeyât-i selâtîn ve meşâhîr-i ricâl, ed. F. Ç. Derin, Istanbul 1978, 85, 114; A. Vandal, *Une ambassade française en Orient*, Paris 1887, 329 ff.

(A.H. de Groot)

MEḤMED PASHA YEGEN, Ḥādjdjī Seyyid (1138-1201/1726-87), Ottoman Grand Vizier from 16 Ramaḍān 1196-25 Muḥarram 1197/25/August-31 December 1782. Of Janissary birth, he died as *Serʿasker* at Köstendje [*q.v.*] on 25 Muḥarram 1202/6 December 1787. (Ed.)

MEḤMED RAʾŪF, Modern Turkish Mehmet Rauf (1875-1931), Turkish novelist of the late 19th and early 20th century. Born in Istanbul and trained as a naval officer, he entered the navy in 1893, was sent to Crete for further education, served as liaison officer in the launches of Foreign Embassies on the Bosphorus, retiring from the navy in 1908. Apart from publishing various periodicals for ladies and some attempts to carry on trade, he devoted his life to his writing.

Already while a student in the naval college he sent his first literary experiments to Khālid Ḍiyāʾ [*q.v.*] in Izmir, who published them in the newspaper *Khidmet*, Later, he contributed to the periodical *Mekteb* and various daily papers. When in 1895, the leading westernising writers formed a group for modern literature [see turk. Literature] around the periodical *Therwet-i Fünūn* [*q.v.*], he soon joined them and published most of his writings there. Through Khālid Ḍiyāʾ, now in Istanbul, he met most of the *Therwet-i Fünūn* school. Most of his novels and collection of short stories, numbering a dozen each, are rather superficial, over-sentimental narratives with one remarkable exception, *Eylül* "September" (1900), which is the first example in Turkish literature, of sustained psychological analysis. This novel stands out not only among the works of Meḥmed Raʾūf, but it is also one of the most outstanding prose productions of the whole period.

Eylül is the love story of Suʿād, a married woman and Nedjīb, a relative and family friend. It is set among the semi-westernised, lower-middle class families of Istanbul at the turn of the century. Thüreyyā is the immature, sporty husband who spends most of his time boating and swimming while his wife tries to find consolation in music and plays the piano for hours on end to escape her boring life. A deep platonic relationship develops between Suʿād and Nedjīb, who shares similar tastes with her. Entire chapters of the novel are devoted to a psychological analysis of the lovers, who, because of their strict upbringing, remain faithful to the bounds of morality. A fire breaks out in the sea-side villa (*yalī*) on the Bosphorus where the young married couple live, and Suʿād, together with Nedjīb who tries to save her, both perish in the flames.

Meḥmed Raʾūf is also the author of several plays; see *Bibl.*

Bibliography: L. Sami Akalın, *Mehmet Rauf, hayatı, sanatı, eserleri*, Istanbul 1953; Sabahat Demirkızdıran, *Mehmet Rauf'un romanlarında kadın tipleri*, 1954, unpubl. thesis, Istanbul University Library no. 2423; Ayla Altındağ, *Mehmet Rauf'un hikâyeciliği*, 1965, unpubl. thesis, Istanbul University Library no. 3756, Cevdet Kudret, *Türk edebiyatında hikâye ve roman*, i^5,Istanbul 1987, 267-77; Kenan Akyüz, *La littérature moderne de Turquie*, in *PTF*, ii, Wiesbaden 1964, 536-7. For a study of his plays, see Metin And in *Varlık*, nos. 686, 688, Istanbul 1967. (Fahir İz)

MEḤMED REʾĪS, Ibn Menemenli, Turkish ship's captain and cartographer from an Aegean seafaring family, author of an 81 × 58 cm chart of the Aegean Sea, showing also Greece and the western coast of Asia Minor (Museo Correr, Venice). Dated 999/1590 and with additional title and author's name in Italian (probably from the 17th century), the chart shows rhumbs and 199 names of coastal towns or islands noted in Turkish.

Similar to the Aegean sea-chart in the atlas of ʿAlī Madjar Reʾīs dating from 1567, the above-mentioned belongs to the portolan tradition. It is more exact than the corresponding maps of Pīrī Reʾīs [*q.v.*], although in some cases differing from both in nomenclature. One should note that all Turkish sea-charts of the Aegean not only differ from the European ones in nomenclature but are also not as standardised as these.

Bibliography: M. Vedovato, *The nautical chart of Mohammed Rais, 1590*, in *Imago Mundi*, viii (1951), 49; W. Brice, C. Imber and R. Lorch, *The Aegean sea-chart of Mehmed Reis ibn Menemenli A.D. 1590/1*, Seminar on early Islamic science, Monograph no. 2, Manchester 1977. (H. Eisenstein)

MEḤMED SAʿĪD GHĀLIB PASHA, Ottoman statesman.

Born in Istanbul in 1177/1763-4, he was the son of Seyyid Aḥmed Efendi, *bash-khalīfe* in the *mektūbī* office of the Grand Vizier. After the death of his father (1188/1774-5), he entered the same office where he became *bash-khalīfe* in 1210/1795. He was appointed *āmedji* [*q.v.*] on 15 Ramaḍān 1213/3 February 1798 and was sent to France (April 1802) to negotiate peace, which had been broken by the French expedition to Egypt (July 1798). He succeeded in signing the Treaty of Paris on 25 June 1802 (for the text of this treaty, see G. Noradounghian, *Recueil d'actes internationaux de l'Empire ottoman*, Paris 1897-1903, ii, 51-4). Back in Istanbul at the beginning of 1803, he became *büyük tedhkiredji* and was nominated *reʾīs ül-küttab* in September 1806. He followed the Ottoman army in the campaign against Russia, but when the news of Selīm III's deposition on 29 May 1807 reached the army, he took refuge with Muṣṭafā Pasha Bayraḳdār [*q.v.*] at Rusčuk. Meanwhile, a few days later, on 15 Djumādā I 1222/21 July 1807, he was appointed *nishāndjī* and charged with the negotiation of an armistice with the Russians. This resulted in the armistice of Slobosia (24 August). Ghālib Efendi was nominated *reʾīs ül-küttāb* for the second time on 19 Safar 1223/15 April 1808. He maintained his position after Muṣṭafā IV's deposition on 28 July, and remained in charge under Maḥmūd II up to the middle of 1811. Then he became *ketkhüdā* of the Grand Vizier. He headed the Ottoman mission in the negotiations with the Russians, aiming at ending the war which had been resumed again in October 1808. Thus he concluded the treaty of Bucharest on 28 May 1812 (for the text of this treaty, see Noradounghian, II, 86-92). He was appointed *reʾīs ül-küttab* for the third time on 30 Muḥarram 1229/22 January 1814, but was dismissed during the *ewāsiṭ-i Radjab*/22 June-8 July.

Ghālib Efendi remained for the following nine years out of Istanbul. He was charged, with the rank of *wazīr* and the title of *pa<u>sh</u>a*, with the administration of different provinces in Anatolia. His banishment was due to Ḥālet Efendi [*q.v.*], a political rival whose influence had become preponderant at the court. He was exiled to Ḳonya in Ramaḍān 1236/June 1827, and could regain favour only after the execution of his rival (during the *ewā<u>kh</u>ir-i Ṣafar* 1238/7-15 November 1822).

<u>Gh</u>ālib Pa<u>sh</u>a was nominated commandant of the European side of the Bosphorus during the *ewāsiṭ-i Muḥarram* 1239/17-26 September 1823. He returned to Istanbul and soon became Grand Vizier (10 Rabīʿ II/14 December). The main problem with which he had to deal was the Greek revolt in the Morea. He charged the *wālī* of Egypt Muḥammad ʿAlī Pa<u>sh</u>a [*q.v.*] to crush the revolt by landing troops in the peninsula. He was dismissed from the Grand Vizierate on 20 Muḥarram 1240/14 September 1824. The cause seems to be his reluctance to agree to the proposal of the Sultan for the abolition of the Janissaries [see YEÑI-ČERI]. Appointed *wālī* of Erzurum and *<u>Sh</u>arḳ ser-ʿaskeri* in Ra<u>dj</u>ab 1240/19 February-20 March 1825, he tried to resist the Russians during the war of 1828, but was not able to prevent the fall of Ḳars (15 July). He was dismissed on <u>Dj</u>umādā II 1244/9 December 1828-6 January 1829 and exiled to Balīkesir, where he died in 1245/1829-30.

<u>Gh</u>ālib Pa<u>sh</u>a was an intelligent and able administrator. His knowledge of international affairs qualified him as the most skilful Ottoman diplomat of his time. He is rightly regarded as the founder of modern Turkish diplomacy.

Bibliography: *Sefāret-nāme-i <u>Gh</u>ālib Efendi*, in *Edebiyyāt-i ʿumūmiyye me<u>dj</u>mūʿasī*, nos. 9-13, 15; Süleymān Fāʾiḳ, *<u>Kh</u>alīfet ül-rüʾesāʾ*, Appx. II, 166-70; *Si<u>dj</u>ill-i ʿo<u>th</u>mānī*, iii, 615-16; Orhan F. Köprülü, *İA*, s.v.; ʿĀṣīm, *Taʾrī<u>kh</u>*, ii, *passim*; <u>Sh</u>ānī-zāde, *Taʾrī<u>kh</u>*, i, *passim*; <u>Dj</u>ewdet, *Taʾri<u>kh</u>*², vi-vii, *passim*; Luṭfī, *Taʾri<u>kh</u>*, i-ii, *passim*; Zinkeisen, vii, *passim*; A. von Prokosch-Osten, *Geschichte des Abfalls der Griechen*, Vienna 1867, i, 226, 240, 302 f., iv, 115 f.; Ismāʿīl Ḥaḳḳī (Uzunçarşılı), *Karesi me<u>sh</u>āhīri*, Istanbul 1339/1925, ii, 137-40; idem, *Amedî Galib Efendinin murahhaslığı*, in *Belleten*, i, 357-410; idem, *Meşhur Rumeli âyanlarından ... Alemdar Mustafa Paşa*, Istanbul 1942, *passim*; J. Puryear, *Napoleon and the Dardanelles*, Berkeley 1951, *passim*; Ismail Soysal, *Fransiz ihtilâli ve Türk-Fransız diplomasi münasebetleri, 1789-1802*, Ankara 1964, 329 ff, 341.

(E. KURAN)

MEḤMED ṢĀLIḤ EFENDI (? - 1175/1762), Ottoman *<u>Sh</u>ay<u>kh</u> al-Islām* of the second half of the 18th century. On his mother's side he was descended from Shaykh Ḥusām al-Dīn ʿU<u>sh</u>shākī, the founder of the ʿU<u>sh</u>shākiyye *ṭarīḳa*, who died in 1001/1592-93, and who is buried in Istanbul at Ḳāsīmpa<u>sh</u>a. His father was Ḳīrīmī ʿAbd Allāh Efendi-zāde Yaḥyā Efendi, who served as *ḳāḍī* of <u>Gh</u>alaṭa and subsequently of Egypt with the rank (*pāye*) of Edirne, being removed from the latter post on 1 <u>Dh</u>u 'l-Ḳaʿda 1126/8 November 1714, and eventually dying in Istanbul in Rabīʿ I 1131/January-February 1719. Ḳīrīmī ʿAbd Allāh Efendi-zāde Yaḥyā Efendi is buried at the Sīt *tekke* outside Edirneḳapīsī, close by the Emīr Bu<u>kh</u>ārī Dergāhī.

As yet we possess no information on the place and date of Meḥmed Ṣāliḥ Efendi's birth. However, it is known that in his youth he attracted the patronage of Yeñi<u>sh</u>ehirli ʿAbd Allāh Efendi, *<u>Sh</u>ay<u>kh</u> al-Islām* (1130-42/1718-30) under Aḥmed III, that he became his patron's son-in-law, and that he studied the religious sciences. Meḥmed Ṣāliḥ Efendi had the fortune to make rapid progress in his career. After spending some years in the *müfetti<u>sh</u>lik*s of the Ḥaremeyn and the Bāb-ī Fetwā, he became *ḳāḍī* of Ḥaleb (Aleppo) with the rank of *ma<u>kh</u>re<u>dj</u>*. In Muḥarram 1148/May-June 1735 he was appointed to the *ḳāḍīlīḳ* of <u>Sh</u>ām, and in 1153/1740-1 to the *ḳāḍīlīk* of Medina. Having completed the term of his appointment, he returned to Istanbul. On 27 <u>Dj</u>umādā II 1159/17 July 1746, he was appointed to the *ḳāḍīlīḳ* of Istanbul. This appointment was terminated on 1 <u>Sh</u>aʿbān 1160/8 August 1747, after he had completed the customary term. He was re-appointed *ḳāḍī* of Istanbul in <u>Sh</u>awwāl 1163/September 1750, and on 3 <u>Dh</u>u 'l-Ḥi<u>dj</u>dja 1163/3 November 1750, at the request of the <u>Sh</u>ay<u>kh</u> al-Islām Sayyid Murtaḍā Efendi, he was additionally granted the rank (*pāye*) of Anadolu by *<u>kh</u>aṭṭ-i hümayūn* of Sultan Maḥmūd. On 7 <u>Sh</u>aʿbān 1167/30 May 1754 he entered into the functions of *Anadolu ḳāḍī ʿaskeri*, and held this post until 10 <u>Sh</u>aʿbān 1168/22 May 1755. On the last day of Ṣafar 1171/12 November 1757 he was appointed *ḳāḍī ʿaskeri* of Rūmeli, and having fulfilled the normal term of the appointment, he was made *<u>Sh</u>ay<u>kh</u> al-Islām* on 16 <u>Dj</u>umāda I 1171/26 January 1758, replacing Dāmād-zāde Fayḍ Allāh Efendi. In this capacity he officiated at the marriage of Muṣṭafā III's sister Ṣāliḥa Sulṭān to the Grand Vizier Ḳodja Rā<u>gh</u>ib Pa<u>sh</u>a at the Ṣāliḥa Sulṭān Sāhilsarāyī in Eyyüb. He was finally removed from office on 5 <u>Dh</u>u 'l-Ḳaʿda 1172/30 June 1759, and given permission to reside in his villa at Ḳanlī<u>dj</u>a.

Meḥmed Ṣāliḥ Efendi died on 1 <u>Sh</u>awwāl 1175/25 April 1762, the first day of <u>Sh</u>eker Bayrāmī. Funeral prayers were held on the following day at the mosque of Fātiḥ Sulṭān Meḥemmed, and he was buried in the cemetery of the *medrese* of *Ḳāḍīʿasker* Meḥmed Efendi. The cemetery is located in the district of Küčük Muṣṭafā Pa<u>sh</u>a, alongside the *Fetwā-<u>kh</u>ānes* of Ḥaydar Maḥallesi, and opposite the mosque of Sinān A<u>gh</u>ā. Meḥmed Ṣālīḥ Efendi was a man of good character and distinguished qualities. His son was the *<u>Sh</u>ay<u>kh</u> al-Islām* Aḥmed Esʿad Efendi.

Bibliography: <u>Sh</u>ay<u>kh</u>ī, Muḥammad Efendi, *Weḳāyiʿ al-fuḍalāʾ*, Istanbul Univ. Library, TY no. 3216, p. 406; Sāmī-<u>Sh</u>ākir-Ṣubḥī, *Weḳāyiʿ-nāme*, Istanbul 1198, ii, 180; Sulaymān ʿIzzi, *Weḳāyiʿ-nāme*, Būlāḳ 1246, i, 21, 27, 64, 69, 71, 106; Müstaḳīm-zāde Sulaymān Saʿd al-Dīn, *Dawḥa-yi ma<u>sh</u>āyi<u>kh</u>-i kibār ve <u>dh</u>eylleri*, Istanbul Univ. Library, TY. no. 9823, 70, 129; idem, *Tuḥfa-yi <u>kh</u>aṭṭāṭīn*, Istanbul 1928, 2; Rifʿat, *Dawḥa-yi ma<u>sh</u>āyi<u>kh</u> maʿa <u>dh</u>eyl*, lith., 100 ff.; Ḥusayn Ayvānsarāyī, *Ḥadīḳat al-<u>dj</u>awāmiʿ*, Istanbul 1281, i, 123; Meḥmed <u>Th</u>urayyā, *Si<u>dj</u>ill-i ʿO<u>th</u>mānī*, Istanbul 1311, iii, 207, 268; <u>Sh</u>ams al-Dīn Sāmī, *Ḳāmūs al-aʿlām*, Istanbul 1311, iv, 2920 ff.; *ʿİlmiyye sālnāmesi*, Istanbul 1334, 520, 569; İ.H. Uzunçarşılı, *Osmanlı tarihi*, Ankara 1983, iv/2, 485; Cahit Baltacı, *XV. - XVI. asırda Osmanlı medreseleri*, Istanbul 1976, 597; Mubahat Kütükoğlu, *1869'da faal İstanbul medreseleri*, Istanbul 1977, 28 ff.; *İA*, art. *Tarikat XII/1*, *XVI*; *Türk Ansiklopedisi*, xxviii, 78, art. *Mehmed Salih Efendi*.

(MÜNIR AKTEPE)

MEḤMED YIRMISEKIZ ČELEBI EFENDI, Ottoman statesman renowned for his diplomatic mission to France in 1132-3/ 1720-1 and for the account of the mission (*sefāret-nāme*) which he left behind, a major contribution to the westernising movement in the Ottoman Empire in its early manifestations.

His biography is known only in part. He was about fifty years old at the time of his mission. He was born at Edirne, and his father was Gürdjü ("the Georgian") Süleymān Agha, *seksondjubashī*, meaning colonel of the 71st regiment of Janissaries. He himself followed a military career, after having, apparently, attended the school for pages of the imperial palace, and he belonged to the 28th regiment, hence the nickname of "Twenty-eight" (*Yirmisekiz*) which he retained. He rose to the rank of *čorbadjī*, then to that of *muḥḍir agha*. But having also acquired a scholastic education which earned him the title of *efendi* (and which is illustrated by poems composed under the name of Fāʾizī, as well as by the Persian verses which adorn his travel narrative), he was assigned to administrative and financial responsibilities in the army: in the role of *ṭopkhāne nāẓirī*, he was charged with the management of the Arsenal. His diplomatic role began with the negotiations over the Treaty of Passarowitz (1718), where he was deputy plenipotentiary with the title of "receiver of taxes of the third order" (*shiḳḳ-i thālith defterdārī*). In this role he acquired, according to Bonnac, ambassador in Constantinople (1716-24) "a fine reputation among the ministers of the Christian princes who were present there". It was as a result of this experience that he was appointed to undertake the mission to France, raised on this occasion to the rank of "chief accountant" (*bash muḥāsebedji*).

The sending to Paris not of a simple emissary as in previous periods, nor of a permanent representative, but at last of a specially accredited ambassador (*elči* [q.v.]), represented a diplomatic innovation, for which the initiative belonged entirely to the Grand Vizier, son-in-law of Aḥmed III, Newshehirli Ibrāhīm Pasha. The latter's ulterior motives were kept secret so as to avoid disturbing foreign powers and perhaps also to avoid friction with conservative elements at home. Officially, the ambassador was entrusted with the task of conveying to the French authorities (King Louis XV, still a minor, and the regent Philippe d'Orléans) the sultan's authorisation of repairs to the cupola of the Church of the Holy Sepulchre, which the French had requested in their role as protectors of the Christians of the East. He was also required to discuss the problem of Maltese piracy and to obtain the release of Ottoman prisoners serving as slaves in the royal galleys. But it is probable that, having experienced the setbacks ratified by the Treaties of Carlowitz (1699 [see ḲARLOFČA] and Passarowitz, the Grand Vizier in fact envisaged a strengthening of the Ottoman Empire against the Habsburgs by means of a more or less close alliance with France (though the latter had been engaged in a system of alliances with Austria since 1718), and he also hoped to acquire information regarding the scientific and technical advances taking place in western Europe and especially in France. A passage which is often quoted from the instructions given to Meḥmed Efendi, required him "to visit fortresses and factories, to make a detailed study of the means of civilisation and education and to compile a report concerning those which may be applied".

The ambassador's journey, made in the company of his son Saʿīd Efendi (himself a future ambassador to Sweden and France, in 1742, and future Grand Vizier) and an entourage of about a hundred persons, lasted a year, from his departure from Istanbul on 7 October 1720 to his return on 8 October 1721. Although dubious at the very principle of his mission, the French authorities received him with respect and considerable pomp, while his public appearances excited much curiosity which is amply reflected in the writings of the diarists and journalists of the time. Arriving at Toulon on 22 November, he had to spend a period of quarantine at Maguelone, and then reached Paris by a circuitous route through the west of the country, initially following the course of the *Canal du Midi*, in order to avoid the south-east which was then the scene of an outbreak of plaque. Arriving in Paris on 8 March 1721, Meḥmed Efendi remained in the capital and its immediate surroundings until 3 August. Returning to Sète via the Rhône valley, he began there on 7 September, his return journey, with a stop-over at La Goulette.

The *Sefāret-nāme*, which is known through numerous editions in Ottoman and modern Turkish and in the French translation by the "jeune de langues", Julien-Claude Galland (nephew of the translator of the *Thousand and one nights*), has not yet been the object of a proper critical edition (see *Bibl.*). It is known that a first draft was composed during the journey itself, and a version presented to the Grand Vizier immediately after his return, followed two years later by a more extended version; from his version, passages regarded as excessively critical of the Secretary of State for Foreign Affairs, the Archbishop of Cambrai, Dubois, were excised at the behest of the Marquis de Bonnac. The account with which we have to do may not perhaps respond to all possible *a priori* expectations of this first discovery of France by an educated Ottoman, this spontaneous encounter between two cultures. But it is necessary to take into account the limited types of experience available to an ambassador, as well as the constraints imposed on a report designed simultaneously to be read by senior officials of the state and to be widely available to the general public. Not only has the author not seen everything, but in a more or less deliberate fashion he refrains from mentioning everything which he actually knows. However, his account, such as it is, remains a no less remarkable document, notable for the curiosity, open mindedness, descriptive qualities and aptitude for judgment which it demonstrates and which place it indisputably above the only surviving precedent, the account of Vienna by Ḳara Meḥmed Pasha in 1665; these qualities were to make it the example to be followed by all subsequent *sefāret-nāme*s.

Meḥmed Efendi pays little attention to manners, beyond noting the curiosity of the French, the astonishing freedom of movement of their women and the respect accorded to them. He is also somewhat sparing of political information, in the sense of French institutions, the personalities of the rulers and the content of his negotiations, which led Bonnac to remark that this was not the account of an ambassador. On the other hand, he writes enthusiastically and pertinently concerning natural phenomena and especially—corresponding to the object of his mission, as noted above—the military, scientific and technical achievements that he witnessed. He shows equal interest and discernement in the artistic domain. He thus provides detailed and vivid descriptions of the *Canal du Midi* and its locks, the Invalides (with the organ, the chapel, the veterans' hospital), military parades and manœuvres on the field of the Sablons, the collection of city models or city plans in relief preserved at that time in the Tuileries, the royal manufacturers of the Gobelin tapestries and the Saint-Gobain mirrors, the "king's garden" (the future Museum of Natural History), the Opera, the Paris observatory, the palaces and landscaped gardens of Saint-Cloud, Meudon, Versailles, Marly (with the famous "machine" drawing water from the Seine) and Chantilly. The ambassador never explicitly advocates imitation of the marvels of the France of Louis XIV and of the Regency (the enormous costs of which he is always at pains to point out), but his role as propagandist is all the more effective in view of his oral commentaries and the numerous artefacts, including 1,000 engravings, which the Grand Vizier sent the dragoman Lenoir to acquire in France following his diplomatic mission, providing a supplement to the information contained in the *sefāret-nāme* and which were addressed moreover to a sympathetic public, the court of Istanbul of the "Age of the tulips" [see LALA DEVRI], which was especially fond of "curiosities" and artistic refinements.

The resulting French influence was manifested most of all in architecture in a style known as *alafranga* (*alla franca*), especially perceptible in the improvements made to the residence of Aḥmed III at the Fresh Waters of Europe, known as Saᶜdābād: the construction of a canal on the model of those of Versailles and Fontainebleau along which the houses of the dignitaries were built contiguously, with the aim of imitating a classical disposition (a procedure called *ḥiṣār yalīlarī*). Similarly, the two elegant fountains built by Aḥmed III have a certain rococo character. It is not known whether the example of the *Canal du Midi* is connected with the resumption under Aḥmed III of work on the canal connecting the Black Sea to the Gulf of Izmir by way of the Sakarya (cf. A. Wāṣīf, *Meḥāsin ül-āthār we-ḥaḳāʾiḳ ül-akhbār*, i, Istanbul 1219/1804-5, 162-3).

Another marked effect of the diplomatic mission was the establishment, in 1727, of the first printing-press using Arabic characters, at the initiative of Ibrāhīm Müteferriḳa [*q.v.*] and Saᶜīd Efendi, who was impressed by examples of printing seen in Paris, a fact mentioned by Saint-Simon (ed. Boislisle, xxxviii, 201-4) but not recorded in his father's account [see MAṬBAᶜA. 2. In Turkey].

The insurrection of 1730 brought a halt—albeit temporary—to this trend which, despite its superficial and even frivolous aspects, represented an important change in attitude towards the West. Affected by the fall of his patrons, Meḥmed Efendi was nevertheless entrusted with the task of conveying to Poland the letter proclaiming the accession of Maḥmūd I (Topkapı Archives, E. 1654). He ended his career as governor of Cyprus, where he died in 1145/1732.

Bibliography: Numerous mss. of the *Sefāret-nāme-yi Fransa*, see Babinger, *GOW*, 326-7, to be completed by F. R. Unat, *Osmanlı sefirleri ve sefaretnâmeleri*, Ankara 1968, 58, and by B.N. suppl. turc. no. 717. There exist various editions in Ottoman Turkish, though without any scientific character: extracts in *Taʾrīkh-i Rāshid*, Istanbul 1282, v, 330-67; *Relation de l'ambassade de Mohammed Efendi* (*texte turk*) *à l'usage des élèves de l'École royale et spéciale des langues orientales vivantes*, ed. P.A. Jaubert, Paris 1841; Meḥmed Čelebi, *Sefāret-nāme-yi Fransa*, Istanbul 1283; *Tacryr ou Relation de Mohammed Efendi, ambassadeur de la Porte en France, 1720, à Ibrahim Pacha, édité et accompagné de notes par Suavi Effendi*, Paris 1872; *Paris sefāret-nāmesi*, Istanbul 1306/1888-9; popular editions in modern Turkish: Mehmed Çelebi, *Yirmisekiz Mehmed Çelebi'nin Fransa seyahatnâmesi*, ed. Ş. Rado and T. Toros, Istanbul 1970, and *Yirmisekiz Çelebi Mehmed Efendi sefâretnâmesi*, ed. A. Uçman, Istanbul 1975. Two contemporary French translations of the travel narrative have been preserved, that of Ph.J. Aubert, French dragoman at Aleppo (*Archives du Ministère des affaires étrangères, Mémoires et documents, Turquie*, xii, fols. 230-99), and the much superior one of J. Cl. Galland published in *Relation de l'ambassade de Mehmet Effendi à la cour de France en 1721, écrite par lui-même et traduite du turc*, Constantinople-Paris 1757. The author of the present article has given a new edition of this version according to more complete mss., annotated and complemented by contemporary texts, in *Mehmed Efendi, Le paradis des infidèles, un ambassadeur ottoman en France sous la Régence*, Paris 1981. Sources: in addition to the French sources cited in the above edition, see Sāmī, Shākir and Ṣubḥī, *Taʾrīkh*, Istanbul 1198/1784, 1-6; Küčük Čelebizāde ᶜĀṣim, *Taʾrīkh*, Istanbul 1282/1865-6, 339 ff.; Rāshid, *op. cit.*, v, 29-30, 213-14, 443-9; Meḥmed Süreyyā, *Sidjill-i ᶜOthmānī*, iv, Istanbul 1311, 266; F.R. Unat, *op. cit.*, reproduces some iconographical documents. Studies: Marquis de Bonnac, *Mémoire historique sur l'ambassade de France à Constantinople*, ed. Ch. Schefer, Paris 1884; E. d'Aubigny, *Un ambassadeur turc á Paris sous la Régence. Ambassade de Méhemet efendi en France, d'après la relation écrite par lui-même et des documents inédits*, in *Revue d'histoire diplomatique*, iii/1 (Paris 1889), 78-91, iii/2, 200-35; A. Gaste, *Retour à Constantinople de l'ambassadeur turc Mehmet Effendi: journal de bord du chevalier de Camilly, juillet 1721-mai 1722*, in *Mémoires de l'Académie nationale des sciences, arts et belles-lettres de Caen*, Caen 1902, 4-141; S.N. Gerçek, *Türk matbaacılığı, I: Müteferrika matbaası*, Istanbul 1939; E.Z. Karal, *Tanzimattan evvel garplılaşma hareketleri*, in *Tanzimat*, Ankara 1940, 13-30; A.H. Tanpınar, *XIX. asır Türk edebiyatı tarihi*, i, Istanbul 1956; A.V. Vitol, *Iz istorii turetsko-frantsuzskikh svyazey* (*posol'stvo Žirmisekiz Čelebi Mekhmeda-Efendi vo Frantsiyu v 1720-1721 gg.*), in *Narodī Azii i Afriki*, iv, Moscow 1976, 123-8; B. Lewis, *The Muslim discovery of Europe*, London 1982; E. Esin, *Le maḥbūbiye, un palais ottoman "alla franca"*, in H. Batu and J.L. Bacqué-Grammont (eds.), *L'Empire ottoman, la république de Turquie et la France*, Paris 1986, 73-86; F. Müge Göçek, *East encounters West. France and the Ottoman Empire in the eighteenth century*, Oxford 1987.
(G. VEINSTEIN)

MEḤMED ZAᶜĪM, Ottoman Turkish historian.

All that we know of his life has to be gleaned from his works. He was born in 1939/1532, for he tells us that at the accession of Sultan Murād III, i.e. in 982/1574, he was 43. At the early age of eleven he took part in the campaign of 950/1543, along with his elder brother Perwāne Agha, who at that time was *Ḳapudjī Bashī*, to the *Sandjaḳ Beg* of Lepanto, Yaḥyā Pasha-Oghlu Aḥmad Beg. When the latter, after the capture of Stuhlweissenburg, was appointed *Sandjaḳ Beg* there, the brothers seemed to have remained in his service, probably till 952/1545, when Aḥmad Beg was summoned to Istanbul, in connection with the plundering of the Stuhlweissenburg churches. In 961/1554 when Sultan Süleymān took the field against Shāh Ṭahmāsp of Persia, Meḥmed Zaᶜīm was a secretary in the service of the governor of Syria, Tekioghlu Meḥmed, and a year later he was secretary to the powerful grand vizier Meḥmed Soḳollu [*q.v.*] and in this capacity compiled the official report of the death of Selīm II and the accession of Murād III which was sent to the governors of Diyārbakr, Aleppo and Baghdād. This office, to which he perhaps succeeded on the promotion (978/1570) of the famous Ferīdūn Aḥmed Beg [*q.v.*], he must have filled till the death of Meḥmed Soḳollu in 987/1579; we hear nothing further about it. He held a great fief (*ziᶜāmet*; hence his epithet Zaᶜīm); he himself says *zuᶜamāʾ-i ᶜatebe-i selāṭīn-i āl-i ᶜothmāniyyeden Meḥmed ile müteᶜāref we shehīr*. Friends requested him to write a history, and he finished it within a year. He began the work in

Muḥarram 985 (beginning of 21 March 1577) and had completed it in Dhu 'l-Ḥidjdja of the same year (beginning of 9 Feb. 1578). The date of his death and the site of his tomb are not known but he is said to have left charitable endowments in Karaferia near Salonika.

He called his book *Humā-yi djāmiʿ al-tawārīkh* and dedicated it to his master Meḥmed Soḳollu. As his sources, he mentions eleven historians from Firdawsī and al-Ṭabarī down to the anonymous *Tawārīkh-i selātīn-i āl-i ʿOthmān* and gives as his main source the *Behdjet al-tawārīkh*, from which, as has been proved, he copied out whole pages without a qualm. The book, which is not yet printed, is divided into a preface and five large sections (*aḳsām*, subdivided into *gurūh*s and then again into *maḳālāt*) and concludes with an epilogue. Rieu and others have given an account of the contents from the manuscripts. In the fourth *gurūh* of the 5th *ḳism* he deals with the Ottomans, and here alone do we have statements of any value, when the author describes from his own experience events from 950/1543 onwards. He brought his story down to the time of writing, and the last event that he mentions took place in the month in which the book was finished.

The passages in the book relating to Hungary have been dealt with by Thúry (*Török történtirók*, ii, 364-89), who also collected the above data for his life; the earlier from 1390 to 1476 are given in extracts and the later from 1521 to 1566 translated in full. Of the other less valuable parts of the book, Diez (*Denkwürdigkeiten von Asien*, i, 212 ff.) has edited a portion of the very early history, dealing with Cain and his descendants, while Von Hammer (*Sur les origines russes*, lxi, 120) edited and translated a portion on the tribal divisions of the Turks, where the Rūs appear as the ninth Turkish tribe. Of the later Ottoman historians, Ibrāhīm Pečewī utilised and quoted from the work of Meḥmed Zaʿīm from the year 949/1542 onwards.

Bibliography: Babinger, *GOW*, 20, 98-9, 193, where further references are given; *İstanbul kütüphaneleri tarih-coğrafya yazmaları kataloğu*, Istanbul 1943, 100 ff. (W. Björkman)

MEHTER (P.), a musical ensemble consisting of combinations of double-reed shawms (*zurna*), trumpets (*boru*), double-headed drum (*ṭabl*), kettle-drums (*naḳḳāre*, *kös*) and metallic percussion instruments. The name (P. "greater") apparently denotes "the greater orchestra". Other terms are: Mehterkhāne, Ṭabl-khāne, Ṭabl-u ʿAlem ("drum and standard"), Mehterān-i Ṭabl-u ʿAlem, Djemāʿat-i Mehterān, and Ṭabl-i Āl-i ʿOthmān ("Drum of the Ottoman House"). The Ottoman *mehter* was an analogue of the wind, brass and percussion ensembles used for official, municipal and military purposes in other Islamic states. Traditions current in Ottoman and in earlier Arabic sources (e.g. Ibn Khaldūn) link the *mehter* to the Turkic and Khurasanian elements in the caliphal armies.

The Ottoman *mehter* was outlawed (and physically destroyed) in 1826. Therefore, information about it is derived from written sources, the most important of which is the *Seyāḥat-nāme* of Ewliyā Čelebi (11th/17th century). Prince Cantemir's history contains a few important passages, and short references are found in a variety of Ottoman and European sources. Another important source lies in Ottoman miniatures which frequently portray the *mehter* musicians. The absence of an authentic oral tradition for the *mehter* is partly compensated by the notations found in the 11th/17th century *Medjmūʿa-yi sāz u söz* by ʿAlī Ufḳī Bey (Alberto Bobowsky) and the *Kitāb-i ʿilm al-mūsīḳī ʿalā wedj al-ḥurūfāt* by Prince Dimitrie Cantemir (1700). A few examples were also preserved in the Hamparsum notation in the late 18th and 19th centuries.

In the capital, the *mehter* was part of the Palace service. The musicians appear to have been originally of *devshirme* [*q.v.*] origin, but not after the early 11th/17th century. They were trained in the Palace school. The names of several *mehter* composers of the Palace have been preserved along with their compositions, e.g. Nefīrī Behrān (10th/16th century) and Zurnazen-bashî Ibrāhīm Agha (11th/17th century). It appears that the *mehterān* trained in the capital were sent to the provinces. Alongside this official *mehter* was another type of ensemble called the *mehter-i bīrūn* which formed part of the urban musicians' guilds. This *mehter* received no salary, but performed at public and private festivities. The *mehter-i bīrūn* differed somewhat in orchestration and in size from the *ṭabl-u ʿalem*, and its repertoire was somewhat distinct. A well-known composer of the *mehter-i bīrūn* was Zurnazen Edirneli Daghī Aḥmed Čelebi (11th/17th century).

The offical *mehter* had three distinct functions: (1) The *mehter* played continuously during battle. The standard (*ʿalem*) was located near the *mehter*, so that silence from the direction of the *mehter* could lead to the Janissaries' abandoning the field. Certain battle signals were given by the percussion of the *mehter* (e.g. *ṭabl-i asāyish* "the drum of repose" for the cessation of fighting). Although the Janissaries entered battle at the pace of the *mehter* music, the *mehter* was not responsible for regulating the movement of troops outside of battle. The march was not a *mehter* genre.

(2) The sultan was greeted every afternoon by a *mehter* performance which was accompanied by prayers for the ruler and the state. In the course of the Ottoman period, this ceremony seems to have become highly ritualised. In addition, the vizier, provincial governors and vassal rulers (such as the khāns of the Crimea and the *voyvod*s of Moldavia) all had their own *mehter* ensembles and were therefore referred to as *ṭabl-u ʿalem ṣāḥibi* (possessor of drum and standard"). The number of musicians in the *mehter* was an indication of the status of the official.

(3) A *mehter* ensemble played every morning and night from a tower within the garden of the Ṭopḳapî Palace, from other towers in the capital and in many other cities of the Empire. These performances occurred before the morning prayer (*ṣabāḥ namāzî*) and after the night prayer (*ʿishāʾ namāzî*).

The basic melody instrument of the *mehter* was the *zurna*, a double-reed shawm with seven holes (6 in front and 1 behind). The official *mehter* used the large instrument known as *ḳaba zurna* which seems to have been identical to the instrument of the same name played today in rural ensembles in central and western Anatolia and Thrace. The *mehter-i bīrūn* preferred the smaller *djurna zurna*. The *ḳaba zurna* had a range of over two octaves and could produce all the notes needed for pre-19th century Ottoman music. Subsidiary to the *zurna* was the trumpet known as *boru* or *nefīr*. Older *borus* were apparently made of bronze, but by the 10th/16th century brass was in use. The *boru* had no holes and could produce five notes within an ambitus of one and a half octaves. Pieces described as *nefīr-i dem* apparently employed the *borus* to hold the drone.

The basic percussion instrument of the *mehter* was the *ṭabl* or *dawul*, a rather large wooden double-headed drum held slantwise by a strap and beaten with two sticks of uneven dimensions and shape, thus producing the bass *düm* and treble *tek* sounds which are essential to the Ottoman conception of rhythm. The

Ottoman *ṭabl* was the ancestor both of the folkloric drum of the same name (called also *ṭapan*, *kas* or *bubandj̲* in the Balkans) and of the European military drum, which has however abandoned the bass-treble distinction during the 19th century.

A secondary percussion instrument was the *naḳḳāre*, a medium-sized kettle-drum made of copper. The two parts of the *naḳḳāra* were tuned differently to produce bass and treble tones, and were struck with sticks (*zaḫme*) of uniform shape. A much larger kettledrum was the *kös*, which could measure one-and-a-half metres at the top. It was also made of copper. The *kös* was taken on campaigns and played at official occasions.

The drum of the *mehter* were supported by two types of brass percussion—the *halīle*s or *zīl*s (cymbals) and the *čewgān*, a crescent-shaped, jingling rattle with bells.

These instruments were played in large groups, with the *zurna*s and *dawul*s in equal numbers, and the other instruments somewhat less numerous. In the early 19th century, Von Hammer reports that a vizier's or pas̲h̲a's *mehter* consisted of 72 pieces: 16 *zurnas*, 16 *ṭabl*s, 11 *borus*, 8 *naḳḳāres*, 7 *halīle*s and 4 *kös*. The sultan's *mehter* (called *mehter-k̲h̲āne-yi k̲h̲āḳānī* or *mehter-k̲h̲āne-yi hümayūn*) was twice that during campaigns.

The *mehter* was conducted by the lead *zurna*-player (*zurna-zen-bas̲h̲ï*), who was therefore termed *mehterbas̲h̲ï*. The *mehter* normally performed in a circular formation. During campaigns or processions (*alay*), the musicians were mounted on horses or camels; the *kös* was taken on a camel or an elephant.

The répertoire of the *mehter* was termed *newbet* or *faṣïl*. Of this répertoire, approximately sixty pieces have survived. This répertoire was related to the instrumental suite (*faṣïl-i sāzendegān*) of Ottoman court music. The dominant forms were the *pes̲h̲rew* and the *semāʿī*, as well as the improvised *taḳsīm*. The *pes̲h̲rew*s and *semāʿī*s of the *mehter* form separate genres which employed somewhat simpler rhythmic cycles and larger melodic leaps than the contemporaneous court music. One performance practice associated exclusively with the *mehter* was the *ḳarabataḳ*: alternation of soft passages played by a partial ensemble with thunderous tutti passages. The *mehter* répertoire is identified in the sources by the names of individual items, e.g. *sandj̲aḳ* ("standard") *atlu* ("horseman"), *alay düzen* ("parade order"), *elči* ("ambassador"), or the term *ḥarbī* ("martial"). During the 18th century, the *mehter* répertoire was broadened to include instrumental versions of the classical vocal forms (*beste*, *naḳïs̲h̲*, *semāʿī*), as well as folk tunes (*ezgi*, *türkü*, *ḳalenderī*).

In 1720 the Porte presented the Polish court with a complete *mehter* ensemble. The gift was very much appreciated, and soon after Russia and then Prussia requested similar ensembles. By the 1770s, many European courts had *mehter* bands, and some sent their bandmasters to Istanbul to study the *mehter*. The main musical result of this cross-cultural exchange appears to have been the introduction of several percussion instruments into European military bands and court orchestras, which gradually led to the augmentation of other instrumental sections and hence a change in orchestral texture. Possible influence of the *mehter* melodies themselves upon European military music of the 18th century has not been adequately researched. In addition, in the South-East European territories under Ottoman domination or influence, the music of the *mehter* was an important factor in the diffusion of Ottoman-Islamic musical principles.

The destruction of the Janissary Corps in 1826 led to the neglect of the *mehter* répertoire, which appears to have been completely forgotten by the end of the 19th century. During the First World War, an attempt was made to revive a version of the *mehter* in accordance with the needs of the modernised Turkish army. Hymns and marches (the latter built on a mixture of Turkish and western musical ideas) were commissioned from classical composers such as Ismāʿīl Ḥaḳḳī (d. 1927), Kâzim Uz (d. 1943) and Ali Riza Şengel (d. 1953). Some private *mehter* ensembles were created during the War of Liberation, but these were not institutionalised during the Republic. In 1952, a new *mehterhane* was established in conjunction with the Military Museum in Istanbul. The costumes and some of the performance practices of this new *mehter* are largely authentic, but its répertoire is drawn almost exclusively from the hybrid *mehter* music of the First World War.

Bibliography: Sources for the *mehter* are few. Almost all Ottoman (but almost no Western) sources for the *mehter* are treated by Haydar Sanal in *Mehter musikisi*, Istanbul 1964. Sanal's book is the major point of reference for any study of the *mehter* and its music. In contains transcriptions of virtually the entire authentic répertoire of the *mehter* found in the works of ʿAlī Ufḳī Bey and Cantemir. Abundant references to Ottoman sources may be found in Sanal's book. Of these, the most important is Evliyā Čelebi's *Seyāḥāt-nāme*, i-v. Several aspects of the *mehter* were treated by Zeki Mehmet Pakalın in *Osmanlı Tarih deyimleri ve terimleri sözlüğü*, ii, Istanbul 1971, 444-51. See also H.G. Farmer, *Turkish influence in military music*, London 1950; K. Signell, *Mozart and the Meḥter*, in *The Consort*, no. 24 (1967), 310-22. (W. FELDMAN)

MEKNÈS [see MIKNĀS].

MELILLA (in modern Arabic: *Mlīlya*, Berber *Tamlilt*, "the white"; in the Arab geographers, *Malīla*), a seaport on the east coast of Morocco on a promontory on the peninsula of Gelʿiyya at the end of which is the Cape Tres Forcas or the Three Forks (*Rās Hurk* of the Arab geographers, now *Rās Werk*).

Melilla probably corresponds to the *Rusadir* of the ancients (cf. *Rhyssadir oppidum et portus* (Pliny, v. 18), *Russadir Colonia* of the Antoninian Itinerary). Leo Africanus says that it had belonged for a time to the Goths and that the Arabs took it from them, but in reality we know nothing of the ancient history of the town.

It is only at the beginning of the 4th/10th century that Melilla appears in the Muslim history of Morocco. In 318/930, the Umayyad Caliph of Spain, ʿAbd al-Raḥmān III al-Nāṣir li-Dīn Allāh, succeeded in detaching from the Fāṭimids the famous Miknāsa chief Mūsā b. Abi 'l-ʿĀfiya, who had established his authority over the basin of the Moulouya and the district of Taza; having seized Melilla, al-Nāṣir built ramparts around it and gave it to his new ally, who thus had at his command a base of defence (*maʿḳil*) against the Fāṭimids of Ifrīḳiya and a port which made communication with Spain easy. Later on, the descendants of his son, al-Būrī b. Mūsā, rebuilt the town, which remained one of the strongholds of the Miknāsa in Morocco down to the time of the decline of the power of the tribe, who were definitively defeated and scattered by the Almoravid Yūsuf b. Tās̲h̲fīn in 462/1070.

But the Miknāsa must have abandoned it before their dynasty was crushed by the Almoravids, for al-Bakrī shows us that by 459/1067 a descendant of the Ḥammūdid Idrīsids of Spain had been summoned to

Melilla and recognised as ruler by the people of the district.

At the period when al-Bakrī wrote (460/1068), Melilla was a town surrounded by a wall of stone; inside was a very strong citadel, a great mosque, a *ḥammām* and markets. The inhabitants belonged to the tribe of the Banū Wartadī (or B. Wartardā), a branch of the Baṭṭūya group of the Ṣanhādja. Melilla had a harbour which was accessible only in summer. It was the terminus of a trade route which connected Sidjilmāsa with the Mediterranean through the valley of the Moulouya and Agarsīf (French *Guercif*). The trade must have been considerable; the principal exports were no doubt those mentioned by Leo Africanus, sc. iron from the mines of the mountains of the Banū Saʿīd and honey from the Kabdāna country; we may also add pearls which were taken from oysters found in the harbour itself. Al-Bakrī notes that the inhabitants made money by granting protection to merchants. The environs of the town were occupied by the Banū Wartadī (who also occupied the stronghold called Ḳulūʿ Gāret), the Maṭmāṭa, the Ahl Kabdān, the Marnīsa of the "White Hill" (*al-Kudya al-bayḍāʾ*) and the Ghassāsa of the massif which ends in Cape Tres Forcas (*Djabal Hurk*). All this region was then independent and had no political link with the kingdom of Fās or that of Nakūr.

But in 472/1080 the Almoravid sovereign Yūsuf b. Tāshfīn took Melilla and added its territory to the Almoravid empire. In 536/1141-2, in the course of the Almoravid pursuit of the Almohads, a body of the latter set out from Tāmsāmān to lay siege to Melilla, which was taken and plundered. In 671/1272, the Marīnid sultan Yaʿḳūb took Melilla from the Almohads, and Ibn Khaldūn simply mentions it as a fortified place. It seems in fact that these three captures of the town had destroyed its commercial importance to the advantage of another town on the west coast of the peninsula of the Gelʿiyya, sc. Ghassāsa, also called *al-Kudya al-bayḍāʾ*, the *Alcudia* of the Portolans; in the 7th/14th century it is this latter town that appears as the Mediterranean port of Fās and Taza, and it was through it that political and commercial relations with eastern Spain and Italy (Genoa and Venice) were carried on.

Leo Africanus reports that in 895/1490, hearing that an attack on it was planned by the Spaniards, the inhabitants abandoned the town and fled to the mountains of the Baṭṭūya; to punish them for this the Waṭṭāsid sultan had the town burned down; when in Muḥarram 903/September 1497 the Spaniards arrived, they were thus able to disembark without resistance and occupied the town, abandoned and half-destroyed. The occupation of Melilla enabled the Spaniards to attack the port of Ghassāsa by land and it was taken in Dhu 'l-Ḳaʿda 911/April 1506. The Moroccans recaptured it in 940/1533, but the dangerous proximity of Melilla henceforth deprived it of importance. The commercial activity of this region was moved farther west to the port of al-Mazimma [see AL-ḤUṢAYMA in Suppl.], and the centre of Muslim resistance in this part of Morocco was henceforth the stronghold of Tāzūṭā, which after having been the capital of the Marīnid fief of the Banū Waṭṭās, became that of a practically independent leader of holy war. After passing into the hands of the Spaniards, Melilla was continuously besieged by the Muslims, mainly by the forces of the leaders of holy war established at Tāzūṭā and at Mdjāw (the *Meggeo* of Leo Africanus). Occupied by the Christians, the town naturally became one of the places in Morocco in which Muslims pretenders and rebels found asylum and support against the central power, especially at the beginning of the Saʿdian dynasty. In 956/1549, it sheltered the dispossessed Waṭṭāsid Abū Ḥassūn, "king" of Bādis; in 956/1550 it welcomed with his family Mawlāy ʿAmar, "king" of Debdū. It was from Melilla that in 1003/1595, the pretender al-Nāṣir b. al-Ghālib bi'llāh set out against his uncle the sultan Aḥmad al-Manṣūr.

Later, Melilla only appears in history in connection with sieges which it had to suffer: sieges by Mawlāy Ismāʿīl in 1098/1687 and 1106/1695; siege in 1188/1774 by Mawlāy Muḥammad b. ʿAbd Allāh; Spanish-Moroccan war of 1893 (Sīdī Waryāsh affair). From 1903 to 1908 the region of Melilla was the scene of struggles between the pretender al-Djīlālī al-Rūgī, established in the *ḳaṣba* of Selwān, and the troops of the sultan ʿAbd al-ʿAzīz; defeated and receiving no support, the latter had to take refuge in Spanish territory and be repatriated. Still more recently in 1921, the same district witnessed the sanguinary battles between the Spaniards and the Rīfans under ʿAbd al-Karīm (Anwāl disaster) (C.R. Pennell, *A country with a government and a flag. The Rif War in Morocco 1921-1926*, Wisbech, England 1986, 166-70, 198). Melilla is for Spain a "place of sovereignty" administratively dependent on the province of Malaga, like Ceuta [see SABTA], which itself depends on that of Cadiz. Before the establishment of the French protectorate, Melilla, constituted a free port, was the landing-place for all the European merchandise (cotton, sugar, tea) intended not only for eastern Morocco but also for the Saharan regions of Morocco and Orania. It has now lost its commercial importance, but its population has considerably increased: 9,000 inhabitants in 1880, and 86,500 on the eve of Moroccan independence. It is also the seat of an important garrison.

Bibliography: Bakrī, index; Leo Africanus, *Description de l'Afrique*, tr. A. Épaulard, 289-90; H. de Castries, *Sources inédites de l'histoire du Maroc, Espagne*, i, pp. i-xxviii: *Melilla au XVème siècle*.

(G.S. COLIN)

MELLĀḤ [see MALLĀḤ].

MEMDŪḤ SHEWKET ESENDAL [see ESENDAL in Suppl.].

MEMON [see AL-MAYMANĪ].

MEMON, the name of one of the three well-known Muslim trading communities of Gudjarāt, the other two being the Bohorās and Khōdjas [*q.vv.*]. They claim to have embraced Islam around the 6th/12th century. Their name, originally derived from *muʾmin* "believer", was later corrupted to *Memon*. They were converted to Islam from the trading Lohana and Kutch Bania castes living in Sindh and Kaččh (Kutch), either by a son or a descendant of ʿAbd al-Ḳādir al-Djīlānī (d. 561/1166 [*q.v.*]). They are devout Sunnīs and follow the Ḥanafī school of law. Most of them, except those who stayed back in Sindh, speak the Kaččhi dialect of Gudjarātī. Following their pre-conversion practice, they do not allow inheritance to their widows and daughters. The most sacred shrine of their *pīr*, after that of ʿAbd al-Ḳādir al-Djīlānī in Baghdād, is that of Khwādja Muʿīn al-Dīn Čishtī [*q.v.*] in Adjmēr (K.B. Faridi, *Gazetteer of the Bombay Presidency, ix/2, Gujarat population, Musalmans and Parsis*, Bombay 1899, 50-7). They celebrate the first ten days of Rabīʿ II by reciting the life history of ʿAbd al-Ḳādir al-Djīlānī at a religious gathering known as *ziyāra madjlis* (S. Edwardes, *The Gazetteer of Bombay City and Island*, Bombay 1909, i, 182-3).

They were a wealthy community living in Surat during the hey-day of the city's prosperity. As Surat sank into insignificance with the rise of Bombay (during the 19th century), they moved to the new city, attracted by its trade and commercial opportunities. After the famine of 1813 in Gudjarāt and Kaččh, they migrated in large numbers and first began to do business in Bombay by opening tailoring establishments in Lohar Chawl. Their status progressed steadily as Bombay advanced in material prosperity, and they indulged in every kind of trade from shopkeeping, broking and peddling to furniture dealing and timber business and included among their number some of the richest individuals in Bombay (Edwardes, *Gazetteer*, i, 178). The Memon Chamber of Commerce, established in 1929 with a view to promote and protect the interests and rights of members in matter of inland and foreign trade, transport, industry, banking and shipping, had over one hundred members (*Modern Bombay and her patriotic citizens*, Bombay 1941, 110-11). With the partition of India in 1947, a considerable number of them migrated to Pakistan, and now some of these are the leading industrialists and the wealthiest merchants of Karachi. They have trade relations with East Africa, the Persian Gulf and the South-East Asia, especially Malaya and Singapore. A conservative, revivalist movement is currently gaining strong support among the Memons of Gudjarāt and Bombay.

Bibliography: In addition to the works cited in the text, see S. Edwardes, *By-ways of Bombay*, Bombay 1912, 82-7, for a description of middle-class Memon daily life; P. and Oliva Strip, *The peoples of Bombay*, Bombay 1944, 33-4. (I. Poonawala)

MEMPHIS [see manf].

MENDERES, the name of three rivers of Anatolia which are known in modern Turkish by this name, usually preceded by the pertinent epithet: Büyük ("Big"), Küçük ("Little"), and Eski ("Old"). They are the classical Maiandros, Kaystros and Skamandros.

1. *Büyük Menderes*. It is part of the geological and hydrological features of western Anatolia that consist of latitudinal mountain chains flanking long valleys, the latter used and enlarged by rivers that flow into the Aegean Sea. These valleys, the mountain slopes along them and the estuaries have in turn been an inviting ground for habitation and economic and cultural development. Büyük Menderes with ancient Miletus, Küçük Menderes with Ephesus, Gediz [*q.v.*] (ancient Hermos) with Izmir, and Bakır Çayı (ancient Kaykos) with Bergama near their estuaries or courses, are the principal ones.

The exact length of the Büyük Menderes depends on which one of its upper arms should be referred to by this name (up to 529 km; drainage area of some 25,000 km^2). The noteworthy fact is that its headwaters reach into the westernmost extension of the inner Anatolian plateau. The stream usually viewed as the beginning of the Büyük Menderes is fed by springs and brooks in the mountainous vicinity of Dinar (ancient Apameia). As it descends from the plateau, this river receives such tributaries as the Kufi Çayı, Banaz Çayı and finally the Çürük Su (ancient Lykos) near Sarayköy.

After Sarayköy, the Büyük Menderes follows the long, widening valley almost due west, at a slower pace, until it is deflected in the vicinity of the ruins of Magnesia-on-the-Maeander by the south-west oriented coastal range of Gümüş Dağı; it then turns south-westward and, avoiding a second obstacle represented by the Samsun Dağı, it enters the sea some 10 km south-west of Balāṭ [*q.v.*] (ancient Miletus). The mountains flanking the Büyük Menderes on the south are cut by several longitudinal valleys used by its principal tributaries from that side: the Vandalas Çayı (ancient Morsynos), Ak Çay (ancient Harpasos), and Çine Suyu (ancient Marsyas). The lower part of the middle course of the Büyük Menderes, roughly between Nazilli and Söke, flows through an alluvial plain marked by a deep and soft soil layer; this and the mild inclination rate with the resulting slowness of the current produces the winding course that has made the term "meander" better known than the river itself. The large amount of silt brought by the Büyük Menderes causes the coastline at its estuary to advance several metres each year. This is illustrated by the fate of ancient Miletus, which in the first millenium before our era was a port on the Latmikos kolpos, a bay to the south-east of the ancient estuary; by the 4th century A.D., the bar created by the silt turned the bay into a lake (the present-day Bafa Gölü is a remnant of this bay) and the port into a town on the river, but several kilometres from the coast (a similar fate threatened in recent centuries the Gulf of Izmir, saved only by a re-routing of the Gediz estuary further north in 1886).

The Büyük Menderes seems to have been little noticed by Islamic geographers. One exception is al-ʿUmarī (d. 750/1349), whose confusion, however, stresses the unfamiliarity of Islamic scholars with this river; he states that the "Mandarus" flows into the Black Sea and is as large as the Nile. The river is briefly mentioned in Pīrī Reʾīs's portolan *Kitāb-i baḥriyye* as "Mendiraz suyi" in the 927/1521 version (Topkapı Sarayı Müzesi, Bağdat Köşkü ms. 337, fol. 22b, text; on the map, 23a, as "Balāṭ suyi"), and as "Ulu Mendirez" in the 932/1526 version (facsim. ed., Istanbul 1935, 209; text; on the map, p. 190, as "Māʾ-i Mendirez"). Kātib Čelebi's [*q.v.*] *Djihān-nümā* (in the addition by Abū Bakr b. Bahrām al-Dimashḳī, second half of the 11th/17th century) has a map of Anatolia (between pp. 629 and 630) but without any trace of the river; the "Nehr-i Mendirez" is, however, briefly discussed on p. 634 of the text, with more detailed discussions of the general area on pp. 636-8. Ewliyā Čelebi [*q.v.*] appears to be the earliest Islamic author who describes the area along the river at some length (*Seyāḥat-nāme*, Istanbul 1935, ix, 148-92). He is followed by European travellers and scholars of the 17th to the 20th centuries; the results are perhaps best exemplified by the field trips and publications of A. Philippson (see *Bibl.*).

The importance of the Büyük Menderes valley, dominated by the warm Mediterranean climate yet also well-watered, has persisted, throughout political and ethnic changes, since antiquity. The fertility of the alluvial plain below and of the higher fringes along the parallel mountains combine to yield abundant as well as varied agricultural, horticultural and industrial crops and products, such as raisins, figs, olives, cereals and cotton. This productivity is reflected in a dense agricultural as well as urban population, handicrafts and commerce. The towns and settlements are mostly located at a certain distance from the river in the more salubrious foothills, the majority being on the northern side. That side has always functioned as one of the principal avenues of trade and travel linking the Aegean coast with the Anatolian interior. Miletus and Ephesus were the chief maritime outlets in antiquity. In the Middle Ages, Miletus, known as Palatia and turkicised as Balāṭ, retained some importance, as it could be reached by smaller ships using the Menderes. For some time toward the end of the 7th/13th century, it served as the point of departure for maritime expeditions of the newly-established Beys of Menteshe [see MENTESHE OGHULLARÏ], but soon trade proved more profitable, and a treaty was concluded with the Venetians by which the latter opened a consulate there (by 1355; the treaty was later confirmed by the Ottoman sultans). Venetians and Genoese sold textiles, soap, tin and lead, and bought such products as alum, rugs, saffron, sesame, honey and wax, nut galls, morocco leather, liquorice, dried raisins, wheat, barley and slaves; they also bought fish, in particular eels from the Bafa lake that could be reached by fishermen (this fishing seems to have survived to this day). Trade at Balāṭ still existed, although at a diminishing rate, in Ewliyā Čelebi's time, when the traveller visited the place in 1082/1671-2; he states that "the saccoleva barges, the barges from Gallipoli and Kos, and the frigates from Syme and Nauplia ... sail into the Menderes river and take on merchandise at this town of Balāṭ" (*Seyāḥat-nāme*, ix, 147). Gradually, Balāṭ was abandoned, due to the continuing silting up of the estuary and to the malaria-infested climate. Another reason may have been the rise of Izmir [*q.v.*] or Smyrna, which in the modern period became the chief maritime outlet for the area. Thus the first railway concession in Anatolia, granted in 1857 to a British company, resulted in a line linking Izmir with Aydın and the Büyük Menderes valley. The railway has recently been joined by a modern and denser highway network.

The traditional assets of the Büyük Menderes valley are being enhanced by modern hydraulic works such as dams, canals and drainage systems, leading to an elimination of malaria-infested stretches on its lower course, expansion of cultivable areas and creation of hydro-electric power (the latter characteristic also of some of the tributaries, such as the Kemer Barajı on the Ak Çay). The valley, especially on its middle and lower course, it thus one of the most densely populated areas of Turkey.

2. *Küçük Menderes*. Unlike the Büyük Menderes, this relatively short (145 km; drainage area of 3,140 km^2) river does not originate in the Anatolian plateau but among the latitudinal mountain ridges closer to the Aegean sea, near the Bozdağ just north of the town of Kiraz (ancient Koloë). It flows south until it reaches the valley between the two mountains chains that separate it, on the north, from the valley of the Gediz and, on the south, from that of the Büyük Menderes. There, near the town of Beydağ, it sharply turns west and follows that course until the hills of Alaman Dağ deflect it south-westward. Having crossed the coastal plain, it enters the sea some 5 km west of the town of Selçuk and the ruins of ancient Ephesus. The latter city was one of the principal ports on the Aegean in antiquity, but the river, like the Büyük Menderes in the case of Miletos, brought silt that ultimately made the coast advance to the point of leaving Ephesos landlocked, despite the reported efforts of the Emperor Hadrian (117-38 A.D.) to re-route the estuary in order to save Ephesus as a harbour.

As in terms of physical geography, in those of human geography too, the Küçük Menderes displays both analogies with its larger namesake and differences from it. The alluvial plain of the valley, the higher slopes along the mountains and the warm Mediterranean climate accompanied by an adequate water supply, make this area yield an abundance and variety of agricultural products; this has spurred dense habitation since antiquity, the growth of towns and handicrafts, and a commerce facilitated by the maritime outlets, exemplified by Ephesus in antiquity, its successor Ayasoluk [*q.v.*] and the latter's successful rival Scalanuova (Kuşadası) in the Middle Ages, and Izmir in the modern period. The valley of the Küçük Menderes, however, does not reach deep enough into the Anatolian interior, and today as in antiquity and the Middle Ages, the principal routes in that direction follow the course of the Büyük Menderes or of the Gediz; the modern railway in the Küçük Menderes valley, an offshoot from the Izmir-Selçuk-Aydın line, stops at Ödemiş near the eastern end of the valley.

3. *Eski Menderes*. The sources of this short river (about 75 km) are on the northern slopes of the Kaz Dağı (ancient Mount Ida) north of the Gulf of Edremit. It enters the Çanakkale Boğazı [see ČANAḲ-ḲALʿE BOGHAZÏ] at its south-western end near Kumkale some 7 km north-west of the ruins of ancient Troy.

Bibliography: In addition to references given in the text, see W.M. Ramsay, *The historical geography of Asia Minor*, London 1890, index s.v. Maeander; W. Tomaschek, *Zur historischen Topographie von Kleinasien im Mittelalter*, in *SBWAW*, Phil.-Hist. Cl., xcciv (1891), 34, 36, 99; G.A. Bean, *Aegean Turkey*, London 1966, 219-20, 225, 232, 245, 253; F. Taeschner, *Das anatolische Wegenetz nach osmanischen Quellen*, Leipzig 1924-6, i, 170-6; A. Philippson, *Reisen und Forschungen im westlichen Kleinasien*, Gotha 1910-15 (in *Petermanns Mitteilungen*, Ergänzungsheft 167, 172, 180, 183; index s.v. Mäander in Heft 183; excellent maps in Heft 167, 172, 180); V. Cuinet, *La Turquie d'Asie*, Paris 1894, iii, 335-685 ("vilâyet de Smyrne"); Ibn Faḍl Allāh al-ʿUmarī, *Masālik al-abṣār*, ed. F. Taeschner, Leipzig 1929, 34 (Fr. tr. Quatremère, in *Notices et extraits*, xiii, 353); Sh. Sāmī, *Ḳāmūs al-aʿlām*, Istanbul 1898, vi, 4446; R. İzbırak, *Türkiye*, Istanbul 1972-3, i, 81-2 and *passim*; D.E. Pitcher, *An historical geography of the Ottoman Empire*, Leiden 1972; W.C. Brice (ed.), *An historical atlas of Islam*, Leiden 1981; *TAVO* (*Tübinger Atlas des Vorderen Orients*), Wiesbaden 1977 ff.; *Pauly-Wissowa, s.vv.* Maiandros, Kaystros, Skamandros; *İA*, s.vv. Menderes, Ayasoluk, Aydın, Balat, Denizli, İzmir, Tire; *Türk Ansiklopedisi*, s.vv. Büyük Menderes, Akçay, Banaz Çayı, Çürük Su, Bafa Gölü, Balat, Aydın, Birgi, Denizli, Kiraz, Kuşadası, Kuyucak, Nazilli, Ödemiş, Sarayköy, Selçuk, Söke, as well as other towns of some importance; *The Times Atlas of the world*, London 1981, ii, plate 36; Ali Tanoğlu, Sırrı Erinç and Erol Tümertekin, *Türkiye atlası*, Istanbul 1961, maps 1/e, 1/f and *passim*. (S. SOUCEK)

MENDERES, ADNAN (1899-1961), Turkish statesman. Born and educated in Izmir, he studied at the Ankara University Faculty of Law, following service in the First World War and Turkey's War of Independence. His political activity commenced upon his joining Ali Fethi Okyar's Free Party in 1930, when he became this party's chairman in Aydın. When the party was closed down, he joined the People's Party (later called Republican People's Party, RPP) and was elected repeatedly to the Grand National Assembly (GNA) in Aydın from 1931 onwards. By 1945, he was a prominent parliamentarian. He then presented to the RPP's parliamentary group a "Four-man Proposal", signed by himself, Celal Bayar, Fuat Köprülü [*q.v.*] and Refik Koraltan, requesting liberalisation. Menderes, Köprülü and Koraltan were ousted from the party and Bayar resigned; together with other breakaways from RPP, they founded the Democrat Party (DP) [see ḤIZB, ii] on 7 January 1946. The DP won 62 GNA seats in that year's elections; Menderes entered as member for Kütahya. A member of DP's Executive Council and second in influence only to Bayar, Menderes orated in the GNA and throughout the country; he smoothed over differences in the DP and was instrumental in leading it to victory in the 1950 elections. The party won again in 1954 and 1957, with comfortable majorities, and ruled the state for a decade (1950-60) with Menderes as Prime Minister, successively heading five different Cabinets.

The DP won the 1950 electoral campaign by representing itself as an agent of change and Menderes began to carry our some of its promises, including: (a) Economics and development: Mechanising agriculture, building roads (largely in rural parts), encouraging industry (chiefly consumer industries), erecting dams (for irrigation and energy production), and reconstructing the larger cities. (b) Social services: Increasing the scope of old-age and life insurance payments, building workers' hospitals and encouraging trade union activities. (c) Cultural: Inaugurating the Aegean University in Izmir, the Middle East Technical University in Ankara and the Atatürk University in Erzurum, and expanding the scope of primary and secondary education. However, Menderes' appeal to private initiative (instead of the RPP's étatism) to finance these projects proved only moderately successful. The United States provided tractors and credits, which sufficed only in part; hence Menderes opted for encouraging foreign investments and loans, which eventually increased Turkey's debt and raised inflation. His foreign policies were definitely pro-Western: he sent Turkish forces to Korea (1950) and joined NATO (1952). However, he was also highly aware of Turkey's need for rapprochement with her neighbours: Turkey signed an *entente* with Greece and Yugoslavia (1953), joined the Baghdad Pact (1954) and worked out the Zürich and London agreements on Cyprus (1959-60).

Although modernisation of Turkey continued in the 1950s, Menderes and the DP were strongly criticised throughout by the RPP and other parties, primarily regarding their domestic policies: overemphasis on a liberal economy and private initiative, preference shown to rural elements and allowing the revival of Islam. In the face of a growing political and economic crisis, Menderes had to withdraw, ironically, from his earlier championship of individual and political liberties: martial law was imposed repeatedly, rival political groups were banned or deterred, the press was muzzled and the military became increasingly politicised in the late 1950s. On 27 May 1960, the military intervened, arresting Menderes and the entire DP leadership. They were tried in Yassıada; Menderes was sentenced to death and executed on 17 September 1961. The trials were considered fair, but many Turks thought the sentences too harsh: the Justice Party, set up in 1961 largely as a successor to the banned DP, took its name from a popular demand to rehabilitate Menderes and the other DP leaders. In the late 1980s, Menderes was rehabilitated in Turkey; streets were being named after him in various localities.

Bibliography: Menderes does not seem to have written memoirs or other works, although his speeches were printed in the parliamentary records and the press, between 1931 and 1960. Some speeches were collected in: Sabahattın Parsadan *et alii*, *Adnan Menderes: siyasî hayatı ve nutukları*, Ankara 1955; A. Kocamemi and V. Ayberk, *D.P.'nin muhteşem zaferi Adnan Menderes'in 1957 seçim nutukları ile Paris NATO konferansındaki tarihi hitabesi*, n.p. 1958; Şükrü Esirci (ed.), *Menderes diyor ki*, Istanbul 1967. For photographs, see Haydar Sönmez (ed.), *Fotoğrafla Menderes albümü*, Istanbul 1967. Personal accounts of Menderes' personality and career are: Samet Ağaoğlu, *Arkadaşım Menderes*, Istanbul 1967; Celâl Bayar, *Başvekilim Adnan Menderes*, Istanbul 1969; Cihad Baban, *Politika galerisi. Büstler portreler*, Istanbul 1970, 127-237; Necip Fazıl Kısakürek, *Benim gözümde Menderes*, Istanbul 1970. Nazlı İlicak (ed.), *15 yıl sonra 27 mayıs yargılanıyor*, Istanbul 1975, is a collection of documents about Menderes' final year in office and the 1960 military intervention. Contemporary accounts of the period, referring to Menderes' activities, are: Demircili (ed.), *Menderes destanı: Türkiyenin mucize adamı*, Ankara 1954; A.E. Yalman, *Turkey in my time*, Norman, Oklahoma 1956: Ahmet Hamdi Başar, *Yaşadığımız devrin içyüzü*, Ankara 1960; Refik Korkud, *Demokratik sistem ve Adnan Menderes*, Ankara 1960; Ömer Altay Egesel, *Tarihin ışığı altında: Menderes nasıl asıldı?* Istanbul 1962; Abdi İpekçi and Ömer Sami Coşar, *İhtilâlin içyüzü*, n.p. [Istanbul] 1965, i; Nimet Arzık, *Menderesi ipe götürenler*, Ankara 1966; Metin Toker, *İsmet Paşayla 10 yıl*, Ankara 1966-7, i-iv; Yakup Kadri Karaosmanoğlu, *Politika'da 45 yıl*, Ankara 1968; Ş. S. Aydemir, *İkinci adam. iii. 1950-1964*, Istanbul 1968; idem, *Menderesin dramı* (*1899-1960*), Istanbul 1969; Ahmet Emin Yalman, *Yakın tarihte gördüklerim ve geçirdiklerim*, Istanbul 1970, iv, 31-358; Samet Ağaoğlu, *Demokrat partinin doğuş ve yükseliş sebepleri: bir soru*, Istanbul 1972; O. Erkanlı, *Anılar... sorunlar... sorumlular*, Istanbul 1973, 345-56; Sadi Kocaş, *Atatürk'ten 12 mart'a*, Istanbul 1977, i-ii; *Yankı* (Ankara weekly), no. 739 (27 May 1985), 12-29; Bekır Tünay, *Menderes devri anıları*, Istanbul n.d. The most detailed biographies are: Mustafa Atalay, *Adnan Menderes ve hayatı*, Ankara 1959; Orhan Cemal Fersoy, *Bir devre adını veren başbakan: Adnan Menderes*, Istanbul 1971; Mükerrem Sarol, *Bilinmeyen Menderes*, Istanbul 1983, i-ii. Studies of the DP evidently discuss M. too; the best is Cem Eroğul, *Demokrat parti (tarihi ve ideolojisi)*, Ankara 1970. For the chronology of events: G. Jäschke, *Die Türkei in den Jahren 1942-1951*, Wiesbaden 1951; idem, *Die Türkei in den Jahren 1952-1961*, Wiesbaden 1965; Halit Tanyeli and Adnan Topsakaloğlu, *İzahlı Demokrat Parti kronolojisi*, *1945-1958*, Istanbul 1958-9; F. Ahmad and B.T. Ahmad, *Türkiye'de çok partili politikanın açıklamalı kronolojisi* (*1945-1971*), Istanbul 1976; Muzaffer Gökman, *50 yılın tutanağı, 1923-1973*, Istanbul 1973. For Menderes' trial on Yassıada: Mithat Perin, *Yassıada ve infazların içyüzü*, Istanbul 1970; Tarık Güryay, *Bir iktidar yargılanıyor*, Istanbul 1971: Samet Ağaoğlu, *Marmarada bir ada*[2], n.p. 1972. See also: Yalman, *The struggle for multi-party government in Turkey*, in *MEJ*, i/1 (Jan. 1947), 46-58; B. Lewis, *Recent developments in Turkey*, in *International Affairs*, xxvii/3 (July 1951), 320-31; idem, *Islamic revival in Turkey*, in *ibid.*, xxviii/1 (Jan. 1952), 38-48; Muammer Aksoy, *Başbakanın hataları ve delilsiz isnatları*, in *Forum* (Ankara), 72 (15 Mar. 1972), 12-14; H.A. Reed, *Secularism and Islam in Turkish politics*, in *Current History*, xxxii/190 (June 1957), 333-8; D.A. Rustow, *Politics and Islam in Turkey 1920-1955*, in R.N. Frye (ed.), *Islam and the West*, The Hague 1957, 69-107; Irfan Orga, *Phoenix ascendant: the rise of modern Turkey*, London 1958, 191-7; P. Stirling, *Religious change in Republican Turkey*, in *MEJ*, xii/4 (Autumn 1958), 395-408; Sabahat Erdemir, *Muhalefette İsmet İnönü* (*1950-1959*), Istanbul 1959; Özcan Ergüder, *Adnan Menderes*, in *Kim* (Istanbul), 40 (27 Feb. 1959), 7; K.H. Karpat,

Turkey's politics: the transition to a multiparty system, Princeton, N.J. 1959, index; Altemur Kiliç, *Turkey and the world*, Washington, D.C. 1959, index; B. Lewis, *Democracy in Turkey*, in *MEA*, x/2 (Feb. 1959), 55-72; Hıfzı Bekata, *Birinci Cumhuriyet biterken*, Istanbul 1960; Fahri Belen, *Demokrasiden diktatörlüğe*, Istanbul 1960; G. Lewis, *Turkey: the end of the first republic*, in *The World Today* (London), xvi/9 (Sept. 1960), 377-86; M. Perlmann, *Upheaval in Turkey*, in *MEA*, xi/6-7 (June-July 1960), 174-9; Ali Fuad Başgil, *La révolution militaire de 1960 en Turquie (ses origines)*, Geneva 1963 (also in Turkish: *27 mayıs ihtilâli ve sebepleri*, Istanbul 1966); Tekin Erer, *On yılın mücadelesi*, Istanbul n.d. [1963]; R.D. Robinson, *The first Turkish republic: a case study in national development*, Cambridge, Mass. 1963, index; W.F. Weiker, *The Turkish revolution, 1960-1961: aspects of military politics*, Washington, D.C. 1963, chs. 1-2; R.E. Ward and D.A. Rustow (eds.), *Political modernization in Japan and Turkey*, Princeton, N.J. 1964, index; F.W. Frey, *The Turkish political elite*, Cambridge Mass. 1965, index; D.J. Simpson, *Development as a process: the Menderes phase in Turkey*, in *MEJ*, xix/2 (Spring 1965), 141-52; Tekin Erer, *Yassıada ve sonrası*, i-ii, Istanbul 1965; idem, *Türkiyede parti kavgaları*[2], Istanbul 1966; D.I. Vdovičenko, *Bor'ba političeskikh partii v Turtsii (1944-1965 gg.)*, Moscow 1967; Samet Ağaoğlu, *Demokrat parti. İnönü-Menderes*, series in *Son Havadis*, 7-21 April 1968; U. Heyd, *Revival of Islam in modern Turkey*, Jerusalem 1968; A. Mango, *Turkey*, London 1968; *Noveyshaya istoriya Turtsii*, Moscow 1968, ch. 7; İsmet Ciritli, *Fifty years of Turkish political development, 1919-1969*, Istanbul 1969, 80-104; G.S. Harris, *The causes of the 1960 revolution in Turkey*, in *MEJ*, xxiv/4 (Autumn 1970), 438-54; Metin Toker, *Tek partiden çok partiye*, n.p. 1970; L.L. and N.P. Roos, *Managers of modernization: organizations and elites in Turkey (1950-1969)*, Cambridge, Mass. 1971; *Meydan-Larousse*, Istanbul, xviii/1972, 607-8, s.v.; Fahir H. Armaoğlu, *Siyasî tarih 1789-1960*, Ankara 1973, 802-19; K.H. Karpat and contributors, *Social change and politics in Turkey*, Leiden 1973, index: Furuzan Tekil, *Politika asları*, Istanbul 1973; J.M. Landau, *Radical politics in modern Turkey*, London 1974, index; G. Lewis, *Modern Turkey*, New York and Washington, D.C. 1974; *New Encyclopaedia Britannica*, Macropaedia, xiii/1974, 792-3, s.v.; *Türkiye 1923-1973 Ansiklopedisi*, Istanbul 1974, iii, 1049-51, s.v.; Müşerref Hekimoğlu, *27 mayısın romani*, Istanbul 1975; Metin Tamkoç, *The warrior diplomats*, Salt Lake City 1976, index; *TA*, xxiii, 494-7; Feroz Ahmad, *The Turkish experiment in democracy 1950-1975*, London 1977, 8-161; W. Kündig-Steiner (ed.), *Die Türkei: Raum und Mensch, Kultur und Wissenschaft in Gegenwart und Vergangenheit*, Tübingen and Basle 1977, index; S.J. and E.K. Shaw, *History of the Ottoman Empire and modern Turkey*, Cambridge 1977, ii, 402-16; Akkan Suver, *Darğacında üç yiğit:Menderes-Zorlu-Polatkan*[4], Istanbul 1979; Weiker, *The modernization of Turkey from Ataturk to the present day*, New York and London 1981, index; Mükerrem Sarol and İsmet Bozdağ (eds.), *100 yaşında Celal Bayar'a armağan*, Istanbul 1982; M.A. Garsatyan *et alii*, *Očerkı istorii Turtsii*, Moscow 1983, 215-31; R.P. Kondakčyan, *Turtsiya: vnutrennyaya politika i Islam*, Erevan 1983, ch. 4; F. Tachau, *Turkey: the politics of authority, democracy and development*, New York 1984, index; K.-D. Grothusen (ed.), *Türkei* (= Südosteuropa Handbuch, iv), Göttingen 1985, index.

(J.M. Landau)

MENEKSHE, Monemvasia, a largely deserted minor fortress town protecting a magnificent harbour on the eastern "finger" of the Peloponnese, situated on top and beneath an impregnable rock, on all but one side surrounded by the sea and connected with the mainland only through a narrow sand bank, through which a ditch was cut, spanned by a drawbridge; hence its name of Μονεμβασία ("Single Entrance"). The Ottoman form of the name is a corruption of the Greek, which was recognised as such by Pīrī Reʾīs. In 16th century Ottoman accounts, the form Benefshe was used alternately with Menekshe and Monvasya. The town has a rich and very eventful history. In the Middle Ages, Menekshe was an impregnable fortress, the "Sacred Rock of Hellenism", the "Gibraltar of Greece" and a notorious pirate's nest. In Ottoman times it was the seat of a minor administrative unit (*nāḥiye*) and a fortress, principally held because of its military importance.

Menekshe, built near the site of the ancient town of Epidauros Limera, was founded in A.D. 582-3 in the first year of the reign of the Byzantine emperor Maurice. Its great days were to come in the 13th century as the main point of entry of the Byzantine forces coming from Constantinople. After the Frankish conquest of the Peloponnese, Monemvasia/Menekshe held out for more than 30 years, only to capitulate to Guillaume Villehardouin after a siege and blockade of three years (1246-8). Fourteen years later, the town returned to the Byzantines as part of the ransom of Prince William of Achaia, captured by the Byzantines in the fateful battle of Pelagonia (near Bitola-Monastır, 1259). From then onwards, Menekshe became the chief springboard of the Byzantines in their long, drawn-out reconquest of the Peloponnese in the course of which Turkish mercenaries from Asia Minor first set foot in the town. In 1292 the town, prosperous through shipping, trade in the famous "Malmsey" wine and piracy, was sacked by Roger de Lluria, the admiral of King James of Aragon. The population found refuge in the impregnable citadel, leaving the apparently open lower suburb to the enemy.

In 1381-2, during the war between the Byzantine lords Cantacuzene and the Despot Theodore, the town made itself independent under the leadership of one of the local noble families, Mamonas. Theodore regained it between 1391 and 1392 and confirmed the town's privileges, dating from the Comneni emperors. Paul Mamonas briefly reoccupied the town in 1394 with help of Ottoman troops of Yīldīrīm Bāyezīd, than active in Central Greece. The Byzantine period came to an end in the autumn of 1463, when Meḥemmed Fātiḥ had occupied the entire Byzantine Peloponnese. The town had been the seat of a Metropolitan of the Orthodox Church and had produced two men of Byzantine letters, the monk Isidore and the famous historian of the Turkish conquest, George Phrantzes. The Metropolitan see survived till the end of the Ottoman period. After the disappearance of Byzantine rule, the town defied the Ottomans and placed itself briefly under Papal protection. At the outbreak of the Ottoman-Venetian War of 1463-79, the citizens of Menekshe exchanged Papal domination for that of Venice, whose fleets were victorious in the first stage of that war. The Republic placed a strong garrison on the rock. By the Ottoman-Venetian Treaty of 1479, Menekshe was to remain in Venetian hands, together with a strip of land on the Peloponnese and the castle of Vatika, from where the ecclesiastical authorities derived most of their dues and the inhabitants had much property and where the corn was grown needed to feed the city. The rock itself produced nothing. During the war of Bāyezīd II with the Signoria (1499 to 1502-3), the Ottomans occupied the last Venetian strongholds on the Peloponnese, Koron, Modon and Navarino and the coastal strip in front of Menekshe. Only Nauplion and Menekshe held out for some decades and were left to Venice in the treaty of 1502-3. After that, all food had to be imported from the Ottoman-controlled mainland. Vatika, now Ottoman, was maintained as a stronghold. The census register T.D. 367 of 1528 (pp. 171-3) mentions a garrison of 36 men and a *Dizdār*, all Muslims, and a Greek auxiliary force of 15 men, who were freed from *djizye* and *ispenče* and the extraordinary taxes in exchange for their services.

During the treaty of 1540, which ended the Ottoman-Venetian war of the 1530s, the last remaining Venetian bases on the Peloponnese were ceded to the Ottomans. The Venetian soldiers, the artillery and all inhabitants who wished to leave, left the town on 24 November 1540. On the following day, the Venetian Podesta Antonio Garzoni handed the town over to the Imperial Dragoman Yūnus Bey under command of Ḳāsim Pasha, *Sandjaḳ Begi* of the Morea. The evacuated inhabitants were settled elsewhere on Venetian territory. Scions of the Mamonas family went to Zante-Zakynthos, others were transplanted to Corfu (Körfez), Cephalonia, Crete or Cyprus. Not a few of them returned and became Ottoman subjects. The acquisition of Menekshe is only briefly mentioned by the Ottoman chroniclers, including Luṭfī Pasha, who had a large share in the negotiations of the treaty. After the Ottoman conquest, the town lost its importance as a trading community and outpost of the West. Its population must have been considerably smaller than in the Byzantine-Venetian period, and its importance largely military. The İcmal Defter T.D. 565 (pp. 79-88) of the *sandjaḳ* of Mezistra (Mistra), from 981/1573-4 mentions a force of 104 men under a *Dizdār* and six gunners under a *Ser-i Ṭopčiyān*. The total tax yield of the town, which was an Imperial *khāṣṣ*, was 28,665 *aḳčes*, of which 6,000 *aḳčes* came from harbour dues. Between 1540 and 1570 the town was part of the *sandjaḳ* of the Morea but after the last-mentioned date was incorporated in the newly-formed *sandjaḳ* of Mezistra, set up after the disastrous Battle of Lepanto with the intention to react more quickly against raids from overseas. In the 1570s, the town seems to have recovered to some extent. The census register T.D. 603 from 991/1583 mentions it as one of the four *ḳaḍā*ʾs of Mezistra, with a total tax yield of 30,000 *aḳčes* and 320 households of non-Muslims as well as 191 bachelors. This brings us, together with the garrison and their families, at a total population of *ca.* 2,500 people, which is relatively large for the small inhabitable space. Seven local Christians had a special status, delivering gunpowder to the castle in exchange for a tax reduction. Not a single Muslim settler is recorded. The greater part of the tax on economic activities was collected from the harbour dues (7,500) and market dues (5,000) leaving 4,725 *aḳčes* for all the other activities. The amounts for flax and wine and olive oil tell us something of the importance of these sectors. Grain had almost entirely to be imported from the mainland. The dues on these agricultural products tell us that the town had regained some property on the mainland.

During the Cretan War (1645-69), Venetian forces tried to capture Menekshe but failed (1653). The lower town, on a low plateau on the sea shore, was on that occasion surrounded by new walls, those which we can still see today. Ewliyā Čelebi, who visited the town in 1667 on his way to Crete, describes the new walls with some detail, calling them the work of Sultan Meḥemmed IV. The dangerous situation created by the war is also reflected in the increase of the garrison of the town: 523 men according to the budget of 1079-80/1669-70, with a group of "New Gunners" and soldiers and gunners for the Western and the Eastern Bulwark mentioned explicitly. The yearly expenditure for this large garrison was defrayed by the *djizye* of the district and the harbour dues of Menekshe itself. The budget also mentions a repair of the walls of the lower town. Ewliyā has left a detailed description of the town as it was in his time. He mentions 500 houses in the citadel and another 1,600 small stone-built ones in the lower town, which must be a gross exaggeration; the enclosed space measures only 4 hectares. In the citadel on the rock was the Mosque of Sultan Süleymān, or Fetḥiyye Djāmiʿ, a converted church. This is the 13th century Byzantine church of St. Sophia, built by the Byzantine Emperor Andronicus II and still preserved. Besides that one, Ewliyā mentions the Mosque of Derwīsh Meḥmed Agha. In the lower town were another two domed mosques and two *mesdjids*, besides two *medreses*, two *mektebs* and fifty shops. The *medreses* do not appear on the official and contemporary list of *medreses* in European Turkey and must be a mistake; Islamic life was not very developed in this outpost.

During the war of 1683-99 with the Christian Powers, the Ottomans lost Menekshe and the entire Morea to Venice. The town surrendered in August 1690 after a fourteen months' siege, the last stronghold in the Morea to give up. Two thousand Turks came out of the fortress, 300 of them soldiers. During Venetian rule, a large number of churches were built in the town, which still exist today (17 of the 25 preserved churches). The Ottoman buildings were destroyed except the church-mosque on the rock. The Venetian census of 1700 mentions 428 families living in the town of Menekshe, altogether 1,622 souls. According to the same source, the town was the chef-lieu of a district numbering 17 villages and 3 monasteries, with a total population of 2,075 families or 8,366 souls. The Ottomans returned as masters of the Morea in 1715, after the swift campaign of the Grand Vizier Dāmād ʿAlī Pasha. The town surrendered again, although it had two years' provisions. When in 1128/1716 an Ottoman census commission described the town, it had only three Muslim inhabitants, of whom two were converts, and 144 grown-up non-Muslim males (*nefer*) (Kuyudu Kadime no. 20, Ankara). The tax account shows that, on the mainland belonging to the town, a considerable quantity of cotton was produced. Wine is no longer mentioned. The town recovered yet again, remaining the chef-lieu of a *ḳaḍā*ʾ and seat of the Greek archbishopric. When Pouqueville visited it at the beginning of the 19th century, it had 2,000 Turkish and Greek inhabitants. The *ḳaḍā*ʾ produced a considerable amount of flax and olive oil for export. Martin Leake, who visited the town in the spring of 1805, mentions that there were 300 houses in the (lower) town and 50 in the castle: all, except about six, were Turkish. Before the Russian invasion of the Morea (1770) there were 150 Greek families, but they, as well as the Greek inhabitants of the villages in the districts, fled after that event to Anatolia (the lands of the Dere Beys) or to the islands. During the Greek War of Independence, Menekshe was starved into submission after a siege of four months (1821). It surrendered on terms. The survivors, some 500 or 700 people, were brought to Asia Minor by ship. After the War and the disappearance of the Muslim community, the town never recovered. Sir Thomas Wyse, British plenipotentiary in Athens, counted during his visit in 1858 no more than a hundred Greek families, half the houses being in ruin. Nowadays, the upper town on the rock is an empty field of ruins, whilst for a long time the lower town was a ghost city in which only a few families lived. The Greek census of 1961 gives only 82 inhabitants. A small fishing village has developed on the mainland, opposite the rock, Recently, tourism has reached the long-isolated place, creating some sort of recovery by rebuilding the ruined houses as holiday homes. Only the mighty walls of Meḥemmed IV and a featureless mosque in the lower town remind one of the Ottoman centuries.

Bibliography: General accounts: W. Miller, *Monemvasia during the Frankish period, 1204-1540* in his *Essays on the Latin Orient*, London 1921, repr. Amsterdam 1964, 231-45: Konstantin E. Kalogeras, *Monemvasia, the Venice of the Peloponnese*, Athens 1955; idem, *Monemvasia, creation of the Byzantines*, Athens, 1961 (both in Greek, patriotic); R. Elliot, *Monemvasia, the Gibraltar of Greece*, London 1971 (popular); E. Xanalatou-Dergalin and A. Kouloglou-Pervolaraki, *Monemvasia*, Athens 1974; R.W. Klaus and U. Steinmüller, *Monemvasia, Geschichte und Stadtbeschreibung*, Berlin 1977. Sources and detailed studies: P. Schreiner, *Notes sur la fondation de Monemvasie*, in *Travaux et Mémoires*, iv, Paris 1970, 471-5; D.A. Zakythinos, *Le Despotat Grec de Morée*, 2 vols., Paris 1932, Athens 1953; V. Laurent, *La Métropole de Monembasie des origines au XVIIe siècle*, in *Echos d'Orient*, xxix, 184-6; *Düstūrnāme-i Enwerī*, ed. Mükrimīn K͟halīl (İnanç), Istanbul 1928; Irène Mélikoff Sayar, *Le Destān d'Umūr Pacha*, Paris 1954, 71, 78, and commentary of P. Lemerle, *L'Emirat d'Aydin, Byzance et l'Occident*, Paris 1957, 83, 102 f.: A. Delatte (ed.), *Les portolans grecs*, Liège, 1947; P. Schreiner, *Die byzantinische Kleinchroniken*, in *Corpus Fontium Historiae Byzantine*, Vienna 1975 (with numerous little-known details); B. Krekić, *O Monemvasij u doba Papskog protektorata*, in *Zbornik Radova, Vizantološog Instituta*, vi, Belgrade (1960), 129-35; W. Lehmann, *Der Friedensvertrag zwischen Venedig und der Türkei von 2. Oktober 1540*, Bonner Orientalische Studien 16, Stuttgart 1936 (full text of an authentic copy of the treaty); Luigi Bonelli, *Il trattato turco-veneto del 1540*, in *Centenario di Michele Amari*, ii, Palermo 1901, 332-63 (preliminary treaty, the original of the text and the receipt of "Yūnus Sūbas͟hī" of 23 Red͟jeb 947/23 November 1540); P. Wittek, *The Castle of the Violets, from Greek Monemvasia to Turkish Menekshe*, in *BSOAS*, xx (1957); Hadschi Chalfa, *Rumeli und Bosna*, tr. J. von Hammer, Vienna 1812, 116-17; *Ali Macar Reis Atlasi*, ed. Fevzi Kurtoğlu, Istanbul 1935; Pīrī Reʾīs, *Kitāb-ī Baḥriyye*, ed. Fevzi Kurtoğlu and Ali Haydar Alpagot, Istanbul 1935 (popular ed. Yavuz Senemoğlu, *Tercüman 1001 temel eser*, Istanbul 1973); Luṭfī Pas͟ha, *Tawārīk͟h-i āl-i ʿOt͟hmān*, ed. ʿAlī, Istanbul 1341, 384 (the Ottoman census registers mentioned in the text are unpublished); Ömer Lûtfi Barkan, *1079-1080 (1669-1670) mâlî yılına ait bir Osmanlı bütçesi ve ekleri*, in *Iktisat Fakültesi Mecmuası*, xvii/1-4 (Ekim 1955), 225-303; Ewliyā Čelebi, *Seyāḥat-nāme*, viii, Istanbul 1928, 350-5; U. Wolfart, *Die Reisen des Evliyā Çelebi durch die Morea*, Munich 1970; *Libro Ristretti delle famiglie e Animi effectiva in cadaun territori del Regno di Morea*, Venice, State Archives, unpubl.; K. Andrews, *Castles of the Morea*, Princeton, N.J. 1953; F.C.H.L. Pouqueville, *Voyage dans la Grèce*, 5 vols., Paris 1820-1 (other details in his *Landreys door Griekenland*, also in other languages, The Hague 1806); G. Finley, *History of Greece under the Othoman and Venetian domination*, Edinburgh, etc. 1856; idem, *History of the Greek Revolution*, 2 vols., Edinburgh 1861; W.M. Leake, *Travels in the Morea*, London 1830; A. Vakalopoulos, *Istoria tou neou Ellinismou*, v, Thessaloniki 1980, 393-4; *Monemvasia*, in *The Greek Religious and Ethnic Encyclopaedia*, Athens 1953, 40-50, with rich bibl.; R. Traquair, *Laconia, the fortresses*: *Monemvasia*, in *Bull. of the Brit. School of Athens*, xii (1905-6), 270-4; A. Kalliga Haris, *I Ekklesiastiki Architektoniki stin Monemvasia kata tin II Enetokratia kai to Katholiko Parekklisi tis Aghias "Annas"*, in Charalambos Bouras (ed.), *Ekklesies stin Ellada meta tin Alosi/Churches in Greece 1453-1850*, Athens 1979, 245-56.

(M. Kiel)

MENEMEN, a town in western Anatolia (population in 1970: 17,514) and administrative centre of a district (*ilçe*) of the same name. The town lies near the left bank of the Gediz [*q.v.*], some 30 km north-north-west of Izmir [*q.v.*], at the inception of the alluvial lowlands formed by the above-mentioned river. The district flanks the Bay of Izmir on the south and that of Çandarlı on the north, but it is separated from the Aegean coast on the west by the *ilçe* of Foça.

The earliest known mention of Menemen is found in Pachymeres (d. 1315), who states that the "Tourkoi" had moved into the "Mainomenou kampos"; this term is reflected in ʿĀs͟hiḳ-Pas͟ha-zāde's [*q.v.*] history as "Menemen owasī". The Turks, led by the Beys of Ṣaruk͟hān [*q.v.*], eventually controlled the area, and Menemen became one of this principality's possessions; the earliest dated building in Menemen would appear to be a mosque erected by the Ṣaruk͟hān Bey Isḥāḳ (Ulu cami or Sünbül Paşa camii, inscription dated 759/1357-8). Menemen continued to be a possession of the Ṣaruk͟hān also for some time after the Ottoman conquest effected early in the reign of Murād I (761-91/1360-89).

The name of Menemen was also pronounced and written as Melemen, whereas that of the district (*ḳaḍāʾ*) appears in Ottoman documents and Ewliyā Čelebi's [*q.v.*] *Seyāḥat-nāme* as Tarḥaniyye or Turḥaniyye (see the latter work for the etymology attributed to these names). Ewliyā Čelebi gives a detailed description of Menemen. The *ḳaḍāʾ*, administered by a *voyvoda*, was part of the *sand͟jaḳ* of Sīg͟hla or Sug͟hla; it was a *k͟hāṣṣ* of the *wālide sulṭān* (possibly since Süleymān's mother Ḥafṣa Sulṭān's time), yielding 400 *yüks* annually; the town had 300 shops and a *bezistān*; in summer it suffered from a mosquito infestation that became proverbial (*Seyāḥat-nāme*, Istanbul 1935, ix, 84-7). The town also had a Bektās͟hī tekke with the tomb of Bekrī Bābā.

Prior to the exchanges of the Republican era, the population of both the town and the district was mixed; Greeks predominated in the town itself (4,683 Rūm, 3,606 Muslims), and Muslims in the *ḳaḍāʾ* as a whole (17,261 Muslims, 7,195 Rūm; there were also smaller numbers of Armenians, Jews, Catholics and "foreigners" (*Sālnāme-yi wilāyet-i Aydīn* for the year 1326 A.H., 416-17 and *passim* for other information).

Menemen's importance lay in its role as an emporium for the agricultural products of its fertile surroundings, and for locally manufactured cloths and rugs. Its market, traditionally held on Mondays, was routinely visited by the merchants of Izmir. The town's strategic location near the convergence of the road (and eventually also a railroad) from Izmir to Manisa and the Anatolian interior, with the coastal road linking Izmir with Bergama, must have been a further factor. Inversely, the *scala* (port for coastal shipping) of Menemen, still mentioned by Chandler (1764) as "lively", disappeared perhaps even before the re-routing of the Gediz in 1886.

Bibliography: In addition to references given in the text, see W.M. Ramsay, *The historical geography of Asia Minor*, London 1890, 108; W. Tomaschek, *Zur historischen Topographie von Kleinasien im Mittelalter*, in *SBWAW*, Phil.-Hist. Cl., xcciv (1891), 28; G.A. Bean, *Aegean Turkey*, London 1966, 42, 97; A. Philippson, *Reisen und Forschungen im westlichen Kleinasien*, Gotha 1910 (in *Petermanns Mitteilungen*, Ergänzungsheft 172, map); V. Cuinet, *La Turquie d'Asie*, Paris 1894, iii, 485-8; Sh. Sāmī, *Ḳāmūs al-aʿlām*, Istanbul 1898, vi, 4454-55; *Türk Ansiklopedisi*, s.v.; F. Giese, *Die altosmanische Chronik des ʿĀşikpaşazāde*, Leipzig 1929, 66; R. Chandler, *Travels in Asia Minor, 1764-1765*, London 1971, 67; M. Çağatay Uluçay, *Saruhan Oğulları ve eserlerine dair vesikalar*, Istanbul 1940-6, ii, 29, 103 n. 402, and *passim*; *The Times Atlas of the World*, London 1981, ii, plate 36; Ali Tanoğlu, Sırrı Erinç and Erol Tümertekin, *Türkiye atlası*, Istanbul 1961, map 1e.

(S. Soucek)

MENEMENLI-ZĀDE MEḤMED ṬĀHIR, minor Turkish poet of the *Therwet-i Fünūn* [*q.v.*] period (1862-1902). He was born in Adana, into a notable family, the son of Hāshim Ḥabīb, director of the telegraphic department in the office of the Grand Vizierate. He was educated in Istanbul and graduated from the school of Political Science in 1883. After serving as Director of Education in Adana, Izmir and Salonica, where he also taught Turkish literature in the local lycées, he became, in Istanbul, director of the secretariat in the Ministry of Education and, at the same time, he taught in the School of Political Science and in the University. He died suddenly at the age of forty. He collected his poems, which follow the language and style of the *Therwet-i Fünūn* school, in various booklets, the most known of which is *Elḥān* ("Melodies") (1885). His *Edebiyyāt-i ʿothmāniyye* ("Ottoman literature") is a didactic book on the rules and technical terms of Turkish literature. Redjāʾi-zāde Maḥmūd Ekrem [*q.v.*], a later *Tanẓīmāt* writer and critic, who had become the leader of young Westernist writers, published in 1886 his *Taḳdīr-i elḥān* ("Appreciation of the melodies") in praise of Menemenli-zāde, where he severely criticised Muʿallim Nādjī [*q.v.*], the leader of the conservatives, who retorted in his *Demdeme* ("Angry talk", 1887) more violently. This famous controversy made Menemenli-zāde Ṭāhir a well-known poet in the late 1880s.

Bibliography: Nejat Birinci, *Menemenli-zade Tahir*, unpubl. thesis in the Library of the Turcological Institute, University of Istanbul 1981, with a full bibl. (see alphabetical hand-list of the Institute). (Fahir İz)

MENGLI GIRĀY I, one of the greatest khāns of the Crimea (Ḳïrïm [*q.v.*]).

As the contemporary sources are controversial, the chronology of his three reigns up to 883/1478-9 cannot be firmly established. On the death of Ḥādjdjī Girāy Khān I (871/1466 [*q.v.*]), disputes arose among his numerous sons about the succession. Mengli Girāy first succeeded in seizing the throne for several months, but finally had to cede it to his oldest brother Nūr Dewlet. Mengli Girāy's second reign probably lasted from 872/1468 to 879/1474-5, when he had to flee to Mangub (Menküp) or Kafa, while Nūr Dewlet and, later, two other pretenders struggled for primacy. In 833/end of 1478 or beginning of 1479, Mengli Girāy regained power and remained khān until his death in Dhu 'l-Ḥidjdja 920/Feb. 1515. Since the leader of the Shīrīn clan, Eminek, in 879/spring 1475 had sought Ottoman intervention in the Crimea's internal strife and help against the menacing Great Horde [see BĀTŪʾIDS], with the result that the Genoese colonies along the Crimean shores had passed under Ottoman control, the khānate was considered as under Ottoman protection. In 889/1484, Mengli Girāy participated in Sultan Bāyezīd II's successful campaign into Moldavia and was recompensed with territorial gains on the Dniepr and Dniestr [see BUDJĀḲ].

No mere Ottoman vassal, Mengli Girāy generally sought to stay on good terms with Muscovy, which he considered an ally against the Great Horde; while for Muscovy, the khān's friendship meant support against the declining Poland-Lithuania. After Mengli Girāy had subjugated the Great Horde in 908/1502, he demanded the traditional tribute from Muscovy and Poland-Lithuania for himself. A Crimean-Russian confrontation, however, broke out only under Mengli Girāy's successors. Mengli Girāy, who was also a patron of the arts, must be considered as the real founder of the Crimean state. He also played a role in the struggle for the throne of the later Sultan Selīm I, his son-in-law (1511-12).

Bibliography: Esp. important is A. Bennigsen *et alii*, eds., *Le Khanat de Crimée dans les Archives du Musée du Palais de Topkapı*, Paris 1978, with further references; the most detailed account to 1502 is B. Spuler, *Die Goldene Horde. Die Mongolen in Russland, 1223-1502*[2], Wiesbaden 1965. See also I. Vásáry, *A contract of the Crimean Khan Mängli Giräy and the inhabitants of Qïrq-yer from 1478/79*, in *CAJ*, xxvi (1982), 289-300; A. Fisher, *The Crimean Tatars*, Stanford 1978 (Hoover Institution Publication, 166); S.M. Solov'ev, *Istoriya Rossii s drevneyshikh vremen*, iii, Moscow 1960, s.v. Mengli-Girej.

(B. Kellner-Heinkele)

MENGÜČEK (Mangūdjak), a Turkmen chief who was the eponym of a minor dynasty which appears in history with his son Isḥāḳ in 512/1118 in eastern Anatolia around the town of Erzindjān [*q.v.*], but including also Diwrigi and Koghonia/Colonia-Ḳara Ḥiṣār Sharḳī.

His territory accordingly lay between that of the Dānishmendids [*q.v.*] on the west, of the Saltuḳids [*q.v.*] of Erzerum on the east, of the Byzantine province of Trebizond on the north and of the Artuḳid principalities [see ARTUḲIDS] on the south; it thus commanded the traditional highway for invasions from Iran into Anatolia. Hardly anything is known of the history of the Mengüčekids. In 1118, menaced by the Artuḳid Balak, Isḥāḳ allied with the military commander of Trebizond, Theodore Gavras; both of these were taken prisoner by the Dānishmendid Ghāzī, Isḥāḳ's father-in-law, who speedily freed him. In the middle of the 6th/12th century, the Mengüčekid principality was divided between two brothers, the younger one receiving the little town of Diwrigi [*q.v.*]. The elder branch acquired some fame under the long reign of Bahrāmshāh (*ca.* 555-617/1160-1220). He made Erzindjān a cultural centre, for which evidence is provided by his protégés, the Persian poets Niẓāmī and Khāḳānī [*q.vv.*] and the Arab scholar ʿAbd al-Laṭīf al-Baghdādī [*q.v.*], who spent 12 years there. The town was, however, also the greatest Armenian centre of eastern Anatolia, still famed for carpet manufacturing in Marco Polo's time. But after Bahrāmshāh's death, the

Mengüčekids were drawn into the complex happenings linked with Djalāl al-Dīn Mankūbirtī's [*q.v.*] invasion, and the Saldjūḳ Kayḳubād I [*q.v.*] annexed their territory, compensating the Mengüčekids with small *iḳṭā*ᶜs. The Diwrigi branch, known through the remarkable mosque constructed by its members, continued there, it seems, till around the time of the Mongol conquest as vassals of the Saldjūḳs.

Bibliography: Houtsma, in *EI*¹, s.v. and *Bibl.* there; O. Turan, in *İA*, s.v.; Van Berchem, *CIA*, iii, 55 ff., for epigraphy and *awḳāf*; Zambaur, *Manuel*, 146; Halil Edhem, *Düwel-i islāmiyye*, 224-6; Cl. Cahen, *Pre-Ottoman Turkey*, London 1968, index; M. Mitchiner, *Oriental coins. The world of Islam*, 176. (Cl. Cahen)

MENSŪKHĀT (A.), pl. of *mensūkh* "annulled", an expression used in the Ottoman Empire, after the abolition of certain early Ottoman army units (*yaya*, *müsellem* [*q.vv.*]), in the 11th/17th century, for the fiefs and other grants these units had previously held. These were referred to as "annulled fiefs" (*mensūkhāt tîmarî*). The Ottoman finance department administering these holdings, the "Bureau of the Annulled [grants]" (*Mensūkhāt ḳalemi*), allotted them, when needed, as fiefs in return for services. When the Ottoman navy was expanded, such holdings were attached to the Admiralty (*Deryā ḳalemi* [see DARYĀ BEGI] and assigned by the *Ḳapudan Pasha* [*q.v.*]. Some appointments were submitted to the Grand Vizier (*Ṣadr-î Aᶜẓam* [*q.v.*]) and marked off in the registers of the naval archives. The possessors of these holdings (*mensūkhat efrādî*) formed a unit whose duties were to guard the coasts and serve on ships. They could pay for exemption from duty when they were called to serve.

Bibliography: İ.H. Uzunçarşılı, *Osmanlı devletinin merkez ve bahriye teşkilatı*, Ankara 1948, 19, 240-1, 382, 422; M.Z. Pakalın, *Osmanlı tarih deyimleri ve terimleri sözlüğü*, Istanbul 1951, 476, 608-11, 627-8; M. Akdağ, *Türkiye'nin iktisadi ve ictimai tarihi*, İstanbul 1979, i, 40; M. Sertoğlu, *Resimli osmanlı tarihi ansiklopedisi*, İstanbul 1958, 206; Gibb and Bowen, i/1, 53-5; Marsigli, *État militaire de l'Empire Ottoman*, i, The Hague 1732, 145, 150-1. (F. Müge Göçek)

MENTESHE-ELI, a region in the south-western part of Anatolia. It derived its name from the Turkish Menteshe-oghullarî [*q.v.*] who established a principality there. There are, however, some claims that the name is of pre-Turkish origin. The region corresponds to classical Caria (today centred on the city of Mughla). There is no doubt that, like other western Anatolian districts, Caria also was occupied by Turkomans towards the end of the 5th/11th century; but later, Byzantine domination was restored there. The Turkomans in the border areas who settled down in Central Anatolia and the western Taurus continued their raids. Moreover, the loss of Rūm Saldjūḳid power in Anatolia in the second half of the 7th/13th century after defeats suffered at the hand of Mongols provided a gradually increasing freedom of movement for the tribal groups who gathered in the frontier areas, so that Turkish pressure on the Byzantine defence line was continuously being increased.

After 659/1261, the region of Caria which stretches inland from the coastal areas was occupied by the Turks. The Turkomans who founded the principality of Menteshe and ultimately gave their name to the region first arrived in this region by sea and occupied the shore line. But to maintain their rule in this region it was necessary to cooperate with the Turks who pressed from the interior towards the shore (see P. Wittek, *Menteşe beyliği*, Turkish tr. O.Ş. Gökyay, Ankara 1944, 46). When John, brother of Michael VIII (1259-82), the Emperor of Byzantium, went on a campaign in this region, he forced the Turks who had settled inland to withdraw to their bases in the mountains; but he never thought of capturing the ports which were held by the Turks in the south-west corner of Caria. It is possible that the founder of the principality of Menteshe was at that time the ruler of the shore region of the Gulf of Makrī (Fetḥiyye). Although in 1278 the Emperor Michael VIII sent an army under the command of his son Andronicus to Anatolia, the regions of Menderes and Caria had already been captured by the Turks. Andronicus's fortification of Tralles (Aydîn) was therefore rendered useless; the Menteshe Beg who had captured Tralles and Nyssa (Sulṭān ḥiṣār) had annexed the territory to his principality. Upon the Ḳaramānids' siege of Konya, Gaykhatu, the Il-Khānid ruler, came to Anatolia in 690/1291 and punished the Turkish principalities which had revolted against him. During Gaykhatu's punitive campaign, the Il-Khānid army entered Menteshe-eli (*Wilāyet-i Menteshe*) and plundered it (see *Taʾrīkh-i Āl-i Saldjūḳ dar Anadolu*, ed. F.N. Uzluk, Ankara 1952, 88, Turkish tr. 62). Following the Byzantine Empire's unsuccessful attempts to reconquer the area in 1296 and 1302, the Turks became the unquestioned masters of Caria. In his description of the principality of Menteshe, Münedjdjim-bashî says that the principality consisted of many cities, namely Balāṭ, Bozöyük, Mīlās, Pedjīn (Bardjīn), Mazîn (Mārīn), Čine, Ṭawās, Būrnāz, Makrī, Köydjeghiz (Köyceğiz) and Mughla, which was the capital (see Münedjdjım-Bashî, *Djāmiᶜ al-duwal*, Nuruosmaniye Libr. no. 3172, fol. 130b; Wittek, *op. cit.*, 172-3). The Föke (Finike) region of Lycia was also included among these names at the beginning of the history of the principality.

Ibn Baṭṭūṭa, who visited this part of Anatolia (*Bilād al-Rūm*) in 732/1333, which he also designated by the name Menteshe-eli, says that Mīlās [*q.v.*] was one of the most beautiful cities of Anatolia, and fruit, gardens and water were abundant. At this time, Ibn Baṭṭūṭa met with Shudjāᶜ al-Dīn Orkhān Beg, the ruler of the principality. He tells us that his residence was at Pedjīn, two miles from Mīlās, and this city, which was rebuilt on a hill, was adorned with beautiful buildings and mosques (see *Riḥla*, ii, 278-80, Eng. tr. Gibb, ii, 428-30, Turkish tr. M. Sharīf, Istanbul 1333-5, i. 321-3). According to Shihāb al-Dīn al-ᶜUmarī, there were 50 cities and 200 fortresses under the control of Orkhān Beg (see *Masālik al-abṣār*, Ayasofya Libr. no. 3146, III, fols. 122a-b). Thus it is clear that Menteshe-eli extended over a large area. In his account, al-ᶜUmarī says that Orkhān Beg's country was located between Dawaz (Ṭawāz), Sakîz and Istanköy. It is clear, then, that the Föke region was also in Menteshe-eli.

Following Bāyazīd I's succession to the throne in 791/1389, an alliance was formed against the Ottomans at the instance of the Ḳaramānids, and the Menteshe Begs also participated in this. Bāyazīd I had moved into Anatolia, and the regions of Balāṭ and Mughla, which were under the rule of the Menteshe principality, soon passed into the hands of the Ottomans. But a line of the dynasty went on to rule in Mīlās and Pedjīn. Following the battle of Ankara (804/1402), the Menteshe-oghullarî regained at the hands of Tīmūr their previous territories. However, this situation did not last. In 827/1424 Murād II annexed Menteshe-eli to Ottoman territory; later,

Menteshe-eli came to be one of the *sandjaks* of the *eyālet* of Anatolia.

Bibliography: In addition to the works given in the text, see İ.H. Uzunçarşılı, *Anadolu beylikleri*, Ankara 1969², 70-83; idem, art. *Menteşe Oğulları*, in *İA*; Besim Darkot, art. *Menteşe*, in *İA*.

(E. Merçil)

MENTESHE-OGHULLARÎ, a Turkish principality founded in the south-west of Anatolia.

The Turkomans who founded this principality came to this region by sea and settled between the shore and Deñizli. However, it is quite difficult to pinpoint the foundation of the principality and the chronology of the early Begs. The Turkomans had captured the Caria (today Muğla) region after 1261, starting from the shores. Menteshe, the founder of the principality, was perhaps the Beg of the shore regions (*Amīr al-Sawāḥil*) in the bay of Makrī (Fethiye). There are also difficulties in establishing the genealogy of Menteshe Beg. His father was said to be *Amīr al-Sawāḥil* Ḥādjdjī Bahāʾ al-Dīn (Bahādîr), who was one of the *amīrs* of the Saldjūḳs (see Shikārī, *Karaman tarihi*, Konya 1946, 11 ff., and Münedjdjim-Bashî, *Djāmiʿ al-duwal*, Nuruosmaniye no. 3172, fol. 131a). However, in the inscriptions of Aḥmed Ghāzī, one of Menteshe's grandsons, his father is mentioned as Eblistan and the father of the latter as Ḳurî or Ḳara Beg. This region had been given as an *iḳṭāʿ* by the rulers of the Anatolian Saldjūḳs to the ancestors of Menteshe Beg. Although in 1278 the Byzantine Emperor Michael VIII sent an army under the command of his son Andronicus and the latter fortified Tralles (Aydın), it was almost useless. In 1282 Menteshe Beg had conquered Tralles and Nyssa (Sulṭān ḥiṣār) and annexed them to his territory. A coin minted in 690/1291 at Mīlās in the name of the Saldjūḳ sultan Masʿūd II leads us to the conclusion that the Menteshe-oghullarî had at first accepted the protection of the Saldjūḳs (see Ismāʿīl Ghālib, *Taḳwīm-i maskūkāt-î Saldjūḳiyya*, Istanbul 1309, 93). Upon the Ḳaramānids' siege of Konya, the Il-Khānid ruler Gaykhatu came to Anatolia to punish them in 690/1291, and during this campaign, the Il-Khānid army plundered the Menteshe-eli. When Alexius Philanthropos, the Byzantine commander, moved south through Menderes (1296), Menteshe Beg was already dead.

After Menteshe Beg, his son Masʿūd became the head of the principality. But his other son Kirmān (Karmān), following or perhaps opposing his brother, continued to rule in Föke (Finike). The historical sources do not clearly explain the relationships between these two brothers. Although in 1300 Masʿūd Beg had seized an important part of Rhodes, later, on 15 August 1308, the Knights Hospitallers recaptured the island (see S. Runciman, *A history of the Crusades*, London 1965, iii, 435; other scholars give the date as 1310). Masʿūd Beg's efforts to regain the island were unsuccessful. His death was probably before 719/1319. Shudjāʿ al-Dīn Orkhān Beg, who inherited the throne after his father, Masʿūd Beg, probably secured power by removing a brother whose name may have been Ibrāhīm. Orkhān Beg was unsuccessful in his struggles against the Knights to capture Rhodes after 1320. Ibn Baṭṭūṭa visited Orkhān Beg in Pedjīn while he was travelling in Anatolia, and has mentioned him as Sultan of Mīlās (see *Riḥla*, ii, 279-80, Eng. tr. Gibb, ii, 429-30, Turkish tr. M. Sharīf, Istanbul 1333-5, i, 321-2). Al-ʿUmarī, on the other hand, gives information about the cities and the number of the soldiers under Orkhān Beg. He also mentions that the Föke branch of the Menteshe principality was in 1330 subject to the Ḥamīd-oghullarî (see *Masālik al-abṣār*, Ayasofya no. 3146, III, fols. 98 a-b and 122 a-b). Orkhān Beg's death was probably before 1344, and his son Ibrāhīm succeeded him.

Ibrāhīm Beg made preparations to help Umur Beg in regaining Izmir, which had fallen into the hands of the Latins, but when Umur Beg fell in battle in 1348, this effort came to nought. The Venetians, with their fleet placed in Balāṭ harbour, threatened Ibrāhīm Beg, who prepared for a campaign against them, but as a result of an agreement made with the assistance of Marino Morosini, the Count of Crete, between the years 1352-5, they were forced to disband. Ibrāhīm Beg died some time before the year 1360. After his death, his three sons reigned in various parts of the principality. It is believed that Mūsā Beg ruled in Pedjīn, Balāṭ and Mīlās; Meḥmed Beg in Mughla and Čine; and Aḥmed Beg ruled, in the south, in Makrī and Marmaris. After Mūsā Beg's death (before 1375), Mīlās and Pedjīn also presumably passed into the hands of Aḥmed Beg. In 1365, as a result of Aḥmed Beg's attacks against the ships between Rhodes and Cyprus, the fleet of Peter I, King of Cyprus, threatened the shores of Aydîn and Menteshe. However, the Venetians, concerned about their people living in Ayasoluḳ and Balāṭ, intervened, and peace was made. Although Aḥmed Beg ruled in Balāṭ for a period, this was not for long. We see that before 1389 Balāṭ and its environment were under the rule of Ghiyāth al-Dīn Maḥmūd, the son of Meḥmed Beg. However, losing the struggle for sovereignty made against his brother Ilyās Beg, he took refuge with the Ottomans. Following the battle of Kosova (1389), Bāyezīd I ascended the Ottoman throne. With the urging of the Ḳaramānids, Ilyās Beg and his father Meḥmed Beg entered into the alliance arranged against the Ottomans in Anatolia. During Bāyezīd I's Anatolian campaign against his alliance, Balāṭ and the lands of the Menteshe principality in Mughla were occupied. Meḥmed and Ilyās Beg fled to Djandār-oghlu Iskandar Beg (in the winter of 1389-90). During this campaign, Aḥmed Beg continued to reign in Mīlās and Pedjīn. His survival was perhaps due to the rugged topography and comparatively impregnable position of the region. Tādj al-Dīn Aḥmed Ghāzī died in Shaʿban 793/July 1391. His territories were later occupied by the Ottomans. Wittek (*Menteşe beyliği*, 86) accepts that, until the Ottoman occupation, Meḥmed Beg ruled in the Menteshe principality, later fleeing to Djandār-oghlu Isfandiyār Beg.

Following the battle of Ankara, Tīmūr, as he did with most of the other principalities, restored Ilyās Beg's territories (1402). After this restoration of the territory, Ilyās Beg continued for a time as vassal of Tīmūr. In the quarrel for sovereignty among Bāyezīd's sons, he made an alliance with the Aydîn-oghullarî and the Ṣarukhān-oghullarî, supporting ʿĪsā Čelebi against Meḥemmed Čelebi. Following Meḥemmed I's victory against this alliance, Ilyās Beg was forced to recognise the sovereignty of the latter (1405). Because Ilyās Beg was inflicting losses upon the Latins in the islands through maritime warfare, in 1403 the Venetians made an agreement with him through the aid of Marco Falieri, the Count of Crete. But later, conflicts between the two sides continued, and as a result of the Venetians' actions, Ilyās Beg was forced to renew the previous agreement with Admiral Ser Pietro Civrano (17 October 1414). In the same year, Ilyās Beg accepted Ottoman rule and in 1415 he had coins minted in the name of Meḥemmed Čelebi. Moreover, he was compelled to send his two sons,

Layt͟h and Aḥmed, to the Ottoman Palace. After the death in 1421 of Ilyās Beg, his sons managed to flee from Edirne and to take up the rule of the principality in Mentes͟he-eli. When Sultan Murād II captured the territory of Mentes͟he, he seized and imprisoned these two brothers, thus putting an end to this principality.

The Mentes͟he-og͟hullarï embellished their country with many fine buildings. Among these are the Ḥād͟jd͟jī Ilyās Mosque at Mīlās (1330), Aḥmed Beg's Medrese at Ped͟jīn (1375), and his Great Mosque at Mīlās (1378) and Ilyās Beg's Great Mosque at Balāṭ (1404). The Mentes͟he-og͟hullarï patronised scholars and men of letters, and under their patronage some works were translated into Turkish. For example, under the patronage of G͟hiyāt͟h al-Dīn Maḥmūd, the *Bāz-nāma* on falconry was translated from Persian into Turkish. A manuscript of this work, located in Milan, was published by Von Hammer under the name of *Falkner-klee* (Pest 1840). In addition to this, there is a short medical book, the *Ilyāsiyye*, which was also translated under the patronage of Ilyās Beg.

Bibliography (in addition to references given in the text): The Mentes͟he principality has been studied in depth by P. Wittek, *Das Fürstentum Mentesche*, Istanbul 1934, repr. 1967, Turkish tr. O.S. Gökyay, *Menteşe beyliği*, Istanbul 1944. See also İ.H. Uzunçarşılı, *Anadolu beylikleri*, Ankara 1969[2], 70-83; idem, *Menteşe-Oğulları*, in *İA*; W. Heyd, *Histoire du commerce du Levant au Moyen-Age*, Turkish tr. E.Z. Karal, *Yakın-doğu ticaret tarihi*, Ankara 1975; Fr. Babinger, *Mentes͟he-Og͟hullarï*, in *EI*[1]; idem, *Mentes͟he-Eli* in *EI*[1]; O. Aslanapa, *Türk sanatı*, Istanbul 1973, ii, 226-30; E.A. Zachariadou, *Trade and Crusade. Venetian Crete and the emirates of Menteshe and Aydin* (*1300-1450*), Venice 1983.

(E. Merçil)

MĒʾŌ, a mixed Indian tribe of largely north-eastern Rād͟jpūt stock, a branch of whom were converted to Islam in the mid-8th/14th century. Their conversion seems to have been nominal, as they are described as offering animal sacrifices to a mother-goddess, worshipping at shrines of the Hindū god of the homestead Bhūmiyā, and following the Pačpiriyā (Pānč Pīr [*q.v.*]), especially Sālār Masʿūd, whose banner was an object of their devotion at the *s͟hab-i barāt* (eve of 14 S͟haʿbān), as well as the K͟hʷād͟ja Ṣāḥib of Ad͟jmēr (Muʿīn al-Dīn Čis͟htī [*q.v.*]); they celebrated Hindū festivals, and followed Hindū practices of exogamous marriage and male inheritance. The Muslim Mēʾō are frequently called Mēwātī; both they and the Hindū Mēʾō were mostly robbers and freebooters, causing much trouble from the times of the early Dihlī sultanates until quelled under Bābur; but there was a resurgence of their turbulence during the decline of the Mug͟hal empire, and in 1857 they were described as "conspicuous for their readiness to take advantage of disorder". See further mēwāt.

Bibliography: W. Crooke, *Tribes and castes of the North-western Provinces and Oudh*, Calcutta 1896, iii, 485 ff.; *Alwar gazetteer*, London 1878, 37 ff., 70; R. V. Weekes (ed.), *Muslim peoples, a world ethnographic survey*[2], London 1984, ii, 517-21.

(J. Burton-Page)

MERCENARY [see d͟jays͟h].

MERCİMEK AHMET [see merd͟jümek].

MERCURY, planet [see ʿuṭārid].

MERCURY, metal [see ziʾbaḳ].

MERD͟JÜMEK, Aḥmed b. Ilyās (Modern Turkish: Mercimek Ahmed), *fl.* first third of the 9th/15th century, the author of a translation into Old Ottoman of the *Ḳābūs-nāme*, a "mirror for princes" composed in Persian prose and occasional verse by Kay Kāʾūs b. Iskandar [*q.v.*] in 475/1082.

Merd͟jümek mentions himself by this name three times in his work (all references are to British Library ms. Or. 3219): introduction (fol. 1b), chapters 11 (fol. 50a) and 31 (fol. 112b). he is not referred to in pre-modern Ottoman biographical or historical works. From his *Ḳābūs-nāme* translation we can glean very little information (none on how he acquired his strange designation Merd͟jümek, Persian for "lentil"). He was a servant or courtier of Sultan Murād II (824-55/1421-51), and his writing shows him to have been well versed in the traditional religious and secular learning of his time. We can only deduce that he was moderate in his habits from his remark that Merd͟jümek never indulged in the "calamitous" practice of morning wine-drinking (fol. 50a).

In Ottoman *ak͟hlāḳ* [*q.v.*] literature, the *Ḳābūs-nāme* held a special place in the 8th/14th and 9th/15th centuries. No less than five completely independent Old Ottoman prose versions composed in this period have survived, of which the latest and best is Merd͟jümek's, completed on 23 S͟haʿban 836/26 April 1432. The translator records that while at Philippopolis in Sultan Murād's service, he found the sultan reading the *Ḳābūs-nāme* in Persian. When Murād complained that an existing Turkish version was dull and unclear, Merd͟jümek immediately undertook a new translation, "complete, without omitting a word; to the best of my ability explaining the more difficult words in it by extended comment so that the readers might enjoy its [full] meaning" (fols. 1b-2a), the book has no independent title; mss. of it are marked by such headings as *Ḳābūs-nāme-yi Türkī* or *Terd͟jeme-yi Ḳābūs-nāme*.

Merd͟jümek showed much greater literary skill than his predecessors. Unlike them, he was neither slavishly literal nor given to cavalier omission. He freely added explanatory comments, as he promised, or he paraphrased, when literalism might have concealed the author's purpose. Occasionally, he further enlivened the text by spontaneously inserting apt Turkish proverbs, or verses of his own composition (e.g. ch. 32, fol. 122a-b), in addition to his usual practice of rendering Kay Kāʾūs's illustrative Persian verses into his own Turkish verse.

At a time when literary Turkish was at a crossroads, with some writers developing a complex and bombastic high *ins͟hāʾ* style, full of Persian literary artifices, and reducing the Turkish lexical material to a minimum in favour of Arabic and Persian loan words, Merd͟jümek chose a manner which was essentially simple, based on spoken Turkish, and lexically mainly Turkish. In subsequent centuries, a minority of writers continued to favour simple Turkish, but most Ottoman writing became increasingly high-flown and Persianised. By the beginning of the 12th/18th century, Merd͟jümek's simplicity of style and vocabulary had come to be considered archaic and uncouth, and the well-known stylist and historian Naẓmī-zāde Murtaḍā (not Muṣṭafā, as in kay kāʾūs, iv, 815, col. 2, l. 3) of Bag͟hdād was commissioned to revise Merd͟jümek's *Ḳābūs-nāme* in accord with contemporary literary taste (1117/1705).

Turkish nationalist currents of the 20th century have enhanced the growing interest in the Turkic elements in Turkey's national language, and have brought a renewed and still continuing appreciation of Merd͟jümek Aḥmed's work.

Bibliography: 1. Manuscripts.—In Ankara, Istanbul, Çorum, London, Oxford, Paris, Leningrad, Berlin, Gotha, Munich and Vienna. See listings in: [Berlin, Staatsbibliothek Preussischer

Kulturbesitz], *Türkische Handschriften*, Teil 2. Beschrieben v. Manfred Götz (= *Verzeichnis der orientalischen Handschriften in Deutschland*, Bd. XIII, 2), Wiesbaden 1968, no. 226, p. 155; supplemented by H. F. Hofman, *Turkish literature: a bio-bibliographical survey*, sect. 3, pt. 1, v. 6, Utrecht 1969, 63. Not noted in them is another B.L. ms., Or. 4130. 2. Editions.—(All in Latin alphabet transcription only) (i) Keykāvūs ibn İskender ibn Ḳābūs, *Ḳābūsnāme. Mercimek Ahmed çevirişi*. Edisyon kritik ve transkripsiyon. [Hazırlayan] Tipi Akçalı [Işıközlü]. İstanbul Üniversitesi Edebiyat Fakültesi, Türk Dili ve Edebiyatı Dalı, Mezuniyet Tezi, Haziran 1966 (unpublished diss.). Based on a ms. in Ankara Millî Kütüphane copied in 941/1534-5 and B.L. ms. Or. 3219, with occasional reference to three Istanbul mss. Includes 15 pp. introd. study; (ii) Keykâvus, Mercimek Ahmet, *Kabusname*... neşr. Orhan Şaik Gökyay, Istanbul 1944, 1966, 1974. Transcription mainly from Ankara, Maarif Ktp. ms. j 5/37, and F. R. Unat's ms. Includes 13 pp. introd. (iii) Keykâvus, (cover: + İlyasoğlu) Mercimek Ahmet, *Kabusname*, hazırlayan ve sadeleştiren Atillâ Özkırımlı. 2 vols. Istanbul (*ca*, 1974); somewhat modernised. Includes introd. study (pp. 9-62) and bibliography (pp. 63-7). (iv) Ahmet Cevat Emre, *Ondördüncü asır yazmalarından nümuneler: Kabusname'den*, in *Türk Dili Belleten*, seri 2, sayı 5-6 (1940) pp. 121-52, numbered 81-112; chs. 7-12, 14, 20, 21 only. 3. Translation (from combined texts of Merdjümek Aḥmed and its revision by Naẓmī-zāde) by H.F. von Diez, *Buch des Kabus, oder, Lehren des... Kjekjawus*... Berlin 1811. 4. Secondary references: E. Birnbaum (ed.), *The Book of Advice... The earliest Old Ottoman... Ḳābūsnāme/Mütercimi meçhul ilk Türkçe Ḳābūsnāme*. Cambridge-Duxbury, Mass. 1981, 6-7; M.F. Köprülü, *Millî edebiyat cereyanın ilk mübeşşirleri*, in idem, *Edebiyat araştırmaları*, Ankara 1966, 278-80; Agâh Sırrı Levend, *Ümmet çağında ahlâk kitaplarımız*, in *Türk Dili Araştırmaları Yıllığı-Belleten, 1963*, Ankara 1964, 89-115; Nihad Sami Banarlı, *Resimli Türk edebiyatı tarihi*, Istanbul (*ca*. 1950 and repr.), 495-6; Âmil Çelebioğlu, *Kabus-nâme tercümesi olan Murad-nâme'ye dair*, in *Türk Kültürü*, xvi, sayı 192, Ekim 1978, 719-28 (an Old Ottoman *mes̲nevī* verse adaptation, completed in 831/1427 by Bedr-i Dils̲h̲ād, who reorganised and expanded it without acknowledging the Persian original).

(E. Birnbaum)

MERGUEZ [see mirkās].

MERGUI, the name of an archipelago, district and town in southern Burma, on the eastern shores of the Bay of Bengal, facing the Andaman Sea.

1. Mergui archipelago. This is a large group of islands (said to number 804), commencing in the north with Tavoy Island (*ca*. 13° 13'N.), and stretching southwards beyond Point Victoria into Thai waters, terminating beyond Ko Chan in *ca*. 8° 50' N. The indigenous population of sea nomads, known to themselves as Moken, to the Burmese as Salôn, to the Thais as Chao Nam or Chao Lay and to the Malays as Oran Laut ("boat people"), numbered 868 according to the 1884 *Mergui District gazetteer*, and were classified as "nature-worshippers" (animistic-shamanistic). Today, they are probably outnumbered by Burmese and Chinese, even on their own islands, and have been partly converted to Theravāda Buddhism in the north of the archipelago, whilst Islam is believed to have made some inroads in the south (Annandale, 1903; Lebar, 1964).

2. Mergui District. This is the southernmost district of Burma and, under the British, of the Tenasserim Division, extending on the mainland from the boundaries of Tavoy District (13° 28' N.) to the mouth of the Pakchan River (9° 58' N.) and the Isthmus of Kra in the south, and including the Burmese part of the Mergui Archipelago. The region is covered in dense jungle, and its economic wealth rests on tin, coal and gold reserves, as well as on the fisheries industry. The main townships are Mergui, Palaw, Tenasserim, Bokpyin and Maliwun. According to the 1921 Census (*1924 Mergui District gazetteer*), the total urban population of Mergui District numbered 25,382, of which 11.69%, or 1,679 persons, returned their religion as Muslim. This comparatively low figure, although representative of the position of Islam in the Mergui District during the 20th century, in fact belies the importance of the region as a channel for the spread of Islam to Thailand and northern South-East Asia during earlier centuries.

3. Mergui Township. This is situated in 12° 26' N. and 98° 36' E., on the Tenasserim Coast, just outside the principal mouth of the Tenasserim River, and protected by the small, hilly island of Palaw which forms a good natural harbour. In 1921 the total population of Mergui municipality was 17,106, of which Buddhists comprised 65.6%, Muslims 14.2%, Hindus 10.4%, and Christians and animists the remainder. The great majority of Mergui's Muslim population are Zerbadī (of mixed Indian-Burmese descent, but identifying strongly with Burma), though there are also a number claiming Arab descent, whilst in the rural areas, Malay Muslims form a strong contingent, numbering 4,239 in the 1911 Census (Yegar, 1972, 118).

As a port in the 20th century, Mergui has survived on the Burmese coastal trade, exporting tin, rubber, pearls, mother-of-pearl, salted fish, ambergris and edible birds' nests. In the past, however, both Mergui and (more particularly) the neighbouring township of Tenasserim were staging posts on an important overland trade route between the Indian Ocean and the South China Sea (Forbes, 1982, *passim*). For several centuries this trade was to be dominated by Muslims, and it was via Mergui and Tenasserim that Islam first penetrated to the heartland of the Thai Kingdom of Ayutthaya (*ca*. 751-1181/1350-1767).

History. The first mention of a trans-peninsular trade route in the Mergui-Tenasserim region occurs in the 1st/7th century *Liang-shu* (Annals of the Liang Dynasty), where reference is made to Tunsun, "an ocean stepping stone" between East and West in the northern part of the Malay Peninsula (Wheatley, 16; Briggs, 257). During this era, the region was chiefly populated by Mons, but trade was apparently dominated by Indian settlers, and was not dependent upon the local inhabitants. Arab shipping is thought to have first penetrated South-East Asian waters during the 5th or 6th centuries A.D. (Tibbetts, 1956, 207), and it is therefore possible that South Arabian voyagers visited the Mergui region even in pre-Islamic times. Early Arab geographical texts, dating from *ca*. 236/850, mention several ports on the western shores of the Malay Peninsula which might possibly be identified with the Mergui region, one of which, Kalāh [see kalah], is described by al-Masʿūdī (in 332/943) as being a "general rendezvous of the Muslim ships of Sīrāf and ʿUmān", and by al-Muhallabī (*ca*. 370/980) as "a prosperous town inhabited by Muslims, Indians and Persians" (Wheatley, 216-20; Tibbetts, 1979, 118-28). Another (perhaps more likely) identification is with Ḳaḳullah, described by Ibn Sa^cīd (d. 685/1286) as standing near a large river "which flows down from a mountain in the north" (the Tenasserim River? - Tibbetts, 1979, 95, 128-35). By the time of Sulaymān al-Mahrī, however, this uncertainty has disappeared, for in his early 10th/16th century *ᶜUmda* (Tibbetts, 1979, 229), the master navigator identifies Mergui as the main port for Tenasserim, and explains that from this landfall both local people and Arabs travel overland, via Tenasserim, to *Shahr-i Naw* (the "new city", or Ayutthaya, capital of the Thai Kingdom of the same name, founded by King Rama T'ibodi in 1350 A.D.).

During the first two centuries of Ayutthayan rule, the Tenasserim trade route—which passed under Thai control in or about 775/1373—was frequented by Muslim and Hindu merchants from South Asia, as well as by Arab and Persian merchants from the Middle East. It seems certain that, after the Portuguese conquest of Malacca in 1511, Muslim usage of the Tenasserim trade route increased in a partly successful attempt to bypass the Portuguese Catholic stranglehold on trade with the Far East. During this period, Muslim traders from Surat, Dābūl, and increasingly, from the Coromandel Coast, came to dominate Ayutthaya's trade with the Indian Ocean, supplying opium, minerals and dyestuffs, but above all cotton cloth, to the Thai Kingdom. Exports from Ayutthaya to the west via the Tenasserim route included aromatic woods and gums—much of which was destined for Yemen and the Ḥidjāz—spices, tin, ivory and porcelain.

A major factor in the rise of Islamic influences over the Mergui-Ayutthaya trade was the establishment of the Muslim Kingdom of Golconda in the mid-10th/16th century [see GOLKONḌĀ]. Merchants trading from the Golcondan capital and chief port of Machilipatanam (or Masulipatam, commonly known in the region as Bandar or "harbour") came rapidly to dominate the export of Indian cotton fabrics to Ayyuthaya, and by the time of the reign of the Thai monarch Phra Narai (*ca.* 1068-1100/1657-88), foreign Muslims, chiefly of South Asian origin but including numbers of Arabs, Persians and even Turks, had attained to positions of great power and prestige within Siam. Nor was the Mergui-Tenasserim route used purely for commerce; Muslim emissaries from Golconda and Iran (Ibrāhīm, 43-52), and possibly from Acheh (Penth, *passim*), are known to have travelled to Ayutthaya by this route, both with the intention of improving trade and, apparently, in the hope of converting the Thai king to Islam (Graham, ii, 294).

By 1679, the South and West Asian Muslim community in Siam had become so numerous and influential that they had their own quarter in Ayutthaya (as distinct from the various Malay Muslim districts), whilst an English factor of the Honourable East India Company was able to report of the Mergui-Tenasserim region: "The Persians and Moors ... are now in effect masters of that part of the country as well as the commerce ... the colonies they have planted in those parts do almost equal the number of the natives, but far exceed them in wealth and power" (White, *IOR* E/3/40). During this period, the governors of Mergui, Tenasserim, Phetchaburi and Bangkok were all Muslims of West or South Asian origin, as were the captains of Phra Narai's merchant vessels trading with Golconda. Indeed, during the first half of the 11th/17th century, Thai trade with the west (that is, with the Bay of Bengal and the Indian Ocean littoral) was almost entirely in Muslim hands, whilst Phra Narai employed a succession of at least three (ostensibly Persian) Muslims as *phraklang*, or foreign minister (the most powerful position at the Thai Court), and even maintained a squadron of Muslim horse guards (de Choisy, 196).

Islamic influence at Ayutthaya entered into sharp decline during the latter part of Narai's reign, particularly following the rise in power of the Greek adventurer, Constant Phaulkon, who came to dominate the Thai royal court in *ca.* 1090/1679 (Hall, 364-74). Phaulkon perceived the "Moors" as political and commercial rivals, and at his behest their position and influence was gradually diminished, whilst that of the Europeans (and particularly of France) was correspondingly increased. During this period, the Muslim merchants dominating the Mergui-Tenasserim region were gradually displaced, and in 1683 an Englishman, Samuel ("Siamese") White, was appointed *s̲h̲āhbandar* of Mergui, with disastrous consequences for non-European regional commerce as a whole. Two years later, as a result of Phaulkon's commercial and political intrigues, war broke out between Siam and Golconda. Shortly thereafter, in 1687, a final blow was dealt to the Mergui-Machilipatanam trade when Golconda succumbed to the advancing armies of the Mug̲h̲al Emperor Awrangzīb [*q.v.*], and its capital was reduced to the status of a fishing village (Alam, 1959, *passim*).

The Mergui-Tenasserim trade route never fully recovered from these setbacks, although Indian Muslim merchants continued to trade with Ayutthaya via Mergui throughout the first half of the 12th/18th century. In *ca.* 1179/1765, however, even this diminished trade was brought to an abrupt end by the Burmese conquest of both Mergui and Tenasserim. Two years later, in 1767, Ayutthaya was itself captured and sacked by the Burmese armies of King Hsinbyushin.

Following the Burmese conquest, the entire Mergui-Tenasserim region as far south as Point Victoria was incorporated within the Burmese empire. The new frontier between Siam and Burma, now much advanced in the latter's favour, remained sealed to trade (Low, iii, 287, 290); besides, the overland portage route from Mergui to Ayutthaya had become increasingly anachronistic, and regional inter-Asian trade had come to be increasingly dominated by European commerce. With the Burmese conquest of 1765, therefore, Mergui ceased to serve as a channel for Muslim commerce and concepts into Siam, and became instead a Burmese backwater. It still retained a substantial Muslim population, however, and it is interesting to note that indigenous Burmese chronicles possibly dating from the late 12th/18th century describe the rebuilding of Mergui in *ca.* 1770, and record the allocation of a special area (the Kakaung quarter) to the township's Muslim population (Kyaw Din, 252-3).

Bibliography: J. Low, *History of Tenasserim*, in *JRAS*, ii (1835), 248-75; iii (1836), 25-54, 287-336; iv (1837), 42-108, 304-32; v (1839), 141-64, 216-63; N. Annandale, *The Coast People of Trang*, in *Fasciculi Malayenses* [*Anthropology*, i, Liverpool, 1903], 53-65; G. White, *Letter to Bantam from a port in Siam, dated 1679 A.D.*, in *Records of the relations between Siam and foreign countries in the 17th Century*, Bangkok 1916, ii, 202-13; original ms. at India Office Records, London E/3/40 (original correspondence, 1679/80); Kyaw Din, *The history of Tenasserim and Mergui*, in *Jnal. of the Burma Research Society*, vii/3 (Dec. 1917), 251-4; W.A. Graham, *Siam*, London 1924, 2 vols.; M. l'Abbé de Choisy, *Journal du voyage de Siam fait en 1685 et 1686*, Paris 1930; W.H. Moreland (ed.),

Relations of Golconda in the early seventeenth century, London 1931; E. Hutchinson, *Journal of Mgr. Lambert, Bishop of Beritus, from Tenasserim to Siam in 1662*, in *Jnal. of the Siam Society*, xxvi (1933), 215-18; M. Collis, *Siamese White*, London, 2nd Penguin ed. 1943; L.P. Briggs, *The Khmer Empire and the Malay Peninsula*, in *Far Eastern Quarterly*, ix (1950), 256-305; idem, *Into hidden Burma*, London 1953; G.R. Tibbetts, *Pre-Islamic Arabia and South-East Asia*, in *Jnal. Malay Branch, Royal Asiatic Society*, xxix/3 (1956), 182-208; Shah Manzoor Alam, *Masulipatam—a metropolitan fort in the 17th century A.D.*, in *The Indian Geographical Jnal.*, xxxiv/3-4 (1959), 33-42; P. Wheatley, *The Golden Khersonese*, Kuala Lumpur 1961; U. Tin Htoo, *The Mergui Archipelago and the Isthmus of Kra*, in *The Guardian* (Rangoon), ix/3 (March 1962), 29-32; E.M. Lebar *et alii*, *Ethnic groups of mainland Southeast Asia*, New Haven 1964; H.G. Penth, *An account in the Hikajat Atjeh on relations between Siam and Atjeh*, in *Felicitation volumes of Southeast-Asian Studies presented to His Highness Prince Dhannivat Kromamun Bidyalabh Bridhyakorn*, Bangkok 1965, i, 55-69; Muḥammad Ibrāhīm, *Safīna-yi Sulaymānī*, Eng. tr. John O'Kane, *The ship of Sulaimān*, London 1972; M. Yegar, *The Muslims of Burma*, Wiesbaden 1972; D.G.E. Hall, *A history of South-East Asia*, 3rd ed. London 1976; Tibbetts, *A study of the Arabic texts containing material on South-East Asia*, Leiden and London 1979; A.D.W. Forbes, *Tenasserim: the Thai kingdom of Ayutthaya's link with the Indian Ocean*, in *Indian Ocean Newsletter*, iii/1 (July 1982). Gazetteers: *The British Burma gazetteer*, Rangoon 1879, *ii. The Mergui Archipelago*; J. Butler, *Gazetteer of the Mergui District*, Rangoon 1884; *Imperial gazetteer of India*², Oxford 1908, xvii, 293-308; G.P. Andrew, *Burma gazetteer: Mergui District*, Rangoon 1912; *Burma gazetteer: Mergui District*, Rangoon 1924. (A.D.W. Forbes)

MERIČ, the Turkish name of a river called Hebros in classical Greek and Maritsa in Bulgarian. It is the principal river of the south-eastern Balkans and, under the Ottomans, of the *eyālet* of the Rumeli. Al-Idrīsī (*Opus geographicum*, Naples 1977, 796 = 4th section of the 5th climate) mentions it as *nahr Mārisū*; on his map of 1154, however, we read *nahr Akhīlū* (K. Miller, *Mappae arabicae*, Bd. I, pt. 2, Blatt V, Bd. II, 122, 126).

From its source in the north-western spur of the Rhodope mountains south of Sofia, the Merič flows eastwards through Bulgaria, forming a broad valley that separates the Balkan mountains to the north from the Rhodope to the south. It touches Turkish territory 20 km west-south-west of Edirne, and for 14 km it flows along the Turkish-Greek border; after a brief stretch inside the Turkish *il* of Edirne, where it is joined by the Tunca as it skirts the province's capital, the Merič turns southwards, and after 8 more km it again forms the border between Turkey and Greece. After having received the important tributary of Ergene, the river flows into the Aegean through a delta, at the eastern mouth of which is the port city of Enez.

It was the Ottomans who integrated the course of the Merič within the *Dār al-Islām*, but the region had experienced Turkish presence long before that: the Turkic Bulgars, then the Pechenegs and Cumans, and finally the forays of the Aydïn [*q.v.*] chieftain Umur Beg, who sailed upstream with his warships to the level of Dimetiḳa (Didymothike) in late 1343 (I. Melikoff-Sayar, *Le destan d'Umur Pacha*, Paris 1954, 41, 101; P. Lemerle, *L'émirat d'Aydin: Byzance et l'Occident*, Paris 1957, 169). Unlike the Turks of Aydïn, the Ottomans under Murād I approached the Merič from landwards and subsequently used the avenue presented by the river's valley for their further conquests in the Balkans. The counter-offensive of 766/1364 resulted in a defeat near the left bank of the Merič, during which the fleeing army sought salvation by crossing the river, a pre-dawn rout remembered by the place-name Ṣïrp Ṣïndïghï "Serbian defeat" (*Die Altosmanische Chronik des ʿĀšïḳpašazāde*, ed. F. Giese, 51).

Before the conquest of Constantinople, Edirne was the principal residence of the Ottoman sultans, and even later the Meṛič witnessed some of the pomp of court life. Thus in 861/1456-7 circumcision festivities of the *shehzādes* Bāyezīd and Muṣṭafā were held on the river island Kirishčiler adasï (*ʿĀšïḳpašazāde*, ed. Giese, 141).

The broad fertile valley of the Merič was appreciated in Byzantine times as one of the granaries of Constantinople; this role was further increasing during the Ottoman rule after the Turks had introduced there the cultivation of rice in the 9th/15th century. The river itself served as a transportation route for these supplies by boat to Enez, from where they were carried by sea-going craft to Istanbul (this role of the Merič ceased only in the 1870s with the construction of a railway from Istanbul). The economic importance of the Merič valley in the Ottoman period was also demonstrated by the prosperity of such cities as Filibe (Plovdiv), Edirne and Enez, and by the creation of Tatar Pazardjïḳ; this town, founded in 890/1485, was settled mainly by Bessarabian Tatars and Ottoman *sipāhīs*; its annual fair, held in July, was frequented by merchants from many parts of the empire. The valley represented an age-old route of communications, transportation and troop movements that continued beyond the Merič to Sofia and Belgrade. In the Ottoman postal organisation, the stages along the Merič pertained to the *orta ḳol* system. The effectiveness of the route was enhanced by the construction and endowment of *khāns* and bridges; especially remarkable is the 10th/16th century bridge known as Djisr-i Muṣṭafā Pasha, with a *khān* on either side, in present-day Svilengrad 40 km west of Edirne.

The Merič acquired a special political significance in the final years of the Ottoman empire when the question of the Turkish-Bulgarian and Turkish-Greek borders arose. With the successful completion of the War of Independence in Anatolia, the Turkish demands that the British authorities persuade the Greeks to withdraw their forces beyond the Merič were met, and the Treaty of Lausanne (July 1923) established the river as the definitive border between Turkey and Greece.

Bibliography: In addition to references given in the text, see Ewliyā Čelebi, *Seyāḥat-nāme*, Istanbul 1314, iii, 420-1; Sh. Sāmī, *Ḳāmūs al-aʿlām*, Istanbul 1898, vi, 4270-1; K. Jireček, *Die Heerstrasse von Belgrad nach Constantinopel*, Prague 1877; M. Tayyib Gökbilgin, *XV-XVI asırlarda Edirne ve Paşa livâsı*, Istanbul 1952, index s.v.; D.E. Pitcher, *An historical geography of the Ottoman Empire*, Leiden 1972; W.C. Brice (ed.), *An historical atlas of Islam*, Leiden 1981, pls. 30-1; *Türk Ansiklopedisi*, s.vv. *Meriç, Enez, Enez-Midye hattı*; Ali Tanoğlu, Sırrı Erinç and Erol Tümertekin, *Türkiye atlası*, Istanbul 1961, map 1a. (S. Soucek)

MERIDA [see mārida].

MERINIDS [see marīnids].

MERKA, the official spelling of Markah (as in al-Idrīsī *et alii*), a settlement which lies in lat. 1° N and 44° E, south of Maḳdishū [*q.v.*] in the Republic of Somalia. It is mentioned *ca.* 943 A.D. by al-Masʿūdī among places in Africa inhabited by the descendants of Kūsh [*q.v.*], but the reading must be considered doubtful because the other places enumerated are in western Africa (cf. *Murūdj*, ed. Pellat, index, s.v. Maranda). Al-Idrīsī (Climate 1, section 6) mentions it as associated with the Hawiyya, one of the groups of the Somali; Ibn Saʿīd (*apud* Abu 'l-Fidāʾ) states that it was their capital, and that it was inhabited by Muslims. In so far as they can be dated by external features, the mosques appear to be of late 18th century date or later. The Friday Mosque, nevertheless, has a dedicatory inscription equivalent to A.D. 1609, and that of Shaykh ʿUthmān to A.D. 1560. The grave in this structure appears to be older, for it incorporates stonework with a cable pattern that may be compared with that in the *miḥrāb* of the mosque at Kizimkazi [*q.v.*], Zanzibar, where the inscription in floriate Kūfic and other decorations are dated by an inscription equivalent to A.D. 1107.

Bibliography: Yāḳūt, *Buldān*, s.v.; E. Cerulli, *Somalia: scritti editi ed inediti*, i, Rome 1957; H.N. Chittick, *An archaeological reconnaissance of the southern Somali coast*, in *Azania*, iv (1969); idem and R.I. Rotberg, eds., *East Africa and the Orient*, New York and London 1975; L.M. Devic, *Le Pays des Zendjs*, Paris 1883; G.S.P. Freeman-Grenville, *Coins from Mogadishu, c. 1300-c. 1700*, in *Numismatic Chronicle* (1963); idem and B.C. Martin, *A preliminary handlist of the Arabic inscriptions of the Eastern African Coast*, in *JRAS* (1973); P.S. Garlake, *The early Islamic architecture of the East African Coast*, Oxford 1966; C. Guillain, *Documents sur l'histoire, la géographie et le commerce de l'Afrique orientale*, Paris 1856, i.

(G.S.P. Freeman-Grenville)

MERKEZ, Shaykh Muṣliḥ al-Dīn b. Muṣṭafā, the head of an Ottoman Ṣūfī order and saint.

Merkez Muṣliḥ al-Dīn Mūsā b. Muṣṭafā b. Ḳïlïdj b. Hadjdar belonged to the village of Ṣarï Maḥmūdlu in the Anatolian district of Lādhikiyya. He was at first a pupil of the Mollā Aḥmad Pasha, son of Khiḍr Beg [*q.v.*], and later of the famous Khalwatī Shaykh Sünbül Sinān Efendi, founder of the Sünbüliyya, a branch of the Khalwatiyya, head of the monastery of Ḳodja Muṣṭafā Pasha in Istanbul (see Bursalï Meḥmed Ṭāhir, *ʿOthmānlı müʾellifleri*, i, 78-9). When the latter died in 936/1529, Merkez Efendi succeeded him in the dignity of Pīr. He held the office of head of a monastery for 23 years and died in the odour of sanctity in 959/1552, aged nearly 90. He was buried in Istanbul in the mosque which bears his name (cf. *Ḥadīḳat al-djawāmiʿ*, i, 230-1; J. von Hammer, *GOR*, ix, 95, no. 495) before the Yeñi Ḳapu. At the tomb of Merkez Efendi there is a much-visited holy well, an *ayazma*, to which one descends by steps. Its reddish water is said to have the miraculous power of healing those sick of a fever (cf. Ewliyā Čelebi, i, 372; von Hammer, *Constantinopolis*, i, 513; idem, *GOR*, *loc. cit.*, following the *Ḥadīḳat al-djawāmiʿ*, *loc. cit.*). Beside it is the cell (*zāwiya*) of Merkez Efendi, of which miraculous stories still circulate among the people. He had many pupils, including his son Aḥmad, famous as the translator of the *Ḳāmūs*, his son-in-law Muṣliḥ al-Dīn (cf. Ewliyā, *loc. cit.*), the poet Ramaḍān Efendi, called Bihishtī, and many others.

Bibliography: In addition to the references in the text, see Ṭashköprüzāde, *Shaḳāʾiḳ al-nuʿmāniyya*, tr. Medjdī, 522-3; *ʿOthmānlï müʾellifleri*, i, 160; Meḥmed Thüreyyā, *Sidjill-i ʿothmānī*, iv, 363; F. Babinger, *GOW*, 44, n. 1; Tahsin Yazıcı, *Fetihten sonra İstanbul'da ilk halvetî şeyhleri*, in *İstanbul Enstitüsü Dergisi*, ii (1956), 104-13; idem, *İA* art. *Merkez Efendi*.

(Fr. Babinger)

MERLIN [see bayzara].

MERSIN, a sea-port on the south coast of Anatolia, capital of the province of Içel with seven districts (1980: 843, 931 inhabitants) and the centre of the Berdan-Ova, where *ca.* 40,000 ha. irrigated fields of cotton, citrus-trees and vegetables are cultivated. These products are exported through an important harbour (1980: 10,452 m^3 wood, 331,145 head of livestock, 74,842 passengers). Beside this, there exists an expanding industry (76 factories, 13,439 labourers) in textiles, chemical products (refinery) and building materials. The regularly-built town, now (1980) with 216,308 inhabitants, was founded in 1832 by Ibrāhīm Pasha [*q.v.*], son of Muḥammad ʿAlī [*q.v.*]; its name derives from the Greek *myrsini* (μυρσίνη) "myrtle", a tree, which grows in the region. To the north-west of Mersin is situated the Neolithic *höyük* of Yümüktepe, which was well-fortified in the 5th millenium B.C. In Hellenistic-Roman times, the harbour town of Zephirium lay in the neighbourhood; not far away to the south-west, the ruins of Soloi, later Pompeiopolis, are to be seen.

Bibliography: V. Cuinet, *La Turquie d'Asie*, Paris 1892, ii, 50 ff.; J. Garstang, *Prehistoric Mersin*, Oxford 1953; L. Rother, *Die Städte des Çukurova: Adana—Mersin—Tarsus*, Tübingen 1971; idem, *Gedanken zur Stadtentwicklung in der Çukurova (Türkei)*, Wiesbaden 1972.

(W. Röllig)

MERSIYE [see marthiya].

MERTOLA [see mīrtula].

MERV [see marw].

MERV-RŪD [see marw al-rūdh].

MĒRWĀRĀ [see rādjāsthān].

MERZIFŪN, also Mārsiwān, modern Turkish spelling Merzifon, a town of north-central Anatolia, lying in lat. 40°52′ and long. 35°35′E. and at an altitude of 750 m./2.464 ft. It is situated on the southern slopes of the Tavşan Dağı, with a rich and fertile plain, the Sulu Ova, on its south, where fruit, vines, nuts, opium poppies, etc. are cultivated, and with the towns of Çorum [see čorum] at 69 km./42 miles to the south-west and of Amasya [*q.v.*] at 49 km./30 miles to the south-east.

The town most probably occupies the site of the ancient Phazemon (Φαζημών) in the district of Phazemonitis; the name is probably a development of Φαζημών. Ibn Bībī (cf. *Recueil de textes relatifs à l'histoire des Seldjoucides*, ed. M. Th. Houtsma, iv, Leiden 1902, 292, 12) also gives the form Bāzīmūn. Little is known of the early history of the town in the Muslim period. It belonged to the kingdom of the Dānishmendids [*q.v.*] and when in 795/1393 Bāyezīd I drove the ruler of Sivas, Mīr Aḥmad, out of the country, the land of "Marsvani", as the Bavarian traveller Hans Schiltenberger (cf. *Hans Schiltbergers Reisebuch*, ed. V. Langmantel, Tübingen 1885, 12) called it, passed to the Ottoman empire. Merzifūn plays a notable part in the history of Ottoman culture as the birthplace and scene of the activities of learned men and authors (cf. A.D. Mordtmann, *Anatolien*, 88); and it was the family place of origin of the celebrated 11th/17th century Ottoman Grand Vizier Ḳara Muṣṭafā Pasha Merzifonlu [*q.v.*].

In Merzifūn there used to be a number of dervish *tekkes* (cf. Ewliyā Čelebi, *Seyāḥet-nāme*, ii, 396 below, where several are mentioned). The saint locally reverenced was Pīr Dede Sulṭān, said to be a pupil of Ḥādjdjī Bektash (Ewliyā, ii, 396).

Monuments there include several mosques converted from Byzantine churches, including the so-called Eski Cami, on the walls of which Christian paintings could be seen till at least the later 19th century (cf. V. Cuinet, *La Turquie d'Asie*, Paris 1892, i, 761); the *madrasa* of Meḥemmed Čelebi (built 817/1414 by one Abū Bekr b. Meḥmed, to which an incongruous clock tower was added in the 19th century); and the complex built by Ḳara Muṣṭafā Pa<u>sh</u>a, with mosque (built in 1077/1666-7), *madrasa* and caravanserai (see G. Goodwin, *A history of Ottoman architecture*, London 1971, 20, 362, 419).

In the 19th century, Merzifūn was the centre of American Protestant missionary enterprise in the *wilāyet* of Sivas (in which Merzifūn was in late Ottoman times situated), with the Anatolia College, a theological seminary, schools and charitable institutions, proselytism being aimed mainly at the local Armenians (Cuinet numbered the town's population at 13,380 Muslims, 5,820 Armenians and 800 Greeks). There were also Roman Catholic Jesuit and Gregorian Armenian schools. Most of these did not survive the First World War and the Armenian massacres, with the consequent liquidation of that ethnic element from the town, as also the Greeks (the 1927 census enumerated only 11,334 inhabitants of Merzifūn), but a small body of American missionaries and a school were still functioning in the late thirties.

Modern Merzifon is the chef-lieu of an *ilçe* or district of the same name in the *il* or province of Amasya, and is noted for its cotton textiles. The population of the town was in 1970 28,210 and that of the district 59,777.

Bibliography: Pauly-Wissowa, xix/2, col. 1909, s.v. *Phazemon*; Ewliyā Čelebi, *Seyāḥat-nāme*, ii, 396 ff., Eng. tr. Von Hammer, ii, 212 ff.; <u>Sh</u>. Sāmī, *Ḳāmūs al-aʿlām*, Istanbul 1315, vi, 4259; *Le Voyage de Monsieur d'Aramon..., escript par .... J. Chesneau*, ed. Ch. Schefer, Paris 1887, 68; J. Morier, *Journey through Persia, Armenia and Asia Minor*, London 1812, 350; *Petermann's Mitteilungen*, 1859, Heft 12; C. Ritter, *Erdkunde von Kleinasien*, i, 179 ff.; W. Ainsworth, *Travels in Asia Minor*, London 1842, i, 33; W. Hamilton, *Researches in Asia Minor*, London 1842, i, 329; A.D. Mordtmann, *Anatolien*, ed. F. Babinger, Hanover 1925, 87 ff.; H.J. van Lennep, *Travels in little-known parts of Asia Minor*, London 1870, i, 82; F. Cumont, *Studia Pontica*, ii, 140; iii, 162; V. Cuinet, *La Turquie d'Asie*, i, 758-62; Naval Intelligence Division, *Admiralty Handbook, Turkey*, London 1942-3, ii, 572; *İA* art. *Merzifon* (Besim Darkot).

(F. Babinger-[C.E. Bosworth])

ME<u>SH</u>ʿALE ("Torch"), a journal published in Turkish, of which eight numbers only appeared between 1 July and 15 October 1928.

It had been founded by <u>D</u>jewdet Ḳudret (Cevdet Kudret Solok), Kenʿān <u>Kh</u>ulūṣī (Kenan Hulusi Koray), Ṣabrī Esʿad (Sabri Esat Siyavuşgil), Waṣfī Māhir (Vasfi Mahir Kocatürk), Ḍiyāʾ ʿO<u>th</u>mān (Ziya Osman Saba) and Yā<u>sh</u>ār Nābī (Yaşar Nabi Nayır) after the unexpected success of an anthology (*Yedi me<u>sh</u>ʿale*, Istanbul 1928) of the above-mentioned authors plus Muʿammar Lütfī. These young writers, the *Me<u>sh</u>ʿale<u>dj</u>iler* (*Meşaleciler*), wished to combat the general, unfavourable judgment pronounced upon the literature of their country through the novel expression of a literary production devoid of the expression of the authors' individual feeling. The contrasting influences, whose action they felt, did not reach maturity, but they certainly felt the need of a call to order, more clearly discernible, it was true, in other Western intellectuals, in order to give a new response to the confused expectations of their national revolution.

Me<u>sh</u>ʿale had the aim of functioning solely in the sphere of literature and art, but its founders were not unaware of social cares, and a few years later, a journal, *Kadro* (1932-5), was to endeavour to shape, within Kemalism, a new political and ideological milieu. *Me<u>sh</u>ʿale* lived though the changes and contrasts of the age, even in its external aspect, since in the latter issues, Latin characters began to replace the Arabic ones, and its decorative designs were always in the style of the twenties of the West, the same elegant and objective artistic style desired by the *Me<u>sh</u>ʿale<u>dj</u>iler* poets, whilst the prose writer Kenʿān <u>Kh</u>ulūṣī was closer to Symbolism.

Under the patronage of Yūsuf Ḍiyāʾ (Yusuf Ziya Ortaç), *Me<u>sh</u>ʿale* provides us with a useful panorama of the Turkish literature of its time, and the foreign authors presented in it confirm the French influence on Turkish culture. That some young people, with the help of writers already well-known, should have endeavoured, by means of journals like *Me<u>sh</u>ʿale* and *Kadro*, to bring about a new cultural atmosphere, shows the desire for social action on the part of the Turkish intellectuals. In their literature, it is always nevertheless more essential to search out the elements of continuity and originality which lie beyond external appearances, together with those enduring elements of faithfulness—sometimes not discernible as such—to tradition.

Bibliography: For the traditional view, see R. Mutluay, *Çağdaş Türk edebiyatı* (*1908-1972*), Istanbul 1973; a new interpretation is furnished in G.E. Carretto, *Saggi su Meşale. Un'avanguardia letteraria turca del 1928*, Venice 1979, which develops further two articles of 1976 and 1977. See also the special number of *Varlık* (*50. yılında Yedi Meşale özel sayısı*), no. 847 (April 1978). On *Kadro*, see Carretto, *Polemiche fra kemalismo, fascismo e communismo negli anni '30*, in *Storia contemporanea*, viii/3 (1977), 205-12, Turkish tr. in *Tarih ve Toplum*, nos. 17-18 (1985).

(G.E. Carretto)

ME<u>SH</u>(H)ED [see mas<u>h</u>had].

ME<u>SH</u>(H)ED ʿALĪ [see al-na<u>dj</u>af].

ME<u>SH</u>(H)ED ḤUSAYN [see karbalāʾ].

ME<u>SH</u>RŪṬA, ME<u>SH</u>RŪṬIYYET [see dustūr].

MESĪḤ MEḤMED PA<u>SH</u>A, <u>Kh</u>ādim (*ca.* 901-98/*ca.* 1495-1589), Ottoman Grand Vizier under Sultan Murād III [*q.v.*].

<u>Kh</u>ādim Mesīḥ made his career as one of the white *a<u>gh</u>a*s in the Sultan's private household (*Enderun* [*q.v.*]) at the time when their influence was still predominant in the palace. At the accession of Murād III (982/1574), he held the office of chief butler (*Kilār<u>dj</u>iba<u>sh</u>ī*). He left the palace service to become *Beglerbegi* of Egypt. He governed that province for five years. His successful administration brought him the appointment as Third Vizier and the recall to Istanbul (989/1581). When the Grand Vizier Özdemiro<u>gh</u>lu ʿO<u>th</u>mān Pa<u>sh</u>a [*q.v.*] left the capital as *Serdār* (20 Ra<u>dj</u>ab 992/28 July 1584), Mesīḥ Pa<u>sh</u>a was made Second Vizier and *Ḳāʾimmaḳām*. Upon the death of the Grand Vizier in 993/1585, Mesīḥ Pa<u>sh</u>a became Grand Vizier, then being about ninety years old. After little more than four months in office he resigned because of a disagreement with the sultan, who refused to replace the *Reʾīs ül-küttāb* Ḥamza Efendi by Küčük Ḥasan Bey, as was the wish of the Grand Vizier (24 Rabīʿ II 994/14 April 1586). Mesīḥ Pa<u>sh</u>a retired from public life. He died three years later and lies buried in the *türbe* in front of the mosque founded by him in 994/1585 in the Karagümrük quarter of Istanbul.

Bibliography: M.C. Baysun, *Reis elküttab Küçük Hasan Bey*, in *TD*, ii (1950-1, publ. 1952, no. 3-4);

ADDENDA AND CORRIGENDA

VOLUME I

P. 847b, **BĀBĪS,** *add* to Bibl.: Abbas Amanat, *Resurrection and renewal. The making of the Babi movement in Iran, 1844-1850*, Ithaca and London 1989.

P. 1007b, **BALŪČISTĀN,** *add* to Bibl.: J. Elfenbein, *A periplus of the "Brahui problem"*, in *Stud. Iranica*, xvi (1987), 215-33.

P. 1345a, **BUST,** *add* to Bibl.: T. Allen, *Notes on Bust*, in *Iran JBIPS*, xxvi (1988), 55-68, xxvii (1989), 57-66, xxviii (1990).

VOLUME III

P. 460b, **HINDŪ-SHĀHĪS,** *add* to Bibl.: Yogendra Mishra, *The Hindu Shahis of Afghanistan and the Punjab*, Patna 1972; Abdur Rahman, *The last two dynasties of the Śāhīs. An analysis of their history, archaeology, coinage and palaeography*, Islamabad 1979.

VOLUME V

P. 375b, **AL-KUMAYT B. ZAYD AL-ASADĪ,** *add* to Bibl.: W. Madelung, *The* Hāshimiyyāt *of al-Kumayt and Hāshimī Shiʿism*, in *SI*, lxx (1989), 5-26.

VOLUME VI

P. 115b, **MAḲĀMA,** *add* to Bibl.: Yūsuf Nūr ʿAwad, *Fann al-maḳāmāt bayn al-mashriḳ wa 'l-maghrib*[2], Mecca 1406/1986; Samīr Maḥmūd al-Durūbī, *Sharḥ maḳāmāt Jalāl al-Dīn al-Suyūṭī al-mutawaffā sanat 911*, 2 vols. Beirut 1409/1989.

P. 453b, **MANŪČIHRĪ,** *add* to Bibl.: W. L. Hanaway, *Blood and wine: sacrifice in Manūchihrī's wine poetry*, in *Iran JBIPS*, xxvi (1988), 69-80.

P. 736b, **MASḲAṬ,** *add* to author's signature "shortened by the Editors".

ISBN 90 04 09298 6

PRINTED IN THE NETHERLANDS

THE ENCYCLOPAEDIA OF ISLAM

NEW EDITION

PREPARED BY A NUMBER OF
LEADING ORIENTALISTS

EDITED BY

C. E. BOSWORTH, E. VAN DONZEL, W. P. HEINRICHS AND CH. PELLAT

ASSISTED BY F. TH. DIJKEMA AND MME S. NURIT

UNDER THE PATRONAGE OF
THE INTERNATIONAL UNION OF ACADEMIES

VOLUME VI

FASCICULE 114A

MESĪḤ MEḤMED PASHA — MIDYŪNA

TUTA SUB AEGIDE PALLAS · 1683 ·

LEIDEN
E.J. BRILL
1990

EXECUTIVE COMMITTEE:

All correspondence on editorial matters should be addressed to the Editorial Secretaries, whose addresses are:

For the English Edition

Dept. of Near Eastern Studies,
The University of Manchester,
Manchester,
England M13 9PL.

For the French Edition

Centre Universitaire
94, avenue des Grésillons
92600 Asnières
France

AUTHORS OF ARTICLES IN THESE FASCICULES

Edith G. Ambros, University of Vienna. 1027.
J. Burton-Page, Church-Knowle, Dorset. 1028, 1029.
G. Dávid. Eötvös Lorand University, Budapest. 1030.
R. H. Davison, Georg Washington University, Washington. 1035.
F. Müge Göçek, University of Michigan, Ann Arbor. 1029, 1030.
A. H. de Groot, University of Leiden. 1025.
H. İnalcik, University of Chicago. 1026.
T. Lewicki, Cracow. 1044.
Ch. Pellat, University of Paris. 1042.
I. H. Siddiqui, Muslim University, Aligarh. 1031.
S. Soucek, New York Public Library. 1037.
J. J. Witkam, University of Leiden. 1031.

Names in square brackets are those of authors of articles reprinted or revised from the first edition of this Encyclopaedia.

İ.H. Danişmend, *Osmanlı tarihi kronolojisi*, iii, Istanbul 1972², 58, 76, 79, 88, 100-2; v, 22; İ.A. Gövsa, *Türk meşhurları ansiklopedisi*, Istanbul n.d., 159; Hammer-Purgstall, *HEO*, vii, 165, 405-6, 206, 226; *Mufassal Osmanlı tarihi*, iii, Istanbul 1959, 1390; ʿO̲t̲h̲mānzāde Aḥmed Tāʾib, *Ḥadīḳat ül-wüzerāʾ* (photo reprint ed.) Freiburg 1969, 41; T. Öz, *İstanbul camileri*, i, Ankara 1962, 83, 104, plate 75; Ibrahīm Pečewī, *Taʾrīk̲h̲*, ii, Istanbul 1283, 18-19; N. Poroy, *İstanbul'da gömülü paşalar*, Istanbul 1947, 19-20; İ.H. Uzunçarşılı, *Osmanlı devletinin saray teşkilâtı*, Ankara 1984², 28, 313, 354-7.

(A.H. de Groot)

MESĪḤ PAS̲H̲A, Ottoman Grand Vizier in 906/1501. Mesīḥ and his elder brother K̲h̲āṣṣ Murād were sons of a brother of Constantine IX Palaeologus (Babinger, *Eine Verfügung*). Apparently Mesīḥ and Murād were captured during the conquest of Constantinople and brought up as pages in Meḥemmed II's seraglio.

The Greek faction under this Sultan first came to power when he decided to conquer the Greek island of Euboea (Eg̲h̲riboz) in 875/1470. Mesīḥ distinguished himself for the first time during this campaign as *sand̲j̲aḳ begi* of Gelibolu [*q.v.*] and admiral of the navy. But soon afterwards he offered, as Venetian documents testify, to surrender Gelibolu, the Ottoman naval base, and the fleet to the Venetians in return for 40,000 gold ducats, aspiring to become ruler over the Morea (Babinger, *Mehmed*, 290). Mesīḥ appears to have been a vizier in late autumn 1476, or in early 1477 (see discussion in Reindl, 280). Two documents (Gökbilgin, 138, 148 n. 153) indicate that he was already second vizier on 19 S̲h̲aʿbān 882/26 November 1477 and also in 883/1478, Meḥmed Pas̲h̲a Ḳaramānī [*q.v.*] being Grand Vizier in both cases. A contemporary source (Donado da Lezze, 112) states that he was a newly-appointed fourth vizier when he was made commander-in-chief of the army and navy against Rhodes in the spring of 995/1480. Having failed at the siege, he was dismissed from the vizierate (Ibn Kemāl, cited by Reindl, 281), but apparently left with the *sand̲j̲aḳ* of Gelibolu as admiral of the navy. During the indecisive period after the death of Meḥemmed II (3 May 1481) Mesīḥ, who belonged to the military *dews̲h̲irme* [*q.v.*] group of Gedik Aḥmed, appeared as a vizier in the *Dīwān*. Bringing Bāyezīd II to the throne, the military *dews̲h̲irme* faction had then full control of the government.

While Gedik Aḥmed, with the support of the Janissaries, acted too independently, Mesīḥ won the trust of the Sultan as an opponent of D̲j̲em [*q.v.*]: when in early summer 887/1482 Gedik Aḥmed, suspected of being pro-D̲j̲em, was imprisoned in the Seraglio, the Janissaries invaded the palace and threatened the Sultan, who sent a group of dignitaries, including Mesīḥ, to negotiate. He succeeded in appeasing the soldiery by accepting all their demands including the promise never to appoint viziers outside the *dews̲h̲irme* (da Lezze, 179-80). This convinced Bāyezīd that he was completely dependent, for his safety on the throne, on the military faction. Mesīḥ, closely co-operating with the seraglio, demonstrated his diplomatic ability and loyalty once again when D̲j̲em took refuge with the Hospitallers of Rhodes. During negotiations, while Gedik Aḥmed proved to be uncompromising, Mesīḥ achieved an agreement to the satisfaction of Bāyezīd, thus becoming the architect of Bāyezīd's policy in respect of the D̲j̲em question. Now members of the military *dews̲h̲irme* (Dāwūd, Mesīḥ and Hersek-og̲h̲lu Aḥmed) dominated the *Dīwān*, while Bāyezīd sent to the most sensitive governorships his eunuch *ḳapî-ag̲h̲as* from the seraglio (Yaḥyā, Yaʿḳūb, ʿAlī, K̲h̲alīl and Fīrūz). Supported by the seraglio, Mesīḥ managed to survive Bāyezīd's bold decision to eliminate Gedik Aḥmed, whom he believed to be a threat to his throne. After his execution (18 November 1482), a new era, that of the seraglio's direct control of government, began. Mesīḥ was second vizier in the *Dīwān* in 888/beg. 9 February 1483 (*Anonymous chronicle*, B.N. Paris, suppl. 1047, fol. 93a; also Yaʿḳūb Pas̲h̲a's *waḳfiyya* dated *awāʾil* Muḥarram 888/mid-February 1483, in Epstein, 290). Mesīḥ had replaced in this post D̲j̲azarī Ḳāsîm Pas̲h̲a, a bureaucrat famous as "the founder of the Ottoman bureaucratic tradition". When Isḥāḳ Pas̲h̲a, Grand Vizier and supporter of Gedik Aḥmed, had to leave the *Dīwān* (in the summer or early autumn 888/1483, see Reindl, 171, 236, 283), Dāwūd Pas̲h̲a, who was already second vizier in 887/beg. 20 February 1482, and apparently favoured by the seraglio faction, became Grand Vizier. It is suggested that Mesīḥ succeeded Isḥāḳ in the grand vizierate (Reindl, 171, 236, 283, on the authority of the contemporary historian Ibn Kemāl), and kept the position until 890/1485. But Mesīḥ is shown in the *Anonymous chronicle*, fol. 93b, as second vizier and Dāwūd as Grand Vizier in 889/beg. 30 January 1484.

In 890/beg. 18 January 1485, Mesīḥ was suddenly dismissed from the vizierate by the sultan, who was infuriated at something which we cannot determine (Ibn Kemāl, cited by Reindl, 283). He was first banished to Filibe as its *subas̲h̲î*, and then was transferred to Kaffa [*q.v.*] as its *sand̲j̲aḳ begi* in 892/1487 (Kaffa, like Salonica, had become an exile for demoted viziers). The customs register of Kaffa dated 892/1487 shows that Mesīḥ then owned a ship which was active in the traffic between Istanbul and Kaffa and at that time his *ketk̲h̲üdā* took for him slaves at Azaḳ. Mesīḥ apparently left Kaffa when Prince Meḥemmed was sent as its governor toward the end of 895/1489 (Reindl, 284). Next we find him in our sources as *sand̲j̲aḳ begi* of Akkerman (Akkerme) in Rabīʿ II 903/beg. 27 November 1497. According to the *Anonymous chronicle*, fols. 118b-121a, he played a major role in stopping a Polish army which invaded Moldavia in 1496-7, in cooperation with the Rumelian and frontier forces and with the Moldavian Voyvode Stephen. Mesīḥ took advantage of this achievement to gain the sultan's favour, sending him 29 standards and enslaved Polish nobles.

The news was welcomed in Istanbul, and Venice was informed as a warning (Sanuto, *I Diarii*, i, 845; Fisher, 56). Mesīḥ's pilgrimage in the summer of 904/1499 seems to be a calculated move to go to Istanbul and exploit his recent success in Moldavia. Actually, considering his experience in naval affairs, his knowledge of western politics and his family connections with Venice (Reindl, 279), he was a man who would be most useful in the war against Venice, which began in June 1499. Shortly after his return from Mecca he was appointed a vizier (*bassà* in Sanuto, quoted by Reindl 285, does not mean necessarily Grand Vizier). In fact, in Rad̲j̲ab 905/February 1500, the Grand Vizier was Yaʿḳūb Pas̲h̲a, Bāyezīd II's first Grand Vizier of palace eunuchs, who came to this post following the death of Čandarlî Ibrāhīm Pas̲h̲a at the end of Muḥarram 905/August 1499. Mesīḥ entered the *Dīwān* as second vizier while his friend Hersek-og̲h̲lu occupied the post of third vizier (*Anonymous chronicle*, fols. 124a). Eunuchs (*ṭawās̲h̲ī*) were never welcomed by the bureaucratic and military factions, but they established supreme authority over government affairs and were particularly favoured by Bāyezīd II. In Muḥarram 906/July-August 1500, Mesīḥ was still mentioned as second vizier (Reindl, 221-2, 354, believes Mesīḥ was made Grand Vizier immediately after Ibrāhīm's death in 1499), and in Ramaḍān 906/March-April 1501 he left Istanbul for Tas̲h̲-ili in Ḳaramān to quell the rebellion of the Warsak tribes which were supporting a Ḳaramānid pretender by the name of Muṣṭafā. There is no doubt that in the spring of 1501 Mesīḥ was appointed Grand Vizier for the first time to lead this important campaign (details in Idrīs Bidlīsī, *Hes̲h̲t bihis̲h̲t*, TKP Library, Hazine 1655). Combining the skills of a general and diplomat, Mesīḥ was able to persuade the tribal chieftains not to give their support to the Ḳaramānid pretender. Soon after his return to Istanbul, a joint Franco-Venetian invasion of the island of Mytilene (Midilli [*q.v.*]) infuriated the sultan, who struck his Grand Vizier with his bow (September 1501). Soon afterwards, Mesīḥ was wounded attending a fire in G̲h̲alaṭa, and died five days later (D̲j̲umāda I 907/November 1501). The mosque bearing his name in Istanbul was converted from a church and is at present in need of repair. Its *waḳfiyya* is dated Rabīᶜ I 907/October 1501 (Ayverdi and Barkan, 142, no. 799). For the *awḳāf* for his mosque and *madrasa* in Gelibolu, see Gölbilgin, 439. Its *waḳfiyya* is dated 888/1478. The names of his three sons, ᶜAlī Beg, Maḥmūd Čelebi and Bali Beg, are known. The latter was *sand̲j̲aḳ begi* of Vulčitrin in Rabīᶜ I 909/ August-September 1503.

Bibliography: Anonymous, *Tawārīk̲h̲-i Āl-i ᶜOt̲h̲mān*, B.N. ms. Supplément turc 1047; Donado da Lezze (J. Maria-Angiolello), *Historia Turchesca*, ed. I. Ursu, Bucharest 1910, 106, 112, 179, 259, 260 (Misit Bassa); Ibn Kemāl (Kemāl Pas̲h̲a-zāde), see Reindl, 19; S.N. Fisher, *The foreign relations of Turkey, 1481-1512*, Urbana 1948; Idrīs-i Bidlīsī, *Hes̲h̲t bihis̲h̲t*, TKP, Hazine 1655; M.T. Gökbilgin, *Edirne ve Paşa lıvâsı*, Istanbul 1952; F. Babinger, *Eine Verfügung des Paläologen Chāṣṣ-Murād*, in *Aufsätze und Abhandlungen*, i, Munich 1962, 344-54; E.H. Ayverdi and Ö.L. Barkan, *Istanbul vakıfları tahrir defteri*, Istanbul 1970; F. Babinger, *Mehmed the Conqueror and his time*, ed. W.C. Hickman, Princeton 1978; R.F. Kreutel, *Der Fromme Sultan Bāyezīd*, Graz, Vienna and Cologne 1978; M.A. Epstein, *The Ottoman Jewish communities and their role in the fifteenth and sixteenth centuries*, Freiburg 1980; H. Reindl, *Männer um Bayezid. Eine prosopographische Studie über die Epoche Bāyezīds II.* (*1481-1512*), Berlin 1983.

(Halil Inalcik)

MESĪḤĪ, an important Ottoman poet of Bāyezīd II's time (886-918/1481-1512), who died after 918/1512, possibly even after 924/1518 (see V.L. Ménage, *An Ottoman manual of provincial correspondence*, in *WZKM*, lxviii [1976], 3-45, and idem, art. on *Gül-i ṣad-berg* in *Osmanlı Araştırmaları*, forthcoming). His given name was ᶜĪsā. Born in Priştina, he came in his youth to Istanbul, where he became a *medrese* student and also soon distinguished himself as a calligrapher. He was able to find favour with the Grand Vizier K̲h̲ādim ᶜAlī Pas̲h̲a, whose *dīwān* secretary he became. However, his patron had frequent cause to be annoyed with him because of his undisciplined, pleasure-oriented life and his lack of conscientiousness in the performance of his official duties, and is reported to have spoken of him as a *s̲h̲eher og̲h̲lanî* ("street arab"). He nevertheless held this position until K̲h̲ādim ᶜAlī Pas̲h̲a fell in 917/1511 fighting the S̲h̲īᶜī rebels under S̲h̲āh Ḳulî. Mesīḥī composed a deeply-felt elegy on his death but, having need of a new protector, ended with a mention of *yeñičeri ag̲h̲asî* Yūnus Pas̲h̲a (cf. İ. Morina, *Mesihi'nin Hadim Ali Paşa'ya yazdığı mersiyesi*, in *Çevren*, viii [1981], no. 31, 55-63). Based on the information given by ᶜĀs̲h̲îḳ Čelebi, it was formerly accepted that Mesīḥī did not succeed in gaining the protection of either Yūnus Pas̲h̲a or the *Nis̲h̲and̲j̲î* Tād̲j̲ī-zāde D̲j̲aᶜfer Čelebi, that he had to be content with a small fief in Bosnia and that his attempts to gain the patronage of Selīm I failed likewise. This assumption should now be revised insofar as Sehī's statement that Mesīḥī was in the service of Yūnus Pas̲h̲a has been shown by Ménage to be the more reliable.

Mesīḥī's place in Ottoman *dīwān* poetry is that of a highly gifted and original poet without an extensive œuvre. His language is relatively plain and clear, his manner devoid of affectation. Some poems and passages of his captivate through their lyricism. There is wealth of charming new images, associations and ideas. A touch of Rumelian dialect here and there is of linguistic interest.

Mesīḥī's lifework comprises: (1) His not especially voluminous *Dīwān* has not yet been printed. Critical editions in typescript form exist, however: Mine Özoğul, *The Divan of the 15th century Ottoman poet Mesīḥī*, Ph. D. thesis, Edinburgh University 1969, and S. Jaber, *Mesîhî'nin hayatı ve dîvânının tenkitli metni*, Ph.D. thesis, Istanbul 1953. Best known in Europe is his *murabbaᶜ* on spring which Sir William Jones published with a Latin translation in *Poeseos Asiaticae commentariorum libri sex*, Leipzig 1774, and which was thereafter repeatedly translated into German, French, Italian, English, Russian and Serbian (cf. F. Bayraktareviç, *Mesîhî'nin dünya edebiyatında yer alan "Bahariye"si*, in *İstanbul Üniversitesi Edebiyat Fakültesi Türk Dili ve Edebiyatı Dergisi*, xxii [1974-6], 213-9; İ. Eren, *"Bahariye"nin Fransizca, Rusça ve Sırpça çevirileri*, in *ibid.*, 221-7. (2) The *met̲h̲newī S̲h̲ehr-engīz* ("rouser of the city") is Mesīḥī's most original work. It is a humorous description of the handsome youths of Edirne, all of whom have Muslim names and are of the lower middle class, with mention of their or their father's profession. (Except for four of the total of 47, two verses are dedicated to each youth.) Cf. on the text, İ. Morina, *XV y.y. büyük Türk şairi Priştine'li Mesihi* (*1470-1513*) [*sic*], in *Çevren*, viii (1981), no. 30, 39-56. Its language is plain, unpretentious and easily understandable. Mesīḥī's *S̲h̲ehr-engīz* became popular and he had numerous followers in this poetic genre. It is generally but not unanimously accepted that the *s̲h̲ehr-engīz* by D̲h̲ātī would appear to date from just about the same time, and that it had no Persian model (cf. Mine Mengi, *Mesîhî'nin hayatı, şairliği ve eserleri*, in *Türkoloji Dergisi*, vi [1974], no. 1, 109-19; A.S. Levend, *Türk edebiyatında şehr-engizler ve şehr-engizlerde İstanbul*, Istanbul 1958; and M. İzzet, *Türk edebiyatında şehrengîzler*, unpubl. Ph.D. thesis, Istanbul 1936). (3) *Gül-i ṣad-berg* ("the many-petalled rose") is an *ins̲h̲āʾ* collection of elegant stylistic samples not without historic interest. Only a very few mss. of this have been reported to exist (cf. the article by Ménage cited above).

Bibliography (in addition to the titles cited above): The *ted̲h̲kires* of Sehī, Laṭīfī, ᶜĀs̲h̲îḳ Čelebi, Ḳînalî-zāde Ḥasan Čelebi, Beyānī and Riyāḍī; ᶜĀlī, *Künh al-ak̲h̲bār*; *Sid̲j̲ill-i ᶜOt̲h̲mānī*, iv, 369; Ḥ. Ḥüsām al-Dīn, *Amasya tārīk̲h̲i*, Istanbul 1927, iii, 260; Müstaḳīm-zāde, *Tuḥfe-yi k̲h̲aṭṭāṭīn*, Istanbul 1928, 566; Ned̲j̲īb ᶜĀṣîm, *Mesīḥī dīwānî*, in *TOEM*, i (1911), 300-8; *ᶜOt̲h̲mānlî müʾellifleri*, ii, 410; Hammer, *Geschichte der osman. Dichtkunst*, i, 297-302; Gibb, *Ottoman Poetry*, ii, 226-56; Nesrin, *Mesîhî*, *hayatı ve eserleri*, unpubl. Ph.D. thesis, Istanbul 1940; A. Karahan, in *İA*, s.v. *Mesihî*.

(Th. Menzel — [E.G. Ambros])

MESOPOTAMIA [see al-Djazīra; al-ʿIrāḳ].

MESSENGER [see rasūl].

MESSIAH [see masīḥ].

METALLURGY [see maʿdin].

METAMORPHOSIS [see maskh].

METAPHOR [see istiʿāra].

METAPHYSICS [see mā baʿd al-ṭabīʿa].

MÉTAYAGE [see khamāsa; muzāraʿa].

METEMPSYCHOSIS [see tanāsukh].

METEOROLOGY [see anwāʾ; āthār ʿulwiyya].

METONYMY [see kināya].

METRICS [see ʿarūḍ].

METROLOGY [see makāyīl; misāḥa; mīzān].

METROPOLIS [see miṣr. b].

MĒWAŔ, the name given in the Indian chronicles to the south-western region of Rādjāsthān [*q.v.*]: approximately the region now known, from its principal town, as Udaypur (although the town of Udaypur [*q.v.*] was not founded until 966/1559), hilly with considerable forest tracts, separated from its Rādjpūt neighbour Mārwāŕ on the west by the Aravallī hills, and bordered on the south by Gudjarāt, on the south-east and east by Mālwā, on the north-east by the Dihlī sultanate (see Map s.v. rādjāsthān). The region is more celebrated for its defences against Islamic forces than for any lasting status as a region under Islamic rule until Bābur's victory at Khānuʾā in 933/1527 over the combined Rādjpūt armies under the Mēwāŕ ruler, and Akbar's conquest of the fort of Čitawŕ forty years later, initiated a period of Mughal sovereignty that was to last for over 200 years.

The first ruling dynasty, the Guhilōt Rādjpūts, is said to have entered Mēwāŕ from Gudjarāt and dominated the region in the 1st/7th century, ruling from the (now derelict) town of Nāgdā some 20 km north of the present Udaypur from where Čitawŕ was conquered; a bardic account credits an early ruler with a successful defence against a powerful Arab general, probably al-Djunayd b. ʿAbd Allāh [*q.v.*], if the chronology can be relied on. A descendant is said to have joined with the Hindū rulers of Gudjarāt in resisting the expansion of the Arab caliphate of Sindh [*q.v.*] beyond Multān [*q.v.*] in the 3rd/9th century. But Mēwāŕ resistance was not only against the Muslim powers: the Čawhāns of Sambhar, the Paramāras of Mālwā, and the Čawlukyas of Gudjarāt were all powerful neighbours who more than once made forays into Mēwāŕ. The Guhilōts stood firm, gradually gaining strength, until the Ghūrid conquest in the north broke the power of the Čawhāns; Mēwāŕ overcame the pretensions of the rival Hindū dynasties, but met with less success against the new Muslim power of Dihlī, for Iltutmish marched on and destroyed Nāgdā, and Čitawŕ became the new Mēwāŕ capital.

By the early 8th/14th century Mēwāŕ was seen as the most powerful of the Rādjpūt states, and its independence as a threat to the prestige of Dihlī; its conquest was undertaken by ʿAlāʾ al-Din Khaldjī, probably partly for strategic reasons and partly in the quest of plunder, although a later age assigned a romantic reason, the outstanding beauty of Ratansen's queen Padminī/Padmāvatī. (Malik Muḥammad Djāyasī [*q.v.*], writing early in the 10th/16th century, made an outstanding love-story of this first sack of Čitawŕ, often interpreted as a Ṣūfistic allegory of the soul; though when he writes *djawhār bhain istirī, purukh bhaé sangrām/pātsāhi gaḍh čūrā, čitawr bhā islām* "the women performed the *djawhār*, the men became warriors (sc. to the death); the king crushed the fort, and Čitawŕ became Islām", he may not be historically accurate (*Padmāvat*, ed. V.Ś. Agrawal, verse 651), for Amīr Khusraw [*q.v.*], who was present with ʿAlāʾ al-Dīn, makes no mention of the *djawhār*, the mass self-immolation of the womenfolk). Čitawŕ fell in 702/1303, by what seems to have been peaceful surrender (epidemic or famine in the garrison have been suggested as the reasons), Ratansen delivering himself personally to ʿAlāʾ al-Dīn; Čitawŕ was then renamed Khiḍrābād and assigned to the young heir-apparent Khiḍr Khān, although the administration lay in the able hands of Maladeva, a Čawhān Rādjpūt in ʿAlāʾ al-Dīn's service who was connected by marriage to the Guhilōt house. Ratansen was dethroned and the succession passed to a cadet branch of the Guhilōts, the Sisodiyas, several princes of whom died in attempting to regain Čitawŕ. After Maladeva's death in 721/1321, the sequence of events is not clear, as the bardic chronicles present a garbled account, often conflating events of the 8th/14th and 10th/16th centuries in a romantic medley. The ruler who emerged was Hammīr, in whose reign Sisodiya rule was restored at Čitawŕ (probably profiting from either the dynastic change at Dihlī from Khaldjīs to Tughluḳids, or from the disaffections *ca.* 739/1338 under Muḥammad b. Tughluḳ's rule); his heroism and chivalry are much extolled, but the Rādjpūt traditions are so much at variance with one another, none of them being compatible with either the few inscriptions or the exiguous references in the Muslim historians, that the chronology of Mēwāŕ until *ca.* 823/1420 must be regarded as obscure; but certainly Hammīr's successor Kshetrasingh successfully withstood an attack by the Mālwā [*q.v.*] ruler Dilāwar Khān Ghūrī.

Early in the 9th/15th century, the discovery of silver and lead mines increased Mēwāŕ's prosperity, and many defensive works were constructed. The long reign of Rāṇā Kumbha, 836-73/1433-68, saw a state at first weakened by interference from the Rāthoŕs of Mārwāŕ in Mēwāŕ affairs (although chronologies are again doubtful, since the bardic accounts of Mēwāŕ do not tally with one another), and by a conflict between Kumbha and his brother Khēm (Kshēma) Karan; nevertheless, some border territories were brought under tribute and garrisoned. Some of these lands had previously acknowledged the suzerainty of Mālwā, which had grown to considerable strength under Maḥmūd Khaldjī I, and which had long annoyed Mēwāŕ by harbouring disaffected Mēwāŕ chieftains and courtiers; but Mēwāŕ had similarly given refuge to ʿUmar Khān, the pretender to Maḥmūd's throne. Conflict between Mēwāŕ and Mālwā was inevitable, and Mālwā forces (often joined by Khēm Karan with an army of Rādjpūt followers) invaded Mēwāŕ on many occasions with varying success (the assertion, however, that Maḥmūd's forces were routed in a battle at Sārangpur [*q.v.*] in 840/1437, and that he himself was taken prisoner to Čitawŕ, does not bear examination), each state erecting a column in token of victory over the other. The Čitawŕ *Kīrttistambhā* inscription, however, seems to refer more to the campaigns against Ḳuṭb al-Dīn Aḥmad Shāh of Gudjarāt; these were occasioned both by border disputes and by Mēwāŕ attacks on Nāgawr [*q.v.*], a pre-conquest site of Islamic learning, for long under the Dihlī sultanate but by now under the rule of the descendants of Shams al-Dīn Dandānī, brother of the first sultan of Gudjarāt. Mālwā and Gudjarāt acted jointly against Mēwāŕ in 861/1457, but without pronounced success; the Rāthoŕs of Mārwāŕ, and Khēm Karan, added to

Mēwāŕ's difficulties by campaigning against Kumbha at the same time. Further forays by the Muslim armies took place over the next few years, with some regions being overrun and laid waste, but little more, and there were no major incursions until after Kumbha's death.

Kumbha was succeeded by the parricide Udaya, who was poorly supported in the state and hence tried to curry favour with his Muslim neighbours by ceding certain border territories; then, less popular than ever, having apparently disorganised the whole state, he was deposed in favour of his younger brother Rāyamalla, 878-915/1473-1509, who was faced with the task of reorganisation while contending with civil war (a renewed attempt by Khēm Karan to come to power), further attacks by Mālwā, now under Ghiyāth al-Dīh Khaldjī, and an insurrection by certain aboriginal tribes. The Mālwā army was worsted, and Mālwā invaded in its turn, Mēwāŕ occupying the Khērwāŕā district. A quarrel between Rāyamalla's sons developed into a war of succession, resolved by the eventual accession of the capable and ambitious Rāṇā Sanga [*q.v.*], 915-35/1509-28. In his first 15 years of rule he consolidated the state; in this time the ascendancy in Mālwā of Mēdinī Rāʾī [*q.v.*] led to Mēwāŕ's involvement against sultan Muẓaffar II of Gudjarāt, who moved to support and reinstate Maḥmūd Khaldjī II. The latter attacked Mēwāŕ in 925/1519, but was badly defeated, taken prisoner to Čitawŕ, and released only after the payment of a large indemnity and the surrender of a son as hostage to the Mēwāŕ court. Next an incident at Īdar [*q.v.*] drew Mēwāŕ into war with Gudjarāt; but Sanga, strengthened by having secured the support of Mālwā by releasing the royal hostage, was apparently able to come to some conciliatory agreement with Gudjarāt. This left him free to pursue his ambitions against the sultanate of Dihlī under Ibrāhīm Lōdī [see LŌDĪS], against whom he had a series of successes and was enabled to enlarge the boundaries of his domains as far as Kalpī and Čāndērī [*q.vv.*]; he or his vassals held lands extending deep into Mālwā; and apparently his authority was acknowledged even by the Rādjpūt rulers of Mārwāŕ and Ambēr. His ambitions towards the conquest of the Dihlī sultanate led him to propose to the Mughal Bābur a simultaneous attack on Ibrāhīm Lōdī. Bābur, of course, carried out his part of the undertaking by his defeat of Ibrāhīm Lōdī at Pānipat in 932/1526, but, contrary to Sanga's expectation, showed every sign of remaining in India. Sanga, by managing to secure the Gudjarāt throne for the exiled prince Bahādur, drove a wedge between Dihlī and Gudjarāt, and it was accordingly against Sanga that Bābur's efforts were now directed, culminating in the battle of Khānuʾā in 933/1527 in which Sanga with a confederated Rādjput army was completely routed. Mēwāŕ as an independently acting kingdom thus lost its power; the subsequent activities of the region are described s.v. RĀDJĀSTHĀN.

Bibliography: The difficulty of reconciling the various bardic accounts has been mentioned in the text; of the many *khyāt*, that of Muhanote Nainsī, in Hindī translation and ed. G.H. Ojha, Banāras 1982, is perhaps the most acceptable. J. Tod, *Annuals and antiquities of Rajasthan*, 3 vols., ed. W. Crooke, Oxford 1920, gives the Mēwāŕ traditions *in extenso* but uncritically. A failure to assess the Mēwāŕ histories *vis-à-vis* the Muslim chronicles appears also in G.H. Ojha, *Rādjpūtānā kā itihās* [in Hindī], Adjmēr 1936-7, and in H.B. Sarda's *Mahārāṇā Sanga*, Adjmēr 1918, and *Mahārāṇā Kumbha*, Adjmēr 1932. For the Muslim sources, see *Bibls.* to GUDJARĀT and MĀLWĀ; also to ĪDAR and MĒDINĪ RĀʾĪ. See also BĀBUR and RĀDJĀSTHĀN.

(J. BURTON-PAGE)

MĒWĀT, a generally imprecisely defined region of India to the south and south-west of Dihlī, the broken country around Alwar, Tidjārā, Bharatpur, Dīg, Rēwāŕī, Mathurā and Gurgāʾōn, "land of the Mēʾō" [*q.v.*], robbers, marauders and cattle thieves.

Punitive excursions under Iltutmish, *ca.* 620/1223, and Balban as *nāʾib* of Nāṣir al-Dīn Maḥmūd in 646/1249 and 658/1260, had only a temporary effect, and Mēwāt was not effectively pacified and controlled until Balban's first regnal year as sultan, 665/1267 (full account in Ḍiyāʾ al-Dīn Baranī, *Taʾrīkh-i Fīrūz Shāhī*, ed. Bibl. Ind., 56 ff.). In the following century, a branch of the Mēʾō were converted to Islam, and their leader Bahādur Nāhar, from his strong *Kōtlā* near Tidjārā, came to be recognised as a powerful noble in the Dihlī court; he supported Abū Bakr, a grandson of Fīrūz Shāh, in the succession struggles after that sultan's death, and was treated as a rebel by later Tughluḳid sultans, although when in 798/1395-6 Khiḍr Khān took refuge with him in Mēwāt he is described as the *muḳtaʿ*. Bahādur Nāhar later opposed Khiḍr when he became suzerain after Tīmūr's invasion, and Mēwāt under him and his successors (now usually known as Khān-zādas) again became a rebel area. The "Sayyid" ruler Mubārak Shāh made attempts to suppress revolt in Mēwāt in 829/1425 and 831/1428 under the twin grandsons of Bahādur, Djalāl Khān and ʿAbd al-Ḳādir Khān ("Djallū" and "Ḳaddū"); Ḳaddū was captured and executed for complicity with the Sharḳī forces of Djawnpur [*q.v.*], but Djallū, after again harrying the Dihlī forces, was eventually compelled to submit and render tribute the following year; a similar sequence of events followed in 836/1432, and on both occasions the Mēwātīs pursued a "scorched earth" policy (fullest account of this period in Yaḥyā b. Aḥmad Sirhindī, *Taʾrīkh-i Mubārak Shāhī*, ed. Bibl. Ind., 148-230 *passim*). Bahlūl Lōdī [*q.v.*] was similarly troubled by Aḥmad Khān Mēwātī both during his struggle to rise to power and after his accession to the Dihlī throne; Aḥmad, compelled to submit, was deprived of seven *parganas* of his *iḳṭāʿ* and compelled to send his uncle Mubārak Khān to Bahlūl's court. In 872/1468 he deserted Bahlūl and allied himself with Ḥusayn Shāh Sharḳī of Djawnpur, although Mēwāt itself remained virtually independent of both sultanates. It remained peaceful for some years thereafter and ʿĀlam Khān Mēwātī served happily under Sikandar Lōdī, even in 908/1502 leading forces against Dholpur in Sikandar's campaign against Gwāliyar, although Mēwāt was not counted as part of the Dihlī sultanate; but in Ibrāhīm Lōdī's reign (923-32/1517-26), when many of his own nobles were in rebellion against him and the hand of the Mughal Bābur was about to fall upon the Dihlī sultanate, Ḥasan Khān of Mēwāt declared his independence. He joined Rāṇā Sanga of Čitawr against Bābur's advance (the *Bābur-nāma*, tr. Beveridge, 523) refers to Ḥasan Khān as an "impious mannikin" and "the sole leader of the trouble and mischief"), and was killed in the battle of Khānuʾā in 933/1527; after this Bābur reduced Mēwāt and entered Alwar; some *parganas* were assigned to Nāhar Khān, Ḥasan's son, who swore allegiance to Bābur, after which Mēwāt seems to have had no further power as a political force, and the strong forts of Alwar and Tidjārā were controlled by Mughal officers. There is no account of Mēwātī intransigence even at the time of Humāyūn's dispossession by Shēr Shāh; the latter struck coin at Alwar.

Mēwāt seems to have remained quiet under Mug͟hal rule in the 11th/17th century. Humāyūn had contracted a matrimonial alliance with a daughter of D̲j̲alāl K̲h̲ān, a cousin of Ḥasan, and another daughter was married to Bayram K̲h̲ān; D̲j̲alāl is described by Abu 'l-Faḍl as a leading *zamīndār* of Hindustān (*Akbar-nāma*, ii, 48 f.). The *Āʾīn-i Akbarī* enumerates 19 *parganas* held by the K̲h̲ān-zādas in Alwar and Tid̲j̲ārā (Bibl. Ind. text, ii, 91-3). Early in the 18th century the D̲j̲āts [*q.v.*] had occupied the southern part of Mēwāt in their rise to power and their assault on Āgrā and Dihlī, as did the Marāthās [*q.v.*] later, and henceforth the history of the region is largely subsumed in that of Alwar and Bharatpur [*q.vv.*].

There seems to be no record of coins struck by the K̲h̲ān-zādas. Of their few monuments in and around Alwar and Tid̲j̲ārā, the tomb of Fatḥ D̲j̲ang in Alwar is of some distinction (954/1547; inscription in the Nāgarī script, which may point to consciousness of Hindū connexions).

Bibliography (in addition to references in the article): Niẓām al-Dīn Bak̲h̲s̲h̲ī, *Ṭabaḳāt-i Akbarī*, ed. Bibl. Ind., i, 302-8, ii, 38; Niʿmat Allāh, *Taʾrīk̲h̲-i K̲h̲ān D̲j̲ahānī*, Dacca 1960, 81 ff.; G.N. Sharma, *Mewar and the Mughal emperors*, 20-7, 37; A.R. Khan, *Chieftains during the reign of Akbar*, Simla 1977, 150 f.; S.H. Hodīvālā, *Studies in Indo-Muslim history*, Bombay 1939, i, 393, takes *kotlā* above as a proper name, not entirely convincingly.

(J. Burton-Page)

MĒWĀTĪ [see Meʾō].

MEWḲŪFATČĪ or Mewḳūfātī, title given to the director of the "Bureau of Retained Revenues" (*Mewḳūfāt ḳalemi*) in the Ottoman finance department. His main task was to manage the *mewḳūf akče*, money accruing from unused state expense allocations, and from vacant fiefs and other grants. The bureau under him also confiscated land not registered in land surveys, allocated depots for state purchases, kept records of contribution units (*ʿawāriḍ-k̲h̲āne* [see ʿawāriḍ], registered relay stations, maintained military depots at all frontiers, allotted food rations and forage, straw and hay rations to soldiers in military campaigns, and provided money to civil servants accompanying the army. In the 12th/18th century, this bureau had four departments: (i) *Ḳalemiyye dāʾiresi*, which collected a 10% registration fee (*ḳalemiyye*) from farmed-out lands; (ii) *Nawul k̲h̲alīfesi*, which kept the books of food depots and of duties paid by bakers in Istanbul; (iii) *Menzil k̲h̲alīfesi*, which managed the relay service; and (iv) *G̲h̲anem kitābeti* which was responsible for the collection of the sheep-tax (*ʿādet-i ag̲h̲nām*).

The *Mewḳūfāt emīni*, a commissioner from the bureau in each *sand̲j̲aḳ* [*q.v.*], was assigned by the *mewḳūfātčī* to gather the yearly revenues accruing from vacant fiefs and other grants, and from fief holders who did not join military campaigns. The *emīn* had agents, *mewḳūfčus*, who went from village to village collecting these revenues. In 1838, after the establishment of the Ottoman finance ministry, the *Mewḳūfāt ḳalemi* was annexed to the bureau handling treasury issues, *Eshām muḥāsebesi ḳalemi* [see ashām].

Bibliography: İ. H. Uzunçarşılı, *Osmanlı devletinin merkez ve bahriye teşkilâtı*, Ankara 1948, 10, 19, 124, 336-48, 353-7, 372, 382: M. Sertoğlu, *Resimli osmanlı tarihi ansiklopedisi*, Istanbul 1958, 112, 159, 208-10, 221-2; M.Z. Pakalın, *Osmanlı tarih deyimleri ve terimleri sözlüğü*, Istanbul 1951, 497-8; M. d'Ohsson, *Tableau général de l'Empire Othoman*, iv, Paris 1791, 267-8; Gibb and Bowen i/1, 51, 130-1, 151, 248; M. Akdağ, *Türkiye'nin iktisadi ve içtimai tarihi*, Istanbul 1979, ii, 78, 337-8, 385-6, 490-1.

(F. Müge Göçek)

MEWLĀNĀ K̲H̲ŪNKĀR [see mawlānā k̲h̲ūnkār].

MEWLEWIYYET or Mollalıḳ, title given to certain judicial districts in the Ottoman Empire. İ.H. Uzunçarşılı located the earliest reference in the 9th/15th century, when *ḳāḍī* [*q.v.*] posts with the highest fee of 500 *akčes* [*q.v.*] were defined as *bes̲h̲yüz akče mewlewiyyetleri*. These posts consisted of Istanbul, Edirne, Bursa, Filibe, Salonika and Sofia. Until the late 9th/15th and early 10th/16th centuries, these *mewlewiyyets* were not ranked. This practice was introduced in the late 10th/16th century after the *s̲h̲ayk̲h̲ al-islām* [*q.v.*] formally became the head of the Ottoman religious hierarchy. The *ḳāḍī* of Istanbul came fourth in rank after the *s̲h̲ayk̲h̲ al-islām* and the Anadolu and Rumeli judges of the army, *ḳāḍī ʿasker* [*q.v.*]. The other *mewlewiyyets* were unranked.

During the 10th/16th and 11th/17th centuries, as the empire expanded, many new *mewlewiyyets* were formed. With minor exceptions, their relative ranks did not change after the 12th/18th century. Uzunçarşılı lists five ranks of *mewlewiyyets* in decreasing importance: (i) *Istanbul ḳāḍīlig̲h̲ī*, the judicial district of Istanbul; (ii) *Ḥaremeyn mewlewiyyetleri*, judicial districts of the two Holy Cities, Mecca and Medina; (iii) *Bilād-ī k̲h̲amse mewlewiyyetleri*, judicial districts of the Five Cities, Edirne, Bursa, Damascus, Egypt and Filibe; (iv) *Bilād-ī ʿas̲h̲ere mewlewiyyetleri*, judicial districts of the Ten Cities, to which an eleventh was later added: Jerusalem, Aleppo, Tīrhala Yeñis̲h̲ehri, Galata, Izmir, Salonika, Eyüb, Üsküdar, Sofia, Crete and Trebizond. (v) *Dewriyye mewlewiyyetleri*, judicial districts held in rotation by *ḳāḍīs* of Marʿas̲h̲, Bag̲h̲dād, Bosnia, Belgrade, Antioch, Kütahya, Beirut, Adana, Van, Rusčuk, Sivas and Čankīrī.

For a *mewlewiyyet* appointment, an applicant was required to graduate from a *madrasa* [*q.v.*], and obtain a license, *id̲j̲āzet-nāme* [see id̲j̲āza]. He could then either teach through all *madrasa* grades or become a *ḳāḍī* in the smallest judicial unit, *ḳaḍāʾ* [*q.v.*], rise to the larger judicial unit of a *sand̲j̲aḳ* [*q.v.*], and then go back and teach through the highest *madrasa* grades. He would then become a candidate for *bilād-ī ʿas̲h̲ere mewlewiyyetleri*, which were also called *mak̲h̲red̲j̲ mewlewiyyetleri* [see mak̲h̲red̲j̲], judicial districts whe.e scholars just "going out" from teaching at *madrasas* were appointed. Appointments were usually for a year. *Mewlewiyyet* appointments were proposed to the Sultan by the Grand Vizier, *ṣadr-ī aʿẓam* [*q.v.*]. Before the 10th/16th century, the *ḳāḍī ʿasker* supplied names of candidates to the Grand Vizier; after then, the *s̲h̲ayk̲h̲ al-islām* provided the list of names.

After the 10th/16th century, the term of the appointment was extended when the number of candidates began to exceed that of available posts in the empire. The title was therefore separated from the post itself. A candidate held the title of *mewlewiyyet pāyesi* for a year before he was appointed to the post itself, *mewlewiyyet manṣībī*. Some who were assigned these posts preferred to reside in the capital, and sent deputies, *nāʾib*, to represent them. During later centuries, titles given without appointments, assignments to sons and to household members of influential families who had not been through the educational system, together with the sale of licenses, brought about a deterioration in *mewlewiyyet* appointments.

Bibliography: İ.H. Uzunçarşılı, *Osmanlı devletinin ilmiye teşkilatı*, Ankara 1965, 38, 46-8, 57, 85-91, 96-102, 110, 117, 263-5, 276-80; M.Z.

Pakalın, *Osmanlı tarih deyimleri ve terimleri sözlüğü*, Istanbul 1951, 519-21; M. Sertoğlu, *Resimli osmanlı tarihi ansiklopedisi*, Istanbul 1958, 45, 130-1,157-8, 194, 209-10, 264, 295; Muṣṭafā Nūrī Pas̲h̲a, *Netāyid̲j̲ ül-wuḳūʿāt*, Istanbul 1327, i, 137-8, ii, 108-12; *ʿİlmiyye sālnāmesi*, Istanbul 1334, 51-5, 59-79, 154-5; M. d'Ohsson, *Tableau général de l'Empire Othoman*, iv, Paris 1791, 530, 541-3, 550-1, 566-8, 573-6; Gibb and Bowen, i/1, 87, 89-91, 105-10, 124-6, 146, 151; M. Akdağ, *Türkiye'nin iktisadi ve içtimai tarihi*, Istanbul 1979, i, 402, ii, 97-9.

(F. Müge Göçek)

MEZÖKERESZTES, the Battle of Mezőkeresztes (Turkish: *Hāčova* or *Ṭābūr muḥārebesi*), the most important encounter between the Habsburg-Hungarian and Ottoman troops during the "long" or 15-years' war.

This took place near a village, south-east of Eger [*q.v.*] in Hungary on 5 Rābīʿ I 1005/26 October 1596. Its immediate antecedent was the capture of Eger by the forces of Meḥemmed III, the first sultan who personally took the field in war after Süleymān I's death. The Imperial troops, which had originally been sent to relieve this important city under attack, now wished to attempt the reconquest of the castle. After some hesitation, a pitched battle was decided on. The Habsburg soldiers were headed by the Archduke Maximilian, but the prince of Transylvania, Zsigmond Báthori, also took part with a considerable army. The number of the confronting soldiers has been exaggerated on both sides. The most realistic figures seem to be 50,000 for the Christian and 100,000 for the Muslim army (possibly varying to a maximum of equal forces on both parts). Technical superiority was on the European side, due to more numerous infantry and more powerful artillery. After some preliminary clashes on 22 and 25 October, the decisive battle was fought on the afternoon of 26 October. As previously, the Christian forces seemed to get the upper hand, but they committed a serious fault by following the fleeing Ottomans and, in the hope of booty, penetrated into their camp. The Turks were thereby able to change the tide of events and in the end secure a victory.

While Meḥemmed III failed further to exploit his favourable position, the Habsburgs were forced to realise that no quick result could be hoped for against the Ottomans. Consequently, warfare continued for several more years. Further events effected the Ottomans adversely. Since many *tīmār* holders did not comply with their duty to arrive at this battle, and some others deserted, the treasury had a good pretext for confiscating *tīmār*s and granting them anew. According to a list of deserters, some 120 *ziʿāmet*s and 550 *tīmār*s passed into the hands of other owners in Rumelia and Hungary (Istanbul, Başbakanlık arşivi, Kâmil Kepeci Tasnifi, 347). Replaced timariots could well be ready to join the D̲j̲elālī rebels [see d̲j̲alālī in Suppl.] thus creating new and lasting difficulties for the state.

Bibliography: The first detailed article on the battle was written by András Komáromy, *A mezőkeresztesi csata 1596-ban* ("The battle of Mezőkeresztes in 1596"), in *Hadtörténelmi Közlemények*, v (1892), 28-67, 157-80, 278-98. More critical is the study by Sándor László Tóth, *A mezőkeresztesi csata története* (*1596. október 26.*) ("The history of the Battle of Mezőkeresztes"), in *Hadtörténelmi Közlemények*, xxx (1983), 553-73. An evaluation of the Ottoman sources was attempted by J. Schmidt, *The Egri-campaign of 1596: military history and the problem of sources*, in *Habsburgisch-osmanische Beziehungen. Beihefte zur WZKM 13*, Vienna 1985, 125-44.

(G. Dávid)

MEZZOMORTO [see ḥusayn pas̲h̲a].

MIʾĀN BHUʾĀ, Masnad-i ʿĀlī, the *wazīr* and *ṣadr* of the Dihlī sultanate during the reign of sultan Sikandar S̲h̲āh Lōdī (894-923/1489-1517).

He was the eldest son of *Masnad-i ʿAlī* K̲h̲awwāṣ K̲h̲ān, who belonged to an old aristocratic family of north India. K̲h̲awwāṣ K̲h̲ān seems to have been elevated to the posts of *wazīr* and *ṣadr* by Sultan Sikandar at the beginning of his reign. Upon his death, sometime towards the close of the 9th/15th century, Miʾān Bhuʾā, who was also adept in learning and statesmanship, was allowed by the sultan to take up the combined charge of the *wizārat* and *ṣadārat* with the specific order that he would retain and take care of the old staff maintained by his late father.

Miʾān Bhuʾā not only came up to the sultan's expectations but also soon began to enjoy great prestige for his administrative talent, strong sense of justice, and patronage of learning and men of piety. As *wazīr* or revenue minister, he ably implemented Sikandar's agrarian policy, which led to the rapid progress of agriculture in the Lōdī lands; peasants were provided with incentives to bring virgin land under the plough (in the words of the contemporary writer, S̲h̲ayk̲h̲ Rizḳ Allāh Mus̲h̲tāḳī, even an inch of land was not left lying fallow) and were protected against exploitation by the state officials, who were forbidden to stay with them and enjoy their hospitability. Forced labour (*bēgār*) was also abolished. As a result, conditions improved in the countryside, and grain and other necessities became cheap.

Since the 9th/15th century, the *ṣadr* (minister for religious affairs) also held the charge of the office of *ḳāḍī 'l-ḳuḍāt* (Chief Justice). Contemporary evidence tends to show that there were two appellate courts in the metropolitan city of Āgra: the first was presided over by the *wazīr*, while the second, being the supreme court, functioned under the personal supervision of the sultan. Generally, the appellant moved to the Supreme Court, if he was not satisified with the judgment given by Miʾān Bhuʾā. The anecdotes contained in the *Wāḳiʿāt-i Mus̲h̲tāḳī* and *Ṭabaḳāt-i Akbarī* cast light on the interest that the *wazīr* and the sultan took in dispensing justice, irrespective of creed, or birth and status of people.

Miʾān Bhuʾā encouraged, in his capacity of *ṣadr*, the scholars and intellectuals who came from abroad to settle in Āgra and Dihlī on a permanent basis and made land-grants to them for their maintenance. Himself interested in learning, he also gathered a fairly large sprinkling of these scholars in his own service and thus emulated his master Sultan Sikandar S̲h̲āh. They undertook at his instance the compilation of works on various themes, literary as well as scientific. The Arabic and Sanskrit classics were collected and transcribed by expert calligraphists and then translated into Persian by capable scholars with the help of Brahmans. Of these translations, the *Maʿdan al-s̲h̲ifāʾ-i-Sikandar S̲h̲āhī*, based on Sanskrit classics such as *Sasrāt*, *Jā Deo karat*, *Rās Ratnāko*, *Suangdhar*, *Čintāma*, etc., is considered an important work on medicine, compiled by Miʾān Bhuʾā himself. The terms and names of the herbs and plants were translated into Persian and, if the equivalent of any term was not found in the Persian language, it was simply transliterated with the necessary explanation. Indirectly emphasising the importance of his work, the Miʾān says in the preface that the medical science imported from the Muslim countries did not suit the constitution of the Indians, due to climatic differences, and he had undertaken the compilation of the work with royal permission, for the Indian system of medicine had been found more effective.

Unfortunately, other books, with the exception of the *Lahdjāt-i Sikandar Shāhī*, compiled by ʿUmar b. Yaḥyā al-Kābulī, a Persian translation of Sanskrit classics and one dealing with Indian music, produced by different scholars employed by Miʾān Bhuʾā, have not survived.

Miʾān Bhuʾā, as a pious Muslim, constructed mosques and made endowments for the benefit of public; the beautiful mosque in Dihlī, popularly known as *mōth kī masdjid*, was constructed at his cost and is known for its attractive features. The shape and proportion of the five main arches of the façade and the domes, the design and grandeur of the doorway and projecting balconies at the sides show that a talented group of craftsmen was employed for its completion. The evidence of the *Maktūbāt-i ḳuddūsī* reveals that its ample facilities included arrangements for students, travellers, teachers and Ṣūfī saints, all of whom got food from the kitchen maintained with the money endowed by Miʾān Bhuʾā.

The followers of Miʾān Bhuʾā also enjoyed prestige in the city. The newly-recruited soldier, no matter whether he was a *suwār* or a foot-soldier, could approach any *ṣarrāf* or money changer and borrow money from him for one or two years, after showing him the *parwāna* or letter of appointment. According to the custom, he was assigned agricultural land in lieu of a cash salary. Miʾān Bhuʾā is said to have had villages and *parganās* of his maintenance *iḳṭāʿ* scattered in different *sarkārs* around Dihlī and Āgra, so that it was possible for him to assign to his retainer maintenance-land in the village of the latter's choice.

Miʾān Bhuʾā retained his position after the death of Sultan Sikandar Lōdī, but subsequently failed to enjoy the confidence of the new Sultan Ibrāhīm Lōdī (923-32/1517-26), who ordered him to be put under arrest and handed over to Malik Ādam Kākar, one of the confidants of the late Sultan and friend of Miʾān Bhuʾā; this was a mild punishment for the aged *wazīr*, for many of his companions were subjected to torture on account of the royal displeaure. Of the mediaeval writers, Shaykh Kabīr Bāṭinī says that the *wazīr* was punished because he did not comply with the royal *farmān* about the grant of money to the royal favourite, the Rāʾī of Gwālior. It may be that, owing to old age, he had become negligent of his duties and the Sultan had become doubtful of his loyalty. This seems to be near the truth, because Mushtāḳī's reference to Miʾān Bhuʾā's imprisonment implies that it occurred before the annexation of Gwālior to the Lōdī empire. On his dismissal, the *ṣadārat* was separated from the *wizārat*; Miʾān Bhuʾā's eldest son, Dilāwar Khān, was assigned the *wizārat*, while Shaykh Farīd Bukhārī, an *ʿālim* and the sultan's teacher, took over as *ṣadr*.

Bibliography: ʿAbd Allāh, *Taʾrīkh-i Dāwūdī*, ʿAlīgaṙh 1969, 36, 70; Firishta, *Gulshan-i Ibrāhīmī* or *Taʾrīkh*, Newal Kishore edn., 178; Miʾān Bhuʾā, *Maʿdan al-shifāʾ-i Sikandar Shāhī* or *Ṭibb-i Sikandarī*, Lucknow 1877; Niʿmat Allāh Harawī, *Taʾrīkh-i Khān-i Djahānī*, ed. Imām al-Dīn, Dacca 1960, 218, 225-7; Niẓām al-Dīn Aḥmad, *Ṭabaḳāt-i Akbarī*, Calcutta 1911. Shaykh Kabīr Bāṭinī, *Afsāna-yi shāhān*, British Library ms. Add. 24,409, fol. 46a-b; Shaykh Rizḳ Allāh Mushtāḳī, *Wāḳiʿāt-i Mushtāḳī*, British Library ms. Or. 1929, fols. 8b, 27a, 33a-b, 45a; ʿUmar b. Yaḥyā al-Kābulī, *Lahdjāt-i Sikandar Shāhi*, Preface, Madras Univ. Library ms. D. no. 518, ms. B. no. 521, fol. 6b; P. Brown, *Indian architecture* (*Islamic period*),3 Bombay, 29-30; I.H. Siddiqui, *Life and culture in the sultanate of Delhi during the Lodi period*, in *IC* (April and July 1982), 127-8, 181-2.

(I.H. Siddiqui)

MIDĀD, the common Arabic word, together with its synonym *ḥibr*, for ink. Derived from the root *m-d-d*, it originally meant "anything that is added to a thing, because of its utility", and therefore one of its more specific meanings is "that with which one writes" (Lane, *Lexicon*, *s.v.*), or "that with which the writer is provided" (*LA*, *s.v.*). There is a single Ḳurʾānic mention of *midād*: "If the sea were ink for the Words of my Lord, the sea would be spent before the Words of my Lord are spent" (XVIII, 109). Tradition has is that on the Day of Judgment, the ink of scholars will be measured with the blood of martyrs, and that both scales of the balance will then be in equilibrium (al-Ḳalḳashandī, *Ṣubḥ*, ii, 461).

In Middle Eastern manuscripts, two types of black ink were generally used, both of which date from pre-Islamic times. One was prepared on the basis of carbon and oil, and the other one from gall-nuts and ferrous components, the former originally being designated as *midād*, the latter as *ḥibr*. Later, the two words were used as synonyms (Grohmann, *Arabische Paläographie*, i, 127). A considerable number of recipes for ink have survived from mediaeval times, many devised by scribes for their personal use and improved for their purpose by trial and error. Numerous recipes have been transmitted by al-Muʿizz b. Bādīs (d. 453/1061 [*q.v.*]) in his *ʿUmdat al-kuttāb*, especially in chs. 2-10. Grohmann (i, 127-131) mentions some from other sources as well. For coloured inks and inks used in secret writings, a whole range of natural ingredients was used, but it is often difficult exactly to identify these ingredients from the literary sources.

As Middle Eastern manuscripts continued to be made till well into the 19th century, it may be assumed that in more recent times imported ink. like imported paper, was used as well. The rise of polychrome manuscripts in the Maghrib in the second half of the 19th century may be explained from such imports. A systematical chemical analysis of the inks used in Middle Eastern manuscripts, both in mediaeval and recent times, has not been undertaken so far. An account of the survival of mediaeval practices in bookmaking, including the handling of ink, in recent times, albeit in a Christian environment , has been given by H.S. Sergew (see Bibl.).

Bibliography: M. Bat-Yehouda-Zerdoun, *La fabrication des encres noires d'après les textes*, in *Codicologica 5. Les matériaux du livre manuscrit*, Leiden 1980, 52-8; G. Endress, *Handschriftenkunde*, in W. Fischer (ed.), *Grundriss der arabischen Philologie*, i, Wiesbaden 1982, 276-7; A. Grohmann, *Arabische Paläographie*, i, Vienna, 1967, 127-31; M. Levey, *Mediaeval Arab bookmaking and its relation to early chemistry and pharmacology*, in *Trans. Amer. Philos. Soc.*, N.S. lii/4, Philadelphia 1962, index *s.v.* Ink; al-Muʿizz b. Bādīs. *ʿUmdat al-kuttāb wa-ʿuddat dhawī al-albāb*, tr. M. Levey in *Mediaeval Arab bookmaking*, 13-50; J. Pedersen, *The Arabic book*, Princeton 1984, 67-9; al-Kalḳashandī, *Ṣubḥ al-aʿshā*, Cairo 1913-19; H.S. Sergew, *Bookmaking in Ethiopia*, Leiden 1981; see also KHAṬṬ; KITĀB; and KITĀBA in Suppl.

(J.J. Witkam)

MIʾDHANA [see MANĀRA].

MIDḤAT PASHA (1822-84), Ottoman provincial governor, twice grand vizier, and father of the 1876 constitution.

Midḥat was born in Istanbul in Ṣafar 1238/October-November 1822, the son of Rusčuklu Ḥādjdjī ʿAlī Efendi-zāde Ḥādjdjī Ḥāfiẓ Meḥmed

E<u>sh</u>ref Efendi. He was named Aḥmed <u>Sh</u>efīḳ. Having memorised the Ḳurʾān at 10, he was then called Ḥāfīẓ <u>Sh</u>efīḳ. In 1833 he moved with his family to Vidin, where his father was an assistant judge. When his family returned to Istanbul the next year, he became an apprentice in the secretariat of the imperial *dīwān*. His talent earned him the name Midḥat, which thereafter replaced his given names. In 1835-6 Midḥat was in Lofča, where his father held another judicial post, before returning to Istanbul in 1836-7. Midḥat had already begun to study Arabic; he now began Persian and attended courses at the Fātiḥ mosque while again working in the secretariat. In 1840 he was transferred to the grand vizier's office.

The bureaucratic career on which Midḥat was now launched falls into four phases: 1840-61, increasingly responsible posts as staff member of commissions and councils and as special investigator; 1861-72, three provincial governorships; 1872-7, two grand-vizierates and constitution-making; 1877-84, exile, two governorships, trial, exile and death. The second and third phases show Midḥat at his most influential.

In 1842-4 Midḥat held a secretarial post in Damascus. Thereafter he was secretary to one of the "commissions of improvement" sent out to the provinces in 1845-7, first in Ḳonya, then Ḳasṭamonu, under Sāmī Baḳīr Pa<u>sh</u>a. During this period, he came on the payroll of the protocol office (*maḍbaṭa odasī*) of the *me<u>dj</u>lis-i wālā-yi aḥkām-i ʿadliyye*, the influential Supreme Council of Judicial Ordinances, and remained in its employ to 1859, even while undertaking special assignments. In 1848 he married. He became chief clerk in the protocol office in 1851. For six months, probably in 1852, Midḥat was in Damascus as commisioner to investigate a dispute between two *ṣarrāf*s over the farm of customs revenues, and to look into alleged misconduct by Ḳībrīslī Meḥmed Pa<u>sh</u>a, commander of the army of Arabia. Midḥat settled the revenue question advantageously to the Treasury. He found misdeeds by Ḳībrīslī Meḥmed in relation to the Druze that led to the commander's removal from his post. When the Supreme Council's paperwork was split in two, Midḥat became second secretary of the Anatolian section.

During the Crimean War, in 1854-5, Midḥat was sent as investigator to the Rumeli *eyālet*. Ḳībrīslī Meḥmed, now grand vizier, may have sent him thither to get his revenge by putting Midḥat in a difficult situation. But Midḥat, working out of Edirne, successfully curbed depredations by *bā<u>sh</u>ī-bozūḳ*s and brigands. On return to Istanbul, Midḥat gave the new grand vizier Re<u>sh</u>īd Pa<u>sh</u>a [*q.v.*] a memorandum containing his ideas on provincial reform. Again in 1855 Midḥat was sent out, this time to Bursa on earthquake relief. In 1856-7, after successfully defending himself against a false charge of illegal participation in the farm of Istanbul fishmarkets, Midḥat was despatched to investigate administration by the *wālī*s of Silistre and Vidin. His vigorous actions in those *eyālet*s led to dismissals of officials, whose friends in the palace got a new investigator appointed. Midḥat, in protest, asked for leave, which was granted by the grand vizier ʿĀlī Pa<u>sh</u>a [*q.v.*]. He then spent six months of 1858 in Paris, London, Brussels and Vienna, improving the French he had recently begun to study, and finally gaining some first-hand knowledge of western Europe. In September 1859 Midḥat became chief secretary of the Supreme Council itself. While in this post he served on the commission to investigate the Ḳūleli affair, an abortive conspiracy in Istanbul against *Tanẓīmāt* [*q.v.*] westernisation.

Midḥat entered on the second phase of his career when he was promoted to vizier and appointed *wālī* of the *eyālet* of Ni<u>sh</u> on 29 January 1861. During his three years in Ni<u>sh</u>, Midḥat displayed the energy, the brusqueness, the secular-mindedness, the egalitarian attitude, the Ottoman patriotism and the honesty that characterised his activity in all posts thereafter. His programme of action was also characteristic. He sought the cooperation of local notables of all creeds. He created a gendarmerie, curbed banditry, and tried also to curb nascent nationalism among the Bulgars. He deferred collection of some onerous taxes. He built roads and bridges, in part by requiring several days of unpaid labour from peasants in the locality. He built barracks, in part with convict labour. He started schools. Because of his success, the Porte joined the Prizren *eyālet* to Ni<u>sh</u> for Midḥat to administer.

The success also led the grand vizier Fuʾād Pa<u>sh</u>a [*q.v.*] to bring Midḥat back to Istanbul in 1864 to draft, with him, a new plan for provincial organisation. The *wilāyet* system, modelled somewhat on French practice, was embodied in a law promulgated on 8 November 1864. It was to be tested in one sizable *wilāyet*, named Tuna (Danube), newly formed of the old *eyālet*s of Silistre, Vidin and Ni<u>sh</u>. Midḥat was appointed its governor on 13 October 1864, even before the new system was official.

Midḥat organised the seven *san<u>dj</u>aḳ*s and 48 *ḳaḍāʾ*s of the Tuna *wilāyet*, including the local *me<u>dj</u>liss*, each containing some non-Muslims, at each administrative level [see BULGARIA]. He embarked on a public works programme, which in his three years produced 3,000 km. of roads and 1,400 bridges by his count; various public buildings, including schools, model farms with imported European machinery, industrial arts training schools for the poor and service on the Danube, and harbour works at the port of Rusčuk, the seat of *wilāyet* government. Tatar and Circassian refugees from Russia were successfully settled in the *wilāyet*, though not without some problems. A modest economic development was aided by such measures, as well as by the increased security which Midḥat established through a gendarmerie and occasional use of regular troops. Midḥat started a few small factories. He wore homespun clothes to boost local products. The measure with the longest lasting consequences was his creation of agricultural credit cooperatives, *menāfiʿ ṣandīklarī*, to lend to peasants at low interest rates. Modern Turkey's Ziraat Bankası is a descendant. Midḥat also created the first official provincial newspaper in the Empire, the *Tuna*, published in Turkish and Bulgarian and beginning on 10 <u>Sh</u>awwāl 1281/8 March 1865; Aḥmed Midḥat [*q.v.*] soon became its editor. Midḥat hoped to win the Bulgarians to Ottomanism through just administration and mixed schools, but the developing Bulgarian nationalism was barely blunted. Midḥat dealt severely with rebels; in 1866 he repressed a premature Russian-financed Bulgarian revolutionary rising. On the whole, the *wilāyet* system had proved workable. In 1867 it was extended to most of the Empire, Midḥat again being brought to Istanbul to consult on revising the regulations.

When in 1868 the Supreme Council was replaced by a Council of State (*<u>Sh</u>ūrā-yi Dewlet*) and a Judicial Council, Midḥat was appointed, on 5 March, to head the former. Its function was to discuss and draft laws. Under Midḥat it elaborated regulations on adoption of the metric system, on nationality, on mining and on a real estate credit bank for small employers. Friction arose between Midḥat and the grand vizier ʿĀlī Pa<u>sh</u>a on both legislative and personal levels. The result was Midḥat's transfer on 27 February 1869 out of his first high national office to the *wilāyet* governorship of Bag͟hdād. He had already in the autumn of 1868 been sent back to Bulgaria by the sultan on an interim 20-day mission to subdue another rebellion.

In ʿIrāḳ, Midḥat's activity, although similar in many ways to that in Bulgaria, was circumscribed by the local tribalism. Midḥat, however, was not only *wālī* but also, extraordinarily, commander of the Sixth Army. He used military force when needed to subdue tribes, to collect taxes and to impose conscription. Success was partial. Midḥat tried to induce tribes to settle. At least one *s͟hayk͟h* exchanged that title for the new one, under the *wilāyet* plan, of *mutaṣarrif* of a *sand͟jaḳ*. Settling tribes was also part of Midḥat's process for bringing land under state control. He applied the Ottoman land code of 1858, furnishing *tapu* deeds that gave freehold right to the cultivator; most such deeds, however, came into the possession of tribal *s͟hayk͟h*s, city merchants or former tax-farmers rather than of ordinary tribesmen or peasants. The marshlands of southern ʿIrāḳ, and date-palm culture, became more prosperous with pacification and settlement. Ottoman control was even extended over Kuwayt and, precariously, into al-Ḥasā and part of Nad͟jd.

Midḥat organised the councils of the *wilāyet* system, and a municipal council for Bag͟hdād also. He appointed a good many ʿIrāḳīs to government offices. He tore down some of the old Bag͟hdād wall to allow city expansion, introduced some paving and street lights, procured fire engines, started a water supply system, and built the only bridge the city possessed before the 20th century. He started wool and cotton mills and an army clothing factory. He established schools, including a military school and a craft training school for orphans, a savings bank, a hospital, and a tramway utilising horse cars to the Kāẓimayn suburb. He promoted regular steamer service on the Euphrates and shipping in the Gulf. The first newspaper in ʿIrāḳ, the official *Zawrāʾ*, in Turkish and Arabic, appeared on 16 June 1869 and semi-weekly thereafter. Midḥat also eased relations with Iran concerning border tribes and currency circulation.

After ʿĀlī Pas͟ha's death, Midḥat clashed with the new grand vizier, Maḥmūd Nedīm Pas͟ha [*q.v.*], especially over the use of *wilāyet* revenues. Midḥat resigned, starting back to Istanbul in May 1872. Maḥmūd Nedīm failed to get Midḥat rusticated to Sivas, but on 26 July got him appointed *wālī* of Edirne in order to keep him out of the capital. Midḥat however obtained an audience of Sultan ʿAbd al-ʿAzīz [*q.v.*] and, supported by other statesmen, persuaded the ruler to oust Maḥmūd Nedīm. Midḥat was appointed grand vizier on 31 July 1872.

Now at the pinnacle of the bureaucracy, Midḥat entered on the third phase of his career. But this grand vizierate lasted only 80 days. From the start, Midḥat was opposed by the Russian ambassador Ignatyev and by the Khedive Ismāʿīl of Egypt, who wanted the privilege of contracting independent foreign loans. Midḥat would not grant it, but ʿAbd al-ʿAzīz did so when bribed. Moreover, Midḥat was impolitic. He implicated the palace and sultan in financial scandals. He once rode on horseback into the third court of the palace, unheard of for any but the sultan. His vigorous action on salary reform, railroad construction, education extension and metric system enforcement remained only beginnings. With his foreign minister K͟halīl S͟herīf Pas͟ha, Midḥat gave thought both to a plan for a constitution and to a plan for federal imperial organisation respecting some of the Balkan lands; but his enemies soon procured his dismissal on 18 October 1872.

For nearly four years, Midḥat was in office only for brief periods: as minister of justice, 12 March to 21 September 1873; as *wālī* of Salonika, 15 October 1873 to 16 February 1874; and as minister of justice again, 21 August to 28 November 1875. He was dismissed from the first two posts; in 1873 this occurred because of revelations that he and the grand vizier of the time, S͟hīrwānī-zāde Meḥmed Rüs͟hdü, were discussing the need for a constitution and a parliament to curb excessive spending, the sultan's included. But in 1875 Midḥat himself resigned as justice minister, with a memorandum to Sultan ʿAbd al-ʿAzīz condemning the administrative confusion under Maḥmūd Nedīm, who was again grand vizier, the financial chaos and default on Ottoman bond interest, and the ineffectual military response to the growing revolt in Bosnia and Herzegovina. During the winter of 1875-6, Midḥat was in touch with groups and individuals in Istanbul who desired change, including members of the *ʿulamāʾ*. On 9 March 1876, a "Manifesto of the Muslim Patriots", probably by Midḥat or his adviser Odian Efendi, went out to European statesmen and was circulated privately in Istanbul; it called for a representative, consultative assembly.

As public discontent mounted in 1876, Midḥat became one of the principal movers of political change. He may have helped to spark demonstrations in Istanbul by *softas* or religious students on 10 and 11 May which resulted in the dismissal of Maḥmūd Nedīm and appointment of Müterd͟jim Meḥmed Rüs͟hdü Pas͟ha as grand vizier. On 19 May, Midḥat was made minister without portfolio. Along with the minister of war Hüseyn ʿAwnī Pas͟ha [*q.v.*] and the military academy director Süleymān Pas͟ha, Midḥat plotted the deposition of the erratic and spendthrift ʿAbd al-ʿAzīz. It was effected, bloodlessly, on 30 May, and Murād V received the oath of homage. Immediately, Midḥat, who on 5 June again became president of the Council of State, began pressing for the elaboration of a constitution. Ḥüseyn ʿAwnī and others opposed him. Serious impediments arose also from unsettling events: the suicide of the ex-sultan ʿAbd al-ʿAzīz on 4 June, the murder by a Circassian officer of Hüseyn ʿAwnī and the foreign minister Rās͟hid at a meeting at Midḥat's house on 15 June, the expanding war against Serbia and Montenegro, and, above all, the nervous breakdown of Murād V, who was never girded. Despite discussions of a constitutional draft by ministers and a *med͟jlis-i ʿumūmī*, progress was minimal. The ministers finally decided that Murād V would have to be replaced by his younger brother, ʿAbd al-Ḥamīd. On about August 27 Midḥat got from ʿAbd al-Ḥamīd a promise that, if enthroned, he would promulgate the constitution without delay. On 31 August Murād was deposed, and was succeeded by ʿAbd al-Ḥamīd II [*q.v.*].

The new sultan was, however, slow to redeem his promise. On 8 October he approved a constitutional commission of leading Muslim and Christian officials, with Midḥat as chairman. The commission considered many models and drafts, including one by Midḥat himself. The draft submitted to ʿAbd al-Ḥamīd in late November incorporated Midḥat's proposal for a prime minister instead of a grand vizier. The sultan was unenthusiastic, and his objections were supported by other ministers and officials, including Aḥmed D͟jewdet [*q.v.*]. Finally, on 6 December the council of ministers approved a revised draft by the commission, which enlarged the sultan's powers and restored the office of grand vizier. ʿAbd al-Ḥamīd accepted the constitution when a clause empowering the sultan to exile dangerous individuals was added. Meḥmed Rüs̲h̲dü then resigned, the sultan appointed Midḥat grand vizier on 19 December, and the constitution was ceremoniously promulgated on 23 December 1876.

Midḥat hoped that the act of promulgation might induce the great-power conference on plans for restructuring Ottoman administration in the Balkans, then meeting in Istanbul, to agree that the new constitutional régime should do it instead. He wanted the powers not only to accept but also to guarantee the constitution, and sent Odian secretly to London to ask support. But the powers treated the constitution as if it were a sham. The conference went ahead to propose drastic changes. Because the election process for the chamber of deputies was not nearly completed, Midḥat convened on 18 January 1877 an unusually large med̲j̲lis-i ʿumūmī, which with patriotic emotion rejected the Constantinople Conference scheme. Midḥat has been blamed for pursuing a hard line with the powers that eventuated in a Russian invasion in late April 1877. But Midḥat sought further negotiation, not war; had he remained in office, he might have avoided war, but he was grand vizier for only 49 days. From the start he and ʿAbd al-Ḥamīd were on a collision course. The sultan rejected proposals by Midḥat; Midḥat failed to carry out orders of the sultan, one of which was to send his constitutionalist friends Nāmi̊ḳ Kemāl [q.v.] and Ḍiyā out of the capital. Those two and others started recruiting a volunteer guard unit that worried the sultan. But basically, ʿAbd al-Ḥamīd feared Midḥat as one who had deposed two sultans and who might try it again. Further, Midḥat conducted himself as if he were a prime minister answerable more to the nation than to the monarch. The sultan also was answerable to the nation, Midḥat believed, and this view was incorporated in the famous letter of 30 January 1877 which Midḥat is said to have written to the sultan, although its authenticity is debated. The sultan may even have believed charges that Midḥat leaned to republicanism. Hence on 5 February, Midḥat was abruptly dismissed and sent in exile to Brindisi on the imperial yacht.

Midḥat visited Naples, Rome, Marseilles, Andalusia, Paris, Plombières, London, Vienna and Scotland. He wrote memoranda to European statesmen, especially British ones, supporting the Ottoman cause in the Russian war of 1877-8. He collected funds for the relief of Muslim refugees from the Balkans. He courted European opinion with a pamphlet defending Ottoman reforms and attacking Russian subversion. Because Midḥat was so popular in Europe, and because of British pressure, ʿAbd al-Hamīd allowed his return to forced residence. Midḥat arrived in Crete on 26 September 1878, going to live with his family in Halepa, outside Ḥanya (Canea). Probably owing to representations by the British ambassador Layard, Midḥat was soon named wālī of Syria. He was transported directly there, without being allowed a visit to Istanbul, and arrived on 28 November.

In his nearly two years as governor of the Syrian wilāyet [see DIMAS̲H̲Ḳ], Midḥat acted much as in Tuna and Bag̲h̲dād. He started schools, including a vocational school, built roads, built a tramway from Tripoli to its port, created a stronger gendarmerie and appointed some Christians to it, appointed some Syrians to the bureaucracy, founded a theatre and a public library, etc. He was less successful in settling tribes and quieting rebellions. With the Druze, he

achieved a standoff; he made the D̲j̲abal Durūz into a new ḳaḍāʾ with its own Druze ḳāʾimaḳām. Midḥat felt that he needed authority over the military and the courts, as well as over the bureaucracy and finance, to be effective. But his requests for broader powers and approval of extensive reforms were refused by the sultan. Twice Midḥat resigned, on 23 October 1879 and 30 May 1880, but the sultan refused consent. ʿAbd al-Ḥamīd was, however, receiving z̲h̲urnals from informers stating that Midḥat sought to be ruler or khedive in an autonomous Syria and was currying local favour to that end. Midḥat in fact opposed any Arab or Syrian separatism, but he may have countenanced some anti-Ottoman agitation to persuade ʿAbd al-Ḥamīd that he needed broader powers. The sultan evidently decided that Midḥat might be a danger in Damascus, and so ordered his transfer to Izmir on 4 August 1880. Midḥat left Syria on 31 August, and again was not allowed a visit to Istanbul.

Midḥat's governorship of Izmir lasted less than a year. It was unremarkable, except for warnings which he received from friends in Istanbul that he might be charged with complicity in the alleged murder of the ex-sultan ʿAbd al-ʿAzīz. Midḥat declined, however, to flee to Europe. At about 2 a.m. on 17 May 1881, troops entered his house to arrest him. Midḥat escaped through a garden gate to the French consulate. The next day, the Paris government refused asylum, and Midḥat agreed to arrest provided that his trial were public, and such an assurance was given. Midḥat was taken by ship to Istanbul and interrogated on board by D̲j̲ewdet Pas̲h̲a, the justice minister, who willingly undertook this mission to apprehend his opponent. Midḥat was confined in the Malta Kiosk in the Yi̊ldi̊z Palace grounds.

The Yi̊ldi̊z trial, though semi-public, was a travesty of justice. The case against Midḥat and nine others was built on weak testimony, presumably obtained through torture, bribery and sycophancy. The trial of the ten began on 27 June 1881. On 28 June, all of them, including Midḥat were found guilty. On 29 June, Midḥat and seven others were sentenced to death. An appeals court, obviously under Palace instructions, confirmed the sentences. But widespread Ottoman and European opinion urged leniency, as did a minority of a special med̲j̲lis convened for review. ʿAbd al-Ḥamīd thereupon converted Midḥat's sentence to life banishment. On 28 July 1881 Midḥat and others were hustled aboard the yacht "ʿIzz ad-Dīn" without even a change of clothing, transported to D̲j̲idda, and thence to imprisonment in a fort in al-Ṭāʾif. There, Midḥat suffered increasingly harsh treatment, and in the early hours of 8 May 1884, he was strangled by soldiers, evidently acting on ʿAbd al-Ḥamīd's orders. His death was reported as due to a carbuncle and other abscesses. He left two widows, three daughters and a son, ʿAlī Ḥaydar. In 1951 his bones were repatriated to Turkey.

Midḥat Pas̲h̲a had proved to be one of the ablest Ottoman administrators of the 19th century. His energy and creativity were most effective in provincial governorships where he had wide authority, although some of his measures were obviously hasty and some were superficial. His forthrightness and arrogance hampered him as grand vizier, especially in dealings with the palace. For his day, he was a liberal; he shared many views with the Yeñi ʿOt̲h̲mānli̊lar or Young Turks, especially on the desirability of a parliament. Without Midḥat, the constitution of 1876 would not have come into existence. Although ambitious for himself, Midḥat fundamentally acted on his belief that the task of a government official was to serve the people and the fatherland.

Bibliography: The principal sources are biographies of his father by ʿAlī Ḥaydar Midḥat, each differing from the others: *Ḥayāt-i siyāsiyyesi*, Istanbul 1325, i, *Tabṣira-yi ʿibret*, ii, *Mirʾāt-i ḥayret* (partly based on memoirs and documents by Midḥat Pas̲h̲a himself); *The life of Midhat Pasha*, London 1903; *Midḥat Pas̲h̲a'nin ḥayātī siyāsiyyesi*, Cairo 1322; *Midhat-pacha*, Paris 1908 (each includes documents by Midḥat Pas̲h̲a). Ali Haydar Midhat, *Hâtıralarım, 1872-1946*, Istanbul 1946, is almost half on his father. Other biographies: L.A. Léouzon-le-Duc, *Midhat-Pacha*, Paris 1877 (eulogistic); A. Clician Vasif, *Son Altesse Midhat-Pacha*, Paris 1909 (by his Croat secretary, laudatory); İbnülemin Mahmud Kemal İnal, *Osmanlı devrinde son sadrıazamlar*, Istanbul 1940-53 (4th printing 1969), 322-414 (with anecdotes, documents, quotations). Mehmed Zeki Pakalın, *Midhat Paşa*, Istanbul 1940 (extensive quotations from older works); M. Tayyib Gökbilgin, art. *Midhat Paşa*, in *İA*, viii, 270-82 (fascicle published in 1958); Bekir Sıtkı Baykal, *Midhat Paşa*, Istanbul 1964 (a short life, illustrations); I.E. Fadeeva, *Midhat-Pas̲h̲a, žizn i deyatel'nost'*, Moscow 1977 (concise but most complete biography, of a "bourgeois" Midḥat, best part on Bulgaria). By Midḥat Pas̲h̲a himself: *The past, present, and future of Turkey*, in *The Nineteenth Century*, iii/18 (June 1878), 981-93 (same as *La Turquie, son passé, son avenir*, Paris 1901; also twice published in Turkish); *Feryād ve figānlar*, Istanbul 1326 (not seen; extensively used by Fadeeva).

Based on archives, especially useful, are works by İ.H. Uzunçarşılı: *Midhat ve Rüştü Paşaların tevkiflerine dair vesikalar*, Ankara 1946: *Midhat Paşa ve Yıldız mahkemesi*, Ankara 1967; *Midhat Paşa ve Taif mahkûmları*, Ankara 1950. Other modern studies based on Ottoman and European documents: B.S. Baykal, *93 meşrutiyeti*, in *Belleten* vi, no. 21-2 (1942), 45-83; idem, *Midhat Paşa'nın gizli bir siyasî teşebbüsü*, in *III. Türk Tarih Kongresi, ... 1943*, Ankara 1948, 470-7; R.H. Davison, *Midhat Paşa and Ottoman foreign relations*, in *Osmanlı Araştırmaları*, v (1985); Nejat Göyünç, *Midhat Paşa'nin Nişvaliliği hakkında notlar ve belgeler*, in *IÜEF Tarih Enstitüsü Dergisi*, xii (1981-2), 279-316; Albertine Jwaideh, *Midhat Pasha and the land system of lower Iraq*, in *St. Antony's Papers*, iii, London 1963, 106-36; Najib E. Saliba, *The achievements of Midhat Pasha as governor of Syria, 1878-1880*, in *IJMES*, ix/3 (August 1978), 307-23; Shimon Shamir, *Midhat Pasha and the anti-Turkish agitation in Syria*, in *MES*, x/2 (May 1974), 115-41; idem, *The modernization of Syria...*, in W. Polk and R. Chambers, eds., *The beginnings of modernization in the Middle East*, Chicago 1968, 351-81; Maria N. Todorova, "*Obs̲h̲čopoleznite kassi*" *na Midhat Pas̲h̲a*, in *Istoričeski Pregled* (Sofia), xxviii/5 (1972), 56-76.

Works by Midḥat's contemporaries: Maḥmūd D̲j̲elāl al-Dīn, *Mirʾāt-ı ḥaḳīḳāt*, 3 vols., Istanbul 1326-7; Cevdet Paşa, *Tezâkir 40 - Tetimme*, ed. C. Baysun, Ankara 1967; Benoît Brunswik, *La vérité sur Midhat Pacha*, Paris 1877 (a tirade against him); A.D. Mordtmann, *Stambul und das moderne Türkentum*, 2 vols., Leipzig 1877-8; Süleymān Pas̲h̲a, *Ḥiss-i inḳilāb*, Istanbul 1326; F. Kanitz, *Donau-Bulgarien und der Balkan*, 3 vols., Leipzig 1875-9. Informative modern studies: M. C. Kuntay, *Namık Kemal*, 2 vols. in 3, Istanbul 1944-56, and the index to it (s.v. Midhat) by Olçay Önertoy, *M.C. Kuntay'ın Namık Kemal adlı eserinin ... indeksi*, Ankara 1965; Davison, *Reform in the Ottoman Empire, 1856-1876*, Princeton 1963; R. Devereux, *The first Ottoman constitutional period*, Baltimore 1963; Enver Ziya Karal, *Osmanlı tarihi*, v-vi, Ankara 1954-6. Further bibliography, including references to the standard older Turkish histories of the period, is conveniently found in the works cited above by Baykal, Davison, Fadeeva and Gökbilgin, and in the *EI*[1] art. s.v. (Fr. Babinger).

(R.H. Davison)

MIDILLI (Turkish form of Μυτιλήνη, Mytilene, the Greek name of its capital), the island of Lesbos in the eastern Aegean alongside the Turkish coast near the entrance to the Gulf of Edremit [*q.v.*] and the town of Ayvalık (Aywalïḳ [*q.v.*]); the straits of Müsellim and Mytilene that separate it from Turkey on the north and east average 10 and 16 km in width.

With an area of 1614 km², Lesbos is the third largest Greek island after Crete and Euboea, and the seventh largest of the Mediterranean. It has a roughly triangular shape, its broad base, *ca.* 70 km long, running from east-south-east to west-north-west, while the line from its apex in the north to the middle of this base measures 47 km. The relatively straight lines of its coast are interrupted by two gulfs on the south and south-east, that of Kallonis (also known by its classical name of Pyrrha), 21 km long, and that of Yeras, 14 km long. The island is well-watered by numerous streams flowing from three groups of mountains, of which Mt. Lepetimnos in the north and Mt. Olympos in the south-east both reach the elevation of 968 m (chart. N.O. 54380, U.S. Naval Oceanographic Office); on days of good visibility, not only Chios to the south, but even Samothrace and Mt. Athos to the north-west can be seen from the former. The geological composition of Lesbos consists partly of volcanic elements, and the island is earthquake-prone; it contains many springs, some hot with beneficial mineral content; several of the latter have been valued since antiquity. The dense oak and pine forests that once grew on Lesbos had dwindled to scattered remnants already in Hellenistic times.

Classical Lesbos was famous for its ideal climate and fertile soil; these assets, combined with an advantageous position near strategic commercial and maritime routes and an enterprising population, led to a remarkable prosperity and to political and cultural achievements (for the island's long and rich classical history, see *Pauly-Wissowa*, xii, 1925, 2107-33, s.v.; *Der Kleine Pauly-Wissowa*, iii, 1969, 585-87, s.v.; A. Philippson, *Die Griechischen Landschaften*, iv, 1959, 233-44; I.D. Kontes, *Lésvos kai he Mikrasiatiké tès perioché*, Athens 1978).

The principal city and port of Lesbos, Mytilene (a name of probably pre-Greek origin), first developed on an islet connected with the island's eastern coast by a possibly man-made isthmus. The city spread to this connecting neck and eventually also to the adjacent coast (see the engraving facing p. 390 of J. Pitton de Tournefort, *Relation d'un voyage du Levant*, i, Amsterdam 1718). In the Middle Ages, Lesbos came to be known by the name of its capital as the island of Mytilene or, through a metathesis, Melitene; this sometimes caused its confusion with the island of Malta or Melita (as shown by the association of the legend about St. Paul and the serpent with Lesbos).

Lesbos seems to have escaped the attention of early Islamic geographers, and it does not appear among the islands of the Aegean on either of al-Idrīsī's maps. On the other hand, Shuʿayb I b. ʿUmar (241-66/855-80) of Crete (Iḳrīts̲h̲ [*q.v.*]) raided the island as part of his forays throughout the Aegean all the way to the Propontis (the Sea of Marmara, Marmara Denizi [*q.v.*]) to the point of making the inhabitants of Eressos (legendary home of the poetess Sappho) abandon their city and move to Mount Athos (A.A. Vasil'ev, *Vizantiya i Arabi*, St. Petersburg 1910, ii, 46-7; French tr. *Byzance et les Arabes*, Brussels 1968, ii/1, 53).

Lesbos came under Muslim rule for the first time in or soon after 1089 and remained so until 1093 as part of the brilliant but short-lived successes of the Turkish *amīr* Čaḳa or Čaḳan (reconstructed from the Greek Tzachas), who founded the earliest Turkish maritime power from his base at Izmir. This Turkish threat was the principal cause of a renaissance of the Byzantine navy, rebuilt by Alexis I Comnenos; Čaḳa himself, however, fell victim to Byzantine diplomacy that contrived his assassination in league with the emperor's relative, the Saldjūḳ sultan Ḳilidj Arslān I, in 1093 (H. Ahrweiler, *Byzance et la mer*, Paris 1966, 184-9; S. Vryonis, *The decline of medieval Hellenism in Asia Minor*, Berkeley 1971, 115; A.N. Kurat, *Çaka*, Istanbul 1936).

By the time that the Aydïn *beg* Umur (1334-48; see P. Lemerle, *L'émirat d'Aydin*, Paris 1957; I. Mélikoff-Sayar, *Le Destan d'Umur Pacha*, Paris 1954; and AYDÏN-OGHLU) repeated and surpassed Čaḳa's exploits (without, however, occupying Lesbos), the growth of Turkish and Latin power in the area made Byzantine hold on the island, among other places, precarious. Thus in 1355 the emperor John V Paleologus gave Lesbos, his sister Mary's dowry, in an act of gratitude and as a practical solution, to his brother-in-law, the Genoese Francesco Gattilusi. This family then ruled Lesbos until its conquest by the Ottomans in 1462 (W. Miller, *Essays on the Latin Orient*, Cambridge 1921, 313-53, ch. "The Gattilusi of Lesbos"; W. Heyd, *Histoire du commerce du Levant*, Leipzig 1885, i, 510-12; E. Armao, *Il giro per il Mar Egeo con Vincenzo Coronelli*, Florence 1951, 110-11). The rule of the Gattilusi was characterised by the pragmatic, commerce-minded goals of Latin, mainly Italian, possessions in the Aegean. Thus when Tīmūr [*q.v.*] occupied Izmir in 1403, the Gattilusis hastened, like the Genoese company of the Mahone on Chios, to send presents and proclaim their loyalty. On the other hand, these Catholic overlords do not seem to have been fully accepted by the mainly Greek Orthodox population, a circumstance that may have facilitated the gradual spread of the Turkish domination.

After the conquest of Constantinople by Meḥemmed II, Dorino Gattiluso (1426-55) managed to conserve his possession by means of a tribute of 3,000 ducats (a sum raised at the accession of Dorino's son Domenico in 1455 to 7,000 ducats). In 1458 Domenico was imprisoned and subsequently murdered by his brother Niccolò. This, as well as irritation at the refuge which both Domenico and Niccolò gave to Catalan corsairs, is often cited as the cause of Meḥemmed's displeasure and eventual conquest, but a more decisive factor may have been the island's economic and strategic importance. Thus in the late summer of 1462, a Turkish fleet under Maḥmūd Pasha [*q.v.*] anchored off Mytilene, while the sultan set up camp on the mainland near Aywalïḳ. Niccolò refused to surrender, but did so after a siege of three weeks. The richer inhabitants were then moved to Istanbul, a number of boys and girls were chosen for imperial service, and the rest of the natives were allowed to stay. The island was surveyed and the population was recorded in Ottoman fiscal registers. Turks, mainly Janissaries who then married local women, were encouraged to settle in the island (Miller, *op. cit.*; F. Babinger, *Mehmed the Conqueror and his time*, Princeton 1978, 210-12, and *passim*; ʿĀshïḳ-pasha-zāde, ed. Giese, 156-57; Neshrī, ed. Taeschner, ii, 280-1; Katib Čelebi, *Tuḥfat al-kibār fī asfār al-biḥār*, Istanbul 1141, 61b). Lesbos became a *sandjaḳ* in the *eyālet* of Rūmili, and an important link in the framework of Ottoman maritime expansion. A minor but significant outcome of the conquest and repopulation of this island was the birth there of the Barbarossa brothers, who later initiated the Ottoman conquest of North Africa [see KHAYR AL-DĪN].

Ottoman rule on Lesbos lasted from 1462 to 1912. It was disturbed, though not disrupted, only at the beginning during the Turco-Venetian wars of 1463-79 and 1499-1502, and again toward the end, when in 1905 four European powers seized its customs and telegraph services in order to pressure the Ottoman government to accept their financial supervision of the *vilāyets* of Selānik, Kosova and Monastir.

In 1434, Lesbos became a *sandjaḳ* in the newly formed *eyālet* of Djazāʾir-i Baḥr-i Safīd [*q.v.*], a province under the jurisdiction of the commander of the Ottoman navy [see ḲAPUDAN PASHA]. This *eyālet* was formed at the appointment of the above-mentioned Khayr al-Dīn to that post. The island maintained this administrative status throughout the history of the *eyālet*—later called *vilāyet*—until the latter's demise concurrent with the end of the Turkish rule on Lesbos in 1912.

The life of the inhabitants does not seem to have been particularly affected by the Turkish rule. The majority remained Greek-speaking and Orthodox, and retained their way of life and religious traditions. European travellers who visited Lesbos during the centuries of the "Tourkokratia" were struck both by the island's features identical with those mentioned in classical sources and by some contrasts. The city of Mytilene, which together with Ephesus, Rodos and Corinth had had the reputation of being among the most beautiful cities of the Greek world, is described by Charles Thomas Newton (1852) as a "strappling, dirty village, the houses much like those of Constantinople constructed of wood on account of earthquakes, with roofs of red tile" (*Travels and discoveries in the Levant*, London 1865, i, 54). The Turkish governor resided with his garrison within the precincts of the citadel on the rocky peninsula; this fortress of Byzantine construction and Genoese additions, on the site of the ancient acropolis, reflected the city's and island's more recent history: according to H.F. Tozer (1886), "in the neighborhood of the entrance, at the summit of the hill, ... a Byzantine eagle, a Frankish coat of arms, and a Turkish inscription are built into the wall close together" (*The islands of the Aegean*, repr. Chicago 1976, 135). Newton (58) estimated the city's population at 8,500, of whom 2,000 were Muslims; there were also two to three hundred foreigners, protected by their diplomatic representatives. The presence of European vice-consuls is already reported by Tournefort (1700; i, 392) and Pococke (1739; *Description of the East*, London 1745, ii, 16). According to Newton, they resided in the "Frankish quarter" near the isthmus; the *sālnāme* of the *vilāyet* of Djazāʾir-i Baḥr-i Safīd, no. 20, for 1321/March 1905-Febr. 1906, 162, lists representatives (mostly vice-consuls acting for their consulates at Izmir) of Great Britain, Austro-Hungary, the United States, Sweden-Norway, Belgium, Greece, Holland, Iran, Spain, France, Italy and Germany. Their presence was due both to the economic importance of the island and to its position on crucial shipping routes. The port of

Mytilene, the busiest of the archipelago, consisted, as in antiquity, of two harbours separated by the isthmus, a northern and a southern one; the northern harbour, protected by a long mole, was the principal one. In 1305/March 1889-Febr. 1890 3,462 ships called there (V. Cuinet, *La Turquie d'Asie* Paris 1894, i, 469). The ratio of the Greek to the Turkish population on the island was about 4 : 1; the *sālnāme*, no. 10 for 1310/March 1894-Febr. 1895, 241, lists 98,882 Ottoman subjects besides a small number of foreigners; of the Ottoman ones, 85,328 were Greek Orthodox and 13,554 were Muslims. In the capital itself, the Turks were, according to Newton, "a decaying and decreasing population" (i, 57); there were, according to him, no very rich Turks except for the Pas͟ha and his son, for the wealthy Lesbiots were the rich landowners of the Greek bourgeoisie. Other sources mention also Greek merchants and bankers. The island's principal source of wealth and article of export were, throughout its history, olives and olive oil, although the fertility of its soil could have yielded an abundance of cereals as well; olive growing was favoured, according to Pococke, because it required little labour, which in turn could be done by women and children, and grain had thus to be imported. Nevertheless, the cultivation of wheat, famous in antiquity, again expanded in the final decades of the Ottoman rule, so that flour mills were second in importance only to olive oil presses (Cuinet, i, 455). Grapes, raisins and wines, as well as figs were also renowned; products derived from sheep and goats, and fishing enriched the Lesbiots' diet; the sardines, molluscs and shellfish of the bay of Kalloni had a specially high reputation. Besides oil pressed from olives and olive stones, the articles of export included soap, valonia, pitch, leather and hides, sponges and salt, and a delicious type of cheese popular in Istanbul. Small-scale shipbuilding and coastal shipping also occupied some inhabitants despite, and in some respects connected with the piracy and brigandage endemic in the Aegean (D.A. Zakythenos, *Corsaires et pirates dans les mers grecques au temps de la domination turque*, Athens 1939). No wheeled carriages were used in the island, transportation being done on pack animals (horses, donkeys, but especially sturdy mules, appreciated for their reliability in the mountainous terrain). A curiosity was small herds of little ponies that lived freely in the interior and were on occasion exported to Istanbul.

The port of Mytilene overshadowed the island's other harbours; from among the latter, the gulf of Yeras, called by Europeans Olivieri, had the reputation of being one of the vastest natural harbours of the Mediterranean. Equally favoured, but of more difficult access, was the gulf of Kalloni. The harbours of Plomari and Sigri on the southern and western coasts, and Molyvo with neighbouring Petra just west of the northern tip of the island, were also active.

There was a Greek Orthodox archbishop in Mytilene, and another in the island's second largest city, Molyvo (Methymna). The Turkish population lived throughout the island in their own quarters and in scattered villages. Numerous mosques and *tekke*s, churches and monasteries are mentioned in the *sālnāme*s. Relations between the two communities were good, and bilingualism was not uncommon. The awareness, among the Greeks, of their history and culture, always maintained by the ecclesiastic élite, spread among the population toward the end of the Ottoman period through an increasing number of schools, some teachers receiving their training also in Athens. Cuinet (i, 450) mentions 157 schools with 7,635 students; there were two high schools in Mytilene, a Greek one with 97 students and a Turkish one with 40 students.

Visitors praised the fresh air of the island enriched with the fragrance of its Mediterranean vegetation, and the climate was salubrious. The only serious ailment was tuberculosis, chiefly limited to the wives, sequestered in their women's quarters, of the more opulent Greek and Turkish inhabitants (Cuinet, i, 451).

In the final decades of the Ottoman period, the *vilāyet* of D͟jazāʾir-i Baḥr-i Safīd (which had by then lost any connection with the office of the commander of the Ottoman navy) consisted of four *sand͟jaḳ*s: Rodos [*q.v.*], Chios (Saḳīz [*q.v.*]), Lesbos and Lemnos (Limni[*q.v.*]). That of Lesbos was divided into four *ḳaḍāʾ*s: of Midilli, Molyvo (Methymna), Pilmar (Plomari) and Yunda; the last-named, known in Greek as Moskonesia or Kekatonesia, consisted of a group of small islets dominated by the larger Alibay Adasī facing Aywalīḳ; this *ḳaḍāʾ* was the only part of the *sand͟jaḳ* that remained Turkish at the conclusion of the Balkan War. The title of the *sand͟jaḳ*'s governor was *mutesarrif*, while the *ḳaḍāʾ*s were administered by *ḳaymaḳām*s, and the *nāḥiye*s by *müdür*s. Lists of government officials in the *sālnāme*s show that majority were Turks, but that Greeks also participated in the administration.

Ottoman rule on Lesbos ended in December 1912, when a Greek fleet landed troops on the island and took control of it (Ali Haydar Emir [Alpagur], *Balkan harbinde Türk filosu*, Istanbul 1932, 249-53). Greek annexation was ratified by the London Conference in May 1913. The Turkish inhabitants left Lesbos as part of the population exchange between the two countries in the 1920s.

Bibliography (apart from works cited in the text): B. Darkot, *İA*, art. *Midilli*; numerous European travel accounts, for whose bibliography see Pauly-Wissowa, cited in the text; numerous portolan texts and charts, best discussed by E. Armao, cited in the text; Pīrī Reʾis, *Kitāb-i Bahriyye*, Istanbul 1935, 130-9, and German tr. of the first version by P. Kahle, *Pīrī Reʾīs; Bahrīje. ii. Übersetzung*, Berlin 1926, 32-42; A. Delatte, *Les Portulans grecs*, Liège 1947, index s.v. *Mytilene*; Ilyās b. K͟hiḍr (Uzun Firdewsī), *Ḳuṭb-nāme, ḳiṣṣa-yi Midilli*, ed. İ. Olgun and İ. Parmaksızoğlu, Ankara 1980; the *ḳānūn-nāme*s listed on p. 66 of H.W. Lowry, *The Ottoman Liva Kanunnames contained in the Defter-i Hakani*, in *Osmanlı araştırmaları. The Journal of Ottoman studies*, ii (Istanbul 1981) (*ḳānūn-nāme*s TT264 from 1548, TT598 from 1581, TT803 from 1671, and TK 2 from 1709; the last-named was published by Ö.L. Barkan, *XV ve XVIıncı asırlarda Osmanlı imperatorluğunda ziraî ekonominin hukukî ve malî esasları, birinci cilt: Kanunlar*, Istanbul 1943, 332-8, and by H. Tuncer, *Osmanlı imparatorluğunda toprak hukuku, arazî kanunları ve kanun açıklamaları*, Ankara 1962, 315-19); İ.H. Uzunçarşılı, *Osmanlı devletinin merkez ve bahriye teşkilâtı*, Ankara 1948, 420-2; S͟h. Sāmī, *Ḳāmūs al-aʿlām*, Istanbul 1898, vi, 4242-3, s.v. *Midilli*; D.E. Pitcher, *An historical geography of the Ottoman empire*, Leiden 1972; A.E. Bakalopoulos, *The Greek nation, 1453-1669*, New Brunswick 1976, index s.vv. *Lesbos* and *Mytilene*; F.W. Hasluck, *Depopulation in the Aegean Islands and the Turkish Conquest*, in the *Annual of the British School of Athens*, xvii (1910-11), 151-81; U.S. Naval Oceanographic Office, *Sailing directions for the Mediterranean*, Publ. no. 132, *Sailing directions for the Eastern Mediterranean*, 303-6.

(S. Soucek)

MIDRĀR (Banū) or MIDRĀRIDS, minor Berber dynasty which was established in Sidjilmās(s)a [*q.v.*] and which enjoyed relative independence until its final collapse in 366/976-7.

The history of this dynasty can be briefly outlined, thanks to al-Bakrī [*q.v.*], who lived in the 5th/11th century and thus possessed quite recent information in order to write the chapter that he devotes to it (*Mughrib*, 148 ff., Fr. tr. 282 ff.), before Ibn ʿIdhārī (7th-8th/13th-14th century [*q.v.*]), Ibn Khaldūn (8th/14th century [*q.v.*]) and several historians of the Maghrib and Mashriḳ were able to take their turn at tackling this; but a number of important episodes of this period were recorded in the works of the *ḳāḍī* al-Nuʿmān [*q.v.*] available today, in particular the *Iftitāḥ al-daʿwa* and the *Kitāb al-Madjālis wa 'l-musāyarāt*, as well as in the *Autobiography* of the chamberlain Djaʿfar b. ʿAlī (see *Bibl.*), although the latter sources, contemporaneous with the events which they relate, express the often biased point of view of the Fāṭimids.

From the start, it is difficult to date the birth of the dynasty which, despite appearances, does not seem to coincide with the foundation of Sidjilmāsa, itself not well established. One tradition links the foundation with a member of the tribe of Miknāsa [*q.v.*], Abu 'l-Ḳāsim Samdjū/Samghū/Samghūn (i.e. Samgū or Samgūn) b. Wāsūl al-Miknāsī, who had adopted the doctrine of the Ṣufrī [*q.v.*] Khāridjites; this man is said to have gathered *ḥadīth*s, in Ifrīḳiya, from ʿIkrima [*q.v.*], the famous *mawlā* of Ibn ʿAbbās, whom legend depicts as the propagator of Khāridjism in the Maghrib, a region where he probably never set foot. The Samgū/Samgūn in question, who, it is said, pastured his flocks on the site of the future town of Sidjilmāsa, gathered around him some Ṣufrīs, and, as soon as the group numbered 40, set out, in 140/757-8, to build houses; the small community surprisingly chose as its chief a negro by the name of ʿĪsā b. Mazyad (rather than Yazīd) al-Aswad, whose father had been converted to Islam, but his conduct so offended those he governed that they tied him to a tree and left him to die in 155/772; he had reigned 15 years (al-Bakrī, 148/286; *Berbères*, i, 261). According to the sources, his successor was the first-mentioned personage, Abu 'l-Ḳāsim Samgū/Samgūn, who reigned 13 years and died in 168/784-5. This tradition, which traces back the foundation of the town and, consequently, of the dynasty, if not of the family, to 140/757-8, is preferred by our first informant, al-Bakrī (149/284); Ibn ʿIdhārī (i, 157) and Ibn Khaldūn (*Berbères*, i, 261) only know of it, while the *Mafākhir al-Barbar* [*q.v.*] (48) reports on the authority of ʿArīb b. Saʿd [*q.v.*] that Abu 'l-Ḳāsim Samḳū ruled over Sidjilmāsa, founded in 140 by his grandfather (*sic*) ʿĪsā b. Yazīd. Al-Bakrī reproduces in any case a second tradition, according to which a smith from Cordova called Midrār, who had taken part in the Revolt of the Suburb (in 202/818 [see ḲURṬUBA]) and was consequently a Rabaḍī, was able to escape and came to settle near the market whose site was to be occupied by the capital of the Midrārids; while suggesting that the first of the two accounts is "more in conformity with the truth", this author nevertheless asserts (149/285) that the rulers of Sidjilmāsa are descendants of the smith Midrār, since they "were subjected to satirical insults on this subject." The *Istibṣār* (204), for its part, draws on the two traditions, which it moreover mixes; it calls Midrār b. ʿAbd Allāh the alleged disciple of ʿIkrima, and says that the Midrār who escaped from Cordova was black, a fact which earned for his descendants gibes or epigrams. As for E. Lévi-Provençal, he admits the Cordovan origin of the founder of Sidjilmāsa (*Hist. Esp. mus.*, i, 170, n. 1).

This latter tradition, which appears seductive in the form in which it is presented by al-Bakrī, does not, however, elude the problem of chronology which is posed, for the impression is given that the town existed as early as the end of the 2nd/ 8th century. In fact, after 168/784-5, al-Bakrī (150/286) and Ibn Khaldūn (i, 262) have a son of Samgū/Samgūn mentioned as reigning by the name of Abu 'l-Wazīr al-Yās b. Abi 'l-Ḳāsim, who was dethroned in 174/790-1 (the date of 170 mentioned by Ibn ʿIdhārī is to be corrected) by his brother Abu 'l-Muntaṣir (sometimes Abū 'l-Manṣūr, but probably wrongly) al-Yasaʿ, who remained on the throne until his death in 208/823-4. This long reign was to be quite brilliant and beneficial, for al-Yasaʿ, who is said to have been of a particularly violent and despotic character, subjugated all the Berbers of the region who resisted him, levied the fifth on the mines of Darʿa [*q.v.*] and had built in 199/814-15 (al-Bakrī, 148/282-3; Jacques-Meunié, i, 201) the town wall with 12 gates in it, of which eight were covered in iron so that the enemy could not set fire to them. It is stated that this wall, the lower part in stone and the upper in unfired brick (Ibn ʿIdhārī, i, 157), was undertaken entirely at his own expense, and that the work force cost him 1,000 measures of grain (*ṭaʿām*) a day. He also adorned the town with a certain number of palaces and public buildings, notably the Friday mosque (al-Bakrī, 148/283; *Berbères*, i, 262; Jacques-Meunié, i, 201).

Given, on the one hand, that the total duration of the dynasty is reckoned at 160 years (al-Bakrī, 149/284; Ibn Idhārī, i, 157; Ibn al-Abbār, *Ḥulla*, i, 191-2) and that, on the other hand, disregarding the Rabaḍī mentioned above, the first Midrār cited is the son of al-Yasaʿ, al-Muntaṣir, who ascended the throne in 208/823-4 (al-Bakrī, 150/286; *Berbères*, i, 262), it is perhaps from this year that we have to date the birth of the Midrārid line, in spite of the fact that, in general, the eponym of dynasties may be the father of the first of their members, that Ibn ʿIdhārī (i, 157) clearly states that it came to an end in 296 after approximately 160 years of rule, that Ibn Khaldūn (i, 260) gives it the name of Banū Wāsūl, which would also take it back to the year 140, and that G.-S. Colin, in the article SIDJILMĀSA IN *EI*[1], makes "the Miknāsī dynasty of the Banū Midrār" begin in 155/771-2, i.e. with the immediate successor of the first ruler of the town, which is in conformity with al-Bakrī's opinion and calculation, but completely disregards the figure of 160 years and the absence of a person called Midrār before 208/823-4. For this reason, we will begin arbitrarily with:

i. Abū Mālik AL-MUNTAṢIR b. al-Yasaʿ, whose surname MIDRĀR (= "one who produces much milk or pours forth abundant rain", etc.), which had no doubt been given him as a title of good omen, served to designate the ruling family whom al-Masʿūdī (*Murūdj*, iv, 39 = § 1367) further named as the Banu 'l-Muntaṣir, which justifies the decision taken. This author estimates the extent of the amīr's dominions—one would wish to know on what basis—at 400 *farsakh*s by 80 (!), and makes one Aḥmad b. al-Muntaṣir the ruler of the land of Asṭūlā (?) which measured, according to him, 400 *farsakh*s by 250. According to Ibn Khurradādhbih (ed. and Fr. tr. M. Hadj-Sadok, 9), the territory of the Banū Midrār included the Darʿa, where a silver mine was located, and the town of Zīz, i.e. it probably exceeded present-day Tafilalt.

Midrār, a nominal vassal of the ʿAbbāsids (in

Tentative genealogy of the Midrārids

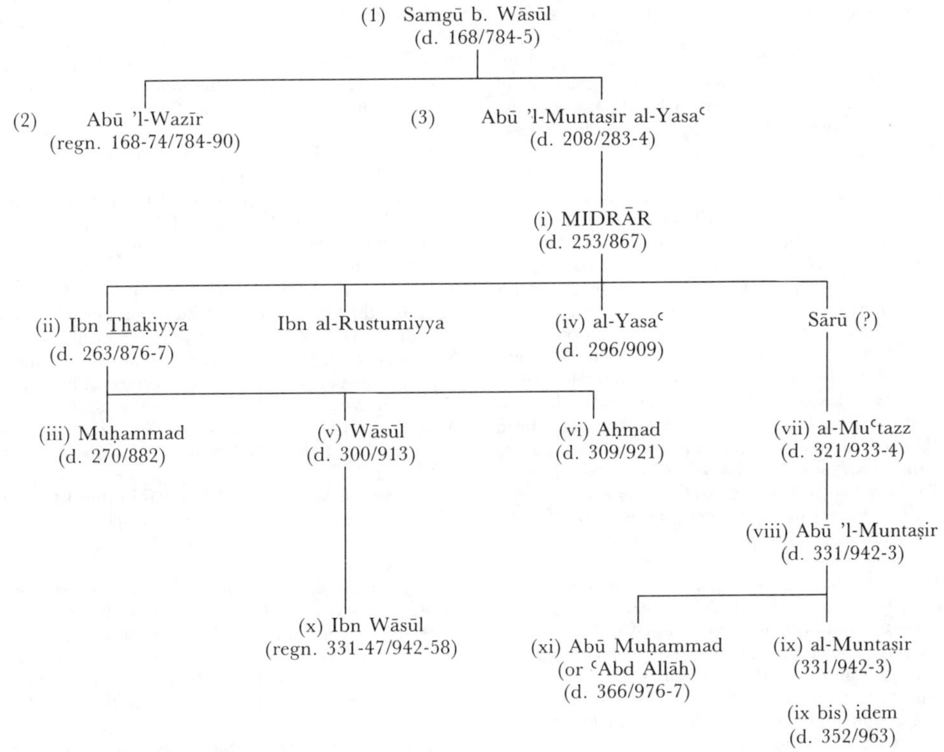

whose name the *k̲h̲uṭba* had been pronounced, at least in the time of the caliphs al-Manṣūr and al-Mahdī, i.e. from 140 to 169/758-85, if we are to believe Ibn K̲h̲aldūn, i, 262) may have acknowledged a certain dependence on Cordova, but no doubt one much less strict, as E. Lévy-Provençal says (*Hist. Esp. Mus.*, i, 281-2), than that of the Rustamids of Tāhart [*q.vv.*], with whom he had moreover some affinities, since, like them, he was a K̲h̲āridjite; he had even married Arwā bint ᶜAbd al-Raḥmān b. Rustam (al-Bakrī, 150/287; *Berbères*, i, 262; G. Marçais, 103-4; Jacques-Meunié, i, 201). It so happens that his reign was troubled by the rivalry of his two sons, both of them with the first name of Maymūn, born to him by the Rustamiyya and another woman by the name of Th̲aḳiyya (? Baḳiyya in Ibn ᶜId̲h̲ārī, i, 157). After having endured three years of dispute, Midrār, who was inclined to favour the former, banished the latter, but was himself dispossessed by the son to whom he had given preference. The population of the town then rebelled, offered the throne to the son of Th̲aḳiyya, who refused it and gave it to Midrār, who made the mistake of appearing firm in his intention to entrust it to Maymūn Ibn al-Rustamiyya. This time, the inhabitants of Sidjilmāsa besieged their sovereign in his palace and gave their allegiance as chief to

ii. Maymūn b. Th̲aḳiyya, called al-Amīr. The deposed dynast died in 253/867, while his son ruled until his death, in 263/876-7, and was succeeded by

iii. his son Muḥammad, who died in Ṣafar 270/August-September 884 (al-Bakrī, 150/287; *Berbères*, i, 263; cf. Ibn ᶜId̲h̲ārī, who does not follow exactly the same order).

It was not long before the principality of Sidjilmāsa, whose tranquility until then appears to have been disturbed only by some purely internal dissensions, entered into the general history of the Mag̲h̲rib and Islam, at the same time losing the autonomy that it had preserved vis-à-vis the Ag̲h̲labids [*q.v.*] of Ḳayrawān and the ᶜAbbāsids of Bag̲h̲dād, of whom the Midrārids were still nominal vassals, as is proved by the letter sent, at the time when the Mahdī ᶜUbayd Allāh was being sought after, most likely not by al-Muᶜtaḍid (279-89/892-902), as is stated by Ibn K̲h̲aldūn (*Muḳaddima*, i, 30; Fr. tr. de Slane, i, 40-1) and the author of the *Istibṣār* (204), but more probably by his successor al-Muktafī (289-95/902-8), to the following *amīr*,

iv. al-Yasaᶜ (sometimes erroneously: ᶜĪsā) b. al-Muntaṣir (or b. Midrār), son of the no. 1 above, who occupied the throne from 270 to 296/882-909.

In fact, on 1 S̲h̲awwāl 292/7 July 905 (see *Autobiography*, 297), following a prediction according to which the awaited Mahdī [*q.v.*] is to appear in Sidjilmāsa, the future founder of the Fāṭimid dynasty, al-Mahdī ᶜUbayd Allāh [*q.v.*] set out in the direction of this small capital with his young son al-Ḳāsim (*Istibṣār*, 204; *Berbères*, i, 263; Terrasse, i, 140; Jacques-Meunié, i, 202). He rented a house there, the Dār Abī Ḥabas̲h̲a (*Autobiogr.*, 302), succeeded in concealing his identity for almost four years and received good treatment from al-Yasaᶜ b. al-Muntaṣir, possibly owing to the presents that he had given him. Besides, he had no doubt been able to make friends among the flourishing ᶜIrāḳī colony resident in the town (cf. Dachraoui, *Califat*, 122, 311). The circumstances in which his true identity was revealed are differently reported by the sources. According to the *Autobiography* of Djaᶜfar b. ᶜAlī (303-4), his son miraculously caused a spring to gush forth in a garden next to his house, and the secret was thus divulged. According to the *Istibṣār* (204), however, he had been denounced by a Jew, while Dachraoui (*Califat*, 123) asserts that al-Yasaʿ was informed of his presence by a letter from Ziyādat Allāh [see AGHLABIDS]. According to Ibn Khaldūn (*Muḳaddima*, i, 30, 33-4; Fr. tr. de Slane, i, 40-1, 45), the letter from Baghdād mentioned above was addressed to the Aghlabids of Ḳayrawān and the Midrārids of Sidjilmāsa ordering them to close their land to ʿUbayd Allāh and his son (whose genealogy, in the opinion of Ibn Khaldūn, was by this act recognised as authentic); al-Yasaʿ then discovered the truth and had the two fugitives imprisoned. Whatever the facts of the matter, at one time or another, the Midrārid put ʿUbayd Allāh, if not in prison, (*Istibṣār*, 202), at least under house arrest in his sister's house and separated him from his son, with whom he could, however, communicate through an intermediary, a young eunuch originally from Aleppo called Ṣandal, whom he had bought locally (*Autobiogr.*, 307 and n. 3). Acting through a Shīʿī from Ḳayrawān in whose company he had travelled (*Autobiogr.*, 305) and who had been authorised to return to Ḳayrawān, he was able to inform of his situation the *dāʿī* Abū ʿAbd Allāh al-Shīʿī, who had just seized Raḳḳāda [*q.v.*]. This *dāʿī* was eager to recruit supporters, hence set out for the West, subdued on his way the Rustamids of Tāhart and arrived before Sidjilmāsa on 6 Dhu 'l-Ḥidjdja 296/26 August 909 (Ibn ʿIdhārī, i, 159; Dachraoui, *Califat*, 122). Abū ʿAbd Allāh scarcely appeared aggressive, and even advised al-Yasaʿ of his peaceful intentions; however, as the latter had had his messengers put to death, he finally took the town by storm. Meanwhile, the Midrārid *amīr* fled, but, on his being caught after a few days, he was killed by his own subjects or died of wounds that he had received (*Autobiogr.*, 319; *Iftitāḥ*, §§ 243-52; *Istibṣār*, 204; *Berbères*, i, 263; Marçais, 134; Terrasse, i, 140; Dachraoui, *Califat*, 124; Jacques-Meunié, i, 202). All the events that are summarised here are recounted in detail in a letter which the *dāʿī* is said to have addressed to Raḳḳāda and which is reproduced in the *Iftitāḥ* (§§ 253-7; see also *Madjālis*, 214). According to the *Autobiography* of Djaʿfar b. ʿAlī (312), al-Yasaʿ took out of the town ʿUbayd Allāh, who himself gave to Abū ʿAbd Allāh the order to seize it, but the chamberlain was then imprisoned, as were all the members of the eminent Shīʿī's entourage; his evidence has however no great value on this point. Once ʿUbayd Allāh and his son had been rescued, Abū ʿAbd Allāh pillaged the town and is said to have dealt severely with the Jews, whom he stripped of their goods and drove out of Sidjilmāsa (but he does appear to have condemned those of them who wished to stay to become cesspool cleaners (*kannāfūn*) and masons (*bannāʾūn*), as the *Istibṣār* (202) reports, for al-Bakrī mentions (149/284) that the former occupation was reserved for lepers). The rest of the population endured a similar fate to such an extent that the *dāʿī* was able to leave for Raḳḳāda carrying with him 120 loads of gold and precious merchandise (*Istibṣār*, 204; Jacques-Meunié, i, 203).

It was in Sidjilmāsa that ʿUbayd Allāh was proclaimed *Imām* (*Autobiogr.*, 316); he stayed there for another 40 days before departing for Ifrīḳiya (Dachraoui, *Califat*, 124). Before his departure, Abū ʿAbd Allāh had designated as governor of the town an officer of the Mazāta [*q.v.*] called Ibrāhīm b. Ghālib (*ʿUyūn al-akhbār*, 24-5; al-Bakrī, 150/288; *Berbères*, i, 263; cf. Ibn ʿIdhārī, i, 206), leaving at his disposal a garrison of 2,000 Kutāma; this figure, mentioned by Dachraoui (124), appears, however, rather exaggerated as, according to al-Bakrī (150/288), this governor was massacred 50 days later, with all his soldiers, by the rebellious townspeople. The latter author (150/287) dates from Dhu 'l-Ḥidjdja 297/August-September 910 the end of the reign of al-Yasaʿ, i.e. there is a difference of a whole year from the date given by the contemporary Shīʿī sources, which is perhaps more reliable; for him (150/288) and for Ibn Khaldūn (i, 263), it was in Rabīʿ I 298/November-December 910 that the rebellious population put on the throne

v. WĀSŪL, i.e. al-Fatḥ (Abu 'l-Fatḥ in Ibn ʿIdhārī, i, 206), son of (ii) Maymūn al-Amīr, who died in Radjab 300/February-March 913 and was succeeded by his brother

vi. AḤMAD, killed in Muḥarram 309/May-June 921, by the governor of Tāhart on behalf of the Mahdī, Maṣāla b. Ḥab(b)ūs, who came to besiege Sidjilmāsa, seized it and installed on the throne a Midrārid prince who was totally devoted to his cause,

vii. AL-MUʿTAZZ, Muḥammad b. Sārū (?) b. Midrār (al-Bakrī, 151/288; *Berbères*, i, 264; Ibn ʿIdhārī, i, 179, 183; Dachraoui, *Califat*, 151). On his death (321/933-4), his son

viii. ABU 'L-MUNTAṢIR (al-Manṣūr in Ibn ʿIdhārī, i, 206) Muḥammad succeeded him and spent the rest of his life in power; he died in 331/942-3 (cf. *Berbères*, i, 264) and his son

ix. AL-MUNTAṢIR Samgū b. (viii) Muḥammad, who was only 13 years old, took his place, but entrusted state affairs to his grandmother, who administered the state for only two months, for a son of (v) Wāsūl,

x. MUḤAMMAD b. (v) al-Fatḥ Wāsūl b. (ii) Maymūn al-Amīr, seized power by force and put the incumbent ruler in prison (*Madjālis*, 389).

The new master of Sidjilmāsa had apparently developed fairly close ties with the Umayyads of Cordova, since he was present in the midst of their troops on 11 Shawwāl 327/1 August 939 at the Battle of Simancas (Lévi-Provençal, *Hist. Esp. mus.*, ii, 58). Thus it is not astonishing that he had repudiated the Ṣufrī Khāridjism to which his ancestors adhered, so as to be converted to the Mālikī Sunnism in force in al-Andalus (al-Bakrī, 151/288). This decision was bound to displease his Fāṭimid suzerain, who endured Khāridjism by force of circumstances and possibly also accepted, however dubious this may be, that the *khuṭba* should be pronounced in the name of the ʿAbbāsids (*Berbères*, i, 264), but was unable to allow a more or less declared allegiance to the Umayyad régime. It is said that he was nevertheless able to govern his principality and to exercise justice there; however, from the testimony of Ibn Ḥawḳal (83/Fr. tr. 79), who was present in Sidjilmāsa in 340/951 and had some dealings with him, "while he called for war [...], he was unable to obtain from the Berbers what he wanted, because those whom he invited to join him on campaign were disinclined to do so, fearing a trick to harm them". There is no mention of whether it was the Fāṭimids against whom he was directing his attack, but it is known that the rulers of Ifrīḳiya grew very angry in 342/953-4, when he had the audacity to proclaim himself caliph, take the title of *Amīr al-Muʾminīn* and the ruling name of al-Shākir li-llāh (*Berbères*, i, 264; Jacques-Meunié, i, 203) and to mint coins (the *mathāḳīl shākiriyya* cited by Ibn Ḥazm, *Naḳṭ al-ʿarūs*, 76; see Colin, in *Hespéris* [1936], 122; Brèthes, 96, no. 773; Jacques-Meunié, i, 226). The Fāṭimid Caliph al-Muʿizz li-dīn Allāh, unable to bear such a mark of insubordination, ordered the general Djawhar [*q.v.*] to go and force the recalcitrant prince to see reason. According to the Shīʿī tradition (*Madjālis*, 338), Djawhar, on arriving near Sidjilmāsa, wrote to the population asking them to surrender Ibn Wāsūl, but they refused. This attitude did nothing to relieve the anxiety of the *amīr*, who hastened to leave the town with his family, his treasures and supporters to go to seek refuge in the neighbouring fortress of Tasegdelt (?); Djawhar then entered the Midrārids' capital, where he had coins minted to replace the *mathākil shākiriyya* (Dachraoui, *Califat*, 232, 344). Ibn Wāsūl, having left his refuge to find out what was happening in the town, was recognised by some members of the Maṭghara [*q.v.*] tribe, who gave him up to Djawhar (on these events, see al-Bakrī, 151/289; *Berbères* i, 264; Jacques-Meunié, i, 203). Contrary to what is said in the art. DJAWHAR, Ibn Wāsūl was not put to death, but made a prisoner (*Mafākhir al-Barbar*, 4) and brought to al-Manṣūriyya, together with the *amīr* of Fās, Aḥmad b. Bakr, captured in the same period, and some sons of notables of Sidjilmāsa (*Madjālis*, 483) taken as hostages. The attack on the town and the capture of Ibn Wāsūl took place in Radjab 347/September-October 958 (al-Bakrī, 151/289). The arrival at al-Manṣūriyya is dated by the *ḳāḍī* al-Nuʿmān (*Madjālis*, 458) to the end of Shaʿban [348?]/November 959, but the dates mentioned by this author do not always appear to be exact. In any case, we are quite well informed on the prisoner's stay with the Fāṭimid caliph, on his internment in a part of the castle (*saḳīfat al-ḳaṣr*), on the ignominious treatment that he experienced when he was taken around in a cage, and also on the *ḳāḍī*'s attempts to convert him, as well as the tenor of the conversations that took place between al-Muʿizz and Ibn Wāsūl (see *Madjālis*, 411-12, 434-5, 458, 460; Ibn ʿIdhārī, i, 222; *Berbères*, i, 263; Ibn al-Athīr, vi, 354; Dachraoui, *Captivité*).

Before leaving Sidjilmāsa, Djawhar had appointed a governor there, but the population were not slow to rebel again and to restore to the throne

ix (for the second time). AL-MUNTAṢIR BI-LLĀH b. (viii) Muḥammad b. (vii) al-Muʿtazz, whose father and grandfather had not been appointed by the Fāṭimid caliph, as al-Nuʿmān (*Madjālis*, 388) claims, but put in power by Maṣāla (see above). According to the same author (*Madjālis*, 389-93), the population, who had killed the governor imposed by Djawhar, made their excuses to al-Muʿizz, but he did not accept them at all and summoned al-Muntaṣir, who made his way to him with 200 men. After a severe reprimand, the caliph nevertheless sent him to govern his town. In 352/963, al-Muntaṣir was dethroned and, according to Ibn Ḥawḳal (107/104), put to death, with the help of a group of twelve men, by his brother

xi. Abū Muḥammad ʿABD ALLĀH (?) b. (viii) Muḥammad b. (vii) al-Muʿtazz, who recognised the suzerainty of the Fāṭimid caliph. This situation lasted until the year 366/976-7, when the chief of the Maghrāwa, Khazrūn b. Falfūl [see MAGHRĀWA], who fought on behalf of Cordova, put an end to the dynasty of the Banū Midrār; the last prince still in power fell on the battlefield, and his head was sent to Cordova (*Berbères*, i, 264-5; Terrasse, i, 169; Jacques-Meunié, i, 206). Lévi Provençal (*Hist. Esp. mus.*, ii, 261), places this event in 369/980, which corresponds better to the total of 160 years proposed by al-Bakrī for the duration of the dynasty.

The descendants of Khazrūn were to be put under the suzerainty of Cordova, to remain then at the head of an independent principality in Arcos [see ARKŪSH] until its annexation by Sevilla.

We have seen that one observer interested in the social and economic situation of the land through which he travelled, Ibn Ḥawḳal, was in 340/951 in Sidjilmāsa, and it is probable that he kept in touch with the course of events that then took place. He states (99-100/98; cf. Jacques-Meunié, i, 203) that in the period when (vii) al-Muʿtazz reigned over the principality, he "levied tariffs on the caravans travelling to the country of the Blacks, as well as the tithe, the land tax and some ancient taxes on the sale and purchase of camels, sheep, cattle, in addition to dues on all merchandise being exported to or imported from Ifrīḳiya, Fās, Spain, Sūs and Aghmāt, and finally other revenues dependent on the administration of the mint. All this amounted to about 400,000 *dīnār*s for the capital and the province". According to this author, the revenue from the town and its province, an area of five days' journey by three, was equal to half of that of the whole Maghrib, and one can understand the interest that the great powers of the period took in the principality. The importance that Ibn Ḥawḳal attributes to the town itself is further reflected by the fact that he calculates the distances from it to other places (91-3/89-92). He passes very favourable judgment on the inhabitants, upon whose commercial activity and wealth he remarks (99-100/97-8); and he is astonished to see "a recognition of debt by which a merchant of Awdaghust admitted himself in debt to an inhabitant of Sidjilmāsa for a sum of 42,000 *dīnārs*" (cf. 61/58, where this observation is already mentioned). Reckoned at 4,06g a *dīnār*, this sum represents a weight in gold of 170.520 kg (Jacques-Meunié, i, 224). One can deduce from the comments of Ibn Ḥawḳal that Sidjilmāsa was, under the Midrārids, the most important caravan centre on the route passing round the desert through the West; the ruler of Egypt, Ibn Ṭūlūn (249-69/863-83 [*q.v.*]) having forbidden caravans and single travellers to follow the routes which led directly to the western Sudan, the eastern merchants passed by Sidjilmāsa, which also benefited from the advantages of eastern and western civilisation, without however leaving behind, at least in this period, the recollection of a really intense cultural activity.

Bibliography: *Autobiography*, see Canard; Bakrī, *Kitāb al-Mughrib bi-dhikr bilād Ifrīḳiya wa 'l-Maghrib/Description de l'Afrique septentrionale*, ed. and Fr. tr. de Slane, 2nd ed. Algiers 1911-13, repr. Paris 1965, Ar. text 148 ff./Fr. tr. 282 ff.; *Berbères* = Ibn Khaldūn, *Kitāb al-ʿIbar*, Fr. tr. de Slane, *Histoire des Berbères et des dynasties musulmanes de l'Afrique septentrionale*, 2nd ed. Paris 1925-34, 1956 (vol. iv and index by H. Pérès), i, 262 ff.; E.W. Bovill, *The golden trade of the Moors*, Oxford 1963; J.D. Brèthes, *Contribution à l'histoire du Maroc par les recherches numismatiques*, Casablanca [1939], 96; M. Canard, *L'Autobiographie d'un chambellan du Mahdî ʿObeidallâh le Fâṭimide*, in *Hespéris*, xxxix/3-4 (1952), 279-324—appx. i: partial Fr. tr. (324-8) of the *Iftitāḥ* of the *ḳāḍī* al-Nuʿmān, appx. ii: partial reproduction (328-9) of the Fagnan tr. of the *Istibṣār* (art. repr., without the appx., in *Miscellanea orientalia*, London 1973, no. V); G.S. Colin, art. SIDJILMĀSA, in *EI*[1]; F. Dachraoui, *La captivité d'Ibn Wāsūl le rebelle de Siǧilmāsa*, in *CT*, iv (1956), 295-9; idem, *Le califat fatimide au Maghreb 296-362/909-973*, Tunis 1981, index; idem (Dashrāwī), *Taʾrīkh al-dawla al-fāṭimiyya bi 'l-Maghrib min K. ʿUyūn al-akhbār wa-funūn al-āthār li 'l-dāʿī Idrīs ʿImād al-Dīn al-Ḳurashī*, Tunis 1981, 24-5; E.F. Gautier, *Les siècles obscurs du Maghreb*, Paris 1927, 292-3; M. Hadj-Sadok, *Description du Maghreb et de l'Europe au IIIe-IXe siècle*, Algiers 1949; Ibn al-Abbār, *al-Ḥulla al-siyarāʾ*, ed. Ḥ. Muʾnis, Cairo 1963; Ibn Ḥawḳal, *K. Ṣūrat al-arḍ*, Fr. tr. Kramers-Wiet, *Configuration de la terre*, Paris-Beirut 1964 [1965], index; Ibn Ḥazm, *Naḳṭ al-ʿarūs*, Cairo 1951, 76; Ibn ʿIdhārī, *Bayān*, ed. Colin and Lévi-Provençal, Leiden 1948-51, i, 156-7; *K. al-Istibṣār*, ed. and partial Fr. tr. S.Z. Abdel-Hamid, Alexandria 1958, 201-5 (Fr. tr. E. Fagnan, *L'Afrique septentrionale au XIᵉ siècle de notre ère*, in *Recueil de notices et mémoires de la Société Archéologique du département de Constantine*, xxxiii (1899) [Paris 1900], 167-70); D. Jacques-Meunié, *Le Maroc saharien des origines à 1670*, Paris 1982, ch. iv; H. Lavoix, *Catalogue des monnaies musulmanes de la Bibliothèque Nationale*, Paris 1891; Leo Africanus, *Description de l'Afrique*, Fr. tr. Épaulard, Paris 1956, 425 n., 429; Lévi-Provençal, *Histoire de l'Espagne musulmane*, Paris-Leiden 1950-3, index; *Mafāk̲h̲ir al-Barbar*, ed. Lévi-Provençal, Rabat 1352/1934, 48; G. Marçais, *La Berbérie musulmane et l'Orient au moyen âge*, Paris 1946; Masʿūdī, *Murūd̲j̲*, iv, 39, 92-3 = §§ 1367, 1420; al-Ḳāḍī al-Nuʿmān, *K. Iftitāḥ al-daʿwa*, ed. and analytical Fr. tr. F. Dachraoui, Tunis 1975, §§ 243-58 (partial Fr. tr. M. Canard, see *Autobiographie*); idem, *K. al-Mad̲j̲ālis wa 'l-musāyarāt*, ed. Ḥ. al-Faḳī, I. S̲h̲abbūḥ and M. al-Yaʿlāwī, Tunis 1978, index; M. Talbi, *L'Émirat aghlabide*, Tunis 1966; H. Terrasse, *Histoire du Maroc*, Casablanca 1949-50, i, 140; *ʿUyūn al-ak̲h̲bār*, see Dachraoui.   (CH. PELLAT)

MIDYŪNA (also MADYŪNA or MEDYŪNA), an important Berber tribe, belonging to the major branch of Butr and descended from the family of Fāṭin, son of Tamzīt (or Tamṣīt), son of Ḍarīs, son of Zaḥīk (Zad̲j̲īk), son of Mādghis al-Abtar. According to Ibn ʿIdhārī, Madyūna was said to be the son of Tamzīt, son of Ḍarī and brother of Maṭmāṭa, Mad̲h̲g̲h̲ara, Ṣadīna, Mag̲h̲īla and Malzūza. According to Ibn K̲h̲aldūn, the Midyūna (Medyūna) were related to the Maṭg̲h̲ara, Ṣadīna, Lamāya, Kūmiya, Mag̲h̲īla, Dūna, Maṭmaṭa, Malzūza, Kas̲h̲āna (Kas̲h̲āta) and Ḍarīsa.

Little is known of the history of the Midyūna. It is very likely that the tribe is derived from the Numidian tribe of Midēni, mentioned by Ptolemy and, if J. Desanges is to believed, resident in Khoumiria at the beginning of the Christian era. Judging from Islamic sources, the Midyūna as such appear only at the beginning of the 2nd/8th century. According to a statement in Ibn K̲h̲aldūn's *Histoire des Berbères*, all of the Midyūna were resident, at this period, in the province of Tlemcen. However, from the start of the 2nd/8th century, various segments of this tribe are encountered, dispersed throughout North Africa, from Libya to Morocco. The earliest mention of the Midyūna found in Arabic sources relates to a significant portion of this clan which, according to Ibn K̲h̲aldūn, moved into Spain "at the time of the first invasion of that country". The historian no doubt refers here to the major expedition of Ṭāriḳ b. Ziyād [*q.v.*], who marched into Spain in 92/711 at the head of 12,000 Berbers and conquered the country in the name of Mūsā b. Nuṣayr. Now, if Ibn K̲h̲aldūn is to be believed, a large proportion of these conquerors was composed of Midyūna warriors, no doubt accompanied by their families. It is for this reason, presumably, that Ibn K̲h̲aldūn states, in this regard, that they soon became very powerful.

Further information regarding the early Midyūna dates from the second half of the 8th century A.D. and relates to certain sections of this tribe inhabiting present-day Algeria, Tunisia and Libya. This is the case of a Midyūna chieftain named D̲j̲arīr b. Masʿūd who took part, with a detachment of the Midyūna, in a major Berber revolt which erupted in 151/168-9 and

which was directed against the Arab governor of the Mag̲h̲rib, ʿUmar b. Ḥafṣ Hazārmard. Among the Berber groups taking part in this revolt, one of the most important was that of Abū Ḳurra al-Īfranī, at the head of 40,000 Ṣufrīs belonging, for the most part, to the Zanātī tribe of the Banū Ifran. The last-named inhabited the western part of Algeria. Originating from the same region were the 6,000 Ibāḍīs commanded by ʿAbd al-Raḥmān b. Rustam of Tāhert (Tiaret) who were among the groups fighting ʿUmar b. Ḥafṣ. Also belonging to these troops were al-Miswar b. Hanī, another Ibāḍī chieftain with a force of 6,000 partisans, and ʿAbd al-Malik b. Ṣanhād̲j̲ī, who brought his 2,000 Ṣufrīs into this coalition. All these detachments laid siege to ʿUmar b. Ḥafṣ at his headquarters in the town of Ṭubna. Joining the Berber rebels at a later stage was Abū Ḥātim al-Malzūzī [*q.v.*], leader of the Ibāḍīs of Tripolitania. The latter succeeded in capturing the town of Ṭubna in 154/771, subsequently setting out in pursuit of ʿUmar b. Ḥafṣ Hazārmard, who made his way towards the east. Abū Ḥātim was preceded by an advance party commanded by D̲j̲arīr b. Masʿūd al-Midyūnī. The latter caught up with ʿUmar b. Ḥafṣ at D̲j̲īd̲j̲il (the present-day Djidjelli) in the land of the Ketāma; in the ensuing battle, D̲j̲arīr b. Masʿūd and his partisans perished, and Abū Ḥātim al-Malzūzī retreated to Tripoli.

Despite the defeat of D̲j̲arīr b. Masʿūd in 754/771 and despite the emigration of a large proportion of the Midyūna of Morocco to Spain with the troops of Ṭāriḳ b. Ziyād in 90-2/709-11, numerous sections of this tribe survived in North Africa, at least until the 8th/14th century, if not later.

The following is the information provided by Arab authors of the Middle Ages regarding these sections:

Morocco: Mention has been made above of the significant group of newly Islamised Midyūna who, taking part in the conquest of Spain by Ṭāriḳ b. Ziyād in 92/711, settled in south-eastern Spain. It is probable that the Midyūna who inhabited the D̲j̲abal Midyūna, a mountain situated to the south of Fās, between this city and that of Ṣufrūy [*q.v.*, present-day Sefrou], and are mentioned by al-Bakrī (5th/11th century), belonged to the same clan. Abu 'l-Fidāʾ (8th/14th century) mentions in his geographical work a D̲j̲abal Midyūna situated to the east of Fās. Could this be the same place as the D̲j̲abal Midyūna situated between Fās and Sefrou? These Midyūna of the region of Fās are also mentioned by Ibn K̲h̲aldūn among numerous other Berber tribes of the Mag̲h̲rib al-Aḳṣā (the Bahlūla, the Fazāz, the G̲h̲iyāt̲h̲a, etc.) as professing Judaism at the beginning of the 3rd/9th century. Later, they converted to Islam, accepting Ṣufrī doctrines at a very early stage. In the second half of this century, during the reign of ʿAlī b. ʿUmar, the Idrīsid prince of Fās, a K̲h̲ārid̲j̲ī Ṣufrī named ʿAbd al-Razzāḳ, a native of the town of Was̲h̲ḳa [*q.v.*, i.e. Huesca] situated in the north-east of Muslim Spain, settled among the Ṣufrī Midyūna inhabiting the mountain of this name to the south of Fās. There he gained numerous partisans. He had courted for his cause numerous neighbouring Berber tribes, for example the G̲h̲iyāt̲h̲a. He had also constructed on the mountain of Salā in the territory of the Midyūna (to the south of Fās) a powerful stronghold, to which he gave the name of Was̲h̲ḳa, in memory of his native city in Spain. According to the author of the *Ḳirṭās* (8th/14th century), this castle was still in existence in 726/1325-6. Subsequently, ʿAbd al-Razzāḳ rebelled against ʿAlī b. ʿUmar. After a number of battles with this prince, he inflicted a decisive victory on him and forced him to abandon the city of Fās and to take refuge in the territory of the Berber tribe of the Awraba, the tribe most loyal to the Idrīsids. The inhabitants of the Andalus quarter of Fās submitted to ʿAbd al-Razzāḳ, but those of the Ḳayrawān quarter refused to heed his demands and brought in, to command them, a son of the Idrīsid prince Yaḥyā b. al-Ḳāsim, surnamed ʿAddām. Nothing is known of the subsequent fate of ʿAbd al-Razzāḳ and his descendents. All that is known is that the latter remained for a period of time faithful to Ṣufrī doctrines and that they also bore the name of Banū Wākil. This family lived for some time in the Maghrib al-Aḳṣā and governed, in all probability, the Midyūna of the region of Fās.

If Ibn Khaldūn is to be believed, the Midyūna of the region of Fās rebelled, in 614-20/1217-23, against the Marīnid prince Abū ʿUthmān Saʿīd, but they were soon defeated by the Marīnids and pledged allegiance to this dynasty.

Besides this fact, nothing definite is known concerning the history of this section of the Midyūna living between Fās and Sefrou, at least as regards the 4th-8th/10th-14th centuries. The last item of information available concerning the Moroccan Midyūna dates from the time of Ibn Khaldūn, who mentions a section of this tribe, still present between Fās and Sefrou, in the vicinity of the important Berber tribe of the Maghīla [*q.v.*] and under its protection.

Algeria: According to Ibn Khaldūn, the original homeland of the Midyūna was located in the central Maghrib, in the province of Tilimsān (Tlemcen). The Midyūna occupied the portion of territory which extends from the Djabal Banī Rāshid (currently Djebel Amour), in the south-east of the High Plateau region, the east of Geryville and north-west of Laghouat, as far as the mountain which stands to the south of Oudjda (west-south-west of Tlemcen) and which still bears the name of Djebel Midïouna. In this early period, that is before the conquest of the central Maghrib by the Zanāta tribes of the Banū Tūdjīn and the Banū Rāshid, the Midyūna of this part of the Maghrib roamed, in nomadic fashion, "the plains and other localities of this region". According to other statements of Ibn Khaldūn, this section of the Midyūna was bordered, to the south-east, by the Banū Īlūmī and the Banū Īfran, to the west, by the Miknāsa, and between them and the sea were the Kūmiya and the Banū Walhāṣa (in the neighbourhood of the town of Ḥunayn). At the time of the conquest of the central Maghrib by the Banū Tūdjīn and the Banū Rāshid, the Midyūna were, says Ibn Khaldūn, much reduced in number; they were also expelled by the invaders from the countryside of Tlemcen and forced to withdraw to the strongholds which they possessed in the Djabal Tasāla and to the south of this mountain (to the south of Oran and to the north-east of Sidi Bel Abbas) and also in the Djabal Midyūna (to the south of Oudjda). A section of the Midyūna is also found in the territory of the tribe of the Beni Khalled (Khelled) in the region of the town of Nedroma. In this area, a village still exists called Dar Midiouna.

In the same region of the province of Tlemcen there existed, in the Middle Ages, another section of the Midyūna. It was based at Tafesra, formerly Tifsart of the Midyūna, a town known from the *Description of Africa* by Leo Africanus (first half of the 16th century). This locality was situated, according to this author, some 15 miles (approx. 27 km) to the south of Tlemcen.

Another canton occupied by the Midyūna is mentioned by de Slane in his *Table géographique* which appears as a supplement to the French translation of the *Histoire des Berbères* of Ibn Khaldūn. It was located to the north-west of the town of Mazouna (east-north-east of Mostaganem). A little to the east of this region, al-Bakrī places the town of al-Khaḍrāʾ, surrounded on all sides by Berber tribes, amongst which this geographer mentions the Midyūna. Al-Khaḍrāʾ was situated on the Chélif, a day's march to the west of the town of Miliana. Al-Bakrī places it in the neighbourhood of Ténès.

Tunisia: An insignificant section of the Midyūna probably inhabited at one time the desert of Ifrīḳiya, in what is now Tunisia. In fact, the Ibāḍī historian and biographer al-Shammākhī (19th/16th century) mentions an Ibāḍī scholar named ʿĪsā b. Ḥamdūn al-Midyūnī al-Hawwārī who lived, during the 5th/11th century, in the *bādiya* (desert) of this country. It seems that this section of Midyūna belonged to the major Berber tribe of Hawwāra [*q.v.*].

Libya: Another section of the tribe of the Midyūna also lived in the canton of Yefren (in the ancient Arab sources: Yafran) situated to the east of Djabal Nafūsa in northern Tripolitania. In fact, in his *Kitāb al-Siyar*, al-Shammākhī speaks of people belonging to the tribe of the Midyūna inhabiting this district in the Middle Ages. Among these people, al-Shammākhī mentions an Ibāḍī Wahbī *shaykh* Abū Yūsuf b. Aḥmad al-Yafranī al-Midyūni who died in 894/1488-9. The same author also says that numerous persons belonging to the tribe of the Midyūna lived, in the 2nd/8th century, among the Berbers of Fazzān. Among these, al-Shammākhī mentions a certain Abu 'l-Ḥasan Djanāw b. Fatā al-Midyūnī who was an Ibāḍī *muftī*.

Spain: It has been noted above that a large number of the Midyūna entered Spain at the time of the first Muslim invasion of Spain led by the Berber Ṭāriḳ b. Ziyād in 92/711. Becoming very powerful and very numerous, the Midyūna of Spain enjoyed considerable influence there and, in 151/768, a group from this tribe embraced the cause of the Berber pretender Shākiyā al-Miknāsī who claimed to be the grandson of Ḥusayn b. ʿAlī. In fact, one of the Midyūna *amīrs* of Spain named Hilāl b. Abziya rose in rebellion at Shantamariyat al-Sharḳ (Santa Maria or Albarracin in south-eastern Spain) against the Umayyad ʿAbd al-Raḥmān al-Dākhil. After the death of Shākiyā, whose revolt lasted nine years, Hilāl b. Abziya pledged submission to ʿAbd al-Raḥmān al-Dākhil and obtained from this *amīr* a commission appointing him chief of the Midyūna of Spain. His power extended over the Berbers established in eastern Spain and in Santa Maria or Albarracin. He was succeeded by Nabith, one of his kinsmen.

Sicily: A section of the Midyūna settled, probably in the 3rd/9th century, on the banks of the river called Selinus in antiquity in south-western Sicily. In fact, this river was later known as *Modiuni*, from the ancient tribal name Madyūna or Midyūna. The relevant group here is probably that section of the tribe of the Midyūna which was formerly resident in Ifrīḳiya and which took part in the conquest of Sicily undertaken in 218/826 by the *ḳāḍī* Asad b. Furāt b. Sinān. Initially Ibāḍīs, these Midyūna were subsequently converted to orthodox doctrines after the death of the *Imām* Abū Ḥātim al-Malzūzī.

Bibliography: Bakrī, *Description de l'Afrique septentrionale*, ed. de Slane, Ar. text 75, 125, Fr. tr. 134; Idrīsī, *Description de l'Afrique et de l'Espagne*, ed. Dozy and De Goeje, Ar. text 57, Fr. tr. 66; Ibn ʿIdhārī, *Bayān*, ed. Dozy (new edn. Colin and Lévi-Provençal), i, 66; Abu 'l-Fidāʾ, *Taḳwīm*, Ar. text ed. Reinaud and de Slane, 66, 123, Fr. tr. Reinaud, ii/1, Paris 1848, 84, 170; Ibn Khaldūn, *Histoire des Berbères*[2], Fr. tr. de Slane, i, 109, 172, 208-8, 221, 236, 250, 259, ii, 566 (Appx.), iii, 293, iv, 1-2, 31, 511, 516 (geographical table); Shammākhī, *Kitāb al-Siyar*, Cairo 1884, 191-2, 136, 382, 563-4, 579; Leo Africanus, *Description de l'Afrique*, Fr. tr. Épaulard, 537 and n. 80; Fournel, *Les Berbers*, Paris 1875-81, i, 423, n. 7, 424, n. *a*, ii, 17-19, 26; R. Basset, *Nédromah et les Traras*, Paris 1901, 89; M. Amari, *Storia dei Musulmani di Sicilia*[2], Catania 1935, ii, 54 (note on p. 53); T. Lewicki, *La répartition des groupements ibāḍites dans l'Afrique du Nord au Moyen Age*, in *RO*, xxi (1957), 340-1; J. Desanges, *Catalogue des tribus africaines de l'antiquité classique à l'Ouest du Nil*, Dakar 1962, 114, 121, 258.

(T. Lewicki)

ISBN 90 04 09358 3

PRINTED IN THE NETHERLANDS